SKY SPORTS

FOOTBALL YEARBOOK 2009-2010

EDITORS: GLENDA ROLLIN AND JACK ROLLIN

D0231233

headline

Copyright © 2009 HEADLINE PUBLISHING GROUP

First published in 2009
by HEADLINE PUBLISHING GROUP

1

Apart from any use permitted under UK copyright law, this publication may only be
reproduced, stored, or transmitted, in any form, or by any means, with prior permission in
writing of the publishers or, in the case of reprographic production, in accordance with
the terms of licences issued by the Copyright Licensing Agency.

This publication contains material that is the copyright and database right of
the FA Premiership, the Football League Limited and PA Sport.
PA Sport is a division of PA News Limited.

Front cover photographs: (left and background) Nicolas Anelka (Chelsea) –
Nigel French/EMPICS Sport/PA Photos; (centre) Nemanja Vidic (Manchester United) –
Jason Cairnduff/Action Images; (right) Gabriel Agbonlahor (Aston Villa) –
Nick Potts/PA Wire/PA Photos.

Spine photograph: Steven Gerrard celebrates his 100th goal for Liverpool –
Shaun Botterill/Getty Images.

Back cover photographs: (above) – Robbie Keane (Tottenham Hotspur) and Robin van
Persie (Arsenal) – *Adam Davy/EMPICS Sport/PA Photos*; (below) Georgios Samaras
(Celtic) and David Weir (Rangers) – *Lynne Cameron/Rangers FC/PA Photos*.

Cataloguing in Publication Data is available from the British Library

CONTENTS

INTERNATIONAL FOOTBALL

NON-LEAGUE FOOTBALL

INFORMATION AND RECORDS

FOREWORD

There are a number of things that signal the start of the season: new kits, new signings and the arrival of the Football Yearbook, a publication we're proud to be associated with at Sky Sports.

I've grown up with football and the Yearbook is part of the game's fabric. It has an iconic look to it; familiar and authoritative. It's a common sight in the office and it's the first source of reference for me when I need to check a fact before a live show or if I need to remind myself of my own career statistics as well.

My pre-seasons have changed and the Yearbook is part of my preparation now. In my playing days I would be running the hills at this time of year; these days I'm more likely to be checking facts in the ultimate source of football information.

My new team-mates are my Sky Sports colleagues: Richard Keys, Andy Gray and Martin Tyler. The buzz is similar to when you're playing – there are still shared goals, a will to succeed and a real sense of teamwork – and we have similar highs after a good show to when I won football matches.

In our pre-season and throughout the 2009–2010 campaign the Yearbook is an essential part of our preparation and match routine.

Jamie Redknapp, Sky Sports

Jamie Redknapp

INTRODUCTION

The 40th edition of the Yearbook, our seventh with sponsors Sky Sports, features a fully comprehensive analysis of the performances of British and Irish clubs in European competitions since 1955 with a statistical summary of the number of matches involved. In addition, a history of the competitions concerned is presented as a prelude to the facts and figures.

To mark the milestone of 40 years for the Yearbook we have reproduced the Golden Boots Awards that were included in the first edition of Rothmans Football Yearbook 1970–71.

With the World Cup finals being held in South Africa next year, there are results of all matches in the qualifying competition to date. For Europe and South America full line-ups are included. Also countries already qualified from other parts of the world are given the same treatment.

Once again the coverage of the Champions League and UEFA Cup is as wide-ranging as ever with the fullest possible details of every match played in the respective tournaments.

There is an extended Daily Round-up of diary events which refer to what happened on any specific day and might well have been overtaken by subsequent events. However nothing is included with hindsight. Transfer figures are often those quoted at the time.

While maintaining the extent of 1,056 pages it has become increasingly difficult to fit in the amount of information which has been added edition upon edition and this particularly affects the English club pages. In an effort to reduce the burden on this area of the book, in the Honours section for each club, for domestic achievements, only winners and runners-up figures are quoted. However, the section devoted to season-by-season records has full details of teams promoted either from their final positions in the League table or via the play-offs. Also on each second page of the relevant club the full record of its history is still easy to find.

Also in the Records Section it should be noted that again through space being at a premium, entries are in the most part divided into Premier League and Football League, the latter records referring to the best performance in any one category irrespective of the status of the division. Thus a Third Division (South) entry from the 1930s might figure at the expense of a lesser achievement from the First Division.

Once again, there is an A to Z index of names with a cross reference to the Players Directory, enabling readers to check on the whereabouts of any specific player during the 2008–09 season. The Who's Who style directory again provides a season-by-season account of individual player's appearances and goals. The fullest possible available details have been provided for players in this section, including all players who appeared in first-class matches.

Throughout the book players sent off are designated thus ■, substitutes in the club pages are 12, 13 and 14 with 15 for the substitute goalkeeper. Squad numbers are not used.

The usual detailed and varied coverage involves Scottish, Welsh and Irish football, amateur, schools, university, reserve team, extensive non-League information, awards, records and an international directory. Women's football, referees and the work of chaplains are also featured.

The Editors would like to express their appreciation of the response from FA Premier League and Football League clubs when requesting information. Thanks are also due to Alan Elliott for checking the Scottish section, Tony Brown for sequences and instances of match results in the records section, Graeme Riley for the statistics for the British and Irish clubs feature in Europe, Ian Nannestad for the obituaries and Andrew Howe on foreign players. Thanks are also due to John English, who provided invaluable and conscientious reading of the proofs.

ACKNOWLEDGEMENTS

The Editors would like to express appreciation of the following individuals and organisations for their co-operation: David Barber, Dawn Keleher and Jill Roberts (Football Association), David C. Thomson (Scottish League), Heather Elliott, Dr Malcolm Brodie, Rev. Nigel Sands, Ken Goldman, Grahame Lloyd, Marshall Gillespie, Sean Creedon, Valery Karpoushkin, Bob Bannister, Martin Cooper and Alan Platt. Special mention, too, of Rhea Halford (Headline Book Publishing). The highest praise is due to the indefatigable, ebullient and loquacious Lorraine Jerram, Headline's Managing Editor for her generosity, expertise, constant support, determined resilience, patience, endearing sincerity, perspicacity and appreciation, not to mention her unfailing humour, stoicism, quick-wit, courtesy, quiet consideration and understated authority.

Finally sincere thanks to John Anderson, Simon Dunnington, Geoff Turner, Brian Tait and the staff at Wearset for their efforts in the production of this book, which was much appreciated throughout the year.

EDITORIAL

It became blindingly obvious that the economic situation was suffering a downturn if you had a cheque returned by the bank stamped "insufficient funds" and you were not absolutely sure whether it was your account or theirs which was in the red.

Not that it seems to have affected either Parliament or the Premier League, but for different reasons. The seemingly bottomless pit of MPs expenses has been impossible to quantify. But in the 2008 summer close season some £540m was spent by the Premiership clubs in the transfer market with a dozen of them beating their previous record.

The January transfer window added another relatively modest £130m when many pundits had forecast a buy-one-get-one-free trade. But the Premier League brushed off the crisis to give a whole new meaning to "Bogof!" Unbelievably there have been unsubstantiated rumours over money-laundering! But as far as we know *The Daily Telegraph* has no cunning plan to blow the whistle on anything about such alleged goings-on.

Manchester United benefited from the £80m sale of Cristiano Ronaldo to Real Madrid and the move was seized upon by FIFA's own Sepp Blatter as an indication of the excellent condition of the game. Not too long ago he was agreeing that Ronaldo was nothing more than a slave. As has been stated before, we get the governments we deserve but can do precious little about football's administrators.

Naturally the Premier League is a transitory organisation, its members flitting in and out. In 2009–10 there will have been 43 different clubs involved in it since its inception in 1992–93. The League has only managed to keep seven of its founders. Departing clubs are given financial compensation and it might be argued that the Premier League does its job in this direction. But they could do more and extend a helping hand way down at the bottom of the pyramid.

A levy of one percent on all transfers in and out affecting Premier League clubs could be used to assist in funding the grass roots of the game. Too much transfer fee money disappears as far as the football industry is concerned. Such a modest cut would be seen as petty cash or chump-change. At least one grass roots organisation attached to a leading club has had to fold. Others less well connected are probably in equally dire straits. The green shoots of recovery are one thing, tending to what is already growing is as important.

There has been much criticism of the behaviour of spectators at the lower levels and finance will not solve that one. The way to improve the situation is to tackle what transpires on the touchlines higher up the echelons. Nothing levels up and the hand-bagging, verbal and otherwise, which can be seen each week would not be aped if measures were taken here.

Abuse of officials is a disgrace and non-productive. You will not tempt more people to take up refereeing and thus improve standards if you do not respect all of them. Constructive criticism is fine, but it has to stop there. Officials who make mistakes must be punished. However, the governing bodies are seemingly against the introduction of technology to solve problems. Indeed we can see this season an experiment of six officials being tried out in the Europa League – the successor to the UEFA Cup.

Give the fourth official the stopwatch to scrap injury time. If coaches were made to sit down as spectators are supposed to do he or she could concentrate on more timely matters.

Also UEFA please note. Leave bleating about foreigners in English football and deal with clubs who ditch their European cup responsibilities when they consider domestic places are more important – and this after they scramble to get into Europe in the first place.

Less important yet odd to understand is the media getting into a series of fits about starts. When Ryan Giggs became the Professional Footballers Association choice as Player of the Year it was pointed out that he had made less than twenty starts in the Premier League. The medium still fails to comprehend that the modern game is at least a 14-a-side affair over the 90 minutes and squad systems rule. Only two percent of players in the four divisions made "starts" and sixty percent of those were goalkeepers! What is the point you are making?

These are cosmetic concerns of course and all part of the hype which fails to focus on the statistics that matter: the score, who played and an accurate timing of the goals. Meaningless minutia includes considering a successful penalty is not a shot on target. Get a grip, people.

On a positive note the SS Fabio Capello is making the right kind of waves in its wake on the way to the Cape of Good Hope or is it Great Expectation? Worryingly of course is another final defeat at Under-21 level to Germany who thus made it a hat-trick with Under-17 and Under-19 levels. The Bundesliga has also overtaken the Premier League for attendances averaging 41,000. Average admission price is 20.79 euros, too.

Plenty to think about but what matters is the desperate need for a restoration of ethics in the game, though it must be emphasised this is not a plea for the rehabilitation of the county immediately east of London.

SKY SPORTS FOOTBALL YEARBOOK HONOURS

For the first time since the inception of the *Sky Sports Football Yearbook* team of the season, the FWA members chose a 4-3-3 formation.

The FWA members chose the following team for the season.

Sky Sports Football Yearbook Team of the Season 2008–09

Mark Schwarzer
(Fulham)

Glen Johnson
(Portsmouth)
(now Liverpool)

Nemanja Vidic
(Manchester U)

Rio Ferdinand
(Manchester U)

Ashley Cole
(Chelsea)

Steven Gerrard
(Liverpool)

Frank Lampard
(Chelsea)

Ashley Young
(Aston Villa)

Cristiano Ronaldo
(Manchester U)
(now Real Madrid)

Fernando Torres
(Liverpool)

Wayne Rooney
(Manchester U)

Manager:
Roy Hodgson *(Fulham)*

Substitutes:
Jamie Carragher *(Liverpool)*
Cesc Fabregas *(Arsenal)*
Xabi Alonso *(Liverpool)*

Fernando Torres leaps to head Liverpool level just after half-time in a thrilling 4-4 draw with Arsenal at Anfield on 21 April 2009. (Action Images/Reuters/Phil Noble)

ROTHMANS GOLDEN BOOTS AWARD 1970

Forty years ago when the first Rothmans Football Yearbook was being prepared, a distinguished panel of twenty-two football journalists was asked to nominate eleven players from the whole of Great Britain to represent Rothmans Golden Boots Award.

The panel's brief was as follows:

The eleven players were asked for in 4-2-4 formation as the talent available was obviously capable of a positive approach to any match without having to worry about too many defensive theories.

There's no doubt that this decision limited the number of votes given to Bobby Charlton and Martin Peters who thrive on the 4-4-2 set up with England.

Gordon Banks
(*Stoke City & England*)
(22 votes)

| David Hay (*Celtic & Scotland*) (10) | Mike England (*Tottenham H & Wales*) (11) | Bobby Moore (*West Ham U & England*) (22) | Terry Cooper (*Leeds U & England*) (21) |

Billy Bremner
(*Leeds U & Scotland*)
(19)

Alan Ball
(*Everton & England*)
(19)

| Jimmy Johnstone (*Celtic & Scotland*) (12) | Geoff Hurst (*West Ham U & England*) (14) | Ron Davies (*Southampton & Wales*) (13) | George Best (*Manchester U & N. Ireland*) (22) |

In fact the players who also received votes but did not manage a place in the team were:

Martin Peters (9), Billy McNeill (7), Francis Lee (6), Terry Hennessy, Paul Reaney (5), Bobby Charlton, Peter Osgood (3), Johnny Giles, Alan Mullery, Brian Labone, Keith Newton, Tommy Gemmell (2), Rod Thomas, Tommy Wright, Colin Stein, Bob McNab, Bobby Moncur, Peter Houseman, Allan Clarke, Ralph Coates, John Greig (1).

The Golden Boots Award concluded:

The selected wingmen, Jimmy Johnstone and George Best, would be able to help out in midfield if necessary – but how often do you think Billy Bremner and Alan Ball would need them?

This team will cause a few arguments, but no one could deny its great potential. Each year the Awards will bring together, if only on paper, the very best of British footballing talent. Just imagine this year's team playing Brazil. There would not be a stadium in the world large enough to do them justice. [!]

FOOTBALL AWARDS 2009

FOOTBALLER OF THE YEAR

The Football Writers' Association Sir Stanley Matthews Trophy for the Footballer of the Year was awarded to Steven Gerrard of Liverpool and England. Ryan Giggs of Manchester United was runner-up and Wayne Rooney, also of Manchester United, came third.

Past Winners

1947–48 Stanley Matthews (Blackpool), 1948–49 Johnny Carey (Manchester U), 1949–50 Joe Mercer (Arsenal), 1950–51 Harry Johnston (Blackpool), 1951–52 Billy Wright (Wolverhampton W), 1952–53 Nat Lofthouse (Bolton W), 1953–54 Tom Finney (Preston NE), 1954–55 Don Revie (Manchester C), 1955–56 Bert Trautmann (Manchester C), 1956–57 Tom Finney (Preston NE), 1957–58 Danny Blanchflower (Tottenham H), 1958–59 Syd Owen (Luton T), 1959–60 Bill Slater (Wolverhampton W), 1960–61 Danny Blanchflower (Tottenham H), 1961–62 Jimmy Adamson (Burnley), 1962–63 Stanley Matthews (Stoke C), 1963–64 Bobby Moore (West Ham U), 1964–65 Bobby Collins (Leeds U), 1965–66 Bobby Charlton (Manchester U), 1966–67 Jackie Charlton (Leeds U), 1967–68 George Best (Manchester U), 1968–69 Dave Mackay (Derby Co) shared with Tony Book (Manchester C), 1969–70 Billy Bremner (Leeds U), 1970–71 Frank McLintock (Arsenal), 1971–72 Gordon Banks (Stoke C), 1972–73 Pat Jennings (Tottenham H), 1973–74 Ian Callaghan (Liverpool), 1974–75 Alan Mullery (Fulham), 1975–76 Kevin Keegan (Liverpool), 1976–77 Emlyn Hughes (Liverpool), 1977–78 Kenny Burns (Nottingham F), 1978–79 Kenny Dalglish (Liverpool), 1979–80 Terry McDermott (Liverpool), 1980–81 Frans Thijssen (Ipswich T), 1981–82 Steve Perryman (Tottenham H), 1982–83 Kenny Dalglish (Liverpool), 1983–84 Ian Rush (Liverpool), 1984–85 Neville Southall (Everton), 1985–86 Gary Lineker (Everton), 1986–87 Clive Allen (Tottenham H), 1987–88 John Barnes (Liverpool), 1988–89 Steve Nicol (Liverpool), 1989–90 John Barnes (Liverpool), 1990–91 Gordon Strachan (Leeds U), 1991–92 Gary Lineker (Tottenham H), 1992–93 Chris Waddle (Sheffield W), 1993–94 Alan Shearer (Blackburn R), 1994–95 Jurgen Klinsmann (Tottenham H), 1995–96 Eric Cantona (Manchester U), 1996–97 Gianfranco Zola (Chelsea), 1997–98 Dennis Bergkamp (Arsenal), 1998–99 David Ginola (Tottenham H), 1999–2000 Roy Keane (Manchester U), 2000–01 Teddy Sheringham (Manchester U), 2001–02 Robert Pires (Arsenal), 2002–03 Thierry Henry (Arsenal), 2003–04 Thierry Henry (Arsenal), 2004–05 Frank Lampard (Chelsea), 2005–06 Thierry Henry (Arsenal), 2006–07 Cristiano Ronaldo (Manchester U), 2007–08 Cristiano Ronaldo (Manchester U), 2008–09 Ryan Giggs (Manchester U).

THE PFA AWARDS 2009

Player of the Year: Ryan Giggs, Manchester U and Wales.
Young Player of the Year: Ashley Young, Aston Villa and England.

OTHER AWARDS

EUROPEAN FOOTBALLER OF THE YEAR 2008

Cristiano Ronaldo, Manchester United and Portugal

WORLD PLAYER OF THE YEAR 2008

Cristiano Ronaldo, Manchester United and Portugal

WOMEN'S PLAYER OF THE YEAR 2008

Marta, Umea and Brazil

SCOTTISH PFA PLAYER OF THE YEAR AWARDS 2009

Player of the Year: Scott Brown, Celtic and Scotland
Young Player of the Year: James McCarthy, Hamilton Academical
First Division Player of the Year: Leigh Griffiths, Livingston
Second Division Player of the Year: Bryan Prunty, Ayr United
Third Division Player of the Year: Bobby Barr, Albion Rovers

SCOTTISH FOOTBALL WRITERS' ASSOCIATION 2009

Player of the Year: Gary Caldwell, Celtic and Scotland
Manager of the Year: Gordon Strachan, Celtic

HISTORY OF EUROPEAN CUPS

EUROPEAN CUP AND CHAMPIONS LEAGUE

The idea of a competition between leading clubs in various European countries seems so obvious that in hindsight it is surprising it did not materialise until 1955. But the credit for the idea of the European Cup belongs solely to Gabriel Hanot, a football writer with the French sports newspaper *L'Equipe*. However, discussions had been held as long ago as 1938 and but for the war, may have happened earlier. In pre-war days several competitions involving various chiefly eastern European countries held sway, notably the Mitropa Cup. There was further talk in the aftermath of hostilities for expansion but nothing more tangible emerged.

Hanot, a former French international who would have played more than 12 times for his country but for the First World War, was of pensionable age by the time UEFA, the European governing body, was formed in 1954. But neither they nor FIFA appeared interested in his plans. So Hanot decided to take a more positive approach than merely conducting the discussion through the columns of his newspaper. He invited delegates from 18 countries to attend a meeting in Paris in the spring of 1955. Only three failed to arrive: Scotland's Hibernian sent a telegram of support, while Sparta Prague and Moscow Dynamo pleaded fixture problems and weather difficulties for their non-acceptance.

The meeting was a total success and plans were drawn up for a tournament to start in the following autumn. FIFA, fearing a threat to its authority, sanctioned the idea with the proviso that clubs entering had to have permission from their national association. UEFA fell in line and agreed to organise it.

Because of the stipulation that clubs had to obtain permission and other factors, Hanot's original 18 was reduced to 12. Chelsea, the Football League champions, were forbidden to enter by the misguided insularity which was so often an English trait. The excuse was 'fixture congestion', Gwardia Warsaw (Poland) replaced them, while PSV Eindhoven of the Netherlands and Denmark's Aarhus took over from Holland Sport and KB Copenhagen respectively. But neither the Czechs nor the Soviets participated. Voros Lobogo replaced Honved from Hungary.

Hibernian, who had finished fifth in the Scottish League, did well to reach the semi-finals. All ties until the final were played on a home and away basis with the aggregate of goals deciding the winner. The first final was appropriately held in Paris and won by Real Madrid, who beat the French entry Reims 4-3.

The competition, which had started with a match between Sporting Lisbon and Partizan Belgrade on 4 September 1955 in the Portuguese capital, had immediately proved an enormous success, producing exciting football and financial rewards for the competitors. Its popularity quickly increased and, after the initial tournament, entry was restricted to national league champions, although the country of the holders could enter their league winners as well.

Real Madrid dominated the early years, winning the first five series and reaching a peak in the 1960 final when they defeated Eintracht Frankfurt (West Germany) 7-3 at Hampden Park, Glasgow before a crowd of 135,000. It took another seven years before the Scots were able to applaud victory of their own, away in Lisbon against Internazionale, the Italian club which had come to epitomise the defensive by-product of the European Cup. Celtic achieved a 2-1 win in what was their first season in the competition.

The following year, Manchester United, who had been England's first representatives in 1956–57, albeit against Football League advice, won it in the country's first successful attempt. They defeated Benfica (Portugal) 4-1 after extra time at Wembley in 1968. These two British successes did more in the overall scheme of the competition than merely provide cause for rejoicing in these islands. They broke the monopoly which the Latin countries had enjoyed, as previously only Spanish, Portuguese and Italian teams had triumphed.

Though AC Milan won their second European Cup in 1969, Feyenoord succeeded for Holland in 1970 and spurred their countrymen from Ajax, whose brand of 'total' football swept aside the negative approach of others, to three successive trophies.

West Germany's Bayern Munich emulated the Dutchmen's feat from 1974 to 1976, before Liverpool stamped their individual style on the European Cup in 1977, one of four trophies to fall to the Anfield club. In fact, English teams did exceptionally well in the years that followed. Nottingham Forest won it in consecutive years and Aston Villa achieved another triumph of their own in 1982. Indeed, the Cup did not leave England after 1977 until 1983.

Unfortunately, England's challenge ended in tragedy at the Heysel Stadium in Brussels in 1985 when a group of rioting Liverpool followers caused the deaths of 39 fans, most of whom were Italian supporters of Juventus. English clubs were banned from European competition as a result.

Although this was the greatest disaster to hit the competition, increased misbehaviour by supporters of various clubs around Europe has brought in its wake the closure of grounds, fines and the suspension of clubs. But the competition has survived and shows no sign of decreasing in its popularity, although the pressures have grown alarmingly as the necessity to win has overshadowed all other aspects.

English clubs were readmitted in 1991 and the clamour for a super league among Europe's elite grew in intensity. The following year in an effort to thwart this ambition, UEFA introduced a Champions League of two divisions into the European Cup after the initial stages from the quarter-final onwards. Further changes followed in 1995 when four groups of four were switched to replace the first and second rounds, with the knock-out stage following. At the same time there was a gradual introduction of a two-tier system of entry, those countries without a history of success in the competition being moved into the UEFA Cup, as further evidence of a shift towards a European elite.

In 1997–98 a further relaxation of the concept that the competition stood for champions came when leading countries were allowed to add their league runners-up, but it did little to satisfy the rich clubs anxious to form a European Super League, some 60 years after the idea was first mooted.

In subsequent years the Champions League has grown in size and importance to almost the exclusion of everything else as a competition for clubs. There has also been a provision for teams knocked out to be given a further lifeline in the UEFA Cup.

One of the more contentious issues surrounding the Champions League has been the grey area of a dividing line between what happened in the European Cup before 1993 and whether all the subsequent records of the Champions League actually have any real connection with what occurred in the past.

English clubs have provided three Champions League winners Manchester United (1999 and 2008) and Liverpool (2005).

EUROPEAN CUP-WINNERS' CUP

The success of the European Cup prompted a call for the winners of national cup competitions to have their own tournament. But not all Europe's members had regularly competed for cups and the initial years had few entries. However, its own momentum convinced those who had been lukewarm about knockout tournaments, to revive their own domestic cups and thus become involved in the Cup-Winners' Cup. It also became possible for the beaten finalists in a national cup to enter, if the winners had already been crowned champions of their league.

Honours had been widespread in this competition, a dozen different countries winning it. Before the ban imposed on them, English clubs had won the Cup-Winners' Cup five times, more than any other country.

It was also the first competition to provide an English club with success in Europe, when Tottenham Hotspur convincingly defeated the holders Atletico Madrid 5-1 in 1963. Two years later West Ham United emulated this feat and at the start of the 1970s, British clubs enjoyed consecutive titles through Manchester City (1970), Chelsea (1971) and Rangers (1972). Manchester United also signalled the return of English clubs to the continent by winning the Cup-Winners' Cup in 1991. Arsenal (1994) and Chelsea (1998) were its last two English successes.

But because of the continuing success of the Champions League, the competition became looked upon as the poor relation in European cup circles and in 1999 it was wound-up.

FAIRS CUP AND UEFA CUP

If Gabriel Hanot had been the instigator of the European Cup, Ernst Thommen, a Swiss vice-president of FIFA, was the man behind the International Inter-Cities Fairs Cup competition, with its lengthy title and unwieldly time-scale. Its initial tournament was spread over three years.

The formation of UEFA provided the opportunity to put the idea of the competition into practice and probably because of their involvement in the Fairs Cup, UEFA reacted coolly to the European Cup. Representatives from 10 countries covering 12 cities met in April 1955 to formulate plans. Initially entrants represented cities that held trade fairs and wherever possible, fixtures were designed to coincide with such events. However, the selection of each city's team was left to the individual country and provided differing interpretations. Barcelona was represented by all but one player from the Barca club, the remaining player coming from Espanol, but in contrast London chose from all professional clubs in the metropolis.

After the second tournament, which took two years, it was decided to hold it every year with one team representing each city. Although the Fairs Cup had increased in size and popularity, losing its original need with the trade fairs, it required a complete relaxation of this rule.

In 1971 the Fairs Cup was replaced by the UEFA Cup and this regularly provided for 64 teams; the number of places per country being decided on previous performance and monitored each season. Since entry is restricted to the highest placed teams in each country, it could be said that the UEFA Cup is second in prestige to the European Cup itself.

This point became even more emphasised when UEFA decided to screen entries for the European Cup, giving the UEFA Cup the champion clubs from an array of countries and increasing the total number of entries to the competition.

With few exceptions, the final had always been decided over two legs even from the earliest Fairs Cup days. But in 1998 it was decided that it would fall in line with the other two competitions and be held at one venue. Liverpool (2001) were the last English winners.

As happened with the Cup-Winners' Cup, the stranglehold which the Champions League held over all other European competitions particularly by the enormous media interest, the UEFA Cup also fell into decline. An attempt to revive it with a cut-down version of the Champions League group stage was not a success. The European governing body then decided to end it, too, in 2009 replacing it with the Europa League, along the lines of the Champions League but with far more teams being allowed in. At the same time the Intertoto Cup was also axed.

EUROPA LEAGUE

For 2009–10 the new competition embraced similar principles to those of the Champions League chiefly copying the group stage with twelve groups of four teams and a lengthy qualifying period initially with 159 teams entering. Whether the media is likely to take much interest remains an uncertainty.

INTERTOTO

Originally started in 1961–62 as a fixture list for summer pools, UEFA took over its organisation in 1995 but found it difficult to persuade many countries to take any serious interest in competing. There was the gradual invitation to allow successful teams to enter the UEFA Cup in the same season. But with the advent of the Europa League it seemed the time to end its existence.

EUROPEAN SUPER CUP

Played annually, with several breaks in continuity, the Super Cup originally involved respective winners of the European Cup and the Cup-Winners' Cup meeting each other, usually on a home and away basis. Finding suitable dates for the matches has remained a problem. In 1974 and 1981 the qualified teams could not agree on dates to meet each other and in 1985 the ban imposed on English teams meant that Everton were unable to play Juventus. On two occasions it was agreed to play just one game, simply because of fixture congestion.

When the Cup-Winners' Cup was scrapped, the winners of the Champions League met the successful team from the UEFA Cup

BRITISH AND IRISH CLUBS IN EUROPE

Key: EC = European Cup; CL = Champions League; FC = Fairs Cup; UE = UEFA Cup; CW = Cup Winners' Cup; IT = Intertoto Cup; SC = Super Cup; W*/L* = won or lost on toss of a coin, drawing of lots, away goals rule or penalty shoot-out.

ABERDEEN

In 1983 they were the first team from Scotland to win both the Cup-Winners' Cup – against Real Madrid after extra time – and Super Cup. In the1970–71 Cup-Winners' Cup against Honved, it was the first such tie in it to be decided by penalty kicks.

	P	W	D	L	F	A	W*	L*	Entries
	109	45	29	35	161	122			27 seasons
EC	12	5	4	3	14	12	2	3	
FC	4	2	1	1	4	4			1
UE	52	15	18	19	62	69	5	15	
CW	39	22	5	12	79	37	1	8	
SC	2	1	1	0	2	0			

Biggest Win: 10-0 v KR, 6-9-1967
Heaviest Defeat: 3-6 v Moenchengladbach, 27-9-1972

ABERYSTWYTH TOWN

Managed home draws with Floriana 1999 and Dinaburg 2004.

	P	W	D	L	F	A	W*	L*	Entries
	4	0	2	2	3	8			2 seasons
IT	4	0	2	2	3	8			2

Heaviest Defeat: 0-4 v Dinaburg, 26-6-2004

AFAN LIDO

Only succumbed to the Latvia team by the narrowest of margins.

	P	W	D	L	F	A	W*	L*	Entries
	2	0	1	1	1	2			1 season
UE	2	0	1	1	1	2			1

Heaviest Defeat: 1-2 v RAF Yelgava, 8-8-1995

AIRDRIEONIANS

Scorer of the lone goal was Kenny Black, later to manage the club which succeeded them – Airdrie United!

	P	W	D	L	F	A	W*	L*	Entries
	2	0	0	2	1	3			1 season
CW	2	0	0	2	1	3			1

Heaviest Defeat: 1-2 v Sparta Prague, 29-9-1992

ARDS

Twice trailing to Standard Liege on 12 September 1973 in the UEFA Cup two penalties gave them a 3-2 win.

	P	W	D	L	F	A	W*	L*	Entries
	12	1	1	10	10	49			5 seasons
EC	2	0	0	2	3	10			1
UE	2	1	0	1	4	8			1
CW	4	0	1	3	2	17			2
IT	4	0	0	4	1	14			1

Biggest Win: 3-2 v Standard Liege, 12-9-1973
Heaviest Defeat: 0-10 v PSV Eindhoven, 18-9-1974

ARSENAL

Had six appearances in European finals. There was Fairs Cup success in 1969–70 despite trailing 3-1 to Anderlecht in away leg, recovered at Highbury in the last 15 minutes to a 3-0 win. In the 1980 Cup-Winners' Cup final against Valencia in Brussels they were beaten on penalties, but won it in 1994 with an Alan Smith goal after 19 minutes. Were unable to retain the cup the following year when a bizarre long-range goal gave Zaragoza an extra time victory. In 1999–2000 failures from the shoot-out cost dearly and defeat after extra time against Galatasaray in the UEFA Cup final. Highest club attendance 73,707 was achieved for a Champions League tie against Lens at Wembley on 25 November 1998. In 2005–06 kept a record ten games without conceding a goal over 995 minutes, but final failure when goalkeeper Jens Lehmann was sent off and despite taking the lead were overtaken by Barcelona. Thierry Henry with 41 goals including 35 in the Champions League is their leading European goal scorer.

	P	W	D	L	F	A	W*	L*	Entries
	205	99	53	53	332	194			24 seasons
EC	10	5	1	4	21	10			2
CL	117	55	32	30	172	111		1	11
FC	24	12	5	7	46	19		1	3
UE	25	12	4	9	45	32	1	2	6
CW	27	15	10	2	48	20	1	1	3
SC	2	0	1	1	0	2			

Biggest Win: 7-0 v Standard Liege, 3-11-1993, v Slavia Prague, 23-10-2007
Heaviest Defeat: 2-5 v Spartak Moscow, 29-9-1982

ASTON VILLA

They are one of four different English teams to win the European Cup. Beat Bayern Munich 1-0 in Rotterdam in 1982 under Tony Barton who had replaced Ron Saunders who resigned at quarter-final stage. Graduated to the 2009 UEFA Cup after winning the Intertoto.

	P	W	D	L	F	A	W*	L*	Entries
	85	39	20	26	120	82			14 seasons
EC	15	9	3	3	24	10	1		2
UE	52	23	13	16	72	54	1	4	11
IT	16	6	4	6	21	17	1		3
SC	2	1	0	1	3	1			

Biggest Win: 5-0 v Guimaraes, 28-9-1983, v Valur, 16-9-1981
Heaviest Defeat: 1-4 v Antwerp, 17-9-1975

ATHLONE TOWN

The UEFA Cup visit of AC Milan to St Mel's Park on 22 October 1975 attracted a crowd of 5874 for the goalless draw.

	P	W	D	L	F	A	W*	L*	Entries
	8	1	4	3	11	19			3 seasons
EC	4	0	2	2	7	14	1	2	
UE	4	1	2	1	4	5			1

Biggest Win: 3-1 v Valerengen, 18-9-1975
Heaviest Defeat: 2-8 v Standard Liege, 28-9-1983

BALLYMENA UNITED

On 17 September 1980 they fought back from being a goal down to beat Vorwaerts of East Germany in the UEFA Cup.

	P	W	D	L	F	A	W*	L*	Entries
	12	1	1	10	3	36			6 seasons
UE	2	1	0	1	2	4			1
CW	8	0	0	8	1	25			4
IT	2	0	1	1	0	7			1

Biggest Win: 2-1 v Vorwaerts, 17-9-1980
Heaviest Defeat: 0-7 v OB, 26-6-2004

BANGOR

Their first goal in Europe was scored in the 25th minute by Richard McEvoy in the Cup-Winners' Cup against Apoel on 18 August 1993.

	P	W	D	L	F	A	W*	L*	Entries
	6	0	1	5	2	14			3 seasons
UE	2	0	0	2	0	6			1
CW	4	0	1	3	2	8			2

Heaviest Defeat: 0-7 v Halmstad, 10-8-2000

BANGOR CITY

Forced Napoli to a third, deciding match in their Cup-Winners' Cup tie in 1962–63.

	P	W	D	L	F	A	W*	L*	Entries
	23	2	2	19	11	54			9 seasons
UE	10	1	0	9	3	32			5
CW	9	1	2	6	5	12		1	3
IT	4	0	0	4	3	10			1

Biggest Win: 2-0 v Napoli, 5-9-1962
Heaviest Defeat: 1-6 v Midtjylland, 17-7-2008

BARRY TOWN

Beat Dinaburg in Latvia 2-1 in the 1996–97 UEFA Cup and drew 0-0 at home to reach the next round.

	P	W	D	L	F	A	W*	L*	Entries
	24	6	3	15	21	61			9 seasons
CL	14	4	1	9	11	38			6
UE	8	2	2	4	10	16	1		2
CW	2	0	0	2	0	7			1

Biggest Win: 3-1 v BVSC-Dreher, 20-8-1996, v Porto, 1-8-2001
Heaviest Defeat: 0-8 v Dynamo Kiev, 22-7-1998, v Porto, 25-7-2001

BIRMINGHAM CITY

Twice Fairs Cup runners-up they played in the first four series. Barcelona attracted a crowd of 40,524 to St Andrews on 29 March 1960 and in 1960–61 home and away wins registered against Internazionale, was a British club record which stood for over 40 years. Suffered defeat to Roma in the 1961 final.

	P	W	D	L	F	A	W*	L*	Entries
	25	14	6	5	51	38			4 seasons
FC	25	14	6	5	51	38			4

Biggest Win: 5-0 v Frem, 7-12-1960
Heaviest Defeat: 2-5 v Espanol, 15-11-1961

BLACKBURN ROVERS

In 2006–07 qualifying for the UEFA Cup was their third such achievement in five seasons and they topped their group. Mike Newell scored a hat-trick in a record nine minutes against Rosenborg in a 1995–96 Champions League match.

	P	W	D	L	F	A	W*	L*	Entries
	30	10	9	11	38	34			7 seasons
CL	6	1	1	4	5	8			1
UE	22	7	8	7	27	26	1		6
IT	2	2	0	0	6	0			1

Biggest Win: 4-0 v Vetra, 28-7-2007
Heaviest Defeat: 0-3 v Spartak Moscow, 22-11-1995

BOHEMIANS

Home and away wins were first successes against Esbjerg (Denmark) in 1976–77 Cup-Winners' Cup.

	P	W	D	L	F	A	W*	L*	Entries
	56	12	12	32	46	98			20 seasons
EC	6	1	2	3	4	13	1		2
CL	8	2	1	5	7	10			2
UE	24	3	7	14	14	42	1	1	11
CW	8	2	2	4	6	13			3
IT	10	4	0	6	15	20			1

Biggest Win: 3-0 v Levadia, 11-7-2001, v BATE Borisov, 23-7-2003
Heaviest Defeat: 0-6 v Dynamo Dresden, 1-11-1978

BOLTON WANDERERS

Drew a UEFA Cup group stage fixture 2-2 against Bayern Munich in 2007–08. They were the first team from a British club to defeat Partizan in Belgrade.

	P	W	D	L	F	A	W*	L*	Entries
	18	6	10	2	18	14			2 seasons
UE	18	6	10	2	18	14			2

Biggest Win: 2-1 v Lokomotiv Plovdiv, 15-9-2005, v Lokomotiv Plovdiv, 29-9-2005
Heaviest Defeat: 1-2 v Marseille. 23-2-2006

BOROUGH UNITED

Gutsy Welsh non-league team attracted 17,613 against Sliema Wanderers at Wrexham and won the Cup-Winners' Cup tie!

	P	W	D	L	F	A	W*	L*	Entries
	4	1	1	2	2	4			1 season
CW	4	1	1	2	2	4			1

Biggest Win: 2-0 v Sliema Wanderers, 3-10-1963
Heaviest Defeat: 0-3 v Slovan Bratislava, 15-12-1963

BRADFORD CITY

Confidently knocked out Atlantas and RKC Wallwijk before losing to Zenit.

	P	W	D	L	F	A	W*	L*	Entries
	6	4	0	2	10	6			1 season
IT	6	4	0	2	10	6			1

Biggest Win: 4-1 v Atlantas, 9-7-2000
Heaviest Defeat: 0-3 v Zenit, 2-8-2000

BRAY WANDERERS

on 22 August 1990 Martin Nugent scored in the 1-1 draw against Trabzonspor in the Cup-Winners' Cup match played at Tolka Park, Dublin.

	P	W	D	L	F	A	W*	L*	Entries
	4	0	1	3	1	11			2 seasons
UE	2	0	0	2	0	8			1
CW	2	0	1	1	1	3			1

Heaviest Defeat: 0-4 Grasshoppers. 12-8-1999, v Grasshoppers, 26-8-1999

BURNLEY

In reaching the quarter-final stage of the Fairs Cup in 1966–67, they accounted for Stuttgart, Lausanne and Napoli.

	P	W	D	L	F	A	W*	L*	Entries
	12	6	3	3	24	13			2 seasons
EC	4	2	0	2	8	8			1
FC	8	4	3	1	16	5			1

Biggest Win: 5-0 v Lausanne, 25-10-1966
Heaviest Defeat: 1-4 v Hamburg, 15-3-1961

CAERSWS

Their Intertoto tie against the Bulgarians gave them a home draw.

	P	W	D	L	F	A	W*	L*	Entries
	2	0	1	1	1	3			1 season
IT	2	0	1	1	1	3			1

Heaviest Defeat: 0-2 v Marek, 22-6-2002

CARDIFF CITY

On 10 March 1971 Real Madrid attracted a crowd of 47,500 to Ninian Park and were rewarded with the only goal of the game from Brian Clark in the 32nd minute of this Cup-Winners' Cup quarter-final.

	P	W	D	L	F	A	W*	L*	Entries
	49	16	14	19	67	61			14 seasons
CW	49	16	14	19	67	61	1	1	14

Biggest Win: 8-0 v Pezoporikos, 16-9-1970
Heaviest Defeat: 2-5 v Standard Liege, 15-9-1993

CARMARTHEN TOWN
Victory over the League of Ireland team came after trailing 2-0 in the away leg of the tie.

	P	W	D	L	F	A	W*	L*	Entries
	10	1	1	8	9	32			4 seasons
UE	6	1	0	5	8	21			2
IT	4	0	1	3	1	11			2

Biggest Win: 5-1 v Longford T, 28-7-2005
Heaviest Defeat: 0-8 v Brann, 19-7-2007

CARRICK RANGERS
It was on 15 September 1976 when two goals from Gary Prenter in the last five minutes turned the game against Aris (Luxembourg) in a Cup-Winners' Cup tie played at Seaview, Belfast into the 3-1 win.

	P	W	D	L	F	A	W*	L*	Entries
	4	1	0	3	7	12			1 season
CW	4	1	0	3	7	12			1

Biggest Win: 3-1 v Aris, 15-9-1976
Heaviest Defeat: 2-5 v Southampton, 20-10-1976

CELTIC
The "Lisbon Lions" were the first British team to win the European Cup in 1966–67 defeating Internazionale of Milan 2-1 in Lisbon. Captained by Billy McNeill all the Scottish players concerned in the final were born within 30 miles of Celtic Park. Three years later when they were finalists again their team had seven survivors and the side was beaten in extra time by Feyenoord. They took Porto to extra time in the UEFA Cup final in 2003.

	P	W	D	L	F	A	W*	L*	Entries
	247	119	44	84	404	257			44 seasons
EC	78	42	15	21	143	73	1	1	15
CL	56	22	9	25	64	70	1	1	9
FC	6	1	3	2	9	10			2
UE	69	33	13	23	113	67	1	2	14
CW	38	21	4	13	75	37		2	8

Biggest Win: 9-0 v KPV, 16-9-1970
Heaviest Defeat: 0-5 v Artmedia, 27-7-2005

CHELSEA
Deprived of entry into the initial European Cup in 1955–56 by the Football League, by the end of the 2007–08 season, despite finishing runners-up to Manchester United, they had become the highest rated club in UEFA's five-year coefficient system of seeding. In 1970–71 the Cup-Winners' Cup was annexed in a replay two days after drawing with Real Madrid. Peter Osgood, who had five goals when Jeunesse Hautcharage was well beaten the following season, scored the winning goal against the Spaniards. The 1998 final saw substitute Gianfranco Zola hit the only goal 17 seconds after appearing against Stuttgart. Gave Barcelona their most difficult Champions League tie in the 2009 semi-final.

	P	W	D	L	F	A	W*	L*	Entries
	155	81	44	30	259	133			18 seasons
CL	87	43	28	16	133	71		3	7
FC	20	10	5	5	33	24		1	3
UE	8	4	1	3	11	10			3
CW	39	23	10	6	81	28	1	1	5
SC	1	1	0	0	1	0			1

Biggest Win: 13-0 v Jeunesse Hautcharage, 29-9-1971
Heaviest Defeat: 0-5 v Barcelona, 25-5-1966

CLIFTONVILLE
On the 26 September 1979 attracted 3500 to Solitude for the visit of Nantes for Cup-Winners' Cup debut.

	P	W	D	L	F	A	W*	L*	Entries
	16	1	2	13	6	55			6 seasons
EC	2	0	0	2	1	13			1
UE	2	0	0	2	0	11			1
CW	2	0	0	2	0	8			1
IT	10	1	2	7	5	23			3

Biggest Win: 1-0 v Dinaburg, 1-7-2007
Heaviest Defeat: 0-8 v Kosice, 29-7-1998

COLERAINE
In consecutive seasons 1969–70 and 1970–71 in the Fairs Cup, Des Dickson scored a total of seven goals including one hat-trick.

	P	W	D	L	F	A	W*	L*	Entries
	36	4	6	26	40	110			15 seasons
EC	2	0	0	2	1	11			1
FC	8	2	1	5	15	23			2
UE	14	1	3	10	8	36			7
CW	8	0	1	7	7	34			4
IT	4	1	1	2	9	6			1

Biggest Win: 5-0 v St Julia, 22-6-2002
Heaviest Defeat: 0-7 v Feyenoord, 18-9-1974

CONWY UNITED
They held Charleroi (Belgium) to a goalless draw at home in the 1996 Intertoto.

	P	W	D	L	F	A	W*	L*	Entries
	4	0	1	3	1	9			1 season
IT	4	0	1	3	1	9			1

Heaviest Defeat: 0-4 v Silkeborg, 20-7-1996

CORK CELTIC
Reached second round of the European Cup beating Cypriot team Omonia in 1974–75.

	P	W	D	L	F	A	W*	L*	Entries
	4	0	1	3	2	10			3 seasons
EC	2	0	0	2	1	7			1
UE	0	0	0	0	0	0			1
CW	2	0	1	1	1	3			1

Heaviest Defeat: 0-5 v Ararat Erevan, 6-11-1974

CORK CITY
Three down in 27 minutes away to Cwmbran in the 1993–94 Champions League lost 3-2, but won tie by winning 2-1 at home.

	P	W	D	L	F	A	W*	L*	Entries
	38	6	9	23	21	55			12 seasons
CL	8	2	1	5	7	12	1		2
UE	16	2	4	10	8	26	1		5
CW	4	1	0	3	2	9			2
IT	16	4	6	6	11	13			4

Biggest Win: 3-1 v Malmö FF, 19-6-2004
Heaviest Defeat: 0-5 v Torpedo Moscow, 13-9-1989

CORK HIBERNIANS
John Lawson scored three of the six goals against the Cypriot team Pezoporikos in the 1972–73 Cup-Winners' Cup.

	P	W	D	L	F	A	W*	L*	Entries
	10	2	1	7	9	21			4 seasons
EC	2	0	0	2	1	7			1
FC	2	0	0	2	1	6			1
CW	6	2	1	3	7	8			2

Biggest Win: 4-1 v Pezoporikos, 13-9-1972
Heaviest Defeat: 0-5 v Moenchengladbach, 15-9-1971

COVENTRY CITY
John O'Rourke scored three goals against Trakia in the 1970–71 Fairs Cup.

	P	W	D	L	F	A	W*	L*	Entries
	4	3	0	1	9	8			1 season
FC	4	3	0	1	9	8			1

Biggest Win: 4-1 v Trakia Plovdiv, 16-9-1970
Heaviest Defeat: 1-6 v Bayern Munich, 20-10-1970

CRUSADERS
Chris Morgan, an 82nd minute substitute against Zhalgiris at Solitude, scored a minute later then hit the winner in the 90th on 24 July 1996 in UEFA Cup!

	P	W	D	L	F	A	W*	L*	Entries
	18	1	3	14	10	58			9 seasons
EC	6	0	0	6	2	27			3
UE	6	1	1	4	3	13			3
CW	6	0	2	4	5	18			3

Biggest Win: 2-1 v Zalgiris, 24-7-1996
Heaviest Defeat: 0-11, v Dinamo Bucharest, 3-10-1973

CRYSTAL PALACE
Also provided Peter Berry and Geoff Truett for London XI in Fairs Cup.

	P	W	D	L	F	A	W*	L*	Entries
	2	0	0	2	0	4			1 season
IT	2	0	0	2	0	4			1

Heaviest Defeat: 0-2 v Samsunspor, 19-7-1998, v Samsunspor, 25-7-1998

CWMBRAN TOWN
Francis Ford scored both goals against Cork City.

	P	W	D	L	F	A	W*	L*	Entries
	12	1	0	11	6	39			6 seasons
CL	2	1	0	1	4	4	1	1	
UE	6	0	0	6	0	21			3
CW	2	0	0	2	2	12			1
IT	2	0	0	2	0	2			1

Biggest Win: 3-2 v Cork City, 18-8-1993
Heaviest Defeat: 0-7 v National Bucharest, 28-8-1997

DERBY COUNTY
Kevin Hector scored 16 European goals including five against Finn Harps in a 1976–77 UEFA Cup game. Semifinalists in 1973 European Cup losing to Juventus.

	P	W	D	L	F	A	W*	L*	Entries
	22	11	4	7	50	29			4 seasons
EC	12	6	2	4	18	12			2
UE	10	5	2	3	32	17	1		2

Biggest Win: 12-0 v Finn Harps, 15-9-1976
Heaviest Defeat: 1-5 v Real Madrid, 5-11-1975

DERRY CITY
The only team to have appeared for two countries.

	P	W	D	L	F	A	W*	L*	Entries
	27	5	5	17	21	53			11 seasons
EC	7	1	1	5	9	23			2
CL	2	0	0	2	0	3			2
UE	12	3	3	6	11	16			4
CW	6	1	1	4	1	11			3

Biggest Win: 5-1 v Lyn, 9-9-1965, v Gretna, 10-8-2006
Heaviest Defeat: 0-9 v Anderlecht, 23-11-1965

DISTILLERY
Held Benfica 3-3 on European Cup debut 1963 in front of 19,326 at Windsor Park.

	P	W	D	L	F	A	W*	L*	Entries
	8	0	1	7	7	23			3 seasons
EC	2	0	1	1	3	8			1
CW	2	0	0	2	1	7			1
IT	4	0	0	4	3	8			1

Heaviest Defeat: 0-5 v Benfica, 2-10-1963

DROGHEDA UNITED
Twice in the UEFA Cup and once in the Champions League they have succeeded in winning a tie.

	P	W	D	L	F	A	W*	L*	Entries
	14	5	4	5	16	27			4 seasons
CL	4	2	1	1	6	5			1
UE	10	3	3	4	10	22		1	3

Biggest Win: 3-0 v Libertas, 2-8-2007
Heaviest Defeat: 0-8 v Tottenham H, 28-9-1983

DRUMCONDRA
There was a Fairs Cup shaker for Bayern Munich beaten by a Billy Dixon goal in 1962–63.

	P	W	D	L	F	A	W*	L*	Entries
	12	3	0	9	11	44			5 seasons
EC	6	1	0	5	3	25			3
FC	6	2	0	4	8	19			2

Biggest Win: 4-1 v Odense XI, 3-10-1962
Heaviest Defeat: 0-8 v Atletico Madrid, 17-9-1958

DUNDALK
Tommy McConville scored 19 European goals. They were the first Irish club to progress three rounds in the European Cup.

	P	W	D	L	F	A	W*	L*	Entries
	40	6	7	27	24	99			16 seasons
EC	18	3	4	11	13	41			7
FC	6	1	1	4	4	25			2
UE	8	0	1	7	0	19			4
CW	8	2	1	5	7	14			3

Biggest Win: 4-0 v Fram, 30-9-1981
Heaviest Defeat: 0-10 v Liverpool, 16-9-1969

DUNDEE
Alan Gilzean had two hat-tricks in the 1962–63 European Cup campaign to the semi-final.

	P	W	D	L	F	A	W*	L*	Entries
	34	16	3	15	63	53			8 seasons
EC	8	5	0	3	20	14			1
FC	8	5	1	2	14	6			1
UE	14	6	0	8	24	24			4
CW	2	0	1	1	3	4			1
IT	2	0	1	1	2	5			1

Biggest Win: 8-1 v Cologne, 5-9-1962
Heaviest Defeat: 1-5 v AC Milan, 24-4-1963

DUNDEE UNITED
Had early success in the 1966–67 Fairs Cup beating Barcelona home and away. They reached the European Cup semi-final stage in 1984. Despite losing to IFK Gothenburg in th 1987 UEFA Cup final, won the FIFA Fair Play Award.

	P	W	D	L	F	A	W*	L*	Entries
	104	45	28	31	162	104			23 seasons
EC	8	5	1	2	14	5	1		1
FC	10	5	1	4	11	12			3
UE	76	32	23	21	128	77	1	3	16
CW	10	3	3	4	9	10			3

Biggest Win: 9-0 v Principat, 30-7-1997
Heaviest Defeat: 0-4 v Antwerp, 17-10-1989, v Vitesse, 7-11-1990

DUNFERMLINE ATHLETIC

Fairs Cup 1962–63 lost 4-0 in Valencia, won 6-2 at home to force replay on neutral territory. They reached the semi-final of the Cup-Winners' Cup 1968–69.

	P	W	D	L	F	A	W*	L*	Entries
	46	23	7	16	87	51			9 seasons
FC	28	16	3	9	49	31			5
UE	4	0	2	2	4	6	2		2
CW	14	7	2	5	34	14			2

Biggest Win: 10-1 v Apoel, 18-9-1968
Heaviest Defeat: 0-4 v Valencia, 12-12-1962

DUNGANNON SWIFTS

Beat Suduva 1-0 with a Mark McAllister goal in 17 minutes in front of 580.

	P	W	D	L	F	A	W*	L*	Entries
	4	1	1	2	2	8			2 season
UE	2	1	0	1	1	4			1
IT	2	0	1	1	1	4			1

Biggest Win: 1-0 v Suduva, 19-7-2007
Heaviest Defeat: 0-4 v Suduva, 2-8-2007

EBBW VALE

Sadly folded after playing Kongsvinger in 1998 Intertoto.

	P	W	D	L	F	A	W*	L*	Entries
	6	0	1	5	3	21			2 seasons
IT	6	0	1	5	3	21			2

Heaviest Defeat: 1-6 v Silkeborg, 19-7-1997, v
Kongsvinger, 20-6-1998

EVERTON

First penalty shoot-out winners in a European Cup match when they beat Moenchengladbach in 1970–71. Beat Rapid Vienna 3-1 in the 1985 Cup-Winners' Cup final after a similar score in the semi-final against Bayern Munich, arguably their finest performance after trailing at half-time by the only goal conceded then in the campaign. Andy Gray, Kevin Sheedy and Trevor Steven were the scorers. In 2007–08 there was a club record run of six successive wins in the UEFA Cup.

	P	W	D	L	F	A	W*	L*	Entries
	61	32	14	15	101	57			14 seasons
EC	8	2	5	1	12	6	1	1	2
CL	2	0	0	2	2	4			1
FC	12	7	2	3	22	15			3
UE	22	12	3	7	40	23		2	6
CW	17	11	4	2	25	9			3

Biggest Win: 6-1 v Brann, 21-2-2008
Heaviest Defeat: 1-5 v Dinamo Bucharest, 15-9-2005

FINN HARPS

In 1974–75 managed to hold Turkish Cup winners Bursaspor to a goalless draw at home.

	P	W	D	L	F	A	W*	L*	Entries
	8	0	1	7	5	37			4 seasons
UE	6	0	0	6	3	33			3
CW	2	0	1	1	2	4			1

Heaviest Defeat: 0-12 v Derby Co, 15-9-1976

FULHAM

More than creditable performance in 2002 Intertoto Cup qualifying for UEFA Cup place and beating Hajduk Split and Dinamo Zagreb to reach its third stage.

	P	W	D	L	F	A	W*	L*	Entries
	14	7	6	1	20	10			1 season
UE	6	3	2	1	9	5			1
IT	8	4	4	0	11	5	1		1

Biggest Win: 3-0 v Dinamo Zagreb, 31-10-2002
Heaviest Defeat: 1-2 v Hertha Berlin, 26-11-2002

GALWAY UNITED

Paul Murphy scored two of their four goals, one as a second half sub against Lyngby.

	P	W	D	L	F	A	W*	L*	Entries
	6	0	0	6	4	19			3 seasons
UE	2	0	0	2	2	8			1
CW	4	0	0	4	2	11			2

Heaviest Defeat: 1-5 v Groningen, 16-9-1986

GLENAVON

13th game in Europe lucky with an 80th minute Stevie Conville goal beating Ilves at Lurgan.

	P	W	D	L	F	A	W*	L*	Entries
	26	2	7	17	15	56			13 seasons
EC	2	0	1	1	0	3			2
UE	12	1	2	9	3	24			5
CW	10	1	3	6	11	25		2	5
IT	2	0	1	1	1	4			1

Biggest Win: 3-2 v Ilves, 17-9-1991
Heaviest Defeat: 2-6 v PSV Eindhoven, 14-9-1977

GLENTORAN

First win in Europe was 1-0 against Arsenal in a 1969–70 Fairs Cup game – scorer Ian Henderson!

	P	W	D	L	F	A	W*	L*	Entries
	86	9	21	56	61	191			38 seasons
EC	20	3	6	11	18	37	1		8
CL	6	0	1	5	2	12			3
FC	8	1	1	6	7	22			4
UE	30	2	6	22	16	74			14
CW	22	3	7	12	18	46	1		9

Biggest Win: 4-0 v Progres, 30-9-1981
Heaviest Defeat: 0-8 v Ajax, 1-10-1975, v Sparta Prague, 22-8-1996

GRETNA

First team from the third rated Scottish division to qualify for Europe. They folded 2008.

	P	W	D	L	F	A	W*	L*	Entries
	2	0	1	1	3	7			1 season
UE	2	0	1	1	3	7			1

Heaviest Defeat: 1-5 v Derry City, 10-8-2006

HAVERFORDWEST COUNTY

Played their home game at Ninian Park with a 612 attendance.

	P	W	D	L	F	A	W*	L*	Entries
	2	0	0	2	1	4			1 season
UE	2	0	0	2	1	4			1

Heaviest Defeat: 1-3 v FH, 29-7-2004

HEART OF MIDLOTHIAN

In 1988–89 they were narrowly beaten by Bayern Munich in the UEFA Cup quarter-finals. For more recent ventures into Europe, Murrayfield has been used as a home ground.

	P	W	D	L	F	A	W*	L*	Entries
	68	26	14	28	90	94			18 seasons
EC	4	1	0	3	4	11			2
CL	4	1	1	2	4	5			1
FC	12	4	4	4	20	20			3
UE	38	17	6	15	46	44		2	10
CW	10	3	3	4	16	14	1	3	

Biggest Win: 5-0 v Lantana, 27-8-1998
Heaviest Defeat: 1-5 v Standard Liege, 3-9-1958

HIBERNIAN

The first Scottish club in Europe despite finishing fifth previous season and reached semi-final. They pushed Roma to a third game in the 1960–61 Fairs Cup semi-final game after beating Barcelona.

	P	W	D	L	F	A	W*	L*	Entries
	82	38	16	28	142	117			19 seasons
EC	6	3	1	2	9	5			1
FC	36	18	5	13	66	60	1	7	
UE	28	11	9	8	38	36	4	9	
CW	6	3	1	2	19	10			1
IT	8	3	1	4	11	8	1	2	

Biggest Win: 9-1 v Rosenborg, 2-10-1974
Heaviest Defeat: 0-6 v Roma, 27-5-1961

HOME FARM

As the first amateur club to win the FAI Cup they competed in the Cup-Winners' Cup and held Lens at home with a Michael Brophy goal.

	P	W	D	L	F	A	W*	L*	Entries
	2	0	1	1	1	7			1 season
CW	2	0	1	1	1	7			1

Heaviest Defeat: 0-6 v Lens, 1-10-1975

INTER CABLETEL CARDIFF

Attracted over 6000 to Ninian Park for the 1997–98 UEFA Cup tie with Celtic.

	P	W	D	L	F	A	W*	L*	Entries
	6	1	0	5	1	18			3 seasons
UE	6	1	0	5	1	18			3

Biggest Win: 1-0 v HIT Gorica, 26-8-1999
Heaviest Defeat: 0-6 v GKS Katowice, 23-8-1994

IPSWICH TOWN

Almost threw away their three goal UEFA Cup final first leg lead over AZ and managed an away goal in Holland to win it. The only English team to have had three different players score as many as four times in European cup matches – Ray Crawford (five goals), Trevor Whymark (twice) and John Wark.

	P	W	D	L	F	A	W*	L*	Entries
	62	36	12	14	120	61			12 seasons
EC	4	3	0	1	16	5			1
UE	52	30	10	12	98	53	5	10	
CW	6	3	2	1	6	3	1	1	

Biggest Win: 10-0 v Floriana, 25-9-1962
Heaviest Defeat: 0-4 v Club Brugge, 5-11-1975

KILMARNOCK

Sensational opening to Fairs Cup 1964–65. Lost 3-0 away to Eintracht Frankfurt, but won 5-1 at home. Semi-finalists 1966–67.

	P	W	D	L	F	A	W*	L*	Entries
	40	14	9	17	50	59			9 seasons
EC	4	1	2	1	4	7			1
FC	20	8	3	9	34	32			4
UE	12	4	2	6	7	14			3
CW	4	1	2	1	5	6			1

Biggest Win: 7-2 v Antwerp, 2-11-1966
Heaviest Defeat: 1-5 v Real Madrid, 1-12-1965

LEEDS UNITED

Losing Fairs Cup finalists in 1967 against Dinamo Zagreb, they beat Ferencvaros a year later over two legs to become the first English winners of the trophy. They won the 13th and last Fairs Cup in 1971 against Juventus. Disallowed effort by Peter Lorimer (30 European goals) in the 1975 final against Bayern Munich led to disturbances by fans and a two-year ban. They had also lost to AC Milan in the 1973 Cup-Winners' Cup final.

	P	W	D	L	F	A	W*	L*	Entries
	148	75	36	37	248	133			18 seasons
EC	17	12	1	4	42	11			3
CL	23	10	5	8	35	31			1
FC	53	28	17	8	92	40	4		5
UE	46	20	10	16	66	48	3		8
CW	9	5	3	1	13	3			1

Biggest Win: 10-0 v Lyn, 17-9-1969
Heaviest Defeat: 3-5 v PSV Eindhoven, 17-10-1995

LEICESTER CITY

Unlucky to be twice paired against Atletico Madrid in two different competitions 30 years apart.

	P	W	D	L	F	A	W*	L*	Entries
	8	2	2	4	11	13			3 seasons
UE	4	0	1	3	3	8			2
CW	4	2	1	1	8	5			1

Biggest Win: 4-1 v Glenavon, 13-9-1961
Heaviest Defeat: 1-3 v Red Star Belgrade, 28-9-2000

LIMERICK UNITED

In 1980–81 Des Kennedy scored in home and away legs against Real Madrid – the only player to achieve that feat during the European Cup that season.

	P	W	D	L	F	A	W*	L*	Entries
	12	0	2	10	7	31			6 seasons
EC	4	0	0	4	4	16			2
UE	2	0	1	1	1	4			1
CW	6	0	1	5	2	11			3

Heaviest Defeat: 0-5 v Young Boys, 31-8-1960

LINFIELD

Quarter-finalists 1967 European Cup losing to CSKA Sofia.

	P	W	D	L	F	A	W*	L*	Entries
	83	12	23	48	81	165			35 seasons
EC	39	4	12	23	43	83	1	1	17
CL	16	2	5	9	11	21	1	1	7
FC	4	1	0	3	3	11			2
UE	18	3	6	9	18	39	1	1	6
CW	6	2	0	4	6	11	1	1	3

Biggest Win: 6-1 v Aris, 14-9-1966
Heaviest Defeat: 0-8 v Red Star Belgrade, 17-9-1969 v PSV Eindhoven, 1-10-1975

LIVERPOOL

Having suffered an extra-time defeat against Borussia Dortmund in the 1966 Cup-Winners' Cup final, eleven years later Bob Paisley became the first manager to win the UEFA Cup and European Cup in successive seasons, the team having beaten Club Brugge the previous year. Their first success in the UEFA Cup had come in 1973 when Moenchengladbach had been defeated. Club Brugge were also victims in the 1978 European Cup victory at Wembley. Then in 1981 the scalp of Real Madrid was added in Paris. Penalties were needed to overcome Roma on their own ground in 1984 before the Heysel Stadium tragedy the following year, defeat against Juventus with a penalty awarded for an infringement outside the area and a ban on English clubs after the rioting which left 39 dead and hundreds injured. A 117th minute sudden death own goal defeated Alaves – who were four times behind – in the 2001 UEFA Cup final. In 2005 they were the first English team involved in Champions League final shoot-out trailing three down to AC Milan at half-time in Istanbul – biggest deficit at the interval – and won penalty shoot-out, after extra time, with goalkeeper Jerzy Dudek saving the crucial spot kick. It was their fifth European Cup win – but failed to repeat their triumph against the same opponents in 2007. UEFA awarded them a Badge of Honour for the five successes. Have succeeded in achieving ten European final appearances and were the first English Super Cup winners. They achieved a record Champions League win in the competition proper, 8-0 v Besiktas in 2007–08. Steven Gerrard with 32 goals has been their top European goalscorer.

	P	W	D	L	F	A	W*	L*	Entries
	300	169	67	64	547	246			36 seasons
EC	77	48	13	16	159	64	2		12
CL	92	49	25	18	153	73	3		7
FC	22	12	4	6	46	15		2	4
UE	73	40	19	14	116	55	4		9
CW	29	16	5	8	57	29			5
SC	7	4	1	2	16	10	1	5	

Biggest Win: 11-0 v Stromsgodset, 17-9-1974
Heaviest Defeat: 1-5 v Ajax, 7-12-1966

LIVINGSTON

In 2002–03 gave a gutsy UEFA Cup display against Sturm Graz, scoring six in the tie against the Austrian team.

	P	W	D	L	F	A	W*	L*	Entries
	4	1	2	1	7	9			1 season
UE	4	1	2	1	7	9	1		1

Biggest Win: 4-3 v Sturm Graz, 3-10-2002
Heaviest Defeat: 2-5 v Sturm Graz, 19-9-2002

LLANELLI

In the 2007 Intertoto against Vetra, Rhys Griffiths' hat-trick almost pulled off a dramatic second leg success in a game played at Carmarthen.

	P	W	D	L	F	A	W*	L*	Entries
	8	3	1	4	10	17			3 seasons
CL	2	1	0	1	1	4			1
UE	4	1	1	2	3	7			1
IT	2	1	0	1	6	6	1	1	

Biggest Win: 5-3 v Vetra, 1-7-2007
Heaviest Defeat: 1-5 v Odense, 24-8-2006

LONDON XI

The 11 London clubs provided various players and managed by Chelsea chairman Joe Mears! Wembley, White Hart Lane, Highbury and Stamford Bridge were home grounds.

	P	W	D	L	F	A	W*	L*	Entries
	8	4	1	3	14	13			1 season
FC	8	4	1	3	14	13			1

Biggest Win: 5-0 v Basle XI, 4-6-1955
Heaviest Defeat: 0-6 v Barcelona, 1-5-1958

LONGFORD TOWN

An outstanding performance was holding the Bulgarian club Litex to a 1-1 draw at home.

	P	W	D	L	F	A	W*	L*	Entries
	6	1	1	4	6	12			3 seasons
UE	6	1	1	4	6	12			3

Biggest Win: 2-0 v Carmarthen T, 14-7-2005
Heaviest Defeat: 1-5 v Carmarthen T, 28-7-2005

MANCHESTER CITY

Defeated Gornik Zabrze (Poland) 2-1 in Vienna for the 1970 Cup-Winners' Cup final with goals from Neil Young and a Franny Lee penalty. They were semi-finalists a year later. Had a roller-coaster ride in the 2009 UEFA Cup to the quarter-finals.

	P	W	D	L	F	A	W*	L*	Entries
	56	29	13	14	90	54			9 seasons
EC	2	0	1	1	1	2			1
UE	36	18	10	8	57	39	2	2	6
CW	18	11	2	5	32	13	1		2

Biggest Win: 5-0 v TNS, 14-8-2003, v Lierse, 26-11-1969
Heaviest Defeat: 1-3 v Moenchengladbach, 20-3-1979, Santander, 18-12-2008, Hamburg, 09-4-2009

MANCHESTER UNITED

In the European Cup final of 1968 at Wembley it was 1-1 heading into extra time when Alex Stepney made a crucial save to send the match into overtime. George Best's 25 yard solo, Brian Kidd on his 19th birthday and Bobby Charlton wrapping it up with his second goal gave them and Sir Matt Busby the first such trophy ten years after the Munich air disaster. In 1999 they had been trailing to a sixth minute free-kick against Bayern Munich, but tirelessly applied themselves until in the most dramatic of finishes, Teddy Sheringham equalised in the 91st minute of injury time and then Ole Gunnar Solskjaer amazingly produced the winner two minutes later! The third such

trophy and the second Champions League success came 40 years after the first European Cup success in Moscow against Chelsea 6-5 on penalties following a 1-1 draw. In 1991 they edged Barcelona 2-1 in the Cup-Winners' Cup final, too. Barcelona gained revenge in the 2009 Champions League final. Ruud Van Nistelrooy scored a record 12 goals in the Champions League during 2002–03.

	P	W	D	L	F	A	W*	L*	Entries
	271	143	73	55	495	259			33 seasons
EC	41	26	7	8	100	45			6
CL	165	88	44	33	290	150	1	3	15
FC	11	6	3	2	29	10			1
UE	20	6	10	4	19	16		4	6
CW	31	16	9	6	55	35	1		5
SC	3	1	0	2	2	3			

Biggest Win: 10-0 v Anderlecht, 26-9-1956
Heaviest Defeat: 0-5 v Sporting Club, 18-3-1964

MERTHYR TYDFIL

Kevin Rogers and Ceri Williams got them off to a good start against Atalanta in the Cup-Winners' Cup 1987–88.

	P	W	D	L	F	A	W*	L*	Entries
	2	1	0	1	2	3			1 season
CW	2	1	0	1	2	3			1

Biggest Win: 2-1 v Atalanta, 16-9-1987
Heaviest Defeat: 0-2 v Atalanta, 30-9-1987

MIDDLESBROUGH

Topped their Group and reached the UEFA Cup final in 2005–06, beaten by Sevilla, after trailing in the first away legs in the quarter and semi-final. Received praise from UEFA for their conduct throughout the season.

	P	W	D	L	F	A	W*	L*	Entries
	25	13	4	8	36	24			2 seasons
UE	25	13	4	8	36	24	2		2

Biggest Win: 4-1 v Basle, 6-4-2006
Heaviest Defeat: 0-4 v Sevilla, 10-5-2006

MILLWALL

Dennis Wise scored both goals against Ferencvaros.

	P	W	D	L	F	A	W*	L*	Entries
	2	0	1	1	2	4			1 season
UE	2	0	1	1	2	4			1

Heaviest Defeat: 1-3 v Ferencvaros, 30-9-2004

MORTON

Norwegian Borge Thorup scored their first Fairs Cup goal.

	P	W	D	L	F	A	W*	L*	Entries
	2	0	0	2	3	9			1 season
FC	2	0	0	2	3	9			1

Heaviest Defeat: 0-5 v Chelsea, 18-9-1968

MOTHERWELL

Lucky mascot Steve Kirk hit five European goals in the 1990s in three games – all won.

	P	W	D	L	F	A	W*	L*	Entries
	10	4	0	6	13	13			4 seasons
UE	8	3	0	5	10	10	1	3	
CW	2	1	0	1	3	3	1	1	

Biggest Win: 4-1 v HB Torshavn, 23-8-1994
Heaviest Defeat: 1-3 v MyPa, 8-8-1995

NEWCASTLE UNITED

Memorable beginning to European competition winning 1968–69 Fairs Cup beating Ujpest Dozsa home and away in final having beaten Rangers in the semi-final. Later Alan Shearer scored 30 European goals.

	P	W	D	L	F	A	W*	L*	Entries
	120	69	22	29	208	119			15 seasons
CL	24	11	3	10	33	33		1	3
FC	24	13	6	5	37	21	2	2	3
UE	58	37	10	11	110	50		2	7
CW	2	1	0	1	2	2		1	1
IT	12	7	3	2	26	13		1	3

Biggest Win: 5-0 v Antwerp, 13-9-1994, v NAC Breda, 24-9-2003
Heaviest Defeat: 1-4 v Sporting Club, 14-4-2005, v Internazionale, 27-11-2002

NEWPORT COUNTY
Reached Cup-Winners' Cup quarter-final against Carl Zeiss Jena drawing 2-2 at home with Tommy Tynan scoring twice.

	P	W	D	L	F	A	W*	L*	Entries
	6	2	3	1	12	3			1 season
CW	6	2	3	1	12	3			1

Biggest Win: 6-0 v Haugar, 4-11-1980
Heaviest Defeat: 0-1 v Carl Zeiss Jena, 18-3-1981

NEWRY TOWN
They did well to progress one round in the 1999 Intertoto. Changed name to Newry City in 2004.

	P	W	D	L	F	A	W*	L*	Entries
	4	2	0	2	3	3			1 season
IT	4	2	0	2	3	3			1

Biggest Win: 2-0 v Hrvatski, 26-6-1999
Heaviest Defeat: 0-2 v Duisburg, 4-7-1999

NEWTOWN
Their Latham Park ground was up to UEFA standard for the 1996–97 UEFA Cup against Skonto. Romilly Brown was their 90th minute consolation goalscorer watched by 2012.

	P	W	D	L	F	A	W*	L*	Entries
	4	0	1	3	1	14			2 seasons
UE	4	0	1	3	1	14			2

Heaviest Defeat: 0-7 v Wisla Krakow, 29-7-1998

NORWICH CITY
Scored twice in 30 minutes to beat Bayern Munich 2-1 in the away leg of a 1993–94 UEFA Cup game, the only English team to win there in Europe.

	P	W	D	L	F	A	W*	L*	Entries
	6	2	2	2	6	4			1 season
UE	6	2	2	2	6	4			1

Biggest Win: 3-0 v Vitesse, 15-9-1993
Heaviest Defeat: 0-1 v Internazionale, 24-11-1993, v Internazionale, 8-12-1993

NOTTINGHAM FOREST
Two European Cup trophies both 1-0, lost only two of 18 matches. In 1979 Martin O'Neill was injured and Trevor Francis scored in his first European outing against Malmo. The next year John Robertson was the marksman and ensured the club had more foreign than domestic league titles! UEFA Cup semi-finalists 1984 losing to Anderlecht – later found guilty of bribing referee!

	P	W	D	L	F	A	W*	L*	Entries
	50	27	10	13	62	42			8 seasons
EC	20	12	4	4	32	14			3
FC	6	3	0	3	8	9		1	2
UE	20	10	5	5	18	16	1		3
SC	4	2	1	1	4	3		1	

Biggest Win: 5-1 v AEK Athens, 1-11-1978
Heaviest Defeat: 1-5 v Valencia, 4-10-1961, v Bayern Munich, 19-3-1996

OMAGH TOWN
Two stints in the Intertoto 1998 and 2003, but sadly the club folded two years later.

	P	W	D	L	F	A	W*	L*	Entries
	4	0	1	3	3	11			2 seasons
IT	4	0	1	3	3	11			2

Heaviest Defeat: 1-7 v Shakhtyor, 28-6-2003

PARTICK THISTLE
Made a useful Fairs Cup start in 1963–64 and seven goals in the tie with Glentoran.

	P	W	D	L	F	A	W*	L*	Entries
	10	4	1	5	16	17			3 seasons
FC	4	3	0	1	10	7			1
UE	2	0	0	2	0	4			1
IT	4	1	1	2	6	6			1

Biggest Win: 4-1 v Glentoran, 16-9-1963
Heaviest Defeat: 0-4 v Spartak Brno, 27-11-1963

PORTADOWN
They reached the second round of the 1974–75 UEFA Cup beating Valur attracting 6000 for the home leg.

	P	W	D	L	F	A	W*	L*	Entries
	28	2	5	21	15	78			13 seasons
EC	4	0	0	4	1	21			2
CL	2	0	1	1	2	3			1
UE	20	1	4	15	8	47			9
CW	2	1	0	1	4	7			1

Biggest Win: 3-2 v OFK Belgrade, 22-11-1962
Heaviest Defeat: 1-8 v Porto, 3-10-1990

PORTSMOUTH
First goal in Europe was scored by Lassana Diarra subsequently transferred to Real Madrid for a record fee.

	P	W	D	L	F	A	W*	L*	Entries
	6	2	2	2	11	10			1 season
UE	6	2	2	2	11	10			1

Biggest Win: 3-0 v Heerenveen, 17-12-2008
Heaviest Defeat: 0-3 v Braga, 23-10-2008

QUEEN OF THE SOUTH
Home leg played at Airdrie and levelled the tie away until the 85th minute!

	P	W	D	L	F	A	W*	L*	Entries
	2	0	0	2	2	4			1 season
UE	2	0	0	2	2	4		1	1

Heaviest Defeat: 1-2 v Nordsjaelland, 14-8-2008, Nordsjaelland, 26-8-2008

QUEENS PARK RANGERS
Stan Bowles scored 11 goals in European matches including two hat-tricks.

	P	W	D	L	F	A	W*	L*	Entries
	12	8	1	3	39	18			2 seasons
UE	12	8	1	3	39	18	1	1	2

Biggest Win: 7-0 v Brann, 29-9-1976
Heaviest Defeat: 0-4 v Partizan Belgrade, 7-11-1984

RAITH ROVERS
1995–96 UEFA Cup victims were GI Gotu and IA Akranes.

	P	W	D	L	F	A	W*	L*	Entries
	6	2	1	3	10	8			1 season
UE	6	2	1	3	10	8			1

Biggest Win: 4-0 v GI Gotu, 8-8-1995
Heaviest Defeat: 0-2 v Bayern Munich, 17-10-1995

RANGERS

Forced to play 13 tiring competitive fixtures in six weeks cost them in the 2008 UEFA Cup final against Zenit in their 48th and record British season in Europe. They were the first British club to reach a European final in 1961 Cup-Winners' Cup, six years later beaten in extra time by Bayern Munich, too. But third time lucky in 1972 when three up in 49 minutes, Willie Waddell's ten men held on to edge Moscow Dynamo in Barcelona. Ally McCoist with 21 goals has been their leading scorer in European matches.

	P	W	D	L	F	A	W*	L*	Entries
	291	127	68	96	448	352			48 seasons
EC	57	26	8	23	94	92	2		14
CL	90	35	26	29	130	105	1		13
FC	18	8	4	6	27	17			3
UE	70	31	19	20	94	70	4	3	14
CW	54	27	11	16	100	62	2	1	10
SC	2	0	0	2	3	6			

Biggest Win: 10-0 v Valletta, 28-9-1983
Heaviest Defeat: 0-6 v Real Madrid, 9-10-1963

RHYL

Edged out Atlantas (Lithuania) on away goals.

	P	W	D	L	F	A	W*	L*	Entries
	12	2	1	9	13	28			4 seasons
CL	2	0	0	2	1	7			1
UE	8	2	1	5	9	12	1	1	3
IT	2	0	0	2	3	9			

Biggest Win: 3-1 v Haka, 19-7-2007
Heaviest Defeat: 0-4 v Skonto, 14-7-2004

SHAMROCK ROVERS

The first Irish team to play in Europe. On 9 November 1966 they had an attendance of 15,462 at Dalymount Park to see a Billy Dixon goal in 61 minutes hold Bayern Munich.

	P	W	D	L	F	A	W*	L*	Entries
	48	10	8	30	45	89			20 seasons
EC	14	0	4	10	7	28	1		7
FC	4	0	2	2	4	6			2
UE	8	2	0	6	8	18			3
CW	16	5	2	9	19	27			6
IT	6	3	0	3	7	10			2

Biggest Win: 4-0 v Fram, 30-9-1982
Heaviest Defeat: 0-7 v Gornik Zabrze, 9-8-1994

SHEFFIELD WEDNESDAY

Gerry Young hit three goals against Roma in the Fairs Cup, so did Bronco Layne v DOS Utrecht.

	P	W	D	L	F	A	W*	L*	Entries
	18	9	2	7	45	30			4 seasons
FC	10	5	0	5	25	18			2
UE	4	2	1	1	13	7			1
IT	4	2	1	1	7	5			1

Biggest Win: 8-1 v Spora, 16-9-1992
Heaviest Defeat: 2-4 v Lyon, 12-9-1961

SHELBOURNE

First Irish club to reach third qualifying round of the UEFA Cup in 2004–05. Once led Rangers 3-0 before losing 5-3 in home leg played in England at Prenton Park for 1998–99 UEFA Cup.

	P	W	D	L	F	A	W*	L*	Entries
	53	9	14	30	47	88			18 seasons
EC	2	0	0	2	1	7			1
CL	18	4	8	6	20	24	1		5
FC	5	1	2	2	3	4			1
UE	12	0	2	10	8	28			6
CW	10	1	1	8	9	20			4
IT	6	3	1	2	6	5			2

Biggest Win: 4-0 v Vetra, 24-6-2006
Heaviest Defeat: 1-5 v Sporting Club, 26-9-1962

SLIGO ROVERS

John Brennan was the 72nd minute marksman for the winner against Floriana.

	P	W	D	L	F	A	W*	L*	Entries
	12	1	3	8	8	25			4 seasons
EC	2	0	0	2	0	6			1
CW	6	1	1	4	5	11			2
IT	4	0	2	2	3	8			1

Biggest Win: 1-0 v Floriana, 25-8-1994
Heaviest Defeat: 0-3 v Haka, 28-9-1983

SOUTHAMPTON

They reached the 1969–70 Fairs Cup third stage but then lost on an away goal in a tie with Newcastle United. Mick Channon scored nine goals in European matches during two spells.

	P	W	D	L	F	A	W*	L*	Entries
	24	8	9	7	38	28			7 seasons
FC	6	2	3	1	11	6	1	1	
UE	12	2	6	4	11	14	1		5
CW	6	4	0	2	16	8			1

Biggest Win: 5-1 v Guimaraes, 12-11-1969
Heaviest Defeat: 2-4 v Sporting Club, 21-10-1981

ST JOHNSTONE

Impressively accounted for Hamburg and Vasas to reach UEFA Cup third round 1971–72.

	P	W	D	L	F	A	W*	L*	Entries
	10	4	2	4	14	15			2 seasons
UE	10	4	2	4	14	15			2

Biggest Win: 3-0 v Hamburg, 29-9-1971
Heaviest Defeat: 1-5 v Zeljeznicar, 8-12-1971

ST MIRREN

Won their first game in the 1980–81 UEFA Cup competition 2-1 away to Elfsborg

	P	W	D	L	F	A	W*	L*	Entries
	14	3	5	6	10	14			4 seasons
UE	10	2	3	5	9	12			3
CW	4	1	2	1	1	2			1

Biggest Win: 3-0 v Slavia Prague, 2-10-1985
Heaviest Defeat: 0-2 v St Etienne, 5-11-1980, v Feyenoord, 28-9-1983, v Mechelen, 4-11-1987

ST PATRICK'S ATHLETIC

First Irish club to make progress in the Intertoto by beating Rijeka the Croatian club. In 2008–09 also reached the UEFA Cup competition proper after two qualifying rounds.

	P	W	D	L	F	A	W*	L*	Entries
	28	5	5	18	22	65			11 seasons
EC	2	0	1	1	1	5			1
CL	4	0	1	3	0	12			2
FC	2	0	0	2	4	9			1
UE	14	3	3	8	10	25			5
CW	2	0	0	2	1	8			1
IT	4	2	0	2	6	6	1	1	1

Biggest Win: 3-1 v Gent, 13-7-2002
Heaviest Defeat: 3-6 v Bordeaux, 11-10-1967

STOKE CITY

In their 1974–75 UEFA Cup tie they only lost out to Ajax on an away goal.

	P	W	D	L	F	A	W*	L*	Entries
	4	1	2	1	4	6			2 seasons
UE	4	1	2	1	4	6	1	2	

Biggest Win: 3-1 v Kaiserslautern, 13-9-1972
Heaviest Defeat: 0-4 v Kaiserslautern, 27-9-1972

SUNDERLAND
Home and away wins over Vasas in 1973–74 Cup-Winners' Cup and had 22,402 at Roker Park.

	P	W	D	L	F	A	W*	L*	Entries
	4	3	0	1	5	3			1 season
CW	4	3	0	1	5	3			1

Biggest Win: 2-0 v Vasas, 19-9-1973
Heaviest Defeat: 0-2 v Sporting Club, 7-11-1973

SWANSEA CITY
Provided eight different scorers against Sliema Wanderers while sub Ian Walsh hit a hat-trick.

	P	W	D	L	F	A	W*	L*	Entries
	18	3	4	11	32	37			7 seasons
CW	18	3	4	11	32	37			7

Biggest Win: 12-0 v Sliema Wanderers, 15-9-1982
Heaviest Defeat: 0-8 v Monaco, 1-10-1991

THE NEW SAINTS
First played as Llansantffraid drawing with Ruch Chorzow in the Cup-Winners' Cup with an Arwel Jones goal at Wrexham. Subsequently became known as TNS, too.

	P	W	D	L	F	A	W*	L*	Entries
	20	1	2	17	10	55			10 seasons
CL	8	1	1	6	6	18	1	4	
UE	10	0	0	10	3	31			5
CW	2	0	1	1	1	6			1

Biggest Win: 3-2 v Ventspils, 17-7-2007
Heaviest Defeat: 2-7 v Amica, 29-8-2002

TON PENTRE
Played against Ruud Van Nistelrooy (Heerenveen).

	P	W	D	L	F	A	W*	L*	Entries
	4	0	0	4	0	16			1 season
IT	4	0	0	4	0	16			1

Heaviest Defeat: 0-7 v Heerenveen, 1-7-1995

TOTTENHAM HOTSPUR
The first British team to win a European title in 1963 beating Atletico Madrid 5-1 and also the first to win the UEFA Cup in 1972 overcoming Wolverhampton Wanderers. In 1973–74 they were beaten by Feyenoord in the UEFA Cup final, but ten years later won 4-3 on penalties after both legs with Anderlecht had been drawn 1-1. Martin Chivers scored 22 European goals in 32 appearances.

	P	W	D	L	F	A	W*	L*	Entries
	131	76	26	29	271	131			17 seasons
EC	8	4	1	3	21	13			1
UE	86	51	20	15	182	71	3	2	9
CW	33	20	5	8	65	34		1	6
IT	4	1	0	3	3	13			1

Biggest Win: 9-0 v íBK, 28-9-1971
Heaviest Defeat: 0-8 v Cologne, 22-7-1995

UNIVERSITY COLLEGE DUBLIN
Goalkeeper Alan O'Neill and his defence kept Everton at bay at Tolka Park on 19 September 1984 watched by 9750.

	P	W	D	L	F	A	W*	L*	Entries
	4	0	3	1	3	4			2 seasons
CW	2	0	1	1	0	1			1
IT	2	0	2	0	3	3		1	1

Heaviest Defeat: 0-1 v Everton, 2-10-1984

WATERFORD UNITED
Lansdowne Road, Dublin housed 48,886 for the visit of Manchester United to see a Denis Law hat-trick in the 1968–69 European Cup.

	P	W	D	L	F	A	W*	L*	Entries
	22	4	1	17	21	61			9 seasons
EC	14	3	0	11	15	47			6
CW	8	1	1	6	6	14			3

Biggest Win: 4-0 v Hibernians, 1-10-1980
Heaviest Defeat: 0-7 v Celtic, 21-10-1970

WATFORD
Lost their first leg UEFA Cup game in Kaiserslautern 3-1 in 1983–84 but won the tie!

	P	W	D	L	F	A	W*	L*	Entries
	6	2	1	3	10	12			1 season
UE	6	2	1	3	10	12			1

Biggest Win: 3-0 v Kaiserslautern, 28-9-1983
Heaviest Defeat: 0-4 v Sparta Prague, 7-12-1983

WEST BROMWICH ALBION
Two quarter-final appearances one in the Cup-Winners' Cup, another ten years later in the 1978–79 UEFA Cup when they beat Valencia 2-0 at home after drawing away.

	P	W	D	L	F	A	W*	L*	Entries
	22	8	5	9	30	27			5 seasons
FC	4	1	1	2	7	9			1
UE	12	5	2	5	15	13			3
CW	6	2	2	2	8	5	1		1

Biggest Win: 5-2 v DOS, 9-11-1966
Heaviest Defeat: 0-3 v Bologna, 1-2-1967

WEST HAM UNITED
England's trio of Bobby Moore, Martin Peters and Geoff Hurst reigned supreme in the Cup-Winners' Cup in the 1965 final at Wembley against Borussia Moenchengladbach. Eleven years later lost to Anderlecht in Brussels.

	P	W	D	L	F	A	W*	L*	Entries
	42	21	8	13	71	52			6 seasons
UE	6	2	1	3	6	7			2
CW	30	15	6	9	58	42	1		4
IT	6	4	1	1	7	3			1

Biggest Win: 5-1 v Castilla, 1-10-1980
Heaviest Defeat: 1-4 v Dinamo Tbilisi, 4-3-1980

WIMBLEDON
Achieved two draws: Kosice away and Beitar Jerusalem at home.

	P	W	D	L	F	A	W*	L*	Entries
	4	0	2	2	1	8			1 season
IT	4	0	2	2	1	8			1

Heaviest Defeat: 0-4 v Bursaspor, 24-6-1995

WOLVERHAMPTON WANDERERS
They were beaten in the first UEFA Cup final in 1972 but probably more famous for their 1954 friendly against Honved won 3-2 after trailing two down. It was one of the sparks which ignited the inauguration of the European Cup. Derek Dougan scored 12 European goals.

	P	W	D	L	F	A	W*	L*	Entries
	32	16	6	10	59	44			7 seasons
EC	8	2	2	4	12	16			2
UE	20	13	3	4	41	23	1		4
CW	4	1	1	2	6	5			1

Biggest Win: 5-0 v FK Austria, 30-11-1960
Heaviest Defeat: 2-5 v Barcelona, 2-3-1960

WREXHAM
With one goal home leg lead found themselves three down in 38 minutes in Portugal for 1984–85 Cup-Winners' Cup before rallying to lose 4-3 but qualify!

	P	W	D	L	F	A	W*	L*	Entries
	28	10	8	10	34	35			8 seasons
CW	28	10	8	10	34	35	1	2	8

Biggest Win: 4-0 v Zurrieq, 1-10-1986
Heaviest Defeat: 2-5 v Magdeburg, 3-10-1979

DAILY ROUND-UP 2008–09

JULY 2008
Ronaldo is a slave ... Ronaldino moves to AC Milan ... Only English in British Olympics.

1   Abramovich to spend £25m. Roberto Di Matteo to be MK Dons boss. Stan Kroenke is on Arsenal board. Steve Round is Everton assistant manager. Wednesday takeover completed.

2   Man City to pay £19m for a Jo job. "Spiderman" Gutierrez – Mallorca to Newcastle. FIFA to pay £57,000 court costs over ISL collapse case. Barry's move to Liverpool still going nowhere.

3   Watford for sale. Philipp Degen to Liverpool. QPR's have Gulf Air tie-up.

4   Newcastle deny club sale. Ronaldo to miss start with injury. Andrea Dossena, Udinese to Liverpool, Marvin Emnes to Boro £3.2m. Andy Cole, 36, to Forest.

5   Adebayor move from Arsenal to Spain seems unlikely. Newcastle USA takeover?

6   Arsenal will need annual £24m for 17 years to pay off £390m Emirates Stadium. Chelsea deny £50m Kaka bid. Yobo brother abducted in Nigeria. Hibs Intertoto shock.

7   Robinho staying say Real. Aleksandar Tunchev, CSKA Sofia to Leicester. Nikola Saric, 17, Herfolge to Liverpool. Scolari faces wanting away players at Chelsea. Newly formed European Club Association replaces G14. Anfield capture Diego Cavalieri £3m from Palmeiras.

8   Scolari "Bridge" debut with CV of 17 trophies, 14 clubs and three national teams: Kuwait, Brazil and Portugal – and offers different "First Choice" job version.

9   Sidwell £5.5m for Villa. Brum get Phillips from WBA. Boateng heading for Hull from Boro. Rooney agent gets 18-month ban. Peter Reid to be Thailand coach.

10   Ronaldo "slave" comment backed by Blatter! Arshavin to stay at home. Liverpool signs Vincent Weijl, 17 – for reserves! Adebayor to AC Milan and Lampard to Inter are not realities. Luton deducted 30 pts! Barton early release denied. Zamora – Pantsil to Fulham in £6.3m deal from Hammers. Belarus ref found drunk in charge – of game!

11   Crouch record £11m Portsmouth capture. Guthrie, Liverpool to Newcastle. Queiroz is Portugal coach. Deco shows his art, training for Chelsea as Lamps may still be Inter bound.

12   Now Platini wants EU to limit foreign transfers! Distin misses Barton trial.

13   Hibs out of Intertoto after Swedish defeat to Elfsborg. Zola predicts Lamps success if he goes to Inter.

14   Arsenal thaw four-year season ticket freeze. Scam on ripping off African youngsters by bogus scouts exposed.

15   Simon Jordan to quit Palace over Bostock sale to Spurs. Llanelli edge it in Ch Lge starter against Ventspils. FA turn down Luton appeal. Vicente Del Bosque is new Spanish manager. Hill-Wood at Arsenal says wages must come down.

16   Ronaldinho – to AC Milan for £19.8m to disappoint Man City as Hleb heads to Barca from Arsenal. Hull arrivals: Halmosi, Boateng, Warner; Marcus Bent to Brum. Kapo to Wigan. Emad Moteab £1.5m record for Bristol C from Al Ahly – then cancelled. Bosingwa £16.2m Chelsea captures already training at Cobham. Ch Lge: Llanelli take 1-0 lead over Ventspils, Drogheda beat Levadia 2-1 but Linfield lost 2-0 at Windsor Park to Dynamo Zagreb.

17   Brazil on standby for WC 2010. Sunderland chases four Spurs. Man City two up in UEFA Cup Faeroes debut to EB/Streymur, St Pat's win 1-0 at Olimps Riga, Glentoran and Cork manage home draws with Metalurgs and Haka respectively, but Cliftonville crash to FC Copenhagen, Bangor ship six against Midtjylland and TNS lose 1-0 at Sudova.

18   Sir Alex says Ron stays, but Spurs unhappy over Berbatov and Keane public bidding. Chelsea and Man Utd charged by FA over end of season fracas. Stoke record capture Kitson £5.5m. Carson to Albion for £3.25m.

19   Sidwell og debut as Intertoto Villa held in Odense.

20   Germany may sub for Ukraine in Euro 2012. England U-19s win, but fail to qualify.

21   Becks boosts LA Galaxy at the gate and shirt sales. Lamps to stay at the Bridge.

22   Eduardo return delayed for Arsenal. McCormick axed by Plymouth after road accident incident. Ch Lge: Llanelli let in four at Ventspils.

23   Scolari gets 4-0 friendly win in China. Valon Behrami costs West Ham £5m. Tainio for Sunderland. Cattermole to Wigan £3.5m. FIFA misled investigation into ISL collapse. Ch Lge: Drogheda eases in 1-0 to go on but draw for Linfield not enough.

24   Olympic 2012 GB team not wanted by Scots, Welsh and Irish!. Blatter blasts 39ers again. Barry to figure in Villa Intertoto. Capello to retire after England job.

25   Saints Dyer gets community service for burglary. Minister in favour of quotas.

26   Bouma suffers horrendous leg injury as Villa beat Odense to qualify for UEFA Cup.

27   Man Utd 2 Pompey 1 in Lagos – of course! Kennedy, Celtic to Norwich. Germany beat Italy 3-1 in UEFA U-19 final.

28   JM admits to extinguishing Lamps. 39ers plan revived. Barton out of jail, Luton out of administration.

29   Nike boot out Barton. Robbie Keane for Liverpool at 19m, Robinson Spurs to Blackburn £3.5m. Everton chief executive Wyness quits. Ch Lge: Kiev takes 2-1 lead at Drogheda.

30   Bentley £17m Rovers to Spurs. Ch Lge: Rangers held by Kaunas at Ibrox. Sorensen free to Stoke. Ben Haim £6m Chelsea to Man City. Kenny Agustien AZ to Brum (loan).

31   Barton faces FA ban. Fair play losers Boro fined £20,000. UEFA Cup: Man City through ok as are St Pat's, but exit for Glentoran, Cork, Bangor, TNS and seven conceding Cliftonville. Mrs Thaksin is guilty of tax evasion.

AUGUST 2008
Lampard cashes in ... Argies stun Brazil in Olympic Final ... USA take ladies prize ... Unwanted record for Derby ... New boys settle in ... Man Utd beaten in Super Cup.

1   Ch Lge draw: McClaren men get Standard, Liverpool at Standard but Rangers will have to survive Kaunas before moving on. UEFA Cup: Man City play Midtjylland, Villa – Hafnarfjordur and Q of S meet Nordsjelland. Thuram retires. Brad Guzan – Chivas USA to Villa. Spitting image for Rooney?

2   SL starts with new boys Annan doing a "Gretna" and winning 4-1 at Cowden. But friendlies leave Rangers stunned 4-0 to Liverpool at Ibrox and Hibs beaten 3-2 by Middlesbrough. Tevez wobbly in Solskjaer benefit as Man Utd lose to Espanyol.

3   Indian big-wig eyes the Toon. Daniel Parejo, 19, is on loan to QPR from Real.

4   FA concern over PL mid-term tournament. Hammers retire Bobby Moore's No.6. Omar Koroma, Banjul Hawks to Pompey. Man Utd Simpson loaned to Blackburn.

5   Ch Lge: Rangers out! – Kaunas last minute winner. CIS Cup: Morton six at Stranraer (three). Rooney hit by Nigeria virus.

6   Ch Lge: Drogheda draw but Kiev go through. Sir Alex and Ron are about to make it up. Rotherham docked 17 points – Bournemouth will be next.

7   Ref Clattenburg suspended over alleged debts. Sir Alex is against quotas. Arsene voices plea to FIFA to challenge Olympic opt-out decision. Everton in stadium row. Shorey to Villa with Boro's Young. Chelsea in Robinho race. Arsenal Ladies beat Everton in Community Shield.

8   Robinho not for sale. Lutons sign 11 players in 24 hours! Lehmann quits German national team. BSP: Barrow tips over Oxford.

9   FL kicks off with Sodje scoring first goal in 30 secs before hamstring injury as Sheff Wed beat Burnley 4-1. Derby continues losing – ten months 23 days and 33 matches at Pride Park – so do Luton. Highest scorers Dagenham hitting Chester for five is watched by the lowest crowd 1434. Promotion returnees Aldershot wins at Accrington, Exeter draws at Darlo. McKenzie hits 100th goal of career for Coventry. Saints Svensson back after 991 days and five ops but they go down in last minute at Cardiff. Phillips, oldest poacher in town, scores 92.07 mins winner for Birmingham. Millwall throw 3-1 lead and loses in odd goal in seven at Oldham. Rotherham wipes off three points, Bournemouth one of their deficit as sub Mulligan scores with first touch for Gills. SPL: Rangers shake off Euro exit with win at Falkirk. SL: Dundee, Partick and Brechin only 100 percent teams after two games! BSP: relegated Wrexham crash five against Stevenage in ten-a-side game, Mansfield fight back to draw at Ebbsfleet. Red cards: SL 6, FL 3, BSP 2.

10   Goalless Community Shield as Man Utd beat Pompey on pens – naturally. Meeting of one up and one down sees Forest and Reading in no-score draw, too. SPL: Celtic needs pen to see off St Mirren.

11   SPL: Hamilton start going top of the table beating Dundee Utd. Thai Man City owner legs it from Bangkok bail.

12   Man Utd line up £28m bid for Berbatov. Crisis club Man City? Cuellar, Rangers to Villa £7.8m. PL eye credit crunch effect on fans. Overmars – ex-retired – gets Go Ahead job. Avram Grant escapes plane crash. Spurs sign another keeper Cesar Sanchez, 36, from Zaragoza. C Cup: Beckford trio as Leeds hit five at Chester; Ellington, too, as Derby beat Lincoln. Even Luton takes out Plymouth. Sheff Wed has best crowd 16,298 but Rotherham clips them on pens. BSP: Barrow boys 4-3 at Altrincham, other newcomer Eastbourne succeeds at Stevenage and Kettering draws at Grays.

13   Not unlucky for Lampard – five year deal £33.8m. Ch Lge: Arsenal twice at Twente; Reina stops Dante's infernal penalty kick as Liverpool draw with Standard. C Cup: four ties – 16 goals!

14   UEFA Cup: Man City suffer humiliating home defeat by Midtjylland Danes, Q of S at home to Danish Nordsjaelland, too; Villa score four in Iceland while St Pat's draw in Sweden. Hull spends record £2,5m on Spurs Gardner. FL increases fees to agents. Pedro Mendes heading for Rangers.

15   Olympic Women's quarter-final winners: Japan, Germany, Brazil and the USA.

16   PL opens with one-nil to the Arsenal against returning WBA – Nasri fastest off the mark as Gunners goal scorer 3ms 42 secs keeping 250th PL clean sheet; Torres 25 yarder wins it for Liverpool at Sunderland; new boys Hull see off Fulham but Stoke find it tough at Bolton in Reyna 200th Trotters outing; Blackburn late win at Everton delights boss Ince; Boro surprise Spurs and Ashton early double for Hammers floors Wigan. FLC: Sharp Blades treble cuts out QPR; Iwelumo braces himself again for Wolves; Pintado the scoring Bull clearly not sub-standard for Swans; Phillips does in old Saints mates for Birmingham. L1: Gill B scores, booked for celebration, then another yellow in Cheltenham win. Oldham derails Leeds; MK Dons give Di Matteo his first win. L2: Thorne again at the double for Bradford; Luton win at Gills; Chester still leaking goals. SPL: Rangers see off Hearts, but Hamilton are still top. SL: No 100 percent teams; Albion sole pointless ones. BSP: Eastbourne three at Oxford, but United double it.

17   Chelsea – also 250th PL clean sheet – four play pleases all but Pompey; punchless Man Utd held by Newcastle; Agbonlahor hat-trick in seven minutes dismisses Man City.

18   Mutu gets union backing to fight £13m fine. Becks – the musical – as LA get Bruce Arena as coach. Transfer window extension by one day. Stuart Pearce fancies leading 2012 GB team for Olympics as its 2008 quarter-final winners are: Brazil, Belgium, Argentina and Nigeria, while Brazil beat Germany 4-1 in Women's semi-final and will meet USA 4-2 conquerors of Japan in the final.

19   U-21s: England edge ten-man Czechs 2-1 Olympic semis: Nigeria beat Belgium 4-1, Agentina stun nine man Brazil 3-0.

20   Cole J saves England blushes in Czech draw while Barwick bows out after Lord T pressure on him. Scots held by Irish, Wales beaten by Georgia and Republic get a draw in Norway. Kazakhstan in England's WC group beat Andorra 3-0. U-21s: Scots win in Lithuania, but Wales lose to Romania. Gunners nab Silvestre. Shevchenko set for AC Milan.

21   FA worried over fans in Barcelona ahead of Andorra game as Barwick gets half a million pay-off. Berbatov autographs a Man Utd shirt! Liam Brady is taken to hospital. Olympic Women: USA edges Brazil for gold in extra time, Germans bronze by beating Japan. BSP: another victory for Wrexham over Oxford.

22   Ho, ho, ho – Robinho for Chelsea? WBA pay record £4.7m for Borja Valero (Mallorca). Brady is given the all clear. Maloney back at Celtic from Villa. Olympic bronze awarded to Brazil 3-0 over Belgium.

23   Cottagers edge shot-shy Arsenal; Liverpool call on Gerrard for 94th min delivery to beat Boro as do Stoke – first top echelon win for 23 years – in seeing off Villa; Black Cats paw Spurs at WHL; Owen Toon raider against Bolton, whose Nolan has five bookings by Given; Hull get a point at Blackburn, Everton, who still need players, three at WBA. FLC: Palace have two dismissed but hold Burnley; super-sub Lupoli levels for Norwich at Cardiff; Derby English League record of 35 with no win, lose at home – again; goals, penalties and a sending-off in Charlton's 4-2 win over Reading; Birmingham only 100 percenters as Barnsley – sole pointless – fall victim. L1: Hughes scores a three for Oldham, keeps them intact, too; Bristol Rovers hit six against pointless Hereford; rebound from pen robs Leeds of win at Yeovil. L2: Rotherham wipe off three more points against leaky Chester; Macc still searching for a point along with Lincoln, Barnet and of course Chester, Exeter first FL win in five years, Shrewsbury, Bradford and Bury make it three wins in three. SPL: Rangers draws with Aberdeen; Celtic get three against pointless Falkirk. SL: Albion achieves first win over Berwick. BSP: Cambridge first win at Eastbourne; Stevenage ship four at Ebbsfleet as do Altrincham at Kidderminster while Histon edge Burton 4-3.

24   Deco delivers stunning free-kick as Chelsea win at Wigan while Elano double helps Man City beat West Ham. Abroad Super Cups: Real with nine men beat Valencia 4-2, Inter needs pens to beat Roma.

25   Fletcher bangs up Pompey for Man Utd, but Berbatov could improve matters. Senderos for AC Milan plus Shevchenko on loan. BSP: Cambridge beaten by Kettering and Salisbury go above on goal difference. GB team for 2012 not wanted by Scots, Irish and Welsh!

26   Ch Lge: Barca shock in Wisla defeat, but go through. UEFA Cup: Q of S out. C Cup: Bolton ko'd by the Cobblers, Owen rescues Newcastle at Coventry in extra time; Hartlepool hand Baggies a defeat; Derby win! Fives for Boro, Reading, Rotherham axe Wolves on pens, hat trick for Ledesma (QPR). CIS Cup: Daly trio for Dundee U, Thistle prick Dundee, St Mirren get seven (Mehmet 3) and Morton clip Hibs.. Vidic wants a less-rainy club than Man Utd..

27   Ch Lge: Liverpool need overtime to beat Standard but Gerrard injured; Arsenal get four against Twente. C Cup: Hammers pushed to extra time by Macclesfield before four-play ends it. CIS up: Inverness goes to pens to oust

Arbroath, but Airdrie are spot-on to dispose of Hearts. Ferdinand A West Ham to Sunderland; Segundo Castillo, Red Star to Everton. Kranjcar is out for three months. Vidic happy at Old Trafford!

28 UEFA Cup: Man City ride luck – get 90 min og and win on pens as Hart saves two; Villa held at home but have mix and match team out. Platini wants to wash out January window. Capello unhappy about losing key players in another country v club issue. English clubs get good Ch Lge pots – Man Utd in same group as Celtic. Wenger can spend £30m.

29 Super Cup: Man Utd seen off by Zenit and Scholes gets two yellows. Villa signs Milner from Newcastle for £12m. Wright-Phillips S goes back to Man City. Reading's Sonko to Stoke, WBA get Jonas Olsson (NEC) for £800,000. Benitez puts Capello in his England place – behind Liverpool needs.

30 Arsenal get three to beat Newcastle, Hammers four play too much for Rovers one as Santa Cruz injured and Roberts pen stopped by Green, Pompey hit a treble at Everton and Yakubu pen saved by James, wheels come off at Hull as Wigan score five, Boro leave it late after mssed chances to beat Stoke and Bolton and Albion settle for goalless dull draw. FLC: Wolves claw back to top with 5-1 over Forest, second-half hat-trick for Doyle at Reading, year without League win for Derby, L1: Graham treble for Carlisle, Demontagnac for Walsall, goal-difference leaders Leicster four play at Cheltenham, Forde pen save helps Millwall first win. L2: Chester first win in style – five goals, Loan-star Clarke four for Darlo in six at Macc, seesaw thriller at the Rec as Shots edge Bradford. Daggers still top on goal difference. SPL: Killie wins at Dundee U makes them top. Falkirk are still searching for a point. SL: Airdrie five over Morton, Alloa five against cash-strapped Stranraer. BSP: Fives for Crawley, Burton, four for Wrexham at Salisbury, Forest Green lead on goal difference.

31 Crisis-club Chelsea? – they are held 1-1 at the Bridge by Spurs; Torres injury as Liverpool draw at Villa. Capello drops Owen, puts Bullard in. SPL: Rangers win Auld Firm derby 4-2 in ten-a-side finish at Celtic.

SEPTEMBER 2008
Robinho £32.5m record transfer ... Keegan resigns at Newcastle ... Walcott treble for England ... Arsenal £318m in debt ... Elgin lose their marbles ... Barnsley parade FL's youngest.

1 Abu Dhabi takeover at Man City as they rob Chelsea of Robinho from Real for record £32.5m; Berbatov goes to Man Utd £30.75m, Roman Pavlyuchenko, Spartak Moscow to Spurs £14m and Corluka from Man City for £8.5m; Albert Riera Espanyol to Liverpool £8m – even hardly poor relations Hull spend £4m on Rangers' Cousin. What recession – as £135m spent on last day of window shopping. Ebbsfleet's 7500 members sell Akinde to Bristol C. Kevin Bond sacked by Bournemouth. Torres out for three weeks. No Owen for England, but Bullard in squad.

2 Keegan "not sacked" after row. Real not sorry to lose Robinho. Man City target Ronaldo. Alan Curbishley may be leaving Upton Park. Bournemouth appoint Jimmy Quinn as manager – he failed to get Cambridge promotion. £540m spent by PL clubs in summer window, 12 breaking club records. J Paint: Essex four play – Daggers home to Barnet, Orient at Southend. BSP: Burton win at Wrexham, Eastbourne beat Forest Green and Stevenage lose again.

3 Curbishley resigns at Hammers – victim of owner power? Delia Smith may sell Norwich. Niemi retires.

4 KK resigns at Newcastle, Poyet tipped as new boss re-uniting with the Wise man. U-21: Scots beat Slovenia 3-1. BSP: Torquay lose at Kiddy.

5 Toon owner Ashley may ban himself from ground. Barton banned six-matches – Rajkovic year for Olympic spitting. Hammers rumours include Donadoni, Bilic. England minus Owen await might of Andorra; Wales one striker to face Azers, Republic to face Georgia in Germany, Scots go to Macedonia and Republic as WC gets going for Europe. U-21: Republic lose in Bulgaria.

6 WC: sub Cole J twice fires nervy England over Andorra; Macedonia strike early to beat pen-denied Scots; Wales leave it late to sub Vokes over Azers; Republic get Georgia off their minds in fine start, but Irish clipped in Slovakia. Shocks elsewhere as France lose in Austria, Italy save themselves at last minute in Cyprus and Tevez is sent off for the Argies held by Paraguay. L1: Leeds hit five against Crewe; sunny Scunny Hooper's hat-trick at the seaside at Brighton; boss Sheridan banned from touchline as nine bookings at Tranmere; another one over the eight as Posh – with Mackail-Smith trio – edge Bristol R 5-4. L2: Daggers lose first time at Brentford; Peter Taylor's Wycombe ahead of it all; Romanian Patulea spurs Lincoln. BSP: Mansfield lead on goal difference after beating Eastbourne, Morison hat-trick for Stevenage. Matt Busby, son of a Man Utd fan, is Pub Team Manager of the Year (Enderby Social).

7 WC: Easy warm-up for Brazil in Chile. SL Cup: away quarterfinal winners: Ross Co, Airdrie, Partick and Morton. BSP: Torquay late, late show. Tolling days for cash-strapped Doncaster Belles.

8 Setanta firm over cash for WC TV highlights. Parry quits Wales. Scots are in crisis. Zola for West Ham. Bill Shorthouse, Wolves star of the 1940s, dies at 86.

9 Capello prefers playing away as fortress Croatia awaits; Essien out for season. Robbie Keane is latest Liverpool burglary sufferer.

10 WC: World-class Walcott treble stops the crowing in Zagreb; Scots win in Iceland; Given heroics earn Republic point in Montenegro; Wales cash-out late in Russia, though Northern Ireland hold the Czechs. Klose hat-trick but Germans held by the Finns; Misimovic treble, too, as Bosnia whack Estonia for seven; France and Italy manage to win. Fall-out from Battle of the Bridge rumbles on. Zola three year contract with Hammers.

11 Capello now firm favourite! Croatia crowd abuse probe. Setanta is under fire from FA. WC: Dunga in danger as Brazil held by ten-man Bolivia.

12 Keegan back at Toon? Berbatov and Robinho ready for expensive debuts. Hartlepool's 4-1 win over Cheltenham means curtains for Town boss Keith Downing.

13 Liverpool break the Man Utd hoodoo – Vidic late red, too; Terry also sees red but Chelsea win moneybags game at Man City after Robinho opening bow shot; Hull surprise strife-torn Toon; Brunt trauma for Zola's day ruined by Baggies; Pompey's Defoe doubles up to deny Boro; Adebayor treble floors Rovers as Jack Wilshere, 16 years 256 days is Gunners youngest in League; Fulham edge Bolton; Wigan ten claw back to draw with Sunderland. FLC: Wolves fight back deflates Charlton; first League win in a year for Derby, first home goals for Palace this term. L1: Stockport joy at Orient, Crossley pen puts Oldham in the mood over MK Dons, Alexander a great winner for Millwall at Leicester. L2: Bradford put Exeter to the sword, Bury secure second place with Lincoln win, Gills swallowed by seven up Shrews, Daggers overcome the Chesterfield nine. SPL: ten-man Rangers edge Killie, Celtic four in 19-min spell ease up at Motherwell, Falkirk first win over Hearts, Dundee Utd still searching. SL: top three in Div 2 still unbeaten. BSP: new leaders in Crawley who surprise Mansfield.

14 Everton win at Stoke with banished Moyes in stand watching.

15 Crisis club Spurs lose to Villa at WHL. Steve Clarke joins Zola at West Ham. AIG collapse threatens Man Utd sponsors. Hasselbaink retires. Grimsby sacks boss Buckley. Cheltenham appoints Martin Allen as manager. Ronaldo – the rotund, Brazilian one – may go to Man City!

16 Ch Lge: Chelsea four play but Big Phil wanted more against Bordeaux, Liverpool look to Gerrard double – now on 99 goals – including pen in Marseille victory. JM has Inter winning at Panathinaikos. UEFA Cup: St Pat's ship two goals at Hertha. FLC: Wolves – best start for 46 years – maintain lead with win over Palace, Birmingham, too, just behind on goal difference. Reading joy of six over Sheff Wed, Plymouth off the bottom with win at Watford.

Terry ban overturned. PL to have more home produced subs. Ashley to sell Toon for £481m. Palace and Watford fined for failing to control players.

17   Ch Lge: Ron as 62nd min sub fails to inspire Man Utd in Villarreal 0-0. Gallas again to Arsenal rescue in draw at Dynamo Kiev, Italian ref sends off wrong Aalborg player, Celtic fail with pen and settle for no goals. FLC: Ipswich draws at Saints, ten-man QPR win at Norwich. John Barnes is Jamaica coach.

18   UEFA Cup: Bent is Wisla's bother as Spurs take narrow lead, Villa ease in away to nine-man Litex, Joy for Jo's double – he missed a sitter and hit the woodwork, too – in Man City win at Omonia, the D men have it for Pompey over Guimaraes, but Everton held by Standard and Motherwell lose to the Nancy boys. Big Phil gets Butch Wilkins in place of Steve Clarke. Home internationals without England. Kroenke joins Arsenal board. Gazza arrested. ITV get part of England deal from Setanta.

19   Arsenal turnover £223m, debt £318.1m Two football hoolies get 15 weeks in jail for last year's Spurs – Chelsea brawl.

20   Arsenal rally to win at Bolton and go head of the class; Liverpool nonplussed by Gerrard's 100th goal ruled out for Kuyt "offside" as Stoke take a precious point; Italian connection helps to topple troubled Toon; sub Chopra double axes Boro – Downing miss pen – for Black Cats; first home win for two-shot Rovers over Fulham. FLC: Reading awarded "own goal" when ball goes for corner against Watford – lino Bannister on the carpet, ref Attwell his aide; hat-trick hunger for hungry Wolves then sees red along with boss McCarthy and goalie Hennessey – but they still win; Brummies beached by Blackpool. L1: nine-man Walsall breeze in at Brighton; sunny Scunny six wins on the trot; Oldham share six with Hartlepool – five goals in ten minutes; Shrimpers net odd goal in seven at Crewe. L2: Bury go top at Barnet; Strevens pen failure hits Daggers at Wycombe; four play Macc continue on goal standard; miss-hit Rhodes sees Millers win over Luton; Bournemouth shake Bradford.. SPL: Wright handball gaffe gives Dundee Utd first win at the Dons. SL: three sent off – Elgin lose their marbles as Albion hit six (Watt, Barr trebles); Livi see off Dundee; McManus trio for East Fife. BSP: Crawley strole on at Oxford. Non-league Four Nations faces axe.

21   Man Utd have better of bruising draw at the Bridge, Hull chuck two goal lead as Everton level it – though another controversial goal involved, Man City six-pack too heavy for Pompey, Spurs held by Wigan and Villa win the midland derby at The Hawthorns. SPL: Rangers home, Celtic away both win games to stay one and two respectively.

22   No replay for Watford. Deco and Ricardo Carvalho are out with injury. BSP: Kettering goes for a Burton. FIFA WC mascot for 2010 is Zakumi – a leopard. Axed: Geraint Williams (Colchester), Lee Sinnott (Port Vale).

23   C Cup: Kid Vela joins the Gunners (average age 19) hat-trick club in joy of six against Sheff Utd; PL casualties are Fulham at Burnley, Hammers at Watford, while Sunderland and Stoke survive on pens; Liverpool stiffs squeak in against Crewe; Possebon breaks leg as Man Utd beat Boro. CIS Cup: St Mirren lose at Dunfermline, but Celtic hit four against Livi. BSP: Mansfield, Wrexham continue to lose ground as Crawley draw at Weymouth keeps them top. Attwell and Bannister are given "time off." Edward Grayson called to the Bar in 1948, champion of sport inside the law and Sky Sports FYB contributor dies at 83.

24   C Cup: Brighton beach moneybags Man City on pens, QPR take out Villa, Spurs pile more misery on the Tyne – only 20,577 turn up as El Tel is courted for the job, Wigan four play too much for Ipswich, Rovers end Everton interest and Pompey let in another four goals to visiting Chelsea. West Ham may have to sell players to pay Sheff Utd over Tevez saga. JM makes 100 career home games without loss. CIS Cup: Partick push Rangers to extra time, Accies win at Motherwell and Killie see off the Dons. Wembley refinanced

25   Sunderland taken over by the Yanks, too. Terry V turns down the Toon. Watford boss Boothrouyd charged by FA over abuse to ref Attwell. Hammers lose Tevez appeal. Croatia fined over Heskey abuse. Jimmy Sirrel, Celtic, Bradford PA and Aldershot player, Notts Co manager of some standing dies at 86.

26   Joe Kinnear is interim Newcastle manager until club is sold! West Ham to appeal against Tevez judgment. Euro 2016 to have 24 finalists, UEFA Cup 2009-10 to be called Europa League; Poland/Ukraine may lose Euro 2012, UEFA to probe alleged fixed cup ties. Colchester win 4-3 at Tranmere, Southend hit three against Orient.

27   Styles gaffe gives Man Utd a pen at Old Trafford and Bolton concede their 500th PL goal; Geovanni "goal of the season" sparks Hull fight-back win at Arsenal; not pretty but pretty good enough for Chelsea three pts at Stoke; Baggies debt to gk Carson for win at Boro; West Ham ride luck for Fulham victory; Villa erase cup shock to beat Sunderland; now Blackburn take it out on Newcastle; Torres double settles Merseyside derby for Liverpool – Cahill late red for Blues. FLC: Hunt boys bag some Swans for Reading; Derby win again – this time at QPR; loanee Primus second Charlton debut in 15 years as Addicks lose to Sheff Wed; better Saints at Donny. L1: seventh heaven for Scunny; Oldham just hold on to unbeaten record but seven booked in Huddersfield game; Leeds leave it late. L2: Bournemouth knocks pts off deficit; Wycombe and Bury are goalless; first win for Barnet at Grimsby. SPL: injury-time Vennegor ends Dons battle at Celtic; Falkirk hit four. SL: Livi whack the Jags; Brechin new leaders in D2, Sten top D3; East Stirling score five. BSP: Crawley see off Kettering; Brian Little parts with Wrexham before Torquay beat them.

28   Defoe does in old Spurs mates and some fans give old boy Campbell stick for Pompey as tottering Tottenham make worst start for 53 years; Wigan pen writes off Man City, but Palacios "lift-off" is controversial. Bidders line up for Newcastle. SPL: Rangers take out Hibs. JM loses first Inter game – to AC Milan.

29   "Sorry" Styles reprieved. Chelsea signs Jeremy Boga, 12, from a Marseille club!

30   Ch Lge: Arsenal take it out on Porto – fourfold; Berbatov breaks Aalborg, but Scholes, Rooney injured; Celtic away day blues again in Villarreal; Real down the Z men in St Petersburg. UEFA Cup: St Pat's outed by Hertha. FLC: Reading first to lower Wolves colours; bottom four all lose – including Donny's fifth straight; sub Reuben Noble-Lazarus 15 years 45 days is Barnsley's youngest FL debutant . L1: Leicester consolidates at top with Colchester win. Mystery "goal" officials are given more R and R.

OCTOBER 2008

Gerrard is a centurion ... Man City want more players ... WAGs to witches? ... Spurs worst ever start ... Barton's get out of jail card ... Redknapp for Tottenham!

1   Ch Lge: Gerrard becomes Liverpool's 16th goal centurion as Keane breaks duck; Chelsea off colour in Cluj draw and lose Drogba with injury; Messi rescues Barca in Donetsk. FA bans two for drug taking. Poland may be axed from WC games over government intervention.

2   UEFA Cup: Everton and Motherwell out, Spurs scrape in with Polish og, but Villa, Pompey and Man City have slightly easier ties as even McClaren's Twente stride on.

3   L1: Drogba back in a month? Oldham tastes initial defeat at Stockport and hattricks apiece Porter – Cox as Hartlepool snatches draw with Swindon after being three down. Sky Sports Victory Shield: England six-hitters in N Ireland.

4   Fabregas rescues Arsenal a point late at Sunderland; Ince whinge at elbow Vidic on gk Brown as Wes of that ilk puts Man Utd ahead and Rooney adds another on his 200th PL outing – while Sir Alex hails it all his best so far this season; Aliadiere hits Boro's 600th PL goal at Wigan but owe it to defence for first away day win in 2008; best PL start for WBA as Fulham lose. FLC: ten Tykes four play downs Donny; the mighty Smith hammers out a

Watford win over Preston; Royals roast Burnley; Derby now win with ten at Ipswich!; Brummies edge QPR to claim top spot as Wolves victims of Swans upping; improving Argyle soar four over Owls; Coventry miss pen but still hit Saints for four. L1: Murray has a hattrick for Brighton, but Cheltenham takes a point with ten men. Shrink visit only gets Hereford the same at home; foxy Leicester edge Huddersfield in five second half scoring spree; Yeovil finish with two late red cards and defeat against Southend; Posh tip up Leeds; Scunny have gk on red but draw at Orient. L2: injury/illness hit Shots stir to snatch point after trailing three down in 69 minutes so Bury's leadership goes to Wycombe winners over Bournemouth; Rotherham points now plus-one after beating Grimsby; Port Vale's sixth successive loss. SPL: Vennegao 20-second injury but Celtic hit four to beat Hamilton; Killie take Hearts third place with 2-1 win. SL: Queens six-hitters lord it over ten-man Livi. BSP: leaders Crawley latest to go for a Burton; winning start for Dean Saunders for Wrexham at FGR. Trophy: four-goal sharpshooters: Scott Barlow (Trafford) at 19, Neil Richmond (Gt Wakering), but Trafford's eight goals top score. Vase: Top of the goal preserves – Tiptree with eight, too.

5   Now Hull add Spurs scalp to their north London belt; some relief for tortured Toon – fight back to earn draw at Everton; Trotters trip to town ends in win at West Ham; Chelsea two better than Villa; Liverpool the hard way at Man City after two down; Pompey's seventh game in 21 days ends with win over Stoke. SPL: one-shot St Mirren finish off Rangers!

6   Man City want more players – having already £74m spent this summer!; Poland back in FIFA fold. Grimsby appoints Mike Newell as manager.

7   Lord Triesman hits out at PL clubs £3b debt, but Richard Scudamore dismisses remarks. UEFA Cup: Man City to face McClaren's Twente in one group, Pompey – AC Milan in another, Villa to meet Ajax in a third version while Spurs have it slightly easier on paper in a fourth on a day when Pavlyuchenko diagnosed with torn ligament. Skrtel back by Christmas for Liverpool. Ref supreme Hackett wants Hawk-Eye vision back. J Paint: Holt five for Shrewsbury in seven-goal romp at Wycombe! BSP: Crawley held by FGR, Wrexham win again. Only three points separate top six.

8   Banks contact three PL clubs over debt – Chelsea £730m in such a state. UEFA may ban such clubs. Terry injured again. West Ham to sell players. Kinnear may face FA charge over language. Paint: Rotherham waters down Leeds.

9   Icy winds from Iceland causing West Ham concern. Dubai millions head for Charlton? League Managers Association hits out at Triesman remarks. 39th step may take five years. Paul Lambert is new Colchester boss. BSP: Torquay held by late Oxford stroke.

10 Kazakhstan ranked 120th already getting written off; Fletcher skippers Scots on his 40th cap v Norway; Liechtenstein 135th in world with Darlington left-back to face Wales; Irish off to Slovenia hoping for clean bill of health. U-21: England edges Wales 3-2 at Ninian Park. Daggers beat Barnet to go second in L2.

11 High five – but all in last 38 mins – help England survive the question marks; debut sub Iwelumo three yard miss of the century curbs Scots in goalless with Norway; Slovenia strikes six minutes from the end finish Irish hopes; Wales labour against Liechtenstein but miss another pen of course (Bellamy this time). Elsewhere: France need to fight back two down to draw in Romania; injury hit Italy draw in Bulgaria; Spain 26 games unbeaten now; Adebayor foursome for Togo! L1: Cheltenham 3-1 down beat Colchester 4-3; nine out of ten wins for Scunny who shoot to top; Kandol return double lifts Millwall. L2: 62 sec lead for Grimsby but Wycombe's finishing ten gets injury time draw; goal-getting Silkmen stitch up the Shots; improving Exeter end Bury run; Gills catch Shrimps five times; Bradford three in last nine minutes edges Stanley. BSP: top four – Crawley, Kettering, Cambridge and Kiddy are all winners again. FA Cup: best gate for Dover v AFC Wimbledon 2710; Michael Lennon four for Nantwich, Craig Davis three pens for Totton; Gavin Cogden hat-trick in Durham's 6-1 win at Stalybridge.

12 FA to look into betting patterns. SLC: Airdrie and Ross Co win semis to reach final. BSP: Torquay win again, Stevenage beaten at Eastbourne.

13 West Ham near new shirt sponsor deal. Community Shield may be sidelined by new PL Cup tournament. BSP: Burton keeps Stags at bay.

14 Ferdinand heralds "new England" with wives and girlfriends banned – WAGS to witches? U-21: England has Huddlestone red-carded and has to settle for Wales draw to qualify; Republic wins friendly in Lithuania. Atletico Madrid must play Liverpool 200 miles from home after racist decision. Moyes signs £15m deal at Everton. Santa Cruz wants Man City role.

15 WC: Despite 23 move equaliser, England batter Belarus as Rooney tunes in twice again to enhance Capello standing; ten man San Marino sunk in Belfast; Wales succumb with just 18 mins left in Germany; Keane early strike enough for Republic; Croatia four but Andorra's Koldo saves Modric pen; Portugal held by Albania; Greece beaten by Swiss; Spain march on;

16 HM Government who muscle in on state of soccer's finances and match-fixing allegations. Torres is injury worry. Dunga under fire as Brazil falter.

17 UEFA to step in over match-fixing allegations. Sheff Utd to block West Ham appeal over Tevez case. Newcastle wants five players. Heskey hankers after Liverpool again.

18 Feast and famine in the PL with 18 goals in four matches, none in three others! Chelsea – with seven first-team players unavailable – still score five goals to defeat Boro at the Riverside. Then there are games of two halves for Walcott inspired Arsenal (200th PL home victory) and Kuyt boosted Liverpool over Everton and ten-man Wigan respectively, though Steve Bruce is unhappy with the late one. Rooney sparks Man Utd four-play against WBA and a thrown coin hits the lino at Villa on Harry Redknapp's 25th managerial celebration. Bolton pre-match fan booze bonanza only leads to goalless hangover as Roberts misses sitter for Rovers; Richardson hits woodwork three times with same free-kick and has goal disallowed, too, as Sunderland draw at Fulham. FLC: Coventry gk lapse, so Wolves back on top as Brummie draw at Burnley; Buzsaky blockbuster gives QPR lift; Derby keep winning; Charlton finish with nine and lose; Saints miss two pens and concede three goals to Watford. L1: Stockport's boss Gannon rages about Colchester. Oldham and Leicester settle for a draw. Scunny roll on, vet Harris is on the ball for Millwall; Lambert's tenth of season for Bristol R. L2: loanee Sigurdsson, 19, debut strike for Shrewsbury; McGleish 97th min pen for Wycombe v Darlo; Bury take Daggers second place; ten Barnet boys win odd goal in seven at Rotherham. SPL: Crock hit Celts win at Caley; Dons dump Falkirk to bottom. SL: six pts separate top eight in Div 1!; Brechin only unbeaten in Lge; Elgin stun Sten in Div 3. BSP: Poppies bloom for Kettering again as Crawley lose at Histon; Torquay nine unbeaten. Trophy goal glut with six packers Boston, Hemel, Soham, Stourbridge; Mark Danks treble for Halesowen in eight goal share at Durham; Michael Chennels four for Windsor; Phil Walsh first half treble for Tiverton.

19 Now Hull nail the Hammers while Spurs in worst-ever start finish with nine in loss at Stoke. FLC: Steel city ends with Blades cut up by the Owls in ten-a-side affair. L2: Vale wins at Chester. Becks to join AC Milan on loan? Inter beat Roma by four.

20 They're playing our Toon – United denied win by late Man City. L2: Darlo edge Bradford in six minute three goal flurry at the close. Seven-game no-in-Dundee dispenses with boss man Alex Rae.

21 Ch Lge: Gunners strafe Fenerbahce with five, Berba duo as Celtic (18th CL away no win) crash at Man Utd; five, too for Lyon in turnaround at Steaua; Villarreal double Aalborg's three; Juve edge Real; Zenit held by BATE.

FLC: ten Wolves bitten five times by Lita treble Canaries, so Birmingham resume at the top after edging Palace; ten-man Saints draw at Sheff Utd; Derby lose at Blackpool, Barnsley beat Sheff Wed. seventh home win for Reading. L1: Scunny held by the Shrimpers; three in six mins Pool get five to Huddersfield's three; Lions paw way to second at Colchester. L2: Rochdale gets six against Chester; Exeter wins at PV; Millers shake Bury at Gigg Lane. Styles weekend gardening leave.

22   Terry rescues Chelsea against Roma; Liverpool held by late Atletico equaliser ; Barca batter Basle five times; Bordeaux down surprise packets Cluj. L2: Spireites skewer pen-missing Shots with high five.

23   UEFA Cup: Spurs implode with O'Hara red-card and defeat at Udinese as ex-boss Jol sees Hamburg victory; McClaren's Twente win; Pompey concede three but Harry R unhappy with ref at Braga; Villa odd goal in three better than Ajax. Barton gets a card – an out of jail one. Rioch sacked by Aalborg. Ex- Polish team boss and MP Wojcik on corruption charges. Dubai group loses interest in Charlton.

24   QPR sacks Iain Dowie, Venables rumoured. L1: Tranmere move up to sixth. L2: Bradford go third after win at Grimsby.

25   Overnight sensation as Ramos and co are sacked by Spurs and Harry Redknapp is appointed! On the field it's a game of two halves as Rio and Man Utd hit high and low spots in draw at Everton, with Roo taken off fearing a red card as Toffees stick to it after the break. Rocket Richardson free and Cisse solo ends Black Cats nightmare against the Toon, but fans invasion mars it all; Hull hand Baggies a lesson; born again McCarthy for Rovers 94th min leveller with Boro. FLC: Centurion Lee's double gaffe gifts Wolves success at Watford. Managerless Rangers stop Reading scoring in no-goals affair. Brum's best start in 133 years with O'Connor duo against Sheff Wed. L1: Scunny just keep the Lions at bay, Delph boy lifts Leeds; on fire Lambert's first half foursome has Shimpers reeling for Bristol R; Posh also have four-play to beat Huddersfield. L2: Bury topped by the Hatters; Wycombe score in last minute for third time in four games; 94th min goal raises Vale; Rotherham makes it seven wins in 13 to stay in the black. SPL: now its baby Sheri (18) for Celtic against Hibs; Boyd brace keeps Rangers in touch at cellar-dwelling Hamilton. S Cup: Sten hit Threave for five in no surprise round. FA Cup: Havant on trail again dumping Crawley while other BSP casualties are Rushden at Evesham, Salisbury at Team Bath and AFC Hornchurch at Weymouth; others await replay fate including Lewes held at Step 5 Leiston; Kiddy five at Kings Lynn. Best gate Wrexham 3115 held by Eastwood.

26   Harry R is Harry Ho Ho Ho! as Xmas comes early for rejuvenated Tottenham over Bolton; Chelsea's 86 game unbeaten home record ends with Liverpool making it a Bridge not too far for them; Pompey struggle without a boss in draw with Fulham; Robinho treble shoots down Stoke for Man City; Arsenal an og and then late win at ten-man finishing Hammers; Villa four play too much for Wigan with sub Carew stripping off to hit a screamer.

27   Harry R appoints Kevin Bond as No.2, Tim Sherwood and David Coles could be added. Vet Cole quits Forest.

28   Relief for Toon as Barton pen kick-starts win over WBA. FLC: caretaker Rangers boss Ainsworth produces crucial win over Birmingham; Jensen heroics give Burnley edge over Reading; Forest end 11-game winless streak at Palace; Southend beach Leeds; Oldham send Scunny a three-goal Alessandra shock; snowstorm abates and Wolves edge out Swans. L1: Leicester beaten at Brighton; Northampton, Walsall called off. L2: Chesterfield have joy of six at Exeter!; Luton, Wycombe abandoned. FA Cup replays: Leiston win at Lewes, Eastwood axe Wrexham; while Telford takes out Northwich first time. CIS: Rangers, Dundee Utd and Falkirk into semis.

29   Now Spurs even share eight goals at Arsenal (Bentley volley against old mates) after twice being two down!; Tony Adams in charge but Portsmouth lose at lack-lustre Liverpool; Boro bounce Man City out; Ron double for Man Utd over West Ham; Chelsea take revenge as Hull are humbled on the Humber; odd goal in five win for Villa against Blackburn; Fellaini again the Everton scoring hero at Bolton; Delap throws Stoke a lifeline for Fuller against Sunderland; Johnson breaks duck twice for Fulham against Wigan. CIS: Celtic complete foursome with win at Killie. Jocky Scott gets Dundee role for third time. Maradona is new Argentine coach! Dropped Greek player commits suicide. Curbs may seek compensation from Hammers.

30   Becks for AC Milan on loan in January. BSP: another Crawley loss this time at Salisbury. Scots girls brave win in Russia not good enough in UEFA Championship play-off.

31   Spanish Novo banned by SFA from playing for Scotland. Sky Sports Victory Shield: England win in Wales.

NOVEMBER 2008

Hull even frighten Man Utd … Managers threaten refs revolt … Ronaldo's century of Man Utd goals … Capello bandwagon rolls on … Rafa's big day for Liverpool … Slump in PL attendances.

1   Stoke put spoke in Gunners wheels as "Chuck" Delap and Fuller finish starts it, then Van Persie sent off, Walcott carted off ends it; Spurs late but still early enough to end Liverpool unbeaten run; Alex with Chelsea's 1000th PL goal, Lampard with his 100th League strike – Cech's 100th clean sheet – Anelka treble, Keane sent to stand for goal protest, so it's high five against the Black Cats; gallant Hull trailing three down, get three but lose and Roo gets another yellow in Man Utd's 400th PL win; on rack Wigan ride their luck to win with Heskey's 100th PL goal; Mido rescues pt for Boro after Turnbull gk heroics against West Ham; Andrews the saviour for ten-man Blackburn at Albion; first home win for Everton, courtesy Saha. FLC: two down Saints win at PNE; initial strikers – I and E-B – help Wolves at Cardiff; Reading hit four at Bristol C; Charlton sliding, Watford score three but lose to Blackpool. L1: Posh 11-game unbeaten run, Orient first win in ten; Cox treble gets pt for Swindon at Scunny; coasting Southend scramble to share six with Colchester; Murray makes a couple for resurging Brighton, but misses pen. L2: Wycombe only undefeated English lose top spot to Darlo after draw at Rotherham; first win in ten for Morecambe as pen-missing again Shots go seven away against Bradford; battling Barnet share six at Bradford. SPL: Boyd 14-min hattrick for Rangers at Caley. SL: Peterhead hit five to end Brechin's unbeaten run and Raith go top. BSP: ten-man Kettering lose to Weymouth; Torquay close to second place. Trophy: another four away goals for Windsor's Chennells!; 22 away wins in 33 ties (one abandoned). Dithering FA must re-apply for Burton Centre.

2   flaky Man City shredded at Bolton. FLC: Attwell at it again in controversial ruling out of Derby winner against ten-finishing Foresters. Kaka misses pen but AC Milan top Serie A. Eleven in a row for bouncing Barca. Moscow mayhem as Spartak and CSKA fans fight, leaving Rubin Kazan to win first Russian title.

3   Toons of glory as Martins double vanquish Villa. Coventry upset Brummies. Managers axed: Boothroyd (Watford), Ward (Carlisle).

4   Ch Lge: Chelsea lose Deco to a red in Roma defeat, Liverpool rescue pt with Gerrard last-ditch pen. Barca's draw enough for last 16. Villa's threesome for Derby day out at Brighton. J Paint: Rotherham surprises Leicester, Shrewsbury hit five against Daggers. SPL: Rangers share six with Dundee Utd. Ternent (Huddersfield) is 13th managerial casualty so far. Attwell to sit it out once more.

5   Ch Lge: Giggs snatches pt for Man Utd at Celtic; Arsenal held by Fenerbahce; by Juve, the Italians beat Real.

6   UEFA Cup: even Bent gets a trio for Pompey over Dinamo Zagreb; Villa win in Prague, Man City edge McClaren's Twente. West Ham up for sale.

7   FA Cup: ten Cobblers hold Leeds. Sky Sports Victory Shield: Scots and Irish draw.

8   It's fantasy football at the Emirates but Nasri double is magic for Arsenal, misery for Man Utd; Keane hits first goal then another for Liverpool on Benitez's 250th in charge against Albion; crisis club Hull? – as Jaaskalainen

heroics help Trotters inflict third defeat in a row; Tony Adams gets first Pompey win at Sunderland; Toffees three in five minutes leave Hammers as late on suckers; Stoke pick up a point at Wigan where Heskey is hamstrung. FLC; Birmingham held at Forest, as Wolves go six points clear; S.Yorks derby flare up in ten-a-side with Sheff U winning at Barnsley; Cardiff nine lose at Rangers; Davis saves pen but Saints lose to Bristol C; another three goals for Reading; Donny still in the toils. FA Cup shocks as Blyth spirit triumphs over Shrews, Histon's Wright piston pips Swindon and Curzon put the curse on Exeter Grecians. Grays hold Carlisle away; Young pen save for Telford but Southend scramble an equaliser. Droylsden sub gk Clancy earns replay at Darlo; Kettering lead for one min in Lincoln draw and 3-1 down Vale hit three in 11 mins to win at Huddersfield. Altrincham survive at Luton; Leiston get another shot at ten-man Fleetwood; Brighton and Hartlepool share six; Scunny beat the Walsall ten. SPL: crock-hit Celts beat the 'Well. SL: ten-a-side as Sten and Sons draw. BSP: Burton take advantage of few games to go top at Northwich.

9 Man City nine beaten by Spurs ten; Fulham put stop to Toon revival as Kinnear unhappy with whistler; on fire Anelka gets two for table-topping Chelsea at Blackburn; Boro please boss Southgate at Villa. FLC: Swans show Sunday best to Watford. FA Cup: Havant, Hornchurch and Team Bath hopes dashed.

10 FA hit out at ref critics. Ipswich fines Norris over support for jailed drink-drive McCormick. Hughes to get Dubai owners backing. FA Cup: Harrold hat-trick ends AFC Dons cup hopes.

11 Managers threaten pre-match go-slow tactics as response to poor ref decisions; C Cup: young Guns too good for Wigan; Tevez pen rescues Man Utd against QPR; Watford get revenge at Swansea; Leeds are Derby's latest victims; Stoke grind the Millers. L1: Leicester regains lead. David Byrne is Swindon caretaker. SPL: Dons climb to fourth place against St Mirren. Hargreaves is out for season. Police corruption net to be widened. Chester sacks Davies.

12 C Cup: Burnley dump Chelsea in shoot-out as Jensen is spot-on saving but Drogba in trouble after coin-throwing incident; return of Santa is present for Blackburn at Sunderland; Spurs quite naturally brush aside "disinterested" Liverpool. SPL: Celtic extends lead as Rangers held at Motherwell. FIFA back the ref respect agenda

13 Drogba faces FA payback for return of coin. Sir Trevor Brooking is unhappy with everything and upsets Lord Mawhinney; Maradona in row with Argentine FA. Celtic fined £42,000 for one-man pitch invasion. Kinnear apologises for ref remark. FA Cup: Tranmere wins Stanley replay. Mark Wright starts third stint as Chester boss.

14 Man City fine Elano for TV criticism of Hughes. Scolari wants coin-throwing fans chucked out. Scunny regain top place at Bristol R.

15 Villa the latest to pop the Gunners bubble; Man Utd celebrate Sir Alex's 50 years in the pro game with 5-0(!) as Ronaldo free kicks 100th and 101st MU goals; Liverpool slip the Bolton despite missed chances and Trotters effort ruled out by ref Styles; Gomes gaffe gives Harry R first defeat at Fulham; ex-Mags Titus B turns Toon tormentor in Wigan leveller; Samba for Rovers but Black Cats call the tune; Anelka double nets his 12th for Chelsea at Albion; Green is Hammers saviour as Pompey held. FLC: Warnock wails over Chopra pen as Palace loses at Cardiff. Weaver woe costs Addicks at Brum and Phillips scores in his 500th game. Reading's crucial win at Sheff Utd; only eighth goal of season gives "dynamic" Donny first win in12; McIndoe spot failure as Bristol C draw; ten-man Saints snared by Wolves; no pen proves Rangers pain against Burnley, three in five mins helps Swans to swoop on Canaries. F1: thirteen lucky for Carlisle, Posh 12 unbeaten; ten-a-side at Tranmere draw with Southend; Huddersfield surprise Leeds. F2: Gills four-play hits Rotherham ten; three in 20 mins for Accrington and on-loan Forte first half treble fortifies foursome Notts. Hunt's first goal since 2006 keeps only unbeaten team Wycombe in front, while last to win Grimsby do it with ten men; Shots miss pen (of course) but finish with ten beating Exeter. SPL: gk McGregor aides nervy Rangers win. SL: Prunty treble for Ayr. BSP: Burton, Torquay, Histon, Kiddy all win. Vase: three year old Dosthill Colts filled in by Coalville five; Barwell gk Lee Castle drop kick goal in six share with Studley; FA Cup surprises Leiston through, too. Inter plough on in Italy.

16 Ireland strikes twice for Man City, but Brazilian Geovanni levels for Hull; Everton fight back to earn Boro draw on Moyes' 250th Toffees League game. FLC: Preston wins the Lancs derby at Blackpool. SPL: Celtic make hard work of Hamilton ten. SLC final: Airdrie beat Ross on pens. Real reel as board call training session but just five players appear and no-show coach Schuster!

17 Capello cracks whip over "injured" players. Bundesliga blueprint to be followed? Drogba holds hand up to coining it. FA Cup: Beckford trio nails Leeds ahead of Cobblers.

18 Walcott dislocates shoulder in training. Maradona dismisses cheat claim with wave of Hand of God. England "B" to bat for England in Berlin. U-21s: England beat Czechs, N Ireland win in Scotland. FA crackdown with Sir Alex, Moyes and Drogba handed various fines. QPR appoint Paulo Sousa as manager. FA Cup: Replay shocks for Darlo at Droylsden and Hatch suffers broken neck while Kettering edges Lincoln. Altrincham miss pen then loses a shoot-out to Luton, Stockport hit Yeovil for five, Grays leads over Carlisle hit by light failure. BSP: Torquay, Histon and Cambridge still winning.

19 Terry seals it in Berlin as Capello makes it five wins in a row; Wales surprise the Danes; Argies off to Maradona win in Scotland; Republic bow to the Poles, Irish need to Hungary. Berbatov suffers hamstring as Bulgaria hammered six by Serbia. Swedish ref Hansson had received death threats after Atletico pen against Liverpool. JM's PL medal thrown to crowd sold on auction for £21,600. Chris Todd has leukaemia. Hull boss Brown misconduct fine.

20 Praise all round for iron-fist Capello! Meanwhile svelte-like Sven is already facing Mexico sacking! UEFA plan to prevent movement of U-18s not favoured by FIFA. Gallas faces Wenger wrath with outburst.

21 Gallas demoted as skipper and dropped. Kinnear tempts Shearer. Phillips at the double helps Brummies in Swans-upping.

22 Big four, big nothing – no goals for them first time over a weekend since 1993, first blank day since 1922 – stats that! Worse as Arsenal even ship three goals at Man City, while Liverpool fail to break down Fulham. Villa bemoans no pen against Man Utd and even Wise turns up to see Newcastle draw at Chelsea. veteran Windass claims og equaliser as his own for Hull at Pompey; Mali man Sidibe late delivery puts Stoke over the Baggies; Bolton two in first ten mins undoes Boro. FLC: new skipper Iwelumo leads Wolves from the front; beaten Reading in a Wright-Phlips state over Saints; Sheff Utd's five so Addicks boss man Alan Pardew has had it; it's a so-and-so for Sousa's Rangers at Watford. F1: King trumps Scunny for Leicester to go top and MK Dons sneak second place at Walsall; Posh 13 no loss. F2: Wycombe claim leadership beating Port Vale as Darlo held at Brentford; Bury back to scoring form; Benson hat-trick in Daggers five star show. SPL: Situ normal as Celtic wins at St Mirren, Rangers home to Dons. SL: Annan hit Elgin for five. BSP: Histon five against Oxford, Burton beat Stevenage, but Torquay have to scrap for draw at Woking. Trophy: Kieran Knight's day for Hayes as his foursome display hits Chelmsford; Hemel give Heybridge the hump; sub Dave Gilroy treble for Bath; AFC Wimbledon eyed by 895 at Worcester and win.

23 Two games, two goals – Hammers with Upson outstanding at Sunderland, Spurs inspired by flying midget Lennon home to Rovers who finish with ten. French bid to hijack PL and get EU backing.

24 Rare goal from Camara points Wigan in right direction against Everton, but the ten-game PL long weekend has yielded a miserable 15 goals. Barnsley wins lively encounter with Burnley by the odd goal in five. Watford

appoints Brendan Rodgers JM protÈgÈ from Chelsea reserve coaching to boss level and Lampard snr is on board, too. Fabregas is new Gunners skipper.

25   Ch Lge: Bendtner winner for relieved Arsenal over Dynamo Kiev, Man Utd draw a blank at Villarreal as both qualify, but Celtic lead then lose to Aalborg and exit Europe; Real, Lyon, Bayern, Porto reach last 16. FLC: Wolves ravage Sheff Utd, Birmingham early strikes put Ipswich off and ten-man Reading get a draw at Cardiff; caretaker Phil Parkinson sees Charlton give Sousa first win for QPR. F1: Leicester squeak in against Crewe, MK Dons see off Hereford and Millwall leave it late to sneak third place as Scunny lose at Tranmere. L2: Wycombe unbeaten in 17 have County in Notts, Darlo lose to Chester, but Bradford beat ten from Chesterfield. Barnsley to take action against Morgan of Sheff Utd over Hume injury. Man City to spend £100m in the transfer window. Trophy: Farnborough strikes replay six against Braintree.

26   Ch Lge: Liverpool record day – Benitez breaks Shankly with 66th Euro game, equals Paisley's 39 such wins and in like vein Gerrard wins with his 30th goal against battling Marseille; Lampard's two yellows leave him red faced as Chelsea struggle for Cluj draw; JM suffers defeat by Panathinaikos but go through with five goal Barca, and Atletico winners over PSV before closed ground, Shakhtar's high five not enough however. FL clubs to vote on four homers in each 16 match squad. Kaka interested in Man City?

27   UEFA Cup: Spurs take out Nijmegen and Man City impress at Schalke, but heartache for Pompey as Milan go from DC (down a couple) to AC (add a couple) to level at Fratton. Torres has hamstring again. Bolton to take Anelka to High Court over image rights. Youth Cup: Chelsea edge Man Utd as Sir Alex watches. *The Daily Telegraph* reveals 11 PL clubs with lower crowds and overall average down 1000 a match day.

28   Wenger dismisses Arsenal crisis talk, Sir Alex jibes and Cech comments as Gallas returns to the fold. French may be losing EU battle over PL. FA Cup: Barrow boys trundle Brentford out of it. Sky Sports Victory Shield: England beat Scots to take it again.

29   Poor Black Cats run over by the Bolton Trotters rare four play; back to back wins for Wigan after Baggies lead; Hull penned in by late Stoke spot kick leveller; another goalless home game for Villa against Fulham plus the Tees-Tyne derby. FLC: Wolves and Brum settle for one a piece; Burnley take the shine off Rams; relief for Forest over Barnsley after three months no home win; nearly ten hours no away goals for QPR held at Palace; Saints Davis holds up Addicks. FA Cup and more shocks as Eastwood chop down Wycombe, Forest Green eat Rochdale and fog-off Droylsden written off at Chesterfield. Blyth earn replay at Bournemouth thanks to roofer gk Bell; Morecambe level with Cheltenham lost in the mist, too; no replay repeat for Grays in daylight defeat by Carlisle; Fryatt treble hits Daggers for Leicester; Hayes injury mars Scunny foursome over Alfreton ten. SPL: Hearts trump Rangers as Celtic edge Caley. BSP: Burton are back on top against Eastbourne. S Cup: East Stirling surprises Livi, Sten stun Clach five times. Spain: Real lose, but Barca win.

30   Wheels off at Chelsea as Van Persie double for firing again Gunners includes offside goal amid Scolari fury; Roo – 100th club goal – divides Mancunian derby, but Ron's two yellows make a red; Moyes 300th Everton game rewarded with win at Spurs; fourth reverse in a row for Rovers at Pompey. Welsh derby finishes ten-a-side as Swans and Cardiff share four. FA Cup: Histon end Leeds hopes, Kettering earns draw at Notts. Inter have six point lead, 250th goal for Juve's Del Piero.

DECEMBER 2008
Burnley surprise Arsenal's youngesters ... Keane texts his resignation ... 700 up for Wenger ... Cracks showing at Chelsea ... Big Sam in at Blackburn ... All play PL Boxing Day!

1   Liverpool in another goalless draw with Hammers, but reach the summit. Three more goals scored by Reading. Watford's chairman Simpson quits.

2   C Cup: Burnley feed on a McDonald double to oust the see-saw young Arsenal; Ellington late pen ends Stoke hopes for Derby for semi places. FA Cup: Cheltenham wins at Morecambe. F2: Wycombe shake off cup defeat to hit Macc for four. Luton and Bournemouth (now zero pts) share six goals. Van Persie lino is on weekend leave! Ronaldo is Euro Player of the Year. Robinho slap on wrist for Man City outburst.

3   UEFA Cup: Man City held but qualify with winners Twente, Galatasaray, Metalist Kharkiv, Standard and Udinese. C Cup: Tevez three (or four?) in Man Utd's five against Rovers three while Spurs recover at Watford to reach semis, too. FA Cup: Miller in the mood for Crewe at Carlisle. FL seek salary cap. U21s: England in Spain, Germany and Finland group.

4   UEFA Cup: calamity James gifts it to Wolfsborg for Pompey; Villa lose at home but still qualify along with AC Milan, Braga, St Etienne, Valencia and CSKA Moscow. Keane texts his resignation to Sunderland. Two charged with racist abuse of Mido.

5   Allardyce Black Cats favourite. Evra four match ban for Chelsea groundsman incident. Greg Abbott is Carlisle boss.

6   Santa Cruz has PL's 400th goal of season but Liverpool sail on at the top; Chelsea record 11 unbeaten away in a row at Bolton; Sunderland rearguard holds up Man Utd until last min man Vidic strikes; Newcastle chuck away Owen's two goals to let Stoke draw; Hull turn tables on Boro; one enough for Arsenal against Wigan; Bullard the key in Fulham draw with Man City. FLC: Rangers ravage the Wolves as Brummies edge Watford to cut lead to three pts; Reading ten too much for Barnsley; Charlton hit the bottom at Blackpool; Burnley with best of five at Sheff Utd. F1: Fryatt second treble in a week batters the Shrimpers; Scunny stunners at MK Dons; Bristol R unable to hold a Kandol at Millwall; Leeds tripped at Tranmere. F2: Wycombe Chairboys last team standing unbeaten have rug pulled under them at Aldershot; "sick note" Anderton signs off with winner in his 477th and last game for Bournemouth against Chester. SPL: another treble for Rangers as they hit Accies for seven and St Mirren climb off the foot. S Cup: Elgin just spear Spartans. SL: Sten beaten at Berwick, East Stirling hit five, but 12 games lost in Scotland to frozen pitches. BSP: Burton, Histon, Kiddy and Crawley win while Torquay held by Cambridge. Vase: trebles for Ryan Blott and Danny Gray as Scarborough hit six; Biggleswade, too.

7   Leaving it late? Everton level in 93rd min, A Young winner for Villa 94th; Miller injury as Baggies held by Pompey. PL rules ok(?) – increasing from 342 ten years ago to 777. SPL: Hibs cause Celtic upset; Real in trouble as Sevilla wins there and Barca is six pts clear. Six in a row for Inter, Bayern catch new boys Hoffenheim at last.

8   Spurs dig in another win at West Ham. Kinnear faces another FA charge. Vet Kuqi sparks Palace over Saints. S Cup: Diack treble for Brechin is tale of two cities at Edinburgh. Hume determined to play again.

9   Ch Lge: Drogba come on to insist Chelsea have the answer against Cluj; Liverpool take the PSV in Eindhoven; Roma send Bordeaux direct to UEFA Cup; Inter defeat in Bremen means Panathinaikos top group and Barca surprised by Shakhtar. FLC: Birmingham seven undefeated but Wolves take it out on the Rams; one again enough for Reading; Charlton beaten once more; QPR miss pen at Sheff Wed and lose. FA Cup: Droylsden hold Chesterfield, Gills and Posh win replays. S Cup: Alloa edge Raith. Real axe Schuster and appoint Spurs failure Ramos!

10   Ch Lge: Man Utd fail to beat Aalborg and Rooney accused of a first-class stamp; Arsenal unable to celebrate Wenger's 700th in charge in losing at Porto; Celtic win but it's too late to save them from the exit; Ramos instant success!; Bayern fine win in Lyon. Last 16: Arsenal, Chelsea, Liverpool, Man Utd, Roma, Barcelona, Panathinaikos, Bayern, Juve, Sporting, Inter, Villarreal, Lyon, Porto, Atletico and Real. FLC: Ipswich, Watford both win.

FA Cup: Kettering's replay win over Notts makes non-league success best for 30 years. MPs on the Morgan trail as FA fail to take action over the Sheff Utd player. Sol Campbell abusers get caught.

11 Ex-boss Grant sneers at Chelsea players. Hughes tells Ince to stand up for himself at Rovers. Lee Clark is Huddersfield manager.

12 Three FL games 18 goals! Another fine mess for Stanley at Lincoln (five), Macc and MK Dons four goals each.

13 Tearaway Tigers force Liverpool into a Gerrard double to make a point; old boy Aliadiere ensures Boro a draw with Arsenal; Gomes comes good to save Spurs from defeat against Man Utd; Ince wince as ragged Rovers show no return at Wigan; caretaker Sbragia's Black Cats four play flattens Baggies; Cahill 92nd min delivery for Toffees wraps it up over Man City; Villa hit fourth place with a foursome over Bolton; Stoke and Fulham – denied a pen call – limp to no goals. FLC: another Watford win; first away goal in 768 mins for QPR at Plymouth; Reading lucky pen riles Norwich; Birmingham late defeat at Preston so Wolves extend lead; Ipswich's ten lose, Sheff Utd ten get a draw; three up in 11 mins Burnley hold off Saints fight back. Fl: Harris equals Teddy Sheri's 111th Millwall goal; McL and M-S (rebound retrieved by McL) miss pens so Posh held by Oldham and Crewe 13th ends misery with win over Swindon ten. Four in a row for slipping Leeds; three adrift at Scunny, Cobblers share eight goals; ten man Cheltenham win at Orient; Leicester two pts clear at top. F2: Grimsby first home win; lights fail for Daggers; Luton get draw at Wycombe; Rochdale make it ten no loss. SPL: Draw men: Celtic home to Hearts, Rangers away at Dundee Utd. SL: St Johnstone, Dunfermline, Partick and Li vi win in Div 1; Rodgers three as East Stirling rise to fourth! S Cup: Locos shunt Vale. Trophy: 17 waterlogged off; Histon finish with nine as Cam Utd win; Johnny Dyer double for Uxbridge accounts for ten finishing AFC Dons. Spain: Barca held up until late by Real.

14 Bridge boos as Chelsea drop two points at home to ex-Blues Zola's Hammers; Newcastle hit three on the coast at Pompey. Is Allardyce for Sunderland? Will Ince survive?

15 Year of Capello caps it all! Rooney escapes stamping ban. Owen's deal at Toon? Portsmouth fined £15,000 by FA over Mwarawari transfers. Scolari will not buy. Charlton foiled by Derby leveller. Danny Wilson heads out of Hartlepool, as Chris Turner moves in. Kettering sponsor alleged to be terrorist outfit! S Cup: Forfar beat the Stranraer nine; Spartans put Elgin to the sword; Ross picks off the Sons of the Rock and Forres eclipse the Star.

16 Big Sam for Rovers as Ince reaches point of no return. Eduardo comeback in Arsenal reserves. FIFA to agree GB team 2012 but can be an all English! FA Cup: Blyth's sports science student stuffs Bournemouth; lights fail and Droylsden fan abuse of lino as Chesterfield lead nullified. Paint: Rotherham, Scunny, Luton and Brighton reach semis. SL: Airdrie slump at Clyde.

17 UEFA Cup: Pompey bow out with a win, Villa with a defeat in Hamburg still qualify. S Cup: Lochee, Lochee unlucky for Ayr. CWC semi: Dep Quito beat Pachuca. Man Utd rapped over Evra evidence. Santa departure key to Blackburn finances. There is a Boardroom shake-up at Arsenal.

18 UEFA Cup: Spurs fight back to level with CSKA Moscow, Man City lose at Santander and have Robinho injured but also qualify. CWC: Man Utd win late goal spree 5-3 with Gamba; Adelaide takes 5th spot beating Al Ahly. FL to ensure four "home-grown" players – in each 16 man squad!

19 Ch Lge draw: JM's Inter get Man Utd, Chelsea paired with Juve, Liverpool against Real and Arsenal face Roma. UEFA Cup: Villa get unbeaten CSKA Moscow, Man City have FC Copenhagen, Spurs to meet Shakhtar Donetsk. Fl: Southend ten sink in the Hartlepool.

20 Slicky Ricky Sbragia's Black Cats send Tigers packing; two in 160 secs and Bolton on way to edging Portsmouth; no Santa but McCarthy gives Big Sam an opening present; Fulham's threesome best of season against Boro; Villa rely on og and gk Friedel. FLC: Swans sixth draw record draw; Doyle on the boil as Reading win crucially at Birmingham to go second; Charlton 14 no win; 12 out injured Sheff Wed lose at Cardiff; first win in seven for Derby; stand-in Collins hero for Wolves. F1: Fryatt's 23rd goal as Foxes spank Posh, Brighton baffled by no pen award and 93rd min loser at Tranmere. MK Dons eighth win in nine hits Leeds for fifth reverse in a row. Loanee Davies has two goals for Stockport in win over Bristol R. F2: Hope gifts Shots two pens as Grimsby draw and Wycombe goes nine pts clear after Shrews victory. Benson's 15th goal of the season as Dagenham defeats Macc. SPL: Boyd beats Hibs for Rangers; Accies shake Motherwell leaving both plus Falkirk and Caley on 17 pts! SL: Fifers and Clyde share eight goals; Raith extend Div 2 lead to four pts; Sten ten lose again at Forfar to late pen. BSP; Burton setting pace as Histon hit by Torquay.

21 Wenger rage over Adebayor dismissal by ref Webb as Liverpool draw at Emirates; Duff stuff gives Toon lift over Spurs; Baggies put slipping Man City to sleep late by Bednar effort. SPL: Celtic keep up momentum at Falkirk. CWC: Man Utd rule the globe (?) with Rooney goal beating Liga de Quito but Vidic sees red. Gary McAllister sacked by Leeds. FA try to mend fences with Sir Alex and Man Utd. Henry rescues win for Barca against Villarreal. Real scrape late win over Valencia ten. Eight League wins in a row for JM but he's not Inter happy!

22 Chelsea held at Everton and Terry red-carded to leave Scolari silent. Fabregas is likely to be out for four months. Simon Grayson is almost certain to become the next Leeds manager.

23 FA Cup: Droylsden dump Chesterfield at fourth attempt. S Cup: Ayr win Lochee replay. Trophy: Burton pushed to pens by Farsley. Man Utd get some Evra concessions.

24 Rangers want to join Atlantic League one day and use reserves in SPL! Gudjon Thordarson is new Crewe manager. Torres nearly fit again.

25 Sir Alex rules out spending in January and hits back at FA over Evra case. Droylsden may be dumped from FA Cup due to suspended player.

26 All play PL! Double strike by Keane is crucial as Liverpool see off Bolton. An early Drogba effort leaves Albion groggy against Chelsea, a Tevez solo success is enough for Man Utd at Stoke but Roo and Ron lucky to escape cards. Villa fight back earns a draw with Arsenal as O'Neill and Wenger deny any spat. Hull springs a five-time leak at Man City and boss Brown conducts a half-time pitch lecture. Everton goes sixth after Cahill strike at Boro. Pompey chimes stifled by blooming bubble-blowing Hammers foursome; Spurs off the goal standard as Fulham take a point with Gomes stopping them; Black Cats and Rovers also scoreless as Roberts misses target; Wigan misery for Toon on Kinnear birthday eve with one sent off another wheeled away. FLC; Calderwood chopped down by Forest after one-goal Donny manage four; gk Federici saves Reading with last kick equaliser against Cardiff; another Swansea draw; fit-again Bristol City take out Watford; Birmingham pen it at Ipswich; Wolves suffer gk gaffe in sharing with Sheff Utd. F1: Leicester held at Leeds so MK Dons close gap with win over Bristol R. Millwall beaten at Posh while Scunny hit Pool for three. Danny Wilson lands the Swindon job. F2: Wycombe have to settle for Exeter draw, so Brentford move second beating Bournemouth with Bury held by Darlo. BSP: Burton ten pts clear after edging York; Torquay snatch second place as Histon draw at Cambridge (6488).

27 SPL: McDonald shows Boyd the way to score as Celtic tip Rangers at Ibrox. SL: three off frozen in Div 3 as Sten held again. Fairclough to go upstairs at Barnet with Ian Hendon appointed manager.

28 Rampaging five goal Liverpool with two-goal Gerrard firing them, savage Toon at St James Park; Fulham catch Chelsea (despite record 19 away undefeated) for a Cottage point; Gallas (!) again Arsenal goal scoring hero against Pompey; Everton unusualy score three to give Sbragia his official debut reverse for Sunderland; seventh now and Wigan pen success at Bolton; late but a West Ham win as Stoke's Fuller sent off for brush with his own Griffin; sub Sturridge sparks Man City into leveller at Blackburn; Spurs revival stopped at the Baggies buffers. FLC; usual late

show for Reading point at Saints; Donny can't stop winning now, but Charlton – 16 without a win – slump on; Cardiff eight unbeaten; Swans draw – of course – but at Birmingham; Paul Jewell quits Derby as their ten lose to Ipswich; Forest clip the Canaries wings. F1: Cheltenham get three – Posh doubles it; Crewe goes crazy at Hartlepool with four; Leeds get a win at Stockport; Scunny downed at Huddersfield. F2: Shots 11-month home record goes as Daggers do them at the death; Holt's 20th goal revives Shrewsbury; another draw for Wycombe, so Brentford cut their lead to five; Rotherham survival now has them with 19 precious points after win at Notts. BSP: Histon get four, Kiddy win at Torquay – who miss pen; Crawley edge Eastbourne; new boss Chris Wilder sees Oxford get five.

29   Gerrard banged up overnight after alleged brawl on Sunday night; Berbatov goal finishes battling Boro. Wolves have to settle for a point at Blackpool. Droylsden expelled from FA Cup.

30   Hull denied pen as ref Bennett changes mind, so Villa go fourth. Jordan Robertson arrested over serious car crash.

31   Madejski gets knighthood, Jimmy Quinn axed by Bournemouth, but Charlton confirm Phil Parkinson. Droylsden appeal fails.

JANUARY 2009
Adverse weather hits fixtures ... Clough the younger at Derby ... Ronaldo FIFA Player of Year ... Kaka on offer at £100m ... Benitez and Sir Alex exchange views ... Robinho goes AWOL.

1   Window opens and Defoe to Spurs looks likely to dawn. Billy Davies appointed at Forest. Bournemouth has Eddie Howe as caretaker. BSP: Burton now 13 pts ahead, but Histon have three games kin hand.

2   FA Cup: Pavlyuchenko double puts Wigan in their place. Man City to secure Bridge from the Stamford version in £11m deal?

3   Global warming? – You're having a laugh with 4 FA Cup, 4 F1, 6 F2, 8 SL and 3 BSP frozen off. FA Cup shocks: megabucks Man City just lumber in the hands of three star Forest at Eastlands; caretaker Turner takes care of Hartlepool in sweeping Stoke out of it; Scolari Oh! No – Southend beach boys earn a replay at Chelsea with birthday boy Clarke snatching it at the death; no seaside busmen's holiday for Blackpool at Torquay either; Forest Green finish with nine but frighten Derby and lose only to a late pen; Kettering flying the non-league flag; weakened Reading lose at Cardiff; reinstated Chesterfield lose again. F2: Wycombe edge Bury on Peter Taylor's 56th birthday. SPL: Celtic held after two goal lead v Dundee Utd; St Mirren's last game at Love Street finishing love-all; Caley now bottom.

4   FA Cup: normal service back as Villa win at Gillingham, Man Utd ease past ten Saints. Cup draw pairs Merseysiders. SPL: Boyd double puts more pressure on Caley. Man City Hughes wants more windows and more signings! Charlton unable to play Christensen in a match because they can't afford it!

5   FA Cup: Blyth thrashed(?) 1-0 by Blackburn. Capello is critical of Gerrard incident. Clough jnr favourite for Derby job. Tevez story still makes news. Are Abramovich and Chelsea to part?

6   C Cup semi: game of two halves as Spurs recover to hit Burnley four times. Defoe paraded before game after signing at £9m making him the most expensive English forward at £35m. Eight games frozen off. Nigel Clough unveiled at Pride Park. Man City wants two teams of stars. Becks – the 38th richest player at £125m – is given his AC Milan debut in Dubai. Abramovich third in rich list now – Sheik Mansour at Man City leads on £15bn. Wembley cut ticket prices. In debt Rangers may see Boyd sold.

7   C Cup semi: Clough watches as Academy boss David Lowe plots Man Utd downfall at Derby. Charlton make loss of £11.5m. Motherwell beat Hearts in one other game played.

8   How much longer before Tevez the movie? Ronaldo car crash writes off Ferrari. Ivan Gazidis is new Arsenal chief exec. Woking game off.

9   Rafa weighs into Sir Alex over practically everything. Scolari is fearful of loss to Man Utd. Santa Cruz could stay at Rovers – until the summer. Reading takes four off Watford to embarrass ex-Academy coach Rodgers. All Welsh games frozen out.

10   Twenty-seven English and Scottish games off. Bendtner 84th minute turns sub zero into win for Arsenal against Bolton, rookie Carroll saves Toon point v Hammers (Bellamy's 100th career goal) and the 128th Tees-Wear derby ends all square. Villa edge Baggies to hold on to third place, off target Hull fourth reverse in a row lose to two on target Everton – one offside plus Fellaini's 10th booking; Liverpool's fifth love-all at Stoke. FLC: Forest still rising, Addicks 17 no win; Preston's Elliott pans old Wolves mates twice; no frills Soton win at Barnsley; Scotland double ends Swans draw habit at Burnley. L1: Leicester five pts clear after three against O's; Leeds losers again hit by an ex-player Bridges; Walsall sack Jimmy Mullen. L2: Bury clips struggling Barnet; MacDonald misses so Brentford draw at ten-man Lincoln. S Cup: Boruc almost gifts Dundee a draw; Ayr holds Killie; Stenousemuir lino treated for hypothermia! SL: Raith downed at Stirling. Trophy: only three games survive including Burton minus Clough beating Salisbury with Roy McFarland i/c.

11   Where are you, Chelsea? – The question is posed as they lose three goals and the points at Man Utd; Tottenham topple it dying moments at Wigan on a bad day for Londoners. Sir Alex reckons Rafa is "disturbed." PL to probe why two games had been called off on Saturday. Raul plays his 500th match for Real and scores. AC Milan gives Becks 90 mins outing.

12   Ronaldo is FIFA Player of the Year. Ten MK Dons held by Colchester, Oldham edge Hartlepool. PL is confident of escaping recession.

13   FA Cup: Wolves win at Brum; Histon seen off by Swans; Pompey replay win at Bristol C; Harris breaks Millwall scoring record; Charlton end misery at Norwich. F2: Luton "reach" zero pts with Chester draw. S Cup: Rangers ease in at St Johnstone; Forfar six puts spanner into Mechanics works. Kaka could become first £100m transfer to Man City.

14   FA Cup: Chelsea recover four play to beat first strike Shrimpers without Drogba; Hull with eight changes still win at Newcastle, but both bosses banished to stand; Palace clip Leicester, but gate is down to 6023 in present climate. PL: Rooney 54 secs winner for Man Utd but then injured against Wigan. Trophy: Pitman's treble shakes Cambridge for Crawley. Norwich sacks manager Glenn Roeder.

15   Italian reports say Kaka move might cost £135m but Wenger rates it "not in the real world." England launches bid for 2018 WC. Bryan Gunn handed Norwich role to end of season.

16   All not well for Rafa? Bellamy walks out on Hammers. Scolari: "love Chelsea or go." Ramon Calderon quits Real Madrid. L1: Hartlepool beat Northampton. BSP: Wrexham get draw at Torquay.

17   Hull rile over ref Wiley as Arsenal late show in the wind and rain is enough; 7th 1-0 win for Man Utd (89 mins 8 secs) – Chelsea equalling ten clean sheets (942 mins) leaving Bolton 7 hours 27 mins goalless; Terry warm-up injury, 400th game Lampard skipper – and Scolari saviour – with 123rd goal in 93rd min edgy win over Stoke; ten Toons lose three goals and points at Blackburn; Man City finish with ten, too, but beat Wigan; Villa – one goal "hands" another outside area "pen" – dismay Sunderland; Baggies send Boro 18th leaving bottom five on 21 pts. FLC: East Anglian revival: Ipswich and Norwich four each and both win!; Wolves chuck lead at Bristol C; on loan Bowyer saves pt at death for Brum at Cardiff; Reading ten crash at Swansea; Clough starts with home defeat against Rangers; two-pens Preston enrage Burnley; good start for Davies as Forest ease over Plymouth; 18 League defeats in a row for Charlton. F1: MK Dons throw away two goal lead at Carlisle and lose; Guinan first half trio as

Hereford bulldoze five over Oldham; Colchester EA revival, too with three and a win. F2: Darlo high five over Luton; Wycombe home record goes in Grimsby win. SPL: late goals rob Falkirk of pt against Rangers in ten-a-side. SL: Cowdenbeath top Div 3 as Sten lose at the Sons. BSP: Burton record 12th successive win. Barca hit five.

18 Spurs held by Pompey at WHL after Bent miss; welcome three pts for Cole fired West Ham against Fulham. SPL: Dons deliver blow to Celtic; Motherwell four play at Dundee Utd.

19 Liverpool held in Mersey derby by late Cahill. Kaka turns down £107m move to Man City. Spain and Portugal in for Iberia 2018 WC bid. Leicester win again at Yeovil. Caley sack manager Craig Brewster. Eddie Howe is new Bournemouth boss.

20 C Cup semi: Man Utd race to comfort zone, then ease to victory over Derby. Robinho goes AWOL and faces £300,000 fine as Kaka father blamed for transfer failure. FA Cup: Donny win the Cheltenham replay. L1: MK Dons held at Posh. Pennant for Portsmouth. Was it a Toon punch-up in training? FA charge Boro over brawl at WBA. Chris Hutchings gets Walsall job.

21 C Cup semi: Spurs – only play when they're losing – recover in extra time three down, to scrape in with two Pavlyuchenko goals at Burnley. Anyway Spurs pay £12m for Palacios from Wigan. No Kaka, but Man City sign Nigel De Jong £17m to add to Bellamy purchase at £14m. Cash-strapped AIG not to renew Man Utd shirt sponsorship. Bryan Gunn gets Norwich post until season's end.

22 Hicks may sell his share at Liverpool to Kuwaiti man. Eduardo ready for return.

23 Bullard to Hull for £5m, Heskey to Villa for £3.5m Sir Alex seeking use of old FA Cup rule allowing extra time in first match. Gerrard court appearance. FA Cup: Forest draw at Derby. Mark Wotte handed Saints role.

24 FA Cup: Swans get two, Pompey a duck as loanee Dyer strikes; Kettering, Torquay denied replays by late reviving four play Fulham and one goal Coventry respectively – but Donny earn another go at Villa; weary Burnley still make Baggies try again; Man Utd fight back to clip Spurs; Watford odd goal in seven win over Palace; Ballack brace for Chelsea; Sheff Utd edge struggling Charlton; Boro leave it late to snare Wolves; Black Cats and Blackburn to battle again; Hull take out Millwall (but some visitors cut up rough); two in a minute Hammers before the interval break Hartlepool though "pen" outside area. FLC: Campbell does in old Brummie mates for Blackpool. F1: on-loan Clarke treble bow for high five Cobblers; bench-man Beckford braces himself for Leeds; four goal Leicester now nine points clear. F2: Wycombe lose again at Bournemouth; Luton ref pelted with missiles as Bradford share six goals there; Forrester three strikes for Notts. SPL: Rangers bench Boyd and drop two points at Aberdeen. Celtic edge Hibs to increase lead. SL: Hamilton, Grehan's three goals as Stirling go on an eight-goal standard at sad Stranraer, which causes Manager Derek Ferguson to resign. BSP: Burton 13th unlucky – they draw with Altrincham.

25 FA Cup: Yet another Mersey derby and naturally finishes one apiece in their 21st such clash as Gerrard again saves the Reds again; Cardiff hold Arsenal; big boys kept apart in cup draw. Kaka two, born-again Becks one for AC Milan. Barca after losing first game have drawn two and won all others.

26 Pompey recruit Mullins from West Ham, another Pele on loan from Porto. The tubby Ronaldo goes to Corinthians. Klaas-Jan Huntelaar , Alax to Real – and Reyes Atletico Madrid to Benfica. Robinho back at Man City and are fined £320,000. BSP: Burton is winning.

27 Van der Sar 1031 mins unbeaten as Man Utd are high-five fliers at ten-man Baggies, the gk beating Cech's record with 11th clean sheet; Heskey already pays some of his fee with Villa winner at Portsmouth; Spurs back scoring and winning as Stoke lose at WHL; Sunderland edge Fulham. FLC: Charlton get first League win since Oct against Palace; Reading og – by Collins (later red-carded) deflates Wolves and Brummie need just one themselves over Derby; Saints fight back earns draw at Norwich; Donny tip up Sheff Utd at the Lane. F1: Orient surprises MK Dons, Leicester held by Brighton, Posh takes four off Crewe. F2: Buzzie Bees too much for Shots, Bury edge Bradford.but ten teams fail to score; Chester nine done in at Vale.

28 Liverpool drop two points at Wigan after leading as new Latic Mido pens them in; Kalou double helps Chelsea over Boro; Bellamy repays some of his Man City fee over Newcastle; Van Persie rescues Arsenal in last minute at Everton; Lancs derby leaves Rovers and Wanderers sharing four goals; Hammers put two more nails into Hull. PL rattles up its 200thm customer. FLC: Cardiff go fourth at Coventry. CIS semi: Celtic 11-10 on pens ends Dundee Utd hopes. MotD gets new three-year deal. Becks scores another goal! Cudicini goes to Spurs, but they have Defoe broken foot in training..

29 Diouf likely to go to Blackburn, N'Zogbia to Wigan after disagreement with Kinnear, Man City offer £20m for Santa Cruz, Birmingham get Carlos Costly, Honduran cap on loan. Wembley get 2011 Ch Lge final.

30 Scolari latest to have a pop at Sir Alex. Norwich net point at Donny

31 Van-man makes it 1122 mins, 12 clean sheets and Ron pen enough for Man Utd against Everton to go five pts clear; first goalless Emirates in 50th PL game then £square with Hammers; Boro (gk Jones a standout) and Blackburn also scoreless as are Villa and Wigan; Stoke's ten with Delap banished hang on to edge Man City; Fulham see off plunging Pompey; sub Bent double not enough to save Spurs at Bolton; Tigers and Baggies share four goals; only six points from 10th to bottom place! FLC: Wolves E-B's 17th goal wobbles Watford; Reading held goalless at QPR; vet Phillips 93rd min leveller again at Sheff Wed; first Derby win for Clough; Saints ten snatch pt off Swans; Blackpool ten make it four in a row losses for Palace; Cardiff 13th unbeaten. L1: Wilbraham trio as MK Dons win 5-3 at Cheltenham (Spencer trio then off!); 20 goal Hooper double puts end to Millwall; Leeds fail at Walsall; Stockport 14 secs Blizzard sweeps to four goals over Hereford. F2: Rhodes 27 min hat-trick for Brentford at Shrews; Frecklington 95th min effort as Lincoln share six with Bournemouth; Thompson 17 min trio for Rochdale sinks Shots. Fleck helps Rangers over Dundee Utd. Trophy: Stevenage four play buckles Burton; Torquay ousted by Southport; Telford takes out Kettering. BS Sth: AFC Dons have 4690 for win over Chelmsford!

FEBRUARY 2009

Arshavin beats the deadline ... Recession-proof PL? ... Scolari out – Hiddink caretaker ... Spain pain for England ... Eduardo returns ... SPL Division 2?

1 Tor-tor Torres late double floors Chelsea with Lampard controversial red as Anfield spurns Spurs £15m for Keane. Black Cats snarl at Toon pen equaliser. Caley with Terry Butcher at the helm hold Celtic goalless. Arshavin expected to arrive and sign for Arsenal. Raul's 307th goal for Real levels with Di Stefano total.

2 Now PL plays extra time for transfer window to let in Arshavin! Keane returns for only £12m! Wolves get Berra from Hearts at £2.5m. Quaresma loan from Inter to Chelsea.

3 Arshavin £15m move after 228 days was 23 hours over deadline. Snow joke as programme decimated but in FA Cup Burnley account for WBA. FLC: E-B treble but Norwich still draw at Wolves. L1: Leicester, MK Dons both win away. L2: Rochdale maintainsrun; Morecambe surprise Brentford. Sky keeps hold on TV coverage. Lamps, Cheltenham Spencer and Dale's Stanton get cards rescinded.

4 FA Cup: Gerrard injured and Gosling is the G-man firing Everton to Mersey glory – but ITV misses the goal!; McCarthy gives Rovers a return in overtime against Sunderland; Clough gets a lift, too, at Nottm Forest of all places. Man City reeling from Robinho nightclub "incident" now reveal facing blackmail.

5   Chris Woods maintains his British gk record 1196 mins for all games is intact; Van-man's was only PL games as he conceded in the CWC v Gamba. Man City has Richards in yet another "incident." Geraint Williams appointed as Orient manager.

6   Recession-proof PL get £1.782m new TV deal which leaves Sky winners, Setanta losers.

7   Pompey 12 mins from defeating Rafa tinkered Liverpool, lose to two in last five mins with sub Torres again the saviour; Scolari under fire as Hull get a draw at the Bridge; Villa consolidate third spot in Rovers win – club record seven away on trot; Toon tonic for hospitalized Kinnear in win at WBA; by Jo, loan star for Everton as Toffees stick it to the Trotters; new boy Given keeps Boro out, Bellamy gets one in; Sunderland rescue ref Styles after he misses obvious hands with two late goals against ten-man Stoke; Wigan and Fulham share no goals in shot-shy one. FLC: tough at the top as Wolves are sent to defeat at Coventry, while Birmingham, Reading held at home by Burnley and Preston; first Owls double over Blades for 95 years in Sheffield derby and first win at Bramall Lane since 1967; Swans 15 unbeaten; Derby win once more. L1: ten-man Oldham holds Leicester goalless – thanks to emergency gk Windass! L2: no hat-trick for ten years so Brentford get two in seven days – MacDonald 24 mins first half, but still snow joke as 19 FL games off. S Cup: Celtic pushed to win by Queen's Park; Caley take out Killie. SL programme hit and only two BSP survive – relegated Wrexham and Mansfield both win, too. Only one Vase escapes.

8   Van man makes it 1212 mins in 13th clean one in PL and overtakes Bobby Clark's 1155 for Aberdeen, too as Hammers lose to a Giggs effort; Eboue out (Wenger's 76th) but Arsenal get a point at Spurs. Tony Adams (103 days) sacked by Portsmouth. S Cup: Rangers frozen out at Forfar. Kaka injured at Milan and LA want to sort out the Becks problem.

9   Scolari – now go! – Abramovich flies in, Big Phil flies out from Bridge of some size and likely to take £10m handshake. Hiddink lined up, Eriksson for Pompey, too? Crucial L1 win for Leeds over Millwall.

10   Dual role for Hiddink – Chelsea (to season end) and Russia . Hint of discontent at the Bridge. Brazil 2 Italy 0 played at the Emirates – of course. England U-21s beaten by Ecuador after two-goal lead.; Republic hold Germans. Posh go third after win at Brighton. Brentford scrape draw at Stanley; four goals for Exeter. BSP: Weymouth shakes Torquay. Karren Brady arrested – again. Kinnear heath query.

11   Spain 29 unbeaten after 2-0 v England, run started 1-0 against them! But sub Becks equals Bobby Moore's 108 caps, but suffers record 17th yellow (plus two reds). Shocks in other friendlies as Norwegians win in Germany, Argies in France, Poles in Wales (local lot?!). WC: Keane double sees off Georgia for Republic, Northern Irish take three off San Marino. Arsenal's Eduardo returns to Croatia victory. Is there a recession? – Man Utd turnover £300m expected, but Real top of the rich table with Chelsea, Arsenal and Liverpool finishing in the top ten. Giggs to sign to 2010. Paul Hart Pompey caretaker with Brian Kidd assistant. Chris Hughton is Toon caretaker too in Kinnear absence.

12   Hiddink upbeat, while Capello assesses the Spanish damage. BSP: Burton losing until snow at Ebbsfleet ends it.

13   Beckford three match ban hits Leeds. Peter Storrie arrested at Portsmouth.

14   FA Cup – draws all round with four of the five needing replays; Blackburn early and very late deny Coventry; Ilunga rescues Hammers against Boro; Gower miss robs Swans against Fulham after own goal gift; Hull force Sheff Utd to play again – but Anelka treble lifts Hiddink boys of Chelsea at Watford after going behind. PL: King James the first to top 536 matches as born again Pompey beat Man City. FLC: Wolves falter at Burnley; as Brum move three pts closer with game in hand after defeating Forest; Charlton win but Saints lose at Bristol C. L1: Leicester scrape a draw with Swindon; MK Dons win, but Posh, Scunny both lose. Windass celebrates with 200th career League goal as Oldham clips Northampton. L2: Only Wycombe of top eight fail to win because they are losers at Bradford. Top half teams moving away. SPL: Hearts consolidate third place beating Dons, because Dundee Utd held by Caley. SL: Nine hit by weather. St Johnstone move further ahead in Div 1, Stranraer hit for another five goals in Div 2 and just East Stirling win only Div 3 survivor against Elgin.

15   FA Cup: Man Utd four play takes care of Derby; Everton signal three-fold intention against Villa. SPL: Celtic grateful for Boruc in goalless derby with Rangers.

16   FA Cup: Eduardo returns with double in Arsenal's four play demolition of Cardiff. Russell Slade and Yeovil part company. Breadline Abramovich loses £6.3bn – down to last £15bn?

17   FLC: Tide turns on Swans after 16 unbeaten run at Watford; Donny keep up improvement; Burnley scrape draw with Coventry. L1: Last gasp Hartlepool snatches a point off Leicester; Leeds loses once more. L2: Gills and Shots share eight goals; Morecambe snatch point at Rochdale; Wycombe win at Daggers. J Paint: Scunthorpe and Luton for final after beating Rotherham and Brighton, respectively on aggregate and penalties. S Cup: Fifers edge Airdrie and, Dons high five over East Fife. BSP: Burton back winning crucially against Wrexham. According to *The Daily Telegraph* 33 managers axed in 193 days – job average now down to 1.47 years, 49 percent of first-time bosses never return and only five PL managers have never been axed. Bullard injury concern, Gerrard hopeful of earlier return.

18   Twenty-two man move and Berbatov touch in, highlights Man Utd's three goal win over Fulham with the Van man coming clean again on 1302 minutes. FLC: Derby foursome rules out Blackpool. UEFA Cup: draw may not suit Villa against CSKA. Aalborg stuns La Coruna. Ian Watmore (Arsenal fan) appointed CEO at FA – mate of Lord Triesman's. Ref Clattenburg can carry on whistling. S Cup: Rangers four play too much for ten Loons at Forfar. WC tickets can only be sold in S. Africa.

19   UEFA Cup: Danes deny Man City win in last minute; Spurs concede two late on in Donetsk; shocks for Marseille against Twente, Fiorentina v Ajax. S Cup replay match: Buddies edge Well. FA thinking of using Twickers for 2018 WC bid as worries continue over S.Africa hosting next year. Internet owned Ebbsfleet hit by recession defectors.

20   Guus gives title to Man Utd as he repeats his short stay vow at Chelsea. SPL are near to a second division.

21   Crisis club Man Utd? They concede a PL goal after 1334 mins – but Van man is not playing. Ron gets a yellow for diving then hits a free-kick beauty against Rovers as MU stay on track. Chelsea shift Villa into fourth place on Guus day, late og gives Pompey point at Stoke and despite Arshavin's delightful debut, Black Cats make it fourth draw for Arsenal and third goalless in the run. Two early strikes – 95 sec burst – and Bolton hold off West Ham; Boro now 495 mins without a goal held by Wigan. FLC: Tough at the top part two: Brummies lose at Coventry, Reading fail at home in 137th anniversary of first game v Reading Grammar School; another Saga double outing as Saints are reborn to beat Preston; Derby do for Forest again; Watford revival carries on at Blackpool. L1: Loanee Bunn pen save helps Leicester's 20th unbeaten; morning departure of boss Micky Adams so Brighton go p.m with win at Millwall!; Leeds win for a change, two down Swindon shunt Scunny four times. L2: first home win since October so Barnet hit Bradford four times; Rochdale's 22nd scoring game in a row but Brentford beat them; already youngest player, now Main Darlo's youngest marksman in 16 years 246 days. SPL: Miller duo puts Rangers in the mood to go top against Killie; Caley just a pt below Falkirk after beating Hibs. SL: Partick, Dundee a little closer to St Johnstone held at QofS; rare Elgin win in Div 3. BSP: Rushden get nine against cash-strapped Weymouth's youth team. Trophy: Stevenage four play upsets FGR; Havant loses at York; Ebbsfleet and Southport draw at Wrexham and Telford respectively. Vase: Whitley Bay axes Stratford.

22 Liverpool unable to beat Man City in Anfield draw as Rafa contract stalls; ten Toons get a point off Everton; Zamora ends 29 hour barren spell as Fulham strike off WBA. FLC: Wolves grateful for gk og in point saving draw with Cardiff. SPL: Celtic held at Motherwell must settle for second place on goal difference. SL: Cellar dwellers Airdrie move point nearer Clyde after beating them.

23 Wilting Hull fall to Spurs. Arteta out for season adds to Toffee injuries. L2: Wycombe 12th draw of season against Rotherham.

24 Ch Lge: JM hopes hit by zero-zero with Man Utd; Roma penned in by Arsenal; Barca level in Lyon as are Porto at Atletico Madrid. FA Cup: Best man for Coventry alters Rovers plans; Zamora unable to stop scoring as Fulham clips the Swans. FLC: Birmingham draws at Palace. L1: Scunny still slipping away; Cheltenham more adrift at the bottom, Millwall, Posh both winners. L2: Bournemouth, Rochdale and Morecambe away day successes. BSP: Histon, Cambridge, Stevenage all win, Torquay share six with FGR; Crawley hit five. FL seeks compensation for Wembley double booking with Ch Lge final 2011. Punters clean up over Rushden nine. Trophy: replay joy for Ebbsfleet, Telford.

25 Ch Lge: Rafa return to Real brings joy in Liverpool victory; Drogba rains on Ranieri's return parade for Juve at Chelsea; buoyant Bayern batter Sporting in nap hand win; Villarreal and Panathinaikos draw. Arsenal's loan repayments concern. FA Cup: Boro come to life in overcoming Hammers. FLC: Cardiff held by Rangers.

26 UEFA Cup: "uninterested" Villa and Spurs lose out to CSKA Moscow and Shakhtar. Is anyone surprised? But it's bella, bella Bellamy as he deigns to put paid to Copenhagen; Becks boys Milan chuck two goal lead and crash out to Werder on Maldini swan song? McClaren's Twente lose s/o to Marseille. Aalborg continues to surprise in ousting La Coruna. FA Cup: boss Blackwell berates ref Walton over Hull goal that exits Sheff Utd. FL relief over diminishing agents fees.

27 Parry to quit Liverpool. O'Neill tries to sweeten Villa away day fans by a meal! FLC: Donny leap over the Rams.

28 Wow! Boro win again – as 526 mins PL goal drought ends – and kill off rekindled Liverpool title dreams. Chelsea (Terry's 35th club goal) still need win by twilight Lamps effort against Wigan. Now it's five draws (four goalless) for Arsenal as Fulham holds them at the Emirates; Everton add luckless, wasteful Albion to their belt. FLC: TLGH at the top pt 3: running-on empty but still leading Wolves eight from poss 33 pts, one win in eleven, beaten at home by Plymouth; Reading no win in four and nine hours since one of them scored bow to Forest after 39 secs. Saints in heaven – defeat Cardiff!; Swans 16th draw L1: MK Dons denied by last min disputed Leicester leveller 17,717 present; Oldham climb over Lions at the New Den; Leeds first win in ten puts more misery on Scunny; Shrimpers nip Posh; Brighton hit by Crewe four play; no win in 13 for Cheltenham. L2: Darlo ten pts deducted lose at Exeter; Wycombe's 13th draw; Bees buzz at top but Bradford droop at Notts. SPL: coin hits Weir at Hamilton but Rangers get the dividend to stay top despite Celtic whacking ten-man St Mirren for seven and missing a pen (Nakamura treble). SL: Partick creep nearer St J held by Dundee. Forfar score five, McLaren (Berwick) four. BSP: Burton have to settle for pt at Woking; wins for Histon, Stevenage and Torquay; Weymouth with new men lose at York. Vase q-finals: Whitley Bay, Glossop get five, Lowestoft four – all winners, Needham and Chalfont draw.

MARCH 2009

Van man suffers puncture ... Burton run ends ... Liverpool rock Man Utd at Old Trafford ... Coppell's 1000th ... Becks hits 109th ... Shearer to guide Newcastle.

1 C Cup final: Surprise! It goes to a s/o and Spurs manage one to Man Utd's four with gk Foster homework paying off. PL: Stoke hit cruising Villa twice 88th and 91st mins to snuff out a point on O'Neill's 57th birthday. Hull's ten lose again at home to Rovers with Geovanni wobbly enraging boss Brown. Hammers emphasise Man City's poor away record with Welsh co-opted Collison goal on St David's Day, but Welshman Bellamy injured; Bolton heaps more problems on the Toon. AC Milan defeat puts pressure on Ancelotti. Real 10 wins on the trot. Hertha are Bundesliga leaders again.

2 Credit crunch hitting FA TV deal with Setanta and ITV in bother. Rafa throws in the title towel. Spurs players did not practise pens! Useful pt for Leeds obtained at Oldham. BSP: Histon and Cambridge share it.

3 If not mountainous at least Arsenal break back with molehill of three at Albion; Liverpool plug away regardless to beat Sunderland and Chelsea look to Drogba again for sailing home tack at Portsmouth. FLC: Wolves fangs are what they used to be – a win pen at Palace; Reading recover, too, victorious at Sheff Wed; Saints unstoppable – three at Ipswich while Norwich shake Rangers; Cardiff keep it up but Preston downed by improving Forest. L1: Leicester held by Stockport, MK Dons abandoned in Cobblers waterlogging, two others postponed. Posh go second after win at Orient; Millwall enjoy Southend outing success. L2: Brentford, Wycombe, Bradford three pointers, Rochdale lose to Barnet, Bury at home to Chesterfield; Bournemouth out of bottom two beating Shots; two called off here as well. BSP: Wrexham lose at Crawley, Stevenage held by FGR, buttTorquay win at Grays. SL: Sten close gap on Div 3 Cowden to three.

4 Van man suffers puncture after 1311 mins as Man Utd fight back to win at Newcastle (Euro record 1390 Danny Verlingen, Club Brugge 1990), but Taylor made remark does not suit Ronaldo; no win in six Villa toiling now at Man City; Spurs goal rush – four against Boro; Cole delivers for West Ham in ten-a-side at Wigan, courtesy ref Attwell; only second win in 19 for Hull late winners at Fulham; artisan Stoke flying after treading on Trotters; Everton goalless pt at Blackburn. FLC: Brum not so glum after clipping Bristol C; Sheff Utd fourth after win at Coventry. FA brushes off finance fears. Labour exchange politics for WC bid. SPL: Weir red for Rangers, Caley in the Black after his penalty win at Ibrox; McDonald double puts Celtic on top with three pt lead. SL: Ayr held but ahead on pts in Div 2, Stranraer ship three to Peterhead.

5 Wenger (76 red cards!) hits out at x-rated tackles! Cole A fined £80 as drunk and disorderly and also fined £164,000 by Chelsea. All is not Attwell with FA. Sheff Utd is still chasing Tevez £45m payout. Jimmy Russo is new Watford chairman.

6 Becks to commute between LA and AC. FA Cup a big TV switch off. Russell Slade gets Brighton post.

7 FA Cup: Determined Drogba digs comfortable victory for Chelsea at Coventry; Tevez sparks four-goal Man Utd at feeble Fulham. PL: King Keane rescues pt for Spurs at Sunderland. FLC: Wolves give Owls the E-B jeebies; one goal enough against Saints for the "Brady bunch" to relieve under-fire McLeish; Reading held at Plymouth; Cardiff hit Donny for three; loanees help Palace over Preston; plunging Charlton lose against Forest. L1: Leicester's four-star shows them 12 pts clear and 56 ahead of victims Cheltenham. Injury time win for Millwall at Huddersfield; Colchester shake Oldham; Leeds caught late in last minute at Bristol R; Posh rule at the 'Pool; MK Dons draw at Swindon; Hooper's 20th League goal relief for Scunny. L2: High fives for Bradford over plummeting Shots, Grimsby (Proudlock 3) – including four in last 12 mins against Lincoln; late again, but one enough for Wycombe; Brentford settle for pt at Rotherham; Bury clip Rochdale in Lancs derby; Luton 16 pts from safety zone after Exeter defeat. S Cup: St Mirren pen banishes seven goal nightmare to edge out Celtic; Falkirk on the spot, too, to dismiss Caley; Fifers and Dons to play it again. SL: ten-man Airdrie and Livi share eight goals; Clyde upset Jags; St J is in another draw. Ayr's five goals hit sad Stranraer. Annan are six-hitters over Elgin. BSP: Cambridge end Burton's 17 match run (4377), but Stevenage unbeaten in 19 after win at Northwich. Barca has a six-point lead over Real. Inter seven ahead in Italy. Lyon just pt in front after loss at Lille; Liverpool loanee Voronin hat trick of goals for Hertha!

Jermaine Jenas of Tottenham Hotspur slides in to challenge Manchester United's Cristiano Ronaldo during the Carling Cup Final at Wembley. United went on to win the Cup in a penalty shoot-out after the game ended 0-0.
(Action Images/Michael Regan)

8   FA Cup: Arsenal three in fifth round win over Burnley – Eduardo with "bad leg" heel volley raises the roof; two in six mins by Everton ends Boro semi-final hopes. S Cup: Five of the best for Rangers against Accies.

9   LA to stop Becks friendly outing for England. English clubs on brink of four teams in last eight of Ch Lge.

10 Ch Lge: Liverpool foursome has Madrid reeling; Drogba the leveller in four goal share with Juve; Bayern take seven off Sporting; Villarreal complete the first four qualifiers against Panathinaikos. FLC: tough at the top again as Wolves, Birmingham, Reading and Sheff Utd only draw and Cardiff lose at struggling Norwich. L1: Beckford threesome for four-goal Leeds against Yeovil; born-again treble shooter Lambert for Bristol R; Posh see off Scunny to consolidate second place, as MK Dons held by Huddersfield. L2: Wycombe beaten at Lincoln and Brentord take advantage against Barnet. SL: Doonhamers damage Dundee, Saints return to winning ways at Clyde. BSP: Histon lose agan, But Cambridge, Torquay both win.

11 Ch Lge: The Special One drops to zero as Man Utd prove too strong for Inter; Roma level it but Gunners prevail in the shoot-out. Sheff Utd are to get compensation over Tevez after all. Inter deny JM punch-up allegation. PL: Blackburn latest winners at Craven Cottage. FLC: Burnley's second half four-play surprises Palace. Shock for Leicester at Tranmere. BSP: Ebbsfleet latest to upset Burton. Blatter stalls on goal-line technology. Arsenal fans were attacked in Italy.

12 UEFA Cup: Man City take useful two-goal lead over Aalborg, remaining seven ties well balanced after first leg matches. Sheff Utd are to get compensation over Tevez after all. Inter deny JM punch-up allegation

13 Terry to become a lifer at Chelsea? Sir Alex perplexed by Rafa remarks about him, while the "Spanish waiter" on eve of 100th PL game admits a perfect run-in is essential for Liverpool.

14 Roof falls in after Ron pen – Man Utd's 700th home PL goal – with Spanish flier Torres igniting Liverpool four play, Vidic gaffes a couple and sees red in worst Old Trafford reverse since FL days in 1992 and even ref Wiley gets three crucial decisions spot on; Ars(enal)havin' a better time – Eboue (!) two! Fulham double their away goals at error-struck Bolton. Hull (boss Brown's 100th for Tigers) and Newcastle – no win in 13 now – draw. Boro's ten salvage pt against Pompey, but Alves fluffs a 94th chance; N'Zogbia solo gem in Wigan win at Sunderland; Everton celebrate Moyes' seven year hitch with victory over Stoke. FLC: Wolves helped by Iwelumo doing in old Charlton mates; Coppell's 999th managerial game ends with Ipswich winning at Reading, but Birmingham take the pts off Donny. Burnley high five finishes Forest; loanee Mooney aids Norwich again; Palace Eagles slick swoop on the Swans; Sheff Utd celebrate £21m Tevez payment plan doubling Derby score. L1: Howard's way for Leicester at Millwall (13,261), but some home fans unhappy; MK Dons four second half goals treble Oldham's couple; 22-goal Beckford hat-trick in Leeds seventh straight win – then sent off! Slade sees Brighton hit ex-club Yeovil for five; Cheltenham end 15 no win run against Hartlepool. L2: Table-topper sees Bees and ten Chairboys share six; Morecambe 11 no loss, but Bradford suffer fourth defeat on trot at Exeter; Macc boss Alexander in new health scare but Bournemouth four pts off drop zone now. SPL: Caley clear water above Falkirk after beating Killie; Hibs win Edinburgh derby. SL: St Johnstone's 22 undefeated run ends at Livi; Airdrie swap bottom place with success over Clyde. Ayr consolidate lead at Raith in Div 2; Gribben three of Berwick four at E Stirling. BSP: Going for a Burton after third defeat in a row as Salisbury wins? Cambridge, Torquay are four goal winners, but saviour Beer goes stale at Weymouth. Trophy: York two ahead of Telford, Stevenage edge Ebbsfleet.

15 Spurs inflict more grief at Villa Park; Chelsea welcome back scorer Essien as Man City away form remains unimpressive. FLC: Cardiff look to McCormack for saving pt at Bristol C. Joe Royle gets temporary job at Oldham as John Sheridan is shown the door. CIS final: Celtic extra time winners over ten-man Rangers.

16 Injury-hit Hammers limp to draw with Baggies. O'Neill touted as Capello successor. FA applies for two WCs.

17 FA Cup: Arsenal shake off Hull lead to win, but simmering turns to accusations in its wake. FLC: Coppell's 1000th milestone of matches as Reading wins at Doncaster; Barnsley welcomes three pts against Palace and rare success for Rangers. L1: Millwall's surprise for the MK Dons, Cheltenham wins again. L2: Bournemouth flying and hit the Bantams badly while Chesterfield upset the Bees. BSP: Burton scores five goals at wilting Weymouth; Barker treble for Histon and Cambridge win at Barrow.

18 Rafa signs five year deal at Anfield. Sir Alex hits at player pundits. Injury time pen gives Cardiff pts over Watford. UEFA Cup: Marseille, Werder Bremen both through. SL: Ayr moves further ahead at East Fife. S Cup: Dunfermline edges Aberdeen in shoot-out.

19　UEFA Cup: Man City Given their life-line in two shoot-out saves at Aalborg; Paris St Germain, Dynamo Kiev, Hamburg, Shakhtar and Udinese – overall winners over Zenit – complete the last eight. Spurs show pre-tax profit of £39.8m. Stranraer saved by partnership with local housing association. BSP: Oxford row on at Kettering.

20　Ch Lge draw: looks good for Man Utd v Porto, Liverpool and Chelsea fifth time on the trot, Barca v Bayern the big one and Villarreal against Arsenal the puzzler, but Walcott injured in training! Sir Alex and Rafa still exchanging views.

21　Fulham's Cottage industry two-much for depleted Man Utd workforce – Scholes (eighth red) hands on, Rooney double yellow as Champions suffer first back-to-back PL defeats in 147 matches; Modric, Gomes inspired Spurs are Derby day winners, Chelsea scarcely at the races; Martins fluffs pen, then levels 13 secs after Arsenal lead before one-in-12 win Newcastle find Van Persie a handful; Crouch brace-full leaps (first his 50th PL goal) peg back Everton; Delap-Shawcross hand and head act, so it's curtains for Boro; Taylor's 50th career goal as Bolton draw at WBA plus another one-a-piece between Rovers and Hammers. FLC: 11 games, 12 goals! – five goalless draws among seven such; Wolves increase lead as lucky Birmingham, ten-man Reading are both held; Swans 19th draw. L1: Super-sub Harris 10 min s/h treble as Millwall come good at Hartlepool; Leicester scrape a draw with Colchester; Oldham still losing; another Attwell ref-gaffe helps Swindon. L2: Strugglers Luton, Grimsby, Barnet, Stanley and Port Vale all win, even Chester get a draw at ten-man Bury; Rochdale steal Wycombe's role with injury-time winner. SPL: Rangers throw two-goal lead as Hearts level; Falkirk takes four off ten-man Caley and with game in hand are just a point adrift. SL: St J move further ahead in Div 1, Raith close gap on Ayr in Div 2 and Cowden are ten pts clear in Div 3. BSP: 97th min winner for Burton at Eastbourne. Trophy: semi-winners York, Stevenage to meet in final

22　On a roll Liverpool flatten Villa's ten with five (Gerrard two pens in trio); one goal enough for Man City over ten-man Sunderland but Robinho is spot off; Wigan edge out one-win-in 14 PL Hull. Cardiff beaten with nine men as Sheff Utd go fourth. SPL: Celtic forced to be content with draw at Dundee Utd. Div 1: Partick and Dundee draw is best result for St J! Barca's six against Malaga – Eto'o hitting his 25th goal.

23　Chelsea will get summer player aid from Guus, JM in bother in Italy over Presidents picking players. Daggers in the dark as floodlights fail.

24　Robinho threatens to sue Pele over drug accusation; Southgate job safe at Boro, Friedel and McCartney red cards rescinded from Sunday. Carlo Ancelotti mentions for Chelsea job. Wada farce – as FIFA and UEFA refuse to toe their drug line. L1: on-form Cox treble for Swindon, Dons held by Crewe, Hereford wins at Carlisle and Cheltenham nearly takes three pts off Oldham. L2: Another Stanley wins but just 1086 in attendance; Bury late draw at Rotherham. SL: Raith reclaim leadership after four goals at Brechin. BSP: crucial draw for Grays at Torquay, Oxford sees off Rushden.

25　Capello concerns over Cole A and Rooney discipline. Capello and Spurs are at odds over King. Emphatic win by Chesterfield over Rochdale. Wigan owner Whelan aims for debt-free club in 18 months. Pele denies Robinho criticism.

26　Liverpool chasing Valencia's Silva; US Congress may investigate bust AIG's £14m shirt payment due to Man Utd. Boro fined for their players' behaviour. Blatter points to the money-orientated PL. Setanta Shield: AFC Telford and Forest Green to meet in final.

27　Capello and Harry R on collision course over King. U21s high five in Norway for England, Wales goalless draw in Luxembourg; Scots to show brave hearts in Holland. Wales worry over Finn pen awards after three misses; Healy to find Irish goal standard again? Russians want to share Guus. Southend just edge ten-man Hartlepool.

28　England all white on the night: Roo two, Becks 109th outing as most capped outfielder, Lamps hits Wembley's 500th, but injuries mount after four play over Slo(w)vakia. WC 2010: Oranje peel off Scots, Wales beached by the Finns, Dunne 40 secs Republic goal but Kilbane og gives Bulgaria a pt; Irish Pole vault aided by Boruc blunders but fans clash afterwards. Elsewhere: Spain with Holland are only 100 percent teams; Portugal struggle to Swedish draw; Plenty of PL scorers around and Adebayor has Togo winner but misses pen, while Sven's Mexicans take out Costa Rica; Scots U21s win in Albania. L1: Beckford's double over Dons for 30 goal target best since Lee Chapman 1990-91; Posh sixth successive success too good for Leicester; Price is right for loanee Lion at Crewe; Hooper brace takes him to 29 for sunny Scunny; Yeovil end eight game no win run. L2: Brentford, Wycombe, Rochdale all held at home, so Bury make ground; Lester duo reaches 20 goals for Chesterfield, first back-to-back score for 80 years there; Morecambe run ended by Luton; Grimsby pen way out of bottom pair against Shots. BSP: Burton open 11 pt lead after four play against Grays; Wrexham lose at Histon, while Torquay, Kiddy both held away, Stevenage and Oxford against each other. SL: Dundee crazy five mins have two sent off and then concede leveller to Ross; Ayr regain Div 2 leadership with four goals at Stranraer (1019). Vase: Chalfont, Glossop share six, Whitley Bay edge Lowestoft in first semis.

29　WC tragedy as 22 die, 132 injured from wall collapse and stampede at Ivory Coast match against Malawi. BSP: ten Barrow boys treble up at Weymouth.

30　Lamps on a nostalgia trip citing today's easy living young pros. Usmanov and Kroenke are Arsenal's two biggest shareholders. Hull version of Fabregas alleged spit spat. BSP: Cambridge close gap on Burton at Woking.

31　Shearer in to guide Toon but not intoxicated to stay over the eight, Wise man leaves. Crouch to return for injury-hit England, Scots reinstate Gordon in goal, Trapattoni relishes Italian return with Republic, Worthington expects another Windsor Park victory but Wales fearful over German invasion. U21s: France surprise England, Irish held by Ukraine, Turkey trot catches Republic, Wales high five over Luxembourg. L1: Colchester surprise for Millwall. L2: Rotherham hit four at Luton, Wycombe's 17th draw. SL: Dundee Dees on their knees conceding another 90th minute leveller at Fifers.

APRIL 2009
Chelsea shock for Liverpool in classic tie ... Everton cup surprise for Man Utd ... Life's a pitch at Wembley ... Keane gets Ipswich job ... Boyd 100th boosts Rangers ... Giggs is PFA choice.

1　Terry pulls Capello out of a draw to preserve 100 percent WC record after Shevy's 40th Ukraine goal in 86 games; Scots freeze out Iceland, Germans roll over Wales, Feeney goal enough for Irish, ten men from third minute but Italy only concede three mins from end to draw with Repubic. Elsewhere Spain recover to keep record in Turkey, Dutch get four against Macedonia. Narrow wins for Russia, France but Bolivia blow out Maradona's Argies with six pack and Poles tear San Marino apart with ten goals. U21s: Scots manage five against Albania. BSP: Kiddy high five at wobbly Woking. Onuoha takes shine off Lamps comments. Sunderland Cisse arrested at a night club venue. Charlton issue threat to 25 staff. Saints admin loophole may save pts deduction.

2　Sven bombed out by Mexico after Honduras defeat! Soton have a month to find buyer. Eriksson in frame for England return job. Gerrard is for court. Ferguson and McGregor on the tartan carpet over alleged drinking spree. Hammers Cole is out for six weeks.

3　Hopes high on the Tyne. Hicks hiccup over loans worries Liverpool. Scottish duo banned internationally. Saints sweat on admin.

4　Four time woodwork rattlers and last min experts Liverpool find it no bar to a 92nd min winner at Fulham to top it; big Al's no Mags Messiah as away day boys Chelsea raid a Toon denied Owen goal; Boro despite ending 679

away blank mins in bother at four play Bolton; Man City's travel record still miserable at 17 unbeaten Arsenal; in the last eight mins Blackburn overcome the pen pain to clip Spurs suffering Gomes gaffe; Stoke's first away win (top flight since 1984!) nails WBA; point a piece for Hull and ten man Pompey; Hammers drag Sunderland nearer the dropping zone. FLC: Fans roll up for crisis Saints (27,228) but fellow suffering Addicks take the points despite Davis pen save while both managers are banished; Norwich foiled by disallowed goal; QPR's tenth goalless draw; Reading held up at Coventry; Blades cut out Ipswich play-off hopes. L1: Leicester caught in late draw by Carlisle; Hereford beached at Blackpool; Colchester's 1971 FA Cup heroes see Leeds revenge; Lions and Dons return to winning ways; Posh close gap with win at Oldham. L2: Exeter go second against Daggers; Barnet's first 2009 away win hits Gills; Pitman treble is goal mine for Bournemouth; Chester first win since Boxing Day. BSP: ten Burton Brewers punch-drunk losers at four star Crawley; Torquay ten unbeaten; Kiddy end Stevenage 24 match run; Cambridge stunned by Forest; ten man (and wrong red) Woking revive at Barrow; Lewes avoid English record 19 straight defeats beating Alty. SPL: Celtic four-play overcomes Accies. SL: Dundee look out of the hunt in Div 1 as Partick and Saints settle for a draw, Raith relegate yo-yo Stranraer – eighth different div in eight years while Dumbarton cut Cowden lead in Div 3. Vase: Glossop (s/o) and Whitley Bay to contest final.

5   Kid Macheda rescues Man Utd with winsome top hitting winner against Villa; Everton four times better than goalless and Zaki AWOL Wigan. Welsh derby finishes level but ref hit by coin at Cardiff. Paint final: Once behind, caught at the death but winners in overtime Luton get some reward for season beating Scunny. SPL: Rangers keep in distance of Celtic leaving Falkirk in bother. Bayern facing wipe out in Barca after conceding five to Wolfsburg to frighten Klinsmann, while the La Liga leaders ease to an Eto'o goal win.

6   Brummies win midland derby against Wolves despite Carsley red. Burton lose again to Torquay. Lazio complain over Macheda snatch. Robinho cleared of civil charge. Villa will keep promise to dine fans on Russian trip.

7   Ch Lge: Now Man Utd caught by late striking Porto in four goal share, while Arsenal virtuoso effort from Adebayor saves their draw at Villarreal, but Fabregas hit by coin. FLC: Plucky Saints get draw at Watford, Sheff Utd consolidates third spot, but handbags out for both bosses in Barnsley match. L1: Leeds held by the Orient, Brighton heaps more doom on Hereford. L2: Wycombe back to winning at Darlo. Five Stanley players mentioned in alleged betting scandal. SL: another draw for St J. BSP: Kiddy finish with nine but draw at FGR; Cambridge beaten at Stevenage.

8   Chelsea leave stunned Liverpool with precious two-goal advantage, Ivanovic heads two, Drogba finishes it off; Barca realise Bayern's worst fears with four goal fest. Cardiff hit Derby for four. SPL: Celtic home, Rangers away both victorious. JM is not for Man City? O'Neill hit by conduct charge.

9   UEFA Cup: Man City 34 secs joy, then more away day gloom in Hamburg; Shakhtar, Werder useful leads, Kiev get draw away to PSG. Man Utd £700m debt despite record turnover! Setanta Shield: AFC Telford surprises FGR in s/o final win. Sousa sacked by QPR. No punch up charge against JM.

10   Another sleepless night for Coppell as Sheff Utd go second at Reading's expense; Wolves need 20 mins to hit Saints for three all round. MK Dons profitable day out at Southend, but Posh held up by Cheltenham and Millwall taken out by Yeovil. Bury clip Shrews, Bradford edged out at Morecambe. Hiddink intends to stay only i/c of Russia's national team at season's end.

11   Big four tally 14 goals – machete Macheda again the super-sub saviour for Man Utd in the odd goal in three carve up at Sunderland; Liverpool foursome blanks Blackburn; Arsenal's quartet recovers h-t deficit at Wigan, but Chelsea four-timers threatened by Bolton's three goals in eight minutes. Boro relief at victory over an increasingly vulnerable Hull; Toon get a point for Big Al at Stoke; even Baggies share four goals at Pompey; Spurs need just one to see off Hammers. FLC: Birmingham's goalless draw at Charlton, but go second again. Blackstock injury-time winner for Forest hits Bristol C. Sir Tom Finney at 87 sees PNE lose derby to Blackpool. Plymouth's four-play derails Coventry; Palace loss to Cardiff and Davis in bother with tackle on Johnson; Ipswich p-o hopes fade against Donny; Norwich slip at Swansea; Barnsley draw at Watford but fans still not happy. L1: Swindon three in 11 s-h mins shake Brighton; Leicester joy is misery for Hereford; ninth successive home win for Leeds. L2: Reid's 19th goal for Rotherham, Wycombe edge out Jackson-wasteful Gills. Veteran Furlong's 200th career goal for Barnet win; four strikers out so Brentford held by Exeter; Rooney the younger on target again for Macc. SPL: Motherwell aim of making the cut hindered by Rangers and Celtic hat at Hearts have just one pt lead over Ibrox men. SL: St J looking more and more in front with Partick, Dundee losing and only improving Morton likely to play catch up. Stranraer end their no-win run at Stirling – their previous away success! Sons only point behind Cowden now in Div 3. BSP: one win or two draws enough for Burton after taking out Histon; Crawley stun Torquay so Cambridge go second; Woking out of bottom four with FGR win, but Weymouth even lose at Lewes. Becks benched by Milan.

12   Villa and Everton share joy of six; another Fulham away win casts doubts on Man City, but heralds possible Euro trip for Cottagers, so it's 40 goals in ten w/e PL games. Marseille go top in France, Barca still in Spanish pole position.

13   FLC: Shaky Wolves still snag Rams; Brummie lead fight for second place in Plymouth draw as Sheff Utd fail to overcome ten-man Forest; Cardiff push ahead with McCormack again the marksman, while another draw disappoints Reading at Blackpool; McGoldrick long-ranger helps Soton but they stay second bottom as Norwich move out with win at Watford and Charlton held by Coventry seem doomed. L1: Stoppage time goal but Howard again leads Leicester against Leeds towards promotion; Posh beaten at The New Den; the new Dons take out Bristol R and Tranmere keep in p-o position against bottom placed Hereford, dumped because Cheltenham beat Yeovil. L2: Luton finally admit relegation after draw with Chesterfield; Brentford win at Bournemouth but lose scorer Powell to a red; crucial win for Exeter over Wycombe; Chester end poor run at Accrington. BSP: Wobbly Burton loses at Kiddy so Cambridge closes gap; Torquay draw but Stevenage wins at Crawley. SPL: Hibees share at St Mirren puts them a pt ahead of Motherwell. Liverpool confident on eve of Hillsborough anniversary of overturning Chelsea deficit; Man Utd and Arsenal equally relaxed of progression in Ch Lge, but Hughes warns of two years wait for pots at Man City.

14   Ch Lge: classic to treasure or what? Swashbuckling Liverpool fall short at Chelsea in share of pieces of eight goals after taking two goal lead watched by 10m TV viewers; Barca ease to draw in Munich. Hicks in dollar default in USA. Vidic is PFA award favourite.

15   Ch Lge: Ronaldo 39 yd vintage strike and it's all over at 64 mph in six minutes in Oporto; Walcott leads Gunners to sink Spanish armada and face semi aganst Man Utd. Now Hammers seal Ilunga stay. Kaka wants Gerrard in Milan. Palace Davis banned for rest of season.

16   UEFA Cup: Man City salvage some pride but slender win is not enough to make mincemeat of Hamburg; Kiev three goals better than PSG, more French gloom as Shakhtar complete double over Marseille, while Werder share six with Udinese to go through to semis. FA Youth Cup: Liverpool in commanding lead at Birmingham. Hughes must achieve pots in one year! Ancelotti in Chelsea frame along with promised £50m bankroll. Now it's the Tesco Cup for kids! Everton express unhappiness over appointment of "Man Utd favouring ref Riley" for semi-final date.

17   Sir Alex has another verbal pop at Rafa. Icelandic banks make a comeback for Hammers. Gerrard is still struggling with injury. BSP: Burton once 19 pts clear now need a pt from last game at Torquay as Oxford beat them. Llanelli draw with Aberystwyth gives Rhyl Welsh title.

18 FA Cup semi: Chelsea's up front superiority plus Fabianski birthday blues is the advantage over Arsenal. PL: Feast is over, now it's famine. Five games, five goals – but at least Heskey's pt saver for Villa against West Ham is the PL's 800th of the season. Boro fail to topple Fulham thanks to old boy Schwarzer and there are single goal wins for homers Pompey (super sub Kanu), Stoke (rule Britannia) and Sunderland (f/h injury strike from Cisse) with Bolton, Blackburn and plunging Hull the losers. FLC: Fifty years to the day they lifted the First Div title, E-B's 25th goal gives Wolves elevation. Preston hit Cardiff for six and Lonergan even saves a pen. Palace's ten beat Derby; Reading booed off in Barnsley draw; Birmingham grateful to sub Jerome for Watford win; Charlton relegated after Blackpool draw; poor Plymouth undone by Donny; "offside" goal pushes Saints to end Sheff Wed 340 home mins goalless; precious win for Forest over Coventry. L1: Bracing air for Foxes Fryatt in a knees-up title celebration for Leicester at Southend. Hereford is relegated at home to Colchester, but Cheltenham still clings on with win at Crewe. Bristol R four play in Disley's 200th game and Lambert's duo brings his 27th goal against ten finishing Millwall; Mackail-Smith's 25th in Posh home win as Dons win at Scunny; Beckford's 32nd goal sparks Leeds to keep Tranmere underneath them; Carlisle ten without a win too. L2: Brentford take out Accrington, Exeter glad of og at Lincoln and Wycombe gain revenge on Shots; Bournemouth put more pressure on Chester and Grimsby ease their situation three fold; Darlo shaker for Rochdale. BSP: Cambridge assured of p-o spot need turnover of five goals and Burton defeat for automatic lift. BSN: Tamworth motoring towards title after Vauxhall victory. BSS: Almost there AFC Dons pull in 3225 at Hampton table-topper finishing all square. SPL: St Mirren win at Motherwell confirms losers miss cut; fiery McDonald taken off as Celtic take advantage of Rangers absence by beating Dons. SL: Clyde close bottom gap beating Airdrie in Div 1; Raith win at Stirling and defeat for Ayr changes top in Div 2; ten man Cowden hold off Dumbarton challenge.

19 FA Cup semi: Sir Alex reject Howard saves two in shoot-out to put Everton into final against Man Utd "reserves" as Moyes wins pre-match pysch over ref Riley who ignores infringement by Jagielka on Welbeck. PL: Toon on the town but it's a loss at Spurs; Robinho back to kick start four-play display for Man City over WBA. Championship: East Anglian derby is no joy for Norwich at Ipswich. SPL: Rangers win but still one pt behind leaders. SL: Q of S surprise St Johnstone. Dutch title for Van Gaal's AZ. Becks is back playing for Milan.

20 FA admits Wembley pitch needs digging up for sixth time! Rafa's little helper Sammy Lee calls for end to general ranting; Moyes points to wins over Liverpool and Man Utd to mock "small club" jibes. PL rejects MPs concerns over finance. Santa Cruz wants away from Ewood. Important win achieved by Burnley over Sheff Utd.

21 Arshavin third to hit four goals at Anfield as Liverpool show the swash but buckle in more pieces of eight this time with Arsenal – is this the sinking of Rafa's title hopes? Reading win at Derby, Cardiff scrapes late draw at Charlton; Barnsley denied win at Coventry with controversial last min pen. Brighton wins at Bristol R. Daggers deal blow to Brentford, but Wycombe need one goal at Luton for victory. BSP: Other results ensure non-playing Woking of relegation, now Weymouth the next most vulnerable. MPs are on the side of Blatter over 6,5 special. Olympic man Simon Clegg is chief exec of Ipswich. UEFA will stop games where racist chants are heard. Klinsmann sacked by Bayern.

22 Man Utd re-ignite superiority against Pompey but Neville and O'Shea injured on Scholes 600th game; Everton extinguish Chelsea's title ambitions in goalless draw. Roy Keane is Ipswich manager elect as Jim Magilton is shown the door.

23 Keane takes over at Portman Road, Zola's 4-yr deal at West Ham. Soton will appeal against pts deduction.

24 Fabregas charged over alleged Hull spit spat. Wembley axe groundsman and dig up pitch – sixth time! Leicester has to settle for Scunny pt (30,542) and Stockport edge Crewe nearer drop. FA Youth Cup: Liverpool repeat semi score v Birmingham. Weymouth relegated from BSP.

25 Shame for Spurs, two goal lead, ref Webb cites a non-pen and Man Utd on way to a double Ron-Roo act in high five response – other title challengers need not apply?; free-falling ten man Hull, no win in nine Lge games and three goals for Liverpool (23 in last seven such); Cech redeems himself with pen save from Noble so Chelsea take the pts at West Ham; Villa once hoping for fourth, now look nervous in fifth as Young A scores at long last (after 18 games) in Bolton draw; Everton home form concern, Jagielka carted off with knee injury and Man City get their second away win – Robinho scoring, too!; Fulham's tenth home win worries Stoke's marathon man Pulis; Baggies first win in 12 PL stuns 2500 travelling Black Cats fans. FLC: Ecstatic invading fans mar Wolves title clincher against Tykes for Barnsley born boss McCarthy. Wallace celebration of winner for PNE gets a sendimg-off as Brummie boss McLeish is shocked over Jerome miss proving costly in ten-a-side. McGoldrick pen miss with Saints leading so Burnley relegates them. Keane soon in top gear for Tractor Boys for their fine win at Cardiff. Two down Watford win at ten-man Coventry. Their 13th home draw costs Bristol City. Cotterill's pen helps as Sheff Utd make it 21 wins in last 23 and ten-man Blackpool and Norwich obtain a valuable pt each. L1: Back-to-back promotion packers Posh make it at Colchester, but MK Dons are dumped into play-off mode by Walsall and Millwall are glad of Alexander duo. Cobblers need a pt to be safe from demotion. Cox (sixth double) – and he now has 30 goals for Swindon; Beckford's 33rd for confident Leeds; Cheltenham draw not enough to avoid the drop and nine-left-at-the-end Carlisle may stay up still themselves. Booth's hits his 149th for Huddersfield, but Brighton take possible safety pt; Skiverton joy at Yeovil survival. L2: Brentford clinch the title at Darlo and drawing Wycombe (18th such) require another pt, Exeter a win for automatic lift-up. Rochdale assured a p-o place. Bradford's first win in ten, ten-man Chesterfield's hopes fade, but fast-finishing Daggers get another threesome. Gills in the same frame, too, but drawing Bury could still clinch straight elevation. Veteran Fletcher's 100th Bournemouth goal clears them and puts Grimsby in theoretical danger as Chester need an avalanche after drawing at the Shots. SC semi: Boyd's 100th Rangers goal in 143 games and News of the World team of the day has ten Ibrox boys and St Mirren gkl Howard – game over! SL: St J win at ten-man Dundee need one win for promotion; Dobbie four goals for Queens in seven hit against Clyde, as Airdrie need a win to send Bully Wee down. In form Dumbarton take over in Div 3. BSS: AFC Dons (4th promotion in 7 years) clinch the title 4722 attending. BSN: Tamworth pt at AFC Telford gives them it, too.

26 Fabregas double leads Boro into more mess; Rovers improve at Wigan's expense. SC semi: Falkirk reaches final disposing of Dunfermline. BSP: Burton finally limp to title and FL status despite Torquay defeat as Cambridge held by Alty; Kiddy fall to Poppies; Oxford attract 10,298 but lose to already doomed Northwich who climb above Weymouth; Stevenage beaten and drawing Histon complete play-off foursome with Cambridge and Torquay.

27 Newcastle held by Pompey to Big Al's dismay. Norwich position plight, Reading's improve with win at Carrow Road. Man City plan bid of £40m for Eto'o. Unfit criticism of Giggs as PFA Player of the Year because of his few "starts." Sale owners of Stockport pay for next game. Graham Turner resigns at Hereford, replaced by John Trewick.

28 Ch Lge semi: Barca kept in Cech by Chelsea's last line. L1: Northampton still not safe as MK Dons win there, but the Iron Scunny boys move into the p-o position. Webb admits pen error.

29 Ch Lge semi: Almunia restricts Man Utd to one goal. Gerrard likely to be back for Liverpool run-in. O'Neill is in favour of Auld Firm in PL.

30 UEFA Cup semis: Ukraine tie tips towards Shakhtar, Germanic one for Hamburg. Man Utd concern over Ferdinand fitness. Stockport in administration and docked ten pts. Dave Penney leaves Darlington for Oldham job.

MAY 2009

Norwegian ref in Fjords of tears over Ch Lge gaffes … Three-in-a-row Man Utd 18th overall title … Shakhtar are last UEFA Cup winners … Newcastle, Middlesbrough join WBA in relegation … Burnley back in top flight … Barca has the final class.

1   Southgate safe at Boro. Kroenke increases his Arsenal share. Skint Setanta? Dave Penney settles in as Oldham boss. BSP p-o: Torquay takes two-goal lead over Histon. Everton are unhappy over final ticket allocation.

2   Giggs, man for all seasons, pushes Man Utd nearer title, Boro the drop; Chelsea 50 secs start in local derby warm up with Fulham before Barca renewal; James gives Arsenal (Bendtner only Gunner scorer in all comps this season – 12th consecutive Ch Lge qualification ahead, too – a helping hand as Pompey finish losers with ten men; Tristan free kick for Hammers nails Stoke; Spurs clip no luck Baggies; Bolton share it goalless at demotion-safe Wigan, thanks to gk Jass on Megson's 50th birthday; Man City's Brazil boys come alive against ragged Rovers, still leaving nine PL clubs in theoretical danger. L1: skipper Byrne's 88th min headed leveller keeps Scunny in the p-o frame, but not ten-man Tranmere. Sub Forster goal ensures Brighton survival against docked and just clear Stockport, but Northampton crash at Leeds to go down after Leicester confirmed Crewe's worst season in 14 years, as Carlisle escape with victory over Millwall, Hartlepool despite drubbing at Bristol R – Lambert's 29th and 50th overall goal. Other highspots: 35 yd Booth's 150th Huddersfield goal; teen sub Ryan Brooke with Oldham winner (Royle's only) in first touch. L2: Wycombe squeak promotion by one goal despite losing to visiting Notts and Bury's injury time pen is winner over Stanley. Exeter confirms two lift-ups in successive years. Shrewsbury deny the Daggers (best Lge gate 4791) p-o; Chester's relegation confirmed by Darlo win and Grimsby pt. Dean Glover parts with Port Vale. SPL: Strachan's 200th i/c and fight back win at Aberdeen; Dundee Utd win at Hibs menaces Hearts third place; Falkirk beating Motherwell puts pressure on other stragglers. SL: St Johnstone are Div 1 champions and SPL entrants; Clyde relegated despite beating Dundee as Airdrie win at Partick; Raith take Div 2 title and promotion as Ayr held by Alloa; Div 3 – Dumbarton almost there as Carcary foursome helps towards six against Elgin. Barca warm-up with amazing 6-2 success at Real! Derbyshire loanee gets two in Olympiakos 4-4 Cup Final ended in 15-14 s/o with AEK for Greek double.

3   North-east hot-bed of gloom as Barton sees red as Newcastle lose to Liverpool and even boss Sbragia is shaken by Black Cats display against Everton. FLC: Birmingham do it the hard way at Reading to join Wolves in automatic promotion, while Sheff Utd are held goalless at Palace; impressive Burnley take four off Bristol C; Preston sneak ahead of Cardiff losers at Sheff Wed after edging QPR to complete p-o quartet. Norwich takes third relegation slot after Burton's hat trick for Charlton. BSN semis: Telford loses 4-3 but beat Alfreton on aggregate; Gateshead held but Southport go out.

4   Even Villa beat Hull now as Geovanni and Cousin have their differences, too. Offer of £62.5 by Man Utd for Ribery – if Ronaldo is sold to Real. Henry is likely to miss out with injury. Hyypia is to join Leverkusen in the summer. BSP p-o: Cambridge takes out Stevenage in extra time, Histon's one is not enough to dislodge Torquay. Women's Cup final: Arsenal beat Sunderland. Welsh Cup final: Bangor winners again over Aberystwyth.

5   Ch Lge semi: Man Utd has more ammunition than the Gunners and Fletcher's red is harsh. Barton's future at St James Park is in doubt. Hammers may be denied Euro entry over licence problems.

6   Ch Lge semi: ref Ovrebo's three no pen gaffes leave tactically flawed Chelsea wringing the Blues as ten-man Barca snatch a 93rd min leveller to save UEFA from a second all-England final! B International: Scots beat N Ireland 2-0; England U-17: held 1-1 by Dutch in Euro finals. Sports Minister wants big four to share wealth – with other PL clubs!

Rangers' Kris Boyd tussles with Celtic's Darren O'Dea during the Clydesdale Scottish Premier League match at Ibrox on 9 May 2009. Rangers were triumphant over their Old Firm rivals winning 1-0 with a 37th-minute goal from Steven Davis. (PA Photos)

Arsenal goalkeeper Lukasz Fabianski dives in vain as Chelsea's Nicolas Anelka (not in picture) scores his side's second goal in the 4-1 defeat of Arsenal at the Emirates Stadium. (PA Photos)

7   Chelsea await UEFA wrath following post-match player behaviour. Norwegian ref smuggled out of country amid death threats. World is apparently savouring final of the two greatest teams. UEFA Cup semis: Werder, Shakhtar to meet in final. Bayern deny Ribery approach. Wembley pitch is already re-laid! L2 play-offs: og gives Bury lead at Shrewsbury, Rochdale held by the Gills. BSS final: Hayes & Y edge out Hampton & R B.

8   Chelsea stands behind Drogba in wake of his semi-behaviour. Henry is likely to miss final. FLC p-o: Preston held by Sheff Utd. L1 p-o: Dons earn draw at Scunny. BSN final: Gateshead edge Telford.

9   Liverpool cling on, go top at West Ham; Gerrard even follows up Green's pen save (5th in last 11) for a brace; Baggies take out out-of-form Latics to leave them level on pts with Toon and Boro. Nine-no-win Hull's slump goes on as Stoke confirms survival there. Blackburn practically safe, too, after beating shot-shy Pompey (Kanu PL sub record 100th bench outing). Sunderland is grateful for Fulop last-ditch save in pt at Bolton. Fulham is dreaming of Europe following disposal of Villa. Everton held by Spurs for whom absentee Palacios was homebound through brother's murder. FLC p-o: Barking Bikey banished so Reading beaten at Burnley with pen king Alexander the score. L1 p-o: Harris with 117th Millwall goal gives them the edge over Leeds, but more fan trouble. SPL: Davis is hero at both ends as Rangers go top at Celtic's expense. Falkirk are two pts nearer to St Mirren beaten by Motherwell after pt at Killie. SL: Sons do it at Annan. Forfar and Sten share eight goals. Real lose at Valencia, Barca on brink. Gomez foursome for Stuttgart gives Bayern chance closing in on Wolfsburg. Trophy final: Stevenage beat York and praises new Wembley pitch.

10   Man Utd win the derby at Old Trafford, but victory over Man City marred scorers Ronaldo (moody for being subbed) and Tevez (demonstrating to board over his future). Arsenal suffer worst home defeat in 32 years and first reverse in 22 PL games as Chelsea's four-play, though Wenger bemoans "diver" Drogba. SPL: Caley and ten-man Hamilton take precious pt apiece to keep away from drop zone. L2 p-o: Daniels pen saving hero as Shrewsbury beat Bury in s/o; Jackson double puts Gills into final to deny Rochdale. Vase final: Whitley Bay two goals better than Glossop and surface given another thumbs up. Euro U-17s: Germany 4 England 0.

11   Toon in tune at last as Big Al's twin subs spin Boro deeper in relegation waters on landmark night: first win from trailing in 14 months, late, legendary Milburn's 85th birthdate and Shearer's own third anniversary of his farewell. FLC p-o: Halford's goal enough to Sheff Utd to end Preston's hopes. Fletcher appeal fails and Tevez decision is delayed at Old Trafford. SL: Wrapped up for the season with champions St Johnstone getting four at Airdrie, Stirling equalling the score against Queen's Park. Spurs drinks ban after King's arrest. PL to agree new financial rules after government pressure.

12   Usmanov intends to pay off some of Arsenal debt, but West Ham has increased concerns. Chelsea lines up Ancelotti deal. Owen is at the career crossroads. PL to give incentives to local talent. FL announces crowd increases – 16.35m overall, 9.9m in the Championship, again Europe's fourth best! Is this second tier? One disagrees. FLC p-o: Burnley completes demolition of Reading and Coppell decides to quit. SPL: Celtic regain lead beating Dundee Utd, third-placed Hearts point at Aberdeen gives them two such lead over United.

13   Almost there, but Man Utd are pushed all the way by invigorated Wigan and need Tevez back-heel and late Carrick strike to fight back. Gerrard is FWA Footballer of the Year, Giggs runner-up. SPL: Rangers miss chance of recapturing lead and have to level at Hibs. Falkirk off the bottom beating Hamilton, St Mirren is in cellar position after losking at Killie. Motherwell and Caley draw. SL Div 1 p-o: Ayr useful two goal lead at Brechin; Div 2: Cowden edge East Stirling away. Barca beat Bilbao in Spanish Cup final.

14   L1 p-o: It's 'ell at Elland for Leeds (37,036) as Millwall gets the Lions share of the draw after Forde's fiesta of a Beckford pen save. Villa's Laursen retires with injury. SL Div 1 p-o: Airdrie useful two-goal lead at Peterhead. Div 2 p-o: Sten takes slender lead over Queen's Park.

15   L1 p-o: Murphy saves two Dons pens in s/o to shoot Scunthorpe into final. Coin thrower only black mark on Leeds fans against Millwall. Rafa thinks Man Utd was not the best team! Arsenal fans are unhappy with fourth place for third year. Barton has one more chance at Newcastle. Campbell chanting abusers found guilty and banned for three years from football grounds.

16   Three-in-a-row Man Utd, 18th overall championship levels with Liverpool, but it's still no goals with Arsenal. Fulham's Euro vision leaves Newcastle with "nul points" and Bassong off the pitch while Big Al is not in tune with ref Webb's whistling. Bolton hits the PL's 900th goal but Hull snatch pressure point to swap places with the Mags. Boro has to make do with one pt, too, though their own player goal famine ends after 464 mins against

Villa. Stoke (now 11th) are like the cat with the cream after free ices given out before the win over Wigan. Saha leads the Everton revival against Hammers. "Dodgy-keeper" Gomes has last laugh as best Tottenham's last line at home conceding just 10 goals (11 in 1919-20) as they recover to beat Man City. SPL: Rangers beat Dons in ten-a-side to top it, Hearts see of Dundee Utd for third place and St Mirren swap places with Falkirk after winning there. Killie safe following win over danger threatened Caley and also save Motherwell clattered Hamilton. SL p-o: Brechin gives Ayr a fright before losing, while the wheels come off for East Stirling with two sent off after conceding to Cowden. Real lose to Villarreal and hand 19th title to Barca. Inter joy again for JM, fourth Serie A title in a row and his record 5th in 7 years in three countries! Wolfsburg move two points away from second place Bayern. Bordeaux back on top in France.

17 End of the year cellar dwelling curse accounts for WBA (the only ones to previously avoid it) as Liverpool win at The Hawthorns. Chelsea eases to win over Rovers and Hiddink given guard of honour for last home appearance. Relegated Chester go into administration. SPL: Hibs hold the title key again with second Auld Firm team draw in four days to thwart Celtic. SL p-o: Airdrie shrug off Peterhead lead, Sten beat Spiders. BSP: Torquay back in the FL at ten-man from 70th min Cambridge's expense after two season's absence.

18 Pompey puts pressure on Black Cats after win but James is injured. FA launches WC 2018 bid with Becks, Gordy B and Rooney at the forefront. Wenger linked with Real, Ancelotti learning English! Juve sack Ranieri. Burton Albion appoints Paul Peschisolido as manager.

19 Home grown Man Utd ties up Brazil player deal. FA's NFC academy factory must produce conveyor belt of talent. Capello worries over injury list – Downing out for six months. Setanta dosh improves. England C lose international Challenge Trophy to Belgium U-21s.

20 UEFA Cup final: Shakhtar are extra time winners over Werder Bremen in the swansong match. Ref Clattenburg is back after ban. Brighton beams again with Tony Bloom in charge. FL want bigger share of TV pot. Darlington appoints Colin Todd as manager.

21 Ronaldo rules out Real. Millwall goes American. Kevin Blackwell is unhappy over ref Dean's appointment for Burnley clash. FA rejects reform measures. Blackpool put in Ian Holloway as manager.

22 UEFA will come down heavily on Chelsea over the Barca rumpus, with Drogba and Bosingwa singled out. Arsenal takes commanding lead in Youth final against Liverpool. Now Ronaldo hints at Real!.

23 Frantic four are nervous on eve of final day. L2 p-o final: Jackson settles in late for Gills over Shrews. SPL: Treble of away day wins and Falkirk relegate Caley, Grafite pencils in Wolfsburg's first Bundesliga title with two goals.

24 Survival/submerging Sunday: All menaced teams fall down, two – Newcastle (after 16 years) and Middlesbrough (11) crucially out of the PL. For Toon it's an og deflected misery at Villa with Edgar handed late red, for Boro a club record 12th successive away defeat at West Ham. But Hull against Man Utd reserves and Sunderland at home to Chelsea (Anelka golden boot 19th PL goal) are both beaten yet live for another season. Sbragia quits. Liverpool (Hyypia farewell) contrive to finish runners-up despite just two defeats all season (at Middlesbrough (!) and Spurs) and avenge the latter despite Keane scoring at Anfield! Arsenal scores four in first half against Stoke. Blackburn (Tugay farewell), Roberts red but hold WBA. Everton consolidate fifth place winning at Fulham. Man City's 13th home win (only MU better) overcomes Bolton. Wigan overtakes Stoke for 11th place defeating Pompey. L1 p-o final: Scunny put a glass on after Paint trophy failure by edging Millwall. SPL: Celtic fail to beat Hearts, so Rangers after three year wait win the title at Dundee Utd, costing them a place in Europe to Aberdeen winners over Hibs, but Dons boss Jimmy Calderwood leaves. SL p-o: Ayr deflates Airdrie. Maldini's 901st and last home game for AC Milan but ends on losing side.

25 FLC p-o final: Burnley (33 years out of top flight) becomes 43rd team to play in the PL with Elliott's 13th min strike unlucky for Sheff Utd. Toon calls for Shearer to stay, but cash remains a problem. Arsenal is unhappy over Walcott in two squads U21 and seniors. JM gets pay rise £8.13m a year. Gordon Strachan quits Celtic. Ferdinand fit for Ch Lge final, Henry doubt for Barca.

26 Superlatives already flowing towards Man Utd. David Moyes is Manager of the Year. Arsenal youngsters wrap up FA Youth Cup title.

27 Ch Lge final: No classic but Barca have the class and it's messy for Man Utd and mesmerising Messi for the Catalans. Al Fahim aims to rescue Pompey with £55m injection. Yankee Ellis Short is in charge of Sunderland, too. Coyle denies Celtic interest. Hiddink praises Ancelotti. Walcott is in for Under-21s.

28 Ronaldo goes coy about Real again. Torres signs 5-year deal at £110,000 a week. All-English team is for Olympics. Southampton is unable to pay players.

29 Cup Final ticket allocation comes under fire, but pitch is perfect. Le Tissier is behind Saints take over. Real renew Ronaldo talk. Accrington faces a winding-up order. Newcastle sacks 120 staff. Liverpool is £80m in the red. Wales gets lucky pen to beat Estonia, Republic held by Nigeria. Mixu Paatelainen quits Hibs.

30 FA Cup Final: Saha's record 25-second goal, then Chelsea take control – Drogba header, Lamps blaster – and make Everton the cup's eighth time record losers. S Cup Final: Galicia born Novo-Scotia wonder strike for Rangers against Galicia gk Dani Mallo ends gallant Falkirk fight. Bordeaux achieves first in France for ten years.

31 Ancelotti says farewell to AC Milan along with Maldini (902nd game) and heads for Chelsea, who say goodbye to GH.

JUNE 2009
Kaka breaks record … Ronaldo tops it at £80m … England seven out of seven … Germans Under-21 crush England.

1 Pressure is already on Ancelotti at Chelsea. Long term injury man Hargreaves facing more delay. Toon sell-off hope.

2 Chelsea target Kaka may be bound for Real to hinder Ronaldo ploy. Barry moves to Man City from Villa for £12m. Drogba is to stay at the Bridge. FA is facing cutbacks. Nigeria beat France but Germany get seven against the UAE.

3 Steve Bruce is appointed manager of Sunderland, Jim Magilton has the QPR job. Agents continue to coin money from the game. Aon replaces AIG as Man Utd shirt sponsors. Corruption investigation into football is still ongoing.

4 Liverpool finances are under scrutiny. Real may yet chase Ronaldo after Kaka deal is done.

5 Setanta is out on a financial limb. Micky Adams is new Port Vale manager, but Tranmere sacks Ronnie Moore. Brendan Rodgers is pencilled in for Reading.

6 WC 2010: Almighty slow start then England rolls over the Kazakhs in Almaty. Sofia so-good and another valuable point obtained by the Republic in Bulgaria. Wales welcome win in Baku over the Azers. Irish give the youngsters a dance date but Italy waltz it. Elsewhere Holland qualify for finals with win in Iceland, but Japan beat them to becoming the first edging Uzbekistan. Aussies and South Korea also book in for the finals. Brazil hits Uruguay for four in ten-a-side finish.

7 Celtic carrys on interest in Tony Mowbray s manager. John Hughes (ex-Falkirk) is appointed by Hibs.

8 Kaka breaks the transfer record in £56m move to Real. The Daily Telegraph compares record of England managers over first 14 matches – Capello level with Winterbottom and Hoddle! U-21s: England hit Azers for seven. West Ham taken over and immediate worries are ended. Ronaldo has suspected hernia.

9   FA to underwrite cost of tube-strike hit fans. Big Al's Toon hopes are fading, Big Phil gets a Uzbekistan role. Wigan is courting Roberto Martinez. Setanta needs a buyer.

10   WC: England six-hitters against Andorra, watched by half-full Wembley. Ukraine put pressure on Croatia after victory against Kazakhstan. Seventh win in a row for Holland. Liverpool's new ground remains in limbo. Real renew Ronaldo pursuit. Confederations Cup kicks-off in S.Africa with Italy beating NZ 4-3.

11   £80m takes Ronaldo to Real at last, busting the Kaka record. Setanta is hopeful of a bale-out. WC shock for Argentina (and Messi) losing to Ecuador, Brazil edges Paraguay.

12   Blatter champions his one-time slave Ronaldo for the money making deal. Setanta supposed to be getting some cash of its own.

13   Barton continues to receive Newcastle payment for image rights. Pompey deny Thaksin takeover move. Story revealed that new FA chief executive Ian Watmore went to Wembley on tube strike day by bus and foot.

14   Carlos Queiroz ex-Man Utd reckons Ronaldo should have stayed at Old Trafford. Confederations Cup starts with no goals South Africa and Iraq. John Barnes is to become Tranmere boss.

15   Euro U-21s: England scrape win over Finns. Con Cup: Italy see off ten-Yanks, but ref Webb in the news with controversial penalty decision which gave Brazil winner against Egypt. Malky Mackay is the new Watford manager.

16   Roberto Martinez finally appointed by Wigan. Euro-U-21s: Swedes hit Belarus for five, Italy and Serbs goalless.

17   Drogba six-match ban, Bosingwa four, Chelsea fined £85,000. Con Cup: Spain record 34th consecutive unbeaten match with win over Iraq, South Africa beat NZ. North Korea qualifys for World Cup finals.

18   Euro U-21s: Spaniards spanked by England, Germans beat Finns. Con Cup: Egypt surprise Italians, Brazil ease over USA. Sir Bobby is unhappy with Ronaldo price tag. Matt Le Tissier likely Saints chairman, but Keegan as boss is unlikely.

19   Setanta loses TV licence. Tevez will not stay at Old Trafford. Chelsea will appeal.

20   Con Cup: Spain continue winning to overcome South Africa, while Iraq and NZ share no goals.

21   Con Cup: Brazil easily beats Italy, whose interest ends as USA similarly defeats Egypt. But Cannavarro equals Maldini's 126 caps.

22   Euro U-21: England settles for draw with Germany. Soton takeover is subject to agreement over point deduction. ESPN the Disney chain succeeds in taking over Setanta's PL rights.

23   FA in hunt to find Setanta successor. Paulo Sousa becomes Swansea manager.

24   Con Cup semi: Pain for Spain as long run ends in defeat by the Yanks.

25   U-21s practice penalties! Con Cup: Brazil edge into final at South Africa's expense.

26   Euro U-21 semis: England wins a shoot-out against the Swedes and face Germany – winners over Italy in final! Ronaldo's deal complete on 1 July. Pompey takeover is stalled.

27   Liverpool despite paying £17m for Glen Johnson has offered Arbeloa a new contract.

28   Con Cup: two-down Brazilians still manage to beat USA in final while Spain edges South Africa for third place.

29   Euro 21 final: England crash out four goals worse off than Germany, but Pearce will stay on as coach. Eto'o expected to turn down Man City advances.

30   Man Utd swoop for Valencia of Wigan at £16m. Saints in a pickle as takeover falters.

LANDMARKS

Reuben Noble-Lazarus (Barnsley) becomes the youngest Football League player at 15 years 45 days.

Ashley Cole (Chelsea) collects his fifth FA Cup winner's medal (three with Arsenal).

Louis Saha scores the fastest FA Cup final goal 25 seconds for Everton v Chelsea.

Robinho breaks the English transfer record in a £32.5 million move from Real Madrid to Manchester City.

Manchester United's Ryan Giggs is the only player to score at least one Premier League goal in each of its 17 seasons.

Edwin Van der Sar of Manchester United breaks the Premier League clean sheet record with an unbeaten 1311 minutes.

Real Madrid pay a world record £80 million for Manchester United's Cristiano Ronaldo.

Portsmouth's David James extends his Premier League record to 547 matches.

Referee Clive Oliver, 48, takes charge of the Gillingham v Shrewsbury Town play-off. His son Michael, 24, a day later controls the Scunthorpe United v Millwall game.

David Beckham becomes England's most capped outfield player with 112 appearances.

Spain's equals Brazil's record of 35 unbeaten matches (32 wins).

ENGLISH LEAGUE TABLES 2008–09

FA BARCLAYCARD PREMIERSHIP

			Home					Away					Total					
		P	W	D	L	F	A	W	D	L	F	A	W	D	L	F	A	GD	Pts
1	Manchester U	38	16	2	1	43	13	12	4	3	25	11	28	6	4	68	24	44	90
2	Liverpool	38	12	7	0	41	13	13	4	2	36	14	25	11	2	77	27	50	86
3	Chelsea	38	11	6	2	33	12	14	2	3	35	12	25	8	5	68	24	44	83
4	Arsenal	38	11	5	3	31	16	9	7	3	37	21	20	12	6	68	37	31	72
5	Everton	38	8	6	5	31	20	9	6	4	24	17	17	12	9	55	37	18	63
6	Aston Villa	38	7	9	3	27	21	10	2	7	27	27	17	11	10	54	48	6	62
7	Fulham	38	11	3	5	28	16	3	8	8	11	18	14	11	13	39	34	5	53
8	Tottenham H	38	10	5	4	21	10	4	4	11	24	35	14	9	15	45	45	0	51
9	West Ham U	38	9	2	8	23	22	5	7	7	19	23	14	9	15	42	45	–3	51
10	Manchester C	38	13	0	6	40	18	2	5	12	18	32	15	5	18	58	50	8	50
11	Wigan Ath	38	8	5	6	17	18	4	4	11	17	27	12	9	17	34	45	–11	45
12	Stoke C	38	10	5	4	22	15	2	4	13	16	40	12	9	17	38	55	–17	45
13	Bolton W	38	7	5	7	21	21	4	3	12	20	32	11	8	19	41	53	–12	41
14	Portsmouth	38	8	3	8	26	29	2	8	9	12	28	10	11	17	38	57	–19	41
15	Blackburn R	38	6	7	6	22	23	4	4	11	18	37	10	11	17	40	60	–20	41
16	Sunderland	38	6	3	10	21	25	3	6	10	13	29	9	9	20	34	54	–20	36
17	Hull C	38	3	5	11	18	36	5	6	8	21	28	8	11	19	39	64	–25	35
18	Newcastle U	38	5	7	7	24	29	2	6	11	16	30	7	13	18	40	59	–19	34
19	Middlesbrough	38	5	9	5	17	20	2	2	15	11	37	7	11	20	28	57	–29	32
20	WBA	38	7	3	9	26	33	1	5	13	10	34	8	8	22	36	67	–31	32

COCA–COLA FOOTBALL LEAGUE CHAMPIONSHIP

			Home					Away					Total					
		P	W	D	L	F	A	W	D	L	F	A	W	D	L	F	A	GD	Pts
1	Wolverhampton W	46	15	5	3	44	21	12	4	7	36	31	27	9	10	80	52	28	90
2	Birmingham C	46	14	5	4	30	17	9	9	5	24	20	23	14	9	54	37	17	83
3	Sheffield U	46	12	6	5	35	22	10	8	5	29	17	22	14	10	64	39	25	80
4	Reading	46	12	5	6	40	17	9	9	5	32	23	21	14	11	72	40	32	77
5	Burnley	46	14	5	4	42	23	7	8	8	30	37	21	13	12	72	60	12	76
6	Preston NE	46	16	3	4	39	20	5	8	10	27	34	21	11	14	66	54	12	74
7	Cardiff C	46	14	5	4	40	23	5	12	6	25	30	19	17	10	65	53	12	74
8	Swansea C	46	11	9	3	40	22	5	11	7	23	28	16	20	10	63	50	13	68
9	Ipswich T	46	8	9	6	30	26	9	6	8	32	27	17	15	14	62	53	9	66
10	Bristol C	46	7	13	3	30	23	8	3	12	24	31	15	16	15	54	54	0	61
11	QPR	46	12	7	4	28	19	3	9	11	14	25	15	16	15	42	44	–2	61
12	Sheffield W	46	11	6	6	26	14	5	7	11	25	44	16	13	17	51	58	–7	61
13	Watford	46	11	6	6	42	32	5	4	14	26	40	16	10	20	68	72	–4	58
14	Doncaster R	46	9	5	9	16	18	8	2	13	26	35	17	7	22	42	53	–11	58
15	Crystal Palace	46	9	8	6	26	19	6	4	13	26	36	15	12	19	52	55	–3	57
16	Blackpool	46	5	8	10	25	33	8	9	6	22	25	13	17	16	47	58	–11	56
17	Coventry C	46	8	8	7	26	26	5	7	11	21	32	13	15	18	47	58	–11	54
18	Derby Co	46	9	7	7	31	26	5	13	5	24	41	14	12	20	55	67	–12	54
19	Nottingham F	46	8	7	8	27	28	5	7	11	23	37	13	14	19	50	65	–15	53
20	Barnsley	46	8	7	8	28	24	5	6	12	17	34	13	13	20	45	58	–13	52
21	Plymouth Arg	46	7	5	11	31	35	6	7	10	13	22	13	12	21	44	57	–13	51
22	Norwich C	46	9	5	9	35	28	3	5	15	22	42	12	10	24	57	70	–13	46
23	Southampton	46	4	10	9	23	29	6	5	12	23	40	10	15	21	46	69	–23	45
24	Charlton Ath	46	6	8	9	33	38	2	7	14	19	36	8	15	23	52	74	–22	39

COCA–COLA FOOTBALL LEAGUE DIVISION 1

			Home				Away					Total						
		P	W	D	L	F	A	W	D	L	F	A	W	D	L	F	A	GD	Pts
1	Leicester C	46	13	9	1	41	16	14	6	3	43	23	27	15	4	84	39	45	96
2	Peterborough U	46	14	6	3	41	22	12	5	6	37	32	26	11	9	78	54	24	89
3	Milton Keynes D	46	12	4	7	42	25	14	5	4	41	22	26	9	11	83	47	36	87
4	Leeds U	46	17	2	4	49	20	9	4	10	28	29	26	6	14	77	49	28	84
5	Millwall	46	13	4	6	30	21	12	3	8	33	32	25	7	14	63	53	10	82
6	Scunthorpe U	46	13	5	5	44	24	9	5	9	38	39	22	10	14	82	63	19	76
7	Tranmere R	46	15	5	3	41	20	6	6	11	21	29	21	11	14	62	49	13	74
8	Southend U	46	13	2	8	29	20	8	6	9	29	41	21	8	17	58	61	-3	71
9	Huddersfield T	46	9	8	6	32	28	9	6	8	30	37	18	14	14	62	65	-3	68
10	Oldham Ath	46	9	9	5	35	24	7	8	8	31	41	16	17	13	66	65	1	65
11	Bristol R	46	11	4	8	44	29	6	8	9	35	32	17	12	17	79	61	18	63
12	Colchester U	46	7	4	12	21	24	11	5	7	37	34	18	9	19	58	58	0	63
13	Walsall	46	10	3	10	34	36	7	7	9	27	30	17	10	19	61	66	-5	61
14	Leyton Orient	46	6	6	11	24	33	9	5	9	21	24	15	11	20	45	57	-12	56
15	Swindon T	46	8	7	8	37	34	4	10	9	31	37	12	17	17	68	71	-3	53
16	Brighton & HA	46	6	6	11	32	40	7	7	9	23	30	13	13	20	55	70	-15	52
17	Yeovil T	46	6	10	7	26	29	6	5	12	15	37	12	15	19	41	66	-25	51
18	Stockport Co*	46	9	7	7	34	28	7	5	11	25	29	16	12	18	59	57	2	50
19	Hartlepool U	46	8	7	8	45	40	5	4	14	21	39	13	11	22	66	79	-13	50
20	Carlisle U	46	8	7	8	36	32	4	7	12	20	37	12	14	20	56	69	-13	50
21	Northampton T	46	8	8	7	38	29	4	5	14	23	36	12	13	21	61	65	-4	49
22	Crewe Alex	46	8	4	11	30	38	4	6	13	29	44	12	10	24	59	82	-23	46
23	Cheltenham T	46	7	6	10	30	38	2	6	15	21	53	9	12	25	51	91	-40	39
24	Hereford U	46	6	4	13	23	28	3	3	17	19	51	9	7	30	42	79	-37	34

Stockport Co deducted 10 points.

COCA–COLA FOOTBALL LEAGUE DIVISION 2

			Home				Away					Total						
		P	W	D	L	F	A	W	D	L	F	A	W	D	L	F	A	GD	Pts
1	Brentford	46	13	8	2	39	15	10	8	5	26	21	23	16	7	65	36	29	85
2	Exeter C	46	13	5	5	36	25	9	8	6	29	25	22	13	11	65	50	15	79
3	Wycombe W	46	11	9	3	32	16	9	9	5	22	17	20	18	8	54	33	21	78
4	Bury	46	14	4	5	36	19	7	11	5	27	24	21	15	10	63	43	20	78
5	Gillingham	46	12	7	4	38	21	9	5	9	20	34	21	12	13	58	55	3	75
6	Rochdale	46	11	6	6	40	24	8	7	8	30	35	19	13	14	70	59	11	70
7	Shrewsbury T	46	14	6	3	41	16	3	12	8	20	28	17	18	11	61	44	17	69
8	Dagenham & R	46	12	3	8	44	24	7	8	8	33	29	19	11	16	77	53	24	68
9	Bradford C	46	11	10	2	39	18	7	3	13	27	37	18	13	15	66	55	11	67
10	Chesterfield	46	8	8	7	32	28	8	7	8	30	29	16	15	15	62	57	5	63
11	Morecambe	46	9	9	5	29	24	6	9	8	24	32	15	18	13	53	56	-3	63
12	Darlington*	46	11	6	6	36	23	9	6	8	25	21	20	12	14	61	44	17	62
13	Lincoln C	46	6	11	6	26	22	8	6	9	27	30	14	17	15	53	52	1	59
14	Rotherham U*	46	11	6	6	32	21	10	6	7	28	25	21	12	13	60	46	14	58
15	Aldershot T	46	9	10	4	36	31	5	2	16	23	49	14	12	20	59	80	-21	54
16	Accrington S	46	9	5	9	25	24	4	6	13	17	35	13	11	22	42	59	-17	50
17	Barnet	46	7	7	9	30	35	4	8	11	26	39	11	15	20	56	74	-18	48
18	Port Vale	46	6	6	11	23	33	7	3	13	21	33	13	9	24	44	66	-22	48
19	Notts Co	46	6	6	11	22	31	5	8	10	27	38	11	14	21	49	69	-20	47
20	Macclesfield T	46	7	4	12	23	37	6	4	13	22	40	13	8	25	45	77	-32	47
21	Bournemouth*	46	11	6	6	28	15	6	6	11	31	36	17	12	17	59	51	8	46
22	Grimsby T	46	6	7	10	31	28	3	7	13	20	41	9	14	23	51	69	-18	41
23	Chester C	46	4	7	12	24	34	4	6	13	19	47	8	13	25	43	81	-38	37
24	Luton T*	46	7	8	8	34	34	6	9	8	24	31	13	17	16	58	65	-7	26

Darlington deducted 10 points, Rotherham U deducted 17 points, Bournemouth deducted 17 points, Luton T deducted 30 points.

FOOTBALL LEAGUE PLAY-OFFS 2008-09

■ Denotes player sent off.

CHAMPIONSHIP FIRST LEG

Friday, 8 May 2009

Preston NE (1) 1 *(St Ledger-Hall 21)*

Sheffield U (0) 1 *(Howard 46)* 19,840

Preston NE: Lonergan; Jones, Nolan, Carter (Nicholson), St Ledger-Hall, Mawene, Sedgwick, McKenna, Parkin, Mellor (Brown C), Wallace.
Sheffield U: Kenny; Naughton, Walker, Montgomery, Morgan, Kilgallon, Halford, Howard, Henderson (Beattie C), Ward (Lupoli), Quinn S.

Saturday, 9 May 2009

Burnley (0) 1 *(Alexander 84 (pen))*

Reading (0) 0 18,853

Burnley: Jensen; Duff, Kalvenes, McCann, Caldwell, Carlisle, Alexander, Gudjonsson (McDonald), Blake, Paterson (Rodriguez), Eagles (Thompson).
Reading: Hahnemann; Rosenior, Harding, Gunnarsson (Cisse), Duberry, Bikey■, Kebe, Matejovsky, Long, Doyle (Kitson), Tabb.

CHAMPIONSHIP SECOND LEG

Monday, 11 May 2009

Sheffield U (0) 1 *(Halford 59)*

Preston NE (0) 0 26,354

Sheffield U: Kenny; Naughton, Walker, Montgomery, Morgan, Kilgallon, Halford (Bromby), Cotterill, Beattie C, Howard, Quinn S.
Preston NE: Lonergan; Jones, Nolan, Nicholson (Carter), St Ledger-Hall, Mawene, Sedgwick (Mellor), McKenna, Brown C (Elliott), Parkin, Wallace.

Tuesday, 12 May 2009

Reading (0) 0

Burnley (0) 2 *(Paterson 51, Thompson 58)* 19,909

Reading: Hahnemann; Rosenior, Harding, Pearce, Duberry, Gunnarsson, Kebe (Kitson), Matejovsky (Hunt S), Church (Little), Long, Tabb.
Burnley: Jensen; Duff, Kalvenes, McCann, Caldwell, Carlisle, Alexander, Thompson (Rodriguez), Blake, Paterson (Gudjonsson), Elliott (Eagles).

CHAMPIONSHIP FINAL (AT WEMBLEY)

Sunday, 24 May 2009

Burnley (1) 1 *(Elliott 13)*

Sheffield U (0) 0 80,518

Burnley: Jensen; Duff, Kalvenes, McCann (Gudjonsson), Caldwell, Carlisle, Alexander, Thompson (Rodriguez), Blake (Eagles), Paterson, Elliott.
Sheffield U: Kenny; Walker, Naughton, Montgomery, Morgan, Kilgallon, Halford, Cotterill (Ward■), Beattie C, Howard (Lupoli), Quinn S (Hendrie).
Referee: M. Dean (Wirral).

LEAGUE 1 FIRST LEG

Friday, 8 May 2009

Scunthorpe U (1) 1 *(Woolford 13)*

Milton Keynes D (1) 1 *(Wilbraham 27)* 6599

Scunthorpe U: Murphy (Lillis); Byrne, Morris, Crosby, Mirfin, McCann, Sparrow, Togwell, Hayes, Hooper (Thompson), Woolford.
Milton Keynes D: Gueret; Regan, Lewington, Leven, Stirling, Llera, Wright (Cummings), Howell, Chadwick (Baldock), Wilbraham, Puncheon.

Saturday, 9 May 2009

Millwall (0) 1 *(Harris 71)*

Leeds U (0) 0 13,228

Millwall: Forde; Dunne, Craig, Abdou, Whitbread, Frampton, Laird (Henry), Bolder, Alexander, Price (Harris), Martin.
Leeds U: Ankergren; Douglas, Parker, Kilkenny, Sodje, Naylor, Snodgrass (Robinson), Howson (Johnson), Beckford, Becchio, Delph.

LEAGUE 1 SECOND LEG

Thursday, 14 May 2009

Leeds U (0) 1 *(Becchio 53)*

Millwall (0) 1 *(Abdu 74)* 37,036

Leeds U: Ankergren; Douglas, Parker (Johnson), Kilkenny (Robinson), Naylor, Sodje, Snodgrass, Howson (Grella), Beckford, Becchio, Delph.
Millwall: Forde; Dunne, Frampton, Abdu, Whitbread, Craig, Henry (Robinson P), Bolder, Alexander, Harris (Grabban), Martin.

Scunthorpe United's Martyn Woolford scores the late winner against Millwall in the League 1 Play-Off Final at Wembley. (PA Photos)

Gillingham's Simeon Jackson (centre left) heads in the winning goal in the final minute of the League 2 Play-Off Final at Wembley. (PA Photos)

Friday, 15 May 2009

Milton Keynes D (0) 0

Scunthorpe U (0) 0 14,479

Milton Keynes D: Gueret; Regan, Lewington, Leven, Stirling, Llera, Wright (Chadwick), Howell (Navarro), Baldock (Flo), Wilbraham, Puncheon.
Scunthorpe U: Murphy; Byrne, Morris, Crosby, Mirfin, McCann, Sparrow, Trotter, Hayes, Thompson (Togwell), Woolford (Forte).
aet; Scunthorpe U won 7-6 on penalties: McCann scored; Leven scored; Hayes scored; Wilbraham scored; Crosby scored; Navarro scored; Byrne missed; Puncheon saved; Trotter scored; Llera scored; Sparrow missed; Stirling missed; Forte scored; Lewington scored; Togwell scored; Gueret scored; Morris scored; Flo missed.

LEAGUE 1 FINAL (AT WEMBLEY)

Sunday, 24 May 2009

Millwall (2) 2 *(Alexander 37, 39)*

Scunthorpe U (1) 3 *(Sparrow 6, 70, Woolford 85)* 59,661

Millwall: Forde; Dunne, Craig, Bolder, Whitbread, Frampton (Robinson P), Grabban (Hackett), Abdou (Laird), Alexander, Harris, Martin.
Scunthorpe U: Murphy; Byrne, Morris, McCann, Mirfin, Crosby, Sparrow, Togwell (Trotter), Hayes, Hooper (Forte), Woolford.
Referee: M. Oliver (Northumberland).

LEAGUE 2 FIRST LEG

Thursday, 7 May 2009

Rochdale (0) 0

Gillingham (0) 0 4450

Rochdale: Fielding; Ramsden, Kennedy, Toner, Stanton, McArdle, Buckley (Thompson), Jones G, Thorpe, Le Fondre (Dagnall), Rundle.
Gillingham: Royce; Fuller, Nutter, Weston, King, Richards, Wright, Barcham, Jackson (McCammon), Oli (Jarrett), Lewis.

Shrewsbury T (0) 0

Bury (0) 1 *(Ashton 81 (og))* 8429

Shrewsbury T: Daniels; Moss, Ashton, Davies, Coughlan, Langmead, Humphrey (Worrall), Murray, Chadwick (Riza), Holt, McIntyre.
Bury: Brown; Haslam, Buchanan, Dawson, Sodje, Futcher, Bennett (Welsh), Barry-Murphy, Jevons, Bishop, Jones.

LEAGUE 2 SECOND LEG

Sunday, 10 May 2009

Bury (0) 0

Shrewsbury T (0) 1 *(McIntyre 88)* 7673

Bury: Brown; Haslam (Racchi), Buchanan, Dawson, Sodje, Futcher, Bennett, Barry-Murphy, Morrell (Hurst), Jevons (Bishop), Jones.
Shrewsbury T: Daniels; Moss, Ashton, Davies, Coughlan, Langmead, Worrall, Murray (Leslie■), Riza (Ashikodi), Holt (Chadwick), McIntyre.
aet; Shrewsbury T won 4-3 on penalties: Barry-Murphy scored; Davies scored; Jones scored; Ashikodi scored; Racchi saved; McIntyre scored; Bennett scored; Worrall scored; Bishop saved.

Gillingham (1) 2 *(Jackson 13, 58 (pen))*

Rochdale (1) 1 *(Dagnall 36)* 9585

Gillingham: Royce; Fuller, Nutter, Weston, King, Richards, Wright (Bentley), Barcham, Jackson (McCammon), Oli (Southall), Lewis.
Rochdale: Fielding; Ramsden, Kennedy, Toner, Stanton, McArdle, Thompson (Buckley), Jones G, Dagnall, Thorpe (Shaw), Rundle (Le Fondre).

LEAGUE 2 FINAL (AT WEMBLEY)

Saturday, 23 May 2009

Gillingham (0) 1 *(Jackson 90)*

Shrewsbury T (0) 0 53,706

Gillingham: Royce; Fuller, Nutter, Weston, King, Richards, Wright, Barcham, Jackson, Oli, Lewis.
Shrewsbury T: Daniels; Moss, Ashton, Davies, Coughlan, Langmead, Humphrey (Ashikodi), Murray (Worrall), Chadwick (Riza), Holt, McIntyre.
Referee: C. Oliver (Northumberland).

LEADING GOALSCORERS 2008–09

	League	Carling Cup	FA Cup	Other	Total
BARCLAYS PREMIERSHIP					
Only goals scored in the same division are included.					
Nicolas Anelka *(Chelsea)*	19	0	4	2	25
Cristiano Ronaldo *(Manchester U)*	18	2	1	5	26
Steven Gerrard *(Liverpool)*	16	0	1	7	24
Fernando Torres *(Liverpool)*	14	0	1	2	17
Frank Lampard *(Chelsea)*	12	2	3	3	20
Darren Bent *(Tottenham H)*	12	1	0	4	17
Dirk Kuyt *(Liverpool)*	12	0	0	3	15
Wayne Rooney *(Manchester U)*	12	0	1	7	20
Robin Van Persie *(Arsenal)*	11	0	4	5	20
John Carew *(Aston Villa)*	11	0	1	3	15
Gabriel Agbonlahor *(Aston Villa)*	11	0	0	1	12
Kevin Davies *(Bolton W)*	11	0	0	0	11
Ricardo Fuller *(Stoke C)*	11	0	0	0	11
In order of total goals:					
Peter Crouch *(Portsmouth)*	10	0	1	4	15
COCA-COLA CHAMPIONSHIP					
Sylvain Ebanks-Blake *(Wolverhampton W)*	25	0	0	0	25
Ross McCormack *(Cardiff C)*	21	1	1	0	23
Jason Scotland *(Swansea C)*	21	0	3	0	24
Kevin Doyle *(Reading)*	18	0	0	0	18
Tommy Smith *(Watford)*	17	0	0	0	17
Rob Hulse *(Derby Co)*	15	0	3	0	18
Chris Iwelumo *(Wolverhampton W)*	14	2	0	0	16
Kevin Phillips *(Birmingham C)*	14	0	0	0	14
Marcus Tudgay *(Sheffield W)*	14	0	0	0	14
Paul Gallagher *(Plymouth Arg)*	13	0	0	0	13
(on loan from Blackburn R).					
COCA-COLA LEAGUE 1					
Simon Cox *(Swindon T)*	29	1	0	2	32
Rickie Lambert *(Bristol R)*	29	0	0	0	29
Matty Fryatt *(Leicester C)*	27	0	4	1	32
Jermaine Beckford *(Leeds U)*	26	4	3	0	33
Gary Hooper *(Scunthorpe U)*	24	0	4	2	30
Craig Mackail-Smith	23	0	3	0	26
(Peterborough U)					
Joel Porter *(Hartlepool U)*	18	3	2	0	23
Lee Hughes *(Oldham Ath)*	18	0	0	0	18
Aaron McLean *(Peterborough U)*	17	0	1	0	18
Paul Hayes *(Scunthorpe U)*	17	0	0	3	20
Aaron Wilbraham *(Milton Keynes D)*	16	0	0	1	17
Luciano Becchio *(Leeds U)*	15	2	0	2	19
Danny Graham *(Carlisle U)*	15	0	1	0	16
Steve Guinan *(Hereford U)*	15	0	0	0	15
COCA-COLA LEAGUE 2					
Grant Holt *(Shrewsbury T)*	20	0	1	7	28
Jack Lester *(Chesterfield)*	20	0	2	1	23
Paul Benson *(Dagenham & R)*	18	0	1	2	21
Reuben Reid *(Rotherham U)*	18	1	0	0	19
Adam Le Fondre *(Rochdale)*	17	0	3	0	20
Simeon Jackson *(Gillingham)*	17	0	1	3	21
John O'Flynn *(Barnet)*	17	0	1	0	18
Brett Pitman *(Bournemouth)*	17	0	0	0	17
Peter Thorne *(Bradford C)*	17	0	0	0	17
Charlie MacDonald *(Brentford)*	16	0	2	0	18
Andy Bishop *(Bury)*	16	0	0	1	17
Ryan Lowe *(Chester C)*	16	2	0	0	18

Other matches consist of European games, J Paint Trophy, Community Shield and Football League play-offs. Players listed in order of League goals total.

REVIEW OF THE SEASON

Manchester United made it three in a row and Sir Alex Ferguson added another trophy to his already outstanding record with the club but without taking anything away from this achievement, just how Liverpool managed to finish merely as runners-up is amazing when you consider their Premier League record in 2008–09.

They were unbeaten at Anfield in the competition, suffered just two away defeats – at Tottenham and Middlesbrough – scored nine more goals than United and what should have been the pinnacle, inflicted a 4-1 defeat on them at Old Trafford. But United sustained just one more reverse the following week at Fulham where they even finished the match with just nine players.

Yet it did not start well for United following an ill-conceived and draining pre-season tour of Africa. They also missed the involvement of the injured Cristiano Ronaldo for the first month of the season. With just one win in the opening four games and losing the first of what was to be a double against Liverpool at Anfield, a clear need for an additional striker and defeat in the European Super Cup by Zenit, it was not the best of openings to retaining the title.

The turning point in the season came after losing at the Emirates Stadium to Arsenal on 8 November. These were to be the last goals Edwin Van der Sar conceded until February in the Premier League and as far as the competition was concerned it carried on almost unhindered until the momentary trauma of Liverpool's visit. Naturally with commitments outside the domestic calendar and the need for the squad system to be used to its fullest potential, United had to call upon the services of no fewer than 33 players. Not one of them succeeded in playing in every match. Nemanja Vidic the central defender turned out 33 times, one of them as substitute, followed by Ronaldo with 32 despite his late start and two of those coming off the bench. He was leading scorer with 18. Wayne Rooney also hit double figures with twelve.

While the Carling Cup was successfully achieved, albeit from the inevitable shoot-out which still plagues the game, the huge disappointment was the failure to retain the Champions League. Manchester United were simply not in any kind of form on the day and would have needed to be at their best against a formidable Barcelona.

For Liverpool it was merely second place despite its impressive results. The failure was in the number of drawn matches of course. Including the victory at Old Trafford, the last eleven matches saw just one draw, the others all wins.

While their assault had been led by Steven Gerrard with 16 goals and Fernando Torres on 14, the Premier's leading marksman was Nicolas Anelka with 19 for Chelsea, who finished third having had a change of manager after mid-season when Felipe Scolari was sacked and Guus Hiddink became interim first team coach at Stamford Bridge, juggling his work with coaching the Russian national team.

Chelsea had been the early pacemakers, but significantly their first three reverses had been at the hands of Liverpool and Arsenal at home, Manchester United away. Liverpool also achieved the double over them and though Hiddink improved matters noticeably it was still third place.

Arsenal had for them an indifferent start and – shades of Liverpool – too many drawn matches in mid-season. Amazingly after winning at Chelsea at the end of November, they lost just one more League game – at home to the Blues! However, Hiddink's one serious mistake was a tactical one in the Champions League semi-final against Barcelona after the epic with Liverpool in the previous round. But there was reward for him and the team with the FA Cup.

Darren Fletcher of Manchester United drives through challenges from Arsenal's Andrey Arshavin (left) and Neves Denilson (right) during the 0-0 Premier League draw at Old Trafford. The single point was enough to ensure United's 11th Premier League title and equalled Liverpool's record haul of 18 titles. (PA Photos)

The top four were thus undisturbed, but at one stage Aston Villa had threatened to break into the quartet. Early in February they were third but defeat at home by Chelsea put them in their place and they won only two more matches at the tail end.

This disappointing run even cost them fifth place as Everton the runners-up in the FA Cup Final secured it with three wins and a draw in the last four games. Defensive problems early in the campaign once put right, it was a satisfactory season at Goodison Park.

Fulham did exceptionally well and Roy Hodgson earned much praise for his handling of affairs at Craven Cottage. Only in one spell in September did they lose three in a row and the scalp of Manchester United gave them late impetus. Something of a Harry Redknapp miracle helped towards Tottenham Hotspur finishing as high as eighth after the worst start in the club's history with just two points out of the first eight fixtures which cost Juande Ramos his job. But there was Carling Cup shoot-out misery.

West Ham United recovered from mid-season lapses which had them fourth from bottom at one time, they lacked striking power, witnessed by fourteen games without scoring. Manchester City with the second best home record were too often found wanting on their travels, yet it was their away form which pulled them out of trouble in the UEFA Cup on several occasions until they reached the quarter-finals.

Wigan Athletic could be satisfied with another solid season in eleventh position, which might have been better when you notice they, too, were hung up with drawn games – sixteen of them. Stoke City confounded their critics in twelfth place. Nine games without a win looked ominous for them before a spirited run-in banished all such fears of relegation.

Bolton Wanderers faltered with only one win in their last eleven and only twice in the term did they managed two wins in a row. Goals were often scarce here, too – an amazing 18 blanks. Portsmouth also underwent managerial movement and a mid-season blip of two points from a possible twenty-seven. Prospects improved in March and April to avoid something worse.

Erratic in the second half of the season, Blackburn Rovers had also only picked up three points from drawn matches from an October downturn which lasted eleven games which had dumped them one off the bottom. Sunderland's Roy Keane quit and relegation was never far removed from the once hot-bed of north-east football and plagued Hull City, Newcastle United plus Middlesbrough, too.

Incredibly Sunderland scraped just one win in their last thirteen outings yet survived. This was nothing compared with Hull's experience, after an impressive start they won only one game from mid-December but somehow, survived. Not so Newcastle and Middlesbrough. West Bromwich Albion had suffered the curse of being bottom at the New Year.

Newcastle had the St James' Park legend Alan Shearer in temporary at the helm, but with only two wins in the second half of the season it was a slow drift into relegation. After 16 November, Middlesbrough contrived just two more wins. Albion had achieved three wins in four matches to be perched ninth in early October. From then on it was free-fall relieved by a brief spurt in December which was not sustained.

Wolverhampton Wanderers, after their best start for 46 years at one stage looking home and dry, started to leak points in February until they put matters right to take the title. They benefited from keeping the number of drawn matches down to reasonable proportions. Runners-up Birmingham City – with their most confident opening of all time perhaps – also had their moments of unease, notably six matches from Boxing Day with just one win, but the situation was tight at the end of the season, too, after losing to Preston North End at home they won their last fixture crucially at Reading.

But it was actually Reading with the biggest slump. From mid-January when settled in second place they won only five matches and the free-scoring first half of the season became a distant memory. Sheffield United overhauled them with a devastating run from late February in which they lost just once – at Burnley. Significantly

Didier Drogba of Chelsea equalizes against Everton in the FA Cup Final at Wembley. An early Louis Saha strike had put the Toffees in front but Chelsea claimed the Cup with Frank Lampard scoring the winner in the 72nd minute.
(Action Images/Tony O'Brien)

Manchester City's Robinho challenges with SV Hamburg's keeper Frank Rost during the UEFA Cup quarter-final second leg tie at The City of Manchester Stadium. Despite a stirring 2-1 victory, City failed to progress with Hamburg winning 4-3 on aggregate. (Action Images/Jason Cairnduff)

Burnley beat them in the play-off final. Five defeats in a row around the turn of the year had threatened to derail the Turf Moor team, but always likely to score goals, they turned it around.

Preston 6-0 winners over Cardiff City with two matches remaining were able to take the last play-off berth which proved the Welsh club's undoing because it was North End which put an end to Cardiff having scored just one more goal! City had picked up just one point from a possible twelve.

Swansea City's problems were definitely in the draw column with no fewer than 20 matches ending thus. Eight of these one-pointers came in a club record row, too. Disappointment, too, for Ipswich Town with just three wins in a row once – at the tail end when the play-offs were out of reach.

One win in the last twelve said much for Bristol City's season of hope and despite being well positioned in January, nine games followed without a win and a mere five points. With nine games without a win and just four goals until the middle of March, this virtually ended any prospects for Queens Park Rangers heading towards the play-offs. Sheffield Wednesday never managed more than two wins in succession and Watford had at best a mid-table look about them. But to have managed fourteenth place was something approaching a miracle for Doncaster Rovers, rock bottom coming up to Christmas having never scored more than one goal in a game and only eleven in total.

Crystal Palace held a strong hand at Christmas in sixth place, but were unable to scrape two wins together and the goals dried up at the same time. Blackpool used more players than any other Championship team yet pulled away from the danger zone from late February. Coventry City had contrived to obtain enough points before failing to win one of the last eight.

Derby County looked in a precarious condition in January but four successive wins put points in the bag so that future problems were not too taxing. Neighbouring Nottingham Forest had similar concerns staying undefeated in the last six games. Barnsley began indifferently and had to arrest another slump in January.

Plymouth Argyle escaped in spite of a sixteen game spell with just one win which ended in February. However Norwich City, Southampton and Charlton Athletic were relegated. Norwich found putting a run of wins beyond them, Southampton with financial worries, too, had a short-lived revival in February which petered out and Charlton went eighteen matches without a win until late January to stay as the cellar dwellers.

Leicester City's solid performance in the middle third of the season was impressive. To be precise, it amounted to half of the season's results in an unbeaten run. Just two defeats on either side of this so the League One title never seemed in doubt. Peterborough United had to build up their momentum and succeeded in depriving Milton Keynes Dons of second place after seven wins in a row. The Dons had looked capable of an automatic place until a spate of drawn matches cost them dearly.

Further disappointment came from the play-offs. Scunthorpe United's experience was totally different. They began well enough then faltered in mid-season before sixth place and a triumph in the play-offs, the final of which saw them end Millwall's aspirations. The Lions had had a confident start and remained there or thereabouts throughout.

Once again Leeds United slipped up this time in the play-offs having lost just one of their last fifteen matches. Tranmere Rovers scraped just one point from the last three outings of hopes of sixth place.

Finishing eighth was creditable enough for Southend United, though they had ideas of the play-offs. Six goals in ten games mid-season pointed to a problem for them. One place lower came Huddersfield Town, their best rating all season. Yet Oldham Athletic's run-in was disastrous. Twelve games with just one win – the last of the campaign – ruined it.

Two wins in a row was all Bristol Rovers could handle at any stage of the season, twelfth spot for Colchester United came after nine unbeaten games at the turn of the year and failure to build upon it. Walsall were stuck in the middle of the table almost the entire second half of the season.

Leyton Orient grasped the task from March when clouds had been gathering in previous months while early in March Swindon Town had dropped to third from the bottom before three wins in succession relieved the pressure.

Brighton & Hove Albion hauled themselves from the drop zone with four wins out of the last five, while Yeovil Town had a brighter second half of the season after just one win in the first ten. Any lingering hopes Stockport County entertained for the play-offs were eclipsed by their ten-point deduction and in the last nine games in which just five goals were scored – four in their only win.

Carlisle United just edged out of the relegation quartet, though half a dozen of other sufferers were close at hand. But it was not surprising as eleven of the last twelve yielded just one win. Hartlepool United finished on the same points above them, a surge in October something at least to remember.

Northampton Town and Crewe Alexandra missed out on the salvage operation and were relegated. Northampton run into trouble from March and Crewe were unable to win any of their last ten games. While Cheltenham Town did overhaul Hereford United – never out of the bottom four – they both completed the relegated foursome.

Brentford showed more staying power in a steady climb throughout the season only slipping out the play-off zone briefly in November. Once heading affairs in mid-February the title looked theirs. Finishing second was an outstanding achievement for Exeter City, newly back from the non-league. Unbeaten in the last eight games they were able to keep Bury out of the play-offs.

Though Wycombe Wanderers took the third automatic spot, they stuttered their way from February inconsistently dropping points when first place had seemed certain. Drawn matches proved costly for Bury. They had seven of them in an unbeaten twelve run-in to the end of the programme.

Not so Gillingham, who survived a setback after a fine February–March and finally defeated Shrewsbury Town in the play-offs. Rochdale lost automatic promotion with only one win in the last eight. Drawn games had cost Shrewsbury dearly. Twelve of them came in away fixtures alone.

Dagenham & Redbridge almost sneaked into the play-offs but were hit by a six-game sequence scoring only in one game. Pacesetters in September, Bradford City collapsed in March until it was too late to make amends. Chesterfield did not score once in the last five games after gradual improvement had been made all season.

Morecambe had a more confident look in the second half of the season, but Darlington were hit by the ten-point deduction which prevented them from at least a chance in the play-offs. Lincoln City had their most productive periods in October and at the turn of the year.

But for the handicap of a 17-point deduction, Rotherham United would probably have made the play-offs, a courageous performance, yet returnees Aldershot Town, still in touch with a possible play-off place at Christmas, fell away badly. Accrington Stanley arrested a slump in February which could have been serious and Barnet fortunately saved their best for April.

Port Vale, seventh at the end of August, slowly lost any impetus and only once dug out two wins in succession. Notts County eleventh in October had to be thankful for others with fewer points as they won just once in a late spell of twelve games.

Macclesfield Town did not score a goal for their first four matches though finding the net was not always a concern. Three times they managed four goals. Bournemouth also shrugged off the 17-points penalty to survive, but Grimsby Town with no such handicap found it harder so to do having gone until the middle of November for their first win.

Chester City clung on until the death but eighteen games without a win to April had proved crucial and they were relegated along with 30-point deducted Luton Town, whose consolation was winning the Johnstone's Paint Trophy. Up from the Blue Square Premier emerge Burton Albion and old Football League friends from a couple of seasons ago Torquay United.

Stephen Quinn of Sheffield United tries to halt Burnley's Wade Elliott during the Championship Play-Off Final at Wembley. Burnley rounded off a magnificent season with a 1-0 victory and passage to the Premier League thanks to Elliott's 13th-minute strike. (Action Images/Alex Morton)

THE FA CHARITY SHIELD WINNERS 1908–2008

1908	Manchester U v QPR	4-0 after 1-1 draw
1909	Newcastle U v Northampton T	2-0
1910	Brighton v Aston Villa	1-0
1911	Manchester U v Swindon T	8-4
1912	Blackburn R v QPR	2-1
1913	Professionals v Amateurs	7-2
1920	WBA v Tottenham H	2-0
1921	Tottenham H v Burnley	2-0
1922	Huddersfield T v Liverpool	1-0
1923	Professionals v Amateurs	2-0
1924	Professionals v Amateurs	3-1
1925	Amateurs v Professionals	6-1
1926	Amateurs v Professionals	6-3
1927	Cardiff C v Corinthians	2-1
1928	Everton v Blackburn R	2-1
1929	Professionals v Amateurs	3-0
1930	Arsenal v Sheffield W	2-1
1931	Arsenal v WBA	1-0
1932	Everton v Newcastle U	5-3
1933	Arsenal v Everton	3-0
1934	Arsenal v Manchester C	4-0
1935	Sheffield W v Arsenal	1-0
1936	Sunderland v Arsenal	2-1
1937	Manchester C v Sunderland	2-0
1938	Arsenal v Preston NE	2-1
1948	Arsenal v Manchester U	4-3
1949	Portsmouth v Wolverhampton W	1-1*
1950	World Cup Team v Canadian Touring Team	4-2
1951	Tottenham H v Newcastle U	2-1
1952	Manchester U v Newcastle U	4-2
1953	Arsenal v Blackpool	3-1
1954	Wolverhampton W v WBA	4-4*
1955	Chelsea v Newcastle U	3-0
1956	Manchester U v Manchester C	1-0
1957	Manchester U v Aston Villa	4-0
1958	Bolton W v Wolverhampton W	4-1
1959	Wolverhampton W v Nottingham F	3-1
1960	Burnley v Wolverhampton W	2-2*
1961	Tottenham H v FA XI	3-2
1962	Tottenham H v Ipswich T	5-1
1963	Everton v Manchester U	4-0
1964	Liverpool v West Ham U	2-2*
1965	Manchester U v Liverpool	2-2*
1966	Liverpool v Everton	1-0
1967	Manchester U v Tottenham H	3-3*
1968	Manchester C v WBA	6-1
1969	Leeds U v Manchester C	2-1
1970	Everton v Chelsea	2-1
1971	Leicester C v Liverpool	1-0
1972	Manchester C v Aston Villa	1-0
1973	Burnley v Manchester C	1-0
1974	Liverpool† v Leeds U	1-1
1975	Derby Co v West Ham U	2-0
1976	Liverpool v Southampton	1-0
1977	Liverpool v Manchester U	0-0*
1978	Nottingham F v Ipswich T	5-0
1979	Liverpool v Arsenal	3-1
1980	Liverpool v West Ham U	1-0
1981	Aston Villa v Tottenham H	2-2*
1982	Liverpool v Tottenham H	1-0
1983	Manchester U v Liverpool	2-0
1984	Everton v Liverpool	1-0
1985	Everton v Manchester U	2-0
1986	Everton v Liverpool	1-1*
1987	Everton v Coventry C	1-0
1988	Liverpool v Wimbledon	2-1
1989	Liverpool v Arsenal	1-0
1990	Liverpool v Manchester U	1-1*
1991	Arsenal v Tottenham H	0-0*
1992	Leeds U v Liverpool	4-3
1993	Manchester U† v Arsenal	1-1
1994	Manchester U v Blackburn R	2-0
1995	Everton v Blackburn R	1-0
1996	Manchester U v Newcastle U	4-0
1997	Manchester U† v Chelsea	1-1
1998	Arsenal v Manchester U	3-0
1999	Arsenal v Manchester U	2-1
2000	Chelsea v Manchester U	2-0
2001	Liverpool v Manchester U	2-1
2002	Arsenal v Liverpool	1-0
2003	Manchester U† v Arsenal	1-1
2004	Arsenal v Manchester U	3-1
2005	Chelsea v Arsenal	2-1
2006	Liverpool v Chelsea	2-1
2007	Manchester U† v Chelsea	1-1
2008	Manchester U† v Portsmouth	0-0

Each club retained shield for six months.   † Won on penalties.

THE FA COMMUNITY SHIELD 2008

Manchester United (0) 0, Portsmouth (0) 0

aet; Manchester U won 3-1 on penalties.

At Wembley Stadium, 10 August 2008, attendance 84,808

Manchester United: Van der Sar; Neville (Brown), Evra, O'Shea (Carrick), Ferdinand, Vidic, Fletcher, Scholes, Giggs, Tevez, Nani (Campbell).

Portsmouth: James; Johnson, Hreidarsson (Lauren), Diarra, Campbell, Distin, Pedro Mendes (Mvemba), Diop, Crouch, Defoe, Kranjcar (Utaka).

Referee: P. Walton (Northants).

ACCRINGTON STANLEY FL Championship 2

FOUNDATION

Accrington Football Club, founder members of the Football League in 1888, were not connected with Accrington Stanley. In fact both clubs ran concurrently between 1891 when Stanley were formed and 1895 when Accrington FC folded. Actually Stanley Villa was the original name, those responsible for forming the club living in Stanley Street and using the Stanley Arms as their meeting place. They became Accrington Stanley in 1893. In 1894–95 they joined the Accrington & District League, playing at Moorhead Park. Subsequently they played in the North-East Lancashire Combination and the Lancashire Combination before becoming founder members of the Third Division (North) in 1921, two years after moving to Peel Park. In 1962 they resigned from the Football League, were wound up, reformed 1963, disbanded in 1966 only to restart as Accrington Stanley (1968), returning to the Lancashire Combination in 1970.

The Fraser Eagle Stadium, Livingstone Road, Accrington, Lancashire BB5 5BX.

Telephone: (0871) 434 1968.

Ticket Office: (01254) 356 950/(01254) 336 954.

Fax: (01254) 356 951.

Website: www.accringtonstanley.co.uk

Email: info@accringtonstanley.co.uk

Ground Capacity: 5,057.

Record Attendance: 4,368 v Colchester U, FA Cup 1st rd, 3 January 2004.

Pitch Measurements: 111yds × 72yds.

Chairman: David O'Neill.

Vice-chairman: Peter Marsden.

Chief Executive: Robert Heys.

Secretary: Hannah Bailey.

Manager: John Coleman.

Assistant Manager: Jimmy Bell.

Physio: Joe Hinnigan.

Club Nickname: 'Reds'.

Colours: All red.

Change Colours: All yellow.

Year Formed: 1891, reformed 1968.

Turned Professional: 1919.

Grounds: 1891, Moorhead Park; 1897, Bell's Ground; 1919, Peel Park; 1970, Crown Inn.

First Football League Game: 27 August 1921, Division 3 (N), v Rochdale (a) L 3-6 – Tattersall; Newton, Baines, Crawshaw, Popplewell, Burkinshaw, Oxley, Makin, Green (1), Hosker (2), Hartles.

HONOURS

Football League: Division 3 (N) – Runners-up 1954–55, 1957–58.

Conference: Champions 2005–06.

FA Cup: 4th rd 1927, 1937, 1959.

Football League Cup: never past 2nd rd.

Northern Premier League: Champions 2002–03.

Northern League: Division 1 – Champions 1999–2000.

North West Counties: Runners-up 1986–87.

Cheshire County League: Division 2 – Champions 1980–81; Runners-up 1979–80.

Lancashire Combination: Champions 1973–74, 1977–78; Runners-up 1971–72, 1975–76.

Lancashire Combination Cup: Winners 1971–72, 1972–73, 1973–74, 1976–77.

SKY SPORTS FACT FILE

During 1956–57 such was the proliferation of Scottish born players at Accrington Stanley that on numerous occasions the only Englishman able to find a place in the team was Bradford born, ex-Hull City forward Paddy Sowden.

Record League Victory: 8–0 v New Brighton, Division 3 (N), 17 March 1934 – Maidment; Armstrong (pen), Price, Dodds, Crawshaw, McCulloch, Wyper, Lennox (2), Cheetham (4), Leedham (1), Watson.

Record Cup Victory: 7–0 v Spennymoor U, FA Cup 2nd rd, 8 December 1938 – Tootill; Armstrong, Whittaker, Latham, Curran, Lee, Parry (2), Chadwick, Jepson (3), McLoughlin (2), Barclay.

Record Defeat: 9–1 v Lincoln C, Division 3 (N), 3 March 1951.

Most League Points (2 for a win): 61, Division 3 (N), 1954–55.

Most League Points (3 for a win): 51, FL 2, 2007–08.

Most League Goals: 96, Division 3 (N), 1954–55.

Highest League Scorer in Season: George Stewart, 35, Division 3 (N), 1955–56; George Hudson, 35, Division 4, 1960–61.

Most League Goals in Total Aggregate: George Stewart, 136, 1954–58.

Most League Goals in One Match: 5, Billy Harker v Gateshead, Division 3 (N), 16 November 1935; George Stewart v Gateshead, Division 3 (N), 27 November 1954.

Most Capped Player: Romuald Boco, (17), Benin.

Most League Appearances: Jim Armstrong, 260, 1927–34.

Youngest League Player: Ian Gibson, 15 years 358 days, v Norwich C, 23 March 1959.

Record Transfer Fee Received: £180,000 from Ipswich T for Gary Roberts, January 2007.

Record Transfer Fee Paid: £85,000 to Swansea C for Ian Craney, January 2008

Football League Record: 1921 Original Member of Division 3 (N); 1958–60 Division 3; 1960–62 Division 4; 2006– FL 2.

MANAGERS

William Cronshaw c.1894
John Haworth 1897–1910
Johnson Haworth c.1916
Sam Pilkingson 1919–24
  (Tommy Booth p-m 1923–24)
Ernie Blackburn 1924–32
Amos Wade 1932–35
John Hacking 1935–49
Jimmy Porter 1949–51
Walter Crook 1951–53
Walter Galbraith 1953–58
George Eastham snr 1958–59
Harold Bodle 1959–60
James Harrower 1960–61
Harold Mather 1962–63
Jimmy Hinksman 1963–64
Terry Neville 1964–65
Ian Bryson 1965
Danny Parker 1965–66
John Coleman May 1999–

LATEST SEQUENCES

Longest Sequence of League Wins: 7, 27.12.1954 – 5.2.1955.

Longest Sequence of League Defeats: 9, 8.3.1030 – 21.4.1930.

Longest Sequence of League Draws: 4, 10.9.1927 – 27.9.1927.

Longest Sequence of Unbeaten League Matches: 11, 27.11.1954 – 5.2.1955.

Longest Sequence Without a League Win: 18, 17.9.1938 – 31.12.1938.

Successive Scoring Runs: 22 from 14.11.1936.

Successive Non-scoring Runs: 5 from 15.3.1930.

TEN YEAR LEAGUE RECORD

		P	W	D	L	F	A	Pts	Pos
1999-2000	U D I	42	25	9	8	96	43	84	1
2000-01	U Pr	44	18	10	16	72	67	64	9
2001-02	U Pr	44	21	9	14	89	64	72	6
2002-03	U Pr	44	30	10	4	97	44	100	1
2003-04	Conf	42	15	13	14	68	61	58	10
2004-05	Conf	42	18	11	13	72	58	65	10
2005-06	Conf	42	28	7	7	76	45	91	1
2006-07	FL 2	46	13	11	22	70	81	50	20
2007-08	FL 2	46	16	3	27	49	83	51	17
2008-09	FL 2	46	13	11	22	42	59	50	16

DID YOU KNOW ?

Amateur goalkeeper Joe Lancaster made just one appearance for Accrington Stanley in 1950–51, but in the previous season had appeared three times in the Manchester United first team, keeping two clean sheets and finishing on the winning side in each game.

ACCRINGTON STANLEY 2008–09 LEAGUE RECORD

Match No.	Date	Venue	Opponents	Result	H/T Score	Lg. Pos.	Goalscorers	Attendance
1	Aug 9	H	Aldershot T	L	0-1	0-1	—		1805
2	16	A	Port Vale	W	2-0	1-0	9	Craney [3], Mullin P [89]	6643
3	23	H	Macclesfield T	W	2-0	0-0	7	Mullin P [50], Ryan [60]	1323
4	30	A	Gillingham	L	0-1	0-0	10		4733
5	Sept 6	A	Exeter C	L	1-2	1-1	12	Clarke [11]	3930
6	13	H	Notts Co	D	1-1	0-0	11	Ryan [90]	1404
7	20	A	Darlington	L	0-3	0-1	15		2814
8	28	H	Rochdale	L	1-3	1-1	17	Miles [2]	2417
9	Oct 4	A	Barnet	L	1-2	1-1	18	Murdock [45]	1899
10	11	H	Bradford C	L	2-3	1-0	19	Ryan [23], Gornell [50]	3012
11	18	A	Luton T	W	2-1	1-1	17	Mullin P [16], Gornell [54]	5492
12	21	H	Shrewsbury T	W	2-1	2-0	—	Gornell [2], Mullin P [6]	1249
13	25	H	Wycombe W	L	0-1	0-0	16		1217
14	28	A	Morecambe	D	1-1	1-0	—	McStay (og) [5]	2044
15	Nov 1	A	Dagenham & R	D	0-0	0-0	16		1433
16	15	H	Bournemouth	W	3-0	3-0	16	Mullin P [3], Gornell [13], Griffiths [20]	1152
17	22	A	Chesterfield	D	1-1	0-1	14	Ryan [86]	3215
18	29	H	Bury	L	1-2	0-2	—	Clarke (pen) [79]	2093
19	Dec 12	A	Lincoln C	L	1-5	1-0	—	Miles [11]	2625
20	20	H	Rotherham U	L	1-3	1-2	19	Proctor [33]	1172
21	26	A	Chester C	L	0-2	0-1	19		2223
22	28	H	Grimsby T	W	3-1	1-1	19	Clarke 3 [11, 59, 84]	1200
23	Jan 3	A	Rochdale	L	1-3	1-1	—	Cavanagh [24]	3126
24	17	A	Bradford C	D	1-1	1-0	20	Ryan [5]	12,172
25	24	H	Barnet	D	1-1	0-1	19	Mullin P [56]	1056
26	27	H	Morecambe	W	1-0	0-0	—	Ryan [57]	1407
27	31	A	Wycombe W	L	1-2	1-1	18	Mullin P [16]	6166
28	Feb 3	A	Shrewsbury T	L	0-2	0-2	—		4134
29	10	H	Brentford	D	1-1	0-0	—	Ryan [48]	1111
30	14	A	Bournemouth	L	0-1	0-0	19		4109
31	21	H	Dagenham & R	D	0-0	0-0	19		1123
32	24	H	Luton T	D	0-0	0-0	—		1033
33	28	A	Aldershot T	L	1-3	0-3	19	Lindfield [62]	2604
34	Mar 7	H	Gillingham	L	0-2	0-1	20		1308
35	10	A	Macclesfield T	W	2-0	1-0	—	Williams [42], Proctor [89]	1746
36	14	A	Notts Co	D	1-1	1-0	19	Ryan [17]	3701
37	17	H	Port Vale	W	2-0	2-0	—	Proctor [4], Ryan [27]	1144
38	21	H	Exeter C	W	2-1	1-1	18	Miles [34], Lindfield [64]	1169
39	24	H	Darlington	W	1-0	1-0	—	Ryan [22]	1086
40	28	A	Rotherham U	D	0-0	0-0	16		2804
41	Apr 4	H	Lincoln C	L	0-2	0-1	17		1139
42	11	A	Grimsby T	W	1-0	0-0	16	Symes [71]	6453
43	13	H	Chester C	L	0-1	0-1	16		1100
44	18	A	Brentford	L	0-3	0-2	17		7135
45	25	H	Chesterfield	W	1-0	0-0	16	Grant [50]	1795
46	May 2	A	Bury	L	0-1	0-0	16		7515

Final League Position: 16

GOALSCORERS

League (42): Ryan 10, Mullin P 7, Clarke 5 (1 pen), Gornell 4, Miles 3, Proctor 3, Lindfield 2, Cavanagh 1, Craney 1, Grant 1, Griffiths 1, Murdock 1, Symes 1, Williams 1, own goal 1.
Carling Cup (2): Craney 1, Mullin P 1.
FA Cup (0).
J Paint Trophy (0).

Arthur K 42	Cavanagh P 28 + 1	Edwards P 46	Proctor A 32 + 5	Murdock C 20 + 3	King C 27	Richardson L 9 + 2	Craney J 2	Clarke J 12 + 3	Mullin P 36	Grant R 6 + 9	Ryan J 41 + 3	Williams R 18 + 5	Onibuje F — + 5	Miles J 42 + 1	Murphy P 1 + 2	Worrall D 1 + 3	Mullin J 25 + 6	Griffiths R 13	Gornell T 10 + 1	Turner C 14 + 8	Charnock K 33 + 1	Higginbotham K 5 + 7	Mahon C — + 2	Blundell G 2	Bell J 5 + 1	Dunbavin I 4	Smith A — + 1	Lindfield C 17 + 3	Kissock J 5	McConville S 2 + 3	Symes M 7	Kay A 1 + 2	Match No.
1	2	3	4[1]	5	6	7[3]	8	9[2]	10	11	12	13	14																				1
1	2	3	4	5	6	7[1]	8	9	10					11	12																		2
1	2	3	4[2]	5	6			9[3]	10		7[1]	12	14	11			13				8												3
1	2	3	4[3]	5[1]	6			9	10		7[2]		14	11	12		13				8												4
1	2	3			6			9	10			5	12	11	4[1]	7	8																5
1	2	4		5	3			9[1]	10			8	13	11[2]			12			7	6												6
1	2	4		5[2]	3[1]			9[3]	10		7	12	13	11						8	6	14											7
1	2	3		5	6			9[1]	10		12			11[2]			8	4	7	13													8
1	2	3	12	5[2]	6			14	10		7	13[4]		11[3]			8	4[1]	9														9
1	2	3	12	5	6				10		7[1]			11			8	4	9														10
1		3		5	2				10		7			11			8	6	9	4													11
1		3[1]		12	6				10		7	5		11			8	4	9[2]	2	13												12
1		2	12		3				10		7	5		11[2]			8	4[1]	9	6	13												13
1		2	12		3				10		7	5		11			8	4[1]	9[2]	6	13												14
1		5			3				10		7	2		11[1]			8	4	9	6	12												15
1		5	4		3	2		12	10		13			8	7	9[1]		6	11[2]														16
1		5	4[1]		3	2			10		7			12			8	11	9	6													17
1		5		12	3[2]	2[1]		14	10		7			11			8	4	6	13	9[3]												18
1	2	3	5						10		12	7		11			8	6	9	4[1]													19
	3	4	5	2[1]				9[2]	10	12	7			11			8	6	13	1													20
12	5	4		3	2[1]			9	10	13	7			11			8[2]	6		1													21
2	5	4		3				9	10		7			11			8	6		1													22
2	5	4						10	9		7			11			8[1]	6		1	12												23
1	5	4	6	3				10	9		7			11			8		2														24
1	2	4	5	3				10	12		7			9			8[1]	6	11														25
1	2	4	5	3	12				10		8			9			7[1]	6	11														26
1	2	4	5	3					10		8			9			12	6	7[2]			13	11[1]										27
1		5	4[1]		3	2			10		8			9			12	6	7[2]			13	11										28
1	2	5		12				3	10		4			11			8	6				9	7[1]										29
1	2	5	4		3[1]				10		7			9[2]			8[3]	6			12	13	11	14									30
1	2	5	4						10		8			8[3]			12	6	13	3		9[2]	11[1]	14									31
1	2	5	4						10		8			11			12	6		3		9	7[1]										32
1	2	5	12						10	13	7			11[2]			8[1]		4[3]	6	14	3		9									33
1	2	3	4						10	12	7	5		11[1]			8[2]		13	6	14	9[3]											34
1	2	5	4						10		7	3		11			8	6				9											35
1	2	5	4						10		7	3		11			12		8[1]	6		9											36
1	2	5	4[1]						10	13	7	3		11			12		8	6		9[2]											37
1		2	4	5							7	3		11			8	6				9								10			38
1		2	4	5							7	3		11			8	6				9								10			39
1		2	4	5							7	3		11			8	6				9		12	10								40
1	2	5	4					8[1]			7	3		11				6				9			10								41
1	2	6	4	5							7	3		11			8					9			10								42
1	2	6	4	5[1]						13	7	3		11[3]			14		8[2]	12		9			10								43
1	2	5	4[1]							12	7	3		11			13		8[2]			9[3]			10	14							44
1	2	5	4					12			11	7[3]	3[1]	10			13		14	6		9					8[2]						45
1	2	5	4[4]							11[1]	7[3]	3		10			13		12	6		9				8[2]				14			46

FA Cup
First Round   Tranmere R   (h) 0-0
                             (a) 0-1

J Paint Trophy
First Round   Tranmere R   (a) 0-1

Carling Cup
First Round   Wolverhampton W   (a) 2-3

ALDERSHOT TOWN   FL Championship 2

FOUNDATION

It was through the initiative of Councillor Jack White, a local newsagent, who immediately captured the interest of the Town Clerk D. Llewellyn Griffiths, that Aldershot Town was formed in 1926. Having established a limited liability company under the chairmanship of Norman Clinton, an Aldershot resident and chairman of the Hampshre County FA, they rented the Recreation Ground from the Aldershot Borough Council. Admitted to the Southern League for 1927–28, they were elected to the Football League in 1932 but were removed from the competition in March 1992 and their record expunged. Re-formed almost immediately as Aldershot Town Football Club.

The EBB Stadium at the Recreation Ground, High Street, Aldershot GU11 1TW.

Telephone: 01252 320211.

Fax: 01252 324347.

Ticket Office: 01252 320211.

Website: www.theshots.co.uk

Ground capacity: 7,100.

Record Attendance: 19,138 v Carlisle U, FA Cup 4th rd (replay), 28 January 1970.

Pitch Measurements: 117yd × 75yd.

Chairman: John McGinty.

Secretary: Graham Hortop.

Manager: Gary Waddock.

Assistant Manager: Martin Kuhl.

Colours: All red with blue and white trim.

Change Colours: All yellow with black trim.

Year Formed: 1926.

Turned Professional: 1927.

Ltd Co.: 1927.

HONOURS

Football League: Best season: 8th, Division 3, 1973–74.

FA Cup: Best season: 5th rd, 1932–33, 5th rd replay, 1978–79.

Football League Cup: Best season: 3rd rd replay, 1984–85.

Blue Square Premier League: Champions 2007–08.

Conference: Runners-up 2003–04.

Isthmian League Division 3: Champions 1992–93.

Isthmian First Division Champions: 1997–98.

Isthmian League Premier Division: Champions 2002–03.

Hampshire Senior Cup: Winners 1928, 1999, 2000, 2002, 2003, 2007.

Setanta Shield: Winners 2008.

Previous Names: 1926, Aldershot Town; c.1937 Aldershot; 1992, Aldershot Town.

Club nickname: 'The Shots'.

Ground: 1927, Recreation Ground.

First Football League Game: 27 August 1932, Division 3 (S), v Southend U (h) L 1–2 – Robb; Wade, McDougall, Lawson, Spence, Middleton, Proud, White, Gamble, Douglas, Fishlock (1).

Record League Victory: 8–1 v Gateshead, Division 4, 13 September 1958 – Marshall; Henry, Jackson, Mundy, Price, Gough, Walters, Stepney (3), Lacey (3), Matthews (2), Tyrer.

SKY SPORTS FACT FILE

On 4 October 2008 Aldershot Town were trailing 3–0 at the Recreation Ground to visiting Bury in the 69th minute. They rallied to reply with three goals, the last two in two minutes with the equaliser coming in the 79th minute, a result which cost Bury top spot.

Record Cup Victory: 7–0 v Chelmsford, FA Cup, 1st rd, 28 November 1931 – Robb; Twine, McDougall (1), Norman Wilson, Gardiner, Middleton (1), Blackbourne, Stevenson (1), Thom (3), Hopkins (1), Edgar.

7–0 v Newport (IW), FA Cup, 2nd rd, 8 December 1945 – Reynolds; Horton, Sheppard, Ray, White, Summerbee, Sinclair, Hold (1), Brooks (5), Fitzgerald, Hobbs (1).

N.B. 11–1 v Kingstonian, FA Cup, 4th qual rd, 16 November 1929 – Mobbs; Thomas, McDougall, Norman Wilson, Gardiner, Middleton (2), Young (1), Common (1), Horton (2), Hopkins (3), Edgar (2).

Record Defeat: – 1–10 v Southend U, Leyland Daf Cup, Pr rd, 6 November 1990.

Most League Points: (2 for a win): 57, Division 4, 1978–79.

Most League Points (3 for a win): 75, Division 4, 1983–84.

Most League Goals: 83, Division 4, 1963–64.

Highest League Scorer in Season: John Dungworth, 26, Division 4, 1978–79.

Most League Goals in Total Aggregate: Jack Howarth, 171, 1965–71 and 1972–77.

Most Capped Player: Louie Soares, 3, Barbados.

Most League Appearances: Murray Brodie, 461, 1970–83.

Youngest League Player: Clive Jackman, 16 years 135 days v Leyton Orient, 16 April 1953.

Record Transfer Fee Received: £150,000 from Wolverhampton W for Tony Lange, July 1989.

Record Transfer Fee Paid: £54,000 to Portsmouth for Colin Garwood, February 1980.

Football League Record: 1932 Elected to Division 3 (S); 1958–73 Division 4; 1973–76 Division 3; 1976–87 Division 4; 1987–89 Division 3; 1989–92 Division 4; 1992–93 Isthmian League Division 3; 1993–94 Isthmian League Division 2; 1994–98 Isthmian League Division 1; 1998–2003 Isthmian League Premier Division; 2003–08 Conference; 2008– FL 2.

MANAGERS
Angus Seed 1927–37
Bill McCracken 1937–49
Gordon Clark 1950–55
Harry Evans 1955–59
Dave Smith 1959–71
(GM from 1967)
Tommy McAnearney 1967–68
Jimmy Melia 1968–72
Tommy McAnearney 1972–81
Len Walker 1981–84
Ron Harris (GM) 1984–85
Len Walker 1985–91
Brian Talbot 1991–92
Ian McDonald 1992
Steve Wignall 1992–95
Steve Wigley 1995–97
George Borg 1997–2002
Terry Brown 2002–07
Gary Waddock May 2007–

LATEST SEQUENCES

Longest Sequence of League Wins: 5, 16.9.1961 – 2.10.61.

Longest Sequence of League Defeats: 9, 20.11.1965 – 5.2.1966.

Longest Sequence of League Draws: 6, 6.10.1962 – 27.10.1962.

Longest Sequence of Unbeaten League Matches: 13, 26.3.1966 – 3.9.1966.

Longest Sequence Without a League Win: 17, 10.10.1936 – 30.1.1937.

Successive Scoring Runs: 29 from 1.4.1961.

Successive Non-scoring Runs: 6 from 22.3.1988.

TEN YEAR LEAGUE RECORD

		P	W	D	L	F	A	Pts	Pos
1999-2000	Isth PR	42	24	5	13	71	51	77	2
2000-01	Isth PR	41	21	11	9	73	39	74	4
2001-02	Isth PR	42	22	7	13	76	51	73	3
2002-03	Isth PR	46	33	6	7	81	36	105	1
2003-04	Conf	42	20	10	12	80	67	70	5
2004-05	Conf	42	21	10	11	68	52	73	4
2005-06	Conf	42	16	6	20	61	74	54	13
2006-07	Conf	46	18	11	17	64	62	65	9
2007-08	B Sq Pr	46	31	8	7	82	48	101	1
2008-09	FL 2	46	14	12	20	59	80	54	15

DID YOU KNOW ?

Aldershot Town ended Wycombe Wanderers' 18-match unbeaten sequence on 6 December 2008 with a 3–2 win at the Recreation Ground. The visitors had previously conceded just eight goals and only two of these in away matches in League 2.

ALDERSHOT TOWN 2008–09 LEAGUE RECORD

Match No.	Date	Venue	Opponents	Result	H/T Score	Lg. Pos.	Goalscorers	Attendance
1	Aug 9	A	Accrington S	W 1-0	1-0	—	Donnelly [43]	1805
2	16	H	Bournemouth	D 1-1	0-0	7	Soares [63]	4564
3	23	A	Shrewsbury T	L 0-1	0-0	12		5422
4	30	H	Bradford C	W 3-2	0-1	8	Harding [48], Morgan [65], Davies [86]	3805
5	Sept 6	H	Darlington	W 2-1	2-1	8	Morgan [7], Soares [27]	3460
6	13	A	Luton T	L 1-3	0-1	7	Grant [51]	6462
7	20	H	Gillingham	W 2-1	0-0	6	Hudson [75], Davies [86]	4198
8	27	A	Notts Co	L 1-2	0-0	7	Charles [52]	6033
9	Oct 4	H	Bury	D 3-3	0-2	8	Elvins [69], Davies (pen) [77], Hylton [79]	3621
10	11	A	Macclesfield T	L 2-4	0-0	10	Hudson [51], Hylton [64]	1857
11	18	H	Brentford	D 1-1	1-0	10	Davies (pen) [14]	5023
12	22	A	Chesterfield	L 1-5	0-2	—	Hudson [50]	3079
13	25	A	Rochdale	L 1-3	0-1	15	Morgan [66]	2750
14	28	H	Port Vale	W 1-0	1-0	—	Soares [13]	3039
15	Nov 1	A	Morecambe	L 0-2	0-0	14		1897
16	15	H	Exeter C	W 1-0	0-0	13	Grant [53]	3784
17	22	A	Chester C	W 1-0	0-0	11	Morgan [63]	1653
18	25	H	Lincoln C	W 2-0	1-0	—	Sandell [36], Davies [60]	2625
19	Dec 6	H	Wycombe W	W 3-2	2-0	10	Hudson 2 [12, 29], Hylton [88]	3915
20	20	H	Grimsby T	D 2-2	0-2	11	Davies 2 (2 pens) [49, 75]	3605
21	26	A	Barnet	W 3-0	1-0	10	Hylton [6], Charles [70], Davies [90]	2729
22	28	H	Dagenham & R	L 1-2	1-1	11	Hudson [16]	3697
23	Jan 17	A	Macclesfield T	D 1-1	0-1	11	Hudson [90]	3018
24	20	H	Notts Co	D 2-2	1-0	—	Harding [6], Davies [76]	2491
25	24	A	Bury	L 1-2	0-2	11	Davies [83]	2558
26	27	A	Brentford	L 0-3	0-2	—		5111
27	31	H	Rochdale	L 2-4	0-4	13	Morgan [75], Davies (pen) [81]	3018
28	Feb 14	A	Exeter C	L 2-3	0-1	14	Robinson [55], Harding [60]	4840
29	17	A	Gillingham	D 4-4	1-1	—	Lindegaard [20], Morgan [57], Bentley (og) [61], Sandell [66]	5974
30	21	H	Morecambe	L 0-2	0-1	14		2872
31	28	H	Accrington S	W 3-1	3-0	14	Hudson [23], Robinson 2 [41, 45]	2604
32	Mar 3	A	Bournemouth	L 0-2	0-1	—		4556
33	7	A	Bradford C	L 0-5	0-2	14		12,465
34	10	A	Shrewsbury T	D 0-0	0-0	—		2090
35	14	H	Luton T	W 2-1	1-1	14	Davies [15], Hudson [49]	3098
36	17	A	Rotherham U	W 2-1	2-0	—	Grant 2 [15, 39]	2769
37	21	H	Darlington	L 0-2	0-1	14		2532
38	28	A	Grimsby T	L 0-1	0-0	14		7095
39	31	H	Chesterfield	D 1-1	0-1	—	Robinson [52]	2482
40	Apr 4	H	Rotherham U	L 0-1	0-1	15		2643
41	7	A	Port Vale	D 0-0	0-0	—		4140
42	11	A	Dagenham & R	L 1-3	1-1	15	Hylton [7]	1586
43	13	H	Barnet	D 1-1	0-1	15	Chalmers [51]	2597
44	18	A	Wycombe W	L 0-3	0-1	15		5440
45	25	H	Chester C	D 2-2	1-1	15	Hudson 2 [14, 56]	3100
46	May 2	A	Lincoln C	W 2-0	1-0	15	Grant [26], Davies [88]	3910

Final League Position: 15

GOALSCORERS

League (59): Davies 13 (5 pens), Hudson 11, Morgan 6, Grant 5, Hylton 5, Robinson 4, Harding 3, Soares 3, Charles 2, Sandell 2, Chalmers 1, Donnelly 1, Elvins 1, Lindegaard 1, own goal 1.
Carling Cup (1): Morgan 1.
FA Cup (4): Hudson 2, Grant 1 (pen), Morgan 1.
Trophy (2): Davies 1 (pen), Elvins 1.

Bull N 30	Starosta B 3	Howell D 14	Harding B 29	Blackburn C 36	Charles A 41	Soares L 30 + 5	Donnelly S 12 + 8	Grant J 28 + 7	Morgan M 22 + 10	Hudson K 35 + 8	Chalmers L 19 + 4	Newman R 10 + 7	Straker A 29 + 3	Hylton D 16 + 13	Day R 16 + 1	Davies S 37 + 4	Osborne J 8	Elvins R 7 + 8	Jaimez-Ruiz M 13 + 1	Mendes J 1 + 5	Sandell A 24 + 5	McCarthy A 3 + 1	Lindegaard A 6	Winfield D 9 + 1	Robinson J 19	Cochrane J 9 + 1	Match No.
1	2	3	4	5	6	7	8²	9	10	11¹	12	13															1
1	2	3¹	4	5	6	7	8²	9³	10	11	13		12	14													2
1	2¹		4	5	6	7	8	9	10	11		3	12														3
1			4²	5	3	2	7¹	9	10³	11	8	13	14	6	12												4
1			4	5¹	6	7	11²	9	10³	8	12	3	14	13	2												5
1			4	6	7	11²	9	10³	13	8	5⁴	3	14	12	2¹												6
1	3¹	4	5	6	7	9	10	11	12	8	2																7
1	3	4	5	6	7	9³	10²	11¹	12	13	8	2	14														8
	3	4	5	6	2	10¹	7	8	9	11	12	1															9
1	3	4	5	6	2	12	13	11	8¹	10	7	9²															10
1	3	8	5	6	7	12	13	4²	9	11¹	2	10	14														11
1	3³	8	5	6	7	12	13	4²	9	11	2	10¹	14														12
1		4	5	3	2	7²	9	12	11	8¹	10	6	13														13
1		4	5	3	7	9	11	10	6	8	2																14
1		4	5	7²	12	9	13	11¹	3	10	6	8	2														15
1			4	6	2	9	10¹	11	3	8⁴	5	7	12														16
1		4	2	6	7	9	10	11	3	5¹	8	12															17
1		4	2	6	7	9	10¹	5	3	8	12	11															18
1		4	2	6	12	10¹	7	13	3	9	5	8	11²														19
1		4	2	6	12	7	3	10	5	8	9¹	11															20
1		4	2	6	12	13	10²	7¹	3	9³	5	8	14	11													21
1		4	5	6	2	10	7	3	9	8	12	11¹															22
1		4	2	6	12	10²	7	3	9¹	5³	8	14	13	11													23
		4	2	6	9²	7	3	12	5	8	13	1	10¹	11													24
		4	2	6	12	13	9	7	3	5¹	8	10	1	11²													25
		4³	2	6	12	8¹	9	11	14	3	13	5	7	10²	1												26
	3		2	6	7	13	9	12	11	4²	10¹	5³	8	1	14												27
		4	6	7	10	12	3¹	8	11	1	2	5	9														28
		4	5	3	7¹	10	12	13	8	11	1	2	6	9²													29
		4¹	5	3	7	10	12	8	11	1	2	6	9														30
1		5	6	10	7	4	13	3	12	11	2³	14	9¹	8²													31
1⁰		5	6	12	10¹	7	8	3	13	11	15	2	9²	4													32
1		4	6	12	10	8¹	3	5	7	11	2	9															33
		2	6	10	12	7	4	3	5	8	1	11¹	9														34
		2	6	9	12	7	4	3	8	1	11	5	10¹														35
		2	6	13	9	12	7²	4³	3	8	1	11	5	10¹	14												36
		2	6	9	12	7	4	3	8	1	11¹	5	10														37
		2	6	7	14	9¹	12	11²	3	13	8	1	5	10	4³												38
		5	6	2³	13	9	12	11	4	3	7	1	14	10¹	8²												39
	8¹		6	13	9³	12	2	5	3	14	7²	1	11	10	4												40
1		6	7²	11	2	5	3	9¹	8	12	13	10	4														41
1		6	7¹	13	14	2²	5	3	9³	8	12	11	10	4													42
1	2		6	12	8	11	4	3¹	7	9	5	10															43
1	3³		6¹	2	4	9	7	12	13	8	14	11	5²	10													44
1⁰		2	11¹	9	7	5	12	8	6	15	3	10	4														45
		2	11	9	7	6	5	8	1	3	10	4															46

FA Cup

First Round	Rotherham U	(h)	1-1
		(a)	3-0
Second Round	Millwall	(a)	0-3

Carling Cup

| First Round | Coventry C | (a) | 1-3 |

J Paint Trophy

| First Round | Swindon T | (h) | 2-2 |

ARSENAL FA Premiership

FOUNDATION

Formed by workers at the Royal Arsenal, Woolwich in 1886, they began as Dial Square (name of one of the workshops), and included two former Nottingham Forest players, Fred Beardsley and Morris Bates. Beardsley wrote to his old club seeking help and they provided the new club with a full set of red jerseys and a ball. The club became known as the 'Woolwich Reds' although their official title soon after formation was Woolwich Arsenal.

Emirates Stadium, Highbury House, Drayton Park, Islington, London N5 1BU.

Telephone: (0207) 619 5003.

Fax: (0207) 704 4001.

Ticket Office: (0207) 619 5000.

Website: www.arsenal.com

Email: info@arsenal.co.uk

Ground Capacity: 60,355.

Record Attendance: 73,295 v Sunderland, Div 1, 9 March 1935.

At Wembley: 73,707 v RC Lens, UEFA Champions League, 25 November 1998.

Pitch Measurements: 105m × 68m.

Chairman: Peter Hill-Wood.

Secretary: David Miles.

Manager: Arsène Wenger.

Assistant Manager: Pat Rice.

Physio: Colin Lewin.

Colours: Red shirts with white trim, white shorts, white stockings with red tops.

Change Colours: Yellow shirts with black sleeves, black shorts, yellow stockings with black trim.

Year Formed: 1886.

Turned Professional: 1891.

Ltd Co: 1893.

Previous Names: 1886, Dial Square; 1886, Royal Arsenal; 1891, Woolwich Arsenal; 1914 Arsenal.

Club Nickname: 'Gunners'.

Grounds: 1886, Plumstead Common; 1887, Sportsman Ground; 1888, Manor Ground; 1890, Invicta Ground; 1893, Manor Ground; 1913, Highbury; 2006, Emirates Stadium.

HONOURS

FA Premier League: Champions 1997–98, 2001–02, 2003–04. Runners-up 1998–99, 1999–2000, 2000–01, 2002–03, 2004–05.

Football League: Division 1 – Champions 1930–31, 1932–33, 1933–34, 1934–35, 1937–38, 1947–48, 1952–53, 1970–71, 1988–89, 1990–91; Runners-up 1925–26, 1931–32, 1972–73; Division 2 – Runners-up 1903–04.

FA Cup: Winners 1930, 1936, 1950, 1971, 1979, 1993, 1998, 2002, 2003, 2005; Runners-up 1927, 1932, 1952, 1972, 1978, 1980, 2001.

Double performed: 1970–71, 1997–98, 2001–02.

Football League Cup: Winners 1987, 1993; Runners-up 1968, 1969, 1988, 2007.

European Competitions: Fairs Cup: 1963–64, 1969–70 (winners), 1970–71. *European Cup:* 1971–72, 1991–92. *UEFA Champions League:* 1998–99, 1999–2000, 2000–01, 2001–02, 2002–03, 2003–04, 2004–05, 2005–06 (runners-up), 2006–07, 2007–08 (q-f), 2008–09 (s-f). *UEFA Cup:* 1978–79, 1981–82, 1982–83, 1996–97, 1997–98, 1999–2000 (runners-up). *European Cup-Winners' Cup:* 1979–80 (runners-up), 1993–94 (winners), 1994–95 (runners-up). *Super Cup:* 1994 (runners up).

SKY SPORTS FACT FILE

On 10 September 2008 against Croatia, Theo Walcott became the third Arsenal player to score a hat-trick for England. Ted Drake hit three against Hungary in 1936 – at Highbury – and Ian Wright even managed four against San Marino in 1993.

First Football League Game: 2 September 1893, Division 2, v Newcastle U (h) D 2–2 – Williams; Powell, Jeffrey; Devine, Buist, Howat; Gemmell, Henderson, Shaw (1), Elliott (1), Booth.

Record League Victory: 12–0 v Loughborough T, Division 2, 12 March 1900 – Orr; McNichol, Jackson; Moir, Dick (2), Anderson (1); Hunt, Cottrell (2), Main (2), Gaudie (3), Tennant (2).

Record Cup Victory: 11–1 v Darwen, FA Cup 3rd rd, 9 January 1932 – Moss; Parker, Hapgood; Jones, Roberts, John; Hulme (2), Jack (3), Lambert (2), James, Bastin (4).

Record Defeat: 0–8 v Loughborough T, Division 2, 12 December 1896.

Most League Points (2 for a win): 66, Division 1, 1930–31.

Most League Points (3 for a win): 90, FA Premier League, 2003–04.

Most League Goals: 127, Division 1, 1930–31.

Highest League Scorer in Season: Ted Drake, 42, 1934–35.

Most League Goals in Total Aggregate: Thierry Henry, 174 (111), 1999–2007.

Most League Goals in One Match: 7, Ted Drake v Aston Villa, Division 1, 14 December 1935.

Most Capped Player: Thierry Henry, 81 (111), France.

Most League Appearances: David O'Leary, 558, 1975–93.

Youngest League Player: Jack Wilshere, 16 years 256 days v Blackburn R, 13 September 2008.

Record Transfer Fee Received: A reported £22,900,000 from Real Madrid for Nicolas Anelka, August 1999.

Record Transfer Fee Paid: £12,800,000 to Marseille for Samir Nasri, July 2008.

Football League Record: 1893 Elected to Division 2; 1904–13 Division 1; 1913–19 Division 2; 1919–92 Division 1; 1992– FA Premier League.

MANAGERS

Sam Hollis 1894–97
Tom Mitchell 1897–98
George Elcoat 1898–99
Harry Bradshaw 1899–1904
Phil Kelso 1904–08
George Morrell 1908–15
Leslie Knighton 1919–25
Herbert Chapman 1925–34
George Allison 1934–47
Tom Whittaker 1947–56
Jack Crayston 1956–58
George Swindin 1958–62
Billy Wright 1962–66
Bertie Mee 1966–76
Terry Neill 1976–83
Don Howe 1984–86
George Graham 1986–95
Bruce Rioch 1995–96
Arsène Wenger September 1996–

LATEST SEQUENCES

Longest Sequence of League Wins: 14, 10.2.2002 – 18.8.2002.

Longest Sequence of League Defeats: 7, 12.2.1977 – 12.3.1977.

Longest Sequence of League Draws: 6, 4.3.1961 – 1.4.1961.

Longest Sequence of Unbeaten League Matches: 49, 7.5.2003 – 24.10.2004.

Longest Sequence Without a League Win: 23, 28.9.1912 – 1.3.1913.

Successive Scoring Runs: 55 from 19.5.2001.

Successive Non-scoring Runs: 6 from 25.2.1987.

TEN YEAR LEAGUE RECORD

		P	W	D	L	F	A	Pts	Pos
1999-2000	PR Lge	38	22	7	9	73	43	73	2
2000-01	PR Lge	38	20	10	8	63	38	70	2
2001-02	PR Lge	38	26	9	3	79	36	87	1
2002-03	PR Lge	38	23	9	6	85	42	78	2
2003-04	PR Lge	38	26	12	0	73	26	90	1
2004-05	PR Lge	38	25	8	5	87	36	83	2
2005-06	PR Lge	38	20	7	11	68	31	67	4
2006-07	PR Lge	38	19	11	8	63	35	68	4
2007-08	PR Lge	38	24	11	3	74	31	83	3
2008-09	PR Lge	38	20	12	6	68	37	72	4

DID YOU KNOW ?

On 21 April 2009 Andrei Arshavin scored all four goals against Liverpool at Anfield. He was the second Arsenal player to achieve this feat on that ground, as Julio Baptista had a quartet in a 6–3 League Cup victory on 9 January 2007.

ARSENAL 2008–09 LEAGUE RECORD

Match No.	Date	Venue	Opponents	Result		H/T Score	Lg. Pos.	Goalscorers	Attendance
1	Aug 16	H	WBA	W	1-0	1-0	—	Nasri [4]	60,071
2	23	A	Fulham	L	0-1	0-1	13		25,276
3	30	H	Newcastle U	W	3-0	2-0	4	Van Persie 2 (1 pen) [18 (p), 41], Denilson [59]	60,067
4	Sept 13	A	Blackburn R	W	4-0	2-0	3	Van Persie [8], Adebayor 3 (1 pen) [45, 81 (p), 90]	23,041
5	20	A	Bolton W	W	3-1	2-1	1	Eboue [26], Bendtner [27], Denilson [87]	22,694
6	27	H	Hull C	L	1-2	0-0	4	McShane (og) [51]	60,037
7	Oct 4	A	Sunderland	D	1-1	0-0	4	Fabregas [90]	40,199
8	18	H	Everton	W	3-1	0-1	4	Nasri [48], Van Persie [70], Walcott [90]	60,064
9	26	A	West Ham U	W	2-0	0-0	4	Faubert (og) [75], Adebayor [90]	34,802
10	29	H	Tottenham H	D	4-4	1-1	—	Silvestre [37], Gallas [46], Adebayor [64], Van Persie [68]	60,043
11	Nov 1	A	Stoke C	L	1-2	0-1	4	Clichy [90]	26,704
12	8	H	Manchester U	W	2-1	1-0	3	Nasri 2 [22, 48]	60,106
13	15	H	Aston Villa	L	0-2	0-0	4		60,047
14	22	A	Manchester C	L	0-3	0-1	5		44,878
15	30	A	Chelsea	W	2-1	0-1	4	Van Persie 2 [59, 62]	41,760
16	Dec 6	H	Wigan Ath	W	1-0	1-0	4	Adebayor [16]	59,317
17	13	A	Middlesbrough	D	1-1	1-1	5	Adebayor [17]	27,320
18	21	H	Liverpool	D	1-1	1-1	5	Van Persie [24]	60,094
19	26	A	Aston Villa	D	2-2	1-0	5	Denilson [40], Diaby [49]	42,585
20	28	H	Portsmouth	W	1-0	0-0	4	Gallas [81]	60,092
21	Jan 10	H	Bolton W	W	1-0	0-0	5	Bendtner [84]	60,068
22	17	A	Hull C	W	3-1	1-0	5	Adebayor [30], Nasri [82], Bendtner [86]	24,924
23	28	A	Everton	D	1-1	0-0	—	Van Persie [90]	37,097
24	31	H	West Ham U	D	0-0	0-0	5		60,109
25	Feb 8	A	Tottenham H	D	0-0	0-0	5		36,021
26	21	H	Sunderland	D	0-0	0-0	5		60,104
27	28	H	Fulham	D	0-0	0-0	5		60,102
28	Mar 3	A	WBA	W	3-1	3-1	—	Bendtner 2 [4, 44], Toure [38]	26,244
29	14	H	Blackburn R	W	4-0	1-0	4	Ooijer (og) [2], Arshavin [65], Eboue 2 (1 pen) [87, 90 (p)]	60,091
30	21	A	Newcastle U	W	3-1	0-0	4	Bendtner [57], Diaby [64], Nasri [67]	49,972
31	Apr 4	H	Manchester C	W	2-0	1-0	4	Adebayor 2 [8, 49]	60,097
32	11	A	Wigan Ath	W	4-1	0-1	4	Walcott [61], Silvestre [71], Arshavin [89], Song Billong [90]	22,954
33	21	A	Liverpool	D	4-4	1-0	—	Arshavin 4 [36, 67, 70, 89]	44,424
34	26	H	Middlesbrough	W	2-0	1-0	4	Fabregas 2 [26, 67]	60,089
35	May 2	A	Portsmouth	W	3-0	2-0	4	Bendtner 2 (1 pen) [13, 41 (p)], Vela [56]	20,418
36	10	H	Chelsea	L	1-4	0-2	4	Bendtner [70]	60,075
37	16	A	Manchester U	D	0-0	0-0	4		75,468
38	24	H	Stoke C	W	4-1	4-1	4	Beattie (og) [10], Van Persie 2 (1 pen) [16 (p), 41], Diaby [18]	60,082

Final League Position: 4

GOALSCORERS

League (68): Van Persie 11 (2 pens), Adebayor 10 (1 pen), Bendtner 9 (1 pen), Arshavin 6, Nasri 6, Denilson 3, Diaby 3, Eboue 3 (1 pen), Fabregas 3, Gallas 2, Silvestre 2, Walcott 2, Clichy 1, Song Billong 1, Toure 1, Vela 1, own goals 4.
Carling Cup (9): Vela 4, Bendtner 2, Simpson 2, Wilshere 1.
FA Cup (13): Van Persie 4, Eduardo 3 (1 pen), Bendtner 1, Eboue 1, Gallas 1, Vela 1, Walcott 1, own goal 1.
Champions League (23): Adebayor 6 (1 pen), Van Persie 5 (3 pens), Gallas 3, Walcott 3, Bendtner 2, Diaby 1, Nasri 1, Ramsey 1, Song Billong 1.

Almunia M 32	Sagna B 34 + 1	Clichy G 30 + 1	Nasri S 28 + 1	Djourou J 13 + 2	Gallas W 23	Eboue E 17 + 11	Denilson 36 + 1	Adebayor E 21 + 5	Bendtner N 17 + 14	Walcott T 16 + 6	Van Persie R 24 + 4	Toure K 26 + 3	Song Billong A 23 + 8	Fabregas F 22	Vela C 2 + 12	Ramsey A 1 + 8	Wilshere J — + 1	Silvestre M 12 + 2	Diaby V 16 + 8	Fabianski L 5 + 1	Hoyte G 1	Gibbs K 6 + 2	Arshavin A 12	Merida Perez F — + 2	Bischoff A — + 1	Randall M — + 1	Mannone V 1	Match No.
1	2	3	4	5	6	7	8	9	10[1]	11[2]	12	13																1
1	2	3	4		6	7	8	9	13	11[2]	10	5[1]	12															2
1	2	3	11		6	7[1]	4[2]	9		12	10[3]	5	13	8	14													3
1	2	3			6	7[2]	4	9		11[1]	10[3]	5	12	8				13	14									4
1	2	3[1]		12	6	7[3]	4	9	10[2]	13		5	11	8					14									5
1	2	3			6	7[1]	4	9	12	11[2]	10	5		8	13													6
1	2	3	12		6		4[1]	9	13	11[2]	10	5	7[3]	8	14													7
1		3	11[2]			7	4	9		12	10	5[1]	2	8				6	13									8
1	14	3	4[2]		6	2		12	9	11[1]	10[3]		7	8				5	13									9
1	2	3	11[2]		6	12	4	9		7[1]	10[3]		13	8				5	14									10
1	2[1]	3					4[2]	9[3]	10	12	13[4]	5	7	8	14			6	11									11
1[6]	2	3	11		6		4	9	7[1]		13	12		8				5	10[2]	15								12
1	2[3]	3	11		6		4	12	9[2]	7		14		8	13			5	10[1]									13
1		3	11	5			4	9			10		7		12	13		6	8[1]				2[2]					14
1	2	3	11	5	6		4	9[1]	12		10		7	8														15
1	2	3	11[1]	5		12[2]	4	9			10	6	7	8				13										16
1	2	3		5	6		4	9	12		10		7	8					11[1]									17
1	2	3	11[1]	5	6	12	4	9			10		7	8[2]				13										18
1	2	12	11[1]		6	7	4				10	5		8[2]		13		3	9									19
1	2	3	11		6	7[2]	4	9	10			13	12					5	8[1]									20
1	2	3	11	5		7[1]	4	9[3]	12		10	6	13						8[2]									21
1	2	3	11	5		7[1]	4	9[2]	12		10	6	13						8									22
1	2[2]	3	11	5	6	13	4	9	12		10		7[1]						8									23
1	2	3	11		6	7[3]	4	9	10[1]		12	5	13						8[2]									24
1	2	3[2]	11		6	7[4]	4	9[1]	12		10	5		8									13					25
1	2	3[1]	11		6	12	4	9			10	5	7[1]	13									14	8[2]				26
1	2[1]	3	11		6	12	4		13		10	5		9[2]					8				7					27
1	2	3	11[3]	5		7[2]	4				10		6[1]	8				13	12				9	14				28
1	2	3	11[1]	5		12	4		9[3]	7[2]		6		8	14	13							10					29
1	2	3	11		6	12	4		9[1]		10	5	13	8									7[2]					30
1	2	3			6	12	4	9[2]	13	11[1]		5	7	8[3]	14								10					31
	2				6[1]		4[2]	14	9	11[3]	13	5	7	8		12				1		3	10					32
	2		11				4[1]		9[2]	12		5	7	8				6	13	1		3	10					33
1			11	12		2	4	14	9	7[2]		5		8[3]				6[1]	13			3	10					34
	2			5		3	4		9[2]	11[1]		6		8	7[3]					1			10	13	12	14		35
	2		11			13	14	12	9[3]	10		5	7[2]	8				6	4[1]	1		3						36
	2		11[1]			14	4		13	12	9	5	6	8					7	1		3[3]	10[2]					37
	2[2]					13	4		12	7[1]	9	5	6	8	14				11			3	10[3]				1	38

FA Cup

Third Round	Plymouth Arg	(h)	3-1
Fourth Round	Cardiff C	(a)	0-0
		(h)	4-0
Fifth Round	Burnley	(h)	3-0
Quarter-Final	Hull C	(h)	2-1
Semi-Final	Chelsea		1-2
(at Wembley)			

Carling Cup

Third Round	Sheffield U	(h)	6-0
Fourth Round	Wigan Ath	(h)	3-0
Quarter-Final	Burnley	(a)	0-2

Champions League

Third Qualifying Round			
	Twente	(a)	2-0
		(h)	4-0
Group G	Dynamo Kiev	(a)	1-1
	Porto	(h)	4-0
	Fenerbahce	(a)	5-2
		(h)	0-0
	Dynamo Kiev	(h)	1-0
	Porto	(a)	0-2
Knock-out Round	Roma	(h)	1-0
		(a)	0-1
Quarter-Final	Villarreal	(a)	1-1
		(h)	3-0
Semi-Final	Manchester U	(a)	0-1
		(h)	1-3

ASTON VILLA   FA Premiership

FOUNDATION

Cricketing enthusiasts of Villa Cross Wesleyan Chapel, Aston, Birmingham decided to form a football club during the winter of 1874–75. Football clubs were few and far between in the Birmingham area and in their first game against Aston Brook St Mary's Rugby team they played one half rugby and the other soccer. In 1876 they were joined by a Scottish soccer enthusiast George Ramsay who was immediately appointed captain and went on to lead Aston Villa from obscurity to one of the country's top clubs in a period of less than 10 years.

Villa Park, Birmingham B6 6HE.
Telephone: (0121) 327 2299.
Fax: (0121) 322 2107.
Ticket Office/Consumer Sales: (0800) 612 0970.
Website: www.avfc.co.uk
Email: postmaster@avfc.co.uk
Ground Capacity: 42,573.
Record Attendance: 76,588 v Derby Co, FA Cup 6th rd, 2 March 1946.
Pitch Measurements: 115yd × 75yd.
Chairman: Randolph Lerner.
Secretary: Sharon Barnhurst.
Manager: Martin O'Neill.
Assistant Managers: John Robertson, Steve Walford.
Physio: Alan Smith.
Colours: Claret body, blue sleeve shirts, white shorts, sky blue stockings.
Change Colours: Laser blue shirts with black sleeves, black shorts, black stockings.
Third Kit: White shirts with thin claret pinstripe, blue shorts, white stockings.
Year Formed: 1874.
Turned Professional: 1885.
Ltd Co.: 1896.
Public Ltd Company: 1969.
Club Nickname: 'The Villans'.
Grounds: 1874, Wilson Road and Aston Park (also used Aston Lower Grounds for some matches); 1876, Wellington Road, Perry Barr; 1897, Villa Park.

HONOURS

FA Premier League: Runners-up 1992–93.
Football League: Division 1 – Champions 1893–94, 1895–96, 1896–97, 1898–99, 1899–1900, 1909–10, 1980–81; Runners-up 1888–89, 1902–03, 1907–08, 1910–11, 1912–13, 1913–14, 1930–31, 1932–33, 1989–90; Division 2 – Champions 1937–38, 1959–60; Runners-up 1974–75, 1987–88; Division 3 – Champions 1971–72.
FA Cup: Winners 1887, 1895, 1897, 1905, 1913, 1920, 1957; Runners-up 1892, 1924, 2000.
Double Performed: 1896–97.
Football League Cup: Winners 1961, 1975, 1977, 1994, 1996; Runners-up 1963, 1971.
European Competitions: European Cup: 1981–82 (winners), 1982–83. UEFA Cup: 1975–76, 1977–78, 1983–84, 1990–91, 1993–94, 1994–95, 1996–97, 1997–98, 1998–99, 2001–02, 2008–09. World Club Championship: 1982. European Super Cup: 1982–83 (winners). Intertoto Cup: 2000, 2001 (winners), 2002, 2008 (winners).

First Football League Game: 8 September 1888, Football League, v Wolverhampton W (a) D 1–1 – Warner; Cox, Coulton; Yates, H. Devey, Dawson; A. Brown, Green (1), Allen, Garvey, Hodgetts.

SKY SPORTS FACT FILE

Gabriel Agbonlahor scored a second-half hat-trick for Aston Villa against Manchester City on 17 August 2008 in a 4–2 win. He was capped for England against Germany in Berlin on 19 November for his first full international appearance.

Record League Victory: 12–2 v Accrington S, Division 1, 12 March 1892 – Warner; Evans, Cox; Harry Devey, Jimmy Cowan, Baird; Athersmith (1), Dickson (2), John Devey (4), L. Campbell (4), Hodgetts (1).

Record Cup Victory: 13–0 v Wednesbury Old Ath, FA Cup 1st rd, 30 October 1886 – Warner; Coulton, Simmonds; Yates, Robertson, Burton (2); R. Davis (1), A. Brown (3), Hunter (3), Loach (2), Hodgetts (2).

Record Defeat: 1–8 v Blackburn R, FA Cup 3rd rd, 16 February 1889.

Most League Points (2 for a win): 70, Division 3, 1971–72.

Most League Points (3 for a win): 78, Division 2, 1987–88.

Most League Goals: 128, Division 1, 1930–31.

Highest League Scorer in Season: 'Pongo' Waring, 49, Division 1, 1930–31.

Most League Goals in Total Aggregate: Harry Hampton, 215, 1904–15.

Most League Goals in One Match: 5, Harry Hampton v Sheffield W, Division 1, 5 October 1912; 5, Harold Halse v Derby Co, Division 1, 19 October 1912; 5, Len Capewell v Burnley, Division 1, 29 August 1925; 5, George Brown v Leicester C, Division 1, 2 January 1932; 5, Gerry Hitchens v Charlton Ath, Division 2, 18 November 1959.

Most Capped Player: Steve Staunton 64 (102), Republic of Ireland.

Most League Appearances: Charlie Aitken, 561, 1961–76.

Youngest League Player: Jimmy Brown, 15 years 349 days v Bolton W, 17 September 1969.

MANAGERS
George Ramsay 1884–1926
(Secretary-Manager)
W. J. Smith 1926–34
(Secretary-Manager)
Jimmy McMullan 1934–35
Jimmy Hogan 1936–44
Alex Massie 1945–50
George Martin 1950–53
Eric Houghton 1953–58
Joe Mercer 1958–64
Dick Taylor 1964–67
Tommy Cummings 1967–68
Tommy Docherty 1968–70
Vic Crowe 1970–74
Ron Saunders 1974–82
Tony Barton 1982–84
Graham Turner 1984–86
Billy McNeill 1986–87
Graham Taylor 1987–90
Dr Jozef Venglos 1990–91
Ron Atkinson 1991–94
Brian Little 1994–98
John Gregory 1998–2002
Graham Taylor OBE 2002–03
David O'Leary 2003–06
Martin O'Neill August 2006–

Record Transfer Fee Received: £12,600,000 from Manchester U for Dwight Yorke, August 1998.

Record Transfer Fee Paid: £12,000,000 to Newcastle U for James Milner, August 2008.

Football League Record: 1888 Founder Member of the League; 1936–38 Division 2; 1938–59 Division 1; 1959–60 Division 2; 1960–67 Division 1; 1967–70 Division 2; 1970–72 Division 3; 1972–75 Division 2; 1975–87 Division 1; 1987–88 Division 2; 1988–92 Division 1; 1992– FA Premier League.

LATEST SEQUENCES

Longest Sequence of League Wins: 9, 15.10.1910 – 10.12.1910.

Longest Sequence of League Defeats: 11, 23.3.1963 – 4.5.1963.

Longest Sequence of League Draws: 6, 12.9.1981 – 10.10.1981.

Longest Sequence of Unbeaten League Matches: 15, 12.3.1949 – 27.8.1949.

Longest Sequence Without a League Win: 12, 27.12.1986 – 25.3.1987.

Successive Scoring Runs: 35 from 10.11.1895.

Successive Non-scoring Runs: 5 from 29.2.1992.

TEN YEAR LEAGUE RECORD

		P	W	D	L	F	A	Pts	Pos
1999-2000	PR Lge	38	15	13	10	46	35	58	6
2000-01	PR Lge	38	13	15	10	46	43	54	8
2001-02	PR Lge	38	12	14	12	46	47	50	8
2002-03	PR Lge	38	12	9	17	42	47	45	16
2003-04	PR Lge	38	15	11	12	48	44	56	6
2004-05	PR Lge	38	12	11	15	45	52	47	10
2005-06	PR Lge	38	10	12	16	42	55	42	16
2006-07	PR Lge	38	11	17	10	43	41	50	11
2007-08	PR Lge	38	16	12	10	71	51	60	6
2008-09	PR Lge	38	17	11	10	54	48	62	6

DID YOU KNOW ?

On 22 October 1980 when Aston Villa beat Brighton & Hove Albion 4–1, it was exactly 48 years to the day that they had held first place in the First Division. In 1932 they had beaten Birmingham City 1–0 in the midlands derby at Villa Park.

ASTON VILLA 2008–09 LEAGUE RECORD

Match No.	Date	Venue	Opponents	Result	H/T Score	Lg. Pos.	Goalscorers	Attendance
1	Aug 17	H	Manchester C	W 4-2	0-0	—	Carew 47, Agbonlahor 3 69, 74, 76	39,955
2	23	A	Stoke C	L 2-3	0-1	6	Carew 63, Laursen 84	27,500
3	31	H	Liverpool	D 0-0	0-0	7		41,647
4	Sept 15	A	Tottenham H	W 2-1	1-0	—	Reo-Coker 5, Young A 54	36,075
5	21	A	WBA	W 2-1	2-1	4	Carew 27, Agbonlahor 29	26,011
6	27	H	Sunderland	W 2-1	2-1	3	Young A 18, Carew 33	38,706
7	Oct 5	A	Chelsea	L 0-2	0-2	5		41,593
8	18	H	Portsmouth	D 0-0	0-0	6		37,660
9	26	A	Wigan Ath	W 4-0	1-0	5	Barry (pen) 22, Agbonlahor 57, Carew 62, Sidwell 90	20,249
10	29	H	Blackburn R	W 3-2	1-1	—	Young L 45, Barry 65, Agbonlahor 87	35,985
11	Nov 3	A	Newcastle U	L 0-2	0-0	—		44,567
12	9	H	Middlesbrough	L 1-2	1-1	5	Sidwell 37	36,672
13	15	A	Arsenal	W 2-0	0-0	5	Clichy (og) 70, Agbonlahor 80	60,047
14	22	H	Manchester U	D 0-0	0-0	4		42,585
15	29	H	Fulham	D 0-0	0-0	5		36,625
16	Dec 7	A	Everton	W 3-2	1-1	5	Sidwell 1, Young A 2 54, 90	31,922
17	13	H	Bolton W	W 4-2	2-1	4	Agbonlahor 2 25, 67, Davies (og) 40, Young A 78	35,134
18	20	A	West Ham U	W 1-0	0-0	3	Neill (og) 78	31,353
19	26	H	Arsenal	D 2-2	0-1	4	Barry (pen) 65, Knight 90	42,585
20	30	A	Hull C	W 1-0	0-0	—	Zayatte (og) 88	24,727
21	Jan 10	H	WBA	W 2-1	2-0	4	Davies 19, Carson (og) 41	41,757
22	17	A	Sunderland	W 2-1	0-1	4	Milner 60, Barry (pen) 80	40,350
23	27	A	Portsmouth	W 1-0	1-0	—	Heskey 21	19,073
24	31	A	Wigan Ath	D 0-0	0-0	4		41,766
25	Feb 7	A	Blackburn R	W 2-0	1-0	3	Milner 27, Agbonlahor 90	24,267
26	21	H	Chelsea	L 0-1	0-1	4		42,585
27	Mar 1	H	Stoke C	D 2-2	1-0	4	Petrov 45, Carew 79	39,641
28	4	A	Manchester C	L 0-2	0-1	—		40,137
29	15	H	Tottenham H	L 1-2	0-1	5	Carew 85	41,205
30	22	A	Liverpool	L 0-5	0-3	5		44,131
31	Apr 5	A	Manchester U	L 2-3	1-1	5	Carew 30, Agbonlahor 58	75,409
32	12	A	Everton	D 3-3	1-2	5	Carew 33, Milner 55, Barry (pen) 66	40,188
33	18	H	West Ham U	D 1-1	1-0	5	Heskey 11	39,534
34	25	A	Bolton W	D 1-1	1-0	5	Young A 43	21,709
35	May 4	H	Hull C	W 1-0	1-0	—	Carew 34	39,607
36	9	A	Fulham	L 1-3	1-1	5	Young A 14	25,660
37	16	A	Middlesbrough	D 1-1	0-1	6	Carew 57	27,261
38	24	H	Newcastle U	W 1-0	1-0	6	Duff (og) 38	42,585

Final League Position: 6

GOALSCORERS

League (54): Agbonlahor 11, Carew 11, Young A 7, Barry 5 (4 pens), Milner 3, Sidwell 3, Heskey 2, Davies 1, Knight 1, Laursen 1, Petrov 1, Reo-Coker 1, Young L 1, own goals 6.
Carling Cup (0).
FA Cup (6): Milner 3 (2 pens), Carew 1, Delfouneso 1, Sidwell 1.
UEFA Cup (15): Barry 3 (1 pen), Carew 2, Delfouneso 2, Laursen 2, Agbonlahor 1, Gardner 1, Harewood 1, Petrov 1, Reo-Coker 1, Young A 1.
Inter-Toto Cup (3): Carew 1, Laursen 1, Young A 1.

Friedel B 38	Young L 33 + 1	Shorey N 19 + 2	Reo-Coker N 19 + 7	Davies C 34 + 1	Laursen M 19	Petrov S 36	Young A 36	Agbonlahor G 35 + 1	Carew J 18 + 9	Barry G 38	Routledge W — + 1	Milner J 31 + 5	Gardner C 3 + 11	Harewood M — + 6	Cuellar C 24 + 4	Sidwell S 11 + 5	Knight Z 13	Heskey E 11 + 3	Delfouneso N — + 4	Guzan B — + 1	Match No.
1	2	3	4	5	6	7	8	9	10	11											1
1	2	3[1]	4	5	6	7	8	9	10	11		12									2
1	2[1]	3[2]	4	5	6	7	8	9	10	11		12	13								3
1	2	3[1]	4	5	6	7	8	9[2]	10[3]	11		12	13	14							4
1	2	3[1]	4	5	6	7[2]	8	9	10[3]	11		12	13	14							5
1	2	3[1]	4	5	6	7	8	9	10[2]	11		12	13								6
1	2[1]	3	4	5[3]	6	7	8	9	10[2]	11		12	13	14							7
1	2	3	4	5	6[1]	7	8	9	10	11		12									8
1	2[2]	3	4	5	6	7[3]	8	9	10	11[1]		12	13	14							9
1	2	3	4[3]	5	6	7[1]	8	9[2]	10	11		12	13	14							10
1	2	3[2]	4[1]	5	6	7	8	9	10	11		12	13								11
1	2	3[1]	4	5	6	7	8	9	10	11		12									12
1	2	3	4	5	6	7	8	9	10	11											13
1	2	3	4	5	6	7	8[1]	9	10	11		12									14
1	2	3	4	5	6	7	8	9	10	11											15
1	2	3	4	5	6	7	8	9	10	11											16
1	2	3	4	5	6	7	8[3]	9[1]	10[2]	11		12	13	14							17
1	2[1]	3	4	5	6	7	8	9	10	11		12									18
1	2	3	4	5	6	7	8	9	10	11											19
1	2	3	4[1]	5	6	7	8	9	10	11		12									20
1	2	3	4[1]	5	6	7	8	9	10	11		12									21
1	2	3	4[1]	5	6	7	8[1]	9	10	11		12									22
1	2	3	4[2]	5	6	7	8	9	10[1]	11		12	13								23
1	2	3	4[1]	5	6	7	8	9	10	11		12									24
1	2[2]	3	4	5	6	7	8	9	10[1]	11		12	13								25
1	2	3	4	5[1]	6	7	8	9	10	11		12									26
1	2	3	4	5	6	7	8	9	10[1]	11		12									27
1	2[2]	3	4	5[1]	6	7	8	9	10	11		12	13								28
1	2	3	4	5	6[1]	7	8	9[3]	10[2]	11		12	13	14							29
1[*]	2[6]	3	4	5	6	7	8	9[1]	10[2]	11		12	13	15							30
1	2	3	4	5	6	7	8	9	10	11[1]		12									31
1	2	3	4	5	6	7	8	9[1]	10	11		12									32
1	2	3	4	5	6	7	8	9[1]	10	11[2]		12	13								33
1	2	3	4	5	6	7	8	9[1]	10	11		12									34
1	2	3	4	5	6	7[2]	8[3]	9	10[1]	11		12	13	14							35
1	2[1]	3[2]	4	5	6	7	8	9	10	11		12	13								36
1	2	3	4	5	6	7	8[1]	9	10	11		12									37
1	2[1]	3	4	5	6	7[2]	8	9	10[3]	11		12	13	14							38

FA Cup

Third Round	Gillingham	(a)	2-1
Fourth Round	Doncaster R	(a)	0-0
		(h)	3-1
Fifth Round	Everton	(a)	1-3

UEFA Cup

Second Qualifying Round

	Hafnarfjordur	(a)	4-1
		(h)	1-1
First Round	Litex	(a)	3-1
		(h)	1-1
Group F	Ajax	(h)	2-1
	Slavia Prague	(a)	1-0
	Zilina	(h)	1-2
	Hamburg	(a)	1-3
Third Round	CSKA Moscow	(h)	1-1
		(a)	0-2

Inter-Toto Cup

Third Round	Odense	(a)	2-2
		(h)	1-0

Carling Cup

Third Round	QPR	(h)	0-1

BARNET

FL Championship 2

FOUNDATION

Barnet Football Club was formed in 1888 as an amateur organisation and they played at a ground in Queen's Road until they disbanded in 1901. A club known as Alston Works FC was then formed and they played at Totteridge Lane until changing to Barnet Alston FC in 1906. They moved to their present ground a year later, combining with The Avenue to form Barnet and Alston in 1912. The club progressed to senior amateur football by way of the Athenian and Isthmian Leagues, turning professional in 1965. It was as a Southern League and Conference club that they made their name.

Underhill Stadium, Barnet Lane, Barnet, Herts EN5 2DN.

Telephone: (020) 8441 6932.

Fax: (020) 8447 0655.

Ticket Office: 0208 449 6325.

Website: www.barnetfc.com

Email: info@barnetfc.com

Ground Capacity: 5,345.

Record Attendance: 11,026 v Wycombe Wanderers, FA Amateur Cup 4th Round 1951–52.

Record Receipts: £31,202 v Portsmouth, FA Cup 3rd Round, 5 January 1991.

Pitch Measurements: 100m × 64m.

Chairman: Anthony Kleanthous.

Secretary: Andrew Adie.

Manager: Ian Hendon.

Physio: Mark Stein.

Colours: All black with amber trim.

Change Colours: White shirts with black trim, red shorts, red stockings.

Year Formed: 1888.

Turned Professional: 1965.

Previous Names: 1906, Barnet Alston FC; 1919, Barnet.

Club Nickname: The Bees.

Grounds: 1888, Queens Road; 1901, Totteridge Lane; 1907, Barnet Lane.

First Football League Game: 17 August 1991, Division 4, v Crewe Alex (h) L 4–7 – Phillips; Blackford, Cooper (Murphy), Horton, Bodley (Stein), Johnson, Showler, Carter (2), Bull (2), Lowe, Evans.

HONOURS

Football League: Division 2 best season: 24th, 1993–94.

FA Amateur Cup: Winners 1946.

FA Trophy: Runners-up 1972.

GM Vauxhall Conference: Winners 1990–91. *Conference:* Winners 2004–05

FA Cup: 4th rd, 2007, 2008.

League Cup: best season: 3rd rd, 2006.

SKY SPORTS FACT FILE

The season before Barnet were elected to the Southern League they accounted for two of that league's teams Stevenage Town and Cambridge United in the FA Cup before narrowly losing 3–2 to Preston North End, the previous runners-up, to an own goal.

Record League Victory: 7–0 v Blackpool, Division 3, 11 November 2000 – Naisbitt; Stockley, Sawyers, Niven (Brown), Heald, Arber (1), Currie (3), Doolan, Richards (2) (McGleish), Cottee (1) (Riza), Toms.

Record Cup Victory: 6–1 v Newport Co, FA Cup 1st rd, 21 November 1970 – McClelland; Lye, Jenkins, Ward, Embery, King, Powell (1), Ferry, Adams (1), Gray, George (3), (1 og).

Record Defeat: 1–9 v Peterborough U, Division 3, 5 September 1998.

Most League Points (3 for a win): 79, Division 3, 1992–93.

Most League Goals: 81, Division 4, 1991–92.

Highest League Scorer in Season: Dougie Freedman, 24, Division 3, 1994–95.

Most League Goals in Total Aggregate: Sean Devine, 47, 1995–99.

Most League Goals in One Match: 4, Dougie Freedman v Rochdale, Division 3, 13 September 1994; 4, Lee Hodges v Rochdale, Division 3, 8 April 1996.

Most Capped Player: Ken Charlery, 4, St Lucia.

Most League Appearances: Paul Wilson, 263, 1991–2000.

Youngest League Player: Kieran Adams, 17 years 71 days v Mansfield T, 31 December 1994.

Record Transfer Fee Received: £800,000 from Crystal Palace for Dougie Freedman, September 1995.

Record Transfer Fee Paid: £130,000 to Peterborough U for Greg Heald, August 1997.

Football League Record: 1991 Promoted to Division 4 from GMVC; 1991–92 Division 4; 1992–93 Division 3; 1993–94 Division 2; 1994–2001 Division 3; 2001–05 Conference; 2005– FL 2.

MANAGERS

Lester Finch
George Wheeler
Dexter Adams
Tommy Coleman
Gerry Ward
Gordon Ferry
Brian Kelly
Bill Meadows 1976–79
Barry Fry 1979–85
Roger Thompson 1985
Don McAllister 1985–86
Barry Fry 1986–93
Edwin Stein 1993
Gary Phillips (Player–Manager) 1993–94
Ray Clemence 1994–96
Alan Mullery (Director of Football) 1996–97
Terry Bullivant 1997
John Still 1997–2000
Tony Cottee 2000–01
John Still 2001–02
Peter Shreeves 2002–03
Martin Allen 2003–04
Paul Fairclough 2004–08
Ian Hendon December 2008–

LATEST SEQUENCES

Longest Sequence of League Wins: 6, 28.8.1993 – 25.9.1999.

Longest Sequence of League Defeats: 11, 8.5.1993 – 2.10.1993.

Longest Sequence of League Draws: 4, 22.1.1994 – 12.2.1994.

Longest Sequence of Unbeaten League Matches: 12, 5.12.1992 – 2.3.1993.

Longest Sequence Without a League Win: 14, 24.4.1993 – 10.10.1993.

Successive Scoring Runs: 12 from 19.3.1995.

Successive Non-scoring Runs: 5 from 12.2.2000.

TEN YEAR LEAGUE RECORD

		P	W	D	L	F	A	Pts	Pos
1999-2000	Div 3	46	21	12	13	59	53	75	6
2000–01	Div 3	46	12	9	25	67	81	45	24
2001–02	Conf	42	19	10	13	64	48	67	5
2002–03	Conf	42	13	14	15	65	68	53	11
2003–04	Conf	42	19	14	9	60	48	71	4
2004–05	Conf	42	26	8	8	90	44	86	1
2005-06	FL 2	46	12	18	16	44	57	54	18
2006-07	FL 2	46	16	11	19	55	70	59	14
2007-08	FL 2	46	16	12	18	56	63	60	12
2008-09	FL 2	46	11	15	20	56	74	48	17

DID YOU KNOW ?

Arthur Morris scored 403 League goals for Barnet in nine seasons from 1927 to 1936 during the club's Athenian League days. Despite this impressive record he was not capped at amateur international level.

BARNET 2008–09 LEAGUE RECORD

Match No.	Date	Venue	Opponents	Result	H/T Score	Lg. Pos.	Goalscorers	Attendance
1	Aug 9	H	Chesterfield	L	1-3	1-0	—	Carew [19]	2237
2	16	A	Rochdale	L	1-3	1-2	19	Birchall [3]	2442
3	23	H	Brentford	L	0-1	0-1	19		2815
4	30	A	Chester C	L	1-5	0-1	20	Akurang [90]	1295
5	Sept 6	A	Lincoln C	L	0-2	0-0	21		3417
6	13	H	Morecambe	D	1-1	1-1	21	Adomah [18]	1776
7	20	H	Bury	L	1-2	0-0	21	Adomah [49]	1995
8	27	A	Grimsby T	W	1-0	1-0	20	Bishop [44]	3713
9	Oct 4	H	Accrington S	W	2-1	1-1	20	O'Flynn [1], Yakubu [75]	1899
10	10	A	Dagenham & R	L	0-2	0-1	—		2629
11	18	A	Rotherham U	W	4-3	2-1	19	Medley [18], Adomah [36], Akurang 2 [57, 62]	3801
12	21	H	Wycombe W	D	1-1	1-0	—	Deverdics [24]	2258
13	25	H	Exeter C	L	0-1	0-0	18		2887
14	28	A	Shrewsbury T	D	2-2	2-2	—	O'Flynn 2 [4, 28]	5163
15	Nov 1	A	Bradford C	D	3-3	2-3	18	O'Flynn [20], Nicolau [32], Adomah [76]	12,510
16	15	H	Notts Co	L	0-4	0-4	20		1934
17	22	H	Macclesfield T	L	1-3	0-1	20	O'Flynn [59]	1579
18	25	A	Port Vale	D	0-0	0-0	—		4617
19	Dec 6	A	Luton T	L	1-3	1-2	20	Ogogo [40]	5536
20	13	H	Gillingham	D	2-2	0-0	20	Leary [46], O'Flynn [71]	2248
21	20	A	Darlington	D	2-2	1-2	20	O'Flynn [19], Yakubu [76]	2770
22	26	H	Aldershot T	L	0-3	0-1	21		2729
23	28	A	Bournemouth	W	2-0	1-0	21	Adomah 2 [24, 70]	4725
24	Jan 10	A	Bury	L	0-1	0-1	—		2402
25	17	H	Dagenham & R	D	1-1	1-0	21	O'Flynn [13]	2366
26	24	A	Accrington S	D	1-1	1-0	21	Furlong [6]	1056
27	27	D	Shrewsbury T	D	0-0	0-0	—		1568
28	31	A	Exeter C	L	1-2	1-1	21	Furlong [45]	4145
29	Feb 10	H	Grimsby T	D	3-3	2-2	—	Bolasie [18], Furlong [20], O'Flynn (pen) [62]	1554
30	14	A	Notts Co	L	0-2	0-1	22		3830
31	21	A	Bradford C	W	4-1	2-0	20	Adomah [25], O'Flynn [41], Bolasie [58], Devera [62]	2445
32	28	A	Chesterfield	D	1-1	1-0	20	Yakubu [33]	3068
33	Mar 3	H	Rochdale	W	2-1	1-1	—	O'Flynn [42], Bolasie [90]	1332
34	7	H	Chester C	W	3-1	0-0	19	O'Flynn 2 (1 pen) [51, 69 (p)], Furlong [74]	2085
35	10	A	Brentford	L	0-1	0-1	—		4742
36	14	A	Morecambe	L	1-2	1-2	20	O'Flynn [34]	1899
37	21	H	Lincoln C	W	3-2	1-1	20	O'Flynn 2 [37, 87], Adomah [63]	1979
38	28	H	Darlington	L	0-1	0-0	20		2069
39	31	A	Wycombe W	D	1-1	1-1	—	Furlong [42]	4066
40	Apr 4	A	Gillingham	W	2-0	1-0	19	Furlong [23], O'Flynn (pen) [54]	6033
41	7	H	Rotherham U	W	2-0	0-0	—	Furlong 2 [70, 81]	1508
42	11	H	Bournemouth	W	1-0	0-0	17	Furlong [51]	3133
43	13	A	Aldershot T	D	1-1	1-0	17	Leary [4]	2597
44	18	H	Luton T	D	1-1	1-0	16	Birchall [45]	2808
45	25	A	Macclesfield T	L	1-2	0-1	17	Adomah [54]	1619
46	May 2	H	Port Vale	L	1-2	0-2	17	Hart [90]	2305

Final League Position: 17

GOALSCORERS

League (56): O'Flynn 17 (3 pens), Adomah 9, Furlong 9, Akurang 3, Bolasie 3, Yakubu 3, Birchall 2, Leary 2, Bishop 1, Carew 1, Devera 1, Deverdics 1, Hart 1, Medley 1, Nicolau 1, Ogogo 1.
Carling Cup (0).
FA Cup (3): Adomah 1, O;Flynn 1, Yakubu 1.
J Paint Trophy (2): Birchall 2.

Harrison L 20+1	Devera J 33+1	Gillet K 28+4	Porter M 18+8	Yakubu I 37+1	Carew A 10	Adomah A 45	Bishop N 41+3	Birchall A 19+20	Akurang C 12+12	St Aimie K 1+2	Medley L 5+13	Deverdics N 22+7	Leary M 24+4	Beckwith R 5	Tabiri J 4+3	Hart D 2+1	Thomas A 2	Charles E —+5	De Magalhaes J 4	Mitchell P 3	Kadoch R 11+1	Nicolau N 12+9	O'Flynn J 32+2	Townsend M 13	Ogogo A 7+2	Burge R 1+1	Breen G 22	Furlong P 21	Black T 5	Bolasie Y 17+3	Lockwood M 12	Hughes M 8+1	Cole J 10	Match No.
1	2	3	4	5	6^3	7	8	9	10	11^2	12	13	14																					1
	2		4^1	5	6	7	8	9^2		12	10		11	1	3	13																		2
1	2		4	5	6^1	7	8	9^3	10^2		12	13	3				11	14																3
1	2	12				7	8	9				13	10^3		6	14	11^2	3		5	4^1													4
15	2	3	4	5	6^1	7	8	9	10^2			13	12							11	16													5
1	2	3		5	6	7	8	9	10^2			13		12							4^1	11												6
1	2	3		5	6	7	8	9^2	10^3				4^1	12		14					11	13												7
1	2	3		5	6	7	8	12	10				4								11	9^1												8
1	2	3	12	5	6	7^1	8	13	10^2				14	4^3							11	9												9
1	2	3		5	6	7	8	9^1	12			13	14	4^3							11^2	10												10
1	2	3	4^6	5		7	8	12	10^1		9^2	11^3	6	14							13													11
1	2	3		5		7	8	12	10^2		9^1	11	6								13	4												12
1	2	3	12	5		7	8	9^1	13		14	11^1	6^2								10	4												13
1	2	3	4	5		7	8	12					10								11	9^1	6											14
1	2	3	4^1	5		7	8	12				13	10								11^2	9	6											15
1		3	4^2	5		7	8	10^1			12	13									11^3	9	6	2	14									16
1		3		5		7	8	10^1			12	11^2	6								13	9	4	2										17
	3	4				7	8	12	10^2		13	11	11	1					5		9^1	6	2											18
	3	12	13			7	8	11^1	10^2		14		6^3	1					5		9	4	2^1											19
		4	5			7	12	10			13	11^1	2	1		8			3		9^2	6												20
	3	4^1	5			7	12	10^3			13	11^2	8	1							14	9	6		2									21
	3	4	5^3			7		10^2	12			13	6							1	11^1	9	8	14	2									22
	3	4	5	6		7			12			11								1		9^1	8	10	2									23
	3	8	5			7	12	13					4							1		9		2^1		6	10^2	11						24
	2	3	5^1			7	8				12	6								1	13	9	4				10	11^2						25
	2	3^4	6			7	4						8							1	12	9^2					5	10	11^1	13				26
	2		4			7	6	12				8^2								1	3	9^1	13				5	10	11^3	14				27
	2		4			7	8	13	12			6								1	3	9^2					5	10^3	11^1	14				28
	2			5		7^2	8		12			13								1		9					6	10^1		11	3	4		29
1	2	12	5^1			7	8	14	13													9					6	10^3		11^2	3	4		30
1	2	12	5			7	4	13				8										9^2					6	10		11^1	3			31
1	2	12	5			7	4		12			8^2										9^1					6	10		11	3	13		32
1^6			5			7	4					8								15		9					6	10		11	3	2		33
	12		5			7^2	4	13	14			8										9					6	10^3		11	3^1	2	1	34
			5			7	4	13	12			8^1										9					6	10		11	3	2^2	1	35
	2		5			7^2	4	13	12			8										9						10^1		11	3	6	1	36
	12		5			7	4	13				8										9^2					6	10		11	3	2^1	1	37
	2^2	12	5			7	4	13				8^1										9					6	10		11	3		1	38
	2	12	5			7^1	4					8										9					6	10		11^1	3		1	39
	2	12	5			7	4	13				8										9^2					6	10		11^1	3		1	40
	2	3	5			7	4	12				8										13	9^1				6	10		11^2			1	41
	2	3	5			7	4	10^2				8^1	12						13								6	9		11			1	42
	2	3	13	5^2		7^1	4	10				8							12								6	9		11			1	43
1	2	3				7	4	10					5		8^1			12									6	9		11				44
	2	3	5			9^1	4	10				6			8^2			13		1	12									11		7		45
	2	3	14				4	12	10^3			9^1	8^2	5		7				1	13				6^4	11								46

FA Cup
First Round   Rochdale   (h)   1-1   (a)   2-3

Carling Cup
First Round   Brighton & HA   (a)   0-4

J Paint Trophy
First Round   Dagenham & R   (a)   2-4

BARNSLEY   FL Championship

FOUNDATION

Many clubs owe their inception to the church and Barnsley are among them, for they were formed in 1887 by the Rev. T. T. Preedy, curate of Barnsley St Peter's and went under that name until it was dropped in 1897 a year before being admitted to the Second Division of the Football League.

Oakwell Stadium, Grove Street, Barnsley, South Yorkshire S71 1ET.
Telephone: (01226) 211 211.
Fax: (01226) 211 444.
Ticket Office: (0871) 22 66 777.
Website: www.barnsleyfc.co.uk
Email: thereds@barnsleyfc.co.uk
Ground Capacity: 23,186.
Record Attendance: 40,255 v Stoke C, FA Cup 5th rd, 15 February 1936.
Pitch Measurements: 110yd × 73yd.
Chairman: Patrick Cryne.
General Manager/Secretary: Albert Donald Rowing.
Manager: Simon Davey.
Assistant Manager: Ryan Kidd.
Physio: Richard Kay.
Colours: Red shirts with white trim, white shorts, red stockings.
Change Colours: Black shirts with red trim, black shorts, black stockings.
Year Formed: 1887.
Turned Professional: 1888.
Ltd Co.: 1899.
Previous Name: 1887, Barnsley St Peter's; 1897, Barnsley.
Club Nickname: 'The Tykes', 'Reds' or 'Colliers'.
Ground: 1887, Oakwell.

HONOURS

Football League: Division 1 – Runners-up 1996–97; Division 3 (N) – Champions 1933–34, 1938–39, 1954–55; Runners-up 1953–54; Division 3 – Runners-up 1980–81; Division 4 – Runners-up 1967–68.
FA Cup: Winners 1912; Runners-up 1910.
Football League Cup: best season: 5th rd, 1982.

First Football League Game: 1 September 1898, Division 2, v Lincoln C (a) L 0–1 – Fawcett; McArtney, Nixon; King, Burleigh, Porteous; Davis, Lees, Murray, McCullough, McGee.
Record League Victory: 9–0 v Loughborough T, Division 2, 28 January 1899 – Greaves; McArtney, Nixon; Porteous, Burleigh, Howard; Davis (4), Hepworth (1), Lees (1), McCullough (1), Jones (2). 9–0 v Accrington S, Division 3 (N), 3 February 1934 – Ellis; Cookson, Shotton; Harper, Henderson, Whitworth; Spence (2), Smith (1), Blight (4), Andrews (1), Ashton (1).
Record Cup Victory: 6–0 v Blackpool, FA Cup 1st rd replay, 20 January 1910 – Mearns; Downs, Ness; Glendinning, Boyle (1), Utley; Bartrop, Gadsby (1), Lillycrop (2), Tufnell (2), Forman. 6–0 v Peterborough U, League Cup 1st rd 2nd leg, 15 September 1981 – Horn; Joyce, Chambers, Glavin (2), Banks, McCarthy, Evans, Parker (2), Aylott (1), McHale, Barrowclough (1).

SKY SPORTS FACT FILE

Before Reuben Courtney Noble-Lazarus became the youngest Football League debutant for Barnsley, the club attempted to play him before he reached the age of 15 in a Carling Cup fixture earlier in the season. An FA age limit prevented such an occurrence.

Record Defeat: 0–9 v Notts Co, Division 2, 19 November 1927.

Most League Points (2 for a win): 67, Division 3 (N), 1938–39.

Most League Points (3 for a win): 82, Division 1, 1999–2000.

Most League Goals: 118, Division 3 (N), 1933–34.

Highest League Scorer in Season: Cecil McCormack, 33, Division 2, 1950–51.

Most League Goals in Total Aggregate: Ernest Hine, 123, 1921–26 and 1934–38.

Most League Goals in One Match: 5, Frank Eaton v South Shields, Division 3 (N), 9 April 1927; 5, Peter Cunningham v Darlington, Division 3 (N), 4 February 1933; 5, Beau Asquith v Darlington, Division 3 (N), 12 November 1938; 5, Cecil McCormack v Luton T, Division 2, 9 September 1950.

Most Capped Player: Gerry Taggart, 35 (50), Northern Ireland.

Most League Appearances: Barry Murphy, 514, 1962–78.

Youngest League Player: Reuben Noble-Lazarus, 15 years 45 days v Ipswich T, 30 September 2008.

Record Transfer Fee Received: £4,500,000 from Blackburn R for Ashley Ward, December 1998.

Record Transfer Fee Paid: £1,500,000 to Partizan Belgrade for Georgi Hristov, July 1997.

Football League Record: 1898 Elected to Division 2; 1932–34 Division 3 (N); 1934–38 Division 2; 1938–39 Division 3 (N); 1946–53 Division 2; 1953–55 Division 3 (N); 1955–59 Division 2; 1959–65 Division 3; 1965–68 Division 4; 1968–72 Division 3; 1972–79 Division 4; 1979–81 Division 3; 1981–92 Division 2; 1992–97 Division 1; 1997–98 FA Premier League; 1998–2002 Division 1; 2002–04 Division 2; 2004–06 FL 1; 2006– FL C.

LATEST SEQUENCES

Longest Sequence of League Wins: 10, 5.3.1955 – 23.4.1955.

Longest Sequence of League Defeats: 9, 14.3.1953 – 25.4.1953.

Longest Sequence of League Draws: 7, 28.3.1911 – 22.4.1911.

Longest Sequence of Unbeaten League Matches: 21, 1.1.1934 – 5.5.1934.

Longest Sequence Without a League Win: 26, 13.12.1952 – 26.8.1953.

Successive Scoring Runs: 44 from 2.10.1926.

Successive Non-scoring Runs: 6 from 7.10.1899.

MANAGERS

Arthur Fairclough 1898–1901
(Secretary-Manager)
John McCartney 1901–04
(Secretary-Manager)
Arthur Fairclough 1904–12
John Hastie 1912–14
Percy Lewis 1914–19
Peter Sant 1919–26
John Commins 1926–29
Arthur Fairclough 1929–30
Brough Fletcher 1930–37
Angus Seed 1937–53
Tim Ward 1953–60
Johnny Steele 1960–71
(continued as General Manager)
John McSeveney 1971–72
Johnny Steele *(General Manager)* 1972–73
Jim Iley 1973–78
Allan Clarke 1978–80
Norman Hunter 1980–84
Bobby Collins 1984–85
Allan Clarke 1985–89
Mel Machin 1989–93
Viv Anderson 1993–94
Danny Wilson 1994–98
John Hendrie 1998–99
Dave Bassett 1999–2000
Nigel Spackman 2001
Steve Parkin 2001–02
Glyn Hodges 2002–03
Gudjon Thordarson 2003–04
Paul Hart 2004–05
Andy Ritchie 2005–06
Simon Davey January 2007–

TEN YEAR LEAGUE RECORD

		P	W	D	L	F	A	Pts	Pos
1999-2000	Div 1	46	24	10	12	88	67	82	4
2000-01	Div 1	46	15	9	22	49	62	54	16
2001-02	Div 1	46	11	15	20	59	86	48	23
2002-03	Div 2	46	13	13	20	51	64	52	19
2003-04	Div 2	46	15	17	14	54	58	62	12
2004-05	FL 1	46	14	19	13	69	64	61	13
2005-06	FL 1	46	18	18	10	62	44	72	5
2006-07	FL C	46	15	5	26	53	85	50	20
2007-08	FL C	46	14	13	19	52	65	55	18
2008-09	FL C	46	13	13	20	45	58	52	20

DID YOU KNOW ?

Little known in the wider football world in 1910 when Barnsley reached the FA Cup final, a gateman at the Crystal Palace ground refused the players entry! Two years later they were better known and winners after a replay, the entire team costing only £200.

BARNSLEY 2008–09 LEAGUE RECORD

Match No.	Date	Venue	Opponents	Result	H/T Score	Lg. Pos.	Goalscorers	Attendance
1	Aug 9	A	QPR	L	1-2	1-2	—	Hume [5]	14,964
2	16	H	Coventry C	L	1-2	1-1	22	Howard [44]	12,987
3	23	A	Birmingham C	L	0-2	0-2	24		17,413
4	30	H	Derby Co	W	2-0	0-0	18	Hume [72], Foster [83]	14,223
5	Sept 13	A	Blackpool	L	0-1	0-0	22		8363
6	16	H	Cardiff C	L	0-1	0-1	—		11,282
7	20	A	Southampton	D	0-0	0-0	24		14,836
8	27	H	Norwich C	D	0-0	0-0	23		12,324
9	30	A	Ipswich T	L	0-3	0-1	—		18,177
10	Oct 4	H	Doncaster R	W	4-1	0-1	22	Foster [54], Campbell-Ryce [60], Macken [73], Hume [87]	15,086
11	18	A	Crystal Palace	L	0-3	0-0	22		16,494
12	21	H	Sheffield W	W	2-1	1-0	—	Hume [4], Campbell-Ryce (pen) [61]	17,784
13	25	H	Bristol C	D	0-0	0-0	21		11,551
14	28	A	Doncaster R	W	1-0	1-0	—	Macken [42]	13,251
15	Nov 1	H	Charlton Ath	W	3-1	3-0	16	Macken 2 [3, 17], Moore [39]	21,527
16	8	H	Sheffield U	L	1-2	0-1	18	Odejayi [87]	19,002
17	15	H	Watford	W	2-1	0-0	15	Mostto [69], Foster [71]	11,285
18	22	A	Preston NE	L	1-2	1-1	17	Campbell-Ryce [33]	12,153
19	24	H	Burnley	W	3-2	1-0	—	Macken [18], Whaley [48], Leon [51]	10,678
20	29	A	Nottingham F	L	0-1	0-1	17		24,974
21	Dec 6	H	Reading	L	0-1	0-0	18		11,938
22	9	A	Swansea C	D	2-2	0-0	—	Macken [49], Campbell-Ryce (pen) [56]	11,442
23	13	A	Wolverhampton W	L	0-2	0-1	19		22,399
24	20	H	Plymouth Arg	W	2-0	1-0	17	Anderson [37], Campbell-Ryce (pen) [90]	10,944
25	26	A	Burnley	W	2-1	1-1	15	Cureton [6], McCann (og) [67]	16,580
26	28	H	Preston NE	D	1-1	1-0	16	Cureton [16]	13,851
27	Jan 10	H	Southampton	L	0-1	0-0	—		11,789
28	17	A	Norwich C	L	0-4	0-0	16		24,685
29	27	H	Ipswich T	L	1-2	0-2	—	Bogdanovic [47]	11,183
30	31	A	Bristol C	L	0-2	0-0	19		15,667
31	Feb 17	A	Sheffield W	W	1-0	1-0	—	Campbell-Ryce [38]	25,820
32	21	H	Charlton Ath	D	0-0	0-0	19		11,668
33	28	H	QPR	W	2-1	2-1	18	Bogdanovic [26], Anderson [43]	11,614
34	Mar 3	A	Cardiff C	L	1-3	0-2	—	Macken [62]	15,902
35	10	H	Birmingham C	D	1-1	0-0	—	Mifsud [82]	11,299
36	14	H	Blackpool	L	0-1	0-0	22		12,228
37	17	A	Crystal Palace	W	3-1	1-1	—	Campbell-Ryce [23], Hills (og) [52], Mifsud [73]	10,885
38	21	A	Derby Co	D	0-0	0-0	19		32,277
39	Apr 4	H	Nottingham F	D	1-1	0-0	20	Campbell-Ryce [46]	19,681
40	7	A	Sheffield U	L	1-2	0-0	—	Bogdanovic [90]	27,061
41	11	A	Watford	D	1-1	0-0	20	Macken [67]	16,052
42	13	H	Swansea C	L	1-3	0-2	21	Bogdanovic (pen) [84]	11,788
43	18	A	Reading	D	0-0	0-0	21		19,420
44	21	C	Coventry C	D	1-1	1-0	—	Bogdanovic [9]	15,035
45	25	H	Wolverhampton W	D	1-1	0-0	21	Macken [58]	18,288
46	May 3	A	Plymouth Arg	W	2-1	1-1	20	Hammill [34], Campbell-Ryce [47]	14,529

Final League Position: 20

GOALSCORERS

League (45): Campbell-Ryce 9 (3 pens), Macken 9, Bogdanovic 5 (1 pen), Hume 4, Foster 3, Anderson 2, Cureton 2, Mifsud 2, Hammill 1, Howard 1, Leon 1, Moore 1, Mostto 1, Odejayi 1, Whaley 1, own goals 2.
Carling Cup (0).
FA Cup (0).

Steele L 10	Devaney M 16 + 10	Hassell B 34 + 6	Foster S 38	Moore D 37 + 1	Howard B 7	El Haimour M 8 + 8	Anderson 33	Hume I 15	Macken J 37 + 8	Van Homoet M 14 + 3	Rigters M 4 + 15	Leon D 15 + 4	Odejayi K 7 + 21	Souza D 32 + 1	Teale G 2 + 1	Mostto M 2 + 7	Kozluk R 36 + 1	Colace R 30 + 4	Campbell-Ryce J 39 + 1	Muller H 36	Noble-Lazarus R — + 2	Whaley S 4	Coulson M — + 2	Cureton J 7 + 1	Butterfield J — + 3	Bogdanovic D 13 + 3	Teimourian A 10 + 1	Hammill A 9 + 5	Mifsud M 11 + 4	Match No.
1	2	3[2]	4	5	6	7[1]	8	9	10[3]	11[1]	12	13	14																	1
1	11	3[1]	4	5	6			9[4]	10			13	8	12	2	7[2]														2
1	11[2]	3[1]	4	5	6	9			10				8	12	2	7	13													3
1	11	13	4	5	6	7[1]		9	10[3]				8[2]	12	2		14	3												4
1	7		4	5	6	11[3]		9[1]	10[2]					12	2	14	13	3	8											5
1			4	5	6			9[1]	10		12	11			2		3	8	7											6
	12	13	4	5	6		11[2]	9	14			10[3]			2		3	8	7[1]	1										7
	12			6	5		8	9	10[2]	11		13			2		3	4[1]	7	1										8
11[3]	12		4	5		6[1]		9	10[2]			13	8		2		3		7	1	14									9
11	12		4	5[2]	6			9[3]				13	10[2]	8[1]	2		3		7	1	14									10
11	5[1]		4			6		9	13		12	10[3]	8[2]		14	2	3		7	1										11
11			4	5		8	9[1]	10[2]	12			13			2		3	6	7	1										12
11[1]			4	5		8	9	10[2]	12			13			2		3	6	7	1										13
11[1]			4	5		8	9[2]	10[3]			13		2		14		3	6	7	1										14
11[1]			4	5		8	9[2]	10[3]	12			13			14		3	6	7	1										15
11	4[3]		5			8[4]	9[2]			12	14		2		13		3	6[1]	7	1	10									16
	12	4	5[1]		6[3]			10	13			11[2]	9	2		14	3	8	7	1										17
12	5	4						10			11[2]	9		8[1]			3	6	7	1		13								18
11[1]	5	4					10	13	12[2]	9[3]			2				3	6	7	1		8	14							19
	5	4			8		10		12	9[1]			2				3	6	7	1			11[2]	13						20
	5	4	12		8		10[2]	3[1]	13				14				6		7	1			11[3]	9						21
	5	4	6				10	3		12			2	8			11		7	1			9[1]							22
	5	4		8			10	3	12	11[1]			2[2]				13	6	7	1			9							23
	6	4	5	12	8		10[3]		2	13	11		14				3		7[1]	1			9[2]							24
	6	4	5		8		10[1]	2	12		11[2]		14				3	13	7	1			9[3]							25
	6	4	5	14	8		10[1]	2	12		11[3]						3[2]	13	7	1			9							26
	6	4	5		8[2]		10	3		11[1]	12			2					7	1			9	13						27
		4	5		8		10	6		9[1]	11[2]	12	2				3		7	1			13							28
11[1]	6		5	4			10	3		12	8[3]	13							7	1		14	9[2]							29
11	4		5		8		10	6		9			2				3		7	1										30
	2	4	5		8		12	3		11									7	1						9[1]	6[2]	13	10	31
	2	4	5		8[2]		12	3		11									7	1						9[1]	6	13	10	32
12	5	4		8			13	2		3							7			1						9[2]	6	11[1]	10	33
	5	4	12		13		14	2[1]		3		8							7	1						9[2]	6[4]	11[3]	10	34
	4	5	12				10[2]	6[1]		2		3		8					7	1						9		13	11	35
12	4		5	6			13	2		3			8[1]						7	1						9[2]		11	10	36
12	2	4	5	13	8		10[5]			3							6		7	1						14		11[1]	9[2]	37
12	2	4	5	14	8[2]		10			13							3[3]	11	7	1						6[1]			9	38
13	2	4	5		8		10										3	11	7[2]	1						12	6		9[1]	39
	2	4	5		8		10										3	11[2]	7	1						13	6	12	9[1]	40
	2	4	5		8		10[5]	13									3	14	7	1						9[1]	6	12	11[2]	41
13	2	4	5		8		10[3]										3	12	7[1]	1						9	6[2]	11	14	42
1	2	4	5		8		10[3]			14							3		7	13						9[1]	6	11[3]	12	43
1	6		5	12	4		10			13			2[1]				3	8	7							9[2]		11		44
1	6		5		4		10						2				3	8	7							9[2]	12	11[1]	13	45
1	13	2	4	5	14		8		10[1]								3	6	7							9[3]		11[2]	12	46

FA Cup
Third Round   West Ham U   (a)   0-3

Carling Cup
First Round   Crewe Alex   (a)   0-2

BIRMINGHAM CITY

FA Premiership

FOUNDATION

In 1875, cricketing enthusiasts who were largely members of Trinity Church, Bordesley, determined to continue their sporting relationships throughout the year by forming a football club which they called Small Heath Alliance. For their earliest games played on waste land in Arthur Street, the team included three Edden brothers and two James brothers.

St Andrews Stadium, Birmingham B9 4NH.
Telephone: 0844 557 1875.
Fax: 0844 557 1975.
Ticket Office: (0844) 557 1875 (then option 2).
Website: www.bcfc.com
Email: reception@bcfc.com
Ground Capacity: 30,079.
Record Attendance: 66,844 v Everton, FA Cup 5th rd, 11 February 1939.
Pitch Measurements: 101m × 68m.
Chairman: David Sullivan (PLC), David Gold (FC).
Vice-chairman: Jack Wiseman.
Managing Director: Karren Brady.
Secretary: Julia Shelton.
Manager: Alex McLeish.
First Team Coaches: Roy Aitken, Andy Watson.
Physio: Tim Williamson.
Colours: Blue shirts with white trim, blue shorts, white stockings.
Change Colours: White shirts with a broad red vertical panel, white shorts, red stockings.
Year Formed: 1875.
Turned Professional: 1885.
Ltd Co.: 1888.
Previous Names: 1875, Small Heath Alliance; 1888, dropped 'Alliance'; 1905, Birmingham; 1945, Birmingham City.
Club Nickname: 'Blues'.
Grounds: 1875, waste ground near Arthur St; 1877, Muntz St, Small Heath; 1906, St Andrews.
First Football League game: 3 September 1892, Division 2, v Burslem Port Vale (h) W 5–1 – Charsley; Bayley, Speller; Ollis, Jenkyns, Devey; Hallam (1), Edwards (1), Short (1), Wheldon (2), Hands.
Record League Victory: 12–0 v Walsall T Swifts, Division 2, 17 December 1892 – Charsley; Bayley, Jones; Ollis, Jenkyns, Devey; Hallam (2), Walton (3), Mobley (3), Wheldon (2), Hands (2). 12–0 v Doncaster R, Division 2, 11 April 1903 – Dorrington; Goldie, Wassell; Beer, Dougherty (1), Howard; Athersmith (1), Leonard (3), McRoberts (1), Wilcox (4), Field (1). Aston, (1 og).

HONOURS

Football League: FL C – Runners-up 2006–07, 2008–09; Division 2 – Champions 1892–93, 1920–21, 1947–48, 1954–55, 1994–95; Runners-up 1893–94, 1900–01, 1902–03, 1971–72, 1984–85; Division 3 Runners-up 1991–92.
FA Cup: Runners-up 1931, 1956.
Football League Cup: Winners 1963; Runners-up 2001.
Leyland Daf Cup: Winners 1991.
Auto Windscreens Shield: Winners 1995.
European Competitions: European Fairs Cup: 1955–58, 1958–60 (runners-up), 1960–61 (runners-up), 1961–62.

SKY SPORTS FACT FILE

The Birmingham City team when still known as Small Heath were particularly harsh on Burton Wanderers in early FA Cup matches. In 1885–86 they beat them 9–2 with Eddie Stanley scoring four goals and in 1888–89 it was 9–0 with the Devey brothers Ted and Will each scoring four times.

Record Cup Victory: 9–2 v Burton W, FA Cup 1st rd,
31 October 1885 – Hedges; Jones, Evetts (1); F. James,
Felton, A. James (1); Davenport (2), Stanley (4), Simms,
Figures, Morris (1).

Record Defeat: 1–9 v Sheffield W, Division 1, 13 December
1930. 1–9 v Blackburn R, Division 1, 5 January 1895.

Most League Points (2 for a win): 59, Division 2, 1947–48.

Most League Points (3 for a win): 89, Division 2, 1994–95.

Most League Goals: 103, Division 2, 1893–94 (only 28 games).

Highest League Scorer in Season: Joe Bradford, 29,
Division 1, 1927–28.

Most League Goals in Total Aggregate: Joe Bradford, 249,
1920–35.

Most League Goals in One Match: 5, Walter Abbott v
Darwen, Division 2, 26 November, 1898; 5, John McMillan v
Blackpool, Division 2, 2 March 1901; 5, James Windridge v
Glossop, Division 2, 23 January 1915.

Most Capped Player: Kenny Cunningham, 32 (72),
Republic of Ireland.

Most League Appearances: Frank Womack, 491, 1908–28.

Youngest League Player: Trevor Francis, 16 years 7 months
v Cardiff C, 5 September 1970.

Record Transfer Fee Received: £6,800,000 from Liverpool
for Jermaine Pennant, July 2006.

Record Transfer Fee Paid: £5,875,000 to Liverpool for
Emile Heskey, July 2004.

Football League Record: 1892 Elected to Division 2;
1894–96 Division 1; 1896–1901 Division 2; 1901–02
Division 1; 1902–03 Division 2; 1903–08 Division 1; 1908–21
Division 2; 1921–39 Division 1; 1946–48 Division 2; 1948–50
Division 1; 1950–55 Division 2; 1955–65 Division 1; 1965–72
Division 2; 1972–79 Division 1; 1979–80 Division 2; 1980–84
Division 1; 1984–85 Division 2; 1985–86 Division 1; 1986–89
Division 2; 1989–92 Division 3; 1992–94 Division 1; 1994–95 Division 2; 1995–2002 Division 1; 2002–06
FA Premier League; 2006–07 FL C; 2007–08 FA Premier League; 2008–09 FL C; 2009– FA Premier
League.

MANAGERS
Alfred Jones 1892–1908
(Secretary-Manager)
Alec Watson 1908–10
Bob McRoberts 1910–15
Frank Richards 1915–23
Billy Beer 1923–27
William Harvey 1927–28
Leslie Knighton 1928–33
George Liddell 1933–39
Harry Storer 1945–48
Bob Brocklebank 1949–54
Arthur Turner 1954–58
Pat Beasley 1959–60
Gil Merrick 1960–64
Joe Mallett 1965
Stan Cullis 1965–70
Fred Goodwin 1970–75
Willie Bell 1975–77
Sir Alf Ramsay 1977–78
Jim Smith 1978–82
Ron Saunders 1982–86
John Bond 1986–87
Garry Pendrey 1987–89
Dave Mackay 1989–91
Lou Macari 1991
Terry Cooper 1991–93
Barry Fry 1993–96
Trevor Francis 1996–2001
Steve Bruce 2001–07
Alex McLeish November 2007–

LATEST SEQUENCES

Longest Sequence of League Wins: 13, 17.12.1892 – 16.9.1893.

Longest Sequence of League Defeats: 8, 28.9.1985 – 23.11.1985.

Longest Sequence of League Draws: 8, 18.9.1990 – 23.10.1990.

Longest Sequence of Unbeaten League Matches: 20, 3.9.1994 – 2.1.1995.

Longest Sequence Without a League Win: 17, 28.9.1985 – 18.1.1986.

Successive Scoring Runs: 24 from 24.9.1892.

Successive Non-scoring Runs: 6 from 1.10.1949.

TEN YEAR LEAGUE RECORD

		P	W	D	L	F	A	Pts	Pos
1999-2000	Div 1	46	22	11	13	65	44	77	5
2000-01	Div 1	46	23	9	14	59	48	78	5
2001-02	Div 1	46	21	13	12	70	49	76	5
2002-03	PR Lge	38	13	9	16	41	49	48	13
2003-04	PR Lge	38	12	14	12	43	48	50	10
2004-05	PR Lge	38	11	12	15	40	46	45	12
2005-06	PR Lge	38	8	10	20	28	50	34	18
2006-07	FL C	46	26	8	12	67	42	86	2
2007-08	PR Lge	38	8	11	19	46	62	35	19
2008-09	FL C	46	23	14	9	54	37	83	2

DID YOU KNOW ?

The oft-made remark that a
good start compensates for a
subsequent slump was born
out for Birmingham in
1900–01 when they were
unbeaten in their opening 15
League games. Despite losing
three of their last five
matches they won promotion
from Division 2.

BIRMINGHAM CITY 2008–09 LEAGUE RECORD

Match No.	Date	Venue	Opponents	Result	H/T Score	Lg. Pos.	Goalscorers	Attendance
1	Aug 9	H	Sheffield U	W 1-0	0-0	—	Phillips 90	24,019
2	16	A	Southampton	W 2-1	0-1	3	O'Connor 49, Phillips 77	18,925
3	23	H	Barnsley	W 2-0	2-0	1	Phillips 13, O'Connor 45	17,413
4	30	A	Norwich C	D 1-1	1-0	3	Larsson 40	24,229
5	Sept13	H	Doncaster R	W 1-0	0-0	2	Jerome 46	18,165
6	16	A	Bristol C	W 2-1	2-0	—	Carey (og) 8, Jerome 24	18,456
7	20	H	Blackpool	L 0-1	0-0	2		20,983
8	27	A	Cardiff C	W 2-1	2-0	2	McFadden 5, Owusu-Abeyie 41	18,304
9	30	A	Derby Co	D 1-1	1-0	—	Owusu-Abeyie 26	29,743
10	Oct 4	H	QPR	W 1-0	1-0	1	Phillips 45	18,498
11	18	A	Burnley	D 1-1	0-1	2	Jerome 77	13,809
12	21	H	Crystal Palace	W 1-0	0-0	—	O'Connor 90	17,706
13	25	H	Sheffield W	W 3-1	3-1	1	O'Connor 2 11, 15, Phillips 38	17,300
14	28	A	QPR	L 0-1	0-0	—		13,594
15	Nov 3	H	Coventry C	L 0-1	0-0	—		17,215
16	8	A	Nottingham F	D 1-1	1-0	2	McFadden 13	21,415
17	15	H	Charlton Ath	W 3-2	1-2	2	McFadden 13, Phillips 50, Queudrue 55	20,071
18	21	A	Swansea C	W 3-2	1-2	—	Bent 42, Phillips 2 74, 79	16,956
19	25	A	Ipswich T	W 2-1	2-0	—	Ridgewell 9, Phillips 14	15,689
20	29	A	Wolverhampton W	D 1-1	0-0	2	Jerome 48	26,329
21	Dec 6	H	Watford	W 3-2	2-1	2	Phillips 8, Bent 18, Jerome 85	18,174
22	9	A	Plymouth Arg	W 1-0	0-0	—	Carsley 62	10,446
23	13	A	Preston NE	L 0-1	0-0	2		10,943
24	20	H	Reading	L 1-3	0-1	3	Phillips 60	19,895
25	26	A	Ipswich T	W 1-0	1-0	3	McFadden (pen) 39	23,536
26	28	H	Swansea C	D 0-0	0-0	3		21,836
27	Jan 17	H	Cardiff C	D 1-1	0-0	3	Bowyer 90	19,853
28	24	A	Blackpool	L 0-2	0-2	—		8105
29	27	H	Derby Co	W 1-0	0-0	—	Carsley 59	15,330
30	31	A	Sheffield W	D 1-1	0-0	3	Phillips 90	18,409
31	Feb 7	H	Burnley	D 1-1	1-1	3	Phillips 37	16,763
32	14	H	Nottingham F	W 2-0	0-0	2	Bent 62, Fahey 75	17,631
33	21	A	Coventry C	L 0-1	0-1	2		22,637
34	24	A	Crystal Palace	D 0-0	0-0	—		12,847
35	Mar 1	A	Sheffield U	L 1-2	0-1	2	Morgan (og) 74	24,232
36	4	H	Bristol C	W 1-0	0-0	—	Queudrue 87	17,551
37	7	H	Southampton	W 1-0	1-0	2	Fahey 45	16,735
38	10	A	Barnsley	D 1-1	0-0	—	Martin Taylor 86	11,299
39	14	A	Doncaster R	W 2-0	2-0	2	Jerome 19, Bouazza 42	11,482
40	21	H	Norwich C	D 1-1	1-0	2	Jerome 38	18,159
41	Apr 6	H	Wolverhampton W	W 2-0	1-0	—	Jerome 45, O'Connor 69	25,935
42	11	A	Charlton Ath	D 0-0	0-0	2		20,022
43	13	H	Plymouth Arg	D 1-1	0-1	2	Queudrue 50	19,323
44	18	A	Watford	W 1-0	0-0	2	Jerome 73	16,180
45	25	H	Preston NE	L 1-2	0-0	2	Fahey 57	24,825
46	May 3	A	Reading	W 2-1	1-0	2	Fahey 19, Phillips 60	24,011

Final League Position: 2

GOALSCORERS

League (54): Phillips 14, Jerome 9, O'Connor 6, Fahey 4, McFadden 4 (1 pen), Bent 3, Queudrue 3, Carsley 2, Owusu-Abeyie 2, Bouazza 1, Bowyer 1, Larsson 1, Ridgewell 1, Martin Taylor 1, own goals 2.
Carling Cup (4): Jerome 1, Nafti 1, O'Connor 1, Owusu-Abeyie 1.
FA Cup (0).

	Taylor Maik 45	Parnaby S 19+2	Murphy D 28+2	Carsley L 41	Taylor Martin 23+1	Ridgewell L 36	Larsson S 35+3	Nafti M 6+5	Bent M 16+17	McFadden J 22+8	McSheffrey G 3+3	Phillips K 24+12	O'Connor G 10+6	Jerome C 25+18	Owusu-Abeyie O 12+7	Kelly S 2+3	Agustien K 13+5	Jaidi R 30	Queudrue F 23+2	Quashie N 8+2	Wilson J —+1	Hunt N 9+2	Johnson D 8+1	Fahey K 15+4	Sinclair S 8+6	Bowyer L 17	Bouazza H 9+7	Costly C 3+5	Carr S 13	De la Cruz U —+1	Doyle C 1+1	Traore D 2+1	Match No.
1	1	2	3	4	5	6	7^3	8	9^2	10	11^1	12	13	14																			1
2	1	2	3	4	5	6	7	8^1	13	10	14	11^2	12	9^3																			2
3	1	2^1	3	4	5	6	7		14	8	13	9^2	10^3		11	12																	3
4	1	2	3	4	5	6	7		13	10	12	9			11^2		8^1																4
5	1	2	3	4	5	6	7	8^8	12	13		9^1		10^3	11^2	14																	5
6	1	2^2	3	4^1	5	6	7		12	10	11			9	14	13	8^3																6
7	1		3^3	4	5	6	7		12	10	11^2	13		9	14	2	8^1																7
8	1	2	3	4		6	7		12	10^1		13	14	9^3	11^2	8	5																8
9	1	2	3	4		6	7		12	10^2		14	13	9^1	11^3	8	5																9
10	1	2	3	4^1		6	7		12		13	9^3	10	14	11^2	8	5																10
11	1	2	3^1	4	5	6	7		12			10	11	9^1		8^1				14													11
12	1	2		4	5	6	7		12			10	11	9^1			8^2		3	13													12
13	1	2		4	5	6	7^1		12		13	14	10^2	11	9^3		8		3														13
14	1	2^3		4	5	6		8^2	12	11	10	9^1	13	7					3			14											14
15	1			4		6	7		12	11	10^1	9^2	13				8^3	5	3	14		2											15
16	1			4	5	3	7		9	10		12		13			8^2	6	11^1			2											16
17	1			4		6	7		12		13	9^3	11	10^2	14		8^8	5	3^1			2											17
18	1			4		6	7	8^2	9	10^3	12	14	11^1	13				5	3			2											18
19	1	12		4^2		6	7		13	9	11	10	14				8^3	5	3^1			2											19
20	1	11		4		6	7		12	9^3		10^2	13	14			8	5	3			2^1											20
21	1	12		4	5		7^3		9^2	10	13	11	14				8	6	3^1			2											21
22	1	7		4	5				10	9^1	12	11	13				8	6	3^2			2											22
23	1	12	11	4		6			10^2	9	13	7^3	14				8	5	3^1			2											23
24	1	2	3	4			7^1		12	11^2	10	9	13				8	6	5														24
25	1	2	3	4		11			12	10^1	9	8					5^2	6					13	7									25
26	1	2	11	4		6			9^1	8	10^2	12	13				3^3	5					14	7									26
27	1		3	4^3		6			12	13	10	9		2^2			5								14	7^1	8	11					27
28	1	2^2		4		6	7		12	13		9					5	3^3							14	11^1	8	10					28
29	1		3	4	5	6	2		10^1	9^2		12					5								11	13	8	7					29
30	1	2^1	3	4^3	5	6			12	13		9	10^2				5								14	11	8	7					30
31	1		3	4	5	6	2		9	10^1		12					6	3							11	13	8	7^2					31
32	1		3	4	5	6	2		10^3	9^1		12					6	6^3							14	11	8	7^2	13			14	32
33	1		3	4^1	5	6	2		10	9^2		11					6	3							11	7	8	12	13				33
34	1		3			6	7^3		10		12					5							14	4	11^2	8	13	9^1	2				34
35	1		3		4	5			10	12		13					6	5						8	7^1	11	9^2	2					35
36	1				4	5	7		10^1	9^2							6	3						11	13	8	12	2					36
37	1				4	5	7		10^1	9^3							6	3						11^2	13	8	14	12	2				37
38	1				4	5	7		9								6	3					8^2	11	13		12	10^1	2				38
39	1				4	6	7		12	9^1							5	3^3						11	13	8	10^2	2	14				39
40	1	12		4		6	7		13	10^2		9					5	3^1						14	8	11^3	2						40
41	1	3		4^8		6	7^3		12	9^1		13	10^2				5							11	8	14	2						41
42	1	3				6	7^1		13	14		12	10^2				5	4						11	8	9^3	2						42
43	1^8	3				6^1	7		13	10		9^2					5	12						4	11^6	8		2	15				43
44			3				7^1		9	12		10^2	13				5	6^3						4	11	8		2		1	14		44
45	1						7^1		9	13		10^2	12				5	6						4	11	8^8		2				3	45
46	1			4	5		12		8^1	9^2	14	10^3					6	7						11	13			2				3	46

FA Cup

Third Round   Wolverhampton W   (h)   0-2

Carling Cup

First Round   Wycombe W   (a)   4-0

Second Round   Southampton   (a)   0-2

BLACKBURN ROVERS   FA Premiership

FOUNDATION

It was in 1875 that some Public School old boys called a meeting at which the Blackburn Rovers club was formed and the colours blue and white adopted. The leading light was John Lewis, later to become a founder of the Lancashire FA, a famous referee who was in charge of two FA Cup Finals, and a vice-president of both the FA and the Football League.

Ewood Park, Blackburn BB2 4JF.

Telephone: 0871 702 1875.

Fax: (01254) 671 042.

Ticket Office: 0871 222 1444.

Website: www.rovers.co.uk

Email: enquiries@rovers.co.uk

Ground Capacity: 31,367.

Record Attendance: 62,522 v Bolton W, FA Cup 6th rd, 2 March 1929.

Pitch Measurements: 105m × 65.8m.

Chairman: John Williams.

Vice-chairman: David Brown.

Managing Director: Tom Finn.

Secretary: Andrew Pincher.

Manager: Sam Allardyce.

Assistant Manager: Neil McDonald.

Physio: Dave Fevre.

Colours: Blue and white halved shirts, white shorts, white stockings.

Change Colours: Black shirts with one white vertical stripe, blue trim, black shorts, black stockings.

Year Formed: 1875.

Turned Professional: 1880.

Ltd Co.: 1897.

Club Nickname: Rovers.

Grounds: 1875, all matches played away; 1876, Oozehead Ground; 1877, Pleasington Cricket Ground; 1878, Alexandra Meadows; 1881, Leamington Road; 1890, Ewood Park.

First Football League Game: 15 September 1888, Football League, v Accrington (h) D 5–5 – Arthur; Beverley, James Southworth; Douglas, Almond, Forrest; Beresford (1), Walton, John Southworth (1), Fecitt (1), Townley (2).

Record League Victory: 9–0 v Middlesbrough, Division 2, 6 November 1954 – Elvy; Suart, Eckersley; Clayton, Kelly, Bell; Mooney (3), Crossan (2), Briggs, Quigley (3), Langton (1).

HONOURS

FA Premier League: Champions 1994–95; Runners-up 1993–94.

Football League: Division 1 – Champions 1911–12, 1913–14; Runners-up 2000–01; Division 2 – Champions 1938–39; Runners-up 1957–58; Division 3 – Champions 1974–75; Runners-up 1979–80.

FA Cup: Winners 1884, 1885, 1886, 1890, 1891, 1928; Runners-up 1882, 1960.

Football League Cup: Winners 2002.

Full Members' Cup: Winners 1987.

European Competitions: European Cup: 1995–96. UEFA Cup: 1994–95, 1998–99, 2002–03, 2003–04, 2006–07, 2007–08. Intertoto Cup: 2007.

SKY SPORTS FACT FILE

In 1935–36 Blackburn Rovers were forced to call upon the services of five different goalkeepers in a run of only nine games, chiefly because of injury: Cliff Binns (broken fibula), Jack Hughes (back), Jim Barron (wrist), then amateurs Kevin Hamill and John Pratt.

Record Cup Victory: 11–0 v Rossendale, FA Cup 1st rd, 13 October 1884 – Arthur; Hopwood, McIntyre; Forrest, Blenkhorn, Lofthouse; Sowerbutts (2), J. Brown (1), Fecitt (4), Barton (3), Birtwistle (1).

Record Defeat: 0–8 v Arsenal, Division 1, 25 February 1933.

Most League Points (2 for a win): 60, Division 3, 1974–75.

Most League Points (3 for a win): 91, Division 1, 2000–01.

Most League Goals: 114, Division 2, 1954–55.

Highest League Scorer in Season: Ted Harper, 43, Division 1, 1925–26.

Most League Goals in Total Aggregate: Simon Garner, 168, 1978–92.

Most League Goals in One Match: 7, Tommy Briggs v Bristol R, Division 2, 5 February 1955.

Most Capped Player: Henning Berg, 58 (100), Norway.

Most League Appearances: Derek Fazackerley, 596, 1970–86.

Youngest League Player: Harry Dennison, 16 years 155 days v Bristol C, 8 April 1911.

Record Transfer Fee Received: £17,000,000 from Tottenham H for David Bentley, July 2008.

Record Transfer Fee Paid: £7,500,000 to Manchester U for Andy Cole, December 2001.

Football League Record: 1888 Founder Member of the League; 1936–39 Division 2; 1946–48 Division 1; 1948–58 Division 2; 1958–66 Division 1; 1966–71 Division 2; 1971–75 Division 3; 1975–79 Division 2; 1979–80 Division 3; 1980–92 Division 2; 1992–99 FA Premier League; 1999–2001 Division 1; 2001– FA Premier League.

LATEST SEQUENCES

Longest Sequence of League Wins: 8, 1.3.1980 – 7.4.1980.

Longest Sequence of League Defeats: 7, 12.3.1966 – 16.4.1966.

Longest Sequence of League Draws: 5, 11.10.1975 – 1.11.1975.

Longest Sequence of Unbeaten League Matches: 23, 30.9.1987 – 27.3.1988.

Longest Sequence Without a League Win: 16, 11.11.1978 – 24.3.1979.

Successive Scoring Runs: 32 from 24.4.1954.

Successive Non-scoring Runs: 4 from 12.12.1908.

MANAGERS

Thomas Mitchell 1884–96
(Secretary-Manager)
J. Walmsley 1896–1903
(Secretary-Manager)
R. B. Middleton 1903–25
Jack Carr 1922–26
(Team Manager under Middleton to 1925)
Bob Crompton 1926–30
(Hon. Team Manager)
Arthur Barritt 1931–36
(had been Secretary from 1927)
Reg Taylor 1936–38
Bob Crompton 1938–41
Eddie Hapgood 1944–47
Will Scott 1947
Jack Bruton 1947–49
Jackie Bestall 1949–53
Johnny Carey 1953–58
Dally Duncan 1958–60
Jack Marshall 1960–67
Eddie Quigley 1967–70
Johnny Carey 1970–71
Ken Furphy 1971–73
Gordon Lee 1974–75
Jim Smith 1975–78
Jim Iley 1978
John Pickering 1978–79
Howard Kendall 1979–81
Bobby Saxton 1981–86
Don Mackay 1987–91
Kenny Dalglish 1991–95
Ray Harford 1995–97
Roy Hodgson 1997–98
Brian Kidd 1998–99
Tony Parkes 1999–2000
Graeme Souness 2000–04
Mark Hughes 2004–08
Paul Ince 2008
Sam Allardyce December 2008–

TEN YEAR LEAGUE RECORD

		P	W	D	L	F	A	Pts	Pos
1999-2000	Div 1	46	15	17	14	55	51	62	11
2000-01	Div 1	46	26	13	7	76	39	91	2
2001-02	PR Lge	38	12	10	16	55	51	46	10
2002-03	PR Lge	38	16	12	10	52	43	60	6
2003-04	PR Lge	38	12	8	18	51	59	44	15
2004-05	PR Lge	38	9	15	14	32	43	42	15
2005-06	PR Lge	38	19	6	13	51	42	63	6
2006-07	PR Lge	38	15	7	16	52	54	52	10
2007-08	PR Lge	38	15	13	10	50	48	58	7
2008-09	PR Lge	38	10	11	17	40	60	41	15

DID YOU KNOW ?

Jimmy Forrest was a man of some stature on and off the field. Five FA Cup final appearances for Blackburn Rovers in the 1880s as a wing-half and the first recognised professional footballer to be fully capped by England making a dozen appearances.

BLACKBURN ROVERS 2008–09 LEAGUE RECORD

Match No.	Date	Venue	Opponents	Result		H/T Score	Lg. Pos.	Goalscorers	Attendance
1	Aug 16	A	Everton	W	3-2	1-1	—	Dunn [22], Santa Cruz [66], Ooijer [90]	38,675
2	23	H	Hull C	D	1-1	1-1	3	Roberts [38]	23,439
3	30	A	West Ham U	L	1-4	1-2	10	Roberts [22]	32,905
4	Sept 13	H	Arsenal	L	0-4	0-2	18		23,041
5	20	H	Fulham	W	1-0	0-0	10	Derbyshire [84]	19,398
6	27	A	Newcastle U	W	2-1	2-0	7	Samba [31], Santa Cruz [41]	44,935
7	Oct 4	H	Manchester U	L	0-2	0-1	10		27,321
8	18	A	Bolton W	D	0-0	0-0	9		24,778
9	25	H	Middlesbrough	D	1-1	0-0	11	McCarthy [90]	17,606
10	29	A	Aston Villa	L	2-3	1-1	—	Warnock [30], Emerton [90]	35,985
11	Nov 1	A	WBA	D	2-2	1-0	13	McCarthy (pen) [13], Andrews [89]	24,976
12	9	H	Chelsea	L	0-2	0-1	15		20,670
13	15	H	Sunderland	L	1-2	1-0	18	Samba [45]	21,798
14	23	A	Tottenham H	L	0-1	0-1	19		35,903
15	30	A	Portsmouth	L	2-3	0-0	19	Derbyshire [62], Tugay [67]	18,111
16	Dec 6	H	Liverpool	L	1-3	0-0	19	Santa Cruz [86]	26,920
17	13	A	Wigan Ath	L	0-3	0-2	19		18,003
18	20	H	Stoke C	W	3-0	3-0	19	McCarthy 2 (1 pen) [9 (pl, 27)], Roberts [18]	23,004
19	26	A	Sunderland	D	0-0	0-0	19		44,680
20	28	H	Manchester C	D	2-2	1-0	19	McCarthy [45], Roberts [84]	25,200
21	Jan 17	H	Newcastle U	W	3-0	0-0	17	McCarthy (pen) [61], Roberts 2 [66, 86]	25,583
22	28	H	Bolton W	D	2-2	0-2	—	Warnock [66], McCarthy [87]	25,205
23	31	A	Middlesbrough	D	0-0	0-0	18		24,303
24	Feb 7	H	Aston Villa	L	0-2	0-1	18		24,267
25	21	A	Manchester U	L	1-2	1-1	18	Santa Cruz [32]	75,000
26	Mar 1	A	Hull C	W	2-1	2-0	17	Warnock [34], Andrews [37]	24,612
27	4	H	Everton	D	0-0	0-0	—		21,445
28	11	A	Fulham	W	2-1	0-0	—	Diouf [69], Roberts [85]	22,259
29	14	A	Arsenal	L	0-4	0-1	15		60,091
30	21	H	West Ham U	D	1-1	0-1	17	Andrews [51]	21,672
31	Apr 4	H	Tottenham H	W	2-1	0-1	14	McCarthy [82], Ooijer [89]	21,891
32	11	A	Liverpool	L	0-4	0-2	16		43,466
33	18	A	Stoke C	L	0-1	0-0	17		27,500
34	26	H	Wigan Ath	W	2-0	1-0	15	McCarthy [45], Nelsen [60]	25,019
35	May 2	A	Manchester C	L	1-3	0-3	15	Andrews [66]	43,967
36	9	H	Portsmouth	W	2-0	1-0	14	Pedersen [31], McCarthy (pen) [58]	24,234
37	17	A	Chelsea	L	0-2	0-1	14		40,804
38	24	H	WBA	D	0-0	0-0	15		28,389

Final League Position: 15

GOALSCORERS

League (40): McCarthy 10 (4 pens), Roberts 7, Andrews 4, Santa Cruz 4, Warnock 3, Derbyshire 2, Ooijer 2, Samba 2, Diouf 1, Dunn 1, Emerton 1, Nelsen 1, Pedersen 1, Tugay 1.
Carling Cup (10): Derbyshire 3, McCarthy 2, Emerton 1, Olsson 1, Santa Cruz 1, Villaneuva 1, own goal 1.
FA Cup (5): McCarthy 1, Mokoena 1, Samba 1, Santa Cruz 1, Villaneuva 1.

Robinson P 35	Ooijer A 30 + 2	Warnock S 37	Mokoena A 9 + 9	Nelsen R 35	Samba C 35	Reid S 4	Dunn D 7 + 8	Santa Cruz R 17 + 3	Roberts J 20 + 6	Pedersen M 32 + 1	McCarthy B 18 + 10	Tugay K 15 + 14	Treacy K 2 + 10	Emerton B 19 + 1	Grella V 15 + 2	Andrews K 27 + 6	Derbyshire M 5 + 12	Simpson D 10 + 2	Villanueva C 6 + 7	Brown J 3 + 1	Olsson M 6 + 3	Fowler R 1 + 2	Khizanishvili Z 3 + 2	Vogel J — + 1	Diouf E 13 + 1	Givet G 14	Doran A — + 3	Match No.
1	2	3	4	5	6	7	8^2	9	10^1	11^3	12	13	14															1
1	2	3	4^1	5	6	7	8^2	9	10^3	11	14	12		13														2
1	2	3		5	6	8		9^2	10	11^1		12		7		4^3	14	13										3
1		3		5	6	8		9	10^1	11^3	12		14	7		4	13	2^2										4
1		3		5	6			9	10^3	11^{11}		12	8^2	7		4	13	2	14									5
	12	3		5	6		9^2	13		4		7		11^1	2	10^3	1	8	14									6
	2	8		5	6		9^1	12	11^3		4^2	14		7	13	10	1	3										7
1	3	11		5	6			10^1		12	4	7		13	14	2	8^3		9^2									8
1	6	11		5			9		12		13	7	4		10^1	2	8	3^2										9
1	2	3^1		5	6		11^3	10^2	12		7		4	13	8	9		14										10
	11			5	6		9	12	10^4	13		7^3	8	4		2^2		3^1		14								11
1		11	12	5			9^3	10			7^1	4^2	13	2	8		3	14	6									12
1	2	3	4		6		9	10^1	11^3		14		8^2	12	7	13			5									13
1	2		4	5	6		9		11^2	10^3		13	7^1	8	12	14		3^8										14
1	2	3		5	6		9		11^2	10^1	4		7	8	12	13												15
1	2	3		5	6		9		11^1	12	4^3	13	7	8	10^2				14									16
1	2	3		5	6	12	9	13	11^1		4^2	14	7	8^3	10													17
1	2	3		5	6	8^1		10	11	9^2	12		7^3	4	13	14												18
1	2	3	12	5^1	6	8^2		10	11	9^3	13		7	4	14													19
1	2	3	12	5	6		10	11	9^2	4^1	7	8	13															20
1	2	3		5	6^1	12	13	10	11	9^2	4^3	7	14	8														21
1	2^1	3	13	5	6		12	10	11^3	9	14	7	8^2	4														22
1	2	3		5	6	12	9	13	11	10^2	14	7^1	8	4^3														23
1	2	3		5	6	8^3	12	10^1	11	9	13	7	4^2										14					24
1	2	3		5		8^2	9		11	12	13	14	7^1	4											10^3	6		25
1^6	2	11	13	5	6		9^1	12	10^4		7	4			15										8^2	3		26
	2	11	13	5	6		9	10		12	14	7^1	4		1										8^3	3^2		27
1	2	11	12	5	6	14	9	10^3	13	4^1	7^2	8													8	3		28
1	2	11^3	4		6	13	9	10	12		7		14		5^1	8									8	3^2		29
1	2^1	11	4	5	6		9	7	10	12															8	3		30
1	13	3	4^3	5	7	12	9^2	11^1	10	14	2														8	6		31
1	6	11	8^1	5	7	10^2			4^3	9	14	2	13													3	12	32
1	2	11	8^2	5	6	13	9	10^1	4		12														7	3		33
1	2	3		5	8	12	11	9^3	4^1	7^2	13	14													10	6		34
1	2	3		5	10^3	11	9^1	4^2	7	13	12														8	6	14	35
1		3	12	5	9	11	10^1	4	7	2															8	6		36
1		3		5^1	10	11^3	14	4	7	2	9				13										8	6^2	12	37
1	5	3	13		10^1	12^4	11	9	4^3	7^2	2		14												8	6		38

FA Cup

Third Round	Blyth Spartans	(a)	1-0
Fourth Round	Sunderland	(a)	0-0
		(h)	2-1
Fifth Round	Coventry C	(h)	2-2
		(a)	0-1

Carling Cup

Second Round	Grimsby T	(h)	4-1
Third Round	Everton	(h)	1-0
Fourth Round	Sunderland	(a)	2-1
Quarter-Final	Manchester U	(a)	3-5

BLACKPOOL

FL Championship

FOUNDATION

Old boys of St John's School who had formed themselves into a football club decided to establish a club bearing the name of their town and Blackpool FC came into being at a meeting at the Stanley Arms Hotel in the summer of 1887. In their first season playing at Raikes Hall Gardens, the club won both the Lancashire Junior Cup and the Fylde Cup.

Bloomfield Road, Seasiders Way, Blackpool FY1 6JJ.
Telephone: (0871) 6221 953.
Fax: (01253) 405 011.
Ticket Office: (0871) 6221 953.
Website: www.blackpoolfc.co.uk
Email: info@blackpoolfc.co.uk
Ground Capacity: 9,491.
Record Attendance: 38,098 v Wolverhampton W, Division 1, 17 September 1955.
Pitch Measurements: 110yd × 74yd.
Chairman: Karl Oyston.
Secretary: Matt Williams.
Manager: Ian Holloway.
First Team Coach: Steve Thompson.
Physio: Phil Horner.

HONOURS

Football League: Division 1 – Runners-up 1955–56; Division 2 – Champions 1929–30; Runners-up 1936–37, 1969–70; Division 4 – Runners-up 1984–85.
FA Cup: Winners 1953; Runners-up 1948, 1951.
Football League Cup: Semi-final 1962.
Anglo-Italian Cup: Winners 1971; Runners-up 1972.
LDV Vans Trophy: Winners 2002, 2004.

Colours: Tangerine shirts with white trim, white shorts, tangerine stockings with white tops.
Change Colours: White shirts with tangerine trim, tangerine shorts, white stockings.
Year Formed: 1887.
Turned Professional: 1887.
Ltd Co.: 1896.
Previous Name: 'South Shore' combined with Blackpool in 1899, twelve years after the latter had been formed on the breaking up of the old 'Blackpool St John's' club.
Club Nickname: 'The Seasiders'.
Grounds: 1887, Raikes Hall Gardens; 1897, Athletic Grounds; 1899, Raikes Hall Gardens; 1899, Bloomfield Road.
First Football League game: 5 September 1896, Division 2, v Lincoln C (a) L 1–3 – Douglas; Parr, Bowman; Stuart, Stirzaker, Norris; Clarkin, Donnelly, R. Parkinson, Mount (1), J. Parkinson.
Record League Victory: 7–0 v Reading, Division 2, 10 November 1928 – Mercer; Gibson, Hamilton, Watson, Wilson, Grant, Ritchie, Oxberry (2), Hampson (5), Tufnell, Neal. 7–0 v Preston NE (away), Division 1, 1 May 1948 – Robinson; Shimwell, Crosland; Buchan, Hayward, Kelly; Hobson, Munro (1), McIntosh (5), McCall, Rickett (1). 7–0 v Sunderland, Division 1, 5 October 1957 – Farm; Armfield, Garrett, Kelly (J), Gratrix, Kelly (H), Matthews, Taylor (2), Charnley (2), Durie (2), Perry (1).

SKY SPORTS FACT FILE

The first Blackpool player to be fully capped by England was centre-forward Harry Bedford, an excellent poacher of goals with over 100 to his credit with the club. In 1922–23 he also scored 32 of the 60 League goals and was capped against Sweden.

Record Cup Victory: 7–1 v Charlton Ath, League Cup 2nd rd, 25 September 1963 – Harvey; Armfield, Martin; Crawford, Gratrix, Cranston; Lea, Ball (1), Charnley (4), Durie (1), Oates (1).

Record Defeat: 1–10 v Small Heath, Division 2, 2 March 1901 and v Huddersfield T, Division 1, 13 December 1930.

Most League Points (2 for a win): 58, Division 2, 1929–30 and Division 2, 1967–68.

Most League Points (3 for a win): 86, Division 4, 1984–85.

Most League Goals: 98, Division 2, 1929–30.

Highest League Scorer in Season: Jimmy Hampson, 45, Division 2, 1929–30.

Most League Goals in Total Aggregate: Jimmy Hampson, 246, 1927–38.

Most League Goals in One Match: 5, Jimmy Hampson v Reading, Division 2, 10 November 1928; 5, Jimmy McIntosh v Preston NE, Division 1, 1 May 1948.

Most Capped Player: Jimmy Armfield, 43, England.

Most League Appearances: Jimmy Armfield, 568, 1952–71.

Youngest League Player: Matty Kay, 16 years 32 days v Scunthorpe U, 13 November 2005.

Record Transfer Fee Received: £1,750,000 from Southampton for Brett Ormerod, December 2001.

Record Transfer Fee Paid: £275,000 to Millwall for Chris Malkin, October 1996.

Football League Record: 1896 Elected to Division 2; 1899 Failed re-election; 1900 Re-elected; 1900–30 Division 2; 1930–33 Division 1; 1933–37 Division 2; 1937–67 Division 1; 1967–70 Division 2; 1970–71 Division 1; 1971–78 Division 2; 1978–81 Division 3; 1981–85 Division 4; 1985–90 Division 3; 1990–92 Division 4; 1992–2000 Division 2; 2000–01 Division 3; 2001–04 Division 2; 2004–07 FL 1; 2007– FL C.

MANAGERS

Tom Barcroft 1903–33
  (Secretary-Manager)
John Cox 1909–11
Bill Norman 1919–23
Maj. Frank Buckley 1923–27
Sid Beaumont 1927–28
Harry Evans 1928–33
  (Hon. Team Manager)
Alex 'Sandy' Macfarlane 1933–35
Joe Smith 1935–58
Ronnie Suart 1958–67
Stan Mortensen 1967–69
Les Shannon 1969–70
Bob Stokoe 1970–72
Harry Potts 1972–76
Allan Brown 1976–78
Bob Stokoe 1978–79
Stan Ternent 1979–80
Alan Ball 1980–81
Allan Brown 1981–82
Sam Ellis 1982–89
Jimmy Mullen 1989–90
Graham Carr 1990
Bill Ayre 1990–94
Sam Allardyce 1994–96
Gary Megson 1996–97
Nigel Worthington 1997–99
Steve McMahon 2000–04
Colin Hendry 2004–06
Simon Grayson 2006–08
Ian Holloway May 2009–

LATEST SEQUENCES

Longest Sequence of League Wins: 9, 21.11.1936 – 1.1.1937.

Longest Sequence of League Defeats: 8, 26.11.1898 – 7.1.1899.

Longest Sequence of League Draws: 5, 4.12.1976 – 1.1.1977.

Longest Sequence of Unbeaten League Matches: 17, 6.4.1968 – 21.9.1968.

Longest Sequence Without a League Win: 19, 19.12.1970 – 24.4.1971.

Successive Scoring Runs: 33 from 23.2.1929.

Successive Non-scoring Runs: 5 from 12.4.1975.

TEN YEAR LEAGUE RECORD

		P	W	D	L	F	A	Pts	Pos
1999-2000	Div 2	46	8	17	21	49	77	41	22
2000-01	Div 2	46	22	6	18	74	58	72	7
2001-02	Div 2	46	14	14	18	66	69	56	16
2002-03	Div 2	46	15	13	18	56	64	58	13
2003-04	Div 2	46	16	11	19	58	65	59	14
2004-05	FL 1	46	15	12	19	54	59	57	16
2005-06	FL 1	46	12	17	17	56	64	53	19
2006-07	FL 1	46	24	11	11	76	49	83	3
2007-08	FL C	46	12	18	16	59	64	54	19
2008-09	FL C	46	13	17	16	47	58	56	16

DID YOU KNOW ?

Though Blackpool managed just one home League win in 1966–67, this isolated victory at Bloomfield Road was little short of amazing. On 22 October 1966 they beat Newcastle United 6–0, the second highest score in the First Division that season.

BLACKPOOL 2008–09 LEAGUE RECORD

Match No.	Date	Venue	Opponents	Result	H/T Score	Lg. Pos.	Goalscorers	Attendance
1	Aug 9	H	Bristol C	L	0-1	0-0	—	8244
2	16	A	Norwich C	D	1-1	0-0	16	Burgess (pen) [55]	23,727
3	23	H	Sheffield U	L	1-3	0-1	21	Kabba [74]	8611
4	30	A	Southampton	W	1-0	1-0	15	Burgess (pen) [45]	15,629
5	Sept 13	H	Barnsley	W	1-0	0-0	12	Kabba [86]	8363
6	16	A	Burnley	L	0-2	0-0	—		13,752
7	20	A	Birmingham C	W	1-0	0-0	10	Taylor-Fletcher [47]	20,983
8	27	H	Coventry C	D	1-1	0-0	13	Burgess [58]	8462
9	30	A	QPR	D	1-1	1-0	—	Taylor-Fletcher [18]	12,500
10	Oct 4	H	Cardiff C	D	1-1	0-0	16	Gow [90]	7328
11	18	H	Doncaster R	D	0-0	0-0	17		11,342
12	21	H	Derby Co	W	3-2	2-0	—	Gow [35], Taylor-Fletcher [43], Burgess [65]	7267
13	25	H	Crystal Palace	D	2-2	0-1	11	Burgess [48], Evatt [65]	7597
14	28	A	Cardiff C	L	0-2	0-0	—		17,570
15	Nov 1	A	Watford	W	4-3	1-2	13	Southern [18], Burgess [56], Taylor-Fletcher [85], Gow [90]	13,516
16	8	H	Ipswich T	L	0-1	0-1	15		7349
17	16	H	Preston NE	L	1-3	1-0	16	Hammill [10]	9643
18	22	A	Wolverhampton W	L	0-2	0-1	18		22,044
19	25	H	Sheffield W	L	0-2	0-0	—		7054
20	29	A	Plymouth Arg	W	2-1	0-0	18	Dickinson 2 [78, 81]	9969
21	Dec 6	H	Charlton Ath	W	2-0	0-0	15	Dickinson 2 [47, 56]	6648
22	9	A	Reading	L	0-1	0-1	—		16,514
23	13	A	Nottingham F	D	0-0	0-0	16		19,103
24	20	A	Swansea C	D	1-1	0-0	16	Gow [74]	7007
25	26	A	Sheffield W	D	1-1	1-0	17	Gow (pen) [48]	25,044
26	29	H	Wolverhampton W	D	2-2	1-1	—	Taylor-Fletcher [10], Edwards [84]	8906
27	Jan 17	A	Coventry C	L	1-2	1-0	17	Campbell [25]	15,551
28	24	H	Birmingham C	W	2-0	2-0	—	Campbell [13], Southern [37]	8105
29	27	H	QPR	L	0-3	0-1	—		6656
30	31	A	Crystal Palace	W	1-0	1-0	15	Campbell (pen) [41]	13,810
31	Feb 7	H	Doncaster R	L	2-3	1-1	15	Vaughan [15], Campbell [55]	7452
32	14	A	Ipswich T	D	1-1	0-0	15	John-Baptiste [28]	19,299
33	18	A	Derby Co	L	1-4	1-1	—	Edwards [31]	26,834
34	21	H	Watford	L	0-2	0-0	17		7451
35	28	A	Bristol C	D	0-0	0-0	20		16,855
36	Mar 3	H	Burnley	L	0-1	0-0	—		7679
37	7	H	Norwich C	W	2-0	0-0	19	Ormerod [55], Adam [74]	7505
38	10	A	Sheffield U	D	2-2	1-1	—	Blackman [42], Campbell [50]	25,273
39	14	A	Barnsley	W	1-0	0-0	18	Small [70]	12,228
40	21	H	Southampton	D	1-1	1-0	18	Campbell (pen) [20]	7947
41	Apr 4	H	Plymouth Arg	L	0-1	0-0	18		8103
42	11	A	Preston NE	W	1-0	1-0	18	Adam [43]	21,273
43	13	H	Reading	D	2-2	1-2	18	Southern [31], Campbell [66]	7722
44	18	A	Charlton Ath	D	2-2	0-0	17	Campbell (pen) [67], Hughes [90]	19,615
45	25	H	Nottingham F	D	1-1	1-1	18	Ormerod [30]	9279
46	May 3	A	Swansea C	W	1-0	1-0	16	Campbell [13]	16,316

Final League Position: 16

GOALSCORERS

League (47): Campbell 9 (3 pens), Burgess 6 (2 pens), Gow 5 (1 pen), Taylor-Fletcher 5, Dickinson 4, Southern 3, Adam 2, Edwards 2, Kabba 2, Ormerod 2, Blackman 1, Evatt 1, Hammill 1, Hughes 1, John-Baptiste 1, Small 1, Vaughan 1.
Carling Cup (0).
FA Cup (0).

Rachubka P 42	Coid D 13+5	Hammill A 14+8	Jorgensen C 21+11	Edwards R 35+1	Evatt I 33	Taylor-Fletcher G 34+4	Southern K 34+1	Burgess B 25+4	Camara M 14	Wright J 3	Vaughan D 26+7	Small W 4+1	Aluko S —+1	Rehman Z —+3	Mahon A 1	Fox D 15+7	Kabba S 12+5	Barker S 42+1	Nardiello D —+2	Martin J 10+5	Hughes L 2+1	Gow A 10+7	Broomes M —+1	McPhee S —+5	Mitchley D —+2	Walton S —+1	Hendrie L 5+1	John-Baptiste A 21	Dickinson L 5+2	Reid K 7	Harte I 4	Owens G 1+7	Campbell D 20	O'Donovan R 11+1	Crainey S 15+2	Nemeth K —+1	Marshall P 1+1	Gilks M 4+1	Ormerod B 7+8	Adam C 13	Blackman N 2+3	Match No.
1	2	3	4²	5	6	7¹	8	9	10	11	12	13																														1
1	2³	11²	8	5	6	7		9	3	10	13		14			4¹	12																									2
1	12	11	4	5	6	7²		9	3¹	8³	14		13			10	2																									3
1	12	11²	8	5	6	7¹		9	3		13		14			4³	10	2																								4
1		11³	8²	5	6	7	12	9	3		13					4¹	10	2	14																							5
1		11	4³	5	6	7¹	8	9	3²		10					2	12	13	14																							6
1		4	5	6	7¹	8	9	3		11²		12				10	2		13																							7
1	12	4	5	6	7	8¹	9	3		11						10	2		13																						8
1		4¹	5	6	7	8	9	3		11²					12	10	2			13																					9
1	11		5	6	7	8	9²	3		4					10¹	2			12		13																				10
1	12	4	5	6	7	8	9²	3		11¹					10	2		13																							11
1	3	12	4	5	6	7¹	8	9			11²					2	13	10																							12
1	3	12	4	5	6	7²	8¹	9		11						2	10			13																					13
1	2	12	4¹	5	6	7	8	9		11						3	10²			13																					14
1	2	12	4	5	6	7	8	9		11¹						3	10																								15
1	12	4³	5	6	7	8	9	3²		11¹		13	14			2	10																								16
1	11	4	5	6	7³	8²	9	3							12	2		10¹		13	14																				17
1	11		5	6	7	8²	12	3			13				9¹			10³	14	4	2																				18
1	11		5	6	7¹	8	13								9	14	3	10	12²	4	2³																				19
1	12		5	6	7¹	8	9					13	10³	2		3		4²				14	11																		20
1	11¹		5	6	12	8	9³						13	2		3	14	4				10²	7																		21
1	11¹		5	6	13	8	9³						12	10²	2	3		4⁸				14	7																		22
1	12	11²	5¹		13	8	9³							4	2	3	14					6	10	7																		23
1	11			6	12	8	9³							4	13	2	3	14				5	10²	7¹																		24
1				5	6	11	8							4		2	3	10					9	7																		25
1				5	6	7³	8	13			14			4		2	12	10					9²	11	3¹																	26
1				5	6	7	8²	9¹			12			4		2									3	13	10	11														27
1		12⁸	5	6	9	8¹								4		2	11³								3	13	10	7²	14													28
1				5	6	9							8	4		2	11²								3¹	13	10	7³	12	14												29
1⁸	2			6	9						11¹			4		3	12								5		10²	7					8⁸	15	13							30
	3			6	9						8			4¹		2									5		10	7²				13	1	12	11⁸							31
		8	5		9						11			4		3									6		10	7	2			1									32
		8	5		9						11¹			4		2									6		10	7	3			1		12							33
		8	5		9						11			4¹		2									6		13	10	7²	3			1		12						34
1	12	4		6¹	7³						11			13		2									5		14	10		3				9²	8						35
1	2	4		7¹							11					6									5		13	10	12	3				9³	8²	14					36
1	2	12				7	4				11¹					6	13								5			10²		3				9	8	13					37
1	2	12				7	8									6	13								5		11¹	10		3					4	9²					38
1	2¹	13	12			8						7²				6	11								5		10			3				14	4	9³					39
1		12	5			8							7	4²		2									6		13	10		3				9³	11¹	14					40
1		12	5			8²	14						11			2					9³	13			6			10¹		3				7	4						41
1		14	5			8	9						11			2								13	6²			10³	7¹	3				12	4						42
1		13	5			8							11			2					9¹				6			10	7²	3				12	4						43
1		13	6			8	9²					11³	7¹			2									5			10		3				12	4						44
1	12	13	6⁸			8						11	7¹			2									5			10		3				9²	4						45
1	2	12				8						11	13			6									5			10	7²	3				9¹	4						46

FA Cup
Third Round   Torquay U   (a)   0-1

Carling Cup
First Round   Macclesfield T   (a)   0-2

BOLTON WANDERERS   FA Premiership

FOUNDATION

In 1874 boys of Christ Church Sunday School, Blackburn Street, led by their master Thomas Ogden, established a football club which went under the name of the school and whose president was Vicar of Christ Church. Membership was 6d (two and a half pence). When their president began to lay down too many rules about the use of church premises, the club broke away and formed Bolton Wanderers in 1877, holding their earliest meetings at the Gladstone Hotel.

The Reebok Stadium, Burnden Way, Lostock, Bolton BL6 6JW.

Telephone: (0844) 871 2932. *Fax:* (01204) 673 773.

Ticket Office: (0844) 871 2932.

Website: www.bwfc.co.uk

Email: reception@bwfc.co.uk

Ground Capacity: 28,101.

Record Attendance: 69,912 v Manchester C, FA Cup 5th rd, 18 February 1933.

Pitch Measurements: 105m × 68m.

Chairman: Phil A. Gartside.

Chief Executive: Allan Duckworth.

Vice-chairman: Brett Warburton.

Secretary: Simon Marland.

Manager: Gary Megson.

Assistant Manager: Chris Evans.

Physio: Nick Worth.

Colours: White shirts with blue shoulder trim, blue shorts, white stockings.

Change Colours: Yellow shirts, black shorts, black stockings.

Year Formed: 1874. *Turned Professional:* 1880. *Ltd Co.:* 1895.

Previous Name: 1874, Christ Church FC; 1877, Bolton Wanderers.

Club Nickname: 'The Trotters'.

Grounds: Park Recreation Ground and Cockle's Field before moving to Pike's Lane ground 1881; 1895, Burnden Park; 1997, Reebok Stadium.

First Football League Game: 8 September 1888, Football League, v Derby Co (h) L 3–6 – Harrison; Robinson, Mitchell; Roberts, Weir, Bullough, Davenport (2), Milne, Coupar, Barbour, Brogan (1).

Record League Victory: 8–0 v Barnsley, Division 2, 6 October 1934 – Jones; Smith, Finney; Goslin, Atkinson, George Taylor; George T. Taylor (2), Eastham, Milsom (1), Westwood (4), Cook, (1 og).

HONOURS

Football League: Division 1 – Champions 1996–97. Division 2 – Champions 1908–09, 1977–78; Runners-up 1899–1900, 1904–05, 1910–11, 1934–35, 1992–93; Division 3 – Champions 1972–73.

FA Cup: Winners 1923, 1926, 1929, 1958; Runners-up 1894, 1904, 1953.

Football League Cup: Runners-up 1995, 2004.

Freight Rover Trophy: Runners-up 1986.

Sherpa Van Trophy: Winners 1989.

European Competitions: UEFA Cup: 2005–06, 2007–08.

SKY SPORTS FACT FILE

In 1910–11 Bolton Wanderers recorded 13 consecutive home wins in Division 2 in a season in which they successfully regained their First Division status as runners-up. They finished two points behind the champions West Bromwich Albion.

Record Cup Victory: 13–0 v Sheffield U, FA Cup 2nd rd, 1 February 1890 – Parkinson; Robinson (1), Jones; Bullough, Davenport, Roberts; Rushton, Brogan (3), Cassidy (5), McNee, Weir (4).

Record Defeat: 1–9 v Preston NE, FA Cup 2nd rd, 10 December 1887.

Most League Points (2 for a win): 61, Division 3, 1972–73.

Most League Points (3 for a win): 98, Division 1, 1996–97.

Most League Goals: 100, Division 1, 1996–97.

Highest League Scorer in Season: Joe Smith, 38, Division 1, 1920–21.

Most League Goals in Total Aggregate: Nat Lofthouse, 255, 1946–61.

Most League Goals in One Match: 5, Tony Caldwell v Walsall, Division 3, 10 September 1983.

Most Capped Player: Mark Fish, 34 (62), South Africa.

Most League Appearances: Eddie Hopkinson, 519, 1956–70.

Youngest League Player: Ray Parry, 15 years 267 days v Wolverhampton W, 13 October 1951.

Record Transfer Fee Received: £15,000,000 from Chelsea for Nicolas Anelka, January 2008.

Record Transfer Fee Paid: £10,000,000 to Toulouse for Johan Elmander, July 2008 (and exchange for Damiel Braaten).

Football League Record: 1888 Founder Member of the League; 1899–1900 Division 2; 1900–03 Division 1; 1903–05 Division 2; 1905–08 Division 1; 1908–09 Division 2; 1909–10 Division 1; 1910–11 Division 2; 1911–33 Division 1; 1933–35 Division 2; 1935–64 Division 1; 1964–71 Division 2; 1971–73 Division 3; 1973–78 Division 2; 1978–80 Division 1; 1980–83 Division 2; 1983–87 Division 3; 1987–88 Division 4; 1988–92 Division 3; 1992–93 Division 2; 1993–95 Division 1; 1995–96 FA Premier League; 1996–97 Division 1; 1997–98 FA Premier League; 1998–2001 Division 1; 2001– FA Premier League.

LATEST SEQUENCES

Longest Sequence of League Wins: 11, 5.11.1904 – 2.1.1905.

Longest Sequence of League Defeats: 11, 7.4.1902 – 18.10.1902.

Longest Sequence of League Draws: 6, 25.1.1913 – 8.3.1913.

Longest Sequence of Unbeaten League Matches: 23, 13.10.1990 – 9.3.1991.

Longest Sequence Without a League Win: 26, 7.4.1902 – 10.1.1903.

Successive Scoring Runs: 24 from 22.11.1996.

Successive Non-scoring Runs: 5 from 3.1.1898.

MANAGERS

Tom Rawthorne 1874–85
(Secretary)
J. J. Bentley 1885–86
(Secretary)
W. G. Struthers 1886–87
(Secretary)
Fitzroy Norris 1887
(Secretary)
J. J. Bentley 1887–95
(Secretary)
Harry Downs 1895–96
(Secretary)
Frank Brettell 1896–98
(Secretary)
John Somerville 1898–1910
Will Settle 1910–15
Tom Mather 1915–19
Charles Foweraker 1919–44
Walter Rowley 1944–50
Bill Ridding 1951–68
Nat Lofthouse 1968–70
Jimmy McIlroy 1970
Jimmy Meadows 1971
Nat Lofthouse 1971
(then Admin. Manager to 1972)
Jimmy Armfield 1971–74
Ian Greaves 1974–80
Stan Anderson 1980–81
George Mulhall 1981–82
John McGovern 1982–85
Charlie Wright 1985
Phil Neal 1985–92
Bruce Rioch 1992–95
Roy McFarland 1995–96
Colin Todd 1996–99
Sam Allardyce 1999–2007
Sammy Lee 2007
Gary Megson October 2007–

TEN YEAR LEAGUE RECORD

		P	W	D	L	F	A	Pts	Pos
1999-2000	Div 1	46	21	13	12	69	50	76	6
2000-01	Div 1	46	24	15	7	76	45	87	3
2001-02	PR Lge	38	9	13	16	44	62	40	16
2002-03	PR Lge	38	10	14	14	41	51	44	17
2003-04	PR Lge	38	14	11	13	48	56	53	8
2004-05	PR Lge	38	16	10	12	49	44	58	6
2005-06	PR Lge	38	15	11	12	49	41	56	8
2006-07	PR Lge	38	16	8	14	47	52	56	7
2007-08	PR Lge	38	9	10	19	36	54	37	16
2008-09	PR Lge	38	11	8	19	41	53	41	13

DID YOU KNOW ?

Gerry McElhinney made his debut for Bolton Wanderers at centre-back on 6 September 1980 against Bristol Rovers. Signed from Distillery he had previously represented Northern Ireland at boxing and Gaelic football and was soon to add similar soccer honours.

BOLTON WANDERERS 2008–09 LEAGUE RECORD

Match No.	Date		Venue	Opponents	Result	H/T Score	Lg. Pos.	Goalscorers	Atten-dance
1	Aug	16	H	Stoke C	W 3-1	3-0	—	Steinsson [34], Davies K [41], Elmander [45]	22,717
2		23	A	Newcastle U	L 0-1	0-0	8		47,711
3		30	H	WBA	D 0-0	0-0	8		20,387
4	Sept	13	A	Fulham	L 1-2	0-2	13	Davies K [82]	23,656
5		20	H	Arsenal	L 1-3	1-2	16	Davies K [14]	22,694
6		27	A	Manchester U	L 0-2	0-0	17		75,484
7	Oct	5	A	West Ham U	W 3-1	2-0	16	Davies K [30], Cahill [34], Taylor [86]	33,715
8		18	H	Blackburn R	D 0-0	0-0	15		24,778
9		26	A	Tottenham H	L 0-2	0-1	17		35,507
10		29	H	Everton	L 0-1	0-0	—		21,692
11	Nov	2	H	Manchester C	W 2-0	0-0	17	Gardner [77], Dunne (og) [88]	21,095
12		8	A	Hull C	W 1-0	0-0	11	Taylor [50]	24,903
13		15	H	Liverpool	L 0-2	0-1	16		24,893
14		22	A	Middlesbrough	W 3-1	2-0	12	Steinsson [8], Taylor [10], Elmander [78]	24,487
15		29	A	Sunderland	W 4-1	3-1	9	Taylor [18], Cahill [21], Elmander 2 [39, 55]	35,457
16	Dec	6	H	Chelsea	L 0-2	0-2	10		22,023
17		13	A	Aston Villa	L 2-4	1-2	11	Elmander [17], Davies K [86]	35,134
18		20	H	Portsmouth	W 2-1	2-1	9	Taylor [1], Gardner [3]	19,884
19		26	A	Liverpool	L 0-3	0-1	10		43,548
20		28	H	Wigan Ath	L 0-1	0-1	11		23,726
21	Jan	10	A	Arsenal	L 0-1	0-0	12		60,068
22		17	H	Manchester U	L 0-1	0-0	13		26,021
23		28	A	Blackburn R	D 2-2	2-0	—	Taylor [15], Davies K [35]	25,205
24		31	H	Tottenham H	W 3-2	1-0	12	Puygrenier [31], Davies K 2 [64, 87]	21,575
25	Feb	7	A	Everton	L 0-3	0-1	14		33,791
26		21	H	West Ham U	W 2-1	2-0	12	Taylor [10], Davies K [11]	21,245
27	Mar	1	H	Newcastle U	W 1-0	0-0	10	Gardner [47]	20,763
28		4	A	Stoke C	L 0-2	0-1	—		26,319
29		14	H	Fulham	L 1-3	1-1	12	Davies K [45]	22,117
30		21	A	WBA	D 1-1	0-0	12	Taylor [67]	25,530
31	Apr	4	H	Middlesbrough	W 4-1	2-1	12	Davies K [6], Cahill [44], Taylor [78], Gardner [84]	20,819
32		11	A	Chelsea	L 3-4	0-1	12	O'Brien A [70], Basham [74], Taylor [78]	41,096
33		18	A	Portsmouth	L 0-1	0-0	13		20,158
34		25	H	Aston Villa	D 1-1	0-1	13	Cohen [60]	21,709
35	May	2	A	Wigan Ath	D 0-0	0-0	12		18,655
36		9	H	Sunderland	D 0-0	0-0	13		24,005
37		16	H	Hull C	D 1-1	1-0	13	Steinsson [26]	25,085
38		24	A	Manchester C	L 0-1	0-1	13		47,202

Final League Position: 13

GOALSCORERS

League (41): Davies K 11, Taylor 10, Elmander 5, Gardner 4, Cahill 3, Steinsson 3, Basham 1, Cohen 1, O'Brien A 1, Puygrenier 1, own goal 1.
Carling Cup (1): Nolan 1.
FA Cup (1): Smolarek 1.

Jaaskelainen J 38	Steinsson G 37	Samuel J 38	Muamba F 33 + 5	O'Brien A 30 + 4	Cahill G 33	O'Brien J 5 + 2	Nolan K 20	Elmander J 30	Davies K 37 + 1	Taylor M 33 + 1	McCann G 30 + 3	Mustapha R 2 + 15	Gardner R 18 + 11	Shittu D 9 + 1	Helguson H — + 1	Vaz Te R — + 2	Smolarek E 1 + 11	Basham C 4 + 7	Obadeyi T — + 3	Makukula A 4 + 2	Puygrenier S 5 + 2	Davies M 8 + 2	Cohen T 3 + 1	Match No.
1	2	3	4	5	6	7	8	9^1	10	11	12													1
1	2	3	4	5	6	7^1	8	9^3	10	11^2	14	12	13											2
1	2	3	4	5		7^1	9		10		8	12	11	6										3
1	2^2	3	4	5		7	8		10		9^1	12	11	6	13									4
1	2	3	4^3	5		7^1	9		10		12	13	11	6		14	8^2							5
1	2	3	4	5	6		8	9^1	10		7		11^2		12	13								6
1	2	3	4^1	5	6	12	7	9^2	10	13	8		11											7
1	2^1	3	4^2	5	6	12	7	9	10	11^3	8	14	13											8
1	2	3	4^1	5	6		8	9^2	10	11	7^4	13	12											9
1	2	3	4	5	6		8	9	10	11		7												10
1	2	3	4	5	6		8		10	11	9	7^1	12											11
1	2	3	4	5	6			9^1	10	11	8		7				12							12
1	2	3	4^1	5	6		8	9	10	11^2	7		12				13							13
1	2	3	4	5	6		8	9^2	10	11^1	7		12				13							14
1	2	3	4	5	6		8	9^2	10	11^1	7		13					13						15
1	2	3^2	4^1	5	6		8	9	10	11	7		12				13							16
1	2	3	4^1	5	6		8	9^2	10	11	7		12				13							17
1	2	3	12	5	6		8	9	10	7	4				11^1									18
1	2	3^1	4	5	6		8	9^3	12	11^2	7	13	10			14								19
1	2	3^2	12	5		8^1	9	10	7	4	13	11^3	6						14					20
1		3	4	5				9^1	10	7	8	12^2	11	6		2	13							21
1	2	3	4		6			10	7				11^2					8	12	9^1	13			22
1	2	3	4	12	6			10	7							-	7		9^1	5	12			23
1	2	3	4	12	6			10	7			11				13			9^2	5^1	8			24
1	7	3	4^2	2	6			10	11			13	14						9^1	5^3	8			25
1	2	3	12	13	6			9^1	10	11	4		7							5^2	8			26
1	2	3	8^1	5	6			9^2	10	11	4		12				13				7			27
1	2^2	3	8^1	5	6			9	10	11	4		12				13				7			28
1	2	3^2	12	5				9	10	7	4	13	11									8^1		29
1	2	3	8		6			9^2	10	7	4		11	12			13			5^1				30
1	2	3	8		6			9^1	10	7	4		11	5			12							31
1	2	3	4	12	6			9^2	10	7	8^3		11	5^1			13					14		32
1	2	3	12	5	6			9	10	7	4		11^1					8						33
1	2	3	8	5^1	6			9	10	7	4		13				12				11^2			34
1	2	3	8	5	6			9	10	7	4	12									11^1			35
1	2	3	8	5	6			9^2	10	7	4	13					12				11^1			36
1	2	3	8^1		6			9^3	10	11^2	4	12		5			13	14	7					37
1	2	3	8	14	6			9^2	10	11^1	4	13		5^2			12		7					38

FA Cup
Third Round   Sunderland   (a)   1-2

Carling Cup
Second Round   Northampton T   (h)   1-2

AFC BOURNEMOUTH   FL Championship 2

FOUNDATION

There was a Bournemouth FC as early as 1875, but the present club arose out of the remnants of the Boscombe St John's club (formed 1890). The meeting at which Boscombe FC came into being was held at a house in Gladstone Road in 1899. They began by playing in the Boscombe and District Junior League.

Dean Court, Kings Park, Bournemouth, Dorset BH7 7AF.

Telephone: (01202) 726 300.

Fax: (01202) 726 373.

Ticket Office: (01202) 726 338.

Website: www.afcb.co.uk

Email: enquiries@afcb.co.uk

Ground Capacity: 10,375 (with temporary stand, 9,776 without).

Record Attendance: 28,799 v Manchester U, FA Cup 6th rd, 2 March 1957.

Pitch Measurements: 105m × 78m.

Chairman: Jeff Mostyn.

Vice-chairman: Steve Sly.

Secretary: Neil Vacher (Football Administrator).

Manager: Eddie Howe.

First Team Coach: Jason Tindall.

Physio: Steve Hard.

Colours: Red shirts with black trim, black shorts, black stockings.

Change Colours: All black with red trim.

Year Formed: 1899.

Turned Professional: 1910.

Ltd Co.: 1914.

Previous Names: 1890, Boscombe St Johns; 1899, Boscombe FC; 1923, Bournemouth & Boscombe Ath FC; 1971, AFC Bournemouth.

Club Nickname: 'Cherries'.

Grounds: 1899, Castlemain Road, Pokesdown; 1910, Dean Court.

First Football League Game: 25 August 1923, Division 3 (S), v Swindon T (a) L 1–3 – Heron; Wingham, Lamb; Butt, C. Smith, Voisey; Miller, Lister (1), Davey, Simpson, Robinson.

Record League Victory: 7–0 v Swindon T, Division 3 (S), 22 September 1956 – Godwin; Cunningham, Keetley; Clayton, Crosland, Rushworth; Siddall (1), Norris (2), Arnott (1), Newsham (2), Cutler (1). 10–0 win v Northampton T at start of 1939–40 expunged from the records on outbreak of war.

HONOURS

Football League: Division 3 – Champions 1986–87; Division 3 (S) – Runners-up 1947–48; Division 4 – Runners-up 1970–71.

FA Cup: best season: 6th rd, 1957.

Football League Cup: best season: 4th rd, 1962, 1964.

Associate Members' Cup: Winners 1984.

Auto Windscreens Shield: Runners-up 1998.

SKY SPORTS FACT FILE

Darren Anderton, 36, made his 477th and final career League appearance (568th domestic) for Bournemouth against Chester City on 6 December 2008. As a substitute he scored the only goal in 88 minutes to put Bournemouth into plus points for the first time.

Record Cup Victory: 11–0 v Margate, FA Cup 1st rd, 20 November 1971 – Davies; Machin (1), Kitchener, Benson, Jones, Powell, Cave (1), Boyer, MacDougall (9 incl. 1p), Miller, Scott (De Garis).

Record Defeat: 0–9 v Lincoln C, Division 3, 18 December 1982.

Most League Points (2 for a win): 62, Division 3, 1971–72.

Most League Points (3 for a win): 97, Division 3, 1986–87.

Most League Goals: 88, Division 3 (S), 1956–57.

Highest League Scorer in Season: Ted MacDougall, 42, 1970–71.

Most League Goals in Total Aggregate: Ron Eyre, 202, 1924–33.

Most League Goals in One Match: 4, Jack Russell v Clapton Orient, Division 3 (S), 7 January 1933; 4, Jack Russell v Bristol C, Division 3 (S), 28 January 1933; 4, Harry Mardon v Southend U, Division 3 (S), 1 January 1938; 4, Jack McDonald v Torquay U, Division 3 (S), 8 November 1947; 4, Ted MacDougall v Colchester U, 18 September 1970; 4, Brian Clark v Rotherham U, 10 October 1972; 4, Luther Blissett v Hull C, 29 November 1988; 4, James Hayter v Bury, Division 2, 21 October 2000.

Most Capped Player: Gerry Peyton, 7 (33), Republic of Ireland.

Most League Appearances: Steve Fletcher, 514, 1992–2007; 2008–09.

Youngest League Player: Jimmy White, 15 years 321 days v Brentford, 30 April 1958.

Record Transfer Fee Received: £800,000 from Everton for Joe Parkinson, March 1994 and £800,000 from Ipswich T for Matt Holland, July 1997.

Record Transfer Fee Paid: £210,000 to Gillingham for Gavin Peacock, August 1989.

Football League Record: 1923 Elected to Division 3 (S) and remained a Third Division club for record number of years until 1970; 1970–71 Division 4; 1971–75 Division 3; 1975–82 Division 4; 1982–87 Division 3; 1987–90 Division 2; 1990–92 Division 3; 1992–2002 Division 2; 2002–03 Division 3; 2003–04 Division 2; 2004–08 FL 1; 2008– FL 2.

MANAGERS

Vincent Kitcher 1914–23
(Secretary-Manager)
Harry Kinghorn 1923–25
Leslie Knighton 1925–28
Frank Richards 1928–30
Billy Birrell 1930–35
Bob Crompton 1935–36
Charlie Bell 1936–39
Harry Kinghorn 1939–47
Harry Lowe 1947–50
Jack Bruton 1950–56
Fred Cox 1956–58
Don Welsh 1958–61
Bill McGarry 1961–63
Reg Flewin 1963–65
Fred Cox 1965–70
John Bond 1970–73
Trevor Hartley 1974–75
John Benson 1975–78
Alec Stock 1979–80
David Webb 1980–82
Don Megson 1983
Harry Redknapp 1983–92
Tony Pulis 1992–94
Mel Machin 1994–2000
Sean O'Driscoll 2000–06
Kevin Bond 2006–08
Jimmy Quinn 2008
Eddie Howe January 2009–

LATEST SEQUENCES

Longest Sequence of League Wins: 7, 22.8.1970 – 23.9.1970.

Longest Sequence of League Defeats: 7, 13.8.1994 – 13.9.1994.

Longest Sequence of League Draws: 5, 25.4.2000 – 12.8.2000.

Longest Sequence of Unbeaten League Matches: 18, 6.3.1982 – 28.8.1982.

Longest Sequence Without a League Win: 14, 6.3.1974 – 27.4.1974.

Successive Scoring Runs: 31 from 28.10.2000.

Successive Non-scoring Runs: 6 from 1.2.1975.

TEN YEAR LEAGUE RECORD

		P	W	D	L	F	A	Pts	Pos
1999-2000	Div 2	46	16	9	21	59	62	57	16
2000-01	Div 2	46	20	13	13	79	55	73	7
2001-02	Div 2	46	10	14	22	56	71	44	21
2002-03	Div 3	46	20	14	12	60	48	74	4
2003-04	Div 2	46	17	15	14	56	51	66	9
2004-05	FL 1	46	20	10	16	77	64	70	8
2005-06	FL 1	46	12	19	15	49	53	55	17
2006-07	FL 1	46	13	13	20	50	64	52	19
2007-08	FL 1	46	17	7	22	62	72	48*	21
2008-09	FL 2	46	17	12	17	59	51	46†	21

10 pts deducted; †17 points deducted.

DID YOU KNOW ?

Boscombe Football Club were drawn in the FA Cup on 8 October 1921 against Bournemouth, an amateur team formerly Rovers, later amalgamated with Wanderers to become Bournemouth Poppies. Boscombe drew 0–0 and won the replay 6–0.

AFC BOURNEMOUTH 2008–09 LEAGUE RECORD

Match No.	Date	Venue	Opponents	Result	H/T Score	Lg. Pos.	Goalscorers	Attendance
1	Aug 9	H	Gillingham	D	1-1	1-0	—	Anderton [42]	5377
2	16	A	Aldershot T	D	1-1	0-0	23	Sappleton [81]	4564
3	23	H	Exeter C	L	0-1	0-0	23		5350
4	30	A	Port Vale	L	1-3	0-1	23	Lindfield [58]	6048
5	Sept 6	A	Notts Co	D	1-1	1-1	23	Pitman [19]	4362
6	13	H	Macclesfield T	L	0-1	0-1	23		3922
7	20	A	Bradford C	W	3-1	1-1	23	Hollands [39], Goulding [54], Pearce [70]	12,824
8	27	H	Darlington	W	3-1	2-1	23	Bartley [15], Austin (og) [37], Pitman [90]	4124
9	Oct 4	A	Wycombe W	L	1-3	0-1	23	Hollands [57]	5005
10	11	H	Rotherham U	D	0-0	0-0	23		4530
11	18	A	Shrewsbury T	L	1-4	0-3	23	Pitman [60]	5738
12	21	H	Dagenham & R	W	2-1	2-0	—	Bradbury [24], Pitman [31]	3554
13	25	H	Lincoln C	L	0-1	0-1	23		4464
14	Nov· 1	H	Chesterfield	D	1-1	0-1	23	Goodall (og) [82]	4082
15	15	A	Accrington S	L	0-3	0-3	23		1152
16	21	H	Grimsby T	D	3-3	1-2	—	Bradbury 2 [6, 89], Anderton [79]	4353
17	25	H	Morecambe	D	0-0	0-0	—		3068
18	Dec 2	A	Luton T	D	3-3	1-1	—	Molesley 2 [20, 51], Tubbs [76]	6773
19	6	H	Chester C	W	1-0	0-0	23	Anderton [88]	4154
20	13	A	Rochdale	D	1-1	1-0	23	Bradbury (pen) [45]	2285
21	20	H	Bury	W	2-0	2-0	23	Igoe [39], Partington [44]	3479
22	26	A	Brentford	L	0-2	0-2	23		6450
23	28	H	Barnet	L	0-2	0-1	23		4725
24	Jan 3	A	Darlington	L	1-2	1-0	—	Hollands [29]	2571
25	17	A	Rotherham U	L	0-1	0-1	23		3270
26	24	H	Wycombe W	W	3-1	2-1	23	Pitman [24], Pearce [32], Thomson [64]	5946
27	27	H	Luton T	D	1-1	1-1	—	Hollands [29]	5230
28	31	A	Lincoln C	D	3-3	1-1	23	Molesley [36], Pitman 2 (2 pens) [65, 77]	3634
29	Feb 7	H	Shrewsbury T	W	1-0	1-0	—	Pitman [23]	4187
30	14	H	Accrington S	W	1-0	0-0	23	Pitman [86]	4109
31	20	A	Chesterfield	L	0-1	0-1	—		3130
32	24	A	Dagenham & R	W	1-0	0-0	—	Molesley [90]	1602
33	28	A	Gillingham	L	0-1	0-0	23		5353
34	Mar 3	H	Aldershot T	W	2-0	1-0	—	Hollands [39], Fletcher [56]	4556
35	7	H	Port Vale	D	0-0	0-0	23		5924
36	10	A	Exeter C	W	3-1	0-1	—	Hollands [56], Pitman 2 [59, 87]	4946
37	14	A	Macclesfield T	W	2-0	0-0	21	Bradbury 2 [50, 70]	1589
38	17	H	Bradford C	W	4-1	3-1	—	Fletcher 2 [4, 39], Goulding 2 [40, 51]	4847
39	21	H	Notts Co	L	0-1	0-1	21		5510
40	28	A	Bury	L	0-1	0-0	21		2762
41	Apr 4	H	Rochdale	W	4-0	2-0	21	Pitman 3 [12, 67, 90], Feeney [25]	5092
42	11	A	Barnet	L	0-1	0-0	21		3133
43	13	H	Brentford	L	0-1	0-1	21		8168
44	18	A	Chester C	W	2-0	1-0	21	Pitman [3], Robinson [79]	3349
45	25	H	Grimsby T	W	2-1	0-1	21	Feeney [47], Fletcher [80]	9008
46	May 2	A	Morecambe	W	4-0	3-0	21	Ward [7], Feeney [36], Pitman 2 [43, 69]	2601

Final League Position: 21

GOALSCORERS

League (59): Pitman 17 (2 pens), Bradbury 6 (1 pen), Hollands 6, Fletcher 4, Molesley 4, Anderton 3, Feeney 3, Goulding 3, Pearce 2, Bartley 1, Igoe 1, Lindfield 1, Partington 1, Robinson 1, Sappleton 1, Thomson 1, Tubbs 1, Ward 1, own goals 2.
Carling Cup (1): Osei-Kuffour 1.
FA Cup (1): Pearce 1.
J Paint Trophy (4): Anderton 1, Goulding 1, Hollands 1, Igoe 1.

Jalal S 41	Garry R 21+4	Bradbury L 28+6	Cooper S 35+2	Pearce J 44	Guyett S 21+4	Igoe S 22+6	Anderton D 17+1	Pitman B 29+10	Osei-Kuffour J 2	Bartley M 27+6	Cummings W 27+5	McQuoid J 5+11	Ward J 16+5	Pettefer C —+1	Sappleton R 1+2	Pryce R 1	Hollands D 39+3	Lindfield C 1+2	Wagstaff S 3+2	Goulding J 14+13	Sturrock B 1+3	Rankine M 3	Molesley M 22+7	Symes M 3+2	Tubbs M 6+2	Partington J 6+5	Preston C 2	Connell A 6+6	Button D 4	Wiggins R 12+1	Thomson J 6	Fletcher S 19+2	Robinson A 16+1	Feeney L 6+8	Tindall J —+2	Webb G —+1	Match No.
1	2	3	4	5	6	7^1	8	9^2	10	11	12	13																									1
1		2	4		6	7^2	8^1	9	10	11	3			5	12	13																					2
		2	4	5	6^1	14	8^2	9		11	3						12	1	7	13	10^3																3
1	6^2	2^1	4	5			8	14		11	3				12		10^3		7	9	13																4
1		2	4	5		7^1	8	9		12	3	13					6			11	10^2																5
1	10	4	5				8	9^1		7^2	2	12	3				6	13	11^3	14																	6
1	9	2	5	6	7^2	8	12			11^2	3	13					4			14	10^1																7
1	3	2	5	6	10	8^1	12			11^2	7	13					4			9^3	14																8
1	9	6	5^2	2	11	8	12			7^3	3		13				4			10^1	14																9
1	9	6	5	2	11^1	8	12			7		13	3				4					10^2															10
1		9		5	6	7^2	8	12			3		$2^\blacksquare$				4			11^1	10	13															11
1		2	11	5	6		8	9^2		7	3	12					4			10^1	13																12
1		3^2	11	5	6	12	8^1	9		7^3	2		13				4			10		14															13
1			6	5	11	7	8	13		12	2		3^1				4^2			14		9^3	10														14
1			6	5	2	7	8^3	9^2		11^1	4		3				12			13		14	10														15
1		9	4	5	$6^\blacksquare$	7^2	8			11	2^1	13^3	3				12						10^3	14													16
1	12	9	6	5		7^2	8			13	2^1	11	3				4						10^1	14													17
1	5	9^3	7	6	2	12		13			11^1	3					4						8^2	14	10												18
1	5	9^3	7	6	2			12	13			11^3	3^1				4						8	14	10^2												19
1		9^1	6		5	13		12			7^3	2	11^2	3			4						8		10	14											20
1	2^1	3		5	6	7					11^3	12	13	14									10	8	4^2	9											21
1	3	9	13	5	6	7		8									12						14	11	4^1	2^3	10^2										22
1	3^2	12	2	5	6	7		8	13								4						11^1	10		9											23
1	12	3	8	5	6			9^3			7	2^1					4			10			11^2	14													24
		2^3	10	5	6^2		9	7				13					$11^\blacksquare$			14			8^1	12	1	3	4										25
	14		6	5		11^3	9	7^1			2						13			8			12		1	3	4^2	10									26
			6	5		7^3	9	11			12	3					4			14			13	1	2	8^1	10^2										27
			6	5			9	11			3						4			8			12		1	2	7^1	10									28
1			6	5		11^1	9	7	12			2^3					4										3	8^2	10	14	13							29
1			5			7^3		9^1			11^2	12					4						13		2			3	8	10	6	14						30
1	12		6^1	5		7^3					11	2					4			14			8			13					9	3	10^2				31
1	6^2			5		7		10			2						4			12			8			11^1					9	3		13			32
1	6			5		7^1					11^3	2					4			13			8			10					9	3	12^2	14			33
1	6	12	4	5			9^1				13	2					7			14			8^2			11^3					10	3					34
1	3		6	5			9	7^2			2						4						8^1		12	13					10	11^3	14				35
1	6		2^1	5	12		9				3	14					4			11^3			8		13						10^1	7					36
1	6	2		5			9				3						4			11			8								10	7					37
1	6	3		5	12		11				13^3	2					4			9^3			8^1								10^2	7	14				38
1	6^3	3^1	12	5			11				13^2	2					4			9			8								10^2	7	14				39
1	6	12	2	5			11				3^3						4			9			8^1					14			10^2	7	13				40
1	6	12	7	5		13	9										4			14			8^1					3			10^3	2	11^2				41
1	2	9	6^3	5	14	12	11										4			10^2			8					3			13	7	8^1				42
1	2^1	14	6	5	12		9										4^2			13			8					3			10^3	7	11				43
1	2	13	6	5			9^3										4			11^1			8					14			10^2	7	12				44
1	6	2		5			9										4			12			8								10^2	7	11^1				45
1		2		5			9^3							8^1	6		4			10^2			12			7					3		13	11		14	46

FA Cup

First Round	Bristol R	(h)	1-0	
Second Round	Blyth S	(h)	0-0	
		(a)	0-1	

Carling Cup

First Round	Cardiff C	(h)	1-2

J Paint Trophy

First Round	Bristol R	(h)	3-0
Second Round	Milton Keynes D	(a)	1-0
Quarter-Final	Colchester U	(h)	0-1

BRADFORD CITY FL Championship 2

FOUNDATION

Bradford was a rugby stronghold around the turn of the century but after Manningham RFC held an archery contest to help them out of financial difficulties in 1903, they were persuaded to give up the handling code and turn to soccer. So they formed Bradford City and continued at Valley Parade. Recognising this as an opportunity of spreading the dribbling code in this part of Yorkshire, the Football League immediately accepted the new club's first application for membership of the Second Division.

Coral Window Stadium, Valley Parade, Bradford, West Yorkshire BD8 7DY.

Telephone: (01274) 773 355.

Fax: (01274) 773 356.

Ticket Office: (01274) 770 012.

Website: www.bradfordcityfc.co.uk

Email: bradfordcityfc@compuserve.com

Ground Capacity: 25,136.

Record Attendance: 39,146 v Burnley, FA Cup 4th rd, 11 March 1911.

Pitch Measurements: 113yd × 70yd.

Joint Chairmen: Julian Rhodes and Mark Lawn.

Director of Operations: David Baldwin.

Secretary: Jon Pollard.

Manager: Stuart McCall.

Assistant Manager: Wayne Jacobs.

Physio: Karen May.

Colours: Claret and amber striped shirts with claret sleeves, black shorts, black stockings.

Change Colours: All white with black trimmed sleeves.

Year Formed: 1903.

Turned Professional: 1903.

Ltd Co.: 1908.

Club Nickname: 'The Bantams'.

Ground: 1903, Valley Parade.

First Football League Game: 1 September 1903, Division 2, v Grimsby T (a) L 0–2 – Seymour; Wilson, Halliday; Robinson, Millar, Farnall; Guy, Beckram, Forrest, McMillan, Graham.

Record League Victory: 11–1 v Rotherham U, Division 3 (N), 25 August 1928 – Sherlaw; Russell, Watson; Burkinshaw (1), Summers, Bauld; Harvey (2), Edmunds (3), White (3), Cairns, Scriven (2).

Record Cup Victory: 11–3 v Walker Celtic, FA Cup 1st rd (replay), 1 December 1937 – Parker; Rookes, McDermott; Murphy, Mackie, Moore; Bagley (1), Whittingham (1), Deakin (4 incl. 1p), Cooke (1), Bartholomew (4).

HONOURS

Football League: Division 1 – Runners-up 1998–99; Division 2 – Champions 1907–08; Division 3 – Champions 1984–85; Division 3 (N) – Champions 1928–29; Division 4 – Runners-up 1981–82.

FA Cup: Winners 1911.

Football League Cup: best season: 5th rd, 1965, 1989.

European Competitions: Intertoto Cup: 2000.

SKY SPORTS FACT FILE

Bradford City had as many as three players who won FA Cup winning medals in their first season with the club: David Taylor, Archie Devine and Frank Thompson. The trio achieved the distinction in 1911 when the new trophy locally manufactured was presented.

Record Defeat: 1–9 v Colchester U, Division 4, 30 December 1961.

Most League Points (2 for a win): 63, Division 3 (N), 1928–29.

Most League Points (3 for a win): 94, Division 3, 1984–85.

Most League Goals: 128, Division 3 (N), 1928–29.

Highest League Scorer in Season: David Layne, 34, Division 4, 1961–62.

Most League Goals in Total Aggregate: Bobby Campbell, 121, 1981–84, 1984–86.

Most League Goals in One Match: 7, Albert Whitehurst v Tranmere R, Division 3 (N), 6 March 1929.

Most Capped Player: Jamie Lawrence (42), Jamaica.

Most League Appearances: Cec Podd, 502, 1970–84.

Youngest League Player: Robert Cullingford, 16 years 141 days v Mansfield T, 22 April 1970.

Record Transfer Fee Received: £2,000,000 from Newcastle U for Des Hamilton, March 1997 and £2,000,000 from Newcastle U for Andrew O'Brien, March 2001.

Record Transfer Fee Paid: £2,500,000 to Leeds U for David Hopkins, July 2000.

Football League Record: 1903 Elected to Division 2; 1908–22 Division 1; 1922–27 Division 2; 1927–29 Division 3 (N); 1929–37 Division 2; 1937–61 Division 3; 1961–69 Division 4; 1969–72 Division 3; 1972–77 Division 4; 1977–78 Division 3; 1978–82 Division 4; 1982–85 Division 3; 1985–90 Division 2; 1990–92 Division 3; 1992–96 Division 2; 1996–99 Division 1; 1999–2001 FA Premier League; 2001–04 Division 1; 2004–07 FL 1; 2007– FL 2.

LATEST SEQUENCES

Longest Sequence of League Wins: 10, 26.11.1983 – 3.2.1984.

Longest Sequence of League Defeats: 8, 21.1.1933 – 11.3.1933.

Longest Sequence of League Draws: 6, 30.1.1976 – 13.3.1976.

Longest Sequence of Unbeaten League Matches: 21, 11.1.1969 – 2.5.1969.

Longest Sequence Without a League Win: 16, 28.8.1948 – 20.11.1948.

Successive Scoring Runs: 30 from 26.12.1961.

Successive Non-scoring Runs: 7 from 18.4.1925.

MANAGERS

Robert Campbell 1903–05
Peter O'Rourke 1905–21
David Menzies 1921–26
Colin Veitch 1926–28
Peter O'Rourke 1928–30
Jack Peart 1930–35
Dick Ray 1935–37
Fred Westgarth 1938–43
Bob Sharp 1943–46
Jack Barker 1946–47
John Milburn 1947–48
David Steele 1948–52
Albert Harris 1952
Ivor Powell 1952–55
Peter Jackson 1955–61
Bob Brocklebank 1961–64
Bill Harris 1965–66
Willie Watson 1966–69
Grenville Hair 1967–68
Jimmy Wheeler 1968–71
Bryan Edwards 1971–75
Bobby Kennedy 1975–78
John Napier 1978
George Mulhall 1978–81
Roy McFarland 1981–82
Trevor Cherry 1982–87
Terry Dolan 1987–89
Terry Yorath 1989–90
John Docherty 1990–91
Frank Stapleton 1991–94
Lennie Lawrence 1994–95
Chris Kamara 1995–98
Paul Jewell 1998–2000
Chris Hutchings 2000
Jim Jefferies 2000–01
Nicky Law 2002–03
Bryan Robson 2003–04
Colin Todd 2004–07
Stuart McCall May 2007–

TEN YEAR LEAGUE RECORD

		P	W	D	L	F	A	Pts	Pos
1999-2000	PR Lge	38	9	9	20	38	68	36	17
2000-01	PR Lge	38	5	11	22	30	70	26	20
2001-02	Div 1	46	15	10	21	69	76	55	15
2002-03	Div 1	46	14	10	22	51	73	52	19
2003-04	Div 1	46	10	6	30	38	69	36	23
2004-05	FL 1	46	17	14	15	64	62	65	11
2005-06	FL 1	46	14	19	13	51	49	61	11
2006-07	FL 1	46	11	14	21	47	65	47	22
2007-08	FL 2	46	17	11	18	63	61	62	10
2008-09	FL 2	46	18	13	15	66	55	67	9

DID YOU KNOW ?

One of the most consistent defenders in the pre-war era was Charlie Bicknell who had one run of 224 consecutive League appearances for Bradford City after being signed from Chesterfield until March 1936 when he was transferred to West Ham United.

BRADFORD CITY 2008–09 LEAGUE RECORD

Match No.	Date	Venue	Opponents	Result	H/T Score	Lg. Pos.	Goalscorers	Attendance
1	Aug 9	H	Notts Co	W 2-1	1-0	—	Thorne 2 [21, 61]	14,038
2	16	A	Macclesfield T	W 2-0	2-0	3	Thorne 2 [10, 14]	2556
3	23	H	Rochdale	W 2-0	2-0	2	Boulding M [20], Thorne [35]	13,154
4	30	A	Aldershot T	L 2-3	1-0	5	McLaren [10], Bullock [68]	3805
5	Sept 6	A	Port Vale	W 2-0	1-0	2	Bullock [17], Thorne [76]	7273
6	13	H	Exeter C	W 4-1	0-1	1	Thorne 2 [54, 68], Boulding M 2 [59, 72]	12,683
7	20	H	Bournemouth	L 1-3	1-1	3	Colbeck [43]	12,824
8	27	A	Shrewsbury T	L 0-2	0-1	5		6517
9	Oct 4	H	Luton T	D 1-1	0-0	6	Conlon [79]	13,083
10	11	A	Accrington S	W 3-2	0-1	3	Boulding M [80], Conlon [88], Thorne [89]	3012
11	18	A	Gillingham	D 2-2	2-0	6	Thorne [21], Colbeck [45]	12,432
12	20	A	Darlington	L 1-2	0-0	—	Daley [85]	3034
13	24	A	Grimsby T	W 3-1	2-0	—	Daley [7], Boulding M [32], Lee G [58]	4470
14	28	H	Bury	W 1-0	0-0	—	Conlon [86]	12,830
15	Nov 1	H	Barnet	D 3-3	3-2	3	Conlon 2 [10, 35], Thorne [29]	12,510
16	15	A	Wycombe W	L 0-1	0-0	6		5002
17	22	A	Rotherham U	W 2-0	0-0	4	O'Brien [71], Law [76]	4586
18	25	H	Chesterfield	W 3-2	2-2	—	Lee G [29], Boulding M [37], Conlon (pen) [73]	12,145
19	Dec 6	H	Dagenham & R	D 1-1	0-0	3	Boulding M [62]	12,145
20	13	A	Brentford	L 1-2	0-0	5	Boulding M [89]	4339
21	20	H	Chester C	D 0-0	0-0	4		12,092
22	26	A	Lincoln C	D 0-0	0-0	4		6156
23	28	H	Morecambe	W 4-0	1-0	3	McLaren [24], Boulding M [62], Law [77], Conlon (pen) [87]	13,105
24	Jan 3	H	Shrewsbury T	D 0-0	0-0	—		12,877
25	17	H	Accrington S	D 1-1	0-1	4	Conlon [51]	12,172
26	24	A	Luton T	D 3-3	0-2	7	McLaren [47], Furman [57], Conlon (pen) [90]	6053
27	27	A	Bury	L 0-1	0-0	—		4112
28	31	H	Grimsby T	W 2-0	0-0	7	Law [75], Jones S [90]	12,816
29	Feb 7	A	Gillingham	W 2-0	1-0	—	Daley [45], Boulding M [70]	4866
30	14	H	Wycombe W	W 1-0	1-0	5	Jones S [43]	12,689
31	17	H	Darlington	D 0-0	0-0	—		12,782
32	21	A	Barnet	L 1-4	0-2	6	Boulding M [56]	2445
33	28	A	Notts Co	L 1-3	0-3	8	Thorne [85]	5138
34	Mar 3	H	Macclesfield T	W 1-0	0-0	—	Furman [60]	11,908
35	7	H	Aldershot T	W 5-0	2-0	4	Thorne 2 [2, 54], Furman [15], Conlon [88], Day (og) [88]	12,465
36	10	A	Rochdale	L 0-3	0-0	—		5500
37	14	A	Exeter C	L 0-1	0-1	8		5253
38	17	A	Bournemouth	L 1-4	1-3	—	Clarke M [25]	4847
39	21	H	Port Vale	L 0-1	0-0	8		12,436
40	28	A	Chester C	D 0-0	0-0	8		2735
41	Apr 4	H	Brentford	D 1-1	0-0	8	Thorne [90]	12,832
42	10	A	Morecambe	L 1-2	1-0	—	Clarke M [37]	4546
43	13	H	Lincoln C	D 1-1	0-0	9	Bullock [65]	12,932
44	18	A	Dagenham & R	L 0-3	0-0	11		1883
45	25	H	Rotherham U	W 3-0	2-0	9	Thorne 2 [12, 32], Jones S [73]	13,242
46	May 2	A	Chesterfield	W 2-0	0-0	9	Furman [54], Boulding M [87]	3859

Final League Position: 9

GOALSCORERS

League (66): Thorne 17, Boulding M 12, Conlon 10 (3 pens), Furman 4, Bullock 3, Daley 3, Jones S 3, Law 3, McLaren 3, Clarke M 2, Colbeck 2, Lee G 2, O'Brien 1, own goal 1.
Carling Cup (0).
FA Cup (3): Boulding M 1, Daley 1, Lee 1.
J Paint Trophy (1): Conlon 1.

Evans R 45	Amison P 25 + 2	Heckingbottom P 9	Bullock L 15 + 8	Lee G 44	Clarke M 42	Daley O 26 + 2	McLaren P 32 + 2	Conlon B 15 + 15	Thorne P 32 + 5	Nix K 6 + 10	Moncur T 11 + 3	Boulding M 35 + 9	Colbeck J 19 + 9	Topp W — + 2	Bower M — + 3	Furman D 26 + 6	Ainge S 1	O'Brien L 34 + 1	Clarke T 4 + 2	Law N 30 + 3	Osborne L 1 + 1	Jones S 25 + 2	O'Grady C — + 2	Rehman Z 16 + 1	Brandon C 4 + 3	Gillespie K 2 + 1	Mullin P 5 + 1	McLaughlin J 1	Boulding R 1	Sharry L — + 1	Match No.
1	2[1]	3	4	5	6	7	8	9[2]	10	11	12	13																			1
1	2	3	4	5	6	7	8		10			9[1]	11	12																	2
1	2	3	4	5	6	7	8[1]	13	10[2]	12	14	9[3]	11																		3
1	2	3	4[2]	5	6[1]	7	8		10	14		9[2]	11	12	13																4
1	2	3	4	5	6	7[1]	8		10	12		9[2]	11	13																	5
1	2	3	4[3]	5	6	7[2]	8	12	10[1]	13		9	11	14																	6
1	2[2]	3	4	5[1]	6	7	8[3]	12	10	13		9	11	14																	7
1		3	4[1]	5	6	7	8	9				13	2[2]	12	11	10															8
1	3			5	6	7	8	12	10[2]			9[2]	11			4	2	13													9
1				5	6		8	12	10	11[1]	2	9	7			4		3													10
1				5	6	7	8	12	10[2]		2	9[1]	11	13		4		3													11
1				5	6	12	8	9	10[2]	11[1]	2	13	7			4		3													12
1	12			5	6	7[2]	8		10		2	9	11[1]			4		3		13											13
1				5		7	8	12	10		2	9[1]				4		3	6	11											14
1				5			8	9	10	12	2	11				4[1]		3	6	7											15
1				5	6	7	8	9	10		2	12						3	4[1]	11											16
1				5	6	7	8[3]	12	10[2]	13	2	9						3	14	11	4[1]										17
1				5	6	7[1]		9	12	11	2	10						3	4	8											18
1				5	6		8	12	10[1]	11	2	9						3	4	7											19
1	2			5	6	7	8	12	10[1]			9						3	4	11											20
1	2			5	6	7	8	9				10						3	4	11											21
1	2			5	6	7	8	9[1]	12			10[2]				13		3	4	11											22
1	2			5	6	12	8	9		13		10[1]				4[2]		3		11	7										23
1	2			5	6	11	8	9				10[1]				4		3		7		12									24
1	2			5	6	7	8	9[2]	12			10[1]				4		3		11		13									25
1	2	14		5	6	7[1]	8	13	10[2]			12				4[3]		3		11		9									26
1	2	4[3]		5	6	11[2]	8	9		13		12				14			7	10[1]		3									27
1				5	6	11[1]		13	10[2]			9	12			4		8	7			2									28
1	2	13		5	6	7[1]		10				9	12			4		8		11[2]		3									29
1	2	12			6	11[2]		10				9[1]	13			4		8	7			5									30
1				12	5	6	11[3]		13	10[2]		9	14			4		3		8	7[1]	2									31
1				5	6			12	13	10		9	7[2]			4		3		8	11[1]	2									32
1		7		5	6			10				9[1]	12			4		3		8	11	2									33
1	2			5	6			9	12	13		10[1]	7[2]			4		3		8	11										34
1	2			5	6			12	10[1]			9[2]	7			4		3		8	11				13						35
1	2[3]		12	5	6			9[2]	10			13	7[1]			4		3		12	11	14									36
1	2	7	5				8[2]		13			9	12			4[1]		3		11	10			6							37
1	2			5	6			9				10				4		8		7		3	11[1]	12							38
1				12	5	6						9				4[1]		3		8	7	2	13	11[2]	10						39
1				12	5	6		8[1]				9				4		3		7	11[2]	2	13		10						40
1				5	6			8[1]	9			12				4		13	14	2	11[2]	7[3]	10								41
1			14	5	6			4	9[1]			12	7					3		8[3]	13	2	11[2]		10						42
1	14		4	5	6			8	9			10[2]	7[1]					3		12	11	2[3]		13							43
1	2		4	5[2]	6			8	9			14		13				3		12	7[3]					11[1]	10				44
1	2	8	5					14	9	7[1]		12			13	4		3		11	10[3]	6[2]									45
	2	8		6						13		9	7			4[3]		3		11[2]	12	5						1	10[1]	14	46

FA Cup
First Round   Milton Keynes D   (a)   2-1
Second Round   Leyton Orient   (h)   1-2

Carling Cup
First Round   Huddersfield T   (a)   0-4

J Paint Trophy
First Round   Leeds U   (a)   1-2

BRENTFORD

FL Championship 1

FOUNDATION

Formed as a small amateur concern in 1889 they were very successful in local circles. They won the championship of the West London Alliance in 1893 and a year later the West Middlesex Junior Cup before carrying off the Senior Cup in 1895. After winning both the London Senior Amateur Cup and the Middlesex Senior Cup in 1898 they were admitted to the Second Division of the Southern League.

Griffin Park, Braemar Road, Brentford, Middlesex TW8 0NT.

Telephone: 0845 3456 442.

Fax: (0208) 568 9940.

Ticket Office: 0845 3456 442.

Website: www.brentfordfc.co.uk

E-mail: enquiries@brentfordfc.co.uk

Ground Capacity: 12,400.

Record Attendance: 38,678 v Leicester C, FA Cup 6th rd, 26 February 1949.

Pitch Measurements: 111yd × 74yd.

Chairman: Greg Dyke.

Acting Chief Executive: David Heath.

Secretary: Lisa Hall.

Manager: Andy Scott.

Assistant Manager: Terry Bullivant.

Physio: Dave Appanah.

HONOURS

Football League: Division 1 best season: 5th, 1935–36; Division 2 – Champions 1934–35; Division 3 – Champions 1991–92, 1998–99; Division 3 (S) – Champions 1932–33, Runners-up 1929–30, 1957–58; Division 4 – Champions 1962–63; FL 2 – Champions 2008–09.

FA Cup: best season: 6th rd, 1938, 1946, 1949, 1989.

Football League Cup: best season: 4th rd, 1983.

Freight Rover Trophy: Runners-up 1985.

LDV Vans Trophy: Runners-up 2001.

Colours: Red and white striped shirts with red sleeves, black shorts, black stockings.

Change Colours: Sky blue shirts with dark blue trim, dark blue shorts, dark blue stockings.

Year Formed: 1889.

Turned Professional: 1899.

Ltd Co.: 1901.

Club Nickname: 'The Bees'.

Grounds: 1889, Clifden Road; 1891, Benns Fields, Little Ealing; 1895, Shotters Field; 1898, Cross Road, S. Ealing; 1900, Boston Park; 1904, Griffin Park.

First Football League Game: 28 August 1920, Division 3, v Exeter C (a) L 0–3 – Young; Hodson, Rosier, Elliott J, Levitt, Amos, Smith, Thompson, Spreadbury, Morley, Henery.

Record League Victory: 9–0 v Wrexham, Division 3, 15 October 1963 – Cakebread; Coote, Jones; Slater, Scott, Higginson; Summers (1), Brooks (2), McAdams (2), Ward (2), Hales (1), (1 og).

Record Cup Victory: 7–0 v Windsor & Eton (away), FA Cup 1st rd, 20 November 1982 – Roche; Rowe, Harris (Booker), McNichol (1), Whitehead, Hurlock (2), Kamara, Joseph (1), Mahoney (3), Bowles, Roberts. *N.B.* 8–0 v Uxbridge, FA Cup, 3rd Qual rd, 31 October 1903.

SKY SPORTS FACT FILE

On 31 January 2009 Justin Rhodes, on loan from Ipswich Town, scored a perfect first-half hat-trick for Brentford at Shrewsbury. Three-in-a-row as well as one with his left foot, one with his right and the third a headed goal, all scored in a 27-minute spell.

Record Defeat: 0–7 v Swansea T, Division 3 (S), 8 November 1924; v Walsall, Division 3 (S), 19 January 1957; v Peterborough U, 24 November 2007.

Most League Points (2 for a win): 62, Division 3 (S), 1932–33 and Division 4, 1962–63.

Most League Points (3 for a win): 85, Division 2, 1994–95, Division 3, 1998–99 and FL 2, 2008–09.

Most League Goals: 98, Division 4, 1962–63.

Highest League Scorer in Season: Jack Holliday, 38, Division 3 (S), 1932–33.

Most League Goals in Total Aggregate: Jim Towers, 153, 1954–61.

Most League Goals in One Match: 5, Jack Holliday v Luton T, Division 3 (S), 28 January 1933; 5, Billy Scott v Barnsley, Division 2, 15 December 1934; 5, Peter McKennan v Bury, Division 2, 18 February 1949.

Most Capped Player: John Buttigieg, 22 (98), Malta.

Most League Appearances: Ken Coote, 514, 1949–64.

Youngest League Player: Danis Salman, 15 years 248 days v Watford, 15 November 1975.

Record Transfer Fee Received: £2,500,000 from Wimbledon for Hermann Hreidarsson, October 1999.

Record Transfer Fee Paid: £750,000 to Crystal Palace for Hermann Hreidarsson, September 1998.

Football League Record: 1920 Original Member of Division 3; 1921–33 Division 3 (S); 1933–35 Division 2; 1935–47 Division 1; 1947–54 Division 2; 1954–62 Division 3 (S); 1962–63 Division 4; 1963–66 Division 3; 1966–72 Division 4; 1972–73 Division 3; 1973–78 Division 4; 1978–92 Division 3; 1992–93 Division 1; 1993–98 Division 2; 1998–99 Division 3; 1999–04 Division 2; 2004–07 FL 1; 2007–09 FL 2; 2009– FL 1.

LATEST SEQUENCES

Longest Sequence of League Wins: 9, 30.4.1932 – 24.9.1932.

Longest Sequence of League Defeats: 9, 20.10.1928 – 25.12.1928.

Longest Sequence of League Draws: 5, 16.3.1957 – 6.4.1957.

Longest Sequence of Unbeaten League Matches: 26, 20.2.1999 – 16.10.1999.

Longest Sequence Without a League Win: 18, 9.9.2006 – 26.12.2006.

Successive Scoring Runs: 26 from 4.3.1963.

Successive Non-scoring Runs: 7 from 7.3.2000.

MANAGERS

Will Lewis 1900–03
(Secretary-Manager)
Dick Molyneux 1902–06
W. G. Brown 1906–08
Fred Halliday 1908–12, 1915–21, 1924–26
(only Secretary to 1922)
Ephraim Rhodes 1912–15
Archie Mitchell 1921–24
Harry Curtis 1926–49
Jackie Gibbons 1949–52
Jimmy Bain 1952–53
Tommy Lawton 1953
Bill Dodgin Snr 1953–57
Malcolm Macdonald 1957–65
Tommy Cavanagh 1965–66
Billy Gray 1966–67
Jimmy Sirrel 1967–69
Frank Blunstone 1969–73
Mike Everitt 1973–75
John Docherty 1975–76
Bill Dodgin Jnr 1976–80
Fred Callaghan 1980–84
Frank McLintock 1984–87
Steve Perryman 1987–90
Phil Holder 1990–93
David Webb 1993–97
Eddie May 1997
Micky Adams 1997–98
Ron Noades 1998–2000
Ray Lewington 2001
Steve Coppell 2001–02
Wally Downes 2002–04
Martin Allen 2004–06
Leroy Rosenior 2006
Scott Fitzgerald 2006–07
Terry Butcher 2007
Andy Scott December 2007–

TEN YEAR LEAGUE RECORD

		P	W	D	L	F	A	Pts	Pos
1999-2000	Div 2	46	13	13	20	47	61	52	17
2000-01	Div 2	46	14	17	15	56	70	59	14
2001-02	Div 2	46	24	11	11	77	43	83	3
2002-03	Div 2	46	14	12	20	47	56	54	16
2003-04	Div 2	46	14	11	21	52	69	53	17
2004-05	FL 1	46	22	9	15	57	60	75	4
2005-06	FL 1	46	20	16	10	72	52	76	3
2006-07	FL 1	46	8	13	25	40	79	37	24
2007-08	FL 2	46	17	8	21	52	70	59	14
2008-09	FL 2	46	23	16	7	65	36	85	1

DID YOU KNOW ?

After a ten-year wait for a treble-scoring Brentford player, hey presto, two come along in a week! On 7 February 2009 Charlie MacDonald scored a 24-minute, first half hat-trick of his own against Chester City at Griffin Park.

BRENTFORD 2008–09 LEAGUE RECORD

Match No.	Date	Venue	Opponents	Result	H/T Score	Lg. Pos.	Goalscorers	Attendance
1	Aug 9	A	Bury	L	0-1	0-1	—	2819
2	16	H	Grimsby T	W	4-0	3-0	8	MacDonald 2 [27, 45], Elder [38], Poole [60]	4009
3	23	A	Barnet	W	1-0	1-0	6	Poole (pen) [10]	2815
4	30	H	Rotherham U	D	0-0	0-0	6		4381
5	Sept 6	H	Dagenham & R	W	2-1	2-0	6	Elder [23], MacDonald [34]	4519
6	13	A	Wycombe W	D	0-0	0-0	6		5799
7	20	H	Lincoln C	D	1-1	1-1	6	Elder [24]	4557
8	27	A	Chesterfield	W	1-0	1-0	4	Bean [7]	3188
9	Oct 4	H	Macclesfield T	W	1-0	1-0	4	MacDonald [15]	4773
10	13	A	Notts Co	D	1-1	1-0	—	Poole [36]	6012
11	18	A	Aldershot T	D	1-1	0-1	5	Poole (pen) [57]	5023
12	21	H	Morecambe	W	3-1	3-1	—	MacDonald [8], Poole [11], Elder [36]	3733
13	25	H	Shrewsbury T	D	1-1	0-0	2	MacDonald [73]	5362
14	28	A	Chester C	L	0-3	0-1	—		1301
15	Nov 1	H	Rochdale	L	1-2	0-2	9	Bowditch [50]	4291
16	15	A	Port Vale	W	3-0	1-0	5	Osborne [45], Bean [67], MacDonald [90]	6058
17	22	H	Darlington	D	1-1	0-0	7	Osborne [90]	4837
18	25	A	Luton T	W	1-0	1-0	—	Elder [29]	5248
19	Dec 13	H	Bradford C	W	2-1	0-0	4	Bean [88], Elder [90]	4339
20	20	A	Gillingham	D	1-1	1-0	3	MacDonald [28]	5521
21	26	H	Bournemouth	W	2-0	2-0	2	Bean 2 [22, 45]	6450
22	28	A	Exeter C	W	2-0	0-0	2	MacDonald (pen) [75], Wood [79]	6791
23	Jan 10	A	Lincoln C	D	2-2	2-1	—	Bean [12], Bowditch [23]	3932
24	17	H	Notts Co	D	1-1	0-1	2	Phillips [90]	5465
25	24	A	Macclesfield T	L	0-2	0-1	2		1942
26	27	H	Aldershot T	W	3-0	2-0	—	Bean [28], MacDonald (pen) [44], Rhodes [87]	5111
27	31	A	Shrewsbury T	W	3-1	3-0	2	Rhodes 3 [2, 17, 29]	5674
28	Feb 3	A	Morecambe	L	0-2	0-1	—		1253
29	7	H	Chester C	W	3-0	3-0	—	MacDonald 3 (1 pen) [21, 35, 45 (p)]	4719
30	10	A	Accrington S	D	1-1	0-0	—	Rhodes [90]	1111
31	14	H	Port Vale	W	2-0	1-0	1	Osborne [45], MacDonald [86]	4702
32	21	A	Rochdale	W	2-1	2-1	1	Rhodes [9], MacDonald [15]	3412
33	28	H	Bury	W	1-0	1-0	1	Bean [39]	6597
34	Mar 3	A	Grimsby T	W	1-0	1-0	—	MacDonald [27]	3001
35	7	A	Rotherham U	D	0-0	0-0	1		3406
36	10	H	Barnet	W	1-0	1-0	—	Bean [8]	4742
37	14	H	Wycombe W	D	3-3	2-2	1	Rhodes [2], Hunt [22], Williams S [81]	10,642
38	17	H	Chesterfield	L	0-1	0-0	—		4541
39	28	H	Gillingham	D	1-1	1-0	1	Hunt [41]	7908
40	Apr 4	A	Bradford C	D	1-1	0-0	1	Clarke [63]	12,832
41	11	H	Exeter C	D	1-1	0-1	1	Clarke [90]	8234
42	13	A	Bournemouth	W	1-0	1-0	1	Clarke [41]	8168
43	18	H	Accrington S	W	3-0	2-0	1	Williams S [8], Dickson [41], Clarke (pen) [54]	7135
44	21	A	Dagenham & R	L	1-3	0-2	—	Spencer [85]	3537
45	25	A	Darlington	W	3-1	2-0	1	Bennett [35], Clarke 2 [43, 54]	3868
46	May 2	H	Luton T	W	2-0	0-0	1	Osborne [73], Newton [90]	10,223

Final League Position: 1

GOALSCORERS

League (65): MacDonald 16 (3 pens), Bean 9, Rhodes 7, Clarke 6 (1 pen), Elder 6, Poole 5 (2 pens), Osborne 4, Bowditch 2, Hunt 2, Williams S 2, Bennett 1, Dickson 1, Newton 1, Phillips 1, Spencer 1, Wood 1.
Carling Cup (0).
FA Cup (4): MacDonald 2, Elder 1, Marvin Williams 1.
J Paint Trophy (4): Poole 2 (1 pen), O'Connor 1, Marvin Williams 1.

Hamer B 45	Newton A 30 + 5	Wood S 37 + 3	O'Connor K 25 + 3	Bennett A 44	Osborne K 19 + 4	Williams Marvin 21 + 13	Bean M 43 + 1	Connell A 1 + 1	Elder N 18 + 9	Poole G 18 + 8	Johnson B 7 + 3	Ademola M — + 8	Phillips M 28 + 5	Wilson J 14	Pead C 5 + 1	MacDonald C 38	Dickson R 31 + 8	Artus F — + 1	Wright J 5	Hails J 22 + 1	Bowditch D 8 + 1	Andersen M 1	Scannell D 1 + 1	Hunt D 10 + 10	Rhodes J 14	Williams S 5 + 6	Smith G 2 + 2	Powell D 3 + 1	Clarke B 8	Spencer D 3 + 2	Brown S — + 1	Match No.
1	2	3^1	4	5	6	7^2	8	9	10	11	12	13																				1
1	2		4	5^1		7^2			10	11	3	13	12	6	8	9																2
1	2		4^1	5		7	12	14	10	11^2	3	13		6	8	9^3																3
1	2			5		7^2	8		10	11^1	3	13		6	4	9	12															4
1	2	12^5		5		7	8		10	11	3			6	4^1	9^2	13															5
1	2			5		7	8		10	11^1	3			6	4	9	12															6
1	2^2	12		5		7^3	4		10	11^1	3	13	14	6		9			8													7
1	2	3		5			8		10^2	11^1		13			4	9	12		7	6												8
1	7^1	3		5		12	8		10	11^2		13		6		9			4	2												9
1	7	3		5		12	8		10	11				6		9			4	2												10
1	7	3	12	5			8^2		10	11		13		6		9			4	2												11
1	2	3	12	5		7^1	8		10	11^2				6		9	13		4													12
1	2	3		5		7	8		10	11^1				6		9	12		4													13
1	2	3^2		5		7	8	14	10^1	11^3	12			6		9	13		4													14
1	2^2	3	4	5		7	8			11	12	13		6^1		9			10													15
1	12	13	4	5	6		8^3		10^1	11^2			14			9	2			7												16
-1	2^2	12	4	5	6		8			11^1		13				9	3			7				10								17
1		3	4	5	6		8		10	11						9	2			7												18
	11		4	5		12	8		10	13			3^2	6		9^3				2	14	1	7^1									19
1	11		4	5	6	12	8		10^4			13	3			9^1	2						7^2									20
1	11		4	5	6	7^1	8						3			9	2							10		12						21
1	11		4	5	6	7	8						3			9	2							10								22
1	6		4	5	7		8			11^1			3			9	2							10		12						23
1		3^1	4	5	6	7	8^2		10^4	11	12	13				9	2															24
1	12		4	5	6	7^1	8			11^2		13				9	3							10	14							25
1			4	5	6	7^2	8			11	12	13				9	3							2^1		10						26
1			4	5	6^1	7^2	8			11	12	13				9	3							2		10						27
1		11^1	4	5	6	7^3	8				12		14			9	3							2^2	13	10						28
1		11	4^2	5	6	7	8				12		14			9^1	3							2	13	10^3						29
1		11	4	5	6	7^1	8				12					9	3							2		10						30
1	12	11	4	5	6	7^1	8^3					13				9	3									10						31
1	12	11	4	5	6	7^1	8					13	14			9^2	3									10^3						32
1		11	4	5	6	7^2	8				12					9	3							2	13	10^1						33
1		11	4	5	6	7^2	8				12					9	3							2	13	10^1						34
1	12	11		5	6	7^1	8					13^3	14			9	3							2		10^2						35
1		11	4^2	5	6		8				12		14			9	3			7^1				2	13	10^3						36
1	7^1	11	4	5	6		8					13				9	3^2							2	4	10	12					37
1	7^1	11^2	4	5	6		8				12	13	14			9	3							2	4	10^3						38
1		11		5	6	2	8					13				5^2	3								4	10^3	12			7^1	14	39
1	7	11		5	6	2	8									3									4		5	10^1	9			40
1				5	6	2	11					13				3			7^2						4	12	8	5	10	9^1		41
1	7^1	11		5	6	2	13					8	12			3									4	9^3	14	5^4	10^2			42
1	7	11^1		5	6	2	13					8	12			3									4	9^2			10^2			43
1	7^1	11		5	6	2	13					8				3									4	9^2		10	12			44
1^6	7	11^2		5	6		8					13				3	2								4	12	10	9^1	15			45
1	7	11		5	6		12					8	13	14	5^1	3^2	2								4	9	10^3					46

FA Cup

First Round	Havant & W	(a)	3-1
Second Round	Barrow	(a)	1-2

Carling Cup

First Round	Swansea C	(a)	0-2

J Paint Trophy

First Round	Yeovil T	(h)	2-2
Second Round	Luton T	(a)	2-2

BRIGHTON & HOVE ALBION FL Championship 1

FOUNDATION

A professional club Brighton United was formed in November 1897 at the Imperial Hotel, Queen's Road, but folded in March 1900 after less than two seasons in the Southern League at the County Ground. An amateur team Brighton & Hove Rangers was then formed by some prominent United supporters and after one season at Withdean, decided to turn semi-professional and play at the County Ground. Rangers were accepted into the Southern League but then also folded June 1901. John Jackson the former United manager organised a meeting at the Seven Stars public house, Ship Street on 24 June 1901 at which a new third club Brighton & Hove United was formed. They took over Rangers' place in the Southern League and pitch at County Ground. The name was changed to Brighton & Hove Albion before a match was played because of objections by Hove FC.

Withdean Stadium, Tongdean Lane, Brighton, East Sussex BN1 5JD.

Telephone: (01273) 695 400 (admin office 44 North Road, Brighton).

Fax: (01273) 648 179 (admin office 44 North Road, Brighton).

Ticket Office: (01273) 776 992 (5/6 Queen's Road).

Website: www.seagulls.co.uk

Email: seagulls@bhafc.co.uk

Ground Capacity: 8,850.

Record Attendance: 36,747 v Fulham, Division 2, 27 December 1958 (at Goldstone Ground).

Pitch Measurements: 110yd × 70yd.

Chairman: Tony Bloom.

Managing Director: Ken Brown.

Chief Executive: Martin Perry.

Secretary: Derek J. Allan.

Manager: Russell Slade.

Assistant Manager: Dean White.

Physio: Jim Joyce.

Colours: Blue and white striped shirts, white sleeves with blue trim, white shorts, white stockings.

Change Colours: Yellow and navy blue striped shirts with blue sleeves, navy blue shorts, navy blue stockings.

Year Formed: 1901. *Turned Professional:* 1901. *Ltd Co.:* 1904.

Grounds: 1901, County Ground; 1902, Goldstone Ground.

Club Nickname: 'The Seagulls'.

First Football League Game: 28 August 1920, Division 3, v Southend U (a) L 0–2 – Hayes; Woodhouse, Little; Hall, Comber, Bentley; Longstaff, Ritchie, Doran, Rodgerson, March.

HONOURS

Football League: Division 1 best season: 13th, 1981–82; Division 2 – Champions 2001–02; Runners-up 1978–79; Division 3 (S) – Champions 1957–58; Runners-up 1953–54, 1955–56; Division 3 – Champions 2000–01; Runners-up 1971–72, 1976–77, 1987–88; Division 4 – Champions 1964–65.

FA Cup: Runners-up 1983.

Football League Cup: best season: 5th rd, 1979.

SKY SPORTS FACT FILE

In 1964–65 Brighton & Hove Albion owed their Fourth Division title to an unbeaten home record which saw them drop just five points. They had to win their last two at the Goldstone Ground to hold off four close challengers for the championship.

Record League Victory: 9–1 v Newport Co, Division 3 (S), 18 April 1951 – Ball; Tennant (1p), Mansell (1p); Willard, McCoy, Wilson; Reed, McNichol (4), Garbutt, Bennett (2), Keene (1). 9–1 v Southend U, Division 3, 27 November 1965 – Powney; Magill, Baxter; Leck, Gall, Turner; Gould (1), Collins (1), Livesey (2), Smith (3), Goodchild (2).

Record Cup Victory: 10–1 v Wisbech, FA Cup 1st rd, 13 November 1965 – Powney; Magill, Baxter; Collins (1), Gall, Turner; Gould, Smith (2), Livesey (3), Cassidy (2), Goodchild (1), (1 og).

Record Defeat: 0–9 v Middlesbrough, Division 2, 23 August 1958.

Most League Points (2 for a win): 65, Division 3 (S), 1955–56 and Division 3, 1971–72.

Most League Points (3 for a win): 92, Division 3, 2000–01.

Most League Goals: 112, Division 3 (S), 1955–56.

Highest League Scorer in Season: Peter Ward, 32, Division 3, 1976–77.

Most League Goals in Total Aggregate: Tommy Cook, 114, 1922–29.

Most League Goals in One Match: 5, Jack Doran v Northampton T, Division 3 (S), 5 November 1921; 5, Adrian Thorne v Watford, Division 3 (S), 30 April 1958.

Most Capped Player: Steve Penney, 17, Northern Ireland.

Most League Appearances: 'Tug' Wilson, 509, 1922–36.

Youngest League Player: Ian Chapman, 16 years 259 days v Birmingham C, 14 February 1987.

Record Transfer Fee Received: £1,500,000 from Tottenham H for Bobby Zamora, July 2003 and £1,500,000 from Celtic for Adam Virgo, July 2005.

Record Transfer Fee Paid: £500,000 to Manchester U for Andy Ritchie, October 1980.

Football League Record: 1920 Original Member of Division 3; 1921–58 Division 3 (S); 1958–62 Division 2; 1962–63 Division 3; 1963–65 Division 4; 1965–72 Division 3; 1972–73 Division 2; 1973–77 Division 3; 1977–79 Division 2; 1979–83 Division 1; 1983–87 Division 2; 1987–88 Division 3; 1988–96 Division 2; 1996–2001 Division 3; 2001–02 Division 2; 2002–03 Division 1; 2003–04 Division 2; 2004–06 FL C; 2006– FL 1.

MANAGERS

John Jackson 1901–05
Frank Scott-Walford 1905–08
John Robson 1908–14
Charles Webb 1919–47
Tommy Cook 1947
Don Welsh 1947–51
Billy Lane 1951–61
George Curtis 1961–63
Archie Macaulay 1963–68
Fred Goodwin 1968–70
Pat Saward 1970–73
Brian Clough 1973–74
Peter Taylor 1974–76
Alan Mullery 1976–81
Mike Bailey 1981–82
Jimmy Melia 1982–83
Chris Cattlin 1983–86
Alan Mullery 1986–87
Barry Lloyd 1987–93
Liam Brady 1993–95
Jimmy Case 1995–96
Steve Gritt 1996–98
Brian Horton 1998–99
Jeff Wood 1999
Micky Adams 1999–2001
Peter Taylor 2001–02
Martin Hinshelwood 2002
Steve Coppell 2002–03
Mark McGhee 2003–06
Dean Wilkins 2006–08
Micky Adams 2008–09
Russell Slade March 2009–

LATEST SEQUENCES

Longest Sequence of League Wins: 9, 2.10.1926 – 20.11.1926.
Longest Sequence of League Defeats: 12, 17.8.2002 – 26.10.2002.
Longest Sequence of League Draws: 6, 16.2.1980 – 15.3.1980.
Longest Sequence of Unbeaten League Matches: 16, 8.10.1930 – 28.1.1931.
Longest Sequence Without a League Win: 15, 21.10.1972 – 27.1.1973
Successive Scoring Runs: 31 from 4.2.1956.
Successive Non-scoring Runs: 6 from 8.11.1924.

TEN YEAR LEAGUE RECORD

		P	W	D	L	F	A	Pts	Pos
1999-2000	Div 3	46	17	16	13	64	46	67	11
2000-01	Div 3	46	28	8	10	73	35	92	1
2001-02	Div 2	46	25	15	6	66	42	90	1
2002-03	Div 1	46	11	12	23	49	67	45	23
2003-04	Div 2	46	22	11	13	64	43	77	4
2004-05	FL C	46	13	12	21	40	65	51	20
2005-06	FL C	46	7	17	22	39	71	38	24
2006-07	FL 1	46	14	11	21	49	58	53	18
2007-08	FL 1	46	19	12	15	58	50	69	7
2008-09	FL 1	46	13	13	20	55	70	52	16

DID YOU KNOW ❓

On 24 September 2008 in a Carling Cup second round match at Withdean, Brighton & Hove Albion beat Manchester City 5–3 on penalties after a 2–2 draw. City's squad featured ten internationals including seven from overseas.

i

BRIGHTON & HOVE ALBION 2008–09 LEAGUE RECORD

Match No.	Date	Venue	Opponents	Result	H/T Score	Lg. Pos.	Goalscorers	Attendance
1	Aug 9	A	Crewe Alex	W 2-1	1-0	—	Virgo [36], Forster [90]	4557
2	16	H	Bristol R	D 1-1	1-0	4	Forster (pen) [10]	6210
3	22	A	Southend U	W 2-0	0-0	—	Murray [74], Forster [89]	7976
4	30	H	Leyton Orient	D 0-0	0-0	4		6675
5	Sept 6	H	Scunthorpe U	L 1-4	0-2	8	Robinson [75]	5529
6	13	A	Yeovil T	D 1-1	0-0	11	Forster (pen) [77]	4451
7	20	H	Walsall	L 0-1	0-1	13		5679
8	27	A	Northampton T	D 2-2	1-0	14	Murray 2 (1 pen) [43 ip], [89]	5389
9	Oct 4	H	Cheltenham T	D 3-3	2-2	14	Murray 3 [1, 7, 47]	5859
10	11	A	Leeds U	L 1-3	0-2	17	Murray [90]	22,726
11	18	H	Hereford U	D 0-0	0-0	17		5608
12	21	A	Peterborough U	D 0-0	0-0	—		5772
13	25	A	Hartlepool U	L 0-1	0-1	18		3962
14	28	H	Leicester C	W 3-2	0-2	—	Johnson 2 [60, 84], Hobbs (og) [89]	6282
15	Nov 1	H	Millwall	W 4-1	1-0	14	Murray 2 [45, 57], Johnson [65], Cox [81]	5973
16	15	A	Carlisle U	L 1-3	0-2	15	Richards [64]	5333
17	22	H	Huddersfield T	L 0-1	0-0	17		6461
18	25	A	Stockport Co	L 0-2	0-1	—		5201
19	Dec 6	A	Oldham Ath	D 1-1	1-1	20	Murray [20]	4803
20	12	H	Milton Keynes D	L 2-4	1-1	—	Johnson [3], Fleetwood [88]	5691
21	20	A	Tranmere R	L 0-1	0-0	21		4885
22	26	H	Colchester U	L 1-2	1-1	21	Forster [21]	6299
23	28	A	Swindon T	W 2-0	1-0	19	Forster 2 (1 pen) [43, 52 ip]	8438
24	Jan 17	H	Leeds U	L 0-2	0-0	20		7096
25	24	A	Cheltenham T	D 2-2	0-1	20	Forster [78], Hinshelwood [90]	3597
26	27	A	Leicester C	D 0-0	0-0	—		17,410
27	31	H	Hartlepool U	W 2-1	0-1	20	Forster [59], Nelson (og) [90]	5784
28	Feb 10	H	Peterborough U	L 2-4	2-2	—	Davies [27], McNulty [45]	5087
29	14	H	Carlisle U	L 0-2	0-2	21		5529
30	21	A	Millwall	W 1-0	0-0	21	Virgo [73]	9226
31	24	A	Northampton T	D 1-1	0-0	—	Elphick [57]	5062
32	28	H	Crewe Alex	L 0-4	0-1	22		6366
33	Mar 7	A	Leyton Orient	L 1-2	1-1	22	Heath [17]	5885
34	10	H	Southend U	L 1-3	1-1	—	Owusu [45]	5035
35	14	H	Yeovil T	W 5-0	2-0	22	Cox 2 [16, 89], Forster 2 [29, 62], Murray (pen) [80]	6291
36	17	A	Walsall	L 0-3	0-3	—		3549
37	21	A	Scunthorpe U	L 0-2	0-1	22		4404
38	28	H	Tranmere R	D 0-0	0-0	22		5819
39	Apr 4	A	Milton Keynes D	L 0-2	0-2	22		15,842
40	7	A	Hereford U	W 2-1	1-0	—	Fraser [9], Owusu [75]	2033
41	11	H	Swindon T	L 2-3	1-0	22	Virgo [38], Dicker [90]	6549
42	13	A	Colchester U	W 1-0	0-0	22	Owusu [57]	4873
43	18	H	Oldham Ath	W 3-1	2-0	22	Cox [26], Owusu 2 [37, 64]	6618
44	21	A	Bristol R	W 2-1	1-1	—	Owusu [43], Andrew [52]	6193
45	25	A	Huddersfield T	D 2-2	1-1	20	Andrew [38], Owusu [66]	14,740
46	May 2	H	Stockport Co	W 1-0	0-0	16	Forster [73]	8618

Final League Position: 16

GOALSCORERS

League (55): Forster 12 (3 pens), Murray 11 (2 pens), Owusu 7, Cox 4, Johnson 4, Virgo 3, Andrew 2, Davies 1, Dicker 1, Elphick 1, Fleetwood 1, Fraser 1, Heath 1, Hinshelwood 1, McNulty 1, Richards 1, Robinson 1, own goals 2.
Carling Cup (7): Virgo 2, Anyinsah 1, Elphick 1, Forster 1, Murray 1, Richards 1.
FA Cup (4): Cox 1, Forster 1, Fraser 1, McLeod 1.
J Paint Trophy (6): Forster 2 (1 pen), Anyinsah 1, Livermore 1, McLeod 1, Virgo 1 (pen).

Kuipers M 28	Whing A 40	Richards M 23	Thomson S 17	Elphick T 38+1	Hawkins C 17	Cox D 32+8	Virgo A 36	Murray G 18+5	Forster N 26+4	McLeod K 11+10	Livermore D 12+4	Hart G 7+4	Owusu L 13+1	Fraser T 18+9	Lynch J —+2	Loft D 7+5	Dicker G 9	Robinson J —+5	Anyinsah J 10+1	El-Abd A 25+6	Dixon J —+1	Thornton K 4+8	Savage R 6	Sullivan J 13	Johnson B 10	Fleetwood S 5+6	Hinshelwood A 11+3	Mayo K —+2	Birchall C 8+1	Jarrett J 11+2	Carole S 5+7	Andrew C 3+6	McNulty J 5	Davies C 10+6	Cook S —+2	Andersen M 5	Borrowdale G 11+1	Heath M 6	Bangura A 6	Match No.
1	2	3	4	5	6	7	8	9	10	11																														1
1	2	3	4	5	8	7^2	6		10			11	9^1	12	13																									2
1	2	3	4	5	8	7^2	8	9	10	11^1	13		12																											3
1	2^1	3	4	5	6	7^2	8	9	10	14	11^3		12	13																										4
1	2	3	4	5	6^1	7		9	10	11^2	8		12		13																									5
1	2	3	4	5	6	7^1	8	9	10^2		13	12		$11^●$																										6
1	2^1	3	4	5		7	8	9	10^3		11^2	12		13	6	14																								7
1	2	3		5	6	12	8	9	13		11^1		7^3							10^2	4	14																		8
1	2	3		5	6		8	9	10		11		12						13	7^2	4^1																			9
1	2	3	4	5	6^1	12	8	9		11^2		7							13	10																				10
1	2^1	3		4	6	7^2	8	9		12		10	5	13	11																									11
1		3	4	5	6		8	9		10^1	12		7	2		13	11^2																							12
1	2^3	3	4	5	6	12	8		10^2			13	9	11					14	7^1																				13
	2	3	4	5	6	12	8		10^1		9			13	7^2	1	11																							14
	2	3	4	5	6	7	8^1	12		13		9		10^3	1	11^2	14																							15
1	2	3		5		7^3		9	12	14	8		13		4^2	6		11	10^1																					16
1	2	3	4	5		6	9	10		7^1		8		11	12																									17
1		3	4	5	6	12	2	9	10		8			11	7^3																									18
1	2	3	4		6	7	$8^●$	9^1	10		5			11	12																									19
	2	3	4	5	6	7^1		9^3	10			12	8^2	13	1	11	14																							20
	2	3		5		7^1	8	12	10^3	9^2			14		6				1	11	$13^{?}$	4																		21
	2	3		5		7^1		9	10^3	13		8^2		6	12	1	11	14	4																					22
	2	3		5		6^1	12	10	11^2	8				1	7	9	4	13																						23
	2		5		13	4	12	10	11^2	7		14	6		1		9^3	3	8^1																					24
	2		5		12	3	10	11^1	13	7		14	6^3		1		9^2	4	8																					25
	2		5			7^1	10	11	8	12			6		1		3	9	4																					26
		5			7^1	2	10	12	11				6		1		3	8^2	4	13	9																			27
		5^2			12	4	10	14	13				6		1		2	8^3	7^1	9	3	11																		28
		5			4	10	12						6		1		2^1	8	7	9	3	11																	29
1	2			5	7	4	10		11^1				6					12	9	8		3																		30
1	2			5	7	$8^●$	10		11^1				6					9^2	4	12		3	13																	31
	2			5^1	7				11				6					12^2	9^3	4	14		3	8	13															32
	2			5				11^2	12				6						4	13		10			1	3	5	7												33
	2			5	7			14					6					12	13	4	8^2		10^3		1	3^1	5	11												34
	2			5	7		14	10^3	3				9^2					4^1	8			13		1		5	11													35
	2	12		5	7			10	3^3				6^1					4	8^2			13		1	14	5	11													36
	2			5	7	8		10^3					6^2								13	9		1	3	$4^●$	11^1													37
1	2				7	6	10^3						9	4			12		5	13		14		8			3^2		11^1											38
1	2				7	6			8^2	9	11^3	4	3							13	14			10	12			5^1												39
1	2			5	7	6		14	12	11	9^3		4							13			8^7			10^1		3												40
1	2			5	7	6		13	11^2	9^1	8^3	4	14													12		10		3										41
1	2			5	7	6		10^1	11	9^2	8^3	4	14													12		13		3										42
1	$2^●$			5^1	7	6		10	11^2	9^3	8	4	12													13		14		3										43
1				5	7^1	6		14	10^3	11	9^2	8	4					2								12		13		3										44
1	2			5	7	6		13	10^1	11	9^3	8	4													12		14		3										45
1	2			5	7^3	6		13	14	10^1	11	9	8	4														12^2		3										46

FA Cup					J Paint Trophy				
First Round	Hartlepool U		(h)	3-3	First Round	Northampton T		(a)	1-0
			(a)	1-2	Second Round	Leyton Orient		(h)	2-2
					Southern Quarter-Final				
Carling Cup						Swindon T		(h)	2-0
First Round	Barnet		(h)	4-0	Southern Semi-Final	Shrewsbury T		(a)	0-0
Second Round	Manchester C		(h)	2-2	Southern Final	Luton T		(h)	0-0
Third Round	Derby Co		(h)	1-4				(a)	1-1

BRISTOL CITY — FL Championship

FOUNDATION

The name Bristol City came into being in 1897 when the Bristol South End club, formed three years earlier, decided to adopt professionalism and apply for admission to the Southern League after competing in the Western League. The historic meeting was held at The Albert Hall, Bedminster. Bristol City employed Sam Hollis from Woolwich Arsenal as manager and gave him £40 to buy players. In 1900 they merged with Bedminster, another leading Bristol club.

Ashton Gate Stadium, Bristol BS3 2EJ.
Telephone: (0871) 222 6666.
Fax: (0117) 9630 700.
Ticket Office: 0871 222 6666 (option 1).
Website: www.bcfc.co.uk
Email: enquiries@bcfc.co.uk
Ground Capacity: 21,804.
Record Attendance: 43,335 v Preston NE, FA Cup 5th rd, 16 February 1935.
Pitch Measurements: 115yd × 75yd.
Chairman: Steve Lansdown.
Vice-chairman: Keith Dawe.
Chief Executive: Colin Sexstone.
Secretary: Michelle McDonald.
Manager: Gary Johnson.
Assistant Manager: Keith Millen.
Physio: Nick Dawes.
Colours: Red shirts with white trim, white shorts, red stockings.

HONOURS

Football League: Division 1 – Runners-up 1906–07; Division 2 – Champions 1905–06; Runners-up 1975–76, 1997–98; FL 1 – Runners-up 2006–07; Division 3 (S) – Champions 1922–23, 1926–27, 1954–55; Runners-up 1937–38; Division 3 – Runners-up 1964–65, 1989–90.
FA Cup: Runners-up 1909.
Football League Cup: Semi-final 1971, 1989.
Welsh Cup: Winners 1934.
Anglo-Scottish Cup: Winners 1978.
Freight Rover Trophy: Winners 1986; Runners-up 1987.
Auto Windscreens Shield: Runners-up 2000.
LDV Vans Trophy: Winners 2003.

Change Colours: White shirts with red trim, red shorts, white stockings.
Year Formed: 1894.
Turned Professional: 1897.
Ltd Co.: 1897. Bristol City Football Club Ltd.
Previous Name: 1894, Bristol South End; 1897, Bristol City.
Club Nickname: 'Robins'.
Grounds: 1894, St John's Lane; 1904, Ashton Gate.
First Football League Game: 7 September 1901, Division 2, v Blackpool (a) W 2–0 – Moles; Tuft, Davies; Jones, McLean, Chambers; Bradbury, Connor, Boucher, O'Brien (2), Flynn.
Record League Victory: 9–0 v Aldershot, Division 3 (S), 28 December 1946 – Eddols; Morgan, Fox; Peacock, Roberts, Jones (1); Chilcott, Thomas, Clark (4 incl. 1p), Cyril Williams (1), Hargreaves (3).

SKY SPORTS FACT FILE

Diminutive left-back Joe Cottle played in 33 consecutive Second Division matches for Bristol City in 1905–06, only one of which was lost. Despite defeat in the opening fixture of the season, City ran out champions. Cottle was capped by England against Ireland.

Record Cup Victory: 11–0 v Chichester C, FA Cup 1st rd, 5 November 1960 – Cook; Collinson, Thresher; Connor, Alan Williams, Etheridge; Tait (1), Bobby Williams (1), Atyeo (5), Adrian Williams (3), Derrick, (1 og).

Record Defeat: 0–9 v Coventry C, Division 3 (S), 28 April 1934.

Most League Points (2 for a win): 70, Division 3 (S), 1954–55.

Most League Points (3 for a win): 91, Division 3, 1989–90.

Most League Goals: 104, Division 3 (S), 1926–27.

Highest League Scorer in Season: Don Clark, 36, Division 3 (S), 1946–47.

Most League Goals in Total Aggregate: John Atyeo, 314, 1951–66.

Most League Goals in One Match: 6, Tommy 'Tot' Walsh v Gillingham, Division 3 (S), 15 January 1927.

Most Capped Player: Billy Wedlock, 26, England.

Most League Appearances: John Atyeo, 597, 1951–66.

Youngest League Player: Marvin Brown, 16 years 105 days v Bristol R, 17 October 1999.

Record Transfer Fee Received: £3,000,000 from Wolverhampton W for Ade Akinbiyi, September 1999.

Record Transfer Fee Paid: £2,250,000 to Crewe Alex for Nicky Maynard, August 2008.

Football League Record: 1901 Elected to Division 2; 1906–11 Division 1; 1911–22 Division 2; 1922–23 Division 3 (S); 1923–24 Division 2; 1924–27 Division 3 (S); 1927–32 Division 2; 1932–55 Division 3 (S); 1955–60 Division 2; 1960–65 Division 3; 1965–76 Division 2; 1976–80 Division 1; 1980–81 Division 2; 1981–82 Division 3; 1982–84 Division 4; 1984–90 Division 3; 1990–92 Division 2; 1992–95 Division 1; 1995–98 Division 2; 1998–99 Division 1; 1999–04 Division 2; 2004–07 FL 1; 2007– FL C.

MANAGERS

Sam Hollis 1897–99
Bob Campbell 1899–1901
Sam Hollis 1901–05
Harry Thickett 1905–10
Frank Bacon 1910–11
Sam Hollis 1911–13
George Hedley 1913–17
Jack Hamilton 1917–19
Joe Palmer 1919–21
Alex Raisbeck 1921–29
Joe Bradshaw 1929–32
Bob Hewison 1932–49
   (under suspension 1938–39)
Bob Wright 1949–50
Pat Beasley 1950–58
Peter Doherty 1958–60
Fred Ford 1960–67
Alan Dicks 1967–80
Bobby Houghton 1980–82
Roy Hodgson 1982
Terry Cooper 1982–88
   (Director from 1983)
Joe Jordan 1988–90
Jimmy Lumsden 1990–92
Denis Smith 1992–93
Russell Osman 1993–94
Joe Jordan 1994–97
John Ward 1997–98
Benny Lennartsson 1998–99
Tony Pulis 1999
Tony Fawthrop 2000
Danny Wilson 2000–04
Brian Tinnion 2004–05
Gary Johnson September 2005–

LATEST SEQUENCES

Longest Sequence of League Wins: 14, 9.9.1905 – 2.12.1905.

Longest Sequence of League Defeats: 7, 3.10.1970 – 7.11.1970.

Longest Sequence of League Draws: 4, 6.11.1999 – 27.11.1999.

Longest Sequence of Unbeaten League Matches: 24, 9.9.1905 – 10.2.1906.

Longest Sequence Without a League Win: 15, 29.4.1933 – 4.11.1933.

Successive Scoring Runs: 25 from 26.12.1905.

Successive Non-scoring Runs: 6 from 10.9.1910.

TEN YEAR LEAGUE RECORD

		P	W	D	L	F	A	Pts	Pos
1999-2000	Div 2	46	15	19	12	59	57	64	9
2000-01	Div 2	46	18	14	14	70	56	68	9
2001-02	Div 2	46	21	10	15	68	53	73	7
2002-03	Div 2	46	24	11	11	79	48	83	3
2003-04	Div 2	46	23	13	10	58	37	82	3
2004-05	FL 1	46	18	16	12	74	57	70	7
2005-06	FL 1	46	18	11	17	66	62	65	9
2006-07	FL 1	46	25	10	11	63	39	85	2
2007-08	FL C	46	20	14	12	54	53	74	4
2008-09	FL C	46	15	16	15	54	54	61	10

DID YOU KNOW ?

When Bristol City reached the FA Cup final in 1908–09 in a ten-match run, they had accounted for three teams who had had outstanding records in the competition in the previous decade – Southampton, Bury and Derby County.

BRISTOL CITY 2008–09 LEAGUE RECORD

Match No.	Date	Venue	Opponents	Result	H/T Score	Lg. Pos.	Goalscorers	Attendance
1	Aug 9	A	Blackpool	W 1-0	0-0	—	Brooker [90]	8244
2	16	H	Derby Co	D 1-1	1-0	7	Maynard [23]	16,389
3	23	A	Coventry C	W 3-0	1-0	3	Adebola [17], McIndoe [54], Brooker [90]	17,994
4	30	H	QPR	D 1-1	1-1	4	Adebola [25]	17,543
5	Sept 13	A	Cardiff C	D 0-0	0-0	5		19,312
6	16	H	Birmingham C	L 1-2	0-2	—	Trundle [79]	18,456
7	20	H	Doncaster R	W 4-1	0-0	5	McIndoe 2 (1 pen) [48 (p), 74], Maynard [57], Sproule [61]	15,960
8	27	A	Wolverhampton W	L 0-2	0-1	6		24,324
9	30	H	Plymouth Arg	D 2-2	0-2	—	Akinde [63], Noble [88]	17,489
10	Oct 4	A	Sheffield U	L 0-3	0-1	13		24,712
11	18	H	Norwich C	W 1-0	0-0	9	McCombe [76]	16,791
12	21	A	Charlton Ath	W 2-0	1-0	—	Trundle [27], Williams [52]	21,207
13	25	A	Barnsley	D 0-0	0-0	6		11,551
14	28	H	Sheffield U	D 0-0	0-0	—		16,798
15	Nov 1	H	Reading	L 1-4	0-2	11	John [90]	18,296
16	8	A	Southampton	W 1-0	0-0	10	Johnson [52]	14,535
17	15	H	Nottingham F	D 2-2	1-1	8	Elliott [38], Fontaine [80]	17,440
18	22	A	Crystal Palace	L 2-4	1-2	11	Adebola [44], Maynard [74]	14,599
19	25	H	Watford	D 1-1	0-0	—	Maynard [71]	15,551
20	29	A	Preston NE	L 0-2	0-1	14		11,161
21	Dec 6	H	Swansea C	D 0-0	0-0	14		16,405
22	10	A	Ipswich T	L 1-3	1-0	—	John [5]	17,749
23	13	A	Sheffield W	D 0-0	0-0	15		15,542
24	20	H	Burnley	L 1-2	0-0	18	Maynard (pen) [52]	16,108
25	26	A	Watford	W 4-2	2-0	14	Maynard 2 [1, 29], Elliott [52], Adebola [90]	15,527
26	28	H	Crystal Palace	W 1-0	1-0	12	Maynard [2]	18,265
27	Jan 17	H	Wolverhampton W	D 2-2	0-1	14	Adebola [58], Maynard [87]	16,749
28	27	A	Plymouth Arg	W 2-0	0-0	—	McIndoe [62], Fontaine [86]	11,438
29	31	H	Barnsley	W 2-0	0-0	11	Williams [65], McIndoe [79]	15,667
30	Feb 3	H	Charlton Ath	W 2-1	0-1	—	Adebola 2 [49, 53]	15,304
31	7	A	Norwich C	W 2-1	2-1	8	Skuse [14], Orr (pen) [45]	24,691
32	14	H	Southampton	W 2-0	1-0	7	Adebola [34], Sproule [90]	17,000
33	17	A	Doncaster R	L 0-1	0-1	—		10,928
34	21	A	Reading	W 2-0	1-0	4	Adebola [26], Skuse [48]	22,462
35	28	H	Blackpool	D 0-0	0-0	6		16,855
36	Mar 4	H	Birmingham C	L 0-1	0-0	—		17,551
37	7	A	Derby Co	L 1-2	0-1	9	Williams [83]	30,824
38	10	H	Coventry C	W 2-0	0-0	—	McAllister [66], Johnson [80]	15,706
39	15	H	Cardiff C	D 1-1	0-0	8	Maynard [71]	17,487
40	21	A	QPR	L 1-2	0-0	9	McIndoe [77]	14,059
41	Apr 4	H	Preston NE	D 1-1	0-0	9	Maynard [59]	16,596
42	11	A	Nottingham F	L 2-3	1-1	9	Sproule [13], Adebola [78]	22,776
43	13	H	Ipswich T	D 1-1	0-0	9	Elliott [49]	16,430
44	18	A	Swansea C	L 0-1	0-1	10		15,327
45	25	H	Sheffield W	D 1-1	1-0	10	Johnson [25]	17,486
46	May 3	A	Burnley	L 0-4	0-2	10		18,005

Final League Position: 10

GOALSCORERS

League (54): Maynard 11 (1 pen), Adebola 10, McIndoe 6 (1 pen), Elliott 3, Johnson 3, Sproule 3, Williams 3, Brooker 2, Fontaine 2, John 2, Skuse 2, Trundle 2, Akinde 1, McAllister 1, McCombe 1, Noble 1, Orr 1 (pen).
Carling Cup (3): Brooker 1, Carey 1, Wilson B 1.
FA Cup (0).

Basso A 43	Orr B 37 + 1	McAllister J 35	Skuse C 29 + 4	Carey L 28	McCombe J 24 + 4	Williams G 24 + 11	Johnson L 43 + 1	Adebola D 32 + 7	Maynard N 34 + 9	McIndoe M 43 + 2	Weale C 3 + 2	Sproule I 18 + 20	Brooker S —+ 4	Wilson B 17 + 3	Fontaine L 41 + 1	Webster A 2 + 3	Trundle L 4 + 15	Elliott M 24 + 4	Noble D 5 + 4	Akinde J 1 + 6	John S 13 + 11	Wilson J —+ 2	Murray S —+ 3	Styvar P 2 + 8	Iriekpen I 4 + 5	Henderson S —+ 1	Match No.
1⁶	2	3	4	5	6	7¹	8	9²	10	11	15	12	13														1
	2	3	4	5	6³	7²	8	9¹	10	11	1	13	12	14													2
1	2	3	4	5¹			8	9³	10²	11		13	14	7	6	12											3
1	2	3³	4¹	5		12	8	9	10	11		13		7²	6	14											4
1	2	3	4	5		12	8	9³	10²	11		13	14	7¹	6												5
1⁶	2²	3	4	5		7¹	8	9	10	11	15	12			6			13									6
	2³	3	4	5		12	8	9	10²	11	1	7¹			6			13	14								7
	12	3	2	5		13	8	9	10	11³	1	7²			6			14	4¹								8
1	2	3	4²				8	9	10³	7¹		11		6	5	13			12	14							9
1	2	3		5			8	9	12	11		7²		6		13	4	10¹									10
1	2	3		5	7¹	8³	9²	12	11			13		14	6		10	4										11
1	2	3		5	7²	8	9¹	12	11			13		14	6		10³	4										12
1	3²			5	7	8	9¹	12	11			2		6	13	10³	4			14							13
1	2			5	7¹	8	9³	12	11			13		3	6	10²	4			14							14
1	2			5		8²		10³	11	7¹		3		6		12	4	13	14	9							15
1	2			5	7²	8	9¹	12	11			13		3	6		4	10³			14						16
1	2	12		5¹	7³	8	9	13	11			3		6		4	10²			14							17
1	2³			5	7¹	8	9	13	11		12	3		6		4	10²			14							18
1	3		5	6	12	8²	13	9	11³			2			14	4	7¹	10									19
1	3²		5	6		8	9³	10	11		12	2		13	14	4	7¹										20
1		4	5	6	12			10²	11	7¹		2		3	13	8		9									21
1		4	5³	6				10¹	11	7		2		3	12	8	13	9	14								22
1	2	4³	5	6¹	14		10	11	7			3		13	8	12	9²										23
1	2³		5	7²	8¹		10	11				3	6	13	4	12	9		14								24
1	2	12	5		8	13	10³	11	7¹			3	6		14	4	9²										25
1	2	14	5	13	8²	12	10³	11	7			3	6		4	9¹											26
1	2	3³	4	5		8	13	10	12	11¹		6			7	14			9²								27
1	2	3	7	5		8	9³	10²	12	11		6			4¹	13			14								28
1	2	3	4	5	12	8	9²		11	7¹		6			13	10²			14								29
1	2	3	4	5	7	8	9²		11			6			13	12	10¹										30
1	2	3¹	4¹	5	7	8	9²	10	11	12		6			13	10²			14								31
1	2	3	4	5	7³	8	9²	10	11¹	12		6			13	12			10¹								32
1	2³	3	4	5	7¹	8		10	11	12		6			13	9²			14								33
1	2	3	4³	5		10	8		11	7¹		6			13	12	14										34
1	2	3¹	4³	5	12	7	8	9	10²	11		6			14												35
1	2	3	4²	5	12	10	8	9³	13	11		7¹			6		14										36
1	2	3		5	4¹	7	8		10²	11		7²			6		9	13									37
1	2	3		5	4	7	8	12	10²	11					6		9¹	13									38
1	2	3	12	5	4	7¹	8	13	10³	11					6		9²	14									39
1	2	3	4	5		8¹	9	10	11			7²			6	12			13								40
1	2	3	4	5	12	8²	9	10³	11			7¹			6	13	14										41
1	2	3⁴	4²	5	14	8³	9	10	11			7			6¹	13								12			42
1⁶	2	3		5	7¹	8	9²	10	11	12					4				13	6	15						43
1	2²	4		5¹	12	8	9	10	11	13					6		7				3						44
1		3	2			10	8	13	9²	11³	7¹				5	14	4			12	6						45
1	2	3¹	4		14	13	8	9	10²	11¹		12			5		7				6						46

FA Cup
Third Round   Portsmouth   (a) 0-0
                           (h) 0-2

Carling Cup
First Round   Peterborough U   (h) 2-1
Second Round Crewe Alex   (a) 1-2

BRISTOL ROVERS — FL Championship 1

FOUNDATION

Bristol Rovers were formed at a meeting in Stapleton Road, Eastville, in 1883. However, they first went under the name of the Black Arabs (wearing black shirts). Changing their name to Eastville Rovers in their second season, they won the Gloucestershire Senior Cup in 1888–89. Original members of the Bristol & District League in 1892, this eventually became the Western League and Eastville Rovers adopted professionalism in 1897.

The Memorial Stadium, Filton Avenue, Horfield, Bristol BS7 0BF.

Telephone: (0117) 909 6648.

Fax: (0117) 907 4312.

Ticket Office: (0117) 909 8848.

Website: www.bristolrovers.co.uk

Email: rodwesson@bristolrovers.co.uk; dave@bristolrovers.co.uk

Ground Capacity: 11,626.

Record Attendance: 12,011 v WBA, FA Cup 6th rd, 9 March 2008 (Memorial Stadium). 9,464 v Liverpool, FA Cup 4th rd, 8 February 1992 (Twerton Park). 38,472 v Preston NE, FA Cup 4th rd, 30 January 1960 (Eastville).

Pitch Measurements: 110yd × 73yd 6in.

Chairman: Nick Higgs.

Secretary: Rod Wesson.

Director of Football: Lennie Lawrence.

First Team Coach: Paul Trollope.

Physio: Phil Kite.

Colours: Blue and white quarters, white shorts, white stockings.

Change Colours: Green shirts, black shorts, green stockings.

Year Formed: 1883. *Turned Professional:* 1897. *Ltd Co.:* 1896.

Previous Names: 1883, Black Arabs; 1884, Eastville Rovers; 1897, Bristol Eastville Rovers; 1898, Bristol Rovers. *Club Nickname:* 'Pirates'.

Grounds: 1883, Purdown; Three Acres, Ashley Hill; Rudgeway, Fishponds; 1897, Eastville; 1986, Twerton Park; 1996, The Memorial Stadium.

First Football League Game: 28 August 1920, Division 3, v Millwall (a) L 0–2 – Stansfield; Bethune, Panes; Boxley, Kenny, Steele; Chance, Bird, Sims, Bell, Palmer.

Record League Victory: 7–0 v Brighton & HA, Division 3 (S), 29 November 1952 – Hoyle; Bamford, Fox; Pitt, Warren, Sampson; McIlvenny, Roost (2), Lambden (1), Bradford (1), Petherbridge (2), (1 og). 7–0 v Swansea T, Division 2, 2 October 1954 – Radford; Bamford, Watkins; Pitt, Muir, Anderson; Petherbridge, Bradford (2), Meyer, Roost (1), Hooper (2), (2 og). 7–0 v Shrewsbury T, Division 3, 21 March 1964 – Hall; Hillard, Gwyn Jones; Oldfield, Stone (1), Mabbutt; Jarman (2), Brown (1), Biggs (1p), Hamilton, Bobby Jones (2).

HONOURS

Football League: Division 2 best season: 4th, 1994–95; Division 3 (S) – Champions 1952–53; Division 3 – Champions 1989–90; Runners-up 1973–74.

FA Cup: best season: 6th rd, 1951, 1958, 2008.

Football League Cup: best season: 5th rd, 1971, 1972.

J Paint Trophy: Runners-up 2007.

SKY SPORTS FACT FILE

On 30 September 1978 Bristol Rovers defender Peter Aitken was cautioned in a Second Division match at Cambridge United in the 92nd minute during time added on for injuries. Sixty seconds later he scored his team's equalising goal.

Record Cup Victory: 6–0 v Merthyr Tydfil, FA Cup 1st rd, 14 November 1987 – Martyn; Alexander (Dryden), Tanner, Hibbitt, Twentyman, Jones, Holloway, Meacham (1), White (2), Penrice (3) (Reece), Purnell.

Most League Points (2 for a win): 64, Division 3 (S), 1952–53.

Most League Points (3 for a win): 93, Division 3, 1989–90.

Most League Goals: 92, Division 3 (S), 1952–53.

Highest League Scorer in Season: Geoff Bradford, 33, Division 3 (S), 1952–53.

Most League Goals in Total Aggregate: Geoff Bradford, 242, 1949–64.

Most League Goals in One Match: 4, Sidney Leigh v Exeter C, Division 3 (S), 2 May 1921; 4, Jonah Wilcox v Bournemouth, Division 3 (S), 12 December 1925; 4, Bill Culley v QPR, Division 3 (S), 5 March 1927; 4, Frank Curran v Swindon T, Division 3 (S), 25 March 1939; 4, Vic Lambden v Aldershot, Division 3 (S), 29 March 1947; 4, George Petherbridge v Torquay U, Division 3 (S), 1 December 1951; 4, Vic Lambden v Colchester U, Division 3 (S), 14 May 1952; 4, Geoff Bradford v Rotherham U, Division 2, 14 March 1959; 4, Robin Stubbs v Gillingham, Division 2, 10 October 1970; 4, Alan Warboys v Brighton & HA, Division 3, 1 December 1973; 4, Jamie Cureton v Reading, Division 2, 16 January 1999.

Most Capped Player: Vitalijs Astafjevs, 31 (142), Latvia.

Most League Appearances: Stuart Taylor, 546, 1966–80.

Youngest League Player: Ronnie Dix, 15 years 173 days v Charlton Ath, 25 February 1928.

Record Transfer Fee Received: £2,100,000 from Fulham for Barry Hayles, November 1998 and £2,100,000 from WBA for Jason Roberts, July 2000.

Record Transfer Fee Paid: £375,000 to QPR for Andy Tillson, November 1992.

Football League Record: 1920 Original Member of Division 3; 1921–53 Division 3 (S); 1953–62 Division 2; 1962–74 Division 3; 1974–81 Division 2; 1981–90 Division 3; 1990–92 Division 2. 1992–93 Division 1; 1993–2001 Division 2; 2001–04 Division 3; 2004–07 FL 2; 2007– FL 1.

MANAGERS

Alfred Homer 1899–1920
  (continued as Secretary to 1928)
Ben Hall 1920–21
Andy Wilson 1921–26
Joe Palmer 1926–29
Dave McLean 1929–30
Albert Prince-Cox 1930–36
Percy Smith 1936–37
Brough Fletcher 1938–49
Bert Tann 1950–68 *(continued as General Manager to 1972)*
Fred Ford 1968–69
Bill Dodgin Snr 1969–72
Don Megson 1972–77
Bobby Campbell 1978–79
Harold Jarman 1979–80
Terry Cooper 1980–81
Bobby Gould 1981–83
David Williams 1983–85
Bobby Gould 1985–87
Gerry Francis 1987–91
Martin Dobson 1991
Dennis Rofe 1992
Malcolm Allison 1992–93
John Ward 1993–96
Ian Holloway 1996–2001
Garry Thompson 2001
Gerry Francis 2001
Garry Thompson 2001–02
Ray Graydon 2002–04
Ian Atkins 2004–05
Paul Trollope September 2005–

LATEST SEQUENCES

Longest Sequence of League Wins: 12, 18.10.1952 – 17.1.1953.
Longest Sequence of League Defeats: 8, 26.10.2002 – 21.12.2002.
Longest Sequence of League Draws: 5, 1.11.1975 – 22.11.1975.
Longest Sequence of Unbeaten League Matches: 32, 7.4.1973 – 27.1.1974.
Longest Sequence Without a League Win: 20, 5.4.1980 – 1.11.1980.
Successive Scoring Runs: 26 from 26.3.1927.
Successive Non-scoring Runs: 6 from 14.10.1922.

TEN YEAR LEAGUE RECORD

		P	W	D	L	F	A	Pts	Pos
1999-2000	Div 2	46	23	11	12	69	45	80	7
2000-01	Div 2	46	12	15	19	53	57	51	21
2001-02	Div 3	46	11	12	23	40	60	45	23
2002-03	Div 3	46	12	15	19	50	57	51	20
2003-04	Div 3	46	14	13	19	50	61	55	15
2004-05	FL 2	46	13	21	12	60	57	60	12
2005-06	FL 2	46	17	9	20	59	67	60	12
2006-07	FL 2	46	20	12	14	49	42	72	6
2007-08	FL 1	46	12	17	17	45	53	53	16
2008-09	FL 1	46	17	12	17	79	61	63	11

DID YOU KNOW ?

Bristol Rovers have had many loyal servants – Ray Warren 20 years from 1936 to 1956, appearance record holder Stuart Taylor 15 years, Harold Jarman 14 years from 1959 to 1973 and Harry Bamford 13 from 1945 before his death in a road accident.

BRISTOL ROVERS 2008–09 LEAGUE RECORD

Match No.	Date	Venue	Opponents	Result	H/T Score	Lg. Pos.	Goalscorers	Attendance
1	Aug 9	H	Carlisle U	L	2-3	1-2	—	Lambert [15], Williams [90]	8285
2	16	A	Brighton & HA	D	1-1	0-1	20	Lambert (pen) [86]	6210
3	23	H	Hereford U	W	6-1	3-0	8	Duffy 2 [3, 22], Lambert 2 [7, 78], Hughes [46], Lines [88]	6735
4	30	A	Leeds U	D	2-2	2-1	11	Lambert [32], Duffy [37]	21,024
5	Sept 6	A	Peterborough U	L	4-5	1-2	15	Elliott [30], Blackett (og) [54], Hughes [74], Lambert [88]	4876
6	13	H	Walsall	L	1-3	0-2	19	Elliott [76]	6609
7	16	A	Cheltenham T	L	1-2	0-2	—	Lambert [50]	4546
8	20	A	Yeovil T	D	2-2	1-2	19	Lambert (pen) [39], Osei-Kuffour [62]	5748
9	27	H	Crewe Alex	D	0-0	0-0	19		5870
10	Oct 4	A	Colchester U	W	1-0	0-0	15	Lambert [53]	4811
11	11	H	Leyton Orient	W	2-1	0-0	11	Coles [61], Hinton [70]	6425
12	18	A	Huddersfield T	D	1-1	0-1	13	Lambert [53]	13,779
13	21	H	Oldham Ath	W	2-0	2-0	—	Lambert [16], Lines [35]	6379
14	25	H	Southend U	W	4-2	3-0	11	Lambert 4 [10, 16, 33, 55]	7055
15	Nov 1	A	Leicester C	L	1-2	0-0	13	Osei-Kuffour [61]	18,941
16	14	H	Scunthorpe U	L	1-2	0-1	—	Lambert [56]	7173
17	22	H	Swindon T	D	2-2	1-1	14	Lambert [26], Lines [90]	8016
18	25	A	Hartlepool U	D	1-1	1-1	—	Hughes [26]	3171
19	Dec 6	A	Millwall	L	2-3	1-2	15	Lambert [19], Osei-Kuffour [79]	8123
20	13	H	Tranmere R	W	2-0	1-0	14	Osei-Kuffour [41], Lines [50]	6217
21	20	A	Stockport Co	L	1-3	1-2	15	Disley [41]	5364
22	26	H	Milton Keynes D	L	1-2	1-1	16	Osei-Kuffour [15]	9002
23	28	A	Northampton T	D	0-0	0-0	16		5557
24	Jan 17	A	Leyton Orient	W	2-1	0-0	17	Hughes [74], Duffy [79]	4262
25	24	H	Colchester U	D	0-0	0-0	17		6634
26	27	H	Cheltenham T	W	3-2	1-1	—	Lambert 2 [21, 85], Duffy [84]	6600
27	31	A	Southend U	L	0-1	0-0	14		7234
28	Feb 14	A	Scunthorpe U	W	2-0	2-0	14	Duffy [21], Osei-Kuffour [31]	4156
29	17	H	Yeovil T	W	3-0	2-0	—	Pipe [19], Duffy [30], Lambert [86]	8049
30	21	H	Leicester C	L	0-1	0-1	14		9138
31	24	A	Oldham Ath	W	2-0	0-0	—	Duffy [48], Anthony [63]	3745
32	28	A	Carlisle U	D	1-1	1-1	14	Hughes [13]	5343
33	Mar 7	H	Leeds U	D	2-2	1-1	14	Hughes [14], Osei-Kuffour [90]	10,293
34	10	A	Hereford U	W	3-0	2-0	—	Lambert 3 (1 pen) [26, 34, 58 (p)]	3199
35	14	A	Walsall	W	5-0	3-0	12	Duffy 2 [3, 58], Disley [6], Lescott 2 [19, 78]	5169
36	17	A	Crewe Alex	W	1-1	0-0	—	Duffy [74]	3879
37	21	H	Peterborough U	L	0-1	0-0	13		7103
38	28	H	Stockport Co	W	2-0	2-0	12	Anthony [4], Lambert (pen) [37]	6214
39	31	H	Huddersfield T	L	1-2	0-0	—	Osei-Kuffour [47]	6286
40	Apr 5	A	Tranmere R	L	0-2	0-1	14		8119
41	10	H	Northampton T	W	1-0	0-0	—	Osei-Kuffour [72]	6666
42	13	A	Milton Keynes D	L	1-2	0-1	12	Elliott [84]	10,251
43	18	H	Millwall	W	4-2	4-1	11	Disley [12], Lambert 2 (1 pen) [32, 45 (p)], Osei-Kuffour [37]	6618
44	21	H	Brighton & HA	L	1-2	1-1	—	Lambert [28]	6193
45	25	A	Swindon T	L	1-2	1-1	12	Duffy [21]	10,977
46	May 2	H	Hartlepool U	W	4-1	2-1	11	Osei-Kuffour [3], Duffy [5], Lambert [46], Lescott [48]	7363

Final League Position: 11

GOALSCORERS

League (79): Lambert 29 (5 pens), Duffy 13, Osei-Kuffour 11, Hughes 6, Lines 4, Disley 3, Elliott 3, Lescott 3, Anthony 2, Coles 1, Hinton 1, Pipe 1, Williams 1, own goal 1.
Carling Cup (0).
FA Cup (0).
J Paint Trophy (0).

Phillips S 46	Pipe D 36+3	Lescott A 43+1	Campbell S 42+2	Anthony B 29+1	Elliott S 39	Lines C 44+1	Disley C 33+11	Lambert R 43+2	Duffy D 28+15	Hughes J 43	Williams A —+4	Rigg S —+8	Hinton C 19+6	Hunt B —+12	Osei-Kuffour J 26+15	Green R 23+3	Coles D 5	Jacobson J 6+16	Reece C 1	Match No.
1	2	3	4	5	6	7^1	8	9	10	11^2	12	13								1
1	2^3	3	4	5	6	7	8	9	10^2	11^1	12		14	13						2
1	2	3	4	5	6	7	8	9^1	10^2	11	13		12							3
1	2	3	4	5	6	7	8	9^2	10^3	11^1	14		12	13						4
1	2	3	4	5	6	7^1	8	9	10^2	11			12	13						5
1	2^3	3	4	5	6	7^3	8	9	10^1	11			12	13	14					6
1	7	3^2	4		6	8^1	12	9	13	11			14		10	2	5^3			7
1	7^2	3	4		6	11	8	9	10^1				12		13	2	5			8
1	12	3	4		6^2	7	8	9	10^3	11			13		14	2^1	5			9
1	2	3	4			7	8	9	10^1	11			6	12			5			10
1	2	3	4	12		7	8	9	10^2	11^3			6	13	14		5^1			11
1	2	3	4	5		7	8	9	10^1	11^2			6		12			13		12
1	2	3	4	5		7	8	9	10^1	11^2			6		12			13		13
1	2	3	4	5		7	8	9	12	11^2			6		10^1			13		14
1	2^1	3^2	4	5		7	8	9	12	11			6		10	14		13^3		15
1		3	4		6	7^1	8	9	13	11			5	12	10^2	2				16
1		3	4		6	7	8^1	9	12	11^2		13	5		10	2				17
1		3	4	5	6		8	9		7				·	10	2		11		18
1		3	4	5	6	7^1	8^2	9	13	11					10	2		12		19
1	2	3	4		6	7	8	9	12	11			5		10^1					20
1	2	3	4		6	7	8^1	9	12	11			5	13	10^2					21
1	2^3	3	4	5	6	7	8^2	9	12	11^1		13			10	14				22
1		3	4		6	7	8	9		11			5		10	2				23
1	13	3	4		6	7^1	8	9	12	11^3			5		10^2	2		14		24
1	12	3	4		6	7	8^1	9		11^2			5		10	2		13		25
1	7	3	4		6	8^1	12	9	13	11^2			5		10^3	2		14		26
1	7^2	3	4		6	13	8	9	12	11^1			5	14	10^3	2				27
1	7	3	4		6	8	12		9^2	11^1		13	5		10^3	2		14		28
1	7^1	3	4		6	8	12	13	9	11^3			5		10^2	2		14		29
1	7^1	3	4		6	8	12	13	9	11^2			5^3		10	2		14		30
1	7	3	4	5	6	8	12	9^1	10^2	11^3				13		2		14		31
1	7	3	4	5	6	8		9	10^1	11				12		2				32
1	7	3^3	4	5	6	8^1	12	10	9	11^2				13		2		14		33
1	7^3	3	12	5	6	4	8^1	9^2	10	11				13		2		14		34
1	7^3	3	12	5	6	4	8^1	9^2	10	11				13		2		14		35
1	7^1	3		5	6	4	8	9	10	11				12		2				36
1	7	2	12	5	6	4^1	8	9	10^3	11^2		13		14		3				37
1		3	4	5	6	8	12	9^2	10	11^1			13	7		2				38
1		12	4	5	6	7	8	9	10					11		2		3^1		39
1	7^2	3^3	4	5	6	8^1	12	9	10	11			13			2		14		40
1	7	3	4	5	6	8		9	12	11					10^1	2				41
1	7	3^1	4	5	6	8	12	9	13	11					10^2	2				42
1	2		4	5	6	7	8	9^1	10^2	3		13	12	11						43
1	2		4	5		7	8	9	10	3			6	11						44
1	2	3	4	5^1	6	7	8	9	12	11					10					45
1	2^1	3	4	5	6	8	12	9	10					14	13	11^2			7^3	46

FA Cup
First Round — Bournemouth — (a) — 0-1

Carling Cup
First Round — Watford — (a) — 0-1

J Paint Trophy
First Round — Bournemouth — (a) — 0-3

BURNLEY

FA Premiership

FOUNDATION

On 18 May 1882 Burnley (Association) Football Club was still known as Burnley Rovers as members of that Rugby Club had decided on that date to play Association Football in the future. It was only a matter of days later that the members met again and decided to drop Rovers from the club's name.

Turf Moor, Harry Potts Way, Burnley, Lancashire BB10 4BX.

Telephone: 0871 221 1882.

Fax: (01282) 700 014.

Ticket Office: 0871 221 1882.

Website: www.burnleyfc.com

Email: info@burnleyfc.com

Ground Capacity: 22,610.

Record Attendance: 54,775 v Huddersfield T, FA Cup 3rd rd, 23 February 1924.

Pitch Measurements: 112yd × 70yd.

Chairman: Barry Kilby.

Vice-chairman: Ray Ingleby.

Manager: Owen Coyle.

Assistant Manager: Sandy Stewart.

Football Secretary: Pauline Scott.

Physio: Andy Mitchell.

Colours: Claret shirts with blue sleeves, white shorts, claret stockings.

Change Colours: White shirts, black shorts, white stockings.

Year Formed: 1882.

Turned Professional: 1883. *Ltd Co.:* 1897.

Previous Names: 1882, Burnley Rovers; 1882, Burnley.

Club Nickname: 'The Clarets'.

Grounds: 1882, Calder Vale; 1883, Turf Moor.

First Football League Game: 8 September 1888, Football League, v Preston NE (a) L 2–5 – Smith; Lang, Bury, Abrahams, Friel, Keenan, Brady, Tait, Poland (1), Gallocher (1), Yates.

Record League Victory: 9–0 v Darwen, Division 1, 9 January 1892 – Hillman; Walker, McFettridge, Lang, Matthews, Keenan, Nicol (3), Bowes, Espie (1), McLardie (3), Hill (2).

Record Cup Victory: 9–0 v Crystal Palace, FA Cup 2nd rd (replay), 10 February 1909 – Dawson; Barron, McLean; Cretney (2), Leake, Moffat; Morley, Ogden, Smith (3), Abbott (2), Smethams (1). 9–0 v New Brighton, FA Cup 4th rd, 26 January 1957 – Blacklaw; Angus, Winton; Seith, Adamson, Miller; Newlands (1), McIlroy (3), Lawson (3), Cheesebrough (1), Pilkington (1). 9–0 v Penrith, FA Cup 1st rd, 17 November 1984 – Hansbury; Miller, Hampton, Phelan, Overson (Kennedy), Hird (3 incl. 1p), Grewcock (1), Powell (2), Taylor (3), Biggins, Hutchison.

HONOURS

Football League: Division 1 – Champions 1920–21, 1959–60; Runners-up 1919–20, 1961–62; Division 2 – Champions 1897–98, 1972–73; Runners-up 1912–13, 1946–47, 1999–2000; Division 3 – Champions 1981–82; Division 4 – Champions 1991–92. Record 30 consecutive Division 1 games without defeat 1920–21.

FA Cup: Winners 1914; Runners-up 1947, 1962.

Football League Cup: Semi-final 1961, 1969, 1983, 2009.

Anglo–Scottish Cup: Winners 1979.

Sherpa Van Trophy: Runners-up 1988.

European Competitions: European Cup: 1960–61. European Fairs Cup: 1966–67.

SKY SPORTS FACT FILE

Few clubs in the modern era can claim to have beaten two of the so-called 'big four' in successive rounds of the Carling Cup. Burnley achieved the remarkable feat of winning a penalty shoot-out at Chelsea, before adding Arsenal to their victims in 2008–09.

Record Defeat: 0–10 v Aston Villa, Division 1, 29 August 1925 and v Sheffield U, Division 1, 19 January 1929.

Most League Points (2 for a win): 62, Division 2, 1972–73.

Most League Points (3 for a win): 88, Division 2, 1999–2000.

Most League Goals: 102, Division 1, 1960–61.

Highest League Scorer in Season: George Beel, 35, Division 1, 1927–28.

Most League Goals in Total Aggregate: George Beel, 179, 1923–32.

Most League Goals in One Match: 6, Louis Page v Birmingham C, Division 1, 10 April 1926.

Most Capped Player: Jimmy McIlroy, 51 (55), Northern Ireland.

Most League Appearances: Jerry Dawson, 522, 1907–28.

Youngest League Player: Tommy Lawton, 16 years 174 days v Doncaster R, 28 March 1936.

Record Transfer Fee Received: £3,250,000 from Glasgow Rangers for Kyle Lafferty, June 2008.

Record Transfer Fee Paid: £1,300,000 to Scunthorpe U for Martin Paterson, June 2008.

Football League Record: 1888 Original Member of the Football League; 1897–98 Division 2; 1898–1900 Division 1; 1900–13 Division 2; 1913–30 Division 1; 1930–47 Division 2; 1947–71 Division 1; 1971–73 Division 2; 1973–76 Division 1; 1976–80 Division 2; 1980–82 Division 3; 1982–83 Division 2; 1983–85 Division 3; 1985–92 Division 4; 1992–94 Division 2; 1994–95 Division 1; 1995–2000 Division 2; 2000–04 Division 1; 2004–09 FL C; 2009– FA Premier League.

LATEST SEQUENCES

Longest Sequence of League Wins: 10, 16.11.1912 – 18.1.1913.

Longest Sequence of League Defeats: 8, 2.1.1995 – 25.2.1995.

Longest Sequence of League Draws: 6, 21.2.1931 – 28.3.1931.

Longest Sequence of Unbeaten League Matches: 30, 6.9.1920 – 25.3.1921.

Longest Sequence Without a League Win: 24, 16.4.1979 – 17.11.1979.

Successive Scoring Runs: 27 from 13.2.1926.

Successive Non-scoring Runs: 6 from 9.8.1997.

MANAGERS

Harry Bradshaw 1894–99
(Secretary-Manager from 1897)
Club Directors 1899–1900
J. Ernest Mangnall 1900–03
(Secretary-Manager)
Spen Whittaker 1903–10
(Secretary-Manager)
John Haworth 1910–24
(Secretary-Manager)
Albert Pickles 1925–31
(Secretary-Manager)
Tom Bromilow 1932–35
Selection Committee 1935–45
Cliff Britton 1945–48
Frank Hill 1948–54
Alan Brown 1954–57
Billy Dougall 1957–58
Harry Potts 1958–70
(General Manager to 1972)
Jimmy Adamson 1970–76
Joe Brown 1976–77
Harry Potts 1977–79
Brian Miller 1979–83
John Bond 1983–84
John Benson 1984–85
Martin Buchan 1985
Tommy Cavanagh 1985–86
Brian Miller 1986–89
Frank Casper 1989–91
Jimmy Mullen 1991–96
Adrian Heath 1996–97
Chris Waddle 1997–98
Stan Ternent 1998–2004
Steve Cotterill 2004–07
Owen Coyle November 2007–

TEN YEAR LEAGUE RECORD

		P	W	D	L	F	A	Pts	Pos
1999-2000	Div 2	46	25	13	8	69	47	88	2
2000-01	Div 2	46	21	9	16	50	54	72	7
2001-02	Div 1	46	21	12	13	70	62	75	7
2002-03	Div 1	46	15	10	21	65	89	55	16
2003-04	Div 1	46	13	14	19	60	77	53	19
2004-05	FL C	46	15	15	16	38	39	60	13
2005-06	FL C	46	14	12	20	46	54	54	17
2006-07	FL C	46	15	12	19	52	49	57	15
2007-08	FL C	46	16	14	16	60	67	62	13
2008-09	FL C	46	21	13	12	72	60	76	5

DID YOU KNOW ?

Februarys were special for hat-tricks in the Burnley career of Dick Smith. They came in League matches 1905 v Port Vale, 1908 v Barnsley and Chesterfield plus 1909 in the FA Cup against Crystal Palace plus four in October 1908 against Gainsborough Trinity!

BURNLEY 2008–09 LEAGUE RECORD

Match No.	Date		Venue	Opponents	Result	H/T Score	Lg. Pos.	Goalscorers	Attendance
1	Aug	9	A	Sheffield W	L	1-4	1-3	—	Paterson [6]	23,793
2		16	H	Ipswich T	L	0-3	0-2	24		11,312
3		23	A	Crystal Palace	D	0-0	0-0	23		14,071
4		30	H	Plymouth Arg	D	0-0	0-0	23		10,032
5	Sept	13	A	Nottingham F	W	2-1	1-0	19	Alexander 2 (1 pen) [25, 70 (p)]	20,504
6		16	H	Blackpool	W	2-0	0-0	—	Paterson [60], Alexander (pen) [76]	13,752
7		20	A	Swansea C	D	1-1	0-0	13	Gudjonsson [59]	13,299
8		27	H	Preston NE	W	3-1	1-1	8	Gudjonsson [33], Caldwell [64], Eagles [90]	16,276
9		30	H	Watford	W	3-2	1-2	—	Alexander (pen) [25], Paterson [46], Elliott [69]	10,033
10	Oct	4	A	Reading	L	1-3	0-1	9	McCann [89]	18,621
11		18	H	Birmingham C	D	1-1	1-0	12	McCann [25]	13,809
12		21	A	Coventry C	W	3-1	0-1	—	Duff [52], Blake [88], Eagles [90]	14,621
13		25	A	Charlton Ath	D	1-1	1-0	8	Thompson [13]	21,884
14		28	H	Reading	W	1-0	0-0	—	Blake [81]	11,538
15	Nov	1	H	Norwich C	W	2-0	0-0	4	Eagles 2 [55, 60]	11,353
16		8	A	Wolverhampton W	L	0-2	0-1	5		23,711
17		15	A	QPR	W	2-1	1-1	4	Blake [34], Mahon [60]	13,226
18		22	H	Doncaster R	D	0-0	0-0	5		12,173
19		24	A	Barnsley	L	2-3	0-1	—	Paterson 2 [69, 73]	10,678
20		29	H	Derby Co	W	3-0	3-0	4	McDonald [6], Paterson 2 [15, 23]	11,552
21	Dec	6	A	Sheffield U	W	3-2	2-1	4	Paterson [19], Alexander (pen) [42], Eagles [79]	24,702
22		9	H	Cardiff C	D	2-2	1-1	—	Blake [14], Thompson [76]	11,230
23		13	H	Southampton	W	3-2	3-0	4	Perry (og) [4], Gudjonsson 2 [7, 11]	11,229
24		20	A	Bristol C	W	2-1	0-0	4	Paterson [57], Thompson [77]	16,108
25		26	H	Barnsley	L	1-2	1-1	4	McCann [38]	16,580
26		28	A	Doncaster R	L	1-2	0-2	5	Paterson [62]	14,020
27	Jan	10	H	Swansea C	L	0-2	0-1	—		13,740
28		17	A	Preston NE	L	1-2	0-0	7	Blake [77]	15,692
29		27	A	Watford	L	0-3	0-1	—		13,193
30		31	H	Charlton Ath	W	2-1	0-1	8	Thompson 2 [76, 90]	14,404
31	Feb	7	A	Birmingham C	D	1-1	1-1	10	Paterson [3]	16,763
32		14	H	Wolverhampton W	W	1-0	1-0	8	McCann [6]	13,515
33		17	H	Coventry C	D	1-1	0-1	—	Eagles [90]	14,595
34		21	A	Norwich C	D	1-1	1-1	8	Thompson [36]	24,363
35		28	H	Sheffield W	L	2-4	0-1	9	McCann 53, Eagles [85]	12,449
36	Mar	3	A	Blackpool	W	1-0	0-0	—	Kalvenes [85]	7679
37		11	H	Crystal Palace	W	4-2	1-2	—	Carlisle [39], Alexander (pen) [83], Thompson [88], Rodriguez [90]	10,312
38		14	H	Nottingham F	W	5-0	2-0	5	Blake [19], Elliott [39], Carlisle [51], Rodriguez [56], Gudjonsson [73]	13,055
39		17	A	Ipswich T	D	1-1	1-0	—	Elliott [19]	18,745
40		21	A	Plymouth Arg	W	2-1	1-1	5	Caldwell [16], Blake [78]	11,246
41	Apr	4	A	Derby Co	D	1-1	0-0	5	McCann [59]	33,010
42		11	H	QPR	W	1-0	0-0	6	Eagles [49]	15,058
43		13	A	Cardiff C	L	1-3	0-0	6	Blake [84]	19,379
44		20	A	Sheffield U	W	1-0	1-0	—	Paterson [23]	14,884
45		25	A	Southampton	D	2-2	1-2	6	Alexander (pen) [32], Carlisle [67]	23,927
46	May	3	H	Bristol C	W	4-0	2-0	5	Alexander 2 (2 pens) [42, 76], Elliott [44], Gudjonsson [86]	18,005

Final League Position: 5

GOALSCORERS

League (72): Paterson 12, Alexander 9 (8 pens), Blake 8, Eagles 8, Thompson 7, Gudjonsson 6, McCann 6, Elliott 4, Carlisle 3, Caldwell 2, Rodriguez 2, Duff 1, Kalvenes 1, Mahon 1, McDonald 1, own goal 1.
Carling Cup (13): Paterson 5, McCann 2, McDonald 2, Rodriguez 2, Akinbiyi 1, Blake 1.
FA Cup (7): Thompson 3, Alexander 1 (pen), Elliott 1, Paterson 1, Rodriguez 1.
Play-Offs (4): Alexander 1 (pen), Elliott 1, Paterson 1, Thompson 1.

Penny D 1	Alexander G 46	Jordan S 26 + 1	McCann C 44	Caldwell S 45	Duff M 22 + 5	Elliott W 41 + 1	Eagles C 30 + 13	Blake R 33 + 13	Paterson M 39 + 4	Van der Schaaf R 1	Gudjonsson J 20 + 19	Akinbiyi A 1 + 10	Jensen B 45	Carlisle C 36	McDonald K 9 + 16	Mahon A — + 8	Kalvenes C 21	Anderson R 4	Thompson S 23 + 11	Rodriguez J 2 + 23	MacDonald A — + 3	Williams R 17	Match No.
1	2	3	4	5	6	7	8	9^2	10	11^1	12	13											1
	2	3	4	5		7	11^3	9^1	10		8^2	12	1	6	13	14							2
	2		4	5	6^1	7	11	12	10^3		13	14	1	8	9^2		3						3
	2		4	5	11^2	9^4	14		10		12	13	1	6	8^3		3^1	7					4
	2	3	4	5		7		12	10^1		13	14	1	6	8^2				11	9^3			5
	2	3	4	5		7		12	10^1		13	14	1	6	11^2				8	9^3			6
	2	3	4	5		7		12	10^1		13		1	6	11^2	14			8	9^3			7
	7	3	4	5	2	11^2	12	13	10^3		8		1	6					9^1	14			8
	7	3	4	5	2	11^1	13	12	10^3		8		1	6					9^2	14			9
	7	3^4	4	5	2^1	11	12	13	10^3		8		1	6					9^2	14			10
	7		4	5	2	11	12	13	10^2		8		1	6			3		9^1				11
	7	4^1		5	2	11	13	12	10		8^2		1	6			3		9^3	14			12
	7	12	4	5^1	2	11	13	14	10^2		8		1	6			3		9^3				13
	2	6	4	5		11	7	12	10^1		8		1		13		3^2		9^3	14			14
	2	3	4	5		11	7		10^1		12	8^2	1	6	13				9^3	14			15
	2	3	4	5		11	7		10^1		12	8^2	1	6^4	13				9^3	14			16
	2	3	4		6	11	7^3		10^2		8	12	1	5	13	14			9^1				17
	2	3	4	5		7	12	11^3	10^2		8^1	13	1	6		14			9^4				18
	7	3	4	5	2^3	11		12	10		8^2	9^1	1	6	13	14							19
	7	3	4	5	2	11^3	9^2		10^1		12		1	6	8				13	14			20
	2	3		5		11	7	9^2	10^1		12		1	4	8		6				13		21
	2	3		5		11^2	7	9	10		4		1	6	8^1		12				13		22
	2	3	4	5		11	7^1	9^3	10^2		8	13	1	6				12			14		23
	7	3	4	5	2	11^3		9^1	10		8^2		1	6					12			13	24
	7	3	4	5	2	11	8	9^1	10				1	6^2	13				12				25
	7	3	4^2	5^4	2	11	8	9^1	10				1	6	13				12				26
	2	3	4	6	5^4	11	7	9^1	10		8^2		1						12	13			27
	7	3	4	5	2		11	12	10		8^1		1	6					9^2	13			28
	2		4	5		11	7	9^2	10^3		8^1		1	6	12		3		13	14			29
	2		4^1	5	6	11	7^3	9	10		12		1		13		3^2		14		8		30
	7		4	5	6	11	12	9^1	10^3				1		13				8^2	14		2	31
	7		4	5	6	11	12	9	10^1				1		14		3^3		8^2	13		2	32
	2	3^2	4	5	6	11	12	9^1	10				1		13				8^3	14	7		33
	7	3	4	5	6	11^1	12	9^2	10				1		13				8^3	14		2	34
	7	3	4	5	6	11^1	12	9	10				1		14				8^2	13		2^3	35
	7		4	5		12	11	9^1	10^2				1	6	8^3		3		13	14		2	36
	2		4^2	5		11	12	9^1	10^3		13		1	6			3		8	14		2	37
	7		4^2	5		11	12	9^1	10		13		1	6			3		8^3	14		2	38
	7		4	5		11	8^1	9	10^2		12		1	6			3		13			2	39
	7		4	5	13	11	8^3	9^1	10^2		12		1	6			3		14			2	40
	7^3		4	5	14	11	8^1	9	10^2		12		1	6			3		13			2	41
	7		4	5		11	8^3	9^1	13		12		1	6	14		3		10^2			2	42
	7^1		4	5	13	11	8	9			12		1	6			3		10^2			2	43
	7		4	5		11	8	9^1	10^2		12		1	6			3		13			2	44
	7		4	5	13	11	8^1	9	10^3		14		1	6			3		12			2^2	45
	7		4	5		11^1	8	9	10^3		12		1	6^2	13		3		14			2	46

FA Cup

Third Round	QPR	(a)	0-0	
		(h)	2-1	
Fourth Round	WBA	(a)	2-2	
		(h)	3-1	
Fifth Round	Arsenal	(a)	0-3	

Play-Offs

Semi-Final	Reading	(h)	1-0	
		(a)	2-0	
Final	Sheffield U		1-0	
(at Wembley)				

Carling Cup

First Round	Bury	(a)	2-0
Second Round	Oldham Ath	(h)	3-0
Third Round	Fulham	(h)	1-0
Fourth Round	Chelsea	(a)	1-1
Quarter-Final	Arsenal	(h)	2-0
Semi-Final	Tottenham H	(a)	1-4
		(h)	3-2

BURTON ALBION   FL Championship 2

FOUNDATION

Once upon a time there were three Football League clubs bearing the name Burton. Then there was none. In reality it had been two. Originally Burton Swifts and Burton Wanderers competed in it until 1901 when they amalgamated to form Burton United. This club disbanded in 1910. There was no senior club representing the town until 1924 when Burton Town, formerly known as Burton All Saints played in the Birmingham & District League, subsequently joining the Midland League in 1935–36. When the Second World War broke out the club fielded a team in a truncated version of the Birmingham & District League taking over from the club's reserves. But it was not revived in peacetime. So it was not until a further decade that a club bearing the name of Burton reappeared. Founded in 1950 Burton Albion made progress from the Birmingham & District League, too, then into the Southern League and because of its geographical situation later had spells in the Northern Premier League. In April 2009 Burton Albion restored the name of the town to the Football League competition as champions of the Blue Square Premier League.

Pirelli Stadium, Princess Way, Burton-on-Trent, Staffordshire DE13 0AR.

Telephone: (01283) 565 938.

Fax: (01283) 523 199.

Website: www.burtonalbionfc.co.uk

Email: bafc@burtonalbionfc.co.uk

Ground Capactiy: 6,350 (2,034 seated).

Record attendance: 6,192 v Oxford U, Blue Square Premier, 17 April 2009.

Chairman: Ben Robinson.

Football Secretary: Fleur Robinson.

Manager: Paul Peschisolido.

Assistant Manager: Gary Rowett.

Physio: Steve Walker.

Club nickname: Brewers.

Grounds: 1950, Wellington Street; 1958, Eton Park; 2005, Pirelli Stadium.

SKY SPORTS FACT FILE

On 8 January 2006 Burton Albion drew 0–0 with Manchester United in an FA Cup third round tie. For the replay 11,000 Brewers fans made the journey and it was the largest contingent of away supporters ever seen at Old Trafford out of a crowd of 53,564.

Year Formed: 1950.

Colours: Yellow shirts with black insert, black shorts, black stockings.

Change Colours: Sky blue shirts with white design, sky blue shorts, white stockings.

Record Victory: 12–1 v Coalville T, Birmingham Senior Cup, 6 September 1954.

Record Defeat: 0–10 v Barnet, Southern League, 7 February 1970.

Record Goalscorer: Richie Barker, 157.

Most Appearances: Darren Stride, 635.

Football League Record: Promoted from Blue Square Premier 2008–09; FL 2 2009–.

MANAGERS

Reg Weston
Eddie Shimwell
Sammy Crooks
Bill Townsend
Peter Taylor
Richie Norman
Reg Gutteridge
Harrold Bodle
Ian Storey-Moore
Neil Warnock
Brian Fidler
Vic Halom
Bobby Hope
Chris Wright
Ken Blair
Frank Upton
Steve Powell
Brian Kenning
John Barton
Nigel Clough
Roy McFarland
Paul Peschisolido

HONOURS

Conference: Champions 2008–09.
FA Cup: 3rd rd 1956, 1985, 2006. *FA Trophy:* Runners-up 1986–87.
Southern League Premier Division: Runners-up 1999–2000, 2000–01.
Division 1 (North): Runners-up 1971–72, 1973–74. *Shared Cup:* 2000.
Southern League Cup: Winners 1964, 1997, 2000; Runners-up 1989.
Northern Premier League: Champions 2001–02. *Northern Premier League Shield:* 1983.
Challenge Cup: Winners 1983; Runners-up 1987. *President's Cup:* Runners-up 1983, 1986. *Birmingham Senior Cup:* Winners 1954, 1997; Runners-up 1970, 1971, 1987.
Staffordshire Senior Cup: Winners 1956; Runners-up 1977. *Midland Floodlit Cup:* Winners 1976; Runners-up 1973.

TEN YEAR LEAGUE RECORD

		P	W	D	L	F	A	Pts	Pos
1999-00	SLPL	42	23	10	9	71	40	79	3
2000-01	SLPL	42	25	13	4	76	36	88	2
2001-02	UNI	44	31	11	2	106	30	104	1
2002-03	Conf	42	13	10	19	52	77	49	16
2003-04	Conf	42	15	7	20	57	59	51*	14
2004-05	Conf	42	13	11	18	50	66	50	16
2005-06	Conf	42	16	12	14	50	52	60	9
2006-07	Conf	46	22	9	15	52	47	75	6
2007-08	Conf	46	23	12	11	79	56	81	5
2008-09	Conf	46	27	7	12	81	52	88	1

*1 pt deducted.

DID YOU KNOW ?

Eddie Shimwell was player-manager of Burton Albion in 1958–59. An England international full-back he had been the first full-back to score in a Wembley FA Cup final, from the penalty spot for Blackpool in the 1948 final against Manchester United.

BURY   FL Championship 2

FOUNDATION

A meeting at the Waggon & Horses Hotel, attended largely by members of Bury Wesleyans and Bury Unitarians football clubs, decided to form a new Bury club. This was officially formed at a subsequent gathering at the Old White Horse Hotel, Fleet Street, Bury on 24 April 1885.

Gigg Lane, Bury BL9 9HR.

Telephone: (0161) 764 4881.

Fax: (0161) 764 5521.

Ticket Office: (0161) 705 2144.

Website: www.buryfc.co.uk

Email: info@buryfc.co.uk

Ground Capacity: 11,669.

Record Attendance: 35,000 v Bolton W, FA Cup 3rd rd, 9 January 1960.

Pitch Measurements: 112yd × 72yd.

Secretary: Jill Neville.

Directors: Ian Harrop, Brian Fenton, Jeremy Rothwell, Margaret Ladkin.

Manager: Alan Knill.

Assistant Manager: Chris Brass.

Physio: Alan Bent.

Colours: White shirts, royal blue shorts, white stockings.

Change Colours: All yellow.

Year Formed: 1885.

Turned Professional: 1885.

Ltd Co.: 1897.

Club Nickname: 'Shakers'.

Ground: 1885, Gigg Lane.

HONOURS

Football League: Division 1 best season: 4th, 1925–26; Division 2 – Champions 1894–95, 1996–97; Runners-up 1923–24; Division 3 – Champions 1960–61; Runners-up 1967–68.

FA Cup: Winners 1900, 1903.

Football League Cup: Semi-final 1963.

First Football League Game: 1 September 1894, Division 2, v Manchester C (h) W 4–2 – Lowe; Gillespie, Davies; White, Clegg, Ross; Wylie, Barbour (2), Millar (1), Ostler (1), Plant.

Record League Victory: 8–0 v Tranmere R, Division 3, 10 January 1970 – Forrest; Tinney, Saile; Anderson, Turner, McDermott; Hince (1), Arrowsmith (1), Jones (4), Kerr (1), Grundy, (1 og).

Record Cup Victory: 12–1 v Stockton, FA Cup 1st rd (replay), 2 February 1897 – Montgomery; Darroch, Barbour; Hendry (1), Clegg, Ross (1); Wylie (3), Pangbourn, Millar (4), Henderson (2), Plant, (1 og).

Record Defeat: 0–10 v Blackburn R, FA Cup pr rd, 1 October 1887. 0–10 v West Ham U, Milk Cup 2nd rd 2nd leg, 25 October 1983.

SKY SPORTS FACT FILE

Bury made a spectacular 7–2 start to the 1946–47 season against Fulham on 31 August with two new signings – Cec Wyles (Everton) and Terry Meaney (Ravensdale). In two weeks both had moved on to Southport and Crewe Alexandra respectively!

Most League Points (2 for a win): 68, Division 3, 1960–61.

Most League Points (3 for a win): 84, Division 4, 1984–85 and Division 2, 1996–97.

Most League Goals: 108, Division 3, 1960–61.

Highest League Scorer in Season: Craig Madden, 35, Division 4, 1981–82.

Most League Goals in Total Aggregate: Craig Madden, 129, 1978–86.

Most League Goals in One Match: 5, Eddie Quigley v Millwall, Division 2, 15 February 1947; 5, Ray Pointer v Rotherham U, Division 2, 2 October 1965.

Most Capped Player: Bill Gorman, 11 (13), Republic of Ireland and (4), Northern Ireland.

Most League Appearances: Norman Bullock, 506, 1920–35.

Youngest League Player: Brian Williams, 16 years 133 days v Stockport Co, 18 March 1972.

Record Transfer Fee Received: £1,100,000 from Ipswich T for David Johnson, November 1997.

Record Transfer Fee Paid: £200,000 to Ipswich T for Chris Swailes, November 1997 and £200,000 to Swindon T for Darren Bullock, February 1999.

Football League Record: 1894 Elected to Division 2; 1895–1912 Division 1; 1912–24 Division 2; 1924–29 Division 1; 1929–57 Division 2; 1957–61 Division 3; 1961–67 Division 2; 1967–68 Division 3; 1968–69 Division 2; 1969–71 Division 3; 1971–74 Division 4; 1974–80 Division 3; 1980–85 Division 4; 1985–96 Division 3; 1996–97 Division 2; 1997–99 Division 1; 1999–2002 Division 2; 2002–04 Division 3; 2004– FL 2.

LATEST SEQUENCES

Longest Sequence of League Wins: 9, 26.9.1960 – 19.11.1960.

Longest Sequence of League Defeats: 8, 18.8.2001 – 25.9.2001.

Longest Sequence of League Draws: 6, 6.3.1999 – 3.4.1999.

Longest Sequence of Unbeaten League Matches: 18, 4.2.1961 – 29.4.1961.

Longest Sequence Without a League Win: 19, 1.4.1911 – 2.12.1911.

Successive Scoring Runs: 24 from 1.9.1894.

Successive Non-scoring Runs: 6 from 11.1.1969.

MANAGERS

T. Hargreaves 1887
(Secretary-Manager)
H. S. Hamer 1887–1907
(Secretary-Manager)
Archie Montgomery 1907–15
William Cameron 1919–23
James Hunter Thompson 1923–27
Percy Smith 1927–30
Arthur Paine 1930–34
Norman Bullock 1934–38
Charlie Dean 1938–44
Jim Porter 1944–45
Norman Bullock 1945–49
John McNeil 1950–53
Dave Russell 1953–61
Bob Stokoe 1961–65
Bert Head 1965–66
Les Shannon 1966–69
Jack Marshall 1969
Colin McDonald 1970
Les Hart 1970
Tommy McAnearney 1970–72
Alan Brown 1972–73
Bobby Smith 1973–77
Bob Stokoe 1977–78
David Hatton 1978–79
Dave Connor 1979–80
Jim Iley 1980–84
Martin Dobson 1984–89
Sam Ellis 1989–90
Mike Walsh 1990–95
Stan Ternent 1995–98
Neil Warnock 1998–99
Andy Preece 2000–04
Graham Barrow 2004–05
Chris Casper 2005–08
Alan Knill February 2008–

TEN YEAR LEAGUE RECORD

		P	W	D	L	F	A	Pts	Pos
1999-2000	Div 2	46	13	18	15	61	64	57	15
2000-01	Div 2	46	16	10	20	45	59	58	16
2001-02	Div 2	46	11	11	24	43	75	44	22
2002-03	Div 3	46	18	16	12	57	56	70	7
2003-04	Div 3	46	15	11	20	54	64	56	12
2004-05	FL 2	46	14	16	16	54	54	58	17
2005-06	FL 2	46	12	17	17	45	57	52*	19
2006-07	FL 2	46	13	11	22	46	61	50	21
2007-08	FL 2	46	16	11	19	58	61	59	13
2008-09	FL 2	46	21	15	10	63	43	78	4

*1 pt deducted.

DID YOU KNOW ?

In 1923–24 Bury won promotion with only 51 points. They scored just eight goals in their first eleven matches. Their programme finished, Derby County needed a 5–0 victory to overtake. The Rams won 4–0 and Bury survived by 0.02 of goal average.

BURY 2008–09 LEAGUE RECORD

Match No.	Date	Venue	Opponents	Result	H/T Score	Lg. Pos.	Goalscorers	Attendance
1	Aug 9	H	Brentford	W	1-0	1-0	—	Bishop [43]	2819
2	16	A	Chesterfield	W	3-1	3-0	4	Futcher [4], Sodje [27], Morrell [40]	3728
3	23	H	Morecambe	W	2-1	2-1	3	Scott [19], Artell (og) [30]	2679
4	30	A	Rochdale	D	1-1	1-0	3	Russell (og) [8]	5492
5	Sept 6	A	Chester C	D	1-1	0-1	3	Bishop (pen) [49]	2327
6	13	H	Lincoln C	W	3-1	1-1	2	Morrell [30], Sodje [50], Bishop (pen) [66]	2663
7	20	A	Barnet	W	2-1	0-0	1	Bishop [75], Morrell [82]	1995
8	27	H	Wycombe W	D	0-0	0-0	1		3597
9	Oct 4	A	Aldershot T	D	3-3	2-0	2	Bishop 2 [24, 57], Scott [30]	3621
10	11	H	Exeter C	L	0-1	0-1	4		3220
11	18	A	Dagenham & R	W	3-1	2-0	2	Dawson [32], Jones [36], Bennett [82]	2364
12	21	H	Rotherham U	L	1-2	1-2	—	Scott [30]	2362
13	25	H	Luton T	L	1-2	0-2	7	Bishop (pen) [53]	3052
14	28	A	Bradford C	L	0-1	0-0	—		12,830
15	Nov 1	A	Notts Co	W	1-0	0-0	7	Cresswell [79]	4391
16	15	H	Grimsby T	L	0-2	0-2	9		2549
17	22	H	Gillingham	W	4-0	2-0	6	Bishop 2 [9, 59], Hurst 2 [40, 63]	2068
18	29	A	Accrington S	W	2-1	2-0	—	Jones [35], Barry-Murphy [38]	2093
19	Dec 6	A	Macclesfield T	D	1-1	1-1	5	Dawson [8]	2431
20	13	H	Port Vale	W	3-0	2-0	2	Futcher [2], Hurst 2 [11, 45]	2651
21	20	A	Bournemouth	L	0-2	0-2	2		3479
22	26	H	Darlington	D	2-2	1-1	3	Brown (og) [31], Bishop (pen) [55]	3454
23	28	A	Shrewsbury T	L	0-1	0-0	6		7127
24	Jan 3	A	Wycombe W	L	1-2	0-0	—	Williamson (og) [90]	4961
25	10	H	Barnet	W	1-0	1-0	—	Jones [37]	2402
26	17	A	Exeter C	D	0-0	0-0	5		4158
27	24	H	Aldershot T	W	2-1	2-0	3	Barry-Murphy [41], Morrell [46]	2558
28	27	H	Bradford C	W	1-0	0-0	—	Morrell [76]	4112
29	31	A	Luton T	W	2-1	0-1	3	Bishop [59], Morrell [66]	5545
30	Feb 7	H	Dagenham & R	D	2-2	2-0	3	Sodje 2 [28, 33]	2530
31	14	A	Grimsby T	W	2-1	0-1	3	Bishop [55], Morrell [65]	3673
32	21	H	Notts Co	W	2-0	1-0	3	Bishop [40], Sodje [84]	2810
33	28	A	Brentford	L	0-1	0-1	4		6597
34	Mar 3	H	Chesterfield	L	1-2	0-2	—	Bishop (pen) [60]	2077
35	7	H	Rochdale	W	2-1	1-0	3	Bennett [19], Jones [84]	7589
36	10	A	Morecambe	D	0-0	0-0	—		2165
37	14	A	Lincoln C	D	1-1	0-1	4	Bishop [82]	3642
38	21	H	Chester C	D	1-1	1-0	5	Morrell [45]	3049
39	24	A	Rotherham U	D	1-1	0-0	—	Sodje [90]	2890
40	28	H	Bournemouth	W	1-0	0-0	2	Morrell [55]	2762
41	Apr 4	A	Port Vale	D	1-1	0-0	3	Bennett [68]	5763
42	10	H	Shrewsbury T	W	2-1	1-0	—	Jevons (pen) [45], Hurst [80]	4850
43	13	A	Darlington	D	2-2	1-1	4	Hurst [8], Sodje [53]	2927
44	18	H	Macclesfield T	W	3-0	1-0	4	Bishop [4], Hurst 2 [57, 75]	3499
45	25	H	Gillingham	D	0-0	0-0	4		8360
46	May 2	H	Accrington S	W	1-0	0-0	4	Jevons (pen) [90]	7515

Final League Position: 4

GOALSCORERS

League (63): Bishop 16 (5 pens), Morrell 9, Hurst 8, Sodje 7, Jones 4, Bennett 3, Scott 3, Barry-Murphy 2, Dawson 2, Futcher 2, Jevons 2 (2 pens), Cresswell 1, own goals 4.
Carling Cup (0).
FA Cup (0).
J Paint Trophy (1): Bishop 1.
Play-Offs (1): own goal 1.

Brown W 35	Scott P 33	Buchanan D 46	Dawson S 42 + 1	Sodje E 40 + 1	Futcher B 33 + 1	Bennett E 46	Barry-Murphy B 41 + 1	Hurst G 16 + 21	Bishop A 39 + 3	Jones M 46	Baker R 6 + 16	Racchi D — + 21	Cresswell R 19 + 6	Morrell A 31 + 10	O'Grady C 3 + 3	Howell D — + 3	Haslam S 13	Belford C — + 1	Tyler M 11	Jevons P 3 + 4	Welsh J 3 + 2	Match No.
1	2²	3	4	5	6	7	8	9¹	10	11³	12	13	14									1
1	2	3	4	5	6	7¹	8	9²		11	13	12	14	10³								2
1	2	3	4	5	6	7¹	8	13	10	11		12		9²								3
1	2	3	4	5	6	7¹	8		10	11	13	12		9²								4
1	2	3	4	5	6	7	8	13	10	11¹	12			9²								5
1	2	3	4	5	6	7	8	12	10	11²	13			9¹								6
1	2	3	4	5¹	6	7	8		10	11		12		9								7
1	2	3	4	5	6	7	8		10	11				9								8
1	2	3	4	5	6	7	8	12	10	11²	13			9¹								9
1	2	3	4¹	5	6³	7	8	13	10	11		12	14	9²								10
1	2	3	4	5	6	7	8	12	10¹	11²		13		9³	14							11
1	2	3	4	5	6¹	7	8		10	11		12		9²	13							12
1	2¹	3	4	5		7	8		10	11²	13	12	6	9								13
1	2	3	4	5		7	8		10	11²	13	6	12	9¹								14
1	2	3	4	5		7	8	12	10²	11			6	9¹	13							15
1	2	3	4	5		7	8³	12	13	11¹		14	6	9²	10							16
1	2	3	4	5	6	7	8¹	9²	10	11		12	13									17
1	2	3	4	5	6	7	8	9²	10¹	11³		14	12				13					18
1	2	3	4	5	6	7	8	9¹	10	11²		12	13									19
1	2	3	4	5	6	7¹		9²	10	11³	8	12		13		14						20
1	2	3	4	5	6	7		9²	10	11³	8³	12		13		14						21
1	2	3	4	5	6	7		9¹	10	11	8	12										22
1		3	4	5⁴	6	7	12	9		11¹	8	13		10²		2						23
1⁰	2	3	4		6	7	9¹	12	8	11		5		10				15				24
	2	3	4		6	7	8		10	11			5	9					1			25
	2	3	4		6	7	8		10	11			5	9					1			26
	2	3	4		6	7	8	12	10	11			5	9¹					1			27
	2	3	4		6	7	8	12	10	11			5	9¹					1			28
	2	3	4	12	6¹	7	8	13	10	11			5	9²					1			29
	2	3	4	5		7	8	12	10	11			6	9¹					1			30
	2	3	4²	5		11	8	12	10	7		13	6	9¹					1			31
	2	3	4	5		11	8	12	10¹	7³	13	14	6	9²					1			32
	2	3	4⁴	5		7	8		10	11¹		12	6	9					1			33
	2	3	6	4		8		12	10	11	7		5	9¹					1			34
		3	4	5		7²	8	12	10	11	13		6	9¹			2		1			35
1		3	4	5		7¹	8	9	10	11		12	6				2					36
1		3	4	5		7	8	12	10	11	13		6	9¹			2²					37
1		3	4	5	12	7	8	13	10²	11³		14	6	9¹			2					38
1		3	4	5	6	7	8	9²	10¹	11		12			13		2					39
1		3	4	5	6	7	8	12		11³	13			9²		14	2			10¹		40
1		3	4	5	6	7³	8	12		11²	13			9¹		14	2			10		41
1		3	4	5	6	7	8	13	12	11³		14		9¹			2			10²		42
1		3	4¹	5	6	7²	8	9³	10		13	12	14				2			11		43
1		3	4	5	6		8	9²	10¹	11³	13	14					2			12	7	44
1		3	12	5	6	4	8	9²	10	11¹							2			13	7	45
1		3	4	5	6	7³	8	9²	10¹	11	13	14					2			12		46

FA Cup
First Round   Gillingham   (h)   0-1

Carling Cup
First Round   Burnley   (h)   0-2

J Paint Trophy
Second Round   Stockport Co   (h)   1-0
Quarter-Final   Darlington   (a)   0-1

Play-Offs
Semi-Final   Shrewsbury T   (a)   1-0
                                                (h)   0-1

CARDIFF CITY   FL Championship

FOUNDATION

Credit for the establishment of a first class professional football club in such a rugby stronghold as Cardiff, is due to members of the Riverside club formed in 1899 out of a cricket club of that name. Cardiff became a city in 1905 and in 1908 the South Wales and Monmouthshire FA granted Riverside permission to call themselves Cardiff City. The club turned professional under that name in 1910.

Ninian Park, Sloper Road, Cardiff CF11 8SX (moving to new ground at Leckwith Road, Cardiff CF11 8AZ).

Telephone: (029) 2022 1001.

Fax: (029) 2034 1148.

Ticket Office: 0845 345 1400.

Website: www.cardiffcityfc.co.uk

Email: club@cardiffcityfc.co.uk

Ground Capacity: 20,324.

Record Attendance: 62,634, Wales v England, 17 October 1959.

Club Record Attendance: 57,893 v Arsenal, Division 1, 22 April 1953.

Pitch Measurements: 110yd × 75yd.

Chairman: Peter Ridsdale.

Secretary: Jason Turner.

Manager: Dave Jones.

Assistant Manager: Terry Burton.

Physio: Sean Connely BHSc MCSP, SRP.

Colours: Blue shirts with yellow trim, white shorts, white stockings.

Change Colours: All dark red with white trim.

Year Formed: 1899.   *Turned Professional:* 1910.

Ltd Co.: 1910.

Previous Names: 1899, Riverside; 1902, Riverside Albion; 1908, Cardiff City.

Club Nickname: 'Bluebirds'.

Grounds: Riverside, Sophia Gardens, Old Park and Fir Gardens. Moved to Ninian Park, 1910.

First Football League Game: 28 August 1920, Division 2, v Stockport Co (a) W 5–2 – Kneeshaw; Brittan, Leyton; Keenor (1), Smith, Hardy; Grimshaw (1), Gill (2), Cashmore, West, Evans (1).

Record League Victory: 9–2 v Thames, Division 3 (S), 6 February 1932 – Farquharson; E. L. Morris, Roberts; Galbraith, Harris, Ronan; Emmerson (1), Keating (1), Jones (1), McCambridge (1), Robbins (5).

Record Cup Victory: 8–0 v Enfield, FA Cup 1st rd, 28 November 1931 – Farquharson; Smith, Roberts; Harris (1), Galbraith, Ronan; Emmerson (2), Keating (3); O'Neill (2), Robbins, McCambridge.

HONOURS

Football League: Division 1 – Runners-up 1923–24; Division 2 – Runners-up 1920–21, 1951–52, 1959–60; Division 3 (S) – Champions 1946–47; Division 3 – Champions 1992–93. Runners-up 1975–76, 1982–83, 2000–01; Division 4 – Runners-up 1987–88.

FA Cup: Winners 1927 (only occasion the Cup has been won by a club outside England); Runners-up 1925, 2008.

Football League Cup: Semi-final 1966.

Welsh Cup: Winners 22 times (joint record).

Charity Shield: Winners 1927.

European Competitions: European Cup-Winners' Cup: 1964–65, 1965–66, 1967–68 (semi-finalists), 1968–69, 1969–70, 1970–71, 1971–72, 1973–74, 1974–75, 1976–77, 1977–78, 1988–89, 1992–93, 1993–94.

SKY SPORTS FACT FILE

Irish international Jimmy McCambridge, born in Northern Ireland with a Scottish name, played for the Welsh club Cardiff City and was signed from the English club Exeter City. Between 1930 and 1932 he scored 53 goals for Cardiff in exactly 100 League and Cup games.

Record Defeat: 2–11 v Sheffield U, Division 1, 1 January 1926.

Most League Points (2 for a win): 66, Division 3 (S), 1946–47.

Most League Points (3 for a win): 86, Division 3, 1982–83.

Most League Goals: 95, Division 3, 2000–01.

Highest League Scorer in Season: Robert Earnshaw, 31, Division 2, 2002–03.

Most League Goals in Total Aggregate: Len Davies, 128, 1920–31.

Most League Goals in One Match: 5, Hugh Ferguson v Burnley, Division 1, 1 September 1928; 5, Walter Robbins v Thames, Division 3 (S), 6 February 1932; 5, William Henderson v Northampton T, Division 3 (S), 22 April 1933.

Most Capped Player: Alf Sherwood, 39 (41), Wales.

Most League Appearances: Phil Dwyer, 471, 1972–85.

Youngest League Player: Bob Adams, 15 years 355 days v Southend U, 18 February 1933.

Record Transfer Fee Received: £5,000,000 from Sunderland for Michael Chopra, August 2006; Aaron Ramsey from Arsenal, June 2008.

Record Transfer Fee Paid: £4,000,000 to Sunderland for Michael Chopra, July 2009.

Football League Record: 1920 Elected to Division 2; 1921–29 Division 2; 1929–31 Division 2; 1931–47 Division 3 (S); 1947–52 Division 2; 1952–57 Division 1; 1957–60 Division 2; 1960–62 Division 1; 1962–75 Division 2; 1975–76 Division 3; 1976–82 Division 2; 1982–83 Division 3; 1983–85 Division 3; 1985–86 Division 3; 1986–88 Division 4; 1988–90 Division 3; 1990–92 Division 4; 1992–93 Division 3; 1993–95 Division 2; 1995–99 Division 3; 1999–2000 Division 2; 2000–01 Division 3; 2001–03 Division 2; 2003–04 Division 1; 2004– FL C.

MANAGERS

Davy McDougall 1910–11
Fred Stewart 1911–33
Bartley Wilson 1933–34
B. Watts-Jones 1934–37
Bill Jennings 1937–39
Cyril Spiers 1939–46
Billy McCandless 1946–48
Cyril Spiers 1948–54
Trevor Morris 1954–58
Bill Jones 1958–62
George Swindin 1962–64
Jimmy Scoular 1964–73
Frank O'Farrell 1973–74
Jimmy Andrews 1974–78
Richie Morgan 1978–81
Graham Williams 1981–82
Len Ashurst 1982–84
Jimmy Goodfellow 1984
Alan Durban 1984–86
Frank Burrows 1986–89
Len Ashurst 1989–91
Eddie May 1991–94
Terry Yorath 1994–95
Eddie May 1995
Kenny Hibbitt *(Chief Coach)* 1995
Phil Neal 1996
Russell Osman 1996–97
Kenny Hibbitt 1996–98
Frank Burrows 1998–99
Billy Ayre 1999–2000
Bobby Gould 2000
Alan Cork 2000–02
Lennie Lawrence 2002–05
Dave Jones May 2005–

LATEST SEQUENCES

Longest Sequence of League Wins: 9, 26.10.1946 – 28.12.1946.

Longest Sequence of League Defeats: 7, 4.11.1933 – 25.12.1933.

Longest Sequence of League Draws: 6, 29.11.1980 – 17.1.1981.

Longest Sequence of Unbeaten League Matches: 21, 21.9.1946 – 1.3.1947.

Longest Sequence Without a League Win: 15, 21.11.1936 – 6.3.1937.

Successive Scoring Runs: 23 from 24.10.1992.

Successive Non-scoring Runs: 8 from 20.12.1952.

TEN YEAR LEAGUE RECORD

		P	W	D	L	F	A	Pts	Pos
1999-2000	Div 2	46	9	17	20	45	67	44	21
2000-01	Div 3	46	23	13	10	95	58	82	2
2001-02	Div 2	46	23	14	9	75	50	83	4
2002-03	Div 2	46	23	12	11	68	43	81	6
2003-04	Div 1	46	17	14	15	68	58	65	13
2004-05	FL C	46	13	15	18	48	51	54	16
2005-06	FL C	46	16	12	18	58	59	60	11
2006-07	FL C	46	17	13	16	57	53	64	13
2007-08	FL C	46	16	16	14	59	55	64	12
2008-09	FL C	46	19	17	10	65	53	74	7

DID YOU KNOW ?

In spite of finishing only 15th in the Second Division that season, in three home matches during December 1957 Cardiff City scored 18 goals, defeating Barnsley 7–0, then Stoke City 5–2 on Boxing Day and finally promotion-chasing Liverpool 6–1.

CARDIFF CITY 2008–09 LEAGUE RECORD

Match No.	Date	Venue	Opponents	Result	H/T Score	Lg. Pos.	Goalscorers	Attendance
1	Aug 9	H	Southampton	W 2-1	1-1	—	Thompson [41], Johnson R [90]	19,749
2	16	A	Doncaster R	D 1-1	0-0	6	McCormack [88]	11,873
3	23	H	Norwich C	D 2-2	1-0	10	McCormack 2 (1 pen) [3, 67 (p)]	18,032
4	30	A	Sheffield U	D 0-0	0-0	12		29,226
5	Sept 13	H	Bristol C	D 0-0	0-0	8		19,312
6	16	A	Barnsley	W 1-0	1-0	—	Whittingham [14]	11,282
7	20	A	Derby Co	D 1-1	0-1	7	McCormack (pen) [69]	28,007
8	27	H	Birmingham C	L 1-2	0-2	11	McCormack [86]	18,304
9	30	H	Coventry C	W 2-1	1-0	—	Bothroyd [31], McCormack (pen) [85]	16,312
10	Oct 4	A	Blackpool	D 1-1	0-0	7	Parry [83]	7328
11	18	H	Charlton Ath	W 2-0	1-0	4	McCormack 2 [18, 52]	17,310
12	21	A	Watford	D 2-2	0-2	—	Bothroyd 2 [72, 75]	13,461
13	25	A	Nottingham F	W 1-0	0-0	4	McCormack (pen) [54]	19,468
14	28	H	Blackpool	W 2-0	0-0	—	Whittingham [83], McCormack [86]	17,570
15	Nov 1	H	Wolverhampton W	L 1-2	1-2	6	McCormack [19]	17,734
16	8	A	QPR	L 0-1	0-0	6		13,347
17	15	H	Crystal Palace	W 2-1	1-1	6	Chopra (pen) [33], Ledley [53]	17,478
18	22	A	Plymouth Arg	L 1-2	0-2	6	Chopra [62]	11,438
19	25	H	Reading	D 2-2	2-1	—	Routledge [10], McCormack (pen) [41]	17,154
20	30	A	Swansea C	D 2-2	1-1	7	Ledley [45], McCormack (pen) [48]	18,053
21	Dec 6	H	Preston NE	W 2-0	1-0	5	Johnson R [42], Chopra (pen) [76]	16,560
22	9	A	Burnley	D 2-2	1-1	—	Bothroyd [26], Routledge [47]	11,230
23	13	A	Ipswich T	W 2-1	2-1	5	Bothroyd [9], Gyepes [26]	19,665
24	20	H	Sheffield W	W 2-0	0-0	5	Johnson R [49], Chopra (pen) [65]	17,600
25	26	A	Reading	D 1-1	0-0	5	Chopra [89]	22,770
26	28	H	Plymouth Arg	W 1-0	0-0	4	Bothroyd [81]	19,145
27	Jan 17	A	Birmingham C	D 1-1	0-0	6	Ledley [61]	19,853
28	28	A	Coventry C	W 2-0	1-0	—	Bothroyd [34], McCormack [61]	14,922
29	31	H	Nottingham F	W 2-0	1-0	4	Parry [18], Bothroyd [87]	18,779
30	Feb 22	A	Wolverhampton W	D 2-2	1-1	6	Chopra [31], Johnson R [48]	22,093
31	25	H	QPR	D 0-0	0-0	—		17,340
32	28	A	Southampton	L 0-1	0-1	7		18,526
33	Mar 3	H	Barnsley	W 3-1	2-0	—	Ledley [4], Chopra [43], Whittingham [88]	15,902
34	7	A	Doncaster R	W 3-0	2-0	4	Chopra [10], Bothroyd [29], Johnson E [60]	17,821
35	10	A	Norwich C	L 0-2	0-0	—		23,706
36	15	H	Bristol C	D 1-1	0-0	6	McCormack [88]	17,487
37	18	H	Watford	W 2-1	1-1	—	Bothroyd [14], McCormack (pen) [90]	17,899
38	22	H	Sheffield U	L 0-3	0-1	6		17,942
39	Apr 5	H	Swansea C	D 2-2	0-1	6	Chopra [54], McCormack (pen) [90]	20,156
40	8	A	Derby Co	W 4-1	1-0	4	Johnson R [16], Rae [61], Bothroyd [63], Johnson E [79]	18,403
41	11	A	Crystal Palace	W 2-0	1-0	4	McCormack 2 (1 pen) [22 (p), 90]	14,814
42	13	H	Burnley	W 3-1	0-0	4	Bothroyd [74], McCormack 2 [85, 90]	19,379
43	18	A	Preston NE	L 0-6	0-2	4		13,692
44	21	A	Charlton Ath	D 2-2	0-1	—	Burke [82], Gyepes [89]	19,390
45	25	H	Ipswich T	L 0-3	0-1	5		19,129
46	May 3	A	Sheffield W	L 0-1	0-0	7		30,658

Final League Position: 7

GOALSCORERS

League (65): McCormack 21 (9 pens), Bothroyd 12, Chopra 9 (3 pens), Johnson R 5, Ledley 4, Whittingham 3, Gyepes 2, Johnson E 2, Parry 2, Routledge 2, Burke 1, Rae 1, Thompson 1.
Carling Cup (4): Parry 2, McCormack 1 (pen), Whittingham 1.
FA Cup (2): Ledley 1, McCormack 1.

Heaton T 21	McNaughton K 39	Kennedy M 35+1	Rae G 39+2	Johnson R 45	Loovens G 1	Whittingham P 23+10	McPhail S 27+5	Thompson S 1+3	McCormack R 32+6	Ledley J 40	Bothroyd J 35+4	Parry P 33+7	Comminges M 10+20	Scimeca R 2+2	Purse D 21+2	Blake D 4+3	Johnson E 5+25	Gyepes G 25+2	Chopra M 23+4	Enckelman P 11+1	Routledge W 9	Burke C 8+6	Konstantopoulos D 6	Owusu-Abeyie Q —+5	Capaldi T 3	Taylor S 8	Match No.
1	2	3	4	5	6	7[2]	8	9[1]	10	11	12	13															1
1	2[2]	3		5		7[3]	8	12	10	11	14	9	13	4[1]	6												2
1		3[1]		6		13	8	14	10[2]	7	9[3]	11	12	4	2	5											3
1	2			5		4	8	12	10[1]	11	9[2]	7	3		6		13										4
1	2		4	5		7	8		12	11	10	9[1]	3		6												5
1	2		4	5		7	8		10[1]	11	12	9	3		6												6
1	2		4	5		7[1]	8		10[2]	11	12	9	3		6		13										7
1	2	12	4	5		7			10	11	9	8[2]	3[1]		6		13										8
1	2	3	4	5		7	8		10	11	9				6												9
1	2[1]	3	4	5		7	8[3]		10	11[2]	9	13	12		6		14										10
1	2	3	4	5		7	8		10		9[2]	11[1]	12		6		13										11
1	2[2]	3	4	5		7[1]	8		10		9	11	13		6		12										12
1	2	3[1]	4	5		13	8		10	11[2]	9	7	12		6[3]		14										13
1	2		4	5		12	8		10	7	9	11[2]	3[1]		6		13										14
1	2		4	5		3	8		10[2]	7	9[1]	11	12		6		13										15
1	2		4	5		7	8			11[2]		12	3		6		9[1]	13	10								16
1	2	3	4[2]	5		7[1]	8			11		12			6		13	9	10								17
1[6]	2[2]	3	4	5			8			11[1]	12				6		13	9	10	15	7						18
		3[1]	4	5			8		10		9[2]		2		12		13	6	11	1	7						19
	2	3	12	5		4			10	11[3]	9[2]	13		14			6	8[1]		1	7						20
	2	3[1]	4	5					10[3]	11	9[2]	8	12	13			6	14		1	7						21
	2	3	4	5						11	9[2]	8[1]	12				13	6	10	1	7						22
	2	3	4	5		13				11	9	8					12[2]	6	10[1]	1	7						23
	2[1]	3	4	5						11	9	8	12				13	6	10[2]	1	7						24
	2	3	4	5		12				11	9	8[1]						6	10	1	7						25
	2	3	4	5		12				11	9	8[1]						6	10	1	7						26
	2	3	4	5		7[3]	12		10	11	9[2]	8[1]					13	6		1		14					27
	2[2]	3	4	5			12		10	11[1]	9	8	13				6			1		7					28
	2	3	4	5					10[3]	11	9	8	12		13		14	6[2]		1		7[1]					29
	2[1]	3	4	5		13			7[2]	11	9	8	12				6		10			14	1				30
	2[1]	3	4	5		13			10	11	8	12			6				9[2]			7[3]	1	14			31
		3	4	5		8[2]			10	11	9		2[1]			12	6					7	1	13			32
		3	4	5		8			12	11		7[2]					2	9	6	10[1]			1	13			33
		3[1]	4	5		8			13	11	9[3]	7	12				2	14	6	10[2]			1				34
			4	5		8[2]			12	11		7					2[3]	9	6	10		13	1	14	3[1]		35
	2			5		8[3]	4		12	11	9[2]	7[1]					13	6	10			14			3	1	36
	2			5		12	4		10	11	9	8[1]						6	13			7[2]			3	1	37
	2	3	4	5			12		10[1]	11	9[3]		13					14	6	8[2]		7[1]			1		38
	2	3[3]	13	5			12	4	10	11	9	7[1]			6			14		8[2]					1		39
	2	3	4	5		7[3]	8		10[2]		9[1]		13					12	6	11		14			1		40
	2	3	4	5[2]			8		10	11	9[3]	12	13					14	6	7[1]					1		41
	2	3	4			12	8		10	11	9[2]				5			13	6	7[1]					1		42
	2	3[2]	4	5		7[1]	8		10	11	9[3]		13					14	6	12					1		43
1		3	4	5[3]					10	11	9	7[2]	2		14		13	6	8[1]			12					44
1	2		4[3]	5			13		10[1]	11	9	8[2]						14	6	12		7					45
1	2	3[1]	4	5		11	8		13		9		12						6	10[2]		7[3]		14			46

FA Cup

Third Round	Reading	(h)	2-0	
Fourth Round	Arsenal	(h)	0-0	
		(a)	0-4	

Carling Cup

First Round	Bournemouth	(a)	2-1	
Second Round	Milton Keynes D	(h)	2-1	
Third Round	Swansea C	(a)	0-1	

CARLISLE UNITED   FL Championship 1

FOUNDATION

Carlisle United came into being in 1903 through the amalgamation of Shaddongate United and Carlisle Red Rose. The new club was admitted to the Second Division of the Lancashire Combination in 1905–06, winning promotion the following season. Devonshire Park was officially opened on 2 September 1905, when St Helens Town were the visitors. Despite defeat in a disappointing 3-2 start, a respectable mid-table position was achieved.

Brunton Park, Warwick Road, Carlisle CA1 1LL.
Telephone: (01228) 526 237.
Fax: (01228) 554 141.
Ticket Office: (01228) 526 237 (option 1).
Website: www.carlisleunited.co.uk
Email: enquiries@carlisleunited.co.uk
Ground Capacity: 16,982.
Record Attendance: 27,500 v Birmingham C, FA Cup 3rd rd, 5 January 1957 and v Middlesbrough, FA Cup 5th rd, 7 February 1970.
Pitch Measurements: 114yd × 74yd.
Chairman: Andrew Jenkins.
Managing Director: John Nixon.
Chief Executive: David Allen.
Secretary: Sarah McKnight.
Manager: Greg Abbott.
First Team Coach: Dennis Booth.   **Physio:** Neil Dalton.
Colours: Blue and white shirts with alternate blue and red sleeves and white trim, blue shorts, blue stockings.
Change Colours: All black with red trim.
Year Formed: 1903.   **Ltd Co.:** 1921.
Previous Name: 1903, Shaddongate United; 1904, Carlisle United.
Club Nicknames: 'Cumbrians' or 'The Blues'.
Grounds: 1903, Milholme Bank; 1905, Devonshire Park; 1909, Brunton Park.
First Football League Game: 25 August 1928, Division 3 (N), v Accrington S (a) W 3–2 – Prout; Coulthard, Cook; Harrison, Ross, Pigg; Agar (1), Hutchison, McConnell (1), Ward (1), Watson.
Record League Victory: 8–0 v Hartlepool U, Division 3 (N), 1 September 1928 – Prout; Smiles, Cook; Robinson (1) Ross, Pigg; Agar (1), Hutchison (1), McConnell (4), Ward (1), Watson. 8–0 v Scunthorpe U, Division 3 (N), 25 December 1952 – MacLaren; Hill, Scott; Stokoe, Twentyman, Waters; Harrison (1), Whitehouse (5), Ashman (2), Duffett, Bond.
Record Cup Victory: 6–0 v Shepshed Dynamo, FA Cup 1st rd, 16 November 1996 – Caig; Hopper, Archdeacon (pen), Walling, Robinson, Pounewatchy, Peacock (1), Conway (1) (Jansen), Smart (McAlindon (1)), Hayward, Aspinall (Thorpe), (2 og).

HONOURS

Football League: Division 1 best season: 22nd, 1974–75; Division 3 – Champions 1964–65, 1994–95; Runners-up 1981–82; Division 4 – Runners-up 1963–64; FL 2 – Champions 2005–06.
FA Cup: best season: 6th rd 1975.
Football League Cup: Semi-final 1970.
Auto Windscreens Shield: Winners 1997; Runners-up 1995.
LDV Vans Trophy: Runners-up 2003, 2006.

SKY SPORTS FACT FILE

On 2 May 2009 Carlisle United ended a miserable run of eleven matches without a win by beating Millwall 2–0 to ensure survival in League 1. Guest of honour for the match was Jimmy Glass, goalkeeping-scorer hero of their salvation in the competition 10 years earlier.

Record Defeat: 1–11 v Hull C, Division 3 (N), 14 January 1939.

Most League Points (2 for a win): 62, Division 3 (N), 1950–51.

Most League Points (3 for a win): 91, Division 3, 1994–95.

Most League Goals: 113, Division 4, 1963–64.

Highest League Scorer in Season: Jimmy McConnell, 42, Division 3 (N), 1928–29.

Most League Goals in Total Aggregate: Jimmy McConnell, 126, 1928–32.

Most League Goals in One Match: 5, Hugh Mills v Halifax T, Division 3 (N), 11 September 1937; 5, Jim Whitehouse v Scunthorpe U, Division 3 (N), 25 December 1952.

Most Capped Player: Eric Welsh, 4, Northern Ireland.

Most League Appearances: Allan Ross, 466, 1963–79.

Youngest League Player: John Slaven, 16 years 162 days v Scunthorpe U, 16 March 2002.

Record Transfer Fee Received: £1,500,000 from Crystal Palace for Matt Jansen, February 1998.

Record Transfer Fee Paid: £140,000 to Blackburn R for Joe Garner, August 2007.

Football League Record: 1928 Elected to Division 3 (N); 1958–62 Division 4; 1962–63 Division 3; 1963–64 Division 4; 1964–65 Division 3; 1965–74 Division 2; 1974–75 Division 1; 1975–77 Division 2; 1977–82 Division 3; 1982–86 Division 2; 1986–87 Division 3; 1987–92 Division 4; 1992–95 Division 3; 1995–96 Division 2; 1996–97 Division 2; 1997–98 Division 2; 1998–04 Division 3; 2004–05 Conference; 2005–06 FL 2; 2006– FL 1.

LATEST SEQUENCES

Longest Sequence of League Wins: 7, 18.2.06 – 8.4.06.

Longest Sequence of League Defeats: 12, 27.9.2003 – 13.12.2003.

Longest Sequence of League Draws: 6, 11.2.1978 – 11.3.1978.

Longest Sequence of Unbeaten League Matches: 19, 1.10.1994 – 11.2.1995.

Longest Sequence Without a League Win: 14, 19.1.1935 – 19.4.1935.

Successive Scoring Runs: 26 from 23.8.1947.

Successive Non-scoring Runs: 5 from 24.8.1968.

MANAGERS

Harry Kirkbride 1904–05 *(Secretary-Manager)*
McCumiskey 1905–06 *(Secretary-Manager)*
Jack Houston 1906–08 *(Secretary-Manager)*
Bert Stansfield 1908–10
Jack Houston 1910–12
Davie Graham 1912–13
George Bristow 1913–30
Billy Hampson 1930–33
Bill Clarke 1933–35
Robert Kelly 1935–36
Fred Westgarth 1936–38
David Taylor 1938–40
Howard Harkness 1940–45
Bill Clark 1945–46 *(Secretary-Manager)*
Ivor Broadis 1946–49
Bill Shankly 1949–51
Fred Emery 1951–58
Andy Beattie 1958–60
Ivor Powell 1960–63
Alan Ashman 1963–67
Tim Ward 1967–68
Bob Stokoe 1968–70
Ian MacFarlane 1970–72
Alan Ashman 1972–75
Dick Young 1975–76
Bobby Moncur 1976–80
Martin Harvey 1980
Bob Stokoe 1980–85
Bryan 'Pop' Robson 1985
Bob Stokoe 1985–86
Harry Gregg 1986–87
Cliff Middlemass 1987–91
Aidan McCaffery 1991–92
David McCreery 1992–93
Mick Wadsworth *(Director of Coaching)* 1993–96
Mervyn Day 1996–97
David Wilkes and John Halpin *(Directors of Coaching)*, and Michael Knighton 1997–99
Nigel Pearson 1998–99
Keith Mincher 1999
Martin Wilkinson 1999–2000
Ian Atkins 2000–01
Roddy Collins 2001–02; 2002–03
Paul Simpson 2003–06
Neil McDonald 2006–07
John Ward 2007–08
Greg Abbott December 2008–

TEN YEAR LEAGUE RECORD

		P	W	D	L	F	A	Pts	Pos
1999-2000	Div 3	46	9	12	25	42	75	39	23
2000-01	Div 3	46	11	15	20	42	65	48	22
2001-02	Div 3	46	12	16	18	49	56	52	17
2002-03	Div 3	46	13	10	23	52	78	49	22
2003-04	Div 3	46	12	9	25	46	69	45	23
2004-05	Conf	42	20	13	9	74	37	73	3
2005-06	FL 2	46	25	11	10	84	42	86	1
2006-07	FL 1	46	19	11	16	54	55	68	8
2007-08	FL 1	46	23	11	12	64	46	80	4
2008-09	FL 1	46	12	14	20	56	69	50	20

DID YOU KNOW ?

Man of many clubs George Cook had two pre-war spells with Carlisle United, playing in their first League match having previously had the same experience for Torquay United! Later he played one game for Tranmere Rovers in a 9–1 victory over Rochdale!

CARLISLE UNITED 2008–09 LEAGUE RECORD

Match No.	Date	Venue	Opponents	Result	H/T Score	Lg. Pos.	Goalscorers	Attendance
1	Aug 9	A	Bristol R	W 3-2	2-1	—	Carlton 2 [19, 80], Bridge-Wilkinson [45]	8285
2	16	H	Crewe Alex	W 4-2	2-1	1	Graham 2 [15, 19], Dobie [59], Hackney [76]	6919
3	23	A	Leyton Orient	D 0-0	0-0	3		3803
4	30	H	Yeovil T	W 4-1	1-1	3	Graham 3 (1 pen) [45, 58, 69 (p)], Madine [90]	6286
5	Sept 6	H	Southend U	W 2-1	0-1	2	Graham (pen) [63], Taylor C [79]	6561
6	13	A	Scunthorpe U	L 1-2	0-0	2	Carlton [77]	5188
7	20	H	Leeds U	L 0-2	0-0	6		12,148
8	27	A	Walsall	L 1-2	0-1	7	Bridge-Wilkinson (pen) [83]	4830
9	Oct 4	H	Tranmere R	L 1-2	0-1	11	Graham [90]	6093
10	11	A	Milton Keynes D	L 1-3	1-1	12	Graham [4]	11,194
11	18	H	Peterborough U	D 3-3	1-1	15	Graham 2 [20, 50], Kavanagh [52]	6074
12	21	A	Hereford U	L 0-1	0-0	—		2300
13	25	A	Colchester U	L 0-5	0-3	17		5152
14	28	H	Hartlepool U	L 0-1	0-1	—		5637
15	Nov 1	A	Stockport Co	L 0-3	0-1	20		6301
16	15	H	Brighton & HA	W 3-1	2-0	18	Bridge-Wilkinson 2 [31, 55], Taylor C [45]	5333
17	22	H	Cheltenham T	W 1-0	0-0	16	Kavanagh [64]	5374
18	25	A	Millwall	L 0-1	0-0	—		6828
19	Dec 6	A	Swindon T	D 1-1	0-0	17	Thirlwell [87]	6787
20	13	H	Leicester C	L 1-2	1-0	17	Graham [27]	7085
21	20	A	Northampton T	L 0-1	0-0	19		4673
22	26	H	Huddersfield T	W 3-0	1-0	17	Graham [12], Bridges [55], Kavanagh [75]	7883
23	28	A	Oldham Ath	D 0-0	0-0	17		6254
24	Jan 10	A	Leeds U	W 2-0	2-0	—	Graham [26], Bridges [35]	22,411
25	17	H	Milton Keynes D	W 3-2	0-2	14	Graham [46], Thirlwell [65], Anyinsah [77]	6298
26	24	A	Tranmere R	L 1-4	0-0	15	Graham [60]	5924
27	27	A	Hartlepool U	D 2-2	2-0	—	Bridge-Wilkinson [12], Taylor C [40]	3765
28	31	H	Colchester U	L 0-2	0-1	18		5745
29	Feb 10	A	Walsall	D 1-1	1-0	—	Thirlwell [19]	4502
30	14	A	Brighton & HA	W 2-0	2-0	15	Anyinsah [24], Keogh [28]	5529
31	21	H	Stockport Co	L 1-2	0-1	17	Neal [53]	5930
32	24	A	Peterborough U	L 0-1	0-0	—		5103
33	28	H	Bristol R	D 1-1	1-1	17	Kavanagh [4]	5343
34	Mar 3	A	Crewe Alex	W 2-1	1-1	—	Taylor G [17], Anyinsah [73]	3759
35	7	A	Yeovil T	D 1-1	0-1	16	Bridges [90]	3892
36	10	H	Leyton Orient	L 1-3	0-2	—	Dobie [78]	4536
37	14	H	Scunthorpe U	D 1-1	1-0	16	Anyinsah [19]	4867
38	21	A	Southend U	L 0-3	0-1	16		7789
39	24	H	Hereford U	L 1-2	1-2	—	Bridges [45]	4223
40	28	H	Northampton T	D 1-1	1-1	18	Neal [37]	5254
41	Apr 4	A	Leicester C	D 2-2	1-0	19	Bridges [32], Dobie [90]	20,159
42	10	H	Oldham Ath	D 1-1	1-0	—	Bridges (pen) [44]	6635
43	13	A	Huddersfield T	L 0-1	0-0	20		12,309
44	18	H	Swindon T	D 1-1	1-0	19	Bridges [8]	5959
45	25	A	Cheltenham T	D 1-1	1-0	21	Harte [19]	4290
46	May 2	H	Millwall	W 2-0	1-0	20	Kavanagh [7], Thirlwell [50]	9470

Final League Position: 20

GOALSCORERS

League (56): Graham 15 (2 pens), Bridges 7 (1 pen), Bridge-Wilkinson 5 (1 pen), Kavanagh 5, Anyinsah 4, Thirlwell 4, Carlton 3, Dobie 3, Taylor C 3, Neal 2, Hackney 1, Harte 1, Keogh 1, Madine 1, Taylor G 1.
Carling Cup (1): Murphy 1.
FA Cup (3): Graham 1, Kavanagh 1, Madine 1.
J Paint Trophy (2): Bridges 1, Madine 1.

Williams B 31	Raven D 41	Horwood E 22+2	Thirlwell P 33+1	Livesey D 27	Murphy P 27+1	Dobie S 11+19	Bridge-Wilkinson M 20+3	Graham D 39+5	Carlton D 12	Hackney S 16+6	Taylor C 37+5	Joyce L 4+3	Bridges M 12+18	Keogh R 31+1	Madine G —+14	Myrie-Williams J 1+7	Kavanagh G 34	Alnwick B 6	Smith J 11+5	Campion D 2	Gowling J 3+1	Smith G 1	Welsh J 2+2	Liddle M 21+1	Krul T 9	Birchall C —+2	Anyinsah J 16+3	Kane T 6+3	Burns M —+1	Lumsdon C 4+3	Neal L 15+1	Taylor G 5	Harte I 3	Morris I 4+2	Rothery G —+1	Match No.
1	2	3	4	5	6	7	8	9^1	10	11^2	12	13																								1
1	2	3	4	5	6	7^2	8	9	10^1	11	12		13																							2
1	2	3	4	5	6	7	8	9^2	10^3	11^1	13			14	12																					3
1	2	3	4	5	6		8	9^3	10	7^1	11^2	13	12		14																					4
1	2	3	4	5	6		8	9^2	10^1	11	7		12		13																					5
1	2	3	4	5	6	12	8	9^1	10	11	7																									6
1	2	3	4	5		12	8	9^1	10^2	11	7^3		14	6			13																			7
1	2	3	4	5		7^2	8	9	10^1	11			12	6			13																			8
1	2	3	4	5		9^1	8	12	10^2	11^3	7		13	6			14																			9
1	2	3		5			8	9		11	7^1		10^2	6	12	13	4																			10
	2	3		5				9^1	10^3	11	7^2		8	6	12	13	4	1	14																	11
	2			5		12		9^2	10	11^1	7		8	6^1	13		4	1		3^3	14															12
	2			5	10			9		11^1	7		8^2		12		4	1	13		3	6														13
	2	3		5		12		9	10^2	13	7						11			6	4^1	1	8													14
	2^3	3					8^2	9		12			14	13	7^1	4		1	11	6	10															15
	2		4	5			8^2	9^1	10	7				6	12		11	1					13	3												16
	2		4	5			8^1	9	10	7				6	12		11							3	1											17
	2		4^1	5			8	9	10^2	7		13		6	12		11							3	1											18
	2		4		6		8^2	9^1		7^3		13	5	12			11		10					3	1	14										19
	2		4^1	5		12		9^3		13	7		10	6	14		11^2		8					3	1											20
	2			5		12	8	9^3		13	7		10^2	6	14		4		11^1					3	1											21
	2			5	6		8	9		13	7^3		10^2	4^1	12		11							3	1	14										22
	2		14	5			8^3	9		13	7		10^2	6	12		4		11^1					3	1											23
	2		4	5	6		8	9		13	7^1		10^2		12		8		11					3	1											24
	2		4	5	6			9		10^2	7				12		11^1							3	1	13										25
1	2	13	4^3	5	6			9		10^1	7	14	12				8		11					3^2												26
1	2		4	5	6		8	9			7			11					10					3												27
1	2	12	4	5	6		8^2	9			7		13	11					10					3^1												28
1	2^2	3^3	4		6			9			7		12	5			8										10^1	13	14	8				11		29
1		3	4		6			9			7		12	5	13		8		2								10^2	2						11^1		30
1		3^1	4		6	12		9			7		13	5			8										10^2	2						11		31
1			4		6	12		9			7		13	5			8							3			10^1	2						11^2		32
1			4		6	12		9^2			7		13	5			8							3			10	2						11^1		33
1	2		4		6	12					7			5			8							3		13	11				10^2	9^1				34
1	2		4		6^2	12					7^3		14	5			8							3		13	10^1					9		11		35
1	6		4			12				14	7^3		13	5			8							3			10^2	2				9^1		11		36
1			4		6	12				10	7		13	5			8							3		7	2				9^1		11^2		37
1	2		4		6^3			9			12		13	5			8		11^1					3			10	14			7^2					38
1	2		4^1				13	9^3			9^3		14	5	12		8		10					3			7^2				11		6			39
1	2	3						9			7		10^2	5			8									13	12				11		6	4^1		40
1	2	3^2			6	12		9			7		10^3	5			11								13		8^1	14						4		41
1	2	3			6	13		9^2			7		10	5	4^3		12		12								11^1	14						8		42
1	2	3^2	4		6	13		9			7^3		10	5	4		11^1										11^1				12	8		14		43
1	2	3	4		6	13		9^2			7		10	5	12																	8^3	11^1	14		44
1	2	3^4	4			12		9^2		14	7^1		10^4	5																		8^2	11	6	13	45
1	2		4		6	12		9^1			7		5														10						11	3		46

FA Cup
First Round   Grays Ath   (h)   1-1
                                      (a)   2-0
Second Round   Crewe Alex   (h)   0-2

Carling Cup
First Round   Shrewsbury T   (a)   1-0
Second Round   QPR   (a)   0-4

J Paint Trophy
Second Round   Rochdale   (a)   2-2

CHARLTON ATHLETIC   FL Championship 1

FOUNDATION

The club was formed on 9 June 1905, by a group of 14- and 15-year-old youths living in streets by the Thames in the area which now borders the Thames Barrier. The club's progress through local leagues was so rapid that after the First World War they joined the Kent League where they spent a season before turning professional and joining the Southern League in 1920. A year later they were elected to the Football League's Division 3 (South).

The Valley, Floyd Road, Charlton, London SE7 8BL.

Telephone: (020) 8333 4000.

Fax: (020) 8333 4001.

Ticket Office: (0871) 226 1905.

Website: www.cafc.co.uk

Email: info@cafc.co.uk

Ground Capacity: 27,111.

Record Attendance: 75,031 v Aston Villa, FA Cup 5th rd, 12 February 1938 (at The Valley).

Pitch Measurements: 101.5m × 65.8m.

Chairman: Richard Murray.

Deputy Chairman: Martin Simons.

Chief Executive: Steve Waggott.

Football Secretary: Chris Parkes.

Manager: Phil Parkinson.

Assistant Manager: Mark Kinsella.

Physio: Steve Allen.

Colours: Red shirts with white trim, white shorts, red stockings.

Change Colours: White shirts with black and red trim, black shorts, black stockings.

Year Formed: 1905.

Turned Professional: 1920.

Ltd Co.: 1919.

Club Nickname: 'Addicks'.

Grounds: 1906, Siemen's Meadow; 1907, Woolwich Common; 1909, Pound Park; 1913, Horn Lane; 1920, The Valley; 1923, Catford (The Mount); 1924, The Valley; 1985, Selhurst Park; 1991, Upton Park; 1992, The Valley.

First Football League Game: 27 August 1921, Division 3 (S), v Exeter C (h) W 1–0 – Hughes; J Mitchell, Goodman; Dowling (1), Hampson, Dunn; Castle, Bailey, Halse, Green, Wilson.

Record League Victory: 8–1 v Middlesbrough, Division 1, 12 September 1953 – Bartram; Campbell, Ellis; Fenton, Ufton, Hammond; Hurst (2), O'Linn (2), Leary (1), Firmani (3), Kiernan.

HONOURS

Football League: Division 1 – Champions 1999–2000; Runners-up Division 2 – Runners-up 1935–36, 1985–86; Division 3 (S) – Champions 1928–29, 1934–35.

FA Cup: Winners 1947; Runners-up 1946.

Football League Cup: Quarter-final 2007.

Full Members' Cup: Runners-up 1987.

SKY SPORTS FACT FILE

England international inside-forward George Stephenson rocketed to three successive promotions in his career. The first was with Preston North End into the First Division in 1933–34 and subsequently two seasons in the company of Charlton Athletic.

Record Cup Victory: 7–0 v Burton A, FA Cup 3rd rd, 7 January 1956 – Bartram; Campbell, Townsend; Hewie, Ufton, Hammond; Hurst (1), Gauld (1), Leary (3), White, Kiernan (2).

Record Defeat: 1–11 v Aston Villa, Division 2, 14 November 1959.

Most League Points (2 for a win): 61, Division 3 (S), 1934–35.

Most League Points (3 for a win): 91, Division 1, 1999–2000.

Most League Goals: 107, Division 2, 1957–58.

Highest League Scorer in Season: Ralph Allen, 32, Division 3 (S), 1934–35.

Most League Goals in Total Aggregate: Stuart Leary, 153, 1953–62.

Most League Goals in One Match: 5, Wilson Lennox v Exeter C, Division 3 (S), 2 February 1929; 5, Eddie Firmani v Aston Villa, Division 1, 5 February 1955; 5, John Summers v Huddersfield T, Division 2, 21 December 1957; 5, John Summers v Portsmouth, Division 2, 1 October 1960.

Most Capped Player: Jonatan Johansson, 42 (88), Finland.

Most League Appearances: Sam Bartram, 579, 1934–56.

Youngest League Player: Jonjo Shevley, 16 years 59 days v Burnley, 26 April 2008.

Record Transfer Fee Received: £16,500,000 from Tottenham H for Darren Bent, May 2007

Record Transfer Fee Paid: £5,380,000 to Ipswich T for Darren Bent, June 2005.

Football League Record: 1921 Elected to Division 3 (S); 1929–33 Division 2; 1933–35 Division 3 (S); 1935–36 Division 2; 1936–57 Division 1; 1957–72 Division 2; 1972–75 Division 3; 1975–80 Division 2; 1980–81 Division 3; 1981–86 Division 2; 1986–90 Division 1; 1990–92 Division 2; 1992–98 Division 1; 1998–99 FA Premier League; 1999–2000 Division 1; 2000–07 FA Premier League; 2007–09 FL C; 2009– FL 1.

MANAGERS

Walter Rayner 1920–25
Alex Macfarlane 1925–27
Albert Lindon 1928
Alex Macfarlane 1928–32
Albert Lindon 1932–33
Jimmy Seed 1933–56
Jimmy Trotter 1956–61
Frank Hill 1961–65
Bob Stokoe 1965–67
Eddie Firmani 1967–70
Theo Foley 1970–74
Andy Nelson 1974–79
Mike Bailey 1979–81
Alan Mullery 1981–82
Ken Craggs 1982
Lennie Lawrence 1982–91
Steve Gritt/Alan Curbishley 1991–95
Alan Curbishley 1995–2006
Iain Dowie 2006
Les Reed 2006
Alan Pardew 2006–08
Phil Parkinson December 2008–

LATEST SEQUENCES

Longest Sequence of League Wins: 12, 26.12.1999 – 7.3.2000.

Longest Sequence of League Defeats: 10, 11.4.1990 – 15.9.1990.

Longest Sequence of League Draws: 6, 13.12.1992 – 16.1.1993.

Longest Sequence of Unbeaten League Matches: 15, 4.10.1980 – 20.12.1980.

Longest Sequence Without a League Win: 18, 18.8.2008 – 17.1.2009.

Successive Scoring Runs: 25 from 26.12.1935.

Successive Non-scoring Runs: 5 from 6.9.1922.

TEN YEAR LEAGUE RECORD

		P	W	D	L	F	A	Pts	Pos
1999-2000	Div 1	46	27	10	9	79	45	91	1
2000-01	PR Lge	38	14	10	14	50	57	52	9
2001-02	PR Lge	38	10	14	14	38	49	44	14
2002-03	PR Lge	38	14	7	17	45	56	49	12
2003-04	PR Lge	38	14	11	13	51	51	53	7
2004-05	PR Lge	38	12	10	16	42	58	46	11
2005-06	PR Lge	38	13	8	17	41	55	47	13
2006-07	PR Lge	38	8	10	20	34	60	34	19
2007-08	FL C	46	17	13	16	63	58	64	11
2008-09	FL C	46	8	15	23	52	74	39	24

DID YOU KNOW ?

On 13 January 2009 a goal by Darren Ambrose, recently returned from a loan spell in East Anglia with Ipswich Town, ended an 18-game run without a win for Charlton Athletic in their FA Cup replay win at Norwich City.

CHARLTON ATHLETIC 2008–09 LEAGUE RECORD

Match No.	Date	Venue	Opponents	Result		H/T Score	Lg. Pos.	Goalscorers	Attendance
1	Aug 9	H	Swansea C	W	2-0	1-0	—	Hudson [3], Gray [85]	21,675
2	16	A	Watford	L	0-1	0-1	12		14,413
3	23	H	Reading	W	4-2	2-1	6	Holland [26], Gray (pen) [42], Varney L [69], Bouazza [72]	20,020
4	30	A	Preston NE	L	1-2	1-0	11	Gray (pen) [19]	12,089
5	Sept13	H	Wolverhampton W	L	1-3	1-0	16	Bailey [3]	21,547
6	16	A	Doncaster R	W	1-0	1-0	—	Gray [3]	10,483
7	20	A	Nottingham F	D	0-0	0-0	9		18,771
8	27	H	Sheffield W	L	1-2	1-2	14	Varney L [20]	20,278
9	30	A	Crystal Palace	L	0-1	0-0	—		16,358
10	Oct 4	H	Ipswich T	W	2-1	1-1	14	Bailey [6], Volz (og) [60]	20,643
11	18	A	Cardiff C	L	0-2	0-1	19		17,310
12	21	A	Bristol C	L	0-2	0-1	—		21,207
13	25	H	Burnley	D	1-1	0-1	20	Todorov [76]	21,884
14	28	A	Ipswich T	D	1-1	0-1	—	Bailey [82]	20,352
15	Nov 1	H	Barnsley	L	1-3	0-3	22	Hudson [75]	21,527
16	8	A	Plymouth Arg	D	2-2	0-1	20	Youga [86], Gray (pen) [89]	10,716
17	15	A	Birmingham C	L	2-3	2-1	20	Bouazza [21], Gray [27]	20,071
18	22	H	Sheffield U	L	2-5	1-3	22	Primus [17], Bouazza [56]	20,328
19	25	A	QPR	L	1-2	1-1	—	Racon [30]	12,286
20	29	H	Southampton	D	0-0	0-0	22		20,831
21	Dec 6	A	Blackpool	L	0-2	0-0	24		6648
22	9	H	Coventry C	L	1-2	0-1	—	Burton (pen) [49]	20,427
23	15	H	Derby Co	D	2-2	1-0	—	Gray [34], Waghorn [64]	20,989
24	20	A	Norwich C	L	0-1	0-0	23		23,827
25	26	H	QPR	D	2-2	0-1	24	Bailey 2 [49, 79]	21,023
26	28	A	Sheffield U	L	1-3	1-0	24	Bouazza [33]	24,717
27	Jan 10	H	Nottingham F	L	0-2	0-2	—		24,553
28	17	A	Sheffield W	L	1-4	0-2	24	Spring [86]	28,766
29	27	H	Crystal Palace	W	1-0	1-0	—	Spring [14]	20,627
30	31	A	Burnley	L	1-2	1-0	24	Bailey [41]	14,404
31	Feb 3	A	Bristol C	L	1-2	1-0	—	Soares [29]	15,304
32	14	H	Plymouth Arg	W	2-0	1-0	24	Racon [33], Bailey [68]	21,876
33	21	A	Barnsley	D	0-0	0-0	24		11,668
34	28	A	Swansea C	D	1-1	0-1	24	Bailey [55]	15,053
35	Mar 3	H	Doncaster R	L	1-2	0-0	24	Bailey [73]	20,815
36	7	H	Watford	L	2-3	2-1	24	Kandol 2 [21, 33]	20,052
37	10	A	Reading	D	2-2	1-0	—	Bailey [16], Hudson [85]	17,875
38	14	A	Wolverhampton W	L	1-2	0-1	24	Zheng-Zhi [51]	24,319
39	21	H	Preston NE	D	0-0	0-0	24		19,215
40	Apr 4	A	Southampton	W	3-2	1-1	24	Shelvey [7], Racon [60], Bailey [69]	27,228
41	11	A	Birmingham C	D	0-0	0-0	24		20,022
42	13	A	Coventry C	D	0-0	0-0	24		16,121
43	18	H	Blackpool	D	2-2	0-0	24	Burton [48], Shelvey [49]	19,615
44	21	H	Cardiff C	D	2-2	1-0	—	Shelvey [35], Bailey [80]	19,390
45	25	A	Derby Co	L	0-1	0-0	24		31,541
46	May 3	H	Norwich C	W	4-2	3-1	24	Bailey [9], Burton 3 [25, 30, 51]	22,020

Final League Position: 24

GOALSCORERS

League (52): Bailey 13, Gray 7 (3 pens), Burton 5 (1 pen), Bouazza 4, Hudson 3, Racon 3, Shelvey 3, Kandol 2, Spring 2, Varney L 2, Holland 1, Primus 1, Soares 1, Todorov 1, Waghorn 1, Youga 1, Zheng-Zhi 1, own goal 1.
Carling Cup (0).
FA Cup (3): Ambrose 1, Dickson 1, Shelvey 1.

Superscript numerals indicate goals scored. Values are the shirt number worn in each match.

Match No.	Weaver N 22	Semedo J 12+6	Youga K 32+1	Racon T 19	Fortune J 17	Hudson M 43	Sam L 28+10	Shelvey J 14+2	Varney L 16+2	Gray A 21+6	Thomas J 1	Holland M 18+16	Basey G 10+9	Bouazza H 22+3	Dickson C 6+15	Bailey N 43	Moutaouakil Y 9+2	Ambrose D 9+12	Cranie M 19	Primus L 19	Todorov S 2+11	Zheng-Zhi 11+2	Wright J 2	McLeod 12	Waghorn M 4+3	Gillespie K 4+2	McEveley J 6	Burton D 12+8	Elliot R 23	Murty G 8	Spring M 12+1	Randolph D 1	Soares T 10+1	Ward D 16	Kandol T 10+3	Butterfield D 12	Tuna T —+2	Wagstaff S —+2	Solly C —+1
1	1	2	3	4	5	6	7^3	8^1	9	10	11^2	12	13	14																									
2	1	2^3	3^4	4^1	5	6	7	8	9	10	11^2	12	13	14																									
3	1	2^1	3	4	5	6	7^2	8	9	10	11	12	13																										
4	1	2^1	3^3	4	5	6	7^2	8	9	10	11	12	13	14																									
5	1	2	3	4	5	6	7^1	8	9	10^2	11	12	13																										
6	1	2	3	4	5	6	7^1	8	9	10	11	12																											
7	1	2^1	3	4	5^3	6	7^2	8	9	10	11	12	13	14																									
8	1	2^1	3	4	5^2	6	7	8	9	10^3	11	12	13	14																									
9	1	2	3	4^1	5	6	7^2	8^3	9	10	11	12	13	14																									
10	1	2^1	3	4^3	5	6	7	8	9	10^2	11	12	13	14																									
11	1	2^1	3	4	5	6	7^2	8	9	10^3	11	12	13	14																									
12	1	2	3	4	5	6	7^1	8	9	10^3	11^2	12	13	14																									
13	1	2	3	4^2	5^1	6	7	8	9	10^3	11	12	13	14																									
14	1	2^1	3	4	5	6	7^2	8	9	10^3	11	12	13	14																									
15	1	2	3	4^2	5	6	7^1	8	9	10	11	12	13																										
16	1	2	3	4^3	5	6	7^2	8	9^1	10	11	12	13	14																									
17	1	2	3^1	4^2	5	6	7^3	8	9	10	11	12	13	14																									
18	1	2	3^2	4	5	6	7	8	9	10^1	11	12	13																										
19	1	2^1	3	4	5	6	7	8	9^2	10	11	12	13																										
20	1	2	3	4^2	5	6	7^1	8	9	10^3	11	12	13	14																									
21	1	2^2	3	4	5	6	7^1	8	9	10^3	11	12	13	14																									
22	1	2	3^1	4	5	6	7^2	8	9^3	10	11	12	13	14																									
23				4	5	6	7^1			10				11	3	8	2	9^2			13							12	1										
24				4^1	5	6	7^2			10				11	3	8	2	9^3			13							12	1						14				
25				4^1	5	6	7			10				11^2	3	8	2	9^3			13							12	1						14				
26				4	5	6	7^1			10				11	3	8	2	9^2			13							12	1										
27				4^1	5	6	7			10					3	8	2	9^2			13							12	1				11^3		14				
28					5	6	7			10				11	3	8^3	2^1	9^2			13							12	1		4				14				
29			3			6	7^2			10^3						8		9		5^1	13							12	1	2	4		11		14				
30			3			6	7^1			10^2						8		9		5								12	1	2	4		11	6	13				
31		11^2	3				7^1			10						8		9		5	13							12	1	2^3	4				14				
32			3			6	7									8		9		5	10^1							12	1	2	4		11						
33			3			6	7									8		9		5	10								1	2	4		11						
34			3			6	7									8		9		5	10^2							12	1	2^1	4		11^3		14	13			
35			3^3			6	7^1									8		9		5	10							12	1	2	4^2		11		14	13			
36			3			6	7^2									8		9^2		5	10							12	1	2	4^1		11		14	13			
37			3			6	7^2									8		9		5	10^1							12	1	2	4^3		11		14	13			
38			3			6	7^2									8		9		5	10^1							12	1	2	4^3		11		14	13			
39			3			6^2	7^1									8		9		5	10							12	1	2^3	4		11		14	13			
40			3			6	7^2									8		9^3		5	10^1							12	1	2	4		11		14	13			
41			3			6	7^2									8		9		5	10							12	1	2	4^1		11			13			
42			3			6	7^2									8		9^3		5	10							12	1	2	4		11^1		14	13			
43			3^2			6	7									8		9^1		5	10							12		2	4		11			13			
44			3			6	7^2									8		9^1		5	10							12	1	2	4		11^3		14	13			
45			3			6	7									8		9		5^2	10^1							12	1	2	4		11			13			
46			3			6	7^3									8		9		5^1	10^2							12	1	2	4		11		14	13			

FA Cup

Third Round	Norwich C	(h)	1-1
		(a)	1-0
Fourth Round	Sheffield U	(a)	1-2

Carling Cup

First Round	Yeovil T	(h)	0-1

CHELSEA

FOUNDATION

Chelsea may never have existed but for the fact that Fulham rejected an offer to rent the Stamford Bridge ground from Mr H. A. Mears who had owned it since 1904. Fortunately he was determined to develop it as a football stadium rather than sell it to the Great Western Railway and got together with Frederick Parker, who persuaded Mears of the financial advantages of developing a major sporting venue. Chelsea FC was formed in 1905, and when admission to the Southern League was denied, they immediately gained admission to the Second Division of the Football League.

Stamford Bridge, Fulham Road, London SW6 1HS.
Telephone: 0871 984 1955.
Fax: (020) 7381 4831.
Ticket Office: 0871 984 1905.
Website: www.chelseafc.com
Ground Capacity: 41,841.
Record Attendance: 82,905 v Arsenal, Division 1, 12 October 1935.
Pitch Measurements: 103m × 67m.
Chairman: Bruce Buck.
Director: Eugene Tenenbaum.
Chief Executive: Peter Kenyon.
Secretary: David Barnard.
Manager: Carlo Ancelotti.
Temporary First Team Coach: Ray Wilkins.
Colours: Reflex blue shirt, reflex blue shorts, white stockings with blue trim.
Change Colours: All black with white trim.
Year Formed: 1905.
Turned Professional: 1905.
Ltd Co.: 1905.
Club Nickname: 'The Blues'.
Ground: 1905, Stamford Bridge.
First Football League Game: 2 September 1905, Division 2, v Stockport Co (a) L 0–1 – Foulke; Mackie, McEwan; Key, Harris, Miller; Moran, J. T. Robertson, Copeland, Windridge, Kirwan.
Record League Victory: 9–2 v Glossop N E, Division 2, 1 September 1906 – Byrne; Walton, Miller; Key (1), McRoberts, Henderson; Moran, McDermott (1), Hilsdon (5), Copeland (1), Kirwan (1).

HONOURS

FA Premier League: Champions 2004–05, 2005–06. Runners-up 2003–04, 2006–07, 2007–08.
Football League: Division 1 – Champions 1954–55; Division 2 – Champions 1983–84, 1988–89; Runners-up 1906–07, 1911–12, 1929–30, 1962–63, 1976–77.
FA Cup: Winners 1970, 1997, 2000, 2007, 2009. Runners-up 1915, 1967, 1994, 2002.
Football League Cup: Winners 1965, 1998, 2005, 2007; Runners-up 1972, 2008.
Full Members' Cup: Winners 1986.
Zenith Data Systems Cup: Winners 1990.
European Competitions: Champions League: 1999–2000, 2003–04 (semi-finals), 2004–05 (semi-finals), 2005–06, 2006–07 (semi-finals), 2007–08 (runners-up), 2008–09 (semi-finals). *European Fairs Cup:* 1958–60, 1965–66, 1968–69. *European Cup-Winners' Cup:* 1970–71 (winners), 1971–72, 1994–95, 1997–98 (winners), 1998–99 (semi-finals). *UEFA Cup:* 2000–01, 2001–02, 2002–03. *Super Cup:* 1998–99 (winners).

SKY SPORTS FACT FILE

1 November 2008 was a red-letter day for Chelsea. Alex scored their 1000th Premier League goal, Frank Lampard hit his 100th, Petr Cech kept his 100th clean sheet and a Nicolas Anelka treble helped defeat Sunderland 5–0.

Record Cup Victory: 13–0 v Jeunesse Hautcharage, ECWC, 1st rd 2nd leg, 29 September 1971 – Bonetti; Boyle, Harris (1), Hollins (1p), Webb (1), Hinton, Cooke, Baldwin (3), Osgood (5), Hudson (1), Houseman (1).

Record Defeat: 1–8 v Wolverhampton W, Division 1, 26 September 1953.

Most League Points (2 for a win): 57, Division 2, 1906–07.

Most League Points (3 for a win): 99, Division 2, 1988–89.

Most League Goals: 98, Division 1, 1960–61.

Highest League Scorer in Season: Jimmy Greaves, 41, 1960–61.

Most League Goals in Total Aggregate: Bobby Tambling, 164, 1958–70.

Most League Goals in One Match: 5, George Hilsdon v Glossop, Division 2, 1 September 1906; 5, Jimmy Greaves v Wolverhampton W, Division 1, 30 August 1958; 5, Jimmy Greaves v Preston NE, Division 1, 19 December 1959; 5, Jimmy Greaves v WBA, Division 1, 3 December 1960; 5, Bobby Tambling v Aston Villa, Division 1, 17 September 1966; 5, Gordon Durie v Walsall, Division 2, 4 February 1989.

Most Capped Player: Marcel Desailly, 67 (116), France.

Most League Appearances: Ron Harris, 655, 1962–80.

Youngest League Player: Ian Hamilton, 16 years 138 days v Tottenham H, 18 March 1967.

Record Transfer Fee Received: £12,000,000 from Rangers for Tore Andre Flo, November 2000; £12,000,000 from Manchester C for Wayne Bridge, January 2009.

Record Transfer Fee Paid: £29,500,000 to AC Milan for Andriy Shevchenko, June 2006.

MANAGERS

John Tait Robertson 1905–07
David Calderhead 1907–33
Leslie Knighton 1933–39
Billy Birrell 1939–52
Ted Drake 1952–61
Tommy Docherty 1961–67
Dave Sexton 1967–74
Ron Suart 1974–75
Eddie McCreadie 1975–77
Ken Shellito 1977–78
Danny Blanchflower 1978–79
Geoff Hurst 1979–81
John Neal 1981–85 *(Director to 1986)*
John Hollins 1985–88
Bobby Campbell 1988–91
Ian Porterfield 1991–93
David Webb 1993
Glenn Hoddle 1993–96
Ruud Gullit 1996–98
Gianluca Vialli 1998–2000
Claudio Ranieri 2000–04
Jose Mourinho 2004–07
Avram Grant 2007–08
Luiz Felipe Scolari 2008–09
Guus Hiddink 2009
Carlo Ancelotti June 2009–

Football League Record: 1905 Elected to Division 2; 1907–10 Division 1; 1910–12 Division 2; 1912–24 Division 1; 1924–30 Division 2; 1930–62 Division 1; 1962–63 Division 2; 1963–75 Division 1; 1975–77 Division 2; 1977–79 Division 1; 1979–84 Division 2; 1984–88 Division 1; 1988–89 Division 2; 1989–92 Division 1; 1992– FA Premier League.

LATEST SEQUENCES

Longest Sequence of League Wins: 10, 19.11.2005 – 15.1.2006.

Longest Sequence of League Defeats: 7, 1.11.1952 – 20.12.1952.

Longest Sequence of League Draws: 6, 20.8.1969 – 13.9.1969.

Longest Sequence of Unbeaten League Matches: 40, 23.10.2004 – 29.10.2005.

Longest Sequence Without a League Win: 21, 3.11.1987 – 2.4.1988.

Successive Scoring Runs: 27 from 29.10.1988.

Successive Non-scoring Runs: 9 from 14.3.1981.

TEN YEAR LEAGUE RECORD

		P	W	D	L	F	A	Pts	Pos
1999-2000	PR Lge	38	18	11	9	53	34	65	5
2000-01	PR Lge	38	17	10	11	68	45	61	6
2001-02	PR Lge	38	17	13	8	66	38	64	6
2002-03	PR Lge	38	19	10	9	68	38	67	4
2003-04	PR Lge	38	24	7	7	67	30	79	2
2004-05	PR Lge	38	29	8	1	72	15	95	1
2005-06	PR Lge	38	29	4	5	72	22	91	1
2006-07	PR Lge	38	24	11	3	64	24	83	2
2007-08	PR Lge	38	25	10	3	65	26	85	2
2008-09	PR Lge	38	25	8	5	68	24	83	3

DID YOU KNOW ?

Dave Webb wore ten different shirt numbers for Chelsea including the goalkeeper's. On that particular occasion on Boxing Day 1970, Peter Bonetti was injured and Steve Sherwood received the return call too late to play. The result – a clean sheet and a 2–0 win.

CHELSEA 2008–09 LEAGUE RECORD

Match No.	Date	Venue	Opponents	Result	H/T Score	Lg. Pos.	Goalscorers	Atten-dance
1	Aug 17	H	Portsmouth	W 4-0	3-0	—	Cole J [12], Anelka [26], Lampard (pen) [45], Deco [89]	41,468
2	24	A	Wigan Ath	W 1-0	1-0	1	Deco [4]	18,139
3	31	H	Tottenham H	D 1-1	1-1	1	Belletti [28]	41,790
4	Sept 13	A	Manchester C	W 3-1	1-1	1	Ricardo Carvalho [16], Lampard [53], Anelka [69]	47,331
5	21	H	Manchester U	D 1-1	0-1	2	Kalou [80]	41,760
6	27	A	Stoke C	W 2-0	1-0	1	Bosingwa [36], Anelka [76]	27,500
7	Oct 5	H	Aston Villa	W 2-0	2-0	1	Cole J [21], Anelka [44]	41,593
8	18	A	Middlesbrough	W 5-0	1-0	1	Kalou 2 [14, 53], Belletti [51], Lampard [63], Malouda [67]	29,221
9	26	H	Liverpool	L 0-1	0-1	2		41,705
10	29	A	Hull C	W 3-0	1-0	—	Lampard [3], Anelka [50], Malouda [75]	24,906
11	Nov 1	H	Sunderland	W 5-0	3-0	1	Alex [27], Anelka 3 [30, 45, 53], Lampard [51]	41,693
12	9	A	Blackburn R	W 2-0	1-0	1	Anelka 2 [40, 68]	20,670
13	15	H	WBA	W 3-0	3-0	1	Bosingwa [34], Anelka 2 [38, 45]	26,322
14	22	H	Newcastle U	D 0-0	0-0	1		41,660
15	30	H	Arsenal	L 1-2	1-0	1	Djourou (og) [31]	41,760
16	Dec 6	A	Bolton W	W 2-0	2-0	2	Anelka [9], Deco [21]	22,023
17	14	H	West Ham U	D 1-1	0-1	2	Anelka [51]	41,675
18	22	A	Everton	D 0-0	0-0	—		35,655
19	26	H	WBA	W 2-0	2-0	2	Drogba [3], Lampard [45]	43,417
20	28	A	Fulham	D 2-2	0-1	2	Lampard 2 [50, 72]	25,462
21	Jan 11	A	Manchester U	L 0-3	0-1	2		75,455
22	17	H	Stoke C	W 2-1	0-0	3	Belletti [88], Lampard [90]	41,788
23	28	H	Middlesbrough	W 2-0	0-0	—	Kalou 2 [58, 81]	40,290
24	Feb 1	A	Liverpool	L 0-2	0-0	3		44,174
25	7	H	Hull C	D 0-0	0-0	4		41,802
26	21	A	Aston Villa	W 1-0	1-0	3	Anelka [19]	42,585
27	28	H	Wigan Ath	W 2-1	1-0	2	Terry [25], Lampard [90]	40,714
28	Mar 3	A	Portsmouth	W 1-0	0-0	—	Drogba [79]	20,326
29	15	H	Manchester C	W 1-0	1-0	2	Essien [18]	41,810
30	21	A	Tottenham H	L 0-1	0-0	3		36,034
31	Apr 4	A	Newcastle U	W 2-0	0-0	3	Lampard [56], Malouda [65]	52,112
32	11	H	Bolton W	W 4-3	1-0	3	Ballack [40], Drogba 2 [48, 63], Lampard (pen) [60]	41,096
33	22	H	Everton	D 0-0	0-0	—		41,556
34	25	A	West Ham U	W 1-0	0-0	3	Kalou [55]	34,749
35	May 2	H	Fulham	W 3-1	2-1	3	Anelka [1], Malouda [10], Drogba [53]	41,801
36	10	A	Arsenal	W 4-1	2-0	3	Alex [28], Anelka [39], Toure (og) [49], Malouda [86]	60,075
37	17	H	Blackburn R	W 2-0	1-0	3	Malouda [4], Anelka [59]	40,804
38	24	A	Sunderland	W 3-2	0-0	3	Anelka [47], Kalou [74], Cole A [86]	42,468

Final League Position: 3

GOALSCORERS

League (68): Anelka 19, Lampard 12 (2 pens), Kalou 7, Malouda 6, Drogba 5, Belletti 3, Deco 3, Alex 2, Bosingwa 2, Cole J 2, Ballack 1, Cole A 1, Essien 1, Ricardo Carvalho 1, Terry 1, own goals 2.
Carling Cup (5): Lampard 2 (1 pen), Drogba 1, Kalou 1, Malouda 1.
FA Cup (17): Anelka 4, Ballack 3, Drogba 3, Lampard 3, Kalou 2, Alex 1, Malouda 1.
Champions League (20): Drogba 5, Lampard 3, Anelka 2, Essien 2, Ivanovic 2, Terry 2, Alex 1, Cole J 1, Kalou 1, Malouda 1.

Cech P 35	Bosingwa J 34	Cole A 33 + 1	Mikel J 33 + 1	Terry J 35	Ricardo Carvalho 11 + 1	Ballack M 22 + 7	Lampard F 37	Anelka N 33 + 4	Deco 17 + 7	Cole J 14	Malouda F 24 + 7	Wright-Phillips S — + 1	Paulo Ferreira 1 + 6	Bridge W 3 + 3	Essien M 10 + 1	Kalou S 17 + 10	Belletti J 5 + 15	Di Santo F — + 8	Alex 22 + 2	Drogba D 15 + 9	Ivanovic B 11 + 5	Cudicini C 2	Sinclair S — + 2	Mineiro — + 1	Stoch M — + 4	Hilario 1	Quaresma R 1 + 3	Mancienne M 2 + 2	Match No.
1	2^3	3	4	5	6	7^1	8	9	10	11^2	12	13	14																1
1	2	3^1		5	6	7	8	9^2	10	11^3	13				12	4	14												2
1	7	3		5	6		8	9^3	10	11^1	12					4	13		2^2	14									3
1	2	3	4	5^4	6		8	9^2	7	10^1	11^3				12	13	14												4
1	2	3	4	5	6^3	7^1	8	9	10	11^2					12	14	13												5
1	2	3	4	5		7^2	8	12		11	13					10^1	14			6	9^3								6
1	2	3	4	5		7	8	9^3	10^1	11^2					12	13	14		6										7
	2		4	5			8^1	9^3	12	11	13	3^2			10	7			6			1	14						8
1	2^3	3	4	5	6		8	9	10	11^1					7^2	12	13	14											9
1	2^3	3	4	5	6		8	9	7^1	10^2	11				12	13	14												10
1	2	3^2	4	5			8	9^3	7	10^1	11	13							6	12				14					11
1	2		4	5		7^2	8	9		11	13	3				10^1	12		6										12
	2		4	5^2	12		8	9^3	7	11	13	3				10^1	14		6			1							13
1	2	3	4	5	12		8	9	7	10^1	11^2	13							6										14
1	2	3	4^1	5	11		8	9	7^2	12	10								6	13									15
1	2^2	3	4	5	11		8	9	7	12	10^1								6	13									16
1	2	3	4^2	5	11^3		8	9	7	10^1	12	13							6	14									17
1	2	3	4	5^4	11		8	9^2	7^3	10^1	14								6	13	12								18
1	2^3	3	4			7	8	9	12	11^1	13					14			6	10^2	5								19
1	2	3	4	12	8	13	7	10^3	11^2						14				6^1	9	5								20
1	2^2	3	4	5	6	7	8	12	10^1	11^3	13					14				9									21
1	2^1	3	4^3		6	7	8	9		11^2	10				12	13			5						14				22
1	2	3	4	5		7	8	9^3	12	11^2					10^1				6	13					14				23
1	2	3	4	5		7	8^8	9^2	12	11^1					10^3				6	13					14				24
	2	3	4^1	5	11^3		8	9	14	10					12				6	13						1	7^2		25
1	2		4	5		7	8	9	12			3			11^1	13			6	10^2									26
1		3	4	5		7	8	9		11^1	12				6	10											13	2^2	27
1	2	3	4^1	5		7^2	8			11					10^3	12			6	9							14	13	28
1	2	3		5	6	11	8	9	7^2	12					4	13				10^1									29
1	2	3		5	11		8	9	12						4^1	7^2			6	10					13				30
1		3	4	5	12		8	9^2		11					7^1	10	13		6		2								31
1		3	4	5	6	7	8^1	13	12	11	10									9^2	2								32
1		3	12	5		7	8	9^2		11^3					4^1	13	14		6	10	2								33
1	3^1	12	4	5	14		8	9		11	13				10^2	7					2						6^3		34
1	2	3	4	5	13		8	9		11					7^2		14		6^1	10^3	12								35
1	2^1	3	4	5	13		8	9		11^2					7				6	10	12								36
1	2	3	4	5			8	9		11					7				6	10									37
1	2	3	4^3	5	12			9		11					8^2	13	7^1		6	10								14	38

FA Cup

Third Round	Southend U	(h)	1-1
		(a)	4-1
Fourth Round	Ipswich T	(h)	3-1
Fifth Round	Watford	(a)	3-1
Quarter-Final	Coventry C	(a)	2-0
Semi-Final	Arsenal		2-1
(at Wembley)			
Final	Everton		2-1
(at Wembley)			

Carling Cup

Third Round	Portsmouth	(a)	4-0
Fourth Round	Burnley	(h)	1-1

Champions League

Group A	Bordeaux	(h)	4-0
	Cluj	(a)	0-0
	Roma	(h)	1-0
		(a)	1-3
	Bordeaux	(a)	1-1
	Cluj	(h)	2-1
Knock-out Round	Juventus	(h)	1-0
		(a)	2-2
Quarter-Final	Liverpool	(a)	3-1
		(h)	4-4
Semi-Final	Barcelona	(a)	0-0
		(h)	1-1

CHELTENHAM TOWN FL Championship 2

FOUNDATION

Although a scratch team representing Cheltenham played a match against Gloucester in 1884, the earliest recorded match for Cheltenham Town FC was a friendly against Dean Close School on 12 March 1892. The School won 4–3 and the match was played at Prestbury (half a mile from Whaddon Road). Cheltenham Town played Wednesday afternoon friendlies at a local cricket ground until entering the Mid Gloucester League. In those days the club played in deep red coloured shirts and were nicknamed 'the Rubies'. The club moved to Whaddon Lane for season 1901–02 and changed to red and white colours two years later.

The Abbey Business Stadium, Whaddon Road, Cheltenham, Gloucestershire GL52 5NA.

Telephone: (01242) 573 558.

Fax: (01242) 224 675.

Ticket Office: (01242) 573 558 (option 1).

Website: www.ctfc.com

Email: info@ctfc.com

Ground Capacity: 7,136.

Record Attendance: at Whaddon Road: 8,326 v Reading, FA Cup 1st rd, 17 November 1956; at Cheltenham Athletic Ground: 10,389 v Blackpool, FA Cup 3rd rd, 13 January 1934.

Pitch Measurements: 112yd × 72yd.

Chairman: Paul Baker.

Vice-chairman: Colin Farmer.

Secretary: Paul Godfrey.

Manager: Martin Allen.

Assistant Manager: Jon Schofield.

Physio: Ian Weston.

Colours: All red with white trim.

Change Colours: All yellow with red trim.

Year Formed: 1892.

Turned Professional: 1932.

Ltd Co.: 1937.

Club Nickname: 'The Robins'.

Grounds: Grafton Cricket Ground, Whaddon Lane, Carter's Field (pre 1932).

HONOURS

Football League: Best Season Division 3 2001–02 (4th).

FA Cup: best season: 5th rd 2002.

Football League Cup: never past 2nd rd.

Football Conference: Champions 1998–99, runners-up 1997–98.

Trophy: Winners 1997–98.

Southern League: Champions 1984–85; *Southern League Cup:* Winners 1957–58, runners-up 1968–69, 1984–85; *Southern League Merit Cup:* Winners 1984–85; *Southern League Championship Shield:* Winners 1985.

Gloucestershire Senior Cup: Winners 1998–99; *Gloucestershire Northern Senior Professional Cup:* Winners 30 times; *Midland Floodlit Cup:* Winners 1985–86, 1986–87, 1987–88; *Mid Gloucester League:* Champions 1896–97; *Gloucester and District League:* Champions 1902–03, 1905–06; *Cheltenham League:* Champions 1910–11, 1913–14; *North Gloucestershire League:* Champions 1913–14; *Gloucestershire Northern Senior League:* Champions 1928–29, 1932–33; *Gloucestershire Northern Senior Amateur Cup:* Winners 1929–30, 1930–31, 1932–33, 1933–34, 1934–35; *Leamington Hospital Cup:* Winners 1934–35.

SKY SPORTS FACT FILE

The first Cheltenham Town player to have joined the club having won international honours was Phil Bach a full-back in 1904 signed as a reinstated amateur. He had been capped by England against Ireland on 18 February 1899 in the 13–2 victory at Sunderland.

Record League Victory: 11–0 v Bourneville Ath,
Birmingham Combination, 29 April 1933 – Davis; Jones;
Williams; Lang (1), Blackburn, Draper; Evans, Hazard (4),
Haycox (4), Goodger (1), Hill (1).

Record Cup Victory: 12–0 v Chippenham R, FA Cup 3rd
qual. rd, 2 November 1935 – Bowles; Whitehouse, Williams;
Lang, Devonport (1), Partridge (2); Perkins, Hackett,
Jones (4), Black (4), Griffiths (1).

Record Defeat: 0–7 v Crystal Palace, League Cup 2nd rd,
2 October 2002.
N.B. 1–10 v Merthyr T, Southern League, 8 March 1952.

Most League Points (2 for a win): 60, Southern League
Division 1, 1963–64.

Most League Points (3 for a win): 78, Division 3, 2001–02.

Most League Goals: 66, Division 3, 2001–02.

Highest League Scorer in Season: Julian Alsop, 20, Division
3, 2001–02.

Most League Goals in Total Aggregate: Martin Devaney,
38, 1999–2005.

Most Capped Player: Grant McCann, 7 (22), Northern
Ireland.

Most League Appearances: Jamie Victory, 258, 1999–.

Record Transfer Fee Received: £400,000 from Colchester U
for Steve Gillespie, July 2008.

Record Transfer Fee Paid: £50,000 to West Ham U for
Grant McCann, January 2003 and £50,000 to Stoke C for
Brian Wilson, March 2004.

Football League Record: 1999 Promoted to Division 3;
2002 Division 2; 2003–04 Division 3; 2004–06 FL 2;
2006–09 FL 1; 2009– FL 2.

MANAGERS

George Blackburn 1932–34
George Carr 1934–37
Jimmy Brain 1937–48
Cyril Dean 1948–50
George Summerbee 1950–52
William Raeside 1952–53
Arch Anderson 1953–58
Ron Lewin 1958–60
Peter Donnelly 1960–61
Tommy Cavanagh 1961
Arch Anderson 1961–65
Harold Fletcher 1965–66
Bob Etheridge 1966–73
Willie Penman 1973–74
Dennis Allen 1974–79
Terry Paine 1979
Alan Grundy 1979–82
Alan Wood 1982–83
John Murphy 1983–88
Jim Barron 1988–90
John Murphy 1990
Dave Lewis 1990–91
Ally Robertson 1991–92
Lindsay Parsons 1992–95
Chris Robinson 1995–97
Steve Cotterill 1997–2002
Graham Allner 2002–03
Bobby Gould 2003
John Ward 2003–07
Keith Downing 2007–08
Martin Allen September 2008–

LATEST SEQUENCES

Longest Sequence of League Wins: 4, 29.4.2006 – 8.8.2006.

Longest Sequence of League Defeats: 7, 27.1.2009 – 28.2.2009.

Longest Sequence of League Draws: 5, 5.4.2003 – 21.4.2003.

Longest Sequence of Unbeaten League Matches: 16, 1.12.2001 – 12.3.2002.

Longest Sequence Without a League Win: 14, 20.12.2008 – 7.3.2009

Successive Scoring Runs: 17 from 16.2.2008.

Successive Non-scoring Runs: 4 from 12.9.1999.

TEN YEAR LEAGUE RECORD

		P	W	D	L	F	A	Pts	Pos
1999-2000	Div 3	46	20	10	16	50	42	70	8
2000-01	Div 3	46	18	14	14	59	52	68	9
2001-02	Div 3	46	21	15	10	66	49	78	4
2002-03	Div 2	46	10	18	18	53	68	48	21
2003-04	Div 3	46	14	14	18	57	71	56	14
2004-05	FL 2	46	16	12	18	51	54	60	14
2005-06	FL 2	46	19	15	12	65	53	72	5
2006-07	FL 1	46	15	9	22	49	61	54	17
2007-08	FL 1	46	13	12	21	42	64	51	19
2008-09	FL 1	46	9	12	25	51	91	39	23

DID YOU KNOW **?**

On 7 September 1963
Cheltenham Town put on
their Saturday best for the
FA Cup preliminary round
tie against Abergavenny
Thursdays. It proved a
memorable day for Billy
James who scored five out of
the seven goals they
registered.

CHELTENHAM TOWN 2008–09 LEAGUE RECORD

Match No.	Date	Venue	Opponents	Result	H/T Score	Lg. Pos.	Goalscorers	Atten-dance
1	Aug 9	A	Northampton T	L	2-4	1-1	—	Gyepes (og) [35], Townsend (pen) [74]	4716
2	16	H	Swindon T	W	2-0	0-0	11	Gill B [62], Myrie-Williams [80]	4975
3	23	A	Oldham Ath	L	0-4	0-1	21		4673
4	30	H	Leicester C	L	0-4	0-1	23		5344
5	Sept 6	H	Huddersfield T	L	1-2	1-0	24	Owusu [42]	3587
6	12	A	Hartlepool U	L	1-4	0-1	—	Owusu [89]	3637
7	16	H	Bristol R	W	2-1	2-0	—	Hayles 2 [19, 30]	4546
8	20	A	Millwall	L	0-2	0-0	22		8009
9	27	H	Stockport Co	D	2-2	1-0	23	Fleetwood [32], Payne [66]	3796
10	Oct 4	A	Brighton & HA	D	3-3	2-2	21	Murray 2 [2, 45], Gallinagh [90]	5859
11	11	H	Colchester U	W	4-3	1-2	18	Kenton [36], Owusu [53], Fleetwood (pen) [57], Hayles [90]	3580
12	18	H	Scunthorpe U	L	1-2	0-1	19	Connor [69]	3682
13	21	A	Tranmere R	L	0-2	0-0	—		4535
14	25	A	Milton Keynes D	L	1-3	1-1	21	Caines [26]	8190
15	Nov 1	H	Leeds U	L	0-1	0-1	22		5726
16	15	A	Hereford U	L	0-3	0-2	23		3761
17	22	A	Carlisle U	L	0-1	0-0	23		5374
18	25	H	Southend U	D	0-0	0-0	—		2908
19	Dec 6	H	Crewe Alex	W	1-0	0-0	23	Diallo [48]	4052
20	13	A	Leyton Orient	W	2-1	1-1	22	Hayles [4], Westlake [78]	4510
21	20	H	Walsall	D	0-0	0-0	22		3656
22	26	A	Yeovil T	D	1-1	1-0	22	Vincent [42]	4989
23	28	H	Peterborough U	L	3-6	0-1	22	Vincent (pen) [48], Hammond [67], Owusu [86]	3976
24	Jan 17	A	Colchester U	L	1-3	0-0	23	Westwood [57]	4183
25	24	H	Brighton & HA	D	2-2	1-0	23	Westlake [7], Westwood [58]	3597
26	27	A	Bristol R	L	2-3	1-1	—	Vincent [11], Owusu [50]	6600
27	31	H	Milton Keynes D	L	3-5	0-3	24	Spencer 3 (1 pen) [68, 75, 81 (p)]	3681
28	Feb 14	H	Hereford U	L	2-3	1-1	24	Owusu 2 [45, 56]	4660
29	17	A	Stockport Co	L	0-1	0-1	—		5041
30	21	A	Leeds U	L	0-2	0-0	24		20,131
31	24	H	Millwall	L	1-3	1-0	—	Duffy (og) [30]	2942
32	28	H	Northampton T	L	0-1	0-1	24		3495
33	Mar 3	A	Swindon T	D	2-2	1-1	—	Hammond 2 [33, 54]	6293
34	7	A	Leicester C	L	0-4	0-2	24		18,939
35	14	H	Hartlepool U	W	2-0	1-0	24	Hammond (pen) [35], Bignall [89]	2945
36	17	H	Tranmere R	W	1-0	1-0	—	Bird [3]	2845
37	21	H	Huddersfield T	D	2-2	2-1	24	Constantine [5], Hammond [18]	11,516
38	24	H	Oldham Ath	D	1-1	1-0	—	Artus [31]	2992
39	28	A	Walsall	D	1-1	1-0	24	Artus [3]	4101
40	Apr 4	A	Leyton Orient	L	0-1	0-1	24		3594
41	10	A	Peterborough U	D	1-1	0-1	—	Hutton [66]	9817
42	13	H	Yeovil T	W	1-0	0-0	23	Artus [51]	3775
43	18	A	Crewe Alex	W	2-1	0-1	23	Finnigan (pen) [58], Connor [84]	4542
44	25	H	Carlisle U	D	1-1	0-1	23	Diallo (pen) [82]	4290
45	28	A	Scunthorpe U	L	0-3	0-2	—		3635
46	May 2	A	Southend U	L	0-2	0-0	23		8192

Final League Position: 23

GOALSCORERS

League (51): Owusu 7, Hammond 5 (1 pen), Hayles 4, Artus 3, Spencer 3 (1 pen), Vincent 3 (1 pen), Connor 2, Diallo 2 (1 pen), Fleetwood 2 (1 pen), Murray 2, Westlake 2, Westwood 2, Bignall 1, Bird 1, Caines 1, Constantine 1, Finnigan 1 (pen), Gallinagh 1, Gill B 1, Hutton 1, Kenton 1, Myrie-Williams 1, Payne 1, Townsend 1 (pen), own goals 2.
Carling Cup (3): Gill B 1, Russell 1, Vincent 1.
FA Cup (6): Vincent 2, Finnigan 1 (pen), Montrose 1, Murray 1, Owusu 1 (pen).
J Paint Trophy (1): Low 1.

Higgs S 10	Gill J 6	Wright A 22+1	Bird D 24+3	Townsend M 23+3	Duff S 18+2	Lindegaard A 11+4	Russell A 19+4	Connor P 18+7	Vincent A 16+13	Armstrong C 3+2	Antonio M 7+2	Gill B —+5	Watkins M 4+8	Myrie-Williams J 5	Hemmings A —+1	Hayles B 11+1	Gallinagh A 30+9	Sinclair D 2+1	Durrant J —+4	Ledgister A —+1	Caines G 5+3	Constantine L 4+2	Low J 13+1	Owusu L 16+6	Berchiche Y 7	Murray S 12+1	Diallo D 27	Brown S P 35	Haynes K 2+2	Montrose L 5	Payne J 9+2	Artus F 9	Fleetwood S 6	Wesolowski J 4	Hutton D 5+2	Kenton D 13	Ridley L 24+3	Rowe-Turner L 1	Lee J 2+1	Westlake I 22	Lewis T —+2	Hayes J 3+3	Spencer D 5+9	Hammond E 17+5	Puddy W 1	Finnigan J 13+4	Emery J —+1	Westwood C 9	Bignall N 8+5	Match No.
1	2	3	4	5	6	7¹	8	9	10	11²	12	13																																						1
1	2	3	4²	5	6	8	12	7¹	11³	13⁴					9	10	14																																	2
1	2	3		5	6	12	8	13	7¹						9	10³	11²	4	14																															3
1	2	3	4	5		14	8	9³	10	6¹	13			11		12	7²																																	4
1	2	3	4	5			8¹		13					11	10²		12				6	7	9																											5
1		3	4	5			8	12	13	14				11²	10¹	2					6	7³	9																											6
1		3	4³	12	6		8	13	14					10	2						5	11	9¹	7²																										7
1		3	12	5			8	9²	14		13			10⁴							6	2¹	11³	7	4																									8
	3			5			8	9¹	12		13				2						14			11	6	1	7²	4	10³																					9
	3			5			8	12	13						14									9¹	7³	2	1	11⁴	10	4	6²																			10
	3		5¹				8	11²						13	12						9	7		6	1	10	4	2																						11
	3							12	11						2						9	7	6	1		8²	10¹	4	5	13																				12
	3				7			9	12						14							13		6	1	4		10³	8²	2	11¹	5																		13
	3							13	12						5					6	9⁴	7		1		8³	10²	2	14		4	11¹																		14
1	3							9¹							2²		12							7	6	4	8	5	11			10	13																	15
1	3	8						9	12						2³							10¹	7	6			11²	5			4	13	14																	16
	3²	8						9	12						5							7¹	6	1		4³	14		11		2	13	10																	17
	3	8						7							5						9	13	6	1		14		2³		4	11¹	12	10²																	18
				13				9¹							10	2						11	6	1		8		5	3		4	12		7²																19
				12	11			9⁴							10²	2						7	6	1		8¹		5	3		4	13																	20
	2²				12										10	6		13						1		8		5	3		4	14	9³	11	7¹															21
12				2	8		9								10²	6						13		1				5³	3		4	14		11	7¹															22
3				8	9										10⁴	2¹		7	12					1				5	6		4	13		11²																23
3				8	9²	10									2						14			1	7¹			6	4			13	12²	5	11															24
	2		6	12	11										14								13	9		1		3	4			10³	7¹	5	8²															25
	2		6	12	8										11	9							1			3	4			10²	7¹	5	13																26
	2¹		6	8	10										12							11³	9			3	4	14⁴			7²	5	13																	27
	8³		6²	7	12										9	5	1						3⁴	4	11	14	13	2	10¹																					28
	3	8	12	7						14			2			10³	9	6¹	1					4	11²	13	5																							29
	3²	13	5	8				11³	14						9¹	6	1						4	12	7	2	10																							30
		8	6				13		11	14					12	5	1						3	4	9²	7¹	2	10³																						31
		8	6				14		11	13					12	5²	1						3	4¹	9	7	2	10³																						32
		2	6				9¹	11²							5		1	8					3	4	12	10	7	3																						33
		2	12	6			13			11²					5	14	8³						1	3	4	9	10	7¹																						34
		8	6				9³			14					12	7							5	1	3	4	11²	10¹				13																		35
		4	6				2								11	7							5	1	3	8	12	10¹				9																		36
		4	6	12²	2				14					8	7⁴			10					5	1	3¹																									37
	3²		6	2			9¹							7	4	8						5	1	13	11		9¹	13	11	37																				38
		6		2	9		7¹		12					4	13	8²	3					5	1	14	11		10³																							39
		6	12	2	9		7²		13					4		8³	3¹					5	1	11	14		10																							40
	12	6	4	2³	9									3		14	11					5	1	7²			8¹																							41
	8	6	5	12	9		13³							4		11	2	1				7	3¹	14	10⁴																								42
	8¹	6	5		9		13							4		14	3²	2³	1			7	11	10				12																						43
		6	5		9		10	12						4			2	1				7	11	3	8¹																									44
		6	5	7			10²							4¹	12		3		1	2³		8	9	11	13	14																								45
		6	5				10							4	13		3³		2²			7		11	9¹		14		1		12																			46

FA Cup

First Round	Oldham Ath	(h)	2-2	
		(a)	1-0	
Second Round	Morecambe	(a)	3-2	
Third Round	Doncaster R	(h)	0-0	
		(a)	0-3	

Carling Cup

First Round	Southend U	(a)	1-0
Second Round	Stoke C	(h)	2-3

J Paint Trophy

Second Round	Walsall	(h)	1-2

CHESTER CITY   Blue Square Premier

FOUNDATION

All students of soccer history have read about the medieval games of football in Chester, but the present club was not formed until 1884 through the amalgamation of King's School Old Boys with Chester Rovers. For many years Chester were overshadowed in Cheshire by Northwich Victoria and Crewe Alexandra who had both won the Senior Cup several times before Chester's first success in 1894–95. The final against Macclesfield saw Chester face the team that had not only beaten them in the previous year's final, but also knocked them out of the FA Cup two seasons in succession. The final was held at the Drill Field, Northwich and Chester had the support of more than 1000 fans. Chester won 2-1.

Deva Stadium, Bumpers Lane, Chester CH1 4LT.

Telephone: (01244) 371 376.

Fax: (01244) 390 265.

Ticket Offfice: (01244) 371 376.

Website: www.chestercityfc.net

Email: info@chestercityfc.net

Ground Capacity: 6,012.

Record Attendance: 20,500 v Chelsea, FA Cup 3rd rd (replay), 16 January 1952 (at Sealand Road).

Pitch Measurements: 115yd × 75yd.

Managing Director: Rob Gray.

Secretary: Tony Allen.

Manager: Mick Wadsworth.

Physio: Ben Holt.

Colours: Blue and white striped shirts, blue shorts, blue stockings.

Change Colours: Yellow shirts with blue sleeves, yellow shorts, yellow stockings.

Year Formed: 1885.

Turned Professional: 1902.

Ltd Co.: 1909.

Previous Name: Chester until 1983.

Club Nickname: 'Blues' and 'City'.

Grounds: 1885, Faulkner Street; 1898, The Old Showground; 1901, Whipcord Lane; 1906, Sealand Road; 1990, Moss Rose Ground, Macclesfield; 1992, Deva Stadium, Bumpers Lane.

First Football League Game: 2 September 1931, Division 3 (N), v Wrexham (a) D 1–1 – Johnson; Herod, Jones; Keeley, Skitt, Reilly; Thompson, Ranson, Jennings (1), Cresswell, Hedley.

Record League Victory: 12–0 v York C, Division 3 (N), 1 February 1936 – Middleton; Common, Hall; Wharton, Wilson, Howarth; Horsman (2), Hughes, Wrightson (4), Cresswell (2), Sargeant (4).

HONOURS

Football League: Division 3 – Runners-up 1993–94; Division 3 (N) – Runners-up 1935–36; Division 4 – Runners-up 1985–86.

Conference: Champions 2003–04.

FA Cup: best season: 5th rd, 1977, 1980.

Football League Cup: Semi-final 1975.

Welsh Cup: Winners 1908, 1933, 1947.

Debenhams Cup: Winners 1977.

SKY SPORTS FACT FILE

On 6 May 1933 Gerry Kelly made a heroic, individual goalscoring effort to save Chester from defeat at Stockport County in an 8–5 reverse. Switched from the right-wing to centre-forward for the first time that season, he rattled up four of their goals.

Record Cup Victory: 6–1 v Darlington, FA Cup 1st rd, 25 November 1933 – Burke; Bennett, Little; Pitcairn, Skitt, Duckworth; Armes (3), Whittam, Mantle (2), Cresswell (1), McLachlan.

Record Defeat: 2–11 v Oldham Ath, Division 3 (N), 19 January 1952.

Most League Points (2 for a win): 56, Division 3 (N), 1946–47 and Division 4, 1964–65.

Most League Points (3 for a win): 84, Division 4, 1985–86.

Most League Goals: 119, Division 4, 1964–65.

Highest League Scorer in Season: Dick Yates, 36, Division 3 (N), 1946–47.

Most League Goals in Total Aggregate: Stuart Rimmer, 135, 1985–88, 1991–98.

Most League Goals in One Match: 5, Tom Jennings v Walsall, Division 3 (N), 30 January 1932; 5, Barry Jepson v York C, Division 4, 8 February 1958.

Most Capped Player: Angus Eve, 35 (117), Trinidad & Tobago.

Most League Appearances: Ray Gill, 406, 1951–62.

Youngest League Player: Aidan Newhouse, 15 years 350 days v Bury, 7 May 1988.

Record Transfer Fee Received: £300,000 from Liverpool for Ian Rush, May 1980.

Record Transfer Fee Paid: £100,000 to Doncaster R for Gregg Blundell, July 2005.

Football League Record: 1931 Elected to Division 3 (N); 1958–75 Division 4; 1975–82 Division 3; 1982–86 Division 4; 1986–92 Division 3; 1992–93 Division 2; 1993–94 Division 3; 1994–95 Division 2; 1995–2000 Division 3; 2000–04 Conference; 2004–09 FL 2; 2009– Blue Square Premier.

MANAGERS

Charlie Hewitt 1930–36
Alex Raisbeck 1936–38
Frank Brown 1938–53
Louis Page 1953–56
John Harris 1956–59
Stan Pearson 1959–61
Bill Lambton 1962–63
Peter Hauser 1963–68
Ken Roberts 1968–76
Alan Oakes 1976–82
Cliff Sear 1982
John Sainty 1982–83
John McGrath 1984
Mick Speight 1985
Harry McNally 1985–92
Graham Barrow 1992–94
Mike Pejic 1994–95
Derek Mann 1995
Kevin Ratcliffe 1995–99
Terry Smith 1999
Ian Atkins 2000
Graham Barrow 2000–01
Gordon Hill 2001
Steve Mungall 2001
Mark Wright 2002–04
Ian Rush 2004–05
Keith Curle 2005–06.
Mark Wright 2006–07
Bobby Williamson 2007–08
Simon Davies 2008
Mark Wright 2008–09
Mick Wadsworth June 2009–

LATEST SEQUENCES

Longest Sequence of League Wins: 8, 12.4.1978 – 26.8.1978.

Longest Sequence of League Defeats: 9, 30.4.1994 – 13.9.1994.

Longest Sequence of League Draws: 6, 11.10.1986 – 1.11.1986.

Longest Sequence of Unbeaten League Matches: 18, 27.10.1934 – 16.2.1935.

Longest Sequence Without a League Win: 25, 19.9.1961 – 3.3.1962.

Successive Scoring Runs: 24 from 31.8.1932.

Successive Non-scoring Runs: 6 from 19.4.2008.

TEN YEAR LEAGUE RECORD

		P	W	D	L	F	A	Pts	Pos
1999-2000	Div 3	46	10	9	27	44	79	39	24
2000-01	Conf.	42	16	14	12	49	43	62	8
2001-02	Conf.	42	15	9	18	54	51	54	14
2002-03	Conf.	42	21	12	9	59	31	75	4
2003-04	Conf.	42	27	11	4	85	34	92	1
2004-05	FL 2	46	12	16	18	43	69	52	20
2005-06	FL 2	46	14	12	20	53	59	54	15
2006-07	FL 2	46	13	14	19	40	48	53	18
2007-08	FL 2	46	12	11	23	51	68	47	22
2008-09	FL 2	46	8	13	25	43	81	37	23

DID YOU KNOW ?

Chester became the first winners of the two-year-surviving Debenhams Cup in 1976–77. Organised for the two clubs who made the most progress having not been exempt at the third round, they defeated Port Vale 4–3 on aggregate.

CHESTER CITY 2008–09 LEAGUE RECORD

Match No.	Date	Venue	Opponents	Result		H/T Score	Lg. Pos.	Goalscorers	Attendance
1	Aug 9	A	Dagenham & R	L	0-6	0-2	—		1434
2	16	H	Wycombe W	L	0-2	0-1	21		1419
3	23	A	Rotherham U	L	1-3	1-3	21	Ellison [18]	3462
4	30	H	Barnet	W	5-1	1-0	16	Ellison [32], Lowe 2 [57, 79], Linwood [62], Roberts [65]	1295
5	Sept 6	H	Bury	D	1-1	1-0	18	Mozika [38]	2327
6	13	A	Grimsby T	W	3-1	1-0	14	Ellison 3 [3, 80, 87]	2950
7	21	H	Shrewsbury T	D	1-1	1-1	14	McManus [43]	2891
8	27	A	Luton T	D	1-1	0-1	13	McManus [77]	5731
9	Oct 4	H	Lincoln C	L	0-2	0-1	15		1962
10	11	A	Chesterfield	D	1-1	1-0	17	Linwood [17]	3042
11	19	H	Port Vale	L	1-2	0-1	18	Lowe [85]	3102
12	21	A	Rochdale	L	1-6	0-2	—	McArdle (og) [53]	2162
13	25	A	Gillingham	L	0-2	0-0	19		4852
14	28	H	Brentford	W	3-0	1-0	—	Lowe 2 [25, 60], Roberts [57]	1301
15	Nov 1	A	Exeter C	L	0-2	0-1	19		4448
16	15	H	Morecambe	L	1-2	0-1	19	Johnson [60]	1647
17	22	H	Aldershot T	L	0-1	0-0	19		1653
18	25	A	Darlington	W	2-1	1-1	—	Lowe [37], Kelly [53]	2416
19	Dec 6	A	Bournemouth	L	0-1	0-0	19		4154
20	13	H	Notts Co	W	2-0	1-0	19	Lowe [12], Roberts [50]	1767
21	20	A	Bradford C	D	0-0	0-0	18		12,092
22	26	H	Accrington S	W	2-0	1-0	17	Lowe 2 (1 pen) [34, 60 (p)]	2223
23	28	A	Macclesfield T	L	1-3	0-1	18	Lowe [56]	2219
24	Jan 13	H	Luton T	D	2-2	1-2	—	Lowe (pen) [37], Ellison [52]	1652
25	17	H	Chesterfield	L	1-3	0-1	18	Mozika [53]	1806
26	24	A	Lincoln C	D	1-1	1-0	18	Barry [31]	3760
27	27	A	Port Vale	L	0-3	0-0	—		4448
28	31	H	Gillingham	L	0-1	0-0	20		1541
29	Feb 3	H	Rochdale	L	0-2	0-0	—		1357
30	7	A	Brentford	L	0-3	0-3	—		4719
31	14	A	Morecambe	L	1-3	0-3	20	Wilson [51]	1795
32	17	A	Shrewsbury T	L	0-1	0-0	—		6133
33	21	H	Exeter C	D	0-0	0-0	21		1640
34	28	H	Dagenham & R	D	2-2	0-2	21	Mannix [86], Roberts [89]	1416
35	Mar 3	A	Wycombe W	L	0-2	0-1	—		3713
36	7	A	Barnet	L	1-3	0-0	21	Ellison [58]	2085
37	10	H	Rotherham U	L	1-5	1-3	—	Ellison [14]	1235
38	14	H	Grimsby T	D	1-1	0-1	22	Lowe [56]	2836
39	21	A	Bury	D	1-1	0-1	23	Lowe [90]	3049
40	28	H	Bradford C	D	0-0	0-0	23		2735
41	Apr 4	A	Notts Co	W	2-1	1-0	23	Mannix [14], Lowe [49]	4025
42	11	H	Macclesfield T	L	0-2	0-2	23		2248
43	13	A	Accrington S	W	1-0	1-0	23	Lowe (pen) [41]	1100
44	18	H	Bournemouth	L	0-2	0-1	23		3349
45	25	A	Aldershot T	D	2-2	1-1	23	Lowe [2], Ellams [63]	3100
46	May 2	H	Darlington	L	1-2	0-0	23	Miller (og) [89]	1945

Final League Position: 23

GOALSCORERS

League (43): Lowe 16 (3 pens), Ellison 8, Roberts 4, Linwood 2, Mannix 2, McManus 2, Mozika 2, Barry 1, Ellams 1, Johnson 1, Kelly 1, Wilson 1, own goals 2.
Carling Cup (2): Lowe 2 (1 pen).
FA Cup (0).
J Paint Trophy (1): Ellison 1.

Danby J 41	Vaughan J 42	Wilson L 34	Harris J 24+7	Butler P 1	Roberts K 44	Partridge R 15+13	Barry A 38+5	Mozika D 21+1	Lowe R 45	Ellison K 39	Mannix D 10+3	Taylor P 2+7	Kelly S 23+4	Linwood P 43	Dinning T 3+1	Hughes M 25+1	Vaughan S 7+1	McManus P 6+3	Rutherford P 5+14	Rule G 18+4	Johnson E 7+3	Jones B 2+13	Owen J 4+3	Ellams L 2+2	Smith P —+5	Spencer J 5	Platt K —+1	Match No.
1	2	3	4^1	5	6	7^2	8	9	10	11	12	13																1
1	2	3	4^2			12	8	9	10	11		13	6	5	7^1													2
1	2	3	7^2		6^1		8	9	10	11		13		5	4		12											3
1	2	3			6			9	10	11			7	5	4	8												4
1	2	3^1			6			9	10	11		8	12	5	7	4												5
1	2				6	7^2	12	9	10^1	11				5	4	8	3	13										6
1	2	3			6	12	7		10^2	11	13		4			8			9^1									7
1	2	12	4■			13	7^2		10	11^3	14			5	6	3	8			9^1								8
1	2	3				12	13	7	10^1	11	14			5	6	4	8^2			9^3								9
1	2	12			6		8	7	10^2	11			4	5		3				9^1	13							10
1					6		8^2	7	10	11	13		4^1	5		3	12	14		9^3		2						11
1	2				6	12	7		10	11				5	4	8	3■			9^1								12
1	2	4			6		8	7	10	11				5		3				9								13
1	2	4			6		3	7	10	11				5		8		12		9^1								14
1	2	4			6		3	7	10	11			12	5^1		8				9								15
1	2	3	4		6	12	7^1		10	11■				5		8		13		9^2								16
1	2	3	12		6		8		10				4	5			7	13	11^2	9^1								17
1	2	3^1	4		6	12	8		10^2	11				5		7			9^1	13	14						18
1	2	3			6	12	8		10	11		13■	4	5			7		9^1								7^2	19
1	2	3	4^1		6	13	8	12	10^2	11				5			7		9									20
1	2	3			6		8	9	10^1	11			4	5			7				12							21
1	2	3			6	7^1	8	9	10^2	11	12			5		4					13							22
1	7	3	4^1		6	12	8		10	11^2		2		5					9		13							23
1	2	3	13		6	7^1	12	9	10	11^2			4	5		8												24
1	2	3			6	7^1	8	9	10	11				5		4						12						25
1	12	3				7^2	8	9^1	10^3	11			6	5	4				14		2	13						26
1		3■	12		6	7^2	8		10	11			4^1	5					13	9^3		2■	14					27
1		3	4		6	7^1	8		10	11			2	5						9	12							28
1	2	3	4			7^1	8		10	11			6	5						9^2	12	13						29
1	2	3	4				8		10	11			6^2	5			7			9^1	12	13						30
1	2^2	9	4		6		8		10^3	11				5			7^1			12	3	13	14					31
1	2	10	4■		6	7^1	8			11	14			5						12	3^3	13	9^2					32
1	2	4			6	7^1	8	9	10	11				5							3	12						33
1	2	4			6	12	8		10	11				5			7			9^1	3^2	13						34
1	2	4^2			6	7^1	8	9^3	10	11				5						12	3	13		14				35
1	2	7	4		6	12	8^2	9^1	10	11	14			5							3^3	13						36
1	2	9	4		6	12	8		10	11				5			7^1				3							37
1	2	9	4		6		8^1		10	11				5			7			12	3							38
1	2	9	4		6		8		10	11				5			7^2			12	3^1	13						39
1	2	9	4		6	7	8		10	11^1				5						12	3							40
1^6	2		4^1		6		8	9	10	11^2							7			12	3	13		15				41
	2	12	4		6	7^3	8	9^1	10				14	5						11	3^2	13				1		42
	2	3	4		6		8		10	11^1				5			7			12		13	9^2			1		43
	2	3	4		6	12	8^2		10	11^1				5			7^3					13	9	14		1		44
	2	3	4			13	8^2		10	11			6	5^1			7			12			9^3	14		1		45
	2	3	4^2		6	7^1	8		10	11				5						12			9			1	13	46

FA Cup
First Round   Milwall   (h)   0-3

Carling Cup
First Round   Leeds U   (h)   2-5

J Paint Trophy
Second Round   Morecambe   (h)   1-1

CHESTERFIELD   FL Championship 2

FOUNDATION

Chesterfield are fourth only to Stoke, Notts County and Nottingham Forest in age for they can trace their existence as far back as 1866, although it is fair to say that they were somewhat casual in the first few years of their history playing only a few friendlies a year. However, their rules of 1871 are still in existence showing an annual membership of 2s (10p), but it was not until 1891 that they won a trophy (the Barnes Cup) and followed this a year later by winning the Sheffield Cup, Barnes Cup and the Derbyshire Junior Cup.

The Recreation Ground, Saltergate, Chesterfield, Derbyshire S40 4SX.

Telephone: (01246) 209 765.

Fax: (01246) 556 799.

Ticket Office: (01246) 209 765.

Website: www.chesterfield-fc.co.uk

Email: reception@chesterfield-fc.co.uk

Ground Capacity: 8,502.

Record Attendance: 30,968 v Newcastle U, Division 2, 7 April 1939.

Pitch Measurements: 111yd × 71yd.

Chairman: Barrie Hubbard.

Vice-chairman: David Jones.

Managing Director: Mike Warner.

Finance Director: Alan Walters.

Manager: John Sheridan.

Assistant Manager: Scott Sellars.

Physio: Jamie Hewitt.

Colours: Blue shirts with white trim, white shorts, white stockings.

Change Colours: Red shirts with white sleeves, red shorts, red stockings.

Year Formed: 1866.

Turned Professional: 1891.

Ltd Co: 1871.

Previous Name: Chesterfield Town.

Club Nicknames: 'Blues' or 'Spireites'.

Grounds: 1867, Drill Field; 1871, Recreation Ground.

First Football League Game: 2 September 1899, Division 2, v Sheffield W (a) L 1–5 – Hancock; Pilgrim, Fletcher; Ballantyne, Bell, Downie; Morley, Thacker, Gooing, Munday (1), Geary.

Record League Victory: 10–0 v Glossop NE, Division 2, 17 January 1903 – Clutterbuck; Thorpe, Lerper; Haig, Banner, Thacker; Tomlinson (2), Newton (1), Milward (3), Munday (2), Steel (2).

Record Cup Victory: 5–0 v Wath Ath (a), FA Cup 1st rd, 28 November 1925 – Birch; Saxby, Dennis; Wass, Abbott, Thompson; Fisher (1), Roseboom (1), Cookson (2), Whitfield (1), Hopkinson.

HONOURS

Football League: Division 2 best season: 4th, 1946–47; Division 3 (N) – Champions 1930–31, 1935–36; Runners-up 1933–34; Division 4 – Champions 1969–70, 1984–85.

FA Cup: Semi-final 1997.

Football League Cup: best season: 4th rd, 1965, 2007.

Anglo-Scottish Cup: Winners 1981.

SKY SPORTS FACT FILE

In the 1980–81 Anglo-Scottish Cup Chesterfield impressively drew 1–1 with Rangers at Ibrox and won the return match 3–0 at Saltergate. Phil Bonnyman, who scored twice in this match, had been given a free transfer by the Glasgow club.

Record Defeat: 0–10 v Gillingham, Division 3, 5 September 1987.

Most League Points (2 for a win): 64, Division 4, 1969–70.

Most League Points (3 for a win): 91, Division 4, 1984–85.

Most League Goals: 102, Division 3 (N), 1930–31.

Highest League Scorer in Season: Jimmy Cookson, 44, Division 3 (N), 1925–26.

Most League Goals in Total Aggregate: Ernie Moss, 161, 1969–76, 1979–81 and 1984–86.

Most League Goals in One Match: 4, Jimmy Cookson v Accrington S, Division 3 (N), 16 January 1926; 4, Jimmy Cookson v Ashington, Division 3 (N), 1 May 1926; 4, Jimmy Cookson v Wigan Borough, Division 3 (N), 4 September 1926; 4, Tommy Lyon v Southampton, Division 2, 3 December 1938.

Most Capped Player: Walter McMillen, 4 (7), Northern Ireland; Mark Williams, 4 (30), Northern Ireland.

Most League Appearances: Dave Blakey, 613, 1948–67.

Youngest League Player: Dennis Thompson, 16 years 160 days v Notts Co, 26 December 1950.

Record Transfer Fee Received: £750,000 from Southampton for Kevin Davies, May 1997.

Record Transfer Fee Paid: £250,000 to Watford for Jason Lee, August 1998.

Football League Record: 1899 Elected to Division 2; 1909 failed re-election; 1921–31 Division 3 (N); 1931–33 Division 2; 1933–36 Division 3 (N); 1936–51 Division 2; 1951–58 Division 3 (N); 1958–61 Division 3; 1961–70 Division 4; 1970–83 Division 3; 1983–85 Division 4; 1985–89 Division 3; 1989–92 Division 4; 1992–95 Division 3; 1995–2000 Division 2; 2000–01 Division 3; 2001–04 Division 2; 2004–07 FL 1; 2007– FL 2.

LATEST SEQUENCES

Longest Sequence of League Wins: 10, 6.9.1933 – 4.11.1933.

Longest Sequence of League Defeats: 9, 22.10.1960 – 27.12.1960.

Longest Sequence of League Draws: 8, 26.11.2005 – 2.1.2006.

Longest Sequence of Unbeaten League Matches: 21, 26.12.1994 – 29.4.1995.

Longest Sequence Without a League Win: 18, 11.9.1999 – 3.1.2000.

Successive Scoring Runs: 46 from 25.12.1929.

Successive Non-scoring Runs: 7 from 23.9.1977.

MANAGERS

E. Russell Timmeus 1891–95 *(Secretary-Manager)*
Gilbert Gillies 1895–1901
E. F. Hind 1901–02
Jack Hoskin 1902–06
W. Furness 1906–07
George Swift 1907–10
G. H. Jones 1911–13
R. L. Weston 1913–17
T. Callaghan 1919
J. J. Caffrey 1920–22
Harry Hadley 1922
Harry Parkes 1922–27
Alec Campbell 1927
Ted Davison 1927–32
Bill Harvey 1932–38
Norman Bullock 1938–45
Bob Brocklebank 1945–48
Bobby Marshall 1948–52
Ted Davison 1952–58
Duggie Livingstone 1958–62
Tony McShane 1962–67
Jimmy McGuigan 1967–73
Joe Shaw 1973–76
Arthur Cox 1976–80
Frank Barlow 1980–83
John Duncan 1983–87
Kevin Randall 1987–88
Paul Hart 1988–91
Chris McMenemy 1991–93
John Duncan 1993–2000
Nicky Law 2000–02
Dave Rushbury 2002–03
Roy McFarland 2003–07
Lee Richardson 2007–09
John Sheridan June 2009–

TEN YEAR LEAGUE RECORD

		P	W	D	L	F	A	Pts	Pos
1999-2000	Div 2	46	7	15	24	34	63	36	24
2000-01	Div 3	46	25	14	7	79	42	80*	3
2001-02	Div 2	46	13	13	20	53	65	52	18
2002-03	Div 2	46	14	8	24	43	73	50	20
2003-04	Div 2	46	12	15	19	49	71	51	20
2004-05	FL 1	46	14	15	17	55	62	57	17
2005-06	FL 1	46	14	14	18	63	73	56	16
2006-07	FL 1	46	12	11	23	45	53	47	21
2007-08	FL 2	46	19	12	15	76	56	69	8
2008-09	FL 2	46	16	15	15	62	57	63	10

*9 pts deducted.

DID YOU KNOW ?

Jack Seagrave was unique in pre-war days for appearing in the most League matches in one season. The maximum was 42, but when he moved from Southport to Chesterfield in 1935 his former club had played two more fixtures – hence 44 appearances.

CHESTERFIELD 2008–09 LEAGUE RECORD

Match No.	Date	Venue	Opponents	Result	H/T Score	Lg. Pos.	Goalscorers	Attendance
1	Aug 9	A	Barnet	W 3-1	0-1	—	Lester 2 [57, 62], Ward [80]	2237
2	16	H	Bury	L 1-3	0-3	10	Kerry [53]	3728
3	23	A	Grimsby T	W 1-0	1-0	8	Ward [42]	3306
4	30	H	Wycombe W	L 0-1	0-1	11		3175
5	Sept 6	H	Rotherham U	W 1-0	0-0	9	Goodall [90]	4951
6	13	A	Dagenham & R	L 0-3	0-1	9		1682
7	20	A	Rochdale	L 1-2	0-0	11	Ward [85]	2884
8	27	H	Brentford	L 0-1	0-1	14		3188
9	Oct 4	A	Morecambe	D 2-2	2-1	13	Robertson [16], Ward (pen) [21]	1734
10	11	H	Chester C	D 1-1	0-1	14	Ward [59]	3042
11	18	A	Lincoln C	L 1-3	0-2	16	Lester [73]	4326
12	22	H	Aldershot T	W 5-1	2-0	—	Lester [24], Ward 3 (1 pen) [41 (p), 53, 76], Niven [73]	3079
13	25	H	Notts Co	W 3-1	1-0	12	Ward [28], Goodall [57], Harsley [90]	4134
14	28	A	Exeter C	W 6-1	2-0	—	Winter [38], Goodall [44], Lester 2 [63, 76], Ward [78], Currie [88]	5093
15	Nov 1	A	Bournemouth	D 1-1	1-0	12	Kerry [34]	4082
16	14	H	Shrewsbury T	D 2-2	0-1	—	Currie [67], Ward (pen) [72]	4099
17	22	H	Accrington S	D 1-1	1-0	12	Lester [14]	3215
18	25	A	Bradford C	L 2-3	2-2	—	Lester [3], Currie [23]	12,145
19	Dec 6	A	Gillingham	L 1-2	0-2	12	Lester [60]	4622
20	12	H	Macclesfield T	L 2-4	1-2	—	Ward 2 [38, 67]	2451
21	20	A	Port Vale	W 1-0	0-0	12	Downes [54]	5011
22	26	H	Luton T	D 2-2	1-0	13	Ward [45], Boden S [82]	4243
23	28	A	Darlington	D 0-0	0-0	13		3352
24	Jan 17	A	Chester C	W 3-1	1-0	13	Wilson (og) [30], Winter [77], Kerry [82]	1806
25	24	A	Morecambe	L 1-2	0-0	14	Gritton [57]	3283
26	28	H	Exeter C	W 2-1	0-1	—	Lester 2 [68, 80]	2894
27	31	H	Notts Co	W 1-0	1-0	11	Talbot [37]	4953
28	Feb 14	A	Shrewsbury T	L 1-2	1-1	12	Boden S [26]	4873
29	20	H	Bournemouth	W 1-0	1-0	—	Lester [37]	3130
30	28	H	Barnet	D 1-1	0-1	12	Hall [74]	3068
31	Mar 3	A	Bury	W 2-1	2-0	—	Downes [2], Lester [40]	2077
32	7	A	Wycombe W	D 1-1	1-0	11	Lester [31]	4809
33	11	H	Grimsby T	W 2-1	0-0	—	Talbot [55], Niven [75]	2999
34	14	H	Dagenham & R	D 1-1	0-0	11	Gritton [77]	3007
35	17	A	Brentford	W 1-0	0-0	—	Gritton [53]	4541
36	21	A	Rotherham U	L 0-3	0-1	10		4658
37	25	H	Rochdale	W 3-0	1-0	—	Lester 2 [34, 61], Robertson [86]	3271
38	28	H	Port Vale	W 2-1	0-0	9	Lester 2 [68, 74]	3511
39	31	A	Aldershot T	D 1-1	1-0	—	Lester [7]	2482
40	Apr 4	A	Macclesfield T	D 1-1	1-1	9	Gritton [8]	2276
41	7	H	Lincoln C	D 1-1	1-0	—	Lester [35]	3419
42	11	H	Darlington	D 0-0	0-0	7		3642
43	13	A	Luton T	D 0-0	0-0	7		6494
44	18	H	Gillingham	L 0-1	0-1	8		3933
45	25	A	Accrington S	L 0-1	0-0	10		1795
46	May 2	H	Bradford C	L 0-2	0-0	10		3859

Final League Position: 10

GOALSCORERS

League (62): Lester 20, Ward 14 (3 pens), Gritton 4, Currie 3, Goodall 3, Kerry 3, Boden S 2, Downes 2, Niven 2, Robertson 2, Talbot 2, Winter 2, Hall 1, Harsley 1, own goal 1.
Carling Cup (0).
FA Cup (6): Lester 2, Ward 2, Winter 2.
J Paint Trophy (2): Kerry 1, Lester 1.

Lee T 28	Picken P 9 + 2	Goodall A 21 + 7	Kerry L 28 + 5	Page R 16	Austin K 27 + 8	Lowry J 37 + 5	Harsley P 7 + 10	Lester J 37	Ward J 23	Robertson G 32 + 6	Niven D 21 + 10	Downes A 40 + 2	Currie D 14 + 13	Carson T 18	Hall D 25	Bowery J — + 3	Winter J 18 + 6	Boden S 3 + 8	Boden L 4	Teixeira V — + 5	Gray D 20 + 5	Till P 14 + 2	Gritton M 19 + 1	Talbot D 17	Wilson J 15 + 1	McDonald C 1 + 1	Montrose L 11 + 1	Algar B 1 + 2	Askham L — + 1	Match No.
1	2	3	4	5	6	7¹	8	9²	10	11	12	13																		1
1	2	3¹	4	5	6	7	8	9²	10	13			12	11																2
	12	3¹	4	5	6	10²	8		9	13	7		2	11	1															3
	12	3²	4		6	7	8³		10	13	11		2¹	9	1	5	14													4
		3	4	5	6	7¹			10			8	2	9	1		12	11												5
		3¹	4¹	5⁸	6	7	13		9	12	11	2	10³	1		8²	14													6
	2	3			6	12	13		10⁴	11	4	5	7²	1		8		9¹												7
	2	3			6	12²	14	9		11¹	4	5	7	1		8		10³	13											8
	2	3			6		12	9	10	11	4	5	7¹	1		13		8²												9
		3	13	5		2		9	10	11¹	6	4	7³	1		12		8²	14											10
		4¹	5	6	7³	8	9	10	13	11	2	12	1	3²		14														11
		3²	4	5	13	7		9¹	10³	11	12	6		1		8		14	2											12
		3	4	5	12	7²	14	9	10	11¹	13	6		1		8³		2												13
		11	4	5	3	7	12	9²	10³		14	6	13	1		8¹		2												14
		11	4	5	3¹	7	13	9	10		12	6		1		8²		2												15
		3	4	5	6¹	7		9	10		2	12	1			8		11												16
		11	4	5	6	7	12	9	10		3		1			8¹		2												17
		11⁸	4	5	3	7		9	10	12		6	8	1		2¹														18
2¹			4	5	3²	7		9	10	11		6	8	1		13	12													19
		11⁸	4	5	3¹		13	9	10	7		6	12	1		8²		2												20
1	3			12	7	4	9	10	11		5	8¹		6		2														21
1	3		4	12	7	8³		10	11		6	9²		5		13	14			2¹										22
1	2		4	3	7		9	11		6		5	8	10																23
1			4	3	8		9	10	11		6	5	12			2¹	7²	13												24
1		13		3³	4	14	9		11	6	12	5	8²			2¹	7	10												25
1		12	4		14	9		3	13	6	5	8²				2	7¹	10	11³											26
1		12	4	13		9		3	14	6	5⁸	8				2	7¹	10³	11²											27
1		11⁸	4	13	12		3		5		8	10				2³	7¹	9		14	6									28
1		12	4	13		9		3	6		5	8²				2	11	10³	7¹		14									29
1		11⁸	4		9		3		6	12	5	8²				2	10	7		13										30
1		4	13	7		9	3	12	6		5					2	10²	11		8¹										31
1	13	4	3	7		9		12	6		5					10¹	11²	2	8											32
1		4¹	3	7		9²		12	5		6	13				10	11	2	8											33
1	12	3	7		9		4	5	6		13	10	11¹	2	8²															34
1		7		9		3	4	6	5		10	11	2	8																35
1	12	7		9		3	4	6¹	13	5		14	10²	11⁸	2	8³														36
1	12		7		9		3	4	6	13	5		8¹	10²	2	11														37
1	12		7³	9		3	4	6	5		14	13	11¹	10	2	8²														38
1	12		7	9²		3	4	6	13	5		14	11³	10	2	8¹														39
1	12		7	9		3	4²	6	13	5		10	11	2	8¹															40
1		7	9		3	4	6	12	5		11	10	8¹	2																41
1		7	9		3	4	6¹	8²	5		13	12	11³	10	2		14													42
1	12	4¹	6	7		9	3	8	13	5³		14	11²	10	2															43
1		6	7	9		3	4	5¹		14	12	11²	10	8	2³	13														44
1	11³	6	7	9⁸		3	4²	14		13	12	5	10¹	8	2															45
1		6	11	3			14	12	9³	5	7²		8	2	4¹	10	13													46

FA Cup

First Round	Mansfield T	(h)	3-1
Second Round	Droylsden	(h)	2-2
		(a)	1-2
reinstated			
Third Round	Ipswich T	(a)	0-3

Carling Cup

First Round	Preston NE	(a)	0-2

J Paint Trophy

First Round	Grimsby T	(h)	2-2

COLCHESTER UNITED   FL Championship 1

FOUNDATION

Colchester United was formed in 1937 when a number of enthusiasts of the much older Colchester Town club decided to establish a professional concern as a limited liability company. The new club continued at Layer Road which had been the amateur club's home since 1909.

Weston Homes Community Stadium, United Way, Colchester, Essex CO4 5UP.

Telephone: (01206) 755 100.

Fax: (01206) 755 112.

Ticket Office: (0845) 437 9089.

Website: www.cu-fc.com

Email: caroline@colchesterunited.net

Ground Capacity: 10,000.

Record Attendance: 19,072 v Reading, FA Cup 1st rd, 27 November 1948.

Pitch Measurements: 106m × 68m.

Chairman: Robbie Cowling.

Chief Executive: Steve Bradshaw.

Football Secretary: Caroline Pugh.

Manager: Paul Lambert.

Assistant Manager: Ian Culverhouse.

Physio: Tony Flynn.

Colours: Royal blue and white striped shirts with white sleeves, royal blue shorts, royal blue stockings.

Change Colours: All yellow.

Year Formed: 1937.

Turned Professional: 1937.

Ltd Co.: 1937.

Club Nickname: 'The U's'.

Grounds: 1937, Layer Road; 2008, Eston Homes Community Stadium.

First Football League Game: 19 August 1950, Division 3 (S), v Gillingham (a) D 0–0 – Wright; Kettle, Allen; Bearryman, Stewart, Elder; Jones, Curry, Turner, McKim, Church.

Record League Victory: 9–1 v Bradford C, Division 4, 30 December 1961 – Ames; Millar, Fowler; Harris, Abrey, Ron Hunt; Foster, Bobby Hunt (4), King (4), Hill (1), Wright.

HONOURS

Football League: FL 1 – Runners-up 2005–06; Division 4 – Runners-up 1961–62.

FA Cup: best season: 6th rd, 1971.

Football League Cup: best season: 5th rd, 1975.

Auto Windscreens Shield: Runners-up 1997.

GM Vauxhall Conference: Winners 1991–92.

FA Trophy: Winners 1992.

SKY SPORTS FACT FILE

Centre-half Reg Stewart, a former millwright, arrived at Colchester United on offer from Sheffield Wednesday at £1,500 in 1949. Signed a year later upon League status arriving at Layer Road for £1,000 he went on to complete 319 League and Cup appearances.

Record Cup Victory: 9-1 v Leamington, FA Cup 1st rd, 5 November 2005 – Davison; Stockley (Garcia), Duguid, Brown (1), Chilvers, Watson (1), Halford (1), Izzet (Danns) (2), Iwelumo (1) (Williams), Cureton (2), Yeates (1).

Record Defeat: 0–8 v Leyton Orient, Division 4, 15 October 1988.

Most League Points (2 for a win): 60, Division 4, 1973–74.

Most League Points (3 for a win): 81, Division 4, 1982–83.

Most League Goals: 104, Division 4, 1961–62.

Highest League Scorer in Season: Bobby Hunt, 38, Division 4, 1961–62.

Most League Goals in Total Aggregate: Martyn King, 130, 1956–64.

Most League Goals in One Match: 4, Bobby Hunt v Bradford C, Division 4, 30 December 1961; 4, Martyn King v Bradford C, Division 4, 30 December 1961; 4, Bobby Hunt v Doncaster R, Division 4, 30 April 1962.

Most Capped Player: Bela Balogh, 2 (9), Hungary.

Most League Appearances: Micky Cook, 613, 1969–84.

Youngest League Player: Lindsay Smith, 16 years 218 days v Grimsby T, 24 April 1971.

Record Transfer Fee Received: £2,500,000 from Reading for Greg Halford, January 2007.

MANAGERS
Ted Fenton 1946–48
Jimmy Allen 1948–53
Jack Butler 1953–55
Benny Fenton 1955–63
Neil Franklin 1963–68
Dick Graham 1968–72
Jim Smith 1972–75
Bobby Roberts 1975–82
Allan Hunter 1982–83
Cyril Lea 1983–86
Mike Walker 1986–87
Roger Brown 1987–88
Jock Wallace 1989
Mick Mills 1990
Ian Atkins 1990–91
Roy McDonough 1991–94
George Burley 1994
Steve Wignall 1995–99
Mick Wadsworth 1999
Steve Whitton 1999–2003
Phil Parkinson 2003–06
Geraint Williams July 2006–08
Paul Lambert October 2008–

Record Transfer Fee Paid: £400,000 to Cheltenham T for Steve Gillespie, July 2008.

Football League Record: 1950 Elected to Division 3 (S); 1958–61 Division 3; 1961–62 Division 4; 1962–65 Division 3; 1965–66 Division 4; 1966–68 Division 3; 1968–74 Division 4; 1974–76 Division 3, 1976–77 Division 4; 1977–81 Division 3; 1981–90 Division 4; 1990–92 GM Vauxhall Conference; 1992–98 Division 3; 1998–04 Division 2; 2004–06 FL 1; 2006–08 FL C; 2008– FL 1.

LATEST SEQUENCES

Longest Sequence of League Wins: 7, 29.11.1968 – 1.2.1969.

Longest Sequence of League Defeats: 8, 9.10.1954 – 4.12.1954.

Longest Sequence of League Draws: 6, 21.3.1977 – 11.4.1977.

Longest Sequence of Unbeaten League Matches: 20, 22.12.1956 – 19.4.1957.

Longest Sequence Without a League Win: 20, 2.3.1968 – 31.8.1968.

Successive Scoring Runs: 24 from 15.9.1962.

Successive Non-scoring Runs: 5 from 7.4.1981.

TEN YEAR LEAGUE RECORD

		P	W	D	L	F	A	Pts	Pos
1999-2000	Div 2	46	14	10	22	59	82	52	18
2000-01	Div 2	46	15	12	19	55	59	57	17
2001-02	Div 2	46	15	12	19	65	76	57	15
2002-03	Div 2	46	14	16	16	52	56	58	12
2003-04	Div 2	46	17	13	16	52	56	64	11
2004-05	FL 1	46	14	17	15	60	50	59	15
2005-06	FL 1	46	22	13	11	58	40	79	2
2006-07	FL C	46	20	9	17	70	56	69	10
2007-08	FL C	46	7	17	22	62	86	38	24
2008-09	FL 1	46	18	9	19	58	58	63	12

DID YOU KNOW ?

Colchester United reached the semi-final of the Southern League Cup in 1938–39. They led 5–1 from the away leg against Norwich City Reserves. Because of fixture congestion the return was fixed for the following season, but on the day after war was declared!

COLCHESTER UNITED 2008–09 LEAGUE RECORD

Match No.	Date	Venue	Opponents	Result	H/T Score	Lg. Pos.	Goalscorers	Attendance
1	Aug 9	A	Hartlepool U	L 2-4	0-2	—	Gillespie 2 (1 pen) [78 (p), 90]	3831
2	16	H	Huddersfield T	D 0-0	0-0	21		5340
3	23	A	Swindon T	W 3-1	2-0	10	Jackson [32], Vernon [45], Wasiu [89]	7031
4	30	H	Oldham Ath	D 2-2	1-0	11	Yeates 2 [42, 63]	4708
5	Sept 13	A	Crewe Alex	L 0-2	0-0	20		3510
6	20	H	Milton Keynes D	L 0-3	0-1	23		4888
7	26	A	Tranmere R	W 4-3	3-1	—	Perkins [4], Yeates [15], Platt [40], Jackson [47]	5713
8	30	H	Leicester C	L 0-1	0-0	—		5133
9	Oct 4	H	Bristol R	L 0-1	0-0	20		4811
10	11	A	Cheltenham T	L 3-4	2-1	21	Wordsworth 2 [20, 43], Jackson [51]	3580
11	18	A	Stockport Co	W 2-1	1-1	18	Perkins [20], Platt [87]	6025
12	21	H	Millwall	L 1-2	1-2	—	Izzet [35]	5506
13	25	H	Carlisle U	W 5-0	3-0	16	Perkins [3], Yeates 2 [14, 31], Hammond [89], Wasiu [90]	5152
14	Nov 1	A	Southend U	D 3-3	1-2	18	Jackson [35], Yeates [71], Wordsworth [81]	8920
15	15	H	Walsall	L 0-2	0-1	20		4071
16	22	A	Peterborough U	L 1-2	0-1	21	Platt [61]	7401
17	25	H	Yeovil T	W 1-0	0-0	—	Easter [55]	3214
18	29	A	Northampton T	W 2-1	2-0	—	Platt [23], Reid [26]	4833
19	Dec 6	H	Hereford U	L 1-2	0-2	16	Easter [71]	4794
20	13	A	Leeds U	W 2-1	1-1	16	Hammond [45], Yeates [66]	19,625
21	20	H	Scunthorpe U	D 0-0	0-0	16		4606
22	26	A	Brighton & HA	W 2-1	1-1	15	Hinshelwood (og) [85], Vernon [87]	6299
23	28	H	Leyton Orient	W 1-0	1-0	11	Gillespie (pen) [39]	6290
24	Jan 12	A	Milton Keynes D	D 1-1	1-0	—	Platt [12]	8408
25	17	H	Cheltenham T	W 3-1	0-0	11	Hammond [62], Gillespie [77], Yeates [88]	4183
26	24	A	Bristol R	D 0-0	0-0	11		6634
27	27	H	Northampton T	W 2-1	0-1	—	Yeates [57], Vernon [58]	3973
28	31	A	Carlisle U	W 2-0	1-0	11	Livesey (og) [11], Perkins [82]	5745
29	Feb 10	H	Tranmere R	L 0-1	0-0	—		3588
30	14	A	Walsall	L 0-2	0-2	11		3719
31	21	A	Southend U	L 0-1	0-1	12		8651
32	24	H	Stockport Co	W 1-0	1-0	—	Tierney [17]	3179
33	28	H	Hartlepool U	D 1-1	1-0	12	Vernon [45]	5158
34	Mar 3	A	Huddersfield T	D 2-2	1-0	—	Hammond 2 (1 pen) [19 (p), 90]	10,580
35	7	A	Oldham Ath	W 1-0	1-0	10	Platt [2]	4591
36	10	A	Swindon T	W 3-2	2-1	—	Platt 2 [2, 45], Perkins [71]	3827
37	14	H	Crewe Alex	L 0-1	0-0	11		4907
38	21	A	Leicester C	D 1-1	1-0	11	Yeates [23]	20,218
39	28	A	Scunthorpe U	L 0-3	0-1	13		4304
40	31	A	Millwall	W 1-0	0-0	—	Platt [84]	8071
41	Apr 4	H	Leeds U	L 0-1	0-1	11		9559
42	11	A	Leyton Orient	L 1-2	1-1	13	Platt [43]	4685
43	13	H	Brighton & HA	L 0-1	0-0	14		4873
44	18	A	Hereford U	W 2-0	2-0	12	Yeates [36], Beckwith (og) [43]	2100
45	25	H	Peterborough U	L 0-1	0-1	14		6532
46	May 2	A	Yeovil T	W 2-0	2-0	12	Vincent [13], Yeates [15]	5237

Final League Position: 12

GOALSCORERS

League (58): Yeates 12, Platt 10, Hammond 5 (1 pen), Perkins 5, Gillespie 4 (2 pens), Jackson 4, Vernon 4, Wordsworth 3, Easter 2, Wasiu 2, Izzet 1, Reid 1, Tierney 1, Vincent 1, own goals 3.
Carling Cup (2): Gillespie 1, Keith 1.
FA Cup (0).
J Paint Trophy (3): Perkins 1, Williams 1, Yeates 1.

Gerken D 21	White J 19+7	Lockwood M 5	Hammond D 38+3	Coyne C 17+2	Reid P 25+1	Yeates M 42+1	Jackson J 22+7	Vernon S 15+18	Gillespie S 8+9	Wordsworth A 9+21	Wasiu A 3+12	Izzet K 39+4	Platt C 39+4	Heath M 11+3	Elito M —+5	Ifil P 5+1	Perkins D 35+3	Borrowdale G 4	Baldwin P 35	Cousins M 9	Hills L 1+1	Williams S 1	Easter J 5	Walker J 16	Tierney M 26	Maybury A 25	Gobern L 5+7	Hackney S 11+6	Guy J 1+3	Trotman N 5+1	Hawley K 4	Vincent A 5+1	Corcoran S —+1	Match No.
1	2	3	4[2]	5	6	7	8	9[3]	10	11[1]	12	13	14																					1
1	2	3			6	7	8	12	10[1]	11[2]		4	9	5	13																			2
1	2	3	12		6	7	8	9[2]		11	13	4[1]	10	5																				3
1		3		5		7	8	9[2]		11[1]	13	4	10	6		2	12																	4
1	2[2]			12	6	7	8	9[3]	14	11		4[1]	10	5		3	13																	5
1	3[3]		12	5	6	7	8	13		10[2]		4[1]	9		14	2	11																	6
1	2		8		6	7[3]	10	12		13		4[2]	9[1]	5	14		11		3															7
1	2		8[1]		6	7	10	12				4	9	5	13		11[2]		3															8
1	2		8		6	7	10	12	13	14		4[2]	9[1]	5			11[3]		3															9
1	2		4		6	7	8			11			9	5			10		3															10
1	2		4		6	7	3		10[2]	11[1]	13	12	9				8		5															11
1	2		8		6	7	3	12				4[2]	9		13		11		5															12
1	2		8	5		7[3]	3	12	10[2]	14	13	4	9[1]				11		6															13
1	2		8	5[1]		7	3	9[2]		14	13	4	10[3]	12			11		6															14
		5	4			7	8[1]	12			13		9			2[2]	11		6			1	3	10										15
1	2[2]		8			7	3			14		4	9	5[1]		12	11		6					13[3]	10									16
1	8	5	12			7	3	13		14		4[3]	9[2]			2[1]	11		6						10									17
			4	5	6	7[2]	8	12		13			9[1]				11		2					10	1	3								18
			4	5	6[3]	7[1]	8		14	12	13		9				11[2]		2					10	1	3								19
			12	5	6	7[1]	8			13	14	4[2]	9				11							10[3]	1	3	2							20
				5		7	8	12	10[2]	13	14	4[1]	9				11[3]		6						1	3	2							21
			14	5		7[2]	8	12	10		13	4	9[1]				11[3]		6						1	3	2							22
			14		6	7[3]	8	12	10[2]		13	4[1]	9				11		5						1	3	2							23
			3		6	7[2]	8	12	10		13	4	9[1]				11		5						1	2								24
			3[1]		6	7	8	12	10[2]		13	4	9				11[3]		5					14	1	2								25
			14		6	7[1]	8	12	10[1]		13	4[3]	9				11[2]		5						1	3	2							26
					6	7[1]	8	12	10		13	4[3]	9[2]	14			11		5						1	3	2							27
					6	7[1]	8	12	10[2]		13	4	9				11		5						1	3	2							28
					6[1]	7	8	12	10		13	4[3]	9[2]	14			11		5						1	3	2							29
					6	7	8	12	10[2]		13	4	9[1]	14			11[3]		5						1	3	2							30
					6[3]	7	8	12	10[1]		13	4	9	14			11[2]		5						1	3	2							31
					6	7[3]	8	12	10[2]		13	4	9[1]	14			11		5						1	3	2							32
					6	7[2]	8[3]	12	10		13	4	9[1]	14			11		5						1	3	2							33
					6[1]	7[2]	8	12	10[3]		13	4	9	14			11		5						1	3	2							34
				5		7[2]	8	12	10[3]		13	4	9[1]	14			11		6						1	3	2							35
				5		7	8	12	10[3]		13	4[1]	9[2]	14			11		6						1	3	2							36
				5		7	8	12	10		13	4[3]	9[1]	14			11		6						1	3	2[2]							37
						7[2]	8	12	10		13	4					11[1]		5						1	3	2	6	9					38
						7	8	12[2]	10		13	4[1]		14			11[3]		5						1	3	2	6	9					39
						7[1]	8	12	10		13	4					11		5						1	3	2	6	9[2]					40
						7[1]	8	12	10		13	4		14			11[2]		5						1	3	2	6	9[3]					41
1						7[1]	8	12			13	4	9	14			11[3]		5						3	2		6	10[2]					42
1	2	3		5	6[1]	7	8	12	10		13	4	9				11[2]																	43
1				5		7	8[1]	12	10		13	4	9	14			11[1]		6						3	2[3]								44
1	2	3		5		7	8[1]	12	10[2]		13	4	9				11		6															45
1				5		7	8	12	10[1]		13	4[2]	9[3]	14			11		6							3	2							46

FA Cup
First Round Leyton Orient (h) 0-1

Carling Cup
First Round Gillingham (a) 1-0
Second Round Ipswich T (a) 1-2

J Paint Trophy
First Round Millwall (a) 1-0
Second Round Gillingham (a) 1-0
Southern Quarter-Finals
  Bournemouth (a) 1-0
Southern Semi-Finals
  Luton T (a) 0-1

COVENTRY CITY FL Championship

FOUNDATION

Workers at Singers' cycle factory formed a club in 1883. The first success of Singers' FC was to win the Birmingham Junior Cup in 1891 and this led in 1894 to their election to the Birmingham and District League. Four years later they changed their name to Coventry City and joined the Southern League in 1908 at which time they were playing in blue and white quarters.

The Ricoh Arena, Phoenix Way, Foleshill, Coventry CV6 6GE.

Telephone: (0844) 873 1883.

Fax: 0870 421 1988.

Ticket Office: (0844) 873 1883 (option 1).

Website: www.ccfc.co.uk

Email: info@ccfc.co.uk

Ground Capacity: 32,609.

Record Attendance: 51,455 v Wolverhampton W, Division 2, 29 April 1967 (at Highfield Road). 28,163 v WBA, FA Cup 5th rd, 16 February 2008 (at Ricoh Arena).

Pitch Measurements: 110yd × 75yd.

Chairman: Ray Ranson.

Vice-chairman: Gary Hoffman.

Secretary: Pam Hindson.

Manager: Chris Coleman.

Assistant Manager: Steve Kean.

Physio: Michael McBride.

HONOURS

Football League: Division 1 best season: 6th, 1969–70; Division 2 – Champions 1966–67; Division 3 – Champions 1963–64; Division 3 (S) – Champions 1935–36; Runners-up 1933–34; Division 4 – Runners-up 1958–59.

FA Cup: Winners 1987.

Football League Cup: Semi-final 1981, 1990.

European Competitions: European Fairs Cup: 1970–71.

Colours: Sky blue and white striped shirts with sky blue sleeves, sky blue shorts, sky blue stockings.

Change Colours: Black with gold trim, black shorts, black stockings.

Year Formed: 1883. *Turned Professional:* 1893. *Ltd Co.:* 1907.

Previous Names: 1883, Singers FC; 1898, Coventry City FC.

Club Nickname: 'Sky Blues'.

Grounds: 1883, Binley Road; 1887, Stoke Road; 1899, Highfield Road; 2005, Ricoh Arena.

First Football League Game: 30 August 1919, Division 2, v Tottenham H (h) L 0–5 – Lindon; Roberts, Chaplin, Allan, Hawley, Clarke, Sheldon, Mercer, Sambrooke, Lowes, Gibson.

Record League Victory: 9–0 v Bristol C, Division 3 (S), 28 April 1934 – Pearson; Brown, Bisby; Perry, Davidson, Frith; White (2), Lauderdale, Bourton (5), Jones (2), Lake.

Record Cup Victory: 8–0 v Rushden & D, League Cup 2nd rd, 2 October 2002 – Debec; Caldwell, Quinn, Betts (1p), Konjic (Shaw), Davenport, Pipe, Safri (Stanford), Mills (2) (Bothroyd (2)), McSheffery (3), Partridge.

Record Defeat: 2–10 v Norwich C, Division 3 (S), 15 March 1930.

SKY SPORTS FACT FILE

Coventry City and in particular George Lowrie were harsh indeed against Newport County on successive Saturdays in January 1947. In the FA Cup third round, City won 5–2, the following week 6–0 in the League, Lowrie scoring a hat-trick in each match.

Most League Points (2 for a win): 60, Division 4, 1958–59 and Division 3, 1963–64.

Most League Points (3 for a win): 66, Division 1, 2001–02.

Most League Goals: 108, Division 3 (S), 1931–32.

Highest League Scorer in Season: Clarrie Bourton, 49, Division 3 (S), 1931–32.

Most League Goals in Total Aggregate: Clarrie Bourton, 171, 1931–37.

Most League Goals in One Match: 5, Clarrie Bourton v Bournemouth, Division 3 (S), 17 October 1931; 5, Arthur Bacon v Gillingham, Division 3 (S), 30 December 1933.

Most Capped Player: Magnus Hedman, 44 (58), Sweden.

Most League Appearances: Steve Ogrizovic, 507, 1984–2000.

Youngest League Player: Ben Mackey, 16 years 167 days v Ipswich T, 12 April 2003.

Record Transfer Fee Received: £13,000,000 from Internazionale for Robbie Keane, July 2000.

Record Transfer Fee Paid: £6,500,000 to Wolverhampton W for Robbie Keane, August 1999; £6,500,000 to Norwich C for Craig Bellamy, August 2000.

Football League Record: 1919 Elected to Division 2; 1925–26 Division 3 (N); 1926–36 Division 3 (S); 1936–52 Division 2; 1952–58 Division 3 (S); 1958–59 Division 4; 1959–64 Division 3; 1964–67 Division 2; 1967–92 Division 1; 1992–2001 FA Premier League; 2001–04 Division 1; 2004– FL C.

LATEST SEQUENCES

Longest Sequence of League Wins: 6, 25.4.1964 – 5.9.1964.

Longest Sequence of League Defeats: 9, 30.8.1919 – 11.10.1919.

Longest Sequence of League Draws: 6, 1.11.2003 – 29.11.2003.

Longest Sequence of Unbeaten League Matches: 25, 26.11.1966 – 13.5.1967.

Longest Sequence Without a League Win: 19, 30.8.1919 – 20.12.1919.

Successive Scoring Runs: 25 from 10.9.1966.

Successive Non-scoring Runs: 11 from 11.10.1919.

MANAGERS

H. R. Buckle 1909–10
Robert Wallace 1910–13
(Secretary-Manager)
Frank Scott-Walford 1913–15
William Clayton 1917–19
H. Pollitt 1919–20
Albert Evans 1920–24
Jimmy Kerr 1924–28
James McIntyre 1928–31
Harry Storer 1931–45
Dick Bayliss 1945–47
Billy Frith 1947–48
Harry Storer 1948–53
Jack Fairbrother 1953–54
Charlie Elliott 1954–55
Jesse Carver 1955–56
George Raynor 1956
Harry Warren 1956–57
Billy Frith 1957–61
Jimmy Hill 1961–67
Noel Cantwell 1967–72
Bob Dennison 1972
Joe Mercer 1972–75
Gordon Milne 1972–81
Dave Sexton 1981–83
Bobby Gould 1983–84
Don Mackay 1985–86
George Curtis 1986–87
(became Managing Director)
John Sillett 1987–90
Terry Butcher 1990–92
Don Howe 1992
Bobby Gould 1992–93
Phil Neal 1993–95
Ron Atkinson 1995–96
(became Director of Football)
Gordon Strachan 1996–2001
Roland Nilsson 2001–02
Gary McAllister 2002–04
Eric Black 2004
Peter Reid 2004–05
Micky Adams 2005–07
Iain Dowie 2007
Chris Coleman February 2008–

TEN YEAR LEAGUE RECORD

		P	W	D	L	F	A	Pts	Pos
1999-2000	PR Lge	38	12	8	18	47	54	44	14
2000-01	PR Lge	38	8	10	20	36	63	34	19
2001-02	Div 1	46	20	6	20	59	53	66	11
2002-03	Div 1	46	12	14	20	46	62	50	20
2003-04	Div 1	46	17	14	15	67	54	65	12
2004-05	FL C	46	13	13	20	61	73	52	19
2005-06	FL C	46	16	15	15	62	65	63	8
2006-07	FL C	46	16	8	22	47	62	56	17
2007-08	FL C	46	14	11	21	52	64	53	21
2008-09	FL C	46	13	15	18	47	58	54	17

DID YOU KNOW ?

Leon McKenzie weighed in with his 100th career goal for Coventry City on the opening day of 2008–09 against Norwich City, his former club. From a renowned boxing family, his father was Clinton McKenzie the one-time British and European champion.

COVENTRY CITY 2008–09 LEAGUE RECORD

Match No.	Date	Venue	Opponents	Result	H/T Score	Lg. Pos.	Goalscorers	Attendance
1	Aug 9	H	Norwich C	W	2-0	0-0	—	Ward (pen) [48], McKenzie [86]	22,607
2	16	A	Barnsley	W	2-1	1-1	1	Eastwood [12], Gray [68]	12,987
3	23	H	Bristol C	L	0-3	0-1	8		17,994
4	30	A	Doncaster R	L	0-1	0-1	13		11,806
5	Sept 13	H	Preston NE	D	0-0	0-0	13		16,544
6	16	A	Sheffield U	D	1-1	1-0	—	Tabb [30]	24,130
7	20	H	QPR	W	1-0	1-0	8	Ward (pen) [15]	16,718
8	27	A	Blackpool	D	1-1	0-0	7	Eastwood [69]	8462
9	30	A	Cardiff C	L	1-2	0-1	—	Dann [89]	16,312
10	Oct 4	H	Southampton	W	4-1	2-0	6	Tabb 2 [19, 87], McKenzie [33], Best [47]	15,518
11	18	A	Wolverhampton W	L	1-2	1-1	15	Mifsud [6]	25,893
12	21	H	Burnley	L	1-3	1-0	—	Ward (pen) [40]	14,621
13	25	H	Derby Co	D	1-1	0-1	17	Morrison [90]	18,430
14	28	A	Southampton	D	1-1	0-0	—	Morrison [75]	14,226
15	Nov 3	A	Birmingham C	W	1-0	0-0	—	Morrison [53]	17,215
16	8	H	Crystal Palace	L	0-2	0-1	17		16,883
17	15	H	Plymouth Arg	L	0-1	0-0	18		18,528
18	22	A	Sheffield W	W	1-0	0-0	15	Morrison [60]	16,119
19	25	H	Swansea C	D	1-1	0-0	—	Fox [87]	15,149
20	Dec 1	A	Reading	L	1-3	1-2	—	Fox [26]	16,803
21	6	H	Nottingham F	D	2-2	2-1	17	Ward [2], Morrison [29]	17,542
22	9	A	Charlton Ath	W	2-1	1-0	—	Simpson [40], Fox [50]	20,427
23	13	A	Watford	L	1-2	0-0	14	Morrison [67]	14,075
24	20	H	Ipswich T	D	2-2	1-1	14	Morrison [1], Eastwood [56]	16,598
25	26	A	Swansea C	D	0-0	0-0	16		17,603
26	28	H	Sheffield W	W	2-0	0-0	14	Morrison [11], Simpson [82]	19,602
27	Jan 10	A	QPR	D	1-1	0-0	—	Fox [73]	13,330
28	17	H	Blackpool	W	2-1	0-1	13	Beuzelin [47], Mifsud [51]	15,551
29	28	H	Cardiff C	L	0-2	0-1	—		14,922
30	31	A	Derby Co	L	1-2	0-2	14	Doyle [53]	29,710
31	Feb 7	H	Wolverhampton W	W	2-1	1-0	14	Doyle [25], McKenzie [75]	21,167
32	17	A	Burnley	D	1-1	1-0	—	Best [44]	14,595
33	21	H	Birmingham C	W	1-0	1-0	13	Dann [2]	22,637
34	28	A	Norwich C	W	2-1	1-0	13	Henderson [19], Fox [73]	24,450
35	Mar 4	H	Sheffield U	L	1-2	0-1	—	Dann [70]	16,300
36	10	A	Bristol C	L	0-2	0-0	—		15,706
37	14	A	Preston NE	L	1-2	1-1	15	Morrison [17]	13,251
38	21	H	Doncaster R	W	1-0	1-0	14	Bell [20]	18,498
39	Apr 4	H	Reading	D	0-0	0-0	14		17,218
40	7	A	Crystal Palace	D	1-1	1-0	—	Gunnarsson [31]	12,898
41	11	A	Plymouth Arg	L	0-4	0-4	15		12,568
42	13	H	Charlton Ath	D	0-0	0-0	14		16,121
43	18	A	Nottingham F	L	0-1	0-0	15		27,856
44	21	A	Barnsley	D	1-1	0-1	—	Ward (pen) [90]	15,035
45	25	H	Watford	L	2-3	1-0	17	Eastwood [10], Simpson [54]	17,195
46	May 3	A	Ipswich T	L	1-2	0-2	17	Morrison [79]	27,225

Final League Position: 17

GOALSCORERS

League (47): Morrison 10, Fox 5, Ward 5 (4 pens), Eastwood 4, Dann 3, McKenzie 3, Simpson 3, Tabb 3, Best 2, Doyle 2, Mifsud 2, Bell 1, Beuzelin 1, Gray 1, Gunnarsson 1, Henderson 1.
Carling Cup (5): Morrison 2, Simpson 2, Dann 1.
FA Cup (6): Best 2, Doyle 1, Gunnarsson 1, McKenzie 1, Ward 1.

Westwood K 46	Wright S 17	Fox D 39	Gunnarsson A 38 + 2	Ward E 33	Dann S 31	Tabb J 21 + 1	Beuzelin G 28 + 7	Morrison C 40 + 5	Eastwood F 37 + 9	Gray J 3	Simpson R 14 + 19	McKenzie L 10 + 9	Thornton K 1 + 3	Mifsud M 19 + 7	Doyle M 34 + 3	Marshall A — + 2	Hall M 15 + 8	Best L 16 + 15	Osbourne I 20 + 5	Turner B 22 + 2	Walker A — + 2	Wynter C 1	Sawyer L 1 + 1	Henderson J 9 + 1	Bell D 8 + 1	McPake J 3 + 1	Cain A — + 5	Grandison J — + 2	Match No.
1	2	3	4	5	6	7¹	8	9	10³	11²	12	13	14																1
1		3	4	5	6	7	2	9¹	10	11³	12	14		8²	13														2
1⁶		3	4	5	6	7	2	9	10²	11	12	13		8¹		15													3
1		3	4	5	6	7	8	9²	10³			13		11	12		2¹	14											4
1		3		5	6	12	8¹	7	10		14	11²		13	4			9³	2										5
1		3	8	5	6		11	7¹	10			9²		13	4			12	2										6
1		3	8	5	6	11¹	12	9	10³			7²		13	4			14	2										7
1		3	8	5	6	7		9²	10			11¹		12	4			13	2										8
1		3	8	5³	6	7¹		9²	10			11		12	4	14	13	2											9
1		3³	8	5	6	7		12	10²			11		13	4	14	9¹	2											10
1		3	8¹	5	6	7	12	13	9			11²		4			10	2											11
1		3	8	5	6	7²	12	14	10		13			11	4¹			9³	2										12
1		3	8	5	6		7³	12	10		13			11	4¹	14		9²	2										13
1		3	8	5	6		7	9	10¹		13			11	4²			12	2										14
1		3	4	5	6	11³	8	9¹	12		13			7		14	10²	2											15
1		3	4	5	6	7²	8¹	9	14		13			11	12			10²	2										16
1		3	8¹	5	6	11	12	9	13		7				4			10²	2										17
1	2	3			6	7		9	10¹		8²			11³	4		13	12	14										18
1	2²	3	12	5	6		7¹	9	10		8			11	4	14		13³											19
1		3	8²	5	6³	7	11	9	10¹					12	4		2	13	14										20
1			2	5		11	8	9	10²		12			7	4¹		3	13	6										21
1		3	4	5		7		9	10¹		8			11			2	12	6										22
1		3	8	5		7		9	10		11			4¹			2	12	6										23
1	2¹	3	4	5		7		9	10		8²	13		11			12		6										24
1	2		8	5			12	9¹	10		7³	14		11²	4		6	13	3										25
1	2	6				7		9¹	12		13	8²		11³	4		5	10		3	14								26
1	2⁴	3	6			7	8	9	12			13		11¹	4			10²	5										27
1		3	6			7	8	9	10²		13	12		11¹	4				5	2									28
1		3	4	6			9	10			8	12	11¹		2			5		7									29
1	2	3		5			8	9	10¹		12			4²	6					13	7	11							30
1	2	3				8	9²	12			10¹			4		13	5			7	11	6							31
1	2	3	8		6		9	12	13					4		10²	5			7	11¹								32
1	2	3	7		6		9¹	12	13	8³				4		10²	5			14	11								33
1	2	3	4	5	6		8	9	12	13						10²				7	11¹								34
1	2	3¹	8		6		13	14	10	9³				4²			12	5		7	11								35
1	2					7	9	10²	12					4	3	8	5			11¹	13	6							36
1	2	12		6		8	9	10²	13					4¹	3		5			7	11								37
1	2	4		6		8³	9	10²	12					3	13	14	5			7¹	11								38
1	2	3	4		6		8	9	11³	12				14	10¹	13	5			7²									39
1		3	8		6		7	9	10¹		11			4			12	2	5										40
1⁶		3	8¹		6		7	9	10		11	12		4	15		2	5											41
1		3		5	6	8²	9	10		11¹		4		2	7		13								12				42
1		3	8	5	6¹	7	9	10	11²			4			2	12									13				43
1		11	8	6		7¹		10	9			4		3	2	5									12				44
1		11⁴	8	6¹			9	10	7²			4		3	2³	5								12	13	14		45
1			8	6		13	9	10	7			4		11³	2²	5								3¹	14	12		46

FA Cup
Third Round	Kidderminster H	(h)	2-0
Fourth Round	Torquay U	(a)	1-0
Fifth Round	Blackburn R	(a)	2-2
		(h)	1-0
Quarter-Final	Chelsea	(h)	0-2

Carling Cup
| First Round | Aldershot T | (h) | 3-1 |
| Second Round | Newcastle U | (h) | 2-3 |

CREWE ALEXANDRA — FL Championship 2

FOUNDATION

The first match played at Crewe was on 1 December 1877 against Basford, the leading North Staffordshire team of that time. During the club's history they have also played in a number of other leagues including the Football Alliance, Football Combination, Lancashire League, Manchester League, Central League and Lancashire Combination. Two former players, Aaron Scragg in 1899 and Jackie Pearson in 1911, had the distinction of refereeing FA Cup finals. Pearson was also capped for England against Ireland in 1892.

The Alexandra Stadium, Gresty Road, Crewe, Cheshire CW2 6EB.

Telephone: (01270) 213 014.

Fax: (01270) 216 320.

Ticket Office: (01270) 252 610.

Website: www.crewealex.net

Email: info@crewealex.net

Ground Capacity: 10,107.

Record Attendance: 20,000 v Tottenham H, FA Cup 4th rd, 30 January 1960.

Pitch Measurements: 112m × 74m.

Chairman: John Bowler.

Vice-chairman: Norman Hassall.

Business Operations Manager: Alison Bowler.

Secretary: Andry Blakemore.

Technical Director: Dario Gradi MBE.

Manager: Gudjon Thordarson.

Assistant Manager: Neil Baker.

Colours: Red shirts with yellow trim, white shorts, red stockings.

Change Colours: Blue shirts with yellow trim, blue shorts, blue stockings.

Year Formed: 1877.

Turned Professional: 1893.

Ltd Co.: 1892.

Club Nickname: 'Railwaymen'.

Ground: 1898, Gresty Road.

First Football League Game: 3 September 1892, Division 2, v Burton Swifts (a) L 1–7 – Hickton; Moore, Cope; Linnell, Johnson, Osborne; Bennett, Pearson (1), Bailey, Barnett, Roberts.

Record League Victory: 8–0 v Rotherham U, Division 3 (N), 1 October 1932 – Foster; Pringle, Dawson; Ward, Keenor (1), Turner (1); Gillespie, Swindells (1), McConnell (2), Deacon (2), Weale (1).

HONOURS

Football League: Division 2 – Runners-up 2002–03.

FA Cup: Semi-final 1888.

Football League Cup: never past 3rd round.

Welsh Cup: Winners 1936, 1937.

SKY SPORTS FACT FILE

On 6 May 1967 Crewe Alexandra drew 1–1 with Halifax Town and thereafter completed 28 unbeaten home League matches at Gresty Road. This sequence took in the entire 1967–68 season and finished well into the following campaign.

Record Cup Victory: 8–0 v Hartlepool U, Auto Windscreens Shield 1st rd, 17 October 1995 – Gayle; Collins (1), Booty, Westwood (Unsworth), Macauley (1), Whalley (1), Garvey (1), Murphy (1), Savage (1) (Rivers (1p)), Lennon, Edwards, (1 og). 8–0 v Doncaster R, LDV Vans Trophy 3rd rd, 10 November 2002 – Bankole; Wright, Walker, Foster, Tierney; Lunt (1), Brammer, Sorvel, Vaughan (1) (Bell); Ashton (3) (Miles), Jack (2) (Jones (1)).

Record Defeat: 2–13 v Tottenham H, FA Cup 4th rd replay, 3 February 1960.

Most League Points (2 for a win): 59, Division 4, 1962–63.

Most League Points (3 for a win): 86, Division 2, 2002–03.

Most League Goals: 95, Division 3 (N), 1931–32.

Highest League Scorer in Season: Terry Harkin, 35, Division 4, 1964–65.

Most League Goals in Total Aggregate: Bert Swindells, 126, 1928–37.

Most League Goals in One Match: 5, Tony Naylor v Colchester U, Division 3, 24 April 1993.

Most Capped Player: Clayton Ince, 38 (73), Trinidad & Tobago.

Most League Appearances: Tommy Lowry, 436, 1966–78.

Youngest League Player: Steve Walters, 16 years 119 days v Peterborough U, 6 May 1988.

Record Transfer Fee Received: £3,400,000 from Norwich C for Dean Ashton, January 2005.

Record Transfer Fee Paid: £650,000 to Torquay U for Rodney Jack, June 1998.

Football League Record: 1892 Original Member of Division 2; 1896 Failed re-election; 1921 Re-entered Division (N); 1958–63 Division 4; 1963–64 Division 3; 1964–68 Division 4; 1968–69 Division 3; 1969–89 Division 4; 1989–91 Division 3; 1991–92 Division 4; 1992–94 Division 3; 1994–97 Division 2; 1997–2002 Division 1; 2002–03 Division 2; 2003–04 Division 1; 2004–06 FL C; 2006–09 FL 1; 2009– FL 2.

MANAGERS

W. C. McNeill 1892–94
(Secretary-Manager)
J. G. Hall 1895–96
(Secretary-Manager)
R. Roberts *(1st team Secretary-Manager)* 1897
J. B. Blomerley 1898–1911
(Secretary-Manager, continued as Hon. Secretary to 1925)
Tom Bailey *(Secretary only)* 1925–38
George Lillycrop *(Trainer)* 1938–44
Frank Hill 1944–48
Arthur Turner 1948–51
Harry Catterick 1951–53
Ralph Ward 1953–55
Maurice Lindley 1956–57
Willie Cook 1957–58
Harry Ware 1958–60
Jimmy McGuigan 1960–64
Ernie Tagg 1964–71
(continued as Secretary to 1972)
Dennis Viollet 1971
Jimmy Melia 1972–74
Ernie Tagg 1974
Harry Gregg 1975–78
Warwick Rimmer 1978–79
Tony Waddington 1979–81
Arfon Griffiths 1981–82
Peter Morris 1982–83
Dario Gradi 1983–2007
Steve Holland 2007–08
Gudjon Thordarson December 2008–

LATEST SEQUENCES

Longest Sequence of League Wins: 7, 30.4.1994 – 3.9.1994.

Longest Sequence of League Defeats: 10, 16.4.1979 – 22.8.1979.

Longest Sequence of League Draws: 5, 31.8.1987 – 18.9.1987.

Longest Sequence of Unbeaten League Matches: 17, 25.3.1995 – 16.9.1995.

Longest Sequence Without a League Win: 30, 22.9.1956 – 6.4.1957.

Successive Scoring Runs: 26 from 7.4.1934.

Successive Non-scoring Runs: 9 from 6.11.1974.

TEN YEAR LEAGUE RECORD

		P	W	D	L	F	A	Pts	Pos
1999-2000	Div 1	46	14	9	23	46	67	51	19
2000-01	Div 1	46	15	10	21	47	62	55	14
2001-02	Div 1	46	12	13	21	47	76	49	22
2002-03	Div 2	46	25	11	10	76	40	86	2
2003-04	Div 1	46	14	11	21	57	66	53	18
2004-05	FL C	46	12	14	20	66	86	50	21
2005-06	FL C	46	9	15	22	57	86	42	22
2006-07	FL 1	46	17	9	20	66	72	60	13
2007-08	FL 1	46	12	14	20	47	65	50	20
2008-09	FL 1	46	12	10	24	59	82	46	22

DID YOU KNOW ?

The long-awaited promotion from Crewe Alexandra in 1962–63 came from a 1–0 win over Exeter City with the goal scored by Frank Lord, who had achieved a club record eight hat-tricks during his service with the club.

CREWE ALEXANDRA 2008–09 LEAGUE RECORD

Match No.	Date	Venue	Opponents	Result	H/T Score	Lg. Pos.	Goalscorers	Attendance
1	Aug 9	H	Brighton & HA	L	1-2	0-1	—	Zola [85]	4557
2	16	A	Carlisle U	L	2-4	1-2	24	McCready [22], Pope [96]	6919
3	23	H	Walsall	W	2-1	2-0	18	Elding [21], Grant [45]	4160
4	30	A	Hereford U	L	0-2	0-0	21		2894
5	Sept 6	A	Leeds U	L	2-5	0-2	23	Zola [89], Bopp [90]	20,075
6	13	H	Colchester U	W	2-0	0-0	17	O'Connor [46], Pope [69]	3510
7	20	H	Southend U	L	3-4	2-2	21	O'Connor [25], Pope [42], Zola [66]	3574
8	27	A	Bristol R	D	0-0	0-0	21		5870
9	Oct 4	H	Northampton T	L	1-3	0-1	22	Pope [56]	3977
10	11	A	Scunthorpe U	L	0-3	0-1	23		4790
11	18	H	Milton Keynes D	D	2-2	2-1	22	O'Hanlon (og) [32], Miller [43]	4055
12	21	A	Yeovil T	L	2-3	0-1	—	Moore [73], Miller [77]	3536
13	24	A	Tranmere R	L	0-2	0-0	—		5790
14	28	H	Peterborough U	D	1-1	0-1	—	Pope [88]	3699
15	Nov 1	A	Huddersfield T	L	2-3	1-2	23	Donaldson 2 [41, 59]	11,679
16	15	H	Leyton Orient	L	0-2	0-0	24		3872
17	22	H	Stockport Co	L	0-3	0-0	24		5337
18	25	A	Leicester C	L	1-2	1-1	—	Zola [30]	16,961
19	Dec 6	A	Cheltenham T	L	0-1	0-0	24		4052
20	13	H	Swindon T	W	1-0	1-0	24	Miller [45]	3941
21	20	A	Millwall	D	0-0	0-0	24		9018
22	26	H	Oldham Ath	L	0-3	0-0	24		5780
23	28	A	Hartlepool U	W	4-1	1-0	24	Brayford [45], Nelson (og) [56], Murphy [61], Miller [83]	3877
24	Jan 17	H	Scunthorpe U	W	3-2	0-1	24	O'Connor (pen) [60], Donaldson [72], O'Donnell [90]	3811
25	24	A	Northampton T	L	1-5	1-2	24	Daniel [30]	4675
26	27	A	Peterborough U	L	2-4	1-0	—	Pope 2 [2, 57]	5782
27	31	H	Tranmere R	W	2-1	0-1	22	Carrington [83], Grant [88]	4936
28	Feb 14	A	Leyton Orient	L	0-1	0-1	23		3705
29	17	A	Southend U	W	1-0	1-0	—	Jones [34]	6614
30	21	H	Huddersfield T	W	3-1	1-1	22	Moore [32], Pope [58], Donaldson [60]	5056
31	24	H	Yeovil T	W	2-0	1-0	—	Donaldson [45], Brayford [79]	3432
32	28	A	Brighton & HA	W	4-0	1-0	19	Jones 2 (1 pen) [24 (p), 84], Schumacher [79], Sigurdsson [89]	6366
33	Mar 3	H	Carlisle U	L	1-2	1-1	—	Donaldson [34]	3759
34	7	H	Hereford U	W	2-1	0-0	19	Jones 2 (1 pen) [56 (p), 82]	5195
35	10	A	Walsall	D	1-1	0-0	—	Schumacher [90]	3604
36	14	A	Colchester U	W	1-0	0-0	18	Zola [63]	4907
37	17	H	Bristol R	D	1-1	0-0	—	Lawrence [70]	3879
38	21	H	Leeds U	L	2-3	0-3	18	Pope 2 [60, 73]	7138
39	24	A	Milton Keynes D	D	2-2	0-2	—	Carrington [78], Sigurdsson (pen) [82]	8454
40	28	A	Millwall	L	0-1	0-0	19		4680
41	Apr 4	A	Swindon T	D	0-0	0-0	20		7165
42	11	H	Hartlepool U	D	0-0	0-0	20		4477
43	13	A	Oldham Ath	D	1-1	0-1	19	Moore [89]	4334
44	18	A	Cheltenham T	L	1-2	1-0	20	Sigurdsson [2]	4542
45	24	A	Stockport Co	L	3-4	1-1	—	Jones [24], Lawrence [80], McManus [90]	7134
46	May 2	H	Leicester C	L	0-3	0-0	22		6982

Final League Position: 22

GOALSCORERS

League (59): Pope 10, Donaldson 6, Jones 6 (2 pens), Zola 5, Miller 4, Moore 3, O'Connor 3 (1 pen), Sigurdsson 3 (1 pen), Brayford 2, Carrington 2, Grant 2, Lawrence 2, Schumacher 2, Bopp 1, Daniel 1, Elding 1, McCready 1, McManus 1, Murphy 1, O'Donnell 1, own goals 2.
Carling Cup (5): Elding 2 (1 pen), O'Connor 2 (1 pen), Moore 1.
FA Cup (7): Miller 3, Donaldson 1, Lawrence 1, Murphy 1, Shelley 1.
J Paint Trophy (3): Jones 1, O'Donnell 1, Schumacher 1.

Collis S 18	Woodards D 35 + 2	Jones B 38	Bailey J 24	McCready C 4 + 1	Baudet J 35	Bopp E 4 + 3	O'Connor M 23	Miller S 18 + 15	Zola C 18 + 9	Grant J 19 + 9	Rix B 1 + 3	Elding A 10 + 6	Moore B 22 + 14	Abbey G 4 + 3	Daniel C 9 + 4	Pope T 17 + 9	O'Donnell D 22 + 2	Donaldson C 28 + 9	Schumacher S 8 + 7	Carrington M 12 + 5	Lawrence D 26	Brayford J 34 + 2	Green S 2	Lunt K 2 + 1	Tomlinson S 9	Murphy L 3 + 6	Shelley D 3	Broomes M 19	Ruddy J 19	Sigurdsson G 14 + 1	Sheehan A 3	Westwood A — + 2	McManus S 3 + 3	Match No.
1	2	3	4	5	6	7^1	8	9^2	10	11^3	12	13	14																					1
1	2	3	4	5^1	6		8	14		11				9^3		7^2	12	13	10															2
1	2	3	4		6		8			11					10^3	7		9	5	12														3
1	2	3	4		6		8^1		14	11					10^3	7		9^2	5	13	12													4
1	2	3	4		6	12			10					8^1	9^2	7		13	5	11														5
1	2	3	4		6		8		10	11^1					9^2	7		13	5		12													6
1	2	3	4		6		8	12	10^2	11^1						7^3		9	5	13	14													7
1	2	3	4		6		8	12	10^2							13	7	9^1	5		14	11^3												8
1	2	3	4^2				8	12	14	13					10^3	7^1		9	5			11	6											9
1	6	3	4			12			9^2	10^3	13						8	5	14	7	11^1		2											10
1	2	3	4		6		8	9	10^1				13				12		11^2		7	5												11
1	2	3	4		6^3		8	9	10^1			12	13					11		7^2	5	14												12
1	2^3	3^1	4^1				8	9		12		10	11^2				5	13	7		6	14												13
1			4				8^2	9^1		11				7	3^3		12	5	10	13	14	6	2											14
1		3	4^1		6			9	12	11			7				13	5	10^2	8		2												15
1		3	4		6		8	12		11		13				9^2		10^1		5	2	7												16
1	2	3	4		6			9		11^2		12				13	5	10^1			7	8^3	14											17
	7^1	3	4		6		8	12	10^2					9			5	13			2	11	1											18
	7	3	4^1		6			11	10^2		12	14		9^3	13	5					2	8	1											19
			4			9^2	8	7		11		10^1		3			5	12			6	2			1	13								20
	3		4			7^1	8^3	9		11^2	12		13		10	5					6	2			1	14								21
	3^2					7^3	8	9		11^1			10		13	5	12		4	6	2				1	14								22
						12	8	9^2					13			3		5	10		4	6	2		1	11	7^1							23
	3	4^1	6			8	9					12			11	13	10			14	5^2	2			1	7^3								24
12	3		6^1			8^2	9					13	11			5	10		4		2				1	7^1								25
4	3					12	13	14				11^3	9^2			10			8	6	2		1			7^1	5							26
4	3					12	13					11^1	9			10			8	6	2					7^2	5	1						27
4^2	3		8^3			7	13	11				12				9^1		10	14	6	2						5	1						28
7	3		4		8	12						10				9^1		11^2		6	2						5	1						29
7	3		4		8							10				9^1		11^2	13	6^2	2						5	1						30
7	3		4		8							11	12			9^2		10	13	6^1	2						5	1						31
7	3		6^1			13						11	4	9^3		12	10^2	8			2						5	1	14					32
8	3	13	6			14		12				9^1	2^2			10	4^3			7							5	1	11					33
7	3		4	6		13	9^2	12				8^1	14		5^3	10				2								1	11					34
7	6		5^2	4		12	10	14				9^3			2^1	11	13			3								1	8					35
7^1	3		4			10	11^2					13				9	12			6	2						5	1	8					36
	3		6				9^1	11				12				10	7			5	2						4	1	8					37
13	3^1		6					11^2				12		9		10	7^1			5	2						4	1	8					38
5			6			12		11^2				13		9^1		10	7				2						4	1	8	3				39
5			6			12						11^1		9		10	7^2				2						4	1	8	3	13			40
7			6			9^2								13		10				5	2						4	1	8	3^1	12	11		41
7	3		6^3			9^2	14					12		13		11				5	2						4	1	8			10^1		42
7	3^3		6^2			12	9					11				10^1				5	2				14		4	1	8			13		43
7	3^2		6			12	9					11^3				10				5	2				14		4^1	1	8			13		44
	3	7^1		6^3			9	13	11			10	14							5	2						4^2	1	8			12		45
1		3	7^3				9					10^2	12			13	6			5	2				14		4		8			11^1		46

FA Cup

First Round	Ebbsfleet U	(h)	1-0
Second Round	Carlisle U	(a)	2-0
Third Round	Millwall	(a)	2-2
		(h)	2-3

Carling Cup

First Round	Barnsley	(h)	2-0
Second Round	Bristol C	(h)	2-1
Third Round	Liverpool	(a)	1-2

J Paint Trophy

| First Round | Macclesfield T | (h) | 3-0 |
| Second Round | Tranmere R | (a) | 0-1 |

CRYSTAL PALACE FL Championship

FOUNDATION

There was a Crystal Palace club as early as 1861 but the present organisation was born in 1905 after the formation of a club by the company that controlled the Crystal Palace (building), had been rejected by the FA who did not like the idea of the Cup Final hosts running their own club. A separate company had to be formed and they had their home on the old Cup Final ground until 1915.

Selhurst Park Stadium, Whitehorse Lane, London SE25 6PU.

Telephone: (020) 8768 6000.

Fax: (020) 8771 5311.

Ticket Office: 0871 200 0071.

Website: www.cpfc.co.uk

Email: info@cpfc.co.uk

Ground Capacity: 26,225.

Record Attendance: 51,482 v Burnley, Division 2, 11 May 1979.

Pitch Measurements: 110yd × 74yd.

Chairman: Simon Jordan.

Vice-chairman: Dominic Jordan.

Chief Executive: Phil Alexander.

Assistant Secretary: Christine Dowdeswell.

Manager: Neil Warnock.

Assistant Manager: Mick Jones.

Physio: Nigel Cox.

Colours: All white with red and blue diagonal stripe shirts.

Change Colours: Yellow shirts with blue trim, blue shorts, yellow stockings.

Year Formed: 1905.

Turned Professional: 1905.

Ltd Co.: 1905.

Club Nickname: 'The Eagles'.

Grounds: 1905, Crystal Palace; 1915, Herne Hill; 1918, The Nest; 1924, Selhurst Park.

First Football League Game: 28 August 1920, Division 3, v Merthyr T (a) L 1–2 – Alderson; Little, Rhodes; McCracken, Jones, Feebury; Bateman, Conner, Smith, Milligan (1), Whibley.

Record League Victory: 9–0 v Barrow, Division 4, 10 October 1959 – Rouse; Long, Noakes; Truett, Evans, McNichol; Gavin (1), Summersby (4 incl. 1p), Sexton, Byrne (2), Colfar (2).

Record Cup Victory: 8–0 v Southend U, Rumbelows League Cup 2nd rd (1st leg), 25 September 1989 – Martyn; Humphrey (Thompson (1)), Shaw, Pardew, Young, Thorn, McGoldrick, Thomas, Bright (3), Wright (3), Barber (Hodges (1)).

HONOURS

Football League: Division 1 – Champions 1993–94; Division 2 – Champions 1978–79; Runners-up 1968–69; Division 3 – Runners-up 1963–64; Division 3 (S) – Champions 1920–21; Runners-up 1928–29, 1930–31, 1938–39; Division 4 – Runners-up 1960–61.

FA Cup: Runners-up 1990.

Football League Cup: Semi-final 1993, 1995, 2001.

Zenith Data Systems Cup: Winners 1991.

European Competition: Intertoto Cup: 1998.

SKY SPORTS FACT FILE

On 9 January 1926 Crystal Palace fielded Michael Hunt, an amateur goalkeeper from North Croydon, at Northampton Town in the FA Cup. Losing 3–0 in 75 minutes, Palace levelled and under pressure had to be saved by Hunt's heroics. They won the replay 2–1.

Record Defeat: 0–9 v Burnley, FA Cup 2nd rd replay, 10 February 1909. 0–9 v Liverpool, Division 1, 12 September 1990.

Most League Points (2 for a win): 64, Division 4, 1960–61.

Most League Points (3 for a win): 90, Division 1, 1993–94.

Most League Goals: 110, Division 4, 1960–61.

Highest League Scorer in Season: Peter Simpson, 46, Division 3 (S), 1930–31.

Most League Goals in Total Aggregate: Peter Simpson, 153, 1930–36.

Most League Goals in One Match: 6, Peter Simpson v Exeter C, Division 3 (S), 4 October 1930.

Most Capped Player: Aleksandrs Kolinko, 23 (82), Latvia.

Most League Appearances: Jim Cannon, 571, 1973–88.

Youngest League Player: John Bostock, 15 years 287 days v Watford, 29 October 2007.

Record Transfer Fee Received: £8,500,000 from Everton for Andy Johnson, May 2006.

Record Transfer Fee Paid: £2,750,000 to RC Strasbourg for Valerien Ismael, January 1998.

Football League Record: 1920 Original Members of Division 3; 1921–25 Division 2; 1925–58 Division 3 (S); 1958–61 Division 4; 1961–64 Division 3; 1964–69 Division 2; 1969–73 Division 1; 1973–74 Division 2; 1974–77 Division 3; 1977–79 Division 2; 1979–81 Division 1; 1981–89 Division 2; 1989–92 Division 1; 1992–93 FA Premier League; 1993–94 Division 1; 1994–95 FA Premier League; 1995–97 Division 1; 1997–98 FA Premier League; 1998–2004 Division 1; 2004–05 FA Premier League; 2005– FL C.

LATEST SEQUENCES

Longest Sequence of League Wins: 8, 9.2.1921 – 26.3.1921.

Longest Sequence of League Defeats: 8, 10.1.1998 – 14.3.1998.

Longest Sequence of League Draws: 5, 21.9.2002 – 19.10.2002.

Longest Sequence of Unbeaten League Matches: 18, 22.2.1969 – 13.8.1969.

Longest Sequence Without a League Win: 20, 3.3.1962 – 8.9.1962.

Successive Scoring Runs: 24 from 27.4.1929.

Successive Non-scoring Runs: 9 from 19.11.1994.

MANAGERS

John T. Robson 1905–07
Edmund Goodman 1907–25
(had been Secretary since 1905 and afterwards continued in this position to 1933)
Alex Maley 1925–27
Fred Mavin 1927–30
Jack Tresadern 1930–35
Tom Bromilow 1935–36
R. S. Moyes 1936
Tom Bromilow 1936–39
George Irwin 1939–47
Jack Butler 1947–49
Ronnie Rooke 1949–50
Charlie Slade and Fred Dawes *(Joint Managers)* 1950–51
Laurie Scott 1951–54
Cyril Spiers 1954–58
George Smith 1958–60
Arthur Rowe 1960–62
Dick Graham 1962–66
Bert Head 1966–72 *(continued as General Manager to 1973)*
Malcolm Allison 1973–76
Terry Venables 1976–80
Ernie Walley 1980
Malcolm Allison 1980–81
Dario Gradi 1981
Steve Kember 1981–82
Alan Mullery 1982–84
Steve Coppell 1984–93
Alan Smith 1993–95
Steve Coppell *(Technical Director)* 1995–96
Dave Bassett 1996–97
Steve Coppell 1997–98
Attilio Lombardo 1998
Terry Venables *(Head Coach)* 1998–99
Steve Coppell 1999–2000
Alan Smith 2000–01
Steve Bruce 2001
Trevor Francis 2001–03
Steve Kember 2003
Iain Dowie 2003–06
Peter Taylor 2006–07
Neil Warnock October 2007–

TEN YEAR LEAGUE RECORD

		P	W	D	L	F	A	Pts	Pos
1999-2000	Div 1	46	13	15	18	57	67	54	15
2000-01	Div 1	46	12	13	21	57	70	49	21
2001-02	Div 1	46	20	6	20	70	62	66	10
2002-03	Div 1	46	14	17	15	59	52	59	14
2003-04	Div 1	46	21	10	15	72	61	73	6
2004-05	PR Lge	38	7	12	19	41	62	33	18
2005-06	FL C	46	21	12	13	67	48	75	6
2006-07	FL C	46	18	11	17	59	51	65	12
2007-08	FL C	46	18	17	11	58	42	71	5
2008-09	FL C	46	15	12	19	52	55	57	15

DID YOU KNOW ?

Despite a stutter of five successive drawn matches, Crystal Palace remained unbeaten in the last 16 League games in the 1920–21 championship winning season. Four of the 19 players used were ever present. Jack Conner with 29 goals outscored his rivals three to one.

CRYSTAL PALACE 2008–09 LEAGUE RECORD

Match No.	Date	Venue	Opponents	Result	H/T Score	Lg. Pos.	Goalscorers	Attendance
1	Aug 9	H	Watford	D	0-0	0-0	—		15,614
2	16	A	Preston NE	L	0-2	0-0	21		14,225
3	23	H	Burnley	D	0-0	0-0	19		14,071
4	30	A	Reading	L	2-4	1-1	22	Carle (pen) [37], Andrew [64]	20,441
5	Sept 13	H	Swansea C	W	2-0	1-0	18	Watson [28], Carle [66]	14,621
6	16	A	Wolverhampton W	L	1-2	1-1	—	Ifill [32]	22,200
7	20	H	Plymouth Arg	L	1-2	0-1	21	McCarthy [85]	14,209
8	27	A	Ipswich T	D	1-1	1-1	22	Moses [25]	19,032
9	30	H	Charlton Ath	W	1-0	0-0	—	Beattie [63]	16,358
10	Oct 4	A	Nottingham F	W	2-0	1-0	18	Ifill [4], Kuqi [81]	22,811
11	18	H	Barnsley	W	3-0	1-0	14	Watson 2 (1 pen) [25 (p), 60], Kuqi [82]	16,494
12	21	A	Birmingham C	L	0-1	0-0	—		17,706
13	25	A	Blackpool	D	2-2	1-0	16	Ifill [28], Beattie [49]	7597
14	28	H	Nottingham F	L	1-2	0-1	—	Kuqi [75]	15,162
15	Nov 1	H	Sheffield W	D	1-1	0-1	17	Watson (pen) [54]	14,650
16	8	A	Coventry C	W	2-0	1-0	16	Hill [9], Watson [53]	16,883
17	15	A	Cardiff C	L	1-2	1-1	17	Scannell [37]	17,478
18	22	H	Bristol C	W	4-2	2-1	14	Oster [11], Scannell [13], Beattie [66], Fonte J [72]	14,599
19	25	A	Norwich C	W	2-1	2-0	—	Beattie [27], Oster [40]	24,034
20	29	H	QPR	D	0-0	0-0	13		16,411
21	Dec 6	A	Derby Co	W	2-1	1-1	9	McCarthy [3], Kuqi [61]	27,203
22	8	H	Southampton	W	3-0	2-0	—	Kuqi [9], Beattie [15], Ifill [75]	13,799
23	13	H	Doncaster R	W	2-1	1-1	8	Kuqi (pen) [21], Lee [89]	13,811
24	20	A	Sheffield U	D	2-2	0-1	7	McCarthy [49], Carle [90]	23,045
25	26	H	Norwich C	W	3-1	2-1	6	Fonte J 2 [6, 31], Butterfield [90]	17,180
26	28	A	Bristol C	L	0-1	0-1	8		18,265
27	Jan 17	H	Ipswich T	L	1-4	1-2	10	Lee [31]	15,348
28	27	A	Charlton Ath	L	0-1	0-1	—		20,627
29	31	H	Blackpool	L	0-1	0-1	12		13,810
30	Feb 17	A	Plymouth Arg	W	3-1	3-0	—	Danns [21], Lee [28], Oster [43]	10,710
31	21	A	Sheffield W	L	0-2	0-0	14		22,687
32	24	H	Birmingham C	D	0-0	0-0	—		12,847
33	28	A	Watford	L	0-2	0-1	14		15,529
34	Mar 3	H	Wolverhampton W	L	0-1	0-0	—		14,907
35	7	H	Preston NE	W	2-1	2-1	13	Stokes [32], Danns [34]	16,340
36	11	A	Burnley	L	2-4	2-1	—	Kuqi [26], Carlisle (og) [35]	10,312
37	14	A	Swansea C	W	3-1	0-0	11	Moses [49], Fonte J [61], Kuqi [90]	13,663
38	17	A	Barnsley	L	1-3	1-1	—	Kuqi [8]	10,885
39	21	H	Reading	D	0-0	0-0	12		14,567
40	Apr 4	A	QPR	D	0-0	0-0	13		15,234
41	7	H	Coventry C	D	1-1	0-1	—	Cadogan [72]	12,898
42	11	H	Cardiff C	L	0-2	0-1	13		14,814
43	13	A	Southampton	L	0-1	0-0	13		23,220
44	18	A	Derby Co	W	1-0	0-0	13	Kuqi [63]	14,736
45	25	A	Doncaster R	L	0-2	0-1	14		12,031
46	May 3	H	Sheffield U	D	0-0	0-0	15		22,824

Final League Position: 15

GOALSCORERS

League (52): Kuqi 10 (1 pen), Beattie 5, Watson 5 (2 pens), Fonte J 4, Ifill 4, Carle 3 (1 pen), Lee 3, McCarthy 3, Oster 3, Danns 2, Moses 2, Scannell 2, Andrew 1, Butterfield 1, Cadogan 1, Hill 1, Stokes 1, own goal 1.
Carling Cup (2): Carle 1, Oster 1.
FA Cup (5): Ifill 2, Danns 1, Hill 1, Scannell 1.

Speroni J 45	Butterfield D 17+9	Hill C 43	Carle N 35+2	McCarthy P 25+2	Lawrence M 28+4	Soares T 4	Derry S 35+4	Scowcroft J 5+5	Moses V 19+8	Scannell S 16+9	Ifill P 27+6	Andrew C 1+6	Oster J 27+4	Hills L 8+6	Djilali K 2+4	Grifitt L 2+3	Fonte J 36+2	Lee A 10+6	Fletcher C —+3	Watson B 18	Thomas S —+1	Kuqi S 20+15	Beattie C 15	Danns N 14+6	Clyne N 25+1	Ertl J 3+9	Wiggins R 1	Flahavan D 1	Fonte R 5+5	Davis C 7	Stokes A 11+2	Comley J 1+3	Cadogan K —+4	Pinney N —+1	Match No.
1	2	3	4	5	6	7	8	9¹	10²	11	12	13																							1
1	2	3	4¹	5	6	7	8	9	13			14	12	11³	10²																				2
1	2	3	4²	5	6	7	8⁸	9⁸			12	11¹		13	10³	14																			3
1	2	3	10	5³	6	7	8²				12		9	11	4¹			14	13																4
1	2	3	10		6		8	9²		12	11¹	13	7³		14		5					4													5
1	2	3	10¹	12	6		8		9²	11³			7	13	5							4	14												6
1	2	3	10¹	12	6		8		13	7		11³	14	5	9²							4													7
1	2	3	7¹	5			8		10	13	11³					6			12	4		14	9²												8
1	2	3	7²	5			8		10¹	12	11				6			13	4		14	9³													9
1	2	3	11	5²	13		8		10¹	7					6			4	12	9	14														10
1		3	8		6	7¹			10		11²	12			5			13	9³		2	14													11
1	2	3	11¹		6		8		10²	7³					5			13	9	12		14													12
1	2	3	10	5	6		8³		12	7²		11¹			4			13	9	14															13
1	2³		11¹	5	6		8		10	7			12			4			13	9²		14	3												14
1		3		5	2		8			12	11	13	7			6			4			10²	9¹							/					15
1		3	12	5	2		8			10¹	11		7²			6			4			9			13										16
	3		5	2⁸		8			12	9	7	11¹			6			4			13	10²				1									17
1		3	8	5						12	10¹	11²	7³			6			4			13	9		2	14									18
1		3	8²	5	12				13		11		14	7		6			4			10³	9¹		2										19
1		3	8¹	5					12		10³	11²	7			14	6		4			13	9		2										20
1	12	3	8²	5					13		11¹		7			6	14		4			10³	9		2										21
1	14	3	8	5					12		11²	13	7³			6		4¹	10			9			2										22
1	14	3	4	5³					8		12	9	7		11¹	6	13		10²			2													23
1	12	3	4	5					8	13	9	11²	7¹			6	14		10³			2													24
1	14	3	4	5³	12				8		9²	11	7			6	10¹		13			2													25
1	7		4		5				8	14	11	9¹	3²			6	10³		13	12	2														26
1	13	3	4		5²				8		10¹	11	7	14		6	9		12			2													27
1	2	3	4¹		5				8	13	9²	11³	7			6	14		10	12															28
1	2	5	4³				8	12	11			7	3			6	9¹		10²	13				14											29
1	14	3					8			9²	11	7³	13			6	10¹		12	4	2				5										30
1	14	3			13		8³	9¹	11			7				6	10		12	4	2				5²										31
1	14	3	8⁸		5			9¹					7²	12		6	11			4	2	13		10³											32
1	8	3			5		9¹		12	11³		7²	13			6	10			4	2			14											33
1		3			5	8	13		11³	10	12	7¹			6	9²				4	2											14			34
1		3		2³		8			12	11¹		7				6			10	4	14	13			5	9²									35
1		3	12			8	13		11		7¹				6	14			10²	4	2				5	9³									36
1		3	4³			8			11²	13	12	2			6				10	5	7	14				9¹									37
1		3	7³			8			11			12	5		6²				10	4¹	2	13				9	14								38
1		3			5		8		11	13		7¹			6				10	4	2			12		9²									39
1		3¹	7		6		8	14	11		13				12				10³	4	2			5	9²										40
1					2		8		11		7¹		3			6				10	4			13	5	9²	12								41
1		3	4	6			8¹		11										10		2				7³	5	9²	12	13	14					42
1		3	8	5	4				9²						6³				10		2				11¹		13	7	12						43
1		3	4	5	6		11⁸											10			2	7		8¹		9	12								44
1		3	8¹	5	6		13						14					10²		4	2	7		11³	9		12								45
1		3	8	5	2		14	11¹					13		6			10		4³	7			12	9²										46

FA Cup
Third Round   Leicester C   (a) 0-0
    (h) 2-1
Fourth Round   Watford   (a) 3-4

Carling Cup
First Round   Hereford U   (h) 2-1
Second Round   Leeds U   (a) 0-4

DAGENHAM & REDBRIDGE   FL Championship 2

FOUNDATION

The roots of Dagenham & Redbridge live firmly in the Essex side of the Greater London area. Though only formed in 1992 their complex origins date back to the 19th century involving Ilford (founded 1881) and Leytonstone (1886) who merged in 1979 to form Leytonstone-Ilford. They and Walthamstow Avenue (1900) joined together in 1988 to becom Redbridge Forest who in turn merged with Dagenham FC (1949) in 1992. Victoria Road has existed as a football ground since 1917. Initially used by Sterling Works, in the summer of 1955 Briggs Sports vacated the premises and Dagenham FC moved in and the pitch was enclosed.

The London Borough of Barking and Dagenham Stadium, Victoria Road, Dagenham, Essex RM10 7XL.

Telephone: (0208) 592 1549.

Fax: (020) 8593 7227.

Ticket Office: (020) 8592 1549 (extension 21).

Website: www.daggers.co.uk

Email: info@daggers.co.uk

Ground Capacity: 6,007.

Record Attendance: 4,791 v Shrewsbury T, FL 2, 2 May 2009.

Pitch Measurements: 100m × 64.5m.

Chairman: David J. Andrews.

Vice-chairman: David E. Ward.

Managing Director: Stephen R. Thompson.

Secretary: Terry Grover.

Manager: John L. Still.

Assistant Manager: Terry W. Harris.

Physio: John Gowens.

Colours: Red and blue striped shirts with red sleeves, white shorts, red stockings.

Change Colours: Yellow shirts, blue shorts, yellow stockings.

Year Formed: 1992.

Ground: 1992, Victoria Road.

Club Nickname: The Daggers.

First Football League Game: 11 August 2007, FL 2 v Stockport Co (a) L 0–1 – Roberts; Foster, Griffiths, Rainford, Uddin, Boardman, Saunders (Strevens), Southam, Benson (Moore), Nurse, Sloma (Huke).

MANAGERS

John Still 1992–94
Dave Cusack 1994–95
Graham Carr 1995–96
Ted Hardy 1996–99
Garry Hill 1999–2004
John Still April 2004–

SKY SPORTS FACT FILE

Dagenham & Redbridge recorded their biggest League win on the first Saturday of 2008–09 in beating Chester City 6–0. Their previous best occurred in the previous term when on 12 February 2008 they accounted for the same opposition 6–2!

Record League Victory: 6–0 v Chester C, FL 2, 9 August 2008 – Roberts; Okuonghae, Griffiths, Arber, Uddin, Taiwo, Saunders (2), Green (1) (Southam), Benson (1) (Nurse), Strevens (1p) (Nwokeji (1)), Gain.

Record Defeat: 0–9 v Hereford U, Conference, 27 February 2004.

Most League Points (3 for a win): 68, FL 2, 2008–09.

Most League Goals: 77, FL 2, 2008–09.

Highest League Scorer in Season: Paul Benson, 28, Conference, 2006–07.

Most League Goals in Total Aggregate: 29, Ben Strevens, 2007–.

Most League Goals in One Match: 3, Paul Benson v Notts Co, FL 2, 22 November 2008.

Most Capped Player: Jon Nurse, 4, Barbados.

Most League Appearances: Ben Strevens, 92, 2007–.

Youngest League Player: Dominic Green, 18 years 93 days v Brentford, 2 October 2007.

Record Transfer Fee Received: Reported figure of £250,000 from Peterborough U for Craig Mackail-Smith and Shane Blackett, January 2007.

Record Transfer Fee Paid: £16,000 to Purfleet for Paul Cobb, 1998.

Football League Record: Promoted from Conference 2006–07; FL 2 2007–.

LATEST SEQUENCES

Longest Sequence of League Wins: 5, 12.2.2008 – 1.3.2008.

Longest Sequence of League Defeats: 4, 27.10.2007 – 17.11.2007.

Longest Sequence of League Draws: 2, 22.3.2008 – 24.3.2008.

Longest Sequence of Unbeaten League Matches: 6, 6.12.2008 – 17.1.2009.

Longest Sequence Without a League Win: 9, 6.10.2007 – 4.12.2007.

Successive Scoring Runs: 16 from 12.4.2008.

Successive Non-scoring Runs: 3 from 12.1.2008.

HONOURS

FA Cup: best season: 3rd rd, 2008.

Conference: Champions – 2006–07. Runners-up – 2001–02.

Isthmian League (Premier): Champions 1999–2000.

Essex Senior Cup: Winners – 1997–98, 2000–01. Runners-up 2001–02.

AS DAGENHAM FC
FA Trophy: Winners 1979–80; Runners-up 1976–77. *Amateur Cup:* Runners-up 1969–70, 1970–71.

AS ILFORD
FA Amateur Cup: Winners 1929, 1930. *Isthmian League:* Champions 1906–07, 1920–21, 1921–22.

AS LEYTONSTONE
FA Amateur Cup: Winners 1947, 1948, 1968. *Isthmian League:* Champions 1918–19, 1937–38, 1938–39, 1946–47, 1947–48, 1949–50, 1950–51, 1951–52, 1965–66.

AS LEYTONSTONE/ILFORD
Isthmian League: Champions 1981–82, 1988–89.

AS WALTHAMSTOW AVENUE
FA Amateur Cup: Winners 1952, 1961. *Isthmian League:* Champions 1945–46, 1948–49, 1952–53, 1954–55. *Athenian League:* Champions 1929–30, 1932–33, 1933–34, 1937–38, 1938–39.

AS REDBRIDGE FOREST
Isthmian League: Winners 1990–91.

TEN YEAR LEAGUE RECORD

		P	W	D	L	F	A	Pts	Pos
1999-00	IPL	42	32	5	5	97	35	101	1
2000-01	Conf	42	23	8	11	71	54	77	3
2001-02	Conf	42	24	12	8	70	47	84	3
2002-03	Conf	42	21	9	12	71	59	72	5
2003-04	Conf	42	15	9	18	59	64	54	13
2004-05	Conf	42	19	8	15	68	60	65	11
2005-06	Conf	42	16	19	16	63	59	58	10
2006-07	Conf	46	28	11	7	93	48	95	1
2007-08	FL 2	46	13	10	23	49	70	49	20
2008-09	FL 2	46	19	11	16	77	53	68	8

DID YOU KNOW ?

On 21 February 2009 veteran Dagenham & Redbridge goalkeeper Tony Roberts aged 39 celebrated his 400th appearance for the club by saving a penalty in the goalless draw away at Accrington Stanley.

DAGENHAM & REDBRIDGE 2008–09 LEAGUE RECORD

Match No.	Date	Venue	Opponents	Result	H/T Score	Lg. Pos.	Goalscorers	Attendance
1	Aug 9	H	Chester C	W 6-0	2-0	—	Green [16], Strevens (pen) [42], Saunders 2 [55, 60], Benson [79], Nwokeji [88]	1434
2	16	A	Lincoln C	W 3-1	0-1	1	Strevens 2 [67, 79], Benson [90]	3581
3	23	H	Port Vale	D 1-1	1-1	4	Benson [5]	1843
4	30	A	Morecambe	W 2-1	0-0	1	Saunders [50], Taiwo [53]	1571
5	Sept 6	A	Brentford	L 1-2	0-2	4	Saunders [50]	4519
6	13	H	Chesterfield	W 3-0	1-0	5	Saunders [2], Nwokeji [87], Benson [88]	1682
7	20	A	Wycombe W	L 1-2	0-1	5	Strevens [58]	4132
8	27	H	Rotherham U	D 1-1	0-0	6	Benson [50]	1805
9	Oct 4	A	Rochdale	W 2-0	1-0	5	Benson [31], Ritchie [68]	2566
10	10	H	Barnet	W 2-0	1-0	—	Ritchie [9], Strevens [62]	2629
11	18	A	Bury	L 1-3	0-2	4	Saunders [90]	2364
12	21	A	Bournemouth	L 1-2	0-2	—	Nurse [72]	3554
13	25	A	Darlington	L 0-3	0-1	9		3070
14	28	H	Grimsby T	W 4-0	2-0	—	Arber [16], Strevens 2 [35, 90], Benson [63]	1622
15	Nov 1	H	Accrington S	D 0-0	0-0	8		1433
16	15	A	Luton T	L 1-2	1-2	10	Okuonghae [33]	5402
17	22	H	Notts Co	W 6-1	3-0	9	Ritchie [9], Strevens [25], Benson 3 [35, 49, 90], Okuonghae [56]	1743
18	25	A	Shrewsbury T	L 1-2	0-0	11	Saunders [78]	4590
19	Dec 6	A	Bradford C	D 1-1	0-0	11	Ritchie [71]	12,145
20	20	A	Macclesfield T	W 4-0	3-0	10	Benson 2 [4, 19], Taiwo [7], Saunders [48]	1909
21	26	H	Gillingham	W 2-0	1-0	7	Strevens [1], Benson [50]	2844
22	28	A	Aldershot T	W 2-1	1-1	4	Taiwo [27], Nurse [87]	3697
23	Jan 3	A	Rotherham U	D 1-1	0-0	—	Ritchie [48]	3307
24	17	A	Barnet	D 1-1	0-1	6	Nwokeji [65]	2366
25	20	H	Exeter C	L 1-2	1-1	—	Strevens [45]	2053
26	24	H	Rochdale	W 3-2	1-2	5	Arber [8], Ritchie [74], Southam [79]	1808
27	27	A	Grimsby T	D 1-1	1-1	—	Nurse [37]	3431
28	31	H	Darlington	L 0-1	0-0	8		1832
29	Feb 7	A	Bury	D 2-2	0-2	—	Nurse [60], Strevens [64]	2530
30	14	H	Luton T	W 2-1	1-0	8	Foster 2 [20, 57]	2310
31	17	A	Wycombe W	L 0-1	0-0	—		2242
32	21	A	Accrington S	D 0-0	0-0	—		1123
33	24	H	Bournemouth	L 0-1	0-0	—		1602
34	28	A	Chester C	D 2-2	2-0	9	Strevens [6], Ritchie [36]	1416
35	Mar 3	H	Lincoln C	L 0-3	0-1	—		1302
36	7	H	Morecambe	L 0-2	0-2	9		1403
37	10	A	Port Vale	W 1-0	1-0	—	Guy [25]	4090
38	14	A	Chesterfield	D 1-1	0-0	9	Saunders [90]	3007
39	28	H	Macclesfield T	W 2-1	0-1	10	Benson [71], Ritchie [83]	1347
40	Apr 4	A	Exeter C	L 1-2	1-1	10	Strevens [36]	5123
41	11	H	Aldershot T	W 3-1	1-1	10	Benson [40], Saunders (pen) [64], Ritchie [67]	1586
42	13	A	Gillingham	L 1-2	1-1	10	Saunders [41]	6945
43	18	H	Bradford C	W 3-0	0-0	9	Saunders [57], Benson [81], Strevens [86]	1883
44	21	H	Brentford	W 3-1	2-0	—	Saunders [20], Taiwo [34], Arber [55]	3537
45	25	A	Notts Co	W 3-0	2-0	7	Saunders [34], Ritchie 2 [44, 88]	4419
46	May 2	H	Shrewsbury T	L 1-2	0-2	8	Benson [53]	4791

Final League Position: 8

GOALSCORERS

League (77): Benson 17, Saunders 14 (1 pen), Strevens 14 (1 pen), Ritchie 11, Nurse 4, Taiwo 4, Arber 3, Nwokeji 3, Foster 2, Okuonghae 2, Green 1, Guy 1, Southam 1.
Carling Cup (1): Taiwo 1.
FA Cup (4): Benson 1, Ritchie 1, Strevens 1, Taiwo 1.
J Paint Trophy (5): Benson 2, Nwokeji 2, Southam 1 (pen).

Roberts T 43	Okuonghae M 45	Griffiths S 43 + 1	Arber M 42	Uddin A 10 + 7	Taiwo S 39 + 1	Saunders S 40	Green D 2	Benson P 31 + 2	Strevens B 46	Gain P 30 + 1	Nwokeji M 3 + 13	Nurse J 16 + 18	Southam G 17 + 13	Graham R 3 + 2	Ritchie M 36 + 1	Foster D 38	Thomas W 1 + 4	Huke S — + 1	Thompson E — + 1	Montgomery G — + 5	Tejan-Sie T — + 1	Palmer A 3	Loft D 10 + 1	Guy J 5 + 4	Hogan D — + 1	Button D 3	Charge D — + 1	Match No.
1	2	3	4	5	6	7	8^3	9^2	10^1	11	12	13	14															1
1	2	3	4	5	6	7	8^1	9	10	11			12															2
1	2	3	4	5	6	7		9	10	11			8^1	12														3
1	2	3	4	5	6	7		9^1	10	11	12	8																4
1	2^1	3	4	5	6	7		9	10^3	11	14	8^2	12	13														5
1	2	3	4^1	5	6	7		9	10	11	13	12			8^2													6
1	2	3		5	6^1	7		9	10	11	13	8	12	4^2														7
1	2	3		5	6	7		9	10	11			4^1	12	8^2	13												8
1	5	3	4		6	8		9	10^2	11		12			7^1	2	13											9
1	5	3	4		6	7		9	10	11		12			8^1	2												10
1	5	3	4		6	7		9^1	10	11		12	13		8^2	2												11
1	5	3^2	4	12	6	7			10	11	14	13	8^1		9^3	2												12
1	5	3	4		6	7			10	11	9^1	12	13		8^2	2												13
1	5	3	4		6^2			9	10	11		12	8^1		7	2	13											14
1	5	3	4		6	7^1		9	10	11	13	12			8^2	2												15
1	5	3	4	12	6	7		9	10	11	14		13		8^3	2^1												16
1^6	5	3	4		6	7^1		9	10^2	11		12			8	2	13	15										17
1	4	3		5	6^1	7		9	10	11		8	12			2												18
1	5	3	4		6	7		9	10	11					8	2												19
1	5	3	4		6	7		9	10^1	11		12			8	2												20
1	5	3	4		6	7^1		9	10	11					8	2												21
1	5	3	4		6			9	10	11	12	7	8^1			2												22
1	5	3	4		6			9	10	11	12		8		7^1	2												23
1		3	4	5	6	7			10		9^1	12^2	8		11	2			13									24
1	5	3	4	12	6^3	7			10		9^1	13	8		11	2^2				14								25
1	5	3^1	4	12	6	7^4		9^2	10			13	8		11	2												26
1	5		4		6			9	10		12	7^1	8		11	2						3						27
1	5		4		6			9	10		12	7^1	8		11	2						3						28
1	5	12	4		6			9	10			7	8^2		11	2						3^1		13				29
1	5	3	4^1	12	6^2	7		9	10			13			11	2							8					30
1	5	3	4			7		9^1	10				8		11	2	12						6					31
1	5	3				7		9	10	11			8			2	4						6	9				32
1	5	3	4			7		9^1	10				8		11	2	12						6					33
1	5	3	4^1	12		7		9	10				8		11	2							6					34
1	5	3	4	12		7		9^1	10				8		11	2							6^1	13				35
1	5	3	4		6	7			10						11	2							8	9				36
1	5	3	4		6	7			10				12		11	2							8	9^1				37
1	5	3	4		6	7			10				12		11	2^1							8	9				38
1	5	3	4		6	7			10^1		12		13		11	2							8^2	9				39
1	5	3	4	6^1	7^3				10		13		8	14	11	2								9^2				40
1	5	3	4		6	7^2		9^1	10				8		11	2				13			12					41
1^6	5^1	3	4	12	6	7		9	10				8^2		11	2				13	15							42
	5	3	4		6	7^2		9^3	10			12	8		11^1	2				14				13		1		43
	5	3	4		6	7		9	10				8		11	2										1		44
	5	3	4		6	7^2		9	10^1			12	8		11^3	2				14						1	13	45
1	5	3	4	6^1	7			9	10			13	8		11	2^2								12				46

FA Cup

First Round	Hereford U	(a)	0-0	
		(h)	2-1	
Second Round	Leicester C	(a)	2-3	

Carling Cup

First Round	Reading	(h)	1-2

J Paint Trophy

First Round	Barnet	(h)	4-2
Second Round	Peterborough U	(a)	1-0
Quarter-Final	Shrewsbury T	(a)	0-5

DARLINGTON   FL Championship 2

FOUNDATION

A football club was formed in Darlington as early as 1861 but the present club began in 1883 and reached the final of the Durham Senior Cup in their first season, losing to Sunderland in a replay after complaining that they had suffered from intimidation in the first. On 5 April 1884, Sunderland had defeated Darlington 4-3. Darlington's objection was upheld by the referee and the replay took place on 3 May. The new referee for the match was Major Marindin, appointed by the Football Association to ensure fair play. Sunderland won 2-0. The following season Darlington won this trophy and for many years were one of the leading amateur clubs in their area.

Northern Echo Darlington Arena, Neasham Road, Darlington DL2 1DL.

Telephone: (01325) 387 000.

Fax: (01325) 387 050.

Ticket Office: 0871 855 1883.

Website: www.darlington-fc.net

Email: reception@darlington-fc.net

Ground Capacity: 25,000.

Record Attendance: 21,023 v Bolton W, League Cup 3rd rd, 14 November 1960.

Pitch Measurements: 112yd × 74yd.

Chairman: George Houghton.

Commercial Director: Christine Balford.

Secretary: Lisa Charlton.

Manager: Colin Todd.

Assistant Manager: Dean Windass.

HONOURS

Football League: Division 2 best season: 15th, 1925–26; Division 3 (N) – Champions 1924–25; Runners-up 1921–22; Division 4 – Champions 1990–91; Runners-up 1965–66.

FA Cup: best season: 5th rd, 1958.

Football League Cup: best season: 5th rd, 1968.

GM Vauxhall Conference: Champions 1989–90.

Colours: Black and white hooped shirts with black sleeves and red trim, black shorts, black stockings.

Change Colours: Red shirts, white shorts, red stockings.

Year Formed: 1883. *Turned Professional:* 1908. *Ltd Co.:* 1891.

Grounds: 1918, Feethams Ground; 2003, Reynolds Arena, Hurworth Moor.

Club Nickname: 'The Quakers'.

First Football League Game: 27 August 1921, Division 3 (N), v Halifax T (h) W 2–0 – Ward; Greaves, Barbour; Dickson (1), Sutcliffe, Malcolm; Dolphin, Hooper (1), Edmunds, Wolstenholme, Winship.

Record League Victory: 9–2 v Lincoln C, Division 3 (N), 7 January 1928 – Archibald; Brooks, Mellen; Kelly, Waugh, McKinnell; Cochrane (1), Gregg (1), Ruddy (3), Lees (3), McGiffen (1).

SKY SPORTS FACT FILE

On 30 August 2008 Darlington were still searching for their first League win of the season. But they rectified the situation at Macclesfield Town with a 6–0 victory. Billy Clarke on loan from Ipswich Town scored four times including three in the second half.

Record Cup Victory: 7–2 v Evenwood T, FA Cup 1st rd, 17 November 1956 – Ward; Devlin, Henderson; Bell (1p), Greener, Furphy; Forster (1), Morton (3), Tulip (2), Davis, Moran.

Record Defeat: 0–10 v Doncaster R, Division 4, 25 January 1964.

Most League Points (2 for a win): 59, Division 4, 1965–66.

Most League Points (3 for a win): 85, Division 4, 1984–85.

Most League Goals: 108, Division 3 (N), 1929–30.

Highest League Scorer in Season: David Brown, 39, Division 3 (N), 1924–25.

Most League Goals in Total Aggregate: Alan Walsh, 90, 1978–84.

Most League Goals in One Match: 5, Tom Ruddy v South Shields, Division 2, 23 April 1927; 5, Maurice Wellock v Rotherham U, Division 3 (N), 15 February 1930.

Most Capped Player: Franz Burgmeier, 5 (53), Liechtenstein.

Most League Appearances: Ron Greener, 442, 1955–68.

Youngest League Player: Curtis Main, 15 years 318 days v Peterborough U, 3 May 2008.

Record Transfer Fee Received: £400,000 from Dundee U for Jason De Vos, October 1998.

Record Transfer Fee Paid: £100,000 to Boston U for Julian Joachim, September 2006 and £100,000 to Swansea C for Pawel Abbott, July 2007.

Football League Record: 1921 Original Member of Division 3 (N); 1925–27 Division 2; 1927–58 Division 3 (N); 1958–66 Division 4; 1966–67 Division 3; 1967–85 Division 4; 1985–87 Division 3; 1987–89 Division 4; 1989–90 GM Vauxhall Conference; 1990–91 Division 4; 1991–2004 Division 3; 2004– FL 2.

LATEST SEQUENCES

Longest Sequence of League Wins: 6, 6.2.2000 – 7.3.2000.

Longest Sequence of League Defeats: 8, 31.8.1985 – 19.10.1985.

Longest Sequence of League Draws: 5, 31.12.1988 – 28.1.1989.

Longest Sequence of Unbeaten League Matches: 17, 27.4.1968 – 19.10.1968.

Longest Sequence Without a League Win: 19, 27.4.1988 – 8.11.1988.

Successive Scoring Runs: 22 from 3.12.1932.

Successive Non-scoring Runs: 7 from 5.9.1975.

MANAGERS

Tom McIntosh 1902–11
W. L. Lane 1911–12
  (Secretary-Manager)
Dick Jackson 1912–19
Jack English 1919–28
Jack Fairless 1928–33
George Collins 1933–36
George Brown 1936–38
Jackie Carr 1938–42
Jack Surtees 1942
Jack English 1945–46
Bill Forrest 1946–50
George Irwin 1950–52
Bob Gurney 1952–57
Dick Duckworth 1957–60
Eddie Carr 1960–64
Lol Morgan 1964–66
Jimmy Greenhalgh 1966–68
Ray Yeoman 1968–70
Len Richley 1970–71
Frank Brennan 1971
Ken Hale 1971–72
Allan Jones 1972
Ralph Brand 1972–73
Dick Conner 1973–74
Billy Horner 1974–76
Peter Madden 1976–78
Len Walker 1978–79
Billy Elliott 1979–83
Cyril Knowles 1983–87
Dave Booth 1987–89
Brian Little 1989–91
Frank Gray 1991–92
Ray Hankin 1992
Billy McEwan 1992–93
Alan Murray 1993–95
Paul Futcher 1995
David Hodgson/Jim Platt
  (Director of Coaching) 1995
Jim Platt 1995–96
David Hodgson 1996–2000
Gary Bennett 2000–01
Tommy Taylor 2001–02
Mick Tait 2003
David Hodgson 2003–06
Dave Penney 2006–09
Colin Todd May 2009–

TEN YEAR LEAGUE RECORD

		P	W	D	L	F	A	Pts	Pos
1999-2000	Div 3	46	21	16	9	66	36	79	4
2000-01	Div 3	46	12	13	21	44	56	49	20
2001-02	Div 3	46	15	11	20	60	71	56	15
2002-03	Div 3	46	12	18	16	58	59	54	14
2003-04	Div 3	46	14	11	21	53	61	53	18
2004-05	FL 2	46	20	12	14	57	49	72	8
2005-06	FL 2	46	16	15	15	58	52	63	8
2006-07	FL 2	46	17	14	15	52	56	65	11
2007-08	FL 2	46	22	12	12	67	40	78	6
2008-09	FL 2	46	20	12	14	61	44	62*	12

10 pts deducted.

DID YOU KNOW ?

Franz Burgmeier, an experienced Liechtenstein international, became the third Darlington player to receive as many as three full international appearances when he played against Wales in the 2010 World Cup qualifying match on 11 October.

DARLINGTON 2008–09 LEAGUE RECORD

Match No.	Date	Venue	Opponents	Result	H/T Score	Lg. Pos.	Goalscorers	Attendance
1	Aug 9	H	Exeter C	D 1-1	1-0	—	Purdie (pen) [40]	3559
2	16	A	Notts Co	D 0-0	0-0	12		4352
3	23	H	Gillingham	L 1-2	0-1	14	Purdie (pen) [78]	2831
4	30	A	Macclesfield T	W 6-0	1-0	12	Clarke B 4 (1 pen) [26, 53, 64 (p), 67], Walker (og) [56], Austin [89]	1554
5	Sept 6	A	Aldershot T	L 1-2	1-2	13	Hulbert [45]	3460
6	13	H	Port Vale	W 2-1	1-1	10	Burgmeier [38], Hatch [77]	3040
7	20	H	Accrington S	W 3-0	1-0	8	Clarke B 2 [32, 57], White [76]	2814
8	27	A	Bournemouth	L 1-3	1-2	10	Hatch [35]	4124
9	Oct 4	H	Shrewsbury T	D 1-1	0-0	10	White [55]	2899
10	11	A	Luton T	W 2-1	1-1	9	Clarke B [15], Blundell [90]	5560
11	18	A	Wycombe W	D 1-1	0-0	9	Kennedy [58]	5345
12	20	H	Bradford C	W 2-1	0-0	—	Austin [84], Burgmeier [90]	3034
13	25	H	Dagenham & R	W 3-0	1-0	6	Hatch 2 [5, 55], Kennedy [51]	3070
14	28	A	Rotherham U	W 1-0	0-0	8	Ravenhill [61]	3322
15	Nov 1	A	Grimsby T	W 2-1	2-0	1	Clarke B [7], Ravenhill [15]	3509
16	15	H	Lincoln C	W 2-0	0-0	1	Hatch [47], Foran [90]	3534
17	22	A	Brentford	D 1-1	0-0	2	Foran [60]	4837
18	25	H	Chester C	L 1-2	1-1	—	Purdie [7]	2416
19	Dec 13	A	Morecambe	L 0-1	0-0	6		1873
20	20	H	Barnet	D 2-2	2-1	6	Hatch 2 [8, 25]	2770
21	26	A	Bury	D 2-2	1-1	9	Miller [44], Foran [72]	3454
22	28	H	Chesterfield	D 0-0	0-0	8		3352
23	Jan 3	H	Bournemouth	W 2-1	0-1	—	Abbott [83], Purdie (pen) [90]	2571
24	17	H	Luton T	W 5-1	4-1	3	Purdie 2 (1 pen) [10 (p), 24], Hatch [26], Austin [28], Blundell [85]	3319
25	24	A	Shrewsbury T	L 0-1	0-1	8		5140
26	27	H	Rotherham U	W 1-0	1-0	—	Carlton [22]	2431
27	31	A	Dagenham & R	W 1-0	0-0	4	Abbott [74]	1832
28	Feb 17	A	Bradford C	D 0-0	0-0	—		12,782
29	21	H	Grimsby T	W 1-0	0-0	7	Main [87]	3418
30	24	H	Rochdale	L 1-2	0-1	—	Abbott [60]	2858
31	28	A	Exeter C	L 0-2	0-0	11		4851
32	Mar 3	H	Notts Co	W 1-0	1-0	—	Hulbert [5]	2450
33	7	H	Macclesfield T	L 1-2	0-1	12	Poole [61]	2995
34	10	A	Gillingham	L 0-1	0-0	—		4730
35	14	A	Port Vale	L 1-3	1-1	13	Carlton [26]	4860
36	17	A	Lincoln C	W 1-0	1-0	—	Carlton [7]	2835
37	21	H	Aldershot T	W 2-0	1-0	12	Main [45], Carlton [72]	2532
38	24	A	Accrington S	L 0-1	0-1	—		1086
39	28	A	Barnet	W 1-0	0-0	11	Abbott [66]	2069
40	Apr 4	H	Morecambe	D 0-0	0-0	12		2560
41	7	H	Wycombe W	L 1-2	0-1	—	Kennedy [60]	2180
42	11	A	Chesterfield	D 0-0	0-0	13		3642
43	13	H	Bury	D 2-2	1-1	13	Kennedy [38], Abbott [74]	2927
44	18	A	Rochdale	W 2-0	1-0	12	Kennedy [4], McArdle (og) [66]	3789
45	25	H	Brentford	L 1-3	0-2	12	Abbott [59]	3868
46	May 2	A	Chester C	W 2-1	0-0	12	Abbott 2 [71, 90]	1945

Final League Position: 12

GOALSCORERS

League (61): Abbott 8, Clarke B 8 (1 pen), Hatch 8, Purdie 6 (4 pens), Kennedy 5, Carlton 4, Austin 3, Foran 3, Blundell 2, Burgmeier 2, Hulbert 2, Main 2, Ravenhill 2, White 2, Miller 1, Poole 1, own goals 2.
Carling Cup (3): Blundell 1, Clarke B 1, Kennedy 1.
FA Cup (0).
J Paint Trophy (3): White 2, Foster 1.

Brown S 22	Purdie R 39 + 1	Fortune C 3 + 4	Ravenhill R 37 + 1	Foster S 34	White A 40	Poole D 18 + 8	Kennedy J 44 + 2	Clarke B 18 + 2	Proudlock A 3 + 5	Griffin A 9 + 8	Hulbert R 9 + 18	Blundell G 2 + 18	Austin N 29 + 4	Miller I 16 + 5	Main C 5 + 13	Burgmeier F 30 + 5	Hatch L 23 + 3	Valentine R 30 + 1	Ryan T 21 + 3	Foran R 7 + 2	Oakes A 10	Flynn M 4	Carole S 3 + 3	Abbott P 15 + 3	Gerken D 7	Carlton D 16 + 1	Tremarco C 2	Gray J 1 + 4	Barnes C 2 + 1	Kazimierczak P 7 + 1	Groves D — + 1	Match No.
1	2	3¹	4¹	5	6	7	8	9	10²	11	12	13	14																			1
1	2		4²	5	6¹	7	8	9	10³	11		13	14	3	12																	2
1	2		4²	5		7	8	9	10¹	11³		13		3	6	12	14															3
1	2		4	5	6	7	8¹	9²			12	13	14	3		11	10³															4
1	2		4	5	6	13	8	9			12		14	7²		10	3¹	11³														5
1	2		4¹	5	6	7³	8	9²			12	13	14	3		11	10															6
1	2		4	5	6	7³	8²	9			12	13	14	3		11	10¹															7
1	2		4	5	6	7¹	8	9			12	13		3²		11	10															8
1	2		4	5	6		8	9¹			12			3		11	10		7													9
1	2		4	5	6	7¹	8	9²			12	13		3		11	10	11														10
1	2			5	6	7	8	9¹			12	13		3		11²	10	4⁴														11
1	7		4	5	6		8²	9¹			12	13		3	2	11	10															12
1	2		4³	5	6		8	9²			12	13	14	3		11	10¹															13
1	2		4	5	6	7	8	9¹			12	13	14	3		11³	10²															14
1	2		4	5	6	7	8¹	9³			12	13	14	3		11²	10															15
1	7		4¹	5⁴	6		8				12	13	14	3	2	11³	10²		9													16
	2		4²		6	7	8				12	13		3		11¹	10	5	9		1											17
1	2²		4¹		6	7	8	9			12	13	14	3³		11	10	5														18
1	2³		4¹	5	6	7	8				12	13	14	3		11¹²	10		9													19
1	2		4	5	6	7²	8				12	13	14	3		11³	10¹		9													20
1	2³		4	5	6	7	8				12	13	14	3		11²	10		9¹													21
1	7		4	5	6		8				12	13	14	3	2³	11²	10		9¹													22
1	2		4	5	6	7²	8¹				12	13	14	3		11	10		9³													23
	7		4	5	6		8				12	13	14	3	2²	11³	10¹				1			9								24
	7		4⁴	5	6		8				12	13		3	2	11	10²				1			9¹								25
	7		4¹	5	6		8				12	13		3	2	11	10				1			9²								26
	7		4	5	6		8				12	13	14	3¹	2	11	10²				1			9²								27
	7		4	5	6		8¹				12	13		3	2	11²	10				1			9								28
	7¹		4	5	6		8				12	13		3	2	11²	10				1			9								29
	7¹		4⁴	5	6		8				12	13	14	3	2	11³	10²				1			9								30
	7		4¹		6⁴		8				12	13	14	3	2	11²	10	5			1			9³								31
	7		4¹	5	6		8				12	13	14	3	2	11³					1			9²		10						32
	7		4	5	6		8				12	13	14	3¹	2	11³								9²	1	10						33
	7	3¹	4	5	6		8				12				2	11								9	1	10						34
	7³		4	5	6		8				12	13	14	3	2	11²								9¹	1	10						35
	7¹		4	5	6		8²				12	13		3	2	11								9	1	10						36
	7		4	5	6		8				12	13		3	2	11¹								9²	1	10						37
	7³		4		6		8¹				12	13	14	3	2	11²		5						9	1	10						38
	2	3	4		6		8				12	13				11¹	10	5						9²	1⁶			7	15			39
	7		4		6		8				12			3	2¹	11		5						9		10				1		40
	7		4		6	13	8				12			3	2	11²		5						9¹		10				1		41
	2		4		6	7	8					13	14	3		11¹	10³	5						9			12²			1		42
	7		4		6		8²				12	13		3	2¹	11	10	5						9						1		43
	2		4		6	7	8				12			3		11	10¹	5						9						1		44
	2		4		6⁴	7²	8				12	13	14	3		11³	10¹	5						9						1		45
	2²		4		6	7¹	8³				12	13	14	3		11	10	5						9						1		46

FA Cup
First Round   Droylsden   (h)   0-0
          (a)   0-1

Carling Cup
First Round   Walsall   (a)   2-1
Second Round   Watford   (a)   1-2

J Paint Trophy
Second Round   Huddersfield T   (h)   1-0
Northern Quarter-Final
          Bury   (h)   1-0
Northern Semi-Final
          Rotherham U   (a)   1-1

DERBY COUNTY — FL Championship

FOUNDATION

Derby County was formed by members of the Derbyshire County Cricket Club in 1884, when football was booming in the area and the cricketers thought that a football club would help boost finances for the summer game. To begin with, they sported the cricket club's colours of amber, chocolate and pale blue, and went into the game at the top immediately entering the FA Cup.

Pride Park Stadium, Derby DE24 8XL.
Telephone: 0871 472 1884.
Fax: (01332) 667 519.
Ticket Office: 0871 472 1884.
Website: www.dcfc.co.uk
Email: derby.county@dcfc.co.uk
Ground Capacity: 33,597.
Record Attendance: Baseball Ground: 41,826 v Tottenham H, Division 1, 20 September 1969. Pride Park: 33,475 Derby Co Legends v Rangers 9 in a Row Legends, 1 May 2006 (Ted McMinn Benefit).
Pitch Measurements: 100.58m × 67.66m.
Chairman of Football Operations: Adam Pearson.
Club Chairman: Andy Appleby.
President and Chief Executive: Tom Glick.
Secretary: Clare Morris.
Manager: Nigel Clough.
Coaches: Gary Crosby, Andy Garner, Martin Taylor.
Physio: Alan Tomlinson.
Colours: White shirts with black trim, black shorts, white stockings.
Change Colours: Green shirts with black trim, black shorts, black stockings.
Year Formed: 1884.
Turned Professional: 1884.
Ltd Co.: 1896.
Club Nickname: 'The Rams'.
Grounds: 1884, Racecourse Ground; 1895, Baseball Ground; 1997, Pride Park.
First Football League Game: 8 September 1888, Football League, v Bolton W (a) W 6–3 – Marshall; Latham, Ferguson, Williamson; Monks, W. Roulstone; Bakewell (2), Cooper (2), Higgins, H. Plackett, L. Plackett (2).
Record League Victory: 9–0 v Wolverhampton W, Division 1, 10 January 1891 – Bunyan; Archie Goodall, Roberts; Walker, Chalmers, Roulstone (1); Bakewell, McLachlan, Johnny Goodall (1), Holmes (2), McMillan (5). 9–0 v Sheffield W, Division 1, 21 January 1899 – Fryer; Methven, Staley; Cox, Archie Goodall, May; Oakden (1), Bloomer (6), Boag, McDonald (1), Allen, (1 og).

HONOURS

Football League: Division 1 – Champions 1971–72, 1974–75; Runners-up 1895–96, 1929–30, 1935–36, 1995–96; Division 2 – Champions 1911–12, 1914–15, 1968–69, 1986–87; Runners-up 1925–26; Division 3 (N) Champions 1956–57; Runners-up 1955–56.
FA Cup: Winners 1946; Runners-up 1898, 1899, 1903.
Football League Cup: Semi-final 1968.
Texaco Cup: Winners 1972.
European Competitions: *European Cup:* 1972–73, 1975–76. *UEFA Cup:* 1974–75, 1976–77. *Anglo-Italian Cup:* Runners-up 1993.

SKY SPORTS FACT FILE

In 1911–12 the Second Division championship was secured by Derby County after a fine unbeaten run at the close of the campaign from 24 February when they dropped only three points from 12 matches. The defence conceded just two goals in the sequence.

Record Cup Victory: 12–0 v Finn Harps, UEFA Cup 1st rd 1st leg, 15 September 1976 – Moseley; Thomas, Nish, Rioch (1), McFarland, Todd (King), Macken, Gemmill, Hector (5), George (3), James (3).

Record Defeat: 2–11 v Everton, FA Cup 1st rd, 1889–90.

Most League Points (2 for a win): 63, Division 2, 1968–69 and Division 3 (N), 1955–56 and 1956–57.

Most League Points (3 for a win): 84, Division 3, 1985–86, Division 3, 1986–87 and FL C, 2006–07.

Most League Goals: 111, Division 3 (N), 1956–57.

Highest League Scorer in Season: Jack Bowers, 37, Division 1, 1930–31; Ray Straw, 37 Division 3 (N), 1956–57.

Most League Goals in Total Aggregate: Steve Bloomer, 292, 1892–1906 and 1910–14.

Most League Goals in One Match: 6, Steve Bloomer v Sheffield W, Division 1, 2 January 1899.

Most Capped Player: Deon Burton, 42 (59), Jamaica.

Most League Appearances: Kevin Hector, 486, 1966–78 and 1980–82.

Youngest League Player: Lee Holmes, 15 years 268 days v Grimsby T, 26 December 2002.

Record Transfer Fee Received: £7,000,000 rising to £9,000,000 for Seth Johnson from Leeds U, October 2001.

Record Transfer Fee Paid: £3,500,000 to Norwich C for Robert Earnshaw, June 2007.

Football League Record: 1888 Founder Member of the Football League; 1907–12 Division 2; 1912–14 Division 1; 1914–15 Division 2; 1915–21 Division 1; 1921–26 Division 2; 1926–53 Division 1; 1953–55 Division 2; 1955–57 Division 3 (N); 1957–69 Division 2; 1969–80 Division 1; 1980–84 Division 2; 1984–86 Division 3; 1986–87 Division 2; 1987–91 Division 1; 1991–92 Division 2; 1992–96 Division 1; 1996–2002 FA Premier League; 2002–04 Division 1; 2004–07 FL C; 2007–08 FA Premier League; 2008– FL C.

MANAGERS

W. D. Clark 1896–1900
Harry Newbould 1900–06
Jimmy Methven 1906–22
Cecil Potter 1922–25
George Jobey 1925–41
Ted Magner 1944–46
Stuart McMillan 1946–53
Jack Barker 1953–55
Harry Storer 1955–62
Tim Ward 1962–67
Brian Clough 1967–73
Dave Mackay 1973–76
Colin Murphy 1977
Tommy Docherty 1977–79
Colin Addison 1979–82
Johnny Newman 1982
Peter Taylor 1982–84
Roy McFarland 1984
Arthur Cox 1984–93
Roy McFarland 1993–95
Jim Smith 1995–2001
Colin Todd 2001–02
John Gregory 2002–03
George Burley 2003–05
Phil Brown 2005–06
Billy Davies 2006–07
Paul Jewell 2007–08
Nigel Clough January 2009–

LATEST SEQUENCES

Longest Sequence of League Wins: 9, 15.3.1969 – 19.4.1969.

Longest Sequence of League Defeats: 8, 12.12.1987 – 10.2.1988.

Longest Sequence of League Draws: 6, 26.3.1927 – 18.4.1927.

Longest Sequence of Unbeaten League Matches: 22, 8.3.1969 – 20.9.1969.

Longest Sequence Without a League Win: 36, 22.9.2007 – 30.8.2008.

Successive Scoring Runs: 29 from 3.12.1960.

Successive Non-scoring Runs: 8 from 30.10.1920.

TEN YEAR LEAGUE RECORD

		P	W	D	L	F	A	Pts	Pos
1999-2000	PR Lge	38	9	11	18	44	57	38	16
2000-01	PR Lge	38	10	12	16	37	59	42	17
2001-02	PR Lge	38	8	6	24	33	63	30	19
2002-03	Div 1	46	15	7	24	55	74	52	18
2003-04	Div 1	46	13	13	20	53	67	52	20
2004-05	FL C	46	22	10	14	71	60	76	4
2005-06	FL C	46	10	20	16	53	67	50	20
2006-07	FL C	46	25	9	12	62	46	84	3
2007-08	PR Lge	38	1	8	29	20	89	11	20
2008-09	FL C	46	14	12	20	55	67	54	18

DID YOU KNOW ?

Injury to goal machine Jack Bowers in September 1934 forced Derby County to seek a comparable alternative. They came up with the legendary Hughie Gallacher! He responded with a debut goal in six minutes and 23 goals from 27 League matches.

DERBY COUNTY 2008–09 LEAGUE RECORD

Match No.	Date		Venue	Opponents	Result		H/T Score	Lg. Pos.	Goalscorers	Attendance
1	Aug	9	H	Doncaster R	L	0-1	0-0	—		33,010
2		16	A	Bristol C	D	1-1	0-1	17	Green [52]	16,389
3		23	H	Southampton	L	0-1	0-0	20		27,032
4		30	A	Barnsley	L	0-2	0-0	24		14,223
5	Sept	13	H	Sheffield U	W	2-1	1-1	20	Kilgallon (og) [24], Hulse [71]	28,473
6		16	A	Swansea C	D	1-1	0-0	—	Pearson [63]	14,003
7		20	H	Cardiff C	D	1-1	1-0	20	Albrechtsen [30]	28,007
8		27	A	QPR	W	2-0	0-0	17	Albrechtsen [80], Villa [89]	14,311
9		30	H	Birmingham C	D	1-1	0-1	—	Davies [87]	29,743
10	Oct	4	A	Norwich C	W	2-1	1-0	15	Hulse [26], Ellington [85]	24,771
11		18	H	Plymouth Arg	W	2-1	1-1	10	Hulse [45], Duguid (og) [52]	28,495
12		21	A	Blackpool	L	2-3	0-2	—	Commons [58], Sterjovski [77]	7267
13		25	H	Coventry C	D	1-1	1-0	14	Hulse [41]	18,430
14		28	H	Norwich C	W	3-1	2-0	—	Green [14], Hulse [29], Kazmierczak [80]	26,621
15	Nov	2	H	Nottingham F	D	1-1	0-0	9	Villa [66]	33,010
16		8	A	Reading	L	0-3	0-1	13		18,724
17		15	H	Sheffield W	W	3-0	1-0	12	Commons [31], Addison [52], Stewart [67]	30,111
18		22	A	Ipswich T	L	0-2	0-1	13		20,239
19		25	H	Preston NE	D	2-2	2-2	—	Hulse [8], Stewart [32]	25,534
20		29	A	Burnley	L	0-3	0-3	15		11,552
21	Dec	6	H	Crystal Palace	L	1-2	1-1	16	Varney [41]	27,203
22		9	A	Wolverhampton W	L	0-3	0-2	—		21,326
23		15	A	Charlton Ath	D	2-2	0-1	—	Ellington 2 (1 pen) [62 (p), 90]	20,989
24		20	H	Watford	W	1-0	0-0	15	Hulse [83]	27,833
25		26	A	Preston NE	L	0-2	0-1	18		13,896
26		28	H	Ipswich T	L	0-1	0-1	18		28,358
27	Jan	17	H	QPR	L	0-2	0-2	20		28,390
28		27	A	Birmingham C	L	0-1	0-0	—		15,330
29		31	H	Coventry C	W	2-1	2-0	18	Hulse [14], Commons [16]	29,710
30	Feb	7	A	Plymouth Arg	W	3-0	1-0	16	Teale [43], Hulse 2 [46, 52]	10,893
31		18	H	Blackpool	W	4-1	1-1	—	Commons 2 [9, 74], Green [87], Barazite [89]	26,834
32		21	H	Nottingham F	W	3-1	1-0	15	Nyatanga [5], Hulse [47], Davies (pen) [67]	29,140
33		27	A	Doncaster R	L	1-2	0-0	—	Savage [50]	14,435
34	Mar	3	H	Swansea C	D	2-2	1-0	—	Porter 2 [14, 48]	26,691
35		7	A	Bristol C	W	2-1	1-0	16	Porter [1], Hulse [85]	30,824
36		10	A	Southampton	D	1-1	0-0	—	Davies [83]	17,567
37		14	H	Sheffield U	L	2-4	0-2	17	Hulse [52], Bannan [69]	27,565
38		21	H	Barnsley	D	0-0	0-0	17		32,277
39	Apr	4	H	Burnley	D	1-1	0-0	17	Connolly [90]	33,010
40		8	A	Cardiff C	L	1-4	0-1	—	Johnson E (og) [90]	18,403
41		11	A	Sheffield W	W	1-0	1-0	17	Hulse [45]	24,392
42		13	H	Wolverhampton W	L	2-3	1-1	17	Kazmierczak [30], Sterjovski [55]	33,079
43		18	A	Crystal Palace	L	0-1	0-0	18		14,736
44		21	H	Reading	L	0-2	0-0	—		31,345
45		25	H	Charlton Ath	W	1-0	0-0	16	Hulse [70]	31,541
46	May	3	A	Watford	L	1-3	0-3	18	Eustace [82]	16,131

Final League Position: 18

GOALSCORERS

League (55): Hulse 15, Commons 5, Davies 3 (1 pen), Ellington 3 (1 pen), Green 3, Porter 3, Albrechtsen 2, Kazmierczak 2, Sterjovski 2, Stewart 2, Villa 2, Addison 1, Bannan 1, Barazite 1, Connolly 1, Eustace 1, Nyatanga 1, Pearson 1, Savage 1, Teale 1, Varney 1, own goals 3.
Carling Cup (14): Ellington 6 (1 pen), Villa 4, Barnes 2 (1 pen), Commons 1, Green 1.
FA Cup (9): Hulse 3, Green 2, Addison 1, Albrechtsen 1, Commons 1, Davies 1 (pen).

Carroll R 16	Mears T 3	McEveley J 13+2	Green P 29	Albrechtsen M 35	Stubbs A 1	Pereplotkins A 2	Kazmierczak P 12+10	Hulse R 42+2	Ellington N 13+14	Commons K 30+4	Savage R 20+2	Connolly P 39+1	Davies S 8+11	Davis C 6+2	Villa E 12+18	Leacock D 10+1	Barazite N 21+9	Stewart J 26	Addison M 28	Pearson S 8+4	Nyatanga L 27+3	Bywater S 30+1	Sterjovski M 6+9	Teale G 24+1	Zadkovich R 2+3	Powell D 5+1	Tomkins J 5+2	Varney L 9+1	Barnes G 1+2	Camara M 1	Todd A 7+4	Porter C 3+2	Eustace J 6+3	Bannan B 6+4	Dudley M —+1	O'Brien M —+1	Match No.
1	2	3	4	5	6²	7³	8¹	9	10	11	12	13	14																								1
1	2	3	4	5		7²	8	9	10¹	11		13		6	12																						2
1	2	3	4	5			8	9³	14	7		11²	6¹	10	12	13																				3
1			4	5			8	9³	13	11¹		2		12	10²	6	14	3	7																	4
1			4	5			8²	9¹	12	11³		2		10	6	13	3	7	14																	5
1	12		4	5			8²	13				2	14	9³	6	11	3	7	10¹																	6
1			4	5			9¹	12				2	13	10	6	7	3	11	8²																	7
1			4	5			9	10²				2	12	13	6	7¹	3	8	11																	8
1			4	5³			9	12				2	13	10¹	6	7	3	8	11²	14																9
1▪			4				12	9	13			2	11²	10⁶	6	7¹	3	8	5	15																10
			4				13	9	10³	12²		2	11¹	6	14	7	3	8	5	1																11
			4					9	10	11		2	5¹	12	6	7²	3	8		1	13															12
			8	9			10²	11				2	12	13	6¹	3	4	5	1	7³	14															13
			4	6			12	9²	10	11		2		13		3	8³	5	1	7¹	14															14
			4				12	9²	10¹	11		2	13		6	14	3	8	5	1	7³															15
			4	5¹				9²	13	11		2	12	10	14	3	8	6	1	7³																16
1			4³				12	9	13	11¹		2		6	10²	7	3	8	5		14															17
1			4				12	9	13	11¹		2		6³	10²	7	3	8	5			14														18
1			4				11	9	12			2			10¹	7	3	8		6																19
1			4				8	9	12	11¹		2					3	7			6	5	10													20
1							8	12	10²	11³		2		13		7¹	3	4				14	6	5	9											21
				5			8²	9¹	12	13		2		10		3	4		1		7	6³	14	11												22
				5			11¹	10	12			2				3	8		1		7	4³	6²	13	9	14										23
				2			8³	12	10	11				13	3	4		5	1		7²	6	9¹	14												24
			4	2				9	10	11				12	3	8		5	1		7¹	6														25
			4	2			13	9¹	10³	11²		12			7	3⁴	8	5	1			6	14													26
1			4	2			9		13					12		8	5					10²	7¹	3	6											27
			4	5			9	10	8	2		7²	3	6			1	13	11¹																	28
12			4	5			9	10	8	2		7²	3	6¹			1	13	11																	29
		3	4	5			9³	10²	8	2		13	7¹	6			1	12	11												14					30
		3	4	5			9³	10	8	2		12	7	6²	13		1		11¹												14					31
		3	4	5			9²	10	8	2	11	13	7¹	6³			1	12													14					32
		3	4¹	5			9	8		2	11				6	1	12	7													10					33
		3	4	5			9	8		2	11				6	1		7													10					34
		3¹		5			12	9		4	2	13		7		6	1	8²	11											14	10³					35
				5			12	9³	13	10	2	14		11		6	1	8²	7	3	4¹															36
				2			9	8	3	10	12	7¹		6		1	11			5	4²	13														37
				3			9	8²	2	10¹	7³			13	5	1	12	11			6	4	14													38
		3		5			13	9	10¹	4	2	12		8²	6	1		11				7														39
		3	6³				9¹	13	8	2	12			5	1	7	11	14	4	10²																40
		3	6				9	10³	14	2	8		5¹	1	13	11		12	4	7²																41
		3¹	6				8²	9	10	4	2	12		1	7³	11	5	13	14																	42
			6				9	10³	4	2	13	8¹	3	1	7²	11	5	12	14																	43
			6				9²	10	4	2	13	14	12	3	1	7	5¹	8																		44
			6				9	10	4²	2	3	7¹	5	1	14	11	13	8³																		45
			9				10	4	2	12	8³	5¹	1	11	7²	6	3	14	13																	46

FA Cup

Third Round	Forest Green R	(a)	4-3
Fourth Round	Nottingham F	(h)	1-1
		(a)	3-2
Fifth Round	Manchester U	(h)	1-4

Carling Cup

First Round	Lincoln C	(h)	3-1
Second Round	Preston NE	(a)	1-0
Third Round	Brighton & HA	(a)	4-1
Fourth Round	Leeds U	(h)	2-1
Quarter-Final	Stoke C	(a)	1-0
Semi-Final	Manchester U	(h)	1-0
		(a)	2-4

DONCASTER ROVERS   FL Championship

FOUNDATION

In 1879, Mr Albert Jenkins assembled a team to play a match against the Yorkshire Institution for the Deaf. The players remained together as Doncaster Rovers, joining the Midland Alliance in 1889 and the Midland Counties League in 1891.

Keepmoat Stadium, Stadium Way, Lakeside, Doncaster, South Yorkshire DN4 5JW.

Telephone: (01302) 764 664.

Fax: (01302) 363 525.

Ticket Office: (01302) 762 576.

Website: www.doncasterroversfc.co.uk

Email: info@doncasterroversfc.co.uk

Ground Capacity: 15,231.

Record Attendance: 37,149 v Hull C, Division 3 (N), 2 October 1948.

Pitch Measurements: 100m × 70m.

Chairman: John Ryan.

Vice-chairman: Dick Watson.

Chief Executive/Secretary: David Morris.

Manager: Sean O'Driscoll.

Assistant Manager: Richard O'Kelly.

Physio: John Dickens.

Colours: Red and white hooped shirts, black shorts, black stockings.

Change Colours: Black shirts with red trim, red shorts, red stockings.

Year Formed: 1879.

Turned Professional: 1885.

Ltd Co.: 1905 & 1920.

Club Nickname: 'Rovers'.

HONOURS

Football League: Best season 2007–08. Division 3 Champions 2003–04; Division 3 (N) Champions – 1934–35, 1946–47, 1949–50; Runners-up: 1937–38, 1938–39; Division 4 Champions 1965–66, 1968–69; Runners-up: 1983–84.

FA Cup: best season 5th rd, 1952, 1954, 1955, 1956.

Football League Cup: best season: 5th rd, 1976.

J Paint Trophy: Winners 2007.

Football Conference: Champions 2002–03

Sheffield County Cup: Winners 1891, 1912, 1936, 1938, 1956, 1968, 1976, 1986.

Midland Counties League: Champions 1897, 1899.

Conference Trophy: Winners 1999, 2000.

Sheffield & Hallamshire Senior Cup: Winners 2001, 2002.

Grounds: 1880–1916, Intake Ground; 1920, Benetthorpe Ground; 1922, Low Pasture, Belle Vue; 2007, Keepmoat Stadium.

First Football League Game: 7 September 1901, Division 2, v Burslem Port Vale (h) D 3–3 – Eggett; Simpson, Layton; Longden, Jones, Wright, Langham, Murphy, Price, Goodson (2), Bailey (1).

Record League Victory: 10–0 v Darlington, Division 4, 25 January 1964: Potter; Raine, Meadows, Windross (1), White, Ripley (2), Robinson, Book (2), Hale (4), Jeffrey, Broadbent (1).

Record Cup Victory: 7–0 v Blyth Spartans, FA Cup 1st rd, 27 November 1937: Imrie; Shaw, Rodgers, McFarlane, Bycroft, Cyril Smith, Burton (1), Killourhy (4), Morgan (2), Malam, Dutton.

SKY SPORTS FACT FILE

In 1934–35 Doncaster Rovers had the unusual experience of not drawing any of their 21 home League games. In fact they divided the spoils only five times away. They called upon just 19 players in winning the Third Division (North) title on goal average.

Record Defeat: 0–12 v Small Heath, Division 2, 11 April 1903.

Most League Points (2 for a win): 72, Division 3 (N), 1946–47.

Most League Points (3 for a win): 92, Division 3, 2003–04.

Most League Goals: 123, Division 3 (N), 1946–47.

Highest League Scorer in Season: Clarrie Jordan, 42, Division 3 (N), 1946–47.

Most League Goals in Total Aggregate: Tom Keetley, 180, 1923–29.

Most League Goals in One Match: 6, Tom Keetley v Ashington, Division 3 (N), 16 February 1929.

Most Capped Player: Len Graham, 14, Northern Ireland.

Most League Appearances: Fred Emery, 417, 1925–36.

Youngest League Player: Alick Jeffrey, 15 years 229 days v Fulham, 15 September 1954.

Record Transfer Fee Received: £275,000 from QPR for Rufus Brevett, February 1991.

Record Transfer Fee Paid: £300,000 to Manchester C for Matthew Mills, July 2008.

Football League Record: 1901 Elected to Division 2; 1903 Failed re-election; 1904 Re-elected; 1905 Failed re-election; 1923 Re-elected to Division 3 (N); 1935–37 Division 2; 1937–47 Division 3 (N); 1947–48 Division 2; 1948–50 Division 3 (N); 1950–58 Division 2; 1958–59 Division 3; 1959–66 Division 4; 1966–67 Division 3; 1967–69 Division 4; 1969–71 Division 3; 1971–81 Division 4; 1981–83 Division 3; 1983–84 Division 4; 1984–88 Division 3; 1988–92 Division 4; 1992–98 Division 3; 1998–2003 Conference; 2003–04 Division 3; 2004–08 FL 1; 2008– FL C.

LATEST SEQUENCES

Longest Sequence of League Wins: 10, 22.1.1947 – 4.4.1947.

Longest Sequence of League Defeats: 9, 14.1.1905 – 1.4.1905.

Longest Sequence of League Draws: 4, 29.10.1932 – 19.11.1932.

Longest Sequence of Unbeaten League Matches: 20, 26.12.1968 – 12.4.1969.

Longest Sequence Without a League Win: 20, 9.8.1997 – 29.11.1997.

Successive Scoring Runs: 27 from 10.11.1934.

Successive Non-scoring Runs: 7 from 27.9.1947.

MANAGERS

Arthur Porter 1920–21
Harry Tufnell 1921–22
Arthur Porter 1922–23
Dick Ray 1923–27
David Menzies 1928–36
Fred Emery 1936–40
Bill Marsden 1944–46
Jackie Bestall 1946–49
Peter Doherty 1949–58
Jack Hodgson & Sid Bycroft
 (*Joint Managers*) 1958
Jack Crayston 1958–59
 (*continued as Secretary-Manager to 1961*)
Jackie Bestall (TM) 1959–60
Norman Curtis 1960–61
Danny Malloy 1961–62
Oscar Hold 1962–64
Bill Leivers 1964–66
Keith Kettleborough 1966–67
George Raynor 1967–68
Lawrie McMenemy 1968–71
Morris Setters 1971–74
Stan Anderson 1975–78
Billy Bremner 1978–85
Dave Cusack 1985–87
Dave Mackay 1987–89
Billy Bremner 1989–91
Steve Beaglehole 1991–93
Ian Atkins 1994
Sammy Chung 1994–96
Kerry Dixon (*Player–Manager*) 1996–97
Dave Cowling 1997
Mark Weaver 1997–98
Ian Snodin 1998–99
Steve Wignall 1999–2001
Dave Penney 2002–06
Sean O'Driscoll September 2006–

TEN YEAR LEAGUE RECORD

		P	W	D	L	F	A	Pts	Pos
1999-2000	Conf.	42	15	9	18	46	48	54	12
2000-01	Conf.	42	15	13	14	47	43	58	9
2001-02	Conf.	42	18	13	11	68	46	67	4
2002-03	Conf.	42	22	12	8	73	47	78	3
2003-04	Div 3	46	27	11	8	79	37	92	1
2004-05	FL 1	46	16	18	12	65	60	66	10
2005-06	FL 1	46	20	9	17	55	51	69	8
2006-07	FL 1	46	16	15	15	52	47	63	11
2007-08	FL 1	46	23	11	12	65	41	80	3
2008-09	FL C	46	17	7	22	42	53	58	14

DID YOU KNOW ?

In 1954–55 Doncaster Rovers reached the fourth round of the FA Cup and drew 0–0 with Aston Villa. It was 2–2 at Villa Park in the replay, 1–1 at Maine Road and 2–2 at Hillsborough. A third replay produced Rovers as winners 3–1 after 510 minutes of the tie.

DONCASTER ROVERS 2008–09 LEAGUE RECORD

Match No.	Date		Venue	Opponents	Result		H/T Score	Lg. Pos.	Goalscorers	Attendance
1	Aug	9	A	Derby Co	W	1-0	0-0	—	Guy [59]	33,010
2		16	H	Cardiff C	D	1-1	0-0	8	Guy [67]	11,873
3		23	A	QPR	L	0-2	0-2	15		15,536
4		30	H	Coventry C	W	1-0	1-0	10	Wellens [31]	11,806
5	Sept	13	A	Birmingham C	L	0-1	0-0	14		18,165
6		16	H	Charlton Ath	L	0-1	0-1	—		10,483
7		20	H	Bristol C	L	1-4	0-0	19	Wellens [69]	15,960
8		27	H	Southampton	L	0-2	0-0	21		10,867
9		30	H	Sheffield U	L	0-2	0-1	—		14,242
10	Oct	4	A	Barnsley	L	1-4	1-0	23	Stock (pen) [11]	15,086
11		18	H	Blackpool	D	0-0	0-0	23		11,342
12		21	A	Reading	L	1-2	0-1	—	Van Nieuwstadt [74]	17,294
13		25	A	Norwich C	L	1-2	0-0	23	Stock (pen) [77]	24,543
14		28	H	Barnsley	L	0-1	0-1	—		13,251
15	Nov	1	H	Swansea C	D	0-0	0-0	24		9534
16		8	A	Sheffield W	L	0-1	0-1	24		20,872
17		15	H	Ipswich T	W	1-0	1-0	24	Martis [42]	10,823
18		22	A	Burnley	D	0-0	0-0	23		12,173
19		25	H	Nottingham F	D	0-0	0-0	—		12,612
20		29	A	Watford	D	1-1	0-1	24	Brooker [70]	14,008
21	Dec	6	H	Plymouth Arg	W	1-0	1-0	22	Stock [37]	10,187
22		9	A	Preston NE	L	0-1	0-0	—		13,152
23		13	A	Crystal Palace	L	1-2	1-1	23	Heffernan [15]	13,811
24		20	H	Wolverhampton W	L	0-1	0-0	24		13,669
25		26	A	Nottingham F	W	4-2	3-0	23	Heffernan 2 [12, 65], Woods M [33], Wellens [45]	26,501
26		28	H	Burnley	W	2-1	2-0	22	Coppinger [37], Stock (pen) [40]	14,020
27	Jan	17	A	Southampton	W	2-1	0-0	22	Woods M [46], Coppinger [81]	15,837
28		27	A	Sheffield U	W	1-0	0-0	—	O'Connor [50]	26,555
29		30	H	Norwich C	D	1-1	1-0	—	Heffernan [23]	12,384
30	Feb	7	A	Blackpool	W	3-2	1-1	19	Stock [26], Hird [54], Coppinger [84]	7452
31		14	H	Sheffield W	W	1-0	1-0	16	Heffernan [31]	14,823
32		17	H	Bristol C	W	1-0	1-0	—	Heffernan [4]	10,928
33		21	A	Swansea C	L	1-3	1-1	16	Coppinger [11]	16,161
34		27	H	Derby Co	W	2-1	0-0	—	Heffernan [56], Wilson [71]	14,435
35	Mar	3	A	Charlton Ath	W	2-1	0-0	—	Coppinger [50], Stock (pen) [78]	20,815
36		7	A	Cardiff C	L	0-3	0-2	15		17,821
37		10	H	QPR	W	2-0	2-0	—	Stewart (og) [23], Heffernan [30]	10,223
38		14	H	Birmingham C	L	0-2	0-2	14		11,482
39		17	H	Reading	L	0-1	0-0	—		10,393
40		21	A	Coventry C	L	0-1	0-1	15		18,498
41	Apr	4	H	Watford	L	1-2	0-2	16	Hayter [85]	12,126
42		11	A	Ipswich T	W	3-1	1-1	16	Roberts [9], Heffernan [74], Hayter [85]	19,918
43		13	H	Preston NE	L	0-2	0-1	16		11,648
44		18	A	Plymouth Arg	W	3-0	2-0	14	Spicer [15], Hayter [33], Heffernan [70]	11,100
45		25	H	Crystal Palace	W	2-0	1-0	13	Shiels [45], Hayter [75]	12,031
46	May	3	A	Wolverhampton W	L	0-1	0-0	14		28,252

Final League Position: 14

GOALSCORERS

League (42): Heffernan 10, Stock 6 (4 pens), Coppinger 5, Hayter 4, Wellens 3, Guy 2, Woods M 2, Brooker 1, Hird 1, Martis 1, O'Connor 1, Roberts 1, Shiels 1, Spicer 1, Van Nieuwstadt 1, Wilson 1, own goal 1.
Carling Cup (0).
FA Cup (4): Stock 2, Hird 1, Price 1.

Sullivan N 46	O'Connor J 31 + 1	Roberts G 27 + 5	Hird S 33 + 4	Mills M 41	Stock B 36	Coppinger J 29 + 3	Wellens R 39	Hayter J 13 + 14	Guy L 19 + 10	Taylor G 11 + 6	Chambers J 34 + 3	Woods M 36 + 5	Van Nieuwstadt J 9 + 7	Lockwood A 12 + 10	Elliott S 3 + 6	Byfield D 3 + 12	Price Jason 11 + 11	Heffernan P 19 + 9	Wilson M 15 + 7	Martis S 5	Spicer J 26 + 4	Brooker S — + 1	Ameobi T — + 1	Shiels D 6 + 6	Fairhurst W — + 3	LuaLua K 2 + 2	Woods G — + 1	Greer G — + 1	Match No.
1	2	3	4	5	6	7^3	8	9^2	10^1	11	12	13	14																1
1	2	3	4	5	6	7	8^1	9^2	10^3	11	12	13		14															2
1	2	3	4	5^1	6	7	8	9	10^2	11^3		13			12	14													3
1	2		4	5	6	7	8^3	9	10^2	11^1	3	13			12	14													4
1^1	2	3^1	4	5	6	7	8	9	10^2	11^3	12		13	14															5
1	2	3	4	5	6	7	8	9^1	10^3	11^2	13	12		14															6
1	2	3	4	5^1	6^2	7	8	9^3	10		13			12	11	14													7
1	2	3	4	5	6	7	8	12	11^2		10^1	9	13																8
1	2	3		5	6		8	12	13		11^3	4	10	9^1	14	7^2													9
1	2	3		5	6	7	8	12	10	9^2	11^1	4	13																10
1		3		5	6	12	13	10^2	2	8	14	4^3	11^1	9	7														11
1	2	12	4		6	7	9^2	10^3	3^1	11	5	13	14	8															12
1	12	3		5	6	7	10^3	2^1	11	4	14	13	9^2	8															13
1	2	3	12	5		7	13	10^3	4	6^1	11	9	14	8^2															14
1	2	3	12	5	6^3	9	11^2	7	10	13	8^1	4	14																15
1	2	3	4	5	6	8	12	13	10^2	9^3	14	7^1	11																16
1	2		4^3	5	6	8	12	13	11	7	9^2	10^1	3	14															17
1	2		4^2	5	6	12	8	13	10^3	3	7	9^1	14	11															18
1	2		5	6	7	8	9^2	10	3	11^3	12	13	4	14															19
1	2	12	5	6	7	8	13	9^3	4	11^2	3^1	10	14																20
1	2		4	5	6^2	7^1	8	12	9^2	3	10	13	14	11															21
1	2		4	5	6	7^1	12	9^2	3	10	8^3	14	13	11															22
1	2		5^4		8^2	12	14	3	7	13	6	10^3		9^1	11														23
1	2		6	8	10^2	12	7	3	5^1	13		9^3	9	13	11	14													24
1	2	12	4	5	6^2	14	8	10^3	3^1	7	9	13	11																25
1	2	12	4	5	6	10	8^1	14	3	7	9^2	13	11^3																26
1	2		4	5	6	9^1	8	10^2	13	3	7	14	12	11^3															27
1	2	12		5	6^2	8	7	10	4	3	14	9^3	13	11^1															28
1	2		4	5	6	9	8	12	3	13	10^2	7	11^1																29
1	2		4	5	6	9	8^1	3	7	13	14	10^2	12	11^3															30
1	2		4	5	6	9^2	8^1	3	7	12	14	10^3	13	11															31
1	2	12	4	5	6	9^3	8	3	7	13	14	10^2	11^1																32
1	2		4	6	9^1	8^4	3	7	5	13	12	10^3	11^2		14														33
1	3	4	5	6	9^2	2	7	12	14	13	10^3	8	11^1																34
1	3	4	5	6	9^3	8	2	7	12	13	10^2	11^1	14																35
1	3	4	5	6^2	9^1	8	12	2	7	10^3	13	11	14																36
1	11	4	5		9^2	8	12	3	7	2	10^1	6	13																37
1	3	4^3	5	6^2	9	8^1	12	2	7	14	10	13	11																38
1	3	5	6	9^1	8	2	7	4	10	11	12																		39
1	3^1	12	5	8	13	2	7	4	10^2	6^3	11	9	14																40
1	3	4^1	5	8^2	14	2	7	6	9	10^3	11	12	13																41
1	3	5	8	13	12	2	7	14	6^3	10^2	4	11^1	9																42
1	3	5	8	9	10^1	2	7^3	6	12	4^2	13	11	14																43
1	3	4	5	8^3	12	2	7	13	14	10	6^1	11	9^2																44
1^6	3	6	8	9	13	2	4	5	11	7^2	12	10^1	15																45
1	3^3	6	8	9	12	2	4	5	11	7^2	13	10^1	14																46

FA Cup

Third Round	Cheltenham T	(a)	0-0
		(h)	3-0
Fourth Round	Aston Villa	(h)	0-0
		(a)	1-3

Carling Cup

First Round	Notts Co	(a)	0-1

EVERTON

FOUNDATION

St Domingo Church Sunday School formed a football club in 1878 which played at Stanley Park. Enthusiasm was so great that in November 1879 they decided to expand membership and changed the name to Everton playing in black shirts with a scarlet sash and nicknamed the 'Black Watch'. After wearing several other colours, royal blue was adopted in 1901.

Goodison Park, Goodison Road, Liverpool L4 4EL.

Telephone: (0871) 663 1878.

Fax: (0151) 286 9112.

Ticket Office: (0871) 663 1878

Website: www.evertonfc.com

Email: everton@evertonfc.com

Ground Capacity: 40,158.

Record Attendance: 78,299 v Liverpool, Division 1, 18 September 1948.

Pitch Measurements: 100.48m × 68m.

Chairman: Bill Kenwright CBE.

Deputy Chairman: Jon Woods.

Chief Executive: Robert Elstone.

Secretary: David Harrison.

Manager: David Moyes.

Assistant Manager: Steve Round.

Head of Sports Medicine: Mick Rathbone Bsc (Hons), MCSP.

Colours: Blue shirts with white trim collar, white shorts, white stockings.

Change Colours: White shirts with dark navy collar, dark navy shorts, dark navy stockings.

Year Formed: 1878.

Turned Professional: 1885.

Ltd Co.: 1892.

Previous Name: 1878, St Domingo FC; 1879, Everton.

Club Nickname: 'The Toffees'.

Grounds: 1878, Stanley Park; 1882, Priory Road; 1884, Anfield Road; 1892, Goodison Park.

First Football League Game: 8 September 1888, Football League, v Accrington (h) W 2–1 – Smalley; Dick, Ross; Holt, Jones, Dobson; Fleming (2), Waugh, Lewis, E. Chadwick, Farmer.

HONOURS

Football League: Division 1 – Champions 1890–91, 1914–15, 1927–28, 1931–32, 1938–39, 1962–63, 1969–70, 1984–85, 1986–87; Runners-up 1889–90, 1894–95, 1901–02, 1904–05, 1908–09, 1911–12, 1985–86; Division 2 – Champions 1930–31; Runners-up 1953–54.

FA Cup: Winners 1906, 1933, 1966, 1984, 1995; Runners-up 1893, 1897, 1907, 1968, 1985, 1986, 1989, 2009.

Football League Cup: Runners-up 1977, 1984.

League Super Cup: Runners-up 1986.

Simod Cup: Runners-up 1989.

Zenith Data Systems Cup: Runners-up 1991.

European Competitions: European Cup: 1963–64, 1970–71. *European Cup-Winners' Cup:* 1966–67, 1984–85 (winners), 1995–96. *European Fairs Cup:* 1962–63, 1964–65, 1965–66. *Champions League:* 2005–06. *UEFA Cup:* 1975–76, 1978–79, 1979–80, 2005–06, 2007–08, 2008–09.

SKY SPORTS FACT FILE

Dave Watson played under five managers at Everton, three times with Howard Kendall, once each with Colin Harvey, Mike Walker, Joe Royle and Walter Smith. There were six managerial changes in his time – and he was caretaker himself in 1996–97!

Record League Victory: 9–1 v Manchester C, Division 1, 3 September 1906 – Scott; Balmer, Crelley; Booth, Taylor (1), Abbott (1); Sharp, Bolton (1), Young (4), Settle (2), George Wilson. 9–1 v Plymouth Arg, Division 2, 27 December 1930 – Coggins; Williams, Cresswell; McPherson, Griffiths, Thomson; Critchley, Dunn, Dean (4), Johnson (1), Stein (4).

Record Cup Victory: 11–2 v Derby Co, FA Cup 1st rd, 18 January 1890 – Smalley; Hannah, Doyle (1); Kirkwood, Holt (1), Parry; Latta, Brady (3), Geary (3), Chadwick, Millward (3).

Record Defeat: 4–10 v Tottenham H, Division 1, 11 October 1958.

Most League Points (2 for a win): 66, Division 1, 1969–70.

Most League Points (3 for a win): 90, Division 1, 1984–85.

Most League Goals: 121, Division 2, 1930–31.

Highest League Scorer in Season: William Ralph 'Dixie' Dean, 60, Division 1, 1927–28 (All-time League record).

Most League Goals in Total Aggregate: William Ralph 'Dixie' Dean, 349, 1925–37.

Most League Goals in One Match: 6, Jack Southworth v WBA, Division 1, 30 December 1893.

Most Capped Player: Neville Southall, 92, Wales.

Most League Appearances: Neville Southall, 578, 1981–98.

Youngest League Player: James Vaughan, 16 years 271 days v Crystal Palace, 10 April 2005.

Record Transfer Fee Received: £23,000,000 rising to £27,000,000 from Manchester U for Wayne Rooney, August 2004.

Record Transfer Fee Paid: £15,000,000 to Standard Liege for Marouane Fellaini, September 2008.

Football League Record: 1888 Founder Member of the Football League; 1930–31 Division 2; 1931–51 Division 1; 1951–54 Division 2; 1954–92 Division 1; 1992– FA Premier League.

MANAGERS

W. E. Barclay 1888–89
(Secretary-Manager)
Dick Molyneux 1889–1901
(Secretary-Manager)
William C. Cuff 1901–18
(Secretary-Manager)
W. J. Sawyer 1918–19
(Secretary-Manager)
Thomas H. McIntosh 1919–35
(Secretary-Manager)
Theo Kelly 1936–48
Cliff Britton 1948–56
Ian Buchan 1956–58
Johnny Carey 1958–61
Harry Catterick 1961–73
Billy Bingham 1973–77
Gordon Lee 1977–81
Howard Kendall 1981–87
Colin Harvey 1987–90
Howard Kendall 1990–93
Mike Walker 1994
Joe Royle 1994–97
Howard Kendall 1997–98
Walter Smith 1998–2002
David Moyes March 2002–

LATEST SEQUENCES

Longest Sequence of League Wins: 12, 24.3.1894 – 13.10.1894.

Longest Sequence of League Defeats: 6, 26.12.1996 – 29.1.1997.

Longest Sequence of League Draws: 5, 4.5.1977 – 16.5.1977.

Longest Sequence of Unbeaten League Matches: 20, 29.4.1978 – 16.12.1978.

Longest Sequence Without a League Win: 14, 6.3.1937 – 4.9.1937.

Successive Scoring Runs: 40 from 15.3.1930.

Successive Non-scoring Runs: 6 from 3.3.1951.

TEN YEAR LEAGUE RECORD

		P	W	D	L	F	A	Pts	Pos
1999-2000	PR Lge	38	12	14	12	59	49	50	13
2000-01	PR Lge	38	11	9	18	45	59	42	16
2001-02	PR Lge	38	11	10	17	45	57	43	15
2002-03	PR Lge	38	17	8	13	48	49	59	7
2003-04	PR Lge	38	9	12	17	45	57	39	17
2004-05	PR Lge	38	18	7	13	45	46	61	4
2005-06	PR Lge	38	14	8	16	34	49	50	11
2006-07	PR Lge	38	15	13	10	52	36	58	6
2007-08	PR Lge	38	19	8	11	55	33	65	5
2008-09	PR Lge	38	17	12	9	55	37	63	5

DID YOU KNOW ?

On 25 January 2009 the fifth round FA Cup meeting at Anfield between Liverpool and Everton was 107 years to the day of the first in the competition. The teams drew 0–0 as they had 2–2 then. The 2009 replay won 1–0 by Everton was the 22nd such clash in the Cup.

EVERTON 2008–09 LEAGUE RECORD

Match No.	Date	Venue	Opponents	Result	H/T Score	Lg. Pos.	Goalscorers	Attendance
1	Aug 16	H	Blackburn R	L 2-3	1-1	—	Arteta [45], Yakubu [64]	38,675
2	23	A	WBA	W 2-1	0-0	9	Osman [65], Yakubu [76]	26,190
3	30	H	Portsmouth	L 0-3	0-2	17		34,418
4	Sept 14	A	Stoke C	W 3-2	1-0	10	Yakubu [41], Anichebe [51], Cahill [77]	27,415
5	21	A	Hull C	D 2-2	0-1	9	Cahill [73], Osman [78]	24,845
6	27	H	Liverpool	L 0-2	0-0	14		39,574
7	Oct 5	H	Newcastle U	D 2-2	2-1	15	Arteta (pen) [17], Fellaini [35]	33,805
8	18	A	Arsenal	L 1-3	1-0	16	Osman [9]	60,064
9	25	H	Manchester U	D 1-1	0-1	14	Fellaini [63]	36,069
10	29	A	Bolton W	W 1-0	0-0	—	Fellaini [90]	21,692
11	Nov 1	H	Fulham	W 1-0	0-0	7	Saha [87]	31,278
12	8	A	West Ham U	W 3-1	0-0	7	Lescott [83], Saha 2 [85, 87]	33,981
13	16	H	Middlesbrough	D 1-1	0-1	7	Yakubu [65]	31,063
14	24	A	Wigan Ath	L 0-1	0-0	—		18,344
15	30	A	Tottenham H	W 1-0	0-0	7	Pienaar [51]	35,742
16	Dec 7	H	Aston Villa	L 2-3	1-1	8	Lescott 2 [30, 89]	31,922
17	13	A	Manchester C	W 1-0	0-0	7	Cahill [90]	41,344
18	22	H	Chelsea	D 0-0	0-0	—		35,655
19	26	A	Middlesbrough	W 1-0	0-0	6	Cahill [51]	30,253
20	28	H	Sunderland	W 3-0	2-0	6	Arteta 2 [10, 27], Gosling [83]	39,146
21	Jan 10	H	Hull C	W 2-0	2-0	6	Fellaini [18], Arteta [45]	37,527
22	19	A	Liverpool	D 1-1	0-0	—	Cahill [87]	44,382
23	28	H	Arsenal	D 1-1	0-0	—	Cahill [61]	37,097
24	31	A	Manchester U	L 0-1	0-1	6		75,399
25	Feb 7	H	Bolton W	W 3-0	1-0	6	Arteta (pen) [40], Jo 2 (1 pen) [49, 90 (p)]	33,791
26	22	A	Newcastle U	D 0-0	0-0	6		47,683
27	28	H	WBA	W 2-0	1-0	6	Cahill [36], Saha [70]	33,898
28	Mar 4	A	Blackburn R	D 0-0	0-0	—		21,445
29	14	H	Stoke C	W 3-1	2-0	6	Jo [18], Lescott [24], Fellaini [90]	36,396
30	21	A	Portsmouth	L 1-2	1-1	6	Baines [4]	20,388
31	Apr 5	H	Wigan Ath	W 4-0	1-0	6	Jo 2 [26, 51], Fellaini [47], Osman [61]	34,427
32	12	A	Aston Villa	D 3-3	2-1	6	Fellaini [19], Cahill [23], Pienaar [53]	40,188
33	22	A	Chelsea	D 0-0	0-0	—		41,556
34	25	H	Manchester C	L 1-2	0-1	6	Gosling [90]	37,791
35	May 3	A	Sunderland	W 2-0	0-0	6	Pienaar [48], Fellaini [71]	41,313
36	9	H	Tottenham H	D 0-0	0-0	6		36,646
37	16	H	West Ham U	W 3-1	1-1	5	Saha 2 (1 pen) [38 (p), 76], Yobo [48]	38,501
38	24	A	Fulham	W 2-0	1-0	5	Osman 2 [45, 88]	25,497

Final League Position: 5

GOALSCORERS

League (55): Cahill 8, Fellaini 8, Arteta 6 (2 pens), Osman 6, Saha 6 (1 pen), Jo 5 (1 pen), Lescott 4, Yakubu 4, Pienaar 3, Gosling 2, Anichebe 1, Baines 1, Yobo 1.
Carling Cup (0).
FA Cup (9): Saha 2, Arteta 1 (pen), Cahill 1, Fellaini 1, Gosling 1, Lescott 1, Osman 1, Rodwell 1.
UEFA Cup (3): Castillo 1, Jagielka 1, Yakubu 1.

Howard T 38	Neville P 36 + 1	Nuno Valente 1 + 1	Yobo J 26 + 1	Lescott J 35 + 1	Jagielka P 33 + 1	Arteta M 26	Rodwell J 9 + 10	Yakubu A 14	Osman L 32 + 2	Baines L 26 + 5	Baxter J 1 + 2	Vaughan J 1 + 12	Anichebe V 5 + 12	Castillo S 5 + 4	Fellaini M 28 + 2	Cahill T 28 + 2	Saha L 10 + 14	Hibbert T 16 + 1	Pienaar S 27 + 1	Van der Meyde A — + 2	Gosling D 6 + 5	Jutkiewicz L — + 1	Jo 11 + 1	Jacobsen L 4 + 1	Match No.
1	2	3¹	4	5	6	7	8	9	10																
1	2	13	4	5	6	7	8	9²	11	11	12														1
1	2		4	5	6	7	8	9	11²	3		10¹	12												2
1	2		4	3	5	11	12	9	3	13		10¹	12												3
1	2		4	12	5	11		9²	7			13	6²		8	7	10¹								4
1	6		4	3	5	11		9	7	3¹		13			6³	8	10	14							5
1				5	6	11									8	10¹	12	2¹							6
1	12			5	6	11	4	9¹	7	3		13	12		8		10¹	2	4²						7
1	2		4	5	6	11		9²	7	3		13			8³		14	2²	10						8
1	2		4	3	5	11¹	12	9²	6			13	12		8		10¹	3							9
1	2		4	3	5	11		9²	6			14			8	13	10³	7							10
1	2		4	3	5	11	6¹		7			13	12		8³	10	14		7¹						11
1	2		4	3	5	11		9²	7³	14		12	10³			8	9²	13							12
1	2¹		4	3	5	11		9	7			13	12		8	6¹	10		14						13
1	2		4	3	5	11		9²	7¹	12		13			8	6	10²								14
1	2²		4	3	5	11			7	12		14			8	6	13³		10	13					15
1	2		4	3	5	11			7	12			9¹		8	6			10						16
1	3		4¹	5	6	11			7				6		8	10			9						17
1	4			6	5	11				12					8	10			2	9	9				18
1	4			6	5	11			7²	3					8	10			2	7		13	14		19
1	4			6	5	11²	13		7	3			12		8¹	10³			2	9					20
1	4			6	5	11			7	3			12		8	10¹			2	9					21
1	4			6	5	11			7	3			9			10			2	8					22
1	4			6	5	11			7	3			12		8	10¹			2	9					23
1	4	12	6	5	11³	13			7	3		12			8¹	10			2	9	14	8	9		24
1	6		4	5	2	11³	8			3¹					10²				2	7¹		9			25
1	6		4		5				12	3		10²	14	13		12			7	9³					26
1	6		4	5	2	8²			7	3		14	8²	10	13	2¹	11			9¹					27
1	6		4	5	2				12	3			12	10	13		11			9¹					28
1	4			6	5	12			7	3			8	10³	13		11		13	9¹	2²				29
1	4			6	5	12			7	3			8		10		11		13	9					30
1	4			6	5				7	3			8³	10	14	2	11²			9²	12				31
1	6		4	5	12				13	7²	3		8	10	13	2¹	11			9³	2¹				32
1	6		4	5					7	3		8		10	14		11	14							33
1	6		4	5					12			3	12	10¹	8²	13	9³	2	11	7³	9²	2¹			34
1	2		4	5	6				12	3		14	8	10	13		11		7¹	9²					35
1	6		4	5					12	7	3		8	10	13		11		14	2					36
1	6¹		4	5				8	7	3		13	8¹	10³	9³		11	12							37
							3	14	13			10	9²	2	11³										38

FA Cup

Third Round	Macclesfield T		(a)	1-0
Fourth Round	Liverpool		(a)	1-1
			(h)	1-0
Fifth Round	Aston Villa		(h)	3-1
Quarter-Final	Middlesbrough		(h)	2-1
Semi-Final	Manchester U			0-0
(at Wembley)				
Final	Chelsea			1-2
(at Wembley)				

Carling Cup

Third Round	Blackburn R	(a)	0-1

UEFA Cup

First Round	Standard Liege	(h)	2-2
		(a)	1-2

EXETER CITY   FL Championship 1

FOUNDATION

Exeter City was formed in 1904 by the amalgamation of St Sidwell's United and Exeter United. The club first played in the East Devon League and then the Plymouth & District League. After an exhibition match between West Bromwich Albion and Woolwich Arsenal which was held to test interest as Exeter was then a rugby stronghold, it was decided to form Exeter City. At a meeting at the Red Lion Hotel in 1908, the club turned professional.

St James Park, Stadium Way, Exeter EX4 6PX.

Telephone: (01392) 411 243.

Fax: (01392) 413 959.

Website: www.exetercityfc.co.uk

Email: reception@exetercityfc.co.uk

Training Ground: (01395) 232784.

Ground Capacity: 8,830.

Record Attendance: 20,984 v Sunderland, FA Cup 6th rd (replay), 4 March 1931.

Record Receipts: £59,862.98 v Aston Villa, FA Cup 3rd rd, 8 January 1994.

Pitch Measurements: 114yd × 73yd.

Chairman: Denise Watts.

Football Secretary: Mike Radford.

Manager: Paul Tisdale.

Sports Therapist: Tamer James.

Secretary: Sally Cooke.

Colours: Red and white broad striped shirts, white sleeves with black trim, black shorts, black stockings.

Change Colours: All blue.

Year Formed: 1904.

Turned Professional: 1908.

Ltd Co.: 1908.

Club Nickname: 'The Grecians'.

Ground: St James Park.

First Football League Game: 28 August 1920, Division 3, v Brentford (h) W 3–0 – Pym; Coleburne, Feebury (1p); Crawshaw, Carrick, Mitton; Appleton, Makin, Wright (1), Vowles (1), Dockray.

Record League Victory: 8–1 v Coventry C, Division 3 (S), 4 December 1926 – Bailey; Pollard, Charlton; Pullen, Pool, Garrett; Purcell (2), McDevitt, Blackmore (2), Dent (2), Compton (2). 8–1 v Aldershot, Division 3 (S), 4 May 1935 – Chesters; Gray, Miller; Risdon, Webb, Angus; Jack Scott (1), Wrightson (1), Poulter (3), McArthur (1), Dryden (1), (1 og).

HONOURS

Football League: Division 3 best season: 8th, 1979–80; Division 3 (S) – Runners-up 1932–33; Division 4 – Champions 1989–90; Runners-up 1976–77. FL 2 – Runners-up 2008–09.

FA Cup: best season: 6th rd replay, 1931, 6th rd 1981.

Football League Cup: never beyond 4th rd.

Division 3 (S) Cup: Winners 1934.

SKY SPORTS FACT FILE

Left-winger Cliff 'Boy' Bastin was developed by Exeter City and apprenticed by them as an electrical engineer as well as a £5 a week professional. At 17 he was transferred to Arsenal for £2,000 and went on to win 21 full England intenational caps.

Record Cup Victory: 14–0 v Weymouth, FA Cup 1st qual rd, 3 October 1908 – Fletcher; Craig, Bulcock; Ambler, Chadwick, Wake; Parnell (1), Watson (1), McGuigan (4), Bell (6), Copestake (2).

Record Defeat: 0–9 v Notts Co, Division 3 (S), 16 October 1948. 0–9 v Northampton T, Division 3 (S), 12 April 1958.

Most League Points (2 for a win): 62, Division 4, 1976–77.

Most League Points (3 for a win): 89, Division 4, 1989–90.

Most League Goals: 88, Division 3 (S), 1932–33.

Highest League Scorer in Season: Fred Whitlow, 33, Division 3 (S), 1932–33.

Most League Goals in Total Aggregate: Tony Kellow, 129, 1976–78, 1980–83, 1985–88.

Most League Goals in One Match: 4, Harold 'Jazzo' Kirk v Portsmouth, Division 3 (S), 3 March 1923; 4, Fred Dent v Bristol R, Division 3 (S), 5 November 1927; 4, Fred Whitlow v Watford, Division 3 (S), 29 October 1932.

Most Capped Player: Dermot Curtis, 1 (17), Eire.

Most League Appearances: Arnold Mitchell, 495, 1952–66.

Youngest League Player: Cliff Bastin, 16 years 31 days v Coventry C, 14 April 1928.

Record Transfer Fee Received: £500,000 from Manchester C for Martin Phillips, November 1995.

Record Transfer Fee Paid: £65,000 to Blackpool for Tony Kellow, March 1980.

Football League Record: 1920 Elected to Division 3; 1921–58 Division 3 (S); 1958–64 Division 4; 1964–66 Division 3; 1966–77 Division 4; 1977–84 Division 3; 1984–90 Division 4; 1990–92 Division 3; 1992–94 Division 2; 1994–2003 Division 3; 2003–08 Conference; 2008–09 FL 2; 2009– FL 1.

MANAGERS

Arthur Chadwick 1910–22
Fred Mavin 1923–27
Dave Wilson 1928–29
Billy McDevitt 1929–35
Jack English 1935–39
George Roughton 1945–52
Norman Kirkman 1952–53
Norman Dodgin 1953–57
Bill Thompson 1957–58
Frank Broome 1958–60
Glen Wilson 1960–62
Cyril Spiers 1962–63
Jack Edwards 1963–65
Ellis Stuttard 1965–66
Jock Basford 1966–67
Frank Broome 1967–69
Johnny Newman 1969–76
Bobby Saxton 1977–79
Brian Godfrey 1979–83
Gerry Francis 1983–84
Jim Iley 1984–85
Colin Appleton 1985–87
Terry Cooper 1988–91
Alan Ball 1991–94
Terry Cooper 1994–95
Peter Fox 1995–2000
Noel Blake 2000–01
John Cornforth 2001–02
Neil McNab 2002–03
Gary Peters 2003
Eamonn Dolan 2003–04
Alex Inglethorpe 2004–06
Paul Tisdale June 2006–

LATEST SEQUENCES

Longest Sequence of League Wins: 7, 23.4.1977 – 20.8.1977.

Longest Sequence of League Defeats: 7, 14.1.1984 – 25.2.1984.

Longest Sequence of League Draws: 6, 13.9.1986 – 4.10.1986.

Longest Sequence of Unbeaten League Matches: 13, 23.8.1986 – 25.10.1986.

Longest Sequence Without a League Win: 18, 21.2.1995 – 19.8.1995.

Successive Scoring Runs: 22 from 15.9.1958.

Successive Non-scoring Runs: 6 from 24.11.1923.

TEN YEAR LEAGUE RECORD

		P	W	D	L	F	A	Pts	Pos
1999-2000	Div 3	46	11	11	24	46	72	44	21
2000-01	Div 3	46	12	14	20	40	58	50	19
2001-02	Div 3	46	14	13	19	48	73	55	16
2002-03	Div 3	46	11	15	20	50	64	48	23
2003-04	Conf	42	19	12	11	71	51	69	6
2004-05	Conf	42	20	11	11	71	50	71	6
2005-06	Conf	42	18	9	15	65	48	63	7
2006-07	Conf	46	22	12	12	67	48	78	5
2007-08	B Sq Pr	46	22	17	7	83	58	83	4
2008-09	FL 2	46	22	13	11	65	50	79	2

DID YOU KNOW

On 12 November 1910 Exeter City wore red and white shirts for the first time in their Southern League fixture with West Ham United in a bid to change the flagging fortunes of the team. They managed a goalless draw and results gradually improved.

EXETER CITY 2008–09 LEAGUE RECORD

Match No.	Date	Venue	Opponents	Result	H/T Score	Lg. Pos.	Goalscorers	Attendance
1	Aug 9	A	Darlington	D	1-1	0-1	—	Seaborne [60]	3559
2	16	H	Shrewsbury T	L	0-1	0-0	13		4916
3	23	A	Bournemouth	W	1-0	0-0	13	Harley [68]	5350
4	30	H	Luton T	L	0-1	0-0	14		5328
5	Sept 6	H	Accrington S	W	2-1	1-1	11	Gill [45], Watson [68]	3930
6	13	A	Bradford C	L	1-4	1-0	13	Gill [38]	12,683
7	20	H	Notts Co	D	2-2	1-0	13	Gill [22], Taylor [87]	4341
8	27	A	Macclesfield T	W	4-1	2-1	11	Stansfield 2 [1, 48], Harley [35], Gill [85]	1854
9	Oct 4	H	Gillingham	W	3-0	3-0	7	Logan [7], Stansfield 2 [39, 43]	4819
10	11	A	Bury	W	1-0	1-0	7	Logan [7]	3220
11	18	H	Grimsby T	D	0-0	0-0	7		5177
12	21	A	Port Vale	W	3-1	2-0	—	Stewart [17], Sercombe [18], Gill [65]	5493
13	25	A	Barnet	W	1-0	0-0	3	Gill [72]	2887
14	28	H	Chesterfield	L	1-6	0-2	—	Stansfield [49]	5093
15	Nov 1	H	Chester C	W	2-0	1-0	4	Stansfield [22], Taylor [88]	4448
16	15	A	Aldershot T	L	0-1	0-0	8		3784
17	22	A	Morecambe	D	1-1	0-1	8	Panther [85]	2003
18	25	H	Rotherham U	D	1-1	1-0	—	Watson [41]	3402
19	Dec 6	H	Lincoln C	W	2-1	0-0	6	McAllister [75], Moxey [90]	3916
20	20	H	Rochdale	W	4-1	2-0	5	Basham 2 (1 pen) [16, 31 (p)], McAllister 2 [84, 87]	4326
21	26	A	Wycombe W	D	1-1	0-1	5	Panther [57]	6094
22	28	H	Brentford	L	0-2	0-0	7		6791
23	Jan 10	A	Notts Co	L	1-2	1-2	—	Stewart (pen) [26]	3832
24	17	H	Bury	D	0-0	0-0	9		4158
25	20	A	Dagenham & R	W	2-1	1-1	—	McAllister 2 [27, 47]	2053
26	24	A	Gillingham	L	0-1	0-0	9		5638
27	28	H	Chesterfield	L	1-2	1-0	—	Moxey [17]	2894
28	31	H	Barnet	W	2-1	1-1	10	Saunders [20], Gill [73]	4145
29	Feb 7	A	Grimsby T	D	2-2	1-1	—	Stewart [8], Harley [79]	3324
30	10	A	Macclesfield T	W	4-0	2-0	—	Stansfield [16], Logan [44], Saunders [73], McAllister [75]	2839
31	14	H	Aldershot T	W	3-2	1-0	6	Stewart [30], Sandell (og) [78], Saunders [80]	4840
32	21	A	Chester C	D	0-0	0-0	8		1640
33	28	H	Darlington	W	2-0	0-0	5	Gill (pen) [72], McAllister [83]	4851
34	Mar 3	A	Shrewsbury T	D	1-1	0-0	—	Stewart [83]	4679
35	7	A	Luton T	W	2-1	2-1	6	Stansfield [4], Sercombe [29]	6460
36	10	H	Bournemouth	L	1-3	1-0	—	Stansfield [13]	4946
37	14	H	Bradford C	W	1-0	1-0	5	Moxey [20]	5253
38	21	A	Accrington S	L	1-2	1-1	6	Stansfield [5]	1169
39	28	A	Rochdale	D	2-2	0-1	6	Stewart 2 (1 pen) [55, 84 (p)]	3364
40	31	H	Port Vale	W	1-0	1-0	—	Prosser [29]	4235
41	Apr 4	H	Dagenham & R	W	2-1	1-1	2	Fleetwood 2 [16, 49]	5123
42	11	A	Brentford	D	1-1	1-0	4	Fleetwood [38]	8234
43	13	H	Wycombe W	W	1-0	0-0	2	Gill [64]	8183
44	18	A	Lincoln C	W	1-0	0-0	2	Burch (og) [88]	3934
45	25	H	Morecambe	D	2-2	0-1	3	Moxey [48], Harley [53]	8544
46	May 2	A	Rotherham U	W	1-0	0-0	2	Logan [71]	6184

Final League Position: 2

GOALSCORERS

League (65): Stansfield 10, Gill 9 (1 pen), McAllister 7, Stewart 7 (2 pens), Harley 4, Logan 4, Moxey 4, Fleetwood 3, Saunders 3, Basham 2 (1 pen), Panther 2, Sercombe 2, Taylor 2, Watson 2, Seaborne 1, own goals 3.
Carling Cup (1): Moxey 1.
FA Cup (2): Basham 1, Moxey 1.
J Paint Trophy (1): Harley 1.

Jones P 46	Tully S 35 + 1	Friend G 4	Edwards R 44	Seaborne D 31 + 2	Taylor M 29 + 2	Gill M 43	Stewart M 35 + 1	Stansfield A 32 + 5	Logan R 18 + 12	Harley R 25 + 6	Panther M 15 + 7	Basham S 12 + 11	McAllister C 8 + 22	Moxey D 41 + 2	Sercombe L 16 + 13	Watson B 4 + 8	Cozic B 14 + 6	Obersteller J 3 + 4	Shephard C — + 2	Murray F 3 + 3	Saunders N 15 + 2	Archibald-Henville T 19	Russell A 7	Fleetwood S 7 + 2	Match No.
1	2	3	4	5	6	7	8	9	10	11															1
1	2	3	4[1]	5	6	7	8	9[2]	10[3]	11	12	13	14												2
1	2	3	4	5	6	7	8	9[1]	10[2]	11				12	13										3
1	2[1]	3[2]	4	5	6	7	8	9[3]	10	11				13	14	12									4
1	2		4	5	6	7	8		10[3]	11[1]	12	13		3	14	9[2]									5
1	2		4[2]	5	6	7	8	9[3]	13	11				3	12	14	10[1]								6
1	2		4	5	6	7	8		12	13	11			3	10[2]	9[1]									7
1	2		4	5	6	7[1]	8	9[2]	10[3]	11				3	13	12	14								8
1	2		4	5	6	7	8[3]	9	10[2]	11[1]				3	13	12	14								9
1	2		4	5	6	7		9[2]	10[1]	11				3	12	13	14	8[3]							10
1	2		4	5	6	7	8[1]	9[3]		11	12			3	10[2]	13	14								11
1	2		4	5	6	7[1]	8	9			12			3	10	11									12
1	2		4	5	6	7	8	9[2]	10[1]					3	12	13	11								13
1	2		4	5	6	7	8[1]	9[3]	10[2]			13		3	12	14	11								14
1	2		4	5	6	7	8	9	10[2]					3	12	11	13								15
1	2		4[3]	5	6		8	9						3	12	10[2]	11		14	7[1]	13				16
1	2		4[2]	5			8[1]	9	10[3]	11		13		3	12	14				7	6				17
1	2			5			8[2]		10	11	12	13		3	4	9[1]	7[3]		14	6					18
1	2		6	5		7	8	9[1]	10[2]	11	12	13		3					14		4[3]				19
1	2		4	5	6	7	13	9[1]	10[2]	11	12			3	14			8[3]							20
1	2		4	5		7	8	9[1]		11	12		6	3	10										21
1	2		4	5		7	8[1]	9[2]	12	11		13	6	3	10[3]				14						22
1	2		4	5		7	8[1]	9[2]		11	12	13	6	3	10[3]				14						23
1	2		4	5		7		9[1]	10	11	12		6	3	8										24
1	2		6	5			8					9	4	3	11	10				7					25
1	2		6	5	13		8	9		14	4		12	11	10[1]							7[3]	3[2]		26
1	2		6	5	12	7		9	8	4[2]	14	10[3]	11	13								3[1]			27
1	2			5	6	7	9[2]		14	12	4	13	10[3]	11	3[1]						8				28
1	2[3]			5	6	8	10	13	14	12	4[1]	9[2]		11							7	3			29
1	12			5	6	7	8	9	10[2]	14	4		13	11[3]							2	3[1]			30
1	2			5	6	7	8[3]	9[2]	10[1]	4	12	13	11							14	3				31
1	2[1]		5	12	6	7	8	9[3]	10	13	4[2]	14									3				32
1				5	6	7	8[2]	9[3]	10			13	14	3	12						11	2[1]	4		33
1				5	6	7	8	13		12	9	10[2]		3[1]							11	2	4		34
1				5	6	7	8	9[1]	10[2]	12	11			3[3]	13						14	2	4		35
1				5	14	6	11	8	9[1]	10[2]	13	11	12	3[1]							2	4			36
1				5	6	7	8	9[1]	12	10[1]	11			3							2	4			37
1			5	3		7	8	9[1]		10[2]	11	6			12						2	4	13		38
1			5	6		7	8	9[3]		10[2]	13	11		3	12						2	4[1]	14		39
1			5	6[■]		7	8	9[2]	12	13	11			3	4						2	10[1]			40
1	2		5			7	8	9[1]	12	13	11			3	4						6	10[2]			41
1	2		5			7	8[1]		12	10	11			3	4						6	9			42
1	2		5			7		12	8	14	10[1]	13[3]	11	3[2]	4						6	9			43
1			5	6	4		12	7		10	11	3[1]		8							2	9			44
1			5	6	8		12	7	13	10[2]	11	4[1]									2	9			45
1	2		5	6	7		13	10	14	12	11	3[1]		8[2]							4	9[3]			46

FA Cup
First Round　　　　　Curzon Ashton　　　(a)　2-3

Carling Cup
First Round　　　　　Southampton　　　(h)　1-3

J Paint Trophy
First Round　　　　　Shrewsbury T　　　(h)　1-2

FULHAM   FA Premiership

FOUNDATION

Churchgoers were responsible for the foundation of Fulham, which first saw the light of day as Fulham St Andrew's Church Sunday School FC in 1879. They won the West London Amateur Cup in 1887 and the championship of the West London League in its initial season of 1892–93. The name Fulham had been adopted in 1888.

Craven Cottage, Stevenage Road, London SW6 6HH
Telephone: 0870 442 1222.
Fax: 0870 442 0236 (Motspur Park).
Ticket Office: 0870 442 1234.
Website: www.fulhamfc.co.uk
Email: enquiries@fulhamfc.com
Ground Capacity: 26,600.
Record Attendance: 49,335 v Millwall, Division 2, 8 October 1938.
Pitch Measurements: 100m × 65m.
Chairman: Mohamed Al Fayed.
Vice-chairman: Omar Fayed.
Chief Executive: Alistair Mackintosh.
Secretary: Darren Preston.
Manager: Roy Hodgson.
Assistant Manager: Mike Kelly.
Head of Sports Medicine and Exercise Science: Mark Taylor.
Colours: White shirts with black trim, black shorts, white stockings.
Change Colours: Red and white halved shirts, white shorts, red stockings.
Year Formed: 1879.
Turned Professional: 1898.
Ltd Co.: 1903.
Reformed: 1987.
Previous Name: 1879, Fulham St Andrew's; 1888, Fulham.
Club Nickname: 'Cottagers'.
Grounds: 1879, Star Road, Fulham; c.1883, Eel Brook Common, 1884, Lillie Road; 1885, Putney Lower Common; 1886, Ranelagh House, Fulham; 1888, Barn Elms, Castelnau; 1889, Purser's Cross (Roskell's Field), Parsons Green Lane; 1891, Eel Brook Common; 1891, Half Moon, Putney; 1895, Captain James Field, West Brompton; 1896, Craven Cottage.
First Football League Game: 3 September 1907, Division 2, v Hull C (h) L 0–1 – Skene; Ross, Lindsay; Collins, Morrison, Goldie; Dalrymple, Freeman, Bevan, Hubbard, Threlfall.
Record League Victory: 10–1 v Ipswich T, Division 1, 26 December 1963 – Macedo; Cohen, Langley; Mullery (1), Keetch, Robson (1); Key, Cook (1), Leggat (4), Haynes, Howfield (3).
Record Cup Victory: 7–0 v Swansea C, FA Cup 1st rd, 11 November 1995 – Lange; Jupp (1), Herrera, Barkus (Brooker (1)), Moore, Angus, Thomas (1), Morgan, Brazil (Hamill), Conroy (3) (Bolt), Cusack (1).

HONOURS

Football League: Division 1 – Champions 2000–01; Division 2 – Champions 1948–49, 1998–99; Runners-up 1958–59; Division 3 (S) – Champions 1931–32; Division 3 – Runners-up 1970–71, 1996–97.
FA Cup: Runners-up 1975.
Football League Cup: best season: 5th rd, 1968, 1971, 2000.
European Competitions: UEFA Cup: 2002–03. *Intertoto Cup:* 2002 (winners)

SKY SPORTS FACT FILE

Fulham used a number of local parks as home grounds before 1896. One was a piece of land behind the 'Half Moon' public house, which was a cricket ground also used by Wasps rugby club during the period 1890 to 1894.

Record Defeat: 0–10 v Liverpool, League Cup 2nd rd 1st leg, 23 September 1986.

Most League Points (2 for a win): 60, Division 2, 1958–59 and Division 3, 1970–71.

Most League Points (3 for a win): 101, Division 2, 1998–99. 101, Division 1, 2000–01.

Most League Goals: 111, Division 3 (S), 1931–32.

Highest League Scorer in Season: Frank Newton, 43, Division 3 (S), 1931–32.

Most League Goals in Total Aggregate: Gordon Davies, 159, 1978–84, 1986–91.

Most League Goals in One Match: 5, Fred Harrison v Stockport Co, Division 2, 5 September 1908; 5, Bedford Jezzard v Hull C, Division 2, 8 October 1955; 5, Jimmy Hill v Doncaster R, Division 2, 15 March 1958; 5, Steve Earle v Halifax T, Division 3, 16 September 1969.

Most Capped Player: Johnny Haynes, 56, England.

Most League Appearances: Johnny Haynes, 594, 1952–70.

Youngest League Player: Matthew Briggs, 16 years 65 days v Middlesbrough, 13 May 2007.

Record Transfer Fee Received: £11,500,000 from Manchester U for Louis Saha, January 2004.

Record Transfer Fee Paid: £11,500,000 to Lyon for Steve Marlet, August 2001.

Football League Record: 1907 Elected to Division 2; 1928–32 Division 3 (S); 1932–49 Division 2: 1949–52 Division 1; 1952–59 Division 2; 1959–68 Division 1; 1968–69 Division 2; 1969–71 Division 3; 1971–80 Division 2; 1980–82 Division 3; 1982–86 Division 2; 1986–92 Division 3; 1992–94 Division 2; 1994–97 Division 3; 1997–99 Division 2; 1999–2001 Division 1; 2001– FA Premier League.

LATEST SEQUENCES

Longest Sequence of League Wins: 12, 7.5.2000 – 18.10.2000.

Longest Sequence of League Defeats: 11, 2.12.1961 – 24.2.1962.

Longest Sequence of League Draws: 6, 14.10.1995 – 18.11.1995.

Longest Sequence of Unbeaten League Matches: 15, 26.1.1999 – 13.4.1999.

Longest Sequence Without a League Win: 15, 25.2.1950 – 23.8.1950.

Successive Scoring Runs: 26 from 28.3.1931.

Successive Non-scoring Runs: 6 from 21.8.1971.

MANAGERS

Harry Bradshaw 1904–09
Phil Kelso 1909–24
Andy Ducat 1924–26
Joe Bradshaw 1926–29
Ned Liddell 1929–31
Jim McIntyre 1931–34
Jimmy Hogan 1934–35
Jack Peart 1935–48
Frank Osborne 1948–64
(was Secretary-Manager or General Manager for most of this period and Team Manager 1953–56)
Bill Dodgin Snr 1949–53
Duggie Livingstone 1956–58
Bedford Jezzard 1958–64
(General Manager for last two months)
Vic Buckingham 1965–68
Bobby Robson 1968
Bill Dodgin Jnr 1968–72
Alec Stock 1972–76
Bobby Campbell 1976–80
Malcolm Macdonald 1980–84
Ray Harford 1984–96
Ray Lewington 1986–90
Alan Dicks 1990–91
Don Mackay 1991–94
Ian Branfoot 1994–96
(continued as General Manager)
Micky Adams 1996–97
Ray Wilkins 1997–98
Kevin Keegan 1998–99
(Chief Operating Officer)
Paul Bracewell 1999–2000
Jean Tigana 2000–03
Chris Coleman 2003–07
Lawrie Sanchez 2007
Roy Hodgson December 2007–

TEN YEAR LEAGUE RECORD

		P	W	D	L	F	A	Pts	Pos
1999-2000	Div 1	46	17	16	13	49	41	67	9
2000-01	Div 1	46	30	11	5	90	32	101	1
2001-02	PR Lge	38	10	14	14	36	44	44	13
2002-03	PR Lge	38	13	9	16	41	50	48	14
2003-04	PR Lge	38	14	10	14	52	46	52	9
2004-05	PR Lge	38	12	8	18	52	60	44	13
2005-06	PR Lge	38	14	6	18	48	58	48	12
2006-07	PR Lge	38	8	15	15	38	60	39	16
2007-08	PR Lge	38	8	12	18	38	60	36	17
2008-09	PR Lge	38	14	11	13	39	34	53	7

DID YOU KNOW ?

On 22 February 2009 there was a double cause for celebration when Fulham entertained West Bromwich Albion. It was manager Roy Hodgson's 50th game in charge of the club and Bobby Zamora ended his goal famine after 1,763 minutes in the 2–0 win.

FULHAM 2008–09 LEAGUE RECORD

Match No.	Date	Venue	Opponents	Result	H/T Score	Lg. Pos.	Goalscorers	Attendance
1	Aug 16	A	Hull C	L	1-2	1-1	—	Seol [8]	24,525
2	23	H	Arsenal	W	1-0	1-0	11	Hangeland [21]	25,276
3	Sept 13	H	Bolton W	W	2-1	2-0	6	Gera [15], Zamora [41]	23,656
4	20	A	Blackburn R	L	0-1	0-0	11		19,398
5	27	H	West Ham U	L	1-2	0-2	15	Murphy (pen) [59]	23,946
6	Oct 4	A	WBA	L	0-1	0-0	17		25,708
7	18	H	Sunderland	D	0-0	0-0	17		25,116
8	26	A	Portsmouth	D	1-1	0-0	16	Dempsey [87]	19,233
9	29	H	Wigan Ath	W	2-0	1-0	—	Johnson 2 [11, 60]	22,500
10	Nov 1	A	Everton	L	0-1	0-0	15		31,278
11	9	H	Newcastle U	W	2-1	1-0	10	Johnson [23], Murphy (pen) [66]	24,740
12	15	H	Tottenham H	W	2-1	1-0	10	Davies [33], Johnson [70]	25,139
13	22	A	Liverpool	D	0-0	0-0	9		43,589
14	29	A	Aston Villa	D	0-0	0-0	10		36,625
15	Dec 6	H	Manchester C	D	1-1	1-1	9	Bullard [27]	24,012
16	13	A	Stoke C	D	0-0	0-0	10		25,287
17	20	H	Middlesbrough	W	3-0	1-0	8	Bullard [41], Murphy (pen) [54], Dempsey [59]	23,722
18	26	A	Tottenham H	D	0-0	0-0	8		35,866
19	28	H	Chelsea	D	2-2	1-0	9	Dempsey 2 [10, 89]	25,462
20	Jan 18	A	West Ham U	L	1-3	1-1	10	Konchesky [22]	31,818
21	27	A	Sunderland	L	0-1	0-0	—		36,539
22	31	H	Portsmouth	W	3-1	1-0	9	Johnson [14], Nevland 2 [71, 80]	23,722
23	Feb 7	A	Wigan Ath	D	0-0	0-0	10		16,499
24	18	A	Manchester U	L	0-3	0-2	—		75.437
25	22	H	WBA	W	2-0	0-0	8	Zamora [61], Johnson [72]	22,394
26	28	A	Arsenal	D	0-0	0-0	9		60,102
27	Mar 4	H	Hull C	L	0-1	0-0	—		23,051
28	11	H	Blackburn R	L	1-2	1-0	—	Dempsey [2]	22,259
29	14	A	Bolton W	W	3-1	1-1	9	Johnson [42], Davies [56], Kamara [88]	22,117
30	21	H	Manchester U	W	2-0	1-0	9	Murphy (pen) [18], Gera [87]	25,652
31	Apr 4	H	Liverpool	L	0-1	0-0	9		25,661
32	12	A	Manchester C	W	3-1	0-1	8	Dempsey 2 [50, 83], Etuhu [59]	39,841
33	18	A	Middlesbrough	D	0-0	0-0	8		30,389
34	25	H	Stoke C	W	1-0	1-0	7	Nevland [29]	25,069
35	May 2	A	Chelsea	L	1-3	1-2	9	Nevland [4]	41,801
36	9	H	Aston Villa	W	3-1	1-1	7	Murphy (pen) [6], Kamara 2 [46, 60]	25,660
37	16	A	Newcastle U	W	1-0	1-0	7	Kamara [41]	52,114
38	24	H	Everton	L	0-2	0-1	7		25,497

Final League Position: 7

GOALSCORERS

League (39): Dempsey 7, Johnson 7, Murphy 5 (5 pens), Kamara 4, Nevland 4, Bullard 2, Davies 2, Gera 2, Zamora 2, Etuhu 1, Hangeland 1, Konchesky 1, Seol 1.
Carling Cup (3): Bullard 1, Gera 1, Murphy 1.
FA Cup (9): Johnson 3, Zamorah 2, Davies 1, Dempsey 1, Murphy 1, own goal 1.

Schwarzer M 38	Pantsil J 37	Konchesky P 36	Murphy D 38	Hughes A 38	Hangeland B 37	Davies S 33	Bullard J 18	Gera Z 20 + 12	Zamora B 32 + 3	Seol K 2 + 2	Dempsey C 28 + 7	Nevland E 4 + 17	Andreasen L — + 6	Kallio T 2 + 1	Baird C 3 + 7	Teimourian A — + 1	Johnson A 30 + 1	Stoor F — + 2	Etuhu D 19 + 2	Dacourt O — + 9	Milsom R — + 1	Brown W — + 1	Kamara D 3 + 9	Gray J — + 1	Smalling C — + 1	Match No.
1	2	3	4^3	5	6	7	8	9	10^1	11^2	12	13	14													1
1	2		4^3	5	6	7	8	9	10	11^2	13			3^1	12	14										2
1	2	3	4	5	6	7	8	11	10^2	12		13					9^1									3
1	2	3	4	5	6	7	8	11	10								9									4
1	2	3	4	5	6	7	8	11	10								9									5
1	2^3	3	4^2	5	6	7	8	11	9^1	12	10		13			14										6
1	2	3	4	5	6	7	8	11^1	10	12							9									7
1	2^2	3	4	5	6	7	8	11^1	10	12	13						9									8
1	2	3	4	5	6	7	8^2	11^1	10	12	14				13		9^3									9
1	2	3	4	5	6	7^3	8^2	11^1	10	12	14				13		9									10
1	2	3	4^3	5	6	7	8	11^1	10^2	12	13				14		9									11
1	2	3	4	5	6	7	8^2	12	10	11^1			13				9									12
1	2	3	4	5	6	7	8^2	12	10	11^1					13		9									13
1	2	3	4	5	6	7	8	12	10^1	11							9									14
1	2	3	4	5	6	7	8		10	11							9									15
1	2	3	4	5	6	7	8	11		10							9									16
1	2	3	4^3	5	6	7	8^2	11^1	12	10			13				9	14								17
1	2	3	4	5		7^1	8^2		10	11	12				6		9	13								18
1	2	3	4^1	5	6	7			10^2		11	13	14		12		9			8^3						19
1	2	3	4	5	6	7^1		12	10^3		11	14	13				9			8^2						20
1	2	3	4	5	6	7^1		12	10		11	13					9			8^2						21
1	2	3	4	5	6	7		12	10^2		11^1	13					9			8						22
1	2	3	4	5	6	7		12	10^2		11^1	13					9			8^3	14					23
1	2^1		4^2	5	6	7		11^3	10		9			3	8				12	13	14					24
1	2	3	4^2	5	6	7		10^1		11	12						9^3		8	13			14			25
1		3	4	5	6	7		12	10		11^1					2^2	9	13	8							26
1	2	3	4	5	6	7		10^1		11							9		8				12			27
1	2	3	4	5^2	6	7^1		11^3		10	12	13					9		8				14			28
1	2	3	4	5	6	7		10^2		11	12						9^1		8				13			29
1	2	3	4^3	5	6	7		12	10^2		11^1						9		8	14			13			30
1	2	3	4^1	5	6	7^2		13	10		11	14					9^3		8	12						31
1	2	3	4^3	5	6	7		12	10^2		11^1						9		8	14			13			32
1	2	3	4	5	6	7^1		12	10		11						9^2		8				13			33
1	2	3^3	4	5	6			11	10^1		7	12			14		9^2		8				13			34
1	2	3	4	5	6			11	10^2		7	9^1							8	13			12			35
1	2	3	4	5	6			11	12		7^2	9^1							8^3	14			10	13		36
1	2	3	4	5	6			11			7	9^1				12			8				10			37
1	2	3	4	5^3	6			11^2	12		7	9^1							8	13			10		14	38

FA Cup

Third Round	Sheffield W	(a)	2-1
Fourth Round	Kettering T	(a)	4-2
Fifth Round	Swansea C	(a)	1-1
		(h)	2-1
Quarter-Final	Manchester U	(h)	0-4

Carling Cup

Second Round	Leicester C	(h)	3-2
Third Round	Burnley	(a)	0-1

GILLINGHAM

FL Championship 1

FOUNDATION

The success of the pioneering Royal Engineers of Chatham excited the interest of the residents of the Medway Towns and led to the formation of many clubs including Excelsior. After winning the Kent Junior Cup and the Chatham District League in 1893, Excelsior decided to go for bigger things and it was at a meeting in the Napier Arms, Brompton, in 1893 that New Brompton FC came into being, buying and developing the ground which is now Priestfield Stadium. Changed name to Gillingham in 1913, when they also changed their strip from black and white stripes to predominantly blue.

KRBS Priestfield Stadium, Redfern Avenue, Gillingham, Kent ME7 4DD.

Telephone: (01634) 300 000.

Fax: (01634) 850 986.

Ticket Office: (01634) 300 000 (option 3).

Website: www.gillinghamfootballclub.com

Email: media@priestfield.com

Ground Capacity: 11,440.

Record Attendance: 23,002 v QPR, FA Cup 3rd rd, 10 January 1948.

Pitch Measurements: 110yd × 70yd.

Chairman: Paul D. P. Scally.

Chief Executive: Mark Jones.

Secretary: Gwen Poynter.

Manager: Mark Stimson.

Assistant Manager: Scott Barrett.

Physio: Paul Smith.

Colours: Blue with white insert.

Change Colours: Yellow with blue insert.

Year Formed: 1893.

Turned Professional: 1894.

Ltd Co.: 1893.

Previous Name: 1893, New Brompton; 1913, Gillingham.

Club Nickname: 'The Gills'.

Ground: 1893, Priestfield Stadium.

HONOURS

Football League: Best season 1999–2000. Division 3 – Runners-up 1995-96; Division 4 – Champions 1963–64; Runners-up 1973–74.

FA Cup: best season: 6th rd, 2000.

Football League Cup: best season: 4th rd, 1964, 1997.

First Football League Game: 28 August 1920, Division 3, v Southampton (h) D 1–1 – Branfield; Robertson, Sissons; Battiste, Baxter, Wigmore; Holt, Hall, Gilbey (1), Roe, Gore.

SKY SPORTS FACT FILE

In 1963–64 Gillingham won the Fourth Division title on goal average having conceded only 30 goals but had to win their last two games while their other rivals had completed fixtures. In fact the Medway club had to play four matches in eight days.

Record League Victory: 10–0 v Chesterfield, Division 3, 5 September 1987 – Kite; Haylock, Pearce, Shipley (2) (Lillis), West, Greenall (1), Pritchard (2), Shearer (2), Lovell, Elsey (2), David Smith (1).

Record Cup Victory: 10–1 v Gorleston, FA Cup 1st rd, 16 November 1957 – Brodie; Parry, Hannaway; Riggs, Boswell, Laing; Payne, Fletcher (2), Saunders (5), Morgan (1), Clark (2).

Record Defeat: 2–9 v Nottingham F, Division 3 (S), 18 November 1950.

Most League Points (2 for a win): 62, Division 4, 1973–74.

Most League Points (3 for a win): 85, Division 2, 1999–2000.

Most League Goals: 90, Division 4, 1973–74.

Highest League Scorer in Season: Ernie Morgan, 31, Division 3 (S), 1954–55; Brian Yeo, 31, Division 4, 1973–74.

Most League Goals in Total Aggregate: Brian Yeo, 135, 1963–75.

Most League Goals in One Match: 6, Fred Cheesmur v Merthyr T, Division 3 (S), 26 April 1930.

Most Capped Player: Mamady Sidibe, 7 (12), Mali.

Most League Appearances: John Simpson, 571, 1957–72.

Youngest League Player: Luke Freeman, 15 years 247 days v Hartlepool U, 24 November 2007.

Record Transfer Fee Received: £1,500,000 from Manchester C for Robert Taylor, November 1999.

Record Transfer Fee Paid: £600,000 to Reading for Carl Asaba, August 1998.

Football League Record: 1920 Original Member of Division 3; 1921 Division 3 (S); 1938 Failed re-election; Southern League 1938–44; Kent League 1944–46; Southern League 1946–50; 1950 Re-elected to Division 3 (S); 1958–64 Division 4; 1964–71 Division 3; 1971–74 Division 4; 1974–89 Division 3; 1989–92 Division 4; 1992–96; Division 3; 1996–2000 Division 2; 2000–04 Division 1; 2004–05 FL C; 2005–08 FL 1; 2008–09 FL 2; 2009– FL 1.

MANAGERS

W. Ironside Groombridge
  1896–1906 *(Secretary-Manager)*
  (previously Financial Secretary)
Steve Smith 1906–08
W. I. Groombridge 1908–19
  (Secretary-Manager)
George Collins 1919–20
John McMillan 1920–23
Harry Curtis 1923–26
Albert Hoskins 1926–29
Dick Hendrie 1929–31
Fred Mavin 1932–37
Alan Ure 1937–38
Bill Harvey 1938–39
Archie Clark 1939–58
Harry Barratt 1958–62
Freddie Cox 1962–65
Basil Hayward 1966–71
Andy Nelson 1971–74
Len Ashurst 1974–75
Gerry Summers 1975–81
Keith Peacock 1981–87
Paul Taylor 1988
Keith Burkinshaw 1988–89
Damien Richardson 1989–92
Glenn Roeder 1992–93
Mike Flanagan 1993–95
Neil Smillie 1995
Tony Pulis 1995–99
Peter Taylor 1999–2000
Andy Hessenthaler 2000–04
Stan Ternent 2004–05
Neale Cooper 2005
Ronnie Jepson 2005–07
Mark Stimson November 2007

LATEST SEQUENCES

Longest Sequence of League Wins: 7, 18.12.1954 – 29.1.1955.
Longest Sequence of League Defeats: 10, 20.9.1988 – 5.11.1988.
Longest Sequence of League Draws: 5, 28.8.1993 – 18.9.1993.
Longest Sequence of Unbeaten League Matches: 20, 13.10.1973 – 10.2.1974.
Longest Sequence Without a League Win: 15, 1.4.1972 – 2.9.1972.
Successive Scoring Runs: 20 from 31.10.1959.
Successive Non-scoring Runs: 6 from 11.2.1961.

TEN YEAR LEAGUE RECORD

		P	W	D	L	F	A	Pts	Pos
1999-2000	Div 2	46	25	10	11	79	48	85	3
2000-01	Div 1	46	13	16	17	61	66	55	13
2001-02	Div 1	46	18	10	18	64	67	64	12
2002-03	Div 1	46	16	14	16	56	65	62	11
2003-04	Div 1	46	14	9	23	48	67	51	21
2004-05	FL C	46	12	14	20	45	66	50	22
2005-06	FL 1	46	16	12	18	50	64	60	14
2006-07	FL 1	46	17	8	21	56	77	59	16
2007-08	FL 1	46	11	13	22	44	73	46	22
2008-09	FL 2	46	21	12	13	58	55	75	5

DID YOU KNOW ?

Midfield player Jackie Briggs made a goalscoring debut for Gillingham in 1946–47 in the 12–1 demolition of Gloucester City. As a former Royal Engineer he helped ex-Army colleague Hughie Russell to his nine goals which thoroughly undermined the opposition.

GILLINGHAM 2008–09 LEAGUE RECORD

Match No.	Date	Venue	Opponents	Result	H/T Score	Lg. Pos.	Goalscorers	Attendance
1	Aug 9	A	Bournemouth	D 1-1	0-1	—	Mulligan [90]	5377
2	16	H	Luton T	L 0-1	0-1	14		5339
3	23	A	Darlington	W 2-1	1-0	10	Jackson [21], Richards [90]	2831
4	30	H	Accrington S	W 1-0	0-0	9	Oli [75]	4733
5	Sept 6	H	Grimsby T	W 3-0	1-0	7	Jackson [34], McCammon [70], Daniels [89]	4912
6	13	A	Shrewsbury T	L 0-7	0-4	8		5319
7	20	A	Aldershot T	L 1-2	0-0	9	Jackson [84]	4198
8	27	H	Port Vale	W 1-0	1-0	8	McCombe (og) [34]	4986
9	Oct 4	A	Exeter C	L 0-3	0-3	9		4819
10	11	H	Morecambe	W 5-0	3-0	8	Bentley [21], Jackson 2 [24, 36], Artell (og) [73], McCammon [80]	4316
11	18	A	Bradford C	D 2-2	0-2	8	Jackson 2 [51, 84]	12,432
12	21	A	Notts Co	D 2-2	1-0	—	Mulligan [39], Southall [63]	4396
13	25	H	Chester C	W 2-0	0-0	8	Barcham [72], Mills [74]	4852
14	28	A	Lincoln C	L 0-2	0-2	—		4396
15	Nov 1	A	Macclesfield T	W 1-0	1-0	10	Miller [18]	1635
16	15	H	Rotherham U	W 4-0	1-0	7	King [6], Miller [58], Richards [78], Cumbers [88]	5304
17	22	A	Bury	L 0-4	0-2	10		2068
18	25	H	Rochdale	D 1-1	1-0	—	Jackson [17]	4029
19	Dec 6	H	Chesterfield	W 2-1	2-0	9	Miller [18], Jackson [45]	4622
20	13	A	Barnet	D 2-2	0-0	9	Barcham [67], Jackson [90]	2248
21	20	H	Brentford	D 1-1	0-1	11	Jackson [60]	5521
22	26	A	Dagenham & R	L 0-2	0-1	11		2844
23	28	H	Wycombe W	D 1-1	0-1	10	Weston [84]	5979
24	Jan 17	A	Morecambe	W 1-0	1-0	10	Weston [19]	2027
25	20	A	Port Vale	W 3-1	0-1	—	Oli [49], Miller [69], Jackson (pen) [72]	4539
26	24	H	Exeter C	W 1-0	0-0	5	Miller [79]	5638
27	27	H	Lincoln C	L 1-2	1-0	—	Jackson (pen) [25]	4525
28	31	A	Chester C	W 1-0	0-0	5	Barcham [79]	1541
29	Feb 7	H	Bradford C	L 0-2	0-1	—		4866
30	14	A	Rotherham U	L 0-2	0-1	10		2757
31	17	H	Aldershot T	D 4-4	1-1	—	Weston [21], McCammon [49], Barcham [55], Miller (pen) [72]	5974
32	21	H	Macclesfield T	W 3-1	1-0	9	King [2], Barcham 2 [74, 88]	4620
33	28	H	Bournemouth	W 1-0	0-0	6	Southall [58]	5353
34	Mar 3	A	Luton T	D 0-0	0-0	—		5739
35	7	A	Accrington S	W 2-0	1-0	7	Jackson [18], Oli [67]	1308
36	10	H	Darlington	W 1-0	0-0	—	Jackson (pen) [90]	4730
37	14	H	Shrewsbury T	D 2-2	1-0	6	Weston [4], Southall [51]	6023
38	17	A	Notts Co	W 1-0	0-0	—	Jackson [58]	3189
39	21	A	Grimsby T	L 0-3	0-1	3		6406
40	28	A	Brentford	D 1-1	0-1	4	Jackson (pen) [59]	7908
41	Apr 4	H	Barnet	L 0-2	0-1	6		6033
42	11	A	Wycombe W	L 0-1	0-1	6		6306
43	13	H	Dagenham & R	W 2-1	1-1	6	McCammon [8], Oli [88]	6945
44	18	A	Chesterfield	W 1-0	1-0	5	McCammon [22]	3933
45	25	H	Bury	D 0-0	0-0	5		8360
46	May 2	A	Rochdale	W 1-0	1-0	5	Weston [20]	3480

Final League Position: 5

GOALSCORERS

League (58): Jackson 17 (4 pens), Barcham 6, Miller 6 (1 pen), McCammon 5, Weston 5, Oli 4, Southall 3, King 2, Mulligan 2, Richards 2, Bentley 1, Cumbers 1, Daniels 1, Mills 1, own goals 2.
Carling Cup (0).
FA Cup (4): Barcham 3, Jackson 1.
J Paint Trophy (0).
Play-Offs (3): Jackson 3 (1 pen).

Royce S 42	Fuller B 37	Nutter J 43 + 2	Weston C 43 + 2	Richards G 26 + 10	King S 43	Bentley M 34 + 5	Crofts A 7 + 2	Jackson S 37 + 4	McCammon M 21 + 10	Miller A 32 + 3	Berry T 2 + 3	Mulligan G 12 + 14	Julian A 4	Mills L 6 + 1	Oli D 20 + 11	Southall N 28 + 8	Daniels C 5	Lewis S 13 + 8	Cumbers L — + 7	Jarrett A 11 + 5	Barcham A 31 + 2	Pugh A — + 1	Payne J — + 1	Peters J 1 + 2	Steer R 3 + 2	Wright J 5	Match No
1	2	3	4²	5	6	7	8	9	10	11¹	12	13															1
	2	3	12		6	7¹	8	9	10			4	13	1	5	11²											2
1	2	3	4²	5	6	13	8	9³	10	7¹		14				11	12										3
1	2	3	4²	5	6¹	12	8	9	10³	13		14				11	7										4
1	2	3	13	5	6			9	14	11	12	10³				7¹		4	8²								5
1	2	3	4	5	6	12	13	9	10²	11¹	14					7³	8										6
1	2	3	4	5	6	7	8	9	10⁴							11¹	12										7
1	2	3	4²	5	6	7	8	9								11	12	13	10¹								8
1	2	3	4¹	5	6	7²	8	9			12					11	10	13									9
1	2	3	4²		6	8		9			12	10¹		5		7		13		11³	14						10
1	2	3	4	13	6	8		9²		12		10¹		5		7				11							11
1	2	3	4	12	6¹	13	11	9³						5		7		14		8²	10						12
1		3	4	2	6			9	10¹	11²				5		7³		13		12	8	14					13
1	2	3	4		6			9	10¹	11				5		7				12	8						14
	2	3	4¹	5	6	8	12	9	11					1		7		13		10²							15
1	2	3	4¹	5	6	8		9³	12	11						7		13	14	10²							16
1	2	3	4³	5	6	8	12	13	11	9²						7¹		14	10								17
1	2	3	4	5³	6	8		9	12	11¹	13					7²		10									18
1	2	3	4	5	6	7		9		11¹		12				13		14	10²	8¹							19
1	2	3	4	5	6	7¹		9		11		12				13		10²	8								20
1	2³	3	4	5	6	8		9		10²						13	12	7¹	11								21
	3	4³	5	6	7			9²		11		13	1			12	2			14	10¹	8					22
1		3	4	5	6			9		11		12				10	2	8	7¹								23
1		3	4		6	5		10²		11		9³				7¹	12	2	13	8	14						24
1		3	4		6	5		10		11		9¹				7	12	2		8							25
1		3	4		6	5		10²		11		9³				7¹		2	13	8		12					26
1		3	4	5		6		9		11		10				7	2	8									27
1		3	4³	12	5¹	6		9		11		13				10²	7	2	8			14					28
1			5²	6	4			9	13	11						10³	12	2	8			7¹	14				29
1	2	3	4	12	5¹	6		9²		11		13				14	7	10³	8								30
1	2		4	5		6		12	13	11¹		9²				10	7		8					3			31
1	2	12	4		5	6		13	9	11						10²	7		8					3¹			32
1	2	12	4²	13	5	6		14	10	11³						9	7		8					3¹			33
1	2	3	4³	12	5	6		9¹	10	11		13				8²	7	14									34
1	2	3	4		5	6		9¹	10³	11²		12				8	7	13					14				35
1	2	3	4	12	5	6¹		9	10	11		13				8³	7²		14								36
1	2	3	4	12	5¹	6		9	10	11		13				7			8²								37
1	2	3	4	12	5	6		9¹	10²	11		13				7			8								38
1	2	3	4¹		5	6		9	10	11		12				7			8								39
1	2	3	4		5	6		9	10	11		12				7¹			8								40
1	2	3	4	13	5	6		9	14	12		10³				7¹		8²			11						41
1	2	3	4	6	5			9	10	11²		13				7¹		12	8								42
1	2	3	4	6	5	13		9	10²			12				11			8						7¹		43
1	2	3	4	6	5	13		9³	10¹			12				14	7		8						11²		44
1	2	3	4	6	5			9	10			12				11			8						7¹		45
	2	3	4¹	5		6				12			1			10	7	11	8						9		46

FA Cup

First Round	Bury	(a)	1-0
Second Round	Stockport Co	(h)	0-0
		(a)	2-1
Third Round	Aston Villa	(h)	1-2

Carling Cup

First Round	Colchester U	(h)	0-1

J Paint Trophy

Second Round	Colchester U	(h)	0-1

Play-Offs

Semi-Final	Rochdale	(a)	0-0
		(h)	2-1
Final	Shrewsbury T		1-0
(at Wembley)			

GRIMSBY TOWN FL Championship 2

FOUNDATION

Grimsby Pelham FC, as they were first known, came into being at a meeting held at the Wellington Arms in September 1878. Pelham is the family name of big landowners in the area, the Earls of Yarborough. The receipts for their first game amounted to 6s. 9d. (approx. 39p). After a year, the club name was changed to Grimsby Town.

Blundell Park, Cleethorpes, North East Lincolnshire DN35 7PY.

Telephone: (01472) 605 050.

Fax: (01472) 693 665.

Ticket Office: (01472) 605 050.

Website: www.gtfc.co.uk

Email: mailbox@gtfc.co.uk

Ground Capacity: 9,106.

Record Attendance: 31,657 v Wolverhampton W, FA Cup 5th rd, 20 February 1937.

Pitch Measurements: 111yd × 75yd.

Chairman: John Fenty.

Chief Executive/Secretary: Ian Fleming.

Manager: Mike Newell.

Assistant Manager: Stuart Watkiss.

Physio: Dave Moore.

Colours: Black and white striped shirts, black shorts, white stockings.

Change Colours: All blue.

Year Formed. 1878.

Turned Professional: 1890. *Ltd Co.:* 1890.

Previous Name: 1878, Grimsby Pelham; 1879, Grimsby Town.

Club Nickname: 'The Mariners'.

Grounds: 1880, Clee Park; 1889, Abbey Park; 1899, Blundell Park.

First Football League Game: 3 September 1892, Division 2, v Northwich Victoria (h) W 2–1 – Whitehouse; Lundie, T. Frith; C. Frith, Walker, Murrell; Higgins, Henderson, Brayshaw, Riddoch (2), Ackroyd.

Record League Victory: 9–2 v Darwen, Division 2, 15 April 1899 – Bagshaw; Lockie, Nidd; Griffiths, Bell (1), Nelmes; Jenkinson (3), Richards (1), Cockshutt (3), Robinson, Chadburn (1).

Record Cup Victory: 8–0 v Darlington, FA Cup 2nd rd, 21 November 1885 – G. Atkinson; J. H. Taylor, H. Taylor; Hall, Kimpson, Hopewell; H. Atkinson (1), Garnham, Seal (3), Sharman, Monument (4).

HONOURS

Football League: Division 1 best season: 5th, 1934–35; Division 2 – Champions 1900–01, 1933–34; Runners-up 1928–29; Division 3 (N) – Champions 1925–26, 1955–56; Runners-up 1951–52; Division 3 – Champions 1979–80; Runners-up 1961–62; Division 4 – Champions 1971–72; Runners-up 1978–79; 1989–90.

FA Cup: Semi-finals, 1936, 1939.

Football League Cup: best season: 5th rd, 1980, 1985.

League Group Cup: Winners 1982.

Auto Windscreen Shield: Winners 1998.

Johnstone's Paint Trophy: Runners-up 2008.

SKY SPORTS FACT FILE

The diminutive Jackie Bestall, skipper of Grimsby Town in the pre-war era, made 427 League appearances for the club. He was 34 years 226 days when he made his England debut against Northern Ireland. He has the smallest street in the area named after him.

Record Defeat: 1–9 v Arsenal, Division 1, 28 January 1931.

Most League Points (2 for a win): 68, Division 3 (N), 1955–56.

Most League Points (3 for a win): 83, Division 3, 1990–91.

Most League Goals: 103, Division 2, 1933–34.

Highest League Scorer in Season: Pat Glover, 42, Division 2, 1933–34.

Most League Goals in Total Aggregate: Pat Glover, 180, 1930–39.

Most League Goals in One Match: 6, Tommy McCairns v Leicester Fosse, Division 2, 11 April 1896.

Most Capped Player: Pat Glover, 7, Wales.

Most League Appearances: John McDermott, 647, 1987– 2007.

Youngest League Player: Tony Ford, 16 years 143 days v Walsall, 4 October 1975.

Record Transfer Fee Received: £1,500,000 from Everton for John Oster, July 1997.

Record Transfer Fee Paid: £500,000 to Preston NE for Lee Ashcroft, August 1998.

Football League Record: 1892 Original Member of Division 2; 1901–03 Division 1; 1903 Division 2; 1910 Failed re-election; 1911 re-elected Division 2; 1920–21 Division 3; 1921–26 Division 3 (N); 1926–29 Division 2; 1929–32 Division 1; 1932–34 Division 2; 1934–48 Division 1; 1948–51 Division 2; 1951–56 Division 3 (N); 1956–59 Division 2; 1959–62 Division 3; 1962–64 Division 2; 1964–68 Division 3; 1968–72 Division 4; 1972–77 Division 3; 1977–79 Division 4; 1979–80 Division 3; 1980–87 Division 2; 1987–88 Division 3; 1988–90 Division 4; 1990–91 Division 3; 1991–92 Division 2; 1992–97 Division 1; 1997–98 Division 2; 1998–2003 Division 1; 2003–04 Division 2; 2004– FL 2.

MANAGERS

H. N. Hickson 1902–20
(Secretary-Manager)
Haydn Price 1920
George Fraser 1921–24
Wilf Gillow 1924–32
Frank Womack 1932–36
Charles Spencer 1937–51
Bill Shankly 1951–53
Billy Walsh 1954–55
Allenby Chilton 1955–59
Tim Ward 1960–62
Tom Johnston 1962–64
Jimmy McGuigan 1964–67
Don McEvoy 1967–68
Bill Harvey 1968–69
Bobby Kennedy 1969–71
Lawrie McMenemy 1971–73
Ron Ashman 1973–75
Tom Casey 1975–76
Johnny Newman 1976–79
George Kerr 1979–82
David Booth 1982–85
Mike Lyons 1985–87
Bobby Roberts 1987–88
Alan Buckley 1988–94
Brian Laws 1994–96
Kenny Swain 1997
Alan Buckley 1997–2000
Lennie Lawrence 2000–01
Paul Groves 2001–04
Nicky Law 2004
Russell Slade 2004–06
Graham Rodger 2006
Alan Buckley 2006–08
Mike Newall October 2008–

LATEST SEQUENCES

Longest Sequence of League Wins: 11, 19.1.1952 – 29.3.1952.

Longest Sequence of League Defeats: 9, 30.11.1907 – 18.1.1908.

Longest Sequence of League Draws: 5, 6.2.1965 – 6.3.1965.

Longest Sequence of Unbeaten League Matches: 19, 16.2.1980 – 30.8.1980.

Longest Sequence Without a League Win: 22, 24.3.2008 – 1.11.2008.

Successive Scoring Runs: 33 from 6.10.1928.

Successive Non-scoring Runs: 6 from 11.3.2000.

TEN YEAR LEAGUE RECORD

		P	W	D	L	F	A	Pts	Pos
1999-2000	Div 1	46	13	12	21	41	67	51	20
2000-01	Div 1	46	14	10	22	43	62	52	18
2001-02	Div 1	46	12	14	20	50	72	50	19
2002-03	Div 1	46	9	12	25	48	85	39	24
2003-04	Div 2	46	13	11	22	55	81	50	21
2004-05	FL 2	46	14	16	16	51	52	58	18
2005-06	FL 2	46	22	12	12	64	44	78	4
2006-07	FL 2	46	17	8	21	57	73	59	15
2007-08	FL 2	46	15	10	21	55	66	55	16
2008-09	FL 2	46	9	14	23	51	69	41	22

DID YOU KNOW ?

On 17 January 2009 Grimsby Town inflicted the first home League defeat of the season on Wycombe Wanderers at Adams Park with a goal by Nathan Jarman in the 24th minute. Wycombe was the last Football League team to lose its home record.

GRIMSBY TOWN 2008–09 LEAGUE RECORD

Match No.	Date	Venue	Opponents	Result	H/T Score	Lg. Pos.	Goalscorers	Attendance
1	Aug 9	H	Rochdale	D	0-0	0-0	—		4213
2	16	A	Brentford	L	0-4	0-3	17		4009
3	23	H	Chesterfield	L	0-1	0-1	17		3306
4	30	A	Lincoln C	D	1-1	1-0	17	Till [38]	4573
5	Sept 6	A	Gillingham	L	0-3	0-1	20		4912
6	13	H	Chester C	L	1-3	0-1	20	North [52]	2950
7	20	A	Morecambe	D	1-1	1-0	20	Till (pen) [10]	1989
8	27	H	Barnet	L	0-1	0-1	21		3713
9	Oct 4	A	Rotherham U	L	1-4	1-0	21	Boshell [29]	3889
10	11	H	Wycombe W	D	1-1	1-0	21	Hegarty [2]	4562
11	18	A	Exeter C	D	0-0	0-0	21		5177
12	21	H	Luton T	D	2-2	1-1	—	Bore [1], Bennett [56]	4021
13	24	H	Bradford C	L	1-3	0-2	—	Trotter [65]	4470
14	28	A	Dagenham & R	L	0-4	0-2	—		1622
15	Nov 1	H	Darlington	L	1-2	0-2	22	Kalala [71]	3509
16	15	A	Bury	W	2-0	2-0	22	Trotter [17], Jarman [22]	2549
17	21	H	Bournemouth	D	3-3	2-1	—	Clarke [42], Bennett [44], Atkinson [61]	4353
18	25	A	Macclesfield T	L	0-1	0-0	—		1182
19	Dec 6	A	Port Vale	L	1-2	0-1	22	Proudlock [85]	5058
20	13	H	Shrewsbury T	W	1-0	0-0	21	Proudlock [53]	3283
21	20	A	Aldershot T	D	2-2	2-0	21	Kalala [2], Hegarty [39]	3605
22	26	H	Notts Co	L	0-1	0-1	22		5432
23	28	A	Accrington S	L	1-3	1-1	22	Proudlock [14]	1200
24	Jan 17	A	Wycombe W	W	1-0	1-0	22	Jarman [24]	4461
25	24	H	Rotherham U	W	3-0	0-0	22	Widdowson [56], Proudlock (pen) [73], Sinclair [84]	4559
26	27	H	Dagenham & R	D	1-1	1-1	—	Elliott [19]	3431
27	31	A	Bradford C	L	0-2	0-0	22		12,816
28	Feb 7	H	Exeter C	D	2-2	1-1	—	Jarman 2 [45, 54]	3324
29	10	A	Barnet	D	3-3	2-2	—	Bennett [25], Elliott [43], Forbes [78]	1554
30	14	H	Bury	L	1-2	1-0	21	Proudlock [31]	3673
31	21	A	Darlington	L	0-1	0-0	22		3418
32	24	H	Morecambe	L	2-3	1-0	—	Forbes 2 [21, 57]	2644
33	28	A	Rochdale	L	0-2	0-2	22		3076
34	Mar 3	H	Brentford	L	0-1	0-1	—		3001
35	7	H	Lincoln C	W	5-1	1-0	22	Proudlock 3 [42, 82, 84], Akpa Akpro 2 [78, 90]	5133
36	11	A	Chesterfield	L	1-2	0-0	—	Bennett [78]	2999
37	14	H	Chester C	D	1-1	1-0	23	Hegarty [21]	2836
38	17	A	Luton T	L	1-2	1-1	—	Bennett [43]	5830
39	21	H	Gillingham	W	3-0	1-0	22	Akpa Akpro [33], Hegarty [58], Conlon [90]	6406
40	28	H	Aldershot T	W	1-0	0-0	22	Conlon (pen) [82]	7095
41	Apr 4	A	Shrewsbury T	D	1-1	0-0	22	Conlon [55]	5535
42	11	H	Accrington S	L	0-1	0-0	22		6453
43	13	A	Notts Co	W	2-0	0-0	22	Atkinson [52], Boshell [79]	5890
44	18	H	Port Vale	W	3-0	2-0	22	Conlon 2 [4, 49], Jarman [21]	6511
45	25	A	Bournemouth	L	1-2	0-0	22	Jarman [41]	9008
46	May 2	H	Macclesfield T	D	0-0	0-0	22		6876

Final League Position: 22

GOALSCORERS

League (51): Proudlock 8 (1 pen), Jarman 6, Bennett 5, Conlon 5 (1 pen), Hegarty 4, Akpa Akpro 3, Forbes 3, Atkinson 2, Boshell 2, Elliott 2, Kalala 2, Till 2 (1 pen), Trotter 2, Bore 1, Clarke 1, North 1, Sinclair 1, Widdowson 1.
Carling Cup (3): Hunt 1, Newey 1, own goal 1.
FA Cup (1): Stockdale 1.
J Paint Trophy (3): Hegarty 1, Jarman 1, North 1.

Barnes P 32	Stockdale R 19+1	Newey T 23+1	Hunt J 21+1	Heywood M 16+2	Hope R 6	Till P 15+1	Heslop S 5+3	Butler M 3	Taylor A 3+3	Llewellyn C 13+15	North D 2+13	Bore P 10+17	Bennett R 45	Hegarty N 32+3	Boshell D 18+6	Clarke J 31+1	Jarman N 25+8	Vidal J 2+1	Trotter L 15	Kamara M 1+1	Aneobi T 2	Nornington G —+1	Kalala J 21	Atkinson R 30+1	Proudlock A 22+6	Akpa Akpro J 19+1	Widdowson J 19+1	Elliot S 9+2	Sinclair D 9	Forbes A 8+7	Henderson W 14	Sweeney P 8	Conlon B 8	Fuller J —+1	Match No.
1	2	3	4	5	6	7	8	9²	10¹	11	12	13																							1
1		3	4	5	6	7	8	9	10²	11¹	12			2	13																				2
1		3	4	5		7¹	8²	9	10	11³	13	12		2	6	14																			3
1		3	4	5		7	8²					13	14	12	2	6¹	11	10	9³																4
1		3	4	5		7	8²					14	13	2	10	11	6¹	9³	12																5
1		3	4	5		7	12			11²	13			2	6¹	10	9	8																	6
1	13	3	4	5		7				12				2	10	11	9	6²	8¹																7
1	2	3	4¹	5		7	12			11²	13		6		14	8	10	9³																	8
1		3	4	5		7²	12				13			2	6	8	10		11		9¹														9
1		3	4	5		7¹	13					10²	6	11		2	9	8	12																10
1		3	4³	5		7				12	13	10	6	11¹		2	9²	8					14												11
1		3	4	5		7				12	13	10	6	11¹		2	9²	8																	12
1		3	4²	5		7					13	12	10	6	11		2	9¹	8																13
1		3	4	5		7²				12	9³	10	6	13	11¹		2	14	8																14
1	2	3		5²		7		9		12				6	10	11¹	8						4	13											15
1	2	3								12	13	5	11³	14	7	9²	8						4⁴	6	10¹										16
1	2	3										12	5	11³	8	4	11	7	9¹					6	10										17
1	2	3											12	5		11	7	9¹					4	6	10										18
1	2							3					12	5		11	7	9¹					4	6	10										19
1	2							3						5	11		7						4	6	10	9									20
1	2							3						5	11		7	12					4	6	10¹	9									21
1	2²							3			12		13	5	8	11¹	7	14					4	6	10³	9									22
1		8¹		12									2	5	3	13	7²	11					4	6	10	9									23
1										12				5			2	7					4	6	10¹	9	3	11	8						24
1										13				12	5		2	7¹					4²	6	10	9	3	11	8						25
1													9	5			2	7					4	6	10		3	11	8						26
1					12								13	5			2	7¹					4⁴		10	9²	3	11	8						27
1		6										12	14	5	13		2	7¹					4	10		3	11	8²	9³						28
1												13	5	12			2	8					4	6	10²	3	11	7	9¹						29
1										11	13		2	5	12		8						4	6	10	3		7¹	9²						30
1		3										10⁴	12	5	11		2	7					4	6	8				9¹						31
1		3										10⁴	12	5	11		2	7					4	6				8	9¹						32
		3³											5	11	12		2	7					4	6	10²	13		14	8¹	9	1				33
										12			5	11³	8		2	7¹					4	6	13	9	3	14	10²	1					34
		3								12			5	8		7	2	13					4¹	6	10²	9	14	11³		1					35
		3								12			5	8		7	2	13					4²	6	10³	9	11¹	14		1					36
		3	4							12			5	8		7¹	2	13						6	10³	9	11²	14		1					37
	2		4²							12			11	13	7¹	5	8							6	9	3		10		1					38
	2		4							11			5	8			6							12	9¹	3				1		7	10		39
	2		4							11¹	12		5	8			6							13	9²	3				1		7	10		40
	2		4							11¹			5	8	12		6								9	3				1		7	10		41
	2		4							11²			5	8			6	12							9¹	3	13			1		7	10		42
	2												5	8	7		6								10	9¹	3	12		1		4	11		43
	2									13			5	8²	11³	14	7							6	10¹	3	12			1		4	9		44
	2		12										5	8	11⁴		7³							6	14	9	3⁴	13		1		4¹	10²		45
	2									11³	7		5	8		3	6	12						9²	13					1		4	10¹	14	46

FA Cup

First Round	Morecambe	(a)	1-2

Carling Cup

First Round	Tranmere R	(h)	2-0
Second Round	Blackburn R	(a)	1-4

J Paint Trophy

First Round	Chesterfield	(a)	2-2
Second Round	Scunthorpe U	(a)	1-2

HARTLEPOOL UNITED   FL Championship 1

FOUNDATION

The inspiration for the launching of Hartlepool United was the West Hartlepool club which won the FA Amateur Cup in 1904–05. They had been in existence since 1881 and their Cup success led in 1908 to the formation of the new professional concern which first joined the North-Eastern League. In those days they were Hartlepools United and won the Durham Senior Cup in their first two seasons.

Victoria Park, Clarence Road, Hartlepool TS24 8BZ.
Telephone: (01429) 272 584.
Fax: (01429) 863 007.
Ticket Office: (01429) 272 584 (option 2).
Website: www.hartlepoolunited.co.uk
Email: enquires@hartlepoolunited.co.uk
Ground Capacity: 7,630.
Record Attendance: 17,426 v Manchester U, FA Cup 3rd rd, 5 January 1957.
Pitch Measurements: 110yd × 74yd.
Chairman: Ken Hodcroft.
Chief Executive: Russ Green.
Senior Administrator: Maureen Smith.
Director of Sport: Chris Turner.
Assistant Coach: Colin West.
Physio: James Haycock.

HONOURS

Football League: FL 2 – Runners-up 2006–07; Division 3 – Runners-up 2002–03; Division 3 (N) – Runners-up 1956–57.
FA Cup: best season: 4th rd, 1955, 1978, 1989, 1993, 2005, 2009.
Football League Cup, best season: 4th rd, 1975.

Colours: White shirts with blue trim, blue shorts, white stockings.
Change Colours: Red and black striped shirts, black shorts, black stockings.
Year Formed: 1908.
Turned Professional: 1908.
Ltd Co.: 1908.
Previous Names: 1908, Hartlepools United; 1968, Hartlepool; 1977, Hartlepool United.
Club Nickname: 'The Pool'.
Ground: 1908, Victoria Park.
First Football League Game: 27 August 1921, Division 3 (N), v Wrexham (a) W 2–0 – Gill; Thomas, Crilly; Dougherty, Hopkins, Short; Kessler, Mulholland (1), Lister (1), Robertson, Donald.
Record League Victory: 10–1 v Barrow, Division 4, 4 April 1959 – Oakley; Cameron, Waugh; Johnson, Moore, Anderson; Scott (1), Langland (1), Smith (3), Clark (2), Luke (2), (1 og).
Record Cup Victory: 6–0 v North Shields, FA Cup 1st rd, 30 November 1946 – Heywood; Brown, Gregory; Spelman, Lambert, Jones; Price, Scott (2), Sloan (4), Moses, McMahon; 6–0 v Gainsborough Trinity (a), FA Cup 1st rd, 10 November 2007 – Budtz; McCunnie, Humphreys, Liddle (1) (Antwi), Nelson, Clark, Moore (1), Sweeney, Barker (2) (Monkhouse), Mackay (Porter 1), Brown (1).

SKY SPORTS FACT FILE

On 3 January 2009 Hartlepool United achieved some measure of revenge in the FA Cup third round when they defeated Stoke City 2–0. At the same stage of the 1953–54 competition they had suffered a 6–2 reverse at the Victoria Ground against the same club.

Record Defeat: 1–10 v Wrexham, Division 4, 3 March 1962.

Most League Points (2 for a win): 60, Division 4, 1967–68.

Most League Points (3 for a win): 88, FL 2, 2006–07.

Most League Goals: 90, Division 3 (N), 1956–57.

Highest League Scorer in Season: William Robinson, 28, Division 3 (N), 1927–28; Joe Allon, 28, Division 4, 1990–91.

Most League Goals in Total Aggregate: Ken Johnson, 98, 1949–64.

Most League Goals in One Match: 5, Harry Simmons v Wigan Borough, Division 3 (N), 1 January 1931; 5, Bobby Folland v Oldham Ath, Division 3 (N), 15 April 1961.

Most Capped Player: Ambrose Fogarty, 1 (11), Republic of Ireland.

Most League Appearances: Wattie Moore, 447, 1948–64.

Youngest League Player: David Foley, 16 years 105 days v Port Vale, 25 August 2003.

Record Transfer Fee Received: £750,000 from Ipswich T for Tommy Miller, July 2001.

Record Transfer Fee Paid: £75,000 to Northampton for Chris Freestone, March 1993; £75,000 to Notts Co for Gary Jones, March 1999; £75,000 to Mansfield T for Darrell Clarke, July 2001.

Football League Record: 1921 Original Member of Division 3 (N); 1958–68 Division 4; 1968–69 Division 3; 1969–91 Division 4; 1991–92 Division 3; 1992–94 Division 2; 1994–2003 Division 3; 2003–04 Division 2; 2004–06 FL 1; 2006–07 FL 2; 2007– FL 1.

LATEST SEQUENCES

Longest Sequence of League Wins: 9, 18.11.2006 – 1.1.2007.

Longest Sequence of League Defeats: 8, 27.1.1993 – 27.2.1993.

Longest Sequence of League Draws: 5, 24.2.2001 – 17.3.2001.

Longest Sequence of Unbeaten League Matches: 23, 18.11.2006 – 30.3.2007.

Longest Sequence Without a League Win: 18, 9.1.1993 – 3.4.1993.

Successive Scoring Runs: 27 from 18.11.2006.

Successive Non-scoring Runs: 11 from 9.1.1993.

MANAGERS

Alfred Priest 1908–12
Percy Humphreys 1912–13
Jack Manners 1913–20
Cecil Potter 1920–22
David Gordon 1922–24
Jack Manners 1924–27
Bill Norman 1927–31
Jack Carr 1932–35
(had been Player-Coach since 1931)
Jimmy Hamilton 1935–43
Fred Westgarth 1943–57
Ray Middleton 1957–59
Bill Robinson 1959–62
Allenby Chilton 1962–63
Bob Gurney 1963–64
Alvan Williams 1964–65
Geoff Twentyman 1965
Brian Clough 1965–67
Angus McLean 1967–70
John Simpson 1970–71
Len Ashurst 1971–74
Ken Hale 1974–76
Billy Horner 1976–83
Johnny Duncan 1983
Mike Docherty 1983
Billy Horner 1984–86
John Bird 1986–88
Bobby Moncur 1988–89
Cyril Knowles 1989–91
Alan Murray 1991–93
Viv Busby 1993
John MacPhail 1993–94
David McCreery 1994–95
Keith Houchen 1995–96
Mick Tait 1996–99
Chris Turner 1999–2002
Mike Newell 2002–03
Neale Cooper 2003–05
Martin Scott 2005–06
Danny Wilson 2006–08
Chris Turner December 2008–

TEN YEAR LEAGUE RECORD

		P	W	D	L	F	A	Pts	Pos
1999-2000	Div 3	46	21	9	16	60	49	72	7
2000-01	Div 3	46	21	14	11	71	54	77	4
2001-02	Div 3	46	20	11	15	74	48	71	7
2002-03	Div 3	46	24	13	9	71	51	85	2
2003-04	Div 2	46	20	13	13	76	61	73	6
2004-05	FL 1	46	21	8	17	76	66	71	6
2005-06	FL 1	46	11	17	18	44	59	50	21
2006-07	FL 2	46	26	10	10	65	40	88	2
2007-08	FL 1	46	15	9	22	63	66	54	15
2008-09	FL 1	46	13	11	22	66	79	50	19

DID YOU KNOW ?

In 1950–51 Eric Wildon came within two goals of Billy Robinson's still standing goal scoring record for Hartlepool United. Discovered in RAF football in the wartime Far East he had been signed in 1947 under the noses of Charlton Athletic, Hull City and Middlesbrough.

HARTLEPOOL UNITED 2008–09 LEAGUE RECORD

Match No.	Date	Venue	Opponents	Result	H/T Score	Lg. Pos.	Goalscorers	Attendance
1	Aug 9	H	Colchester U	W 4-2	2-0	—	Brown 2 [13, 14], Boland [66], Jones [76]	3831
2	16	A	Tranmere R	L 0-1	0-1	9		5418
3	23	H	Stockport Co	L 0-1	0-0	16		3945
4	30	A	Peterborough U	W 2-1	0-0	7	Monkhouse [58], Barker [59]	5728
5	Sept 6	A	Millwall	L 0-2	0-2	14		7207
6	12	H	Cheltenham T	W 4-1	1-0	—	Brown [20], Gallinagh (og) [48], Monkhouse [62], MacKay [87]	3637
7	20	H	Oldham Ath	D 3-3	0-2	9	Monkhouse [48], Sweeney [49], Porter (pen) [53]	4507
8	27	A	Leicester C	L 0-1	0-1	12		18,578
9	Oct 3	H	Swindon T	D 3-3	0-2	—	Porter 3 [53, 82, 90]	4018
10	10	A	Northampton T	L 0-1	0-1	—		5277
11	18	H	Walsall	W 3-2	0-2	14	Sweeney [72], Robson [76], Brown [83]	4142
12	21	H	Huddersfield T	W 5-3	2-3	—	Kyle 2 [26, 86], Brown [40], Porter 2 (1 pen) [83 (p), 89]	3771
13	25	H	Brighton & HA	W 1-0	1-0	12	Kyle [12]	3962
14	28	A	Carlisle U	W 1-0	1-0	—	Brown [28]	5637
15	Nov 1	A	Leyton Orient	L 0-1	0-0	10		3638
16	15	H	Milton Keynes D	L 1-3	0-2	12	O'Hanlon (og) [47]	4021
17	22	A	Leeds U	L 1-4	1-1	12	Porter [25]	21,182
18	25	H	Bristol R	D 1-1	1-1	—	Nelson [6]	3171
19	Dec 6	H	Yeovil T	D 0-0	0-0	13		3393
20	13	A	Hereford U	D 1-1	0-1	13	Beckwith (og) [48]	2490
21	19	H	Southend U	W 3-0	2-0	—	Kyle 2 [4, 61], Robson [36]	3123
22	26	A	Scunthorpe U	L 0-3	0-1	13		5347
23	28	H	Crewe Alex	L 1-4	0-1	15	Porter [48]	3877
24	Jan 12	A	Oldham Ath	L 1-2	0-1	—	Lomax (og) [67]	4211
25	16	H	Northampton T	W 2-0	1-0	—	Porter 2 [5, 56]	3814
26	27	H	Carlisle U	D 2-2	0-2	—	Monkhouse [59], Porter [85]	3765
27	31	A	Brighton & HA	L 1-2	1-0	16	Nelson [20]	5784
28	Feb 3	A	Huddersfield T	D 1-1	1-1	—	Jones [37]	9294
29	7	H	Walsall	D 2-2	1-1	—	Gerrard (og) [36], Porter [64]	3286
30	14	A	Milton Keynes D	L 1-3	1-1	17	Lange [36]	8657
31	17	H	Leicester C	D 2-2	1-1	—	Porter (pen) [32], Monkhouse [90]	4068
32	21	A	Leyton Orient	L 0-1	0-0	16		3678
33	24	A	Swindon T	W 1-0	0-0	—	Clark (pen) [90]	6010
34	28	A	Colchester U	D 1-1	0-1	15	Nelson [71]	5158
35	Mar 3	H	Tranmere R	W 2-1	0-0	—	Nelson [69], Clark (pen) [83]	3033
36	7	H	Peterborough U	L 1-2	1-1	15	Monkhouse [38]	3722
37	10	A	Stockport Co	L 1-2	0-0	—	MacKay [85]	4790
38	14	A	Cheltenham T	L 0-2	0-1	15		2945
39	21	H	Millwall	L 2-3	2-0	15	Sweeney 2 [23, 25]	3601
40	27	A	Southend U	L 2-3	1-3	—	Porter (pen) [33], Jones [62]	7227
41	Apr 4	H	Hereford U	W 4-2	2-2	16	Porter 2 (1 pen) [9, 14 (p)], Collins [78], Sweeney [81]	3579
42	11	A	Crewe Alex	D 0-0	0-0	18		4477
43	13	H	Scunthorpe U	L 2-3	1-1	18	Nelson [18], Nardiello [77]	3998
44	18	H	Yeovil T	W 3-2	2-1	18	Porter 2 (1 pen) [13 (p), 45], Nardiello [72]	4232
45	25	H	Leeds U	L 0-1	0-0	18		6402
46	May 2	A	Bristol R	L 1-4	1-2	19	Nardiello [28]	7363

Final League Position: 19

GOALSCORERS

League (66): Porter 18 (6 pens), Brown 6, Monkhouse 6, Kyle 5, Nelson 5, Sweeney 5, Jones 3, Nardiello 3, Clark 2 (2 pens), MacKay 2, Robson 2, Barker 1, Boland 1, Collins 1, Lange 1, own goals 5.
Carling Cup (8): Porter 3, Foley 2, Barker 1, Brown 1, Monkhouse 1.
FA Cup (10): Mackay 2, Porter 2 (1 pen), Brown 1, Foley 1, Liddle 1, Monkhouse 1, Nelson 1, own goal 1.
J Paint Trophy (0).

Lee-Barrett A 37	Sweeney A 43 + 1	Humphreys R 39 + 6	Liddle G 37 + 6	Nelson M 46	Collins S 40	Jones R 36	Boland W 3	Porter J 37 + 1	Brown J 18	Monkhouse A 41 + 3	Foley D 4 + 19	Robson M 14 + 15	Barker R — + 8	McCunnie J 10 + 5	Power A — + 4	MacKay M 9 + 14	Kyle K 15	Clark B 35	Budtz J 9 + 1	Rowell J 3 + 3	Henderson L 2 + 6	Nardiello D 8 + 4	Lange R 2 + 1	Guy L 4	Parker K 9	Skarz J 5 + 2	Match No.
1	2	3	4	5	6	7	8	9^3	10^1	11^2	12	13	14														1
1	2	3	4	5	6	7^1	8^2	9	10	11^3	12	14	13														2
1	2	3	4	5	6	7^1	8^2	9	10	11^3	12		14	13													3
1	8	3	4	5	6	7		9^2	10^3	11^1	13	12	14	2													4
1	7	3	4	5^1	6			9	10	11^3	13	8^2	14	2	12												5
1	7	3	4	5	6	8		9^1	10^3	11^2	13	12		2		14											6
1	7	3	4	5	6	8		9	10^3	11^1	13	12		2^2		14											7
1	7^2	3	4^1	5	6	8		9^2	10	11	12	13		2		14											8
1	12	3	4	5	6	7^2		9	10	11	13			2^1		8											9
1	2	3^1		5	6	7		9	10	11^2	12	13				8		4									10
1	2	3		5	6	7		9^1	10	11^2	13	12				8		4									11
1	2^1	3	12	5	6	7		9	10	11^2	13					8		4									12
1	2	3	12	5	6	7		9	10^1	11						8		4									13
1	2	3	12	5	6	7		9^1	10	11^2	13					8		4									14
1	2	3^2	12	5	6	7^1		9^3	10	11	14	13				8		4									15
1	2^3	3	12	5	6^1	7		9^1	10	11^3	13	14				8		4									16
1	2	12	13	5	6^1	7		9	10	11^2					3	8		4									17
1	2	12	4	5		7		9	10^2	11^1	13				3	8		6									18
	2	3	4	5	6	7		9^1	12	11		10				8			1								19
	2^3	3	4	5	6			12	13	11		14		9^2	10	8^1			1	7							20
	2	3	4	5	6	7		9^2	12	11	13				10	8^1			1								21
1	2	3		5	6	7		9^2		11	12	13			10			4	8^1								22
1	2	3	4	5	6	7		9		11^2	12	13	14		10^3				8^1								23
1		3	4	5	6	7^2		9^1	12	11				2	10	8	13										24
1		3	4	5			8^3	9^2	12	11		7^1		2	10	14	13	6									25
1	2	3	4	5		7		9	12	11					10^1	8		6									26
1	2^1	3	4	5		7		9	12	11					10	8		6									27
1	7	3	4	5		8		9^1	12	11				2	10^4			6									28
1	7	3	4	5				9	12	11				2	10^1	8		6									29
1	2	3	4	5	6			7^1	12	11	13				10	8^2									9		30
1	2	3	4	5	6	7		9		11	12^2				10	8^1							13				31
1	2	3	4	5	6	7		9^2		11	12				10^1	8							13				32
1	2	3	4	5	6	7		9^2		11	12	13			10^1	8											33
1	2	3	4	5	6	7^1		9		11	12				10	8											34
1	2	3	4	5	6	7^2		9^1		11	12				10	8							13				35
1	2	3	4	5	6	7		9^1		11	12				10	8											36
1	2	3	4	5	6	7^1		9		11	12				10	8											37
1	2	3	4	5	6	7		9^2		11	12	13			10	8^1											38
1	8	3	6	5		7		9		11	12			2	10^1			4									39
1^8	7^6	3^2	2	5	6			9		11	12				10	8^1	15	4				13					40
	7	3^3	2	5	6			9		11	12				10^1	8^2		4	1		14		13				41
	7	13	2	5	6					11	12				10^2	8		4	1						9^1	3	42
	7		2	5	6					11	12				10^2	8^3		4	1		14		13		9^1	3	43
	7	12	2	5	6					11					10	8		4^1	1				13		9^2	3	44
	7	12	2	5^2	6					11					10	8^1		4	1		14		13		9^3	3	45
	7	12	2	5^1	6					11					10	8^2		4	1				13		9	3	46

FA Cup

First Round	Brighton & HA	(a)	3-3	
		(h)	2-1	
Second Round	Fleetwood T	(a)	3-2	
Third Round	Stoke C	(h)	2-0	
Fourth Round	West Ham U	(h)	0-2	

Carling Cup

First Round	Scunthorpe U	(h)	3-0
Second Round	WBA	(h)	3-1
Third Round	Leeds U	(a)	2-3

J Paint Trophy

First Round	Leicester C	(h)	0-3

HEREFORD UNITED　　FL Championship 2

FOUNDATION

Two local teams RAOC and St Martins amalgamated in 1924 under the chairmanship of Dr. E.W. Maples to form Hereford United and joined the Birmingham Combination. The first game at Edgar Street was against Atherstone Town on 24 August 1924, the visitors winnning 3-2. The players used the Wellington Hotel as a changing room. They graduated to the Birmingham League four years later and the Southern League in 1939.

Athletic Ground, Edgar Street, Hereford HR4 9JU.

Telephone: (08442) 761 939.

Fax: (08442) 761 982.

Ticket Office: (08442) 761 939.

Website: www.herefordunited.co.uk

Email: hufc1939@hotmail.com

Ground capacity: 7,149.

Record Attendance: 18,114 v Sheffield W, FA Cup 3rd rd, 4 January 1958.

Pitch measurements: 100m × 72m.

HONOURS

Football League: Division 2 best season: 22nd, 1976–77; Division 3 – Champions 1975–76; Division 4 – Runners-up 1972–73.

FA Cup: best season: 4th rd, 1972, 1974, 1977, 1982, 1990, 1992, 2008.

Football League Cup: best season: 3rd rd, 1975.

Welsh Cup: Winners 1990.

Conference (runners-up): 2003–04, 2004–05.

Chairman and Director of Football: Graham Turner.

Secretary: Mrs Joan Fennessy.

Manager: John Trewick.

Physio: Jamie Pitman.

Colours: White shirts, black shorts, white stockings.

Change colours: Yellow shirts with blue sleeves, blue shorts, blue stockings.

Year Formed: 1924.

Turned Professional: 1924.

Ltd Co.: 1939.

Club Nickname: 'United'.

Ground: 1924, Edgar Street.

First Football League game: 12 August 1972, Division 4, v Colchester U (a) L 0-1 – Potter; Mallender, Naylor; Jones, McLaughlin, Tucker; Slattery, Hollett, Owen, Radford, Wallace.

SKY SPORTS FACT FILE

Hereford United is the last English club to win the Welsh Cup having defeated Wrexham 2–1 in the 1990 final. It was the club's fourth appearance in the final having previously lost twice to Cardiff City and once to Swansea City, respectively in 1968, 1976 and 1981.

Record League Victory: 6–0 v Burnley (away), Division 4, 24 January 1987 – Rose; Rodgerson, Devine, Halliday, Pejic, Dalziel, Harvey (1p), Wells, Phillips (3), Kearns (2), Spooner.

Record Cup Victory: 6–1 v QPR, FA Cup 2nd rd, 7 December 1957 – Sewell; Tomkins, Wade; Masters, Niblett, Horton (2p); Reg Bowen (1), Clayton (1), Fidler, Williams (1), Cyril Beech (1).

Record Defeat: 0–7 v Middlesbrough, Coca-Cola Cup 2nd rd, 1st leg, 18 September 1996.

Most League Points (2 for a win): 63, Division 3, 1975–76.

Most League Points (3 for a win): 88, FL 2, 2007–08.

Most League Goals: 86, Division 3, 1975–76.

Highest League Scorer in Season: Dixie McNeil, 35, 1975–76.

Most League Goals in Total Aggregate: Stewart Phillips, 93, 1980–88, 1990–91.

Most Capped Player: Trevor Benjamin, 2, Jamaica.

Most League Appearances: Mel Pejic, 412, 1980–92.

MANAGERS
Eric Keen 1939
George Tranter 1948–49
Alex Massie 1952
George Tranter 1953–55
Joe Wade 1956–62
Ray Daniels 1962–63
Bob Dennison 1963–67
John Charles 1967–71
Colin Addison 1971–74
John Sillett 1974–78
Mike Bailey 1978–79
Frank Lord 1979–82
Tommy Hughes 1982–83
Johnny Newman 1983–87
Ian Bowyer 1987–90
Colin Addison 1990–91
John Sillett 1991–92
Greg Downs 1992–94
John Layton 1994–95
Graham Turner 1995–2009
John Trewick April 2009–

Record Transfer Fee Received: £440,000 from QPR for Darren Peacock, December 1990.

Record Transfer Fee Paid: £80,000 to Walsall for Dean Smith, June 1994.

Football League Record: 1972 Elected to Division 4; 1973–76 Division 3; 1976–77 Division 2; 1977–78 Division 3; 1978–92 Division 4; 1992–97 Division 3; 1997–2006 Vauxhall Conference; 2006–08 FL 2; 2008–09 FL 1; 2009– FL 2.

LATEST SEQUENCES

Longest Sequence of League Wins: 6, 2.4.1996 – 20.4.1996.

Longest Sequence of League Defeats: 8, 7.2.1987 – 18.3.1987.

Longest Sequence of League Draws: 6, 12.4.1975 – 23.8.1975.

Longest Sequence of Unbeaten League Matches: 14, 21.10.1972 – 17.1.1973.

Longest Sequence Without a League Win: 13, 19.11.1977 – 25.2.1978.

Successive Scoring Runs: 23 from 20.9.1975.

Successive Non-scoring Runs: 6 from 10.3.2007.

TEN YEAR LEAGUE RECORD

		P	W	D	L	F	A	Pts	Pos
1999-2000	Conf	42	15	14	13	61	52	59	8
2000-01	Conf	42	14	15	13	60	46	57	11
2001-02	Conf	42	14	10	18	50	53	52	17
2002-03	Conf	42	19	7	16	64	51	64	6
2003-04	Conf	42	28	7	7	103	44	91	2
2004-05	Conf	42	21	11	10	68	41	74	2
2005-06	Conf	42	22	14	6	59	33	80	2
2006-07	FL 2	46	14	13	19	45	53	55	16
2007-08	FL 2	46	26	10	10	72	41	88	3
2008-09	FL 1	46	9	7	30	42	79	34	24

DID YOU KNOW ?

On 17 January 2009 Steve Guinan's first half-hat-trick against Oldham Athletic avenged a 4–0 defeat earlier in the season at Oldham. His first goal was also the 1,500th achieved by Hereford United in their two spells in the Football League.

HEREFORD UNITED 2008–09 LEAGUE RECORD

Match No.	Date	Venue	Opponents	Result		H/T Score	Lg. Pos.	Goalscorers	Attendance
1	Aug 9	A	Leyton Orient	L	1-2	1-2	—	Beckwith [14]	4727
2	16	H	Yeovil T	L	1-2	0-2	22	Hudson-Odoi [82]	3476
3	23	A	Bristol R	L	1-6	0-3	24	Guinan [90]	6735
4	30	H	Crewe Alex	W	2-0	0-0	22	O'Leary [48], Hudson-Odoi [56]	2894
5	Sept 5	H	Swindon T	D	1-1	0-1	—	Hudson-Odoi [68]	4061
6	13	A	Southend U	L	0-1	0-1	23		6393
7	20	H	Scunthorpe U	L	1-2	1-0	24	Chadwick (pen) [25]	3004
8	27	A	Leeds U	L	0-1	0-0	24		25,676
9	Oct 4	H	Walsall	D	0-0	0-0	24		3900
10	12	A	Oldham Ath	L	0-4	0-3	24		5468
11	18	A	Brighton & HA	D	0-0	0-0	24		5608
12	21	H	Carlisle U	W	1-0	0-0	—	Williams [60]	2300
13	25	H	Stockport Co	L	0-1	0-0	23		3210
14	28	A	Millwall	L	0-1	0-0	—		9071
15	Nov 1	A	Peterborough U	L	0-2	0-1	24		6087
16	15	H	Cheltenham T	W	3-0	2-0	22	Guinan 2 [15, 26], Gwynne [55]	3761
17	22	H	Northampton T	L	0-2	0-0	22		3061
18	25	A	Milton Keynes D	L	0-3	0-0	—		7189
19	Dec 6	A	Colchester U	W	2-1	2-0	22	Guinan [29], Ainsworth [39]	4794
20	13	H	Hartlepool U	D	1-1	1-0	23	Guinan [18]	2490
21	20	A	Huddersfield T	L	0-2	0-0	23		13,070
22	26	H	Tranmere R	D	2-2	1-1	23	Diagouraga [45], Guinan [66]	3495
23	28	A	Leicester C	L	1-2	0-1	23	Broadhurst [79]	22,920
24	Jan 17	H	Oldham Ath	W	5-0	4-0	22	Guinan 3 [3, 10, 41], Ainsworth 2 [27, 62]	3342
25	24	A	Walsall	D	1-1	0-1	22	Guinan (pen) [59]	4438
26	27	H	Millwall	L	0-2	0-0	—		3001
27	31	A	Stockport Co	L	1-4	1-2	23	Hewson [26]	5586
28	Feb 14	A	Cheltenham T	W	3-2	1-1	22	Brandy [13], Hewson 2 [67, 80]	4660
29	17	H	Leeds U	W	2-0	1-0	—	Myrie-Williams [39], Brandy [63]	6120
30	21	H	Peterborough U	L	0-1	0-1	23		3217
31	28	H	Leyton Orient	W	2-1	2-1	23	Brandy [6], Guinan (pen) [16]	3286
32	Mar 7	A	Crewe Alex	L	1-2	0-0	23	Diagouraga [79]	5195
33	10	H	Bristol R	L	0-3	0-2	—		3199
34	14	H	Southend U	L	0-1	0-0	23		2663
35	17	A	Scunthorpe U	L	0-3	0-2	—		3672
36	21	A	Swindon T	L	0-3	0-1	23		7129
37	24	A	Carlisle U	W	2-1	2-1	—	Guinan [7], Smith [24]	4223
38	28	H	Huddersfield T	L	0-1	0-0	23		2979
39	Apr 4	A	Hartlepool U	L	2-4	2-2	23	Brandy [11], Pugh [28]	3579
40	7	H	Brighton & HA	L	1-2	0-1	—	Taylor [90]	2033
41	11	H	Leicester C	L	1-3	1-1	23	Guinan (pen) [29]	4389
42	13	A	Tranmere R	L	1-2	0-2	24	Guinan (pen) [90]	5945
43	18	H	Colchester U	L	0-2	0-2	24		2100
44	21	H	Yeovil T	D	2-2	1-0	—	Myrie-Williams [27], Guinan [61]	3780
45	25	A	Northampton T	L	1-2	0-1	24	Williams [51]	5518
46	May 2	H	Milton Keynes D	L	0-1	0-0	24		3224

Final League Position: 24

GOALSCORERS

League (42): Guinan 15 (4 pens), Brandy 4, Ainsworth 3, Hewson 3, Hudson-Odoi 3, Diagouraga 2, Myrie-Williams 2, Williams 2, Beckwith 1, Broadhurst 1, Chadwick 1 (pen), Gwynne 1, O'Leary 1, Pugh 1, Smith 1, Taylor 1.
Carling Cup (1): Ashikodi 1.
FA Cup (1): Taylor 1.
J Paint Trophy (1): Done 1.

Randolph D 13	Rose R 40 + 2	Threlfall R 3	Diaguraga T 45	Beckwith D 22 + 3	Oji S 4	Johnson S 8 + 21	Smith B 29 + 8	Astikodi M 4 + 2	Done M 24 + 12	Taylor K 38 + 1	Hudson-Odoi B 10 + 6	Guinan S 40 + 3	Samson C 10 + 1	Macleod J 2 + 4	Easton C 9 + 3	O'Leary S 11 + 4	Jackson R 24 + 1	Williams A 19 + 7	Broadhurst K 23 + 2	Chadwick N 5 + 5	N'Gotty B 8	Gwynne S 17 + 4	Murray M 3	Ainsworth L 7	Weale C 1	Gowling J 13	Hewson S 9 + 1	Myrie-Williams J 15	Gulacsi P 18	Brandy F 14 + 1	Antwi-Birago G 5	Dennehy D 3	Pugh M 8 + 1	Veiga J 1	Jones C 1 + 2	Match No.
1	2	3	4	5	6	7	8[2]	9[1]	10	11	12	13																								1
	2	3	4	5	6	7[1]	8	9[3]	13			14	10		1	12	11[2]																			2
	2	3	4	5	6	7[2]	8	9[3]	13			14	10		1	12	11[1]																			3
1	2		4	5	6	13	8		10[1]	3	11[2]	9			12	7																				4
1	2		4	5			8		12	3	10	9			7	6	11[1]																			5
1	2		4	5		12	8[2]		14	3	7	10			13	11[1]	6	9[3]																		6
1			4	5			12	8		10	3	7				11[1]	2		6	9																7
1	3		4			8[2]	12	14	10	13	7[1]				11	2		6	9[3]	5																8
1	3		4			12		9[1]		11	7				8	2	10	6		5																9
1	3		4			12			11	7[1]	10				8[4]	2	9	6		5																10
1	2	8				11	12	9[2]		3		5	10[1]	6	13	4	7																			11
1	3		4				8	12	10	11		2			9[1]	6		5	7																	12
1	3		4			12	8		13	10[3]	11	2[1]			9[2]	6	14	5	7																	13
1	2		4			7[3]	8	13		3	10[1]	12	11[2]	14		6	9[4]	5																		14
1	2		4	14			8	12		3	10	9			11[1]	13	6		5[3]	7[2]																15
		4	5				8	12		3	10[2]	11		7	9[1]	6		13	2	1																16
	2	4	5				8	12		10[3]	9[2]	11[1]		3	13	6	14			1	7															17
		4	5	7		8	12		11[1]	3	13	15		2	9	6	10[2]	16																		18
		4	5		13	8			11[2]	3		2	9			12	7[1]	1	6																	19
	2	4[1]	5			8			11	3		10	1		12	9						7		6												20
	2	4	5	12		8			11[2]	3		10	1			9[1]	13					7		6												21
	2	4	5			8			11	3		10	1			9						7		6												22
	2	4				8			11	3		10	1			12	5	9[1]				7		6												23
	2	4					12		11[2]	3		10	1			9	6		13			7		5	8[1]											24
	2	4				12	8		11	3		10	1			9[1]	6					5		7												25
	2	4				12	8		11	3		10	1			9	6					5		7[1]												26
	3	4				12			11[2]			10	1			2	9[1]	6				13		5	8	7										27
	2	4	5[1]	14	12				3	10		13[3]								7		6[2]	8	11	1	9										28
	5	4		12					3	10		2								7			8	11	1	9[1]	6									29
	5	4		13	12				3	10		2								7[2]			8	11[1]	1	9	6									30
	5	4							11	3		10				2	13	12		7			8		1	9[2]	6[1]									31
	5	4		13	12				11	3		10				2				7[1]			8[6]		1	9[2]	6									32
	14	4[2]	12	13		8			11	3[3]		10				2		6		7[1]					1	9	5[1]									33
	3	4	5	12					11			10				2				7[1]					1	8	9	6								34
	3	4	5	11					12			10		7		8[2]	2								1	13	9[1]	6								35
	3	4	5	13	12				11			10		7[2]		2									1	8[1]	9	6								36
	2	4	5	7	8				11[2]	3		10				12	6			13					1		9[1]									37
	2	4	5[1]	14	8				3			10			12[2]	13	6			11					1		9			7[3]						38
	5	4		8[2]					3	10		13			2[1]	12	6			7					1		9			11	1					39
	5	4		14	8[2]				13	3		10			12	2	6			7[1]					1		9			11[3]						40
	5	4		13	8				12	3		10			2	6				7					1		9[2]			11[1]						41
	5	4		12	8				9[2]	3		10		13	6					2						7	1			11[1]						42
	12	4	5						13	9		3[1]	10		8[3]	2				6					7		1			11[2]					14	43
	6	5							8	11[2]		3	10		14	12				9					2		7[3]	1					13		4[1]	44
	5	4	12						8	13		3	10			9				2						6[1]	7	1		11[2]						45
	5	4							8[2]	9[1]		3	10			2				6							7	1	12	11					13	46

FA Cup
First Round — Dagenham & R — (h) 0-0 / (a) 1-2

Carling Cup
First Round — Crystal Palace — (a) 1-2

J Paint Trophy
Second Round — Swindon T — (h) 1-2

HUDDERSFIELD TOWN FL Championship 1

FOUNDATION

A meeting, attended largely by members of the Huddersfield & District FA, was held at the Imperial Hotel in 1906 to discuss the feasibility of establishing a football club in this rugby stronghold. However, it was not until a man with both the enthusiasm and the money to back the scheme came on the scene, that real progress was made. This benefactor was Mr Hilton Crowther and it was at a meeting at the Albert Hotel in 1908, that the club formally came into existence with a capital of £2,000 and joined the North-Eastern League.

The Galpharm Stadium, Stadium Way, Leeds Road, Huddersfield HD1 6PX.
Telephone: 0870 4444 677.
Fax: (01484) 484 101.
Ticket Office: 0870 4444 552.
Website: www.htafc.com
Email: info@htafc.com
Ground Capacity: 24,554.
Record Attendance: 67,037 v Arsenal, FA Cup 6th rd, 27 February 1932 (at Leeds Road); 23,678 v Liverpool, FA Cup 3rd rd, 12 December 1999 (at Alfred McAlpine Stadium).
Pitch Measurements: 115yd × 76yd.
Chairman: Ken Davy.
Secretary: Ann Hough.
Manager: Lee Clark.
Assistant Manager: Terry McDermott.
Physio: Dave Buckby.

HONOURS

Football League: Division 1 – Champions 1923–24, 1924–25, 1925–26; Runners-up 1926–27, 1927–28, 1933–34; Division 2 – Champions 1969–70; Runners-up 1919–20, 1952–53; Division 4 – Champions 1979–80.

FA Cup: Winners 1922; Runners-up 1920, 1928, 1930, 1938.

Football League Cup: Semi-final 1968.

Autoglass Trophy: Runners-up 1994.

Colours: Blue and white striped shirts, white shorts, black stockings.
Change Colours: Red shirts with white trim and black sleeves, black shorts, black stockings.
Year Formed: 1908. *Turned Professional:* 1908. *Ltd Co.:* 1908. *Club Nickname:* 'The Terriers'.
Grounds: 1908, Leeds Road; 1994, The Alfred McAlpine Stadium (renamed the Galpharm Stadium 2004).
First Football League Game: 3 September 1910, Division 2, v Bradford PA (a) W 1–0 – Mutch; Taylor, Morris; Beaton, Hall, Bartlett; Blackburn, Wood, Hamilton (1), McCubbin, Jee.
Record League Victory: 10–1 v Blackpool, Division 1, 13 December 1930 – Turner; Goodall, Spencer; Redfern, Wilson, Campbell; Bob Kelly (1), McLean (4), Robson (3), Davies (1), Smailes (1).
Record Cup Victory: 7–0 v Lincoln U, FA Cup 1st rd, 16 November 1991 – Clarke; Trevitt, Charlton, Donovan (2), Mitchell, Doherty, O'Regan (1), Stapleton (1) (Wright), Roberts (2), Onuora (1), Barnett (Ireland). *N.B.* 11-0 v Heckmondwike (a), FA Cup pr rd, 18 September 1909 – Doggart; Roberts, Ewing; Hooton, Stevenson, Randall; Kenworthy (2), McCreadie (1), Foster (4), Stacey (4), Jee.

SKY SPORTS FACT FILE

On 2 May 2009 Andy Booth signed off as a Huddersfield Town player with his 150th League and Cup goal for the club in the 1–1 draw with Leyton Orient. He achieved his total in two spells and ranks with George Brown and Jimmy Glazzard as club scoring legends.

Record Defeat: 1–10 v Manchester C, Division 2, 7 November 1987.

Most League Points (2 for a win): 66, Division 4, 1979–80.

Most League Points (3 for a win): 82, Division 3, 1982–83.

Most League Goals: 101, Division 4, 1979–80.

Highest League Scorer in Season: Sam Taylor, 35, Division 2, 1919–20; George Brown, 35, Division 1, 1925–26.

Most League Goals in Total Aggregate: George Brown, 142, 1921–29; Jimmy Glazzard, 142, 1946–56.

Most League Goals in One Match: 5, Dave Mangnall v Derby Co, Division 1, 21 November 1931; 5, Alf Lythgoe v Blackburn R, Division 1, 13 April 1935.

Most Capped Player: Jimmy Nicholson, 31 (41), Northern Ireland.

Most League Appearances: Billy Smith, 520, 1914–34.

Youngest League Player: Denis Law, 16 years 303 days v Notts Co, 24 December 1956.

Record Transfer Fee Received: £2,750,000 from Ipswich T for Marcus Stewart, February 2000.

Record Transfer Fee Paid: £1,200,000 to Bristol R for Marcus Stewart, July 1996.

Football League Record: 1910 Elected to Division 2; 1920–52 Division 1; 1952–53 Division 2; 1953–56 Division 1; 1956–70 Division 2; 1970–72 Division 1; 1972–73 Division 2; 1973–75 Division 3; 1975–80 Division 4; 1980–83 Division 3; 1983–88 Division 2; 1988–92 Division 3; 1992–95 Division 2; 1995–2001 Division 1; 2001–03 Division 2; 2003–04 Division 3; 2004– FL 1.

LATEST SEQUENCES

Longest Sequence of League Wins: 11, 5.4.1920 – 4.9.1920.

Longest Sequence of League Defeats: 7, 8.10.1955 – 19.11.1955.

Longest Sequence of League Draws: 6, 3.3.1987 – 3.4.1987.

Longest Sequence of Unbeaten League Matches: 27, 24.1.1925 – 17.10.1925.

Longest Sequence Without a League Win: 22, 4.12.1971 – 29.4.1972.

Successive Scoring Runs: 27 from 12.3.2005.

Successive Non-scoring Runs: 7 from 22.1.1972.

MANAGERS

Fred Walker 1908–10
Richard Pudan 1910–12
Arthur Fairclough 1912–19
Ambrose Langley 1919–21
Herbert Chapman 1921–25
Cecil Potter 1925–26
Jack Chaplin 1926–29
Clem Stephenson 1929–42
David Steele 1943–47
George Stephenson 1947–52
Andy Beattie 1952–56
Bill Shankly 1956–59
Eddie Boot 1960–64
Tom Johnston 1964–68
Ian Greaves 1968–74
Bobby Collins 1974
Tom Johnston 1975–78
 (had been General Manager since 1975)
Mike Buxton 1978–86
Steve Smith 1986–87
Malcolm Macdonald 1987–88
Eoin Hand 1988–92
Ian Ross 1992–93
Neil Warnock 1993–95
Brian Horton 1995–97
Peter Jackson 1997–99
Steve Bruce 1999–2000
Lou Macari 2000–02
Mick Wadsworth 2002–03
Peter Jackson 2003–07
Andy Ritchie 2007–08
Stan Ternent 2008
Lee Clark December 2008–

TEN YEAR LEAGUE RECORD

		P	W	D	L	F	A	Pts	Pos
1999-2000	Div 1	46	21	11	14	62	49	74	8
2000-01	Div 1	46	11	15	20	48	57	48	22
2001-02	Div 2	46	21	15	10	65	47	78	6
2002-03	Div 2	46	11	12	23	39	61	45	22
2003-04	Div 3	46	23	12	11	68	52	81	4
2004-05	FL 1	46	20	10	16	74	65	70	9
2005-06	FL 1	46	19	16	11	72	59	73	4
2006-07	FL 1	46	14	17	15	60	69	59	15
2007-08	FL 1	46	20	6	20	50	62	66	10
2008-09	FL 1	46	18	14	14	62	65	68	9

DID YOU KNOW ?

Huddersfield Town achieved their first double over West Yorkshire rivals Leeds United since 1930–31 with a 1–0 victory on 14 February 2009 at Galpharm in front of a crowd of 20,928. Huddersfield had won 2–1 at Elland Road earlier in the season.

HUDDERSFIELD TOWN 2008–09 LEAGUE RECORD

Match No.	Date	Venue	Opponents	Result	H/T Score	Lg. Pos.	Goalscorers	Atten-dance
1	Aug 9	H	Stockport Co	D 1-1	1-1	—	Booth 30	15,578
2	16	A	Colchester U	D 0-0	0-0	17		5340
3	23	H	Milton Keynes D	L 1-3	0-2	23	Roberts 83	13,189
4	30	A	Millwall	L 1-2	1-1	24	Dickinson 18	7513
5	Sept 6	A	Cheltenham T	W 2-1	0-1	17	Clarke N 57, Craney 67	3587
6	13	H	Tranmere R	L 1-2	1-1	22	Dickinson 16	12,128
7	20	H	Northampton T	W 3-2	1-1	15	Booth 34, Flynn 2 64, 78	12,414
8	27	A	Oldham Ath	D 1-1	1-0	15	Craney 29	7418
9	Oct 4	H	Leicester C	L 2-3	0-0	17	Roberts 69, Dickinson 77	16,212
10	11	A	Swindon T	W 3-1	2-0	15	Dickinson 6, Roberts 26, Flynn 69	7071
11	18	H	Bristol R	D 1-1	1-0	16	Flynn 7	13,779
12	21	A	Hartlepool U	L 3-5	3-2	—	Dickinson 2 8, 44, Craney 38	3771
13	25	A	Peterborough U	L 0-4	0-2	19		7064
14	28	H	Yeovil T	D 0-0	0-0	—		10,719
15	Nov 1	H	Crewe Alex	W 3-2	2-1	16	Butler 20, Craney 39, Parker 88	11,679
16	15	A	Leeds U	W 2-1	0-1	14	Skarz 46, Collins 90	32,028
17	22	A	Brighton & HA	W 1-0	0-0	13	Collins 50	6461
18	25	H	Leyton Orient	L 0-1	0-1	—		10,414
19	Dec 6	H	Walsall	W 2-1	1-0	12	Roberts (pen) 26, Collins 90	11,827
20	13	A	Southend U	W 1-0	0-0	10	Craney 48	8382
21	20	H	Hereford U	W 2-0	0-0	10	Clarke N 70, Roberts 77	13,070
22	26	A	Carlisle U	L 0-3	0-1	10		7883
23	28	H	Scunthorpe U	W 2-0	0-0	10	Goodwin 65, Roberts 90	15,228
24	Jan 3	H	Oldham Ath	D 1-1	0-1	—	Collins 66	16,950
25	10	A	Northampton T	D 1-1	0-0	—	Jevons 65	5110
26	17	H	Swindon T	W 2-1	0-0	8	Collins 51, Butler 60	13,414
27	24	A	Leicester C	L 2-4	1-1	10	Jevons 6, Parker 51	21,311
28	27	A	Yeovil T	L 0-1	0-1	—		3703
29	31	H	Peterborough U	W 1-0	1-0	10	Collins 36	14,480
30	Feb 3	H	Hartlepool U	D 1-1	1-1	—	Nelson (og) 9	9294
31	14	H	Leeds U	W 1-0	1-0	9	Clarke N 18	20,928
32	21	A	Crewe Alex	L 1-3	1-1	10	Berrett 30	5056
33	28	A	Stockport Co	D 1-1	1-0	10	Collins 16	7739
34	Mar 3	H	Colchester U	D 2-2	0-1	—	Pilkington 51, Roberts 66	10,580
35	7	H	Millwall	L 1-2	0-0	11	Roberts 74	13,196
36	10	A	Milton Keynes D	D 1-1	0-0	—	Butler 80	9707
37	14	A	Tranmere R	L 1-3	1-1	13	Booth 23	5515
38	21	H	Cheltenham T	D 2-2	1-2	14	Cadamarteri 40, Butler 90	11,516
39	28	A	Hereford U	W 1-0	0-0	14	Collins 72	2979
40	31	H	Bristol R	W 2-1	0-0	—	Pilkington 70, Cadamarteri 78	6286
41	Apr 4	H	Southend U	L 0-1	0-0	12		12,203
42	10	A	Scunthorpe U	W 2-1	1-1	—	Clarke T 26, Roberts 54	5543
43	13	H	Carlisle U	W 1-0	0-0	9	Booth 78	12,309
44	18	A	Walsall	W 3-2	2-2	9	Booth 2 43, 46, Kelly 62	3951
45	25	H	Brighton & HA	D 2-2	1-1	9	Booth 16, Collins 57	14,740
46	May 2	A	Leyton Orient	D 1-1	1-0	9	Booth 24	5371

Final League Position: 9

GOALSCORERS

League (62): Collins 9, Roberts 9 (1 pen), Booth 8, Dickinson 6, Craney 5, Butler 4, Flynn 4, Clarke N 3, Cadamarteri 2, Jevons 2, Parker 2, Pilkington 2, Berrett 1, Clarke T 1, Goodwin 1, Kelly 1, Skarz 1, own goal 1.
Carling Cup (5): Roberts 2, Flynn 1, Williams 1, Worthington 1.
FA Cup (3): Collins 1, Craney 1, Williams 1.
J Paint Trophy (0).

Glennon M 18	Holdsworth A 30 + 4	Unsworth D 4	Goodwin J 35 + 2	Butler A 42	Lucketti C 12 + 1	Collins M 34 + 2	Flynn M 18 + 7	Cadamarteri D 24 + 8	Booth A 9 + 11	Roberts G 43	Worthington J 12 + 7	Beckett L — + 1	Williams R 31 + 4	Craney J 23 + 11	Dickinson L 13	Parker K 14 + 6	Clarke N 38	Jevons P 12 + 11	Skarz J 9	Jones S 2 + 2	Berrett J 8 + 1	Broadbent D — + 1	Smithies A 27	Kamara M — + 2	Clarke T 11 + 4	Ainsworth L 7 + 7	Pilkington A 16	Werling D — + 3	Jurkiewicz L 6 + 1	Kelly M 7	Eastwood S 1	Match No.
1	2	3	4	5	6	7	8^1	9	10^2	11	12	13																				1
1	2		4	5	6		8	9	10	11	7		3																			2
1	2		4^1	5	6		8^2	9	12	11	13		3	7	10^3	14																3
1	4	3		5	14	6	9^1			11	7^3			8	10	12^2	2	13														4
1	2	3			6	7	8			11				4	10	12	5	9^1														5
1	2	3^2			6	7	8	12		11	13		14	4^1	9	10^2	5															6
1		2		5			8		10^1	11	7			4	9	12	6		3													7
1		2		5			8			11	7			4	9		6	10	3													8
1		2		5			8	12		11	7			4^1	9	13	6	10^2	3													9
1	12	2		5			8	9^2		11	7			4	10^1		6	13	3													10
1		2		5	12		8			11	7^1		13	4^3	9	14	6			3^2	10											11
1	12	2^3		5			8			11	7^1		13	4	9		6	14		3^2	10											12
1	2	4		5			8			11	7^1		3	10	9		6	12														13
1	12	2^1		5			8			11	7^2		3	4	9	10	6				13											14
1	2	12		5			8^3			11	7^1		3	4	9^2	10	6	13		14												15
1	2		8	5		7	13			11^3	12		14	4^1	9^2		6		3	10												16
1	2			5			8	12		11^2	7			4	9^1		6	13	3	10												17
1	2		8	5		7	13			11	12			4^1	9^2		6		3	10^3	14											18
	2		8	5		7	9			11			3^1	4			6	10					1		12							19
	2		7	5			8^2	9		11^1			3	4			6	10					1		12	13						20
	2		8	5		7		12		11	13		3	4^1	9^2		6	14		10^3			1									21
	2		8	5		7		12		11	13		3^3	4^1	9^2		6	14		10			1									22
	2		4	5		7	8			11			3	12	9^2		6	10^2					1			13						23
	2		4	5		7	8			11			3	12	9		6	10^1					1									24
	2		4	5		7	8	12		11			3	13	9^2		6	10^1					1									25
	2		4	5		7	13		8	11			3	12	9^1		6	10^2					1									26
	2		4	5		7	8				11		3	12	9^1		6	10					1									27
	2		4^1	5		7	8						3	12	9^2		6	10					1			13	11					28
	2		4	5			8		9				3	12			6	10^1					1		13	7^3	11^2	14				29
	2		4	5			8					11^3	3^2	12	9		6	10^1					1			7	11	13				30
	2		4	5			8					11^3	3	12			6	13					1		9^2	7	14	10^1				31
	2		4	5			8	12			11		3	14			6	13		10^1			1		7^3			9^2				32
	2		4	5	13		8	10^3		12	11^2		3				6						1		14	7		9^1				33
	2		4^1	5	6		8	9^3		13	11		3	12									1		14	7		10^2				34
	2			5	6		8	12		11			3	4			13						1		14	9^2	7^3	10^1				35
	2			5	6		8	12		9^2	11		3	10^1									1		4	7		13				36
2^1	12			5	6		8	9		13	11^2		3	10^3									1		4	14	7					37
	4^2			5	6		8	9		13	11^3		3										1		2	14	7	10^1				38
				5	4	8	9	12		11^2			3				6				13		1		2	7^1	10					39
			4	5		7	8^1	10		12	11						6						1		2		9		3			40
			4^2	5		8	13	9		12	11						6						1		2	7^1	10		3			41
			4	5		8	9^1	12		11			3				6						1			7	10		2			42
			4^2	5		8	13	9		12	11		3				6						1			7	10^1		2			43
			4	5		8^1	12	9	10	11			3				6						1			7			2			44
				5	7	8	9	10^1		11			3				6						1		4	12			2			45
	12			5		8		9	10^2	11			3				6								4	13	7		2^1		1	46

FA Cup
First Round   Port Vale   (h)   3-4

Carling Cup
First Round   Bradford C   (h)   4-0
Second Round   Sheffield U   (h)   1-2

J Paint Trophy
Second Round   Darlington   (a)   0-1

HULL CITY   FA Premiership

FOUNDATION

The enthusiasts who formed Hull City in 1904 were brave men indeed. More than that they were audacious for they immediately put the club on the map in this Rugby League fortress by obtaining a three-year agreement with the Hull Rugby League club to rent their ground! They had obtained quite a number of conversions to the dribbling code, before the Rugby League forbade the use of any of their club grounds by Association Football clubs. By that time, Hull City were well away having entered the FA Cup in their initial season and the Football League, Second Division after only a year.

Kingston Communications Stadium, Walton Street, Hull, East Yorkshire HU3 6HU.

Telephone: 0870 837 0003.

Fax: (01482) 304 882.

Ticket Office: 0870 837 0004.

Website: www.hullcityafc.net

Email: info@hulltigers.com

Ground Capacity: 25,404.

Record Attendance: KC Stadium: 25,512 v Sunderland, FL C, 28 October 2007. Boothferry Park: 55,019 v Manchester U, FA Cup 6th rd, 26 February 1949.

Pitch Measurements: 100.5m × 67.5m.

Chairman/Chief Executive: Paul Duffen.

Football Secretary: Phil Hough.

Manager: Phil Brown.

Assistant Manager: Brian Horton.

Physio: Simon Maltby.

Colours: Black and amber striped shirts, black shorts, black stockings.

Change Colours: Grey shirts with black trim, black shorts, black stockings.

Year Formed: 1904. *Turned Professional:* 1905.

Ltd Co.: 1905.

Club Nickname: 'The Tigers'.

HONOURS

Football League: Best season 2007–08, Championship 1 runners-up 2004–05; Division 3 (N) – Champions 1932–33, 1948–49; Division 3 – Champions 1965–66; Runners-up 1958–59, 2003–04; Division 4 – Runners-up 1982–83.

FA Cup: Semi-final 1930.

Football League Cup: best season: 4th, 1974, 1976, 1978.

Associate Members' Cup: Runners-up 1984.

Grounds: 1904, Boulevard Ground (Hull RFC); 1905, Anlaby Road (Hull CC); 1944, Boulevard Ground; 1946, Boothferry Park; 2002, Kingston Communications Stadium.

First Football League Game: 2 September 1905, Division 2, v Barnsley (h) W 4–1 – Spendiff; Langley, Jones; Martin, Robinson, Gordon (2); Rushton, Spence (1), Wilson (1), Howe, Raisbeck.

Record League Victory: 11–1 v Carlisle U, Division 3 (N), 14 January 1939 – Ellis; Woodhead, Dowen; Robinson (1), Blyth, Hardy; Hubbard (2), Richardson (2), Dickinson (2), Davies (2), Cunliffe (2).

SKY SPORTS FACT FILE

The first Third Division team to win promotion and reach the sixth round of the FA Cup in the same season was Hull City in 1948–49. The average attendance at Boothferry Park that season for their Northern Section matches was an impressive 36,763.

Record Cup Victory: 8–2 v Stalybridge Celtic (a), FA Cup 1st rd, 26 November 1932 – Maddison; Goldsmith, Woodhead; Gardner, Hill (1), Denby; Forward (1), Duncan, McNaughton (1), Wainscoat (4), Sargeant (1).

Record Defeat: 0–8 v Wolverhampton W, Division 2, 4 November 1911.

Most League Points (2 for a win): 69, Division 3, 1965–66.

Most League Points (3 for a win): 90, Division 4, 1982–83.

Most League Goals: 109, Division 3, 1965–66.

Highest League Scorer in Season: Bill McNaughton, 39, Division 3 (N), 1932–33.

Most League Goals in Total Aggregate: Chris Chilton, 195, 1960–71.

Most League Goals in One Match: 5, Ken McDonald v Bristol C, Division 2, 17 November 1928; 5, Simon 'Slim' Raleigh v Halifax T, Division 3 (N), 26 December 1930.

Most Capped Player: Theo Whitmore, 28 (105), Jamaica.

Most League Appearances: Andy Davidson, 520, 1952–67.

Youngest League Player: Matthew Edeson, 16 years 63 days v Fulham, 10 October 1992.

Record Transfer Fee Received: £1,000,000 from Crystal Palace for Leon Cort, June 2006.

Record Transfer Fee Paid: £5,000,000 to Fulham for Jimmy Bullard, January 2009.

Football League Record: 1905 Elected to Division 2; 1930–33 Division 3 (N); 1933–36 Division 2; 1936–49 Division 3 (N); 1949–56 Division 2; 1956–58 Division 3 (N); 1958–59 Division 3; 1959–60 Division 2; 1960–66 Division 3; 1966–78 Division 2; 1978–81 Division 3; 1981–83 Division 4; 1983–85 Division 3; 1985–91 Division 2; 1991–92 Division 3; 1992–96 Division 2; 1996–2004 Division 3; 2004–05 FL 1; 2005–08 FL C; 2008– FA Premier League.

LATEST SEQUENCES

Longest Sequence of League Wins: 10, 23.2.1966 – 20.4.1966.

Longest Sequence of League Defeats: 8, 7.4.1934 – 8.9.1934.

Longest Sequence of League Draws: 5, 30.3.1929 – 15.4.1929.

Longest Sequence of Unbeaten League Matches: 19, 13.3.2001 – 22.9.2001.

Longest Sequence Without a League Win: 27, 27.3.1989 – 4.11.1989.

Successive Scoring Runs: 26 from 10.4.1990.

Successive Non-scoring Runs: 6 from 13.11.1920.

MANAGERS

James Ramster 1904–05
(Secretary-Manager)
Ambrose Langley 1905–13
Harry Chapman 1913–14
Fred Stringer 1914–16
David Menzies 1916–21
Percy Lewis 1921–23
Bill McCracken 1923–31
Haydn Green 1931–34
John Hill 1934–36
David Menzies 1936
Ernest Blackburn 1936–46
Major Frank Buckley 1946–48
Raich Carter 1948–51
Bob Jackson 1952–55
Bob Brocklebank 1955–61
Cliff Britton 1961–70
(continued as General Manager to 1971)
Terry Neill 1970–74
John Kaye 1974–77
Bobby Collins 1977–78
Ken Houghton 1978–79
Mike Smith 1979–82
Bobby Brown 1982
Colin Appleton 1982–84
Brian Horton 1984–88
Eddie Gray 1988–89
Colin Appleton 1989
Stan Ternent 1989–91
Terry Dolan 1991–97
Mark Hateley 1997–98
Warren Joyce 1998–2000
Brian Little 2000–02
Jan Molby 2002
Peter Taylor 2002–06
Phil Parkinson 2006
Phil Brown *(after caretaker role December 2006)* January 2007–

TEN YEAR LEAGUE RECORD

		P	W	D	L	F	A	Pts	Pos
1999-2000	Div 3	46	15	14	17	43	43	59	14
2000-01	Div 3	46	19	17	10	47	39	74	6
2001-02	Div 3	46	16	13	17	57	51	61	11
2002-03	Div 3	46	14	17	15	58	53	59	13
2003-04	Div 3	46	25	13	8	82	44	88	2
2004-05	FL 1	46	26	8	12	80	53	86	2
2005-06	FL C	46	12	16	18	49	55	52	18
2006-07	FL C	46	13	10	23	51	67	49	21
2007-08	FL C	46	21	12	13	65	47	75	3
2008-09	PR Lge	38	8	11	19	39	64	35	17

DID YOU KNOW ?

On 20 December 2008 the much travelled Nick Barmby became the fourth different player in Premier League history to score goals for six different teams when he scored against Sunderland. Les Ferdinand, Andy Cole and Marcus Bent had preceded him.

HULL CITY 2008–09 LEAGUE RECORD

Match No.	Date	Venue	Opponents	Result		H/T Score	Lg. Pos.	Goalscorers	Attendance
1	Aug 16	H	Fulham	W	2-1	1-1	—	Geovanni [22], Folan [81]	24,525
2	23	A	Blackburn R	D	1-1	1-1	4	Garcia [40]	23,439
3	30	H	Wigan Ath	L	0-5	0-2	12		24,282
4	Sept 13	A	Newcastle U	W	2-1	1-0	4	King 2 (1 pen) [34 (pl), 55]	50,242
5	21	H	Everton	D	2-2	1-0	7	Turner [18], Neville (og) [50]	24,845
6	27	A	Arsenal	W	2-1	0-0	6	Geovanni [62], Cousin [66]	60,037
7	Oct 5	A	Tottenham H	W	1-0	1-0	3	Geovanni [9]	36,062
8	19	H	West Ham U	W	1-0	0-0	3	Turner [51]	24,896
9	25	A	WBA	W	3-0	0-0	3	Zayatte [47], Geovanni [62], King [66]	26,323
10	29	H	Chelsea	L	0-3	0-1	—		24,906
11	Nov 1	L	Manchester U	L	3-4	1-3	6	Cousin [23], Mendy [69], Geovanni (pen) [82]	75,398
12	8	H	Bolton W	L	0-1	0-0	6		24,903
13	16	H	Manchester C	D	2-2	1-2	6	Cousin [14], Geovanni [60]	24,902
14	22	A	Portsmouth	D	2-2	0-1	6	Turner [54], Windass [89]	20,240
15	29	A	Stoke C	D	1-1	1-0	6	King [45]	27,500
16	Dec 6	H	Middlesbrough	W	2-1	0-0	6	Turnbull (og) [82], King (pen) [85]	24,912
17	13	A	Liverpool	D	2-2	2-2	6	McShane [12], Carragher (og) [22]	43,835
18	20	H	Sunderland	L	1-4	1-1	6	Barmby [19]	24,917
19	26	A	Manchester C	L	1-5	0-4	7	Fagan [80]	45,196
20	30	H	Aston Villa	L	0-1	0-0	—		24,727
21	Jan 10	A	Everton	L	0-2	0-2	8		37,527
22	17	H	Arsenal	L	1-3	0-1	9	Cousin [65]	24,924
23	28	A	West Ham U	L	0-2	0-1	—		34,340
24	31	H	WBA	D	2-2	1-0	11	Mendy [44], Fagan [69]	24,879
25	Feb 7	A	Chelsea	D	0-0	0-0	12		41,802
26	23	H	Tottenham H	L	1-2	1-1	—	Turner [27]	24,742
27	Mar 1	H	Blackburn R	L	1-2	0-2	13	Ashbee [79]	24,612
28	4	A	Fulham	W	1-0	0-0	—	Manucho [90]	23,051
29	14	H	Newcastle U	D	1-1	1-1	13	Geovanni [9]	24,914
30	22	A	Wigan Ath	L	0-1	0-0	13		17,689
31	Apr 4	H	Portsmouth	D	0-0	0-0	15		24,802
32	11	A	Middlesbrough	L	1-3	1-2	15	Manucho [9]	32,255
33	18	A	Sunderland	L	0-1	0-1	16		42,855
34	25	H	Liverpool	L	1-3	0-1	17	Geovanni [72]	24,942
35	May 4	A	Aston Villa	L	0-1	0-1	—		39,607
36	9	H	Stoke C	L	1-2	0-1	17	Dawson [90]	24,932
37	16	A	Bolton W	D	1-1	0-1	17	Fagan [47]	25,085
38	24	H	Manchester U	L	0-1	0-1	17		24,945

Final League Position: 17

GOALSCORERS

League (39): Geovanni 8 (1 pen), King 5 (2 pens), Cousin 4, Turner 4, Fagan 3, Manucho 2, Mendy 2, Ashbee 1, Barmby 1, Dawson 1, Folan 1, Garcia 1, McShane 1, Windass 1, Zayatte 1, own goals 3.
Carling Cup (1): Windass 1.
FA Cup (7): Ashbee 1, Barmby 1, Cousin 1, Halmosi 1, Turner 1, Zayatte 1, own goal 1.

Myhill B 28	Ricketts S 27 + 2	Dawson A 25	Ashbee I 31	Turner M 38	Gardner A 6	Garcia R 13 + 10	Boateng G 21 + 2	Geovanni 32 + 2	King M 19 + 1	Barmby N 13 + 8	Fagan C 15 + 7	Folan C 2 + 13	Halmosi P 4 + 14	Mendy B 15 + 13	Marney D 26 + 5	Brown W 1	Windass D 1 + 4	McShane P 17	Hughes B 1 + 5	Zayatte K 31 + 1	Cousin D 18 + 9	Giannakopoulos S — + 2	Doyle N 2 + 1	Kilbane K 15 + 1	France R 1 + 1	Manucho 6 + 7	Duke M 10	Bullard J — + 1	Match No.
1	2	3	4	5	6	7¹	8	9	10²	11³	12	13	14																1
1	2	3¹	4	5	6	7²		9³	10	13	11	14			12		8												2
1	2	3²	4	5		7¹		9³		12	11	10			13	8	6	14											3
1		3	4	5	6	7¹	8²	9	10³	11	12				13		14	2											4
1		3	4	5		7¹	8	9³	10²	14	11	12	13					2		6									5
1		3	4	5		7	8¹	9²	10	11³	12	13			14			2		6									6
1		3	4	5		7	8	9³	10¹	11²	12	13	14					2		6									7
1		3	4	5		7	8²	9¹	10	11³	12	13	14					2		6									8
1	12	3¹	4³	5			8	9	10	11²	13				14			2		6									9
1		3	4	5		7¹	8²	9	10³	11	12	13						2		6									10
1		3		5		7	8¹	9	10²	11	12	13	14					2	4³	6									11
1	12	3¹	4	5			8²	9³	10	11		13			14			2		6									12
1	3		4	5		7	8¹	9²	10	11	12	13						2		6									13
1	3		4	5		7³	8¹	9	10²	11	12	13	14					2		6									14
1	3		4	5		7	8³	9¹	10	11²	12	13			14			2		6									15
1	3		4	5		7³	8	9¹	10	11²	12	13						2		6	14								16
1	3		4	5		7	8¹	9	10	11³	12	13						2²		6									17
1	3▪		4	5		7²	8¹	9³	10	11	12				13		14	2		6									18
1			4	5		7	8³	9¹	10	11²	12	13					14	2		6			3						19
1	2		4	5		7³	8	9¹	10²	11	12	13	14					3		6									20
1	3		4	5		7	8¹	9	10	11³	12	13	14					2²		6									21
1	6		4	5		7	8²	9	10¹	11³	12	13	14									2	3						22
	2	3	4	5		7¹	8²	9	10³	11	12	13	14							6					1				23
	2	3	4	5		7	8¹	9	10	11	12									6					1				24
	2	3	4	5		7	8	9	10¹	11	12									6					1				25
	2	3	4	5		7	8	9²	10³	11	12	13	14							6¹					1				26
		3	4	5		7	8▪	9¹	10	11³	12	13	14					2²		6					1				27
	2		4	5	8	7¹		9	10³	11²	12	13	14							6			3		1				28
	2		4	5	8	7¹		9³	10²	11	12	13	14							6			3		1				29
	2	3¹		5		7	8	9³	10	11	12	13	14					4		6²					1				30
	2³		4	5		7	8²	9¹	10	11	12	13	14							6					1				31
	2	3	4	5		7¹	8²	9³	10	11	12	13	14							6					1				32
1	2	3		5		7¹	8	9²	10	11	12	13	14					4³		6									33
1	2			4³		7¹	8	9▪	10²	11	12	13	14							6			3						34
1	2	3	4¹	5		7	8		10²	13	12									6	9	14		11³					35
1	2	3		5		7¹	8	9²	10	11	12	13	14					4		6³									36
1	2	6	4	5		7	8¹	9³	10	11²	12	13	14										3						37
1	2	6	4	5		7³	8	9	10²	11¹	12	13	14										3						38

FA Cup

Third Round	Newcastle U	(h)	0-0
		(a)	1-0
Fourth Round	Millwall	(h)	2-0
Fifth Round	Sheffield U	(a)	1-1
		(h)	2-1
Quarter-Final	Arsenal	(a)	1-2

Carling Cup

Second Round	Swansea C	(a)	1-2

IPSWICH TOWN

FL Championship

FOUNDATION

Considering that Ipswich Town only reached the Football League in 1938, many people outside of East Anglia may be surprised to learn that this club was formed at a meeting held in the Town Hall as far back as 1878 when Mr T. C. Cobbold, MP, was voted president. Originally it was the Ipswich Association FC to distinguish it from the older Ipswich Football Club which played rugby. These two amalgamated in 1888 and the handling game was dropped in 1893.

Portman Road, Ipswich, Suffolk IP1 2DA.

Telephone: (01473) 400 500.

Fax: (01473) 400 040.

Ticket Office: 0870 1110 555.

Website: www.itfc.co.uk

Email: enquiries@itfc.co.uk

Ground Capacity: 30,311.

Record Attendance: 38,010 v Leeds U, FA Cup 6th rd, 8 March 1975.

Pitch Measurements: 102.46m × 66m.

Chairman: Marcus Evans.

Chief Executive: Simon Clegg CBE.

Secretary: Sally Webb.

Manager: Roy Keane.

First Team Coach: Tony Loughlan.

Physio: Matt Byard.

Colours: Blue and white thin striped shirts, blue sleeves, white shorts, blue stockings.

Change Colours: All dark red.

Year Formed: 1878.

Turned Professional: 1936.

Ltd Co.: 1936.

Club Nicknames: 'Blues' or 'Town' or 'Tractor Boys'.

Grounds: 1878, Broom Hill and Brook's Hall; 1884, Portman Road.

Record League Victory: 7–0 v Portsmouth, Division 2, 7 November 1964 – Thorburn; Smith, McNeil; Baxter, Bolton, Thompson; Broadfoot (1), Hegan (2), Baker (1), Leadbetter, Brogan (3). 7–0 v Southampton, Division 1, 2 February 1974 – Sivell; Burley, Mills (1), Morris, Hunter, Beattie (1), Hamilton (2), Viljoen, Johnson, Whymark (2), Lambert (1) (Woods). 7–0 v WBA, Division 1, 6 November 1976 – Sivell; Burley, Mills, Talbot, Hunter, Beattie (1), Osborne, Wark (1), Mariner (1) (Bertschin), Whymark (4), Woods.

HONOURS

Football League: Division 1 – Champions 1961–62; Runners-up 1980–81, 1981–82; Division 2 – Champions 1960–61, 1967–68, 1991–92; Division 3 (S) – Champions 1953–54, 1956–57.

FA Cup: Winners 1978.

Football League Cup: Semi-final 1982, 1985.

Texaco Cup: Winners 1973.

European Competitions: *European Cup:* 1962–63. *European Cup-Winners' Cup:* 1978–79. *UEFA Cup:* 1973–74, 1974–75, 1975–76, 1977–78, 1979–80, 1980–81 (winners), 1981–82, 1982–83, 2001–02, 2002–03.

SKY SPORTS FACT FILE

In 1980–81 Ipswich Town finished as runners-up four points behind the First Division champions Aston Villa. But they did have the consolation of beating them home and away during the season 1–0 at Portman Road, 2–1 at Villa Park.

First Football League Game: 27 August 1938, Division 3 (S), v Southend U (h) W 4–2 – Burns; Dale, Parry; Perrett, Fillingham, McLuckie; Williams, Davies (1), Jones (2), Alsop (1), Little.

Record Cup Victory: 10–0 v Floriana, European Cup prel. rd, 25 September 1962 – Bailey; Malcolm, Compton; Baxter, Laurel, Elsworthy (1); Stephenson, Moran (2), Crawford (5), Phillips (2), Blackwood.

Record Defeat: 1–10 v Fulham, Division 1, 26 December 1963.

Most League Points (2 for a win): 64, Division 3 (S), 1953–54 and 1955–56.

Most League Points (3 for a win): 87, Division 1, 1999–2000.

Most League Goals: 106, Division 3 (S), 1955–56.

Highest League Scorer in Season: Ted Phillips, 41, Division 3 (S), 1956–57.

MANAGERS
Mick O'Brien 1936–37
Scott Duncan 1937–55
(continued as Secretary)
Alf Ramsey 1955–63
Jackie Milburn 1963–64
Bill McGarry 1964–68
Bobby Robson 1969–82
Bobby Ferguson 1982–87
Johnny Duncan 1987–90
John Lyall 1990–94
George Burley 1994–2002
Joe Royle 2002–06
Jim Magilton 2006–09
Roy Keane April 2009–

Most League Goals in Total Aggregate: Ray Crawford, 204, 1958–63 and 1966–69.

Most League Goals in One Match: 5, Alan Brazil v Southampton, Division 1, 16 February 1981.

Most Capped Player: Allan Hunter, 47 (53), Northern Ireland.

Most League Appearances: Mick Mills, 591, 1966–82.

Youngest League Player: Jason Dozzell, 16 years 56 days v Coventry C, 4 February 1984.

Record Transfer Fee Received: £6,000,000 from Newcastle U for Kieron Dyer, July 1999 and £6,000,000 from Arsenal for Richard Wright, July 2001.

Record Transfer Fee Paid: £5,000,000 to Sampdoria for Matteo Sereni, August 2001.

Football League Record: 1938 Elected to Division 3 (S); 1954–55 Division 2; 1955–57 Division 3 (S); 1957–61 Division 2; 1961–64 Division 1; 1964–68 Division 2; 1968–86 Division 1; 1986–92 Division 2; 1992–95 FA Premier League; 1995–2000 Division 1; 2000–02 FA Premier League; 2002–04 Division 1; 2004– FL C.

LATEST SEQUENCES

Longest Sequence of League Wins: 8, 23.9.1953 – 31.10.1953.

Longest Sequence of League Defeats: 10, 4.9.1954 – 16.10.1954.

Longest Sequence of League Draws: 7, 10.11.1990 – 21.12.1990.

Longest Sequence of Unbeaten League Matches: 23, 8.12.1979 – 26.4.1980.

Longest Sequence Without a League Win: 21, 28.8.1963 – 14.12.1963.

Successive Scoring Runs: 31 from 7.3.2004.

Successive Non-scoring Runs: 7 from 28.2.1995.

TEN YEAR LEAGUE RECORD

		P	W	D	L	F	A	Pts	Pos
1999-2000	Div 1	46	25	12	9	71	42	87	3
2000-01	PR Lge	38	20	6	12	57	42	66	5
2001-02	PR Lge	38	9	9	20	41	64	36	18
2002-03	Div 1	46	19	13	14	80	64	70	7
2003-04	Div 1	46	21	10	15	84	72	73	5
2004-05	FL C	46	24	13	9	85	56	85	3
2005-06	FL C	46	14	14	18	53	66	56	15
2006-07	FL C	46	18	8	20	64	59	62	14
2007-08	FL C	46	18	15	13	65	56	69	8
2008-09	FL C	46	17	15	14	62	53	66	9

DID YOU KNOW ?

Noel Parkinson made senior appearances for Ipswich Town before his League debut on loan to Bristol Rovers in 1979–80. At 18 years of age he was twice a playing substitute in the UEFA Cup against Skeid Oslo, initially on 19 September 1979.

IPSWICH TOWN 2008–09 LEAGUE RECORD

Match No.	Date	Venue	Opponents	Result	H/T Score	Lg. Pos.	Goalscorers	Attendance
1	Aug 9	H	Preston NE	L	1-2	1-2	—	Lisbie [2]	22,307
2	16	A	Burnley	W	3-0	2-0	10	Trotter [34], Lisbie [41], Jordan (og) [88]	11,312
3	23	H	Wolverhampton W	L	0-2	0-1	16		21,483
4	30	A	Watford	L	1-2	1-0	17	Counago [2]	16,345
5	Sept 13	H	Reading	W	2-0	0-0	15	Stead [63], Walters [86]	21,366
6	17	A	Southampton	D	2-2	1-1	—	Garvan [20], Quinn [50]	14,916
7	20	A	Sheffield W	D	0-0	0-0	16		17,198
8	27	H	Crystal Palace	D	1-1	1-1	16	Stead [23]	19,032
9	30	H	Barnsley	W	3-0	1-0	—	Stead [20], Garvan [66], Campo [69]	18,177
10	Oct 4	A	Charlton Ath	L	1-2	1-1	17	Cranie (og) [34]	20,643
11	18	A	Swansea C	D	2-2	1-0	18	Counago 2 [43, 82]	20,026
12	21	A	Nottingham F	D	1-1	0-1	—	Miller (pen) [52]	19,455
13	25	A	Plymouth Arg	W	3-1	2-0	13	Garvan 2 [28, 42], Lisbie [48]	12,294
14	28	H	Charlton Ath	D	1-1	1-0	—	Garvan [37]	20,352
15	Nov 1	H	QPR	W	2-0	0-0	8	Stead 2 [73, 75]	20,966
16	8	A	Blackpool	W	1-0	1-0	8	Norris [42]	7349
17	15	A	Doncaster R	L	0-1	0-1	11		10,823
18	22	H	Derby Co	W	2-0	1-0	8	Counago [27], Walters [66]	20,239
19	25	A	Birmingham C	L	1-2	0-2	—	Bruce [84]	15,689
20	29	H	Sheffield U	D	1-1	1-0	11	Miller (pen) [41]	19,785
21	Dec 7	A	Norwich C	L	0-2	0-0	13		25,472
22	10	H	Bristol C	W	3-1	0-1	—	Walters [49], Counago [51], Fontaine (og) [56]	17,749
23	13	H	Cardiff C	L	1-2	1-2	12	Stead [42]	19,665
24	20	A	Coventry C	D	2-2	1-1	12	Lisbie 2 [12, 65]	16,598
25	26	H	Birmingham C	L	0-1	0-1	13		23,536
26	28	A	Derby Co	W	1-0	1-0	10	Walters [14]	28,358
27	Jan 10	H	Sheffield W	D	1-1	0-0	10	Counago [66]	22,213
28	17	A	Crystal Palace	W	4-1	2-1	11	Garvan [19], Norris [28], Lisbie [69], Hill (og) [89]	15,348
29	27	A	Barnsley	W	2-1	2-0	—	Stead 2 [8, 10]	11,183
30	31	H	Plymouth Arg	D	0-0	0-0	10		20,333
31	Feb 7	A	Swansea C	L	0-3	0-1	11		14,020
32	14	H	Blackpool	D	1-1	1-1	11	Miller [34]	19,299
33	18	H	Nottingham F	W	2-1	1-0	—	Perch (og) [14], Wright D [60]	19,930
34	21	A	QPR	W	3-1	1-1	10	Stead [14], Counago [61], Walters [70]	13,904
35	28	H	Preston NE	L	2-3	1-2	10	Miller 2 [31, 63]	12,709
36	Mar 3	A	Southampton	L	0-3	0-1	—		20,040
37	10	A	Wolverhampton W	D	0-0	0-0	—		22,227
38	14	A	Reading	W	1-0	0-0	10	Stead [47]	20,592
39	17	H	Burnley	D	1-1	0-1	—	Giovani [73]	18,745
40	21	H	Watford	D	0-0	0-0	10		21,434
41	Apr 4	A	Sheffield U	L	0-2	0-2	11		25,315
42	11	H	Doncaster R	L	1-3	1-1	11	Garvan [12]	19,918
43	13	A	Bristol C	D	1-1	0-0	11	Giovani (pen) [90]	16,430
44	19	H	Norwich C	W	3-2	1-1	9	Quinn [24], Giovani (pen) [62], Stead [89]	28,274
45	25	A	Cardiff C	W	3-0	1-0	9	Counago [34], Norris [51], Stead [90]	19,129
46	May 3	H	Coventry C	W	2-1	2-0	9	Giovani [24], Counago [26]	27,225

Final League Position: 9

GOALSCORERS

League (62): Stead 12, Counago 9, Garvan 7, Lisbie 6, Miller 5 (2 pens), Walters 5, Giovani 4 (2 pens), Norris 3, Quinn 2, Bruce 1, Campo 1, Trotter 1, Wright D 1, own goals 5.
Carling Cup (7): Haynes 2, Counago 1, Lee 1, Lisbie 1, Miller 1, Walters 1.
FA Cup (4): Bruce 1, Counago 1, Stead 1, Walters 1 (pen).

Wright R 46	Smith T 2	Wright D 34	Garvan O 22+15	McAuley G 35	Balkestein P 15+5	Haynes D 8+16	Sumulikoski V 22+4	Lisbie K 24+17	Counago P 26+18	Quinn A 28+6	Miller T 26+6	Rhodes J —+2	Lee A 2+1	Bruce A 25	Thatcher B 20	Naylor R 20+3	Trotter L 2+1	Walters J 30+6	Volz M 20+2	Campo I 14+3	Stead J 26+13	Norris D 35+2	Ambrose D 6+3	Harding D 1	Civelli L 8	Bowditch D —+1	Giovani 6+2	Wickham C —+2	Peters J 2+1	Richards M 1	Match No.
1	2	3	4	5	6	7¹	8	9	10²	11¹	12	13	14																		1
1		12		5		13	8	9²	14				4	10	2	3		6				7¹	11³								2
1		13		5		7¹	8²	9	14				4	10³	2⁴	3		6		12		11									3
1				5		14	12	9³	10²	8	13				3	6	11¹	7	2	4											4
1	2	4	5²	13		12	10³	11	8					6		7	3	14	9¹												5
1	3	4	5		12	13	14	11	8¹					6		7	2	10²	9³												6
1	3	4	5		8	12		11						6		7	2	10¹	9												7
1	3	12	5		8³	9	13		4					2	6		11	14	10²	7¹											8
1	3	4¹	5	13		14	10²	11						2	6	7³		8	9	12											9
1	3	12	5		13	14	11	8³						6	9	2	4¹	10²	7												10
1	3	12	5		13	10	11²	14						6	7	2	4³	9¹	8												11
1	3	4	5		12	8³	13	10²	11¹	7				6	9	2		14													12
1	3	4²	5		8	10³	12	11	13					6	9¹	2		14	7*												13
1	3	4	5		12	8	9	13	11¹					6	7	2		10²													14
1	3	4	5		8	9²	12	11¹						6	10	2		13	7												15
1	3	4	5		8	9²		11¹	12					6	10	2		13	7												16
1	3	4		8	9¹	12	11³							5	6	10²	2	13	7	14											17
1	2	4		8	12	10³		13						5	3	6		9¹		14	7²	11									18
1	2	4		12	8¹	13	10²	14						5	3	6		7		9³		11									19
1	3		5		8	12	10	13	4³					6		14		2		9¹	7	11²									20
1	3	4²	5		12	8		10³						6	13	9	2		14	7	11¹										21
1	3	12	5		8	13	10²							6*	14	11	2		9³	7	4¹										22
1		12	5	13	14	4¹		10²						3*	6	11	2		9³	7	8										23
1	3		5		8²	9	12	11³	4					6	13²			10¹	7	14											24
1			5		8²	9	12	11³	6					3	13	2¹	4	10	7	14											25
1		5	12		8	9²	13	11	6					3¹		10	2	4		7											26
1		12	5		8	9³	10		4¹	2	3			11		13	6²	14	7												27
1	4	5	6	8¹		12	10³	13	11	2				9²		14	7			3											28
1	2	14	5	6		13	8²	12	11	4				3		9¹		10³	7												29
1	3	4	5	6		13		12	10	8				2		11		9²	7¹												30
1	2	4²	5	6		13		8	12	11	10			3		9¹		14	7³												31
1	2	4¹	5		7	12		10		8				6	3			9								11²	13				32
1	2	12	5		7²			10¹	11	4				6	3			13		9	14					8³					33
1	2	12	5			14		10¹	11	4				6	3			13		9³	7					8²					34
1	3		5	12				14	10	11	4			6		13	2¹			9³	7²					8					35
1	3	12	5	6				14	10	11¹	4			2		13				9³	7					8²					36
1	2			6				10²	12	11	4			3		9¹		5		13	7					8					37
1	2	12	5	6				10²	13	11¹	4			3		9³					7					8	14				38
1	2	12	5					9²	13	14	4³			3			6	10			7¹					8	11				39
1	2²	12	5	13	14				10	11	4¹			3			6	9			7					8³					40
1		4		5	13	8		10	12	11				2	3			14	6³	9¹	7²										41
1	2	4		5		8¹		13	10²	14				3	9			6			7³						11	12			42
1	2¹			5		4	9	10³	11					6	3			8²	12		7						13	14			43
1				5	13	4	9	10³	11					2	3¹			6	14		7						8²	12			44
1		4		5	13		9	10²	14					2¹				6	12		7						11	8³	3		45
1	3	4		5	12	14	8³	10²	13					6				9			7						11¹	2			46

FA Cup

Third Round	Chesterfield	(h)	3-0
Fourth Round	Chelsea	(a)	1-3

Carling Cup

First Round	Leyton Orient	(h)	4-1
Second Round	Colchester U	(h)	2-1
Third Round	Wigan Ath	(h)	1-4

LEEDS UNITED   FL Championship 1

FOUNDATION

Immediately the Leeds City club (founded in 1904) was wound up by the FA in October 1919, following allegations of illegal payments to players, a meeting was called by a Leeds solicitor, Mr Alf Masser, at which Leeds United was formed. They joined the Midland League playing their first game in that competition in November 1919. It was in this same month that the new club had discussions with the directors of a virtually bankrupt Huddersfield Town who wanted to move to Leeds in an amalgamation. But Huddersfield survived even that crisis.

Elland Road, Leeds, West Yorkshire LS11 0ES.

Telephone: (0871) 334 1919.

Fax: (0113) 367 6050.

Ticket Office: 0871 334 1992.

Website: www.leedsunited.com

Email: reception@leedsunited.com

Ground Capacity: 39,457.

Record Attendance: 57,892 v Sunderland, FA Cup 5th rd (replay), 15 March 1967.

Pitch Measurements: 115yd × 76yd.

Chairman: Ken Bates.

Chief Executive: Shaun Harvey.

Manager: Simon Grayson.

Assistant Managers: Glynn Snodin, Ian Miller.

Physio: Harvey Sharman.

Colours: All white with one vertical blue stripe and blue trim sleeves, white shorts, white stockings.

Change Colours: Turquoise and navy blue stripe shirts, navy shorts, navy stockings

Year Formed: 1919, as Leeds United after disbandment (by FA order) of Leeds City (formed in 1904).

Turned Professional: 1920.

Ltd Co.: 1920.

Club Nickname: 'The Whites'.

Ground: 1919, Elland Road.

First Football League Game: 28 August 1920, Division 2, v Port Vale (a) L 0–2 – Down; Duffield, Tillotson; Musgrove, Baker, Walton; Mason, Goldthorpe, Thompson, Lyon, Best.

HONOURS

Football League: Division 1 – Champions 1968–69, 1973–74, 1991–92; Runners-up 1964–65, 1965–66, 1969–70, 1970–71, 1971–72; Division 2 – Champions 1923–24, 1963–64, 1989–90; Runners-up 1927–28, 1931–32, 1955–56.

FA Cup: Winners 1972; Runners-up 1965, 1970, 1973.

Football League Cup: Winners 1968; Runners-up 1996.

European Competitions: European Cup: 1969–70, 1974–75 (runners-up). *Champions League:* 1992–93, 2000–01 (semi-finalists). *European Cup-Winners' Cup:* 1972–73 (runners-up). *European Fairs Cup:* 1965–66, 1966–67 (runners-up), 1967–68 (winners), 1968–69, 1970–71 (winners). *UEFA Cup:* 1971–72, 1973–74, 1979–80, 1995–96, 1998–99, 1999–2000 (semi-finalists), 2001–02, 2002–03.

SKY SPORTS FACT FILE

On 24 November 1956 Leeds United were three goals down at half-time to Arsenal. They pulled one back through John Charles after 64 minutes, Bob Forrest added a second three minutes later and finally Charles levelled in the 84th minute. All three goals were headed.

Record League Victory: 8–0 v Leicester C, Division 1, 7 April 1934 – Moore; George Milburn, Jack Milburn; Edwards, Hart, Copping; Mahon (2), Firth (2), Duggan (2), Furness (2), Cochrane.

Record Cup Victory: 10–0 v Lyn (Oslo), European Cup 1st rd 1st leg, 17 September 1969 – Sprake; Reaney, Cooper, Bremner (2), Charlton, Hunter, Madeley, Clarke (2), Jones (3), Giles (2) (Bates), O'Grady (1).

Record Defeat: 1–8 v Stoke C, Division 1, 27 August 1934.

Most League Points (2 for a win): 67, Division 1, 1968–69.

Most League Points (3 for a win): 85, Division 2, 1989–90.

Most League Goals: 98, Division 2, 1927–28.

Highest League Scorer in Season: John Charles, 42, Division 2, 1953–54.

Most League Goals in Total Aggregate: Peter Lorimer, 168, 1965–79 and 1983–86.

Most League Goals in One Match: 5, Gordon Hodgson v Leicester C, Division 1, 1 October 1938.

Most Capped Player: Lucas Radebe, 58 (70), South Africa.

Most League Appearances: Jack Charlton, 629, 1953–73.

Youngest League Player: Peter Lorimer, 15 years 289 days v Southampton, 29 September 1962.

Record Transfer Fee Received: £30,000,000 from Manchester U for Rio Ferdinand, July 2002.

Record Transfer Fee Paid: £18,000,000 to West Ham United for Rio Ferdinand, November 2000.

MANAGERS

Dick Ray 1919–20
Arthur Fairclough 1920–27
Dick Ray 1927–35
Bill Hampson 1935–47
Willis Edwards 1947–48
Major Frank Buckley 1948–53
Raich Carter 1953–58
Bill Lambton 1958–59
Jack Taylor 1959–61
Don Revie OBE 1961–74
Brian Clough 1974
Jimmy Armfield 1974–78
Jock Stein CBE 1978
Jimmy Adamson 1978–80
Allan Clarke 1980–82
Eddie Gray MBE 1982–85
Billy Bremner 1985–88
Howard Wilkinson 1988–96
George Graham 1996–98
David O'Leary 1998–2002
Terry Venables 2002–03
Peter Reid 2003
Eddie Gray *(Caretaker)* 2003–04
Kevin Blackwell 2004–06
Dennis Wise 2006–08
Gary McAllister 2008
Simon Grayson December 2008–

Football League Record: 1920 Elected to Division 2; 1924–27 Division 1; 1927–28 Division 2; 1928–31 Division 1; 1931–32 Division 2; 1932–47 Division 1; 1947–56 Division 2; 1956–60 Division 1; 1960–64 Division 2; 1964–82 Division 1; 1982–90 Division 2; 1990–92 Division 1; 1992–2004 FA Premier League; 2004–07 FL C; 2007– FL 1.

LATEST SEQUENCES

Longest Sequence of League Wins: 9, 26.9.1931 – 21.11.1931.

Longest Sequence of League Defeats: 6, 28.12.2003 – 7.2.2004.

Longest Sequence of League Draws: 5, 19.4.1997 – 9.8.1997.

Longest Sequence of Unbeaten League Matches: 34, 26.10.1968 – 26.8.1969.

Longest Sequence Without a League Win: 17, 1.2.1947 – 26.5.1947.

Successive Scoring Runs: 30 from 27.8.1927.

Successive Non-scoring Runs: 6 from 30.1.1982.

TEN YEAR LEAGUE RECORD

		P	W	D	L	F	A	Pts	Pos
1999-2000	PR Lge	38	21	6	11	58	43	69	3
2000-01	PR Lge	38	20	8	10	64	43	68	4
2001-02	PR Lge	38	18	12	8	53	37	66	5
2002-03	PR Lge	38	14	5	19	58	57	47	15
2003-04	PR Lge	38	8	9	21	40	79	33	19
2004-05	FL C	46	14	18	14	49	52	60	14
2005-06	FL C	46	21	15	10	57	38	78	5
2006-07	FL C	46	13	7	26	46	72	36*	24
2007-08	FL 1	46	27	10	9	72	38	76†	5
2008-09	FL 1	46	26	6	14	77	49	84	4

10 pts deducted; †15 pts deducted.

DID YOU KNOW ❓

On a goals-per-game ratio, veteran Gordon Hodgson was outstanding as a Leeds United centre-forward. A South African-born England international aged 34 when signed from Liverpool in March 1937 he scored 53 goals in 86 games.

LEEDS UNITED 2008–09 LEAGUE RECORD

Match No.	Date	Venue	Opponents	Result	H/T Score	Lg. Pos.	Goalscorers	Attendance
1	Aug 9	A	Scunthorpe U	W 2-1	0-0	—	Showunmi [61], Beckford [80]	8315
2	16	H	Oldham Ath	L 0-2	0-0	13		24,631
3	23	A	Yeovil T	D 1-1	1-0	12	Becchio [1]	6580
4	30	H	Bristol R	D 2-2	1-2	14	Elliott (og) [5], Beckford [77]	21,024
5	Sept 6	H	Crewe Alex	W 5-2	2-0	6	Delph [26], Sheehan [36], Douglas [49], Beckford [67], Robinson [82]	20,075
6	13	A	Swindon T	W 3-1	1-1	4	Beckford 2 [22, 84], Kilkenny [50]	13,001
7	20	A	Carlisle U	W 2-0	1-0	3	Becchio [31], Beckford [86]	12,148
8	27	H	Hereford U	W 1-0	0-0	3	Robinson [72]	25,676
9	Oct 4	A	Peterborough U	L 0-2	0-0	4		13,191
10	11	H	Brighton & HA	W 3-1	2-0	4	Becchio [44], Beckford 2 [45, 89]	22,726
11	18	A	Millwall	L 1-3	0-1	5	Becchio [31]	13,041
12	21	H	Leyton Orient	W 2-1	2-1	—	Purches (og) [38], Becchio [45]	18,990
13	25	H	Walsall	W 3-0	0-0	2	Becchio [46], Delph 2 [65, 86]	22,422
14	28	A	Southend U	L 0-1	0-1	—		10,132
15	Nov 1	A	Cheltenham T	W 1-0	1-0	2	Becchio [7]	5726
16	15	H	Huddersfield T	L 1-2	1-0	6	Snodgrass [4]	32,028
17	22	H	Hartlepool U	W 4-1	1-1	6	Beckford 2 [15, 90], Delph [50], Becchio [64]	21,182
18	25	A	Northampton T	L 1-2	0-1	—	Beckford [69]	6008
19	Dec 6	A	Tranmere R	L 1-2	1-1	7	Showunmi [11]	8700
20	13	A	Colchester U	L 1-2	1-1	8	Snodgrass [34]	19,625
21	20	A	Milton Keynes D	L 1-3	0-2	9	Snodgrass [49]	17,073
22	26	H	Leicester C	D 1-1	0-1	9	Snodgrass [90]	33,580
23	28	A	Stockport Co	W 3-1	1-1	9	Becchio [19], Delph [73], Christie [86]	10,273
24	Jan 10	H	Carlisle U	L 0-2	0-2	—		22,411
25	17	A	Brighton & HA	W 2-0	0-0	9	Trundle [61], Delph [82]	7096
26	24	H	Peterborough U	W 3-1	0-0	7	Beckford 2 [62, 71], Howson [90]	22,766
27	27	H	Southend U	W 2-0	2-0	—	Rui Marques [6], Naylor [11]	20,392
28	31	A	Walsall	L 0-1	0-1	7		8920
29	Feb 9	H	Millwall	W 2-0	1-0	—	Beckford 2 [32, 90]	19,314
30	14	A	Huddersfield T	L 0-1	0-1	7		20,928
31	17	A	Hereford U	L 0-2	0-1	—		6120
32	21	H	Cheltenham T	W 2-0	0-0	8	Howson 2 [54, 65]	20,131
33	28	H	Scunthorpe U	W 3-2	2-1	6	Beckford 2 [33, 69], Johnson [38]	24,921
34	Mar 2	A	Oldham Ath	D 1-1	0-0	—	Becchio [53]	7835
35	7	A	Bristol R	D 2-2	1-1	7	Becchio [27], Snodgrass [58]	10,293
36	10	H	Yeovil T	W 4-0	2-0	—	Beckford 3 [25, 51, 58], Kilkenny [43]	18,847
37	14	H	Swindon T	W 1-0	0-0	5	Beckford [87]	21,765
38	21	A	Crewe Alex	W 3-2	3-0	5	Kilkenny [27], Becchio [30], Snodgrass [32]	7138
39	28	H	Milton Keynes D	W 2-0	1-0	5	Beckford 2 [37, 54]	27,649
40	Apr 4	A	Colchester U	W 1-0	1-0	5	Becchio [29]	9559
41	7	A	Leyton Orient	D 2-2	1-0	—	Snodgrass 2 (1 pen) [19, 60 (p)]	6943
42	11	H	Stockport Co	W 1-0	1-0	5	Howson [9]	24,967
43	13	A	Leicester C	L 0-1	0-0	5		25,507
44	18	H	Tranmere R	W 3-1	2-1	5	Beckford [15], Kilkenny [26], Becchio [56]	24,360
45	25	A	Hartlepool U	W 1-0	0-0	5	Beckford [60]	6402
46	May 2	H	Northampton T	W 3-0	1-0	4	Becchio [44], Beckford [59], Snodgrass [90]	34,214

Final League Position: 4

GOALSCORERS

League (77): Beckford 26, Becchio 15, Snodgrass 9 (1 pen), Delph 6, Howson 4, Kilkenny 4, Robinson 2, Showunmi 2, Christie 1, Douglas 1, Johnson 1, Naylor 1, Rui Marques 1, Sheehan 1, Trundle 1, own goals 2.
Carling Cup (13): Beckford 4, Becchio 2, Robinson 2, Showunmi 2, Snodgrass 2, Douglas 1.
FA Cup (6): Beckford 3, Parker 1, Robinson 1 (pen), own goal 1.
J Paint Trophy (4): Becchio 1, Howson 1, Robinson 1 (pen), Showunmi 1.
Play-Offs (1): Becchio 1.

Ankergren C 33	Richardson F 21+2	Sheehan A 11	Howson J 26+14	Huntington P 4	Rui Marques M 32	Prutton D 8+8	Snodgrass R 25+17	Beckford J 32+2	Showunmi E 3+5	Robinson A 20+12	Becchio L 40+5	Hughes A 18+9	Delph F 40+2	Douglas J 42+1	Lucas D 13	Michalik L 15+4	Johnson B 7+8	Kilkenny N 27+3	Telfer P 14	White A 5	Parker B 23+1	Christie M 1+3	Assoumani M 1	Trundle L 7+3	Dickinson C 7	Naylor R 22	Grella M —+11	Sodje S 5	Dickinson L 4+4	Match No.
1	2	3	4	5	6	7	8	9	10[1]	11[2]	12	13																		1
1	2	3	4[1]	5	6	7	8	9	10[2]	11	13			12																2
1	2	3	4[2]	5	6	7	8[1]	9	14	11[3]	10			13	12															3
	2		13	5			14	9	12		10[3]	8[2]	11	7	1	6	3[1]	4												4
	2	3	12				14	9		13	10[3]	7[1]	11	8	1	6[4]		4[2]	5											5
	2	3[4]	12		6	13	14	9[3]			10[1]	11	8	7	1			4[2]	5											6
	2		12		6		13	9		14	10[3]	11	8	7	1			4[2]	5	3[1]										7
	2		4		6		12	9		11[1]	10	13	8	7	1				5	3[2]										8
1	2		4[1]		6		12	9		11	10		8[2]	7	13				5		3[3]	14								9
	2				6			9			10	8	11	7	1	5		4			3									10
	2				6		12	9	13		10	11[2]	8	7	1	5		4[1]			3									11
	2		8				12	9		13	10[1]		11	7	1	6		4[2]	5		3									12
1	2		8				12	13	9	14	10[2]		11[1]	7		6		4[3]	5		3									13
1	2		8				12	9		13	10		11[1]	7		6		4[2]	5		3									14
1	2		8[3]				12	13	9[2]	14	10		11	7		6		4[1]	5		3									15
1	2		12				13	9	14	8	10		11[1]	7		6		4[3]	5		3									16
							7	12	9		8	10[1]	2	11	4	1	6		5		3									17
	13						7	12	9[2]		11	10	2	4	8[1]	1	6		5		3									18
	2	3	4[1]		6	7	8		9		10			11	1		12	5												19
	3				6	7[4]	9			12	10	2[1]	11	8	1			4[2]	5			13								20
12	3	8[2]			6		9			13	10		11	7	1	5[1]		4					2							21
1	2	3	12		6	7[3]	13	9		11[1]	10	14	4	8[2]		5														22
1	2	3	12		6	13	8[1]	9[3]		10	11[2]	4	7			5			14											23
1	2	3[1]			6		8		13	10	11[2]	4	7		5	12						9[3]		14						24
1	2[2]		12		6			13	10	8	4	7				11[1]			14			9[3]			3	5				25
1			13		6		14	12		8[3]	10[1]	2	4	7				11				9[2]			3	5				26
1			14		6		12	9[2]		8[1]	13	2	4	7				11				10[3]			3	5				27
1			14		6		12	9[2]		8	13	2	4	7[3]				11[1]				10			3	5				28
1			13		6		8[2]	9		11[3]	12	2	4	7					14			10[1]			3	5				29
1			13		6[1]		8			11	9	2[2]	4	7				12				10[3]			3	5	14			30
1			8		6	12	7[2]			11	9		4		13						3[1]	10[3]	2			5	14			31
1			8		6		10[2]			11	9[3]	2[1]	4	7				12			3			13		5	14			32
1			8[4]		6		10	9		11[3]		4	2					13	14	7[1]	3	12[2]		5						33
1					6		7	9		10		4	2					11	8		3					5				34
1	4				6	12	7	9		10		11	2					8[1]			3					5				35
1			8		6		7	9		10[2]		11	2					12	4[1]		3					5	13			36
1			8		6		7	9[4]		10[3]		11	2					12	4[1]		3[2]					5	13		14	37
1			8		6[1]		7			10		11	2					12	13	4[2]	3					5	14		9[3]	38
1			8				7[3]	9		10	12	11	2					13		4[1]	3					5		6[2]	14	39
1			8				7[2]	9		12	10[3]	13	11	2				4[1]			3					5		6	14	40
1			8	6			7			12	10	13	11	2				4[2]			3					5	13		9[1]	41
1			8	6			7			12	10[1]		11	2				4			3					5	13		9[2]	42
1			8				7			12	10[1]	13	11	2				4[2]			3					5	14	6	9[3]	43
1			8				7[1]	9[3]		11[2]	10	13		2				12	4		3					5	14	6		44
1			8				9[2]			7[1]	10	13		2				11	4[3]		3					5	12	6	14	45
1	13		8	6			12	9[3]		7	10		11	2				4[1]			3[2]					5	14			46

FA Cup

First Round	Northampton T	(h)	1-1
		(a)	5-2
Second Round	Histon	(a)	0-1

J Paint Trophy

First Round	Bradford C	(h)	2-1
Second Round	Rotherham U	(a)	2-4

Carling Cup

First Round	Chester C	(a)	5-2
Second Round	Crystal Palace	(h)	4-0
Third Round	Hartlepool U	(h)	3-2
Fourth Round	Derby Co	(a)	1-2

Play-Offs

Semi-Final	Millwall	(a)	0-1
		(h)	1-1

LEICESTER CITY   FL Championship

FOUNDATION

In 1884 a number of young footballers who were mostly old boys of Wyggeston School, held a meeting at a house on the Roman Fosse Way and formed Leicester Fosse FC. They collected 9d (less than 4p) towards the cost of a ball, plus the same amount for membership. Their first professional, Harry Webb from Stafford Rangers, was signed in 1888 for 2s 6d (12p) per week, plus travelling expenses.

Walkers Stadium, Filbert Way, Leicester LE2 7FL.
Telephone: 0844 815 6000.
Fax: (0116) 229 4549.
Ticket Office: 0844 815 5000.
Website: www.lcfc.co.uk
Email: customer.relations@lcfc.co.uk
Ground Capacity: 32,312.
Record Attendance: 47,298 v Tottenham H, FA Cup 5th rd, 18 February 1928.
Pitch Measurements: 110yd × 74yd.
Chairman: Milan Mandaric.
Chief Executive: Lee Hoos.
Secretary: Andrew Neville.
Manager: Nigel Pearson.
Assistant Managers: Craig Shakespeare, Steve Walsh.
Physio: Dave Rennie.
Colours: Blue shirts with white trim, white shorts, blue stockings with white trim.
Change Colours: Mustard shirts with white trim and alternative blue sleeve, blue shorts, mustard stockings.
Year Formed: 1884.
Turned Professional: 1888.   *Ltd Co:* 1897.
Previous Name: 1884, Leicester Fosse; 1919, Leicester City.
Club Nickname: 'Foxes'.
Grounds: 1884, Victoria Park; 1887, Belgrave Road; 1888, Victoria Park; 1891, Filbert Street; 2002, Walkers Stadium.
First Football League Game: 1 September 1894, Division 2, v Grimsby T (a) L 3–4 – Thraves; Smith, Bailey; Seymour, Brown, Henrys; Hill, Hughes, McArthur (1), Skea (2), Priestman.
Record League Victory: 10–0 v Portsmouth, Division 1, 20 October 1928 – McLaren; Black, Brown; Findlay, Carr, Watson; Adcock, Hine (3), Chandler (6), Lochhead, Barry (1).
Record Cup Victory: 8–1 v Coventry C (a), League Cup 5th rd, 1 December 1964 – Banks; Sjoberg, Norman (2); Roberts, King, McDerment; Hodgson (2), Cross, Goodfellow, Gibson (1), Stringfellow (2), (1 og).

HONOURS

Football League: Division 1 – Runners-up 1928–29; Division 2 – Champions 1924–25, 1936–37, 1953–54, 1956–57, 1970–71, 1979–80; Runners-up 1907–08; FL 1 – Champions 2008–09.

FA Cup: Runners-up 1949, 1961, 1963, 1969.

Football League Cup: Winners 1964, 1997, 2000; Runners-up 1965, 1999.

European Competitions: *European Cup-Winners' Cup:* 1961–62. *UEFA Cup:* 1997–98, 2000–01.

SKY SPORTS FACT FILE

On 6 December 2008 Matty Fryatt scored his second hat-trick in a week for Leicester City in the 3–0 win over Southend United. It took his League and Cup goals to 22, the first City player to reach 20 before Christmas since Derek Dougan in 1966.

Record Defeat: 0–12 (as Leicester Fosse) v Nottingham F, Division 1, 21 April 1909.

Most League Points (2 for a win): 61, Division 2, 1956–57.

Most League Points (3 for a win): 96, FL 1, 2008–09.

Most League Goals: 109, Division 2, 1956–57.

Highest League Scorer in Season: Arthur Rowley, 44, Division 2, 1956–57.

Most League Goals in Total Aggregate: Arthur Chandler, 259, 1923–35.

Most League Goals in One Match: 6, John Duncan v Port Vale, Division 2, 25 December 1924; 6, Arthur Chandler v Portsmouth, Division 1, 20 October 1928.

Most Capped Player: John O'Neill, 39, Northern Ireland.

Most League Appearances: Adam Black, 528, 1920–35.

Youngest League Player: Dave Buchanan, 16 years 192 days v Oldham Ath, 1 January 1979.

Record Transfer Fee Received: £11,000,000 from Liverpool for Emile Heskey, March 2000.

Record Transfer Fee Paid: £5,000,000 to Wolverhampton W for Ade Akinbiyi, July 2000.

Football League Record: 1894 Elected to Division 2; 1908–09 Division 1; 1909–25 Division 2; 1925–35 Division 1; 1935–37 Division 2; 1937–39 Division 1; 1946–54 Division 2; 1954–55 Division 1; 1955–57 Division 2; 1957–69 Division 1; 1969–71 Division 2; 1971–78 Division 1; 1978–80 Division 2; 1980–81 Division 1; 1981–83 Division 2; 1983–87 Division 1; 1987–92 Division 2; 1992–94 Division 1; 1994–95 FA Premier League; 1995–96 Division 1; 1996–2002 FA Premier League; 2002–03 Division 1; 2003–04 FA Premier League; 2004–08 FL C; 2008–09 FL 1; 2009– FL C.

LATEST SEQUENCES

Longest Sequence of League Wins: 7, 28.2.1993 – 27.3.1993.

Longest Sequence of League Defeats: 8, 17.3.2001 – 28.4.2001.

Longest Sequence of League Draws: 6, 21.8.1976 – 18.9.1976.

Longest Sequence of Unbeaten League Matches: 23, 1.11.2008 – 7.3.2009.

Longest Sequence Without a League Win: 18, 12.4.1975 – 1.11.1975.

Successive Scoring Runs: 31 from 12.11.1932.

Successive Non-scoring Runs: 7 from 21.11.1987.

MANAGERS

Frank Gardner 1884–92
Ernest Marson 1892–94
J. Lee 1894–95
Henry Jackson 1895–97
William Clark 1897–98
George Johnson 1898–1912
Jack Bartlett 1912–14
Louis Ford 1914–15
Harry Linney 1915–19
Peter Hodge 1919–26
Willie Orr 1926–32
Peter Hodge 1932–34
Arthur Lochhead 1934–36
Frank Womack 1936–39
Tom Bromilow 1939–45
Tom Mather 1945–46
John Duncan 1946–49
Norman Bullock 1949–55
David Halliday 1955–58
Matt Gillies 1958–68
Frank O'Farrell 1968–71
Jimmy Bloomfield 1971–77
Frank McLintock 1977–78
Jock Wallace 1978–82
Gordon Milne 1982–86
Bryan Hamilton 1986–87
David Pleat 1987–91
Gordon Lee 1991
Brian Little 1991–94
Mark McGhee 1994–95
Martin O'Neill 1995–2000
Peter Taylor 2000–01
Dave Bassett 2001–02
Micky Adams 2002–04
Craig Levein 2004–06
Robert Kelly 2006–07
Martin Allen 2007
Gary Megson 2007
Ian Holloway 2007–08
Nigel Pearson June 2008–

TEN YEAR LEAGUE RECORD

		P	W	D	L	F	A	Pts	Pos
1999-2000	PR Lge	38	16	7	15	55	55	55	8
2000-01	PR Lge	38	14	6	18	39	51	48	13
2001-02	PR Lge	38	5	13	20	30	64	28	20
2002-03	Div 1	46	26	14	6	73	40	92	2
2003-04	PR Lge	38	6	15	17	48	65	33	18
2004-05	FL C	46	12	21	13	49	46	57	15
2005-06	FL C	46	13	15	18	51	59	54	16
2006-07	FL C	46	13	14	19	49	64	53	19
2007-08	FL C	46	12	16	18	42	45	52	22
2008-09	FL 1	46	27	15	4	84	39	96	1

DID YOU KNOW ?

Between 1990 and 2000 Leicester City appeared at Wembley on seven different occasions. Three of these were in the League Cup final and four in the Football League play-offs. They are also one of two to win the Charity Shield without League or Cup honours.

LEICESTER CITY 2008–09 LEAGUE RECORD

Match No.	Date	Venue	Opponents	Result	H/T Score	Lg. Pos.	Goalscorers	Attendance
1	Aug 9	H	Milton Keynes D	W 2-0	1-0	—	Fryatt 2 (1 pen) 24 (p), 83	23,351
2	16	A	Stockport Co	D 0-0	0-0	3		7151
3	23	H	Tranmere R	W 3-1	1-0	2	Howard 33, Fryatt 2 52, 90	17,798
4	30	A	Cheltenham T	W 4-0	1-0	1	Dyer 2 3, 80, Oakley 54, Fryatt 77	5344
5	Sept 13	H	Millwall	L 0-1	0-1	6		19,591
6	20	A	Leyton Orient	W 3-1	1-1	5	Dyer 11, Fryatt 87, King A 90	6448
7	27	H	Hartlepool U	W 1-0	1-0	5	Oakley 3	18,578
8	30	A	Colchester U	W 1-0	0-0	—	Dyer 49	5133
9	Oct 4	A	Huddersfield T	W 3-2	0-0	1	Fryatt 2 (1 pen) 5, 65 (p), Dyer 90	16,212
10	18	A	Oldham Ath	D 1-1	0-0	2	Howard 54	8901
11	21	H	Walsall	D 2-2	1-1	—	King A 34, Tunchev 73	17,178
12	25	A	Northampton T	D 0-0	0-0	4		22,795
13	28	A	Brighton & HA	L 2-3	2-0	—	Fryatt 2 35, 42	6282
14	Nov 1	H	Bristol R	W 2-1	0-0	5	Fryatt 2 87, 90	18,941
15	11	H	Yeovil T	W 1-0	1-0	—	Dyer 25	16,528
16	15	A	Swindon T	D 2-2	0-0	2	Oakley 57, Fryatt 74	9499
17	22	A	Scunthorpe U	W 2-1	1-1	1	Dyer 22, King A 81	7957
18	25	H	Crewe Alex	W 2-1	1-1	—	Fryatt 15, King A 72	16,961
19	Dec 6	H	Southend U	W 3-0	1-0	1	Fryatt 3 (1 pen) 6, 76, 80 (p)	16,836
20	13	A	Carlisle U	W 2-1	0-1	1	King A 60, Berner 69	7085
21	20	H	Peterborough U	W 4-0	2-0	1	Morgan (og) 6, Fryatt 38, King A 70, Howard 90	23,390
22	26	A	Leeds U	D 1-1	0-0	1	Oakley 24	33,580
23	28	H	Hereford U	W 2-1	1-0	1	Howard 9, King A 71	22,920
24	Jan 10	H	Leyton Orient	W 3-0	2-0	—	Oakley 9, Davies 37, Dickov (pen) 84	18,240
25	19	A	Yeovil T	W 2-0	0-0	—	Howard 57, Mattock 88	4569
26	24	H	Huddersfield T	W 4-2	1-1	1	Morrison 11, Berner 59, Fryatt 63, Hobbs 73	21,311
27	27	H	Brighton & HA	D 0-0	0-0	—		17,410
28	31	A	Northampton T	W 2-1	1-1	1	Howard (pen) 21, Dyer 73	7028
29	Feb 3	A	Walsall	W 4-1	2-0	1	Fryatt 12, King A 34, Cleverley 47, Howard 52	5634
30	7	H	Oldham Ath	D 0-0	0-0	1		22,328
31	14	H	Swindon T	D 1-1	0-1	1	King A 86	19,926
32	17	A	Hartlepool U	D 2-2	1-1	1	Howard 2 (1 pen) 28, 80 (p)	4068
33	21	A	Bristol R	W 1-0	1-0	1	Fryatt 20	9138
34	28	A	Milton Keynes D	D 2-2	1-1	1	Fryatt 5, Gradel 90	17,717
35	Mar 3	H	Stockport Co	D 1-1	1-1	—	Gilbert 2	16,378
36	7	H	Cheltenham T	W 4-0	2-0	1	Howard 15, Fryatt 22, Cleverley 67, Oakley 70	18,939
37	11	A	Tranmere R	L 0-2	0-0	—		6032
38	14	A	Millwall	W 1-0	1-0	1	Howard 22	13,261
39	21	H	Colchester U	D 1-1	0-1	1	Dickov 67	20,218
40	28	A	Peterborough U	L 0-2	0-1	1		14,110
41	Apr 4	H	Carlisle U	D 2-2	0-1	1	Oakley 52, Fryatt 88	20,159
42	11	A	Hereford U	W 3-1	1-1	1	Oakley 35, Dyer 74, Howard 86	4389
43	13	H	Leeds U	W 1-0	0-0	1	Howard 90	25,507
44	18	A	Southend U	W 2-0	0-0	1	Fryatt 2 (1 pen) 60 (p), 70	10,089
45	24	H	Scunthorpe U	D 2-2	1-0	—	Morrison 2 16, 77	30,542
46	May 2	A	Crewe Alex	W 3-0	0-0	1	Berner 56, Dyer 66, Fryatt 68	6982

Final League Position: 1

GOALSCORERS

League (84): Fryatt 27 (4 pens), Howard 13 (2 pens), Dyer 10, King A 9, Oakley 8, Berner 3, Morrison 3, Cleverley 2, Dickov 2 (1 pen), Davies 1, Gilbert 1, Gradel 1, Hobbs 1, Mattock 1, Tunchev 1, own goal 1.
Carling Cup (3): Dickov 1, Howard 1, King A 1.
FA Cup (7): Fryatt 4 (1 pen), Dyer 1, Gradel 1, King A 1.
J Paint Trophy (3): Adams 1, Fryatt 1, Howard 1.

Henderson P 6	Gilbert K 33+1	Mattock J 25+6	King A 45	Morrison M 32+3	Tunchev A 19+1	Gradel M 16+11	Oakley M 45	Howard S 40+1	Fryatt M 46	Dyer L 43+1	Dickov P 4+16	Hobbs J 39+5	Martin D 25	Porter L 1	Adams N 4+8	Powell C 12+5	Campbell D 2+5	Kisnorbo P 5+3	Berner B 21+11	Hayles B 1+9	Edworthy M 5	Davies M 5+2	Cleverley T 10+5	Brown W 7+2	Pentney C —+1	Chambers A —+1	Bunn M 3	Stockdale D 8	Warner T 4	Ajdarevic A —+5	Match No.
1	2	3	4	5	6^2	7	8	9^1	10	11	12	13																			1
1	2		4	5	6	7^1	8	9	10	11	12	3																			2
	2		4	5		7^1	8	9	10	3	13	6	1	11^2	12																3
	2		4	5	6^1	13	8	9	10^3	11	7^2	3	1				12	14													4
	2^1		4	5	12	7^3	8	9	10	11	13	6	1				3^2	14													5
	2^1		4	5	6	7^2	8	9^3	10	11	12		1		13	3	14														6
	2		4		6		8	9	10	11		5	1		7	3															7
	2		4		6		8	9	10	11		5	1		7	3															8
	2		4	12	6	13	8	9	10^1	11		5	1		7^2	3															9
	2		4	5^2	12		8	9	10	11^3		6	1		7^1	3		13	14												10
	2^2	12	4		6	7	8	9	10	11^3		5	1			3^1		13	14												11
		3^2	4		6	7	8	9^1	10	11		2	1					5	13	12											12
			4		6	7^1		9	10	11		2	1		12	3		5	8												13
1		3	4		6	7^2	8	9^1	10	11		2^3			13			5	14	12											14
1		3	4	5	6		8	9	10^2	11		12					13		7				2^1								15
1		3	4	5	6		8	9	10^1	11		12					13		7				2								16
1		3^3	4	5	6	12	8		10^1	11					13		14	9	7				2^2								17
		3	4	5	6	12	8^1	13	10	11		14	1					9^2	7				2^3								18
	2		4	13	6^2		8	9	10^3	11		14	1		5	3			7^1				12								19
	2		4	5			8	9	10^2	11		6	1		13	3^1			7				12								20
	2		4		6		8	9	10	11		12	1			3		5	7												21
		3	4		6		8	9	10	11		12	1					5	7				2								22
	2	12	4		6		8	9	10^2	11^3			1		13	3^1		5	7	14											23
	2	12	4		6	14	8	9	10^2	11^3			1		13	3^1		5	7												24
	2	12	4	5			8	9	10^2	11^1		6	1			3			7				13								25
	2^1	12	4	5			8	9^2	10	11		6	1			3	13		7												26
	2	12	4	5			8		10	11		6	1			3^1	13	9^2	7												27
	2	3^1	4	5			8	9	10	11		6	1				12		7												28
	2^3	3	4	5			8	9	10^2	11^1		6	1		13		12		7				14								29
	2^3	3^2	4	5		14	8	9	10	11^3		6	1		13		12		7												30
	2	3	4	5			8	9	10	11^1		6	1^6				12		7^2									15	13		31
	12	3	4	5^1			8	9	10	11^2		6					13		7				2				1				32
	2	3	4	12			8^2	9	10	11^1		6^8					13	5	7								1				33
	2	3^1	4	5		12	8	9	10	11^3							13		7				14	6^2			1				34
	2	3	4	5			8	9^1	10	11		6				7^2	12						13					1			35
	2	3^3	4	5		11	8^1	9^2	10			6			14	12	13		7									1			36
	2	3^2	4^1	5		13	8	9	10			6				11	12		7									1			37
	2	3	4	5			8	9^2	10	11^1		6					12	13	7									1			38
	2	3	4	5		11^1	8		10	13	12	6						9					7^2					1			39
	2	3	4		7			9	10	11^1		6			12			5	8^2				13					1			40
	2^1	3	4			7^2	8	9	10	11		6				5								12				1		13	41
		3	4	2		12	8	9	10^2	11^3		6			13				7^1				5					1		14	42
		3^2	4	2		7	8	9	10^1	11		12			6				13				5						1		43
		3^2	4	2		7^3	8		10	11		6					13	9^1	12				5						1	14	44
			4	5		7^3	8	9	10	11		6			14	3^1			12			2^2							1	13	45
		3^1	4^2	2		12	8	9	10	11^3		6			14				7				5						1	13	46

FA Cup

First Round	Stevenage B	(h)	3-0
Second Round	Dagenham & R	(h)	3-2
Third Round	Crystal Palace	(h)	0-0
		(a)	1-2

Carling Cup

First Round	Stockport Co	(h)	1-0
Second Round	Fulham	(a)	2-3

J Paint Trophy

First Round	Hartlepool U	(a)	3-0
Second Round	Lincoln C	(h)	0-0
Quarter-Final	Rotherham U	(a)	0-2

LEYTON ORIENT   FL Championship 1

FOUNDATION

There is some doubt about the foundation of Leyton Orient, and, indeed, some confusion with clubs like Leyton and Clapton over their early history. As regards the foundation, the most favoured version is that Leyton Orient was formed originally by members of Homerton Theological College who established Glyn Cricket Club in 1881 and then carried on through the following winter playing football. Eventually many employees of the Orient Shipping Line became involved and so the name Orient was chosen in 1888.

Matchroom Stadium, Brisbane Road, Leyton, London E10 5NF.

Telephone: 0871 310 1881.

Fax: 0871 310 1882.

Ticket Office: 0871 310 1883.

Website: www.leytonorient.com

Email: info@leytonorient.net

Ground Capacity: 9,300

Record Attendance: 34,345 v West Ham U, FA Cup 4th rd, 25 January 1964.

Pitch Measurements: 110yd × 76yd.

Chairman: Barry Hearn.

Vice-chairman: Nick Levene.

Chief Executive: Matthew Porter.

Secretary: Lindsey Martin.

Manager: Geraint Williams.

Assistant Manager: Kevin Nugent.

Physio: Lewis Manning.

Colours: Red shirts with white insert and striped sleeves, red shorts, red stockings.

Change Colours: All blue.

Year Formed: 1881. *Turned Professional:* 1903. *Ltd Co.:* 1906.

Previous Names: 1881, Glyn Cricket and Football Club; 1886, Eagle Football Club; 1888, Orient Football Club; 1898, Clapton Orient; 1946, Leyton Orient; 1966, Orient; 1987, Leyton Orient.

Club Nickname: 'The O's'.

Grounds: 1884, Glyn Road; 1896, Whittles Athletic Ground; 1900, Millfields Road; 1930, Lea Bridge Road; 1937, Brisbane Road.

First Football League Game: 2 September 1905, Division 2, v Leicester Fosse (a) L 1–2 – Butler; Holmes, Codling; Lamberton, Boden, Boyle; Kingaby (1), Wootten, Leigh, Evenson, Bourne.

Record League Victory: 8–0 v Crystal Palace, Division 3 (S), 12 November 1955 – Welton; Lee, Earl; Blizzard, Aldous, McKnight; White (1), Facey (3), Burgess (2), Heckman, Hartburn (2). 8–0 v Rochdale, Division 4, 20 October 1987 – Wells; Howard, Dickenson (1), Smalley (1), Day, Hull, Hales (2), Castle (Sussex), Shinners (2), Godfrey (Harvey), Comfort (2). 8–0 v Colchester U,

HONOURS

Football League: Division 1 best season: 22nd, 1962–63; Division 2 – Runners-up 1961–62; Division 3 – Champions 1969–70; Division 3 (S) – Champions 1955–56; Runners-up 1954–55.

FA Cup: Semi-final 1978.

Football League Cup: best season: 5th rd, 1963.

SKY SPORTS FACT FILE

In 1914, 41 players and staff of Clapton Orient joined the Footballers Battalion of the Middlesex Regiment, the first to volunteer en masse. Richard Madden, George Scott and William Jones subsequently lost their lives in the ensuing First World War.

Division 4, 15 October 1988 – Wells; Howard, Dickenson, Hales (1p), Day (1), Sitton (1), Baker (1), Ward, Hull (3), Juryeff, Comfort (1). 8–0 v Doncaster R, Division 3, 28 December 1997 – Hyde; Channing, Naylor, Smith (1p), Hicks, Clark, Ling, Joseph R, Griffiths (3) (Harris), Richards (2) (Baker (1)), Inglethorpe (1) (Simpson).

Record Cup Victory: 9–2 v Chester, League Cup 3rd rd, 15 October 1962 – Robertson; Charlton, Taylor; Gibbs, Bishop, Lea; Deeley (1), Waites (3), Dunmore (2), Graham (3), Wedge.

Record Defeat: 0–8 v Aston Villa, FA Cup 4th rd, 30 January 1929.

Most League Points (2 for a win): 66, Division 3 (S), 1955–56.

Most League Points (3 for a win): 81, FL 2, 2005–06.

Most League Goals: 106, Division 3 (S), 1955–56.

Highest League Scorer in Season: Tom Johnston, 35, Division 2, 1957–58.

Most League Goals in Total Aggregate: Tom Johnston, 121, 1956–58, 1959–61.

Most League Goals in One Match: 4, Wally Leigh v Bradford C, Division 2, 13 April 1906; 4, Albert Pape v Oldham Ath, Division 2, 1 September 1924; 4, Peter Kitchen v Millwall, Division 3, 21 April 1984.

Most Capped Players: Tunji Banjo, 7 (7), Nigeria; John Chiedozie, 7 (9), Nigeria; Tony Grealish, 7 (45), Republic of Ireland.

Most League Appearances: Peter Allen, 432, 1965–78.

Youngest League Player: Paul Went, 15 years 327 days v Preston NE, 4 September 1965.

Record Transfer Fee Received: £1,000,000 from Fulham for Gabriel Zakuani, July 2006.

Record Transfer Fee Paid: £175,000 to Wigan Ath for Paul Beesley, October 1989.

Football League Record: 1905 Elected to Division 2; 1929–56 Division 3 (S); 1956–62 Division 2; 1962–63 Division 1; 1963–66 Division 2; 1966–70 Division 3; 1970–82 Division 2; 1982–85 Division 3; 1985–89 Division 4; 1989–92 Division 3; 1992–95 Division 2; 1995–2004 Division 3; 2004–06 FL 2; 2006– FL 1.

LATEST SEQUENCES

Longest Sequence of League Wins: 10, 21.1.1956 – 30.3.1956.

Longest Sequence of League Defeats: 9, 1.4.1995 – 6.5.1995.

Longest Sequence of League Draws: 6, 30.11.1974 – 28.12.1974.

Longest Sequence of Unbeaten League Matches: 13, 30.10.1954 – 19.2.1955.

Longest Sequence Without a League Win: 23, 6.10.1962 – 13.4.1963.

Successive Scoring Runs: 24 from 3.5.2003.

Successive Non-scoring Runs: 8 from 19.11.1994.

MANAGERS

Sam Omerod 1905–06
Ike Ivenson 1906
Billy Holmes 1907–22
Peter Proudfoot 1922–29
Arthur Grimsdell 1929–30
Peter Proudfoot 1930–31
Jimmy Seed 1931–33
David Pratt 1933–34
Peter Proudfoot 1935–39
Tom Halsey 1939
Bill Wright 1939–45
Willie Hall 1945
Bill Wright 1945–46
Charlie Hewitt 1946–48
Neil McBain 1948–49
Alec Stock 1949–59
Les Gore 1959–61
Johnny Carey 1961–63
Benny Fenton 1963–64
Dave Sexton 1965
Dick Graham 1966–68
Jimmy Bloomfield 1968–71
George Petchey 1971–77
Jimmy Bloomfield 1977–81
Paul Went 1981
Ken Knighton 1981–83
Frank Clark 1983–91
   (Managing Director)
Peter Eustace 1991–94
Chris Turner/John Sitton 1994–95
Pat Holland 1995–96
Tommy Taylor 1996–2001
Paul Brush 2001–03
Martin Ling 2004–08
Geraint Williams February 2009–

TEN YEAR LEAGUE RECORD

		P	W	D	L	F	A	Pts	Pos
1999-2000	Div 3	46	13	13	20	47	52	52	19
2000-01	Div 3	46	20	15	11	59	51	75	5
2001-02	Div 3	46	13	13	20	55	71	52	18
2002-03	Div 3	46	14	11	21	51	61	53	18
2003-04	Div 3	46	13	14	19	48	65	53	19
2004-05	FL 2	46	16	15	15	65	67	63	11
2005-06	FL 2	46	22	15	9	67	51	81	3
2006-07	FL 1	46	12	15	19	61	77	51	20
2007-08	FL 1	46	16	12	18	49	63	60	14
2008-09	FL 1	46	15	11	20	45	57	56	14

DID YOU KNOW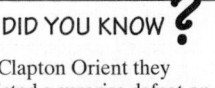

As Clapton Orient they inflicted a surprise defeat on the much fancied Newcastle United in a fifth round FA Cup tie at Millfields Road on 20 February 1926. John Galbraith scored in 23 minutes, then Donald Cock three minutes before the break sealed a memorable win.

LEYTON ORIENT 2008–09 LEAGUE RECORD

Match No.	Date	Venue	Opponents	Result	H/T Score	Lg. Pos.	Goalscorers	Attendance
1	Aug 9	H	Hereford U	W 2-1	2-1	—	Melligan [23], Boyd (pen) [45]	4727
2	16	A	Peterborough U	L 0-3	0-1	16		6643
3	23	H	Carlisle U	D 0-0	0-0	14		3803
4	30	A	Brighton & HA	D 0-0	0-0	16		6675
5	Sept 6	A	Walsall	W 2-0	0-0	9	Terry [73], Boyd (pen) [80]	4838
6	13	H	Stockport Co	L 0-3	0-2	13		4473
7	20	H	Leicester C	L 1-3	1-1	17	Chambers [44]	6448
8	26	A	Southend U	L 0-3	0-2	—		9261
9	Oct 4	H	Scunthorpe U	D 2-2	0-2	19	Boyd [59], Purches [67]	4244
10	11	A	Bristol R	L 1-2	0-0	20	Demetriou [46]	6425
11	18	H	Tranmere R	L 0-1	0-1	21		5568
12	21	A	Leeds U	L 1-2	1-2	—	Morgan D [36]	18,990
13	25	A	Yeovil T	D 0-0	0-0	22		4320
14	28	H	Milton Keynes D	L 1-2	0-2	—	Mkandawire [90]	3869
15	Nov 1	H	Hartlepool U	W 1-0	0-0	21	Boyd [81]	3638
16	15	A	Crewe Alex	W 2-0	0-0	19	Mkandawire [56], Boyd [74]	3872
17	22	H	Millwall	D 0-0	0-0	20		6951
18	25	A	Huddersfield T	W 1-0	1-0	—	Boyd [2]	10,414
19	Dec 6	A	Northampton T	D 1-1	1-1	18	Melligan [42]	5039
20	13	H	Cheltenham T	L 1-2	1-1	18	Boyd (pen) [33]	4510
21	20	A	Oldham Ath	D 1-1	0-1	17	Demetriou [72]	6839
22	26	H	Swindon T	L 1-2	0-1	20	Mkandawire [79]	4349
23	28	A	Colchester U	L 0-1	0-1	21		6290
24	Jan 10	A	Leicester C	L 0-3	0-2	—		18,240
25	17	H	Bristol R	L 1-2	0-0	21	Boyd [56]	4262
26	20	H	Southend U	D 1-1	1-0	—	Boyd [11]	3835
27	24	A	Scunthorpe U	L 1-2	0-1	21	Morgan D [58]	4230
28	27	A	Milton Keynes D	W 2-1	1-1	—	Morgan D [23], Purches [63]	8170
29	31	H	Yeovil T	L 0-1	0-0	21		4597
30	Feb 7	A	Tranmere R	D 0-0	0-0	—		4892
31	14	H	Crewe Alex	W 1-0	1-0	19	Purches [11]	3705
32	21	A	Hartlepool U	W 1-0	0-0	20	Mkandawire [83]	3678
33	28	A	Hereford U	L 1-2	1-2	21	Mkandawire [44]	3286
34	Mar 3	H	Peterborough U	L 2-3	1-3	—	McGleish 2 (1 pen) [42 (p), 56]	3381
35	7	H	Brighton & HA	W 2-1	1-1	20	McGleish (pen) [45], Thornton [88]	5885
36	10	A	Carlisle U	W 3-1	2-0	—	Daniels [29], McGleish [35], Church [50]	4536
37	14	A	Stockport Co	W 1-0	0-0	17	Church [53]	5835
38	21	H	Walsall	L 0-1	0-1	17		3969
39	28	H	Oldham Ath	W 2-1	0-1	15	McGleish (pen) [60], Demetriou [84]	4034
40	Apr 4	A	Cheltenham T	W 1-0	1-0	15	Morgan D [25]	3594
41	7	H	Leeds U	D 2-2	0-2	—	Church 2 [65, 85]	6943
42	11	H	Colchester U	W 2-1	1-1	15	Daniels [45], McGleish [80]	4685
43	13	A	Swindon T	W 1-0	1-0	15	Demetriou [3]	7735
44	18	H	Northampton T	L 1-3	1-0	15	Crowe (og) [24]	4665
45	25	A	Millwall	L 1-2	0-0	15	Church [47]	11,414
46	May 2	H	Huddersfield T	D 1-1	0-1	14	Morgan D [65]	5371

Final League Position: 14

GOALSCORERS

League (45): Boyd 9 (3 pens), McGleish 6 (3 pens), Church 5, Mkandawire 5, Morgan D 5, Demetriou 4, Purches 3, Daniels 2, Melligan 2, Chambers 1, Terry 1, Thornton 1, own goal 1.
Carling Cup (1): Boyd 1.
FA Cup (4): Demetriou 2, Granville 1, Melligan 1 (pen).
J Paint Trophy (6): Boyd 2 (2 pens), Jarvis 2, Chambers 1, Melligan 1.

Morris G 26	Purches S 42	Granville D 12	Chambers A 33	Mkandawire T 36	Saah B 14 + 1	Melligan J 25 + 10	Terry P 24 + 4	Boyd A 27 + 6	Jarvis R 15 + 16	Demetriou J 42 + 1	Gray W 6 + 10	Thornton S 26 + 4	Pires L — + 6	Palmer A 7 + 3	Dawkins S 2 + 9	Thelwell A 23 + 5	Ashworth L 1 + 2	Jeffery L — + 1	Morgan D 18 + 14	Cave-Brown A 10 + 3	Parkin S 12 + 1	Daniels C 21	Baker H 2 + 2	Jones J 20	Spence J 20	Smith J 15 + 1	McGleish S 15 + 1	Church D 12 + 1	Match No.
1	2	3	4	5	6	7	8^2	9^3	10^1	11	12	13	14																1
1	2	3^1	4	5	6	7^2		9	13	11	10^3	8		12	14														2
1	2	3^1	4		6		8	9	10^3	11	7^2		14	12	13	5													3
1	2		3		6	12	8	9	10	11				4	7^1	5													4
1	2		4		6	7	8	9	10	11				3		5													5
1	2		4		6	7^3	8	9	10^1	11		12	3		5^2	13	14												6
1	2		4		6	7^1	8	9	10	11		3		5		12													7
1	2		4		6	7	8^2	9^1	10	11		3^3	12	5		13	14												8
1	2		4		6	7	8	9	12	11		13	10^1	5		3^2													9
1	2		4		6	7^2	8	9	10^1	11		12	5	14	13	3^3													10
1	2		4		6	12	8^1	9	10^2	11		14	13	5		7^3	3												11
1	2		4	5		7	8	9^2	12	11^3		14	3	13	6		10^1												12
1	2	3	4	5			12	8	9^1	13	11			6		7	10^2												13
1	2	3	4	5			12	8^3	9^2	13	11	14		6		7^1	10												14
1	2	3	4	5	6	7		12		11		8		9		10^1													15
1	2	3	4	5	6^1	7		9		11		8		12		10													16
1	2	3	4	5		7^2		9^1	12	11		8		13	6	14	10^3												17
1	2	3	4	5		7^3		9^2	12	11		8		13	6	14	10^1												18
1	2		4	5		7^2		9	13	11		8	3	6		10^1	12												19
1	2	3^1	4	5		7		9	12			8	6	11		10													20
1		3	4	5		7		9^2	13	11		8	6	12	2	10^1													21
1	2	3^2	4	5		7^1		9	12	11		8	6	13		10													22
1	2		4	5	6	12		9^3	7^1	11		8	13		14	3	10^2												23
1	2			5		7^2		9	12	11			4		8	6	10^1	3	13	13									24
1	2		4	5		7		9	12	11		8^2		6		13	10^1	3											25
1	2		4	5			13	9	8^2	11			6		10	12		3	7^1										26
		3	4	5		12	8^2	9	11			13			10	2				7^1	1	6							27
		3		5		7^3	4	12	10	11		14		13	9^1	2^2		8		1	6								28
	2^2		4	5		7^3	12	9	8	11				13	10^1			3	14	1	6								29
	2		4	5			8	12	9^1	11		13			10^2			3		1	6	7							30
	2		4	5			9^2	12	11			8			13			3		1	6	7^1	10						31
			4	5				11		8				6				3		1	2	7	10	9					32
			4	5			12	11		8				6^2		14	13	3		1	2	7^1	10	9^3					33
	3		4	5				11	12	8				13	2			3		1	6	7^2	10	9^1					34
	2		4^1	5		7^2	12		11^3	13	8			14				3		1	6		10	9					35
	2			5			4		11	12	8							3		1	6	7	10	9					36
	2			5			4		11	12	8							3		1	6	7	10	9^1					37
	2			5^1		14	8^3		11	13	6			12				3		1	4	7^2	10	9					38
	2			4			14	8^2	12	11	9^1	4		6			13^3	3		1	5	7	10						39
	2^1			5			14	4		11	13			12			8^2	3		1	6	7	10	9^3					40
				5	14	12			11^1	10^2	4						8^3	2^1	3	1	6	7	13	9					41
	2			5		7^1	8	13		12	4							3		1	6	11^2	10	9					42
	2			5		7	8		11	9	4^1							3		1	6	12	10^2	13					43
	2			5		7^2		13		12	4					11		3		1	6	8	10	9^1					44
	2			5			8		13	12	4					11		3		1	6	7	10^2	9^1					45
	2			5			12		13	11	9	4^1				8		3		1	6	7	10^2						46

FA Cup
First Round — Colchester U — (a) — 1-0
Second Round — Bradford C — (a) — 2-1
Third Round — Sheffield U — (h) — 1-4

Carling Cup
First Round — Ipswich T — (a) — 1-4

J Paint Trophy
First Round — Southend U — (a) — 4-2
Second Round — Brighton & HA — (a) — 2-2

LINCOLN CITY   FL Championship 2

FOUNDATION

The original Lincoln Football Club was established in the early
1860s and was one of the first provisional clubs to affiliate to the
Football Association. In their early years, they regularly played
matches against the famous Sheffield Club and later became
known as Lincoln Lindum. The present organisation was formed
at a public meeting held in the Monson Arms Hotel in June 1884
and won the Lincolnshire Cup in only their third season. They
were founder members of the Midland League in 1889 and that
competition's first champions.

Sincil Bank Stadium, Sincil Bank, Lincoln LN5 8LD.
Telephone: 0870 899 2005.
Fax: (01522) 880 020.
Ticket Office: 0870 899 1976.
Website: www.redimps.com
Email: lcfc@redimps.com
Ground Capacity: 10,059.
Record Attendance: 23,196 v Derby Co, League Cup
4th rd, 15 November 1967.
Pitch Measurements: 100m × 65m.
Chairman: Steff Wright.
Vice-chairman: David Beck.
Chief Executive: Dave Roberts.
Football Secretary: Fran Martin.
Manager: Peter Jackson.
Assistant Manager: Iffy Onuora.
Physio: Michael Wait.
Colours: Red and white striped shirts, red sleeves, black shorts, red stockings.
Change Colours: White shirts, red shorts, white stockings.
Year Formed: 1884.
Turned Professional: 1892.
Ltd Co.: 1895.
Club Nickname: 'The Red Imps'.
Grounds: 1883, John O'Gaunt's; 1894, Sincil Bank.
First Football League Game: 3 September 1892, Division 2, v Sheffield U (a) L 2–4 – W. Gresham;
Coulton, Neill; Shaw, Mettam, Moore; Smallman, Irving (1), Cameron (1), Kelly, J. Gresham.
Record League Victory: 11–1 v Crewe Alex, Division 3 (N), 29 September 1951 – Jones; Green (1p);
Varney; Wright, Emery, Grummett (1); Troops (1), Garvey, Graver (6), Whittle (1), Johnson (1).
Record Cup Victory: 8–1 v Bromley, FA Cup 2nd rd, 10 December 1938 – McPhail; Hartshorne,
Corbett; Bean, Leach, Whyte (1); Hancock, Wilson (1), Ponting (3), Deacon (1), Clare (2).

HONOURS

Football League: Division 2 best
season: 5th, 1901–02; Division 3 (N) –
Champions 1931–32, 1947–48,
1951–52; Runners-up 1927–28,
1930–31, 1936–37; Division 4 –
Champions 1975–76; Runners-up
1980–81.

FA Cup: best season: 1st rd of Second
Series (5th rd equivalent), 1887,
2nd rd (5th rd equivalent), 1890, 1902.

Football League Cup: best season:
4th rd, 1968.

GM Vauxhall Conference: Champions
1987–88.

SKY SPORTS FACT FILE

Initially playing at Sincil Bank as a wartime guest from
Sheffield United, Jimmy Hutchinson arrived in
November 1946 on a £750 transfer from Bournemouth.
He was top scorer in 1947–48 with 32 League goals
almost three times more than any colleague's total.

Record Defeat: 3–11 v Manchester C, Division 2, 23 March 1895.

Most League Points (2 for a win): 74, Division 4, 1975–76.

Most League Points (3 for a win): 77, Division 3, 1981–82.

Most League Goals: 121, Division 3 (N), 1951–52.

Highest League Scorer in Season: Allan Hall, 41, Division 3 (N), 1931–32.

Most League Goals in Total Aggregate: Andy Graver, 143, 1950–55 and 1958–61.

Most League Goals in One Match: 6, Frank Keetley v Halifax T, Division 3 (N), 16 January 1932; 6, Andy Graver v Crewe Alex, Division 3 (N), 29 September 1951.

Most Capped Player: Gareth McAuley, 5 (16), Northern Ireland.

Most League Appearances: Grant Brown, 407, 1989–2002.

Youngest League Player: Shane Nicholson, 16 years 172 days v Burnley, 22 November 1986.

Record Transfer Fee Received: £750,000 from Liverpool for Jack Hobbs, August 2005.

Record Transfer Fee Paid: £75,000 to Carlisle U for Dean Walling, October 1997 and £75,000 to Bury for Tony Battersby, August 1998.

Football League Record: 1892 Founder member of Division 2. Remained in Division 2 until 1920 when they failed re-election but also missed seasons 1908–09 and 1911–12 when not re-elected. 1921–32 Division 3 (N); 1932–34 Division 2; 1934–48 Division 3 (N); 1948–49 Division 2; 1949–52 Division 3 (N); 1952–61 Division 2; 1961–62 Division 3; 1962–76 Division 4; 1976–79 Division 3; 1979–81 Division 4; 1981–86 Division 3; 1986–87 Division 4; 1987–88 GM Vauxhall Conference; 1988–92 Division 4; 1992–98 Division 3; 1998–99 Division 2; 1999–2004 Division 3; 2004– FL 2.

MANAGERS

David Calderhead 1900–07
John Henry Strawson 1907–14
   (had been Secretary)
George Fraser 1919–21
David Calderhead Jnr. 1921–24
Horace Henshall 1924–27
Harry Parkes 1927–36
Joe McClelland 1936–46
Bill Anderson 1946–65
   (General Manager to 1966)
Roy Chapman 1965–66
Ron Gray 1966–70
Bert Loxley 1970–71
David Herd 1971–72
Graham Taylor 1972–77
George Kerr 1977–78
Willie Bell 1977–78
Colin Murphy 1978–85
John Pickering 1985
George Kerr 1985–87
Peter Daniel 1987
Colin Murphy 1987–90
Allan Clarke 1990
Steve Thompson 1990–93
Keith Alexander 1993–94
Sam Ellis 1994–95
Steve Wicks *(Head Coach)* 1995
John Beck 1995–98
Shane Westley 1998
John Reames 1998–99
Phil Stant 2000–01
Alan Buckley 2001–02
Keith Alexander 2002–06
John Schofield 2006–07
Peter Jackson October 2007–

LATEST SEQUENCES

Longest Sequence of League Wins: 10, 1.9.1930 – 18.10.1930.

Longest Sequence of League Defeats: 12, 21.9.1896 – 9.1.1897.

Longest Sequence of League Draws: 5, 21.2.1981 – 7.3.1981.

Longest Sequence of Unbeaten League Matches: 18, 11.3.1980 – 13.9.1980.

Longest Sequence Without a League Win: 19, 22.8.1978 – 23.12.1978.

Successive Scoring Runs: 37 from 1.3.1930.

Successive Non-scoring Runs: 5 from 15.11.1913.

TEN YEAR LEAGUE RECORD

		P	W	D	L	F	A	Pts	Pos
1999-2000	Div 3	46	15	14	17	67	69	59	15
2000-01	Div 3	46	12	15	19	58	66	51	18
2001-02	Div 3	46	10	16	20	44	62	46	22
2002-03	Div 3	46	18	16	12	46	37	70	6
2003-04	Div 3	46	19	17	10	68	47	74	7
2004-05	FL 2	46	20	12	14	64	47	72	6
2005-06	FL 2	46	15	21	10	65	53	66	7
2006-07	FL 2	46	21	11	14	70	59	74	5
2007-08	FL 2	46	18	4	24	61	77	58	15
2008-09	FL 2	46	14	17	15	53	52	59	13

DID YOU KNOW ?

On 12 December 2008 Lincoln City were trailing 1–0 at home to Accrington Stanley from a first half goal. They levelled in the 68th minute and then went on to hit five goals, the last two coming in time added on for injuries.

LINCOLN CITY 2008–09 LEAGUE RECORD

Match No.	Date	Venue	Opponents	Result		H/T Score	Lg. Pos.	Goalscorers	Attendance
1	Aug 9	A	Rotherham U	L	0-1	0-1	—		4748
2	16	H	Dagenham & R	L	1-3	1-0	18	John-Lewis [18]	3581
3	23	A	Wycombe W	L	0-1	0-1	18		4112
4	30	H	Grimsby T	D	1-1	0-1	19	Frecklington (pen) [73]	4573
5	Sept 6	H	Barnet	W	2-0	0-0	16	N'Guessan [74], Patulea [87]	3417
6	13	A	Bury	L	1-3	1-1	19	Buchanan (og) [37]	2663
7	20	A	Brentford	D	1-1	1-1	19	Patulea [30]	4557
8	27	H	Morecambe	D	1-1	1-1	19	Frecklington [20]	5003
9	Oct 4	A	Chester C	W	2-0	1-0	14	Kovacs [45], Patulea [57]	1962
10	10	H	Rochdale	D	1-1	0-0	—	Hone [86]	4510
11	18	H	Chesterfield	W	3-1	2-0	13	Oakes [17], Patulea [30], Kovacs [56]	4326
12	21	A	Macclesfield T	W	2-1	1-1	—	Beevers [45], Frecklington [82]	1247
13	25	A	Bournemouth	W	1-0	1-0	11	John-Lewis [24]	4464
14	28	H	Gillingham	W	2-0	2-0	—	Frecklington [12], N'Guessan [14]	4396
15	Nov 1	H	Port Vale	L	0-1	0-1	11		4793
16	15	A	Darlington	L	0-2	0-0	12		3534
17	22	H	Shrewsbury T	D	0-0	0-0	13		3517
18	25	A	Aldershot T	L	0-2	0-1	—		2625
19	Dec 6	A	Exeter C	L	1-2	0-0	13	John-Lewis [51]	3916
20	12	H	Accrington S	W	5-1	0-1	—	Patulea 2 [68, 89], Brown A [77], Wright [83], Frecklington (pen) [90]	2625
21	20	A	Notts Co	W	1-0	1-0	12	Patulea [32]	4568
22	26	A	Bradford C	D	0-0	0-0	12		6156
23	28	H	Luton T	L	2-3	1-2	12	John-Lewis [38], Patulea [90]	6643
24	Jan 10	A	Brentford	D	2-2	1-2	—	N'Guessan [6], Elding [86]	3932
25	17	A	Rochdale	D	2-2	0-1	12	Kennedy (og) [48], N'Guessan [62]	2897
26	24	H	Chester C	D	1-1	0-1	12	Frecklington [48]	3760
27	27	A	Gillingham	W	2-1	0-1	—	Horsfield [52], N'Guessan [90]	4525
28	31	H	Bournemouth	D	3-3	1-1	12	N'Guessan [19], Beevers [86], Frecklington [90]	3634
29	Feb 10	A	Morecambe	D	1-1	0-1	—	Green [83]	1471
30	20	A	Port Vale	W	1-0	1-0	—	N'Guessan [12]	5097
31	28	A	Rotherham U	L	0-1	0-0	13		4336
32	Mar 3	A	Dagenham & R	W	3-0	1-0	—	Brown A [44], Elding [84], Kovacs [87]	1302
33	7	A	Grimsby T	L	1-5	0-1	13	N'Guessan (pen) [60]	5133
34	10	H	Wycombe W	W	1-0	0-0	—	Elding [49]	2562
35	14	H	Bury	D	1-1	1-0	12	Wright [30]	3642
36	17	H	Darlington	L	0-1	0-1	—		2835
37	21	A	Barnet	L	2-3	1-1	13	O'Connor [15], Patulea [66]	1979
38	28	H	Notts Co	D	1-1	0-0	13	Mullarkey [67]	4027
39	31	H	Macclesfield T	W	1-0	1-0	—	Patulea [27]	2478
40	Apr 4	A	Accrington S	W	2-0	1-0	11	Kerr 2 [4, 50]	1139
41	7	A	Chesterfield	D	1-1	0-1	—	Patulea [52]	3419
42	11	H	Luton T	D	0-0	0-0	11		4664
43	13	A	Bradford C	D	1-1	0-0	12	Hutchinson [47]	12,932
44	18	H	Exeter C	L	0-1	0-0	13		3934
45	25	A	Shrewsbury T	D	0-0	0-0	13		6740
46	May 2	H	Aldershot T	L	0-2	0-1	13		3910

Final League Position: 13

GOALSCORERS

League (53): Patulea 11, N'Guessan 8 (1 pen), Frecklington 7 (2 pens), John-Lewis 4, Elding 3, Kovacs 3, Beevers 2, Brown A 2, Kerr 2, Wright 2, Green 1, Hone 1, Horsfield 1, Hutchinson 1, Mullarkey 1, O'Connor 1, Oakes 1, own goals 2.
Carling Cup (1): Wright 1.
FA Cup (2): John-Lewis 1, N'Guessan 1.
J Paint Trophy (0).

Burch R 46	Green P 33	Brown A 33+6	Kovacs J 45	Beevers L 43+1	Kerr S 45	John-Lewis L 21+6	Oakes S 21+7	Wright B 15+18	Gall K 6+3	King G 2+3	Frecklington L 25+2	N'Guessan D 43+2	Graham D 2+7	Sinclair F 21+2	Clarke S 13+10	Mullarkey S 7+11	Hone D 17+2	Patulea A 17+14	Duffy A —+1	Elding A 15	Horsfield G 14+3	Swaibu M 10	O'Connor M 9+1	Miller K —+1	Hutchinson A 3+1	Adams N —+2	Colman-Carr L —+1	Match No.
1	2	3	4	5	6	7^1	8	9^3	10	11^2	12	13	14															1
1	2	3	4	12	6	7^2		9^3	10	13	8	11	14	5^1														2
1	2	3^1	4	5	6^2	7		9^3	10	14	8	11	12		13													3
1	2	3	4			7	6	9	10^2		8	11	12	5	13													4
1	2		4	5	6^1	13	8	9^3	10^2		7	11		3			12	14										5
1	2		4	5	6^1	7	8	9^2	12		10	11		3	13													6
1^0	2^2		4	5	6	7		12			8	11		3	10	13	9^1	15										7
1	12		4	5	6	7					8	11		2^1	9	3	10											8
1	2	12	4	5	6	7					8^1	11			10	3	9											9
1	2	12	4^1	5	6	7^3	13		14		8	11			10^2	3	9											10
1	2	3	4		6	7	8^2	12			10	11		13	5^4	9^1												11
1	2		4	5	6	7	8^1	13			10	11		3	12	9^2												12
1	2	3	4		6	7	8	12			10^2	11		13	5	9^1												13
1	2	3	4		6^3	7	8	12			10^2	11		14	13	5	9^1											14
1	2	12	4	3	6	7	8^1	13	14			11^3			10	5	9^2											15
1	2	14	4	3	6			12	10^3		8	11	13	7^1		5	9^2											16
1	2	9^1	4	3	6	7^2	8	12			10	11	13				5											17
1	2	9	4	3	6	7^1	8	12			10^2	11	13				5											18
1	2	12		3	6	7^1	8				10	11^4	9^2	4	5	13												19
1	2	11	4	3	6	7^3	8^1	12			10		9^2	14	5	13												20
1	2	11	4	3	6			12	14	10^1	8^3	13		7	5	9^2												21
1		11^2	4	3	6			12	13		8	10		2	7	5	9^1											22
1		11	4	3	6	7^2		12			8^1	10		2	9	5	13											23
1	2^4	11	4	3	6		8^1				12			7	5	13	10						9^2					24
1		11	4	3	6			12			8	7		2^2	13	5^1	10						9					25
1		3	4	2	6			12			8	7		5	11^1	13	10						9^2					26
1		3	4	2	6			12	13		8^2	11		5	7	14	10						9^3					27
1	2^1	11	4	3	6^2				13		8	7		5	12	14	10						9^3					28
1	2	3	4		6	9^2	8					11		7^1	13		12			10	5							29
1	2	3	4	5	6	11^1	8	9^3						7	13	14	12			10^2								30
1	2	7	4	3	6		8	12				11		5	13					10^2			9^1					31
1	2	11	4	3	6		8^1	13						7	5		12			10			9^2					32
1		11	4	5	6		8	14						7	3^1	2^2	12			10	13		9^3					33
1	2	11	4	3	6		9							7^2	5		12			10	8^1	13						34
1	2	11	4	3	6		9^1							7	5		12			10^4	8							35
1	2	11^2	4	3	6			10	13					7	5		12				8		9^1					36
1	2	11	4	3	6			10^1						7	5		9				8		12					37
1		3	4	2	6						10		11^2	7			12	13		5			9	8^1				38
1		3	4	2	6									7			8	11		10	5		9					39
1		3	4^2	2	6			12						7^1				11		10	5	8	9				13	40
1		3	4	2	6				14					7			13	11^3		9^1	10	12	5	8^2				41
1	2	11^2	4	3	6			9^1						7			13			10	5	8			12			42
1	2	11	4	3	6	12	13							7^1			14			10^3	5	8			9^2			43
1	2	11	4	3	6			12						7	8					10^2	5				9^1	13		44
1	2	3	4		6			11^3	13					7	8		14			10^2	5				9^1	12		45
1		3	4	2	6		8^2	9						7			11	12		10^1	5							46

FA Cup
First Round Kettering T (a) 1-1
 (h) 1-2

Carling Cup
First Round Derby Co (a) 1-3

J Paint Trophy
Second Round Leicester C (a) 0-0

LIVERPOOL   FA Premiership

FOUNDATION

But for a dispute between Everton FC and their landlord at Anfield in 1892, there may never have been a Liverpool club. This dispute persuaded the majority of Evertonians to quit Anfield for Goodison Park, leaving the landlord, Mr John Houlding, to form a new club. He originally tried to retain the name 'Everton' but when this failed, he founded Liverpool Association FC on 15 March 1892.

Anfield Stadium, Anfield Road, Liverpool L4 0TH.

Telephone: (0151) 260 1433.

Fax: (0151) 260 8813.

Ticket Office: (0151) 260 8680.

Website: www.liverpoolfc.tv

Email: customercontact@liverpoolfc.tv or customerservices@liverpoolfc.tv

Ground Capacity: 45,522.

Record Attendance: 61,905 v Wolverhampton W, FA Cup 4th rd, 2 February 1952.

Pitch Measurements: 101m × 68m.

Chairmen: George Gillett Jnr and Tom Hicks.

Secretary: Ian Silvester.

Manager: Rafael Benitez.

Assistant Manager: Sammy Lee.

Physio: Rob Price.

Colours: All red with white trim.

Change Colours: Grey with red trim.

Year Formed: 1892.

Turned Professional: 1892.

Ltd Co.: 1892.

Club Nicknames: 'Reds' or 'Pool'.

Ground: 1892, Anfield.

First Football League Game: 2 September 1893, Division 2, v Middlesbrough Ironopolis (a) W 2–0 – McOwen; Hannah, McLean; Henderson, McQue (1), McBride; Gordon, McVean (1), M. McQueen, Stott, H. McQueen.

HONOURS

Football League: Division 1 – Champions 1900–01, 1905–06, 1921–22, 1922–23, 1946–47, 1963–64, 1965–66, 1972–73, 1975–76, 1976–77, 1978–79, 1979–80, 1981–82, 1982–83, 1983–84, 1985–86, 1987–88, 1989–90 (Liverpool have a record number of 18 League Championship wins); Runners-up 1898–99, 1909–10, 1968–69, 1973–74, 1974–75, 1977–78, 1984–85, 1986–87, 1988–89, 1990–91, 2001–02; Division 2 – Champions 1893–94, 1895–96, 1904–05, 1961–62; FA Premier League – Runners-up 2001–02, 2008–09.

FA Cup: Winners 1965, 1974, 1986, 1989, 1992, 2001, 2006; Runners-up 1914, 1950, 1971, 1977, 1988, 1996.

Football League Cup: Winners 1981, 1982, 1983, 1984, 1995, 2001, 2003; Runners-up 1978, 1987, 2005.

League Super Cup: Winners 1986.

European Competitions: European Cup: 1964–65, 1966–67, 1973–74, 1976–77 (winners), 1977–78 (winners), 1978–79, 1979–80, 1980–81 (winners), 1981–82, 1982–83, 1983–84 (winners), 1984–85 (runners-up). *Champions League:* 2001–02, 2002–03, 2004–05 (winners), 2005–06, 2006–07 (runners-up), 2007–08 (s-f), 2008–09 (q-f). *European Cup-Winners' Cup:* 1965–66 (runners-up), 1971–72, 1974–75, 1992–93, 1996–97 (s-f). *European Fairs Cup:* 1967–68, 1968–69, 1969–70, 1970–71. *UEFA Cup:* 1972–73 (winners), 1975–76 (winners), 1991–92, 1995–96, 1997–98, 1998–99, 2000–01 (winners), 2002–03, 2003–04. *Super Cup:* 1977 (winners), 1978, 1984, 2001 (winners), 2005 (winners). *World Club Championship:* 1981 (runners-up), 1984 (runners-up). *FIFA Club World Championship:* 2005 (runners-up).

SKY SPORTS FACT FILE

On 1 October 2008 Steven Gerrard became the 16th different Liverpool player to reach a century of goals. The first such centurion was Sam Raybould who scored his 100th League and Cup goal against Newcastle United in a 3–2 away win on 25 November 1905.

Record League Victory: 10–1 v Rotherham T, Division 2, 18 February 1896 – Storer; Goldie, Wilkie; McCartney, McQue, Holmes; McVean (3), Ross (2), Allan (4), Becton (1), Bradshaw.

Record Cup Victory: 11–0 v Stromsgodset Drammen, ECWC 1st rd 1st leg, 17 September 1974 – Clemence; Smith (1), Lindsay (1p), Thompson (2), Cormack (1), Hughes (1), Boersma (2), Hall, Heighway (1), Kennedy (1), Callaghan (1).

Record Defeat: 1–9 v Birmingham C, Division 2, 11 December 1954.

Most League Points (2 for a win): 68, Division 1, 1978–79.

Most League Points (3 for a win): 90, Division 1, 1987–88.

Most League Goals: 106, Division 2, 1895–96.

Highest League Scorer in Season: Roger Hunt, 41, Division 2, 1961–62.

Most League Goals in Total Aggregate: Roger Hunt, 245, 1959–69.

Most League Goals in One Match: 5, Andy McGuigan v Stoke C, Division 1, 4 January 1902; 5, John Evans v Bristol R, Division 2, 15 September 1954; 5, Ian Rush v Luton T, Division 1, 29 October 1983.

Most Capped Player: Ian Rush, 67 (73), Wales.

Most League Appearances: Ian Callaghan, 640, 1960–78.

Youngest League Player: Max Thompson, 17 years 128 days v Tottenham H, 8 May 1974.

Record Transfer Fee Received: £15,000,000 from Tottenham H for Robbie Keane, February 2009.

Record Transfer Fee Paid: £22,000,000 to Atletico Madrid for Fernando Torres, July 2007.

Football League Record: 1893 Elected to Division 2; 1894–95 Division 1; 1895–96 Division 2; 1896–1904 Division 1; 1904–05 Division 2; 1905–54 Division 1; 1954–62 Division 2; 1962–92 Division 1; 1992– FA Premier League.

MANAGERS

W. E. Barclay 1892–96
Tom Watson 1896–1915
David Ashworth 1920–23
Matt McQueen 1923–28
George Patterson 1928–36
(continued as Secretary)
George Kay 1936–51
Don Welsh 1951–56
Phil Taylor 1956–59
Bill Shankly 1959–74
Bob Paisley 1974–83
Joe Fagan 1983–85
Kenny Dalglish 1985–91
Graeme Souness 1991–94
Roy Evans 1994–98
(then Joint Manager)
Gerard Houllier 1998–2004
Rafael Benitez June 2004–

LATEST SEQUENCES

Longest Sequence of League Wins: 12, 21.4.1990 – 6.10.1990.

Longest Sequence of League Defeats: 9, 29.4.1899 – 14.10.1899.

Longest Sequence of League Draws: 6, 19.2.1975 – 19.3.1975.

Longest Sequence of Unbeaten League Matches: 31, 4.5.1987 – 16.3.1988.

Longest Sequence Without a League Win: 14, 12.12.1953 – 20.3.1954.

Successive Scoring Runs: 29 from 27.4.1957.

Successive Non-scoring Runs: 5 from 22.12.1906.

TEN YEAR LEAGUE RECORD

		P	W	D	L	F	A	Pts	Pos
1999-2000	PR Lge	38	19	10	9	51	30	67	4
2000-01	PR Lge	38	20	9	9	71	39	69	3
2001-02	PR Lge	38	24	8	6	67	30	80	2
2002-03	PR Lge	38	18	10	10	61	41	64	5
2003-04	PR Lge	38	16	12	10	55	37	60	4
2004-05	PR Lge	38	17	7	14	52	41	58	5
2005-06	PR Lge	38	25	7	6	57	25	82	3
2006-07	PR Lge	38	20	8	10	57	27	68	3
2007-08	PR Lge	38	21	13	4	67	28	76	4
2008-09	PR Lge	38	25	11	2	77	27	86	2

DID YOU KNOW ?

On 14 March 2009 Liverpool beat Manchester United 4–1. It was their highest win at Old Trafford since 21 November 1936 when a Fred Howe hat-trick helped towards a 5–2 victory. Liverpool finished 18th that season, United were relegated.

LIVERPOOL 2008–09 LEAGUE RECORD

Match No.	Date	Venue	Opponents	Result	H/T Score	Lg. Pos.	Goalscorers	Attendance
1	Aug 16	A	Sunderland	W 1-0	0-0	—	Torres 83	43,259
2	23	H	Middlesbrough	W 2-1	0-0	2	Pogatetz (og) 86, Gerrard 90	43,168
3	31	A	Aston Villa	D 0-0	0-0	2		41,647
4	Sept 13	H	Manchester U	W 2-1	1-1	2	Brown (og) 27, Babel 77	44,192
5	20	H	Stoke C	D 0-0	0-0	3		43,931
6	27	A	Everton	W 2-0	0-0	2	Torres 2 59, 62	39,574
7	Oct 5	A	Manchester C	W 3-2	0-2	2	Torres 2 55, 73, Kuyt 90	47,280
8	18	H	Wigan Ath	W 3-2	1-2	2	Kuyt 2 37, 85, Riera 80	43,868
9	26	A	Chelsea	W 1-0	1-0	1	Alonso 10	41,705
10	29	H	Portsmouth	W 1-0	0-0	—	Gerrard (pen) 76	43,378
11	Nov 1	A	Tottenham H	L 1-2	1-0	2	Kuyt 3	36,183
12	8	H	WBA	W 3-0	2-0	2	Keane 2 34, 43, Arbeloa 90	43,451
13	15	A	Bolton W	W 2-0	1-0	2	Kuyt 28, Gerrard 73	24,893
14	22	H	Fulham	D 0-0	0-0	2		43,589
15	Dec 1	H	West Ham U	D 0-0	0-0	—		41,169
16	6	A	Blackburn R	W 3-1	0-0	1	Alonso 69, Benayoun 79, Gerrard 90	26,920
17	13	H	Hull C	D 2-2	2-2	1	Gerrard 2 24, 32	43,835
18	21	A	Arsenal	D 1-1	1-1	1	Keane 42	60,094
19	26	H	Bolton W	W 3-0	1-0	1	Riera 26, Keane 2 53, 58	43,548
20	28	A	Newcastle U	W 5-1	2-1	1	Gerrard 2 31, 66, Hyypia 36, Babel 50, Alonso (pen) 77	52,114
21	Jan 10	A	Stoke C	D 0-0	0-0	1		27,500
22	19	H	Everton	D 1-1	0-0	—	Gerrard 68	44,382
23	28	H	Wigan Ath	D 1-1	1-0	—	Benayoun 41	21,237
24	Feb 1	H	Chelsea	W 2-0	0-0	2	Torres 2 89, 90	44,174
25	7	A	Portsmouth	W 3-2	0-0	2	Fabio Aurelio 69, Kuyt 85, Torres 90	20,524
26	22	H	Manchester C	D 1-1	0-0	2	Kuyt 78	44,259
27	28	A	Middlesbrough	L 0-2	0-1	3		33,724
28	Mar 3	H	Sunderland	W 2-0	0-0	—	N'Gog 52, Benayoun 65	41,587
29	14	A	Manchester U	W 4-1	2-1	3	Torres 28, Gerrard (pen) 44, Fabio Aurelio 77, Dossena 90	75,569
30	22	H	Aston Villa	W 5-0	3-0	2	Kuyt 8, Riera 33, Gerrard 3 (2 pens) 39 ipl, 50, 65 ipl	44,131
31	Apr 4	A	Fulham	W 1-0	0-0	2	Benayoun 90	25,661
32	11	H	Blackburn R	W 4-0	2-0	2	Torres 2 5, 33, Agger 83, N'Gog 90	43,466
33	21	H	Arsenal	D 4-4	0-1	—	Torres 2 49, 72, Benayoun 2 56, 90	44,424
34	25	A	Hull C	W 3-1	1-0	2	Alonso 45, Kuyt 2 63, 89	24,942
35	May 3	H	Newcastle U	W 3-0	2-0	2	Benayoun 22, Kuyt 26, Lucas 87	44,121
36	9	A	West Ham U	W 3-0	2-0	2	Gerrard 2 2, 38, Babel 84	34,951
37	17	A	WBA	W 2-0	1-0	2	Gerrard 28, Kuyt 63	26,138
38	24	H	Tottenham H	W 3-1	1-0	2	Torres 31, Hutton (og) 64, Benayoun 81	43,937

Final League Position: 2

GOALSCORERS

League (77): Gerrard 16 (4 pens), Torres 14, Kuyt 12, Benayoun 8, Keane 5, Alonso 4 (1 pen), Babel 3, Riera 3, Fabio Aurelio 2, N'Gog 2, Agger 1, Arbeloa 1, Dossena 1, Hyypia 1, Lucas 1, own goals 3.
Carling Cup (4): Agger 1, Hyypia 1, Lucas 1, Plessis 1.
FA Cup (3): Gerrard 1, Riera 1, Torres 1.
Champions League (22): Gerrard 7 (3 pens), Kuyt 3, Keane 2, Torres 2, Babel 1, Benayoun 1, Dossena 1, Fabio Aurelio 1, Lucas 1, N'Gog 1, Riera 1, Xabi Alonso 1 (pen).

Reina J 38	Arbeloa A 29	Dossena A 12 + 4	Plessis D 1	Carragher J 38	Hypia S 12 + 4	Kuyt D 36 + 2	Gerrard S 30 + 1	Torres F 20 + 4	Keane R 16 + 3	Benayoun Y 21 + 11	Alonso X 27 + 6	Fabio Aurelio 19 + 5	El Zhar N 1 + 14	Skrtel M 20 + 1	Babel R 6 + 21	Mascherano J 27	Lucas 13 + 12	N'Gog D 2 + 12	Riera A 24 + 4	Pennant J 2 + 1	Agger D 15 + 3	Insua E 9 + 1	Match No.
1	2	3	4[1]	5	6	7	8	9	10[3]	11[2]	12	13	14										1
1	2[1]	3[2]		5		7	8	9	10	11[3]	4	13	12	6	14								2
1	2	3		5		7[1]		9[3]	10[2]	13	4	12		6		8	11	14					3
1	2			5	12	9	13		10	7[2]	4	3		6	14	8[1]			11[3]				4
1	2	3		5		7	8	9	10[1]	12	4			6		13					11[2]		5
1	2	3		5		7	8	9	10[3]		4[1]	13		6			12		11[2]	14			6
1	2	12		5		7	8	9	13	14	10	3[1]		6		4[2]			11[3]				7
1	2[2]	3[3]		5	12	9	8		10[1]	13	4		14			11					7	6	8
1	2			5	12	10[3]	8	9[2]		4		3				13	7	14	11[1]		6		9
1	2			5	6	9	10[1]		12	13	4	3		11[3]		8		14	7[2]				10
1	2	3		5		7		9	10[2]	12	4			13		8			11[1]		6		11
1	2			5		9	8[1]	13	10[2]	7	12	3	14			4			11[3]		6		12
1				2	6	9[2]	8	12	10[1]	14	4	3				7	13		11[3]			5	13
1	2			5		7[3]		9	10		12	3	14	13		4[1]	8		11[2]		6		14
1	2	3		5	6	9	8	10[2]	7		4					12	13		11[1]				15
1	2			5	6	9	10			7[2]	4		14	11[3]		8[1]	12	13			3		16
1	2	3		5	6	9	10			7[2]	4			13		12	8[3]	14	11[1]				17
1	2			5		7		9	10[2]		4			13		12	8[3]	14	11[1]		6	3	18
1				2	6	9[3]	8[1]		10	7		13				4	12	14	11[2]		5	3	19
1				2	6	9[2]	10[3]			7[1]	12			13		11	4	8	14		5	3	20
1				2	6	10		9	12	7[2]		3		5		13	4	8	11[1]				21
1				2	6	7	8	9[2]	10[1]	12	4	3		5		14	13		11[3]				22
1	2			5	12	10[2]		9[3]	13	7[1]		3		6		11	4	8	14				23
1	2			5		7	10	9[3]	12		4	3		6		13	8[2]	14	11[1]				24
1	2	3[2]		5	14	12		7	13	11	4			10[1]		8		9[3]			6		25
1	2	3[1]		5		10		9		7	12			13		6	14	4[3]	8		11[2]		26
1		2[1]		6		10	8[2]	12		4		3		9[3]	5	11	7	13	14				27
1				5		10	8[1]			7[2]	4	13		6		12	2	14	9[3]		11	3	28
1		12		2	6	10	8[3]	9[2]				3	14	5		13	4	7	11[1]				29
1	2[1]			5		10	8[3]	9		4[2]		3		6		7	13	14	11	12			30
1	2	11[1]		5		10[2]	8[3]	9		13	4			6		12	7			14	3		31
1	2			5		10[2]	9[1]			13	4[3]			12		8	14	7	11		6	3	32
1	2			5		10[2]		9		7	4	3		13		12	8		11[1]		6		33
1	2	14		5		10[3]		9		7[2]	4	12		6		8[3]	11	13				3	34
1	2			5		10		9		7	4[2]	3		12		8[3]	13	14	11[1]		6		35
1	2	14		5		10	8	9[2]		7[3]		3[1]		6		13	4		11	12			36
1	2			5		10	8	9[2]		11[3]	12	13				4[1]	7	14			6	3	37
1				2	14	10[1]	8[3]	9[2]		11	4	3		6		7	13	12				5	38

FA Cup

Third Round	Preston NE	(a)	2-0
Fourth Round	Everton	(h)	1-1
		(a)	0-1

Carling Cup

Third Round	Crewe Alex	(h)	2-1
Fourth Round	Tottenham H	(a)	2-4

Champions League

Third Qualifying Round

	Standard Liege	(a)	0-0
		(h)	1-0
Group D	Marseille	(a)	2-1
	PSV Eindhoven	(h)	3-1
	Atletico Madrid	(a)	1-1
		(h)	1-1
	Marseille	(h)	1-0
	PSV Eindhoven	(a)	3-1
Knock-out Round	Real Madrid	(a)	1-0
		(h)	4-0
Quarter-Final	Chelsea	(h)	1-3
		(a)	4-4

LUTON TOWN　　　　Blue Square Premier

FOUNDATION

Formed by an amalgamation of two leading local clubs, Wanderers and Excelsior a works team, at a meeting in Luton Town Hall in April 1885. The Wanderers had three months earlier changed their name to Luton Town Wanderers and did not take too kindly to the formation of another Town club but were talked around at this meeting. Wanderers had already appeared in the FA Cup and the new club entered in its inaugural season.

Kenilworth Road Stadium, 1 Maple Road, Luton, Beds LU4 8AW.

Telephone: (01582) 416 976.

Fax: (01582) 405 070.

Ticket Office: (01582) 416 976.

Website: www.lutontown.co.uk

Email: info@ltfc.co.uk

Ground Capacity: 10,226.

Record Attendance: 30,069 v Blackpool, FA Cup 6th rd replay, 4 March 1959.

Pitch Measurements: 110yd × 72yd.

Chairman: Nick Owen.

Managing Director/Acting Secretary: Gary Sweet.

Manager: Mick Harford.

First Team Coaches: Alan Neilson, Kevin Watson.

Physio: Harry Scott-Stackman.

HONOURS

Football League: Championship 1 – Winners 2004–05; Division 1 best season: 7th, 1986–87; Division 2 – Champions 1981–82; Runners-up 1954–55, 1973–74; Division 3 – Runners-up 1969–70, 2001–02; Division 4 – Champions 1967–68; Division 3 (S) – Champions 1936–37; Runners-up 1935–36.

FA Cup: Runners-up 1959.

Football League Cup: Winners 1988; Runners-up 1989.

Simod Cup: Runners-up 1988.

Johnstone's Paint Trophy: Winners 2009.

Colours: White shirts with amber trim, black shorts, white stockings.

Change Colours: All black with amber trim.

Year Formed: 1885.

Turned Professional: 1890.

Ltd Co.: 1897.

Club Nickname: 'The Hatters'.

Grounds: 1885, Excelsior, Dallow Lane; 1897, Dunstable Road; 1905, Kenilworth Road.

First Football League Game: 4 September 1897, Division 2, v Leicester Fosse (a) D 1–1 – Williams; McCartney, McEwen; Davies, Stewart, Docherty; Gallacher, Coupar, Birch, McInnes, Ekins (1).

Record League Victory: 12–0 v Bristol R, Division 3 (S), 13 April 1936 – Dolman; Mackey, Smith; Finlayson, Nelson, Godfrey; Rich, Martin (1), Payne (10), Roberts (1), Stephenson.

Record Cup Victory: 9–0 v Clapton, FA Cup 1st rd (replay after abandoned game), 30 November 1927 – Abbott; Kingham, Graham; Black, Rennie, Fraser; Pointon, Yardley (4), Reid (2), Woods (1), Dennis (2).

SKY SPORTS FACT FILE

In 1921–22 Luton Town provided three players for one international match despite them being a Third Division (South) team. On 22 October at Windsor Park, Ernie Simms led the England attack, while Allan Mathieson and Louis Bookman formed the Irish left wing.

Record Defeat: 0–9 v Small Heath, Division 2, 12 November 1898.

Most League Points (2 for a win): 66, Division 4, 1967–68.

Most League Points (3 for a win): 98, FL 1 2004–05.

Most League Goals: 103, Division 3 (S), 1936–37.

Highest League Scorer in Season: Joe Payne, 55, Division 3 (S), 1936–37.

Most League Goals in Total Aggregate: Gordon Turner, 243, 1949–64.

Most League Goals in One Match: 10, Joe Payne v Bristol R, Division 3 (S), 13 April 1936.

Most Capped Player: Mal Donaghy, 58 (91), Northern Ireland.

Most League Appearances: Bob Morton, 495, 1948–64.

Youngest League Player: Mike O'Hara, 16 years 32 days v Stoke C, 1 October 1960.

Record Transfer Fee Received: £3,000,000 from WBA for Curtis Davies, August 2005.

Record Transfer Fee Paid: £850,000 to Odense for Lars Elstrup, August 1989.

Football League Record: 1897 Elected to Division 2; 1900 Failed re-election; 1920 Division 3; 1921–37 Division 3 (S); 1937–55 Division 2; 1955–60 Division 1; 1960–63 Division 2; 1963–65 Division 3; 1965–68 Division 4; 1968–70 Division 3; 1970–74 Division 2; 1974–75 Division 1; 1975–82 Division 2; 1982–96 Division 1; 1996–2001 Division 2; 2001–02 Division 3; 2002–04 Division 2; 2004–05 FL 1; 2005–07 FL C; 2007–08 FL 1; 2008–09 FL 2; 2009– Blue Square Premier.

MANAGERS

Charlie Green 1901–28
(Secretary-Manager)
George Thomson 1925
John McCartney 1927–29
George Kay 1929–31
Harold Wightman 1931–35
Ted Liddell 1936–38
Neil McBain 1938–39
George Martin 1939–47
Dally Duncan 1947–58
Syd Owen 1959–60
Sam Bartram 1960–62
Bill Harvey 1962–64
George Martin 1965–66
Allan Brown 1966–68
Alec Stock 1968–72
Harry Haslam 1972–78
David Pleat 1978–86
John Moore 1986–87
Ray Harford 1987–89
Jim Ryan 1990–91
David Pleat 1991–95
Terry Westley 1995
Lennie Lawrence 1995–2000
Ricky Hill 2000
Lil Fuccillo 2000
Joe Kinnear 2001–03
Mike Newell 2003–07
Kevin Blackwell 2007–08
Mick Harford January 2008–

LATEST SEQUENCES

Longest Sequence of League Wins: 12, 19.2.2002 – 6.4.2002.

Longest Sequence of League Defeats: 8, 11.11.1899 – 6.1.1900.

Longest Sequence of League Draws: 5, 28.8.1971 – 18.9.1971.

Longest Sequence of Unbeaten League Matches: 19, 8.4.1969 – 7.10.1969.

Longest Sequence Without a League Win: 16, 9.9.1964 – 6.11.1964.

Successive Scoring Runs: 25 from 24.10.1931.

Successive Non-scoring Runs: 5 from 10.4.1973.

TEN YEAR LEAGUE RECORD

		P	W	D	L	F	A	Pts	Pos
1999-2000	Div 2	46	17	10	19	61	65	61	13
2000-01	Div 2	46	9	13	24	52	80	40	22
2001-02	Div 3	46	30	7	9	96	48	97	2
2002-03	Div 2	46	17	14	15	67	62	65	9
2003-04	Div 2	46	17	15	14	69	66	66	10
2004-05	FL 1	46	29	11	6	87	48	98	1
2005-06	FL C	46	17	10	19	66	67	61	10
2006-07	FL C	46	10	10	26	53	81	40	23
2007-08	FL 1	46	11	10	25	43	63	33*	24
2008-09	FL 2	46	13	17	16	58	65	26†	24

*10 pts deducted; †30 points deducted.

DID YOU KNOW ?

On 2 September 1980 in a League Cup second round second leg match at Reading, Seamus Heath made his only first team appearance for Luton Town. In the next round against Manchester City, Herbert Smith emulated his achievement as a playing substitute.

LUTON TOWN 2008–09 LEAGUE RECORD

Match No.	Date	Venue	Opponents	Result	H/T Score	Lg. Pos.	Goalscorers	Attendance
1	Aug 9	H	Port Vale	L	1-3	1-2	—	Parkin [35]	7149
2	16	A	Gillingham	W	1-0	1-0	24	Parkin [3]	5339
3	23	H	Notts Co	D	1-1	0-0	24	Martin [49]	6085
4	30	A	Exeter C	W	1-0	0-0	24	Parkin [47]	5328
5	Sept 6	A	Macclesfield T	L	1-2	0-1	24	Charles [90]	2349
6	13	H	Aldershot T	W	3-1	1-0	24	Spillane [17], Hall [89], Martin [90]	6462
7	20	A	Rotherham U	L	0-1	0-0	24		4095
8	27	H	Chester C	D	1-1	1-0	24	Hall [41]	5731
9	Oct 4	A	Bradford C	D	1-1	0-0	24	Spillane [86]	13,083
10	11	H	Darlington	L	1-2	1-1	24	Gnakpa [31]	5560
11	18	H	Accrington S	L	1-2	1-1	24	Hall [34]	5492
12	21	A	Grimsby T	D	2-2	1-1	—	Craddock 2 (1 pen) [24 (p), 90]	4021
13	25	A	Bury	W	2-1	2-0	24	Craddock [35], Roper [44]	3052
14	Nov 1	A	Shrewsbury T	L	0-3	0-1	24		6188
15	15	H	Dagenham & R	W	2-1	2-1	24	Davis [7], McVeigh [41]	5402
16	22	H	Rochdale	L	0-2	0-1	24		2901
17	25	H	Brentford	L	0-1	0-1	—		5248
18	Dec 2	H	Bournemouth	D	3-3	1-1	—	Garry (og) [18], Gallen [56], McVeigh (pen) [85]	6773
19	6	H	Barnet	W	3-1	2-1	24	McVeigh [11], Martin [15], Townsend (og) [88]	5536
20	13	A	Wycombe W	D	0-0	0-0	24		5567
21	20	H	Morecambe	D	1-1	0-0	24	Spillane [51]	5664
22	26	A	Chesterfield	D	2-2	0-1	24	Craddock [56], Roper [90]	4243
23	28	H	Lincoln C	W	3-2	2-1	24	Martin 2 [31, 33], Roper [50]	6643
24	Jan 13	A	Chester C	D	2-2	2-1	—	Martin [22], Emanuel [27]	1652
25	17	A	Darlington	L	1-5	1-4	24	Martin [30]	3319
26	24	H	Bradford C	D	3-3	2-0	24	Hall 2 [4, 90], Wasiu [37]	6053
27	27	A	Bournemouth	D	1-1	1-1	—	Hollands (og) [11]	5230
28	31	H	Bury	L	1-2	1-0	24	Hall [36]	5545
29	Feb 14	A	Dagenham & R	L	1-2	0-1	24	Henderson [58]	2310
30	21	H	Shrewsbury T	W	3-1	2-1	24	Craddock [15], Parkin [35], Hall [73]	5661
31	24	A	Accrington S	D	0-0	0-0	—		1033
32	28	A	Port Vale	W	3-1	0-0	24	Hall [43], Gallen [52], Martin [63]	5689
33	Mar 3	H	Gillingham	D	0-0	0-0	—		5739
34	7	H	Exeter C	L	1-2	1-2	24	Craddock [39]	6460
35	10	A	Notts Co	W	2-0	2-0	—	Martin [25], Craddock (pen) [45]	2886
36	14	A	Aldershot T	L	1-2	1-1	24	Craddock [35]	3098
37	17	H	Grimsby T	W	2-1	1-1	—	Bower [45], Hall [89]	5830
38	21	H	Macclesfield T	W	1-0	0-0	24	Craddock (pen) [69]	5363
39	28	A	Morecambe	W	2-1	1-1	24	Martin [43], Gallen [59]	2599
40	31	A	Rotherham U	L	2-4	1-2	—	Martin [42], Hall [70]	5975
41	Apr 11	A	Lincoln C	D	0-0	0-0	24		4664
42	13	H	Chesterfield	D	0-0	0-0	24		6494
43	18	A	Barnet	D	1-1	0-1	24	Jarvis [49]	2808
44	21	H	Wycombe W	L	0-1	0-0	—		6553
45	25	H	Rochdale	D	1-1	1-0	24	Craddock (pen) [33]	7025
46	May 2	A	Brentford	L	0-2	0-0	24		10,223

Final League Position: 24

GOALSCORERS

League (58): Martin 11, Craddock 10 (4 pens), Hall 10, Parkin 4, Gallen 3, McVeigh 3 (1 pen), Roper 3, Spillane 3, Bower 1, Charles 1, Davis 1, Emanuel 1, Gnakpa 1, Henderson 1, Jarvis 1, Wasiu 1, own goals 3.
Carling Cup (3): Chambers 1, Jarvis 1, Plummer 1.
FA Cup (1): Spillane 1.
J Paint Trophy (8): Craddock 2, Gnakpa 2, Martin 2, Hall 1, Jarvis 1.

Brill D 23	Gnakpa C 19+8	Davis S 22+2	Nicholls K 16+3	Roper I 18+1	Pilkington G 18	Hall A 35+7	Jarvis R 31+4	Martin C 39+1	Parkin S 15+8	Emanuel L 17+3	Plummer T —+5	Klein-Davies J —+1	Spillane M 35+4	Keane K 40	Watson K 2+4	Charles R —+10	Logan C 22	Pugh M 3+1	Worley H 6+2	Asafu-Adjaye E 17+2	Howells J 14+14	McVeigh P 9+4	O'Connor G 3	Andrews W 1+6	Craddock T 27	Patrick J —+2	Gallen K 26+3	Talbot D 4+3	Beavan G 3+1	Henderson I 14+5	Wasiu A 2+3	Bower M 16	Price L 1	Livermore D 8	Match No.
1	2	3²	4	5	6	7	8¹	9	10	11	12	13																							1
1	2	3	4		6	7	8	9²	10			13		5	11¹	12																			2
1	2	3	4		6	7¹	8²	9	10	11		13		5		12																			3
1	2	3	4		6		8	9¹	10	11				5	7	12																			4
1	4²	3¹			6	13	8³	9	10	11	14			5	2	7	12																		5
	2				6¹	7	8²	9	10	3	13			5	4	12	14	1		11³															6
1	2²					7³	8¹	9	10	3				5	4	12	13	11	6	14															7
	2	3				7	8¹	9		11				5	6		12	1	10	4															8
	2	3²				7	8¹	9		11³				5	4		12	1		6	10	13	14												9
	6					7	8	9						5	10		12	1	13	4	2¹	3		11²											10
				5		7	8¹	9						2	6		1		4		3	12	11²	13	10										11
	2	3¹		6		7³	8	9²	13					5	4		1			11	12			10	14										12
	2	3¹		6		7	8³	9						5	4		1	13		11	12		14	10²											13
	2²			6			8	9¹						5	7		1	4		3	11		12	10	13										14
	2	3¹	4²	5		13	12	9						6	7		1			11	8			10											15
	2			5		7	8	9						6	3		1	12		11¹	4²			10	13										16
	2	6²		5		7	12							4	3		1			8	11	13		10	9¹										17
	2		4¹		6	13	12	9		11³				5	8²		1			3	7			10	14										18
12				5	6²	13	8	9						2	4		1			3	7	14		10¹	11³										19
				5		4	8	9						6	2		1			3	7	11¹		10	12										20
14				5		7	8	9³						6	2¹		1		12	3	4	13		10	11²										21
12				5		7	8³	13		11²				6¹	2		1			3	9		4	10	14										22
12				5			8	9¹		11				6	2		1			13			4	10	7²	3	*								23
				5			8	9		3¹				2	4		1			12			11	10	6	7									24
				5		12	8³	9						6	4		1			2	13		11	10¹	3²	7	14								25
	3	13	5			4	8	9▪	14					6			1			2	12			10²		11¹	7³								26
	12	4³	5¹			7	8²		9					2			1			3	13				10	14	11	6							27
12	3²	4				7			9					5¹			1			2	13			10³		8	14	6							28
12		4³	5			7¹	8		13					2			1			3			9	10		11²	14	6	1						29
1	4¹	3				7	8	11²	10					5	14					2	12		9³	13				6							30
1	3					4	8	9²	10					5						2	12		11	13		7¹		6							31
1	13	3				4	8²	9	10					14	5					2	12		11	10³		7¹		6							32
1	3					4		9	10					5						2	12		11	8		7¹		6							33
1	3					4		9²	10					12	5	14				2	13		11	8¹		7³		6							34
1	3	12				4		9						7	5					2	13		11	10²		8		11¹	6						35
1	3	12				4³		9	13	14				7	5					2¹			10	8		11²		6							36
1		7				4	12	8²	11³	14	3			2	5					9			10	13		6¹									37
1	12	7				5	8		11	10²	3¹			2	4					9			13			6									38
1		7				5	4	12	9¹		3			2						11	10					6		8							39
1		7				5	4		8	12	3¹			2						9	10					6		11							40
1	13	7				5	14	9			3¹			12	4					2			11	10²		6		8³							41
1	3¹	7				5	4		10					13	8					2			9			12	6²	11							42
1	3	7▪				5	8	10³		13				6¹	4					2	14		9²			12		11							43
1	3					5	4	8²	9		12			6	2					‘			10	13		7¹		11							44
1						6	4		9	12				2	5					3			10	8		7			11¹						45
1		14	6³	4			9		12					2	5	13				3			10²	8		7¹			11						46

FA Cup
First Round   Altrincham   (h)   0-0
    (a)   0-0
Second Round   Southend U   (a)   1-3

Carling Cup
First Round   Plymouth Arg   (h)   2-0
Second Round   Reading   (a)   1-5

J Paint Trophy
Second Round   Brentford   (h)   2-2
Southern Quarter-Final   Walsall   (a)   1-0
Southern Semi-Final   Colchester U   (h)   1-0
Southern Final   Brighton & HA   (a)   0-0
    (h)   1-1
Final (at Wembley)   Scunthorpe U   3-2

MACCLESFIELD TOWN   FL Championship 2

FOUNDATION

From the mid-19th Century until 1874, Macclesfield Town FC played under rugby rules. In 1891 they moved to the Moss Rose and finished champions of the Manchester & District League in 1906 and 1908. By 1911, they had carried off the Cheshire Senior Cup five times. Macclesfield were founder members of the Cheshire County League in 1919.

Moss Rose Ground, London Road, Macclesfield, Cheshire SK11 7SP.

Telephone: (01625) 264 686.

Fax: (01625) 264 692.

Ticket Office: (01625) 264 686.

Website: www.mtfc.co.uk

Email: office@mtfc.co.uk

Ground Capacity: 6,141.

Record Attendance: 9,008 v Winsford U, Cheshire Senior Cup 2nd rd, 4 February 1948.

Pitch Measurements: 100m × 60m.

Chairman: Mike Rance.

Vice-chairman: Andy Scott.

Chief Executive: Patrick Nelson.

Company Secretary: Barrie Darcey.

Manager: Keith Alexander.

Assistant Manager: Gary Simpson.

Physio: Nick Reid.

Colours: Blue shirts with white design, white shorts, blue stockings.

Change Colours: White shirts, blue shorts, white stockings

Year formed: 1874.

Club Nickname: 'The Silkmen'.

Grounds: 1874, Rostron Field; 1891, Moss Rose.

First Football League Game: 9 August 1997, Division 3, v Torquay U (h) W 2–1 – Price; Tinson, Rose, Payne (Edey), Howarth, Sodje (1), Askey, Wood, Landon (1) (Power), Mason, Sorvel.

HONOURS

Football League: Division 3 – Runners-up 1997–98.

FA Cup: best season: 3rd rd, 1968, 1988, 2002, 2003, 2004, 2007, 2009.

Football League Cup: never past 2nd rd.

Vauxhall Conference: Champions 1994–95, 1996–97.

FA Trophy: Winners 1969–70, 1995–96; Runners-up 1988–89.

Bob Lord Trophy: Winners 1993–94; Runners-up 1995–96, 1996–97.

Vauxhall Conference Championship Shield: Winners 1996, 1997, 1998.

Northern Premier League: Winners 1968–69, 1969–70, 1986–87; Runners-up 1984–85.

Northern Premier League Challenge Cup: Winners 1986–87; Runners-up 1969–70, 1970–71, 1982–83.

Northern Premier League Presidents Cup: Winners 1986–87; Runners-up 1984–85.

Cheshire Senior Cup: Winners 20 times; Runners-up 11.

SKY SPORTS FACT FILE

The captain of Macclesfield Town's successful 1930 Cheshire Cup winning team was Scottish born inside-left Billy Johnston signed from Manchester United. He spent two years with them before resuming his Football League career at Old Trafford.

Record League Victory: 6–0 v Stockport Co, FL 1, 26 December 2005 – Fettis; Harsley, Sandwith, Morley, Swailes (Teague), Navarro, Whitaker (Miles (1)), Bullock (1), Parkin (2), Wijnhard (2) (Townson), McIntyre.

Record Win: 15–0 v Chester St Marys, Cheshire Senior Cup, 2nd rd, 16 February 1886.

Record Defeat: 1–13 v Tranmere R reserves, 3 May 1929.

Most League Points (3 for a win): 82, Division 3, 1997–98.

Most League Goals: 66, Division 3, 1999–2000.

Highest League Scorer in Season: Jon Parkin, 22, FL 2, 2004–05.

Most League Goals in Total Aggregate: Matt Tipton, 45, 2002–05; 2006–07.

Most Capped Player: George Abbey, 10, Nigeria.

Most League Appearances: Darren Tinson, 263, 1997–2003.

Youngest League Player: Peter Griffiths, 18 years 44 days v Reading, 26 September 1998.

Record Transfer Fee Received: £300,000 from Stockport Co for Rickie Lambert, April 2002.

Record Transfer Fee Paid: £40,000 to Bury for Danny Swailes, January 2005.

Football League Record: 1997 Promoted to Division 3; 1998–99 Division 2; 1999–2004 Division 3; 2004– FL 2.

MANAGERS

Since 1967
Keith Goalen 1967–68
Frank Beaumont 1968–72
Billy Haydock 1972–74
Eddie Brown 1974
John Collins 1974
Willie Stevenson 1974
John Collins 1975–76
Tony Coleman 1976
John Barnes 1976
Brian Taylor 1976
Dave Connor 1976–78
Derek Partridge 1978
Phil Staley 1978–80
Jimmy Williams 1980–81
Brian Booth 1981–85
Neil Griffiths 1985–86
Roy Campbell 1986
Peter Wragg 1986–93
Sammy McIlroy 1993–2000
Peter Davenport 2000
Gil Prescott 2001
David Moss 2001–03
John Askey 2003–04
Brian Horton 2004–06
Paul Ince 2006–07
Ian Brightwell 2007–08
Keith Alexander February 2008–

LATEST SEQUENCES

Longest Sequence of League Wins: 6, 25.1.2005 – 26.2.2005.

Longest Sequence of League Defeats: 6, 26.12.1998 – 6.2.1999.

Longest Sequence of League Draws: 5, 5.5.2007 – 1.9.2007.

Longest Sequence of Unbeaten League Matches: 8, 16.10.1999 – 27.11.1999.

Longest Sequence Without a League Win: 19, 5.8.2006 – 25.11.2006.

Successive Scoring Runs: 14 from 11.10.2003.

Successive Non-scoring Runs: 5 from 18.12.1998.

TEN YEAR LEAGUE RECORD

		P	W	D	L	F	A	Pts	Pos
1999-2000	Div 3	46	18	11	17	66	61	65	13
2000-01	Div 3	46	14	14	18	51	62	56	14
2001-02	Div 3	46	15	13	18	41	52	58	13
2002-03	Div 3	46	14	12	20	57	63	54	16
2003-04	Div 3	46	13	13	20	54	69	52	20
2004-05	FL 2	46	22	9	15	60	49	75	5
2005-06	FL 2	46	12	18	16	60	71	54	17
2006-07	FL 2	46	12	12	22	55	77	48	22
2007-08	FL 2	46	11	17	18	47	64	50	19
2008-09	FL 2	46	13	8	25	45	77	47	20

DID YOU KNOW ?

A few days before he was appointed player-manager of Macclesfield Town in May 1960, Stoke City's Frank Bowyer made a guest appearance for the club in a benefit match for Roger Wood. Macclesfield won 7–2.

MACCLESFIELD TOWN 2008–09 LEAGUE RECORD

Match No.	Date		Venue	Opponents	Result		H/T Score	Lg. Pos.	Goalscorers	Attendance
1	Aug	9	A	Shrewsbury T	L	0-4	0-1	—		5812
2		16	H	Bradford C	L	0-2	0-2	20		2556
3		23	A	Accrington S	L	0-2	0-0	20		1323
4		30	H	Darlington	L	0-6	0-1	21		1554
5	Sept	6	H	Luton T	W	2-1	1-0	19	Yeo [12], Morgan [61]	2349
6		13	A	Bournemouth	W	1-0	1-0	16	Evans [2]	3922
7		20	A	Port Vale	W	4-1	1-1	12	Dunfield [36], Yeo 2 (1 pen) [75 (p), 83], Reid I [86]	6645
8		27	H	Exeter C	L	1-4	1-2	15	Yeo [45]	1854
9	Oct	4	A	Brentford	L	0-1	0-1	16		4773
10		11	A	Aldershot T	W	4-2	0-0	13	Evans [48], Thomas 2 [55, 58], Green [83]	1857
11		18	A	Notts Co	D	1-1	0-0	15	Yeo [66]	4600
12		21	H	Lincoln C	L	1-2	1-1	—	Yeo [5]	1247
13		25	H	Rotherham U	L	1-2	0-1	17	Green [90]	2020
14	Nov	1	H	Gillingham	L	0-1	0-1	20		1635
15		15	A	Rochdale	D	1-1	0-0	18	Brown [81]	3013
16		22	A	Barnet	W	3-1	1-0	18	Gritton [15], Green [87], Brown [89]	1579
17		25	A	Grimsby T	W	1-0	0-0	—	Brown [68]	1182
18	Dec	2	A	Wycombe W	L	0-4	0-2	—		3770
19		6	H	Bury	D	1-1	1-1	16	Gritton [6]	2431
20		12	A	Chesterfield	W	4-2	2-1	—	Gritton 2 [23, 57], Bell [25], Evans [77]	2451
21		20	A	Dagenham & R	L	0-4	0-3	14		1909
22		26	A	Morecambe	L	1-4	1-2	16	Reid I [3]	2578
23		28	H	Chester C	W	3-1	1-0	14	Brown [6], Evans (pen) [76], Gritton [85]	2219
24	Jan	17	A	Aldershot T	D	1-1	1-0	15	Evans [21]	3018
25		24	H	Brentford	W	2-0	1-0	15	Sinclair [45], Evans (pen) [58]	1942
26		27	H	Wycombe W	D	0-0	0-0	—		1306
27		31	A	Rotherham U	L	0-2	0-1	15		2945
28	Feb	10	A	Exeter C	L	0-4	0-2	—		2839
29		14	H	Rochdale	L	0-1	0-1	16		2396
30		17	H	Notts Co	D	1-1	1-0	—	Yeo [26]	1370
31		21	A	Gillingham	L	1-3	0-1	16	Evans (pen) [80]	4620
32		25	H	Port Vale	L	0-2	0-0	—		2267
33		28	H	Shrewsbury T	W	3-0	1-0	16	Cansdell-Sherriff (og) [21], Evans (pen) [53], Brown [90]	2553
34	Mar	3	A	Bradford C	L	0-1	0-0	—		11,908
35		7	A	Darlington	W	2-1	1-0	16	Evans 2 (1 pen) [40, 67 (p)]	2995
36		10	A	Accrington S	L	0-2	0-1	—		1746
37		14	H	Bournemouth	L	0-2	0-0	17		1589
38		21	A	Luton T	L	0-1	0-0	19		5363
39		28	A	Dagenham & R	L	1-2	1-0	19	Rooney [38]	1347
40		31	A	Lincoln C	L	0-1	0-1	—		2478
41	Apr	4	H	Chesterfield	D	1-1	1-1	20	Evans [15]	2276
42		11	A	Chester C	W	2-0	2-0	20	Rooney [8], Evans [29]	2248
43		13	H	Morecambe	L	0-1	0-0	20		1773
44		18	A	Bury	L	0-3	0-1	20		3499
45		25	H	Barnet	W	2-1	1-0	18	Brown [2], Dennis [82]	1619
46	May	2	A	Grimsby T	D	0-0	0-0	20		6876

Final League Position: 20

GOALSCORERS

League (45): Evans 12 (5 pens), Yeo 7 (1 pen), Brown 6, Gritton 5, Green 3, Reid I 2, Rooney 2, Thomas 2, Bell 1, Dennis 1, Dunfield 1, Morgan 1, Sinclair 1, own goal 1.
Carling Cup (3): Brisley 1, Evans 1, Gritton 1.
FA Cup (5): Green 2, Brisley 1, Dunfield 1, Gritton 1.
J Paint Trophy (0).

Brain J 46	Deen A 19+9	Brisley S 38	Hessey S 29+4	Walker R 14+1	Dunfield T 19+1	Tolley J 14+2	Morgan P 38+1	Gritton M 13+8	Green F 9+15	Thomas D 24+16	Reid I 30+8	Evans G 35+5	Yeo S 22+11	Bell L 37+4	McDonald C 2	Hadfield J 14+2	Jennings J 13+5	Flynn M 23+5	Rooney J 10+4	Harvey N —+5	Brown N 29+1	Sinclair E 14+3	Elliott T 4+2	Fraser-Allen K —+2	Bains R 1+1	Daniel C 8	Dennis K —+3	Millar C —+2	Liburd P 1	Mukendi V —+1	Match No.
1	2	3	4[1]	5[3]	6	7	8	9	10[2]	11	12	13	14																		1
1	2	3[1]	4[2]	5		7	6	9	14	11[3]	12	10	13	8																	2
1	6		5[2]	12	7[3]	3	9	13	11	2	10			8	4[1]	14															3
1	2	3	4	5	13	7[2]		12	10	11		9		8	6[1]																4
1		3	13		6		5			11[1]	7	9[3]	10[2]	8		2	4	14	12												5
1	12	3	13		6		5	14		11[3]	2	9	10[2]	8		4[1]	7														6
1	12	3	13		6		5	14	9[3]	11[2]	4		10	8		7[1]	2														7
1	12	3	13		6		5	14	10	11	4		9	8[2]		7[3]	2[1]														8
1	12	3	4		6		5[1]	9[2]	13	11	2		10	7		8[3]		14													9
1		3	4		6		5	12	13	11[3]	2	9[3]	10[2]	8		7	14														10
1		3	4		6		5		7		2	9	10[1]	8		11		12													11
1		3	4		6		5	12	9[1]	11	2		10	8		7[2]		13													12
1		3	4		6		5[1]	9	13	11[3]	2		10	8[2]		12	7	14													13
1	2	3	4		6			9[1]	10	11[2]		5	12	8[3]			7	13	14												14
1	11		4		6		5	13	14	12	2	9[2]	10[3]			7[1]		8													15
1		3	4		6		5	11	12	13	2[3]	9[1]	10[2]	14		8		7													16
1		3	4		6		5	9[1]	10	11	2[2]	12		13		8		7													17
1	12	3[2]	4[1]		6		5	9	10	14	13	11[3]		8		2		7													18
1	3	5	4		6			9[2]	12	11[3]	14	13	10[1]	8		2		7													19
1	3	5	4		6			9[3]	12	11[1]	2	13	10[2]	8		14		7													20
1	3	5	4[3]		6[2]		14	9		11	2	10	12	8		13		7[1]													21
1	3[2]	6[1]					5	9		11	2	10	12	8		13	4	7													22
1	13		4	3	6		5	14		12	2	9	10[3]	8[2]		7[1]		11													23
1	12		4	6		8	5			2	10[1]	13	7[3]			3	14	11	9[2]												24
1			4	6		7	5		12	11[1]	2	10[3]	14			3	13	8	9[2]												25
1			4	6		7	5		13	11[2]	2[1]	10				3	12	8	9[3]	14											26
1			4	6		7	5		12		2	10[1]		13		11[2]	3[3]	8	9	14											27
1	13	6	4			8[1]	5		12	2	10			11		3[2]		7	9												28
1		6	4[1]				5		11	2	12	13	7			3		8	9	10[2]											29
1		6					5		12	13	2	9	10[2]	7		3	4	11			8[1]										30
1		6[1]		4			5	14	12			9	10[3]	7		3[2]	2	11			8										31
1	3		6			12	5			11[3]	2	10	13	8		7[1]		4			9[2]	14									32
1	2	4	6				5		12	14	11[3]	10[1]	7			8		3			13	9[2]									33
1		3	2[1]	6[3]			5		13	12	11	10[2]	8			4		7			9		14								34
1		3	4				5[1]		14	13	11	10[3]	8			6	2[1]	7			9[2]							12			35
1		3	4[2]				5		13	12	8	10	7[3]			6	2[1]	14			11	9									36
1	3	6					5		11		10	12	13			4[2]		8			7	9[1]		2							37
1	3	6					5		12		10		7[1]			4	2	8	13	11		9[2]									38
1	3	6					5		12		10		7[1]			4	2	9			11	13			8[2]						39
1	3	2	6				5		12		10	13	8[3]			4		9[1]			7	14		11[2]							40
1	3	2		4[1]			5				10	8[2]	7			12		9			6	13			11						41
1	3	2		4			5		13	12		8[2]	10[1]	7				9			6				11						42
1	3			4			5		12	2	10			7		8					6	9[2]					11[1]	13			43
1	12	3	4[1]		6					11	2	8		7		9		5										10			44
1	3	5								2	8			7		4[1]	12	10[2]			6	9					11[3]	13	14		45
1	3		5			8[2]				2	10[1]					4		7	9[3]							11	13	14	6	12	46

FA Cup

First Round	Harlow T	(a)	2-0
Second Round	Port Vale	(a)	3-1
Third Round	Everton	(h)	0-1

Carling Cup

First Round	Blackpool	(h)	2-0
Second Round	West Ham U	(a)	1-4

J Paint Trophy

First Round	Crewe Alex	(a)	0-3

MANCHESTER CITY   FA Premiership

FOUNDATION

Manchester City was formed as a Limited Company in 1894 after their predecessors Ardwick had been forced into bankruptcy. However, many historians like to trace the club's lineage as far back as 1880 when St Mark's Church, West Gorton added a football section to their cricket club. They amalgamated with Gorton Athletic in 1884 as Gorton FC. Because of a change of ground they became Ardwick in 1887.

The City of Manchester Stadium, SportCity, Manchester M11 3FF.
Telephone: 0870 062 1894.
Fax: (0161) 438 7999.
Ticket Office: 0870 062 1894 (option 2).
Club Museum and Ground Tours: 0870 062 1894.
Website: www.mcfc.co.uk
Email: mcfc@mcfc.co.uk
Ground Capacity: 47,726.
Record Attendance: (at Maine Road) 85,569 v Stoke C, FA Cup 6th rd, 3 March 1934 (British record for any game outside London or Glasgow); (at City of Manchester Stadium) 47,304 v Chelsea, FA Premier League, 28 February 2004.
Pitch Measurements: 105m × 68m.
Chairman: Khaldoon Al Mubarak.
Chief Executive: Garry Cook.
Secretary: Bernard Halford.
Manager: Mark Hughes.
Assistant Manager: Mark Bowen.
Physio: Ally Beattie.
Colours: Sky blue shirts with white detail, white shorts with sky blue detail, white stockings with sky blue tops.
Change Colours: Red, white and black striped shirts with black sleeves, black shorts with white trim, white stockings with black, red and white trim.
Year Formed: 1887 as Ardwick FC; 1894 as Manchester City.
Turned Professional: 1887 as Ardwick FC. *Ltd Co.:* 1894.
Previous Names: 1887, Ardwick FC (formed through the amalgamation of West Gorton and Gorton Athletic, the latter having been formed in 1880); 1894, Manchester City.
Club Nicknames: 'Blues' or 'The Citizens'.
Grounds: 1880, Clowes Street; 1881, Kirkmanshulme Cricket Ground; 1882, Queens Road; 1884, Pink Bank Lane; 1887, Hyde Road (1894–1923 as City); 1923, Maine Road; 2003, City of Manchester Stadium.
First Football League Game: 3 September 1892, Division 2, v Bootle (h) W 7–0 – Douglas; McVickers, Robson; Middleton, Russell, Hopkins; Davies (3), Morris (2), Angus (1), Weir (1), Milarvie.
Record League Victory: 10–1 v Huddersfield T, Division 2, 7 November 1987 – Nixon; Gidman, Hinchcliffe, Clements, Lake, Redmond, White (3), Stewart (3), Adcock (3), McNab (1), Simpson.

HONOURS

Football League: Division 1 – Champions 1936–37, 1967–68, 2001–02; Runners-up 1903–04, 1920–21, 1976–77, 1999–2000; Division 2 – Champions 1898–99, 1902–03, 1909–10, 1927–28, 1946–47, 1965–66; Runners-up 1895–96, 1950–51, 1987–88.
FA Cup: Winners 1904, 1934, 1956, 1969; Runners-up 1926, 1933, 1955, 1981.
Football League Cup: Winners 1970, 1976; Runners-up 1974.
European Competitions: European Cup: 1968–69. *European Cup-Winners' Cup:* 1969–70 (winners), 1970–71. *UEFA Cup:* 1972–73, 1976–77, 1977–78, 1978–79, 2003–04, 2008–09.

SKY SPORTS FACT FILE

Eric Westwood played for Manchester Boys v Southampton in 1932–33 at Maine Road and The Dell. His League debut for Manchester City on 5 November 1938 was against Southampton at Maine Road. His next game at The Dell was against Southampton!

Record Cup Victory: 10–1 v Swindon T, FA Cup 4th rd, 29 January 1930 – Barber; Felton, McCloy; Barrass, Cowan, Heinemann; Toseland, Marshall (5), Tait (3), Johnson (1), Brook (1).

Record Defeat: 1–9 v Everton, Division 1, 3 September 1906.

Most League Points (2 for a win): 62, Division 2, 1946–47.

Most League Points (3 for a win): 99, Division 1, 2001–02.

Most League Goals: 108, Division 2, 1926–27, 108, Division 1, 2001–02.

Highest League Scorer in Season: Tommy Johnson, 38, Division 1, 1928–29.

Most League Goals in Total Aggregate: Tommy Johnson, 158, 1919–30.

Most League Goals in One Match: 5, Fred Williams v Darwen, Division 2, 18 February 1899; 5, Tom Browell v Burnley, Division 2, 24 October 1925; 5, Tom Johnson v Everton, Division 1, 15 September 1928; 5, George Smith v Newport Co, Division 2, 14 June 1947.

Most Capped Player: Colin Bell, 48, England.

Most League Appearances: Alan Oakes, 565, 1959–76.

Youngest League Player: Glyn Pardoe, 15 years 314 days v Birmingham C, 11 April 1962.

Record Transfer Fee Received: £21,000,000 from Chelsea for Shaun Wright-Phillips, July 2005.

Record Transfer Fee Paid: £32,500,000 to Real Madrid for Robinho, September 2008.

Football League Record: 1892 Ardwick elected founder member of Division 2; 1894 Newly-formed Manchester C elected to Division 2; Division 1 1899–1902, 1903–09, 1910–26, 1928–38, 1947–50, 1951–63, 1966–83, 1985–87, 1989–92; Division 2 1902–03, 1909–10, 1926–28, 1938–47, 1950–51, 1963–66, 1983–85, 1987–89; 1992–96 FA Premier League; 1996–98 Division 1; 1998–99 Division 2; 1999–2000 Division 1; 2000–01 FA Premier League; 2001–02 Division 1; 2002– FA Premier League.

LATEST SEQUENCES

Longest Sequence of League Wins: 9, 8.4.1912 – 28.9.1912.

Longest Sequence of League Defeats: 8, 23.8.1995 – 14.10.1995.

Longest Sequence of League Draws: 6, 5.4.1913 – 6.9.1913.

Longest Sequence of Unbeaten League Matches: 22, 16.11.1946 – 19.4.1947.

Longest Sequence Without a League Win: 17, 26.12.1979 – 7.4.1980.

Successive Scoring Runs: 44 from 3.10.1936.

Successive Non-scoring Runs: 6 from 30.1.1971.

MANAGERS

Joshua Parlby 1893–95
  (Secretary-Manager)
Sam Omerod 1895–1902
Tom Maley 1902–06
Harry Newbould 1906–12
Ernest Magnall 1912–24
David Ashworth 1924–25
Peter Hodge 1926–32
Wilf Wild 1932–46
  (continued as Secretary to 1950)
Sam Cowan 1946–47
John 'Jock' Thomson 1947–50
Leslie McDowall 1950–63
George Poyser 1963–65
Joe Mercer 1965–71
  (continued as General Manager to 1972)
Malcolm Allison 1972–73
Johnny Hart 1973
Ron Saunders 1973–74
Tony Book 1974–79
Malcolm Allison 1979–80
John Bond 1980–83
John Benson 1983
Billy McNeill 1983–86
Jimmy Frizzell 1986–87
  (continued as General Manager)
Mel Machin 1987–89
Howard Kendall 1990
Peter Reid 1990–93
Brian Horton 1993–95
Alan Ball 1995–96
Steve Coppell 1996
Frank Clark 1996–98
Joe Royle 1998–2001
Kevin Keegan 2001–05
Stuart Pearce 2005–07
Sven-Göran Eriksson 2007–08
Mark Hughes June 2008–

TEN YEAR LEAGUE RECORD

		P	W	D	L	F	A	Pts	Pos
1999-2000	Div 1	46	26	11	9	78	40	89	2
2000-01	PR Lge	38	8	10	20	41	65	34	18
2001-02	Div 1	46	31	6	9	108	52	99	1
2002-03	PR Lge	38	15	6	17	47	54	51	9
2003-04	PR Lge	38	9	14	15	55	54	41	16
2004-05	PR Lge	38	13	13	12	47	39	52	8
2005-06	PR Lge	38	13	4	21	43	48	43	15
2006-07	PR Lge	38	11	9	18	29	44	42	14
2007-08	PR Lge	38	15	10	13	45	53	55	9
2008-09	PR Lge	38	15	5	18	58	50	50	10

DID YOU KNOW ?

Record transfer fees are nothing new to Manchester City. In November 1902 they broke the British record when they paid Preston North End £450 for full-back Johnny McMahon. He quickly went on to collect a Second Division championship medal.

MANCHESTER CITY 2008–09 LEAGUE RECORD

Match No.	Date	Venue	Opponents	Result	H/T Score	Lg. Pos.	Goalscorers	Attendance
1	Aug 17	A	Aston Villa	L	2-4	0-0	—	Elano (pen) [64], Corluka [89]	39,955
2	24	H	West Ham U	W	3-0	0-0	7	Sturridge [65], Elano 2 [70, 76]	36,635
3	31	A	Sunderland	W	3-0	1-0	3	Ireland [45], Wright-Phillips 2 [50, 58]	39,622
4	Sept 13	H	Chelsea	L	1-3	1-1	5	Robinho [13]	47,331
5	21	H	Portsmouth	W	6-0	2-0	5	Jo [13], Dunne [20], Robinho [57], Wright-Phillips [68], Evans [78], Gelson [83]	40,238
6	28	A	Wigan Ath	L	1-2	1-2	8	Kompany [22]	18,214
7	Oct 5	H	Liverpool	L	2-3	2-0	11	Ireland [19], Garrido [41]	47,280
8	20	A	Newcastle U	D	2-2	1-1	—	Robinho (pen) [14], Ireland [86]	45,908
9	26	H	Stoke C	W	3-0	1-0	8	Robinho 3 [14, 47, 72]	44,624
10	29	A	Middlesbrough	L	0-2	0-0	—		25,731
11	Nov 2	A	Bolton W	L	0-2	0-0	10		21,095
12	9	H	Tottenham H	L	1-2	1-1	13	Robinho [16]	41,893
13	16	A	Hull C	D	2-2	2-1	12	Ireland 2 [37, 45]	24,902
14	22	H	Arsenal	W	3-0	1-0	11	Ireland [45], Robinho [56], Sturridge (pen) [90]	44,878
15	30	H	Manchester U	L	0-1	0-1	14		47,320
16	Dec 6	A	Fulham	D	1-1	1-1	14	Mwaruwari [6]	24,012
17	13	H	Everton	L	0-1	0-0	17		41,344
18	21	A	WBA	L	1-2	0-0	18	Carson (og) [86]	25,010
19	26	H	Hull C	W	5-1	4-0	15	Caicedo 2 [15, 27], Robinho 2 [28, 36], Ireland [82]	45,196
20	28	A	Blackburn R	D	2-2	0-1	13	Sturridge [88], Robinho [90]	25,200
21	Jan 17	H	Wigan Ath	W	1-0	0-0	11	Zabaleta [53]	41,262
22	28	H	Newcastle U	W	2-1	1-0	—	Wright-Phillips [17], Bellamy [77]	42,280
23	31	A	Stoke C	L	0-1	0-1	10		27,236
24	Feb 7	H	Middlesbrough	W	1-0	0-0	9	Bellamy [51]	40,558
25	14	A	Portsmouth	L	0-2	0-0	—		20,018
26	22	A	Liverpool	D	1-1	0-0	10	Bellamy [51]	44,259
27	Mar 1	A	West Ham U	L	0-1	0-0	11		34,562
28	4	H	Aston Villa	W	2-0	1-0	—	Elano (pen) [24], Wright-Phillips [89]	40,137
29	15	A	Chelsea	L	0-1	0-1	10		41,810
30	22	H	Sunderland	W	1-0	0-0	10	Richards [56]	43,017
31	Apr 4	A	Arsenal	L	0-2	0-1	10		60,097
32	12	H	Fulham	L	1-3	1-0	11	Ireland [28]	39,841
33	19	H	WBA	W	4-2	2-1	10	Robinho [8], Onuoha [21], Elano (pen) [56], Sturridge [90]	40,072
34	25	A	Everton	W	2-1	1-0	9	Robinho [35], Ireland [54]	37,791
35	May 2	H	Blackburn R	W	3-1	3-0	8	Caicedo [27], Robinho [34], Elano (pen) [45]	43,967
36	10	A	Manchester U	L	0-2	0-2	10		75,464
37	16	A	Tottenham H	L	1-2	0-1	10	Bojinov [65]	36,000
38	24	H	Bolton W	W	1-0	1-0	10	Caicedo [8]	47,202

Final League Position: 10

GOALSCORERS

League (58): Robinho 14 (1 pen), Ireland 9, Elano 6 (4 pens), Wright-Phillips 5, Caicedo 4, Sturridge 4 (1 pen), Bellamy 3, Bojinov 1, Corluka 1, Dunne 1, Evans 1, Garrido 1, Gelson 1, Jo 1, Kompany 1, Mwaruwari 1, Onuoha 1, Richards 1, Zabaleta 1, own goal 1.
Carling Cup (2): Gelson 1, Ireland 1.
FA Cup (0).
UEFA Cup (24): Caicedo 3, Ireland 3, Wright-Phillips 3, Bellamy 2, Elano 2 (1 pen), Jo 2, Mwaruwari 2, Petkov 2, Hamann 1, Onuoha 1, Robinho 1, Vassell 1, own goal 1.

Hart J 23	Corluka V 3	Garrido J 11+2	Ben Haim T 8+1	Richards M 33+1	Johnson M 3	Etuhu K 2+2	Gelson 3+14	Elano 21+7	Evans C 3+13	Petrov M 4+5	Ireland S 34+1	Sturridge D 3+13	Hamann D 5+4	Ball M 8	Kompany V 34	Dunne R 31	Wright-Phillips S 27	Jo 6+3	Zabaleta P 26+3	Robinho 30+1	Onuoha N 20+3	Vassell D 6+2	Mwaruwari B 7+1	Schmeichel K —+1	Caicedo F 10+7	Bridge W 16	De Jong N 16	Bellamy C 7+1	Given S 15	Logan S 1	Bojinov V 2+6	Berti G —+1	Weiss V —+1	Match No.
1	2	3	4	5	6	7	8^1	9	10^2	11	12	13																						1
1	2		4	5^1	8	13		9^3	14	11^2	7	10	12		3	6																		2
1	2	13	5^2	6^3			14	12		7					8	3	11	4	10^1	9														3
1				5			12			7	13	8^1	3^2		6	4	11	9	2	10														4
1	3			5			12	8	13		7^1	14			4	6	11	9^2	2	10^3														5
1	3			5			12	10^2	14		11	13			4^1	6	7	9^3	2	8														6
1	3			5			12	10^2	14	13	11				4	6	7	9^1	2^1	8^3														7
1	3^2	5	2^3					12			11	13	8^1		4	6	7	9		10	14													8
1	3^3	5	2				12	10	9^2		11	13			6	4^1	7			8	14													9
1		5	3				12	9^1	13		11	10^2			4	6	7			8	2													10
1		5	3					9^1	10^2		11	13	12		4	6	7			2	8													11
1	3		5				4^5				11		12		6^6	7			2	8		10^1	9											12
1^6	3	6	5								11				4		7	12	2	8		10	9^1	15										13
1	3		5				12				11	13	14		4	6	7		2	8^3		10^1	9^2											14
1	3		2^2				12				11	13	4^1		5	6	7		14	8		10^3	9											15
1		5						12			11		8	3	4	6	7		2			10	9^1											16
1		5					10				11			3	4	6	7	12	2	8^2		13	9^1											17
1		5		8							11			3	4	6	7		2			10	9^1	12										18
1		5^1		13	9						11^2			3	4	6	7	14	2	8	12			10^3										19
1			12					9^2			11	14		3	4	6	7		2	8	5^1	13		10^3										20
1	12	5					10					9^1		4	6^6	7			2	8	3			11										21
1			2	13	12			10			4					11^3		7^2	8	5				14	3	6^1	9							22
1			2		12			10			4					11		7^1	8	5				13	3	6^2	9							23
			2					10			4					11		7	8^1	5				12	3	6	9	1					24
						9	12			11			4				7^1	8^2	5					13	3	6	10	1	2				25
			2							11				4	6		7	10^1	5					12	3	8	9	1					26
			2^2				12				11				4	6	7	10		5				13	3	8^3	9^1	1		14			27
							12	9^3	13		11				4	6	7		2	5				10^2	3	8^1		1		14			28
			2	13				9^2	12	4					6	11		7	10^3	5				8^1	3		1	14					29
	14		2^3				12	9							4^1	6	7		3	10	5			8	13		1	11^2					30
			2	12	13								14		4^2	6	11		7	10^3	5			3^1	8	9	1						31
	3		2	8^3			12	10^2	11	14					6		7	13	5				4	1		9^1							32
				13	9^2				14	7	12			4	6			2	10^3	5				11^1	3	8	1						33
			2^1	12	9^3	14	13	7						4	6			10	5				11^2	3	8	1						34
			2				9^2			13	7			4	6			10	5				11^1	3	8	1	12						35
			2				9	14	13	7				4	6			10^3	5				11^1	3	8^2	1	12						36
			2				9^1			11^2	7			4	6		12		5	13				10^3	3	8	1	14					37
			2					7^1						4^2	6	11		13	10	5				9	3^3	8	1	14	12				38

FA Cup
Third Round   Nottingham F   (h)   0-3

Carling Cup
Second Round   Brighton & HA   (a)   2-2

UEFA Cup

First Qualifying Round	EB/Streymur	(a)	2-0
		(h)	2-0
Second Qualifying Round	Midtjylland	(h)	0-1
		(a)	1-0
First Round	Omonia	(a)	2-1
		(h)	2-1
Group A	Twente	(h)	3-2
	Schalke	(a)	2-0
	Paris St Germain	(h)	0-0
	Santander	(a)	1-3
Third Round	FC Copenhagen	(a)	2-2
		(h)	2-1
Fourth Round	Aalborg	(h)	2-0
		(a)	0-2
Quarter-Finals	Hamburg	(a)	1-3
		(h)	2-1

MANCHESTER UNITED   FA Premiership

FOUNDATION

Manchester United was formed as comparatively recently as 1902 after their predecessors, Newton Heath, went bankrupt. However, it is usual to give the date of the club's foundation as 1878 when the dining room committee of the carriage and waggon works of the Lancashire and Yorkshire Railway Company formed Newton Heath L and YR Cricket and Football Club. They won the Manchester Cup in 1886 and as Newton Heath FC were admitted to the Second Division in 1892.

Old Trafford, Sir Matt Busby Way, Manchester M16 0RA.

Telephone: (0161) 868 8000.

Fax: (0161) 868 8804.

Ticket Office: (0161) 868 8000.

Website: www.manutd.com

Email: enquiries@manutd.co.uk

Ground Capacity: 75,769.

Record Attendance: 76,962 Wolverhampton W v Grimsby T, FA Cup semi-final, 25 March 1939.

Club Record Attendance: 76,098 v Blackburn R, FA Premier League, 31 March 2007.

Pitch Measurements: 105m × 68m.

Chief Executive: David Gill.

Secretary: Ken Ramsden.

Manager: Sir Alex Ferguson CBE.

Assistant Manager: Mick Phelan.

Physio: Rob Swire.

Colours: Red shirts, white shorts, black stockings.

Change Colours: White shirts with red and blue trim, blue shorts with white trim, white stockings.

Year Formed: 1878 as Newton Heath LYR; 1902, Manchester United.

Turned Professional: 1885. **Ltd Co.:** 1907.

Previous Name: 1880, Newton Heath; 1902, Manchester United.

Club Nickname: 'Red Devils'.

Grounds: 1880, North Road, Monsall Road; 1893, Bank Street; 1910, Old Trafford (played at Maine Road 1941–49).

First Football League Game: 3 September 1892, Division 1, v Blackburn R (a) L 3–4 – Warner; Clements, Brown; Perrins, Stewart, Erentz; Farman (1), Coupar (1), Donaldson (1), Carson, Mathieson.

HONOURS

FA Premier League – Champions 1992–93, 1993–94, 1995–96, 1996–97, 1998–99, 1999–2000, 2000–01, 2002–03, 2006–07, 2007–08, 2008–09; Runners-up 1994–95, 1997–98, 2005–06.

Football League: Division 1 – Champions 1907–08, 1910–11, 1951–52, 1955–56, 1956–57, 1964–65, 1966–67; Runners-up 1946–47, 1947–48, 1948–49, 1950–51, 1958–59, 1963–64, 1967–68, 1979–80, 1987–88, 1991–92. Division 2 – Champions 1935–36, 1974–75; Runners-up 1896–97, 1905–06, 1924–25, 1937–38.

FA Cup: Winners 1909, 1948, 1963, 1977, 1983, 1985, 1990, 1994, 1996, 1999, 2004; Runners-up 1957, 1958, 1976, 1979, 1995, 2005, 2007.

Football League Cup: Winners 1992, 2006, 2009; Runners-up 1983, 1991, 1994, 2003.

European Competitions: *European Cup:* 1956–57 (s-f), 1957–58 (s-f), 1965–66 (s-f), 1967–68 (winners), 1968–69 (s-f). *Champions League:* 1993–94, 1994–95, 1996–97 (s-f), 1997–98, 1998–99 (winners), 1999–2000, 2000–01, 2001–02 (s-f), 2002–03, 2003–04, 2004–05, 2005–06, 2006–07 (s-f), 2007–08 (winners), 2008–09 (runners-up). *European Cup-Winners' Cup:* 1963–64, 1977–78, 1983–84, 1990–91 (winners). 1991–92. *Inter Cities Fairs Cup:* 1964–65. *UEFA Cup:* 1976–77, 1980–81, 1982–83, 1984–85, 1992–93, 1995–96. *Super Cup:* 1991 (winners), 1999 (runners-up), 2008 (runners-up). *Inter-Continental Cup:* 1999 (winners), 1968 (runners-up). *FIFA World Club Cup:* 2008 (winners).

SKY SPORTS FACT FILE

On 15 November, the day Sir Alex Ferguson celebrated 50 years in professional football, Cristiano Ronaldo scored his 100th and 101st goals for Manchester United and appropriately, the team recorded a 5–0 victory over Stoke City.

Record League Victory (as Newton Heath): 10–1 v Wolverhampton W, Division 1, 15 October 1892 – Warner; Mitchell, Clements; Perrins, Stewart (3), Erentz; Farman (1), Hood (1), Donaldson (3), Carson (1), Hendry (1).

Record League Victory (as Manchester U): 9–0 v Ipswich T, FA Premier League, 4 March 1995 – Schmeichel; Keane (1) (Sharpe), Irwin, Bruce (Butt), Kanchelskis, Pallister, Cole (5), Ince (1), McClair, Hughes (2), Giggs.

Record Cup Victory: 10–0 v RSC Anderlecht, European Cup prel. rd 2nd leg, 26 September 1956 – Wood; Foulkes, Byrne; Colman, Jones, Edwards; Berry (1), Whelan (2), Taylor (3), Viollet (4), Pegg.

Record Defeat: 0–7 v Blackburn R, Division 1, 10 April 1926; 0–7 v Aston Villa, Division 1, 27 December 1930; 0–7 v Wolverhampton W, Division 2, 26 December 1931.

Most League Points (2 for a win): 64, Division 1, 1956–57.

Most League Points (3 for a win): 92, FA Premier League, 1993–94.

Most League Goals: 103, Division 1, 1956–57 and 1958–59.

Highest League Scorer in Season: Dennis Viollet, 32, 1959–60.

Most League Goals in Total Aggregate: Bobby Charlton, 199, 1956–73.

Most Capped Player: Bobby Charlton, 106, England.

Most League Appearances: Bobby Charlton, 606, 1956–73.

Youngest League Player: Jeff Whitefoot, 16 years 105 days v Portsmouth, 15 April 1950.

Record Transfer Fee Received: £80,000,000 from Real Madrid for Cristiano Ronaldo, June 2009.

Record Transfer Fee Paid: £30,750,000 to Tottenham H for Dimitar Berbatov, September 2008.

Football League Record: 1892 Newton Heath elected to Division 1; 1894–1906 Division 2; 1906–22 Division 1; 1922–25 Division 2; 1925–31 Division 1; 1931–36 Division 2; 1936–37 Division 1; 1937–38 Division 2; 1938–74 Division 1; 1974–75 Division 2; 1975–92 Division 1; 1992– FA Premier League.

MANAGERS

J. Ernest Mangnall 1903–12
John Bentley 1912–14
John Robson 1914–21
  (Secretary-Manager from 1916)
John Chapman 1921–26
Clarence Hilditch 1926–27
Herbert Bamlett 1927–31
Walter Crickmer 1931–32
Scott Duncan 1932–37
Walter Crickmer 1937–45
  (Secretary-Manager)
Matt Busby 1945–69
  (continued as General Manager then Director)
Wilf McGuinness 1969–70
Sir Matt Busby 1970–71
Frank O'Farrell 1971–72
Tommy Docherty 1972–77
Dave Sexton 1977–81
Ron Atkinson 1981–86
Sir Alex Ferguson November 1986–

LATEST SEQUENCES

Longest Sequence of League Wins: 14, 15.10.1904 – 3.1.1905.

Longest Sequence of League Defeats: 14, 26.4.1930 – 25.10.1930.

Longest Sequence of League Draws: 6, 30.10.1988 – 27.11.1988.

Longest Sequence of Unbeaten League Matches: 29, 26.12.1998 – 25.9.1999.

Longest Sequence Without a League Win: 16, 19.4.1930 – 25.10.1930.

Successive Scoring Runs: 36 from 3.12.2007.

Successive Non-scoring Runs: 5 from 22.2.1902.

TEN YEAR LEAGUE RECORD

		P	W	D	L	F	A	Pts	Pos
1999-2000	PR Lge	38	28	7	3	97	45	91	1
2000-01	PR Lge	38	24	8	6	79	31	80	1
2001-02	PR Lge	38	24	5	9	87	45	77	3
2002-03	PR Lge	38	25	8	5	74	34	83	1
2003-04	PR Lge	38	23	6	9	64	35	75	3
2004-05	PR Lge	38	22	11	5	58	26	77	3
2005-06	PR Lge	38	25	8	5	72	34	83	2
2006-07	PR Lge	38	28	5	5	83	27	89	1
2007-08	PR Lge	38	27	6	5	80	22	87	1
2008-09	PR Lge	38	28	6	4	68	24	90	1

DID YOU KNOW ?

Two weeks before Ronaldo hit his century for Manchester United, the club achieved its 400th Premier League victory in beating Hull City 4–3 at Old Trafford, the first team to reach this milestone in the competition's 17th season.

MANCHESTER UNITED 2008–09 LEAGUE RECORD

Match No.	Date	Venue	Opponents	Result	H/T Score	Lg. Pos.	Goalscorers	Attendance
1	Aug 17	H	Newcastle U	D 1-1	1-1	—	Fletcher [24]	75,512
2	25	A	Portsmouth	W 1-0	1-0	—	Fletcher [32]	20,540
3	Sept 13	A	Liverpool	L 1-2	1-1	14	Tevez [3]	44,192
4	21	A	Chelsea	D 1-1	1-0	15	Park [18]	41,760
5	27	H	Bolton W	W 2-0	0-0	11	Ronaldo (pen) [60], Rooney [77]	75,484
6	Oct 4	A	Blackburn R	W 2-0	1-0	8	Brown [31], Rooney [64]	27,321
7	18	H	WBA	W 4-0	0-0	5	Rooney [56], Ronaldo [69], Berbatov [71], Nani [90]	75,451
8	25	A	Everton	D 1-1	1-0	6	Fletcher [22]	36,069
9	29	H	West Ham U	W 2-0	2-0	—	Ronaldo 2 [14, 30]	75,397
10	Nov 1	H	Hull C	W 4-3	3-1	3	Ronaldo 2 [3, 44], Carrick [29], Vidic [57]	75,398
11	8	A	Arsenal	L 1-2	0-1	4	Rafael [90]	60,106
12	15	H	Stoke C	W 5-0	2-0	5	Ronaldo 2 [3, 89], Carrick [45], Berbatov [49], Welbeck [84]	75,369
13	22	A	Aston Villa	D 0-0	0-0	3		42,585
14	30	A	Manchester C	W 1-0	1-0	3	Rooney [42]	47,320
15	Dec 6	H	Sunderland	W 1-0	0-0	3	Vidic [90]	75,400
16	13	A	Tottenham H	D 0-0	0-0	3		35,882
17	26	A	Stoke C	W 1-0	0-0	3	Tevez [83]	27,500
18	29	H	Middlesbrough	W 1-0	0-0	—	Berbatov [69]	75,294
19	Jan 11	H	Chelsea	W 3-0	1-0	3	Vidic [45], Rooney [63], Berbatov [87]	75,455
20	14	A	Wigan Ath	W 1-0	1-0	—	Rooney [1]	73,917
21	17	A	Bolton W	W 1-0	0-0	1	Berbatov [90]	26,021
22	27	A	WBA	W 5-0	2-0	—	Berbatov [22], Tevez [44], Vidic [60], Ronaldo 2 [65, 73]	26,105
23	31	H	Everton	W 1-0	1-0	1	Ronaldo (pen) [44]	75,399
24	Feb 8	A	West Ham U	W 1-0	0-0	1	Giggs [62]	34,958
25	18	H	Fulham	W 3-0	2-0	—	Scholes [12], Berbatov [30], Rooney [63]	75,437
26	21	H	Blackburn R	W 2-1	1-1	1	Rooney [23], Ronaldo [60]	75,000
27	Mar 4	A	Newcastle U	W 2-1	1-1	—	Rooney [20], Berbatov [56]	51,636
28	14	H	Liverpool	L 1-4	1-2	1	Ronaldo (pen) [23]	75,569
29	21	A	Fulham	L 0-2	0-1	1		25,652
30	Apr 5	H	Aston Villa	W 3-2	1-1	1	Ronaldo 2 [14, 80], Macheda [90]	75,409
31	11	A	Sunderland	W 2-1	1-0	1	Scholes [19], Macheda [76]	45,408
32	22	A	Portsmouth	W 2-0	1-0	1	Rooney [9], Carrick [82]	74,895
33	25	H	Tottenham H	W 5-2	0-2	1	Ronaldo 2 (1 pen) [57 (p), 68], Rooney 2 [67, 71], Berbatov [79]	75,458
34	May 2	A	Middlesbrough	W 2-0	1-0	1	Giggs [25], Park [51]	33,767
35	10	H	Manchester C	W 2-0	2-0	1	Ronaldo [18], Tevez [45]	75,464
36	13	A	Wigan Ath	W 2-1	0-1	—	Tevez [61], Carrick [86]	21,286
37	16	H	Arsenal	D 0-0	0-0	1		75,468
38	24	A	Hull C	W 1-0	1-0	1	Gibson [24]	24,945

Final League Position: 1

GOALSCORERS

League (68): Ronaldo 18 (4 pens), Rooney 12, Berbatov 9, Tevez 5, Carrick 4, Vidic 4, Fletcher 3, Giggs 2, Macheda 2, Park 2, Scholes 2, Brown 1, Gibson 1, Nani 1, Rafael 1, Welbeck 1.
Carling Cup (13): Tevez 6 (2 pens), Nani 3, Ronaldo 2, Giggs 1, O'Shea 1.
FA Cup (13): Gibson 2, Nani 2 (1 pen), Tevez 2, Welbeck 2, Berbatov 1, Park 1, Ronaldo 1, Rooney 1, Scholes 1.
Champions League (18): Berbatov 4, Ronaldo 4, Rooney 4, Tevez 2, Giggs 1, O'Shea 1, Park 1, Vidic 1.
FIFA Club World Cup (6): Rooney 3, Fletcher 1, Ronaldo 1, Vidic 1.
Community Shield (0).
Super Cup (1): Vidic 1.

Van der Sar E 33	Brown W 6+2	Evra P 28	Carrick M 24+4	Ferdinand R 24	Vidic N 33+1	Fletcher D 25+1	Scholes P 14+7	Rooney W 25+5	Campbell F 1	Giggs R 15+13	O'Shea J 20+10	Possebon R —+3	Rafael 12+4	Anderson 1+6	Tevez C 18+11	Nani 7+6	Hargreaves O 1+1	Berbatov D 29+2	Kuszczak T 3+1	Neville G 13+3	Evans J 16+1	Ronaldo C 31+2	Park J 21+4	Gibson D 1+2	Manucho —+1	Welbeck D 1+2	Eckersley R —+2	Tosic Z —+2	Macheda F 2+2	Foster B 2	De Laet R 1	Martin L 1	Match No.
1	2	3	4[1]	5	6	7	8	9		10[3]	11[2]	12	13	14																			1
1	2	3	11	5	6	7	8	9			12			4[1]	10																		2
1	2	3	4[1]	5	6[s]	7	8[2]	10		11[3]	12	13			9					14													3
1[6]		3	4	5	6	7	8[1]	10		11[2]	12	13		15	9					2													4
1		3	4[1]	5	6		8	10[2]		11	12	13		14	9					2		7[3]											5
1	2	3[1]	4	5	6	7	8			11[2]	12	13			9							10[3]	14										6
1	3[1]		4[2]	5	6	7	8			11	12	13	2[3]		9	14						10											7
1	2	3	4[3]	5	6	7	8[1]			11	12	13			10[2]	14																	8
	3		4	5	6	7	8[1]			11[2]	12	13	2[3]		10	14			1														9
1	3	4[1]		5	6	7		8[2]		11[3]	12	13			10	14				2													10
1	3	4	2[2]	5	6	7		8[1]		11	12	13			10[3]	14																	11
1	3	4	5		6		8[1]			11[2]			2		9	12				7		10[3]	13	14									12
1	3	4		5	6	7[1]	8	9			11		2		10[2]	12	13																13
1	3	4	7[s]	5	6		8	10		11[2]	12	13	2		9[1]																		14
1	3	4	7[1]	5	6		8[3]	10		11[2]	12		2		14	13						9											15
1		4	7	5	6		8[1]	12		11		13	3		10[2]					2		9											16
1	12		4	6		7	8[1]	11					3[2]		10		13			2	5												17
1			4	6		7[3]	8			11	5	13	2[1]		10	14		9		12													18
1	3[1]		4		6	7	8	9		11[2]	5	13	2		10	12																	19
1			4	6		7	8[3]	10[1]		11[2]	5		3		9	12		13		2	14												20
1			4	6		7	8[2]	12		11[1]	5	13	3		10					2		9											21
1	12		4	5[1]	6	7	8	11					3		10	13		9[3]		2[2]			14										22
1	12		4	5	6	7	8[2]	11				13	3		10			9		2[1]													23
1			4	5	6	7	8			11	12		3		10[1]			9		2													24
1	3	4[3]	5	6		8	12					2[2]			10		13	9[1]		7	11	14											25
	3	4	5	12		8[2]	10	13					2		14	11[3]		9[1]	1	6[1]	7												26
1	3	4	5	6		8	10	12			2				9[1]					7	11												27
1	3	4[1]	5	6[s]		13	9	12			2		8[2]		10	14					7	11[3]											28
1	3		5			10	8[s]	12[s]		11	2[2]	13			9[1]				6	7	4												29
1	3	4				8		9		5	10[2]	11[1]	2		6	7					13			12									30
	4		6			8	7	3		14	10[3]	9[2]	2		5	12		11[1]				13	1										31
1	3	14	6	7		8	10			11	12[2]	13	4[3]		2[1]	5		9															32
1	3	4	5	6		8[2]	13	10		14	2[3]		12		11[1]			9		7													33
	3[3]		6			8	10	11		2	14	12	13		9			5			4[2]			7[1]	1								34
1	3		6			8	13	12		11	14	10			9			5[3]		7[1]	4[2]												35
1	3	4	6			8[2]	10	13			2		11[1]	12	9[3]			5		7	14												36
1	3	4	6			8	9[2]	11[1]			2	13	10[1]		5			7		12													37
	6					7				13	2[1]		11		1	5				4	8[3]	12	14	9		3[2]	10						38

FA Cup

Third Round	Southampton	(a)	3-0
Fourth Round	Tottenham H	(h)	2-1
Fifth Round	Derby Co	(a)	4-1
Quarter-Final	Fulham	(a)	4-0
Semi-Final	Everton		0-0
(at Wembley)			

FIFA Club World Cup *(in Japan)*

Semi-Final	Gamba Osaka	5-3
Final	Liga Deportiva	1-0

Carling Cup

Third Round	Middlesbrough	(h)	3-1
Fourth Round	QPR	(h)	1-0
Quarter-Final	Blackburn R	(h)	5-3
Semi-Final	Derby Co	(a)	0-1
		(h)	4-2
Final *(at Wembley)*	Tottenham H		0-0

Community Shield

(at Wembley)	Portsmouth	0-0

Champions League

Group E	Villarreal	(h)	0-0
	Aalborg	(a)	3-0
	Celtic	(h)	3-0
		(a)	1-1
	Villarreal	(a)	0-0
	Aalborg	(h)	2-2
Knock-out Round	Internazionale	(a)	0-0
		(h)	2-0
Quarter-Final	Porto	(h)	2-2
		(a)	1-0
Semi-Final	Arsenal	(h)	1-0
		(a)	3-1
Final *(in Rome)*	Barcelona		0-2

Super Cup

(in Monaco)	Zenit	1-2

MIDDLESBROUGH   FL Championship

FOUNDATION

A previous belief that Middlesbrough Football Club was founded at a tripe supper at the Corporation Hotel has proved to be erroneous. In fact, members of Middlesbrough Cricket Club were responsible for forming it at a meeting in the gymnasium of the Albert Park Hotel in 1875.

Riverside Stadium, Middlesbrough TS3 6RS.

Telephone: (0844) 499 6789.

Fax: (01642) 757 690.

Ticket Office: (0844) 499 1234

Website: www.mfc.co.uk

Email: enquiries@mfc.co.uk

Ground Capacity: 35,100.

Record Attendance: Ayresome Park: 53,536 v Newcastle U, Division 1, 27 December 1949. Riverside Stadium: 34,814 v Newcastle U, FA Premier League, 5 March 2003.

Pitch Measurements: 105m × 68m.

Chairman: Steve Gibson.

Chief Executive: Keith Lamb.

Secretary: Karen Nelson.

Manager: Gareth Southgate.

Physio: Grant Downie.

Colours: Red shirts with white chestband, red shorts, red stockings.

Change Colours: Black and blue striped shirts, black shorts, black stockings.

Year Formed: 1876; reformed 1986.

Turned Professional: 1889; became amateur 1892, and professional again, 1899.

Ltd Co: 1892.

Club Nickname: 'Boro'.

Grounds: 1877, Old Archery Ground, Albert Park; 1879, Breckon Hill; 1882, Linthorpe Road Ground; 1903, Ayresome Park; 1995, Riverside Stadium.

First Football League Game: 2 September 1899, Division 2, v Lincoln C (a) L 0–3 – Smith; Shaw, Ramsey; Allport, McNally, McCracken; Wanless, Longstaffe, Gettins, Page, Pugh.

Record League Victory: 9–0 v Brighton & HA, Division 2, 23 August 1958 – Taylor; Bilcliff, Robinson; Harris (2p), Phillips, Walley; Day, McLean, Clough (5), Peacock (2), Holliday.

Record Cup Victory: 7–0 v Hereford U, Coca-Cola Cup 2nd rd, 1st leg, 18 September 1996 – Miller; Fleming (1), Branco (1), Whyte, Vickers, Whelan, Emerson (1), Mustoe, Stamp, Juninho, Ravanelli (4).

HONOURS

Football League: Division 1 – Champions 1994–95; Runners-up 1997–98; Division 2 – Champions 1926–27, 1928–29, 1973–74; Runners-up 1901–02, 1991–92; Division 3 – Runners-up 1966–67, 1986–87.

FA Cup: Runners-up 1997.

Football League Cup: Winners 2004; Runners-up 1997, 1998.

Amateur Cup: Winners 1895, 1898.

Anglo-Scottish Cup: Winners 1976.

Zenith Data Systems Cup: Runners-up 1990.

European Competitions: *UEFA Cup:* 2004–05, 2005–06 (runners-up).

SKY SPORTS FACT FILE

On 4 October 2008 an 89th minute strike by Jeremie Aliadiere gave Middlesbrough a 1–0 victory at Wigan Athletic. It was the club's first away victory in 2008 and registered the 600th goal scored by the club in the Premier League.

Record Defeat: 0–9 v Blackburn R, Division 2, 6 November 1954.

Most League Points (2 for a win): 65, Division 2, 1973–74.

Most League Points (3 for a win): 94, Division 3, 1986–87.

Most League Goals: 122, Division 2, 1926–27.

Highest League Scorer in Season: George Camsell, 59, Division 2, 1926–27 (Second Division record).

Most League Goals in Total Aggregate: George Camsell, 325, 1925–39.

Most League Goals in One Match: 5, John Wilkie v Gainsborough T, Division 2, 2 March 1901; 5, Andy Wilson v Nottingham F, Division 1, 6 October 1923; 5, George Camsell v Manchester C, Division 2, 25 December 1926; 5, George Camsell v Aston Villa, Division 1, 9 September 1935; 5, Brian Clough v Brighton & HA, Division 2, 22 August 1958.

Most Capped Player: Wilf Mannion, 26, England.

Most League Appearances: Tim Williamson, 563, 1902–23.

Youngest League Player: Stephen Bell, 16 years 323 days v Southampton, 30 January 1982; Sam Lawrie, 16 years 323 days v Arsenal, 3 November 1951.

Record Transfer Fee Received: £12,000,000 from Atletico Madrid for Juninho, July 1997.

Record Transfer Fee Paid: £12,000,000 to Heerenveen for Afonso Alves, January 2008.

Football League Record: 1899 Elected to Division 2; 1902–24 Division 1; 1924–27 Division 2; 1927–28 Division 1; 1928–29 Division 2; 1929–54 Division 1; 1954–66 Division 2; 1966–67 Division 3; 1967–74 Division 2; 1974–82 Division 1; 1982–86 Division 2; 1986–87 Division 3; 1987–88 Division 2; 1988–89 Division 1; 1989–92 Division 2; 1992–93 FA Premier League; 1993–95 Division 1; 1995–97 FA Premier League; 1997–98 Division 1; 1998–2009 FA Premier League; 2009– FL C.

MANAGERS

John Robson 1899–1905
Alex Mackie 1905–06
Andy Aitken 1906–09
J. Gunter 1908–10
  (Secretary-Manager)
Andy Walker 1910–11
Tom McIntosh 1911–19
Jimmy Howie 1920–23
Herbert Bamlett 1923–26
Peter McWilliam 1927–34
Wilf Gillow 1934–44
David Jack 1944–52
Walter Rowley 1952–54
Bob Dennison 1954–63
Raich Carter 1963–66
Stan Anderson 1966–73
Jack Charlton 1973–77
John Neal 1977–81
Bobby Murdoch 1981–82
Malcolm Allison 1982–84
Willie Maddren 1984–86
Bruce Rioch 1986–90
Colin Todd 1990–91
Lennie Lawrence 1991–94
Bryan Robson 1994–2001
Steve McClaren 2001–06
Gareth Southgate June 2006–

LATEST SEQUENCES

Longest Sequence of League Wins: 9, 16.2.1974 – 6.4.1974.

Longest Sequence of League Defeats: 8, 26.12.1995 – 17.2.1996.

Longest Sequence of League Draws: 8, 3.4.1971 – 1.5.1971.

Longest Sequence of Unbeaten League Matches: 24, 8.9.1973 – 19.1.1974.

Longest Sequence Without a League Win: 19, 3.10.1981 – 6.3.1982.

Successive Scoring Runs: 26 from 21.9.1946.

Successive Non-scoring Runs: 5 from 17.1.2009.

TEN YEAR LEAGUE RECORD

		P	W	D	L	F	A	Pts	Pos
1999-2000	PR Lge	38	14	10	14	46	52	52	12
2000-01	PR Lge	38	9	15	14	44	44	42	14
2001-02	PR Lge	38	12	9	17	35	47	45	12
2002-03	PR Lge	38	13	10	15	48	44	49	11
2003-04	PR Lge	38	13	9	16	44	52	48	11
2004-05	PR Lge	38	14	13	11	53	46	55	7
2005-06	PR Lge	38	12	9	17	48	58	45	14
2006-07	PR Lge	38	12	10	16	44	49	46	12
2007-08	PR Lge	38	10	12	16	43	53	42	13
2008-09	PR Lge	38	7	11	20	28	57	32	19

DID YOU KNOW ?

The first two floodlight friendly matches held at Ayresome Park featured the club's two most notable neighbours. On 16 October Middlesbrough defeated Sunderland 2–0 with Brian Clough scoring once and two weeks later they accounted for Newcastle United 3–0.

MIDDLESBROUGH 2008–09 LEAGUE RECORD

Match No.	Date	Venue	Opponents	Result		H/T Score	Lg. Pos.	Goalscorers	Attendance
1	Aug 16	H	Tottenham H	W	2-1	0-0	—	Wheater [71], Mido [86]	32,623
2	23	A	Liverpool	L	1-2	0-0	10	Mido [70]	43,168
3	30	H	Stoke C	W	2-1	1-0	6	Alves [37], Tuncay [85]	27,627
4	Sept 13	A	Portsmouth	L	1-2	1-0	8	Mido [24]	19,425
5	20	A	Sunderland	L	0-2	0-0	12		38,388
6	27	H	WBA	L	0-1	0-0	16		26,248
7	Oct 4	A	Wigan Ath	W	1-0	0-0	12	Aliadiere [89]	16,806
8	18	H	Chelsea	L	0-5	0-1	13		29,221
9	25	A	Blackburn R	D	1-1	0-0	12	Alves [74]	17,606
10	29	H	Manchester C	W	2-0	0-0	12	Alves (pen) [53], O'Neil [90]	25,731
11	Nov 1	H	West Ham U	D	1-1	0-1	8	Mido [83]	25,164
12	9	A	Aston Villa	W	2-1	1-1	8	Tuncay 2 [34, 88]	36,672
13	16	A	Everton	D	1-1	1-0	8	O'Neil [8]	31,063
14	22	H	Bolton W	L	1-3	0-2	10	Pogatetz [77]	24,487
15	29	H	Newcastle U	D	0-0	0-0	12		32,160
16	Dec 6	A	Hull C	L	1-2	0-0	12	Tuncay [79]	24,912
17	13	H	Arsenal	D	1-1	1-1	12	Aliadiere [29]	27,320
18	20	A	Fulham	L	0-3	0-1	14		23,722
19	26	H	Everton	L	0-1	0-0	17		30,253
20	29	A	Manchester U	L	0-1	0-0	—		75,294
21	Jan 10	H	Sunderland	D	1-1	1-0	16	Alves [45]	29,310
22	17	A	WBA	L	0-3	0-1	18		25,557
23	28	A	Chelsea	L	0-2	0-0	—		40,290
24	31	H	Blackburn R	D	0-0	0-0	19		24,303
25	Feb 7	A	Manchester C	L	0-1	0-0	19		40,558
26	21	H	Wigan Ath	D	0-0	0-0	19		24,020
27	28	H	Liverpool	W	2-0	1-0	18	Xabi Alonso (og) [32], Tuncay [63]	33,724
28	Mar 4	A	Tottenham H	L	0-4	0-3	—		35,761
29	14	H	Portsmouth	D	1-1	0-1	19	King [90]	24,281
30	21	A	Stoke C	L	0-1	0-0	19		26,442
31	Apr 4	A	Bolton W	L	1-4	1-2	19	O'Neil [38]	20,819
32	11	H	Hull C	W	3-1	2-1	19	Tuncay [3], Bates [29], King [90]	32,255
33	18	H	Fulham	D	0-0	0-0	18		30,389
34	26	A	Arsenal	L	0-2	0-1	18		60,089
35	May 2	H	Manchester U	L	0-2	0-1	19		33,767
36	11	A	Newcastle U	L	1-3	1-1	—	Beye (og) [3]	51,252
37	16	H	Aston Villa	D	1-1	1-0	19	Tuncay [14]	27,261
38	24	A	West Ham U	L	1-2	0-1	19	O'Neil [50]	34,007

Final League Position: 19

GOALSCORERS
League (28): Tuncay 7, Alves 4 (1 pen), Mido 4, O'Neil 4, Aliadiere 2, King 2, Bates 1, Pogatetz 1, Wheater 1, own goals 2.
Carling Cup (6): Johnson A 2, Aliadiere 1, Digard 1, Emnes 1, Mido 1.
FA Cup (8): Alves 3, Downing 2, Emnes 1, Tuncay 1, Wheater 1.

Jones B 16	Wheater D 31 + 1	Taylor A 20 + 6	O'Neil G 28 + 1	Huth R 23 + 1	Pogatetz E 27	Aliadiere J 27 + 2	Shawky M 11 + 2	Alves A 24 + 7	Tuncay S 30 + 3	Downing S 37	Mido 5 + 8	Digard D 15 + 8	Turnbull R 22	Hoyte J 17 + 5	Riggott C 17	Johnson A 10 + 16	Grounds J 2	Johnson J — + 1	Emnes M 3 + 12	Arca J 14 + 4	Hines S — + 1	McMahon T 13	Bates M 15 + 2	Walker J 2 + 4	King M 9 + 4	Bennett J — + 1	Franks J — + 1	Match No.
1	2	3	4	5	6	7	8	9^{1}	10^{2}	11	12	13																1
	2	3^{1}	4	5	6	7	8	9^{2}	10^{3}	11	13	14	1	12														2
	6	12	4	5	3	7	8^{2}	9^{3}	10	11	14	13	1	2^{1}														3
				12	4	5	3	7	9	11	10^{2}	8^{1}	1	2	6	13												4
			2	3	4	5	6	7	12	9	11	8^{1}	1	13	10^{2}													5
			6	3	4	5	7^{2}	8^{1}	9	11	10	12	1	2	13													6
					5	4	7	8^{1}	9^{2}	11	10	12	1	2	6	13	3											7
				5	3	4	7	8^{2}	12	11	10	13	1	6	9^{1}	2^{3}	14											8
				2	3	4	5	7	9	10^{1}	11	8	1	6	12													9
				2	3	4	5	7	9	10	11^{1}	8^{2}	1	6	12	13												10
			2^{2}	3	4	5	7	9^{1}	10	11	12	8^{3}	1	13	6	14												11
					3	4	5	7	9^{1}	10	11	8	1	2	6	12												12
					12	3	4	5	9^{3}	10	11	7	1	2	6^{1}	13	14	8^{2}										13
				5	3^{3}	4	6	7^{1}	9^{2}	10	11	8	1	2	12	13	14											14
				5	3	6	7^{1}	9	10	11	12	4	1	2	8													15
					5^{4}	3	6	7	9	10	11	4^{1}	1	2	8	12												16
						5	3	9	12	10	11	4^{1}	1	6	7^{2}	13	8	2										17
					12	5^{1}	3	9	8	10	11	13	1	6	7^{3}	14	4^{2}	2										18
					3	4^{3}	5	7^{2}	12	10^{1}	11	9	1	6	13	14	8	2										19
						5	4	3	7^{1}	9	10	11	1	6	12	8	2											20
						5	3	9^{1}	10	11	12	8^{3}	1	6	13	7	2	14	4^{2}									21
			5	3	7^{1}	13	8	9	10	11	12	4^{8}	1	6^{2}	2^{3}	14												22
							5	4	8^{2}	12	13	11	1	6	7	2	9	10^{1}										23
1	2	5	3	12	10^{1}	11	6	7	13	8	4	9^{2}																24
1	2	12	5	3	9	13	11	4^{1}	14	6^{3}	7^{2}	8	10															25
1	6	4	5	3	12	9	13	11	8^{3}	2	7^{2}	10^{1}	14															26
1	6	4	5	3	9^{3}	10^{1}	11	2	12	8^{2}	7	13	14															27
1	6	13	4	5^{2}	3	9^{3}	10	11	2^{1}	12	8	7	14															28
1	6	14	5	3^{3}	7^{2}	12	10	11	13	8^{1}	2	4^{8}	9															29
1	4	3^{3}	7	5	6	8	12	10	11	14	13	2^{3}	9^{1}															30
1	6	12	4	5	3^{1}	8^{2}	9	10	11	2	13	7																31
1	6	3	5	7^{2}	9^{1}	10	11	12	13	2	4	8																32
1	6	3	5	7	9^{1}	10	11	12	2	4	8																	33
1	6	3	4	5	9^{3}	10	11	13	12	14	2^{2}	7	8^{1}															34
1	6	4^{3}	5	9	13	10	11	12	3	14	2^{1}	7	8^{2}															35
1	3^{3}	4	5	13	8^{2}	9^{1}	10	11	2	14	7	6	12															36
1	6	4^{2}	5	10	11^{1}	3	7	9	8	2	13	12																37
1	6	4	5	10	3	11	9^{3}	8^{2}	2^{1}	7	13	12	14															38

FA Cup

Third Round	Barrow	(h)	2-1
Fourth Round	Wolverhampton W	(a)	2-1
Fifth Round	West Ham U	(a)	1-1
		(h)	2-0
Quarter-Final	Everton	(a)	1-2

Carling Cup

Second Round	Yeovil T	(h)	5-1
Third Round	Manchester U	(a)	1-3

MILLWALL   FL Championship 1

FOUNDATION

Formed in 1885 as Millwall Rovers by employees of Morton & Co, a jam and marmalade factory in West Ferry Road. The founders were predominantly Scotsmen. Their first headquarters was The Islanders pub in Tooke Street, Millwall. Their first trophy was the East End Cup in 1887.

The Den, Zampa Road, London SE16 3LN.

Telephone: (020) 7232 1222.

Fax: (020) 7231 3663.

Ticket Office: (020) 7231 9999.

Website: www.millwallfc.co.uk

Email: questions@millwallplc.com

Ground Capacity: 19,734.

Record Attendance: 20,093 v Arsenal, FA Cup 3rd rd, 10 January 1994.

Pitch Measurements: 105m × 68m.

Chairman: John G Berylson.

Executive Deputy Chairman: Heather Rabbatts.

Chief Operating Officer: Andy Ambler.

Secretary: Yvonne Haines.

Manager: Kenny Jackett.

Assistant Manager: Joe Gallen.

Physio: Bobby Bacic.

Colours: Royal blue shirts with white detail, white shorts, royal blue stockings.

Change Colours: White shirts, black shorts, black stockings

Year Formed: 1885. *Turned Professional:* 1893. *Ltd Co.:* 1894.

Previous Names: 1885, Millwall Rovers; 1889, Millwall Athletic; 1899, Millwall; 1985, Millwall Football & Athletic Company.

Club Nickname: 'The Lions'.

Grounds: 1885, Glengall Road, Millwall; 1886, Back of 'Lord Nelson'; 1890, East Ferry Road; 1901, North Greenwich; 1910, The Den, Cold Blow Lane; 1993, The Den, Bermondsey.

First Football League Game: 28 August 1920, Division 3, v Bristol R (h) W 2–0 – Lansdale; Fort, Hodge; Voisey (1), Riddell, McAlpine; Waterall, Travers, Broad (1), Sutherland, Dempsey.

Record League Victory: 9–1 v Torquay U, Division 3 (S), 29 August 1927 – Lansdale, Tilling, Hill, Amos, Bryant (3), Graham, Chance, Hawkins (3), Landells (1), Phillips (2), Black. 9–1 v Coventry C, Division 3 (S), 19 November 1927 – Lansdale, Fort, Hill, Amos, Collins (1), Graham, Chance, Landells (4), Cock (2), Phillips (2), Black.

HONOURS

Football League: Division 1 best season: 3rd, 1993–94; Division 2 – Champions 1987–88, 2000–01; Division 3 (S) – Champions 1927–28, 1937–38; Runners-up 1952–53; Division 3 – Runners-up 1965–66, 1984–85; Division 4 – Champions 1961–62; Runners-up 1964–65.

FA Cup: Runners-up 2004; Semi-final 1900, 1903, 1937 (first Division 3 side to reach semi-final).

Football League Cup: best season: 5th rd, 1974, 1977, 1995.

Football League Trophy: Winners 1983.

Auto Windscreens Shield: Runners-up 1999.

European Competitions: UEFA Cup: 2004–05.

SKY SPORTS FACT FILE

On 13 January 2009 in a third round FA Cup replay at Crewe Alexandra, Neil Harris broke Teddy Sheringham's record for Millwall with his 112th League and Cup goal. Not an unlucky date because on 13 December he had equalled the total at Walsall.

Record Cup Victory: 7–0 v Gateshead, FA Cup 2nd rd, 12 December 1936 – Yuill; Ted Smith, Inns; Brolly, Hancock, Forsyth; Thomas (1), Mangnall (1), Ken Burditt (2), McCartney (2), Thorogood (1).

Record Defeat: 1–9 v Aston Villa, FA Cup 4th rd, 28 January 1946.

Most League Points (2 for a win): 65, Division 3 (S), 1927–28 and Division 3, 1965–66.

Most League Points (3 for a win): 93, Division 2, 2000–01.

Most League Goals: 127, Division 3 (S), 1927–28.

Highest League Scorer in Season: Richard Parker, 37, Division 3 (S), 1926–27.

Most League Goals in Total Aggregate: Neil Harris, 101, 1995–2004; 2006–07.

Most League Goals in One Match: 5, Richard Parker v Norwich C, Division 3 (S), 28 August 1926.

Most Capped Player: Eamonn Dunphy, 22 (23), Republic of Ireland.

Most League Appearances: Barry Kitchener, 523, 1967–82.

Youngest League Player: Moses Ashikodi, 15 years 240 days v Brighton & HA, 22 February 2003.

Record Transfer Fee Received: £2,300,000 from Liverpool for Mark Kennedy, March 1995.

Record Transfer Fee Paid: £800,000 to Derby Co for Paul Goddard, December 1989.

Football League Record: 1920 Original Members of Division 3; 1921 Division 3 (S); 1928–34 Division 2; 1934–38 Division 3 (S); 1938–48 Division 2; 1948–58 Division 3 (S); 1958–62 Division 4; 1962–64 Division 3; 1964–65 Division 4; 1965–66 Division 3; 1966–75 Division 2; 1975–76 Division 3; 1976–79 Division 2; 1979–85 Division 3; 1985–88 Division 2; 1988–90 Division 1; 1990–92 Division 2; 1992–96 Division 1; 1996–2001 Division 2; 2001–04 Division 1; 2004–06 FL C; 2006– FL 1.

LATEST SEQUENCES

Longest Sequence of League Wins: 10, 10.3.1928 – 25.4.1928.

Longest Sequence of League Defeats: 11, 10.4.1929 – 16.9.1929.

Longest Sequence of League Draws: 5, 22.12.1973 – 12.1.1974.

Longest Sequence of Unbeaten League Matches: 19, 22.8.1959 – 31.10.1959.

Longest Sequence Without a League Win: 20, 26.12.1989 – 5.5.1990.

Successive Scoring Runs: 22 from 8.12.1923.

Successive Non-scoring Runs: 6 from 20.12.1947.

MANAGERS

F. B. Kidd 1894–99
 (Hon. Treasurer/Manager)
E. R. Stopher 1899–1900
 (Hon. Treasurer/Manager)
George Saunders 1900–11
 (Hon. Treasurer/Manager)
Herbert Lipsham 1911–19
Robert Hunter 1919–33
Bill McCracken 1933–36
Charlie Hewitt 1936–40
Bill Voisey 1940–44
Jack Cock 1944–48
Charlie Hewitt 1948–56
Ron Gray 1956–57
Jimmy Seed 1958–59
Reg Smith 1959–61
Ron Gray 1961–63
Billy Gray 1963–66
Benny Fenton 1966–74
Gordon Jago 1974–77
George Petchey 1978–80
Peter Anderson 1980–82
George Graham 1982–86
John Docherty 1986–90
Bob Pearson 1990
Bruce Rioch 1990–92
Mick McCarthy 1992–96
Jimmy Nicholl 1996–97
John Docherty 1997
Billy Bonds 1997–98
Keith Stevens May 1998–2000
 (then Joint Manager)
(plus Alan McLeary 1999–2000)
Mark McGhee 2000–03
Dennis Wise 2003–05
Steve Claridge 2005
Colin Lee 2005–06
Nigel Spackman 2006
Willie Donachie 2006–07
Kenny Jackett November 2007–

TEN YEAR LEAGUE RECORD

		P	W	D	L	F	A	Pts	Pos
1999-2000	Div 2	46	23	13	10	76	50	82	5
2000-01	Div 2	46	28	9	9	89	38	93	1
2001-02	Div 1	46	22	11	13	69	48	77	4
2002-03	Div 1	46	19	9	18	59	69	66	9
2003-04	Div 1	46	18	15	13	55	48	69	10
2004-05	FL C	46	18	12	16	51	45	66	10
2005-06	FL C	46	8	17	21	35	61	40	23
2006-07	FL 1	46	19	9	18	59	62	66	10
2007-08	FL 1	46	14	10	22	45	60	52	17
2008-09	FL 1	46	25	7	14	63	53	82	5

DID YOU KNOW ?

The first chairman of Millwall was a local GP Dr William Murray-Leslie who had been capped by Northern Ireland. On 5 February 1887 while attached to the YMCA he played at centre-half against England at Bramall Lane, Sheffield as Willie Leslie.

MILLWALL 2008–09 LEAGUE RECORD

Match No.	Date	Venue	Opponents	Result	H/T Score	Lg. Pos.	Goalscorers	Attendance
1	Aug 9	A	Oldham Ath	L 3-4	2-1	—	Kandol [1], Hazell (og) [14], Grabban [56]	5367
2	16	H	Southend U	D 1-1	0-1	19	Brkovic [90]	8114
3	23	A	Northampton T	D 0-0	0-0	22		4402
4	30	H	Huddersfield T	W 2-1	1-1	11	Kandol [37], Grabban [62]	7513
5	Sept 6	H	Hartlepool U	W 2-0	2-0	7	Grabban [3], Alexander [41]	7207
6	13	A	Leicester C	W 1-0	1-0	5	Alexander [20]	19,591
7	20	H	Cheltenham T	W 2-0	0-0	4	Alexander (pen) [70], Martin [81]	8009
8	28	A	Swindon T	W 2-1	1-0	4	Easter [24], Grabban [75]	7589
9	Oct 4	H	Milton Keynes D	L 0-4	0-2	6		9871
10	11	A	Tranmere R	W 3-1	2-0	5	Kandol 2 [8, 13], Abdou [60]	5863
11	18	H	Leeds U	W 3-1	1-1	3	Martin [38], Harris 2 [59, 88]	13,041
12	21	A	Colchester U	W 2-1	2-1	—	Grabban [8], Robinson [22]	5506
13	25	A	Scunthorpe U	L 2-3	0-2	3	Harris [62], Craig [69]	5670
14	28	H	Hereford U	W 1-0	0-0	—	Grabban [86]	9071
15	Nov 1	A	Brighton & HA	L 1-4	0-1	3	Kandol [49]	5973
16	15	H	Stockport Co	W 1-0	0-0	3	Martin [76]	9030
17	22	A	Leyton Orient	D 0-0	0-0	4		6951
18	25	H	Carlisle U	W 1-0	0-0	—	Kandol [90]	6828
19	Dec 6	H	Bristol R	W 3-2	2-1	2	Kandol 2 [5, 18], Alexander [72]	8123
20	13	A	Walsall	W 2-1	1-1	2	Harris [16], Frampton [89]	3790
21	20	H	Crewe Alex	D 0-0	0-0	3		9018
22	26	A	Peterborough U	L 0-1	0-1	3		9351
23	28	H	Yeovil T	D 1-1	1-1	3	Robinson [3]	9042
24	Jan 17	H	Tranmere R	W 1-0	0-0	3	Laird [73]	8257
25	27	A	Hereford U	W 2-0	0-0	—	Craig [65], Laird [90]	3001
26	31	H	Scunthorpe U	L 1-2	0-0	5	Alexander [64]	8868
27	Feb 9	A	Leeds U	L 0-2	0-1	—		19,314
28	14	A	Stockport Co	D 2-2	1-0	6	McLeod 2 (1 pen) [17, 53 (p)]	5461
29	17	H	Swindon T	D 1-1	0-1	—	Henry [90]	7104
30	21	H	Brighton & HA	L 0-1	0-0	6		9226
31	24	A	Cheltenham T	W 3-1	0-1	—	Henry (pen) [50], Grimes [60], Laird [89]	2942
32	28	H	Oldham Ath	L 2-3	0-2	5	Harris (pen) [56], Grimes [68]	8551
33	Mar 3	A	Southend U	W 1-0	0-0	—	Alexander [39]	7620
34	7	A	Huddersfield T	W 2-1	0-0	4	Laird [69], Henry [90]	13,196
35	10	H	Northampton T	W 1-0	1-0	—	Alexander [35]	6685
36	14	H	Leicester C	L 0-1	0-1	4		13,261
37	17	A	Milton Keynes D	W 1-0	1-0	—	Laird [20]	12,238
38	21	A	Hartlepool U	W 3-2	0-2	3	Harris 3 [62, 67, 72]	3601
39	28	H	Crewe Alex	W 1-0	0-0	3	Price [90]	4680
40	31	H	Colchester U	L 0-1	0-1	—		8071
41	Apr 4	A	Walsall	W 3-1	2-1	3	Price [18], Alexander 2 [45, 54]	8800
42	10	A	Yeovil T	L 0-2	0-1	—		6230
43	13	H	Peterborough U	W 2-0	1-0	3	Martin (pen) [25], Price [58]	10,518
44	18	A	Bristol R	L 2-4	1-4	4	Abdou 2 [28, 78]	6618
45	25	H	Leyton Orient	W 2-1	0-0	3	Alexander 2 [70, 87]	11,414
46	May 2	A	Carlisle U	L 0-2	0-1	5		9470

Final League Position: 5

GOALSCORERS

League (63): Alexander 11 (1 pen), Harris 8 (1 pen), Kandol 8, Grabban 6, Laird 5, Martin 4 (1 pen), Abdou 3, Henry 3 (1 pen), Price 3, Craig 2, Grimes 2, McLeod 2 (1 pen), Robinson 2, Brkovic 1, Easter 1, Frampton 1, own goal 1.
Carling Cup (0).
FA Cup (11): Alexander 2, Grimes 2, Harris 2, Barron 1, Frampton 1, Grabban 1, Laird 1, Whitbread 1.
J Paint Trophy (0).
Play-Offs (4): Alexander 2, Abdou 1, Harris 1.

Forde D 46	Dunne A 20 + 4	Craig T 43 + 1	Laird M 30 + 8	Robinson P 26	Whitbread Z 34 + 4	Abdou N 31 + 5	Fuseini A 11 + 6	Kandol T 16 + 2	Grabban L 29 + 2	Martin D 37 + 7	Frampton A 32 + 5	Hackett C 15 + 7	Alexander G 29 + 6	Brkovic A 3 + 3	Harris N 20 + 15	Smith R — + 1	Moore K 2 + 4	Grimes A 4 + 13	Forbes A — + 2	Easter J 2 + 3	Noel-Williams G 1	Spiller D — + 2	Bolder A 28	Bignot M 1	Barron S 7 + 7	McLeod 15 + 2	Duffy R 11 + 1	Henry J 15 + 1	Pericard V 2	Price J 6 + 2	Match No.
1	2²	3	4	5▪	6	7¹	8	9³	10	11	12	13	14																		1
1		3	4	5	6	13	8²	9	10³	11¹		2	12	7	14																2
1		2	4¹	5	6	12			11¹	3	7	9	8	10	13																3
1		3		5	6	7		9	10	12	2	11		4		8¹															4
1		3		5	6	4	8		7²	11	12	2¹	9	14	10³		13														5
1	12	3		5	6	4	8	9▪	7¹	11²		2	10	13																	6
1		3		5	6	4	7		10	11		2	9	8¹			12														7
1		3	12	5		4	8¹		7	11	6	2	9								10▪										8
1		3	14	5	6	4	8³		10	11²		2	9		13		12		7¹												9
1		3	4	5	6	8			10³	7	11²	12	2¹	9			13	14													10
1	12	2	4	5	6	8			7¹	11	3		10		9																11
1		3	4¹	5	6	8	12	9	7²	11	13	2		10³					14												12
1		2	4	5	6	8		9	7	11³	3¹	12		13		14		10²													13
1		3	4	5	6¹	8▪		9³	7	13	12	2		10		11²		14													14
1		3	4²			8	9	7	11¹	6		2		10			12	13													15
1	2	3	4	5				9¹	7³	13	6	8²	12		10								14	11							16
1	2		4²	5¹		13		9³	7	11	6	12	14		10								8	3							17
1	2³	3	4	5				12	7	11²	6	13	9¹		10			14					8								18
1	2	3	12	5		4¹		9	7²	11	6	13	10³		14								8								19
1	2	3	4	5	13			9	11³		6	7¹		10	12²	14							8								20
1	2	3	4	5	12			9²	7³	11	6¹		13		10		14						8								21
1	2	3▪		5	6	4		9²	7³	12			10		13		11¹						8		14						22
1	2		13	5	6	3		12		11²		7³	10		9¹		14						8		4						23
1	2	12	4	5	6	13	8²	9³	7	11¹	3				10											14					24
1	2	3	4	5	13	8			7	11²	6		9		12										10¹						25
1	2	3	4	5²	13			7¹	11	6	12	9		10³											14						26
1	12	3			5	4	7³		11	6		9		13		14							8		10²	2¹					27
1	2	3			5	4			11▪	6			12		9¹								8		13	10	7²				28
1	12	3			5	7		9²		6			10		13								8		11	2¹	4				29
1		3	13		5	4²			11³	12			10		14								8		7	2¹	6	9			30
1		3	12		5	4			11	6			13		14								8¹		10³	2	7	9²			31
1		3	4		5	8¹	12		11³	6		13		10²		9									14	2	7				32
1		3	4		5	2			11³	6		9	12	13	10²							8		14		7¹				33
1		3	4		5	2			11	6		9										8		12	10¹	7				34
1		3	4¹		5	6			11	2		9²		12								8		14	7³	10				35
1		3	4³		5	10	13		11	6		9¹		12	14							8²			2	7				36
1		3	4			10			11	6		9										8		5	2	7				37
1		3	4		5		14		10³	13	6	9		12								8		11	2¹	7²				38
1	2	3	4		5		12		11	6		9		10²								8				7¹			13	39
1	2	3	4		5			12	11	6		9²		13								8				7¹			10	40
1	2	3	4		5	12			7	11¹	6	9										8							10	41
1	2▪	3	4		5	11			7³	12	6²	9		13								8¹		14					10	42
1		3	4		5	7	12		11			9										8		6		2¹			10	43
1	2	3	4²		5³	7			11			9▪	12									8		6		14	13	10		44
1	2	3	14		5	4			13	11²	6		9		12							8³				7		10¹		45
1	2	3	14			4			7²	13	6		9		10¹							8³		5		11	12			46

FA Cup

First Round	Chester C	(a)	3-0
Second Round	Aldershot T	(h)	3-0
Third Round	Crewe Alex	(h)	2-2
		(a)	3-2
Fourth Round	Hull C	(a)	0-2

Carling Cup

First Round	Northampton T	(h)	0-1

J Paint Trophy

First Round	Colchester U	(h)	0-1

Play-Offs

Semi-Final	Leeds U	(h)	1-0
		(a)	1-1
Final	Scunthorpe U		2-3
(at Wembley)			

MILTON KEYNES DONS FL Championship 1

FOUNDATION

Old boys from Central School formed this club as Wimbledon Old Centrals in 1889. Their earliest successes were in the Clapham League before switching to the Southern Suburban League in 1902. In July 2004 Wimbledon became MK Dons and relocated to Milton Keynes.

Stadiummk, Stadium Way West, Milton Keynes MK1 1ST.

Telephone: (01908) 622 922.

Fax: (01908) 622 933.

Ticket Office: (01908) 622 900.

Website: www.mkdons.com

Email: info@mkdons.com

Ground Capacity: 21,189.

Record Attendance: 30,115 v Manchester U, FA Premier League, 9 May 1993 (at Selhurst Park).

Pitch Measurements: 105m × 68m.

Chairman: Pete Winkelman.

Head of Football Operations: Kirstine Nicholson.

Manager: Paul Ince.

Physio: Simon Crampton.

Colours: White shirts, white shorts, white stockings with black tops.

Change Colours: All red with white top stockings.

Year Formed: 1889.

Turned Professional: 1964.

Ltd Co.: 1964.

Previous Names: 1899, Wimbledon Old Centrals; 1905, Wimbledon; 2004, Milton Keynes Dons.

Grounds: 1899, Plough Lane; 1991, Selhurst Park; 2003, The National Hockey Stadium; 2007, Stadiummk.

Club Nicknames: 'The Dons', 'The Crazy Gang'.

First Football League Game: 20 August 1977, Division 4, v Halifax T (h) D 3–3 – Guy; Bryant (1), Galvin, Donaldson, Aitken, Davies, Galliers, Smith, Connell (1), Holmes, Leslie (1).

HONOURS

As Wimbledon
FA Premier League: best season: 6th, 1993–94.

Football League: Division 3 – Runners-up 1983–84; Division 4 – Champions 1982–83.

FA Cup: Winners 1988.

Football League Cup: Semi-final 1996–97, 1998–99.

League Group Cup: Runners-up 1982.

Amateur Cup: Winners 1963; Runners-up 1935, 1947.

European Competitions: *Intertoto Cup:* 1995.

As Milton Keynes Dons
Football League: FL 2 – Champions 2007–08.

Johnstone's Paint Trophy: Winners 2008.

SKY SPORTS FACT FILE

The first match at the 22,000 capacity stadiummk was on 18 July 2007 with Milton Keynes Dons opposing a Chelsea XI. A restricted crowd of 4,477 witnessed the 4–3 win by the MK Dons. Queen Elizabeth II officially opened the ground on 29 November.

Record League Victory: 6–0 v Newport Co, Division 3, 3 September 1983 – Beasant; Peters, Winterburn, Galliers, Morris, Hatter, Evans (2), Ketteridge (1), Cork (3 incl. 1p), Downes, Hodges (Driver).

Record Cup Victory: 7–2 v Windsor & Eton, FA Cup 1st rd, 22 November 1980 – Beasant; Jones, Armstrong, Galliers, Mick Smith (2), Cunningham (1), Ketteridge, Hodges, Leslie, Cork (1), Hubbick (3).

Record Defeat: 0–8 v Everton, League Cup 2nd rd, 29 August 1978.

Most League Points (2 for a win): 61, Division 4, 1978–79.

Most League Points (3 for a win): 98, Division 4, 1982–83; as MK Dons 97, FL 2, 2007–08

Most League Goals: 97, Division 3, 1983–84; as MK Dons 83, FL 1, 2008–09.

Highest League Scorer in Season: Alan Cork, 29, 1983–84.

Most League Goals in Total Aggregate: Alan Cork, 145, 1977–92.

MANAGERS
Les Henley 1955–71
Mike Everitt 1971–73
Dick Graham 1973–74
Allen Batsford 1974–78
Dario Gradi 1978–81
Dave Bassett 1981–87
Bobby Gould 1987–90
Ray Harford 1990–91
Peter Withe 1991
Joe Kinnear 1992–99
Egil Olsen 1999–2000
Terry Burton 2000–02
Stuart Murdock 2002–04
Danny Wilson 2004–06
Martin Allen 2006–07
Paul Ince 2007–08
Roberto Di Matteo 2008–09
Paul Ince June 2009–

Most League Goals in One Match: 4, Alan Cork v Torquay U, Division 4, 28 February 1979.

Most Capped Player: Kenny Cunningham, 40 (72), Republic of Ireland.

Most League Appearances: Alan Cork, 430, 1977–92.

Youngest League Player: Kevin Gage, 17 years 15 days v Bury, 2 May 1981.

Record Transfer Fee Received: £7,000,000 from Newcastle U for Carl Cort, July 2000.

Record Transfer Fee Paid: £7,500,000 to West Ham U for John Hartson, January 1999.

Football League Record: 1977 Elected to Division 4; 1979–80 Division 3; 1980–81 Division 4; 1981–82 Division 3; 1982–83 Division 4; 1983–84 Division 3; 1984–86 Division 2; 1986–92 Division 1; 1992–2000 FA Premier League; 2000–04 Division 1; 2004–06 FL 1; 2006–08 FL 2; 2008– FL 1.

LATEST SEQUENCES (as Milton Keynes Dons)

Longest Sequence of League Wins: 8, 7.9.2007 – 20.10.2007.

Longest Sequence of League Defeats: 4, 10.8.2004 – 28.8.2004.

Longest Sequence of League Draws: 4, 21.2.2009 – 10.3.2009.

Longest Sequence of Unbeaten League Matches: 18, 29.1.2008 – 3.5.2008.

Longest Sequence Without a League Win: 10, 2.10.2004 – 7.12.2004.

Successive Scoring Runs: 18 from 7.4.2007.

Successive Non-scoring Runs: 4, 17.12.2005–2.1.2006.

TEN YEAR LEAGUE RECORD

		P	W	D	L	F	A	Pts	Pos
1999-2000	PR Lge	38	7	12	19	46	74	33	18
2000-01	Div 1	46	17	18	11	71	50	69	8
2001-02	Div 1	46	18	13	15	63	57	67	9
2002-03	Div 1	46	18	11	17	76	73	65	10
2003-04	Div 1	46	8	5	33	41	89	29	24
2004-05	FL 1	46	12	15	19	54	68	51	20
2005-06	FL 1	46	12	14	20	45	66	50	22
2006-07	FL 2	46	25	9	12	76	58	84	4
2007-08	FL 2	46	29	10	7	82	37	97	1
2008-09	FL 1	46	26	9	11	83	47	87	3

DID YOU KNOW ?

On 15 November 2008 Daniel Powell became the youngest goalscorer for Milton Keynes Dons when he came on as an 84th-minute substitute against Hartlepool United. Aged 17 years 248 days at the time his injury-time goal ensured a 3–1 win.

MILTON KEYNES DONS FC 2008–09 LEAGUE RECORD

Match No.	Date	Venue	Opponents	Result	H/T Score	Lg. Pos.	Goalscorers	Attendance
1	Aug 9	A	Leicester C	L 0-2	0-1	—		23,351
2	16	H	Northampton T	W 1-0	0-0	15	Wilbraham 66	12,078
3	23	A	Huddersfield T	W 3-1	2-0	5	Stirling 16, Leven 38, Baldock 64	13,189
4	30	H	Swindon T	L 1-2	0-0	9	Stirling 65	8846
5	Sept 6	H	Yeovil T	W 3-0	1-0	5	Leven 2 21, 78, Baldock 53	7959
6	13	A	Oldham Ath	L 0-2	0-1	9		5530
7	20	A	Colchester U	W 3-0	1-0	8	Wilbraham 2, Baldock 2 88, 90	4888
8	27	H	Peterborough U	L 1-2	0-0	9	Gerba 63	10,876
9	Oct 4	A	Millwall	W 4-0	2-0	8	O'Hanlon 9, Baldock 2 45, 90, Robinson (og) 62	9871
10	11	H	Carlisle U	W 3-1	1-1	6	Leven 2 (1 pen) 38, 90 (p), Llera 62	11,194
11	18	A	Crewe Alex	D 2-2	1-2	7	Baldock 15, Chadwick 79	4055
12	21	H	Stockport Co	L 1-2	1-0	—	Gerba 45	6931
13	25	H	Cheltenham T	W 3-1	1-1	5	Gerba 2 9, 80, Baldock (pen) 55	8190
14	28	A	Leyton Orient	W 2-1	2-0	—	Chadwick 2 19, 23	3869
15	Nov 1	H	Tranmere R	W 1-0	0-0	4	Gallen 81	8185
16	15	H	Hartlepool U	W 3-1	2-0	4	Lewington 37, Wright 39, Powell 90	4021
17	22	A	Walsall	W 3-0	1-0	2	Johnson 6, Gerba 59, Wright 87	5026
18	25	H	Hereford U	W 3-0	0-0	—	Leven (pen) 61, Wright 63, Johnson 88	7189
19	Dec 6	H	Scunthorpe U	L 0-2	0-0	3		11,550
20	12	A	Brighton & HA	W 4-2	1-1	—	Llera 26, Johnson 46, Leven 69, Puncheon 90	5691
21	20	H	Leeds U	W 3-1	2-0	2	O'Hanlon 11, Wilbraham 2 17, 55	17,073
22	26	A	Bristol R	W 2-1	1-1	2	Wilbraham 14, Anthony (og) 59	9002
23	28	H	Southend U	W 2-0	1-0	2	O'Hanlon 8, Baldock 58	10,432
24	Jan 12	H	Colchester U	D 1-1	0-1	—	Wilbraham 65	8408
25	17	A	Carlisle U	L 2-3	2-0	2	Wilbraham 2 15, 39	6298
26	20	A	Peterborough U	D 0-0	0-0	—		8982
27	27	H	Leyton Orient	L 1-2	1-1	—	Chadwick 19	8170
28	31	A	Cheltenham T	W 5-3	3-0	2	Johnson 2 17, 71, Wilbraham 3 44, 45, 59	3681
29	Feb 3	A	Stockport Co	W 1-0	1-0	—	Wilbraham 36	4891
30	14	H	Hartlepool U	W 3-1	1-1	2	Gerba 2 37, 90, Lewington 86	8657
31	21	A	Tranmere R	D 1-1	0-0	2	Leven (pen) 74	5625
32	28	H	Leicester C	D 2-2	1-1	2	Leven 2 36, 63	17,717
33	Mar 7	A	Swindon T	D 1-1	1-1	3	Wilbraham 27	7453
34	10	H	Huddersfield T	D 1-1	0-0	—	Baldock 59	9707
35	14	H	Oldham Ath	W 6-2	2-2	3	Wilbraham 33, Puncheon 42, Baldock 2 53, 58, Navarro 81, Gerba 90	10,621
36	17	H	Millwall	L 0-1	0-1	—		12,238
37	21	A	Yeovil T	D 0-0	0-0	4		4028
38	24	H	Crewe Alex	D 2-2	2-0	—	Wilbraham 15, Puncheon 19	8454
39	28	A	Leeds U	L 0-2	0-1	4		27,649
40	Apr 4	H	Brighton & HA	W 2-0	2-0	4	Gerba 29, Puncheon 40	15,842
41	10	A	Southend U	W 2-0	0-0	—	Wright 2 59, 90	10,241
42	13	H	Bristol R	W 2-1	1-0	4	Gerba 29, Chadwick 51	10,251
43	18	A	Scunthorpe U	W 1-0	1-0	3	Chadwick 35	4873
44	25	H	Walsall	L 0-1	0-0	4		12,094
45	28	A	Northampton T	W 1-0	1-0	—	Wilbraham 34	6054
46	May 2	A	Hereford U	W 1-0	0-0	3	Howell 85	3224

Final League Position: 3

GOALSCORERS

League (83): Wilbraham 16, Baldock 12 (1 pen), Gerba 10, Leven 10 (3 pens), Chadwick 6, Johnson 5, Wright 5, Puncheon 4, O'Hanlon 3, Lewington 2, Llera 2, Stirling 2, Gallen 1, Howell 1, Navarro 1, Powell 1, own goals 2.
Carling Cup (2): Baldock 1, O'Hanlon 1.
FA Cup (1): Johnson 1.
J Paint Trophy (0).
Play-Offs (1): Wilbraham 1.

Gueret W 44	Regan C 24+3	Lewington D 40	Andrews K 1	O'Hanlon S 40	Stirling J 21+11	Wright M 29+3	Navarro A 32+6	Baldock S 32+8	Wilbraham A 29+4	Sturm F 2+3	Leven P 37+3	Chicksen A —+1	Johnson J 19+14	Swailes D 1	Cummings S 29+3	Gallen K 1+5	Belson F 9+4	McDermott D —+1	Llera M 34	Gerba A 16+8	Chadwick L 21+3	Abbey N —+1	Puncheon J 26+1	Price L 2	Howell L 9+6	Powell D —+7	N'Gala B 1+2	Flo T 2+11	Magnay C —+2	Gleeson S 5	Match No.
1	2	3	4	5	6	7	8^1	9^3	10	11^2	12	13	14																		1
1	2	3		5	12	7	8	9^3	10	11^2	4				6^3	13	14														2
1	2	3		5	6	7	12	9^2	10		8		13		11		4^1														3
1	2	3		5	6	7^1		9^2	10		8		12		11	13	4														4
1	2	3		5	6	7	12	9	10	13	4				11^2		8^1														5
$1^∎$	2^1	3		5	6	7^2		9	10		4		12		11		8	13													6
1	2	3		5		7	8	12	10		4				11				6	9^1											7
1	2	3		5		7	8	12	10^1		4				11				6	9											8
1		3		5		7	8	9	12		4				2				6	10			11^1								9
1	12	3		5	13	7	8	9			4				2				6	10^2			11^1								10
1		3		5	12	7^2	8	9			4	13			2	14			6^1	10^3	11										11
1		3		5		7^1	8	9			4		12		2	13			6	10^2	11										12
$1^∎$		3		5	6	7^6	12	9			4				2		8^1			10	11^2	15	13								13
		3		5	6	7^2	8	12			4	14			$2^∎$					10^3	9		11^1	1	13						14
	2	3		5	6		12	9			4						13	8^1		10	7		11	1							15
1		3		5		7	8		12	4	9^2	2							6	10^1			11		13						16
1		3^3		5		7	8	12	13	4	9^1	2							6	10^2			11			14					17
1	3^3			5		7^1	8	9	10^2	4		12	2						6	13			11			14					18
1	3^3			5		7^2	8	9	14	4		13	2							10^1			11			6	12				19
1				5	2	7^1	8	12	10^3		4^2	9	3						6				11	13		14					20
1				5	2^3	12	8	9^1	10^2		4	7	3						6				11	14	13						21
1				5	3	7	8	9^2	10^3		4	11^1	2						$6^∎$					13	12	14					22
1		3		5	6	7^1	8	9	10^3		4	11^2	2											13	12	14					23
1		3		5	13	12		9^3	10		4^1	7	2^2						6			$11^∎$	8		14						24
1		3		5		7^1	8	9	10	12	4	11	2						6												25
1		3		5	13		8	7	10		4	9^1	2						6^2	12			11								26
1		3		5^2	2	12	8	9	10			7							6^3	11			4^1	13	14						27
1	2^3	3		5		8	4^2	10^1		9			13						6	12	7		11					14			28
1	5	3		2		8		10		9^2			4						6	12	7^1		11		13						29
1	2	3		5		8	9^3		12	4									6	10	7^2		11^1					13	14		30
1	2	3		5		8	12	10	4	9							7		6				11^1								31
1	2	3		5	12		8	13	10	4		14							6^3		7^1		11^2								32
1	12	$3^∎$		5	6		8	7	10	4	9^2	2									11^1				13						33
1				5	3		8	9^2	10	4	12	2			6	13	7^1		11												34
1		3		5		8^2	9^3	10	4	12	2	13			6	14	7^1		11												35
1		3		5		8		10	4	9^2	2				6	12	7^1		11				13								36
1		3		5		8		10	4	9	2	7^1			6	13	12		11^2												37
1	2	3		5			9	10	4	12					6		7^1		11	8											38
1	2^3	3		5	12		8	9	10	4	14	7^1			6^2	13			11												39
1	2	3		5	12	7^1		9		4					6	10			11^2	13				8							40
1	2	3		5	12	9							14		6	10^2	8^1		11^3	4			13		7						41
1	2	3		5	12	9	14								6	10^2	8^1		11^3	4			13		7						42
1	2	3		5		7^3		12				14			6	10^2	9^1		11	4			13		8						43
1	2	3		5^1	12	7		9	13	14					6				11	4^3			10^2		8						44
1	2	3			5	7^1	8	9^2	10		13				6	12	11														45
1	14	3		5	7^1	13	9		4^2	12	2				6	11^3			8				10								46

FA Cup
First Round — Bradford C — (h) — 1-2

Carling Cup
First Round — Norwich C — (h) — 1-0
Second Round — Cardiff C — (a) — 1-2

J Paint Trophy
Second Round — Bournemouth — (h) — 0-1

Play-Offs
Semi-Final — Scunthorpe U — (a) — 1-1 / (h) — 0-0

MORECAMBE

FOUNDATION

Several attempts to start a senior football club in a rugby stronghold finally succeeded on 7 May 1920 at the West View Hotel, Morecambe and a team competed in the Lancashire Combination for 1920–21. The club shared with a local cricket club at Woodhill Lane for the first season and a crowd of 3,000 watched the first game. The club moved to Roseberry Park the name of which was changed to Christie Park after J.B. Christie who as President had purchased the ground.

Christie Park, Lancaster Road, Morecambe LA4 5TJ.

Telephone: (01524) 411797.

Fax: (01524) 832 230.

Ticket Office: (01524) 411797.

Website: www.morecambefc.com

Email: office@morecambefc.com

Ground Capacity: 6,030.

Pitch Measurements: 103m × 70m.

Record Attendance: 9,383 v Weymouth, FA Cup 3rd rd, 6 January 1962.

Chairman: Peter McGuigan.

Vice-chairman: Graham Hodgson.

Chief Executive: Rod Taylor.

Secretary: Neil Marsdin.

Manager: Sammy McIlroy.

Assistant Manager: Mark Lillis.

Physio: David Edge.

Colours: Red shirts with white sleeves, white shorts, red stockings.

Change Colours: All royal blue with black trim.

Year Formed: 1920.

HONOURS

FA Cup: best season: 3rd rd, 1962, 2001, 2003.

League Cup: best season: 3rd rd, 2008.

Northern Premier League: Runners-up – 1994–95.

Presidents Cup: Winners – 1991–92.

FA Trophy: Winners 1973–74.

Lancs Senior Cup: Winners 1967–68.

Lancs Combination: Champions – 1924–25, 1961–62, 1962–63, 1967–68. Runners-up – 1925–26.

Lancs Combination Cup: Winners – 1926–27, 1945–46, 1964–65, 1966–67, 1967–68. Runners-up – 1923–24, 1924–25, 1962–63.

Lancs Junior Cup: Winners – 1927, 1928, 1962, 1963, 1969, 1986, 1987, 1994, 1996, 1999, 2004.

SKY SPORTS FACT FILE

Between 1958 and 1966 centre-forward Keith Borrowdale scored 18 FA Cup goals for Morecambe. During his service with the club he hit 289 in all competitions from 1956 to 1968. He played over 450 matches, captained the team and was an accountant.

Club Nickname: The Shrimps.

Grounds: 1920, Woodhill Lane; 1921, Christie Park.

First Football League game: 11 August 2007, FL 2, v Barnet (h) D 0–0 – Lewis; Yates, Adams, Artell, Bentley, Stanley, Baker (Burns), Sorvel, Twiss (Newby), Curtis, Hunter (Thompson).

Record League Victory: 16-0 v Rossendale U, Lancashire Combination, September 1967.

Most League Points (3 for a win): 63, FL 2 2008–09.

Most League Goals: 59, FL 2, 2007–08.

Highest League Scorer in Season: Justin Jackson, 29, 1999–2000.

Most League Goals in Total Aggregate: Stuart Drummond, 12, 2007–.

Most League Goals in One Match: 3, Jon Newby v Rotherham U, FL 2, 29 March 2008.

Most League Appearances: Jim Bentley, 88, 2007–.

Record Transfer Fee Received: undisclosed from Rushden & D for Justin Jackson, June 2000.

Record Transfer Fee Paid: undisclosed to Southport for Carl Baker, July 2007.

Football League Record: 2006–07 Promoted from Conference; 2007– FL2.

MANAGERS

Jimmy Milne 1947–48
Albert Dainty 1955–56
Ken Horton 1956–61
Joe Dunn 1961–64
Geoff Twentyman 1964–65
Ken Waterhouse 1965–69
Ronnie Clayton 1969–70
Gerry Irving/Ronnie Mitchell 1970
Ken Waterhouse 1970–72
Dave Roberts 1972–75
Alan Spavin 1975–76
Johnny Johnson 1976–77
Tommy Ferber 1977–78
Mick Hogarth 1978–79
Don Curbage 1979–81
Jim Thompson 1981
Les Rigby 1981–84
Sean Gallagher 1984–85
Joe Wojciechowicz 1985–88
Eric Whalley 1988
Billy Wright 1988–89
Lawrie Milligan 1989
Bryan Griffiths 1989–93
Leighton James 1994
Jim Harvey 1994–2006
Sammy McIlroy May 2006–

LATEST SEQUENCES

Longest Sequence of League Wins: 3, 17.11.2007 – 4.12.2007.

Longest Sequence of League Defeats: 4, 23.2.2008 – 12.3.2008.

Longest Sequence of League Draws: 4, 13.9.2008 – 4.10.2008.

Longest Sequence of Unbeaten League Matches: 12, 31.1.2009 – 21.3.2009.

Longest Sequence Without a League Win: 10, 5.4.2008 – 30.8.2008.

Successive Scoring Runs: 6 from 2.10.2007.

Successive Non-scoring Runs: 2 from 15.1.2008.

TEN YEAR LEAGUE RECORD

		P	W	D	L	F	A	Pts	Pos
1999-2000	Conf	42	18	16	8	70	48	70	3
2000-01	Conf	42	11	12	19	64	66	45	19
2001-02	Conf	42	17	11	14	63	67	62	6
2002-03	Conf	42	23	9	10	86	42	78	2
2003-04	Conf	42	20	7	15	66	66	67	7
2004-05	Conf	42	19	14	9	69	50	71	7
2005-06	Conf	42	22	8	12	68	41	74	5
2006-07	Conf	46	23	12	11	64	46	81	3
2007-08	FL 2	46	16	12	18	59	63	60	11
2008-09	FL 2	46	15	18	13	53	56	63	11

DID YOU KNOW ?

On successive Saturdays early in 2009 Brentford had had two players scoring hat-tricks. In between these events they played at Morecambe on 3 February, neither treble marksman figured in the statistics with Morecambe finishing worthy 2–0 winners.

MORECAMBE 2008–09 LEAGUE RECORD

Match No.	Date	Venue	Opponents	Result	H/T Score	Lg. Pos.	Goalscorers	Attendance
1	Aug 9	A	Wycombe W	D	1-1	0-1	—	Artell [66]	4021
2	16	H	Rotherham U	L	1-3	0-2	16	Wainwright [77]	2606
3	23	A	Bury	L	1-2	1-2	16	Howe [14]	2679
4	30	H	Dagenham & R	L	1-2	0-0	18	O'Carroll [79]	1571
5	Sept 6	H	Shrewsbury T	W	1-0	1-0	17	Howe [4]	2318
6	13	A	Barnet	D	1-1	1-1	18	O'Carroll [42]	1776
7	20	H	Grimsby T	D	1-1	0-1	18	Curtis [75]	1989
8	27	A	Lincoln C	D	1-1	1-1	16	Stanley [45]	5003
9	Oct 4	H	Chesterfield	D	2-2	1-2	17	Drummond [6], Howe [85]	1734
10	11	A	Gillingham	L	0-5	0-3	18		4316
11	18	H	Rochdale	D	1-1	0-1	20	Taylor [48]	2572
12	21	A	Brentford	L	1-3	1-3	—	Drummond [5]	3733
13	25	A	Port Vale	L	1-2	0-0	20	Bentley [81]	5629
14	28	H	Accrington S	D	1-1	0-1	—	Stanley [50]	2044
15	Nov 1	H	Aldershot T	W	2-0	0-0	17	Drummond [56], McGivern [69]	1897
16	15	A	Chester C	W	2-1	1-0	17	Stanley [32], Howe (pen) [56]	1647
17	22	H	Exeter C	D	1-1	1-0	17	Howe [22]	2003
18	25	A	Bournemouth	D	0-0	0-0	—		3068
19	Dec 6	A	Notts Co	L	0-1	0-1	18		3671
20	13	H	Darlington	W	1-0	0-0	17	Howe [67]	1873
21	20	A	Luton T	D	1-1	0-0	16	Carlton [57]	5664
22	26	H	Macclesfield T	W	4-1	2-1	14	McStay [17], Carlton [24], Drummond [63], Howe [79]	2578
23	28	A	Bradford C	L	0-4	0-1	16		13,105
24	Jan 17	A	Gillingham	L	0-1	0-1	17		2027
25	24	A	Chesterfield	W	2-1	0-0	16	Howe [54], Stanley [65]	3283
26	27	A	Accrington S	L	0-1	0-0	—		1407
27	31	H	Port Vale	D	1-1	1-1	17	Stanley [4]	1823
28	Feb 3	H	Brentford	W	2-0	1-0	—	Twiss [23], Howe [89]	1253
29	10	H	Lincoln C	D	1-1	1-0	—	Bentley [19]	1471
30	14	H	Chester C	W	3-1	3-0	13	Taylor [15], Curtis 2 [32, 44]	1795
31	17	A	Rochdale	D	1-1	0-0	—	Twiss [90]	3347
32	21	A	Aldershot T	W	2-0	1-0	13	Curtis [45], Drummond [54]	2872
33	24	A	Grimsby T	W	3-2	0-1	—	Twiss [63], O'Carroll [81], Hunter [90]	2644
34	28	H	Wycombe W	D	0-0	0-0	10		2005
35	Mar 7	A	Dagenham & R	W	2-0	2-0	10	O'Carroll [13], Drummond [15]	1403
36	10	H	Bury	D	0-0	0-0	—		2165
37	14	H	Barnet	W	2-1	2-1	10	Artell [33], Curtis [38]	1899
38	21	A	Shrewsbury T	D	0-0	0-0	11		5426
39	28	H	Luton T	L	1-2	1-1	12	Drummond [21]	2599
40	Apr 4	A	Darlington	D	0-0	0-0	13		2560
41	10	H	Bradford C	W	2-1	0-1	—	Drummond [56], Howe [75]	4546
42	13	A	Macclesfield T	W	1-0	0-0	11	Artell [85]	1773
43	18	H	Notts Co	W	1-0	0-0	10	Duffy [72]	2161
44	21	A	Rotherham U	L	2-3	0-1	—	O'Carroll [52], Bentley [90]	2078
45	25	A	Exeter C	D	2-2	1-0	11	Drummond 2 [9, 79]	8544
46	May 2	H	Bournemouth	L	0-4	0-3	11		2601

Final League Position: 11

GOALSCORERS

League (53): Drummond 10, Howe 10 (1 pen), Curtis 5, O'Carroll 5, Stanley 5, Artell 3, Bentley 3, Twiss 3, Carlton 2, Taylor 2, Duffy 1, Hunter 1, McGivern 1, McStay 1, Wainwright 1.
Carling Cup (0).
FA Cup (4): Taylor 2, Howe 1 (pen), McStay 1.
J Paint Trophy (2): Drummond 1, Howe 1.

Roche B 46	Parrish A 10+3	Adams D 39	Carr M 4+3	Artell D 35+2	Bentley J 45	Wainwright N 32+6	Hunter G 23+6	Howe R 35+2	Blinkhorn M 5+6	McLachlan F 21+6	Curtis W 23+9	O'Carroll D 15+14	Drummond S 41+3	McStay H 17+3	McCann R 11+2	Stanley C 22+2	Smith D —+2	Twiss M 26+2	Taylor A 7+10	Yates A 32	McGivern R 5	Carlton D 8	Duffy M 4+5	Match No.
1	2	3	4^2	5	6	7^1	8	9	10^3	11	12	13	14											1
1	2	3	4	5	6	7	8	9	10	11^1	12													2
1		3	4^2	5	6	7		9	10	11	12	13	2	8^1										3
1		3	4^3	5	6	7	14	9	10	11	12	13	2^1	8^2										4
1		3		5	6	7	8^1	9^2	13	11	10	4		2	12									5
1	2			5	6	7^1	8	9		11	10	4		3		12								6
1	2			5	6	7^3	8	9			12	10^1	4	3	14	13		11^2						7
1	12	3^1		5	6	13	8	9			14	10^3	4	2	7			11^2						8
1	2			5	6	12	8^1	9	13	7^2	11		3	4	10^3	14								9
1	2	3		5	6	12	8^2	9	10	11		7^1	4	13										10
1		3			6	7^1	12	9	11	13	8	5	4		10^2					2				11
1		3			6	7^1		9	11	13	8	5	12	4	10^2					2				12
1		3			6			9	7	12	11^2	5	13	8	10^1				4	2				13
1		3			6			9		11	12		8	5	4				10^1	2		7		14
1		3			6			9^1		11	10	13	8	5	4				12^2	2		7		15
1	2	3^4		13	6	12		9^3		7^2	8	5	4			14		11^1			10			16
1				5	6^1	12		9		11^2	13	8	2	3	4			7			10			17
1	12	3		5	6			9		11	8		2		4			7^1			10			18
1	2^1	3	13		6	12		9		11	8	5	4^2		7						10			19
1		3		5	6	7		9		11	8	5	4					12		2	10^1			20
1		3	12	13	6	7^2		9		11	8^1	5	4							2	10			21
1		3	12		6	7^2		9		11	8^1	5	4	13	14					2	10^3			22
1		3			6	7		9		11^1	8	5	4					12		2	10			23
1		3		5	6	7^3	12	9	13	8^1	14		4					11	10^2	2				24
1		3		5	6	7		9	12	8	11		4					10^1		2				25
1		3		5	6	7^2	12	9^3	13	8^1	14	11	4					10		2				26
1		3		5	6	7		9		8^1	12	11	4					10		2				27
1		3		5	6	7	12	9^2		8	13	11	4					10^1		2				28
1		3		5	6	7	12	9		8^2	13	11	4^1					10		2				29
1		3		5	6	7	8	10	12				4					11	9^1	2				30
1		3		5	6	7	8	12	10				4					11	9^1	2				31
1		3		5	6	7	8	9^1	10	12			4					11		2				32
1		3		5	6	7^1	8	10	9				4					11	12	2^2		13		33
1		3		5	6	7^1	8	10	9				4					11		2		12		34
1				5	6	7^1	8	12	10	9			4	3				11		2				35
1	12			5	6	7^3	8	10	9^2				4	2^1				11	13	3		14		36
1		3		5	6	7^1	8	13	12	10^2	9		4					11		2				37
1		3		5	6	7	8	9	10				4					11		2				38
1		3		5	6		8	9	10^1	12			4					11		2		7		39
1		3		5	6	7	8	9	12	10			4					11^1		2				40
1		3		5	6	7^1	8^2	9	12	10			4		13			11		2				41
1		3		5	6	7^1	8	13	10^2	9^3			4		14			11		2		12		42
1		3		5	6	7^1	8	9	14	10^3			4					11^2	13	2		12		43
1		3		5	6		8	9	12	10			4					11^1		2		7		44
1		3		5	6		12	7	10	9^1			4					11		2			8	45
1	2	3		5	6		13	7^3	10	9^2			4		14			11^1	12				8	46

FA Cup

First Round	Grimsby T	(h)	2-1
Second Round	Cheltenham T	(h)	2-3

Carling Cup

First Round	Nottingham F	(a)	0-4

J Paint Trophy

First Round	Oldham Ath	(a)	1-1
Second Round	Chester C	(a)	1-1
Northern Quarter-Final	Tranmere R	(a)	0-1

NEWCASTLE UNITED FL Championship

FOUNDATION

It stemmed from a newly formed club called Stanley in 1881.
In October 1882 they changed their name to Newcastle East End to
avoid confusion with two other local clubs, Stanley Nops and
Stanley Albion. Shortly afterwards another club Rosewood merged
with them. Newcastle West End had been formed in August 1882
and they played on a pitch which was part of the Town Moor.
Moved to Brandling Park 1885 and St James' Park 1886 (home of
Newcastle Rangers). West End went out of existence after a bad
run and the remaining committee men invited East End to move to
St James' Park. They accepted and, at a meeting in Bath Lane Hall
in 1892, changed their name to Newcastle United.

St James' Park, Newcastle-upon-Tyne NE1 4ST.

Telephone: (0191) 201 8400.

Fax: (0191) 201 8600.

Ticket Office: (0844) 372 1892.

Website: www.nufc.co.uk

Email: admin@nufc.co.uk

Ground Capacity: 52,387.

Record Attendance: 68,386 v Chelsea, Division 1,
3 September 1930.

Pitch Measurements: 105m × 68m.

Managing Director: Derek Llambias.

Exec Director Operations: David Williamson.

Manager: TBC.

First Team Coaches: Chris Hughton, Paul Barron.

Physio: Derek Wright.

Colours: Black and white striped shirts, black shorts with
white trim, black stockings.

Change Colours: Yellow and white striped shirts, yellow
shorts, yellow stockings with white trim.

Year Formed: 1881.

Turned Professional: 1889.

Ltd Co.: 1890.

Previous Names: 1881, Stanley; 1882, Newcastle East End; 1892, Newcastle United.

Club Nickname: 'The Magpies'.

Grounds: 1881, South Byker; 1886, Chillingham Road, Heaton; 1892, St James' Park.

First Football League Game: 2 September 1893, Division 2, v Royal Arsenal (a) D 2–2 – Ramsay;
Jeffery, Miller; Crielly, Graham, McKane; Bowman, Crate (1), Thompson, Sorley (1), Wallace.
Graham and not Crate scored according to some reports.

HONOURS

FA Premier League: Runners-up
1995–96, 1996–97; *Football League:*
Division 1 – Champions 1904–05,
1906–07, 1908–09, 1926–27, 1992–93;
Division 2 – Champions 1964–65;
Runners-up 1897–98, 1947–48.

FA Cup: Winners 1910, 1924, 1932,
1951, 1952, 1955; Runners-up 1905,
1906, 1908, 1911, 1974, 1998, 1999.

Football League Cup: Runners-up 1976.

Texaco Cup: Winners 1974, 1975.

*European Competitions: Champions
League:* 1997–98, 2002–03, 2003–04.
European Fairs Cup: 1968–69 (winners),
1969–70, 1970–71. *UEFA Cup:* 1977–78,
1994–95, 1996–97, 1999–2000, 2003–04
(semi-final), 2004–05, 2006–07.
European Cup Winners' Cup: 1998–99.
Anglo-Italian Cup: Winners 1972–73.
Intertoto Cup: 2001 (runners-up), 2005,
2006 (winners).

SKY SPORTS FACT FILE

In the Newcastle United squad which won the First
Division championship in 1904–05 there were nine
international players. They had just one point to spare
over runners-up Everton. The previous season they had
finished third a point ahead of United.

Record League Victory: 13–0 v Newport Co, Division 2, 5 October 1946 – Garbutt; Cowell, Graham; Harvey, Brennan, Wright; Milburn (2), Bentley (1), Wayman (4), Shackleton (6), Pearson.

Record Cup Victory: 9–0 v Southport (at Hillsborough), FA Cup 4th rd, 1 February 1932 – McInroy; Nelson, Fairhurst; McKenzie, Davidson, Weaver (1); Boyd (1), Jimmy Richardson (3), Cape (2), McMenemy (1), Lang (1).

Record Defeat: 0–9 v Burton Wanderers, Division 2, 15 April 1895.

Most League Points (2 for a win): 57, Division 2, 1964–65.

Most League Points (3 for a win): 96, Division 1, 1992–93.

Most League Goals: 98, Division 1, 1951–52.

Highest League Scorer in Season: Hughie Gallacher, 36, Division 1, 1926–27.

Most League Goals in Total Aggregate: Jackie Milburn, 177, 1946–57.

Most League Goals in One Match: 6, Len Shackleton v Newport Co, Division 2, 5 October 1946.

Most Capped Player: Shay Given, 82 (96), Republic of Ireland.

Most League Appearances: Jim Lawrence, 432, 1904–22.

Youngest League Player: Steve Watson, 16 years 223 days v Wolverhampton W, 10 November 1990.

Record Transfer Fee Received: £13,650,000 from Real Madrid for Jonathan Woodgate, August 2004.

Record Transfer Fee Paid: £16,000,000 to Real Madrid for Michael Owen, September 2005.

Football League Record: 1893 Elected to Division 2; 1898–1934 Division 1; 1934–48 Division 2; 1948–61 Division 1; 1961–65 Division 2; 1965–78 Division 1; 1978–84 Division 2; 1984–89 Division 1; 1989–92 Division 2; 1992–93 Division 1; 1993–2009 FA Premier League; 2009– FL C.

MANAGERS

Frank Watt 1895–32
(Secretary-Manager)
Andy Cunningham 1930–35
Tom Mather 1935–39
Stan Seymour 1939–47
(Hon. Manager)
George Martin 1947–50
Stan Seymour 1950–54
(Hon. Manager)
Duggie Livingstone 1954–56
Stan Seymour 1956–58
(Hon. Manager)
Charlie Mitten 1958–61
Norman Smith 1961–62
Joe Harvey 1962–75
Gordon Lee 1975–77
Richard Dinnis 1977
Bill McGarry 1977–80
Arthur Cox 1980–84
Jack Charlton 1984
Willie McFaul 1985–88
Jim Smith 1988–91
Ossie Ardiles 1991–92
Kevin Keegan 1992–97
Kenny Dalglish 1997–98
Ruud Gullit 1998–99
Sir Bobby Robson 1999–2004
Graeme Souness 2004–06
Glenn Roeder 2006–07
Sam Allardyce 2007–08
Kevin Keegan 2008
Joe Kinnear 2008–09
Alan Shearer 2009

LATEST SEQUENCES

Longest Sequence of League Wins: 13, 25.4.1992 – 18.10.1992.

Longest Sequence of League Defeats: 10, 23.8.1977 – 15.10.1977.

Longest Sequence of League Draws: 4, 20.1.1990 – 24.2.1990.

Longest Sequence of Unbeaten League Matches: 14, 22.4.1950 – 30.9.1950.

Longest Sequence Without a League Win: 21, 14.1.1978 – 23.8.1978.

Successive Scoring Runs: 25 from 15.4.1939.

Successive Non-scoring Runs: 6 from 31.12.1938.

TEN YEAR LEAGUE RECORD

		P	W	D	L	F	A	Pts	Pos
1999-2000	PR Lge	38	14	10	14	63	54	52	11
2000-01	PR Lge	38	14	9	15	44	50	51	11
2001-02	PR Lge	38	21	8	9	74	52	71	4
2002-03	PR Lge	38	21	6	11	63	48	69	3
2003-04	PR Lge	38	13	17	8	52	40	56	5
2004-05	PR Lge	38	10	14	14	47	57	44	14
2005-06	PR Lge	38	17	7	14	47	42	58	7
2006-07	PR Lge	38	11	10	17	38	47	43	13
2007-08	PR Lge	38	11	10	17	45	65	43	12
2008-09	PR Lge	38	7	13	18	40	59	34	18

DID YOU KNOW ?

The highest number of goals scored in a Newcastle United match was 18 in Canada on 1 June 1949. United won 16–2 with Jackie Milburn scoring six, George Robledo five. All ten tour games were won scoring 79 against 15. Milburn had 31, Robledo 19.

NEWCASTLE UNITED 2008–09 LEAGUE RECORD

Match No.	Date	Venue	Opponents	Result	H/T Score	Lg. Pos.	Goalscorers	Attendance
1	Aug 17	A	Manchester U	D 1-1	1-1	—	Martins [22]	75,512
2	23	H	Bolton W	W 1-0	0-0	5	Owen [71]	47,711
3	30	A	Arsenal	L 0-3	0-2	11		60,067
4	Sept 13	H	Hull C	L 1-2	0-1	16	Xisco [82]	50,242
5	20	A	West Ham U	L 1-3	0-2	19	Owen [67]	34,743
6	27	H	Blackburn R	L 1-2	0-2	19	Owen (pen) [51]	44,935
7	Oct 5	A	Everton	D 2-2	1-2	18	Taylor S [45], Duff [47]	33,805
8	20	H	Manchester C	D 2-2	1-1	—	Ameobi [44], Dunne (og) [63]	45,908
9	25	A	Sunderland	L 1-2	1-1	19	Ameobi [30]	47,936
10	28	H	WBA	W 2-1	2-0	—	Barton (pen) [10], Martins [42]	45,801
11	Nov 3	A	Aston Villa	W 2-0	0-0	—	Martins 2 [60, 83]	44,567
12	9	A	Fulham	L 1-2	0-1	18	Ameobi [57]	24,740
13	15	H	Wigan Ath	D 2-2	0-1	17	Owen [80], Martins [87]	47,657
14	22	A	Chelsea	D 0-0	0-0	17		41,660
15	29	H	Middlesbrough	D 0-0	0-0	17		32,160
16	Dec 6	H	Stoke C	D 2-2	2-0	16	Owen 2 [8, 24]	47,422
17	14	A	Portsmouth	W 3-0	0-0	14	Owen [52], Martins [77], Guthrie [89]	19,416
18	21	H	Tottenham H	W 2-1	1-1	12	N'Zogbia [12], Duff [90]	47,982
19	26	A	Wigan Ath	L 1-2	0-1	12	Guthrie (pen) [88]	20,266
20	28	H	Liverpool	L 1-5	1-2	14	Edgar [45]	52,114
21	Jan 10	H	West Ham U	D 2-2	1-1	11	Owen [19], Carroll [78]	47,571
22	17	A	Blackburn R	L 0-3	0-0	14		25,583
23	28	A	Manchester C	L 1-2	0-1	—	Carroll [81]	42,280
24	Feb 1	H	Sunderland	D 1-1	0-1	15	Ameobi (pen) [69]	52,084
25	7	A	WBA	W 3-2	3-1	13	Duff [2], Lovenkrands [9], Taylor S [41]	25,817
26	22	H	Everton	D 0-0	0-0	14		47,683
27	Mar 1	A	Bolton W	L 0-1	0-0	15		20,763
28	4	H	Manchester U	L 1-2	1-1	—	Lovenkrands [9]	51,636
29	14	A	Hull C	D 1-1	1-1	16	Taylor S [38]	24,914
30	21	H	Arsenal	L 1-3	0-0	18	Martins [56]	49,972
31	Apr 4	H	Chelsea	L 0-2	0-0	18		52,112
32	11	A	Stoke C	D 1-1	0-1	18	Carroll [81]	27,500
33	19	A	Tottenham H	L 0-1	0-1	19		35,850
34	27	H	Portsmouth	D 0-0	0-0	—		47,481
35	May 3	A	Liverpool	L 0-3	0-2	18		44,121
36	11	H	Middlesbrough	W 3-1	1-1	—	Taylor S [9], Martins [71], Lovenkrands [86]	51,252
37	16	H	Fulham	L 0-1	0-1	18		52,114
38	24	A	Aston Villa	L 0-1	0-1	18		42,585

Final League Position: 18

GOALSCORERS

League (40): Martins 8, Owen 8 (1 pen), Ameobi 4 (1 pen), Taylor S 4, Carroll 3, Duff 3, Lovenkrands 3, Guthrie 2 (1 pen), Barton 1 (pen), Edgar 1, N'Zogbia 1, Xisco 1, own goal 1.
Carling Cup (4): Owen 2, Milner 1, own goal 1.
FA Cup (0).

Given S 22	Beye H 22 + 1	N'Zogbia C 14 + 4	Butt N 33	Coloccini F 34	Taylor S 25 + 2	Milner J 2	Guthrie D 21 + 3	Martins O 21 + 3	Duff D 28 + 2	Gutierrez J 23 + 7	Owen M 21 + 7	Geremi 11 + 4	Jose Enrique 24 + 2	Bassong S 26 + 4	Barton J 6 + 3	Edgar D 7 + 4	Ameobi S 14 + 8	Gonzalez I — + 2	Xisco 3 + 2	Cacapa C 4 + 2	Carroll A 5 + 9	Viduka M 6 + 6	LuaLua K — + 3	Harper S 16	Lovenkrands P 8 + 4	Nolan K 10 + 1	Taylor R 8 + 2	Smith A 4 + 2	Match No.
1	2	3	4	5	6	7	8	9	10	11																			1
1	2	3	4	5	6	7	8	9^1	10^2	11	12	13																	2
1	2^3	11	4	5	6		8		7^2	10			3^1	12	13	14	9												3
1		3	4	5	6		$8^⁕$		10	7		12					2^1	9^2	13	11									4
1		3	4	5	6			11	9	7		12					2^1	13	10	8^2									5
1		11^2	4	5	6		8	9	7^1		2	13	12		10		3												6
1		11	4	5	2		8	10	9	7^1	3^2	13		12						6									7
1	$2^⁕$	12	4	5	6	8	9^1	11		7		3					10^2				13								8
1	2		4^3	5	6	8	9	11	12	7^1	13	3^2	14		10														9
1	2			5	6	8	9^1	7	11^2		13	3	4	10^3		12	14												10
1	2		4	5	6		9^2	11	7	12		3	8	10^1		13													11
1	2		4	5			9	11	7^1	12		3	8	10		6													12
1	2	12	4	5		13	9	11	7^3	14		3^1	6	8^2	10														13
1	2	12	4	5		8	9^2	11	7^1	10		3	6		13														14
1	2	11	4	5		8	9^1		7	10		3	6			12													15
1	2	11		5	12	4^1	9^3		8	10	7^2	3	6	13	14														16
1	2	11	4	5		8	9^1		7	10		3	6	12															17
1	2	11	4	5		8		12	7	10		3^1	6	9^2		13													18
1	2^1	3	4	5	12	8		11	7	9^2		$6^⁕$	13		14	10^3													19
1		11	4^1	5	6	8		10	7	9^3	12	3^2	2	13	14														20
1		12		5	2	4		10	11	9	7^1	3	6	8															21
1		11^2	$4^⁕$	5		8		7^1	12	9		3	6	13	2	10													22
			5	6				11	12	9^1	7^2	3	4	8^3	2		10				13			1	14				23
			4	5^1	2			11	7		3	6		12	9		10^2				13	8		1					24
			4	5	6			11			3	2		9^2	12		13				10^1	8	7	1					25
			4	5	2		13	11^1	12		3	6		9^2							10^3	$8^⁕$	7	1	14				26
			4^1	5	2		9^2	7		12	3	6		10			13				11	8		1					27
				5	2		9	8		7	3	6		13			12				11	4^2	10^1	1					28
			4	5	2		9	11	10^1	7	3	6		12							13	8^2		1					29
	13		4	5	2^1		9	11		12	3	6^2	14								10^3	8	7	1					30
	6		4	5		13	9^3	12	7	10	3		14								11^1	8^2	2	1					31
	5	4			7^1		11	12	10		6	2	9^2	13							8	3		1					32
	3	4	5^1		13	11	7	10		6		9^2	14								8^3	2	12	1					33
	2	4^3	5	12	9	11	14	10	3^1	6			13	8^2								7		1					34
	2	4	5		9^2	11	12	14	6	$8^⁕$		10^3		3^1	13							7		1					35
	2	4	5	7	13	3	11^1	9^2	6	14	10^3		12	8										1					36
	2	4	5	7^1	9	3	11^2		$6^⁕$	14	10^3	13	8	12										1					37
		4	5	6	7	9	3		13	12	$2^⁕$	14	10^3	11^1	8^2									1					38

FA Cup
Third Round   Hull C   (a) 0-0   (h) 0-1

Carling Cup
Second Round   Coventry C   (a) 3-2
Third Round   Tottenham H   (h) 1-2

NORTHAMPTON TOWN FL Championship 2

FOUNDATION

Formed in 1897 by school teachers connected with the Northampton and District Elementary Schools' Association, they survived a financial crisis at the end of their first year when they were £675 in the red and became members of the Midland League – a fast move indeed for a new club. They achieved Southern League membership in 1901.

Sixfields Stadium, Upton Way, Northampton NN5 5QA.

Telephone: (01604) 683 700.

Fax: (01604) 751 613.

Ticket Office: (01604) 683 777.

Website: www.ntfc.co.uk

Email: paula.kane@ntfc.co.uk

Ground Capacity: 7,300.

Record Attendance: (at County Ground): 24,523 v Fulham, Division 1, 23 April 1966; (at Sixfields Stadium): 7,557 v Manchester C, Division 2, 26 September 1998.

Pitch Measurements: 116yd × 72yd.

Chairman: David Cardoza.

Secretary: Norman Howells.

Manager: Stuart Gray.

Coaches: Ian Sampson, Jim Barron.

Physio: Stuart Barker.

Colours: Claret shirts with yellow inserts, white shorts and stockings.

Change Colours: All black with white inserts and trim on sleeves.

Year Formed: 1897.

Turned Professional: 1901.

Ltd Co.: 1901.

Grounds: 1897, County Ground; 1994, Sixfields Stadium.

Club Nickname: 'The Cobblers'.

First Football League Game: 28 August 1920, Division 3, v Grimsby T (a) L 0–2 – Thorpe; Sproston, Hewison; Jobey, Tomkins, Pease; Whitworth, Lockett, Thomas, Freeman, MacKechnie.

Record League Victory: 10–0 v Walsall, Division 3 (S), 5 November 1927 – Hammond; Watson, Jeffs; Allen, Brett, Odell; Daley, Smith (3), Loasby (3), Hoten (1), Wells (3).

Record Cup Victory: 10–0 v Sutton T, FA Cup prel rd, 7 December 1907 – Cooch; Drennan, Lloyd Davies, Tirrell (1), McCartney, Hickleton, Badenock (3), Platt (3), Lowe (1), Chapman (2), McDiarmid.

HONOURS

Football League: Division 1 best season: 21st, 1965–66; Division 2 – Runners-up 1964–65; Division 3 – Champions 1962–63; Division 3 (S) – Runners-up 1927–28, 1949–50; Division 4 – Champions 1986–87; Runners-up 1975–76; FL 2 – Runners-up 2005–06.

FA Cup: best season: 5th rd, 1934, 1950, 1970.

Football League Cup: best season: 5th rd, 1965, 1967.

SKY SPORTS FACT FILE

On 13 December 2008 Northampton Town found themselves 3–1 down in 32 minutes at Scunthorpe United, 4–1 adrift in the 51st minute but rallied to scored twice in four minutes and then level the scores at four-all with just five minutes of the match remaining.

Record Defeat: 0–11 v Southampton, Southern League, 28 December 1901.

Most League Points (2 for a win): 68, Division 4, 1975–76.

Most League Points (3 for a win): 99, Division 4, 1986–87.

Most League Goals: 109, Division 3, 1962–63 and Division 3 (S), 1952–53.

Highest League Scorer in Season: Cliff Holton, 36, Division 3, 1961–62.

Most League Goals in Total Aggregate: Jack English, 135, 1947–60.

Most League Goals in One Match: 5, Ralph Hoten v Crystal Palace, Division 3 (S), 27 October 1928.

Most Capped Player: Edwin Lloyd Davies, 12 (16), Wales.

Most League Appearances: Tommy Fowler, 521, 1946–61.

Youngest League Player: Adrian Mann, 16 years 297 days v Bury, 5 May 1984.

Record Transfer Fee Received: £265,000 from Watford for Richard Hill, July 1987.

Record Transfer Fee Paid: £165,000 to Oldham Ath for Josh Low, July 2003.

Football League Record: 1920 Original Member of Division 3; 1921 Division 3 (S); 1958–61 Division 4; 1961–63 Division 3; 1963–65 Division 2; 1965–66 Division 1; 1966–67 Division 2; 1967–69 Division 3; 1969–76 Division 4; 1976–77 Division 3; 1977–87 Division 4; 1987–90 Division 3; 1990–92 Division 4; 1992–97 Division 3; 1997–99 Division 2; 1999–2000 Division 3; 2000–03 Division 2; 2003–04 Division 3; 2004–06 FL 2; 2006–09 FL 1; 2009– FL 2.

LATEST SEQUENCES

Longest Sequence of League Wins: 8, 27.8.1960 – 19.9.1960.

Longest Sequence of League Defeats: 8, 26.10.1935 – 21.12.1935.

Longest Sequence of League Draws: 6, 18.9.1983 – 15.10.1983.

Longest Sequence of Unbeaten League Matches: 21, 27.9.1986 – 6.2.1987.

Longest Sequence Without a League Win: 18, 26.3.1969 – 20.9.1969.

Successive Scoring Runs: 27 from 23.8.1986.

Successive Non-scoring Runs: 7 from 7.4.1939.

MANAGERS

Arthur Jones 1897–1907
(Secretary-Manager)
Herbert Chapman 1907–12
Walter Bull 1912–13
Fred Lessons 1913–19
Bob Hewison 1920–25
Jack Tresadern 1925–30
Jack English 1931–35
Syd Puddefoot 1935–37
Warney Cresswell 1937–39
Tom Smith 1939–49
Bob Dennison 1949–54
Dave Smith 1954–59
David Bowen 1959–67
Tony Marchi 1967–68
Ron Flowers 1968–69
Dave Bowen 1969–72
(continued as General Manager and Secretary to 1985 when joined the board)
Billy Baxter 1972–73
Bill Dodgin Jnr 1973–76
Pat Crerand 1976–77
Bill Dodgin Jnr 1977
John Petts 1977–78
Mike Keen 1978–79
Clive Walker 1979–80
Bill Dodgin Jnr 1980–82
Clive Walker 1982–84
Tony Barton 1984–85
Graham Carr 1985–90
Theo Foley 1990–92
Phil Chard 1992–93
John Barnwell 1993–95
Ian Atkins 1995–99
Kevin Wilson 1999–2001
Kevan Broadhurst 2001–03
Terry Fenwick 2003
Martin Wilkinson 2003
Colin Calderwood 2003–06
John Gorman 2006
Stuart Gray January 2007–

TEN YEAR LEAGUE RECORD

		P	W	D	L	F	A	Pts	Pos
1999-2000	Div 3	46	25	7	14	63	45	82	3
2000-01	Div 2	46	15	12	19	46	59	57	18
2001-02	Div 2	46	14	7	25	54	79	49	20
2002-03	Div 2	46	10	9	27	40	79	39	24
2003-04	Div 3	46	22	9	15	58	51	75	6
2004-05	FL 2	46	20	12	14	62	51	72	7
2005-06	FL 2	46	22	17	7	63	37	83	2
2006-07	FL 1	46	15	14	17	48	51	59	14
2007-08	FL 1	46	17	15	14	60	55	66	9
2008-09	FL 1	46	12	13	21	61	65	49	21

DID YOU KNOW ?

The Northampton Town player immortalised by Walter Tull Way was only the second black player in the League. Signed from Tottenham Hotspur in October 1911 he was commissioned in the Army, was decorated and died in action in 1918.

NORTHAMPTON TOWN 2008–09 LEAGUE RECORD

Match No.	Date	Venue	Opponents	Result	H/T Score	Lg. Pos.	Goalscorers	Attendance
1	Aug 9	H	Cheltenham T	W 4-2	1-1	—	Doig [42], Akinfenwa 2 (2 pens) [64, 68], Constantine [77]	4716
2	16	A	Milton Keynes D	L 0-1	0-0	10		12,078
3	23	H	Millwall	D 0-0	0-0	9		4402
4	30	A	Tranmere R	L 1-4	1-3	18	Gilligan [10]	5034
5	Sept 13	H	Peterborough U	·D 1-1	1-1	21	Larkin [43]	6520
6	16	A	Stockport Co	D 1-1	1-0	—	Hawley [5]	4974
7	20	A	Huddersfield T	L 2-3	1-1	20	Goodwin (og) [25], Davis [90]	12,414
8	27	H	Brighton & HA	D 2-2	0-1	20	Akinfenwa 2 [77, 90]	5389
9	Oct 4	A	Crewe Alex	W 3-1	1-0	16	Jackman [45], Akinfenwa (pen) [64], Osman [70]	3977
10	10	H	Hartlepool U	W 1-0	1-0	—	Hawley [17]	5277
11	18	H	Yeovil T	W 3-0	2-0	10	Jackman [17], Akinfenwa [20], Crowe [81]	5217
12	21	A	Swindon T	L 1-2	0-0	—	Coke [90]	6653
13	25	A	Leicester C	D 0-0	0-0	14		22,795
14	Nov 1	A	Walsall	L 1-3	0-2	15	Constantine [70]	4377
15	15	H	Oldham Ath	L 0-1	0-0	16		5067
16	22	A	Hereford U	W 2-0	0-0	15	Jackman [49], Gilligan [61]	3061
17	25	H	Leeds U	W 2-1	1-0	—	Davis [28], Bignall [87]	6008
18	29	H	Colchester U	L 1-2	0-2	—	Jackman [53]	4833
19	Dec 6	H	Leyton Orient	D 1-1	1-1	14	Davis [2]	5039
20	13	A	Scunthorpe U	D 4-4	1-3	15	McGleish [24], Coke [53], Jackman 2 [57, 85]	3976
21	20	H	Carlisle U	W 1-0	0-0	12	Crowe [63]	4673
22	26	A	Southend U	L 0-1	0-0	14		7767
23	28	A	Bristol R	D 0-0	0-0	14		5557
24	Jan 10	H	Huddersfield T	D 1-1	1-1	—	Akinfenwa [90]	5110
25	16	A	Hartlepool U	L 0-2	0-1	—		3814
26	24	H	Crewe Alex	W 5-1	2-1	12	Clarke 3 (1 pen) [2, 55, 70 (p)], Jackman [18], Davis [57]	4675
27	27	A	Colchester U	L 1-2	1-0	—	Akinfenwa [18]	3973
28	31	H	Leicester C	L 1-2	1-1	15	Constantine [16]	7028
29	Feb 14	A	Oldham Ath	L 1-2	0-1	18	Akinfenwa [67]	4629
30	21	H	Walsall	L 0-2	0-0	18		4528
31	24	A	Brighton & HA	D 1-1	1-0	—	Gilligan [45]	5062
32	28	H	Cheltenham T	W 1-0	1-0	16	Crowe [45]	3495
33	Mar 7	H	Tranmere R	D 1-1	0-1	17	Holt [52]	4546
34	10	A	Millwall	L 0-1	0-1	—		6685
35	14	A	Peterborough U	L 0-1	0-1	19		8881
36	21	H	Stockport Co	W 4-0	2-0	19	Akinfenwa [12], Osman [45], Guttridge [72], Vernon [79]	4814
37	24	H	Swindon T	L 3-4	1-3	—	Akinfenwa [3], Jackman [68], Anya [87]	5025
38	28	A	Carlisle U	D 1-1	1-1	20	Guttridge [41]	5254
39	31	A	Yeovil T	L 0-1	0-0	—		3884
40	Apr 10	A	Bristol R	L 0-1	0-0	—		6666
41	13	H	Southend U	L 2-3	0-1	21	Akinfenwa [50], Prijovic [80]	5190
42	18	A	Leyton Orient	W 3-1	0-1	21	Akinfenwa [71], Prijovic [73], Anya [90]	4665
43	21	A	Scunthorpe U	D 3-3	1-1	—	Crowe [38], Anya [60], Hughes [76]	4416
44	25	H	Hereford U	W 2-1	1-0	19	Holt [29], Crowe [69]	5518
45	28	H	Milton Keynes D	L 0-1	0-1	—		6054
46	May 2	A	Leeds U	L 0-3	0-1	21		34,214

Final League Position: 21

GOALSCORERS

League (61): Akinfenwa 13 (3 pens), Jackman 8, Crowe 5, Davis 4, Anya 3, Clarke 3 (1 pen), Constantine 3, Gilligan 3, Coke 2, Guttridge 2, Hawley 2, Holt 2, Osman 2, Prijovic 2, Bignall 1, Doig 1, Hughes 1, Larkin 1, McGleish 1, Vernon 1, own goal 1.
Carling Cup (5): Akinfenwa 2 (1 pen), Crowe 1, Guttridge 1, Larkin 1.
FA Cup (3): Crowe 2, McGleish 1.
J Paint Trophy (0).

Bunn M 3	Gyepes G 2	Crowe J 42 + 1	Gilligan R 23 + 8	Hughes M 41	Doig C 26 + 2	Davis L 21 + 8	Guttridge L 23 + 2	Constantine L 21 + 11	Akinfenwa A 29 + 4	Jackman D 42 + 1	Holt A 28 + 13	Larkin C 9 + 12	Coke G 25 + 7	Osman A 34 + 2	Benjamin J — + 4	Little M 9	Dolman L 9 + 5	Henderson I — + 3	Dunn C 29	Hawley K 11	Fielding F 12	McGleish S 7 + 2	Dyer A 5 + 3	Walker K 9	Bignall N 1 + 4	Todd A 7	Rodgers P 9 + 2	Clarke B 5	Zieler R 2	Anya 16 + 8	Magnay C 2	Prijovic A 3 + 7	Vernon S 4 + 2	Hodgkiss J 4 + 1	Watts A 3 + 2	Match No.
1	2	3	4	5	6	7^1	8	9	10^2	11	12	13																								1
1	2	3	4^1	5	6^2	7	8^3	9	10	11	12	13	14																							2
1	2		4	5	6	13	8^2		10		11	3^1	9	7																						3
	2^1		4^3	5	6^2	12			10		3	11		9		8	7	13	14	1																4
	3^4		4^3	5		7^1	8	13		11	12	9^2	14			2	6		1	10																5
			4		6		8^2		12	3	11	9^1	13	7		2	5		1	10																6
	3	12	6		13	8	14	10^3	11^2	9^1		7		2	5		1	4																		7
	3		5		6	8	12	10	13	11^2	4^1	14	7^3	2					9	1																8
	2	13	5		6	8	12	10^1	3	11			7	4					9^2	1																9
	3^1	13	5	14	7^3	8^2		10	11	4		12	6	2					9	1																10
	6	12	5	13		7	14	10^3	3	11	4^1		8	2^2					9	1																11
	2	4^1	5	6		8	9	12	3	11^3			13	7^2		14			10	1																12
	2	4^2	5	6			12	10^1	3	11			8	7			13		9	1																13
	2	4^3	5	6			10		3^2	11			7	8^1		12			9	1	13	14														14
	2	7	5			12	10		3	11				6^1					9^2	1	13	8^3	4	14												15
	2	7	5			11	8^1	10	3				12	6						1	9^2		4	13												16
	2	7				4	8^1	9^2	3	12			11							1	10		5	13	6											17
	2	7^1	4				8	9	3	12			11				13			1	10		5^3	14	6											18
	2	7^1	4				8		3	13		12	11							1	10		6	9^2	5											19
	2	12	4^2	6			9	3	13	3			11	7						1	10^1		5		8											20
	2		8^1	4			9	12	3	13			11	7						1	10^2		5		6											21
	2^1		5			8^2	14	9	10^3	3		12	13	11	7^8					1			4		6											22
	2	7	5			8^1		13	10	3		12		11						1	9^2		4		6											23
	2^8	4^2	6				9	10	3^1	11	12	7	8	13	5		1																			24
		3^2	4	5	14		9	10		11	8^1	6^3	7	13	2		1					12														25
		14	6	5	4^1		9	10^2	3	12	13	7	8				1								2	11^3										26
	12		6	5	4^3		11	10^2	3	13	14	7	8				1								2^8	9^1										27
	2	12	6	5	4^3		7^2		3	11	10^1		8	14		13	1									9										28
	2		6	5			10	3	11	12	4^3	8^2		13	1							14			7^1	9										29
	2	7	5	6			10	3	11	12	4			8											9^1	1										30
	2	7	5	6			9	10^8		11				8										4		3		1								31
	2	7	5	6			9		11	10				8					1				4		3		12									32
	5		6				9		3	11	7	4	10						1				8^1		2		12									33
	2	6^1	5	13	10^2	9		3	11^3	12	4	8							1								14	7								34
	2	6	5^3	13		12		3	11^1	9	4	8							1							14	10	7^2								35
	2	6	6^1	11		7		10^2	3	3	12		4^2	8					1				12			13	9	14								36
	6	5	11^1	7			10	3	12		4^2	8							1				2			13	9^3	14								37
	6		5	11	7^2		10^1	3	12		4	8							1								13	9	2							38
	7		5	6	11^1		10	3		12	4	8							1							13	14	9^2	2^3							39
	7	4^2		6	12		10	3	11		8	8^1							1							13	14	9	2^3	5						40
	7	8^2	4	6			10	3	11			14							1				12			13	9^3	2^1	5							41
	7	13	5	6		4		10^2	3	11^1			8						1							2	9	12								42
	7		5	6		4^2	13	10^1	3	11			8						1							2^3	9	12		14						43
	7		5	6^1		8^2	14	10^3	3	11			4						1								9	13		12	2					44
	2	4^1	5^3			7	13	12	3	11			8		6				1								9	10^2		14						45
	2		5			13	4	9	10	3	11^2	12		7					6	1								8^1								46

FA Cup

First Round	Leeds U	(a)	1-1	
		(h)	2-5	

Carling Cup

First Round	Millwall	(a)	1-0	
Second Round	Bolton W	(a)	2-1	
Third Round	Sunderland	(a)	2-2	

J Paint Trophy

First Round	Brighton & HA	(h)	0-1

NORWICH CITY   FL Championship 1

FOUNDATION

Formed in 1902, largely through the initiative of two local schoolmasters who called a meeting at the Criterion Cafe, they were shocked by an FA Commission which in 1904 declared the club professional and ejected them from the FA Amateur Cup. However, this only served to strengthen their determination. New officials were appointed and a professional club established at a meeting in the Agricultural Hall in March 1905.

Carrow Road, Norwich NR1 1JE.

Telephone: (01603) 760 760.

Fax: (01603) 613 886.

Ticket Office: (0844) 826 1902.

Website: www.canaries.co.uk

Email: reception@ncfc-canaries.co.uk

Ground Capacity: 26,034.

Record Attendance: 43,984 v Leicester C, FA Cup 6th rd, 30 March 1963.

Pitch Measurements: 105m × 67m.

Chairman: Roger Munby.

Chief Executive: David McNally.

Director of Finance and Operations: Sam Gordon.

Secretary: Kevan Platt.

Manager: Bryan Gunn.

Assistant Manager: Ian Butterworth.

Colours: Yellow shirts with two thin green stripes, green shorts, yellow stockings.

Change Colours: All white.

Year Formed: 1902.

Turned Professional: 1905.

Ltd Co.: 1905.

Club Nickname: 'The Canaries'.

Grounds: 1902, Newmarket Road; 1908, The Nest, Rosary Road; 1935, Carrow Road.

First Football League Game: 28 August 1920, Division 3, v Plymouth Arg (a) D 1–1 – Skermer; Gray, Gadsden; Wilkinson, Addy, Martin; Laxton, Kidger, Parker, Whitham (1), Dobson.

Record League Victory: 10–2 v Coventry C, Division 3 (S), 15 March 1930 – Jarvie; Hannah, Graham; Brown, O'Brien, Lochhead (1); Porter (1), Anderson, Hunt (5), Scott (2), Slicer (1).

Record Cup Victory: 8–0 v Sutton U, FA Cup 4th rd, 28 January 1989 – Gunn; Culverhouse, Bowen, Butterworth, Linighan, Townsend (Crook), Gordon, Fleck (3), Allen (4), Phelan, Putney (1).

HONOURS

FA Premier League: best season: 3rd 1992–93.

Football League: Division 1 – Champions 2003–04; Division 2 – Champions 1971–72, 1985–86; Division 3 (S) – Champions 1933–34; Division 3 – Runners-up 1959–60.

FA Cup: Semi-finals 1959, 1989, 1992.

Football League Cup: Winners 1962, 1985; Runners-up 1973, 1975.

European Competitions: UEFA Cup: 1993–94.

SKY SPORTS FACT FILE

On 31 August 1935 the Canaries flew from The Nest to their new headquarters at Carrow Road for the visit of West Ham United. Norwich City won 4–3 in front of a crowd of 29,779 with two goals from Jack Vinall, one each from Billy Warnes and Doug Lochhead.

Record Defeat: 2–10 v Swindon T, Southern League, 5 September 1908.

Most League Points (2 for a win): 64, Division 3 (S), 1950–51.

Most League Points (3 for a win): 94, Division 1, 2003–04.

Most League Goals: 99, Division 3 (S), 1952–53.

Highest League Scorer in Season: Ralph Hunt, 31, Division 3 (S), 1955–56.

Most League Goals in Total Aggregate: Johnny Gavin, 122, 1945–54, 1955–58.

Most League Goals in One Match: 5, Tommy Hunt v Coventry C, Division 3 (S), 15 March 1930; 5, Roy Hollis v Walsall, Division 3 (S), 29 December 1951.

Most Capped Player: Mark Bowen, 35 (41), Wales.

Most League Appearances: Ron Ashman, 592, 1947–64.

Youngest League Player: Ryan Jarvis, 16 years 282 days v Walsall, 19 April 2003.

Record Transfer Fee Received: £7,250,000 from West Ham U for Dean Ashton, January 2006.

Record Transfer Fee Paid: £3,400,000 to Crewe Alex for Dean Ashton, January 2005.

Football League Record: 1920 Original Member of Division 3; 1921 Division 3 (S): 1934–39 Division 2; 1946–58 Division 3 (S); 1958–60 Division 3; 1960–72 Division 2; 1972–74 Division 1; 1974–75 Division 2; 1975–81 Division 1; 1981–82 Division 2; 1982–85 Division 1; 1985–86 Division 2; 1986–92 Division 1; 1992–95 FA Premier League; 1995–2004 Division 1; 2004–05 FA Premier League; 2005–09 FL C; 2009– FL 1.

LATEST SEQUENCES

Longest Sequence of League Wins: 10, 23.11.1985 – 25.1.1986.

Longest Sequence of League Defeats: 7, 1.4.1995 – 6.5.1995.

Longest Sequence of League Draws: 7, 15.1.1994 – 26.2.1994.

Longest Sequence of Unbeaten League Matches: 20, 31.8.1950 – 30.12.1950.

Longest Sequence Without a League Win: 25, 22.9.1956 – 23.2.1957.

Successive Scoring Runs: 25 from 31.8.1963.

Successive Non-scoring Runs: 5 from 21.2.1925.

MANAGERS

John Bowman 1905–07
James McEwen 1907–08
Arthur Turner 1909–10
Bert Stansfield 1910–15
Major Frank Buckley 1919–20
Charles O'Hagan 1920–21
Albert Gosnell 1921–26
Bert Stansfield 1926
Cecil Potter 1926–29
James Kerr 1929–33
Tom Parker 1933–37
Bob Young 1937–39
Jimmy Jewell 1939
Bob Young 1939–45
Cyril Spiers 1946–47
Duggie Lochhead 1947–50
Norman Low 1950–55
Tom Parker 1955–57
Archie Macaulay 1957–61
Willie Reid 1961–62
George Swindin 1962
Ron Ashman 1962–66
Lol Morgan 1966–69
Ron Saunders 1969–73
John Bond 1973–80
Ken Brown 1980–87
Dave Stringer 1987–92
Mike Walker 1992–94
John Deehan 1994–95
Martin O'Neill 1995
Gary Megson 1995–96
Mike Walker 1996–98
Bruce Rioch 1998–2000
Bryan Hamilton 2000
Nigel Worthington 2001–06
Peter Grant 2006–07
Glenn Roeder 2007–09
Bryan Gunn January 2009–

TEN YEAR LEAGUE RECORD

		P	W	D	L	F	A	Pts	Pos
1999-2000	Div 1	46	14	15	17	45	50	57	12
2000-01	Div 1	46	14	12	20	46	58	54	15
2001-02	Div 1	46	22	9	15	60	51	75	6
2002-03	Div 1	46	19	12	15	60	49	69	8
2003-04	Div 1	46	28	10	8	79	39	94	1
2004-05	PR Lge	38	7	12	19	42	77	33	19
2005-06	FL C	46	18	8	20	56	65	62	9
2006-07	FL C	46	16	9	21	56	71	57	16
2007-08	FL C	46	15	10	21	49	59	55	17
2008-09	FL C	46	12	10	24	57	70	46	22

DID YOU KNOW ?

Norwich City became the fourth Third Division club to reach the FA Cup semi-final in 1959. On the way they accounted for Manchester United 3–0 at Carrow Road. The club topped this particular feat in 1967 when they won a Cup tie 2–1 at Old Trafford.

NORWICH CITY 2008–09 LEAGUE RECORD

Match No.	Date		Venue	Opponents	Result		H/T Score	Lg. Pos.	Goalscorers	Attendance
1	Aug	9	A	Coventry C	L	0-2	0-0	—		22,607
2		16	H	Blackpool	D	1-1	0-0	19	Russell [74]	23,727
3		23	A	Cardiff C	D	2-2	0-1	18	Lupoli 2 [77, 81]	18,032
4		30	H	Birmingham C	D	1-1	0-1	19	Russell [46]	24,229
5	Sept	13	A	Plymouth Arg	W	2-1	1-0	17	Lupoli [15], Sibierski [59]	11,185
6		17	H	QPR	L	0-1	0-1	—		24,249
7		20	H	Sheffield U	W	1-0	0-0	11	Croft [90]	24,175
8		27	A	Barnsley	D	0-0	0-0	15	.	12,324
9		30	A	Southampton	L	0-2	0-1	—		14,480
10	Oct	4	H	Derby Co	L	1-2	0-0	21	Clingan (pen) [51]	24,771
11		18	A	Bristol C	L	0-1	0-0	21		16,791
12		21	H	Wolverhampton W	W	5-2	2-1	—	Ikeme (og) [28], Lita 3 [39, 58, 70], Croft [75]	24,351
13		25	H	Doncaster R	W	2-1	0-0	18	Sibierski [83], Lita [90]	24,543
14		28	A	Derby Co	L	1-3	0-2	—	Kennedy [64]	26,621
15	Nov	1	A	Burnley	L	0-2	0-0	19		11,353
16		8	H	Preston NE	D	2-2	1-1	19	Lita [14], Kennedy [62]	23,225
17		15	H	Swansea C	L	2-3	1-1	19	Lupoli [28], Rangel (og) [61]	24,262
18		22	A	Nottingham F	W	2-1	1-1	19	Pattison [23], Cohen (og) [73]	18,566
19		25	H	Crystal Palace	L	1-2	0-2	—	Pattison [61]	24,034
20		29	A	Sheffield W	L	2-3	1-0	21	Clingan (pen) [43], Lita [62]	18,883
21	Dec	7	H	Ipswich T	W	2-0	0-0	19	Croft [61], Pattison [82]	25,472
22		10	A	Watford	L	1-2	0-1	—	Croft [61]	13,268
23		13	A	Reading	L	0-2	0-0	20		19,382
24		20	H	Charlton Ath	W	1-0	0-0	20	Lita [60]	23,827
25		26	A	Crystal Palace	L	1-3	1-2	20	Doherty [19]	17,180
26		28	H	Nottingham F	L	2-3	0-2	20	Breckin (og) [73], Garner (og) [90]	25,475
27	Jan	10	A	Sheffield U	L	0-1	0-1	—		27,267
28		17	H	Barnsley	W	4-0	0-0	19	Hoolahan [55], Cureton [74], Clingan (pen) [88], Russell [90]	24,685
29		27	H	Southampton	D	2-2	2-0	—	Fotheringham [40], Hoolahan [42]	25,271
30		30	A	Doncaster R	D	1-1	0-1	—	Grounds [61]	12,384
31	Feb	3	A	Wolverhampton W	D	3-3	1-1	—	Croft [32], Cort [47], Doherty [66]	21,654
32		7	H	Bristol C	L	1-2	1-2	20	Grounds [24]	24,691
33		14	A	Preston NE	L	0-1	0-1	20		12,033
34		21	H	Burnley	D	1-1	1-1	22	Cureton [20]	24,363
35		28	A	Coventry C	L	1-2	0-1	23	Grounds [53]	24,450
36	Mar	3	H	QPR	W	1-0	0-0	—	Russell [68]	13,533
37		7	A	Blackpool	L	0-2	0-0	23		7505
38		10	H	Cardiff C	W	2-0	0-0	—	Mooney [49], McDonald [90]	23,706
39		14	H	Plymouth Arg	W	1-0	0-0	20	Mooney [53]	25,064
40		21	A	Birmingham C	D	1-1	0-1	20	Clingan [53]	18,159
41	Apr	4	H	Sheffield W	L	0-1	0-0	21		25,385
42		11	A	Swansea C	L	1-2	1-1	22	Lee [33]	15,783
43		13	H	Watford	W	2-0	1-0	20	Rose (og) [15], Doherty [85]	25,487
44		19	A	Ipswich T	L	2-3	1-1	22	Mooney [16], Clingan (pen) [90]	28,274
45		27	A	Reading	L	0-2	0-0	—		25,041
46	May	3	A	Charlton Ath	L	2-4	1-3	22	Lee [45], Clingan [61]	22,020

Final League Position: 22

GOALSCORERS

League (57): Lita 7, Clingan 6 (4 pens), Croft 5, Lupoli 4, Russell 4, Doherty 3, Grounds 3, Mooney 3, Pattison 3, Cureton 2, Hoolahan 2, Kennedy 2, Lee 2, Sibierski 2, Cort 1, Fotheringham 1, McDonald 1, own goals 6.
Carling Cup (0).
FA Cup (1): Lupoli 1.

	Marshall D 46	Omozusi E 20 + 1	Stefanovic D 12	Shackell J 15	Kennedy J 15 + 1	Clingan S 40	Croft L 34 + 7	Fotheringham M 20 + 7	Cureton J 10 + 12	Lupoli A 7 + 10	Hoolahan W 27 + 5	Koroma O 2 + 3	Russell D 31 + 7	Bertrand R 37 + 1	Pattison M 18 + 6	Osemobor J 35 + 2	Sibierski A 13 + 2	Grounds J 14 + 2	Drury A 10 + 1	Lita L 16	Bell D 12 + 7	Doherty G 32 + 2	Cort C 7 + 5	Gow A 8 + 5	Killen C — + 4	Carney D 4 + 5	Daley L — + 3	Mooney D 8 + 1	Leijer A 1 + 3	McDonald C 1 + 6	Lappin S 4 + 1	Lee A 6 + 1	Smith K 1 + 1	Match No.
1	1	2	3	4	5	6²	7	8	9	10¹	11	12	13																					1
2	1	2	4		5	6	12	8	9²	10³	11	13	14	3	7¹																			2
3	1	5	4		2	6¹	13	8	9³	12	11²	14	10	3	7																			3
4	1		4		5	6	12	8	13	10²	11		9	3	7¹	2																		4
5	1	2	6		5		12	8	13	10²	11³		4¹	3	7		9	14																5
6	1	2	6		5³		12	8	13	10¹	11²		4	3	7		9	14																6
7	1	5					7	8	14	13³	12		10	11	4²	2	9	6	3¹															7
8	1	5	6				7²	8	12		13		10	11	4¹	2	9	3																8
9	1	5	6⁴				7²	8	12	14	13	10³	4	11		2	9¹	3																9
10	1	5				8	7²	12			13		11³	4	3	2¹	9		6	10	14													10
11	1	2			5	6	7²	12				8	3	11		9¹		4³	10	13	14													11
12	1	2	4			6	7³		12	13	11		8	3		9¹		10²	14	5														12
13	1	2	4		12	6	7³		13		11²		8	3		9		10	14	5¹														13
14	1	2	4		5	6	7				11¹		8	3	12	9²		10	13															14
15	1	2¹			5	6	7²	8³	14				9			3	10	11	4															15
16	1	4³			5	6	7²		12				8⁴	3	13	2	9¹		10	11	14													16
17	1				5	6		8²	12	10¹	13		3	11	2			9	7	4														17
18	1	2¹			5	6	7	12			11²		3	10	13			9	8	4⁴														18
19	1				5	6	7	12	13	14			3¹	11	2	9³		4	10	8²														19
20	1			5⁴		6	7			10		12	11	2	13	3¹	9	8²	4															20
21	1	5				6	7³	12		13	10²		14	3	11	2		9	8¹	4														21
22	1	5				6	7					10	3	11	2			9	8	4														22
23	1	12			5¹	6	7	8				9	3	11²	2			10	4	13														23
24	1	5				6	7	12		10²			11²	2	3	9	8	4	13															24
25	1	5				6		8		7¹		12	3	11²	2	9	10	4	13															25
26	1	5				6	7		8			12	3	11²	2	13	9	10¹	4															26
27	1					6	7	8	10	11			3		2	9¹	5		12	4														27
28	1					6	7³	8	9²	13	11¹		10	3	12	2	5		14	4														28
29	1					6	7	8	8³	9¹	12	11²	10	3	13	2	5		4	14														29
30	1					6	7	8	8	9¹	12	11²	10³	3	13	2	5		4	14														30
31	1					6	7		9¹		8	11³		2		5	3		4	10²	12	13	14											31
32	1					6	7²	12	9¹		11		8		2	5	3		4⁴	10³	13	14												32
33	1	6					7	8	12		11³		4	2		3			5	9¹	10²	13	14											33
34	1	4				6	7	8	9³		11¹		12	2		3			5	10²		13		14										34
35	1	4				6	7	8¹	9²		11		12	2		3			5	10			13											35
36	1	4				6	7		10¹		8		11	2		3			5	9	12													36
37	1	4				6	7³		10¹		8		11²	2		3			5	9	12		13	14										37
38	1	4²				6	7¹		11		8		3	2		5			10	12	9³		13	14										38
39	1	4				6	7²		11¹		8⁴		3	2		5			10³	12	9		13	14										39
40	1	4				6					3			2		5	8		11	9			7	10										40
41	1	4				6	7¹						3	2		5	10³	8²	9			13	11	12	14									41
42	1	4				6	12		8³	11			2	3¹		5	14		9		13	7²	10											42
43	1	4				6	12		8	3³			2	14		5	7²	11¹	9			13	10											43
44	1	4				6	7¹		8	3			2	5		11	9	12	10															44
45	1	4²				6			8	3			2	5		11	7¹	12	13	9	10													45
46	1	4				7			8	2			5			9	6¹	12	11	10	3													46

FA Cup
Third Round   Charlton Ath   (a) 1-1
               (h) 0-1

Carling Cup
First Round   Milton Keynes D   (a) 0-1

NOTTINGHAM FOREST   FL Championship

FOUNDATION

One of the oldest football clubs in the world, Nottingham Forest was formed at a meeting in the Clinton Arms in 1865. Known originally as the Forest Football Club, the game which first drew the founders together was 'shinney', a form of hockey. When they determined to change to football in 1865, one of their first moves was to buy a set of red caps to wear on the field.

The City Ground, Nottingham NG2 5FJ.
Telephone: (0115) 982 4444.
Fax: (0115) 982 4455.
Ticket Office: 0871 226 1980.
Website: www.nottinghamforest.co.uk
Email: info@nottinghamforest.co.uk
Ground Capacity: 30,576.
Record Attendance: 49,946 v Manchester U, Division 1, 28 October 1967.
Pitch Measurements: 112yd × 76yd.
Chairman: Nigel Doughty.
Chief Executive: Mark Arthur.
Finance Director: John Pelling.
Manager: Billy Davies.
Assistant Manager: David Kelly.
Physios: Steve Devine, Andy Hunt.
Colours: White shirts with red trim, white shorts, red stockings.
Change Colours: White shirts, red shorts, white stockings.
Year Formed: 1865.
Turned Professional: 1889.
Ltd Co.: 1982.
Club Nickname: 'Reds'.

HONOURS

Football League: Division 1 – Champions 1977–78, 1997–98; Runners-up 1966–67, 1978–79; FL 1 – Runners-up 2007–08. Division 2 – Champions 1906–07, 1921–22; Runners-up 1956–57; Division 3 (S) – Champions 1950–51.

FA Cup: Winners 1898, 1959; Runners-up 1991.

Football League Cup: Winners 1978, 1979, 1989, 1990; Runners-up 1980, 1992.

Anglo-Scottish Cup: Winners 1977;

Simod Cup: Winners 1989.

Zenith Data Systems Cup: Winners: 1992.

European Competitions: *European Cup:* 1978–79 (winners), 1979–80 (winners), 1980–81. *European Fairs Cup:* 1961–62, 1967–68. *UEFA Cup:* 1983–84, 1984–85, 1995–96. *Super Cup:* 1979–80 (winners), 1980–81 (runners-up). *World Club Championship:* 1980.

Grounds: 1865, Forest Racecourse; 1879, The Meadows; 1880, Trent Bridge Cricket Ground; 1882, Parkside, Lenton; 1885, Gregory, Lenton; 1890, Town Ground; 1898, City Ground.

First Football League Game: 3 September 1892, Division 1, v Everton (a) D 2–2 – Brown; Earp, Scott; Hamilton, A. Smith, McCracken; McCallum, W. Smith, Higgins (2), Pike, McInnes.

Record League Victory: 12–0 v Leicester Fosse, Division 1, 12 April 1909 – Iremonger; Dudley, Maltby; Hughes (1), Needham, Armstrong; Hooper (3), Marrison, West (3), Morris (2), Spouncer (3 incl. 1p).

Record Cup Victory: 14–0 v Clapton (away), FA Cup 1st rd, 17 January 1891 – Brown; Earp, Scott; A. Smith, Russell, Jeacock; McCallum (2), 'Tich' Smith (1), Higgins (5), Lindley (4), Shaw (2).

Record Defeat: 1–9 v Blackburn R, Division 2, 10 April 1937.

SKY SPORTS FACT FILE

Nottingham Forest have had the better of FA Cup exchanges with Manchester City, but on 3 January 2009 achieved their finest performance when they won 3–0 at Eastlands. This brought their tally to four successes out of five meetings in the Cup.

Most League Points (2 for a win): 70, Division 3 (S), 1950–51.

Most League Points (3 for a win): 94, Division 1, 1997–98.

Most League Goals: 110, Division 3 (S), 1950–51.

Highest League Scorer in Season: Wally Ardron, 36, Division 3 (S), 1950–51.

Most League Goals in Total Aggregate: Grenville Morris, 199, 1898–1913.

Most League Goals in One Match: 4, Enoch West v Sunderland, Division 1, 9 November 1907; 4, Tommy Gibson v Burnley, Division 2, 25 January 1913; 4, Tom Peacock v Port Vale, Division 2, 23 December 1933; 4, Tom Peacock v Barnsley, Division 2, 9 November 1935; 4, Tom Peacock v Port Vale, Division 2, 23 November 1935; 4, Tom Peacock v Doncaster R, Division 2, 26 December 1935; 4, Tommy Capel v Gillingham, Division 3 (S), 18 November 1950; 4, Wally Ardron v Hull C, Division 2, 26 December 1952; 4, Tommy Wilson v Barnsley, Division 2, 9 February 1957; 4, Peter Withe v Ipswich T, Division 1, 4 October 1977.

Most Capped Player: Stuart Pearce, 76 (78), England.

Most League Appearances: Bob McKinlay, 614, 1951–70.

Youngest League Player: Craig Westcarr, 16 years 257 days v Burnley, 13 October 2001.

Record Transfer Fee Received: £8,500,000 from Liverpool for Stan Collymore, June 1995.

Record Transfer Fee Paid: £3,500,000 to Celtic for Pierre van Hooijdonk, March 1997.

Football League Record: 1892 Elected to Division 1; 1906–07 Division 2; 1907–11 Division 1; 1911–22 Division 2; 1922–25 Division 1; 1925–49 Division 2; 1949–51 Division 3 (S); 1951–57 Division 2; 1957–72 Division 1; 1972–77 Division 2; 1977–92 Division 1; 1992–93 FA Premier League; 1993–94 Division 1; 1994–97 FA Premier League; 1997–98 Division 1; 1998–99 FA Premier League; 1999–2004 Division 1; 2004–05 FL C; 2005–08 FL 1; 2008– FL C.

MANAGERS

Harry Radford 1889–97
(Secretary-Manager)
Harry Haslam 1897–1909
(Secretary-Manager)
Fred Earp 1909–12
Bob Masters 1912–25
John Baynes 1925–29
Stan Hardy 1930–31
Noel Watson 1931–36
Harold Wightman 1936–39
Billy Walker 1939–60
Andy Beattie 1960–63
Johnny Carey 1963–68
Matt Gillies 1969–72
Dave Mackay 1972
Allan Brown 1973–75
Brian Clough 1975–93
Frank Clark 1993–96
Stuart Pearce 1996–97
Dave Bassett 1997–98 *(previously General Manager from February)*
Ron Atkinson 1998–99
David Platt 1999–2001
Paul Hart 2001–04
Joe Kinnear 2004
Gary Megson 2005
Colin Calderwood 2006–08
Billy Davies January 2009–

LATEST SEQUENCES

Longest Sequence of League Wins: 7, 9.5.1979 – 1.9.1979.

Longest Sequence of League Defeats: 14, 21.3.1913 – 27.9.1913.

Longest Sequence of League Draws: 7, 29.4.1978 – 2.9.1978.

Longest Sequence of Unbeaten League Matches: 42, 26.11.1977 – 25.11.1978.

Longest Sequence Without a League Win: 19, 8.9.1998 – 16.1.1999.

Successive Scoring Runs: 22 from 28.3.1931.

Successive Non-scoring Runs: 7 from 13.12.2003.

TEN YEAR LEAGUE RECORD

		P	W	D	L	F	A	Pts	Pos
1999-2000	Div 1	46	14	14	18	53	55	56	14
2000-01	Div 1	46	20	8	18	55	53	68	11
2001-02	Div 1	46	12	18	16	50	51	54	16
2002-03	Div 1	46	20	14	12	82	50	74	6
2003-04	Div 1	46	15	15	16	61	58	60	14
2004-05	FL C	46	9	17	20	42	66	44	23
2005-06	FL 1	46	19	12	15	67	52	69	7
2006-07	FL 1	46	23	13	10	65	41	82	4
2007-08	FL 1	46	22	16	8	64	32	82	2
2008-09	FL C	46	13	14	19	50	65	53	19

DID YOU KNOW ?

During 1935–36 Nottingham Forest finished 19th in the Second Division, failed to score in 15 League games yet hit three sixes and a nine in other games. In three of these high scoring victories Tom Peacock scored four goals in each from his total of 20.

NOTTINGHAM FOREST 2008–09 LEAGUE RECORD

Match No.	Date	Venue	Opponents	Result	H/T Score	Lg. Pos.	Goalscorers	Attendance
1	Aug 10	H	Reading	D 0-0	0-0	—		21,571
2	16	A	Swansea C	L 1-3	1-1	20	Perch [35]	16,811
3	23	H	Watford	W 3-2	2-1	14	Martin [10], Earnshaw [35], Tyson [69]	20,005
4	30	A	Wolverhampton W	L 1-5	0-4	16	Stearman (og) [55]	25,301
5	Sept 13	H	Burnley	L 1-2	0-1	21	Earnshaw [52]	20,504
6	16	A	Preston NE	L 1-2	0-0	—	Mawene (og) [67]	13,145
7	20	H	Charlton Ath	D 0-0	0-0	23		18,771
8	27	A	Plymouth Arg	L 0-1	0-1	24		12,594
9	30	A	Sheffield W	L 0-1	0-0	—		20,823
10	Oct 4	H	Crystal Palace	L 0-2	0-1	24		22,811
11	18	A	QPR	L 1-2	0-0	24	McGugan [84]	15,122
12	21	H	Ipswich T	D 1-1	1-0	—	McCleary [31]	19,455
13	25	H	Cardiff C	L 0-1	0-0	24		19,468
14	28	A	Crystal Palace	W 2-1	1-0	—	Cohen [28], Thornhill [81]	15,162
15	Nov 2	A	Derby Co	L 1-1	0-0	23	Villa (og) [55]	33,010
16	8	H	Birmingham C	D 1-1	0-1	23	Perch [52]	21,415
17	15	A	Bristol C	D 2-2	1-1	23	Garner [11], Tyson [47]	17,440
18	22	H	Norwich C	L 1-2	1-1	24	Anderson [38]	18,566
19	25	A	Doncaster R	D 0-0	0-0	—		12,612
20	29	H	Barnsley	W 1-0	1-0	23	Garner [36]	24,974
21	Dec 6	A	Coventry C	D 2-2	1-2	23	Earnshaw [27], Garner [61]	17,542
22	9	H	Sheffield U	L 0-1	0-1	—		19,541
23	13	H	Blackpool	D 0-0	0-0	22		19,103
24	20	A	Southampton	W 2-0	1-0	22	Morgan [42], Garner [75]	26,580
25	26	H	Doncaster R	L 2-4	0-3	22	Hird (og) [68], Garner [85]	26,501
26	28	A	Norwich C	W 3-2	2-0	21	Thornhill [17], McGugan [30], Earnshaw [89]	25,475
27	Jan 10	A	Charlton Ath	W 2-0	2-0	—	Tyson [34], Earnshaw [36]	24,553
28	17	H	Plymouth Arg	W 2-0	1-0	18	Earnshaw [24], Anderson [51]	20,392
29	27	H	Sheffield W	W 2-1	1-1	—	Tyson [34], Chambers [75]	22,618
30	31	A	Cardiff C	L 0-2	0-1	17		18,779
31	Feb 7	H	QPR	D 2-2	1-1	18	McGugan (pen) [45], Cohen [67]	25,859
32	14	A	Birmingham C	L 0-2	0-0	19		17,631
33	18	A	Ipswich T	L 1-2	0-1	—	Tyson [77]	19,930
34	21	H	Derby Co	L 1-3	0-1	21	Earnshaw [87]	29,140
35	28	A	Reading	W 1-0	0-0	21	McGugan [61]	21,196
36	Mar 3	H	Preston NE	W 2-1	0-0	—	Earnshaw 2 [58, 71]	17,568
37	7	A	Swansea C	D 1-1	0-0	20	McGugan [76]	20,475
38	10	A	Watford	L 1-2	1-2	—	Thornhill [17]	14,730
39	14	A	Burnley	L 0-5	0-2	21		13,055
40	21	H	Wolverhampton W	L 0-1	0-0	22		24,510
41	Apr 4	A	Barnsley	D 1-1	0-0	22	Earnshaw [68]	19,681
42	11	H	Bristol C	W 3-2	1-1	21	Earnshaw [32], Garner [83], Blackstock [90]	22,776
43	13	A	Sheffield U	D 0-0	0-0	22		28,374
44	18	H	Coventry C	W 1-0	0-0	20	Perch [46]	27,856
45	25	A	Blackpool	D 1-1	1-1	20	Blackstock [9]	9279
46	May 3	H	Southampton	W 3-1	0-1	19	Garner [73], Chambers [87], Earnshaw [90]	29,008

Final League Position: 19

GOALSCORERS

League (50): Earnshaw 12, Garner 7, McGugan 5 (1 pen), Tyson 5, Perch 3, Thornhill 3, Anderson 2, Blackstock 2, Chambers 2, Cohen 2, Martin 1, McCleary 1, Morgan 1, own goals 4.
Carling Cup (5): Earnshaw 3, Cohen 1, Newbold 1.
FA Cup (6): Earnshaw 2, Tyson 2 (1 pen), Cohen 1, Garner 1

Smith P 28	Chambers L 32+7	Bennett J 10+2	Perch J 36+1	Morgan W 42	Wilson K 35+1	Moussi G 14+1	McGugan L 25+8	Earnshaw R 26+6	Davies A 3+10	Cohen C 41	Sinclair E —+3	McCleary G 14+25	Martin L 9+4	Newbold A —+4	Breckin I 17+6	Tyson N 28+7	Cole A 5+5	Heath J 9+1	Thornhill M 13+11	Lynch J 20+3	Anderson P 24+2	Fletcher C 4+1	Camp L 15	Garner J 19+9	Byrne M —+1	Moloney B 9+3	Reid J —+1	Osbourne J 7+1	McSheffrey G 4	Gunter C 8	Turner I 3	Blackstock D 6	Match No.
1	2	3	4	5	6	7	8¹	9	10²	11	12	13																					1
1	2	3	4	5	6	7²	8	9		11¹		12	10	13																			2
1	2	3	4	5			9³	8		14	11¹	10²			6	12	13																3
1	2¹	3	4²	5	12	7		9		11		13	10		6	8³	14																4
1	2¹		4	5	6	7		9		11		12	8			10	13	3²															5
1	12		4	5¹	6	7		9		8		11	2³		3	13	10²		14														6
1	2³	3	4	5	6	7	9²	8		12		11¹	10			13			14														7
1	2	3	4¹	5¹	6	7			13	8		12	11²			10	9																8
1	2²	3³	4		6	12				11		13	14		5	9	10		8	7¹													9
1	12	3	4	5	2	7¹			13	8		11	9²			10	14			6³													10
1	2	3³		5	6		12	13		8		11				9	10		14		7¹	4²											11
	2	3³		5	6		12			8		11²		13		9	10¹		14		7	4	1										12
	12		2	5	6¹		8	13		10		11							14	3	7³	4	1	9²									13
	2		4	5			8	9²		11	12				6	13			14	3	7¹		1	10³									14
	12		2	5			8⁴	9		11³					6	13			14	3	7	4¹	1	10²									15
	2		4	5	6		8			10	12	13							3	11	7¹		1	9²									16
	2		4	5	6		8			10	12								3	11²	7	13	1	9¹									17
	2		4	5	6		8			10	12	13							3²	11¹	7		1	9									18
	2		4	5	6		8³			11²	12	13				10			3		7		1	9¹	14								19
			4	5	6		8	10¹		11	12								13	3	7²		1	9³		2	14						20
	12		4	5	6		8	10²		11						13			14	3	7		1	9		2¹							21
			4	5	6		8	10²		11	12	13							3		7³		1	9²		2¹							22
	12		4	5	6		8	10		11		13							14	3¹	7³		1	9²		2							23
	12		4	5	6		8	10³		11		13							14	3	7²		1	9		2¹							24
	12		4	5	6³		8	10		11		13							14	3¹	7²		1	9		2							25
	2		4²	5			8			11	12					10	6		9¹	3³	7		1	13	14								26
1	2		4	5			8			10²	12				6				3	11	7			9¹		13							27
1	2		4	5			8			10	3				6				9¹	11	7			12									28
1	2		4		5		8	10³		11¹						7²			6	9	3			12	14			13					29
1	2		4	5	3		8¹			11						7²			6	9	10			13		12							30
1	2			5	6		8			11	12	14				13			9³	4	7²			10¹				3					31
1	2		4	5	6		8			11		13				14	12		9³		7¹			10³				3²					32
1			4	5	3²		8			11		14					12		6	9	7¹			10³		2							33
1	2¹		4	5			8	10		11	12	13							6	9	3			7²									34
1	2			5	6	4	8³	10²		11	12					13			9¹	14	3	7											35
1	2			5	6		8³	9²		11		10				13	12		14	3¹	7							4					36
1	2		12		6	7	13	9		8		14		5					3		11³							4¹	10²				37
1	2			5	6	4³	8			13		7				12²	9		11	3¹								14	10				38
1	2		4	5			12			10		8				7³	9		13					14				6¹	11²	3			39
			4	5	6		8³	9		11		12							13		3			10¹				14	7²	2	1		40
	13			5	6		8¹	9		11		12									7²			3				4	2	1		10	41
			4³	5	6		11¹	14		9²		8				12					3			7				13	2	1		10	42
1	2		4	5	3⁴			14				8³				13			6		12			9²				7		11		10¹	43
1	6		4	5			8²			11		12							13		7¹			9				3		2		10	44
1	2		4	5				14		13		8³				12			6¹		3			9				11²	7			10	45
1	5					4²	8	9		14		11				7³			6		3			13		12				2		10¹	46

FA Cup

Third Round	Manchester C	(a)	3-0
Fourth Round	Derby Co	(a)	1-1
		(h)	2-3

Carling Cup

First Round	Morecambe	(h)	4-0
Second Round	Sunderland	(h)	1-2

NOTTS COUNTY   FL Championship 2

FOUNDATION

According to the official history of Notts County 'the true date of Notts' foundation has to be the meeting at the George Hotel on 7 December 1864'. However, there is documented evidence of continuous play from 1862, when club members played organised matches amongst themselves in The Park in Nottingham.

Meadow Lane Stadium, Meadow Lane, Nottingham NG2 3HJ.

Telephone: (0115) 952 9000.

Fax: (0115) 955 3994.

Ticket Office: (0115) 955 7204.

Website: www.nottscountyfc.co.uk

Email: info@nottscountyfc.co.uk

Ground Capacity: 20,300.

Record Attendance: 47,310 v York C, FA Cup 6th rd, 12 March 1955.

Pitch Measurements: 113yd × 72yd.

Chairman: Peter Trembling.

Director: Peter Willett.

Secretary and General Manager: Tony Cuthbert.

Manager: Ian McParland.

Assistant Manager: Dave Kevan.

Physio: Paul Godfrey.

Colours: Black and white striped shirts, black shorts, black stockings.

Change Colours: Tan and blue halved shirts, tan shorts, blue stockings.

Year Formed: 1862* (*see Foundation*). *Turned Professional:* 1885. *Ltd Co.:* 1890.

Club Nickname: 'Magpies'.

Grounds: 1862, The Park; 1864, The Meadows; 1877, Beeston Cricket Ground; 1880, Castle Ground; 1883, Trent Bridge; 1910, Meadow Lane.

First Football League Game: 15 September 1888, Football League, v Everton (a) L 1–2 – Holland; Guttridge, McLean; Brown, Warburton, Shelton; Hodder, Harker, Jardine, Moore (1), Wardle.

Record League Victory: 11–1 v Newport Co, Division 3 (S), 15 January 1949 – Smith; Southwell, Purvis; Gannon, Baxter, Adamson; Houghton (1), Sewell (4), Lawton (4), Pimbley, Johnston (2).

Record Cup Victory: 15–0 v Rotherham T (at Trent Bridge), FA Cup 1st rd, 24 October 1885 – Sherwin; Snook, H. T. Moore; Dobson (1), Emmett (1), Chapman; Gunn (1), Albert Moore (2), Jackson (3), Daft (2), Cursham (4), (1 og).

Record Defeat: 1–9 v Blackburn R, Division 1, 16 November 1889. 1–9 v Aston Villa, Division 1, 29 September 1888. 1–9 v Portsmouth, Division 2, 9 April 1927.

HONOURS

Football League: Division 1 best season: 3rd, 1890–91, 1900–01; Division 2 – Champions 1896–97, 1913–14, 1922–23; Runners-up 1894–95, 1980–81; Division 3 (S) – Champions 1930–31, 1949–50; Runners-up 1936–37; Division 3 – Champions 1997–98; Runners-up 1972–73; Division 4 – Champions 1970–71; Runners-up 1959–60.

FA Cup: Winners 1894; Runners-up 1891.

Football League Cup: best season: 5th rd, 1964, 1973, 1976.

Anglo-Italian Cup: Winners 1995; Runners-up 1994.

SKY SPORTS FACT FILE

On 31 March 1894 when Notts County beat Bolton Wanderers 4–1 there were two firsts for the FA Cup final. Jimmy Logan hit a hat-trick and the winners were the first from a club outside the top division to achieve the feat.

Most League Points (2 for a win): 69, Division 4, 1970–71.

Most League Points (3 for a win): 99, Division 3, 1997–98.

Most League Goals: 107, Division 4, 1959–60.

Highest League Scorer in Season: Tom Keetley, 39, Division 3 (S), 1930–31.

Most League Goals in Total Aggregate: Les Bradd, 125, 1967–78.

Most League Goals in One Match: 5, Robert Jardine v Burnley, Division 1, 27 October 1888; 5, Daniel Bruce v Port Vale, Division 2, 26 February 1895; 5, Bertie Mills v Barnsley, Division 2, 19 November 1927.

Most Capped Player: Kevin Wilson, 15 (42), Northern Ireland.

Most League Appearances: Albert Iremonger, 564, 1904–26.

Youngest League Player: Tony Bircumshaw, 16 years 54 days v Brentford, 3 April 1961.

Record Transfer Fee Received: £2,500,000 from Derby Co for Craig Short, September 1992.

Record Transfer Fee Paid: £685,000 to Sheffield U for Tony Agana, November 1991.

Football League Record: 1888 Founder Member of the Football League; 1893–97 Division 2; 1897–1913 Division 1; 1913–14 Division 2; 1914–20 Division 1; 1920–23 Division 2; 1923–26 Division 1; 1926–30 Division 2; 1930–31 Division 3 (S); 1931–35 Division 2; 1935–50 Division 3 (S); 1950–58 Division 2; 1958–59 Division 3; 1959–60 Division 4; 1960–64 Division 3; 1964–71 Division 4; 1971–73 Division 3; 1973–81 Division 2; 1981–84 Division 1; 1984–85 Division 2; 1985–90 Division 3; 1990–91 Division 2; 1991–95 Division 1; 1995–97 Division 2; 1997–98 Division 3; 1998–2004 Division 2; 2004– FL 2.

LATEST SEQUENCES

Longest Sequence of League Wins: 10, 3.12.1997 – 31.1.1998.

Longest Sequence of League Defeats: 7, 3.9.1983 – 16.10.1983.

Longest Sequence of League Draws: 6, 16.8.2008 – 20.9.2008.

Longest Sequence of Unbeaten League Matches: 19, 26.4.1930 – 6.12.1930.

Longest Sequence Without a League Win: 20, 3.12.1996 – 31.3.1997.

Successive Scoring Runs: 35 from 26.4.1930.

Successive Non-scoring Runs: 5 from 30.11.1912.

MANAGERS

Albert Fisher 1913–27
Horace Henshall 1927–34
Charlie Jones 1934
David Pratt 1935
Percy Smith 1935–36
Jimmy McMullan 1936–37
Harry Parkes 1938–39
Tony Towers 1939–42
Frank Womack 1942–43
Major Frank Buckley 1944–46
Arthur Stollery 1946–49
Eric Houghton 1949–53
George Poyser 1953–57
Tommy Lawton 1957–58
Frank Hill 1958–61
Tim Coleman 1961–63
Eddie Lowe 1963–65
Tim Coleman 1965–66
Jack Burkitt 1966–67
Andy Beattie *(General Manager)* 1967
Billy Gray 1967–68
Jack Wheeler (*Caretaker Manager*) 1968–69
Jimmy Sirrel 1969–75
Ron Fenton 1975–77
Jimmy Sirrel 1978–82 *(continued as General Manager to 1984)*
Howard Wilkinson 1982–83
Larry Lloyd 1983–84
Richie Barker 1984–85
Jimmy Sirrel 1985–87
John Barnwell 1987–88
Neil Warnock 1989–93
Mick Walker 1993–94
Russell Slade 1994–95
Howard Kendall 1995
Colin Murphy 1995 *(continued as General Manager to 1996)*
Steve Thompson 1996
Sam Allardyce 1997–99
Gary Brazil 1999–2000
Jocky Scott 2000–01
Gary Brazil 2001
Billy Dearden 2002–04
Gary Mills 2004
Ian Richardson 2004–05
Gudjon Thordarson 2005–06
Steve Thompson 2006–07
Ian McParland October 2007–

TEN YEAR LEAGUE RECORD

		P	W	D	L	F	A	Pts	Pos
1999-2000	Div 2	46	18	11	17	61	55	65	8
2000-01	Div 2	46	19	12	15	62	66	69	8
2001-02	Div 2	46	13	11	22	59	71	50	19
2002-03	Div 2	46	13	16	17	62	70	55	15
2003-04	Div 2	46	10	12	24	50	78	42	23
2004-05	FL 2	46	13	13	20	46	62	52	19
2005-06	FL 2	46	12	16	18	48	63	52	21
2006-07	FL 2	46	16	14	16	55	53	62	13
2007-08	FL 2	46	10	18	18	37	53	48	21
2008-09	FL 2	46	11	14	21	49	69	47	19

DID YOU KNOW ?

Scoring just 46 goals from 42 League matches and acquiring only 53 points would seem little evidence of a promotion-winning team, but in 1922–23 Notts County finished as Second Division champions. Both figures were the lowest for a title-achieving team.

NOTTS COUNTY 2008–09 LEAGUE RECORD

Match No.	Date		Venue	Opponents	Result		H/T Score	Lg. Pos.	Goalscorers	Atten- dance
1	Aug	9	A	Bradford C	L	1-2	0-1	—	Butcher [73]	14,038
2		16	H	Darlington	D	0-0	0-0	15		4352
3		23	A	Luton T	D	1-1	0-0	15	Forrester (pen) [53]	6085
4		30	H	Shrewsbury T	D	2-2	1-0	15	Edwards [39], Butcher [75]	4697
5	Sept	6	H	Bournemouth	D	1-1	1-1	15	Forrester [12]	4362
6		13	A	Accrington S	D	1-1	0-0	17	Canham [89]	1404
7		20	A	Exeter C	D	2-2	0-1	17	Johnson [58], Canham [90]	4341
8		27	H	Aldershot T	W	2-1	0-0	12	Johnson [56], Butcher [90]	6033
9	Oct	4	A	Port Vale	W	2-1	1-0	11	Forrester [6], Weston [66]	6247
10		13	H	Brentford	D	1-1	0-1	—	Forrester (pen) [65]	6012
11		18	H	Macclesfield T	D	1-1	0-0	11	Facey [48]	4600
12		21	A	Gillingham	D	2-2	0-1	—	Butcher [65], Facey [79]	4396
13		25	A	Chesterfield	L	1-3	0-1	14	Facey [60]	4134
14		28	H	Rochdale	L	1-2	0-0	—	Forrester (pen) [47]	3610
15	Nov	1	H	Bury	L	0-1	0-0	15		4391
16		15	H	Barnet	W	4-0	4-0	15	Butcher [7], Forte 3 [14, 32, 45]	1934
17		22	A	Dagenham & R	L	1-6	0-3	16	Forte [86]	1743
18		25	H	Wycombe W	L	0-2	0-0	—		2964
19	Dec	6	H	Morecambe	W	1-0	1-0	15	Canham [45]	3671
20		13	A	Chester C	L	0-2	0-1	16		1767
21		20	H	Lincoln C	L	0-1	0-1	17		4568
22		26	A	Grimsby T	W	1-0	1-0	15	Facey [37]	5432
23		28	H	Rotherham U	L	0-3	0-1	17		6686
24	Jan	10	A	Exeter C	W	2-1	2-1	—	Facey [32], Strachan [39]	3832
25		17	A	Brentford	D	1-1	1-0	14	Facey [12]	5465
26		20	A	Aldershot T	D	2-2	0-1	—	Clapham [66], Hamshaw [78]	2491
27		24	H	Port Vale	W	4-2	1-0	13	Weston [32], Forrester 3 (1 pen) [55, 65, 81 (p)]	4447
28		27	H	Rochdale	L	0-3	0-1	—		2289
29		31	H	Chesterfield	L	0-1	0-1	14		4953
30	Feb	14	H	Barnet	W	2-0	1-0	15	Hamshaw [43], Clapham [62]	3830
31		17	A	Macclesfield T	D	1-1	0-1	—	Hamshaw [72]	1370
32		21	A	Bury	L	0-2	0-1	15		2810
33		28	H	Bradford C	W	3-1	3-0	15	Forte 2 [11, 31], Facey [45]	5138
34	Mar	3	A	Darlington	L	0-1	0-1	—		2450
35		7	A	Shrewsbury T	L	2-3	1-2	15	Butcher [16], Forte [85]	5192
36		10	H	Luton T	L	0-2	0-2	—		2886
37		14	H	Accrington S	D	1-1	0-1	16	Facey [73]	3701
38		17	H	Gillingham	L	0-1	0-0	—		3189
39		21	A	Bournemouth	W	1-0	1-0	16	Weston [39]	5510
40		28	A	Lincoln C	D	1-1	0-0	17	Facey [64]	4027
41	Apr	4	H	Chester C	L	1-2	0-1	16	Edwards [88]	4025
42		11	A	Rotherham U	L	1-2	0-1	18	Forte [75]	2945
43		13	H	Grimsby T	L	0-2	0-0	18		5890
44		18	A	Morecambe	L	0-1	0-0	18		2161
45		25	H	Dagenham & R	L	0-3	0-2	20		4419
46	May	2	A	Wycombe W	W	2-1	1-0	19	Thompson 2 [30, 90]	9625

Final League Position: 19

GOALSCORERS

League (49): Facey 9, Forrester 8 (4 pens), Forte 8, Butcher 6, Canham 3, Hamshaw 3, Weston 3, Clapham 2, Edwards 2, Johnson 2, Thompson 2, Strachan 1.
Carling Cup (1): Weston 1.
FA Cup (3): Butcher 1, Canham 1, Smith 1.
J Paint Trophy (1): Butcher 1.

Pilkington K 25	Beardsley J 11	Mayo P 10 + 2	Nowland A 16 + 4	Edwards M 42 + 1	Johnson M 29	Hamshaw M 39 + 2	Butcher R 29 + 5	Facey D 44 + 1	Forrester J 27 + 3	Weston M 44	Canham S 7 + 16	MacKenzie N — + 1	Weir-Daley S — + 10	Smith J 6 + 7	Hoult R 16	Tann A 9 + 5	Fairclough B 2 + 6	Clapham J 40	Strachan G 13 + 5	Thompson J 35	Neal L 4	Forte J 15 + 3	Hanson M 5	Wedderburn N 3 + 6	Hunt S 8 + 3	Picken P 22	Lillis J 5	Richards M — + 1	Match No.
1	2	3	4	5	6	7	8	9[1]	10	11	12																		1
1	2	3	4[1]	5	6	7	8	9	10[2]	11				12	13														2
1	2	3	4[1]	5	6	7	8	9	10	11				12															3
1	2	3		5	6	7	8	9	10	11				4															4
	2	3		5	6[1]	7	8	9	10	11						4	1	12											5
	2	3		5	6	7[2]	8	9[1]	10	11	12					4	1		13										6
	2				6	7	8	9	10[1]	11	12					4[2]	1	5	3				13						7
	2			5	6	7	8	9	10[2]	11	14			13	12	1			4[1]	3									8
				5	6	7	8	9	10[1]	11						12	1	2	3	4									9
				5	6	7	8	9	10[1]	11	12						1	2	3	4									10
	12	13		5		7	8	9	10[3]	11	14						1	2[1]	3	4[2]	6								11
	6[2]	4		5		7	8	9	10[1]	11				12	13		1	2	3										12
	12	4		5	6[1]	7	8	9	10[2]	11					13		1	2	3										13
	2	4[2]		5		7	8	9	10[1]	11				12	13		1		3		6								14
	2[1]			5		7	8	9	10[2]	11				12	13		1		3		6	4							15
	3	12		5		7[1]	8	9[2]		11		13					1		2		6	4	10						16
	2	3	4[1]	5			8	9						12			1		11		6	7	10						17
	3			5			8	9	10[1]					12			1		2		7	6	4	11					18
				5				9						11	10[1]	12	4	1	3	13	6		7	2	8[2]				19
	12	6	7					9	13[9]	11	10[2]					4	1		3	8	5					2[1]			20
1		13	5	6	7			9		11	10[1]	12							3	8[2]	4				2				21
1			5	6[1]	7			9		11	10								3	8	4		2		12				22
1		12	5		7			9		11	10	13							3	8[1]	4		2[2]		6				23
1			4[3]	5	6	7		9	10[1]	11	12								3	8[2]			13	14	2				24
1			4[2]	5	6	7		9[1]	10	11	12							3		8				13	2				25
			4	5		7		10[1]	11	9						12	3			8			6	2			1		26
			4	5	6	7[2]		9	10[1]	11						13	3			8			12	2			1		27
			4	5[1]		7		9	10[2]	11						13	3			8			12	6	2		1		28
			4[2]	5	6	7		9	10[1]	11	12						3			8			13	2			1		29
			5	6[1]	7	13		9[3]		11	14					12	10[2]	3		8			4	2			1		30
1			5	6[2]	7	12	9			11	14					13		3		8		10[3]	4[1]	2					31
1			5	6	7[1]	8[2]	9	12	11							3	13	4		10			2						32
1			4[3]	5	6			12	9	10[1]	11					2[2]	3	13	8		7		14						33
1			4[1]	5				12	9[2]	10	11	13				6	3			8	7			2					34
1				6	12	8	9		7							5	11[1]	4		10		3	2						35
1					7	8	9		11							5	3	4		10			6	2					36
1			4[1]	5	6	7	12	9		11							3	8		10			6	2[1]					37
1				5		7	8	9		11	12						3	4		10			6	2[1]					38
1				5	6	7[2]	8	9	10[1]	11							3	12	4	13				2					39
1				5	6	7[1]	8	9	10[2]	11						13	3	4		12				2					40
1				5	6[2]	7	8	9	10[3]	11	12					13	3[1]	4		14				2					41
1				6		7	8	9		11						5	3	4		10				2					42
1				5	6[1]	7	8	9		11	12						3	4		10				2					43
1				5		12	8	9		11							3	7[1]	4	10			6	2					44
1				5	6[2]	7	10[1]	9	14	11						12	3[3]	8	4				13	2					45
1				5		7		13		11	9[2]					14	10[3]	3	8[1]	4				6	2		12		46

FA Cup

First Round	Sutton U	(a)	1-0
Second Round	Kettering T	(h)	1-1
		(a)	1-2

Carling Cup

First Round	Doncaster R	(h)	1-0
Second Round	Wigan Ath	(a)	0-4

J Paint Trophy

First Round	Scunthorpe U	(a)	1-2

OLDHAM ATHLETIC FL Championship 1

FOUNDATION

It was in 1895 that John Garland, the landlord of the Featherstall and Junction Hotel, decided to form a football club. As Pine Villa they played in the Oldham Junior League. In 1899 the local professional club, Oldham County, went out of existence and one of the liquidators persuaded Pine Villa to take over their ground at Sheepfoot Lane and change their name to Oldham Athletic.

Boundary Park, Furtherwood Road, Oldham OL1 2PA.

Telephone: 0871 226 2235.

Fax: 0871 226 1715.

Ticket Office: 0871 226 1653.

Website: www.oldhamathletic.co.uk

Email: enquiries@oldhamathletic.co.uk

Ground Capacity: 13,624.

Record Attendance: 46,471 v Sheffield W, FA Cup 4th rd, 25 January 1930.

Pitch Measurements: 106yd × 72yd.

Chairman: Simon Blitz.

Managing Director: Simon Corney.

Chief Executive/Secretary: Alan Hardy.

Manager: Dave Penney.

Assistant Manager: Martin Gray.

Physio: Marc Czuczman.

Colours: Blue shirts with white design, blue shorts, white stockings.

Change Colours: Yellow shirts with black design, black shorts, black stockings.

Year Formed: 1895.

Turned Professional: 1899.

Ltd Co.: 1906.

Previous Name: 1895, Pine Villa; 1899, Oldham Athletic.

Club Nickname: 'The Latics'.

Grounds: 1895, Sheepfoot Lane; 1900, Hudson Field; 1906, Sheepfoot Lane; 1907, Boundary Park.

First Football League Game: 9 September 1907, Division 2, v Stoke (a) W 3–1 – Hewitson; Hodson, Hamilton; Fay, Walders, Wilson; Ward, W. Dodds (1), Newton (1), Hancock, Swarbrick (1).

Record League Victory: 11–0 v Southport, Division 4, 26 December 1962 – Bollands; Branagan, Marshall; McCall, Williams, Scott; Ledger (1), Johnstone, Lister (6), Colquhoun (1), Whitaker (3).

HONOURS

Football League: Division 1 – Runners-up 1914–15; Division 2 – Champions 1990–91; Runners-up 1909–10; Division 3 (N) – Champions 1952–53; Division 3 – Champions 1973–74; Division 4 – Runners-up 1962–63.

FA Cup: Semi-final 1913, 1990, 1994.

Football League Cup: Runners-up 1990.

SKY SPORTS FACT FILE

With promotion guaranteed in 1990–91, Oldham Athletic had also-promoted Sheffield Wednesday as visitors in a championship vying contest. Wednesday were two up, the Latics levelled and Neil Redfearn converted a 92nd-minute penalty to ensure the title.

Record Cup Victory: 10–1 v Lytham, FA Cup 1st rd, 28 November 1925 – Gray; Wynne, Grundy; Adlam, Heaton, Naylor (1), Douglas, Pynegar (2), Ormston (2), Barnes (3), Watson (2).

Record Defeat: 4–13 v Tranmere R, Division 3 (N), 26 December 1935.

Most League Points (2 for a win): 62, Division 3, 1973–74.

Most League Points (3 for a win): 88, Division 2, 1990–91.

Most League Goals: 95, Division 4, 1962–63.

Highest League Scorer in Season: Tom Davis, 33, Division 3 (N), 1936–37.

Most League Goals in Total Aggregate: Roger Palmer, 141, 1980–94.

Most League Goals in One Match: 7, Eric Gemmell v Chester, Division 3 (N), 19 January 1952.

Most Capped Player: Gunnar Halle, 24 (64), Norway.

Most League Appearances: Ian Wood, 525, 1966–80.

Youngest League Player: Wayne Harrison, 15 years 11 months v Notts Co, 27 October 1984.

Record Transfer Fee Received: £1,700,000 from Aston Villa for Earl Barrett, February 1992.

Record Transfer Fee Paid: £750,000 to Aston Villa for Ian Olney, June 1992.

Football League Record: 1907 Elected to Division 2; 1910–23 Division 1; 1923–35 Division 2; 1935–53 Division 3 (N); 1953–54 Division 2; 1954–58 Division 3 (N); 1958–63 Division 4; 1963–69 Division 3; 1969–71 Division 4; 1971–74 Division 3; 1974–91 Division 2; 1991–92 Division 1; 1992–94 FA Premier League; 1994–97 Division 1; 1997–2004 Division 2; 2004– FL 1.

MANAGERS

David Ashworth 1906–14
Herbert Bamlett 1914–21
Charlie Roberts 1921–22
David Ashworth 1923–24
Bob Mellor 1924–27
Andy Wilson 1927–32
Jimmy McMullan 1933–34
Bob Mellor 1934–45
    (continued as Secretary to 1953)
Frank Womack 1945–47
Billy Wootton 1947–50
George Hardwick 1950–56
Ted Goodier 1956–58
Norman Dodgin 1958–60
Jack Rowley 1960–63
Les McDowall 1963–65
Gordon Hurst 1965–66
Jimmy McIlroy 1966–68
Jack Rowley 1968–69
Jimmy Frizzell 1970–82
Joe Royle 1982–94
Graeme Sharp 1994–97
Neil Warnock 1997–98
Andy Ritchie 1998–2001
Mick Wadsworth 2001–02
Iain Dowie 2002–03
Brian Talbot 2004–05
Ronnie Moore 2005–06
John Sheridan 2006–09
Joe Royle 2009
Dave Penney April 2009–

LATEST SEQUENCES

Longest Sequence of League Wins: 10, 12.1.1974 – 12.3.1974.

Longest Sequence of League Defeats: 8, 15.12.1934 – 2.2.1935.

Longest Sequence of League Draws: 5, 26.12.1982 – 15.1.1983.

Longest Sequence of Unbeaten League Matches: 20, 1.5.1990 – 10.11.1990.

Longest Sequence Without a League Win: 17, 4.9.1920 – 18.12.1920.

Successive Scoring Runs: 25 from 15.1.1927.

Successive Non-scoring Runs: 6 from 4.2.1922.

TEN YEAR LEAGUE RECORD

		P	W	D	L	F	A	Pts	Pos
1999-2000	Div 2	46	16	12	18	50	55	60	14
2000-01	Div 2	46	15	13	18	53	65	58	15
2001-02	Div 2	46	18	16	12	77	65	70	9
2002-03	Div 2	46	22	16	8	68	38	82	5
2003-04	Div 2	46	12	21	13	66	60	57	15
2004-05	FL 1	46	14	10	22	60	73	52	19
2005-06	FL 1	46	18	11	17	58	60	65	10
2006-07	FL 1	46	21	12	13	69	47	75	6
2007-08	FL 1	46	18	13	15	58	46	67	8
2008-09	FL 1	46	16	17	13	66	65	65	10

DID YOU KNOW ?

Oldham Athletic became the first team to change their colours in the name of charity when on 2 March 2009 they ditched their blue shirts for neon pink in the aid of Link 4 Pink for the local Breast Unit at the Royal Oldham hospital.

OLDHAM ATHLETIC 2008–09 LEAGUE RECORD

Match No.	Date	Venue	Opponents	Result	H/T Score	Lg. Pos.	Goalscorers	Attendance
1	Aug 9	H	Millwall	W 4-3	1-2	—	Liddell 2 (1 pen) 3, 74 (p), Alessandra 80, Taylor 85	5367
2	16	A	Leeds U	W 2-0	0-0	2	Taylor 2 51, 65	24,631
3	23	H	Cheltenham T	W 4-0	1-0	1	Hughes 3 45, 50, 62, Whitaker 85	4673
4	30	A	Colchester U	D 2-2	0-1	2	Taylor 64, Smalley 88	4708
5	Sept 6	A	Tranmere R	W 1-0	1-0	1	Hazell 35	6802
6	13	H	Milton Keynes D	W 2-0	1-0	1	Hughes 8, Allott 90	5530
7	20	A	Hartlepool U	D 3-3	2-0	1	Hughes 23, Taylor 2 44, 58	4507
8	27	H	Huddersfield T	D 1-1	0-1	1	Liddell 50	7418
9	Oct 3	A	Stockport Co	L 1-3	1-0	—	Liddell 24	8360
10	12	H	Hereford U	W 4-0	3-0	3	Hughes 4, Liddell (pen) 15, Jones D 36, Whitaker 90	5468
11	18	H	Leicester C	D 1-1	0-0	4	Whitaker 69	8901
12	21	A	Bristol R	L 0-2	0-2	—		6379
13	25	A	Swindon T	L 0-2	0-2	7		6756
14	28	H	Scunthorpe U	W 3-0	1-0	—	Alessandra 3 26, 50, 60	6057
15	Nov 1	A	Yeovil T	L 0-2	0-0	7		5318
16	15	A	Northampton T	W 1-0	0-0	7	Liddell (pen) 76	5067
17	22	A	Southend U	W 2-1	0-0	7	Taylor 67, Hughes 71	7041
18	25	H	Walsall	W 3-2	2-2	—	Allott 15, Hughes 2 38, 89	3936
19	Dec 6	H	Brighton & HA	D 1-1	1-1	6	Liddell (pen) 9	4803
20	13	A	Peterborough U	D 2-2	1-2	6	Hughes 2 40, 59	6219
21	20	H	Leyton Orient	D 1-1	1-0	6	Liddell (pen) 34	6839
22	26	A	Crewe Alex	W 3-0	0-0	5	Byfield 57, Hughes 2 68, 85	5780
23	28	H	Carlisle U	D 0-0	0-0	5		6254
24	Jan 3	A	Huddersfield T	D 1-1	1-0	—	Allott 6	16,950
25	12	H	Hartlepool U	W 2-1	1-0	—	Hughes 21, Smalley 52	4211
26	17	A	Hereford U	L 0-5	0-4	5		3342
27	24	H	Stockport Co	W 3-1	2-1	3	Whitaker 3, Hughes 18, Taylor 56	7605
28	27	A	Scunthorpe U	L 0-2	0-2	—		4447
29	31	H	Swindon T	D 0-0	0-0	6		4712
30	Feb 7	A	Leicester C	D 0-0	0-0	—		22,328
31	14	H	Northampton T	W 2-1	1-0	5	Hazell 8, Windass 60	4629
32	21	A	Yeovil T	D 2-2	2-2	4	Smalley 12, Forbes (og) 39	4150
33	24	H	Bristol R	L 0-2	0-0	—		3745
34	28	A	Millwall	W 3-2	2-0	4	Smalley 5, Hughes 10, Taylor 90	8551
35	Mar 2	H	Leeds U	D 1-1	0-0	—	Hughes 51	7835
36	7	H	Colchester U	L 0-1	0-1	5		4591
37	14	A	Milton Keynes D	L 2-6	2-2	8	Maher 4, Hughes 40	10,621
38	21	H	Tranmere R	L 0-2	0-0	8		7489
39	24	A	Cheltenham T	D 1-1	0-1	—	Whitaker 90	2992
40	28	A	Leyton Orient	L 1-2	1-0	9	Whitaker 34	4034
41	Apr 4	H	Peterborough U	L 1-2	1-1	9	Taylor 43	5083
42	10	A	Carlisle U	D 1-1	0-1	—	Eardley 89	6635
43	13	H	Crewe Alex	D 1-1	1-0	10	Hazell 41	4334
44	18	A	Brighton & HA	L 1-3	0-2	10	Alessandra 62	6618
45	25	H	Southend U	D 1-1	0-0	10	Eardley (pen) 51	4830
46	May 2	A	Walsall	W 2-1	1-1	10	Smalley 44, Brooke 74	4807

Final League Position: 10

GOALSCORERS

League (66): Hughes 18, Taylor 10, Liddell 8 (5 pens), Whitaker 6, Alessandra 5, Smalley 5, Allott 3, Hazell 3, Eardley 2 (1 pen), Brooke 1, Byfield 1, Jones D 1, Maher 1, Windass 1, own goal 1.
Carling Cup (0).
FA Cup (2): Taylor 1, Whitaker 1.
J Paint Trophy (1): Whitaker 1.

Crossley M 21	Eardley N 31 + 3	Lomax K 27	Maher K 21 + 7	Hazell R 43	Gregan S 38 + 2	Liddell A 18 + 14	Allott M 44 + 1	O'Grady C 3 + 10	Davies C 5 + 7	Taylor C 42	Alessandra L 12 + 20	Hughes L 36 + 1	Whitaker D 30 + 9	Smalley D 22 + 12	Byrne R 3 + 1	Stam S 11 + 2	Jones D 23	Fleming G 17 + 1	Ormerod B 2 + 3	Byfield D 8	Lee K 6 + 1	Windass D 9 + 2	Golbourne S 7 + 1	Budtz J 3	Hines S 4	Kabba S 7 + 1	Supple S 5	Westlake I 5	Ferreira F — + 1	Wolfenden M 1 + 4	Black P 2 + 1	Brooke R — + 1	Match No.
1	2	3	4[3]	5	6	7	8	9[1]	10[2]	11	12	13	14																				1
1	2	3	12	5	6	7[2]	8	14		11			9[1]	10[3]	4	13																	2
1	2	3	13	5	6	7[1]	8[2]	14		11			9	10[3]	4	12																	3
1	2	3		5	6	7[1]	8	13		11			9[2]	10	4	12																	4
1	2	3		5	6	7[1]	8	13	10	11			9[2]		4	12																	5
1	2	3	12	5	6	7[2]	8[1]	14		11			9	10[3]	4	13																	6
1	2	3		5	6[4]	7[3]	8	12	13	11			9[2]	10[1]	4	14																	7
1	2	3		5		7[2]	8	12		11			9[1]	10	4	13	6																8
1	2			5		7[1]	8	9[2]	10	11		13			4	12	6	3															9
1[6]	2			5		7[1]	8		10	11		13	9[2]		4	12	6	3	15														10
1	2			5	6	12	8	10[2]		11			9		4		7	3[1]		13													11
1	2[1]			5	6		8	12		11		13	9		4		7	3		10[2]													12
1	2	12		5	6	7[2]	8[1]	14		11			9		4	13		3		10[3]													13
1	2			5	6	7[1]	8			11			9[2]	10	4	12		3		13													14
1	2[1]	12		5	6	7[2]	8			11			9[3]	10	4	13		3		14													15
1	2		4	5	13	12[4]	8			11			9[4]			7[1]	6	3		10													16
1	2		4	5		7	8			11			9				6	3		10													17
1	2		4[1]	5		7	8	13		11			9			12	6	3		10[2]													18
1	2	12		5	6[3]	7[1]	8[2]	9		11		13		10	4	14		3															19
	2	3		5	12		8			11			9		4		6	1	7[1]	10													20
	2	3		5		7[2]	8	14		11	12		9		4[3]	13	6	1		10[1]													21
	2	3	4	5	12		8	13		11	14		9				6[1]	1		10[3]	7[2]												22
	2	3	4[2]	5	6	12	8			11	14		9			13		1		10[3]	7[1]												23
	2	3	4[1]	5	6	12	8	13	7	11			9					1		10[2]													24
	2	3	4	5	6	13	8	12		11	14		9[1]				7[2]	1		10[3]													25
	2	3	4[1]	5	6	12	8[2]	13		11			9				7	1		10													26
		3		5	6	12	8	13		11			9[2]		4		7[1]	1	2	10													27
	2			5	6	12	8			11		13	9		4[1]		7	1		10[2]	3												28
	2			5	6		8			11	12		9		4		7	1		10[1]	3												29
	2		4	5	6		8			11	12		9[1]				7	1[4]		10	3												30
	2		4[1]	5	6	12	8			11		13	9					1		10[2]	3					7							31
12			4[1]	5	6	13	8			11			9				7	1	2	10[2]	3												32
12				5	6	13	8			11	14		9[2]		4		7	1	2	10[3]	3[1]												33
	2		4	5	6		8			11	12		9				7	1			3					10[1]							34
	2		4	5	6	12	8			11		13	9[3]				7[1]	1			3	14				10[2]							35
	2		4	5	6	11[2]	8[1]	13					9	12			7	1			3	14				10[3]							36
	2		4[1]		6	13	8			11[2]	14		9	12			7	1			3					10[3]		5					37
	2				6		8			11[2]			9				7[1]	1		10	3				4	13	12	5[4]					38
	2		4[1]	5	6		8			11		13	9[2]	12			7[3]	1		10						14							39
				5	6	12	8			11[1]			9	10	4			1	2		3					7							40
	2		4	5	6		8			11			9[1]	10				1			3					7		12					41
	2		4[1]	5	6		8	13		11				12			7	1		10[4]		14				9[2]					3[3]		42
	2	13		5	6		8			11	4[3]			10				1			3		7[2]			9[1]				12	14		43
1	2			5	6		8	13		11			9	12	4		7				3[1]									10[2]			44
1	2		4	5	6		8						9[1]	12						10	3	11[2]							7	13			45
12	2		4	5	6		8					10[3]	9					1			7[2]					11				13	3[1]	14	46

FA Cup

First Round — Cheltenham T (a) 2-2
(h) 0-1

Carling Cup

First Round — Rochdale (a) 0-0
Second Round — Burnley (a) 0-3

J Paint Trophy

First Round — Morecambe (h) 1-1

PETERBOROUGH UNITED   FL Championship

FOUNDATION

The old Peterborough & Fletton club, founded in 1923, was suspended by the FA during season 1932–33 and disbanded. Local enthusiasts determined to carry on and in 1934 a new professional club, Peterborough United, was formed and entered the Midland League the following year. Peterborough's first success came in 1939–40, but from 1955–56 to 1959–60 they won five successive titles. During the 1958–59 season they were undefeated in the Midland League. They reached the third round of the FA Cup, won the Northamptonshire Senior Cup, the Maunsell Cup and were runners-up in the East Anglian Cup.

London Road, Peterborough PE2 8AL.

Telephone: (01733) 563 947.

Fax: (01733) 344 140.

Ticket Office: (01733) 865 674.

Website: www.theposh.com

Email: info@theposh.com

Ground Capacity: 15,460.

Record Attendance: 30,096 v Swansea T, FA Cup 5th rd, 20 February 1965.

Pitch Measurements: 112yd × 71yd.

Chairman: Darragh MacAnthony.

Chief Executive: Bob Symns.

Secretary: Karen Turner.

Player-Manager: Darren Ferguson.

Assistant Manager: Kevin Russell.

Physio: Keith Oakes.

Colours: Blue shirts with white design, white shorts, blue stockings.

Change Colours: All black.

Year Formed: 1934.

Turned Professional: 1934.

Ltd Co.: 1934.

Club Nickname: 'The Posh'.

Ground: 1934, London Road Stadium.

First Football League Game: 20 August 1960, Division 4, v Wrexham (h) W 3–0 – Walls; Stafford, Walker; Rayner, Rigby, Norris; Hails, Emery (1), Bly (1), Smith, McNamee (1).

Record League Victory: 9–1 v Barnet (a) Division 3, 5 September 1998 – Griemink; Hooper (1), Drury (Farell), Gill, Bodley, Edwards, Davies, Payne, Grazioli (5), Quinn (2) (Rowe), Houghton (Etherington) (1).

HONOURS

Football League: Division 1 best season: 10th, 1992–93; Division 2 1991–92 (play-offs); FL 1 – Runners-up 2008–09; FL 2 – Runners-up 2007–08; Division 4 – Champions 1960–61, 1973–74.

FA Cup: best season: 6th rd, 1965.

Football League Cup: Semi-final 1966.

SKY SPORTS FACT FILE

In successive home Midland League matches in December 1938, Peterborough United defeated Denaby United 7–0 and Boston United 12–0. In the second of these matches centre-forward Charlie MacCartney, signed from Darlington, scored five goals.

Record Cup Victory: 7–0 v Harlow T, FA Cup 1st rd, 16 November 1991 – Barber; Luke, Johnson, Halsall (1), Robinson D, Welsh, Sterling (1) (Butterworth), Cooper G (2 incl. 1p), Riley (1) (Culpin (1)), Charlery (1), Kimble.

Record Defeat: 1–8 v Northampton T, FA Cup 2nd rd (2nd replay), 18 December 1946.

Most League Points (2 for a win): 66, Division 4, 1960–61.

Most League Points (3 for a win): 92, FL 2, 2007–08.

Most League Goals: 134, Division 4, 1960–61.

Highest League Scorer in Season: Terry Bly, 52, Division 4, 1960–61.

Most League Goals in Total Aggregate: Jim Hall, 122, 1967–75.

Most League Goals in One Match: 5, Guiliano Grazioli v Barnet, Division 3, 5 September 1998.

Most Capped Player: James Quinn, 9 (50), Northern Ireland.

Most League Appearances: Tommy Robson, 482, 1968–81.

Youngest League Player: Matthew Etherington, 15 years 262 days v Brentford, 3 May 1997.

Record Transfer Fee Received: £700,000 from Tottenham H for Simon Davies, December 1999.

Record Transfer Fee Paid: £400,000 to Norwich C for Joe Lewis, January 2008.

Football League Record: 1960 Elected to Division 4; 1961–68 Division 3, when they were demoted for financial irregularities; 1968–74 Division 4; 1974–79 Division 3; 1979–91 Division 4; 1991–92 Division 3; 1992–94 Division 1; 1994–97 Division 2; 1997–2000 Division 3; 2000–04 Division 2; 2004–05 FL 1; 2005–08 FL 2; 2008–09 FL 1; 2009– FL C.

MANAGERS

Jock Porter 1934–36
Fred Taylor 1936–37
Vic Poulter 1937–38
Sam Madden 1938–48
Jack Blood 1948–50
Bob Gurney 1950–52
Jack Fairbrother 1952–54
George Swindin 1954–58
Jimmy Hagan 1958–62
Jack Fairbrother 1962–64
Gordon Clark 1964–67
Norman Rigby 1967–69
Jim Iley 1969–72
Noel Cantwell 1972–77
John Barnwell 1977–78
Billy Hails 1978–79
Peter Morris 1979–82
Martin Wilkinson 1982–83
John Wile 1983–86
Noel Cantwell 1986–88 *(continued as General Manager)*
Mick Jones 1988–89
Mark Lawrenson 1989–90
Dave Booth 1990–91
Chris Turner 1991–92
Lil Fuccillo 1992–93
John Still 1994–95
Mick Halsall 1995–96
Barry Fry 1996–2005
Mark Wright 2005–06
Keith Alexander 2006–07
Darren Ferguson January 2007–

LATEST SEQUENCES

Longest Sequence of League Wins: 9, 1.2.1992 – 14.3.1992.

Longest Sequence of League Defeats: 6, 16.12.2006 – 21.1.2007.

Longest Sequence of League Draws: 8, 18.12.1971 – 12.2.1972.

Longest Sequence of Unbeaten League Matches: 17, 17.12.1960 – 8.4.1961.

Longest Sequence Without a League Win: 17, 23.9.1978 – 30.12.1978.

Successive Scoring Runs: 33 from 20.9.1960.

Successive Non-scoring Runs: 6 from 13.8.2002.

TEN YEAR LEAGUE RECORD

		P	W	D	L	F	A	Pts	Pos
1999-2000	Div 3	46	22	12	12	63	54	78	5
2000-01	Div 2	46	15	14	17	61	66	59	12
2001-02	Div 2	46	15	10	21	64	59	55	17
2002-03	Div 2	46	14	16	16	51	54	58	11
2003-04	Div 2	46	12	16	18	58	58	52	18
2004-05	FL 1	46	9	12	25	49	73	39	23
2005-06	FL 2	46	17	11	18	57	49	62	9
2006-07	FL 2	46	18	11	17	70	61	65	10
2007-08	FL 2	46	28	8	10	84	43	92	2
2008-09	FL 1	46	26	11	9	78	54	89	2

DID YOU KNOW ?

Peterborough United started the 1939–40 season with an 8–0 win against Notts County reserves in the Midland League. Jack Haycox, signed from Northampton Town, scored four and Posh followed with two 4–0 successes before the competition was stopped.

PETERBOROUGH UNITED 2008–09 LEAGUE RECORD

Match No.	Date	Venue	Opponents	Result	H/T Score	Lg. Pos.	Goalscorers	Attendance
1	Aug 9	A	Southend U	L 0-1	0-0	—		8665
2	16	H	Leyton Orient	W 3-0	1-0	8	Mackail-Smith 2 [44, 69], McLean [50]	6643
3	23	A	Scunthorpe U	L 0-1	0-1	15		4217
4	30	H	Hartlepool U	L 1-2	0-0	20	Boyd [78]	5728
5	Sept 6	H	Bristol R	W 5-4	2-1	12	Mackail-Smith 3 (1 pen) [16, 51 (p), 65], McLean [23], Rendell [83]	4876
6	13	A	Northampton T	D 1-1	1-1	14	Boyd [15]	6520
7	20	H	Tranmere R	D 2-2	1-2	14	Mackail-Smith [41], Zakuani [77]	5735
8	27	A	Milton Keynes D	W 2-1	0-0	10	Mackail-Smith (pen) [73], Green [75]	10,876
9	Oct 4	H	Leeds U	W 2-0	0-0	9	Boyd [47], Mackail-Smith [90]	13,191
10	11	A	Walsall	W 2-1	2-0	7	Batt [2], Whelpdale [43]	4792
11	18	A	Carlisle U	D 3-3	1-1	8	Lee [34], Mackail-Smith 2 (1 pen) [60 (p), 90]	6074
12	21	H	Brighton & HA	D 0-0	0-0	—		5772
13	25	H	Huddersfield T	W 4-0	2-0	6	McLean 2 [12, 63], Boyd [24], Whelpdale [55]	7064
14	28	A	Crewe Alex	D 1-1	1-0	6	McLean [14]	3699
15	Nov 1	H	Hereford U	W 2-0	1-0	6	Mackail-Smith 2 [35, 68]	6087
16	15	A	Yeovil T	W 1-0	1-0	5	McLean [36]	4001
17	22	H	Colchester U	W 2-1	1-0	5	Mackail-Smith [45], Boyd [63]	7401
18	25	A	Swindon T	D 2-2	1-1	—	McGovern (og) [20], Batt [90]	6616
19	Dec 6	A	Stockport Co	W 3-1	1-0	4	Raynes (og) [22], Mackail-Smith [62], Tunnicliffe (og) [75]	6148
20	13	H	Oldham Ath	D 2-2	2-1	4	McLean 2 [12, 37]	6219
21	20	A	Leicester C	L 0-4	0-2	7		23,390
22	26	H	Millwall	W 1-0	1-0	6	McLean [23]	9351
23	28	A	Cheltenham T	W 6-3	1-0	4	Boyd [3], Lee [60], Mackail-Smith [63], Wright (og) [75], McLean [87], Whelpdale [90]	3976
24	Jan 17	H	Walsall	W 1-0	1-0	4	Whelpdale [6]	5705
25	20	H	Milton Keynes D	D 0-0	0-0	—		8982
26	24	A	Leeds U	L 1-3	0-0	4	Mackail-Smith [79]	22,766
27	27	H	Crewe Alex	W 4-2	0-1	—	Boyd 2 [50, 87], McLean [53], Keates [69]	5782
28	31	A	Huddersfield T	L 0-1	0-1	4		14,480
29	Feb 10	A	Brighton & HA	W 4-2	2-2	—	Mackail-Smith [38], McLean 2 [42, 76], Keates (pen) [65]	5087
30	14	H	Yeovil T	L 1-3	0-2	3	McLean [56]	6129
31	17	A	Tranmere R	D 1-1	1-1	—	Mackail-Smith [37]	4862
32	21	A	Hereford U	W 1-0	1-0	3	McLean [3]	3217
33	24	H	Carlisle U	W 1-0	0-0	—	McLean [69]	5103
34	28	H	Southend U	L 1-2	1-1	3	Keates (pen) [6]	7341
35	Mar 3	A	Leyton Orient	W 3-2	3-1	—	Whelpdale [6], Torres [12], Martin [45]	3381
36	7	A	Hartlepool U	W 2-1	1-1	2	Keates [11], Boyd [48]	3722
37	10	H	Scunthorpe U	W 2-1	0-1	—	Whelpdale [63], Mackail-Smith [86]	5637
38	14	H	Northampton T	W 1-0	1-0	2	Lee [33]	8881
39	21	A	Bristol R	W 1-0	0-0	2	McLean [70]	7103
40	28	H	Leicester C	W 2-0	1-0	2	Lee [44], Whelpdale [79]	14,110
41	Apr 4	A	Oldham Ath	W 2-1	1-1	2	Mackail-Smith 2 [26, 86]	5083
42	10	H	Cheltenham T	D 1-1	1-0	—	McLean [36]	9817
43	13	A	Millwall	L 0-2	0-1	2		10,518
44	18	H	Stockport Co	W 1-0	1-0	2	Mackail-Smith [25]	8333
45	25	A	Colchester U	W 1-0	1-0	2	Lee [40]	6532
46	May 2	H	Swindon T	D 2-2	1-2	2	Mackail-Smith [40], Keates [90]	10,886

Final League Position: 2

GOALSCORERS

League (78): Mackail-Smith 23 (3 pens), McLean 18, Boyd 9, Whelpdale 7, Keates 5 (2 pens), Lee 5, Batt 2, Green 1, Martin 1, Rendell 1, Torres 1, Zakuani 1, own goals 4.
Carling Cup (1): Boyd 1.
FA Cup (4): Mackail-Smith 3, McLean 1.
J Paint Trophy (0).

Lewis J 46	Martin R 46	Williams T 22 + 3	Lee C 39 + 5	Morgan C 26 + 1	Westwood C 10 + 6	Whelpdale C 29 + 10	Keates D 37 + 1	Mackail-Smith C 43 + 3	McLean A 39 + 3	Boyd G 46	Torres S 10 + 5	Blackett S 7 + 4	Hyde M 5 + 4	Charnock K 2	Day J 5	Hatch L — + 1	Coutts P 34 + 3	Rendell S 2 + 1	Zakuani G 32	Green D 3 + 13	Batt S 10 + 20	Crofts A 4 + 5	Blanchett D 2 + 1	Chester J 5	Frecklington L 2 + 5	Wright B — + 1	McKeown J — + 1	Match No.
1	2	3	4	5	6	7¹	8	9	10	11	12																	1
1	2	12	4³	5	6	13	8	9	10	11	7²	3¹	14															2
1	2	13	4			12	8	9	10	11	7³	6		5¹	3²	14												3
1	2			12	5	13	8²	9	10	11	7	6	4¹				3											4
1	2	4²			6	12	8	9	10³	11	7¹	5					3			13	14							5
1	2			5		7²	8	9		11	12				3		4¹	10	6	13								6
1	2	4¹		5		7		9		11					3		8	10²	6	12	13							7
1	2	3	12	5	13	7³		9		11					4		8		6²	14	10¹							8
1	2	3	12	5	13			9		11					4		8¹		6	7²	10							9
1	2	3	4			7¹	13	9	12	11		6		5			8²		10									10
1	2	3⁴		5	12	7²		9	13	11			14		4¹		8		6		10							11
1	2	3	4	5		7¹		9	12	11							8		6	13	10²							12
1	2	3	4	5		7		9	10³	11	13					12	8¹		6		14							13
1	2	3	4¹	5		7³		9	10²	11	13					12	8		6		14							14
1	2	3	4	5		7²		9	10¹	11	12						8		6		13							15
1	2	3	4²	5	12		8	9¹	10	11	7³	13							6		14							16
1	2	3	4²	5			8	9	10	11	7¹						6			12	13							17
1	2	3		5	12		8	9	10	11	7²						6¹			13	4							18
1	2¹	3	12	5			8	9	10	11²							6		13	7	4							19
1	2³	3	12	5			8	9	10	11							6		13	7²	4							20
1	2		4	5	3¹	7	8	9³	10	11	12								13	14	6²							21
1	2	3	4	5		7¹	8	9	10	11²							6³		13	12	14							22
1	2	3	4	5		7	8	9	10	11							6¹			12								23
1	2	3		5		7	8	9	10	11							4		6									24
1	2	3		5		7¹	8	9	10	11							4		6		12							25
1	2	3		5		7¹	8	9	10	11							4		6		12							26
1	2			5		7¹	8³	9²	10	11							4		6	13	12	14	3					27
1	2	3		5¹		7²	8³	9	10	11							4		6	13	12	14						28
1	2	3				12	8	9²	10	11							4		6		7¹			5	13			29
1	2			5¹		12	8	9	10	11							4		6	13	7²				3			30
1	2	3				7¹	8	9	10	11							4		6					5	12			31
1	2	3²				12	8	9	10	11							4		6	13				5	7¹			32
1	2	3				12	8	9	10	11	13						4		6²					5	7¹			33
1	2	3²	4			7¹	8	9	10	11	12	6					4							5	13			34
1	2	3	6	5		7¹	8	12	10	11²	9						4			13								35
1	2		6	5		7	8	12	10	11	9¹						4		3									36
1	2	13	3	5²		7	8	12	10	11	9¹						4		6									37
1	2	3		5	12	7	8	9²	10	11¹							4		6	13								38
1	2	3¹	6	5		7	8	9	10	11	12						4											39
1	2	3		5		7	8	9¹	10	11							4		6		12							40
1	2	3⁴		5	12	7²	8	9	10	11						14	4		6¹	13								41
1	2		6	5			8	9	10	11		3					4			12	7¹							42
1	2			5	12	7²	8	9	10	11³		3¹					4		6	14	13							43
1	2	3		5	6	12	8	9	10	11							4²				7¹				13			44
1	2	3		5		7	8¹	9	10²	11							4		6	13					12			45
1⁶	2	3		5			8	9¹	10	11							4		6	13	7²				12		15	46

FA Cup

First Round	AFC Hornchurch	(a)	1-0
Second Round	Tranmere R	(h)	0-0
		(a)	2-1
Third Round	WBA	(a)	1-1
		(h)	0-2

Carling Cup

First Round	Bristol C	(a)	1-2
Second Round			

J Paint Trophy

Second Round	Dagenham & R	(h)	0-1

PLYMOUTH ARGYLE FL Championship

FOUNDATION

The club was formed in September 1886 as the Argyle Football Club by former public and private school pupils who wanted to continue playing the game. The meeting was held in a room above the Borough Arms (a Coffee House), Bedford Street, Plymouth. It was common then to choose a local street/terrace as a club name and Argyle or Argyll was a fashionable name throughout the land due to Queen Victoria's great interest in Scotland.

Home Park, Plymouth, Devon PL2 3DQ.
Telephone: (01752) 562 561.
Fax: (01752) 606 167.
Ticket Office: 0845 338 7232.
Website: www.pafc.co.uk
Email: argyle@pafc.co.uk
Ground Capacity: 21,118.
Record Attendance: 43,596 v Aston Villa, Division 2, 10 October 1936.
Pitch Measurements: 112yd × 73yd.
Chairman: Paul Stapleton.
Vice-chairman: Robert Dennerly.
Chief Executive: Michael Dunford.
Secretary: Carole Rowntree.
Manager: Paul Sturrock.
Assistant Manager: Kevin Summerfield.
Physio: Paul Maxwell.
Colours: Green shirts with one white sleeve, white shorts, black stockings.
Change Colours: Tangerine shirts, green shorts, tangerine stockings.
Year Formed: 1886.
Turned Professional: 1903.
Ltd Co.: 1903.
Previous Name: 1886, Argyle Athletic Club; 1903, Plymouth Argyle.
Club Nickname: 'The Pilgrims'.
Ground: 1886, Home Park.
First Football League Game: 28 August 1920, Division 3, v Norwich C (h) D 1–1 – Craig; Russell, Atterbury; Logan, Dickinson, Forbes; Kirkpatrick, Jack, Bowler, Heeps (1), Dixon.
Record League Victory: 8–1 v Millwall, Division 2, 16 January 1932 – Harper; Roberts, Titmuss; Mackay, Pullan, Reed; Grozier, Bowden (2), Vidler (3), Leslie (1), Black (1), (1 og). 8–1 v Hartlepool U (a), Division 2, 7 May 1994 – Nicholls; Patterson (Naylor), Hill, Burrows, Comyn, McCall (1), Barlow, Castle (1), Landon (3), Marshall (1), Dalton (2).

HONOURS

Football League: Division 2 – Champions 2003–04; Division 3 (S) – Champions 1929–30, 1951–52; Runners-up 1921–22, 1922–23, 1923–24, 1924–25, 1925–26, 1926–27 (record of six consecutive years); Division 3 – Champions 1958–59, 2001–02; Runners-up 1974–75, 1985–86.
FA Cup: Semi-final 1984.
Football League Cup: Semi-final 1965, 1974.

SKY SPORTS FACT FILE

On 6 December 1930 Plymouth Argyle – no win in eight matches – hosted Tottenham Hotspur. In 30 minutes Argyle lost goalkeeper Harry Cann injured. Fred Titmuss took over but goals from Tommy Grozier and Sammy Black (his 100th) sealed victory.

Record Cup Victory: 6–0 v Corby T, FA Cup 3rd rd, 22 January 1966 – Leiper; Book, Baird; Williams, Nelson, Newman; Jones (1), Jackson (1), Bickle (3), Piper (1), Jennings.

Record Defeat: 0–9 v Stoke C, Division 2, 17 December 1960.

Most League Points (2 for a win): 68, Division 3 (S), 1929–30.

Most League Points (3 for a win): 102, Division 3, 2001–02.

Most League Goals: 107, Division 3 (S), 1925–26 and 1951–52.

Highest League Scorer in Season: Jack Cock, 32, Division 3 (S), 1926–27.

Most League Goals in Total Aggregate: Sammy Black, 180, 1924–38.

Most League Goals in One Match: 5, Wilf Carter v Charlton Ath, Division 2, 27 December 1960.

Most Capped Player: Moses Russell, 20 (23), Wales.

Most League Appearances: Kevin Hodges, 530, 1978–92.

Youngest League Player: Lee Phillips, 16 years 43 days v Gillingham, 29 October 1996.

Record Transfer Fee Received: £3,000,000 from Hull C for Peter Halmosi, July 2008.

Record Transfer Fee Paid: £500,000 to Cardiff C for Steve MacLean, January 2008; £500,000 to QPR for Simon Walton, August 2008.

Football League Record: 1920 Original Member of Division 3; 1921–30 Division 3 (S); 1930–50 Division 2; 1950–52 Division 3 (S); 1952–56 Division 2; 1956–58 Division 3 (S); 1958–59 Division 3; 1959–68 Division 2; 1968–75 Division 3; 1975–77 Division 2; 1977–86 Division 3; 1986–95 Division 2; 1995–96 Division 3; 1996–98 Division 2; 1998–2002 Division 3; 2002–04 Division 2; 2004– FL C.

MANAGERS

Frank Brettell 1903–05
Bob Jack 1905–06
Bill Fullerton 1906–07
Bob Jack 1910–38
Jack Tresadern 1938–47
Jimmy Rae 1948–55
Jack Rowley 1955–60
Neil Dougall 1961
Ellis Stuttard 1961–63
Andy Beattie 1963–64
Malcolm Allison 1964–65
Derek Ufton 1965–68
Billy Bingham 1968–70
Ellis Stuttard 1970–72
Tony Waiters 1972–77
Mike Kelly 1977–78
Malcolm Allison 1978–79
Bobby Saxton 1979–81
Bobby Moncur 1981–83
Johnny Hore 1983–84
Dave Smith 1984–88
Ken Brown 1988–90
David Kemp 1990–92
Peter Shilton 1992–95
Steve McCall 1995
Neil Warnock 1995–97
Mick Jones 1997–98
Kevin Hodges 1998–2000
Paul Sturrock 2000–04
Bobby Williamson 2004–05
Tony Pulis 2005–06
Ian Holloway 2006–07
Paul Sturrock November 2007–

LATEST SEQUENCES

Longest Sequence of League Wins: 9, 8.3.1986 – 12.4.1986.

Longest Sequence of League Defeats: 9, 12.10.1963 – 7.12.1963.

Longest Sequence of League Draws: 5, 26.2.2000 – 14.3.2000.

Longest Sequence of Unbeaten League Matches: 22, 20.4.1929 – 21.12.1929.

Longest Sequence Without a League Win: 13, 27.4.1963 – 2.10.1963.

Successive Scoring Runs: 39 from 15.4.1939.

Successive Non-scoring Runs: 5 from 20.9.1947.

TEN YEAR LEAGUE RECORD

		P	W	D	L	F	A	Pts	Pos
1999-2000	Div 3	46	16	18	12	55	51	66	12
2000-01	Div 3	46	15	13	18	54	61	58	12
2001-02	Div 3	46	31	9	6	71	28	102	1
2002-03	Div 2	46	17	14	15	63	52	65	8
2003-04	Div 2	46	26	12	8	85	41	90	1
2004-05	FL C	46	14	11	21	52	64	53	17
2005-06	FL C	46	13	17	16	39	46	56	14
2006-07	FL C	46	17	16	13	63	62	67	11
2007-08	FL C	46	17	13	16	60	50	64	10
2008-09	FL C	46	13	12	21	44	57	51	21

DID YOU KNOW ?

Unusual names from the proliferation of foreign players in the last two decades are no longer a novelty. But in pre-war days there was ex-Royal Navy seaman Jack Demmelweek who had two spells with Plymouth Argyle as an outside-right from 1928 and 1931.

PLYMOUTH ARGYLE 2008–09 LEAGUE RECORD

Match No.	Date	Venue	Opponents	Result	H/T Score	Lg. Pos.	Goalscorers	Attendance
1	Aug 9	H	Wolverhampton W	D 2-2	1-1	—	Fallon [7], Seip [55]	14,789
2	16	A	Reading	L 0-2	0-1	18		19,202
3	23	H	Swansea C	L 0-1	0-1	22		9203
4	30	A	Burnley	D 0-0	0-0	21		10,032
5	Sept 13	H	Norwich C	L 1-2	0-1	24	Gallagher [90]	11,185
6	16	A	Watford	W 2-1	1-0	—	Duguid [30], Summerfield (pen) [72]	13,237
7	20	A	Crystal Palace	W 2-1	1-0	18	Gallagher 2 [28, 56]	14,209
8	27	H	Nottingham F	W 1-0	1-0	12	Fallon [41]	12,594
9	30	A	Bristol C	D 2-2	2-0	—	Mackie [6], Fallon [18]	17,489
10	Oct 4	H	Sheffield W	W 4-0	3-0	5	Beevers (og) [15], Gallagher [25], Mackie [30], Seip [90]	10,795
11	18	A	Derby Co	L 1-2	1-1	13	Gallagher [8]	28,495
12	21	H	Preston NE	W 1-0	1-0	—	Fallon [18]	9824
13	25	H	Ipswich T	L 1-3	0-2	10	Cathcart [79]	12,294
14	28	A	Sheffield W	W 1-0	1-0	—	MacLean [23]	16,515
15	Nov 1	A	Sheffield U	L 0-2	0-0	12		25,601
16	8	H	Charlton Ath	D 2-2	1-0	11	Doumbe [39], Mpenza [90]	10,716
17	15	A	Coventry C	W 1-0	0-0	9	Noone [87]	18,528
18	22	H	Cardiff C	W 2-1	2-0	7	Mpenza [39], Gallagher [41]	11,438
19	25	A	Southampton	D 0-0	0-0	—		14,895
20	29	H	Blackpool	L 1-2	0-0	9	Gallagher [67]	9969
21	Dec 6	A	Doncaster R	L 0-1	0-1	11		10,187
22	9	H	Birmingham C	L 0-1	0-0	—		10,446
23	13	H	QPR	D 1-1	0-1	13	MacLean [83]	10,747
24	20	A	Barnsley	L 0-2	0-1	13		10,944
25	26	H	Southampton	W 2-0	1-0	12	Fallon [38], Summerfield (pen) [52]	15,197
26	28	A	Cardiff C	L 0-1	0-0	15		19,145
27	Jan 17	A	Nottingham F	L 0-2	0-1	15		20,392
28	27	H	Bristol C	L 0-2	0-0	—		11,438
29	31	A	Ipswich T	D 0-0	0-0	16		20,333
30	Feb 3	A	Preston NE	D 1-1	1-1	—	Mackie [13]	10,660
31	7	H	Derby Co	L 0-3	0-1	17		10,893
32	14	A	Charlton Ath	L 0-2	0-1	18		21,876
33	17	H	Crystal Palace	L 1-3	0-3	—	Sawyer [68]	10,710
34	21	H	Sheffield U	D 2-2	0-0	20	Fletcher [49], Gallagher [70]	10,044
35	28	A	Wolverhampton W	W 1-0	1-0	19	Gallagher [1]	25,710
36	Mar 3	H	Watford	W 2-1	1-0	—	Gallagher 2 (1 pen) [35 (p), 73]	9529
37	7	H	Reading	D 2-2	1-1	17	Gallagher [20], Mackie [56]	14,014
38	10	A	Swansea C	L 0-1	0-0	—		13,103
39	14	A	Norwich C	L 0-1	0-0	19		25,064
40	21	H	Burnley	L 1-2	1-1	21	Judge [17]	11,246
41	Apr 4	A	Blackpool	W 1-0	0-0	19	Sawyer [86]	8103
42	11	H	Coventry C	W 4-0	4-0	19	Barnes [15], Mackie [26], Judge [27], Seip [37]	12,568
43	13	A	Birmingham C	D 1-1	1-0	19	Gallagher (pen) [26]	19,323
44	18	H	Doncaster R	L 0-3	0-2	19		11,100
45	25	A	QPR	D 0-0	0-0	19		14,779
46	May 3	H	Barnsley	L 1-2	1-1	21	Sawyer [12]	14,529

Final League Position: 21

GOALSCORERS

League (44): Gallagher 13 (2 pens), Fallon 5, Mackie 5, Sawyer 3, Seip 3, Judge 2, MacLean 2, Mpenza 2, Summerfield 2 (2 pens), Barnes 1, Cathcart 1, Doumbe 1, Duguid 1, Fletcher 1, Noone 1, own goal 1.
Carling Cup (0).
FA Cup (1): Duguid 1.

Stack G 5	Duguid K 39	Barker C 38+2	Walton S 12+1	Doumbe S 21+3	Seip M 41	Clark C 30+6	Summerfield L 28+1	Fallon R 26+18	Easter J 2+2	Mackie J 35+8	Timar K 13+8	Paterson J 7+10	Puncheon J 5+1	McNamee D 5+5	MacLean S 11+10	Gallagher P 36+4	Noone C 3+18	Mpenza E 3+6	Folly Y 6+5	Larrieu R 41	Cathcart C 30+1	Marin N 1+5	Sawyer G 13	Gray D 14	Judge A 15+2	Barnes A 12+3	Fletcher C 13	Douala R 1+1	Donnelly G —+2	Match No.
1	2	3	4	5^1	6	7^2	8^3	9	10	11	12	13	14																	1
1	2	3	4^2	5	6^1	7	8	9		10^3	12				11	13	14													2
1	2	3	4	5	6	7	8^1	10^2		13	14				11	12	9^3													3
1	2	3	4		6	7	8^3	13		5	14	11				9^2	10^1	12												4
1	2	3	4^3	12	6	7		13	10^2			5^4				11^1		9	14	8										5
	2	12		5	6	7	8	9		10		3^1				11^2	13			1	4									6
	2	3^1		5	6	7	8	9		10^3	12					11^2	14			1	4									7
	2	3		5	6	7^2	8	9		10^3	12					11	13			1	4^1	14								8
	2	3		5	6	7	8^3	9^1		10^3	12				14	13				1	4									9
	2	3		5	6	7^3	8	9		10^1		12				11^2	13			1	4	14								10
	2	3^1		5	6	7^2	8	9		10^3		12				11	13			1	4	14								11
	2	3		5^1	6	7	8	9		10		12				11				1	4									12
	2	3			6	7	8^1	9^3		10^2					5	12	11	14		1	4	13								13
	2	3	14		6	7	8	12				13	10^2		5^3	9^1	11			1	4									14
	2	3		5^3	6	7^2	8	12		13	4				14	9^1	11			1		10^1								15
	2	3		5	6	7	8^2	10		12					9^1	11^3	13	14		1	4									16
	2	3		5	6	7	8	9		11^2					12		13	10^1		1	4									17
2^3	3			5	6	7	8	9		12					13	11^1		10^2	14	1	4									18
	3			5	6	7	8	9^1		11^2					10	12	13		4	1	2									19
	3			5	6	7	8	9^3		12					13	11	14	10^2	4^1	1	2									20
	3			5^1	6	7	8	12		13		11^3			10	9^2	14		4	1	2									21
	3	4			6	2	8^1	9		7	5	11^2			12	10	13			1										22
	3	4			6	2	8	9		7^3	5	11^2			12	10^1	13			1		14								23
	3	4^*			6	2^2	8			7^1	5	11^3		12	9	10	14			1	13									24
	2	3			6	7	8	9		12				4	13	10^2	11^1			1	5									25
		2^2	6			8	12	10	5			11^3	13^4	9		14			7^1	1	4		3							26
	7	3^1			6	13	8^3	9		11						12	10^2	14	4	1	5			2						27
	7	3		5^3	6	4	8	10		11	13					9^1	12	14		1	2^2									28
	7	3	4	12	6	8^2		10		11	5			2^1		9				1					13					29
	7	3^2	4	12			8	13	9	11	5			2^1		10^3	14			1	6									30
	7		4	2^1		12		9^2		11	5					10				1	6		3		8	13				31
	2	3	4			7^1	8^2	12		10	5	13				9				1	6				11					32
	7		2					10¹		4	5	11			9^2	12	13			1	6		3		8^3	14				33
	7	5						9		11^3		13				10^1	12			1	6		3	2	8^2	14	4			34
	7	3			6	8		12		11						9^2				1	5		2	13	10^1	4				35
	7	3			6	13		12		11						9^1				1	5		2	8^2	10	4				36
	7				6			12		11	13	14				9^1				1	5^2		3	2	8^3	10	4			37
	2				6			12		10	5	14		13		8^2				1			3^3	7	11	9^1	4			38
	2	3^3			6			12		8		14				10	13			1	5			7	11^2	9^1	4			39
	7				6			12		11^2						13	10	14		1	5		3	2	8^3	9^1	4			40
	7	12			6	13		14		11						10^3				1	5^1		3	2	8^2	9	4			41
	7	5			6	12		13		11^2						10				1			3	2	8^1	9^3	4	14		42
	7	5			6			12		11^1						10				1			3	2	8	9	4			43
	7	5			6	14		13		11						10^3				1			3	2	8^2	9^1	4		12	44
	7	5			6			12		11						10				1			3	2	8	9^1	4			45
	7	5			6			12								11	13			1			3	2	8^3	9^2	4	10^1	14	46

FA Cup
Third Round   Arsenal   (a)   1-3

Carling Cup
First Round   Luton T   (a)   0-2

PORTSMOUTH

FA Premiership

FOUNDATION

At a meeting held in his High Street, Portsmouth offices in 1898, solicitor Alderman J. E. Pink and five other business and professional men agreed to buy some ground close to Goldsmith Avenue for £4,950 which they developed into Fratton Park in record breaking time. A team of professionals was signed up by manager Frank Brettell and entry to the Southern League obtained for the new club's September 1899 kick-off.

Fratton Park, Frogmore Road, Portsmouth, Hampshire PO4 8RA.

Telephone: (02392) 731 204.

Fax: (02392) 734 129.

Ticket Office: (0844) 847 1898.

Website: www.pompeyfc.co.uk

Email: info@pompeyfc.co.uk

Ground Capacity: 20,688.

Record Attendance: 51,385 v Derby Co, FA Cup 6th rd, 26 February 1949.

Pitch Measurements: 100m × 65m.

Owner: Alexander Gaydamak.

Chief Executive: Peter Storrie.

Secretary: Paul Weld.

Manager: Paul Hart.

Assistant Manager: Brian Kidd.

Physio: Gary Sadler MCSP, SROP.

Colours: Blue shirts with yellow trim, blue shorts, blue stockings.

Change Colours: White shirts, blue sleeves with white trim, white shorts with blue trim, white stockings.

Year Formed: 1898.

Turned Professional: 1898.

Ltd Co.: 1898.

Club Nickname: 'Pompey'.

Ground: 1898, Fratton Park.

First Football League Game: 28 August 1920, Division 3, v Swansea T (h) W 3–0 – Robson; Probert, Potts; Abbott, Harwood, Turner; Thompson, Stringfellow (1), Reid (1), James (1), Beedie.

Record League Victory: 9–1 v Notts Co, Division 2, 9 April 1927 – McPhail; Clifford, Ted Smith; Reg Davies (1), Foxall, Moffat; Forward (1), Mackie (2), Haines (3), Watson, Cook (2).

Record Cup Victory: 7–0 v Stockport Co, FA Cup 3rd rd, 8 January 1949 – Butler; Rookes, Ferrier; Scoular, Flewin, Dickinson; Harris (3), Barlow, Clarke (2), Phillips (2), Froggatt.

HONOURS

Football League: Division 1 – Champions 1948–49, 1949–50, 2002–03; Division 2 – Runners-up 1926–27, 1986–87; Division 3 (S) – Champions 1923–24; Division 3 – Champions 1961–62, 1982–83.

FA Cup: Winners 1939, 2008; Runners-up 1929, 1934.

Football League Cup: best season: 5th rd, 1961, 1986.

European Competitions: UEFA Cup: 2008–09.

SKY SPORTS FACT FILE

The 31st August 1946 was a milestone day for Portsmouth and two outstanding wing-halves at the club. Jimmy Dickinson signed in January 1944 made his League debut, Jimmy Guthrie signed from Dundee nine years earlier became the fifth chairman of the PFA.

Record Defeat: 0–10 v Leicester C, Division 1, 20 October 1928.

Most League Points (2 for a win): 65, Division 3, 1961–62.

Most League Points (3 for a win): 98, Division 1, 2002–03.

Most League Goals: 97, Division 1, 2002–03.

Highest League Scorer in Season: Guy Whittingham, 42, Division 1, 1992–93.

Most League Goals in Total Aggregate: Peter Harris, 194, 1946–60.

Most League Goals in One Match: 5, Alf Strange v Gillingham, Division 3, 27 January 1923; 5, Peter Harris v Aston Villa, Division 1, 3 September 1958.

Most Capped Player: Jimmy Dickinson, 48, England.

Most League Appearances: Jimmy Dickinson, 764, 1946–65.

Youngest League Player: Clive Green, 16 years 259 days v Wrexham, 21 August 1976.

Record Transfer Fee Received: £20,000,000 from Real Madrid for Lassana Diarra, January 2009.

Record Transfer Fee Paid: Reported fee of £11,000,000 to Liverpool for Peter Crouch, July 2008.

Football League Record: 1920 Original Member of Division 3; 1921 Division 3 (S); 1924–27 Division 2; 1927–59 Division 1; 1959–61 Division 2; 1961–62 Division 3; 1962–76 Division 2; 1976–78 Division 3; 1978–80 Division 4; 1980–83 Division 3; 1983–87 Division 2; 1987–88 Division 1; 1988–92 Division 2; 1992–2003 Division 1; 2003– FA Premier League.

MANAGERS

Frank Brettell 1898–1901
Bob Blyth 1901–04
Richard Bonney 1905–08
Bob Brown 1911–20
John McCartney 1920–27
Jack Tinn 1927–47
Bob Jackson 1947–52
Eddie Lever 1952–58
Freddie Cox 1958–61
George Smith 1961–70
Ron Tindall 1970–73
  (General Manager to 1974)
John Mortimore 1973–74
Ian St John 1974–77
Jimmy Dickinson 1977–79
Frank Burrows 1979–82
Bobby Campbell 1982–84
Alan Ball 1984–89
John Gregory 1989–90
Frank Burrows 1990–91
Jim Smith 1991–95
Terry Fenwick 1995–98
Alan Ball 1998–99
Tony Pulis 2000
Steve Claridge 2000–01
Graham Rix 2001–02
Harry Redknapp 2002–04
Velimir Zajec 2004–05
Alain Perrin 2005
Harry Redknapp 2005–08
Tony Adams 2008–09
Paul Hart February 2009–

LATEST SEQUENCES

Longest Sequence of League Wins: 7, 17.8.2002 – 17.9.2002.

Longest Sequence of League Defeats: 9, 21.10.1975 – 6.12.1975.

Longest Sequence of League Draws: 5, 16.12.2000 – 13.1.2001.

Longest Sequence of Unbeaten League Matches: 15, 18.4.1924 – 18.10.1924.

Longest Sequence Without a League Win: 25, 29.11.1958 – 22.8.1959.

Successive Scoring Runs: 23 from 30.8.1930.

Successive Non-scoring Runs: 6 from 14.1.1939.

TEN YEAR LEAGUE RECORD

		P	W	D	L	F	A	Pts	Pos
1999-2000	Div 1	46	13	12	21	55	66	51	18
2000-01	Div 1	46	10	19	17	47	59	49	20
2001-02	Div 1	46	13	14	19	60	72	53	17
2002-03	Div 1	46	29	11	6	97	45	98	1
2003-04	PR Lge	38	12	9	17	47	54	45	13
2004-05	PR Lge	38	10	9	19	43	59	39	16
2005-06	PR Lge	38	10	8	20	37	62	38	17
2006-07	PR Lge	38	14	12	12	45	42	54	9
2007-08	PR Lge	38	16	9	13	48	40	57	8
2008-09	PR Lge	38	10	11	17	38	57	41	14

DID YOU KNOW ?

When Portsmouth won the FA Cup in 2008 their seven goals from six matches during the campaign was the fewest by any club since Wanderers in 1872 with four in only three games and the following year when given a bye to the final itself!

PORTSMOUTH 2008–09 LEAGUE RECORD

Match No.	Date	Venue	Opponents	Result	H/T Score	Lg. Pos.	Goalscorers	Attendance
1	Aug 17	A	Chelsea	L 0-4	0-3	—		41,468
2	25	H	Manchester U	L 0-1	0-1	—		20,540
3	30	A	Everton	W 3-0	2-0	16	Defoe 2 [12, 69], Johnson [40]	34,418
4	Sept 13	H	Middlesbrough	W 2-1	0-1	9	Defoe 2 [59, 86]	19,425
5	21	A	Manchester C	L 0-6	0-2	13		40,238
6	28	H	Tottenham H	W 2-0	1-0	9	Defoe (pen) [34], Crouch [68]	20,352
7	Oct 5	H	Stoke C	W 2-1	1-0	7	Crouch [25], Defoe [51]	19,248
8	18	A	Aston Villa	D 0-0	0-0	7		37,660
9	26	H	Fulham	D 1-1	0-0	7	Crouch [61]	19,233
10	29	A	Liverpool	L 0-1	0-0	—		43,378
11	Nov 1	H	Wigan Ath	L 1-2	0-1	9	Kranjcar [82]	18,416
12	8	H	Sunderland	W 2-1	0-1	9	Belhadj [51], Defoe (pen) [90]	37,712
13	15	A	West Ham U	D 0-0	0-0	9		32,328
14	22	H	Hull C	D 2-2	1-0	8	Crouch [20], Johnson [63]	20,240
15	30	A	Blackburn R	W 3-2	0-0	8	Crouch [49], Defoe [53], Davis [79]	18,111
16	Dec 7	A	WBA	D 1-1	0-1	7	Crouch [58]	24,964
17	14	H	Newcastle U	L 0-3	0-0	8		19,416
18	20	A	Bolton W	L 1-2	1-2	10	Crouch [20]	19,884
19	26	H	West Ham U	L 1-4	1-1	11	Belhadj [8]	20,102
20	28	A	Arsenal	L 0-1	0-0	12		60,092
21	Jan 18	A	Tottenham H	D 1-1	0-0	12	Nugent [59]	36,011
22	27	H	Aston Villa	L 0-1	0-1	—		19,073
23	31	A	Fulham	L 1-3	0-0	16	Nugent [84]	23,722
24	Feb 7	H	Liverpool	L 2-3	0-0	16	Nugent [62], Hreidarsson [78]	20,524
25	14	H	Manchester C	W 2-0	0-0	—	Johnson [70], Hreidarsson [75]	20,018
26	21	A	Stoke C	D 2-2	0-0	15	Kranjcar [75], Shawcross (og) [90]	26,354
27	Mar 3	H	Chelsea	L 0-1	0-0	—		20,326
28	14	A	Middlesbrough	D 1-1	1-0	17	Crouch [30]	24,281
29	21	H	Everton	W 2-1	1-1	15	Crouch 2 [22, 76]	20,388
30	Apr 4	A	Hull C	D 0-0	0-0	16		24,802
31	11	H	WBA	D 2-2	1-0	14	Kaboul [33], Kranjcar [65]	20,376
32	18	H	Bolton W	W 1-0	0-0	14	Kanu [78]	20,158
33	22	A	Manchester U	L 0-2	0-1	—		74,895
34	27	A	Newcastle U	D 0-0	0-0	—		47,481
35	May 2	H	Arsenal	L 0-3	0-2	14		20,418
36	9	A	Blackburn R	L 0-2	0-1	15		24,234
37	18	H	Sunderland	W 3-1	0-0	—	Utaka [60], Bardsley (og) [68], Traore A [88]	20,398
38	24	A	Wigan Ath	L 0-1	0-1	14		17,696

Final League Position: 14

GOALSCORERS
League (38): Crouch 10, Defoe 8 (2 pens), Johnson 3, Kranjcar 3, Nugent 3, Belhadj 2, Hreidarsson 2, Davis 1, Kaboul 1, Kanu 1, Traore A 1, Utaka 1, own goals 2.
Carling Cup (0).
FA Cup (2): Crouch 1, Kranjcar 1.
UEFA Cup (11): Crouch 4, Defoe 2, Diarra 1, Hreidarsson 1, Kaboul 1, Kanu 1, Mvuemba 1.
Community Shield (0).

James D 36	Kaboul Y 17+3	Hreidarsson H 19+4	Diarra L 11+1	Campbell S 32	Distin S 38	Johnson G 29	Diop P 15+1	Crouch P 38	Defoe J 17+2	Kranjcar N 16+5	Mvuemba A 1+5	Thomas J —+3	Davis S 31+1	Utaka J 4+14	Traore A 14+5	Belhadj N 21+8	Pamarot N 11+5	Little G 4+1	Hughes R 17+3	Kanu N 3+14	Nugent D 13+3	Wilson M 2+1	Mullins H 15+2	Pennant J 9+4	Basinas A 3	Gekas T —+1	Begovic A 2	Primus L —+1	Match No.
1	2	3	4^1	5	6	7	8	9	10	11^2	12	13																	1
1	2	·	4	5	6	3	8	9	10			13	7^1	12	11^2														2
1	2	14	4	5	6	3	8	9	10^1			13	7^2	12	11^3														3
1	2^3	12	4	5	6	3	8^2	9	10				7	13	11^1	14													4
1	8^2		4	5	6	2^3	12	9	10				7^1	13	11	3	14												5
1	12		4	5	6	2		9	10^1					13	11	3		8	7^2										6
1	12			5	6	2	8	9	10				4		11^3	3			7										7
1				5	6	2	8	9	10^2			13		12	$4^{\blacksquare}$	11^3	14	3	7^1										8
1	5	4^2			6		8	9	10				12	13	11^1	3	2		7										9
1	5	4^3			6		8	9	10^1			13	7	12	11^2	3	2			14									10
1			4	5	6	2	8^2	9	10			13	7	12	11^1	3^3	14												11
1			4	5	6	2	8	9^3	10^2			13	7	12	11^1	3	14												12
1	5	4^1			6	2	8	9^2	10			13	7	12	11	3													13
1	5		4		6	2	8	9	10^2			13		12	11^1	3	14		7^3										14
1			4	5	6	2	8	9^3	10			13	7^1	12	11^2	3	14												15
1			4		6	2	8	9^2	10			13	7^1	12	11	3			8^2										16
1			4	5	6	2		9	10			13	7^1	12	11	3			8^2										17
1	3	12	4	5	6	2	8^2	9	10			13			11				7^1										18
1			4	5	6	2		9	10^2			13		12	11	3		8	7^1										19
1			4	5	6	2	8^3	9				13		12	11	3	14		7^2		10^1								20
1	11^3	12	4	5	6	2	8	9				13				3			7^1	14	10^2								21
1	12	3		5^1	6	2		9					8	13		$11^{\blacksquare}$					10^2		4	7					22
1	5^1	3			6	2		9					8	13		11^2				12	10^3	14	4	7					23
1	3			5	6	2		9					8			11				12	10		4^1	7					24
1	3			5	6	2		9								11				12	10	13	4	7^1	8^2				25
1	3			5	6	2		9								11^2	14			12	10^1	13	4	7	8^3				26
1	3			5	6	2		9					8			11				12	10		4	7^1					27
1	3			5	6	2		9					8	13	14	11^3				12	10^1		4	7^2					28
1	2	3		5	6	7		9					8			11				12	10^1		4						29
1	2	3		5	6	$7^{\blacksquare}$		9					8	13		11^2				12	10^1		4						30
1	2	3		5	6			9					8			11				12	10^1		4	7^2	13				31
1	2^3	3		5	6	7		9					8	13		11^2	14			12	10^1		4						32
1	3			5	6	2		9					7			11			8	12	10^1		4						33
1	3			5	6	2		9					8			11			7	12	10^1		4						34
1	3^1			5	6	$2^{\blacksquare}$		9					8	13		11				12	10		4	7^2					35
1	2^3	3		5	6	7		9					8	13		11^1				12	10^2		4			14			36
	12	3		5	6	2		9^3					8	13		11^1			7		10^2		4				1	14	37
	2^1	3		5	6			9					8	13		11				12	10		4	7^2			1		38

FA Cup

Third Round	Bristol C	(h)	0-0	
		(a)	2-0	
Fourth Round	Swansea C	(h)	0-2	

UEFA Cup

First Round	Guimaraes	(h)	2-0
		(a)	2-2
Group E	Braga	(a)	0-3
	AC Milan	(h)	2-2
	Wolfsburg	(a)	2-3
	Heerenveen	(h)	3-0

Carling Cup

Third Round	Chelsea	(h)	0-4

Community Shield
(at Wembley)	Manchester U	0-0

PORT VALE   FL Championship 2

FOUNDATION

Formed in 1876 as Port Vale, adopting the prefix 'Burslem' in 1884
upon moving to that part of the city. It was dropped in 1909.

**Vale Park, Hamil Road, Burslem, Stoke-on-Trent
ST6 1AW.**

Telephone: (01782) 655 800.

Fax: (01782) 834 981.

Ticket Office: (01782) 655 832.

Website: www.port-vale.co.uk

Email: enquiries@port-vale.co.uk

Ground Capacity: 18,982.

Record Attendance: 49,768 v Aston Villa, FA Cup 5th rd,
20 February 1960.

Pitch Measurements: 114yd × 75yd.

Chairman/Chief Executive: Bill Bratt.

Vice-chairmen: Dave Smith, Peter Jackson.

Secretary: Bill Lodey.

Manager: Micky Adams.

Physio: John Bower.

Colours: Black and white striped shirts, black shorts, black stockings.

Change Colours: Dark blue shirts with light blue trim, dark blue shorts, blue stockings.

Year Formed: 1876.

Turned Professional: 1885.

Ltd Co.: 1911.

Previous Names: 1876, Port Vale; 1884, Burslem Port Vale; 1909, Port Vale.

Club Nickname: 'Valiants'.

Grounds: 1876, Limekin Lane, Longport; 1881, Westport; 1884, Moorland Road, Burslem; 1886,
Athletic Ground, Cobridge; 1913, Recreation Ground, Hanley; 1950, Vale Park.

First Football League Game: 3 September 1892, Division 2, v Small Heath (a) L 1–5 – Frail; Clutton,
Elson; Farrington, McCrindle, Delves; Walker, Scarratt, Bliss (1), Jones. (Only 10 men).

Record League Victory: 9–1 v Chesterfield, Division 2, 24 September 1932 – Leckie; Shenton, Poyser;
Sherlock, Round, Jones; McGrath, Mills, Littlewood (6), Kirkham (2), Morton (1).

Record Cup Victory: 7–1 v Irthlingborough, FA Cup 1st rd, 12 January 1907 – Matthews; Dunn,
Hamilton; Eardley, Baddeley, Holyhead; Carter, Dodds (2), Beats, Mountford (2), Coxon (3).

Record Defeat: 0–10 v Sheffield U, Division 2, 10 December 1892. 0–10 v Notts Co, Division 2,
26 February 1895.

HONOURS

Football League: Division 2 –
Runners-up 1993–94; Division 3 (N) –
Champions 1929–30, 1953–54;
Runners-up 1952–53; Division 4 –
Champions 1958–59.

FA Cup: Semi-final 1954, when in
Division 3.

Football League Cup: best season:
4th rd 2007.

Autoglass Trophy: Winners 1993.

Anglo-Italian Cup: Runners-up 1996.

LDV Vans Trophy: Winners 2001.

SKY SPORTS FACT FILE

As Port Vale tried to make a return to the Football
League in 1909–10 they re-signed a former half-back Joe
Brough from Tottenham Hotspur now as a striker. He
scored on his debut, hit 43 goals in the season and was
then snapped up by Liverpool.

Most League Points (2 for a win): 69, Division 3 (N), 1953–54.

Most League Points (3 for a win): 89, Division 2, 1992–93.

Most League Goals: 110, Division 4, 1958–59.

Highest League Scorer in Season: Wilf Kirkham 38, Division 2, 1926–27.

Most League Goals in Total Aggregate: Wilf Kirkham, 154, 1923–29, 1931–33.

Most League Goals in One Match: 6, Stewart Littlewood v Chesterfield, Division 2, 24 September 1922.

Most Capped Player: Chris Birchall, 22 (32), Trinidad & Tobago.

Most League Appearances: Roy Sproson, 761, 1950–72.

Youngest League Player: Malcolm McKenzie, 15 years 347 days v Newport Co, 12 April 1966.

Record Transfer Fee Received: £2,000,000 from Wimbledon for Gareth Ainsworth, October 1998.

Record Transfer Fee Paid: £500,000 to York C for Jon McCarthy, August 1995 and £500,000 to Lincoln C for Gareth Ainsworth, September 1997.

Football League Record: 1892 Original Member of Division 2. Failed re-election in 1896; Re-elected 1898; Resigned 1907; Returned in Oct, 1919, when they took over the fixtures of Leeds City; 1929–30 Division 3 (N); 1930–36 Division 2; 1936–38 Division 3 (N); 1938–52 Division 3 (S); 1952–54 Division 3 (N); 1954–57 Division 2; 1957–58 Division 3 (S); 1958–59 Division 4; 1959–65 Division 3; 1965–70 Division 4; 1970–78 Division 3; 1978–83 Division 4; 1983–84 Division 3; 1984–86 Division 4; 1986–89 Division 3; 1989–94 Division 2; 1994–2000 Division 1; 2000–04 Division 2; 2004–08 FL 1; 2008– FL 2.

LATEST SEQUENCES

Longest Sequence of League Wins: 8, 8.4.1893 – 30.9.1893.

Longest Sequence of League Defeats: 9, 9.3.1957 – 20.4.1957.

Longest Sequence of League Draws: 6, 26.4.1981 – 12.9.1981.

Longest Sequence of Unbeaten League Matches: 19, 5.5.1969 – 8.11.1969.

Longest Sequence Without a League Win: 17, 7.12.1991 – 21.3.1992.

Successive Scoring Runs: 22 from 12.9.1992.

Successive Non-scoring Runs: 4 from 10.2.1896.

MANAGERS

Sam Gleaves 1896–1905
  (Secretary-Manager)
Tom Clare 1905–11
A. S. Walker 1911–12
H. Myatt 1912–14
Tom Holford 1919–24
  (continued as Trainer)
Joe Schofield 1924–30
Tom Morgan 1930–32
Tom Holford 1932–35
Warney Cresswell 1936–37
Tom Morgan 1937–38
Billy Frith 1945–46
Gordon Hodgson 1946–51
Ivor Powell 1951
Freddie Steele 1951–57
Norman Low 1957–62
Freddie Steele 1962–65
Jackie Mudie 1965–67
Sir Stanley Matthews
  (General Manager) 1965–68
Gordon Lee 1968–74
Roy Sproson 1974–77
Colin Harper 1977
Bobby Smith 1977–78
Dennis Butler 1978–79
Alan Bloor 1979
John McGrath 1980–83
John Rudge 1984–99
Brian Horton 1999–2004
Martin Foyle 2004–07
Lee Sinnott 2007–08
Dean Glover 2008–09
Micky Adams June 2009–

TEN YEAR LEAGUE RECORD

		P	W	D	L	F	A	Pts	Pos
1999-2000	Div 1	46	7	15	24	48	69	36	23
2000-01	Div 2	46	16	14	16	55	49	62	11
2001-02	Div 2	46	16	10	20	51	62	58	14
2002-03	Div 2	46	14	11	21	54	70	53	17
2003-04	Div 2	46	21	10	15	73	63	73	7
2004-05	FL 1	46	17	5	24	49	59	56	18
2005-06	FL 1	46	16	12	18	49	54	60	13
2006-07	FL 1	46	18	6	22	64	65	60	12
2007-08	FL 1	46	9	11	26	47	81	38	23
2008-09	FL 2	46	13	9	24	44	66	48	18

DID YOU KNOW ?

When Harry O'Grady made what was to be his only League appearance for Port Vale on 25 January 1930 he embarked on one-club, one-season moves in eight years: Southampton, Leeds United, Barnsley, Bury, Millwall, Carlisle United and Accrington Stanley!

PORT VALE 2008–09 LEAGUE RECORD

Match No.	Date	Venue	Opponents	Result	H/T Score	Lg. Pos.	Goalscorers	Attendance
1	Aug 9	A	Luton T	W 3-1	2-1	—	Dodds 25, Taylor 45, Richards 58	7149
2	16	H	Accrington S	L 0-2	0-1	11		6643
3	23	A	Dagenham & R	D 1-1	1-1	9	Richards 7	1843
4	30	H	Bournemouth	W 3-1	1-0	7	Richards 15, Richman 64, McCombe 66	6048
5	Sept 6	H	Bradford C	L 0-2	0-1	10		7273
6	13	A	Darlington	L 1-2	1-1	12	Rodgers 28	3040
7	20	H	Macclesfield T	L 1-4	1-1	16	Dodds 44	6645
8	27	H	Gillingham	L 0-1	0-1	18		4986
9	Oct 4	H	Notts Co	L 1-2	0-1	19	Prosser 48	6247
10	11	A	Shrewsbury T	W 2-1	1-0	16	Dodds 19, Richards 90	7162
11	19	A	Chester C	W 2-1	1-0	14	Richards 11, Richman 78	3102
12	21	A	Exeter C	L 1-3	0-2	—	Rodgers 86	5493
13	25	H	Morecambe	W 2-1	0-0	13	Rodgers 80, Richards 90	5629
14	28	A	Aldershot T	L 0-1	0-1	—		3039
15	Nov 1	A	Lincoln C	W 1-0	1-0	13	Howland 26	4793
16	15	H	Brentford	L 0-3	0-1	14		6058
17	22	A	Wycombe W	L 2-4	0-2	15	Richards (pen) 51, Brown S 66	4521
18	25	H	Barnet	D 0-0	0-0	—		4617
19	Dec 6	H	Grimsby T	W 2-1	1-0	14	Richards 28, Richman 88	5058
20	13	A	Bury	L 0-3	0-3	15		2651
21	20	H	Chesterfield	L 0-1	0-0	15		5011
22	26	A	Rotherham U	L 0-1	0-0	18		4350
23	28	H	Rochdale	W 2-1	0-0	15	Glover 74, Thompson 90	5720
24	Jan 17	H	Shrewsbury T	D 1-1	1-1	16	Thompson 9	7068
25	20	H	Gillingham	L 1-3	1-0	—	Richards 28	4539
26	24	A	Notts Co	L 2-4	0-1	17	Richman 51, Dodds 73	4447
27	27	H	Chester C	W 3-0	0-0	—	Glover 59, Taylor 73, Lawrie 89	4448
28	31	A	Morecambe	D 1-1	1-1	16	Richman 43	1823
29	Feb 14	A	Brentford	L 0-2	0-1	17		4702
30	20	H	Lincoln C	L 0-1	0-1	—		5097
31	25	A	Macclesfield T	W 2-0	0-0	—	Ahmed 85, Dodds 90	2267
32	28	H	Luton T	L 1-3	1-1	17	McCombe 26	5689
33	Mar 7	A	Bournemouth	D 0-0	0-0	17		5924
34	10	H	Dagenham & R	L 0-1	0-1	—		4090
35	14	H	Darlington	W 3-1	1-1	18	Dodds 45, Taylor 51, Richards 78	4860
36	17	A	Accrington S	L 0-2	0-2	—		1144
37	21	A	Bradford C	W 1-0	0-0	17	Howland 49	12,436
38	28	A	Chesterfield	L 1-2	0-0	18	Marshall 77	3511
39	31	A	Exeter C	L 0-1	0-1	—		4235
40	Apr 4	H	Bury	D 1-1	0-0	18	Lawrie 57	5763
41	7	H	Aldershot T	D 0-0	0-0	—		4140
42	11	A	Rochdale	L 0-1	0-1	19		3100
43	13	H	Rotherham U	D 0-0	0-0	19		4814
44	18	A	Grimsby T	L 0-3	0-2	19		6511
45	25	H	Wycombe W	D 1-1	0-0	19	Collins 61	6047
46	May 2	A	Barnet	W 2-1	2-0	18	Dodds 11, Glover 45	2305

Final League Position: 18

GOALSCORERS

League (44): Richards 10 (1 pen), Dodds 7, Richman 5, Glover 3, Rodgers 3, Taylor 3, Howland 2, Lawrie 2, McCombe 2, Thompson 2, Ahmed 1, Brown S 1, Collins 1, Marshall 1, Prosser 1.
Carling Cup (1): Rodgers 1.
FA Cup (5): Dodds 3, Howland 1, Richards 1.
J Paint Trophy (0):

Anyon J 36	Stockley S 21 + 1	Collins L 39	Griffith A 37 + 1	McCombe J 30 + 1	Slater C 6	Taylor R 10 + 10	Davidson R 15 + 8	Richards M 30	Perry K 9 + 6	Dodds L 37 + 7	Rodgers L 10 + 5	Howland D 35 + 5	Tudor S 3 + 2	Richman S 20 + 17	Prosser L 24 + 2	Glover D 11 + 12	Taiwo T 2 + 2	Martin C 10 + 1	Lawrie J 8 + 10	Edwards P 29 + 2	McCrory D 10 + 2	Brammer D 13	Brown S 18	Owen G 12	MacKenzie N 2	Thompson S 5 + 12	Ahmed A 4 + 1	Gall K 7	Marshall P 13	Malbon A — + 1	Match No.
1	2	3	4	5	6	7¹	8	9	10²	11	12	13																			1
1	2	3	4	5¹	6	13	8	9	10²	11	7³	12	14																		2
1	2ᵃ	3	4	5	6		8²	9	12	11	10³	13		7¹	14																3
1		3	4	5	6		8²	9	14	11³	10	2		7¹		12	13														4
1	2¹	3	4	5	6	13		9	14	11²	10³	8		7	12																5
1		3	4	5		12	13	9	14	11¹	10	8		2³	6	7²															6
		3	4		6	12	13	9		11³	10	8	14	2¹	5	7²		1													7
1	2	3	4	5			8	9	12	13	10¹			11³	7²	6			14												8
1	2	3	4	5²			8	9	11	10	12			7¹	6				13												9
1	2	5¹	11				8¹	9	10	12	4			7²	13	6				3³	14										10
1	2		4	5			8	9	11	12	10¹			13	6					3²	7										11
1	2	5	8²			10		9		7³	12	4¹		13	6	14				11	3										12
1		5		2		12		9		7¹	10	4		8	6	13				11²	3										13
1		5	8			12		9³		7	10	4		2¹	6	14	13			3	11²										14
1		3	10			12		9		7	13	4		2²	5	11	6			8¹											15
1	6	2	5				8⁴	9		7	11	4		13	12	10²				3¹											16
1	6	2					9	10	4	7	5			11	3					8											17
1	5	2					9	11	4	7	12			10¹	3					8	6										18
1	2	5					8	9		11				12	10²					3		7	6			4¹	13				19
1	2	5	12				8	9²		11¹		13		7³		10					3		7	6		4	14				20
		5	2				8	9⁴	12	13		4			11²	1					3		7	6		10¹					21
1		3	2	5			8	10		9²		4¹		6	12					13	11³	7		14							22
1		3	2	5				10¹		4				6	9⁴					11	8	7		12							23
1		2	4	5			12			11⁸	9			3	6					8	7		10¹								24
1		3	2	5				10		11²		4¹		12	6		14	13		8	7		9³								25
1	5	2					13	9		4²		11¹	10	14		3		8		7³	6		12								26
1	5	2					14	12		4³		7		10	13					8¹	11	6	9²								27
1	5	2					12			9		8		4¹	7					10	3	11	6								28
1	6	2					12	8	10	9				4	5					11	3					7¹					29
1	5	2	13							10²		11³		14		9¹		8	3		4	6		12		7					30
1		3	2	5				9²		12				4	14	6				13	11		8¹			7	10³				31
1		3	2	5				9²		12				4	6¹					13	11	8				7	10				32
1		3	2	5				9		12		4		13	14					11³		7²	6				10¹	8			33
1	13	2	5					9		11		4		12						3		7²	6¹				10	8			34
1		2	5				11¹	9²		7		4		12	6					3			13			10	8				35
1		2	5				11¹			7		4³		12	6	9²				3			13		14	10	8				36
1	2	7	5				11²	9		12		4		13	6					3							10¹	8			37
1⁶	2	4	5				10²	9¹		7		8		12	6				15	13	3							11			38
	2	11	5					9		4³		12		6	14			1	13	3		8²	7¹					10			39
	2	6	5				11²	9		4		12						1	10	3		7¹					13	8			40
	2	6	5				11¹	9		4		12						1	10	3		7						8			41
	2	6	5				11²	9		4		12	13					1	10	3		7¹						8			42
	2	6	4	5			11¹	13		10		9³		7²				1	12	3		14						8			43
	2	4	5				11¹			10³		9²	7	12	14			1		3		6				13		8			44
	2	6	5				12			13				7²	11			1	10	3		4					9¹	8			45
	2		5				12			11²		4		7³	6	9		1	10¹	3		8				13				14	46

FA Cup
First Round   Huddersfield T   (a)   4-3
Second Round   Macclesfield T   (h)   1-3

Carling Cup
First Round   Sheffield U   (a)   1-3

J Paint Trophy
First Round   Stockport Co   (a)   0-1

PRESTON NORTH END · FL Championship

FOUNDATION

North End Cricket and Rugby Club which was formed in 1863, indulged in most sports before taking up soccer in about 1879. In 1881 they decided to stick to football to the exclusion of other sports and even a 16–0 drubbing by Blackburn Rovers in an invitation game at Deepdale, a few weeks after taking this decision, did not deter them for they immediately became affiliated to the Lancashire FA.

Deepdale Stadium, Sir Tom Finney Way, Deepdale, Preston PR1 6RU.

Telephone: (0844) 856 1964.

Fax: (01772) 693 366.

Ticket Office: (0844) 856 1966.

Website: www.pne.com

Email: enquiries@pne.com

Ground Capacity: 23,408.

Record Attendance: 42,684 v Arsenal, Division 1, 23 April 1938.

Pitch Measurements: 110yd × 77yd.

Chairman: Derek Shaw.

Vice-chairman: David Taylor.

Secretary: Janet Parr.

Manager: Alan Irvine.

Assistant Manager: Rob Kelly.

Physio: Matt Radcliffe.

Colours: White shirts, blue shorts, white stockings.

Change Colours: Yellow shirts with blue sleeves, yellow shorts, yellow stockings.

Year Formed: 1881.

Turned Professional: 1885. *Ltd Co.:* 1893.

Club Nicknames: 'The Lilywhites' or 'North End'.

Ground: 1881, Deepdale.

HONOURS

Football League: Division 1 – Champions 1888–89 (first champions) 1889–90; Runners-up 1890–91, 1891–92, 1892–93, 1905–06, 1952–53, 1957–58; Division 2 – Champions 1903–04, 1912–13, 1950–51, 1999–2000; Runners-up 1914–15, 1933–34; Division 3 – Champions 1970–71, 1995–96; Division 4 – Runners-up 1986–87.

FA Cup: Winners 1889, 1938; Runners-up 1888, 1922, 1937, 1954, 1964.

Football League Cup: best season: 4th rd, 2003.

Double Performed: 1888–89.

Football League Cup: best season: 4th rd, 1963, 1966, 1972, 1981.

First Football League Game: 8 September 1888, Football League, v Burnley (h) W 5–2 – Trainer; Howarth, Holmes; Robertson, W. Graham, J. Graham; Gordon (1), Ross (2), Goodall, Dewhurst (2), Drummond.

Record League Victory: 10–0 v Stoke, Division 1, 14 September 1889 – Trainer; Howarth, Holmes; Kelso, Russell (1), Graham; Gordon, Jimmy Ross (2), Nick Ross (3), Thomson (2), Drummond (2).

Record Cup Victory: 26–0 v Hyde, FA Cup 1st rd, 15 October 1887 – Addison; Howarth, Nick Ross; Russell (1), Thomson (5), Graham (1); Gordon (5), Jimmy Ross (8), John Goodall (1), Dewhurst (3), Drummond (2).

Record Defeat: 0–7 v Blackpool, Division 1, 1 May 1948.

Most League Points (2 for a win): 61, Division 3, 1970–71.

SKY SPORTS FACT FILE

In 1965–66 Preston North End had 16 Scottish-born players on their staff. Both manager Jimmy Milne and reserve team trainer Willie Cunningham were from north of the border, too and the club's Scottish scout was appropriately named Jimmy Scott!

Most League Points (3 for a win): 95, Division 2, 1999–2000.

Most League Goals: 100, Division 2, 1927–28 and Division 1, 1957–58.

Highest League Scorer in Season: Ted Harper, 37, Division 2, 1932–33.

Most League Goals in Total Aggregate: Tom Finney, 187, 1946–60.

Most League Goals in One Match: 4, Jimmy Ross v Stoke, Division 1, 6 October 1888; 4, Nick Ross v Derby Co, Division 1, 11 January 1890; 4, George Drummond v Notts Co, Division 1, 12 December 1891; 4, Frank Becton v Notts Co, Division 1, 31 March 1893; 4, George Harrison v Grimsby T, Division 2, 3 November 1928; 4, Alex Reid v Port Vale, Division 2, 23 February 1929; 4, James McClelland v Reading, Division 2, 6 September 1930; 4, Dick Rowley v Notts Co, Division 2, 16 April 1932; 4, Ted Harper v Burnley, Division 2, 29 August 1932; 4, Ted Harper v Lincoln C, Division 2, 11 March 1933; 4, Charlie Wayman v QPR, Division 2, 25 December 1950; 4, Alex Bruce v Colchester U, Division 3, 28 February 1978.

Most Capped Player: Tom Finney, 76, England.

Most League Appearances: Alan Kelly, 447, 1961–75.

Youngest League Player: Steve Doyle, 16 years 166 days v Tranmere R, 15 November 1974.

Record Transfer Fee Received: £6,000,000 from Portsmouth for David Nugent, August 2007.

Record Transfer Fee Paid: £1,500,000 to Manchester U for David Healy, December 2000.

Football League Record: 1888 Founder Member of League; 1901–04 Division 2; 1904–12 Division 1; 1912–13 Division 2; 1913–14 Division 1; 1914–15 Division 2; 1919–25 Division 1; 1925–34 Division 2; 1934–49 Division 1; 1949–51 Division 2; 1951–61 Division 1; 1961–70 Division 2; 1970–71 Division 3; 1971–74 Division 2; 1974–78 Division 3; 1978–81 Division 2; 1981–85 Division 3; 1985–87 Division 4; 1987–92 Division 3; 1992–93 Division 2; 1993–96 Division 3; 1996–2000 Division 2; 2000–04 Division 1; 2004– FL C.

MANAGERS

Charlie Parker 1906–15
Vincent Hayes 1919–23
Jim Lawrence 1923–25
Frank Richards 1925–27
Alex Gibson 1927–31
Lincoln Hayes 1931–32
Run by committee 1932–36
Tommy Muirhead 1936–37
Run by committee 1937–49
Will Scott 1949–53
Scot Symon 1953–54
Frank Hill 1954–56
Cliff Britton 1956–61
Jimmy Milne 1961–68
Bobby Seith 1968–70
Alan Ball Sr 1970–73
Bobby Charlton 1973–75
Harry Catterick 1975–77
Nobby Stiles 1977–81
Tommy Docherty 1981
Gordon Lee 1981–83
Alan Kelly 1983–85
Tommy Booth 1985–86
Brian Kidd 1986
John McGrath 1986–90
Les Chapman 1990–92
Sam Allardyce 1992 (*Caretaker*)
John Beck 1992–94
Gary Peters 1994–98
David Moyes 1998–2002
Kelham O'Hanlon 2002
    (*Caretaker*)
Craig Brown 2002–04
Billy Davies 2004–06
Paul Simpson 2006–07
Alan Irvine November 2007–

LATEST SEQUENCES

Longest Sequence of League Wins: 14, 25.12.1950 – 27.3.1951.

Longest Sequence of League Defeats: 8, 22.9.1984 – 27.10.1984.

Longest Sequence of League Draws: 6, 24.2.1979 – 20.3.1979.

Longest Sequence of Unbeaten League Matches: 23, 8.9.1888 – 14.9.1889.

Longest Sequence Without a League Win: 15, 14.4.1923 – 20.10.1923.

Successive Scoring Runs: 30 from 15.11.1952.

Successive Non-scoring Runs: 6 from 8.4.1897.

TEN YEAR LEAGUE RECORD

		P	W	D	L	F	A	Pts	Pos
1999-2000	Div 2	46	28	11	7	74	37	95	1
2000-01	Div 1	46	23	9	14	64	52	78	4
2001-02	Div 1	46	20	12	14	71	59	72	8
2002-03	Div 1	46	16	13	17	68	70	61	12
2003-04	Div 1	46	15	14	17	69	71	59	15
2004-05	FL C	46	21	12	13	67	58	75	5
2005-06	FL C	46	20	20	6	59	30	80	4
2006-07	FL C	46	22	8	16	64	53	74	7
2007-08	FL C	46	15	11	20	50	56	56	15
2008-09	FL C	46	21	11	14	66	54	74	6

DID YOU KNOW

A fact often overlooked in the record-breaking 1950–51 season for Preston North End was their 3,000th League goal. On 7 October Ken Horton's goal in the 2–1 win over Luton Town registered this milestone. They used the services of just 18 players in the season.

PRESTON NORTH END 2008–09 LEAGUE RECORD

Match No.	Date		Venue	Opponents	Result		H/T Score	Lg. Pos.	Goalscorers	Atten- dance
1	Aug	9	A	Ipswich T	W	2-1	2-1	—	McKenna [21], Whaley [34]	22,307
2		16	H	Crystal Palace	W	2-0	0-0	2	Nicholson [58], Chaplow [90]	14,225
3		23	A	Sheffield W	D	1-1	0-1	4	Chaplow [77]	17,963
4		30	H	Charlton Ath	W	2-1	0-1	2	Mellor [58], Nicholson [66]	12,089
5	Sept	13	A	Coventry C	D	0-0	0-0	3		16,544
6		16	H	Nottingham F	W	2-1	0-0	—	Mawene [50], Mellor [59]	13,145
7		20	A	Wolverhampton W	L	1-3	0-1	3	Mellor (pen) [90]	17,567
8		27	A	Burnley	L	1-3	1-1	4	Nicholson [22]	16,276
9		30	H	Swansea C	L	0-2	0-1	—		10,558
10	Oct	4	A	Watford	L	1-2	1-2	12	St Ledger-Hall [5]	14,087
11		18	H	Reading	W	2-1	0-1	8	Ingimarsson (og) [55], Elliott [81]	12,316
12		21	A	Plymouth Arg	L	0-1	0-1	—		9824
13		25	A	Sheffield U	L	0-1	0-0	15		24,445
14		28	H	Watford	W	2-0	1-0	—	Jones [43], Wallace [68]	11,234
15	Nov	1	H	Southampton	L	2-3	2-0	14	Jones [36], Elliott [42]	11,508
16		8	A	Norwich C	D	2-2	1-1	14	Brown C [2], Mellor [81]	23,225
17		16	A	Blackpool	W	3-1	0-1	13	Brown C 2 [55, 77], Mellor [68]	9643
18		22	H	Barnsley	W	2-1	1-1	10	Chaplow [21], St Ledger-Hall [88]	12,153
19		25	A	Derby Co	D	2-2	2-2	—	Davidson (pen) [21], Mellor [29]	25,534
20		29	H	Bristol C	W	2-0	1-0	6	Elliott [30], Wallace [56]	11,161
21	Dec	6	A	Cardiff C	L	0-2	0-1	8		16,560
22		9	H	Doncaster R	W	1-0	0-0	—	Parkin [82]	13,152
23		13	H	Birmingham C	W	1-0	0-0	6	Parkin [90]	10,943
24		20	A	QPR	L	2-3	1-2	8	Sedgwick [28], Davidson (pen) [60]	14,103
25		26	H	Derby Co	W	2-0	1-0	7	St Ledger-Hall [30], Parkin [68]	13,896
26		28	A	Barnsley	D	1-1	0-1	7	Wallace [73]	13,851
27	Jan	10	A	Wolverhampton W	W	3-1	2-1	—	Elliott 2 [24, 61], St Ledger-Hall [41]	26,138
28		17	H	Burnley	W	2-1	0-0	5	Davidson (pen) [53], Mellor (pen) [85]	15,692
29		27	A	Swansea C	L	1-4	0-2	—	Brown C [90]	14,774
30		31	H	Sheffield U	D	0-0	0-0	6		14,889
31	Feb	3	H	Plymouth Arg	D	1-1	1-1	—	Parkin [43]	10,660
32		7	A	Reading	D	0-0	0-0	6		19,570
33		14	A	Norwich C	W	1-0	1-0	4	Parkin [41]	12,033
34		21	A	Southampton	L	1-3	0-3	5	Wallace [73]	14,790
35		28	H	Ipswich T	W	3-2	2-1	4	Davidson (pen) [6], Parkin [41], Elliott [61]	12,709
36	Mar	3	A	Nottingham F	L	1-2	0-0	—	Parkin [63]	17,568
37		7	A	Crystal Palace	L	1-2	1-2	6	Jones [29]	16,340
38		10	H	Sheffield W	D	1-1	0-1	—	Parkin [90]	12,381
39		14	H	Coventry C	W	2-1	1-1	7	Turner (og) [38], Parkin [72]	13,251
40		21	A	Charlton Ath	D	0-0	0-0	7		19,215
41	Apr	4	A	Bristol C	D	1-1	0-0	7	Mawene [69]	16,596
42		11	H	Blackpool	L	0-1	0-1	8		21,273
43		13	A	Doncaster R	W	2-0	1-0	8	Brown C [26], Mellor [72]	11,648
44		18	H	Cardiff C	W	6-0	2-0	8	Mellor 2 [17, 41], Parkin [51], Kennedy (og) [54], Brown C [75], Williamson [86]	13,692
45		25	A	Birmingham C	W	2-1	0-0	7	McKenna [69], Wallace [89]	24,825
46	May	3	A	QPR	W	2-1	1-0	6	Parkin [37], St Ledger-Hall [74]	18,264

Final League Position: 6

GOALSCORERS

League (66): Parkin 11, Mellor 10 (2 pens), Brown C 6, Elliott 6, St Ledger-Hall 5, Wallace 5, Davidson 4 (4 pens), Chaplow 3, Jones 3, Nicholson 3, Mawene 2, McKenna 2, Sedgwick 1, Whaley 1, Williamson 1, own goals 3.
Carling Cup (2): Mellor 2.
FA Cup (0).
Play-Offs (1): St Ledger-Hall 1.

Lonergan A 46	St Ledger-Hall S 46	Davidson C 18 + 2	Chaplow R 21 + 4	Mawene Y 38 + 3	Whaley S 7 + 14	Sedgwick S 38 + 2	Nicholson B 27 + 10	Mellor N 20 + 13	Jones B 44	McKenna P 44	Hawley K — + 5	Hart M 5 + 1	Hill M 1	Wallace R 34 + 5	Carter D 8 + 10	Parkin J 30 + 9	Elliott S 23 + 14	Brown C 15 + 15	McEveley J 7	Jarrett J — + 3	Brown W 6	Nolan E 18 + 3	Davies A 5	Williamson L 5	Chilvers L — + 1	Match No.
1	2	3	4	5	6	7	8	9^1	10	11	12															1
1	5	3^1	4	6	11	7	9	10	2	8			12													2
1	2		4	5	6^2	7	8^1	9	10	11	13			3	12											3
1	6		4	5	12	7^1	8	9^2	2	11^3	13	3			14	10										4
1	5	12	4^1	6		7^3	8	9	2	11^2		3		14	13	10										5
1	5			6		7^1	4	9^2	2	8		3		12	11	10	13									6
1	5			6	12	7^2	4	9	2	8^1		3		13	11	10^3	14									7
1	5	12	13	6		7	8	9	2	11		3^1		4^2	10^3		14									8
1	5			6^2		7^1	8	9	2	11				12	4^3	13	14	10	3							9
1	5			6		7	8^1	9^2	2	4^3				11	12	13	10	3	14							10
1	5			6	12	7^1	8	13	2	4				11^3	10	9^2		3	14							11
1	5			6	12	7^1	8	13	2	4^3				11	10^2	9		3	14							12
1	5			6	12	7^1	8	13	2	4				11	10	9^2		3								13
1	2			6	13		8	12	4	7				11^2	10	9^1		3			5					14
1	2			6			12	8^1	13	4	7			11	10^3	9^2	14	3			5					15
1	2^3	3	12	6		14	8^1	13	4	7				11		10^2	9				5					16
1	6	3	4			7		10^2	2	8				11		12	9				5					17
1	6	3	4			7^2	12	10	2	8				11^1		14	13	9^3			5					18
1	6	3	4			7		10^2	2	8				11		12	9				5					19
1	5	3	4	6		7^1	12	10^2	2	8				11		14	13	9^3								20
1	5	3	4	6		7^1	12	10^3	2	8^2				11		13	14	9								21
1	5	3	4	6		7^1	12		2^3	8				11		13	10	9^2				14				22
1	5	3	4^1	6		7	12			8	14			11		13	10^3	9^2				2				23
1	5	3		6	12	7^1	8			4				11		10		9				2				24
1	5	3	4^1	6		7	12	9^3	2	8				11		10^2	14	13								25
1	5	3	4	6			7	12	2	8				11		13	10^1	9^2								26
1	5		4^1	6		7	12	13	2	8				11		10^3	9^2	14			3					27
1	5	3	4^1	6		7	12	13	2	8				11		10	9^2									28
1	5	3^3	4^1	6	12		8		2	7				11		10	9^2	13			14					29
1	5		4^1	6		7	8		2	11				12	10	9^2	13				3					30
1	5		12	6	13	7^1	8^2		2	4				11		10	9^3	14			3					31
1	5			6		7	8		2	4				11		10	9^1	12			3					32
1	5		4^3	13	12	7^1	8		2	11				14	10^2		9				3	6				33
1	5		13	12		7^3	8^2		2	4				11		10	9	14				3	6^1				34
1	5^2	3	4	6	7			2	8	11				10^1	9	12					13					35
1	5	3	4^3	7			8^2		2	10				11	14	9^1	13	12				6				36
1	5	3		12		8^1	14	7		13				11	4		9^2	10^3				2	6			37
1	5		12			7	13	14	2	8				11^2	4^3	10	9					3	6^1			38
1	5		6	12		7^1	4^3	13	2	8				11	14	10	9^2					3				39
1	5		6	4^1	7			2		11				8	10	9	12					3				40
1	5		6			7			2	8				11	12	10	9					3		4^1		41
1	5		6	12		7^1		13	2	8				11	14	10	9^2					3		4^3		42
1	5		6			7^3		10^2	2	8				11	14	12	13	9^1				3		4		43
1	5		6			7		10^2	2	8^3				11	14	12	13	12				3		4		44
1	5		6	13		7^2		9^3	2	8				11^4		10^1		12				3		4^4	14	45
1	5		6	4^2	7		13	10^1	2	8				11		9^3	14	12				3				46

FA Cup
Third Round   Liverpool   (h)   0-2

Carling Cup
First Round   Chesterfield   (h)   2-0
Second Round   Derby Co   (h)   0-1

Play-Offs
Semi-Final   Sheffield U   (h)   1-1
                                (a)   0-1

QUEENS PARK RANGERS   FL Championship

FOUNDATION

There is an element of doubt about the date of the foundation of this club, but it is believed that in either 1885 or 1886 it was formed through the amalgamation of Christchurch Rangers and St Jude's Institute FC. The leading light was George Wodehouse, whose family maintained a connection with the club until comparatively recent times. Most of the players came from the Queen's Park district so this name was adopted after a year as St Jude's Institute.

Loftus Road Stadium, South Africa Road, Shepherds Bush, London W12 7PA.

Telephone: (020) 8743 0262

Fax: (020) 8749 0994

Ticket Office: 08444 777077

Website: www.qpr.co.uk

Ground Capacity: 18,682.

Record Attendance: 35,353 v Leeds U, Division 1, 27 April 1974.

Pitch Measurements: 110yd × 73yd.

Chairman: Gianni Paladini.

Manager: Jim Magilton.

Physio: Paul Hunter.

Colours: Blue and white hooped shirts, white shorts, white stockings.

Change Colours: All red with blue design on shirts.

Year Formed: 1885* (*see Foundation*).

Turned Professional: 1898. *Ltd Co.:* 1899.

HONOURS

Football League: Division 1 – Runners-up 1975–76; Division 2 – Champions 1982–83; Runners-up 1967–68, 1972–73, 2003–04; Division 3 (S) – Champions 1947–48; Runners-up 1946–47; Division 3 – Champions 1966–67.

FA Cup: Runners-up 1982.

Football League Cup: Winners 1967; Runners-up 1986. (In 1966–67 won Division 3 and Football League Cup).

European Competitions: UEFA Cup: 1976–77, 1984–85.

Previous Names: 1885, St Jude's; 1887, Queens Park Rangers. *Club Nicknames:* 'Rangers' or 'Rs'.

Grounds: 1885* (*see Foundation*), Welford's Fields; 1888–99; London Scottish Ground, Brondesbury, Home Farm, Kensal Rise Green, Gun Club Wormwood Scrubs, Kilburn Cricket Ground; 1899, Kensal Rise Athletic Ground; 1901, Latimer Road, Notting Hill; 1904, Agricultural Society, Park Royal; 1907, Park Royal Ground; 1917, Loftus Road; 1931, White City; 1933, Loftus Road; 1962, White City; 1963, Loftus Road.

First Football League Game: 28 August 1920, Division 3, v Watford (h) L 1–2 – Price; Blackman, Wingrove; McGovern, Grant, O'Brien; Faulkner, Birch (1), Smith, Gregory, Middlemiss.

Record League Victory: 9–2 v Tranmere R, Division 3, 3 December 1960 – Drinkwater; Woods, Ingham; Keen, Rutter, Angell; Lazarus (2), Bedford (2), Evans (2), Andrews (1), Clark (2).

Record Cup Victory: 8–1 v Bristol R (away), FA Cup 1st rd, 27 November 1937 – Gilfillan; Smith, Jefferson; Lowe, James, March; Cape, Mallett, Cheetham (3), Fitzgerald (3) Bott (2). 8–1 v Crewe Alex, Milk Cup 1st rd, 3 October 1983 – Hucker; Neill, Dawes, Waddock (1), McDonald (1), Fenwick, Micklewhite (1), Stewart (1), Allen (1), Stainrod (3), Gregory.

SKY SPORTS FACT FILE

Queens Park Rangers gave goalkeeper Reg Allen (Corona FC) a trial, nine reserve games, one in the Brentford Hospital Cup. They signed him in March 1938. After excellent wartime Army service and 254 peacetime appearances he was then sold to Manchester United for £12,000.

Record Defeat: 1–8 v Mansfield T, Division 3, 15 March 1965. 1–8 v Manchester U, Division 1, 19 March 1969.

Most League Points (2 for a win): 67, Division 3, 1966–67.

Most League Points (3 for a win): 85, Division 2, 1982–83.

Most League Goals: 111, Division 3, 1961–62.

Highest League Scorer in Season: George Goddard, 37, Division 3 (S), 1929–30.

Most League Goals in Total Aggregate: George Goddard, 172, 1926–34.

Most League Goals in One Match: 4, George Goddard v Merthyr T, Division 3 (S), 9 March 1929; 4, George Goddard v Swindon T, Division 3 (S), 12 April 1930; 4, George Goddard v Exeter C, Division 3 (S), 20 December 1930; 4, George Goddard v Watford, Division 3 (S), 19 September 1931; 4, Tom Cheetham v Aldershot, Division 3 (S), 14 September 1935; 4, Tom Cheetham v Aldershot, Division 3 (S), 12 November 1938.

Most Capped Player: Alan McDonald, 52, Northern Ireland.

Most League Appearances: Tony Ingham, 519, 1950–63.

Youngest League Player: Frank Sibley, 16 years 97 days v Bristol C, 10 March 1964.

Record Transfer Fee Received: £6,000,000 from Newcastle U for Les Ferdinand, June 1995.

Record Transfer Fee Paid: £2,350,000 to Stoke C for Mike Sheron, July 1997.

Football League Record: 1920 Original Members of Division 3; 1921–48 Division 3 (S); 1948–52 Division 2; 1952–58 Division 3 (S); 1958–67 Division 3; 1967–68 Division 2; 1968–69 Division 1; 1969–73 Division 2; 1973–79 Division 1; 1979–83 Division 2; 1983–92 Division 1; 1992–96 FA Premier League; 1996–2001 Division 1; 2001–04 Division 2; 2004– FL C.

LATEST SEQUENCES

Longest Sequence of League Wins: 8, 7.11.1931 – 28.12.1931.

Longest Sequence of League Defeats: 9, 25.2.1969 – 5.4.1969.

Longest Sequence of League Draws: 6, 29.1.2000 – 5.3.2000.

Longest Sequence of Unbeaten League Matches: 20, 11.3.1972 – 23.9.1972.

Longest Sequence Without a League Win: 20, 7.12.1968 – 7.4.1969.

Successive Scoring Runs: 33 from 9.12.1961.

Successive Non-scoring Runs: 6 from 18.3.1939.

MANAGERS

James Cowan 1906–13
Jimmy Howie 1913–20
Ned Liddell 1920–24
Will Wood 1924–25
  (had been Secretary since 1903)
Bob Hewison 1925–31
John Bowman 1931
Archie Mitchell 1931–33
Mick O'Brien 1933–35
Billy Birrell 1935–39
Ted Vizard 1939–44
Dave Mangnall 1944–52
Jack Taylor 1952–59
Alec Stock 1959–65
  (General Manager to 1968)
Bill Dodgin Jnr 1968
Tommy Docherty 1968
Les Allen 1968–71
Gordon Jago 1971–74
Dave Sexton 1974–77
Frank Sibley 1977–78
Steve Burtenshaw 1978–79
Tommy Docherty 1979–80
Terry Venables 1980–84
Gordon Jago 1984
Alan Mullery 1984
Frank Sibley 1984–85
Jim Smith 1985–88
Trevor Francis 1988–90
Don Howe 1990–91
Gerry Francis 1991–94
Ray Wilkins 1994–96
Stewart Houston 1996–97
Ray Harford 1997–98
Gerry Francis 1998–2001
Ian Holloway 2001–06
Gary Waddock 2006
John Gregory 2006–07
Luigi Di Canio 2007–08
Iain Dowie 2008
Paulo Sousa 2008–09
Jim Magilton June 2009–

TEN YEAR LEAGUE RECORD

		P	W	D	L	F	A	Pts	Pos
1999-2000	Div 1	46	16	18	12	62	53	66	10
2000-01	Div 1	46	7	19	20	45	75	40	23
2001-02	Div 2	46	19	14	13	60	49	71	8
2002-03	Div 2	46	24	11	11	69	45	83	4
2003-04	Div 2	46	22	17	7	80	45	83	2
2004-05	FL C	46	17	11	18	54	58	62	11
2005-06	FL C	46	12	14	20	50	65	50	21
2006-07	FL C	46	14	11	21	54	68	53	18
2007-08	FL C	46	14	16	16	60	66	58	14
2008-09	FL C	46	15	16	15	42	44	61	11

DID YOU KNOW

William Steer scored 27 goals for Queens Park Rangers in 45 League and Cup matches during their injury-hit 1909–10 campaign, three times as many as any other member of the team. Despite winning just one of the last 14 games they still finished third!

QUEENS PARK RANGERS 2008–09 LEAGUE RECORD

Match No.	Date	Venue	Opponents	Result		H/T Score	Lg. Pos.	Goalscorers	Atten- dance
1	Aug 9	H	Barnsley	W	2-1	2-1	—	Hall 2 [29, 31]	14,964
2	16	A	Sheffield U	L	0-3	0-2	15		25,273
3	23	H	Doncaster R	W	2-0	2-0	9	Blackstock [5], Ledesma [28]	15,536
4	30	A	Bristol C	D	1-1	1-1	9	Blackstock [18]	17,543
5	Sept 14	H	Southampton	W	4-1	1-0	4	Blackstock 2 [1, 77], Stewart [63], Agyemang [90]	13,770
6	17	A	Norwich C	W	1-0	1-0	—	Rowlands [33]	24,249
7	20	A	Coventry C	L	0-1	0-1	4		16,718
8	27	H	Derby Co	L	0-2	0-0	5		14,311
9	30	H	Blackpool	D	1-1	0-1	—	Blackstock [79]	12,500
10	Oct 4	A	Birmingham C	L	0-1	0-1	11		18,498
11	18	H	Nottingham F	W	2-1	0-0	7	Balanta [48], Buzsaky [60]	15,122
12	21	A	Swansea C	D	0-0	0-0	—		13,475
13	25	A	Reading	D	0-0	0-0	9		20,571
14	28	H	Birmingham C	W	1-0	0-0	—	Di Carmine [54]	13,594
15	Nov 1	A	Ipswich T	L	0-2	0-0	7		20,966
16	8	H	Cardiff C	W	1-0	0-0	7	Mahon [80]	13,347
17	15	H	Burnley	L	1-2	1-1	10	Blackstock [14]	13,226
18	22	A	Watford	L	0-3	0-3	12		16,201
19	25	H	Charlton Ath	W	2-1	1-1	—	Blackstock 2 [17, 80]	12,286
20	29	A	Crystal Palace	D	0-0	0-0	10		16,411
21	Dec 6	H	Wolverhampton W	W	1-0	0-0	7	Rowlands [63]	13,416
22	9	A	Sheffield W	L	0-1	0-0	—		14,792
23	13	A	Plymouth Arg	D	1-1	1-0	9	Helguson [16]	10,747
24	20	H	Preston NE	W	3-2	2-1	9	Helguson 2 [16, 34], Blackstock [86]	14,103
25	26	A	Charlton Ath	D	2-2	0-0	9	Cook [18], Blackstock [68]	21,023
26	28	H	Watford	D	0-0	0-0	9		16,196
27	Jan 10	H	Coventry C	D	1-1	0-0	—	Blackstock [87]	13,330
28	17	A	Derby Co	W	2-0	2-0	8	Routledge [22], Leigertwood [36]	28,390
29	27	A	Blackpool	W	3-0	1-0	—	Helguson 2 (1 pen) [17, 58 (p)], Ephraim [90]	6656
30	31	H	Reading	D	0-0	0-0	7		17,120
31	Feb 7	A	Nottingham F	D	2-2	1-1	9	Alberti 2 [45, 48]	25,859
32	21	H	Ipswich T	L	1-3	1-1	11	Di Carmine [3]	13,904
33	25	H	Cardiff C	D	0-0	0-0	—		17,340
34	28	A	Barnsley	L	1-2	1-2	11	Delaney [35]	11,614
35	Mar 3	H	Norwich C	L	0-1	0-0	—		13,533
36	7	H	Sheffield U	D	0-0	0-0	11		13,718
37	10	A	Doncaster R	L	0-2	0-2	—		10,223
38	14	A	Southampton	D	0-0	0-0	12		18,691
39	17	H	Swansea C	W	1-0	1-0	—	Leigertwood [30]	12,288
40	21	H	Bristol C	W	2-1	0-0	11	Lopez [65], Taarabt [81]	14,059
41	Apr 4	H	Crystal Palace	D	0-0	0-0	10		15,234
42	11	A	Burnley	L	0-1	0-0	10		15,058
43	13	H	Sheffield W	W	3-2	0-1	10	Vine [62], Mahon [74], Stewart [88]	13,742
44	18	A	Wolverhampton W	L	0-1	0-0	11		27,511
45	25	H	Plymouth Arg	D	0-0	0-0	11		14,779
46	May 3	A	Preston NE	L	1-2	0-1	11	Agyemang [57]	18,264

Final League Position: 11

GOALSCORERS

League (42): Blackstock 11, Helguson 5 (1 pen), Agyemang 2, Alberti 2, Di Carmine 2, Hall 2, Leigertwood 2, Mahon 2, Rowlands 2, Stewart 2, Balanta 1, Buzsaky 1, Cook 1, Delaney 1, Ephraim 1, Ledesma 1, Lopez 1, Routledge 1, Taarabt 1, Vine 1.
Carling Cup (8): Ledesma 3, Stewart 2, Balanta 1, Blackstock 1, Delaney 1.
FA Cup (1): Di Carmine 1.

Cerny R 42	Ramage P 30+1	Delaney D 35+2	Mahon G 29+6	Hall F 18+6	Gorkss K 30+1	Agyemang P 11+9	Leigertwood M 36+6	Cook L 28+6	Blackstock D 26+10	Ledesma E 11+6	Parejo D 10+4	Alberti M 6+6	Connolly M 31+4	Balanta A 2+8	Di Carmine S 15+12	Stewart D 37	Rowlands M 20+4	Ephraim H 16+11	Buzsaky A 5+6	Tommasi D 5+2	Helguson H 15+5	Routledge W 18+1	Camp L 4	Miller L 11+2	Rose R —+2	Lopez J 7+3	German A —+3	Taarabt A 5+2	Vine R 3+2	Match No.
1	2	3	4	5	6	7¹	8	9	10	11²	12	13																		1
1	2			5	6		8	9¹	10	11	4	12	3	7²	13															2
1	6	2	4	5¹		8	11²	10	9	7³	12	13	3				14													3
1	2	3	4		12	8	9²	10	7⁸	11¹	5	6			13															4
1	2	3	7		12	8	9	10		6²	5	4	13		11¹															5
1	2	3	4		12	13	8	11¹	10²	9³	5⁹	6	7				14													6
1	2²	3	4	5	12	8	11	10¹	9³	13		6	7				14													7
1		3	4¹	5	13	12	14	10	9²	8		2		6	7		11³													8
1	6	2	4³	5	13	12	11	10	9²	8¹			3	7			14													9
1	2²	3	4³	5		9	8	11	10	12	13		6	7¹			14													10
1	6	2	12	5²		8	11	10		13	9³	14	3	7	4¹															11
1	6³	2	4	5		8	11²	10	13	12		14	3	7¹	9															12
1		6		5		8	11	12	10²	2		13	9¹	3	7	4														13
1		12		5	2⁸	11¹	10³	8		3	9²		6	7		13	14	4												14
1	3			5		11	12	13	8		2		9¹	6	7		10²	4												15
1	2		12	5	13	11	10	8³		4	9²		3	7			14	6¹												16
1	2	12	13	5	14	11	10		3¹	9		6	7	8³			4²													17
1	2	3	4³	5⁹		9	8		10²	7¹	12	13	6				11	14												18
1	2	3	14		6	12	8		10	13	7²	9¹	5				11	4³												19
1	2	3	4		6	7²	8		10¹		9³	13	5	12			11	14												20
1	2	3	4		6	7	12²	10¹	13	5		8	11				14	9³												21
1	5	2³	4²	14	6	9	8	12		13			3	7	11¹		10													22
1	2¹	3	4	12	6	9²	8	11³	13		5	7	14				10													23
1	2²	3³	4¹	14	6	9	12	10	13		5	7	11		8															24
1	2		5	6		8	11¹	10	12		4²	3	9³	7			13	14												25
1	6	2	4¹	5		9	12	11²	13			3	7	8			10													26
1	2²		12	6	4³	10	13		3	14	5		8		11¹						9	7								27
1		3	4	6		8	10³	14	2	13	5		11¹		12						9²	7								28
1		3	4	14	6	8	11	12	2³		5		13								9¹	7	1	10²						29
1		3	4²	6		8	11³	12	2	14	5		13								9¹	7	1	10						30
1		3	4	6		8	12	10³	2	14	9¹		5		13							7	1	11²						31
1		3¹	4	5	6	8	11	12	2	13	9³		14									7	1	10²						32
1		3	4¹	6		8	11	12	14	2	13				5						9²	7		10³						33
1		3		6		8	10	4³	2	12	5		9¹								7	11²					13	14		34
1		3	12	6¹		8	10	2	14	5		13					9³					7		4²		11				35
1		3	6	8¹		10	14	2		13	9²				5		12					7		4³		11				36
1		3	4	6³	8¹	10	11²		2	9			5									7		12			13	14		37
1		3	12	6		8	10	2			5		11²									7		9¹			14	13		38
1		3	12	5¹	6	8	7	2		9²			10								13		14	11³			4			39
1		2	3	6		8	12	4³	5²	9¹			10								13		14	11	7					40
1		3	2	6		8	12	5		14	9³		11									7		4¹			10²	13		41
1		5	3	6		8	12	14	2	9¹			11²									7					13	4	10³	42
1		5	4³	6		14	11	2	3	13	9										9	7				8²	10¹		12	43
1		3	4	6		14	11¹	2	5	13	9										9	7				8³		12	10²	44
1		13	4	6		10³	5	11¹	2	12	3	9									9	7				8²		14		45
1		2	3	4²	6	9¹	8	5		13	11						11					7					12	10		46

FA Cup

Third Round	Burnley	(h)	0-0
		(a)	1-2

Carling Cup

First Round	Swindon T	(a)	3-2
Second Round	Carlisle U	(h)	4-0
Third Round	Aston Villa	(a)	1-0
Fourth Round	Manchester U	(a)	0-1

READING   FL Championship

FOUNDATION

Reading was formed as far back as 1871 at a public meeting held at the Bridge Street Rooms. They first entered the FA Cup as early as 1877 when they amalgamated with the Reading Hornets. The club was further strengthened in 1889 when Earley FC joined them. They were the first winners of the Berks and Bucks Cup in 1878–79.

Madejski Stadium, Junction 11, M4, Reading, Berkshire RG2 0FL.

Telephone: (0844) 249 1871.

Fax: (0118) 968 1101.

Ticket Office: (0844) 249 1871.

Website: www.readingfc.co.uk

Email: customerservice@readingfc.co.uk

Ground Capacity: 24,082.

Record Attendance: Madejski Stadium: 24,122 v Aston Villa, Premiershp, 10 February 2007. Elm Park: 33,042 v Brentford, FA Cup 5th rd, 19 February 1927.

Pitch Measurements: 105m × 68m.

Chairman: John Madejski OBE, DL.

Vice-chairman: Ian Wood-Smith.

Chief Executive: Nigel Howe.

Secretary: Sue Hewett.

Director of Football: Nick Hammond

Manager: Brendan Rodgers.

Physio: Jon Fearn MMACP, MCSP.

HONOURS

FA Premier League: Best season – 8th 2006–07.
Football League: FL C – Champions 2005–06; Division 1 – Runners-up 1994–95; Division 2 – Champions 1993–94; Runners-up 2001–02; Division 3 – Champions 1985–86; Division 3 (S) – Champions 1925–26; Runners-up 1931–32, 1934–35, 1948–49, 1951–52; Division 4 – Champions 1978–79.
FA Cup: Semi-final 1927.
Football League Cup: best season: 5th rd, 1996.
Simod Cup: Winners 1988.

Colours: Blue and white hooped shirts, white shorts, blue stockings.

Change Colours: Tan shirts, blue shorts, tan stockings.

Year Formed: 1871.

Turned Professional: 1895. *Ltd Co.:* 1895.

Club Nickname: 'The Royals'.

Grounds: 1871, Reading Recreation; Reading Cricket Ground; 1882, Coley Park; 1889, Caversham Cricket Ground; 1896, Elm Park; 1998, Madejski Stadium.

First Football League Game: 28 August 1920, Division 3, v Newport Co (a) W 1–0 – Crawford; Smith, Horler; Christie, Mavin, Getgood; Spence, Weston, Yarnell, Bailey (1), Andrews.

Record League Victory: 10–2 v Crystal Palace, Division 3 (S), 4 September 1946 – Groves; Glidden, Gulliver; McKenna, Ratcliffe, Young; Chitty, Maurice Edelston (3), McPhee (4), Barney (1), Deverell (2).

SKY SPORTS FACT FILE

On 31 October 1931 Reading defeated Mansfield Town 4–1 at Elm Park and had completed 19 successive home wins in Division Three (South) until 1 October 1932 when they were held to a 2–2 draw by Aldershot in front of an attendance of 10,778.

Record Cup Victory: 6–0 v Leyton, FA Cup 2nd rd, 12 December 1925 – Duckworth; Eggo, McConnell; Wilson, Messer, Evans; Smith (2), Braithwaite (1), Davey (1), Tinsley, Robson (2).

Record Defeat: 0–18 v Preston NE, FA Cup 1st rd, 1893–94.

Most League Points (2 for a win): 65, Division 4, 1978–79.

Most League Points (3 for a win): 106, Championship, 2005–06.

Most League Goals: 112, Division 3 (S), 1951–52.

Highest League Scorer in Season: Ronnie Blackman, 39, Division 3 (S), 1951–52.

Most League Goals in Total Aggregate: Ronnie Blackman, 158, 1947–54.

Most League Goals in One Match: 6, Arthur Bacon v Stoke C, Division 2, 3 April 1931.

Most Capped Player: Jimmy Quinn, 17 (46), Northern Ireland.

Most League Appearances: Martin Hicks, 500, 1978–91.

Youngest League Player: Peter Castle, 16 years 49 days v Watford, 30 April 2003.

Record Transfer Fee Received: £5,500,000 from Stoke C for Dave Kitson, July 2008.

Record Transfer Fee Paid: Undisclosed to Nantes for Emerse Fae, August 2007.

Football League Record: 1920 Original Member of Division 3; 1921–26 Division 3 (S); 1926–31 Division 2; 1931–58 Division 3 (S); 1958–71 Division 3; 1971–76 Division 4; 1976–77 Division 3; 1977–79 Division 4; 1979–83 Division 3; 1983–84 Division 4; 1984–86 Division 3; 1986–88 Division 2; 1988–92 Division 3; 1992–94 Division 2; 1994–98 Division 1; 1998–2002 Division 2; 2002–04 Division 1; 2004–06 FL C; 2006–08 FA Premier League; 2008– FL C.

MANAGERS

Thomas Sefton 1897–1901
  (Secretary-Manager)
James Sharp 1901–02
Harry Matthews 1902–20
Harry Marshall 1920–22
Arthur Chadwick 1923–25
H. S. Bray 1925–26
  *(Secretary only since 1922 and
  1926–35)*
Andrew Wylie 1926–31
Joe Smith 1931–35
Billy Butler 1935–39
John Cochrane 1939
Joe Edelston 1939–47
Ted Drake 1947–52
Jack Smith 1952–55
Harry Johnston 1955–63
Roy Bentley 1963–69
Jack Mansell 1969–71
Charlie Hurley 1972–77
Maurice Evans 1977–84
Ian Branfoot 1984–89
Ian Porterfield 1989–91
Mark McGhee 1991–94
Jimmy Quinn/Mick Gooding
  1994–97
Terry Bullivant 1997–98
Tommy Burns 1998–99
Alan Pardew 1999–2003
Steve Coppell 2003–09
Brendan Rodgers June 2009–

LATEST SEQUENCES

Longest Sequence of League Wins: 13, 17.8.1985 – 19.10.1985.

Longest Sequence of League Defeats: 8, 29.12.2007 – 24.2.2008.

Longest Sequence of League Draws: 6, 23.3.2002 – 20.4.2002.

Longest Sequence of Unbeaten League Matches: 33, 9.8.2005 – 14.2.2006.

Longest Sequence Without a League Win: 14, 30.4.1927 – 29.10.1927.

Successive Scoring Runs: 32 from 1.10.1932.

Successive Non-scoring Runs: 6 from 13.4.1925.

TEN YEAR LEAGUE RECORD

		P	W	D	L	F	A	Pts	Pos
1999-2000	Div 2	46	16	14	16	57	63	62	10
2000-01	Div 2	46	25	11	10	86	52	86	3
2001-02	Div 2	46	23	15	8	70	43	84	2
2002-03	Div 1	46	25	4	17	61	46	79	4
2003-04	Div 1	46	20	10	16	55	57	70	9
2004-05	FL C	46	19	13	14	51	44	70	7
2005-06	FL C	46	31	13	2	99	32	106	1
2006-07	PR Lge	38	16	7	15	52	47	55	8
2007-08	PR Lge	38	10	6	22	41	66	36	18
2008-09	FL C	46	21	14	11	72	40	77	4

DID YOU KNOW ?

Reading were the first in the Third Division to reach 5,000 goals. Against Wycombe Wanderers on 22 September 2001 Adrian Williams was the milestone scorer. But a commemorative citation was given to Darius Henderson – the 5,001st two minutes later!

READING 2008–09 LEAGUE RECORD

Match No.	Date	Venue	Opponents	Result		H/T Score	Lg. Pos.	Goalscorers	Attendance
1	Aug 10	A	Nottingham F	D	0-0	0-0	—		21,571
2	16	H	Plymouth Arg	W	2-0	1-0	5	Sonko 2 [13, 50]	19,202
3	23	A	Charlton Ath	L	2-4	1-2	18	Sonko [45], Hunt S (pen) [54]	20,020
4	30	H	Crystal Palace	W	4-2	1-1	6	Harper [18], Doyle 3 [67, 68, 89]	20,441
5	Sept 13	A	Ipswich T	L	0-2	0-0	9		21,366
6	16	H	Sheffield W	W	6-0	3-0	—	Doyle 3 [5, 9, 62], Bikey [30], Hunt N 2 [50, 64]	18,159
7	20	A	Watford	D	2-2	1-0	6	Eustace (og) [13], Hunt S (pen) [87]	14,761
8	27	H	Swansea C	W	4-0	3-0	3	Hunt N [19], Doyle 2 [26, 90], Hunt S [40]	20,093
9	30	A	Wolverhampton W	W	3-0	1-0	—	Hennessey (og) [4], Bikey [71], Cisse [88]	24,302
10	Oct 4	H	Burnley	W	3-1	1-0	3	Hunt N [4], Hunt S [52], Long [64]	18,621
11	18	A	Preston NE	L	1-2	1-0	3	Hunt S (pen) [27]	12,316
12	21	H	Doncaster R	W	2-1	1-0	—	Bikey [18], Doyle [76]	17,294
13	25	H	QPR	D	0-0	0-0	3		20,571
14	28	A	Burnley	L	0-1	0-0	—		11,538
15	Nov 1	A	Bristol C	W	4-1	2-0	3	Doyle 2 [14, 47], Hunt N [16], Cisse [54]	18,296
16	8	H	Derby Co	W	3-0	1-0	3	Hunt N [20], Doyle 2 [68, 75]	18,724
17	15	A	Sheffield U	W	2-0	2-0	3	Cisse [5], Doyle [44]	25,065
18	22	H	Southampton	L	1-2	0-1	3	Kebe [57]	23,121
19	25	A	Cardiff C	D	2-2	1-2	—	Doyle [16], Gunnarsson [50]	17,154
20	Dec 1	H	Coventry C	W	3-1	2-1	—	Hunt N 2 [32, 62], Cisse [37]	16,803
21	6	A	Barnsley	W	1-0	1-0	3	Gunnarsson [64]	11,938
22	9	H	Blackpool	W	1-0	1-0	—	Ingimarsson [27]	16,514
23	13	H	Norwich C	W	2-0	0-0	3	Hunt S (pen) [84], Long [86]	19,382
24	20	A	Birmingham C	W	3-1	1-0	2	Hunt N [13], Doyle [66], Cisse [82]	19,895
25	26	H	Cardiff C	D	1-1	0-0	2	Federici [90]	22,770
26	28	A	Southampton	D	1-1	0-0	2	Long [84]	20,142
27	Jan 9	H	Watford	W	4-0	1-0	—	Armstrong [38], Hunt N [67], Doyle [68], Lita [89]	18,072
28	17	A	Swansea C	L	0-2	0-1	2		15,197
29	27	H	Wolverhampton W	W	1-0	1-0	—	Collins (og) [2]	23,009
30	31	A	QPR	D	0-0	0-0	2		17,120
31	Feb 7	H	Preston NE	D	0-0	0-0	2		19,570
32	21	H	Bristol C	L	0-2	0-1	3		22,462
33	28	H	Nottingham F	L	0-1	0-0	3		21,196
34	Mar 3	A	Sheffield W	W	2-1	1-0	—	Doyle [56], Long [81]	19,268
35	7	A	Plymouth Arg	D	2-2	1-1	3	Pearce [22], Kebe [80]	14,014
36	10	H	Charlton Ath	D	2-2	0-1	—	Long 2 (1 pen) [47 (p), 67]	17,875
37	14	H	Ipswich T	L	0-1	0-0	3		20,592
38	17	A	Doncaster R	W	1-0	0-0	—	Kitson [82]	10,393
39	21	A	Crystal Palace	D	0-0	0-0	3		14,567
40	Apr 4	A	Coventry C	D	0-0	0-0	3		17,218
41	10	H	Sheffield U	L	0-1	0-0	—		20,756
42	13	A	Blackpool	D	2-2	2-1	5	Hunt N [10], Karacan [24]	7722
43	18	H	Barnsley	D	0-0	0-0	5		19,420
44	21	A	Derby Co	W	2-0	0-0	—	Kitson [56], Long [73]	31,345
45	27	A	Norwich C	W	2-0	0-0	—	Long 2 [68, 78]	25,041
46	May 3	H	Birmingham C	L	1-2	0-1	4	Matejovsky [61]	24,011

Final League Position: 4

GOALSCORERS

League (72): Doyle 18, Hunt N 11, Long 9 (1 pen), Hunt S 6 (4 pens), Cisse 5, Bikey 3, Sonko 3, Gunnarsson 2, Kebe 2, Kitson 2, Armstrong 1, Federici 1, Harper 1, Ingimarsson 1, Karacan 1, Lita 1, Matejovsky 1, Pearce 1, own goals 3.
Carling Cup (9): Henry 4 (1 pen), Hunt N 2, Hunt S 1, Karacan 1, Pearce 1.
FA Cup (0).
Play-Offs (0).

Hahnemann M 32	Rosenior L 42	Hunt S 41 + 5	Ingimarsson I 26	Sonko I 3	Harper J 28 + 6	Kebe J 38 + 3	Matejovsky M 11 + 11	Lita L 6 + 4	Doyle K 39 + 2	Convey B 3 + 3	Cisse K 24 + 12	Kelly J 4 + 3	Hunt N 27 + 10	Long S 11 + 26	Pearce A 13 + 3	Armstrong C 40	Karacan J 15	Bikey A 23 + 2	Gunnarsson B 13 + 14	Henry J 3 + 4	Duberry M 27	Federici A 14 + 1	Tabb J 6 + 3	Little G 6 + 3	Kitson D 9 + 1	Harding D 3	Match No.
1	2	3	4	5	6	7	8[1]	9	10	11	12																1
1	2	11	4	5	6	3			9[2]	10[3]	7[1]	8	12	13	14												2
1	2	3	4	5	6	7			9[3]	10[2]	11[1]	8	12	13	14												3
1	2	11	4		6	7			10		12		9[1]			5		3	8								4
1	2	11	4		6	7			10		12	13	9[2]			5		3[1]	8[3]		14						5
1	2	11[2]			6	7			10[1]		13	14	9[3]	12		5		3	8		4						6
1	2	11			6	7			10				9[1]	12		5		3	8		4						7
1	2	11	4			7[3]			10		12		9[2]	13	3	6		5	8[1]		14						8
1	2	11	4			7			10[3]		12		9[2]	13	3	8[1]		5	6		14						9
1	2	11	4			7			10		12	13	9[3]	14	3[2]	8[1]		5	6								10
1	2	11	4		12	7			10[2]		14	9	13		3	8[1]		5	6[3]								11
1	2	11	4		12	7			10		13	9[3]	14		3	8[2]		5	6[1]								12
1	2	11	4		12	7[3]			10		13	9	14		3	8[2]		5	6[1]								13
1	2	11	4		6	7			10		8		9		3	5											14
1	2	11	4		6[2]	7	12		10[3]		8		9[1]	14	3	5		13									15
1	2	11	4		6[2]	7	12		10		8[1]		9	14	3	5		13									16
1	2	11	4		6	7[2]			10		8		9[1]	12	3	5		13									17
1	2	11	4		6[3]	7	12		10		8[1]		9[2]	13	3	5		14									18
1	2	11	4		6	7			10		8		9[1]		3	5[1]		12									19
1	2	11	4		6	7[3]			10		8[2]		9[1]	12	3	13		14	5								20
1	2	11	4		6	7[1]			10		8		9[1]		3	12		5									21
1[6]	2	11	4			8			10	12			9[2]	13	3	6		7[1]	5		15						22
	2	11	4		6[2]	8			10		7[3]		9[1]	12	3	13		14	5			1					23
	2	11	4		6				10		8		9[1]	12	3	13		7[2]	5			1					24
	2	11	4		6	12			10		8		9[2]	13	3	7[1]			5			1					25
	2	11	4		12	7	8[1]		10		14	13	9		3[2]	6[3]			5			1					26
	2	11	4		6	7	12		10[1]		8[2]		9[3]	14	3	13			5			1					27
	2[1]	11	4		6[3]	7[2]	12	13	10		8		9[1]		3	14			5			1					28
		11			6	7	13		10[2]		8	2	9[1]	12	4	3			14			5[3]	1				29
	2	11			6	7[1]		9	10		8				4	3			12			5	1				30
	2	11			6[1]	7[2]	12	9	10[3]		8		13	14	4	3			5				1				31
	2	11			6[3]	7	12	9	10		8[1]		13		4[2]	3			14			5	1				32
	2	11				7[3]	8	12	10		13		9		4	3[1]		6[2]				5	1	14			33
	2	11				12	8		10		13		9[3]	14	4	3		6[2]				5	1	7[1]			34
	2	11				12	7	8	10		6[1]		9		4[2]	3			13			5	1				35
	2	11[3]				12	8		10		6[2]		13	9	4	3			5			1		14	7[1]		36
1	2[2]	11[1]			6	12	13		14				9[3]	4	3	8			5					7	10		37
1	2	12			6	7[1]	8		10				13	3	4	11			5					9[2]			38
1	2[1]	12			6	7[1]	8[3]		10		13		14	3	4	11[2]			5					9			39
1		13			6[2]	12			8	2	14	10		3	4	5			11[3]				7[1]	9			40
1		11			7[2]	8[3]	10		4[1]	2	14			3	6	5			12				13	9			41
1		11			7[1]				2	9	10[2]		3	4	6	5			8				13	12	9		42
1	2	11[2]			7				14		9[1]	12		3	4[3]	6			5				8	13	10		43
1	2	12			11[3]	14			10		13			4	6[2]	5			8				7[1]	9		3	44
1	2	12			7	13			8[2]		10	14		4	6	5			11[1]				9[3]			3	45
1	2	11			7	12			13		10			4[1]	6	5			8				9			3[2]	46

FA Cup
Third Round   Cardiff C   (a)   0-2

Carling Cup
First Round   Dagenham & R   (a)   2-1
Second Round   Luton T   (h)   5-1
Third Round   Stoke C   (a)   2-2

Play-Offs
Semi-Final   Burnley   (a)   0-1
    (h)   0-2

ROCHDALE

FOUNDATION

Considering the love of rugby in their area, it is not surprising that Rochdale had difficulty in establishing an Association Football club. The earlier Rochdale Town club formed in 1900 went out of existence in 1907 when the present club was immediately established and joined the Manchester League, before graduating to the Lancashire Combination in 1908.

Spotland Stadium, Sandy Lane, Rochdale OL11 5DS.

Telephone: (0870) 822 1907.

Fax: (01706) 648 466.

Ticket Office: (01706) 648 466.

Website: www.rochdaleafc.co.uk

Email: office@rochdaleafc.co.uk

Ground Capacity: 10,199.

Record Attendance: 24,231 v Notts Co, FA Cup 2nd rd, 10 December 1949.

Pitch Measurements: 114yd × 76yd.

Chairman: Chris Dunphy.

Chief Executive/Secretary: Colin Garlick.

Manager: Keith Hill.

Assistant Manager: David Flitcroft.

Physio: Andy Thorpe.

Colours: Black and blue striped shirts, white shorts, blue stockings.

Change Colours: White shirts, blue shorts, white stockings.

Year Formed: 1907.

Turned Professional: 1907.

Ltd Co.: 1910.

Club Nickname: 'The Dale'.

Ground: 1907, St Clements Playing Fields (original name Spotland).

First Football League Game: 27 August 1921, Division 3 (N), v Accrington Stanley (h) W 6–3 – Crabtree; Nuttall, Sheehan; Hill, Farrer, Yarwood; Hoad, Sandiford, Dennison (2), Owens (3), Carney (1).

Record League Victory: 8–1 v Chesterfield, Division 3 (N), 18 December 1926 – Hill; Brown, Ward; Hillhouse, Parkes, Braidwood; Hughes, Bertram, Whitehurst (5), Schofield (2), Martin (1).

Record Cup Victory: 8–2 v Crook T, FA Cup 1st rd, 26 November 1927 – Moody; Hopkins, Ward; Braidwood, Parkes, Barker; Tompkinson, Clennell (3) Whitehurst (4), Hall, Martin (1).

HONOURS

Football League: Division 3 best season: 9th, 1969–70; Division 3 (N) – Runners-up 1923–24, 1926–27.

FA Cup: best season: 5th rd, 1990, 2003.

Football League Cup: Runners-up 1962 (record for 4th Division club).

SKY SPORTS FACT FILE

Jack Livesey scored for Rochdale after 20 seconds at New Brighton on 11 September 1948 in a 2–1 win. This remained the club's quickest goal until Steve Johnson scored in just 14 seconds against York City on 13 December 1983 in a 2–0 FA Cup success.

Record Defeat: 1–9 v Tranmere R, Division 3 (N), 25 December 1931.

Most League Points (2 for a win): 62, Division 3 (N), 1923–24.

Most League Points (3 for a win): 80, FL 2, 2007–08.

Most League Goals: 105, Division 3 (N), 1926–27.

Highest League Scorer in Season: Albert Whitehurst, 44, Division 3 (N), 1926–27.

Most League Goals in Total Aggregate: Reg Jenkins, 119, 1964–73.

Most League Goals in One Match: 6, Tommy Tippett v Hartlepools U, Division 3 (N), 21 April 1930.

Most Capped Player: Leo Bertos, 6 (23), New Zealand.

Most League Appearances: Gary Jones, 345, 1998–2001; 2003–.

Youngest League Player: Zac Hughes, 16 years 105 days v Exeter C, 19 September 1987.

Record Transfer Fee Received: £400,000 from West Ham U for Stephen Bywater, August 1998.

Record Transfer Fee Paid: £150,000 to Stoke C for Paul Connor, March 2001.

Football League Record: 1921 Elected to Division 3 (N); 1958–59 Division 3; 1959–69 Division 4; 1969–74 Division 3; 1974–92 Division 4; 1992–2004 Division 3; 2004– FL 2.

LATEST SEQUENCES

Longest Sequence of League Wins: 8, 29.9.1969 – 3.11.1969.

Longest Sequence of League Defeats: 17, 14.11.1931 – 12.3.1932.

Longest Sequence of League Draws: 6, 17.8.1968 – 14.9.1968.

Longest Sequence of Unbeaten League Matches: 20, 15.9.1923 – 19.1.1924.

Longest Sequence Without a League Win: 28, 14.11.1931 – 29.8.1932.

Successive Scoring Runs: 29 from 8.1.1927.

Successive Non-scoring Runs: 9 from 14.3.1980.

MANAGERS

Billy Bradshaw 1920
Run by committee 1920–22
Tom Wilson 1922–23
Jack Peart 1923–30
Will Cameron 1930–31
Herbert Hopkinson 1932–34
Billy Smith 1934–35
Ernest Nixon 1935–37
Sam Jennings 1937–38
Ted Goodier 1938–52
Jack Warner 1952–53
Harry Catterick 1953–58
Jack Marshall 1958–60
Tony Collins 1960–68
Bob Stokoe 1967–68
Len Richley 1968–70
Dick Conner 1970–73
Walter Joyce 1973–76
Brian Green 1976–77
Mike Ferguson 1977–78
Doug Collins 1979
Bob Stokoe 1979–80
Peter Madden 1980–83
Jimmy Greenhoff 1983–84
Vic Halom 1984–86
Eddie Gray 1986–88
Danny Bergara 1988–89
Terry Dolan 1989–91
Dave Sutton 1991–94
Mick Docherty 1995–96
Graham Barrow 1996–99
Steve Parkin 1999–2001
John Hollins 2001–02
Paul Simpson 2002–03
Alan Buckley 2003–04
Steve Parkin 2004–06
Keith Hill January 2007–

TEN YEAR LEAGUE RECORD

		P	W	D	L	F	A	Pts	Pos
1999-2000	Div 3	46	18	14	14	57	54	68	10
2000-01	Div 3	46	18	17	11	59	48	71	8
2001-02	Div 3	46	21	15	10	65	52	78	5
2002-03	Div 3	46	12	16	18	63	70	52	19
2003-04	Div 3	46	12	14	20	49	58	50	21
2004-05	FL 2	46	16	18	12	54	48	66	9
2005-06	FL 2	46	14	14	18	66	69	56	14
2006-07	FL 2	46	18	12	16	70	50	66	9
2007-08	FL 2	46	23	11	12	77	54	80	5
2008-09	FL 2	46	19	13	14	70	59	70	6

DID YOU KNOW ?

On 31 January 2009, hat-tricks-are-us Rochdale added another one to their list when Joe Thompson produced a treble of goals in a 17-minute first half spell at Aldershot. It was his first such feat for the club and Rochdale went on to win 4–1.

ROCHDALE 2008–09 LEAGUE RECORD

Match No.	Date	Venue	Opponents	Result	H/T Score	Lg. Pos.	Goalscorers	Attendance
1	Aug 9	A	Grimsby T	D	0-0	0-0	—	4213
2	16	H	Barnet	W	3-1	2-1	5	Rundle [39], Dagnall [45], Shaw [72]	2442
3	23	A	Bradford C	L	0-2	0-2	11		13,154
4	30	H	Bury	D	1-1	0-1	13	Le Fondre (pen) [66]	5492
5	Sept 6	H	Wycombe W	L	0-1	0-1	14		2880
6	13	A	Rotherham U	D	2-2	1-0	15	Rhodes [43], Buckley [51]	3569
7	20	A	Chesterfield	W	2-1	0-0	10	Buckley [67], Kennedy [90]	2884
8	28	A	Accrington S	W	3-1	1-1	9	Le Fondre (pen) [38], Buckley [57], Rhodes [90]	2417
9	Oct 4	H	Dagenham & R	L	0-2	0-1	12		2566
10	10	A	Lincoln C	D	1-1	1-0	—	Rundle [26]	4510
11	18	A	Morecambe	D	1-1	1-0	12	Dagnall [19]	2572
12	21	H	Chester C	W	6-1	2-0	—	Dagnall 3 [14, 32, 58], Thorpe [62], Le Fondre 2 [68, 69]	2162
13	25	H	Aldershot T	W	3-1	1-0	10	Rundle [27], Thompson [81], Buckley [90]	2750
14	28	A	Notts Co	W	2-1	0-0	—	Thorpe 2 [63, 73]	3610
15	Nov 1	A	Brentford	W	2-1	0-0	6	McArdle [31], Buckley [40]	4291
16	15	H	Macclesfield T	D	1-1	0-0	4	Rundle [66]	3013
17	22	H	Luton T	W	2-0	1-0	3	Thorpe [2], Le Fondre (pen) [59]	2901
18	25	A	Gillingham	D	1-1	0-1	—	Le Fondre [61]	4029
19	Dec 13	H	Bournemouth	D	1-1	0-1	7	Le Fondre [67]	2285
20	20	A	Exeter C	L	1-4	0-2	9	Keltie (pen) [90]	4326
21	26	H	Shrewsbury T	W	2-1	0-0	6	McEvilly 2 [67, 83]	4159
22	28	A	Port Vale	L	1-2	0-0	9	Le Fondre (pen) [82]	5720
23	Jan 3	H	Accrington S	W	3-1	1-1	—	Le Fondre (pen) [22], Buckley [56], Higginbotham [87]	3126
24	17	H	Lincoln C	D	2-2	1-0	8	Le Fondre [26], McEvilly [84]	2897
25	24	A	Dagenham & R	L	2-3	2-1	10	Kennedy [16], Adams [21]	1808
26	27	H	Notts Co	W	3-0	1-0	—	Buckley [45], Dagnall [72], Le Fondre [90]	2289
27	31	A	Aldershot T	W	4-2	4-0	6	Thompson 3 [17, 23, 34], Toner [45]	3018
28	Feb 3	A	Chester C	W	2-0	0-0	—	Thompson [55], McEvilly [65]	1357
29	14	A	Macclesfield T	W	1-0	1-0	4	Kennedy (pen) [45]	2396
30	17	H	Morecambe	D	1-1	0-0	—	Buckley [50]	3347
31	21	H	Brentford	L	1-2	1-2	5	Kennedy (pen) [37]	3412
32	24	A	Darlington	W	2-1	1-0	—	Le Fondre [28], Rundle [62]	2858
33	28	H	Grimsby T	W	2-0	2-0	2	Rundle [5], Le Fondre [12]	3076
34	Mar 3	A	Barnet	L	1-2	1-1	—	McEvilly [45]	1332
35	7	A	Bury	L	1-2	0-1	5	Buckley [90]	7589
36	10	H	Bradford C	W	3-0	0-0	—	McArdle [49], Le Fondre 2 (2 pens) [56, 74]	5500
37	14	H	Rotherham U	L	1-2	0-0	3	Le Fondre [75]	3201
38	21	A	Wycombe W	W	1-0	0-0	2	Le Fondre [90]	6055
39	25	A	Chesterfield	L	0-3	0-1	—		3271
40	28	H	Exeter C	D	2-2	1-0	3	Thorpe [27], Le Fondre [83]	3364
41	Apr 4	A	Bournemouth	L	0-4	0-2	5		5092
42	11	H	Port Vale	W	1-0	1-0	5	Buckley [36]	3100
43	13	A	Shrewsbury T	D	1-1	0-0	5	Dagnall [73]	6234
44	18	H	Darlington	L	0-2	0-1	6		3789
45	25	A	Luton T	D	1-1	0-1	6	Rundle [56]	7025
46	May 2	H	Gillingham	L	0-1	0-1	6		3480

Final League Position: 6

GOALSCORERS

League (70): Le Fondre 18 (7 pens), Buckley 10, Dagnall 7, Rundle 7, McEvilly 5, Thompson 5, Thorpe 5, Kennedy 4 (2 pens), McArdle 2, Rhodes 2, Adams 1, Higginbotham 1, Keltie 1 (pen), Shaw 1, Toner 1.
Carling Cup (0):
FA Cup (4): Le Fondre 3, Dagnall 1.
J Paint Trophy (2): Dagnall 1, Thorpe 1.
Play-Offs (1): Dagnall 1.

Russell S 23	Ramsden S 25 + 3	Kennedy T 45	Keltie C 26 + 5	Stanton N 39	McArdle R 41	Wiseman S 30 + 2	Jones G 28	Dagnall C 25 + 15	Le Fondre A 28 + 16	Rundle A 32 + 12	Higginbotham K 3 + 4	Thorpe L 18 + 10	Toner C 32 + 5	Shaw J 5 + 1	Buckley W 28 + 9	Lambert K —+ 1	Rhodes J 5	Thompson J 21 + 9	Holness M 4 + 4	McEvilly L 4 + 12	Jones M 7 + 2	Fielding F 23	Adams N 12 + 2	Madine G 1 + 2	Newey T 1 + 1	Flitcroft D —+ 1	Match No.
1	2	3	4	5	6	7^1	8	9	10^2	11	12	13															1
1	2	3	4	5	6		8	9^2	13	11	7^1	14	12	10^3													2
1	2^1	3	4	5	6	12	8	9	13	11		14	7^2	10^3													3
1		3	4	5	6	2	8	9	10	11				7													4
1	2	3		5	6		8	9^3	10	11	14	12	4^2	7^1	13												5
1	2	3	4	5	6		8	12	10^2	11		13	14	7^3			9^1										6
1	2	3	4	5	6		8	12	10^1	11				7			9										7
1	2^2	3	4	5	6	13	8	12	10^1	11				7^3			9	14									8
1		3	4^1	5	6	2	8	13	10^2	11^3		12		7			9	14									9
1		3		5	6		8	12	13	11		10	4	7^2			9^1		2								10
1		3		5^1	6		8	9^2	13	11^3		10	4		14			7	12								11
1		3	12	5	6	2	8^1	9^2	13	14		10^3	4		7			11									12
1		3		5^1	6	2	8	9^2	13	11^3		10	4		14			7	12								13
1		3		5	6	2	8	9^1	12	11		10	4		13			7^2									14
1		3		5	6	2	8	9^1	12	11		10	4		7^2			13									15
1		3		5	6	2	8	9^1	12	11		10	4		13			7^2									16
1		3	4	5	6	2	8^2	12	9^1	11		10	13		7^3			14									17
1		3	4	5	6	2^2		9	11^1			10	8		12			7	13								18
1	2	3	4	5				12	9	11^1			8	13	7					6	10^2						19
1	5	3	4		6	2^8		14	10^1	11^3			8	9	7^2					13	12						20
1	2	3	4	5	6			12	10^1	11			8^3	9^2	7					13	14						21
1	2	3	4^3	5	6			9^1	12			11^2	7	8				13		10	14						22
1		3	4	5	6	2		12	9^2	11		13	8		7						10^1						23
	2	3	12	5	6		8	13	9^2	11				4^1	10			7^3			14	1		1			24
	2	3	4	5	6		8	13	10^2	14				9				7^3			12	1	11^1	1			25
		3		5	6	2	8	9	13	12				4	10^2			7				1	11^1				26
14		3		5^8	6	2	8	9^1	12	13				4	10^2			7				1	11^3				27
		3		5	6	2	8	9^3	12	13				4	11^1			10	14			1	7^2				28
		3		5	6	2	8	9^1	12	13				4	10^2			7	14			1	11^3				29
5		3			6	2	8	9^2	12			13	4		10^1			7				1	11				30
		3	12	5	6	2	8	9	13					4^1	10			7^3			14	1	11^2				31
6		3	12	5		2	8^1		9	11		10	4									1	7				32
6		3	8	5		2		12	9^1	11		10^3	4		13			14				1	7^2				33
	2	3	4	5		6		12^8	9^1	11^3			13	8	14						10^2	1	7				34
6		3	12	5		2		9		13		10^3	4^1		11			8			14	1	7^2				35
12	3^1		4	5	6	2						10		9^2	11^3			7				1	13	8	14		36
		3	4	5	6	2			10	11^2		12	9^3					7^1				1	14	8		13	37
5		3	4		6	2			11^2	10		12			9^3			13				1	8	7^1		14	38
5		3	4^1		6	2		7	10^3	11			13		12			14				1	8	9^2			39
		3		5	6	2			9^1	12		11	10		4			7				1	8				40
5		3			6	2		12	10	11^3			9	4	13			7^1				1	8^2		14		41
	2	3	4		6			9	10^2	14	7^1		8		11^3			12	5			1	13				42
	2	3	4	5	6			9	10	13			12	8	11^2			7^1				1					43
	2	3	4	5	6			9	10	11			12	8				7^1				1					44
	2	3	7^1	5	6		8	9^2	10	12		11^3	4		14			13				1					45
	12		6^1			2	4			11^3		10	9					7^2	5	14	8	1			3	13	46

FA Cup

First Round	Barnet	(a)	1-1	
		(h)	3-2	
Second Round	Forest Green R	(a)	0-2	

Carling Cup

First Round	Oldham Ath	(h)	0-0

J Paint Trophy

Second Round	Carlisle U	(h)	2-2
Quarter-Final	Scunthorpe U	(a)	0-1

Play-Offs

Semi-Final	Gillingham	(h)	0-0
		(a)	1-2

ROTHERHAM UNITED   FL Championship 2

FOUNDATION

Rotherham were formed in 1870 before becoming Town in the late 1880s. Thornhill United were founded in 1877 and changed their name to Rotherham County in 1905. The Town amalgamated with Rotherham County to form Rotherham United in 1925.

Don Valley Stadium, Worksop Road, Sheffield, South Yorkshire S9 3TL.
Telephone: (08444) 140 737.
Ticket Office: (08444) 140 737.
Website: www.themillers.co.uk
Email: office@rotherhamunited.net
Ground Capacity: 25,000.
Record Attendance: 25,170 v Sheffield U, Division 2, 13 December 1952.
Pitch Measurements. 108yd × 72yd.
Chairman: Tony Stewart.
Chief Operating Officer: Paul Douglas.
Secretary: J. Pilmner.
Manager: Mark Robins.
Assistant Manager: John Breckin.
Physio: Denis Circuit.
Colours: Red shirts with white design, white shorts, red stockings.
Change Colours: Yellow shirts with black trim, black shorts, yellow stockings.
Year Formed: 1870.
Turned Professional: 1905.
Ltd Co.: 1920.
Club Nickname: 'The Merry Millers'.
Previous Names: 1877, Thornhill United; 1905, Rotherham County; 1925, amalgamated with Rotherham Town under Rotherham United.
Grounds: 1870, Red House Ground; 1907, Millmoor; 2008, Don Valley Stadium.
First Football League Game: 2 September 1893, Division 2, Rotherham T v Lincoln C (a) D 1–1 – McKay; Thickett, Watson; Barr, Brown, Broadhead; Longden, Cutts, Leatherbarrow, McCormick, Pickering, (1 og). 30 August 1919, Division 2, Rotherham Co v Nottingham F (h) W 2–0 – Branston; Alton, Baines; Bailey, Coe, Stanton; Lee (1), Cawley (1), Glennon, Lees, Lamb.
Record League Victory: 8–0 v Oldham Ath, Division 3 (N), 26 May 1947 – Warnes; Selkirk, Ibbotson; Edwards, Horace Williams, Danny Williams; Wilson (2), Shaw (1), Ardron (3), Guest (1), Hainsworth (1).
Record Cup Victory: 6–0 v Spennymoor U, FA Cup 2nd rd, 17 December 1977 – McAlister; Forrest, Breckin, Womble, Stancliffe, Green, Finney, Phillips (3), Gwyther (2) (Smith), Goodfellow, Crawford (1). 6–0 v Wolverhampton W, FA Cup 1st rd, 16 November 1985 – O'Hanlon; Forrest, Dungworth, Gooding (1), Smith (1), Pickering, Birch (2), Emerson, Tynan (1), Simmons (1), Pugh. 6–0 v Kings Lynn, FA Cup 2nd rd, 6 December 1997 – Mimms; Clark, Hurst (Goodwin), Garner (1) (Hudson) (1), Warner (Bass), Richardson (1), Berry (1), Thompson, Druce (1), Glover (1), Roscoe.

HONOURS

Football League: Division 2 – runners-up 2000–01; Division 3 – Champions 1980–81; Runners-up 1999–2000; Division 3 (N) – Champions 1950–51; Runners-up 1946–47, 1947–48, 1948–49; Division 4 – Champions 1988–89; Runners-up 1991–92.
FA Cup: best season: 5th rd, 1953, 1968.
Football League Cup: Runners-up 1961.
Auto Windscreens Shield: Winners 1996.

SKY SPORTS FACT FILE

Andy Smailes initially had a month's trial with Rotherham United towards the end of a lengthy career as a midfield player in August 1929. It turned out to be the start of a 30-year attachment to the club. Appointed trainer in 1933 he retired in October 1958.

Record Defeat: 1–11 v Bradford C, Division 3 (N), 25 August 1928.

Most League Points (2 for a win): 71, Division 3 (N), 1950–51.

Most League Points (3 for a win): 91, Division 2, 2000–01.

Most League Goals: 114, Division 3 (N), 1946–47.

Highest League Scorer in Season: Wally Ardron, 38, Division 3 (N), 1946–47.

Most League Goals in Total Aggregate: Gladstone Guest, 130, 1946–56.

Most League Goals in One Match: 4, Roland Bastow v York C, Division 3 (N), 9 November 1935; 4, Roland Bastow v Rochdale, Division 3 (N), 7 March 1936; 4, Wally Ardron v Crewe Alex, Division 3 (N), 5 October 1946; 4, Wally Ardron v Carlisle U, Division 3 (N), 13 September 1947; 4, Wally Ardron v Hartlepools U, Division 3 (N), 13 October 1948; 4, Ian Wilson v Liverpool, Division 2, 2 May 1955; 4, Carl Gilbert v Swansea C, Division 3, 28 September 1971; 4, Carl Airey v Chester, Division 3, 31 August 1987; 4, Shaun Goater v Hartlepool U, Division 3, 9 April 1994; 4, Lee Glover v Hull C, Division 3, 28 December 1997; 4, Darren Byfield v Millwall, Division 1, 10 August 2002.

Most Capped Player: Shaun Goater, 14 (36), Bermuda.

Most League Appearances: Danny Williams, 459, 1946–62.

Youngest League Player: Kevin Eley, 16 years 72 days v Scunthorpe U, 15 May 1984.

Record Transfer Fee Received: £850,000 from Cardiff C for Alan Lee, August 2003.

Record Transfer Fee Paid: £150,000 to Millwall for Tony Towner, August 1980; £150,000 to Port Vale for Lee Glover, August 1996; £150,000 to Burnley for Alan Lee, September 2000; £150,000 to Reading for Martin Butler, September 2003.

Football League Record: 1893 Rotherham Town elected to Division 2; 1896 Failed re-election; 1919 Rotherham County elected to Division 2; 1923–51 Division 3 (N); 1951–68 Division 2; 1968–73 Division 3; 1973–75 Division 4; 1975–81 Division 3; 1981–83 Division 2; 1983–88 Division 3; 1988–89 Division 4; 1989–91 Division 3; 1991–92 Division 4; 1992–97 Division 2; 1997–2000 Division 3; 2000–01 Division 2; 2001–04 Division 1; 2004–05 FL C; 2005–07 FL 1; 2007– FL 2.

MANAGERS

Billy Heald 1925–29 *(Secretary only for long spell)*
Stanley Davies 1929–30
Billy Heald 1930–33
Reg Freeman 1934–52
Andy Smailes 1952–58
Tom Johnston 1958–62
Danny Williams 1962–65
Jack Mansell 1965–67
Tommy Docherty 1967–68
Jimmy McAnearney 1968–73
Jimmy McGuigan 1973–79
Ian Porterfield 1979–81
Emlyn Hughes 1981–83
George Kerr 1983–85
Norman Hunter 1985–87
Dave Cusack 1987–88
Billy McEwan 1988–91
Phil Henson 1991–94
Archie Gemmill/John McGovern 1994–96
Danny Bergara 1996–97
Ronnie Moore 1997–2005
Mick Harford 2005
Alan Knill 2005–07
Mark Robins April 2007–

LATEST SEQUENCES

Longest Sequence of League Wins: 9, 2.2.1982 – 6.3.1982.

Longest Sequence of League Defeats: 8, 7.4.1956 – 18.8.1956.

Longest Sequence of League Draws: 6, 13.10.1969 – 22.11.1969.

Longest Sequence of Unbeaten League Matches: 18, 13.10.1969 – 7.2.1970.

Longest Sequence Without a League Win: 21, 9.5.2004 – 20.11.2004.

Successive Scoring Runs: 30 from 3.4.1954.

Successive Non-scoring Runs: 6 from 21.8.2004.

TEN YEAR LEAGUE RECORD

		P	W	D	L	F	A	Pts	Pos
1999-2000	Div 3	46	24	12	10	72	36	84	2
2000-01	Div 2	46	27	10	9	79	55	91	2
2001-02	Div 1	46	10	19	17	52	66	49	21
2002-03	Div 1	46	15	14	17	62	62	59	15
2003-04	Div 1	46	13	15	18	53	61	54	17
2004-05	FL C	46	5	14	27	35	69	29	24
2005-06	FL 1	46	12	16	18	52	62	52	20
2006-07	FL 1	46	13	9	24	58	75	38	23
2007-08	FL 2	46	21	11	14	62	58	64*	9
2008-09	FL 2	46	21	12	13	60	46	58†	14

10 pts deducted; †17 points deducted.

DID YOU KNOW ?

When Rotherham United entertained Brentford on 20 December 1980, the match was preceded by a circus act at Millmoor. But it did not herald sending in the clowns as the Merry Millers won 4–1 in the Third Division championship-winning season for them.

ROTHERHAM UNITED 2008–09 LEAGUE RECORD

Match No.	Date		Venue	Opponents	Result		H/T Score	Lg. Pos.	Goalscorers	Atten- dance
1	Aug	9	H	Lincoln C	W	1-0	1-0	—	Reid [44]	4748
2		16	A	Morecambe	W	3-1	2-0	22	Lynch 2 [8, 90], Taylor R [40]	2606
3		23	H	Chester C	W	3-1	3-1	22	Sharps [2], Reid [14], Rhodes [27]	3462
4		30	A	Brentford	D	0-0	0-0	22		4381
5	Sept	6	A	Chesterfield	L	0-1	0-0	22		4951
6		13	H	Rochdale	D	2-2	0-1	22	McArdle (og) [77], Reid [90]	3569
7		20	H	Luton T	W	1-0	0-0	22	Rhodes [61]	4095
8		27	A	Dagenham & R	D	1-1	0-0	22	Burchill [84]	1805
9	Oct	4	H	Grimsby T	W	4-1	0-1	22	Reid [49], Hudson [57], Cummins [69], Barker [80]	3889
10		11	A	Bournemouth	D	0-0	0-0	22		4530
11		18	H	Barnet	L	3-4	1-2	22	Fenton [7], Sharps [70], Burchill (pen) [81]	3801
12		21	A	Bury	W	2-1	2-1	—	Reid [2], Broughton [11]	2362
13		25	A	Macclesfield T	W	2-1	1-0	21	Tonge [5], Sharps [89]	2020
14		28	H	Darlington	L	0-1	0-0	—		3322
15	Nov	1	H	Wycombe W	D	0-0	0-0	21		3471
16		15	A	Gillingham	L	0-4	0-1	21		5304
17		22	H	Bradford C	L	0-2	0-0	22		4586
18		25	A	Exeter C	D	1-1	0-1	—	Reid (pen) [66]	3402
19	Dec	6	A	Shrewsbury T	L	0-1	0-0	21		5314
20		20	A	Accrington S	W	3-1	2-1	22	Burchill 2 (1 pen) [6 (p), 11], Broughton [88]	1172
21		26	H	Port Vale	W	1-0	0-0	20	Broughton [67]	4350
22		28	A	Notts Co	W	3-0	1-0	20	Reid [5], Broughton [47], Cummins [52]	6686
23	Jan	3	H	Dagenham & R	D	1-1	0-0	—	Sharps [90]	3307
24		17	H	Bournemouth	W	1-0	1-0	19	Hudson [18]	3270
25		24	A	Grimsby T	L	0-3	0-0	20		4559
26		27	A	Darlington	L	0-1	0-1	—		2431
27		31	H	Macclesfield T	W	2-0	1-0	19	Hudson [12], Reid [76]	2945
28	Feb	14	H	Gillingham	W	2-0	1-0	18	Clarke [25], Green [81]	2757
29		23	A	Wycombe W	D	0-0	0-0	—		3739
30		28	A	Lincoln C	W	1-0	0-0	18	Cummins [65]	4336
31	Mar	7	H	Brentford	D	0-0	0-0	18		3406
32		10	A	Chester C	W	5-1	3-1	—	Reid 3 (1 pen) [26 (p), 50, 72], Cummins [38], Broughton [45]	1235
33		14	A	Rochdale	W	2-1	0-0	15	Reid [50], Taylor R [71]	3201
34		17	H	Aldershot T	L	1-2	0-2	—	Clarke [78]	2769
35		21	H	Chesterfield	W	3-0	1-0	15	Reid 2 [38, 55], Mills [83]	4658
36		24	H	Bury	D	1-1	0-0	—	Reid (pen) [83]	2890
37		28	H	Accrington S	D	0-0	0-0	15		2804
38		31	A	Luton T	W	4-2	2-1	—	Reid [11], Broughton [38], Harrison [53], Hudson [87]	5975
39	Apr	4	A	Aldershot T	W	1-0	1-0	14	Reid [11]	2643
40		7	A	Barnet	L	0-2	0-0	—		1508
41		11	H	Notts Co	W	2-1	1-0	14	Hudson [44], Reid [69]	2945
42		13	A	Port Vale	D	0-0	0-0	14		4814
43		18	H	Shrewsbury T	L	1-2	0-1	14	Taylor R [70]	3196
44		21	H	Morecambe	W	3-2	1-0	—	Taylor R [45], Taylor J [80], Burchill (pen) [89]	2078
45		25	A	Bradford C	L	0-3	0-2	14		13,242
46	May	2	H	Exeter C	L	0-1	0-0	14		6184

Final League Position: 14

GOALSCORERS

League (60): Reid 18 (3 pens), Broughton 6, Burchill 5 (3 pens), Hudson 5, Cummins 4, Sharps 4, Taylor R 4, Clarke 2, Lynch 2, Rhodes 2, Barker 1, Fenton 1, Green 1, Harrison 1, Mills 1, Taylor J 1, Tonge 1, own goal 1.
Carling Cup (5): Broughton 1, Fenton 1, Harrison 1, Reid 1, Rhodes 1.
FA Cup (1): Cummins 1.
J Paint Trophy (7): Broughton 2, Fenton 1, Harrison 1, Hudson 1, Sharps 1, Tonge 1.

Warrington A 38	Lynch M 7 + 1	Green J 29 + 2	Harrison D 27 + 6	Sharps I 45	Joseph M 13 + 12	Mills P 34 + 1	Hudson D 35 + 7	Taylor R 16 + 17	Rhodes A 14 + 4	Reid R 38 + 3	Cummins M 30 + 5	Holmes P 2 + 1	Fenton N 45	Broughton D 33 + 7	Burchill M 10 + 14	Yates J — + 3	Nicholas A 19	Tonge D 39	Barker R 4 + 9	Garcia O 2	Stockdale D 8	Cann S — + 1	Taylor J 9 + 6	Thomas S 2	Clarke J 7 + 4	Brogan S — + 1	Match No.
1	2	3	4	5	6	7	8	9	10^1	11^2	12	13															1
1	2	3	4	5		7	8	9	10	11			6														2
1	2	3	4	5			8		10^2	11	7		6	9^1	12	13											3
1	2		4	5		7	8	13	10^1	11			6	9^2	12		3										4
1	2	13	4	5^1		7	8	9^3	14	11	12		6^2		10		3										5
1	2		4^1	5		7	8^2	9^3	13	11	12		6	14	10		3										6
1	2^1	12	4	5		7	13		10	11	8^2		6	9			3										7
1			4^1	5		7^2		12	10	11	8		6	9^3	13	14	3	2									8
1				5		7	8		10	11^1	4		6	9^2	12		3	2	13								9
1		12		5	13	7	8^1		10	11	4		6^2	9^3			3	2	14								10
1				5		7	8^1		10	11	4		6	9^2	12		3	2	13								11
1			4	5	12	7			10	11^1	8		6	9^2			3	2	13								12
1			4	$5^▪$	12	7			10		8		6	9^2	11^1		3	2	13								13
1			4	5	7^1	12			10	13	8		6	9^3	11^2		3	2	14								14
1			4	5	12	7		13	10	11^2	8		6^1	9^3			3	2	14	10							15
1			$4^▪$	5		7		12			11^2	8	6	14		13	3	2	9^3	10^1							16
	3		5	2			4	10^1		8	11		6	9				7	12		1						17
	4		5	3^3		8	10^2	14	13	7	11		6	12				2	9^1		1						18
	10^9	12	5	2^1		8	13		11^2	4			6	$9^▪$			3	7		$1^▪$	15						19
	7	4	5	2		8	13			11			6	12	10^2			3	9^1	1							20
	11	4	5	$2^▪$		8	12			7			6	13	10^1			3	9^2	1							21
13	3	4	5			8	12			11^1	10^2		6	9				7	2	1							22
	11	4	5			8	12			10	7		6	9^2			3^1	2	13	1							23
	4	12	5			11	13			10^3	8		6	9^2	14		3	2		1		7^1					24
1	11^2	4	5	13		8	10						6	9	12		3^1	2			7						25
1		5^1		8^2	4	12	10	11					6	9	13		3	2			7						26
1	7	12	5	13	8	4		10^2	11				6	9				2			3^1						27
1	3		5	12	7	4	13	8					6					2			11	10^2	9^1				28
1	3		5	7	8	4		13	11		6	12						2					9^1	10^2			29
1	3		5	12	7	4	13		11^2	8			6	9				2						10^1			30
1	3		5		7	4	12		8^1	11			6	9				2						10			31
1	3	13	5	12	7^2	4	14		11	8			6	9^3				2^1						10			32
1	3	4	5			7	10		11	8			6	9^1	12			2									33
1	3	4^1	5		12	8	9		7	11			6		10^2			2						13			34
1	3^1		5	12	4	8^3	13		10	11			6	9				2				14	7^2				35
1	3		5		8	4	12		11	7^2			6	9				2				13	10^1				36
1	3^1		5	12	8	4	7		10	11^3			6	9^2	13			2				14					37
1		4	5	3	8	12	13		11				6	9^2	10^1			2				7					38
1		4^1	5	3	8	12	14		11	13			6	9^3	10^2			2				7					39
1		4	5	3	8				14	11^3	12		6	9	10^2			2				7^1	13				40
1	3		5		8	4	10^1		11	7			6	9	12			2						13			41
1	3	12	5	14	8	4	10^2		11	7^1			6	9^3				2						13			42
1	3	4	5		7^2	8	10		11				6	9^1				2				13	12				43
1	3	4	5	9	8^2	10			11^1		12		6		12			2				13					44
1	3	4	5	8^1	7	12	9		11^3				6	13	14			2				10^2					45
1	3	4	5		7	8^2	10		11^3				6	9^1	12			$2^▪$				13			14	46

FA Cup

First Round	Aldershot T	(a)	1-1
		(h)	0-3

Carling Cup

First Round	Sheffield W	(a)	2-2
Second Round	Wolverhampton W	(h)	0-0
Third Round	Southampton	(h)	3-1
Fourth Round	Stoke C	(a)	0-2

J Paint Trophy

Second Round	Leeds U	(h)	4-2
Northern Quarter-Final	Leicester C	(h)	2-0
Northern Semi-Final	Darlington	(h)	1-1
Northern Final	Scunthorpe U	(a)	0-2
		(h)	0-1

SCUNTHORPE UNITED   FL Championship

FOUNDATION

The year of foundation for Scunthorpe United has often been quoted as 1910, but the club can trace its history back to 1899 when Brumby Hall FC, who played on the Old Showground, consolidated their position by amalgamating with some other clubs and changing their name to Scunthorpe United. The year 1910 was when that club amalgamated with North Lindsey United as Scunthorpe and Lindsey United. The link is Mr W. T. Lockwood whose chairmanship covers both years.

Glanford Park, Doncaster Road, Scunthorpe DN15 8TD.

Telephone: (0871) 221 1899.

Fax: (01724) 857 986.

Ticket Office: (0871) 221 1899.

Website: www.scunthorpe-united.co.uk

Email: admin@scunthorpe-united.co.uk

Ground Capacity: 9,088.

Record Attendance: Old Showground: 23,935 v Portsmouth, FA Cup 4th rd, 30 January 1954. Glanford Park: 8,906 v Nottingham F, FL 1, 10 March 2007.

Pitch Measurements: 112yd × 72yd.

Chairman: Steve Wharton.

Vice-chairman: Rex Garton.

Chief Executive/Secretary: Jamie Hammond BA (Hons).

Manager: Nigel Adkins B.Sc (Hons).

Assistant Manager: Andy Crosby.

Physio: Alex Dalton.

Colours: Claret shirts with blue design, white cuffs on sleeves, claret shorts, claret stockings.

Change Colours: All white with blue inserts and claret cuffs on sleeves.

Year Formed: 1899.

Turned Professional: 1912.

Ltd Co.: 1912.

Club Nickname: 'The Iron'.

Previous Names: Amalgamated first with Brumby Hall then North Lindsey United to become Scunthorpe & Lindsey United, 1910; dropped '& Lindsey' in 1958.

Grounds: 1899, Old Showground; 1988, Glanford Park.

First Football League Game: 19 August 1950, Division 3 (N), v Shrewsbury T (h) D 0–0 – Thompson; Barker, Brownsword; Allen, Taylor, McCormick; Mosby, Payne, Gorin, Rees, Boyes.

HONOURS

Football League: FL 1 – Champions 2006–07; FL 2 – Runners-up 2004–05; Division 3 (N) – Champions 1957–58.

FA Cup: best season: 5th rd, 1958, 1970.

Football League Cup: never past 3rd rd.

Johnstone's Paint Trophy: Runners-up 2008–09.

SKY SPORTS FACT FILE

Jack Brownsword missed only three penalties in 14 years for Scunthorpe United ironically after stepping in after Tim Bowers had had a spot kick saved but had been ordered to have it retaken in the second game of 1947–48 against Scarborough Town.

Record League Victory: 8–1 v Luton T, Division 3, 24 April 1965 – Sidebottom; Horstead, Hemstead; Smith, Neale, Lindsey; Bramley (1), Scott, Thomas (5), Mahy (1), Wilson (1). 8–1 v Torquay U (a), Division 3, 28 October 1995 – Samways; Housham, Wilson, Ford (1), Knill (1), Hope (Nicholson), Thornber, Bullimore (Walsh), McFarlane (4) (Young), Eyre (2), Paterson.

Record Cup Victory: 9–0 v Boston U, FA Cup 1st rd, 21 November 1953 – Malan; Hubbard, Brownsword; Sharpe, White, Bushby; Mosby (1), Haigh (3), Whitfield (2), Gregory (1), Mervyn Jones (2).

Record Defeat: 0–8 v Carlisle U, Division 3 (N), 25 December 1952.

Most League Points (2 for a win): 66, Division 3 (N), 1956–57, 1957–58.

Most League Points (3 for a win): 91, FL 1, 2006–07.

Most League Goals: 88, Division 3 (N), 1957–58.

Highest League Scorer in Season: Barrie Thomas, 31, Division 2, 1961–62.

Most League Goals in Total Aggregate: Steve Cammack, 110, 1979–81, 1981–86.

Most League Goals in One Match: 5, Barrie Thomas v Luton T, Division 3, 24 April 1965.

Most Capped Player: Dave Mulligan, 1(20), New Zealand.

Most League Appearances: Jack Brownsword, 595, 1950–65.

Youngest League Player: Mike Farrell, 16 years 240 days v Workington, 8 November 1975.

Record Transfer Fee Received: £2,000,000 from Sheffield U for Billy Sharp, July 2007.

Record Transfer Fee Paid: £425,000 to Stoke C for Martin Paterson, July 2007.

Football League Record: 1950 Elected to Division 3 (N); 1958–64 Division 2; 1964–68 Division 3; 1968–72 Division 4; 1972–73 Division 3; 1973–83 Division 4; 1983–84 Division 3; 1984–92 Division 4; 1992–99 Division 3; 1999–2000 Division 2; 2000–04 Division 3; 2004–05 FL 2; 2005–07 FL 1; 2007–08 FL C; 2008–09 FL 1; 2009– FL C.

MANAGERS

Harry Allcock 1915–53
(Secretary-Manager)
Tom Crilly 1936–37
Bernard Harper 1946–48
Leslie Jones 1950–51
Bill Corkhill 1952–56
Ron Suart 1956–58
Tony McShane 1959
Bill Lambton 1959
Frank Soo 1959–60
Dick Duckworth 1960–64
Fred Goodwin 1964–66
Ron Ashman 1967–73
Ron Bradley 1973–74
Dick Rooks 1974–76
Ron Ashman 1976–81
John Duncan 1981–83
Allan Clarke 1983–84
Frank Barlow 1984–87
Mick Buxton 1987–91
Bill Green 1991–93
Richard Money 1993–94
David Moore 1994–96
Mick Buxton 1996–97
Brian Laws 1997–2004; 2004–06
Nigel Adkins December 2006–

LATEST SEQUENCES

Longest Sequence of League Wins: 7, 27.1.2007 – 3.3.2007.

Longest Sequence of League Defeats: 8, 29.11.1997 – 20.1.1998.

Longest Sequence of League Draws: 6, 2.1.1984 – 25.2.1984.

Longest Sequence of Unbeaten League Matches: 19, 22.12.2006 – 6.4.2007.

Longest Sequence Without a League Win: 14, 22.3.1975 – 6.9.1975.

Successive Scoring Runs: 24 from 13.1.2007.

Successive Non-scoring Runs: 7 from 19.4.1975.

TEN YEAR LEAGUE RECORD

		P	W	D	L	F	A	Pts	Pos
1999-2000	Div 2	46	9	12	25	40	74	39	23
2000-01	Div 3	46	18	11	17	62	52	65	10
2001-02	Div 3	46	19	14	13	74	56	71	8
2002-03	Div 3	46	19	15	12	68	49	72	5
2003-04	Div 3	46	11	16	19	69	72	49	22
2004-05	FL 2	46	22	14	10	69	42	80	2
2005-06	FL 1	46	15	15	16	68	73	60	12
2006-07	FL 1	46	26	13	7	73	35	91	1
2007-08	FL C	46	11	13	22	46	69	46	23
2008-09	FL 1	46	22	10	14	82	63	76	6

DID YOU KNOW ?

On 29 October 1938 Scunthorpe United had a remarkable 11–3 FA Cup third qualifying round win over Lysaghts Sports. Harry Johnson had five (his second of the tournament) and Samson Nightingale hit four. In six ties United scored 31 goals (Johnson 15).

SCUNTHORPE UNITED 2008–09 LEAGUE RECORD

Match No.	Date	Venue	Opponents	Result	H/T Score	Lg. Pos.	Goalscorers	Attendance
1	Aug 9	H	Leeds U	L	1-2	0-0	—	Hooper [57]	8315
2	16	A	Walsall	L	1-2	1-1	23	Thompson [2]	4162
3	23	H	Peterborough U	W	1-0	1-0	17	Hayes (pen) [44]	4217
4	30	A	Stockport Co	W	3-0	1-0	6	Hooper 2 [30, 47], McCann [58]	6348
5	Sept 6	A	Brighton & HA	W	4-1	2-0	4	Woolford [4], Hooper 3 [45, 55, 68]	5529
6	13	H	Carlisle U	W	2-1	0-0	3	Sparrow [62], Hayes [73]	5188
7	20	A	Hereford U	W	2-1	0-1	2	Togwell [53], Hooper [58]	3004
8	27	H	Yeovil T	W	2-0	1-0	2	Iriekpen [27], Forbes (og) [63]	4829
9	Oct 4	A	Leyton Orient	D	2-2	2-0	2	Iriekpen [26], Hayes [45]	4244
10	11	H	Crewe Alex	W	3-0	1-0	1	Woolford [35], Hayes [67], Iriekpen [80]	4790
11	18	A	Cheltenham T	W	2-1	1-0	1	Hooper [34], Sparrow [90]	3682
12	21	H	Southend U	D	1-1	0-0	—	Hayes (pen) [79]	4324
13	25	H	Millwall	W	3-2	2-0	1	Hooper [5], Hayes (pen) [16], Sparrow [51]	5670
14	28	A	Oldham Ath	L	0-3	0-1	—		6057
15	Nov 1	H	Swindon T	D	3-3	1-1	1	McCann [27], Woolford [50], Hayes [59]	4744
16	14	A	Bristol R	W	2-1	1-0	—	McCann [40], Iriekpen [62]	7173
17	22	H	Leicester C	L	1-2	1-1	3	Hayes [32]	7957
18	25	A	Tranmere R	L	0-2	0-1	—		4564
19	Dec 6	H	Milton Keynes D	W	2-0	0-0	4	Morris [77], Thompson [83]	11,550
20	13	H	Northampton T	D	4-4	3-1	5	May 2 [13, 51], Hooper 2 [19, 32]	3976
21	20	A	Colchester U	D	0-0	0-0	4		4606
22	26	H	Hartlepool U	W	3-0	1-0	4	McCann [32], Hooper [47], Hayes (pen) [90]	5347
23	28	A	Huddersfield T	L	0-2	0-0	6		15,228
24	Jan 13	A	Yeovil T	W	2-1	2-0	—	Togwell [26], Hooper [45]	3275
25	17	A	Crewe Alex	L	2-3	1-0	6	Hayes [19], O'Donnell (og) [70]	3811
26	24	H	Leyton Orient	W	2-1	1-0	5	Hayes [44], Thompson [64]	4230
27	27	H	Oldham Ath	W	2-0	2-0	—	McCann [26], Hooper [33]	4447
28	31	A	Millwall	W	2-1	0-0	3	Hooper 2 [73, 88]	8868
29	Feb 14	H	Bristol R	L	0-2	0-2	4		4156
30	21	A	Swindon T	L	2-4	2-0	5	Hooper [26], Lansbury [39]	6852
31	24	A	Southend U	L	0-2	0-0	—		6028
32	28	A	Leeds U	L	2-3	1-2	7	Hooper 2 [42, 52]	24,921
33	Mar 3	H	Walsall	D	1-1	0-0	—	Odejayi [79]	3423
34	7	H	Stockport Co	W	2-1	2-1	6	Hurst [6], Hooper [14]	4890
35	10	A	Peterborough U	L	1-2	1-0	—	Lansbury [39]	5637
36	14	A	Carlisle U	D	1-1	0-1	7	Hayes [69]	4867
37	17	H	Hereford U	W	3-0	2-0	—	Hooper [7], Hurst [19], Hayes [79]	3672
38	21	H	Brighton & HA	W	2-0	1-0	6	Hooper [42], McCann (pen) [90]	4404
39	28	H	Colchester U	W	3-0	1-0	6	Hooper 2 [36, 59], Lansbury [69]	4304
40	Apr 10	A	Huddersfield T	L	1-2	1-1	—	Woolford [19]	5543
41	13	A	Hartlepool U	W	3-2	1-1	7	McCann [8], Hayes 2 [55, 80]	3998
42	18	H	Milton Keynes D	L	0-1	0-1	7		4873
43	21	A	Northampton T	D	3-3	1-1	—	Trotter [45], McCann (pen) [49], Sparrow [68]	4416
44	24	A	Leicester C	D	2-2	0-1	—	Hayes [57], McCann (pen) [66]	30,542
45	28	A	Cheltenham T	W	3-0	2-0	—	Hayes [36], Byrne [40], Lansbury [67]	3635
46	May 2	H	Tranmere R	D	1-1	0-1	6	Byrne [88]	8029

Final League Position: 6

GOALSCORERS

League (82): Hooper 24, Hayes 17 (4 pens), McCann 9 (3 pens), Iriekpen 4, Lansbury 4, Sparrow 4, Woolford 4, Thompson 3, Byrne 2, Hurst 2, May 2, Togwell 2, Morris 1, Odejayi 1, Trotter 1, own goals 2.
Carling Cup (0).
FA Cup (7): Hooper 4, Hurst 1, May 1, Togwell 1.
J Paint Trophy (12): Hayes 3, Hooper 2, McCann 1, May 1, Mirfin 1, Morris 1, Pearce 1, Togwell 1, Woolford 1.
Play-Offs (4): Sparrow 2, Woolford 2.

Lillis J 4+1	Byrne C 43	Williams M 26	Morris 14+16	Milne K 1	Iriekpen I 14+2	Thompson G 15+9	McCann G 43	Hayes P 39+5	Hooper G 45	Hurst K 13+7	Forte J 1+7	Sparrow M 27+9	May B 5+18	Mirfin D 32+1	Togwell S 34+6	Wright A 17+11	Murphy J 42	Pearce K 36+3	Woolford M 32+7	Lansbury H 12+4	Mills J 13+1	Crosby A 3+1	Trotter L 4+8	Odejayi K 1+5	Match No.
1	2	3	4	5	6	7	8[3]	9[1]	10	11[2]	12	13	14												1
1	2	3	12		6	7	8	9[2]	10[3]	11[1]		13	14	5	4										2
	2	3	12		6	7	4	9[3]	10[2]	11[1]	14	13		5		8	1								3
	2	3			6	7[1]	4	9[3]	10	11[2]	12	13	14	5		8	1								4
	2	3			6	7[1]	4	9	10[3]	11[2]	12	13	14	5		8	1								5
	2	3	12		6	7[2]	4	9	10	11[3]		13	14	5		8	1								6
	2	3	12		6	7	4[1]	9[2]	10	11		13		5		8	1								7
	2	3			6	7	4	9[1]	10	11	12			5		8	1								8
15	2	3			6	7	4	9[1]	10	11[6]	12			5		8	1								9
	2	3			6	7	4[1]	9[2]	10	11	12	13	14	5		8[3]	1								10
	2	3			6	7	4	9[1]	10[3]	11[2]	12	13	14	5		8	1								11
	2	3	12		6	7	4	9[1]	10	11				5		8	1								12
	2	3			6	7	4	9[1]	10[2]	11	12	13		5		8	1								13
	2	3				7	4[1]	9[2]	10	11	12	13	14	5[3]		8	1								14
	2	3	12		6	7	4	9	10[2]	11[1]		13		5		8	1								15
	2	3			6	7	4	9[2]	10[3]	11[1]		13	14	5		8	1								16
	2	3			6	7[2]	4	9	10	11	12	13		5	8[1]		1								17
	2	3	12		6	7	4	9[3]	10	11[2]		13	14	5		8[1]	1								18
	2	3			6	7	4	9[2]	10	11[3]	12	13	14	5[1]		8	1								19
	2	3			6	7	4	9	10	11				5		8	1								20
	2	3	12		6	7[1]	4	9	10	11[2]		13		5		8	1								21
	2	3	12		6	7[2]	4	9[1]	10[3]	11		13	14	5		8	1								22
	2	3	12		6[3]	7	4[1]	9	10	11[2]		13	14	5		8	1								23
	2	3			6	7	4	9[2]	10[3]	11[1]	12	13	14	5		8	1								24
	2	3			6	7[1]	4[2]	9	10	11	12	13	14	5		8[3]	1								25
	2				6	7	4[3]	9	10[2]	11	12	13	14	5		8[1]	1				3				26
	2				6	7	4[1]	9[2]	10[3]	11	12	13	14	5		8	1				3				27
	2				6	7[3]	4	9[1]	10	11[2]	12	13	14	5		8	1				3				28
	2				6	7[1]	4	9	10	11[3]	12	13	14	5		8	1				3[2]				29
	2				6	7	4	9[2]	10[1]	11[3]	12	13	14	5		8	1				3				30
	2				6	7[2]	4	9	10		12	13	14	5		8[3]	1		11[1]		3				31
	2				6	7	4		10		12	13	14	5[2]		8	1		11[1]		3			9[3]	32
	2[2]						4	9[1]	10		12	13		5		8	1	6	11	7	3				33
	2						4[2]	9	10		12	13	14	5		8	1	6	11[3]	7[1]	3				34
	2						4	9	10[3]		12	13	14	5		8	1	6	11	7[1]	3[2]				35
	2						4	9[3]	10		12	13	14	5		8	1	6	11[2]	7[1]	3				36
	2						4	9	10		12	13	14	5		8	1	6[2]	11[1]	7[3]	3				37
	2[1]						4	9[2]	10		12	13	14	5		8	1	6	11	7[3]	3				38
	2						4	9	10[2]		12	13	14	5		8	1	6	11[3]	7[1]		3			39
	2						4	9[2]	10[1]		12	13	14	5		8	1	6	11[2]	7[1]		3			40
	2						4	9	10[3]		12	13	14	5		8	1	6	11[2]	7[1]		3			41
	2						4	9	10		12	13	14	5			1	6	11[1]	7[3]		3		8[2]	42
	2						4	9	10					5			1	6	11	7		3		8	43
	2[1]						4	9	10[2]		12	13	14	5			1	6	11[3]	7		3		8	44
1	2	3[1]					4	9	10[2]		12	13	14	5[3]		8		6	11	7					45
1	2						4	9	10		12	13	14	5		8		6[3]		7[2]		3[1]			46

FA Cup

First Round	Walsall	(a)	3-1
Second Round	Alfreton T	(h)	4-0
Third Round	Watford	(a)	0-1

Carling Cup

First Round	Hartlepool U	(a)	0-3

Play-Offs

Semi-Final	Milton Keynes D	(h)	1-1
		(a)	0-0
Final (*at Wembley*)	Millwall		3-2

J Paint Trophy

First Round	Notts Co	(h)	2-1
Second Round	Grimsby T	(h)	2-1
Northern Quarter-Final	Rochdale	(h)	1-0
Northern Semi-Final	Tranmere R	(h)	2-1
Northern Final	Rotherham U	(h)	2-0
		(a)	1-0
Final (*at Wembley*)	Luton T		2-3

SHEFFIELD UNITED   FL Championship

FOUNDATION

In March 1889, Yorkshire County Cricket Club formed Sheffield United six days after an FA Cup semi-final between Preston North End and West Bromwich Albion had finally convinced Charles Stokes, a member of the cricket club, that the formation of a professional football club would prove successful at Bramall Lane. The United's first secretary, Mr J. B. Wostinholm was also secretary of the cricket club.

Bramall Lane Ground, Cherry Street, Bramall Lane, Sheffield S2 4SU.

Telephone: (0871) 995 1899.

Fax: 0871 663 2430.

Ticket Office: (0871) 995 1889.

Website: www.sufc.co.uk

Email: info@sufc.co.uk

Ground Capacity: 32,500.

Record Attendance: 68,287 v Leeds U, FA Cup 5th rd, 15 February 1936.

Pitch Measurements: 101.1m × 62.2m.

Chairman: Kevin McCabe.

Vice-chairman: Chris Steer.

Chief Executive: Jason Rockett.

Secretary: Donna Fletcher.

Manager: Kevin Blackwell.

Assistant Manager: Sam Ellis.

Physio: Dennis Pettitt.

Colours: Red and white striped shirts, black shorts, black stockings.

Change Colours: Black shirts, black shorts, black stockings.

Year Formed: 1889. *Turned Professional:* 1889. *Ltd Co.:* 1899.

Club Nickname: 'The Blades'.

Ground: 1889, Bramall Lane.

First Football League Game: 3 September 1892, Division 2, v Lincoln C (h) W 4–2 – Lilley; Witham, Cain; Howell, Hendry, Needham (1); Wallace, Dobson, Hammond (3), Davies, Drummond.

Record League Victory: 10–0 v Burslem Port Vale (a), Division 2, 10 December 1892 – Howlett; Witham, Lilley; Howell, Hendry, Needham; Drummond (1), Wallace (1), Hammond (4), Davies (2), Watson (2).

Record Cup Victory: 6–1 v Lincoln C, League Cup, 22 August 2000 – Tracey; Uhlenbeek, Weber, Woodhouse (Ford), Murphy, Sandford, Devlin (pen), Ribeiro (Santos), Bent (3), Kelly (1) (Thompson), Jagielka, og (1). 6–1 v Loughborough, FA Cup 4th qualifying rd, 6 December 1890; 6–1 v Scarborough (a), FA Cup 1st qualifying rd, 5 October 1889.

Record Defeat: 0–13 v Bolton W, FA Cup 2nd rd, 1 February 1890.

HONOURS

Football League: FL C – Runners-up 2005–06; Division 1 – Champions 1897–98; Runners-up 1896–97, 1899–1900; Division 2 – Champions 1952–53; Runners-up 1892–93, 1938–39, 1960–61, 1970–71, 1989–90; Division 4 – Champions 1981–82.

FA Cup: Winners 1899, 1902, 1915, 1925; Runners-up 1901, 1936.

Football League Cup: semi-final 2003.

SKY SPORTS FACT FILE

After two relegations in three seasons, Sheffield United won the Fourth Division championship in 1981–82. They suffered only four defeats in the campaign and on 3 April scored four goals in only six minutes to overturn Torquay United 4–1.

Most League Points (2 for a win): 60, Division 2, 1952–53.

Most League Points (3 for a win): 96, Division 4, 1981–82.

Most League Goals: 102, Division 1, 1925–26.

Highest League Scorer in Season: Jimmy Dunne, 41, Division 1, 1930–31.

Most League Goals in Total Aggregate: Harry Johnson, 205, 1919–30.

Most League Goals in One Match: 5, Harry Hammond v Bootle, Division 2, 26 November 1892; 5, Harry Johnson v West Ham U, Division 1, 26 December 1927.

Most Capped Player: Billy Gillespie, 25, Northern Ireland.

Most League Appearances: Joe Shaw, 629, 1948–66.

Youngest League Player: Steve Hawes, 17 years 47 days v WBA, 2 September 1995.

Record Transfer Fee Received: £4,000,000 from Everton for Phil Jagielka, July 2007.

Record Transfer Fee Paid: £4,000,000 to Everton for James Beattie, August 2007.

Football League Record: 1892 Elected to Division 2; 1893–1934 Division 1; 1934–39 Division 2; 1946–49 Division 1; 1949–53 Division 2; 1953–56 Division 1; 1956–61 Division 2; 1961–68 Division 1; 1968–71 Division 2; 1971–76 Division 1; 1976–79 Division 2; 1979–81 Division 1; 1981–82 Division 4; 1982–84 Division 3; 1984–88 Division 2; 1988–89 Division 3; 1989–90 Division 2; 1990–92 Division 1; 1992–94 FA Premier League; 1994–2004 Division 1; 2004–06 FL C; 2006–07 FA Premier League; 2007– FL C.

MANAGERS

J. B. Wostinholm 1889–99
  (Secretary-Manager)
John Nicholson 1899–1932
Ted Davison 1932–52
Reg Freeman 1952–55
Joe Mercer 1955–58
Johnny Harris 1959–68
  (continued as General Manager to 1970)
Arthur Rowley 1968–69
Johnny Harris *(General Manager resumed Team Manager duties)* 1969–73
Ken Furphy 1973–75
Jimmy Sirrel 1975–77
Harry Haslam 1978–81
Martin Peters 1981
Ian Porterfield 1981–86
Billy McEwan 1986–88
Dave Bassett 1988–95
Howard Kendall 1995–97
Nigel Spackman 1997–98
Steve Bruce 1998–99
Adrian Heath 1999
Neil Warnock 1999–2007
Bryan Robson 2007–08
Kevin Blackwell February 2008–

LATEST SEQUENCES

Longest Sequence of League Wins: 8, 14.9.1960 – 22.10.1960.

Longest Sequence of League Defeats: 7, 19.8.1975 – 20.9.1975.

Longest Sequence of League Draws: 6, 6.5.2001 – 8.9.2001.

Longest Sequence of Unbeaten League Matches: 22, 2.9.1899 – 13.1.1900.

Longest Sequence Without a League Win: 19, 27.9.1975 – 7.2.1976.

Successive Scoring Runs: 34 from 30.3.1956.

Successive Non-scoring Runs: 6 from 4.12.1993.

TEN YEAR LEAGUE RECORD

		P	W	D	L	F	A	Pts	Pos
1999-2000	Div 1	46	13	15	18	59	71	54	16
2000-01	Div 1	46	19	11	16	52	49	68	10
2001-02	Div 1	46	15	15	16	53	54	60	13
2002-03	Div 1	46	23	11	12	72	52	80	3
2003-04	Div 1	46	20	11	15	65	56	71	8
2004-05	FL C	46	18	13	15	57	56	67	8
2005-06	FL C	46	26	12	8	76	46	90	2
2006-07	PR Lge	38	10	8	20	32	55	38	18
2007-08	FL C	46	17	15	14	56	51	66	9
2008-09	FL C	46	22	14	10	64	39	80	3

DID YOU KNOW ?

During 1892–93, their first season in the Football League, Sheffield United played a benefit match at Hull on 9 February under floodlights! It was in aid of medical charities and was against Grimsby Town. United ran out 2–0 winners.

SHEFFIELD UNITED 2008–09 LEAGUE RECORD

Match No.	Date	Venue	Opponents	Result	H/T Score	Lg. Pos.	Goalscorers	Attendance
1	Aug 9	A	Birmingham C	L 0-1	0-0	—		24,019
2	16	H	QPR	W 3-0	2-0	11	Sharp 3 [3, 13, 51]	25,273
3	23	A	Blackpool	W 3-1	1-0	5	Quinn S [21], Speed (pen) [57], Halford [78]	8611
4	30	H	Cardiff C	D 0-0	0-0	5		29,226
5	Sept 13	A	Derby Co	L 1-2	1-1	7	Henderson [26]	28,473
6	16	H	Coventry C	D 1-1	0-1	—	Sharp [56]	24,130
7	20	A	Norwich C	L 0-1	0-0	15		24,175
8	27	H	Watford	W 2-1	1-0	10	Speed [1], Beattie J [66]	24,427
9	30	A	Doncaster R	W 2-0	1-0	—	Roberts (og) [14], Quinn S [60]	14,242
10	Oct 4	H	Bristol C	W 3-0	1-0	4	Beattie J 2 [45, 69], Fontaine (og) [56]	24,712
11	19	A	Sheffield W	L 0-1	0-1	6		30,441
12	21	H	Southampton	D 0-0	0-0	—		25,642
13	25	H	Preston NE	W 1-0	1-0	5	Ehiogu [50]	24,445
14	28	A	Bristol C	D 0-0	0-0	—		16,798
15	Nov 1	H	Plymouth Arg	W 2-0	0-0	5	Beattie J 2 (1 pen) [49 (p), 57]	25,601
16	8	A	Barnsley	W 2-1	1-0	4	Beattie J 2 (1 pen) [20, 85 (p)]	19,002
17	15	H	Reading	L 0-2	0-2	5		25,065
18	22	A	Charlton Ath	W 5-2	3-1	4	Beattie J [7], Speed [29], Kilgallon [45], Youga (og) [48], Quinn S [53]	20,328
19	25	H	Wolverhampton W	L 1-3	0-1	—	Spring [75]	27,111
20	29	A	Ipswich T	D 1-1	0-1	5	Beattie J (pen) [90]	19,785
21	Dec 6	H	Burnley	L 2-3	1-2	6	Beattie J (pen) [36], Quinn S [87]	24,702
22	9	A	Nottingham F	W 1-0	1-0	—	Howard [31]	19,541
23	13	A	Swansea C	D 1-1	0-0	7	Morgan [87]	14,744
24	20	H	Crystal Palace	D 2-2	1-1	6	Dyer [41], Beattie J (pen) [88]	23,045
25	26	A	Wolverhampton W	D 1-1	1-1	8	Beattie J [22]	27,106
26	28	H	Charlton Ath	W 3-1	0-1	6	Quinn S 2 [65, 79], Webber [72]	24,717
27	Jan 10	H	Norwich C	W 1-0	1-0	—	Henderson [17]	27,267
28	17	A	Watford	W 2-0	0-0	4	Webber [52], Henderson [67]	14,555
29	27	H	Doncaster R	L 0-1	0-0	—		26,555
30	31	A	Preston NE	D 0-0	0-0	5		14,889
31	Feb 3	A	Southampton	W 2-1	1-0	—	Halford [35], Ward [90]	13,257
32	7	H	Sheffield W	L 1-2	1-2	5	Lupoli [5]	30,786
33	21	A	Plymouth Arg	D 2-2	0-0	7	Webber [63], Halford [72]	10,044
34	Mar 1	H	Birmingham C	W 2-1	1-0	5	Webber [44], Cotterill (pen) [83]	24,232
35	4	A	Coventry C	W 2-1	1-0	—	Bromby [46], Morgan [54]	16,300
36	7	A	QPR	D 0-0	0-0	5		13,718
37	10	H	Blackpool	D 2-2	1-1	—	Coid (og) [5], Cotterill (pen) [73]	25,273
38	14	H	Derby Co	W 4-2	2-0	4	Naughton [7], Henderson 2 [21, 62], Beattie C [90]	27,565
39	22	A	Cardiff C	W 3-0	1-0	4	Cotterill (pen) [25], Ward [46], Quinn S [87]	17,942
40	Apr 4	H	Ipswich T	W 2-0	2-0	4	Halford [19], Henderson [27]	25,315
41	7	A	Barnsley	W 2-1	0-0	—	O'Toole [82], Lupoli [87]	27,061
42	10	A	Reading	W 1-0	0-0	—	Howard [59]	20,756
43	13	H	Nottingham F	D 0-0	0-0	3		28,374
44	20	A	Burnley	L 0-1	0-1	—		14,884
45	25	H	Swansea C	W 1-0	1-0	3	Cotterill (pen) [37]	28,010
46	May 3	A	Crystal Palace	D 0-0	0-0	3		22,824

Final League Position: 3

GOALSCORERS

League (64): Beattie J 12 (5 pens), Quinn S 7, Henderson 6, Cotterill 4 (4 pens), Halford 4, Sharp 4, Webber 4, Speed 3 (1 pen), Howard 2, Lupoli 2, Morgan 2, Ward 2, Beattie C 1, Bromby 1, Dyer 1, Ehiogu 1, Kilgallon 1, Naughton 1, O'Toole 1, Spring 1, own goals 4.
Carling Cup (5): Henderson 1, Hendrie 1, Naughton 1, Quinn 1, Webber 1 (pen).
FA Cup (8): Halford 3, Sharp 2, Hendrie 1, Naughton 1, Webber 1.
Play-Offs (2): Halford 1, Howard 1.

Kenny P 44	Jihai S 11+1	Naysmith G 37+2	Speed G 17	Morgan C 40+1	Kilgallon M 39+1	Halford G 31+10	Tonge M 4	Henderson D 25+7	Sharp B 17+5	Quinn S 43	Webber D 21+15	Stead J —+1	Ehiogu U 11+5	Cotterill D 17+7	Geary D —+1	Spring M 8+3	Beattie J 21+2	Montgomery N 26+2	Gillespie K —+1	Naughton K 39+1	Hendrie L —+5	Dyer N 3+4	Howard B 22+4	Stokes A 5+7	Bennett 12	Bromby L 6+6	Ward J 7+9	Lupoli A 2+7	Beattie C 1+12	OToole J 5+4	Walker K 2	Match No.
1	2	3	4	5	6	7	8	9²	10¹	11	12	13																				1
1	2	3	4	5¹	6	7²	8	9	10³	11	14		12	13																		2
1	2¹	3	4		6	7²	8	9	10³	11	14		5		12	13																3
1	2	3	4		6	7¹	8²	9	10³	11	13		5	12			14															4
1	2	3	4	5	6	7¹		9	10³	11	13			12			14	8²														5
1	2⁵	3	4	5	6	12			10²	11	13			7¹			9³	8	14													6
1		3	4	5	6	2			10¹	11²	12			7³			9	8		14	13											7
1		3	4	5	6	7		12	10	11	8²	13					9¹			2³	14											8
1		3	4	5	6	7³		12	10	11	8²	14					9¹	13		2												9
1		3	4		6				10	11	8¹	5	7²				9			2	12	13										10
1		3	4	12	6⁵				10²	11	13	5	7¹				9			2			8³	14								11
1		3	4²	5					11	10		6	7¹	12			9			2			8	13								12
1	12	3¹		5		13			14	11	7²	6				4	9³			2			8	10								13
1	2			5		12			11	7²		6				4	9			3		13	8	10¹								14
1	2		4	5		13			12	11	8²	6				7	9			3			10¹									15
1	2		4	5	12	13			11³	8²		6⁵				7	9	14		3			10¹									16
1	2		4	5	6	12		14	13	11¹						7²	9			3			8	10³								17
1	2¹	12	4	5	6	7		14	10²	11	13					9²				3			8									18
1		3	4³	5	6	7		12	10¹	11²	13					14	9			2			8									19
1		3		5	6	7³		14	10¹	11	12					4⁵	9			2		13	8									20
1		3		5	6	7²		12	10¹	11		13				4³	9			2			8	14								21
1		3		5	6	7		10		11	12	13				9²	4			2			8¹									22
1	3²			5	6	7¹		10⁵		11	12	14				4	9			2			8	13³								23
1				5	6	12			11	10²		3	13			9	4			2		7³	8¹	14								24
	12			5	6				11	10²		3¹	13			9	4			2		7	8		1							25
		3		5	6			12	11	10						9	4			2		7	8¹		1							26
1		3		5	6	12		8	10²	11	9¹	7³					4			2				13	14							27
1		3		5	6	7²		10		11	9¹						4			2			8	12	13							28
1		3		5	6	7³		8	10²	11¹	9						4			2	14		12			13						29
1		3		5¹	6	7		10		11	9						4			2			8		12							30
1		3			6	7		10⁵		11	9¹						4			2			8		5	12						31
1		3			6	7		12		11	9¹						4			2	13		8²		5	14	10³					32
1		3		5	6¹	7			11	9²		8					4			2				12	13	10³	14					33
1		3		5	6	7¹		10²	11	9³		8					4			2				12	14	13						34
1		3		5	6	13		9	11		8²						4			7	10¹			2³		14	12					35
1		3		5	6	2		10³	11	9¹							4			7	8²			13		12	14					36
1		3		5	6	7¹		10²	11	9³		8					4			2				14	13	12						37
1		3		5	6	12		10	11		8³						7	13		2¹	9²			14	4							38
1		3		5	6	2³		9¹	11		8²						7				14	13		12	10							39
1		3		5	6³	2		9	11²		8¹						7		14	10	12	13										40
1		3		5				7	9		8¹						4			6	10²	12	13	11								41
1		3		5	6	7		9			13						4			2	8³	14	10²	12	11¹							42
1		3		5				7	9		11¹						4			2	13	8²	6	10³	14	12						43
1	3¹			5	6	7		10	11²								4			2	13		12	14	9³	8						44
1				5	6	7²		9	11	12	8³						4			3	10¹	14		13	2							45
1				5	6	7		9¹	11³	14	8						4			3	10²	12	13		2							46

FA Cup

Third Round	Leyton Orient	(a)	4-1
Fourth Round	Charlton Ath	(h)	2-1
Fifth Round	Hull C	(h)	1-1
		(a)	1-2

Carling Cup

First Round	Port Vale	(h)	3-1
Second Round	Huddersfield T	(a)	2-1
Third Round	Arsenal	(a)	0-6

Play-Offs

Semi-Final	Preston NE	(a)	1-1
		(h)	1-0
Final	Burnley		0-1
(at Wembley)			

SHEFFIELD WEDNESDAY   FL Championship

FOUNDATION

Sheffield being one of the principal centres of early Association Football, this club was formed as long ago as 1867 by the Sheffield Wednesday Cricket Club (formed 1825) and their colours from the start were blue and white. The inaugural meeting was held at the Adelphi Hotel and the original committee included Charles Stokes who was subsequently a founder member of Sheffield United.

Hillsborough, Sheffield S6 1SW.

Telephone: (0871) 995 1867.

Fax: (0114) 221 2122.

Ticket Office: (0871) 900 1867.

Website: www.swfc.co.uk

Email: enquiries@swfc.co.uk

Ground Capacity: 39,812.

Record Attendance: 72,841 v Manchester C, FA Cup 5th rd, 17 February 1934.

Pitch Measurements: 110yd × 71yd.

Chairman: Lee Strafford.

Chief Executive: Nick Parker.

Company Secretary: Paul Johnson.

Operations Manager: John Rutherford

Manager: Brian Laws.

Assistant Manager: Russ Wilcox.

Physio: Mark Palmer.

Colours: Blue and white striped shirts, black shorts, black stockings.

Change Colours: White shirts with blue design, blue shorts, white stockings.

Year Formed: 1867 (fifth oldest League club).

Turned Professional: 1887.

Ltd Co.: 1899.

Former Names: The Wednesday until 1929.

Club Nickname: 'The Owls'.

Grounds: 1867, Highfield; 1869, Myrtle Road; 1877, Sheaf House; 1887, Olive Grove; 1899, Owlerton (since 1912 known as Hillsborough). Some games were played at Endcliffe in the 1880s. Until 1895 Bramall Lane was used for some games.

First Football League Game: 3 September 1892, Division 1, v Notts Co (a) W 1–0 – Allan; Tom Brandon (1), Mumford; Hall, Betts, Harry Brandon; Spiksley, Brady, Davis, R. N. Brown, Dunlop.

Record League Victory: 9–1 v Birmingham, Division 1, 13 December 1930 – Brown; Walker, Blenkinsop; Strange, Leach, Wilson; Hooper (3), Seed (2), Ball (2), Burgess (1), Rimmer (1).

HONOURS

Football League: Division 1 – Champions 1902–03, 1903–04, 1928–29, 1929–30; Runners-up 1960–61; Division 2 – Champions 1899–1900, 1925–26, 1951–52, 1955–56, 1958–59; Runners-up 1949–50, 1983–84.

FA Cup: Winners 1896, 1907, 1935; Runners-up 1890, 1966, 1993.

Football League Cup: Winners 1991; Runners-up 1993.

European Competitions: European Fairs Cup: 1961–62, 1963–64. UEFA Cup: 1992–93. Intertoto Cup: 1995.

SKY SPORTS FACT FILE

Tom Cawley who had an exemplary disciplinary record was wrongly sent off playing for Sheffield Wednesday v Lincoln City in 1888. The referee realising his error called the player back onto the pitch but the player declined on a matter of principle!

Record Cup Victory: 12–0 v Halliwell, FA Cup 1st rd, 17 January 1891 – Smith; Thompson, Brayshaw; Harry Brandon (1), Betts, Cawley (2); Winterbottom, Mumford (2), Bob Brandon (1), Woolhouse (5), Ingram (1).

Record Defeat: 0–10 v Aston Villa, Division 1, 5 October 1912.

Most League Points (2 for a win): 62, Division 2, 1958–59.

Most League Points (3 for a win): 88, Division 2, 1983–84.

Most League Goals: 106, Division 2, 1958–59.

Highest League Scorer in Season: Derek Dooley, 46, Division 2, 1951–52.

Most League Goals in Total Aggregate: Andrew Wilson, 199, 1900–20.

Most League Goals in One Match: 6, Doug Hunt v Norwich C, Division 2, 19 November 1938.

Most Capped Player: Nigel Worthington, 50 (66), Northern Ireland.

Most League Appearances: Andrew Wilson, 501, 1900–20.

Youngest League Player: Peter Fox, 15 years 269 days v Orient, 31 March 1973.

Record Transfer Fee Received: £2,750,000 from Blackburn R for Paul Warhurst, September 1993.

Record Transfer Fee Paid: £4,500,000 to Celtic for Paolo Di Canio, August 1997.

Football League Record: 1892 Elected to Division 1; 1899–1900 Division 2; 1900–20 Division 1; 1920–26 Division 2; 1926–37 Division 1; 1937–50 Division 2; 1950–51 Division 1; 1951–52 Division 2; 1952–55 Division 1; 1955–56 Division 2; 1956–58 Division 1; 1958–59 Division 2; 1959–70 Division 1; 1970–75 Division 2; 1975–80 Division 3; 1980–84 Division 2; 1984–90 Division 1; 1990–91 Division 2; 1991–92 Division 1; 1992–2000 FA Premier League; 2000–03 Division 1; 2003–04 Division 2; 2004–05 FL 1; 2005– FL C.

MANAGERS

Arthur Dickinson 1891–1920
(Secretary-Manager)
Robert Brown 1920–33
Billy Walker 1933–37
Jimmy McMullan 1937–42
Eric Taylor 1942–58
(continued as General Manager to 1974)
Harry Catterick 1958–61
Vic Buckingham 1961–64
Alan Brown 1964–68
Jack Marshall 1968–69
Danny Williams 1969–71
Derek Dooley 1971–73
Steve Burtenshaw 1974–75
Len Ashurst 1975–77
Jackie Charlton 1977–83
Howard Wilkinson 1983–88
Peter Eustace 1988–89
Ron Atkinson 1989–91
Trevor Francis 1991–95
David Pleat 1995–97
Ron Atkinson 1997–98
Danny Wilson 1998–2000
Peter Shreeves (Acting) 2000
Paul Jewell 2000–01
Peter Shreeves 2001
Terry Yorath 2001–02
Chris Turner 2002–04
Paul Sturrock 2004–06
Brian Laws November 2006–

LATEST SEQUENCES

Longest Sequence of League Wins: 9, 23.4.1904 – 15.10.1904.

Longest Sequence of League Defeats: 8, 9.9.2000 – 17.10.2000.

Longest Sequence of League Draws: 7, 15.3.2008 – 14.4.2008.

Longest Sequence of Unbeaten League Matches: 19, 10.12.1960 – 8.4.1961.

Longest Sequence Without a League Win: 20, 11.1.1975 – 30.8.1975.

Successive Scoring Runs: 40 from 14.11.1959.

Successive Non-scoring Runs: 8 from 8.3.1975.

TEN YEAR LEAGUE RECORD

		P	W	D	L	F	A	Pts	Pos
1999-2000	PR Lge	38	8	7	23	38	70	31	19
2000-01	Div 1	46	15	8	23	52	71	53	17
2001-02	Div 1	46	12	14	20	49	71	50	20
2002-03	Div 1	46	10	16	20	56	73	46	22
2003-04	Div 2	46	13	14	19	48	64	53	16
2004-05	FL 1	46	19	15	12	77	59	72	5
2005-06	FL C	46	13	13	20	39	52	52	19
2006-07	FL C	46	20	11	15	70	66	71	9
2007-08	FL C	46	14	13	19	54	55	55	16
2008-09	FL C	46	16	13	17	51	58	61	12

DID YOU KNOW ?

On 7 February 2009 in the 123rd competitive Steel City derby, Sheffield Wednesday beat Sheffield United 2–1. It was the Owls' first win at Bramall Lane since 1967 and the first double achieved against the Blades since 1913–14.

SHEFFIELD WEDNESDAY 2008–09 LEAGUE RECORD

Match No.	Date	Venue	Opponents	Result		H/T Score	Lg. Pos.	Goalscorers	Attendance
1	Aug 9	H	Burnley	W	4-1	3-1	—	Tudgay 2 [1, 66], Sodje 2 [4, 17]	23,793
2	16	A	Wolverhampton W	L	1-4	1-1	13	Esajas [15]	22,491
3	23	H	Preston NE	D	1-1	1-0	11	McAllister [20]	17,963
4	30	A	Swansea C	D	1-1	0-1	14	Watson [70]	16,702
5	Sept 13	H	Watford	W	2-0	1-0	6	Tudgay [22], Spurr [55]	17,066
6	16	A	Reading	L	0-6	0-3	—		18,159
7	20	H	Ipswich T	D	0-0	0-0	14		17,198
8	27	A	Charlton Ath	W	2-1	2-1	9	Small [39], Tudgay [42]	20,278
9	30	H	Nottingham F	W	1-0	0-0	—	Esajas [48]	20,823
10	Oct 4	A	Plymouth Arg	L	0-4	0-3	10		10,795
11	19	H	Sheffield U	W	1-0	1-0	5	Watson [35]	30,441
12	21	A	Barnsley	L	1-2	0-1	—	Clarke (pen) [69]	17,784
13	25	A	Birmingham C	L	1-3	1-3	12	Esajas [14]	17,300
14	28	H	Plymouth Arg	L	0-1	0-1	—		16,515
15	Nov 1	A	Crystal Palace	D	1-1	1-0	15	Clarke [7]	14,650
16	8	H	Doncaster R	W	1-0	1-0	12	Clarke [43]	20,872
17	15	A	Derby Co	L	0-3	0-1	14		30,111
18	22	H	Coventry C	L	0-1	0-0	16		16,119
19	25	A	Blackpool	W	2-0	0-0	—	Tudgay [61], Burton [86]	7054
20	29	A	Norwich C	W	3-2	0-1	12	McMahon [51], Clarke [55], Tudgay [72]	18,883
21	Dec 6	A	Southampton	D	1-1	0-1	12	Tudgay [87]	15,440
22	9	H	QPR	W	1-0	0-0	—	Clarke [75]	14,792
23	13	H	Bristol C	D	0-0	0-0	10		15,542
24	20	A	Cardiff C	L	0-2	0-0	11		17,600
25	26	H	Blackpool	D	1-1	0-1	11	Slusarski [65]	25,044
26	28	A	Coventry C	L	0-2	0-0	13		19,602
27	Jan 10	A	Ipswich T	D	1-1	0-0	—	Watson [52]	22,213
28	17	H	Charlton Ath	W	4-1	2-0	12	Potter [16], Tudgay 2 (1 pen) [38, 90 lpl], Jeffers [63]	28,766
29	27	A	Nottingham F	L	1-2	1-1	—	Johnson [27]	22,618
30	31	H	Birmingham C	D	1-1	0-0	13	Buxton [57]	18,409
31	Feb 7	A	Sheffield U	W	2-1	2-1	12	Spurr [1], Tudgay [29]	30,786
32	14	A	Doncaster R	L	0-1	0-1	12		14,823
33	17	H	Barnsley	L	0-1	0-1	—		25,820
34	21	H	Crystal Palace	W	2-0	0-0	12	McAllister [80], Clarke [90]	22,687
35	28	A	Burnley	W	4-2	1-0	12	Tudgay 2 [19, 69], Clarke 2 [79, 82]	12,449
36	Mar 3	H	Reading	L	1-2	1-0	—	McAllister [45]	19,268
37	7	H	Wolverhampton W	L	0-1	0-1	12		23,703
38	10	A	Preston NE	D	1-1	1-0	—	Jeffers [30]	12,381
39	14	A	Watford	D	2-2	1-1	13	Tudgay [20], Jeffers (pen) [90]	16,294
40	21	H	Swansea C	D	0-0	0-0	13		22,564
41	Apr 4	A	Norwich C	W	1-0	0-0	12	Johnson [48]	25,385
42	11	H	Derby Co	L	0-1	0-1	12		24,392
43	13	A	QPR	L	2-3	1-0	12	Mahon (og) [35], Tudgay (pen) [53]	13,742
44	18	H	Southampton	W	2-0	1-0	12	Varney 2 [24, 73]	24,145
45	25	A	Bristol C	D	1-1	0-1	12	Potter [88]	17,486
46	May 3	H	Cardiff C	W	1-0	0-0	12	Johnson [71]	30,658

Final League Position: 12

GOALSCORERS

League (51): Tudgay 14 (2 pens), Clarke 8 (1 pen), Esajas 3, Jeffers 3 (1 pen), Johnson 3, McAllister 3, Watson 3, Potter 2, Sodje 2, Spurr 2, Varney 2, Burton 1, Buxton 1, McMahon 1, Slusarski 1, Small 1, own goal 1.
Carling Cup (2): Esajas 2.
FA Cup (1): Spurr 1.

Grant L 46	Hinds R 13 + 1	Spurr T 41	McAllister S 37 + 3	Beevers M 30 + 4	Wood R 42	O'Connor J 35 + 6	Tudgay M 42	Sodje A 2 + 9	Burton D 9 + 8	Johnson J 29 + 8	Clarke L 20 + 9	Smith J 3 + 9	Watson S 15 + 7	Boden L 2 + 10	Esajas E 18 + 4	McMahon T 14 + 1	Gilbert P 8	Small W 6 + 13	Jeffers F 20 + 11	Buxton L 32	Simek F 4 + 2	Slusarski B 4 + 3	Modest N 1 + 3	Lekaj R — + 2	Gray M 13	Potter D 17	Varney L 3 + 1	Match No.
1	2	3	4	5	6	7³	8	9¹	10	11²	12	13	14															1
1	2	3	4	5	6		8		10	9³	13	12	7¹	14	11²													2
1		3	4	5	6	7	8		10²	9¹	13	12			11	2												3
1		3	4	5	6	7	9		10³	13	14	8²	12		11¹	2												4
1		3	4¹		6	7	9	12	10²	13		2		11³	8	5	14											5
1		3	4¹		6	7	9	10³	8	12		11²	2	5	13	14												6
1		3	4³		6	7	9	12	10²		8	11¹	2	5	13	14												7
1		3	4		6	11	9	12	10¹		13	7²	14	2	5	8³												8
1		3	4	12	6¹	7	9	10			11	2	5	8²	13													9
1		3	4	5		7	9	10²	12	13	6	11¹	2	8³	14													10
1		3	4	5	6	8¹	9	13	10³	11¹	7	12	2	14														11
1		3	4	5		9¹	12	13	8	14	2²	11	7²	10³	6													12
1		3	4		6	12	9²	10¹	8¹	7	11	2	13	5														13
1		3	4		6³	12	13	8	9	7	11¹	2	10²	5	14													14
1		3	4	5	6	8	9	12	13	10¹	7	11²	2															15
1		3	4	5	6	8	9	12	13	10¹	7	11²	14	2³														16
1		3	4²	5	6	8	11	9¹	12	13	10³	7	2	14														17
1			4	5	6	11	7	12	8	10¹	13	3	9²	2														18
1			4¹	5	6	7	8	10	11²	9	12	13	3	2														19
1		12	5	6	4	8	10	7¹	11	3	9²	2	13															20
1			4	5	6	8	7	10	11¹	12	9²	3	2	13														21
1		3	4	5	6	7	8	10	14	11¹	12	9²	2³	13														22
1		3	4	5	6	8	7	10	12	13	9¹	2	11²															23
1		3	4	5	6	7	8	12	10	2	9²	11¹	13															24
1		3	12	5	6	8³	11	4	13	7¹	9²	2	10	14														25
1		3	4¹	5	6	8²	10	7	13	11³	12	2	9	14														26
1		3	4	5	6		10	7	8	9	2	12	11¹															27
1		3	12	5	6	8	10	7²	14	13	9³	2	11	4¹														28
1		3		5	6	4³	10²	7¹	12	14	13	9⁴	2	11	8													29
1		3		5	6	4	9	7¹	10	12	2	11	8															30
1		3		5	6	4	9	7¹	10	12	2	11	8															31
1		3		5	6	4	9	7	10	2	11	8																32
1	5	3		6	4	9	7¹	10³	14	12	13	2	11²	8														33
1	6	3	4	5	12	10	7¹	14	13	9²	2	11³	8															34
1	6	3	4¹	5	12	9	7²	10	13	14	2	11³	8															35
1		3	4	5	6	12	9	7³	10	13	14	2	11²	8¹														36
1	5	3	4	6	8²	9	12	7	10³	13	14	2	11¹															37
1		3	4	5	6	12	9	13	11¹	10²	2	7	8															38
1	14	3¹	4	5	6	7³	9	8	13	10	2	12	11²															39
1	5	3	4²	6	7	9	11	12	10¹	2	8	13																40
1	5	3⁴	4	13	6	9	12	11²	10¹	2	8	7																41
1	5	4	6	7¹	9	13	11³	12	14	10²	2	3	8															42
1	5	3	12	6¹	4	9	14	13	10³	11²	2	8	7															43
1	5	3	4	6	13	9	12	11²	10¹	2	8	7																44
1	5	3	4	6	13	7	12	10	11¹	9²	2	8																45
1	5¹	3	4³	12	6	7	9	11	13	10²	2	14	8															46

FA Cup
Third Round   Fulham   (h)   1-2

Carling Cup
First Round   Rotherham U   (h)   2-2

SHREWSBURY TOWN — FL Championship 2

FOUNDATION

Shrewsbury School having provided a number of the early England and Wales international players it is not surprising that there was a Town club as early as 1876 which won the Birmingham Senior Cup in 1879. However, the present Shrewsbury Town club was formed in 1886 and won the Welsh FA Cup as early as 1891.

ProStar Stadium, Oteley Road, Shrewsbury, Shropshire SY2 6ST.

Telephone: (0871) 811 8800.

Fax: (0871) 811 8801.

Ticket Office: (01743) 273 943.

Website: www.shrewsburytown.com

Email: ian@shrewsburytown.co.uk

Ground Capacity: 10,000.

Record Attendance: 18,917 v Walsall, Division 3, 26 April 1961 (Gay Meadow); 8,429 v Bury, FL 2 Play-off semi final, 7 May 2009 (ProStar Stadium).

Pitch Measurements: 114yd × 73yd.

Chairman: Roland Wycherley.

Vice-chairman: Keith Sayfritz.

Managing Director: Rob Bickerton.

Secretary/General Manager: Jonathan Harris.

Manager: Paul Simpson.

Assistant Manager: John McMahon.

Physio: Nathan Ring.

Colours: Blue shirts with amber design, blue shorts, blue stockings.

Change Colours: All black with red and white design on shirts.

Year Formed: 1886.

Turned Professional: 1896.

Ltd Co.: 1936.

HONOURS

Football League: Division 2 best season: 8th, 1983–84, 1984–85; Division 3 – Champions 1978–79, 1993–94; Division 4 – Runners-up 1974–75.

FA Cup: best season: 6th rd, 1979, 1982.

Football League Cup: Semi-final 1961.

Welsh Cup: Winners 1891, 1938, 1977, 1979, 1984, 1985; Runners-up 1931, 1948, 1980.

Auto Windscreens Shield: Runners-up 1996.

Club Nickname: 'Town', 'Blues' or 'Salop'. The name 'Salop' is a colloquialism for the county of Shropshire. Since Shrewsbury is the only club in Shropshire, cries of 'Come on Salop' are frequently used!

Grounds: 1886, Old Shrewsbury Racecourse; 1910, Gay Meadow; 2007, The New Stadium.

First Football League Game: 19 August 1950, Division 3 (N), v Scunthorpe U (a) D 0–0 – Egglestone; Fisher, Lewis; Wheatley, Depear, Robinson; Griffin, Hope, Jackson, Brown, Barker.

Record League Victory: 7–0 v Swindon T, Division 3 (S), 6 May 1955 – McBride; Bannister, Skeech; Wallace, Maloney, Candlin; Price, O'Donnell (1), Weigh (4), Russell, McCue (2).

SKY SPORTS FACT FILE

On 7 October 2008 Shrewsbury Town won 7–0 at Wycombe Wanderers in a Johnstone's Paint Trophy second round match, Five of the goals were scored by Grant Holt including a perfect three in a row in six minutes during the last ten minutes.

Record Cup Victory: 11–2 v Marine, FA Cup 1st rd,
11 November 1995 – Edwards, Seabury (Dempsey (1)),
Withe (1), Evans (1), Whiston (2), Scott (1), Woods,
Stevens (1), Spink (3) (Anthrobus), Walton, Berkley, (1 og).

Record Defeat: 1–8 v Norwich C, Division 3 (S), 13 September
1952; 1–8 v Coventry C, Division 3, 22 October 1963.

Most League Points (2 for a win): 62, Division 4, 1974–75.

Most League Points (3 for a win): 79, Division 3, 1993–94.

Most League Goals: 101, Division 4, 1958–59.

Highest League Scorer in Season: Arthur Rowley, 38,
Division 4, 1958–59.

Most League Goals in Total Aggregate: Arthur Rowley, 152,
1958–65 (thus completing his League record of 434 goals).

Most League Goals in One Match: 5, Alf Wood v
Blackburn R, Division 3, 2 October 1971.

Most Capped Player: Jimmy McLaughlin, 5 (12), Northern
Ireland; Bernard McNally, 5, Northern Ireland.

Most League Appearances: Mickey Brown, 418, 1986–91;
1992–94; 1996–2001.

Youngest League Player: Graham French, 16 years 177 days
v Reading, 30 September 1961.

Record Transfer Fee Received: £600,000 from Manchester
C for Joe Hart, May 2006.

Record Transfer Fee Paid: £170,000 to Nottingham F for
Grant Holt, June 2008.

Football League Record: 1950 Elected to Division 3 (N);
1951–58 Division 3 (S); 1958–59 Division 4; 1959–74
Division 3; 1974–75 Division 4; 1975–79 Division 3; 1979–89
Division 2; 1989–94 Division 3; 1994–97 Division 2;
1997–2003 Division 3; 2003–04 Conference; 2004– FL 2.

MANAGERS

W. Adams 1905–12
(Secretary-Manager)
A. Weston 1912–34
(Secretary-Manager)
Jack Roscamp 1934–35
Sam Ramsey 1935–36
Ted Bousted 1936–40
Leslie Knighton 1945–49
Harry Chapman 1949–50
Sammy Crooks 1950–54
Walter Rowley 1955–57
Harry Potts 1957–58
Johnny Spuhler 1958
Arthur Rowley 1958–68
Harry Gregg 1968–72
Maurice Evans 1972–73
Alan Durban 1974–78
Richie Barker 1978
Graham Turner 1978–84
Chic Bates 1984–87
Ian McNeill 1987–90
Asa Hartford 1990–91
John Bond 1991–93
Fred Davies 1994–97
(previously Caretaker-Manager 1993–94)
Jake King 1997–99
Kevin Ratcliffe 1999–2003
Jimmy Quinn 2003–04
Gary Peters 2004–08
Paul Simpson March 2008–

LATEST SEQUENCES

Longest Sequence of League Wins: 7, 28.10.1995 – 16.12.1995.

Longest Sequence of League Defeats: 11, 9.4.2003 – 14.8.2004.

Longest Sequence of League Draws: 6, 30.10.1963 – 14.12.1963.

Longest Sequence of Unbeaten League Matches: 16, 30.10.1993 – 26.2.1994.

Longest Sequence Without a League Win: 18, 8.3.2003 – 14.8.2004.

Successive Scoring Runs: 28 from 7.9.1960.

Successive Non-scoring Runs: 6 from 1.1.1991.

TEN YEAR LEAGUE RECORD

		P	W	D	L	F	A	Pts	Pos
1999-2000	Div 3	46	9	13	24	40	67	40	22
2000-01	Div 3	46	15	10	21	49	65	55	15
2001-02	Div 3	46	20	10	16	64	53	70	9
2002-03	Div 3	46	9	14	23	62	92	41	24
2003-04	Conf.	42	20	14	8	67	42	74	3
2004-05	FL 2	46	11	16	19	48	53	49	21
2005-06	FL 2	46	16	13	17	55	55	61	10
2006-07	FL 2	46	18	17	11	68	46	71	7
2007-08	FL 2	46	12	14	20	56	65	50	18
2008-09	FL 2	46	17	18	11	61	44	69	7

DID YOU KNOW ?

The only existing League
club Shrewsbury Town have
not played in any competitive
or friendly fixture is
Tottenham Hotspur. The
closest they came was in a
1993–94 League Cup tie
when beaten by Blackburn
Rovers, who met Spurs in the
next round.

SHREWSBURY TOWN 2008–09 LEAGUE RECORD

Match No.	Date	Venue	Opponents	Result	H/T Score	Lg. Pos.	Goalscorers	Attendance
1	Aug 9	H	Macclesfield T	W 4-0	1-0	—	Cansdell-Sherriff [31], Holt (pen) [51], Coughlan [79], Hibbert [85]	5812
2	16	A	Exeter C	W 1-0	0-0	2	Murray [71]	4916
3	23	H	Aldershot T	W 1-0	0-0	1	Holt [79]	5422
4	30	A	Notts Co	D 2-2	0-1	2	Hibbert [47], Symes [88]	4697
5	Sept 6	A	Morecambe	L 0-1	0-1	5		2318
6	13	H	Gillingham	W 7-0	4-0	4	Jackson [27], Hibbert [30], Davies 2 [42, 87], Coughlan [45], Cansdell-Sherriff [52], Holt (pen) [58]	5319
7	21	A	Chester C	D 1-1	1-1	4	Holt (pen) [29]	2891
8	27	H	Bradford C	W 2-0	1-0	3	Davies [6], Walker [90]	6517
9	Oct 4	A	Darlington	D 1-1	0-0	3	Thornton [71]	2899
10	11	H	Port Vale	L 1-2	0-1	5	Symes [89]	7162
11	18	H	Bournemouth	W 4-1	3-0	3	Sigurdsson [22], Davies 2 [33, 41], Walker [90]	5738
12	21	A	Accrington S	L 1-2	0-2	—	Davies [68]	1249
13	25	A	Brentford	D 1-1	0-0	5	Humphrey [80]	5362
14	28	H	Barnet	D 2-2	2-2	—	Holt [31], Davies [33]	5163
15	Nov 1	H	Luton T	W 3-0	1-0	5	Murray [4], Davies [76], Holt [87]	6188
16	14	A	Chesterfield	D 2-2	1-0	—	Holt 2 (1 pen) [45 (p), 54]	4099
17	22	A	Lincoln C	D 0-0	0-0	5		3517
18	25	H	Dagenham & R	W 2-1	0-0	—	White [50], Holt (pen) [90]	4590
19	Dec 6	H	Rotherham U	W 1-0	0-0	2	Holt [72]	5314
20	13	A	Grimsby T	L 0-1	0-0	3		3283
21	20	H	Wycombe W	L 0-1	0-0	6		6160
22	26	A	Rochdale	L 1-2	0-0	7	Holt [59]	4159
23	28	H	Bury	W 1-0	0-0	5	Holt [76]	7127
24	Jan 3	A	Bradford C	D 0-0	0-0	—		12,877
25	17	A	Port Vale	D 1-1	1-1	7	Walker [28]	7068
26	24	H	Darlington	W 1-0	1-0	6	Walker [5]	5140
27	27	A	Barnet	D 0-0	0-0	—		1568
28	31	H	Brentford	L 1-3	0-3	9	Holt [68]	5674
29	Feb 3	H	Accrington S	W 2-0	2-0	—	Coughlan [20], Holt (pen) [40]	4134
30	7	A	Bournemouth	L 0-1	0-1	—		4187
31	14	A	Chesterfield	W 2-1	1-1	7	Jackson [19], Davies [53]	4873
32	17	H	Chester C	W 1-0	0-0	—	Walker [57]	6133
33	21	A	Luton T	L 1-3	1-2	4	Davies [20]	5661
34	28	A	Macclesfield T	L 0-3	0-1	7		2553
35	Mar 3	H	Exeter C	D 1-1	0-0	—	Holt (pen) [51]	4679
36	7	H	Notts Co	W 3-2	2-1	8	Ashikodi [20], Holt (pen) [38], Coughlan [71]	5192
37	10	A	Aldershot T	D 0-0	0-0	—		2090
38	14	A	Gillingham	D 2-2	0-1	7	Holt 2 (1 pen) [79 (p), 90]	6023
39	21	H	Morecambe	D 0-0	0-0	7		5426
40	28	A	Wycombe W	D 1-1	0-1	7	Davies [75]	4803
41	Apr 4	H	Grimsby T	D 1-1	0-0	7	Davies [58]	5535
42	10	A	Bury	L 1-2	0-1	—	Chadwick [55]	4850
43	13	H	Rochdale	D 1-1	0-0	8	Holt [47]	6234
44	18	A	Rotherham U	W 2-1	1-0	7	Chadwick [44], Sharps (og) [76]	3196
45	25	H	Lincoln C	D 0-0	0-0	8		6740
46	May 2	A	Dagenham & R	W 2-1	2-0	7	Holt [19], Humphrey [33]	4791

Final League Position: 7

GOALSCORERS
League (61): Holt 20 (9 pens), Davies 12, Walker 5, Coughlan 4, Hibbert 3, Cansdell-Sherriff 2, Chadwick 2, Humphrey 2, Jackson 2, Murray 2, Symes 2, Ashikodi 1, Sigurdsson 1, Thornton 1, White 1, own goal 1.
Carling Cup (0).
FA Cup (1): Holt 1.
J Paint Trophy (14): Holt 7, McIntyre 2, Cansdell-Sherriff 1, Coughlan 1, Davies 1, Leslie 1, Walker 1.
Play-Offs (1): McIntyre 1.

Daniels L 38	Herd B 20 + 1	Tierney M 18	Davies B 42	Jackson M 21	Coughlan G 42	Cansdell-Sherriff S 27 + 4	Murray P 31 + 1	Walker R 16 + 11	Holt G 43	McIntyre K 25 + 1	Hibbert D 9 + 14	Hindmarch S — + 3	Humphrey C 24 + 13	Langmead K 29 + 4	Ashton N 24 + 7	Moss D 28 + 1	Symes M 1 + 7	Pugh M — + 7	Thornton S 5	Sigurdsson G 4 + 1	Garner G 4	Leslie S 12 + 15	White J 3 + 6	Gilks M 4	Hunt D — + 2	Labadie J 1	Chadwick N 9 + 6	Dunfield T 15 + 2	Worrall D 7 + 2	Ashikodi M 4 + 4	Riza O — + 2	Match No.
1	2	3	4	5	6	7	8²	9¹	10³	11	12	13	14																			1
1	2	3	4	5		7	8¹	9²	10	11	12	13		6																		2
1	2	3	4¹	5		7		9²	10	11	13		6	12	8																	3
1	2	3	4	5		7			10	11²	9			12	6	8¹	13															4
1	2	3	4	5	6	7²			10	11	9		8¹		13		12															5
1	2	3	4	5¹	6	7			10	11²	9³	14		12	13		8															6
1	2	3	4	5	6³	7²		12	10	11	9¹			13	14		8															7
1	2	3	4	5	6	7¹		13	10	11	9²			12			8															8
1	2	3	4	5	6	7¹		13	10	11	9²			12			8															9
1	2	3	4	5	6	7³	9¹		11	10²				13	12		14	8														10
1	2	3	4¹	5	6	7		13	10	11	9²			12			8															11
1	2	3²	4	5	6	7		13	10	11	9¹			12			8															12
	2	3	4	5	6	7¹		9²	10	11			12		13		8		1													13
	2	3	4	5	6	7¹	13	9	10	11			12				14		8²	1												14
	2	3	4	5	6		8¹	9	10	11				7²		12	1	13														15
	2	3		5			8²	9¹	10	11				7	6	4³	13		1	14	12											16
		3		5			8¹	9⁴	10	11				7²	6	4	2				12	13	1									17
		3	4	5			8²		10	11	12				6	7	2					9¹	1	13								18
			4	5	3	7			10	11	12				6	8²	2					13	9¹	1								19
			4	5	3		8		10	11²	12				6	7¹	2					9	1	13								20
1			4	5		7¹	8	9²	10	11³					6	3	2	14				12	13									21
1			4	5	3		8²	9³	10	11				7¹	6		2	13				12	14									22
1			4	5	3		8²	12	11		13			7³	6		2	9¹				10	14									23
1				5	3		8¹		10	11				7²	6	12	2					9	13				4					24
1	6²			5	3	7		9³		11¹				4	10	12	2			13⁴		8					14					25
1	4¹			5	3		8³		10²			13		7	6	11	2			14		9					12					26
1				5	12		8¹	9³	10			13		7	6	3	2					11²					14	4				27
1	11			5			8¹	9²	10			13		7	6	3	2					12					4					28
1	8	6		5¹					10			13		7	12	3	2			14		11³					9²	4				29
1	8	6		5	12				13	10			14	7²	3	2⁴						11					9³	4¹				30
1	2	7	6	5			8		10				12		11²	3				13							9¹	4				31
1	2	11	6	5			12		10					7		3	8										9¹	4				32
1	2	11	6	5			8¹	9³	10					7²		3				14		12					13	4				33
1	2²	11		5	3		8	12	10			13			6												4	7	9¹			34
1	11²			5	3		8¹		10					12	6		2					13					14	4	7	9³		35
1	11			5	3		8¹		10					12	6		2					13					14	4²	7	9³		36
1	7¹			5	3		8²		10					12	6	11	2					13						4	9			37
1	11			5	3	7³	8²		10					12	6	3	2					13						4	9¹	14		38
1	11³			5			8¹	13	10					7	6	3	2					12						4	14	9²		39
1	11			5			8		10					7	6	3	2					12					13	4¹	9²			40
1	12	11		5			8		10					7	6	3	2¹					13						4²	9³	14		41
1			4	5			8¹		10		14			7	6	3	2					11²					9³	12	13			42
1			4	5			8³		10		12			7²	6	3	2					11					9¹	13	14			43
1			4	5	13		8¹		10					7²	6	3	2					11					9			12		44
1			4	5			8	12	10		13			7²	6	3	2					11					9¹					45
1			4	5	12		8¹		10	11				7³	6	3	2					11					9²	14	13			46

FA Cup

First Round	Blyth S		(a)	1-3

Carling Cup

First Round	Carlisle U		(h)	0-1

Play-Offs

Semi-Final	Bury		(h)	0-1
			(a)	1-0
Final (at Wembley)	Gillingham			0-1

J Paint Trophy

First Round	Exeter C		(a)	2-1
Second Round	Wycombe W			7-0
Southern Quarter-Final	Dagenham & R		(h)	5-0
Southern Semi-Final	Brighton & HA		(h)	0-0

SOUTHAMPTON

FL Championship 1

FOUNDATION

The club was formed by members of the St Mary's Church of England Young Men's Association at a meeting of the Y.M.A. in November 1885 and it was named as such. For the sake of brevity this was usually shortened to St Mary's Y.M.A. The rector Canon Albert Basil Orme Wilberforce was elected president. The name was changed to plain St Mary's during 1887–88 and did not become Southampton St Mary's until 1894, the inaugural season in the Southern League.

St Mary's Stadium, Britannia Road, Southampton SO14 5FP.

Telephone: (0845) 688 9448.

Fax: (0845) 688 9445

Ticket Office: (0845) 688 9288.

Website: www.saintsfc.co.uk

Email: sfc@saintsfc.co.uk

Ground Capacity: 32,689.

Record Attendance: 32,104 v Liverpool, FA Premier League, 18 January 2003.

Pitch Measurements: 112yd × 72yd.

Football Secretary: Ros Wheeler.

Manager: Alan Pardew.

Physio: Mo Gimpel.

Colours: Red and white striped shirts, black shorts, white stockings.

Change Colours: All flint with white cuffs on sleeves.

Year Formed: 1885.

Turned Professional: 1894. *Ltd Co.:* 1897.

Previous Name: 1885, St Mary's Young Men's Association; 1887–88, St Mary's; 1894–95 Southampton St Mary's; 1897, Southampton.

Club Nickname: 'The Saints'.

Grounds: 1885, 'The Common' (from 1887 also used the County Cricket Ground and Antelope Cricket Ground); 1889, Antelope Cricket Ground; 1896 The County Cricket Ground; 1898, The Dell; 2001, St Mary's.

First Football League Game: 28 August 1920, Division 3, v Gillingham (a) D 1–1 – Allen; Parker, Titmuss; Shelley, Campbell, Turner; Barratt, Dominy (1), Rawlings, Moore, Foxall.

Record League Victory: 9–3 v Wolverhampton W, Division 2, 18 September 1965 – Godfrey; Jones, Williams; Walker, Knapp, Huxford; Paine (2), O'Brien (1), Melia, Chivers (4), Sydenham (2).

HONOURS

Football League: Division 1 – Runners-up 1983–84; Division 2 – Runners-up 1965–66, 1977–78; Division 3 (S) – Champions 1921–22; Division 3 – Champions 1959–60; Runners-up 1920–21.

FA Cup: Winners 1976; Runners-up 1900, 1902, 2003.

Football League Cup: Runners-up 1979.

Zenith Data Systems Cup: Runners-up 1992.

European Competitions: *European Fairs Cup:* 1969–70. *UEFA Cup:* 1971–72, 1981–82, 1982–83, 1984–85, 2003–04. *European Cup-Winners' Cup:* 1976–77.

SKY SPORTS FACT FILE

There were just 19 goals scored in ten Premier League matches on the penultimate weekend in February 1998. Southampton were top scorers on the occasion beating Blackburn Rovers 3–0 with two goals from Egil Ostenstad and one from David Hirst.

Record Cup Victory: 7–1 v Ipswich T, FA Cup 3rd rd, 7 January 1961 – Reynolds; Davies, Traynor, Conner, Page, Huxford, Paine (1), O'Brien (3 incl. 1p), Reeves, Mulgrew (2), Penk (1).

Record Defeat: 0–8 v Tottenham H, Division 2, 28 March 1936; 0–8 v Everton, Division 1, 20 November 1971.

Most League Points (2 for a win): 61, Division 3 (S), 1921–22 and Division 3, 1959–60.

Most League Points (3 for a win): 77, Division 1, 1983–84.

Most League Goals: 112, Division 3 (S), 1957–58.

Highest League Scorer in Season: Derek Reeves, 39, Division 3, 1959–60.

Most League Goals in Total Aggregate: Mike Channon, 185, 1966–77, 1979–82.

Most League Goals in One Match: 5, Charlie Wayman v Leicester C, Division 2, 23 October 1948.

Most Capped Player: Peter Shilton, 49 (125), England.

Most League Appearances: Terry Paine, 713, 1956–74.

Youngest League Player: Theo Walcott, 16 years 143 days v Wolverhampton W, 6 August 2005.

Record Transfer Fee Received: Up to £10,000,000 from Arsenal for Theo Walcott, January 2006.

Record Transfer Fee Paid: £4,000,000 to Derby Co for Rory Delap, July 2001.

Football League Record: 1920 Original Member of Division 3; 1921–22 Division 3 (S); 1922–53 Division 2; 1953–58 Division 3 (S); 1958–60 Division 3; 1960–66 Division 2; 1966–74 Division 1; 1974–78 Division 2; 1978–92 Division 1; 1992–2005 FA Premier League; 2005–09 FL C; 2009– FL 1.

LATEST SEQUENCES

Longest Sequence of League Wins: 6, 3.3.1992 – 4.4.1992.

Longest Sequence of League Defeats: 5, 16.8.1998 – 12.9.1998.

Longest Sequence of League Draws: 8, 29.8.2005 – 15.10.2005.

Longest Sequence of Unbeaten League Matches: 19, 5.9.1921 – 31.12.1921.

Longest Sequence Without a League Win: 20, 30.8.1969 – 27.12.1969.

Successive Scoring Runs: 28 from 10.2.2008.

Successive Non-scoring Runs: 5 from 1.9.1937.

MANAGERS

Cecil Knight 1894–95
(Secretary-Manager)
Charles Robson 1895–97
Er Arnfield 1897–1911
(Secretary-Manager)
(continued as Secretary)
George Swift 1911–12
Er Arnfield 1912–19
Jimmy McIntyre 1919–24
Arthur Chadwick 1925–31
George Kay 1931–36
George Gross 1936–37
Tom Parker 1937–43
J. R. Sarjantson stepped down from the board to act as Secretary-Manager 1943–47 with the next two listed being team Managers during this period
Arthur Dominy 1943–46
Bill Dodgin Snr 1946–49
Sid Cann 1949–51
George Roughton 1952–55
Ted Bates 1955–73
Lawrie McMenemy 1973–85
Chris Nicholl 1985–91
Ian Branfoot 1991–94
Alan Ball 1994–95
Dave Merrington 1995–96
Graeme Souness 1996–97
Dave Jones 1997–2000
Glenn Hoddle 2000–01
Stuart Gray 2001
Gordon Strachan 2001–04
Paul Sturrock 2004
Steve Wigley 2004
Harry Redknapp 2004–05
George Burley 2005–08
Nigel Pearson 2008
Jan Poortvliet 2008–09
Mark Wotte 2009
Alan Pardew July 2009–

TEN YEAR LEAGUE RECORD

		P	W	D	L	F	A	Pts	Pos
1999-2000	PR Lge	38	12	8	18	45	62	44	15
2000-01	PR Lge	38	14	10	14	40	48	52	10
2001-02	PR Lge	38	12	9	17	46	54	45	11
2002-03	PR Lge	38	13	13	12	43	46	52	8
2003-04	PR Lge	38	12	11	15	44	45	47	12
2004-05	PR Lge	38	6	14	18	45	66	32	20
2005-06	FL C	46	13	19	14	49	50	58	12
2006-07	FL C	46	21	12	13	77	53	75	6
2007-08	FL C	46	13	15	18	56	72	54	20
2008-09	FL C	46	10	15	21	46	69	45	23

DID YOU KNOW ?

Varied individual scoring feats achieved in Southampton colours have included Joe Rogers 10 goals v Wiltshire Regiment 1895, Alf Whittingham (Bradford City guest) 8 v Luton T 1945, Albert Brown 7 v Northampton T 1901 and Doug McGibbon 6 v Chelsea 1945.

SOUTHAMPTON 2008–09 LEAGUE RECORD

Match No.	Date	Venue	Opponents	Result	H/T Score	Lg. Pos.	Goalscorers	Attendance
1	Aug 9	A	Cardiff C	L	1-2	1-1	—	McGoldrick [45]	19,749
2	16	H	Birmingham C	L	1-2	1-0	23	Perry [43]	18,925
3	23	A	Derby Co	W	1-0	0-0	17	McGoldrick [58]	27,032
4	30	H	Blackpool	L	0-1	0-1	20		15,629
5	Sept14	A	QPR	L	1-4	0-1	23	Lallana [53]	13,770
6	17	H	Ipswich T	D	2-2	1-1	—	Surman [12], Pekhart [68]	14,916
7	20	H	Barnsley	D	0-0	0-0	22		14,836
8	27	A	Doncaster R	W	2-0	0-0	20	Mills (og) [50], Surman (pen) [58]	10,867
9	30	H	Norwich C	W	2-0	1-0	—	Robertson [29], McGoldrick (pen) [64]	14,480
10	Oct 4	A	Coventry C	L	1-4	0-2	20	Surman [63]	15,518
11	18	H	Watford	L	0-3	0-3	20		17,454
12	21	A	Sheffield U	D	0-0	0-0	—		25,642
13	25	A	Swansea C	L	0-3	0-1	22		15,564
14	28	H	Coventry C	D	1-1	0-0	—	McGoldrick [68]	14,226
15	Nov 1	A	Preston NE	W	3-2	0-2	20	Pearce [64], Surman [69], McGoldrick [90]	11,508
16	8	H	Bristol C	L	0-1	0-0	21		14,535
17	15	H	Wolverhampton W	L	1-2	1-2	21	Pearce [21]	17,812
18	22	A	Reading	W	2-1	1-0	20	Wright-Phillips 2 [14, 49]	23,121
19	25	H	Plymouth Arg	D	0-0	0-0	—		14,895
20	29	A	Charlton Ath	D	0-0	0-0	19		20,831
21	Dec 6	H	Sheffield W	D	1-1	1-0	20	Wright-Phillips [14]	15,440
22	8	A	Crystal Palace	L	0-3	0-2	—		13,799
23	13	A	Burnley	L	2-3	0-3	21	Skacel [49], Surman [61]	11,229
24	20	H	Nottingham F	L	0-2	0-1	21		26,580
25	26	A	Plymouth Arg	L	0-2	0-1	21		15,197
26	28	H	Reading	D	1-1	0-0	23	McGoldrick [74]	20,142
27	Jan 10	A	Barnsley	W	1-0	0-0	—	McGoldrick [76]	11,789
28	17	H	Doncaster R	L	1-2	0-0	23	Saganowski [90]	15,837
29	27	A	Norwich C	D	2-2	0-2	—	McLaggon [57], Saganowski [78]	25,271
30	31	H	Swansea C	D	2-2	1-1	23	Saganowski 2 [17, 76]	17,823
31	Feb 3	H	Sheffield U	L	1-2	0-1	—	Surman [89]	13,257
32	14	A	Bristol C	L	0-2	0-1	23		17,000
33	21	H	Preston NE	W	3-1	3-0	23	Surman [19], Saganowski 2 [29, 42]	14,790
34	28	H	Cardiff C	W	1-0	1-0	22	McGoldrick (pen) [11]	18,526
35	Mar 3	A	Ipswich T	W	3-0	1-0	—	Euell 2 [30, 85], Paterson [88]	20,040
36	7	A	Birmingham C	L	0-1	0-1	22		16,735
37	10	H	Derby Co	D	1-1	0-0	—	Perry [59]	17,567
38	14	H	QPR	D	0-0	0-0	23		18,691
39	21	A	Blackpool	D	1-1	0-1	23	McGoldrick [69]	7947
40	Apr 4	H	Charlton Ath	L	2-3	1-1	23	McGoldrick [17], Wright-Phillips [84]	27,228
41	7	A	Watford	D	2-2	1-1	—	Saeijs 2 [13, 89]	16,066
42	10	A	Wolverhampton W	L	0-3	0-3	—		24,636
43	13	H	Crystal Palace	W	1-0	0-0	23	McGoldrick [67]	23,220
44	18	A	Sheffield W	L	0-2	0-1	23		24,145
45	25	H	Burnley	D	2-2	2-1	23	Wright-Phillips [11], McGoldrick [44]	23,927
46	May 3	A	Nottingham F	L	1-3	1-0	23	Wright-Phillips [16]	29,008

Final League Position: 23

GOALSCORERS

League (46): McGoldrick 12 (2 pens), Surman 7 (1 pen), Saganowski 6, Wright-Phillips 6, Euell 2, Pearce 2, Perry 2, Saeijs 2, Lallana 1, McLaggon 1, Paterson 1, Pekhart 1, Robertson 1, Skacel 1, own goal 1.
Carling Cup (6): Holmes 2, McGoldrick 2 (1 pen), John 1, Lallana 1.
FA Cup (0).

Davis K 46	James L 40+1	Thomson J 6+4	Holmes L 11	Perry C 30+2	Svensson M 4	Surman A 44	Schneiderlin M 23+7	McGoldrick D 45+1	Lallana A 34+6	Gillett S 23+4	Dyer N 1+3	Wright-Phillips B 16+17	Wotton P 18+11	John S 4+3	Cork J 22+1	White J 2+1	Pekhart T 2+7	Lancashire O 10+1	Mills J 6+2	Robertson J 8+2	Paterson M 1+10	Smith R 7+6	Skacel R 28	Euell J 18+6	Pearce A 6+3	Gobern O 4+2	Gasmi R —+4	McLaggon K 1+6	Saganowski M 14+5	Saeijs J 20	Molyneux L 4	Liptak Z —+7	Match No.
1	2	3¹	4²	5	6	7	8³	9	10	11	12	13	14																				1
1	2	12	4	5	6	3	8	7	10	11				9¹																			2
1	2¹		4³	5	6	3	8	9	10	11		13	14	12	7²																		3
1	2		4	5	6	3	8¹	9	10	7²	14				13	12		11³															4
1	2	4¹				3	8²	9	10	11	12		7		6		13	5⁴															5
1	2					5	3	12	9	10	7¹	11²	13	4	8³	6		14															6
1	12			5				9	10	11	6	8¹	4	13	2	7		3²															7
1	2	12				11	8¹	9³	7			4	10²	6	14	13	5	3															8
1	2			5		11		9	10		12		4	7¹	6	3	8²	13															9
1	2¹			5		11		9	10³	12		13	4²	7	14	6	3	8															10
1	2¹	12				11		9	10				6	4	13	5	3	8	7²														11
1	12			5		3	13	10	6		8¹	14	7³	2	4⁴	9²		11															12
1	2			5		3	8¹	9	10	6		7²		4	12	13	11																13
1	2	4²				3¹	8	9	10⁵			12	6	5	14				13	11	7												14
1	2²	4¹				3	8	9		12		13		10	5				7³	11	6	14											15
1	4²					11		9	10			13	6¹	2	14	3			7	12	5	8³											16
1		12				11	8³	9	10			13		2	6¹	14			3	4⁴	5	7²											17
1	2			5		3	4	7	10			8		6					9¹	12		11											18
1	2			6		11	4	8²	7			10		5					9¹	12	3			13									19
1	2			6		11	4¹	7	8			10³	12	5					9²	14	3		13										20
1	2			5		11		7¹	8	12		10		4					9²	13	3		6										21
1	2			5		11		7	8			10³	12	4				13	9²		3		6¹	14									22
1	2²			5		11	4¹	9	7			10		6				13			3	8	12										23
1	2	7²		5		11		9¹	10			12		4							3	8	6	13									24
1	2	10³				11		9		7¹		6			5			12	8²	3		13	4	14									25
1	2	8³	5					9		7		13		6				10¹	11²	3	12		4	14									26
1	8	7	2			11	4	9		10²	12													13	5¹	6	3						27
1	2	4¹	5²			11	8	9	13			7							12						10	6	3						28
1	2	8³	5					9	10	11¹		4									7²		12		14	13	6	3					29
1	2			5		11	12	9	10²	7		4						13					14		14	8¹	6	3⁴					30
1	2			5		3	12	9	10	7²		13		4¹				14							11³	8	6						31
1	2			5		11	7¹	9	12	13		4²											3	8		14	10³	6					32
1	2			5		11		9²	8³	7		12	13										3	4					10¹	6		14	33
1	2			5		11	12	9²	7¹	4		13											3	8					10³	6		14	34
1	2			5		11	4¹	9²		7		12											13	3	8³				10	6		14	35
1	2			5		11	4³	9²		7													13	12	3¹	8			10	6		14	36
1	2			5		11¹	4²	9	13	7								12					14	3	8				10³	6			37
1	2	13		5		11		9	8²	7		12											3	4					10¹	6			38
1	2¹			5		11	4²	9	12	7		14	13										3	8²					10	6			39
1	2³			5		11²		9	7¹			13	4					12					3	8					10	6		14	40
1	2			5		11		9	13			10¹	4²					7					3	8³					12	6		14	41
1	2			5		11	8³	9²	14			12	4					7					3¹	13					10	6			42
1	2			5		11	13	9³	7			10²						3					8¹	12					6	14			43
1	2			5		11	14	9	7²			10³						13					3¹	8					12	6			44
1	2			5		11	14	9³	7²	3¹		10	4					13					8						12	6			45
1	2			5		3	8³	9	7	4		10¹						13					11			14	12		6²				46

FA Cup
Third Round   Manchester U   (h)   0-3

Carling Cup
First Round   Exeter C   (a)   3-1
Second Round   Birmingham C   (h)   2-0
Third Round   Rotherham U   (a)   1-3

SOUTHEND UNITED FL Championship 1

FOUNDATION

The leading club in Southend around the turn of the century was Southend Athletic, but they were an amateur concern. Southend United was a more ambitious professional club when they were founded in 1906, employing Bob Jack as secretary-manager and immediately joining the Second Division of the Southern League.

Roots Hall Stadium, Victoria Avenue, Southend-on-Sea, Essex SS2 6NQ.

Telephone: (01702) 304 050.

Fax: (01702) 304 124.

Ticket Office: (08444) 770 077.

Website: www.southendunited.co.uk

Email: info@southend-united.co.uk

Ground Capacity: 12,260.

Record Attendance: 31,090 v Liverpool, FA Cup 3rd rd, 10 January 1979.

Pitch Measurements: 110yd × 76yd.

Chairman: Ronald Martin.

Chief Executive: Geoffrey King.

Secretary: Mrs Helen Norbury.

Manager: Steve Tilson.

Assistant Manager: Paul Brush.

Physio: John Stannard.

Club Nickname: 'The Blues' or 'The Shrimpers'.

Colours: Navy blue shirts, sky blue neck, black sleeves, black shorts, black stockings.

Change Colours: Red shirts with white trim, red shorts, red stockings.

Year Formed: 1906.

Turned Professional: 1906. *Ltd Co.:* 1919.

Grounds: 1906, Roots Hall, Prittlewell; 1920, Kursaal; 1934, Southend Stadium; 1955, Roots Hall Football Ground.

First Football League Game: 28 August 1920, Division 3, v Brighton & HA (a) W 2–0 – Capper; Reid, Newton; Wileman, Henderson, Martin; Nicholls, Nuttall, Fairclough (2), Myers, Dorsett.

Record League Victory: 9–2 v Newport Co, Division 3 (S), 5 September 1936 – McKenzie; Nelson, Everest (1); Deacon, Turner, Carr; Bolan, Lane (1), Goddard (4), Dickinson (2), Oswald (1).

Record Cup Victory: 10–1 v Golders Green, FA Cup 1st rd, 24 November 1934 – Moore; Morfitt, Kelly; Mackay, Joe Wilson, Carr (1); Lane (1), Johnson (5), Cheesmuir (2), Deacon (1), Oswald. 10–1 v Brentwood, FA Cup 2nd rd, 7 December 1968 – Roberts; Bentley, Birks; McMillan (1) Beesley, Kurila; Clayton, Chisnall, Moore (4), Best (5), Hamilton. 10–1 v Aldershot, Leyland Daf Cup Prel rd, 6 November 1990 – Sansome; Austin, Powell, Cornwell, Prior (1), Tilson (3), Cawley, Butler, Ansah (1), Benjamin (1), Angell (4).

HONOURS

Football League: FL 1 – Champions 2005–06; Division 1 best season: 13th, 1994–95; Division 3 – Runners-up 1990–91; Division 4 – Champions 1980–81; Runners-up 1971–72, 1977–78.

FA Cup: best season: old 3rd rd, 1921; 5th rd, 1926, 1952, 1976, 1993.

Football League Cup: Quarter final 2007.

LDV Vans Trophy: Runners-up 2004, 2005.

SKY SPORTS FACT FILE

When Southend United were drawn to play Chelsea at Stamford Bridge in the third round of the FA Cup on 3 January 2009 it was only their second such Cup meeting. Chelsea had won 5–2 back in 1913. Peter Clarke on his 27th birthday earned a replay.

Record Defeat: 1–9 v Brighton & HA, Division 3, 27 November 1965.

Most League Points (2 for a win): 67, Division 4, 1980–81.

Most League Points (3 for a win): 85, Division 3, 1990–91.

Most League Goals: 92, Division 3 (S), 1950–51.

Highest League Scorer in Season: Jim Shankly, 31, 1928–29; Sammy McCrory, 1957–58, both in Division 3 (S).

Most League Goals in Total Aggregate: Roy Hollis, 122, 1953–60.

Most League Goals in One Match: 5, Jim Shankly v Merthyr T, Division 3 (S), 1 March 1930.

Most Capped Player: George Mackenzie, 9, Eire.

Most League Appearances: Sandy Anderson, 452, 1950–63.

Youngest League Player: Phil O'Connor, 16 years 76 days v Lincoln C, 26 December 1969.

Record Transfer Fee Received: £4,200,000 from Nottingham F for Stan Collymore, June 1993.

Record Transfer Fee Paid: £750,000 to Crystal Palace for Stan Collymore, November 1992.

Football League Record: 1920 Original Member of Division 3; 1921–58 Division 3 (S); 1958–66 Division 3; 1966–72 Division 4; 1972–76 Division 3; 1976–78 Division 4; 1978–80 Division 3; 1980–81 Division 4; 1981–84 Division 3; 1984–87 Division 4; 1987–89 Division 3; 1989–90 Division 4; 1990–91 Division 3; 1991–92 Division 2; 1992–97 Division 1; 1997–98 Division 2; 1998–2004 Division 3; 2004–05 FL 2; 2005–06 FL 1; 2006–07 FL C; 2007– FL 1.

LATEST SEQUENCES

Longest Sequence of League Wins: 8, 29.8.2005 – 9.10.2005.

Longest Sequence of League Defeats: 6, 29.8.1987 – 19.9.1987.

Longest Sequence of League Draws: 6, 30.1.1982 – 19.2.1982.

Longest Sequence of Unbeaten League Matches: 16, 20.2.1932 – 29.8.1932.

Longest Sequence Without a League Win: 17, 31.12.1983 – 14.4.1984.

Successive Scoring Runs: 24 from 23.3.1929.

Successive Non-scoring Runs: 6 from 28.10.1933.

MANAGERS

Bob Jack 1906–10
George Molyneux 1910–11
O. M. Howard 1911–12
Joe Bradshaw 1912–19
Ned Liddell 1919–20
Tom Mather 1920–21
Ted Birnie 1921–34
David Jack 1934–40
Harry Warren 1946–56
Eddie Perry 1956–60
Frank Broome 1960
Ted Fenton 1961–65
Alvan Williams 1965–67
Ernie Shepherd 1967–69
Geoff Hudson 1969–70
Arthur Rowley 1970–76
Dave Smith 1976–83
Peter Morris 1983–84
Bobby Moore 1984–86
Dave Webb 1986–87
Dick Bate 1987
Paul Clark 1987–88
Dave Webb *(General Manager)* 1988–92
Colin Murphy 1992–93
Barry Fry 1993
Peter Taylor 1993–95
Steve Thompson 1995
Ronnie Whelan 1995–97
Alvin Martin 1997–99
Alan Little 1999–2000
David Webb 2000–01
Rob Newman 2001–03
Steve Wignall 2003–04
Steve Tilson May 2004–

TEN YEAR LEAGUE RECORD

		P	W	D	L	F	A	Pts	Pos
1999-2000	Div 3	46	15	11	20	53	61	56	16
2000-01	Div 3	46	15	18	13	55	53	63	11
2001-02	Div 3	46	15	13	18	51	54	58	12
2002-03	Div 3	46	17	3	26	47	59	54	17
2003-04	Div 3	46	14	12	20	51	63	54	17
2004-05	FL 2	46	22	12	12	65	46	78	4
2005-06	FL 1	46	23	13	10	72	43	82	1
2006-07	FL C	46	10	12	24	47	80	42	22
2007-08	FL 1	46	22	10	14	70	55	76	6
2008-09	FL 1	46	21	8	17	58	61	71	8

DID YOU KNOW ?

Southend United met neighbours Colchester United initially in 1950–51 on the opposition's elevation to the League. Southend won 4–2 at the Greyhound Stadium on 14 October after a Reg Davies goal in 90 seconds and 3–1 at Layer Road on 24 February.

SOUTHEND UNITED 2008–09 LEAGUE RECORD

Match No.	Date	Venue	Opponents	Result		H/T Score	Lg. Pos.	Goalscorers	Attendance
1	Aug 9	H	Peterborough U	W	1-0	0-0	—	Clarke [76]	8665
2	16	A	Millwall	D	1-1	1-0	7	Revell [7]	8114
3	22	H	Brighton & HA	L	0-2	0-0	—		7976
4	30	A	Walsall	L	2-5	1-1	19	Robson-Kanu [33], Barnard [87]	3843
5	Sept 6	A	Carlisle U	L	1-2	1-0	22	Freedman [22]	6561
6	13	H	Hereford U	W	1-0	1-0	16	Barnard [29]	6393
7	20	A	Crewe Alex	W	4-3	2-2	12	Freedman 2 [4, 69], Baudet (og) [21], Grant [88]	3574
8	26	H	Leyton Orient	W	3-0	2-0	—	Barnard [1], Sawyer [12], Freedman [70]	9261
9	Oct 4	A	Yeovil T	W	2-1	1-0	7	Barnard (pen) [24], Robson-Kanu [86]	4008
10	11	H	Stockport Co	D	1-1	1-0	9	Barnard [19]	7125
11	18	H	Swindon T	W	2-1	1-0	6	Revell [11], Laurent [71]	7965
12	21	A	Scunthorpe U	D	1-1	0-0	—	Barrett [47]	4324
13	25	A	Bristol R	L	2-4	0-3	10	Clarke [70], Laurent [75]	7055
14	28	H	Leeds U	W	1-0	1-0	—	Harding [18]	10,132
15	Nov 1	H	Colchester U	D	3-3	2-1	9	Clarke [8], Laurent [13], Christophe [90]	8920
16	15	A	Tranmere R	D	2-2	2-2	8	Revell [10], Betsy [35]	5019
17	22	H	Oldham Ath	L	1-2	0-0	9	Walker [53]	7041
18	25	A	Cheltenham T	D	0-0	0-0	—		2908
19	Dec 6	A	Leicester C	L	0-3	0-1	11		16,836
20	13	H	Huddersfield T	L	0-1	0-0	12		8382
21	19	A	Hartlepool U	L	0-3	0-2	—		3123
22	26	H	Northampton T	W	1-0	0-0	12	Stanislas [90]	7767
23	28	A	Milton Keynes D	L	0-2	0-1	13		10,432
24	Jan 17	A	Stockport Co	L	1-3	0-2	16	Revell [62]	5762
25	20	A	Leyton Orient	D	1-1	0-1	—	Walker [90]	3835
26	24	H	Yeovil T	L	0-1	0-1	16		6409
27	27	A	Leeds U	L	0-2	0-2	—		20,392
28	31	H	Bristol R	W	1-0	0-0	13	Freedman [57]	7234
29	Feb 14	H	Tranmere R	W	2-1	1-0	13	Robinson T [3], Betsy [90]	6507
30	17	H	Crewe Alex	L	0-1	0-1	—		6614
31	21	A	Colchester U	W	1-0	1-0	13	Moussa [14]	8651
32	24	H	Scunthorpe U	W	2-0	0-0	—	Robinson T [54], McCormack [87]	6028
33	28	A	Peterborough U	W	2-1	1-1	13	Christophe [25], Blackett (og) [63]	7341
34	Mar 3	H	Millwall	L	0-1	0-0	—		7620
35	7	H	Walsall	W	2-0	0-0	12	Betsy [50], Robinson T [72]	6973
36	10	A	Brighton & HA	W	3-1	1-1	—	Barnard 2 [23, 85], Robinson T [89]	5035
37	14	A	Hereford U	W	1-0	0-0	10	Robinson T (pen) [87]	2663
38	17	A	Swindon T	L	0-3	0-2	—		6269
39	21	H	Carlisle U	W	3-0	1-0	9	Clarke [14], Scannell [69], McCormack [80]	7789
40	27	H	Hartlepool U	W	3-2	3-1	—	Barnard (pen) [17], Moussa [19], Robinson T [43]	7227
41	Apr 4	A	Huddersfield T	W	1-0	0-0	8	Barnard (pen) [63]	12,203
42	10	H	Milton Keynes D	L	0-2	0-0	—		10,241
43	13	A	Northampton T	W	3-2	1-0	8	Christophe [38], Robinson T [56], Barnard [60]	5190
44	18	H	Leicester C	L	0-2	0-0	8		10,089
45	25	A	Oldham Ath	D	1-1	0-0	8	Barnard [60]	4830
46	May 2	H	Cheltenham T	W	2-0	0-0	8	Barrett [54], Christophe [89]	8192

Final League Position: 8

GOALSCORERS

League (58): Barnard 11 (3 pens), Robinson T 7 (1 pen), Freedman 5, Christophe 4, Clarke 4, Revell 4, Betsy 3, Laurent 3, Barrett 2, McCormack 2, Moussa 2, Robson-Kanu 2, Walker 2, Grant 1, Harding 1, Sawyer 1, Scannell 1, Stanislas 1, own goals 2.
Carling Cup (0).
FA Cup (9): Stanislaus 2, Walker 2, Barrett 1, Christophe 1, Clarke 1, Francis 1, Laurent 1.
J Paint Trophy (2): Sawyer 2.

Mildenhall S 34	Francis S 37 + 8	Harding D 19	Bailey N 1	Clarke P 43	Barrett A 45	Moussa F 25 + 1	Walker J 9 + 8	Furlong P 1 + 2	Barnard L 24 + 11	Scannell D 6 + 13	Betsy K 28 + 13	Grant A 23 + 12	Revell A 19 + 4	Ademeno C 1 + 1	Sankofa O 23 + 4	Robson-Kanu H 12 + 2	Sawyer L 11 + 1	Christophe J 29 + 4	Freedman D 12 + 4	Joyce 12 + 1	Federici A 10	McCormack A 26 + 8	Laurent F 10 + 11	Milsom R 6	Feeney L — + 1	Stanislas J 6	Herd J 5 + 1	O'Keefe S 1 + 2	Robinson T 20 + 1	Dervite D 18	Match No.
1	2	3	4	5	6	7	8^{2}	9^{3}	10	11^{1}	12	13	14																		1
1	2	3		5	6	7	12		10		8	4	9^{1}	11^{2}	13																2
1	2	3		5	6	7^{4}			10		8	4	9^{1}			11	12														3
1	2	3		5	6		13		10	12	8	4	9^{2}			11^{1}	7														4
1	2	3		5	6		12	14	10^{3}		11^{2}	4	13				7^{1}	8	9												5
1	2	3		5	6		8^{3}		10^{1}	12	7	13				14	11^{2}	4	9												6
	2	3		5	6		8^{3}		10^{1}	11	13	12				14	7^{2}	4	9	1											7
	2	3		5	6				10		7	12	13			11^{1}	8^{3}	4	9^{2}	1		14									8
	2	3		5	6		12		10^{1}		7	13	9			11	8^{2}	4^{3}		1		14									9
	2	3^{4}		5	6				10		7		9^{2}			12	11	8^{1}	4	1		13									10
		3		5	6				10		7	12	9^{3}		2	11^{1}	8^{2}	4		1		13	14								11
		3		5	6		12		10^{1}		7		9^{3}		2	11	8^{2}	4		1		13	14								12
		3		5	6				10^{3}		12	7^{1}	13	9	2	11		4		1		8^{2}	14								13
	2	3		5	6		12				7	13	9^{3}			11	8^{2}	4		1		14	10^{1}								14
	2	3^{2}		5	6		12				7		9	13		11^{3}	8	4		1		14	10^{1}								15
	2	3		5	6						7^{1}	12	9			11	8^{2}	4		1		13	10^{6}								16
	2	3		5	6				10		7	12	9^{2}	13				4^{1}		1		8		11							17
1	7	3		5	6						9		10		2			4				8		11							18
1	2	3		5	6		12				7^{2}		9									8	10^{1}	4		13	11				19
1	2	3		5	6		12		13		7		9^{1}						14			8	10^{3}	4		11^{2}					20
1	2	3		5	6^{6}				10^{1}		7^{2}	12	9	13								8	14	4		11^{3}					21
1	6			5			12		13		7		9		2^{2}						10	8	4^{1}			11	3				22
1	2^{2}	3		5	6		12		13		7		9^{1}					4			10	8				11					23
1	13			5^{6}	6	14	12					4	9^{1}		2			7			10	8^{3}				11^{2}	3				24
1	5				6	11	13		12		7	4^{2}	9^{3}		2							8	10^{1}				3		14		25
1	5				6	11		9	10	14	7^{1}	4			2^{3}							8^{2}					3		13	12	26
1	5				6	8	10^{2}		12	13	7				2			4									3	11^{1}	9		27
1		6		5	3	11			12	13					2			7				10^{1}					8^{2}		9	4	28
1		7		5	3	11			12						2^{1}			4				10					8	13	9^{2}	6	29
1		7		5	3	11			12	13					2^{3}			4				10^{2}					8	14	9^{1}	6	30
1		13		5	3	11			12	14	7^{2}				2			4				8	10^{1}						9^{3}	6	31
1		13		5	3	11			12	14	7^{2}				2			4				8	10^{1}						9^{3}	6	32
1		13		5	3	11			10^{2}		12	7			2			4				8							9^{1}	6	33
1		12		5	3	11				13		7			2^{1}			4^{3}				8	10^{2}			14			9	6	34
1		12		5	3	11^{3}			10^{1}	14		7			2^{2}			4				8	13						9	6	35
1^{6}		13		5	3	11			10			7^{2}			2			4				8^{1}							9	6	36
				5	3	11			10^{2}		12	7^{1}			2			4			1	8					13		9	6	37
1		12		5	3	11			10^{2}	14		7			2^{1}			4				8^{3}	13						9	6	38
1	2			5	3	11			12	13		7^{1}						4	14			8^{3}	10^{2}						9	6	39
1	2			5	3	11			10^{2}		12	7^{1}		6				4				8	13						9		40
1	2			5	3	11			10		12	7^{1}						4				8							9	6	41
1	2			5	3	11			10^{2}	14	12	7^{3}						4				8	13						9^{1}	6	42
1	2			5	3	11			10		12	7^{1}						4				8							9	6	43
1	2			5	3	11			10			7^{1}	13^{3}					4^{2}	14			8	12						9	6	44
1	7			5	3	11			12						2			4				10^{1}	8						9	6	45
1	2			5	3	11			10^{3}	12	14							4^{2}	13			8	7^{1}						9	6	46

FA Cup

First Round	AFC Telford U	(a)	2-2
		(h)	2-0
Second Round	Luton T	(h)	3-1
Third Round	Chelsea	(a)	1-1
		(h)	1-4

Carling Cup

First Round	Cheltenham T	(h)	0-1

J Paint Trophy

First Round	Leyton Orient	(h)	2-4

STOCKPORT COUNTY   FL Championship 1

FOUNDATION

Formed at a meeting held at Wellington Road South by members of Wycliffe Congregational Chapel in 1883, they called themselves Heaton Norris Rovers until changing to Stockport County in 1890, a year before joining the Football Combination.

Edgeley Park, Hardcastle Road, Edgeley, Stockport, Cheshire SK3 9DD.

Telephone: (0161) 286 8888 (ext 257).

Fax: (0161) 429 7392.

Ticket Office: 0845 688 5799.

Website: www.stockportcounty.com

Email: fans@stockportcounty.com

Ground Capacity: 10,641.

Record Attendance: 27,833 v Liverpool, FA Cup 5th rd, 11 February 1950.

Pitch Measurements: 104m × 66m.

Chairman: Martin Reid.

Chief Executive: Sean Connolly.

Acting Secretary: Rachael Moss.

Manager: Gary Ablett.

Assistant Manager: Peter Ward.

Physio: Rodger Wylde.

Colours: Reflex blue shirts with one broad white band, reflex blue shorts, white stockings.

Change Colours: All black.

Year Formed: 1883.

Turned Professional: 1891.

Ltd Co.: 1908.

Previous Names: 1883, Heaton Norris Rovers; 1888, Heaton Norris; 1890, Stockport County.

Club Nicknames: 'County' or 'Hatters'.

Grounds: 1883 Heaton Norris Recreation Ground; 1884 Heaton Norris Wanderers Cricket Ground; 1885 Chorlton's Farm, Chorlton's Lane; 1886 Heaton Norris Cricket Ground; 1887 Wilkes' Field, Belmont Street; 1889 Nursery Inn, Green Lane; 1902 Edgeley Park.

First Football League Game: 1 September 1900, Division 2, v Leicester Fosse (a) D 2–2 – Moores; Earp, Wainwright; Pickford, Limond, Harvey; Stansfield, Smith (1), Patterson, Foster, Betteley (1).

Record League Victory: 13–0 v Halifax T, Division 3 (N), 6 January 1934 – McGann; Vincent (1p), Jenkinson; Robinson, Stevens, Len Jones; Foulkes (1), Hill (3), Lythgoe (2), Stevenson (2), Downes (4).

Record Cup Victory: 5–0 v Lincoln C, FA Cup 1st rd, 11 November 1995 – Edwards; Connelly, Todd, Bennett, Flynn, Gannon (Dinning), Beaumont, Oliver, Ware, Eckhardt (3), Armstrong (1) (Mike), Chalk, (1 og).

HONOURS

Football League: Division 1 best season: 8th, 1997–98; Division 2 – Runners-up 1996–97; Division 3 (N) – Champions 1921–22, 1936–37; Runners-up 1928–29, 1929-30, 1996–97; Division 4 – Champions 1966–67; Runners-up 1990–91.

FA Cup: best season: 5th rd, 1935, 1950, 2001.

Football League Cup: Semi-final 1997.

Autoglass Trophy: Runners-up 1992, 1993.

SKY SPORTS FACT FILE

On 6 May 1933 Stockport County won a last game of season 13-goal thriller with visiting Chester. County's 8–5 win just pipped their opponents for third place. Four players equally shared the goals: Percy Downes, Jabez Foulkes, Alf Lythgoe and Bert Humpish.

Record Defeat: 1–8 v Chesterfield, Division 2, 19 April 1902.

Most League Points (2 for a win): 64, Division 4, 1966–67.

Most League Points (3 for a win): 85, Division 2, 1993–94.

Most League Goals: 115, Division 3 (N), 1933–34.

Highest League Scorer in Season: Alf Lythgoe, 46, Division 3 (N), 1933–34.

Most League Goals in Total Aggregate: Jack Connor, 132, 1951–56.

Most League Goals in One Match: 5, Joe Smith v Southport, Division 3 (N), 7 January 1928; 5, Joe Smith v Lincoln C, Division 3 (N), 15 September 1928; 5, Frank Newton v Nelson, Division 3 (N), 21 September 1929; 5, Alf Lythgoe v Southport, Division 3 (N), 25 August 1934; 5, Billy McNaughton v Mansfield T, Division 3 (N), 14 December 1935; 5, Jack Connor v Workington, Division 3 (N), 8 November 1952; 5, Jack Connor v Carlisle U, Division 3 (N), 7 April 1956.

Most Capped Player: Jarkko Wiss, 9 (43), Finland.

Most League Appearances: Andy Thorpe, 489, 1978–86, 1988–92.

Youngest League Player: Paul Turnbull, 16 years 97 days v Wrexham, 30 April 2005.

Record Transfer Fee Received: £1,600,000 from Middlesbrough for Alun Armstrong, February 1998.

Record Transfer Fee Paid: £800,000 to Nottingham F for Ian Moore, July 1998.

Football League Record: 1900 Elected to Division 2; 1904 Failed re-election; 1905–21 Division 2; 1921–22 Division 3 (N); 1922–26 Division 2; 1926–37 Division 3 (N); 1937–38 Division 2; 1938–58 Division 3 (N); 1958–59 Division 3; 1959–67 Division 4; 1967–70 Division 3; 1970–91 Division 4; 1991–92 Division 3; 1992–97 Division 2; 1997–2002 Division 1; 2002–04 Division 2; 2004–05 FL 1; 2005–08 FL 2; 2008– FL 1.

LATEST SEQUENCES

Longest Sequence of League Wins: 9, 13.1.2007 – 3.3.2007.

Longest Sequence of League Defeats: 10, 24.11.2001 – 13.01.2002.

Longest Sequence of League Draws: 7, 17.3.1989 – 14.4.1989.

Longest Sequence of Unbeaten League Matches: 18, 28.1.1933 – 28.8.1933.

Longest Sequence Without a League Win: 19, 28.12.1999 – 22.4.2000.

Successive Scoring Runs: 27 from 20.10.2007.

Successive Non-scoring Runs: 7 from 10.3.1923.

MANAGERS

Fred Stewart 1894–1911
Harry Lewis 1911–14
David Ashworth 1914–19
Albert Williams 1919–24
Fred Scotchbrook 1924–26
Lincoln Hyde 1926–31
Andrew Wilson 1932–33
Fred Westgarth 1934–36
Bob Kelly 1936–38
George Hunt 1938–39
Bob Marshall 1939–49
Andy Beattie 1949–52
Dick Duckworth 1952–56
Billy Moir 1956–60
Reg Flewin 1960–63
Trevor Porteous 1963–65
Bert Trautmann *(General Manager)* 1965–66
Eddie Quigley *(Team Manager)* 1965–66
Jimmy Meadows 1966–69
Wally Galbraith 1969–70
Matt Woods 1970–71
Brian Doyle 1972–74
Jimmy Meadows 1974–75
Roy Chapman 1975–76
Eddie Quigley 1976–77
Alan Thompson 1977–78
Mike Summerbee 1978–79
Jimmy McGuigan 1979–82
Eric Webster 1982–85
Colin Murphy 1985
Les Chapman 1985–86
Jimmy Melia 1986
Colin Murphy 1986–87
Asa Hartford 1987–89
Danny Bergara 1989–95
Dave Jones 1995–97
Gary Megson 1997–99
Andy Kilner 1999–2001
Carlton Palmer 2001–03
Sammy McIlroy 2003–04
Chris Turner 2004–05
Jim Gannon 2006–09
Gary Ablett July 2009–

TEN YEAR LEAGUE RECORD

		P	W	D	L	F	A	Pts	Pos
1999-2000	Div 1	46	13	15	18	55	67	54	17
2000-01	Div 1	46	11	18	17	58	65	51	19
2001-02	Div 1	46	6	8	32	42	102	26	24
2002-03	Div 2	46	15	10	21	65	70	55	14
2003-04	Div 2	46	11	19	16	62	70	52	19
2004-05	FL 1	46	6	8	32	49	98	26	24
2005-06	FL 2	46	11	19	16	57	78	52	22
2006-07	FL 2	46	21	8	17	65	54	71	8
2007-08	FL 2	46	24	10	12	72	54	82	4
2008-09	FL 1	46	16	12	18	59	57	50*	18

* 10 points deducted.

DID YOU KNOW ?

On 31 January 2009 Dominic Blizzard swept in with the opening goal after just 14 seconds of the League game with Hereford United. It was the fastest goal scored by a Stockport County player in the competition and they went on to win 4–1.

STOCKPORT COUNTY 2008–09 LEAGUE RECORD

Match No.	Date	Venue	Opponents	Result	H/T Score	Lg. Pos.	Goalscorers	Attendance
1	Aug 9	A	Huddersfield T	D	1-1	1-1	—	Rowe T [45]	15,578
2	16	H	Leicester C	D	0-0	0-0	18		7151
3	23	A	Hartlepool U	W	1-0	0-0	7	Rowe T [90]	3945
4	30	H	Scunthorpe U	L	0-3	0-1	17		6348
5	Sept 13	A	Leyton Orient	W	3-0	2-0	12	Saah (og) [13], McNulty [45], Rowe T [70]	4473
6	16	H	Northampton T	D	1-1	0-1	—	McSweeney [76]	4974
7	20	H	Swindon T	D	1-1	1-0	10	Gleeson [32]	5536
8	27	A	Cheltenham T	D	2-2	0-1	11	Thompson [55], Raynes [90]	3796
9	Oct 3	H	Oldham Ath	W	3-1	0-1	—	Turnbull [47], Thompson [68], Raynes [82]	8360
10	11	A	Southend U	D	1-1	0-1	10	McSweeney [64]	7125
11	18	A	Colchester U	L	1-2	1-1	12	McNeil [42]	6025
12	21	A	Milton Keynes D	W	2-1	0-1	—	Taylor [57], Lewington (og) [90]	6931
13	25	A	Hereford U	W	1-0	0-0	9	Rowe T [90]	3210
14	28	H	Tranmere R	D	0-0	0-0	—		6121
15	Nov 1	H	Carlisle U	W	3-0	1-0	8	Baker 2 [7, 70], Gleeson [63]	6301
16	15	A	Millwall	L	0-1	0-0	9		9030
17	22	A	Crewe Alex	W	3-0	0-0	8	Davies [48], Pilkington A [66], Thompson [90]	5337
18	25	H	Brighton & HA	W	2-0	1-0	—	Blizzard [33], Davies (pen) [86]	5201
19	Dec 6	H	Peterborough U	L	1-3	0-0	8	Pilkington A [52]	6148
20	13	A	Yeovil T	W	4-2	3-2	7	Mullins 2 [24, 45], Rowe T [44], Baker [89]	3687
21	20	H	Bristol R	W	3-1	2-1	5	Davies 3 [27, 45, 90]	5364
22	26	A	Walsall	L	0-1	0-0	7		5496
23	28	H	Leeds U	L	1-3	1-1	7	Mullins [3]	10,273
24	Jan 13	A	Swindon T	D	1-1	0-0	—	Pilkington A [73]	6002
25	17	H	Southend U	W	3-1	2-0	7	Pilkington A 2 [20, 38], Rowe T [84]	5762
26	24	A	Oldham Ath	L	1-3	1-2	8	Johnson [40]	7605
27	27	A	Tranmere R	L	1-2	0-0	—	Johnson [90]	5259
28	31	H	Hereford U	W	4-1	2-1	8	Blizzard [1], McNeil [33], Mainwaring [52], McSweeney [76]	5586
29	Feb 3	H	Milton Keynes D	L	0-1	0-1	—		4891
30	14	H	Millwall	D	2-2	0-1	10	McNeil [79], Johnson [83]	5461
31	17	H	Cheltenham T	W	1-0	1-0	—	Johnson [31]	5041
32	21	A	Carlisle U	W	2-1	1-0	7	Blizzard [6], Rowe T [70]	5930
33	24	A	Colchester U	L	0-1	0-1	—		3179
34	28	H	Huddersfield T	D	1-1	0-1	8	Clarke (og) [90]	7739
35	Mar 3	A	Leicester C	D	1-1	1-1	—	O'Grady [5]	16,378
36	7	A	Scunthorpe U	L	1-2	1-2	8	Raynes [21]	4890
37	10	H	Hartlepool U	W	2-1	0-0	—	McSweeney [55], Vincent [65]	4790
38	14	H	Leyton Orient	L	0-1	0-0	9		5835
39	21	A	Northampton T	L	0-4	0-2	10		4814
40	28	A	Bristol R	L	0-2	0-2	10		6214
41	Apr 4	H	Yeovil T	D	0-0	0-0	10		5664
42	11	A	Leeds U	L	0-1	0-1	12		24,967
43	13	H	Walsall	L	1-2	0-1	13	Tansey [76]	5274
44	18	A	Peterborough U	L	0-1	0-1	14		8333
45	24	H	Crewe Alex	W	4-3	1-1	—	Vincent [13], O'Grady [49], Johnson 2 [65, 82]	7134
46	May 2	A	Brighton & HA	L	0-1	0-0	18		8618

Final League Position: 18

GOALSCORERS

League (59): Rowe T 7, Johnson 6, Davies 5 (1 pen), Pilkington A 5, McSweeney 4, Baker 3, Blizzard 3, McNeil 3, Mullins 3, Raynes 3, Thompson 3, Gleeson 2, O'Grady 2, Vincent 2, Mainwaring 1, McNulty 1, Tansey 1, Taylor 1, Turnbull 1, own goals 3.
Carling Cup (0).
FA Cup (7): Davies 1, Dicker 1, Gleeson 1, McNeil 1, Pilkington A 1, Rose 1, Vincent 1.
J Paint Trophy (1): McSweeney 1.

Williams O 33	Mullins J 31 + 2	Rose M 23 + 4	Raynes M 34 + 1	McNulty J 26	Owen G 8	Pilkington A 22 + 2	Dicker G 22 + 3	Rowe T 42 + 2	Thompson P 12 + 7	Gleeson S 17 + 4	McNeil M 15 + 4	Baker C 15 + 7	Blizzard D 30 + 1	McSweeney L 28 + 8	Turnbull P 15 + 19	Mainwaring M 17 + 4	Vincent J 8 + 8	Tunnicliffe J 27 + 3	Forster F 6	Kane T 3	Fojut J 3	Johnson O 9 + 15	Taylor J 5 + 3	Davies C 9	Mooney D 2	Thompson J 6 + 3	Threlfall R 1 + 1	Tansey G 9 + 3	Pilkington D — + 3	O'Grady C 17 + 1	Ennis P — + 2	Logan C 7	Rowe D — + 3	Halls A 4 + 1	Fisher T — + 1	Match No.
1	2	3¹	4	5	6	7²	8	9	10	11	12	13																								1
1	2	13	5	3	6	12	8²	9	10	11		7¹	4																							2
1		2¹	5	3	6	7	8	9		11		10²	4	12	13																					3
1			6	3	5	7	8¹					10³	11²	4	2	9	12	13	14																	4
1			4	5	6	7¹	8²	9	10³	14				11	2	13	12	3																		5
1	2		5	3	6	7	8²	9¹	12	11			4	10³	13	14																				6
1	2		5	3	6	7		12	9³	13	11		8¹	4²	10	14																				7
1	2	12	5	3	6¹	7	8			10	11²		13	9³	4		14																			8
1	12	3²	5		6			7³	8	9	10		14	2¹	11			4																		9
	12		5	3		7	8		9²		11		13	14	10			4	1		2³	6¹														10
			4²	5		12	8³	3	9	11		10¹		7	2			13				1		6	14											11
		2				7¹		13	9	11		8³		12	10²	14						5	1	3	6		4									12
		2			6	7	12	9	10²	11¹		4³	13	14	5							1		3		8										13
			6	3	5	7	8¹	9²	10	11				13	2			4				1		12												14
		6	14	3		8		9	13	11³		7¹		2	4			5				1	12	10²												15
1		5	11	3		7¹		9				13	12	4	2			8				6		10²												16
1	2³	3			6	7		12	9¹			13		10	4			14				5					8	11²								17
1	2		5	3		7¹		12		11²		10		4	13							6						9								18
1		3³	12	5²	6	7	8¹	9		11				4	2							14				13		10								19
1	2	3		5		7³		9		11¹		12		4	13							6				14	8	10²								20
1	2	3		5		7²	8	9	14	13		11¹		4	12							6						10³								21
1	2	3³		5		7	8¹	9	12	13		11²		4	14							6						10								22
1	2	3²		5		7		9	12	8		11³		4	13			14				6						10¹								23
1	2	4³		5		7		3				12	10²	8	14	11						6				13				9¹						24
1		3	4	5		7		9				10¹	8²	2³	12	11						6					14			13						25
1	2		5	3				9				10¹		4	11	13		7				6³					8²	12		14						26
1	2		5	3				9				10¹		4		7	11	8²				6						12		13						27
1	2	12	5					9				10		4³	6²	7	8	14				11				3¹		13								28
1	2	3¹	5					9				10		4	6	11²	8	12				7								13						29
1			5	3				7				9			12	4	2	8¹				6						11		10						30
1			5	3				8				7²			10	4	2	13				12				6		11¹		9						31
1	2		5					8				3			10	4	13	7²				12				6		11¹		9						32
1	2	3¹	5					8²				9		4	7	12	11³	14				6				13				10						33
1		3	5					8²	11			9		4¹	2	12	7					6				13				10						34
1	2	3	5					8				9		11	4¹		7²					6				12		13		10						35
1	2	3²	5					8				9		11¹	4		7					6				13		12		10						36
1			6	3	5							9		11	2	12	8	7												4¹		10				37
1		3	5									9		10	6	2¹	12	8³				7²	14			13				4		11				38
1		3	5									9		11	4	2³	13	8²				6¹	12							7		10	14			39
			5									9			6	4	2¹	13				8³	3²			11	14			7	12	10		1		40
		5¹	3	4								9		8	2							11	12							6	7	10		1		41
		3	5									9		4	7³	11	2¹	13				6								8²		10	1	14	12	42
			5	3					9²					4	12							13				6				8³		10	13	1	14 2	43
			5	3					9					4	7	14	11					12				6				8²		10³	1	13	2¹	44
			5									3			8	7	9					11				6		4		10¹		1	2	12		45
		6¹	5									3			8	7	11					9				4		12		10		1	2			46

FA Cup
First Round — Yeovil T — (a) 1-1
(h) 5-0
Second Round — Gillingham — (a) 0-0
(h) 1-2

Carling Cup
First Round — Leicester C — (a) 0-1

J Paint Trophy
First Round — Port Vale — (h) 1-0
Second Round — Bury — (a) 0-1

STOKE CITY   FA Premiership

FOUNDATION

The date of the formation of this club has long been in doubt. The year 1863 was claimed, but more recent research by Wade Martin has uncovered nothing earlier than 1868, when a couple of Old Carthusians, who were apprentices at the local works of the old North Staffordshire Railway Company, met with some others from that works, to form Stoke Ramblers. It should also be noted that the old Stoke club went bankrupt in 1908 when a new club was formed.

Britannia Stadium, Stanley Matthews Way, Stoke-on-Trent, Staffs ST4 4EG.

Telephone: (0871) 663 2008.

Fax: (01782) 592 210.

Ticket Office: (0871) 663 2007.

Website: www.stokecityfc.com

Email: info@stokecityfc.com

Ground Capacity: 28,383.

Record Attendance: 51,380 v Arsenal, Division 1, 29 March 1937 (at Victoria Ground).

Pitch Measurements: 100m × 64m.

Chairman: Peter Coates.

Chief Executive: Tony Scholes.

Football Administrator: Eddie Harrison.

Manager: Tony Pulis.

Assistant Manager: Dave Kemp.

Physio: Dave Watson.

HONOURS

Football League: Division 1 best season: 4th, 1935–36, 1946–47; FL C – Runners-up 2007–08; Division 2 – Champions 1932–33, 1962–63, 1992–93; Runners-up 1921–22; Division 3 (N) – Champions 1926–27.

FA Cup: Semi-finals 1899, 1971, 1972.

Football League Cup: Winners 1972; Runners-up 1964.

Autoglass Trophy: Winners: 1992.

Auto Windscreens Shield: Winners: 2000.

European Competitions: UEFA Cup: 1972–73, 1974–75.

Colours: Red and white striped shirts, white shorts, royal blue stockings.

Change Colours: Yellow shirts, royal blue shorts, yellow stockings.

Year Formed: 1863* (*see Foundation*). *Turned Professional:* 1885. *Ltd Co.:* 1908.

Previous Names: 1868, Stoke Ramblers; 1870, Stoke; 1925, Stoke City.

Club Nickname: 'The Potters'.

Grounds: 1875, Sweeting's Field; 1878, Victoria Ground (previously known as the Athletic Club Ground); 1997, Britannia Stadium.

First Football League Game: 8 September 1888, Football League, v WBA (h) L 0–2 – Rowley; Clare, Underwood; Ramsey, Shutt, Smith; Sayer, McSkimming, Staton, Edge, Tunnicliffe.

Record League Victory: 10–3 v WBA, Division 1, 4 February 1937 – Doug Westland; Brigham, Harbot; Tutin, Turner (1p), Kirton; Matthews, Antonio (2), Freddie Steele (5), Jimmy Westland, Johnson (2).

Record Cup Victory: 7–1 v Burnley, FA Cup 2nd rd (replay), 20 February 1896 – Clawley; Clare, Eccles; Turner, Grewe, Robertson; Willie Maxwell, Dickson, A. Maxwell (3), Hyslop (4), Schofield.

SKY SPORTS FACT FILE

On 8 March 1978 Brendan O'Callaghan was making his debut for Stoke City against Hull City after a transfer from Doncaster Rovers. He came on as a substitute and within ten seconds scored what proved to be the only goal of the match.

Record Defeat: 0–10 v Preston NE, Division 1, 14 September 1889.

Most League Points (2 for a win): 63, Division 3 (N), 1926–27.

Most League Points (3 for a win): 93, Division 2, 1992–93.

Most League Goals: 92, Division 3 (N), 1926–27.

Highest League Scorer in Season: Freddie Steele, 33, Division 1, 1936–37.

Most League Goals in Total Aggregate: Freddie Steele, 142, 1934–49.

Most League Goals in One Match: 7, Neville Coleman v Lincoln C, Division 2, 23 February 1957.

Most Capped Player: Gordon Banks, 36 (73), England.

Most League Appearances: Eric Skeels, 506, 1958–76.

Youngest League Player: Peter Bullock, 16 years 163 days v Swansea C, 19 April 1958.

Record Transfer Fee Received: £3,000,000 from Manchester U for Ritchie De Laat, January 2009.

Record Transfer Fee Paid: £5,500,000 to Reading for Dave Kitson, July 2008.

Football League Record: 1888 Founder Member of Football League; 1890 Not re-elected; 1891 Re-elected; relegated in 1907, and after one year in Division 2, resigned for financial reasons; 1919 re-elected to Division 2; 1922–23 Division 1; 1923–26 Division 2; 1926–27 Division 3 (N); 1927–33 Division 2; 1933–53 Division 1; 1953–63 Division 2; 1963–77 Division 1; 1977–79 Division 2; 1979–85 Division 1; 1985–90 Division 2; 1990–92 Division 3; 1992–93 Division 2; 1993–98 Division 1; 1998–2002 Division 2; 2002–04 Division 1; 2004–08 FL C; 2008– FA Premier League.

LATEST SEQUENCES

Longest Sequence of League Wins: 8, 30.3.1895 – 21.9.1895.

Longest Sequence of League Defeats: 11, 6.4.1985 – 17.8.1985.

Longest Sequence of League Draws: 5, 21.3.1987 – 11.4.1987.

Longest Sequence of Unbeaten League Matches: 25, 5.9.1992 – 20.2.1993.

Longest Sequence Without a League Win: 17, 22.4.1989 – 14.10.1989.

Successive Scoring Runs: 21 from 24.12.1921.

Successive Non-scoring Runs: 8 from 29.12.1984.

MANAGERS

Tom Slaney 1874–83
(Secretary-Manager)
Walter Cox 1883–84
(Secretary-Manager)
Harry Lockett 1884–90
Joseph Bradshaw 1890–92
Arthur Reeves 1892–95
William Rowley 1895–97
H. D. Austerberry 1897–1908
A. J. Barker 1908–14
Peter Hodge 1914–15
Joe Schofield 1915–19
Arthur Shallcross 1919–23
John 'Jock' Rutherford 1923
Tom Mather 1923–35
Bob McGrory 1935–52
Frank Taylor 1952–60
Tony Waddington 1960–77
George Eastham 1977–78
Alan A'Court 1978
Alan Durban 1978–81
Richie Barker 1981–83
Bill Asprey 1984–85
Mick Mills 1985–89
Alan Ball 1989–91
Lou Macari 1991–93
Joe Jordan 1993–94
Lou Macari 1994–97
Chic Bates 1997–98
Chris Kamara 1998
Brian Little 1998–99
Gary Megson 1999
Gudjon Thordarson 1999–2002
Steve Cotterill 2002
Tony Pulis 2002–05
Johan Boskamp 2005–06
Tony Pulis June 2006–

TEN YEAR LEAGUE RECORD

		P	W	D	L	F	A	Pts	Pos
1999-2000	Div 2	46	23	13	10	68	42	82	6
2000-01	Div 2	46	21	14	11	74	49	77	5
2001-02	Div 2	46	23	11	12	67	40	80	5
2002-03	Div 1	46	12	14	20	45	69	50	21
2003-04	Div 1	46	18	12	16	58	55	66	11
2004-05	FL C	46	17	10	19	36	38	61	12
2005-06	FL C	46	17	7	22	54	63	58	13
2006-07	FL C	46	19	16	11	62	41	73	8
2007-08	FL C	46	21	16	9	69	55	79	2
2008-09	PR Lge	38	12	9	17	38	55	45	12

DID YOU KNOW ?

From December 1935 until September 1936 Stoke City fielded the same goalkeeper, two full-backs and three halves in 30 successive League matches. They included newcomers goalkeeper Norman Wilkinson, full-back Bill Winstanley and wing-half Frank Soo.

STOKE CITY 2008–09 LEAGUE RECORD

Match No.	Date	Venue	Opponents	Result		H/T Score	Lg. Pos.	Goalscorers	Attendance
1	Aug 16	A	Bolton W	L	1-3	0-3	—	Fuller [90]	22,717
2	23	H	Aston Villa	W	3-2	1-0	14	Lawrence (pen) [30], Fuller [80], Sidibe [90]	27,500
3	30	A	Middlesbrough	L	1-2	0-1	15	Hoyte (og) [71]	27,627
4	Sept14	H	Everton	L	2-3	0-1	19	Olofinjana [55], Jagielka (og) [63]	27,415
5	20	A	Liverpool	D	0-0	0-0	18		43,931
6	27	H	Chelsea	L	0-2	0-1	18		27,500
7	Oct 5	A	Portsmouth	L	1-2	0-1	19	Fuller [48]	19,248
8	19	H	Tottenham H	W	2-1	1-1	18	Higginbotham (pen) [19], Delap [53]	27,500
9	26	A	Manchester C	L	0-3	0-1	18		44,624
10	29	H	Sunderland	W	1-0	0-0	—	Fuller [73]	26,731
11	Nov 1	H	Arsenal	W	2-1	1-0	12	Fuller [11], Olofinjana [73]	26,704
12	8	A	Wigan Ath	D	0-0	0-0	12		15,881
13	15	A	Manchester U	L	0-5	0-2	15		75,369
14	22	H	WBA	W	1-0	0-0	14	Sidibe [84]	26,613
15	29	H	Hull C	D	1-1	0-1	13	Fuller (pen) [73]	27,500
16	Dec 6	A	Newcastle U	D	2-2	0-2	13	Sidibe [60], Diagne-Faye [90]	47,422
17	13	H	Fulham	D	0-0	0-0	13		25,287
18	20	A	Blackburn R	L	0-3	0-3	15		23,004
19	26	H	Manchester U	L	0-1	0-0	18		27,500
20	28	A	West Ham U	L	1-2	1-0	18	Diagne-Faye [4]	34,477
21	Jan 10	H	Liverpool	D	0-0	0-0	17		27,500
22	17	A	Chelsea	L	1-2	0-0	19	Delap [60]	41,788
23	27	A	Tottenham H	L	1-3	0-3	—	Beattie [57]	36,072
24	31	H	Manchester C	W	1-0	1-0	17	Beattie [45]	27,236
25	Feb 7	A	Sunderland	L	0-2	0-0	17		38,350
26	21	H	Portsmouth	D	2-2	0-0	17	Beattie 2 (1 pen) [78 (p), 80]	26,354
27	Mar 1	A	Aston Villa	D	2-2	0-1	19	Shawcross [88], Whelan [90]	39,641
28	4	H	Bolton W	W	2-0	1-0	—	Beattie [14], Fuller [73]	26,319
29	14	A	Everton	L	1-3	0-2	18	Shawcross [52]	36,396
30	21	H	Middlesbrough	W	1-0	0-0	16	Shawcross [84]	26,442
31	Apr 4	A	WBA	W	2-0	1-0	13	Fuller [2], Beattie [49]	26,277
32	11	H	Newcastle U	D	1-1	0-0	13	Diagne-Faye [33]	27,500
33	18	H	Blackburn R	W	1-0	0-0	12	Lawrence [75]	27,500
34	25	A	Fulham	L	0-1	0-1	12		25,069
35	May 2	H	West Ham U	L	0-1	0-1	13		27,500
36	9	A	Hull C	W	2-1	1-0	12	Fuller [41], Lawrence [73]	24,932
37	16	H	Wigan Ath	W	2-0	0-0	11	Fuller [69], Beattie [76]	25,641
38	24	A	Arsenal	L	1-4	1-4	12	Fuller (pen) [31]	60,082

Final League Position: 12

GOALSCORERS

League (38): Fuller 11 (2 pens), Beattie 7 (1 pen), Diagne-Faye 3, Lawrence 3 (1 pen), Shawcross 3, Sidibe 3, Delap 2, Olofinjana 2, Higginbotham 1 (pen), Whelan 1, own goals 2.
Carling Cup (7): Whelan 2, Cresswell 1, Parkin 1, Pericard 1, Pugh 1, Sidibe 1.
FA Cup (0).

Sorensen T 35+1	Wilkinson A 20+2	Griffin A 17+3	Olofinjana S 14+4	Cort L 9+2	Shawcross R 28+2	Delap R 34	Whelan G 21+5	Sidibe M 17+5	Kitson D 10+6	Cresswell R 11+18	Dickinson C 3+2	Lawrence L 18+2	Fuller R 25+9	Diagne-Faye A 36	Faye A 18+3	Diao S 18+2	Higginbotham D 28	Tonge M 1+9	Sonko 17+7	Simonsen S 3+2	Soares T 5+2	Pugh D 9+8	Pericard V 1+3	Davies A —+2	Etherington M 12+2	Beattie J 16	Kelly S 2+4	Camara H —+4	Match No.
1	2^1	3	4	5	6	7	8^2	9^3	10	11	12	13	14																1
1		2	4	5	14	7		13	9^2		3	11	10^3		6		8^1	12											2
1	12	2	4	5		7		14	9^2	13	3^1	11	10^3		6		8												3
1		2	4	5		7	12	9^1	13	11^2		10	8^3			3	14		6										4
1		2	4	12		7		9	10^2	14		11^3	13	6			8	3			5^1								5
1		2	4	5			9^2	10^1	11			7^3	12	6	13	8	3	14											6
1		2	4	5	7^2		12	9^1	13			10	6		8	3	11^{13}	1	14										7
1^6		2	4		12	7		9	10^2			13	6		8	3		5^1	15	11									8
1		2	4		5	7	12	9^3	14	13		10	6		11^1	3		8^2											9
1		2	4^2		5	7		9	12			10^1	6	13	11	3	14		8^3										10
1		2	4		5	7	12	9^2	13	14		10^3	6	8	11^1	3													11
1		2	4^1		5	7	12	9^2	13	14		10	6	8^3	11	3													12
1	14	2^3	4^1		5	7		9	13	12		10^2	6	8	11	3													13
1		2		12	5^1	7		9	10^2	13			6	4	11	3	14		8^3										14
1		2		5		7		9				10	6	4	11	3	12		8^1										15
1		2			7^1	13	9		10			12	6	4^3	11^2	3	14	5		8									16
1	2				7^2	8	9^1		12			10	6	4		3	13	5		11^{13}	14								17
		12		2	7^2	8			11			10	6	4^1		3	14	5	1	13		9^3							18
1	2^4	12		5	7^3	8			9^2			10	6	4^1		3				11	13	14							19
1	2^2	4		5	7	8			9			10^4	6			3				11^1	12	13							20
1	2			5	7	8	9^2	10		12			6	4		3				13		11^1							21
1	2	12		5	7	8	13	10					6	4^3	3^1			14				14			11^2	9			22
1	2^1	12		5	7	8		10		13			6^3	4^2	3				14		3				11	9			23
1	2	12		5	7^1	8			13				10^2	6	4^1				14		3				11^3	9			24
1	2^2			5^1		8			7				10^3	6		4			12			13			11^8	9	3	14	25
1	2			5			10^1	12		7^2			6	4	8	3	13					11			9				26
1^6	3			2		12	10		7	13			4^1	8	6		5	15		11^2			9						27
1	2^3			5	11	4	9^2		7	13	6	12	8^1	3		14									10				28
1	2			5	11^2	4	9^1		7^3	12	6			8^2	3							13	10				14		29
1	2^3			5	11	4	12		7^1	10	6			8^2	3							13	9	14					30
1	2	14		5	8	4		13		7^1		10^3	6			3						12			11	9^2			31
1	2^3			5	8	4		12		7		10	6			3						13			11^2	9^1	14		32
1	2^1			5	8	4		13		7		10	6			3		14				13			11^3	9^2	12		33
1				5	8	4			9^2	14		7	10	6					13			3^3			11		2^1	12	34
1	2^3	13		5	8	4				7		10	6			14						3^2			11	9^1	12		35
1	2		5	3	8	4				12		7	10^3	6		13									11^2	9^1	14		36
1	2		5^1	3	8	4				14		7	10	6	13							12			11^2	9^3			37
15	2		5	11	4		13	3		7			10^2	6		8^1			1^6			12			9				38

FA Cup
Third Round   Hartlepool U   (a)   0-2

Carling Cup
Second Round   Cheltenham T   (a)   3-2
Third Round   Reading   (h)   2-2
Fourth Round   Rotherham U   (h)   2-0
Quarter-Final   Derby Co   (h)   0-1

SUNDERLAND

FA Premiership

FOUNDATION

A Scottish schoolmaster named James Allan, working at Hendon Board School, took the initiative in the foundation of Sunderland in 1879 when they were formed as The Sunderland and District Teachers' Association FC at a meeting in the Adults School, Norfolk Street. Due to financial difficulties, they quickly allowed members from outside the teaching profession and so became Sunderland AFC in October 1880.

Stadium of Light, Sunderland, Tyne and Wear SR5 1SU.

Telephone: (0871) 911 1200.

Fax: (0191) 551 5123.

Ticket Office: (0871) 911 1973.

Website: www.safc.com

Email: enquiries@safc.com

Ground Capacity: 49,000.

Record Attendance: Stadium of Light: 48,353 v Liverpool, FA Premier League, 13 April 2002. FA Premier League figure (46,062). Roker Park: 75,118 v Derby Co, FA Cup 6th rd replay, 8 March 1933.

Pitch Measurements: 105m × 68m.

Chairman: Niall Quinn.

Vice-chairman: John Hays.

Chief Executive: Steve Walton.

Club Secretary: Margaret Byrne.

Manager: Steve Bruce.

Head of Sports Therapy: Pete Friar.

HONOURS

Football League: FL C – Champions 2004–05, 2006–07; Division 1 – Champions 1891–92, 1892–93, 1894–95, 1901–02, 1912–13, 1935–36, 1995–96, 1998–99; Runners-up 1893–94, 1897–98, 1900–01, 1922–23, 1934–35; Division 2 – Champions 1975–76; Runners-up 1963–64, 1979–80. Division 3 – Champions 1987–88.

FA Cup: Winners 1937, 1973; Runners-up 1913, 1992.

Football League Cup: Runners-up 1985.

European Competitions: European Cup-Winners' Cup: 1973–74.

Colours: Red and white striped shirts, black shorts, black stockings.

Change Colours: All white with black sleeves.

Year Formed: 1879. *Turned Professional:* 1886. *Ltd Co.:* 1906.

Club Nickname: Black Cats.

Previous Name: 1879, Sunderland and District Teacher's AFC; 1880, Sunderland.

Grounds: 1879, Blue House Field, Hendon; 1882, Groves Field, Ashbrooke; 1883, Horatio Street; 1884, Abbs Field, Fulwell; 1886, Newcastle Road; 1898, Roker Park; 1997, Stadium of Light.

First Football League Game: 13 September 1890, Football League, v Burnley (h) L 2–3 – Kirtley; Porteous, Oliver; Wilson, Auld, Gibson; Spence (1), Miller, Campbell (1), Scott, D. Hannah.

Record League Victory: 9–1 v Newcastle U (a), Division 1, 5 December 1908 – Roose; Forster, Melton; Daykin, Thomson, Low; Mordue (1), Hogg (3), Brown, Holley (3), Bridgett (2).

Record Cup Victory: 11–1 v Fairfield, FA Cup 1st rd, 2 February 1895 – Doig; McNeill, Johnston; Dunlop, McCreadie (1), Wilson; Gillespie (1), Millar (5), Campbell, Hannah (3), Scott (1).

SKY SPORTS FACT FILE

The two most prolific scorers in Sunderland history were Charlie Buchan (222 League and Cup goals) and Bobby Gurney (228). They each enjoyed 13 seasons as the club's leading scorers. Buchan spanned the First World War, Gurney from 1929–30 onwards.

Record Defeat: 0–8 v Sheff Wed, Division 1, 26 December 1911. 0–8 v West Ham U, Division 1, 19 October 1968. 0–8 v Watford, Division 1, 25 September 1982.

Most League Points (2 for a win): 61, Division 2, 1963–64.

Most League Points (3 for a win): 105, Division 1, 1998–99 (Football League Record).

Most League Goals: 109, Division 1, 1935–36.

Highest League Scorer in Season: Dave Halliday, 43, Division 1, 1928–29.

Most League Goals in Total Aggregate: Charlie Buchan, 209, 1911–25.

Most League Goals in One Match: 5, Charlie Buchan v Liverpool, Division 1, 7 December 1919; 5, Bobby Gurney v Bolton W, Division 1, 7 December 1935; 5, Dominic Sharkey v Norwich C, Division 2, 20 February 1962.

Most Capped Player: Charlie Hurley, 38 (40), Republic of Ireland.

Most League Appearances: Jim Montgomery, 537, 1962–77.

Youngest League Player: Derek Forster, 15 years 184 days v Leicester C, 22 August 1964.

Record Transfer Fee Received: £5,500,000 from Leeds U for Michael Bridges, July 1999.

Record Transfer Fee Paid: £9,000,000 to Hearts for Craig Gordon, August 2007.

Football League Record: 1890 Elected to Division 1; 1958–64 Division 2; 1964–70 Division 1; 1970–76 Division 2; 1976–77 Division 1; 1977–80 Division 2; 1980–85 Division 1; 1985–87 Division 1; 1987–88 Division 3; 1988–90 Division 2; 1990–91 Division 1; 1991–92 Division 2; 1992–96 Division 1; 1996–97 FA Premier League; 1997–99 Division 1; 1999–2003 FA Premier League; 2003–04 Division 1; 2004–05 FL C; 2005–06 FA Premier League; 2006–07 FL C; 2007– FA Premier League.

MANAGERS

Tom Watson 1888–96
Bob Campbell 1896–99
Alex Mackie 1899–1905
Bob Kyle 1905–28
Johnny Cochrane 1928–39
Bill Murray 1939–57
Alan Brown 1957–64
George Hardwick 1964–65
Ian McColl 1965–68
Alan Brown 1968–72
Bob Stokoe 1972–76
Jimmy Adamson 1976–78
Ken Knighton 1979–81
Alan Durban 1981–84
Len Ashurst 1984–85
Lawrie McMenemy 1985–87
Denis Smith 1987–91
Malcolm Crosby 1992–93
Terry Butcher 1993
Mick Buxton 1993–95
Peter Reid 1995–2002
Howard Wilkinson 2002–03
Mick McCarthy 2003–06
Niall Quinn 2006
Roy Keane 2006–08
Ricky Sbragia 2008–09
Steve Bruce June 2009–

LATEST SEQUENCES

Longest Sequence of League Wins: 13, 14.11.1891 – 2.4.1892.

Longest Sequence of League Defeats: 17, 18.1.2003 – 16.8.2003.

Longest Sequence of League Draws: 6, 26.3.1949 – 19.4.1949.

Longest Sequence of Unbeaten League Matches: 19, 3.5.1998 – 14.11.1998.

Longest Sequence Without a League Win: 22, 21.12.2002 – 16.8.2003.

Successive Scoring Runs: 29 from 8.11.1997.

Successive Non-scoring Runs: 10 from 27.11.1976.

TEN YEAR LEAGUE RECORD

		P	W	D	L	F	A	Pts	Pos
1999-2000	PR Lge	38	16	10	12	57	56	58	7
2000-01	PR Lge	38	15	12	11	46	41	57	7
2001-02	PR Lge	38	10	10	18	29	51	40	17
2002-03	PR Lge	38	4	7	27	21	65	19	20
2003-04	Div 1	46	22	13	11	62	45	79	3
2004-05	FL C	46	29	7	10	76	41	94	1
2005-06	PR Lge	38	3	6	29	26	69	15	20
2006-07	FL C	46	27	7	12	76	47	88	1
2007-08	PR Lge	38	11	6	21	36	59	39	15
2008-09	PR Lge	38	9	9	20	34	54	36	16

DID YOU KNOW ?

The highest attendance at Roker Park for a floodlit match was achieved on 10 January 1962 for an FA Cup replay with Southampton. The 58,527 spectators present saw Sunderland win 3–0 with two goals from George Herd, one from Willie McPheat.

SUNDERLAND 2008–09 LEAGUE RECORD

Match No.	Date	Venue	Opponents	Result		H/T Score	Lg. Pos.	Goalscorers	Attendance
1	Aug 16	H	Liverpool	L	0-1	0-0	—		43,259
2	23	A	Tottenham H	W	2-1	0-0	12	Richardson [55], Cisse [83]	36,064
3	31	H	Manchester C	L	0-3	0-1	18		39,622
4	Sept 13	A	Wigan Ath	D	1-1	0-0	17	Bramble (og) [15]	18,015
5	20	H	Middlesbrough	W	2-0	0-0	8	Chopra 2 [81, 90]	38,388
6	27	A	Aston Villa	L	1-2	1-2	13	Cisse [10]	38,706
7	Oct 4	H	Arsenal	D	1-1	0-0	14	Leadbitter [86]	40,199
8	18	A	Fulham	D	0-0	0-0	12		25,116
9	25	H	Newcastle U	W	2-1	1-1	9	Cisse [20], Richardson [75]	47,936
10	29	A	Stoke C	L	0-1	0-0	—		26,731
11	Nov 1	A	Chelsea	L	0-5	0-3	14		41,693
12	8	H	Portsmouth	L	1-2	1-0	19	Cisse [4]	37,712
13	15	A	Blackburn R	W	2-1	0-1	9	Jones [49], Cisse [71]	21,798
14	23	H	West Ham U	L	0-1	0-1	16		35,222
15	29	H	Bolton W	L	1-4	1-3	18	Cisse [11]	35,457
16	Dec 6	A	Manchester U	L	0-1	0-0	18		75,400
17	13	H	WBA	W	4-0	3-0	18	Jones 2 [22, 24], Reid [40], Cisse (pen) [47]	36,280
18	20	A	Hull C	W	4-1	1-1	13	Malbranque [10], Zayatte (og) [78], Jones [84], Cisse [90]	24,917
19	26	H	Blackburn R	D	0-0	0-0	14		44,680
20	28	A	Everton	L	0-3	0-2	15		39,146
21	Jan 10	A	Middlesbrough	D	1-1	0-1	13	Jones [82]	29,310
22	17	H	Aston Villa	L	1-2	1-0	15	Collins [11]	40,350
23	27	H	Fulham	W	1-0	0-0	—	Jones [55]	36,539
24	Feb 1	A	Newcastle U	D	1-1	1-0	13	Cisse [32]	52,084
25	7	H	Stoke C	W	2-0	0-0	11	Jones [78], Healy [90]	38,350
26	21	A	Arsenal	D	0-0	0-0	11		60,104
27	Mar 3	A	Liverpool	L	0-2	0-0	—		41,587
28	7	H	Tottenham H	D	1-1	1-0	—	Richardson [3]	37,894
29	14	H	Wigan Ath	L	1-2	1-2	14	Leadbitter [41]	39,266
30	22	A	Manchester C	L	0-1	0-0	14		43,017
31	Apr 4	A	West Ham U	L	0-2	0-1	17		34,761
32	11	H	Manchester U	L	1-2	0-1	17	Jones [55]	45,408
33	18	H	Hull C	W	1-0	1-0	15	Cisse [45]	42,855
34	25	A	WBA	L	0-3	0-1	16		26,256
35	May 3	H	Everton	L	0-2	0-0	16		41,313
36	9	A	Bolton W	D	0-0	0-0	16		24,005
37	18	A	Portsmouth	L	1-3	0-0	—	Jones [59]	20,398
38	24	H	Chelsea	L	2-3	0-0	16	Richardson [53], Jones [90]	42,468

Final League Position: 16

GOALSCORERS

League (34): Cisse 10 (1 pen), Jones 10, Richardson 4, Chopra 2, Leadbitter 2, Collins 1, Healy 1, Malbranque 1, Reid 1, own goals 2.
Carling Cup (5): Stokes 2, Bardsley 1, Healy 1, Jones 1.
FA Cup (3): Cisse 1, Healy 1, Jones 1.

Gordon C 12	Chimbonda P 13	Bardsley P 27+1	Tainio T 18+3	Nosworthy N 16	Collins D 35	Malbranque S 34+2	Reid A 20+12	Murphy D 6+17	Diouf E 11+3	Richardson K 31+1	Edwards C 6+16	Whitehead D 30+4	Chopra M 1+5	Higginbotham D 1	Miller L 1+2	Cisse D 29+6	Leadbitter G 12+11	Healy D —+10	Stokes A —+2	McCartney G 16	Ferdinand A 31	Yorke D 4+3	Fulop M 26	Jones K 25+4	Waghorn M 1	Henderson J —+1	McShane P —+3	Ben Haim T 5	Davenport C 7+1	Match No.
1	2	3	4^2	5	6	7^1	8	9	10^3	11	12	13	14																	1
1	2			5	3	7	8^1	9	10	11^2			4			6	12	13												2
1	2	3		5	6	7	8	13	10^1	11						9^3	4^2	12	14											3
1	2		4	5		7^1	12	10	11	8						9				3	6									4
1	2		4^3	5		7	12	13	10^1	11		8	14			9^2				3	6									5
1	2				6	7	13	12	10^1	11^3		4			8^2	9	14			3	5									6
1	2				6	7^3	8	12	11	10		14				9^1	13			3	5	4^2								7
1	2				6	7	12	13	11			4	10^3			9^2	8^1	14		3	5									8
	2		12		6	7^1	13		10^2	11		8				9				3	5	4^3	1	14						9
	2				6	7^1	12		10	11		8	13			9^2				3	5	4^3	1	14						10
	2		4	5		7^3	12			11	8	13								3	6		1	10^2	9^1	14				11
	2			5	3	7^2	8^1	9^3	14	11	4	10	13					12			6		1							12
	2		4^1	5	3	7^2	12			11		8				9^3	13				6	14	1	10						13
	2			5	3	7^3	8^1		12	13	11	14	4			9					6		1	10^2						14
1	3	2	12	5	6	7^1	8^2			11^3		4	13			9						14		10						15
	2	3	12		6	7	8		10	13		11^2				9^3					5	4^1	1	14						16
	2		4	5	3	7^2	8^1			11		13				9	12				6		1	10						17
	2		4^3	5	3	7	8^1			11^2	13	12				9	14				6		1	10						18
	2		4^1	5	3	7	8			11^3	13	12				9^2	14				6		1	10						19
		3	4^1	5	6	7^3	8			11		14			2	9^2	13	12					1	10						20
	2			5	3	7^3	12		8^1	11^2		14	4			9	13				6		1	10						21
	2		12	4	5^3		3^1			11^2		13				9					6		1	10		14				22
	2		4^1	5		7	8^2			13		11				9	12			3^3	6		1	10		14				23
	2			5		7^1	8^2	12		11		4	14			9^3	13			3	6		1	10						24
	2				6	7^2	8^1	12		11		13	4			9^3	14			3	5		1	10						25
			4^3		6	7	8^1	12		11		13	10				14			3	5		1	9^2			2			26
					6	7^3	8	12		11		14	4			13	10^2			3	5		1	9^1			2			27
	2				6	7	8^3	12		11^2		14	4			9^1	13			3			1	10				5		28
	2				6	7^3	11^1	12				14	4			9	8	13		3			1	10				5^2		29
	2			5		11	12	9^3	7			4	13			8				3^4	6		1	10^2			14			30
1	2				3	7^2			10^1	11	13	4	9				8				6		12						5	31
1	2		4^3		3	11	2^1	13	7	9	8										6	14	10	12					5^1	32
1	2		4		3	13	11^1	14	12	7^2	9^3	8									6			10					5	33
	2		4^3		3	13	8^1	11	7^2	12	9					14					6		1	10					5	34
	2				3	7^2	11	13	4	9^1	8					12					6		1	10					5	35
	2		4^2		3	7	13	11	8	12	10										6		1	9^1					5	36
	2		4^2		3	7^1	14	11	12	8	13	10^3									6		1	9					5	37
	2		4^1		3	7^2	12	14	11^3	8	10	13									6		1	9					5	38

FA Cup

Third Round	Bolton W	(h)	2-1
Fourth Round	Blackburn R	(h)	0-0
		(a)	1-2

Carling Cup

Second Round	Nottingham F	(a)	2-1
Third Round	Northampton T	(h)	2-2
Fourth Round	Blackburn R	(h)	1-2

SWANSEA CITY FL Championship

FOUNDATION

The earliest Association Football in Wales was played in the Northern part of the country and no international took place in the South until 1894, when a local paper still thought it necessary to publish an outline of the rules and an illustration of the pitch markings. There had been an earlier Swansea club, but this has no connection with Swansea Town (now City) formed at a public meeting in June 1912.

Liberty Stadium, Morfa, Swansea SA1 2FA.
Telephone: (01792) 616 600.
Fax: (01792) 616 606.
Ticket Office: (0870) 040 0004.
Website: www.swanseacity.net
Email: info@swanseacityfc.co.uk
Ground Capacity: 20,520.
Record Attendance: 32,796 v Arsenal, FA Cup 4th rd, 17 February 1968 (at Vetch Field).
Pitch Measurements: 115yd × 74yd.
Chairman: Huw Jenkins.
Vice-chairman: Leigh Dineen.
General Manager: Alun Cowie.
Secretary: Jackie Rockey.
Manager: Paulo Sousa.
Assistant Manager: Graeme Jones.
Physio: Richard Evans B.Sc.
Colours: All white.
Change Colours: Royal blue shirts with navy sleeves, navy shorts, navy stockings.
Year Formed: 1912. *Turned Professional:* 1912.
Ltd Co.: 1912.
Previous Name: 1912, Swansea Town; 1970, Swansea City.
Club Nicknames: 'The Swans', 'The Jacks'.
Grounds: 1912, Vetch Field; 2005, Liberty Stadium.
First Football League Game: 28 August 1920, Division 3, v Portsmouth (a) L 0–3 – Crumley; Robson, Evans; Smith, Holdsworth, Williams; Hole, I. Jones, Edmundson, Rigsby, Spottiswood.
Record League Victory: 8–0 v Hartlepool U, Division 4, 1 April 1978 – Barber; Evans, Bartley, Lally (1) (Morris), May, Bruton, Kevin Moore, Robbie James (3 incl. 1p), Curtis (3), Toshack (1), Chappell.
Record Cup Victory: 12–0 v Sliema W (Malta), ECWC 1st rd 1st leg, 15 September 1982 – Davies; Marustik, Hadziabdic (1), Irwin (1), Kennedy, Rajkovic (1), Loveridge (2) (Leighton James), Robbie James, Charles (2), Stevenson (1), Latchford (1) (Walsh (3)).

HONOURS

Football League: Division 1 best season: 6th, 1981–82; FL 1 – Champions 2007–08; Division 3 (S) – Champions 1924–25, 1948–49; Division 3 – Champions 1999–2000.
FA Cup: Semi-finals 1926, 1964.
Football League Cup: best season: 4th rd, 1965, 1977, 2009.
Welsh Cup: Winners 11 times; Runners-up 8 times.
Autoglass Trophy: Winners 1994, 2006.
Football League Trophy: Winners 2006.
European Competitions: European Cup-Winners' Cup: 1961–62, 1966–67, 1981–82, 1982–83, 1983–84, 1989–90, 1991–92.

SKY SPORTS FACT FILE

In 2005–06 Swansea City players achieved home and away hat-tricks against the same opposition. Lee Trundle scored three on 29 October in the home fixture against Chesterfield, while Leon Knight repeated the feat at Saltergate on 6 May.

Record Defeat: 0–8 v Liverpool, FA Cup 3rd rd, 9 January 1990. 0–8 v Monaco, ECWC, 1st rd 2nd leg, 1 October 1991.

Most League Points (2 for a win): 62, Division 3 (S), 1948–49.

Most League Points (3 for a win): 92, FL 1, 2007–08.

Most League Goals: 90, Division 2, 1956–57.

Highest League Scorer in Season: Cyril Pearce, 35, Division 2, 1931–32.

Most League Goals in Total Aggregate: Ivor Allchurch, 166, 1949–58, 1965–68.

Most League Goals in One Match: 5, Jack Fowler v Charlton Ath, Division 3S, 27 December 1924.

Most Capped Player: Ivor Allchurch, 42 (68), Wales.

Most League Appearances: Wilfred Milne, 585, 1919–37.

Youngest League Player: Nigel Dalling, 15 years 289 days v Southport, 6 December 1974.

Record Transfer Fee Received: £1,000,000 from Bristol C for Lee Trundle, July 2007.

Record Transfer Fee Paid: £400,000 to Stockport Co for Ashley Williams, May 2008.

Football League Record: 1920 Original Member of Division 3; 1921–25 Division 3 (S); 1925–47 Division 2; 1947–49 Division 3 (S); 1949–65 Division 2; 1965–67 Division 3; 1967–70 Division 4; 1970–73 Division 3; 1973–78 Division 4; 1978–79 Division 3; 1979–81 Division 2; 1981–83 Division 1; 1983–84 Division 2; 1984–86 Division 3; 1986–88 Division 4; 1988–92 Division 3; 1992–96 Division 2; 1996–2000 Division 3;-2000–01 Division 2; 2001–04 Division 3; 2004–05 FL 2; 2005–08 FL 1; 2008– FL C.

LATEST SEQUENCES

Longest Sequence of League Wins: 9, 27.11.1999 – 22.01.2000.

Longest Sequence of League Defeats: 9, 26.1.1991 – 19.3.1991.

Longest Sequence of League Draws: 8, 25.11.2008 – 28.12.2008.

Longest Sequence of Unbeaten League Matches: 19, 19.10.1970 – 9.3.1971.

Longest Sequence Without a League Win: 15, 25.3.1989 – 2.9.1989.

Successive Scoring Runs: 27 from 28.8.1947.

Successive Non-scoring Runs: 6 from 6.2.1996.

MANAGERS

Walter Whittaker 1912–14
William Bartlett 1914–15
Joe Bradshaw 1919–26
Jimmy Thomson 1927–31
Neil Harris 1934–39
Haydn Green 1939–47
Bill McCandless 1947–55
Ron Burgess 1955–58
Trevor Morris 1958–65
Glyn Davies 1965–66
Billy Lucas 1967–69
Roy Bentley 1969–72
Harry Gregg 1972–75
Harry Griffiths 1975–77
John Toshack 1978–83
(resigned October re-appointed in December) 1983–84
Colin Appleton 1984
John Bond 1984–85
Tommy Hutchison 1985–86
Terry Yorath 1986–89
Ian Evans 1989–90
Terry Yorath 1990–91
Frank Burrows 1991–95
Bobby Smith 1995
Kevin Cullis 1996
Jan Molby 1996–97
Micky Adams 1997
Alan Cork 1997–98
John Hollins 1998–2001
Colin Addison 2001–02
Nick Cusack 2002
Brian Flynn 2002–04
Kenny Jackett 2004–07
Roberto Martinez 2007–09
Paulo Sousa June 2009–

TEN YEAR LEAGUE RECORD

		P	W	D	L	F	A	Pts	Pos
1999-2000	Div 3	46	24	13	9	51	30	85	1
2000-01	Div 2	46	8	13	25	47	73	37	23
2001-02	Div 3	46	13	12	21	53	77	51	20
2002-03	Div 3	46	12	13	21	48	65	49	21
2003-04	Div 3	46	15	14	17	58	61	59	10
2004-05	FL 2	46	24	8	14	62	43	80	3
2005-06	FL 1	46	18	17	11	78	55	71	6
2006-07	FL 1	46	20	12	14	69	53	72	7
2007-08	FL 1	46	27	11	8	82	42	92	1
2008-09	FL C	46	16	20	10	63	50	68	8

DID YOU KNOW ?

Signed from Birmingham in 1922, Yorkshire born Harry Deacon scored four times for Swansea Town against Blackpool on 27 August 1928. However, he was unable to secure both points for his team as the match ended in a 5–5 draw.

SWANSEA CITY 2008–09 LEAGUE RECORD

Match No.	Date	Venue	Opponents	Result	H/T Score	Lg. Pos.	Goalscorers	Attendance
1	Aug 9	A	Charlton Ath	L	0-2	0-1	—		21,675
2	16	H	Nottingham F	W	3-1	1-1	14	Smith (og)[9], Bodde[71], Pintado[86]	16,811
3	23	A	Plymouth Arg	W	1-0	1-0	7	Scotland[44]	9203
4	30	H	Sheffield W	D	1-1	1-0	7	Bodde[36]	16,702
5	Sept13	A	Crystal Palace	L	0-2	0-1	10		14,621
6	16	H	Derby Co	D	1-1	0-0	—	Williams[76]	14,003
7	20	H	Burnley	D	1-1	0-0	12	Bodde[90]	13,299
8	27	A	Reading	L	0-4	0-3	18		20,093
9	30	A	Preston NE	W	2-0	1-0	—	Bodde[19], Gomez (pen)[80]	10,558
10	Oct 4	H	Wolverhampton W	W	3-1	2-1	8	Gomez[1], Scotland 2[41,57]	17,556
11	18	A	Ipswich T	D	2-2	0-1	11	Bodde[49], Gomez[69]	20,026
12	21	H	QPR	D	0-0	0-0	—		13,475
13	25	H	Southampton	W	3-0	1-0	7	Pratley[12], Gomez[58], Butler[72]	15,564
14	28	A	Wolverhampton W	L	1-2	0-1	—	Pratley[49]	21,988
15	Nov 1	A	Doncaster R	D	0-0	0-0	10		9534
16	9	H	Watford	W	3-1	1-1	9	Bodde[34], Scotland[59], Bauza[90]	13,891
17	15	A	Norwich C	W	3-2	1-1	7	Scotland[43], Pratley[47], Bodde[48]	24,262
18	21	H	Birmingham C	L	2-3	2-1	—	Gomez[2], Jaidi (og)[45]	16,956
19	25	A	Coventry C	D	1-1	0-0	—	Gomez[67]	15,149
20	30	H	Cardiff C	D	2-2	1-1	8	Pratley[19], Pintado[61]	18,053
21	Dec 6	A	Bristol C	D	0-0	0-0	10		16,405
22	9	H	Barnsley	D	2-2	0-0	—	Scotland 2[66,90]	11,442
23	13	H	Sheffield U	D	1-1	0-0	11	Scotland (pen)[56]	14,744
24	20	A	Blackpool	D	1-1	0-0	10	Scotland[67]	7007
25	26	H	Coventry C	D	0-0	0-0	10		17,603
26	28	A	Birmingham C	D	0-0	0-0	11		21,836
27	Jan 10	A	Burnley	W	2-0	1-0	—	Scotland 2 (1 pen)[35(p),86]	13,740
28	17	H	Reading	W	2-0	1-0	9	Scotland[45], Orlandi[89]	15,197
29	27	H	Preston NE	W	4-1	2-0	—	Gomez[2], Scotland[29], Bauza[69], Tate[87]	14,774
30	31	A	Southampton	D	2-2	1-1	9	Gomez[33], Pintado[65]	17,823
31	Feb 7	H	Ipswich T	W	3-0	1-0	7	Scotland 2[3,73], Gomez[85]	14,020
32	17	A	Watford	L	0-2	0-2	—		13,727
33	21	H	Doncaster R	W	3-1	1-1	9	Scotland (pen)[28], Gomez 2[71,90]	16,161
34	28	H	Charlton Ath	D	1-1	1-0	8	Dyer[42]	15,053
35	Mar 3	A	Derby Co	D	2-2	0-1	—	Rangel[55], Pintado[87]	26,691
36	7	A	Nottingham F	D	1-1	0-0	8	Scotland[61]	20,475
37	10	A	Plymouth Arg	W	1-0	0-0	—	Scotland (pen)[78]	13,103
38	14	H	Crystal Palace	L	1-3	0-0	9	Pintado[66]	13,663
39	17	A	QPR	L	0-1	0-1	—		12,288
40	21	A	Sheffield W	D	0-0	0-0	8		22,564
41	Apr 5	A	Cardiff C	D	2-2	1-1	8	Dyer[11], Allen[88]	20,156
42	11	H	Norwich C	W	2-1	1-1	7	Scotland 2 (1 pen)[29,50(p)]	15,783
43	13	A	Barnsley	W	3-1	2-0	7	Williams[2], Gomez[36], Scotland[67]	11,788
44	18	H	Bristol C	W	1-0	1-0	7	Monk[25]	15,327
45	25	A	Sheffield U	L	0-1	0-1	8		28,010
46	May 3	H	Blackpool	L	0-1	0-1	8		16,316

Final League Position: 8

GOALSCORERS

League (63): Scotland 21 (5 pens), Gomez 12 (1 pen), Bodde 7, Pintado 5, Pratley 4, Bauza 2, Dyer 2, Williams 2, Allen 1, Butler 1, Monk 1, Orlandi 1, Rangel 1, Tate 1, own goals 2.
Carling Cup (5): Gomes 2 (1 pen), MacDonald 2, Pintado 1.
FA Cup (6): Scotland 3 (1 pen), Bauza 1, Dyer 1, Pintado 1.

De Vries D 40	Collins M 2 + 1	Painter M 11	Britton L 42 + 1	Monk G 40	Williams A 46	Gower M 32 + 4	Bodde F 17	Butler T 20 + 9	Bauza G 4 + 11	Pratley D 33 + 4	Brandy F — + 14	Gomez J 38 + 6	Scotland J 39 + 6	Rangel A 39 + 1	Pintado G 9 + 31	Bessone F 13 + 2	Orlandi A 6 + 5	Macdonald S 2 + 3	Tudur Jones O 4 + 5	Krysiak A 2	Tate A 21 + 4	Konstantopoulos D 4	Allen J 17 + 6	O'Halloran S 2	Dyer N 13 + 4	Serran A 10 + 3	Match No.
1	2	3	4	5	6	7^2	8	9	10^1	11^3	12	14	13														1
1	2^1	3	4	5	6	7	8	9^2		11		13	10^3	12	14												2
1		3	4	5	6	7	8	9		11^1	12	10^2		2	13												3
1		3	4	5	6	7	8	9^2		11	13	12	10^3	2	14												4
1		3^3	4	5	6	7^1	8	9		11	13	10^2		2	12	14											5
1		3	4	5	6	7^1	8	9		11^2	14	12	10^3	2	13												6
1			4	5	6	12	8			11^2		13	14	2	9	3	7^3	10^1									7
1			4	5	6	12	8	9^1			13	7	10^2	2	11	3											8
1		3	4^1	5	6	7	8	9^3	12		13	11		2	10^2				14								9
1		3	4	5	6	7^1		12	8		9	10^2		2	13	11^3			14								10
1		3	4	5	6	7^1	8	12		11^3		9	13	2	10^2				14								11
1^6		3	4	5	6	7	8	12		11		9^1	10	2							15						12
		3^3	4^2	5	6		8	9		11	13	7	10^1	2	12					1	14						13
			4^2	5	6	7^1	8	12		11		9	10	2	13	3				1							14
			4^1	5	6	7	8		12	11		9	10^2	2	13	3							1				15
			4	5	6	7^2	8		12	11^1	14	9	10^3	2	13	3							1				16
			4	5	6	7^2	8			11	12	9	10^1	2	13	3							1				17
			4^1	5	6	7	8^2		13	11	14	9	12	2	10^3	3							1				18
1				5	6	7^1		12	13	11		8	10^2	2	9	3		4									19
1			4^4	5	6	7		9^2		11		10	2	12	13	3^1		13	8								20
1				5	6	7^1		8^3		11		9	10	2	12	3^2		4			13		14				21
1			4^1	5	6	7^2		9			12	11	10	2	13				8^3				14	3			22
1			4	5	6			9		11	12	7	10^2	2	13						14		8^1	3^3			23
1			4	5	6			9^1		11	12	7	10	2	13						3		8^2				24
1			4	5	6	12		9^1		11		7	10	2	13						3		8^2				25
1			4	5	6	9^1		12		11	14	7	13	2	10^3						3		8^2				26
1			4	5	6	7				11		9^1	10	2	12						3		8^2		13		27
1				5	6	7^2				11		8	10	2	12		13				3		4		9^1		28
1			4^3	5	6	7				12	11^1	8	10^2	2	13				14		3				9		29
1			4	5	6	7^2		12				9	10	2	13	11					3		8^1				30
1			4	5	2	7^1		12	13			9	10		14						3		8^3		11^2	6	31
1			4	5	6			11	12			7^1	10			13	14				3^2		8		9^3	2	32
1			4		6	7			12			9	10	2					13		3		8^1		11^2	5	33
1			4	5^3	6	7^2		13	8^1	12		11	10	2							3				9	14	34
1			4^1		6			11		12		9^3	10	2	13		14				3		8		7^2	5	35
1			4		6	7^3			11^2	12		9	10^1	2	13						3		8		14	5	36
1			4		6			7		11		8	10^2	2	12						3		13		9^1	5	37
1	13		4		6	7^1			11			8	10	2	12		14				3^2				9^3	5	38
1			12	5	6			7	10	11		8^3	13	2	9^2								4^1		14	3	39
1			4	5	6	7				11^1		9	10	2	12	3							8				40
1			4	5	6	7^1			11			8	10	2^6	14						3		12		9^3	13	41
1			4	5	6				11	10		13	2	7^1	12						3		8		9^2		42
1			4	5	6	7^3			13	11		8	10^2	9^1							3		12		14	2	43
1			4	5	6				12			7	10	2^3		11^2	13				3		8^1		9	14	44
1			4	5	6			14		11		7	10	2	13	12					3^3		8^2		9^1		45
1			4^1		5	14		11				9	10	13	6^3	7	8^2				3		12		2		46

FA Cup

Third Round	Histon	(a)	2-1
Fourth Round	Portsmouth	(a)	2-0
Fifth Round	Fulham	(h)	1-1
		(a)	1-2

Carling Cup

First Round	Brentford	(h)	2-0
Second Round	Hull C	(h)	2-1
Third Round	Cardiff C	(h)	1-0
Fourth Round	Watford	(h)	0-1

SWINDON TOWN   FL Championship 1

FOUNDATION

It is generally accepted that Swindon Town came into being in 1881, although there is no firm evidence that the club's founder, Rev. William Pitt, captain of the Spartans (an offshoot of a cricket club) changed his club's name to Swindon Town before 1883, when the Spartans amalgamated with St Mark's Young Men's Friendly Society.

The County Ground, County Road, Swindon, Wiltshire SN1 2ED.

Telephone: 0871 423 6433.

Fax: (0844) 880 1112.

Ticket Office: 0871 223 2300.

Website: www.swindontownfc.co.uk

Email: enquiries@swindontownfc.co.uk

Ground Capacity: 14,225.

Record Attendance: 32,000 v Arsenal, FA Cup 3rd rd, 15 January 1972.

Pitch Measurements: 110yd × 70yd.

Chairman: Andrew Fitton.

Chief Executive: Nicholas Watkins.

Secretary: Louise Fletcher.

Manager: Danny Wilson.

Assistant Manager: Peter Shirtliff.

Physio: Dick Mackey.

Colours: All red with white inserts on shirt.

Change Colours: Blue shirts with white trim, white shorts, blue stockings.

Year Formed: 1881* (*see Foundation*).

Turned Professional: 1894.

Ltd Co.: 1894.

Club Nickname: 'Robins'.

Grounds: 1881, The Croft; 1896, County Ground.

First Football League Game: 28 August 1920, Division 3, v Luton T (h) W 9–1 – Nash; Kay, Macconachie; Langford, Hawley, Wareing; Jefferson (1), Fleming (4), Rogers, Batty (2), Davies (1), (1 og).

Record League Victory: 9–1 v Luton T, Division 3 (S), 28 August 1920 – Nash; Kay, Macconachie; Langford, Hawley, Wareing; Jefferson (1), Fleming (4), Rogers, Batty (2), Davies (1), (1 og).

HONOURS

Football League: Best season 1992–93. Division 2 – Champions 1995–96; Division 3 – Runners-up 1962–63, 1968–69; Division 4 – Champions 1985–86 (with record 102 points).

FA Cup: Semi-finals 1910, 1912.

Football League Cup: Winners 1969.

Anglo-Italian Cup: Winners 1970.

SKY SPORTS FACT FILE

In successive FA Cup seasons, Swindon Town accounted for north London's big two clubs. In 1909–10 they beat Tottenham Hotspur 1–0 with a Harold Fleming goal and the following term toppled Arsenal when Bob Jefferson again scored the solitary effort.

Record Cup Victory: 10–1 v Farnham U Breweries (away), FA Cup 1st rd (replay), 28 November 1925 – Nash; Dickenson, Weston, Archer, Bew, Adey; Denyer (2), Wall (1), Richardson (4), Johnson (3), Davies.

Record Defeat: 1–10 v Manchester C, FA Cup 4th rd (replay), 25 January 1930.

Most League Points (2 for a win): 64, Division 3, 1968–69.

Most League Points (3 for a win): 102, Division 4, 1985–86.

Most League Goals: 100, Division 3 (S), 1926–27.

Highest League Scorer in Season: Harry Morris, 47, Division 3 (S), 1926–27.

Most League Goals in Total Aggregate: Harry Morris, 216, 1926–33.

Most League Goals in One Match: 5, Harry Morris v QPR, Division 3 (S), 18 December 1926; 5, Harry Morris v Norwich C, Division 3 (S), 26 April 1930; 5, Keith East v Mansfield T, Division 3, 20 November 1965.

Most Capped Player: Rod Thomas, 30 (50), Wales.

Most League Appearances: John Trollope, 770, 1960–80.

Youngest League Player: Paul Rideout, 16 years 107 days v Hull C, 29 November 1980.

Record Transfer Fee Received: £1,500,000 from Manchester C for Kevin Horlock, January 1997.

Record Transfer Fee Paid: £800,000 to West Ham U for Joey Beauchamp, August 1994.

Football League Record: 1920 Original Member of Division 3; 1921–58 Division 3 (S); 1958–63 Division 3; 1963–65 Division 2; 1965–69 Division 3; 1969–74 Division 2; 1974–82 Division 3; 1982–86 Division 4; 1986–87 Division 3; 1987–92 Division 2; 1992–93 Division 1; 1993–94 FA Premier League; 1994–95 Division 1; 1995–96 Division 2; 1996–2000 Division 1; 2000–04 Division 2; 2004–06 FL 1; 2006–07 FL 2; 2007– FL 1.

MANAGERS

Sam Allen 1902–33
Ted Vizard 1933–39
Neil Harris 1939–41
Louis Page 1945–53
Maurice Lindley 1953–55
Bert Head 1956–65
Danny Williams 1965–69
Fred Ford 1969–71
Dave Mackay 1971–72
Les Allen 1972–74
Danny Williams 1974–78
Bobby Smith 1978–80
John Trollope 1980–83
Ken Beamish 1983–84
Lou Macari 1984–89
Ossie Ardiles 1989–91
Glenn Hoddle 1991–93
John Gorman 1993–94
Steve McMahon 1994–99
Jimmy Quinn 1999–2000
Colin Todd 2000
Andy King 2000–01
Roy Evans 2001
Andy King 2002–06
Iffy Onuora 2006
Dennis Wise 2006
Paul Sturrock 2006–07
Maurice Malpas 2008
Danny Wilson December 2008–

LATEST SEQUENCES

Longest Sequence of League Wins: 8, 12.1.1986 – 15.3.1986.

Longest Sequence of League Defeats: 8, 29.8.2005 – 8.10.2005.

Longest Sequence of League Draws: 6, 22.11.1991 – 28.12.1991.

Longest Sequence of Unbeaten League Matches: 22, 12.1.1986 – 23.8.86.

Longest Sequence Without a League Win: 19, 30.10.1999 – 4.3.2000.

Successive Scoring Runs: 31 from 17.4.1926.

Successive Non-scoring Runs: 5 from 16.11.1963.

TEN YEAR LEAGUE RECORD

		P	W	D	L	F	A	Pts	Pos
1999-2000	Div 1	46	8	12	26	38	77	36	24
2000-01	Div 2	46	13	13	20	47	65	52	20
2001-02	Div 2	46	15	14	17	46	56	59	13
2002-03	Div 2	46	16	12	18	59	63	60	10
2003-04	Div 2	46	20	13	13	76	58	73	5
2004-05	FL 1	46	17	12	17	66	68	63	12
2005-06	FL 1	46	11	15	20	46	65	48	23
2006-07	FL 2	46	25	10	11	58	38	85	3
2007-08	FL 1	46	16	13	17	63	56	61	13
2008-09	FL 1	46	12	17	17	68	71	53	15

DID YOU KNOW ?

In addition to fielding the Football League's youngest pair of full-backs – 18-year-olds John Trollope and Terry Wollen – against Peterborough United on 18 November 1961, the Swindon Town goalkeeper that day was Michael O'Hara, aged 17.

SWINDON TOWN 2008–09 LEAGUE RECORD

Match No.	Date	Venue	Opponents	Result	H/T Score	Lg. Pos.	Goalscorers	Attendance
1	Aug 9	H	Tranmere R	W	3-1	2-0	—	Paynter [5], Cox [37], McGovern [51]	7975
2	16	A	Cheltenham T	L	0-2	0-0	12		4975
3	23	H	Colchester U	L	1-3	0-2	19	Cox (pen) [67]	7031
4	30	A	Milton Keynes D	W	2-1	0-0	10	Paynter [52], Cox (pen) [90]	8846
5	Sept 5	A	Hereford U	D	1-1	1-0	—	Ifil [45]	4061
6	13	H	Leeds U	L	1-3	1-1	15	Cox [45]	13,001
7	20	A	Stockport Co	D	1-1	0-1	16	Easton [49]	5536
8	28	H	Millwall	L	1-2	0-1	17	Smith J [47]	7589
9	Oct 3	A	Hartlepool U	D	3-3	2-0	—	Cox 3 [5, 39, 52]	4018
10	11	H	Huddersfield T	L	1-3	0-2	19	Easton [88]	7071
11	18	A	Southend U	L	1-2	0-1	20	Paynter [60]	7965
12	21	H	Northampton T	W	2-1	0-0	—	Paynter [48], Cox [61]	6653
13	25	H	Oldham Ath	W	2-0	2-0	15	Morrison [25], Smith J (pen) [34]	6756
14	Nov 1	A	Scunthorpe U	D	3-3	1-1	17	Cox 3 (1 pen) [15, 52, 80 (p)]	4744
15	15	H	Leicester C	D	2-2	0-0	17	Cox [84], Corr [85]	9499
16	22	A	Bristol R	D	2-2	1-1	18	Kanyuka [39], Corr [53]	8016
17	25	H	Peterborough U	D	2-2	1-1	—	Smith J [10], Cox [81]	6616
18	29	A	Walsall	L	1-2	0-1	—	Paynter [90]	3844
19	Dec 6	H	Carlisle U	D	1-1	0-0	19	Murphy (og) [50]	6787
20	13	A	Crewe Alex	L	0-1	0-1	19		3941
21	20	H	Yeovil T	L	2-3	1-2	20	Timlin [45], McGovern [47]	7072
22	26	A	Leyton Orient	W	2-1	1-0	18	Peacock [1], Smith J (pen) [61]	4349
23	28	H	Brighton & HA	L	0-2	0-1	20		8438
24	Jan 13	A	Stockport Co	D	1-1	0-0	—	Smith J [62]	6002
25	17	A	Huddersfield T	L	1-2	0-0	18	Cox [90]	13,414
26	27	H	Walsall	W	3-2	2-0	—	Amankwaah [6], Cox [29], Paynter [49]	6100
27	31	A	Oldham Ath	D	0-0	0-0	19		4712
28	Feb 14	A	Leicester C	D	1-1	1-0	20	Cox [38]	19,926
29	17	A	Millwall	D	1-1	1-0	—	Paynter [43]	7104
30	21	H	Scunthorpe U	W	4-2	0-2	19	Timlin [62], Wright (og) [71], Robson-Kanu [82], Peacock [85]	6852
31	24	H	Hartlepool U	L	0-1	0-0	—		6010
32	28	A	Tranmere R	L	0-1	0-0	20		5153
33	Mar 3	H	Cheltenham T	D	2-2	1-1	—	Robson-Kanu [32], Amankwaah [66]	6293
34	7	H	Milton Keynes D	D	1-1	1-1	21	Paynter [18]	7453
35	10	A	Colchester U	L	2-3	1-2	—	Cox (pen) [38], Robson-Kanu [64]	3827
36	14	A	Leeds U	L	0-1	0-0	21		21,765
37	17	H	Southend U	W	3-0	2-0	—	Robson-Kanu [13], Cox 2 (2 pens) [19, 90]	6269
38	21	A	Hereford U	W	3-0	1-0	20	Cox 2 [29, 46], Paynter [76]	7129
39	24	A	Northampton T	W	4-3	3-1	—	Cox 3 [18, 31, 79], Paynter [40]	5025
40	28	A	Yeovil T	L	0-1	0-1	16		5476
41	Apr 4	H	Crewe Alex	D	0-0	0-0	18		7165
42	11	A	Brighton & HA	W	3-2	0-1	17	Greer [47], Paynter [50], Cox [58]	6549
43	13	H	Leyton Orient	L	0-1	0-1	17		7735
44	18	A	Carlisle U	D	1-1	0-1	17	Tudur Jones [90]	5959
45	25	H	Bristol R	W	2-1	1-1	16	Cox 2 [4, 81]	10,977
46	May 2	A	Peterborough U	D	2-2	2-1	15	Cox 2 [17, 42]	10,886

Final League Position: 15

GOALSCORERS

League (68): Cox 29 (6 pens), Paynter 11, Smith J 5 (2 pens), Robson-Kanu 4, Amankwaah 2, Corr 2, Easton 2, McGovern 2, Peacock 2, Timlin 2, Greer 1, Ifil 1, Kanyuka 1, Morrison 1, Tudur Jones 1, own goals 2.
Carling Cup (2): Cox 1, Paynter 1.
FA Cup (0).
J Paint Trophy (4): Cox 2, Ifil 1, Peacock 1.

Brezovan P 21	Smith J 34+4	Casal K 4+1	Nalis L 18+6	Ifil J 28+2	Aljofree H 17+1	McGovern J 22+4	Timlin M 38+3	Paynter B 42	Cox S 45	McNamee A 30+13	Peacock L 17+10	Easton C 14+9	Morrison S 18+2	Marshall M —+12	Kanyuka P 16	Smith P 25	Amankwaah K 26+5	Corr B 2+9	Pook M 11+3	Joyce B 1	Kennedy C 3+1	Sturrock B 2+8	Vincent J 18	Allen C 2+2	Greer G 19	Robson-Kanu H 20	Razak H —+3	Lescinel J 2+3	Tudur Jones O 11	Macklin L —+2	Match No.
1	2	3	4	5	6	7²	8	9¹	10	11	12	13																			1
1	2	3	4		6	7	8¹	9²	10	11		13			5	12															2
1	2		4³	5	6	7¹	8²	9	10	11		13	14		12	3															3
	2	3¹	4	5	6		8	9³	10	11²	14	7			13	1	12														4
	3		4	5	6		8	9²	10	11¹		13	7		12	1	2														5
	2		8	5	6	7²	12	9	10	11	4¹				13	1	3														6
	3	4		6	7	8¹	9³	10²	12	13	11	5			13	1	2	14													7
	3			8²	6	7¹		9	10	11	12	4	5		13	1	2														8
	3¹	12	7	5		8	9	10		11	4	6			1	2															9
1	3		4¹	5		8	9²	10	12	11	7	6			2	13															10
1	2	3¹		6	7	8	9²	10	12	11		5							13		4										11
1	2			6	7	3	9	10	11²	8¹	12	5							13		4										12
1	2			6	7	3	9¹	10	11	8		5							12		4										13
	2			6	7	3	9	10	11²	8	12	5			1				13		4¹										14
	2	4				3	9	10	11¹	8		5			6	1			12		7										15
	2	4		12	13	3	9		11¹			5			6	1			10		8	7²									16
	2	12		6	7	3	9¹	10	11	8		5			1				4												17
	2	12		6	7	3¹	9	10	13	8	4²	5			1				11												18
	2			5	6	7²		9	10	11	8				1	12			4			3¹	13								19
	2			5	6	7¹	12	9³	10	11³	8²	13			1				4			3	14								20
	2			5	6¹	7	8	9	10	11²	4	12			1				13			3³	14								21
1	2	8		5		7	3	9	10			4			6							12	11¹								22
1	2	8²		5		7	3	9	10	13		4			6							12	11¹								23
1	2			5		7	3²	9¹	10	11³	8	4			6	13						14	12								24
1	2			5		7¹	3	9³	10	12	8	13			6	11						4²	14								25
1		8		5		7²	12	9³	10	13			14		2										3¹	4	6	11			26
1				5		7		9³	10	13	12	4¹			2										3	8	6	11²	14		27
1	2			5			8	9	10			4				7									3	6		11			28
1	2			5			8	9²	10	12		4				7									3	6³	13	11¹	14		29
1	2			5			8	9³	10	13	12	14				4									3¹	6		11	7²		30
1	2			5			8	9²	10	12	13	4³				7¹									3	6	14	11			31
1	2	14		5			8	9²	10	12	13	4³				7¹									3	6		11			32
1	2			5			8²	9	10	11		4				12									3¹	6	13	7			33
1		4	12				8	9	10	11²						5¹									2	3	6	7	13		34
1							8	9	10	11						5	12								2	3	6	7¹	13	4²	35
		12					8	9	10	11¹						5				1					2	3	6	7		4	36
		12					8	9²	10	11						5	14			1					2	13	3	6	7³	4¹	37
12		13					8	9	10	11³						5	14			1					2	3¹	6	7		4²	38
	3	12					8	9	10	11²						5	13			1					2		6	7¹		4	39
	3	4²	12				8	9	10	11						5¹				1					2	13	14	6	7³		40
12				5			8	9	10	11										1					2	3¹	6	7²13		4	41
				5			8	9	10	11		12								1					2	3	6	7¹	4²13		42
				5		14	8	9	10	11¹										1					2³	3²	6	7	13 4	12	43
3¹				5			8	9	10	11	13									1					2²		6	7	12 4		44
14				5			8¹	9	10	11³							12			1					2	3	6	7²		4	45
				5	6	7¹	8²	9	10³	11		13	14				12			1					2				4		46

FA Cup
First Round   Histon   (a)   0-1

Carling Cup
First Round   QPR   (h)   2-3

J Paint Trophy
First Round   Aldershot T   (a)   2-2
Second Round   Hereford U   (a)   2-1
Southern Quarter-Final   Brighton & HA   (a)   0-1

TORQUAY UNITED   FL Championship 2

FOUNDATION

The idea of establishing a Torquay club was agreed by old boys of Torquay College and Torbay College, while sitting in Princess Gardens listening to the band. A proper meeting was subsequently held at Tor Abbey Hotel at which officers were elected. This was on 1 May 1899 and the club's first competition was the Eastern League (later known as the East Devon League). As an amateur club it played at Teignmouth Road, Torquay Recreation Ground and Cricket Field Road before settling down for four years at Torquay Cricket Ground where the rugby club now plays. They became Torquay United in 1921 after merging with Babbacombe FC.

Plainmoor Ground, Torquay, Devon TQ1 3PS.
Telephone: (01803) 328 666.
Fax: (01803) 323 976.
Ticket Office: (01803) 328 666.
Website: www.torquayunited.com
Email: reception@torquayunited.com
Ground Capacity: 6,117.
Record Attendance: 21,908 v Huddersfield T, FA Cup 4th rd, 29 January 1955.
Pitch Measurements: 110yd × 74yd.
Chairman: Alex Rowe.
Vice-chairman: Simon Baker.
Chief Executive: Colin Lee.
Secretary: Ann Sandford.
Manager: Paul Buckle.
First Team Coach: Shaun North.
Physio: Damien Davey.
Colours: All yellow with blue insert.
Change Colours: All white with blue design.
Year Formed: 1899.
Turned Professional: 1921.
Ltd Co.: 1921.
Previous Name: 1910, Torquay Town; 1921, Torquay United.
Club Nickname: 'The Gulls'.
Grounds: 1899, Teignmouth Road; 1900, Torquay Recreation Ground; 1904, Cricket Field Road; 1906, Torquay Cricket Ground; 1910, Plainmoor Ground.
First Football League Game: 27 August 1927, Division 3 (S), v Exeter C (h) D 1–1 – Millsom; Cook, Smith; Wellock, Wragg, Connor, Mackey, Turner (1), Jones, McGovern, Thomson.

HONOURS

Football League: Division 3 (S) – Runners-up 1956–57.
FA Cup: best season: 4th rd, 1949, 1955, 1971, 1983, 1990, 2009.
Football League Cup: never past 3rd rd.
Sherpa Van Trophy: Runners-up 1989.

SKY SPORTS FACT FILE

Promotion from the Blue Square Premier in 2009 gave Torquay United manager Paul Buckle something of a unique hat trick. He was previously in charge of Exeter City and a former Aldershot Town player, both of which teams had joined the Football League a year earlier.

Record League Victory: 9–0 v Swindon T, Division 3 (S), 8 March 1952 – George Webber; Topping, Ralph Calland; Brown, Eric Webber, Towers; Shaw (1), Marchant (1), Northcott (2), Collins (3), Edds (2).

Record Cup Victory: 7–1 v Northampton T, FA Cup 1st rd, 14 November 1959 – Gill; Penford, Downs; Bettany, George Northcott, Rawson; Baxter, Cox, Tommy Northcott (1), Bond (3), Pym (3).

Record Defeat: 2–10 v Fulham, Division 3 (S), 7 September 1931. 2–10 v Luton T, Division 3 (S), 2 September 1933.

Most League Points (2 for a win): 60, Division 4, 1959–60.

Most League Points (3 for a win): 81, Division 3, 2003–04.

Most League Goals: 89, Division 3 (S), 1956–57.

Highest League Scorer in Season: Sammy Collins, 40, Division 3 (S), 1955–56.

Most League Goals in Total Aggregate: Sammy Collins, 204, 1948–58.

Most League Goals in One Match: 5, Robin Stubbs v Newport Co, Division 4, 19 October 1963.

Most Capped Player: Rodney Jack, (71), St Vincent.

Most League Appearances: Dennis Lewis, 443, 1947–59.

Youngest League Player: David Byng, 16 years 36 days v Walsall, 14 August 1993.

Record Transfer Fee Received: £400,000 from Crystal Palace for Matthew Greg, October 1998.

Record Transfer Fee Paid: £500,000 to Crewe Alex for Rodney Jack, August 1998.

Football League Record: 1927 Elected to Division 3 (S); 1958–60 Division 4; 1960–62 Division 3; 1962–66 Division 4; 1966–72 Division 3; 1972–91 Division 4; 1991–2004 Division 3; 2004–05 FL 1; 2005–07 FL 2; 2007–09 Blue Square Pr; 2009– FL 2.

LATEST SEQUENCES

Longest Sequence of League Wins: 8, 24.1.1998 – 3.3.1998.

Longest Sequence of League Defeats: 8, 30.9.1995 – 18.11.1995.

Longest Sequence of League Draws: 8, 25.10.1969 – 13.12.1969.

Longest Sequence of Unbeaten League Matches: 15, 5.5.1990 – 3.11.1990.

Longest Sequence Without a League Win: 19, 23.9.2006 – 20.1.2007.

Successive Scoring Runs: 19 from 3.10.1953.

Successive Non-scoring Runs: 7 from 8.1.1972.

MANAGERS

Percy Mackrill 1927–29
A. H. Hoskins 1929
 (Secretary-Manager)
Frank Womack 1929–32
Frank Brown 1932–38
Alf Steward 1938–40
Billy Butler 1945–46
Jack Butler 1946–47
John McNeil 1947–50
Bob John 1950
Alex Massie 1950–51
Eric Webber 1951–65
Frank O'Farrell 1965–68
Alan Brown 1969–71
Jack Edwards 1971–73
Malcolm Musgrove 1973–76
Mike Green 1977–81
Frank O'Farrell 1981–82
 (continued as General Manager to 1983)
Bruce Rioch 1982–84
Dave Webb 1984–85
John Sims 1985
Stuart Morgan 1985–87
Cyril Knowles 1987–89
Dave Smith 1989–91
John Impey 1991–92
Ivan Golac 1992
Paul Compton 1992–93
Don O'Riordan 1993–95
Eddie May 1995–96
Kevin Hodges *(Head Coach)* 1996–98
Wes Saunders 1998–2001
Roy McFarland 2001–02
Leroy Rosenior 2002–06
Ian Atkins 2006
Lubos Kubik 2006–07
Keith Curle 2007
Leroy Rosenior 2007
Paul Buckle June 2007–

TEN YEAR LEAGUE RECORD

		P	W	D	L	F	A	Pts	Pos
1999-2000	Div 3	46	19	12	15	62	52	69	9
2000-01	Div 3	46	12	13	21	52	77	49	21
2001-02	Div 3	46	12	15	19	46	63	51	19
2002-03	Div 3	46	16	18	12	71	71	66	9
2003-04	Div 3	46	23	12	11	68	44	81	3
2004-05	FL 1	46	12	15	19	55	79	51	21
2005-06	FL 2	46	13	13	20	53	66	52	20
2006-07	FL 2	46	7	14	25	36	63	35	24
2007-08	Conf	46	26	8	12	83	57	86	3
2008-09	Conf	46	23	14	9	72	47	83	4

DID YOU KNOW ?

Though holding neither most League appearance or goals records for Torquay United, Tommy Northcott made 443 League and Cup appearances and scored 150 goals in all such competitions in two spells at the club between 1948 to 1952 and 1957 to 1965.

TOTTENHAM HOTSPUR   FA Premiership

FOUNDATION

The Hotspur Football Club was formed from an older cricket club in 1882. Most of the founders were old boys of St John's Presbyterian School and Tottenham Grammar School. The Casey brothers were well to the fore as the family provided the club's first goalposts (painted blue and white) and their first ball. They soon adopted the local YMCA as their meeting place, but after a couple of moves settled at the Red House, which is still their headquarters, although now known simply as 748 High Road.

White Hart Lane, Bill Nicholson Way, 748 High Road, Tottenham, London N17 0AP.

Telephone: (0844) 499 5000.

Fax: (020) 8365 5005.

Ticket Office: 0844 844 0102.

Website: www.spursfc.com

Email: email@spursfc.com

Ground Capacity: 36,534.

Record Attendance: 75,038 v Sunderland, FA Cup 6th rd. 5 March 1938.

Pitch Measurements: 100m × 67m.

Executive Chairman: Daniel Levy.

Secretary: John Alexander.

Manager: Harry Redknapp.

Assistant Manager: Kevin Bond.

Head of Medical Services: Wayne Diesel.

Colours: White shirts with black inserts and trim on sleeves, black shorts, white stockings with two black hoops.

Change Colours: All light blue.

Year Formed: 1882.

Turned Professional: 1895.

Ltd Co.: 1898.

Previous Name: 1882, Hotspur Football Club; 1884, Tottenham Hotspur.

Club Nickname: 'Spurs'.

Grounds: 1882, Tottenham Marshes; 1888, Northumberland Park; 1899, White Hart Lane.

First Football League Game: 1 September 1908, Division 2, v Wolverhampton W (h) W 3–0 – Hewitson; Coquet, Burton; Morris (1), D. Steel, Darnell; Walton, Woodward (2), Macfarlane, R. Steel, Middlemiss.

HONOURS

Football League: Division 1 – Champions 1950–51, 1960–61; Runners-up 1921–22, 1951–52, 1956–57, 1962–63; Division 2 – Champions 1919–20, 1949–50; Runners-up 1908–09, 1932–33.

FA Cup: Winners 1901 (as non-League club), 1921, 1961, 1962, 1967, 1981, 1982, 1991; Runners-up 1987.

Football League Cup: Winners 1971, 1973, 1999, 2008; Runners-up 1982, 2002, 2009.

European Competitions: *European Cup:* 1961–62. *European Cup-Winners' Cup:* 1962–63 (winners), 1963–64, 1967–68, 1981–82, 1982–83, 1991–92. *UEFA Cup:* 1971–72 (winners), 1972–73, 1973–74 (runners-up), 1983–84 (winners), 1984–85, 1999–2000, 2006–07, 2007–08, 2008–09. *Intertoto Cup:* 1995.

SKY SPORTS FACT FILE

Welshman Willie Evans played in an England amateur international trial match before his birthplace was realised. He signed for Tottenham Hotspur and became a marksman winger achieving the unusual feat of converting 11 penalties in 1932–33.

Record League Victory: 9–0 v Bristol R, Division 2, 22 October 1977 – Daines; Naylor, Holmes, Hoddle (1), McAllister, Perryman, Pratt, McNab, Moores (3), Lee (4), Taylor (1).

Record Cup Victory: 13–2 v Crewe Alex, FA Cup 4th rd (replay), 3 February 1960 – Brown; Hills, Henry; Blanchflower, Norman, Mackay; White, Harmer (1), Smith (4), Allen (5), Jones (3 incl. 1p).

Record Defeat: 0–8 v Cologne, UEFA Intertoto Cup, 22 July 1995.

Most League Points (2 for a win): 70, Division 2, 1919–20.

Most League Points (3 for a win): 77, Division 1, 1984–85.

Most League Goals: 115, Division 1, 1960–61.

Highest League Scorer in Season: Jimmy Greaves, 37, Division 1, 1962–63.

Most League Goals in Total Aggregate: Jimmy Greaves, 220, 1961–70.

Most League Goals in One Match: 5, Ted Harper v Reading, Division 2, 30 August 1930; 5, Alf Stokes v Birmingham C, Division 1, 18 September 1957; 5, Bobby Smith v Aston Villa, Division 1, 29 March 1958.

Most Capped Player: Pat Jennings, 74 (119), Northern Ireland.

Most League Appearances: Steve Perryman, 655, 1969–86.

Youngest League Player: Ally Dick, 16 years 301 days v Manchester C, 20 February 1982.

Record Transfer Fee Received: £19,000,000 from Liverpool for Robbie Keane, July 2008.

Record Transfer Fee Paid: £17,000,000 to Blackburn R for David Bentley, July 2008.

Football League Record: 1908 Elected to Division 2; 1909–15 Division 1; 1919–20 Division 2; 1920–28 Division 1; 1928–33 Division 2; 1933–35 Division 1; 1935–50 Division 2; 1950–77 Division 1; 1977–78 Division 2; 1978–92 Division 1; 1992– FA Premier League.

MANAGERS

Frank Brettell 1898–99
John Cameron 1899–1906
Fred Kirkham 1907–08
Peter McWilliam 1912–27
Billy Minter 1927–29
Percy Smith 1930–35
Jack Tresadern 1935–38
Peter McWilliam 1938–42
Arthur Turner 1942–46
Joe Hulme 1946–49
Arthur Rowe 1949–55
Jimmy Anderson 1955–58
Bill Nicholson 1958–74
Terry Neill 1974–76
Keith Burkinshaw 1976–84
Peter Shreeves 1984–86
David Pleat 1986–87
Terry Venables 1987–91
Peter Shreeves 1991–92
Doug Livermore 1992–93
Ossie Ardiles 1993–94
Gerry Francis 1994–97
Christian Gross *(Head Coach)* 1997–98
George Graham 1998–2001
Glenn Hoddle 2001–03
David Pleat *(Caretaker)* 2003–04
Jacques Santini 2004
Martin Jol 2004–07
Juande Ramos 2007–08
Harry Redknapp October 2008–

LATEST SEQUENCES

Longest Sequence of League Wins: 13, 23.4.1960 – 1.10.1960.

Longest Sequence of League Defeats: 7, 1.1.1994 – 27.2.1994.

Longest Sequence of League Draws: 6, 9.1.1999 – 27.2.1999.

Longest Sequence of Unbeaten League Matches: 22, 31.8.1949 – 31.12.1949.

Longest Sequence Without a League Win: 16, 29.12.1934 – 13.4.1935.

Successive Scoring Runs: 32 from 24.2.1962.

Successive Non-scoring Runs: 6 from 28.12.1985.

TEN YEAR LEAGUE RECORD

		P	W	D	L	F	A	Pts	Pos
1999-2000	PR Lge	38	15	8	15	57	49	53	10
2000-01	PR Lge	38	13	10	15	47	54	49	12
2001-02	PR Lge	38	14	8	16	49	53	50	9
2002-03	PR Lge	38	14	8	16	51	62	50	10
2003-04	PR Lge	38	13	6	19	47	57	45	14
2004-05	PR Lge	38	14	10	14	47	41	52	9
2005-06	PR Lge	38	18	11	9	53	38	65	5
2006-07	PR Lge	38	17	9	12	57	54	60	5
2007-08	PR Lge	38	11	13	14	66	61	46	11
2008-09	PR Lge	38	14	9	15	45	45	51	8

DID YOU KNOW ?

In a fifth round FA Cup replay at White Hart Lane on 22 February 1937, Everton were leading Tottenham Hotspur 3–1 with four minutes left. Arthur Rowe tripped Dixie Dean in the area but a linesman had flagged for an earlier throw-in. Spurs scored to win 4–3!

TOTTENHAM HOTSPUR 2008–09 LEAGUE RECORD

Match No.	Date	Venue	Opponents	Result	H/T Score	Lg. Pos.	Goalscorers	Attendance
1	Aug 16	A	Middlesbrough	L 1-2	0-0	—	Huth (og) [90]	32,623
2	23	H	Sunderland	L 1-2	0-0	17	Jenas [73]	36,064
3	31	A	Chelsea	D 1-1	1-1	19	Bent [45]	41,790
4	Sept 15	H	Aston Villa	L 1-2	0-1	—	Bent [87]	36,075
5	21	H	Wigan Ath	D 0-0	0-0	20		35,808
6	28	A	Portsmouth	L 0-2	0-1	20		20,352
7	Oct 5	A	Hull C	L 0-1	0-1	20		36,062
8	19	A	Stoke C	L 1-2	1-1	20	Bent [25]	27,500
9	26	H	Bolton W	W 2-0	1-0	20	Pavlyuchenko [17], Bent (pen) [76]	35,507
10	29	A	Arsenal	D 4-4	1-1	—	Bentley [13], Bent [67], Jenas [89], Lennon [90]	60,043
11	Nov 1	H	Liverpool	W 2-1	0-1	19	Carragher (og) [70], Pavlyuchenko [90]	36,183
12	9	A	Manchester C	W 2-1	1-1	16	Bent 2 [29, 64]	41,893
13	15	A	Fulham	L 1-2	0-1	19	Campbell [81]	25,139
14	23	H	Blackburn R	W 1-0	1-0	15	Pavlyuchenko [9]	35,903
15	30	H	Everton	L 0-1	0-0	16		35,742
16	Dec 8	A	West Ham U	W 2-0	0-0	—	King [68], O'Hara [90]	34,277
17	13	H	Manchester U	D 0-0	0-0	15		35,882
18	21	A	Newcastle U	L 1-2	1-1	16	Modric [29]	47,982
19	26	H	Fulham	D 0-0	0-0	16		35,866
20	28	A	WBA	L 0-2	0-0	16		26,344
21	Jan 11	A	Wigan Ath	L 0-1	0-0	18		17,500
22	18	H	Portsmouth	D 1-1	0-0	16	Defoe [70]	36,011
23	27	H	Stoke C	W 3-1	3-0	—	Lennon [8], Defoe [21], Dawson [25]	36,072
24	31	A	Bolton W	L 2-3	0-1	14	Bent 2 [73, 75]	21,575
25	Feb 8	H	Arsenal	D 0-0	0-0	15		36,021
26	23	A	Hull C	W 2-1	1-1	—	Lennon [17], Woodgate [86]	24,742
27	Mar 4	H	Middlesbrough	W 4-0	3-0	—	Keane [9], Pavlyuchenko [14], Lennon 2 [40, 79]	35,761
28	7	A	Sunderland	D 1-1	0-1	—	Keane [89]	37,894
29	15	A	Aston Villa	W 2-1	1-0	11	Jenas [5], Bent [50]	41,205
30	21	H	Chelsea	W 1-0	0-0	11	Modric [50]	36,034
31	Apr 4	A	Blackburn R	L 1-2	1-0	11	Keane (pen) [30]	21,891
32	11	H	West Ham U	W 1-0	0-0	9	Pavlyuchenko [65]	35,969
33	19	H	Newcastle U	W 1-0	1-0	9	Bent [24]	35,850
34	25	A	Manchester U	L 2-5	2-0	10	Bent [29], Modric [32]	75,458
35	May 2	H	WBA	W 1-0	1-0	10	Jenas [43]	35,836
36	9	A	Everton	D 0-0	0-0	8		36,646
37	16	H	Manchester C	W 2-1	1-0	8	Defoe [29], Keane (pen) [86]	36,000
38	24	A	Liverpool	L 1-3	0-1	8	Keane [77]	43,937

Final League Position: 8

GOALSCORERS

League (45): Bent 12 (1 pen), Keane 5 (2 pens), Lennon 5, Pavlyuchenko 5, Jenas 4, Defoe 3, Modric 3, Bentley 1, Campbell 1, Dawson 1, King 1, O'Hara 1, Woodgate 1, own goals 2.
Carling Cup (14): Pavlyuchenko 6 (1 pen), Campbell 2, O'Hara 2, Bent 1, Dawson 1, Defoe 1, own goal 1.
FA Cup (4): Pavlyuchenko 3 (1 pen), Modric 1.
UEFA Cup (11): Bent 4, Huddlestone 2, Bentley 1, Giovani 1, Modric 1, O'Hara 1, own goal 1.

Gomes H 34	Zokora D 24+5	Assou-Ekotto B 29	Woodgate J 34	Modric L 34	Dawson M 13+3	Lennon A 26+9	Jenas J 28+4	Giovani 2+4	Bent D 21+12	Bentley D 20+5	O'Hara J 6+9	Bale G 12+4	Berbatov D —+1	King L 24	Huddlestone T 14+8	Gunter C 2+1	Corluka V 33+1	Pavlyuchenko R 19+9	Campbell F 1+9	Gilberto 1	Hutton A 5+3	Boateng K —+1	Defoe J 6+2	Cudicini C 4	Chimbonda P 1+2	Palacios W 11	Taarabt A —+1	Keane R 14	Match No.
1	2	3¹	4	5	6	7²	8	9³	10	11	12	13	14																1
1	2	3¹	4	5		7²	8	13	10	9		11		6	12														2
1	2		4	5		13	8	9²	10	7³	14	11		6	12	3¹													3
1	4¹	11²		5	6³	7	13	14	10		12		3		8		2	9											4
1	2	3		5		12	8		10	7¹	4	11²	13	6				9³	14										5
1	4²	3		5	6	12	8	13	14	7		11					2	9³	10¹										6
1	4	11		5		7³	8	14	12	13		3		6			2²	9¹	10										7
1	4	11		5	12■	7	8		10			9²	3■	6¹	13		2												8
1		3	11		12	8	13	7	10¹					6	4		5	9²	2										9
1		3	10	5		12	8	13	7		11¹			4	14		6	9²	2³										10
1	4	3³	10¹	5		12		9	7	11²				6	8		2	13	14										11
1	4	3■	10¹	5		12	11		9	7				6	8		2												12
1	4		10²	5		12	8	9³	7			3		6	11¹		2	13	14										13
1		3		5		7	8		10	11¹	12			6	4		2	9²	13										14
1	4	3¹		5		7			10²	11		12		6	8³		2	9	13		14								15
1	4	3	10	5		7	8		12	11²	13			6			2	9¹											16
1	4	3	10	5³	6	7	8²		12	11	13				14		2	9¹											17
1	4	3	10		5	7				11				6	8		2	9¹	12										18
1	4	3	10	5		7	12	9²	11³					6	8¹		2	13	14										19
1	4³	3■		5	6	7	8	9	11²	13	12						2		14										20
1	4	8²	5	6¹	13	12		14		7		11		3			2	9³					10						21
1	4	8	5	12	7		13	14	11	3³				6¹			2	9²					10						22
	4	3	8	5	6	7¹			11						12		2	9²	13		10	1							23
	4¹	3	10²	5	6	7	12		13	11					2³			9			1		14	8					24
		3	11	5	6	7³	8		12						2²			9¹			1		13	4	14	10			25
	12	3	11	5²	13	7¹	8		10³					6			2	14			1		4			9			26
1	2	3	11³	5	6	7	8²		12		14				13			9¹					4			10			27
1			11	5		7	8²		9	12				6	13		2³	14					3	4¹		10			28
1	2¹	3	11²	5		7	8		9	13				6			12							4		10			29
1	12	3	11²	5		7¹	8		9	13				6			2							4		10			30
1	12	3	11	5		7¹	8		9					6			2							4■		10			31
1	12	3	11	5		7	8¹	9²						6	4		2	13								10			32
1		3	11	5	6¹	7		9²							8		2				12		13	4		10			33
1		3	11¹	5		7	8		9		12			6	13		2							4		10²			34
1		3	11	5		7	8							6			2	9¹					12	4		10			35
1		11¹	5			8					3			6	4		2	12		7	9					10			36
1	13	3	11	5¹		8²								6	4		2	9³	14	12	10		7						37
1	4	3	7			8¹				14	12	11³		6			5	13			2		10²			9			38

FA Cup

Third Round	Wigan Ath	(h)	3-1
Fourth Round	Manchester U	(a)	1-2

Carling Cup

Third Round	Newcastle U	(a)	2-1
Fourth Round	Liverpool	(h)	4-2
Quarter-Final	Watford	(a)	2-1
Semi-Final	Burnley	(h)	4-1
		(a)	2-3
Final	Manchester U		0-0
(at Wembley)			

UEFA Cup

First Round	Wisla	(h)	2-1
		(a)	1-1
Group D	Udinese	(a)	0-2
	Dinamo Zagreb	(h)	4-0
	NEC Nijmegen	(a)	1-0
	Spartak Moscow	(h)	2-2
Third Round	Shakhter Donetsk	(a)	0-2
		(h)	1-1

TRANMERE ROVERS   FL Championship 1

FOUNDATION

Formed in 1884 as Belmont they adopted their present title the following year and eventually joined their first league, the West Lancashire League in 1889–90, the same year as their first success in the Wirral Challenge Cup. The club almost folded in 1899–1900 when all the players left en bloc to join a rival club, but they survived the crisis and went from strength to strength winning the 'Combination' title in 1907–08 and the Lancashire Combination in 1913–14. They joined the Football League in 1921 from the Central League.

Prenton Park, Prenton Road West, Birkenhead, Merseyside CH42 9PY.

Telephone: (0871) 221 2001.

Fax: (0151) 608 6144.

Ticket Office: (0871) 221 2001.

Website: www.tranmererovers.co.uk

Email: info@tranmererovers.co.uk

Ground Capacity: 16,587.

Record Attendance: 24,424 v Stoke C, FA Cup 4th rd, 5 February 1972.

Pitch Measurements: 100yd × 70yd.

Chairperson: Lorraine Rogers.

Chief Executive/Secretary: Mick Horton.

Manager: John Barnes.

Assistant Manager: Peter Shirtliff.

Physio: Les Parry.

Colours: All white with one sky blue sleeve and one dark blue cuff on reverse.

Change Colours: All navy blue with sky blue collar.

Year Formed: 1884.

Turned Professional: 1912.

Ltd Co.: 1920.

Previous Name: 1884, Belmont AFC; 1885, Tranmere Rovers.

Club Nickname: 'The Rovers'.

Grounds: 1884, Steeles Field; 1887, Ravenshaws Field/Old Prenton Park; 1912, Prenton Park.

First Football League Game: 27 August 1921, Division 3 (N), v Crewe Alex (h) W 4–1 – Bradshaw; Grainger, Stuart (1); Campbell, Milnes (1), Heslop; Moreton, Groves (1), Hyam, Ford (1), Hughes.

Record League Victory: 13–4 v Oldham Ath, Division 3 (N), 26 December 1935 – Gray; Platt, Fairhurst; McLaren, Newton, Spencer; Eden, MacDonald (1), Bell (9), Woodward (2), Urmson (1).

HONOURS

Football League Division 1 best season: 4th, 1992–93; Division 3 (N) – Champions 1937–38; Division 4 – Runners-up 1988–89.

FA Cup: best season: 6th rd, 2000, 2001, 2004.

Football League Cup: Runners-up, 2000.

Welsh Cup: Winners 1935; Runners-up 1934.

Leyland Daf Cup: Winners 1990; Runners-up 1991.

SKY SPORTS FACT FILE

In 1930–31 Tranmere Rovers produced three players who had each scored more than 20 League goals in the season. Jack Kennedy hit 34, Ernie Dixon 31 and the unusually named Farewell Watts 27. This came from a total of 111 in Division 3 (North).

Record Cup Victory: 13–0 v Oswestry U, FA Cup 2nd prel rd, 10 October 1914 – Ashcroft; Stevenson, Bullough, Hancock, Taylor, Holden (1), Moreton (1), Cunningham (2), Smith (5), Leck (3), Gould (1).

Record Defeat: 1–9 v Tottenham H, FA Cup 3rd rd (replay), 14 January 1953.

Most League Points (2 for a win): 60, Division 4, 1964–65.

Most League Points (3 for a win): 80, Division 4, 1988–89; Division 3, 1989–90; Division 2, 2002–03.

Most League Goals: 111, Division 3 (N), 1930–31.

Highest League Scorer in Season: Bunny Bell, 35, Division 3 (N), 1933–34.

Most League Goals in Total Aggregate: Ian Muir, 142, 1985–95.

Most League Goals in One Match: 9, Bunny Bell v Oldham Ath, Division 3 (N), 26 December 1935.

Most Capped Player: John Aldridge, 30 (69), Republic of Ireland.

Most League Appearances: Harold Bell, 595, 1946–64 (incl. League record 401 consecutive appearances).

Youngest League Player: Iain Hume, 16 years 167 days v Swindon T, 15 April 2000.

Record Transfer Fee Received: £2,500,000 from WBA for Jason Koumas, August 2002.

Record Transfer Fee Paid: £450,000 to Aston Villa for Shaun Teale, August 1995.

Football League Record: 1921 Original Member of Division 3 (N): 1938–39 Division 2; 1946–58 Division 3 (N); 1958–61 Division 3; 1961–67 Division 4; 1967–75 Division 3; 1975–76 Division 4; 1976–79 Division 3; 1979–89 Division 4; 1989–91 Division 3; 1991–92 Division 2; 1992–2001 Division 1; 2001–04 Division 2; 2004– FL 1.

MANAGERS

Bert Cooke 1912–35
Jackie Carr 1935–36
Jim Knowles 1936–39
Bill Ridding 1939–45
Ernie Blackburn 1946–55
Noel Kelly 1955–57
Peter Farrell 1957–60
Walter Galbraith 1961
Dave Russell 1961–69
Jackie Wright 1969–72
Ron Yeats 1972–75
John King 1975–80
Bryan Hamilton 1980–85
Frank Worthington 1985–87
Ronnie Moore 1987
John King 1987–96
John Aldridge 1996–2001
Dave Watson 2001–02
Ray Mathias 2002–03
Brian Little 2003–06
Ronnie Moore 2006–09
John Barnes June 2009–

LATEST SEQUENCES

Longest Sequence of League Wins: 9, 9.2.1990 – 19.3.1990.

Longest Sequence of League Defeats: 8, 29.10.1938 – 17.12.1938.

Longest Sequence of League Draws: 5, 26.12.1997 – 31.1.1998.

Longest Sequence of Unbeaten League Matches: 18, 16.3.1970 – 4.9.1970.

Longest Sequence Without a League Win: 16, 8.11.1969 – 14.3.1970.

Successive Scoring Runs: 32 from 24.2.1934.

Successive Non-scoring Runs: 7 from 20.12.1997.

TEN YEAR LEAGUE RECORD

		P	W	D	L	F	A	Pts	Pos
1999-2000	Div 1	46	15	12	19	57	68	57	13
2000-01	Div 1	46	9	11	26	46	77	38	24
2001-02	Div 2	46	16	15	15	63	60	63	12
2002-03	Div 2	46	23	11	12	66	57	80	7
2003-04	Div 2	46	17	16	13	59	56	67	8
2004-05	FL 1	46	22	13	11	73	55	79	3
2005-06	FL 1	46	13	15	18	50	52	54	18
2006-07	FL 1	46	18	13	15	58	53	67	9
2007-08	FL 1	46	18	11	17	52	47	65	11
2008-09	FL 1	46	21	11	14	62	49	74	7

DID YOU KNOW ?

The official opening of Prenton Park's all-seater version on 11 March 1995 included the parading of former favourites including Mark Palios (!), Dave Hickson, George Yardley and Harold Atkinson. Moreover Tranmere Rovers then beat Grimsby Town 2–0.

TRANMERE ROVERS 2008–09 LEAGUE RECORD

Match No.	Date	Venue	Opponents	Result	H/T Score	Lg. Pos.	Goalscorers	Attendance
1	Aug 9	A	Swindon T	L 1-3	0-2	—	Savage [85]	7975
2	16	H	Hartlepool U	W 1-0	1-0	14	Curran [23]	5418
3	23	A	Leicester C	L 1-3	0-1	20	Shuker [80]	17,798
4	30	H	Northampton T	W 4-1	3-1	8	Savage [35], Kay [38], Curran [45], Moore [90]	5034
5	Sept 6	H	Oldham Ath	L 0-1	0-1	13		6802
6	13	A	Huddersfield T	W 2-1	1-1	10	Sonko [39], Shotton [49]	12,128
7	20	A	Peterborough U	D 2-2	2-1	11	Greenacre 2 [7, 30]	5735
8	26	H	Colchester U	L 3-4	1-3	—	Kay [12], Taylo Andyr [76], Shotton [78]	5713
9	Oct 4	A	Carlisle U	W 2-1	1-0	12	Moore [1], Shotton [80]	6093
10	11	H	Millwall	L 1-3	0-2	14	Savage [90]	5863
11	18	H	Leyton Orient	W 1-0	1-0	11	Shuker [39]	5568
12	21	H	Cheltenham T	W 2-0	0-0	—	Savage [69], Sonko [89]	4535
13	24	H	Crewe Alex	W 2-0	0-0	—	Jennings [51], Shuker [74]	5790
14	28	A	Stockport Co	D 0-0	0-0	—		6121
15	Nov 1	A	Milton Keynes D	L 0-1	0-0	11		8185
16	15	H	Southend U	D 2-2	2-2	11	Moore [8], Savage [14]	5019
17	22	A	Yeovil T	L 0-1	0-1	11		3445
18	25	H	Scunthorpe U	W 2-0	1-0	—	Sonko [41], Shotton [75]	4564
19	Dec 6	H	Leeds U	W 2-1	1-1	9	Kay [17], Moore [49]	8700
20	13	A	Bristol R	L 0-2	0-1	9		6217
21	20	H	Brighton & HA	W 1-0	0-0	8	Kay [90]	4885
22	26	A	Hereford U	D 2-2	1-1	8	Sonko 2 [37, 61]	3495
23	28	H	Walsall	W 2-1	1-0	8	Goodison [42], Kay [90]	5913
24	Jan 17	A	Millwall	L 0-1	0-0	10		8257
25	24	H	Carlisle U	W 4-1	0-0	9	Moore 2 [48, 77], Edds [53], Jennings [66]	5924
26	27	H	Stockport Co	W 2-1	0-0	—	Edds [57], Moore (pen) [90]	5259
27	31	A	Crewe Alex	L 1-2	1-0	9	Kay [26]	4936
28	Feb 7	H	Leyton Orient	D 0-0	0-0	—		4892
29	10	A	Colchester U	W 1-0	0-0	—	Shotton [50]	3588
30	14	A	Southend U	L 1-2	0-1	8	Moore (pen) [63]	6507
31	17	H	Peterborough U	D 1-1	1-1	—	Barnett [16]	4862
32	21	H	Milton Keynes D	D 1-1	0-0	9	Gornell [83]	5625
33	28	H	Swindon T	W 1-0	0-0	9	Kay [48]	5153
34	Mar 3	A	Hartlepool U	L 1-2	0-0	—	Chorley [70]	3033
35	7	A	Northampton T	D 1-1	1-0	9	Savage [32]	4546
36	11	H	Leicester C	W 2-0	0-0	—	Kay [47], Jennings (pen) [83]	6032
37	14	H	Huddersfield T	W 3-1	1-1	6	Kay 2 [6, 53], Savage [50]	5515
38	17	A	Cheltenham T	L 0-1	0-1	—		2845
39	21	A	Oldham Ath	W 2-0	0-0	7	Barnett [57], Moore (pen) [75]	7489
40	28	A	Brighton & HA	D 0-0	0-0	7		5819
41	Apr 5	H	Bristol R	W 2-0	1-0	7	Cresswell [37], Moore [64]	8119
42	11	A	Walsall	W 1-0	0-0	6	Savage [80]	4206
43	13	H	Hereford U	W 2-1	2-0	6	Savage [8], Barnett [27]	5945
44	18	A	Leeds U	L 1-3	1-2	6	Sodje (og) [27]	24,360
45	25	H	Yeovil T	D 1-1	0-0	6	Kay [78]	8306
46	May 2	A	Scunthorpe U	D 1-1	1-0	7	Curran [39]	8029

Final League Position: 7

GOALSCORERS

League (62): Kay 11, Moore 10 (3 pens), Savage 9, Shotton 5, Sonko 5, Barnett 3, Curran 3, Jennings 3 (1 pen), Shuker 3, Edds 2, Greenacre 2, Chorley 1, Cresswell 1, Goodison 1, Gornell 1, Taylor Andy 1, own goal 1.
Carling Cup (0).
FA Cup (2): Kay 1, Shuker 1.
J Paint Trophy (4): Moore 1, Shotton 1, Shuker 1, Sonko 1.

Achterberg J 7	Antwi-Birago G 4+1	Taylor Andy 38+1	O'Callaghan G 4+2	Chorley B 45	Kay A 44	Jennings S 44	Barnett C 25+4	Moore I 40+2	Savage B 38+4	Curran C 7+8	Sonko E 29+9	Coyne D 39	Goodison I 33	Edds G 22+12	Shuker C 23+5	Greenacre C 6+7	Shotton R 33	Cresswell A 8+5	Holmes D 1	Wilson M 4+1	Gornell T 4+6	Johnson J 4	Macauley J —+1	Henry P 1	Mayor D 3	Burns R —+2	Taylor Ash —+1	Match No.
1	2	3	4[1]	5	6	7	8	9	10	11	12																	1
	2	3	4[1]	5	8	7		9[2]	12	11	10	1	6	13														2
		3	4[1]	5	8	7			10	11	9[2]	1	6	2	12	13												3
		3		5	6	8		12	10	11[2]	9	1	4	2	7[1]	13												4
		3		5	6	7		12	10	11[2]	9	1		2	8[1]	13	4											5
		3		5	6	7		9	10	12	11	1	4			8[1]	2											6
		3		5	6	7		9	10	12	11	1	4			8[1]	2											7
		3	12	5	6	7[3]		9	10	13	11[1]	1	4		14	8[2]	2											8
		3	4[1]	5	8	7		9	10[2]		11	1	6	12		13	2											9
6		3		5	4	7[1]		9	10			1		12	8	11	2											10
		3	12	5	6	7		9	10	13		1	4	11[1]	8[2]		2											11
		3		5	6	7		9	10	12		1	4	11[1]	8		2											12
		3		5	6	7	12	9	10[2]	14		1	4	11[1]	8[3]	13	2											13
	12	3[4]		5	6	7	13	9[3]	10	14		1	4[1]	11[2]	8		2											14
				5	6	7	8	9	10[2]	12		1		11	4[1]	13	2	3										15
				5	6	7[4]		9	10			1	4	11	8		2	3										16
	2	3		5		7[2]	8		10	12	11	1			9[3]	13		14	4	6								17
		3		5	6	7	12		10		11[1]	1	4	13			2			8	9[2]							18
		3		5	6	7		9	10		11[2]	1	4	12	13	8[1]	2											19
		3		5	6	7		9	10[2]		11[1]	1	4	12	13	8	2											20
		3		5	6	7		9	10			1	4	11[1]		8	2				12							21
		3		5	6	7			10	12	11	1	4			8	2			8	9[1]							22
		3		5	6	7		9	10		11[1]	1	4	12		8	2											23
		3		5	6	7		9	10		11	1	4			8	2											24
		3		5	6[1]	7	8[2]	9	10		11	1	4	12			2						13					25
		3		5	6	7	8[1]	9	10	12	11	1	4				2											26
		3		5	6	7	8	9	10[2]	13	11	1	4[1]	12			2											27
		3		5	6	7	8	9	10	12	11[1]	1	4				2											28
		3		5	6	7	8	9	10		11	1	4				2											29
1		3[1]		5	6	7	8	9	10		11		4				2	12										30
1				5	6	7	8	9	10		11[1]		4	12			2	3										31
1				5	6	7	8[2]	9[3]	10	13			4[1]	12	11		2	3				14						32
1		3		5	6	7	8	9	10[2]				4[8]	12	11[1]		2					13						33
1		3		5	6		8	9	10		11		4				2	12						7[1]				34
1		3		5	6	11	8	9	10				4				2								7			35
		3		5	6	11	8		10			1	4				2					9			7			36
		3		5	6	11	8		10	12		1	4		13		2					9[1]			7[2]			37
		3		5	6	7[1]	8[2]	9	10	13	11	1	4	12			2											38
				5	6	7	8	9	10		11	1	4				2	3										39
				5	6	7	8	9[1]	10	12	11	1	4				2	3										40
				5	6	7	8	9[1]	10	12	11	1	4				2	3										41
	12			5	6	7[3]	8[2]	9	10	13	11	1	4		14		2	3[1]										42
		3		5	6	7[1]	8	9	10		11	1	4[8]	12			2											43
		3		5	6	7	8[1]	9	10[3]	12	11[2]	1	4				2	14								13		44
		3		5	6	7	8[2]	9	10		11[1]	1	4				2	12								13		45
		3		5	6[2]	7	8[1]	9	10		11	1	4				2[4]	12									13	46

FA Cup

First Round	Accrington S	(a)	0-0
		(h)	1-0
Second Round	Peterborough U	(a)	0-0
		(h)	1-2

Carling Cup

First Round	Grimsby T	(a)	0-2

J Paint Trophy

First Round	Accrington S	(h)	1-0
Second Round	Crewe Alex	(h)	1-0
Northern Quarter-Final	Morecambe	(h)	1-0
Northern Semi-Final	Scunthorpe U	(a)	1-2

WALSALL — FL Championship 1

FOUNDATION

Two of the leading clubs around Walsall in the 1880s were Walsall Swifts (formed 1877) and Walsall Town (formed 1879). The Swifts were winners of the Birmingham Senior Cup in 1881, while the Town reached the 4th round (5th round modern equivalent) of the FA Cup in 1883. These clubs amalgamated as Walsall Town Swifts in 1888, becoming simply Walsall in 1895.

Banks's Stadium, Bescot Crescent, Walsall WS1 4SA.

Telephone: 0871 221 0442.

Fax: (01922) 613 202.

Ticket Office: 0871 663 0111 or 0871 663 0222.

Website: www.saddlers.co.uk

Email: info@walsallfc.co.uk

Ground Capacity: 11,300.

Record Attendance: 11,037 v Wolverhampton W, Division 1, 11 January 2003.

Pitch Measurements: 110yd × 73yd.

Chairman: Jeff Bonser.

Secretary: Roy Whalley.

Manager: Chris Hutchings.

Assistant Manager: Martin O'Connor.

Physio: Jon Whitney.

Colours: Red shirts with white cuffs on sleeves, white shorts, red stockings with white tops.

Change Colours: All black.

Year Formed: 1888.

Turned Professional: 1888.

Ltd Co.: 1921.

Previous Names: Walsall Swifts (founded 1877) and Walsall Town (founded 1879) amalgamated in 1888 and were known as Walsall Town Swifts until 1895.

Club Nickname: 'The Saddlers'.

Grounds: 1888, Fellows Park; 1990, Bescot Stadium.

First Football League Game: 3 September 1892, Division 2, v Darwen (h) L 1–2 – Hawkins; Withington, Pinches; Robinson, Whitrick, Forsyth; Marshall, Holmes, Turner, Gray (1), Pangbourn.

Record League Victory: 10–0 v Darwen, Division 2, 4 March 1899 – Tennent; E. Peers (1), Davies; Hickinbotham, Jenkyns, Taggart; Dean (3), Vail (2), Aston (4), Martin, Griffin.

Record Cup Victory: 7–0 v Macclesfield T (a), FA Cup 2nd rd, 6 December 1997 – Walker; Evans, Marsh, Viveash (1), Ryder, Peron, Boli (2 incl. 1p) (Ricketts), Porter (2), Keates, Watson (Platt), Hodge (2 incl. 1p).

Record Defeat: 0–12 v Small Heath, 17 December 1892. 0–12 v Darwen, 26 December 1896, both Division 2.

HONOURS

Football League: Division 2: Runners-up, 1998–99; FL 2 – Champions 2006–07; Division 3 – Runners-up 1960–61, 1994–95; Division 4 – Champions 1959–60; Runners-up 1979–80.

FA Cup: best season: 5th rd, 1939, 1975, 1978, 1987, 2002, 2003 and last 16 1889.

Football League Cup: Semi-final 1984.

SKY SPORTS FACT FILE

Arthur Campey was converted by Walsall from right-back to centre-forward and had an immediate goal scoring reward. In 1914–15 he achieved five hat-tricks including a treble in the FA Cup and five goals in the same competition.

Most League Points (2 for a win): 65, Division 4, 1959–60.

Most League Points (3 for a win): 89, FL 2, 2006–07.

Most League Goals: 102, Division 4, 1959–60.

Highest League Scorer in Season: Gilbert Alsop, 40, Division 3 (N), 1933–34 and 1934–35.

Most League Goals in Total Aggregate: Tony Richards, 184, 1954–63; Colin Taylor, 184, 1958–63, 1964–68, 1969–73.

Most League Goals in One Match: 5, Gilbert Alsop v Carlisle U, Division 3 (N), 2 February 1935; 5, Bill Evans v Mansfield T, Division 3 (N), 5 October 1935; 5, Johnny Devlin v Torquay U, Division 3 (S), 1 September 1949.

Most Capped Player: Mick Kearns, 15 (18), Republic of Ireland.

Most League Appearances: Colin Harrison, 467, 1964–82.

Youngest League Player: Geoff Morris, 16 years 218 days v Scunthorpe U, 14 September 1965.

Record Transfer Fee Received: £750,000 from Coventry C for Scott Dann, January 2008.

Record Transfer Fee Paid: £175,000 to Birmingham C for Alan Buckley, June 1979.

Football League Record: 1892 Elected to Division 2; 1895 Failed re-election; 1896–1901 Division 2; 1901 Failed re-election; 1921 Original Member of Division 3 (N); 1927–31 Division 3 (S); 1931–36 Division 3 (N); 1936–58 Division 3 (S); 1958–60 Division 4; 1960–61 Division 3; 1961–63 Division 2; 1963–79 Division 3; 1979–80 Division 4; 1980–88 Division 3; 1988–89 Division 2; 1989–90 Division 3; 1990–92 Division 4; 1992–95 Division 3; 1995–99 Division 2; 1999–2000 Division 1; 2000–01 Division 2; 2001–04 Division 1; 2004–06 FL 1; 2006–07 FL 2; 2007– FL 1.

LATEST SEQUENCES

Longest Sequence of League Wins: 7, 10.10.1959 – 21.11.1959.

Longest Sequence of League Defeats: 15, 29.10.1988 – 4.2.1989.

Longest Sequence of League Draws: 5, 7.5.1988 – 17.9.1988.

Longest Sequence of Unbeaten League Matches: 21, 6.11.1979 – 22.3.1980.

Longest Sequence Without a League Win: 18, 15.10.1988 – 4.2.1989.

Successive Scoring Runs: 27 from 9.2.1928.

Successive Non-scoring Runs: 5 from 8.10.1927.

MANAGERS

H. Smallwood 1888–91
(Secretary-Manager)
A. G. Burton 1891–93
J. H. Robinson 1893–95
C. H. Ailso 1895–96
(Secretary-Manager)
A. E. Parsloe 1896–97
(Secretary-Manager)
L. Ford 1897–98 *(Secretary-Manager)*
G. Hughes 1898–99
(Secretary-Manager)
L. Ford 1899–1901
(Secretary-Manager)
J. E. Shutt 1908–13
(Secretary-Manager)
Haydn Price 1914–20
Joe Burchell 1920–26
David Ashworth 1926–27
Jack Torrance 1927–28
James Kerr 1928–29
Sid Scholey 1929–30
Peter O'Rourke 1930–32
Bill Slade 1932–34
Andy Wilson 1934–37
Tommy Lowes 1937–44
Harry Hibbs 1944–51
Tony McPhee 1951
Brough Fletcher 1952–53
Major Frank Buckley 1953–55
John Love 1955–57
Billy Moore 1957–64
Alf Wood 1964
Reg Shaw 1964–68
Dick Graham 1968
Ron Lewin 1968–69
Billy Moore 1969–72
John Smith 1972–73
Doug Fraser 1973–77
Dave Mackay 1977–78
Alan Ashman 1978
Frank Sibley 1979
Alan Buckley 1979–86
Neil Martin *(Joint Manager with Buckley)* 1981–82
Tommy Coakley 1986–88
John Barnwell 1989–90
Kenny Hibbitt 1990–94
Chris Nicholl 1994–97
Jan Sorensen 1997–98
Ray Graydon 1998–2002
Colin Lee 2002–04
Paul Merson 2004–06
Kevin Broadhurst 2006
Richard Money 2006–08
Jimmy Mullen 2008
Chris Hutchings January 2009–

TEN YEAR LEAGUE RECORD

		P	W	D	L	F	A	Pts	Pos
1999-2000	Div 1	46	11	13	22	52	77	46	22
2000-01	Div 2	46	23	12	11	79	50	81	4
2001-02	Div 1	46	13	12	21	51	71	51	18
2002-03	Div 1	46	15	9	22	57	69	54	17
2003-04	Div 1	46	13	12	21	45	65	51	22
2004-05	FL 1	46	16	12	18	65	69	60	14
2005-06	FL 1	46	11	14	21	47	70	47	24
2006-07	FL 2	46	25	14	7	66	34	89	1
2007-08	FL 1	46	16	16	14	52	46	64	12
2008-09	FL 1	46	17	10	19	61	66	61	13

DID YOU KNOW ?

On 16 December 1957 the opening of the Fellows Park floodlights attracted a crowd of 6,196 for the friendly visit of Falkirk. A hat-trick from Tom Brownlee and one each from Ken Hodgkisson and Tony Richards saw Walsall eased to a 5–1 win.

WALSALL 2008–09 LEAGUE RECORD

Match No.	Date	Venue	Opponents	Result	H/T Score	Lg. Pos.	Goalscorers	Attendance
1	Aug 9	A	Yeovil T	D 1-1	0-1	—	Ibehre [77]	4518
2	16	H	Scunthorpe U	W 2-1	1-1	5	Reich [12], Ibehre [89]	4162
3	23	A	Crewe Alex	L 1-2	0-2	11	Hughes [59]	4160
4	30	H	Southend U	W 5-2	1-1	5	Reich [23], Grant (og) [48], Demontagnac 3 [50, 69, 84]	3843
5	Sept 6	H	Leyton Orient	L 0-2	0-0	10		4838
6	13	A	Bristol R	W 3-1	2-0	7	Ricketts 2 (1 pen) [10, 90 (p)], Roberts [24]	6609
7	20	A	Brighton & HA	W 1-0	1-0	7	Mattis [44]	5679
8	27	H	Carlisle U	W 2-1	1-0	6	Mattis [45], Ibehre [64]	4830
9	Oct 4	A	Hereford U	D 0-0	0-0	5		3900
10	11	H	Peterborough U	L 1-2	0-2	8	Deeney [90]	4792
11	18	H	Hartlepool U	L 2-3	2-0	9	Ricketts [5], Ibehre [13]	4142
12	21	A	Leicester C	D 2-2	1-1	—	Nicholls [11], Ricketts [47]	17,178
13	25	A	Leeds U	L 0-3	0-0	13		22,422
14	Nov 1	H	Northampton T	W 3-1	2-0	12	Palmer [17], Gerrard [22], Deeney [63]	4377
15	15	A	Colchester U	W 2-0	1-0	10	Mattis [16], Ricketts [62]	4071
16	22	H	Milton Keynes D	L 0-3	0-1	10		5026
17	25	A	Oldham Ath	L 2-3	2-2	—	Ricketts [23], Nicholls [25]	3936
18	29	H	Swindon T	W 2-1	1-0	—	Ricketts [17], Nicholls [89]	3844
19	Dec 6	A	Huddersfield T	L 1-2	0-1	10	Nicholls [49]	11,827
20	13	H	Millwall	L 1-2	1-1	11	Nicholls [28]	3790
21	20	A	Cheltenham T	D 0-0	0-0	13		3656
22	26	H	Stockport Co	W 1-0	0-0	11	Weston [64]	5496
23	28	A	Tranmere R	L 1-2	0-1	12	Reich (pen) [54]	5913
24	Jan 17	A	Peterborough U	L 0-1	0-1	13		5705
25	24	H	Hereford U	D 1-1	1-0	13	Deeney [33]	4438
26	27	A	Swindon T	L 2-3	0-2	—	Ibehre [75], Deeney [77]	6100
27	31	H	Leeds U	W 1-0	1-0	12	Deeney [7]	8920
28	Feb 3	H	Leicester C	L 1-4	0-2	—	Mattis [84]	5634
29	7	A	Hartlepool U	D 2-2	1-1	—	Deeney [10], Williams S [82]	3286
30	10	A	Carlisle U	D 1-1	0-1	—	Ricketts (pen) [84]	4502
31	14	H	Colchester U	W 2-0	2-0	12	Ricketts [17], Deeney [42]	3719
32	21	A	Northampton T	W 2-0	0-0	11	Hughes [83], Ibehre [90]	4528
33	28	H	Yeovil T	W 2-0	1-0	11	Deeney [52], Nicholls [76]	3916
34	Mar 3	A	Scunthorpe U	D 1-1	0-0	—	Deeney [84]	3423
35	7	A	Southend U	L 0-2	0-0	13		6973
36	10	H	Crewe Alex	D 1-1	0-0	—	Deeney [57]	3604
37	14	H	Bristol R	L 0-5	0-3	14		5169
38	17	H	Brighton & HA	W 3-0	3-0	—	Bradley [14], Deeney [30], Gerrard [39]	3549
39	21	A	Leyton Orient	W 1-0	1-0	12	Bradley [45]	3969
40	28	H	Cheltenham T	D 1-1	0-1	11	Townsend (og) [67]	4101
41	Apr 4	A	Millwall	L 1-3	1-2	13	Ibehre [29]	8800
42	11	H	Tranmere R	L 0-1	0-0	14		4206
43	13	A	Stockport Co	W 2-1	1-0	11	Gerrard [11], Logan (og) [90]	5274
44	18	H	Huddersfield T	L 2-3	2-2	13	Ibehre 2 [14, 28]	3951
45	25	A	Milton Keynes D	W 1-0	0-0	11	Ibehre [61]	12,094
46	May 2	H	Oldham Ath	L 1-2	1-1	13	Deeney [2]	4807

Final League Position: 13

GOALSCORERS

League (61): Deeney 12, Ibehre 10, Ricketts 9 (2 pens), Nicholls 6, Mattis 4, Demontagnac 3, Gerrard 3, Reich 3 (1 pen), Bradley 2, Hughes 2, Palmer 1, Roberts 1, Weston 1, Williams S 1, own goals 3.
Carling Cup (1): Ricketts 1.
FA Cup (1): Ricketts 1.
J Paint Trophy (2): Ibehre 1, Ricketts 1.

Ince C 36	Roberts S 15	Sansara N 7 + 3	Taundry R 27 + 11	Gerrard A 42	Palmer C 41 + 3	Nicholls A 38 + 7	Hughes S 32	Ricketts M 25 + 3	Ibehre J 35 + 4	Zaaboub S 24 + 5	Reich M 9 + 10	Boertien P 25 + 6	Demontagnac I 2 + 8	Smith M 22 + 4	Deeney T 37 + 8	Bradley M 16 + 12	Weston R 30 + 1	Mattis D 33 + 4	Gilmartin R 10 + 1	Grigg W — + 1	Adkins S — + 1	Davies R — + 3	Williams S — + 5	Shroot R — + 5	Craddock J — + 2	Match No.
1	2	3	4	5	6	7²	8¹	9³	10	11	12	13	14													1
1			4	5	2	7¹	8		10	11¹²	9	3	12	6	13											2
1			4	5	2	7¹	8		10	11¹²	9	3	13	6	12											3
1		2¹	4	5	6	14	8²		10³		9	3	11	12	7	13										4
1		2¹	4	5	6		8³	13	10		9	3	11	12	7²	14										5
1	2	3	4	5³	14	7		9	10¹		11²		12		13		6	8								6
1	6	3⁴	4	5	12	7²	8		10³		9¹	13			14		2⁸	11								7
1	2		4	5	6	7¹	8	9²	10			3	12		13			11								8
1	2		4	5	6	7¹	8	9²	10			3	12		13			11								9
	2		4	5	6	12	8	9	10¹		11³	3²	13		14		7		1							10
1	2		4⁷	5	6	12		9	10			3	13	11¹	14		7³	8								11
1	2		4¹	5	6	7		9²	10³			14	3	11	12	13		8								12
1	2		4	5	6	7¹		9	10	12	13	3		11²				8								13
1	2		4	5	6	12	8	9²	10		13	3		11¹	14		7³									14
1	6		4	5	3	7	8³	9		13	14	12		10²			2¹	11								15
1⁶			4	5	6	7¹	8²	9		12		3	11	13	2	10	15									16
			4²	5	3	7	8	9		12	13			6	11¹	14	2	10³	1							17
	6²		14	5		7	8	9¹		12	10³	3		13	11	4	2		1							18
	2¹			5	6	7	8³	9	10	14	12			11	4²	3	13		1							19
1		3¹	13	5	6	7	8³	9	10		12			11	4²	2	14									20
1		3	4	5	6	7		9						11	10	2	8¹			12						21
1		12	4	5	6	7		9⁸	10		13			11²	8¹	2	3									22
1		3	4	5	6	7		10			9			11			2	8								23
1		3	4	5	2²	7		10		12				6	11¹	8		9				13				24
1			4	5	2	3		9	11¹	12				6	10	8	7									25
1			4	5	2	3		9	11					6	10	7¹		8				12				26
1		12	4	5	2	7²		9¹	11			3			10		6	8					13			27
1			4¹	5	2	7²		9	11			3			10	12	6	8					13			28
1				5	2	7	4	9²	11			3			10	12	6	8¹					13			29
				5	2	7	8	12	9²	11		3			10¹	6	4		1				13			30
1		13		5	2	7	8	9		11²		3		12	10³	6	4¹						14			31
1		12		5	2	7¹	8	9	13	11		3		6	10²	4³							14			32
1	14	12		5²	2	7	4¹	9	13	11³		3		6	10			8								33
1		13			2	7	4	9¹	12	11²		3		6	10		5	8								34
1					2	7²	6	9⁸	12	11¹		3		5	10		4	8						13		35
1					2	7	6	9		11¹		3		5	10		4	8						12		36
1				5		7²	4¹	9	11			3		6	10	12	2	8					13			37
1		13		5¹	12	7		9²	11³			3		6	10	4	2	8					14			38
1		12			2	7¹		9²	11			3		6	10	4	5	8					13			39
		12		5	3	7²	4	9	11¹					6	10		2	8	1					13		40
			4	5	3	7	8	12	9					6¹	10		2	11	1							41
				5	3	7¹	8	9	10	11²				6	12	4	2		1			13				42
				5	3	12	4	9²	10	11¹				6	7	13	2	8	1							43
		13		5	3	12	8	9¹	10	11				6	7	4³	2⁴	14	1							44
1		13		5	3	12	7³	9²	11					6	10	4¹	2	8				14				45
1			4	5	3	9	7³			11²	12			6	10	14	2¹	8						13		46

FA Cup
First Round — Scunthorpe U — (h) 1-3

Carling Cup
First Round — Darlington — (h) 1-2

J Paint Trophy
Second Round — Cheltenham T — (a) 2-1
Quarter-Final — Luton T — (h) 0-1

WATFORD   FL Championship

FOUNDATION

The club was formed as Watford Rovers in 1881. The name was changed to West Herts in 1893 and then the name Watford was adopted after rival club Watford St Mary's was absorbed in 1898.

Vicarage Road Stadium, Vicarage Road, Watford, Hertsfordshire, WD18 0ER.

Telephone: 0845 442 1881.

Fax: (01923) 496 001.

Ticket Office: 0845 442 1881.

Website: www.watfordfc.com

Email: yourvoice@watfordfc.com

Ground Capacity: 19,920.

Record Attendance: 34,099 v Manchester U, FA Cup 4th rd (replay), 3 February 1969.

Pitch Measurements: 114 yd × 73yd.

Chairman: Graham Simpson.

Chief Executive: Mark Ashton.

Secretary: Michelle Ives.

Manager: Malky Mackay.

Assistant Manager: Sean Dyche.

Physio: Andy Rolls.

Colours: Yellow shirts with red collar, black shorts, yellow stockings.

Change Colours: All red.

Year Formed: 1881.

Turned Professional: 1897.

Ltd Co.: 1909.

Club Nickname: 'The Hornets'.

Previous Names: 1881, Watford Rovers; 1893, West Herts; 1898, Watford.

Grounds: 1883, Vicarage Meadow, Rose and Crown Meadow; 1889, Colney Butts; 1890, Cassio Road; 1922, Vicarage Road.

First Football League Game: 28 August 1920, Division 3, v QPR (a) W 2–1 – Williams; Horseman, F. Gregory; Bacon, Toone, Wilkinson; Bassett, Ronald (1), Hoddinott, White (1), Waterall.

Record League Victory: 8–0 v Sunderland, Division 1, 25 September 1982 – Sherwood; Rice, Rostron, Taylor, Terry, Bolton, Callaghan (2), Blissett (4), Jenkins (2), Jackett, Barnes.

Record Cup Victory: 10–1 v Lowestoft T, FA Cup 1st rd, 27 November 1926 – Yates; Prior, Fletcher (1); F. Smith, 'Bert' Smith, Strain; Stephenson, Warner (3), Edmonds (3), Swan (1), Daniels (1), (1 og).

Record Defeat: 0–10 v Wolverhampton W, FA Cup 1st rd (replay), 24 January 1912.

HONOURS

Football League: Division 1 – Runners-up 1982–83; Division 2 – Champions 1997–98; Runners-up 1981–82; Division 3 – Champions 1968–69; Runners-up 1978–79; Division 4 – Champions 1977–78.

FA Cup: Runners-up 1984, semi-finals 1970, 1984, 1987, 2003, 2007.

Football League Cup: Semi-final 1979.

European Competitions: UEFA Cup: 1983–84.

SKY SPORTS FACT FILE

When Eddie Mummery scored five of the Watford goals in their 8–2 win over Newport County on 5 January 1924 with a goalscoring record which stands today, it was at the time the biggest victory achieved by the club but subsequently overtaken.

Most League Points (2 for a win): 71, Division 4, 1977–78.

Most League Points (3 for a win): 88, Division 2, 1997–98.

Most League Goals: 92, Division 4, 1959–60.

Highest League Scorer in Season: Cliff Holton, 42, Division 4, 1959–60.

Most League Goals in Total Aggregate: Luther Blissett, 148, 1976–83, 1984–88, 1991–92.

Most League Goals in One Match: 5, Eddie Mummery v Newport Co, Division 3 (S), 5 January 1924.

Most Capped Player: John Barnes, 31 (79), England and Kenny Jackett, 31, Wales.

Most League Appearances: Luther Blissett, 415, 1976–83, 1984–88, 1991–92.

Youngest League Player: Keith Mercer, 16 years 125 days v Tranmere R, 16 February 1973.

Record Transfer Fee Received: £9,600,000 from Aston V for Ashley Young, January 2007.

Record Transfer Fee Paid: £3,250,000 to WBA for Nathan Ellington, August 2007.

Football League Record: 1920 Original Member of Division 3; 1921–58 Division 3 (S); 1958–60 Division 4; 1960–69 Division 3; 1969–72 Division 2; 1972–75 Division 3; 1975–78 Division 4; 1978–79 Division 3; 1979–82 Division 2; 1982–88 Division 1; 1988–92 Division 2; 1992–96 Division 1; 1996–98 Division 2; 1998–99 Division 1; 1999–2000 FA Premier League; 2000–04 Division 1; 2004–06 FL C; 2006–07 FA Premier League; 2007– FL C.

LATEST SEQUENCES

Longest Sequence of League Wins: 7, 28.8.2000 – 14.10.2000.

Longest Sequence of League Defeats: 9, 26.12.1972 – 27.2.1973.

Longest Sequence of League Draws: 7, 30.11.1996 – 27.1.1997.

Longest Sequence of Unbeaten League Matches: 22, 1.10.1996 – 1.3.1997.

Longest Sequence Without a League Win: 19, 27.11.1971 – 8.4.1972.

Successive Scoring Runs: 22 from 20.8.1985.

Successive Non-scoring Runs: 7 from 18.12.1971.

MANAGERS

John Goodall 1903–10
Harry Kent 1910–26
Fred Pagnam 1926–29
Neil McBain 1929–37
Bill Findlay 1938–47
Jack Bray 1947–48
Eddie Hapgood 1948–50
Ron Gray 1950–51
Haydn Green 1951–52
Len Goulden 1952–55
   (General Manager to 1956)
Johnny Paton 1955–56
Neil McBain 1956–59
Ron Burgess 1959–63
Bill McGarry 1963–64
Ken Furphy 1964–71
George Kirby 1971–73
Mike Keen 1973–77
Graham Taylor 1977–87
Dave Bassett 1987–88
Steve Harrison 1988–90
Colin Lee 1990
Steve Perryman 1990–93
Glenn Roeder 1993–96
Kenny Jackett 1996–97
Graham Taylor 1997–2001
Gianluca Vialli 2001–02
Ray Lewington 2002–05
Adrian Boothroyd 2005–08
Brendan Rodgers 2008–09
Malky Mackay June 2009–

TEN YEAR LEAGUE RECORD

		P	W	D	L	F	A	Pts	Pos
1999-2000	PR Lge	38	6	6	26	35	77	24	20
2000-01	Div 1	46	20	9	17	76	67	69	9
2001-02	Div 1	46	16	11	19	62	56	59	14
2002-03	Div 1	46	17	9	20	54	70	60	13
2003-04	Div 1	46	15	12	19	54	68	57	16
2004-05	FL C	46	12	16	18	52	59	52	18
2005-06	FL C	46	22	15	9	77	53	81	3
2006-07	PR Lge	38	5	13	20	29	59	28	20
2007-08	FL C	46	18	16	12	62	56	70	6
2008-09	FL C	46	16	10	20	68	72	58	13

DID YOU KNOW ?

In terms of a goal per game ratio, George James' record with Watford was outstanding. Signed from Reading in 1929 after eight seasons at West Bromwich Albion where he had an England trial, this centre-forward registered 67 League goals in 83 matches.

WATFORD 2008–09 LEAGUE RECORD

Match No.	Date		Venue	Opponents	Result	H/T Score	Lg. Pos.	Goalscorers	Attendance
1	Aug	9	A	Crystal Palace	D	0-0	0-0	—	15,614
2		16	H	Charlton Ath	W	1-0	1-0	9	Smith [28]	14,413
3		23	A	Nottingham F	L	2-3	1-2	13	Smith 2 [22, 61]	20,005
4		30	H	Ipswich T	W	2-1	0-1	8	Eustace [56], O'Toole [87]	16,345
5	Sept	13	A	Sheffield W	L	0-2	0-1	11		17,066
6		16	H	Plymouth Arg	L	1-2	0-1	—	O'Toole [83]	13,237
7		20	H	Reading	D	2-2	0-1	17	Smith [57], O'Toole [64]	14,761
8		27	A	Sheffield U	L	1-2	0-1	19	O'Toole [56]	24,427
9		30	A	Burnley	L	2-3	2-1	—	Hoskins 2 [6, 45]	10,033
10	Oct	4	H	Preston NE	W	2-1	2-1	19	Harley [12], Smith [21]	14,087
11		18	A	Southampton	W	3-0	3-0	16	Priskin 2 [10, 41], Eustace [30]	17,454
12		21	H	Cardiff C	D	2-2	2-0	—	O'Toole [2], Hoskins [24]	13,461
13		25	H	Wolverhampton W	L	2-3	1-2	19	Rasiak [21], O'Toole [47]	16,386
14		28	A	Preston NE	L	0-2	0-1	—		11,234
15	Nov	1	H	Blackpool	L	3-4	2-1	21	Hoskins [4], Rasiak [36], Smith (pen) [68]	13,516
16		9	A	Swansea C	L	1-3	1-1	22	Williamson L [33]	13,891
17		15	A	Barnsley	L	1-2	0-0	22	Smith [52]	11,285
18		22	H	QPR	W	3-0	3-0	21	Smith (pen) [26], Ward [34], Williamson L [45]	16,201
19		25	A	Bristol C	D	1-1	0-0	—	Smith [72]	15,551
20		29	H	Doncaster R	D	1-1	1-0	20	Smith [31]	14,008
21	Dec	6	A	Birmingham C	L	2-3	1-2	21	Priskin [7], Jenkins [89]	18,174
22		10	H	Norwich C	W	2-1	1-0	—	Priskin [16], Smith [64]	13,268
23		13	H	Coventry C	W	2-1	0-0	17	Smith (pen) [62], O'Toole [72]	14,075
24		20	A	Derby Co	L	0-1	0-0	19		27,833
25		26	H	Bristol C	L	2-4	0-2	19	Rasiak [49], Elliott (og) [65]	15,527
26		28	A	QPR	D	0-0	0-0	19		16,196
27	Jan	9	A	Reading	L	0-4	0-1	—		18,072
28		17	H	Sheffield U	L	0-2	0-0	21		14,555
29		27	H	Burnley	W	3-0	1-0	—	McAnuff [2], Priskin 2 [78, 90]	13,193
30		31	A	Wolverhampton W	L	1-3	0-1	22	Mariappa [81]	23,571
31	Feb	17	H	Swansea C	W	2-0	2-0	—	Priskin [23], Smith [33]	13,727
32		21	A	Blackpool	W	2-0	0-0	18	Williamson M [54], Priskin [85]	7451
33		28	H	Crystal Palace	W	2-0	1-0	17	Cowie [22], Fonte J (og) [72]	15,529
34	Mar	3	A	Plymouth Arg	L	1-2	0-1	—	Smith [59]	9529
35		7	A	Charlton Ath	W	3-2	1-2	18	Cowie [17], Rasiak [56], Priskin [83]	20,052
36		10	H	Nottingham F	W	2-1	2-1	—	Rasiak [5], Priskin [43]	14,730
37		14	H	Sheffield W	D	2-2	1-1	16	Beevers (og) [45], McAnuff [56]	16,294
38		18	A	Cardiff C	L	1-2	1-1	—	Smith (pen) [10]	17,899
39		21	A	Ipswich T	D	0-0	0-0	16		21,434
40	Apr	4	A	Doncaster R	W	2-1	0-0	15	Hird (og) [13], Cowie [18]	12,126
41		7	H	Southampton	D	2-2	1-1	—	Cauna [21], Priskin [66]	16,066
42		11	H	Barnsley	D	1-1	0-0	14	Smith [88]	16,052
43		13	A	Norwich C	L	0-2	0-1	15		25,487
44		18	A	Birmingham C	L	0-1	0-0	16		16,180
45		25	H	Coventry C	W	3-2	0-1	15	Smith [58], Rasiak [61], Priskin [74]	17,195
46	May	3	H	Derby Co	W	3-1	3-0	1	McAnuff [14], Rasiak 2 [28, 41]	16,131

Final League Position: 13

GOALSCORERS

League (68): Smith 17 (4 pens), Priskin 12, Rasiak 8, O'Toole 7, Hoskins 4, Cowie 3, McAnuff 3, Eustace 2, Williamson L 2, Cauna 1, Harley 1, Jenkins 1, Mariappa 1, Ward 1, Williamson M 1, own goals 4.
Carling Cup (6): Francis 1, Hoskins 1, O'Toole 1, Priskin 1, Williamson L 1, own goal 1.
FA Cup (6): Rasiak 2, Cork 1, DeMerit 1, Hoskins 1, Priskin 1.

Poom M 7	Doyley L 35+2	Sadler M 15	Eustace J 14+3	Bromby L 19+3	DeMerit J 31+1	McAnuff J 34+6	Williamson L 26+8	Priskin T 32+4	Smith T 43+1	Harley J 32+5	Robinson T —+3	Francis D —+4	Mariappa A 37+2	Rasiak G 12+9	Hoskins W 16+16	Parkes J 1	O'Toole J 14+8	Henderson L —+5	Ainsworth L 1+6	Loach S 30+1	Bangura A —+2	Lee R 9+1	Sodje S 1	Ward D 9	Jenkins R 28+1	Bridcutt L 4+2	Young L —+1	Hoyte G 6+1	Cork J 18+1	Williamson M 17	Cowie D 10	Cauna A 2+3	Rose D 3+4	Stepanov A —+1	Hodson L —+1	Match No.
1	2	3	4	5	6	7^1	8	9^2	10	11	12	13																								1
1	2	3	4	5	6	7^3	8^1	9^2	10	11			12	14	13																					2
1	2	3	4	5	6	7^1	8^2	14	10	11^3			13	9	12																					3
1	2		4	5	6	7	8^2	9^2	10	11			13				3^1	12	14																	4
1	2		4	5	6	7^2	8	9	10	3				12				11^1	13																	5
1	2^1		4	5	6	7^2	8	9^2	10	3				12	14			11	13																	6
16			4	5	6	7^1	8		10	3			2	9			11^2	12	15	13																7
			4^1	5		12	8		10	3			2	9			11	13	7^3	16	15	6														8
	11	4^1	5			8^2	12	10	3				2	9			7	13		1	6															9
	3		12	6^1		8	9^2	10	11				2	7^3			4	13		14	1	5														10
	12	3	4	5		8	9^2	10	7				2^1	11^3			14	13		1		6														11
	3	12	5		14	8^1	9^4	10^3	11				2	13	7^2		4			1		6														12
2^2	3	4	5		12			10	11^1				6	9	8^3		7	13	14	1																13
2^3	3	4^2		5	12	13		10	11^1				9	8			7	14		1		6														14
2	3	4		5		12		10	11				9	8			7^1			1		6														15
	3	12	5^3	6	7	8	13	10		14			9^2	11^1			2			1		4														16
3			5	6	7	8	9^3	10	11^2				2	14	13		12			1					4^1											17
3			6	7^1	8^2	9	10	11				2		12		13			1					5	4											18
3		12	6	7^3	8	9^2	10	11				2		13		14			1					5^1	4											19
12			6	7	8	9	10	3				2		11^2		13			1					4	5^1											20
2	3^2	4^1	5		12		9	10	11			6		13			14		1					8	7^3											21
2	3^1	12	5			8	9	10	11			6		13					1					4	7^2											22
2	3^3			5	12	8	9	10	11^2	13		6		7					1					4^1	14											23
3		5	12	7	8	9^2	10	11				2^1		13		6^3			1					4	14											24
	3^3	5	6	7	8		10	11^1			2	9	12			4^2			1					13	14											25
3		12	5	7	8	9^2	10	11			2	13							1					4	6^1											26
		6	7	8	9	10	11			5	12								1					4^1			2	3								27
		6	7	8^1		10	11			5	9	12							1					4			2	3								28
3			7	12	14	10	13			5	9^2	11^3							1					8			2^1	4	6							29
3			7	12	9^2	10				5	13	11							1					8			2^1	4	6							30
3			5	7	12	9^2	10	11			2								1					11^1				4	6	8						31
3			5	7	13	9^2	10	12			2								1					11				4	6	8^1						32
3			5^1	7			10	12			2	9^2	13						1					11				4	6	8						33
3				8	9	12	11^3			5	13	10^1							1					4		2		6	7^2	14						34
2			7	13	9^2	10^1	3			5	12								1					11				4	6	8						35
2			7	12	9		3			5	10^1								1					11				4	6	8						36
2			7	10^1	9		3			5		12							1					11				4	6	8						37
2		5	7		9	10				3									1					11				4	6	8^1						38
2		5^2	7		9	10				3	12								1					11	13	4	6	8^1								39
3		5	7		9^3	10	13			2		14							1					11				4	6	8^1	12^2					40
3		5	7		9^2	10				2									1					11				4	6		8^1	12	13			41
3		5	7		9^2	10				2		13							1					11				4	6		8^1	12				42
3		5	7			10	11			2		9							1					8				12	6			4^1				43
3		5	7			10	13			2	12	9^1							1					11				4	6			8^2				44
3		5	7		9^2	10				2	8								1					11^1				4	6		13	12				45
3			6	7		9	10			5	11	14							1						2^1	4^3				13	8^2		12			46

FA Cup

Third Round	Scunthorpe U	(h)	1-0
Fourth Round	Crystal Palace	(h)	4-3
Fifth Round	Chelsea	(h)	1-3

Carling Cup

First Round	Bristol R	(h)	1-0
Second Round	Darlington	(h)	2-1
Third Round	West Ham U	(h)	1-0
Fourth Round	Swansea C	(a)	1-0
Quarter-Final	Tottenham H	(h)	1-2

WEST BROMWICH ALBION FL Championship

FOUNDATION

There is a well known story that when employees of Salter's Spring Works in West Bromwich decided to form a football club, they had to send someone to the nearby Association Football stronghold of Wednesbury to purchase a football. A weekly subscription of 2d (less than 1p) was imposed and the name of the new club was West Bromwich Strollers.

The Hawthorns, West Bromwich, West Midlands B71 4LF.

Telephone: 0871 271 1100.

Fax: 0871 271 9861.

Ticket Office: 0871 271 9780.

Website: www.wbafc.co.uk

Email: enquiries@wbafc.co.uk

Ground Capacity: 28,003.

Record Attendance: 64,815 v Arsenal, FA Cup 6th rd, 6 March 1937.

Pitch Measurements: 115yd × 74yd.

Chairman: Jeremy Peace.

Legal Director/Secretary: Darren Eales.

Head Coach: Roberto Di Matteo.

Assistant Head Coach: Eddie Newton.

Physio: Richie Rawlins.

Colours: Navy blue and white striped shirts, white shorts, white stockings.

Change Colours: Yellow shirts, navy blue shorts, yellow stockings.

Year Formed: 1878.

Turned Professional: 1885.

Ltd Co.: 1892.

Plc: 1996.

Previous Name: 1878, West Bromwich Strollers; 1881, West Bromwich Albion.

Club Nicknames: 'Throstles', 'Baggies', 'Albion'.

Grounds: 1878, Coopers Hill; 1879, Dartmouth Park; 1881, Bunns Field, Walsall Street; 1882, Four Acres (Dartmouth Cricket Club); 1885, Stoney Lane; 1900, The Hawthorns.

First Football League Game: 8 September 1888, Football League, v Stoke (a) W 2–0 – Roberts; J. Horton, Green; E. Horton, Perry, Bayliss; Bassett, Woodhall (1), Hendry, Pearson, Wilson (1).

Record League Victory: 12–0 v Darwen, Division 1, 4 April 1892 – Reader; J. Horton, McCulloch; Reynolds (2), Perry, Groves; Bassett (3), McLeod, Nicholls (1), Pearson (4), Geddes (1), (1 og).

HONOURS

Football League: Division 1 – Champions 1919–20; Runners-up 1924–25, 1953–54, 2001–02, 2003–04; FLC – Champions 2007–08; Division 2 – Champions 1901–02, 1910–11; Runners-up 1930–31, 1948–49.

FA Cup: Winners 1888, 1892, 1931, 1954, 1968; Runners-up 1886, 1887, 1895, 1912, 1935.

Football League Cup: Winners 1966; Runners-up 1967, 1970.

European Competitions: European Cup-Winners' Cup: 1968–69. *European Fairs Cup:* 1966–67. *UEFA Cup:* 1978–79, 1979–80, 1981–82.

SKY SPORTS FACT FILE

On 4 March 1933 when West Bromwich Albion entertained Newcastle United, eighteen of the players on the pitch were in possession of FA Cup winning medals. Ten of these belonged to Albion players who won the match 3–2 at The Hawthorns.

Record Cup Victory: 10–1 v Chatham (away), FA Cup 3rd rd, 2 March 1889 – Roberts; J. Horton, Green; Timmins (1), Charles Perry, E. Horton; Bassett (2), Perry (1), Bayliss (2), Pearson, Wilson (3), (1 og).

Record Defeat: 3–10 v Stoke C, Division 1, 4 February 1937.

Most League Points (2 for a win): 60, Division 1, 1919–20.

Most League Points (3 for a win): 89, Division 1, 2001–02.

Most League Goals: 105, Division 2, 1929–30.

Highest League Scorer in Season: William 'Ginger' Richardson, 39, Division 1, 1935–36.

Most League Goals in Total Aggregate: Tony Brown, 218, 1963–79.

Most League Goals in One Match: 6, Jimmy Cookson v Blackpool, Division 2, 17 September 1927.

Most Capped Player: Stuart Williams, 33 (43), Wales.

Most League Appearances: Tony Brown, 574, 1963–80.

Youngest League Player: Charlie Wilson, 16 years 73 days v Oldham Ath, 1 October 1921.

Record Transfer Fee Received: £8,000,000 from Aston Villa for Curtis Davies, July 2008.

Record Transfer Fee Paid: £4,700,000 to Mallorca for Borja Valero, August 2008.

Football League Record: 1888 Founder Member of Football League; 1901–02 Division 2; 1902–04 Division 1; 1904–11 Division 2; 1911–27 Division 1; 1927–31 Division 2; 1931–38 Division 1; 1938–49 Division 2; 1949–73 Division 1; 1973–76 Division 2; 1976–86 Division 1; 1986–91 Division 2; 1991–92 Division 3; 1992–93 Division 2; 1993–2002 Division 1; 2002–03 FA Premier League; 2003–04 Division 1; 2004–06 FA Premier League; 2006–08 FL C; 2008–09 FA Premier League; 2009– FL C.

LATEST SEQUENCES

Longest Sequence of League Wins: 11, 5.4.1930 – 8.9.1930.

Longest Sequence of League Defeats: 11, 28.10.1995 – 26.12.1995.

Longest Sequence of League Draws: 5, 30.8.1999 – 3.10.1999.

Longest Sequence of Unbeaten League Matches: 17, 7.9.1957 – 7.12.1957.

Longest Sequence Without a League Win: 15, 16.10.2004 – 25.9.2004.

Successive Scoring Runs: 36 from 26.4.1958.

Successive Non-scoring Runs: 4 from 15.2.1913.

MANAGERS

Louis Ford 1890–92
(Secretary-Manager)
Henry Jackson 1892–94
(Secretary-Manager)
Edward Stephenson 1894–95
(Secretary-Manager)
Clement Keys 1895–96
(Secretary-Manager)
Frank Heaven 1896–1902
(Secretary-Manager)
Fred Everiss 1902–48
Jack Smith 1948–52
Jesse Carver 1952
Vic Buckingham 1953–59
Gordon Clark 1959–61
Archie Macaulay 1961–63
Jimmy Hagan 1963–67
Alan Ashman 1967–71
Don Howe 1971–75
Johnny Giles 1975–77
Ronnie Allen 1977
Ron Atkinson 1978–81
Ronnie Allen 1981–82
Ron Wylie 1982–84
Johnny Giles 1984–85
Ron Saunders 1986–87
Ron Atkinson 1987–88
Brian Talbot 1988–91
Bobby Gould 1991–92
Ossie Ardiles 1992–93
Keith Burkinshaw 1993–94
Alan Buckley 1994–97
Ray Harford 1997
Denis Smith 1997–2000
Brian Little 2000
Gary Megson 2000–04
Bryan Robson 2004–06
Tony Mowbray 2006–09
Roberto Di Matteo June 2009–

TEN YEAR LEAGUE RECORD

		P	W	D	L	F	A	Pts	Pos
1999-2000	Div 1	46	10	19	17	43	60	49	21
2000-01	Div 1	46	21	11	14	60	52	74	6
2001-02	Div 1	46	27	8	11	61	29	89	2
2002-03	PR Lge	38	6	8	24	29	65	26	19
2003-04	Div 1	46	25	11	10	64	42	86	2
2004-05	PR Lge	38	6	16	16	36	61	34	17
2005-06	PR Lge	38	7	9	22	31	58	30	19
2006-07	FL C	46	22	10	14	81	55	76	4
2007-08	FL C	46	23	12	11	88	55	81	1
2008-09	PR Lge	38	8	8	22	36	67	32	20

DID YOU KNOW ?

Goalkeeper Bob Roberts, often referred to as 'Long Bob', was the first West Bromwich Albion player to be capped for England against Scotland on 19 March 1887. A previously failed outfield player he was in the Baggies' first League game and FA Cup tie.

WEST BROMWICH ALBION 2008–09 LEAGUE RECORD

Match No.	Date	Venue	Opponents	Result	H/T Score	Lg. Pos.	Goalscorers	Attendance
1	Aug 16	A	Arsenal	L	0-1	0-1	—		60,071
2	23	H	Everton	L	1-2	0-0	18	Bednar (pen) [89]	26,190
3	30	A	Bolton W	D	0-0	0-0	20		20,387
4	Sept 13	H	West Ham U	W	3-2	2-2	15	Morrison [3], Bednar (pen) [37], Brunt [83]	26,213
5	21	H	Aston Villa	L	1-2	1-2	17	Morrison [24]	26,011
6	27	A	Middlesbrough	W	1-0	0-0	12	Olsson [53]	26,248
7	Oct 4	H	Fulham	W	1-0	0-0	9	Bednar [61]	25,708
8	18	A	Manchester U	L	0-4	0-0	10		75,451
9	25	H	Hull C	L	0-3	0-0	13		26,323
10	28	A	Newcastle U	L	1-2	0-2	—	Miller [65]	45,801
11	Nov 1	A	Blackburn R	D	2-2	0-1	18	Bednar [56], Miller [62]	24,976
12	8	A	Liverpool	L	0-3	0-2	20		43,451
13	15	H	Chelsea	L	0-3	0-3	20		26,322
14	22	A	Stoke C	L	0-1	0-0	20		26,613
15	29	A	Wigan Ath	L	1-2	0-0	20	Miller [47]	17,054
16	Dec 7	H	Portsmouth	D	1-1	1-0	20	Greening [39]	24,964
17	13	A	Sunderland	L	0-4	0-3	20		36,280
18	21	H	Manchester C	W	2-1	0-0	20	Moore [69], Bednar [90]	25,010
19	26	A	Chelsea	L	0-2	0-2	20		43,417
20	28	H	Tottenham H	W	2-0	0-0	20	Bednar [83], Beattie [90]	26,344
21	Jan 10	A	Aston Villa	L	1-2	0-2	20	Morrison [49]	41,757
22	17	H	Middlesbrough	W	3-0	1-0	20	McMahon (og) [4], Fortune [54], Koren [67]	25,557
23	27	A	Manchester U	L	0-5	0-2	—		26,105
24	31	A	Hull C	D	2-2	0-1	20	Simpson [53], Brunt (pen) [73]	24,879
25	Feb 7	H	Newcastle U	L	2-3	1-3	20	Fortune 2 [4, 73]	25,817
26	22	A	Fulham	L	0-2	0-0	20		22,394
27	28	A	Everton	L	0-2	0-1	20		33,898
28	Mar 3	A	Arsenal	L	1-3	1-3	—	Brunt [7]	26,244
29	16	A	West Ham U	D	0-0	0-0	—		30,842
30	21	H	Bolton W	D	1-1	0-0	20	Shittu (og) [82]	25,530
31	Apr 4	H	Stoke C	L	0-2	0-1	20		26,277
32	11	A	Portsmouth	D	2-2	0-1	20	Greening [48], Brunt [62]	20,376
33	19	H	Manchester C	L	2-4	1-2	20	Brunt 2 [37, 54]	40,072
34	25	H	Sunderland	W	3-0	1-0	20	Olsson [40], Brunt [58], Menseguez [88]	26,256
35	May 2	A	Tottenham H	L	0-1	0-1	20		35,836
36	9	H	Wigan Ath	W	3-1	1-1	20	Fortune 2 [8, 73], Brunt [59]	24,741
37	17	H	Liverpool	L	0-2	0-1	20		26,138
38	24	A	Blackburn R	D	0-0	0-0	20		28,389

Final League Position: 20

GOALSCORERS

League (36): Brunt 8 (1 pen), Bednar 6 (2 pens), Fortune 5, Miller 3, Morrison 3, Greening 2, Olsson 2, Beattie 1, Koren 1, Menseguez 1, Moore 1, Simpson 1, own goals 2.
Carling Cup (1): Koren 1.
FA Cup (6): Kim 1, Koren 1, Olsson 1, Robinson 1, Simpson 1, Zuiverloon 1.

Carson S 35	Hoefkens C 6+4	Robinson P 35	Morrison J 29+1	Barnett L 10+1	Meite A 18	Brunt C 28+6	Kim D 9+7	Cech M 3+5	Miller I 11+4	Greening J 33+1	Beattie C 1+6	MacDonald S —+5	Bednar R 12+14	Zuiverloon G 33	Koren R 34+1	Borja Valero 27+3	Olsson J 28	Moore L 5+16	Donk R 14+2	Teixeira F 1+9	Dorrans G 5+3	Simpson J 9+4	Pele 1+2	Fortune M 17	Menseguez J 3+4	Martis S 6+1	Mulumbu Y 2+4	Wood C —+2	Kiely D 3	Match No.
1	2	3	4	5	6	7^1	8	9^2	10^3	11	12	13	14																	1
1		3	4	5	6	7	8^1		10^3	11	14	12	13	2	9^2															2
1	12	3	4	5	6^1	9	13	10	11	14				2	8^3	7^2														3
1	2	3	7^2	5	8	13	12	11	9^1	4	10^3	6	14																	4
1		3	4	5	7^2	13	12	11	9^1	2	8	10^3	6	14																5
1		3	4^1			10^2	12	14	11	13^3	9	2	8	7	6		5													6
1		3	4^1			12	10^2	11	9	2	8	7	6	13	5															7
1		3	4		10			12	11	9^1	2	8^2	7	6	13	5														8
1		3	4^2		12			10^3	11	14	9	2	8^1	7	6	13	5													9
1		3	4		10^1			12	11	9^2	2	8	7	6	13	5														10
1	12	3	4^2		13			10^3	11	9	2	8	7	6	14	5^1														11
1		3			12	8^3		10^1	11	9^2	2	4	7	6	13	5	14													12
1		3	4^3		5^2		12	10	11	9^1	2	8	7	6	13	14														13
1		3			5	10	8^2	9	11	12	2	4	7^1	6	13															14
1		3	4^1		5	10^2		9	11	13	2	8	7	6	12															15
1		3	4		5	10		9^2	11	12	2	8	7^1	6	13															16
1		3	4^1		5	10^2	13		11	14	12	2	8	7	6	9^3														17
1		3	4		5	12	7^3	11^1	13	9	2	8		6	10^2	14														18
1		3	4	12	5^1	10	7^2	11	9^3	13	2	8		6	14															19
1	12		4	5	8^3	3		11	13	10	2^1		7^2	6	9		14													20
1	2	3	4^1	5		12	14	11		13		8	7^3	6	9^2			10												21
1	2	3	5^3		8			11	12			4	7	13	6	9^2	14	10^1												22
1	2	3^4	12		11	13				14	4^1	8	7	5	10^3	6	9^2													23
1		3	4^1		6	11	12			13	2	8	7^3	5	10	14	9^2													24
1	2	3	4	5	6	10^1	11^3			12	8	7^2		13	14	9														25
1		3	4^3	5	6	12				13	2	8	7	11^1	10		9^2	14												26
1		3	4		6	11	12				2	8	7^1	13	5	14	10^2	9^3												27
1		3	4^2		6	7^1			11		2	8	9	5	13			10	12	7	14									28
1		3	4^1			10^9			11		2	8		5	13	12	7	14	9^2	6										29
1	3^3	4		7		11	13				2^1	8	12	6		14	10^2	9	5											30
1	3^1	4		8		11^3	13				2	12	7	5		14	10^2	9	6											31
1	13	3	4^1		6	10^3			11		2^2	8		5		7				9				14	12					32
1		3	4^3		5	10			11		2	8^1	13	6		7^2	12			9				14						33
1		3			6^1	8			11		2	4		5		7^3	10^2			9	14	12	13							34
1		3^1				8			11		2	4	7^3	5		14			12		9	13	6	10^2						35
					10	3^2			11		2		7	5	13		4^1	14			9	8^3	6	12			1			36
						8			11		2	6	12	5	13	3					9	10	4^1	7^2			1			37
		3				8	12		11		2	4	7^1	6		5					9	10^2			13		1			38

FA Cup

Third Round	Peterborough U	(h)	1-1
		(a)	2-0
Fourth Round	Burnley	(h)	2-2
		(a)	1-3

Carling Cup

Second Round	Hartlepool U	(a)	1-3

WEST HAM UNITED FA Premiership

FOUNDATION

Thames Iron Works FC was formed by employees of this famous shipbuilding company in 1895 and entered the FA Cup in their initial season at Chatham and the London League in their second. The committee wanted to introduce professional players, so Thames Iron Works was wound up in June 1900 and relaunched a month later as West Ham United.

The Boleyn Ground, Upton Park, Green Street, London E13 9AZ.

Telephone: (020) 8548 2748.

Fax: (020) 8548 2758.

Ticket Office: 0870 112 2700.

Website: www.whufc.co.uk

Email: yourcomments@westhamunited.co.uk

Ground Capacity: 35,303.

Record Attendance: 42,322 v Tottenham H, Division 1, 17 October 1970.

Pitch Measurements: 100.58m × 66.84m.

Chairman: Andrew Bernhardt.

Chief Executive: Scott Duxbury.

Secretary: Peter Barnes.

Manager: Gianfranco Zola.

First Team Coach: Steve Clarke.

Physio: George Cooper.

Colours: Claret shirts with light blue sleeves and white collar, white shorts, white stockings.

Change Colours: Dark blue shirts with broad royal blue stripe, dark blue shorts, dark blue stockings.

Year Formed: 1895.

Turned Professional: 1900.

Ltd Co.: 1900.

Previous Name: 1895, Thames Iron Works FC; 1900, West Ham United.

Club Nicknames: 'The Hammers', 'The Irons'.

Grounds: 1895, Memorial Recreation Ground, Canning Town; 1904, Boleyn Ground.

First Football League Game: 30 August 1919, Division 2, v Lincoln C (h) D 1–1 – Hufton; Cope, Lee; Lane, Fenwick, McCrae; D. Smith, Moyes (1), Puddefoot, Morris, Bradshaw.

HONOURS

Football League: Division 2 – Champions 1957–58, 1980–81; Runners-up 1922–23, 1990–91.

FA Cup: Winners 1964, 1975, 1980; Runners-up 1923, 2006.

Football League Cup: Runners-up 1966, 1981.

European Competitions: *European Cup-Winners' Cup:* 1964–65 (winners), 1965–66, 1975–76 (runners-up), 1980–81. *UEFA Cup:* 1999–2000; 2006–07. *Intertoto Cup:* 1999 (winners).

SKY SPORTS FACT FILE

West Ham United goalkeeper Peter Grotier at the age of 18 played for four different club sides in five matches in 1969 starting with the A team, then reserves, youth team, reserves again and finally as his debut for the first team at Tottenham Hotspur on 19 April.

Record League Victory: 8–0 v Rotherham U, Division 2, 8 March 1958 – Gregory; Bond, Wright; Malcolm, Brown, Lansdowne; Grice, Smith (2), Keeble (2), Dick (4), Musgrove. 8–0 v Sunderland, Division 1, 19 October 1968 – Ferguson; Bonds, Charles; Peters, Stephenson, Moore (1); Redknapp, Boyce, Brooking (1), Hurst (6), Sissons.

Record Cup Victory: 10–0 v Bury, League Cup 2nd rd (2nd leg), 25 October 1983 – Parkes; Stewart (1), Walford, Bonds (Orr), Martin (1), Devonshire (2), Allen, Cottee (4), Swindlehurst, Brooking (2), Pike.

Record Defeat: 2–8 v Blackburn R, Division 1, 26 December 1963.

Most League Points (2 for a win): 66, Division 2, 1980–81.

Most League Points (3 for a win): 88, Division 1, 1992–93.

Most League Goals: 101, Division 2, 1957–58.

Highest League Scorer in Season: Vic Watson, 42, Division 1, 1929–30.

Most League Goals in Total Aggregate: Vic Watson, 298, 1920–35.

Most League Goals in One Match: 6, Vic Watson v Leeds U, Division 1, 9 February 1929; 6, Geoff Hurst v Sunderland, Division 1, 19 October 1968.

Most Capped Player: Bobby Moore, 108, England.

Most League Appearances: Billy Bonds, 663, 1967–88.

Youngest League Player: Billy Williams, 16 years 221 days v Blackpool, 6 May 1922.

Record Transfer Fee Received: £18,000,000 from Leeds U for Rio Ferdinand, November 2000.

Record Transfer Fee Paid: £9,000,000 to Brescia for Savio Nsereko, January 2009.

Football League Record: 1919 Elected to Division 2; 1923–32 Division 1; 1932–58 Division 2; 1958–78 Division 1; 1978–81 Division 2; 1981–89 Division 1; 1989–91 Division 2; 1991–93 Division 1; 1993–2003 FA Premier League; 2003–04 Division 1; 2004–05 FL C; 2005– FA Premier League.

MANAGERS

Syd King 1902–32
Charlie Paynter 1932–50
Ted Fenton 1950–61
Ron Greenwood 1961–74
   (continued as General Manager to 1977)
John Lyall 1974–89
Lou Macari 1989–90
Billy Bonds 1990–94
Harry Redknapp 1994–2001
Glenn Roeder 2001–03
Alan Pardew 2003–06
Alan Curbishley 2006–08
Gianfranco Zola September 2008–

LATEST SEQUENCES

Longest Sequence of League Wins: 9, 19.10.1985 – 14.12.1985.

Longest Sequence of League Defeats: 9, 28.3.1932 – 29.8.1932.

Longest Sequence of League Draws: 5, 15.10.2003 – 1.11.2003.

Longest Sequence of Unbeaten League Matches: 27, 27.12.80 – 10.10.81.

Longest Sequence Without a League Win: 17, 31.1.1976 – 21.8.1976.

Successive Scoring Runs: 27 from 5.10.1957.

Successive Non-scoring Runs: 5 from 1.5.1971.

TEN YEAR LEAGUE RECORD

		P	W	D	L	F	A	Pts	Pos
1999-2000	PR Lge	38	15	10	13	52	53	55	9
2000-01	PR Lge	38	10	12	16	45	50	42	15
2001-02	PR Lge	38	15	8	15	48	57	53	7
2002-03	PR Lge	38	10	12	16	42	59	42	18
2003-04	Div 1	46	19	17	10	67	45	74	4
2004-05	FL C	46	21	10	15	66	56	73	6
2005-06	PR Lge	38	16	7	15	52	55	55	9
2006-07	PR Lge	38	12	5	21	35	59	41	15
2007-08	PR Lge	38	13	10	15	42	50	49	10
2008-09	PR Lge	38	14	9	15	42	45	51	9

DID YOU KNOW ?

When West Ham United won promotion to the First Division in 1922–23 they called upon the services of 26 different players. Only one of them was an ever present and had been signed from Sunderland. This inside-forward was called Billy Moore!

WEST HAM UNITED 2008–09 LEAGUE RECORD

Match No.	Date	Venue	Opponents	Result	H/T Score	Lg. Pos.	Goalscorers	Attendance
1	Aug 16	H	Wigan Ath	W 2-1	2-0	—	Ashton 2 [3, 10]	32,758
2	24	A	Manchester C	L 0-3	0-0	15		36,635
3	30	H	Blackburn R	W 4-1	2-1	5	Davenport [12], Samba (og) [20], Cole [89], Bellamy [90]	32,905
4	Sept 13	A	WBA	L 2-3	2-2	7	Noble [29], Neill [35]	26,213
5	20	H	Newcastle U	W 3-1	2-0	6	Di Michele 2 [8, 37], Etherington [53]	34,743
6	27	A	Fulham	W 2-1	2-0	5	Cole [43], Etherington [45]	23,946
7	Oct 5	H	Bolton W	L 1-3	0-2	6	Cole [69]	33,715
8	19	A	Hull C.	L 0-1	0-0	8		24,896
9	26	H	Arsenal	L 0-2	0-0	10		34,802
10	29	A	Manchester U	L 0-2	0-2	—		75,397
11	Nov 1	A	Middlesbrough	D 1-1	1-0	11	Mullins [21]	25,164
12	8	H	Everton	L 1-3	0-0	14	Collison [60]	33,981
13	15	H	Portsmouth	D 0-0	0-0	14		32,328
14	23	A	Sunderland	W 1-0	1-0	13	Behrami [20]	35,222
15	Dec 1	A	Liverpool	D 0-0	0-0	—		41,169
16	8	H	Tottenham H	L 0-2	0-0	—		34,277
17	14	A	Chelsea	D 1-1	1-0	16	Bellamy [33]	41,675
18	20	H	Aston Villa	L 0-1	0-0	17		31,353
19	26	A	Portsmouth	W 4-1	1-0	13	Collison [20], Cole [67], Bellamy 2 [70, 83]	20,102
20	28	H	Stoke C	W 2-1	0-1	10	Cole [51], Tristan [88]	34,477
21	Jan 10	A	Newcastle U	D 2-2	1-1	10	Bellamy [29], Cole [55]	47,571
22	18	H	Fulham	W 3-1	1-1	8	Di Michele [7], Noble (pen) [60], Cole [76]	31,818
23	28	A	Hull C	W 2-0	1-0	—	Di Michele [33], Cole [51]	34,340
24	31	A	Arsenal	D 0-0	0-0	8		60,109
25	Feb 8	H	Manchester U	L 0-1	0-0	8		34,958
26	21	A	Bolton W	L 1-2	0-2	9	Parker [66]	21,245
27	Mar 1	H	Manchester C	W 1-0	1-0	7	Collison [71]	34,562
28	4	A	Wigan Ath	W 1-0	1-0	—	Cole [34]	14,169
29	16	H	WBA	D 0-0	0-0	—		30,842
30	21	A	Blackburn R	D 1-1	1-0	8	Noble [35]	21,672
31	Apr 4	H	Sunderland	W 2-0	1-0	7	Stanislas [42], Tomkins [53]	34,761
32	11	A	Tottenham H	L 0-1	0-0	7		35,969
33	18	A	Aston Villa	D 1-1	0-1	7	Tristan [85]	39,534
34	25	H	Chelsea	L 0-1	0-0	8		34,749
35	May 2	H	Stoke C	W 1-0	1-0	7	Tristan [33]	27,500
36	9	H	Liverpool	L 0-3	0-2	9		34,951
37	16	A	Everton	L 1-3	1-1	9	Kovac [24]	38,501
38	24	H	Middlesbrough	W 2-1	1-0	9	Cole [33], Stanislas [58]	34,007

Final League Position: 9

GOALSCORERS

League (42): Cole 10, Bellamy 5, Di Michele 4, Collison 3, Noble 3 (1 pen), Tristan 3, Ashton 2, Etherington 2, Stanislas 2, Behrami 1, Davenport 1, Kovac 1, Mullins 1, Neill 1, Parker 1, Tomkins 1, own goal 1.
Carling Cup (4): Bowyer 1, Cole 1, Hines 1, Reid 1.
FA Cup (6): Ilunga 2, Noble 2 (2 pens), Behrami 1, Cole 1.

Green R 38	Behrami V 24	Neill L 34	Noble M 28 + 1	Upson M 37	Davenport C 7	Faubert J 15 + 5	Parker S 28	Cole C 26 + 1	Ashton D 4	Etherington M 8 + 5	Boa Morte L 13 + 14	Mullins H 5 + 12	Sears F 4 + 13	McCartney G — + 1	Bellamy C 13 + 3	Ilunga H 35	Di Michele D 22 + 8	Collins J 17 + 1	Bowyer L 4 + 2	Collison J 16 + 4	Tristan D 8 + 6	Spector J 4 + 5	Dyer K 1 + 6	Nsereko S 1 + 9	Tomkins J 11 + 1	Kovac R 8 + 1	Lopez W — + 5	Stanislas J 7 + 2	Payne J — + 2	Match No.
1	2	3	4	5	6	7^1	8^2	9	10^3	11	12	13	14																	1
1	2	3	4^4	5	6	7	8	9^2	10	11^1	12	14	13^3																	2
1	2	3	4^1	5	6	7^2	8	9	10^3	11	12	13	14																	3
1	7^1	2	4	5	6^1	12	8	9	10^3	13	11^2					3	14													4
1	2	6	4	5		7	8^2	9^3		11^1	12	13	14			3	10													5
1	2	6	4	5		7	8^1	9		11^2	12	13				3	10^3													6
1	2	6	4	5		7	8	9		11^1			12			3	10^2													7
1	2	6	4	5		7^2	8	9		11^1						3	13	10												8
1				5		7	8^2	9^8			12	13	2	14		10	3	11^1	6	4^3										9
1	2^1			5		7					11^3	4	13			9	3	10	6	8^2	14									10
1	2			5		7					12	11^2	4			10^1	9	3	6	13	8	14								11
1	2	5^3				7	4^2				12	11^1	10			9	3	13	6	8	14									12
1	7	2		5		12	8^3	9		13			14		11^2	10	3^1		6		4									13
1	11	2		5		7^1	4	9			12	13			4	10^3	3	14	6	8^2										14
1	11	2		5		7^1	8	9			12	4				10	3	13	6											15
1	7	2	12	5		11^1	8^3	9					4^2			10	3	13	6		14									16
1	11	2	4^2	5	6		8	9			12	13				10^3	3	14		7^1										17
1	11^2	2	4	5	6		8^1	9				12				10^3	3		13	7^3	14									18
1	11	2^1	4^2	5	6	12	8	9^3			13					10^3	3			7	14									19
1	7			5		2	8^1	9			11	12				10^3	3	6		4^2	13	14								20
1	11	2	4^2	5			8	9			12	13				10^3	3	14	6	7^1										21
1	7	2	4^1	5		12	8	9				13				10^3	3	6	11^2		14									22
1	7	2	4^2	5		12	8	9				13				10^3	3	6	11^1		14									23
1	7	2	4^2	5			8	9				12				10^1	3	6	11		13									24
1	7^1	2	4^2	5			8	9								10	3	6	11	12	13									25
1	7		4	5			8	9			12					6^3	3	10	11^2	2^1	13	14								26
1	7^2	2	4	5			8	9								10^3	3	11	12	13	6	4^1	14							27
1		2	4	5			8^3	9^4								10^2	3	7^1	12	13	6	11	14							28
1		2	4^1	5^2			8				12					10	3		13	11^3	6	7		14						29
1		2	4				8				11^1					10^3	3	9^2	5	14		6	7	12		13				30
1		2	4	5							11					10^2	12	3	7^1	13	9	6		14	8^3					31
1		2	8	5							11^1		14			10	3	9^3	6	12	13	4^2			7					32
1		2	8	5							11		14			10^3	3	6^1	9	12	13	4			7^2					33
1		2	4	5							11^3		13			10^2	3	9	8^1	14	6	12			7					34
1		2	4^2	5							11^1					10^3	3	12	9		6	8	13	7						35
1		2	4	5							11^3		13			10^2	3	12	9		6	8		7^1	14					36
1		2	4	5				12			11					10^2	3	7	9^1	13		6^8	8^3	14						37
1	6	4^1	5					9^2			11					3	14	7^3	13	2	12		8	10						38

FA Cup

Third Round	Barnsley	(h)	3-0
Fourth Round	Hartlepool U	(a)	2-0
Fifth Round	Middlesbrough	(h)	1-1
		(a)	0-2

Carling Cup

Second Round	Macclesfield T	(h)	4-1
Third Round	Watford	(a)	0-1

WIGAN ATHLETIC
FA Premiership

FOUNDATION

Following the demise of Wigan Borough and their resignation from the Football League in 1931, a public meeting was called in Wigan at the Queen's Hall in May 1932 at which a new club, Wigan Athletic, was founded in the hope of carrying on in the Football League. With this in mind, they bought Springfield Park for £2,250, but failed to gain admission to the Football League until 46 years later.

JJB Stadium, Robin Park, Newtown, Wigan, Lancashire WN5 0UZ.

Telephone: (01942) 774 000.

Fax: (01942) 770 477.

Ticket Office: (0871) 663 3552.

Website: www.wiganathletic.tv

Email: latics@jjbstadium.co.uk

Ground Capacity: 25,138.

Record Attendance: 27,526 v Hereford U, 12 December 1953 (at Springfield Park).

Pitch Measurements: 105m × 68m.

Chairman: David Whelan.

Vice-chairman: Phillip Williams.

Chief Executive: Brenda Spencer.

Secretary: Stuart Hayton.

Manager: Roberto Martinez.

Assistant Manager: Graeme Jones.

Physio: David Galley.

Colours: Blue and white shirts with blue sleeves, blue shorts, white stockings.

Change Colours: Fluo yellow shirts with black trim, black shorts, black stockings.

Year Formed: 1932.

Grounds: 1932, Springfield Park; 1999, JJB Stadium.

Club Nickname: 'The Latics'.

First Football League Game: 19 August 1978, Division 4, v Hereford U (a) D 0–0 – Brown; Hinnigan, Gore, Gillibrand, Ward, Davids, Corrigan, Purdie, Houghton, Wilkie, Wright.

Record League Victory: 7–1 v Scarborough, Division 3, 11 March 1997 – Butler L, Butler J, Sharp (Morgan), Greenall, McGibbon (Biggins (1)), Martinez (1), Diaz (2), Jones (Lancashire (1)), Lowe (2), Rogers, Kilford.

Record Cup Victory: 6–0 v Carlisle U (away), FA Cup 1st rd, 24 November 1934 – Caunce; Robinson, Talbot; Paterson, Watson, Tufnell; Armes (2), Robson (1), Roberts (2), Felton, Scott (1).

HONOURS

Football League: Championship – Runners-up 2004–05; Division 2 Champions, 2002–03; Division 3 Champions, 1996–97.

FA Cup: best season: 6th rd, 1987.

Football League Cup: Runners up: 2006.

Freight Rover Trophy: Winners 1985.

Auto Windscreens Shield: Winners 1999.

SKY SPORTS FACT FILE

By the time Wigan Athletic had reached their 100th Football League appearance on 27 September 1980 against Mansfield Town, only two players had been ever-present. Tommy Gore and Jeff Wright had joined the club within a week of each other in 1974.

Record Defeat: 1–6 v Bristol R, Division 3, 3 March 1990.

Most League Points (2 for a win): 55, Division 4, 1978–79 and 1979–80.

Most League Points (3 for a win): 100, Division 2, 2002–03.

Most League Goals: 84, Division 3, 1996–97.

Highest League Scorer in Season: Graeme Jones, 31, Division 3, 1996–97.

Most League Goals in Total Aggregate: Andy Liddell, 70, 1998–2004.

Most League Goals in One Match: Not more than three goals by one player.

Most Capped Player: Lee McCulloch, 11 (15), Scotland.

Most League Appearances: Kevin Langley, 317, 1981–86, 1990–94.

Youngest League Player: Steve Nugent, 16 years 132 days v Leyton Orient, 16 September 1989.

Record Transfer Fee Received: £12,000,000 from Tottenham H for Wilson Palacios, March 2009.

Record Transfer Fee Paid: £6,000,000 to Newcastle U for Charles N'Zogbia, February 2009.

Football League Record: 1978 Elected to Division 4; 1982–92 Division 3; 1992–93 Division 2; 1993–97 Division 3; 1997–2003 Division 2; 2003–04 Division 1; 2004–05 FL C; 2005– FA Premier League.

LATEST SEQUENCES

Longest Sequence of League Wins: 11, 2.11.2002 – 18.1.2003.

Longest Sequence of League Defeats: 8, 13.12.2006 – 30.1.2007.

Longest Sequence of League Draws: 6, 11.12.2001 – 5.1.2002.

Longest Sequence of Unbeaten League Matches: 25, 8.5.1999 – 3.1.2000.

Longest Sequence Without a League Win: 14, 9.5.1989 – 17.10.1989.

Successive Scoring Runs: 24 from 27.4.1996.

Successive Non-scoring Runs: 4 from 15.4.1995.

MANAGERS

Charlie Spencer 1932–37
Jimmy Milne 1946–47
Bob Pryde 1949–52
Ted Goodier 1952–54
Walter Crook 1954–55
Ron Suart 1955–56
Billy Cooke 1956
Sam Barkas 1957
Trevor Hitchen 1957–58
Malcolm Barrass 1958–59
Jimmy Shirley 1959
Pat Murphy 1959–60
Allenby Chilton 1960
Johnny Ball 1961–63
Allan Brown 1963–66
Alf Craig 1966–67
Harry Leyland 1967–68
Alan Saunders 1968
Ian McNeill 1968–70
Gordon Milne 1970–72
Les Rigby 1972–74
Brian Tiler 1974–76
Ian McNeill 1976–81
Larry Lloyd 1981–83
Harry McNally 1983–85
Bryan Hamilton 1985–86
Ray Mathias 1986–89
Bryan Hamilton 1989–93
Dave Philpotts 1993
Kenny Swain 1993–94
Graham Barrow 1994–95
John Deehan 1995–98
Ray Mathias 1998–99
John Benson 1999–2000
Bruce Rioch 2000–01
Steve Bruce 2001
Paul Jewell 2001–07
Chris Hutchings 2007
Steve Bruce 2007–09
Roberto Martinez June 2009–

TEN YEAR LEAGUE RECORD

		P	W	D	L	F	A	Pts	Pos
1999-2000	Div 2	46	22	17	7	72	38	83	4
2000-01	Div 2	46	19	18	9	53	42	75	6
2001-02	Div 2	46	16	16	14	66	51	64	10
2002-03	Div 2	46	29	13	4	68	25	100	1
2003-04	Div 1	46	18	17	11	60	45	71	7
2004-05	FL C	46	25	12	9	79	35	87	2
2005-06	PR Lge	38	15	6	17	45	52	51	10
2006-07	PR Lge	38	10	8	20	37	59	38	17
2007-08	PR Lge	38	10	10	18	34	51	40	14
2008-09	PR Lge	38	12	9	17	34	45	45	11

DID YOU KNOW ?

Harry Lyon was the leading goalscorer for Wigan Athletic in their Cheshire League days during the early 1960s. He hit 174 for the club in this competition and overall remains the club's leading FA Cup marksman with 20 goals. He also kept goal in two Cup finals!

WIGAN ATHLETIC 2008–09 LEAGUE RECORD

Match No.	Date	Venue	Opponents	Result	H/T Score	Lg. Pos.	Goalscorers	Attendance
1	Aug 16	A	West Ham U	L	1-2	0-2	—	Zaki [47]	32,758
2	24	H	Chelsea	L	0-1	0-1	19		18,139
3	30	A	Hull C	W	5-0	2-0	13	Ricketts (og) [5], Valencia [13], Zaki 2 [63, 81], Heskey [68]	24,282
4	Sept 13	H	Sunderland	D	1-1	0-1	11	Zaki [78]	18,015
5	21	A	Tottenham H	D	0-0	0-0	14		35,808
6	28	H	Manchester C	W	2-1	2-1	10	Valencia [16], Zaki (pen) [34]	18,214
7	Oct 4	H	Middlesbrough	L	0-1	0-0	13		16,806
8	18	A	Liverpool	L	2-3	2-1	14	Zaki 2 [29, 45]	43,868
9	26	H	Aston Villa	L	0-4	0-1	15		20,249
10	29	A	Fulham	L	0-2	0-1	—		22,500
11	Nov 1	H	Portsmouth	W	2-1	1-0	16	Zaki (pen) [45], Heskey [90]	18,416
12	8	H	Stoke C	D	0-0	0-0	17		15,881
13	15	A	Newcastle U	D	2-2	1-0	16	Taylor [3], Bramble [89]	47,657
14	24	H	Everton	W	1-0	0-0	—	Camara [51]	18,344
15	29	H	WBA	W	2-1	0-0	11	Camara [61], Boyce [87]	17,054
16	Dec 6	A	Arsenal	L	0-1	0-1	11		59,317
17	13	H	Blackburn R	W	3-0	2-0	9	Heskey [10], Valencia [12], Cattermole [77]	18,003
18	26	H	Newcastle U	W	2-1	1-0	9	Taylor [29], Zaki (pen) [73]	20,266
19	28	A	Bolton W	W	1-0	1-0	7	Zaki (pen) [44]	23,726
20	Jan 11	H	Tottenham H	W	1-0	0-0	7	Figueroa [90]	17,500
21	14	A	Manchester U	L	0-1	0-1	—		73,917
22	17	A	Manchester C	L	0-1	0-0	7		41,262
23	28	H	Liverpool	D	1-1	0-1	—	Mido (pen) [83]	21,237
24	31	A	Aston Villa	D	0-0	0-0	7		41,766
25	Feb 7	H	Fulham	D	0-0	0-0	7		16,499
26	21	A	Middlesbrough	D	0-0	0-0	7		24,020
27	28	A	Chelsea	L	1-2	0-1	8	Kapo [82]	40,714
28	Mar 4	H	West Ham U	L	0-1	0-1	—		14,169
29	14	A	Sunderland	W	2-1	2-1	8	Watson [12], N'Zogbia [45]	39,266
30	22	H	Hull C	W	1-0	0-0	7	Watson [84]	17,689
31	Apr 5	A	Everton	L	0-4	0-1	8		34,427
32	11	H	Arsenal	L	1-4	1-0	10	Mido [18]	22,954
33	26	A	Blackburn R	L	0-2	0-1	11		25,019
34	May 2	H	Bolton W	D	0-0	0-0	11		18,655
35	9	A	WBA	L	1-3	1-1	11	Rodallega [17]	24,741
36	13	H	Manchester U	L	1-2	1-0	—	Rodallega [28]	21,286
37	16	A	Stoke C	L	0-2	0-0	12		25,641
38	24	H	Portsmouth	W	1-0	1-0	11	Rodallega [26]	17,696

Final League Position: 11

GOALSCORERS

League (34): Zaki 10 (4 pens), Heskey 3, Rodallega 3, Valencia 3, Camara 2, Mido 2 (1 pen), Taylor 2, Watson 2, Boyce 1, Bramble 1, Cattermole 1, Figueroa 1, Kapo 1, N'Zogbia 1, own goal 1.
Carling Cup (8): Camara 3, Cattermole 1, Kapo 1, Kupisz 1, Scharner 1, Zaki 1.
FA Cup (1): Camara 1.

Kirkland C 32	Melchiot M 33+1	Figueroa M 38	Palacios W 21	Boyce E 26+1	Scharner P 27+2	Valencia L 31	Cattermole L 33	Heskey E 20	Kapo O 10+9	Zaki A 22+7	De Ridder D 5+13	Koumas J 5+11	Sibierski A —+3	Pollitt M 3	Camara H 3+14	Bramble T 35	Kilbane K 3+7	Brown M 18+7	Taylor R 11+1	Mido 10+2	Rodallega H 9+6	Watson B 6+4	N'Zogbia C 13	Edman E —+2	Kingson R 3+1	Routledge J —+1	McManaman C —+1	Cho W 1	Match No.
1	2^{1}	3	4	5	6^{2}	7	8^{3}	9	10	11	12	13	14																1
	2^{1}	3	4^{2}	5		7	8	9	13	10	14	11^{3}		1	12	6													2
1	2	3	4	5		7	8^{1}	9^{2}	12	10						13	6	11^{3}	14										3
1	2	3	4^{1}	5	14	7	8^{4}	9	12	10^{3}						6		11^{2}											4
1	2	3	4	5	8	7		9	12	10^{2}	11^{1}				13	6													5
1	2	3	4	5		7	8^{1}	9	10	11					6	12													6
1	2	3	4^{3}		6	7	8	9	10^{1}	11^{2}	12		14		13	5													7
1	2	3	4^{1}		6	7^{4}	8	9^{3}	10^{2}	11	12					5	14	13											8
1		3	4	2	6	7^{2}	8^{3}	9	10^{1}	11	12					5	14	13											9
1	2	3^{1}	4^{2}	5	6	7	8^{3}	9	10		12	13	14					11											10
1	2	3	4	5		7	8	9	10^{1}	11	12					6													11
1	2	3	4	5		7	8	9^{1}	10	11	12					6													12
1		3	4	5^{5}	11	7	8	9^{2}	10^{3}		12	13	14		6	13	14	2^{1}											13
1		3	4		6	7	8	9	10^{1}		12				2	5		11											14
1	12	3^{3}	4	5	6	7	8	9	10			13	14			6	14	11^{2}	2^{1}										15
1	2	3	4	5^{3}	6	7	8^{2}	9	10^{1}		12	13	14			6		11											16
1	2^{2}	3			6	7^{1}	8	9^{3}	10		12	13	14		5		4	11											17
1	2	3	4^{2}		6	7	8	9^{1}	10		12	13	14		5			11^{3}											18
	2	3	4		6	7	8	9^{1}	10^{3}		12	13	14	1	12	5	13	11^{2}											19
1	2	3	4		6	7	8	9	10							5		11											20
1	2	3	4		6	7	8^{3}	9	10^{1}		12	13	14			5		11^{2}											21
1	2	3^{1}	4		6	7	8	9	10		12	13	14			5^{3}		11^{2}											22
	2	3		5	6		8		10^{3}		7^{1}	12		1		13	4	11^{2}	9	14									23
1	2	3		5	4^{2}		8		7^{1}	10						6		11	9	12		13							24
1	2	3		6	7^{3}	8					12	13				5	4^{2}				9^{1}	10	14	11					25
1	2	3		5			8	9^{2}	10^{1}		12				6	4			7			13	11						26
1	2	3		5	6		8^{2}	9	10^{1}		12					4	7					13	11						27
1	2	3		5	12	7	8^{4}		10^{2}						6^{3}		4^{1}				9	13	14	11					28
1	2	3		5	4	7					12				6						9^{1}	10	11	8					29
1	2	3		5	4^{1}						12	13	14		6		8				9^{2}	10	7	11^{3}					30
1	2	3		5	8	7^{2}						13			6		10^{1}				9	12	4	11					31
1	2	3^{1}	4	5	8	7					12	13	14		6		11^{2}				9^{1}	10	4^{3}						32
1		3^{2}		2	6	7	8		14	12	13				5						9^{1}	10	4^{3}	11					33
1	2^{1}	3		5	12	6^{2}	7	8		14					5	4	9^{3}	10					11	13					34
1^{6}	2	3		6	7	8	9	12^{2}	13						5	4		10				11^{1}		15					35
	2	3		5		7	8								4	10	12	9	11^{1}										36
	2	3^{3}		5	6		8								4	10^{2}	13	9	12	11	14	1					7^{1}		37
	2	3		5		7	8		10^{2}						4	6		9				11^{1}			1	13	12		38

FA Cup
Third Round   Tottenham H   (a)   1-3

Carling Cup
Second Round   Notts Co   (h)   4-0
Third Round   Ipswich T   (a)   4-1
Fourth Round   Arsenal   (a)   0-3

WOLVERHAMPTON WANDERERS   FA Premiership

FOUNDATION

Enthusiasts of the game at St Luke's School, Blakenhall formed a club in 1877. In the same neighbourhood a cricket club called Blakenhall Wanderers had a football section. Several St Luke's footballers played cricket for them and shortly before the start of the 1879–80 season the two amalgamated and Wolverhampton Wanderers FC was brought into being.

Molineux, Waterloo Road, Wolverhampton WV1 4QR.
Telephone: (0871) 222 2220.

Fax: (01902) 687 006.

Ticket Office: (0871) 222 1877.

Website: wolves.co.uk

Email: info@wolves.co.uk

Ground Capacity: 28,565.

Record Attendance: 61,315 v Liverpool, FA Cup 5th rd, 11 February 1939.

Pitch Measurements: 110yd × 75yd.

Chairman: Steve Morgan OBE.

Chief Executive: Jez Moxey.

Secretary: Richard Skirrow.

Manager: Mick McCarthy.

Assistant Manager: Terry Connor.

Physio: Steve Kemp.

Colours: Old gold shirts with black trim, black shorts, old gold stockings with black tops.

Change Colours: All black with light green cuffs on sleeves and collar.

Year Formed: 1877* (*see Foundation*).

Turned Professional: 1888.

Ltd Co.: 1923 (but current club is WWFC (1986) Ltd).

Previous Names: 1879, St Luke's combined with Wanderers Cricket Club to become Wolverhampton Wanderers (1923) Ltd. New limited companies followed in 1982 and 1986 (current).

Club Nickname: 'Wolves'.

Grounds: 1877, Windmill Field; 1879, John Harper's Field; 1881, Dudley Road; 1889, Molineux.

First Football League Game: 8 September 1888, Football League, v Aston Villa (h) D 1–1 – Baynton; Baugh, Mason; Fletcher, Allen, Lowder; Hunter, Cooper, Anderson, White, Cannon, (1 og).

Record League Victory: 10–1 v Leicester C, Division 1, 15 April 1938 – Sidlow; Morris, Dowen; Galley, Cullis, Gardiner; Maguire (1), Horace Wright, Westcott (4), Jones (1), Dorsett (4).

HONOURS

Football League: Division 1 – Champions 1953–54, 1957–58, 1958–59; Runners-up 1937–38, 1938–39, 1949–50, 1954–55, 1959–60; Division 2 – Champions 1931–32, 1976–77; Runners-up 1966–67, 1982–83; FL C – Champions 2008–09; Division 3 (N) – Champions 1923–24; Division 3 – Champions 1988–89; Division 4 – Champions 1987–88.

FA Cup: Winners 1893, 1908, 1949, 1960; Runners-up 1889, 1896, 1921, 1939.

Football League Cup: Winners 1974, 1980.

Texaco Cup: Winners 1971.

Sherpa Van Trophy: Winners 1988.

European Competitions: *European Cup:* 1958–59, 1959–60. *European Cup-Winners' Cup:* 1960–61. *UEFA Cup:* 1971–72 (runners-up), 1973–74, 1974–75, 1980–81.

SKY SPORTS FACT FILE

On 20 December 2008 substitute Neill Collins was upgraded to a starter when centre-back Michael Mancienne fell ill with a severe migraine in the pre-match warm-up against Doncaster Rovers. Collins then scored the only goal of the match in the 81st minute.

Record Cup Victory: 14–0 v Crosswell's Brewery, FA Cup 2nd rd, 13 November 1886 – I. Griffiths; Baugh, Mason; Pearson, Allen (1), Lowder; Hunter (4), Knight (2), Brodie (4), B. Griffiths (2), Wood. Plus one goal 'scrambled through'.

Record Defeat: 1–10 v Newton Heath, Division 1, 15 October 1892.

Most League Points (2 for a win): 64, Division 1, 1957–58.

Most League Points (3 for a win): 92, Division 3, 1988–89.

Most League Goals: 115, Division 2, 1931–32.

Highest League Scorer in Season: Dennis Westcott, 38, Division 1, 1946–47.

Most League Goals in Total Aggregate: Steve Bull, 250, 1986–99.

Most League Goals in One Match: 5, Joe Butcher v Accrington, Division 1, 19 November 1892; 5, Tom Phillipson v Barnsley, Division 2, 26 April 1926; 5, Tom Phillipson v Bradford C, Division 2, 25 December 1926; 5, Billy Hartill v Notts Co, Division 2, 12 October 1929; 5, Billy Hartill v Aston Villa, Division 1, 3 September 1934.

Most Capped Player: Billy Wright, 105, England (70 consecutive).

Most League Appearances: Derek Parkin, 501, 1967–82.

Youngest League Player: Jimmy Mullen, 16 years 43 days v Leeds U, 18 February 1939.

Record Transfer Fee Received: £6,000,000 from Coventry C for Robbie Keane, August 1999.

Record Transfer Fee Paid: £3,500,000 to Bristol C for Ade Akinbiyi, September 1999.

MANAGERS

George Worrall 1877–85
  (Secretary-Manager)
John Addenbrooke 1885–1922
George Jobey 1922–24
Albert Hoskins 1924–26
  (had been Secretary since 1922)
Fred Scotchbrook 1926–27
Major Frank Buckley 1927–44
Ted Vizard 1944–48
Stan Cullis 1948–64
Andy Beattie 1964–65
Ronnie Allen 1966–68
Bill McGarry 1968–76
Sammy Chung 1976–78
John Barnwell 1978–81
Ian Greaves 1982
Graham Hawkins 1982–84
Tommy Docherty 1984–85
Bill McGarry 1985
Sammy Chapman 1985–86
Brian Little 1986
Graham Turner 1986–94
Graham Taylor 1994–95
Mark McGhee 1995–98
Colin Lee 1998–2000
Dave Jones 2001–04
Glenn Hoddle 2004–06
Mick McCarthy July 2006–

Football League Record: 1888 Founder Member of Football League: 1906–23 Division 2; 1923–24 Division 3 (N); 1924–32 Division 2; 1932–65 Division 1; 1965–67 Division 2; 1967–76 Division 1; 1976–77 Division 2; 1977–82 Division 1; 1982–83 Division 2; 1983–84 Division 1; 1984–85 Division 2; 1985–86 Division 3; 1986–88 Division 4; 1988–89 Division 3; 1989–92 Division 2; 1992–2003 Division 1; 2003–04 FA Premier League; 2004–09 FL C; 2009– FA Premier League.

LATEST SEQUENCES

Longest Sequence of League Wins: 8, 15.10.1988 – 26.11.1988.
Longest Sequence of League Defeats: 8, 5.12.1981 – 13.2.1982.
Longest Sequence of League Draws: 6, 22.4.1995 – 20.8.1995.
Longest Sequence of Unbeaten League Matches: 21, 15.1.2005 – 13.8.2005.
Longest Sequence Without a League Win: 19, 1.12.1984 – 6.4.1985.
Successive Scoring Runs: 41 from 20.12.1958.
Successive Non-scoring Runs: 7 from 2.2.1985.

TEN YEAR LEAGUE RECORD

		P	W	D	L	F	A	Pts	Pos
1999-2000	Div 1	46	21	11	14	64	48	74	7
2000-01	Div 1	46	14	13	19	45	48	55	12
2001-02	Div 1	46	25	11	10	76	43	86	3
2002-03	Div 1	46	20	16	10	81	44	76	5
2003-04	PR Lge	38	7	12	19	38	77	33	20
2004-05	FL C	46	15	21	10	72	59	66	9
2005-06	FL C	46	16	19	11	50	42	67	7
2006-07	FL C	46	22	10	14	59	56	76	5
2007-08	FL C	46	18	16	12	53	48	70	7
2008-09	FL C	46	27	9	10	80	52	90	1

DID YOU KNOW ?

On 18 April 2009 Wolverhampton Wanderers' 1–0 win over Queens Park Rangers ensured their promotion to the Premier League. It was 50 years to the day that they had beaten Luton Town 5–0 at Molineux to win the First Division title.

WOLVERHAMPTON WANDERERS 2008–09 LEAGUE RECORD

Match No.	Date	Venue	Opponents	Result	H/T Score	Lg. Pos.	Goalscorers	Attendance
1	Aug 9	A	Plymouth Arg	D 2-2	1-1	—	Kightly [19], Vokes [78]	14,789
2	16	H	Sheffield W	W 4-1	1-1	4	Iwelumo 2 [28, 59], Ebanks-Blake (pen) [54], Edwards D [90]	22,491
3	23	A	Ipswich T	W 2-0	1-0	2	Ebanks-Blake [21], Edwards D [78]	21,483
4	30	H	Nottingham F	W 5-1	4-0	1	Jones David [14], Morgan (og) [29], Kightly 2 [43, 62], Iwelumo [45]	25,301
5	Sept 13	A	Charlton Ath	W 3-1	0-1	1	Ebanks-Blake (pen) [61], Vokes 2 [81, 87]	21,547
6	16	H	Crystal Palace	W 2-1	1-1	—	Ebanks-Blake [1], Keogh [58]	22,200
7	20	A	Preston NE	W 3-1	1-0	1	Iwelumo 3 (1 pen) [36, 66, 72 (p)]	17,567
8	27	H	Bristol C	W 2-0	1-0	1	Kightly [17], Ebanks-Blake [68]	24,324
9	30	H	Reading	L 0-3	0-1	—		24,302
10	Oct 4	A	Swansea C	L 1-3	1-2	2	Keogh [16]	17,556
11	18	H	Coventry C	W 2-1	1-1	1	Kightly [42], Ebanks-Blake [59]	25,893
12	21	A	Norwich C	L 2-5	1-2	—	Collins [41], Ebanks-Blake (pen) [67]	24,351
13	25	A	Watford	W 3-2	2-1	2	Iwelumo [1], Jones David [40], Gray [71]	16,386
14	28	H	Swansea C	W 2-1	1-0	—	Ebanks-Blake 2 [45, 57]	21,988
15	Nov 1	A	Cardiff C	W 2-1	2-1	1	Iwelumo [4], Ebanks-Blake [8]	17,734
16	8	H	Burnley	W 2-0	1-0	1	Kightly 2 [31, 75]	23,711
17	15	A	Southampton	W 2-1	2-1	1	Iwelumo [8], Jones David [17]	17,812
18	22	H	Blackpool	W 2-0	1-0	1	Iwelumo 2 [30, 66]	22,044
19	25	A	Sheffield U	W 3-1	1-0	—	Iwelumo 2 [5, 59], Ebanks-Blake [63]	27,111
20	29	H	Birmingham C	D 1-1	0-0	1	Ebanks-Blake [74]	26,329
21	Dec 6	A	QPR	L 0-1	0-0	1		13,416
22	9	H	Derby Co	W 3-0	2-0	—	Ebanks-Blake 2 (1 pen) [2 (p), 58], Edwards D [40]	21,326
23	13	H	Barnsley	W 2-0	1-0	1	Hassell (og) [19], Foley [86]	22,399
24	20	A	Doncaster R	W 1-0	0-0	1	Collins [81]	13,669
25	26	H	Sheffield U	D 1-1	1-1	1	Collins [19]	27,106
26	29	A	Blackpool	D 2-2	1-1	—	Ebanks-Blake (pen) [4], Jarvis [70]	8906
27	Jan 10	H	Preston NE	L 1-3	1-2	—	Ebanks-Blake [20]	26,138
28	17	A	Bristol C	D 2-2	1-0	1	Collins [45], Jarvis [54]	16,749
29	27	A	Reading	L 0-1	0-1	—		23,009
30	31	H	Watford	W 3-1	1-0	1	Ebanks-Blake [23], Keogh [67], Vokes [90]	23,571
31	Feb 3	H	Norwich C	D 3-3	1-1	—	Ebanks-Blake 3 [25, 54, 56]	21,654
32	7	A	Coventry C	L 1-2	0-1	1	Vokes [72]	21,167
33	14	A	Burnley	L 0-1	0-1	1		13,515
34	22	H	Cardiff C	D 2-2	1-1	1	Ebanks-Blake [11], Konstantopoulos (og) [81]	22,093
35	28	H	Plymouth Arg	L 0-1	0-1	1		25,710
36	Mar 3	A	Crystal Palace	W 1-0	0-0	—	Ebanks-Blake (pen) [74]	14,907
37	7	A	Sheffield W	W 1-0	1-0	1	Ebanks-Blake [5]	23,703
38	10	H	Ipswich T	D 0-0	0-0	—		22,227
39	14	H	Charlton Ath	W 2-1	1-0	1	Iwelumo [36], Ebanks-Blake [79]	24,319
40	21	A	Nottingham F	W 1-0	0-0	1	Kightly [76]	24,510
41	Apr 6	A	Birmingham C	L 0-2	0-1	—		25,935
42	10	H	Southampton	W 3-0	3-0	—	Vokes [1], Craddock [6], Jones David (pen) [19]	24,636
43	13	A	Derby Co	W 3-2	1-1	1	Keogh 2 [7, 87], Jarvis [74]	33,079
44	18	H	QPR	W 1-0	0-0	1	Ebanks-Blake [46]	27,511
45	25	A	Barnsley	D 1-1	0-0	1	Reid [84]	18,288
46	May 3	H	Doncaster R	W 1-0	0-0	1	Stearman [90]	28,252

Final League Position: 1

GOALSCORERS

League (80): Ebanks-Blake 25 (6 pens), Iwelumo 14 (1 pen), Kightly 8, Vokes 6, Keogh 5, Collins 4, Jones David 4 (1 pen), Edwards D 3, Jarvis 3, Craddock 1, Foley 1, Gray 1, Reid 1, Stearman 1, own goals 3.
Carling Cup (3): Iwelumo 2, Davies 1.
FA Cup (3): Vokes 2, Keogh 1.

Hennessey W 34 + 1	Foley K 45	Elokobi G 3 + 1	Jones David 31 + 3	Craddock J 17	Stearman R 32 + 5	Kightly M 37 + 1	Henry K 42 + 1	Keogh A 21 + 21	Ebanks-Blake S 41	Ward S 38 + 4	Jarvis M 21 + 7	Iwelumo C 25 + 6	Vokes S 4 + 32	Collins N 20 + 3	Edwards D 23 + 21	Ward D — + 1	Gray M 4 + 4	Shackell J 3 + 9	Ikeme C 12	Friend G 4 + 2	Edwards C 5 + 1	Mancienne M 8 + 2	Hill M 13	Quashie N 3	Reid K 3 + 5	Berra C 15	Harewood M 2 + 3	Hemmings A — + 2	Match No.
1	2	3	4	5	6	7	8	9^{1}	10^{3}	11^{2}	12	13	14																1
1	2	3	4	5^{1}	6	7^{2}	8	14	10	11^{3}	9	12	13																2
1	2	3^{1}	4		6	7^{2}	8	13	10^{3}	11	9			5	12	14													3
1	2		4		6	7^{1}	8	14	10^{3}	3	11^{2}	9		5	13		12												4
1	2		4		6	7	8	9^{2}	10^{3}	11^{1}		12		5	14		13												5
1	2		4^{1}		6	7	8	9	10^{3}	3	11^{2}			5	12		13	14											6
1●	2		4^{2}		6	7	8	12	10^{1}	3	11^{3}	9●		5	13			14											7
	2		4		6	7^{3}	8	9	10^{1}	3	11^{2}	12		5			13	14	1										8
1	2	3			6	7^{1}	4	9	10	11^{3}	8^{2}	12		5			13	14											9
	2		4		6		8	9	10		12			5	7			13	1	3^{1}	11^{2}								10
	2		4		6	7	8	9^{1}	10^{3}	3^{2}	11			5	12		13		1		14								11
	2		12		6●	7^{1}	8	13	10	3	9^{3}			5	4		14		1		11^{2}								12
	2		4			7	8	12	10^{1}	3	9^{2}	13		5	14				1	6		11^{3}							13
	2		4			7^{2}	8	12	10	3	9			5	13				1		6^{1}	11^{3}	14						14
	2		4		6	7^{2}	8	12	10^{1}	11	9			14	13		3^{3}		1	5									15
	2		4		6	7	8	12	10^{2}	3	9^{1}	13		14					1	5		11^{3}							16
	2		4		6	7^{2}	8	12	10^{1}	3	9	13		14					1	5		11^{3}							17
	2		4		6^{3}	7		12	10^{1}	3	9^{2}	13		5	8		11		14	1									18
15	2		4^{1}		6	7	8		10	3	9			5	11^{2}							12	16	13					19
1	2		4^{3}		6	7	8	12	10^{1}	3	9^{2}			13			4			5		11^{1}							20
1	2	11^{3}			6	7	8	12	10^{1}	3	9^{2}	14		13			4			5									21
1	2				6	7^{2}	8	9	10^{1}	11^{3}		14		12	13		4			5	3								22
1	2		12		6	7^{3}	8	9^{2}	10	11		14		13			4^{1}			5	3								23
1	2				6	7	8	9^{2}	10^{1}	11		14		13	12		4			5	3								24
1	2				6	7	8	12	10^{1}	3^{3}	11^{2}	9		13	5		4				14								25
1	2		12		6		8		10	11	9^{3}	14		13			4			7^{1}	3^{2}	5							26
	2					7	8	12	10	3	11	9^{2}		13	5		4		1			6^{1}							27
1	2		4		6	7	8	9	10^{1}		11^{2}	12		5	14		13				3^{3}								28
1	2				6	7	8	9^{1}	10	3	11^{2}	12		13	5		14				4^{3}								29
1	2		4	5	6	7^{3}	8	9	10^{2}	3		12		13			14								11^{1}				30
1	2		4	5	6	7^{2}	8	9^{3}	10	3	11^{1}	12		13											14				31
1	2				6	7^{3}	8^{2}		10	3	11	9^{1}		12			13							4	14	5			32
1	2				6	7	8		10	3	11	12	9^{1}				13							4^{2}		5			33
1	2			5	12	7	8	9^{2}	10	3^{1}	11^{3}			13									4		14	6			34
1	2			5		7	8	9^{3}	10	3^{1}				13						14			4		12	11^{2}	6		35
1	2			5	12	7^{1}	8		10^{2}		9^{3}			14			13					4			11	3	6		36
1	2		8	5	12	7^{1}			10^{2}	14	9						13					4			11^{3}	3	6		37
1	2		8	5	12				10	11	9^{3}			14			13				7^{1}	4			3^{2}		6		38
1	2		8	5	12	7	14		10^{2}	11^{3}	9						13					4^{1}				3	6		39
1	2		4^{3}	5		7	8	12	10	11^{1}	9^{2}			13								14				3	6		40
1	2			5		7	8	12		11	9^{1}			13							4^{3}		14		3^{2}	6	10		41
1	2^{3}			5	14	7	8	9	10^{5}	11^{1}				13									14		4	3	6	12	42
1	2			5		7	8	9	10^{1}	11			14				13				3^{3}				4^{2}	6	12	43
1	2			5	14	7^{2}	8	9	10^{1}	3^{3}	11						13								4	6	12	44
1	2			5			8	9^{3}		3	11^{1}	7	12				13								4	6	10^{2}	14	45
1	7	14		5	2		8	9	10^{2}	3	11^{1}	12									4^{3}					6		13	46

FA Cup

Third Round	Birmingham C	(a)	2-0
Fourth Round	Middlesbrough	(h)	1-2

Carling Cup

First Round	Accrington S	(h)	3-2
Second Round	Rotherham U	(a)	0-0

WYCOMBE WANDERERS FL Championship 1

FOUNDATION

In 1887 a group of young furniture trade workers called a meeting at the Steam Engine public house with the aim of forming a football club and entering junior football. It is thought that they were named after the famous FA Cup winners, The Wanderers who had visited the town in 1877 for a tie with the original High Wycombe club. It is also possible that they played informally before their formation, although there is no proof of this.

Adams Park, Hillbottom Road, Sands, High Wycombe HP12 4HJ.

Telephone: (01494) 472 100.

Fax: (01494) 527 633.

Ticket Office: (01494) 441 118.

Website: www.wwfc.com

Email: wwfc@wwfc.com

Ground Capacity: 10,000.

Record Attendance: 9,921 v Fulham, FA Cup 3rd rd, 9 January 2002.

Pitch Measurements: 115yd × 75yd.

Chairman: Ivor L. Beeks.

Managing Director: Steve Hayes.

Secretary: Keith Allen.

Manager: Peter Taylor.

Assistant Manager: Ian Culverhouse.

First Team Coach: Junior Lewis.

Physio: Shay Connolly.

Colours: Light blue and dark blue quartered shirts, light blue shorts, light blue stockings.

Change Colours: Red and white quartered shirts, red shorts, red stockings.

Year Formed: 1887.

Turned Professional: 1974.

Club Nicknames: 'Chairboys' (after High Wycombe's tradition of furniture making), 'The Blues'.

Grounds: 1887, The Rye; 1893, Spring Meadow; 1895, Loakes Park; 1899, Daws Hill Park; 1901, Loakes Park; 1990, Adams Park.

First Football League Game: 14 August 1993, Division 3 v Carlisle U (a) D 2–2: Hyde; Cousins, Horton (Langford), Kerr, Crossley, Ryan, Carroll, Stapleton, Thompson, Scott, Guppy (1) (Hutchinson), (1 og).

Record League Victory: 5–0 v Burnley, Division 2, 15 April 1997 – Parkin; Cousins, Bell, Kavanagh, McCarthy, Forsyth, Carroll (2p) (Simpson), Scott (Farrell), Stallard (1), McGavin (1) (Read (1)), Brown.

HONOURS

Football League: Division 2 best season: 6th, 1994–95.

FA Amateur Cup: Winners 1931.

FA Trophy: Winners 1991, 1993.

GM Vauxhall Conference: Winners 1992–93.

FA Cup: semi-final 2001.

Football League Cup: semi-final 2007.

SKY SPORTS FACT FILE

Centre-forward Fred 'Sonny' Rouse – who drove a horse bus – was the first Wycombe Wanderers player to follow a professional career after leaving the club from 1902 with Grimsby Town, Stoke, Chelsea, Everton and West Bromwich Albion.

Record Cup Victory: 5–0 v Hitchin T (a), FA Cup 2nd rd, 3 December 1994 – Hyde; Cousins, Brown, Crossley, Evans, Ryan (1), Carroll, Bell (1), Thompson, Garner (3) (Hemmings), Stapleton (Langford).

Record Defeat: 0–5 v Walsall, Auto Windscreens Shield 1st rd, 7 November 1995.

Most League Points (3 for a win): 78, Division 2, 1994–95; 78, FL 2, 2007–08; 78, FL 2, 2008–09.

Most League Goals: 72, FL 2, 2005–06.

Highest League Goalscorer in Season: Scott McGleish, 25, 2007–08.

Most League Goals in Total Aggregate: Nathan Tyson, 42, 2004–06.

Most League Goals in One Match: 3, Miquel Desouza v Bradford C, Division 2, 2 September 1995; 3, John Williams v Stockport Co, Division 2, 24 February 1996; 3, Mark Stallard v Walsall, Division 2, 21 October 1997; 3, Sean Devine v Reading, Division 2, 2 October 1999; 3, Sean Divine v Bury, Division 2, 26 February 2000; 3, Nathan Tyson v Lincoln C, FL 2, 5 March 2005; 3, Nathan Tyson v Kidderminster H, FL 2, 2 April 2005; 3, Nathan Tyson v Stockport Co, FL 2, 10 September 2005; 3, Kevin Betsy v Mansfield T, FL 2, 24 September 2005; 3, Scott McGleish v Mansfield T, FL 2, 8 January 2008.

Most Capped Player: Mark Rogers, 7, Canada.

Most League Appearances: Steve Brown, 371, 1994–2004.

Youngest League Player: Ikechi Anya, 16 years 279 days v Scunthorpe U, 8 October 2004.

Record Transfer Fee Received: £600,000 from Nottingham F for Nathan Tyson, January 2006.

Record Transfer Fee Paid: £200,000 to Barnet for Sean Devine, 15 April 1999.

Football League Record: 1993 Promoted to Division 3 from GM Vauxhall Conference; 1993–94 Division 3; 1994–2004 Division 2; 2004–09 FL 2; 2009– FL 1.

MANAGERS

First coach appointed 1951. *Prior to Brian Lee's appointment in 1969 the team was selected by a Match Committee which met every Monday evening.*

James McCormack 1951–52
Sid Cann 1952–61
Graham Adams 1961–62
Don Welsh 1962–64
Barry Darvill 1964–68
Brian Lee 1969–76
Ted Powell 1976–77
John Reardon 1977–78
Andy Williams 1978–80
Mike Keen 1980–84
Paul Bence 1984–86
Alan Gane 1986–87
Peter Suddaby 1987–88
Jim Kelman 1988–90
Martin O'Neill 1990–95
Alan Smith 1995–96
John Gregory 1996–98
Neil Smillie 1998–99
Lawrie Sanchez 1999–2003
Tony Adams 2003–04
John Gorman 2004–06
Paul Lambert 2006–08
Peter Taylor May 2008–

LATEST SEQUENCES

Longest Sequence of League Wins: 6, 19.8.2006 – 16.9.2006.

Longest Sequence of League Defeats: 6, 18.3.2006 – 17.4.2006.

Longest Sequence of League Draws: 5, 24.1.2004 – 21.2.2004.

Longest Sequence of Unbeaten League Matches: 21, 6.8.2005 – 10.12.2005.

Longest Sequence Without a League Win: 13, 16.8.2003 – 18.10.2003 and 10.1.2004 – 20.3.2004.

Successive Scoring Runs: 15 from 28.12.2004.

Successive Non-scoring Runs: 5 from 15.10.1996.

TEN YEAR LEAGUE RECORD

		P	W	D	L	F	A	Pts	Pos
1999-2000	Div 2	46	16	13	17	56	53	61	12
2000-01	Div 2	46	15	14	17	46	53	59	13
2001-02	Div 2	46	17	13	16	58	64	64	11
2002-03	Div 2	46	13	13	20	59	66	52	18
2003-04	Div 2	46	6	19	21	50	75	37	24
2004-05	FL 2	46	17	14	15	58	52	65	10
2005-06	FL 2	46	18	17	11	72	56	71	6
2006-07	FL 2	46	16	14	16	52	47	62	12
2007-08	FL 2	46	22	12	12	56	42	78	7
2008-09	FL 2	46	20	18	8	54	33	78	3

DID YOU KNOW ?

The foundation of their Isthmian League title in 1971–72 was a run of eleven successive wins from 25 September to 13 November. Five of the Wycombe Wanderers reached double figures in scoring from an impressive total of 102 goals.

WYCOMBE WANDERERS 2008–09 LEAGUE RECORD

Match No.	Date		Venue	Opponents	Result	H/T Score	Lg. Pos.	Goalscorers	Attendance
1	Aug	9	H	Morecambe	D 1-1	1-0	—	Spence [34]	4021
2		16	A	Chester C	W 2-0	1-0	6	Mousinho [26], McGleish (pen) [67]	1419
3		23	H	Lincoln C	W 1-0	1-0	5	Woodman [15]	4112
4		30	A	Chesterfield	W 1-0	1-0	4	Williamson [4]	3175
5	Sept	6	A	Rochdale	W 1-0	1-0	1	Zebroski [31]	2880
6		13	H	Brentford	D 0-0	0-0	3		5799
7		20	H	Dagenham & R	W 2-1	1-0	2	Williamson 2 [34, 68]	4132
8		27	A	Bury	D 0-0	0-0	2		3597
9	Oct	4	H	Bournemouth	W 3-1	1-0	1	Harrold [40], Zebroski [60], McGleish [84]	5005
10		11	A	Grimsby T	D 1-1	0-1	1	Johnson [90]	4562
11		18	H	Darlington	D 1-1	1-0	1	McGleish (pen) [90]	5345
12		21	A	Barnet	D 1-1	0-1	—	Zebroski [68]	2258
13		25	A	Accrington S	W 1-0	0-0	1	Zebroski [90]	1217
14	Nov	1	A	Rotherham U	D 0-0	0-0	2		3471
15		15	H	Bradford C	W 1-0	0-0	2	Hunt [70]	5002
16		22	H	Port Vale	W 4-2	2-0	1	Harrold 2 (1 pen) [23 (p), 82], Zebroski 2 [45, 65]	4521
17		25	A	Notts Co	W 2-0	0-0	—	Harrold [47], Spence [65]	2964
18	Dec	2	H	Macclesfield T	W 4-0	2-0	—	Vieira 2 [11, 51], Balanta [45], Johnson [71]	3770
19		6	A	Aldershot T	L 2-3	0-2	1	Balanta [76], Phillips [90]	3915
20		13	H	Luton T	D 0-0	0-0	1		5567
21		20	A	Shrewsbury T	W 1-0	0-0	1	Harrold [55]	6160
22		26	H	Exeter C	D 1-1	1-0	1	Harrold (pen) [6]	6094
23		28	A	Gillingham	D 1-1	1-0	1	Lewis (og) [31]	5979
24	Jan	3	A	Bury	W 2-1	1-0	—	Harrold [37], Balanta [63]	4961
25		17	H	Grimsby T	L 0-1	0-1	1		4461
26		24	A	Bournemouth	L 1-3	1-2	1	Harrold [9]	5946
27		27	A	Macclesfield T	D 0-0	0-0	—		1306
28		31	H	Accrington S	W 2-1	1-1	1	Murdock (og) [24], Harrold [80]	6166
29	Feb	14	A	Bradford C	L 0-1	0-1	2		12,689
30		17	A	Dagenham & R	W 1-0	0-0	—	Pittman [50]	2242
31		23	H	Rotherham U	D 0-0	0-0	—		3739
32		28	A	Morecambe	D 0-0	0-0	2		2005
33	Mar	3	H	Chester C	W 2-0	1-0	—	Phillips [26], Pittman [66]	3713
34		7	H	Chesterfield	D 1-1	0-1	2	Pittman [90]	4809
35		10	A	Lincoln C	L 0-1	0-0	—		2562
36		14	A	Brentford	D 3-3	2-2	2	Akinde 2 [15, 49], Mousinho [40]	10,642
37		21	H	Rochdale	L 0-1	0-0	4		6055
38		28	H	Shrewsbury T	D 1-1	1-0	5	Holt [29]	4803
39		31	H	Barnet	D 1-1	1-1	—	Akinde [19]	4066
40	Apr	7	A	Darlington	W 2-1	1-0	—	Akinde [39], Zebroski [90]	2180
41		11	H	Gillingham	W 1-0	1-0	2	Akinde [41]	6306
42		13	A	Exeter C	L 0-1	0-0	3		8183
43		18	H	Aldershot T	W 3-0	1-0	3	Akinde [7], Newman (og) [52], Phillips [67]	5440
44		21	A	Luton T	W 1-0	0-0	—	Akinde [56]	6553
45		25	A	Port Vale	D 1-1	0-0	2	Sawyer [80]	6047
46	May	2	H	Notts Co	L 1-2	0-1	3	McCracken [52]	9625

Final League Position: 3

GOALSCORERS

League (54): Harrold 9 (2 pens), Akinde 7, Zebroski 7, Balanta 3, McGleish 3 (2 pens), Phillips 3, Pittman 3, Williamson 3, Johnson 2, Mousinho 2, Spence 2, Vieira 2, Holt 1, Hunt 1, McCracken 1, Sawyer 1, Woodman 1, own goals 3.
Carling Cup (0).
FA Cup (4): Harrold 3, Phillips 1.
J Paint Trophy (0).

Shearer S 29	Crooks L 2	Woodman C 46	Doherty T 34	Johnson L 29	Williamson M 22	Spence L 21+9	Grant G 9+1	Zebroski C 31+2	McGleish S 10+5	Holt G 33	Mousinho J 21+13	Antwi W 4+2	McCracken D 39	Rice R —+1	Ashton N —+11	Vieira M 2+12	Church S 6+3	Harrold M 28+9	Phillips M 18+19	Moussa F 7+2	Hunt L 20	Balanta A 9+2	Bloomfield M 15+5	Casement C 12	Moncur T —+2	Oliver L 1+7	Pittman J 11+6	Young J 15	Beavon S 2+6	Stech M 2	Akinde J 11	Sawyer L 8+1	Sinclair F 9	Match No.
1	2²	3	4	5	6	7	8	9	10	11¹	12	13																						1
1		3	4²	5	6	7	8¹	9³	10		11		2			12	13	14																2
1		3	4	5	6	7¹	8	9	10		11		2			12																		3
1		3	4	5	6		8¹	9	10²	11	7					13	12																	4
1		3	4¹	5	6	7	8	9	10²		11		2			13	12																	5
1		3	4	5	6	7¹	8²	9	10³		11		2			12	14	13																6
1¹		3	4	5	6	7¹	8²	9			11		2		12	10*	13																	7
1		3	4	5	6	7	8¹	9	10²		11		2			13	12																	8
1		3	4	5	6	7¹	13	9	12		11		2			10³	8²																	9
1		3	4*	5	6	12	8	9	13	7²	11³		2¹			10	14																	10
1		3	5¹		6	7²		8*	10	11	12		2		14	9	13	4³																11
1		3			6		8	12	11	7²				5		10	9¹	13	4	2														12
1		3			6		8		11	7²				5	12	10¹	9	13	4	2														13
1		3	4		6		11		7					5	12	10¹	9	13	8²	2														14
1		3			6	4¹	8		11	7				5		9	10			2	12													15
1		3			6	12	8		11	7				5	13	9²	4³	14	2	10¹														16
1		3	4		6	7	11							5		9	12	8	2	10¹														17
1		3	4³	5			8			11²				6	13	9		12	7	2	10¹	14												18
1		3	4		6	8			11²				5		9³	12	13	7¹	2	10	14													19
1		3	4		6	12			11				5	14	10³	9	7²	13	2		8¹													20
1		3	4	5		12			11	13			6	14	10³	9	7¹		2		8²													21
1		3	4	5		12			11	13			6	14	10	7³		2²	9	8¹														22
1		3	4²	5	6	7			8	13	2³		12			9	11			10¹	14													23
1	2	3		5	6	4			11	12			13		9	7¹			10*	8														24
1		3	4	5³	6		7	10	11²				9	13				12	8¹	2	14													25
1		3	4³	5			7	11	12				14	6			9	13	10²	8¹	2													26
1		3	4	5				8	10¹	11			6		12	9	7			2														27
1		3	4	5	'			8	14	11	13		6		12	9²	7¹			10³	2													28
1		3	4	5				7*			11¹	12	6			9	13			8²	2³				14	10								29
		3	4	5				11	7				6		12	9				8	2				10¹	1								30
		3	4	5	12			11					6			9	7³			8¹	2²		13	10	1	14								31
		3	4	5	8³			11	12				6	14		9	7²				2		13	1	10¹									32
		3	4	5	12			11		8	'		6	13		14	7¹				2		9²	1	10³									33
		3	4	5²	12			11¹		8			6	13		10	7				2³		9	1	14									34
		3	4	5	7	8³		11¹	6	2²	12		9	14				13	10	1														35
		3	4*	5	7			11	8¹	6			9	12²				2	13	14				1	10³									36
		3		5	7¹	13		11	12	6			9	8²	2			14					1	10³	4									37
		3			12			11	7	5			9		8	2²	13	14	1					10³	4¹	6								38
		3			8			11	7				12	13	2	4³		5	9¹	1				10²	14	6								39
		3			7			11	14	5			13	12	2	8			9²	1				10¹	4³	6								40
		3	4³		7			13		5			9¹	12	2	8		14		1				10	11²	6								41
		3	4³		9¹			11		5			7	2				14	12	1	13			10	8²	6								42
		3			12			11²	13	5			7	2	8				9¹	1	14			10³	4	6								43
		3²			4			11	8	5			7¹	2	14		13	9³	1	12			10		6									44
		3	4		9			11¹		5			14	2	8³		13	1	12				10²	7	6									45
		3	4		8			11		5			12	2	13			9¹	1				10	7²	6									46

FA Cup
First Round — AFC Wimbledon   (a)   4-1
Second Round — Eastwood T   (a)   0-2

Carling Cup
First Round — Birmingham C   (h)   0-4

J Paint Trophy
Second Round — Shrewsbury T   (h)   0-7

YEOVIL TOWN FL Championship 1

FOUNDATION

One of the prime movers of Yeovil football was Ernest J. Sercombe. His association with the club began in 1895 as a playing member of Yeovil Casuals, of which team he became vice-captain and in his last season 1899–1900, he was chosen to play for Somerset against Devon. Upon the reorganisation of the club, he became secretary of the old Yeovil Town FC and with the amalgamation with Petters United in 1914, he continued to serve until his resignation in 1930.

Huish Park, Lufton Way, Yeovil, Somerset BA22 8YF.

Telephone: (01935) 423 662.

Fax: (01935) 473 956.

Ticket Office: (01935) 847 888.

Website: www.ytfc.net

Email: jcotton@ytfc.co.uk

Ground Capacity: 9,665.

Record Attendance: 9,527 v Leeds U, FL 1, 25 April 2008 (16,318 v Sunderland at Huish).

Pitch Measurements: 110m × 69m.

Chairman: John R. Fry.

Chief Executive: Martyn Starnes.

Secretary: Jean Cotton.

Manager: Terry Skiverton.

Assistant Manager: Nathan Jones.

Colours: Green and white hooped shirts, green shorts, white stockings.

Change Colours: Black shirts with one green sleeve, green shorts, black stockings.

Year Formed: 1895.

Turned Professional: 1921.

Ltd Co.: 1923.

Club Nickname: 'Glovers'.

Previous Names: 1895, Yeovil Casuals; 1907, Yeovil Town; 1915, Yeovil & Petters United; 1946, Yeovil Town.

Grounds: 1895, Pen Mill Ground; 1921, Huish; 1990, Huish Park.

HONOURS

FL Championship 2 winners 2004–05.

Conference: Champions 2002–03.

FA Cup: 5th rd 1949.

League Cup: never past 2nd rd.

Southern League: Champions 1954–55, 1963–64, 1970–71; Runners-up: 1923–24, 1931–32, 1934–35, 1969–70, 1972–73.

Southern League Cup: Winners 1948–49, 1954–55, 1960–61, 1965–66; Runners-up: 1946–47, 1955–56.

Isthmian League: Winners 1987–88; Runners-up: 1985–86, 1986–87, 1996–97.

AC Delco Cup: Winners 1987–88.

Bob Lord Trophy: Winners 1989–90.

FA Trophy: Winners 2002.

London Combination: Runners-up 1930–31, 1932–33.

SKY SPORTS FACT FILE

In a comparatively few years since they attained Football League status, Yeovil Town have had the unusual record of fielding players who have won international honours with a variety of foreign countries: Antigua, Canada, DR Congo, Ghana, Latvia and Nigeria.

First Football League Game: 9 August 2003, Division 3 v Rochdale (a) W 3-1: Weale; Williams (Lindegaard), Crittenden, Lockwood, O'Brien, Pluck (Rodrigues), Gosling (El Kholti), Way, Jackson, Gall (2), Johnson (1).

Record League Victory: 10–0 v Kidderminster H, Southern League, 27 December 1955. 10–0 v Bedford T, Southern League, 4 March 1961.

Record Cup Victory: 12–1 v Westbury United, FA Cup 1st qual rd, 1923–24.

Record Defeat: 0–8 v Manchester United, FA Cup 5th rd, 12 February 1949.

Most League Points (3 for a win): 83, FL 2, 2004–05.

Most League Goals: 90, FL 2, 2004–05.

Highest League Goalscorer in Season: Phil Jevons, 27, 2004–05

Most League Goals in Total Aggregate: Phil Jevons, 42, 2004–06

Most Capped Player: Andrejs Stolcers, 1 (81) Latvia and Arron Davies, 1, Wales.

Most League Appearances: Terry Skiverton, 195, 2003–.

Record Transfer Fee Received: Undisclosed from Nottingham F for Arron Davies, July 2007.

Record Transfer Fee Paid: Undisclosed to Atletico Penarol de Rafaela (Argentina) for Pablo Bastianini, August 2005.

Football League Record: 2003 Promoted to Division 3 from Conference; 2003–04 Division 3; 2004–05 FL 2; 2005– FL 1.

LATEST SEQUENCES

Longest Sequence of League Wins: 7, 7.12.2004 – 15.1.2005.

Longest Sequence of League Defeats: 5, 29.10.05 – 6.12.05.

Longest Sequence of Unbeaten League Matches: 7, 7.12.2004 – 15.1.2005.

Longest Sequence Without a League Win: 6, 6.8.05 – 29.8.05.

Successive Scoring Runs: 22 from 30.10.2004.

Successive Non-scoring Runs: 3 from 21.1.2006.

MANAGERS

Jack Gregory 1922–28
Tommy Lawes 1928–29
Dave Pratt 1929–33
Louis Page 1933–35
Dave Halliday 1935–38
Billy Kingdon 1938–46
Alec Stock 1946–49
George Patterson 1949–51
Harry Lowe 1951–53
Ike Clarke 1953–57
Norman Dodgin 1957
Jimmy Baldwin 1957–60
Basil Hayward 1960–64
Glyn Davies 1964–65
Joe McDonald 1965–67
Ron Saunders 1967–69
Mike Hughes 1969–72
Cecil Irwin 1972–75
Stan Harland 1975–81
Barry Lloyd 1978–81
Malcolm Allison 1981
Jimmy Giles 1981–83
Trevor Finnigan/Mike Hughes 1983
Steve Coles 1983–84
Ian McFarlane 1984
Gerry Gow 1984–87
Brian Hall 1987–90
Clive Whitehead 1990–91
Steve Rutter 1991–93
Brian Hall 1994–95
Graham Roberts 1995–98
Colin Lippiatt 1998–99
Steve Thompson 1999–2000
Dave Webb 2000
Gary Johnson 2001–05
Steve Thompson 2005–06
Russell Slade 2006–09
Terry Skiverton February 2009–

TEN YEAR LEAGUE RECORD

		P	W	D	L	F	A	Pts	Pos
1999-2000	Conf.	42	18	10	14	60	63	64	7
2000-01	Conf.	42	24	8	10	73	50	80	2
2001-02	Conf.	42	19	13	10	66	53	70	3
2002-03	Conf.	42	28	11	3	100	37	95	1
2003-04	Div 3	46	23	5	18	70	57	74	8
2004-05	FL 2	46	25	8	13	90	65	83	1
2005-06	FL 1	46	15	11	20	54	62	56	15
2006-07	FL 1	46	23	10	13	55	39	79	5
2007-08	FL 1	46	14	10	22	38	59	52	18
2008-09	FL 1	46	12	15	19	41	66	51	17

DID YOU KNOW

On 9 May 1949 Yeovil Town won their first Southern League Cup. Barry Town, Torquay United Reserves, Bath City and Hereford United were beaten, then in the final faced Colchester United. Yeovil won 3–0 with Chris Coffey scoring twice, Eric Bryant once.

YEOVIL TOWN 2008–09 LEAGUE RECORD

Match No.	Date		Venue	Opponents	Result		H/T Score	Lg. Pos.	Goalscorers	Attendance
1	Aug	9	H	Walsall	D	1-1	1-0	—	Tomlin [10]	4518
2		16	A	Hereford U	W	2-1	2-0	6	Schofield [19], Warne [22]	3476
3		23	H	Leeds U	D	1-1	0-1	6	Owusu [62]	6580
4		30	A	Carlisle U	L	1-4	1-1	15	Tomlin [16]	6286
5	Sept	6	A	Milton Keynes D	L	0-3	0-1	19		7959
6		13	H	Brighton & HA	D	1-1	0-0	18	Way [80]	4451
7		20	H	Bristol R	D	2-2	2-1	18	Skiverton [6], Roberts [45]	5748
8		27	A	Scunthorpe U	L	0-2	0-1	22		4829
9	Oct	4	H	Southend U	L	1-2	0-1	23	Schofield [88]	4008
10		18	A	Northampton T	L	0-3	0-2	23		5217
11		21	H	Crewe Alex	W	3-2	1-0	—	Schofield 2 [45, 66], Way [85]	3536
12		25	H	Leyton Orient	D	0-0	0-0	20		4320
13		28	A	Huddersfield T	D	0-0	0-0	—		10,719
14	Nov	1	A	Oldham Ath	W	2-0	0-0	19	Brown A [62], Warne [65]	5318
15		11	A	Leicester C	L	0-1	0-1	—		16,528
16		15	H	Peterborough U	L	0-1	0-1	21		4001
17		22	H	Tranmere R	W	1-0	1-0	19	Skiverton [23]	3445
18		25	A	Colchester U	L	0-1	0-0	—		3214
19	Dec	6	A	Hartlepool U	D	0-0	0-0	21		3393
20		13	H	Stockport Co	L	2-4	2-3	21	Smith [26], Warne [43]	3687
21		20	A	Swindon T	W	3-2	2-1	18	Alcock [10], Peltier [28], Ifil (og) [72]	7072
22		26	H	Cheltenham T	D	1-1	0-1	19	Rodgers [75]	4989
23		28	A	Millwall	D	1-1	1-1	18	Rodgers [37]	9042
24	Jan	13	A	Scunthorpe U	L	1-2	0-2	—	McCollin [90]	3275
25		19	H	Leicester C	L	0-2	0-0	—		4569
26		24	A	Southend U	W	1-0	1-0	18	Brown A [6]	6409
27		27	H	Huddersfield T	W	1-0	1-0	—	Macdonald [45]	3703
28		31	A	Leyton Orient	W	1-0	0-0	17	Tomlin [90]	4597
29	Feb	14	A	Peterborough U	W	3-1	2-0	16	Warne [31], Brown A [33], Macdonald [69]	6129
30		17	A	Bristol R	L	0-3	0-2	—		8049
31		21	H	Oldham Ath	D	2-2	2-2	15	Tomlin 2 [16, 33]	4150
32		24	A	Crewe Alex	L	0-2	0-1	—		3432
33		28	A	Walsall	L	0-2	0-0	18		3916
34	Mar	7	H	Carlisle U	D	1-1	1-0	18	Roberts [31]	3892
35		10	A	Leeds U	L	0-4	0-2	—		18,847
36		14	A	Brighton & HA	L	0-5	0-2	20		6291
37		21	H	Milton Keynes D	D	0-0	0-0	21		4028
38		28	H	Swindon T	W	1-0	1-0	21	Obika [33]	5476
39		31	A	Northampton T	W	1-0	0-0	—	Obika [79]	3884
40	Apr	4	A	Stockport Co	D	0-0	0-0	17		5664
41		10	H	Millwall	W	2-0	1-0	—	Obika [40], Tomlin [49]	6230
42		13	A	Cheltenham T	L	0-1	0-0	16		3775
43		18	H	Hartlepool U	L	2-3	1-2	18	Tomlin [7], Townsend [57]	4232
44		21	H	Hereford U	D	2-2	0-1	—	Rodgers [78], Weale [90]	3780
45		25	A	Tranmere R	D	1-1	0-0	17	Obika [67]	8306
46	May	2	H	Colchester U	L	0-2	0-2	17		5237

Final League Position: 17

GOALSCORERS

League (41): Tomlin 7, Obika 4, Schofield 4, Warne 4, Brown A 3, Rodgers 3, Macdonald 2, Roberts 2, Skiverton 2, Way 2, Alcock 1, McCollin 1, Owusu 1, Peltier 1, Smith 1, Townsend 1, Weale 1, own goal 1.
Carling Cup (2): Tomlin 1, Warne 1.
FA Cup (1): Skiverton 1.
J Paint Trophy (2): Bircham 1, Tomlin 1 (pen).

Begovic A 14	Peltier L 34+1	Smith N 32+1	Bircham M 3	Skiverton T 25	Forbes T 38	Downes A 15+9	Way D 15	Tomlin G 29+13	Warne P 38+6	Schofield D 34+5	Owusu L —+4	Murtagh K 16+10	Alcock C 25+5	McCollin A —+11	Jones N 14+7	Roberts G 27+3	Dayton J —+2	Welsh A 23+14	Brown A 16+7	Owen R 7	Rendell S 5	Wagenaar J 22+1	Noel-Williams G 6	Rodgers L 10+12	Macdonald S 4	Prijovic A 4	Worthington J 9	Hutchins D 8+1	Weale C 10	Townsend A 10	Obika J 10	Noble D 2	Maguire D 1	Match No.
1	2	3	4	5	6	7²	8	9	10¹	11	12	13																						1
1	2	3		5	6	7	8³	9¹	10²	11	12	4	14	13																				2
1	2			5	6	7¹	8²	9	10	11³	14	4	13			3		12																3
1	2		4	5	6		8	9³	10				14	7²	12	3		11¹	13															4
1	2		4¹	5	6			12	10³	11		8		14		3	7	13	9²															5
1	2²			5	6		8¹	9	10	11	12	13	14			3		7	4³															6
1	2	3		5	6	7³	8¹	13	10	11	12		14					9	4²															7
1	2			5	6	7²	8	12	10	11				13		3		9	4¹															8
1	2			5			8	9	10	11■				12		3	4■	7¹	6															9
1				5	2■		8	9¹	10²	11		4		13		3		12		6	7													10
1				5			8	12	10	11		4	2			3		7		6	9													11
1				5			8	12	10¹	11		13	2			3	4	7		6	9²													12
1	12						8	13	14	11		7²	2			3	4	10³		5	6	9¹												13
1	4						12	8	10¹	11					2	3		7		5	6	9												14
	7	3		5	2³	10²	8			13	11¹		14			4		12		6		1		9										15
	7	3¹		5		13	8		10²	2³		12				4		14		6		1		8²										16
	3			5	6	7¹		9	10	11		2				12	4	13				1	8²											17
	7	3		5²	6	8¹		10³	11			2				4		12	13			1	9	14										18
	4	3		5	6	7²		14	8	11		2¹				13	12					1	9	10³										19
	2	3		5	6	7¹		9³	10²	11				13		4	12	14				1		8										20
	4	3		5	6			12	8	11		2				7						1	9¹	10										21
	7	3		5	6	12		9³	10²	11		2				4¹		13	14			1		8										22
	7	3		5	6	8		9¹		11		2	12			4		10				1												23
		3		5³	6	8		10¹	9²	11		2	13	14		4¹		7³	12			1												24
		3			6	8³		9²	11		12	2	13	14		4¹		7	5			1		10										25
	4²	3			6	8■		12	9¹	11		13	2			7³		14	5			1		10										26
		3			6			14	13	11		4	2			12		8¹	5			1		10³	7	9²								27
		3			6			12	10	11		2				8		5				1			4	9¹	7							28
	4	3		5²				12	10			14	2			13		11² 6				1			8	9¹	7							29
	4	3			6			12	10¹	13		2				11		5				1		14	8³	9²	7							30
	4	3			6		12	9	10²	11		2				8¹		5				1		13			7							31
	4	3			6		12	9³	10²	11		2				8	5¹					1		14			7							32
	4	13			6		12	9	10			2³	3			14		11²	5			1		8¹			7							33
					6			9	10	11		3				4		8¹	5			1		12			7	2						34
	5				6	8		9¹	12	11²	14					3	4	10	13³			1					7							35
	7	3		5	6	13		9	15	12		2²				4		10¹				1■		8⁶			11							36
	2	3		5³	6	12		10¹	11²			7				4								13				14	1	8	9			37
	5	3			6			10²	8¹		12					4								13				2	1	11	9	7		38
	5	3			6			10³	8²			12				4		13						14				2	1	11	9	7		39
	5	3			6			10²	8	12		7				4								13				2	1	11	9			40
	5	3			6			10²	8			7				4		12						13				2	1	11	9			41
	5	3			6			10²	8¹	14		7				4■		12						13				2³	1	11	9			42
	5	3			6			10	8¹	13		7				12		14										2	1	11³	9		4²	43
	5	3			6			10	8¹	7		4				12	6	13										2	1	11	9²			44
		3			6			10	8	7		4	2			12		5										1	11	9				45
		3			6	13		10	12	7		4	2			8²		5		15								1⁶	11	9¹				46

FA Cup
First Round — Stockport Co — (h) — 1-1
(a) — 0-5

Carling Cup
First Round — Charlton Ath — (a) — 1-0
Second Round — Middlesbrough — (a) — 1-5

J Paint Trophy
First Round — Brentford — (a) — 2-2

ENGLISH LEAGUE PLAYERS DIRECTORY

Players listed represent those with their clubs during the 2008–09 season.

Players are listed alphabetically on pages 561–567.

The number alongside each player corresponds to the team number heading. (Abbey, George 28 = team 28 (Crewe Alex))

ACCRINGTON S (1)

ARTHUR, Kenny (G) 309 0
H: 6 3 W: 13 08 b.Bellshill 7-12-78
1997-98	Partick T	19	0		
1998-99	Partick T	26	0		
1999-2000	Partick T	4	0		
2000-01	Partick T	34	0		
2001-02	Partick T	23	0		
2002-03	Partick T	35	0		
2003-04	Partick T	22	0		
2004-05	Partick T	35	0		
2005-06	Partick T	24	0		
2006-07	Partick T	21	0	243	0
2007-08	Accrington S	24	0		
2008-09	Accrington S	42	0	66	0

BELL, James (M) 8 0
H: 6 0 W: 12 00 b.Liverpool 24-11-89
Source: Scholar.
| 2007-08 | Accrington S | 2 | 0 | | |
| 2008-09 | Accrington S | 6 | 0 | 8 | 0 |

CAVANAGH, Paul (D) 74 6
H: 5 11 W: 11 09 b.Liverpool 14-10-81
Source: Liverpool Scholar.
2006-07	Accrington S	26	4		
2007-08	Accrington S	19	1		
2008-09	Accrington S	29	1	74	6

DUNBAVIN, Ian (G) 146 0
H: 6 1 W: 12 10 b.Knowsley 27-5-80
Source: Trainee.
1998-99	Liverpool	0	0		
1999-2000	Liverpool	0	0		
1999-2000	Shrewsbury T	7	0		
2000-01	Shrewsbury T	22	0		
2001-02	Shrewsbury T	34	0		
2002-03	Shrewsbury T	33	0		
2003-04	Shrewsbury T	0	0	96	0
From Halifax T.
2006-07	Accrington S	23	0		
2007-08	Accrington S	23	0		
2008-09	Accrington S	4	0	50	0

EDWARDS, Phil (D) 110 2
H: 5 8 W: 11 03 b.Bootle 8-11-85
Source: Scholar.
2005-06	Wigan Ath	0	0		
2006-07	Accrington S	33	1		
2007-08	Accrington S	31	1		
2008-09	Accrington S	46	0	110	2

GRANT, Robert (M) 23 1
H: 5 11 W: 12 00 b.Blackpool 27-3-87
Source: Scholar.
2006-07	Accrington S	1	0		
2007-08	Accrington S	7	0		
2008-09	Accrington S	15	1	23	1

KING, Chris (D) 27 0
H: 5 8 W: 10 01 b.Liverpool 14-11-80
| 2008-09 | Accrington S | 27 | 0 | 27 | 0 |

McCONVILLE, Sean (F) 5 0
H: 5 11 W: 11 09 b.Burscough 6-3-89
Source: Skelmersdale U.
| 2008-09 | Accrington S | 5 | 0 | 5 | 0 |

MILES, John (F) 199 25
H: 5 10 W: 10 08 b.Fazackerley 28-9-81
Source: Trainee.
1998-99	Liverpool	0	0		
1999-2000	Liverpool	0	0		
2000-01	Liverpool	0	0		
2001-02	Liverpool	0	0		
2001-02	Stoke C	1	0	1	0
2002-03	Crewe Alex	5	1	5	1
2002-03	Macclesfield T	8	4		
2003-04	Macclesfield T	29	6		
2004-05	Macclesfield T	30	3		
2005-06	Macclesfield T	25	4		
2006-07	Macclesfield T	30	4	122	21
2007-08	Accrington S	16	0		
2007-08	Milton Keynes D	12	0	12	0
2008-09	Accrington S	43	3	59	3

MULLIN, John (M) 404 31
H: 6 0 W: 11 10 b.Bury 11-8-75
Source: School.
1992-93	Burnley	0	0		
1993-94	Burnley	6	1		
1994-95	Burnley	12	1		
1995-96	Sunderland	10	1		
1996-97	Sunderland	10	1		
1997-98	Sunderland	6	0		
1997-98	Preston NE	7	0	7	0
1997-98	Burnley	6	0		
1998-99	Sunderland	9	2	35	4
1999-2000	Burnley	37	5		
2000-01	Burnley	36	3		
2001-02	Burnley	4	0	101	10
2001-02	Rotherham U	34	2		
2002-03	Rotherham U	34	3		
2003-04	Rotherham U	38	4		
2004-05	Rotherham U	31	1		
2005-06	Rotherham U	43	2	180	12
2006-07	Tranmere R	40	5		
2007-08	Tranmere R	10	0	50	5
2008-09	Accrington S	31	0	31	0

MULLIN, Paul (F) 131 33
H: 6 0 W: 12 01 b.Bury 16-3-74
Source: Clitheroe, Darwen, Radcliffe Borough.
2006-07	Accrington S	46	14		
2007-08	Accrington S	43	12		
2008-09	Accrington S	36	7	125	33
2008-09	Bradford C	6	0	6	0

MURDOCH, Colin (D) 325 14
H: 6 2 W: 13 00 b.Ballymena 2-7-75
Source: Trainee. *Honours:* Northern Ireland Schools, Youth, B, 34 full caps, 1 goal.
1992-93	Manchester U	0	0		
1993-94	Manchester U	0	0		
1994-95	Manchester U	0	0		
1995-96	Manchester U	0	0		
1996-97	Manchester U	0	0		
1997-98	Preston NE	27	1		
1998-99	Preston NE	33	1		
1999-2000	Preston NE	33	2		
2000-01	Preston NE	37	0		
2001-02	Preston NE	23	2		
2002-03	Preston NE	24	0	177	6
2003-04	Hibernian	32	3		
2004-05	Hibernian	5	0	37	3
2004-05	Crewe Alex	16	0	16	0
2005-06	Rotherham U	39	2		
2006-07	Rotherham U	4	0	43	2
2007-08	Shrewsbury T	29	2	29	2
2008-09	Accrington S	23	1	23	1

MURPHY, Peter (M) 5 0
H: 6 0 W: 11 10 b.Liverpool 13-2-90
Source: Scholar.
| 2007-08 | Accrington S | 2 | 0 | | |
| 2008-09 | Accrington S | 3 | 0 | 5 | 0 |

ONIBUJE, Fola (F) 34 2
H: 6 7 W: 12 00 b.Lagos 25-9-84
Source: Charlton Ath Juniors.
2002-03	Preston NE	0	0		
2003-04	Preston NE	0	0		
2003-04	Huddersfield T	2	0	2	0
2004-05	Barnsley	3	0	3	0
2004-05	Peterborough U	2	0	2	0
From Cambridge U.
2006-07	Swindon T	14	2	14	2
2006-07	Brentford	2	0	2	0
2006-07	Wycombe W	5	0	5	0
2007-08	Shrewsbury T	0	0		
2007-08	Macclesfield T	1	0	1	0
2008-09	Accrington S	5	0	5	0

PROCTOR, Andy (M) 123 16
H: 6 0 W: 12 04 b.Blackburn 13-3-83
Source: Great Harwood T.
2006-07	Accrington S	43	3		
2007-08	Accrington S	43	10		
2008-09	Accrington S	37	3	123	16

RICHARDSON, Leam (D) 191 1
H: 5 7 W: 11 04 b.Leeds 19-11-79
Source: Trainee.
1997-98	Blackburn R	0	0		
1998-99	Blackburn R	0	0		
1999-2000	Blackburn R	0	0		
2000-01	Bolton W	12	0		
2001-02	Bolton W	1	0		
2001-02	Notts Co	21	0	21	0
2002-03	Bolton W	0	0	13	0
2002-03	Blackpool	20	0		
2003-04	Blackpool	28	0		
2004-05	Blackpool	23	0	71	0
2006-07	Accrington S	38	0		
2007-08	Accrington S	37	1		
2008-09	Accrington S	11	0	86	1

RYAN, James (M) 48 10
H: 5 8 W: 11 08 b.Maghull 6-9-88
Source: Scholar. *Honours:* Eire Under-21.
2006-07	Liverpool	0	0		
2007-08	Liverpool	0	0		
2007-08	Shrewsbury T	4	0	4	0
2008-09	Accrington S	44	10	44	10

SMITH, Andrew (F) 2 0
H: 5 10 W: 11 02 b.Burnley 22-12-89
Source: Scholar.
| 2007-08 | Accrington S | 1 | 0 | | |
| 2008-09 | Accrington S | 1 | 0 | 2 | 0 |

TURNER, Chris (F) 23 0
H: 5 10 W: 11 10 b.Manchester 12-8-87
Source: Scholar.
| 2007-08 | Accrington S | 1 | 0 | | |
| 2008-09 | Accrington S | 22 | 0 | 23 | 0 |

WILLIAMS, Robbie (D) 92 4
H: 5 10 W: 12 00 b.Liverpool 12-4-79
Source: St Dominics.
2006-07	Accrington S	43	3		
2007-08	Accrington S	26	0		
2008-09	Accrington S	23	1	92	4

ALDERSHOT T (2)

BLACKBURN, Chris (D) 44 0
H: 6 0 W: 12 00 b.Crewe 2-8-82
Source: Scholarship.
| 1999-2000 | Chester C | 1 | 0 | 1 | 0 |
From Morecambe.
| 2007-08 | Swindon T | 7 | 0 | 7 | 0 |
| 2008-09 | Aldershot T | 36 | 0 | 36 | 0 |

BULL, Nikki (G) 30 0
H: 6 2 W: 12 08 b.Hastings 2-10-81
Source: Scholarship.
1999-2000	QPR	0	0		
2000-01	QPR	0	0		
2001-02	QPR	0	0		
2008-09	Aldershot T	30	0	30	0

CHALMERS, Lewis (M) 23 1
H: 6 0 W: 12 04 b.Manchester 4-2-86
Source: Altrincham.
| 2008-09 | Aldershot T | 23 | 1 | 23 | 1 |

CHARLES, Anthony (D) 98 2
H: 6 1 W: 12 07 b.Isleworth 11-3-81
Source: Brook House.
| 1999-2000 | Crewe Alex | 0 | 0 | | |
From Brookhouse.
| 2000-01 | Crewe Alex | 0 | 0 | | |

From Hayes, Aldershot T, Farnborough T

2004-05	Barnet	0	0	
2005-06	Barnet	40	0	
2006-07	Barnet	17	0	**57** **0**
2008-09	Aldershot T	41	2	**41** **2**

COCHRANE, Justin (M)   **132** **4**
H: 5 11   W: 11 07   b.Hackney 26-1-82
Source: Scholarship.

1999-2000	QPR	0	0	
2000-01	QPR	1	0	
2001-02	QPR	0	0	
2002-03	QPR	0	0	**1** **0**

From Hayes.

2003-04	Crewe Alex	39	0	
2004-05	Crewe Alex	29	0	
2005-06	Crewe Alex	4	0	**72** **0**
2005-06	Gillingham	5	1	**5** **1**
2006-07	Rotherham U	31	1	**31** **1**
2007-08	Yeovil T	12	2	**12** **2**
2007-08	Millwall	1	0	**1** **0**

From Rushden & D.

2008-09	Aldershot T	10	0	**10** **0**

DAY, Rhys (D)   **129** **12**
H: 6 1   W: 12 08   b.Bridgend 31-8-82
Source: Scholarship. *Honours:* Wales Under-21.

1999-2000	Manchester C	0	0	
2000-01	Manchester C	0	0	
2001-02	Manchester C	0	0	
2001-02	*Blackpool*	9	0	**9** **0**
2002-03	Manchester C	0	0	
2002-03	Mansfield T	23	1	
2003-04	Mansfield T	41	6	
2004-05	Mansfield T	18	3	
2005-06	Mansfield T	21	2	**103** **12**
2008-09	Aldershot T	17	0	**17** **0**

DONNELLY, Scott (M)   **33** **1**
H: 5 8   W: 11 10   b.Hammersmith 25-12-87
Source: Scholar.

2004-05	QPR	2	0	
2005-06	QPR	8	0	
2006-07	QPR	3	0	**13** **0**

From Wealdstone.

2008-09	Aldershot T	20	1	**20** **1**

ELVINS, Rob (F)   **20** **1**
H: 6 2   W: 12 04   b.Alvechurch 17-9-86
Source: Scholar.

2005-06	WBA	0	0	
2006-07	WBA	0	0	
2006-07	*Cheltenham T*	5	0	**5** **0**
2008-09	Aldershot T	15	1	**15** **1**

GRANT, John (F)   **61** **7**
H: 5 11   W: 10 08   b.Manchester 9-8-81
Source: Trainee.

1999-2000	Crewe Alex	4	0	
2000-01	Crewe Alex	2	0	
2001-02	Crewe Alex	1	0	**7** **0**
2001-02	*Rushden & D*	0	0	

From Here U, Telfd U

2004-05	Shrewsbury T	19	2	**19** **2**

From Halifax T

2008-09	Aldershot T	35	5	**35** **5**

HARDING, Ben (M)   **80** **9**
H: 5 10   W: 11 02   b.Carshalton 6-9-84
Source: Scholar.

2001-02	Wimbledon	0	0	
2002-03	Wimbledon	0	0	
2003-04	Wimbledon	15	0	**15** **0**
2004-05	Milton Keynes D	26	4	
2005-06	Milton Keynes D	10	2	
2006-07	Milton Keynes D	0	0	**36** **6**
2008-09	Aldershot T	29	3	**29** **3**

HOWELL, Dean (D)   **26** **0**
H: 6 1   W: 12 05   b.Burton-on-Trent 29-11-80
Source: Trainee.

1999-2000	Notts Co	1	0	**1** **0**
2000-01	Crewe Alex	1	0	**1** **0**
2000-01	Rochdale	3	0	**3** **0**

From Southport, Morecambe, Halifax T

2005-06	Colchester U	4	0	**4** **0**

From Halifax, Weymth, Grays, Rushden

2008-09	Aldershot T	14	0	**14** **0**
2008-09	Bury	3	0	**3** **0**

HUDSON, Kirk (F)   **44** **11**
H: 5 8   W: 10 00   b.Rochford 12-12-86
Source: Ipswich T Scholar, Celtic.

2005-06	Bournemouth	1	0	**1** **0**
2008-09	Aldershot T	43	11	**43** **11**

HYLTON, Danny (F)   **29** **5**
H: 6 0   W: 11 13   b.London 25-2-89
Source: Youth.

2008-09	Aldershot T	29	5	**29** **5**

JAIMEZ-RUIZ, Mikhael (G)   **14** **0**
H: 6 0   W: 12 02   b.Merida 12-7-84
Source: Northwood.

2008-09	Aldershot T	14	0	**14** **0**

MELLETTI, Jason (D)   **0** **0**
b. 18-9-87

2008-09	Aldershot T	0	0	

MENDES, Junior (F)   **322** **52**
H: 5 10   W: 11 00   b.Balham 15-9-76
Source: Trainee. *Honours:* Montserrat full caps.

1995-96	Chelsea	0	0	
1995-96	St Mirren	0	0	
1996-97	St Mirren	36	3	
1997-98	St Mirren	29	9	
1998-99	St Mirren	22	4	
1998-99	*Carlisle U*	6	1	**6** **1**
1999-2000	St Mirren	33	5	
2000-01	Dunfermline Ath	13	0	**13** **0**
2001-02	Rushden & D	0	0	
2002-03	St Mirren	17	6	**137** **27**
2002-03	Mansfield T	18	1	
2003-04	Mansfield T	39	11	**57** **12**
2004-05	Huddersfield T	25	5	
2005-06	Huddersfield T	5	0	**30** **5**
2005-06	*Northampton T*	12	2	**12** **2**
2005-06	*Grimsby T*	15	0	**15** **0**
2006-07	Notts Co	37	5	**37** **5**
2007-08	*Lincoln C*	9	0	**9** **0**
2008-09	Aldershot T	6	0	**6** **0**

MORGAN, Marvin (F)   **32** **6**
H: 6 4   W: 12 08   b.Manchester 13-4-83
Source: Wealdstone, Yeading, Woking.

2008-09	Aldershot T	32	6	**32** **6**

NEWMAN, Ricky (D)   **376** **13**
H: 5 10   W: 12 06   b.Guildford 5-8-70
Source: Trainee.

1987-88	Crystal Palace	0	0	
1988-89	Crystal Palace	0	0	
1989-90	Crystal Palace	0	0	
1990-91	Crystal Palace	0	0	
1991-92	Crystal Palace	0	0	
1991-92	*Maidstone U*	10	1	**10** **1**
1992-93	Crystal Palace	2	0	
1993-94	Crystal Palace	11	0	
1994-95	Crystal Palace	35	3	**48** **3**
1995-96	Millwall	36	1	
1996-97	Millwall	41	3	
1997-98	Millwall	35	1	
1998-99	Millwall	24	0	
1999-2000	Millwall	14	0	**150** **5**
1999-2000	*Reading*	7	1	
2000-01	Reading	39	0	
2001-02	Reading	0	0	
2002-03	Reading	28	0	
2003-04	Reading	30	0	
2004-05	Reading	30	1	**121** **1**
2005-06	Brentford	30	3	**30** **3**
2008-09	Aldershot T	17	0	**17** **0**

OSBORNE, Junior (D)   **10** **0**
H: 5 11   W: 11 13   b.Watford 12-2-88
Source: Scholar.

2004-05	Watford	1	0	
2005-06	Watford	1	0	
2006-07	Watford	0	0	
2007-08	Watford	0	0	**2** **0**
2008-09	Aldershot T	8	0	**8** **0**

SANDELL, Andy (M)   **65** **5**
H: 5 11   W: 11 09   b.Calne 8-9-83
Source: Bath C.

2005-06	Bristol R	0	0	
2006-07	Bristol R	36	3	
2008-09	Bristol R	0	0	**36** **3**

From Salisbury C.

2008-09	Aldershot T	29	2	**29** **2**

SOARES, Louie (D)   **56** **4**
H: 5 11   W: 13 05   b.Reading 8-1-85
Source: Scholar. *Honours:* Barbados 3 full caps.

2004-05	Reading	0	0	
2004-05	Bristol R	1	0	**1** **0**
2005-06	Barnet	20	1	**20** **1**
2008-09	Aldershot T	35	3	**35** **3**

STRAKER, Anthony (D)   **32** **0**
H: 5 9   W: 11 11   b.Ealing 23-9-88
Source: Crystal Palace Scholar.

2008-09	Aldershot T	32	0	**32** **0**

WINFIELD, Dave (D)   **10** **0**
H: 6 3   W: 13 08   b.Aldershot 24-2-88
Source: Youth.

2008-09	Aldershot T	10	0	**10** **0**

ARSENAL (3)

ADEBAYOR, Emmanuel (F)   **226** **79**
H: 6 4   W: 11 08   b.Lome 26-2-84
Source: Lome. *Honours:* Togo 40 full caps, 16 goals.

2001-02	Metz	10	2	
2002-03	Metz	34	13	**44** **15**
2003-04	Monaco	31	8	
2004-05	Monaco	34	9	
2005-06	Monaco	13	1	**78** **18**
2005-06	Arsenal	13	4	
2006-07	Arsenal	29	8	
2007-08	Arsenal	36	24	
2008-09	Arsenal	26	10	**104** **46**

ALMUNIA, Manuel (G)   **205** **0**
H: 6 3   W: 13 00   b.Pamplona 19-5-77

1997-98	Osasuna B	31	0	
1998-99	Osasuna B	13	0	**44** **0**
1999-2000	Cartagonova	3	0	**3** **0**
2000-01	Sabadell	25	0	**25** **0**
2001-02	Celta Vigo	0	0	
2001-02	Eibar	35	0	**35** **0**
2002-03	Recreativo	2	0	**2** **0**
2003-04	Albacete	24	0	**24** **0**
2004-05	Arsenal	10	0	
2005-06	Arsenal	0	0	
2006-07	Arsenal	1	0	
2007-08	Arsenal	29	0	
2008-09	Arsenal	32	0	**72** **0**

ARSHAVIN, Andrei (F)   **250** **57**
H: 5 9   W: 9 11   b.St Petersburg 29-5-81
Honours: Russia 44 full caps, 15 goals.

1999	Zenit	0	0	
2000	Zenit	10	0	
2001	Zenit	29	4	
2002	Zenit	30	4	
2003	Zenit	27	5	
2004	Zenit	28	6	
2005	Zenit	29	9	
2006	Zenit	28	7	
2007	Zenit	30	10	
2008	Zenit	27	6	**238** **51**
2008-09	Arsenal	12	6	**12** **6**

BARAZITE, Nacer (M)   **30** **1**
H: 6 2   W: 13 01   b.Arnhem 27-5-90
Source: Scholar. *Honours:* Holland Youth.

2007-08	Arsenal	0	0	
2008-09	Arsenal	0	0	
2008-09	*Derby Co*	30	1	**30** **1**

BARTLEY, Kyle (D)   **0** **0**
b.Manchester 22-5-91
Source: Scholar.

2008-09	Arsenal	0	0	

BENDTNER, Nicklas (F)   **100** **25**
H: 6 2   W: 13 00   b.Copenhagen 16-1-88
Source: From Scholar. *Honours:* Denmark Youth, Under-21, 26 full caps, 8 goals.

2005-06	Arsenal	0	0	
2006-07	Arsenal	0	0	
2006-07	*Birmingham C*	42	11	**42** **11**
2007-08	Arsenal	27	5	
2008-09	Arsenal	31	9	**58** **14**

BISCHOFF, Amaury (M)   **63** **6**
H: 5 9   W: 10 03   b.Colmar 31-3-87
Source: Colmar, Strasbourg. *Honours:* Portugal Under-21.

2005-06	Werder Bremen II	34	4	

2006-07	Werder Bremen II	27	2		
2006-07	Werder Bremen	0	0		
2007-08	Werder Bremen II	1	0	62	6
2007-08	Werder Bremen	0	0		
2008-09	Arsenal	1	0	1	0

BOTHELO, Pedro (D)   0   0
H: 6 2 W: 13 00 b.Salvador 14-12-89
Source: Salamanca.

2007-08	Arsenal	0	0		
2008-09	Arsenal	0	0		

CLICHY, Gael (D)   130   1
H: 5 9 W: 10 04 b.Toulouse 26-7-85
Source: From Cannes. Honours: France Under-21, B.

2003-04	Arsenal	12	0		
2004-05	Arsenal	15	0		
2005-06	Arsenal	7	0		
2006-07	Arsenal	27	0		
2007-08	Arsenal	38	0		
2008-09	Arsenal	31	1	130	1

COQUELIN, Francis (M)   0   0
H: 5 10 W: 11 08 b.Laval 13-5-91
Source: Laval.

2008-09	Arsenal	0	0	

CRUISE, Thomas (D)   0   0
b.London 9-3-91
Source: Scholar.

2008-09	Arsenal	0	0	

DENILSON (M)   72   3
H: 5 10 W: 10 10 b.Sao Paulo 16-2-88
Honours: Brazil Youth, Under-20.

2005	Sao Paulo	10	0		
2006	Sao Paulo	2	0	12	0
2006-07	Arsenal	10	0		
2007-08	Arsenal	13	0		
2008-09	Arsenal	37	3	60	3

DIABY, Vassiriki (M)   73   7
H: 6 2 W: 12 04 b.Paris 11-5-86
Honours: France Youth, Under-21, 3 full caps.

2004-05	Auxerre	5	0		
2005-06	Auxerre	5	1	10	1
2005-06	Arsenal	12	1		
2006-07	Arsenal	12	1		
2007-08	Arsenal	15	1		
2008-09	Arsenal	24	3	63	6

DJOUROU, Johan (D)   58   0
H: 6 2 W: 12 05 b.Ivory Coast 18-1-87
Source: Scholar. Honours: Switzerland Youth, Under-20, Under-21, 24 full caps, 1 goal.

2004-05	Arsenal	0	0		
2005-06	Arsenal	7	0		
2006-07	Arsenal	21	0		
2007-08	Arsenal	2	0		
2007-08	Birmingham C	13	0	13	0
2008-09	Arsenal	15	0	45	0

DUNNE, James (M)   0   0
b.Farnborough 18-9-89
Source: Scholar.

2007-08	Arsenal	0	0	
2008-09	Arsenal	0	0	
2008-09	Nottingham F	0	0	

EBOUE, Emmanuel (D)   164   7
H: 5 10 W: 11 08 b.Abidjan 4-6-83
Honours: Ivory Coast 41 full caps.

2002-03	Beveren	23	0		
2003-04	Beveren	30	2		
2004-05	Beveren	17	2	70	4
2004-05	Arsenal	1	0		
2005-06	Arsenal	18	0		
2006-07	Arsenal	24	0		
2007-08	Arsenal	23	0		
2008-09	Arsenal	28	3	94	3

EDUARDO (F)   143   87
H: 5 10 W: 10 03 b.Rio 25-2-83
Source: Bangu. Honours: Croatia Under-21, 24 full caps, 14 goals.

2001-02	Dinamo Zagreb	4	0		
2002-03	Inter Zapresic	15	10	15	10
2003-04	Dinamo Zagreb	24	9		
2004-05	Dinamo Zagreb	22	10		
2005-06	Dinamo Zagreb	29	20		
2006-07	Dinamo Zagreb	32	34	111	73
2007-08	Arsenal	17	4		
2008-09	Arsenal	0	0	17	4

EMMANUEL-THOMAS, Jay (M)   0   0
b.Forest Gate 27-12-90
Source: Scholar. Honours: England Youth.

2008-09	Arsenal	0	0	

FABIANSKI, Lukasz (G)   62   0
H: 6 3 W: 13 01 b.Costrzyn nad Odra 18-4-85
Honours: Poland Under-21, 14 full caps.

2005-06	Legia	30	0		
2006-07	Legia	23	0	53	0
2007-08	Arsenal	3	0		
2008-09	Arsenal	6	0	9	0

FABREGAS, Francesc (M)   160   17
H: 5 11 W: 11 00 b.Vilessoc de Mar 4-5-87
Source: Barcelona. Honours: Spain Youth, Under-21, 41 full caps, 1 goal.

2003-04	Arsenal	0	0		
2004-05	Arsenal	33	2		
2005-06	Arsenal	35	3		
2006-07	Arsenal	38	2		
2007-08	Arsenal	32	7		
2008-09	Arsenal	22	3	160	17

FONTE, Rui (F)   10   0
H: 6 0 W: 12 13 b.Lisbon 23-9-90
Source: Scholar. Honours: Portugal Youth, Under-21.

2007-08	Arsenal	0	0		
2008-09	Arsenal	0	0		
2008-09	Crystal Palace	10	0	10	0

FREEMAN, Luke (F)   1   0
H: 6 0 W: 10 00 b.London 22-3-92
Source: Scholar.

2007-08	Gillingham	1	0	1	0
2008-09	Arsenal	0	0		

FRIMPONG, Emmanuel (M)   0   0
H: 5 11 W: 10 07 b.Ghana 10-1-92
Source: Scholar.

2008-09	Arsenal	0	0	

GALLAS, William (D)   337   23
H: 6 0 W: 12 12 b.Asnieres 17-8-77
Honours: France Under-21, 72 full caps, 2 goals.

1996-97	Caen	18	0	18	0
1997-98	Marseille	3	0		
1998-99	Marseille	30	0		
1999-2000	Marseille	22	0		
2000-01	Marseille	30	2	85	2
2001-02	Chelsea	30	1		
2002-03	Chelsea	38	4		
2003-04	Chelsea	29	0		
2004-05	Chelsea	28	2		
2005-06	Chelsea	34	5		
2006-07	Chelsea	0	0	159	12
2006-07	Arsenal	21	3		
2007-08	Arsenal	31	4		
2008-09	Arsenal	23	2	75	9

GIBBS, Kieran (D)   15   0
H: 5 10 W: 10 02 b.Lambeth 26-9-89
Source: Scholar. Honours: England Youth, Under-21.

2007-08	Arsenal	0	0		
2007-08	Norwich C	7	0	7	0
2008-09	Arsenal	8	0	8	0

GILBERT, Kerrea (D)   65   1
H: 5 6 W: 11 03 b.Hammersmith 28-2-87
Source: Scholar. Honours: England Youth.

2005-06	Arsenal	2	0		
2006-07	Arsenal	0	0		
2006-07	Cardiff C	24	0	24	0
2007-08	Arsenal	0	0		
2007-08	Southend U	5	0	5	0
2008-09	Arsenal	0	0	2	0
2008-09	Leicester C	34	1	34	1

HENDERSON, Conor (M)   0   0
H: 6 1 W: 11 13 b.Sidcup 8-9-91
Source: Scholar. Honours: Eire Youth.

2008-09	Arsenal	0	0	

HOYTE, Gavin (D)   8   0
H: 5 11 W: 11 00 b.Waltham Forest 6-6-90
Source: Scholar. Honours: England Youth.

2007-08	Arsenal	0	0		
2008-09	Arsenal	1	0	1	0
2008-09	Watford	7	0	7	0

LANSBURY, Henri (M)   16   4
H: 6 0 W: 13 06 b.Enfield 12-10-90
Source: Scholar. Honours: England Youth.

2007-08	Arsenal	0	0		
2008-09	Arsenal	0	0		
2008-09	Scunthorpe U	16	4	16	4

MANNONE, Vito (G)   3   0
H: 6 0 W: 11 08 b.Desio 2-3-88
Source: Atalanta.

2005-06	Arsenal	0	0		
2006-07	Arsenal	0	0		
2006-07	Barnsley	2	0	2	0
2007-08	Arsenal	0	0		
2008-09	Arsenal	1	0	1	0

MERIDA PEREZ, Fran (M)   2   0
H: 5 11 W: 13 00 b.Barcelona 4-3-90
Source: Scholar.

2006-07	Arsenal	0	0		
2007-08	Arsenal	0	0		
2008-09	Arsenal	2	0	2	0

MURPHY, Rhys (F)   0   0
H: 6 1 W: 11 13 b.Shoreham 6-11-90
Honours: England Youth.

2007-08	Arsenal	0	0	
2008-09	Arsenal	0	0	

NASRI, Samir (M)   150   17
H: 5 9 W: 11 11 b.Marseille 26-6-87
Honours: France Youth, Under-21, 15 full caps, 2 goals.

2004-05	Marseille	24	1		
2005-06	Marseille	30	1		
2006-07	Marseille	37	3		
2007-08	Marseille	30	6	121	11
2008-09	Arsenal	29	6	29	6

NORDTVEIT, Havard (D)   9   0
H: 6 2 W: 11 09 b.Vats 21-6-90
Honours: Norway Youth.

2007	Haugesund	9	0	9	0
2007-08	Arsenal	0	0		
2008-09	Arsenal	0	0		

On loan to Lillestrom

OGOGO, Abu (D)   9   1
H: 5 8 W: 10 02 b.Epsom 3-11-89
Source: Scholar.

2007-08	Arsenal	0	0		
2008-09	Arsenal	0	0		
2008-09	Barnet	9	1	9	1

RAMSEY, Aaron (M)   25   1
H: 5 9 W: 10 07 b.Caerphilly 26-12-90
Source: School. Honours: Wales Youth, Under-21, 6 full caps.

2006-07	Cardiff C	1	0		
2007-08	Cardiff C	15	1	16	1
2008-09	Arsenal	9	0	9	0

RANDALL, Mark (M)   12   0
H: 6 0 W: 12 12 b.Milton Keynes 28-9-89
Source: Scholar.

2006-07	Arsenal	0	0		
2007-08	Arsenal	1	0		
2007-08	Burnley	10	0	10	0
2008-09	Arsenal	1	0	2	0

RASMUSSEN, Jonas (M)   0   0
b.Denmark 1-8-91
Source: Scholar.

2008-09	Arsenal	0	0	

RODGERS, Paul (D)   11   0
H: 5 10 W: 10 10 b.Edmonton 6-10-89
Source: Scholar.

2007-08	Arsenal	0	0		
2008-09	Arsenal	0	0		
2008-09	Northampton T	11	0	11	0

ROSICKY, Tomas (M)   234   36
H: 5 10 W: 10 10 b.Prague 4-10-80
Honours: Czech Republic Under-21, 67 full caps, 18 goals.

1998-99	Sparta Prague	3	0		
1999-2000	Sparta Prague	24	5		
2000-01	Sparta Prague	14	3	41	8
2000-01	Borussia Dortmund	15	0		
2001-02	Borussia Dortmund	30	5		
2002-03	Borussia Dortmund	30	3		
2003-04	Borussia Dortmund	30	9		
2004-05	Borussia Dortmund	27	4		
2005-06	Borussia Dortmund	28	5	149	19
2006-07	Arsenal	26	3		

2007-08	Arsenal	18	6		
2008-09	Arsenal	0	0	44	9

SAGNA, Bakari (D)   151   1
H: 5 10 W: 11 05 b.Sens 14-2-83
Source: Auxerre B. *Honours:* France
Under-21, 10 full caps.

2004-05	Auxerre	26	0		
2005-06	Auxerre	23	0		
2006-07	Auxerre	38	0	87	0
2007-08	Arsenal	29	1		
2008-09	Arsenal	35	0	64	1

SENDEROS, Philippe (D)   90   7
H: 6 1 W: 13 10 b.Geneva 14-2-85
Honours: Switzerland Youth, Under-20,
Under-21, 31 full caps, 3 goals.

2001-02	Servette	3	0		
2002-03	Servette	23	3	26	3
2003-04	Arsenal	0	0		
2004-05	Arsenal	13	0		
2005-06	Arsenal	20	2		
2006-07	Arsenal	14	0		
2007-08	Arsenal	17	2		
2008-09	Arsenal	0	0	64	4

On loan to AC Milan

SILVESTRE, Mikael (D)   330   9
H: 6 0 W: 13 12 b.Chambray les Tours
9-8-77
Honours: France Youth, Under-21, 40 full
caps, 2 goals.

1995-96	Rennes	1	0		
1996-97	Rennes	16	0		
1997-98	Rennes	32	0	49	0
1998-99	Internazionale	18	1	18	1
1999-2000	Manchester U	31	0		
2000-01	Manchester U	30	1		
2001-02	Manchester U	35	0		
2002-03	Manchester U	34	1		
2003-04	Manchester U	34	0		
2004-05	Manchester U	35	2		
2005-06	Manchester U	33	1		
2006-07	Manchester U	14	1		
2007-08	Manchester U	3	0	249	6
2008-09	Arsenal	14	2	14	2

SIMPSON, Jay (M)   54   7
H: 5 11 W: 13 04 b.Enfield 1-12-88
Source: Scholar.

2007-08	Arsenal	0	0		
2007-08	*Millwall*	41	6	41	6
2008-09	Arsenal	0	0		
2008-09	*WBA*	13	1	13	1

SONG BILLONG, Alexandre (M)   59   1
H: 5 11 W: 12 04 b.Douala 9-9-87
Source: Bastia. *Honours:* France Youth,
Cameroon Youth. Cameroon 12 full caps.

2005-06	Arsenal	5	0		
2006-07	Arsenal	2	0		
2006-07	*Charlton Ath*	12	0	12	0
2007-08	Arsenal	9	0		
2008-09	Arsenal	31	1	47	1

STEER, Rene (D)   5   0
H: 5 8 W: 13 00 b.Luton 31-1-90
Source: Scholar.

2007-08	Arsenal	0	0		
2008-09	Arsenal	0	0		
2008-09	*Gillingham*	5	0	5	0

SUNU, Gilles (F)   0   0
b.Chateauroux 30-3-91
Source: Scholar.

2007-08	Arsenal	0	0		
2008-09	Arsenal	0	0		

SZCZESNY, Wojciech (G)   0   0
H: 5 10 W: 11 11 b.Warsaw 18-4-90
Source: Scholar.

2007-08	Arsenal	0	0		
2008-09	Arsenal	0	0		

TOURE, Kolo (D)   225   9
H: 5 10 W: 13 08 b.Sokoura Bouake
19-3-81
Source: ASEC Mimosas. *Honours:* Ivory
Coast 68 full caps, 2 goals.

2001-02	Arsenal	0	0		
2002-03	Arsenal	26	2		
2003-04	Arsenal	37	1		
2004-05	Arsenal	35	0		
2005-06	Arsenal	33	0		
2006-07	Arsenal	35	3		

2007-08	Arsenal	30	2		
2008-09	Arsenal	29	1	225	9

TRAORE, Armand (D)   22   1
H: 6 1 W: 12 12 b.Paris 8-10-89
Source: Monaco. *Honours:* France Youth.

2006-07	Arsenal	0	0		
2007-08	Arsenal	3	0		
2008-09	Arsenal	0	0	3	0
2008-09	*Portsmouth*	19	1	19	1

VAN DEN BERG, Vincent (M)   5   0
b.Holland 19-1-89
Source: Heerenveen.

2006-07	Arsenal	0	0		
2007-08	*Go Ahead*	5	0	5	0
2007-08	Arsenal	0	0		
2008-09	Arsenal	0	0		

VAN PERSIE, Robin (F)   176   53
H: 6 0 W: 11 00 b.Rotterdam 6-8-83
Honours: Holland Under-17, 31 full caps, 13
goals.

2001-02	Feyenoord	10	0		
2002-03	Feyenoord	23	8		
2003-04	Feyenoord	28	6	61	14
2004-05	Arsenal	26	5		
2005-06	Arsenal	24	5		
2006-07	Arsenal	22	11		
2007-08	Arsenal	15	7		
2008-09	Arsenal	28	11	115	39

VELA, Carlos (F)   78   12
H: 5 9 W: 10 05 b.Cancun 1-3-89
Source: Guadalajara. *Honours:* Mexico
Youth, Under-20, 14 full caps, 4 goals.

2005-06	Arsenal	0	0		
2006-07	Arsenal	0	0		
2006-07	*Salamanca*	31	8	31	8
2007-08	Arsenal	0	0		
2007-08	*Osasuna*	33	3	33	3
2008-09	Arsenal	14	1	14	1

WALCOTT, Theo (F)   84   10
H: 5 9 W: 11 01 b.Compton 16-3-89
Source: Scholar. *Honours:* England Youth,
Under-21, B, 8 full caps, 3 goals.

2005-06	Southampton	21	4	21	4
2005-06	Arsenal	0	0		
2006-07	Arsenal	16	0		
2007-08	Arsenal	25	4		
2008-09	Arsenal	22	2	63	6

WATT, Sanchez (M)   0   0
b.London 14-2-91
Source: Scholar.

2008-09	Arsenal	0	0		

WILSHERE, Jack (M)   1   0
H: 5 7 W: 11 03 b.Stevenage 1-1-92
Source: From Scholar. *Honours:* England
Youth.

2008-09	Arsenal	1	0	1	0

Scholars
Ayling, Luke David; Byles, Sam Frank;
Deacon, Roarie; Eastmond, Craig Leon;
Evina, Cedric David; Freeman, Luke
Anthony; Obed, Rhema; Shea, James.

ASTON VILLA (4)

AGBONLAHOR, Gabriel (F)   130   32
H: 5 11 W: 12 05 b.Birmingham 13-10-86
Source: Scholar. *Honours:* England Under-20,
Under-21, 2 full caps.

2005-06	Aston Villa	9	1		
2005-06	*Watford*	2	0	2	0
2005-06	*Sheffield W*	8	0	8	0
2006-07	Aston Villa	38	9		
2007-08	Aston Villa	37	11		
2008-09	Aston Villa	36	11	120	32

ALBRIGHTON, Marc (M)   0   0
H: 6 2 W: 12 06 b.Sutton Coldfield
18-11-89
Source: Scholar. *Honours:* England Youth.

2008-09	Aston Villa	0	0		

BAKER, Nathan (D)   0   0
H: 6 2 W: 11 11 b. 23-4-91
Source: Scholar. *Honours:* England Youth.

2008-09	Aston Villa	0	0		

BANNAN, Barry (D)   10   1
H: 5 10 W: 10 08 b.Glasgow 1-12-89
Source: Scholar. *Honours:* Scotland
Under-21.

2008-09	Aston Villa	0	0		
2008-09	*Derby Co*	10	1	10	1

BARRY, Gareth (D)   365   41
H: 5 11 W: 12 06 b.Hastings 23-2-81
Source: Trainee. *Honours:* England Youth, B,
Under-21, 30 full caps, 2 goals.

1997-98	Aston Villa	2	0		
1998-99	Aston Villa	32	2		
1999-2000	Aston Villa	30	1		
2000-01	Aston Villa	30	0		
2001-02	Aston Villa	20	0		
2002-03	Aston Villa	35	3		
2003-04	Aston Villa	36	3		
2004-05	Aston Villa	34	7		
2005-06	Aston Villa	36	3		
2006-07	Aston Villa	35	8		
2007-08	Aston Villa	37	9		
2008-09	Aston Villa	38	5	365	41

BEVAN, David (G)   0   0
H: 6 2 W: 13 00 b.Cork 24-6-89
Source: Scholar.

2007-08	Aston Villa	0	0		
2008-09	Aston Villa	0	0		

BOUMA, Wilfred (D)   334   38
H: 5 10 W: 13 01 b.Helmond 15-6-78
Honours: Holland 35 full caps, 2 goals.

1994-95	PSV Eindhoven	1	0		
1995-96	PSV Eindhoven	4	0		
1996-97	PSV Eindhoven	1	0		
1996-97	MVV	18	7		
1997-98	MVV	33	6	51	13
1998-99	Fortuna Sittard	33	5	33	5
1999-2000	PSV Eindhoven	27	9		
2000-01	PSV Eindhoven	20	0		
2001-02	PSV Eindhoven	27	3		
2002-03	PSV Eindhoven	27	1		
2003-04	PSV Eindhoven	32	5		
2004-05	PSV Eindhoven	28	1	167	19
2005-06	Aston Villa	20	0		
2006-07	Aston Villa	25	0		
2007-08	Aston Villa	38	1		
2008-09	Aston Villa	0	0	83	1

CAREW, John (F)   284   110
H: 6 5 W: 14 11 b.Lorenskog 5-9-79
Source: Lorenskog. *Honours:* Norway Youth,
Under-21, 77 full caps, 21 goals.

1998	Valerenga	18	7		
1999	Valerenga	15	7	33	14
1999	Rosenborg	8	10		
2000	Rosenborg	10	8	18	18
2000-01	Valencia	37	11		
2001-02	Valencia	15	1		
2002-03	Valencia	32	8	84	20
2003-04	Roma	20	8	20	8
2004-05	Besiktas	24	13	24	13
2005-06	Lyon	26	9		
2006-07	Lyon	9	1	35	10
2006-07	Aston Villa	11	3		
2007-08	Aston Villa	32	13		
2008-09	Aston Villa	27	11	70	27

CLARK, Ciaran (D)   0   0
H: 6 2 W: 12 00 b.Harrow 26-9-89
Source: Scholar. *Honours:* England Youth.

2008-09	Aston Villa	0	0		

COLLINS, James (F)   0   0
b. 1-12-90
Source: Scholar.

2008-09	Aston Villa	0	0		

COLLINS, Jordan (F)   0   0
H: 5 7 W: 11 08 b.Birmingham 11-3-89
Source: Scholar.

2007-08	Aston Villa	0	0		
2008-09	Aston Villa	0	0		

CUELLAR, Carlos (D)   224   10
H: 6 3 W: 13 03 b.Madrid 23-8-81

2000-01	Calahorra	27	0	27	0
2001-02	Numancia	23	1		
2002-03	Numancia	39	3	62	4
2003-04	Osasuna	5	0		
2004-05	Osasuna	14	0		
2005-06	Osasuna	29	1		
2006-07	Osasuna	23	1	71	2

2007-08	Rangers	36	4	**36**	**4**
2008-09	Aston Villa	28	0	**28**	**0**

DAU, Thomas (G)   **0　0**
b.Austria 9-8-91
Source: Scholar.

2008-09	Aston Villa	0	0

DAVIES, Curtis (D)   **168　6**
H: 6 2　W: 11 13　b.Waltham Forest 15-3-85
Source: From Scholar. Honours: England Under-21.

2003-04	Luton T	6	0		
2004-05	Luton T	44	1		
2005-06	Luton T	6	1	**56**	**2**
2005-06	WBA	33	2		
2006-07	WBA	32	0		
2007-08	WBA	0	0	**65**	**2**
2007-08	*Aston Villa*	12	1		
2008-09	Aston Villa	35	1	**47**	**2**

DELFOUNESO, Nathan (F)   **4　0**
H: 6 1　W: 12 04　b.Birmingham 2-2-91
Source: Scholar. Honours: England Youth.

2007-08	Aston Villa	0	0		
2008-09	Aston Villa	4	0	**4**	**0**

FORRESTER, Harry (M)   **0　0**
b. 2-1-91

2007-08	Aston Villa	0	0
2008-09	Aston Villa	0	0

FRIEDEL, Brad (G)   **389　1**
H: 6 3　W: 14 00　b.Lakewood 18-5-71
Honours: USA 82 full caps.

1996	Columbus Crew	9	0		
1997	Columbus Crew	29	0	**38**	**0**
1997-98	Liverpool	11	0		
1998-99	Liverpool	12	0		
1999-2000	Liverpool	2	0		
2000-01	Liverpool	0	0	**25**	**0**
2000-01	Blackburn R	27	0		
2001-02	Blackburn R	36	0		
2002-03	Blackburn R	37	0		
2003-04	Blackburn R	36	1		
2004-05	Blackburn R	38	0		
2005-06	Blackburn R	38	0		
2006-07	Blackburn R	38	0		
2007-08	Blackburn R	38	0	**288**	**1**
2008-09	Aston Villa	38	0	**38**	**0**

GARDNER, Craig (M)   **58　5**
H: 5 10　W: 11 13　b.Solihull 25-11-86
Source: Scholar. Honours: England Under-21.

2004-05	Aston Villa	0	0		
2005-06	Aston Villa	8	0		
2006-07	Aston Villa	13	2		
2007-08	Aston Villa	23	3		
2008-09	Aston Villa	14	0	**58**	**5**

GUZAN, Brad (G)   **80　0**
H: 6 4　W: 14 11　b.Chicago 9-9-84
Honours: USA 13 full caps.

2005	Chivas USA	24	0		
2006	Chivas USA	13	0		
2007	Chivas USA	27	0		
2008	Chivas USA	15	0	**79**	**0**
2008-09	Aston Villa	1	0	**1**	**0**

HALFHUID, Arsenio (M)   **0　0**
b.Voorburg 9-11-91
Source: Excelsior.

2008-09	Aston Villa	0	0

HAREWOOD, Marlon (F)   **364　104**
H: 6 1　W: 13 07　b.Hampstead 25-8-79
Source: Trainee.

1996-97	Nottingham F	0	0		
1997-98	Nottingham F	1	0		
1998-99	Nottingham F	23	1		
1998-99	*Ipswich T*	6	1	**6**	**1**
1999-2000	Nottingham F	34	4		
2000-01	Nottingham F	33	3		
2001-02	Nottingham F	28	11		
2002-03	Nottingham F	44	20		
2003-04	Nottingham F	19	12	**182**	**63**
2003-04	West Ham U	28	13		
2004-05	West Ham U	45	17		
2005-06	West Ham U	37	14		
2006-07	West Ham U	32	3	**142**	**47**
2007-08	Aston Villa	23	5		
2008-09	Aston Villa	6	0	**29**	**5**
2008-09	*Wolverhampton W*	5	0	**5**	**0**

HERD, Chris (M)   **15　2**
H: 5 9　W: 11 04　b.Melbourne 4-4-89
Source: Scholar.

2007-08	Aston Villa	0	0		
2007-08	*Port Vale*	11	2	**11**	**2**
2007-08	*Wycombe W*	4	0	**4**	**0**
2008-09	Aston Villa	0	0		

HESKEY, Emile (F)   **468　110**
H: 6 2　W: 13 12　b.Leicester 11-1-78
Source: Trainee. Honours: England Youth, Under-21, B, 53 full caps, 7 goals.

1994-95	Leicester C	1	0		
1995-96	Leicester C	30	7		
1996-97	Leicester C	35	10		
1997-98	Leicester C	35	10		
1998-99	Leicester C	30	6		
1999-2000	Leicester C	23	7	**154**	**40**
1999-2000	Liverpool	12	3		
2000-01	Liverpool	36	14		
2001-02	Liverpool	35	9		
2002-03	Liverpool	32	6		
2003-04	Liverpool	35	7	**150**	**39**
2004-05	Birmingham C	34	10		
2005-06	Birmingham C	34	4	**68**	**14**
2006-07	Wigan Ath	34	8		
2007-08	Wigan Ath	28	4		
2008-09	Wigan Ath	20	3	**82**	**15**
2008-09	Aston Villa	14	2	**14**	**2**

HOFBAUER, Dominik (M)   **0　0**
b.Eggenberg 19-9-90
Source: Scholar.

2007-08	Aston Villa	0	0
2008-09	Aston Villa	0	0

HOGG, Jonathan (M)   **0　0**
H: 5 7　W: 10 05　b.Middlesbrough 6-12-88
Source: Scholar.

2007-08	Aston Villa	0	0
2008-09	Aston Villa	0	0

KNIGHT, Zat (D)   **198　5**
H: 6 6　W: 15 02　b.Solihull 2-5-80
Source: Rushall Olympic. Honours: England Under-21, 2 full caps.

1998-99	Fulham	0	0		
1999-2000	Fulham	0	0		
1999-2000	*Peterborough U*	8	0	**8**	**0**
2000-01	Fulham	0	0		
2001-02	Fulham	10	0		
2002-03	Fulham	17	0		
2003-04	Fulham	31	0		
2004-05	Fulham	35	1		
2005-06	Fulham	30	0		
2006-07	Fulham	23	2		
2007-08	Fulham	4	0	**150**	**3**
2007-08	Aston Villa	27	1		
2008-09	Aston Villa	13	1	**40**	**2**

LAURSEN, Martin (D)   **217　13**
H: 6 2　W: 12 05　b.Farvoug 26-7-77
Honours: Denmark Youth, Under-21, 53 full caps, 2 goals.

1995-96	Silkeborg	1	0		
1996-97	Silkeborg	12	0		
1997-98	Silkeborg	22	1	**35**	**1**
1998-99	Verona	6	0		
1999-2000	Verona	19	2		
2000-01	Verona	31	0	**56**	**2**
2001-02	AC Milan	22	2		
2002-03	AC Milan	10	0		
2003-04	AC Milan	10	0	**42**	**2**
2004-05	Aston Villa	12	1		
2005-06	Aston Villa	1	0		
2006-07	Aston Villa	14	0		
2007-08	Aston Villa	38	6		
2008-09	Aston Villa	19	1	**84**	**8**

LICHAJ, Eric (M)   **0　0**
H: 5 11　W: 12 07　b.Denvers Grove 17-11-88
Source: Univ of North Carolina, Chicago Magic.

2007-08	Aston Villa	0	0
2008-09	Aston Villa	0	0

LOWRY, Shane (D)   **0　0**
H: 6 1　W: 13 01　b.Perth 12-6-89
Source: Scholar. Honours: Eire Under-21.

2007-08	Aston Villa	0	0
2008-09	Aston Villa	0	0

LUND, Eric (D)   **0　0**
H: 6 1　W: 12 00　b.Gothenburg 6-11-88
Source: Scholar.

2006-07	Aston Villa	0	0
2007-08	Aston Villa	0	0
2008-09	Aston Villa	0	0

McGURK, Adam (F)   **0　0**
H: 5 9　W: 12 13　b.St Helier 24-1-89
Source: Scholar.

2005-06	Aston Villa	0	0
2006-07	Aston Villa	0	0
2007-08	Aston Villa	0	0
2008-09	Aston Villa	0	0

MIKAELSSON, Tobias (F)   **6　0**
H: 6 3　W: 11 04　b.Jorlanda 17-11-88
Source: Scholar.

2005-06	Aston Villa	0	0		
2006-07	Aston Villa	0	0		
2007-08	*Port Vale*	6	0	**6**	**0**
2008-09	Aston Villa	0	0		

MILNER, James (M)   **211　17**
H: 5 9　W: 11 00　b.Leeds 4-1-86
Source: Trainee. Honours: FA Schools, Youth, England Under-20, Under-21.

2002-03	Leeds U	18	2		
2003-04	Leeds U	30	3	**48**	**5**
2003-04	*Swindon T*	6	2	**6**	**2**
2004-05	Newcastle U	25	1		
2005-06	Newcastle U	3	0		
2005-06	*Aston Villa*	27	1		
2006-07	Newcastle U	35	3		
2007-08	Newcastle U	29	2		
2008-09	Newcastle U	2	0	**94**	**6**
2008-09	Aston Villa	36	3	**63**	**4**

O'HALLORAN, Stephen (D)   **14　0**
H: 6 0　W: 11 07　b.Cork 29-11-87
Source: Scholar. Honours: Eire Under-21, 2 full caps.

2005-06	Aston Villa	0	0		
2006-07	Aston Villa	0	0		
2006-07	*Wycombe W*	11	0	**11**	**0**
2007-08	Aston Villa	0	0		
2007-08	*Southampton*	1	0	**1**	**0**
2008-09	Aston Villa	0	0		
2008-09	*Swansea C*	2	0	**2**	**0**

OSBOURNE, Isaiah (M)   **27　0**
H: 6 2　W: 12 07　b.Birmingham 5-11-87
Source: Scholar.

2005-06	Aston Villa	0	0		
2006-07	Aston Villa	11	0		
2007-08	Aston Villa	8	0		
2008-09	Aston Villa	0	0	**19**	**0**
2008-09	*Nottingham F*	8	0	**8**	**0**

PARISH, Elliot (G)   **0　0**
b.Northampton 20-5-90
Source: Scholar. Honours: England Youth.

2008-09	Aston Villa	0	0

PETROV, Stilian (M)   **360　60**
H: 5 11　W: 11 09　b.Sofia 5-7-79
Source: FC Montana. Honours: Bulgaria 87 full caps, 8 goals.

1997-98	CSKA Sofia	10	0		
1998-99	CSKA Sofia	29	3	**39**	**3**
1999-2000	Celtic	29	1		
2000-01	Celtic	28	7		
2001-02	Celtic	27	6		
2002-03	Celtic	34	12		
2003-04	Celtic	35	6		
2004-05	Celtic	37	11		
2005-06	Celtic	37	10	**227**	**53**
2006-07	Aston Villa	30	2		
2007-08	Aston Villa	36	1		
2008-09	Aston Villa	36	1	**94**	**4**

REO-COKER, Nigel (M)   **240　18**
H: 5 8　W: 12 03　b.Southwark 14-5-84
Source: Scholar. Honours: England Youth, Under-20, Under-21.

2001-02	Wimbledon	1	0		
2002-03	Wimbledon	32	2		
2003-04	Wimbledon	25	4	**58**	**6**
2003-04	West Ham U	15	2		
2004-05	West Ham U	39	3		
2005-06	West Ham U	31	5		
2006-07	West Ham U	35	1	**120**	**11**
2007-08	Aston Villa	36	0		
2008-09	Aston Villa	26	1	**62**	**1**

ROOME, Matthew (M)   0   0
b.Burton 12-10-89
Source: Scholar.

| 2008-09 | Aston Villa | 0 | 0 | | |

SALIFOU, Moustapha (M)   67   3
H: 5 11   W: 10 12   b.Lome 1-6-83
Source: From Modele de Lome. *Honours:*
Togo 39 full caps, 4 goals.

2002-03	Oberhausen	11	1		
2003-04	Oberhausen	6	0		
2004-05	Oberhausen	16	0	33	1
2005-06	Stade Brest	7	0	7	0
2006-07	FC Wil	19	2		
2007-08	FC Wil	4	0	23	2
2007-08	Aston Villa	4	0		
2008-09	Aston Villa	0	0	4	0

SHOREY, Nicky (D)   303   10
H: 5 9   W: 10 08   b.Romford 19-2-81
Source: Trainee. *Honours:* England B, 2 full
caps.

1999-2000	Leyton Orient	7	0		
2000-01	Leyton Orient	8	0	15	0
2000-01	Reading	0	0		
2001-02	Reading	32	0		
2002-03	Reading	43	2		
2003-04	Reading	35	2		
2004-05	Reading	44	3		
2005-06	Reading	40	2		
2006-07	Reading	37	1		
2007-08	Reading	36	2	267	12
2008-09	Aston Villa	21	0	21	0

SIDWELL, Steve (M)   241   41
H: 5 10   W: 11 00   b.Wandsworth 14-12-82
Source: Scholar. *Honours:* England Under-20,
Under-21.

2001-02	Arsenal	0	0		
2001-02	*Brentford*	30	4	30	4
2002-03	Arsenal	0	0		
2002-03	*Brighton & HA*	12	5	12	5
2002-03	Reading	13	2		
2003-04	Reading	43	8		
2004-05	Reading	44	5		
2005-06	Reading	33	10		
2006-07	Reading	35	4	168	29
2007-08	Chelsea	15	0	15	0
2008-09	Aston Villa	16	3	16	3

SIEGRIST, Benjamin (G)   0   0
b.Basle 31-1-92
Source: Scholar.

| 2008-09 | Aston Villa | 0 | 0 | | |

SIMMONDS, Sam (D)   0   0
b.Birmingham 17-3-90
Source: Scholar.

| 2008-09 | Aston Villa | 0 | 0 | | |

STIEBER, Zoltan (M)   15   1
H: 5 8   W: 9 10   b.Savar 16-10-88
Source: From Scholar. *Honours:* Hungary
Youth.

2006-07	Aston Villa	0	0		
2007-08	Aston Villa	0	0		
2007-08	*Yeovil T*	15	1	15	1
2008-09	Aston Villa	0	0		

TAYLOR, Stuart (G)   68   0
H: 6 5   W: 13 07   b.Romford 28-11-80
Source: Trainee. *Honours:* FA Schools,
England Youth, Under-21.

1998-99	Arsenal	0	0		
1999-2000	Arsenal	0	0		
1999-2000	*Bristol R*	4	0	4	0
2000-01	Arsenal	0	0		
2000-01	Crystal Palace	10	0	10	0
2000-01	*Peterborough U*	6	0	6	0
2001-02	Arsenal	10	0		
2002-03	Arsenal	8	0		
2003-04	Arsenal	0	0		
2004-05	Arsenal	0	0	18	0
2004-05	*Leicester C*	10	0	10	0
2005-06	Aston Villa	2	0		
2006-07	Aston Villa	6	0		
2007-08	Aston Villa	4	0		
2008-09	Aston Villa	0	0	12	0
2008-09	*Cardiff C*	8	0	8	0

WEIMANN, Andreas (F)   0   0
b.Vienna 5-8-91
Source: Scholar.

| 2008-09 | Aston Villa | 0 | 0 | | |

WILLIAMS, Sam (M)   35   6
H: 5 11   W: 10 08   b.London 9-6-87
Source: Scholar.

2004-05	Aston Villa	0	0		
2005-06	Aston Villa	0	0		
2005-06	*Wrexham*	15	2	15	2
2006-07	Aston Villa	0	0		
2006-07	*Brighton & HA*	3	1	3	1
2007-08	Aston Villa	0	0		
2008-09	Aston Villa	0	0		
2008-09	*Colchester U*	1	0	1	0
2008-09	*Walsall*	5	1	5	1
2008-09	*Brentford*	11	2	11	2

YOUNG, Ashley (M)   184   37
H: 5 10   W: 10 03   b.Stevenage 9-7-85
Source: Juniors. *Honours:* England Under-21,
5 full caps.

2002-03	Watford	0	0		
2003-04	Watford	5	3		
2004-05	Watford	34	0		
2005-06	Watford	39	13		
2006-07	Watford	20	3	98	19
2006-07	Aston Villa	13	2		
2007-08	Aston Villa	37	9		
2008-09	Aston Villa	36	7	86	18

YOUNG, Luke (D)   314   6
H: 6 0   W: 12 04   b.Harlow 19-7-79
Source: Trainee. *Honours:* England Youth,
Under-21, 7 full caps.

1997-98	Tottenham H	0	0		
1998-99	Tottenham H	15	0		
1999-2000	Tottenham H	20	0		
2000-01	Tottenham H	23	0	58	0
2001-02	Charlton Ath	34	0		
2002-03	Charlton Ath	32	0		
2003-04	Charlton Ath	24	0		
2004-05	Charlton Ath	36	2		
2005-06	Charlton Ath	32	1		
2006-07	Charlton Ath	29	1	187	4
2007-08	Middlesbrough	35	1	35	1
2008-09	Aston Villa	34	1	34	1

Scholars
Berry, Durrell Joel; Blythe, Richard John;
Bradley, Daniel David; Clifton, James;
Collins, James Steven; Deeney, Ellis John
Paul; Dyer, Jack Robert; Flanagan, Callum
Reiss; Gardner, Gary; Grocott, William;
Lampkin, Jason Severiano; Love, Ben Jake;
Poyser, Kofi Ray; Roberts, Tomos Daniel;
Simmonds, Ryan; Stieber, Andras.

BARNET (5)

ADOMAH, Albert (F)   67   14
H: 6 1   W: 11 08   b.Harrow 13-12-87
Source: Harrow Borough.

| 2007-08 | Barnet | 22 | 5 | | |
| 2008-09 | Barnet | 45 | 9 | 67 | 14 |

AKURANG, Cliff (F)   45   10
H: 6 2   W: 12 03   b.Histon 27-2-81
Source: Chesham U, Hitchin T, Thurrock,
Heybridge S, Dagenham & R, Histon.

| 2007-08 | Barnet | 21 | 7 | | |
| 2008-09 | Barnet | 24 | 3 | 45 | 10 |

BECKWITH, Rob (G)   33   0
H: 6 1   W: 13 12   b.Hackney 12-9-84
Source: Scholar.

2002-03	Luton T	4	0		
2003-04	Luton T	13	0		
2004-05	Luton T	0	0		
2005-06	Luton T	0	0		
2005-06	*Chesterfield*	2	0	2	0
2006-07	Luton T	0	0	17	0
2007-08	Barnet	9	0		
2008-09	Barnet	5	0	14	0

BIRCHALL, Adam (F)   152   25
H: 5 7   W: 10 09   b.Maidstone 2-12-84
Source: Trainee. *Honours:* Wales Under-21.

2002-03	Arsenal	0	0		
2003-04	Arsenal	0	0		
2004-05	Arsenal	0	0		
2004-05	*Wycombe W*	12	4	12	4
2005-06	Mansfield T	31	2		
2006-07	Mansfield T	5	0	36	2
2006-07	Barnet	23	6		
2007-08	Barnet	42	11		
2008-09	Barnet	39	2	104	19

BISHOP, Neil (M)   83   3
H: 6 1   W: 12 10   b.Stockton 7-8-81
Source: Billingham T, Gateshead,
Spennymoor U, Whitby T, Scarborough,
York C.

| 2007-08 | Barnet | 39 | 2 | | |
| 2008-09 | Barnet | 44 | 1 | 83 | 3 |

BLACK, Tommy (M)   205   19
H: 5 7   W: 11 10   b.Chigwell 26-11-79
Source: Trainee.

1998-99	Arsenal	0	0		
1999-2000	Arsenal	1	0	1	0
1999-2000	*Carlisle U*	5	1	5	1
1999-2000	*Bristol C*	4	0	4	0
2000-01	Crystal Palace	40	4		
2001-02	Crystal Palace	25	0		
2002-03	Crystal Palace	36	6		
2003-04	Crystal Palace	25	0		
2004-05	Crystal Palace	0	0		
2004-05	*Sheffield U*	4	1	4	1
2005-06	Crystal Palace	1	0		
2005-06	*Gillingham*	17	5	17	5
2006-07	Crystal Palace	0	0	127	10
2006-07	*Bradford C*	4	0	4	0
2007-08	Southend U	38	2		
2008-09	Southend U	0	0	38	2
2008-09	Barnet	5	0	5	0

BREEN, Gary (D)   527   13
H: 6 3   W: 13 03   b.Hendon 12-12-73
Source: Charlton Ath. *Honours:* Eire
Under-21, 63 full caps, 7 goals.

1991-92	Maidstone U	19	0	19	0
1992-93	Gillingham	29	0		
1993-94	Gillingham	22	0	51	0
1994-95	Peterborough U	44	1		
1995-96	Peterborough U	25	0	69	1
1995-96	Birmingham C	18	1		
1996-97	Birmingham C	22	1	40	2
1996-97	Coventry C	9	0		
1997-98	Coventry C	30	1		
1998-99	Coventry C	25	0		
1999-2000	Coventry C	21	0		
2000-01	Coventry C	31	1		
2001-02	Coventry C	30	0	146	2
2002-03	West Ham U	14	0	14	0
2003-04	Sunderland	32	4		
2004-05	Sunderland	40	2		
2005-06	Sunderland	35	1	107	7
2006-07	Wolverhampton W	40	1		
2007-08	Wolverhampton W	19	0	59	1
2008-09	Barnet	22	0	22	0

BURGE, Ryan (M)   2   0
H: 5 10   W: 10 03   b.Cheltenham 12-10-88
Source: Scholar.

2005-06	Birmingham C	0	0		
2006-07	Birmingham C	0	0		
2007-08	Birmingham C	0	0		
2008-09	Barnet	2	0	2	0

CAREW, Ashley (M)   43   2
H: 6 0   W: 11 00   b.Lambeth 17-12-85
Source: Scholar.

2006-07	Barnet	0	0		
2007-08	Barnet	33	1		
2008-09	Barnet	10	1	43	2

CARPENTER, Phil (M)   0   0
H: 5 11   W: 11 10   b.Barnet 15-1-90

| 2008-09 | Barnet | 0 | 0 | | |

CHARLES, Elliott (F)   5   0
H: 6 2   W: 13 00   b.Enfield 23-12-90
Source: Scholar.

| 2008-09 | Barnet | 5 | 0 | 5 | 0 |

DE MAGALHAES, Jeremy (D)   101   1
H: 6 0   W: 12 02   b.Paris 21-11-83

2002-03	Laval	7	0		
2003-04	Laval	19	0		
2004-05	Laval	26	0		
2005-06	Laval	19	0		
2006-07	Laval	4	1	75	1
2007-08	Cannes	22	0	22	0
2008-09	Barnet	4	0	4	0

DEVERA, Joe (D)   101   1
H: 6 2   W: 12 00   b.Southgate 6-2-87

2005-06	Barnet	0	0		
2006-07	Barnet	26	0		
2007-08	Barnet	41	0		
2008-09	Barnet	34	1	101	1

DEVERDICS, Nicky (M) — 60 4
H: 5 11 W: 12 04 b.Gateshead 24-11-87
Source: Newcastle U Scholar, Gateshead.

Season	Club	Apps	Gls	Tot A	Tot G
2006-07	Gretna	6	1		
2007-08	Gretna	25	2	31	3
2008-09	Barnet	29	1	29	1

GILLET, Kenny (M) — 63 0
H: 5 10 W: 12 04 b.Bordeaux 3-1-86
Source: Caen.

Season	Club	Apps	Gls	Tot A	Tot G
2007-08	Barnet	31	0		
2008-09	Barnet	32	0	63	0

HARRISON, Lee (G) — 362 0
H: 6 2 W: 11 13 b.Billericay 12-9-71
Source: Trainee.

Season	Club	Apps	Gls	Tot A	Tot G
1990-91	Charlton Ath	0	0		
1991-92	Charlton Ath	0	0		
1991-92	Fulham	0	0		
1991-92	Gillingham	2	0	2	0
1992-93	Charlton Ath	0	0		
1992-93	Fulham	0	0		
1993-94	Fulham	0	0		
1994-95	Fulham	7	0		
1995-96	Fulham	5	0	12	0
1996-97	Barnet	21	0		
1997-98	Barnet	46	0		
1998-99	Barnet	43	0		
1999-2000	Barnet	43	0		
2000-01	Barnet	30	0		
2001-02	Barnet	0	0		
2002-03	Peterborough U	12	0		
2002-03	Leyton Orient	6	0		
2003-04	Leyton Orient	20	0		
2004-05	Leyton Orient	34	0	60	0
2005-06	Peterborough U	6	0	18	0
2006-07	Barnet	28	0		
2007-08	Barnet	38	0		
2008-09	Barnet	21	0	270	0

HART, Danny (M) — 5 1
H: 5 10 W: 11 09 b.London 26-4-89
Source: Boreham Wood.

Season	Club	Apps	Gls	Tot A	Tot G
2007-08	Barnet	2	0		
2008-09	Barnet	3	1	5	1

HENDON, Ian (D) — 418 25
H: 6 1 W: 13 02 b.Ilford 5-12-71
Source: Trainee. *Honours:* England Youth, Under-21.

Season	Club	Apps	Gls	Tot A	Tot G
1989-90	Tottenham H	0	0		
1990-91	Tottenham H	2	0		
1991-92	Tottenham H	2	0		
1991-92	Portsmouth	4	0	4	0
1991-92	Leyton Orient	4	0		
1992-93	Tottenham H	0	0		
1992-93	Barnsley	6	0	6	0
1993-94	Leyton Orient	36	2		
1994-95	Leyton Orient	29	0		
1994-95	Birmingham C	4	0	4	0
1995-96	Leyton Orient	38	2		
1996-97	Leyton Orient	28	1	137	5
1996-97	Notts Co	12	0		
1997-98	Notts Co	38	0		
1998-99	Notts Co	32	6	82	6
1998-99	Northampton T	7	0		
1999-2000	Northampton T	44	2		
2000-01	Northampton T	9	1	60	3
2000-01	Sheffield W	31	2		
2001-02	Sheffield W	9	0		
2002-03	Sheffield W	9	0	49	2
2002-03	Peterborough U	7	1	7	1
2004-05	Barnet	0	0		
2005-06	Barnet	35	4		
2006-07	Barnet	26	4		
2007-08	Barnet	4	0		
2008-09	Barnet	0	0	65	8

HUGHES, Mark (M) — 143 6
H: 5 10 W: 12 05 b.Dungannon 16-9-83
Source: Scholar. *Honours:* Northern Ireland Schools, Youth, Under-21, Under-23, 2 full caps.

Season	Club	Apps	Gls	Tot A	Tot G
2001-02	Tottenham H	0	0		
2002-03	Tottenham H	0	0		
2003-04	Tottenham H	0	0		
2004-05	Tottenham H	0	0		
2004-05	Northampton T	3	0	3	0
2004-05	Oldham Ath	27	0		
2005-06	Oldham Ath	33	1		
2006-07	Oldham Ath	0	0	60	1

From Thurrock.

Season	Club	Apps	Gls	Tot A	Tot G
2006-07	Chesterfield	2	1	2	1

From Stevenage B.

Season	Club	Apps	Gls	Tot A	Tot G
2007-08	Chester C	43	4		
2008-09	Chester C	26	0	69	4
2008-09	Barnet	9	0	9	0

KADOCH, Ran (G) — 58 0
H: 6 0 W: 12 06 b.Israel 4-10-85
Source: Sektzia Nes Tziona.

Season	Club	Apps	Gls	Tot A	Tot G
2006-07	Hapoel Ra'anana	22	0	22	0
2007-08	Sektzia Nes Tziona	24	0	24	0
2008-09	Barnet	12	0	12	0

LEARY, Michael (M) — 119 6
H: 6 0 W: 11 11 b.Ealing 17-4-83
Source: Scholar.

Season	Club	Apps	Gls	Tot A	Tot G
2001-02	Luton T	0	0		
2002-03	Luton T	0	0		
2003-04	Luton T	14	2		
2004-05	Luton T	8	0		
2005-06	Luton T	0	0		
2005-06	Bristol R	13	0	13	0
2005-06	Walsall	15	1	15	1
2006-07	Luton T	0	0	22	2
2006-07	Torquay U	2	0	2	0
2006-07	Brentford	17	0	17	0
2007-08	Barnet	22	1		
2008-09	Barnet	28	2	50	3

MEDLEY, Luke (F) — 27 3
H: 6 1 W: 13 03 b.Greenwich 21-6-89
Source: Tottenham H Scholar.

Season	Club	Apps	Gls	Tot A	Tot G
2007-08	Bradford C	9	2	9	2
2008-09	Barnet	18	1	18	1

NICOLAU, Nicky (D) — 117 5
H: 5 8 W: 10 03 b.Camden 12-10-83
Source: Trainee.

Season	Club	Apps	Gls	Tot A	Tot G
2002-03	Arsenal	0	0		
2003-04	Arsenal	0	0		
2003-04	Southend U	9	0		
2004-05	Southend U	22	1	31	1
2005-06	Swindon T	5	0	5	0
2006-07	Barnet	22	1		
2007-08	Barnet	38	2		
2008-09	Barnet	21	1	81	4

O'FLYNN, John (F) — 34 17
H: 5 11 W: 11 11 b.Cobh 11-7-82
Source: Peterborough U Scholar, Cork C.
Honours: Eire Under-21.

Season	Club	Apps	Gls	Tot A	Tot G
2008-09	Barnet	34	17	34	17

PORTER, Max (M) — 56 1
H: 5 10 W: 12 04 b.Hornchurch 29-6-87
Source: Bishop's Stortford.

Season	Club	Apps	Gls	Tot A	Tot G
2007-08	Barnet	30	1		
2008-09	Barnet	26	0	56	1

ST AIMIE, Kieron (M) — 13 0
H: 6 1 W: 13 00 b.Brent 4-5-89

Season	Club	Apps	Gls	Tot A	Tot G
2006-07	QPR	0	0		
2007-08	QPR	0	0		
2007-08	Barnet	10	0		
2008-09	Barnet	3	0	13	0

TABIRI, Joe (M) — 7 0
H: 5 9 W: 11 09 b.Kingsbury 16-10-89

Season	Club	Apps	Gls	Tot A	Tot G
2008-09	Barnet	7	0	7	0

YAKUBU, Ismail (D) — 121 7
H: 6 1 W: 13 09 b.Kano 8-4-85
Source: Trainee.

Season	Club	Apps	Gls	Tot A	Tot G
2005-06	Barnet	26	1		
2006-07	Barnet	29	1		
2007-08	Barnet	28	2		
2008-09	Barnet	38	3	121	7

BARNSLEY (6)

ADAM, Jamil (M) — 1 0
H: 5 10 W: 10 00 b.Bolton 5-6-91
Source: Scholar.

Season	Club	Apps	Gls	Tot A	Tot G
2007-08	Barnsley	1	0		
2008-09	Barnsley	0	0	1	0

ANDERSON (M) — 125 6
H: 6 2 W: 12 11 b.Sao Paulo 29-8-82
Honours: Brazil 4 full caps.

Season	Club	Apps	Gls	Tot A	Tot G
2003	Santiago Wanderers	18	2	18	2
2003-04	Santander	8	0		
2004-05	Santander	30	2	38	2
2005-06	Malaga	15	0	15	0
2006-07	Everton	1	0		
2007-08	Everton	0	0	1	0
2007-08	Barnsley	20	0		
2008-09	Barnsley	33	2	53	2

BOGDANOVIC, Daniel (F) — 16 5
H: 6 2 W: 11 02 b.Misurata 26-3-80
Source: Sliema W, Naxxar Lions, Valletta, Marsaxlokk, Cisco Roma, Lokomotiv Sofia.
Honours: Malta 24 full caps, 1 goal.

Season	Club	Apps	Gls	Tot A	Tot G
2008-09	Barnsley	16	5	16	5

BUTTERFIELD, Jacob (D) — 6 0
H: 5 10 W: 11 00 b.Manchester 10-6-90
Source: Scholar.

Season	Club	Apps	Gls	Tot A	Tot G
2007-08	Barnsley	3	0		
2008-09	Barnsley	3	0	6	0

CAMPBELL-RYCE, Jamal (M) — 208 16
H: 5 7 W: 12 03 b.Lambeth 6-4-83
Source: Scholar. *Honours:* Jamaica 15 full caps.

Season	Club	Apps	Gls	Tot A	Tot G
2002-03	Charlton Ath	1	0		
2002-03	Leyton Orient	17	2	17	2
2003-04	Charlton Ath	2	0		
2003-04	Wimbledon	4	0	4	0
2004-05	Charlton Ath	0	0	3	0
2004-05	Chesterfield	14	0	14	0
2004-05	Rotherham U	24	0		
2005-06	Rotherham U	7	0	31	0
2005-06	Southend U	13	0		
2005-06	Colchester U	4	0	4	0
2006-07	Southend U	43	2		
2007-08	Southend U	2	0	58	2
2007-08	Barnsley	37	3		
2008-09	Barnsley	40	9	77	12

COLACE, Roberto (M) — 34 0
H: 5 10 W: 11 07 b.Buenos Aires 6-1-84
Honours: Argentina Youth.

Season	Club	Apps	Gls	Tot A	Tot G
2008-09	Barnsley	34	0	34	0

COULSON, Michael (F) — 16 0
H: 5 10 W: 10 00 b.Scarborough 4-4-88
Source: Scarborough.

Season	Club	Apps	Gls	Tot A	Tot G
2006-07	Barnsley	2	0		
2007-08	Barnsley	12	0		
2008-09	Barnsley	2	0	16	0

DEVANEY, Martin (M) — 342 53
H: 5 11 W: 12 00 b.Cheltenham 1-6-80
Source: Trainee.

Season	Club	Apps	Gls	Tot A	Tot G
1997-98	Coventry C	0	0		
1998-99	Coventry C	0	0		
1999-2000	Cheltenham T	26	6		
2000-01	Cheltenham T	34	10		
2001-02	Cheltenham T	25	1		
2002-03	Cheltenham T	40	6		
2003-04	Cheltenham T	40	5		
2004-05	Cheltenham T	38	10	203	38
2005-06	Watford	0	0		
2005-06	Barnsley	38	6		
2006-07	Barnsley	41	5		
2007-08	Barnsley	34	4		
2008-09	Barnsley	26	0	139	15

EL HAIMOUR, Mounir (M) — 78 13
H: 5 9 W: 10 03 b.Limoges 29-10-80

Season	Club	Apps	Gls	Tot A	Tot G
2000-01	Chatellerault	0	0		
2001-02	Chatellerault	0	0		
2002-03	Champagne Sports	22	12	22	12
2003-04	Yverdon	0	0		
2004-05	Yverdon	0	0		
2004	Alania	9	0	9	0
2005-06	Yverdon	0	0		
2006-07	Schaffhausen	26	1	26	1
2006-07	Chateauroux	1	0	1	0
2007-08	Neuchatel Xamax	4	0	4	0
2008-09	Barnsley	16	0	16	0

FOSTER, Stephen (D) — 314 19
H: 6 0 W: 11 05 b.Warrington 10-9-80
Source: Trainee. *Honours:* England Schools.

Season	Club	Apps	Gls	Tot A	Tot G
1998-99	Crewe Alex	1	0		
1999-2000	Crewe Alex	0	0		
2000-01	Crewe Alex	30	0		
2001-02	Crewe Alex	34	5		
2002-03	Crewe Alex	35	4		
2003-04	Crewe Alex	45	2		
2004-05	Crewe Alex	34	1		
2005-06	Crewe Alex	39	3	218	15
2006-07	Burnley	17	0		
2007-08	Burnley	0	0	17	0
2007-08	Barnsley	41	1		
2008-09	Barnsley	38	3	79	4

HASSELL, Bobby (D) 326 7
H: 5 10 W: 12 00 b.Derby 4-6-80
Source: Trainee.

1997-98	Mansfield T	9	0	
1998-99	Mansfield T	3	0	
1999-2000	Mansfield T	11	1	
2000-01	Mansfield T	40	1	
2001-02	Mansfield T	43	1	
2002-03	Mansfield T	20	0	
2003-04	Mansfield T	34	0	160 3
2004-05	Barnsley	39	0	
2005-06	Barnsley	28	2	
2006-07	Barnsley	39	2	
2007-08	Barnsley	20	0	
2008-09	Barnsley	40	0	166 4

HESLOP, Simon (M) 9 0
H: 5 11 W: 11 00 b.York 1-5-87
Source: Scholar.

2005-06	Barnsley	0	0	
2006-07	Barnsley	1	0	
2007-08	Barnsley	0	0	
2008-09	Barnsley	0	0	1 0
2008-09	*Grimsby T*	8	0	8 0

HUME, Iain (F) 287 69
H: 5 7 W: 11 02 b.Brampton 31-10-83
Source: Juniors. *Honours:* Canada Youth, Under-20, 26 full caps, 2 goals.

1999-2000	Tranmere R	3	0	
2000-01	Tranmere R	10	0	
2001-02	Tranmere R	14	0	
2002-03	Tranmere P.	35	6	
2003-04	Tranmere R	40	10	
2004-05	Tranmere R	42	15	
2005-06	Tranmere R	6	1	150 32
2005-06	Leicester C	37	9	
2006-07	Leicester C	45	13	
2007-08	Leicester C	40	11	122 33
2008-09	Barnsley	15	4	15 4

KOZLUK, Rob (D) 305 2
H: 5 8 W: 10 02 b.Mansfield 5-8-77
Source: Trainee. *Honours:* England Under-21.

1995-96	Derby Co	0	0	
1996-97	Derby Co	0	0	
1997-98	Derby Co	9	0	
1998-99	Derby Co	7	0	16 0
1998-99	Sheffield U	10	0	
1999-2000	Sheffield U	39	0	
2000-01	Sheffield U	27	0	
2000-01	*Huddersfield T*	14	0	14 0
2001-02	Sheffield U	8	0	
2002-03	Sheffield U	32	1	
2003-04	Sheffield U	42	1	
2004-05	Sheffield U	9	0	
2004-05	*Preston NE*	1	0	1 0
2005-06	Sheffield U	27	0	
2006-07	Sheffield U	19	0	213 2
2007-08	Barnsley	24	0	
2008-09	Barnsley	37	0	61 0

LEON, Diego (M) 81 6
H: 5 7 W: 10 10 b.Palencia 16-1-84

2005-06	Real Madrid	0	0	
2005-06	*Arm Bielefeld*	14	1	14 1
2006-07	Grasshoppers	30	3	30 3
2007-08	Barnsley	18	1	
2008-09	Barnsley	19	1	37 2

LETHEREN, Kyle (G) 0 0
H: 6 2 W: 12 02 b.Llanelli 26-12-87
Source: Swansea C Scholar. *Honours:* Wales Under-21.

2006-07	Barnsley	0	0
2007-08	Barnsley	0	0
2008-09	Barnsley	0	0
2008-09	*Doncaster R*	0	0

MACKEN, Jon (F) 359 92
H: 5 11 W: 12 04 b.Manchester 7-9-77
Source: Trainee. *Honours:* England Youth. Eire 1 full cap.

1996-97	Manchester U	0	0	
1997-98	Preston NE	29	6	
1998-99	Preston NE	42	8	
1999-2000	Preston NE	44	22	
2000-01	Preston NE	38	19	
2001-02	Preston NE	31	8	184 63
2001-02	Manchester C	8	5	
2002-03	Manchester C	5	0	
2003-04	Manchester C	15	1	
2004-05	Manchester C	23	1	51 7

2005-06	Crystal Palace	24	2	
2006-07	Crystal Palace	1	0	25 2
2006-07	Ipswich T	14	4	14 4
2006-07	Derby Co	8	0	
2007-08	Derby Co	3	0	11 0
2007-08	Barnsley	29	7	
2008-09	Barnsley	45	9	74 16

McGRORY, Scott (F) 0 0
H: 5 11 W: 10 11 b.Aberdeen 5-4-87
Source: Scholar.

2006-07	Barnsley	0	0
2007-08	Barnsley	0	0
2008-09	Barnsley	0	0

MOORE, Darren (D) 522 30
H: 6 2 W: 15 07 b.Birmingham 22-4-74
Source: Trainee. *Honours:* Jamaica 3 full caps.

1991-92	Torquay U	5	1	
1992-93	Torquay U	31	2	
1993-94	Torquay U	37	2	
1994-95	Torquay U	30	3	103 8
1995-96	Doncaster R	35	2	
1996-97	Doncaster R	41	5	76 7
1997-98	Bradford C	18	0	
1998-99	Bradford C	44	3	
1999-2000	Bradford C	0	0	62 3
1999-2000	Portsmouth	25	1	
2000-01	Portsmouth	32	1	
2001-02	Portsmouth	2	0	59 2
2001-02	WBA	32	2	
2002-03	WBA	29	2	
2003-04	WBA	22	2	
2004-05	WBA	16	0	
2005-06	WBA	5	0	104 6
2005-06	Derby Co	14	1	
2006-07	Derby Co	35	2	
2007-08	Derby Co	31	0	80 3
2008-09	Barnsley	38	1	38 1

MOSSTTO, Miguel (F) 23 2
H: 5 10 W: 11 11 b.Ica 11-1-79
Source: Universitario, Coronel Bolognesi, Cienciano. *Honours:* Peru 10 full caps, 1 goal.

2007-08	Barnsley	14	1	
2008-09	Barnsley	9	1	23 2

To Total Clean Futbol January 2009

MULLER, Heinz (G) 138 0
H: 6 4 W: 15 04 b.Frankfurt-on-Main 30-5-78
Source: FSV Frankfurt.

1999-2000	Hanover	4	0	4 0
2000-01	Arm Bielefeld	0	0	
2001-02	Arm Bielefeld	1	0	1 0
2002-03	St Pauli	16	0	16 0
2003-04	Regensberg	4	0	4 0
2004	Odd Grenland	7	0	7 0
2005	Lillestrom	5	0	
2006	Lillestrom	24	0	
2007	Lillestrom	13	0	42 0
2007-08	Barnsley	28	0	
2008-09	Barnsley	36	0	64 0

NOBLE-LAZARUS, Reuben (F) 2 0
H: 5 11 W: 13 07 b.Huddersfield 16-8-93

2008-09	Barnsley	2	0	2 0

ODEJAYI, Kayode (F) 227 35
H: 6 2 W: 12 02 b.Ibadon 21-2-82
Source: Scholar. *Honours:* Nigeria 1 full cap.

1999-2000	Bristol C	3	0	
2000-01	Bristol C	3	0	
2001-02	Bristol C	0	0	
2002-03	Bristol C	0	0	6 0
2003-04	Cheltenham T	30	5	
2004-05	Cheltenham T	32	1	
2005-06	Cheltenham T	41	11	
2006-07	Cheltenham T	45	13	148 30
2007-08	Barnsley	39	3	
2008-09	Barnsley	28	1	67 4
2008-09	*Scunthorpe U*	6	1	6 1

POTTER, Luke (D) 1 0
H: 6 2 W: 12 07 b.Barnsley 13-7-89
Source: Scholar.

2006-07	Barnsley	1	0	
2007-08	Barnsley	0	0	
2008-09	Barnsley	0	0	1 0

SOUZA, Dennis (M) 174 6
H: 6 3 W: 13 05 b.Sao Paulo 1-9-80
Source: Matsubara, Roda JC.

2000-01	Harelbeke	0	0
2002-03	RAEC Mons	25	1

2003-04	KBHZ	31	0	31 0
2004-05	Standard	0	0	
2004-05	RAEC Mons	8	0	
2005-06	RAEC Mons	16	1	49 2
2006-07	Charleroi	16	2	16 2
2007-08	Barnsley	45	2	
2008-09	Barnsley	33	0	78 2

STEELE, Luke (G) 65 0
H: 6 2 W: 12 00 b.Peterborough 24-9-84
Source: Scholar. *Honours:* England Youth, Under-20.

2001-02	Peterborough U	2	0	2 0
2001-02	Manchester U	0	0	
2002-03	Manchester U	0	0	
2003-04	Manchester U	0	0	
2004-05	Manchester U	0	0	
2004-05	Coventry C	32	0	
2005-06	Manchester U	0	0	
2006-07	WBA	0	0	
2006-07	Coventry C	5	0	37 0
2007-08	WBA	2	0	2 0
2007-08	*Barnsley*	14	0	
2008-09	Barnsley	10	0	24 0

VAN HOMOET, Marciano (D) 64 1
H: 5 9 W: 11 11 b.Rotterdam 7-3-84

2004-05	Sparta Rotterdam	23	1	
2005-06	Sparta Rotterdam	5	0	
2006-07	Sparta Rotterdam	0	0	28 1
2007-08	Barnsley	19	0	
2008-09	Barnsley	17	0	36 0

BIRMINGHAM C (7)

AGUSTIEN, Kemy (M) 129 7
H: 5 10 W: 11 05 b.Tilburg 2-6-86
Honours: Holland Under-21.

2004-05	Willem II	21	1	
2005-06	Willem II	34	2	55 3
2006-07	Roda JC	31	2	31 2
2007-08	AZ	25	2	25 2

On loan from AZ.

2008-09	Birmingham C	18	0	18 0

ALUKO, Sone (F) 21 3
H: 5 8 W: 9 11 b.Birmingham 19-2-89
Source: Scholar. *Honours:* England Schools, Youth.

2005-06	Birmingham C	0	0	
2006-07	Birmingham C	0	0	
2007-08	*Aberdeen*	20	3	20 3
2007-08	Birmingham C	0	0	
2008-09	Birmingham C	0	0	
2008-09	*Blackpool*	1	0	1 0

Transferred to Aberdeen September 2008

AYDILEK, Semih (F) 0 0
H: 6 1 W: 11 13 b.Frankfurt 16-1-89
Source: Eintracht Frankfurt.

2007-08	Birmingham C	0	0
2008-09	*Motherwell*	0	0
2008-09	Birmingham C	0	0

BENT, Marcus (F) 465 93
H: 6 2 W: 13 03 b.Hammersmith 19-5-78
Source: Trainee. *Honours:* England Under-21.

1995-96	Brentford	12	1	
1996-97	Brentford	34	3	
1997-98	Brentford	24	4	70 8
1997-98	Crystal Palace	16	5	
1998-99	Crystal Palace	12	0	28 5
1998-99	Port Vale	15	0	
1999-2000	Port Vale	8	1	23 1
1999-2000	Sheffield U	32	15	
2000-01	Sheffield U	16	5	48 20
2000-01	Blackburn R	28	8	
2001-02	Blackburn R	9	0	37 8
2001-02	Ipswich T	25	9	
2002-03	Ipswich T	32	11	
2003-04	Ipswich T	4	1	61 21
2003-04	Leicester C	33	9	33 9
2004-05	Everton	37	6	
2005-06	Everton	18	1	55 7
2005-06	Charlton Ath	13	2	
2006-07	Charlton Ath	30	1	
2007-08	Charlton Ath	3	1	46 4
2007-08	Wigan Ath	31	7	31 7
2008-09	Birmingham C	33	3	33 3

CARR, Stephen (D)   317 8
H: 5 9   W: 11 13   b.Dublin 29-8-76
Source: Trainee. *Honours:* Eire Schools, Youth, Under-21, 44 full caps.

Season	Club				
1993-94	Tottenham H	1	0		
1994-95	Tottenham H	0	0		
1995-96	Tottenham H	0	0		
1996-97	Tottenham H	26	0		
1997-98	Tottenham H	38	0		
1998-99	Tottenham H	37	0		
1999-2000	Tottenham H	34	3		
2000-01	Tottenham H	28	3		
2001-02	Tottenham H	0	0		
2002-03	Tottenham H	30	0		
2003-04	Tottenham H	32	1	226	7
2004-05	Newcastle U	26	1		
2005-06	Newcastle U	19	0		
2006-07	Newcastle U	23	0		
2007-08	Newcastle U	10	0		
2008-09	Newcastle U	0	0	78	1
2008-09	Birmingham C	13	0	13	0

CARSLEY, Lee (M)   438 33
H: 5 10   W: 12 04   b.Birmingham 28-2-74
Source: Trainee. *Honours:* Eire 39 full caps.

Season	Club				
1992-93	Derby Co	0	0		
1993-94	Derby Co	0	0		
1994-95	Derby Co	23	2		
1995-96	Derby Co	35	1		
1996-97	Derby Co	24	0		
1997-98	Derby Co	34	1		
1998-99	Derby Co	22	1	138	5
1998-99	Blackburn R	8	0		
1999-2000	Blackburn R	30	10		
2000-01	Blackburn R	8	0	46	10
2000-01	Coventry C	21	2		
2001-02	Coventry C	26	2	47	4
2001-02	Everton	8	1		
2002-03	Everton	24	3		
2003-04	Everton	21	2		
2004-05	Everton	36	4		
2005-06	Everton	5	0		
2006-07	Everton	38	1		
2007-08	Everton	34	1	166	12
2008-09	Birmingham C	41	2	41	2

COSTLY, Carlos (F)   57 13
H: 6 3   W: 10 00   b.San Pedro Sula 17-7-82
Honours: Honduras 24 full caps, 9 goals.

Season	Club				
2006-07	Belchatow	11	6		
2007-08	Belchatow	26	5		
2008-09	Belchatow	12	2	49	13
2008-09	Birmingham C	8	0	8	0

DE LA CRUZ, Ulises (D)   305 27
H: 5 8   W: 12 10   b.Piqulucho 8-2-74
Source: Cruzeiro. *Honours:* Ecuador Youth, Under-23, 90 full caps, 5 goals.

Season	Club				
1996	Aucas	32	3	32	3
1997	LDU Quito	38	4		
1998	LDU Quito	42	7		
1999	LDU Quito	22	4		
1999	Cruzeiro	4	0	4	0
2000	LDU Quito	30	5	132	20
2001-02	Hibernian	32	2	32	2
2002-03	Aston Villa	20	1		
2003-04	Aston Villa	28	0		
2004-05	Aston Villa	34	0		
2005-06	Aston Villa	7	0	89	1
2006-07	Reading	9	1		
2007-08	Reading	6	0		
2008-09	Reading	0	0	15	1
2008-09	Birmingham C	1	0	1	0

DOYLE, Colin (G)   41 0
H: 6 5   W: 14 05   b.Cork 12-8-85
Honours: Eire Youth, Under-21, 1 full cap.

Season	Club				
2004-05	Birmingham C	0	0		
2004-05	Chester C	0	0		
2004-05	Nottingham F	3	0	3	0
2005-06	Birmingham C	0	0		
2005-06	Millwall	14	0	14	0
2006-07	Birmingham C	19	0		
2007-08	Birmingham C	3	0		
2008-09	Birmingham C	2	0	24	0

FAHEY, Keith (M)   130 21
H: 5 10   W: 12 07   b.Dublin 15-1-83

Season	Club		
1999-2000	Aston Villa	0	0
2000-01	Aston Villa	0	0
2001-02	Aston Villa	0	0
2002-03	Aston Villa	0	0
2003-04	Aston Villa	0	0
2005	St Patrick's Ath	14	3
2005	Drogheda U	14	2
2006	Drogheda U	8	0	22	2
2006	St Patrick's Ath	13	3
2007	St Patrick's Ath	32	1
2008	St Patrick's Ath	30	8	89	15
2008-09	Birmingham C	19	4	19	4

JAIDI, Radhi (D)   129 14
H: 6 2   W: 14 00   b.Tunis 30-8-75
Source: Esperance. *Honours:* Tunisia 101 full caps, 7 goals.

Season	Club				
2004-05	Bolton W	27	5		
2005-06	Bolton W	16	3	43	8
2006-07	Birmingham C	38	6		
2007-08	Birmingham C	18	0		
2008-09	Birmingham C	30	0	86	6

JEROME, Cameron (F)   187 47
H: 6 1   W: 13 06   b.Huddersfield 14-8-86
Honours: England Under-21.

Season	Club				
2004-05	Cardiff C	29	6		
2005-06	Cardiff C	44	18	73	24
2005-06	Birmingham C	0	0		
2006-07	Birmingham C	38	7		
2007-08	Birmingham C	33	7		
2008-09	Birmingham C	43	9	114	23

JOHNSON, Damien (M)   258 7
H: 5 9   W: 11 09   b.Lisburn 18-11-78
Source: Trainee. *Honours:* Northern Ireland Youth, Under-21, 52 full caps.

Season	Club				
1995-96	Blackburn R	0	0		
1996-97	Blackburn R	0	0		
1997-98	Blackburn R	0	0		
1997-98	Nottingham F	6	0	6	0
1998-99	Blackburn R	21	1		
1999-2000	Blackburn R	16	1		
2000-01	Blackburn R	16	0		
2001-02	Blackburn R	7	1	60	3
2001-02	Birmingham C	8	1		
2002-03	Birmingham C	30	1		
2003-04	Birmingham C	35	1		
2004-05	Birmingham C	36	0		
2005-06	Birmingham C	31	0		
2006-07	Birmingham C	26	1		
2007-08	Birmingham C	17	0		
2008-09	Birmingham C	9	0	192	4

JOYCE, David (D)   0 0
H: 5 10   W: 12 13   b.County Mayo 8-8-90
Source: Scholar.

Season	Club		
2007-08	Birmingham C	0	0
2008-09	Birmingham C	0	0

KELLY, Stephen (D)   152 2
H: 6 0   W: 11 10   b.Dublin 6-9-83
Source: Juniors. *Honours:* Eire Youth, Under-21, 14 full caps.

Season	Club				
2000-01	Tottenham H	0	0		
2001-02	Tottenham H	0	0		
2002-03	Tottenham H	0	0		
2002-03	Southend U	10	0	10	0
2002-03	QPR	7	0	7	0
2003-04	Tottenham H	11	0		
2003-04	Watford	13	0	13	0
2004-05	Tottenham H	17	2		
2005-06	Tottenham H	9	0	37	2
2006-07	Birmingham C	36	0		
2007-08	Birmingham C	38	0		
2008-09	Birmingham C	5	0	79	0
2008-09	Stoke C	6	0	6	0

KRYSIAK, Artur (G)   7 0
H: 6 1   W: 12 00   b.Lodz 11-8-89
Source: LKS Lodz. *Honours:* Poland Youth.

Season	Club				
2006-07	Birmingham C	0	0		
2007-08	Gretna	4	0	4	0
2007-08	Birmingham C	0	0		
2008-09	Birmingham C	0	0		
2008-09	Motherwell	1	0	1	0
2008-09	Swansea C	2	0	2	0

LARSSON, Sebastian (M)   119 11
H: 5 11   W: 11 02   b.Eskilstuna 6-6-85
Source: Trainee. *Honours:* Sweden Under-21, 14 full caps.

Season	Club				
2002-03	Arsenal	0	0		
2003-04	Arsenal	0	0		
2004-05	Arsenal	0	0		
2005-06	Arsenal	3	0		
2006-07	Arsenal	0	0	3	0
2006-07	Birmingham C	43	4		
2007-08	Birmingham C	35	6		
2008-09	Birmingham C	38	1	116	11

McFADDEN, James (M)   214 45
H: 6 0   W: 12 11   b.Glasgow 14-4-83
Honours: Scotland Under-21, B, 42 full caps, 13 goals.

Season	Club				
2000-01	Motherwell	6	0		
2001-02	Motherwell	24	10		
2002-03	Motherwell	30	13		
2003-04	Motherwell	3	3	63	26
2003-04	Everton	23	0		
2004-05	Everton	23	1		
2005-06	Everton	32	6		
2006-07	Everton	19	2		
2007-08	Everton	12	2	109	11
2007-08	Birmingham C	12	4		
2008-09	Birmingham C	30	4	42	8

McKERR, Michael (D)   16 0
b. 23-2-84
Source: Scholar. *Honours:* Northern Ireland Youth.

Season	Club				
2006-07	Glenavon	6	0		
2007-08	Glenavon	10	0	16	0
2007-08	Birmingham C	0	0		
2008-09	Birmingham C	0	0		

McPIKE, James (F)   0 0
H: 5 10   W: 11 02   b.Birmingham 4-10-88
Source: Scholar.

Season	Club		
2005-06	Birmingham C	0	0
2006-07	Birmingham C	0	0
2007-08	Birmingham C	0	0
2008-09	Birmingham C	0	0

McSHEFFREY, Gary (F)   253 71
H: 5 8   W: 10 06   b.Coventry 13-8-82
Source: Trainee. *Honours:* England Youth, Under-20.

Season	Club				
1998-99	Coventry C	1	0		
1999-2000	Coventry C	3	0		
2000-01	Coventry C	0	0		
2001-02	Stockport Co	5	1	5	1
2001-02	Coventry C	8	1		
2002-03	Coventry C	29	4		
2003-04	Coventry C	19	11		
2003-04	Luton T	18	9		
2004-05	Coventry C	37	12		
2004-05	Luton T	5	1	23	10
2005-06	Coventry C	43	15		
2006-07	Coventry C	3	1	143	44
2006-07	Birmingham C	40	13		
2007-08	Birmingham C	32	3		
2008-09	Birmingham C	6	0	78	16
2008-09	Nottingham F	4	0	4	0

MILOJEVIC, Stefan (M)   0 0
H: 5 9   W: 11 03   b.Paris 6-2-89

Season	Club		
2007-08	Birmingham C	0	0
2008-09	Birmingham C	0	0

MOSES-GARVEY, Aaron (F)   0 0
H: 5 8   W: 11 13   b.Birmingham 6-9-89
Source: Scholar.

Season	Club		
2007-08	Birmingham C	0	0
2008-09	Birmingham C	0	0

MURPHY, David (D)   174 7
H: 6 1   W: 12 03   b.Hartlepool 1-3-84
Source: Scholar. *Honours:* England Youth.

Season	Club				
2001-02	Middlesbrough	5	0		
2002-03	Middlesbrough	8	0		
2003-04	Middlesbrough	0	0	13	0
2003-04	Barnsley	10	2	10	2
2004-05	Hibernian	27	1		
2005-06	Hibernian	30	1		
2006-07	Hibernian	33	0		
2007-08	Hibernian	17	2	107	4
2007-08	Birmingham C	14	1		
2008-09	Birmingham C	30	0	44	1

MUTCH, Jordon (M)   0 0
H: 5 9   W: 10 03   b.Birmingham 2-12-91
Source: Derby Co. *Honours:* England Youth.

Season	Club		
2007-08	Birmingham C	0	0
2008-09	Birmingham C	0	0

NAFTI, Mehdi (M)   236 4
H: 5 10   W: 12 02   b.Toulouse 28-11-78
Honours: Tunisia 41 full caps, 1 goal.

Season	Club				
1998-99	Toulouse	11	0		
1999-2000	Toulouse	13	1	24	1
2000-01	Santander B	21	0	21	0
2000-01	Santander	3	0		

2001-02	Santander	30	0		
2002-03	Santander	31	2		
2003-04	Santander	31	1		
2004-05	Santander	16	0	111	3
2004-05	Birmingham C	10	0		
2005-06	Birmingham C	1	0		
2006-07	Birmingham C	32	0		
2007-08	Birmingham C	26	0		
2008-09	Birmingham C	11	0	80	0

O'BRIEN, James (M)　　　0　0
b.Dublin 8-6-90
Source: Scholar. *Honours:* Eire Youth.

2007-08	Birmingham C	0	0
2008-09	Birmingham C	0	0

O'CONNOR, Garry (F)　　　179　56
H: 6 1　W: 12 02　b.Edinburgh 7-5-83
Honours: Scotland Under-21, 15 full caps, 5 goals.

2000-01	Hibernian	1	0		
2001-02	Hibernian	4	1		
2002-03	Hibernian	19	10		
2003-04	Hibernian	24	6		
2004-05	Hibernian	35	13		
2005-06	Hibernian	24	11	107	41
2006	Lokomotiv Moscow	24	7		
2007	Lokomotiv Moscow	9	0	33	7
2007-08	Birmingham C	23	2		
2008-09	Birmingham C	16	6	39	8

PARNABY, Stuart (M)　　　131　2
H: 5 11　W: 11 00　b.Durham 19-7-82
Source: Trainee. *Honours:* England Youth, Under-20, Under-21.

1999-2000	Middlesbrough	0	0		
2000-01	Middlesbrough	0	0		
2000-01	*Halifax T*	6	0	6	0
2001-02	Middlesbrough	0	0		
2002-03	Middlesbrough	21	0		
2003-04	Middlesbrough	13	0		
2004-05	Middlesbrough	19	0		
2005-06	Middlesbrough	20	2		
2006-07	Middlesbrough	18	0	91	2
2007-08	Birmingham C	13	0		
2008-09	Birmingham C	21	0	34	0

PEARCE, Krystian (D)　　　59　1
H: 6 1　W: 13 05　b.Birmingham 5-1-90
Source: Scholar. *Honours:* England Youth.

2006-07	Birmingham C	0	0		
2007-08	Birmingham C	0	0		
2007-08	*Port Vale*	12	0	12	0
2007-08	*Notts Co*	8	1	8	1
2008-09	Birmingham C	0	0		
2008-09	*Scunthorpe U*	39	0	39	0

PHILLIPS, Kevin (F)　　　461　215
H: 5 7　W: 11 00　b.Hitchin 25-7-73
Source: Baldock T. *Honours:* England B, 8 full caps.

1994-95	Watford	16	9		
1995-96	Watford	27	11		
1996-97	Watford	16	4	59	24
1997-98	Sunderland	43	29		
1998-99	Sunderland	26	23		
1999-2000	Sunderland	36	30		
2000-01	Sunderland	34	14		
2001-02	Sunderland	37	11		
2002-03	Sunderland	32	6	208	113
2003-04	Southampton	34	12		
2004-05	Southampton	30	10	64	22
2005-06	Aston Villa	23	4		
2006-07	Aston Villa	0	0	23	4
2006-07	WBA	36	16		
2007-08	WBA	35	22	71	38
2008-09	Birmingham C	36	14	36	14

QUEUDRUE, Franck (D)　　　262　17
H: 6 1　W: 12 01　b.Paris 27-8-78
Source: Meaux. *Honours:* France B.

1999-2000	Lens	16	1		
2000-01	Lens	24	1		
2001-02	Lens	2	0	42	2
2001-02	Middlesbrough	28	2		
2002-03	Middlesbrough	31	1		
2003-04	Middlesbrough	31	0		
2004-05	Middlesbrough	31	5		
2005-06	Middlesbrough	29	3	150	11
2006-07	Fulham	29	1	29	1
2007-08	Birmingham C	16	0		
2008-09	Birmingham C	25	3	41	3

RIDGEWELL, Liam (D)　　　155　8
H: 5 10　W: 10 03　b.Bexley 21-7-84
Source: Scholar. *Honours:* England Youth, Under-20, Under-21.

2001-02	Aston Villa	0	0		
2002-03	Aston Villa	0	0		
2002-03	*Bournemouth*	5	0	5	0
2003-04	Aston Villa	11	0		
2004-05	Aston Villa	15	0		
2005-06	Aston Villa	32	5		
2006-07	Aston Villa	21	1	79	6
2007-08	Birmingham C	35	1		
2008-09	Birmingham C	36	1	71	2

SAMMONS, Ashley (M)　　　0　0
b.Solihull 10-11-91
Source: Scholar. *Honours:* England Youth.

2008-09	Birmingham C	0	0

SHROOT, Robin (M)　　　5　0
H: 5 9　W: 11 05　b.London 26-3-88
Source: Staines T, AFC Wimbledon, Harrow Borough. *Honours:* Northern Ireland Under-21.

2008-09	Birmingham C	0	0		
2008-09	*Walsall*	5	0	5	0

TAYLOR, Maik (G)　　　484　0
H: 6 4　W: 14 02　b.Hildesheim 4-9-71
Source: Farnborough T. *Honours:* Northern Ireland Under-21, B, 77 full caps.

1995-96	Barnet	45	0		
1996-97	Barnet	25	0	70	0
1996-97	Southampton	18	0		
1997-98	Southampton	0	0	18	0
1997-98	Fulham	28	0		
1998-99	Fulham	46	0		
1999-2000	Fulham	46	0		
2000-01	Fulham	44	0		
2001-02	Fulham	1	0		
2002-03	Fulham	19	0		
2003-04	Fulham	0	0	184	0
2003-04	Birmingham C	34	0		
2004-05	Birmingham C	38	0		
2005-06	Birmingham C	34	0		
2006-07	Birmingham C	27	0		
2007-08	Birmingham C	34	0		
2008-09	Birmingham C	45	0	212	0

TAYLOR, Martin (D)　　　206　8
H: 6 4　W: 15 00　b.Ashington 9-11-79
Source: Trainee. *Honours:* England Youth, Under-21.

1997-98	Blackburn R	0	0		
1998-99	Blackburn R	3	0		
1999-2000	Blackburn R	6	0		
1999-2000	*Darlington*	4	0	4	0
1999-2000	*Stockport Co*	7	0	7	0
2000-01	Blackburn R	16	3		
2001-02	Blackburn R	19	0		
2002-03	Blackburn R	33	2		
2003-04	Blackburn R	11	0	88	5
2003-04	Birmingham C	12	1		
2004-05	Birmingham C	7	0		
2005-06	Birmingham C	21	0		
2006-07	Birmingham C	31	0		
2007-08	Birmingham C	4	0		
2007-08	*Norwich C*	8	1	8	1
2008-09	Birmingham C	24	1	99	2

WILSON, Jared (D)　　　17　0
H: 5 8　W: 10 10　b.Cheltenham 24-11-89
Source: Scholar.

2007-08	Birmingham C	0	0		
2008-09	Birmingham C	1	0	1	0
2008-09	*Chesterfield*	16	0	16	0

BLACKBURN R (8)

ANDREWS, Keith (M)　　　233　25
H: 6 0　W: 12 04　b.Dublin 13-9-80
Source: Trainee. *Honours:* Eire Youth, 6 full caps, 1 goal.

1997-98	Wolverhampton W	0	0		
1998-99	Wolverhampton W	0	0		
1999-2000	Wolverhampton W	2	0		
2000-01	Wolverhampton W	22	0		
2000-01	*Oxford U*	4	1	4	1
2001-02	Wolverhampton W	11	0		
2002-03	Wolverhampton W	9	0		
2003-04	Wolverhampton W	1	0		
2003-04	*Stoke C*	16	0	16	0

2003-04	*Walsall*	10	2	10	2
2004-05	Wolverhampton W	20	0	65	0
2005-06	Hull C	26	0		
2006-07	Hull C	3	0	29	0
2006-07	Milton Keynes D	34	6		
2007-08	Milton Keynes D	41	12		
2008-09	Milton Keynes D	1	0	76	18
2008-09	Blackburn R	33	4	33	4

ARESTIDOU, Andreas (G)　　　0　0
b. 6-12-89
Source: Scholar.

2007-08	Blackburn R	0	0
2008-09	Blackburn R	0	0

BATESON, Jonathan (D)　　　0　0
b. 20-9-89
Source: Scholar.

2008-09	Blackburn R	0	0

BLACKMAN, Nick (F)　　　17　2
H: 6 2　W: 11 08　b.Whitefield 11-11-89
Source: Scholar.

2006-07	Macclesfield T	1	0		
2007-08	Macclesfield T	11	1		
2008-09	Macclesfield T	0	0	12	1
2008-09	Blackburn R	0	0		
2008-09	*Blackpool*	5	1	5	1

BOWEN, Jordan (M)　　　0　0
Source: Scholar.

2008-09	Blackburn R	0	0

BROWN, Jason (G)　　　131　0
H: 6 0　W: 15 07　b.Southwark 18-5-82
Source: From Charlton Ath Scholar.
Honours: Wales Youth, Under-21, 2 full caps.

2000-01	Gillingham	0	0		
2001-02	Gillingham	10	0		
2002-03	Gillingham	39	0		
2003-04	Gillingham	22	0		
2004-05	Gillingham	16	0		
2005-06	Gillingham	39	0	126	0
2006-07	Blackburn R	1	0		
2007-08	Blackburn R	0	0		
2008-09	Blackburn R	4	0	5	0

BUNN, Mark (G)　　　93　0
H: 6 0　W: 12 02　b.Camden 16-11-84
Source: Scholar.

2004-05	Northampton T	0	0		
2005-06	Northampton T	0	0		
2006-07	Northampton T	42	0		
2007-08	Northampton T	45	0		
2008-09	Northampton T	3	0	90	0
2008-09	Blackburn R	0	0		
2008-09	*Leicester C*	3	0	3	0

BUSSMANN, Bjorn (G)　　　0　0
H: 6 0　W: 12 00　b.Germany 18-3-91
Source: Scholar.

2007-08	Blackburn R	0	0
2008-09	Blackburn R	0	0

DERBYSHIRE, Matt (F)　　　91　20
H: 5 10　W: 11 01　b.Gt Harwood 14-4-86
Source: Gt Harwood T. *Honours:* England Under-21.

2003-04	Blackburn R	0	0		
2004-05	Blackburn R	1	0		
2005-06	Blackburn R	0	0		
2005-06	*Plymouth Arg*	12	0	12	0
2005-06	*Wrexham*	16	10	16	10
2006-07	Blackburn R	22	5		
2007-08	Blackburn R	23	3		
2008-09	Blackburn R	17	2	63	10

On loan to Olympiakos

DIOUF, El Hadji (F)　　　294　44
H: 5 11　W: 11 11　b.Dakar 15-1-81
Honours: Senegal 57 full caps, 16 goals.

1998-99	Sochaux	15	0	15	0
1999-2000	Rennes	28	1	28	1
2000-01	Lens	28	8		
2001-02	Lens	26	10	54	18
2002-03	Liverpool	29	3		
2003-04	Liverpool	26	0		
2004-05	Liverpool	0	0	55	3
2004-05	*Bolton W*	27	9		
2005-06	Bolton W	20	3		
2006-07	Bolton W	33	5		
2007-08	Bolton W	34	4	114	21
2008-09	Sunderland	14	0	14	0
2008-09	Blackburn R	14	1	14	1

DORAN, Aaron (M) 3 0
H: 5 7 W: 11 13 b.Ireland 13-5-91
Source: Scholar. *Honours:* Eire Youth.

2007-08	Blackburn R	0	0	
2008-09	Blackburn R	3	0	3 0

DUNN, David (M) 251 39
H: 5 9 W: 12 03 b.Gt Harwood 27-12-79
Source: Trainee. *Honours:* England Youth, Under-21, 1 full cap.

1997-98	Blackburn R	0	0	
1998-99	Blackburn R	15	1	
1999-2000	Blackburn R	22	2	
2000-01	Blackburn R	42	12	
2001-02	Blackburn R	29	7	
2002-03	Birmingham C	28	8	
2003-04	Birmingham C	21	2	
2004-05	Birmingham C	11	2	
2005-06	Birmingham C	15	2	
2006-07	Birmingham C	11	1	58 7
2006-07	Blackburn R	11	0	
2007-08	Blackburn R	31	1	
2008-09	Blackburn R	15	1	193 32

EMERTON, Brett (M) 377 36
H: 6 1 W: 13 05 b.Bankstown 22-2-79
Honours: Australia Youth, Under-20, Under-23, 69 full caps, 17 goals.

1996-97	Sydney Olympic	18	2	
1997-98	Sydney Olympic	24	3	
1998-99	Sydney Olympic	21	2	
1999-2000	Sydney Olympic	31	9	94 16
2000-01	Feyenoord	28	2	
2001-02	Feyenoord	31	6	
2002-03	Feyenoord	33	3	92 11
2003-04	Blackburn R	37	2	
2004-05	Blackburn R	37	4	
2005-06	Blackburn R	30	1	
2006-07	Blackburn R	34	0	
2007-08	Blackburn R	33	1	
2008-09	Blackburn R	20	1	191 9

FIELDING, Frank (G) 71 0
H: 5 11 W: 12 00 b.Blackburn 4-4-88
Source: Scholar. *Honours:* England Youth, Under-21.

2006-07	Blackburn R	0	0	
2007-08	Blackburn R	0	0	
2007-08	Wycombe W	36	0	36 0
2008-09	Blackburn R	0	0	
2008-09	Northampton T	12	0	12 0
2008-09	Rochdale	23	0	23 0

FLYNN, Jonathan (D) 0 0
H: 5 10 W: 11 00 b.Ballymena 18-11-89
Source: Ballymena U. *Honours:* Northern Ireland Under-21.

2007-08	Blackburn R	0	0
2008-09	Blackburn R	0	0

FOWLER, Robbie (F) 392 167
H: 5 10 W: 12 05 b.Liverpool 9-4-75
Source: Trainee. *Honours:* England Youth, B, Under-21, 26 full caps, 7 goals.

1991-92	Liverpool	0	0	
1992-93	Liverpool	0	0	
1993-94	Liverpool	28	12	
1994-95	Liverpool	42	25	
1995-96	Liverpool	38	28	
1996-97	Liverpool	32	18	
1997-98	Liverpool	20	9	
1998-99	Liverpool	25	14	
1999-2000	Liverpool	14	3	
2000-01	Liverpool	27	8	
2001-02	Liverpool	10	3	
2001-02	Leeds U	22	12	
2002-03	Leeds U	8	2	30 14
2002-03	Manchester C	13	2	
2003-04	Manchester C	31	7	
2004-05	Manchester C	32	11	
2005-06	Manchester C	4	1	80 21
2005-06	Liverpool	14	5	
2006-07	Liverpool	16	3	266 128
2007-08	Cardiff C	13	4	
2008-09	Cardiff C	0	0	13 4
2008-09	Blackburn R	3	0	3 0

Transferred to North Queensbury Ferry

GALLAGHER, Paul (F) 163 31
H: 6 1 W: 11 00 b.Glasgow 9-8-84
Source: Trainee. *Honours:* Scotland Under-21, B, 1 full cap.

2002-03	Blackburn R	1	0
2003-04	Blackburn R	26	3

2004-05	Blackburn R	16	2	
2005-06	Blackburn R	1	0	
2005-06	Stoke C	37	11	
2006-07	Blackburn R	16	1	
2007-08	Blackburn R	0	0	
2007-08	Preston NE	19	1	19 1
2007-08	Stoke C	7	0	44 11
2008-09	Blackburn R	0	0	60 6
2008-09	Plymouth Arg	40	13	40 13

GIVET, Gael (D) 221 8
H: 5 11 W: 11 11 b.Arles 9-10-81
Honours: France 13 full caps.

2000-01	Monaco	1	0	
2001-02	Monaco	23	2	
2002-03	Monaco	23	1	
2003-04	Monaco	33	2	
2004-05	Monaco	34	0	
2005-06	Monaco	32	2	
2006-07	Monaco	32	1	178 8
2007-08	Marseille	29	0	
2008-09	Marseille	0	0	29 0
2008-09	Blackburn R	14	0	14 0

GRELLA, Vince (M) 285 7
H: 6 0 W: 12 06 b.Melbourne 5-10-79
Honours: Australia Under-20, Under-23, 40 full caps.

1996-97	Canberra Cosmos	14	1	14 1
1997-98	Carlton SC	22	2	
1998-99	Carlton SC	1	0	23 2
1998-99	Empoli	5	0	
1999-2000	Empoli	0	0	
1999-2000	Ternana	9	0	
2000-01	Ternana	18	0	27 0
2001-02	Empoli	32	0	
2002-03	Empoli	31	1	
2003-04	Empoli	24	0	
2004-05	Empoli	0	0	92 1
2004-05	Parma	23	0	
2005-06	Parma	35	1	
2006-07	Parma	26	1	84 2
2007-08	Torino	28	1	28 1
2008-09	Blackburn R	17	0	17 0

GRIFFITHS, Rostyn (M) 25 1
H: 6 2 W: 12 08 b.Stoke 10-3-88
Source: Scholar. *Honours:* Australia Youth.

2005-06	Blackburn R	0	0	
2006-07	Blackburn R	0	0	
2007-08	Blackburn R	0	0	
2007-08	Gretna	12	0	12 0
2008-09	Blackburn R	0	0	
2008-09	Accrington S	13	1	13 1

GUNNING, Gavin (D) 0 0
b.Dublin 26-1-91
Source: Scholar. *Honours:* Eire Youth.

2007-08	Blackburn R	0	0
2008-09	Blackburn R	0	0

HANLEY, Grant (D) 0 0
b. 20-11-91
Source: Scholar.

2008-09	Blackburn R	0	0

HAWORTH, Andrew (M) 0 0
H: 5 11 W: 11 10 b.Lancaster 28-11-88
Source: Scholar.

2007-08	Blackburn R	0	0
2008-09	Blackburn R	0	0

HODGE, Bryan (M) 26 0
H: 5 11 W: 11 07 b.Hamilton 23-9-87
Source: Scholar.

2004-05	Blackburn R	0	0	
2005-06	Blackburn R	0	0	
2006-07	Blackburn R	0	0	
2006-07	Mansfield T	9	0	9 0
2007-08	Blackburn R	0	0	
2007-08	Millwall	10	0	10 0
2007-08	Darlington	7	0	7 0
2008-09	Blackburn R	0	0	

HOILETT, David (M) 0 0
Source: Scholar.

2008-09	Blackburn R	0	0

JUDGE, Alan (F) 17 2
H: 5 6 W: 11 03 b.Dublin 11-11-88
Honours: Eire Under-21.

2006-07	Blackburn R	0	0	
2007-08	Blackburn R	0	0	
2008-09	Blackburn R	0	0	
2008-09	Plymouth Arg	17	2	17 2

KANE, Tony (D) 16 0
H: 5 11 W: 11 00 b.Belfast 29-8-87
Source: Scholar. *Honours:* Eire Under-21, Northern Ireland Youth, Under-21.

2004-05	Blackburn R	0	0	
2005-06	Blackburn R	0	0	
2006-07	Blackburn R	0	0	
2006-07	Stockport Co	4	0	
2007-08	Blackburn R	0	0	
2007-08	Blackburn R	0	0	
2008-09	Stockport Co	3	0	7 0
2008-09	Carlisle U	9	0	9 0

KAVANAGH, Conor (D) 0 0
b.Limerick 8-1-90

2007-08	Blackburn R	0	0
2008-09	Blackburn R	0	0

KHIZANISHVILI, Zurab (D) 191 6
H: 6 1 W: 12 08 b.Tbilisi 6-10-81
Honours: Georgia 59 full caps, 1 goal.

1998-99	Dynamo Tbilisi B	17	3	17 3
1998-99	Dynamo Tbilisi	2	1	2 1
1999-2000	Tbilisi	9	0	9 0
1999-2000	Lokomotivi	5	1	
2000-01	Lokomotivi	11	0	16 1
2000-01	Dundee	6	0	
2001-02	Dundee	18	0	
2002-03	Dundee	19	0	43 0
2003-04	Rangers	26	0	
2004-05	Rangers	16	0	
2005-06	Rangers	0	0	42 0
2005-06	Blackburn R	26	1	
2006-07	Blackburn R	18	0	
2007-08	Blackburn R	13	0	
2008-09	Blackburn R	5	0	62 1

MARROW, Alex (M) 0 0
b. 21-1-90

2007-08	Blackburn R	0	0
2008-09	Blackburn R	0	0

MARSHALL, Marcus (F) 0 0
H: 5 10 W: 11 06 b.Hammersmith 7-10-89

2007-08	Blackburn R	0	0
2008-09	Blackburn R	0	0

McCARTHY, Benni (F) 339 155
H: 6 0 W: 12 08 b.Ciudad de Cabo 11-12-77
Honours: South Africa 70 caps, 30 goals.

1995-96	Seven Stars	29	27	
1996-97	Seven Stars	20	12	49 39
1997-98	Cape Town Spurs	7	4	7 4
1997-98	Ajax	17	9	
1998-99	Ajax	19	11	36 20
1999-2000	Celta Vigo	31	8	
2000-01	Celta Vigo	19	0	
2001-02	Celta Vigo	2	0	
2001-02	Porto	11	12	
2002-03	Celta Vigo	14	2	66 10
2003-04	Porto	29	20	
2004-05	Porto	23	11	
2005-06	Porto	23	3	86 46
2006-07	Blackburn R	36	18	
2007-08	Blackburn R	31	8	
2008-09	Blackburn R	28	10	95 36

McCUBBIN, Martin (F) 0 0
b. 7-3-90
Source: Scholar.

2008-09	Blackburn R	0	0

MOKOENA, Aaron (D) 167 2
H: 6 2 W: 14 00 b.Johannesburg 25-11-80
Honours: South Africa 89 full caps, 1 goal.

2000-01	Ajax	0	0	
2000-01	Antwerp	6	0	
2001-02	Antwerp	13	1	
2002-03	Antwerp	29	1	48 2
2003-04	Genk	18	0	18 0
2004-05	Blackburn R	16	0	
2005-06	Blackburn R	22	0	
2006-07	Blackburn R	27	0	
2007-08	Blackburn R	18	0	
2008-09	Blackburn R	18	0	101 0

MORRISSEY, Gearoid (M) 0 0
b. 17-11-91
Source: Scholar. *Honours:* Eire Youth.

2008-09	Blackburn R	0	0

NELSEN, Ryan (D) 196 8
H: 5 11 W: 14 02 b.Christchurch, NZ 18-10-77
Honours: New Zealand Under-23, 34 full caps, 7 goals.

2001	DC United	19	0	
2002	DC United	20	4	
2003	DC United	25	1	
2004	DC United	17	2	81 7
2004-05	Blackburn R	15	0	
2005-06	Blackburn R	31	0	
2006-07	Blackburn R	22	0	
2007-08	Blackburn R	22	0	
2008-09	Blackburn R	35	1	115 1

O'KEEFE, Josh (M) 0 0
H: 6 1 W: 11 05 b.Whalley 22-12-88
Source: Scholar. *Honours:* Eire Under-21.

2005-06	Blackburn R	0	0
2006-07	Blackburn R	0	0
2007-08	Blackburn R	0	0
2008-09	Blackburn R	0	0

OLSSON, Martin (D) 11 0
H: 5 7 W: 12 12 b.Sweden 17-5-88
Source: Hogaborg. *Honours:* Sweden Under-21.

2005-06	Blackburn R	0	0	
2006-07	Blackburn R	0	0	
2007-08	Blackburn R	2	0	
2008-09	Blackburn R	9	0	11 0

OOIJER, Andre (D) 378 34
H: 6 0 W: 11 13 b.Amsterdam 11-7-74
Source: SDW, SDZ, Ajax.Holland 40 full caps, 2 goals.

1994-95	Volendam	32	4	32 4
1995-96	Roda JC	23	1	
1996-97	Roda JC	33	2	
1997-98	Roda JC	19	6	75 9
1997-98	PSV Eindhoven	12	2	
1998-99	PSV Eindhoven	21	2	
1999-2000	PSV Eindhoven	18	1	
2000-01	PSV Eindhoven	20	2	
2001-02	PSV Eindhoven	26	5	
2002-03	PSV Eindhoven	32	3	
2003-04	PSV Eindhoven	15	2	
2004-05	PSV Eindhoven	24	2	
2005-06	PSV Eindhoven	24	0	192 19
2006-07	Blackburn R	20	0	
2007-08	Blackburn R	27	0	
2008-09	Blackburn R	32	2	79 2

PATERSON, Kris (D) 0 0
b. 28-9-89
Source: Scholar.

2008-09	Blackburn R	0	0

PEDERSEN, Morten (F) 322 69
H: 5 11 W: 11 00 b.Vadso 8-9-81
Honours: Norway Youth, Under-21, 50 full caps, 10 goals.

2004	Tromso	18	7	
1997	Norlid	21	0	
1998	Pola	20	4	20 4
1999	Norlid	19	0	40 0
2000	Tromso	10	3	
2001	Tromso	26	5	
2002	Tromso	23	18	
2003	Tromso	26	8	103 41
2004-05	Blackburn R	19	4	
2005-06	Blackburn R	34	9	
2006-07	Blackburn R	36	6	
2007-08	Blackburn R	37	4	
2008-09	Blackburn R	33	1	159 24

PEZZONI, Kevin (D) 0 0
b. 22-3-89

2006-07	Blackburn R	0	0
2007-08	Blackburn R	0	0
2008-09	Blackburn R	0	0

POTTS, Michael (F) 0 0
b. 26-11-91
Source: Scholar.

2008-09	Blackburn R	0	0

REID, Steven (M) 248 24
H: 6 0 W: 12 07 b.Kingston 10-3-81
Source: From Trainee. *Honours:* England Youth. Eire Under-21, 23 full caps, 2 goals.

1997-98	Millwall	1	0
1998-99	Millwall	25	0
1999-2000	Millwall	21	0
2000-01	Millwall	37	7
2001-02	Millwall	35	5
2002-03	Millwall	20	6 139 18
2003-04	Blackburn R	16	0
2004-05	Blackburn R	28	2
2005-06	Blackburn R	34	4
2006-07	Blackburn R	3	0
2007-08	Blackburn R	24	0
2008-09	Blackburn R	4	0 109 6

RIGTERS, Maceo (F) 79 5
H: 5 10 W: 14 07 b.Amsterdam 22-1-84
Honours: Holland Under-21.

2005-06	NAC Breda	24	2	
2006-07	NAC Breda	32	3	56 5
2007-08	Blackburn R	2	0	
2007-08	Norwich C	2	0	2 0
2008-09	Blackburn R	0	0	2 0
2008-09	Barnsley	19	0	19 0

ROBERTS, Jason (F) 357 121
H: 6 0 W: 14 01 b.Park Royal 25-1-78
Source: Hayes. *Honours:* Grenada 22 full caps, 12 goals.

1993-94	Wolverhampton W	0	0	
1997-98	Torquay U	14	6	14 6
1997-98	Bristol C	3	1	3 1
1998-99	Bristol R	37	16	
1999-2000	Bristol R	41	22	78 38
2000-01	WBA	43	14	
2001-02	WBA	14	7	
2002-03	WBA	32	3	
2003-04	WBA	0	0	89 24
2003-04	Portsmouth	10	1	10 1
2003-04	Wigan Ath	14	8	
2004-05	Wigan Ath	45	21	
2005-06	Wigan Ath	34	8	93 37
2006-07	Blackburn R	18	4	
2007-08	Blackburn R	26	3	
2008-09	Blackburn R	26	7	70 14

ROBERTS, Joe (M) 0 0
b. 9-9-89
Source: Academy.

2008-09	Blackburn R	0	0

ROBINSON, Paul (G) 267 1
H: 6 1 W: 14 07 b.Beverley 15-10-79
Source: From Trainee. *Honours:* England Under-21, 41 full caps.

1996-97	Leeds U	0	0	
1997-98	Leeds U	0	0	
1998-99	Leeds U	5	0	
1999-2000	Leeds U	0	0	
2000-01	Leeds U	16	0	
2001-02	Leeds U	0	0	
2002-03	Leeds U	38	0	
2003-04	Leeds U	36	0	95 0
2003-04	Tottenham H	0	0	
2004-05	Tottenham H	36	0	
2005-06	Tottenham H	38	0	
2006-07	Tottenham H	38	1	
2007-08	Tottenham H	25	0	137 1
2008-09	Blackburn R	35	0	35 0

SAMBA, Christopher (D) 106 6
H: 6 5 W: 13 03 b.Creteil 28-3-84
Source: Issy-les-Moulineaux, Rouen.Congo 20 full caps.

2001-02	Sedan	1	0	
2002-03	Sedan	0	0	
2003-04	Sedan	3	0	4 0
2004-05	Hertha Berlin	0	0	
2005-06	Hertha Berlin	12	0	
2006-07	Hertha Berlin	8	0	20 0
2006-07	Blackburn R	14	2	
2007-08	Blackburn R	33	2	
2008-09	Blackburn R	35	2	82 6

SANTA CRUZ, Julio (F) 0 0
H: 6 0 W: 12 04 b.Asuncion 12-5-90
Source: Cerro Porteno.

2008-09	Blackburn R	0	0

SANTA CRUZ, Roque (F) 220 57
H: 6 2 W: 13 12 b.Asuncion 16-8-81
Honours: Paraguay Under-20, 64 full caps, 20 goals.

1998-99	Olimpia	9	3	9 3
1999-2000	Bayern Munich	28	5	
2000-01	Bayern Munich	19	5	
2001-02	Bayern Munich	22	5	
2002-03	Bayern Munich	14	5	
2003-04	Bayern Munich	28	5	
2004-05	Bayern Munich	4	0	
2005-06	Bayern Munich	13	4	
2006-07	Bayern Munich	26	2	154 31
2007-08	Blackburn R	37	19	
2008-09	Blackburn R	20	4	57 23

TREACY, Keith (M) 16 0
H: 6 0 W: 13 02 b.Dublin 13-9-88
Source: Scholar. *Honours:* Eire Under-21.

2005-06	Blackburn R	0	0	
2006-07	Blackburn R	0	0	
2006-07	Stockport Co	4	0	4 0
2007-08	Blackburn R	0	0	
2008-09	Blackburn R	12	0	12 0

TUGAY, Kerimoglu (M) 550 48
H: 5 9 W: 11 07 b.Istanbul 24-8-70
Honours: Turkey Youth, Under-21, Under-23, 93 full caps, 2 goals.

1988-89	Galatasaray	16	0	
1989-90	Galatasaray	23	0	
1990-91	Galatasaray	12	0	
1991-92	Galatasaray	26	3	
1992-93	Galatasaray	25	6	
1993-94	Galatasaray	25	12	
1994-95	Galatasaray	23	1	
1995-96	Galatasaray	30	3	
1996-97	Galatasaray	33	4	
1997-98	Galatasaray	30	2	
1998-99	Galatasaray	22	2	
1999-2000	Galatasaray	10	1	275 34
1999-2000	Rangers	16	1	
2000-01	Rangers	26	3	42 4
2001-02	Blackburn R	33	3	
2002-03	Blackburn R	37	1	
2003-04	Blackburn R	36	1	
2004-05	Blackburn R	21	0	
2005-06	Blackburn R	27	1	
2006-07	Blackburn R	30	1	
2007-08	Blackburn R	20	2	
2008-09	Blackburn R	29	1	233 10

VILLANUEVA, Carlos (F) 153 55
H: 5 9 W: 11 02 b.La Serena 5-2-86
Honours: Chile 12 full caps, 1 goal.

2003	La Serena	15	5	15 5
2004	Audax Italiano	11	1	
2005	Audax Italiano	32	3	
2006	Audax Italiano	28	17	
2007	Audax Italiano	37	24	
2008	Audax Italiano	17	5	125 50
2008-09	Blackburn R	13	0	13 0

VOGEL, Johann (M) 339 20
H: 5 10 W: 11 03 b.Geneva 8-3-77
Honours: Switzerland Under-21, 94 full caps, 2 goals.

1992-93	Grasshoppers	3	0	
1993-94	Grasshoppers	4	0	
1994-95	Grasshoppers	23	0	
1995-96	Grasshoppers	24	0	
1996-97	Grasshoppers	28	3	
1997-98	Grasshoppers	24	5	
1998-99	Grasshoppers	27	5	133 13
1999-2000	PSV Eindhoven	31	2	
2000-01	PSV Eindhoven	30	1	
2001-02	PSV Eindhoven	25	1	
2002-03	PSV Eindhoven	32	1	
2003-04	PSV Eindhoven	24	1	
2004-05	PSV Eindhoven	27	1	169 7
2005-06	AC Milan	13	0	13 0
2006-07	Betis	17	0	
2007-08	Betis	0	0	17 0
2007-08	Blackburn R	6	0	
2008-09	Blackburn R	1	0	7 0

WARNOCK, Stephen (D) 183 10
H: 5 7 W: 11 09 b.Ormskirk 12-12-81
Source: Trainee. *Honours:* England Schools, Youth, 1 full cap.

1998-99	Liverpool	0	0	
1999-2000	Liverpool	0	0	
2000-01	Liverpool	0	0	
2001-02	Liverpool	0	0	
2002-03	Liverpool	0	0	
2002-03	Bradford C	12	1	12 1
2003-04	Coventry C	44	3	44 3
2004-05	Liverpool	19	0	
2005-06	Liverpool	20	1	
2006-07	Liverpool	1	0	40 1
2006-07	Blackburn R	13	1	
2007-08	Blackburn R	37	1	
2008-09	Blackburn R	37	3	87 5

WINNARD, Dean (D)　　0　0
H: 5 9　W: 10 04　b.Wigan 20-8-89
2006-07	Blackburn R	0	0
2007-08	Blackburn R	0	0
2008-09	Blackburn R	0	0

Scholars
Hall, Michael James Angelo; Jones, Philip Anthony; Kean, Jacob Kendall; Lowe, Jason John; Morris, Joshua Francis; O'Connor, Callum Anthony; Parry, Andrew James; Swann, Joshua James.

BLACKPOOL (9)

ADAM, Charlie (M)　　111　22
H: 6 1　W: 12 00　b.Dundee 10-12-85
Honours: Scotland Under-21, B, 2 full caps.
2004-05	Rangers	1	0		
2004-05	*Ross Co*	10	2		
2004-05	*Ross Co*	0	0	10	2
2005-06	Rangers	1	0		
2005-06	*St Mirren*	29	5	29	5
2006-07	Rangers	32	11		
2007-08	Rangers	16	2		
2008-09	Rangers	9	0	59	13
2008-09	Blackpool	13	2	13	2

BARKER, Shaun (D)　　257　12
H: 6 2　W: 12 08　b.Nottingham 19-9-82
Source: Scholar.
2002-03	Rotherham U	11	0		
2003-04	Rotherham U	36	2		
2004-05	Rotherham U	33	2		
2005-06	Rotherham U	43	3	123	7
2006-07	Blackpool	45	3		
2007-08	Blackpool	46	2		
2008-09	Blackpool	43	0	134	5

BAYLISS, Ashton (D)　　0　0
Source: Scholar.
2007-08	Blackpool	0	0
2008-09	Blackpool	0	0

BROOMES, Marlon (D)　　208　4
H: 6 0　W: 12 12　b.Birmingham 28-11-77
Source: Trainee. *Honours:* England Schools, Youth, Under-21.
1994-95	Blackburn R	0	0		
1995-96	Blackburn R	0	0		
1996-97	Blackburn R	0	0		
1996-97	*Swindon T*	12	1	12	1
1997-98	Blackburn R	4	0		
1998-99	Blackburn R	13	0		
1999-2000	Blackburn R	13	1		
2000-01	Blackburn R	1	0		
2000-01	*QPR*	5	0	5	0
2001-02	Blackburn R	0	0	31	1
2001-02	*Grimsby T*	15	0	15	0
2001-02	*Sheffield W*	19	0	19	0
2002-03	Preston NE	28	0		
2003-04	Preston NE	30	0		
2004-05	Preston NE	11	0	69	0
2005-06	Stoke C	37	2		
2006-07	Stoke C	0	0		
2007-08	Stoke C	0	0	37	2
2008-09	Blackpool	1	0	1	0
2008-09	*Crewe Alex*	19	0	19	0

BURGESS, Ben (F)　　259　78
H: 6 3　W: 14 04　b.Buxton 9-11-81
Source: Trainee. *Honours:* Eire Youth, Under-21.
1998-99	Blackburn R	0	0		
1999-2000	Blackburn R	2	0		
2000-01	Blackburn R	0	0		
2000-01	*Northern Spirit*	27	16	27	16
2001-02	Blackburn R	0	0	2	0
2001-02	*Brentford*	43	17	43	17
2002-03	Stockport Co	19	4	19	4
2002-03	*Oldham Ath*	7	0	7	0
2002-03	Hull C	7	4		
2003-04	Hull C	44	18		
2004-05	Hull C	2	0		
2005-06	Hull C	14	2		
2006-07	Hull C	3	0	70	24
2006-07	Blackpool	27	2		
2007-08	Blackpool	35	9		
2008-09	Blackpool	29	6	91	17

COID, Danny (D)　　263　9
H: 5 11　W: 11 07　b.Liverpool 3-10-81
Source: Trainee.
1998-99	Blackpool	1	0		
1999-2000	Blackpool	21	1		
2000-01	Blackpool	46	1		
2001-02	Blackpool	27	3		
2002-03	Blackpool	36	1		
2003-04	Blackpool	35	3		
2004-05	Blackpool	35	0		
2005-06	Blackpool	13	0		
2006-07	Blackpool	18	0		
2007-08	Blackpool	13	0		
2008-09	Blackpool	18	0	263	9

CRAINEY, Stephen (D)　　155　9
H: 5 9　W: 9 11　b.Glasgow 22-6-81
Honours: Scotland B, Under-21, 6 full caps.
1999-2000	Celtic	9	0		
2000-01	Celtic	2	0		
2001-02	Celtic	15	0		
2002-03	Celtic	13	0		
2003-04	Celtic	2	0	41	0
2003-04	*Southampton*	5	0	5	0
2004-05	Leeds U	9	0		
2005-06	Leeds U	24	0		
2006-07	Leeds U	19	0	52	0
2007-08	Blackpool	40	1		
2008-09	Blackpool	17	0	57	1

EDWARDS, Rob (D)　　162　5
H: 6 1　W: 11 10　b.Telford 25-12-82
Source: Trainee. *Honours:* Wales Youth, 15 full caps.
1999-2000	Aston Villa	0	0		
2000-01	Aston Villa	0	0		
2001-02	Aston Villa	0	0		
2002-03	Aston Villa	8	0		
2003-04	Aston Villa	0	0	8	0
2003-04	*Crystal Palace*	7	1	7	1
2003-04	*Derby Co*	11	1	11	1
2004-05	Wolverhampton W	17	0		
2005-06	Wolverhampton W	42	0		
2006-07	Wolverhampton W	33	0		
2007-08	Wolverhampton W	8	1	100	1
2008-09	Blackpool	36	2	36	2

EVATT, Ian (D)　　262　10
H: 6 3　W: 13 12　b.Coventry 19-11-81
Source: Trainee.
1998-99	Derby Co	0	0		
1999-2000	Derby Co	0	0		
2000-01	Derby Co	1	0		
2001-02	*Northampton T*	11	0	11	0
2001-02	Derby Co	3	0		
2002-03	Derby Co	30	0	34	0
2003-04	Chesterfield	43	5		
2004-05	Chesterfield	41	4	84	9
2005-06	QPR	27	0		
2006-07	QPR	0	0	27	0
2006-07	Blackpool	44	0		
2007-08	Blackpool	29	0		
2008-09	Blackpool	33	1	106	1

FLYNN, Mike (D)　　658　25
H: 6 0　W: 11 00　b.Oldham 23-2-69
Source: Trainee.
1986-87	Oldham Ath	0	0		
1987-88	Oldham Ath	31	1		
1988-89	Oldham Ath	9	0	40	1
1988-89	Norwich C	0	0		
1989-90	Norwich C	0	0		
1989-90	Preston NE	23	1		
1990-91	Preston NE	35	1		
1991-92	Preston NE	43	3		
1992-93	Preston NE	35	2	136	7
1992-93	Stockport Co	10	0		
1993-94	Stockport Co	46	1		
1994-95	Stockport Co	43	2		
1995-96	Stockport Co	46	6		
1996-97	Stockport Co	46	2		
1997-98	Stockport Co	34	1		
1998-99	Stockport Co	46	1		
1999-2000	Stockport Co	46	1		
2000-01	Stockport Co	44	0		
2001-02	Stockport Co	26	2	387	16
2001-02	*Stoke C*	13	0	13	0
2001-02	Barnsley	7	0		
2002-03	Barnsley	14	0	21	0
2002-03	Blackpool	21	0		
2003-04	Blackpool	30	1		
2004-05	Blackpool	43	0		
2005-06	Blackpool	0	0		

2006-07	Blackpool	0	0		
2007-08	Blackpool	0	0		
2008-09	Blackpool	0	0	57	1
2008-09	*Darlington*	4	0	4	0

FOX, David (M)　　98　7
H: 5 9　W: 11 08　b.Leek 13-12-83
Source: Scholar. *Honours:* England Youth, Under-20.
2000-01	Manchester U	0	0		
2001-02	Manchester U	0	0		
2002-03	Manchester U	0	0		
2003-04	Manchester U	0	0		
2004-05	Manchester U	0	0		
2004-05	*Shrewsbury T*	4	1	4	1
2005-06	Manchester U	0	0		
2005-06	Blackpool	7	1		
2006-07	Blackpool	37	4		
2007-08	Blackpool	28	1		
2008-09	Blackpool	22	0	94	6

GILKS, Matthew (G)　　185　0
H: 6 3　W: 13 12　b.Rochdale 4-6-82
Source: Scholar.
2000-01	Rochdale	3	0		
2001-02	Rochdale	19	0		
2002-03	Rochdale	20	0		
2003-04	Rochdale	12	0		
2004-05	Rochdale	30	0		
2005-06	Rochdale	46	0		
2006-07	Rochdale	46	0	176	0
2007-08	Norwich C	0	0		
2008-09	Blackpool	5	0	5	0
2008-09	*Shrewsbury T*	4	0	4	0

GREEN, Stuart (M)　　195　33
H: 5 10　W: 11 01　b.Whitehaven 15-6-81
Source: Trainee.
1999-2000	Newcastle U	0	0		
2000-01	Newcastle U	0	0		
2001-02	Newcastle U	0	0		
2001-02	*Carlisle U*	16	3		
2002-03	Newcastle U	0	0		
2002-03	*Carlisle U*	28	6		
2002-03	*Carlisle U*	10	2	26	5
2003-04	Hull C	42	6		
2004-05	Hull C	29	8		
2005-06	Hull C	38	4		
2006-07	Hull C	0	0	137	24
2006-07	*Crystal Palace*	14	2		
2007-08	*Crystal Palace*	10	2	24	4
2007-08	Blackpool	6	0		
2008-09	Blackpool	0	0	6	0
2008-09	*Crewe Alex*	2	0	2	0

JOHN-BAPTISTE, Alex (D)　　195　6
H: 6 0　W: 11 11　b.Sutton-in-Ashfield 31-1-86
Source: Scholar.
2002-03	Mansfield T	4	0		
2003-04	Mansfield T	17	0		
2004-05	Mansfield T	41	1		
2005-06	Mansfield T	41	1		
2006-07	Mansfield T	46	3		
2007-08	Mansfield T	25	0	174	5
2008-09	Blackpool	21	1	21	1

JORGENSEN, Claus (M)　　306　38
H: 5 10　W: 10 06　b.Holstebro 27-4-76
Source: Resen-Humlum, Struer BK, Holstebro, Aarhus, AC Horsens. *Honours:* Faeroes 10 full caps, 1 goal.
1999-2000	Bournemouth	44	6		
2000-01	Bournemouth	43	8		
2001-02	Bradford C	18	1		
2002-03	Bradford C	32	11	50	12
2003-04	Coventry C	8	0		
2003-04	*Bournemouth*	17	0	104	14
2004-05	Coventry C	17	3		
2005-06	Coventry C	27	3	52	6
2006-07	Blackpool	31	2		
2007-08	Blackpool	37	4		
2008-09	Blackpool	32	0	100	6

KAY, Matty (M)　　1　0
H: 5 9　W: 11 00　b.Blackpool 12-10-89
2005-06	Blackpool	1	0		
2006-07	Blackpool	0	0		
2007-08	Blackpool	0	0		
2008-09	Blackpool	0	0	1	0

MARTIN, Joe (M)   16   0
H: 6 0   W: 12 13   b.Dagenham 29-11-88
Source: Scholar. *Honours:* England Youth.

Season	Club				
2005-06	Tottenham H	0	0		
2006-07	Tottenham H	0	0		
2007-08	Tottenham H	0	0		
2007-08	*Blackpool*	1	0		
2008-09	Blackpool	15	0	16	0

McPHEE, Stephen (F)   220   50
H: 5 7   W: 10 08   b.Glasgow 5-6-81
Honours: Scotland Under-21.

Season	Club				
1998-99	Coventry C	0	0		
1999-2000	Coventry C	0	0		
2000-01	Coventry C	0	0		
2001-02	Port Vale	44	11		
2002-03	Port Vale	40	3		
2003-04	Port Vale	46	25	130	39
2004-05	Beira Mar	31	5	31	5
2005-06	Hull C	4	0		
2006-07	Hull C	12	0		
2007-08	Hull C	19	2	35	2
2007-08	Blackpool	19	4		
2008-09	Blackpool	5	0	24	4

MERELLA, Dominic (M)   0   0
b.Chorley 31-12-89
Source: Scholar.

Season	Club		
2008-09	Blackpool	0	0

MITCHLEY, Daniel (F)   2   0
H: 5 10   W: 10 08   b.Liverpool 7-10-89
Source: Scholar.

Season	Club				
2007-08	Blackpool	0	0		
2008-09	Blackpool	2	0	2	0

NARDIELLO, Daniel (F)   145   33
H: 5 11   W: 11 04   b.Coventry 22-10-82
Source: Trainee. *Honours:* Wales 3 full caps.

Season	Club				
1999-2000	Manchester U	0	0		
2000-01	Manchester U	0	0		
2001-02	Manchester U	0	0		
2002-03	Manchester U	0	0		
2003-04	Manchester U	0	0		
2003-04	*Swansea C*	4	0	4	0
2003-04	*Barnsley*	16	7		
2004-05	Manchester U	0	0		
2004-05	*Barnsley*	28	7		
2005-06	Barnsley	34	5		
2006-07	Barnsley	30	9		
2007-08	QPR	8	0	8	0
2007-08	*Barnsley*	11	2	119	30
2008-09	Blackpool	2	0	2	0
2008-09	*Hartlepool U*	12	3	12	3

ORMEROD, Brett (F)   334   76
H: 5 11   W: 11 12   b.Blackburn 18-10-76
Source: Blackburn R Trainee, Accrington S.

Season	Club				
1996-97	Blackpool	4	0		
1997-98	Blackpool	9	2		
1998-99	Blackpool	40	8		
1999-2000	Blackpool	13	5		
2000-01	Blackpool	41	17		
2001-02	Blackpool	21	13		
2001-02	Southampton	18	1		
2002-03	Southampton	31	5		
2003-04	Southampton	22	5		
2004-05	Southampton	9	0		
2004-05	*Leeds U*	6	0	6	0
2004-05	*Wigan Ath*	6	2	6	2
2005-06	Southampton	19	1	99	12
2005-06	Preston NE	15	4		
2006-07	Preston NE	29	8		
2007-08	Preston NE	18	1		
2007-08	*Nottingham F*	13	2	13	2
2008-09	Preston NE	0	0	62	13
2008-09	*Oldham Ath*	5	0	5	0
2008-09	Blackpool	15	2	143	47

RACHUBKA, Paul (G)   207   0
H: 6 1   W: 13 05   b.San Luis Opispo 21-5-81
Source: Trainee. *Honours:* England Youth, Under-20.

Season	Club				
1999-2000	Manchester U	0	0		
2000-01	Manchester U	1	0		
2001-02	Manchester U	0	0	1	0
2001-02	*Oldham Ath*	16	0	16	0
2002-03	Charlton Ath	0	0		
2003-04	Charlton Ath	0	0		
2003-04	*Huddersfield T*	13	0		
2004-05	Charlton Ath	0	0		
2004-05	*Milton Keynes D*	4	0	4	0
2004-05	*Northampton T*	10	0	10	0
2004-05	Huddersfield T	29	0		
2005-06	Huddersfield T	34	0		
2006-07	Huddersfield T	0	0	76	0
2006-07	*Peterborough U*	4	0	4	0
2006-07	*Blackpool*	8	0		
2007-08	Blackpool	46	0		
2008-09	Blackpool	42	0	96	0

SOUTHERN, Keith (M)   239   22
H: 5 10   W: 12 06   b.Gateshead 24-4-81
Source: Trainee.

Season	Club				
1998-99	Everton	0	0		
1999-2000	Everton	0	0		
2000-01	Everton	0	0		
2001-02	Everton	0	0		
2002-03	Everton	0	0		
2002-03	Blackpool	38	1		
2003-04	Blackpool	28	2		
2004-05	Blackpool	27	6		
2005-06	Blackpool	42	2		
2006-07	Blackpool	39	5		
2007-08	Blackpool	30	3		
2008-09	Blackpool	35	3	239	22

STEINBORS, Pavels (G)   0   0
H: 6 2   W: 13 00   b.Latvia 21-9-85
Source: FK Jurmala.

Season	Club		
2007-08	Blackpool	0	0
2008-09	Blackpool	0	0

TAYLOR-FLETCHER, Gary (F)   268   60
H: 6 0   W: 11 00   b.Liverpool 4-6-81
Source: Northwich Vic. *Honours:* England Schools.

Season	Club				
2000-01	Hull C	5	0	5	0
2001-02	Leyton Orient	9	0		
2002-03	Leyton Orient	12	1	21	1
2003-04	Lincoln C	42	16		
2004-05	Lincoln C	38	11	80	27
2005-06	Huddersfield T	43	10		
2006-07	Huddersfield T	39	11	82	21
2007-08	Blackpool	42	6		
2008-09	Blackpool	38	5	80	11

VAUGHAN, David (M)   225   20
H: 5 7   W: 11 00   b.Rhuddlan 18-2-83
Source: Scholar. *Honours:* Wales Youth, Under-20, Under-21, 14 full caps.

Season	Club				
2000-01	Crewe Alex	1	0		
2001-02	Crewe Alex	13	0		
2002-03	Crewe Alex	32	3		
2003-04	Crewe Alex	31	0		
2004-05	Crewe Alex	44	6		
2005-06	Crewe Alex	34	5		
2006-07	Crewe Alex	29	4		
2007-08	Crewe Alex	1	0	185	18
2007-08	Real Sociedad	7	1	7	1
2008-09	Blackpool	33	1	33	1

WRIGHT, Jermaine (M)   413   21
H: 5 9   W: 11 09   b.Greenwich 21-10-75
Source: Trainee. *Honours:* England Youth.

Season	Club				
1992-93	Millwall	0	0		
1993-94	Millwall	0	0		
1994-95	Millwall	0	0		
1994-95	Wolverhampton W	6	0		
1995-96	Wolverhampton W	7	0		
1995-96	*Doncaster R*	13	0	13	0
1996-97	Wolverhampton W	3	0		
1997-98	Wolverhampton W	4	0	20	0
1997-98	Crewe Alex	5	0		
1998-99	Crewe Alex	44	5	49	5
1999-2000	Ipswich T	34	1		
2000-01	Ipswich T	37	2		
2001-02	Ipswich T	29	1		
2002-03	Ipswich T	39	1		
2003-04	Ipswich T	45	5	184	10
2004-05	Leeds U	35	3		
2005-06	Leeds U	3	0	38	3
2005-06	*Millwall*	15	2	15	2
2005-06	*Southampton*	13	0		
2006-07	Southampton	42	1		
2007-08	Southampton	36	0	91	1
2008-09	Blackpool	3	0	3	0

BOLTON W (10)

AL-HABSI, Ali (G)   72   0
H: 6 4   W: 15 02   b.Oman 30-12-81
Source: Al-Nasser, Al-Mudhaibi. *Honours:* Oman 66 full caps.

Season	Club				
2003	Lyn	13	0		
2004	Lyn	24	0		
2005	Lyn	25	0	62	0
2005-06	Bolton W	0	0		
2006-07	Bolton W	0	0		
2007-08	Bolton W	10	0		
2008-09	Bolton W	0	0	10	0

BASHAM, Chris (M)   24   1
H: 5 11   W: 12 08   b.Stafford 20-7-88
Source: Scholar.

Season	Club				
2007-08	Bolton W	0	0		
2007-08	*Rochdale*	13	0	13	0
2008-09	Bolton W	11	1	11	1

BOGDAN, Adam (G)   0   0
H: 6 4   W: 14 02   b.Budapest 27-9-87
Source: Vasas.

Season	Club		
2007-08	Bolton W	0	0
2008-09	Bolton W	0	0

CAHILL, Gary (D)   117   7
H: 6 2   W: 12 06   b.Dronfield 19-12-85
Source: From Trainee. *Honours:* England Youth, Under-20, Under-21.

Season	Club				
2003-04	Aston Villa	0	0		
2004-05	Aston Villa	0	0		
2004-05	*Burnley*	27	1	27	1
2005-06	Aston Villa	7	1		
2006-07	Aston Villa	20	0		
2007-08	Aston Villa	1	0	28	1
2007-08	*Sheffield U*	16	2	16	2
2007-08	Bolton W	13	0		
2008-09	Bolton W	33	3	46	3

COHEN, Tamir (M)   113   7
H: 5 11   W: 11 09   b.Israel 4-3-84
Honours: Israel 10 full caps.

Season	Club				
2002-03	Maccabi Tel Aviv	13	0		
2003-04	Maccabi Tel Aviv	30	2		
2004-05	Maccabi Tel Aviv	22	2		
2005-06	Maccabi Tel Aviv	16	0		
2006-07	Maccabi Tel Aviv	3	0	84	4
2006-07	Maccabi Netanya	15	1	15	1
2007-08	Bolton W	10	1		
2008-09	Bolton W	4	1	14	2

DAVIES, Kevin (F)   478   91
H: 6 0   W: 12 10   b.Sheffield 26-3-77
Source: Trainee. *Honours:* England Youth, Under-21.

Season	Club				
1993-94	Chesterfield	24	4		
1994-95	Chesterfield	41	11		
1995-96	Chesterfield	30	4		
1996-97	Chesterfield	34	3	129	22
1996-97	Southampton	0	0		
1997-98	Southampton	25	9		
1998-99	Blackburn R	21	1		
1999-2000	Blackburn R	2	0	23	1
1999-2000	Southampton	23	6		
2000-01	Southampton	27	1		
2001-02	Southampton	23	2		
2002-03	Southampton	9	1	107	19
2002-03	*Millwall*	9	3	9	3
2003-04	Bolton W	38	9		
2004-05	Bolton W	35	8		
2005-06	Bolton W	37	7		
2006-07	Bolton W	30	8		
2007-08	Bolton W	32	3		
2008-09	Bolton W	38	11	210	46

DAVIES, Mark (M)   44   2
H: 5 11   W: 11 08   b.Wolverhampton 18-2-88
Source: Scholar. *Honours:* England Youth.

Season	Club				
2004-05	Wolverhampton W	0	0		
2005-06	Wolverhampton W	20	1		
2006-07	Wolverhampton W	7	0		
2007-08	Wolverhampton W	0	0		
2008-09	Wolverhampton W	0	0	27	1
2008-09	*Leicester C*	7	1	7	1
2008-09	Bolton W	10	0	10	0

DZEMAILI, Blerim (M)   108   9
H: 5 10   W: 11 07   b.Tetovo 12-4-86
Honours: Switzerland 7 full caps.

Season	Club				
2003-04	Zurich	30	2		
2004-05	Zurich	23	1		
2005-06	Zurich	34	3		
2006-07	Zurich	21	3	108	9
2007-08	Bolton W	0	0		
2008-09	Bolton W	0	0		

On loan to Torino September 2008

ELMANDER, Johan (F)   304 80
H: 6 1 W: 11 13 b.Alingsas 27-5-81
Honours: Sweden Under-21, 41 full caps, 11 goals.

1997	Holmalund	5	0		
1998	Holmalund	19	5	24	5
1999	Orgryte	18	2		
2000	Orgryte	21	2	39	4
2000-01	Feyenoord	16	2		
2001-02	Feyenoord	22	1		
2002	Djurgaarden	8	5		
2002-03	Feyenoord	1	0	39	3
2003	Djurgaarden	11	7	19	12
2003-04	*NAC Breda*	31	7	31	7
2004-05	Brondby	27	9		
2005-06	Brondby	31	13	58	22
2006-07	Toulouse	32	11		
2007-08	Toulouse	32	11	64	22
2008-09	Bolton W	30	5	30	5

FOJUT, Jaroslaw (D)   20 2
H: 6 2 W: 13 00 b.Legionowo 17-10-87
Source: Scholar. *Honours:* Poland Youth.

2005-06	Bolton W	1	0		
2006-07	Bolton W	0	0		
2007-08	Bolton W	0	0		
2007-08	*Luton T*	16	2	16	2
2008-09	Bolton W	0	0	1	0
2008-09	*Stockport Co*	3	0	3	0

Transferred to Slask Wroclaw Jan 2009

GARDNER, Ricardo (D)   312 19
H: 5 9 W: 11 00 b.St Andrews 25-9-78
Source: Harbour View. *Honours:* Jamaica 58 full caps, 4 goals.

1998-99	Bolton W	30	2		
1999-2000	Bolton W	29	5		
2000-01	Bolton W	32	3		
2001-02	Bolton W	31	3		
2002-03	Bolton W	32	2		
2003-04	Bolton W	22	0		
2004-05	Bolton W	33	0		
2005-06	Bolton W	30	0		
2006-07	Bolton W	18	0		
2007-08	Bolton W	26	0		
2008-09	Bolton W	29	4	312	19

HARSANYI, Zoltan (D)   11 1
H: 6 1 W: 12 00 b.Bratislava 1-6-87
Honours: Slovakia Youth, Under-20.

2006-07	Senec	11	1	11	1
2006-07	Bolton W	0	0		
2007-08	Bolton W	0	0		
2008-09	Bolton W	0	0		

HUNT, Nicky (D)   139 1
H: 6 1 W: 13 07 b.Westhoughton 3-9-83
Source: Scholar. *Honours:* England Under-21.

2000-01	Bolton W	1	0		
2001-02	Bolton W	0	0		
2002-03	Bolton W	0	0		
2003-04	Bolton W	31	1		
2004-05	Bolton W	29	0		
2005-06	Bolton W	20	0		
2006-07	Bolton W	33	0		
2007-08	Bolton W	14	0		
2008-09	Bolton W	0	0	128	1
2008-09	*Birmingham C*	11	0	11	0

JAASKELAINEN, Jussi (G)   501 0
H: 6 3 W: 12 10 b.Vaasa 19-4-75
Honours: Finland Youth, Under-21, 51 full caps.

1992	MP	6	0		
1993	MP	6	0		
1994	MP	26	0		
1995	MP	26	0	64	0
1996	VPS	27	0		
1997	VPS	27	0	54	0
1997-98	Bolton W	0	0		
1998-99	Bolton W	34	0		
1999-2000	Bolton W	34	0		
2000-01	Bolton W	27	0		
2001-02	Bolton W	34	0		
2002-03	Bolton W	38	0		
2003-04	Bolton W	38	0		
2004-05	Bolton W	36	0		
2005-06	Bolton W	38	0		
2006-07	Bolton W	38	0		
2007-08	Bolton W	28	0		
2008-09	Bolton W	38	0	383	0

MAKUKULA, Ariza (F)   137 43
H: 6 3 W: 13 05 b.Kinshasa 4-3-81
Honours: Portugal Under-21, 4 full caps, 1 goal.

1999-2000	Guimaraes	0	0		
2000-01	Salamanca	2	0		
2000-01	Leganes	13	4	13	4
2001-02	Salamanca	39	21	41	21
2002-03	Nantes	18	1	18	1
2003-04	Valladolid	18	8	18	8
2004-05	Sevilla	13	1		
2005-06	Sevilla	0	0	13	1
2006-07	Tarragona	12	1	12	1
2007-08	Maritimo	13	7	13	7
2007-08	Benfica	3	0		
2008-09	Benfica	0	0	3	0
2008-09	Bolton W	6	0	6	0

McCANN, Gavin (M)   301 2
H: 5 11 W: 11 00 b.Blackpool 10-1-78
Source: Trainee. *Honours:* England 1 full cap.

1995-96	Everton	0	0		
1996-97	Everton	0	0		
1997-98	Everton	11	0		
1998-99	Everton	0	0	11	0
1998-99	Sunderland	11	0		
1999-2000	Sunderland	24	4		
2000-01	Sunderland	22	3		
2001-02	Sunderland	29	0		
2002-03	Sunderland	30	1	116	8
2003-04	Aston Villa	28	0		
2004-05	Aston Villa	20	1		
2005-06	Aston Villa	32	1		
2006-07	Aston Villa	30	1	110	3
2007-08	Bolton W	31	1		
2008-09	Bolton W	33	0	64	1

MUAMBA, Fabrice (M)   109 2
H: 6 1 W: 11 10 b.DR Congo 6-4-88
Source: Scholar. *Honours:* England Youth, Under-21.

2005-06	Arsenal	0	0		
2006-07	Arsenal	0	0		
2006-07	Birmingham C	34	0		
2007-08	Birmingham C	37	2	71	2
2008-09	Bolton W	38	0	38	0

MUSTAPHA, Riga (F)   229 55
H: 5 10 W: 11 00 b.Accra 10-10-81
Honours: Holland Under-21.

1998-99	Vitesse	1	0		
1999-2000	Vitesse	7	0		
2000-01	Roosendaal	8	0	8	0
2001-02	Vitesse	6	1		
2002-03	Vitesse	17	0	31	1
2003-04	Sparta Rotterdam	32	4		
2004-05	Sparta Rotterdam	36	22	68	26
2005-06	Levante	38	11		
2006-07	Levante	33	9		
2007-08	Levante	34	8	105	28
2008-09	Bolton W	17	0	17	0

O'BRIEN, Andy (D)   351 10
H: 6 2 W: 11 13 b.Harrogate 29-6-79
Source: Trainee. *Honours:* England Youth, Under-21, Eire Under-21, 26 full caps, 1 goal.

1996-97	Bradford C	22	2		
1997-98	Bradford C	26	0		
1998-99	Bradford C	31	0		
1999-2000	Bradford C	36	1		
2000-01	Bradford C	18	0	133	3
2000-01	Newcastle U	9	1		
2001-02	Newcastle U	34	2		
2002-03	Newcastle U	26	0		
2003-04	Newcastle U	28	1		
2004-05	Newcastle U	23	2	120	6
2005-06	Portsmouth	29	0		
2006-07	Portsmouth	3	0		
2007-08	Portsmouth	0	0	32	0
2007-08	Bolton W	32	0		
2008-09	Bolton W	34	1	66	1

O'BRIEN, Joey (M)   65 2
H: 5 11 W: 10 13 b.Dublin 17-2-86
Source: Scholar. *Honours:* Eire Youth, Under-21, 3 full caps.

2004-05	Bolton W	0	0		
2004-05	*Sheffield W*	15	2	15	2
2005-06	Bolton W	23	0		
2006-07	Bolton W	0	0		
2007-08	Bolton W	19	0		
2008-09	Bolton W	7	0	50	0

OBADEYI, Temitope (F)   3 0
H: 5 10 W: 11 09 b.Coventry 29-10-89
Source: Coventry C. *Honours:* England Youth.

2006-07	Bolton W	0	0		
2007-08	Bolton W	0	0		
2008-09	Bolton W	3	0	3	0

PUYGRENIER, Sebastien (D)   160 12
H: 6 2 W: 13 12 b.Limoges 28-1-82

2002-03	Rennes	3	0	3	0
2003-04	Nancy	27	0		
2004-05	Nancy	19	0		
2005-06	Nancy	32	1		
2006-07	Nancy	30	6		
2007-08	Nancy	33	3	141	10
2008	Zenit	9	1	9	1

On loan from Zenit.

2008-09	Bolton W	7	1	7	1

SAMUEL, JLloyd (D)   235 2
H: 5 11 W: 11 04 b.Trinidad 29-3-81
Source: Charlton Ath Trainee. *Honours:* England Youth, Under-20, Under-21.

1998-99	Aston Villa	0	0		
1999-2000	Aston Villa	9	0		
2000-01	Aston Villa	3	0		
2001-02	*Gillingham*	8	0	8	0
2001-02	Aston Villa	23	0		
2002-03	Aston Villa	38	0		
2003-04	Aston Villa	38	2		
2004-05	Aston Villa	35	0		
2005-06	Aston Villa	19	0		
2006-07	Aston Villa	4	0	169	2
2007-08	Bolton W	20	0		
2008-09	Bolton W	38	0	58	0

SHITTU, Dan (D)   265 27
H: 6 2 W: 16 03 b.Lagos 2-9-80
Honours: Nigeria 16 full caps.

1999-2000	Charlton Ath	0	0		
2000-01	Charlton Ath	0	0		
2000-01	*Blackpool*	17	2	17	2
2001-02	Charlton Ath	0	0		
2001-02	QPR	27	2		
2002-03	QPR	43	7		
2003-04	QPR	20	0		
2004-05	QPR	34	4		
2005-06	QPR	45	4	169	17
2006-07	Watford	30	1		
2007-08	Watford	39	7	69	8
2008-09	Bolton W	10	0	10	0

SINCLAIR, James (F)   2 0
H: 5 6 W: 10 05 b.Newcastle 22-10-87
Source: Scholar.

2005-06	Bolton W	0	0		
2006-07	Bolton W	2	0		
2007-08	Bolton W	0	0		
2008-09	Bolton W	0	0	2	0

SISSONS, Robert (M)   0 0
H: 5 8 W: 11 02 b.Stockport 29-9-88
Source: Scholar. *Honours:* England Youth.

2005-06	Bolton W	0	0	
2006-07	Bolton W	0	0	
2007-08	Bolton W	0	0	
2008-09	Bolton W	0	0	

SMOLAREK, Ebi (M)   194 41
H: 5 10 W: 10 10 b.Lodz 9-1-81
Honours: Poland 39 full caps, 19 goals.

2000-01	Feyenoord	25	3		
2001-02	Feyenoord	19	2		
2002-03	Feyenoord	0	0		
2003-04	Feyenoord	21	7		
2004-05	Feyenoord	3	0	68	12
2004-05	Borussia Dortmund	15	3		
2005-06	Borussia Dortmund	34	13		
2006-07	Borussia Dortmund	30	9		
2007-08	Santander	33	4	33	4
2007-08	Borussia Dortmund	2	0	81	25
2008-09	Bolton W	12	0	12	0

STEINSSON, Gretar Rafn (D)   195 23
H: 6 2 W: 12 04 b.Siglufjordur 9-1-82
Honours: Iceland 33 full caps, 4 goals.

1999	IA Akranes	1	0		
2000	IA Akranes	13	0		
2001	IA Akranes	18	6		
2002	IA Akranes	17	2		
2003	IA Akranes	11	2		
2004	IA Akranes	17	2	76	12
2004-05	Young Boys	14	3		

2005-06	Young Boys	7	0	21	3
2005-06	AZ	20	4		
2006-07	AZ	25	1	45	5
2007-08	Bolton W	16	0		
2008-09	Bolton W	37	3	53	3

TAYLOR, Matthew (D)   358   52
H: 5 11   W: 12 03   b.Oxford 27-11-81
Source: Trainee. *Honours:* England Youth, Under-21.

1998-99	Luton T	0	0		
1999-2000	Luton T	41	4		
2000-01	Luton T	45	1		
2001-02	Luton T	43	11	129	16
2002-03	Portsmouth	35	7		
2003-04	Portsmouth	30	0		
2004-05	Portsmouth	32	1		
2005-06	Portsmouth	34	6		
2006-07	Portsmouth	35	8		
2007-08	Portsmouth	13	1	179	23
2007-08	Bolton W	16	3		
2008-09	Bolton W	34	10	50	13

VAZ TE, Ricardo (F)   64   3
H: 6 2   W: 12 07   b.Lisbon 1-10-86
Source: Trainee. *Honours:* Portugal Youth, Under-20, Under-21.

2003-04	Bolton W	1	0		
2004-05	Bolton W	7	0		
2005-06	Bolton W	22	3		
2006-07	Bolton W	25	0		
2006-07	*Hull C*	6	0	6	0
2007-08	Bolton W	1	0		
2008-09	Bolton W	2	0	58	3

WARD, Daniel (M)   0   0

2008-09	Bolton W	0	0

WOOLFE, Nathan (M)   0   0
H: 5 11   W: 12 05   b.Florida 6-10-88
Source: Scholar.

2007-08	Bolton W	0	0
2008-09	Bolton W	0	0

Scholars
Bennett, Rhys Gordon; Blakeman, Adam John; Brocklehurst, Tom Matthew; Campbell, Javlon; Carlisle, Matthew James; Eckersley, Thomas Scott; Lainton, Robert; McDonald, Stuart Robert; McGeechan, Maison Sean; Michail, Marcos; Mooy, Aaron Frank; O'Halloran, Michael Francis; Pawley, George; Riley, Joseph; Sheridan, Samuel; Spencer, Grant Paul; Stokes, Christopher Martin Thomas.

BOURNEMOUTH (11)

ANDERTON, Darren (M)   471   57
H: 6 1   W: 12 05   b.Southampton 3-3-72
Source: Trainee. *Honours:* England Youth, Under-21, B, 30 full caps, 7 goals.

1989-90	Portsmouth	0	0		
1990-91	Portsmouth	20	0		
1991-92	Portsmouth	42	7	62	7
1992-93	Tottenham H	34	6		
1993-94	Tottenham H	37	6		
1994-95	Tottenham H	37	5		
1995-96	Tottenham H	8	2		
1996-97	Tottenham H	16	3		
1997-98	Tottenham H	15	0		
1998-99	Tottenham H	32	3		
1999-2000	Tottenham H	22	3		
2000-01	Tottenham H	23	2		
2001-02	Tottenham H	35	3		
2002-03	Tottenham H	20	0		
2003-04	Tottenham H	20	1	299	34
2004-05	Birmingham C	20	3		
2005-06	Birmingham C	0	0	20	3
2005-06	Wolverhampton W	24	1	24	1
2006-07	Bournemouth	28	6		
2007-08	Bournemouth	20	3		
2008-09	Bournemouth	18	3	66	12

BARTLEY, Marvyn (M)   53   2
H: 6 1   W: 12 04   b.Reading 4-7-86
Source: Hampton & Richmond B.

2007-08	Bournemouth	20	1		
2008-09	Bournemouth	33	1	53	2

BRADBURY, Lee (F)   451   91
H: 6 0   W: 12 07   b.Isle of Wight 3-7-75
Source: Cowes. *Honours:* England Under-21.

1995-96	Portsmouth	12	0		
1995-96	*Exeter C*	14	5	14	5
1996-97	Portsmouth	42	15		
1997-98	Manchester C	27	7		
1998-99	Manchester C	13	3	40	10
1998-99	Crystal Palace	22	4		
1998-99	*Birmingham C*	7	0	7	0
1999-2000	Crystal Palace	10	2	32	6
1999-2000	Portsmouth	35	10		
2000-01	Portsmouth	39	10		
2001-02	Portsmouth	22	7		
2002-03	Portsmouth	3	1		
2002-03	*Sheffield W*	11	3	11	3
2003-04	Portsmouth	0	0	153	43
2003-04	*Derby Co*	7	0	7	0
2003-04	Walsall	8	1	8	1
2004-05	Oxford U	41	4		
2005-06	Oxford U	22	5	63	9
2005-06	Southend U	15	1		
2006-07	Southend U	31	4		
2007-08	Southend U	1	0	47	5
2007-08	Bournemouth	35	3		
2008-09	Bournemouth	34	6	69	9

CONNELL, Alan (F)   176   36
H: 6 0   W: 12 00   b.Enfield 5-2-83
Source: Ipswich T Trainee.

2002-03	Bournemouth	13	6		
2003-04	Bournemouth	7	0		
2004-05	Bournemouth	34	2		
2005-06	Torquay U	22	7	22	7
2006-07	Hereford U	44	9	44	9
2007-08	Brentford	42	12		
2008-09	Brentford	2	0	44	12
2008-09	Bournemouth	12	0	66	8

COOPER, Shaun (D)   169   1
H: 5 10   W: 10 05   b.Newport (IW) 5-10-83
Source: School.

2000-01	Portsmouth	0	0		
2001-02	Portsmouth	7	0		
2002-03	Portsmouth	0	0		
2003-04	Portsmouth	0	0		
2003-04	*Leyton Orient*	9	0	9	0
2004-05	Portsmouth	0	0		
2004-05	*Kidderminster H*	10	0	10	0
2005-06	Portsmouth	0	0	7	0
2005-06	Bournemouth	35	0		
2006-07	Bournemouth	33	0		
2007-08	Bournemouth	38	1		
2008-09	Bournemouth	37	0	143	1

CUMMINGS, Warren (D)   214   7
H: 5 9   W: 11 05   b.Aberdeen 15-10-80
Source: Trainee. *Honours:* Scotland Under-21, 1 full cap.

1999-2000	Chelsea	0	0		
2000-01	Chelsea	0	0		
2000-01	*Bournemouth*	10	1		
2000-01	WBA	3	0		
2001-02	Chelsea	0	0		
2001-02	*WBA*	14	0	17	0
2002-03	Chelsea	0	0		
2002-03	Bournemouth	20	0		
2003-04	Bournemouth	42	2		
2004-05	Bournemouth	30	2		
2005-06	Bournemouth	0	0		
2006-07	Bournemouth	31	0		
2007-08	Bournemouth	32	2		
2008-09	Bournemouth	32	0	197	7

FEENEY, Liam (M)   15   3
H: 5 10   W: 12 02   b.Hammersmith 21-1-87
Source: Salisbury C.
On loan from Salisbury C.

2008-09	Southend U	1	0	1	0
2008-09	Bournemouth	14	3	14	3

FLETCHER, Steve (F)   584   101
H: 6 2   W: 14 09   b.Hartlepool 26-7-72
Source: Trainee.

1990-91	Hartlepool U	14	2		
1991-92	Hartlepool U	18	2	32	4
1992-93	Bournemouth	31	4		
1993-94	Bournemouth	36	6		
1994-95	Bournemouth	40	6		
1995-96	Bournemouth	7	1		
1996-97	Bournemouth	35	7		
1997-98	Bournemouth	42	12		
1998-99	Bournemouth	39	8		
1999-2000	Bournemouth	36	7		
2000-01	Bournemouth	45	9		
2001-02	Bournemouth	2	0		
2002-03	Bournemouth	35	5		
2003-04	Bournemouth	41	9		
2004-05	Bournemouth	36	9		
2005-06	Bournemouth	27	4		
2006-07	Bournemouth	41	1		
2007-08	Chesterfield	38	5	38	5

From Crawley T.

2008-09	Bournemouth	21	4	514	92

GARRY, Ryan (D)   34   0
H: 6 0   W: 11 05   b.Hornchurch 29-9-83
Source: Scholar. *Honours:* England Youth, Under-20.

2001-02	Arsenal	0	0		
2002-03	Arsenal	1	0		
2003-04	Arsenal	0	0		
2004-05	Arsenal	0	0		
2005-06	Arsenal	0	0		
2006-07	Arsenal	0	0	1	0
2007-08	Bournemouth	8	0		
2008-09	Bournemouth	25	0	33	0

GOULDING, Jeff (F)   27   3
H: 6 2   W: 11 11   b.Sutton 13-5-84
Source: Croydon, Egham T, Aldershot T, Hayes, Yeading, Fisher Ath.

2008-09	Bournemouth	27	3	27	3

GUYETT, Scott (D)   136   2
H: 6 2   W: 13 06   b.Ascot 20-1-76
Source: Brisbane C, Gresley R, Southport.

2001-02	Oxford U	22	0	22	0

From Chester C.

2004-05	Yeovil T	18	2		
2005-06	Yeovil T	21	0		
2006-07	Yeovil T	16	0		
2007-08	Yeovil T	34	0	89	2
2008-09	Bournemouth	25	0	25	0

HOLLANDS, Danny (M)   122   12
H: 6 2   W: 11 11   b.Ashford 6-11-85
Source: Trainee.

2003-04	Chelsea	0	0		
2004-05	Chelsea	0	0		
2005-06	Chelsea	0	0		
2005-06	*Torquay U*	10	1	10	1
2006-07	Bournemouth	37	4		
2007-08	Bournemouth	42	6	112	11

IGOE, Sammy (M)   437   30
H: 5 6   W: 10 00   b.Staines 30-9-75
Source: Trainee.

1993-94	Portsmouth	0	0		
1994-95	Portsmouth	1	0		
1995-96	Portsmouth	22	0		
1996-97	Portsmouth	40	2		
1997-98	Portsmouth	31	3		
1998-99	Portsmouth	40	5		
1999-2000	Portsmouth	26	1	160	11
1999-2000	Reading	6	0		
2000-01	Reading	31	6		
2001-02	Reading	35	1		
2002-03	Reading	15	0	87	7
2003-04	*Luton T*	2	0	2	0
2003-04	Swindon T	36	5		
2004-05	Swindon T	43	4	79	9
2005-06	*Millwall*	5	0	5	0
2005-06	Bristol R	11	1		
2006-07	Bristol R	40	1		
2007-08	Bristol R	21	0	72	2
2007-08	*Hereford U*	4	0	4	0
2008-09	Bristol R	28	1	28	1

JALAL, Shwan (G)   61   0
H: 6 2   W: 14 02   b.Baghdad 14-8-83
Source: Hastings T.

2001-02	Tottenham H	0	0		
2002-03	Tottenham H	0	0		
2003-04	Tottenham H	0	0		

From Woking.

2006-07	*Sheffield W*	0	0		
2006-07	Peterborough U	1	0		
2007-08	Peterborough U	7	0		
2007-08	*Morecambe*	12	0	12	0
2008-09	Peterborough U	0	0	8	0
2008-09	Bournemouth	41	0	41	0

McQUOID, Josh (M)   23   0
H: 5 9 W: 10 10 b.Southampton 15-12-89
Source: Scholar. *Honours:* Northern Ireland Under-21, B.

Season	Club	App	Gls	Tot	
2006-07	Bournemouth	2	0		
2007-08	Bournemouth	5	0		
2008-09	Bournemouth	16	0	23	0

MOLESLEY, Mark (M)   29   4
H: 6 1 W: 12 07 b.Hillingdon 11-3-81
From Hayes, Cam C, Ald T, Steve B, Grays

Season	Club	App	Gls	Tot	
2008-09	Bournemouth	29	4	29	4

PARTINGTON, Joe (M)   17   2
H: 5 11 W: 11 13 b.Portsmouth 1-4-90
Source: Scholar. *Honours:* Wales Youth, Under-21.

Season	Club	App	Gls	Tot	
2007-08	Bournemouth	6	1		
2008-09	Bournemouth	11	1	17	2

PEARCE, Jason (D)   77   3
H: 5 11 W: 12 00 b.Hillingdon 6-12-87
Source: Scholar.

Season	Club	App	Gls	Tot	
2006-07	Portsmouth	0	0		
2007-08	Bournemouth	33	1		
2008-09	Bournemouth	44	2	77	3

PETTEFER, Carl (M)   103   1
H: 5 7 W: 10 02 b.Burnham 22-3-81
Source: Trainee.

Season	Club	App	Gls	Tot	
1998-99	Portsmouth	0	0		
1999-2000	Portsmouth	0	0		
2000-01	Portsmouth	1	0		
2001-02	Portsmouth	2	0		
2002-03	Portsmouth	0	0		
2002-03	Exeter C	31	1	31	1
2003-04	Portsmouth	0	0	3	0
2003-04	Southend U	11	0		
2004-05	Southend U	46	0		
2005-06	Southend U	11	0	68	0
From Oxford U.					
2008-09	Bournemouth	1	0	1	0

PITMAN, Brett (M)   126   29
H: 6 0 W: 11 00 b.Jersey 31-1-88

Season	Club	App	Gls	Tot	
2005-06	Bournemouth	19	1		
2006-07	Bournemouth	29	5		
2007-08	Bournemouth	39	6		
2008-09	Bournemouth	39	17	126	29

PRESTON, Carl (M)   2   0
H: 5 7 W: 11 04 b.Poole 25-4-91

Season	Club	App	Gls	Tot	
2008-09	Bournemouth	2	0	2	0

PRYCE, Ryan (G)   5   0
H: 6 0 W: 11 09 b.Bournemouth 20-9-89
Source: Scholar.

Season	Club	App	Gls	Tot	
2007-08	Bournemouth	4	0		
2008-09	Bournemouth	1	0	5	0

RANKINE, Michael (F)   24   1
H: 6 1 W: 14 12 b.Doncaster 15-1-85
Source: Armthorpe W, Barrow, Scunthorpe U, Doncaster R, Barrow.

Season	Club	App	Gls	Tot	
2004-05	Scunthorpe U	21	1		
2005-06	Scunthorpe U	0	0	21	1
From Alfreton T, Rushden & D.					
2008-09	Bournemouth	3	0	3	0

ROBINSON, Anton (M)   17   1
H: 5 9 W: 10 03 b.Harrow 17-2-86
Source: Millwall Scholar.
From Ex C, Eastb B, Fish A, Weymouth.

Season	Club	App	Gls	Tot	
2008-09	Bournemouth	17	1	17	1

TINDALL, Jason (M)   173   6
H: 6 1 W: 11 09 b.Stepney 15-11-77
Source: Trainee.

Season	Club	App	Gls	Tot	
1996-97	Charlton Ath	0	0		
1997-98	Charlton Ath	0	0		
1998-99	Bournemouth	17	1		
1999-2000	Bournemouth	8	0		
2000-01	Bournemouth	45	1		
2001-02	Bournemouth	44	3		
2002-03	Bournemouth	27	1		
2003-04	Bournemouth	19	0		
2004-05	Bournemouth	0	0		
2005-06	Bournemouth	11	0		
From Weymouth.					
2008-09	Bournemouth	2	0	173	6

TUBBS, Matt (F)   8   1
H: 5 9 W: 11 00 b.Salisbury 15-7-84
Source: Bolton W Scholar.
On loan from Salisbury C.

Season	Club	App	Gls	Tot	
2008-09	Bournemouth	8	1	8	1

WEBB, George (M)   1   0
H: 5 10 W: 11 06 b.Poole 1-5-91

Season	Club	App	Gls	Tot	
2008-09	Bournemouth	1	0	1	0

YOUNG, Neil (D)   429   4
H: 5 9 W: 12 04 b.Harlow 31-8-73
Source: Trainee.

Season	Club	App	Gls	Tot	
1991-92	Tottenham H	0	0		
1992-93	Tottenham H	0	0		
1993-94	Tottenham H	0	0		
1994-95	Bournemouth	32	0		
1995-96	Bournemouth	41	0		
1996-97	Bournemouth	44	0		
1997-98	Bournemouth	44	2		
1998-99	Bournemouth	44	1		
1999-2000	Bournemouth	37	0		
2000-01	Bournemouth	7	0		
2001-02	Bournemouth	11	0		
2002-03	Bournemouth	32	1		
2003-04	Bournemouth	10	0		
2004-05	Bournemouth	30	0		
2005-06	Bournemouth	42	0		
2006-07	Bournemouth	34	0		
2007-08	Bournemouth	21	0		
2008-09	Bournemouth	0	0	429	4

BRADFORD C (12)

AINGE, Simon (D)   14   0
H: 6 1 W: 12 02 b.Shipley 18-2-88
Source: Scholar.

Season	Club	App	Gls	Tot	
2005-06	Bradford C	0	0		
2006-07	Bradford C	9	0		
2007-08	Bradford C	4	0		
2008-09	Bradford C	1	0	14	0

ARNISON, Paul (D)   199   4
H: 5 10 W: 10 12 b.Hartlepool 18-9-77
Source: Trainee.

Season	Club	App	Gls	Tot	
1995-96	Newcastle U	0	0		
1996-97	Newcastle U	0	0		
1997-98	Newcastle U	0	0		
1998-99	Newcastle U	0	0		
1999-2000	Newcastle U	0	0		
1999-2000	Hartlepool U	8	1		
2000-01	Hartlepool U	27	1		
2001-02	Hartlepool U	19	0		
2002-03	Hartlepool U	19	1		
2003-04	Hartlepool U	4	0	77	3
2003-04	Carlisle U	26	1		
2004-05	Carlisle U	0	0		
2005-06	Carlisle U	41	0		
2006-07	Carlisle U	11	0		
2007-08	Carlisle U	17	0	95	1
2008-09	Bradford C	27	0	27	0

BOULDING, Mick (F)   311   87
H: 5 10 W: 11 05 b.Sheffield 8-2-76
Source: Hallam.

Season	Club	App	Gls	Tot	
1999-2000	Mansfield T	33	6		
2000-01	Mansfield T	33	6		
2001-02	Mansfield T	0	0		
2001-02	Grimsby T	35	11		
2002-03	Aston Villa	0	0		
2002-03	Sheffield U	6	0	6	0
2002-03	Grimsby T	12	4		
2003-04	Grimsby T	27	12	74	27
2003-04	Barnsley	6	0		
2004-05	Barnsley	29	10	35	10
2004-05	Cardiff C	4	0	4	0
2005-06	Rotherham U	0	0		
2006-07	Mansfield T	39	5		
2007-08	Mansfield T	43	21	148	38
2008-09	Bradford C	44	12	44	12

BOULDING, Rory (F)   21   0
H: 6 0 W: 12 02 b.Sheffield 21-7-88
Source: Ilkeston T.

Season	Club	App	Gls	Tot	
2006-07	Mansfield T	9	0		
2007-08	Mansfield T	11	0	20	0
2008-09	Bradford C	1	0	1	0

BOWER, Mark (D)   283   15
H: 5 10 W: 11 00 b.Bradford 23-1-80
Source: Trainee.

Season	Club	App	Gls	Tot	
1997-98	Bradford C	3	0		
1998-99	Bradford C	0	0		
1999-2000	Bradford C	0	0		
1999-2000	York C	15	1		
2000-01	Bradford C	0	0		
2000-01	York C	21	1	36	2
2001-02	Bradford C	10	2		
2002-03	Bradford C	37	0		
2003-04	Bradford C	14	0		
2004-05	Bradford C	46	2		
2005-06	Bradford C	45	2		
2006-07	Bradford C	46	3		
2007-08	Bradford C	27	3		
2008-09	Bradford C	3	0	231	12
2008-09	Luton T	16	1	16	1

BRANDON, Chris (M)   297   33
H: 5 8 W: 10 00 b.Bradford 7-4-76
Source: Bradford PA.

Season	Club	App	Gls	Tot	
1999-2000	Torquay U	42	5		
2000-01	Torquay U	2	0		
2001-02	Torquay U	27	3	71	8
2002-03	Chesterfield	36	7		
2003-04	Chesterfield	43	4	79	11
2004-05	Huddersfield T	44	6		
2005-06	Huddersfield T	40	3		
2006-07	Huddersfield T	23	1		
2006-07	*Blackpool*	5	2	5	2
2007-08	Huddersfield T	28	2	135	12
2008-09	Bradford C	7	0	7	0

BULLOCK, Lee (M)   308   39
H: 6 0 W: 11 04 b.Stockton 22-5-81
Source: Trainee.

Season	Club	App	Gls	Tot	
1999-2000	York C	24	0		
2000-01	York C	33	3		
2001-02	York C	40	8		
2002-03	York C	39	6		
2003-04	York C	35	7	171	24
2003-04	*Cardiff C*	11	3		
2004-05	Cardiff C	21	3	32	6
2005-06	Hartlepool U	31	4		
2006-07	Hartlepool U	25	1		
2007-08	Hartlepool U	1	0	57	5
2007-08	*Mansfield T*	5	0	5	0
2007-08	*Bury*	8	0	8	0
2007-08	Bradford C	12	1		
2008-09	Bradford C	23	3	35	4

CLARKE, Matthew (D)   307   18
H: 6 3 W: 13 00 b.Leeds 18-12-80
Source: Wolverhampton W Trainee.

Season	Club	App	Gls	Tot	
1999-2000	Halifax T	19	0		
2000-01	Halifax T	19	1		
2001-02	Halifax T	31	1	69	2
2002-03	Darlington	38	3		
2003-04	Darlington	45	4		
2004-05	Darlington	43	3		
2005-06	Darlington	43	3		
2006-07	Bradford C	8	0		
2006-07	*Darlington*	2	0	171	13
2007-08	Darlington	17	1		
2008-09	Bradford C	42	2	67	3

COLBECK, Joe (M)   110   10
H: 5 10 W: 10 12 b.Bradford 29-11-86
Source: Scholar.

Season	Club	App	Gls	Tot	
2004-05	Bradford C	0	0		
2005-06	Bradford C	11	0		
2006-07	Bradford C	32	0		
2007-08	Bradford C	33	6		
2007-08	*Darlington*	6	2	6	2
2008-09	Bradford C	28	2	104	8

CONLON, Barry (F)   397   109
H: 6 3 W: 14 00 b.Drogheda 1-10-78
Source: QPR Trainee. *Honours:* Eire Under-21.

Season	Club	App	Gls	Tot	
1997-98	Manchester C	7	0		
1997-98	*Plymouth Arg*	13	2	13	2
1998-99	Manchester C	0	0	7	0
1998-99	Southend U	34	7	34	7
1999-2000	York C	40	11		
2000-01	York C	8	0	48	11
2000-01	Colchester U	26	8	26	8
2001-02	Darlington	35	10		
2002-03	Darlington	41	15		
2003-04	Darlington	39	14		
2004-05	Barnsley	24	6		
2005-06	Barnsley	11	1	35	7
2005-06	*Rotherham U*	3	1	3	1
2006-07	Darlington	19	6	134	45
2006-07	Mansfield T	17	6	17	6
2007-08	Bradford C	42	7		
2008-09	Bradford C	30	10	72	17
2008-09	*Grimsby T*	8	5	8	5

CONVEY, Matthew (G)   0   0
H: 6 1 W: 11 12 b.Oman 5-11-89
Source: Scholar.

Season	Club	App	Gls	Tot	
2008-09	Bradford C	0	0		

DALEY, Omar (M) 103 9
H: 5 10 W: 11 03 b.Kingston, Jamaica 25-4-81
Source: From Portmore U. *Honours:* Jamaica Under-20, 61 full caps, 6 goals.

Season	Club	App	Gls	Tot App	Tot Gls
2003-04	Reading	6	0	6	0
2004-05	Preston NE	14	0	14	0

From Charleston B, Portmore U.

Season	Club	App	Gls	Tot App	Tot Gls
2006-07	Bradford C	14	2		
2007-08	Bradford C	41	4		
2008-09	Bradford C	28	3	83	9

EVANS, Rhys (G) 242 0
H: 6 1 W: 13 12 b.Swindon 27-1-82
Source: Trainee. *Honours:* England Schools, Youth, Under-20, Under-21.

Season	Club	App	Gls	Tot App	Tot Gls
1998-99	Chelsea	0	0		
1999-2000	Chelsea	0	0		
1999-2000	*Bristol R*	4	0	4	0
2000-01	Chelsea	0	0		
2001-02	Chelsea	0	0		
2001-02	*QPR*	11	0	11	0
2002-03	Chelsea	0	0		
2002-03	*Leyton Orient*	7	0	7	0
2003-04	Swindon T	41	0		
2004-05	Swindon T	45	0		
2005-06	Swindon T	32	0	118	0
2006-07	Blackpool	32	0		
2007-08	Blackpool	0	0	32	0
2007-08	*Bradford C*	4	0		
2007-08	Millwall	21	0	21	0
2008-09	Bradford C	45	0	49	0

FURMAN, Dean (M) 33 4
H: 6 0 W: 11 08 b.Cape Town 22-6-88
Source: Chelsea Scholar.

Season	Club	App	Gls	Tot App	Tot Gls
2007-08	Rangers	1	0	1	0
2008-09	Bradford C	32	4	32	4

GILLESPIE, Keith (M) 396 27
H: 5 10 W: 11 03 b.Larne 18-2-75
Source: Trainee. *Honours:* Northern Ireland Schools, Youth, Under-21, 86 full caps, 2 goals.

Season	Club	App	Gls	Tot App	Tot Gls
1992-93	Manchester U	0	0		
1993-94	Manchester U	0	0		
1993-94	*Wigan Ath*	8	4		
1994-95	Manchester U	9	1	9	1
1994-95	Newcastle U	17	2		
1995-96	Newcastle U	28	4		
1996-97	Newcastle U	32	1		
1997-98	Newcastle U	29	4		
1998-99	Newcastle U	7	0	113	11
1998-99	Blackburn R	16	1		
1999-2000	Blackburn R	22	2		
2000-01	Blackburn R	18	0		
2000-01	*Wigan Ath*	5	0	13	4
2001-02	Blackburn R	32	2		
2002-03	Blackburn R	25	0	113	5
2003-04	Leicester C	12	0		
2004-05	Leicester C	30	2	42	2
2005-06	Sheffield U	30	0		
2006-07	Sheffield U	31	2		
2007-08	Sheffield U	35	2		
2008-09	Sheffield U	1	0	97	4
2008-09	*Charlton Ath*	6	0	6	0
2008-09	Bradford C	3	0	3	0

HECKINGBOTTOM, Paul (D) 351 11
H: 6 0 W: 13 01 b.Barnsley 17-7-77
Source: Manchester U Trainee.

Season	Club	App	Gls	Tot App	Tot Gls
1995-96	Sunderland	0	0		
1996-97	Sunderland	0	0		
1997-98	Sunderland	0	0		
1997-98	*Scarborough*	29	0	29	0
1998-99	Sunderland	0	0		
1998-99	*Hartlepool U*	5	1	5	1
1998-99	Darlington	10	0		
1999-2000	Darlington	45	1		
2000-01	Darlington	18	1		
2001-02	Darlington	42	3	115	5
2002-03	Norwich C	15	0	15	0
2003-04	Bradford C	43	0		
2004-05	Sheffield W	38	4		
2005-06	Sheffield W	4	0	42	4
2005-06	Barnsley	18	1		
2006-07	Barnsley	31	0		
2007-08	Barnsley	0	0	49	1
2007-08	Bradford C	44	0		
2008-09	Bradford C	9	0	96	0

LEE, Graeme (D) 398 31
H: 6 2 W: 13 07 b.Middlesbrough 31-5-78
Source: Trainee.

Season	Club	App	Gls	Tot App	Tot Gls
1995-96	Hartlepool U	6	0		
1996-97	Hartlepool U	24	0		
1997-98	Hartlepool U	37	3		
1998-99	Hartlepool U	24	3		
1999-2000	Hartlepool U	38	7		
2000-01	Hartlepool U	6	0		
2001-02	Hartlepool U	39	4		
2002-03	Hartlepool U	45	2		
2003-04	Sheffield W	30	3		
2004-05	Sheffield W	22	1		
2005-06	Sheffield W	15	1	67	5
2005-06	Doncaster R	20	1		
2006-07	Doncaster R	39	4		
2007-08	Doncaster R	1	0	60	5
2007-08	*Hartlepool U*	3	0	222	19
2007-08	*Shrewsbury T*	5	0	5	0
2008-09	Bradford C	44	2	44	2

McLAREN, Paul (M) 454 24
H: 6 0 W: 13 04 b.High Wycombe 17-11-76
Source: Trainee.

Season	Club	App	Gls	Tot App	Tot Gls
1993-94	Luton T	1	0		
1994-95	Luton T	0	0		
1995-96	Luton T	12	1		
1996-97	Luton T	24	0		
1997-98	Luton T	43	0		
1998-99	Luton T	23	0		
1999-2000	Luton T	29	1		
2000-01	Luton T	35	2	167	4
2001-02	Sheffield W	35	2		
2002-03	Sheffield W	36	4		
2003-04	Sheffield W	2	2	96	8
2004-05	Rotherham U	33	1		
2005-06	Rotherham U	39	3	72	4
2006-07	Tranmere R	42	1		
2007-08	Tranmere R	43	4	85	5
2008-09	Bradford C	34	3	34	3

McLAUGHLIN, Jon (G) 1 0
H: 6 2 W: 13 00 b.Edinburgh 9-9-87
Source: Harrogate Railway.

Season	Club	App	Gls	Tot App	Tot Gls
2008-09	Bradford C	1	0	1	0

NIX, Kyle (F) 56 6
H: 5 6 W: 9 10 b.Sydney 21-1-86
Source: Manchester U Trainee. *Honours:* FA Schools, England Youth, Under-20.

Season	Club	App	Gls	Tot App	Tot Gls
2002-03	Aston Villa	0	0		
2003-04	Aston Villa	0	0		
2004-05	Aston Villa	0	0		
2005-06	Sheffield U	0	0		
2005-06	*Barnsley*	0	0		
2006-07	Sheffield U	0	0		
2007-08	Bradford C	40	6		
2008-09	Bradford C	16	0	56	6

O'BRIEN, Luke (D) 37 1
H: 5 9 W: 12 01 b.Halifax 11-9-88
Source: Scholar.

Season	Club	App	Gls	Tot App	Tot Gls
2007-08	Bradford C	2	0		
2008-09	Bradford C	35	1	37	1

OSBORNE, Leon (F) 3 0
H: 5 10 W: 10 10 b.Doncaster 28-10-89
Source: Scholar.

Season	Club	App	Gls	Tot App	Tot Gls
2006-07	Bradford C	1	0		
2007-08	Bradford C	0	0		
2008-09	Bradford C	2	0	3	0

SHARRY, Luke (M) 1 0
H: 5 10 W: 12 12 b.Leeds 9-3-90
Source: Scholar.

Season	Club	App	Gls	Tot App	Tot Gls
2008-09	Bradford C	1	0	1	0

TAYLFORTH, Sean (F) 1 0
H: 5 11 W: 10 03 b.Middlewich 10-3-89
Source: Scholar.

Season	Club	App	Gls	Tot App	Tot Gls
2007-08	Bradford C	1	0		
2008-09	Bradford C	0	0	1	0

THORNE, Peter (F) 478 170
H: 6 1 W: 13 13 b.Manchester 21-6-73
Source: Trainee.

Season	Club	App	Gls	Tot App	Tot Gls
1991-92	Blackburn R	0	0		
1992-93	Blackburn R	0	0		
1993-94	Blackburn R	0	0		
1993-94	*Wigan Ath*	11	0	11	0
1994-95	Blackburn R	0	0		
1994-95	Swindon T	20	9		
1995-96	Swindon T	26	10		
1996-97	Swindon T	31	8	77	27
1997-98	Stoke C	36	12		
1998-99	Stoke C	34	9		
1999-2000	Stoke C	45	24		
2000-01	Stoke C	38	16		
2001-02	Stoke C	5	4	158	65
2001-02	Cardiff C	26	8		
2002-03	Cardiff C	46	13		
2003-04	Cardiff C	23	13		
2004-05	Cardiff C	31	12	126	46
2005-06	Norwich C	21	1		
2006-07	Norwich C	15	0	36	1
2007-08	Bradford C	33	14		
2008-09	Bradford C	37	17	70	31

TOPP, Willy (F) 13 0
H: 5 9 W: 11 04 b.Temuco 4-3-86
Source: Univ Catolica. *Honours:* Chile Youth.

Season	Club	App	Gls	Tot App	Tot Gls
2007-08	Bradford C	11	0		
2008-09	Bradford C	2	0	13	0

WAITE, Jamie (G) 0 0
H: 6 2 W: 13 02 b.Plymouth 20-2-86
Source: Rotherham U, Milton Keynes D, St Albans.

Season	Club	App	Gls	Tot App	Tot Gls
2006-07	Milton Keynes D	0	0		
2007-08	Bradford C	0	0		
2008-09	Bradford C	0	0		

WETHERALL, David (D) 506 30
H: 6 3 W: 13 12 b.Sheffield 14-3-71
Source: School. *Honours:* England Schools.

Season	Club	App	Gls	Tot App	Tot Gls
1989-90	Sheffield W	0	0		
1990-91	Sheffield W	0	0		
1991-92	Leeds U	1	0		
1992-93	Leeds U	13	1		
1993-94	Leeds U	32	1		
1994-95	Leeds U	38	3		
1995-96	Leeds U	34	4		
1996-97	Leeds U	29	0		
1997-98	Leeds U	34	3		
1998-99	Leeds U	21	0	202	12
1999-2000	Bradford C	38	2		
2000-01	Bradford C	18	1		
2001-02	Bradford C	19	2		
2002-03	Bradford C	17	0		
2003-04	Bradford C	34	1		
2004-05	Bradford C	45	4		
2005-06	Bradford C	46	5		
2006-07	Bradford C	41	1		
2007-08	Bradford C	46	2		
2008-09	Bradford C	0	0	304	18

BRENTFORD (13)

ADEMOLA, Moses (F) 8 0
H: 5 6 W: 10 08 b.Lewisham 9-8-89
Source: Croydon Ath.

Season	Club	App	Gls	Tot App	Tot Gls
2008-09	Brentford	8	0	8	0

BEAN, Marcus (M) 163 14
H: 5 11 W: 11 06 b.Hammersmith 2-11-84
Source: Scholar.

Season	Club	App	Gls	Tot App	Tot Gls
2002-03	QPR	7	0		
2003-04	QPR	31	1		
2004-05	QPR	20	1		
2004-05	*Swansea C*	8	0		
2005-06	QPR	9	0	67	2
2005-06	*Swansea C*	9	1	17	1
2005-06	Blackpool	17	1		
2006-07	Blackpool	6	0		
2007-08	Blackpool	0	0	23	1
2007-08	*Rotherham U*	12	1	12	1
2008-09	Brentford	44	9	44	9

BROWN, Sebastian (G) 0 0
H: 6 2 W: 13 07 b. 24-11-89
Source: Scholar.

Season	Club	App	Gls	Tot App	Tot Gls
2008-09	Brentford	0	0		

BROWN, Simon (G) 240 0
H: 6 2 W: 15 00 b.Chelmsford 3-12-76
Source: Trainee.

Season	Club	App	Gls	Tot App	Tot Gls
1995-96	Tottenham H	0	0		
1996-97	Tottenham H	0	0		
1997-98	Tottenham H	0	0		
1997-98	*Lincoln C*	1	0	1	0
1998-99	Tottenham H	0	0		
1998-99	*Fulham*	0	0		
1999-2000	Colchester U	38	0		
2000-01	Colchester U	18	0		
2001-02	Colchester U	19	0		
2002-03	Colchester U	27	0		
2003-04	Colchester U	40	0	142	0

2004-05	Hibernian	36	0	
2005-06	Hibernian	8	0	
2006-07	Hibernian	4	0	48 0
2007-08	Brentford	26	0	
2008-09	Brentford	1	0	27 0
2008-09	Darlington	22	0	22 0

CHARLES, Darius (M)   37 1
H: 6 1   W: 13 05   b.Ealing 10-12-87
Source: Scholar.

2004-05	Brentford	1	0	
2005-06	Brentford	2	0	
2006-07	Brentford	17	1	
2007-08	Brentford	17	0	
2008-09	Brentford	0	0	37 1

DICKSON, Ryan (M)   84 2
H: 5 10   W: 11 05   b.Saltash 14-12-86
Source: Scholar.

2004-05	Plymouth Arg	3	0	
2005-06	Plymouth Arg	0	0	
2006-07	Plymouth Arg	2	0	
2006-07	Torquay U	9	1	9 1
2007-08	Plymouth Arg	0	0	5 0
2007-08	Brentford	31	0	
2008-09	Brentford	39	1	70 1

ELDER, Nathan (F)   66 12
H: 6 1   W: 13 12   b.Hornchurch 5-4-85
Source: Billericay T.

2006-07	Brighton & HA	13	1	
2007-08	Brighton & HA	9	1	22 2
2007-08	Brentford	17	4	
2008-09	Brentford	27	6	44 10

HALLS, John (M)   115 3
H: 6 0   W: 11 11   b.Islington 14-2-82
Source: Scholar. *Honours:* England Youth, Under-20.

2000-01	Arsenal	0	0	
2001-02	Arsenal	0	0	
2001-02	Colchester U	6	0	6 0
2002-03	Arsenal	0	0	
2003-04	Arsenal	0	0	
2003-04	Stoke C	34	0	
2004-05	Stoke C	22	0	
2005-06	Stoke C	13	2	69 2
2005-06	Reading	1	1	
2006-07	Reading	0	0	
2007-08	Reading	1	0	
2007-08	*Preston NE*	4	0	4 0
2007-08	*Crystal Palace*	5	0	5 0
2007-08	*Sheffield U*	6	0	6 0
2008-09	Reading	0	0	2 1
2008-09	Brentford	23	0	23 0

HUNT, David (M)   189 8
H: 5 11   W: 11 09   b.Dulwich 10-9-82
Source: Scholar.

2002-03	Crystal Palace	2	0	2 0
2003-04	Leyton Orient	38	1	
2004-05	Leyton Orient	27	0	65 1
2005-06	Northampton T	4	0	
2005-06	Northampton T	40	3	
2006-07	Northampton T	29	0	73 3
2007-08	Shrewsbury T	27	2	
2008-09	Shrewsbury T	2	0	29 2
2008-09	Brentford	20	2	20 2

IDE, Charlie (M)   46 7
H: 5 9   W: 11 00   b.Sunbury 10-5-88

2004-05	Brentford	1	0	
2005-06	Brentford	0	0	
2006-07	Brentford	26	7	
2007-08	Brentford	19	0	
2008-09	Brentford	0	0	46 7

JOHNSON, Brett (D)   36 0
H: 6 1   W: 13 00   b.Hammersmith 15-8-85
Source: Ashford T, Aldershot T.

2005-06	Northampton T	6	0	
2006-07	Northampton T	4	0	
2007-08	Northampton T	16	0	26 0
2008-09	Brentford	10	0	10 0

MACDONALD, Charlie (F)   88 21
H: 5 8   W: 12 10   b.Southwark 13-2-81
Source: Trainee.

1998-99	Charlton Ath	0	0	
1999-2000	Charlton Ath	3	0	
2000-01	Charlton Ath	3	0	
2000-01	*Cheltenham T*	8	2	8 2
2001-02	Charlton Ath	2	1	
2001-02	*Torquay U*	5	0	5 0
2001-02	Colchester U	4	1	4 1

2002-03	Charlton Ath	0	0	
2003-04	Charlton Ath	0	0	
2004-05	Charlton Ath	0	0	
2005-06	Charlton Ath	0	0	
2006-07	Charlton Ath	0	0	8 1
2007-08	Southend U	25	1	25 1
2008-09	Brentford	38	16	38 16

MONTAGUE, Ross (F)   14 1
H: 6 0   W: 12 11   b.Twickenham 1-11-88
Source: Scholar.

2006-07	Brentford	4	0	
2007-08	Brentford	10	1	
2008-09	Brentford	0	0	14 1

NEWTON, Adam (M)   288 11
H: 5 10   W: 11 00   b.Ascot 4-12-80
Source: West Ham U Trainee. *Honours:* England Under-21. St Kitts & Nevis 2 full caps, 1 goal.

1999-2000	West Ham U	2	0	
1999-2000	*Portsmouth*	3	0	3 0
2000-01	West Ham U	0	0	
2000-01	*Notts Co*	20	1	20 1
2001-02	West Ham U	0	0	2 0
2001-02	*Leyton Orient*	10	1	10 1
2002-03	Peterborough U	36	2	
2003-04	Peterborough U	37	2	
2004-05	Peterborough U	30	0	
2005-06	Peterborough U	40	3	
2006-07	Peterborough U	43	1	
2007-08	Peterborough U	32	0	218 8
2008-09	Brentford	35	1	35 1

O'CONNOR, Kevin (F)   301 25
H: 5 11   W: 12 00   b.Blackburn 24-2-82
Source: Trainee. *Honours:* Eire Youth, Under-21.

1999-2000	Brentford	6	0	
2000-01	Brentford	11	1	
2001-02	Brentford	25	0	
2002-03	Brentford	45	5	
2003-04	Brentford	43	1	
2004-05	Brentford	37	2	
2005-06	Brentford	30	7	
2006-07	Brentford	39	6	
2007-08	Brentford	37	3	
2008-09	Brentford	28	0	301 25

OSBORNE, Karleigh (D)   75 5
H: 6 2   W: 12 04   b.Southall 19-3-88
Source: Scholar.

2004-05	Brentford	1	0	
2005-06	Brentford	1	0	
2006-07	Brentford	21	0	
2007-08	Brentford	29	1	
2008-09	Brentford	23	4	75 5

PEAD, Craig (M)   173 3
H: 5 9   W: 11 06   b.Bromsgrove 15-9-81
Source: Trainee. *Honours:* England Youth, Under-20.

1998-99	Coventry C	0	0	
1999-2000	Coventry C	0	0	
2000-01	Coventry C	0	0	
2001-02	Coventry C	1	0	
2002-03	Coventry C	24	2	
2003-04	Coventry C	17	1	
2004-05	Coventry C	0	0	42 3
2004-05	*Notts Co*	5	0	5 0
2004-05	Walsall	8	0	
2005-06	Walsall	39	0	
2006-07	Walsall	41	0	88 0
2007-08	Brentford	32	0	
2008-09	Brentford	6	0	38 0

PHILLIPS, Mark (D)   108 2
H: 6 2   W: 11 00   b.Lambeth 27-1-82
Source: Scholarship.

1999-2000	Millwall	0	0	
2000-01	Millwall	0	0	
2001-02	Millwall	1	0	
2002-03	Millwall	7	0	
2003-04	Millwall	0	0	
2004-05	Millwall	25	1	
2005-06	Millwall	22	0	
2006-07	Millwall	12	0	
2006-07	*Darlington*	8	0	8 0
2007-08	Millwall	0	0	67 1
2008-09	Brentford	33	1	33 1

POOLE, Glenn (M)   77 19
H: 5 7   W: 11 04   b.Essex 3-2-81
Source: Thurrock, Grays Ath.

2006-07	Rochdale	6	0	6 0
2007-08	Brentford	45	14	
2008-09	Brentford	26	5	71 19

POWELL, Darren (D)   241 11
H: 6 2   W: 13 07   b.Hammersmith 10-3-76
Source: Hampton.

1998-99	Brentford	33	2	
1999-2000	Brentford	36	2	
2000-01	Brentford	18	1	
2001-02	Brentford	41	1	
2002-03	Crystal Palace	39	1	
2003-04	Crystal Palace	10	0	
2004-05	Crystal Palace	6	1	55 2
2004-05	*West Ham U*	5	1	5 1
2005-06	Southampton	25	1	
2006-07	Southampton	8	0	
2007-08	Southampton	10	1	
2008-09	Southampton	0	0	43 2
2008-09	*Derby Co*	6	0	6 0
2008-09	Brentford	4	0	132 6

SMITH, Gary (M)   115 9
H: 5 8   W: 10 09   b.Middlesbrough 30-1-84
Source: Trainee.

2002-03	Middlesbrough	0	0	
2003-04	Middlesbrough	0	0	
2003-04	*Wimbledon*	11	3	11 3
2004-05	Milton Keynes D	23	1	
2005-06	Milton Keynes D	25	3	
2006-07	Milton Keynes D	23	1	71 5
2007-08	Brentford	29	1	
2008-09	Brentford	4	0	33 1

WILLIAMS, Marvin (M)   110 8
H: 5 11   W: 11 06   b.London 12-8-87
Source: Scholar.

2005-06	Millwall	22	4	
2006-07	Millwall	29	3	51 7
2006-07	*Torquay U*	2	1	2 1
2007-08	Yeovil T	23	0	23 0
2008-09	Brentford	34	0	34 0

WOOD, Sam (M)   40 1
H: 6 0   W: 11 05   b.London 9-8-86
Source: Bromley.

2008-09	Brentford	40	1	40 1

BRIGHTON & HA (14)

BIRCHALL, Chris (M)   127 9
H: 5 7   W: 13 05   b.Stafford 5-5-84
Source: Scholar. *Honours:* Trinidad & Tobago 35 full caps, 4 goals.

2001-02	Port Vale	1	0	
2002-03	Port Vale	2	0	
2003-04	Port Vale	10	0	
2004-05	Port Vale	34	6	
2005-06	Port Vale	31	1	78 7
2006-07	Coventry C	28	2	
2007-08	Coventry C	1	0	
2007-08	*St Mirren*	9	0	9 0
2008-09	Coventry C	0	0	29 2
2008-09	*Carlisle U*	2	0	2 0
2008-09	Brighton & HA	9	0	9 0

CAROLE, Sebastien (M)   115 6
H: 5 7   W: 11 05   b.Pontoise 8-9-82
Source: Monaco.

2003-04	West Ham U	1	0	1 0
2004-05	Chateauroux	11	1	11 1
2005-06	Brighton & HA	40	2	
2006-07	Leeds U	17	0	
2007-08	Leeds U	28	3	
2008-09	Leeds U	0	0	45 3
2008-09	*Darlington*	6	0	6 0
2008-09	Brighton & HA	12	0	52 2

COMPTON, Jack (M)   0 0
H: 5 8   W: 10 07   b.Cardiff 2-9-88
Source: West Bromwich Albion Scholar.

2008-09	Brighton & HA	0	0	

COOK, Steve (D)   2 0
H: 6 1   W: 12 13   b.Hastings 19-4-91
Source: Scholar.

2008-09	Brighton & HA	2	0	2 0

COX, Dean (M) 125 16
H: 5 4 W: 9 08 b.Cuckfield 12-8-87
Source: Scholar.
2005-06	Brighton & HA	1	0	
2006-07	Brighton & HA	42	6	
2007-08	Brighton & HA	42	6	
2008-09	Brighton & HA	40	4	125 16

DAVIES, Craig (F) 140 24
H: 6 2 W: 13 05 b.Burton-on-Trent 9-1-86
Source: Manchester C.Wales Youth,
Under-21, 5 full caps.
2004-05	Oxford U	28	6		
2005-06	Oxford U	20	2	48	8
2005-06	Verona	0	0		
2006-07	Wolverhampton W	23	0	23	0
2007-08	Oldham Ath	32	10		
2008-09	Oldham Ath	12	0	44	10
2008-09	*Stockport Co*	9	5	9	5
2008-09	Brighton & HA	16	1	16	1

DIXON, Jonny (F) 78 7
H: 5 9 W: 11 01 b.Murcia 16-1-84
Source: Scholar.
2002-03	Wycombe W	22	5		
2003-04	Wycombe W	8	0		
2004-05	Wycombe W	16	1		
2005-06	Wycombe W	17	0		
2006-07	Wycombe W	10	1	73	7
From Aldershot T.					
2007-08	Brighton & HA	4	0		
2008-09	Brighton & HA	1	0	5	0

EL-ABD, Adam (D) 164 2
H: 5 10 W: 13 05 b.Brighton 11-9-84
Source: Scholar.
2003-04	Brighton & HA	11	0		
2004-05	Brighton & HA	16	0		
2005-06	Brighton & HA	29	0		
2006-07	Brighton & HA	42	1		
2007-08	Brighton & HA	35	1		
2008-09	Brighton & HA	31	0	164	2

ELPHICK, Tommy (M) 82 3
H: 5 11 W: 11 07 b.Brighton 7-9-87
Source: Scholar.
2005-06	Brighton & HA	1	0		
2006-07	Brighton & HA	3	0		
2007-08	Brighton & HA	39	2		
2008-09	Brighton & HA	39	1	82	3

FOGDEN, Wes (F) 3 0
H: 5 8 W: 10 04 b.Brighton 12-4-88
Source: Scholar.
2006-07	Brighton & HA	0	0		
2007-08	Brighton & HA	3	0		
2008-09	Brighton & HA	0	0	3	0

FORSTER, Nicky (F) 561 174
H: 5 9 W: 11 05 b.Caterham 8-9-73
Source: Horley T. *Honours:* England
Under-21.
1992-93	Gillingham	26	6		
1993-94	Gillingham	41	18	67	24
1994-95	Brentford	46	24		
1995-96	Brentford	38	5		
1996-97	Brentford	25	10	109	39
1996-97	Birmingham C	7	3		
1997-98	Birmingham C	28	3		
1998-99	Birmingham C	33	5	68	11
1999-2000	Reading	36	10		
2000-01	Reading	9	1		
2001-02	Reading	42	19		
2002-03	Reading	40	16		
2003-04	Reading	30	7		
2004-05	Reading	30	7	187	60
2005-06	Ipswich T	20	7		
2006-07	Ipswich T	4	1	24	8
2006-07	Hull C	35	5	35	5
2007-08	Brighton & HA	41	15		
2008-09	Brighton & HA	30	12	71	27

FRASER, Tom (M) 79 2
H: 5 10 W: 11 00 b.Brighton 5-12-87
Source: Bognor Regis T.
2006-07	Brighton & HA	28	1		
2007-08	Brighton & HA	24	0		
2008-09	Brighton & HA	27	1	79	2

GARGAN, Sam (F) 1 0
H: 6 3 W: 11 12 b.Hurstpierpoint 24-6-88
Source: Scholar.
2007-08	Brighton & HA	1	0		
2008-09	Brighton & HA	0	0	1	0

GATTING, Joe (D) 44 4
H: 5 11 W: 12 04 b.Brighton 25-11-87
Source: Scholar.
2005-06	Brighton & HA	12	0		
2006-07	Brighton & HA	23	4		
2007-08	Brighton & HA	9	0		
2008-09	Brighton & HA	0	0	44	4

HART, Gary (F) 353 44
H: 5 9 W: 12 03 b.Harlow 21-9-76
Source: Stansted.
1998-99	Brighton & HA	44	12		
1999-2000	Brighton & HA	43	9		
2000-01	Brighton & HA	45	7		
2001-02	Brighton & HA	39	4		
2002-03	Brighton & HA	36	4		
2003-04	Brighton & HA	42	3		
2004-05	Brighton & HA	26	2		
2005-06	Brighton & HA	35	1		
2006-07	Brighton & HA	25	2		
2007-08	Brighton & HA	7	0		
2008-09	Brighton & HA	11	0	353	44

HAWKINS, Colin (D) 260 20
H: 6 1 W: 12 06 b.Galway 17-8-77
Honours: Eire Youth, Under-20, Under-21.
1995-96	Coventry C	0	0		
1996-97	Coventry C	0	0		
1997-98	St Patrick's Ath	32	4		
1998-99	St Patrick's Ath	26	7		
1999-2000	St Patrick's Ath	27	2	85	13
From Doncaster R					
2001-02	Bohemians	9	1		
2002-03	Bohemians	21	2		
2003	Bohemians	30	1		
2004	Bohemians	29	1	89	5
2005	Shelbourne	26	0		
2006	Shelbourne	25	2	51	2
2006-07	Coventry C	13	0		
2007-08	Coventry C	0	0	13	0
2007-08	*Chesterfield*	5	0	5	0
2008-09	Brighton & HA	17	0	17	0

HINSHELWOOD, Adam (D) 99 2
H: 5 10 W: 12 10 b.Oxford 8-1-84
Source: Scholar.
2002-03	Brighton & HA	7	0		
2003-04	Brighton & HA	17	0		
2004-05	Brighton & HA	38	1		
2005-06	Brighton & HA	11	0		
2006-07	Brighton & HA	11	0		
2007-08	Brighton & HA	1	0		
2008-09	Brighton & HA	14	1	99	2

JARRETT, Jason (M) 244 9
H: 6 1 W: 13 10 b.Bury 14-9-79
Source: Trainee.
1998-99	Blackpool	2	0		
1999-2000	Blackpool	0	0	2	0
1999-2000	Wrexham	1	0	1	0
2000-01	Bury	25	2		
2001-02	Bury	37	2	62	4
2001-02	Wigan Ath	5	0		
2002-03	Wigan Ath	35	0		
2003-04	Wigan Ath	41	1		
2004-05	Wigan Ath	14	0	95	1
2004-05	*Stoke C*	2	0	2	0
2005-06	Norwich C	11	0	11	0
2005-06	*Plymouth Arg*	7	0	7	0
2005-06	*Preston NE*	10	1		
2006-07	Preston NE	5	0		
2006-07	*Hull C*	3	0	3	0
2006-07	*Leicester C*	13	0	13	0
2007-08	Preston NE	0	0		
2007-08	*QPR*	2	0	2	0
2007-08	*Oldham Ath*	15	3	15	3
2008-09	Preston NE	3	0	18	1
2008-09	Brighton & HA	13	0	13	0

KUIPERS, Michels (G) 246 0
H: 6 2 W: 14 03 b.Amsterdam 26-6-74
Source: SDW Amsterdam.
1998-99	Bristol R	1	0		
1999-2000	Bristol R	0	0	1	0
2000-01	Brighton & HA	34	0		
2001-02	Brighton & HA	39	0		
2002-03	Brighton & HA	21	0		
2003-04	Brighton & HA	10	0		
2003-04	*Hull C*	3	0	3	0
2004-05	Brighton & HA	30	0		
2005-06	Brighton & HA	5	0		
2005-06	*Boston U*	15	0	15	0
2006-07	Brighton & HA	14	0		

2007-08	Brighton & HA	46	0		
2008-09	Brighton & HA	28	0	227	0

LIVERMORE, David (M) 352 18
H: 5 11 W: 12 02 b.Edmonton 20-5-80
Source: Trainee.
1998-99	Arsenal	0	0		
1999-2000	Millwall	32	2		
2000-01	Millwall	39	3		
2001-02	Millwall	43	0		
2002-03	Millwall	41	2		
2003-04	Millwall	36	1		
2004-05	Millwall	41	2		
2005-06	Millwall	41	2	273	12
2006-07	Hull C	25	4		
2007-08	Hull C	20	1	45	5
2007-08	*Oldham Ath*	10	1	10	1
2008-09	Brighton & HA	16	0	16	0
2008-09	*Luton T*	8	0	8	0

LOFT, Doug (M) 50 2
H: 6 0 W: 12 01 b.Maidstone 25-12-86
Source: Hastings U.
2005-06	Brighton & HA	3	1		
2006-07	Brighton & HA	11	1		
2007-08	Brighton & HA	13	0		
2008-09	Brighton & HA	12	0	39	2
2008-09	*Dagenham & R*	11	0	11	0

LOUIS, Kane (F) 0 0
H: 5 9 W: 10 10 b.Brighton 21-5-90
Source: Scholar.
2008-09	Brighton & HA	0	0		

LYNCH, Joel (G) 102 2
H: 6 1 W: 12 10 b.Eastbourne 3-10-87
Source: From Scholar. *Honours:* England
Youth.
2005-06	Brighton & HA	16	1		
2006-07	Brighton & HA	39	0		
2007-08	Brighton & HA	22	1		
2008-09	Brighton & HA	2	0	79	2
2008-09	*Nottingham F*	23	0	23	0

MAYO, Kerry (D) 368 12
H: 5 10 W: 12 08 b.Haywards Heath
21-9-77
Source: Trainee.
1996-97	Brighton & HA	24	0		
1997-98	Brighton & HA	44	6		
1998-99	Brighton & HA	25	1		
1999-2000	Brighton & HA	31	1		
2000-01	Brighton & HA	45	1		
2001-02	Brighton & HA	33	0		
2002-03	Brighton & HA	41	1		
2003-04	Brighton & HA	33	0		
2004-05	Brighton & HA	27	1		
2005-06	Brighton & HA	18	1		
2006-07	Brighton & HA	30	0		
2007-08	Brighton & HA	15	0		
2008-09	Brighton & HA	2	0	368	12

McLEOD, Kevin (M) 189 20
H: 5 11 W: 11 00 b.Liverpool 12-9-80
Source: Trainee.
1998-99	Everton	0	0		
1999-2000	Everton	0	0		
2000-01	Everton	5	0		
2001-02	Everton	0	0		
2002-03	Everton	0	0		
2002-03	*QPR*	8	2		
2003-04	Everton	0	0	5	0
2003-04	QPR	35	3		
2004-05	QPR	24	1	67	6
2004-05	Swansea C	11	0		
2005-06	Swansea C	29	7		
2006-07	Swansea C	4	0	44	7
2006-07	Colchester U	24	3		
2007-08	Colchester U	28	4	52	7
2008-09	Brighton & HA	21	0	21	0

McNULTY, Jim (D) 76 3
H: 6 1 W: 12 00 b.Liverpool 13-2-85
Source: Scholar. *Honours:* Scotland Youth.
2003-04	Wrexham	0	0		
2004-05	Wrexham	0	0		
2005-06	Wrexham	0	0		
2006-07	Macclesfield T	15	0		
2007-08	Macclesfield T	19	1	34	1
2007-08	Stockport Co	11	0		
2008-09	Stockport Co	26	1	37	1
2008-09	Brighton & HA	5	1	5	1

MURRAY, Glenn (F)   136 51
H: 6 1 W: 12 12 b.Maryport 25-9-83
Source: Wilmington Hammerheads, Workington.

2005-06	Carlisle U	26	3		
2006-07	Carlisle U	1	0	27	3
2006-07	*Stockport Co*	11	3	11	3
2006-07	Rochdale	31	16		
2007-08	Rochdale	23	9	54	25
2007-08	Brighton & HA	21	9		
2008-09	Brighton & HA	23	11	44	20

PEARSON, Andy (D)   0 0
H: 6 2 W: 13 10 b.Brighton 19-9-89
Source: Scholar.

| 2008-09 | Brighton & HA | 0 | 0 | | |

ROBINSON, Jake (F)   142 17
H: 5 7 W: 10 10 b.Brighton 23-10-86
Source: Scholar.

2003-04	Brighton & HA	9	0		
2004-05	Brighton & HA	10	1		
2005-06	Brighton & HA	27	1		
2006-07	Brighton & HA	38	6		
2007-08	Brighton & HA	34	4		
2008-09	Brighton & HA	5	1	123	13
2008-09	*Aldershot T*	19	4	19	4

ROYCE, Dan (M)   0 0
H: 5 9 W: 11 13 b.Chichester 26-11-89
Source: Scholar.

| 2008-09 | Brighton & HA | 0 | 0 | | |

SULLIVAN, John (G)   13 0
H: 5 10 W: 11 04 b.Brighton 8-3-88
Source: From Scholar. Honours: England Youth.

2005-06	Brighton & HA	0	0		
2006-07	Brighton & HA	0	0		
2007-08	Brighton & HA	0	0		
2008-09	Brighton & HA	13	0	13	0

THOMSON, Steve (M)   262 7
H: 5 8 W: 10 04 b.Glasgow 23-1-78
Source: Trainee. Honours: Scotland Youth.

1995-96	Crystal Palace	0	0		
1996-97	Crystal Palace	0	0		
1997-98	Crystal Palace	0	0		
1998-99	Crystal Palace	16	0		
1999-2000	Crystal Palace	21	0		
2000-01	Crystal Palace	18	0		
2001-02	Crystal Palace	23	0		
2002-03	Crystal Palace	27	1	105	1
2003-04	Peterborough U	35	1		
2004-05	Peterborough U	31	2	66	3
2005-06	Falkirk	32	1		
2006-07	Falkirk	22	2	54	3
2007-08	Brighton & HA	20	0		
2008-09	Brighton & HA	17	0	37	0

Transferred to St Mirren January 2009

VIRGO, Adam (D)   179 14
H: 6 2 W: 13 12 b.Brighton 25-1-83
Source: Juniors. Honours: Scotland B.

2000-01	Brighton & HA	6	0		
2001-02	Brighton & HA	6	0		
2002-03	Brighton & HA	3	0		
2002-03	*Exeter C*	9	0	9	0
2003-04	Brighton & HA	22	1		
2004-05	Brighton & HA	36	8		
2005-06	Celtic	10	0		
2006-07	Celtic	0	0	10	0
2006-07	Coventry C	15	1		
2007-08	Coventry C	0	0	15	1
2007-08	*Colchester U*	36	1	36	1
2008-09	Brighton & HA	36	3	109	12

WHING, Andrew (D)   200 2
H: 6 0 W: 12 00 b.Birmingham 20-9-84
Source: Scholar.

2002-03	Coventry C	14	0		
2003-04	Coventry C	28	1		
2004-05	Coventry C	16	1		
2005-06	Coventry C	32	0		
2006-07	Coventry C	16	0	106	2
2006-07	*Brighton & HA*	12	0		
2007-08	Brighton & HA	42	0		
2008-09	Brighton & HA	40	0	94	0

WILLS, Kane (M)   0 0
H: 5 9 W: 12 02 b.Shoreham 25-3-90
Source: Scholar.

| 2008-09 | Brighton & HA | 0 | 0 | | |

BRISTOL C (15)

ADEBOLA, Dele (F)   534 126
H: 6 3 W: 12 08 b.Lagos 23-6-75
Source: Trainee.

1992-93	Crewe Alex	6	0		
1993-94	Crewe Alex	0	0		
1994-95	Crewe Alex	30	8		
1995-96	Crewe Alex	29	8		
1996-97	Crewe Alex	27	7		
1997-98	Crewe Alex	27	7	124	39
1997-98	Birmingham C	17	7		
1998-99	Birmingham C	39	13		
1999-2000	Birmingham C	42	5		
2000-01	Birmingham C	31	6		
2001-02	Birmingham C	0	0	129	31
2001-02	*Oldham Ath*	5	0	5	0
2002-03	Crystal Palace	39	5 ·	39	5
2003-04	Coventry C	28	2		
2003-04	*Burnley*	3	1	3	1
2004-05	Coventry C	25	5		
2004-05	*Bradford C*	15	3	15	3
2005-06	Coventry C	44	12		
2006-07	Coventry C	40	8		
2007-08	Coventry C	26	4	163	31
2007-08	Bristol C	17	6		
2008-09	Bristol C	39	10	56	16

AKINDE, John (F)   18 8
H: 6 2 W: 10 01 b.Gravesend 8-7-89
Source: Ebbsfleet U.

| 2008-09 | Bristol C | 7 | 1 | 7 | 1 |
| 2008-09 | *Wycombe W* | 11 | 7 | 11 | 7 |

ARTUS, Frankie (M)   10 3
H: 6 0 W: 11 02 b.Bristol 27-9-88
Source: Scholar.

2005-06	Bristol C	0	0		
2006-07	Bristol C	0	0		
2007-08	Bristol C	0	0		
2008-09	Bristol C	0	0		
2008-09	*Brentford*	1	0	1	0
2008-09	*Cheltenham T*	9	3	9	3

BASSO, Adriano (G)   161 0
H: 6 1 W: 11 07 b.Jundiai 18-4-75
Source: Woking.

2005-06	Bristol C	29	0		
2006-07	Bristol C	45	0		
2007-08	Bristol C	44	0		
2008-09	Bristol C	43	0	161	0

CAREY, Louis (D)   486 10
H: 5 10 W: 11 00 b.Bristol 20-1-77
Source: Trainee. Honours: Scotland Under-21.

1995-96	Bristol C	23	0		
1996-97	Bristol C	42	0		
1997-98	Bristol C	38	0		
1998-99	Bristol C	41	0		
1999-2000	Bristol C	22	0		
2000-01	Bristol C	46	3		
2001-02	Bristol C	35	0		
2002-03	Bristol C	24	1		
2003-04	Bristol C	41	1		
2004-05	Coventry C	23	0	23	0
2004-05	Bristol C	14	0		
2005-06	Bristol C	38	3		
2006-07	Bristol C	38	2		
2007-08	Bristol C	33	0		
2008-09	Bristol C	28	0	463	10

ELLIOTT, Marvin (M)   217 11
H: 6 0 W: 12 02 b.Wandsworth 15-9-84
Source: Scholar.

2001-02	Millwall	0	0		
2002-03	Millwall	1	0		
2003-04	Millwall	21	0		
2004-05	Millwall	41	1		
2005-06	Millwall	39	2		
2006-07	Millwall	42	0	144	3
2007-08	Bristol C	45	5		
2008-09	Bristol C	28	3	73	8

FONTAINE, Liam (D)   151 2
H: 5 11 W: 11 09 b.Beckenham 7-1-86
Source: Trainee. Honours: England Youth, Under-20.

2003-04	Fulham	0	0		
2004-05	Fulham	1	0		
2004-05	*Yeovil T*	15	0		
2005-06	Fulham	0	0	1	0
2005-06	*Yeovil T*	10	0	25	0

2005-06	*Bristol C*	15	0		
2006-07	Bristol C	30	0		
2007-08	Bristol C	38	1		
2008-09	Bristol C	42	2	125	3

HENDERSON, Stephen (G)   2 0
H: 6 3 W: 11 00 b.Dublin 2-5-88
Source: Scholar. Honours: Eire Under-21.

2005-06	Aston Villa	0	0		
2006-07	Aston Villa	0	0		
2007-08	Bristol C	1	0		
2008-09	Bristol C	1	0	2	0

IRIEKPEN, Izzy (D)   183 14
H: 6 1 W: 12 02 b.East London 14-5-82
Source: Trainee. Honours: England Youth.

1998-99	West Ham U	0	0		
1999-2000	West Ham U	0	0		
2000-01	West Ham U	0	0		
2001-02	West Ham U	0	0		
2002-03	West Ham U	0	0		
2002-03	*Leyton Orient*	5	1	5	1
2002-03	*Cambridge U*	13	1	13	1
2003-04	Swansea C	34	1		
2004-05	Swansea C	29	2		
2005-06	Swansea C	28	0		
2006-07	Swansea C	32	4	123	7
2007-08	Scunthorpe U	17	1		
2008-09	Scunthorpe U	16	4	33	5
2008-09	Bristol C	9	0	9	0

JOHNSON, Lee (M)   245 23
H: 5 6 W: 10 07 b.Newmarket 7-6-81
Source: Trainee.

1998-99	Watford	0	0		
1999-2000	Watford	0	0		
2000-01	Brighton & HA	0	0		
2000-01	Brentford	0	0		
2001-02	Brentford	0	0		
2003-04	Yeovil T	45	5		
2004-05	Yeovil T	44	7		
2005-06	Yeovil T	26	2	115	14
2005-06	Hearts	4	0	4	0
2006-07	Bristol C	42	5		
2007-08	Bristol C	40	1		
2008-09	Bristol C	44	3	126	9

MAGEE, Mark (M)   0 0
Source: Scholar.

| 2008-09 | Bristol C | 0 | 0 | | |

MAYNARD, Nicky (F)   102 42
H: 5 11 W: 11 00 b.Winsford 11-12-86
Source: Scholar.

2005-06	Crewe Alex	1	1		
2006-07	Crewe Alex	31	16		
2007-08	Crewe Alex	27	14	59	31
2008-09	Bristol C	43	11	43	11

McALLISTER, Jamie (D)   355 3
H: 5 10 W: 11 00 b.Glasgow 26-4-78
Honours: Scotland 1 full cap.

1995-96	Q of S	2	0		
1996-97	Q of S	6	0		
1997-98	Q of S	15	0		
1998-99	Q of S	27	0	50	0
1999-2000	Aberdeen	34	0		
2000-01	Aberdeen	25	0		
2001-02	Aberdeen	29	0		
2002-03	Aberdeen	29	0	117	0
2003-04	Livingston	34	1	34	1
2004-05	Hearts	30	0		
2005-06	Hearts	17	0	47	0
2006-07	Bristol C	31	1		
2007-08	Bristol C	41	0		
2008-09	Bristol C	35	1	107	2

McCOMBE, Jamie (D)   253 16
H: 6 5 W: 12 05 b.Scunthorpe 1-1-83
Source: Scholar.

2001-02	Scunthorpe U	17	0		
2002-03	Scunthorpe U	31	1		
2003-04	Scunthorpe U	15	0	63	1
2003-04	Lincoln C	8	0		
2004-05	Lincoln C	41	3		
2005-06	Lincoln C	38	4	87	7
2006-07	Bristol C	41	4		
2007-08	Bristol C	34	3		
2008-09	Bristol C	28	1	103	8

McINDOE, Michael (M)   304 47
H: 5 8 W: 11 00 b.Edinburgh 2-12-79
Source: Trainee. Honours: Scotland B.

| 1997-98 | Luton T | 0 | 0 | | |
| 1998-99 | Luton T | 22 | 0 | | |

1999-2000	Luton T	17	0	**39**	**0**

Fr Hereford, Yeovil

2003-04	Doncaster R	45	10		
2004-05	Doncaster R	44	10		
2005-06	Doncaster R	33	8	**122**	**28**
2005-06	*Derby Co*	8	0	**8**	**0**
2006-07	Barnsley	18	4	**18**	**4**
2006-07	Wolverhampton W	27	3	**27**	**3**
2007-08	Bristol C	45	6		
2008-09	Bristol C	45	6	**90**	**12**

MURRAY, Scott (M)   **405**   **81**
H: 5 9   W: 11 00   b.Aberdeen 26-5-74
Source: Fraserburgh. *Honours:* Scotland B.

1993-94	Aston Villa	0	0		
1994-95	Aston Villa	0	0		
1995-96	Aston Villa	3	0		
1996-97	Aston Villa	1	0		
1997-98	Aston Villa	0	0	**4**	**0**
1997-98	Bristol C	23	0		
1998-99	Bristol C	32	3		
1999-2000	Bristol C	41	6		
2000-01	Bristol C	46	10		
2001-02	Bristol C	37	8		
2002-03	Bristol C	45	19		
2003-04	Reading	34	5	**34**	**5**
2003-04	Bristol C	6	0		
2004-05	Bristol C	42	8		
2005-06	Bristol C	37	10		
2006-07	Bristol C	28	7		
2007-08	Bristol C	14	3		
2008-09	Bristol C	3	0	**354**	**74**
2008-09	*Cheltenham T*	13	2	**13**	**2**

MYRIE-WILLIAMS, Jennison (F)   **91**   **8**
H: 5 11   W: 12 08   b.London 17-5-88
Source: Scholar.

2005-06	Bristol C	1	0		
2006-07	Bristol C	25	2		
2007-08	Bristol C	0	0		
2007-08	*Cheltenham T*	12	0		
2007-08	*Tranmere R*	25	3	**25**	**3**
2008-09	Bristol C	0	0	**26**	**2**
2008-09	*Cheltenham T*	5	1	**17**	**1**
2008-09	*Carlisle U*	8	0	**8**	**0**
2008-09	*Hereford U*	15	2	**15**	**2**

NOBLE, David (M)   **162**   **13**
H: 6 0   W: 12 04   b.Hitchin 2-2-82
Source: Scholar. *Honours:* England Youth, Under-20. Scotland Under-21, B.

2000-01	Arsenal	0	0		
2001-02	Arsenal	0	0		
2001-02	*Watford*	15	1	**15**	**1**
2002-03	Arsenal	0	0		
2002-03	West Ham U	0	0		
2003-04	West Ham U	3	0	**3**	**0**
2003-04	Boston U	14	2		
2004-05	Boston U	32	3		
2005-06	Boston U	11	0	**57**	**5**
2005-06	Bristol C	24	1		
2006-07	Bristol C	26	3		
2007-08	Bristol C	26	2		
2008-09	Bristol C	9	1	**85**	**7**
2008-09	*Yeovil T*	2	0	**2**	**0**

ORR, Bradley (M)   **194**   **10**
H: 6 0   W: 11 11   b.Liverpool 1-11-82
Source: Scholar.

2001-02	Newcastle U	0	0		
2002-03	Newcastle U	0	0		
2003-04	Newcastle U	0	0		
2003-04	*Burnley*	4	0	**4**	**0**
2004-05	Bristol C	37	0		
2005-06	Bristol C	38	1		
2006-07	Bristol C	35	4		
2007-08	Bristol C	42	4		
2008-09	Bristol C	38	1	**190**	**10**

PLUMMER, Tristan (F)   **5**   **0**
H: 5 6   W: 10 07   b.Bristol 30-1-90
Source: Scholar. *Honours:* England Youth.

2007-08	Bristol C	0	0		
2008-09	Bristol C	0	0		
2008-09	*Luton T*	5	0	**5**	**0**

RIBEIRO, Christian (D)   **0**   **0**
H: 5 11   W: 12 02   b.Neath 14-12-89
Source: Scholar. *Honours:* Wales Youth, Under-21.

2006-07	Bristol C	0	0		
2007-08	Bristol C	0	0		
2008-09	Bristol C	0	0		

SKUSE, Cole (M)   **145**   **4**
H: 6 1   W: 11 05   b.Bristol 29-3-86
Source: Scholar.

2004-05	Bristol C	7	0		
2005-06	Bristol C	38	2		
2006-07	Bristol C	42	0		
2007-08	Bristol C	25	0		
2008-09	Bristol C	33	2	**145**	**4**

SPROULE, Ivan (M)   **142**   **56**
H: 5 8   W: 11 09   b.Castlederg 18-2-81
Source: Omagh Town, Institute. *Honours:* Northern Ireland 11 full caps, 1 goal.

2005-06	Hibernian	32	4		
2006-07	Hibernian	32	7	**64**	**11**
2007-08	Bristol C	40	2		
2008-09	Bristol C	38	3	**78**	**5**

STYVAR, Peter (F)   **10**   **0**
H: 5 11   W: 12 04   b.Roznava 13-8-80
Source: Lokomotiv Kosice, Sport Podbrezova, Ozeta Trencin, Teplice, Chomutov (loan), Prestejov (loan), Usti dad Labem, Trencin, Zilina. *Honours:* Slovakia 2 full caps.

2008-09	Bristol C	10	0	**10**	**0**

TRUNDLE, Lee (F)   **301**   **112**
H: 6 0   W: 11 06   b.Liverpool 10-10-76
Source: Rhyl.

1999-2000	Wrexham	14	8		
2001-02	Wrexham	36	8		
2002-03	Wrexham	44	11	**94**	**27**
2003-04	Swansea C	31	16		
2004-05	Swansea C	42	22		
2005-06	Swansea C	36	20		
2006-07	Swansea C	34	19	**143**	**77**
2007-08	Bristol C	35	5		
2008-09	Bristol C	19	2	**54**	**7**
2008-09	*Leeds U*	10	1	**10**	**1**

WEALE, Chris (G)   **119**   **1**
H: 6 2   W: 13 03   b.Yeovil 9-2-82
Source: Juniors.

2003-04	Yeovil T	35	0		
2004-05	Yeovil T	38	0		
2005-06	Yeovil T	25	0		
2006-07	Bristol C	1	0		
2007-08	Hereford U	1	0		
2007-08	Bristol C	3	0		
2008-09	Bristol C	5	0	**9**	**0**
2008-09	*Hereford U*	1	0	**2**	**0**
2008-09	*Yeovil T*	10	1	**108**	**1**

WEBSTER, Andy (D)   **175**   **7**
H: 6 0   W: 11 13   b.Dundee 23-4-82
Honours: Scotland Under-21, B, 22 full caps, 1 goal.

1999-2000	Arbroath	4	0		
2000-01	Arbroath	13	1	**17**	**1**
2000-01	Hearts	4	0		
2001-02	Hearts	26	1		
2002-03	Hearts	21	1		
2003-04	Hearts	32	2		
2004-05	Hearts	35	1		
2005-06	Hearts	30	1	**148**	**6**
2006-07	Wigan Ath	4	0		
2007-08	Wigan Ath	0	0	**4**	**0**
2007-08	*Rangers*	1	0	**1**	**0**

On loan from Rangers.

2008-09	*Bristol C*	5	0	**5**	**0**

WILLIAMS, Gavin (M)   **154**   **18**
H: 5 10   W: 11 05   b.Pontypridd 20-6-80
Source: Hereford U. *Honours:* Wales 2 full caps.

2003-04	Yeovil T	42	9		
2004-05	Yeovil T	13	2	**55**	**11**
2004-05	West Ham U	10	1		
2005-06	West Ham U	0	0	**10**	**1**
2005-06	Ipswich T	12	1		
2006-07	Ipswich T	29	2		
2007-08	Ipswich T	13	0	**54**	**3**
2008-09	Bristol C	35	3	**35**	**3**

WILSON, Brian (D)   **188**   **15**
H: 5 10   W: 11 00   b.Manchester 9-5-83
Source: Scholar.

2001-02	Stoke C	1	0		
2002-03	Stoke C	3	0		
2003-04	Stoke C	2	0	**6**	**0**
2003-04	Cheltenham T	14	0		
2004-05	Cheltenham T	43	3		
2005-06	Cheltenham T	43	9		
2006-07	Cheltenham T	25	2	**125**	**14**
2006-07	Bristol C	19	0		
2007-08	Bristol C	18	1		
2008-09	Bristol C	20	0	**57**	**1**

WILSON, James (D)   **16**   **0**
H: 6 2   W: 11 05   b.Chepstow 26-2-89
Source: Scholar. *Honours:* Wales Youth, Under-21.

2005-06	Bristol C	0	0		
2006-07	Bristol C	0	0		
2007-08	Bristol C	0	0		
2008-09	Bristol C	2	0	**2**	**0**
2008-09	*Brentford*	14	0	**14**	**0**

BRISTOL R (16)

ANTHONY, Byron (D)   **73**   **3**
H: 6 1   W: 11 02   b.Newport 20-9-84
Source: Scholar. *Honours:* Wales Youth, Under-21.

2003-04	Cardiff C	0	0		
2004-05	Cardiff C	0	0		
2005-06	Cardiff C	0	0		
2006-07	Bristol R	23	0		
2007-08	Bristol R	20	1		
2008-09	Bristol R	30	2	**73**	**3**

CAMPBELL, Stuart (M)   **388**   **14**
H: 5 10   W: 10 08   b.Corby 9-12-77
Source: Trainee. *Honours:* Scotland Under-21.

1996-97	Leicester C	10	0		
1997-98	Leicester C	11	0		
1998-99	Leicester C	12	0		
1999-2000	Leicester C	4	0		
1999-2000	*Birmingham C*	2	0	**2**	**0**
2000-01	Leicester C	0	0	**37**	**0**
2000-01	Grimsby T	38	2		
2001-02	Grimsby T	33	3		
2002-03	Grimsby T	45	6		
2003-04	Grimsby T	39	1	**155**	**12**
2004-05	Bristol R	25	0		
2005-06	Bristol R	38	1		
2006-07	Bristol R	41	1		
2007-08	Bristol R	46	0		
2008-09	Bristol R	44	0	**194**	**2**

COLES, Danny (D)   **211**   **7**
H: 6 1   W: 11 05   b.Bristol 31-10-81
Source: Scholarship.

1999-2000	Bristol C	1	0		
2000-01	Bristol C	2	0		
2001-02	Bristol C	23	0		
2002-03	Bristol C	39	2		
2003-04	Bristol C	45	2		
2004-05	Bristol C	38	1	**148**	**5**
2005-06	Hull C	9	0		
2006-07	Hull C	21	0		
2007-08	Hull C	1	0	**31**	**0**
2007-08	*Hartlepool U*	3	0	**3**	**0**
2007-08	Bristol R	24	1		
2008-09	Bristol R	5	1	**29**	**2**

DISLEY, Craig (M)   **344**   **41**
H: 5 10   W: 10 13   b.Worksop 24-8-81
Source: Trainee.

1999-2000	Mansfield T	5	0		
2000-01	Mansfield T	24	0		
2001-02	Mansfield T	36	7		
2002-03	Mansfield T	42	4		
2003-04	Mansfield T	34	5	**141**	**16**
2004-05	Bristol R	28	4		
2005-06	Bristol R	42	8		
2006-07	Bristol R	45	4		
2007-08	Bristol R	44	4		
2008-09	Bristol R	44	3	**203**	**25**

DUFFY, Darryl (F)   **170**   **56**
H: 5 11   W: 12 01   b.Glasgow 16-4-84
Honours: Scotland Under-21, B.

2003-04	Rangers	1	0	**1**	**0**
2003-04	*Brechin C*	8	3	**8**	**3**
2004-05	Falkirk	35	17		
2005-06	Falkirk	21	9	**56**	**26**
2005-06	Hull C	15	3		
2006-07	Hull C	9	0	**24**	**3**
2006-07	*Hartlepool U*	10	5	**10**	**5**
2006-07	Swansea C	8	5		
2007-08	Swansea C	20	1	**28**	**6**
2008-09	Bristol R	43	13	**43**	**13**

ELLIOTT, Steve (D)   298   16
H: 6 1   W: 14 00   b.Derby 29-10-78
Source: Trainee. *Honours:* England Under-21.

Season	Club	App	Gls	Tot App	Tot Gls
1996-97	Derby Co	0	0		
1997-98	Derby Co	3	0		
1998-99	Derby Co	11	0		
1999-2000	Derby Co	20	0		
2000-01	Derby Co	6	0		
2001-02	Derby Co	6	0		
2002-03	Derby Co	23	1		
2003-04	Derby Co	4	0	73	1
2003-04	Blackpool	28	0	28	0
2004-05	Bristol R	41	2		
2005-06	Bristol R	45	2		
2006-07	Bristol R	39	5		
2007-08	Bristol R	33	3		
2008-09	Bristol R	39	3	197	15

FRASER, James (M)   0   0
H: 5 9   W: 12 07   b.Brighton 26-4-89
Source: Scholar.

Season	Club	App	Gls
2007-08	Bristol R	0	0
2008-09	Bristol R	0	0

GREEN, Mike (G)   0   0
H: 6 1   W: 13 01   b.Bristol 23-7-89
Source: Scholar.

Season	Club	App	Gls
2006-07	Bristol R	0	0
2007-08	Bristol R	0	0
2008-09	Bristol R	0	0

GREEN, Ryan (M)   106   0
H: 5 7   W: 10 10   b.Cardiff 20-10-80
Source: Danes Court. *Honours:* Wales Youth, Under-21, 2 full caps.

Season	Club	App	Gls	Tot App	Tot Gls
1997-98	Wolverhampton W	0	0		
1998-99	Wolverhampton W	1	0		
1999-2000	Wolverhampton W	7	0		
2000-01	Wolverhampton W	0	0		
2000-01	*Torquay U*	10	0	10	0
2001-02	Wolverhampton W	0	0	8	0
2001-02	Millwall	13	0	13	0
2002-03	Cardiff C	0	0		
2002-03	Sheffield W	4	0	4	0

From Hereford U.

Season	Club	App	Gls	Tot App	Tot Gls
2006-07	Bristol R	33	0		
2007-08	Bristol R	12	0		
2008-09	Bristol R	26	0	71	0

GROVES, Matt (F)   1   0
H: 5 8   W: 11 07   b.Bristol 11-12-88
Source: Scholar.

Season	Club	App	Gls	Tot App	Tot Gls
2007-08	Bristol R	1	0		
2008-09	Bristol R	0	0	1	0

HALDANE, Lewis (F)   147   15
H: 6 0   W: 11 03   b.Trowbridge 13-3-85
Source: Scholar. *Honours:* Wales Under-21.

Season	Club	App	Gls	Tot App	Tot Gls
2003-04	Bristol R	27	5		
2004-05	Bristol R	13	0		
2005-06	Bristol R	30	3		
2006-07	Bristol R	45	6		
2007-08	Bristol R	32	1		
2008-09	Bristol R	0	0	147	15

HARWOOD, Liam (D)   0   0

Season	Club	App	Gls
2008-09	Bristol R	0	0

HINTON, Craig (D)   326   6
H: 6 0   W: 12 00   b.Wolverhampton 26-11-77
Source: Trainee.

Season	Club	App	Gls	Tot App	Tot Gls
1996-97	Birmingham C	0	0		
1997-98	Birmingham C	0	0		
2000-01	Kidderminster H	46	2		
2001-02	Kidderminster H	41	0		
2002-03	Kidderminster H	44	0		
2003-04	Kidderminster H	42	1	173	3
2004-05	Bristol R	38	0		
2005-06	Bristol R	36	0		
2006-07	Bristol R	30	0		
2007-08	Bristol R	24	2		
2008-09	Bristol R	25	1	153	3

HUGHES, Jeff (D)   173   16
H: 6 1   W: 11 00   b.Larne 29-5-85
Source: Larne Tech Old Boys. *Honours:* Northern Ireland Under-21, 2 full caps.

Season	Club	App	Gls	Tot App	Tot Gls
2003-04	Larne	21	1		
2004-05	Larne	29	0	50	1
2005-06	Lincoln C	22	2		
2006-07	Lincoln C	41	6	63	8
2007-08	Crystal Palace	10	0	10	0
2007-08	*Peterborough U*	7	1	7	1
2008-09	Bristol R	43	6	43	6

HUNT, Ben (F)   12   0
H: 6 1   W: 12 07   b.Southwark 23-1-90
Source: West Ham U Scholar.

Season	Club	App	Gls	Tot App	Tot Gls
2008-09	Bristol R	12	0	12	0

JACOBSON, Joe (D)   80   2
H: 5 11   W: 12 06   b.Cardiff 17-11-86
Source: Scholar. *Honours:* Wales Under-21.

Season	Club	App	Gls	Tot App	Tot Gls
2005-06	Cardiff C	1	0		
2006-07	Cardiff C	0	0	1	0
2006-07	*Accrington S*	6	1	6	1
2006-07	*Bristol R*	11	0		
2007-08	Bristol R	40	1		
2008-09	Bristol R	22	0	73	1

KITE, Alex (D)   0   0
H: 6 0   W: 12 05   b.Kent 7-3-89
Source: Scholar.

Season	Club	App	Gls
2007-08	Bristol R	0	0
2008-09	Bristol R	0	0

KLEIN-DAVIES, Josh (F)   11   1
H: 5 11   W: 13 09   b.Bristol 6-7-89
Source: Bristol C Scholar. *Honours:* Wales Youth.

Season	Club	App	Gls	Tot App	Tot Gls
2007-08	Bristol R	10	1		
2008-09	Bristol R	0	0	10	1
2008-09	*Luton T*	1	0	1	0

LAMBERT, Ricky (F)   336   105
H: 6 2   W: 14 08   b.Liverpool 16-2-82
Source: Trainee.

Season	Club	App	Gls	Tot App	Tot Gls
1999-2000	Blackpool	3	0		
2000-01	Blackpool	0	0	3	0
2000-01	Macclesfield T	9	0		
2001-02	Macclesfield T	35	8	44	8
2001-02	Stockport Co	0	0		
2002-03	Stockport Co	29	2		
2003-04	Stockport Co	40	12		
2004-05	Stockport Co	29	4	98	18
2004-05	Rochdale	15	6		
2005-06	Rochdale	46	22		
2006-07	Rochdale	3	0	64	28
2006-07	Bristol R	36	8		
2007-08	Bristol R	46	14		
2008-09	Bristol R	45	29	127	51

LANGLEY, Richard (M)   265   30
H: 6 0   W: 11 04   b.Harlesden 27-12-79
Source: Trainee. *Honours:* England Youth, Jamaica 12 full caps, 2 goals.

Season	Club	App	Gls	Tot App	Tot Gls
1996-97	QPR	0	0		
1997-98	QPR	0	0		
1998-99	QPR	8	1		
1999-2000	QPR	41	3		
2000-01	QPR	26	1		
2001-02	QPR	18	3		
2002-03	QPR	39	9		
2003-04	QPR	1	1		
2003-04	Cardiff C	44	6		
2004-05	Cardiff C	25	2		
2005-06	Cardiff C	0	0	69	8
2005-06	QPR	33	3	166	21
2006-07	Luton T	29	1		
2007-08	Luton T	1	0	30	1
2008-09	Bristol R	0	0		

LESCOTT, Aaron (M)   297   4
H: 5 8   W: 10 09   b.Birmingham 2-12-78
Source: Trainee. *Honours:* England Schools.

Season	Club	App	Gls	Tot App	Tot Gls
1996-97	Aston Villa	0	0		
1997-98	Aston Villa	0	0		
1998-99	Aston Villa	0	0		
1999-2000	Aston Villa	0	0		
1999-2000	*Lincoln C*	5	0	5	0
2000-01	Aston Villa	0	0		
2000-01	Sheffield W	30	0		
2001-02	Sheffield W	7	0	37	0
2001-02	Stockport Co	17	0		
2002-03	Stockport Co	41	1		
2003-04	Stockport Co	14	0	72	1
2003-04	*Bristol R*	8	0		
2004-05	Bristol R	26	0		
2005-06	Bristol R	37	0		
2006-07	Bristol R	34	0		
2007-08	Bristol R	34	0		
2008-09	Bristol R	44	3	183	3

LINES, Chris (M)   83   7
H: 6 2   W: 12 00   b.Bristol 30-11-85
Source: Youth.

Season	Club	App	Gls	Tot App	Tot Gls
2005-06	Bristol R	4	0		
2006-07	Bristol R	7	0		
2007-08	Bristol R	27	3		
2008-09	Bristol R	45	4	83	7

MAHDI, Adam (M)   0   0
H: 5 8   W: 11 00   b.London 2-12-89
Source: Scholar.

Season	Club	App	Gls
2007-08	Bristol R	0	0
2008-09	Bristol R	0	0

OSEI-KUFFOUR, Jo (F)   283   66
H: 5 8   W: 11 11   b.Edmonton 17-11-81
Source: Scholar.

Season	Club	App	Gls	Tot App	Tot Gls
2000-01	Arsenal	0	0		
2001-02	Arsenal	0	0		
2001-02	*Swindon T*	11	2	11	2
2002-03	Torquay U	30	5		
2003-04	Torquay U	41	10		
2004-05	Torquay U	34	6		
2005-06	Torquay U	43	8	148	29
2006-07	Brentford	39	12	39	12
2007-08	Bournemouth	42	12		
2008-09	Bournemouth	2	0	44	12
2008-09	Bristol R	41	11	41	11

PARRINELLO, Tom (D)   0   0
H: 5 6   W: 10 07   b.Parkway 11-11-89
Source: Scholar.

Season	Club	App	Gls
2006-07	Bristol R	0	0
2007-08	Bristol R	0	0
2008-09	Bristol R	0	0

PHILLIPS, Steve (G)   393   0
H: 6 1   W: 11 10   b.Bath 6-5-78
Source: Paulton R.

Season	Club	App	Gls	Tot App	Tot Gls
1996-97	Bristol C	0	0		
1997-98	Bristol C	0	0		
1998-99	Bristol C	15	0		
1999-2000	Bristol C	21	0		
2000-01	Bristol C	42	0		
2001-02	Bristol C	22	0		
2002-03	Bristol C	46	0		
2003-04	Bristol C	46	0		
2004-05	Bristol C	46	0		
2005-06	Bristol C	19	0	257	0
2006-07	Bristol R	44	0		
2007-08	Bristol R	46	0		
2008-09	Bristol R	46	0	136	0

PIPE, David (M)   241   8
H: 5 9   W: 12 01   b.Caerphilly 5-11-83
Source: Scholar. *Honours:* Wales Youth, Under-21, 1 full cap.

Season	Club	App	Gls	Tot App	Tot Gls
2000-01	Coventry C	0	0		
2001-02	Coventry C	0	0		
2002-03	Coventry C	21	1		
2003-04	Coventry C	0	0	21	1
2003-04	Notts Co	18	0		
2004-05	Notts Co	41	2		
2005-06	Notts Co	43	2		
2006-07	Notts Co	39	0	141	4
2007-08	Bristol R	40	2		
2008-09	Bristol R	39	1	79	3

REECE, Charlie (M)   2   0
H: 5 11   W: 11 03   b.Birmingham 8-9-88
Source: Scholar.

Season	Club	App	Gls	Tot App	Tot Gls
2007-08	Bristol R	1	0		
2008-09	Bristol R	1	0	2	0

RIGG, Sean (F)   57   2
H: 5 9   W: 12 01   b.Bristol 1-10-88
Source: Forest Green R.

Season	Club	App	Gls	Tot App	Tot Gls
2006-07	Bristol R	18	1		
2007-08	Bristol R	31	1		
2008-09	Bristol R	8	0	57	2

WALKER, Richard (F)   305   78
H: 6 0   W: 12 04   b.Sutton Coldfield 8-11-77
Source: Trainee.

Season	Club	App	Gls	Tot App	Tot Gls
1995-96	Aston Villa	0	0		
1996-97	Aston Villa	0	0		
1997-98	Aston Villa	1	0		
1998-99	Aston Villa	0	0		
1998-99	*Cambridge U*	21	3	21	3
1999-2000	Aston Villa	5	2		
2000-01	Aston Villa	0	0		
2000-01	*Blackpool*	18	3		
2001-02	Aston Villa	0	0	6	2
2001-02	*Wycombe W*	12	3	12	3
2001-02	Blackpool	21	8		
2002-03	Blackpool	32	4		
2003-04	Blackpool	0	0	80	15
2003-04	*Northampton T*	12	4	12	4
2003-04	Oxford U	4	0	4	0

Season	Club	App	Gls	Tot App	Tot Gls
2004-05	Bristol R	27	10		
2005-06	Bristol R	46	20		
2006-07	Bristol R	46	12		
2007-08	Bristol R	24	4		
2008-09	Bristol R	0	0	143	46
2008-09	Shrewsbury T	27	5	27	5

WHITE, Joe (F)   0   0
b. 9-2-90

Season	Club	App	Gls	Tot App	Tot Gls
2008-09	Bristol R	0	0		

WILLIAMS, Andy (F)   112   15
H: 5 11   W: 11 09   b.Hereford 14-8-86
Source: Pershore College.

Season	Club	App	Gls	Tot App	Tot Gls
2006-07	Hereford U	41	8		
2007-08	Bristol R	41	4		
2008-09	Bristol R	4	1	45	5
2008-09	Hereford U	26	2	67	10

BURNLEY (17)

AKINBIYI, Ade (F)   479   136
H: 6 1   W: 13 08   b.Hackney 10-10-74
Source: Trainee. Honours: Nigeria 1 full cap.

Season	Club	App	Gls	Tot App	Tot Gls
1992-93	Norwich C	0	0		
1993-94	Norwich C	2	0		
1993-94	Hereford U	4	2	4	2
1994-95	Norwich C	13	0		
1994-95	Brighton & HA	7	4	7	4
1995-96	Norwich C	22	3		
1996-97	Norwich C	12	0	49	3
1996-97	Gillingham	19	7		
1997-98	Gillingham	44	21	63	28
1998-99	Bristol C	44	19		
1999-2000	Bristol C	3	2	47	21
1999-2000	Wolverhampton W	37	16	37	16
2000-01	Leicester C	37	9		
2001-02	Leicester C	21	2	58	11
2001-02	Crystal Palace	14	2		
2002-03	Crystal Palace	10	1		
2002-03	Stoke C	4	2		
2003-04	Crystal Palace	0	0	24	3
2003-04	Stoke C	30	10		
2004-05	Stoke C	29	7	63	19
2004-05	Burnley	10	4		
2005-06	Burnley	29	12		
2005-06	Sheffield U	15	3		
2006-07	Sheffield U	3	0	18	3
2006-07	Burnley	20	2		
2007-08	Burnley	39	8		
2008-09	Burnley	11	0	109	26

Transferred to Houston Dynamo April 2009

ALEXANDER, Graham (D)   750   95
H: 5 10   W: 12 07   b.Coventry 10-10-71
Source: Trainee. Honours: Scotland B, 38 full caps.

Season	Club	App	Gls	Tot App	Tot Gls
1989-90	Scunthorpe U	0	0		
1990-91	Scunthorpe U	1	0		
1991-92	Scunthorpe U	36	5		
1992-93	Scunthorpe U	41	5		
1993-94	Scunthorpe U	41	4		
1994-95	Scunthorpe U	40	4	159	18
1995-96	Luton T	37	1		
1996-97	Luton T	45	2		
1997-98	Luton T	39	8		
1998-99	Luton T	29	4	150	15
1998-99	Preston NE	10	0		
1999-2000	Preston NE	46	6		
2000-01	Preston NE	34	5		
2001-02	Preston NE	45	6		
2002-03	Preston NE	45	10		
2003-04	Preston NE	45	9		
2004-05	Preston NE	42	7		
2005-06	Preston NE	40	3		
2006-07	Preston NE	42	6		
2007-08	Preston NE	3	0	352	52
2007-08	Burnley	43	1		
2008-09	Burnley	46	9	89	10

BERISHA, Besart (M)   65   21
H: 5 11   W: 11 12   b.Pristina 29-7-85
Honours: Albania 9 full caps, 3 goals.

Season	Club	App	Gls	Tot App	Tot Gls
2004-05	Hamburg	0	0		
2004-05	Aalborg	2	0	2	0
2005-06	Hamburg	0	0		
2005-06	Horsens	33	11		
2006-07	Hamburg	11	1	11	1
2007-08	Burnley	0	0		
2008	Rosenborg	8	4	8	4
2008	Horsens	11	5	44	16
2008-09	Burnley	0	0		

BLAKE, Robbie (F)   531   142
H: 5 9   W: 12 00   b.Middlesbrough 4-3-76
Source: Trainee.

Season	Club	App	Gls	Tot App	Tot Gls
1994-95	Darlington	9	0		
1995-96	Darlington	29	11		
1996-97	Darlington	30	10	68	21
1996-97	Bradford C	5	0		
1997-98	Bradford C	34	8		
1998-99	Bradford C	39	16		
1999-2000	Bradford C	28	2		
2000-01	Bradford C	21	4		
2000-01	Nottingham F	11	1	11	1
2001-02	Bradford C	26	10	153	40
2001-02	Burnley	10	0		
2002-03	Burnley	41	13		
2003-04	Burnley	45	19		
2004-05	Burnley	24	10		
2004-05	Birmingham C	11	2	11	2
2005-06	Leeds U	41	11		
2006-07	Leeds U	36	8	77	19
2007-08	Burnley	45	9		
2008-09	Burnley	46	8	211	59

CALDWELL, Steven (D)   223   10
H: 6 2   W: 13 12   b.Stirling 12-9-80
Source: Trainee. Honours: Scotland Youth, Under-21, B, 9 full caps.

Season	Club	App	Gls	Tot App	Tot Gls
1997-98	Newcastle U	0	0		
1998-99	Newcastle U	0	0		
1999-2000	Newcastle U	0	0		
2000-01	Newcastle U	9	0		
2001-02	Newcastle U	0	0		
2001-02	Blackpool	6	0	6	0
2001-02	Bradford C	9	0	9	0
2002-03	Newcastle U	14	1		
2003-04	Newcastle U	5	0	28	1
2003-04	Leeds U	13	1	13	1
2004-05	Sunderland	41	4		
2005-06	Sunderland	24	0		
2006-07	Sunderland	11	0	76	4
2006-07	Burnley	17	0		
2007-08	Burnley	29	2		
2008-09	Burnley	45	2	91	4

CARLISLE, Clarke (D)   334   25
H: 6 2   W: 14 11   b.Preston 14-10-79
Source: Trainee. Honours: England Under-21.

Season	Club	App	Gls	Tot App	Tot Gls
1997-98	Blackpool	11	2		
1998-99	Blackpool	39	1		
1999-2000	Blackpool	43	4	93	7
2000-01	QPR	27	3		
2001-02	QPR	0	0		
2002-03	QPR	36	2		
2003-04	QPR	33	1	96	6
2004-05	Leeds U	35	4	35	4
2005-06	Watford	32	3		
2006-07	Watford	4	0		
2006-07	Luton T	5	0	5	0
2007-08	Watford	0	0	36	3
2007-08	Burnley	33	2		
2008-09	Burnley	36	3	69	5

DUFF, Michael (D)   363   16
H: 6 1   W: 11 08   b.Belfast 11-1-78
Source: Trainee. Honours: Northern Ireland 22 full caps.

Season	Club	App	Gls	Tot App	Tot Gls
1999-2000	Cheltenham T	31	2		
2000-01	Cheltenham T	39	5		
2001-02	Cheltenham T	45	3		
2002-03	Cheltenham T	44	2		
2003-04	Cheltenham T	42	0	201	12
2004-05	Burnley	42	0		
2005-06	Burnley	41	0		
2006-07	Burnley	44	2		
2007-08	Burnley	8	1		
2008-09	Burnley	27	1	162	4

EAGLES, Chris (M)   119   17
H: 5 10   W: 11 07   b.Hemel Hempstead 19-11-85
Source: Trainee. Honours: England Youth.

Season	Club	App	Gls	Tot App	Tot Gls
2003-04	Manchester U	0	0		
2004-05	Manchester U	0	0		
2004-05	Watford	13	1		
2005-06	Manchester U	0	0		
2005-06	Sheffield W	25	3	25	3
2005-06	Watford	17	3	30	4
2006-07	Manchester U	2	1		
2006-07	NEC Nijmegen	15	1	15	1
2007-08	Manchester U	4	0	6	1
2008-09	Burnley	43	8	43	8

ELLIOTT, Wade (M)   386   44
H: 5 10   W: 10 03   b.Southampton 14-12-78
Source: Bashley.

Season	Club	App	Gls	Tot App	Tot Gls
1999-2000	Bournemouth	12	3		
2000-01	Bournemouth	36	9		
2001-02	Bournemouth	46	8		
2002-03	Bournemouth	44	4		
2003-04	Bournemouth	39	3		
2004-05	Bournemouth	43	4	220	31
2005-06	Burnley	36	3		
2006-07	Burnley	42	4		
2007-08	Burnley	46	2		
2008-09	Burnley	42	4	166	13

GUDJONSSON, Joey (M)   248   28
H: 5 9   W: 12 04   b.Akranes 25-5-80
Honours: Iceland Youth, Under-21, 34 full caps, 1 goal.

Season	Club	App	Gls	Tot App	Tot Gls
1998-99	Genk	5	0	5	0
1999-2000	MVV	19	5	19	5
2000-01	RKC	31	4	31	4
2001-02	Betis	11	0	11	0
2002-03	Aston Villa	11	2	11	2
2003-04	Wolverhampton W	11	0	11	0
2004-05	Leicester C	35	2		
2005-06	Leicester C	42	8	77	10
2006-07	AZ	5	0	5	0
2006-07	Burnley	11	0		
2007-08	Burnley	28	1		
2008-09	Burnley	39	6	78	7

JENSEN, Brian (G)   254   0
H: 6 1   W: 12 04   b.Copenhagen 8-6-75
Source: Hvidovre, B93.

Season	Club	App	Gls	Tot App	Tot Gls
1997-98	AZ	0	0		
1998-99	AZ	1	0	1	0
1999-2000	WBA	12	0		
2000-01	WBA	33	0		
2001-02	WBA	1	0		
2002-03	WBA	0	0	46	0
2003-04	Burnley	46	0		
2004-05	Burnley	27	0		
2005-06	Burnley	39	0		
2006-07	Burnley	31	0		
2007-08	Burnley	19	0		
2008-09	Burnley	45	0	207	0

JONES, Steve (F)   261   50
H: 5 10   W: 10 05   b.Derry 25-10-76
Source: Leigh RMI. Honours: Northern Ireland B, 29 full caps, 1 goal.

Season	Club	App	Gls	Tot App	Tot Gls
2001-02	Rochdale	9	1	9	1
2001-02	Crewe Alex	6	0		
2002-03	Crewe Alex	31	9		
2003-04	Crewe Alex	45	15		
2004-05	Crewe Alex	36	10		
2005-06	Crewe Alex	41	5		
2006-07	Burnley	41	5		
2007-08	Burnley	17	1		
2007-08	Crewe Alex	4	1	163	40
2008-09	Burnley	0	0	58	6
2008-09	Huddersfield T	4	0	4	0
2008-09	Bradford C	27	3	27	3

JORDAN, Stephen (D)   112   7
H: 6 1   W: 13 00   b.Warrington 6-3-82
Source: Scholarship.

Season	Club	App	Gls	Tot App	Tot Gls
1998-99	Manchester C	0	0		
1999-2000	Manchester C	0	0		
2000-01	Manchester C	0	0		
2001-02	Manchester C	0	0		
2002-03	Manchester C	1	0		
2002-03	Cambridge U	11	0	11	0
2003-04	Manchester C	2	0		
2004-05	Manchester C	19	0		
2005-06	Manchester C	18	0		
2006-07	Manchester C	13	0	53	0
2007-08	Burnley	21	0		
2008-09	Burnley	27	0	48	0

KALVENES, Christian (D)   141   7
H: 6 0   W: 11 11   b.Bergen 8-3-77

Season	Club	App	Gls	Tot App	Tot Gls
2000	Sogndal	6	0		
2001	Sogndal	22	3		
2002	Sogndal	18	0		
2003	Sogndal	21	1	67	4
2004	Brann	0	0		
2005	Brann	4	0		
2006	Brann	1	0	5	0
2006-07	Dundee U	29	1		
2007-08	Dundee U	19	1	48	2
2008-09	Burnley	21	1	21	1

KAY, Adam (M)   3   0
H: 5 10   W: 11 00   b.Burnley 29-9-89
Source: Scholar.
2008-09	Burnley	0	0
2008-09	*Accrington S*	3	0	3 0

MACDONALD, Alex (F)   5   0
H: 5 7   W: 11 04   b.Warrington 14-4-90
Source: Scholar. *Honours:* Scotland Youth.
2007-08	Burnley	2	0
2008-09	Burnley	3	0	5 0

MAHON, Alan (M)   298   30
H: 5 8   W: 12 03   b.Dublin 4-4-78
Source: Crumplin U. *Honours:* Eire School, Youth, Under-21, 2 full caps.
1994-95	Tranmere R	0	0
1995-96	Tranmere R	2	0
1996-97	Tranmere R	25	2
1997-98	Tranmere R	18	1
1998-99	Tranmere R	39	6
1999-2000	Tranmere R	36	4	120 13
2000-01	Sporting Lisbon	0	1	1 0
2000-01	Blackburn R	18	0
2001-02	Blackburn R	13	1
2002-03	Blackburn R	2	0
2002-03	*Cardiff C*	15	2	15 2
2003-04	Blackburn R	3	0	36 1
2003-04	*Ipswich T*	11	1	11 1
2003-04	Wigan Ath	14	1
2004-05	Wigan Ath	27	7
2005-06	Wigan Ath	6	1	47 9
2005-06	Burnley	8	0
2006-07	Burnley	25	2
2007-08	Burnley	26	1
2008-09	Burnley	8	1	67 4
2008-09	*Blackpool*	1	0	1 0

McCANN, Chris (M)   140   18
H: 6 1   W: 11 11   b.Dublin 21-7-87
Source: Scholar. *Honours:* Eire Youth.
2005-06	Burnley	23	2
2006-07	Burnley	38	5
2007-08	Burnley	35	5
2008-09	Burnley	44	6	140 18

McDONALD, Kevin (M)   116   15
H: 6 2   W: 13 03   b.Carnoustie 4-11-88
Honours: Scotland Youth, Under-21.
2005-06	Dundee	26	3
2006-07	Dundee	31	2
2007-08	Dundee	34	9	91 14
2008-09	Burnley	25	1	25 1

PATERSON, Martin (F)   113   32
H: 5 9   W: 10 11   b.Tunstall 13-5-87
Source: Scholar. *Honours:* Northern Ireland Youth, Under-21, 8 full caps.
2004-05	Stoke C	3	0
2005-06	Stoke C	3	0
2006-07	Stoke C	9	1	15 1
2006-07	*Grimsby T*	15	6	15 6
2007-08	Scunthorpe U	40	13	40 13
2008-09	Burnley	43	12	43 12

PENNY, Diego (G)   180   0
H: 6 5   W: 12 00   b.Lima 22-4-84
Honours: Peru 6 full caps.
2004	Cor Bolognesi	39	0
2005	Cor Bolognesi	47	0
2006	Cor Bolognesi	38	0
2007	Cor Bolognesi	40	0
2008	Cor Bolognesi	15	0	179 0
2008-09	Burnley	1	0	1 0

RODRIGUEZ, Jay (F)   37   5
H: 6 0   W: 12 00   b.Burnley 27-7-89
Source: Scholar.
2007-08	Burnley	1	0
2007-08	*Stirling Alb*	11	3	11 3
2008-09	Burnley	25	2	26 2

THOMPSON, Steven (F)   322   58
H: 6 2   W: 12 05   b.Paisley 14-10-78
Source: Dundee U BC. *Honours:* Scotland Under-21, 16 full caps, 3 goals.
1996-97	Dundee U	1	0
1997-98	Dundee U	8	0
1998-99	Dundee U	15	1
1999-2000	Dundee U	27	1
2000-01	Dundee U	31	4
2001-02	Dundee U	32	6
2002-03	Dundee U	20	6	134 18
2002-03	Rangers	8	2
2003-04	Rangers	16	8

2004-05	Rangers	19	5
2005-06	Rangers	14	2	57 17
2005-06	Cardiff C	14	4
2006-07	Cardiff C	43	6
2007-08	Cardiff C	36	5
2008-09	Cardiff C	4	1	97 16
2008-09	Burnley	34	7	34 7

VAN DER SCHAAF, Remco (D)   206   10
H: 6 01   W: 12 02   b.Groningen 28-2-79
Honours: Holland Under-21.
1997-98	Vitesse	3	0
1998-99	Vitesse	22	0
1999-2000	Vitesse	14	1
1999-2000	Fortuna Sittard	4	0	4 0
2000-01	Vitesse	26	0
2001-02	Vitesse	27	4
2002-03	PSV Eindhoven	17	0
2003-04	PSV Eindhoven	18	0
2004-05	PSV Eindhoven	4	0	39 0
2005-06	Vitesse	27	2
2006-07	Vitesse	14	0
2007-08	Vitesse	29	3	162 10
2008-09	Burnley	1	0	1 0

On loan to Brøndby.

BURY (18)

ANANE, Ricky (D)   0   0
H: 6 1   W: 12 03   b.Manchester 12-1-91
Source: Scholar.
2008-09	Bury	0	0

BAKER, Richie (M)   93   6
H: 5 10   W: 11 05   b.Burnley 29-12-87
Source: Preston NE Scholar.
2006-07	Bury	39	5
2007-08	Bury	32	1
2008-09	Bury	22	0	93 6

BARRY-MURPHY, Brian (M)   346   15
H: 5 10   W: 13 01   b.Cork 27-7-78
Honours: Eire Youth, Under-21.
1995-96	Cork City	13	0
1996-97	Cork City	25	0
1997-98	Cork City	15	1
1998-99	Cork City	27	1	80 2
1999-2000	Preston NE	1	0
2000-01	Preston NE	14	0
2001-02	Preston NE	4	0
2001-02	*Southend U*	8	1	8 1
2002-03	Preston NE	0	2	21 0
2002-03	*Hartlepool U*	7	0	7 0
2002-03	Sheffield W	17	0
2003-04	Sheffield W	41	0	58 0
2004-05	Bury	45	6
2005-06	Bury	40	3
2006-07	Bury	14	0
2007-08	Bury	31	1
2008-09	Bury	42	2	172 12

BELFORD, Cameron (G)   2   0
H: 6 1   W: 11 10   b.Nuneaton 16-10-88
2006-07	Coventry C	0	0
2007-08	Bury	1	0
2008-09	Bury	1	0	2 0

BISHOP, Andy (F)   184   60
H: 6 0   W: 10 10   b.Stone 19-10-82
Source: Scholar.
2002-03	Walsall	0	0
2002-03	*Kidderminster H*	29	5
2003-04	*Kidderminster H*	11	2	40 7
2003-04	*Rochdale*	10	1	10 1
2003-04	*Yeovil T*	5	2	5 2

From York C.
2006-07	Bury	43	15
2007-08	Bury	44	19
2008-09	Bury	42	16	129 50

BROWN, Wayne (G)   226   0
H: 6 0   W: 13 11   b.Southampton 14-1-77
Source: Trainee.
1993-94	Bristol C	1	0
1994-95	Bristol C	0	0
1995-96	Bristol C	0	0	1 0

From Weston-S-Mare
1996-97	Chester C	2	0
1997-98	Chester C	13	0
1998-99	Chester C	23	0
1999-2000	Chester C	46	0
2000-01	Chester C	0	0

2001-02	Chester C	0	0
2004-05	Chester C	23	0
2005-06	Chester C	0	0	107 0
2006-07	Hereford U	39	0
2007-08	Hereford U	44	0	83 0
2008-09	Bury	35	0	35 0

BUCHANAN, David (M)   148   0
H: 5 7   W: 11 03   b.Rochdale 6-5-86
Source: Scholar. *Honours:* Northern Ireland Youth, Under-21.
2004-05	Bury	3	0
2005-06	Bury	23	0
2006-07	Bury	41	0
2007-08	Bury	35	0
2008-09	Bury	46	0	148 0

BULLARD, Tom (M)   0   0
2008-09	Bury	0	0

CRESSWELL, Ryan (D)   49   2
H: 5 9   W: 10 05   b.Rotherham 22-12-87
Source: Scholar.
2006-07	Sheffield U	0	0
2007-08	Sheffield U	0	0
2007-08	*Rotherham U*	3	0	3 0
2007-08	*Morecambe*	2	0	2 0
2007-08	*Macclesfield T*	19	1	19 1
2008-09	Bury	25	1	25 1

DAWSON, Stephen (M)   160   6
H: 5 9   W: 11 09   b.Dublin 4-12-85
Source: Scholar. *Honours:* Eire Under-21.
2003-04	Leicester C	0	0
2004-05	Leicester C	0	0
2005-06	Mansfield T	40	1
2006-07	Mansfield T	34	1
2007-08	Mansfield T	43	2	117 4
2008-09	Bury	43	2	43 2

DEAN, James (F)   4   0
H: 5 10   W: 12 00   b.Cardiff 16-3-89
Source: Northwich Vic.
2007-08	Bury	4	0
2008-09	Bury	0	0	4 0

DORNEY, Jack (M)   7   0
H: 5 9   W: 10 00   b.Ashton-under-Lyne 9-1-90
Source: Scholar.
2007-08	Bury	7	0
2008-09	Bury	0	0	7 0

FUTCHER, Ben (D)   263   20
H: 6 7   W: 12 05   b.Manchester 20-2-81
Source: Trainee.
1999-2000	Oldham Ath	5	0
2000-01	Oldham Ath	5	0
2001-02	Oldham Ath	0	0	10 0

From Stalybridge C, Doncaster R
2002-03	Lincoln C	43	8
2003-04	Lincoln C	43	2
2004-05	Lincoln C	35	3	121 13
2005-06	Boston U	14	0	14 0
2005-06	Grimsby T	15	2
2006-07	Grimsby T	4	0	19 2
2006-07	*Peterborough U*	25	3	25 3
2007-08	Bury	40	0
2008-09	Bury	34	2	74 2

HASLAM, Steven (M)   197   3
H: 5 11   W: 10 10   b.Sheffield 6-9-79
Source: Trainee. *Honours:* England Schools, Youth.
1996-97	Sheffield W	0	0
1997-98	Sheffield W	0	0
1998-99	Sheffield W	2	0
1999-2000	Sheffield W	23	0
2000-01	Sheffield W	27	1
2001-02	Sheffield W	41	0
2002-03	Sheffield W	26	1
2003-04	Sheffield W	25	0	144 2
2004-05	Northampton T	3	0
2005-06	Northampton T	0	0
2006-07	Northampton T	0	0	3 0

From Halifax T.
2007-08	Bury	37	1
2008-09	Bury	13	0	50 1

HURST, Glynn (F)   374   117
H: 5 10   W: 11 06   b.Barnsley 17-1-76
Source: Tottenham H Trainee.
1994-95	Barnsley	2	0
1995-96	Barnsley	5	0
1995-96	*Swansea C*	2	1	2 1

Season	Club	A	G	Tot A	Tot G
1996-97	Barnsley	1	0	**8**	**0**
1996-97	*Mansfield T*	6	0	**6**	**0**
1998-99	Ayr U	34	18		
1999-2000	Ayr U	25	14	**59**	**32**
2000-01	Stockport Co	11	0		
2001-02	Stockport Co	15	4	**26**	**4**
2001-02	Chesterfield	23	9		
2002-03	Chesterfield	32	7		
2003-04	Chesterfield	29	13	**84**	**29**
2004-05	Notts Co	41	14		
2005-06	Notts Co	18	9	**59**	**23**
2005-06	Shrewsbury T	16	3		
2006-07	Shrewsbury T	0	0	**16**	**3**
2006-07	Bury	35	11		
2007-08	Bury	42	6		
2008-09	Bury	37	8	**114**	**25**

JONES, Mike (M)   **69 6**
H: 5 11   W: 12 04   b.Birkenhead 15-8-87
Source: Scholar.

Season	Club	A	G	Tot A	Tot G
2005-06	Tranmere R	1	0		
2006-07	Tranmere R	0	0		
2006-07	*Shrewsbury T*	13	1	**13**	**1**
2007-08	Tranmere R	9	1	**10**	**1**
2008-09	Tranmere R	46	4	**46**	**4**

MORGAN, Paul (D)   **271 3**
H: 6 0   W: 11 05   b.Belfast 23-10-78
Source: Trainee. *Honours:* Northern Ireland Under-21.

Season	Club	A	G	Tot A	Tot G
1997-98	Preston NE	0	0		
1998-99	Preston NE	0	0		
1999-2000	Preston NE	0	0		
2000-01	Preston NE	0	0		
2001-02	Lincoln C	34	1		
2002-03	Lincoln C	45	0		
2003-04	Lincoln C	41	0		
2004-05	Lincoln C	39	0		
2005-06	Lincoln C	20	0		
2006-07	Lincoln C	33	1	**212**	**2**
2007-08	Bury	20	0		
2008-09	Bury	0	0	**20**	**0**
2008-09	*Macclesfield T*	39	1	**39**	**1**

MORRELL, Andy (F)   **327 87**
H: 5 11   W: 12 00   b.Doncaster 28-9-74
Source: Newcastle Blue Star.

Season	Club	A	G	Tot A	Tot G
1998-99	Wrexham	7	0		
1999-2000	Wrexham	13	1		
2000-01	Wrexham	20	3		
2001-02	Wrexham	25	2		
2002-03	Wrexham	45	34	**110**	**40**
2003-04	Coventry C	30	9		
2004-05	Coventry C	34	6		
2005-06	Coventry C	34	2		
2006-07	Coventry C	0	0	**98**	**17**
2006-07	Blackpool	40	16		
2007-08	Blackpool	38	5	**78**	**21**
2008-09	Bury	41	9	**41**	**9**

RACCHI, Danny (D)   **27 0**
H: 5 8   W: 10 04   b.Halifax 22-11-87
Source: Scholar.

Season	Club	A	G	Tot A	Tot G
2006-07	Huddersfield T	3	0		
2007-08	Huddersfield T	3	0	**6**	**0**
2008-09	Bury	21	0	**21**	**0**

ROUSE, Domaine (F)   **8 0**
H: 5 6   W: 10 10   b.Stretford 4-7-89
Source: Scholar.

Season	Club	A	G	Tot A	Tot G
2006-07	Bury	2	0		
2007-08	Bury	6	0		
2008-09	Bury	0	0	**8**	**0**

SCOTT, Paul (D)   **215 15**
H: 5 11   W: 12 00   b.Wakefield 5-11-79
Source: Trainee.

Season	Club	A	G	Tot A	Tot G
1998-99	Huddersfield T	0	0		
1999-2000	Huddersfield T	0	0		
2000-01	Huddersfield T	0	0		
2001-02	Huddersfield T	0	0		
2002-03	Huddersfield T	13	0		
2003-04	Huddersfield T	19	2		
2004-05	Huddersfield T	0	0	**32**	**2**
2004-05	Bury	23	0		
2005-06	Bury	41	2		
2006-07	Bury	46	2		
2007-08	Bury	40	6		
2008-09	Bury	33	3	**183**	**13**

SODJE, Efe (D)   **392 27**
H: 6 1   W: 12 00   b.Greenwich 5-10-72
Source: Delta Steel Pioneer, Stevenage Bor.
Honours: Nigeria 9 full caps, 1 goal.

Season	Club	A	G	Tot A	Tot G
1997-98	Macclesfield T	41	3		
1998-99	Macclesfield T	42	3	**83**	**6**
1999-2000	Luton T	9	0	**9**	**0**
1999-2000	Colchester U	3	0	**3**	**0**
2000-01	Crewe Alex	32	0		
2001-02	Crewe Alex	36	2		
2002-03	Crewe Alex	30	1	**98**	**3**
2003-04	Huddersfield T	39	4		
2004-05	Huddersfield T	28	1	**67**	**5**
2004-05	Yeovil T	6	2		
2005-06	Yeovil T	19	1	**25**	**3**
2005-06	Southend U	13	1		
2006-07	Southend U	24	1	**37**	**2**
2007-08	Gillingham	13	0	**13**	**0**
2007-08	Bury	16	1		
2008-09	Bury	41	7	**57**	**8**

CARDIFF C (19)

BLAKE, Darcy (M)   **26 0**
H: 5 10   W: 12 05   b.Caerphilly 13-12-88
Source: Scholar. *Honours:* Wales Youth, Under-21.

Season	Club	A	G	Tot A	Tot G
2005-06	Cardiff C	1	0		
2006-07	Cardiff C	10	0		
2007-08	Cardiff C	8	0		
2008-09	Cardiff C	7	0	**26**	**0**

BOTHROYD, Jay (F)   **225 45**
H: 6 3   W: 14 13   b.Islington 7-5-82
Source: Trainee. *Honours:* England Schools, Youth, Under-20, Under-21.

Season	Club	A	G	Tot A	Tot G
1999-2000	Arsenal	0	0		
2000-01	Coventry C	8	0		
2001-02	Coventry C	31	6		
2002-03	Coventry C	33	8	**72**	**14**
2003-04	*Perugia*	26	4	**26**	**4**
2004-05	Blackburn R	11	1	**11**	**1**
2005-06	Charlton Ath	18	2	**18**	**2**
2006-07	Wolverhampton W	33	9		
2007-08	Wolverhampton W	22	3	**55**	**12**
2007-08	*Stoke C*	4	0	**4**	**0**
2008-09	Cardiff C	39	12	**39**	**12**

BROWN, Jon (M)   **2 0**
H: 5 10   W: 11 04   b.Llanelli 17-4-90
Source: Scholar. *Honours:* Wales Youth, Under-21.

Season	Club	A	G	Tot A	Tot G
2007-08	Cardiff C	2	0		
2008-09	Cardiff C	0	0	**2**	**0**

BURKE, Chris (M)   **109 12**
H: 5 9   W: 10 10   b.Glasgow 2-12-83
Honours: Scotland Under-21, B, 2 full caps.

Season	Club	A	G	Tot A	Tot G
2001-02	Rangers	2	1		
2002-03	Rangers	9	0		
2003-04	Rangers	20	3		
2004-05	Rangers	12	0		
2005-06	Rangers	27	3		
2006-07	Rangers	22	2		
2007-08	Rangers	11	2		
2008-09	Rangers	1	0	**95**	**11**
2008-09	Cardiff C	14	1	**14**	**1**

CAPALDI, Tony (D)   **188 12**
H: 6 0   W: 11 08   b.Porsgrunn 12-8-81
Source: Trainee. *Honours:* Northern Ireland Youth, Under-21, 22 full caps.

Season	Club	A	G	Tot A	Tot G
1999-2000	Birmingham C	0	0		
2000-01	Birmingham C	0	0		
2001-02	Birmingham C	0	0		
2002-03	Birmingham C	0	0		
2002-03	Plymouth Arg	1	0		
2003-04	Plymouth Arg	33	7		
2004-05	Plymouth Arg	35	2		
2005-06	Plymouth Arg	41	3		
2006-07	Plymouth Arg	31	0	**141**	**12**
2007-08	Cardiff C	44	0		
2008-09	Cardiff C	3	0	**47**	**0**

COMMINGES, Miguel (D)   **156 0**
H: 5 9   W: 11 03   b.Les Abymes 16-3-82

Season	Club	A	G	Tot A	Tot G
2002-03	Amiens	12	0	**12**	**0**
2003-04	Reims	29	0		
2004-05	Reims	21	0		
2005-06	Reims	11	0		
2006-07	Reims	13	0	**74**	**0**
2007-08	Swindon T	40	0	**40**	**0**
2008-09	Swindon T	30	0	**30**	**0**

DENNEHY, Darren (D)   **3 0**
H: 6 3   W: 11 11   b.Republic of Ireland 21-9-88
Source: Scholar. *Honours:* Eire Under-21.

Season	Club	A	G	Tot A	Tot G
2005-06	Everton	0	0		
2006-07	Everton	0	0		
2007-08	Everton	0	0		
2008-09	Cardiff C	0	0		
2008-09	Hereford U	3	0	**3**	**0**

ENCKELMAN, Peter (G)   **161 0**
H: 6 2   W: 12 05   b.Turku 10-3-77
Source: TPS Turku. *Honours:* Finland Under-21, 11 full caps.

Season	Club	A	G	Tot A	Tot G
1995	TPS Turku	6	0		
1996	TPS Turku	24	0		
1997	TPS Turku	25	0		
1998	TPS Turku	24	0	**79**	**0**
1998-99	Aston Villa	0	0		
1999-2000	Aston Villa	10	0		
2000-01	Aston Villa	0	0		
2001-02	Aston Villa	9	0		
2002-03	Aston Villa	33	0		
2003-04	Aston Villa	0	0	**52**	**0**
2004-05	Blackburn R	2	0		
2005-06	Blackburn R	0	0		
2006-07	Blackburn R	0	0		
2007-08	Blackburn R	0	0	**2**	**0**
2007-08	*Cardiff C*	16	0		
2008-09	Cardiff C	12	0	**28**	**0**

FEENEY, Warren (F)   **260 70**
H: 5 8   W: 12 04   b.Belfast 17-1-81
Source: Trainee. *Honours:* Northern Ireland Schools, Youth, Under-21, 32 full caps, 5 goals.

Season	Club	A	G	Tot A	Tot G
1997-98	Leeds U	0	0		
1998-99	Leeds U	0	0		
1999-2000	Leeds U	0	0		
2000-01	Leeds U	0	0		
2000-01	Bournemouth	10	4		
2001-02	Bournemouth	37	13		
2002-03	Bournemouth	21	7		
2003-04	Bournemouth	40	12	**108**	**36**
2004-05	Stockport Co	31	15	**31**	**15**
2004-05	Luton T	6	0		
2005-06	Luton T	42	6		
2006-07	Luton T	29	2	**77**	**8**
2007-08	*Cardiff C*	6	0		
2007-08	Cardiff C	5	0		
2007-08	*Swansea C*	10	5	**10**	**5**
2008-09	Dundee U	23	6	**23**	**6**
2008-09	Cardiff C	0	0	**11**	**0**

FLOOD, Willo (M)   **109 4**
H: 5 7   W: 10 05   b.Dublin 10-4-85
Source: Trainee. *Honours:* Eire Youth, Under-21.

Season	Club	A	G	Tot A	Tot G
2001-02	Manchester C	0	0		
2002-03	Manchester C	0	0		
2003-04	Manchester C	0	0		
2003-04	*Rochdale*	6	0	**6**	**0**
2004-05	Manchester C	9	1		
2005-06	Manchester C	5	0	**14**	**1**
2005-06	*Coventry C*	8	1	**8**	**1**
2006-07	Cardiff C	25	1		
2007-08	Cardiff C	0	0		
2007-08	*Dundee U*	36	1		
2008-09	*Dundee U*	20	0	**56**	**1**
2008-09	Cardiff C	0	0	**25**	**1**

Transferred to Celtic January 2009

GYEPES, Gabor (D)   **176 14**
H: 6 3   W: 13 01   b.Hungary 26-6-81
Honours: Hungary 22 full caps, 1 goal.

Season	Club	A	G	Tot A	Tot G
1999-2000	Ferencvaros	2	0		
2000-01	Ferencvaros	29	2		
2001-02	Ferencvaros	33	3		
2002-03	Ferencvaros	17	2		
2003-04	Ferencvaros	7	0		
2004-05	Ferencvaros	26	5	**114**	**12**
2005-06	Wolverhampton W	20	0		
2006-07	Wolverhampton W	0	0	**20**	**0**
2007-08	Northampton T	13	0		
2008-09	Northampton T	2	0	**15**	**0**
2008-09	Cardiff C	27	2	**27**	**2**

JOHNSON, Roger (D) 276 31
H: 6 3 W: 11 00 b.Ashford 28-4-83
Source: Trainee.

1999-2000	Wycombe W	1	0	
2000-01	Wycombe W	1	0	
2001-02	Wycombe W	7	1	
2002-03	Wycombe W	33	3	
2003-04	Wycombe W	28	2	
2004-05	Wycombe W	42	6	
2005-06	Wycombe W	45	7	157 19
2006-07	Cardiff C	32	2	
2007-08	Cardiff C	42	5	
2008-09	Cardiff C	45	5	119 12

KENNEDY, Mark (M) 403 32
H: 5 11 W: 11 09 b.Dublin 15-5-76
Source: Belvedere, Trainee. Honours: Eire
Schools, Youth, Under-21, 34 full caps, 3
goals.

1992-93	Millwall	1	0	
1993-94	Millwall	12	4	
1994-95	Millwall	30	5	43 9
1994-95	Liverpool	6	0	
1995-96	Liverpool	4	0	
1996-97	Liverpool	5	0	
1997-98	Liverpool	1	0	16 0
1997-98	QPR	8	2	8 2
1997-98	Wimbledon	4	0	
1998-99	Wimbledon	17	0	21 0
1999-2000	Manchester C	41	8	
2000-01	Manchester C	25	0	66 8
2001-02	Wolverhampton W	35	5	
2002-03	Wolverhampton W	31	3	
2003-04	Wolverhampton W	31	2	
2004-05	Wolverhampton W	30	0	
2005-06	Wolverhampton W	40	2	167 10
2006-07	Crystal Palace	38	1	
2007-08	Crystal Palace	8	0	46 1
2008-09	Cardiff C	36	0	36 0

LEDLEY, Joe (M) 197 22
H: 6 0 W: 11 07 b.Cardiff 23-1-87
Source: Scholar. Honours: Wales Youth,
Under-21, 29 full caps, 2 goals.

2004-05	Cardiff C	28	3	
2005-06	Cardiff C	42	3	
2006-07	Cardiff C	46	2	
2007-08	Cardiff C	41	10	
2008-09	Cardiff C	40	4	197 22

LOOVENS, Glenn (D) 162 5
H: 6 1 W: 12 11 b.Doetinchem 22-9-83
Honours: Holland Youth, Under-21.

2001-02	Feyenoord	8	0	
2002-03	Feyenoord	12	0	
2003-04	Feyenoord	1	0	
2003-04	Excelsior	24	2	24 2
2004-05	Feyenoord	6	0	27 0
2004-05	De Graafschap	11	0	11 0
2005-06	Cardiff C	33	2	
2006-07	Cardiff C	30	1	
2007-08	Cardiff C	36	0	
2008-09	Cardiff C	19	0	100 3

Transferred to Celtic August 2008

MARSHALL, David (G) 129 0
H: 6 3 W: 13 04 b.Glasgow 5-3-85
Source: Celtic Youth. Honours: Scotland
Youth, Under-21, B, 2 full caps.

2003-04	Celtic	11	0	
2004-05	Celtic	18	0	
2005-06	Celtic	4	0	
2006-07	Celtic	2	0	35 0
2006-07	Norwich C	2	0	
2007-08	Norwich C	46	0	
2008-09	Norwich C	46	0	94 0
2008-09	Cardiff C	0	0	

MATTHEWS, Adam (M) 0 0
H: 5 10 W: 11 02 b.Swansea 13-1-92
Source: Scholar.

2008-09	Cardiff C	0	0	

McCORMACK, Ross (F) 116 38
H: 5 9 W: 11 00 b.Glasgow 18-8-86
Honours: Scotland Youth, Under-21, B, 3 full
caps, 1 goal.

2003-04	Rangers	2	1	
2004-05	Rangers	1	0	
2005-06	Rangers	8	1	11 2
2005-06	Doncaster R	19	4	19 4
2006-07	Motherwell	12	2	
2007-08	Motherwell	36	9	48 11
2008-09	Cardiff C	38	21	38 21

McNAUGHTON, Kevin (D) 291 4
H: 5 10 W: 10 06 b.Dundee 28-8-82
Honours: Scotland Under-21, 4 full caps.

1999-2000	Aberdeen	0	0	
2000-01	Aberdeen	33	0	
2001-02	Aberdeen	34	0	
2002-03	Aberdeen	22	1	
2003-04	Aberdeen	17	0	
2004-05	Aberdeen	35	2	
2005-06	Aberdeen	34	0	175 3
2006-07	Cardiff C	42	0	
2007-08	Cardiff C	35	1	
2008-09	Cardiff C	39	0	116 1

McPHAIL, Stephen (M) 283 10
H: 5 8 W: 11 04 b.Westminster 9-12-79
Source: Trainee. Honours: Eire Youth, B,
Under-21, 10 full caps, 1 goal.

1996-97	Leeds U	0	0	
1997-98	Leeds U	4	0	
1998-99	Leeds U	17	0	
1999-2000	Leeds U	24	2	
2000-01	Leeds U	7	0	
2001-02	Leeds U	1	0	
2001-02	Millwall	3	0	3 0
2002-03	Leeds U	13	0	
2003-04	Leeds U	12	1	78 3
2003-04	Nottingham F	14	0	14 0
2004-05	Barnsley	36	2	
2005-06	Barnsley	34	2	70 4
2006-07	Cardiff C	43	0	
2007-08	Cardiff C	43	3	
2008-09	Cardiff C	32	0	118 3

MORRIS, Aaron (D) 0 0
H: 6 1 W: 12 05 b.Cardiff 30-12-89
Source: Scholar. Honours: Wales Youth,
Under-21.

2008-09	Cardiff C	0	0	

OWUSU-ABEYIE, Quincy (F) 70 7
H: 5 11 W: 11 10 b.Amsterdam 15-4-86
Source: Scholar. Honours: Holland Youth,
Under-21, Ghana 12 full caps, 1 goal.

2003-04	Arsenal	0	0	
2004-05	Arsenal	1	0	
2005-06	Arsenal	4	0	5 0
2006	Spartak Moscow	21	1	21 1
2007-08	Celta Vigo	20	4	20 4
2008-09	Birmingham C	19	2	19 2
2008-09	Cardiff C	5	0	5 0

Transferred to Spartak Moscow May 2009

PARRY, Paul (M) 191 24
H: 5 11 W: 12 12 b.Chepstow 19-8-80
Source: Hereford U. Honours: Wales 12 full
caps, 1 goal.

2003-04	Cardiff C	17	1	
2004-05	Cardiff C	24	4	
2005-06	Cardiff C	27	1	
2006-07	Cardiff C	42	6	
2007-08	Cardiff C	41	10	
2008-09	Cardiff C	40	2	191 24

PURSE, Darren (D) 415 27
H: 6 2 W: 12 08 b.Stepney 14-2-77
Source: Trainee. Honours: England
Under-21.

1993-94	Leyton Orient	5	0	
1994-95	Leyton Orient	38	3	
1995-96	Leyton Orient	12	0	55 3
1996-97	Oxford U	31	1	
1997-98	Oxford U	28	4	59 5
1997-98	Birmingham C	8	0	
1998-99	Birmingham C	20	0	
1999-2000	Birmingham C	38	2	
2000-01	Birmingham C	37	3	
2001-02	Birmingham C	36	3	
2002-03	Birmingham C	20	1	
2003-04	Birmingham C	9	0	168 9
2004-05	WBA	22	0	22 0
2005-06	Cardiff C	39	5	
2006-07	Cardiff C	31	4	
2007-08	Cardiff C	18	1	
2008-09	Cardiff C	23	0	111 10

RAE, Gavin (D) 326 31
H: 5 11 W: 10 04 b.Aberdeen 28-11-77
Source: Hermes J. Honours: Scotland
Under-21, 13 full caps.

1995-96	Dundee	6	0	
1996-97	Dundee	17	2	
1997-98	Dundee	6	0	
1998-99	Dundee	30	1	
1999-2000	Dundee	35	4	
2000-01	Dundee	32	4	
2001-02	Dundee	36	6	
2002-03	Dundee	37	4	
2003-04	Dundee	13	2	212 23
2003-04	Rangers	10	2	
2004-05	Rangers	0	0	
2005-06	Rangers	8	0	
2006-07	Rangers	10	1	28 3
2007-08	Cardiff C	45	4	
2008-09	Cardiff C	41	1	86 5

SAK, Erwin (G) 0 0
H: 6 0 W: 12 00 b.Lublin 15-2-90
Source: Sokol Pniewi.

2007-08	Cardiff C	0	0	
2008-09	Cardiff C	0	0	

SCIMECA, Riccardo (D) 354 16
H: 6 1 W: 12 09 b.Leamington Spa 13-6-75
Source: Trainee. Honours: England
Under-21, B.

1993-94	Aston Villa	0	0	
1994-95	Aston Villa	0	0	
1995-96	Aston Villa	17	0	
1996-97	Aston Villa	17	0	
1997-98	Aston Villa	21	0	
1998-99	Aston Villa	18	2	73 2
1999-2000	Nottingham F	38	0	
2000-01	Nottingham F	36	4	
2001-02	Nottingham F	37	0	
2002-03	Nottingham F	40	3	151 7
2003-04	Leicester C	29	1	29 1
2004-05	WBA	33	0	
2005-06	WBA	2	0	35 0
2005-06	Cardiff C	18	1	
2006-07	Cardiff C	35	5	
2007-08	Cardiff C	9	0	
2008-09	Cardiff C	4	0	66 6

WHITTINGHAM, Peter (D) 167 13
H: 5 10 W: 9 13 b.Nuneaton 8-9-84
Source: Trainee. Honours: England Youth,
Under-20, Under-21.

2002-03	Aston Villa	4	0	
2003-04	Aston Villa	32	0	
2004-05	Aston Villa	13	1	
2004-05	Burnley	7	0	7 0
2005-06	Aston Villa	4	0	
2005-06	Derby Co	11	0	11 0
2006-07	Aston Villa	3	0	56 1
2006-07	Cardiff C	19	4	
2007-08	Cardiff C	41	5	
2008-09	Cardiff C	33	3	93 12

CARLISLE U (20)

ALDRED, Tom (D) 0 0
H: 6 2 W: 13 02 b.Bolton 11-9-90
Source: Scholar.

2008-09	Carlisle U	0	0	

ANYINSAH, Joe (M) 66 7
H: 5 8 W: 11 00 b.Bristol 8-10-84
Source: Scholar.

2001-02	Bristol C	0	0	
2002-03	Bristol C	0	0	
2003-04	Bristol C	0	0	
2004-05	Bristol C	7	0	7 0
2005-06	Preston NE	3	0	
2005-06	Bury	3	0	3 0
2006-07	Preston NE	3	0	
2007-08	Preston NE	0	0	
2007-08	Carlisle U	12	3	
2007-08	Crewe Alex	8	0	8 0
2008-09	Preston NE	0	0	6 0
2008-09	Brighton & HA	11	0	11 0
2008-09	Carlisle U	19	4	31 7

BLAKE, Jonny (M) 0 0
H: 5 8 W: 11 00 b.Carlisle 4-2-91
Source: Scholar.

2008-09	Carlisle U	0	0	

BRIDGE-WILKINSON, Marc (M) 309 56
H: 5 6 W: 11 00 b.Coventry 16-3-79
Source: Trainee.

1996-97	Derby Co	0	0	
1997-98	Derby Co	0	0	
1998-99	Derby Co	1	0	
1998-99	Carlisle U	7	0	
1999-2000	Derby Co	0	0	1 0

2000-01	Port Vale	42	9		
2001-02	Port Vale	19	6		
2002-03	Port Vale	31	9		
2003-04	Port Vale	32	7	124	31
2004-05	Stockport Co	22	2	22	2
2004-05	*Bradford C*	12	3		
2005-06	Bradford C	36	5		
2006-07	Bradford C	39	4	87	12
2007-08	Carlisle U	45	6		
2008-09	Carlisle U	23	5	75	11

BURNS, Michael (D)   1 0
H: 5 10 W: 11 07 b.Huyton 4-10-88
Source: Liverpool Scholar.

2007-08	Bolton W	0	0		
2008-09	Bolton W	0	0		
2008-09	Carlisle U	1	0	1	0

CAMPION, Darren (D)   4 0
H: 5 11 W: 12 00 b.Birmingham 17-10-88
Source: Scholar.

2007-08	Carlisle U	2	0		
2008-09	Carlisle U	2	0	4	0

CARLTON, Danny (F)   68 9
H: 5 11 W: 12 04 b.Leeds 22-12-83
Source: Morecambe.

2007-08	Carlisle U	31	0		
2008-09	Carlisle U	12	3	43	3
2008-09	*Morecambe*	8	2	8	2
2008-09	*Darlington*	17	4	17	4

COOK, Andy (F)   0 0
H: 6 1 W: 11 04 b.Bishop Auckland 18-10-90
Source: Scholar.

2008-09	Carlisle U	0	0		

DOBIE, Scott (F)   354 58
H: 6 1 W: 12 05 b.Workington 10-10-78
Source: From Trainee. *Honours:* Scotland 6 full caps, 1 goal.

1996-97	Carlisle U	2	1		
1997-98	Carlisle U	23	0		
1998-99	Carlisle U	33	6		
1998-99	*Clydebank*	6	0	6	0
1999-2000	Carlisle U	34	7		
2000-01	Carlisle U	44	10		
2001-02	WBA	43	10		
2002-03	WBA	31	5		
2003-04	WBA	31	5		
2004-05	WBA	5	1	110	21
2004-05	Millwall	16	3	16	3
2004-05	Nottingham F	12	1		
2005-06	Nottingham F	8	2		
2006-07	Nottingham F	19	0		
2007-08	Nottingham F	2	0	41	3
2007-08	Carlisle U	15	4		
2008-09	Carlisle U	30	3	181	31

GALL, Kevin (F)   263 27
H: 5 9 W: 10 08 b.Merthyr 4-2-82
Source: Trainee. *Honours:* Wales Schools, Youth, Under-21.

1998-99	Newcastle U	0	0		
1999-2000	Newcastle U	0	0		
2000-01	Newcastle U	0	0		
2000-01	Bristol R	10	2		
2001-02	Bristol R	31	3		
2002-03	Bristol R	9	0	50	5
2003-04	Yeovil T	43	8		
2004-05	Yeovil T	43	3		
2005-06	Yeovil T	37	2	123	13
2006-07	Carlisle U	45	8		
2007-08	Carlisle U	21	0		
2007-08	*Darlington*	8	0	8	0
2008-09	Carlisle U	0	0	66	9
2008-09	*Lincoln C*	9	0	9	0
2008-09	*Port Vale*	7	0	7	0

GOWLING, Josh (D)   113 1
H: 6 3 W: 12 08 b.Coventry 29-11-83
Source: WBA Scholar.

2004-05	Herfolge	13	0	13	0
2005-06	Bournemouth	13	0		
2006-07	Bournemouth	33	1		
2007-08	Bournemouth	37	0	83	1
2008-09	Carlisle U	4	0	4	0
2008-09	*Hereford U*	13	0	13	0

GRAHAM, Danny (F)   145 40
H: 5 11 W: 12 05 b.Gateshead 12-8-85
Source: Trainee. *Honours:* England Youth, Under-20.

2003-04	Middlesbrough	0	0		
2003-04	*Darlington*	9	2	9	2
2004-05	Middlesbrough	11	1		
2005-06	Middlesbrough	3	0		
2005-06	Derby Co	14	0	14	0
2005-06	Leeds U	3	0	3	0
2006-07	Middlesbrough	1	0	15	1
2006-07	Blackpool	4	1	4	1
2006-07	Carlisle U	11	7		
2007-08	Carlisle U	45	14		
2008-09	Carlisle U	44	15	100	36

HARTE, Ian (D)   258 30
H: 5 11 W: 12 06 b.Drogheda 31-8-77
Source: Trainee. *Honours:* Eire 63 full caps, 11 goals.

1995-96	Leeds U	4	0		
1996-97	Leeds U	14	2		
1997-98	Leeds U	12	0		
1998-99	Leeds U	35	4		
1999-2000	Leeds U	33	6		
2000-01	Leeds U	29	7		
2001-02	Leeds U	36	5		
2002-03	Leeds U	27	3		
2003-04	Leeds U	23	1	213	28
2004-05	Levante	24	1		
2005-06	Levante	0	0		
2006-07	Levante	6	0	30	1
2007-08	Sunderland	8	0	8	0
2008-09	Blackpool	4	0	4	0
2008-09	Carlisle U	3	1	3	1

HORWOOD, Evan (D)   89 1
H: 6 0 W: 10 06 b.Billingham 10-3-86
Source: Scholar.

2004-05	Sheffield U	0	0		
2004-05	Stockport Co	10	0	10	0
2005-06	Sheffield U	0	0		
2005-06	Scunthorpe U	0	0		
2005-06	Chester C	1	0	1	0
2006-07	Sheffield U	0	0		
2006-07	Darlington	20	0	20	0
2007-08	Sheffield U	0	0		
2007-08	Gretna	15	1	15	1
2007-08	Carlisle U	19	0		
2008-09	Carlisle U	24	0	43	0

JOYCE, Luke (M)   26 2
H: 5 11 W: 12 03 b.Bolton 9-7-87
Source: Scholar.

2005-06	Wigan Ath	0	0		
2005-06	Carlisle U	0	0		
2006-07	Carlisle U	16	1		
2007-08	Carlisle U	3	1		
2008-09	Carlisle U	7	0	26	2

KAVANAGH, Graham (M)   507 74
H: 5 10 W: 13 03 b.Dublin 2-12-73
Source: Home Farm. *Honours:* Eire Schools, Youth, Under-21, B, 16 full caps, 1 goal.

1991-92	Middlesbrough	0	0		
1992-93	Middlesbrough	0	0		
1993-94	Middlesbrough	11	2		
1993-94	*Darlington*	5	0	5	0
1994-95	Middlesbrough	7	0		
1995-96	Middlesbrough	7	1		
1996-97	Middlesbrough	0	0	35	3
1996-97	Stoke C	38	4		
1997-98	Stoke C	44	5		
1998-99	Stoke C	36	11		
1999-2000	Stoke C	45	7		
2000-01	Stoke C	43	8	206	35
2001-02	Cardiff C	43	13		
2002-03	Cardiff C	44	5		
2003-04	Cardiff C	27	7		
2004-05	Cardiff C	28	3	142	28
2004-05	Wigan Ath	11	0		
2005-06	Wigan Ath	35	0		
2006-07	Wigan Ath	2	0	48	0
2006-07	Sunderland	14	1		
2007-08	Sunderland	0	0		
2007-08	Sheffield W	23	2	23	2
2008-09	Sunderland	0	0	14	1
2008-09	Carlisle U	34	5	34	5

KEOGH, Richard (D)   101 5
H: 6 0 W: 11 02 b.Harlow 11-8-86
Source: Scholar. *Honours:* Eire Under-21.

2004-05	Stoke C	0	0		
2005-06	Bristol C	9	1		
2005-06	*Wycombe W*	3	0	3	0
2006-07	Bristol C	31	2		
2007-08	Bristol C	0	0	40	3
2007-08	*Huddersfield T*	9	1	9	1

2007-08	*Carlisle U*	7	0		
2007-08	*Cheltenham T*	10	0	10	0
2008-09	Carlisle U	32	1	39	1

LIVESEY, Danny (D)   166 11
H: 6 3 W: 13 01 b.Salford 31-12-84
Source: Trainee.

2002-03	Bolton W	2	0		
2003-04	Bolton W	0	0		
2003-04	Notts Co	11	0	11	0
2003-04	Rochdale	13	0	13	0
2004-05	Bolton W	0	0	2	0
2004-05	Blackpool	1	0	1	0
2005-06	Carlisle U	36	4		
2006-07	Carlisle U	31	1		
2007-08	Carlisle U	45	6		
2008-09	Carlisle U	27	0	139	11

LUMSDON, Chris (M)   233 23
H: 5 11 W: 10 06 b.Newcastle 15-12-79
Source: Trainee.

1997-98	Sunderland	1	0		
1998-99	Sunderland	0	0		
1999-2000	Sunderland	1	0		
1999-2000	*Blackpool*	6	1	6	1
2000-01	Sunderland	0	0		
2000-01	*Crewe Alex*	16	0	16	0
2001-02	Sunderland	0	0	2	0
2001-02	Barnsley	32	7		
2002-03	Barnsley	25	3		
2003-04	Barnsley	28	3		
2004-05	Barnsley	0	0	85	13
2005-06	Carlisle U	38	7		
2006-07	Carlisle U	39	2		
2007-08	Carlisle U	40	0		
2008-09	Carlisle U	7	0	124	9

MADINE, Gary (F)   28 1
H: 6 1 W: 12 00 b.Gateshead 24-8-90
Source: Scholar.

2007-08	Carlisle U	11	0		
2008-09	Carlisle U	14	1	25	1
2008-09	*Rochdale*	3	0	3	0

MURPHY, Peter (M)   284 11
H: 5 10 W: 12 10 b.Dublin 27-10-80
Source: Trainee. *Honours:* Eire Youth, Under-21, 1 full cap.

1998-99	Blackburn R	0	0		
1999-2000	Blackburn R	0	0		
2000-01	Blackburn R	0	0		
2000-01	*Halifax T*	21	1	21	1
2001-02	Blackburn R	0	0		
2001-02	Carlisle U	40	0		
2002-03	Carlisle U	40	2		
2003-04	Carlisle U	35	1		
2004-05	Carlisle U	0	0		
2005-06	Carlisle U	44	2		
2006-07	Carlisle U	40	2		
2007-08	Carlisle U	36	3		
2008-09	Carlisle U	28	0	263	10

NEAL, Lewis (M)   155 9
H: 5 10 W: 11 02 b.Leicester 14-7-81
Source: Juniors.

1998-99	Stoke C	0	0		
1999-2000	Stoke C	0	0		
2000-01	Stoke C	1	0		
2001-02	Stoke C	11	0		
2002-03	Stoke C	16	0		
2003-04	Stoke C	19	1		
2004-05	Stoke C	23	1	70	2
2005-06	Preston NE	24	2		
2006-07	Preston NE	24	1		
2007-08	Preston NE	17	2		
2008-09	Preston NE	0	0	65	5
2008-09	*Notts Co*	4	0	4	0
2008-09	Carlisle U	16	2	16	2

RAVEN, David (D)   132 1
H: 6 0 W: 11 04 b.Birkenhead 10-3-85
Source: Scholar. *Honours:* England Youth, Under-20.

2001-02	Liverpool	0	0		
2002-03	Liverpool	0	0		
2003-04	Liverpool	0	0		
2004-05	Liverpool	1	0		
2005-06	Liverpool	0	0	1	0
2005-06	*Tranmere R*	11	0	11	0
2006-07	Carlisle U	36	0		
2007-08	Carlisle U	43	1		
2008-09	Carlisle U	41	0	120	1

ROTHERY, Gavin (M)　　1　0
H: 5 9　W: 10 12　b.Morley 22-9-87
Source: Scholar. *Honours:* England Youth.

2005-06	Leeds U	0	0		
From York C.					
2008-09	Carlisle U	1	0	1	0

SMITH, Grant (M)　　110　15
H: 6 1　W: 12 07　b.Irvine 5-5-80

1998-99	Reading	0	0		
1999-2000	Reading	0	0		
2000-01	Reading	0	0		
2001-02	*Halifax T*	11	0	11	0
2001-02	Sheffield U	7	0		
2002-03	Sheffield U	3	0	10	0
2002-03	*Plymouth Arg*	5	1	5	1
2003-04	Swindon T	7	0		
2004-05	Swindon T	30	10	37	10
2005-06	Bristol C	11	0		
2005-06	*Walsall*	13	3	13	3
2006-07	Bristol C	0	0	11	0
2006-07	Dundee U	6	0		
2007-08	Dundee U	0	0	6	0
2007-08	Carlisle U	16	1		
2008-09	Carlisle U	1	0	17	1

SMITH, Jeff (M)　　163　9
H: 5 11　W: 11 10　b.Middlesbrough 28-6-80
Source: Trainee.

1998-99	Hartlepool U	3	0		
1999-2000	Hartlepool U	0	0	3	0
From Bishop Auckland					
2000-01	Bolton W	1	0		
2001-02	*Macclesfield T*	8	2	8	2
2001-02	Bolton W	1	0		
2002-03	Bolton W	0	0		
2003-04	Bolton W	0	0	2	0
2003-04	*Scunthorpe U*	1	0	1	0
2003-04	*Rochdale*	1	0	1	0
2003-04	*Preston NE*	5	0	5	0
2004-05	Port Vale	34	1		
2005-06	Port Vale	27	1		
2006-07	Port Vale	27	3	88	5
2006-07	Carlisle U	17	1		
2007-08	Carlisle U	22	1		
2008-09	Carlisle U	16	0	55	2

TAYLOR, Cleveland (M)　　237　18
H: 5 8　W: 10 07　b.Leicester 9-9-83
Source: Scholar. *Honours:* Jamaica Youth.

2001-02	Bolton W	0	0		
2002-03	Bolton W	0	0		
2002-03	*Exeter C*	3	0	3	0
2003-04	Bolton W	0	0		
2003-04	Scunthorpe U	20	3		
2004-05	Scunthorpe U	44	6		
2005-06	Scunthorpe U	45	3		
2006-07	Scunthorpe U	45	3		
2007-08	Scunthorpe U	20	0	174	15
2007-08	Carlisle U	18	0		
2008-09	Carlisle U	42	3	60	3

THIRLWELL, Paul (M)　　217　5
H: 5 11　W: 12 08　b.Springwell 13-2-79
Source: Trainee. *Honours:* England Under-21.

1996-97	Sunderland	0	0		
1997-98	Sunderland	0	0		
1998-99	Sunderland	2	0		
1999-2000	Sunderland	8	0		
1999-2000	*Swindon T*	12	0	12	0
2000-01	Sunderland	5	0		
2001-02	Sunderland	14	0		
2002-03	Sunderland	19	0		
2003-04	Sunderland	29	0	77	0
2004-05	Sheffield U	30	1	30	1
2005-06	Derby Co	21	0		
2006-07	Derby Co	0	0	21	0
2006-07	Carlisle U	30	0		
2007-08	Carlisle U	13	0		
2008-09	Carlisle U	34	4	77	4

WILLIAMS, Ben (G)　　180　0
H: 6 0　W: 13 01　b.Manchester 27-8-82
Source: Scholar. *Honours:* England Schools.

2001-02	Manchester U	0	0		
2002-03	Manchester U	0	0		
2002-03	Coventry C	0	0		
2002-03	*Chesterfield*	14	0	14	0
2003-04	Manchester U	0	0		
2004-05	Crewe Alex	10	0		
2004-05	Crewe Alex	23	0		
2005-06	Crewe Alex	17	0		
2006-07	Crewe Alex	39	0		
2007-08	Crewe Alex	46	0	135	0
2008-09	Carlisle U	31	0	31	0

CHARLTON ATH (21)

AMBROSE, Darren (M)　　188　26
H: 6 0　W: 11 00　b.Harlow 29-2-84
Source: Scholar. *Honours:* England Youth, Under-20, Under-21.

2001-02	Ipswich T	1	0		
2002-03	Ipswich T	29	8		
2002-03	Newcastle U	1	0		
2003-04	Newcastle U	24	2		
2004-05	Newcastle U	12	3	37	5
2005-06	Charlton Ath	28	3		
2006-07	Charlton Ath	26	3		
2007-08	Charlton Ath	37	7		
2008-09	Charlton Ath	21	0	112	13
2008-09	*Ipswich T*	9	0	39	8

ARTER, Harry (M)　　0　0
H: 5 9　W: 11 07　b.Sidcup 23-12-89
Source: Scholar. *Honours:* Eire Youth.

2007-08	Charlton Ath	0	0
2008-09	Charlton Ath	0	0

BAILEY, Nicky (M)　　177　34
H: 5 10　W: 12 06　b.Hammersmith 10-6-84
Source: Sutton U.

2005-06	Barnet	45	7		
2006-07	Barnet	44	5	89	12
2007-08	Southend U	44	9		
2008-09	Southend U	1	0	45	9
2008-09	Charlton Ath	43	13	43	13

BASEY, Grant (D)　　35　1
H: 6 2　W: 13 12　b.Farnborough 30-11-88
Source: Scholar. *Honours:* Wales Under-21.

2007-08	Charlton Ath	8	1		
2007-08	*Brentford*	8	0	8	0
2008-09	Charlton Ath	19	0	27	1

BURTON, Deon (F)　　430　94
H: 5 9　W: 11 09　b.Ashford 25-10-76
Source: Trainee. *Honours:* Jamaica 51 full caps, 9 goals.

1993-94	Portsmouth	2	0		
1994-95	Portsmouth	7	2		
1995-96	Portsmouth	32	7		
1996-97	Portsmouth	21	1		
1996-97	*Cardiff C*	5	2	5	2
1997-98	Derby Co	29	3		
1998-99	Derby Co	21	9		
1998-99	*Barnsley*	3	0	3	0
1999-2000	Derby Co	19	4		
2000-01	Derby Co	32	5		
2001-02	Derby Co	17	1		
2001-02	*Stoke C*	12	2	12	2
2002-03	Derby Co	7	3	125	25
2002-03	Portsmouth	15	4		
2003-04	Portsmouth	1	0	78	14
2003-04	*Walsall*	3	0	3	0
2003-04	*Swindon T*	4	1	4	1
2004-05	Brentford	40	10	40	10
2005-06	Rotherham U	24	12	24	12
2005-06	Sheffield W	17	3		
2006-07	Sheffield W	42	12		
2007-08	Sheffield W	40	7		
2008-09	Sheffield W	17	1	116	23
2008-09	Charlton Ath	20	5	20	5

CHRISTENSEN, Martin (D)　　0　0
H: 5 11　W: 12 10　b.Ishoj 23-12-87
Source: Herfolge. *Honours:* Denmark Youth, Under-21.

2007-08	Charlton Ath	0	0
2008-09	Charlton Ath	0	0
On loan to Lyngby			

DICKSON, Chris (F)　　38　7
H: 5 11　W: 11 09　b.East Dulwich 28-12-84
Source: Dulwich H. *Honours:* Ghana 1 full cap.

2006-07	Charlton Ath	0	0		
2007-08	Charlton Ath	2	0		
2007-08	*Crewe Alex*	3	0	3	0
2007-08	*Gillingham*	12	7	12	7
2008-09	Charlton Ath	21	0	23	0

ELLIOT, Rob (G)　　35　0
H: 6 3　W: 14 10　b.Chatham 30-4-86
Source: Scholar.

2004-05	Charlton Ath	0	0		
2004-05	*Notts Co*	4	0	4	0
2005-06	Charlton Ath	0	0		
2006-07	Charlton Ath	0	0		
2006-07	*Accrington S*	7	0	7	0
2007-08	Charlton Ath	1	0		
2008-09	Charlton Ath	23	0	24	0

FLEETWOOD, Stuart (F)　　64　9
H: 5 10　W: 12 07　b.Gloucester 23-4-86
Source: Scholar. *Honours:* Wales Youth, Under-21.

2003-04	Cardiff C	2	0		
2004-05	Cardiff C	6	0		
2005-06	Cardiff C	0	0	8	0
2006-07	*Hereford U*	27	3	27	3
2006-07	*Accrington S*	3	0	3	0
2008-09	Charlton Ath	0	0		
From Forest Green R.					
2008-09	*Cheltenham T*	6	2	6	2
2008-09	*Brighton & HA*	11	1	11	1
2008-09	*Exeter C*	9	3	9	3

FORTUNE, Jon (D)　　198　8
H: 6 2　W: 12 12　b.Islington 23-8-80
Source: Trainee.

1998-99	Charlton Ath	0	0		
1999-2000	Charlton Ath	0	0		
1999-2000	*Mansfield T*	4	0		
2000-01	Charlton Ath	0	0		
2000-01	*Mansfield T*	14	0	18	0
2001-02	Charlton Ath	19	0		
2002-03	Charlton Ath	26	1		
2003-04	Charlton Ath	28	2		
2004-05	Charlton Ath	31	2		
2005-06	Charlton Ath	11	0		
2006-07	Charlton Ath	8	0		
2006-07	*Stoke C*	14	1	14	1
2007-08	Charlton Ath	26	2		
2008-09	Charlton Ath	17	0	166	7

GIBBS, Cory (D)　　106　6
H: 6 3　W: 12 12　b.Fort Lauderdale 14-1-80
Source: Brown Univ. *Honours:* USA Under-23, 19 full caps.

2001-02	St Pauli II	5	1	5	1
2001-02	St Pauli	25	1		
2002-03	St Pauli	21	0		
2003-04	St Pauli	14	3	60	4
2004	Dallas Burn	21	0	21	0
2004-05	Feyenoord	15	1	15	1
2005-06	Den Haag	5	0	5	0
2006-07	Charlton Ath	0	0		
2007-08	Charlton Ath	0	0		
2008-09	Charlton Ath	0	0		

GRAY, Andy (F)　　369　85
H: 6 1　W: 13 00　b.Harrogate 15-11-77
Source: Trainee. *Honours:* Scotland Youth, B, 2 full caps.

1995-96	Leeds U	15	0		
1996-97	Leeds U	7	0		
1997-98	Leeds U	0	0		
1997-98	*Bury*	6	1	6	1
1998-99	Leeds U	0	0	22	0
1998-99	Nottingham F	8	0		
1998-99	*Preston NE*	5	0	5	0
1998-99	*Oldham Ath*	4	0	4	0
1999-2000	Nottingham F	22	0		
2000-01	Nottingham F	18	0		
2001-02	Nottingham F	16	1	64	1
2002-03	Bradford C	44	15		
2003-04	Bradford C	33	5	77	20
2003-04	Sheffield U	14	9		
2004-05	Sheffield U	43	15		
2005-06	Sheffield U	1	1	58	25
2005-06	Sunderland	21	1	21	1
2005-06	Burnley	9	3		
2006-07	Burnley	35	14		
2007-08	Burnley	25	11	69	28
2007-08	Charlton Ath	16	2		
2008-09	Charlton Ath	27	7	43	9

HOLLAND, Matt (M)　　554　69
H: 5 10　W: 12 03　b.Bury 11-4-74
Source: Trainee. *Honours:* Eire B, 49 full caps, 5 goals.

1992-93	West Ham U	0	0
1993-94	West Ham U	1	0
1994-95	West Ham U	0	0

1994-95	Bournemouth	16	1		
1995-96	Bournemouth	43	10		
1996-97	Bournemouth	45	7	104	18
1997-98	Ipswich T	46	10		
1998-99	Ipswich T	46	5		
1999-2000	Ipswich T	46	10		
2000-01	Ipswich T	38	3		
2001-02	Ipswich T	38	3		
2002-03	Ipswich T	45	7	259	38
2003-04	Charlton Ath	38	6		
2004-05	Charlton Ath	32	3		
2005-06	Charlton Ath	23	1		
2006-07	Charlton Ath	33	1		
2007-08	Charlton Ath	31	1		
2008-09	Charlton Ath	34	1	191	13

HUDSON, Mark (D)   178   10
H: 6 1   W: 12 01   b.Guildford 30-3-82
Source: Trainee.

1998-99	Fulham	0	0		
1999-2000	Fulham	0	0		
2000-01	Fulham	0	0		
2001-02	Fulham	0	0		
2002-03	Fulham	0	0		
2003-04	Fulham	0	0		
2003-04	*Oldham Ath*	15	0	15	0
2003-04	*Crystal Palace*	14	0		
2004-05	Crystal Palace	7	1		
2005-06	Crystal Palace	15	0		
2006-07	Crystal Palace	39	4		
2007-08	Crystal Palace	45	2	120	7
2008-09	Crystal Palace	43	3	43	3

JENSEN, Mikkel (M)   0   0
b.Herfolge 25-12-90
Source: Herfolge. *Honours:* Denmark
Under-21.

2008-09	Charlton Ath	0	0		

KOUADIO, Konan (M)   0   0
b.Abidjan 31-12-88
Source: ASEC Mimosas.

2007-08	Charlton Ath	0	0		
2008-09	Charlton Ath	0	0		

McLEOD, Izale (F)   191   61
H: 6 1   W: 11 02   b.Birmingham 15-10-84
Source: Scholar. *Honours:* England Youth.

2002-03	Derby Co	29	3		
2003-04	Derby Co	10	1	39	4
2003-04	*Sheffield U*	7	0	7	0
2004-05	Milton Keynes D	43	16		
2005-06	Milton Keynes D	39	17		
2006-07	Milton Keynes D	34	21	116	54
2007-08	Charlton Ath	18	1		
2007-08	*Colchester U*	2	0	2	0
2008-09	Charlton Ath	2	0	20	1
2008-09	*Millwall*	7	2	7	2

MOUTAOUAKIL, Yassin (D)   21   0
H: 5 10   W: 11 05   b.Nice 18-7-86
Honours: France Youth, Under-21.

2006-07	Chateauroux	0	0		
2007-08	Charlton Ath	10	0		
2008-09	Charlton Ath	11	0	21	0

RACON, Thierry (M)   59   6
H: 5 10   W: 10 02   b.Villeneuve-St-Georges
1-5-84

2004-05	Lorient	28	3	28	3
2005-06	Guingamp	0	0		
2006-07	Guingamp	4	0		
2007-08	Charlton Ath	8	0	8	0
2008-09	Charlton Ath	19	3	23	3

RANDOLPH, Darren (G)   33   0
H: 6 2   W: 14 00   b.Dublin 12-5-87
Source: Ardmore R Scholar, Eire B,
Under-21.

2004-05	Charlton Ath	0	0		
2005-06	Charlton Ath	0	0		
2006-07	Charlton Ath	1	0		
2006-07	*Gillingham*	3	0	3	0
2007-08	Charlton Ath	1	0		
2007-08	*Bury*	14	0	14	0
2008-09	Charlton Ath	1	0	3	0
2008-09	*Hereford U*	13	0	13	0

SAM, Lloyd (F)   92   2
H: 5 10   W: 11 00   b.Leeds 27-9-84
Honours: England Youth, Under-20.

2002-03	Charlton Ath	0	0		
2003-04	Charlton Ath	0	0		
2003-04	*Leyton Orient*	10	0	10	0

2004-05	Charlton Ath	1	0		
2005-06	Charlton Ath	2	0		
2006-07	Charlton Ath	7	0		
2006-07	*Sheffield W*	4	0	4	0
2006-07	*Southend U*	2	0	2	0
2007-08	Charlton Ath	28	2		
2008-09	Charlton Ath	38	0	76	2

SEMEDO, Jose (D)   110   2
H: 6 0   W: 12 08   b.Setubal 11-1-85
Honours: Portugal Under-21.

2004-05	Sporting Lisbon	0	0		
2004-05	*Casa Pia*	34	2	34	2
2005-06	*Feirense*	18	0	18	0
2006-07	*Cagliari*	3	0	3	0
2007-08	Charlton Ath	37	0		
2008-09	Charlton Ath	18	0	55	0

SHELVEY, Jonjo (M)   18   3
H: 6 1   W: 11 02   b.Romford 27-2-92
Honours: England Youth.

2007-08	Charlton Ath	2	0		
2008-09	Charlton Ath	16	3	18	3

SINCLAIR, Dean (M)   112   10
H: 5 10   W: 11 03   b.St Albans 17-12-84
Source: Scholar.

2002-03	Norwich C	2	0		
2003-04	Norwich C	0	0	2	0
2004-05	Barnet	0	0		
2005-06	Barnet	44	2		
2006-07	Barnet	42	6	86	8
2007-08	Charlton Ath	12	1		
2007-08	*Cheltenham T*	12	1		
2008-09	Charlton Ath	0	0		
2008-09	*Cheltenham T*	3	0	15	1
2008-09	*Grimsby T*	9	1	9	1

SOLLY, Chris (D)   1   0
H: 5 8   W: 10 07   b.Rochester 20-1-91
Source: Scholar.

2008-09	Charlton Ath	1	0	1	0

SPRING, Matthew (M)   390   47
H: 5 11   W: 12 05   b.Harlow 17-11-79
Source: Trainee.

1997-98	Luton T	12	0		
1998-99	Luton T	45	3		
1999-2000	Luton T	45	6		
2000-01	Luton T	41	4		
2001-02	Luton T	42	6		
2002-03	Luton T	41	5		
2003-04	Luton T	24	1		
2004-05	Leeds U	13	1		
2005-06	Leeds U	0	0	13	1
2005-06	Watford	39	8		
2006-07	Watford	6	0	45	8
2006-07	Luton T	14	1		
2007-08	Luton T	44	9		
2008-09	Luton T	0	0	308	35
2008-09	*Sheffield U*	11	1	11	1
2008-09	Charlton Ath	13	2	13	2

THOMAS, Aswad (D)   15   2
H: 5 11   W: 12 08   b.Westminster 9-8-89
Source: Scholar.

2007-08	Charlton Ath	0	0		
2007-08	*Accrington S*	13	2	13	2
2008-09	Charlton Ath	0	0		
2008-09	*Barnet*	2	0	2	0

TODOROV, Svetoslav (F)   199   76
H: 5 8   W: 11 11   b.Dobrich 30-8-78
Honours: Bulgaria Youth, 42 full caps, 6 goals.

1996-97	Dobrudzha	12	2	12	2
1997-98	Litets Lovech	19	9		
1998-99	Litets Lovech	11	2		
1999-2000	Litets Lovech	26	19		
2000-01	Litets Lovech	15	7	71	37
2000-01	West Ham U	8	1		
2001-02	West Ham U	6	0	14	1
2001-02	Portsmouth	3	1		
2002-03	Portsmouth	45	26		
2003-04	Portsmouth	1	0		
2004-05	Portsmouth	0	0		
2005-06	Portsmouth	24	4		
2006-07	Portsmouth	4	2	77	33
2006-07	*Wigan Ath*	5	0	5	0
2007-08	Charlton Ath	7	2		
2008-09	Charlton Ath	13	1	20	3

TUNA, Tamer (F)   2   0
H: 5 9   W: 11 05   b.Bexley 19-10-91
Source: Scholar.

2008-09	Charlton Ath	2	0	2	0

WAGSTAFF, Scott (F)   9   0
H: 5 10   W: 10 03   b.Maidstone 31-3-90
Source: Scholar.

2007-08	Charlton Ath	2	0		
2008-09	Charlton Ath	2	0	4	0
2008-09	*Bournemouth*	5	0	5	0

WEAVER, Nick (G)   254   0
H: 6 4   W: 14 07   b.Sheffield 2-3-79
Source: Trainee. *Honours:* England
Under-21.

1995-96	Mansfield T	1	0		
1996-97	Mansfield T	0	0	1	0
1996-97	Manchester C	0	0		
1997-98	Manchester C	0	0		
1998-99	Manchester C	45	0		
1999-2000	Manchester C	45	0		
2000-01	Manchester C	31	0		
2001-02	Manchester C	25	0		
2002-03	Manchester C	0	0		
2003-04	Manchester C	0	0		
2004-05	Manchester C	1	0		
2005-06	Manchester C	0	0		
2005-06	*Sheffield W*	14	0	14	0
2006-07	Manchester C	25	0	172	0
2007-08	Charlton Ath	45	0		
2008-09	Charlton Ath	22	0	67	0

WRIGHT, Josh (M)   44   1
H: 6 1   W: 11 07   b.Tower Hamlets 6-11-89
Source: Scholar. *Honours:* England Youth.

2007-08	Charlton Ath	0	0		
2007-08	*Barnet*	32	1	32	1
2008-09	Charlton Ath	2	0	2	0
2008-09	*Brentford*	5	0	5	0
2008-09	*Gillingham*	5	0	5	0

YOUGA, Kelly (D)   78   2
H: 6 1   W: 12 00   b.Bangui 22-9-85
Source: Lyon.

2005-06	Charlton Ath	0	0		
2005-06	*Bristol C*	4	0	4	0
2006-07	Charlton Ath	0	0		
2006-07	*Bradford C*	11	0	11	0
2007-08	Charlton Ath	11	0		
2007-08	*Scunthorpe U*	19	1	19	1
2008-09	Charlton Ath	33	1	44	1

YUSSUF, Rashid (M)   0   0
H: 6 1   W: 10 07   b.Poplar 23-9-89
Source: Scholar.

2007-08	Charlton Ath	0	0		
2008-09	Charlton Ath	0	0		

ZHENG-ZHI (M)   187   52
H: 5 11   W: 11 11   b.Shenyang 20-8-80
Honours: China 48 full caps, 12 goals.

2001	Shenzhen	23	3		
2002	Shenzhen	22	6		
2003	Shenzhen	16	3		
2004	Shenzhen	16	2	77	14
2005	Shandong Luneng	17	8		
2006	Shandong Luneng	26	21	43	29
2006-07	Charlton Ath	12	1		
2007-08	Charlton Ath	42	7		
2008-09	Charlton Ath	13	1	67	9

CHELSEA (22)

ALEX (D)   199   27
H: 6 2   W: 14 00   b.Niteroi 17-6-82
Honours: Brazil 12 full caps.

2002	Santos	25	3		
2003	Santos	34	9		
2004	Santos	4	0	63	12
2004-05	PSV Eindhoven	27	3		
2005-06	PSV Eindhoven	28	2		
2006-07	PSV Eindhoven	29	6	84	11
2007-08	Chelsea	28	2		
2008-09	Chelsea	24	2	52	4

ANELKA, Nicolas (F)   385   132
H: 6 1   W: 13 03   b.Versailles 14-3-79
Honours: France Youth, Under-21, 57 full
caps, 12 goals.

1995-96	Paris St Germain	2	0		
1996-97	Paris St Germain	8	1		
1996-97	Arsenal	4	0		

1997-98	Arsenal	26	6		
1998-99	Arsenal	35	17	65	23
1999-2000	Real Madrid	19	2	19	2
2000-01	Paris St Germain	27	8		
2001-02	Paris St Germain	12	2	49	11
2001-02	Liverpool	20	4	20	4
2002-03	Manchester C	38	14		
2003-04	Manchester C	32	16		
2004-05	Manchester C	19	7	89	37
2004-05	Fenerbahce	14	4		
2005-06	Fenerbahce	25	10	39	14
2006-07	Bolton W	35	11		
2007-08	Bolton W	18	10	53	21
2007-08	Chelsea	14	1		
2008-09	Chelsea	37	19	51	20

BALLACK, Michael (M)   371 105
H: 6 2   W: 12 08   b.Gorlitz 26-9-76
Source: Motor Karl-Marx-Stadt.Germany
Under-21, 92 full caps, 41 goals.

1995-96	Chemnitzer	15	0		
1996-97	Chemnitzer	34	10	49	10
1997-98	Kaiserslautern A	17	8	17	8
1997-98	Kaiserslautern	16	0		
1998-99	Kaiserslautern	30	4	46	4
1999-2000	Leverkusen	23	3		
2000-01	Leverkusen	27	7		
2001-02	Leverkusen	29	17	79	27
2002-03	Bayern Munich	26	10		
2003-04	Bayern Munich	28	7		
2004-05	Bayern Munich	27	13		
2005-06	Bayern Munich	26	13	107	43
2006-07	Chelsea	26	5		
2007-08	Chelsea	18	7		
2008-09	Chelsea	29	1	73	13

BELLETTI, Juliano (D)   265 20
H: 5 9   W: 10 12   b.Casacvel 20-6-76
Honours: Brazil 23 full caps, 2 goals.

1994	Cruzeiro	5	0		
1995	Cruzeiro	17	0	22	0
1996	Sao Paulo	13	1		
1997	Sao Paulo	12	1		
1998	Sao Paulo	4	1		
1999	Atletico Mineiro	17	5	17	5
2000	Sao Paulo	11	0		
2001	Sao Paulo	14	1		
2002	Sao Paulo	0	0	54	4
2002-03	Villarreal	31	3		
2003-04	Villarreal	28	3	59	6
2004-05	Barcelona	31	0		
2005-06	Barcelona	26	0		
2006-07	Barcelona	13	0	70	0
2007-08	Chelsea	23	2		
2008-09	Chelsea	20	3	43	5

BERTRAND, Ryan (D)   82 0
H: 5 10   W: 11 00   b.Southwark 5-8-89
Source: Scholar. *Honours:* England Youth,
Under-21.

2006-07	Chelsea	0	0		
2006-07	Bournemouth	5	0	5	0
2007-08	Chelsea	0	0		
2007-08	Oldham Ath	21	0	21	0
2007-08	Norwich C	18	0		
2008-09	Chelsea	0	0		
2008-09	Norwich C	38	0	56	0

BORINI, Fabio (F)   0 0
H: 5 10   W: 11 02   b.Bentivoglio 23-3-91
Source: Scholar.

2008-09	Chelsea	0	0		

BOSINGWA, Jose (D)   193 5
H: 6 0   W: 12 08   b.Kinshasa 24-8-82
Honours: Portugal Under-21, 18 full caps.

2000-01	Freamunde	11	0	11	0
2001-02	Boavista	15	0		
2002-03	Boavista	26	0	41	0
2003-04	Porto	13	1		
2004-05	Porto	25	1		
2005-06	Porto	21	0		
2006-07	Porto	25	0		
2007-08	Porto	23	1	107	3
2008-09	Chelsea	34	2	34	2

BRIDCUTT, Liam (M)   15 0
H: 5 9   W: 11 07   b.Reading 8-5-89
Source: Scholar.

2007-08	Chelsea	0	0		
2007-08	Yeovil T	9	0	9	0
2008-09	Chelsea	0	0		
2008-09	Watford	6	0	6	0

CECH, Petr (G)   278 0
H: 6 5   W: 14 07   b.Plzen 20-5-82
Honours: Czech Republic Youth, Under-20,
Under-21, 67 full caps.

1998-99	Viktoria Plzen	0	0		
1999-2000	Chmel	1	0		
2000-01	Chmel	26	0	27	0
2001-02	Sparta Prague	26	0	26	0
2002-03	Rennes	37	0		
2003-04	Rennes	38	0	75	0
2004-05	Chelsea	35	0		
2005-06	Chelsea	34	0		
2006-07	Chelsea	20	0		
2007-08	Chelsea	26	0		
2008-09	Chelsea	35	0	150	0

CLIFFORD, Conor (M)   0 0
H: 5 8   W: 10 08   b.Dublin 1-10-91
Source: Scholar. *Honours:* Eire Youth.

2008-09	Chelsea	0	0		

COLE, Ashley (D)   254 11
H: 5 8   W: 10 05   b.Stepney 20-12-80
Source: Trainee. *Honours:* England Schools,
Youth, Under-21, B, 74 full caps.

1998-99	Arsenal	0	0		
1999-2000	Arsenal	1	0		
1999-2000	Crystal Palace	14	1	14	1
2000-01	Arsenal	17	3		
2001-02	Arsenal	29	2		
2002-03	Arsenal	31	1		
2003-04	Arsenal	32	0		
2004-05	Arsenal	35	2		
2005-06	Arsenal	11	0		
2006-07	Arsenal	0	0	156	8
2006-07	Chelsea	23	0		
2007-08	Chelsea	27	1		
2008-09	Chelsea	34	1	84	2

COLE, Joe (M)   283 35
H: 5 9   W: 11 09   b.Romford 8-11-81
Source: Trainee. *Honours:* England Schools,
Youth, Under-21, B, 53 full caps, 10 goals.

1998-99	West Ham U	8	0		
1999-2000	West Ham U	22	1		
2000-01	West Ham U	30	5		
2001-02	West Ham U	30	0		
2002-03	West Ham U	36	4	126	10
2003-04	Chelsea	35	1		
2004-05	Chelsea	28	8		
2005-06	Chelsea	34	7		
2006-07	Chelsea	13	0		
2007-08	Chelsea	33	7		
2008-09	Chelsea	14	2	157	25

CORK, Jack (D)   83 2
H: 6 0   W: 10 12   b.Carshalton 25-6-89
Source: Scholar. *Honours:* England Youth,
Under-21.

2006-07	Chelsea	0	0		
2006-07	Bournemouth	7	0	7	0
2007-08	Chelsea	0	0		
2007-08	Scunthorpe U	34	2	34	2
2008-09	Chelsea	0	0		
2008-09	Southampton	23	0	23	0
2008-09	Watford	19	0	19	0

CUMMINGS, Shaun (F)   32 0
H: 6 0   W: 11 10   b.Hammersmith 25-2-89

2007-08	Chelsea	0	0		
2008-09	Chelsea	0	0		
2008-09	Milton Keynes D	32	0	32	0

DECO (M)   325 63
H: 5 9   W: 11 07   b.Sao Paulo 27-8-77
Honours: Portugal 63 full caps, 5 goals.

1997-98	Alverca	32	13	32	13
1998-99	Salgueiros	9	2	9	2
1998-99	Porto	6	0		
1999-2000	Porto	23	1		
2000-01	Porto	31	6		
2001-02	Porto	30	13		
2002-03	Porto	30	10		
2003-04	Porto	28	2	148	32
2004-05	Barcelona	35	8		
2005-06	Barcelona	29	3		
2006-07	Barcelona	30	1		
2007-08	Barcelona	18	1	112	13
2008-09	Chelsea	24	3	24	3

DI SANTO, Franco (F)   63 13
H: 6 4   W: 13 01   b.Mendoza 7-4-89
Source: Audax Italiano. *Honours:* Argentina
Under-20.

2006	Audax Italiano	18	6		
2007	Audax Italiano	37	7	55	13
2007-08	Chelsea	0	0		
2008-09	Chelsea	8	0	8	0

DROGBA, Didier (F)   278 104
H: 6 2   W: 14 05   b.Abidjan 11-3-78
Honours: Ivory Coast 54 full caps, 35 goals.

1998-99	Le Mans	2	0		
1999-2000	Le Mans	30	6		
2000-01	Le Mans	11	0		
2001-02	Le Mans	21	5	64	11
2001-02	Guingamp	11	3		
2002-03	Guingamp	34	17	45	20
2003-04	Marseille	35	18	35	18
2004-05	Chelsea	26	10		
2005-06	Chelsea	29	12		
2006-07	Chelsea	36	20		
2007-08	Chelsea	19	8		
2008-09	Chelsea	24	5	134	55

ESSIEN, Michael (M)   239 29
H: 5 10   W: 13 06   b.Accra 3-12-82
Honours: Ghana 44 full caps, 8 goals.

2000-01	Bastia	13	1		
2001-02	Bastia	24	4		
2002-03	Bastia	29	6	66	11
2003-04	Lyon	34	3		
2004-05	Lyon	37	4	71	7
2005-06	Chelsea	31	2		
2006-07	Chelsea	33	2		
2007-08	Chelsea	27	6		
2008-09	Chelsea	11	1	102	11

FERNANDES, Ricardo (M)   0 0
b.Portugal 20-4-78
Source: Scholar.

2006-07	Chelsea	0	0		
2007-08	Chelsea	0	0		
2008-09	Chelsea	0	0		

FERREIRA, Fabio (M)   1 0
b.Barreiro 3-5-89
Source: Scholar. *Honours:* Portugal Youth.

2006-07	Chelsea	0	0		
2007-08	Chelsea	0	0		
2008-09	Chelsea	0	0		
2008-09	Morecambe	0	0		
2008-09	Oldham Ath	1	0	1	0

GORDON, Ben (D)   0 0
H: 5 11   W: 12 06   b.Bradford 2-3-91
Source: Scholar.

2008-09	Chelsea	0	0		

HILARIO (G)   170 0
H: 6 2   W: 13 05   b.San Pedro da Cova
21-10-75
Honours: Portugal Under-21, B.

1997-98	Porto	3	0		
1998-99	Amadora	27	0	27	0
1999-2000	Porto	19	0		
2000-01	Porto	0	0		
2001-02	Varzim	24	0	24	0
2002-03	Porto	0	0	22	0
2002-03	Academica	10	0	10	0
2003-04	Nacional	29	0		
2004-05	Nacional	32	0		
2005-06	Nacional	11	0	72	0
2006-07	Chelsea	11	0		
2007-08	Chelsea	3	0		
2008-09	Chelsea	1	0	15	0

HUTCHINSON, Sam (M)   1 0
H: 6 0   W: 11 07   b.Windsor 3-8-89
Source: Scholar. *Honours:* England Youth.

2006-07	Chelsea	1	0		
2007-08	Chelsea	0	0		
2008-09	Chelsea	0	0	1	0

IVANOVIC, Branislav (M)   144 12
H: 6 0   W: 12 04   b.Sremska Mitreovica
22-2-84
Honours: Serbia Under-21, 23 full caps, 4
goals.

2002-03	Sremska	19	2	19	2
2003-04	OFK Belgrade	13	0		
2004-05	OFK Belgrade	27	2		
2005-06	OFK Belgrade	15	3	55	5
2006	Lokomotiv Moscow	28	2		
2007	Lokomotiv Moscow	26	3	54	5

2007-08	Chelsea	0	0		
2008-09	Chelsea	16	0	16	0

KAKUTA, Gael (F)   0 0
H: 5 8 W: 10 03 b.Lille 21-6-91
Source: Scholar.

2008-09	Chelsea	0	0		

KALOU, Salomon (F)   168 60
H: 6 0 W: 12 02 b.Oume 5-8-85
Source: From Oume, ASEC Abidjan.
Honours: Ivory Coast 18 full caps, 10 goals.

2003-04	Excelsior	11	4	11	4
2003-04	Feyenoord	2	0		
2004-05	Feyenoord	31	20		
2005-06	Feyenoord	34	15	67	35
2006-07	Chelsea	33	7		
2007-08	Chelsea	30	7		
2008-09	Chelsea	27	7	90	21

LAMPARD, Frank (M)   441 108
H: 6 0 W: 14 02 b.Romford 20-6-78
Source: Trainee. *Honours:* England Youth,
Under-21, B, 71 full caps, 17 goals.

1994-95	West Ham U	0	0		
1995-96	West Ham U	2	0		
1995-96	*Swansea C*	9	1	9	1
1996-97	West Ham U	13	0		
1997-98	West Ham U	31	5		
1998-99	West Ham U	38	5		
1999-2000	West Ham U	34	7		
2000-01	West Ham U	30	7	148	24
2001-02	Chelsea	37	5		
2002-03	Chelsea	38	6		
2003-04	Chelsea	38	10		
2004-05	Chelsea	38	13		
2005-06	Chelsea	35	16		
2006-07	Chelsea	37	11		
2007-08	Chelsea	24	10		
2008-09	Chelsea	37	12	284	83

MAGNAY, Carl (D)   4 0
H: 6 0 W: 11 13 b.Durham 27-1-89

2006-07	Chelsea	0	0		
2007-08	Chelsea	0	0		
2008-09	Chelsea	0	0		
2008-09	*Milton Keynes D*	2	0	2	0
2008-09	*Northampton T*	2	0	2	0

MALOUDA, Florent (M)   341 53
H: 6 0 W: 11 06 b.Cayenne 13-6-80
Honours: France 45 full caps, 3 goals.

1996-97	Chateauroux	2	0		
1997-98	Chateauroux	1	0		
1998-99	Chateauroux	28	3		
1999-2000	Chateauroux	28	2	59	5
2000-01	Guingamp	23	1		
2001-02	Guingamp	32	4		
2002-03	Guingamp	37	10	92	15
2003-04	Lyon	35	4		
2004-05	Lyon	37	5		
2005-06	Lyon	31	6		
2006-07	Lyon	35	10	138	25
2007-08	Chelsea	21	2		
2008-09	Chelsea	31	6	52	8

MANCIENNE, Michael (D)   72 0
H: 6 0 W: 11 09 b.Isleworth 8-1-88
Source: Scholar. *Honours:* England Youth,
Under-21.

2005-06	Chelsea	0	0		
2006-07	Chelsea	0	0		
2006-07	*QPR*	28	0		
2007-08	Chelsea	0	0		
2007-08	*QPR*	30	0	58	0
2008-09	Chelsea	4	0	4	0
2008-09	*Wolverhampton W*	10	0	10	0

MELLIS, Jacob (D)   0 0
H: 6 0 W: 11 08 b.Nottingham 8-1-91
Source: Scholar. *Honours:* England Youth.

2008-09	Chelsea	0	0		

MIKEL, John Obi (M)   91 1
H: 6 0 W: 13 05 b.Plateau State 22-4-87
Source: Plateau U. *Honours:* Nigeria Youth,
25 full caps, 2 goals.

2005	Lyn	6	1	6	1
2006-07	Chelsea	22	0		
2007-08	Chelsea	29	0		
2008-09	Chelsea	34	0	85	0

MINEIRO (M)   301 18
H: 5 6 W: 10 05 b.Porto Alegre 2-8-75
Source: Rio Branco. *Honours:* Brazil 25 full
caps.

1997	Guarani	24	0		
1998	Guarani	0	0	24	0
1998	Ponte Preta	21	3		
1999	Ponte Preta	23	2		
2000	Ponte Preta	26	1		
2001	Ponte Preta	25	0		
2002	Ponte Preta	9	0		
2003	Ponte Preta	0	0	104	6
2003	Sao Caetano	38	0		
2004	Sao Caetano	41	3	79	3
2005	Sao Paulo	30	4		
2006	Sao Paulo	27	3	57	7
2006-07	Hertha Berlin	10	1		
2007-08	Hertha Berlin	26	1	36	2
2008-09	Chelsea	1	0	1	0

MODUBI, Michael (M)   0 0
b.Polokwane 22-4-85

2007-08	Chelsea	0	0		
2008-09	Chelsea	0	0		

NIELSEN, Morten (F)   0 0
H: 6 3 W: 13 12 b.Copenhagen 24-2-90
Source: Scholar.

2007-08	Chelsea	0	0		
2008-09	Chelsea	0	0		

NTUKA, Pule (M)   0 0
b.South Africa 10-5-85
Source: Westerlo.

2007-08	Chelsea	0	0		
2008-09	Chelsea	0	0		

OFORI-TWUMASI, Nana (D)   0 0
H: 5 8 W: 11 09 b.Accra 15-5-90
Source: Scholar.

2007-08	Chelsea	0	0		
2008-09	Chelsea	0	0		

PAIM, Fabio (F)   0 0
b.Portugal 15-2-88
On loan from Sporting Lisbon.

2008-09	Chelsea	0	0		

PAULO FERREIRA (D)   264 4
H: 6 0 W: 11 13 b.Cascais 18-1-79
Honours: Portugal Under-21, 55 full caps.

1997-98	Estoril	1	0		
1998-99	Estoril	16	0		
1999-2000	Estoril	18	2	35	2
2000-01	Vitoria Setubal	34	2		
2001-02	Vitoria Setubal	34	0	68	2
2002-03	Porto	30	0		
2003-04	Porto	32	0	62	0
2004-05	Chelsea	29	0		
2005-06	Chelsea	21	0		
2006-07	Chelsea	24	0		
2007-08	Chelsea	18	0		
2008-09	Chelsea	7	0	99	0

PHILLISKIRK, Daniel (M)   0 0
b.Oldham 10-4-91
Source: Scholar.

2008-09	Chelsea	0	0		

PIZARRO, Claudio (F)   336 138
H: 6 0 W: 12 06 b.Lima 3-10-78
Honours: Peru 53 full caps, 13 goals.

1995-96	Dep Pesquero	25	8		
1996-97	Dep Pesquero	16	3	41	11
1997-98	Alianza	22	7		
1998-99	Alianza	22	18	44	25
1999-2000	Werder Bremen	25	10		
2000-01	Werder Bremen	31	19	56	29
2001-02	Bayern Munich	30	15		
2002-03	Bayern Munich	31	15		
2003-04	Bayern Munich	31	11		
2004-05	Bayern Munich	23	11		
2005-06	Bayern Munich	26	11		
2006-07	Bayern Munich	33	8	174	71
2007-08	Chelsea	21	2		
2008-09	Chelsea	0	0	21	2

QUARESMA, Ricardo (M)   212 34
H: 5 8 W: 11 09 b.Lisbon 29-9-83
Honours: Portugal Youth, Under-21, 25 full
caps, 3 goals.

2001-02	Sporting Lisbon	28	3		
2002-03	Sporting Lisbon	31	5	59	8
2003-04	Barcelona	22	1	22	1
2004-05	Porto	32	5		

2005-06	Porto	29	5		
2006-07	Porto	26	6		
2007-08	Porto	27	8	114	24
2008-09	Internazionale	13	1	13	1
2008-09	Chelsea	4	0	4	0

RAJKOVIC, Slobodan (D)   83 2
H: 6 5 W: 14 00 b.Belgrade 3-3-89
Honours: Serbia Under-21, 2 full caps.

2004-05	OFK Belgrade	26	1		
2005-06	Chelsea	0	0		
2005-06	*OFK Belgrade*	25	0		
2006-07	Chelsea	0	0		
2006-07	*OFK Belgrade*	11	0	62	1
2007-08	Chelsea	0	0		
2007-08	*PSV Eindhoven*	13	0	13	0
2008-09	Chelsea	0	0		
2008-09	*Twente*	8	1	8	1

RICARDO CARVALHO (D)   261 14
H: 6 0 W: 12 04 b.Amarante 18-5-78
Honours: Portugal Under-21, 53 full caps, 4
goals.

1996-97	Leca	0	0		
1997-98	Leca	22	1	22	1
1998-99	Porto	1	0		
1999-2000	Vitoria Setubal	25	2	25	2
2000-01	Alverca	29	1	29	1
2001-02	Porto	25	0		
2002-03	Porto	17	1		
2003-04	Porto	29	2	72	3
2004-05	Chelsea	25	1		
2005-06	Chelsea	24	1		
2006-07	Chelsea	31	3		
2007-08	Chelsea	21	1		
2008-09	Chelsea	12	1	113	7

SAHAR, Ben (F)   24 3
H: 5 10 W: 12 05 b.Holon 10-8-89
Honours: Israel Under-21, 7 full caps, 2 goals.

2006-07	Chelsea	3	0		
2007-08	Chelsea	0	0		
2007-08	*QPR*	9	0	9	0
2007-08	*Sheffield W*	12	3	12	3
2008-09	Chelsea	0	0	3	0
2008-09	*Portsmouth*	3	0		

SARKI, Emmanuel (M)   7 0
b.Nigeria 26-12-87

2005-06	Chelsea	0	0		
2005-06	*Westerlo*	7	0	7	0
2006-07	Chelsea	0	0		
2007-08	Chelsea	0	0		
2008-09	Chelsea	0	0		

SAWYER, Lee (M)   23 2
H: 5 10 W: 10 03 b.Leytonstone 10-9-89
Source: Scholar. *Honours:* England Youth.

2007-08	Chelsea	0	0		
2008-09	Chelsea	0	0		
2008-09	*Southend U*	12	1	12	1
2008-09	*Coventry C*	2	0	2	0
2008-09	*Wycombe W*	9	1	9	1

SHEVCHENKO, Andriy (F)   373 196
H: 6 0 W: 11 05 b.Dvirkivshchyna 29-9-76
Honours: Ukraine Youth, Under-21, 81 full
caps, 37 goals.

1994-95	Dynamo Kiev	16	1		
1995-96	Dynamo Kiev	31	16		
1996-97	Dynamo Kiev	20	6		
1997-98	Dynamo Kiev	23	19		
1998-99	Dynamo Kiev	28	18	118	60
1999-2000	AC Milan	32	24		
2000-01	AC Milan	34	24		
2001-02	AC Milan	29	14		
2002-03	AC Milan	24	5		
2003-04	AC Milan	32	24		
2004-05	AC Milan	29	17		
2005-06	AC Milan	28	19	208	127
2006-07	Chelsea	30	4		
2007-08	Chelsea	17	5		
2008-09	Chelsea	0	0	47	9
On loan to AC Milan August 2008					

SINCLAIR, Scott (F)   54 5
H: 5 10 W: 10 00 b.Bath 26-3-89
Source: Bristol R Schoolboy, England Youth.

2004-05	Bristol R	2	0	2	0
2005-06	Chelsea	0	0		
2006-07	Chelsea	2	0		
2006-07	*Plymouth Arg*	15	2	15	2
2007-08	Chelsea	1	0		
2007-08	*QPR*	9	1	9	1

2007-08	Charlton Ath	3	0	3	0
2007-08	Crystal Palace	6	2	6	2
2008-09	Chelsea	2	0	5	0
2008-09	Birmingham C	14	0	14	0

SMITH, Jimmy (M) 67 6
H: 6 0　W: 10 03　b.Newham 7-1-87
Source: Scholar. Honours: England Youth.

2004-05	Chelsea	0	0		
2005-06	Chelsea	1	0		
2006-07	Chelsea	0	0		
2006-07	QPR	29	6	29	6
2007-08	Chelsea	0	0		
2007-08	Norwich C	9	0	9	0
2008-09	Chelsea	0	0	1	0
2008-09	Sheffield W	12	0	12	0
2008-09	Leyton Orient	16	0	16	0

STOCH, Miroslav (F) 4 0
H: 5 6　W: 10 01　b.Nitra 19-10-89
Source: Scholar. Honours: Slovakia 4 full caps, 1 goal.

| 2007-08 | Chelsea | 0 | 0 | | |
| 2008-09 | Chelsea | 4 | 0 | 4 | 0 |

TAIWO, Tom (M) 4 0
H: 5 8　W: 10 07　b.Leeds 27-2-90
Source: Scholar.

2007-08	Chelsea	0	0		
2008-09	Chelsea	0	0		
2008-09	Port Vale	4	0	4	0

TAYLOR, Rhys (G) 0 0
H: 6 2　W: 12 08　b.Neath 7-4-90
Honours: Wales Under-21.

| 2007-08 | Chelsea | 0 | 0 | | |
| 2008-09 | Chelsea | 0 | 0 | | |

TEJERA RODRIQUEZ, Sergio (M) 0 0
H: 5 11　W: 10 10　b.Barcelona 28-5-90
Source: Scholar.

| 2007-08 | Chelsea | 0 | 0 | | |
| 2008-09 | Chelsea | 0 | 0 | | |

TERRY, John (D) 278 17
H: 6 1　W: 14 02　b.Barking 7-12-80
Source: From Trainee. Honours: England Under-21, 53 full caps, 6 goals.

1997-98	Chelsea	0	0		
1998-99	Chelsea	2	0		
1999-2000	Chelsea	0	0		
1999-2000	Nottingham F	6	0	6	0
2000-01	Chelsea	22	1		
2001-02	Chelsea	33	1		
2002-03	Chelsea	20	3		
2003-04	Chelsea	33	2		
2004-05	Chelsea	36	3		
2005-06	Chelsea	36	4		
2006-07	Chelsea	28	1		
2007-08	Chelsea	23	1		
2008-09	Chelsea	35	1	272	17

TORE, Gokhan (M) 0 0
H: 5 9　W: 11 09　b.Cologne 20-1-92
Source: Leverkusen.

| 2008-09 | Chelsea | 0 | 0 | | |

VAN AANHOLT, Patrick (D) 0 0
H: 5 9　W: 10 08　b.S'Hertogenbosch 3-7-88

| 2007-08 | Chelsea | 0 | 0 | | |
| 2008-09 | Chelsea | 0 | 0 | | |

WOODS, Michael (M) 0 0
H: 6 0　W: 12 07　b.York 6-4-90
Source: Scholar. Honours: England Youth. Scotland B.

2006-07	Chelsea	0	0		
2007-08	Chelsea	0	0		
2008-09	Chelsea	0	0		

Scholars
Ahamed, Nikki; Djalo, Aliu; Haxhia, Aldi; Hayden, Thomas William; Heimann, Niclas; Mitrovic, Marko; Nouble, Frank Herman; Phillip, Adam; Sala, Jacopo; Sebek, Jan; Van, Homoet Bruma Jeffrey Kevin; Walker, Samuel Colin.

CHELTENHAM T (23)

ARMSTRONG, Craig (M) 349 9
H: 5 11　W: 12 09　b.South Shields 23-5-75
Source: Trainee.

| 1992-93 | Nottingham F | 0 | 0 | | |

1993-94	Nottingham F	0	0		
1994-95	Nottingham F	0	0		
1994-95	Burnley	4	0	4	0
1995-96	Nottingham F	0	0		
1995-96	Bristol R	14	0	14	0
1996-97	Nottingham F	0	0		
1996-97	Gillingham	10	0		
1996-97	Watford	15	0	15	0
1997-98	Nottingham F	18	0		
1998-99	Nottingham F	22	0	40	0
1998-99	Huddersfield T	13	1		
1999-2000	Huddersfield T	39	0		
2000-01	Huddersfield T	44	3		
2001-02	Huddersfield T	11	1	107	5
2001-02	Sheffield W	8	0		
2002-03	Sheffield W	17	1		
2003-04	Sheffield W	10	0		
2003-04	Grimsby T	9	1	9	1
2004-05	Sheffield W	0	0	35	1
2004-05	Bradford C	7	0	7	0
2005-06	Cheltenham T	34	2		
2006-07	Cheltenham T	42	0		
2007-08	Gillingham	13	0	23	0
2007-08	Cheltenham T	14	0		
2008-09	Cheltenham T	5	0	95	2

BIRD, David (M) 212 8
H: 5 9　W: 12 00　b.Gloucester 26-12-84
Source: Cinderford T.

2001-02	Cheltenham T	0	0		
2002-03	Cheltenham T	14	0		
2003-04	Cheltenham T	24	0		
2004-05	Cheltenham T	34	0		
2005-06	Cheltenham T	36	1		
2006-07	Cheltenham T	31	2		
2007-08	Cheltenham T	46	4		
2008-09	Cheltenham T	27	1	212	8

BROWN, Scott P (G) 47 0
H: 6 2　W: 13 01　b.Wolverhampton 26-4-85
Source: Wolverhampton W Trainee. From Welshpool T

2003-04	Bristol C	0	0		
2004-05	Cheltenham T	0	0		
2005-06	Cheltenham T	1	0		
2006-07	Cheltenham T	11	0		
2007-08	Cheltenham T	0	0		
2008-09	Cheltenham T	35	0	47	0

CAINES, Gavin (D) 143 7
H: 6 1　W: 12 00　b.Birmingham 20-9-83
Source: Scholar.

2003-04	Walsall	0	0		
2004-05	Cheltenham T	29	2		
2005-06	Cheltenham T	39	2		
2006-07	Cheltenham T	39	0		
2007-08	Cheltenham T	28	2		
2008-09	Cheltenham T	8	1	143	7

CONNOLLY, Adam (M) 32 1
H: 5 9　W: 12 04　b.Manchester 10-4-86
Source: Scholar.

2004-05	Cheltenham T	4	0		
2005-06	Cheltenham T	5	1		
2006-07	Cheltenham T	8	0		
2007-08	Cheltenham T	15	0		
2008-09	Cheltenham T	0	0	32	1

CONNOR, Paul (F) 326 70
H: 6 2　W: 11 08　b.Bishop Auckland 12-1-79
Source: Trainee.

1996-97	Middlesbrough	0	0		
1997-98	Middlesbrough	0	0		
1997-98	Hartlepool U	5	0	5	0
1998-99	Middlesbrough	0	0		
1998-99	Stoke C	3	2		
1999-2000	Stoke C	26	5		
2000-01	Stoke C	7	0	36	7
2000-01	Cambridge U	13	5	13	5
2000-01	Rochdale	14	10		
2001-02	Rochdale	17	1		
2002-03	Rochdale	39	12		
2003-04	Rochdale	24	5	94	28
2003-04	Swansea C	12	5		
2004-05	Swansea C	40	10		
2005-06	Swansea C	13	1	65	16
2005-06	Leyton Orient	16	5		
2006-07	Leyton Orient	18	2	34	7
2007-08	Cheltenham T	15	1		
2008-09	Cheltenham T	25	2	79	7

DIALLO, Drissa (D) 167 5
H: 6 1　W: 11 13　b.Nouadhibou 4-1-73
Honours: Guinea full caps.

2002-03	Burnley	14	1	14	1
2003-04	Ipswich T	19	0		
2004-05	Ipswich T	26	0	45	0
2005-06	Sheffield W	11	0	11	0
2006-07	Milton Keynes D	40	0		
2007-08	Milton Keynes D	30	2		
2008-09	Milton Keynes D	0	0	70	2
2008-09	Cheltenham T	27	2	27	2

DUFF, Shane (D) 182 2
H: 6 1　W: 12 10　b.Wroughton 2-4-82
Source: Juniors. Honours: Northern Ireland Under-21.

2000-01	Cheltenham T	0	0		
2001-02	Cheltenham T	0	0		
2002-03	Cheltenham T	18	0		
2003-04	Cheltenham T	15	1		
2004-05	Cheltenham T	45	1		
2005-06	Cheltenham T	20	0		
2006-07	Cheltenham T	34	0		
2007-08	Cheltenham T	30	0		
2008-09	Cheltenham T	20	0	182	2

DURRANT, Jack (D) 4 0
H: 6 0　W: 11 03　b.Bristol 6-5-91
Source: Scholar.

| 2008-09 | Cheltenham T | 4 | 0 | 4 | 0 |

EMERY, Josh (M) 1 0
H: 5 6　W: 10 10　b.Ledbury 30-9-90
Source: Scholar.

| 2008-09 | Cheltenham T | 1 | 0 | 1 | 0 |

FINNIGAN, John (M) 363 23
H: 5 8　W: 10 09　b.Wakefield 29-3-76
Source: Trainee.

1992-93	Nottingham F	0	0		
1993-94	Nottingham F	0	0		
1994-95	Nottingham F	0	0		
1995-96	Nottingham F	0	0		
1996-97	Nottingham F	0	0		
1997-98	Nottingham F	0	0		
1997-98	Lincoln C	6	0		
1998-99	Lincoln C	37	1		
1999-2000	Lincoln C	37	2		
2000-01	Lincoln C	40	0		
2001-02	Lincoln C	23	0	143	3
2001-02	Cheltenham T	12	2		
2002-03	Cheltenham T	37	1		
2003-04	Cheltenham T	33	1		
2004-05	Cheltenham T	32	3		
2005-06	Cheltenham T	39	4		
2006-07	Cheltenham T	40	7		
2007-08	Cheltenham T	10	1		
2008-09	Cheltenham T	17	1	220	20

GALLINAGH, Andy (D) 67 1
H: 5 8　W: 11 08　b.Sutton Coldfield 16-3-85
Source: Stratford T.

2004-05	Cheltenham T	0	0		
2005-06	Cheltenham T	1	0		
2006-07	Cheltenham T	1	0		
2007-08	Cheltenham T	26	0		
2008-09	Cheltenham T	39	1	67	1

GILL, Ben (M) 7 1
H: 5 9　W: 10 11　b.Harrow 9-10-87
Source: Scholar.

2005-06	Watford	0	0		
2006-07	Watford	0	0		
2007-08	Cheltenham T	2	0		
2008-09	Cheltenham T	5	1	7	1

GILL, Jerry (D) 282 0
H: 5 11　W: 12 00　b.Clevedon 8-9-70
Source: Yeovil T.

1997-98	Birmingham C	3	0		
1998-99	Birmingham C	3	0		
1999-2000	Birmingham C	11	0		
2000-01	Birmingham C	29	0		
2001-02	Birmingham C	14	0		
2002-03	Birmingham C	0	0	60	0
2002-03	Northampton T	41	0		
2003-04	Northampton T	0	0	41	0
2003-04	Cheltenham T	7	0		
2004-05	Cheltenham T	44	0		
2005-06	Cheltenham T	42	0		
2006-07	Cheltenham T	39	0		
2007-08	Cheltenham T	43	0		
2008-09	Cheltenham T	6	0	181	0

HAMMOND, Elvis (F) 122 15
H: 5 10 W: 11 02 b.Accra 6-10-80
Source: Trainee. *Honours:* Ghana 1 full cap.

1999-2000	Fulham	0	0		
2000-01	Fulham	0	0		
2001-02	Fulham	0	0		
2001-02	*Bristol R*	7	0	7	0
2002-03	Fulham	10	0		
2003-04	Fulham	0	0		
2003-04	*Norwich C*	4	0	4	0
2004-05	Fulham	0	0		
2004-05	RBC Roosendaal	14	2	14	2
2005-06	Fulham	0	0	11	0
2005-06	Leicester C	33	3		
2006-07	Leicester C	31	5		
2007-08	Leicester C	0	0	64	8
2008-09	Cheltenham T	22	5	22	5

HAYNES, Kyle (D) 4 0
H: 5 11 W: 11 02 b.Wolverhampton 29-12-91
Source: Scholar.

2008-09	Cheltenham T	4	0	4	0

HIGGS, Shane (G) 247 0
H: 6 3 W: 14 06 b.Oxford 13-5-77
Source: Trainee.

1994-95	Bristol R	0	0		
1995-96	Bristol R	0	0		
1996-97	Bristol R	2	0		
1997-98	Bristol R	8	0	10	0
From Worcester C.					
1999-2000	Cheltenham T	0	0		
2000-01	Cheltenham T	1	0		
2001-02	Cheltenham T	1	0		
2002-03	Cheltenham T	10	0		
2003-04	Cheltenham T	42	0		
2004-05	Cheltenham T	46	0		
2005-06	Cheltenham T	45	0		
2006-07	Cheltenham T	36	0		
2007-08	Cheltenham T	46	0		
2008-09	Cheltenham T	10	0	237	0
2008-09	*Wolverhampton W*	0	0		

LEDGISTER, Aaron (M) 1 0
H: 5 10 W: 11 07 b.Hong Kong 15-11-88
Source: Bristol C.

2007-08	Cheltenham T	0	0		
2008-09	Cheltenham T	1	0	1	0

LEE, Jake (F) 3 0
H: 6 0 W: 12 07 b.Cirencester 18-9-91

2008-09	Cheltenham T	3	0	3	0

LEWIS, Theo (F) 2 0
H: 5 10 W: 10 12 b.Oxford 10-8-91
Source: Scholar.

2008-09	Cheltenham T	2	0	2	0

LINDEGAARD, Andy (M) 151 6
H: 5 8 W: 11 04 b.Taunton 10-9-80
Source: Westland Sp.

2003-04	Yeovil T	23	2		
2004-05	Yeovil T	29	1		
2005-06	Yeovil T	23	0		
2006-07	Yeovil T	14	0	89	3
2007-08	Cheltenham T	41	2		
2008-09	Cheltenham T	15	0	56	2
2008-09	*Aldershot T*	6	1	6	1

LOW, Josh (M) 289 28
H: 6 2 W: 14 03 b.Bristol 15-2-79
Source: Trainee. *Honours:* Wales Youth, Under-21.

1995-96	Bristol R	1	0		
1996-97	Bristol R	3	0		
1997-98	Bristol R	10	0		
1998-99	Bristol R	8	0	22	0
1999-2000	Leyton Orient	5	1	5	1
1999-2000	Cardiff C	17	2		
2000-01	Cardiff C	36	4		
2001-02	Cardiff C	22	0		
2002-03	Cardiff C	0	0	75	6
2002-03	Oldham Ath	21	3	21	3
2003-04	Northampton T	33	3		
2004-05	Northampton T	34	7		
2005-06	Northampton T	35	5	102	15
2006-07	Leicester C	16	0	16	0
2006-07	Peterborough U	19	1		
2007-08	Peterborough U	15	2		
2008-09	Peterborough U	0	0	34	3
2008-09	Cheltenham T	14	0	14	0

OWUSU, Lloyd (F) 389 119
H: 6 2 W: 14 00 b.Slough 12-12-76
Source: Slough T. *Honours:* Ghana 2 full caps.

1998-99	Brentford	46	22		
1999-2000	Brentford	41	12		
2000-01	Brentford	33	10		
2001-02	Brentford	44	20		
2002-03	Sheffield W	32	4		
2003-04	Sheffield W	20	5	52	9
2003-04	Reading	16	4		
2004-05	Reading	25	6	41	10
2005-06	Brentford	42	12		
2006-07	Brentford	7	0	213	76
2007-08	Yeovil T	43	9		
2008-09	Yeovil T	4	1	47	10
2008-09	Cheltenham T	22	7	22	7
2008-09	*Brighton & HA*	14	7	14	7

PUDDY, Will (G) 1 0
H: 5 10 W: 11 07 b.Warminster 4-10-87
Source: Scholar.

2005-06	Cheltenham T	0	0		
2006-07	Cheltenham T	0	0		
2007-08	Cheltenham T	0	0		
2008-09	Cheltenham T	1	0	1	0

RIDLEY, Lee (D) 156 2
H: 5 9 W: 11 11 b.Scunthorpe 5-12-81
Source: Scholar.

2000-01	Scunthorpe U	2	0		
2001-02	Scunthorpe U	4	0		
2002-03	Scunthorpe U	11	0		
2003-04	Scunthorpe U	18	1		
2004-05	Scunthorpe U	44	0		
2005-06	Scunthorpe U	3	1		
2006-07	Scunthorpe U	18	0	100	2
2007-08	Cheltenham T	8	0		
2007-08	*Darlington*	6	0	6	0
2007-08	*Lincoln C*	15	0	15	0
2008-09	Cheltenham T	27	0	35	0

RUSSELL, Alex (M) 448 52
H: 5 10 W: 11 07 b.Crosby 17-3-73
Source: Burscough.

1994-95	Rochdale	7	1		
1995-96	Rochdale	25	0		
1996-97	Rochdale	39	9		
1997-98	Rochdale	31	4	102	14
1998-99	Cambridge U	37	6		
1999-2000	Cambridge U	15	0		
2000-01	Cambridge U	29	2	81	8
2001-02	Torquay U	33	7		
2002-03	Torquay U	39	9		
2003-04	Torquay U	43	2		
2004-05	Torquay U	38	3	153	21
2005-06	Bristol C	27	4		
2006-07	Bristol C	28	2		
2007-08	Bristol C	1	0	56	6
2007-08	*Northampton T*	13	1	13	1
2008-09	*Cheltenham T*	23	0	36	2
2008-09	*Exeter C*	7	0	7	0

SPENCER, Damien (F) 248 37
H: 6 1 W: 14 00 b.Ascot 19-9-81
Source: Scholarship.

1999-2000	Bristol C	9	1		
2000-01	Bristol C	4	0		
2000-01	*Exeter C*	6	0	6	0
2001-02	Bristol C	0	0	13	1
2002-03	Cheltenham T	30	6		
2003-04	Cheltenham T	36	9		
2004-05	Cheltenham T	41	8		
2005-06	Cheltenham T	46	3		
2006-07	Cheltenham T	27	3		
2007-08	Cheltenham T	30	3		
2008-09	Cheltenham T	14	3	224	35
2008-09	*Brentford*	5	1	5	1

TOWNSEND, Michael (D) 113 3
H: 6 1 W: 13 12 b.Walsall 17-5-86
Source: Wolverhampton W scholar.

2004-05	Cheltenham T	0	0		
2005-06	Cheltenham T	31	0		
2006-07	Cheltenham T	30	1		
2007-08	Cheltenham T	13	1		
2008-09	Cheltenham T	26	1	100	3
2008-09	*Barnet*	13	0	13	0

WATKINS, Marley (M) 12 0
H: 5 10 W: 10 04 b.London 17-10-90
Source: Scholar.

2008-09	Cheltenham T	12	0	12	0

WESTLAKE, Ian (M) 199 20
H: 5 10 W: 11 06 b.Clacton 10-7-83
Source: Scholar.

2002-03	Ipswich T	4	0		
2003-04	Ipswich T	39	6		
2004-05	Ipswich T	45	7		
2005-06	Ipswich T	26	2	114	15
2006-07	Leeds U	27	0		
2007-08	Leeds U	20	1		
2007-08	*Brighton & HA*	11	2	11	2
2008-09	Leeds U	0	0	47	1
2008-09	Cheltenham T	22	2	22	2
2008-09	*Oldham Ath*	5	0	5	0

WRIGHT, Alan (D) 559 8
H: 5 4 W: 9 09 b.Ashton-under-Lyme 28-9-71
Source: Trainee. *Honours:* England Schools, Youth, Under-21.

1987-88	Blackpool	1	0		
1988-89	Blackpool	16	0		
1989-90	Blackpool	24	0		
1990-91	Blackpool	45	0		
1991-92	Blackpool	12	0	98	0
1991-92	Blackburn R	33	1		
1992-93	Blackburn R	24	0		
1993-94	Blackburn R	12	0		
1994-95	Blackburn R	5	0	74	1
1994-95	Aston Villa	8	0		
1995-96	Aston Villa	38	2		
1996-97	Aston Villa	38	1		
1997-98	Aston Villa	37	0		
1998-99	Aston Villa	38	0		
1999-2000	Aston Villa	32	1		
2000-01	Aston Villa	36	1		
2001-02	Aston Villa	23	0		
2002-03	Aston Villa	10	0	260	5
2003-04	Middlesbrough	2	0	2	0
2003-04	Sheffield U	21	1		
2004-05	Sheffield U	14	0		
2005-06	Sheffield U	6	0		
2005-06	*Derby Co*	7	0	7	0
2006-07	Sheffield U	1	0		
2006-07	*Leeds U*	1	0	1	0
2006-07	*Cardiff C*	7	0	7	0
2006-07	*Doncaster R*	3	0	3	0
2006-07	*Nottingham F*	9	0	9	0
2007-08	Sheffield U	0	0	42	1
2007-08	Cheltenham T	33	1		
2008-09	Cheltenham T	23	0	56	1

CHESTER C (24)

ALLISON, Wayne (F) 752 171
H: 6 0 W: 14 13 b.Huddersfield 16-10-68
Source: Trainee.

1986-87	Halifax T	8	4		
1987-88	Halifax T	35	4		
1988-89	Halifax T	41	15	84	23
1989-90	Watford	7	0	7	0
1990-91	Bristol C	37	6		
1991-92	Bristol C	43	10		
1992-93	Bristol C	39	4		
1993-94	Bristol C	39	15		
1994-95	Bristol C	37	13	195	48
1995-96	Swindon T	44	17		
1996-97	Swindon T	41	11		
1997-98	Swindon T	16	3	101	31
1997-98	Huddersfield T	27	6		
1998-99	Huddersfield T	44	9		
1999-2000	Huddersfield T	3	0	74	15
1999-2000	Tranmere R	40	16		
2000-01	Tranmere R	36	6		
2001-02	Tranmere R	27	4	103	26
2002-03	Sheffield U	34	6		
2003-04	Sheffield U	39	1	73	7
2004-05	Chesterfield	38	6		
2005-06	Chesterfield	32	11		
2006-07	Chesterfield	36	4		
2007-08	Chesterfield	9	0	115	21
2008-09	Chester C	0	0		

BARRY, Anthony (M) 107 1
H: 5 7 W: 10 00 b.Liverpool 29-5-86
Source: Everton.

2004-05	Coventry C	0	0		
From Accrington S.					
2005-06	Yeovil T	4	0		
2006-07	Yeovil T	24	0		
2007-08	Yeovil T	36	0	64	0
2008-09	Chester C	43	1	43	1

BUTLER, Paul (D)   **597 26**
H: 6 2 W: 13 00 b.Manchester 2-11-72
Source: Trainee. *Honours:* Eire B, 1 full cap.

1990-91	Rochdale	2	0	
1991-92	Rochdale	25	0	
1992-93	Rochdale	16	2	
1993-94	Rochdale	38	2	
1994-95	Rochdale	39	3	
1995-96	Rochdale	38	3	**158 10**
1996-97	Bury	41	2	
1997-98	Bury	43	2	**84 4**
1998-99	Sunderland	44	2	
1999-2000	Sunderland	32	1	
2000-01	Sunderland	3	0	**79 3**
2000-01	Wolverhampton W	12	0	
2001-02	Wolverhampton W	43	1	
2002-03	Wolverhampton W	32	1	
2003-04	Wolverhampton W	37	1	**124 3**
2004-05	Leeds U	39	0	
2005-06	Leeds U	44	3	
2006-07	Leeds U	16	1	**99 4**
2006-07	*Milton Keynes D*	17	0	**17 0**
2007-08	Chester C	35	2	
2008-09	Chester C	1	0	**36 2**

DANBY, John (G)   **181 0**
H: 6 2 W: 14 06 b.Stoke 20-9-83
Source: Juniors.

2001-02	Kidderminster H	2	0	
2002-03	Kidderminster H	0	0	
2003-04	Kidderminster H	9	0	
2004-05	Kidderminster H	37	0	
2005-06	Kidderminster H	0	0	**48 0**
2006-07	Chester C	46	0	
2007-08	Chester C	46	0	
2008-09	Chester C	41	0	**133 0**

DINNING, Tony (M)   **454 55**
H: 6 0 W: 13 05 b.Wallsend 12-4-75
Source: Trainee.

1993-94	Newcastle U	0	0	
1994-95	Stockport Co	40	1	
1995-96	Stockport Co	10	1	
1996-97	Stockport Co	20	2	
1997-98	Stockport Co	30	4	
1998-99	Stockport Co	41	5	
1999-2000	Stockport Co	44	12	
2000-01	Stockport Co	6	0	
2000-01	Wolverhampton W	31	6	
2001-02	Wolverhampton W	4	0	**35 6**
2001-02	Wigan Ath	33	5	
2001-02	*Stoke C*	5	0	**5 0**
2002-03	Wigan Ath	38	7	
2003-04	Wigan Ath	13	0	
2003-04	*Walsall*	5	0	**5 0**
2003-04	*Blackpool*	10	3	**10 3**
2004-05	Wigan Ath	0	0	**84 12**
2004-05	*Ipswich T*	7	0	**7 0**
2004-05	*Bristol C*	19	0	**19 0**
2004-05	Port Vale	7	3	
2005-06	Port Vale	35	2	**42 5**
2006-07	Stockport Co	32	2	
2007-08	Stockport Co	0	0	**223 27**
2007-08	Chester C	20	2	
2008-09	Chester C	4	0	**24 2**

ELLAMS, Lloyd (F)   **4 1**
H: 6 2 W: 12 00 b.Chester 11-1-91
Source: Scholar.

2008-09	Chester C	4	1	**4 1**

HARRIS, Jay (M)   **104 2**
H: 5 7 W: 11 06 b.Liverpool 15-4-87

2005-06	Everton	0	0	
2005-06	Everton	0	0	
2006-07	Accrington S	32	2	
2007-08	Accrington S	41	0	**73 2**
2008-09	Chester C	31	0	**31 0**

JOHNSON, Eddie (F)   **122 18**
H: 5 10 W: 13 05 b.Chester 20-9-84
Source: Scholar. *Honours:* England Youth, Under-20.

2001-02	Manchester U	0	0	
2002-03	Manchester U	0	0	
2003-04	Manchester U	0	0	
2004-05	Manchester U	0	0	
2004-05	*Coventry C*	26	5	**26 5**
2005-06	Manchester U	0	0	
2005-06	*Crewe Alex*	22	5	**22 5**
2006-07	Bradford C	32	3	
2007-08	Bradford C	32	4	
2008-09	Bradford C	0	0	**64 7**
2008-09	Chester C	10	1	**10 1**

JONES, Ben (F)   **15 0**
H: 6 0 W: 12 00 b.Deeside 11-9-92

2008-09	Chester C	15	0	**15 0**

KELLY, Shaun (D)   **39 1**
H: 6 1 W: 11 04 b.Southampton 4-7-86
Source: Scholar.

2006-07	Chester C	2	0	
2007-08	Chester C	10	0	
2008-09	Chester C	27	1	**39 1**

LINWOOD, Paul (D)   **175 4**
H: 6 2 W: 13 03 b.Birkenhead 24-10-83
Source: Scholar.

2001-02	Tranmere R	0	0	
2002-03	Tranmere R	0	0	
2003-04	Tranmere R	20	0	
2004-05	Tranmere R	10	0	
2005-06	Tranmere R	14	0	**44 0**
2005-06	*Wrexham*	9	0	**9 0**
2006-07	Chester C	37	1	
2007-08	Chester C	42	1	
2008-09	Chester C	43	2	**122 4**

LOWE, Ryan (F)   **290 65**
H: 5 10 W: 12 08 b.Liverpool 18-9-78
Source: Burscough.

2000-01	Shrewsbury T	30	4	
2001-02	Shrewsbury T	38	7	
2002-03	Shrewsbury T	39	9	
2003-04	Shrewsbury T	0	0	
2004-05	Shrewsbury T	30	3	**137 23**
2004-05	Chester C	8	4	
2005-06	Chester C	32	10	
2005-06	Crewe Alex	37	8	
2006-07	Crewe Alex	37	8	
2007-08	Crewe Alex	27	4	**64 12**
2007-08	*Stockport Co*	0	0	
2008-09	Chester C	45	16	**85 30**

MANNIX, David (M)   **26 2**
H: 5 8 W: 11 06 b.Winsford 24-9-85
Source: Trainee. *Honours:* England Under-20.

2003-04	Liverpool	0	0	
2004-05	Liverpool	0	0	
2005-06	Liverpool	0	0	
2006-07	Liverpool	0	0	
2006-07	*Accrington S*	1	0	
2007-08	Liverpool	0	0	
2007-08	Accrington S	12	0	**13 0**
2008-09	Chester C	13	2	**13 2**

McMANUS, Paul (F)   **28 3**
H: 5 6 W: 10 00 b.Liverpool 22-4-90
Source: Scholar.

2007-08	Chester C	19	1	
2008-09	Chester C	9	2	**28 3**

MITCHELL, Andy (F)   **4 0**
H: 6 0 W: 12 03 b.Liverpool 18-4-90
Source: Scholar.

2007-08	Chester C	4	0	
2008-09	Chester C	0	0	**4 0**

MOZIKA, Damien (M)   **50 2**
H: 6 0 W: 11 13 b.Corbell-Essonnes 15-4-87

2006-07	*Nancy*	0	0	
2007-08	*Louhans*	28	0	**28 0**
2008-09	Chester C	22	2	**22 2**

OWEN, James (M)   **7 0**
H: 5 9 W: 10 07 b.Caernarfon 14-1-91
Source: Scholar.

2008-09	Chester C	7	0	**7 0**

PALETHORPE, Philip (G)   **1 0**
H: 6 2 W: 11 08 b.Wallasey 17-9-86
Source: Scholar.

2003-04	Tranmere R	0	0	
2004-05	Tranmere R	0	0	
2005-06	Tranmere R	0	0	
2006-07	Chester C	0	0	
2007-08	Chester C	1	0	
2008-09	Chester C	0	0	**1 0**

PARTRIDGE, Richie (M)   **148 13**
H: 5 8 W: 11 00 b.Dublin 12-9-80
Source: Trainee. *Honours:* Eire Youth, Under-21.

1998-99	Liverpool	0	0	
1999-2000	Liverpool	0	0	
2000-01	Liverpool	0	0	
2000-01	*Bristol R*	6	1	**6 1**
2001-02	Liverpool	0	0	
2002-03	Liverpool	0	0	
2002-03	*Coventry C*	27	4	**27 4**
2003-04	Liverpool	0	0	
2004-05	Liverpool	0	0	
2005-06	Sheffield W	18	0	**18 0**
2006-07	Rotherham U	33	3	**33 3**
2007-08	Chester C	36	5	
2008-09	Chester C	28	0	**64 5**

PLATT, Kristian (D)   **1 0**
H: 6 2 W: 11 13 b.Birkenhead 11-10-92
Source: Scholar.

2008-09	Chester C	1	0	**1 0**

ROBERTS, Kevin (D)   **81 7**
H: 6 2 W: 14 00 b.Liverpool 17-8-89
Source: Scholar.

2006-07	Chester C	0	0	
2007-08	Chester C	37	3	
2008-09	Chester C	44	4	**81 7**

RULE, Glenn (M)   **26 0**
H: 5 11 W: 11 07 b.Birkenhead 30-11-89
Source: Scholar.

2007-08	Chester C	4	0	
2008-09	Chester C	22	0	**26 0**

RUTHERFORD, Paul (M)   **57 1**
H: 5 9 W: 11 07 b.Moreton 10-7-87
Source: Greenleas.

2005-06	Chester C	6	0	
2006-07	Chester C	9	0	
2007-08	Chester C	23	1	
2008-09	Chester C	19	0	**57 1**

SMITH, Paul (M)   **5 0**
H: 5 9 W: 11 09 b.Liverpool 13-3-91
Source: Scholar.

2008-09	Chester C	5	0	**5 0**

TAYLOR, Paul (M)   **9 0**
H: 5 11 W: 11 02 b.Liverpool 4-11-87
on loan from Vauxhall M.

2008-09	Chester C	9	0	**9 0**

VAUGHAN, James (D)   **78 0**
H: 5 10 W: 12 09 b.Liverpool 6-12-86
Source: Scholar.

2004-05	Tranmere R	0	0	
2005-06	Chester C	0	0	
2006-07	Chester C	6	0	
2007-08	Chester C	30	0	
2008-09	Chester C	42	0	**78 0**

VAUGHAN, Stephen (D)   **73 0**
H: 5 6 W: 11 11 b.Liverpool 22-1-85
Source: Scholar.

2001-02	Liverpool	0	0	
2002-03	Liverpool	0	0	
2003-04	Liverpool	0	0	
2004-05	Chester C	21	0	
2005-06	Chester C	17	0	
2006-07	Chester C	20	0	
2006-07	*Boston U*	7	0	**7 0**
2007-08	Chester C	0	0	
2008-09	Chester C	8	0	**66 0**

WILSON, Laurence (M)   **130 5**
H: 5 10 W: 10 09 b.Huyton 10-10-86
Source: Scholar. *Honours:* England Youth.

2004-05	Everton	0	0	
2005-06	Everton	0	0	
2005-06	*Mansfield T*	15	1	**15 1**
2006-07	Chester C	41	1	
2007-08	Chester C	40	2	
2008-09	Chester C	34	1	**115 · 4**

CHESTERFIELD (25)

ALGAR, Ben (M)   **5 0**
H: 6 1 W: 12 00 b.Dronfield 3-12-89

2007-08	Chesterfield	2	0	
2008-09	Chesterfield	3	0	**5 0**

ASKHAM, Lee (M)   **1 0**
H: 5 10 W: 11 02 b.Killamarsh 25-2-90
Source: Scholar.

2008-09	Sheffield U	0	0	
2008-09	Chesterfield	1	0	**1 0**

AUSTIN, Kevin (D) — 458 5
H: 6 1 W: 14 08 b.Hackney 12-2-73
Source: Saffron Walden. Honours: Trinidad & Tobago 1 full cap.

Season	Club				
1993-94	Leyton Orient	30	0		
1994-95	Leyton Orient	39	2		
1995-96	Leyton Orient	40	1	109	3
1996-97	Lincoln C	44	1		
1997-98	Lincoln C	46	0		
1998-99	Lincoln C	39	1	129	2
1999-2000	Barnsley	3	0		
2000-01	Barnsley	0	0	3	0
2000-01	Brentford	3	0	3	0
2001-02	Cambridge U	6	0	6	0
2002-03	Bristol R	33	0		
2003-04	Bristol R	23	0	56	0
2004-05	Swansea C	42	0		
2005-06	Swansea C	26	0		
2006-07	Swansea C	30	0		
2007-08	Swansea C	19	0	117	0
2008-09	Chesterfield	35	0	35	0

BODEN, Scott (F) — 11 2
H: 5 11 W: 11 00 b.Sheffield 19-12-89
Source: IFK Marlehamn.

Season	Club				
2008-09	Chesterfield	11	2	11	2

BOWERY, Jordan (F) — 3 0
H: 6 1 W: 12 00 b.Nottingham 2-7-91
Source: Scholar.

Season	Club				
2008-09	Chesterfield	3	0	3	0

CURRIE, Darren (M) — 531 60
H: 5 11 W: 12 07 b.Hampstead 29-11-74
Source: Trainee.

Season	Club				
1993-94	West Ham U	0	0		
1994-95	West Ham U	0	0		
1994-95	Shrewsbury T	17	2		
1995-96	West Ham U	0	0		
1995-96	Leyton Orient	10	0	10	0
1995-96	Shrewsbury T	13	2		
1996-97	Shrewsbury T	37	2		
1997-98	Shrewsbury T	16	4	83	10
1997-98	Plymouth Arg	7	0	7	0
1998-99	Barnet	38	4		
1999-2000	Barnet	44	5		
2000-01	Barnet	45	10	127	19
2001-02	Wycombe W	46	3		
2002-03	Wycombe W	38	4		
2003-04	Wycombe W	42	7	126	14
2004-05	Brighton & HA	22	2	22	2
2004-05	Ipswich T	24	3		
2005-06	Ipswich T	46	5		
2006-07	Ipswich T	13	1	83	9
2006-07	Coventry C	8	0	8	0
2006-07	Derby Co	7	1	7	1
2007-08	Luton T	31	2	31	2
2008-09	Chesterfield	27	3	27	3

DOWNES, Aaron (D) — 158 9
H: 6 2 W: 13 02 b.Mudgee 15-5-85
Honours: Australia Youth, Under-20, Under-21, Under-23.

Season	Club				
2004-05	Chesterfield	9	2		
2005-06	Chesterfield	22	0		
2006-07	Chesterfield	45	3		
2007-08	Chesterfield	40	2		
2008-09	Chesterfield	42	2	158	9

GOODALL, Alan (D) — 177 12
H: 5 7 W: 11 08 b.Birkenhead 2-12-81
Source: Bangor C.

Season	Club				
2004-05	Rochdale	34	2		
2005-06	Rochdale	40	3		
2006-07	Rochdale	46	3	120	8
2007-08	Luton T	29	1	29	1
2008-09	Chesterfield	28	3	28	3

GRAY, Dan (M) — 25 0
H: 6 0 W: 11 00 b.Mansfield 23-11-89
Source: Scholar.

Season	Club				
2008-09	Chesterfield	25	0	25	0

GRITTON, Martin (F) — 304 62
H: 6 1 W: 12 02 b.Glasgow 1-6-78
Source: Porthleven.

Season	Club				
1998-99	Plymouth Arg	2	0		
1999-2000	Plymouth Arg	30	6		
2000-01	Plymouth Arg	10	1		
2001-02	Plymouth Arg	2	0		
2002-03	Plymouth Arg	0	0	44	7
2002-03	Torquay U	43	13		
2003-04	Torquay U	31	4		
2004-05	Torquay U	19	6	93	23
2004-05	Grimsby T	23	4		
2005-06	Grimsby T	26	2	49	6
2005-06	Lincoln C	10	1		
2006-07	Lincoln C	17	2	27	3
2006-07	Mansfield T	19	6	19	6
2007-08	Macclesfield T	31	8		
2008-09	Macclesfield T	21	5	52	13
2008-09	Chesterfield	20	4	20	4

HALL, Danny (D) — 146 2
H: 6 0 W: 12 02 b.Ashton-under-Lyne 14-11-83
Source: Scholar.

Season	Club				
2002-03	Oldham Ath	2	0		
2003-04	Oldham Ath	31	1		
2004-05	Oldham Ath	21	0		
2005-06	Oldham Ath	10	0	64	1
2006-07	Shrewsbury T	27	0		
2007-08	Shrewsbury T	15	0	42	0
2007-08	Gretna	15	0	15	0
2008-09	Chesterfield	25	1	25	1

HARSLEY, Paul (M) — 429 36
H: 5 8 W: 11 05 b.Scunthorpe 29-5-78
Source: Trainee.

Season	Club				
1996-97	Grimsby T	0	0		
1997-98	Scunthorpe U	15	1		
1998-99	Scunthorpe U	34	0		
1999-2000	Scunthorpe U	46	3		
2000-01	Scunthorpe U	33	1	128	5
2001-02	Halifax T	45	11	45	11
2002-03	Northampton T	45	2		
2003-04	Northampton T	14	0	59	2
2003-04	Macclesfield T	16	2		
2004-05	Macclesfield T	46	3		
2005-06	Macclesfield T	45	6	107	11
2006-07	Port Vale	32	1		
2007-08	Port Vale	41	5	73	6
2008-09	Chesterfield	17	1	17	1

KERRY, Lloyd (M) — 53 6
H: 6 2 W: 12 04 b.Chesterfield 22-1-88
Source: Scholar.

Season	Club				
2006-07	Sheffield U	0	0		
2006-07	Torquay U	7	1	7	1
2007-08	Sheffield U	0	0		
2007-08	Chesterfield	13	2		
2008-09	Chesterfield	33	3	46	5

LEE, Tommy (G) — 102 0
H: 6 2 W: 12 00 b.Keighley 3-1-86
Source: Scholar.

Season	Club				
2005-06	Manchester U	0	0		
2005-06	Macclesfield T	11	0		
2006-07	Macclesfield T	34	0		
2007-08	Macclesfield T	18	0	63	0
2007-08	Rochdale	11	0	11	0
2008-09	Chesterfield	28	0	28	0

LESTER, Jack (F) — 436 106
H: 5 9 W: 12 08 b.Sheffield 8-10-75
Source: Trainee. Honours: England Schools.

Season	Club				
1994-95	Grimsby T	7	0		
1995-96	Grimsby T	5	0		
1996-97	Grimsby T	19	0		
1996-97	Doncaster R	11	1	11	1
1997-98	Grimsby T	40	4		
1998-99	Grimsby T	33	4		
1999-2000	Grimsby T	26	4	133	17
1999-2000	Nottingham F	15	2		
2000-01	Nottingham F	19	7		
2001-02	Nottingham F	32	5		
2002-03	Nottingham F	33	7		
2003-04	Sheffield U	32	12		
2004-05	Sheffield U	12	0	44	12
2004-05	Nottingham F	3	1		
2005-06	Nottingham F	38	5		
2006-07	Nottingham F	35	6	175	33
2007-08	Chesterfield	36	23		
2008-09	Chesterfield	37	20	73	43

LOWRY, Jamie (D) — 92 6
H: 6 0 W: 12 00 b.Newquay 18-3-87
Source: Scholar.

Season	Club				
2006-07	Chesterfield	8	0		
2007-08	Chesterfield	42	6		
2008-09	Chesterfield	42	0	92	6

NIVEN, Derek (M) — 217 15
H: 5 11 W: 12 05 b.Falkirk 12-12-83
Source: Stenhousemuir.

Season	Club				
2000-01	Raith R	1	0	1	0
2001-02	Bolton W	0	0		
2002-03	Bolton W	0	0		
2003-04	Bolton W	0	0		
2003-04	Chesterfield	22	1		
2004-05	Chesterfield	38	1		
2005-06	Chesterfield	42	5		
2006-07	Chesterfield	45	3		
2007-08	Chesterfield	38	3		
2008-09	Chesterfield	31	2	216	15

PAGE, Robert (D) — 436 5
H: 6 0 W: 12 05 b.Llwynpia 3-9-74
Source: Trainee. Honours: Wales Schools, Youth, Under-21, B, 41 full caps.

Season	Club				
1992-93	Watford	0	0		
1993-94	Watford	4	0		
1994-95	Watford	5	0		
1995-96	Watford	19	0		
1996-97	Watford	36	0		
1997-98	Watford	41	0		
1998-99	Watford	39	0		
1999-2000	Watford	36	1		
2000-01	Watford	36	1		
2001-02	Watford	0	0	216	2
2001-02	Sheffield U	43	0		
2002-03	Sheffield U	34	0		
2003-04	Sheffield U	30	1	107	1
2004-05	Cardiff C	9	0	9	0
2004-05	Coventry C	9	0		
2005-06	Coventry C	32	1		
2006-07	Coventry C	29	0		
2007-08	Coventry C	0	0	70	1
2007-08	Huddersfield T	18	1	18	1
2008-09	Chesterfield	16	0	16	0

PICKEN, Phil (D) — 141 2
H: 5 9 W: 10 07 b.Droylsden 12-11-85
Source: Scholar.

Season	Club				
2004-05	Manchester U	0	0		
2005-06	Manchester U	0	0		
2005-06	Chesterfield	32	1		
2006-07	Chesterfield	39	1		
2007-08	Chesterfield	37	0		
2008-09	Chesterfield	11	0	119	2
2008-09	Notts Co	22	0	22	0

ROBERTSON, Gregor (D) — 162 4
H: 6 0 W: 12 04 b.Edinburgh 19-1-84
Honours: Scotland Under-21.

Season	Club				
2000-01	Nottingham F	0	0		
2001-02	Nottingham F	0	0		
2002-03	Nottingham F	0	0		
2003-04	Nottingham F	16	0		
2004-05	Nottingham F	20	0	36	0
2005-06	Rotherham U	35	1		
2006-07	Rotherham U	18	0	53	1
2007-08	Chesterfield	35	1		
2008-09	Chesterfield	38	2	73	3

TEIXEIRA, Val (M) — 37 9
H: 6 1 W: 12 03 b.Lisbon 26-4-77
Source: Rhode Island Stingrays, Sanjoanese (loan), New Hampshire Phantoms.

Season	Club				
2008	CP Baltimore	17	4		
2009	CP Baltimore	15	5	32	9
2008-09	Chesterfield	5	0	5	0

WHATSIZE, Dan (G) — 0 0
b.Leicester 14-8-90
Source: Scholar.

Season	Club				
2008-09	Chesterfield	0	0		

WINTER, Jamie (M) — 49 2
H: 5 10 W: 13 10 b.Dundee 4-8-85
Source: Scholar.

Season	Club				
2002-03	Leeds U	0	0		
2003-04	Leeds U	0	0		
2004-05	Leeds U	0	0		
2005-06	Leeds U	0	0		
2006-07	Leeds U	0	0		
2007-08	Chesterfield	25	0		
2008-09	Chesterfield	24	2	49	2

COLCHESTER U (26)

BALDWIN, Pat (D) — 185 1
H: 6 3 W: 12 07 b.City of London 12-11-82
Source: Chelsea Academy.

Season	Club				
2002-03	Colchester U	19	0		
2003-04	Colchester U	4	0		
2004-05	Colchester U	38	0		
2005-06	Colchester U	25	0		
2006-07	Colchester U	38	1		

Season	Club				
2007-08	Colchester U	26	0		
2008-09	Colchester U	35	0	185	1

CORCORAN, Sam (M)   1   0
H: 5 11 W: 12 02 b.Enfield 5-2-91
Source: Scholar.

Season	Club				
2008-09	Colchester U	1	0	1	0

COUSINS, Mark (G)   11   0
H: 6 2 W: 12 02 b.Chelmsford 9-1-87
Source: Scholar.

Season	Club				
2005-06	Colchester U	0	0		
2006-07	Colchester U	0	0		
2007-08	Colchester U	2	0		
2008-09	Colchester U	9	0	11	0

COYNE, Chris (D)   285   15
H: 6 2 W: 13 10 b.Brisbane 20-12-78
Source: Perth SC. *Honours:* Australia Youth, Under-23, 7 full caps.

Season	Club				
1995-96	West Ham U	0	0		
1996-97	West Ham U	0	0		
1997-98	West Ham U	0	0		
1998-99	West Ham U	1	0	1	0
1998-99	Brentford	7	0	7	0
1998-99	Southend U	1	0	1	0
1999-2000	Dundee	2	0		
2000-01	Dundee	18	0	20	0
2001-02	Luton T	31	3		
2002-03	Luton T	40	1		
2003-04	Luton T	44	2		
2004-05	Luton T	40	5		
2005-06	Luton T	30	2		
2006-07	Luton T	18	1		
2007-08	Luton T	18	0	221	14
2007-08	Colchester U	16	1		
2008-09	Colchester U	19	0	35	1

ELITO, Medy (M)   16   1
H: 6 2 W: 13 00 b.Kinshasa 20-3-90
Source: Scholar. *Honours:* England Youth.

Season	Club				
2007-08	Colchester U	11	1		
2008-09	Colchester U	5	0	16	1

GERKEN, Dean (G)   116   0
H: 6 3 W: 12 08 b.Rochford 22-5-85
Source: Scholar.

Season	Club				
2003-04	Colchester U	1	0		
2004-05	Colchester U	13	0		
2005-06	Colchester U	7	0		
2006-07	Colchester U	27	0		
2007-08	Colchester U	40	0		
2008-09	Colchester U	21	0	109	0
2008-09	Darlington	7	0	7	0

GILLESPIE, Steven (F)   115   34
H: 5 9 W: 11 02 b.Liverpool 4-6-84
Source: Liverpool Schools.

Season	Club				
2004-05	Bristol C	8	0		
2004-05	Cheltenham T	12	5		
2005-06	Bristol C	4	1	12	1
2005-06	Cheltenham T	14	5		
2006-07	Cheltenham T	23	5		
2007-08	Cheltenham T	37	14	86	29
2008-09	Colchester U	17	4	17	4

GUY, Jamie (M)   60   4
H: 6 1 W: 13 00 b.Barking 1-8-87
Source: Scholar.

Season	Club				
2004-05	Colchester U	2	0		
2005-06	Colchester U	2	0		
2006-07	Colchester U	32	3		
2007-08	Colchester U	11	0		
2008-09	Colchester U	4	0	51	3
2008-09	Dagenham & R	9	1	9	1

HACKNEY, Simon (M)   130   17
H: 5 8 W: 9 13 b.Manchester 5-2-84
Source: Woodley Sports.

Season	Club				
2005-06	Carlisle U	30	6		
2006-07	Carlisle U	18	2		
2007-08	Carlisle U	43	8		
2008-09	Carlisle U	22	1	113	17
2008-09	Colchester U	17	0	17	0

HAMMOND, Dean (M)   198   26
H: 6 0 W: 11 09 b.Hastings 7-3-83
Source: Scholar.

Season	Club				
2002-03	Brighton & HA	4	0		
2003-04	Brighton & HA	0	0		
2003-04	Leyton Orient	8	0	8	0
2004-05	Brighton & HA	30	4		
2005-06	Brighton & HA	41	4		
2006-07	Brighton & HA	37	8		
2007-08	Brighton & HA	24	5	136	21
2007-08	Colchester U	13	0		
2008-09	Colchester U	41	5	54	5

HEATH, Matt (D)   168   12
H: 6 4 W: 13 13 b.Leicester 1-11-81
Source: Trainee.

Season	Club				
2000-01	Leicester C	0	0		
2001-02	Leicester C	5	0		
2002-03	Leicester C	11	3		
2003-04	Leicester C	13	0		
2003-04	Stockport Co	8	0	8	0
2004-05	Leicester C	22	3	51	6
2005-06	Coventry C	25	1		
2006-07	Coventry C	7	0	32	1
2006-07	Leeds U	26	3		
2007-08	Leeds U	26	1	52	4
2007-08	Colchester U	5	0		
2008-09	Colchester U	14	0	19	0
2008-09	Brighton & HA	6	1	6	1

IFIL, Phil (D)   57   0
H: 5 10 W: 12 02 b.Willesden 18-11-86
Honours: England Youth, Under-20.

Season	Club				
2004-05	Tottenham H	2	0		
2005-06	Tottenham H	0	0		
2005-06	Millwall	16	0	16	0
2006-07	Tottenham H	1	0		
2007-08	Tottenham H	0	0	3	0
2007-08	Southampton	12	0	12	0
2007-08	Colchester U	20	0		
2008-09	Colchester U	6	0	26	0

IZZET, Kem (M)   299   18
H: 5 7 W: 10 05 b.Mile End 29-9-80
Source: Trainee.

Season	Club				
1998-99	Charlton Ath	0	0		
1999-2000	Charlton Ath	0	0		
2000-01	Charlton Ath	0	0		
2000-01	Colchester U	6	1		
2001-02	Colchester U	40	3		
2002-03	Colchester U	45	8		
2003-04	Colchester U	44	3		
2004-05	Colchester U	4	0		
2005-06	Colchester U	33	0		
2006-07	Colchester U	45	1		
2007-08	Colchester U	39	1		
2008-09	Colchester U	43	1	299	18

JACKSON, Johnnie (M)   174   17
H: 6 1 W: 12 00 b.Camden 15-8-82
Source: Trainee. *Honours:* England Youth, Under-20.

Season	Club				
1999-2000	Tottenham H	0	0		
2000-01	Tottenham H	0	0		
2001-02	Tottenham H	0	0		
2002-03	Tottenham H	0	0		
2002-03	Swindon T	13	1	13	1
2002-03	Colchester U	8	0		
2003-04	Tottenham H	11	1		
2003-04	Coventry C	5	2	5	2
2004-05	Tottenham H	8	0		
2004-05	Watford	15	0	15	0
2005-06	Tottenham H	1	0	20	1
2005-06	Derby Co	6	0	6	0
2006-07	Colchester U	32	2		
2007-08	Colchester U	46	7		
2008-09	Colchester U	29	4	115	13

KUEVI-HAMMOND, James (D)   0   0
b.London 11-11-89
Source: Scholar.

Season	Club				
2008-09	Colchester U	0	0		

LOCKWOOD, Matt (D)   419   51
H: 5 11 W: 11 10 b.Southend 17-10-76
Source: Trainee.

Season	Club				
1994-95	QPR	0	0		
1995-96	QPR	0	0		
1996-97	Bristol R	39	1		
1997-98	Bristol R	24	0	63	1
1998-99	Leyton Orient	37	3		
1999-2000	Leyton Orient	41	6		
2000-01	Leyton Orient	32	7		
2001-02	Leyton Orient	24	2		
2002-03	Leyton Orient	43	5		
2003-04	Leyton Orient	25	2		
2004-05	Leyton Orient	43	6		
2005-06	Leyton Orient	42	8		
2006-07	Leyton Orient	41	11	328	50
2007-08	Nottingham F	11	0	11	0
2008-09	Colchester U	5	0	5	0
2008-09	Barnet	12	0	12	0

MAYBURY, Alan (D)   248   7
H: 5 8 W: 11 08 b.Dublin 8-8-78
Source: Trainee. *Honours:* Eire Youth, Under-21, B, 10 full caps.

Season	Club				
1995-96	Leeds U	1	0		
1996-97	Leeds U	0	0		
1997-98	Leeds U	12	0		
1998-99	Leeds U	0	0		
1998-99	Reading	8	0	8	0
1999-2000	Leeds U	0	0		
2000-01	Leeds U	0	0		
2000-01	Crewe Alex	6	0	6	0
2001-02	Leeds U	1	0	14	0
2001-02	Hearts	27	0		
2002-03	Hearts	35	2		
2003-04	Hearts	33	2		
2004-05	Hearts	15	0	110	4
2004-05	Leicester C	17	2		
2005-06	Leicester C	40	1		
2006-07	Leicester C	27	0		
2007-08	Leicester C	1	0		
2008-09	Leicester C	0	0	85	3
2008-09	Colchester U	25	0	25	0

PERKINS, David (D)   96   9
H: 5 6 W: 11 06 b.St Asaph 21-6-82

Season	Club				
2006-07	Rochdale	18	0		
2007-08	Rochdale	40	4	58	4
2008-09	Colchester U	38	5	38	5

PLATT, Clive (F)   443   88
H: 6 4 W: 12 07 b.Wolverhampton 27-10-77
Source: Trainee.

Season	Club				
1995-96	Walsall	4	2		
1996-97	Walsall	1	0		
1997-98	Walsall	20	1		
1998-99	Walsall	7	1		
1999-2000	Walsall	0	0	32	4
1999-2000	Rochdale	41	9		
2000-01	Rochdale	43	8		
2001-02	Rochdale	43	7		
2002-03	Rochdale	42	6	169	30
2003-04	Notts Co	19	3	19	3
2003-04	Peterborough U	18	2		
2004-05	Peterborough U	19	4	37	6
2004-05	Milton Keynes D	20	3		
2005-06	Milton Keynes D	40	6		
2006-07	Milton Keynes D	42	18	102	27
2007-08	Colchester U	41	8		
2008-09	Colchester U	43	10	84	18

QUINTYN, Fabian (F)   0   0
b.London 16-11-89
Source: Scholar.

Season	Club				
2008-09	Colchester U	0	0		

RAFTER, Michael (M)   0   0

Season	Club				
2008-09	Colchester U	0	0		

REID, Paul (D)   213   7
H: 6 2 W: 11 08 b.Carlisle 18-2-82
Source: Trainee. *Honours:* England Youth, Under-20.

Season	Club				
1998-99	Carlisle U	0	0		
1999-2000	Carlisle U	19	0		
2000-01	Rangers	0	0		
2001-02	Rangers	0	0		
2001-02	Preston NE	1	1	1	1
2002-03	Rangers	0	0		
2002-03	Northampton T	0	0		
2003-04	Northampton T	33	2	52	2
2004-05	Barnsley	41	3		
2005-06	Barnsley	33	0		
2006-07	Barnsley	37	0		
2007-08	Barnsley	3	0	114	3
2007-08	Carlisle U	1	0	20	0
2008-09	Colchester U	26	1	26	1

TIERNEY, Marc (D)   142   2
H: 5 11 W: 11 04 b.Manchester 7-9-86
Source: Trainee.

Season	Club				
2003-04	Oldham Ath	2	0		
2004-05	Oldham Ath	11	0		
2005-06	Oldham Ath	19	0		
2006-07	Oldham Ath	5	0	37	0
2006-07	Shrewsbury T	18	0		
2007-08	Shrewsbury T	43	1		
2008-09	Shrewsbury T	10	0	79	1
2008-09	Colchester U	26	1	26	1

VERNON, Scott (F) 212 50
H: 6 1 W: 11 06 b.Manchester 13-12-83
Source: Scholar.

2002-03	Oldham Ath	8	1		
2003-04	Oldham Ath	45	12		
2004-05	Oldham Ath	22	7	75	20
2004-05	*Blackpool*	4	3		
2005-06	Blackpool	17	1		
2005-06	*Colchester U*	7	1		
2006-07	Blackpool	38	11		
2007-08	Blackpool	15	4	74	19
2007-08	Colchester U	17	5		
2008-09	Colchester U	33	4	57	10
2008-09	*Northampton*	6	1	6	1

VINCENT, Ashley (F) 116 9
H: 5 10 W: 11 05 b.Oldbury 26-5-85
Source: Wolverhampton W Scholar.

2004-05	Cheltenham T	26	1		
2005-06	Cheltenham T	13	2		
2006-07	Cheltenham T	5	0		
2007-08	Cheltenham T	37	2		
2008-09	Cheltenham T	29	3	110	8
2008-09	Colchester U	6	1	6	1

WASIU, Akanni-Sunday (F) 62 7
H: 6 1 W: 11 11 b.Nigeria 18-3-84

2004-05	Szczakowianka	15	1	15	1
2006	Vilnius	18	3		
2007	Vilnius	9	0	27	3
From St Albans C.					
2008-09	*Colchester U*	15	2	15	2
2008-09	*Luton T*	5	1	5	1

WHITE, John (D) 118 0
H: 6 0 W: 12 01 b.Maldon 26-7-86
Source: Scholar.

2004-05	Colchester U	20	0	
2005-06	Colchester U	35	0	
2006-07	Colchester U	16	0	
2007-08	Colchester U	21	0	
2008-09	Colchester U	26	0	118 0

WORDSWORTH, Anthony (M) 33 3
H: 6 1 W: 12 00 b.Camden 3-1-89
Source: Scholar.

2007-08	Colchester U	3	0		
2008-09	Colchester U	30	3	33	3

YEATES, Mark (F) 146 26
H: 5 8 W: 13 03 b.Dublin 11-1-85
Source: Trainee. *Honours:* Eire Youth, Under-21.

2002-03	Tottenham H	0	0		
2003-04	Tottenham H	1	0		
2003-04	*Brighton & HA*	9	0	9	0
2004-05	Tottenham H	2	0		
2004-05	*Swindon T*	4	0	4	0
2005-06	Tottenham H	0	0		
2005-06	*Colchester U*	44	5		
2006-07	Tottenham H	0	0	3	0
2006-07	*Hull C*	5	0	5	0
2006-07	*Leicester C*	9	1	9	1
2007-08	Colchester U	29	8		
2008-09	Colchester U	43	12	116	25

COVENTRY C (27)

BELL, David (M) 230 18
H: 5 10 W: 11 05 b.Kettering 21-1-84
Source: Trainee. *Honours:* Eire Youth, Under-21.

2001-02	Rushden & D	0	0		
2002-03	Rushden & D	30	3		
2003-04	Rushden & D	37	1		
2004-05	Rushden & D	40	3		
2005-06	Rushden & D	14	3	121	10
2005-06	Luton T	9	0		
2006-07	Luton T	34	3		
2007-08	Luton T	32	4	75	7
2007-08	*Leicester C*	6	0	6	0
2008-09	Norwich C	19	0	19	0
2008-09	Coventry C	9	1	9	1

BEST, Leon (F) 128 29
H: 6 1 W: 13 03 b.Nottingham 19-9-86
Source: Scholar. *Honours:* Eire Youth, Under-21, 2 full caps.

2004-05	Southampton	3	0		
2004-05	*QPR*	5	0	5	0
2005-06	Southampton	3	0		
2005-06	*Sheffield W*	13	2	13	2

2006-07	Southampton	9	4	15	4
2006-07	*Bournemouth*	15	3	15	3
2006-07	*Yeovil T*	15	10	15	10
2007-08	Coventry C	34	8		
2008-09	Coventry C	31	2	65	10

BEUZELIN, Guillaume (M) 262 22
H: 6 0 W: 11 13 b.Le Havre 14-4-79
Source: Scholar.

1999-2000	Le Havre	24	4		
2000-01	Le Havre	7	0		
2001-02	*Beauvais*	35	3	35	3
2002-03	Le Havre	36	1		
2003-04	Le Havre	26	3	93	8
2004-05	Hibernian	26	4		
2005-06	Hibernian	21	5		
2006-07	Hibernian	25	1		
2007-08	Hibernian	27	0	99	10
2008-09	Coventry C	35	1	35	1

CAIN, Ashley (M) 5 0
H: 6 2 W: 12 06 b.Nuneaton 27-9-90
Source: Scholar.

2008-09	Coventry C	5	0	5	0

DANN, Scott (D) 106 10
H: 6 2 W: 12 00 b.Liverpool 14-2-87
Source: From Scholar. *Honours:* England Under-21.

2004-05	Walsall	1	0		
2005-06	Walsall	0	0		
2006-07	Walsall	30	4		
2007-08	Walsall	28	3	59	7
2007-08	Coventry C	16	0		
2008-09	Coventry C	31	3	47	3

DOYLE, Micky (M) 247 19
H: 5 10 W: 11 02 b.Dublin 8-7-81
Source: Celtic. *Honours:* Eire Under-21, 1 full cap.

2003-04	Coventry C	40	5		
2004-05	Coventry C	44	2		
2005-06	Coventry C	44	0		
2006-07	Coventry C	40	3		
2007-08	Coventry C	42	7		
2008-09	Coventry C	37	2	247	19

EASTWOOD, Freddy (F) 192 60
H: 5 11 W: 12 04 b.Epsom 29-10-83
Source: West Ham U Trainee, Grays Ath.
Honours: Wales 10 full caps, 4 goals.

2004-05	Southend U	33	19		
2005-06	Southend U	40	23		
2006-07	Southend U	42	11	115	53
2007-08	Wolverhampton W	31	3	31	3
2008-09	Coventry C	46	4	46	4

FOX, Daniel (D) 167 13
H: 5 11 W: 12 06 b.Crewe 29-5-86
Source: Scholar. *Honours:* England Under-21.

2004-05	Everton	0	0		
2004-05	*Stranraer*	11	1	11	1
2005-06	Walsall	33	0		
2006-07	Walsall	44	3		
2007-08	Walsall	22	3	99	6
2007-08	Coventry C	18	1		
2008-09	Coventry C	39	5	57	6

GRANDISON, Jermaine (D) 2 0
H: 6 4 W: 13 03 b.Birmingham 15-12-90
Source: Scholar.

2008-09	Coventry C	2	0	2	0

GUNNARSSON, Aron (M) 41 1
H: 5 9 W: 11 00 b.Akureyri 22-9-89
Honours: Iceland Under-21, 12 full caps.

2007-08	AZ	1	0	1	0
2008-09	Coventry C	40	1	40	1

HALL, Marcus (D) 342 3
H: 6 1 W: 12 02 b.Coventry 24-3-76
Source: Trainee. *Honours:* England Under-21, B.

1994-95	Coventry C	5	0		
1995-96	Coventry C	25	0		
1996-97	Coventry C	13	0		
1997-98	Coventry C	25	1		
1998-99	Coventry C	5	0		
1999-2000	Coventry C	9	0		
2000-01	Coventry C	21	0		
2001-02	Coventry C	29	1		
2002-03	Nottingham F	1	0	1	0
2002-03	Stoke C	24	0		
2003-04	Stoke C	35	0		
2004-05	Stoke C	20	1	79	1
2004-05	Coventry C	10	0		

HILDRETH, Lee (M) 1 0
H: 6 0 W: 11 02 b.Nuneaton 22-11-88
Source: Scholar.

2005-06	Coventry C	39	0		
2006-07	Coventry C	40	0		
2007-08	Coventry C	18	0		
2008-09	Coventry C	23	0	262	2

2006-07	Coventry C	1	0		
2007-08	Coventry C	0	0		
2008-09	Coventry C	0	0	1	0

IRELAND, Daniel (G) 0 0
H: 6 2 W: 13 00 b.Sydney 20-1-89
Source: Academy.

2007-08	Coventry C	0	0	
2008-09	Coventry C	0	0	

KONSTANTOPOULOS, Dimitrios (G) 148 0
H: 6 4 W: 14 02 b.Kalamata 29-11-78
Source: Farense. *Honours:* Greece Under-21.

2003-04	Hartlepool U	0	0		
2004-05	Hartlepool U	25	0		
2005-06	Hartlepool U	46	0		
2006-07	Hartlepool U	46	0	117	0
2007-08	Coventry C	21	0		
2008-09	Coventry C	0	0	21	0
2008-09	*Swansea C*	4	0	4	0
2008-09	*Cardiff C*	6	0	6	0

KYLE, Kevin (F) 177 23
H: 6 4 W: 14 07 b.Stranraer 7-6-81
Source: Ayr Boswell. *Honours:* Scotland Under-21, B, 9 full caps, 1 goal.

1998-99	Sunderland	0	0		
1999-2000	Sunderland	0	0		
2000-01	Sunderland	3	0		
2000-01	*Huddersfield T*	4	0	4	0
2000-01	*Darlington*	5	1	5	1
2000-01	*Rochdale*	6	0	6	0
2001-02	Sunderland	6	0		
2002-03	Sunderland	17	0		
2003-04	Sunderland	44	10		
2004-05	Sunderland	6	0		
2005-06	Sunderland	13	1		
2006-07	Sunderland	2	0	91	11
2006-07	Coventry C	31	3		
2007-08	Coventry C	13	2		
2007-08	*Wolverhampton W*	12	1	12	1
2008-09	Coventry C	0	0	44	5
2008-09	*Hartlepool U*	15	5	15	5
Transferred to Kilmarnock January 2009					

MARSHALL, Andy (G) 390 0
H: 6 3 W: 14 08 b.Bury St Edmunds 14-4-75
Source: Trainee. *Honours:* England Youth, Under-21.

1993-94	Norwich C	0	0		
1994-95	Norwich C	21	0		
1995-96	Norwich C	3	0		
1996-97	Norwich C	7	0		
1996-97	*Bournemouth*	11	0	11	0
1996-97	*Gillingham*	5	0	5	0
1997-98	Norwich C	42	0		
1998-99	Norwich C	37	0		
1999-2000	Norwich C	44	0		
2000-01	Norwich C	41	0	195	0
2001-02	Ipswich T	13	0		
2002-03	Ipswich T	40	0		
2003-04	Ipswich T	0	0	53	0
2003-04	Millwall	16	0		
2004-05	Millwall	22	0		
2005-06	Millwall	29	0	67	0
2006-07	Coventry C	41	0		
2007-08	Coventry C	16	0		
2008-09	Coventry C	2	0	59	0

McKENZIE, Leon (F) 332 92
H: 5 11 W: 12 11 b.Croydon 17-5-78
Source: Trainee.

1995-96	Crystal Palace	12	0		
1996-97	Crystal Palace	21	2		
1997-98	Crystal Palace	3	0		
1997-98	*Fulham*	3	0	3	0
1998-99	Crystal Palace	16	1		
1998-99	*Peterborough U*	14	8		
1999-2000	Crystal Palace	25	4		
2000-01	Crystal Palace	8	0	85	7
2000-01	Peterborough U	30	13		
2001-02	Peterborough U	30	18		
2002-03	Peterborough U	11	5		
2003-04	Peterborough U	19	9	104	53
2003-04	Norwich C	18	9		

2004-05	Norwich C	37	7		
2005-06	Norwich C	20	4		
2006-07	Norwich C	4	0	79	20
2006-07	Coventry C	31	7		
2007-08	Coventry C	11	2		
2008-09	Coventry C	19	3	61	12

McPAKE, James (D) 116 9
H: 6 2 W: 12 08 b.Airdrie 2-6-84
2003-04	Livingston	1	0		
2004-05	Livingston	15	2		
2005-06	Livingston	15	0		
2005-06	Morton	11	2	11	2
2006-07	Livingston	33	3		
2007-08	Livingston	19	0		
2008-09	Livingston	18	2	101	7
2008-09	Coventry C	4	0	4	0

MIFSUD, Michael (F) 232 91
H: 5 6 W: 10 00 b.Pieta 17-4-81
Honours: Malta 65 full caps, 20 goals.
1997-98	Sliema Wanderers	7	1		
1998-99	Sliema Wanderers	22	8		
1999-2000	Sliema Wanderers	26	21		
2000-01	Sliema Wanderers	25	30	80	60
2001-02	Kaiserslautern	5	0		
2002-03	Kaiserslautern	16	2		
2003-04	Kaiserslautern	0	0	21	2
2004	Lillestrom	9	0		
2005	Lillestrom	2	0		
2006	Lillestrom	19	11	30	11
2006-07	Coventry C	19	4		
2007-08	Coventry C	41	10		
2008-09	Coventry C	26	2	86	16
2008-09	Barnsley	15	2	15	2

MORRISON, Clinton (F) 413 127
H: 6 0 W: 12 00 b.Tooting 14-5-79
Source: Trainee. *Honours:* Eire Under-21, 36 full caps, 9 goals.
1996-97	Crystal Palace	0	0		
1997-98	Crystal Palace	1	1		
1998-99	Crystal Palace	37	12		
1999-2000	Crystal Palace	29	13		
2000-01	Crystal Palace	45	14		
2001-02	Crystal Palace	45	22		
2002-03	Birmingham C	28	6		
2003-04	Birmingham C	32	4		
2004-05	Birmingham C	26	4		
2005-06	Birmingham C	1	0	87	14
2005-06	Crystal Palace	40	13		
2006-07	Crystal Palace	41	12		
2007-08	Crystal Palace	43	16	281	103
2008-09	Coventry C	45	10	45	10

OSBOURNE, Isaac (M) 109 0
H: 5 10 W: 11 11 b.Birmingham 22-6-86
Source: Scholar.
2002-03	Coventry C	2	0		
2003-04	Coventry C	0	0		
2004-05	Coventry C	9	0		
2005-06	Coventry C	10	0		
2006-07	Coventry C	19	0		
2006-07	Crewe Alex	2	0	2	0
2007-08	Coventry C	42	0		
2008-09	Coventry C	25	0	107	0

SIMMONDS, Donovan (F) 22 1
H: 5 11 W: 11 00 b.Walthamstow 12-10-88
Source: Charlton Ath.
2007-08	Coventry C	0	0		
2007-08	Gillingham	3	0		
2007-08	Gillingham	0	0	3	0
2008-09	Coventry C	0	0		
2008-09	Kilmarnock	19	1	19	1

SIMPSON, Robbie (F) 61 4
H: 6 1 W: 11 11 b.Stevenage 15-3-85
Source: Cambridge U.
| 2007-08 | Coventry C | 28 | 1 | | |
| 2008-09 | Coventry C | 33 | 3 | 61 | 4 |

THORNTON, Kevin (M) 62 2
H: 5 7 W: 11 00 b.Drogheda 9-7-86
Source: Scholar. *Honours:* Eire Youth.
2003-04	Coventry C	0	0		
2004-05	Coventry C	0	0		
2005-06	Coventry C	16	0		
2006-07	Coventry C	11	1		
2007-08	Coventry C	19	1		
2008-09	Coventry C	4	0	50	2
2008-09	Brighton & HA	12	0	12	0

TURNER, Ben (D) 54 0
H: 6 4 W: 14 04 b.Birmingham 21-1-88
Source: Scholar. *Honours:* England Youth.
2005-06	Coventry C	1	0		
2006-07	Coventry C	1	0		
2006-07	Peterborough U	8	0	8	0
2006-07	Oldham Ath	1	0	1	0
2007-08	Coventry C	19	0		
2008-09	Coventry C	24	0	45	0

WALKER, Adam (M) 2 0
H: 5 6 W: 9 00 b.Coventry 22-1-91
Source: Scholar.
| 2008-09 | Coventry C | 2 | 0 | 2 | 0 |

WARD, Elliot (D) 143 15
H: 6 2 W: 13 00 b.Harrow 19-1-85
Source: Scholar.
2001-02	West Ham U	0	0		
2002-03	West Ham U	0	0		
2003-04	West Ham U	0	0		
2004-05	West Ham U	11	0		
2004-05	Bristol R	3	0	3	0
2005-06	West Ham U	4	0	15	0
2005-06	Plymouth Arg	16	1	16	1
2006-07	Coventry C	39	3		
2007-08	Coventry C	37	6		
2008-09	Coventry C	33	5	109	14

WESTWOOD, Keiren (G) 173 0
H: 6 1 W: 13 10 b.Manchester 23-10-84
Source: Scholar. *Honours:* Eire 1 full cap.
2001-02	Manchester C	0	0		
2002-03	Manchester C	0	0		
2003-04	Manchester C	0	0		
2003-04	Oldham Ath	0	0		
2004-05	Manchester C	0	0		
2005-06	Manchester C	0	0		
2005-06	Carlisle U	35	0		
2006-07	Carlisle U	46	0		
2007-08	Carlisle U	46	0	127	0
2008-09	Coventry C	46	0	46	0

WRIGHT, Stephen (D) 162 2
H: 6 0 W: 12 06 b.Liverpool 8-2-80
Source: Trainee. *Honours:* England Youth, Under-21.
1997-98	Liverpool	0	0		
1998-99	Liverpool	0	0		
1999-2000	Liverpool	0	0		
1999-2000	Crewe Alex	23	0	23	0
2000-01	Liverpool	2	0		
2001-02	Liverpool	12	0	14	0
2002-03	Sunderland	26	0		
2003-04	Sunderland	22	1		
2004-05	Sunderland	39	1		
2005-06	Sunderland	2	0		
2006-07	Sunderland	3	0		
2007-08	Sunderland	0	0	92	2
2007-08	Stoke C	16	0	16	0
2008-09	Coventry C	17	0	17	0

WYNTER, Curtis (D) 1 0
H: 6 3 W: 13 02 b.Birmingham 24-6-91
Source: Scholar.
| 2008-09 | Coventry C | 1 | 0 | 1 | 0 |

CREWE ALEX (28)

ABBEY, George (D) 192 2
H: 5 10 W: 12 04 b.Port Harcourt 20-10-78
Source: Sharks. *Honours:* Nigeria 16 full caps.
1999-2000	Macclesfield T	18	0		
2000-01	Macclesfield T	18	0		
2001-02	Macclesfield T	17	0		
2002-03	Macclesfield T	22	1		
2003-04	Macclesfield T	25	0		
2004-05	Macclesfield T	0	0	100	1
2004-05	Port Vale	18	0		
2005-06	Port Vale	20	0		
2006-07	Port Vale	24	1	62	1
2007-08	Crewe Alex	23	0		
2008-09	Crewe Alex	7	0	30	0

BAILEY, James (M) 25 0
H: 6 0 W: 12 05 b.Bollington 18-9-88
Source: Scholar.
2006-07	Crewe Alex	0	0		
2007-08	Crewe Alex	1	0		
2008-09	Crewe Alex	24	0	25	0

BAUDET, Julien (D) 248 16
H: 6 2 W: 13 07 b.Grenoble 13-1-79
Source: Toulouse.
2001-02	Oldham Ath	20	1		
2002-03	Oldham Ath	24	2	44	3
2003-04	Rotherham U	11	0	11	0
2004-05	Notts Co	39	5		
2005-06	Notts Co	42	6	81	11
2006-07	Crewe Alex	42	1		
2007-08	Crewe Alex	35	1		
2008-09	Crewe Alex	35	0	112	2

BOPP, Eugene (M) 123 15
H: 5 11 W: 12 03 b.Kiev 5-9-83
Source: Bayern Munich.
2000-01	Nottingham F	0	0		
2001-02	Nottingham F	19	1		
2002-03	Nottingham F	13	2		
2003-04	Nottingham F	15	1		
2004-05	Nottingham F	18	3		
2005-06	Nottingham F	12	1	77	8
2006-07	Rotherham U	29	5	29	5
2007-08	Crewe Alex	10	1		
2008-09	Crewe Alex	7	1	17	2

BRAYFORD, John (D) 36 2
H: 5 8 W: 11 02 b.Stoke 29-12-87
Source: Burton Alb.
| 2008-09 | Crewe Alex | 36 | 2 | 36 | 2 |

CARRINGTON, Mark (M) 29 2
H: 6 0 W: 11 00 b.Warrington 4-5-87
Source: Scholar.
2006-07	Crewe Alex	3	0		
2007-08	Crewe Alex	9	0		
2008-09	Crewe Alex	17	2	29	2

CLEMENTS, Chris (M) 0 0
H: 5 9 W: 10 05 b.Birmingham 6-2-90
Source: Scholar.
| 2008-09 | Crewe Alex | 0 | 0 | | |

COLLIS, Steve (G) 82 0
H: 6 3 W: 12 05 b.Harrow 18-3-81
Source: Barnet Juniors.
1999-2000	Barnet	0	0		
2000-01	Nottingham F	0	0		
2001-02	Nottingham F	0	0		
2003-04	Yeovil T	11	0		
2004-05	Yeovil T	9	0		
2005-06	Yeovil T	23	0	43	0
2006-07	Southend U	1	0		
2007-08	Southend U	20	0	21	0
2008-09	Crewe Alex	18	0	18	0

DANIEL, Colin (M) 22 1
H: 5 11 W: 11 06 b.Crewe 15-2-88
Source: Eastwood T.
2007-08	Crewe Alex	0	0		
2007-08	Crewe Alex	1	0		
2008-09	Crewe Alex	13	1	14	1
2008-09	Macclesfield T	8	0	8	0

DANVILLE, Luke (D) 0 0
Source: Scholar.
| 2008-09 | Crewe Alex | 0 | 0 | | |

DONALDSON, Clayton (F) 56 11
H: 6 1 W: 11 07 b.Bradford 7-2-84
Source: Scholar.
2002-03	Hull C	2	0		
2003-04	Hull C	0	0		
2004-05	Hull C	0	0	2	0
From York C					
2007-08	Hibernian	17	5	17	5
2008-09	Crewe Alex	37	6	37	6

ELDING, Anthony (F) 112 34
H: 6 1 W: 12 02 b.Boston 16-4-82
Source: Trainee.
2002-03	Boston U	8	0		
From Stevenage B, Kettering T.					
2006-07	Boston U	19	5	27	5
2006-07	Stockport Co	20	11		
2007-08	Stockport Co	25	13	45	24
2007-08	Leeds U	9	1	9	1
2008-09	Crewe Alex	16	1	16	1
2008-09	Lincoln C	15	3	15	3

GRANT, Joel (F) 35 2
H: 6 0 W: 12 01 b.Hammersmith 26-8-87
Source: Scholar.
| 2005-06 | Watford | 7 | 0 | | |
| 2006-07 | Watford | 0 | 0 | 7 | 0 |

From Aldershot T.

2008-09	Crewe Alex	28	2	28	2

JONES, Billy (D) **144** **6**
H: 6 1 W: 11 05 b.Chatham 26-3-83
Source: Trainee.

2000-01	Leyton Orient	1	0		
2001-02	Leyton Orient	16	0		
2002-03	Leyton Orient	24	0		
2003-04	Leyton Orient	31	0		
2004-05	Leyton Orient	0	0	**72**	**0**
2004-05	Kidderminster H	12	0		
2005-06	Kidderminster H	0	0		
2006-07	Kidderminster H	0	0	**12**	**0**
2007-08	Crewe Alex	22	0		
2008-09	Crewe Alex	38	6	**60**	**6**

LAWRENCE, Dennis (D) **303** **23**
H: 6 7 W: 11 13 b.Trinidad 1-8-74
Source: Defence Force. *Honours:* Trinidad & Tobago 85 full caps, 5 goals.

2000-01	Wrexham	3	0		
2001-02	Wrexham	32	2		
2002-03	Wrexham	32	1		
2003-04	Wrexham	45	5		
2004-05	Wrexham	44	4		
2005-06	Wrexham	39	2		
2006-07	Wrexham	3	0	**198**	**14**
2006-07	Swansea C	39	5		
2007-08	Swansea C	40	2		
2008-09	Swansea C	0	0	**79**	**7**
2008-09	Crewe Alex	26	2	**26**	**2**

LEGZDINS, Adam (G) **0** **0**
H: 6 1 W: 14 02 b.Stafford 28-11-86
Source: Scholar.

2006-07	Birmingham C	0	0		
2007-08	Birmingham C	0	0		
2008-09	Crewe Alex	0	0		

LEITCH-SMITH, AJ (F) **0** **0**
Source: Scholar.

2008-09	Crewe Alex	0	0		

McCREADY, Chris (D) **157** **3**
H: 6 1 W: 12 05 b.Ellesmere Port 5-9-81
Source: Scholar.

2000-01	Crewe Alex	0	0		
2001-02	Crewe Alex	1	0		
2002-03	Crewe Alex	8	0		
2003-04	Crewe Alex	22	0		
2004-05	Crewe Alex	20	0		
2005-06	Crewe Alex	25	0		
2006-07	Tranmere R	42	1	**42**	**1**
2007-08	Crewe Alex	34	1		
2008-09	Crewe Alex	5	1	**115**	**2**

McMANUS, Scott (D) **23** **3**
H: 6 0 W: 11 00 b.Prestwich 28-5-89

2006-07	Stenhousemuir	11	2		
2007-08	Stenhousemuir	6	0	**17**	**2**

From Curzon Ashton.

2008-09	Crewe Alex	6	1	**6**	**1**

MELLOR, Kelvin (D) **0** **0**
Source: Nantwich T.

2007-08	Crewe Alex	0	0		
2008-09	Crewe Alex	0	0		

MILLER, Shaun (F) **55** **8**
H: 5 10 W: 11 08 b.Alsager 25-9-87
Source: Scholar.

2006-07	Crewe Alex	7	3		
2007-08	Crewe Alex	15	1		
2008-09	Crewe Alex	33	4	**55**	**8**

MOORE, Byron (M) **69** **6**
H: 6 0 W: 10 06 b.Stoke 24-8-88
Source: Scholar.

2006-07	Crewe Alex	0	0		
2007-08	Crewe Alex	33	3		
2008-09	Crewe Alex	36	3	**69**	**6**

MURPHY, Luke (M) **9** **1**
H: 6 1 W: 11 05 b.Alsager 21-10-89
Source: Scholar.

2008-09	Crewe Alex	9	1	**9**	**1**

O'CONNOR, Michael (M) **87** **4**
H: 6 1 W: 11 08 b.Belfast 6-10-87
Source: From Scholar. *Honours:* Northern Ireland Youth, Under-21, B, 6 full caps.

2005-06	Crewe Alex	2	0		
2006-07	Crewe Alex	29	0		
2007-08	Crewe Alex	23	0		
2008-09	Crewe Alex	23	3	**77**	**3**
2008-09	*Lincoln C*	10	1	**10**	**1**

O'DONNELL, Daniel (D) **76** **3**
H: 6 2 W: 11 11 b.Livepool 10-3-86
Source: Scholar.

2004-05	Liverpool	0	0		
2005-06	Liverpool	0	0		
2006-07	Liverpool	0	0		
2006-07	*Crewe Alex*	25	1		
2007-08	Crewe Alex	27	1		
2008-09	Crewe Alex	24	1	**76**	**3**

POPE, Tom (M) **56** **17**
H: 6 3 W: 11 03 b.Stoke 27-8-85
Source: Lancaster C.

2005-06	Crewe Alex	0	0		
2006-07	Crewe Alex	4	0		
2007-08	Crewe Alex	26	7		
2008-09	Crewe Alex	26	10	**56**	**17**

RIX, Ben (M) **143** **4**
H: 5 9 W: 11 13 b.Wolverhampton 11-12-82
Source: Scholar.

2000-01	Crewe Alex	0	0		
2001-02	Crewe Alex	21	0		
2002-03	Crewe Alex	23	0		
2003-04	Crewe Alex	26	2		
2004-05	Crewe Alex	0	0		
2005-06	Crewe Alex	2	0		
2005-06	*Bournemouth*	11	0	**11**	**0**
2006-07	Crewe Alex	31	2		
2007-08	Crewe Alex	25	0		
2008-09	Crewe Alex	4	0	**132**	**4**

Transferred to Nea Salamis January 2009

SCHUMACHER, Steven (M) **162** **16**
H: 5 10 W: 11 00 b.Liverpool 30-4-84
Source: Scholar. *Honours:* England Youth.

2000-01	Everton	0	0		
2001-02	Everton	0	0		
2002-03	Everton	0	0		
2003-04	Everton	0	0		
2003-04	*Carlisle U*	4	0	**4**	**0**
2004-05	Bradford C	43	6		
2005-06	Bradford C	30	1		
2006-07	Bradford C	44	6	**117**	**13**
2007-08	Crewe Alex	26	1		
2008-09	Crewe Alex	15	2	**41**	**3**

SHELLEY, Danny (D) **3** **0**
H: 5 9 W: 10 08 b.Stoke 29-12-90
Source: Scholar.

2008-09	Crewe Alex	3	0	**3**	**0**

THOMPSON, Josh (F) **0** **0**
Source: Scholar.

2008-09	Crewe Alex	0	0		

TOMLINSON, Stuart (G) **20** **0**
H: 6 1 W: 11 02 b.Chester 10-5-85
Source: Scholar.

2002-03	Crewe Alex	1	0		
2003-04	Crewe Alex	1	0		
2004-05	Crewe Alex	0	0		
2005-06	Crewe Alex	2	0		
2006-07	Crewe Alex	7	0		
2007-08	Crewe Alex	0	0		
2008-09	Crewe Alex	9	0	**20**	**0**

WESTWOOD, Ashley (D) **2** **0**
H: 5 10 W: 11 00 b.Nantwich 1-4-90
Source: Scholar.

2008-09	Crewe Alex	2	0	**2**	**0**

WOODARDS, Danny (M) **84** **0**
H: 5 11 W: 11 01 b.Forest Gate 7-10-83
Source: Trainee.

2003-04	Chelsea	0	0		
2004-05	Chelsea	0	0		
2005-06	Chelsea	0	0		

From Exeter C.

2006-07	Crewe Alex	11	0		
2007-08	Crewe Alex	36	0		
2008-09	Crewe Alex	37	0	**84**	**0**

ZOLA, Calvin (F) **148** **26**
H: 6 3 W: 14 06 b.Kinshasa 31-12-84
Source: Scholar.

2001-02	Newcastle U	0	0		
2002-03	Newcastle U	0	0		
2003-04	Newcastle U	0	0		
2003-04	*Oldham Ath*	25	5	**25**	**5**
2004-05	Tranmere R	15	2		
2005-06	Tranmere R	22	4		
2006-07	Tranmere R	29	5		
2007-08	Tranmere R	30	5	**96**	**16**
2008-09	Crewe Alex	27	5	**27**	**5**

CRYSTAL PALACE (29)

ANDREW, Calvin (F) **82** **8**
H: 6 0 W: 12 11 b.Luton 19-12-86
Source: Scholar.

2004-05	Luton T	8	0		
2005-06	Luton T	1	1		
2005-06	*Grimsby T*	8	1	**8**	**1**
2005-06	*Bristol C*	3	0	**3**	**0**
2006-07	Luton T	7	1		
2007-08	Luton T	39	2	**55**	**4**
2008-09	Crystal Palace	7	1	**7**	**1**
2008-09	*Brighton & HA*	9	2	**9**	**2**

BUTTERFIELD, Danny (D) **331** **9**
H: 5 10 W: 11 06 b.Boston 21-11-79
Source: Trainee. *Honours:* England Youth.

1997-98	Grimsby T	7	0		
1998-99	Grimsby T	12	0		
1999-2000	Grimsby T	29	0		
2000-01	Grimsby T	30	1		
2001-02	Grimsby T	46	2	**124**	**3**
2002-03	Crystal Palace	46	1		
2003-04	Crystal Palace	45	4		
2004-05	Crystal Palace	7	0		
2005-06	Crystal Palace	13	0		
2006-07	Crystal Palace	28	0		
2007-08	Crystal Palace	30	0		
2008-09	Crystal Palace	26	1	**195**	**6**
2008-09	*Charlton Ath*	12	0	**12**	**0**

CADOGAN, Kieron (M) **4** **1**
H: 6 4 W: 12 07 b.Tooting 3-8-90
Source: Scholar.

2007-08	Crystal Palace	0	0		
2008-09	Crystal Palace	4	1	**4**	**1**

CARLE, Nick (F) **235** **30**
H: 5 9 W: 12 04 b.Sydney 23-11-81
Honours: Australia Youth, Under-20, Under-23, 8 full caps.

1997-98	Sydney Olympic	16	3		
1998-99	Sydney Olympic	11	3		
1999-2000	Sydney Olympic	24	1		
2000-01	Sydney Olympic	23	2		
2001-02	Sydney Olympic	12	3	**86**	**12**
2001-02	Troyes	5	0		
2002-03	Troyes	0	0	**5**	**0**
2003-04	Marconi Stallions	24	6		
2004	Ryde City	7	1	**7**	**1**
2004-05	Marconi Stallions	0	0	**24**	**6**
2005-06	Newcastle U Jets	22	3		
2006-07	Newcastle U Jets	23	4	**45**	**7**
2007-08	Genclerbirligi	14	1	**14**	**1**
2007-08	Bristol C	17	0	**17**	**0**
2008-09	Crystal Palace	37	3	**37**	**3**

CLYNE, Nathaniel (D) **26** **0**
H: 5 9 W: 10 07 b.Stockwell 5-4-91
Source: Scholar.

2008-09	Crystal Palace	26	0	**26**	**0**

COMLEY, James (M) **4** **0**
H: 5 10 W: 12 09 b.Holloway 24-1-91
Source: Scholar.

2008-09	Crystal Palace	4	0	**4**	**0**

DANNS, Neil (M) **152** **27**
H: 5 10 W: 10 12 b.Liverpool 23-11-82
Source: Scholar.

2000-01	Blackburn R	0	0		
2001-02	Blackburn R	0	0		
2002-03	Blackburn R	2	0		
2003-04	Blackpool	12	2	**12**	**2**
2003-04	Blackburn R	1	0		
2003-04	*Hartlepool U*	9	1	**9**	**1**
2004-05	Blackburn R	0	0	**3**	**0**
2004-05	Colchester U	32	11		
2005-06	Colchester U	41	8	**73**	**19**
2006-07	Birmingham C	29	3		
2007-08	Birmingham C	2	0	**31**	**3**
2007-08	Crystal Palace	4	0		
2008-09	Crystal Palace	20	2	**24**	**2**

DAYTON, James (M) **2** **0**
H: 5 8 W: 10 01 b.Enfield 12-12-88
Source: Scholar.

2007-08	Crystal Palace	0	0		
2008-09	Crystal Palace	0	0		
2008-09	*Yeovil T*	2	0	**2**	**0**

DERRY, Shaun (M) — 430 11
H: 5 10　W: 10 13　b.Nottingham 6-12-77
Source: Trainee.

Season	Club	Apps	Gls	Tot A	Tot G
1995-96	Notts Co	12	0		
1996-97	Notts Co	39	2		
1997-98	Notts Co	28	2	79	4
1997-98	Sheffield U	12	0		
1998-99	Sheffield U	26	0		
1999-2000	Sheffield U	34	0	72	0
1999-2000	Portsmouth	9	1		
2000-01	Portsmouth	28	0		
2001-02	Portsmouth	12	0	49	1
2002-03	Crystal Palace	39	1		
2003-04	Crystal Palace	37	2		
2004-05	Crystal Palace	7	0		
2004-05	*Nottingham F*	7	0	7	0
2004-05	Leeds U	7	2		
2005-06	Leeds U	41	0		
2006-07	Leeds U	23	1		
2007-08	Leeds U	0	0	71	3
2007-08	Crystal Palace	30	0		
2008-09	Crystal Palace	39	0	152	3

DJILALI, Kieran (M) — 6 0
H: 6 3　W: 13 02　b.London 1-1-91
Source: Scholar.

Season	Club	Apps	Gls	Tot A	Tot G
2008-09	Crystal Palace	6	0	6	0

ERTL, Johannes (D) — 129 6
H: 6 2　W: 12 08　b.Graz 13-11-82
Honours: Austria 7 full caps.

Season	Club	Apps	Gls	Tot A	Tot G
2003-04	Kalzdorf	11	3	11	3
2004-05	Sturm Graz	26	0		
2005-06	Sturm Graz	27	0		
2006-07	Sturm Graz	5	0	58	0
2006-07	FK Austria	24	1		
2007-08	FK Austria	24	2	48	3
2008-09	Crystal Palace	12	0	12	0

FLAHAVAN, Darryl (G) — 292 0
H: 5 11　W: 12 05　b.Southampton 9-9-77
Source: Trainee.
From Woking.

Season	Club	Apps	Gls	Tot A	Tot G
2000-01	Southend U	29	0		
2001-02	Southend U	41	0		
2002-03	Southend U	41	0		
2003-04	Southend U	37	0		
2004-05	Southend U	28	0		
2005-06	Southend U	43	0		
2006-07	Southend U	46	0		
2007-08	Southend U	26	0	291	0
2008-09	Crystal Palace	1	0	1	0
2008-09	*Leeds U*				

FLETCHER, Carl (M) — 326 27
H: 5 10　W: 11 07　b.Camberley 7-4-80
Source: Trainee. *Honours:* Wales 36 full caps, 1 goal.

Season	Club	Apps	Gls	Tot A	Tot G
1997-98	Bournemouth	1	0		
1998-99	Bournemouth	1	0		
1999-2000	Bournemouth	25	3		
2000-01	Bournemouth	43	6		
2001-02	Bournemouth	35	5		
2002-03	Bournemouth	42	1		
2003-04	Bournemouth	40	2		
2004-05	Bournemouth	6	2	193	19
2004-05	West Ham U	32	2		
2005-06	West Ham U	12	1	44	3
2005-06	Watford	3	0	3	0
2006-07	Crystal Palace	37	3		
2007-08	Crystal Palace	28	1		
2008-09	Crystal Palace	3	0	68	4
2008-09	*Nottingham F*	5	0	5	0
2008-09	*Plymouth Arg*	13	1	13	1

FLINDERS, Scott (G) — 52 0
H: 6 4　W: 13 00　b.Rotherham 12-6-86
Source: Scholar. *Honours:* England Youth, Under-20.

Season	Club	Apps	Gls	Tot A	Tot G
2004-05	Barnsley	11	0		
2005-06	Barnsley	3	0	14	0
2006-07	Crystal Palace	8	0		
2006-07	*Gillingham*	9	0	9	0
2006-07	*Brighton & HA*	12	0	12	0
2007-08	Crystal Palace	0	0		
2007-08	*Yeovil T*	9	0	9	0
2008-09	Crystal Palace	0	0	8	0

FONTE, Jose (D) — 140 8
H: 6 2　W: 12 08　b.Penafiel 22-12-83
Source: Sporting Lisbon, Salgueiros.
Honours: Portugal Under-21.

Season	Club	Apps	Gls	Tot A	Tot G
2004-05	Felgueiros	28	1	28	1
2005-06	Setubal	15	0	15	0
2005-06	Benfica	1	0	1	0
2005-06	Pacos	11	1	11	1
2006-07	Amadora	25	1	25	1
2007-08	Crystal Palace	22	1		
2008-09	Crystal Palace	38	4	60	5

GRIFFITT, Leandre (M) — 46 3
H: 5 8　W: 11 04　b.Maubeuge 21-5-84
Source: Amiens.

Season	Club	Apps	Gls	Tot A	Tot G
2003-04	Southampton	5	2		
2004-05	Southampton	2	0	7	2
2004-05	*Leeds U*	1	0	1	0
2004-05	*Rotherham U*	2	0	2	0
2005-06	Elfsborg	7	1		
2006-07	Elfsborg	12	0		
2006-07	Norrkoping	9	0		
2007-08	Elfsborg	2	0	21	1
2007-08	Norrkoping	1	0	10	0
2008-09	Crystal Palace	5	0	5	0

HILL, Clint (D) — 308 24
H: 6 0　W: 11 06　b.Liverpool 19-10-78
Source: Trainee.

Season	Club	Apps	Gls	Tot A	Tot G
1997-98	Tranmere R	14	0		
1998-99	Tranmere R	33	4		
1999-2000	Tranmere R	29	5		
2000-01	Tranmere R	34	5		
2001-02	Tranmere R	30	2	140	16
2002-03	Oldham Ath	17	1	17	1
2003-04	Stoke C	12	0		
2004-05	Stoke C	32	1		
2005-06	Stoke C	13	0		
2006-07	Stoke C	18	2		
2007-08	Stoke C	5	0	80	3
2007-08	Crystal Palace	28	3		
2008-09	Crystal Palace	43	1	71	4

HILLS, Lee (D) — 28 1
H: 5 10　W: 11 11　b.Croydon 3-4-90
Source: Scholar. *Honours:* England Youth.

Season	Club	Apps	Gls	Tot A	Tot G
2007-08	Crystal Palace	12	1		
2008-09	Crystal Palace	14	0	26	1
2008-09	*Colchester U*	2	0	2	0

IFILL, Paul (M) — 331 57
H: 6 0　W: 12 09　b.Brighton 20-10-79
Source: Trainee. *Honours:* England Youth, Barbados 10 full caps, 6 goals.

Season	Club	Apps	Gls	Tot A	Tot G
1998-99	Millwall	15	1		
1999-2000	Millwall	44	11		
2000-01	Millwall	35	6		
2001-02	Millwall	40	4		
2002-03	Millwall	45	6		
2003-04	Millwall	33	8		
2004-05	Millwall	18	4	230	40
2005-06	Sheffield U	39	9		
2006-07	Sheffield U	3	0	42	9
2006-07	Crystal Palace	13	2		
2007-08	Crystal Palace	13	2		
2008-09	Crystal Palace	33	4	59	8

KUDJODJI, Ben (F) — 1 0
H: 6 0　W: 11 11　b.Luton 23-4-89
Source: Scholar.

Season	Club	Apps	Gls	Tot A	Tot G
2007-08	Crystal Palace	1	0		
2008-09	Crystal Palace	0	0	1	0

KUQI, Shefki (F) — 426 112
H: 6 2　W: 13 13　b.Albania 10-11-76
Source: Trepka, Miki. *Honours:* Albania 8 full caps, 1 goal, Finland 56 full caps, 8 goals.

Season	Club	Apps	Gls	Tot A	Tot G
1995	MP	24	3		
1996	MP	26	7	50	10
1997	HJK Helsinki	25	6		
1998	HJK Helsinki	22	1		
1999	HJK Helsinki	25	11	72	18
From Jokerit					
2000-01	Stockport Co	17	6		
2001-02	Stockport Co	18	5	35	11
2001-02	Sheffield W	17	6		
2002-03	Sheffield W	40	8		
2003-04	Sheffield W	7	5	64	19
2003-04	Ipswich T	36	11		
2004-05	Ipswich T	43	19		
2005-06	Blackburn R	33	7		
2006-07	Blackburn R	1	0	34	7
2006-07	Crystal Palace	35	7		
2007-08	Crystal Palace	8	0		
2007-08	Fulham	10	0	10	0
2007-08	*Ipswich T*	4	0	83	30
2008-09	Crystal Palace	35	10	78	17

LAWRENCE, Matt (D) — 465 6
H: 6 1　W: 12 12　b.Northampton 19-6-74
Source: Grays Ath. *Honours:* England Schools.

Season	Club	Apps	Gls	Tot A	Tot G
1995-96	Wycombe W	3	0		
1996-97	Wycombe W	13	1		
1996-97	Fulham	15	0		
1997-98	Fulham	43	0		
1998-99	Fulham	1	0	59	0
1998-99	Wycombe W	34	2		
1999-2000	Wycombe W	29	2	79	5
1999-2000	Millwall	9	0		
2000-01	Millwall	45	0		
2001-02	Millwall	26	0		
2002-03	Millwall	33	0		
2003-04	Millwall	36	0		
2004-05	Millwall	44	0		
2005-06	Millwall	31	0	224	0
2006-07	Crystal Palace	34	0		
2007-08	Crystal Palace	37	1		
2008-09	Crystal Palace	32	0	103	1

LEE, Alan (F) — 356 87
H: 6 2　W: 13 09　b.Galway 21-8-78
Source: Trainee. *Honours:* Eire Under-21, 10 full caps.

Season	Club	Apps	Gls	Tot A	Tot G
1995-96	Aston Villa	0	0		
1996-97	Aston Villa	0	0		
1997-98	Aston Villa	0	0		
1998-99	Aston Villa	0	0		
1998-99	*Torquay U*	7	2	7	2
1998-99	*Port Vale*	11	2	11	2
1999-2000	Burnley	15	0		
2000-01	Burnley	0	0	15	0
2000-01	Rotherham U	31	13		
2001-02	Rotherham U	38	9		
2002-03	Rotherham U	41	15		
2003-04	Rotherham U	1	0	111	37
2003-04	Cardiff C	23	3		
2004-05	Cardiff C	38	5		
2005-06	Cardiff C	25	2	86	10
2005-06	Ipswich T	14	4		
2006-07	Ipswich T	41	16		
2007-08	Ipswich T	45	11		
2008-09	Ipswich T	3	0	103	31
2008-09	Crystal Palace	16	3	16	3
2008-09	*Norwich C*	7	2	7	2

McCARTHY, Patrick (D) — 146 8
H: 6 2　W: 13 07　b.Dublin 31-5-83
Source: Scholar. *Honours:* Eire Youth, B, Under-21.

Season	Club	Apps	Gls	Tot A	Tot G
2000-01	Manchester C	0	0		
2001-02	Manchester C	0	0		
2002-03	Manchester C	0	0		
2002-03	*Boston U*	12	0	12	0
2002-03	*Notts Co*	6	0	6	0
2003-04	Manchester C	0	0		
2004-05	Manchester C	0	0		
2004-05	Leicester C	12	0		
2005-06	Leicester C	38	2		
2006-07	Leicester C	22	1	72	3
2007-08	Charlton Ath	29	2	29	2
2008-09	Crystal Palace	27	3	27	3

MOSES, Victor (F) — 40 5
H: 5 10　W: 11 07　b.Lagos 12-12-90
Source: Scholar. *Honours:* England Youth.

Season	Club	Apps	Gls	Tot A	Tot G
2007-08	Crystal Palace	13	3		
2008-09	Crystal Palace	27	2	40	5

N'DIAYE, Alassane (M) — 0 0
Season	Club	Apps	Gls	Tot A	Tot G
2008-09	Crystal Palace	0	0		

OSTER, John (M) — 281 22
H: 5 9　W: 10 08　b.Boston 8-12-78
Source: Trainee. *Honours:* Wales Youth, Under-21, B, 13 full caps.

Season	Club	Apps	Gls	Tot A	Tot G
1996-97	Grimsby T	24	3		
1997-98	Everton	31	1		
1998-99	Everton	9	0	40	1
1999-2000	Sunderland	10	0		
2000-01	Sunderland	8	0		
2001-02	Sunderland	0	0		
2001-02	*Barnsley*	2	0	2	0
2002-03	Sunderland	3	0		
2002-03	*Grimsby T*	17	6	41	9
2003-04	Sunderland	38	5		
2004-05	Sunderland	9	0	68	5
2004-05	*Leeds U*	8	1	8	1
2004-05	*Burnley*	15	1	15	1
2005-06	Reading	33	1		
2006-07	Reading	25	1		

| 2007-08 | Reading | 18 | 0 | 76 | 2 |
| 2008-09 | Crystal Palace | 31 | 3 | 31 | 3 |

PINNEY, Nathaniel (F) 1 0
H: 6 0 W: 12 05 b.South Norwood 16-11-90
Source: Scholar.

| 2008-09 | Crystal Palace | 1 | 0 | 1 | 0 |

ROBINSON, Ashley (F) 6 0
H: 5 9 W: 14 01 b. *Honours:* 5-12-89
Source: Scholar.

| 2007-08 | Crystal Palace | 6 | 0 | | |
| 2008-09 | Crystal Palace | 0 | 0 | 6 | 0 |

SCANNELL, Sean (F) 48 4
H: 5 9 W: 11 07 b.Cork 21-3-89
Source: Scholar. *Honours:* Eire Youth, Under-21.

| 2007-08 | Crystal Palace | 23 | 2 | | |
| 2008-09 | Crystal Palace | 25 | 2 | 48 | 4 |

SCOWCROFT, James (F) 468 88
H: 6 1 W: 14 07 b.Bury St Edmunds 15-11-75
Source: Trainee. *Honours:* England Under-21.

1994-95	Ipswich T	0	0		
1995-96	Ipswich T	23	2		
1996-97	Ipswich T	41	9		
1997-98	Ipswich T	31	6		
1998-99	Ipswich T	32	13		
1999-2000	Ipswich T	41	13		
2000-01	Ipswich T	34	4		
2001-02	Leicester C	24	5		
2002-03	Leicester C	43	10		
2003-04	Leicester C	35	5		
2004-05	Leicester C	31	4	133	24
2004-05	*Ipswich T*	9	0	211	47
2005-06	Coventry C	41	3	41	3
2006-07	Crystal Palace	35	5		
2007-08	Crystal Palace	38	9		
2008-09	Crystal Palace	10	0	83	14

SPERONI, Julian (G) 200 0
H: 6 0 W: 11 00 b.Buenos Aires 18-5-79
Honours: Argentina Under-20, Under-21.

1999-2000	Platense	2	0		
2000-01	Platense	0	0	2	0
2001-02	Dundee	17	0		
2002-03	Dundee	38	0		
2003-04	Dundee	37	0	92	0
2004-05	Crystal Palace	6	0		
2005-06	Crystal Palace	4	0		
2006-07	Crystal Palace	5	0		
2007-08	Crystal Palace	46	0		
2008-09	Crystal Palace	45	0	106	0

THOMAS, Simon (F) 3 0
H: 5 6 W: 12 02 b.Stratford 21-7-84
Source: Thurrock, Aveley, Wivenhoe T, Redbridge, Boreham Wood.

| 2008-09 | Crystal Palace | 1 | 0 | 1 | 0 |
| 2008-09 | *Rotherham U* | 2 | 0 | 2 | 0 |

WIGGINS, Rhoys (D) 14 0
H: 5 8 W: 11 05 b.Uxbridge 4-11-87
Source: Scholar. *Honours:* Wales Youth, Under-21.

2006-07	Crystal Palace	0	0		
2007-08	Crystal Palace	0	0		
2008-09	Crystal Palace	1	0	1	0
2008-09	Bournemouth	13	0	13	0

WILKINSON, David (G) 0 0
H: 5 11 W: 12 00 b.Croydon 17-4-88
Source: Scholar.

2006-07	Crystal Palace	0	0		
2007-08	Crystal Palace	0	0		
2008-09	Crystal Palace	0	0		

DAGENHAM & R (30)

ALAILE, Michael (D) 0 0
H: 6 0 W: 12 09 b. 23-11-88

| 2008-09 | Dagenham & R | 0 | 0 | | |

ARABA, Hakeem (D) 0 0
H: 5 11 W: 12 02 b.London 23-12-88
Source: Scholar.

| 2008-09 | Dagenham & R | 0 | 0 | | |

ARBER, Mark (D) 367 28
H: 6 1 W: 11 09 b.Johannesburg 9-10-77
Source: Trainee.

1995-96	Tottenham H	0	0		
1996-97	Tottenham H	0	0		
1997-98	Tottenham H	0	0		
1998-99	Tottenham H	0	0		
1998-99	Barnet	35	2		
1999-2000	Barnet	45	6		
2000-01	Barnet	45	7		
2001-02	Barnet	0	0	125	15
2002-03	Peterborough U	25	2		
2003-04	Peterborough U	44	3		
2004-05	Oldham Ath	14	1	14	1
2004-05	Peterborough U	21	0		
2005-06	Peterborough U	46	2		
2006-07	Peterborough U	34	1		
2007-08	Peterborough U	0	0	170	8
2007-08	*Dagenham & R*	16	1		
2008-09	Dagenham & R	42	3	58	4

BENSON, Paul (F) 55 23
H: 6 1 W: 11 01 b.Rochford 12-10-79
Source: White Notley.

| 2007-08 | Dagenham & R | 22 | 6 | | |
| 2008-09 | Dagenham & R | 33 | 17 | 55 | 23 |

BINGHAM, Billy (D) 0 0
H: 5 11 W: 11 02 b.London 15-7-90
Source: Crystal Palace.

| 2008-09 | Dagenham & R | 0 | 0 | | |

CHARGE, Daniel (M) 1 0
H: 5 11 W: 11 00 b.Woodford 1-1-90
Source: Scholar.

| 2007-08 | Dagenham & R | 0 | 0 | | |
| 2008-09 | Dagenham & R | 1 | 0 | 1 | 0 |

COOK, Anthony (D) 1 0
H: 5 7 W: 11 02 b.London 10-8-89
Source: Croydon Ath.

| 2007-08 | Dagenham & R | 1 | 0 | | |
| 2008-09 | Dagenham & R | 0 | 0 | 1 | 0 |

DEAN, Harle (M) 0 0
H: 6 0 W: 11 10 b.Basingstoke 26-7-91
Source: Scholar.

| 2008-09 | Dagenham & R | 0 | 0 | | |

ERSKINE, Emmanuel (F) 0 0
H: 6 1 W: 13 06 b.London 13-1-89
Source: Wingate & Finchley.

| 2007-08 | Dagenham & R | 0 | 0 | | |
| 2008-09 | Dagenham & R | 0 | 0 | | |

FOSTER, Danny (D) 70 3
H: 5 10 W: 12 10 b.Enfield 23-9-84
Source: Trainee.

2002-03	Tottenham H	0	0		
2003-04	Tottenham H	0	0		
2004-05	Tottenham H	0	0		
2005-06	Tottenham H	0	0		
2006-07	Tottenham H	0	0		
2007-08	Dagenham & R	32	1		
2008-09	Dagenham & R	38	2	70	3

GAIN, Peter (M) 347 31
H: 5 9 W: 11 07 b.Hammersmith 11-11-76
Source: Trainee.

1995-96	Tottenham H	0	0		
1996-97	Tottenham H	0	0		
1997-98	Tottenham H	0	0		
1998-99	Tottenham H	0	0		
1998-99	Lincoln C	4	0		
1999-2000	Lincoln C	32	0		
2000-01	Lincoln C	24	5		
2001-02	Lincoln C	42	2		
2002-03	Lincoln C	43	5		
2003-04	Lincoln C	42	7		
2004-05	Lincoln C	40	0	227	21
2005-06	Peterborough U	37	3		
2006-07	Peterborough U	34	6		
2007-08	Peterborough U	0	0	71	9
2007-08	Dagenham & R	18	1		
2008-09	Dagenham & R	31	0	49	1

GRAHAM, Richard (M) 63 3
H: 5 10 W: 11 10 b.Newry 5-8-79
Source: Trainee. *Honours:* Northern Ireland Youth, Under-21.

1996-97	QPR	0	0		
1997-98	QPR	0	0		
1998-99	QPR	2	0		
1999-2000	QPR	0	0		
2000-01	QPR	0	0	2	0

From Chesham, Billericay, Kettering

2004-05	Barnet	0	0		
2005-06	Barnet	15	1		
2006-07	Barnet	34	2	49	3
2007-08	Dagenham & R	7	0		
2008-09	Dagenham & R	5	0	12	0

GRIFFITHS, Scott (D) 85 0
H: 5 9 W: 11 08 b.London 27-11-85
Source: Aveley.

| 2007-08 | Dagenham & R | 41 | 0 | | |
| 2008-09 | Dagenham & R | 44 | 0 | 85 | 0 |

HOGAN, David (G) 1 0
H: 6 0 W: 13 10 b.Harlow 31-5-89

| 2008-09 | Dagenham & R | 1 | 0 | 1 | 0 |

HUKE, Shane (M) 66 3
H: 5 11 W: 12 07 b.Reading 2-10-85
Source: Scholar.

2003-04	Peterborough U	0	0		
2004-05	Peterborough U	8	0		
2005-06	Peterborough U	3	0		
2006-07	Peterborough U	18	1	29	1
2007-08	Peterborough U	36	2		
2008-09	Dagenham & R	1	0	37	2

KALIPHA, Kayan (F) 0 0
Source: MK Dons, Harrow B.

| 2007-08 | Dagenham & R | 0 | 0 | | |
| 2008-09 | Dagenham & R | 0 | 0 | | |

MONTGOMERY, Graeme (M) 5 0
H: 6 1 W: 12 00 b.Dagenham 3-3-88
Source: Wealdstone.

| 2008-09 | Dagenham & R | 5 | 0 | 5 | 0 |

NURSE, Jon (F) 64 5
H: 5 9 W: 12 04 b.Barbados 28-3-81
Source: From Stevenage B. *Honours:* Barbados 4 full caps.

| 2007-08 | Dagenham & R | 30 | 1 | | |
| 2008-09 | Dagenham & R | 34 | 4 | 64 | 5 |

NWOKEJI, Mark (M) 16 3
H: 5 11 W: 11 05 b.London 30-1-82
Source: Harlow T, Leatherhead, Chesham U, Walton & Hersham, St Albans C, Staines T.

| 2008-09 | Dagenham & R | 16 | 3 | 16 | 3 |

OKUONGHAE, Magnus (D) 77 3
H: 6 3 W: 13 04 b.Nigeria 16-2-86
Source: Scholar.

2003-04	Rushden & D	1	0		
2004-05	Rushden & D	0	0		
2005-06	Rushden & D	21	1		
2006-07	Rushden & D	0	0	22	1
2007-08	Dagenham & R	10	0		
2008-09	Dagenham & R	45	2	55	2

PATTERSON, Marlon (D) 6 0
H: 5 9 W: 11 10 b.London 24-6-83
Source: Yeading.

| 2007-08 | Dagenham & R | 6 | 0 | | |
| 2008-09 | Dagenham & R | 0 | 0 | 6 | 0 |

ROBERTS, Tony (G) 216 0
H: 6 0 W: 13 11 b.Holyhead 4-8-69
Source: Trainee. *Honours:* Wales Under-21, 2 full caps.

1987-88	QPR	1	0		
1988-89	QPR	0	0		
1989-90	QPR	5	0		
1990-91	QPR	12	0		
1991-92	QPR	1	0		
1992-93	QPR	28	0		
1993-94	QPR	16	0		
1994-95	QPR	31	0		
1995-96	QPR	5	0		
1996-97	QPR	13	0		
1997-98	QPR	10	0	122	0
1998-99	Millwall	8	0	8	0

From St Albans C.

| 2007-08 | Dagenham & R | 43 | 0 | | |
| 2008-09 | Dagenham & R | 43 | 0 | 86 | 0 |

ROCHESTER, Kraig (M) 0 0
H: 6 1 W: 13 01 b.London 3-11-88
Source: Leicester C.

| 2007-08 | Dagenham & R | 0 | 0 | | |
| 2008-09 | Dagenham & R | 0 | 0 | | |

SAUNDERS, Sam (M)   62 14
H: 5 6   W: 11 04   b.London 29-10-82
Source: Welling U, Hastings T, Ashford T, Carshalton Ath.

2007-08	Dagenham & R	22	0		
2008-09	Dagenham & R	40	14	62	14

SOUTHAM, Glen (M)   75 3
H: 5 7   W: 11 10   b.Enfield 27-8-80
Source: Bishop's Stortford.

2007-08	Dagenham & R	45	2		
2008-09	Dagenham & R	30	1	75	3

STREVENS, Ben (M)   161 38
H: 6 1   W: 12 00   b.Edgware 24-5-80
Source: Wingate & Finchley.

1998-99	Barnet	0	0		
1999-2000	Barnet	6	0		
2000-01	Barnet	28	4		
2001-02	Barnet	0	0		
2002-03	Barnet	0	0		
2003-04	Barnet	0	0		
2004-05	Barnet	0	0		
2005-06	Barnet	35	5		
2006-07	Barnet	0	0	69	9

From Crawley T.

2007-08	Dagenham & R	46	15		
2008-09	Dagenham & R	46	14	92	29

TAIWO, Soloman (M)   50 4
H: 6 1   W: 13 02   b.Lagos 29-4-85
Source: Sutton U.

2007-08	Dagenham & R	10	0		
2008-09	Dagenham & R	40	4	50	4

TEJAN-SIE, Thomas (F)   1 0
H: 5 6   W: 11 08   b.London 23-11-88
Source: Leicester C Scholar, Wingate & Finchley.

2007-08	Dagenham & R	0	0		
2008-09	Dagenham & R	1	0	1	0

THOMAS, Wesley (F)   5 0
H: 5 10   W: 11 00   b.Barking 23-1-87
Source: QPR Youth, Waltham Forest, Thurrock, Fisher Ath.

2008-09	Dagenham & R	5	0	5	0

THOMPSON, Ed (G)   4 0
H: 5 10   W: 12 02   b.Enfield 8-1-83
Source: Wingate & Finchley.

2007-08	Dagenham & R	3	0		
2008-09	Dagenham & R	1	0	4	0

UDDIN, Anwar (D)   77 2
H: 5 11   W: 11 10   b.Whitechapel 1-11-81
Source: West Ham U Scholar.

2001-02	West Ham U	0	0		
2001-02	Sheffield W	0	0		
2002-03	Bristol R	18	1		
2003-04	Bristol R	1	0		
2004-05	Bristol R	0	0		
2005-06	Bristol R	0	0		
2006-07	Bristol R	0	0	19	1
2007-08	Dagenham & R	41	1		
2008-09	Dagenham & R	17	0	58	1

DARLINGTON (31)

ABBOTT, Pawel (F)   213 78
H: 6 2   W: 13 10   b.York 5-5-82
Source: LKS Lodz. *Honours:* Poland Under-21.

2000-01	Preston NE	0	0		
2001-02	Preston NE	0	0		
2002-03	Preston NE	16	4		
2002-03	Bury	17	6	17	6
2003-04	Preston NE	9	2	25	6
2003-04	Huddersfield T	13	5		
2004-05	Huddersfield T	44	26		
2005-06	Huddersfield T	36	12		
2006-07	Huddersfield T	18	5	111	48
2006-07	Swansea C	18	1	18	1
2007-08	Darlington	24	9		
2008-09	Darlington	18	8	42	17

AUSTIN, Neil (D)   210 5
H: 5 10   W: 11 09   b.Barnsley 26-4-83
Source: Trainee. *Honours:* England Youth, Under-20.

1999-2000	Barnsley	0	0		
2000-01	Barnsley	0	0		
2001-02	Barnsley	0	0		
2002-03	Barnsley	34	0		
2003-04	Barnsley	37	0		
2004-05	Barnsley	15	0		
2005-06	Barnsley	38	0		
2006-07	Barnsley	24	0	148	0
2007-08	Darlington	29	2		
2008-09	Darlington	33	3	62	5

BARNES, Corey (F)   3 0
H: 5 8   W: 10 08   b.Sunderland 1-1-92
Source: Scholar.

2008-09	Darlington	3	0	3	0

BLUNDELL, Greg (F)   215 51
H: 5 10   W: 11 06   b.Liverpool 3-10-77
Source: Tranmere R Trainee, Vauxhall M, Northwich Vic.

2003-04	Doncaster R	44	18		
2004-05	Doncaster R	41	9	85	27
2005-06	Chester C	30	7		
2006-07	Chester C	27	6	57	13
2006-07	Darlington	15	3		
2007-08	Darlington	36	6		
2008-09	Darlington	20	2	71	11
2008-09	Accrington S	2	0	2	0

BURGMEIER, Franz (M)   220 31
H: 5 9   W: 11 07   b.Triesen 7-4-82
Honours: Liechtenstein 19 full caps, 3 goals.

2001-02	Vaduz	26	5		
2002-03	Vaduz	31	8		
2003-04	Vaduz	31	5		
2004-05	Vaduz	27	9	115	27
2005-06	Aarau	35	1	35	1
2006-07	Basle	18	1	18	1
2007-08	Thun	17	0	17	0
2008-09	Darlington	35	2	35	2

FORTUNE, Clayton (D)   108 2
H: 6 3   W: 13 10   b.Forest Gate 10-11-82
Source: Tottenham H Scholar.

2000-01	Bristol C	0	0		
2001-02	Bristol C	1	0		
2002-03	Bristol C	10	0		
2003-04	Bristol C	6	0		
2004-05	Bristol C	30	0		
2005-06	Bristol C	6	0	53	0
2005-06	Port Vale	25	2		
2006-07	Leyton Orient	9	0		
2006-07	Port Vale	13	0	38	2
2007-08	Leyton Orient	1	0	10	0
2008-09	Darlington	7	0	7	0

FOSTER, Steve (D)   435 15
H: 6 1   W: 13 00   b.Mansfield 3-12-74
Source: Trainee.

1993-94	Mansfield T	5	0	5	0

From Telford U, Woking

1997-98	Bristol R	34	0		
1998-99	Bristol R	43	1		
1999-2000	Bristol R	43	1		
2000-01	Bristol R	44	4		
2001-02	Bristol R	33	1	197	7
2002-03	Doncaster R	0	0		
2003-04	Doncaster R	44	1		
2004-05	Doncaster R	34	1		
2005-06	Doncaster R	17	0	95	2
2005-06	Scunthorpe U	18	0		
2006-07	Scunthorpe U	44	0	62	0
2007-08	Darlington	42	2		
2008-09	Darlington	34	0	76	2

GRAY, Josh (F)   5 0
H: 6 1   W: 11 12   b.South Shields 22-7-91
Source: Scholar.

2008-09	Darlington	5	0	5	0

GRIFFIN, Adam (D)   179 9
H: 5 7   W: 10 04   b.Salford 26-8-84
Source: Scholar.

2001-02	Oldham Ath	1	0		
2002-03	Oldham Ath	0	0		
2003-04	Oldham Ath	26	1		
2004-05	Oldham Ath	35	2		
2005-06	Oldham Ath	0	0	62	3
2005-06	Oxford U	9	0	9	0
2005-06	Stockport Co	21	2		
2006-07	Stockport Co	42	3		
2007-08	Stockport Co	28	1	91	6
2008-09	Darlington	17	0	17	0

GROVES, Danny (M)   1 0
H: 6 2   W: 12 00   b.Darlington 12-10-90
Source: Scholar.

2008-09	Darlington	1	0	1	0

HARDMAN, Lewis (D)   1 0
H: 5 10   W: 11 00   b.Sunderland 12-4-85
Source: Scholar.

2006-07	Darlington	1	0		
2007-08	Darlington	0	0		
2008-09	Darlington	0	0	1	0

HULBERT, Robin (M)   169 3
H: 5 9   W: 12 02   b.Plymouth 14-3-80
Source: Trainee. *Honours:* England Schools, Youth.

1997-98	Swindon T	1	0		
1997-98	Newcastle U	0	0		
1998-99	Swindon T	16	0		
1999-2000	Swindon T	12	0	29	0
1999-2000	Bristol C	2	0		
2000-01	Bristol C	19	0		
2001-02	Bristol C	11	0		
2002-03	Bristol C	7	0		
2002-03	Shrewsbury T	7	0	7	0
2003-04	Bristol C	0	0	39	0
2004-05	Port Vale	24	0		
2005-06	Port Vale	1	0		
2006-07	Port Vale	20	1		
2007-08	Port Vale	22	0	67	1
2008-09	Darlington	27	2	27	2

KAZIMIERCZAK, Prezemek (G)   17 0
H: 6 0   W: 12 02   b.Lodz 22-2-88
Source: Scholar.

2006-07	Bolton W	0	0		
2006-07	Accrington S	8	0	8	0
2007-08	Bolton W	0	0		
2007-08	Darlington	1	0		
2008-09	Darlington	8	0	9	0

KENNEDY, Jason (M)   106 10
H: 6 1   W: 13 02   b.Stockton 11-9-86
Source: Scholar.

2004-05	Middlesbrough	1	0		
2005-06	Middlesbrough	3	0		
2006-07	Middlesbrough	0	0		
2006-07	Boston U	13	1	13	1
2006-07	Bury	12	0	12	0
2007-08	Middlesbrough	0	0	4	0
2007-08	Livingston	18	2	18	2
2007-08	Darlington	13	2		
2008-09	Darlington	46	5	59	7

LIVERSEDGE, Nick (G)   0 0
H: 6 1   W: 11 07   b.Huddersfield 18-7-88
Source: Scholar.

2007-08	Darlington	0	0		
2008-09	Darlington	0	0		

MAIN, Curtis (F)   19 2
H: 5 9   W: 12 02   b.South Shields 20-6-92
Source: Scholar.

2007-08	Darlington	1	0		
2008-09	Darlington	18	2	19	2

MILLER, Ian (M)   69 4
H: 6 2   W: 12 02   b.Colchester 23-11-83

2006-07	Ipswich T	1	0		
2006-07	Boston U	12	0	12	0
2006-07	Darlington	7	1		
2007-08	Ipswich T	0	0	1	0
2007-08	Darlington	28	2		
2008-09	Darlington	21	1	56	4

OAKES, Andy (G)   117 0
H: 6 3   W: 12 04   b.Northwich 11-1-77
Source: Burnley Trainee.

1995-96	Bury	0	0		
1996-97	Bury	0	0		
1997-98	Bury	0	0		

From Winsford U.

1998-99	Hull C	19	0	19	0
1999-2000	Derby Co	0	0		
1999-2000	Port Vale	0	0		
2000-01	Derby Co	6	0		
2001-02	Derby Co	20	0		
2002-03	Derby Co	7	0		
2003-04	Derby Co	10	0		
2004-05	Derby Co	0	0	43	0
2004-05	Bolton W	1	0	1	0
2004-05	Walsall	9	0		
2005-06	Walsall	25	0	34	0
2006-07	Swansea C	4	0	4	0
2007-08	Darlington	6	0		
2008-09	Darlington	10	0	16	0

POCKLINGTON, Scott (G)   0   0
H: 6 2   W: 13 00   b.Bishop Auckland
18-9-90
Source: Scholar.

2008-09	Darlington	0	0		

POOLE, David (M)   108   9
H: 5 8   W: 12 00   b.Manchester 25-11-84
Source: Trainee.

2002-03	Manchester U	0	0		
2003-04	Manchester U	0	0		
2004-05	Manchester U	0	0		
2005-06	Yeovil T	25	2		
2006-07	Yeovil T	4	0	29	2
2006-07	Stockport Co	31	4		
2007-08	Stockport Co	22	2	53	6
2008-09	Darlington	26	1	26	1

RYAN, Tim (D)   190   11
H: 5 10   W: 11 00   b.Stockport 10-12-74
Source: Trainee.

1992-93	Scunthorpe U	1	0		
1993-94	Scunthorpe U	1	0		
1994-95	Scunthorpe U	0	0	2	0
From Buxton.					
1996-97	Doncaster R	28	0		
From Southport.					
2003-04	Doncaster R	42	2		
2004-05	Doncaster R	39	4		
2005-06	Doncaster R	7	0	116	6
2005-06	Peterborough U	7	0	7	0
2006-07	Boston U	23	4	23	4
2006-07	Darlington	5	1		
2007-08	Darlington	13	0		
2008-09	Darlington	24	0	42	1

TREMARCO, Carl (D)   64   1
H: 5 8   W: 11 11   b.Liverpool 11-10-85
Source: Scholar.

2003-04	Tranmere R	0	0		
2004-05	Tranmere R	3	0		
2005-06	Tranmere R	18	1		
2006-07	Tranmere R	23	0		
2007-08	Tranmere R	8	0	52	1
2007-08	Wrexham	10	0		
2008-09	Wrexham	0	0	10	0
On loan from Wrexham.					
2008-09	*Darlington*	2	0	2	0

VALENTINE, Ryan (D)   258   6
H: 5 10   W: 11 05   b.Wrexham 19-8-82
Source: Trainee. *Honours:* Wales Youth, Under-21.

1999-2000	Everton	0	0		
2000-01	Everton	0	0		
2001-02	Everton	0	0		
2002-03	Darlington	43	1		
2003-04	Darlington	40	2		
2004-05	Darlington	36	1		
2005-06	Darlington	43	0		
2006-07	Wrexham	34	2		
2007-08	Wrexham	14	0	48	2
2007-08	Darlington	17	0		
2008-09	Darlington	31	0	210	4

WHITE, Alan (D)   414   22
H: 6 0   W: 13 04   b.Darlington 22-3-76
Source: Derby Co Schoolboy.

1994-95	Middlesbrough	0	0		
1995-96	Middlesbrough	0	0		
1996-97	Middlesbrough	0	0		
1997-98	Middlesbrough	0	0		
1997-98	Luton T	28	1		
1998-99	Luton T	33	1		
1999-2000	Luton T	19	1	80	3
1999-2000	Colchester U	4	0		
2000-01	Colchester U	32	0		
2001-02	Colchester U	33	3		
2002-03	Colchester U	41	0		
2003-04	Colchester U	33	1	143	4
2004-05	Leyton Orient	26	0	26	0
2004-05	Boston U	11	0		
2005-06	Boston U	37	4	48	4
2006-07	Notts Co	35	5	35	5
2006-07	*Peterborough U*	7	3	7	3
2007-08	Darlington	35	1		
2008-09	Darlington	40	2	75	3

DERBY CO (32)

ADDISON, Miles (D)   31   1
H: 6 2   W: 13 03   b.London 7-1-89
Source: Scholar.

2005-06	Derby Co	2	0		
2006-07	Derby Co	0	0		
2007-08	Derby Co	1	0		
2008-09	Derby Co	28	1	31	1

ALBRECHTSEN, Martin (D)   314   9
H: 6 1   W: 12 13   b.Copenhagen 31-3-80
Source: Denmark Youth, Under-21, 4 full caps.

1998-99	Aalborg	9	1		
1999-2000	Aalborg	31	1		
2000-01	Aalborg	30	0		
2001-02	Aalborg	19	1	89	3
2001-02	FC Copenhagen	14	0		
2002-03	FC Copenhagen	27	0		
2003-04	FC Copenhagen	31	0	72	0
2004-05	WBA	24	0		
2005-06	WBA	31	1		
2006-07	WBA	31	1		
2007-08	WBA	32	2	118	4
2008-09	Derby Co	35	2	35	2

ATKINS, Ross (G)   0   0
H: 6 0   W: 13 00   b.Derby 3-11-89
Source: Scholar.

2008-09	Derby Co	0	0		

BARNES, Giles (M)   82   10
H: 6 0   W: 12 10   b.Barking 5-8-88
Source: From Scholar. *Honours:* England Youth.

2005-06	Derby Co	19	1		
2006-07	Derby Co	39	8		
2007-08	Derby Co	21	0		
2008-09	Derby Co	3	0	82	10
2008-09	Fulham	0	0		

BUXTON, Jake (D)   151   5
H: 6 1   W: 13 05   b.Sutton-in-Ashfield 4-3-85
Source: Scholar.

2002-03	Mansfield T	3	0		
2003-04	Mansfield T	9	1		
2004-05	Mansfield T	30	1		
2005-06	Mansfield T	39	0		
2006-07	Mansfield T	30	1		
2007-08	Mansfield T	40	2		
2008-09	Mansfield T	0	0	151	5
From Burton Alb.					
2008-09	Derby Co	0	0		

BYWATER, Steve (G)   182   0
H: 6 2   W: 12 10   b.Manchester 7-6-81
Source: Trainee. *Honours:* England Youth, Under-20, Under-21.

1997-98	Rochdale	0	0		
1998-99	West Ham U	0	0		
1999-2000	West Ham U	4	0		
1999-2000	*Wycombe W*	2	0	2	0
1999-2000	*Hull C*	4	0	4	0
2000-01	West Ham U	1	0		
2001-02	West Ham U	0	0		
2001-02	*Wolverhampton W*	0	0		
2001-02	*Cardiff C*	0	0		
2002-03	West Ham U	0	0		
2003-04	West Ham U	17	0		
2004-05	West Ham U	36	0		
2005-06	West Ham U	1	0		
2005-06	*Coventry C*	14	0	14	0
2006-07	West Ham U	1	0	59	0
2006-07	Derby Co	37	0		
2007-08	Derby Co	18	0		
2007-08	*Ipswich T*	17	0	17	0
2008-09	Derby Co	31	0	86	0

CAMARA, Mo (D)   337   2
H: 5 11   W: 11 03   b.Conakry 25-6-75
Honours: Guinea 79 full caps.

1993-94	Beauvais	19	0		
1994-95	Beauvais	31	0		
1995-96	Troyes	13	0	13	0
1996-97	Beauvais	35	0	54	0
1997-98	Le Havre	14	0		
1998-99	Lille	34	2	34	2
1999-2000	Le Havre	2	0	16	0
2000-01	Wolverhampton W	18	0		
2001-02	Wolverhampton W	27	0		
2002-03	Wolverhampton W	0	0	45	0

2003-04	Burnley	45	0		
2004-05	Burnley	45	0	90	0
2005-06	Celtic	18	0		
2006-07	Celtic	1	0	19	0
2006-07	Derby Co	19	0		
2007-08	Derby Co	1	0		
2007-08	*Norwich C*	21	0	21	0
2008-09	Derby Co	1	0	21	0
2008-09	*Blackpool*	14	0	14	0
2008-09	*St Mirren*	10	0	10	0

CARROLL, Roy (G)   291   0
H: 6 2   W: 13 12   b.Enniskillen 30-9-77
Source: Trainee. *Honours:* Northern Ireland Youth, Under-21, 19 full caps.

1995-96	Hull C	23	0		
1996-97	Hull C	23	0	46	0
1996-97	*Wigan Ath*	0	0		
1997-98	Wigan Ath	29	0		
1998-99	Wigan Ath	43	0		
1999-2000	Wigan Ath	34	0		
2000-01	Wigan Ath	29	0	135	0
2001-02	Manchester U	7	0		
2002-03	Manchester U	10	0		
2003-04	Manchester U	6	0		
2004-05	Manchester U	26	0	49	0
2005-06	West Ham U	19	0		
2006-07	West Ham U	12	0	31	0
2007-08	Rangers	0	0		
2007-08	Derby Co	14	0		
2008-09	Derby Co	16	0	30	0

COMMONS, Kris (M)   213   42
H: 5 6   W: 9 08   b.Mansfield 30-8-83
Source: Scholar. *Honours:* Scotland 4 full caps.

2000-01	Stoke C	0	0		
2001-02	Stoke C	0	0		
2002-03	Stoke C	8	1		
2003-04	Stoke C	33	4	41	5
2004-05	Nottingham F	30	6		
2005-06	Nottingham F	37	8		
2006-07	Nottingham F	32	9		
2007-08	Nottingham F	39	9	138	32
2008-09	Derby Co	34	5	34	5

CONNOLLY, Paul (D)   202   2
H: 6 0   W: 11 09   b.Liverpool 29-9-83
Source: Scholar.

2000-01	Plymouth Arg	1	0		
2001-02	Plymouth Arg	0	0		
2002-03	Plymouth Arg	2	0		
2003-04	Plymouth Arg	29	0		
2004-05	Plymouth Arg	19	0		
2005-06	Plymouth Arg	31	0		
2006-07	Plymouth Arg	38	0		
2007-08	Plymouth Arg	42	1	162	1
2008-09	Derby Co	40	1	40	1

DAVIES, Steve (F)   79   8
H: 6 0   W: 12 00   b.Liverpool 29-12-87
Source: Scholar.

2005-06	Tranmere R	22	2		
2006-07	Tranmere R	28	1		
2007-08	Tranmere R	10	2	60	5
2008-09	Derby Co	19	3	19	3

DAVIS, Claude (D)   149   4
H: 6 3   W: 14 04   b.Kingston, Jam 6-3-79
Source: Portmore U. *Honours:* Jamaica 62 full caps, 2 goals.

2003-04	Preston NE	22	1		
2004-05	Preston NE	32	0		
2005-06	Preston NE	40	3	94	4
2006-07	Sheffield U	21	0	21	0
2007-08	Derby Co	19	0		
2008-09	Derby Co	8	0	27	0
2008-09	*Crystal Palace*	7	0	7	0

DICKINSON, Liam (F)   122   43
H: 6 4   W: 11 07   b.Salford 4-10-85
Source: Woodley Sports.

2005-06	Stockport Co	21	7		
2006-07	Stockport Co	33	7		
2007-08	Stockport Co	40	19	94	33
2008-09	*Huddersfield T*	13	6	13	6
2008-09	*Blackpool*	7	4	7	4
2008-09	*Leeds U*	8	0	8	0
2008-09	Derby Co	0	0		

DUDLEY, Mark (D)   1   0
H: 5 10   W: 12 02   b.Doncaster 29-1-90
Source: Scholar.

2008-09	Derby Co	1	0	1	0

GREEN, Paul (M)   227   28
H: 5 9   W: 10 02   b.Pontefract 10-4-83
Source: Scholar.

Season	Club				
2003-04	Doncaster R	43	8		
2004-05	Doncaster R	42	7		
2005-06	Doncaster R	34	3		
2006-07	Doncaster R	41	2		
2007-08	Doncaster R	38	5	198	25
2008-09	Derby Co	29	3	29	3

HANSON, Mitch (D)   5   0
H: 6 1   W: 13 07   b.Derby 2-9-88
Source: Scholar.

Season	Club				
2007-08	Derby Co	0	0		
2008-09	Derby Co	0	0		
2008-09	*Notts Co*	5	0	5	0

HULSE, Rob (F)   300   97
H: 6 1   W: 12 04   b.Crewe 25-10-79
Source: Trainee.

Season	Club				
1998-99	Crewe Alex	0	0		
1999-2000	Crewe Alex	4	1		
2000-01	Crewe Alex	33	11		
2001-02	Crewe Alex	41	12		
2002-03	Crewe Alex	38	22	116	46
2003-04	WBA	33	10		
2004-05	WBA	5	0	38	10
2004-05	Leeds U	13	6		
2005-06	Leeds U	39	12	52	18
2006-07	Sheffield U	29	8		
2007-08	Sheffield U	21	0	50	8
2008-09	Derby Co	44	15	44	15

KAZMIERCZAK, Przemyslaw (M)   135   17
H: 6 3   W: 12 08   b.Leczyca 5-5-82
Source: LKS Lodz, Gornik Leczna, Piotrcovia. *Honours:* Poland 9 full caps, 1 goal.

Season	Club				
2003-04	Pogon	24	5		
2004-05	Pogon	25	2		
2005-06	Pogon	24	3		
2006-07	Pogon	0	0	73	10
2006-07	*Boavista*	29	5	29	5
2007-08	Porto	11	0	11	0
2008-09	Derby Co	22	2	22	2

LEACOCK, Dean (D)   97   0
H: 6 2   W: 12 04   b.Croydon 10-6-84
Source: Trainee. *Honours:* England Youth, Under-20.

Season	Club				
2002-03	Fulham	0	0		
2003-04	Fulham	4	0		
2004-05	Fulham	0	0		
2004-05	*Coventry C*	13	0	13	0
2005-06	Fulham	5	0		
2006-07	Fulham	0	0	9	0
2006-07	Derby Co	38	0		
2007-08	Derby Co	26	0		
2008-09	Derby Co	11	0	75	0

McEVELEY, James (D)   123   4
H: 6 1   W: 13 03   b.Liverpool 11-2-85
Source: Trainee. *Honours:* England Under-20, Under-21. Scotland B, 3 full caps.

Season	Club				
2002-03	Blackburn R	9	0		
2003-04	Blackburn R	0	0		
2003-04	*Burnley*	4	0	4	0
2004-05	Blackburn R	5	0		
2004-05	*Gillingham*	10	1	10	1
2005-06	Blackburn R	0	0		
2005-06	*Ipswich T*	19	1	19	1
2006-07	Blackburn R	4	0	18	0
2006-07	Derby Co	15	0		
2007-08	Derby Co	29	2		
2008-09	Derby Co	15	0	59	2
2008-09	*Preston NE*	7	0	7	0
2008-09	*Charlton Ath*	6	0	6	0

MEARS, Tyrone (D)   117   6
H: 5 11   W: 11 10   b.Stockport 18-2-83
Source: Manchester C Juniors.

Season	Club				
2000-01	Manchester C	0	0		
2001-02	Manchester C	1	0	1	0
2002-03	Preston NE	22	1		
2003-04	Preston NE	12	1		
2004-05	Preston NE	4	0		
2005-06	Preston NE	32	2	70	4
2006-07	West Ham U	5	0	5	0
2007-08	*Derby Co*	13	1		
2007-08	Derby Co	25	1		
2008-09	Derby Co	3	0	41	2

On loan to Marseille August 2008

MENDY, Arnaud (F)   0   0
H: 6 3   W: 13 10   b.Evreux 10-2-90

Season	Club		
2008-09	Derby Co	0	0

NYATANGA, Lewin (D)   125   6
H: 6 2   W: 12 08   b.Burton 18-8-88
Source: Scholar. *Honours:* Wales Under-21, 27 full caps.

Season	Club				
2005-06	Derby Co	24	1		
2006-07	Derby Co	7	1		
2006-07	*Sunderland*	11	0	11	0
2006-07	*Barnsley*	10	1		
2007-08	Derby Co	2	1		
2007-08	*Barnsley*	41	1	51	2
2008-09	Derby Co	30	1	63	4

O'BRIEN, Mark (D)   1   0
H: 5 11   W: 12 02   b.Dublin 20-11-92
Source: Cherry Orchard.

Season	Club				
2008-09	Derby Co	1	0	1	0

PEARSON, Stephen (M)   185   19
H: 6 0   W: 11 01   b.Lanark 2-10-82
Honours: Scotland Under-21, B, 10 full caps.

Season	Club				
2000-01	Motherwell	6	0		
2001-02	Motherwell	27	2		
2002-03	Motherwell	29	6		
2003-04	Motherwell	18	4	80	12
2003-04	Celtic	17	3		
2004-05	Celtic	8	0		
2005-06	Celtic	18	2		
2006-07	Celtic	13	1	56	6
2006-07	Derby Co	9	0		
2007-08	Derby Co	24	0		
2007-08	*Stoke C*	4	0	4	0
2008-09	Derby Co	12	1	45	1

PEREPLOTKINS, Andrejs (M)   27   5
H: 5 7   W: 10 07   b.Kharkiv 27-12-84
Honours: Latvia 14 full caps.

Season	Club				
2002-03	Metalist Kharkiv	0	0		
2003	Fili Moscow	0	0		
2003-04	Anderlecht	7	2	7	2
2004	Bohemian	18	3	18	3
2004	Skonto Riga	0	0		
2005	Skonto Riga	0	0		
2006	Skonto Riga	0	0		
2007	Skonto Riga	0	0		
2008	Skonto Riga	0	0		
2008-09	Derby Co	2	0	2	0

On loan to Skonto Riga

PORTER, Chris (F)   201   72
H: 6 1   W: 12 09   b.Wigan 12-12-83
Source: School.

Season	Club				
2002-03	Bury	2	0		
2003-04	Bury	37	9		
2004-05	Bury	32	9	71	18
2005-06	Oldham Ath	31	7		
2006-07	Oldham Ath	35	21	66	28
2007-08	Motherwell	37	14		
2008-09	Motherwell	22	9	59	23
2008-09	Derby Co	5	3	5	3

PRICE, Lewis (G)   83   0
H: 6 3   W: 13 05   b.Bournemouth 19-7-84
Source: Southampton Academy. *Honours:* Wales Youth, Under-21, 6 full caps.

Season	Club				
2002-03	Ipswich T	0	0		
2003-04	Ipswich T	1	0		
2004-05	Ipswich T	8	0		
2004-05	*Cambridge U*	6	0	6	0
2005-06	Ipswich T	25	0		
2006-07	Ipswich T	34	0	68	0
2007-08	Derby Co	6	0		
2008-09	Derby Co	0	0	6	0
2008-09	*Milton Keynes D*	2	0	2	0
2008-09	*Luton T*	1	0	1	0

PRIJOVIC, Aleksander (F)   14   2
H: 6 3   W: 13 01   b.St Gallen 21-4-90
Honours: Serbia Youth.

Season	Club				
2008-09	Derby Co	0	0		
2008-09	*Yeovil T*	4	0	4	0
2008-09	*Northampton T*	10	2	10	2

RICHARDS, Matthew (M)   0   0
H: 5 9   W: 11 07   b.Derby 1-12-89
Source: Scholar.

Season	Club		
2006-07	Derby Co	0	0
2007-08	Derby Co	0	0
2008-09	Derby Co	0	0

SAVAGE, Robbie (M)   451   31
H: 5 11   W: 11 00   b.Wrexham 18-10-74
Source: Trainee. *Honours:* Wales Schools, Youth, Under-21, 39 full caps, 2 goals.

Season	Club				
1993-94	Manchester U	0	0		
1994-95	Crewe Alex	6	2		
1995-96	Crewe Alex	30	7		
1996-97	Crewe Alex	41	1	77	10
1997-98	Leicester C	35	2		
1998-99	Leicester C	34	1		
1999-2000	Leicester C	35	1		
2000-01	Leicester C	33	4		
2001-02	Leicester C	35	0	172	8
2002-03	Birmingham C	33	4		
2003-04	Birmingham C	31	3		
2004-05	Birmingham C	18	4	82	11
2004-05	Blackburn R	9	0		
2005-06	Blackburn R	34	1		
2006-07	Blackburn R	21	0		
2007-08	Blackburn R	12	0	76	1
2007-08	Derby Co	16	0		
2008-09	Derby Co	22	1	38	1
2008-09	*Brighton & HA*	6	0	6	0

SIMMONS, Paris (F)   1   0
H: 5 10   W: 11 12   b.London 2-1-90

Season	Club				
2007-08	Derby Co	1	0		
2008-09	Derby Co	0	0	1	0
2008-09	*Lincoln C*	0	0		

STERJOVSKI, Mile (M)   295   66
H: 6 1   W: 12 08   b.Wollongong 27-5-79
Honours: Australia Under-20, Under-23, 40 full caps, 8 goals.

Season	Club				
1995-96	Wollongong Wolves	2	0		
1996-97	Wollongong Wolves	0	0	2	0
1997-98	Sydney United	11	2		
1998-99	Sydney United	26	18	37	20
1999-2000	Parramatta Power	31	11	31	11
2000-01	Lille	22	4		
2001-02	Lille	25	6		
2002-03	Lille	22	5		
2003-04	Lille	21	0	90	15
2004-05	Basle	28	1		
2005-06	Basle	32	7		
2006-07	Basle	34	7	94	15
2007-08	Genclerbirligi	14	3	14	3
2007-08	Derby Co	21	0		
2008-09	Derby Co	15	2	27	2

STEWART, Jordan (D)   245   10
H: 6 0   W: 12 09   b.Birmingham 3-3-82
Source: Trainee. *Honours:* England Youth, Under-21.

Season	Club				
1999-2000	Leicester C	1	0		
1999-2000	*Bristol R*	4	0	4	0
2000-01	Leicester C	0	0		
2001-02	Leicester C	12	0		
2002-03	Leicester C	37	4		
2003-04	Leicester C	25	1		
2004-05	Leicester C	35	1	110	6
2005-06	Watford	35	0		
2006-07	Watford	31	0		
2007-08	Watford	39	2	105	2
2008-09	Derby Co	26	2	26	2

STUBBS, Alan (D)   496   19
H: 6 2   W: 14 02   b.Kirkby 6-10-71
Source: Trainee. *Honours:* England B.

Season	Club				
1990-91	Bolton W	23	0		
1991-92	Bolton W	32	1		
1992-93	Bolton W	42	2		
1993-94	Bolton W	41	1		
1994-95	Bolton W	39	1		
1995-96	Bolton W	25	4	202	9
1996-97	Celtic	20	0		
1997-98	Celtic	29	1		
1998-99	Celtic	23	1		
1999-2000	Celtic	23	0		
2000-01	Celtic	11	1	106	3
2001-02	Everton	31	2		
2002-03	Everton	35	0		
2003-04	Everton	27	0		
2004-05	Everton	31	1		
2005-06	Sunderland	10	1	10	1
2005-06	Everton	14	0		
2006-07	Everton	23	2		
2007-08	Everton	8	1	169	6
2007-08	Derby Co	8	0		
2008-09	Derby Co	1	0	9	0

TEALE, Gary (F)   406 37

H: 5 11   W: 12 02   b.Glasgow 21-7-78
Honours: Scotland Under-21, B, 13 full caps.

Season	Club				
1996-97	Clydebank	33	6		
1997-98	Clydebank	27	6		
1998-99	Clydebank	8	2	68	14
1998-99	Ayr U	23	4		
1999-2000	Ayr U	32	0		
2000-01	Ayr U	29	5		
2001-02	Ayr U	18	4	102	13
2001-02	Wigan Ath	23	1		
2002-03	Wigan Ath	38	2		
2003-04	Wigan Ath	28	2		
2004-05	Wigan Ath	37	3		
2005-06	Wigan Ath	24	0		
2006-07	Wigan Ath	12	0	162	8
2006-07	Derby Co	16	1		
2007-08	Derby Co	18	0		
2007-08	Plymouth Arg	12	0	12	0
2008-09	Derby Co	25	1	59	2
2008-09	Barnsley	3	0	3	0

TODD, Andy (D)   289 11

H: 5 11   W: 13 04   b.Derby 21-9-74
Source: Trainee.

Season	Club				
1991-92	Middlesbrough	0	0		
1992-93	Middlesbrough	0	0		
1993-94	Middlesbrough	3	0		
1994-95	Middlesbrough	5	0	8	0
1994-95	*Swindon T*	13	0	13	0
1995-96	Bolton W	12	2		
1996-97	Bolton W	15	0		
1997-98	Bolton W	25	0		
1998-99	Bolton W	20	0		
1999-2000	Bolton W	12	0	84	2
1999-2000	Charlton Ath	12	0		
2000-01	Charlton Ath	23	1		
2001-02	Charlton Ath	5	0	40	1
2001-02	*Grimsby T*	12	3	12	3
2002-03	Blackburn R	12	1		
2003-04	Blackburn R	19	0		
2003-04	*Burnley*	7	0	7	0
2004-05	Blackburn R	26	1		
2005-06	Blackburn R	22	2		
2006-07	Blackburn R	9	0	88	4
2007-08	Derby Co	19	1		
2008-09	Derby Co	11	0	30	1
2008-09	*Northampton T*	7	0	7	0

VARNEY, Luke (F)   166 40

H: 5 11   W: 11 00   b.Leicester 28-9-82
Source: Quorn.

Season	Club				
2002-03	Crewe Alex	0	0		
2003-04	Crewe Alex	8	1		
2004-05	Crewe Alex	26	4		
2005-06	Crewe Alex	27	5		
2006-07	Crewe Alex	34	17	95	27
2007-08	Charlton Ath	39	8		
2008-09	Charlton Ath	18	2	57	10
2008-09	*Sheffield W*	4	2	4	2
2008-09	Derby Co	10	1	10	1

VILLA, Emanuel (F)   207 65

H: 6 0   W: 12 00   b.Capital Federal 24-2-82

Season	Club				
2001-02	Huracan	18	8		
2002-03	Huracan	28	3	46	11
2003-04	Atletico Rafaela	25	9	25	9
2004-05	Rosario Central	32	14		
2005-06	Atlas	16	10		
2005-06	Rosario Central	10	4	42	18
2006-07	Tecos UAG	17	7	17	7
2006-07	Atlas	15	5	31	15
2007-08	Derby Co	16	3		
2008-09	Derby Co	30	2	46	5

ZADKOVICH, Ruben (M)   14 1

H: 5 11   W: 11 00   b.Australia 23-5-86
Source: Wollongong R, QPR, Sydney.
Honours: Australia Under-20, 1 full cap.

Season	Club				
2004-05	Notts Co	8	1		
2005-06	Notts Co	1	0		
2006-07	Notts Co	0	0		
2007-08	Notts Co	0	0	9	1
2008-09	Derby Co	5	0	5	0

DONCASTER R (33)

AMEOBI, Tomi (F)   12 0

H: 6 3   W: 12 10   b.Newcastle 16-8-88
Source: Scholar.

Season	Club				
2007-08	Leeds U	0	0		
2007-08	*Scunthorpe U*	9	0	9	0
2008-09	Doncaster R	1	0	1	0
2008-09	*Grimsby T*	2	0	2	0

BROOKER, Stephen (F)   248 78

H: 6 0   W: 14 00   b.Newport Pagnell 21-5-81
Source: Trainee.

Season	Club				
1999-2000	Watford	1	0		
2000-01	Watford	0	0	1	0
2000-01	Port Vale	23	8		
2001-02	Port Vale	41	9		
2002-03	Port Vale	26	5		
2003-04	Port Vale	32	8		
2004-05	Port Vale	9	5	131	35
2004-05	Bristol C	33	16		
2005-06	Bristol C	37	16		
2006-07	Bristol C	23	2		
2007-08	Bristol C	4	1		
2007-08	*Cheltenham T*	14	5	14	5
2008-09	Bristol C	4	2	101	37
2008-09	Doncaster R	1	1	1	1

BYFIELD, Darren (F)   341 86

H: 5 11   W: 12 07   b.Sutton Coldfield 29-9-76
Source: Trainee. *Honours:* Jamaica 7 full caps.

Season	Club				
1993-94	Aston Villa	0	0		
1994-95	Aston Villa	0	0		
1995-96	Aston Villa	0	0		
1996-97	Aston Villa	0	0		
1997-98	Aston Villa	7	0		
1998-99	Aston Villa	0	0		
1998-99	*Preston NE*	5	1	5	1
1999-2000	Aston Villa	0	0	7	0
1999-2000	*Northampton T*	6	1	6	1
1999-2000	*Cambridge U*	4	0	4	0
1999-2000	*Blackpool*	3	0	3	0
2000-01	Walsall	40	9		
2001-02	Walsall	37	4	77	13
2001-02	Rotherham U	3	2		
2002-03	Rotherham U	37	13		
2003-04	Rotherham U	28	7	68	22
2003-04	*Sunderland*	17	5	17	5
2004-05	Gillingham	38	6		
2005-06	Gillingham	29	13	67	19
2006-07	Millwall	31	16		
2007-08	Millwall	0	0	31	16
2007-08	Bristol C	33	8	33	8
2008-09	Doncaster R	15	0	15	0
2008-09	*Oldham Ath*	8	1	8	1

CHAMBERS, James (D)   231 0

H: 5 10   W: 11 11   b.West Bromwich 20-11-80
Source: Trainee. *Honours:* England Youth.

Season	Club				
1998-99	WBA	0	0		
1999-2000	WBA	12	0		
2000-01	WBA	31	0		
2001-02	WBA	5	0		
2002-03	WBA	8	0		
2003-04	WBA	17	0		
2004-05	WBA	0	0	73	0
2005-06	Watford	40	0		
2005-06	Watford	38	0		
2006-07	Watford	12	0	90	0
2006-07	*Cardiff C*	7	0	7	0
2007-08	Leicester C	24	0	24	0
2008-09	Doncaster R	37	0	37	0

COPPINGER, James (F)   245 27

H: 5 7   W: 10 03   b.Middlesbrough 10-1-81
Source: Darlington Trainee. *Honours:* England Youth.

Season	Club				
1997-98	Newcastle U	0	0		
1998-99	Newcastle U	0	0		
1999-2000	Newcastle U	0	0		
1999-2000	*Hartlepool U*	10	3		
2000-01	Newcastle U	1	0		
2001-02	Newcastle U	0	0	1	0
2001-02	*Hartlepool U*	14	2	24	5
2002-03	Exeter C	43	5		
2003-04	Exeter C	0	0	43	5
2004-05	Doncaster R	31	0		
2005-06	Doncaster R	36	5		
2006-07	Doncaster R	39	4		
2007-08	Doncaster R	39	3		
2008-09	Doncaster R	32	5	177	17

ELLIOTT, Stuart (M)   389 116

H: 5 10   W: 11 09   b.Belfast 23-7-78
Honours: Northern Ireland Under-21, B, 39 full caps, 4 goals.

Season	Club				
1994-95	Glentoran	0	0		
1995-96	Glentoran	1	0		
1996-97	Glentoran	8	1		
1997-98	Glentoran	22	5		
1998-99	Glentoran	31	7		
1999-2000	Glentoran	34	16	96	29
2000-01	Motherwell	33	10		
2001-02	Motherwell	37	10	70	20
2002-03	Hull C	36	12		
2003-04	Hull C	42	14		
2004-05	Hull C	36	27		
2005-06	Hull C	40	7		
2006-07	Hull C	32	5		
2007-08	Hull C	7	0	193	65
2007-08	Doncaster R	10	0		
2008-09	Doncaster R	9	0	19	0
2008-09	*Grimsby T*	11	2	11	2

FAIRHURST, Waide (F)   3 0

H: 5 10   W: 10 07   b.Sheffield 7-5-89
Source: Scholar.

Season	Club				
2008-09	Doncaster R	3	0	3	0

GREER, Gordon (D)   173 6

H: 6 2   W: 12 05   b.Glasgow 14-12-80
Source: From Port Glasgow. *Honours:* Scotland B.

Season	Club				
2000-01	Clyde	30	0	30	0
2000-01	Blackburn R	0	0		
2001-02	Blackburn R	0	0		
2002-03	Blackburn R	0	0		
2002-03	*Stockport Co*	5	1	5	1
2003-04	Kilmarnock	25	0		
2004-05	Kilmarnock	22	1		
2005-06	Kilmarnock	27	2		
2006-07	Kilmarnock	33	0	107	3
2007-08	Doncaster R	11	1		
2008-09	Doncaster R	1	0	12	1
2008-09	*Swindon T*	19	1	19	1

GUY, Lewis (F)   138 18

H: 5 10   W: 10 07   b.Penrith 27-8-85
Source: Trainee. *Honours:* England Youth, Under-20.

Season	Club				
2002-03	Newcastle U	0	0		
2003-04	Newcastle U	0	0		
2004-05	Newcastle U	0	0		
2004-05	Doncaster R	9	3		
2005-06	Doncaster R	31	3		
2006-07	Doncaster R	36	4		
2007-08	Doncaster R	29	6		
2008-09	Doncaster R	29	2	134	18
2008-09	*Hartlepool U*	4	0	4	0

HAYTER, James (F)   419 105

H: 5 9   W: 10 13   b.Newport (IW) 9-4-79
Source: Trainee.

Season	Club				
1996-97	Bournemouth	2	0		
1997-98	Bournemouth	5	0		
1998-99	Bournemouth	20	2		
1999-2000	Bournemouth	31	2		
2000-01	Bournemouth	40	11		
2001-02	Bournemouth	44	7		
2002-03	Bournemouth	45	9		
2003-04	Bournemouth	44	14		
2004-05	Bournemouth	39	19		
2005-06	Bournemouth	46	20		
2006-07	Bournemouth	42	10	358	94
2007-08	Doncaster R	34	7		
2008-09	Doncaster R	27	4	61	11

HEFFERNAN, Paul (F)   237 77

H: 5 10   W: 11 00   b.Dublin 29-12-81
Source: Newton.

Season	Club				
1999-2000	Notts Co	2	0		
2000-01	Notts Co	1	0		
2001-02	Notts Co	23	6		
2002-03	Notts Co	36	10		
2003-04	Notts Co	38	20	100	36
2004-05	Bristol C	27	5	27	5
2005-06	Doncaster R	26	8		
2006-07	Doncaster R	29	11		
2007-08	Doncaster R	27	7		
2008-09	Doncaster R	28	10	110	36

HIRD, Samuel (D)   63 1

H: 5 7   W: 10 12   b.Askern 7-9-87
Source: Scholar.

Season	Club				
2005-06	Leeds U	0	0		
2006-07	Leeds U	0	0		
2006-07	*Doncaster R*	5	0		
2007-08	Doncaster R	4	0		
2007-08	*Grimsby T*	17	0	17	0
2008-09	Doncaster R	37	1	46	1

LOCKWOOD, Adam (D) — 187 12

H: 6 0 W: 12 07 b.Wakefield 26-10-81
Source: Reading Trainee.

Season	Club	Apps	Gls	Tot A	Tot G
2003-04	Yeovil T	43	4		
2004-05	Yeovil T	10	0		
2005-06	Yeovil T	20	0	73	4
2005-06	*Torquay U*	9	3	9	3
2006-07	Doncaster R	44	2		
2007-08	Doncaster R	39	3		
2008-09	Doncaster R	22	0	105	5

MILLS, Matthew (D) — 106 6

H: 6 3 W: 12 12 b.Swindon 14-7-86
Source: Scholar. Honours: England Youth.

Season	Club	Apps	Gls	Tot A	Tot G
2004-05	Southampton	0	0		
2004-05	*Coventry C*	4	0	4	0
2004-05	*Bournemouth*	12	3	12	3
2005-06	Southampton	4	0	4	0
2005-06	Manchester C	1	0		
2006-07	Manchester C	1	0		
2006-07	*Colchester U*	9	0	9	0
2007-08	Manchester C	0	0	2	0
2007-08	Doncaster R	34	3		
2008-09	Doncaster R	41	0	75	3

NELTHORPE, Craig (M) — 17 1

H: 5 10 W: 11 00 b.Doncaster 10-6-87
Source: Scholar.

Season	Club	Apps	Gls	Tot A	Tot G
2004-05	Doncaster R	1	0		
2005-06	Doncaster R	1	0		
2006-07	Doncaster R	6	1		
2007-08	Doncaster R	2	0		
2007-08	*Darlington*	7	0	7	0
2008-09	Doncaster R	0	0	10	1

O'CONNOR, James (D) — 170 3

H: 5 10 W: 12 05 b.Birmingham 20-11-84
Source: Scholar.

Season	Club	Apps	Gls	Tot A	Tot G
2003-04	Aston Villa	0	0		
2004-05	Aston Villa	0	0		
2004-05	*Port Vale*	13	0	13	0
2004-05	Bournemouth	6	0		
2005-06	Bournemouth	39	1	45	1
2006-07	Doncaster R	40	1		
2007-08	Doncaster R	40	0		
2008-09	Doncaster R	32	1	112	2

PRICE, Jason (M) — 384 62

H: 6 2 W: 11 05 b.Pontypridd 12-4-77
Source: Aberaman Ath. Honours: Wales Under-21.

Season	Club	Apps	Gls	Tot A	Tot G
1995-96	Swansea C	0	0		
1996-97	Swansea C	2	0		
1997-98	Swansea C	34	3		
1998-99	Swansea C	28	4		
1999-2000	Swansea C	39	6		
2000-01	Swansea C	41	4	144	17
2001-02	Brentford	15	1	15	1
2001-02	Tranmere R	24	7		
2002-03	Tranmere R	25	4	49	11
2003-04	Hull C	33	9		
2004-05	Hull C	27	2		
2005-06	Hull C	15	2	75	13
2005-06	Doncaster R	11	4		
2006-07	Doncaster R	31	6		
2007-08	Doncaster R	29	7		
2008-09	Doncaster R	22	0	93	17
2008-09	*Millwall*	8	3	8	3

ROBERTS, Gareth (D) — 380 18

H: 5 8 W: 11 12 b.Wrexham 6-2-78
Source: Trainee. Honours: Wales Under-21, B, 9 full caps.

Season	Club	Apps	Gls	Tot A	Tot G
1995-96	Liverpool	0	0		
1996-97	Liverpool	0	0		
1997-98	Liverpool	0	0		
1998-99	Liverpool	0	0		
1999-2000	Tranmere R	37	1		
2000-01	Tranmere R	34	0		
2001-02	Tranmere R	45	2		
2002-03	Tranmere R	37	4		
2003-04	Tranmere R	44	1		
2004-05	Tranmere R	40	3		
2005-06	Tranmere R	44	2	281	13
2006-07	Doncaster R	30	1		
2007-08	Doncaster R	37	3		
2008-09	Doncaster R	32	1	99	5

SHIELS, Dean (M) — 130 25

H: 5 11 W: 9 10 b.Magherfelt 1-2-85
Source: Arsenal Scholar. Honours: Northern Ireland Under-21, 4 full caps.

Season	Club	Apps	Gls	Tot A	Tot G
2002-03	Arsenal	0	0		
2003-04	Arsenal	0	0		
2004-05	*Hibernian*	37	5		
2005-06	*Hibernian*	16	2		
2006-07	*Hibernian*	24	7		
2007-08	*Hibernian*	22	7		
2008-09	*Hibernian*	19	3	118	24
2008-09	Doncaster R	12	1	12	1

SMITH, Benjamin (G) — 22 0

H: 6 1 W: 12 11 b.Newcastle 5-9-86
Source: Newcastle U Scholar.

Season	Club	Apps	Gls	Tot A	Tot G
2005-06	Stockport Co	0	0		
2006-07	Doncaster R	13	0		
2007-08	Doncaster R	0	0		
2007-08	*Lincoln C*	9	0	9	0
2008-09	Doncaster R	0	0	13	0

SPICER, John (M) — 142 11

H: 5 11 W: 11 07 b.Romford 13-9-83
Source: Scholar. Honours: England Schools, Youth, Under-20.

Season	Club	Apps	Gls	Tot A	Tot G
2001-02	Arsenal	0	0		
2002-03	Arsenal	0	0		
2003-04	Arsenal	0	0		
2004-05	Arsenal	0	0		
2004-05	Bournemouth	39	6		
2005-06	Bournemouth	4	0	43	6
2005-06	Burnley	34	3		
2006-07	Burnley	11	1		
2007-08	Burnley	24	0	69	4
2008-09	Doncaster R	30	1	30	1

STOCK, Brian (M) — 265 31

H: 5 11 W: 11 02 b.Winchester 24-12-81
Source: Trainee. Honours: Wales Under-21.

Season	Club	Apps	Gls	Tot A	Tot G
1999-2000	Bournemouth	5	0		
2000-01	Bournemouth	1	0		
2001-02	Bournemouth	26	2		
2002-03	Bournemouth	27	2		
2003-04	Bournemouth	19	3		
2004-05	Bournemouth	41	6		
2005-06	Bournemouth	26	3	145	16
2005-06	Preston NE	6	1		
2006-07	Preston NE	2	0	8	1
2006-07	Doncaster R	36	3		
2007-08	Doncaster R	40	5		
2008-09	Doncaster R	36	6	112	14

SULLIVAN, Neil (G) — 453 0

H: 6 2 W: 12 00 b.Sutton 24-2-70
Source: Trainee. Honours: Scotland 28 full caps.

Season	Club	Apps	Gls	Tot A	Tot G
1988-89	Wimbledon	0	0		
1989-90	Wimbledon	0	0		
1990-91	Wimbledon	1	0		
1991-92	Wimbledon	1	0		
1991-92	*Crystal Palace*	1	0	1	0
1992-93	Wimbledon	1	0		
1993-94	Wimbledon	2	0		
1994-95	Wimbledon	11	0		
1995-96	Wimbledon	16	0		
1996-97	Wimbledon	36	0		
1997-98	Wimbledon	38	0		
1998-99	Wimbledon	38	0		
1999-2000	Wimbledon	37	0	181	0
2000-01	Tottenham H	35	0		
2001-02	Tottenham H	29	0		
2002-03	Tottenham H	0	0	64	0
2003-04	Chelsea	4	0	4	0
2004-05	Leeds U	46	0		
2005-06	Leeds U	42	0		
2006-07	Leeds U	7	0	95	0
2006-07	*Doncaster R*	16	0		
2007-08	Doncaster R	46	0		
2008-09	Doncaster R	46	0	108	0

TAYLOR, Gareth (F) — 498 123

H: 6 2 W: 13 07 b.Weston-Super-Mare 25-2-73
Source: Southampton Trainee. Honours: Wales Under-21, 15 full caps, 1 goal.

Season	Club	Apps	Gls	Tot A	Tot G
1991-92	Bristol R	1	0		
1992-93	Bristol R	0	0		
1993-94	Bristol R	0	0		
1994-95	Bristol R	39	12		
1995-96	Bristol R	7	4	47	16
1995-96	Crystal Palace	20	1	20	1
1995-96	Sheffield U	10	2		
1996-97	Sheffield U	34	12		
1997-98	Sheffield U	28	10		
1998-99	Sheffield U	12	1	84	25
1998-99	Manchester C	26	4		
1999-2000	Manchester C	17	5		
1999-2000	*Port Vale*	4	0	4	0
1999-2000	*QPR*	6	1	6	1
2000-01	Manchester C	0	0	43	9
2000-01	*Burnley*	15	4		
2001-02	Burnley	40	16		
2002-03	Burnley	40	16		
2003-04	Burnley	0	0	95	36
2003-04	Nottingham F	34	8		
2004-05	Nottingham F	36	7		
2005-06	Nottingham F	20	4	90	19
2005-06	*Crewe Alex*	15	4	15	4
2006-07	Tranmere R	37	7		
2007-08	Tranmere R	23	3	60	10
2008-09	Doncaster R	12	1		
2008-09	Doncaster R	17	0	29	1
2008-09	*Carlisle U*	5	1	5	1

VAN NIEUWSTADT, Jos (D) — 198 4

H: 5 9 W: 12 10 b.Waalwijk 19-11-79

Season	Club	Apps	Gls	Tot A	Tot G
1998-99	Willem II	1	0		
1999-2000	Willem II	6	0		
2000-01	Willem II	19	0		
2001-02	Willem II	33	0		
2002-03	Willem II	20	1		
2003-04	Willem II	23	0		
2004-05	Willem II	20	1		
2005-06	Willem II	17	0	139	2
2006-07	Excelsior	32	1		
2007-08	Excelsior	11	0	43	1
2008-09	Doncaster R	16	1	16	1

WELLENS, Richard (M) — 359 33

H: 5 9 W: 11 06 b.Manchester 26-3-80
Source: Trainee. Honours: England Youth.

Season	Club	Apps	Gls	Tot A	Tot G
1996-97	Manchester U	0	0		
1997-98	Manchester U	0	0		
1998-99	Manchester U	0	0		
1999-2000	Manchester U	0	0		
1999-2000	Blackpool	8	0		
2000-01	Blackpool	36	8		
2001-02	Blackpool	36	1		
2002-03	Blackpool	39	1		
2003-04	Blackpool	41	3		
2004-05	Blackpool	28	3	188	16
2005-06	Oldham Ath	45	4		
2006-07	Oldham Ath	42	4	87	8
2007-08	Doncaster R	45	6		
2008-09	Doncaster R	39	3	84	9

WILSON, Mark (M) — 151 10

H: 5 10 W: 12 07 b.Scunthorpe 9-2-79
Source: Trainee. Honours: England Schools, Youth, Under-21.

Season	Club	Apps	Gls	Tot A	Tot G
1995-96	Manchester U	0	0		
1996-97	Manchester U	0	0		
1997-98	Manchester U	0	0		
1997-98	*Wrexham*	13	4	13	4
1998-99	Manchester U	0	0		
1999-2000	Manchester U	3	0		
2000-01	Manchester U	0	0	3	0
2001-02	Middlesbrough	10	0		
2002-03	Middlesbrough	6	0		
2002-03	*Stoke C*	4	0	4	0
2003-04	Middlesbrough	0	0		
2003-04	*Swansea C*	12	2	12	2
2003-04	*Sheffield W*	3	0	3	0
2004-05	Middlesbrough	0	0	16	0
2004-05	*Doncaster R*	3	0		
2004-05	Livingston	5	0	5	0
2006	Dallas	12	1	12	1
2006-07	Doncaster R	22	1		
2007-08	Doncaster R	31	1		
2008-09	Doncaster R	22	1	78	3
2008-09	*Tranmere R*	5	0	5	0

WOODS, Gary (G) — 1 0

H: 6 1 W: 11 00 b.Kettering 1-10-90
Source: Scholar.

Season	Club	Apps	Gls	Tot A	Tot G
2008-09	Manchester U	0	0		
2008-09	Doncaster R	1	0	1	0

WOODS, Martin (M) — 109 6

H: 5 11 W: 11 13 b.Airdrie 1-1-86
Source: Trainee. Honours: Scotland Youth, Under-21.

Season	Club	Apps	Gls	Tot A	Tot G
2002-03	Leeds U	0	0		
2003-04	Leeds U	0	0		
2004-05	Leeds U	1	0	1	0
2004-05	*Hartlepool U*	6	0	6	0
2005-06	Sunderland	7	0	7	0
2006-07	Rotherham U	36	4	36	4
2007-08	Doncaster R	15	0		
2007-08	*Yeovil T*	3	0	3	0
2008-09	Doncaster R	41	2	56	2

EVERTON (34)

AGARD, Kieran (F)   0   0
b.Newham 10-10-89
Source: Scholar.

2006-07	Everton	0	0
2007-08	Everton	0	0
2008-09	Everton	0	0

AKPAN, Hope (M)   0   0
b.Liverpool 14-8-91
Source: Scholar.

2007-08	Everton	0	0
2008-09	Everton	0	0

ANICHEBE, Victor (F)   65   6
H: 6 1   W: 13 00   b.Nigeria 23-4-88
Source: From Scholar. *Honours:* Nigeria
Under-23, 4 full caps, 1 goal.

2005-06	Everton	2	1
2006-07	Everton	19	3
2007-08	Everton	27	1
2008-09	Everton	17	1	65	6

ARTETA, Mikel (M)   225   33
H: 5 9   W: 10 08   b.San Sebastian 26-3-82
Honours: Spain Youth, Under-21.

2000-01	Barcelona B	0	0
2000-01	Paris St Germain	6	1
2001-02	Paris St Germain	25	1	31	2
2002-03	Rangers	27	4
2003-04	Rangers	23	8	50	12
2004-05	Real Sociedad	14	1	14	1
2004-05	Everton	12	1
2005-06	Everton	29	1
2006-07	Everton	35	9
2007-08	Everton	28	1
2008-09	Everton	26	6	130	18

BAINES, Leighton (D)   198   5
H: 5 8   W: 11 00   b.Liverpool 11-12-84
Source: Trainee. *Honours:* England
Under-21.

2002-03	Wigan Ath	6	0
2003-04	Wigan Ath	26	0
2004-05	Wigan Ath	41	1
2005-06	Wigan Ath	37	0
2006-07	Wigan Ath	35	3
2007-08	Wigan Ath	0	0	145	4
2007-08	Everton	22	0
2008-09	Everton	31	1	53	1

BARNETT, Moses (D)   0   0
b.London 3-12-90
Source: Arsenal.

2007-08	Everton	0	0
2008-09	Everton	0	0

BAXTER, Jose (F)   3   0
H: 5 9   W: 11 07   b.Bootle 7-2-92
Source: From Academy. *Honours:* England
Youth.

2008-09	Everton	3	0	3	0

CAHILL, Tim (M)   348   89
H: 5 10   W: 10 12   b.Sydney 6-12-79
Source: Sydney U. *Honours:* Western Samoa
Youth, Australia Under-23, 32 full caps, 14
goals.

1997-98	Millwall	1	0
1998-99	Millwall	36	6
1999-2000	Millwall	45	12
2000-01	Millwall	41	9
2001-02	Millwall	43	13
2002-03	Millwall	11	3
2003-04	Millwall	40	9	217	52
2004-05	Everton	33	11
2005-06	Everton	32	6
2006-07	Everton	18	5
2007-08	Everton	18	7
2008-09	Everton	30	8	131	37

CASTILLO, Segundo (M)   237   38
H: 5 10   W: 12 02   b.Quito 15-5-82
Honours: Ecuador 41 full caps, 2 goals.

2000	Espoli	8	0
2001	Espoli	28	2
2002	Espoli	30	9	66	11
2003	El Nacional	14	0
2004	El Nacional	32	0
2005	El Nacional	48	8
2006	El Nacional	19	3	113	11
2006-07	Red Star Belgrade	23	8

2007-08	Red Star Belgrade	26	8	49	16
2008-09	Everton	9	0	9	0

CODLING, Lewis (F)   0   0
b.Bootle 11-11-90
Source: Scholar.

2008-09	Everton	0	0

COLEMAN, Seamus (D)   0   0
b.Donegal 11-10-88
Source: From Sligo R. *Honours:* Eire
Under-21, Under-23.

2008-09	Everton	0	0

CRAIG, Nathan (M)   0   0
b.Bangor 25-10-91
Source: Scholar. *Honours:* Wales Under-21.

2008-09	Everton	0	0

DUFFY, Shane (D)   0   0
b.County Derry 1-1-92
Source: Scholar.

2008-09	Everton	0	0

FELLAINI, Marouane (M)   89   14
H: 6 4   W: 13 05   b.Brussels 22-11-87
Honours: Belgium 16 full caps, 2 goals.

2006-07	Standard Liege	29	0
2007-08	Standard Liege	30	6	59	6
2008-09	Everton	30	8	30	8

GOSLING, Dan (M)   33   4
H: 6 0   W: 11 00   b.Brixham 2-2-90
Source: Scholar. *Honours:* England Youth.

2006-07	Plymouth Arg	12	2
2007-08	Plymouth Arg	10	0	22	2
2007-08	Everton	0	0
2008-09	Everton	11	2	11	2

HIBBERT, Tony (D)   181   0
H: 5 9   W: 11 05   b.Liverpool 20-2-81
Source: Trainee.

1998-99	Everton	0	0
1999-2000	Everton	0	0
2000-01	Everton	3	0
2001-02	Everton	10	0
2002-03	Everton	24	0
2003-04	Everton	25	0
2004-05	Everton	36	0
2005-06	Everton	29	0
2006-07	Everton	13	0
2007-08	Everton	24	0
2008-09	Everton	17	0	181	0

HOWARD, Tim (G)   240   0
H: 6 3   W: 14 12   b.North Brunswick 6-3-79
Source: USA Under-21, Under-23, 43 full
caps.

1998	NY/NJ MetrStars	1	0
1999	NY/NJ MetrStars	9	0
2000	NY/NJ MetrStars	9	0
2001	NY/NJ MetrStars	26	0
2002	NY/NJ MetrStars	27	0
2003	NY/NJ MetrStars	13	0	85	0
2003-04	Manchester U	32	0
2004-05	Manchester U	12	0
2005-06	Manchester U	1	0
2006-07	Manchester U	0	0	45	0
2006-07	Everton	36	0
2007-08	Everton	36	0
2008-09	Everton	38	0	110	0

IRVING, John (M)   0   0
H: 5 10   W: 11 00   b.Liverpool 17-9-88
Source: Scholar.

2005-06	Everton	0	0
2006-07	Everton	0	0
2007-08	Everton	0	0
2008-09	Everton	0	0

JACOBSEN, Lars (D)   254   0
H: 5 11   W: 12 02   b.Odense 29-9-79
Honours: Denmark Youth, Under-21, 22 full
caps.

1996-97	Odense	5	0
1997-98	Odense	15	0
1998-99	Odense	0	0
1999-2000	Odense	27	1
2000-01	Odense	32	0
2001-02	Odense	32	1	111	2
2002-03	Hamburg II	5	0
2002-03	Hamburg	12	1
2003-04	Hamburg II	1	0	6	0
2003-04	Hamburg	10	0	22	1
2003-04	FC Copenhagen	13	0
2004-05	FC Copenhagen	27	0

2005-06	FC Copenhagen	33	3
2006-07	FC Copenhagen	30	0	103	3
2007-08	Nuremberg	7	0	7	0
2008-09	Everton	5	0	5	0

JAGIELKA, Phil (D)   322   19
H: 6 0   W: 13 01   b.Manchester 17-8-82
Source: Scholar. *Honours:* England Youth,
Under-20, Under-21, B, 3 full caps.

1999-2000	Sheffield U	1	0
2000-01	Sheffield U	15	0
2001-02	Sheffield U	23	3
2002-03	Sheffield U	42	0
2003-04	Sheffield U	43	3
2004-05	Sheffield U	46	0
2005-06	Sheffield U	46	8
2006-07	Sheffield U	38	4	254	18
2007-08	Everton	34	1
2008-09	Everton	34	0	68	1

JUTKIEWICZ, Lucas (F)   49   5
H: 6 1   W: 12 11   b.Southampton 20-3-89
Source: Scholar.

2005-06	Swindon T	5	0
2006-07	Swindon T	33	5	38	5
2007-08	Everton	0	0
2007-08	Everton	0	0
2007-08	Plymouth Arg	3	0	3	0
2008-09	Everton	1	0	1	0
2008-09	Huddersfield T	7	0	7	0

KINSELLA, Gerard (M)   0   0
b. 30-11-90
Source: Scholar.

2008-09	Everton	0	0

KISSOCK, John (M)   16   0
H: 5 6   W: 11 00   b.Fazackerley 1-12-89
Source: Scholar.

2006-07	Everton	0	0
2007-08	Gretna	11	0	11	0
2007-08	Everton	0	0
2008-09	Everton	0	0
2008-09	Accrington S	5	0	5	0

KRENN, George (M)   0   0
b.Austria 4-10-90
Source: Scholar.

2007-08	Everton	0	0
2008-09	Everton	0	0

LESCOTT, Jolean (D)   324   27
H: 6 2   W: 13 00   b.Birmingham 16-8-82
Source: Trainee. *Honours:* England Youth,
Under-20, Under-21, B, 7 full caps.

1999-2000	Wolverhampton W	0	0
2000-01	Wolverhampton W	37	2
2001-02	Wolverhampton W	44	5
2002-03	Wolverhampton W	44	1
2003-04	Wolverhampton W	0	0
2004-05	Wolverhampton W	41	4
2005-06	Wolverhampton W	46	1	212	13
2006-07	Everton	38	2
2007-08	Everton	38	8
2008-09	Everton	36	4	112	14

McARDLE, Lee (M)   0   0
Source: Scholar.

2008-09	Everton	0	0

McCARTEN, James (D)   0   0
b.Netherton 8-11-90
Source: Scholar.

2008-09	Everton	0	0

NASH, Carlo (G)   243   0
H: 6 5   W: 14 01   b.Bolton 13-9-73
Source: Clitheroe.

1996-97	Crystal Palace	21	0
1997-98	Crystal Palace	0	0	21	0
1998-99	Stockport Co	43	0
1999-2000	Stockport Co	38	0
2000-01	Stockport Co	8	0	89	0
2000-01	Manchester C	6	0
2001-02	Manchester C	23	0
2002-03	Manchester C	9	0	38	0
2003-04	Middlesbrough	1	0
2004-05	Middlesbrough	2	0	3	0
2004-05	Preston NE	7	0
2005-06	Preston NE	46	0
2006-07	Preston NE	29	0	82	0
2007-08	Wigan Ath	0	0
2007-08	Stoke C	10	0	10	0
2008-09	Wigan Ath	0	0
2008-09	Everton	0	0

NEVILLE, Phil (M)   406   8
H: 5 11   W: 12 00   b.Bury 21-1-77
Source: Trainee. Honours: England Schools, Youth, B, Under-21, 59 full caps.

1994-95	Manchester U	2	0		
1995-96	Manchester U	24	0		
1996-97	Manchester U	18	0		
1997-98	Manchester U	30	1		
1998-99	Manchester U	28	0		
1999-2000	Manchester U	29	0		
2000-01	Manchester U	29	1		
2001-02	Manchester U	28	2		
2002-03	Manchester U	25	1		
2003-04	Manchester U	31	0		
2004-05	Manchester U	19	0	263	6
2005-06	Everton	34	0		
2006-07	Everton	35	1		
2007-08	Everton	37	2		
2008-09	Everton	37	0	143	3

NUNO VALENTE (D)   280   4
H: 6 0   W: 12 03   b.Lisbon 12-9-74
Honours: Portugal Under-21, 33 full caps, 1 goal.

1993-94	Portimonense	26	1	26	1
1994-95	Sporting Lisbon	9	0		
1995-96	Sporting Lisbon	9	0		
1996-97	Maritimo	30	0	30	0
1997-98	Sporting Lisbon	6	0		
1998-99	Sporting Lisbon	12	1	36	1
1999-2000	Uniao Leiria	28	0		
2000-01	Uniao Leiria	31	2		
2001-02	Uniao Leiria	28	0	87	2
2002-03	Porto	21	0		
2003-04	Porto	27	0		
2004-05	Porto	8	0	56	0
2005-06	Everton	20	0		
2006-07	Everton	14	0		
2007-08	Everton	9	0		
2008-09	Everton	2	0	45	0

O'KANE, Eunan (M)   0   0
b.County Derry 10-7-90
Honours: Northern Ireland Youth, Under-21.

| 2007-08 | Everton | 0 | 0 | | |
| 2008-09 | Everton | 0 | 0 | | |

OSMAN, Leon (F)   195   27
H: 5 8   W: 10 09   b.Billinge 17-5-81
Source: Trainee. Honours: England Schools, Youth.

1998-99	Everton	0	0		
1999-2000	Everton	0	0		
2000-01	Everton	0	0		
2001-02	Everton	0	0		
2002-03	Everton	2	0		
2002-03	Carlisle U	12	1	12	1
2003-04	Everton	4	1		
2003-04	Derby Co	17	3	17	3
2004-05	Everton	29	6		
2005-06	Everton	35	3		
2006-07	Everton	34	3		
2007-08	Everton	28	4		
2008-09	Everton	34	6	166	23

PIENAAR, Steven (M)   175   20
H: 5 10   W: 10 06   b.Westbury 17-3-82
Honours: South Africa 43 full caps.

2001-02	Ajax	8	1		
2002-03	Ajax	31	5		
2003-04	Ajax	16	3		
2004-05	Ajax	24	4		
2005-06	Ajax	15	2	94	15
2006-07	Bor Dortmund	25	0	25	0
2007-08	Everton	28	2		
2008-09	Everton	28	3	56	5

RODWELL, Jack (D)   21   0
H: 6 2   W: 12 08   b.Birkdale 11-3-91
Source: Scholar. Honours: England Youth, Under-21.

| 2007-08 | Everton | 2 | 0 | | |
| 2008-09 | Everton | 19 | 0 | 21 | 0 |

RUDDY, John (G)   100   0
H: 6 3   W: 12 07   b.St Ives 24-10-86
Source: Scholar. Honours: England Youth.

2003-04	Cambridge U	1	0		
2004-05	Cambridge U	38	0	39	0
2005-06	Everton	1	0		
2005-06	Walsall	5	0	5	0
2005-06	Rushden & D	3	0	3	0
2005-06	Chester C	4	0	4	0
2006-07	Everton	0	0		

2006-07	Stockport Co	11	0		
2006-07	Wrexham	5	0	5	0
2006-07	Bristol C	1	0	1	0
2007-08	Everton	0	0		
2007-08	Stockport Co	12	0	23	0
2008-09	Everton	0	0	1	0
2008-09	Crewe Alex	19	0	19	0

SAHA, Louis (F)   285   93
H: 6 1   W: 12 08   b.Paris 8-8-78
Honours: France Youth, Under-21, 18 full caps, 4 goals.

1997-98	Metz	21	1		
1998-99	Metz	3	0		
1998-99	Newcastle U	11	1	11	1
1999-2000	Metz	23	4	47	5
2000-01	Fulham	43	27		
2001-02	Fulham	36	8		
2002-03	Fulham	17	5		
2003-04	Fulham	21	13	117	53
2003-04	Manchester U	12	7		
2004-05	Manchester U	14	1		
2005-06	Manchester U	19	7		
2006-07	Manchester U	24	8		
2007-08	Manchester U	17	5		
2008-09	Manchester U	0	0	86	28
2008-09	Everton	24	6	24	6

SHEPPARD, Karl (F)   0   0
b.Shelbourne 14-2-91
Source: Scholar.

| 2007-08 | Everton | 0 | 0 | | |
| 2008-09 | Everton | 0 | 0 | | |

SINNOTT, Cory (D)   0   0
b.Liverpool 21-8-90
Source: Scholar.

| 2007-08 | Everton | 0 | 0 | | |
| 2008-09 | Everton | 0 | 0 | | |

SPENCER, Scott (F)   3   0
H: 5 11   W: 12 08   b.Manchester 1-1-89
Source: Oldham Ath Scholar.

2006-07	Everton	0	0		
2007-08	Everton	0	0		
2007-08	Yeovil T	0	0		
2007-08	Macclesfield T	3	0	3	0
2008-09	Everton	0	0		

STEWART, Michael (M)   0   0
b.Warrington 3-1-91
Source: Scholar.

| 2007-08 | Everton | 0 | 0 | | |
| 2008-09 | Everton | 0 | 0 | | |

STUBHAUG, Lars (G)   0   0
b.Haugesund 18-4-90
Source: Vard-Haugesund.

2006-07	Everton	0	0		
2007-08	Everton	0	0		
2008-09	Everton	0	0		

TURNER, Iain (G)   48   0
H: 6 3   W: 12 10   b.Stirling 26-1-84
Source: Riverside BC. Honours: Scotland Youth, Under-21, B.

2002-03	Stirling A	14	0	14	0
2003-04	Everton	0	0		
2003-04	Everton	0	0		
2004-05	Everton	0	0		
2004-05	Doncaster R	8	0	8	0
2005-06	Everton	3	0		
2005-06	Wycombe W	3	0	3	0
2006-07	Everton	1	0		
2006-07	Crystal Palace	5	0	5	0
2006-07	Sheffield W	11	0	11	0
2007-08	Everton	0	0		
2008-09	Everton	0	0	4	0
2008-09	Nottingham F	3	0	3	0

VAN DER MEYDE, Andy (M)   175   22
H: 5 10   W: 12 04   b.Arnhem 30-9-79
Honours: Holland 18 full caps, 1 goal.

1997-98	Ajax	4	0		
1998-99	Ajax	1	0		
1999-2000	Twente	32	2	32	2
2000-01	Ajax	27	3		
2001-02	Ajax	30	5		
2002-03	Ajax	29	11	91	19
2003-04	Internazionale	14	1		
2004-05	Internazionale	18	0	32	1
2005-06	Everton	10	0		
2006-07	Everton	8	0		
2007-08	Everton	0	0		
2008-09	Everton	2	0	20	0

VAUGHAN, James (F)   38   6
H: 5 11   W: 13 00   b.Birmingham 14-7-88
Source: Scholar. Honours: England Youth, Under-21.

2004-05	Everton	2	1		
2005-06	Everton	1	0		
2006-07	Everton	14	4		
2007-08	Everton	8	1		
2008-09	Everton	13	0	38	6

WALLACE, James (M)   0   0
b.Fazackerly 19-12-91
Source: Scholar.

| 2008-09 | Everton | 0 | 0 | | |

YAKUBU, Ayegbeni (F)   256   101
H: 6 0   W: 14 07   b.Benin City 22-11-82
Source: From Julius Berger. Honours: Nigeria Under-21, Under-23, 41 full caps, 17 goals.

1999-2000	Gil Vicente	0	0		
1999-2000	Hapoel Kfar-Sava	23	6	23	6
2000-01	Maccabi Haifa	14	3		
2001-02	Maccabi Haifa	22	13	36	16
2002-03	Portsmouth	14	7		
2003-04	Portsmouth	37	16		
2004-05	Portsmouth	30	12	81	35
2005-06	Middlesbrough	34	13		
2006-07	Middlesbrough	37	12		
2007-08	Everton	2	0	73	25
2007-08	Everton	29	15		
2008-09	Everton	14	4	43	19

YOBO, Joseph (D)   274   9
H: 6 1   W: 13 00   b.Kano 6-9-80
Source: Mechelen. Honours: Nigeria B, 60 full caps, 4 goals.

1998-99	Standard Liege	0	0		
1999-2000	Standard Liege	18	0		
2000-01	Standard Liege	30	2	48	2
2001-02	Marseille	23	0	23	0
2002-03	Everton	24	0		
2003-04	Everton	28	2		
2004-05	Everton	27	0		
2005-06	Everton	29	1		
2006-07	Everton	38	2		
2007-08	Everton	30	1		
2008-09	Everton	27	1	203	7

Scholars
Davies, Adam; Forshaw, Adam; McAleny, Conor Michael; Nolan, Jon Anthony; Nsiala, Aristote.

EXETER C (35)

BASHAM, Steve (F)   263   57
H: 6 0   W: 12 04   b.Southampton 2-12-77
Source: Trainee.

1996-97	Southampton	6	0		
1997-98	Southampton	9	0		
1997-98	Wrexham	5	0	5	0
1998-99	Southampton	4	1	19	1
1998-99	Preston NE	17	10		
1999-2000	Preston NE	24	2		
2000-01	Preston NE	11	2		
2001-02	Preston NE	16	1	68	15
2002-03	Oxford U	31	8		
2003-04	Oxford U	38	14		
2004-05	Oxford U	39	9		
2005-06	Oxford U	40	8	148	39
2008-09	Exeter C	23	2	23	2

BENNETT, Scott (D)   0   0
H: 5 10   W: 12 10   b.Truro 30-11-90
Source: Scholar.

| 2008-09 | Exeter C | 0 | 0 | | |

BULL, Ronnie (D)   123   2
H: 5 7   W: 10 12   b.Hackney 26-12-80
Source: Trainee.

1998-99	Millwall	1	0		
1999-2000	Millwall	9	0		
2000-01	Millwall	2	0		
2001-02	Millwall	26	0		
2002-03	Millwall	12	0		
2003-04	Millwall	0	0	50	0
2003-04	Yeovil T	7	0	7	0
2003-04	Brentford	20	0	20	0
2004-05	Grimsby T	27	2		
2005-06	Grimsby T	0	0	27	2
From New Zealand Knights					
2005-06	Rushden & D	19	0		

Exeter C (continued)

Season	Club	App	Gls	Tot App	Tot Gls
2006-07	Rushden & D	0	0		
2007-08	Rushden & D	0	0	19	0
2008-09	Exeter C	0	0		

COZIC, Bertrand (M) 56 1
H: 5 10 W: 12 06 b.Quimper 18-5-78
Source: Team Bath.

Season	Club	App	Gls	Tot App	Tot Gls
2003-04	Cheltenham T	7	1	7	1
From Hereford U					
2004-05	Northampton T	14	0	14	0
2004-05	Kidderminster H	15	0	15	0
From Aldershot T.					
2008-09	Exeter C	20	0	20	0

EDWARDS, Rob (D) 535 15
H: 6 0 W: 12 02 b.Kendal 1-1-73
Source: Trainee. *Honours:* Wales Youth, Under-21, B, 4 full caps.

Season	Club	App	Gls	Tot App	Tot Gls
1989-90	Carlisle U	12	0		
1990-91	Carlisle U	36	5	48	5
1990-91	Bristol C	0	0		
1991-92	Bristol C	20	1		
1992-93	Bristol C	18	0		
1993-94	Bristol C	38	2		
1994-95	Bristol C	30	0		
1995-96	Bristol C	19	0		
1996-97	Bristol C	31	0		
1997-98	Bristol C	37	2		
1998-99	Bristol C	23	0	216	5
1999-2000	Preston NE	41	2		
2000-01	Preston NE	42	0		
2001-02	Preston NE	36	2		
2002-03	Preston NE	26	0		
2003-04	Preston NE	24	0	169	4
2004-05	Blackpool	26	1		
2005-06	Blackpool	32	0	58	1
2008-09	Exeter C	44	0	44	0

GILL, Matthew (M) 251 14
H: 5 11 W: 11 10 b.Cambridge 8-11-80
Source: Trainee.

Season	Club	App	Gls	Tot App	Tot Gls
1997-98	Peterborough U	2	0		
1998-99	Peterborough U	26	0		
1999-2000	Peterborough U	20	1		
2000-01	Peterborough U	17	1		
2001-02	Peterborough U	12	2		
2002-03	Peterborough U	41	1		
2003-04	Peterborough U	33	0	151	5
2004-05	Notts Co	43	0		
2005-06	Notts Co	14	0	57	0
2008-09	Exeter C	43	9	43	9

HARLEY, Ryan (D) 33 4
H: 5 11 W: 11 00 b.Bristol 22-1-85
Source: Scholar.

Season	Club	App	Gls	Tot App	Tot Gls
2004-05	Bristol C	2	0		
2005-06	Bristol C	0	0	2	0
2008-09	Exeter C	31	4	31	4

JONES, Paul (G) 46 0
H: 6 3 W: 13 00 b.Maidstone 28-6-86
Source: Leyton Orient Scholar.

Season	Club	App	Gls	Tot App	Tot Gls
2008-09	Exeter C	46	0	46	0

JORDAN, Nick (G) 0 0

Season	Club	App	Gls	Tot App	Tot Gls
2008-09	Exeter C	0	0		

LOGAN, Richard (F) 185 37
H: 6 1 W: 12 05 b.Bury St Edmunds 4-1-82
Source: Trainee. *Honours:* England Youth.

Season	Club	App	Gls	Tot App	Tot Gls
1998-99	Ipswich T	2	0		
1999-2000	Ipswich T	1	0		
2000-01	Ipswich T	0	0		
2000-01	*Cambridge U*	5	1	5	1
2001-02	Ipswich T	0	0		
2001-02	*Torquay U*	16	4	16	4
2002-03	Ipswich T	0	0	3	0
2002-03	Boston U	27	10		
2003-04	Boston U	8	0	35	10
2003-04	Peterborough U	29	7		
2004-05	Peterborough U	26	4		
2004-05	*Shrewsbury T*	5	1	5	1
2005-06	Peterborough U	28	4	83	15
2005-06	*Lincoln C*	8	2	8	2
From Weymouth.					
2008-09	Exeter C	30	4	30	4

McALLISTER, Craig (F) 30 7
H: 6 1 W: 11 03 b.Glasgow 28-6-80
Source: Basingstoke T, Stevenage B, Woking, Grays Ath, Oxford U.

Season	Club	App	Gls	Tot App	Tot Gls
2008-09	Exeter C	30	7	30	7

MOXEY, Dean (D) 43 4
H: 6 2 W: 11 00 b.Exeter 14-1-86
Source: Scholar.

Season	Club	App	Gls	Tot App	Tot Gls
2008-09	Exeter C	43	4	43	4

MURRAY, Fred (D) 132 0
H: 5 10 W: 11 12 b.Clonmel 22-5-82
Source: Trainee.

Season	Club	App	Gls	Tot App	Tot Gls
1998-99	Blackburn R	0	0		
1999-2000	Blackburn R	0	0		
2000-01	Blackburn R	0	0		
2001-02	Blackburn R	0	0		
2001-02	Cambridge U	21	0		
2002-03	Cambridge U	29	0		
2003-04	Cambridge U	38	0	88	0
2004-05	Northampton T	38	0	38	0
From Stafford R, Stevenage B.					
2008-09	Exeter C	6	0	6	0

OBERSTELLER, Jack (D) 7 0
b. 10-10-88
Source: Millwall Scholar, Crawley T.

Season	Club	App	Gls	Tot App	Tot Gls
2007-08	Wycombe W	0	0		
2008-09	Exeter C	7	0	7	0

OSMAN, Ben (M) 0 0
b.Southampton 24-9-90
Source: Scholar.

Season	Club	App	Gls	Tot App	Tot Gls
2008-09	Exeter C	0	0		

OSMAN, Toby (F) 0 0
H: 5 11 W: 10 12 b.Southampton 24-9-90
Source: Birmingham C Scholar.

Season	Club	App	Gls	Tot App	Tot Gls
2008-09	Exeter C	0	0		

PANTHER, Manny (F) 63 5
H: 6 0 W: 13 07 b.Glasgow 11-5-84

Season	Club	App	Gls	Tot App	Tot Gls
2001-02	St Johnstone	7	0		
2002-03	St Johnstone	4	0	11	0
2003-04	Partick T	8	0		
2004-05	Partick T	14	2	22	2
2004-05	Brechin C	8	1	8	1
From York C.					
2008-09	Exeter C	22	2	22	2

PATTISON, Jack (M) 0 0

Season	Club	App	Gls	Tot App	Tot Gls
2008-09	Exeter C	0	0		

SAUNDERS, Neil (M) 17 3
H: 5 11 W: 11 02 b.Dagenham 7-5-83
Source: Watford Scholar, Harlow T.

Season	Club	App	Gls	Tot App	Tot Gls
2001-02	Watford	0	0		
2002-03	Watford	0	0		
From Barnet, Team Bath.					
2008-09	Exeter C	17	3	17	3

SEABORNE, Danny (D) 33 1
H: 6 0 W: 11 10 b.Barnstaple 5-3-87

Season	Club	App	Gls	Tot App	Tot Gls
2008-09	Exeter C	33	1	33	1

SERCOMBE, Liam (M) 29 2
H: 5 10 W: 10 10 b.Exeter 25-4-90

Season	Club	App	Gls	Tot App	Tot Gls
2008-09	Exeter C	29	2	29	2

SHEPHARD, Chris (M) 2 0
H: 6 3 W: 13 03 b.Exeter 25-12-88

Season	Club	App	Gls	Tot App	Tot Gls
2008-09	Exeter C	2	0	2	0

STANSFIELD, Adam (F) 69 16
H: 5 11 W: 11 02 b.Plymouth 10-9-78
Source: Elmore.

Season	Club	App	Gls	Tot App	Tot Gls
2003-04	Yeovil T	32	6	32	6
From Hereford U.					
2008-09	Exeter C	37	10	37	10

STEWART, Marcus (F) 615 197
H: 5 10 W: 11 00 b.Bristol 7-11-72
Source: Trainee. *Honours:* England Schools, Football League.

Season	Club	App	Gls	Tot App	Tot Gls
1991-92	Bristol R	33	5		
1992-93	Bristol R	38	11		
1993-94	Bristol R	29	5		
1994-95	Bristol R	27	15		
1995-96	Bristol R	44	21	171	57
1996-97	Huddersfield T	20	7		
1997-98	Huddersfield T	41	15		
1998-99	Huddersfield T	43	22		
1999-2000	Huddersfield T	29	14	133	58
1999-2000	Ipswich T	10	2		
2000-01	Ipswich T	34	19		
2001-02	Ipswich T	28	6		
2002-03	Ipswich T	3	0	75	27
2002-03	Sunderland	19	1		
2003-04	Sunderland	40	14		
2004-05	Sunderland	43	16	102	31
2005-06	Bristol C	27	5		
2005-06	Preston NE	4	0	4	0
2006-07	Bristol C	0	0	27	5
2006-07	Yeovil T	31	8		
2007-08	Yeovil T	36	4	67	12
2008-09	Exeter C	36	7	36	7

TAYLOR, Matthew (D) 31 2
H: 6 0 W: 12 04 b.Chorley 30-1-82
Source: Burscough, Rossendale U, Matlock T, Hucknall T, Guiseley, Team Bath.

Season	Club	App	Gls	Tot App	Tot Gls
2008-09	Exeter C	31	2	31	2

TULLY, Steve (D) 142 3
H: 5 8 W: 11 02 b.Paignton 10-2-80
Source: Trainee.

Season	Club	App	Gls	Tot App	Tot Gls
1997-98	Torquay U	9	0		
1998-99	Torquay U	37	2		
1999-2000	Torquay U	13	0		
2000-01	Torquay U	29	1		
2001-02	Torquay U	18	0	106	3
From Weymouth.					
2008-09	Exeter C	36	0	36	0

WATSON, Ben (F) 12 2
H: 5 10 W: 10 11 b.Shoreham 6-12-85
Source: Grays Ath.

Season	Club	App	Gls	Tot App	Tot Gls
2008-09	Exeter C	12	2	12	2

FULHAM (36)

ANDERSON, Joe (D) 0 0
b. 13-10-89
Source: Scholar.

Season	Club	App	Gls	Tot App	Tot Gls
2008-09	Fulham	0	0		

ANDREASEN, Leon (D) 171 23
H: 6 1 W: 13 03 b.Aarhus 23-4-83
Honours: Denmark Youth, Under-20, Under-21, 15 full caps, 2 goals.

Season	Club	App	Gls	Tot App	Tot Gls
2001-02	Aarhus	17	3		
2002-03	Aarhus	32	8		
2003-04	Aarhus	25	3		
2004-05	Aarhus	31	3	105	17
2005-06	Werder Bremen	18	0		
2006-07	Werder Bremen	4	0		
2006-07	Mainz	15	4	15	4
2007-08	Werder Bremen	10	2	32	2
2007-08	Fulham	13	0		
2008-09	Fulham	6	0	19	0

BAIRD, Chris (D) 114 3
H: 5 10 W: 11 11 b.Ballymoney 25-2-82
Source: Scholar. *Honours:* Northern Ireland Youth, Under-21, 40 full caps.

Season	Club	App	Gls	Tot App	Tot Gls
2000-01	Southampton	0	0		
2001-02	Southampton	0	0		
2002-03	Southampton	3	0		
2003-04	Southampton	4	0		
2003-04	*Walsall*	10	0	10	0
2003-04	*Watford*	8	0	8	0
2004-05	Southampton	0	0		
2005-06	Southampton	17	0		
2006-07	Southampton	44	3	68	3
2007-08	Fulham	18	0		
2008-09	Fulham	10	0	28	0

BOUAZZA, Hameur (F) 157 17
H: 5 10 W: 12 01 b.Evry 22-2-85
Source: Scholar. *Honours:* Algeria 8 full caps, 1 goal.

Season	Club	App	Gls	Tot App	Tot Gls
2003-04	Watford	9	1		
2004-05	Watford	28	1		
2005-06	Watford	14	1		
2005-06	*Swindon T*	13	2	13	2
2006-07	Watford	32	6	83	9
2007-08	Fulham	20	1		
2008-09	Fulham	0	0	20	1
2008-09	*Charlton Ath*	25	4	25	4
2008-09	*Birmingham C*	16	1	16	1

BRIGGS, Matthew (D) 1 0
H: 6 1 W: 11 12 b.Wandsworth 6-3-91
Source: School. *Honours:* England Youth.

Season	Club	App	Gls	Tot App	Tot Gls
2006-07	Fulham	1	0		
2007-08	Fulham	0	0		
2008-09	Fulham	0	0	1	0

BROWN, Wayne (M) 12 1
H: 5 9 W: 12 05 b.Kingston 6-8-88
Source: Scholar.

Season	Club	App	Gls	Tot App	Tot Gls
2006-07	Fulham	0	0		
2007-08	Fulham	0	0		
2007-08	*Brentford*	11	1	11	1

2008-09 Fulham 1 0 **1 0**
On loan to TPS Turku

DACOURT, Olivier (M) **377 13**
H: 5 10 W: 11 07 b.Kourou 25-9-74
Honours: France 9 full caps.

Season	Club	Apps	Gls		
1992-93	Strasbourg	6	0		
1993-94	Strasbourg	8	0		
1994-95	Strasbourg	18	0		
1995-96	Strasbourg	34	0		
1996-97	Strasbourg	31	1		
1997-98	Strasbourg	30	3	**127**	**4**
1998-99	Everton	30	2	**30**	**2**
1999-2000	Lens	26	2	**26**	**2**
2000-01	Leeds U	33	3		
2001-02	Leeds U	17	0		
2002-03	Leeds U	7	0	**57**	**3**
2002-03	Roma	18	0		
2003-04	Roma	27	1		
2004-05	Roma	23	0		
2005-06	Roma	26	1	**94**	**2**
2006-07	Internazionale	24	0		
2007-08	Internazionale	9	0		
2008-09	Internazionale	1	0	**34**	**0**
2008-09	Fulham	9	0	**9**	**0**

DAVIES, Simon (M) **315 29**
H: 5 10 W: 11 07 b.Haverfordwest 23-10-79
Source: Trainee. *Honours:* Wales Youth, Under-21, B, 57 full caps, 6 goals.

Season	Club	Apps	Gls		
1997-98	Peterborough U	6	0		
1998-99	Peterborough U	43	4		
1999-2000	Peterborough U	16	2	**65**	**6**
1999-2000	Tottenham H	3	0		
2000-01	Tottenham H	13	2		
2001-02	Tottenham H	31	4		
2002-03	Tottenham H	36	5		
2003-04	Tottenham H	17	2		
2004-05	Tottenham H	21	0	**121**	**13**
2005-06	Everton	30	1		
2006-07	Everton	15	0	**45**	**1**
2006-07	Fulham	14	2		
2007-08	Fulham	37	5		
2008-09	Fulham	33	2	**84**	**9**

DEMPSEY, Clint (M) **158 40**
H: 6 1 W: 12 02 b.Nacogdoches 9-3-83
Source: Furman Univ. *Honours:* USA Under-21, 56 full caps, 14 goals.

Season	Club	Apps	Gls		
2004	New England Rev	24	7		
2005	New England Rev	30	11		
2006	New England Rev	23	8	**77**	**26**
2006-07	Fulham	10	1		
2007-08	Fulham	36	6		
2008-09	Fulham	35	7	**81**	**14**

ETHERIDGE, Neil (G) **0 0**
H: 6 3 W: 14 00 b.Enfield 7-2-90
Source: Scholar.

Season	Club	Apps	Gls
2008-09	Fulham	0	0

ETUHU, Dickson (M) **249 25**
H: 6 2 W: 13 04 b.Kano 8-6-82
Source: From Scholar. *Honours:* Nigeria 7 full caps.

Season	Club	Apps	Gls		
1999-2000	Manchester C	0	0		
2000-01	Manchester C	0	0		
2001-02	Manchester C	12	0	**12**	**0**
2001-02	Preston NE	16	3		
2002-03	Preston NE	39	6		
2003-04	Preston NE	31	3		
2004-05	Preston NE	35	3		
2005-06	Preston NE	13	2	**134**	**17**
2005-06	Norwich C	19	0		
2006-07	Norwich C	43	6	**62**	**6**
2007-08	Sunderland	20	1		
2008-09	Sunderland	0	0	**20**	**1**
2008-09	Fulham	21	1	**21**	**1**

FODERINGHAM, Wesley (G) **0 0**
b.Hammersmith 14-1-91
Source: Scholar.

Season	Club	Apps	Gls
2008-09	Fulham	0	0

GERA, Zoltan (M) **298 59**
H: 6 0 W: 11 11 b.Pecs 22-4-79
Source: From Hakarny. *Honours:* Hungary 59 full caps, 18 goals.

Season	Club	Apps	Gls		
1999-2000	Pecsi	15	4	**15**	**4**
2000-01	Ferencvaros	32	7		
2001-02	Ferencvaros	27	8		
2002-03	Ferencvaros	26	6		
2003-04	Ferencvaros	30	11	**115**	**32**
2004-05	WBA	38	6		
2005-06	WBA	15	2		
2006-07	WBA	40	5		
2007-08	WBA	43	8	**136**	**21**
2008-09	WBA	32	2	**32**	**2**

GRAY, Julian (M) **225 17**
H: 6 1 W: 11 00 b.Lewisham 21-9-79
Source: Trainee.

Season	Club	Apps	Gls		
1998-99	Arsenal	0	0		
1999-2000	Arsenal	1	0	**1**	**0**
2000-01	Crystal Palace	23	1		
2001-02	Crystal Palace	43	2		
2002-03	Crystal Palace	35	5		
2003-04	Crystal Palace	24	2	**125**	**10**
2003-04	*Cardiff C*	9	0	**9**	**0**
2004-05	Birmingham C	32	2		
2005-06	Birmingham C	21	1		
2006-07	Birmingham C	7	0	**60**	**3**
2007-08	Coventry C	26	3		
2008-09	Coventry C	3	1	**29**	**4**
2008-09	Fulham	1	0	**1**	**0**

HANGELAND, Brede (D) **229 10**
H: 6 4 W: 13 05 b.Houston 20-6-81
Honours: Norway Under-21, 53 full caps.

Season	Club	Apps	Gls		
2000	Vidar	0	0		
2001	Viking	22	0		
2002	Viking	26	2		
2003	Viking	26	1		
2004	Viking	14	3		
2005	Viking	26	0	**114**	**6**
2005-06	FC Copenhagen	13	1		
2006-07	FC Copenhagen	32	0		
2007-08	FC Copenhagen	18	2	**63**	**3**
2007-08	Fulham	15	0		
2008-09	Fulham	37	1	**52**	**1**

HOESEN, Danny (F) **0 0**
b. 15-1-91
Source: Fortuna Sittard.

Season	Club	Apps	Gls
2008-09	Fulham	0	0

HUGHES, Aaron (D) **327 1**
H: 6 0 W: 11 02 b.Cookstown 8-11-79
Source: From Trainee. *Honours:* Northern Ireland Youth, B, 66 full caps.

Season	Club	Apps	Gls		
1996-97	Newcastle U	0	0		
1997-98	Newcastle U	4	0		
1998-99	Newcastle U	14	0		
1999-2000	Newcastle U	27	2		
2000-01	Newcastle U	35	0		
2001-02	Newcastle U	34	0		
2002-03	Newcastle U	35	1		
2003-04	Newcastle U	34	0		
2004-05	Newcastle U	22	1	**205**	**4**
2005-06	Aston Villa	35	0		
2006-07	Aston Villa	19	0	**54**	**0**
2007-08	Fulham	30	0		
2008-09	Fulham	38	0	**68**	**0**

JOHN, Collins (F) **146 33**
H: 5 11 W: 12 13 b.Zwandru 17-10-85
Source: Holland Youth, Under-21, 2 full caps.

Season	Club	Apps	Gls		
2002-03	Twente	17	2		
2003-04	Twente	18	9	**35**	**11**
2003-04	Fulham	8	4		
2004-05	Fulham	27	4		
2005-06	Fulham	35	11		
2006-07	Fulham	23	1		
2007-08	Fulham	2	0		
2007-08	*Leicester C*	11	2	**11**	**2**
2007-08	*Watford*	5	0	**5**	**0**
2008-09	Fulham	0	0	**95**	**20**

On loan to NEC Nijmegen September 2008

JOHNSON, Andy (F) **315 104**
H: 5 7 W: 10 09 b.Bedford 10-2-81
Source: Trainee. *Honours:* England Youth, Under-20, 8 full caps.

Season	Club	Apps	Gls		
1997-98	Birmingham C	0	0		
1998-99	Birmingham C	4	0		
1999-2000	Birmingham C	22	1		
2000-01	Birmingham C	34	4		
2001-02	Birmingham C	23	3	**83**	**8**
2002-03	Crystal Palace	28	11		
2003-04	Crystal Palace	42	27		
2004-05	Crystal Palace	37	21		
2005-06	Crystal Palace	33	13	**140**	**74**
2006-07	Everton	32	11		
2007-08	Everton	29	6	**61**	**17**
2008-09	Fulham	31	7	**31**	**7**

JOHNSON, Eddie (F) **166 43**
H: 6 0 W: 12 02 b.Bunnell 31-3-84
Honours: USA 34 full caps, 11 goals.

Season	Club	Apps	Gls		
2001	Dallas Burn	10	2		
2002	Dallas Burn	14	2		
2003	Dallas Burn	22	3		
2004	Dallas Burn	26	12		
2005	Dallas Burn	15	5	**87**	**24**
2006	Kansas City Wizards	19	2		
2007	Kansas City Wizards	24	15	**43**	**17**
2007-08	Fulham	6	0		
2008-09	Fulham	0	0	**6**	**0**
2008-09	*Cardiff C*	30	2	**30**	**2**

KALLIO, Tony (D) **212 24**
H: 6 4 W: 13 05 b.Tampere 9-8-78
Source: HJK Helsinki. *Honours:* Finland 48 full caps, 2 goals.

Season	Club	Apps	Gls		
1997	Jazz	1	0	**1**	**0**
1997	Tampere U	19	1		
1998	Tampere U	19	2	**38**	**3**
1998	HJK Helsinki	9	0		
2000	HJK Helsinki	19	1		
2001	HJK Helsinki	32	5		
2002	HJK Helsinki	26	7		
2003	HJK Helsinki	0	0	**86**	**13**
2004	Molde	7	2		
2005	Molde	22	3		
2006	Molde	24	1	**53**	**6**
2006-07	Young Boys	15	0		
2007-08	Young Boys	16	2	**31**	**2**
2007-08	Fulham	0	0		
2008-09	Fulham	3	0	**3**	**0**

KAMARA, Diomansy (F) **212 52**
H: 6 0 W: 11 05 b.Paris 8-11-80
Honours: Senegal 45 full caps, 9 goals.

Season	Club	Apps	Gls		
1999-2000	Catanzaro	11	4		
2000-01	Catanzaro	23	5	**34**	**9**
2001-02	Chievo	0	0		
2001-02	Modena	24	4		
2002-03	Modena	29	5	**53**	**9**
2004-05	Portsmouth	25	4	**25**	**4**
2005-06	WBA	26	1		
2006-07	WBA	34	20	**60**	**21**
2007-08	Fulham	28	5		
2008-09	Fulham	12	4	**40**	**9**

KONCHESKY, Paul (D) **289 7**
H: 5 10 W: 11 07 b.Barking 15-5-81
Source: Trainee. *Honours:* England Youth, Under-20, Under-21, 2 full caps.

Season	Club	Apps	Gls		
1997-98	Charlton Ath	3	0		
1998-99	Charlton Ath	2	0		
1999-2000	Charlton Ath	8	0		
2000-01	Charlton Ath	23	0		
2001-02	Charlton Ath	34	1		
2002-03	Charlton Ath	30	3		
2003-04	Charlton Ath	21	0		
2003-04	*Tottenham H*	12	0	**12**	**0**
2004-05	Charlton Ath	28	1	**149**	**5**
2005-06	West Ham U	37	1		
2006-07	West Ham U	22	0	**59**	**1**
2007-08	Fulham	33	0		
2008-09	Fulham	36	1	**69**	**1**

LARIBI, Karim (D) **0 0**
b.Tunisi
Source: Internazionale Academy.

Season	Club	Apps	Gls
2007-08	Fulham	0	0
2008-09	Fulham	0	0

LEIJER, Adrian (D) **65 1**
H: 6 1 W: 12 08 b.Dubbo 25-3-86
Honours: Australia Youth, Under-20, Under-23, 1 full cap.

Season	Club	Apps	Gls		
2003-04	Melbourne Knights	20	0		
2004-05	Melbourne Knights	0	0	**20**	**0**
2005-06	Melbourne Victory	20	1		
2006-07	Melbourne Victory	21	0	**41**	**1**
2007-08	Fulham	0	0		
2008-09	Fulham	0	0		
2008-09	*Norwich C*	4	0	**4**	**0**

MILSOM, Robert (D) **13 0**
H: 5 10 W: 11 05 b.Redhill 2-1-87
Source: Scholar.

Season	Club	Apps	Gls		
2005-06	Fulham	0	0		
2006-07	Fulham	0	0		
2007-08	Fulham	0	0		
2007-08	*Brentford*	6	0	**6**	**0**
2008-09	Fulham	1	0	**1**	**0**
2008-09	*Southend U*	6	0	**6**	**0**

MOSCATIELLO, Luca (M)   0   0
b. 25-5-91
Source: Internazionale.
| 2008-09 | Fulham | 0 | 0 | | |

MURPHY, Danny (M)   469   71
H: 5 10   W: 11 09   b.Chester 18-3-77
Source: From Trainee. Honours: England Schools, Youth, Under-21, 9 full caps, 1 goal.
1993-94	Crewe Alex	12	2		
1994-95	Crewe Alex	35	5		
1995-96	Crewe Alex	42	10		
1996-97	Crewe Alex	45	10		
1997-98	Liverpool	16	0		
1998-99	Liverpool	1	0		
1998-99	Crewe Alex	16	1	150	28
1999-2000	Liverpool	23	3		
2000-01	Liverpool	27	4		
2001-02	Liverpool	36	6		
2002-03	Liverpool	36	7		
2003-04	Liverpool	31	5	170	25
2004-05	Charlton Ath	38	3		
2005-06	Charlton Ath	18	4	56	7
2005-06	Tottenham H	16	0		
2006-07	Tottenham H	12	1		
2007-08	Tottenham H	0	0	22	1
2007-08	Fulham	33	5		
2008-09	Fulham	38	5	71	10

NEVLAND, Erik (F)   283 129
H: 5 10   W: 11 12   b.Stavanger 10-11-77
Honours: Norway 8 full caps.
1996	Viking	1	0		
1997	Viking	13	5		
1997-98	Manchester U	1	0	1	0
1998	Viking	8	3		
1999	IFK Gothenburg	4	0	4	0
2000	Viking	20	14		
2001	Viking	37	18		
2002	Viking	27	23		
2003	Viking	25	11		
2004	Viking	23	6	154	80
2004-05	Groningen	20	16		
2005-06	Groningen	29	8		
2006-07	Groningen	31	13		
2007-08	Groningen	15	6	95	43
2007-08	Fulham	8	2		
2008-09	Fulham	21	4	29	6

OMOZUSI, Elliot (D)   29   0
H: 5 11   W: 12 09   b.Hackney 15-12-88
Source: Scholar. Honours: England Youth.
2005-06	Fulham	0	0		
2006-07	Fulham	0	0		
2007-08	Fulham	8	0		
2008-09	Fulham	0	0	8	0
2008-09	Norwich C	21	0	21	0

OSEI-GYAN, King (M)   12   0
H: 5 9   W: 10 03   b.Ghana 22-12-88
2006-07	Fulham	0	0		
2007-08	Fulham	0	0		
2007-08	Beerschot	12	0	12	0
2008-09	Fulham	0	0		

OWUSU, Daniel (M)   0   0
H: 5 8   W: 10 03   b.Ghana 13-6-89
Source: Scholar.
| 2007-08 | Fulham | 0 | 0 | | |
| 2008-09 | Fulham | 0 | 0 | | |

PANTSIL, John (D)   144   0
H: 5 10   W: 12 08   b.Berekum 15-6-81
Source: Liberty Professionals, Berkum Arsenals. Honours: Ghana Youth, Under-20, 52 full caps.
2002-03	Maccabi Tel Aviv	17	0		
2003-04	Maccabi Tel A	29	0	46	0
2004-05	Hapoel Tel Aviv	15	1		
2005-06	Hapoel Tel A	27	2	42	3
2006-07	West Ham U	5	0		
2007-08	West Ham U	14	0	19	0
2008-09	Fulham	37	0	37	0

SAUNDERS, Matthew (M)   0   0
H: 5 11   W: 11 05   b.Chertsey 12-9-89
Source: Scholar.
| 2008-09 | Fulham | 0 | 0 | | |

SCHWARZER, Mark (G)   482   0
H: 6 4   W: 14 07   b.Sydney 6-10-72
Honours: Australia Youth, Under-20, Under-23, 66 full caps.
| 1990-91 | Marconi Stallions | 1 | 0 | | |
| 1991-92 | Marconi Stallions | 9 | 0 | | |

1992-93	Marconi Stallions	23	0		
1993-94	Marconi Stallions	25	0	58	0
1994-95	Dynamo Dresden	2	0	2	0
1995-96	Kaiserslautern	4	0		
1996-97	Kaiserslautern	0	0	4	0
1996-97	Bradford C	13	0	13	0
1996-97	Middlesbrough	7	0		
1997-98	Middlesbrough	35	0		
1998-99	Middlesbrough	34	0		
1999-2000	Middlesbrough	37	0		
2000-01	Middlesbrough	31	0		
2001-02	Middlesbrough	21	0		
2002-03	Middlesbrough	38	0		
2003-04	Middlesbrough	36	0		
2004-05	Middlesbrough	31	0		
2005-06	Middlesbrough	27	0		
2006-07	Middlesbrough	36	0		
2007-08	Middlesbrough	34	0	367	0
2008-09	Fulham	38	0	38	0

SEOL, Ki-Hyun (F)   211   41
H: 6 0   W: 11 07   b.South Korea 8-1-79
Honours: South Korea 77 full caps, 18 goals.
2000-01	Antwerp	25	10	25	10
2001-02	Anderlecht	20	3		
2002-03	Anderlecht	32	12		
2003-04	Anderlecht	19	3	71	18
2004-05	Wolverhampton W	37	4		
2005-06	Wolverhampton W	32	4	69	8
2006-07	Reading	27	4		
2007-08	Reading	3	0	30	4
2007-08	Fulham	12	0		
2008-09	Fulham	4	1	16	1
On loan to Al-Halil

SMALLING, Chris (D)   1   0
H: 6 4   W: 14 02   b.Greenwich 22-11-89
Honours: England Youth.
| 2008-09 | Fulham | 1 | 0 | 1 | 0 |

STOCKDALE, David (G)   64   0
H: 6 3   W: 13 04   b.Leeds 20-9-85
Source: Scholar.
2002-03	York C	1	0		
2003-04	York C	0	0		
2004-05	York C	0	0		
2005-06	York C	0	0	1	0
2006-07	Darlington	6	0		
2007-08	Darlington	41	0	47	0
2008-09	Fulham	0	0		
2008-09	Rotherham U	8	0	8	0
2008-09	Leicester C	8	0	8	0

STOOR, Fredrik (D)   74   2
H: 6 0   W: 12 06   b.Stockholm 28-2-84
Honours: Sweden 10 full caps.
2002	Hammarby	0	0		
2003	Hammarby	1	0		
2004	Hammarby	7	0		
2005	Hammarby	20	1		
2006	Hammarby	23	1	51	2
2007	Rosenborg	21	0	21	0
2008-09	Fulham	2	0	2	0

TEIMOURIAN, Andranik (M)   32   2
H: 5 11   W: 11 07   b.Tehran 6-3-83
Source: Ararat, Keshavirz, Esteghal, Oghab, ABV Moslem. Honours: Iran 34 full caps, 2 goals.
2006-07	Bolton W	17	2		
2007-08	Bolton W	3	0	20	2
2008-09	Fulham	1	0	1	0
2008-09	Barnsley	11	0	11	0

UWEZU, Michael (M)   0   0
H: 5 6   W: 12 02   b.Nigeria 12-12-90
| 2008-09 | Fulham | 0 | 0 | | |

VOLZ, Moritz (D)   157   3
H: 5 10   W: 11 07   b.Siegen 21-1-83
Source: Schalke. Honours: Germany Youth, Under-21.
1999-2000	Arsenal	0	0		
2000-01	Arsenal	0	0		
2001-02	Arsenal	0	0		
2002-03	Wimbledon	10	1	10	1
2003-04	Arsenal	0	0		
2003-04	Fulham	33	0		
2004-05	Fulham	31	0		
2005-06	Fulham	33	0		
2006-07	Fulham	29	2		
2007-08	Fulham	9	0		
2008-09	Fulham	0	0	125	2

WATTS, Adam (D)   7   0
H: 6 1   W: 11 09   b.London 4-3-88
Source: Scholar.
2006-07	Fulham	0	0		
2006-07	Milton Keynes D	2	0	2	0
2007-08	Fulham	0	0		
2008-09	Fulham	0	0		
2008-09	Northampton T	5	0	5	0

ZAMORA, Bobby (F)   310 108
H: 6 1   W: 11 11   b.Barking 16-1-81
Source: Trainee. Honours: England Under-21.
1999-2000	Bristol R	4	0	4	0
1999-2000	Brighton & HA	6	6		
2000-01	Brighton & HA	43	28		
2001-02	Brighton & HA	41	28		
2002-03	Brighton & HA	35	14	125	76
2003-04	Tottenham H	16	0	16	0
2003-04	West Ham U	17	5		
2004-05	West Ham U	34	7		
2005-06	West Ham U	34	6		
2006-07	West Ham U	32	11		
2007-08	West Ham U	13	1	130	30
2008-09	Fulham	35	2	35	2

ZUBERBUHLER, Pascal (G)   465   0
H: 6 5   W: 15 08   b.Frauenfeld 8-1-71
Honours: Switzerland 51 full caps.
1991-92	Grasshoppers	9	0		
1992-93	Grasshoppers	21	0		
1993-94	Grasshoppers	0	0		
1994-95	Grasshoppers	33	0		
1995-96	Grasshoppers	24	0		
1996-97	Grasshoppers	36	0		
1997-98	Grasshoppers	28	0		
1998-99	Grasshoppers	36	0	187	0
1999-2000	Basle	36	0		
2000-01	Basle	3	0		
2000-01	Leverkusen	13	0	13	0
2000-01	Aarau	2	0	2	0
2001-02	Basle	36	0		
2002-03	Basle	35	0		
2003-04	Basle	35	0		
2004-05	Basle	33	0		
2005-06	Basle	36	0	214	0
2006-07	WBA	15	0	15	0
2007-08	Neuchatel Xamax	34	0	34	0
2008-09	Fulham	0	0		

Scholars
Bettinelli, Marcus; Briggs, Matthew; Dunn, James Patrick Christopher; Harris, Courtney; Jones, Reece Nicholas; Marsh-Brown, Keanu; Quinn, Padraig; Smith, Alex; Thomas, Lewis Hadley.

GILLINGHAM (37)

BARCHAM, Andy (F)   58   7
H: 5 8   W: 11 10   b.Basildon 16-12-86
Source: Scholar.
2005-06	Tottenham H	0	0		
2006-07	Tottenham H	0	0		
2007-08	Tottenham H	0	0		
2007-08	Leyton Orient	25	1	25	1
2008-09	Tottenham H	0	0		
2008-09	Gillingham	33	6	33	6

BENTLEY, Mark (M)   206   19
H: 6 2   W: 13 04   b.Hertford 7-1-78
Source: Enfield, Aldershot T, Gravesend & N, Dagenham & R.
2003-04	Southend U	21	2		
2004-05	Southend U	39	5		
2005-06	Southend U	33	5	93	12
2006-07	Gillingham	41	4		
2007-08	Gillingham	33	2		
2008-09	Gillingham	39	1	113	7

BERRY, Tyrone (F)   30   0
H: 5 8   W: 10 03   b.Brixton 11-3-87
Source: Scholar.
2004-05	Crystal Palace	0	0		
2005-06	Crystal Palace	0	0		
2005-06	Notts Co	5	0	5	0
2005-06	Rushden & D	20	0	20	0
From Crawley T, Stevenage B.					
2008-09	Gillingham	5	0	5	0

English League Players – Gillingham (37) — 478

CLOHESSY, Sean (D)   43 1
H: 5 11 W: 12 07 b.Croydon 12-12-86
Source: Arsenal Scholar.

2005-06	Gillingham	20	1		
2006-07	Gillingham	6	0		
2007-08	Gillingham	17	0		
2008-09	Gillingham	0	0	43	1

COGAN, Barry (F)   79 4
H: 5 9 W: 9 0 b.Sligo 4-11-84
Source: Scholar. *Honours:* Eire Under-21.

2001-02	Millwall	0	0		
2002-03	Millwall	0	0		
2003-04	Millwall	3	0		
2004-05	Millwall	7	0		
2005-06	Millwall	14	0	24	0
2006-07	Barnet	39	3	39	3
2007-08	Gillingham	16	1		
2008-09	Gillingham	0	0	16	1

CROFTS, Andrew (D)   183 17
H: 5 10 W: 12 09 b.Chatham 29-5-84
Source: Trainee. *Honours:* Wales Youth, Under-21, 12 full caps.

2000-01	Gillingham	1	0		
2001-02	Gillingham	0	0		
2002-03	Gillingham	0	0		
2003-04	Gillingham	8	0		
2004-05	Gillingham	27	2		
2005-06	Gillingham	45	2		
2006-07	Gillingham	43	8		
2007-08	Gillingham	41	5		
2008-09	Gillingham	9	0	174	17
2008-09	*Peterborough U*	9	0	9	0

CUMBERS, Luis (M)   14 1
H: 6 0 W: 11 10 b.Chelmsford 6-9-88
Source: Scholar.

2006-07	Gillingham	1	0		
2007-08	Gillingham	6	0		
2008-09	Gillingham	7	1	14	1

FULLER, Barry (M)   62 1
H: 5 10 W: 11 10 b.Ashford 25-9-84
Source: Scholar.

2004-05	Charlton Ath	0	0		
2005-06	Charlton Ath	0	0		
2005-06	*Barnet*	15	1	15	1
From Stevenage B.					
2007-08	Gillingham	10	0		
2008-09	Gillingham	37	0	47	0

HOWARD, Charlie (M)   1 0
H: 6 0 W: 15 00 b.London 26-11-89
Source: Scholar.

2007-08	Gillingham	1	0		
2008-09	Gillingham	0	0	1	0

JACKSON, Simeon (M)   76 26
H: 5 10 W: 10 12 b.Kingston, Jamaica 28-3-87
Source: Scholar. *Honours:* Canada Youth, 1 full cap, 1 goal.

2004-05	Rushden & D	3	0		
2005-06	Rushden & D	14	5		
2006-07	Rushden & D	0	0		
2007-08	Rushden & D	0	0	17	5
2007-08	Gillingham	18	4		
2008-09	Gillingham	41	17	59	21

JARRETT, Albert (M)   65 3
H: 6 1 W: 10 07 b.Sierra Leone 23-10-84
Source: Dulwich Hamlet. *Honours:* Sierra Leone 5 full caps.

2002-03	Wimbledon	0	0		
2003-04	Wimbledon	9	0	9	0
2004-05	Brighton & HA	12	1		
2005-06	Brighton & HA	11	0	23	1
2005-06	*Swindon T*	6	0	6	0
2006-07	Watford	1	0		
2006-07	*Boston U*	5	2	5	2
2006-07	*Milton Keynes D*	5	0	5	0
2007-08	Watford	0	0		
2008-09	Watford	0	0	1	0
2008-09	Watford	16	0	16	0

JULIAN, Alan (G)   20 0
H: 6 2 W: 13 07 b.Ashford 11-3-83
Source: Trainee. *Honours:* Northern Ireland Youth, Under-21.

2001-02	Brentford	0	0		
2002-03	Brentford	3	0		
2003-04	Brentford	13	0		
2004-05	Brentford	0	0		
2005-06	Brentford	0	0		
2006-07	Brentford	0	0		
2007-08	Brentford	0	0	16	0
From Stevenage B.					
2008-09	Gillingham	4	0	4	0

KING, Simon (D)   164 4
H: 6 0 W: 13 00 b.Oxford 11-4-83
Source: Scholar.

2000-01	Oxford U	2	0		
2001-02	Oxford U	2	0		
2002-03	Oxford U	0	0		
2003-04	Oxford U	0	0		
2004-05	Oxford U	0	0	4	0
2005-06	Barnet	32	0		
2006-07	Barnet	43	2	75	2
2007-08	Gillingham	42	0		
2008-09	Gillingham	43	2	85	2

LEWIS, Stuart (M)   35 0
H: 5 10 W: 11 06 b.Welwyn 15-10-87
Source: Scholar. *Honours:* England Youth.

2005-06	Tottenham H	0	0		
2006-07	Tottenham H	0	0		
2006-07	Barnet	4	0	4	0
From Stevenage B.					
2007-08	Gillingham	10	0		
2008-09	Gillingham	21	0	31	0

McCAMMON, Mark (F)   230 30
H: 6 2 W: 14 05 b.Barnet 7-8-78
Source: Cambridge C. *Honours:* Barbados 5 full caps, 4 goals.

1997-98	Cambridge U	2	0		
1998-99	Cambridge U	2	0	4	0
1998-99	Charlton Ath	0	0		
1999-2000	Charlton Ath	4	0	4	0
1999-2000	*Swindon T*	4	0	4	0
2000-01	Brentford	24	3		
2001-02	Brentford	14	0		
2002-03	Brentford	37	7	75	10
2002-03	Millwall	7	2		
2003-04	Millwall	7	0		
2004-05	Millwall	8	0	22	2
2004-05	Brighton & HA	18	3		
2005-06	Brighton & HA	7	0	25	3
2005-06	*Bristol C*	11	4	11	4
2006-07	Doncaster R	22	2		
2007-08	Doncaster R	32	4	54	6
2008-09	Gillingham	31	5	31	5

MILLER, Adam (M)   80 9
H: 5 11 W: 11 06 b.Hemel Hempstead 19-2-82
Source: Aldershot T.

2004-05	QPR	14	0		
2005-06	QPR	1	0	15	0
2005-06	*Peterborough U*	2	0	2	0
From Stevenage B					
2007-08	Gillingham	28	3		
2008-09	Gillingham	35	6	63	9

MULLIGAN, Gary (M)   131 19
H: 6 1 W: 12 03 b.Dublin 23-4-85
Source: Scholar.

2002-03	Wolverhampton W	0	0		
2003-04	Wolverhampton W	0	0		
2004-05	Wolverhampton W	1	0	1	0
2004-05	*Rushden & D*	13	3	13	3
2005-06	Sheffield U	0	0		
2005-06	*Port Vale*	10	1	10	1
2005-06	*Gillingham*	13	1		
2006-07	Gillingham	38	7		
2007-08	Gillingham	30	5		
2008-09	Gillingham	26	2	107	15

MURPHY, Tom (M)   0 0
H: 5 11 W: 10 12 b.Gillingham 19-12-91
Source: Scholar.

2008-09	Gillingham	0	0		

NUTTER, John (D)   70 0
H: 6 2 W: 12 10 b.Burnham 13-6-82
Source: Blackburn R Scholar.

2000-01	Wycombe W	1	0		
2001-02	Wycombe W	0	0		
2007-08	Wycombe W	0	0	1	0
From Ald'shot T, Grays Ath, Stevenage B					
2007-08	Gillingham	24	1		
2008-09	Gillingham	45	0	69	1

OLI, Dennis (F)   81 9
H: 6 0 W: 12 00 b.Newham 28-1-84
Source: Scholar.

2001-02	QPR	2	0		
2002-03	QPR	18	0		
2003-04	QPR	3	0	23	0
2004-05	Swansea C	1	0	1	0
2004-05	Cambridge U	4	1		
2005-06	Cambridge U	0	0		
2006-07	Cambridge U	0	0	4	1
From Grays Ath.					
2007-08	Gillingham	22	4		
2008-09	Gillingham	31	4	53	8

PAYNE, Jack (M)   2 0
H: 5 9 W: 9 02 b.Gravesend 5-12-91
Source: Scholar.

2008-09	Gillingham	2	0	2	0

PUGH, Andy (F)   6 0
H: 5 9 W: 12 02 b.Gravesend 28-1-89
Source: Scholar.

2006-07	Gillingham	3	0		
2007-08	Gillingham	2	0		
2008-09	Gillingham	1	0	6	0

RICHARDS, Garry (D)   90 5
H: 6 3 W: 13 00 b.Romford 11-6-86
Source: Scholar.

2005-06	Colchester U	15	0		
2006-07	Colchester U	5	1	20	1
2006-07	*Brentford*	10	1	10	1
2007-08	*Southend U*	10	0	10	0
2007-08	Gillingham	14	1		
2008-09	Gillingham	36	2	50	3

ROYCE, Simon (G)   342 0
H: 6 2 W: 12 10 b.Forest Gate 9-9-71
Source: Heybridge Swifts.

1991-92	Southend U	1	0		
1992-93	Southend U	3	0		
1993-94	Southend U	6	0		
1994-95	Southend U	13	0		
1995-96	Southend U	46	0		
1996-97	Southend U	43	0		
1997-98	Southend U	37	0	149	0
1998-99	Charlton Ath	8	0		
1999-2000	Charlton Ath	0	0		
2000-01	Leicester C	19	0		
2001-02	Leicester C	0	0		
2001-02	*Brighton & HA*	6	0	6	0
2001-02	*Manchester C*	0	0		
2002-03	Leicester C	0	0	19	0
2002-03	QPR	16	0		
2003-04	Charlton Ath	1	0		
2004-05	Charlton Ath	0	0	9	0
2004-05	*Luton T*	2	0	2	0
2004-05	QPR	13	0		
2005-06	QPR	30	0		
2006-07	QPR	20	0	79	0
2006-07	*Gillingham*	3	0		
2007-08	Gillingham	33	0		
2008-09	Gillingham	42	0	78	0

SOUTHALL, Nicky (M)   634 66
H: 5 11 W: 12 04 b.Stockton 28-1-72
Source: Trainee.

1990-91	Hartlepool U	0	0		
1991-92	Hartlepool U	22	3		
1992-93	Hartlepool U	39	6		
1993-94	Hartlepool U	40	9		
1994-95	Hartlepool U	37	6	138	24
1995-96	Grimsby T	33	2		
1996-97	Grimsby T	34	3		
1997-98	Grimsby T	5	0	72	5
1997-98	Gillingham	23	2		
1998-99	Gillingham	42	4		
1999-2000	Gillingham	45	9		
2000-01	Gillingham	44	2		
2001-02	Bolton W	18	1		
2002-03	Bolton W	0	0	18	1
2002-03	*Norwich C*	9	0	9	0
2002-03	Gillingham	24	1		
2003-04	Gillingham	35	0		
2004-05	Gillingham	33	1		
2005-06	Nottingham F	40	8		
2006-07	Nottingham F	27	5	67	13
2006-07	Gillingham	15	0		
2007-08	Gillingham	33	1		
2008-09	Gillingham	36	3	330	23

THURGOOD, Stuart (M)   91 1
H: 5 8 W: 12 03 b.Enfield 4-11-81
From Shimizu S-Pulse

2000-01	Southend U	13	1		
2001-02	Southend U	39	0		
2002-03	Southend U	27	0		
2003-04	Southend U	0	0	79	1

From Grays Ath

2007-08	Gillingham	12	0		
2008-09	Gillingham	0	0	12	0

WALDER, Danny (D)   0 0
b.Chatham 3-9-89
Source: Scholar.

2008-09	Gillingham	0	0

WESTON, Curtis (M)   90 7
H: 5 11 W: 11 09 b.Greenwich 24-1-87

2003-04	Millwall	1	0		
2004-05	Millwall	3	0		
2005-06	Millwall	0	0	4	0
2006-07	Swindon T	27	1	27	1
2007-08	Leeds U	7	1		
2007-08	Scunthorpe U	7	0	7	0
2008-09	Leeds U	0	0	7	1
2008-09	Gillingham	45	5	45	5

WYNTER, Tom (M)   0 0
H: 5 7 W: 11 11 b.Lewisham 20-6-90
Source: Scholar.

2008-09	Gillingham	0	0

GRIMSBY T (38)

AKPA AKPRO, Jean-Louis (F)   72 9
H: 6 0 W: 10 12 b.Toulouse 4-1-85

2004-05	Toulouse	13	0		
2005-06	Toulouse	14	3		
2006-07	Toulouse	10	1		
2007-08	Brest	15	2	15	2
2007-08	Toulouse	0	0	37	4
2008-09	Grimsby T	20	3	20	3

ATKINSON, Rob (D)   65 0
H: 6 1 W: 12 00 b.Beverley 29-4-87
Source: Scholar.

2003-04	Barnsley	1	0		
2004-05	Barnsley	1	0		
2005-06	Barnsley	0	0		
2006-07	Barnsley	6	0		
2007-08	Barnsley	0	0		
2007-08	Rochdale	2	0	2	0
2007-08	Grimsby T	24	1		
2008-09	Barnsley	0	0	8	0
2008-09	Grimsby T	31	2	55	3

BARNES, Phil (G)   270 0
H: 6 1 W: 11 01 b.Sheffield 2-3-79
Source: Trainee.

1996-97	Rotherham U	2	0	2	0
1997-98	Blackpool	1	0		
1998-99	Blackpool	1	0		
1999-2000	Blackpool	12	0		
2000-01	Blackpool	34	0		
2001-02	Blackpool	30	0		
2002-03	Blackpool	44	0		
2003-04	Blackpool	19	0	141	0
2004-05	Sheffield U	1	0		
2004-05	Torquay U	5	0	5	0
2005-06	Sheffield U	0	0	1	0
2005-06	QPR	1	0	1	0
2006-07	Grimsby T	46	0		
2007-08	Grimsby T	42	0		
2008-09	Grimsby T	32	0	120	0

BENNETT, Ryan (M)   90 6
H: 6 2 W: 11 00 b.Orsett 6-3-90
Source: Scholar. *Honours:* England Youth.

2006-07	Grimsby T	5	0		
2007-08	Grimsby T	40	1		
2008-09	Grimsby T	45	5	90	6

BOLLAND, Paul (M)   302 19
H: 5 10 W: 10 12 b.Bradford 23-12-79
Source: Trainee.

1997-98	Bradford C	10	0		
1998-99	Bradford C	2	0	12	0
1998-99	Notts Co	13	0		
1999-2000	Notts Co	25	1		
2000-01	Notts Co	7	0		
2001-02	Notts Co	19	0		
2002-03	Notts Co	29	3		
2003-04	Notts Co	39	1		
2004-05	Grimsby T	40	1	172	6
2005-06	Grimsby T	44	4		
2006-07	Grimsby T	39	5		
2007-08	Grimsby T	35	4		
2008-09	Grimsby T	0	0	118	13

BORE, Peter (M)   76 11
H: 5 11 W: 11 04 b.Grimsby 4-11-87
Source: Scholar.

2006-07	Grimsby T	32	8		
2007-08	Grimsby T	17	2		
2008-09	Grimsby T	27	1	76	11

BOSHELL, Danny (M)   202 13
H: 5 11 W: 11 09 b.Bradford 30-5-81
Source: Trainee.

1998-99	Oldham Ath	0	0		
1999-2000	Oldham Ath	8	0		
2000-01	Oldham Ath	18	1		
2001-02	Oldham Ath	4	0		
2002-03	Oldham Ath	2	0		
2003-04	Oldham Ath	22	0		
2004-05	Oldham Ath	16	1	70	2
2004-05	Bury	6	0	6	0
2005-06	Stockport Co	33	1	33	1
2006-07	Grimsby T	29	2		
2007-08	Grimsby T	40	6		
2008-09	Grimsby T	24	2	93	10

BUTLER, Martin (F)   450 127
H: 5 11 W: 11 09 b.Wordsley 15-9-74
Source: Trainee.

1993-94	Walsall	15	3		
1994-95	Walsall	8	0		
1995-96	Walsall	28	4		
1996-97	Walsall	23	1		
1997-98	Cambridge U	31	10		
1998-99	Cambridge U	46	17		
1999-2000	Cambridge U	26	14	103	41
1999-2000	Reading	17	4		
2000-01	Reading	45	24		
2001-02	Reading	17	2		
2002-03	Reading	21	2		
2003-04	Reading	3	0	103	32
2003-04	Rotherham U	37	15		
2004-05	Rotherham U	21	6		
2005-06	Rotherham U	39	7	97	28
2006-07	Walsall	44	11		
2007-08	Walsall	5	1	123	20
2007-08	Grimsby T	21	6		
2008-09	Grimsby T	3	0	24	6

CLARKE, Jamie (D)   210 8
H: 6 2 W: 12 03 b.Sunderland 18-9-82
Source: Scholar.

2001-02	Mansfield T	1	0		
2002-03	Mansfield T	21	1		
2003-04	Mansfield T	12	0	34	1
2004-05	Rochdale	41	1		
2005-06	Rochdale	22	0	63	1
2005-06	Boston U	15	1		
2006-07	Boston U	37	2	52	3
2007-08	Grimsby T	29	2		
2008-09	Grimsby T	32	1	61	3

FULLER, Josh (M)   1 0
H: 5 9 W: 11 00 b.Grimsby 9-2-92
Source: Scholar.

2008-09	Grimsby T	1	0	1	0

HEGARTY, Nick (M)   83 8
H: 5 10 W: 11 00 b.Hemsworth 25-6-86
Source: Scholar.

2004-05	Grimsby T	1	0		
2005-06	Grimsby T	2	0		
2006-07	Grimsby T	15	0		
2007-08	Grimsby T	30	4		
2008-09	Grimsby T	35	4	83	8

HEYWOOD, Matt (D)   298 12
H: 6 3 W: 14 00 b.Chatham 26-8-79
Source: Trainee.

1998-99	Burnley	13	0		
1999-2000	Burnley	0	0		
2000-01	Burnley	0	0	13	0
2000-01	Swindon T	21	2		
2001-02	Swindon T	44	3		
2002-03	Swindon T	46	1		
2003-04	Swindon T	40	1		
2004-05	Swindon T	32	1	183	8
2005-06	Bristol C	24	2	24	2
2006-07	Brentford	28	1		
2007-08	Brentford	32	1	60	2
2008-09	Grimsby T	18	0	18	0

HOPE, Richard (D)   376 12
H: 6 2 W: 12 06 b.Stockton 22-6-78
Source: Trainee.

1995-96	Blackburn R	0	0
1996-97	Blackburn R	0	0

1996-97	Darlington	20	0		
1997-98	Darlington	35	1		
1998-99	Darlington	8	0	63	1
1998-99	Northampton T	19	0		
1999-2000	Northampton T	17	0		
2000-01	Northampton T	33	0		
2001-02	Northampton T	43	6		
2002-03	Northampton T	23	1	135	7
2003-04	York C	36	2	36	2
2004-05	Chester C	28	0	28	0
2005-06	Shrewsbury T	42	2		
2006-07	Shrewsbury T	33	0	75	2
2007-08	Wrexham	33	0	33	0
2008-09	Grimsby T	6	0	6	0

HUNT, James (M)   440 20
H: 5 8 W: 10 03 b.Derby 17-12-76
Source: Trainee.

1994-95	Notts Co	0	0		
1995-96	Notts Co	10	1		
1996-97	Notts Co	9	0	19	1
1997-98	Northampton T	21	0		
1998-99	Northampton T	35	2		
1999-2000	Northampton T	37	1		
2000-01	Northampton T	41	1		
2001-02	Northampton T	38	4	172	8
2002-03	Oxford U	39	1		
2003-04	Oxford U	41	2	80	3
2004-05	Bristol R	41	4		
2005-06	Bristol R	40	1		
2006-07	Bristol R	14	1	95	6
2006-07	Grimsby T	15	2		
2007-08	Grimsby T	37	0		
2008-09	Grimsby T	22	0	74	2

JARMAN, Nathan (F)   57 6
H: 5 11 W: 11 03 b.Scunthorpe 19-9-86
Source: Scholar.

2004-05	Barnsley	6	0		
2005-06	Barnsley	9	0		
2005-06	Bury	2	0	2	0
2006-07	Barnsley	0	0		
2007-08	Barnsley	0	0	15	0
2007-08	Grimsby T	7	0		
2008-09	Grimsby T	33	6	40	6

LLEWELLYN, Chris (F)   383 47
H: 5 11 W: 11 06 b.Swansea 29-8-79
Source: Trainee. *Honours:* Wales Schools, Youth, Under-21, B, 6 full caps, 1 goal.

1996-97	Norwich C	0	0		
1997-98	Norwich C	15	4		
1998-99	Norwich C	31	2		
1999-2000	Norwich C	36	3		
2000-01	Norwich C	42	8		
2001-02	Norwich C	13	0		
2002-03	Norwich C	5	0	142	17
2002-03	Bristol R	14	3	14	3
2003-04	Wrexham	46	8		
2004-05	Wrexham	45	7		
2005-06	Hartlepool U	29	0	29	0
2006-07	Wrexham	39	9		
2007-08	Wrexham	40	3	170	27
2008-09	Wrexham	28	0	28	0

LUND, Jonny (G)   0 0
H: 5 10 W: 11 10 b.Leeds 1-11-88
Source: Scholar.

2006-07	Leeds U	0	0
2007-08	Leeds U	0	0
2008-09	Grimsby T	0	0

MONTGOMERY, Gary (G)   50 0
H: 5 11 W: 13 08 b.Leamington Spa 8-10-82
Source: Scholar.

2000-01	Coventry C	0	0		
2001-02	Coventry C	0	0		
2001-02	Crewe Alex	0	0		
2001-02	Kidderminster H	2	0	2	0
2002-03	Coventry C	8	0	8	0
2003-04	Rotherham U	4	0		
2004-05	Rotherham U	1	0		
2005-06	Rotherham U	24	0		
2006-07	Rotherham U	6	0	35	0
2007-08	Grimsby T	5	0		
2008-09	Grimsby T	0	0	5	0

NEWEY, Tom (D)   232 7
H: 5 10 W: 10 02 b.Sheffield 31-10-82
Source: Scholar.

2000-01	Leeds U	0	0
2001-02	Leeds U	0	0
2002-03	Leeds U	0	0

2002-03	Cambridge U	6	0	
2002-03	Darlington	7	1	7 1
2003-04	Leyton Orient	34	2	
2004-05	Leyton Orient	20	1	54 3
2004-05	Cambridge U	16	0	22 0
2005-06	Grimsby T	38	1	
2006-07	Grimsby T	43	1	
2007-08	Grimsby T	42	1	
2008-09	Grimsby T	24	0	147 3
2008-09	Rochdale	2	0	2 0

NORMINGTON, Grant (M) 1 0
H: 5 8 W: 12 08 b.Hull 9-5-90
Source: Scholar.

2008-09	Grimsby T	1	0	1 0

NORTH, Danny (F) 64 16
H: 5 9 W: 12 08 b.Grimsby 7-9-87
Source: Scholar.

2004-05	Grimsby T	1	0	
2005-06	Grimsby T	1	0	
2006-07	Grimsby T	20	6	
2007-08	Grimsby T	27	9	
2008-09	Grimsby T	15	1	64 16

PROUDLOCK, Adam (F) 239 47
H: 6 0 W: 13 07 b.Wellington 9-5-81
Source: Trainee.

1999-2000	Wolverhampton W	0	0	
2000-01	*Clyde*	4	4	4 4
2000-01	Wolverhampton W	35	8	
2001-02	Wolverhampton W	19	3	
2001-02	*Nottingham F*	3	0	3 0
2002-03	Wolverhampton W	17	2	
2002-03	*Tranmere R*	5	0	5 0
2002-03	Sheffield W	5	2	
2003-04	Wolverhampton W	0	0	71 13
2003-04	Sheffield W	30	3	
2004-05	Sheffield W	14	6	
2005-06	Sheffield W	6	0	55 11
2005-06	Ipswich T	9	0	
2006-07	Ipswich T	0	0	9 0
2006-07	Stockport Co	23	3	
2007-08	Stockport Co	33	8	56 11
2008-09	Darlington	8	0	8 0
2008-09	Grimsby T	28	8	28 8

RANKIN, Isiah (F) 256 44
H: 5 10 W: 11 00 b.London 22-5-78
Source: Trainee.

1995-96	Arsenal	0	0	
1996-97	Arsenal	0	0	
1997-98	Arsenal	1	0	1 0
1997-98	Colchester U	11	5	11 5
1998-99	Bradford C	27	4	
1999-2000	Bradford C	9	0	
1999-2000	*Birmingham C*	13	4	13 4
2000-01	Bradford C	1	0	37 4
2000-01	*Bolton W*	16	2	16 2
2000-01	Barnsley	9	1	
2001-02	Barnsley	9	1	
2002-03	Barnsley	9	1	
2003-04	Barnsley	20	5	47 8
2003-04	Grimsby T	12	4	
2004-05	Brentford	41	8	
2005-06	Brentford	37	7	78 15
2006-07	Grimsby T	20	2	
2006-07	*Macclesfield T*	4	0	4 0
2007-08	Grimsby T	17	0	
2008-09	Grimsby T	0	0	49 6

STOCKDALE, Robbie (D) 248 3
H: 6 0 W: 11 03 b.Middlesbrough 30-11-79
Source: Trainee. *Honours:* England
Under-21. Scotland B, 5 full caps.

1997-98	Middlesbrough	1	0	
1998-99	Middlesbrough	19	0	
1999-2000	Middlesbrough	11	1	
2000-01	Middlesbrough	0	0	
2000-01	*Sheffield W*	6	0	6 0
2001-02	Middlesbrough	28	1	
2002-03	Middlesbrough	14	0	
2003-04	Middlesbrough	2	0	75 2
2003-04	*West Ham U*	7	0	7 0
2003-04	*Rotherham U*	16	1	
2004-05	Rotherham U	27	0	43 1
2004-05	Hull C	14	0	
2005-06	Hull C	0	0	14 0
2005-06	*Darlington*	3	0	3 0
2006-07	Tranmere R	36	0	
2007-08	Tranmere R	44	0	80 0
2008-09	Grimsby T	20	0	20 0

TAYLOR, Andy (F) 43 7
H: 6 2 W: 13 00 b.Caistor 30-10-88
Source: Scholar.

2005-06	Grimsby T	0	0	
2006-07	Grimsby T	11	2	
2007-08	Grimsby T	26	5	
2008-09	Grimsby T	6	0	43 7

TILL, Peter (M) 116 5
H: 5 11 W: 11 04 b.Walsall 7-9-85
Source: Scholar.

2005-06	Birmingham C	0	0	
2005-06	*Scunthorpe U*	8	0	8 0
2005-06	*Boston U*	16	1	16 1
2006-07	Birmingham C	0	0	
2006-07	*Leyton Orient*	4	0	4 0
2006-07	Grimsby T	22	0	
2007-08	Grimsby T	34	2	
2008-09	Grimsby T	16	2	72 4
2008-09	*Chesterfield*	16	0	16 0

WHITTLE, Justin (D) 399 6
H: 6 1 W: 12 12 b.Derby 18-3-71
Source: Celtic.

1994-95	Stoke C	0	0	
1995-96	Stoke C	8	0	
1996-97	Stoke C	37	0	
1997-98	Stoke C	20	0	
1998-99	Stoke C	14	1	79 1
1998-99	Hull C	24	1	
1999-2000	Hull C	38	0	
2000-01	Hull C	38	0	
2001-02	Hull C	36	0	
2002-03	Hull C	39	1	
2003-04	Hull C	18	0	193 2
2004-05	Grimsby T	40	1	
2005-06	Grimsby T	32	0	
2006-07	Grimsby T	37	1	
2007-08	Grimsby T	18	1	
2008-09	Grimsby T	0	0	127 3

HARTLEPOOL U (39)

BOLAND, Willie (M) 336 4
H: 5 9 W: 12 04 b.Ennis 6-8-75
Source: Trainee. *Honours:* Eire Youth, B, Under-21.

1992-93	Coventry C	1	0	
1993-94	Coventry C	27	0	
1994-95	Coventry C	12	0	
1995-96	Coventry C	3	0	
1996-97	Coventry C	1	0	
1997-98	Coventry C	19	0	
1998-99	Coventry C	0	0	63 0
1999-2000	Cardiff C	28	1	
2000-01	Cardiff C	25	1	
2001-02	Cardiff C	42	1	
2002-03	Cardiff C	41	0	
2003-04	Cardiff C	37	0	
2004-05	Cardiff C	21	0	
2005-06	Cardiff C	15	0	209 3
2006-07	Hartlepool U	27	0	
2007-08	Hartlepool U	34	0	
2008-09	Hartlepool U	3	1	64 1

BROWN, James (F) 93 23
H: 5 11 W: 11 00 b.Newcastle 3-1-87
Source: Cramlington Jun.

2004-05	Hartlepool U	0	0	
2005-06	Hartlepool U	4	1	
2006-07	Hartlepool U	36	6	
2007-08	Hartlepool U	35	10	
2008-09	Hartlepool U	18	6	93 23

BUDTZ, Jan (G) 72 0
H: 6 0 W: 13 05 b.Denmark 20-4-79
Source: B1909 Odense.

2004-05	Nordsjaelland	0	0	
2005-06	Doncaster R	20	0	
2006-07	Doncaster R	7	0	27 0
2006-07	*Wolverhampton W*	4	0	4 0
2007-08	Hartlepool U	28	0	
2008-09	Hartlepool U	10	0	38 0
2008-09	*Oldham Ath*	3	0	3 0

CLARK, Ben (D) 159 6
H: 6 1 W: 13 11 b.Shotley Bridge 24-1-83
Source: Manchester U Trainee. *Honours:*
England Youth, Under-20.

2000-01	Sunderland	0	0	
2001-02	Sunderland	0	0	
2002-03	Sunderland	1	0	
2003-04	Sunderland	5	0	
2004-05	Sunderland	2	0	8 0
2004-05	Hartlepool U	25	0	
2005-06	Hartlepool U	32	0	
2006-07	Hartlepool U	40	3	
2007-08	Hartlepool U	19	1	
2008-09	Hartlepool U	35	2	151 6

COLLINS, Sam (D) 331 16
H: 6 2 W: 14 03 b.Pontefract 5-6-77
Source: Trainee.

1994-95	Huddersfield T	0	0	
1995-96	Huddersfield T	0	0	
1996-97	Huddersfield T	4	0	
1997-98	Huddersfield T	10	0	
1998-99	Huddersfield T	23	0	37 0
1999-2000	Bury	19	0	
2000-01	Bury	34	2	
2001-02	Bury	29	0	82 2
2002-03	Port Vale	44	5	
2003-04	Port Vale	43	4	
2004-05	Port Vale	33	2	
2005-06	Port Vale	15	0	135 11
2005-06	Hull C	17	0	
2006-07	Hull C	6	0	
2007-08	Hull C	0	0	23 0
2007-08	*Swindon T*	4	0	4 0
2008-09	Hartlepool U	10	2	
2008-09	Hartlepool U	40	1	50 3

COOK, Mark (G) 0 0
H: 6 1 W: 12 01 b.North Shields 7-9-88

2008-09	Hartlepool U	0	0	

FOLEY, David (F) 96 0
H: 5 4 W: 8 09 b.South Shields 12-5-87
Source: Scholar.

2003-04	Hartlepool U	1	0	
2004-05	Hartlepool U	2	0	
2005-06	Hartlepool U	11	0	
2006-07	Hartlepool U	25	0	
2007-08	Hartlepool U	34	0	
2008-09	Hartlepool U	23	0	96 0

HUMPHREYS, Richie (M) 454 41
H: 5 11 W: 12 07 b.Sheffield 30-11-77
Source: Trainee. *Honours:* England Youth,
Under-21.

1995-96	Sheffield W	5	0	
1996-97	Sheffield W	29	3	
1997-98	Sheffield W	7	0	
1998-99	Sheffield W	19	1	
1999-2000	Sheffield W	0	0	
1999-2000	*Scunthorpe U*	6	2	6 2
1999-2000	*Cardiff C*	9	2	9 2
2000-01	Sheffield W	7	0	67 4
2000-01	Cambridge U	7	3	7 3
2001-02	Hartlepool U	46	5	
2002-03	Hartlepool U	46	11	
2003-04	Hartlepool U	46	3	
2004-05	Hartlepool U	46	3	
2005-06	Hartlepool U	46	2	
2006-07	Hartlepool U	38	3	
2006-07	*Port Vale*	7	0	7 0
2007-08	Hartlepool U	45	3	
2008-09	Hartlepool U	45	0	358 30

JONES, Richie (M) 55 3
H: 6 0 W: 11 00 b.Manchester 26-9-86
Source: Scholar. *Honours:* England Youth.

2004-05	Manchester U	0	0	
2005-06	Manchester U	0	0	
2006-07	Manchester U	0	0	
2006-07	*Colchester U*	6	0	6 0
2006-07	*Barnsley*	4	0	4 0
2007-08	*Yeovil T*	9	0	9 0
2008-09	Hartlepool U	36	3	36 3

LANGE, Rune (F) 301 168
H: 6 2 W: 13 04 b.Tromso 24-6-77
Honours: Norway Youth, Under-21, 1 full
cap.

1993	Floya	10	6	
1994	Floya	22	33	32 39
1995	Tromsdalen	21	4	
1996	Tromsdalen	21	11	
1997	Tromsdalen	12	15	54 30
1997	Tromso	9	4	
1998	Tromso	26	20	
1999	Tromso	26	12	
2000	Tromso	11	3	
2000-01	Trabzonspor	12	5	12 5
2000-01	Club Brugge	4	0	

2001-02	Club Brugge	33	19		
2002-03	Club Brugge	12	4		
2003-04	Club Brugge	25	12		
2004-05	Club Brugge	32	15		
2005-06	Club Brugge	2	2	108	52
2006	Valerenga	6	0		
2007	Valerenga	11	2	17	2
2008	Tromso	3	0	75	39
2008-09	Hartlepool U	3	1	3	1

LEE-BARRETT, Arran (G) 55 0
H: 6 2 W: 14 01 b.Ipswich 28-2-84
Source: Norwich C Scholar.

2002-03	Cardiff C	0	0		
2003-04	Cardiff C	0	0		
2004-05	Cardiff C	0	0		
2005-06	Cardiff C	0	0		

From Weymouth

2006-07	Coventry C	0	0		
2007-08	Hartlepool U	18	0		
2008-09	Hartlepool U	37	0	55	0

LIDDLE, Gary (D) 126 5
H: 6 1 W: 12 06 b.Middlesbrough 15-6-86
Source: Trainee. Honours: England Youth.

2003-04	Middlesbrough	0	0		
2004-05	Middlesbrough	0	0		
2005-06	Middlesbrough	0	0		
2006-07	Hartlepool U	42	3		
2007-08	Hartlepool U	41	2		
2008-09	Hartlepool U	43	0	126	5

MACKAY, Michael (F) 48 7
H: 6 0 W: 11 06 b.Durham 11-10-82
Source: Consett.

2006-07	Hartlepool U	1	0		
2007-08	Hartlepool U	24	5		
2008-09	Hartlepool U	23	2	48	7

McCUNNIE, Jamie (D) 203 1
H: 5 10 W: 10 11 b.Airdrie 15-4-83
Source: Dundee U BC. Honours: Scotland Under-21.

2000-01	Dundee U	15	0		
2001-02	Dundee U	28	0		
2002-03	Dundee U	18	0	61	0
2003-04	Ross Co	35	0		
2004-05	Ross Co	27	0	62	0
2005-06	Dunfermline Ath	22	0		
2006-07	Dunfermline Ath	14	0	36	0
2007-08	Hartlepool U	29	1		
2008-09	Hartlepool U	15	0	44	1

MONKHOUSE, Andy (M) 233 26
H: 6 1 W: 11 06 b.Leeds 23-10-80
Source: Trainee.

1998-99	Rotherham U	5	1		
1999-2000	Rotherham U	0	0		
2000-01	Rotherham U	12	0		
2001-02	Rotherham U	38	2		
2002-03	Rotherham U	20	0		
2003-04	Rotherham U	27	3		
2004-05	Rotherham U	14	2		
2005-06	Rotherham U	12	1	128	9
2006-07	Swindon T	10	2	10	2
2006-07	Hartlepool U	26	7		
2007-08	Hartlepool U	25	2		
2008-09	Hartlepool U	44	6	95	15

NELSON, Michael (D) 331 22
H: 6 2 W: 11 06 b.Gateshead 15-3-82
Source: Bishop Auckland.

2000-01	Bury	2	1		
2001-02	Bury	31	2		
2002-03	Bury	39	5	72	8
2003-04	Hartlepool U	40	3		
2004-05	Hartlepool U	43	1		
2005-06	Hartlepool U	43	2		
2006-07	Hartlepool U	42	1		
2007-08	Hartlepool U	45	2		
2008-09	Hartlepool U	46	5	259	14

PORTER, Joel (F) 281 87
H: 5 9 W: 11 13 b.Adelaide 25-12-78
Honours: Australia 4 full caps, 5 goals.

1998-99	West Adelaide	20	3	20	3
2000-01	Melbrne Knights	30	12		
2001-02	Melbrne Knights	26	12	56	24
2002-03	Sydney Olympic	32	8	32	8
2003-04	Hartlepool U	27	3		
2004-05	Hartlepool U	39	14		
2005-06	Hartlepool U	8	3		
2006-07	Hartlepool U	22	5		
2007-08	Hartlepool U	39	9		
2008-09	Hartlepool U	38	18	173	52

POWER, Alan (M) 4 0
H: 5 7 W: 11 06 b.Dublin 23-1-88
Source: Scholar. Honours: Eire Under-21.

2005-06	Nottingham F	0	0		
2006-07	Nottingham F	0	0		
2007-08	Nottingham F	0	0		
2008-09	Hartlepool U	4	0	4	0

ROBSON, Matty (D) 135 9
H: 5 10 W: 11 02 b.Durham 23-1-85
Source: Scholar.

2002-03	Hartlepool U	0	0		
2003-04	Hartlepool U	23	1		
2004-05	Hartlepool U	27	2		
2005-06	Hartlepool U	19	1		
2006-07	Hartlepool U	20	2		
2007-08	Hartlepool U	17	1		
2008-09	Hartlepool U	29	2	135	9

ROWELL, Jonny (M) 6 0
H: 5 7 W: 11 02 b.Newcastle 10-9-89

| 2007-08 | Hartlepool U | 0 | 0 | | |
| 2008-09 | Hartlepool U | 6 | 0 | 6 | 0 |

SWEENEY, Anthony (M) 211 32
H: 6 0 W: 11 07 b.Stockton 5-9-83
Source: Scholar.

2001-02	Hartlepool U	2	0		
2002-03	Hartlepool U	4	0		
2003-04	Hartlepool U	11	1		
2004-05	Hartlepool U	44	13		
2005-06	Hartlepool U	35	5		
2006-07	Hartlepool U	35	4		
2007-08	Hartlepool U	36	4		
2008-09	Hartlepool U	44	5	211	32

TAIT, Joe (D) 0 0
H: 6 2 W: 11 12 b.Middlesbrough 4-2-90
Source: Scholar.

| 2008-09 | Hartlepool U | 0 | 0 | | |

TURNBULL, Stephen (M) 33 0
H: 5 10 W: 11 00 b.South Shields 7-1-87
Source: Scholar.

2004-05	Hartlepool U	2	0		
2005-06	Hartlepool U	21	0		
2006-07	Hartlepool U	0	0		
2006-07	Bury	5	0	5	0
2006-07	Rochdale	4	0	4	0
2007-08	Hartlepool U	1	0		
2008-09	Hartlepool U	0	0	24	0

TYMON, Matty (F) 0 0
H: 5 11 W: 12 04 b.Middlesbrough 15-4-90
Source: Scholar.

| 2008-09 | Hartlepool U | 0 | 0 | | |

YOUNG, Martin (M) 0 0
H: 5 11 W: 11 07 b.Hartlepool 8-9-88
Source: Scholar.

| 2007-08 | Hartlepool U | 0 | 0 | | |
| 2008-09 | Hartlepool U | 0 | 0 | | |

HEREFORD U (40)

BECKWITH, Dean (D) 96 3
H: 6 3 W: 13 04 b.Southwark 18-9-83
Source: Scholar.

2003-04	Gillingham	0	0		
2004-05	Gillingham	1	0	1	0
2006-07	Hereford U	32	0		
2007-08	Hereford U	38	2		
2008-09	Hereford U	25	1	95	3

BREEN, Garry (D) 0 0
H: 6 2 W: 13 10 b.Kilkenny 17-3-89
Source: Scholar. Honours: Eire Under-21.

2006-07	Manchester C	0	0		
2007-08	Manchester C	0	0		
2008-09	Hereford U	0	0		

BROADHURST, Karl (D) 240 4
H: 6 1 W: 11 07 b.Portsmouth 18-3-80
Source: Trainee.

1998-99	Bournemouth	0	0		
1999-2000	Bournemouth	16	0		
2000-01	Bournemouth	30	0		
2001-02	Bournemouth	23	0		
2002-03	Bournemouth	21	1		
2003-04	Bournemouth	39	1		
2004-05	Bournemouth	29	1		
2005-06	Bournemouth	7	0		
2006-07	Bournemouth	27	0	192	3
2007-08	Hereford U	23	0		
2008-09	Hereford U	25	1	48	1

D'AGOSTINO, Michael (M) 25 0
H: 5 9 W: 11 08 b.Vancouver 7-1-87
Source: Kentucky Wildcats, Whitecaps.
Honours: Canada Youth.

2007-08	Blackpool	0	0		
2007-08	Cheltenham T	25	0	25	0
2008-09	Hereford U	0	0		

DIAGOURAGA, Toumani (M) 102 4
H: 6 2 W: 11 05 b.Corbeil-Essones 10-6-87
Source: Scholar.

2004-05	Watford	0	0		
2005-06	Watford	1	0		
2005-06	Swindon T	8	0	8	0
2006-07	Watford	0	0		
2006-07	Rotherham U	7	0	7	0
2007-08	Watford	0	0	1	0
2007-08	Hereford U	41	2		
2008-09	Hereford U	45	2	86	4

DONE, Matt (M) 102 4
H: 5 10 W: 10 04 b.Oswestry 22-6-88
Source: Scholar.

2005-06	Wrexham	6	0		
2006-07	Wrexham	34	1		
2007-08	Wrexham	26	0	66	1
2008-09	Hereford U	36	0	36	0

EASTON, Clint (M) 274 12
H: 5 11 W: 11 00 b.Barking 1-10-77
Source: Trainee. Honours: England Youth.

1996-97	Watford	17	1		
1997-98	Watford	12	0		
1998-99	Watford	7	0		
1999-2000	Watford	17	0		
2000-01	Watford	11	0	64	1
2001-02	Norwich C	14	1		
2002-03	Norwich C	26	2		
2003-04	Norwich C	10	2	50	5
2004-05	Wycombe W	33	1		
2005-06	Wycombe W	44	1	77	2
2006-07	Gillingham	32	1	32	1
2007-08	Hereford U	39	3		
2008-09	Hereford U	12	0	51	3

FITZPATRICK, Jordan (M) 1 0
H: 6 0 W: 12 00 b.Stourbridge 15-6-88
Source: Wolverhampton W Scholar.

2006-07	Hereford U	1	0		
2007-08	Hereford U	0	0		
2008-09	Hereford U	0	0	1	0

GUINAN, Stephen (F) 265 52
H: 6 1 W: 13 02 b.Birmingham 24-12-75
Source: Trainee.

1992-93	Nottingham F	0	0		
1993-94	Nottingham F	0	0		
1994-95	Nottingham F	0	0		
1995-96	Nottingham F	2	0		
1995-96	Darlington	3	1	3	1
1996-97	Nottingham F	2	0		
1996-97	Burnley	6	0	6	0
1997-98	Nottingham F	2	0		
1997-98	Crewe Alex	3	0	3	0
1998-99	Nottingham F	0	0		
1998-99	Halifax T	12	2	12	2
1999-99	Plymouth Arg	11	7		
1999-2000	Nottingham F	1	0	7	0
1999-2000	Scunthorpe U	3	1	3	1
1999-2000	Cambridge U	6	0	6	0
1999-2000	Plymouth Arg	8	2		
2000-01	Plymouth Arg	22	1		
2001-02	Plymouth Arg	0	0	41	10
2001-02	Shrewsbury T	5	0		
2002-03	Shrewsbury T	0	0		
2003-04	Shrewsbury T	0	0	5	0
2004-05	Cheltenham T	43	6		
2005-06	Cheltenham T	30	7		
2006-07	Cheltenham T	19	0	92	13
2006-07	Hereford U	16	7		
2007-08	Hereford U	28	0		
2008-09	Hereford U	43	15	87	25

GWYNNE, Sam (M) 36 1
H: 5 9 W: 11 11 b.Hereford 17-12-87
Source: Scholar.

2006-07	Hereford U	0	0		
2007-08	Hereford U	15	0		
2008-09	Hereford U	21	1	36	1

HUDSON-ODOI, Bradley (F)   16   3
H: 5 8   W: 11 11   b.Ghana 29-11-88
Source: Fulham Scholar. *Honours:* Ghana Under-20.
2008-09   Hereford U   16   3   16   3

JACKSON, Richard (D)   194   0
H: 5 8   W: 12 10   b.Whitby 18-4-80
Source: Trainee.
1997-98   Scarborough   2   0
1998-99   Scarborough   20   0   22   0
1998-99   Derby Co   0   0
1999-2000   Derby Co   2   0
2000-01   Derby Co   2   0
2001-02   Derby Co   7   0
2002-03   Derby Co   21   0
2003-04   Derby Co   36   0
2004-05   Derby Co   19   0
2005-06   Derby Co   26   0
2006-07   Derby Co   5   0   118   0
2007-08   Luton T   29   0
2008-09   Luton T   0   0   29   0
2008-09   Hereford U   25   0   25   0

JOHNSON, Simon (F)   182   22
H: 5 9   W: 11 09   b.West Bromwich 9-3-83
Source: Scholar. *Honours:* England Youth, Under-20.
2000-01   Leeds U   0   0
2001-02   Leeds U   0   0
2002-03   Leeds U   4   0
2002-03   *Hull C*   12   2   12   2
2003-04   Leeds U   5   0
2003-04   *Blackpool*   4   1   4   1
2004-05   Leeds U   2   0   11   0
2004-05   *Sunderland*   5   0   5   0
2004-05   *Doncaster R*   11   3   11   3
2004-05   *Barnsley*   11   2   11   2
2005-06   Darlington   42   7
2006-07   Darlington   24   2   66   9
2007-08   Hereford U   33   5
2008-09   Hereford U   29   0   62   5

JONES, Craig (M)   3   0
H: 6 1   W: 12 02   b.Hereford 12-12-89
Source: Cardiff C.
2007-08   Hereford U   0   0
2008-09   Hereford U   3   0   3   0

MACLEOD, Jack (D)   6   0
H: 5 8   W: 10 00   b.Epsom 3-8-88
Source: Millwall Scholar, Carshalton Ath.
2007-08   Hereford U   0   0
2008-09   Hereford U   6   0   6   0

McCLENAHAN, Trent (D)   103   2
H: 5 11   W: 12 00   b.Sydney 4-2-85
Source: Scholar. *Honours:* Australia Under-20, Under-23.
2004-05   West Ham U   2   0
2004-05   *Milton Keynes D*   8   0
2005-06   West Ham U   0   0   2   0
2005-06   *Milton Keynes D*   29   0   37   0
2006-07   Hereford U   26   1
2007-08   Hereford U   38   1
2008-09   Hereford U   0   0   64   2

O'LEARY, Stephen (M)   81   7
H: 6 0   W: 11 09   b.Barnet 12-2-85
Source: Scholar. *Honours:* Eire Youth.
2003-04   Luton T   5   1
2004-05   Luton T   17   1
2005-06   Luton T   0   0
2005-06   *Tranmere R*   21   3   21   3
2006-07   Luton T   7   1
2007-08   Luton T   16   0   45   3
2008-09   Hereford U   15   1   15   1

OJI, Sam (D)   26   0
H: 6 0   W: 14 05   b.Westminster 9-10-85
Source: Arsenal Scholar.
2003-04   Birmingham C   0   0
2004-05   Birmingham C   0   0
2005-06   Birmingham C   0   0
2005-06   *Doncaster R*   4   0   4   0
2006-07   Birmingham C   0   0
2006-07   *Bristol R*   5   0   5   0
2007-08   Birmingham C   0   0
2007-08   Leyton Orient   13   0   13   0
2008-09   Hereford U   4   0   4   0

PALMER, Marcus (F)   4   0
H: 6 0   W: 11 07   b.Gloucester 22-12-88
Source: Cheltenham T Scholar.
2006-07   Hereford U   3   0

2007-08   Hereford U   1   0
2008-09   Hereford U   0   0   4   0

ROSE, Richard (D)   173   2
H: 6 0   W: 12 04   b.Pembury 8-9-82
Source: Trainee.
2000-01   Gillingham   4   0
2001-02   Gillingham   3   0
2002-03   Gillingham   2   0
2002-03   *Bristol R*   9   0   9   0
2003-04   Gillingham   17   0
2004-05   Gillingham   18   0
2005-06   Gillingham   14   0   58   0
2006-07   Hereford U   33   1
2007-08   Hereford U   31   1
2008-09   Hereford U   42   0   106   2

SAMSON, Craig (G)   104   0
H: 6 2   W: 12 07   b.Irvine 1-4-84
Honours: Scotland Under-21.
2003-04   Kilmarnock   1   0
2003-04   *Queen of the S*   12   0   12   0
2004-05   Kilmarnock   0   0   1   0
2004-05   *St Johnstone*   12   0   12   0
2005-06   Dundee U   8   0   8   0
2006-07   Ross Co   29   0   29   0
2007-08   Dundee   31   0   31   0
2008-09   Hereford U   11   0   11   0

SMITH, Ben (M)   124   11
H: 5 9   W: 11 09   b.Chelmsford 23-11-78
Source: Yeovil T.
2001-02   Southend U   1   0   1   0
From Hereford U
2004-05   Shrewsbury T   12   3
2005-06   Shrewsbury T   12   1   24   4
From Weymouth.
2006-07   Hereford U   18   1
2007-08   Hereford U   44   5
2008-09   Hereford U   37   1   99   7

TAYLOR, Kris (M)   150   8
H: 5 9   W: 11 05   b.Stafford 12-1-84
Source: Scholar. *Honours:* England Schools, Youth.
2000-01   Manchester U   0   0
2001-02   Manchester U   0   0
2002-03   Manchester U   0   0
2002-03   Walsall   0   0
2003-04   Walsall   11   1
2004-05   Walsall   12   2
2005-06   Walsall   22   2
2006-07   Walsall   35   1   80   6
2007-08   Hereford U   31   1
2008-09   Hereford U   39   1   70   2

VEIGA, Jose Manuel (G)   272   0
H: 6 2   W: 12 13   b.Lisbon 18-12-76
Source: Benfica. *Honours:* Cape Verde full caps.
1996-97   Alverca   14   0
1997-98   Alverca   33   0   47   0
1998-99   Levante   38   0
1999-2000   Levante   40   0
2000-01   Levante   30   0
2001-02   Levante   22   0   130   0
2001-02   Valladolid   0   0
2002-03   Amadora   33   0
2003-04   Amadora   28   0
2004-05   Amadora   31   0   92   0
2005-06   Olhanse   2   0   2   0
From Tamworth, Atherstone T.
2008-09   Hereford U   1   0   1   0

HUDDERSFIELD T (41)

AINSWORTH, Lionel (F)   67   7
H: 5 9   W: 9 10   b.Nottingham 1-10-87
Source: Scholar. *Honours:* England Youth.
2005-06   Derby Co   2   0
2006-07   Derby Co   0   0   2   0
2006-07   *Bournemouth*   7   0   7   0
2006-07   *Wycombe W*   7   0   7   0
2007-08   Hereford U   15   4
2007-08   Watford   8   0
2008-09   Watford   7   0   15   0
2008-09   *Hereford U*   7   3   22   7
2008-09   Huddersfield T   14   0   14   0

BECKETT, Luke (F)   353   145
H: 5 11   W: 11 02   b.Sheffield 25-11-76
Source: Trainee.
1995-96   Barnsley   0   0
1996-97   Barnsley   0   0
1997-98   Barnsley   0   0
1998-99   Chester C   28   11
1999-2000   Chester C   46   14   74   25
2000-01   Chesterfield   41   16
2001-02   Chesterfield   21   6   62   22
2001-02   Stockport Co   19   7
2002-03   Stockport Co   42   27
2003-04   Stockport Co   8   4
2004-05   Stockport Co   15   7   84   45
2004-05   Sheffield U   5   0
2004-05   *Huddersfield T*   7   6
2004-05   *Oldham Ath*   9   6
2005-06   Sheffield U   0   0   5   0
2005-06   *Oldham Ath*   34   18   43   24
2006-07   Huddersfield T   41   15
2007-08   Huddersfield T   36   8
2008-09   Huddersfield T   1   0   85   29

BERRETT, James (M)   26   2
H: 5 10   W: 10 13   b.Halifax 13-1-89
Source: Scholar. *Honours:* Eire Youth, Under-21.
2006-07   Huddersfield T   2   0
2007-08   Huddersfield T   15   1
2008-09   Huddersfield T   9   1   26   2

BOOTH, Andy (F)   531   162
H: 6 0   W: 12 06   b.Huddersfield 6-12-73
Source: Trainee. *Honours:* England Under-21.
1991-92   Huddersfield T   3   0
1992-93   Huddersfield T   5   2
1993-94   Huddersfield T   26   10
1994-95   Huddersfield T   46   26
1995-96   Huddersfield T   43   16
1996-97   Sheffield W   35   10
1997-98   Sheffield W   23   7
1998-99   Sheffield W   34   6
1999-2000   Sheffield W   23   2
2000-01   Sheffield W   18   3   133   28
2000-01   *Tottenham H*   4   0   4   0
2000-01   *Huddersfield T*   8   3
2001-02   Huddersfield T   36   11
2002-03   Huddersfield T   33   6
2003-04   Huddersfield T   37   13
2004-05   Huddersfield T   29   10
2005-06   Huddersfield T   36   13
2006-07   Huddersfield T   34   7
2007-08   Huddersfield T   38   9
2008-09   Huddersfield T   20   8   394   134

BROADBENT, Daniel (M)   6   0
H: 5 10   W: 12 00   b.Leeds 2-3-90
Source: Scholar. *Honours:* England Youth.
2006-07   Huddersfield T   0   0
2007-08   Huddersfield T   5   0
2008-09   Huddersfield T   1   0   6   0

BUTLER, Andy (D)   181   20
H: 6 0   W: 13 00   b.Doncaster 4-11-83
Source: Scholar.
2003-04   Scunthorpe U   35   2
2004-05   Scunthorpe U   37   10
2005-06   Scunthorpe U   16   1
2006-07   Scunthorpe U   11   1
2006-07   *Grimsby T*   4   0   4   0
2007-08   Scunthorpe U   36   2   135   16
2008-09   Huddersfield T   42   4   42   4

CADAMARTERI, Danny (F)   269   28
H: 5 7   W: 13 05   b.Bradford 12-10-79
Source: Trainee. *Honours:* England Youth, Under-21.
1996-97   Everton   1   0
1997-98   Everton   26   4
1998-99   Everton   30   4
1999-2000   Everton   17   1
1999-2000   *Fulham*   5   1   5   1
2000-01   Everton   16   4
2001-02   Everton   3   0   93   13
2001-02   Bradford C   14   2
2002-03   Bradford C   20   0
2003-04   Bradford C   18   3
2004-05   Leeds U   0   0
2004-05   Sheffield U   21   1   21   1
2005-06   Bradford C   39   2
2006-07   Bradford C   0   0   91   7
2006-07   *Doncaster R*   6   1   6   1

2006-07	Leicester C	9	0	9	0
2007-08	Huddersfield T	12	3		
2008-09	Huddersfield T	32	2	44	5

CLARKE, Nathan (D) 246 7
H: 6 2 W: 12 00 b.Halifax 30-11-83
Source: Scholar.

2001-02	Huddersfield T	36	1		
2002-03	Huddersfield T	3	0		
2003-04	Huddersfield T	26	1		
2004-05	Huddersfield T	37	0		
2005-06	Huddersfield T	46	0		
2006-07	Huddersfield T	16	0		
2007-08	Huddersfield T	44	2		
2008-09	Huddersfield T	38	3	246	7

CLARKE, Tom (D) 62 2
H: 6 0 W: 11 02 b.Halifax 21-12-87
Source: Scholar. *Honours:* England Youth.

2004-05	Huddersfield T	12	0		
2005-06	Huddersfield T	17	1		
2006-07	Huddersfield T	9	0		
2007-08	Huddersfield T	3	0		
2008-09	Huddersfield T	15	1	56	2
2008-09	*Bradford C*	6	0	6	0

CODMAN, Daniel (D) 0 0
H: 6 1 W: 10 13 b.Huddersfield 1-6-90
Source: Scholar.

2008-09	Huddersfield T	0	0		

COLLINS, Michael (M) 145 16
H: 6 0 W: 11 00 b.Halifax 30-4-86
Source: From Scholar. *Honours:* Eire Youth, Under-21.

2004-05	Huddersfield T	8	0		
2005-06	Huddersfield T	17	1		
2006-07	Huddersfield T	43	4		
2007-08	Huddersfield T	41	2		
2008-09	Huddersfield T	36	9	145	16

CRANEY, Ian (M) 116 18
H: 5 10 W: 12 00 b.Liverpool 21-7-82
Source: Runcorn, Altrincham.

2006-07	Accrington S	18	5		
2006-07	Swansea C	27	0		
2007-08	Swansea C	1	0	28	0
2007-08	Accrington S	34	7		
2008-09	Accrington S	2	1	54	13
2008-09	Huddersfield T	34	5	34	5

DENTON, Tom (F) 0 0
H: 6 6 b.Shepley 24-7-89
Source: Wakefield.

2008-09	Huddersfield T	0	0		

EASTWOOD, Simon (G) 1 0
H: 6 2 W: 13 00 b.Luton 26-6-89
Source: From Scholar. *Honours:* England Youth.

2005-06	Huddersfield T	0	0		
2006-07	Huddersfield T	0	0		
2007-08	Huddersfield T	0	0		
2008-09	Huddersfield T	1	0	1	0

FLYNN, Michael (M) 194 28
H: 5 10 W: 13 04 b.Newport 17-10-80
Source: Barry T.

2002-03	Wigan Ath	17	1		
2003-04	Wigan Ath	8	0		
2004-05	Wigan Ath	13	1	38	2
2004-05	*Blackpool*	6	0		
2004-05	Gillingham	16	3		
2005-06	Gillingham	36	6		
2006-07	Gillingham	45	10	97	19
2007-08	Blackpool	28	3	34	3
2008-09	*Darlington*	3	0		
2008-09	Huddersfield T	25	4	25	4

GLENNON, Matty (G) 262 0
H: 6 2 W: 14 08 b.Stockport 8-10-78
Source: Trainee.

1997-98	Bolton W	0	0		
1998-99	Bolton W	0	0		
1999-2000	Bolton W	0	0		
1999-2000	*Port Vale*	0	0		
1999-2000	*Stockport Co*	0	0		
2000-01	Bolton W	0	0		
2000-01	*Bristol R*	1	0	1	0
2000-01	Carlisle U	29	0		
2001-02	Hull C	26	0		
2002-03	Hull C	9	0	35	0
2002-03	Carlisle U	32	0		
2003-04	Carlisle U	44	0		
2004-05	Carlisle U	0	0	105	0

2005-06	St Johnstone	12	0	12	0
2006-07	Huddersfield T	46	0		
2007-08	Huddersfield T	45	0		
2008-09	Huddersfield T	18	0	109	0

GOODWIN, Jim (M) 224 14
H: 5 9 W: 12 01 b.Waterford 20-11-81
Source: Tramore. *Honours:* Eire Under-21, B, 1 full cap.

2001-02	Celtic	0	0		
2002-03	Stockport Co	33	3		
2003-04	Stockport Co	34	4		
2004-05	Stockport Co	36	0	103	7
2005-06	Scunthorpe U	13	2		
2006-07	Scunthorpe U	31	1		
2007-08	Scunthorpe U	40	3	84	6
2008-09	Huddersfield T	37	1	37	1

HOLDSWORTH, Andy (D) 231 6
H: 5 9 W: 11 02 b.Pontefract 29-1-84
Source: Scholar.

2003-04	Huddersfield T	36	0		
2004-05	Huddersfield T	40	0		
2005-06	Huddersfield T	42	1		
2006-07	Huddersfield T	35	2		
2007-08	Huddersfield T	44	3		
2008-09	Huddersfield T	34	0	231	6

JEVONS, Phil (F) 273 85
H: 5 11 W: 12 00 b.Liverpool 1-8-79
Source: Trainee.

1996-97	Everton	0	0		
1997-98	Everton	0	0		
1998-99	Everton	1	0		
1999-2000	Everton	3	0		
2000-01	Everton	4	0	8	0
2001-02	Grimsby T	31	6		
2002-03	Grimsby T	3	0		
2002-03	*Hull C*	24	3	24	3
2003-04	Grimsby T	29	12	63	18
2004-05	Yeovil T	46	27		
2005-06	Yeovil T	38	15	84	42
2006-07	Bristol C	41	11		
2007-08	Bristol C	2	0	43	11
2007-08	Huddersfield T	21	7		
2008-09	Huddersfield T	23	2	44	9
2008-09	*Bury*	7	2	7	2

KAMARA, Malvin (M) 157 10
H: 5 11 W: 13 00 b.Southwark 17-11-83
Source: Scholar. *Honours:* Sierra Leone 1 full cap.

2002-03	Wimbledon	2	0		
2003-04	Wimbledon	27	2	29	2
2004-05	Milton Keynes D	25	1		
2005-06	Milton Keynes D	23	2	48	3
2006-07	Cardiff C	15	1	15	1
2006-07	Port Vale	18	1	18	1
2007-08	Huddersfield T	43	3		
2008-09	Huddersfield T	2	0	45	3
2008-09	*Grimsby T*	2	0	2	0

KILLOCK, Shane (D) 1 0
H: 6 0 W: 12 04 b.Huddersfield 12-3-89
Source: Ossett Albion.

2007-08	Huddersfield T	1	0		
2008-09	Huddersfield T	0	0	1	0

LUCKETTI, Chris (D) 605 21
H: 6 1 W: 13 06 b.Rochdale 28-9-71
Source: Trainee.

1988-89	Rochdale	1	0		
1989-90	Rochdale	0	0	1	0
1990-91	Stockport Co	0	0		
1991-92	Halifax T	36	0		
1992-93	Halifax T	42	2	78	2
1993-94	Bury	27	1		
1994-95	Bury	39	3		
1995-96	Bury	42	1		
1996-97	Bury	38	0		
1997-98	Bury	46	2		
1998-99	Bury	43	1	235	8
1999-2000	Huddersfield T	26	0		
2000-01	Huddersfield T	40	1		
2001-02	Huddersfield T	2	0		
2001-02	Preston NE	40	2		
2002-03	Preston NE	43	2		
2003-04	Preston NE	37	1		
2004-05	Preston NE	41	4		
2005-06	Preston NE	28	1	189	10
2005-06	*Sheffield U*	3	0		
2006-07	Sheffield U	8	0		
2007-08	Sheffield U	6	0	17	0

2007-08	*Southampton*	4	0	4	0
2008-09	Huddersfield T	13	0	81	1

NOVAK, Lee (F) 0 0
H: 6 0 W: 12 04 b.Newcastle 28-9-88
Source: Gateshead.

				0	0
2008-09	Huddersfield T	0	0		

PARKER, Keigan (F) 302 57
H: 5 7 W: 10 05 b.Livingston 8-6-82
Source: St Johnstone BC. *Honours:* Scotland Youth, Under-21.

1998-99	St Johnstone	2	0		
1999-2000	St Johnstone	10	2		
2000-01	St Johnstone	37	9		
2001-02	St Johnstone	21	1		
2002-03	St Johnstone	31	1		
2003-04	St Johnstone	31	8	132	21
2004-05	Blackpool	35	9		
2005-06	Blackpool	40	12		
2006-07	Blackpool	45	13		
2007-08	Blackpool	21	0	141	34
2008-09	Huddersfield T	20	2	20	2
2008-09	*Hartlepool U*	9	0	9	0

PILKINGTON, Anthony (M) 93 18
H: 5 11 W: 12 00 b.Blackburn 3-11-87
Source: Atherton CW. *Honours:* Eire Under-21.

2006-07	Stockport Co	24	5		
2007-08	Stockport Co	29	6		
2008-09	Stockport Co	24	5	77	16
2008-09	Huddersfield T	16	2	16	2

ROBERTS, Gary (F) 115 20
H: 5 10 W: 11 09 b.Chester 18-3-84
Source: Denbigh T, Bangor C.

2006-07	Accrington S	14	8	14	8
2006-07	Ipswich T	33	2		
2007-08	Ipswich T	21	1	54	3
2007-08	*Crewe Alex*	4	0	4	0
2008-09	Huddersfield T	43	9	43	9

SKARZ, Joe (D) 60 1
H: 5 10 W: 11 04 b.Huddersfield 13-7-89
Source: Scholar.

2006-07	Huddersfield T	17	0		
2007-08	Huddersfield T	27	0		
2008-09	Huddersfield T	9	1	53	1
2008-09	*Hartlepool U*	7	0	7	0

SMITHIES, Alex (G) 29 0
H: 6 1 W: 10 01 b.Huddersfield 25-3-90
Source: Scholar. *Honours:* England Youth.

2006-07	Huddersfield T	0	0		
2007-08	Huddersfield T	2	0		
2008-09	Huddersfield T	27	0	29	0

SPENCER, James (F) 0 0
Source: Scholar.

2008-09	Huddersfield T	0	0		

UNSWORTH, Dave (D) 449 45
H: 6 1 W: 13 07 b.Chorley 16-10-73
Source: From Trainee. *Honours:* England Youth, Under-21, 1 full cap.

1991-92	Everton	2	1		
1992-93	Everton	3	0		
1993-94	Everton	8	0		
1994-95	Everton	38	3		
1995-96	Everton	31	2		
1996-97	Everton	34	5		
1997-98	West Ham U	32	2	32	2
1998-99	Aston Villa	0	0		
1998-99	Everton	34	1		
1999-2000	Everton	33	6		
2000-01	Everton	29	5		
2001-02	Everton	33	3		
2002-03	Everton	33	5		
2003-04	Everton	26	3	304	34
2004-05	Portsmouth	15	2		
2004-05	*Ipswich T*	16	1	16	1
2005-06	Portsmouth	0	0	15	2
2005-06	Sheffield U	34	4		
2006-07	Sheffield U	5	0	39	4
2006-07	Wigan Ath	10	1	10	1
2007-08	Burnley	29	1	29	1
2008-09	Huddersfield T	4	0	4	0

WERLING, Dominik (M) 75 4
H: 5 8 W: 12 08 b.Ludwigshafen 13-12-82

2003-04	Bielefeld II	20	0	20	0
2004-05	Union Berlin	9	0	9	0
2005-06	Crailsheim	26	3	26	3

Season	Club				
2006-07	Sakarya	0	0		
2007-08	Barnsley	17	1		
2008-09	Barnsley	0	0	17	1
2008-09	Huddersfield T	3	0	3	0

WILLIAMS, Robbie (D)   135 10
H: 5 10 W: 11 13 b.Pontefract 2-10-84
Source: Scholar.

Season	Club				
2002-03	Barnsley	8	0		
2003-04	Barnsley	4	1		
2004-05	Barnsley	17	1		
2005-06	Barnsley	22	2		
2006-07	Barnsley	15	0		
2006-07	*Blackpool*	9	4	9	4
2007-08	Barnsley	0	0	66	4
2007-08	Huddersfield T	25	2		
2008-09	Huddersfield T	35	0	60	2

WORTHINGTON, Jon (M)   222 12
H: 5 9 W: 11 05 b.Dewsbury 16-4-83
Source: Scholar.

Season	Club				
2001-02	Huddersfield T	0	0		
2002-03	Huddersfield T	22	0		
2003-04	Huddersfield T	39	3		
2004-05	Huddersfield T	39	3		
2005-06	Huddersfield T	41	4		
2006-07	Huddersfield T	28	2		
2007-08	Huddersfield T	25	0		
2008-09	Huddersfield T	19	0	213	12
2008-09	*Yeovil T*	9	0	9	0

HULL C (42)

ASHBEE, Ian (M)   428 20
H: 6 1 W: 13 07 b.Birmingham 6-9-76
Source: Trainee. Honours: England Youth.

Season	Club				
1994-95	Derby Co	1	0		
1995-96	Derby Co	0	0		
1996-97	Derby Co	0	0	1	0
1996-97	Cambridge U	18	0		
1997-98	Cambridge U	27	1		
1998-99	Cambridge U	31	4		
1999-2000	Cambridge U	45	1		
2000-01	Cambridge U	44	3		
2001-02	Cambridge U	38	2	203	11
2002-03	Hull C	31	1		
2003-04	Hull C	39	2		
2004-05	Hull C	40	1		
2005-06	Hull C	6	0		
2006-07	Hull C	35	1		
2007-08	Hull C	42	3		
2008-09	Hull C	31	1	224	9

ATKINSON, Will (M)   16 0
H: 5 10 W: 10 07 b.Driffield 14-10-88
Source: Scholar.

Season	Club				
2006-07	Hull C	0	0		
2007-08	Hull C	0	0		
2007-08	*Port Vale*	4	0	4	0
2007-08	*Mansfield T*	12	0	12	0
2008-09	Hull C	0	0		

BARMBY, Nick (F)   429 73
H: 5 7 W: 11 03 b.Hull 11-2-74
Source: Trainee. Honours: England Schools, Youth, Under-21, B, 23 full caps, 4 goals.

Season	Club				
1991-92	Tottenham H				
1992-93	Tottenham H	22	6		
1993-94	Tottenham H	27	5		
1994-95	Tottenham H	9	8	87	20
1995-96	Middlesbrough	32	7		
1996-97	Middlesbrough	10	1	42	8
1996-97	Everton	25	4		
1997-98	Everton	30	2		
1998-99	Everton	24	3		
1999-2000	Everton	37	9	116	18
2000-01	Liverpool	26	2		
2001-02	Liverpool	6	0	32	2
2002-03	Leeds U	19	4		
2003-04	*Nottingham F*	6	1	6	1
2003-04	Leeds U	6	0	25	4
2004-05	Hull C	39	9		
2005-06	Hull C	26	5		
2006-07	Hull C	20	4		
2007-08	Hull C	15	1		
2008-09	Hull C	21	1	121	20

BENNETT, James (M)   0 0
H: 5 10 W: 12 03 b.Beverley 4-9-88
Source: Scholar.

Season	Club				
2006-07	Hull C	0	0		
2007-08	Hull C	0	0		
2008-09	Hull C	0	0		
2008-09	*Lincoln C*	0	0		

BOATENG, George (M)   432 17
H: 5 9 W: 12 06 b.Nkawkaw 5-9-75
Honours: Holland Under-21, 4 full caps.

Season	Club				
1994-95	Excelsior	9	0	9	0
1995-96	Feyenoord	24	1		
1996-97	Feyenoord	26	0		
1997-98	Feyenoord	18	0	68	1
1997-98	Coventry C	14	1		
1998-99	Coventry C	33	4	47	5
1999-2000	Aston Villa	33	2		
2000-01	Aston Villa	33	1		
2001-02	Aston Villa	37	1	103	4
2002-03	Middlesbrough	28	0		
2003-04	Middlesbrough	35	0		
2004-05	Middlesbrough	25	3		
2005-06	Middlesbrough	26	2		
2006-07	Middlesbrough	35	1		
2007-08	Middlesbrough	33	1	182	7
2008-09	Hull C	23	0	23	0

BRIDGES, Michael (F)   253 60
H: 6 1 W: 10 11 b.North Shields 5-8-78
Source: Trainee. Honours: England Schools, Youth, Under-21.

Season	Club				
1995-96	Sunderland	15	4		
1996-97	Sunderland	25	3		
1997-98	Sunderland	9	1		
1998-99	Sunderland	30	8		
1999-2000	Leeds U	34	19		
2000-01	Leeds U	7	0		
2001-02	Leeds U	0	0		
2002-03	Leeds U	5	0		
2003-04	Leeds U	10	0	56	19
2003-04	*Newcastle U*	6	0	6	0
2004-05	Bolton W	0	0		
2004-05	Sunderland	19	1	98	17
2005-06	*Bristol C*	11	0	11	0
2005-06	Carlisle U	25	15		
2006-07	Carlisle U	5	0		
2006-07	Hull C	15	2		
2007-08	Hull C	7	0		
2008-09	Hull C	0	0	22	2
2008-09	*Carlisle U*	30	7	60	22

BROWN, Wayne (D)   298 11
H: 6 0 W: 12 06 b.Barking 20-8-77
Source: Trainee.

Season	Club				
1995-96	Ipswich T	0	0		
1996-97	Ipswich T	0	0		
1997-98	Ipswich T	1	0		
1997-98	*Colchester U*	2	0		
1998-99	Ipswich T	1	0		
1999-2000	Ipswich T	25	0		
2000-01	Ipswich T	4	0		
2000-01	*QPR*	2	0	2	0
2001-02	Ipswich T	0	0		
2001-02	*Wimbledon*	17	1	17	1
2001-02	*Watford*	11	3		
2002-03	Ipswich T	9	0	40	0
2002-03	Watford	13	1		
2003-04	Watford	12	0	36	4
2003-04	*Gillingham*	4	1	4	1
2003-04	Colchester U	16	0		
2004-05	Colchester U	40	1		
2005-06	Colchester U	38	2		
2006-07	Colchester U	46	1	142	4
2007-08	Hull C	41	1		
2008-09	Hull C	1	0	42	1
2008-09	*Preston NE*	6	0	6	0
2008-09	*Leicester C*	9	0	9	0

BULLARD, Jimmy (M)   251 27
H: 5 10 W: 11 05 b.Newham 23-10-78
Source: Corinthian, Dartford, Gravesend & N.

Season	Club				
1998-99	West Ham U	0	0		
1999-2000	West Ham U	0	0		
2000-01	West Ham U	0	0		
2001-02	Peterborough U	40	8		
2002-03	Peterborough U	26	3	66	11
2002-03	Wigan Ath	17	1		
2003-04	Wigan Ath	46	2		
2004-05	Wigan Ath	46	3		
2005-06	Wigan Ath	36	4	145	10
2005-06	Fulham	0	0		
2006-07	Fulham	4	2		
2007-08	Fulham	17	2		
2008-09	Fulham	18	2	39	6
2008-09	Hull C	1	0	1	0

COOPER, Liam (D)   0 0
H: 6 2 W: 13 07 b.Hull 30-8-91
Source: Scholar. Honours: Scottish Youth.

Season	Club				
2008-09	Hull C	0	0		

COUSIN, Daniel (F)   364 94
H: 6 2 W: 12 13 b.Libreville 7-2-77
Honours: Gabon 9 full caps, 2 goals.

Season	Club				
1997-98	Martigues	36	5	36	5
1998-99	Niort	22	1		
1999-2000	Niort	24	4	46	5
2000-01	Le Mans	29	6		
2001-02	Le Mans	33	12		
2002-03	Le Mans	33	15		
2003-04	Le Mans	33	11	128	44
2004-05	Lens	37	9		
2005-06	Lens	33	13		
2006-07	Lens	30	4		
2007-08	Lens	1	0	101	26
2008-09	*Rangers*	26	10	26	10
2008-09	Hull C	27	4	27	4

DAWSON, Andy (D)   372 15
H: 5 9 W: 11 02 b.Northallerton 20-10-78
Source: Trainee.

Season	Club				
1995-96	Nottingham F	0	0		
1996-97	Nottingham F	0	0		
1997-98	Nottingham F	0	0		
1998-99	Nottingham F	0	0		
1998-99	Scunthorpe U	24	0		
1999-2000	Scunthorpe U	43	2		
2000-01	Scunthorpe U	41	4		
2001-02	Scunthorpe U	44	0		
2002-03	Scunthorpe U	43	2	195	8
2003-04	Hull C	33	3		
2004-05	Hull C	34	0		
2005-06	Hull C	18	0		
2006-07	Hull C	38	2		
2007-08	Hull C	29	1		
2008-09	Hull C	25	1	177	7

DEVITT, Jamie (F)   0 0
H: 5 10 W: 10 05 b.Dublin 6-6-90
Source: Cherry Orchard BC, Hull C Scholar.
Honours: Eire Youth.

Season	Club				
2007-08	Hull C	0	0		
2008-09	Hull C	0	0		

DOYLE, Nathan (M)   54 0
H: 5 11 W: 12 06 b.Derby 12-1-87
Source: Scholar. Honours: England Youth, Under-20.

Season	Club				
2003-04	Derby Co	2	0		
2004-05	Derby Co	3	0		
2005-06	Derby Co	4	0		
2005-06	*Notts Co*	12	0	12	0
2006-07	Derby Co	0	0	9	0
2006-07	*Bradford C*	28	0	28	0
2006-07	Hull C	1	0		
2007-08	Hull C	1	0		
2008-09	Hull C	3	0	5	0

DUKE, Matt (G)   26 0
H: 6 5 W: 13 04 b.Sheffield 16-7-77
Source: Alfreton T.

Season	Club				
1999-2000	Sheffield U	0	0		
2000-01	Sheffield U	0	0		
2001-02	Sheffield U	0	0		
2004-05	Hull C	2	0		
2005-06	Hull C	2	0		
2005-06	*Stockport Co*	3	0	3	0
2005-06	*Wycombe W*	5	0	5	0
2006-07	Hull C	1	0		
2007-08	Hull C	3	0		
2008-09	Hull C	10	0	18	0

EKRA, Yann (F)   0 0
b. 10-12-90
Honours: France Youth.

Season	Club				
2008-09	Hull C	0	0		

FAGAN, Craig (F)   219 37
H: 5 11 W: 11 11 b.Birmingham 11-12-82
Source: Scholar.

Season	Club				
2001-02	Birmingham C	0	0		
2002-03	Birmingham C	1	0		
2002-03	*Bristol C*	6	1	6	1
2003-04	Birmingham C	0	0	1	0
2003-04	Colchester U	37	9		
2004-05	Colchester U	26	8	63	17
2004-05	Hull C	12	4		
2005-06	Hull C	41	5		
2006-07	Hull C	27	6		
2006-07	Derby Co	17	1		

2007-08	Derby Co	22	0	39 1
2007-08	Hull C	8	0	
2008-09	Hull C	22	3	110 18

FEATHERSTONE, Nicky (F)   **8 0**
H: 5 6 W: 11 02 b.North Ferriby 22-9-88
Source: Scholar.

2006-07	Hull C	2	0	
2007-08	Hull C	6	0	
2008-09	Hull C	0	0	8 0

FOLAN, Caleb (F)   **168 26**
H: 6 2 W: 14 07 b.Leeds 26-10-82
Source: Trainee. *Honours:* Eire 4 full caps.

1999-2000	Leeds U	0	0	
2000-01	Leeds U	0	0	
2001-02	Leeds U	0	0	
2001-02	Rushden & D	6	0	6 0
2001-02	Hull C	1	0	
2002-03	Leeds U	0	0	
2002-03	Chesterfield	13	1	
2003-04	Chesterfield	7	0	
2004-05	Chesterfield	32	6	
2005-06	Chesterfield	27	0	
2006-07	Chesterfield	23	8	102 15
2006-07	Wigan Ath	13	2	
2007-08	Wigan Ath	2	0	15 2
2007-08	Hull C	29	8	
2008-09	Hull C	15	1	45 9

FRANCE, Ryan (M)   **133 6**
H: 5 11 W: 11 11 b.Sheffield 13-12-80
Source: Alfreton T.

2003-04	Hull C	28	2	
2004-05	Hull C	31	2	
2005-06	Hull C	35	2	
2006-07	Hull C	24	0	
2007-08	Hull C	13	0	
2008-09	Hull C	2	0	133 6

GARCIA, Richard (F)   **177 26**
H: 5 11 W: 12 01 b.Perth 4-9-81
Source: Trainee. *Honours:* Australia Under-23, 5 full caps.

1998-99	West Ham U	0	0	
1999-2000	West Ham U	0	0	
2000-01	West Ham U	0	0	
2000-01	Leyton Orient	18	4	18 4
2001-02	West Ham U	8	0	
2002-03	West Ham U	0	0	
2003-04	West Ham U	7	0	
2004-05	West Ham U	1	0	16 0
2004-05	Colchester U	24	4	
2005-06	Colchester U	22	5	
2006-07	Colchester U	36	7	82 16
2007-08	Hull C	38	5	
2008-09	Hull C	23	1	61 6

GARDNER, Anthony (D)   **161 6**
H: 6 3 W: 14 00 b.Stone 19-9-80
Source: Trainee. *Honours:* England Under-21, 1 full cap.

1998-99	Port Vale	15	1	
1999-2000	Port Vale	26	3	41 4
1999-2000	Tottenham H	0	0	
2000-01	Tottenham H	0	0	
2001-02	Tottenham H	15	0	
2002-03	Tottenham H	12	1	
2003-04	Tottenham H	33	0	
2004-05	Tottenham H	17	0	
2005-06	Tottenham H	17	0	
2006-07	Tottenham H	8	0	
2007-08	Everton	0	0	
2007-08	Tottenham H	4	1	114 2
2008-09	Hull C	6	0	6 0

GARDNER, Steven (D)   **0 0**
H: 5 9 W: 10 09 b.Hull 12-5-90
Source: Scholar.

2008-09	Hull C	0	0	

GEOVANNI (F)   **252 42**
H: 5 8 W: 10 08 b.Acaiaca 11-1-80
Honours: Brazil 4 full caps, 1 goal.

1997	Cruzeiro	7	0	
1998	America	15	1	15 1
1999	Cruzeiro	21	2	
2000	Cruzeiro	22	9	
2001-02	Barcelona	21	1	
2002-03	Barcelona	5	0	26 1
2002-03	Benfica	17	2	
2003-04	Benfica	21	5	
2004-05	Benfica	31	6	
2005-06	Benfica	25	3	94 16

2006	Cruzeiro	12	2	
2007	Cruzeiro	2	0	64 13
2007-08	Manchester C	19	3	19 3
2008-09	Hull C	34	8	34 8

GIANNAKOPOULOS, Stelios (M)   **445 116**
H: 5 8 W: 11 00 b.Athens 12-7-74
Honours: Greece 76 full caps, 12 goals.

1992-93	Ethnikos	32	6	32 6
1993-94	Paniliakos	26	9	
1994-95	Paniliakos	31	10	
1995-96	Paniliakos	27	7	84 26
1996-97	Olympiakos	31	7	
1997-98	Olympiakos	31	3	
1998-99	Olympiakos	23	7	
1999-2000	Olympiakos	29	10	
2000-01	Olympiakos	26	11	
2001-02	Olympiakos	21	11	
2002-03	Olympiakos	29	15	190 64
2003-04	Bolton W	31	2	
2004-05	Bolton W	34	7	
2005-06	Bolton W	34	9	
2006-07	Bolton W	23	0	
2007-08	Bolton W	15	2	
2008-09	Bolton W	0	0	137 20
2008-09	Hull C	2	0	2 0

Transferred to Larissa January 2009

HALMOSI, Peter (M)   **271 39**
H: 5 10 W: 10 12 b.Szombathely 25-9-79
Honours: Hungary 25 full caps.

1998-99	Haladas	2	0	
1999-2000	Haladas	26	2	
2000-01	Haladas	14	2	
2001-02	Haladas	38	2	80 6
2002-03	Grez	17	3	17 3
2003-04	Debrecen	29	5	
2004-05	Debrecen	28	5	
2005-06	Debrecen	26	7	
2006-07	Debrecen	14	1	97 18
2006-07	Plymouth Arg	16	4	
2007-08	Plymouth Arg	43	8	59 12
2008-09	Hull C	18	0	18 0

HUGHES, Bryan (M)   **457 52**
H: 5 10 W: 11 08 b.Liverpool 19-6-76
Source: Trainee.

1993-94	Wrexham	11	0	
1994-95	Wrexham	38	9	
1995-96	Wrexham	22	0	
1996-97	Wrexham	23	3	94 12
1996-97	Birmingham C	11	0	
1997-98	Birmingham C	40	5	
1998-99	Birmingham C	28	3	
1999-2000	Birmingham C	45	10	
2000-01	Birmingham C	45	4	
2001-02	Birmingham C	31	7	
2002-03	Birmingham C	22	2	
2003-04	Birmingham C	26	3	248 34
2004-05	Charlton Ath	17	1	
2005-06	Charlton Ath	33	3	
2006-07	Charlton Ath	24	1	74 5
2007-08	Hull C	35	1	
2008-09	Hull C	6	0	41 1

KENDALL, Ryan (F)   **0 0**
H: 5 7 W: 10 09 b.Hull 14-9-89
Source: Scholar.

2008-09	Hull C	0	0	

KILBANE, Kevin (M)   **462 32**
H: 6 1 W: 13 05 b.Preston 1-2-77
Source: From Trainee. *Honours:* Eire Under-21, 96 full caps, 7 goals.

1993-94	Preston NE	0	0	
1994-95	Preston NE	0	0	
1995-96	Preston NE	11	1	
1996-97	Preston NE	36	2	47 3
1997-98	WBA	43	4	
1998-99	WBA	44	6	
1999-2000	WBA	19	5	106 15
1999-2000	Sunderland	20	1	
2000-01	Sunderland	30	4	
2001-02	Sunderland	28	2	
2002-03	Sunderland	30	1	
2003-04	Sunderland	5	0	113 8
2003-04	Everton	30	3	
2004-05	Everton	38	1	
2005-06	Everton	34	0	
2006-07	Everton	2	0	104 4
2006-07	Wigan Ath	31	1	
2007-08	Wigan Ath	35	1	

2008-09	Wigan Ath	10	0	76 2
2008-09	Hull C	16	0	16 0

LAMPLOUGH, Joe (D)   **0 0**
b.Hull 18-2-90
Source: Scholar.

2008-09	Hull C	0	0	

LAW, Bill (F)   **0 0**
b.Beverley 25-4-90
Source: Scholar.

2008-09	Hull C	0	0	

MARNEY, Dean (M)   **144 10**
H: 5 10 W: 11 09 b.Barking 31-1-84
Source: From Scholar. *Honours:* England Under-21.

2002-03	Tottenham H	0	0	
2002-03	Swindon T	9	0	9 0
2003-04	Tottenham H	3	0	
2003-04	QPR	2	0	2 0
2004-05	Tottenham H	5	2	
2004-05	Gillingham	3	0	3 0
2005-06	Tottenham H	0	0	8 2
2005-06	Norwich C	13	0	13 0
2006-07	Hull C	37	2	
2007-08	Hull C	41	6	
2008-09	Hull C	30	2	109 8

McNAMARA, Nick (M)   **0 0**
b. 11-12-89
Source: Scholar.

2008-09	Hull C	0	0	

MENDY, Bernard (D)   **272 6**
H: 5 11 W: 12 02 b.Evreux 20-8-81
Honours: France 3 full caps.

1998-99	Caen	4	0	
1999-2000	Caen	30	2	34 2
2000-01	Paris St Germain	19	0	
2001-02	Paris St Germain	21	1	
2002-03	Bolton W	21	0	21 0
2003-04	Paris St Germain	33	0	
2004-05	Paris St Germain	29	0	
2005-06	Paris St Germain	36	0	
2006-07	Paris St Germain	28	0	
2007-08	Paris St Germain	23	1	189 2
2008-09	Hull C	28	2	28 2

MYHILL, Boaz (G)   **249 0**
H: 6 3 W: 14 06 b.Modesto 9-11-82
Source: Scholar. *Honours:* England Youth, Under-20, Wales 5 full caps.

2000-01	Aston Villa	0	0	
2001-02	Aston Villa	0	0	
2001-02	Stoke C	0	0	
2002-03	Aston Villa	0	0	
2002-03	Bristol C	0	0	
2002-03	Bradford C	2	0	2 0
2002-03	Aston Villa	0	0	
2003-04	Macclesfield T	15	0	15 0
2003-04	Stockport Co	2	0	2 0
2003-04	Hull C	23	0	
2004-05	Hull C	45	0	
2005-06	Hull C	45	0	
2006-07	Hull C	46	0	
2007-08	Hull C	43	0	
2008-09	Hull C	28	0	230 0

OXLEY, Mark (G)   **0 0**
H: 5 11 W: 11 05 b. 2-6-90
Source: Rotherham U Scholar. *Honours:* England Youth.

2008-09	Hull C	0	0	

PEDERSEN, Henrik (F)   **286 88**
H: 6 1 W: 13 03 b.Copenhagen 10-6-75
Honours: Denmark 3 full caps.

1995-96	Silkeborg	12	4	
1996-97	Silkeborg	2	0	
1997-98	Silkeborg	15	9	
1998-99	Silkeborg	33	16	
1999-2000	Silkeborg	28	13	
2000-01	Silkeborg	32	20	122 62
2001-02	Bolton W	11	0	
2002-03	Bolton W	33	7	
2003-04	Bolton W	33	7	
2004-05	Bolton W	27	6	
2005-06	Bolton W	21	1	
2006-07	Bolton W	18	1	
2007-08	Bolton W	0	0	143 22
2007-08	Hull C	21	4	
2008-09	Hull C	0	0	21 4

PLUMMER, Matthew (D) 0 0
H: 6 1 W: 12 01 b.Hull 18-1-89
Source: Scholar.

2006-07	Hull C	0	0		
2007-08	Hull C	0	0		
2008-09	Hull C	0	0		

RICKETTS, Sam (D) 244 3
H: 6 1 W: 12 01 b.Aylesbury 11-10-81
Source: Trainee. *Honours:* Wales 34 full caps.

1999-2000	Oxford U	0	0		
2000-01	Oxford U	14	0		
2001-02	Oxford U	29	1		
2002-03	Oxford U	2	0	45	1
From Telford U					
2004-05	Swansea C	42	0		
2005-06	Swansea C	44	1	86	1
2006-07	Hull C	40	1		
2007-08	Hull C	44	0		
2008-09	Hull C	29	0	113	1

SATELLE, Darragh (F) 0 0

| 2008-09 | Hull C | 0 | 0 | | |

SIMPSON, Liam (M) 0 0
Source: Scholar.

| 2008-09 | Hull C | 0 | 0 | | |

TURNER, Michael (D) 223 16
H: 6 4 W: 13 05 b.Lewisham 9-11-83
Source: Scholar.

2001-02	Charlton Ath	0	0		
2002-03	Charlton Ath	0	0		
2002-03	*Leyton Orient*	7	1	7	1
2003-04	Charlton Ath	0	0		
2004-05	Charlton Ath	0	0		
2004-05	Brentford	45	1		
2005-06	Brentford	46	2	91	3
2006-07	Hull C	43	3		
2007-08	Hull C	44	5		
2008-09	Hull C	38	4	125	12

WARNER, Tony (G) 291 0
H: 6 4 W: 15 06 b.Liverpool 11-5-74
Source: School. *Honours:* Trinidad & Tobago 1 full cap.

1993-94	Liverpool	0	0		
1994-95	Liverpool	0	0		
1995-96	Liverpool	0	0		
1996-97	Liverpool	0	0		
1997-98	Liverpool	0	0		
1997-98	*Swindon T*	2	0	2	0
1998-99	Liverpool	0	0		
1998-99	*Celtic*	3	0	3	0
1998-99	*Aberdeen*	6	0	6	0
1999-2000	Millwall	45	0		
2000-01	Millwall	35	0		
2001-02	Millwall	46	0		
2002-03	Millwall	46	0		
2003-04	Millwall	28	0	200	0
2004-05	Cardiff C	26	0		
2005-06	Cardiff C	0	0	26	0
2005-06	Fulham	18	0		
2006-07	Fulham	0	0		
2006-07	*Leeds U*	13	0	13	0
2006-07	*Norwich C*	13	0	13	0
2007-08	Fulham	3	0	21	0
2007-08	*Barnsley*	3	0	3	0
2008-09	Hull C	0	0		
2008-09	*Leicester C*	4	0	4	0

WELSH, John (M) 69 3
H: 5 7 W: 12 02 b.Liverpool 10-1-84
Source: Scholar. *Honours:* England Youth, Under-20, Under-21.

2000-01	Liverpool	0	0		
2001-02	Liverpool	0	0		
2002-03	Liverpool	0	0		
2003-04	Liverpool	1	0		
2004-05	Liverpool	3	0		
2005-06	Liverpool	0	0	4	0
2005-06	Hull C	32	2		
2006-07	Hull C	18	1		
2007-08	Hull C	0	0		
2007-08	*Chester C*	6	0	6	0
2008-09	Hull C	0	0	50	3
2008-09	*Carlisle U*	4	0	4	0
2008-09	*Bury*	5	0	5	0

WINDASS, Dean (F) 628 199
H: 5 10 W: 12 03 b.North Ferriby 1-4-69
Source: N Ferriby U.

1991-92	Hull C	32	6		
1992-93	Hull C	41	7		
1993-94	Hull C	43	23		
1994-95	Hull C	44	17		
1995-96	Hull C	16	4		
1995-96	Aberdeen	20	6		
1996-97	Aberdeen	29	10		
1997-98	Aberdeen	24	5	73	21
1998-99	Oxford U	33	15	33	15
1998-99	Bradford C	12	3		
1999-2000	Bradford C	38	10		
2000-01	Bradford C	24	3		
2000-01	Middlesbrough	8	2		
2001-02	Middlesbrough	27	1		
2001-02	*Sheffield W*	2	0	2	0
2002-03	Middlesbrough	2	0	37	3
2002-03	Sheffield U	20	6	20	6
2003-04	Bradford C	36	6		
2004-05	Bradford C	41	27		
2005-06	Bradford C	40	16		
2006-07	Bradford C	25	11	216	76
2006-07	*Hull C*	18	8		
2007-08	Hull C	37	11		
2008-09	Hull C	5	1	236	77
2008-09	*Oldham Ath*	11	1	11	1

WOODHEAD, Tom (G) 0 0
H: 5 10 W: 12 00 b.Beverley 9-5-90
Source: Scholar.

| 2007-08 | Hull C | 0 | 0 | | |
| 2008-09 | Hull C | 0 | 0 | | |

ZAYATTE, Kamil (D) 33 1
H: 6 2 W: 13 10 b.Conakry 7-3-85
Honours: Guinea 19 full caps, 2 goals.

2005-06	Lens	0	0		
2006-07	Lens	1	0	1	0
2008-09	Hull C	32	1	32	1

Scholars
Cairney, Thomas; Cullen, Mark; Deagle, Dean; East, Daniel; Emerton, Daniel James; Fox, Joseph Charles; Hanley, Nathan; Holohan, Gavan; Leonard, John; Overment, Richard Kenneth; Wilkinson, Daniel; Wright, Lee Robert.

IPSWICH T (43)

BALKESTEIN, Pim (D) 20 0
H: 6 3 W: 11 06 b.Gouda 29-4-87

| 2008-09 | Ipswich T | 20 | 0 | 20 | 0 |

BOWDITCH, Dean (F) 121 15
H: 5 11 W: 11 05 b.Bishops Stortford 15-6-86
Source: Trainee. *Honours:* FA Schools, England Youth.

2002-03	Ipswich T	5	0		
2003-04	Ipswich T	16	4		
2004-05	Ipswich T	21	3		
2004-05	*Burnley*	10	1	10	1
2005-06	Ipswich T	21	0		
2005-06	*Wycombe W*	11	1	11	1
2006-07	Ipswich T	9	1		
2006-07	*Brighton & HA*	3	1		
2007-08	Ipswich T	0	0		
2007-08	*Northampton T*	10	2	10	2
2007-08	*Brighton & HA*	5	0	8	1
2008-09	Ipswich T	1	0	73	8
2008-09	*Brentford*	9	2	9	2

BRUCE, Alex (D) 137 1
H: 6 0 W: 11 06 b.Norwich 28-9-84
Source: Trainee. *Honours:* Eire B, Under-21, 2 full caps.

2002-03	Blackburn R	0	0		
2003-04	Blackburn R	0	0		
2004-05	Blackburn R	0	0		
2004-05	*Oldham Ath*	12	0	12	0
2004-05	Birmingham C	0	0		
2004-05	*Sheffield W*	6	0	6	0
2005-06	*Birmingham C*	6	0	6	0
2005-06	*Tranmere R*	11	0	11	0
2006-07	Ipswich T	41	0		
2007-08	Ipswich T	36	0		
2008-09	Ipswich T	25	1	102	1

CAMPO, Ivan (M) 358 21
H: 6 1 W: 12 10 b.San Sebastian 21-2-74
Honours: Spain 4 full caps.

1993-94	Alaves	11	1		
1994-95	Alaves	23	1		
1995-96	Alaves	11	0	45	2
1995-96	Valladolid	24	2	24	2
1996-97	Valencia	7	1	7	1
1997-98	Mallorca	33	1	33	1
1998-99	Real Madrid	27	1		
1999-2000	Real Madrid	20	0		
2000-01	Real Madrid	10	0		
2001-02	Real Madrid	3	0	60	1
2002-03	Bolton W	31	2		
2003-04	Bolton W	38	4		
2004-05	Bolton W	27	0		
2005-06	Bolton W	15	2		
2006-07	Bolton W	34	4		
2007-08	Bolton W	27	1	172	13
2008-09	Ipswich T	17	1	17	1

CASEMENT, Chris (M) 21 0
H: 6 0 W: 12 02 b.Belfast 12-1-88
Source: Scholar. *Honours:* Northern Ireland Youth, Under-21, B, 2 full caps.

2005-06	Ipswich T	5	0		
2006-07	Ipswich T	0	0		
2007-08	Ipswich T	3	0		
2008-09	Ipswich T	0	0	8	0
2008-09	*Hamilton A*	1	0	1	0
2008-09	*Wycombe W*	12	0	12	0

CIVELLI, Luciano (M) 78 8
H: 6 2 W: 13 01 b.Buenos Aires 6-10-86

2005-06	Banfield	1	0		
2006-07	Banfield	18	0		
2007-08	Banfield	34	6		
2008-09	Banfield	17	2	70	8
2008-09	Ipswich T	8	0	8	0

CLARKE, Billy (F) 96 21
H: 5 7 W: 10 01 b.Cork 13-12-87
Source: Scholar. *Honours:* Eire Youth, Under-21.

2004-05	Ipswich T	0	0		
2005-06	Ipswich T	2	0		
2005-06	*Colchester U*	6	0	6	0
2006-07	Ipswich T	27	3		
2007-08	*Falkirk*	8	1	8	1
2007-08	Ipswich T	20	0		
2008-09	Ipswich T	0	0	49	3
2008-09	*Darlington*	20	8	20	8
2008-09	*Northampton T*	5	3	5	3
2008-09	*Brentford*	8	6	8	6

COUNAGO, Pablo (F) 283 67
H: 5 11 W: 11 06 b.Pontevedra 9-8-79

1998-99	Numancia	13	1	13	1
1998-99	Celta Vigo	1	0		
1999-2000	Huelva	26	4	26	4
2000-01	Celta Vigo	8	0	9	0
2001-02	Ipswich T	13	0		
2002-03	Ipswich T	39	17		
2003-04	Ipswich T	29	11		
2004-05	Ipswich T	19	3		
2004-05	Malaga	27	3		
2006-07	Malaga	21	7	48	10
2007-08	Ipswich T	43	12		
2008-09	Ipswich T	44	9	187	52

GARVAN, Owen (M) 139 13
H: 6 0 W: 10 07 b.Dublin 29-1-88
Source: Scholar. *Honours:* Eire Youth, Under-21.

2005-06	Ipswich T	32	3		
2006-07	Ipswich T	27	1		
2007-08	Ipswich T	43	2		
2008-09	Ipswich T	37	7	139	13

HARDING, Dan (D) 182 3
H: 6 0 W: 11 11 b.Gloucester 23-12-83
Source: Scholar. *Honours:* England Under-21.

2002-03	Brighton & HA	1	0		
2003-04	Brighton & HA	23	0		
2004-05	Brighton & HA	43	1	67	0
2005-06	Leeds U	20	0	20	0
2006-07	Ipswich T	42	0		
2007-08	Ipswich T	30	1		
2008-09	Ipswich T	1	0	73	1
2008-09	*Southend U*	19	1	19	1
2008-09	*Reading*	3	0	3	0

HAYNES, Danny (F) 119 19
H: 5 11 W: 12 04 b.London 19-1-88
Source: Scholar. *Honours:* England Youth.

2005-06	Ipswich T	19	3		
2006-07	Ipswich T	31	7		
2006-07	*Millwall*	5	2	5	2
2007-08	Ipswich T	40	7		
2008-09	Ipswich T	24	0	114	17

LISBIE, Kevin (F) 262 45
H: 5 10 W: 11 06 b.Hackney 17-10-78
Source: Trainee. *Honours:* England Youth. Jamaica 10 full caps, 2 goals.

Season	Club				
1996-97	Charlton Ath	25	1		
1997-98	Charlton Ath	17	1		
1998-99	Charlton Ath	1	0		
1998-99	*Gillingham*	7	4	**7**	**4**
1999-2000	Charlton Ath	0	0		
1999-2000	*Reading*	2	0	**2**	**0**
2000-01	Charlton Ath	18	0		
2000-01	*QPR*	2	0	**2**	**0**
2001-02	Charlton Ath	22	5		
2002-03	Charlton Ath	32	4		
2003-04	Charlton Ath	9	4		
2004-05	Charlton Ath	17	1		
2005-06	Charlton Ath	6	0		
2005-06	Norwich C	6	1	**6**	**1**
2005-06	Derby Co	7	1	**7**	**1**
2006-07	Charlton Ath	8	0	**155**	**16**
2007-08	Colchester U	42	17	**42**	**17**
2008-09	Ipswich T	41	6	**41**	**6**

McAULEY, Gareth (D) 181 13
H: 6 3 W: 13 00 b.Larne 5-12-79
Source: Coleraine. *Honours:* Northern Ireland Schools, B, 16 full caps, 1 goal.

Season	Club				
2004-05	Lincoln C	37	3		
2005-06	Lincoln C	35	5	**72**	**8**
2006-07	Leicester C	30	3		
2007-08	Leicester C	44	2	**74**	**5**
2008-09	Ipswich T	35	0	**35**	**0**

McLOUGHLIN, Ian (M) 0 0
2008-09 Ipswich T 0 0

MILLER, Tommy (M) 363 78
H: 6 0 W: 11 07 b.Easington 8-1-79
Source: Trainee.

Season	Club				
1997-98	Hartlepool U	13	1		
1998-99	Hartlepool U	34	4		
1999-2000	Hartlepool U	44	14		
2000-01	Hartlepool U	46	16		
2001-02	Hartlepool U	0	0	**137**	**35**
2001-02	Ipswich T	8	0		
2002-03	Ipswich T	30	6		
2003-04	Ipswich T	34	11		
2004-05	Ipswich T	45	13		
2005-06	Sunderland	29	3		
2006-07	Sunderland	4	0	**33**	**3**
2006-07	*Preston NE*	7	0	**7**	**0**
2007-08	Ipswich T	37	5		
2008-09	Ipswich T	32	5	**186**	**40**

MURPHY, Paul (M) 0 0
H: 5 9 W: 11 00 b.19-3-91
Source: Scholar. *Honours:* Eire Youth.
2008-09 Ipswich T 0 0

NORRIS, David (M) 278 32
H: 5 7 W: 11 06 b.Stamford 22-2-81
Source: Boston U.

Season	Club				
1999-2000	Bolton W	0	0		
2000-01	Bolton W	0	0		
2001-02	Bolton W	0	0		
2001-02	*Hull C*	6	1	**6**	**1**
2002-03	Bolton W	0	0		
2002-03	Plymouth Arg	33	6		
2003-04	Plymouth Arg	45	5		
2004-05	Plymouth Arg	35	3		
2005-06	Plymouth Arg	45	2		
2006-07	Plymouth Arg	41	6		
2007-08	Plymouth Arg	27	5	**226**	**27**
2007-08	Ipswich T	9	1		
2008-09	Ipswich T	37	3	**46**	**4**

PETERS, Jaime (M) 61 3
H: 5 7 W: 10 12 b.Pickering 4-5-87
Source: Moor Green. *Honours:* Canada Youth, Under-20, Under-23, 16 full caps, 1 goal.

Season	Club				
2005-06	Ipswich T	13	0		
2006-07	Ipswich T	23	2		
2007-08	Ipswich T	5	0		
2007-08	*Yeovil T*	14	1	**14**	**1**
2008-09	Ipswich T	3	0	**44**	**2**
2008-09	*Gillingham*	3	0	**3**	**0**

QUINN, Alan (M) 310 30
H: 5 9 W: 10 06 b.Dublin 13-6-79
Source: Cherry Orchard. *Honours:* Eire Youth, Under-21, 8 full caps.

Season	Club				
1997-98	Sheffield W	1	0		
1998-99	Sheffield W	1	0		
1999-2000	Sheffield W	19	3		
2000-01	Sheffield W	37	2		
2001-02	Sheffield W	38	2		
2002-03	Sheffield W	37	5		
2003-04	Sheffield W	24	4	**157**	**16**
2003-04	*Sunderland*	6	0	**6**	**0**
2004-05	Sheffield U	43	7		
2005-06	Sheffield U	27	4		
2006-07	Sheffield U	19	0		
2007-08	Sheffield U	8	0	**97**	**11**
2007-08	Ipswich T	16	1		
2008-09	Ipswich T	34	2	**50**	**3**

REASON, Jai (M) 0 0
H: 5 11 W: 12 13 b.Southend 9-1-90
Source: Scholar.
2008-09 Ipswich T 0 0

RHODES, Jordan (F) 29 10
H: 6 1 W: 11 03 b.Oldham 5-2-90
Source: Academy.

Season	Club				
2007-08	Ipswich T	8	1		
2008-09	Ipswich T	2	0	**10**	**1**
2008-09	*Rochdale*	5	2	**5**	**2**
2008-09	*Brentford*	14	7	**14**	**7**

ROBINSON, Kurt (D) 0 0
H: 5 8 W: 11 00 b.Basildon 21-10-89
Source: Southend U.

Season	Club				
2007-08	Ipswich T	0	0		
2008-09	Ipswich T	0	0		
2008-09	*Northampton T*	0	0		

SMITH, Tommy (D) 2 0
H: 6 2 W: 12 02 b.Macclesfield 31-3-90
Source: Scholar.

Season	Club				
2007-08	Ipswich T	0	0		
2008-09	Ipswich T	2	0	**2**	**0**

STEAD, Jon (F) 240 55
H: 6 3 W: 13 03 b.Huddersfield 7-4-83
Source: Scholar. *Honours:* England Under-21.

Season	Club				
2001-02	Huddersfield T	0	0		
2002-03	Huddersfield T	42	6		
2003-04	Huddersfield T	26	16	**68**	**22**
2003-04	Blackburn R	13	6		
2004-05	Blackburn R	29	2	**42**	**8**
2005-06	Sunderland	30	1		
2006-07	Sunderland	5	1	**35**	**2**
2006-07	*Derby Co*	17	3	**17**	**3**
2006-07	Sheffield U	14	5		
2007-08	Sheffield U	24	3		
2008-09	Sheffield U	1	0	**39**	**8**
2008-09	Ipswich T	39	12	**39**	**12**

SUMULIKOSKI, Velice (M) 199 7
H: 6 0 W: 12 02 b.Macedonia 24-1-81
Honours: Macedonia 56 full caps, 1 goal.

Season	Club				
1999-2000	Publikum	21	2		
2000-01	Publikum	28	1		
2001-02	Publikum	7	0	**56**	**3**
2001-02	Slovacko	13	0		
2002-03	Slovacko	29	2		
2003-04	Slovacko	13	0	**55**	**2**
2004	Zenit	25	0		
2005	Zenit	16	1		
2006	Zenit	5	0	**46**	**1**
2007-08	Ipswich T	16	1		
2008-09	Ipswich T	26	0	**42**	**1**

SUPPLE, Shane (G) 43 0
H: 6 0 W: 11 13 b.Dublin 4-5-87
Source: Scholar. *Honours:* Eire Youth, Under-21.

Season	Club				
2004-05	Ipswich T	0	0		
2005-06	Ipswich T	22	0		
2006-07	Ipswich T	12	0		
2007-08	*Falkirk*	4	0	**4**	**0**
2007-08	Ipswich T	0	0		
2008-09	Ipswich T	0	0	**34**	**0**
2008-09	*Oldham Ath*	5	0	**5**	**0**

THATCHER, Ben (D) 330 2
H: 5 10 W: 12 07 b.Swindon 30-11-75
Source: Trainee. *Honours:* England Youth, Under-21, Wales 7 full caps.

Season	Club				
1992-93	Millwall	0	0		
1993-94	Millwall	8	0		
1994-95	Millwall	40	1		
1995-96	Millwall	42	0	**90**	**1**
1996-97	Wimbledon	9	0		
1997-98	Wimbledon	26	0		
1998-99	Wimbledon	31	0		
1999-2000	Wimbledon	20	0	**86**	**0**
2000-01	Tottenham H	12	0		
2001-02	Tottenham H	12	0		
2002-03	Tottenham H	12	0	**36**	**0**
2003-04	Leicester C	29	1	**29**	**1**
2004-05	Manchester C	18	0		
2005-06	Manchester C	18	0		
2006-07	Manchester C	11	0	**47**	**0**
2006-07	Charlton Ath	11	0		
2007-08	Charlton Ath	11	0	**22**	**0**
2008-09	Ipswich T	20	0	**20**	**0**

TROTTER, Liam (M) 40 5
H: 6 2 W: 12 02 b.Ipswich 24-8-88
Source: Scholar.

Season	Club				
2005-06	Ipswich T	1	0		
2006-07	Ipswich T	0	0		
2006-07	*Millwall*	2	0	**2**	**0**
2007-08	Ipswich T	7	1		
2008-09	Ipswich T	3	1	**11**	**2**
2008-09	*Grimsby T*	15	2	**15**	**2**
2008-09	*Scunthorpe U*	12	1	**12**	**1**

UPSON, Edward (M) 0 0
H: 5 10 W: 11 07 b.Bury St Edmunds 21-11-89
Source: Scholar. *Honours:* England Youth.

Season	Club				
2006-07	Ipswich T	0	0		
2007-08	Ipswich T	0	0		
2008-09	Ipswich T	0	0		

WALTERS, Jon (F) 219 43
H: 6 0 W: 12 06 b.Birkenhead 20-9-83
Source: Blackburn R Scholar. *Honours:* Eire Youth, Under-21, B.

Season	Club				
2001-02	Bolton W	0	0		
2002-03	Bolton W	4	0		
2002-03	Hull C	11	5		
2003-04	Bolton W	0	0	**4**	**0**
2003-04	*Barnsley*	8	0	**8**	**0**
2003-04	Hull C	16	1		
2004-05	Hull C	21	1	**48**	**7**
2004-05	*Scunthorpe U*	3	0	**3**	**0**
2005-06	Wrexham	38	5	**38**	**5**
2006-07	Chester C	26	9	**26**	**9**
2006-07	Ipswich T	16	4		
2007-08	Ipswich T	40	13		
2008-09	Ipswich T	36	5	**92**	**22**

WICKHAM, Connor (F) 2 0
H: 6 0 W: 14 01 b.Ipswich 31-3-93
Honours: England Youth.
2008-09 Ipswich T 2 0 **2** **0**

WRIGHT, David (D) 355 7
H: 5 11 W: 11 01 b.Warrington 1-5-80
Source: Trainee. *Honours:* England Youth.

Season	Club				
1997-98	Crewe Alex	3	0		
1998-99	Crewe Alex	20	1		
1999-2000	Crewe Alex	45	0		
2000-01	Crewe Alex	42	0		
2001-02	Crewe Alex	30	0		
2002-03	Crewe Alex	31	1		
2003-04	Crewe Alex	40	1	**211**	**3**
2004-05	Wigan Ath	31	0		
2005-06	Wigan Ath	2	0		
2005-06	Norwich C	5	0	**5**	**0**
2006-07	Wigan Ath	12	0	**45**	**0**
2006-07	Ipswich T	19	1		
2007-08	Ipswich T	41	2		
2008-09	Ipswich T	34	1	**94**	**4**

WRIGHT, Richard (G) 365 0
H: 6 2 W: 14 00 b.Ipswich 5-11-77
Source: Trainee. *Honours:* England Schools, Youth, Under-21, 2 full caps.

Season	Club				
1994-95	Ipswich T	3	0		
1995-96	Ipswich T	23	0		
1996-97	Ipswich T	40	0		
1997-98	Ipswich T	46	0		
1998-99	Ipswich T	46	0		
1999-2000	Ipswich T	46	0		
2000-01	Ipswich T	36	0		
2001-02	Arsenal	12	0	**12**	**0**
2002-03	Everton	33	0		
2003-04	Everton	4	0		
2004-05	Everton	7	0		
2005-06	Everton	15	0		
2006-07	Everton	1	0	**60**	**0**
2007-08	West Ham U	0	0		
2007-08	*Southampton*	7	0	**7**	**0**
2008-09	Ipswich T	46	0	**286**	**0**

LEEDS U (44)

ANKERGREN, Casper (G) 176 0
H: 6 3 W: 14 07 b.Koge 9-11-79
Source: Koge. *Honours:* Denmark Youth, Under-21.

2001-02	Brondby	1	0	
2002-03	Brondby	16	0	
2003-04	Brondby	1	0	
2004-05	Brondby	32	0	
2005-06	Brondby	18	0	
2006-07	Brondby	18	0	86 0
2006-07	Leeds U	14	0	
2007-08	Leeds U	43	0	
2008-09	Leeds U	33	0	90 0

ASSOUMANI, Mansour (D) 75 4
H: 6 2 W: 11 13 b.Nice 30-1-83

2001-02	Montpellier	1	0	
2002-03	Montpellier	15	1.	
2003-04	Montpellier	27	1	
2004-05	Montpellier	15	2	
2005-06	Montpellier	15	0	74 4
2006-07	Saarebruck	0	0	
2007-08	Siegen	0	0	
2008-09	Leeds U	1	0	1 0

BECCHIO, Luciano (F) 145 47
H: 6 2 W: 13 02 b.Cordoba 28-12-83
Source: Boca Juniors.

2003-04	Mallorca B	0	0	
2004-05	Mallorca B	0	0	
2004-05	*Murcia*	16	3	16 3
2005-06	Terrassa	24	2	24 2
2006-07	Barcelona Athletic	10	0	10 0
2006-07	*Merida*	12	5	
2007-08	Merida	38	22	50 27
2008-09	Leeds U	45	15	45 15

BECKFORD, Jermaine (F) 106 55
H: 6 2 W: 13 02 b.London 9-12-83
Source: Wealdstone.

2005-06	Leeds U	5	0	
2006-07	Leeds U	5	0	
2006-07	*Carlisle U*	4	1	4 1
2006-07	*Scunthorpe U*	18	8	18 8
2007-08	Leeds U	40	20	
2008-09	Leeds U	34	26	84 46

CARTMAN, Nathan (M) 0 0
b. 4-11-89
Source: Scholar.

2008-09	Leeds U	0	0

CHRISTIE, Malcolm (F) 163 38
H: 6 0 W: 12 06 b.Peterborough 11-4-79
Source: From Nuneaton B. *Honours:* England Under-21.

1998-99	Derby Co	2	0	
1999-2000	Derby Co	21	5	
2000-01	Derby Co	34	8	
2001-02	Derby Co	35	9	
2002-03	Derby Co	24	8	116 30
2002-03	Middlesbrough	4	0	
2003-04	Middlesbrough	10	1	
2004-05	Middlesbrough	2	1	
2005-06	Middlesbrough	6	0	
2006-07	Middlesbrough	13	1	
2007-08	Middlesbrough	0	0	
2008-09	Middlesbrough	0	0	43 7
2008-09	Leeds U	4	1	4 1

DARVILLE, Liam (D) 0 0
b. 26-10-90
Source: Scholar. *Honours:* England Youth.

2008-09	Leeds U	0	0

DELPH, Fabian (D) 44 6
H: 5 8 W: 11 00 b.Bradford 5-5-91
Source: Scholar. *Honours:* England Youth, Under-21.

2006-07	Leeds U	1	0	
2007-08	Leeds U	1	0	
2008-09	Leeds U	42	6	44 6

DOUGLAS, Jonathan (M) 191 15
H: 5 11 W: 11 11 b.Monaghan 22-11-81
Source: Trainee. *Honours:* Eire Under-21, 8 full caps.

1999-2000	Blackburn R	0	0	
2000-01	Blackburn R	0	0	
2001-02	Blackburn R	0	0	
2002-03	Blackburn R	1	0	
2002-03	*Chesterfield*	7	1	7 1

2003-04	Blackpool	16	3	16 3
2003-04	Blackburn R	14	1	
2004-05	Blackburn R	1	0	
2004-05	*Gillingham*	10	0	10 0
2005-06	Blackburn R	0	0	
2005-06	*Leeds U*	40	5	
2006-07	Blackburn R	0	0	16 1
2006-07	Leeds U	35	1	
2007-08	Leeds U	24	3	
2008-09	Leeds U	43	1	142 10

ELLIOTT, Tom (F) 9 0
H: 5 10 W: 11 02 b.Leeds 9-9-89
Source: School.

2006-07	Leeds U	3	0	
2007-08	Leeds U	0	0	
2008-09	Leeds U	0	0	3 0
2008-09	*Macclesfield T*	6	0	6 0

GARDNER, Scott (M) 1 0
H: 5 9 W: 11 04 b.Luxembourg 1-4-88
Source: Scholar. *Honours:* England Youth.

2005-06	Leeds U	0	0	
2006-07	Leeds U	0	0	
2007-08	Leeds U	1	0	
2008-09	Leeds U	0	0	1 0

GRELLA, Mike (F) 11 0
H: 5 11 W: 12 02 b.Glen Cove 23-1-87
Source: Duke University. *Honours:* USA Youth.

2008-09	Leeds U	11	0	11 0

HOTCHKISS, Oliver (M) 0 0
b.Houghton-le-Spring 27-9-89
Source: Scholar.

2007-08	Leeds U	0	0
2008-09	Leeds U	0	0

HOWSON, Jonathan (M) 75 8
H: 5 11 W: 12 01 b.Morley 21-5-88
Source: Scholar.

2006-07	Leeds U	9	1	
2007-08	Leeds U	26	3	
2008-09	Leeds U	40	4	75 8

HUGHES, Andy (M) 448 39
H: 5 11 W: 12 01 b.Stockport 2-1-78
Source: Trainee.

1995-96	Oldham Ath	15	1	
1996-97	Oldham Ath	8	0	
1997-98	Oldham Ath	10	0	33 1
1997-98	Notts Co	15	2	
1998-99	Notts Co	30	3	
1999-2000	Notts Co	35	7	
2000-01	Notts Co	30	5	110 17
2001-02	Reading	39	6	
2002-03	Reading	43	9	
2003-04	Reading	43	3	
2004-05	Reading	41	0	166 18
2005-06	Norwich C	36	2	
2006-07	Norwich C	36	0	72 2
2007-08	Leeds U	40	1	
2008-09	Leeds U	27	0	67 1

HUNTINGTON, Paul (D) 32 2
H: 6 3 W: 12 08 b.Carlisle 17-9-87
Source: Scholar. *Honours:* England Youth.

2005-06	Newcastle U	0	0	
2006-07	Newcastle U	11	1	
2007-08	Newcastle U	0	0	11 1
2007-08	Leeds U	17	1	
2008-09	Leeds U	4	0	21 1

JOHNSON, Brad (M) 100 16
H: 6 0 W: 12 10 b.Hackney 28-4-87
Source: Cambridge U Juniors.

2004-05	Cambridge U	1	0	1 0
2005-06	Northampton T	3	0	
2006-07	Northampton T	27	5	
2007-08	Northampton T	23	3	53 8
2007-08	Leeds U	21	3	
2008-09	Leeds U	15	1	36 4
2008-09	*Brighton & HA*	10	4	10 4

KANDOL, Tresor (F) 159 37
H: 6 0 W: 13 07 b.Banga 30-8-81
Source: Trainee. *Honours:* DR Congo 1 full cap.

1998-99	Luton T	4	0	
1999-2000	Luton T	4	0	
2000-01	Luton T	13	3	21 3
2001-02	Bournemouth	12	0	12 0

From Thurrock, Dagenham

2005-06	*Darlington*	7	2	7 2

From Dagenham & R.

2005-06	Barnet	13	4	
2006-07	Barnet	16	6	29 10
2006-07	Leeds U	18	1	
2007-08	Leeds U	41	11	
2008-09	Leeds U	0	0	59 12
2008-09	Millwall	18	8	18 8
2008-09	*Charlton Ath*	13	2	13 2

KENTON, Darren (D) 259 12
H: 5 10 W: 12 06 b.Wandsworth 13-9-78
Source: Trainee.

1997-98	Norwich C	11	0	
1998-99	Norwich C	22	1	
1999-2000	Norwich C	26	1	
2000-01	Norwich C	29	2	
2001-02	Norwich C	33	4	
2002-03	Norwich C	37	1	158 9
2002-03	Southampton	0	0	
2003-04	Southampton	7	0	
2004-05	Southampton	9	0	
2004-05	*Leicester C*	10	0	
2005-06	Southampton	13	0	29 0
2006-07	Leicester C	23	2	
2007-08	Leicester C	10	0	43 2
2007-08	Leeds U	16	0	
2008-09	Leeds U	0	0	16 0
2008-09	*Cheltenham T*	13	1	13 1

KILKENNY, Neil (M) 119 10
H: 5 8 W: 10 08 b.Enfield 19-12-85
Source: Arsenal Trainee. *Honours:* England Youth, Under-20, Australia Under-23, 2 full caps.

2003-04	Birmingham C	0	0	
2004-05	Birmingham C	0	0	
2004-05	*Oldham Ath*	27	4	
2005-06	Birmingham C	18	0	
2006-07	Birmingham C	8	0	
2007-08	Birmingham C	0	0	26 0
2007-08	*Oldham Ath*	20	1	47 5
2007-08	Leeds U	16	1	
2008-09	Leeds U	30	4	46 5

LEES, Thomas (M) 0 0

2008-09	Leeds U	0	0

LUCAS, David (G) 228 0
H: 6 1 W: 13 07 b.Preston 23-11-77
Source: Trainee. *Honours:* England Youth.

1995-96	Preston NE	1	0	
1995-96	*Darlington*	6	0	
1996-97	Preston NE	2	0	
1996-97	*Darlington*	7	0	13 0
1996-97	*Scunthorpe U*	6	0	6 0
1997-98	Preston NE	6	0	
1998-99	Preston NE	30	0	
1999-2000	Preston NE	6	0	
2000-01	Preston NE	29	0	
2001-02	Preston NE	24	0	
2002-03	Preston NE	21	0	
2003-04	Preston NE	2	0	121 0
2003-04	*Sheffield W*	17	0	
2004-05	Sheffield W	34	0	
2005-06	Sheffield W	18	0	
2006-07	Sheffield W	0	0	69 0
2006-07	Barnsley	3	0	
2007-08	Barnsley	0	0	3 0
2007-08	Leeds U	3	0	
2008-09	Leeds U	13	0	16 0

MADDEN, Simon (D) 0 0
H: 5 9 W: 11 10 b.Dublin 1-5-88
Source: Shelbourne.

2005-06	Leeds U	0	0
2006-07	Leeds U	0	0
2007-08	Leeds U	0	0
2008-09	Leeds U	0	0

MARTIN, Alan (G) 0 0
H: 6 0 W: 11 11 b.Glasgow 1-1-89
Source: Motherwell. *Honours:* Scotland Youth, Under-21.

2007-08	Leeds U	0	0
2008-09	Leeds U	0	0

MICHALIK, Lubomir (D) 74 4
H: 6 4 W: 13 00 b.Cadca 13-8-83
Source: Cadca, Martin. *Honours:* Slovakia 4 full caps, 2 goals.

2005-06	Senec	8	1	
2006-07	Senec	12	1	20 2
2006-07	*Leeds U*	7	1	
2006-07	Bolton W	4	1	

2007-08	Bolton W	7	0	11	1
2007-08	Leeds U	17	0		
2008-09	Leeds U	19	0	43	1

NAYLOR, Richard (D)   357 38
H: 6 1 W: 13 07 b.Leeds 28-2-77
Source: Trainee.

1995-96	Ipswich T	0	0		
1996-97	Ipswich T	27	4		
1997-98	Ipswich T	5	2		
1998-99	Ipswich T	30	5		
1999-2000	Ipswich T	36	8		
2000-01	Ipswich T	13	1		
2001-02	Ipswich T	14	1		
2001-02	*Millwall*	3	0	3	0
2001-02	*Barnsley*	8	0	8	0
2002-03	Ipswich T	17	2		
2003-04	Ipswich T	39	5		
2004-05	Ipswich T	46	6		
2005-06	Ipswich T	42	3		
2006-07	Ipswich T	25	0		
2007-08	Ipswich T	7	0		
2008-09	Ipswich T	23	0	324	37
2008-09	Leeds U	22	1	22	1

PARKER, Ben (D)   85 0
H: 5 11 W: 11 06 b.Pontefract 8-11-87
Source: Scholar. *Honours:* England Youth.

2004-05	Leeds U	0	0		
2005-06	Leeds U	0	0		
2006-07	Leeds U	0	0		
2006-07	*Bradford C*	39	0	39	0
2007-08	Leeds U	9	0		
2007-08	*Darlington*	13	0	13	0
2008-09	Leeds U	24	0	33	0

PRUTTON, David (M)   296 16
H: 5 10 W: 13 00 b.Hull 12-9-81
Source: Trainee. *Honours:* England Youth, Under-21.

1998-99	Nottingham F	0	0		
1999-2000	Nottingham F	34	2		
2000-01	Nottingham F	42	1		
2001-02	Nottingham F	43	3		
2002-03	Nottingham F	24	1		
2002-03	Southampton	12	0		
2003-04	Southampton	27	1		
2004-05	Southampton	23	1		
2005-06	Southampton	17	0		
2006-07	Southampton	3	1	82	3
2006-07	*Nottingham F*	12	2	155	9
2007-08	Leeds U	43	4		
2008-09	Leeds U	16	0	59	4

RICHARDSON, Frazer (D)   162 4
H: 5 11 W: 11 12 b.Rotherham 29-10-82
Source: Trainee. *Honours:* England Youth, Under-20.

1999-2000	Leeds U	0	0		
2000-01	Leeds U	0	0		
2001-02	Leeds U	0	0		
2002-03	Leeds U	0	0		
2002-03	*Stoke C*	7	0		
2003-04	Leeds U	4	0		
2003-04	*Stoke C*	6	1	13	1
2004-05	Leeds U	38	1		
2005-06	Leeds U	23	1		
2006-07	Leeds U	22	0		
2007-08	Leeds U	39	1		
2008-09	Leeds U	23	0	149	3

ROBINSON, Andy (M)   224 45
H: 5 8 W: 11 04 b.Birkenhead 3-11-79
Source: Cammell Laird.

2002-03	Tranmere R	0	0		
2003-04	Swansea C	37	8		
2004-05	Swansea C	37	8		
2005-06	Swansea C	39	12		
2006-07	Swansea C	39	7		
2007-08	Swansea C	40	8	192	43
2008-09	Leeds U	32	2	32	2

ROSS, Damian (G)   0 0
b.Bishop Auckland

2007-08	Leeds U	0	0		
2008-09	Leeds U	0	0		

RUI MARQUES, Manuel (D)   201 4
H: 5 11 W: 11 13 b.Luanda 3-9-77
Source: Benfica. *Honours:* Angola 7 full caps.

1998-99	Baden	27	0	27	0
1999-2000	SSV Ulm	32	0	32	0
2000-01	Hertha	1	0	1	0
2000-01	Stuttgart	12	0		
2001-02	Stuttgart	23	0		
2002-03	Stuttgart	12	0		
2003-04	Stuttgart	0	0	47	0
2004-05	Maritimo	8	0	8	0
2005-06	Leeds U	0	0		
2005-06	*Hull C*	1	0	1	0
2006-07	Leeds U	17	0		
2007-08	Leeds U	36	3		
2008-09	Leeds U	32	1	85	4

SHEEHAN, Alan (D)   57 3
H: 5 11 W: 11 02 b.Athlone 14-9-86
Source: Scholar. *Honours:* Eire Youth, Under-21.

2004-05	Leicester C	1	0		
2005-06	Leicester C	2	0		
2006-07	Leicester C	0	0		
2006-07	*Mansfield T*	10	0	10	0
2007-08	Leicester C	20	1	23	1
2007-08	*Leeds U*	10	1		
2008-09	Leeds U	11	1	21	2
2008-09	*Crewe Alex*	3	0	3	0

SHOWUNMI, Enoch (F)   170 29
H: 6 3 W: 14 11 b.Kilburn 21-4-82
Source: Willesden Constantine. *Honours:* Nigeria 2 full caps.

2003-04	Luton T	26	7		
2004-05	Luton T	35	6		
2005-06	Luton T	41	1	102	14
2006-07	Bristol C	33	10		
2007-08	Bristol C	17	3	50	13
2007-08	*Sheffield W*	10	0	10	0
2008-09	Leeds U	8	2	8	2

SNODGRASS, Robert (F)   135 29
H: 6 0 W: 12 02 b.Glasgow 7-9-87
Honours: Scotland Youth, Under-21.

2003-04	Livingston	0	0		
2004-05	Livingston	17	2		
2005-06	Livingston	27	4		
2006-07	Livingston	6	0		
2006-07	*Stirling A*	12	5	12	5
2007-08	Livingston	31	9	81	15
2008-09	Leeds U	42	9	42	9

SWEENEY, Peter (M)   126 7
H: 6 0 W: 12 11 b.Glasgow 25-9-84
Source: Scholar. *Honours:* Scotland Youth, Under-21, B.

2001-02	Millwall	1	0		
2002-03	Millwall	5	1		
2003-04	Millwall	29	2		
2004-05	Millwall	24	2	59	5
2005-06	Stoke C	17	1		
2006-07	Stoke C	13	1		
2006-07	*Yeovil T*	8	0	8	0
2007-08	Stoke C	5	0	35	2
2007-08	*Walsall*	7	0	7	0
2008-09	Leeds U	9	0		
2008-09	*Grimsby T*	8	0	8	0

TELFER, Paul (D)   552 27
H: 5 10 W: 11 13 b.Edinburgh 21-10-71
Source: Trainee. *Honours:* Scotland Under-21, B, 1 full cap.

1988-89	Luton T	0	0		
1989-90	Luton T	0	0		
1990-91	Luton T	1	0		
1991-92	Luton T	20	1		
1992-93	Luton T	32	2		
1993-94	Luton T	45	7		
1994-95	Luton T	46	9	144	19
1995-96	Coventry C	31	1		
1996-97	Coventry C	34	0		
1997-98	Coventry C	33	3		
1998-99	Coventry C	32	2		
1999-2000	Coventry C	30	0		
2000-01	Coventry C	31	0		
2001-02	Coventry C	0	0	191	6
2001-02	Southampton	28	1		
2002-03	Southampton	33	0		
2003-04	Southampton	37	0		
2004-05	Southampton	30	0	128	1
2005-06	Celtic	36	1		
2006-07	Celtic	21	0	57	1
2007-08	Bournemouth	18	0	18	0
2008-09	Leeds U	14	0	14	0

WEBB, Jonathan (D)   0 0
H: 5 10 W: 11 02 b.Wetherby 15-1-90

2008-09	Leeds U	0	0		

WHITE, Aidan (D)   5 0
H: 5 7 W: 10 00 b.Otley 10-10-91
Source: Scholar. *Honours:* England Youth.

2008-09	Leeds U	5	0	5	0

WILKINSON, Ross (D)   0 0
b. 15-10-89
Source: Scholar.

2008-09	Leeds U	0	0		

LEICESTER C (45)

ADAMS, Nicky (F)   103 15
H: 5 10 W: 11 00 b.Bolton 16-10-86
Source: Scholar. *Honours:* Wales Under-21.

2005-06	Bury	15	1		
2006-07	Bury	19	1		
2007-08	Bury	43	12	77	14
2008-09	Leicester C	12	0	12	0
2008-09	*Rochdale*	14	1	14	1

BERNER, Bruno (M)   216 9
H: 6 1 W: 12 13 b.Zurich 21-11-77
Honours: Switzerland Youth, Under-20, Under-21, 16 full caps.

1997-98	Grasshoppers	2	0		
1998-99	Grasshoppers	21	0		
1999-2000	Grasshoppers	6	1		
1999-2000	Oviedo	1	1	1	1
2000-01	Grasshoppers	27	1		
2001-02	Grasshoppers	16	0	72	2
2002-03	Freiburg	31	2		
2003-04	Freiburg	33	1		
2004-05	Freiburg	12	0	76	3
2005-06	Basle	17	0		
2006-07	Basle	15	0	32	0
2006-07	Blackburn R	1	0		
2007-08	Blackburn R	2	0		
2008-09	Blackburn R	0	0	3	0
2008-09	Leicester C	32	3	32	3

BESWICK, Ryan (M)   0 0
b.Walton-on-Thames 12-1-88

2007-08	Leicester C	0	0		
2008-09	Leicester C	0	0		

BURNS, Robbie (M)   2 0
H: 6 0 W: 11 12 b.Milton Keynes 15-11-90
Source: Scholar.

2008-09	Leicester C	0	0		
2008-09	*Tranmere R*	2	0	2	0

CAMPBELL, Dudley (F)   121 31
H: 5 10 W: 11 00 b.London 12-11-81
Source: Aston Villa Trainee, QPR, Chesham U, Stevenage B, Yeading.

2005-06	Brentford	23	9	23	9
2005-06	Birmingham C	11	0		
2006-07	Birmingham C	32	9	43	9
2007-08	Leicester C	28	4		
2008-09	Leicester C	7	0	35	4
2008-09	*Blackpool*	20	9	20	9

CHAMBERS, Ashley (F)   6 0
H: 5 10 W: 11 06 b.Leicester 1-3-90
Source: Scholar. *Honours:* England Schools, Youth.

2005-06	Leicester C	0	0		
2006-07	Leicester C	0	0		
2007-08	Leicester C	5	0		
2008-09	Leicester C	1	0	6	0

CISAK, Aleksander (G)   0 0
H: 6 3 W: 14 11 b.Krakow 19-5-89
Source: Scholar.

2006-07	Leicester C	0	0		
2007-08	Leicester C	0	0		
2008-09	Leicester C	0	0		

CLEMENCE, Stephen (M)   242 12
H: 6 0 W: 12 09 b.Liverpool 31-3-78
Source: Trainee. *Honours:* England Schools, Youth, Under-21.

1994-95	Tottenham H	0	0		
1995-96	Tottenham H	0	0		
1996-97	Tottenham H	0	0		
1997-98	Tottenham H	17	0		
1998-99	Tottenham H	18	0		
1999-2000	Tottenham H	20	1		
2000-01	Tottenham H	29	1		
2001-02	Tottenham H	6	0		
2002-03	Tottenham H	0	0	90	2
2002-03	Birmingham C	15	2		

2003-04	Birmingham C	35	2	
2004-05	Birmingham C	22	0	
2005-06	Birmingham C	15	0	
2006-07	Birmingham C	34	4	121 8
2007-08	Leicester C	31	2	
2008-09	Leicester C	0	0	31 2

COX, Lee (D)   **0 0**
Source: Scholar.

2007-08	Leicester C	0	0
2008-09	Leicester C	0	0
2008-09	Yeovil T	0	0

DICKOV, Paul (F)   **395 96**
H: 5 6 W: 10 06 b.Livingston 1-11-72
Source: Trainee. Honours: Scotland Schools, Youth, Under-21, 10 full caps, 1 goal.

1992-93	Arsenal	3	2	
1993-94	Arsenal	1	0	
1993-94	Luton T	15	1	15 1
1993-94	Brighton & HA	8	5	8 5
1994-95	Arsenal	9	0	
1995-96	Arsenal	7	1	
1996-97	Arsenal	1	0	21 3
1996-97	Manchester C	29	5	
1997-98	Manchester C	30	9	
1998-99	Manchester C	35	10	
1999-2000	Manchester C	34	5	
2000-01	Manchester C	21	4	
2001-02	Manchester C	7	0	
2001-02	Leicester C	12	4	
2002-03	Leicester C	42	17	
2003-04	Leicester C	35	11	
2004-05	Blackburn R	29	9	
2005-06	Blackburn R	21	5	50 14
2006-07	Manchester C	16	0	
2007-08	Manchester C	0	0	172 33
2007-08	Crystal Palace	9	0	9 0
2007-08	Blackpool	11	6	11 6
2008-09	Leicester C	20	2	109 34

DYER, Lloyd (M)   **185 29**
H: 5 8 W: 10 03 b.Birmingham 13-9-82
Source: Aston Villa Juniors.

2001-02	WBA	0	0	
2002-03	WBA	0	0	
2003-04	WBA	17	2	
2003-04	Kidderminster H	7	1	7 1
2004-05	WBA	4	0	
2004-05	Coventry C	6	0	6 0
2005-06	WBA	0	0	21 2
2005-06	QPR	15	0	15 0
2005-06	Millwall	6	0	6 0
2006-07	Milton Keynes D	41	5	
2007-08	Milton Keynes D	45	11	86 16
2008-09	Leicester C	44	10	44 10

EDWORTHY, Marc (D)   **446 2**
H: 5 10 W: 11 11 b.Barnstaple 24-12-72
Source: Trainee.

1990-91	Plymouth Arg	0	0	
1991-92	Plymouth Arg	15	0	
1992-93	Plymouth Arg	15	0	
1993-94	Plymouth Arg	12	0	
1994-95	Plymouth Arg	27	1	69 1
1995-96	Crystal Palace	44	0	
1996-97	Crystal Palace	45	0	
1997-98	Crystal Palace	34	0	
1998-99	Crystal Palace	3	0	126 0
1998-99	Coventry C	22	0	
1999-2000	Coventry C	10	0	
2000-01	Coventry C	24	1	
2001-02	Coventry C	20	0	76 1
2002-03	Wolverhampton W	22	0	22 0
2003-04	Norwich C	43	0	
2004-05	Norwich C	28	0	71 0
2005-06	Derby Co	30	0	
2006-07	Derby Co	38	0	
2007-08	Derby Co	9	0	77 0
2008-09	Leicester C	5	0	5 0

FRYATT, Matty (F)   **207 66**
H: 5 10 W: 11 00 b.Nuneaton 5-3-86
Source: Scholar. Honours: England Youth.

2002-03	Walsall	0	0	
2003-04	Walsall	11	1	
2003-04	Carlisle U	10	1	10 1
2004-05	Walsall	36	15	
2005-06	Walsall	23	11	70 27
2005-06	Leicester C	19	6	
2006-07	Leicester C	32	3	
2007-08	Leicester C	30	2	
2008-09	Leicester C	46	27	127 38

GRADEL, Max (M)   **61 10**
H: 5 8 W: 12 03 b.Ivory Coast 30-9-87

2005-06	Leicester C	0	0	
2006-07	Leicester C	0	0	
2007-08	Leicester C	0	0	
2007-08	Bournemouth	34	9	34 9
2008-09	Leicester C	27	1	27 1

HAYES, Jonathan (M)   **35 0**
H: 5 7 W: 11 00 b.Dublin 9-7-87
Source: Scholar. Honours: Eire Under-21.

2004-05	Reading	0	0	
2005-06	Reading	0	0	
2006-07	Reading	0	0	
2006-07	Milton Keynes D	11	0	11 0
2007-08	Leicester C	7	0	
2007-08	Northampton T	11	0	11 0
2008-09	Leicester C	0	0	7 0
2008-09	Cheltenham T	6	0	6 0

HAYLES, Barry (F)   **398 113**
H: 5 11 W: 12 11 b.Lambeth 17-5-72
Source: Stevenage Bor. Honours: Jamaica 10 full caps.

1997-98	Bristol R	45	23	
1998-99	Bristol R	17	9	62 32
1998-99	Fulham	30	8	
1999-2000	Fulham	35	5	
2000-01	Fulham	35	18	
2001-02	Fulham	35	8	
2002-03	Fulham	14	1	
2003-04	Fulham	26	4	175 44
2004-05	Sheffield U	4	0	4 0
2004-05	Millwall	32	12	
2005-06	Millwall	23	4	55 16
2006-07	Plymouth Arg	39	13	
2007-08	Plymouth Arg	23	2	62 15
2007-08	Leicester C	18	2	
2008-09	Leicester C	10	0	28 2
2008-09	Cheltenham T	12	4	12 4

HENDERSON, Paul (G)   **237 0**
H: 6 1 W: 12 06 b.Sydney 22-4-76

1998-99	Northern Spirit	30	0	
1999-2000	Northern Spirit	14	0	
2000-01	Northern Spirit	21	0	
2001-02	Northern Spirit	13	0	
2002-03	Northern Spirit	33	0	
2003-04	Northern Spirit	23	0	134 0
2004-05	Bradford C	40	0	40 0
2005-06	Leicester C	15	0	
2006-07	Leicester C	28	0	
2007-08	Leicester C	14	0	
2008-09	Leicester C	6	0	63 0

HOBBS, Jack (D)   **56 2**
H: 6 3 W: 13 05 b.Portsmouth 18-8-88
Source: Scholar. Honours: England Youth.

2004-05	Lincoln C	1	0	1 0
2005-06	Liverpool	0	0	
2006-07	Liverpool	0	0	
2007-08	Liverpool	2	0	
2007-08	Scunthorpe U	9	1	9 1
2008-09	Liverpool	0	0	2 0
2008-09	Leicester C	44	1	44 1

HOWARD, Steve (F)   **565 176**
H: 6 3 W: 15 00 b.Durham 10-5-76
Source: Tow Law T. Honours: Scotland B.

1995-96	Hartlepool U	39	7	
1996-97	Hartlepool U	32	8	
1997-98	Hartlepool U	43	7	
1998-99	Hartlepool U	28	5	142 27
1998-99	Northampton T	12	0	
1999-2000	Northampton T	41	10	
2000-01	Northampton T	33	8	86 18
2000-01	Luton T	12	3	
2001-02	Luton T	42	24	
2002-03	Luton T	41	22	
2003-04	Luton T	34	14	
2004-05	Luton T	40	18	
2005-06	Luton T	43	14	212 95
2006-07	Derby Co	43	16	
2007-08	Derby Co	20	1	63 17
2007-08	Leicester C	21	6	
2008-09	Leicester C	41	13	62 19

KING, Andy (M)   **56 10**
H: 6 0 W: 11 10 b.Luton 29-10-88
Source: Scholar. Honours: Wales Youth, Under-21, 1 full cap.

2007-08	Leicester C	11	1	
2008-09	Leicester C	45	9	56 10

KING, Craig (F)   **81 6**
H: 5 11 W: 11 12 b.Chesterfield 6-10-90
Source: Scholar. Honours: Scotland Youth.

2005-06	The New Saints	33	2	
2006-07	The New Saints	18	1	
2007-08	The New Saints	30	3	81 6
2008-09	Leicester C	0	0	

KISHISHEV, Radostin (D)   **396 19**
H: 5 11 W: 12 03 b.Bourgas 30-7-74
Honours: Bulgaria 78 full caps.

1991-92	Chernomorets	6	1	
1992-93	Chernomorets	23	2	
1993-94	Chernomorets	23	1	52 4
1994-95	Neftochimik	14	0	
1995-96	Neftochimik	30	0	
1996-97	Neftochimik	30	6	
1997-98	Neftochimik	1	0	75 6
1997-98	Bursaspor	20	3	20 3
1997-98	Litets Lovech	5	0	
1998-99	Litets Lovech	26	2	
1999-2000	Litets Lovech	15	2	46 4
2000-01	Charlton Ath	27	0	
2001-02	Charlton Ath	3	0	
2002-03	Charlton Ath	34	2	
2003-04	Charlton Ath	33	0	
2004-05	Charlton Ath	31	0	
2005-06	Charlton Ath	37	0	
2006-07	Charlton Ath	14	0	179 2
2006-07	Leeds U	10	0	
2007-08	Leicester C	7	0	
2007-08	Leeds U	7	0	17 0
2008-09	Leicester C	0	0	7 0

Transferred to Litex January 2009

KISNORBO, Patrick (D)   **241 13**
H: 6 1 W: 11 11 b.Melbourne 24-3-81
Honours: Australia Schools, Under-20, Under-23, 14 full caps.

2000-01	South Melbourne	25	0	
2001-02	South Melbourne	23	2	
2002-03	South Melbourne	19	1	67 3
2003-04	Hearts	31	0	
2004-05	Hearts	17	1	48 1
2005-06	Leicester C	37	1	
2006-07	Leicester C	40	5	
2007-08	Leicester C	41	3	
2008-09	Leicester C	8	0	126 9

LACZKO, Zsolt (F)   **9 0**
H: 6 0 W: 12 11 b.Szeged 18-12-86
Source: Ferencvaros, Olympiakos. Honours: Hungary Under-21.

2007-08	Leicester C	9	0	
2008-09	Leicester C	0	0	9 0

LOGAN, Conrad (G)   **94 0**
H: 6 2 W: 14 00 b.Letterkenny 18-4-86
Source: Scholar. Honours: Eire Youth.

2003-04	Leicester C	0	0	
2004-05	Leicester C	0	0	
2005-06	Leicester C	0	0	
2005-06	Boston U	13	0	13 0
2006-07	Leicester C	18	0	
2007-08	Leicester C	0	0	
2007-08	Stockport Co	34	0	
2008-09	Leicester C	0	0	18 0
2008-09	Luton T	22	0	22 0
2008-09	Stockport Co	7	0	41 0

MAGUNDA, Joseph (D)   **0 0**
b.Leamington 16-4-89

2007-08	Leicester C	0	0
2008-09	Leicester C	0	0

MATTOCK, Joe (D)   **66 1**
H: 5 11 W: 12 05 b.Leicester 15-5-90
Source: Scholar. Honours: England Youth, Under-21.

2006-07	Leicester C	4	0	
2007-08	Leicester C	31	0	
2008-09	Leicester C	31	1	66 1

McKAY, Billy (F)   **0 0**
b.Corby 22-10-88
Honours: Northern Ireland Under-21.

2007-08	Leicester C	0	0
2008-09	Leicester C	0	0

MORRISON, Michael (D)   **35 3**
H: 6 0 W: 12 00 b.Bury St Edmunds 3-3-88
Source: Cambridge U.

2008-09	Leicester C	35	3	35 3

N'GOTTY, Bruno (D)   586 25
H: 6 1   W: 13 07   b.Lyon 10-6-71
Honours: France Youth, Under-21, Under-23, B, 6 full caps.

1989-90	Lyon	27	0		
1990-91	Lyon	37	2		
1991-92	Lyon	36	1		
1992-93	Lyon	36	3		
1993-94	Lyon	36	3		
1994-95	Lyon	35	3	207	12
1995-96	Paris St Germain	24	1		
1996-97	Paris St Germain	30	4		
1997-98	Paris St Germain	26	2	80	7
1998-99	AC Milan	25	1		
1999-2000	AC Milan	9	0	34	1
1999-2000	Venezia	16	0	16	0
2000-01	Marseille	30	0	30	0
2001-02	Bolton W	26	1		
2002-03	Bolton W	23	1		
2003-04	Bolton W	33	2		
2004-05	Bolton W	37	0		
2005-06	Bolton W	29	0	148	4
2006-07	Birmingham C	25	1	25	1
2007-08	Leicester C	38	0		
2008-09	Leicester C	0	0	38	0
2008-09	Hereford U	8	0	8	0

O'NEILL, Luke (D)   0 0
H: 6 0   W: 11 04   b.Slough 20-8-91
Source: Scholar. *Honours:* England Youth.

2008-09	Leicester C	0	0

OAKLEY, Matthew (M)   382 31
H: 5 10   W: 12 06   b.Peterborough 17-8-77
Source: Trainee. *Honours:* England Under-21.

1994-95	Southampton	1	0		
1995-96	Southampton	10	0		
1996-97	Southampton	28	3		
1997-98	Southampton	33	1		
1998-99	Southampton	22	2		
1999-2000	Southampton	31	3		
2000-01	Southampton	35	1		
2001-02	Southampton	27	1		
2002-03	Southampton	31	0		
2003-04	Southampton	7	0		
2004-05	Southampton	7	1		
2005-06	Southampton	29	2	261	14
2006-07	Derby Co	37	6		
2007-08	Derby Co	19	3	56	9
2007-08	Leicester C	20	0		
2008-09	Leicester C	45	8	65	8

ODHIAMBO, Eric (F)   9 0
H: 5 9   W: 11 02   b.Oxford 12-5-89
Source: Scholar.

2006-07	Leicester C	0	0		
2007-08	Leicester C	0	0		
2007-08	Dundee U	4	0	4	0
2007-08	Southend U	5	0	5	0
2008-09	Leicester C	0	0		
2008-09	Brentford	0	0		
Transferred to Inverness CT January 2009

PENTNEY, Carl (G)   1 0
H: 6 0   W: 12 00   b.Leicester 3-2-88

2007-08	Leicester C	0	0
2008-09	Leicester C	1	0	1	0

PORTER, Levi (F)   39 3
H: 5 4   W: 10 05   b.Leicester 6-4-87
Source: Scholar. *Honours:* England Youth.

2005-06	Leicester C	0	0
2006-07	Leicester C	34	3
2007-08	Leicester C	4	0
2008-09	Leicester C	1	0	39	3

POWELL, Chris (D)   665 6
H: 5 11   W: 11 12   b.Lambeth 8-9-69
Source: Trainee. *Honours:* England 5 full caps.

1987-88	Crystal Palace	0	0		
1988-89	Crystal Palace	3	0		
1989-90	Crystal Palace	0	0	3	0
1989-90	Aldershot	11	0	11	0
1990-91	Southend U	45	1		
1991-92	Southend U	44	0		
1992-93	Southend U	42	2		
1993-94	Southend U	46	0		
1994-95	Southend U	44	0		
1995-96	Southend U	27	0	248	3
1995-96	Derby Co	19	0		
1996-97	Derby Co	35	0		
1997-98	Derby Co	37	1	91	1

1998-99	Charlton Ath	38	0		
1999-2000	Charlton Ath	40	0		
2000-01	Charlton Ath	33	0		
2001-02	Charlton Ath	36	1		
2002-03	Charlton Ath	37	0		
2003-04	Charlton Ath	16	0		
2004-05	Charlton Ath	0	0		
2004-05	West Ham U	36	0	36	0
2005-06	Charlton Ath	27	0		
2006-07	Watford	15	0	15	0
2007-08	Charlton Ath	17	1	244	2
2008-09	Leicester C	17	0	17	0

ROWE-TURNER, Lathanial (D)   1 0
H: 6 1   W: 13 00   b.Leicester 12-11-89
Source: Scholar.

2007-08	Leicester C	0	0		
2008-09	Leicester C	0	0		
2008-09	Cheltenham T	1	0	1	0

SAPPLETON, Reneil (M)   4 1
H: 5 10   W: 11 13   b.Kingston 8-12-89

2007-08	Leicester C	1	0		
2008-09	Leicester C	0	0	1	0
2008-09	Bournemouth	3	1	3	1

TUNCHEV, Aleksandar (D)   231 25
H: 6 2   W: 13 03   b.Pazardzhik 10-7-81
Honours: Bulgaria 25 full caps, 1 goal.

1998-99	Pazardzhik	6	0		
1999-2000	Pazardzhik	14	2		
1999-2000	Iskar	15	1	15	1
2000-01	Pazardzhik	18	3	38	5
2001-02	Belasitsa	30	3	30	3
2002-03	Lokomotiv Plovdiv	1	0		
2003-04	Lokomotiv Plovdiv	25	1		
2004-05	Lokomotiv Plovdiv	28	0		
2005-06	Lokomotiv Plovdiv	11	2	65	4
2005-06	CSKA Sofia	10	1		
2006-07	CSKA Sofia	27	7		
2007-08	CSKA Sofia	26	3	63	11
2008-09	Leicester C	20	1	20	1

VERMA, Aman (M)   0 0
H: 5 8   W: 11 11   b.Sydney 25-8-87
Source: Scholar. *Honours:* Australia Youth, Under-20.

2004-05	Leicester C	0	0		
2005-06	Leicester C	5	0		
2006-07	Leicester C	19	0		
2007-08	Leicester C	22	0		
2008-09	Leicester C	0	0	46	0
2008-09	Dundee U	8	0	8	0
2008-09	Cheltenham T	4	0	4	0

WORLEY, Harry (D)   21 0
H: 6 3   W: 13 00   b.Warrington 25-11-88
Source: Scholar.

2005-06	Chelsea	0	0		
2006-07	Chelsea	0	0		
2006-07	Doncaster R	10	0	10	0
2007-08	Chelsea	0	0		
2007-08	Carlisle U	1	0	1	0
2007-08	Leicester C	2	0		
2008-09	Leicester C	0	0	2	0
2008-09	Luton T	8	0	8	0

LEYTON ORIENT (46)

ASHWORTH, Luke (D)   3 0
H: 6 2   W: 12 08   b.Bolton 4-12-89

2008-09	Wigan	0	0
2008-09	Leyton Orient	3	0	3	0

BAKER, Harry (M)   4 0
H: 5 11   W: 12 04   b.Bexley Heath 20-9-90
Source: Scholar.

2008-09	Leyton Orient	4	0	4	0

BOYD, Adam (F)   254 81
H: 5 9   W: 10 12   b.Hartlepool 25-5-82
Source: Scholarship.

1999-2000	Hartlepool U	4	1		
2000-01	Hartlepool U	5	0		
2001-02	Hartlepool U	29	9		
2002-03	Hartlepool U	22	5		
2003-04	Hartlepool U	18	12		
2003-04	Boston U	14	4	14	4
2004-05	Hartlepool U	45	22		
2005-06	Hartlepool U	21	4	144	53

2006-07	Luton T	19	1	19	1
2007-08	Leyton Orient	44	14		
2008-09	Leyton Orient	33	9	77	23

CAVE-BROWN, Andrew (D)   13 0
H: 5 10   W: 12 02   b.Gravesend 5-8-88
Source: Scholar. *Honours:* Scotland Youth.

2005-06	Norwich C	0	0
2006-07	Norwich C	0	0
2007-08	Norwich C	0	0
2008-09	Leyton Orient	13	0	13	0

CHAMBERS, Adam (D)   185 9
H: 5 10   W: 11 12   b.Sandwell 20-11-80
Source: Trainee. *Honours:* England Youth.

1998-99	WBA	0	0		
1999-2000	WBA	0	0		
2000-01	WBA	11	1		
2001-02	WBA	32	0		
2002-03	WBA	13	0		
2003-04	WBA	0	0		
2003-04	Sheffield W	11	0	11	0
2004-05	WBA	0	0	56	1
2004-05	Kidderminster H	2	0	2	0
2006-07	Leyton Orient	38	4		
2007-08	Leyton Orient	45	3		
2008-09	Leyton Orient	33	1	116	8

DANIELS, Charlie (M)   59 5
H: 6 1   W: 12 12   b.Harlow 7-9-86
Source: Scholar.

2005-06	Tottenham H	0	0		
2006-07	Tottenham H	0	0		
2006-07	Chesterfield	2	0	2	0
2007-08	Tottenham H	0	0		
2007-08	Leyton Orient	31	2		
2008-09	Tottenham H	0	0		
2008-09	Gillingham	5	1	5	1
2008-09	Leyton Orient	21	2	52	4

DEMETRIOU, Jason (M)   104 9
H: 5 11   W: 10 08   b.Newham 18-11-87
Source: Scholar.

2005-06	Leyton Orient	3	0		
2006-07	Leyton Orient	15	2		
2007-08	Leyton Orient	43	3		
2008-09	Leyton Orient	43	4	104	9

GRANVILLE, Danny (D)   355 19
H: 6 0   W: 12 00   b.Islington 19-1-75
Source: Trainee. *Honours:* England Under-21.

1993-94	Cambridge U	11	5		
1994-95	Cambridge U	16	2		
1995-96	Cambridge U	35	0		
1996-97	Cambridge U	37	0	99	7
1996-97	Chelsea	5	0		
1997-98	Chelsea	13	0	18	0
1998-99	Leeds U	9	0		
1999-2000	Leeds U	0	0	9	0
1999-2000	Manchester C	35	2		
2000-01	Manchester C	19	0		
2000-01	Norwich C	6	0	6	0
2001-02	Manchester C	16	1	70	3
2001-02	Crystal Palace	16	0		
2002-03	Crystal Palace	35	3		
2003-04	Crystal Palace	21	3		
2004-05	Crystal Palace	35	3		
2005-06	Crystal Palace	15	0	122	9
2006-07	Crystal Palace	15	0	122	9
2007-08	Colchester U	19	0	19	0
2008-09	Leyton Orient	12	0	12	0

GRAY, Wayne (F)   292 53
H: 5 10   W: 11 05   b.Dulwich 7-11-80
Source: Trainee.

1998-99	Wimbledon	0	0		
1999-2000	Wimbledon	1	0		
1999-2000	Swindon T	12	2	12	2
2000-01	Wimbledon	11	0		
2000-01	Port Vale	3	0	3	0
2001-02	Wimbledon	15	5		
2001-02	Brighton & HA	4	1	4	1
2002-03	Wimbledon	30	2		
2003-04	Wimbledon	33	4	75	6
2004-05	Southend U	44	11		
2005-06	Southend U	39	9	83	20
2006-07	Yeovil T	46	11	46	11
2007-08	Leyton Orient	38	8		
2008-09	Leyton Orient	16	0	69	13

JARVIS, Ryan (F)   106   12
H: 6 1   W: 11 11   b.Fakenham 11-7-86
Source: Scholar. Honours: FA Schools, England Youth.

Season	Club				
2002-03	Norwich C	3	0		
2003-04	Norwich C	12	1		
2004-05	Norwich C	4	1		
2004-05	Colchester U	6	0	6	0
2005-06	Norwich C	4	1		
2006-07	Norwich C	5	0		
2006-07	Leyton Orient	14	6		
2007-08	Norwich C	1	0	29	3
2007-08	Kilmarnock	9	1	9	1
2007-08	Notts Co	17	2	17	2
2008-09	Leyton Orient	31	0	45	6

JONES, Jamie (G)   20   0
H: 6 2   W: 14 05   b.Kirkby 18-2-89
Source: Scholar.

Season	Club				
2007-08	Everton	0	0		
2008-09	Leyton Orient	20	0	20	0

MELLIGAN, John (M)   246   33
H: 5 9   W: 11 02   b.Dublin 11-2-82
Source: Trainee. Honours: Eire Youth, Under-21.

Season	Club				
2000-01	Wolverhampton W	0	0		
2001-02	Wolverhampton W	0	0		
2001-02	Bournemouth	8	0	8	0
2002-03	Wolverhampton W	2	0		
2002-03	Kidderminster H	29	10		
2003-04	Wolverhampton W	0	0	2	0
2003-04	Kidderminster H	5	1	34	11
2003-04	Doncaster R	21	2	21	2
2004-05	Cheltenham T	29	2		
2005-06	Cheltenham T	42	6		
2006-07	Cheltenham T	43	7	114	15
2007-08	Leyton Orient	32	3		
2008-09	Leyton Orient	35	2	67	5

MKANDAWIRE, Tamika (D)   110   10
H: 6 1   W: 12 03   b.Malawi 28-5-83
Source: Scholar.

Season	Club				
2002-03	WBA	0	0		
2003-04	WBA	0	0		
2006-07	Hereford U	39	2	39	2
2007-08	Leyton Orient	35	3		
2008-09	Leyton Orient	36	5	71	8

MORRIS, Glenn (G)   113   0
H: 6 0   W: 12 03   b.Woolwich 20-12-83
Source: Scholar.

Season	Club				
2001-02	Leyton Orient	2	0		
2002-03	Leyton Orient	23	0		
2003-04	Leyton Orient	27	0		
2004-05	Leyton Orient	12	0		
2005-06	Leyton Orient	4	0		
2006-07	Leyton Orient	3	0		
2007-08	Leyton Orient	16	0		
2008-09	Leyton Orient	26	0	113	0

PALMER, Aiden (D)   50   0
H: 5 8   W: 10 10   b.Enfield 2-1-87
Source: Scholar.

Season	Club				
2004-05	Leyton Orient	5	0		
2005-06	Leyton Orient	3	0		
2006-07	Leyton Orient	6	0		
2007-08	Leyton Orient	23	0		
2008-09	Leyton Orient	10	0	47	0
2008-09	Dagenham & R	3	0	3	0

PIRES, Loick (F)   7   0
H: 6 3   W: 13 02   b.Lisbon 20-11-89
Source: Scholar.

Season	Club				
2007-08	Leyton Orient	1	0		
2008-09	Leyton Orient	6	0	7	0

PURCHES, Stephen (D)   323   14
H: 5 11   W: 11 13   b.Ilford 14-1-80

Season	Club				
1998-99	West Ham U	0	0		
1999-2000	West Ham U	0	0		
2000-01	Bournemouth	34	0		
2001-02	Bournemouth	41	2		
2002-03	Bournemouth	44	3		
2003-04	Bournemouth	42	3		
2004-05	Bournemouth	14	1		
2005-06	Bournemouth	26	0		
2006-07	Bournemouth	43	1	244	10
2007-08	Leyton Orient	37	1		
2008-09	Leyton Orient	42	3	79	4

SAAH, Brian (M)   93   1
H: 6 3   W: 12 03   b.Rush Green 16-12-86
Source: Scholar.

Season	Club				
2003-04	Leyton Orient	6	0		
2004-05	Leyton Orient	12	0		
2005-06	Leyton Orient	3	0		
2006-07	Leyton Orient	32	0		
2007-08	Leyton Orient	25	1		
2008-09	Leyton Orient	15	0	93	1

SHIELDS, Solomon (M)   1   0
H: 5 10   W: 12 00   b.Leyton 14-10-89
Source: Scholar.

Season	Club				
2006-07	Leyton Orient	1	0		
2007-08	Leyton Orient	0	0		
2008-09	Leyton Orient	0	0	1	0

TERRY, Paul (M)   206   11
H: 5 10   W: 12 06   b.Barking 3-4-79
Source: Dagenham & R.

Season	Club				
2003-04	Yeovil T	34	1		
2004-05	Yeovil T	39	6		
2005-06	Yeovil T	42	1		
2006-07	Yeovil T	20	2	135	10
2007-08	Leyton Orient	43	0		
2008-09	Leyton Orient	28	1	71	1

THELWELL, Alton (D)   136   2
H: 6 0   W: 12 05   b.Islington 5-9-80
Source: Trainee. Honours: England Under-21.

Season	Club				
1998-99	Tottenham H	0	0		
1999-2000	Tottenham H	0	0		
2000-01	Tottenham H	16	0		
2001-02	Tottenham H	2	0		
2002-03	Tottenham H	0	0	18	0
2003-04	Hull C	26	1		
2004-05	Hull C	3	0		
2005-06	Hull C	9	0		
2006-07	Hull C	2	0	40	1
2006-07	Leyton Orient	22	1		
2007-08	Leyton Orient	28	0		
2008-09	Leyton Orient	28	0	78	1

THORNTON, Sean (M)   188   17
H: 5 10   W: 11 00   b.Drogheda 18-5-83
Source: Scholar. Honours: Eire Youth, Under-21.

Season	Club				
2001-02	Tranmere R	11	1	11	1
2002-03	Sunderland	11	1		
2002-03	Blackpool	3	0	3	0
2003-04	Sunderland	22	4		
2004-05	Sunderland	16	4	49	9
2005-06	Doncaster R	29	2		
2006-07	Doncaster R	30	0	59	2
2007-08	Leyton Orient	31	3		
2008-09	Leyton Orient	30	1	61	4
2008-09	Shrewsbury T	5	1	5	1

LINCOLN C (47)

ADAMS, Nathan (M)   2   0
H: 5 7   W: 11 00   b.Lincoln 6-10-91
Source: Scholar.

Season	Club				
2008-09	Lincoln C	2	0	2	0

BEEVERS, Lee (D)   238   12
H: 6 2   W: 11 07   b.Doncaster 4-12-83
Source: From Scholar. Honours: Wales Youth, Under-21.

Season	Club				
2000-01	Ipswich T	0	0		
2001-02	Ipswich T	0	0		
2002-03	Ipswich T	0	0		
2002-03	Boston U	1	0		
2003-04	Boston U	40	2		
2004-05	Boston U	31	1	72	3
2004-05	Lincoln C	8	0		
2005-06	Lincoln C	33	1		
2006-07	Lincoln C	44	5		
2007-08	Lincoln C	37	1		
2008-09	Lincoln C	44	2	166	9

BROWN, Aaron (M)   283   20
H: 5 10   W: 11 11   b.Bristol 14-3-80
Source: Trainee. Honours: England Schools.

Season	Club				
1997-98	Bristol C	0	0		
1998-99	Bristol C	14	0		
1999-2000	Bristol C	13	2		
1999-2000	Exeter C	5	1	5	1
2000-01	Bristol C	35	2		
2001-02	Bristol C	36	1		
2002-03	Bristol C	32	2		
2003-04	Bristol C	30	5	160	12
2004-05	QPR	1	0		
2004-05	Torquay U	5	0	5	0
2005-06	QPR	2	0	3	0
2005-06	Cheltenham T	3	0	3	0
2005-06	Swindon T	27	2		
2006-07	Swindon T	30	2	57	4
2007-08	Gillingham	11	1	11	1
2008-09	Lincoln C	39	2	39	2

BURCH, Rob (G)   54   0
H: 6 2   W: 12 13   b.Yeovil 8-10-83
Source: Trainee. Honours: England Under-20.

Season	Club				
2002-03	Tottenham H	0	0		
2003-04	Tottenham H	0	0		
2004-05	Tottenham H	0	0		
2004-05	West Ham U	0	0		
2005-06	Tottenham H	0	0		
2005-06	Bristol C	0	0		
2006-07	Tottenham H	0	0		
2006-07	Barnet	6	0	6	0
2007-08	Sheffield W	2	0	2	0
2008-09	Lincoln C	46	0	46	0

CLARKE, Shane (D)   39   0
H: 6 1   W: 13 03   b.Lincoln 7-11-87
Source: Scholar.

Season	Club				
2006-07	Lincoln C	0	0		
2007-08	Lincoln C	16	0		
2008-09	Lincoln C	23	0	39	0

COLMAN-CARR, Luca (D)   1   0
H: 5 8   W: 11 02   b.Epsom 11-1-91
Source: Scholar.

Season	Club				
2008-09	Lincoln C	1	0	1	0

DUFFY, Ayden (M)   5   0
H: 5 8   W: 10 12   b.Kettering 16-11-86
Source: Scholar.

Season	Club				
2006-07	Lincoln C	0	0		
2007-08	Lincoln C	4	0		
2008-09	Lincoln C	1	0	5	0

GRAHAM, David (F)   291   69
H: 5 10   W: 11 02   b.Edinburgh 6-10-78
Source: Rangers SABC. Honours: Scotland Under-21.

Season	Club				
1995-96	Rangers	0	0		
1996-97	Rangers	0	0		
1997-98	Rangers	0	0		
1998-99	Rangers	3	0	3	0
1998-99	Dunfermline Ath	21	2		
1999-2000	Dunfermline Ath	15	2		
2000-01	Dunfermline Ath	4	0	40	4
2000-01	Torquay U	4	0		
2001-02	Torquay U	36	8		
2002-03	Torquay U	34	15		
2003-04	Torquay U	45	22		
2004-05	Wigan Ath	30	1		
2005-06	Wigan Ath	0	0	30	1
2005-06	Sheffield W	24	2		
2005-06	Huddersfield T	16	9	16	9
2006-07	Sheffield W	4	0	28	2
2006-07	Bradford C	22	3	22	3
2006-07	Torquay U	7	0	127	47
2007-08	Gillingham	16	3	16	3
2008-09	Lincoln C	9	0	9	0

GREEN, Paul (D)   85   3
H: 5 8   W: 10 04   b.Birmingham 15-4-87
Source: Scholar.

Season	Club				
2005-06	Aston Villa	0	0		
2006-07	Aston Villa	0	0		
2006-07	Lincoln C	16	1		
2007-08	Lincoln C	36	1		
2008-09	Lincoln C	33	1	85	3

HONE, Daniel (D)   42   2
H: 6 2   W: 12 00   b.Croydon 15-9-89
Source: Scholar.

Season	Club				
2007-08	Lincoln C	23	1		
2008-09	Lincoln C	19	1	42	2

HORSFIELD, Geoff (F)   331   79
H: 6 0   W: 11 07   b.Barnsley 1-11-73

Season	Club				
1992-93	Scarborough	6	1		
1993-94	Scarborough	6	0	12	1
From Witton Alb					
1998-99	Halifax T	10	7	10	7
1998-99	Fulham	28	15		
1999-2000	Fulham	31	7	59	22
2000-01	Birmingham C	34	7		
2001-02	Birmingham C	40	11		
2002-03	Birmingham C	31	5		
2003-04	Birmingham C	3	0	108	23
2003-04	Wigan Ath	16	7	16	7
2003-04	WBA	20	7		
2004-05	WBA	29	3		

2005-06	WBA	18	4		
2005-06	*Sheffield U*	3	0		
2006-07	WBA	0	0	67	14
2006-07	Sheffield U	0	0		
2006-07	*Leeds U*	14	2	14	2
2006-07	*Leicester C*	13	2	13	2
2007-08	Sheffield U	0	0		
2007-08	*Scunthorpe U*	12	0	12	0
2008-09	Sheffield U	0	0	3	0
2008-09	Lincoln C	17	1	17	1

HUTCHINSON, Andrew (F) 4 1
H: 5 7 W: 12 00 b.Lincoln 10-3-92
Source: Scholar.

2008-09	Lincoln C	4	1	4	1

JOHN-LEWIS, Leneli (M) 48 7
H: 5 10 W: 11 10 b.Hammersmith 17-5-89
Source: Scholar.

2006-07	Lincoln C	0	0		
2007-08	Lincoln C	21	3		
2008-09	Lincoln C	27	4	48	7

KERR, Scott (M) 167 8
H: 5 9 W: 10 07 b.Leeds 11-12-81
Source: Scholar.

2000-01	Bradford C	1	0	1	0
2001-02	Hull C	0	0		
2002-03	Hull C	0	0		
2003-04	Hull C	0	0		
2004-05	Hull C	0	0		

From Scarborough.

2005-06	Lincoln C	41	2		
2006-07	Lincoln C	44	3		
2007-08	Lincoln C	36	1		
2008-09	Lincoln C	45	2	166	8

KING, Gary (M) 11 1
H: 5 10 W: 11 04 b.Grimsby 27-1-90
Source: Scholar.

2007-08	Lincoln C	6	1		
2008-09	Lincoln C	5	0	11	1

KOVACS, Janos (D) 102 5
H: 6 4 W: 14 10 b.Budapest 11-9-85
Source: MTK. *Honours:* Hungary Under-20.

2005-06	Chesterfield	9	0		
2006-07	Chesterfield	7	0		
2007-08	Chesterfield	41	2	57	2
2008-09	Lincoln C	45	3	45	3

MILLER, Kern (D) 1 0
H: 5 9 W: 11 03 b.Skegness 2-9-91
Source: Scholar.

2008-09	Lincoln C	1	0	1	0

MULLARKEY, Sam (F) 18 1
H: 5 11 W: 12 03 b.Sleaford 24-9-87
Source: Scholar.

2004-05	Nottingham F	0	0		
2005-06	Nottingham F	0	0		
2006-07	Nottingham F	0	0		

From Grantham T.

2008-09	Lincoln C	18	1	18	1

N'GUESSAN, Dany (M) 114 20
H: 6 0 W: 12 13 b.Ivry-sur-Seine 11-8-87
Source: Auxerre, Rangers.

2006-07	Boston U	23	5	23	5
2006-07	Lincoln C	9	0		
2007-08	Lincoln C	37	7		
2008-09	Lincoln C	45	8	91	15

OAKES, Stefan (M) 255 13
H: 6 1 W: 13 07 b.Leicester 6-9-78
Source: Trainee.

1997-98	Leicester C	0	0		
1998-99	Leicester C	3	0		
1999-2000	Leicester C	22	1		
2000-01	Leicester C	13	0		
2001-02	Leicester C	21	1		
2002-03	Leicester C	5	0	64	2
2002-03	Crewe Alex	7	0	7	0
2003-04	Walsall	5	0	5	0
2003-04	Notts Co	14	0		
2004-05	Notts Co	31	5	45	5
2005-06	Wycombe W	37	2		
2006-07	Wycombe W	35	0		
2007-08	Wycombe W	34	3	106	5
2008-09	Lincoln C	28	1	28	1

PATULEA, Adrian (F) 31 11
H: 5 10 W: 11 04 b.Targoviste 10-11-84
Source: Petrolul.

2008-09	Lincoln C	31	11	31	11

PEMBLETON, Martin (M) 6 0
H: 5 7 W: 10 09 b.Scunthorpe 1-6-90
Source: Scholar.

2007-08	Lincoln C	6	0		
2008-09	Lincoln C	0	0	6	0

SINCLAIR, Frank (D) 505 12
H: 5 8 W: 12 09 b.Lambeth 3-12-71
Source: Trainee. *Honours:* Jamaica 28 full caps, 1 goal.

1989-90	Chelsea	0	0		
1990-91	Chelsea	4	0		
1991-92	Chelsea	8	1		
1991-92	WBA	6	1	6	1
1992-93	Chelsea	32	0		
1993-94	Chelsea	35	0		
1994-95	Chelsea	35	3		
1995-96	Chelsea	13	1		
1996-97	Chelsea	20	1		
1997-98	Chelsea	22	1	169	7
1998-99	Leicester C	31	1		
1999-2000	Leicester C	34	0		
2000-01	Leicester C	17	0		
2001-02	Leicester C	35	0		
2002-03	Leicester C	33	1		
2003-04	Leicester C	14	1	164	3
2004-05	Burnley	36	1		
2005-06	Burnley	37	0		
2006-07	Burnley	19	0	92	1
2006-07	*Huddersfield T*	13	0		
2007-08	Huddersfield T	29	0	42	0
2008-09	Lincoln C	23	0	23	0
2008-09	*Wycombe W*	9	0	9	0

SWAIBU, Moses (D) 10 0
H: 6 2 W: 11 11 b.Croydon 9-5-89
Source: Scholar.

2007-08	Crystal Palace	0	0		
2008-09	Crystal Palace	0	0		
2008-09	Lincoln C	10	0	10	0

WARLOW, Owain (M) 22 0
H: 6 0 W: 12 00 b.Treforest 3-7-88
Source: Scholar. *Honours:* Wales Under-21.

2006-07	Lincoln C	5	0		
2007-08	Lincoln C	17	0		
2008-09	Lincoln C	0	0	22	0

WRIGHT, Ben (F) · 190 49
H: 6 1 W: 13 07 b.Munster 1-7-80

1998-99	Bristol C	0	0		
1999-2000	Bristol C	2	0		
2000-01	Bristol C	0	0	2	0
2001	Viking	22	0		
2002	Viking	18	1	40	1
2003	Start	30	13		
2004	Start	29	15		
2005	Start	9	1		
2006	Moss	11	2	11	2
2007	Start	2	0	70	29
2007-08	Lincoln C	34	15		
2008-09	Lincoln C	33	2	67	17

LIVERPOOL (48)

AGGER, Daniel (D) 88 8
H: 6 2 W: 12 06 b.Hvidovre 12-12-84
Honours: Denmark Youth, Under-20, Under-21, 27 full caps, 3 goals.

2004-05	Brondby	26	5		
2005-06	Brondby	8	0	34	5
2005-06	Liverpool	4	0		
2006-07	Liverpool	27	2		
2007-08	Liverpool	5	0		
2008-09	Liverpool	18	1	54	3

AJDAREVIC, Astrit (M) 9 1
H: 6 1 W: 11 08 b.Kosovo 17-4-90

2006-07	Falkenberg	4	1	4	1
2006-07	Liverpool	0	0		
2007-08	Liverpool	0	0		
2008-09	Liverpool	0	0		
2008-09	*Leicester C*	5	0	5	0

AMOO, David (F) 0 0
b.London 23-4-91

2007-08	Liverpool	0	0		
2008-09	Liverpool	0	0		

ANDERSON, Paul (M) 57 9
H: 5 9 W: 10 04 b.Leicester 23-7-88
Source: Scholar. *Honours:* England Youth.

2005-06	Hull C	0	0		
2005-06	Liverpool	0	0		
2006-07	Liverpool	0	0		
2007-08	Liverpool	0	0		
2007-08	*Swansea C*	31	7	31	7
2008-09	Liverpool	0	0		
2008-09	*Nottingham F*	26	2	26	2

ANTWI-BIRAGO, Godwin (D) 46 1
H: 6 1 W: 13 09 b.Tafu 7-6-88
Source: San Gregorio.

2005-06	Liverpool	0	0		
2006-07	Liverpool	0	0		
2006-07	*Accrington S*	9	0	9	0
2007-08	Liverpool	0	0		
2007-08	*Hartlepool U*	27	1	27	1
2008-09	Liverpool	0	0		
2008-09	*Tranmere R*	5	0	5	0
2008-09	*Hereford U*	5	0	5	0

ARBELOA, Alvaro (D) 173 3
H: 6 0 W: 12 06 b.Salamanca 17-1-83
Honours: Spain Under-21, 9 full caps.

2003-04	Real Madrid B	22	0		
2004-05	Real Madrid B	28	1	50	1
2004-05	Real Madrid	0	0	2	0
2005-06	R M Castilla	34	0	34	0
2006-07	La Coruna	21	0	21	0
2006-07	Liverpool	9	1		
2007-08	Liverpool	28	0		
2008-09	Liverpool	29	1	66	2

AYALA, Daniel (M) 0 0
H: 6 3 W: 13 03 b.Sevilla 7-11-90

2007-08	Liverpool	0	0		
2008-09	Liverpool	0	0		

BABEL, Ryan (F) 130 21
H: 6 1 W: 12 04 b.Amsterdam 19-12-86
Honours: Holland Under-21, 33 full caps, 5 goals.

2003-04	Ajax	1	0		
2004-05	Ajax	20	7		
2005-06	Ajax	25	2		
2006-07	Ajax	27	5	73	14
2007-08	Liverpool	30	4		
2008-09	Liverpool	27	3	57	7

BENAYOUN, Yossi (M) 346 101
H: 5 10 W: 11 00 b.Beer Sheva 6-6-80
Honours: Israel 72 full caps, 19 goals.

1997-98	Hapoel Beer Sheva	25	15	25	15
1998-99	Maccabi Haifa	29	16		
1999-2000	Maccabi Haifa	38	19		
2000-01	Maccabi Haifa	37	13		
2001-02	Maccabi Haifa	26	7	130	55
2002-03	Santander	31	4		
2003-04	Santander	35	7		
2004-05	Santander	0	0	66	11
2004-05	West Ham U	34	5		
2005-06	West Ham U	29	3	63	8
2007-08	Liverpool	30	4		
2008-09	Liverpool	32	8	62	12

BOUZANIS, Dean (G) 0 0
H: 6 1 W: 13 06 b.Sydney 2-10-90
Source: St George Saints, Sydney.

2007-08	Liverpool	0	0		
2008-09	Liverpool	0	0		

BROUWER, Jordy (F) 0 0
H: 6 2 W: 12 05 b.Den Haag 26-2-88
Source: Ajax.

2006-07	Liverpool	0	0		
2007-08	Liverpool	0	0		
2008-09	Liverpool	0	0		

BRUNA, Gerardo (M) 0 0
H: 5 8 W: 10 02 b.Mendoza 29-1-91

2007-08	Liverpool	0	0		
2008-09	Liverpool	0	0		

CARRAGHER, Jamie (D) 398 3
H: 5 9 W: 12 01 b.Liverpool 28-1-78
Source: Trainee. *Honours:* England Youth, Under-21, B, 34 full caps.

1995-96	Liverpool	0	0		
1996-97	Liverpool	2	1		
1997-98	Liverpool	20	0		
1998-99	Liverpool	34	1		
1999-2000	Liverpool	36	0		
2000-01	Liverpool	34	0		

2001-02	Liverpool	33	0		
2002-03	Liverpool	35	0		
2003-04	Liverpool	22	0		
2004-05	Liverpool	38	0		
2005-06	Liverpool	36	0		
2006-07	Liverpool	35	1		
2007-08	Liverpool	35	0		
2008-09	Liverpool	38	0	398	3

CAVALIERI, Diego (G) 66 0
H: 6 3 W: 13 07 b.Sao Paulo 1-12-82

2001	Palmeiras	0	0		
2002	Palmeiras	0	0		
2003	Palmeiras	0	0		
2004	Palmeiras	3	0		
2005	Palmeiras	0	0		
2006	Palmeiras	25	0		
2007	Palmeiras	38	0		
2008	Palmeiras	0	0	66	0
2008-09	Liverpool	0	0		

COLLINS, Michael (F) 0 0
b. 12-7-90
Source: Scholar.

2007-08	Liverpool	0	0
2008-09	Liverpool	0	0

COOPER, Alex (M) 0 0

2008-09	Liverpool	0	0

CROWTHER, Ryan (M) 2 0
H: 5 11 W: 11 00 b.Stockport 17-9-88
Source: Scholar.

2005-06	Stockport Co	1	0		
2006-07	Stockport Co	1	0	2	0
2007-08	Liverpool	0	0		
2008-09	Liverpool	0	0		

DALLA VALLE, Lauri (M) 0 0

2008-09	Liverpool	0	0

DARBY, Stephen (D) 0 0
H: 5 9 W: 10 00 b.Liverpool 6-10-88
Source: Scholar. Honours: England Youth.

2006-07	Liverpool	0	0
2007-08	Liverpool	0	0
2008-09	Liverpool	0	0

DEGEN, Philipp (D) 167 5
H: 6 0 W: 12 10 b.Holstein 15-2-83
Honours: Switzerland Under-21, 30 full caps.

2001-02	Basle	3	0		
2002-03	Basle	16	0		
2002-03	Aarau	16	0	16	0
2003-04	Basle	33	4		
2004-05	Basle	31	0	83	4
2005-06	Bor Dortmund	31	1		
2006-07	Bor Dortmund	27	0		
2007-08	Bor Dortmund	10	0	68	1
2008-09	Liverpool	0	0		

DOSSENA, Andrea (D) 199 6
H: 5 11 W: 12 06 b.Lodi 11-9-81
Honours: Italy Youth, 10 full caps.

2001-02	Verona	2	0		
2002-03	Verona	21	1		
2003-04	Verona	37	1		
2004-05	Verona	39	1	99	3
2005-06	Treviso	21	0	21	0
2006-07	Udinese	28	0		
2007-08	Udinese	35	2	63	2
2008-09	Liverpool	16	1	16	1

DURAN VAZQUEZ, Francisco (M) 0 0
H: 5 10 W: 12 04 b.Malaga 28-4-88
Source: Malaga.

2006-07	Liverpool	0	0
2007-08	Liverpool	0	0
2008-09	Liverpool	0	0

ECCLESTON, Nathan (F) 0 0
H: 5 10 W: 12 00 b.Manchester 30-12-90
Source: Scholar.

2007-08	Liverpool	0	0
2008-09	Liverpool	0	0

EL ZHAR, Nabil (F) 18 0
H: 5 9 W: 11 05 b.Ales 27-8-86
Source: From St Etienne. Honours: France Youth, Morocco Under-20, 7 full caps, 2 goals.

2006-07	Liverpool	3	0		
2007-08	Liverpool	0	0		
2008-09	Liverpool	15	0	18	0

FABIO AURELIO (M) 205 17
H: 5 10 W: 11 11 b.Sao Carlos 24-9-79
Honours: Brazil Youth, Under-20, Under-21.

1997	Sao Paulo	15	1		
1998	Sao Paulo	11	1		
1998	Santos	0	0		
1999	Sao Paulo	23	1		
2000	Sao Paulo	4	0	53	3
2000-01	Valencia	7	0		
2001-02	Valencia	15	1		
2002-03	Valencia	26	8		
2003-04	Valencia	2	0		
2004-05	Valencia	21	0		
2005-06	Valencia	24	2	95	11
2006-07	Liverpool	17	0		
2007-08	Liverpool	16	1		
2008-09	Liverpool	24	2	57	3

FLORA, Vitor (F) 0 0
H: 5 10 W: 12 03 b.Sao Joaquim da Barra 21-2-90
Source: Botafogo.

2008-09	Liverpool	0	0

FLYNN, Ryan (M) 0 0
H: 5 8 W: 10 00 b.Scotland 4-9-88
Source: Scholar.

2006-07	Liverpool	0	0
2007-08	Hereford U	0	0
2007-08	Liverpool	0	0
2008-09	Liverpool	0	0

GERRARD, Steven (M) 333 71
H: 6 0 W: 12 05 b.Whiston 30-5-80
Source: Trainee. Honours: England Youth, Under-21, 74 full caps, 14 goals.

1997-98	Liverpool	0	0		
1998-99	Liverpool	12	0		
1999-2000	Liverpool	29	1		
2000-01	Liverpool	33	7		
2001-02	Liverpool	28	3		
2002-03	Liverpool	34	5		
2003-04	Liverpool	34	4		
2004-05	Liverpool	30	7		
2005-06	Liverpool	32	10		
2006-07	Liverpool	36	7		
2007-08	Liverpool	34	11		
2008-09	Liverpool	31	16	333	71

GULACSI, Peter (G) 18 0
H: 6 3 W: 13 01 b.Budapest 6-5-90
Source: MTK. Honours: Hungary Youth.

2007-08	Liverpool	0	0		
2008-09	Hereford U	18	0	18	0

HAMMILL, Adam (M) 74 3
H: 5 11 W: 11 07 b.Liverpool 25-1-88
Source: Scholar. Honours: England Youth.

2005-06	Liverpool	0	0		
2006-07	Dunfermline Ath	13	1	13	1
2007-08	Liverpool	0	0		
2007-08	Southampton	25	0	25	0
2008-09	Liverpool	0	0		
2008-09	Blackpool	22	1	22	1
2008-09	Barnsley	14	1	14	1

HANSEN, Martin (G) 0 0
H: 6 2 W: 12 07 b.Glostrup 15-6-90
Source: Brondby.

2007-08	Liverpool	0	0
2008-09	Liverpool	0	0

HIGHDALE, Sean (M) 0 0
b.Liverpool 4-3-91

2007-08	Liverpool	0	0
2008-09	Liverpool	0	0

HUTH, Ronald (D) 0 0
H: 6 2 W: 14 01 b.Asuncion 30-10-89
Source: Tacuary.

2006-07	Liverpool	0	0
2007-08	Liverpool	0	0
2008-09	Liverpool	0	0

HYYPIA, Sami (D) 481 28
H: 6 3 W: 13 09 b.Porvoo 7-10-73
Source: KuMu. Honours: Finland Youth, Under-21, 99 full caps, 5 goals.

1993	MyPa 47	12	0		
1994	MyPa 47	25	0		
1995	MyPa 47	26	3	63	3
1995-96	Willem II	14	0		
1996-97	Willem II	30	1		
1997-98	Willem II	30	0		
1998-99	Willem II	26	2	100	3
1999-2000	Liverpool	38	2		
2000-01	Liverpool	35	3		
2001-02	Liverpool	37	3		
2002-03	Liverpool	36	3		
2003-04	Liverpool	38	4		
2004-05	Liverpool	32	2		
2005-06	Liverpool	36	1		
2006-07	Liverpool	23	2		
2007-08	Liverpool	27	1		
2008-09	Liverpool	16	1	318	22

INSUA, Emiliano (D) 15 0
H: 5 10 W: 12 08 b.Buenos Aires 7-1-89
Source: Boca Juniors. Honours: Argentina Youth, Under-20, Under-23.

2006-07	Liverpool	2	0		
2007-08	Liverpool	3	0		
2008-09	Liverpool	10	0	15	0

IRWIN, Steven (D) 0 0
H: 5 8 W: 10 06 b.Liverpool 29-9-90
Source: Scholar.

2007-08	Liverpool	0	0
2008-09	Liverpool	0	0

ITANDJE, Charles (G) 179 0
H: 6 3 W: 13 01 b.Paris 2-11-82
Honours: France Under-21.

2000-01	Red Star 93	9	0	9	0
2001-02	Lens	0	0		
2002-03	Lens	22	0		
2003-04	Lens	35	0		
2004-05	Lens	38	0		
2005-06	Lens	37	0		
2006-07	Lens	38	0	170	0
2007-08	Liverpool	0	0		
2008-09	Liverpool	0	0		

KACANIKLIC, Alexander (M) 0 0
H: 5 11 W: 10 05 b.Sweden 13-8-91
Source: Scholar.

2008-09	Liverpool	0	0

KELLY, Martin (D) 7 1
H: 6 3 W: 12 02 b.Bolton 27-4-90
Source: From Scholar. Honours: England Youth.

2007-08	Liverpool	0	0		
2008-09	Liverpool	0	0		
2008-09	Huddersfield T	7	1	7	1

KUYT, Dirk (F) 365 149
H: 6 0 W: 12 02 b.Katwijk 22-7-80
Source: Quick Boys.Holland 53 full caps, 12 goals.

1998-99	Utrecht	28	5		
1999-2000	Utrecht	32	6		
2000-01	Utrecht	32	13		
2001-02	Utrecht	34	7		
2002-03	Utrecht	34	20	160	51
2003-04	Feyenoord	34	20		
2004-05	Feyenoord	34	29		
2005-06	Feyenoord	33	22	101	71
2006-07	Liverpool	34	12		
2007-08	Liverpool	32	3		
2008-09	Liverpool	38	12	104	27

LETO, Sebastian (M) 45 7
H: 6 2 W: 12 04 b.San Vicente 30-8-86

2006	Lanus	27	5		
2007	Lanus	18	2	45	7
2007-08	Liverpool	0	0		
2008-09	Liverpool	0	0		

LINDFIELD, Craig (F) 33 4
H: 6 0 W: 10 05 b.Wirral 7-9-88
Source: Scholar. Honours: England Youth.

2006-07	Liverpool	0	0		
2007-08	Liverpool	0	0		
2007-08	Notts Co	3	1	3	1
2007-08	Chester C	7	0	7	0
2008-09	Liverpool	0	0		
2008-09	Bournemouth	3	1	3	1
2008-09	Accrington S	20	2	20	2

LUCAS (M) 76 5
H: 5 10 W: 11 09 b.Dourados 9-1-87
Honours: Brazil Under-20, 2 full caps.

2005	Gremio	3	0		
2006	Gremio	30	4	33	4
2007-08	Liverpool	18	0		
2008-09	Liverpool	25	1	43	1

MACKAY-STEVEN, Gary (M)   0   0
H: 5 9   W: 11 03   b.Wick 31-8-90
Source: Ross Co.

| 2007-08 | Liverpool | 0 | 0 | | |
| 2008-09 | Liverpool | 0 | 0 | | |

MARTIN, David (G)   52   0
H: 6 1   W: 13 04   b.Romford 22-1-86
Source: From Scholar. *Honours:* England Youth, Under-20.

2003-04	Wimbledon	2	0	2	0
2004-05	Milton Keynes D	15	0		
2005-06	Milton Keynes D	0	0	15	0
2005-06	Liverpool	0	0		
2006-07	Liverpool	0	0		
2006-07	*Accrington S*	10	0	10	0
2007-08	Liverpool	0	0		
2008-09	Liverpool	0	0		
2008-09	*Leicester C*	25	0	25	0

MASCHERANO, Javier (M)   117   1
H: 5 7   W: 10 05   b.San Lorenzo 8-6-84
Honours: Argentina Youth, Under-20, Under-23, 49 full caps, 2 goals.

2003-04	River Plate	21	0		
2004-05	River Plate	25	0	46	0
2005	Corinthians	7	0	7	0
2006-07	West Ham U	5	0	5	0
2006-07	Liverpool	7	0		
2007-08	Liverpool	25	1		
2008-09	Liverpool	27	0	59	1

MENDY, Emmanuel (D)   0   0
H: 5 7   W: 11 09   b.Medina Gounass 30-3-90
Source: Murcia.

| 2008-09 | Liverpool | 0 | 0 | | |

MIHAYLOV, Nikolay (G)   44   0
H: 6 3   W: 14 00   b.Bulgaria 28-6-88

2004-05	Levski	10	0		
2005-06	Levski	21	0		
2006-07	Levski	13	0	44	0
2007-08	Liverpool	0	0		
2008-09	Liverpool	0	0		

N'GOG, David (F)   32   3
H: 6 3   W: 12 04   b.Paris 1-4-89
Honours: France Youth, Under-21.

2006-07	Paris St Germain	4	0		
2007-08	Paris St Germain	14	1	18	1
2008-09	Liverpool	14	2	14	2

NEMETH, Kristian (F)   38   14
H: 5 10   W: 11 07   b.Gyor 5-1-89

2005-06	MTK	13	2		
2006-07	MTK	24	12	37	14
2007-08	Liverpool	0	0		
2008-09	Liverpool	0	0		
2008-09	*Blackpool*	1	0	1	0

PACHECO, Daniel (F)   0   0
H: 5 6   W: 10 07   b.Malaga 5-1-91

| 2007-08 | Liverpool | 0 | 0 | | |
| 2008-09 | Liverpool | 0 | 0 | | |

PALETTA, Gabriel (D)   45   5
H: 6 3   W: 12 08   b.Longchamps 15-2-86
Honours: Argentina Under-20.

2004-05	Banfield	9	2		
2005-06	Banfield	33	3	42	5
2006-07	Liverpool	3	0		
2007-08	Liverpool	0	0		
2008-09	Liverpool	0	0	3	0

PALSSON, Victor (M)   0   0
H: 6 1   b.Iceland 30-4-91
Source: Aarhus. *Honours:* Iceland Youth.

| 2008-09 | Liverpool | 0 | 0 | | |

PENNANT, Jermaine (M)   187   12
H: 5 9   W: 10 06   b.Nottingham 15-1-83
Honours: England Schools, Youth, Under-21.

1998-99	Notts Co	0	0		
1998-99	Arsenal	0	0		
1999-2000	Arsenal	0	0		
2000-01	Arsenal	0	0		
2001-02	Arsenal	0	0		
2001-02	*Watford*	9	2		
2002-03	Arsenal	5	3		
2002-03	*Watford*	12	0	21	2
2003-04	Arsenal	0	0		
2003-04	*Leeds U*	36	2	36	2
2004-05	Arsenal	7	0	12	3
2004-05	Birmingham C	12	0		
2005-06	Birmingham C	38	2	50	2

2006-07	Liverpool	34	1		
2007-08	Liverpool	18	2		
2008-09	Liverpool	3	0	55	3
2008-09	*Portsmouth*	13	0	13	0

PEPPER, Adam (M)   0   0
| 2008-09 | Liverpool | 0 | 0 | | |

PLESSIS, Damien (M)   19   0
H: 6 3   W: 12 02   b.Neuvy-sous-Bois 5-3-88
Honours: France Youth.

2005-06	Lyon B	7	0		
2006-07	Lyon B	9	0	16	0
2007-08	Liverpool	2	0		
2008-09	Liverpool	1	0	3	0

POURIE, Marvin (F)   0   0
H: 6 0   W: 12 00   b.Germany 8-1-91

| 2007-08 | Liverpool | 0 | 0 | | |
| 2008-09 | Liverpool | 0 | 0 | | |

PUTTERILL, Ray (M)   0   0
H: 5 8   W: 12 03   b.Liverpool 2-3-89
Source: Scholar.

| 2007-08 | Liverpool | 0 | 0 | | |
| 2008-09 | Liverpool | 0 | 0 | | |

REINA, Jose (G)   275   0
H: 6 2   W: 14 06   b.Madrid 31-8-82
Honours: Spain Youth, Under-21, 15 full caps.

1999-2000	Barcelona B	30	0	30	0
2000-01	Barcelona	19	0		
2001-02	Barcelona	11	0	30	0
2002-03	Villarreal	33	0		
2003-04	Villarreal	38	0		
2004-05	Villarreal	0	0	71	0
2005-06	Liverpool	33	0		
2006-07	Liverpool	35	0		
2007-08	Liverpool	38	0		
2008-09	Liverpool	38	0	144	0

RIERA, Alberto (M)   260   33
H: 6 1   W: 12 01   b.Manacor 15-4-82
Honours: Spain Under-21, 13 full caps, 3 goals.

2000-01	Mallorca B	31	6		
2000-01	Mallorca	3	1		
2001-02	Mallorca	8	1		
2001-02	Mallorca B	16	5	47	11
2002-03	Mallorca	35	4	46	6
2003-04	Bordeaux	32	2		
2004-05	Bordeaux	21	2	53	4
2005-06	Espanyol	8	0		
2005-06	*Manchester C*	15	1	15	1
2006-07	Espanyol	28	4		
2007-08	Espanyol	35	4	71	8
2008-09	Liverpool	28	3	28	3

ROBERTS, Michael (M)   0   0
b.Liverpool 5-12-91

| 2008-09 | Liverpool | 0 | 0 | | |

ROQUE, Miguel (D)   4   0
H: 6 2   W: 12 03   b.Lleida 8-7-88
Source: EU Lleida.

2005-06	Liverpool	0	0		
2006-07	Liverpool	0	0		
2006-07	*Oldham Ath*	4	0	4	0
2007-08	Liverpool	0	0		
2008-09	Liverpool	0	0		

SAN JOSE DOMINGUEZ, Mikel (D) 0   0
H: 6 0   W: 12 04   b.Pamplona 30-5-89
Source: Athletic Bilbao.

| 2007-08 | Liverpool | 0 | 0 | | |
| 2008-09 | Liverpool | 0 | 0 | | |

SARIC, Nikola (F)   0   0
H: 6 0   W: 11 08   b.Sarajevo 6-1-91
Source: Herfolge. *Honours:* Denmark Youth.

| 2008-09 | Liverpool | 0 | 0 | | |

SIMON, Andras (F)   1   0
H: 6 0   W: 11 05   b.Salgotarjan 30-3-90

2006-07	MTK	1	0	1	0
2007-08	Liverpool	0	0		
2008-09	Liverpool	0	0		

SKRTEL, Martin (D)   144   3
H: 6 3   W: 12 10   b.Handlova 15-12-84
Honours: Slovakia 32 full caps, 5 goals.

2002-03	Trencin	1	0		
2003-04	Trencin	34	0	35	0
2004	Zenit	7	0		
2005	Zenit	18	1		
2006	Zenit	26	1		

2007	Zenit	23	1	74	3
2007-08	Liverpool	14	0		
2008-09	Liverpool	21	0	35	0

SPEARING, Jay (D)   0   0
H: 5 6   W: 11 01   b.Wallasey 25-11-88
Source: Scholar.

2006-07	Liverpool	0	0		
2007-08	Liverpool	0	0		
2008-09	Liverpool	0	0		

THRELFALL, Robbie (D)   14   0
H: 5 11   W: 11 00   b.Liverpool 25-11-88
Source: Scholar. *Honours:* England Youth.

2006-07	Liverpool	0	0		
2007-08	Liverpool	0	0		
2007-08	*Hereford U*	9	0		
2008-09	Liverpool	0	0		
2008-09	*Hereford U*	3	0	12	0
2008-09	*Stockport Co*	2	0	2	0

TORRES, Fernando (F)   231   113
H: 5 9   W: 12 03   b.Madrid 20-3-84
Honours: Spain 67 full caps, 22 goals.

2002-03	Atletico Madrid	29	13		
2003-04	Atletico Madrid	35	19		
2004-05	Atletico Madrid	38	16		
2005-06	Atletico Madrid	36	13		
2006-07	Atletico Madrid	36	14	174	75
2007-08	Liverpool	33	24		
2008-09	Liverpool	24	14	57	38

VORONIN, Andrei (F)   213   70
H: 5 11   W: 11 08   b.Odessa 21-7-79
Honours: Ukraine 53 full caps, 6 goals.

1997-98	M Gladbach	7	1		
1998-99	M Gladbach	0	0		
1999-2000	M Gladbach	2	0	9	1
2000-01	Mainz	10	1		
2001-02	Mainz	34	8		
2002-03	Mainz	31	20	75	29
2003-04	Cologne	19	4	19	4
2004-05	Leverkusen	31	14		
2005-06	Leverkusen	29	7		
2006-07	Leverkusen	31	10	91	31
2007-08	Liverpool	19	5		
2008-09	Liverpool	0	0	19	5

On loan to Hertha Berlin

WEIJL, Vincent (M)   0   0
H: 6 0   W: 12 04   b.Amsterdam 11-11-90

| 2008-09 | Liverpool | 0 | 0 | | |

XABI ALONSO (M)   272   24
H: 6 0   W: 12 02   b.Tolosa 25-11-81
Honours: Spain Under-21, 61 full caps, 5 goals.

1999-2000	Real Sociedad	0	0		
2000-01	Eibar	14	0	14	0
2000-01	Real Sociedad	18	0		
2001-02	Real Sociedad	29	3		
2002-03	Real Sociedad	33	3		
2003-04	Real Sociedad	35	3	115	9
2004-05	Liverpool	24	2		
2005-06	Liverpool	35	3		
2006-07	Liverpool	32	4		
2007-08	Liverpool	19	2		
2008-09	Liverpool	33	4	143	15

Scholars
Buchtmann, Christopher; Chamberlain, Deale; Duyan, Hakan Ashworth; Ellison, James; Ince, Thomas; Oldfield, Christopher.

LUTON T (49)

ANDREWS, Wayne (F)   191   39
H: 5 10   W: 11 06   b.Paddington 25-11-77
Source: Trainee.

1995-96	Watford	1	0		
1996-97	Watford	25	4		
1997-98	Watford	2	0		
1998-99	Watford	0	0	28	4
1998-99	*Cambridge U*	2	0	2	0
1998-99	*Peterborough U*	10	5	10	5

From Aldershot T, Chesham U

2001-02	Oldham Ath	0	0		
2002-03	Oldham Ath	37	11	37	11
2003-04	Colchester U	41	12		
2004-05	Colchester U	5	2	46	14
2004-05	Crystal Palace	9	0		
2005-06	Crystal Palace	24	1	33	1
2006-07	Coventry C	3	1		

2006-07	Sheffield W	9	1	9 1
2006-07	Bristol C	7	2	7 2
2007-08	Coventry C	7	0	
2007-08	Leeds U	1	0	1 0
2007-08	Bristol R	1	0	1 0
2008-09	Coventry U	0	0	10 1
2008-09	Luton T	7	0	7 0

ASAFU-ADJAYE, Ed (D) 26 0
H: 5 11 W: 12 04 b.Southwark 22-12-88
Source: Scholar.

2007-08	Luton T	7	0
2008-09	Luton T	19	0 26 0

BEAVAN, George (D) 6 0
H: 5 9 W: 12 02 b.Luton 12-1-90
Source: Scholar.

2007-08	Luton T	2	0
2008-09	Luton T	4	0 6 0

BRILL, Dean (G) 89 0
H: 6 2 W: 14 05 b.Luton 2-12-85
Source: Scholar.

2003-04	Luton T	5	0
2004-05	Luton T	0	0
2005-06	Luton T	5	0
2006-07	Luton T	11	0
2006-07	*Gillingham*	8	0 8 0
2007-08	Luton T	37	0
2008-09	Luton T	23	0 81 0

CHARLES, Ryan (F) 17 2
H: 6 0 W: 12 00 b.Enfield 30-9-89
Source: Scholar.

2007-08	Luton T	7	1
2008-09	Luton T	10	1 17 2

CRADDOCK, Tom (F) 36 11
H: 5 11 W: 11 10 b.Durham 14-10-86
Source: Scholar.

2005-06	Middlesbrough	1	0
2006-07	Middlesbrough	0	0
2006-07	*Wrexham*	1	1 1 1
2007-08	Middlesbrough	3	0
2007-08	*Hartlepool U*	4	0 4 0
2008-09	Middlesbrough	0	0 4 0
2008-09	Luton T	27	10 27 10

DAVIS, Sol (D) 316 3
H: 5 7 W: 12 04 b.Cheltenham 4-9-79
Source: Trainee.

1997-98	Swindon T	6	0
1998-99	Swindon T	25	0
1999-2000	Swindon T	29	0
2000-01	Swindon T	36	0
2001-02	Swindon T	21	0
2002-03	Swindon T	0	0 117 0
2002-03	Luton T	34	0
2003-04	Luton T	36	0
2004-05	Luton T	45	2
2005-06	Luton T	21	0
2006-07	Luton T	24	0
2007-08	Luton T	15	0
2008-09	Luton T	24	1 199 3

EMANUEL, Lewis (D) 219 7
H: 5 8 W: 12 01 b.Bradford 14-10-83
Source: Scholar. *Honours:* England Schools, Youth. Eire B.

2001-02	Bradford C	9	0
2002-03	Bradford C	29	0
2003-04	Bradford C	28	2
2004-05	Bradford C	36	0
2005-06	Bradford C	37	2 139 4
2006-07	Luton T	40	2
2007-08	Luton T	17	2
2007-08	*Brentford*	3	0 3 0
2008-09	Luton T	20	1 77 5

GALLEN, Kevin (F) 484 115
H: 5 11 W: 13 05 b.Hammersmith 21-9-75
Source: Trainee. *Honours:* England Schools, Youth, Under-21.

1992-93	QPR	0	0
1993-94	QPR	0	0
1994-95	QPR	37	10
1995-96	QPR	30	8
1996-97	QPR	2	3
1997-98	QPR	27	3
1998-99	QPR	44	8
1999-2000	QPR	31	4
2000-01	Huddersfield T	38	10 38 10
2001-02	Barnsley	9	2 9 2
2001-02	QPR	25	7
2002-03	QPR	42	13

2003-04	QPR	45	17	
2004-05	QPR	46	10	
2005-06	QPR	18	4	
2006-07	QPR	18	3	365 90
2006-07	*Plymouth Arg*	13	1	13 1
2007-08	Milton Keynes D	24	8	
2008-09	Milton Keynes D	6	1	30 9
2008-09	Luton T	29	3	29 3

GNAKPA, Claude (D) 55 1
H: 6 0 W: 13 05 b.Marseille 9-6-83
Source: Montpellier, Santander, Alaves, Vaduz.

2006-07	Swindon T	0	0
2007-08	Peterborough U	28	0 28 0
2008-09	Luton T	27	1 27 1

HALL, Asa (M) 69 13
H: 6 2 W: 11 09 b.Sandwell 29-11-86
Source: Scholar. *Honours:* England Youth, Under-20.

2004-05	Birmingham C	0	0
2005-06	Birmingham C	0	0
2005-06	*Boston U*	12	0 12 0
2006-07	Birmingham C	0	0
2007-08	Birmingham C	0	0
2007-08	*Shrewsbury T*	15	3 15 3
2008-09	Luton T	42	10 42 10

HENDERSON, Ian (F) 131 8
H: 5 10 W: 11 06 b.Thetford 24-1-85
Source: Scholar. *Honours:* England Youth, Under-20.

2002-03	Norwich C	20	1
2003-04	Norwich C	19	4
2004-05	Norwich C	3	0
2005-06	Norwich C	24	1
2006-07	Norwich C	2	0 68 6
2006-07	*Rotherham U*	18	1 18 1
2007-08	Northampton T	23	0
2008-09	Northampton T	3	0 26 0
2008-09	Luton T	19	1 19 1

HOWELLS, Jake (M) 29 0
H: 5 9 W: 11 08 b.St Albans 18-4-91
Source: Scholar.

2007-08	Luton T	1	0
2008-09	Luton T	28	0 29 0

JARVIS, Rossi (D) 56 1
H: 5 11 W: 11 12 b.Fakenham 11-3-88
Source: Scholar. *Honours:* England Youth.

2005-06	Norwich C	3	0
2006-07	Norwich C	0	0
2006-07	*Torquay U*	4	0 4 0
2006-07	*Rotherham U*	10	0 10 0
2007-08	Norwich C	4	0 7 0
2008-09	Luton T	35	1 35 1

KEANE, Keith (M) 129 4
H: 5 9 W: 12 02 b.Luton 20-11-86
Source: Scholar. *Honours:* Eire Youth, Under-21.

2003-04	Luton T	15	1
2004-05	Luton T	17	0
2005-06	Luton T	10	1
2006-07	Luton T	19	1
2007-08	Luton T	28	1
2008-09	Luton T	40	0 129 4

McVEIGH, Paul (F) 265 43
H: 5 7 W: 11 00 b.Belfast 6-12-77
Source: Trainee. *Honours:* Northern Ireland Schools, Youth, Under-21, 20 full caps.

1995-96	Tottenham H	0	0
1996-97	Tottenham H	3	1
1997-98	Tottenham H	0	0
1998-99	Tottenham H	0	0
1999-2000	Tottenham H	0	0 3 1
1999-2000	Norwich C	1	0
2000-01	Norwich C	11	1
2001-02	Norwich C	42	8
2002-03	Norwich C	44	14
2003-04	Norwich C	44	5
2004-05	Norwich C	17	1
2005-06	Norwich C	36	7
2006-07	Norwich C	21	0 216 36
2006-07	*Burnley*	8	3 8 3
2007-08	Luton T	25	0
2008-09	Luton T	13	3 38 3

MORGAN, Dean (M) 239 26
H: 5 11 W: 13 00 b.Enfield 3-10-83
Source: Scholar.

2000-01	Colchester U	4	0

2001-02	Colchester U	30	0	
2002-03	Colchester U	37	6	
2003-04	Colchester U	0	0	71 6
2003-04	Reading	13	1	
2004-05	Reading	18	2	31 3
2005-06	Luton T	36	6	
2006-07	Luton T	36	4	
2007-08	Luton T	16	1	
2007-08	*Southend U*	8	0	8 0
2007-08	*Crewe Alex*	9	1	9 1
2008-09	Luton T	0	0	88 11
2008-09	*Leyton Orient*	32	5	32 5

NICHOLLS, Kevin (M) 269 33
H: 5 10 W: 11 13 b.Newham 2-1-79
Source: Trainee. *Honours:* England Youth.

1995-96	Charlton Ath	0	0
1996-97	Charlton Ath	6	1
1997-98	Charlton Ath	6	0
1998-99	Charlton Ath	0	0 12 1
1998-99	*Brighton & HA*	4	1 4 1
1999-2000	Wigan Ath	8	0
2000-01	Wigan Ath	20	0 28 0
2001-02	Luton T	42	7
2002-03	Luton T	36	5
2003-04	Luton T	21	2
2004-05	Luton T	44	12
2005-06	Luton T	32	5
2006-07	Leeds U	13	0 13 0
2007-08	Preston NE	18	0 18 0
2008-09	Luton T	19	0 194 31

O'CONNOR, Gareth (M) 245 35
H: 5 10 W: 11 00 b.Dublin 10-11-78
Source: Bohemians.

1998-99	Shamrock R	8	0 8 0
1999-2000	Bohemians	22	4 22 4
2000-01	Bournemouth	22	1
2001-02	Bournemouth	28	0
2002-03	Bournemouth	41	8
2003-04	Bournemouth	37	2
2004-05	Bournemouth	40	13
2005-06	Burnley	29	7
2006-07	Burnley	8	0
2007-08	Burnley	1	0
2007-08	*Bournemouth*	6	0 174 24
2008-09	Burnley	0	0 38 7
2008-09	Luton T	3	0 3 0

PARKIN, Sam (F) 271 94
H: 6 2 W: 13 00 b.Roehampton 14-3-81
Honours: England Schools. Scotland B.

1998-99	Chelsea	0	0
1999-2000	Chelsea	0	0
2000-01	Chelsea	0	0
2000-01	Millwall	7	4 7 4
2000-01	*Wycombe W*	8	1 8 1
2000-01	*Oldham Ath*	7	3 7 3
2001-02	Chelsea	0	0
2001-02	*Northampton T*	40	4 40 4
2002-03	Swindon T	43	25
2003-04	Swindon T	40	19
2004-05	Swindon T	41	23 124 67
2005-06	Ipswich T	20	5
2006-07	Ipswich T	2	0 22 5
2006-07	Luton T	8	1
2007-08	Luton T	19	5
2008-09	Luton T	23	4 50 10
2008-09	*Leyton Orient*	13	0 13 0

PATRICK, Jordan (F) 2 0
H: 5 8 W: 11 00 b.Luton 10-10-92

2008-09	Luton T	2	0 2 0

PILKINGTON, George (D) 249 11
H: 5 11 W: 12 05 b.Rugeley 7-11-81
Source: Scholar. *Honours:* England Youth.

1998-99	Everton	0	0
1999-2000	Everton	0	0
2000-01	Everton	0	0
2001-02	Everton	0	0
2002-03	Everton	0	0
2002-03	*Exeter C*	7	0 7 0
2003-04	Port Vale	44	1
2004-05	Port Vale	43	0
2005-06	Port Vale	46	2
2006-07	Port Vale	46	6
2007-08	Port Vale	45	2 224 11
2008-09	Luton T	18	0 18 0

ROPER, Ian (D) 344 10
H: 6 3 W: 14 00 b.Nuneaton 20-6-77
Source: Trainee.

1994-95	Walsall	0	0

1995-96	Walsall	5	0		
1996-97	Walsall	11	0		
1997-98	Walsall	21	0		
1998-99	Walsall	32	1		
1999-2000	Walsall	34	1		
2000-01	Walsall	25	0		
2001-02	Walsall	27	0		
2002-03	Walsall	40	0		
2003-04	Walsall	33	0		
2004-05	Walsall	26	0		
2005-06	Walsall	25	0		
2006-07	Walsall	27	4		
2007-08	Walsall	19	1	325	7
2008-09	Luton T	19	3	19	3

TALBOT, Drew (F)   98   10
H: 5 10 W: 11 00 b.Barnsley 19-7-86
Source: Trainee.

2003-04	Sheffield W	0	0		
2004-05	Sheffield W	21	4		
2005-06	Sheffield W	0	0		
2006-07	Sheffield W	8	0	29	4
2006-07	Scunthorpe U	3	1	3	1
2006-07	Luton T	15	3		
2007-08	Luton T	27	0		
2008-09	Luton T	7	0	49	3
2008-09	Chesterfield	17	2	17	2

UNDERWOOD, Paul (M)   177   6
H: 5 9 W: 12 13 b.Wimbledon 16-8-73
Source: Enfield.

2001-02	Rushden & D	40	0		
2002-03	Rushden & D	40	1		
2003-04	Rushden & D	30	0	110	1
2003-04	Luton T	1	0		
2004-05	Luton T	37	5		
2005-06	Luton T	29	0		
2006-07	Luton T	0	0		
2007-08	Luton T	0	0		
2008-09	Luton T	0	0	67	5

WATSON, Kevin (M)   402   13
H: 6 0 W: 12 06 b.Hackney 3-1-74
Source: Trainee.

1991-92	Tottenham H	0	0		
1992-93	Tottenham H	5	0		
1993-94	Tottenham H	0	0		
1993-94	Brentford	3	0	3	0
1994-95	Tottenham H	0	0		
1994-95	Bristol C	2	0	2	0
1994-95	Barnet	13	0	13	0
1995-96	Tottenham H	0	0	5	0
1996-97	Swindon T	27	1		
1997-98	Swindon T	18	0		
1998-99	Swindon T	18	0	63	1
1999-2000	Rotherham U	44	1		
2000-01	Rotherham U	46	5		
2001-02	Rotherham U	19	1	109	7
2001-02	Reading	12	1		
2002-03	Reading	32	1		
2003-04	Reading	22	0	66	2
2004-05	Colchester U	44	2		
2005-06	Colchester U	44	0		
2006-07	Colchester U	40	1		
2007-08	Colchester U	7	0	135	3
2008-09	Luton T	6	0	6	0

MACCLESFIELD T (50)

BAINS, Rikki (D)   5   0
H: 6 1 W: 13 00 b.Coventry 3-2-88
Source: Scholar.

2006-07	Coventry C	0	0		
2006-07	Accrington S	3	0	3	0

From Tamworth, Corby.

2008-09	Macclesfield T	2	0	2	0

BELL, Lee (M)   118   5
H: 5 11 W: 12 04 b.Crewe 26-1-83
Source: Scholar.

2000-01	Crewe Alex	0	0		
2001-02	Crewe Alex	0	0		
2002-03	Crewe Alex	17	1		
2003-04	Crewe Alex	3	0		
2004-05	Crewe Alex	17	0		
2005-06	Crewe Alex	17	2		
2006-07	Crewe Alex	0	0	54	3
2007-08	Mansfield T	23	1	23	1
2008-09	Macclesfield T	41	1	41	1

BRAIN, Jonny (G)   143   0
H: 6 3 W: 13 05 b.Carlisle 11-2-83
Source: Newcastle U Trainee.

2003-04	Port Vale	32	0		
2004-05	Port Vale	27	0		
2005-06	Port Vale	0	0	59	0
2006-07	Macclesfield T	9	0		
2007-08	Macclesfield T	29	0		
2008-09	Macclesfield T	46	0	84	0

BRISLEY, Shaun (M)   48   2
H: 6 2 W: 12 02 b.Stockport 6-5-90
Source: Scholar.

2007-08	Macclesfield T	10	2		
2008-09	Macclesfield T	38	0	48	2

BROWN, Nat (F)   200   14
H: 6 2 W: 12 05 b.Sheffield 15-6-81
Source: Trainee.

1999-2000	Huddersfield T	0	0		
2000-01	Huddersfield T	0	0		
2001-02	Huddersfield T	0	0		
2002-03	Huddersfield T	38	0		
2003-04	Huddersfield T	21	0		
2004-05	Huddersfield T	17	0	76	0
2005-06	Lincoln C	39	7		
2006-07	Lincoln C	28	1		
2007-08	Lincoln C	27	0	94	8

on loan from Wrexham

2008-09	Macclesfield T	30	6	30	6

CHALMERS, Aaron (M)   2   0
H: 5 10 W: 12 08 b.Manchester 2-2-91
Source: Scholar.

2007-08	Oldham Ath	2	0	2	0
2008-09	Macclesfield T	0	0		

DEEN, Ahmed (M)   33   0
H: 5 9 W: 11 05 b.Sierra Leone 30-6-85
Source: Leicester C Scholar. *Honours:* Sierra Leone 10 full caps.

2004-05	Peterborough U	5	0	5	0

From Aldershot T, St Albans C.

2008-09	Macclesfield T	28	0	28	0

DENNIS, Kristian (F)   4   1
H: 5 11 W: 11 00 b.Macclesfield 12-3-90
Source: Scholar.

2007-08	Macclesfield T	1	0		
2008-09	Macclesfield T	3	1	4	1

EVANS, Gary (F)   82   19
H: 6 0 W: 12 08 b.Macclesfield 26-4-88
Source: Crewe Alex.

2007-08	Macclesfield T	42	7		
2008-09	Macclesfield T	40	12	82	19

FLYNN, Matthew (D)   28   0
H: 6 0 W: 11 08 b.Warrington 10-5-89
Source: Warrington T.

2007-08	Macclesfield T	0	0		
2008-09	Macclesfield T	28	0	28	0

GREEN, Francis (F)   318   51
H: 5 9 W: 11 04 b.Nottingham 25-4-80
Source: Ilkeston T.

1997-98	Peterborough U	4	1		
1998-99	Peterborough U	7	1		
1999-2000	Peterborough U	20	1		
2000-01	Peterborough U	32	6		
2001-02	Peterborough U	23	3		
2002-03	Peterborough U	19	2		
2003-04	Peterborough U	3	0	108	14
2003-04	Lincoln C	35	7		
2004-05	Lincoln C	37	8		
2005-06	Lincoln C	28	3	100	18
2005-06	Boston U	6	1		
2006-07	Boston U	39	4	45	5
2007-08	Macclesfield T	41	11		
2008-09	Macclesfield T	24	3	65	14

HADFIELD, Jordan (M)   69   1
H: 5 10 W: 11 04 b.Swinton 12-8-87
Source: Trainee.

2004-05	Stockport Co	1	0		
2005-06	Stockport Co	0	0	1	0
2006-07	Macclesfield T	37	1		
2007-08	Macclesfield T	2	0		
2007-08	Milton Keynes D	13	0	13	0
2008-09	Macclesfield T	16	0	55	1

HARVEY, Neil (F)   5   0
H: 6 1 W: 12 04 b.London 6-8-83
Source: Retford U. *Honours:* Barbados 4 full caps, 2 goals.

2008-09	Macclesfield T	5	0	5	0

HESSEY, Sean (D)   199   2
H: 5 11 W: 12 08 b.Whiston 19-9-78
Source: Liverpool Trainee.

1997-98	Wigan Ath	0	0		
1997-98	Leeds U	0	0		
1997-98	Huddersfield T	1	0		
1998-99	Huddersfield T	10	0	11	0
1999-2000	Kilmarnock	11	0		
2000-01	Kilmarnock	6	0		
2001-02	Kilmarnock	15	0		
2002-03	Kilmarnock	5	0		
2003-04	Kilmarnock	7	1	44	1
2003-04	Blackpool	6	0	6	0
2004-05	Chester C	34	1		
2005-06	Chester C	19	0		
2006-07	Chester C	26	0		
2007-08	Chester C	0	0	79	1
2008-09	Macclesfield T	33	0	59	0

HIRST, Chris (M)   0   0
H: 5 11 W: 10 00 b.Stockport 24-9-88

2008-09	Macclesfield T	0	0		

JENNINGS, James (D)   38   0
H: 5 10 W: 11 02 b.Manchester 2-9-87
Source: Scholar.

2006-07	Macclesfield T	9	0		
2007-08	Macclesfield T	11	0		
2008-09	Macclesfield T	18	0	38	0

LIBURD, Patrece (D)   1   0
H: 5 9 W: 11 05 b.Basseterr 1-3-88
Source: Nottingham F, Worcester C, Dorchester T. *Honours:* St Kitts 1 full cap.

2008-09	Macclesfield T	1	0	1	0

MILLAR, Christian (M)   4   0
H: 5 11 W: 11 00 b.Stoke 23-11-89

2007-08	Macclesfield T	2	0		
2008-09	Macclesfield T	2	0	4	0

MUKENDI, Vinny (F)   1   0
H: 6 2 W: 12 00 b.Bury 12-3-92
Source: Scholar.

2008-09	Macclesfield T	1	0	1	0

REID, Izak (M)   71   4
H: 5 5 W: 10 05 b.Sheffield 8-7-87
Source: Scholar.

2006-07	Macclesfield T	8	0		
2007-08	Macclesfield T	25	2		
2008-09	Macclesfield T	38	2	71	4

ROONEY, John (F)   16   2
H: 5 10 W: 12 00 b.Liverpool 17-12-90
Source: Scholar.

2007-08	Macclesfield T	2	0		
2008-09	Macclesfield T	14	2	16	2

TEAGUE, Andrew (D)   44   2
H: 6 2 W: 12 00 b.Preston 5-2-86
Source: Scholar.

2004-05	Macclesfield T	5	0		
2005-06	Macclesfield T	25	1		
2006-07	Macclesfield T	13	1		
2007-08	Macclesfield T	1	0		
2008-09	Macclesfield T	0	0	44	2

THOMAS, Danny (M)   248   18
H: 5 7 W: 10 10 b.Leamington Spa 1-5-81
Source: Trainee.

1997-98	Nottingham F	0	0		
1997-98	Leicester C	0	0		
1998-99	Leicester C	0	0		
1999-2000	Leicester C	3	0		
2000-01	Leicester C	0	0		
2001-02	Leicester C	0	0	3	0
2001-02	Bournemouth	12	0		
2002-03	Bournemouth	37	2		
2003-04	Bournemouth	10	0	59	2
2003-04	Boston U	8	3		
2004-05	Boston U	39	3		
2005-06	Boston U	35	2		
2006-07	Boston U	0	0	82	8
2006-07	Shrewsbury T	6	0	6	0
2006-07	Hereford U	15	2	15	2
2007-08	Macclesfield T	43	4		
2008-09	Macclesfield T	40	2	83	6

TOLLEY, Jamie (M) 223 17
H: 6 1 W: 11 03 b.Ludlow 12-5-83
Source: Scholarship. *Honours:* Wales Under-21.

1999-2000	Shrewsbury T	2	0	
2000-01	Shrewsbury T	24	2	
2001-02	Shrewsbury T	23	1	
2002-03	Shrewsbury T	39	3	
2003-04	Shrewsbury T	0	0	
2004-05	Shrewsbury T	36	4	
2005-06	Shrewsbury T	36	4	160 14
2006-07	Macclesfield T	23	1	
2007-08	Macclesfield T	24	2	
2008-09	Macclesfield T	16	0	63 3

TOWNS, Matt (G) 0 0
H: 6 1 b.Macclesfield 12-9-82

2008-09	Macclesfield T	0	0

WALKER, Richard (D) 144 6
H: 6 2 W: 12 08 b.Stafford 17-9-80
Source: Brook House.

1999-2000	Crewe Alex	0	0	
2000-01	Crewe Alex	3	0	
2001-02	Crewe Alex	1	0	
2002-03	Crewe Alex	35	2	
2003-04	Crewe Alex	20	1	
2004-05	Crewe Alex	23	2	
2005-06	Crewe Alex	18	1	100 6
2006-07	Port Vale	16	0	
2006-07	*Wrexham*	3	0	3 0
2007-08	Port Vale	0	0	16 0
2007-08	Macclesfield T	10	0	
2008-09	Macclesfield T	15	0	25 0

YEO, Simon (F) 224 59
H: 5 10 W: 11 08 b.Stockport 20-10-73
Source: Hyde U.

2002-03	Lincoln C	37	5	
2003-04	Lincoln C	41	11	
2004-05	Lincoln C	44	21	
From New Zealand Knights				
2005-06	Lincoln C	12	5	134 42
2006-07	Peterborough U	13	2	13 2
2006-07	Chester C	15	4	
2007-08	Chester C	21	4	36 8
2007-08	Bury	8	0	8 0
2008-09	Macclesfield T	33	7	33 7

MANCHESTER C (51)

BALL, David (F) 0 0
b.Whitefield 14-12-89
Source: Scholar.

2007-08	Manchester C	0	0
2008-09	Manchester C	0	0

BALL, Michael (D) 238 9
H: 5 11 W: 11 12 b.Liverpool 2-10-79
Source: Trainee. *Honours:* England Schools, Youth, Under-21, 1 full cap.

1996-97	Everton	5	0	
1997-98	Everton	25	1	
1998-99	Everton	37	3	
1999-2000	Everton	25	1	
2000-01	Everton	29	3	121 8
2001-02	Rangers	8	0	
2002-03	Rangers	0	0	
2003-04	Rangers	32	1	
2004-05	Rangers	15	0	
2005-06	Rangers	2	0	57 1
2005-06	PSV Eindhoven	12	0	
2006-07	PSV Eindhoven	0	0	12 0
2006-07	Manchester C	12	0	
2007-08	Manchester C	28	0	
2008-09	Manchester C	8	0	48 0

BELLAMY, Craig (F) 309 102
H: 5 9 W: 10 12 b.Cardiff 13-7-79
Source: Trainee. *Honours:* Wales Schools, Youth, Under-21, 56 full caps, 16 goals.

1996-97	Norwich C	3	0	
1997-98	Norwich C	36	13	
1998-99	Norwich C	40	17	
1999-2000	Norwich C	4	2	
2000-01	Norwich C	1	0	84 32
2000-01	Coventry C	34	6	34 6
2001-02	Newcastle U	27	9	
2002-03	Newcastle U	29	7	
2003-04	Newcastle U	14	5	
2004-05	Newcastle U	21	7	93 27
2004-05	*Celtic*	12	7	12 7

2005-06	Blackburn R	27	13	27 13
2006-07	Liverpool	27	7	27 7
2007-08	West Ham U	8	2	
2008-09	West Ham U	16	5	24 7
2008-09	Manchester C	8	3	8 3

BEN HAIM, Tal (D) 201 3
H: 5 11 W: 11 09 b.Rishon Le Zion 31-3-82
Source: Maccabi Tel Aviv. *Honours:* Israel Under-21, 49 full caps.

2000-01	Maccabi Tel Aviv	1	0	
2001-02	Maccabi Tel Aviv	29	1	
2002-03	Maccabi Tel Aviv	30	0	
2003-04	Maccabi Tel Aviv	26	1	86 2
2004-05	Bolton W	21	1	
2005-06	Bolton W	35	0	
2006-07	Bolton W	32	0	88 1
2007-08	Chelsea	13	0	13 0
2008-09	Manchester C	9	0	9 0
2008-09	Sunderland	5	0	5 0

BENALI, Ahmed (M) 0 0
b.Libya 7-2-92
Source: Scholar.

2008-09	Manchester C	0	0

BERTI, Glauber (D) 52 0
H: 6 2 W: 12 01 b.Sao Jose do Rio Preto 5-8-83

2005-06	Nuremberg	12	0	
2006-07	Nuremberg	20	0	
2007-08	Nuremberg	19	0	51 0
2008-09	Manchester C	1	0	1 0

BOJINOV, Valeri (F) 130 30
H: 5 10 W: 12 04 b.Oriahovizca 15-2-86
Honours: Bulgaria 21 full caps, 5 goals.

2001-02	Lecce	2	0	
2002-03	Lecce	15	2	
2003-04	Lecce	28	3	
2004-05	Lecce	20	11	65 16
2004-05	Fiorentina	9	2	
2005-06	Fiorentina	27	6	36 8
2006-07	Juventus	18	5	18 5
2007-08	Manchester C	3	0	
2008-09	Manchester C	8	1	11 1

BOYATA, Anga (M) 0 0
Source: Scholar.

2008-09	Manchester C	0	0

BRIDGE, Wayne (D) 267 9
H: 5 10 W: 12 13 b.Southampton 5-8-80
Source: From Trainee. *Honours:* England Youth, Under-21, 33 full caps, 1 goal.

1997-98	Southampton	0	0	
1998-99	Southampton	23	0	
1999-2000	Southampton	19	1	
2000-01	Southampton	38	0	
2001-02	Southampton	38	0	
2002-03	Southampton	34	1	152 2
2003-04	Chelsea	33	1	
2004-05	Chelsea	15	0	
2005-06	Chelsea	0	0	
2005-06	Fulham	12	0	12 0
2006-07	Chelsea	22	0	
2007-08	Chelsea	11	0	
2008-09	Chelsea	6	0	87 1
2008-09	Manchester C	16	0	16 0

BROWN, Matthew (D) 0 0
Source: Scholar.

2007-08	Manchester C	0	0
2008-09	Manchester C	0	0

CAICEDO, Felipe (F) 72 15
H: 6 1 W: 12 08 b.Guayaquil 5-9-88
Source: Rocafuerte. *Honours:* Ecuador 27 full caps, 3 goals.

2006-07	Basle	27	7	
2007-08	Basle	18	4	45 11
2007-08	Manchester C	10	0	
2008-09	Manchester C	17	4	27 4

CLAYTON, Adam (M) 0 0
H: 5 9 W: 11 11 b.Manchester 14-1-89
Source: Scholar.

2007-08	Manchester C	0	0
2008-09	Manchester C	0	0

CUNNINGHAM, Gregory (M) 0 0
b. 31-1-91
Source: Scholar.

2008-09	Manchester C	0	0

DALY, Ian (F) 0 0
b.Dublin 20-3-90
Source: From Scholar. *Honours:* Eire Youth.

2007-08	Manchester C	0	0
2008-09	Manchester C	0	0

DALY, Michael (M) 0 0

2006-07	Manchester C	0	0
2007-08	Manchester C	0	0
2008-09	Manchester C	0	0

DE JONG, Nigel (D) 178 11
H: 5 8 W: 11 05 b.Amsterdam 30-11-84
Honours: Holland 34 full caps, 1 goal.

2002-03	Ajax	17	0	
2003-04	Ajax	32	1	
2004-05	Ajax	31	5	
2005-06	Hamburg	12	1	
2005-06	Ajax	16	2	96 8
2006-07	Hamburg	18	1	
2007-08	Hamburg	29	1	
2008-09	Hamburg	7	0	66 3
2008-09	Manchester C	16	0	16 0

DUNNE, Richard (D) 354 8
H: 6 2 W: 15 10 b.Dublin 21-9-79
Source: Trainee. *Honours:* Eire Schools, Youth, Under-21, B, 52 full caps, 7 goals.

1996-97	Everton	7	0	
1997-98	Everton	3	0	
1998-99	Everton	16	0	
1999-2000	Everton	31	0	
2000-01	Everton	3	0	60 0
2000-01	Manchester C	25	0	
2001-02	Manchester C	43	1	
2002-03	Manchester C	29	0	
2003-04	Manchester C	29	0	
2004-05	Manchester C	35	2	
2005-06	Manchester C	32	3	
2006-07	Manchester C	38	1	
2007-08	Manchester C	36	0	
2008-09	Manchester C	31	1	294 8

ELANO (M) 242 61
H: 5 9 W: 10 03 b.Iracemapolis 14-6-81
Source: Guarani, Internacional. *Honours:* Brazil 34 full caps, 6 goals.

2001	Santos	24	2	
2002	Santos	28	8	
2003	Santos	39	8	
2004	Santos	40	15	131 33
2004-05	Shakhter Donetsk	13	4	
2005-06	Shakhter Donetsk	25	5	
2006-07	Shakhter Donetsk	11	5	49 14
2007-08	Manchester C	34	8	
2008-09	Manchester C	28	6	62 14

ETUHU, Kelvin (F) 18 3
H: 5 11 W: 11 02 b.Kano 30-5-88
Source: Scholar.

2005-06	Manchester C	0	0	
2006-07	Manchester C	0	0	
2006-07	*Rochdale*	4	2	4 2
2007-08	Manchester C	6	1	
2007-08	*Leicester C*	4	0	4 0
2008-09	Manchester C	4	0	10 1

EVANS, Ched (F) 44 11
H: 6 0 W: 12 00 b.Rhyl 28-12-88
Source: Scholar. *Honours:* Wales Under-21, 10 full caps, 2 goals.

2006-07	Manchester C	0	0	
2007-08	Manchester C	0	0	
2007-08	*Norwich C*	28	10	28 10
2008-09	Manchester C	16	1	16 1

GARRIDO, Javier (M) 126 2
H: 5 10 W: 11 11 b.Irun 15-3-85
Honours: Spain Under-21.

2004-05	Real Sociedad	28	0	
2005-06	Real Sociedad	33	0	
2006-07	Real Sociedad	25	1	86 1
2007-08	Manchester C	27	0	
2008-09	Manchester C	13	1	40 1

GELSON (M) 142 4
H: 6 0 W: 11 03 b.Cape Verde Isl 2-9-86
Honours: Switzerland Under-21, 17 full caps, 1 goal.

2002-03	Sion	6	0	
2003-04	Sion	28	0	
2004-05	Sion	9	0	
2005-06	Sion	22	0	
2006-07	Sion	34	1	99 1

| 2007-08 | Manchester C | 26 | 2 | | |
| 2008-09 | Manchester C | 17 | 1 | 43 | 3 |

GIVEN, Shay (G) 393 0
H: 6 0 W: 13 03 b.Lifford 20-4-76
Source: Celtic. Honours: Eire Youth,
Under-21, 96 full caps.

1994-95	Blackburn R	0	0		
1994-95	Swindon T	0	0		
1995-96	Blackburn R	0	0		
1995-96	Swindon T	5	0	5	0
1995-96	Sunderland	17	0	17	0
1996-97	Blackburn R	2	0	2	0
1997-98	Newcastle U	24	0		
1998-99	Newcastle U	31	0		
1999-2000	Newcastle U	14	0		
2000-01	Newcastle U	34	0		
2001-02	Newcastle U	38	0		
2002-03	Newcastle U	38	0		
2003-04	Newcastle U	38	0		
2004-05	Newcastle U	36	0		
2005-06	Newcastle U	38	0		
2006-07	Newcastle U	22	0		
2007-08	Newcastle U	19	0		
2008-09	Newcastle U	22	0	354	0
2008-09	Manchester C	15	0	15	0

HAMANN, Dietmar (M) 373 18
H: 6 2 W: 13 00 b.Waldasson 27-8-73
Source: Wacker Munich. Honours: Germany
Youth, Under-21, 59 full caps, 5 goals.

1993-94	Bayern Munich	5	1		
1994-95	Bayern Munich	30	0		
1995-96	Bayern Munich	20	2		
1996-97	Bayern Munich	22	1		
1997-98	Bayern Munich	28	2	105	6
1998-99	Newcastle U	23	4	23	4
1999-2000	Liverpool	28	1		
2000-01	Liverpool	30	2		
2001-02	Liverpool	31	1		
2002-03	Liverpool	30	2		
2003-04	Liverpool	25	2		
2004-05	Liverpool	30	0		
2005-06	Liverpool	17	0	191	8
2006-07	Manchester C	16	0		
2007-08	Manchester C	29	0		
2008-09	Manchester C	9	0	54	0

HART, Joe (G) 113 0
H: 6 3 W: 13 03 b.Shrewsbury 19-4-87
Source: Scholar, England Youth, Under-21, 1
full cap.

2004-05	Shrewsbury T	6	0		
2005-06	Shrewsbury T	46	0	52	0
2006-07	Manchester C	1	0		
2006-07	Tranmere R	6	0	6	0
2006-07	Blackpool	5	0	5	0
2007-08	Manchester C	26	0		
2008-09	Manchester C	23	0	50	0

HARTLEY, Gregory (M) 0 0
Source: Scholar.

| 2008-09 | Manchester C | 0 | 0 | | |

IBRAHIM, Abdisalam (M) 0 0
Source: Scholar.

| 2008-09 | Manchester C | 0 | 0 | | |

IRELAND, Stephen (F) 116 14
H: 5 8 W: 10 07 b.Cork 22-8-86
Source: From Scholar. Honours: Eire Youth,
Under-21, 6 full caps, 4 goals.

2005-06	Manchester C	24	0		
2006-07	Manchester C	24	1		
2007-08	Manchester C	33	4		
2008-09	Manchester C	35	9	116	14

JO (F) 155 49
H: 5 9 W: 11 00 b.Sao Paulo 20-3-87
Honours: Brazil Under-23, 3 full caps.

2003	Corinthians	14	1		
2004	Corinthians	42	8		
2005	Corinthians	25	4	81	13
2006	CSKA Moscow	18	14		
2007	CSKA Moscow	27	13		
2008	CSKA Moscow	8	3	53	30
2008-09	Manchester C	9	1	9	1
2008-09	Everton	12	5	12	5

JOHANSEN, Tobias (G) 0 0
b.Tonsberg 29-8-90
Source: Scholar.

| 2007-08 | Manchester C | 0 | 0 | | |
| 2008-09 | Manchester C | 0 | 0 | | |

JOHNSON, Michael (M) 36 2
H: 6 1 W: 12 07 b.Urmston 3-3-88
Source: Scholar. Honours: England Youth,
Under-21.

2005-06	Manchester C	0	0		
2006-07	Manchester C	10	0		
2007-08	Manchester C	23	2		
2008-09	Manchester C	3	0	36	2

KAY, Scott (D) 0 0
b.Denton 18-9-89
Source: Scholar.

| 2007-08 | Manchester C | 0 | 0 | | |
| 2008-09 | Manchester C | 0 | 0 | | |

KOMPANY, Vincent (D) 124 6
H: 6 3 W: 13 05 b.Brussels 10-4-86
Honours: Belgium 28 full caps.

2004-05	Anderlecht	29	2		
2005-06	Anderlecht	32	2	61	4
2006-07	Hamburg	6	0		
2007-08	Hamburg	22	1		
2008-09	Hamburg	1	0	29	1
2008-09	Manchester C	34	1	34	1

LOGAN, Shaleum (M) 17 2
H: 6 1 W: 12 07 b.Manchester 6-11-88
Source: Scholar.

2006-07	Manchester C	0	0		
2007-08	Manchester C	0	0		
2007-08	Grimsby T	5	2	5	2
2007-08	Scunthorpe U	4	0	4	0
2007-08	Stockport Co	7	0	7	0
2008-09	Manchester C	1	0	1	0

MAK, Robert (M) 0 0
Source: Scholar.

| 2008-09 | Manchester C | 0 | 0 | | |

MANCINI, Filippo (F) 0 0
b.Genoa 13-10-90
Source: Internazionale.

| 2007-08 | Manchester C | 0 | 0 | | |
| 2008-09 | Manchester C | 0 | 0 | | |

MARSHALL, Paul (M) 15 1
H: 6 1 W: 12 03 b.Manchester 9-7-89
Source: Scholar.

2007-08	Manchester C	0	0		
2008-09	Manchester C	0	0		
2008-09	Blackpool	2	0	2	0
2008-09	Port Vale	13	1	13	1

MARTIN, Richard (G) 0 0
H: 6 2 W: 12 13 b.Chelmsford 1-9-87
Source: Scholar.

2005-06	Brighton & HA	0	0		
2006-07	Brighton & HA	0	0		
2007-08	Manchester C	0	0		
2008-09	Manchester C	0	0		

McDERMOTT, Donal (F) 1 0
H: 6 6 W: 12 00 b.Dublin 19-10-89
Source: Scholar. Honours: Eire Youth.

2007-08	Manchester C	0	0		
2008-09	Manchester C	0	0		
2008-09	Milton Keynes D	1	0	1	0

McDONALD, Clayton (D) 4 0
H: 6 6 W: 16 05 b.Liverpool 26-12-88
Source: Scholar.

2007-08	Manchester C	0	0		
2008-09	Manchester C	0	0		
2008-09	Macclesfield T	2	0	2	0
2008-09	Chesterfield	2	0	2	0

McGIVERN, Ryan (D) 5 1
H: 5 10 W: 11 07 b.Newry 8-1-90
Source: Scholar. Honours: Northern Ireland
Youth, B, 6 full caps.

2007-08	Manchester C	0	0		
2008-09	Manchester C	0	0		
2008-09	Morecambe	5	1	5	1

MEE, Ben (D) 0 0
b.Sale 21-9-89
Source: Scholar. Honours: England Youth.

| 2007-08 | Manchester C | 0 | 0 | | |
| 2008-09 | Manchester C | 0 | 0 | | |

MENTEL, Filip (G) 0 0
b.Bratislava 2-2-90
Source: Scholar.

| 2007-08 | Manchester C | 0 | 0 | | |
| 2008-09 | Manchester C | 0 | 0 | | |

MILLS, Danny (D) 321 7
H: 5 11 W: 12 13 b.Norwich 18-5-77
Source: Trainee. Honours: England Youth,
Under-21, 19 full caps.

1994-95	Norwich C	0	0		
1995-96	Norwich C	14	0		
1996-97	Norwich C	32	0		
1997-98	Norwich C	20	0	66	0
1997-98	Charlton Ath	9	1		
1998-99	Charlton Ath	36	2		
1999-2000	Leeds U	17	1		
2000-01	Leeds U	23	0		
2001-02	Leeds U	28	1		
2002-03	Leeds U	33	1		
2003-04	Leeds U	0	0	101	3
2003-04	Middlesbrough	28	0	28	0
2004-05	Manchester C	32	0		
2005-06	Manchester C	18	1		
2006-07	Manchester C	1	0		
2006-07	Hull C	9	0	9	0
2007-08	Manchester C	0	0		
2007-08	Charlton Ath	19	0	64	3
2007-08	Derby Co	2	0	2	0
2008-09	Manchester C	0	0	51	1

MOORE, Karl (M) 6 0
H: 5 7 W: 9 12 b.Dublin 9-11-88
Source: Scholar. Honours: Eire Under-21.

2006-07	Manchester C	0	0		
2007-08	Manchester C	0	0		
2008-09	Manchester C	0	0		
2008-09	Millwall	6	0	6	0

MORRIS, Benjamin (M) 0 0
Source: Scholar.

| 2008-09 | Manchester C | 0 | 0 | | |

MWARUWARI, Benjamin (F) 233 63
H: 6 2 W: 12 03 b.Harare 13-8-78
Honours: Zimbabwe 33 full caps, 9 goals.

1999-2000	Jomo Cosmos	15	7		
2000-01	Jomo Cosmos	30	13	45	20
2001-02	Grasshoppers	25	1	25	1
2002-03	Auxerre	27	7		
2003-04	Auxerre	3	0		
2004-05	Auxerre	31	11		
2005-06	Auxerre	11	1	72	19
2005-06	Portsmouth	16	1		
2006-07	Portsmouth	31	6		
2007-08	Portsmouth	23	12	70	19
2007-08	Manchester C	13	3		
2008-09	Manchester C	8	1	21	4

NIELSEN, Gunnar (G) 0 0
H: 6 3 W: 14 00 b.Faeroes 7-10-86
Source: Frem. Honours: Faeroes Under-21.

| 2007-08 | Blackburn R | 0 | 0 | | |
| 2008-09 | Manchester C | 0 | 0 | | |

NIMELY-TCHUIMENI, Alex (F) 0 0
b.Monrovia 11-5-91
Source: Mighty Barolle, Cotonsport Garoua,
Manchester C Scholar. Honours: Liberia
Youth.

| 2008-09 | Manchester C | 0 | 0 | | |

OBENG, Curtis (D) 0 0
H: 5 8 W: 10 08 b.Manchester 14-2-89
Source: Scholar. Honours: England Youth.

| 2007-08 | Manchester C | 0 | 0 | | |
| 2008-09 | Manchester C | 0 | 0 | | |

ONUOHA, Nedum (D) 84 2
H: 6 2 W: 12 04 b.Warri 12-11-86
Source: Scholar. Honours: England Youth,
Under-20, Under-21.

2004-05	Manchester C	17	0		
2005-06	Manchester C	10	0		
2006-07	Manchester C	18	0		
2007-08	Manchester C	16	1		
2008-09	Manchester C	23	1	84	2

PETROV, Martin (F) 290 58
H: 6 0 W: 12 02 b.Vzatza 15-1-79
Honours: Bulgaria 76 full caps, 16 goals.

1996-97	CSKA Sofia	3	0		
1997-98	CSKA Sofia	4	0	7	0
1998-99	Servette	12	2		
1999-2000	Servette	31	9		
2000-01	Servette	32	11	75	22
2001-02	Wolfsburg	32	6		
2002-03	Wolfsburg	26	2		
2003-04	Wolfsburg	28	8		
2004-05	Wolfsburg	30	12	116	28
2005-06	Atletico Madrid	36	1		

2006-07	Atletico Madrid	13	2	**49**	**3**
2007-08	Manchester C	34	5	
2008-09	Manchester C	9	0	**43**	**5**

POOLE, James (F)   **0**   **0**
b.Stockport 20-3-90
Source: Scholar.
2008-09   Manchester C   0   0

RAMSEY, Christopher (M)   **0**   **0**
Source: Scholar. *Honours:* Northern Ireland Youth.
2008-09   Manchester C   0   0

RICHARDS, Micah (D)   **100**   **2**
H: 5 11   W: 13 00   b.Birmingham 24-6-88
Source: Scholar. *Honours:* England Youth, Under-21, 11 full caps, 1 goal.

2005-06	Manchester C	13	0	
2006-07	Manchester C	28	1	
2007-08	Manchester C	25	0	
2008-09	Manchester C	34	1	**100**	**2**

ROBINHO (F)   **230**   **79**
H: 5 8   W: 10 00   b.Sao Vicente 25-1-84
Honours: Brazil Under-23, 70 full caps, 18 goals.

2002	Santos	24	7	
2003	Santos	32	9	
2004	Santos	37	21	
2005	Santos	5	3	**98**	**40**
2005-06	Real Madrid	37	8	
2006-07	Real Madrid	32	6	
2007-08	Real Madrid	32	11	**101**	**25**
2008-09	Manchester C	31	14	**31**	**14**

SCHMEICHEL, Kasper (G)   **79**   **0**
H: 6 1   W: 13 00   b.Denmark 5-11-86
Source: Scholar. *Honours:* Denmark Youth, Under-20, Under-21.

2003-04	Manchester C	0	0	
2004-05	Manchester C	0	0	
2005-06	Manchester C	0	0	
2005-06	Darlington	4	0	**4**	**0**
2005-06	Bury	15	0	
2006-07	Manchester C	0	0	
2006-07	Falkirk	15	0	**15**	**0**
2006-07	Bury	14	0	**29**	**0**
2007-08	Manchester C	7	0	
2007-08	Cardiff C	14	0	**14**	**0**
2007-08	Coventry C	9	0	**9**	**0**
2008-09	Manchester C	1	0	**8**	**0**

STURRIDGE, Daniel (F)   **21**   **5**
H: 6 2   W: 12 00   b.Manchester 1-9-89
Source: Scholar. *Honours:* England Youth.

2006-07	Manchester C	2	0	
2007-08	Manchester C	3	1	
2008-09	Manchester C	16	4	**21**	**5**

TRIPPIER, Keiran (D)   **0**   **0**
b.Bury
Source: Scholar. *Honours:* England Youth.
2007-08   Manchester C   0   0
2008-09   Manchester C   0   0

TSIAKLIS, Angelos (M)   **0**   **0**
Source: Scholar.
2008-09   Manchester C   0   0

TUTTE, Andrew (M)   **0**   **0**
Source: Scholar. *Honours:* England Youth.
2007-08   Manchester C   0   0
2008-09   Manchester C   0   0

VASSELL, Darius (F)   **265**   **52**
H: 5 9   W: 13 00   b.Birmingham 13-6-80
Source: Trainee. *Honours:* England Youth, Under-21, 22 full caps, 6 goals.

1998-99	Aston Villa	6	0	
1999-2000	Aston Villa	11	0	
2000-01	Aston Villa	23	4	
2001-02	Aston Villa	36	12	
2002-03	Aston Villa	33	8	
2003-04	Aston Villa	32	9	
2004-05	Aston Villa	21	2	**162**	**35**
2005-06	Manchester C	36	8	
2006-07	Manchester C	32	3	
2007-08	Manchester C	27	6	
2008-09	Manchester C	8	0	**103**	**17**

VIDAL, Javan (D)   **16**   **0**
H: 5 10   W: 10 10   b.Manchester 10-5-89
Source: Scholar. *Honours:* England Youth.
2007-08   Manchester C   0   0
2008-09   Manchester C   0   0

2008-09	*Aberdeen*	13	0	**13**	**0**
2007-08	*Grimsby T*	3	0	**3**	**0**

WABARA, Reece (D)   **0**   **0**
b. 28-12-91
2008-09   Manchester C   0   0

WEISS, Vladimir (M)   **1**   **0**
H: 5 9   W: 10 10   b.Bratislava 30-11-89
Source: Scholar.
2007-08   Manchester C   0   0
2008-09   Manchester C   1   0   **1**   **0**

WILLIAMSON, Samuel (D)   **1**   **0**
H: 5 8   W: 11 09   b.Macclesfield 15-10-87
Source: Scholar.
2006-07   Manchester C   0   0
2007-08   Manchester C   1   0
2008-09   Manchester C   0   0   **1**   **0**

WRIGHT-PHILLIPS, Shaun (F)   **262**   **35**
H: 5 5   W: 10 01   b.Lewisham 25-10-81
Source: Scholar. *Honours:* England Under-21, 25 full caps, 4 goals.

1998-99	Manchester C	0	0	
1999-2000	Manchester C	4	0	
2000-01	Manchester C	15	0	
2001-02	Manchester C	35	8	
2002-03	Manchester C	31	1	
2003-04	Manchester C	34	7	
2004-05	Manchester C	34	10	
2005-06	Chelsea	27	0	
2006-07	Chelsea	27	2	
2007-08	Chelsea	27	2	
2008-09	Chelsea	1	0	**82**	**4**
2008-09	Manchester C	27	5	**180**	**31**

ZABALETA, Pablo (D)   **175**   **12**
H: 5 8   W: 10 12   b.Buenos Aires 16-1-85
Honours: Argentina Youth, Under-23, 7 full caps.

2002-03	San Lorenzo	11	0	
2003-04	San Lorenzo	27	3	
2004-05	San Lorenzo	28	5	**66**	**8**
2005-06	Espanyol	27	2	
2006-07	Espanyol	21	0	
2007-08	Espanyol	32	1	**80**	**3**
2008-09	Manchester C	29	1	**29**	**1**

Scholars
Chantler, Christopher Steven; Dean, Nathan; Elabdellaoui, Omar; Grandison, Kingsley John Jordon; Guidetti, John Alberto; Helan, Jeremy; Johansen, Eirik Holmen; Kapsalopodas, Anastasios; Mitchell, Andrew; Paris, James Michael; Redshaw, Jack; Smith, Thomas George; Tse, Sean Ka Keung; Wood, James Robert Fraser.

MANCHESTER U (52)

AMOS, Ben (G)   **0**   **0**
H: 6 1   W: 13 00   b.Macclesfield 10-4-90
Source: Scholar. *Honours:* England Youth.
2007-08   Manchester U   0   0
2008-09   Manchester U   0   0

ANDERSON (M)   **64**   **0**
H: 5 8   W: 10 07   b.Porto Alegre 13-4-88

2004-05	Gremio	5	1	**5**	**1**
2005-06	Porto	3	0	
2006-07	Porto	15	2	**18**	**2**
2007-08	Manchester U	24	0	
2008-09	Manchester U	17	0	**41**	**0**

BERBATOV, Dimitar (F)   **305**   **130**
H: 6 2   W: 12 06   b.Blagoevgrad 30-1-81
Honours: Bulgaria 71 full caps, 41 goals.

1998-99	CSKA Sofia	11	3	
1999-2000	CSKA Sofia	27	14	
2000-01	CSKA Sofia	12	8	**50**	**25**
2000-01	Leverkusen	6	0	
2001-02	Leverkusen	24	8	
2002-03	Leverkusen	24	4	
2003-04	Leverkusen	33	16	
2004-05	Leverkusen	33	20	
2005-06	Leverkusen	34	21	**154**	**69**
2006-07	Tottenham H	33	12	
2007-08	Tottenham H	36	15	
2008-09	Tottenham H	1	0	**70**	**27**
2008-09	Manchester U	31	9	**31**	**9**

BRADY, Robert (F)   **0**   **0**
b.Belfast 14-1-92
Source: Scholar.
2008-09   Manchester U   0   0

BRANDY, Febian (F)   **48**   **7**
H: 5 5   W: 10 00   b.Manchester 4-2-89
Source: From Scholar. *Honours:* England Youth.

2006-07	Manchester U	0	0	
2007-08	Manchester U	0	0	
2007-08	Swansea C	19	3	
2008-09	Manchester U	0	0	
2008-09	Swansea C	14	0	**33**	**3**
2008-09	Hereford U	15	4	**15**	**4**

BROWN, Wes (D)   **206**   **3**
H: 6 1   W: 13 08   b.Manchester 13-10-79
Source: Trainee. *Honours:* England Schools, Youth, Under-21, 21 full caps, 1 goal.

1996-97	Manchester U	0	0	
1997-98	Manchester U	2	0	
1998-99	Manchester U	14	0	
1999-2000	Manchester U	0	0	
2000-01	Manchester U	28	0	
2001-02	Manchester U	17	0	
2002-03	Manchester U	22	0	
2003-04	Manchester U	17	0	
2004-05	Manchester U	21	1	
2005-06	Manchester U	19	0	
2006-07	Manchester U	22	0	
2007-08	Manchester U	36	1	
2008-09	Manchester U	8	1	**206**	**3**

BRYAN, Antonio (F)   **0**   **0**
b.Manchester 4-10-89
Source: Scholar.
2008-09   Manchester U   0   0

CAMPBELL, Frazier (F)   **46**   **16**
H: 5 11   W: 12 04   b.Huddersfield 13-9-87
Source: From Scholar. *Honours:* England Youth, Under-21.

2005-06	Manchester U	0	0	
2006-07	Manchester U	0	0	
2007-08	Manchester U	1	0	
2007-08	Hull C	34	15	**34**	**15**
2008-09	Manchester U	1	0	**2**	**0**
2008-09	*Tottenham H*	10	1	**10**	**1**

CARRICK, Michael (M)   **300**   **19**
H: 6 1   W: 11 10   b.Wallsend 28-7-81
Source: Trainee. *Honours:* England Youth, Under-21, B, 17 full caps.

1998-99	West Ham U	0	0	
1999-2000	West Ham U	8	1	
1999-2000	Swindon T	6	2	**6**	**2**
1999-2000	Birmingham C	2	0	**2**	**0**
2000-01	West Ham U	33	1	
2001-02	West Ham U	30	2	
2002-03	West Ham U	30	1	
2003-04	West Ham U	35	1	
2004-05	West Ham U	0	0	**136**	**6**
2004-05	Tottenham H	29	0	
2005-06	Tottenham H	35	2	**64**	**2**
2006-07	Manchester U	33	3	
2007-08	Manchester U	31	2	
2008-09	Manchester U	28	4	**92**	**9**

CATHCART, Craig (D)   **44**   **3**
H: 6 2   W: 11 06   b.Belfast 6-2-89
Source: Scholar. *Honours:* Northern Ireland Youth, Under-21.

2005-06	Manchester U	0	0	
2006-07	Manchester U	0	0	
2007-08	Manchester U	0	0	
2007-08	Antwerp	13	2	**13**	**2**
2008-09	Manchester U	0	0	
2008-09	Plymouth Arg	31	1	**31**	**1**

CHESTER, James (D)   **5**   **0**
H: 5 11   W: 11 04   b.Warrington 23-1-89
Source: Scholar.

2007-08	Manchester U	0	0	
2008-09	Manchester U	0	0	
2008-09	Peterborough U	5	0	**5**	**0**

CLEVERLEY, Tom (M)   **15**   **2**
H: 5 9   W: 10 07   b.Basingstoke 12-8-89
Source: Scholar. *Honours:* England Youth.

2007-08	Manchester U	0	0	
2008-09	Manchester U	0	0	
2008-09	Leicester C	15	2	**15**	**2**

DE LAET, Ritchie (D)　　1　0
H: 6 1　W: 12 02　b.Belgium 28-11-88
Source: Antwerp. *Honours:* Belgium 2 full caps.

2007-08	Stoke C	0	0	
2008-09	Stoke C	0	0	
2008-09	Manchester U	1	0	1　0

DONG FANGZHOU (M)　　93　54
H: 6 1　W: 11 09　b.Liaoning 23-1-85
Source: China Under-23, 13 full caps, 1 goal.

2002	Dalian Saidelong	14	20	14　20
2003	Dalian Shide	8	0	8　0
2003-04	Manchester U	0	0	
2003-04	*Antwerp*	9	1	
2004-05	*Antwerp*	19	6	
2005-06	*Antwerp*	28	18	
2006-07	*Antwerp*	14	9	70　34
2006-07	Manchester U	1	0	
2007-08	Manchester U	0	0	
2008-09	Manchester U	0	0	1　0

DRINKWATER, Daniel (M)　　0　0
b.Manchester 5-3-90
Source: Scholar. *Honours:* England Youth.

2008-09	Manchester U	0	0

ECKERSLEY, Richard (D)　　2　0
H: 5 9　W: 11 09　b.Worsley 12-3-89
Source: Scholar.

2006-07	Manchester U	0	0	
2007-08	Manchester U	0	0	
2008-09	Manchester U	2	0	2　0

ECKERSLEY, Richard (D)　　0　0
b.Salford 12-3-89
Source: Scholar.

2007-08	Manchester U	0	0
2008-09	Manchester U	0	0

EIKREM, Magnus (M)　　0　0
b.Molde 8-8-90
Source: Scholar.

2008-09	Manchester U	0	0

EVANS, Corry (M)　　0　0
H: 5 8　W: 10 12　b.Belfast 30-7-90
Source: From Scholar. *Honours:* Northern Ireland Under-21, B, 1 full cap.

2007-08	Manchester U	0	0
2008-09	Manchester U	0	0

EVANS, Jonny (D)　　64　3
H: 6 2　W: 12 02　b.Belfast 3-1-88
Source: Scholar. *Honours:* Northern Ireland Schools, Youth, Under-21, 17 full caps, 1 goal.

2004-05	Manchester U	0	0	
2005-06	Manchester U	0	0	
2006-07	Manchester U	0	0	
2006-07	*Antwerp*	14	2	14　2
2006-07	*Sunderland*	18	1	
2007-08	Manchester U	0	0	
2007-08	*Sunderland*	15	0	33　1
2008-09	Manchester U	17	0	17　0

EVRA, Patrice (D)　　282　6
H: 5 8　W: 11 10　b.Dakar 15-5-81
Honours: France 20 full caps.

1998-99	Marsala	24	3	24　3
1999-2000	Monza	3	0	3　0
2000-01	Nice	5	0	
2001-02	Nice	34	1	39　1
2002-03	Monaco	36	1	
2003-04	Monaco	33	0	
2004-05	Monaco	36	0	
2005-06	Monaco	15	0	120　1
2005-06	Manchester U	11	0	
2006-07	Manchester U	24	1	
2007-08	Manchester U	33	0	
2008-09	Manchester U	28	0	96　1

FABIO (M)　　0　0
H: 5 8　W: 10 03　b.Rio de Janeiro 9-7-90
Source: Fluminense.

2008-09	Manchester U	0	0

FERDINAND, Rio (D)　　399　10
H: 6 2　W: 13 12　b.Peckham 7-11-78
Source: From Trainee. *Honours:* England Youth, Under-21, B, 73 full caps, 3 goals.

1995-96	West Ham U	1	0	
1996-97	West Ham U	15	2	
1996-97	*Bournemouth*	10	0	· 10　0
1997-98	West Ham U	35	0	
1998-99	West Ham U	31	0	
1999-2000	West Ham U	33	0	
2000-01	West Ham U	12	0	127　2
2000-01	Leeds U	23	2	
2001-02	Leeds U	31	0	54　2
2002-03	Manchester U	28	0	
2003-04	Manchester U	20	0	
2004-05	Manchester U	31	0	
2005-06	Manchester U	37	3	
2006-07	Manchester U	33	1	
2007-08	Manchester U	35	2	
2008-09	Manchester U	24	0	208　6

FLETCHER, Darren (M)　　133　10
H: 6 0　W: 11 09　b.Edinburgh 1-2-84
Source: Scholar. *Honours:* Scotland Under-21, B, 42 full caps, 4 goals.

2000-01	Manchester U	0	0	
2001-02	Manchester U	0	0	
2002-03	Manchester U	0	0	
2003-04	Manchester U	22	0	
2004-05	Manchester U	18	3	
2005-06	Manchester U	27	1	
2006-07	Manchester U	24	3	
2007-08	Manchester U	16	0	
2008-09	Manchester U	26	3	133　10

FOSTER, Ben (G)　　95　0
H: 6 2　W: 12 08　b.Leamington Spa 3-4-83
Source: Racing Club Warwick. *Honours:* England 2 full caps.

2000-01	Stoke C	0	0	
2001-02	Stoke C	0	0	
2002-03	Stoke C	0	0	
2003-04	Stoke C	0	0	
2004-05	Stoke C	0	0	
2004-05	*Kidderminster H*	2	0	2　0
2004-05	*Wrexham*	17	0	17　0
2005-06	*Watford*	44	0	
2006-07	Manchester U	0	0	
2006-07	*Watford*	29	0	73　0
2007-08	Manchester U	1	0	
2008-09	Manchester U	2	0	3　0

GALBRAITH, Daniel (F)　　0　0
H: 5 9　W: 10 03　b.Manchester 5-3-90
Source: Scholar.

2007-08	Manchester U	0	0
2008-09	Manchester U	0	0

GIBSON, Darron (M)　　24　2
H: 6 0　W: 12 04　b.Londonderry 25-10-87
Source: Scholar. *Honours:* Eire Youth, Under-21, 5 full caps.

2005-06	Manchester U	0	0	
2006-07	Manchester U	0	0	
2007-08	Manchester U	0	0	
2007-08	*Wolverhampton W*	21	1	21　1
2008-09	Manchester U	3	1	3　1

GIGGS, Ryan (F)　　563　103
H: 5 11　W: 11 02　b.Cardiff 29-11-73
Source: School. *Honours:* England Schools, Wales Youth, Under-21, 64 full caps, 12 goals.

1990-91	Manchester U	2	1	
1991-92	Manchester U	38	4	
1992-93	Manchester U	41	9	
1993-94	Manchester U	38	13	
1994-95	Manchester U	29	1	
1995-96	Manchester U	33	11	
1996-97	Manchester U	26	3	
1997-98	Manchester U	29	8	
1998-99	Manchester U	24	3	
1999-2000	Manchester U	30	6	
2000-01	Manchester U	31	5	
2001-02	Manchester U	25	7	
2002-03	Manchester U	36	8	
2003-04	Manchester U	33	7	
2004-05	Manchester U	32	5	
2005-06	Manchester U	27	3	
2006-07	Manchester U	30	4	
2007-08	Manchester U	31	3	
2008-09	Manchester U	28	2	563　103

GRAY, David (F)　　15　0
H: 5 11　W: 11 02　b.Edinburgh 4-5-88
Source: Scholar. *Honours:* Scotland Under-21.

2005-06	Manchester U	0	0	
2006-07	Manchester U	0	0	
2007-08	Manchester U	0	0	
2007-08	*Crewe Alex*	1	0	1　0
2008-09	*Plymouth Arg*	14	0	14　0

HARGREAVES, Owen (M)　　170　7
H: 5 11　W: 11 07　b.Calgary 20-1-81
Source: Calgary Foothills. *Honours:* England Under-21, B, 42 full caps.

2000-01	Bayern Munich	14	0	
2001-02	Bayern Munich	29	0	
2002-03	Bayern Munich	25	1	
2003-04	Bayern Munich	25	2	
2004-05	Bayern Munich	27	1	
2005-06	Bayern Munich	16	1	
2006-07	Bayern Munich	9	0	145　5
2007-08	Manchester U	23	2	
2008-09	Manchester U	2	0	25　2

HEATON, Tom (G)　　35　0
H: 6 1　W: 13 12　b.Chester 15-4-86
Source: Trainee. *Honours:* England Youth, Under-21.

2003-04	Manchester U	0	0	
2004-05	Manchester U	0	0	
2005-06	Manchester U	0	0	
2005-06	*Swindon T*	14	0	14　0
2006-07	Manchester U	0	0	
2007-08	Manchester U	0	0	
2008-09	Manchester U	0	0	
2008-09	*Cardiff C*	21	0	21　0

HEWSON, Sam (M)　　10　3
H: 5 8　W: 11 00　b.Bolton 28-11-88
Source: Scholar.

2007-08	Manchester U	0	0	
2008-09	Manchester U	0	0	
2008-09	*Hereford U*	10	3	10　3

JAMES, Matthew (M)　　0　0
b.Bacup 22-7-91
Source: Scholar. *Honours:* England Youth.

2007-08	Manchester U	0	0
2008-09	Manchester U	0	0

KING, Joshua (F)　　0　0
b.Oslo 15-1-92
Source: Scholar.

2008-09	Manchester U	0	0

KUSZCZAK, Tomasz (G)　　50　0
H: 6 3　W: 13 03　b.Krosno Odrzansia 20-3-82
Source: From Uerdingen. *Honours:* Poland Youth, Under-21, 6 full caps.

2001-02	Hertha Berlin	0	0	
2002-03	Hertha Berlin	0	0	
2003-04	Hertha Berlin	0	0	
2004-05	WBA	3	0	
2005-06	WBA	28	0	
2006-07	WBA	0	0	31　0
2006-07	*Manchester U*	6	0	
2007-08	Manchester U	9	0	
2008-09	Manchester U	4	0	19　0

LEA, Michael (D)　　0　0
b.Salford 4-11-87
Source: Scholar.

2007-08	Manchester U	0	0
2008-09	Manchester U	0	0

MACHEDA, Federico (F)　　4　2
H: 6 0　W: 11 13　b.Rome 22-8-91
Source: Scholar.

2008-09	Manchester U	4	2	4　2

MANUCHO (F)　　21　6
H: 6 2　W: 13 00　b.Luanda 7-3-83
Source: Benfica de Luanda, Petro Atletico. *Honours:* Angola 23 full caps, 7 goals.

2007-08	*Panathinaikos*	7	4	7　4
2007-08	Manchester U	0	0	
2008-09	Manchester U	1	0	1　0
2008-09	*Hull C*	13	2	13　2

MARTIN, Lee (M)　　52　4
H: 5 10　W: 10 03　b.Taunton 9-2-87
Source: Scholar. *Honours:* England Youth.

2004-05	Manchester U	0	0	
2005-06	Manchester U	0	0	
2006-07	Manchester U	0	0	
2006-07	*Rangers*	7	0	7　0
2006-07	*Stoke C*	13	1	13　1
2007-08	Manchester U	0	0	
2007-08	*Plymouth Arg*	12	2	12　2
2007-08	*Sheffield U*	6	0	6　0
2008-09	Manchester U	1	0	1　0
2008-09	*Nottingham F*	13	1	13　1

NANI (M) 97 13
H: 5 9 W: 10 04 b.Amadora 17-11-86
Honours: Portugal Under-21, 26 full caps, 4 goals.

2005-06	Sporting Lisbon	29	4
2006-07	Sporting Lisbon	29	5	58	9
2007-08	Manchester U	26	3
2008-09	Manchester U	13	1	39	4

NEVILLE, Gary (D) 380 5
H: 5 11 W: 12 10 b.Bury 18-2-75
Source: Trainee. *Honours:* England Youth, 85 full caps.

1992-93	Manchester U	0	0
1993-94	Manchester U	1	0
1994-95	Manchester U	18	0
1995-96	Manchester U	31	0
1996-97	Manchester U	31	1
1997-98	Manchester U	34	0
1998-99	Manchester U	34	1
1999-2000	Manchester U	22	0
2000-01	Manchester U	32	1
2001-02	Manchester U	34	0
2002-03	Manchester U	32	6
2003-04	Manchester U	30	2
2004-05	Manchester U	22	0
2005-06	Manchester U	25	0
2006-07	Manchester U	24	0
2007-08	Manchester U		
2008-09	Manchester U	16	0	380	5

O'SHEA, John (D) 231 10
H: 6 3 W: 13 07 b.Waterford 30-4-81
Source: Waterford. *Honours:* Eire Youth, Under-21, 54 full caps, 1 goal.

1998-99	Manchester U	0	0
1999-2000	Manchester U	0	0
1999-2000	*Bournemouth*	10	1	10	1
2000-01	Manchester U	0	0
2001-02	Manchester U	9	0
2002-03	Manchester U	32	0
2003-04	Manchester U	33	2
2004-05	Manchester U	23	2
2005-06	Manchester U	34	1
2006-07	Manchester U	32	4
2007-08	Manchester U	28	0
2008-09	Manchester U	30	0	221	0

PARK, Ji-Sung (M) 224 33
H: 5 9 W: 11 06 b.Seoul 25-2-81
Honours: South Korea 80 full caps, 10 goals.

2000	Kyoto Purple S	13	1
2001	Kyoto Purple S	9	0
2002	Kyoto Purple S	25	7	76	11
2002-03	PSV Eindhoven	8	0
2003-04	PSV Eindhoven	28	6
2004-05	PSV Eindhoven	28	7	64	13
2005-06	Manchester U	33	1
2006-07	Manchester U	14	5
2007-08	Manchester U	12	1
2008-09	Manchester U	25	2	84	9

PETRUCCI, Davide (F) 0 0
b.Rome 5-10-91
Source: Scholar.

2008-09	Manchester U	0	0

POSSEBON, Rodrigo (M) 3 0
H: 6 0 W: 11 13 b.Porto Alegre 13-2-89
Source: From Internacional. *Honours:* Italy Youth.

2007-08	Manchester U	0	0
2008-09	Manchester U	3	0	3	0

RAFAEL (D) 16 1
H: 6 3 W: 12 08 b.Petropolis 9-7-90
Source: Fluminense. *Honours:* Brazil Youth.

2008-09	Manchester U	16	1	16	1

RONALDO, Cristiano (M) 221 87
H: 6 1 W: 13 02 b.Funchal 5-2-85
Honours: Portugal Youth, Under-21, 64 full caps, 22 goals.

2002-03	Sporting Lisbon	25	3	25	3
2003-04	Manchester U	29	4
2004-05	Manchester U	33	5
2005-06	Manchester U	33	9
2006-07	Manchester U	34	17
2007-08	Manchester U	34	31
2008-09	Manchester U	33	18	196	84

ROONEY, Wayne (F) 224 80
H: 5 10 W: 12 13 b.Liverpool 24-10-85
Source: Scholar. *Honours:* FA Schools, England Youth, 52 full caps, 24 goals.

2002-03	Everton	33	6
2003-04	Everton	34	9	67	15
2004-05	Manchester U	29	11
2005-06	Manchester U	36	16
2006-07	Manchester U	35	14
2007-08	Manchester U	27	12
2008-09	Manchester U	30	12	157	65

SCHOLES, Paul (M) 416 98
H: 5 7 W: 11 00 b.Salford 16-11-74
Source: Trainee. *Honours:* England Youth, 66 full caps, 14 goals.

1992-93	Manchester U	0	0
1993-94	Manchester U	0	0
1994-95	Manchester U	17	5
1995-96	Manchester U	26	10
1996-97	Manchester U	24	3
1997-98	Manchester U	31	8
1998-99	Manchester U	31	6
1999-2000	Manchester U	31	9
2000-01	Manchester U	32	6
2001-02	Manchester U	35	8
2002-03	Manchester U	33	14
2003-04	Manchester U	28	9
2004-05	Manchester U	33	9
2005-06	Manchester U	20	2
2006-07	Manchester U	30	6
2007-08	Manchester U	24	1
2008-09	Manchester U	21	2	416	98

SIMPSON, Danny (D) 37 0
H: 5 9 W: 11 05 b.Eccles 4-1-87
Source: Scholar.

2005-06	Manchester U	0	0
2006-07	Manchester U	0	0
2006-07	*Sunderland*	14	0	14	0
2007-08	Manchester U	3	0
2007-08	*Ipswich T*	8	0	8	0
2008-09	Manchester U	0	0	3	0
2008-09	*Blackburn R*	12	0	12	0

TEVEZ, Carlos (F) 193 72
H: 5 8 W: 11 11 b.Cuidadela 5-2-84
Source: All Boys. *Honours:* Argentina Youth, Under-20, Under-23, 47 full caps, 8 goals.

2001-02	Boca Juniors	11	1
2002-03	Boca Juniors	32	11
2003-04	Boca Juniors	23	12
2004-05	Boca Juniors	9	2	75	26
2005	Corinthians	29	20	29	20
2006-07	West Ham U	26	7	26	7
2007-08	Manchester U	34	14
2008-09	Manchester U	29	5	63	19

TOSIC, Zoran (M) 83 16
H: 5 7 W: 10 10 b.Zrenjanin 24-4-87
Honours: Serbia Under-21, 13 full caps.

2005-06	Buducnost	7	0	7	0
2006-07	Banat Zrenjanin	25	2	25	2
2007-08	Partizan Belgrade	32	8
2008-09	Partizan Belgrade	17	6	49	14
2008-09	Manchester U	2	0	2	0

VAN DER SAR, Edwin (G) 551 1
H: 6 5 W: 14 11 b.Voorhout 29-10-70
Honours: Holland 128 full caps.

1990-91	Ajax	9	0
1991-92	Ajax	19	0
1992-93	Ajax	19	0
1993-94	Ajax	32	0
1994-95	Ajax	33	0
1995-96	Ajax	33	0
1996-97	Ajax	33	0
1997-98	Ajax	33	1	192	1
1998-99	Juventus	34	0
1999-2000	Juventus	32	0
2000-01	Juventus	34	0	100	0
2001-02	Fulham	37	0
2002-03	Fulham	19	0
2003-04	Fulham	37	0
2004-05	Fulham	34	0	127	0
2005-06	Manchester U	38	0
2006-07	Manchester U	32	0
2007-08	Manchester U	29	0
2008-09	Manchester U	33	0	132	0

VIDIC, Nemanja (D) 236 30
H: 6 1 W: 13 02 b.Uzice 21-10-81
Honours: Serbia 40 full caps, 2 goals.

2000-01	Subotica	27	6	27	6

2001-02	Red Star Belgrade	22	2
2002-03	Red Star Belgrade	26	5
2003-04	Red Star Belgrade	20	5	68	12
2004	Spartak Moscow	12	2
2005	Spartak Moscow	27	2	39	4
2005-06	Manchester U	11	0
2006-07	Manchester U	25	3
2007-08	Manchester U	32	1
2008-09	Manchester U	34	4	102	8

WELBECK, Danny (F) 3 1
H: 6 1 W: 11 07 b.Manchester 26-11-90
Source: Scholar. *Honours:* England Youth, Under-21.

2007-08	Manchester U	0	0
2008-09	Manchester U	3	1	3	1

ZIELER, Ron-Robert (G) 2 0
H: 6 1 W: 11 07 b.Cologne 12-2-89
Source: Scholar.

2006-07	Manchester U	0	0
2007-08	Manchester U	0	0
2008-09	Manchester U	0	0
2008-09	*Northampton T*	2	0	2	0

Scholars
Ajose, Nicholas; Brown, Reece; Devlin, Conor; Dudgeon, Joseph Patrick; James, Matthew; Moffatt, Scott Lee; Norwood, Oliver James; Stewart, Cameron Reece; Wootton, Scott James.

MIDDLESBROUGH (53)

ALIADIERE, Jeremie (F) 108 10
H: 6 0 W: 11 00 b.Rambouillet 30-3-83
Source: Scholar. *Honours:* France Youth, Under-21.

1999-2000	Arsenal	0	0
2000-01	Arsenal	0	0
2001-02	Arsenal	1	0
2002-03	Arsenal	3	1
2003-04	Arsenal	10	0
2004-05	Arsenal	4	0
2005-06	Celtic	0	0
2005-06	*West Ham U*	7	0	7	0
2005-06	*Wolverhampton W*	14	2	14	2
2006-07	Arsenal	11	0	29	1
2007-08	Middlesbrough	29	5
2008-09	Middlesbrough	29	2	58	7

ALVES, Afonso (F) 175 107
H: 6 1 W: 11 09 b.Belo Horizonte 30-1-81
Honours: Brazil 8 full caps, 1 goal.

2002	Orgryte	18	13
2003	Orgryte	21	10	39	23
2004	Malmo	24	12
2005	Malmo	24	14
2006	Malmo	7	3	55	29
2006-07	Heerenveen	31	34
2007-08	Heerenveen	8	11	39	45
2007-08	Middlesbrough	11	6
2008-09	Middlesbrough	31	4	42	10

ARCA, Julio (M) 256 22
H: 5 9 W: 11 13 b.Quilmes 31-1-81
Honours: Argentina Youth, Under-21.

1999-2000	Argentinos Jun	9	0
2000-01	Argentinos Jun	17	1	36	1
2000-01	Sunderland	27	2
2001-02	Sunderland	22	1
2002-03	Sunderland	13	0
2003-04	Sunderland	31	4
2004-05	Sunderland	40	9
2005-06	Sunderland	24	1	157	17
2006-07	Middlesbrough	21	2
2007-08	Middlesbrough	24	2
2008-09	Middlesbrough	18	0	63	4

BATES, Matthew (D) 45 1
H: 5 10 W: 12 03 b.Stockton 10-12-86
Source: Scholar. *Honours:* England Youth, Under-20.

2003-04	Middlesbrough	0	0
2004-05	Middlesbrough	2	0
2004-05	*Darlington*	4	0	4	0
2005-06	Middlesbrough	16	0
2006-07	Middlesbrough	1	0
2006-07	*Ipswich T*	2	0	2	0
2007-08	Middlesbrough	0	0

| 2007-08 | Norwich C | 3 | 0 | 3 | 0 |
| 2008-09 | Middlesbrough | 17 | 1 | 36 | 1 |

BENNETT, Joe (D) 1 0
H: 5 10 W: 10 04 b.Rochdale 28-3-90
Source: Scholar.

| 2008-09 | Middlesbrough | 1 | 0 | 1 | 0 |

DIGARD, Didier (M) 111 3
H: 6 0 W: 11 13 b.Gisors 12-7-86
Honours: France Under-21.

2004-05	Le Havre	15	0		
2005-06	Le Havre	30	2		
2006-07	Le Havre	27	1	72	3
2007-08	Paris St Germain	16	0	16	0
2008-09	Middlesbrough	23	0	23	0

DOWNING, Stewart (M) 188 20
H: 5 11 W: 10 04 b.Middlesbrough 22-7-84
Source: Scholar. Honours: England Youth, Under-21, B, 23 full caps.

2001-02	Middlesbrough	3	0		
2002-03	Middlesbrough	2	0		
2003-04	Middlesbrough	20	0		
2003-04	Sunderland	7	3	7	3
2004-05	Middlesbrough	35	5		
2005-06	Middlesbrough	12	1		
2006-07	Middlesbrough	34	2		
2007-08	Middlesbrough	38	9		
2008-09	Middlesbrough	37	0	181	17

EMNES, Marvin (M) 71 9
H: 5 11 W: 10 06 b.Rotterdam 27-5-88
Honours: Holland Under-21.

2005-06	Sparta Rotterdam	11	1		
2006-07	Sparta Rotterdam	16	0		
2007-08	Sparta Rotterdam	29	8	56	9
2008-09	Middlesbrough	15	0	15	0

FRANKS, Jonathan (F) 1 0
H: 5 9 W: 11 03 b.Stockton 8-4-90
Source: Scholar. Honours: England Youth.

| 2007-08 | Middlesbrough | 0 | 0 | | |
| 2008-09 | Middlesbrough | 1 | 0 | 1 | 0 |

GOULON, Herold (M) 0 0
H: 6 4 W: 14 07 b.Paris 12-6-88

2005-06	Lyon	0	0		
2006-07	Middlesbrough	0	0		
2007-08	Middlesbrough	0	0		
2008-09	Middlesbrough	0	0		

GROUNDS, Jonathan (D) 23 3
H: 6 1 W: 13 10 b.Thornaby 2-2-88
Source: Scholar.

2007-08	Middlesbrough	5	0		
2008-09	Middlesbrough	2	0	7	0
2008-09	Norwich C	16	3	16	3

HINES, Seb (D) 6 0
H: 6 1 W: 12 02 b.Wetherby 29-5-88
Source: Scholar. Honours: England Youth.

2005-06	Middlesbrough	0	0		
2006-07	Middlesbrough	0	0		
2007-08	Middlesbrough	1	0		
2008-09	Middlesbrough	1	0	2	0
2008-09	Derby Co	0	0		
2008-09	Oldham Ath	4	0	4	0

HOYTE, Justin (D) 83 2
H: 5 11 W: 11 00 b.Waltham Forest 20-11-84
Source: Scholar. Honours: England Youth, Under-20, Under-21.

2002-03	Arsenal	1	0		
2003-04	Arsenal	1	0		
2004-05	Arsenal	5	0		
2005-06	Arsenal	0	0		
2005-06	Sunderland	27	1	27	1
2006-07	Arsenal	22	1		
2007-08	Arsenal	5	0	34	1
2008-09	Middlesbrough	22	0	22	0

HUTH, Robert (D) 91 2
H: 6 3 W: 14 07 b.Berlin 18-8-84
Source: Scholar. Honours: Germany Youth, Under-21, 19 full caps, 2 goals.

2001-02	Chelsea	1	0		
2002-03	Chelsea	2	0		
2003-04	Chelsea	16	0		
2004-05	Chelsea	10	0		
2005-06	Chelsea	13	0	42	0
2006-07	Middlesbrough	12	1		
2007-08	Middlesbrough	13	1		
2008-09	Middlesbrough	24	0	49	2

JOHNSON, Adam (M) 87 7
H: 5 8 W: 10 00 b.Sunderland 14-7-87
Source: Scholar. Honours: England Youth, Under-21.

2004-05	Middlesbrough	0	0		
2005-06	Middlesbrough	13	1		
2006-07	Middlesbrough	12	0		
2007-08	Leeds U	5	0	5	0
2007-08	Middlesbrough	19	1		
2007-08	Watford	12	5	12	5
2008-09	Middlesbrough	26	0	70	2

JOHNSON, John (D) 5 0
H: 6 0 W: 12 00 b.Middlesbrough 16-9-88
Source: Scholar.

2007-08	Middlesbrough	0	0		
2008-09	Middlesbrough	1	0	1	0
2008-09	Tranmere R	4	0	4	0

JONES, Brad (G) 69 0
H: 6 3 W: 12 01 b.Armadale 19-3-82
Source: Trainee. Honours: Australia Under-20, Under-23, 1 full cap.

1998-99	Middlesbrough	0	0		
1999-2000	Middlesbrough	0	0		
2000-01	Middlesbrough	0	0		
2001-02	Middlesbrough	0	0		
2002	Shelbourne	2	0	2	0
2002-03	Middlesbrough	0	0		
2002-03	Stockport Co	1	0	1	0
2003-04	Middlesbrough	1	0		
2003-04	Blackpool	5	0		
2003-04	Rotherham U	0	0		
2004-05	Middlesbrough	5	0		
2004-05	Blackpool	12	0	17	0
2005-06	Middlesbrough	9	0		
2006-07	Middlesbrough	2	0		
2006-07	Sheffield W	15	0	15	0
2007-08	Middlesbrough	1	0		
2008-09	Middlesbrough	16	0	34	0

KNIGHT, David (G) 5 0
H: 6 0 W: 11 07 b.Sunderland 15-1-87
Source: Scholar. Honours: England Youth.

2004-05	Middlesbrough	0	0		
2005-06	Middlesbrough	0	0		
2005-06	Darlington	3	0	3	0
2006-07	Middlesbrough	0	0		
2006-07	Oldham Ath	2	0	2	0
2007-08	Swansea C	0	0		
2008-09	Middlesbrough	0	0		

McMAHON, Tony (D) 47 1
H: 5 10 W: 11 04 b.Bishop Auckland 24-3-86
Source: Scholar. Honours: England Youth.

2003-04	Middlesbrough	0	0		
2004-05	Middlesbrough	13	0		
2005-06	Middlesbrough	3	0		
2006-07	Middlesbrough	0	0		
2007-08	Middlesbrough	1	0		
2007-08	Blackpool	2	0	2	0
2008-09	Middlesbrough	13	0	30	0
2008-09	Sheffield W	15	1	15	1

MIDO (F) 188 68
H: 6 2 W: 14 09 b.Cairo 23-2-83
Honours: Egypt 50 full caps, 19 goals.

1999-2000	Zamalek	4	3	4	3
2000-01	Gent	21	11	21	11
2001-02	Ajax	24	12		
2002-03	Ajax	16	9	40	21
2002-03	Celta Vigo	8	4	8	4
2003-04	Marseille	22	7	22	7
2004-05	Roma	8	0	8	0
2004-05	Tottenham H	9	2		
2005-06	Tottenham H	27	11		
2006-07	Tottenham H	12	1		
2007-08	Tottenham H	0	0	48	14
2007-08	Middlesbrough	12	2		
2008-09	Middlesbrough	13	4	25	6
2008-09	Wigan Ath	12	2	12	2

O'NEIL, Gary (M) 246 21
H: 5 10 W: 11 00 b.Bromley 18-5-83
Source: Scholar. Honours: England Youth, Under-20, Under-21.

1999-2000	Portsmouth	1	0		
2000-01	Portsmouth	10	1		
2001-02	Portsmouth	33	1		
2002-03	Portsmouth	31	3		
2003-04	Portsmouth	0	0		
2003-04	Walsall	7	0	7	0
2004-05	Portsmouth	24	2		
2004-05	Cardiff C	9	1	9	1
2005-06	Portsmouth	36	6		
2006-07	Portsmouth	35	1		
2007-08	Portsmouth	2	0	175	16
2007-08	Middlesbrough	26	0		
2008-09	Middlesbrough	29	4	55	4

OWENS, Graeme (M) 12 0
H: 5 10 W: 11 06 b.Cramlington 1-6-88

2007-08	Middlesbrough	0	0		
2007-08	Chesterfield	4	0	4	0
2008-09	Middlesbrough	0	0		
2008-09	Blackpool	8	0	8	0

POGATETZ, Emanuel (D) 233 6
H: 6 2 W: 13 05 b.Steinbock 16-1-83
Honours: Austria 37 full caps, 2 goals.

1999-2000	Sturm Graz	0	0		
2000-01	Karntern	33	0	33	0
2001-02	Leverkusen B	23	0		
2001-02	Leverkusen	0	0		
2002-03	Leverkusen B	3	0	26	0
2002-03	Leverkusen	0	0		
2002-03	Aarau	11	0	11	0
2003-04	Graz	31	1		
2004-05	Graz	22	1	53	2
2005-06	Middlesbrough	24	1		
2006-07	Middlesbrough	35	2		
2007-08	Middlesbrough	24	0		
2008-09	Middlesbrough	27	1	110	4

PORRITT, Nathan (F) 0 0
H: 5 9 W: 12 00 b.Middlesbrough 9-1-90
Source: Scholar.

| 2008-09 | Middlesbrough | 0 | 0 | | |

RIGGOTT, Chris (D) 198 10
H: 6 2 W: 13 09 b.Derby 1-9-80
Source: From Trainee. Honours: England Youth, Under-21.

1998-99	Derby Co	0	0		
1999-2000	Derby Co	1	0		
2000-01	Derby Co	31	3		
2001-02	Derby Co	37	0		
2002-03	Derby Co	22	2	91	5
2002-03	Middlesbrough	5	2		
2003-04	Middlesbrough	17	0		
2004-05	Middlesbrough	21	2		
2005-06	Middlesbrough	22	0		
2006-07	Middlesbrough	6	0		
2007-08	Middlesbrough	10	1		
2007-08	Stoke C	9	0	9	0
2008-09	Middlesbrough	17	0	98	5

SHAWKY, Mohamed (M) 18 0
H: 5 11 W: 11 11 b.Port Said 5-10-81
Source: Al Ahly. Honours: Egypt Under-21, 59 full caps, 5 goals.

| 2007-08 | Middlesbrough | 5 | 0 | | |
| 2008-09 | Middlesbrough | 13 | 0 | 18 | 0 |

SMALLWOOD, Richard (M) 0 0
H: b.Redcar 29-12-90
Source: Scholar. Honours: England Youth.

| 2008-09 | Middlesbrough | 0 | 0 | | |

STEELE, Jason (G) 0 0
H: 6 2 W: 12 07 b.Stockton 18-8-90
Source: Scholar. Honours: England Youth.

| 2007-08 | Middlesbrough | 0 | 0 | | |
| 2008-09 | Middlesbrough | 0 | 0 | | |

TAYLOR, Andrew (D) 116 0
H: 5 10 W: 11 04 b.Hartlepool 1-8-86
Source: Trainee. Honours: England Youth, Under-20, Under-21.

2003-04	Middlesbrough	0	0		
2004-05	Middlesbrough	0	0		
2005-06	Middlesbrough	13	0		
2005-06	Bradford C	24	0	24	0
2006-07	Middlesbrough	34	0		
2007-08	Middlesbrough	19	0		
2008-09	Middlesbrough	26	0	92	0

TUNCAY, Sanli (F) 284 104
H: 5 10 W: 11 00 b.Sakarya 16-1-82
Honours: Turkey 66 full caps, 19 goals.

2000-01	Sakarya	31	16		
2001-02	Sakarya	35	16	66	32
2002-03	Fenerbahce	29	9		
2003-04	Fenerbahce	31	19		
2004-05	Fenerbahce	31	7		
2005-06	Fenerbahce	27	13		
2006-07	Fenerbahce	33	9	151	57

2007-08	Middlesbrough	34	8	
2008-09	Middlesbrough	33	7	67 15

TURNBULL, Ross (G) 91 0
H: 6 4 W: 15 00 b.Bishop Auckland 4-1-85
Source: Trainee. Honours: England Youth, Under-20.

2002-03	Middlesbrough	0	0	
2003-04	Middlesbrough	0	0	
2003-04	Darlington	1	0	1 0
2003-04	Barnsley	3	0	
2004-05	Middlesbrough	0	0	
2004-05	Bradford C	2	0	2 0
2004-05	Barnsley	23	0	26 0
2005-06	Middlesbrough	2	0	
2005-06	Crewe Alex	29	0	29 0
2006-07	Middlesbrough	0	0	
2007-08	Middlesbrough	3	0	
2007-08	Cardiff C	6	0	6 0
2008-09	Middlesbrough	22	0	27 0

WALKER, Josh (M) 21 0
H: 5 11 W: 11 13 b.Newcastle 21-2-89
Source: Scholar. Honours: England Schools, Youth.

2005-06	Middlesbrough	1	0	
2006-07	Middlesbrough	0	0	
2006-07	Bournemouth	6	0	6 0
2007-08	Aberdeen	8	0	8 0
2007-08	Middlesbrough	0	0	
2008-09	Middlesbrough	6	0	7 0

WHEATER, David (D) 97 8
H: 6 5 W: 12 12 b.Redcar 14-2-87
Source: Scholar. Honours: England Youth, Under-21.

2004-05	Middlesbrough	0	0	
2005-06	Middlesbrough	6	0	
2005-06	Doncaster R	7	1	7 1
2006-07	Middlesbrough	2	1	
2006-07	Wolverhampton W	1	0	1 0
2007-08	Darlington	15	2	15 2
2007-08	Middlesbrough	34	3	
2008-09	Middlesbrough	32	1	74 5

WILLIAMS, Rhys (D) 17 0
H: 6 2 W: 11 05 b.Perth 14-7-88
Source: Scholar. Honours: Wales Under-21.

2006-07	Middlesbrough	0	0	
2007-08	Middlesbrough	0	0	
2008-09	Middlesbrough	0	0	
2008-09	Burnley	17	0	17 0

Scholars
Bassi, Derrick Singh; Corker, Ashley; Cronesberry, James Liam; Edwards, Kieran; Gray, James; Hawkins, Daniel; Martin, Gary; Oliver, Kyle Michael; Otte, Patrick James; Park, Cameron; Robinson, Jordan; Roushias, Onisiforos; Saiko, Shaun; Sellars, Conor Joseph; Shead, Philip Adam; Weldon, Paul Lewis.

MILLWALL (54)

ABDOU, Nadjim (M) 173 7
H: 5 10 W: 11 02 b.Martigues 13-7-84

2002-03	Martigues	26	1	26 1
2003-04	Sedan	17	0	
2004-05	Sedan	32	2	
2005-06	Sedan	14	0	
2006-07	Sedan	17	0	80 2
2007-08	Plymouth Arg	31	1	31 1
2008-09	Millwall	36	3	36 3

ALEXANDER, Gary (F) 392 116
H: 6 0 W: 13 04 b.Lambeth 15-8-79
Source: Trainee.

1998-99	West Ham U	0	0	
1999-2000	West Ham U	0	0	
1999-2000	Exeter C	37	16	37 16
2000-01	Swindon T	37	7	37 7
2001-02	Hull C	43	17	
2002-03	Hull C	25	6	68 23
2002-03	Leyton Orient	17	2	
2003-04	Leyton Orient	44	15	
2004-05	Leyton Orient	28	9	
2005-06	Leyton Orient	46	14	
2006-07	Leyton Orient	44	12	179 52
2007-08	Millwall	36	7	
2008-09	Millwall	35	11	71 18

BARRON, Scott (D) 44 0
H: 5 9 W: 9 08 b.Preston 2-9-85
Source: Scholar.

2003-04	Ipswich T	0	0	
2004-05	Ipswich T	0	0	
2005-06	Ipswich T	15	0	
2006-07	Ipswich T	0	0	15 0
2006-07	Wrexham	3	0	3 0
2007-08	Millwall	12	0	
2008-09	Millwall	14	0	26 0

BIGNOT, Marcus (D) 394 4
H: 5 7 W: 11 04 b.Birmingham 22-8-74
Source: Kidderminster H.

1997-98	Crewe Alex	42	0	
1998-99	Crewe Alex	26	0	
1999-2000	Crewe Alex	27	0	95 0
2000-01	Bristol R	26	1	26 1
2000-01	QPR	9	1	
2001-02	QPR	45	0	
2002-03	Rushden & D	33	0	
2003-04	Rushden & D	35	2	68 2
2003-04	QPR	6	0	
2004-05	QPR	43	0	
2005-06	QPR	44	0	
2006-07	QPR	33	0	
2007-08	QPR	2	0	182 1
2007-08	Millwall	22	0	
2008-09	Millwall	1	0	23 0

BOLDER, Adam (M) 267 15
H: 5 9 W: 10 08 b.Hull 25-10-80
Source: Trainee.

1998-99	Hull C	1	0	
1999-2000	Hull C	19	0	20 0
1999-2000	Derby Co	0	0	
2000-01	Derby Co	2	0	
2001-02	Derby Co	11	0	
2002-03	Derby Co	45	6	
2003-04	Derby Co	24	1	
2004-05	Derby Co	36	2	
2005-06	Derby Co	35	2	
2006-07	Derby Co	13	0	166 11
2006-07	QPR	16	0	
2007-08	QPR	24	2	
2007-08	Sheffield W	13	2	13 2
2008-09	QPR	0	0	40 2
2008-09	Millwall	28	0	28 0

BOWES, Gary (F) 1 0
H: 5 11 W: 12 00 b.Ilford 14-2-80
Source: Scholar.

2007-08	Millwall	1	0	
2008-09	Millwall	0	0	1 0

BRKOVIC, Ahmet (M) 294 42
H: 5 8 W: 11 11 b.Dubrovnik 23-9-74
Source: Dubrovnik.

1999-2000	Leyton Orient	29	5	
2000-01	Leyton Orient	40	3	
2001-02	Leyton Orient	0	0	69 8
2001-02	Luton T	21	1	
2002-03	Luton T	36	3	
2003-04	Luton T	32	1	
2004-05	Luton T	42	15	
2005-06	Luton T	42	8	
2006-07	Luton T	20	3	
2007-08	Luton T	1	0	194 31
2007-08	Millwall	25	2	
2008-09	Millwall	6	1	31 3

CRAIG, Tony (D) 155 5
H: 6 0 W: 10 03 b.Greenwich 20-4-85
Source: Scholar.

2002-03	Millwall	2	1	
2003-04	Millwall	9	0	
2004-05	Millwall	10	0	
2004-05	Wycombe W	14	0	14 0
2005-06	Millwall	28	0	
2006-07	Millwall	30	1	
2007-08	Crystal Palace	13	0	13 0
2007-08	Millwall	5	1	
2008-09	Millwall	44	2	128 5

DUFFY, Richard (D) 110 2
H: 5 9 W: 10 03 b.Swansea 30-8-85
Source: Scholar. Honours: Wales Youth, Under-21, 13 full caps.

2002-03	Swansea C	0	0	
2003-04	Swansea C	18	1	
2003-04	Portsmouth	1	0	
2004-05	Portsmouth	0	0	
2004-05	Burnley	7	1	7 1
2004-05	Coventry C	14	0	

2005-06	Portsmouth	0	0	
2005-06	Coventry C	32	0	
2006-07	Portsmouth	0	0	
2006-07	Coventry C	13	0	
2006-07	Swansea C	11	0	29 1
2007-08	Portsmouth	0	0	
2007-08	Coventry C	2	0	61 0
2008-09	Portsmouth	0	0	1 0
2008-09	Millwall	12	0	12 0

DUNNE, Alan (D) 147 12
H: 5 10 W: 10 13 b.Dublin 23-8-82
Source: Trainee.

1999-2000	Millwall	0	0	
2000-01	Millwall	0	0	
2001-02	Millwall	1	0	
2002-03	Millwall	4	0	
2003-04	Millwall	8	0	
2004-05	Millwall	19	3	
2005-06	Millwall	40	0	
2006-07	Millwall	32	6	
2007-08	Millwall	19	3	
2008-09	Millwall	24	0	147 12

EBSWORTH, Darren (D) 0 0
H: 5 10 W: 10 02 b.London 23-8-90
Source: Scholar.

2007-08	Millwall	0	0	
2008-09	Millwall	0	0	

EDWARDS, Preston (G) 1 0
H: 6 0 W: 12 07 b.Cheshunt 5-9-89
Source: Scholar.

2006-07	Millwall	0	0	
2007-08	Millwall	1	0	
2008-09	Millwall	0	0	1 0

FORBES, Adrian (F) 317 37
H: 5 8 W: 11 10 b.Greenford 23-1-79
Source: Trainee. Honours: England Youth.

1996-97	Norwich C	10	0	
1997-98	Norwich C	33	4	
1998-99	Norwich C	15	0	
1999-2000	Norwich C	25	1	
2000-01	Norwich C	29	3	112 8
2001-02	Luton T	40	4	
2002-03	Luton T	5	1	
2003-04	Luton T	27	9	72 14
2004-05	Swansea C	40	7	
2005-06	Swansea C	29	4	69 11
2006-07	Blackpool	34	1	
2007-08	Blackpool	2	0	36 1
2007-08	Millwall	11	0	
2008-09	Millwall	2	0	13 0
2008-09	Grimsby T	15	3	15 3

FORDE, David (G) 69 0
H: 6 3 W: 13 06 b.Galway 20-12-79
Source: Barry T.

2001-02	West Ham U	0	0	
2002-03	West Ham U	0	0	
2003-04	West Ham U	0	0	
2004-05	West Ham U	0	0	
2005-06	West Ham U	0	0	
2006-07	Cardiff C	7	0	
2007-08	Cardiff C	0	0	7 0
2007-08	Luton T	5	0	5 0
2007-08	Bournemouth	11	0	11 0
2008-09	Millwall	46	0	46 0

FRAMPTON, Andrew (D) 229 6
H: 5 11 W: 10 10 b.Wimbledon 3-9-79
Source: Trainee.

1998-99	Crystal Palace	6	0	
1999-2000	Crystal Palace	9	0	
2000-01	Crystal Palace	10	0	
2001-02	Crystal Palace	2	0	
2002-03	Crystal Palace	1	0	28 0
2002-03	Brentford	15	0	
2003-04	Brentford	16	0	
2004-05	Brentford	35	0	
2005-06	Brentford	36	3	
2006-07	Brentford	32	1	134 4
2007-08	Millwall	30	1	
2008-09	Millwall	37	1	67 2

FUSEINI, Ali (M) 61 2
H: 5 6 W: 9 10 b.Ghana 7-12-88
Source: Scholar.

2006-07	Millwall	7	0	
2007-08	Millwall	37	2	
2008-09	Millwall	17	0	61 2

GRABBAN, Lewis (F) 69 10
H: 6 0 W: 11 03 b.Croydon 12-1-88
Source: Scholar.

2005-06	Crystal Palace	0	0	
2006-07	Crystal Palace	8	1	
2006-07	*Oldham Ath*	9	0	9 0
2007-08	Crystal Palace	2	0	10 1
2007-08	*Motherwell*	6	0	6 0
2007-08	Millwall	13	3	
2008-09	Millwall	31	6	44 9

GRIMES, Ashley (M) 21 2
H: 6 0 W: 11 02 b.Swinton 9-12-86
Source: Scholar.

2006-07	Manchester C	0	0	
2006-07	*Swindon T*	4	0	4 0
2007-08	Manchester C	0	0	
2008-09	Millwall	17	2	17 2

HACKETT, Chris (M) 188 12
H: 6 0 W: 12 08 b.Oxford 1-3-83
Source: Scholarship.

1999-2000	Oxford U	2	0	
2000-01	Oxford U	16	2	
2001-02	Oxford U	15	0	
2002-03	Oxford U	12	0	
2003-04	Oxford U	22	1	
2004-05	Oxford U	37	4	
2005-06	Oxford U	21	2	125 9
2005-06	*Hearts*	2	0	2 0
2006-07	Millwall	33	3	
2007-08	Millwall	6	0	
2008-09	Millwall	22	0	61 3

HARRIS, Neil (F) 388 117
H: 5 10 W: 12 08 b.Orsett 12-7-77
Source: Cambridge C.

1997-98	Millwall	3	0	
1998-99	Millwall	39	15	
1999-2000	Millwall	38	25	
2000-01	Millwall	42	27	
2001-02	Millwall	21	4	
2002-03	Millwall	40	12	
2003-04	Millwall	38	9	
2004-05	Millwall	12	1	
2004-05	*Cardiff C*	3	1	3 1
2004-05	Nottingham F	13	0	
2005-06	Nottingham F	1	0	
2005-06	*Gillingham*	36	6	36 6
2006-07	Nottingham F	19	1	33 1
2006-07	Millwall	21	5	
2007-08	Millwall	27	3	
2008-09	Millwall	35	8	316 109

LAIRD, Marc (M) 68 7
H: 6 1 W: 10 07 b.Edinburgh 23-1-86
Source: Trainee.

2003-04	Manchester C	0	0	
2004-05	Manchester C	0	0	
2005-06	Manchester C	0	0	
2006-07	Manchester C	0	0	
2006-07	*Northampton T*	6	0	6 0
2007-08	Manchester C	0	0	
2007-08	*Port Vale*	7	1	7 1
2007-08	Millwall	17	1	
2008-09	Millwall	38	5	55 6

MARTIN, David (M) 69 6
H: 5 9 W: 10 10 b.Erith 3-6-85
Source: Dartford.

2006-07	Crystal Palace	5	0	
2007-08	Crystal Palace	9	0	14 0
2007-08	Millwall	11	2	
2008-09	Millwall	44	4	55 6

MORISON, Steven (F) 23 3
H: 6 2 W: 13 07 b.Enfield 29-8-83
Source: Scholar.

2001-02	Northampton T	1	0	
2002-03	Northampton T	13	1	
2003-04	Northampton T	5	1	
2004-05	Northampton T	4	1	23 3

From Stevenage B.

2008-09	Millwall	0	0

NOEL-WILLIAMS, Gifton (F) 323 65
H: 6 3 W: 13 06 b.Islington 21-1-80
Source: Trainee. Honours: England Youth.

1996-97	Watford	25	2
1997-98	Watford	38	7
1998-99	Watford	26	10
1999-2000	Watford	3	0
2000-01	Watford	32	8
2001-02	Watford	29	6

2002-03	Watford	16	0	169 33
2003-04	Stoke C	42	10	
2004-05	Stoke C	46	13	88 23
2005-06	Burnley	29	2	
2005-06	*Brighton & HA*	7	2	7 2
2006-07	Burnley	23	5	52 7
2008-09	Millwall	1	0	1 0

From Elche.

2008-09	*Yeovil T*	6	0	6 0

Transferred to Austin Aztex

O'CONNOR, Patrick (M) 0 0
H: 6 1 W: 13 00 b.Croydon 5-9-90
Source: Scholar.

2008-09	Millwall	0	0

PIDGELEY, Lenny (G) 84 0
H: 6 4 W: 14 09 b.Isleworth 7-2-84
Source: From Scholar. Honours: England Under-20.

2003-04	Chelsea	0	0	
2003-04	*Watford*	27	0	27 0
2004-05	Chelsea	1	0	
2005-06	Chelsea	1	0	2 0
2005-06	*Millwall*	0	0	
2006-07	Millwall	42	0	
2007-08	Millwall	13	0	
2008-09	Millwall	0	0	55 0

ROBINSON, Paul (D) 176 8
H: 6 1 W: 11 09 b.Barnet 7-1-82
Source: Scholar.

2000-01	Millwall	0	0	
2001-02	Millwall	0	0	
2002-03	Millwall	14	0	
2003-04	Millwall	9	0	
2004-05	Millwall	0	0	
2004-05	*Torquay U*	12	0	12 0
2005-06	Millwall	32	0	
2006-07	Millwall	38	3	
2007-08	Millwall	45	3	
2008-09	Millwall	26	2	164 8

SENDA, Danny (M) 352 10
H: 5 10 W: 10 02 b.Harrow 17-4-81
Source: Southampton Trainee. Honours: England Youth.

1998-99	Wycombe W	6	0	
1999-2000	Wycombe W	27	1	
2000-01	Wycombe W	31	2	
2001-02	Wycombe W	43	0	
2002-03	Wycombe W	41	2	
2003-04	Wycombe W	40	0	
2004-05	Wycombe W	44	4	
2005-06	Wycombe W	44	0	276 9
2006-07	Millwall	36	0	
2007-08	Millwall	40	1	
2008-09	Millwall	0	0	76 1

SPILLER, Danny (M) 137 7
H: 5 8 W: 11 00 b.Maidstone 10-10-81
Source: Trainee.

2000-01	Gillingham	0	0	
2001-02	Gillingham	1	0	
2002-03	Gillingham	10	0	
2003-04	Gillingham	39	6	
2004-05	Gillingham	22	0	
2005-06	Gillingham	32	0	
2006-07	Gillingham	25	0	129 6
2007-08	Millwall	6	1	
2008-09	Millwall	2	0	8 1

TAYLOR, Lyle (F) 0 0
b.Staines

2007-08	Millwall	0	0
2008-09	Millwall	0	0

WALKER, Lawrie (G) 0 0
b.Bedford 14-10-89
Source: Milton Keynes D Scholar.

2008-09	Millwall	0	0

WHITBREAD, Zak (D) 100 3
H: 6 2 W: 12 07 b.Houston 4-3-84
Honours: USA Under-23.

2002-03	Liverpool	0	0	
2003-04	Liverpool	0	0	
2004-05	Liverpool	0	0	
2005-06	*Millwall*	25	0	
2006-07	Millwall	14	0	
2007-08	Millwall	23	3	
2008-09	Millwall	38	0	100 3

MILTON KEYNES D (55)

ABBEY, Nathan (G) 209 0
H: 6 1 W: 11 13 b.Islington 11-7-78
Source: Trainee.

1995-96	Luton T	0	0	
1996-97	Luton T	0	0	
1997-98	Luton T	0	0	
1998-99	Luton T	2	0	
1999-2000	Luton T	33	0	
2000-01	Luton T	20	0	
2001-02	Chesterfield	46	0	46 0
2002-03	Northampton T	5	0	5 0
2003-04	Luton T	0	0	55 0
2003-04	Macclesfield T	0	0	
2003-04	Ipswich T	0	0	
2003-04	Burnley	0	0	
2004-05	Boston U	44	0	
2005-06	Boston U	17	0	61 0
2005-06	Leyton Orient	0	0	
2005-06	Bristol C	1	0	1 0
2006-07	Torquay U	24	0	24 0
2006-07	Brentford	16	0	16 0
2007-08	Milton Keynes D	0	0	
2008-09	Milton Keynes D	1	0	1 0

BALDOCK, Sam (F) 46 12
H: 5 7 W: 10 07 b.Bedford 15-3-89
Source: Scholar.

2005-06	Milton Keynes D	0	0	
2006-07	Milton Keynes D	1	0	
2007-08	Milton Keynes D	5	0	
2008-09	Milton Keynes D	40	12	46 12

BELSON, Flavien (M) 23 0
H: 6 2 W: 12 02 b.Le Havre 22-2-87

2005-06	Metz	4	0	
2006-07	Metz	0	0	
2007-08	Metz	6	0	10 0
2008-09	Milton Keynes D	13	0	13 0

CARAYOL, Mustapha (M) 0 0
H: 5 10 W: 11 11 b.Gambia 10-4-90

2007-08	Milton Keynes D	0	0
2008-09	Milton Keynes D	0	0

CHADWICK, Luke (M) 200 22
H: 5 11 W: 11 08 b.Cambridge 18-11-80
Source: Trainee. Honours: England Youth, Under-21.

1998-99	Manchester U	0	0	
1999-2000	Manchester U	0	0	
2000-01	Manchester U	16	2	
2001-02	Manchester U	8	0	
2002-03	Manchester U	1	0	
2002-03	*Reading*	15	1	15 1
2003-04	Manchester U	0	0	25 2
2003-04	*Burnley*	36	5	36 5
2004-05	West Ham U	32	1	
2005-06	West Ham U	0	0	32 1
2005-06	Stoke C	36	2	
2006-07	Stoke C	15	3	51 5
2006-07	Norwich C	4	1	
2007-08	Norwich C	13	1	
2008-09	Norwich C	0	0	17 2
2008-09	Milton Keynes D	24	6	24 6

CHICKSEN, Adam (D) 1 0
H: 5 8 W: 11 09 b.Coventry 27-9-91

2008-09	Milton Keynes D	1	0	1 0

DOBSON, Craig (M) 3 0
H: 5 7 W: 10 06 b.Chingford 23-1-84
Source: Crystal Palace scholar. Honours: Jamaica 1 full cap.

2003-04	Cheltenham T	2	0	2 0

From Barnet, Camb C, Stevenage.

2007-08	Milton Keynes D	1	0	
2008-09	Milton Keynes D	0	0	1 0
2008-09	*Wycombe W*	0	0	

FLO, Tore Andre (F) 407 140
H: 6 4 W: 13 08 b.Strin 15-6-73
Honours: Norway Under-21, 76 full caps, 39 goals.

1994	Sogndal	22	5	22 5
1995	Tromso	26	18	26 18
1996	Brann	24	19	
1997	Brann	16	9	40 28
1997-98	Chelsea	34	11	
1998-99	Chelsea	30	10	
1999-2000	Chelsea	34	10	
2000-01	Chelsea	14	3	112 34

2000-01	Rangers	19	11	
2001-02	Rangers	30	17	
2002-03	Rangers	4	0	53 28
2002-03	Sunderland	29	4	29 4
2003-04	Siena	33	8	
2004-05	Siena	32	7	65 15
2005	Valerenga	8	0	
2006	Valerenga	16	4	24 4
2006-07	Leeds U	1	1	
2007-08	Leeds U	22	3	
2008-09	Leeds U	0	0	23 4
2008-09	Milton Keynes D	13	0	13 0

GERBA, Ali (F)   184 59
H: 6 0   W: 14 05   b.Montreal 4-9-81
Honours: Canada 23 full caps, 11 goals.

2000	Montreal Impact	17	6	
2001	Miami Fusion	0	0	
2002	Pittsburg Riverhounds	19	1	19 1
2002-03	Toronto Lynx	25	6	
2003-04	Montreal Impact	7	1	
2004-05	Toronto Lynx	32	17	57 23
2005	Montreal Impact	8	5	32 12
2005	Sundsvall	11	5	11 5
2006-07	IFK Gothenburg	5	0	5 0
2006	Odd Grenland	10	1	10 1
2007	Horsens	15	4	15 4
2008	Ingolstadt	11	3	11 3
2008-09	Milton Keynes D	24	10	24 10

GUERET, Willy (G)   236 0
H: 6 1   W: 13 02   b.Saint Claude 3-8-73
Source: Le Mans.

2000-01	Millwall	11	0	
2001-02	Millwall	1	0	
2002-03	Millwall	0	0	
2003-04	Millwall	2	0	14 0
2004-05	Swansea C	44	0	
2005-06	Swansea C	46	0	
2006-07	Swansea C	42	0	132 0
2007-08	Milton Keynes D	46	0	
2008-09	Milton Keynes D	44	0	90 0

HOWELL, Luke (D)   24 1
H: 5 10   W: 10 05   b.Cuckfield 5-1-87
Source: Scholar.

2006-07	Gillingham	1	0	1 0
2007-08	Milton Keynes D	8	0	
2008-09	Milton Keynes D	15	1	23 1

JOHNSON, Jemal (F)   115 17
H: 5 8   W: 11 09   b.New Jersey 3-5-84
Source: Scholar.

2001-02	Blackburn R	0	0	
2002-03	Blackburn R	0	0	
2003-04	Blackburn R	0	0	
2004-05	Blackburn R	3	0	
2005-06	Blackburn R	3	0	
2005-06	Preston NE	3	1	3 1
2005-06	Darlington	9	3	9 3
2006-07	Blackburn R	0	0	6 0
2006-07	Wolverhampton W	20	3	
2006-07	Leeds U	5	0	5 0
2007-08	Wolverhampton W	0	0	20 3
2007-08	Milton Keynes D	39	5	
2008-09	Milton Keynes D	33	5	72 10

LEVEN, Peter (M)   147 21
H: 5 11   W: 12 13   b.Glasgow 27-9-83
Source: Rangers.

2004-05	Kilmarnock	32	4	
2005-06	Kilmarnock	6	0	
2006-07	Kilmarnock	27	1	65 5
2007-08	Chesterfield	42	6	42 6
2008-09	Milton Keynes D	40	10	40 10

LEWINGTON, Dean (D)   246 7
H: 5 11   W: 11 07   b.Kingston 18-5-84
Source: Scholar.

2002-03	Wimbledon	1	0	
2003-04	Wimbledon	28	1	29 1
2004-05	Milton Keynes D	43	2	
2005-06	Milton Keynes D	44	1	
2006-07	Milton Keynes D	45	1	
2007-08	Milton Keynes D	45	0	
2008-09	Milton Keynes D	40	2	217 6

LLERA, Miguel (D)   34 2
H: 6 3   W: 13 12   b.Seville 7-8-79

2008-09	Milton Keynes D	34	2	34 2

MITCHELL, Paul (M)   162 0
H: 5 9   W: 12 01   b.Manchester 26-8-81
Source: Trainee.

2000-01	Wigan Ath	1	0	
2000-01	Halifax T	11	0	11 0
2001-02	Wigan Ath	23	0	
2002-03	Wigan Ath	27	0	
2003-04	Wigan Ath	12	0	
2004-05	Wigan Ath	1	0	64 0
2004-05	Swindon T	7	0	7 0
2004-05	Milton Keynes D	13	0	
2005-06	Milton Keynes D	39	0	
2006-07	Milton Keynes D	20	0	
2006-07	Wrexham	5	0	5 0
2007-08	Milton Keynes D	0	0	
2008-09	Milton Keynes D	0	0	72 0
2008-09	Barnet	3	0	3 0

NAVARRO, Alan (M)   210 9
H: 5 10   W: 11 07   b.Liverpool 31-5-81
Source: Trainee.

1998-99	Liverpool	0	0	
1999-2000	Liverpool	0	0	
2000-01	Liverpool	0	0	
2000-01	Crewe Alex	8	1	
2001-02	Liverpool	0	0	
2001-02	Crewe Alex	7	0	15 1
2001-02	Tranmere R	21	1	
2002-03	Tranmere R	5	0	
2003-04	Tranmere R	19	0	
2004-05	Tranmere R	0	0	
2004-05	Chester C	3	0	3 0
2004-05	Macclesfield T	11	1	
2005-06	Tranmere R	0	0	45 1

From Accrington S.

2005-06	Macclesfield T	27	0	
2006-07	Macclesfield T	32	2	70 3
2007-08	Milton Keynes D	39	3	
2008-09	Milton Keynes D	38	1	77 4

O'HANLON, Sean (D)   218 20
H: 6 1   W: 12 05   b.Southport 2-1-83
Honours: England Schools, Youth, Under-20.

1999-2000	Everton	0	0	
2000-01	Everton	0	0	
2001-02	Everton	0	0	
2002-03	Everton	0	0	
2003-04	Everton	0	0	
2003-04	Swindon T	19	2	
2004-05	Swindon T	40	3	
2005-06	Swindon T	40	4	99 9
2006-07	Milton Keynes D	36	4	
2007-08	Milton Keynes D	43	4	
2008-09	Milton Keynes D	40	3	119 11

POWELL, Daniel (F)   7 1
H: 5 11   W: 13 03   b.Luton 12-3-91
Source: Scholar.

2008-09	Milton Keynes D	7	1	7 1

REGAN, Carl (D)   216 3
H: 5 11   W: 11 12   b.Liverpool 14-1-80
Source: From Trainee. *Honours:* England Youth.

1997-98	Everton	0	0	
1998-99	Everton	0	0	
1999-2000	Everton	0	0	
2000-01	Barnsley	27	0	
2001-02	Barnsley	10	0	
2002-03	Barnsley	0	0	37 0
2002-03	Hull C	38	0	
2003-04	Hull C	0	0	
2004-05	Hull C	0	0	38 0
2004-05	Chester C	6	0	
2005-06	Chester C	41	0	47 0
2006-07	Macclesfield T	38	2	
2007-08	Macclesfield T	20	0	58 2
2007-08	Milton Keynes D	9	1	
2008-09	Milton Keynes D	27	0	36 1

STIRLING, Jude (D)   130 5
H: 6 2   W: 11 12   b.Enfield 29-6-82
Source: Trainee.

1999-2000	Luton T	0	0	
2000-01	Luton T	9	0	
2001-02	Luton T	1	0	10 0

From Tamworth.

2005-06	Oxford U	10	0	10 0

From Stevenage B, Hornchurch, Tamworth

2005-06	Lincoln C	6	0	6 0
2006-07	Peterborough U	22	0	22 0
2006-07	Milton Keynes D	16	1	

2007-08	Milton Keynes D	34	2	
2008-09	Milton Keynes D	32	2	82 5

STURM, Florian (M)   5 0
H: 5 10   W: 11 05   b.Worgl 6-5-82
Honours: Austria Under-21.

2008-09	Milton Keynes D	5	0	5 0

SWAILES, Danny (D)   299 22
H: 6 3   W: 12 06   b.Bolton 1-4-79
Source: Trainee.

1997-98	Bury	0	0	
1998-99	Bury	0	0	
1999-2000	Bury	24	3	
2000-01	Bury	11	0	
2001-02	Bury	28	1	
2002-03	Bury	39	3	
2003-04	Bury	42	5	
2004-05	Bury	20	1	164 13
2004-05	Macclesfield T	17	0	
2005-06	Macclesfield T	39	2	
2006-07	Macclesfield T	38	3	
2007-08	Macclesfield T	0	0	94 5
2007-08	Milton Keynes D	40	4	
2008-09	Milton Keynes D	1	0	41 4

WILBRAHAM, Aaron (F)   331 77
H: 6 3   W: 12 04   b.Knutsford 21-10-79
Source: Trainee.

1997-98	Stockport Co	7	1	
1998-99	Stockport Co	26	0	
1999-2000	Stockport Co	26	4	
2000-01	Stockport Co	36	12	
2001-02	Stockport Co	21	3	
2002-03	Stockport Co	15	7	
2003-04	Stockport Co	41	8	172 35
2004-05	Hull C	19	2	19 2
2004-05	Oldham Ath	4	2	4 2
2005-06	Milton Keynes D	31	4	
2005-06	Bradford C	5	1	5 1
2006-07	Milton Keynes D	32	7	
2007-08	Milton Keynes D	35	10	
2008-09	Milton Keynes D	33	16	131 37

WRIGHT, Mark (M)   190 27
H: 5 11   W: 11 00   b.Wolverhampton 24-2-82
Source: Scholar.

2000-01	Walsall	4	0	
2001-02	Walsall	0	0	
2002-03	Walsall	5	0	
2003-04	Walsall	11	2	
2004-05	Walsall	37	2	
2005-06	Walsall	30	2	
2006-07	Walsall	37	3	124 9
2007-08	Milton Keynes D	34	13	
2008-09	Milton Keynes D	32	5	66 18

MORECAMBE (56)

ADAMS, Danny (D)   336 2
H: 5 8   W: 13 08   b.Manchester 3-1-76
Source: Altrincham.

2000-01	Macclesfield T	37	0	
2001-02	Macclesfield T	39	0	
2002-03	Macclesfield T	45	1	
2003-04	Macclesfield T	27	0	148 1
2003-04	Stockport Co	12	0	
2004-05	Stockport Co	27	1	39 1
2004-05	Huddersfield T	5	0	
2005-06	Huddersfield T	40	0	
2006-07	Huddersfield T	23	0	68 0
2007-08	Morecambe	42	0	
2008-09	Morecambe	39	0	81 0

ALLEN, Damien (M)   70 1
H: 5 11   W: 11 04   b.Cheadle 1-8-86
Source: Trainee.

2004-05	Stockport Co	21	1	
2005-06	Stockport Co	22	0	
2006-07	Stockport Co	7	0	50 1
2006-07	Antwerp	0	0	
2007-08	Morecambe	20	0	
2008-09	Morecambe	0	0	20 0

ARTELL, Dave (D)   263 19
H: 6 3   W: 14 01   b.Rotherham 22-11-80
Source: Trainee.

1999-2000	Rotherham U	1	0	
2000-01	Rotherham U	36	4	
2001-02	Rotherham U	0	0	
2002-03	Rotherham U	0	0	37 4

2002-03	*Shrewsbury T*	28	1	28	1
2003-04	Mansfield T	26	3		
2004-05	Mansfield T	19	2	45	5
2005-06	Chester C	37	2		
2006-07	Chester C	43	1	80	3
2007-08	Morecambe	36	3		
2008-09	Morecambe	37	3	73	6

BELL, Matthew (D)   0   0
b.Lancaster 9-10-89
Source: Scholar.

2008-09	Morecambe	0	0

BENTLEY, Jim (D)   88   9
H: 6 1   W: 13 00   b.Liverpool 11-6-76
Source: Trainee.

1993-94	Manchester C	0	0		
1994-95	Manchester C	0	0		
1995-96	Manchester C	0	0		
1996-97	Manchester C	0	0		
1997-98	Manchester C	0	0		
1998-99	Manchester C	0	0		
2007-08	Morecambe	43	6		
2008-09	Morecambe	45	3	88	9

BLINKHORN, Matthew (F)   108   15
H: 5 11   W: 10 10   b.Blackpool 2-3-85
Source: Scholar.

2001-02	Blackpool	3	0		
2002-03	Blackpool	7	2		
2003-04	Blackpool	12	1		
2004-05	Blackpool	4	0		
2004-05	*Luton T*	2	0	2	0
2005-06	Blackpool	16	2		
2006-07	Blackpool	2	0	44	5
2006-07	*Bury*	10	0	10	0
2007-08	Morecambe	41	10		
2008-09	Morecambe	11	0	52	10

CARR, Michael (D)   18   0
H: 5 11   W: 12 04   b.Crewe 6-12-83
Source: Scholar.

2002-03	Macclesfield T	4	0		
2003-04	Macclesfield T	7	0		
2004-05	Macclesfield T	0	0	11	0

From Northwich Vic.

2008-09	Morecambe	7	0	7	0

CURTIS, Wayne (M)   68   7
H: 6 0   W: 12 00   b.Barrow 6-3-80
Source: Holker Old Boys.

2007-08	Morecambe	36	2		
2008-09	Morecambe	32	5	68	7

DAVIES, Scott (G)   10   0
H: 6 0   W: 11 00   b.Blackpool 27-2-87

2007-08	Morecambe	10	0		
2008-09	Morecambe	0	0	10	0

DRUMMOND, Stuart (M)   216   31
H: 6 2   W: 13 08   b.Preston 11-12-75
Source: Morecambe.

2004-05	Chester C	45	6		
2005-06	Chester C	42	6	87	12
2006-07	Shrewsbury T	44	4		
2007-08	Shrewsbury T	23	3	67	7
2007-08	Morecambe	18	2		
2008-09	Morecambe	44	10	62	12

DUFFY, Mark (M)   9   1
H: 5 9   W: 11 05   b.Liverpool 7-10-85
Source: Vauxhall M, Prescot C, Southport.

2008-09	Morecambe	9	1	9	1

EDGE, Lewis (G)   4   0
H: 6 1   W: 12 10   b.Lancaster 12-1-87
Source: Scholar.

2003-04	Blackpool	1	0		
2004-05	Blackpool	1	0		
2005-06	Blackpool	1	0		
2006-07	Blackpool	1	0		
2006-07	*Bury*	1	0	1	0
2007-08	Morecambe	0	0	3	0
2008-09	Morecambe	0	0		

HOWARD, Mike (D)   232   2
H: 5 6   W: 10 07   b.Birkenhead 2-12-78
Source: Tranmere R Trainee.

1997-98	Swansea C	0	0		
1998-99	Swansea C	39	1		
1999-2000	Swansea C	40	0		
2000-01	Swansea C	41	0		
2001-02	Swansea C	42	1		
2002-03	Swansea C	38	0		
2003-04	Swansea C	25	0		
2004-05	Swansea C	0	0		
2005-06	Swansea C	0	0		
2006-07	Swansea C	0	0	228	2
2007-08	Morecambe	4	0		
2008-09	Morecambe	0	0	4	0

HUNTER, Garry (M)   67   2
H: 5 7   W: 10 03   b.Morecambe 1-1-85
Source: Scholar.

2007-08	Morecambe	38	1		
2008-09	Morecambe	29	1	67	2

LLOYD, Paul (M)   7   0
H: 5 9   W: 10 11   b.Preston 26-3-87

2007-08	Morecambe	7	0		
2008-09	Morecambe	0	0	7	0

McCANN, Ryan (M)   122   8
H: 5 8   W: 11 03   b.Bellshill 15-9-82

1999-2000	Celtic	1	0		
2000-01	Celtic	0	0		
2001-02	Celtic	0	0		
2002-03	Celtic	0	0	1	0
2002-03	St Johnstone	17	3		
2003-04	Hartlepool U	4	0		
2004-05	Hartlepool U	0	0	4	0
2004-05	St Johnstone	26	3		
2005-06	St Johnstone	16	0	59	6
2006-07	Clyde	21	0	21	0
2007	Bohemians	10	2	10	2
2007-08	Queen of the S	14	0	14	0
2008-09	Morecambe	13	0	13	0

McLACHLAN, Fraser (M)   110   4
H: 5 11   W: 12 07   b.Manchester 9-11-82
Source: Scholar.

2001-02	Stockport Co	11	1		
2002-03	Stockport Co	22	0		
2003-04	Stockport Co	20	3		
2004-05	Stockport Co	0	0	53	4
2004-05	Mansfield T	21	0		
2005-06	Mansfield T	8	0	29	0
2007-08	Morecambe	1	0		
2008-09	Morecambe	27	0	28	0

McSTAY, Henry (D)   46   1
H: 6 0   W: 11 11   b.Co Armagh 6-3-85
Source: Scholar. *Honours:* Eire Under-21.

2001-02	Leeds U	0	0		
2002-03	Leeds U	0	0		
2003-04	Leeds U	0	0		
2004-05	Leeds U	0	0		
2005-06	Leeds U	0	0		
2006-07	Leeds U	0	0		
2007-08	Antwerp	13	0	13	0
2007-08	Morecambe	13	0		
2008-09	Morecambe	20	1	33	1

O'CARROLL, Diarmuid (F)   44   7
H: 5 11   W: 11 11   b.Killarney 16-3-87
Source: Home Farm.

2006-07	Celtic	0	0		
2006-07	*Ross Co*	15	2	15	2
2007-08	Celtic	0	0		
2008-09	Morecambe	29	5	29	5

PARRISH, Andy (D)   56   1
H: 6 0   W: 11 00   b.Bolton 22-6-88
Source: Scholar.

2005-06	Bury	8	0		
2006-07	Bury	9	0		
2007-08	Bury	26	1	43	1
2008-09	Morecambe	13	0	13	0

ROCHE, Barry (G)   185   0
H: 6 5   W: 14 08   b.Dublin 6-4-82
Source: Trainee.

1999-2000	Nottingham F	0	0		
2000-01	Nottingham F	2	0		
2001-02	Nottingham F	0	0		
2002-03	Nottingham F	1	0		
2003-04	Nottingham F	8	0		
2004-05	Nottingham F	2	0	13	0
2005-06	Chesterfield	41	0		
2006-07	Chesterfield	40	0		
2007-08	Chesterfield	45	0	126	0
2008-09	Morecambe	46	0	46	0

STANLEY, Craig (M)   65   7
H: 5 8   W: 10 08   b.Bedworth 3-3-83
Source: Scholar.

2002-03	Walsall	0	0
2003-04	Walsall	0	0
2004-05	Walsall	0	0
2005-06	Walsall	0	0
2006-07	Walsall	0	0

2007-08	Morecambe	41	2		
2008-09	Morecambe	24	5	65	7

TAYLOR, Aaron (F)   17   2
H: 5 8   W: 11 11   b.Morecambe 9-3-90

2008-09	Morecambe	17	2	17	2

TWISS, Michael (M)   94   12
H: 5 11   W: 13 03   b.Salford 28-12-77
Source: Scholar.

1996-97	Manchester U	0	0		
1997-98	Manchester U	0	0		
1998-99	*Sheffield U*	12	1	12	1
1999-2000	Manchester U	0	0		
2000-01	Port Vale	18	2		
2001-02	Port Vale	0	0	18	2
2007-08	Morecambe	36	6		
2008-09	Morecambe	28	3	64	9

WAINWRIGHT, Neil (M)   324   32
H: 6 0   W: 12 00   b.Warrington 4-11-77
Source: Trainee.

1996-97	Wrexham	0	0		
1997-98	Wrexham	11	3	11	3
1998-99	Sunderland	2	0		
1999-2000	Sunderland	0	0		
1999-2000	*Darlington*	17	4		
2000-01	Sunderland	0	0		
2000-01	*Halifax T*	13	0	13	0
2001-02	Sunderland	0	0	2	0
2001-02	Darlington	35	4		
2002-03	Darlington	33	1		
2003-04	Darlington	35	7		
2004-05	Darlington	38	4		
2005-06	Darlington	39	3		
2006-07	Darlington	41	5		
2007-08	Darlington	14	0	252	28
2007-08	*Shrewsbury T*	3	0	3	0
2007-08	*Mansfield T*	5	0	5	0
2008-09	Morecambe	38	1	38	1

YATES, Adam (D)   76   0
H: 5 10   W: 10 07   b.Stoke 28-5-83
Source: Scholar.

2000-01	Crewe Alex	0	0		
2001-02	Crewe Alex	0	0		
2002-03	Crewe Alex	0	0		
2003-04	Crewe Alex	0	0		
2004-05	Crewe Alex	0	0		
2005-06	Crewe Alex	0	0		
2006-07	Crewe Alex	0	0		
2007-08	Morecambe	44	0		
2008-09	Morecambe	32	0	76	0

NEWCASTLE U (57)

ADJEI, Samuel (M)   0   0
H: 6 1   W: 12 00   b.Ghana 18-1-92
Source: Jonkoping.

2008-09	Newcastle U	0	0

AMEOBI, Shola (F)   196   32
H: 6 3   W: 11 13   b.Zaria 12-10-81
Source: From Trainee. *Honours:* England Under-21.

1998-99	Newcastle U	0	0		
1999-2000	Newcastle U	0	0		
2000-01	Newcastle U	20	2		
2001-02	Newcastle U	15	0		
2002-03	Newcastle U	28	5		
2003-04	Newcastle U	26	7		
2004-05	Newcastle U	31	2		
2005-06	Newcastle U	30	9		
2006-07	Newcastle U	12	3		
2007-08	Newcastle U	6	0		
2007-08	*Stoke C*	6	0	6	0
2008-09	Newcastle U	22	4	190	32

BARTON, Joey (M)   162   17
H: 5 11   W: 12 05   b.Huyton 2-9-82
Source: Scholar. *Honours:* England Under-21, 1 full cap.

2001-02	Manchester C	0	0		
2002-03	Manchester C	7	1		
2003-04	Manchester C	28	1		
2004-05	Manchester C	31	1		
2005-06	Manchester C	31	6		
2006-07	Manchester C	33	6	130	15
2007-08	Newcastle U	23	1		
2008-09	Newcastle U	9	1	32	2

BASSONG, Sebastien (D)   109 1
H: 6 2   W: 11 07   b.Paris 9-7-86
Honours: France Under-21.

2005-06	Metz	23	0		
2006-07	Metz	37	1		
2007-08	Metz	19	0	79	1
2008-09	Newcastle U	30	0	30	0

BEYE, Habib (D)   314 11
H: 6 0   W: 12 06   b.Paris 19-10-77
Honours: Senegal 41 full caps, 1 goal.

1997-98	Paris St Germain	0	0		
1998-99	Strasbourg	23	0		
1999-2000	Strasbourg	33	1		
2000-01	Strasbourg	31	3		
2001-02	Strasbourg	20	3		
2002-03	Strasbourg	26	1		
2003-04	Strasbourg	1	0	134	8
2003-04	Marseille	22	0		
2004-05	Marseille	37	1		
2005-06	Marseille	29	1		
2006-07	Marseille	36	0		
2007-08	Marseille	4	0	128	2
2007-08	Newcastle U	29	1		
2008-09	Newcastle U	23	0	52	1

BUTT, Nicky (M)   411 29
H: 5 10   W: 11 05   b.Manchester 21-1-75
Source: Trainee. *Honours:* England Schools, Youth, Under-21, 39 full caps.

1992-93	Manchester U	1	0		
1993-94	Manchester U	1	0		
1994-95	Manchester U	22	1		
1995-96	Manchester U	32	2		
1996-97	Manchester U	26	5		
1997-98	Manchester U	33	3		
1998-99	Manchester U	31	2		
1999-2000	Manchester U	32	3		
2000-01	Manchester U	28	3		
2001-02	Manchester U	25	1		
2002-03	Manchester U	18	0		
2003-04	Manchester U	21	1	270	21
2004-05	Newcastle U	18	1		
2005-06	*Birmingham C*	24	3	24	3
2006-07	Newcastle U	31	1		
2007-08	Newcastle U	35	3		
2008-09	Newcastle U	33	0	117	5

CACAPA, Claudio (D)   218 10
H: 6 0   W: 12 01   b.Lavras 29-5-76
Honours: Brazil 4 full caps.

1997	Atletico Mineiro	6	0		
1998	Atletico Mineiro	15	0		
1999	Atletico Mineiro	29	1		
2000	Atletico Mineiro	18	1	68	2
2000-01	Lyon	6	1		
2001-02	Lyon	15	0		
2002-03	Lyon	36	2		
2003-04	Lyon	15	1		
2004-05	Lyon	21	1		
2005-06	Lyon	26	2		
2006-07	Lyon	6	0	125	7
2007-08	Newcastle U	19	1		
2008-09	Newcastle U	6	0	25	1

CARROLL, Andy (F)   33 4
H: 6 4   W: 11 00   b.Gateshead 6-1-89
Source: Scholar. *Honours:* England Youth.

2006-07	Newcastle U	4	0		
2007-08	Newcastle U	4	0		
2007-08	*Preston NE*	11	1	11	1
2008-09	Newcastle U	14	3	22	3

COLOCCINI, Fabricio (D)   252 16
H: 6 0   W: 12 04   b.Cordoba 22-1-82
Honours: Argentina 32 full caps, 1 goal.

1998-99	Boca Juniors	1	1		
1999-2000	Boca Juniors	1	0	2	1
1999-2000	AC Milan	0	0		
2000-01	AC Milan	0	0		
2000-01	San Lorenzo	19	3	19	3
2001-02	Alaves	33	6	33	6
2002-03	Atletico Madrid	27	0	27	0
2003-04	Villarreal	31	1	31	1
2004-05	AC Milan	1	0	1	0
2004-05	La Coruna	15	1		
2005-06	La Coruna	26	0		
2006-07	La Coruna	26	0		
2007-08	La Coruna	38	4	105	5
2008-09	Newcastle U	34	0	34	0

DANQUAH, Frank (F)   0 0
H: 5 11   W: 11 07   b.Amsterdam 4-10-89
Source: Scholar.

2008-09	Newcastle U	0	0		

DONALDSON, Ryan (F)   0 0
H: 5 9   W: 11 00   b. *Honours:* 1-5-91
Source: Scholar.

2008-09	Newcastle U	0	0		

DONINGER, Mark (M)   0 0
b.Newcastle 19-10-89

2007-08	Newcastle U	0	0		
2008-09	Newcastle U	0	0		

DUFF, Damien (F)   333 45
H: 5 9   W: 12 06   b.Ballyboden 2-3-79
Source: Lourdes Celtic. *Honours:* Eire Schools, Youth, Under-20, B, 74 full caps, 7 goals.

1995-96	Blackburn R	0	0		
1996-97	Blackburn R	1	0		
1997-98	Blackburn R	26	4		
1998-99	Blackburn R	28	1		
1999-2000	Blackburn R	39	5		
2000-01	Blackburn R	32	1		
2001-02	Blackburn R	32	7		
2002-03	Blackburn R	26	9	184	27
2003-04	Chelsea	23	5		
2004-05	Chelsea	30	6		
2005-06	Chelsea	28	3	81	14
2006-07	Newcastle U	22	1		
2007-08	Newcastle U	16	0		
2008-09	Newcastle U	30	3	68	4

EDGAR, David (D)   19 2
H: 6 2   W: 12 13   b.Ontario 19-5-87
Source: Scholar. *Honours:* Canada Youth, Under-20.

2005-06	Newcastle U	0	0		
2006-07	Newcastle U	3	1		
2007-08	Newcastle U	5	0		
2008-09	Newcastle U	11	1	19	2

FERGUSON, Shane (M)
Source: Scholar. *Honours:* Northern Ireland Under-21, B, 1 full cap.

2008-09	Newcastle U	0	0		

FORSTER, Fraser (G)   6 0
H: 6 4   W: 12 00   b.Hexham 17-3-88
Source: Scholar.

2007-08	Newcastle U	0	0		
2008-09	Newcastle U	0	0		
2008-09	*Stockport Co*	6	0	6	0

GEREMI (M)   255 21
H: 5 9   W: 13 01   b.Bafoussam 20-12-78
Source: Racing Bafousam. *Honours:* Cameroon 72 full caps, 10 goals.

1997	Cerro Porteno	6	0	6	0
1997-98	Genclerbirligi	28	4		
1998-99	Genclerbirligi	29	5	57	9
1999-2000	Real Madrid	20	0		
2000-01	Real Madrid	16	0		
2001-02	Real Madrid	9	0	45	0
2002-03	Middlesbrough	33	7	33	7
2003-04	Chelsea	25	1		
2004-05	Chelsea	13	0		
2005-06	Chelsea	15	2		
2006-07	Chelsea	19	1	72	4
2007-08	Newcastle U	27	1		
2008-09	Newcastle U	15	0	42	1

GODSMARK, Jonny (M)   0 0
H: 5 6   W: 10 01   b.Guide Post 3-9-89
Source: Scholar.

2008-09	Newcastle U	0	0		

GONZALEZ, Ignacio (M)   157 45
H: 5 11   W: 11 07   b.Montevideo 14-5-82
Honours: Uruguay 17 full caps.

2002	Danubio	24	3		
2003	Danubio	34	4		
2004	Danubio	14	4		
2005	Danubio	16	0		
2005-06	Danubio	28	13		
2006-07	Danubio	25	13		
2007-08	Danubio	9	7	150	44
2007-08	Monaco	5	1	5	1
2008-09	Newcastle U	2	0	2	0

GUTHRIE, Danny (M)   62 2
H: 5 9   W: 11 06   b.Shrewsbury 18-4-87
Source: Scholar. *Honours:* England Schools, Youth.

2004-05	Liverpool	0	0		
2005-06	Liverpool	0	0		
2006-07	Liverpool	3	0		
2006-07	*Southampton*	10	0	10	0
2007-08	Liverpool	0	0	3	0
2007-08	*Bolton W*	25	0	25	0
2008-09	Newcastle U	24	2	24	2

GUTIERREZ, Jonas (M)   224 6
H: 6 0   W: 11 07   b.Buenos Aires 5-7-82
Honours: Argentina 11 full caps, 1 goal.

2001-02	Velez Sarsfield	17	0		
2002-03	Velez Sarsfield	21	1		
2003-04	Velez Sarsfield	27	0		
2004-05	Velez Sarsfield	33	0	98	1
2005-06	Mallorca	30	2		
2006-07	Mallorca	36	3		
2007-08	Mallorca	30	0	96	5
2008-09	Newcastle U	30	0	30	0

HARPER, Steve (G)   128 0
H: 6 2   W: 13 10   b.Easington 14-3-75
Source: Seaham Red Star.

1993-94	Newcastle U	0	0		
1994-95	Newcastle U	0	0		
1995-96	Newcastle U	0	0		
1995-96	*Bradford C*	1	0	1	0
1996-97	Newcastle U	0	0		
1996-97	*Stockport Co*	0	0		
1997-98	Newcastle U	0	0		
1997-98	*Hartlepool U*	15	0	15	0
1997-98	*Huddersfield T*	24	0	24	0
1998-99	Newcastle U	8	0		
1999-2000	Newcastle U	18	0		
2000-01	Newcastle U	5	0		
2001-02	Newcastle U	0	0		
2002-03	Newcastle U	0	0		
2003-04	Newcastle U	0	0		
2004-05	Newcastle U	2	0		
2005-06	Newcastle U	0	0		
2006-07	Newcastle U	18	0		
2007-08	Newcastle U	21	0		
2008-09	Newcastle U	16	0	88	0

JOSE ENRIQUE (D)   105 1
H: 6 0   W: 12 00   b.Valencia 23-1-86
Honours: Spain Under-21.

2004-05	Levante	19	1	19	1
2005-06	Valencia	0	0		
2005-06	*Celta Vigo*	14	0	14	0
2006-07	*Villarreal*	23	0	23	0
2007-08	Newcastle U	23	0		
2008-09	Newcastle U	26	0	49	0

KADAR, Tamas (D)   0 0
H: 6 0   W: 12 10   b.Veszprem 14-3-90

2007-08	Newcastle U	0	0		
2008-09	Newcastle U	0	0		

KRUL, Tim (G)   31 0
H: 6 2   W: 11 08   b.Den Haag 3-4-88
Source: Academy. *Honours:* Holland Youth, Under-21.

2005-06	Newcastle U	0	0		
2006-07	Newcastle U	0	0		
2007-08	*Falkirk*	22	0	22	0
2007-08	Newcastle U	0	0		
2008-09	Newcastle U	0	0		
2008-09	*Carlisle U*	9	0	9	0

LOVENKRANDS, Peter (F)   220 54
H: 5 11   W: 11 02   b.Copenhagen 29-1-80
Honours: Denmark Youth, 21 full caps, 1 goal.

1998-99	AB Copenhagen	18	2		
1999-2000	AB Copenhagen	14	5	32	7
2000-01	Rangers	8	0		
2001-02	Rangers	18	2		
2002-03	Rangers	28	9		
2003-04	Rangers	25	8		
2004-05	Rangers	17	3		
2005-06	Rangers	33	14	129	36
2006-07	Schalke	24	6		
2007-08	Schalke	20	0		
2008-09	Schalke B	3	2	44	6
2008-09	Newcastle U	12	3	12	3

LUALUA, Kazenga (F) 9 0
H: 5 11 W: 12 00 b.Kinshasa 10-12-90
Source: Scholar.

2007-08	Newcastle U	2	0	
2008-09	Newcastle U	3	0	5 0
2008-09	*Doncaster R*	4	0	4 0

MARTINS, Obafemi (F) 178 55
H: 5 9 W: 10 07 b.Lagos 28-10-84
Honours: Nigeria 21 full caps, 13 goals.

2000-01	Reggiana	2	0	2 0
2001-02	Internazionale	0	0	
2002-03	Internazionale	4	1	
2003-04	Internazionale	25	7	
2004-05	Internazionale	31	11	
2005-06	Internazionale	28	8	88 27
2006-07	Newcastle U	33	11	
2007-08	Newcastle U	31	9	
2008-09	Newcastle U	24	8	88 28

McLAUGHLIN, Patrick (M) 0 0
b.Larne 14-1-91

2007-08	Newcastle U	0	0
2008-09	Newcastle U	0	0

NGO BAHENG, Wesley (F) 0 0
H: 5 11 W: 11 06 b.Blanc Mesnil 23-9-89

2007-08	Newcastle U	0	0
2008-09	Newcastle U	0	0

NOLAN, Kevin (M) 307 40
H: 6 0 W: 14 00 b.Liverpool 24-6-82
Source: Scholar. *Honours:* England Youth,
Under-20, Under-21.

1999-2000	Bolton W	4	0	
2000-01	Bolton W	31	1	
2001-02	Bolton W	35	8	
2002-03	Bolton W	33	1	
2003-04	Bolton W	37	9	
2004-05	Bolton W	36	4	
2005-06	Bolton W	36	9	
2006-07	Bolton W	31	3	
2007-08	Bolton W	33	5	
2008-09	Bolton W	20	0	296 40
2008-09	Newcastle U	11	0	11 0

OWEN, Michael (F) 323 157
H: 5 8 W: 10 12 b.Chester 14-12-79
Source: Trainee. *Honours:* England Schools,
Youth, Under-21, B, 89 full caps, 40 goals.

1996-97	Liverpool	2	1	
1997-98	Liverpool	36	18	
1998-99	Liverpool	30	18	
1999-2000	Liverpool	27	11	
2000-01	Liverpool	28	16	
2001-02	Liverpool	29	19	
2002-03	Liverpool	35	19	
2003-04	Liverpool	29	16	216 118
2004-05	Real Madrid	36	13	36 13
2005-06	Newcastle U	11	7	
2006-07	Newcastle U	3	0	
2007-08	Newcastle U	29	11	
2008-09	Newcastle U	28	8	71 26

RANGER, Nile (F) 0 0
H: 6 2 W: 13 03 b.London 11-4-91
Source: Southampton Scholar. *Honours:*
England Youth.

2008-09	Newcastle U	0	0

ROZEHNAL, David (D) 223 5
H: 6 3 W: 12 04 b.Stembeck 5-7-80
Honours: Czech Republic Under-21, 42 full
caps.

1999-2000	Olomouc	4	0	
2000-01	Olomouc	10	1	
2001-02	Olomouc	28	1	
2002-03	Olomouc	26	0	70 2
2003-04	FC Brugge	26	0	
2004-05	FC Brugge	24	1	50 1
2005-06	Paris St Germain	37	2	
2006-07	Paris St Germain	37	2	75 2
2007-08	Lazio	7	0	7 0
2007-08	Newcastle U	21	0	
2008-09	Newcastle U	0	0	21 0

SMITH, Alan (F) 272 45
H: 5 10 W: 12 04 b.Rothwell 28-10-80
Source: Trainee. *Honours:* England Youth,
Under-21, B, 19 full caps, 1 goal.

1997-98	Leeds U	21	7
1998-99	Leeds U	22	7
1999-2000	Leeds U	26	4
2000-01	Leeds U	33	11
2001-02	Leeds U	23	4

2002-03	Leeds U	33	3	
2003-04	Leeds U	35	9	172 38
2004-05	Manchester U	31	6	
2005-06	Manchester U	21	1	
2006-07	Manchester U	9	0	61 7
2007-08	Newcastle U	33	0	
2008-09	Newcastle U	6	0	39 0

SODERBERG, Ole (D) 0 0
b.Norrkoping 20-7-90
Source: BK Hacken.

2007-08	Newcastle U	0	0
2008-09	Newcastle U	0	0

TAYLOR, Ryan (M) 164 20
H: 5 8 W: 10 04 b.Liverpool 19-8-84
Source: Scholar. *Honours:* England Youth,
Under-21.

2001-02	Tranmere R	0	0	
2002-03	Tranmere R	25	1	
2003-04	Tranmere R	30	5	
2004-05	Tranmere R	43	8	98 14
2005-06	Wigan Ath	11	0	
2006-07	Wigan Ath	16	1	
2007-08	Wigan Ath	17	3	
2008-09	Wigan Ath	12	2	56 6
2008-09	Newcastle U	10	0	10 0

TAYLOR, Steven (D) 117 7
H: 6 2 W: 13 01 b.Greenwich 23-1-86
Source: Trainee. *Honours:* FA Schools,
Youth, England Under-20, Under-21, B.

2002-03	Newcastle U	0	0	
2003-04	Newcastle U	1	0	
2003-04	*Wycombe W*	6	0	6 0
2004-05	Newcastle U	13	0	
2005-06	Newcastle U	12	0	
2006-07	Newcastle U	27	2	
2007-08	Newcastle U	31	1	
2008-09	Newcastle U	27	4	111 7

TOZER, Ben (D) 2 0
H: 6 1 W: 12 11 b.Plymouth 1-3-90
Source: Scholar.

2007-08	Swindon T	2	0	2 0
2007-08	Newcastle U	0	0	
2008-09	Newcastle U	0	0	

VIDUKA, Mark (F) 409 202
H: 6 2 W: 15 01 b.Melbourne 9-10-75
Honours: Australia Youth, Under-20,
Under-23, 43 full caps, 11 goals.

1992-93	Melbourne Knights	4	2	
1993-94	Melbourne Knights	20	17	
1994-95	Melbourne Knights	24	21	48 40
1995-96	Croatia Zagreb	27	12	
1996-97	Croatia Zagreb	25	18	
1997-98	Croatia Zagreb	25	8	
1998-99	Croatia Zagreb	7	2	84 40
1998-99	Celtic	9	5	
1999-2000	Celtic	28	25	37 30
2000-01	Leeds U	34	17	
2001-02	Leeds U	33	11	
2002-03	Leeds U	33	20	
2003-04	Leeds U	30	11	130 59
2004-05	Middlesbrough	16	5	
2005-06	Middlesbrough	27	7	
2006-07	Middlesbrough	29	14	72 26
2007-08	Newcastle U	26	7	
2008-09	Newcastle U	12	0	38 7

XISCO (F) 76 26
H: 6 0 W: 13 03 b.Palma 26-6-86

2004-05	La Coruna	7	2	
2005-06	La Coruna	12	1	
2006-07	*Vecindario*	27	13	27 13
2007-08	La Coruna	25	9	44 12
2008-09	Newcastle U	5	1	5 1

ZAMBLERA, Fabio (F) 0 0
H: 6 3 W: 14 09 b.Atalanta 7-4-90
Source: Atalanta. *Honours:* Italy Youth.

2007-08	Newcastle U	0	0
2008-09	Newcastle U	0	0

Scholars
Airey, Philip; Ameobi, Samuel; Archer,
Richard Houston; Dummett, Paul; Ferguson,
Shane; Folan, Stephen; Grieve, Matthew
Andrias; Henderson, Jeffrey; Inman,
Bradden; Leadbetter, Daniel William; Lough,
Darren; McCrudden, Michael; McDermott,
Greg; Morris, Callum Edward; Newton,
Conor; Tavernier, James Henry; Taylor,
James Edward; Vuckic, Haris; Williams,
Daniel Lewis.

NORTHAMPTON T (58)

AKINFENWA, Adebayo (F) 187 57
H: 5 11 W: 13 07 b.Nigeria 10-5-82

2001	Atlantas	19	4	
2002	Atlantas	4	1	23 5
From Barry T				
2003-04	Boston U	3	0	3 0
2003-04	Leyton Orient	1	0	1 0
2003-04	Rushden & D	0	0	
2003-04	Doncaster R	9	4	9 4
2004-05	Torquay U	37	14	37 14
2005-06	Swansea C	34	9	
2006-07	Swansea C	25	5	
2007-08	Swansea C	0	0	59 14
2007-08	Millwall	7	0	7 0
2007-08	Northampton T	15	7	
2008-09	Northampton T	33	13	48 20

ANYA, Ikechi (M) 32 3
H: 5 5 W: 11 04 b.Glasgow 3-1-88
Source: Scholar.

2004-05	Wycombe W	3	0	
2005-06	Wycombe W	2	0	
2006-07	Wycombe W	13	0	
2007-08	Wycombe W	0	0	
2008-09	Wycombe W	0	0	18 0
2008-09	Northampton T	14	3	14 3

BENJAMIN, Joe (F) 4 0
H: 5 11 W: 11 05 b.Woodford 8-10-90
Source: Scholar.

2008-09	Northampton T	4	0	4 0

COKE, Gilles (M) 122 12
H: 6 0 W: 11 11 b.London 3-6-86
Source: Kingstonian.

2004-05	Mansfield T	9	0	
2005-06	Mansfield T	40	4	
2006-07	Mansfield T	21	1	70 5
2007-08	Northampton T	20	5	
2008-09	Northampton T	32	2	52 7

CONSTANTINE, Leon (F) 248 74
H: 6 2 W: 12 00 b.Hackney 24-2-78
Source: Edgware T.

2000-01	Millwall	1	0	
2001-02	Millwall	0	0	1 0
2001-02	*Leyton Orient*	10	3	10 3
2002-03	Brentford	17	0	17 0
2003-04	Southend U	43	21	43 21
2004-05	Peterborough U	11	1	11 1
2004-05	Torquay U	27	9	
2005-06	Torquay U	15	1	42 10
2005-06	Port Vale	30	10	
2006-07	Port Vale	42	22	
2007-08	Port Vale	0	0	72 32
2007-08	Leeds U	4	1	4 1
2007-08	*Oldham Ath*	8	2	8 2
2008-09	Northampton T	32	3	32 3
2008-09	Cheltenham T	6	1	6 1

CROWE, Jason (D) 343 23
H: 5 9 W: 10 09 b.Sidcup 30-9-78
Source: Trainee. *Honours:* England Schools,
Youth.

1995-96	Arsenal	0	0	
1996-97	Arsenal	0	0	
1997-98	Arsenal	0	0	
1998-99	Arsenal	0	0	
1998-99	*Crystal Palace*	8	0	8 0
1999-2000	Portsmouth	25	0	
2000-01	Portsmouth	23	0	
2000-01	*Brentford*	9	0	9 0
2001-02	Portsmouth	22	1	
2002-03	Portsmouth	16	4	86 5
2003-04	Grimsby T	32	0	
2004-05	Grimsby T	37	4	69 4
2005-06	Northampton T	41	2	
2006-07	Northampton T	43	3	
2007-08	Northampton T	44	4	
2008-09	Northampton T	43	5	171 14

DAVIS, Liam (M) 47 4
H: 5 9 W: 11 07 b.Wandsworth 23-11-86
Source: Scholar.

2005-06	Coventry C	2	0
2006-07	Coventry C	3	0

2006-07	Peterborough U	7	0	**7**	**0**
2007-08	Coventry C	6	0	**11**	**0**
2008-09	Northampton T	29	4	**29**	**4**

DOIG, Chris (D)   **206 5**
H: 6 2   W: 12 06   b.Dumfries 13-2-81
Source: Trainee. *Honours:* Scotland Schools, Youth, Under-21.

1997-98	Nottingham F	0	0		
1998-99	Nottingham F	2	0		
1999-2000	Nottingham F	11	0		
2000-01	Nottingham F	15	0		
2001-02	Nottingham F	8	1		
2002-03	Nottingham F	10	0		
2003-04	Nottingham F	10	0		
2003-04	*Northampton T*	9	0		
2004-05	Nottingham F	21	0	**77**	**1**
2005-06	Northampton T	38	2		
2006-07	Northampton T	39	0		
2007-08	Northampton T	15	1		
2008-09	Northampton T	28	1	**129**	**4**

DOLMAN, Liam (D)   **45 1**
H: 6 0   W: 14 05   b.Brixworth 26-9-87
Source: Scholar.

2005-06	Northampton T	0	0		
2006-07	Northampton T	1	0		
2007-08	Northampton T	30	1		
2008-09	Northampton T	14	0	**45**	**1**

DUNN, Chris (G)   **30 0**
H: 6 5   W: 13 11   b.Brentwood 23-10-87
Source: Scholar.

2006-07	Northampton T	0	0		
2007-08	Northampton T	1	0		
2008-09	Northampton T	29	0	**30**	**0**

DYER, Alex (M)   **14 1**
H: 5 8   W: 11 07   b.Wordsley 1-6-90
Source: Scholar.

| 2007-08 | Northampton T | 6 | 1 | | |
| 2008-09 | Northampton T | 8 | 0 | **14** | **1** |

GILLIGAN, Ryan (M)   **116 11**
H: 5 10   W: 11 07   b.Swindon 18-1-87
Source: Watford Scholar.

2005-06	Northampton T	23	4		
2006-07	Northampton T	24	0		
2007-08	Northampton T	38	4		
2008-09	Northampton T	31	3	**116**	**11**

GUTTRIDGE, Luke (M)   **256 25**
H: 5 6   W: 9 07   b.Barnstaple 27-3-82
Source: Trainee.

1999-2000	Torquay U	1	0		
2000-01	Torquay U	0	0	**1**	**0**
2000-01	Cambridge U	1	1		
2001-02	Cambridge U	29	2		
2002-03	Cambridge U	43	3		
2003-04	Cambridge U	46	11		
2004-05	Cambridge U	17	0	**136**	**17**
2004-05	*Southend U*	5	0		
2005-06	Southend U	41	5		
2006-07	Southend U	17	0	**63**	**5**
2006-07	Leyton Orient	17	1	**17**	**1**
2007-08	Colchester U	14	0	**14**	**0**
2008-09	Northampton T	25	2	**25**	**2**

HOLT, Andy (M)   **404 28**
H: 6 1   W: 12 07   b.Stockport 21-5-78
Source: Trainee.

1996-97	Oldham Ath	1	0		
1997-98	Oldham Ath	14	1		
1998-99	Oldham Ath	43	5		
1999-2000	Oldham Ath	46	3		
2000-01	Oldham Ath	20	1	**124**	**10**
2000-01	Hull C	10	2		
2001-02	Hull C	30	0		
2002-03	Hull C	6	0		
2002-03	*Barnsley*	7	0	**7**	**0**
2002-03	*Shrewsbury T*	9	0	**9**	**0**
2003-04	Hull C	25	1	**71**	**3**
2004-05	Wrexham	45	6		
2005-06	Wrexham	36	3	**81**	**9**
2006-07	Northampton T	35	2		
2007-08	Northampton T	36	2		
2008-09	Northampton T	41	2	**112**	**6**

HUGHES, Mark (D)   **97 5**
H: 6 1   W: 13 03   b.Liverpool 9-12-86
Source: Scholar.

2004-05	Everton	0	0		
2005-06	Everton	0	0		
2005-06	*Stockport Co*	3	1	**3**	**1**
2006-07	Everton	1	0	**1**	**0**

2006-07	Northampton T	17	2		
2007-08	Northampton T	35	1		
2008-09	Northampton T	41	1	**93**	**4**

JACKMAN, Danny (D)   **222 15**
H: 5 4   W: 10 00   b.Worcester 3-1-83
Source: Scholar.

2000-01	Aston Villa	0	0		
2001-02	Aston Villa	0	0		
2001-02	*Cambridge U*	7	1	**7**	**1**
2002-03	Aston Villa	0	0		
2003-04	Aston Villa	0	0		
2004-05	Stockport Co	27	2		
2004-05	Stockport Co	33	2	**60**	**4**
2005-06	Gillingham	4	0		
2006-07	Gillingham	31	1	**73**	**1**
2007-08	Northampton T	39	1		
2008-09	Northampton T	43	8	**82**	**9**

LARKIN, Colin (F)   **262 45**
H: 5 9   W: 11 07   b.Dundalk 27-4-82
Source: Trainee.

1998-99	Wolverhampton W	0	0		
1999-2000	Wolverhampton W	1	0		
2000-01	Wolverhampton W	2	0		
2001-02	Wolverhampton W	0	0	**3**	**0**
2001-02	*Kidderminster H*	33	6	**33**	**6**
2002-03	Mansfield T	22	7		
2003-04	Mansfield T	37	7		
2004-05	Mansfield T	33	11	**92**	**25**
2005-06	Chesterfield	41	7		
2006-07	Chesterfield	39	4	**80**	**11**
2007-08	Northampton T	33	2		
2008-09	Northampton T	21	1	**54**	**3**

OSMAN, Abdul (M)   **54 3**
H: 6 0   W: 11 00   b.Accra 27-2-87
Source: Hampton & Richmond B, Maidenhead U.

| 2007-08 | Gretna | 18 | 1 | **18** | **1** |
| 2008-09 | Northampton T | 36 | 2 | **36** | **2** |

TAYLOR, Greg (M)   **0 0**
H: 6 1   W: 12 01   b.Bedford 15-1-90
Source: Scholar.

| 2008-09 | Northampton T | 0 | 0 | | |

NORWICH C (59)

ADEYEMI, Thomas (M)   **0 0**
H: 6 1   W: 12 04   b.Norwich 24-10-91
Source: Scholar.

| 2008-09 | Norwich C | 0 | 0 | | |

CLINGAN, Sammy (M)   **161 10**
H: 5 11   W: 11 06   b.Belfast 13-1-84
Source: From Scholar. *Honours:* Northern Ireland Schools, Youth, Under-21, Under-23, 21 full caps.

2001-02	Wolverhampton W	0	0		
2002-03	Wolverhampton W	0	0		
2003-04	Wolverhampton W	0	0		
2004-05	Wolverhampton W	0	0		
2004-05	*Chesterfield*	15	2		
2005-06	Wolverhampton W	0	0		
2005-06	*Chesterfield*	21	1	**36**	**3**
2005-06	Nottingham F	15	0		
2006-07	Nottingham F	28	0		
2007-08	Nottingham F	42	1	**85**	**1**
2008-09	Norwich C	40	6	**40**	**6**

CORT, Carl (F)   **221 56**
H: 6 4   W: 12 04   b.Southwark 1-11-77
Source: Trainee. *Honours:* England Under-21.

1996-97	Wimbledon	7	0		
1996-97	*Lincoln C*	6	1	**6**	**1**
1997-98	Wimbledon	22	4		
1998-99	Wimbledon	16	3		
1999-2000	Wimbledon	34	9	**73**	**16**
2000-01	Newcastle U	13	6		
2001-02	Newcastle U	8	1		
2002-03	Newcastle U	0	0		
2003-04	Newcastle U	0	0	**22**	**7**
2003-04	Wolverhampton W	16	5		
2004-05	Wolverhampton W	37	15		
2005-06	Wolverhampton W	31	11		
2006-07	Wolverhampton W	10	0	**94**	**31**
2007-08	Leicester C	14	0		
2008-09	Leicester C	0	0	**14**	**0**
2008-09	Norwich C	12	1	**12**	**1**

CROFT, Lee (F)   **158 10**
H: 5 11   W: 13 00   b.Wigan 21-6-85
Source: Scholar. *Honours:* England Youth, Under-20.

2002-03	Manchester C	0	0		
2003-04	Manchester C	0	0		
2004-05	Manchester C	7	0		
2004-05	*Oldham Ath*	12	0	**12**	**0**
2005-06	Manchester C	21	1	**28**	**1**
2006-07	Norwich C	36	3		
2007-08	Norwich C	41	1		
2008-09	Norwich C	41	5	**118**	**9**

CURETON, Jamie (F)   **512 184**
H: 5 8   W: 10 07   b.Bristol 28-8-75
Source: Trainee. *Honours:* England Youth.

1992-93	Norwich C	0	0		
1993-94	Norwich C	0	0		
1994-95	Norwich C	17	4		
1995-96	Norwich C	12	2		
1995-96	*Bournemouth*	5	0	**5**	**0**
1996-97	Norwich C	0	0		
1996-97	Bristol R	38	11		
1997-98	Bristol R	43	13		
1998-99	Bristol R	46	25		
1999-2000	Bristol R	46	22		
2000-01	Bristol R	1	1	**174**	**72**
2000-01	Reading	43	26		
2001-02	Reading	38	15		
2002-03	Reading	27	9	**108**	**50**
From Busan Icons.					
2003-04	QPR	13	2		
2004-05	QPR	30	4	**43**	**6**
2005-06	Swindon T	30	7	**30**	**7**
2005-06	Colchester U	8	4		
2006-07	Colchester U	44	23	**52**	**27**
2007-08	Norwich C	41	12		
2008-09	Norwich C	22	2	**92**	**20**
2008-09	*Barnsley*	8	2	**8**	**2**

DALEY, Luke (F)   **3 0**
H: 5 11   W: 11 00   b.Northampton 10-11-89
Source: Scholar.

| 2007-08 | Norwich C | 0 | 0 | | |
| 2008-09 | Norwich C | 3 | 0 | **3** | **0** |

DOHERTY, Gary (D)   **298 22**
H: 6 3   W: 13 13   b.Carndonagh 31-1-80
Source: Trainee. *Honours:* Eire Youth, Under-20, Under-21, 34 full caps, 4 goals.

1997-98	Luton T	10	0		
1998-99	Luton T	20	6		
1999-2000	Luton T	40	6	**70**	**12**
1999-2000	Tottenham H	2	0		
2000-01	Tottenham H	22	3		
2001-02	Tottenham H	7	0		
2002-03	Tottenham H	15	1		
2003-04	Tottenham H	17	0		
2004-05	Tottenham H	1	0	**64**	**4**
2004-05	Norwich C	20	2		
2005-06	Norwich C	42	1		
2006-07	Norwich C	34	0		
2007-08	Norwich C	34	0		
2008-09	Norwich C	34	3	**164**	**6**

DRURY, Adam (D)   **407 5**
H: 5 10   W: 11 09   b.Cambridge 29-8-78
Source: Scholar.

1995-96	Peterborough U	1	0		
1996-97	Peterborough U	5	1		
1997-98	Peterborough U	31	0		
1998-99	Peterborough U	40	0		
1999-2000	Peterborough U	42	1		
2000-01	Peterborough U	29	0	**148**	**2**
2000-01	Norwich C	6	0		
2001-02	Norwich C	35	0		
2002-03	Norwich C	45	2		
2003-04	Norwich C	42	0		
2004-05	Norwich C	33	1		
2005-06	Norwich C	39	0		
2006-07	Norwich C	39	0		
2007-08	Norwich C	9	0		
2008-09	Norwich C	11	0	**259**	**3**

EAGLE, Robert (M)   **10 0**
H: 5 7   W: 10 08   b.Leiston 23-2-87
Source: Scholar.

2006-07	Norwich C	10	0		
2007-08	Norwich C	0	0		
2008-09	Norwich C	0	0	**10**	**0**

FOTHERINGHAM, Mark (M)   145   7
H: 5 7   W: 12 00   b.Dundee 22-10-83
Honours: Scotland Youth, Under-20, Under-21, B.

Season	Club				
1999-2000	Celtic	2	0		
2000-01	Celtic	1	0		
2001-02	Celtic	0	0		
2002-03	Celtic	0	0	3	0
2003-04	Dundee	24	4		
2004-05	Dundee	27	0	51	4
2005-06	Freiburg	9	0	9	0
2006-07	Aarau	13	0	13	0
2006-07	Norwich C	14	0		
2007-08	Norwich C	28	2		
2008-09	Norwich C	27	1	69	3

GOW, Alan (M)   193   44
H: 6 0   W: 11 00   b.Clydebank 9-10-82
Honours: Scotland B.

Season	Club				
2000-01	Clydebank	3	0		
2001-02	Clydebank	5	0	8	0
2002-03	Airdrie U	27	5		
2003-04	Airdrie U	32	12		
2004-05	Airdrie U	26	9	85	26
2005-06	Falkirk	34	6		
2006-07	Falkirk	36	7	70	13
2007-08	Rangers	0	0		

on loan from Rangers.

Season	Club				
2008-09	Blackpool	17	5	17	5
2008-09	Norwich C	13	0	13	0

HOOLAHAN, Wes (M)   238   24
H: 5 6   W: 10 03   b.Dublin 10-8-83
Honours: Eire Under-21, 1 full cap.

Season	Club				
2001-02	Shelbourne	20	3		
2002-03	Shelbourne	23	0		
2004	Shelbourne	31	2		
2005	Shelbourne	29	4	103	9
2005-06	Livingston	16	0	16	0
2006-07	Blackpool	42	8		
2007-08	Blackpool	45	5	87	13
2008-09	Norwich C	32 ·	2	32	2

KENNEDY, John (D)   44   3
H: 6 01   W: 12 06   b.Airdrie 18-8-83
Honours: Scotland Under-21, 1 full cap.

Season	Club				
1999-2000	Celtic	5	0		
2000-01	Celtic	1	0		
2001-02	Celtic	0	0		
2002-03	Celtic	12	1		
2003-04	Celtic	0	0		
2004-05	Celtic	0	0		
2006-07	Celtic	3	0		
2007-08	Celtic	7	0	28	1

on loan from Celtic.

Season	Club				
2008-09	Norwich C	16	2	16	2

KILLEN, Chris (F)   151   43
H: 6 1   W: 11 07   b.Wellington 8-10-81
Source: Miramar R. *Honours:* New Zealand Under-20, Under-23, 27 full caps, 10 goals.

Season	Club				
1998-99	Manchester C	0	0		
1999-2000	Manchester C	0	0		
2000-01	Manchester C	0	0		
2000-01	Wrexham	12	3	12	3
2001-02	Port Vale	9	6	9	6
2001-02	Manchester C	3	0	3	0
2002-03	Oldham Ath	27	3		
2003-04	Oldham Ath	13	2		
2004-05	Oldham Ath	26	10		
2005-06	Oldham Ath	12	2	78	17
2005-06	Hibernian	7	3		
2006-07	Hibernian	18	13	25	16
2007-08	Celtic	20	1	20	1

On loan from Celtic.

Season	Club				
2008-09	Norwich C	4	0	4	0

LAPPIN, Simon (M)   200   13
H: 5 11   W: 9 06   b.Glasgow 25-1-83
Honours: Scotland Under-21.

Season	Club				
2001-02	St Mirren	1	0		
2002-03	St Mirren	34	0		
2003-04	St Mirren	24	4		
2004-05	St Mirren	34	1		
2005-06	St Mirren	35	3		
2006-07	St Mirren	24	1	152	9
2006-07	Norwich C	14	1		
2007-08	Motherwell	14	2	14	2
2007-08	Norwich C	15	1		
2008-09	Norwich C	5	0	34	2

LATHROPE, Damon (M)   0   0
H: 5 8   W: 10 02   b.Stevenage 28-10-89
Source: Scholar.

Season	Club				
2007-08	Norwich C	0	0		
2008-09	Norwich C	0	0		

MARTIN, Chris (F)   65   15
H: 6 2   W: 12 06   b.Beccles 4-11-88
Source: From Scholar. *Honours:* England Youth.

Season	Club				
2006-07	Norwich C	18	4		
2007-08	Norwich C	7	0		
2008-09	Norwich C	0	0	25	4
2008-09	Luton T	40	11	40	11

McDONALD, Cody (F)   7   1
H: 5 10   W: 11 03   b.Witham 30-5-86
Source: Dartford.

Season	Club				
2008-09	Norwich C	7	1	7	1

OTSEMOBOR, John (D)   161   5
H: 5 10   W: 12 07   b.Liverpool 23-3-83
Source: From Trainee. *Honours:* England Youth, Under-20.

Season	Club				
1999-2000	Liverpool	0	0		
2000-01	Liverpool	0	0		
2001-02	Liverpool	0	0		
2002-03	Liverpool	0	0		
2002-03	*Hull C*	9	3	9	3
2003-04	Liverpool	4	0		
2003-04	*Bolton W*	1	0	1	0
2004-05	Liverpool	0	0	4	0
2004-05	*Crewe Alex*	14	1		
2005-06	Rotherham U	10	0	10	0
2005-06	Crewe Alex	16	0		
2006-07	Crewe Alex	27	0	57	1
2007-08	Norwich C	43	1		
2008-09	Norwich C	37	0	80	1

PATTISON, Matt (M)   61   3
H: 5 9   W: 11 00   b.Johannesburg 27-10-86
Source: Scholar.

Season	Club				
2005-06	Newcastle U	3	0		
2006-07	Newcastle U	7	0		
2007-08	Newcastle U	0	0	10	0
2007-08	Norwich C	27	0		
2008-09	Norwich C	24	3	51	3

RENTON, Kris (F)   3   0
H: 6 3   W: 12 06   b.Musselburgh 12-7-90
Source: Scholar.

Season	Club				
2006-07	Norwich C	3	0		
2007-08	Norwich C	0	0		
2008-09	Norwich C	0	0	3	0

RUDD, Declan (G)   0   0
H: 6 3   W: 12 06   b.Norwich 16-1-91
Source: Scholar.

Season	Club				
2008-09	Norwich C	0	0		

RUSSELL, Darel (M)   380   31
H: 5 10   W: 11 09   b.Mile End 22-10-80
Source: From Trainee. *Honours:* England Youth.

Season	Club				
1997-98	Norwich C	1	0		
1998-99	Norwich C	13	1		
1999-2000	Norwich C	33	4		
2000-01	Norwich C	41	2		
2001-02	Norwich C	23	0		
2002-03	Norwich C	21	0		
2003-04	Stoke C	46	4		
2004-05	Stoke C	45	2		
2005-06	Stoke C	37	3		
2006-07	Stoke C	43	7	171	16
2007-08	Norwich C	39	4		
2008-09	Norwich C	38	4	209	15

SMITH, Korey (M)   2   0
H: 5 9   W: 11 01   b.Hatfield 31-1-91
Source: Scholar.

Season	Club				
2008-09	Norwich C	2	0	2	0

SPILLANE, Michael (M)   52   3
H: 5 9   W: 11 10   b.Jersey 23-3-89
Source: From Scholar. *Honours:* Eire Youth, Under-21.

Season	Club				
2005-06	Norwich C	2	0		
2006-07	Norwich C	5	0		
2007-08	Norwich C	6	0		
2008-09	Norwich C	0	0	13	0
2008-09	Luton T	39	3	39	3

STEFANOVIC, Dejan (D)   343   20
H: 6 2   W: 13 01   b.Belgrade 28-10-74
Honours: Serbia-Montenegro 23 full caps.

Season	Club				
1992-93	Red Star Belgrade	14	0		
1993-94	Red Star Belgrade	2	0		
1994-95	Red Star Belgrade	30	9	46	9
1995-96	Sheffield W	6	0		
1996-97	Sheffield W	29	2		
1997-98	Sheffield W	20	2		
1998-99	Sheffield W	11	0	66	4
1999-2000	Perugia	0	0		
1999-2000	OFK Belgrade	0	0		
1999-2000	Vitesse	14	0		
2000-01	Vitesse	27	1		
2001-02	Vitesse	25	3		
2002-03	Vitesse	28	0	94	4
2003-04	Portsmouth	32	3		
2004-05	Portsmouth	32	0		
2005-06	Portsmouth	28	0		
2006-07	Portsmouth	20	0		
2007-08	Portsmouth	0	0	112	3
2007-08	Fulham	13	0	13	0
2008-09	Norwich C	12	0	12	0

NOTTINGHAM F (60)

BENCHERIF, Hamza (D)   12   1
H: 5 9   W: 12 03   b.Paris 9-2-88
Source: Scholar.

Season	Club				
2006-07	Nottingham F	0	0		
2007-08	*Lincoln C*	12	1	12	1
2008-09	Nottingham F	0	0		

BENGELLOUN, Tarik (M)   0   0
b.Paris 8-2-91
Source: Scholar.

Season	Club				
2008-09	Nottingham F	0	0		

BENNETT, Julian (D)   145   11
H: 6 1   W: 13 00   b.Nottingham 17-12-84
Source: Scholar.

Season	Club				
2003-04	Walsall	1	0		
2004-05	Walsall	31	2		
2005-06	Walsall	11	1	51	3
2005-06	Nottingham F	18	2		
2006-07	Nottingham F	30	2		
2007-08	Nottingham F	34	4		
2008-09	Nottingham F	12	0	94	8

BRECKIN, Ian (D)   583   26
H: 6 2   W: 13 05   b.Rotherham 24-2-75
Source: Trainee.

Season	Club				
1993-94	Rotherham U	10	0		
1994-95	Rotherham U	41	2		
1995-96	Rotherham U	39	1		
1996-97	Rotherham U	42	3	132	6
1997-98	Chesterfield	43	1		
1998-99	Chesterfield	44	2		
1999-2000	Chesterfield	38	1		
2000-01	Chesterfield	45	3		
2001-02	Chesterfield	42	1	212	8
2002-03	Wigan Ath	9	0		
2003-04	Wigan Ath	45	0		
2004-05	Wigan Ath	42	0	96	0
2005-06	Nottingham F	46	8		
2006-07	Nottingham F	46	3		
2007-08	Nottingham F	28	1		
2008-09	Nottingham F	23	0	143	12

BYRNE, Mark (M)   2   0
H: 5 9   W: 11 00   b.Dublin 9-11-88

Season	Club				
2006-07	Nottingham F	0	0		
2007-08	Nottingham F	1	0		
2008-09	Nottingham F	1	0	2	0

CHAMBERS, Luke (D)   219   9
H: 6 1   W: 11 13   b.Kettering 29-8-85
Source: Scholar.

Season	Club				
2002-03	Northampton T	1	0		
2003-04	Northampton T	24	0		
2004-05	Northampton T	27	0		
2005-06	Northampton T	43	0		
2006-07	Northampton T	29	1	124	1
2006-07	Nottingham F	14	0		
2007-08	Nottingham F	42	6		
2008-09	Nottingham F	39	2	95	8

COHEN, Chris (M)   174   11
H: 5 11   W: 10 11   b.Norwich 5-3-87
Source: Scholar. *Honours:* England Youth.

Season	Club				
2003-04	West Ham U	7	0		
2004-05	West Ham U	11	0		

2005-06	West Ham U	0	0	18	0
2005-06	*Yeovil T*	30	1		
2006-07	*Yeovil T*	44	6	74	7
2007-08	Nottingham F	41	2		
2008-09	Nottingham F	41	2	82	4

COLE, Andy (F)   509 229
H: 5 11 W: 12 11 b.Nottingham 15-10-71
Source: Trainee. Honours: England Schools, Youth, Under-21, B, 15 full caps, 1 goal. Football League.

1989-90	Arsenal	0	0		
1990-91	Arsenal	1	0		
1991-92	Arsenal	0	0	1	0
1991-92	*Fulham*	13	3		
1991-92	*Bristol C*	12	8		
1992-93	*Bristol C*	29	12	41	20
1992-93	Newcastle U	12	12		
1993-94	Newcastle U	40	34		
1994-95	Newcastle U	18	9	70	55
1994-95	Manchester U	18	12		
1995-96	Manchester U	34	11		
1996-97	Manchester U	20	6		
1997-98	Manchester U	33	15		
1998-99	Manchester U	32	17		
1999-2000	Manchester U	28	19		
2000-01	Manchester U	19	9		
2001-02	Manchester U	11	4	195	93
2001-02	Blackburn R	15	9		
2002-03	Blackburn R	34	7		
2003-04	Blackburn R	34	11	83	27
2004-05	Fulham	31	12	44	15
2005-06	Manchester C	22	9	22	9
2006-07	Portsmouth	18	3		
2006-07	*Birmingham C*	5	1	5	1
2007-08	Portsmouth	0	0	18	3
2007-08	*Sunderland*	7	0	7	0
2007-08	*Burnley*	13	6	13	6
2008-09	Nottingham F	10	0	10	0

DAVIES, Arron (M)   137 23
H: 5 9 W: 11 00 b.Cardiff 22-6-84
Source: Trainee. Honours: Wales Under-21, 1 full cap.

2002-03	Southampton	0	0		
2003-04	Southampton	0	0		
2003-04	*Barnsley*	4	0	4	0
2004-05	Southampton	0	0		
2004-05	*Yeovil T*	23	8		
2005-06	*Yeovil T*	39	8		
2006-07	*Yeovil T*	39	6	101	22
2007-08	Nottingham F	19	1		
2008-09	Nottingham F	13	0	32	1

DIAGNE, Tony (D)   0 0
b.Meulan 17-9-90
Source: Scholar.

2008-09	Nottingham F	0	0

DORNAT, Mickael (M)   0 0
b.Cagnes-sur-Mer 10-3-90

2008-09	Nottingham F	0	0

EARNSHAW, Robert (F)   323 139
H: 5 6 W: 9 09 b.Mulfulira 6-4-81
Source: Trainee. Honours: Wales Youth, Under-21, 45 full caps, 14 goals.

1997-98	Cardiff C	5	0		
1998-99	Cardiff C	5	1		
1998-99	*Middlesbrough*	0	0		
1999-2000	Cardiff C	6	1		
1999-2000	*Morton*	3	2	3	2
2000-01	Cardiff C	36	19		
2001-02	Cardiff C	30	11		
2002-03	Cardiff C	46	31		
2003-04	Cardiff C	46	21		
2004-05	Cardiff C	4	1	178	85
2004-05	WBA	31	11		
2005-06	WBA	12	1	43	12
2005-06	Norwich C	15	8		
2006-07	Norwich C	30	19	45	27
2007-08	Derby Co	22	1	22	1
2008-09	Nottingham F	32	12	32	12

GAMBLE, Paddy (G)   0 0
H: 6 4 W: 10 12 b.Nottingham 1-9-88
Source: Scholar. Honours: England Youth.

2005-06	Nottingham F	0	0
2006-07	Nottingham F	0	0
2007-08	Nottingham F	0	0
2008-09	Nottingham F	0	0

GARNER, Joe (F)   77 26
H: 5 10 W: 11 02 b.Blackburn 12-4-88
Source: Scholar. Honours: England Schools, Youth.

2004-05	Blackburn R	0	0		
2005-06	Blackburn R	0	0		
2006-07	Blackburn R	0	0		
2006-07	*Carlisle U*	18	5		
2007-08	*Carlisle U*	31	14	49	19
2008-09	Nottingham F	28	7	28	7

GIBBONS, Robert (M)   0 0
b.Dublin 8-10-91
Source: Scholar.

2008-09	Nottingham F	0	0

HEATH, Joe (D)   10 0
H: 5 11 W: 11 11 b.Birkenhead 4-10-88

2005-06	Nottingham F	0	0		
2006-07	Nottingham F	0	0		
2007-08	Nottingham F	0	0		
2008-09	Nottingham F	10	0	10	0

McCLEARY, Garath (F)   47 2
H: 5 10 W: 12 06 b.Oxford 15-5-87
Source: Bromley.

2007-08	Nottingham F	8	1		
2008-09	Nottingham F	39	1	47	2

McGUGAN, Lewis (M)   79 13
H: 5 9 W: 11 06 b.Long Eaton 25-10-88
Source: Scholar.

2006-07	Nottingham F	13	2		
2007-08	Nottingham F	33	6		
2008-09	Nottingham F	33	5	79	13

MITCHELL, Aaron (D)   0 0
b.Nottingham 5-2-90
Source: Scholar.

2007-08	Nottingham F	0	0
2008-09	Nottingham F	0	0

MOLONEY, Brendan (M)   24 1
H: 6 1 W: 11 12 b.Enfield 18-1-89
Source: Scholar. Honours: Eire Under-21.

2005-06	Nottingham F	0	0		
2006-07	Nottingham F	1	0		
2007-08	Nottingham F	2	0		
2007-08	*Chesterfield*	9	1	9	1
2008-09	Nottingham F	12	0	15	0

MORGAN, Wes (D)   245 8
H: 6 2 W: 14 00 b.Nottingham 21-1-84
Source: Scholar.

2002-03	Nottingham F	0	0		
2002-03	*Kidderminster H*	5	1	5	1
2003-04	Nottingham F	32	2		
2004-05	Nottingham F	43	1		
2005-06	Nottingham F	43	2		
2006-07	Nottingham F	38	0		
2007-08	Nottingham F	42	1		
2008-09	Nottingham F	42	1	240	7

MOUSSI, Guy (M)   106 2
H: 6 1 W: 12 11 b.Paris 23-1-85

2004-05	Angers	15	1		
2005-06	Angers	9	0		
2006-07	Angers	32	0		
2007-08	Angers	35	1	91	2
2008-09	Nottingham F	15	0	15	0

NEWBOLD, Adam (F)   0 0
H: 6 0 W: 12 00 b.Nottingham 16-11-89
Source: Scholar.

2006-07	Nottingham F	0	0		
2007-08	Nottingham F	0	0		
2008-09	Nottingham F	4	0	4	0

PERCH, James (D)   173 11
H: 5 11 W: 11 05 b.Mansfield 29-9-85
Source: Scholar.

2002-03	Nottingham F	0	0		
2003-04	Nottingham F	0	0		
2004-05	Nottingham F	22	0		
2005-06	Nottingham F	38	3		
2006-07	Nottingham F	46	5		
2007-08	Nottingham F	30	0		
2008-09	Nottingham F	37	3	173	11

REDMOND, Shane (G)   0 0
H: 6 0 W: 12 10 b.Dublin 23-3-89
Source: Scholar. Honours: Eire Under-21.

2006-07	Nottingham F	0	0
2007-08	Nottingham F	0	0
2008-09	Nottingham F	0	0

REID, James (D)   1 0
H: 5 10 W: 11 04 b.Ashbourne 28-2-90
Source: Scholar. Honours: England Youth.

2007-08	Nottingham F	0	0		
2008-09	Nottingham F	1	0	1	0

ROBERTS, Dale (M)   0 0
H: 6 3 W: 11 06 b.Horden 22-10-86
Source: Scholar.

2005-06	Nottingham F	0	0
2006-07	Nottingham F	0	0
2007-08	Nottingham F	0	0
2008-09	Nottingham F	0	0

RODNEY, Nialle (F)   0 0
b. 28-2-91

2008-09	Nottingham F	0	0

SHARPE, Thomas (D)   0 0
b.Nottingham 12-10-88
Source: Scholar.

2007-08	Nottingham F	0	0
2008-09	Nottingham F	0	0

SINCLAIR, Emile (F)   36 2
H: 6 0 W: 11 04 b.Leeds 20-12-87
Source: Scholar.

2007-08	Nottingham F	12	1		
2007-08	*Brentford*	4	0	4	0
2008-09	Nottingham F	3	0	15	1
2008-09	*Macclesfield T*	17	1	17	1

SMITH, Paul (G)   221 0
H: 6 3 W: 14 00 b.Epsom 17-12-79
Source: Walton & Hersham.

1998-99	Charlton Ath	0	0		
1998-99	*Brentford*	0	0		
1999-2000	Charlton Ath	0	0		

From Carshalton Ath.

2000-01	Brentford	2	0		
2001-02	Brentford	18	0		
2002-03	Brentford	43	0		
2003-04	Brentford	24	0	87	0
2003-04	Southampton	0	0		
2004-05	Southampton	6	0		
2005-06	Southampton	9	0	15	0
2006-07	Nottingham F	45	0		
2007-08	Nottingham F	46	0		
2008-09	Nottingham F	28	0	119	0

STAPLES, Reece (M)   0 0
b.Nottingham 10-9-90
Source: Scholar.

2006-07	Nottingham F	0	0
2007-08	Nottingham F	0	0
2008-09	Nottingham F	0	0

TAIT, Richard (D)   0 0
b.Gallashields 2-12-89
Source: Curzon Ashton.

2007-08	Nottingham F	0	0
2008-09	Nottingham F	0	0

THORNHILL, Matt (M)   38 5
H: 5 9 W: 12 00 b.Nottingham 11-10-88
Source: Scholar.

2007-08	Nottingham F	14	2		
2008-09	Nottingham F	24	3	38	5

TYSON, Nathan (F)   251 76
H: 5 10 W: 10 02 b.Reading 4-5-82
Source: Trainee. Honours: England Under-20.

1999-2000	Reading	1	0		
2000-01	Reading	0	0		
2001-02	Reading	1	0		
2001-02	*Swansea C*	11	1	11	1
2001-02	*Cheltenham T*	8	1	8	1
2002-03	Reading	23	1		
2003-04	Reading	8	0	33	1
2003-04	Wycombe W	21	9		
2004-05	Wycombe W	42	22		
2005-06	Wycombe W	15	11	78	42
2005-06	Nottingham F	28	10		
2006-07	Nottingham F	24	7		
2007-08	Nottingham F	34	9		
2008-09	Nottingham F	35	5	121	31

WHITEHURST, Ryan (F)   0 0
b.Nuthall 6-9-89
Source: Scholar.

2008-09	Nottingham F	0	0

WILSON, Kelvin (D) 183 4
H: 6 2 W: 12 12 b.Nottingham 3-9-85
Source: Scholar.

2003-04	Notts Co	3	0	
2004-05	Notts Co	41	2	
2005-06	Notts Co	34	1	78 3
2005-06	*Preston NE*	6	0	
2006-07	Preston NE	21	1	27 1
2007-08	Nottingham F	42	0	
2008-09	Nottingham F	36	0	78 0

NOTTS CO (61)

BEARDSLEY, Jason (D) 11 0
H: 6 0 W: 11 00 b.Burton 12-7-89
Source: Scholar.

2007-08	Derby Co	0	0	
2008-09	Derby Co	0	0	
2008-09	Notts Co	11	0	11 0

BUTCHER, Richard (M) 267 38
H: 6 0 W: 13 01 b.Peterborough 22-1-81
Source: Kettering T.

2002-03	Lincoln C	26	3	
2003-04	Lincoln C	32	6	
2004-05	Lincoln C	46	2	
2005-06	Oldham Ath	36	4	36 4
2005-06	*Lincoln C*	4	1	108 12
2006-07	Peterborough U	43	4	43 4
2007-08	Notts Co	46	12	
2008-09	Notts Co	34	6	80 18

CANHAM, Sean (F) 23 3
H: 6 1 W: 13 01 b.Exeter 26-9-84
Source: Exeter City Scholar, Team Bath.

2008-09	Notts Co	23	3	23 3

CLAPHAM, Jamie (M) 393 13
H: 5 9 W: 11 09 b.Lincoln 7-12-75
Source: Trainee.

1994-95	Tottenham H	0	0	
1995-96	Tottenham H	0	0	
1996-97	Tottenham H	1	0	
1996-97	*Leyton Orient*	6	0	6 0
1996-97	*Bristol R*	5	0	5 0
1997-98	Tottenham H	0	0	1 0
1997-98	Ipswich T	22	0	
1998-99	Ipswich T	46	3	
1999-2000	Ipswich T	46	2	
2000-01	Ipswich T	35	2	
2001-02	Ipswich T	32	2	
2002-03	Ipswich T	26	1	207 10
2002-03	Birmingham C	16	0	
2003-04	Birmingham C	25	0	
2004-05	Birmingham C	27	0	
2005-06	Birmingham C	16	1	84 1
2006-07	Wolverhampton W	26	0	
2007-08	Wolverhampton W	0	0	26 0
2007-08	*Leeds U*	13	0	13 0
2007-08	Leicester C	11	0	
2008-09	Leicester C	0	0	11 0
2008-09	Notts Co	40	2	40 2

EDWARDS, Mike (D) 378 20
H: 6 0 W: 12 10 b.Hessle 25-4-80
Source: Trainee.

1997-98	Hull C	21	0	
1998-99	Hull C	30	0	
1999-2000	Hull C	40	1	
2000-01	Hull C	42	4	
2001-02	Hull C	39	1	
2002-03	Hull C	6	0	178 6
2002-03	*Colchester U*	5	0	5 0
2003-04	Grimsby T	33	1	33 1
2004-05	Notts Co	9	0	
2005-06	Notts Co	46	7	
2006-07	Notts Co	45	3	
2007-08	Notts Co	19	1	
2008-09	Notts Co	43	2	162 13

FACEY, Delroy (F) 308 57
H: 6 0 W: 15 02 b.Huddersfield 22-4-80
Source: Trainee.

1996-97	Huddersfield T	3	0	
1997-98	Huddersfield T	3	0	
1998-99	Huddersfield T	20	3	
1999-2000	Huddersfield T	2	0	
2000-01	Huddersfield T	34	10	
2001-02	Huddersfield T	13	2	
2002-03	Huddersfield T	0	0	
2002-03	*Bradford C*	6	1	6 1
2002-03	Bolton W	9	1	
2003-04	Bolton W	1	0	10 1
2003-04	*Burnley*	14	5	14 5
2003-04	WBA	9	0	9 0
2004-05	Hull C	21	4	21 4
2004-05	*Huddersfield T*	4	0	79 15
2004-05	Oldham Ath	6	0	
2005-06	Oldham Ath	3	0	9 0
2005-06	Tranmere R	37	8	37 8
2006-07	Rotherham U	40	10	40 10
2007-08	Gillingham	32	3	32 3
2007-08	*Wycombe W*	6	1	6 1
2008-09	Notts Co	45	9	45 9

FAIRCLOUGH, Ben (F) 8 0
H: 5 6 W: 9 10 b.Nottingham 18-4-89
Source: Nottingham F Scholar.

2008-09	Notts Co	8	0	8 0

FORRESTER, Jamie (F) 496 148
H: 5 7 W: 11 00 b.Bradford 1-11-74
Source: Auxerre. *Honours:* England Schools, Youth.

1992-93	Leeds U	6	0	
1993-94	Leeds U	3	0	
1994-95	Leeds U	0	0	
1994-95	*Southend U*	5	0	5 0
1994-95	*Grimsby T*	9	1	
1995-96	Leeds U	0	0	9 0
1995-96	Grimsby T	28	5	
1996-97	Grimsby T	13	1	50 7
1996-97	Scunthorpe U	10	6	
1997-98	Scunthorpe U	45	11	
1998-99	Scunthorpe U	46	20	101 37
1999-2000	Utrecht	1	0	1 0
1999-2000	Walsall	5	0	5 0
1999-2000	*Northampton T*	10	6	
2000-01	Northampton T	43	17	
2001-02	Northampton T	43	17	
2002-03	Northampton T	25	5	121 45
2002-03	Hull C	11	3	
2003-04	Hull C	21	4	32 7
2004-05	Bristol R	35	7	
2005-06	Bristol R	17	2	52 9
2005-06	Lincoln C	9	5	
2006-07	Lincoln C	41	18	
2007-08	Lincoln C	40	12	90 35
2008-09	Notts Co	30	8	30 8

HAMSHAW, Matt (M) 239 16
H: 5 10 W: 11 08 b.Rotherham 1-1-82
Source: Trainee. *Honours:* England Youth, Under-20.

1998-99	Sheffield W	0	0	
1999-2000	Sheffield W	0	0	
2000-01	Sheffield W	18	0	
2001-02	Sheffield W	21	0	
2002-03	Sheffield W	15	1	
2003-04	Sheffield W	0	0	
2004-05	Sheffield W	20	1	74 2
2005-06	Stockport Co	39	5	39 5
2006-07	Mansfield T	40	4	
2007-08	Mansfield T	45	2	85 6
2008-09	Notts Co	41	3	41 3

HOULT, Russell (G) 423 0
H: 6 3 W: 14 09 b.Ashby 22-11-72
Source: Trainee.

1990-91	Leicester C	0	0	
1991-92	Leicester C	0	0	
1991-92	*Lincoln C*	2	0	
1991-92	*Blackpool*	0	0	
1992-93	Leicester C	10	0	
1993-94	Leicester C	0	0	
1993-94	*Bolton W*	4	0	4 0
1994-95	Leicester C	0	0	10 0
1994-95	*Lincoln C*	15	0	17 0
1994-95	Derby Co	15	0	
1995-96	Derby Co	41	0	
1996-97	Derby Co	32	0	
1997-98	Derby Co	2	0	
1998-99	Derby Co	23	0	
1999-2000	Derby Co	10	0	123 0
1999-2000	Portsmouth	18	0	
2000-01	Portsmouth	22	0	40 0
2000-01	WBA	13	0	
2001-02	WBA	45	0	
2002-03	WBA	37	0	
2003-04	WBA	44	0	
2004-05	WBA	36	0	
2005-06	WBA	1	0	
2005-06	*Nottingham F*	8	0	8 0
2006-07	WBA	14	0	190 0
2006-07	Stoke C	0	0	
2007-08	Stoke C	1	0	1 0
2007-08	*Notts Co*	14	0	
2008-09	Notts Co	16	0	30 0

HUNT, Stephen (D) 102 4
H: 6 2 W: 13 00 b.Southampton 11-11-84
Source: Southampton Scholar.

2004-05	Colchester U	20	1	
2005-06	Colchester U	2	0	22 1
2006-07	Notts Co	32	1	
2007-08	Notts Co	37	2	
2008-09	Notts Co	11	0	80 3

JOHNSON, Michael (D) 561 20
H: 5 11 W: 11 12 b.Nottingham 4-7-73
Source: Trainee. *Honours:* Jamaica 14 full caps.

1991-92	Notts Co	5	0	
1992-93	Notts Co	37	0	
1993-94	Notts Co	34	0	
1994-95	Notts Co	31	0	
1995-96	Notts Co	0	0	
1995-96	Birmingham C	33	0	
1996-97	Birmingham C	35	0	
1997-98	Birmingham C	38	3	
1998-99	Birmingham C	45	5	
1999-2000	Birmingham C	34	2	
2000-01	Birmingham C	39	2	
2001-02	Birmingham C	32	1	
2002-03	Birmingham C	6	0	
2003-04	Birmingham C	0	0	262 13
2003-04	Derby Co	39	1	
2004-05	Derby Co	36	1	
2005-06	Derby Co	31	1	
2006-07	Derby Co	29	1	
2007-08	Derby Co	3	0	138 4
2007-08	*Sheffield W*	13	0	13 0
2007-08	*Notts Co*	12	1	
2008-09	Notts Co	29	2	148 3

MACKENZIE, Neil (M) 283 21
H: 6 2 W: 12 05 b.Birmingham 15-4-76
Source: WBA schoolboy.

1996-97	Stoke C	22	1	
1997-98	Stoke C	12	0	
1998-99	Stoke C	6	0	
1998-99	*Cambridge U*	4	1	
1999-2000	Stoke C	2	0	42 1
1999-2000	Cambridge U	22	0	
2000-01	Cambridge U	16	0	
2000-01	Kidderminster H	23	3	23 3
2001-02	Blackpool	14	1	14 1
2002-03	Mansfield T	24	1	
2003-04	Mansfield T	32	2	
2004-05	Mansfield T	15	1	71 4
2004-05	Macclesfield T	18	0	
2005-06	Macclesfield T	6	1	24 1
2005-06	Scunthorpe U	14	2	
2006-07	Scunthorpe U	24	2	38 4
2006-07	Hereford U	7	0	7 0
2007-08	Notts Co	29	6	
2008-09	Notts Co	1	0	30 6
2008-09	*Port Vale*	2	0	2 0

MAYO, Paul (D) 241 11
H: 5 11 W: 11 09 b.Lincoln 13-10-81
Source: Scholarship.

1999-2000	Lincoln C	19	0	
2000-01	Lincoln C	27	0	
2001-02	Lincoln C	14	0	
2002-03	Lincoln C	15	0	
2003-04	Lincoln C	31	6	
2003-04	Watford	12	0	
2004-05	Watford	13	0	25 0
2005-06	Lincoln C	28	3	
2006-07	Lincoln C	34	1	168 10
2007-08	Notts Co	29	0	
2007-08	*Darlington*	7	1	7 1
2008-09	Notts Co	12	0	41 0

NOWLAND, Adam (M) 191 15
H: 5 11 W: 11 06 b.Preston 6-7-81
Source: Trainee.

1997-98	Blackpool	1	0	
1998-99	Blackpool	37	2	
1999-2000	Blackpool	21	3	
2000-01	Blackpool	10	0	69 5
2001-02	Wimbledon	7	0	
2002-03	Wimbledon	24	2	
2003-04	Wimbledon	25	3	56 5
2003-04	West Ham U	11	0	
2004-05	West Ham U	4	1	15 1
2004-05	*Gillingham*	3	1	

2004-05	Nottingham F	5	0		
2005-06	Nottingham F	0	0	5	0
2005-06	Preston NE	13	3		
2006-07	Preston NE	1	0		
2007-08	Preston NE	0	0	14	3
2007-08	Gillingham	5	0	8	1
2007-08	*Stockport Co*	4	0	4	0
2008-09	Notts Co	20	0	20	0

PILKINGTON, Kevin (G) 360 0
H: 6 1 W: 13 00 b.Hitchin 8-3-74
Source: Trainee. *Honours:* England Schools.

1992-93	Manchester U	0	0		
1993-94	Manchester U	0	0		
1994-95	Manchester U	1	0		
1995-96	Manchester U	3	0		
1995-96	Rochdale	6	0	6	0
1996-97	Manchester U	0	0		
1996-97	*Rotherham U*	17	0	17	0
1997-98	Manchester U	2	0		
1998-99	Manchester U	0	0	6	0
1998-99	Port Vale	8	0		
1999-2000	Port Vale	15	0	23	0
2000-01	Macclesfield T	0	0		
2000-01	Wigan Ath	0	0		
2000-01	Mansfield T	2	0		
2001-02	Mansfield T	45	0		
2002-03	Mansfield T	32	0		
2003-04	Mansfield T	46	0		
2004-05	Mansfield T	42	0	167	0
2005-06	Notts Co	45	0		
2006-07	Notts Co	39	0		
2007-08	Notts Co	32	0		
2008-09	Notts Co	25	0	141	0

RAVENHILL, Ricky (M) 206 17
H: 5 10 W: 11 02 b.Doncaster 16-1-81
Source: Barnsley Trainee.

2003-04	Doncaster R	36	3		
2004-05	Doncaster R	35	3		
2005-06	Doncaster R	27	3	98	9
2006-07	Chester C	3	0	3	0
2006-07	Grimsby T	17	2	17	2
2006-07	Darlington	15	1		
2007-08	Darlington	35	3		
2008-09	Darlington	38	2	88	6
2008-09	Notts Co	0	0		

SMITH, Jay (M) 128 11
H: 5 7 W: 12 00 b.Lambeth 24-9-81
Source: Scholar.

2000-01	Aston Villa	0	0		
2001-02	Aston Villa	0	0		
2002-03	Aston Villa	0	0		
2002-03	Southend U	31	5		
2003-04	Southend U	18	1		
2004-05	Southend U	0	0		
2005-06	Southend U	13	1		
2005-06	*Oxford U*	6	0	6	0
2006-07	Southend U	0	0	62	7
2006-07	Notts Co	27	4		
2007-08	Notts Co	20	0		
2008-09	Notts Co	13	0	60	4

STRACHAN, Gavin (M) 157 11
H: 5 10 W: 11 07 b.Aberdeen 23-12-78
Source: Trainee. *Honours:* Scotland Youth, Under-21.

1996-97	Coventry C	0	0		
1997-98	Coventry C	9	0		
1998-99	Coventry C	0	0		
1998-99	*Dundee*	6	0	6	0
1999-2000	Coventry C	3	0		
2000-01	Coventry C	2	0		
2001-02	Coventry C	1	0		
2002-03	Coventry C	1	0	16	0
2002-03	*Peterborough U*	2	0		
2002-03	Southend U	7	0	7	0
2003-04	Hartlepool U	36	5		
2004-05	Hartlepool U	29	1		
2005-06	Hartlepool U	9	1		
2005-06	*Stockport Co*	4	0	4	0
2006-07	Hartlepool U	4	0	78	7
2006-07	Peterborough U	16	3		
2007-08	Peterborough U	3	0	21	3
2007-08	Notts Co	7	0		
2008-09	Notts Co	18	1	25	1

TANN, Adam (D) 212 7
H: 6 0 W: 11 05 b.Fakenham 12-5-82
Source: Scholar. *Honours:* England Youth.

1999-2000	Cambridge U	0	0		
2000-01	Cambridge U	1	0		
2001-02	Cambridge U	25	0		
2002-03	Cambridge U	25	1		
2003-04	Cambridge U	34	2		
2004-05	Cambridge U	36	1	121	4

From Gravesend & N.

2005-06	Notts Co	5	0		
2005-06	Leyton Orient	10	1		
2006-07	Leyton Orient	21	1	31	2
2007-08	Notts Co	41	1		
2008-09	Notts Co	14	0	60	1

THOMPSON, John (D) 183 9
H: 6 0 W: 12 01 b.Dublin 12-10-81
Source: Home Farm. *Honours:* Eire Youth, Under-21, 1 full cap.

1999-2000	Nottingham F	0	0		
2000-01	Nottingham F	0	0		
2001-02	Nottingham F	8	0		
2002-03	Nottingham F	20	3		
2003-04	Nottingham F	32	1		
2004-05	Nottingham F	20	0		
2005-06	Nottingham F	35	3		
2006-07	Nottingham F	14	0	129	7
2006-07	*Tranmere R*	12	0	12	0
2007-08	Oldham Ath	7	0		
2008-09	Oldham Ath	0	0	7	0
2008-09	Notts Co	35	2	35	2

WEIR-DALEY, Spencer (F) 70 12
H: 5 9 W: 10 11 b.Leicester 5-9-85
Source: Scholar.

2003-04	Nottingham F	0	0		
2004-05	Nottingham F	0	0		
2005-06	Nottingham F	6	1		
2006-07	Nottingham F	1	0	7	1
2006-07	*Macclesfield F*	7	2	7	2
2006-07	*Lincoln C*	11	5	11	5
2006-07	*Bradford C*	5	1	5	1
2007-08	Notts Co	30	3		
2008-09	Notts Co	10	0	40	3

WESTON, Myles (F) 73 3
H: 5 11 W: 12 05 b.Lewisham 12-3-88
Source: Scholar.

2006-07	Charlton Ath	0	0		
2006-07	*Notts Co*	4	0		
2007-08	Notts Co	25	0		
2008-09	Notts Co	44	3	73	3

OLDHAM ATH (62)

ALESSANDRA, Lewis (F) 47 7
H: 5 9 W: 11 07 b.Oldham 8-2-89
Source: Scholar.

2007-08	Oldham Ath	15	2		
2008-09	Oldham Ath	32	5	47	7

ALLOTT, Mark (M) 462 49
H: 5 11 W: 11 07 b.Middleton 3-10-77
Source: Trainee.

1995-96	Oldham Ath	0	0		
1996-97	Oldham Ath	5	1		
1997-98	Oldham Ath	22	2		
1998-99	Oldham Ath	41	7		
1999-2000	Oldham Ath	32	10		
2000-01	Oldham Ath	39	7		
2001-02	Oldham Ath	15	4		
2001-02	Chesterfield	21	4		
2002-03	Chesterfield	33	0		
2003-04	Chesterfield	40	2		
2004-05	Chesterfield	45	2		
2005-06	Chesterfield	43	3		
2006-07	Chesterfield	39	0	221	11
2007-08	Oldham Ath	42	4		
2008-09	Oldham Ath	45	3	241	38

BELL, Josh (G) 0 0
H: 6 1 W: 13 03 b.Stockport 22-1-90
Source: Scholar.

2008-09	Oldham Ath	0	0		

BLACK, Paul (D) 5 0
H: 6 0 W: 12 10 b.Middleton 18-5-90
Source: Scholar.

2007-08	Oldham Ath	2	0		
2008-09	Oldham Ath	3	0	5	0

BROOKE, Ryan (F) 1 1
H: 6 1 W: 11 07 b.Crewe 4-10-90
Source: Scholar.

2008-09	Oldham Ath	1	1	1	1

BYRNE, Ritchie (D) 73 1
H: 6 1 W: 12 05 b.Dublin 24-9-81
Honours: Eire B.

2003-04	Dunfermline Ath	13	0		
2004-05	Dunfermline Ath	6	0	19	0
2004-05	Aberdeen	13	1		
2005-06	Aberdeen	19	0		
2006-07	Aberdeen	5	0		
2007-08	Aberdeen	13	0	50	1
2008-09	Oldham Ath	4	0	4	0

Transferred to Inverness CT January 2009

CROSSLEY, Mark (G) 447 1
H: 6 3 W: 15 09 b.Barnsley 16-6-69
Source: Trainee. *Honours:* England Under-21, B, Wales B, 8 full caps.

1987-88	Nottingham F	0	0		
1988-89	Nottingham F	2	0		
1989-90	Nottingham F	8	0		
1989-90	*Manchester U*	0	0		
1990-91	Nottingham F	38	0		
1991-92	Nottingham F	36	0		
1992-93	Nottingham F	37	0		
1993-94	Nottingham F	37	0		
1994-95	Nottingham F	42	0		
1995-96	Nottingham F	38	0		
1996-97	Nottingham F	33	0		
1997-98	Nottingham F	0	0		
1997-98	*Millwall*	13	0	13	0
1998-99	Nottingham F	12	0		
1999-2000	Nottingham F	20	0	303	0
2000-01	Middlesbrough	5	0		
2001-02	Middlesbrough	18	0		
2002-03	Middlesbrough	0	0	23	0
2002-03	*Stoke C*	12	0	12	0
2003-04	Fulham	1	0		
2004-05	Fulham	6	0		
2005-06	Fulham	13	0		
2006-07	Fulham	0	0	20	0
2006-07	*Sheffield W*	17	1	17	1
2007-08	Oldham Ath	38	0		
2008-09	Oldham Ath	21	0	59	0

EARDLEY, Neal (M) 113 10
H: 5 11 W: 11 10 b.Llandudno 6-11-88
Source: Scholar. *Honours:* Wales Under-21, 10 full caps.

2005-06	Oldham Ath	1	0		
2006-07	Oldham Ath	36	2		
2007-08	Oldham Ath	42	6		
2008-09	Oldham Ath	34	2	113	10

FLEMING, Greg (G) 48 0
H: 5 11 W: 12 09 b.Edinburgh 27-9-86
Source: Livingston. *Honours:* Scotland Under-21.

2006-07	Gretna	2	0		
2007-08	Gretna	28	0	30	0
2008-09	Oldham Ath	18	0	18	0

GREGAN, Sean (M) 573 18
H: 6 2 W: 14 00 b.Guisborough 29-3-74
Source: Trainee.

1991-92	Darlington	17	0		
1992-93	Darlington	17	1		
1993-94	Darlington	23	1		
1994-95	Darlington	25	2		
1995-96	Darlington	38	0		
1996-97	Darlington	16	0	136	4
1996-97	Preston NE	21	1		
1997-98	Preston NE	35	2		
1998-99	Preston NE	41	3		
1999-2000	Preston NE	33	3		
2000-01	Preston NE	41	2		
2001-02	Preston NE	41	1	212	12
2002-03	WBA	36	1		
2003-04	WBA	43	1		
2004-05	WBA	0	0	79	2
2004-05	Leeds U	35	0		
2005-06	Leeds U	28	0		
2006-07	Leeds U	1	0	64	0
2006-07	Oldham Ath	27	0		
2007-08	Oldham Ath	15	0		
2008-09	Oldham Ath	40	0	82	0

HAZELL, Reuben (D) 275 9
H: 5 11 W: 12 05 b.Birmingham 24-4-79
Source: Trainee.

1996-97	Aston Villa	0	0		
1997-98	Aston Villa	0	0		
1998-99	Aston Villa	0	0		
1999-2000	Tranmere R	23	1		
2000-01	Tranmere R	13	0		

2001-02	Tranmere R	6	0	42	1
2001-02	Torquay U	19	0		
2002-03	Torquay U	46	1		
2003-04	Torquay U	19	1		
2004-05	Torquay U	0	0	84	2
2005-06	Chesterfield	33	0		
2006-07	Chesterfield	39	2		
2007-08	Chesterfield	0	0	72	2
2007-08	Oldham Ath	34	1		
2008-09	Oldham Ath	43	3	77	4

HUGHES, Lee (F) 311 130
H: 5 10 W: 12 00 b.Smethwick 22-5-76
Source: Kidderminster H.

1997-98	WBA	37	14		
1998-99	WBA	42	31		
1999-2000	WBA	36	12		
2000-01	WBA	41	21		
2001-02	Coventry C	38	14		
2002-03	Coventry C	4	1	42	15
2002-03	WBA	23	0		
2003-04	WBA	32	11		
2004-05	WBA	0	0		
2005-06	WBA	0	0		
2006-07	WBA	0	0	211	89
2007-08	Oldham Ath	18	7		
2008-09	Oldham Ath	37	18	55	25
2008-09	Blackpool	3	1	3	1

KALALA, Jean-Paul (M) 102 8
H: 5 10 W: 12 02 b.Lubumbashi 16-2-82
Honours: DR Congo 6 full caps.

2003-04	Nice	2	0		
2004-05	Nice	0	0	2	0
2005-06	Grimsby T	21	5		
2006-07	Yeovil T	38	1	38	1
2007-08	Oldham Ath	20	0		
2008-09	Oldham Ath	0	0	20	0
2008-09	*Grimsby T*	21	2	42	7

LEE, Kieran (D) 15 0
H: 6 1 W: 12 00 b.Tameside 22-6-88
Source: Scholar.

2006-07	Manchester U	1	0		
2007-08	Manchester U	0	0	1	0
2007-08	QPR	7	0	7	0
2008-09	Oldham Ath	7	0	7	0

LIDDELL, Andy (F) 573 136
H: 5 7 W: 11 11 b.Leeds 28-6-73
Source: Trainee. Honours: Scotland Under-21.

1990-91	Barnsley	0	0		
1991-92	Barnsley	1	0		
1992-93	Barnsley	21	2		
1993-94	Barnsley	22	1		
1994-95	Barnsley	39	13		
1995-96	Barnsley	43	9		
1996-97	Barnsley	38	8		
1997-98	Barnsley	26	1		
1998-99	Barnsley	8	0	198	34
1998-99	Wigan Ath	28	10		
1999-2000	Wigan Ath	41	8		
2000-01	Wigan Ath	37	9		
2001-02	Wigan Ath	34	18		
2002-03	Wigan Ath	37	16		
2003-04	Wigan Ath	40	9	217	70
2004-05	Sheffield U	33	3	33	3
2005-06	Oldham Ath	29	9		
2006-07	Oldham Ath	46	10		
2007-08	Oldham Ath	18	2		
2008-09	Oldham Ath	32	8	125	29

LOMAX, Kelvin (D) 77 0
H: 5 11 W: 12 03 b.Bury 12-11-86
Source: Scholar.

2003-04	Oldham Ath	1	0		
2004-05	Oldham Ath	9	0		
2005-06	Oldham Ath	0	0		
2006-07	Oldham Ath	9	0		
2007-08	Oldham Ath	21	0		
2007-08	*Rochdale*	10	0	10	0
2008-09	Oldham Ath	27	0	67	0

MAHER, Kevin (M) 418 23
H: 6 0 W: 12 13 b.Ilford 17-10-76
Source: Trainee. Honours: Eire Under-21.

1995-96	Tottenham H	0	0		
1996-97	Tottenham H	0	0		
1997-98	Tottenham H	0	0		
1997-98	Southend U	18	1		
1998-99	Southend U	34	4		
1999-2000	Southend U	24	0		
2000-01	Southend U	41	2		

2001-02	Southend U	36	5		
2002-03	Southend U	42	2		
2003-04	Southend U	42	1		
2004-05	Southend U	42	1		
2005-06	Southend U	44	1		
2006-07	Southend U	41	5		
2007-08	Southend U	19	0	383	22
2007-08	*Gillingham*	7	0	7	0
2008-09	Oldham Ath	28	1	28	1

O'GRADY, Chris (F) 145 20
H: 6 3 W: 12 04 b.Nottingham 25-1-86
Source: Trainee. Honours: England Youth.

2002-03	Leicester C	1	0		
2003-04	Leicester C	0	0		
2004-05	Leicester C	0	0		
2004-05	*Notts Co*	9	0	9	0
2005-06	Leicester C	13	1		
2005-06	*Rushden & D*	22	4	22	4
2006-07	Leicester C	10	0	24	1
2006-07	Rotherham U	13	4		
2007-08	Rotherham U	38	9	51	13
2008-09	Oldham Ath	13	0	13	0
2008-09	*Bury*	6	0	6	0
2008-09	*Bradford C*	2	0	2	0
2008-09	*Stockport Co*	18	2	18	2

PURDIE, Rob (M) 123 12
H: 5 9 W: 11 06 b.Leicester 28-9-82
Source: Leicester C.

2006-07	Hereford U	44	6	44	6
2007-08	Darlington	39	0		
2008-09	Darlington	40	6	79	6
2008-09	Oldham Ath	0	0		

SMALLEY, Deane (M) 73 7
H: 6 0 W: 11 10 b.Chadderton 5-9-88
Source: Scholar.

2006-07	Oldham Ath	2	0		
2007-08	Oldham Ath	37	2		
2008-09	Oldham Ath	34	5	73	7

STAM, Stefan (D) 97 1
H: 6 2 W: 13 02 b.Amersfoort 14-9-79
Honours: Holland Under-21.

2004-05	Oldham Ath	13	0		
2005-06	Oldham Ath	13	0		
2006-07	Oldham Ath	22	1		
2007-08	Oldham Ath	36	0		
2008-09	Oldham Ath	13	0	97	1

STEPHENS, Dale (M) 9 1
H: 5 7 W: 11 04 b.Bolton 12-12-87
Source: Scholar.

2006-07	Bury	3	0		
2007-08	Bury	6	1	9	1
2008-09	Oldham Ath	0	0		

TAYLOR, Chris (M) 142 19
H: 5 11 W: 11 00 b.Oldham 20-12-86
Source: Scholar.

2005-06	Oldham Ath	14	0		
2006-07	Oldham Ath	44	4		
2007-08	Oldham Ath	42	5		
2008-09	Oldham Ath	42	10	142	19

WHITAKER, Danny (M) 296 43
H: 5 10 W: 11 00 b.Manchester 14-11-80
Source: Wilmslow Sports.

2000-01	Macclesfield T	0	0		
2001-02	Macclesfield T	16	2		
2002-03	Macclesfield T	41	10		
2003-04	Macclesfield T	36	5		
2004-05	Macclesfield T	36	2		
2005-06	Macclesfield T	44	4	171	23
2006-07	Port Vale	45	7		
2007-08	Port Vale	41	7	86	14
2008-09	Oldham Ath	39	6	39	6

WOLFENDEN, Matthew (F) 39 2
H: 5 9 W: 11 02 b.Oldham 23-7-87
Source: Scholar.

2003-04	Oldham Ath	1	0		
2004-05	Oldham Ath	1	0		
2005-06	Oldham Ath	1	0		
2006-07	Oldham Ath	6	0		
2007-08	Oldham Ath	25	2		
2008-09	Oldham Ath	5	0	39	2

PETERBOROUGH U (63)

APPIAH, Kwesi (F) 0 0
b.London 12-8-90
Source: Ebbsfleet U.

| 2008-09 | Peterborough U | 0 | 0 | | |

BATT, Shaun (F) 30 2
H: 6 3 W: 12 08 b.Harlow 22-2-87
Source: Fisher Ath.

| 2008-09 | Peterborough U | 30 | 2 | 30 | 2 |

BLACKETT, Shane (D) 35 0
H: 6 0 W: 12 11 b.Luton 26-6-81
Source: Arlesey, Dagenham & R.

2006-07	Peterborough U	13	0		
2007-08	Peterborough U	11	0		
2008-09	Peterborough U	11	0	35	0

BLANCHETT, Danny (D) 7 1
H: 5 11 W: 11 12 b.Wembley 12-3-88
Source: Northwood, Hendon, Harrow Borough, Cambridge C.

2006-07	Peterborough U	3	1		
2007-08	Peterborough U	1	0		
2008-09	Peterborough U	3	0	7	1

BONHAM-BARRETT, Craig (D) 0 0

| | Source: Peterborough U | 0 | 0 | | |

BOYD, George (M) 112 27
H: 5 10 W: 11 07 b.Chatham 2-10-85
Source: Stevenage B. Honours: Scotland B.

2006-07	Peterborough U	20	6		
2007-08	Peterborough U	46	12		
2008-09	Peterborough U	46	9	112	27

CHARNOCK, Kieran (D) 46 0
H: 6 1 W: 13 07 b.Preston 3-8-84
Source: Scholar.

2002-03	Wigan Ath	0	0		
2003-04	Wigan Ath	0	0		
2004-05	Wigan Ath	0	0		
2005-06	Wigan Ath	0	0		
2006-07	Wigan Ath	0	0		

From Southport, Northwich Vic.

2007-08	Peterborough U	10	0		
2008-09	Peterborough U	2	0	12	0
2008-09	*Accrington S*	34	0	34	0

COUTTS, Paul (M) 37 0
H: 5 9 W: 11 11 b.Aberdeen 22-7-88
Source: Cove R. Honours: Scotland Under-21.

| 2008-09 | Peterborough U | 37 | 0 | 37 | 0 |

DAY, Jamie (M) 97 5
H: 5 9 W: 10 07 b.Wycombe 7-5-86
Source: Scholar.

2003-04	Peterborough U	0	0		
2004-05	Peterborough U	1	0		
2005-06	Peterborough U	25	1		
2006-07	Peterborough U	24	1		
2007-08	Peterborough U	42	3		
2008-09	Peterborough U	5	0	97	5

FRECKLINGTON, Lee (M) 131 21
H: 5 8 W: 11 00 b.Lincoln 8-9-85
Source: Scholar. Honours: Eire B.

2003-04	Lincoln C	0	0		
2004-05	Lincoln C	3	0		
2005-06	Lincoln C	18	2		
2006-07	Lincoln C	42	8		
2007-08	Lincoln C	34	4		
2008-09	Lincoln C	27	7	124	21
2008-09	Peterborough U	7	0	7	0

GREEN, Dominic (F) 30 2
H: 5 6 W: 11 02 b.London 5-7-89
Source: Scholar.

2007-08	Dagenham & R	12	0		
2008-09	Dagenham & R	2	1	14	1
2008-09	Peterborough U	16	1	16	1

HATCH, Liam (F) 125 21
H: 6 4 W: 13 09 b.Hitchin 3-4-84
Source: Herne Bay, Gravesend & N.

2005-06	Barnet	35	2		
2006-07	Barnet	31	3		
2007-08	Barnet	21	6	87	11
2007-08	Peterborough U	11	0		
2008-09	Peterborough U	1	0	12	2
2008-09	*Darlington*	26	8	26	8

HOWE, Rene (F)   72 20
H: 6 0   W: 14 03   b.Bedford 22-10-86
Source: Kettering T.

2007-08	Peterborough U	15	1	
2007-08	*Rochdale*	20	9	20 9
2008-09	Peterborough U	0	0	15 1
2008-09	*Morecambe*	37	10	37 10

HYDE, Micah (M)   526 38
H: 5 10   W: 11 02   b.Newham 10-11-74
Source: Trainee. *Honours:* Jamaica 16 full caps, 1 goal.

1993-94	Cambridge U	18	2	
1994-95	Cambridge U	27	0	
1995-96	Cambridge U	24	4	
1996-97	Cambridge U	38	7	107 13
1997-98	Watford	40	4	
1998-99	Watford	44	2	
1999-2000	Watford	34	3	
2000-01	Watford	26	6	
2001-02	Watford	39	4	
2002-03	Watford	37	4	
2003-04	Watford	33	1	253 24
2004-05	Burnley	38	1	
2005-06	Burnley	41	0	
2006-07	Burnley	23	0	102 1
2006-07	Peterborough U	18	0	
2007-08	Peterborough U	37	0	
2008-09	Peterborough U	9	0	64 0

KEATES, Dean (M)   410 49
H: 5 6   W: 10 06   b.Walsall 30-6-78
Source: Trainee.

1996-97	Walsall	2	0	
1997-98	Walsall	33	1	
1998-99	Walsall	43	2	
1999-2000	Walsall	35	1	
2000-01	Walsall	33	4	
2001-02	Walsall	13	1	
2002-03	Hull C	36	4	
2003-04	Hull C	14	0	50 4
2003-04	Kidderminster H	8	2	
2004-05	Kidderminster H	41	5	49 7
2005-06	Lincoln C	21	4	21 4
2005-06	Walsall	14	2	
2006-07	Walsall	39	13	212 24
2007-08	Peterborough U	40	5	
2008-09	Peterborough U	38	5	78 10

LEE, Charlie (M)   91 11
H: 5 11   W: 11 07   b.Whitechapel 5-1-87
Source: Scholar.

2005-06	Tottenham H	0	0	
2006-07	Tottenham H	0	0	
2006-07	*Millwall*	5	0	5 0
2007-08	Peterborough U	42	6	
2008-09	Peterborough U	44	5	86 11

LEWIS, Joe (G)   92 0
H: 6 5   W: 12 10   b.Bury St Edmunds 6-10-87
Source: Scholar. *Honours:* England Youth, Under-21.

2004-05	Norwich C	0	0	
2005-06	Norwich C	0	0	
2006-07	Norwich C	0	0	
2006-07	*Stockport Co*	5	0	5 0
2007-08	Norwich C	0	0	
2007-08	*Morecambe*	19	0	19 0
2007-08	Peterborough U	22	0	
2008-09	Peterborough U	46	0	68 0

MACKAIL-SMITH, Craig (F)   97 43
H: 6 3   W: 12 04   b.Hertford 25-2-84
Source: Dagenham & R.

2006-07	Peterborough U	15	8	
2007-08	Peterborough U	36	12	
2008-09	Peterborough U	46	23	97 43

MARTIN, Russell (M)   162 6
H: 6 0   W: 11 08   b.Brighton 4-1-86

2004-05	Wycombe W	7	0	
2005-06	Wycombe W	23	3	
2006-07	Wycombe W	42	2	
2007-08	Wycombe W	44	0	116 5
2008-09	Peterborough U	46	1	46 1

McKEOWN, James (G)   2 0
H: 6 1   W: 13 07   b.Sutton Coldfield 24-7-89
Source: Scholar.

2005-06	Walsall	0	0	
2006-07	Walsall	0	0	
2007-08	Peterborough U	1	0	
2008-09	Peterborough U	1	0	2 0

McLEAN, Aaron (F)   143 56
H: 5 9   W: 10 10   b.Hammersmith 25-5-83
Source: Trainee.

1999-2000	Leyton Orient	3	0	
2000-01	Leyton Orient	2	1	
2001-02	Leyton Orient	27	1	
2002-03	Leyton Orient	8	0	40 2

From Aldershot T, Grays Ath.

2006-07	Peterborough U	16	7	
2007-08	Peterborough U	45	29	
2008-09	Peterborough U	42	18	103 54

MORGAN, Craig (D)   187 4
H: 6 0   W: 11 04   b.St Asaph 18-6-85
Source: Scholar. *Honours:* Wales Youth, Under-21, 15 full caps.

2001-02	Wrexham	29	0	
2002-03	Wrexham	6	1	
2003-04	Wrexham	18	0	
2004-05	Wrexham	36	0	
2005-06	Milton Keynes D	40	0	
2006-07	Milton Keynes D	3	0	43 0
2006-07	Wrexham	1	0	53 1
2006-07	Peterborough U	23	1	
2007-08	Peterborough U	41	2	
2008-09	Peterborough U	27	0	91 3

POTTER, Alfie (M)   2 0
H: 5 7   W: 9 06   b. 9-1-89
Source: Millwall.

2007-08	Peterborough U	2	0	
2008-09	Peterborough U	0	0	2 0

RENDELL, Scott (F)   18 4
H: 6 1   W: 13 00   b.Ashford 21-10-86
Source: Aldershot T, Forest Green R, Crawley T.
On loan from Cambridge U.

2007-08	Peterborough U	10	3	
2008-09	Peterborough U	3	1	13 4
2008-09	Yeovil T	5	0	5 0

ROWE, Tommy (M)   72 13
H: 5 11   W: 12 11   b.Manchester 1-5-89
Source: Scholar.

2006-07	Stockport Co	4	0	
2007-08	Stockport Co	24	6	
2008-09	Stockport Co	44	7	72 13
2008-09	Peterborough U	0	0	

TORRES, Sergio (M)   101 7
H: 6 2   W: 12 04   b.Mar del Plata 8-11-83
Source: Basingstoke T.

2005-06	Wycombe W	24	1	
2006-07	Wycombe W	20	0	
2007-08	Wycombe W	42	5	86 6
2008-09	Wycombe W	15	1	15 1

TYLER, Mark (G)   424 0
H: 6 0   W: 12 09   b.Norwich 2-4-77
Source: Trainee. *Honours:* England Youth, Under-20.

1994-95	Peterborough U	5	0	
1995-96	Peterborough U	5	0	
1996-97	Peterborough U	3	0	
1997-98	Peterborough U	46	0	
1998-99	Peterborough U	27	0	
1999-2000	Peterborough U	32	0	
2000-01	Peterborough U	40	0	
2001-02	Peterborough U	44	0	
2002-03	Peterborough U	29	0	
2003-04	Peterborough U	43	0	
2004-05	Peterborough U	46	0	
2005-06	Peterborough U	40	0	
2006-07	Peterborough U	41	0	
2007-08	Peterborough U	17	0	
2008-09	Peterborough U	0	0	413 0
2008-09	*Bury*	11	0	11 0

WESTWOOD, Chris (D)   385 15
H: 5 11   W: 12 10   b.Dudley 13-2-77
Source: Trainee.

1995-96	Wolverhampton W	0	0	
1996-97	Wolverhampton W	0	0	
1997-98	Wolverhampton W	4	1	
1998-99	Wolverhampton W	0	0	4 1
1998-99	Hartlepool U	4	0	
1999-2000	Hartlepool U	37	0	
2000-01	Hartlepool U	46	1	
2001-02	Hartlepool U	35	1	
2002-03	Hartlepool U	46	1	
2003-04	Hartlepool U	45	0	
2004-05	Hartlepool U	37	4	250 7
2005-06	Walsall	29	3	
2006-07	Walsall	40	2	69 5
2007-08	Peterborough U	37	0	
2008-09	Peterborough U	16	0	53 0
2008-09	*Cheltenham T*	9	2	9 2

WHELPDALE, Chris (M)   74 10
H: 6 0   W: 12 08   b.Harold Wood 27-1-87
Source: Billericay T.

2006-07	Peterborough U	0	0	
2007-08	Peterborough U	35	3	
2008-09	Peterborough U	39	7	74 10

WILLIAMS, Tom (M)   232 4
H: 5 11   W: 12 06   b.Carshalton 8-7-80
Source: Walton & Hersham. *Honours:* Cyprus 1 full cap.

1999-2000	West Ham U	0	0	
2000-01	West Ham U	0	0	
2000-01	*Peterborough U*	2	0	
2001-02	Peterborough U	34	2	
2001-02	Birmingham C	4	0	
2002-03	Birmingham C	0	0	
2002-03	QPR	26	1	
2003-04	Birmingham C	0	0	4 0
2003-04	QPR	5	0	31 1
2003-04	*Peterborough U*	21	1	
2004-05	Barnsley	39	0	39 0
2005-06	Gillingham	13	0	13 0
2005-06	Swansea C	17	0	
2006-07	Swansea C	29	0	46 0
2007-08	Wycombe W	10	0	10 0
2007-08	Peterborough U	7	0	
2008-09	Peterborough U	25	0	89 3

WRIGHT, Ben (F)   1 0
H: 6 2   W: 13 05   b.Basingstoke 20-8-88
Source: Basingstoke T, Hampton & Richmond B.

2008-09	Peterborough U	1	0	1 0

ZAKUANI, Gaby (D)   147 4
H: 6 1   W: 12 13   b.DR Congo 31-5-86
Source: Scholar. *Honours:* DR Congo 1 full cap.

2002-03	Leyton Orient	1	0	
2003-04	Leyton Orient	10	2	
2004-05	Leyton Orient	33	0	
2005-06	Leyton Orient	43	1	87 3
2006-07	Fulham	9	0	
2007-08	Fulham	0	0	
2007-08	*Stoke C*	19	0	28 0
2008-09	Fulham	0	0	
2008-09	Peterborough U	32	1	32 1

PLYMOUTH ARG (64)

BARKER, Chris (D)   379 3
H: 6 2   W: 13 08   b.Sheffield 2-3-80
Source: Alfreton.

1998-99	Barnsley	0	0	
1999-2000	Barnsley	29	0	
2000-01	Barnsley	40	0	
2001-02	Barnsley	44	3	113 3
2002-03	Cardiff C	40	0	
2003-04	Cardiff C	39	0	
2004-05	*Stoke C*	4	0	4 0
2004-05	Cardiff C	39	0	
2005-06	Cardiff C	41	0	
2006-07	Cardiff C	0	0	159 0
2006-07	*Colchester U*	38	0	38 0
2007-08	QPR	25	0	25 0
2008-09	Plymouth Arg	40	0	40 0

BARNES, Ashley (F)   15 1
H: 6 0   W: 12 00   b.Bath 30-10-89
Source: Paulton R.

2006-07	Plymouth Arg	0	0	
2007-08	Plymouth Arg	0	0	
2008-09	Plymouth Arg	15	1	15 1

BOLASIE, Yannick (M)   20 3
H: 6 2   W: 13 02   b.DR Congo 24-5-89

2008-09	Plymouth Arg	0	0	
2008-09	*Barnet*	20	3	20 3

CLARK, Chris (F)   229 8
H: 5 7   W: 10 05   b.Aberdeen 15-9-80

1999-2000	Aberdeen	2	0	
2000-01	Aberdeen	24	0	
2001-02	Aberdeen	8	0	
2002-03	Aberdeen	25	1	
2003-04	Aberdeen	23	1	

2004-05	Aberdeen	31	2		
2005-06	Aberdeen	31	3		
2006-07	Aberdeen	37	1	181	8
2007-08	Plymouth Arg	12	0		
2008-09	Plymouth Arg	36	0	48	0

DONNELLY, George (F)   **2   0**
H: 6 2   W: 13 03   b.Plymouth 28-5-88
Source: Skelmersdale U.

2008-09	Plymouth Arg	2	0	2	0

DOUALA, Rudolphe (F)   **234 34**
H: 5 9   W: 11 11   b.Douala 25-9-78
Honours: Cameroon 11 full caps, 1 goal.

1998-99	Boavista	26	5		
1999-2000	Boavista	14	1	40	6
2000-01	Desportes Aves	28	4	28	4
2001-02	Gil Vicente	32	4	32	4
2002-03	Uniao Leiria	33	5		
2003-04	Uniao Leiria	33	10	66	15
2004-05	Sporting Lisbon	22	4		
2005-06	Sporting Lisbon	25	1	47	5
2006-07	Portsmouth	7	0	7	0
2007-08	St Etienne	12	0	12	0
2008-09	Plymouth Arg	2	0	2	0

DOUMBE, Stephen (D)   **179   6**
H: 6 1   W: 12 05   b.Paris 28-10-79
Source: Paris St Germain. *Honours:* France Youth.

2001-02	Hibernian	0	0		
2002-03	Hibernian	12	0		
2003-04	Hibernian	33	2	45	2
2004-05	Plymouth Arg	26	2		
2005-06	Plymouth Arg	43	1		
2006-07	Plymouth Arg	29	0		
2007-08	Plymouth Arg	12	0		
2008-09	Plymouth Arg	24	1	134	4

DUGUID, Karl (M)   **424 43**
H: 5 11   W: 11 06   b.Hitchin 21-3-78
Source: Trainee.

1995-96	Colchester U	16	1		
1996-97	Colchester U	20	3		
1997-98	Colchester U	21	3		
1998-99	Colchester U	33	4		
1999-2000	Colchester U	41	12		
2000-01	Colchester U	41	5		
2001-02	Colchester U	41	4		
2002-03	Colchester U	27	3		
2003-04	Colchester U	30	2		
2004-05	Colchester U	0	0		
2005-06	Colchester U	35	0		
2006-07	Colchester U	43	5		
2007-08	Colchester U	37	0	385	42
2008-09	Plymouth Arg	39	1	39	1

EASTER, Jermaine (F)   **199 51**
H: 5 9   W: 12 02   b.Cardiff 15-1-82
Source: Trainee. *Honours:* Wales Youth, 7 full caps.

2000-01	Wolverhampton W	0	0		
2000-01	Hartlepool U	4	0		
2001-02	Hartlepool U	12	0		
2002-03	Hartlepool U	8	0		
2003-04	Hartlepool U	3	0	27	2
2003-04	*Cambridge U*	15	2		
2004-05	Cambridge U	24	6	39	8
2004-05	Boston U	9	3	9	3
2005-06	Stockport Co	19	8	19	8
2005-06	Wycombe W	15	2		
2006-07	Wycombe W	38	17		
2007-08	Wycombe W	6	2	59	21
2007-08	Plymouth Arg	32	6		
2008-09	Plymouth Arg	4	0	36	6
2008-09	*Millwall*	5	1	5	1
2008-09	*Colchester U*	5	2	5	2

FALLON, Rory (F)   **273 58**
H: 6 2   W: 11 09   b.Gisbourne 20-3-82
Source: North Shore U. *Honours:* England Youth.

1998-99	Barnsley	0	0		
1999-2000	Barnsley	0	0		
2000-01	Barnsley	1	0		
2001-02	Barnsley	5	0		
2001-02	*Shrewsbury T*	11	0	11	0
2002-03	Barnsley	26	7		
2003-04	Barnsley	16	4	52	11
2003-04	Swindon T	19	6		
2004-05	Swindon T	31	3		
2004-05	*Yeovil T*	6	1	6	1
2005-06	Swindon T	25	12	75	21
2005-06	Swansea C	17	4		

2006-07	Swansea C	24	8	41	12
2006-07	Plymouth Arg	15	1		
2007-08	Plymouth Arg	29	7		
2008-09	Plymouth Arg	44	5	88	13

FOLLY, Yoann (M)   **85   0**
H: 5 9   W: 11 04   b.Togo 6-6-85
Source: St Etienne. *Honours:* France Youth, Under-21. Togo 1 full cap.

2003-04	Southampton	9	0		
2004-05	Southampton	3	0		
2004-05	*Nottingham F*	1	0	1	0
2004-05	*Preston NE*	2	0	2	0
2005-06	Southampton	2	0	14	0
2005-06	*Sheffield W*	14	0		
2006-07	Sheffield W	29	0		
2007-08	Sheffield W	10	0	53	0
2007-08	Plymouth Arg	4	0		
2008-09	Plymouth Arg	11	0	15	0

HEAD, Liam (F)   **0   0**
b. 26-1-92
Source: Scholar.

2008-09	Plymouth Arg	0	0		

LARRIEU, Romain (G)   **259   0**
H: 6 4   W: 13 01   b.Mont-de-Marsan 31-8-76
Source: Montpellier, ASOA Valence.
Honours: France Youth.

2000-01	Plymouth Arg	15	0		
2001-02	Plymouth Arg	45	0		
2002-03	Plymouth Arg	43	0		
2003-04	Plymouth Arg	6	0		
2004-05	Plymouth Arg	23	0		
2005-06	Plymouth Arg	45	0		
2006-07	Plymouth Arg	6	0		
2006-07	*Gillingham*	14	0	14	0
2007-08	Plymouth Arg	15	0		
2007-08	*Yeovil T*	6	0	6	0
2008-09	Plymouth Arg	41	0	239	0

MACLEAN, Steve (F)   **181 61**
H: 5 11   W: 12 06   b.Edinburgh 23-8-82
Honours: Scotland Under-21.

2002-03	Rangers	3	0	3	0
2003-04	Scunthorpe U	42	23	42	23
2004-05	Sheffield W	36	18		
2005-06	Sheffield W	6	2		
2006-07	Sheffield W	41	12	83	32
2007-08	Cardiff C	15	1	15	1
2007-08	Plymouth Arg	17	3		
2008-09	Plymouth Arg	21	2	38	5

MACKIE, Jamie (F)   **72   8**
H: 5 8   W: 11 00   b.Dorking 22-9-85
Source: Leatherhead.

2003-04	Wimbledon	13	0	13	0
2004-05	Milton Keynes D	3	0	3	0
	From Exeter C				
2007-08	Plymouth Arg	13	3		
2008-09	Plymouth Arg	43	5	56	8

MARIN, Nicolas (F)   **159 18**
H: 5 7   W: 11 00   b.Marseille 29-8-80

2001-02	Auxerre	1	0		
2002-03	Auxerre	1	0	2	0
2003-04	St Etienne	34	6		
2004-05	St Etienne	26	3	60	9
2005-06	Sedan	33	3		
2006-07	Sedan	28	5	61	8
2007-08	Lorient	30	1	30	1
2008-09	Plymouth Arg	6	0	6	0
	On loan to Lorient				

McCRORY, Damien (M)   **12   0**
H: 6 2   W: 12 10   b.Limerick 22-2-90
Honours: Eire Youth.

2008-09	Plymouth Arg	0	0		
2008-09	*Port Vale*	12	0	12	0

McNAMEE, David (D)   **156   4**
H: 5 11   W: 11 02   b.Glasgow 10-10-80
Source: St Mirren BC. *Honours:* Scotland B, 4 full caps.

1997-98	St Mirren	1	0		
1998-99	St Mirren	31	0	32	0
1998-99	Blackburn R	0	0		
1999-2000	Blackburn R	0	0		
2000-01	Blackburn R	0	0		
2001-02	Blackburn R	0	0		
2002-03	Livingston	12	0		
2003-04	Livingston	30	3		
2004-05	Livingston	29	1		
2005-06	Livingston	14	0	85	4
2006-07	Coventry C	16	0		

2007-08	Coventry C	13	0	29	0
2008-09	Plymouth Arg	10	0	10	0

MPENZA, Emile (F)   **256 94**
H: 5 9   W: 10 12   b.Zellik 4-7-78
Honours: Belgium 54 full caps, 17 goals.

1995-96	Kortrijk	0	0		
1996-97	Mouscron	31	12	31	12
1997-98	Standard Liege	20	6		
1998-99	Standard Liege	17	10		
1999-2000	Standard Liege	11	4		
1999-2000	Schalke	15	6		
2000-01	Schalke	27	13		
2001-02	Schalke	16	4		
2002-03	Schalke	21	5	79	28
2003-04	Standard Liege	28	21	76	41
2004-05	Hamburg	26	5		
2005-06	Hamburg	10	1	36	6
	From Al Rayyan.				
2006-07	Manchester C	10	3		
2007-08	Manchester C	15	2		
2008-09	Manchester C	0	0	25	5
2008-09	Plymouth Arg	9	2	9	2

NOONE, Craig (M)   **21   1**
H: 6 3   W: 12 07   b.Southport 17-11-87
Source: Skelmersdale U, Burscough, Southport.

2008-09	Plymouth Arg	21	1	21	1

PATERSON, Jim (M)   **238 11**
H: 5 11   W: 12 13   b.Airdrie 25-9-79
Source: Dundee U BC. *Honours:* Scotland Under-21.

1998-99	Dundee U	15	0		
1999-2000	Dundee U	8	1		
2000-01	Dundee U	6	1		
2001-02	Dundee U	27	2		
2002-03	Dundee U	33	1		
2003-04	Dundee U	16	0	105	5
2004-05	Motherwell	35	3		
2005-06	Motherwell	19	1		
2006-07	Motherwell	34	1		
2007-08	Motherwell	20	0	108	5
2007-08	Plymouth Arg	8	1		
2008-09	Plymouth Arg	17	0	25	1

PUNCHEON, Jason (M)   **145 20**
H: 5 9   W: 12 05   b.Croydon 26-6-86
Source: Scholar.

2003-04	Wimbledon	8	0	8	0
2004-05	Milton Keynes D	25	1		
2005-06	Milton Keynes D	1	0		
2006-07	Barnet	37	5		
2007-08	Barnet	41	10	78	15
2008-09	Plymouth Arg	6	0	6	0
2008-09	*Milton Keynes D*	27	4	53	5

SAWYER, Gary (D)   **66   4**
H: 6 0   W: 11 08   b.Bideford 5-7-85
Source: Scholar.

2004-05	Plymouth Arg	0	0		
2005-06	Plymouth Arg	0	0		
2006-07	Plymouth Arg	22	0		
2007-08	Plymouth Arg	31	1		
2008-09	Plymouth Arg	13	3	66	4

SAXTON, Lloyd (G)   **0   0**
H: 5 11   W: 12 03   b.Alsager 18-4-90
Source: Scholar.

2008-09	Plymouth Arg	0	0		

SEIP, Marcel (D)   **234   8**
H: 6 0   W: 11 03   b.Winschoten 5-4-82

1999-2000	Veendam	9	0		
2000-01	Veendam	18	0	27	0
2001-02	Heerenveen	0	0		
2002-03	Heerenveen	6	0		
2003-04	Heerenveen	31	1		
2004-05	Heerenveen	30	1		
2005-06	Heerenveen	28	0	95	2
2006-07	Plymouth Arg	37	2		
2007-08	Plymouth Arg	34	1		
2008-09	Plymouth Arg	41	3	112	6

SMITH, Dan (M)   **4   0**
H: 5 10   W: 10 07   b.Saltash 5-10-88
Source: Scholar.

2007-08	Plymouth Arg	2	0		
2008-09	Plymouth Arg	0	0	2	0
2008-09	*Morecambe*	2	0	2	0

STACK, Graham (G) 46 0
H: 6 2 W: 12 07 b.Hampstead 26-9-81
Honours: Eire Youth, Under-21.

2000-01	Arsenal	0	0	
2001-02	Arsenal	0	0	
2002-03	Arsenal	0	0	
2003-04	Arsenal	0	0	
2004-05	Arsenal	0	0	
2004-05	*Millwall*	26	0	26 0
2005-06	Arsenal	0	0	
2005-06	Reading	1	0	
2006-07	Reading	0	0	
2006-07	*Leeds U*	12	0	12 0
2007-08	Reading	0	0	1 0
2007-08	*Wolverhampton W*	2	0	
2008-09	Plymouth Arg	5	0	5 0
2008-09	Blackpool	0	0	
2008-09	*Wolverhampton W*	0	0	2 0

SUMMERFIELD, Luke (M) 68 4
H: 6 0 W: 11 00 b.Ivybridge 6-12-87
Source: Scholar.

2004-05	Plymouth Arg	1	0	
2005-06	Plymouth Arg	0	0	
2006-07	Plymouth Arg	23	1	
2006-07	*Bournemouth*	8	1	8 1
2007-08	Plymouth Arg	7	0	
2008-09	Plymouth Arg	29	2	60 3

TIMAR, Krisztian (D) 149 11
H: 6 3 W: 13 08 b.Budapest 4-10-79
Source: Ferencvaros, MTK, Elore. *Honours:*
Hungary Youth, Under-21, Under-23, 3 full
caps.

2001-02	Videoton	31	4	
2002-03	Videoton	15	0	46 4
2003	Jokerit	0	0	
2003-04	Tatabanya	0	0	
2004-05	Nyiregyhaza	12	0	12 0
2005-06	Ferencvaros	23	3	23 3
2006-07	Plymouth Arg	9	1	
2007-08	Plymouth Arg	38	3	
2008-09	Plymouth Arg	21	0	68 4

WALTON, Simon (D) 88 6
H: 6 1 W: 13 05 b.Sherburn-in-Elmet
13-9-87
Source: Scholar. *Honours:* England Youth.

2004-05	Leeds U	30	3	
2005-06	Leeds U	4	0	34 3
2006-07	Charlton Ath	0	0	
2006-07	*Ipswich T*	19	3	19 3
2006-07	*Cardiff C*	6	0	6 0
2007-08	QPR	5	0	5 0
2007-08	*Hull C*	10	0	10 0
2008-09	Plymouth Arg	13	0	13 0
2008-09	*Blackpool*	1	0	1 0

PORT VALE (65)

ANYON, Joe (G) 102 0
H: 6 1 W: 12 11 b.Poulton-le-Fylde
29-12-86
Source: Scholar.

2005-06	Port Vale	0	0	
2006-07	Port Vale	22	0	
2007-08	Port Vale	44	0	
2008-09	Port Vale	36	0	102 0

BRAMMER, Dave (M) 455 22
H: 5 8 W: 12 00 b.Bromborough 28-2-75
Source: Trainee.

1992-93	Wrexham	2	0	
1993-94	Wrexham	22	2	
1994-95	Wrexham	14	1	
1995-96	Wrexham	11	2	
1996-97	Wrexham	21	1	
1997-98	Wrexham	33	4	
1998-99	Wrexham	34	2	137 12
1998-99	Port Vale	9	0	
1999-2000	Port Vale	29	0	
2000-01	Port Vale	35	3	
2001-02	Crewe Alex	30	2	
2002-03	Crewe Alex	41	1	
2003-04	Crewe Alex	16	1	87 4
2004-05	Stoke C	43	1	
2005-06	Stoke C	40	1	
2006-07	Stoke C	22	0	105 2
2006-07	Millwall	17	1	
2007-08	Millwall	23	0	

BROWN, Scott (M) 105 6
H: 5 9 W: 10 03 b.Runcorn 8-5-85
Source: Scholar. *Honours:* England Youth.

2001-02	Everton	0	0	
2002-03	Everton	0	0	
2003-04	Everton	0	0	
2004-05	Bristol C	19	0	
2005-06	Bristol C	29	1	
2006-07	Bristol C	15	4	63 5
2006-07	Cheltenham T	4	0	
2007-08	Cheltenham T	20	0	
2008-09	Cheltenham T	0	0	24 0
2008-09	Port Vale	18	1	18 1

CHAPMAN, Luke (M) 1 0
H: 6 1 W: 11 10 b.Cannock 10-3-91
Source: Scholar.

2007-08	Port Vale	1	0	
2008-09	Port Vale	0	0	1 0

COLLINS, Lee (D) 55 1
H: 6 1 W: 11 10 b.Telford 23-9-83
Source: Scholar. *Honours:* England Youth.

2006-07	Wolverhampton W	0	0	
2007-08	Wolverhampton W	0	0	
2007-08	*Hereford U*	16	0	16 0
2008-09	Wolverhampton W	0	0	
2008-09	Port Vale	39	1	39 1

DAVIDSON, Ross (M) 26 0
H: 6 2 W: 11 05 b.Burton 6-9-89
Source: Scholar.

2007-08	Port Vale	3	0	
2008-09	Port Vale	23	0	26 0

DODDS, Louis (F) 97 18
H: 5 10 W: 12 04 b.Leicester 8-10-86
Source: Scholar.

2005-06	Leicester C	0	0	
2006-07	Leicester C	0	0	
2006-07	*Rochdale*	12	2	12 2
2007-08	Leicester C	0	0	
2007-08	*Lincoln C*	41	9	41 9
2008-09	Port Vale	44	7	44 7

EDWARDS, Paul (M) 243 9
H: 5 11 W: 10 12 b.Manchester 1-1-80
Source: Altrincham.

2001-02	Swindon T	20	0	20 0
2002-03	Wrexham	38	4	
2003-04	Wrexham	41	0	79 4
2004-05	Blackpool	28	3	28 3
2005-06	Oldham Ath	34	0	
2006-07	Oldham Ath	26	0	60 0
2007-08	Port Vale	25	2	
2008-09	Port Vale	31	0	56 2

GLOVER, Danny (M) 38 4
H: 6 0 W: 11 02 b.Crewe 24-10-89
Source: Scholar.

2007-08	Port Vale	15	1	
2008-09	Port Vale	23	3	38 4

GRIFFITH, Anthony (M) 48 0
H: 6 0 W: 12 00 b.Huddersfield 28-10-86
Source: Glasshoughton W.

2005-06	Doncaster R	4	0	
2005-06	*Oxford U*	0	0	
2006-07	Doncaster R	2	0	
2006-07	*Darlington*	4	0	4 0
2007-08	Doncaster R	0	0	6 0
2007-08	Doncaster R	0	0	
2008-09	Port Vale	38	0	38 0

HOWLAND, David (M) 57 3
H: 5 11 W: 10 08 b.Ballynahinch 17-9-86
Source: Scholar. *Honours:* Northern Ireland
Under-21.

2004-05	Birmingham C	0	0	
2005-06	Birmingham C	0	0	
2006-07	Birmingham C	0	0	
2007-08	Birmingham C	0	0	
2007-08	*Port Vale*	17	1	
2008-09	Port Vale	40	2	57 3

LAWRIE, James (F) 24 2
H: 6 0 W: 12 05 b.Belfast 18-12-90
Source: Scholar. *Honours:* Northern Ireland
Under-21, B, 1 full cap.

2007-08	Port Vale	6	0	
2008-09	Port Vale	18	2	24 2

MALBON, Anthony (M) 1 0
H: 5 8 W: 11 00 b.Stoke 14-10-91
Source: Scholar.

2008-09	Port Vale	1	0	1 0

MARTIN, Chris (G) 13 0
H: 6 0 W: 13 05 b.Mansfield 21-7-90
Source: Scholar.

2007-08	Port Vale	2	0	
2008-09	Port Vale	11	0	13 0

McCOMBE, John (D) 72 2
H: 6 2 W: 13 00 b.Pontefract 7-5-85
Source: Scholar.

2002-03	Huddersfield T	1	0	
2003-04	Huddersfield T	0	0	
2004-05	Huddersfield T	5	0	
2005-06	Huddersfield T	1	0	
2005-06	*Torquay U*	0	0	
2006-07	Huddersfield T	7	0	14 0
2007-08	Hereford U	27	0	27 0
2008-09	Port Vale	31	2	31 2

OWEN, Gareth (D) 153 1
H: 6 1 W: 11 07 b.Cheadle 21-9-82
Source: Scholar. *Honours:* Wales Youth.

2001-02	Stoke C	0	0	
2002-03	Stoke C	0	0	
2003-04	Stoke C	3	0	
2003-04	*Oldham Ath*	15	1	
2004-05	Stoke C	2	0	5 0
2004-05	*Torquay U*	5	0	5 0
2004-05	*Oldham Ath*	9	0	
2005-06	Oldham Ath	17	0	
2006-07	Oldham Ath	0	0	41 1
2006-07	*Stockport Co*	39	0	
2007-08	Stockport Co	36	0	
2008-09	Stockport Co	8	0	83 0
2008-09	*Yeovil T*	7	0	7 0
2008-09	Port Vale	12	0	12 0

PERRY, Kyle (F) 31 0
H: 6 4 W: 14 05 b.Birmingham 5-3-86
Source: Chasetown.

2007-08	Port Vale	16	0	
2008-09	Port Vale	15	0	31 0

PROSSER, Luke (M) 31 1
H: 6 2 W: 12 04 b.Enfield 28-5-88
Source: Scholar.

2005-06	Port Vale	0	0	
2006-07	Port Vale	0	0	
2007-08	Port Vale	5	0	
2008-09	Port Vale	26	1	31 1

RICHARDS, Marc (F) 217 52
H: 6 2 W: 12 06 b.Wolverhampton 8-7-82
Source: Trainee. *Honours:* England Youth,
Under-20.

1999-2000	Blackburn R	0	0	
2000-01	Blackburn R	0	0	
2001-02	Blackburn R	0	0	
2001-02	*Crewe Alex*	4	0	4 0
2001-02	*Oldham Ath*	5	0	5 0
2001-02	*Halifax T*	5	0	5 0
2002-03	Blackburn R	0	0	
2002-03	Swansea C	17	7	17 7
2003-04	Northampton T	41	8	
2004-05	Northampton T	12	2	
2004-05	*Rochdale*	5	2	5 2
2005-06	Northampton T	0	0	53 10
2005-06	Barnsley	38	12	
2006-07	Barnsley	31	6	69 18
2007-08	Port Vale	29	5	
2008-09	Port Vale	30	10	59 15

RICHMAN, Simon (M) 43 5
H: 5 11 W: 11 12 b.Ormskirk 2-6-90
Source: Scholar.

2007-08	Port Vale	6	0	
2008-09	Port Vale	37	5	43 5

SLATER, Chris (D) 11 0
H: 6 0 W: 13 03 b.Dudley 14-1-84
Source: Chasetown.

2007-08	Port Vale	5	0	
2008-09	Port Vale	6	0	11 0

STOCKLEY, Sam (D) 449 6
H: 6 0 W: 12 08 b.Tiverton 5-9-77
Source: Trainee.

1996-97	Southampton	0	0	
1996-97	Barnet	21	0	
1997-98	Barnet	41	0	
1998-99	Barnet	41	0	

1999-2000	Barnet	34	1		
2000-01	Barnet	45	1	**182**	**2**
2001-02	Oxford U	41	0		
2002-03	Oxford U	0	0	**41**	**0**
2002-03	Colchester U	33	1		
2003-04	Colchester U	44	0		
2004-05	Colchester U	37	1		
2005-06	Colchester U	27	1	**141**	**3**
2005-06	Blackpool	7	0	**7**	**0**
2006-07	Wycombe W	34	1		
2007-08	Wycombe W	22	0	**56**	**1**
2008-09	Port Vale	22	0	**22**	**0**

TAYLOR, Rob (D) 　　**20 3**
H: 6 0　W: 12 08　b.Shrewsbury 16-1-85
Source: Ludlow T, Stourport Swifts, Solihull B, Redditch U, Nuneaton B.

2008-09	Port Vale	20	3	**20**	**3**

THOMPSON, Steve (F) 　　**17 2**
H: 5 7　W: 11 11　b.Peterlee 15-4-89
Source: Scholar.

2008-09	Port Vale	17	2	**17**	**2**

TUDOR, Shane (M) 　　**207 27**
H: 5 7　W: 11 12　b.Wolverhampton 10-2-82
Source: Trainee.

1999-2000	Wolverhampton W	0	0		
2000-01	Wolverhampton W	1	0		
2001-02	Wolverhampton W	0	0	**1**	**0**
2001-02	Cambridge U	32	3		
2002-03	Cambridge U	27	9		
2003-04	Cambridge U	36	3		
2004-05	Cambridge U	26	6	**121**	**21**
2005-06	Leyton Orient	33	4		
2006-07	Leyton Orient	33	2	**66**	**6**
2007-08	Shrewsbury T	0	0		
2007-08	Port Vale	14	0		
2008-09	Port Vale	5	0	**19**	**0**

PORTSMOUTH (66)

ASHDOWN, Jamie (G) 　　**72 0**
H: 6 1　W: 13 05　b.Reading 30-11-80
Source: Scholar.

1999-2000	Reading	0	0		
2000-01	Reading	1	0		
2001-02	Reading	1	0		
2001-02	Arsenal	0	0		
2002-03	Reading	1	0		
2002-03	Bournemouth	2	0	**2**	**0**
2003-04	Reading	10	0	**13**	**0**
2003-04	Rushden & D	19	0	**19**	**0**
2004-05	Portsmouth	16	0		
2005-06	Portsmouth	17	0		
2006-07	Portsmouth	0	0		
2006-07	Norwich C	2	0	**2**	**0**
2007-08	Portsmouth	3	0		
2008-09	Portsmouth	0	0	**36**	**0**

BASINAS, Angelos (M) 　　**291 28**
H: 5 11　W: 11 13　b.Chalkida 31-1-76
Honours: Greece 100 full caps, 7 goals.

1995-96	Panathinaikos	1	0		
1996-97	Panathinaikos	1	0		
1997-98	Panathinaikos	26	1		
1998-99	Panathinaikos	21	0		
1999-2000	Panathinaikos	29	4		
2000-01	Panathinaikos	25	3		
2001-02	Panathinaikos	22	4		
2002-03	Panathinaikos	24	5		
2003-04	Panathinaikos	26	7		
2004-05	Panathinaikos	24	3		
2005-06	Panathinaikos	0	0	**199**	**27**
2005-06	Mallorca	14	0		
2006-07	Mallorca	29	0		
2007-08	Mallorca	32	1	**75**	**1**
2008-09	AEK Athens	14	0	**14**	**0**
2008-09	Portsmouth	3	0	**3**	**0**

BEGOVIC, Asmir (G) 　　**29 0**
H: 6 5　W: 13 01　b.Trebinje 20-6-87
Source: La Louviere. *Honours:* Canada Under-20.

2006-07	Portsmouth	0	0		
2006-07	Macclesfield T	3	0	**3**	**0**
2007-08	Portsmouth	0	0		
2007-08	Bournemouth	8	0	**8**	**0**
2007-08	Yeovil T	2	0		
2008-09	Portsmouth	2	0	**2**	**0**
2008-09	Yeovil T	14	0	**16**	**0**

BELHADJ, Nadir (D) 　　**223 9**
H: 5 9　W: 10 07　b.Saint-Claude 18-6-82
Honours: France Youth. Algeria 31 full caps, 4 goals.

2002-03	Gueugnon	28	1		
2003-04	Gueugnon	36	1	**64**	**2**
2004-05	Sedan	31	1		
2005-06	Sedan	34	2		
2006-07	Sedan	37	2	**102**	**5**
2007-08	Lyon	9	0	**9**	**0**
2007-08	Lens	19	0	**19**	**0**
2008-09	Portsmouth	29	2	**29**	**2**

CAMPBELL, Sol (D) 　　**485 20**
H: 6 2　W: 15 07　b.Plaistow 18-9-74
Source: Trainee. *Honours:* England Youth, Under-21, B, 73 full caps, 1 goal.

1992-93	Tottenham H	1	1		
1993-94	Tottenham H	34	0		
1994-95	Tottenham H	30	0		
1995-96	Tottenham H	31	1		
1996-97	Tottenham H	38	0		
1997-98	Tottenham H	34	0		
1998-99	Tottenham H	37	6		
1999-2000	Tottenham H	29	0		
2000-01	Tottenham H	21	2	**255**	**10**
2001-02	Arsenal	31	2		
2002-03	Arsenal	33	2		
2003-04	Arsenal	35	1		
2004-05	Arsenal	16	1		
2005-06	Arsenal	20	2	**135**	**8**
2006-07	Portsmouth	32	1		
2007-08	Portsmouth	31	1		
2008-09	Portsmouth	32	0	**95**	**2**

CIFTCI, Nadir (F) 　　**0 0**
H: 6 1　W: 13 00　b.Karacan 12-2-92
Source: Scholar.

2008-09	Portsmouth	0	0

COLLINS, Joe (M) 　　**0 0**
b.Southampton 29-10-90
Source: Scholar.

2008-09	Portsmouth	0	0

COWAN-HALL, Paris (F) 　　**0 0**
b.London 5-10-90
Source: Scholar.

2008-09	Portsmouth	0	0

CRANIE, Martin (D) 　　**58 0**
H: 6 1　W: 12 09　b.Yeovil 23-9-86
Source: From Scholar. *Honours:* England Youth, Under-20, Under-21.

2003-04	Southampton	1	0		
2004-05	Southampton	3	0		
2004-05	Bournemouth	3	0	**3**	**0**
2005-06	Southampton	11	0		
2006-07	Southampton	1	0	**16**	**0**
2006-07	Yeovil T	12	0	**12**	**0**
2007-08	Portsmouth	2	0		
2007-08	QPR	6	0	**6**	**0**
2008-09	Portsmouth	0	0	**2**	**0**
2008-09	Charlton Ath	19	0	**19**	**0**

CROUCH, Peter (F) 　　**281 82**
H: 6 7　W: 13 03　b.Macclesfield 30-1-81
Source: Trainee. *Honours:* England Youth, Under-20, Under-21, B, 34 full caps, 16 goals.

1998-99	Tottenham H	0	0		
1999-2000	Tottenham H	0	0		
2000-01	QPR	42	10	**42**	**10**
2001-02	Portsmouth	37	18		
2001-02	Aston Villa	7	2		
2002-03	Aston Villa	14	0		
2003-04	Aston Villa	16	4	**37**	**6**
2003-04	Norwich C	15	4	**15**	**4**
2004-05	Southampton	27	12	**27**	**12**
2005-06	Liverpool	32	8		
2006-07	Liverpool	32	9		
2007-08	Liverpool	21	5	**85**	**22**
2008-09	Portsmouth	38	10	**75**	**28**

DAVIS, Sean (M) 　　**272 16**
H: 5 10　W: 12 00　b.Clapham 20-9-79
Source: Trainee. *Honours:* England Under-21.

1996-97	Fulham	1	0		
1997-98	Fulham	0	0		
1998-99	Fulham	6	0		
1999-2000	Fulham	26	0		
2000-01	Fulham	40	0		
2001-02	Fulham	30	0		
2002-03	Fulham	28	3		
2003-04	Fulham	24	5	**155**	**14**
2004-05	Tottenham H	15	0		
2005-06	Tottenham H	0	0	**15**	**0**
2005-06	Portsmouth	17	1		
2006-07	Portsmouth	31	0		
2007-08	Portsmouth	22	0		
2008-09	Portsmouth	32	1	**102**	**2**

DIARRA, Lassana (M) 　　**44 1**
H: 5 8　W: 11 02　b.Paris 10-3-85
Source: Le Havre. *Honours:* France Youth, Under-21, Under-23, 20 full caps.

2005-06	Chelsea	3	0		
2006-07	Chelsea	10	0		
2007-08	Chelsea	0	0	**13**	**0**
2007-08	Arsenal	7	0	**7**	**0**
2007-08	Portsmouth	12	1		
2008-09	Portsmouth	12	0	**24**	**1**

Transferred to Real Madrid January 2009

DIOP, Papa Bouba (M) 　　**211 23**
H: 6 4　W: 14 12　b.Dakar 28-1-78
Source: Espoir, Jaraaf, Vevey Sports.
Honours: Senegal 58 full caps, 10 goals.

1999-2000	Neuchatel Xamax	0	0		
2000-01	Neuchatel Xamax	18	4	**18**	**4**
2000-01	Grasshoppers	11	1		
2001-02	Grasshoppers	18	4	**29**	**5**
2001-02	Lens	5	0		
2002-03	Lens	16	3		
2003-04	Lens	26	3	**47**	**6**
2004-05	Fulham	29	6		
2005-06	Fulham	22	2		
2006-07	Fulham	23	0		
2007-08	Fulham	2	0	**76**	**8**
2007-08	Portsmouth	25	0		
2008-09	Portsmouth	16	0	**41**	**0**

DISTIN, Sylvain (D) 　　**367 9**
H: 6 3　W: 14 06　b.Bagnolet 16-12-77

1998-99	Tours	26	3	**26**	**3**
1999-2000	Gueugnon	33	1	**33**	**1**
2000-01	Paris St Germain	28	0	**28**	**0**
2001-02	Newcastle U	28	0	**28**	**0**
2002-03	Manchester C	34	0		
2003-04	Manchester C	38	2		
2004-05	Manchester C	38	1		
2005-06	Manchester C	31	0		
2006-07	Manchester C	37	2	**178**	**5**
2007-08	Portsmouth	36	0		
2008-09	Portsmouth	38	0	**74**	**0**

GAZET DUCHATTELIER, Ryan (M) **0 0**
b.Richmond, Aus 17-2-91
Source: Scholar.

2007-08	Portsmouth	0	0
2008-09	Portsmouth	0	0

GEKAS, Theofanis (F) 　　**278 119**
H: 5 10　b.Larissa 23-5-80
Honours: Greece 38 full caps, 14 goals.

1998-99	Larissa	8	1		
1999-2000	Larissa	24	5		
2000-01	Larissa	29	10	**61**	**16**
2001-02	Kallithea	26	14		
2002-03	Kallithea	29	9		
2003-04	Kallithea	28	13		
2004-05	Kallithea	16	10	**99**	**46**
2004-05	Panathinaikos	13	8		
2005-06	Panathinaikos	28	15	**41**	**23**
2006-07	Bochum	32	21	**32**	**21**
2007-08	Leverkusen	29	11		
2008-09	Leverkusen	15	2	**44**	**13**
2008-09	Portsmouth	1	0	**1**	**0**

HREIDARSSON, Hermann (D) 　　**457 24**
H: 6 3　W: 12 12　b.Reykjavik 11-7-74
Honours: Iceland Under-21, 85 full caps, 5 goals.

1993	IBV	2	0		
1994	IBV	18	2		
1995	IBV	18	1		
1996	IBV	17	2		
1997	IBV	11	0	**66**	**5**
1997-98	Crystal Palace	30	2		
1998-99	Crystal Palace	7	0	**37**	**2**
1998-99	Brentford	33	4		
1999-2000	Brentford	8	2	**41**	**6**
1999-2000	Wimbledon	24	1	**24**	**1**
2000-01	Ipswich T	36	1		
2001-02	Ipswich T	38	1		
2002-03	Ipswich T	28	0	**102**	**2**
2002-03	Charlton Ath	0	0		
2003-04	Charlton Ath	33	2		

2004-05	Charlton Ath	34	1		
2005-06	Charlton Ath	34	0		
2006-07	Charlton Ath	31	0	132	3
2007-08	Portsmouth	32	3		
2008-09	Portsmouth	23	2	55	5

HUGHES, Richard (M)   **253 15**
H: 6 0   W: 13 03   b.Glasgow 25-6-79
Source: Atalanta. *Honours:* Scotland Youth, Under-21, 5 full caps.

1997-98	Arsenal	0	0		
1998-99	Bournemouth	44	2		
1999-2000	Bournemouth	21	2		
2000-01	Bournemouth	44	8		
2001-02	Bournemouth	22	2	131	14
2002-03	Portsmouth	6	0		
2002-03	*Grimsby T*	12	1	12	1
2003-04	Portsmouth	11	0		
2004-05	Portsmouth	16	0		
2005-06	Portsmouth	26	0		
2006-07	Portsmouth	18	0		
2007-08	Portsmouth	13	0		
2008-09	Portsmouth	20	0	110	0

HURST, James (D)   **0 0**
b.Sutton Coldfield 31-1-92
Source: Scholar.

2008-09	Portsmouth	0	0

JAMES, David (G)   **663 0**
H: 6 5   W: 15 07   b.Welwyn 1-8-70
Source: From Trainee. *Honours:* England Youth, Under-21, B, 48 full caps.

1988-89	Watford	0	0		
1989-90	Watford	0	0		
1990-91	Watford	46	0		
1991-92	Watford	43	0	89	0
1992-93	Liverpool	29	0		
1993-94	Liverpool	14	0		
1994-95	Liverpool	42	0		
1995-96	Liverpool	38	0		
1996-97	Liverpool	38	0		
1997-98	Liverpool	27	0		
1998-99	Liverpool	26	0	214	0
1999-2000	Aston Villa	29	0		
2000-01	Aston Villa	38	0	67	0
2001-02	West Ham U	38	0		
2002-03	West Ham U	26	0		
2003-04	West Ham U	27	0	91	0
2003-04	Manchester C	17	0		
2004-05	Manchester C	38	0		
2005-06	Manchester C	38	0	93	0
2006-07	Portsmouth	38	0		
2007-08	Portsmouth	35	0		
2008-09	Portsmouth	36	0	109	0

JOHNSON, Glen (D)   **149 7**
H: 6 0   W: 13 04   b.Greenwich 23-8-84
Source: Scholar. *Honours:* England Youth, Under-20, Under-21, 15 full caps.

2001-02	West Ham U	0	0		
2002-03	West Ham U	15	0	15	0
2002-03	*Millwall*	8	0	8	0
2003-04	Chelsea	19	3		
2004-05	Chelsea	17	0		
2005-06	Chelsea	4	0		
2006-07	Chelsea	0	0		
2006-07	*Portsmouth*	26	0		
2007-08	Chelsea	2	0	42	3
2007-08	Portsmouth	29	1		
2008-09	Portsmouth	29	3	84	4

KABOUL, Younes (D)   **93 7**
H: 6 2   W: 13 07   b.St-Julien-en-Genevois 4-1-86
Honours: France Under-21.

2004-05	Auxerre	12	1		
2005-06	Auxerre	9	0		
2006-07	Auxerre	31	2	52	3
2007-08	Tottenham H	21	3	21	3
2008-09	Portsmouth	20	1	20	1

KANU, Nwankwo (F)   **376 93**
H: 6 5   W: 12 08   b.Owerri 1-8-76
Honours: Nigeria 73 full caps, 13 goals.

1991-92	Federation Works	30	9	30	9
1992-93	Iwanyanwu	30	6	30	6
1993-94	Ajax	6	2		
1994-95	Ajax	18	10		
1995-96	Ajax	30	13	54	25
1996-97	Internazionale	0	0		
1997-98	Internazionale	11	1		
1998-99	Internazionale	1	0	12	1
1998-99	Arsenal	12	6		

1999-2000	Arsenal	31	12		
2000-01	Arsenal	27	3		
2001-02	Arsenal	23	3		
2002-03	Arsenal	16	5		
2003-04	Arsenal	10	1	119	30
2004-05	WBA	28	2		
2005-06	WBA	25	5	53	7
2006-07	Portsmouth	36	10		
2007-08	Portsmouth	25	4		
2008-09	Portsmouth	17	1	78	15

KILBEY, Tom (M)   **0 0**
H: 6 3   W: 13 08   b.Waltham Forest 19-10-90
Source: Millwall.

2007-08	Portsmouth	0	0
2008-09	Portsmouth	0	0

KOROMA, Omar (F)   **5 0**
H: 5 10   W: 12 00   b.Banjul 22-10-89
Source: Banjul Hawks. *Honours:* Gambia Under-20, 2 full caps.

2008-09	Portsmouth	0	0		
2008-09	*Norwich C*	5	0	5	0

KRANJCAR, Niko (M)   **214 42**
H: 6 3   W: 12 13   b.Zagreb 13-8-84
Honours: Croatia Youth, Under-21, 48 full caps, 7 goals.

2001-02	Dynamo Zagreb	24	3		
2002-03	Dynamo Zagreb	21	4		
2003-04	Dynamo Zagreb	24	10		
2004-05	Dynamo Zagreb	16	2	85	19
2004-05	Hajduk Split	13	1		
2005-06	Hajduk Split	32	10		
2006-07	Hajduk Split	5	3	50	14
2006-07	Portsmouth	24	2		
2007-08	Portsmouth	34	4		
2008-09	Portsmouth	21	3	79	9

LAUREN, Etame-Mayer (D)   **327 24**
H: 5 11   W: 11 07   b.Londi Kribi 19-1-77
Honours: Cameroon 25 full caps, 8 goals.

1995-96	Utrera	30	5	30	5
1996-97	Sevilla B	17	3	17	3
1997-98	Levante	34	6	34	6
1998-99	Mallorca	32	1		
1999-2000	Mallorca	30	3	62	4
2000-01	Arsenal	18	2		
2001-02	Arsenal	27	2		
2002-03	Arsenal	27	1		
2003-04	Arsenal	32	0		
2004-05	Arsenal	33	1		
2005-06	Arsenal	22	0		
2006-07	Arsenal	0	0	159	6
2006-07	Portsmouth	10	0		
2007-08	Portsmouth	15	0		
2008-09	Portsmouth	0	0	25	0

LITTLE, Glen (M)   **371 40**
H: 6 3   W: 13 00   b.Wimbledon 15-10-75
Source: Trainee.

1994-95	Crystal Palace	0	0		
1995-96	Crystal Palace	0	0		
1996-97	Glentoran	6	2	6	2
1996-97	Burnley	9	0		
1997-98	Burnley	24	4		
1998-99	Burnley	34	5		
1999-2000	Burnley	41	3		
2000-01	Burnley	34	3		
2001-02	Burnley	37	9		
2002-03	Burnley	33	5		
2002-03	*Reading*	6	1		
2003-04	Burnley	34	3	246	32
2003-04	*Bolton W*	4	0	4	0
2004-05	Reading	35	0		
2005-06	Reading	35	5		
2006-07	Reading	24	0		
2007-08	Reading	2	0		
2008-09	Portsmouth	5	0	5	0
2008-09	*Reading*	8	0	110	6

MANTYLA, Tero (D)   **0 0**
b.Finland 18-4-91
Source: Scholar.

2007-08	Portsmouth	0	0
2008-09	Portsmouth	0	0

MBUYI-MUTOMBO, Andrea (F)   **14 3**
H: 6 1   W: 11 13   b.Brussels 6-12-90
Source: Anderlecht, FC Brussels. *Honours:* Belgium Youth.

2008-09	*Waregem*	14	3	14	3
2008-09	Portsmouth	0	0		

MULLINS, Hayden (D)   **419 22**
H: 5 11   W: 11 12   b.Reading 27-3-79
Source: Trainee. *Honours:* England Under-21.

1996-97	Crystal Palace	0	0		
1997-98	Crystal Palace	0	0		
1998-99	Crystal Palace	40	5		
1999-2000	Crystal Palace	45	10		
2000-01	Crystal Palace	41	1		
2001-02	Crystal Palace	43	0		
2002-03	Crystal Palace	43	2		
2003-04	Crystal Palace	10	0	222	18
2003-04	West Ham U	27	0		
2004-05	West Ham U	37	1		
2005-06	West Ham U	35	0		
2006-07	West Ham U	30	2		
2007-08	West Ham U	34	0		
2008-09	West Ham U	17	1	180	4
2008-09	Portsmouth	17	0	17	0

MVUEMBA, Arnold (M)   **54 2**
H: 5 8   W: 10 07   b.Alencon 28-1-85
Honours: France Under-21.

2003-04	Rennes	8	0		
2004-05	Rennes	8	0		
2005-06	Rennes	16	1		
2006-07	Rennes	1	0	33	1
2006-07	Portsmouth	7	1		
2007-08	Portsmouth	8	0		
2008-09	Portsmouth	6	0	21	1

NLUNDULU, Gael (F)   **0 0**
b.France 29-4-92
Source: Scholar. *Honours:* France Youth.

2008-09	Portsmouth	0	0

NUGENT, Dave (F)   **213 54**
H: 5 11   W: 12 13   b.Liverpool 2-5-85
Source: Scholar. *Honours:* England Youth, Under-20, Under-21, 1 full cap, 1 goal.

2001-02	Bury	5	0		
2002-03	Bury	31	4		
2003-04	Bury	26	3		
2004-05	Bury	26	11	88	18
2004-05	Preston NE	18	8		
2005-06	Preston NE	32	10		
2006-07	Preston NE	44	15	94	33
2007-08	Portsmouth	15	0		
2008-09	Portsmouth	16	3	31	3

O'BRIEN, Liam (G)   **0 0**
b.Brent 30-11-91
Source: Scholar.

2008-09	Portsmouth	0	0

PAMAROT, Noe (D)   **239 12**
H: 5 11   W: 13 07   b.Fontenay-sous-Bois 14-4-79
Source: Martigues, Nice.

1997-98	Martigues	25	2		
1998-99	Martigues	0	0	25	2
1999-2000	Nice	0	0		
1999-2000	Portsmouth	2	0		
2000-01	Nice	23	0		
2001-02	Nice	33	3		
2002-03	Nice	33	1		
2003-04	Nice	33	2	122	6
2004-05	Tottenham H	23	1		
2005-06	Tottenham H	2	0	25	1
2005-06	Portsmouth	8	0		
2006-07	Portsmouth	23	2		
2007-08	Portsmouth	18	1		
2008-09	Portsmouth	16	0	67	3

PELE (M)   **28 0**
H: 6 1   W: 12 00   b.Oporto 14-9-87
Honours: Portugal Youth, Under-21.

2006-07	Guimaraes	11	0	11	0
2007-08	Internazionale	15	0	15	0
2008-09	Porto	2	0	2	0
2008-09	Portsmouth	0	0		

PRIMUS, Linvoy (D)   **434 14**
H: 5 10   W: 12 04   b.Forest Gate 14-9-73
Source: Trainee.

1992-93	Charlton Ath	4	0		
1993-94	Charlton Ath	0	0		
1994-95	Barnet	39	0		
1995-96	Barnet	42	4		
1996-97	Barnet	46	3	127	7
1997-98	Reading	36	1		
1998-99	Reading	31	0		
1999-2000	Reading	28	0	95	1
2000-01	Portsmouth	23	0		

2001-02	Portsmouth	22	2		
2002-03	Portsmouth	40	0		
2003-04	Portsmouth	21	0		
2004-05	Portsmouth	35	1		
2005-06	Portsmouth	20	0		
2006-07	Portsmouth	36	2		
2007-08	Portsmouth	0	0		
2008-09	Portsmouth	1	0	198	5
2008-09	*Charlton Ath*	10	1	14	1

REYNOLDS, Callum (D) 0 0
b.Luton 10-11-89
Source: Rushden & D Scholar.

2007-08	Portsmouth	0	0
2008-09	Portsmouth	0	0

RITCHIE, Matt (M) 37 11
H: 5 8 W: 11 00 b.Gosport 10-9-89

2008-09	Portsmouth	0	0		
2008-09	*Dagenham & R*	37	11	37	11

SONGO'O, Frank (M) 34 1
H: 6 2 W: 12 06 b.Yaounde 14-5-87
Source: Barcelona. *Honours:* France Youth.

2005-06	Portsmouth	2	0		
2006-07	Portsmouth	0	0		
2006-07	*Bournemouth*	4	0	4	0
2006-07	*Preston NE*	6	0	6	0
2007-08	Portsmouth	1	0		
2007-08	*Crystal Palace*	9	0	9	0
2007-08	*Sheffield W*	12	1	12	1
2008-09	Portsmouth	0	0	3	0

STEWART, Jon (M) 0 0
H: 6 1 W: 13 09 b.Harlesden 13-3-89
Source: Weymouth.

2008-09	Portsmouth	0	0

SUBOTIC, Danijel (F) 0 0
H: 6 2 W: 12 00 b.Doboj 31-1-89
Source: Basle.

2007-08	Portsmouth	0	0
2008-09	Portsmouth	0	0

THOMAS, Jerome (M) 116 10
H: 5 9 W: 11 09 b.Wembley 23-3-83
Source: Scholar. *Honours:* England Youth, Under-20, Under-21.

2001-02	Arsenal	0	0		
2001-02	*QPR*	4	1		
2002-03	Arsenal	0	0		
2002-03	*QPR*	6	2	10	3
2003-04	Arsenal	1	0		
2003-04	Charlton Ath	1	0		
2004-05	Charlton Ath	24	3		
2005-06	Charlton Ath	25	1		
2006-07	Charlton Ath	20	3		
2007-08	Charlton Ath	32	0		
2008-09	Charlton Ath	1	0	103	7
2008-09	Portsmouth	3	0	3	0

TRAORE, Djimi (D) 149 0
H: 6 2 W: 12 07 b.Saint-Ouen 1-3-80
Source: Laval. *Honours:* France Youth, Under-21, Mali 5 full caps, 1 goal.

1998-99	Liverpool	0	0		
1999-2000	Liverpool	0	0		
2000-01	Liverpool	8	0		
2001-02	Liverpool	0	0		
2001-02	*Lens*	19	0	19	0
2002-03	Liverpool	32	0		
2003-04	Liverpool	7	0		
2004-05	Liverpool	26	0		
2005-06	Liverpool	15	0	88	0
2006-07	*Charlton Ath*	11	0	11	0
2006-07	Portsmouth	10	0		
2007-08	*Rennes*	15	0	15	0
2007-08	Portsmouth	3	0		
2008-09	Portsmouth	0	0	13	0
2008-09	*Birmingham C*	3	0	3	0

UTAKA, John (F) 212 52
H: 5 9 W: 11 02 b.Enugu 8-1-82
Source: Ismaily, Al Saad. *Honours:* Nigeria 39 full caps, 5 goals.

2002-03	Lens	36	8		
2003-04	Lens	32	4		
2004-05	Lens	34	12	102	24
2005-06	Rennes	28	11		
2006-07	Rennes	35	11	63	22
2007-08	Portsmouth	29	5		
2008-09	Portsmouth	18	1	47	6

WARD, Joel (D) 21 1
H: 6 2 W: 11 13 b.Emsworth 29-10-89
Source: Scholar.

2008-09	Portsmouth	0	0		
2008-09	*Bournemouth*	21	1	21	1

WILSON, Marc (M) 35 3
H: 6 2 W: 12 07 b.Belfast 17-8-87
Source: Scholar. *Honours:* Eire Under-21.

2005-06	Portsmouth	0	0		
2005-06	*Yeovil T*	2	0	2	0
2006-07	Portsmouth	0	0		
2006-07	*Bournemouth*	19	3		
2007-08	Portsmouth	0	0		
2007-08	*Bournemouth*	7	0	26	3
2007-08	*Luton T*	4	0	4	0
2008-09	Portsmouth	3	0	3	0

Scholars
Bogard, Daniel Robert; Carter, Maximillian Louis; Goddard, Billy; Gregory, Peter; Hughes, Jordan Gary; Martin, Ellis; Navas, Alors Pablo; Pack, Marlon; Ryan, Perry Dean; Smith, Mark James; Smith, Tommy Ben; Sowah, Lennard; Watts, Nicholas James.

PRESTON NE (67)

APPIAH, Philip (M) 0 0
b.Toronto
Source: Fulham.

2008-09	Preston NE	0	0

BARTON, Adam (M) 0 0
H: 5 11 W: 12 01 b.Blackburn 7-1-91
Source: Scholar.

2008-09	Preston NE	0	0

BROWN, Chris (F) 166 32
H: 6 3 W: 13 01 b.Doncaster 11-12-84
Source: From Trainee. *Honours:* England Youth.

2002-03	Sunderland	0	0		
2003-04	Sunderland	0	0		
2003-04	*Doncaster R*	22	10	22	10
2004-05	Sunderland	37	5		
2005-06	Sunderland	13	1		
2005-06	*Hull C*	13	1	13	1
2006-07	Sunderland	16	3	66	9
2006-07	Norwich C	4	0		
2007-08	Norwich C	14	1	18	1
2007-08	Preston NE	17	5		
2008-09	Preston NE	30	6	47	11

CARTER, Darren (M) 165 12
H: 6 2 W: 12 11 b.Solihull 18-12-83
Source: Scholar. *Honours:* England Youth, Under-20.

2001-02	Birmingham C	13	1		
2002-03	Birmingham C	12	0		
2003-04	Birmingham C	5	0		
2004-05	Birmingham C	15	2	45	3
2004-05	*Sunderland*	10	1	10	1
2005-06	WBA	20	1		
2006-07	WBA	33	3	53	4
2007-08	Preston NE	39	4		
2008-09	Preston NE	18	0	57	4

CHAPLOW, Richard (M) 157 15
H: 5 9 W: 9 03 b.Accrington 2-2-85
Source: Scholar. *Honours:* England Youth, Under-20, Under-21.

2002-03	Burnley	5	0		
2003-04	Burnley	39	5		
2004-05	Burnley	21	2	65	7
2004-05	WBA	4	0		
2005-06	WBA	7	0		
2005-06	*Southampton*	11	1	11	1
2006-07	WBA	28	1		
2007-08	WBA	5	0	44	1
2007-08	Preston NE	12	3		
2008-09	Preston NE	25	3	37	6

CHILVERS, Liam (D) 203 5
H: 6 2 W: 12 03 b.Chelmsford 6-11-81
Source: Scholar.

2000-01	Arsenal	0	0		
2000-01	*Northampton T*	7	0	7	0
2001-02	Arsenal	0	0		
2001-02	*Notts Co*	9	1	9	1
2002-03	Arsenal	0	0		
2002-03	*Colchester U*	6	0		
2003-04	Arsenal	0	0		

2003-04	*Colchester U*	32	0		
2004-05	Colchester U	41	1		
2005-06	Colchester U	34	2	113	3
2006-07	Preston NE	45	2		
2007-08	Preston NE	28	0		
2008-09	Preston NE	1	0	74	2

COLLINS, Dominic (D) 0 0
b.Preston 15-4-91
Source: Scholar.

2008-09	Preston NE	0	0

DAVIDSON, Callum (D) 331 20
H: 5 10 W: 11 08 b.Stirling 25-6-76
Source: From 'S' Form. *Honours:* Scotland Under-21, 17 full caps.

1994-95	St Johnstone	7	1		
1995-96	St Johnstone	2	0		
1996-97	St Johnstone	20	2		
1997-98	St Johnstone	15	1	44	4
1997-98	Blackburn R	1	0		
1998-99	Blackburn R	34	1		
1999-2000	Blackburn R	30	0	65	1
2000-01	Leicester C	28	1		
2001-02	Leicester C	30	0		
2002-03	Leicester C	30	1		
2003-04	Leicester C	13	0	101	2
2004-05	Preston NE	19	1		
2005-06	Preston NE	27	4		
2006-07	Preston NE	15	0		
2007-08	Preston NE	40	4		
2008-09	Preston NE	20	4	121	13

ELLIOTT, Stephen (F) 149 32
H: 5 8 W: 11 07 b.Dublin 6-1-84
Source: School. *Honours:* Eire Youth, Under-21, 9 full caps, 1 goal.

2000-01	Manchester C	0	0		
2001-02	Manchester C	0	0		
2002-03	Manchester C	0	0		
2003-04	Manchester C	2	0	2	0
2004-05	Sunderland	42	15		
2005-06	Sunderland	15	2		
2006-07	Sunderland	24	5	81	22
2007-08	Wolverhampton W	29	4		
2008-09	Wolverhampton W	0	0	29	4
2008-09	Preston NE	37	6	37	6

FAIRHURST, Nathan (M) 0 0
Source: Scholar.

2008-09	Preston NE	0	0

HART, Michael (M) 181 0
H: 5 10 W: 11 06 b.Airdrie 10-2-80

1998-99	Aberdeen	14	0		
1999-2000	Aberdeen	3	0		
1999-2000	*Livingston*	3	0		
1999-2000	*Morton*	10	0	10	0
2000-01	Aberdeen	0	0		
2000-01	*Livingston*	22	0		
2001-02	*Livingston*	21	0		
2002-03	*Livingston*	11	0	57	0
2002-03	Aberdeen	8	0		
2003-04	Aberdeen	11	0		
2004-05	Aberdeen	32	0		
2005-06	Aberdeen	4	0		
2006-07	Aberdeen	34	0	106	0
2007-08	Preston NE	2	0		
2008-09	Preston NE	6	0	8	0

HAWLEY, Karl (F) 152 48
H: 5 8 W: 12 02 b.Walsall 6-12-81
Source: Scholar.

2000-01	Walsall	0	0		
2001-02	Walsall	1	0		
2002-03	Walsall	0	0		
2002-03	*Raith R*	17	7		
2003-04	Walsall	0	0	1	0
2003-04	*Raith R*	11	2	28	9
2004-05	Carlisle U	0	0		
2005-06	Carlisle U	46	22		
2006-07	Carlisle U	32	12	78	34
2007-08	Preston NE	25	3		
2008-09	Preston NE	5	0	30	3
2008-09	*Northampton T*	11	2	11	2
2008-09	*Colchester U*	4	0	4	0

HENDERSON, Wayne (G) 87 0
H: 5 11 W: 12 02 b.Dublin 16-9-83
Source: Scholar. *Honours:* Eire Youth, Under-21, 6 full caps.

2000-01	Aston Villa	0	0
2001-02	Aston Villa	0	0
2002-03	Aston Villa	0	0

Season	Club	Apps	Gls	Tot Apps	Tot Gls
2003-04	Aston Villa	0	0		
2003-04	*Wycombe W*	3	0	3	0
2004-05	Aston Villa	0	0		
2004-05	*Notts Co*	11	0	11	0
2005-06	Aston Villa	0	0		
2005-06	Brighton & HA	32	0		
2006-07	Brighton & HA	20	0	52	0
2006-07	Preston NE	4	0		
2007-08	Preston NE	3	0		
2008-09	Preston NE	0	0	7	0
2008-09	*Grimsby T*	14	0	14	0

JONES, Billy (M) 205 11
H: 5 11 W: 13 00 b.Shrewsbury 24-3-87
Source: Scholar. *Honours:* England Youth, Under-20.

Season	Club	Apps	Gls	Tot Apps	Tot Gls
2003-04	Crewe Alex	27	1		
2004-05	Crewe Alex	20	0		
2005-06	Crewe Alex	44	6		
2006-07	Crewe Alex	41	1	132	8
2007-08	Preston NE	29	0		
2008-09	Preston NE	44	3	73	3

LONERGAN, Andrew (G) 139 1
H: 6 4 W: 13 02 b.Preston 19-10-83
Source: Scholar. *Honours:* Eire Youth, England Youth, Under-20.

Season	Club	Apps	Gls	Tot Apps	Tot Gls
2000-01	Preston NE	1	0		
2001-02	Preston NE	0	0		
2002-03	Preston NE	0	0		
2002-03	*Darlington*	2	0	2	0
2003-04	Preston NE	8	0		
2004-05	Preston NE	23	1		
2005-06	Preston NE	0	0		
2005-06	*Wycombe W*	2	0	2	0
2006-07	Preston NE	13	0		
2007-08	Preston NE	43	0		
2008-09	Preston NE	46	0	134	1

MAWENE, Youl (D) 216 9
H: 6 2 W: 12 06 b.Caen 16-7-79

Season	Club	Apps	Gls	Tot Apps	Tot Gls
1999-2000	Lens	6	0	6	0
2000-01	Derby Co	8	0		
2001-02	Derby Co	17	1		
2002-03	Derby Co	0	0		
2003-04	Derby Co	30	0	55	1
2004-05	Preston NE	46	2		
2005-06	Preston NE	30	1		
2006-07	Preston NE	0	0		
2007-08	Preston NE	38	3		
2008-09	Preston NE	41	2	155	8

MAYOR, Danny (M) 3 0
H: 6 0 W: 11 12 b.Leyland 18-10-90
Source: Scholar.

Season	Club	Apps	Gls	Tot Apps	Tot Gls
2008-09	Preston NE	0	0		
2008-09	*Tranmere R*	3	0	3	0

McKENNA, Paul (M) 422 30
H: 5 7 W: 11 12 b.Eccleston 20-10-77
Source: Trainee.

Season	Club	Apps	Gls	Tot Apps	Tot Gls
1995-96	Preston NE	0	0		
1996-97	Preston NE	5	1		
1997-98	Preston NE	5	0		
1998-99	Preston NE	36	0		
1999-2000	Preston NE	24	2		
2000-01	Preston NE	44	5		
2001-02	Preston NE	38	4		
2002-03	Preston NE	41	3		
2003-04	Preston NE	39	6		
2004-05	Preston NE	39	3		
2005-06	Preston NE	41	2		
2006-07	Preston NE	33	2		
2007-08	Preston NE	33	0		
2008-09	Preston NE	44	2	422	30

MELLOR, Neil (F) 105 25
H: 6 0 W: 13 05 b.Sheffield 4-11-82
Source: Scholar.

Season	Club	Apps	Gls	Tot Apps	Tot Gls
2001-02	Liverpool	0	0		
2002-03	Liverpool	3	0		
2003-04	Liverpool	0	0		
2003-04	*West Ham U*	16	2	16	2
2004-05	Liverpool	9	2		
2005-06	Liverpool	0	0		
2005-06	*Wigan Ath*	3	1	3	1
2006-07	Liverpool	0	0	12	2
2006-07	Preston NE	5	1		
2007-08	Preston NE	36	9		
2008-09	Preston NE	33	10	74	20

MURPHY, Andrew (G) 0 0
H: 6 4 W: 14 00 b. 22-9-88
Source: Scholar.

Season	Club	Apps	Gls
2007-08	Preston NE	0	0
2008-09	Preston NE	0	0

NEAL, Chris (G) 1 0
H: 6 2 W: 12 04 b.St Albans 23-10-85
Source: Scholar.

Season	Club	Apps	Gls	Tot Apps	Tot Gls
2004-05	Preston NE	1	0		
2005-06	Preston NE	0	0		
2006-07	Preston NE	0	0		
2007-08	*Morecambe*	0	0		
2007-08	Preston NE	0	0		
2008-09	Preston NE	0	0	1	0

NICHOLSON, Barry (M) 321 39
H: 5 7 W: 9 01 b.Dumfries 24-8-78
Honours: Scotland Under-21, 3 full caps.

Season	Club	Apps	Gls	Tot Apps	Tot Gls
1995-96	Rangers	0	0		
1996-97	Rangers	0	0		
1997-98	Rangers	0	0		
1998-99	Rangers	6	0		
1999-2000	Rangers	2	0	8	0
2000-01	Dunfermline Ath	36	3		
2001-02	Dunfermline Ath	37	7		
2002-03	Dunfermline Ath	38	5		
2003-04	Dunfermline Ath	36	5		
2004-05	Dunfermline Ath	27	3	174	23
2005-06	Aberdeen	33	2		
2006-07	Aberdeen	31	6		
2007-08	Aberdeen	38	5	102	13
2008-09	Preston NE	37	3	37	3

NOLAN, Eddie (D) 36 0
H: 6 0 W: 13 05 b.Waterford 5-8-88
Source: Scholar. *Honours:* Eire Under-21, 1 full cap.

Season	Club	Apps	Gls	Tot Apps	Tot Gls
2005-06	Blackburn R	0	0		
2006-07	Blackburn R	0	0		
2006-07	*Stockport Co*	4	0	4	0
2007-08	Blackburn R	0	0		
2007-08	*Hartlepool U*	11	0	11	0
2008-09	Blackburn R	0	0		
2008-09	Preston NE	21	0	21	0

PARKIN, Jon (F) 271 71
H: 6 4 W: 13 07 b.Barnsley 30-12-81
Source: Scholarship.

Season	Club	Apps	Gls	Tot Apps	Tot Gls
1998-99	Barnsley	2	0		
1999-2000	Barnsley	0	0		
2000-01	Barnsley	4	0		
2001-02	Barnsley	4	0	10	0
2001-02	*Hartlepool U*	1	0	1	0
2001-02	York C	18	2		
2002-03	York C	41	10		
2003-04	York C	15	2	74	14
2003-04	Macclesfield T	12	1		
2004-05	Macclesfield T	42	22		
2005-06	Macclesfield T	11	7	65	30
2005-06	Hull C	18	5		
2006-07	Hull C	29	6	47	11
2006-07	*Stoke C*	6	3		
2007-08	Stoke C	29	2		
2008-09	Stoke C	0	0	35	5
2008-09	Preston NE	39	11	39	11

SEDGWICK, Chris (M) 438 28
H: 5 11 W: 11 10 b.Sheffield 28-4-80
Source: Trainee.

Season	Club	Apps	Gls	Tot Apps	Tot Gls
1997-98	Rotherham U	4	0		
1998-99	Rotherham U	33	4		
1999-2000	Rotherham U	38	5		
2000-01	Rotherham U	21	2		
2001-02	Rotherham U	44	1		
2002-03	Rotherham U	43	1		
2003-04	Rotherham U	40	2		
2004-05	Rotherham U	20	2	243	17
2004-05	Preston NE	24	3		
2005-06	Preston NE	46	4		
2006-07	Preston NE	43	1		
2007-08	Preston NE	42	2		
2008-09	Preston NE	40	1	195	11

ST LEDGER-HALL, Sean (D) 203 8
H: 6 0 W: 11 09 b.Solihull 28-12-84
Source: Scholar. *Honours:* Eire 2 full caps.

Season	Club	Apps	Gls	Tot Apps	Tot Gls
2002-03	Peterborough U	1	0		
2003-04	Peterborough U	2	0		
2004-05	Peterborough U	33	0		
2005-06	Peterborough U	43	1	79	1
2006-07	Preston NE	41	1		
2007-08	Preston NE	37	1		
2008-09	Preston NE	46	5	124	7

TROTMAN, Neal (D) 27 1
H: 6 3 W: 13 08 b.Levenshulme 11-3-87
Source: Burnley Scholar.

Season	Club	Apps	Gls	Tot Apps	Tot Gls
2006-07	Oldham Ath	1	0		
2007-08	Oldham Ath	17	1	18	1
2007-08	Preston NE	3	0		
2008-09	Preston NE	0	0	3	0
2008-09	*Colchester U*	6	0	6	0

WALLACE, Ross (M) 129 14
H: 5 6 W: 9 12 b.Dundee 23-5-85
Source: Celtic S Form. *Honours:* Scotland Youth, Under-21, B.

Season	Club	Apps	Gls	Tot Apps	Tot Gls
2001-02	Celtic	0	0		
2002-03	Celtic	0	0		
2003-04	Celtic	8	1		
2004-05	Celtic	16	0		
2005-06	Celtic	11	0		
2006-07	Celtic	2	0	37	1
2006-07	Sunderland	32	6		
2007-08	Sunderland	21	2		
2008-09	Sunderland	0	0	53	8
2008-09	Preston NE	39	5	39	5

WHALEY, Simon (M) 197 26
H: 5 10 W: 11 11 b.Bolton 7-6-85
Source: Scholar.

Season	Club	Apps	Gls	Tot Apps	Tot Gls
2002-03	Bury	2	0		
2003-04	Bury	10	1		
2004-05	Bury	38	3		
2005-06	Bury	23	7	73	11
2005-06	Preston NE	16	3		
2006-07	Preston NE	40	6		
2007-08	Preston NE	43	4		
2008-09	Preston NE	21	1	120	14
2008-09	*Barnsley*	4	1	4	1

QPR (68)

AGYEMANG, Patrick (F) 325 59
H: 6 1 W: 12 00 b.Walthamstow 29-9-80
Source: Trainee. *Honours:* Ghana 3 full caps, 1 goal.

Season	Club	Apps	Gls	Tot Apps	Tot Gls
1998-99	Wimbledon	0	0		
1999-2000	Wimbledon	0	0		
1999-2000	*Brentford*	12	0	12	0
2000-01	Wimbledon	29	4		
2001-02	Wimbledon	33	4		
2002-03	Wimbledon	33	5		
2003-04	Wimbledon	26	7	121	20
2003-04	Gillingham	20	6		
2004-05	Gillingham	13	2	33	8
2004-05	Preston NE	27	4		
2005-06	Preston NE	42	6		
2006-07	Preston NE	31	7		
2007-08	Preston NE	22	4	122	21
2007-08	QPR	17	8		
2008-09	QPR	20	2	37	10

AINSWORTH, Gareth (M) 424 89
H: 5 10 W: 12 05 b.Blackburn 10-5-73
Source: Blackburn R Trainee.

Season	Club	Apps	Gls	Tot Apps	Tot Gls
1991-92	Preston NE	5	0		
1992-93	Cambridge U	4	1	4	1
1992-93	Preston NE	26	0		
1993-94	Preston NE	38	11		
1994-95	Preston NE	16	1		
1995-96	Preston NE	2	0		
1995-96	Lincoln C	31	12		
1996-97	Lincoln C	46	22		
1997-98	Lincoln C	6	3	83	37
1997-98	Port Vale	40	5		
1998-99	Port Vale	15	5	55	10
1998-99	Wimbledon	8	0		
1999-2000	Wimbledon	2	2		
2000-01	Wimbledon	12	2		
2001-02	Wimbledon	2	0		
2001-02	*Preston NE*	5	1	92	13
2002-03	Wimbledon	12	2	36	6
2002-03	*Walsall*	5	1	5	1
2002-03	*Cardiff C*	9	0	9	0
2003-04	QPR	29	6		
2004-05	QPR	22	2		
2005-06	QPR	43	9		
2006-07	QPR	22	1		
2007-08	QPR	24	3		
2008-09	QPR	0	0	140	21

ALBERTI, Matteo (M) — 12 2
H: 5 10 W: 11 05 b.Chievo Verona 4-8-88
Source: Chievo Verona.

Season	Club				
2008-09	QPR	12	2	12	2

BALANTA, Angelo (F) — 32 5
H: 5 10 W: 11 11 b.Colombia 1-7-90
Source: Scholar.

Season	Club				
2007-08	QPR	11	1		
2008-09	QPR	10	1	21	2
2008-09	*Wycombe W*	11	3	11	3

BLACKSTOCK, Dexter (F) — 167 43
H: 6 2 W: 13 00 b.Oxford 20-5-86
Source: Scholar. *Honours:* England Youth, Under-20, Under-21.

Season	Club				
2004-05	Southampton	9	1		
2004-05	*Plymouth Arg*	14	4	14	4
2005-06	Southampton	19	3	28	4
2005-06	*Derby Co*	9	3	9	3
2006-07	QPR	39	13		
2007-08	QPR	35	6		
2008-09	QPR	36	11	110	30
2008-09	*Nottingham F*	6	2	6	2

BORROWDALE, Gary (D) — 135 0
H: 6 0 W: 12 01 b.Sutton 16-7-85
Source: Scholar. *Honours:* England Youth, Under-20.

Season	Club				
2002-03	Crystal Palace	13	0		
2003-04	Crystal Palace	23	0		
2004-05	Crystal Palace	7	0		
2005-06	Crystal Palace	30	0		
2006-07	Crystal Palace	25	0	98	0
2007-08	Coventry C	21	0		
2008-09	Coventry C	0	0	21	0
2008-09	*Colchester U*	4	0	4	0
2008-09	QPR	0	0		
2008-09	*Brighton & HA*	12	0	12	0

BROWN, Lee (M) — 0 0
Source: Scholar.

Season	Club				
2008-09	QPR	0	0		

BUZSAKY, Akos (M) — 134 19
H: 5 11 W: 11 09 b.Hungary 7-5-82
Source: From MTK, Porto. *Honours:* Hungary Under-21, 13 full caps, 1 goal.

Season	Club				
2004-05	Plymouth Arg	15	1		
2005-06	Plymouth Arg	34	4		
2006-07	Plymouth Arg	36	3		
2007-08	Plymouth Arg	11	0	96	8
2007-08	QPR	27	10		
2008-09	QPR	11	1	38	11

CAMP, Lee (G) — 180 0
H: 5 11 W: 11 11 b.Derby 22-8-84
Source: Scholar. *Honours:* England Youth, Under-20, Under-21.

Season	Club				
2002-03	Derby Co	1	0		
2003-04	Derby Co	0	0		
2003-04	*QPR*	12	0		
2004-05	Derby Co	45	0		
2005-06	Derby Co	40	0		
2006-07	Derby Co	3	0	89	0
2006-07	*Norwich C*	3	0	3	0
2006-07	QPR	11	0		
2007-08	QPR	46	0		
2008-09	QPR	4	0	73	0
2008-09	*Nottingham F*	15	0	15	0

CERNY, Radek (G) — 58 0
H: 6 1 W: 14 02 b.Prague 18-2-74
Source: Slavia Prague. *Honours:* Czech Republic 3 full caps.

Season	Club				
2004-05	Tottenham H	3	0		
2005-06	Tottenham H	0	0		
2006-07	Tottenham H	0	0		
2007-08	Tottenham H	13	0	16	0
2008-09	QPR	42	0	42	0

COLE, Jake (G) — 16 0
H: 6 2 W: 13 00 b.Hammersmith 11-9-85
Source: Scholar.

Season	Club				
2005-06	QPR	3	0		
2006-07	QPR	3	0		
2007-08	QPR	0	0		
2008-09	QPR	0	0	6	0
2008-09	*Barnet*	10	0	10	0

CONNOLLY, Matthew (D) — 76 3
H: 6 1 W: 11 03 b.Barnet 24-9-87
Source: Scholar. *Honours:* England Youth.

Season	Club				
2005-06	Arsenal	0	0		
2006-07	Arsenal	0	0		
2006-07	*Bournemouth*	5	1	5	1
2007-08	Arsenal	0	0		
2007-08	*Colchester U*	16	2	16	2
2007-08	QPR	20	0		
2008-09	QPR	35	0	55	0

COOK, Lee (M) — 241 19
H: 5 8 W: 11 10 b.Hammersmith 3-8-82
Source: Aylesbury U.

Season	Club				
1999-2000	Watford	0	0		
2000-01	Watford	4	0		
2001-02	Watford	10	0		
2002-03	Watford	4	0		
2002-03	*York C*	7	1	7	1
2002-03	*QPR*	13	1		
2003-04	Watford	41	7	59	7
2004-05	QPR	42	2		
2005-06	QPR	40	4		
2006-07	QPR	37	3		
2007-08	Fulham	0	0		
2007-08	Charlton Ath	9	0	9	0
2008-09	Fulham	0	0		
2008-09	QPR	34	1	166	11

CROWTHER, Reece (M) — 0 0
H: 6 5 W: 11 01 b.California 28-11-88
Source: Scholar.

Season	Club				
2008-09	QPR	0	0		

DELANEY, Damien (D) — 307 8
H: 6 3 W: 14 00 b.Cork 20-7-81
Source: From Cork. *Honours:* Eire 2 full caps.

Season	Club				
2000-01	Leicester C	5	0		
2001-02	Leicester C	3	0		
2001-02	*Stockport Co*	12	1	12	1
2001-02	*Huddersfield T*	2	0	2	0
2002-03	Leicester C	0	0	8	0
2002-03	*Mansfield T*	7	0	7	0
2002-03	Hull C	30	1		
2003-04	Hull C	46	2		
2004-05	Hull C	43	1		
2005-06	Hull C	46	0		
2006-07	Hull C	37	1		
2007-08	Hull C	22	0	224	5
2007-08	QPR	17	1		
2008-09	QPR	37	1	54	2

DI CARMINE, Samuel (F) — 30 2
H: 6 2 W: 12 04 b.Florence 20-9-88

Season	Club				
2006-07	Fiorentina	2	0		
2007-08	Fiorentina	1	0	3	0
2008-09	QPR	27	2	27	2

EPHRAIM, Hogan (F) — 77 5
H: 5 9 W: 10 06 b.Islington 31-3-88
Source: Scholar. *Honours:* England Youth.

Season	Club				
2004-05	West Ham U	0	0		
2005-06	West Ham U	0	0		
2006-07	West Ham U	0	0		
2006-07	*Colchester U*	21	1	21	1
2007-08	West Ham U	0	0		
2007-08	QPR	29	3		
2008-09	QPR	27	1	56	4

FLOOD, Christopher (M) — 0 0

Season	Club				
2008-09	QPR	0	0		

GERMAN, Antonio (F) — 3 0
H: 5 10 W: 12 03 b.Wembley 26-12-91
Source: Scholar.

Season	Club				
2008-09	QPR	3	0	3	0

GORKSS, Kaspars (D) — 192 11
H: 6 3 W: 13 05 b.Riga 6-11-81
Honours: Latvia 25 full caps, 2 goals.

Season	Club				
2002	Auda Riga	28	0	28	0
2003	Oster	8	0		
2004	Oster	24	1	32	1
2005	Assyriska	23	0	23	0
2006	Ventspils	28	5	28	5
2006-07	Blackpool	10	0		
2007-08	Blackpool	40	5	50	5
2008-09	QPR	31	0	31	0

HALL, Fitz (D) — 193 10
H: 6 3 W: 13 00 b.Leytonstone 20-12-80
Source: Barnet Trainee, Chesham U.

Season	Club				
2001-02	Oldham Ath	4	1		
2002-03	Oldham Ath	40	4	44	5
2003-04	Southampton	11	0	11	0
2004-05	Crystal Palace	36	2		
2005-06	Crystal Palace	39	1	75	3
2006-07	Wigan Ath	24	0		
2007-08	Wigan Ath	1	0	25	0
2007-08	QPR	14	0		
2008-09	QPR	24	2	38	2

HELGUSON, Heidar (F) — 302 92
H: 5 10 W: 12 09 b.Akureyri 22-8-77
Source: Throttur. *Honours:* Iceland Youth, Under-21, 43 full caps, 8 goals.

Season	Club				
1998	Lillestrom	19	2		
1999	Lillestrom	25	16	44	18
1999-2000	Watford	16	6		
2000-01	Watford	33	8		
2001-02	Watford	34	6		
2002-03	Watford	30	11		
2003-04	Watford	22	8		
2004-05	Watford	39	16	174	55
2005-06	Fulham	27	8		
2006-07	Fulham	30	4	57	12
2007-08	Bolton W	6	2		
2008-09	Bolton W	1	0	7	2
2008-09	QPR	20	5	20	5

LEDESMA, Emmanuel (M) — 18 1
H: 5 11 W: 12 02 b.Quilmes 24-5-88

Season	Club				
2007-08	Genoa	1	0	1	0
2008-09	QPR	17	1	17	1

Transferred to Genoa February 2009

LEIGERTWOOD, Mikele (D) — 226 10
H: 6 1 W: 11 04 b.Enfield 12-11-82
Source: Scholar.

Season	Club				
2001-02	Wimbledon	1	0		
2001-02	*Leyton Orient*	8	0	8	0
2002-03	Wimbledon	28	0		
2003-04	Wimbledon	37	2	56	2
2003-04	Crystal Palace	12	0		
2004-05	Crystal Palace	20	1		
2005-06	Crystal Palace	27	0	59	1
2006-07	Sheffield U	19	0		
2007-08	Sheffield U	2	0	21	0
2007-08	QPR	40	5		
2008-09	QPR	42	2	82	7

LOPEZ, Jordi (M) — 86 3
H: 6 0 W: 12 02 b.Barcelona 28-2-81

Season	Club				
2003-04	Real Madrid	2	0	2	0
2004-05	Sevilla	18	1		
2005-06	Sevilla	19	1	37	2
2006-07	Mallorca	23	0	23	0
2007-08	Santander	14	0	14	0
2008-09	QPR	10	1	10	1

MAGUIRE, Danny (M) — 1 0
H: 6 10 W: 12 00 b. 9-9-89
Source: Scholar.

Season	Club				
2008-09	QPR	0	0		
2008-09	*Yeovil T*	1	0	1	0

MAHON, Gavin (M) — 392 18
H: 5 11 W: 13 07 b.Birmingham 2-1-77
Source: Trainee.

Season	Club				
1995-96	Wolverhampton W	0	0		
1996-97	Hereford U	11	1		
1997-98	Hereford U	0	0		
1998-99	Hereford U	0	0	11	1
1998-99	Brentford	29	4		
1999-2000	Brentford	37	3		
2000-01	Brentford	40	1		
2001-02	Brentford	35	0	141	8
2001-02	Watford	6	0		
2002-03	Watford	17	0		
2003-04	Watford	32	2		
2004-05	Watford	43	0		
2005-06	Watford	38	3		
2006-07	Watford	34	1		
2007-08	Watford	19	0	189	6
2007-08	QPR	16	1		
2008-09	QPR	35	2	51	3

MILLER, Liam (M) — 151 12
H: 5 7 W: 10 05 b.Cork 13-2-81
Honours: Eire Under-21, 20 full caps, 1 goal.

Season	Club				
1999-2000	Celtic	1	0		
2000-01	Celtic	0	0		
2001-02	Celtic	0	0		
2001-02	*Aarhus*	18	6	18	6
2002-03	Celtic	0	0		
2003-04	Celtic	25	2	26	2
2004-05	Manchester U	8	0		
2005-06	Manchester U	1	0	9	0
2005-06	*Leeds U*	28	1	28	1
2006-07	Sunderland	30	2		
2007-08	Sunderland	24	1		
2008-09	Sunderland	3	0	57	3
2008-09	QPR	13	0	13	0

O'BRIEN, Matthew (M) 0 0
2008-09 QPR 0 0

OASTLER, Joseph (D) 0 0
Source: Scholar.
2008-09 QPR 0 0

PAREJO, Daniel (M) 51 11
H: 5 11 W: 11 11 b.Madrid 16-4-89
Honours: Spain Youth, Under-21.
2006-07 Real Madrid Castilla 4 1
2007-08 Real Madrid Castilla33 10 37 11
2008-09 QPR 14 0 14 0
On loan to Real Madrid B

PUTNINS, Elvijs (M) 0 0
2008-09 QPR 0 0

RAMAGE, Peter (D) 82 0
H: 6 3 W: 11 02 b.Whitley Bay 22-11-83
Source: Trainee.
2003-04 Newcastle U 0 0
2004-05 Newcastle U 4 0
2005-06 Newcastle U 23 0
2006-07 Newcastle U 21 0
2007-08 Newcastle U 3 0 51 0
2008-09 QPR 31 0 31 0

REHMAN, Zesh (D) 111 2
H: 6 2 W: 12 08 b.Birmingham 14-10-83
Source: Scholar. *Honours:* England Youth, Pakistan 6 full caps.
2001-02 Fulham 0 0
2002-03 Fulham 0 0
2003-04 Fulham 1 0
2003-04 *Brighton & HA* 11 2
2004-05 Fulham 17 0
2005-06 Fulham 3 0 21 0
2005-06 *Norwich C* 5 0 5 0
2006-07 QPR 25 0
2006-07 *Brighton & HA* 8 0 19 2
2007-08 QPR 21 0
2008-09 QPR 0 0 46 0
2008-09 *Blackpool* 3 0 3 0
2008-09 *Bradford C* 17 0 17 0

ROSE, Romone (M) 3 0
H: 5 9 W: 11 05 b.Pennsylvania 19-1-90
Source: Scholar.
2007-08 QPR 1 0
2008-09 QPR 2 0 3 0

ROUTLEDGE, Wayne (M) 182 13
H: 5 6 W: 11 02 b.Sidcup 7-1-85
Source: Scholar. *Honours:* England Youth, Under-20, Under-21.
2001-02 Crystal Palace 2 0
2002-03 Crystal Palace 26 4
2003-04 Crystal Palace 44 6
2004-05 Crystal Palace 38 0 110 10
2005-06 Tottenham H 3 0
2005-06 *Portsmouth* 13 0 13 0
2006-07 Tottenham H 0 0
2006-07 *Fulham* 24 0 24 0
2007-08 Tottenham H 2 0 5 0
2007-08 Aston Villa 1 0
2008-09 Aston Villa 1 0 2 0
2008-09 *Cardiff C* 9 2 9 2
2008-09 QPR 19 1 19 1

ROWLANDS, Martin (M) 337 53
H: 5 9 W: 10 10 b.Hammersmith 8-2-79
Source: Farnborough T. *Honours:* Eire Under-21, 3 full caps.
1998-99 Brentford 36 4
1999-2000 Brentford 40 6
2000-01 Brentford 32 2
2001-02 Brentford 23 7
2002-03 Brentford 18 1 149 20
2003-04 QPR 42 10
2004-05 QPR 35 3
2005-06 QPR 14 2
2006-07 QPR 29 10
2007-08 QPR 44 6
2008-09 QPR 24 2 188 33

STEWART, Damion (D) 144 9
H: 6 3 W: 13 10 b.Jamaica 18-8-80
Source: Harbour View. *Honours:* Jamaica 50 full caps, 3 goals.
2005-06 Bradford C 23 1 23 1
2006-07 QPR 45 1
2007-08 QPR 39 5
2008-09 QPR 37 2 121 8

TOMMASI, Damiano (M) 7 0
H: 5 11 W: 11 07 b.Verona 17-5-74
Honours: Italy Under-21, 32 full caps, 2 goals.
2008-09 QPR 7 0 7 0
Transferred to Tianjin Teda

VINE, Rowan (F) 247 55
H: 5 11 W: 12 10 b.Basingstoke 21-9-82
Source: Scholar.
2000-01 Portsmouth 2 0
2001-02 Portsmouth 11 0
2002-03 Portsmouth 0 0
2002-03 Brentford 42 10 42 10
2003-04 Portsmouth 0 0
2003-04 Colchester U 35 6 35 6
2004-05 Portsmouth 0 0 13 0
2004-05 *Luton T* 45 9
2005-06 *Luton T* 31 10
2006-07 *Luton T* 26 12 102 31
2006-07 Birmingham C 17 1
2007-08 Birmingham C 0 0 17 1
2007-08 QPR 33 6
2008-09 QPR 5 1 38 7

READING (69)

ANDERSEN, Mikkel (G) 6 0
H: 6 5 W: 12 08 b.Copenhagen 17-12-88
Source: AB Copenhagen. *Honours:* Denmark Youth.
2006-07 Reading 0 0
2007-08 Reading 0 0
2008-09 Reading 0 0
2008-09 *Brentford* 1 0 1 0
2008-09 *Brighton & HA* 5 0 5 0

ANTONIO, Michael (M) 9 0
H: 6 0 W: 11 11 b.London 28-3-90
Source: Tooting & M.
2008-09 Reading 0 0
2008-09 *Cheltenham T* 9 0 9 0

ARMSTRONG, Chris (D) 238 7
H: 5 9 W: 11 00 b.Newcastle 5-8-82
Source: Scholar. *Honours:* England Under-20. Scotland B.
2000-01 Bury 22 1
2001-02 Bury 11 0 33 1
2001-02 Oldham Ath 32 0
2002-03 Oldham Ath 33 1 65 1
2003-04 Sheffield U 12 1
2004-05 Sheffield U 0 0
2005-06 Sheffield U 24 2
2005-06 *Blackpool* 5 0 5 0
2006-07 Sheffield U 27 0
2007-08 Sheffield U 32 3
2008-09 Sheffield U 0 0 95 6
2008-09 Reading 40 1 40 1

BENNETT, Alan (D) 65 2
H: 6 2 W: 12 08 b.Kilkenny 4-10-81
Honours: Eire Under-21, B, 2 full caps.
2006-07 Reading 0 0
2007-08 Reading 0 0
2007-08 *Southampton* 10 0 10 0
2008-09 *Brentford* 11 1
2008-09 Reading 0 0
2008-09 *Brentford* 44 1 55 2

BIGNALL, Nicholas (F) 18 2
H: 5 10 W: 11 12 b.Reading 11-7-90
Source: Scholar.
2008-09 Reading 0 0
2008-09 *Northampton T* 5 1 5 1
2008-09 *Cheltenham T* 13 1 13 1

BIKEY, Andre (D) 89 7
H: 6 0 W: 12 08 b.Douala 8-1-85
Source: Espanyol, Marco. *Honours:* Cameroon 10 full caps, 1 goal.
2003-04 Pacos de Ferreira 2 0 2 0
2004-05 Dep Aves 0 0
2005 Shinnik 11 1 11 1
2005 Loko Moscow 9 0
2006 Loko Moscow 5 0 14 0
2006-07 Reading 15 0
2007-08 Reading 22 3
2008-09 Reading 25 3 62 6

BOZANIC, Ollie (M) 0 0
H: 6 0 W: 12 00 b.Melbourne 8-1-89
Source: Central Coast M. *Honours:* Australia Youth, Under-20.
2006-07 Reading 0 0
2007-08 Reading 0 0
2008-09 Reading 0 0

BRYANT, Mitchell (M) 0 0
Source: Scholar.
2008-09 Reading 0 0

CHURCH, Simon (F) 40 6
H: 6 0 W: 13 04 b.Amersham 10-12-88
Source: From Scholar. *Honours:* Wales Under-21, 2 full caps.
2007-08 Reading 0 0
2007-08 *Crewe Alex* 12 1 12 1
2007-08 *Yeovil T* 6 0 6 0
2008-09 Reading 0 0
2008-09 *Wycombe W* 9 0 9 0
2008-09 *Leyton Orient* 13 5 13 5

CISSE, Kalifa (M) 106 6
H: 6 2 W: 12 11 b.Orleans 1-9-84
Source: Toulouse. *Honours:* Mali 1 full cap.
2004-05 Estoril 6 0 6 0
2005-06 Boavista 15 0
2006-07 Boavista 27 0 42 0
2007-08 Reading 22 1
2008-09 Reading 36 5 58 6

CONVEY, Bobby (M) 98 7
H: 5 8 W: 10 12 b.Philadelphia 27-5-83
Source: DC United. *Honours:* USA Youth, Under-21, 46 full caps, 1 goal.
2004-05 Reading 18 0
2005-06 Reading 45 7
2006-07 Reading 9 0
2007-08 Reading 20 0
2008-09 Reading 6 0 98 7

DAVIES, Scott (M) 41 13
H: 5 11 W: 12 00 b.Aylesbury 10-3-88
Source: Scholar.
2006-07 Reading 0 0
2007-08 Reading 0 0
2008-09 Reading 0 0
2008-09 *Aldershot T* 41 13 41 13

DOYLE, Kevin (F) 197 75
H: 5 11 W: 12 06 b.Adamstown 18-9-83
Source: Adamstown, Wexford, St Patrick's Ath. *Honours:* Eire Under-21, 26 full caps, 6 goals.
2004 Cork C 32 13
2005 Cork C 11 7 43 20
2005-06 Reading 45 18
2006-07 Reading 32 13
2007-08 Reading 36 6
2008-09 Reading 41 18 154 55

DUBERRY, Michael (D) 294 6
H: 6 1 W: 13 10 b.Enfield 14-10-75
Source: Trainee. *Honours:* England Under-21.
1993-94 Chelsea 1 0
1994-95 Chelsea 0 0
1995-96 Chelsea 22 0
1995-96 *Bournemouth* 7 0 7 0
1996-97 Chelsea 15 1
1997-98 Chelsea 23 0
1998-99 Chelsea 25 0 86 1
1999-2000 Leeds U 13 1
2000-01 Leeds U 5 0
2001-02 Leeds U 3 0
2002-03 Leeds U 14 0
2003-04 Leeds U 19 3
2004-05 Leeds U 4 0 58 4
2004-05 Stoke C 25 0
2005-06 Stoke C 41 1
2006-07 Stoke C 29 0 95 1
2006-07 Reading 8 0
2007-08 Reading 13 0
2008-09 Reading 27 0 48 0

FEDERICI, Adam (G) 27 1
H: 6 2 W: 14 02 b.Nowra 31-1-85
Honours: Australia Youth, Under-20, Under-21.
2005-06 Reading 0 0
2006-07 Reading 2 0
2007-08 Reading 0 0
2008-09 Reading 15 1 17 1
2008-09 *Southend U* 10 0 10 0

GOLBOURNE, Scott (M) 63 1
H: 5 8   W: 11 08   b.Bristol 29-2-88
Source: Scholar. *Honours:* England Youth.

2004-05	Bristol C	9	0	
2005-06	Bristol C	5	0	14 0
2005-06	Reading	1	0	
2006-07	Reading	0	0	
2006-07	Wycombe W	34	1	34 1
2007-08	Reading	1	0	
2007-08	Bournemouth	5	0	5 0
2008-09	Reading	0	0	2 0
2008-09	Oldham Ath	8	0	8 0

GUNNARSSON, Brynjar (M) 337 31
H: 6 1   W: 12 01   b.Reykjavik 16-10-75
Honours: Iceland Youth, Under-21, 70 full caps, 4 goals.

1995	KR	16	1	
1996	KR	18	0	
1997	KR	16	0	50 1
1998	Moss	5	2	5 2
1999-2000	Stoke C	22	1	
2000-01	Stoke C	46	5	
2001-02	Stoke C	23	5	
2002-03	Stoke C	40	5	
2003-04	Nottingham F	13	0	13 0
2003-04	*Stoke C*	3	0	134 16
2004-05	Watford	36	3	36 3
2005-06	Reading	29	4	
2006-07	Reading	23	3	
2007-08	Reading	20	0	
2008-09	Reading	27	2	99 9

HAHNEMANN, Marcus (G) 355 0
H: 6 3   W: 13 03   b.Seattle 15-6-72
Honours: USA 7 full caps.

1997	Colorado Rapids	25	0	
1998	Colorado Rapids	28	0	
1999	Colorado Rapids	13	0	66 0
1999-2000	Fulham	0	0	
2000-01	Fulham	2	0	
2001-02	Fulham	0	0	2 0
2001-02	*Rochdale*	5	0	5 0
2001-02	*Reading*	6	0	
2002-03	Reading	41	0	
2003-04	Reading	36	0	
2004-05	Reading	46	0	
2005-06	Reading	45	0	
2006-07	Reading	38	0	
2007-08	Reading	38	0	
2008-09	Reading	32	0	282 0

HAMER, Ben (G) 65 0
H: 5 11   W: 12 04   b.Chard 20-11-87
Source: Crawley T.

2006-07	Reading	0	0	
2007-08	Reading	0	0	
2007-08	*Brentford*	20	0	
2008-09	Reading	0	0	
2008-09	*Brentford*	45	0	65 0

HARPER, James (M) 312 25
H: 5 10   W: 11 02   b.Chelmsford 9-11-80
Source: Trainee.

1999-2000	Arsenal	0	0	
2000-01	Arsenal	0	0	
2000-01	*Cardiff C*	3	0	3 0
2000-01	Reading	12	1	
2001-02	Reading	26	1	
2002-03	Reading	36	2	
2003-04	Reading	39	1	
2004-05	Reading	41	3	
2005-06	Reading	45	7	
2006-07	Reading	38	3	
2007-08	Reading	38	6	
2008-09	Reading	34	1	309 25

HENRY, James (M) 38 7
H: 6 1   W: 11 11   b.Reading 10-6-89
Source: Scholar. *Honours:* England Youth.

2006-07	Reading	0	0	
2006-07	*Nottingham F*	1	0	1 0
2007-08	Reading	0	0	
2007-08	*Bournemouth*	11	4	11 4
2007-08	*Norwich C*	3	0	3 0
2008-09	Reading	7	0	7 0
2008-09	*Millwall*	16	3	16 3

HUNT, Noel (F) 181 42
H: 5 8   W: 11 05   b.Waterford 26-12-82
Honours: Eire Under-21, B, 2 full caps.

2002-03	Dunfermline Ath	12	1	
2003-04	Dunfermline Ath	13	2	
2004-05	Dunfermline Ath	23	1	

2005-06	Dunfermline Ath	32	4	80 8
2006-07	Dundee U	28	10	
2007-08	Dundee U	36	13	64 23
2008-09	Reading	37	11	37 11

HUNT, Steve (M) 295 42
H: 5 9   W: 10 10   b.Port Laoise 1-8-80
Source: Trainee. *Honours:* Eire Under-21, B, 20 full caps, 1 goal.

1999-2000	Crystal Palace	3	0	
2000-01	Crystal Palace	0	0	3 0
2001-02	Brentford	35	4	
2002-03	Brentford	42	7	
2003-04	Brentford	40	11	
2004-05	Brentford	19	3	136 25
2005-06	Reading	38	2	
2006-07	Reading	35	4	
2007-08	Reading	37	5	
2008-09	Reading	46	6	156 17

ILLUGASON, Viktor (F) 9 1
H: 6 1   W: 12 08   b.Reykjavik 25-1-90
Source: Scholar. *Honours:* Iceland Youth.

2006	Breidablik	9	1	9 1
2006-07	Reading	0	0	
2007-08	Reading	0	0	
2008-09	Reading	0	0	

Transferred to Valur

INGIMARSSON, Ivar (D) 439 34
H: 6 0   W: 12 07   b.Reykjavik 20-8-77
Honours: Iceland Youth, Under-21, 30 full caps.

1995	Valur	12	0	
1996	Valur	17	2	
1997	Valur	16	3	45 5
1998	IBV	18	1	
1999	IBV	18	4	36 5
1999-2000	Torquay U	4	1	4 1
1999-2000	Brentford	25	1	
2000-01	Brentford	42	3	
2001-02	Brentford	46	6	113 10
2002-03	Wolverhampton W	13	2	
2002-03	*Brighton & HA*	15	0	15 0
2003-04	Wolverhampton W	0	0	13 2
2003-04	Reading	25	1	
2004-05	Reading	44	3	
2005-06	Reading	46	2	
2006-07	Reading	38	2	
2007-08	Reading	34	2	
2008-09	Reading	26	1	213 11

KARACAN, Jem (M) 35 2
H: 5 10   W: 11 13   b.Lewisham 21-2-89
Source: Scholar.

2006-07	Reading	0	0	
2007-08	*Bournemouth*	13	1	13 1
2007-08	*Millwall*	7	0	7 0
2008-09	Reading	15	1	15 1

KEBE, Jimmy (M) 80 9
H: 6 2   W: 11 07   b.Vitry-sur-Seine 19-1-84
Honours: Mali 8 full caps, 3 goals.

2005-06	Lens	0	0	
2006-07	*Chateauroux*	18	2	18 2
2007-08	Lens	0	0	
2007-08	*Boulogne*	16	5	16 5
2007-08	Reading	5	0	
2008-09	Reading	41	2	46 2

KELLY, Julian (D) 7 0
H: 5 8   W: 11 04   b.London 6-9-89
Source: Arsenal Scholar.

2008-09	Reading	7	0	7 0

LITA, Leroy (F) 192 61
H: 5 7   W: 11 12   b.DR Congo 28-12-84
Source: From Scholar. *Honours:* England Under-21.

2002-03	Bristol C	15	2	
2003-04	Bristol C	26	5	
2004-05	Bristol C	44	24	85 31
2005-06	Reading	26	11	
2006-07	Reading	33	7	
2007-08	Reading	14	1	
2007-08	*Charlton Ath*	8	3	8 3
2008-09	Reading	10	1	83 20
2008-09	*Norwich C*	16	7	16 7

LONG, Shane (F) 99 17
H: 5 10   W: 11 02   b.Gortnahoe 22-1-87
Honours: Eire Youth, B, Under-21, 10 full caps, 3 goals.

2005	Cork C	1	0	1 0
2005-06	Reading	11	3	

2006-07	Reading	21	2	
2007-08	Reading	29	3	
2008-09	Reading	37	9	98 17

LYSKOV, Tom (M) 0 0
b. 20-7-91

2007-08	Reading	0	0	
2008-09	Reading	0	0	

MATEJOVSKY, Marek (M) 125 8
H: 5 10   W: 11 00   b.Brandys nad Labem 20-12-81
Honours: Czech Republic 13 full caps, 1 goal.

2000-01	Jablonec	1	0	
2001-02	Jablonec	4	0	
2002-03	Jablonec	1	0	6 0
2003-04	Mlada Boleslav	0	0	
2004-05	Mlada Boleslav	28	1	
2005-06	Mlada Boleslav	26	5	
2006-07	Mlada Boleslav	29	0	83 6
2007-08	Reading	14	1	
2008-09	Reading	22	1	36 2

McCARTHY, Alex (G) 4 0
H: 6 4   W: 11 12   b.Guildford 3-12-89

2008-09	Reading	0	0	
2008-09	*Aldershot T*	4	0	4 0

MOONEY, David (F) 113 46
H: 6 2   W: 12 06   b.Dublin 30-10-84
Source: Shamrock R, Longford T. *Honours:* Eire Under-23.

2005	Shamrock R	14	2	14 2
2005	Longford T	13	4	
2006	Longford T	21	3	
2007	Longford T	32	19	66 26
2008	Cork City	22	15	22 15
2008-09	Reading	0	0	
2008-09	*Stockport Co*	2	0	2 0
2008-09	*Norwich C*	9	3	9 3

MURTY, Graeme (D) 431 9
H: 5 10   W: 11 10   b.Saltburn 13-11-74
Source: Trainee. *Honours:* Scotland B, 4 full caps.

1992-93	York C	0	0	
1993-94	York C	1	0	
1994-95	York C	20	2	
1995-96	York C	35	2	
1996-97	York C	27	2	
1997-98	York C	34	1	117 7
1998-99	Reading	9	0	
1999-2000	Reading	17	0	
2000-01	Reading	23	1	
2001-02	Reading	43	0	
2002-03	Reading	44	0	
2003-04	Reading	38	0	
2004-05	Reading	41	0	
2005-06	Reading	40	1	
2006-07	Reading	23	0	
2007-08	Reading	28	0	
2008-09	Reading	0	0	306 2
2008-09	*Charlton Ath*	8	0	8 0

PEARCE, Alex (D) 62 4
H: 6 0   W: 11 10   b.Wallingford 9-11-88
Source: Scholar. *Honours:* Scotland Youth, Under-21.

2006-07	Reading	0	0	
2006-07	*Northampton T*	15	1	15 1
2007-08	Reading	0	0	
2007-08	*Bournemouth*	11	0	11 0
2007-08	*Norwich C*	11	0	11 0
2008-09	Reading	16	1	16 1
2008-09	*Southampton*	9	2	9 2

ROBSON-KANU, Hal (F) 42 9
H: 5 7   W: 11 08   b.Acton 21-5-89
Honours: England Youth.

2007-08	Reading	0	0	
2007-08	*Southend U*	8	3	
2008-09	Reading	0	0	
2008-09	*Southend U*	14	2	22 5
2008-09	*Swindon T*	20	4	20 4

ROSENIOR, Liam (D) 170 2
H: 5 10   W: 11 05   b.Wandsworth 9-7-84
Source: Scholar. *Honours:* England Youth, Under-20, Under-21.

2001-02	Bristol C	1	0	
2002-03	Bristol C	21	2	
2003-04	Bristol C	0	0	22 2
2003-04	Fulham	0	0	
2003-04	*Torquay U*	10	0	10 0
2004-05	Fulham	17	0	

2005-06	Fulham	24	0		
2006-07	Fulham	38	0		
2007-08	Fulham	0	0	79	0
2007-08	Reading	17	0		
2008-09	Reading	42	0	59	0

SIGURDSSON, Gylfi (M)   20   4
H: 6 1   W: 12 02   b.Reykjavik 9-9-89
Source: Scholar. Honours: Iceland Youth, Under-21.

2007-08	Reading	0	0		
2008-09	Reading	0	0		
2008-09	Shrewsbury T	5	1	5	1
2008-09	Crewe Alex	15	3	15	3

SODJE, Sam (D)   126   15
H: 6 0   W: 12 00   b.Greenwich 29-5-79
Source: Stevenage B, Margate. Honours: Nigeria 4 full caps.

2004-05	Brentford	40	7		
2005-06	Brentford	43	5	83	12
2006-07	Reading	3	0		
2006-07	WBA	7	1	7	1
2007-08	Reading	0	0		
2007-08	Charlton Ath	27	2	27	2
2008-09	Reading	0	0	3	0
2008-09	Watford	1	0	1	0
2008-09	Leeds U	5	0	5	0

SPENCE, Daniel (M)   0   0
H: 6 2   W: 12 07   b.Reading 22-10-89
Source: Scholar.

2008-09	Reading	0	0		

TABB, Jay (M)   232   31
H: 5 7   W: 10 00   b.Tooting 21-2-84
Source: From Trainee. Honours: Eire Under-21.

2000-01	Brentford	2	0		
2001-02	Brentford	3	0		
2002-03	Brentford	5	0		
2003-04	Brentford	36	9		
2004-05	Brentford	40	5		
2005-06	Brentford	42	6	128	20
2006-07	Coventry C	31	3		
2007-08	Coventry C	42	5		
2008-09	Coventry C	22	3	95	11
2008-09	Reading	9	0	9	0

VASILEV, Radoslav (F)   0   0
H: 6 2   W: 12 07   b.Sofia 12-10-90
Source: Slavia Sofia. Honours: Bulgaria Youth.

2008-09	Reading	0	0		

ROCHDALE (70)

BOWYER, George (M)   1   0
H: 6 0   W: 10 02   b.Stockport 11-11-90
Source: Scholar.

2007-08	Rochdale	1	0		
2008-09	Rochdale	0	0	1	0

BUCKLEY, Will (F)   44   10
H: 6 0   W: 13 00   b.Burnley 12-8-88
Source: Curzon Ashton.

2007-08	Rochdale	7	0		
2008-09	Rochdale	37	10	44	10

D'LARYEA, Nathan (D)   7   0
H: 5 10   W: 12 02   b.Manchester 3-9-85
Source: Trainee.

2003-04	Manchester C	0	0		
2004-05	Manchester C	0	0		
2005-06	Manchester C	0	0		
2006-07	Manchester C	0	0		
2006-07	Macclesfield T	1	0	1	0
2007-08	Rochdale	6	0		
2008-09	Rochdale	0	0	6	0

DAGNALL, Chris (F)   151   41
H: 5 8   W: 12 03   b.Liverpool 15-4-86
Source: Scholar.

2003-04	Tranmere R	10	1		
2004-05	Tranmere R	23	6		
2005-06	Tranmere R	6	0	39	7
2005-06	Rochdale	21	3		
2006-07	Rochdale	37	17		
2007-08	Rochdale	14	7		
2008-09	Rochdale	40	7	112	34

DAWSON, Craig (M)   0   0
Source: Radcliffe B.

2008-09	Rochdale	0	0		

FLITCROFT, David (M)   453   28
H: 5 11   W: 14 05   b.Bolton 14-1-74
Source: Trainee.

1991-92	Preston NE	0	0		
1992-93	Preston NE	8	2		
1993-94	Preston NE	0	0	8	2
1993-94	Lincoln C	2	0	2	0
1993-94	Chester C	8	1		
1994-95	Chester C	32	0		
1995-96	Chester C	9	1		
1996-97	Chester C	32	6		
1997-98	Chester C	44	4		
1998-99	Chester C	42	6	167	18
1999-2000	Rochdale	43	2		
2000-01	Rochdale	41	0		
2001-02	Rochdale	35	0		
2002-03	Rochdale	41	2		
2003-04	Macclesfield T	15	0	15	0
2003-04	Bury	17	0		
2004-05	Bury	36	3		
2005-06	Bury	43	1		
2006-07	Bury	4	0		
2007-08	Bury	0	0	100	4
2008-09	Rochdale	1	0	161	4

HIGGINBOTHAM, Kallum (F)   52   4
H: 5 11   W: 10 10   b.Manchester 15-6-89

2007-08	Rochdale	33	3		
2008-09	Rochdale	7	1	40	4
2008-09	Accrington S	12	0	12	0

HOLNESS, Marcus (D)   27   0
H: 6 0   W: 12 02   b.Swinton 8-12-88
Source: Scholar.

2007-08	Oldham Ath	0	0		
2007-08	Rochdale	19	0		
2008-09	Rochdale	8	0	27	0

JONES, Gary (M)   409   50
H: 5 11   W: 12 05   b.Birkenhead 3-6-77
Source: Caernarfon T.

1997-98	Swansea C	8	0	8	0
1997-98	Rochdale	17	2		
1998-99	Rochdale	20	0		
1999-2000	Rochdale	39	7		
2000-01	Rochdale	44	8		
2001-02	Rochdale	20	5		
2001-02	Barnsley	25	1		
2002-03	Barnsley	31	1		
2003-04	Barnsley	0	0	56	2
2003-04	Rochdale	26	4		
2004-05	Rochdale	39	8		
2005-06	Rochdale	42	4		
2006-07	Rochdale	27	3		
2007-08	Rochdale	43	7		
2008-09	Rochdale	28	0	345	48

JONES, Mark (M)   137   22
H: 5 11   W: 11 02   b.Wrexham 15-8-83
Source: Scholar. Honours: Wales Under-21, 2 full caps.

2002-03	Wrexham	1	0		
2003-04	Wrexham	13	1		
2004-05	Wrexham	26	3		
2005-06	Wrexham	42	13		
2006-07	Wrexham	30	5		
2007-08	Wrexham	16	0		
2008-09	Wrexham	0	0	128	22
2008-09	Rochdale	9	0	9	0

KELTIE, Clark (M)   192   10
H: 5 11   W: 11 08   b.Newcastle 31-8-83
Source: Shildon.

2001-02	Darlington	1	0		
2002-03	Darlington	30	3		
2003-04	Darlington	31	1		
2004-05	Darlington	21	0		
2005-06	Darlington	24	0		
2006-07	Darlington	27	1		
2007-08	Darlington	27	4	161	9
2008-09	Rochdale	31	1	31	1

KENNEDY, Tom (D)   231   11
H: 5 10   W: 11 01   b.Bury 24-6-85
Source: Scholar.

2002-03	Bury	0	0		
2003-04	Bury	27	0		
2004-05	Bury	46	1		
2005-06	Bury	33	4		
2006-07	Bury	37	0	143	5
2007-08	Rochdale	43	2		
2008-09	Rochdale	45	4	88	6

LAMBERT, Kyle (M)   1   0
H: 5 10   W: 11 08   b.Preston 26-3-90
Source: Scholar.

2008-09	Rochdale	1	0	1	0

LE FONDRE, Adam (F)   160   55
H: 5 9   W: 11 04   b.Stockport 2-12-86
Source: Trainee.

2004-05	Stockport Co	20	4		
2005-06	Stockport Co	22	6		
2006-07	Stockport Co	21	7	63	17
2006-07	Rochdale	7	4		
2007-08	Rochdale	46	16		
2008-09	Rochdale	44	18	97	38

McARDLE, Rory (D)   129   5
H: 6 1   W: 11 11   b.Doncaster 1-5-87
Source: Scholar. Honours: Northern Ireland Youth, Under-21.

2004-05	Sheffield W	0	0		
2005-06	Sheffield W	0	0		
2005-06	Rochdale	19	1		
2006-07	Sheffield W	1	0	1	0
2006-07	Rochdale	25	0		
2007-08	Rochdale	43	2		
2008-09	Rochdale	41	2	128	5

McEVILLY, Lee (F)   170   47
H: 6 0   W: 13 00   b.Liverpool 15-4-82
Source: Burscough. Honours: Northern Ireland Under-21, 1 full cap.

2001-02	Rochdale	18	4		
2002-03	Rochdale	37	15		
2003-04	Rochdale	30	6		
From Accrington S					
2005-06	Wrexham	23	7		
2006-07	Wrexham	28	7	51	14
2007-08	Accrington S	11	0	11	0
2007-08	Rochdale	7	3		
From Cambridge U.					
2008-09	Rochdale	16	5	108	33

RAMSDEN, Simon (D)   181   6
H: 6 0   W: 12 06   b.Bishop Auckland 17-12-81
Source: Scholar.

2000-01	Sunderland	0	0		
2001-02	Sunderland	0	0		
2002-03	Sunderland	0	0		
2002-03	Notts Co	32	0	32	0
2003-04	Sunderland	0	0		
2004-05	Grimsby T	25	0		
2005-06	Grimsby T	12	0	37	0
2005-06	Rochdale	15	1		
2006-07	Rochdale	34	3		
2007-08	Rochdale	35	2		
2008-09	Rochdale	28	0	112	6

RUNDLE, Adam (F)   229   26
H: 5 8   W: 11 02   b.Durham 8-7-84
Source: Scholar.

2001-02	Darlington	12	0		
2002-03	Darlington	5	0	17	0
2002-03	Carlisle U	21	1		
2003-04	Carlisle U	23	0		
2004-05	Carlisle U	0	0	44	1
2004-05	Mansfield T	18	4		
2005-06	Mansfield T	35	5	53	9
2006-07	Rochdale	29	4		
2007-08	Rochdale	42	5		
2008-09	Rochdale	44	7	115	16

RUSSELL, Sam (G)   156   0
H: 6 0   W: 10 13   b.Middlesbrough 4-10-82
Source: Scholar.

2000-01	Middlesbrough	0	0		
2001-02	Middlesbrough	0	0		
2002-03	Middlesbrough	0	0		
2002-03	Darlington	1	0		
2003-04	Middlesbrough	0	0		
2003-04	Scunthorpe U	10	0	10	0
2004-05	Darlington	46	0		
2005-06	Darlington	30	0		
2006-07	Darlington	31	0	108	0
2007-08	Rochdale	15	0		
2008-09	Rochdale	23	0	38	0

SHAW, Jon (F)   32   3
H: 6 0   W: 13 01   b.Sheffield 10-11-83
Source: Scholar.

2002-03	Sheffield W	1	0		
2003-04	Sheffield W	14	2		
2003-04	York C	8	0	8	0
2004-05	Sheffield W	3	0	18	2

From Burton Alb, Halifax T.

2008-09	Rochdale	6	1	**6**	**1**

SPENCER, James (G) 116
H: 6 3 W: 15 04 b.Stockport 11-4-85
Source: Trainee.

2001-02	Stockport Co	2	0
2002-03	Stockport Co	1	0
2003-04	Stockport Co	15	0
2004-05	Stockport Co	24	0
2005-06	Stockport Co	34	0
2006-07	Stockport Co	15	0	**91**	**0**
2007-08	Rochdale	20	0		
2008-09	Rochdale	0	0	**20**	**0**
2008-09	*Chester C*	5	0	**5**	**0**

STANTON, Nathan (D) 338 0
H: 5 9 W: 12 06 b.Nottingham 6-5-81
Source: Trainee. *Honours:* England Youth.

1997-98	Scunthorpe U	1	0
1998-99	Scunthorpe U	4	0
1999-2000	Scunthorpe U	34	0
2000-01	Scunthorpe U	38	0
2001-02	Scunthorpe U	42	0
2002-03	Scunthorpe U	42	0
2003-04	Scunthorpe U	33	0
2004-05	Scunthorpe U	21	0
2005-06	Scunthorpe U	22	0	**237**	**0**
2006-07	Rochdale	35	0		
2007-08	Rochdale	27	0		
2008-09	Rochdale	39	0	**101**	**0**

THOMPSON, Joe (M) 55 6
H: 6 0 W: 9 07 b.Rochdale 5-3-89
Source: Scholar.

2005-06	Rochdale	1	0
2006-07	Rochdale	13	0
2007-08	Rochdale	11	1
2008-09	Rochdale	30	5	**55**	**6**

THORPE, Lee (F) 430 98
H: 6 0 W: 11 06 b.Wolverhampton 14-12-75
Source: Trainee.

1993-94	Blackpool	1	0
1994-95	Blackpool	1	0
1995-96	Blackpool	1	0
1996-97	Blackpool	9	0	**12**	**0**
1997-98	Lincoln C	44	14		
1998-99	Lincoln C	38	8		
1999-2000	Lincoln C	42	16		
2000-01	Lincoln C	31	7		
2001-02	Lincoln C	37	13	**192**	**58**
2001-02	Leyton Orient	0	0		
2002-03	Leyton Orient	38	8		
2003-04	Leyton Orient	17	4	**55**	**12**
2003-04	Grimsby T	6	0	**6**	**0**
2003-04	Bristol R	10	1		
2004-05	Bristol R	25	3	**35**	**4**
2004-05	Swansea C	15	3		
2005-06	Swansea C	3	0	**18**	**3**
2005-06	*Peterborough U*	6	0	**6**	**0**
2006-07	*Torquay U*	10	3		
2006-07	Torquay U	41	8	**51**	**11**
2007-08	Brentford	19	4	**19**	**4**
2007-08	Rochdale	8	1		
2008-09	Rochdale	28	5	**36**	**6**

TONER, Ciaran (M) 218 19
H: 6 1 W: 12 02 b.Craigavon 30-6-81
Source: Trainee. *Honours:* Northern Ireland Schools, Youth, Under-21, 2 full caps.

1999-2000	Tottenham H	0	0
2000-01	Tottenham H	0	0
2001-02	Tottenham H	0	0
2001-02	*Peterborough U*	6	0	**6**	**0**
2001-02	Bristol R	6	0	**6**	**0**
2001-02	Leyton Orient	0	0		
2002-03	Leyton Orient	25	1		
2003-04	Leyton Orient	27	1	**52**	**2**
2004-05	Lincoln C	15	2	**15**	**2**
2004-05	*Cambridge U*	8	0	**8**	**0**
2005-06	Grimsby T	31	3		
2006-07	Grimsby T	33	8		
2007-08	Grimsby T	30	3	**94**	**14**
2008-09	Rochdale	37	1	**37**	**1**

WISEMAN, Scott (D) 85 1
H: 6 0 W: 11 06 b.Hull 9-10-85
Source: Scholar. *Honours:* England Youth, Under-20.

2003-04	Hull C	2	0
2004-05	Hull C	3	0

2004-05	*Boston U*	2	0	**2**	**0**
2005-06	Hull C	11	0		
2006-07	Hull C	0	0	**16**	**0**
2006-07	*Rotherham U*	18	1	**18**	**1**
2007-08	*Darlington*	10	0		
2007-08	Darlington	7	0	**17**	**0**
2008-09	Rochdale	32	0	**32**	**0**

ROTHERHAM U (71)

BARKER, Richard (F) 434 111
H: 6 0 W: 14 03 b.Sheffield 30-5-75
Source: Trainee. *Honours:* England Schools.

1993-94	Sheffield W	0	0		
1994-95	Sheffield W	0	0		
1995-96	Sheffield W	0	0		
1995-96	*Doncaster R*	6	0	**6**	**0**
1996-97	Sheffield W	0	0		
From Linfield					
1997-98	Brighton & HA	17	2		
1998-99	Brighton & HA	43	10	**60**	**12**
1999-2000	Macclesfield T	35	16		
2000-01	Macclesfield T	23	7	**58**	**23**
2000-01	Rotherham U	19	1		
2001-02	Rotherham U	35	3		
2002-03	Rotherham U	37	7		
2003-04	Rotherham U	32	1		
2004-05	Rotherham U	17	0		
2004-05	Mansfield T	28	10		
2005-06	Mansfield T	43	18		
2006-07	Mansfield T	24	12	**95**	**40**
2006-07	Hartlepool U	18	9		
2007-08	Hartlepool U	36	13		
2008-09	Hartlepool U	8	1	**62**	**23**
2008-09	Rotherham U	13	1	**153**	**13**

BROGAN, Stephen (D) 56 3
H: 5 7 W: 10 04 b.Rotherham 12-4-88
Source: Scholar.

2005-06	Rotherham U	3	0		
2006-07	Rotherham U	23	0		
2007-08	Rotherham U	29	3		
2008-09	Rotherham U	1	0	**56**	**3**

BROUGHTON, Drewe (F) 356 64
H: 6 3 W: 12 01 b.Hitchin 25-10-78
Source: Trainee.

1996-97	Norwich C	8	1		
1997-98	Norwich C	1	0		
1997-98	Wigan Ath	4	0	**4**	**0**
1998-99	Norwich C	0	0	**9**	**1**
1998-99	Brentford	1	0	**1**	**0**
1998-99	Peterborough U	25	7		
1999-2000	Peterborough U	10	1		
2000-01	Peterborough U	0	0	**35**	**8**
2000-01	Kidderminster H	19	7		
2001-02	Kidderminster H	38	8		
2002-03	Kidderminster H	37	4	**94**	**19**
2003-04	Southend U	35	2		
2004-05	Southend U	9	0	**44**	**2**
2004-05	Rushden & D	21	6		
2004-05	Wycombe W	3	0	**3**	**0**
2005-06	Rushden & D	37	10	**58**	**16**
2006-07	Chester C	14	2	**14**	**2**
2006-07	*Boston U*	25	8	**25**	**8**
2007-08	Milton Keynes D	13	0	**13**	**0**
2007-08	Wrexham	16	2	**16**	**2**
2008-09	Rotherham U	40	6	**40**	**6**

BURCHILL, Mark (F) 199 55
H: 5 8 W: 11 09 b.Broxburn 18-8-80
Source: Celtic BC. *Honours:* Scotland Schools, Under-21, 6 full caps.

1997-98	Celtic	0	0		
1998-99	Celtic	21	9		
1999-2000	Celtic	0	0		
2000-01	Celtic	2	1	**23**	**10**
2000-01	*Birmingham C*	13	4	**13**	**4**
2001-02	*Ipswich T*	7	1		
2001-02	Ipswich T	0	0	**7**	**1**
2001-02	Portsmouth	6	4		
2002-03	Portsmouth	18	4		
2003-04	Portsmouth	0	0		
2003-04	Wigan Ath	4	0	**4**	**0**
2003-04	*Sheffield W*	5	0	**5**	**0**
2004-05	Portsmouth	0	0	**24**	**8**
2004-05	*Rotherham U*	3	1		
2004-05	Hearts	12	3	**12**	**3**
2005-06	Dunfermline Ath	31	12		
2006-07	Dunfermline Ath	20	0		
2007-08	Dunfermline Ath	33	11	**84**	**23**

2008-09	Rotherham U	24	5	**27**	**6**

CAHILL, Tom (F) 7 0
H: 5 10 W: 12 08 b.Derby 21-11-86
Source: Matlock T.

2007-08	Rotherham U	7	0		
2008-09	Rotherham U	0	0	**7**	**0**

CANN, Steven (G) 1 0
H: 6 3 W: 13 01 b.Benoni 20-1-88
Source: Scholar. *Honours:* Wales Youth.

2006-07	Derby Co	0	0		
2007-08	Rotherham U	0	0		
2008-09	Rotherham U	1	0	**1**	**0**

CLARKE, Jamie (F) 26 7
H: 5 10 W: 11 11 b.Sunderland 11-9-88
Source: Scholar.

2007-08	Blackburn R	0	0		
2008-09	Blackburn R	0	0		
2008-09	*Accrington S*	15	5	**15**	**5**
2008-09	Rotherham U	11	2	**11**	**2**

CUMMINS, Michael (M) 369 45
H: 6 0 W: 13 06 b.Dublin 1-6-78
Source: Trainee. *Honours:* Eire Youth, Under-21.

1995-96	Middlesbrough	0	0		
1996-97	Middlesbrough	0	0		
1997-98	Middlesbrough	0	0		
1998-99	Middlesbrough	1	0		
1999-2000	Middlesbrough	1	0	**2**	**0**
1999-2000	Port Vale	12	1		
2000-01	Port Vale	45	2		
2001-02	Port Vale	46	8		
2002-03	Port Vale	30	4		
2003-04	Port Vale	42	4		
2004-05	Port Vale	39	2		
2005-06	Port Vale	39	10	**253**	**31**
2006-07	Darlington	39	4		
2007-08	Darlington	40	6	**79**	**10**
2008-09	Rotherham U	35	4	**35**	**4**

ELLISON, Kevin (M) 232 36
H: 6 0 W: 12 00 b.Liverpool 23-2-79
Source: Altrincham.

2000-01	Leicester C	1	0		
2001-02	Leicester C	0	0	**1**	**0**
2001-02	Stockport Co	11	0		
2002-03	Stockport Co	23	1		
2003-04	Stockport Co	14	1	**48**	**2**
2003-04	*Lincoln C*	11	0	**11**	**0**
2004-05	Chester C	24	9		
2004-05	Hull C	16	1		
2005-06	Hull C	23	1	**39**	**2**
2006-07	Tranmere R	34	4	**34**	**4**
2007-08	Chester C	36	11		
2008-09	Chester C	39	8	**99**	**28**
2008-09	Rotherham U	0	0		

FENTON, Nick (D) 384 20
H: 6 0 W: 10 02 b.Preston 23-11-79
Source: Trainee. *Honours:* England Youth.

1996-97	Manchester C	0	0		
1997-98	Manchester C	0	0		
1998-99	Manchester C	15	0		
1999-2000	Manchester C	0	0		
1999-2000	Notts Co	13	1		
1999-2000	*Bournemouth*	8	0		
2000-01	Manchester C	0	0	**15**	**0**
2000-01	*Bournemouth*	5	0	**13**	**0**
2000-01	Notts Co	30	2		
2001-02	Notts Co	42	3		
2002-03	Notts Co	40	3		
2003-04	Notts Co	43	1	**168**	**10**
2004-05	Doncaster R	38	1		
2005-06	Doncaster R	25	2		
2006-07	Doncaster R	0	0	**63**	**3**
2006-07	Grimsby T	38	4		
2007-08	Grimsby T	42	2	**80**	**6**
2008-09	Rotherham U	45	1	**45**	**1**

GARCIA, Omar (F) 2 0
H: 6 2 W: 12 08 b.Logrono 9-7-83
Source: Logrones, Alfaro, Logrones.

2008-09	Rotherham U	2	0	**2**	**0**

GREEN, Jamie (F) 40 2
H: 5 7 W: 10 07 b.Rossington 18-8-89
Source: Scholar.

2007-08	Rotherham U	9	1		
2008-09	Rotherham U	31	1	**40**	**2**

HAGGARTY, David (M)   1 0
H: 6 2   W: 13 07   b.Sheffield 28-3-91
Source: Scholar.
2007-08	Rotherham U	1	0	
2008-09	Rotherham U	0	0	1 0

HARRISON, Danny (M)   201 10
H: 5 11   W: 12 04   b.Liverpool 4-11-82
Source: Scholar.
2001-02	Tranmere R	1	0	
2002-03	Tranmere R	12	0	
2003-04	Tranmere R	32	2	
2004-05	Tranmere R	32	0	
2005-06	Tranmere R	35	2	
2006-07	Tranmere R	12	1	124 5
2007-08	Rotherham U	44	4	
2008-09	Rotherham U	33	1	77 5

HOLMES, Peter (M)   147 14
H: 5 11   W: 11 13   b.Bishop Auckland 18-11-80
Source: Trainee. *Honours:* England Schools, Youth.
1997-98	Sheffield W	0	0	
1998-99	Sheffield W	0	0	
1999-2000	Sheffield W	0	0	
2000-01	Luton T	18	1	
2001-02	Luton T	7	1	
2002-03	Luton T	17	1	
2003-04	Luton T	16	3	
2004-05	Luton T	19	3	
2005-06	Luton T	23	2	
2006-07	Luton T	5	0	105 11
2006-07	*Chesterfield*	10	1	10 1
2006-07	*Lincoln C*	5	0	5 0
2007-08	Rotherham U	24	2	
2008-09	Rotherham U	3	0	27 2

HUDSON, Danny (M)   90 10
H: 5 9   W: 11 07   b.Mexborough 25-6-79
Source: Trainee.
1997-98	Rotherham U	10	0	
1998-99	Rotherham U	26	4	
1999-2000	Rotherham U	7	1	
2000-01	Rotherham U	5	0	
2001-02	Rotherham U	0	0	
2002-03	Rotherham U	0	0	
2003-04	Rotherham U	0	0	
2004-05	Rotherham U	0	0	
2005-06	Rotherham U	0	0	
2006-07	Rotherham U	0	0	
2007-08	Rotherham U	0	0	
2008-09	Rotherham U	42	5	90 10

HUDSON, Mark (M)   205 25
H: 5 10   W: 11 03   b.Bishop Auckland 24-10-80
Source: Trainee.
1999-2000	Middlesbrough	0	0	
2000-01	Middlesbrough	3	0	
2001-02	Middlesbrough	2	0	
2002-03	Middlesbrough	0	0	5 0
2002-03	*Carlisle U*	15	1	15 1
2002-03	Chesterfield	24	3	
2003-04	Chesterfield	35	2	
2004-05	Chesterfield	34	4	93 9
2005-06	Huddersfield T	29	3	
2006-07	Huddersfield T	32	3	61 6
2007-08	Rotherham U	31	9	
2008-09	Rotherham U	0	0	31 9

JOSEPH, Marc (D)   391 7
H: 6 0   W: 12 05   b.Leicester 10-11-76
Source: Trainee.
1995-96	Cambridge U	12	0	
1996-97	Cambridge U	8	0	
1997-98	Cambridge U	41	0	
1998-99	Cambridge U	29	0	
1999-2000	Cambridge U	33	0	
2000-01	Cambridge U	30	0	153 0
2001-02	Peterborough U	44	2	
2002-03	Peterborough U	17	0	61 2
2002-03	Hull C	23	0	
2003-04	Hull C	32	1	
2004-05	Hull C	29	0	
2005-06	Hull C	5	0	89 1
2005-06	*Bristol C*	3	0	3 0
2005-06	Blackpool	16	0	
2006-07	Blackpool	8	0	24 0
2007-08	Rotherham U	36	4	
2008-09	Rotherham U	25	0	61 4

LYNCH, Mark (D)   86 2
H: 5 11   W: 11 03   b.Manchester 2-9-81
Source: Trainee.
1999-2000	Manchester U	0	0	
2000-01	Manchester U	0	0	
2001-02	Manchester U	0	0	
2001-02	*St Johnstone*	20	0	20 0
2002-03	Manchester U	0	0	
2003-04	Manchester U	0	0	
2004-05	Sunderland	11	0	11 0
2005-06	Hull C	16	0	
2006-07	Hull C	0	0	16 0
2006-07	Yeovil T	17	0	
2007-08	Yeovil T	14	0	31 0
2008-09	Rotherham U	8	2	8 2

MILLS, Pablo (D)   187 4
H: 5 9   W: 11 04   b.Birmingham 27-5-84
Source: Trainee. *Honours:* England Youth.
2002-03	Derby Co	16	0	
2003-04	Derby Co	19	0	
2004-05	Derby Co	22	0	
2005-06	Derby Co	1	0	58 0
2005-06	*Milton Keynes D*	16	1	16 1
2005-06	*Walsall*	14	0	14 0
2006-07	Rotherham U	31	1	
2007-08	Rotherham U	33	1	
2008-09	Rotherham U	35	1	99 3

NEWSHAM, Mark (F)   48 7
H: 5 10   W: 9 11   b.Hatfield 24-3-87
Source: Scholar.
2004-05	Rotherham U	4	0	
2005-06	Rotherham U	3	0	
2006-07	Rotherham U	16	3	
2007-08	Rotherham U	25	4	
2008-09	Rotherham U	0	0	48 7

NICHOLAS, Andrew (D)   150 4
H: 6 2   W: 12 08   b.Liverpool 10-10-83
Honours: Liverpool Trainee.
2003-04	Swindon T	31	1	
2004-05	Swindon T	16	0	
2004-05	*Chester C*	5	0	5 0
2005-06	Swindon T	33	0	
2006-07	Swindon T	35	2	
2007-08	Swindon T	11	1	126 4
2008-09	Rotherham U	19	0	19 0

REID, Reuben (F)   78 22
H: 6 0   W: 12 02   b.Bristol 26-7-88
Source: Scholar.
2005-06	Plymouth Arg	1	0	
2006-07	Plymouth Arg	6	0	
2006-07	*Rochdale*	2	0	2 0
2006-07	*Torquay U*	7	2	7 2
2007-08	Plymouth Arg	0	0	7 0
2007-08	*Wycombe W*	11	1	11 1
2007-08	Brentford	10	1	10 1
2008-09	Rotherham U	41	18	41 18

RHODES, Alex (F)   107 10
H: 5 9   W: 10 04   b.Cambridge 23-1-82
Source: Newmarket T.
2003-04	Brentford	3	1	
2004-05	Brentford	22	3	
2005-06	Brentford	17	1	
2006-07	Brentford	15	0	57 5
2006-07	*Swindon T*	4	0	4 0
2007-08	Bradford C	28	3	
2007-08	Bradford C	0	0	
2008-09	Bradford C	0	0	28 3
2008-09	Rotherham U	18	2	18 2

SHARPS, Ian (D)   286 14
H: 6 3   W: 14 07   b.Warrington 23-10-80
Source: Trainee.
1998-99	Tranmere R	1	0	
1999-2000	Tranmere R	0	0	
2000-01	Tranmere R	0	0	
2001-02	Tranmere R	29	0	
2002-03	Tranmere R	30	3	
2003-04	Tranmere R	27	1	
2004-05	Tranmere R	44	1	
2005-06	Tranmere R	39	1	170 6
2006-07	Rotherham U	38	2	
2007-08	Rotherham U	33	2	
2008-09	Rotherham U	45	4	116 8

TAYLOR, Jason (M)   119 7
H: 6 1   W: 11 03   b.Ashton-under-Lyne 28-1-87
Source: Scholar.
2005-06	Oldham Ath	0	0	
2005-06	*Stockport Co*	9	0	

2006-07	Stockport Co	45	1	
2007-08	Stockport Co	42	4	
2008-09	Stockport Co	8	1	104 6
2008-09	Rotherham U	15	1	15 1

TAYLOR, Ryan (F)   79 10
H: 6 2   W: 10 10   b.Rotherham 4-5-88
Source: Scholar.
2005-06	Rotherham U	1	0	
2006-07	Rotherham U	10	0	
2007-08	Rotherham U	35	6	
2008-09	Rotherham U	33	4	79 10

TODD, Andrew (M)   81 10
H: 6 0   W: 11 03   b.Nottingham 22-2-79
Source: Eastwood T.
1995-96	Nottingham F	0	0	
1996-97	Nottingham F	0	0	
1997-98	Nottingham F	0	0	
1998-99	Nottingham F	0	0	
1998-99	Scarborough	1	0	1 0

From Etwd T, Wksop, Hucknall, Burton Alb
2006-07	Accrington S	46	10	
2007-08	Rotherham U	13	0	
2007-08	*Accrington S*	21	0	67 10
2008-09	Rotherham U	0	0	13 0

TONGE, Dale (D)   124 1
H: 5 10   W: 10 06   b.Doncaster 7-5-85
Source: Scholar.
2003-04	Barnsley	1	0	
2004-05	Barnsley	14	0	
2005-06	Barnsley	24	0	
2006-07	Barnsley	6	0	45 0
2006-07	*Gillingham*	3	0	3 0
2007-08	Rotherham U	37	0	
2008-09	Rotherham U	39	1	76 1

WARRINGTON, Andy (G)   254 0
H: 6 3   W: 12 13   b.Sheffield 10-6-76
Source: Trainee.
1994-95	York C	0	0	
1995-96	York C	6	0	
1996-97	York C	27	0	
1997-98	York C	17	0	
1998-99	York C	11	0	61 0
2003-04	Doncaster R	46	0	
2004-05	Doncaster R	34	0	
2005-06	Doncaster R	9	0	
2006-07	Doncaster R	0	0	89 0
2006-07	Bury	20	0	20 0
2007-08	Rotherham U	46	0	
2008-09	Rotherham U	38	0	84 0

YATES, Jamie (F)   26 3
H: 5 7   W: 10 11   b.Sheffield 24-12-88
Source: Scholar.
2006-07	Rotherham U	3	0	
2007-08	Rotherham U	20	3	
2008-09	Rotherham U	3	0	26 3

SCUNTHORPE U (72)

BARACLOUGH, Ian (M)   604 40
H: 6 1   W: 12 09   b.Leicester 4-12-70
Source: Trainee.
1988-89	Leicester C	0	0	
1989-90	Leicester C	0	0	
1989-90	*Wigan Ath*	9	2	9 2
1990-91	Leicester C	0	0	
1990-91	*Grimsby T*	4	0	
1991-92	Grimsby T	0	0	
1992-93	Grimsby T	1	0	5 0
1992-93	Lincoln C	36	5	
1993-94	Lincoln C	37	5	73 10
1994-95	Mansfield T	36	3	
1995-96	Mansfield T	11	2	47 5
1995-96	Notts Co	35	2	
1996-97	Notts Co	38	2	
1997-98	Notts Co	38	6	
1997-98	QPR	8	0	
1998-99	QPR	43	1	
1999-2000	QPR	45	0	
2000-01	QPR	29	0	125 1
2001-02	Notts Co	33	3	
2002-03	Notts Co	34	2	
2003-04	Notts Co	34	0	212 15
2004-05	Scunthorpe U	45	3	
2005-06	Scunthorpe U	38	3	
2006-07	Scunthorpe U	33	1	
2007-08	Scunthorpe U	17	0	
2008-09	Scunthorpe U	0	0	133 7

BYRNE, Cliff (D) 205 5
H: 6 0 W: 12 11 b.Dublin 27-4-82
Honours: Eire Youth, Under-21.
1999-2000	Sunderland	0	0		
2000-01	Sunderland	0	0		
2001-02	Sunderland	0	0		
2002-03	Sunderland	0	0		
2002-03	*Scunthorpe U*	13	0		
2003-04	Scunthorpe U	39	1		
2004-05	Scunthorpe U	29	1		
2005-06	Scunthorpe U	32	1		
2006-07	Scunthorpe U	24	0		
2007-08	Scunthorpe U	25	0		
2008-09	Scunthorpe U	43	2	205	5

CROSBY, Andy (D) 623 39
H: 6 2 W: 13 13 b.Rotherham 3-3-73
Source: Leeds U Trainee.
1991-92	Doncaster R	22	0		
1992-93	Doncaster R	29	0		
1993-94	Doncaster R	0	0	51	0
1993-94	Darlington	25	0		
1994-95	Darlington	35	0		
1995-96	Darlington	45	1		
1996-97	Darlington	42	1		
1997-98	Darlington	34	1	181	3
1998-99	Chester C	41	4	41	4
1999-2000	Brighton & HA	36	3		
2000-01	Brighton & HA	34	2		
2001-02	Brighton & HA	2	0	72	5
2001-02	Oxford U	23	1		
2002-03	Oxford U	46	6		
2003-04	Oxford U	42	5	111	12
2004-05	Scunthorpe U	44	3		
2005-06	Scunthorpe U	42	3		
2006-07	Scunthorpe U	39	5		
2007-08	Scunthorpe U	38	4		
2008-09	Scunthorpe U	4	0	167	15

FORTE, Jonathan (M) 159 26
H: 6 0 W: 12 12 b.Sheffield 25-7-86
Source: Scholar. *Honours:* England Youth.
Barbados 2 full caps.
2003-04	Sheffield U	7	0		
2004-05	Sheffield U	22	1		
2005-06	Sheffield U	1	0		
2005-06	*Doncaster R*	13	4		
2005-06	*Rotherham U*	11	4	11	4
2006-07	Sheffield U	0	0	30	1
2006-07	*Doncaster R*	41	5	54	9
2007-08	Scunthorpe U	38	4		
2008-09	Scunthorpe U	8	0	46	4
2008-09	*Notts Co*	18	8	18	8

HAYES, Paul (F) 262 65
H: 6 0 W: 12 12 b.Dagenham 20-9-83
Source: Norwich C Scholar.
2002-03	Scunthorpe U	18	8		
2003-04	Scunthorpe U	35	2		
2004-05	Scunthorpe U	46	18		
2005-06	Barnsley	45	6		
2006-07	Barnsley	30	5	75	11
2006-07	*Huddersfield T*	4	1	4	1
2007-08	Scunthorpe U	40	8		
2008-09	Scunthorpe U	44	17	183	53

HOOPER, Gary (M) 100 39
H: 5 10 W: 12 07 b.Loughton 26-1-88
Source: Grays Ath.
2006-07	Southend U	19	0		
2006-07	*Leyton Orient*	4	2	4	2
2007-08	Southend U	13	2	32	2
2007-08	*Hereford U*	19	11	19	11
2008-09	Scunthorpe U	45	24	45	24

HURST, Kevan (M) 150 12
H: 5 10 W: 11 07 b.Chesterfield 27-8-85
Source: Sheffield U Scholar.
2003-04	*Boston U*	7	1	7	1
2004-05	Sheffield U	1	0		
2004-05	*Stockport Co*	14	1	14	1
2005-06	Sheffield U	0	0		
2005-06	*Chesterfield*	37	4		
2006-07	Sheffield U	0	0	1	0
2006-07	*Chesterfield*	25	3	62	7
2006-07	*Scunthorpe U*	13	0		
2007-08	Scunthorpe U	33	1		
2008-09	Scunthorpe U	20	2	66	3

LILLIS, Josh (G) 14 0
H: 6 0 W: 12 08 b.Derby 24-6-87
Source: Scholar.
2006-07	Scunthorpe U	1	0		
2007-08	Scunthorpe U	3	0		

2008-09	Scunthorpe U	5	0	9	0
2008-09	*Notts Co*	5	0	5	0

MAY, Ben (F) 193 26
H: 6 3 W: 12 12 b.Gravesend 10-3-84
Source: Juniors.
2000-01	Millwall	0	0		
2001-02	Millwall	0	0		
2002-03	Millwall	10	1		
2002-03	*Colchester U*	6	0		
2003-04	Millwall	0	0		
2003-04	*Brentford*	41	7		
2004-05	Millwall	8	1		
2004-05	*Colchester U*	14	1	20	1
2004-05	*Brentford*	10	1	51	8
2005-06	Millwall	39	10		
2006-07	Millwall	13	2		
2007-08	Millwall	8	0	78	14
2007-08	Scunthorpe U	21	1		
2008-09	Scunthorpe U	23	2	44	3

McCANN, Grant (M) 297 48
H: 5 10 W: 11 00 b.Belfast 14-4-80
Source: Trainee. *Honours:* Northern Ireland
Youth, Under-21, 22 full caps, 3 goals.
1998-99	West Ham U	0	0		
1999-2000	West Ham U	0	0		
2000-01	West Ham U	1	0		
2000-01	*Notts Co*	2	0	2	0
2000-01	*Cheltenham T*	30	3		
2001-02	West Ham U	3	0		
2002-03	West Ham U	0	0	4	0
2002-03	Cheltenham T	27	6		
2003-04	Cheltenham T	43	8		
2004-05	Cheltenham T	39	4		
2005-06	Cheltenham T	39	8		
2006-07	Cheltenham T	15	5	193	34
2006-07	Barnsley	22	1		
2007-08	Barnsley	19	3	41	4
2007-08	Scunthorpe U	14	1		
2008-09	Scunthorpe U	43	9	57	10

MILNE, Kenny (D) 208 12
H: 6 2 W: 12 08 b.Alloa 26-8-79
Honours: Scotland Under-21.
1997-98	Hearts	1	0		
1998-99	Hearts	0	0		
1998-99	*Cowdenbeath*	23	6		
1999-2000	Hearts	1	0		
2000-01	Hearts	7	0		
2001-02	Hearts	4	0	13	0
2001-02	*Cowdenbeath*	9	0	32	6
2002-03	Partick T	12	0		
2003-04	Partick T	25	1		
2004-05	Partick T	30	1	67	2
2005-06	Falkirk	33	2		
2006-07	Falkirk	34	1		
2007-08	Falkirk	28	1	95	4
2008-09	Scunthorpe U	1	0	1	0

MIRFIN, David (D) 194 9
H: 6 3 W: 13 00 b.Sheffield 18-4-85
Source: Scholar.
2002-03	Huddersfield T	1	0		
2003-04	Huddersfield T	21	2		
2004-05	Huddersfield T	41	4		
2005-06	Huddersfield T	31	1		
2006-07	Huddersfield T	38	1		
2007-08	Huddersfield T	29	1	161	9
2008-09	Scunthorpe U	33	0	33	0

MORRIS, Ian (D) 109 10
H: 6 0 W: 11 05 b.Dublin 27-2-87
Source: Scholar. *Honours:* Eire Under-21.
2003-04	Leeds U	0	0		
2004-05	Leeds U	0	0		
2005-06	Leeds U	0	0		
2005-06	*Blackpool*	30	3	30	3
2006-07	Leeds U	0	0		
2006-07	Scunthorpe U	28	3		
2007-08	Scunthorpe U	25	3		
2008-09	Scunthorpe U	20	1	73	7
2008-09	*Carlisle U*	6	0	6	0

MURPHY, Joe (G) 239 0
H: 6 2 W: 13 06 b.Dublin 21-8-81
Source: Trainee. *Honours:* Eire Youth,
Under-21, 1 full cap.
1999-2000	Tranmere R	21	0		
2000-01	Tranmere R	20	0		
2001-02	Tranmere R	22	0	63	0
2002-03	WBA	2	0		
2003-04	WBA	3	0		
2004-05	WBA	0	0	5	0

2004-05	*Walsall*	25	0		
2005-06	Sunderland	0	0		
2005-06	*Walsall*	14	0	39	0
2006-07	Scunthorpe U	45	0		
2007-08	Scunthorpe U	45	0		
2008-09	Scunthorpe U	42	0	132	0

SLOCOMBE, Sam (G) 0 0
H: 6 0 W: 11 11 b.Scunthorpe 5-6-88
Source: Bottesford T.
2008-09	Scunthorpe U	0	0		

SPARROW, Matt (M) 306 36
H: 5 11 W: 10 06 b.Wembley 3-10-81
Source: Scholar.
1999-2000	Scunthorpe U	11	0		
2000-01	Scunthorpe U	11	4		
2001-02	Scunthorpe U	24	1		
2002-03	Scunthorpe U	42	9		
2003-04	Scunthorpe U	38	3		
2004-05	Scunthorpe U	44	5		
2005-06	Scunthorpe U	39	5		
2006-07	Scunthorpe U	29	4		
2007-08	Scunthorpe U	32	1		
2008-09	Scunthorpe U	36	4	306	36

THOMPSON, Gary (M) 64 10
H: 6 0 W: 14 02 b.Kendal 24-11-80
Source: Scholar.
2007-08	Morecambe	40	7	40	7
2008-09	Scunthorpe U	24	3	24	3

TOGWELL, Sam (D) 146 6
H: 5 11 W: 12 04 b.Beaconsfield 14-10-84
Source: Scholar.
2002-03	Crystal Palace	1	0		
2003-04	Crystal Palace	0	0		
2004-05	Crystal Palace	0	0		
2004-05	*Oxford U*	4	0	4	0
2004-05	*Northampton T*	8	0	8	0
2005-06	Crystal Palace	0	0	1	0
2005-06	*Port Vale*	27	2	27	2
2006-07	Barnsley	44	1		
2007-08	Barnsley	22	1	66	2
2008-09	Scunthorpe U	40	2	40	2

WILCOX, Joe (D) 0 0
H: 6 1 W: 11 05 b.Northampton 18-4-89
Source: Scholar.
2007-08	Scunthorpe U	0	0		
2008-09	Scunthorpe U	0	0		

WILLIAMS, Marcus (D) 129 0
H: 5 8 W: 10 07 b.Doncaster 8-4-86
Source: Scholar.
2003-04	Scunthorpe U	1	0		
2004-05	Scunthorpe U	4	0		
2005-06	Scunthorpe U	29	0		
2006-07	Scunthorpe U	35	0		
2007-08	Scunthorpe U	34	0		
2008-09	Scunthorpe U	26	0	129	0

WINN, Peter (M) 4 0
H: 6 0 W: 11 09 b.Cleethorpes 19-12-88
Source: Scholar.
2006-07	Scunthorpe U	0	0		
2007-08	Scunthorpe U	4	0		
2008-09	Scunthorpe U	0	0	4	0

WOOLFORD, Martyn (M) 39 4
H: 6 0 W: 11 09 b.Castleford 13-10-85
Source: Glasshoughton W, Frickley Ath,
York C.
2008-09	Scunthorpe U	39	4	39	4

WRIGHT, Andrew (M) 30 0
H: 6 1 W: 13 07 b.Southport 15-1-85
Source: Scholar.
2001-02	Liverpool	0	0		
2002-03	Liverpool	0	0		
2003-04	Liverpool	0	0		
2004-05	Liverpool	0	0		
2005-06	Liverpool	0	0		
2006-07	Liverpool	0	0		
	From West Virginia Univ.				
2007-08	Scunthorpe U	2	0		
2008-09	Scunthorpe U	28	0	30	0

SHEFFIELD U (73)

ABDI, Liban (F)   0   0
b.Burco 5-10-88
Source: Newport Pagnell T, Buckingham T.
Honours:

Season	Club	A	G
2006-07	Sheffield U	0	0
2007-08	Sheffield U	0	0
2008-09	Sheffield U	0	0

ANNERSON, Jamie (G)   0   0
H: 6 2 W: 13 02 b.Sheffield 21-6-88
Source: Scholar. Honours: England Youth.

Season	Club	A	G
2005-06	Sheffield U	0	0
2006-07	Sheffield U	0	0
2007-08	*Rotherham U*	0	0
2007-08	*Chesterfield*	0	0
2007-08	Sheffield U	0	0
2008-09	Sheffield U	0	0
2008-09	*Rotherham U*	0	0

BENNETT, Ian (G)   385   0
H: 6 0 W: 12 10 b.Worksop 10-10-71
Source: Newcastle U Trainee.

Season	Club	A	G	A	G
1991-92	Peterborough U	7	0		
1992-93	Peterborough U	46	0		
1993-94	Peterborough U	19	0	72	0
1993-94	Birmingham C	22	0		
1994-95	Birmingham C	46	0		
1995-96	Birmingham C	24	0		
1996-97	Birmingham C	40	0		
1997-98	Birmingham C	45	0		
1998-99	Birmingham C	10	0		
1999-2000	Birmingham C	21	0		
2000-01	Birmingham C	45	0		
2001-02	Birmingham C	18	0		
2002-03	Birmingham C	10	0		
2003-04	Birmingham C	6	0		
2004-05	Birmingham C	0	0	287	0
2004-05	*Sheffield U*	5	0		
2004-05	*Coventry C*	6	0	6	0
2005-06	Leeds U	4	0		
2006-07	Leeds U	0	0	4	0
2006-07	Sheffield U	2	0		
2007-08	Sheffield U	7	0		
2008-09	Sheffield U	2	0	16	0

CARNEY, David (M)   76   9
H: 5 11 W: 11 00 b.Sydney 30-11-83
Source: Scholar. Honours: Australia Under-20, 19 full caps, 2 goals.

Season	Club	A	G	A	G
2000-01	Everton	0	0		
2001-02	Everton	0	0		
2002-03	Everton	0	0		
2003-04	Oldham Ath	0	0		
2004-05	Hamilton A	8	0	8	0
2005-06	Sydney FC	24	6		
2006-07	Sydney FC	14	1	38	7
2007-08	Sheffield U	21	2		
2008-09	Sheffield U	0	0	21	2
2008-09	*Norwich C*	9	0	9	0

CHANOT, Maxime (D)   0   0
H: 6 1 W: 13 00 b.Nancy 21-11-89
Source: Nancy, Reims.

Season	Club	A	G
2007-08	Sheffield U	0	0
2008-09	Sheffield U	0	0

CHAPMAN, Adam (M)   0   0
b.Doncaster 29-11-89
Source: Scholar. Honours: Northern Ireland Under-21.

Season	Club	A	G
2008-09	Sheffield U	0	0

COTTERILL, David (F)   120   13
H: 5 9 W: 11 02 b.Cardiff 4-12-87
Source: Scholar. Honours: Wales Youth, Under-21, 13 full caps.

Season	Club	A	G	A	G
2004-05	Bristol C	12	0		
2005-06	Bristol C	45	7		
2006-07	Bristol C	5	1	62	8
2006-07	Wigan Ath	16	1		
2007-08	Wigan Ath	2	0	18	1
2007-08	*Sheffield U*	16	0		
2008-09	Sheffield U	24	4	40	4

EHIOGU, Ugo (D)   406   22
H: 6 2 W: 14 10 b.Hackney 3-11-72
Source: Trainee. Honours: England Under-21, B, 4 full caps, 1 goal.

Season	Club	A	G	A	G
1990-91	WBA	2	0	2	0
1991-92	Aston Villa	8	0		
1992-93	Aston Villa	4	0		
1993-94	Aston Villa	17	0		
1994-95	Aston Villa	39	3		
1995-96	Aston Villa	36	1		
1996-97	Aston Villa	38	3		
1997-98	Aston Villa	37	2		
1998-99	Aston Villa	25	2		
1999-2000	Aston Villa	31	1		
2000-01	Aston Villa	2	0	237	12
2000-01	Middlesbrough	21	3		
2001-02	Middlesbrough	29	1		
2002-03	Middlesbrough	32	3		
2003-04	Middlesbrough	16	0		
2004-05	Middlesbrough	10	0		
2005-06	Middlesbrough	18	0		
2006-07	Middlesbrough	0	0	126	7
2006-07	*Leeds U*	6	1	6	1
2006-07	Rangers	9	1		
2007-08	Rangers	0	0	9	1
2007-08	Sheffield U	10	0		
2008-09	Sheffield U	16	1	26	1

GEARY, Derek (D)   204   1
H: 5 6 W: 10 00 b.Dublin 19-6-80
Source: Rivermont BC.

Season	Club	A	G	A	G
1997-98	Sheffield W	0	0		
1998-99	Sheffield W	0	0		
1999-2000	Sheffield W	0	0		
2000-01	Sheffield W	5	0		
2001-02	Sheffield W	32	0		
2002-03	Sheffield W	26	0		
2003-04	Sheffield W	41	0	104	0
2004-05	*Stockport Co*	13	0	13	0
2004-05	Sheffield U	19	1		
2005-06	Sheffield U	20	0		
2006-07	Sheffield U	26	0		
2007-08	Sheffield U	21	0		
2008-09	Sheffield U	1	0	87	1

HABER, Justin (G)   0   0
H: 5 11 W: 12 00 b.Malta 9-6-81
Source: Floriana, Dobrudzha (loan), Birkirkara, US Quevilly, Virton, Marsaxlokk, Haidari. Honours: Malta 35 full caps.

Season	Club	A	G
2008-09	Sheffield U	0	0

HENDERSON, Darius (F)   260   62
H: 6 3 W: 14 03 b.Sutton 7-9-81
Source: Trainee.

Season	Club	A	G	A	G
1999-2000	Reading	6	0		
2000-01	Reading	4	0		
2001-02	Reading	38	7		
2002-03	Reading	22	4		
2003-04	Reading	1	0	71	11
2003-04	*Brighton & HA*	10	2	10	2
2003-04	Gillingham	0	0		
2004-05	Gillingham	32	9	36	9
2004-05	*Swindon T*	6	5	6	5
2005-06	Watford	30	14		
2006-07	Watford	35	3		
2007-08	Watford	40	12	105	29
2008-09	Sheffield U	32	6	32	6

HENDRIE, Lee (M)   311   32
H: 5 10 W: 11 00 b.Birmingham 18-5-77
Source: Trainee. Honours: England Youth, Under-21, B, 1 full cap.

Season	Club	A	G	A	G
1993-94	Aston Villa	0	0		
1994-95	Aston Villa	0	0		
1995-96	Aston Villa	3	0		
1996-97	Aston Villa	4	0		
1997-98	Aston Villa	17	3		
1998-99	Aston Villa	32	3		
1999-2000	Aston Villa	29	1		
2000-01	Aston Villa	32	6		
2001-02	Aston Villa	29	2		
2002-03	Aston Villa	27	4		
2003-04	Aston Villa	32	2		
2004-05	Aston Villa	29	5		
2005-06	Aston Villa	16	1		
2006-07	Aston Villa	1	0	251	27
2006-07	*Stoke C*	28	3	28	3
2007-08	Sheffield U	12	1		
2008-09	*Leicester C*	9	1	9	1
2008-09	Sheffield U	5	0	17	1
2008-09	*Blackpool*	6	0	6	0

HOWARD, Brian (M)   217   38
H: 5 8 W: 11 00 b.Winchester 23-1-83
Source: Trainee. Honours: England Schools, Youth, Under-20.

Season	Club	A	G	A	G
1999-2000	Southampton	0	0		
2000-01	Southampton	0	0		
2001-02	Southampton	0	0		
2002-03	Southampton	0	0		
2003-04	*Swindon T*	35	4		
2004-05	*Swindon T*	35	5	70	9
2005-06	Barnsley	31	5		
2006-07	Barnsley	42	8		
2007-08	Barnsley	41	13		
2008-09	Barnsley	7	1	121	27
2008-09	Sheffield U	26	2	26	2

JIHAI, Sun (D)   165   3
H: 5 9 W: 12 02 b.Dalian 30-9-77
Source: Dalian Wanda. Honours: China 71 full caps, 1 goal.

Season	Club	A	G	A	G
1998-99	Crystal Palace	23	0	23	0

From Dalian Wanda.

Season	Club	A	G	A	G
2001-02	Manchester C	7	0		
2002-03	Manchester C	28	2		
2003-04	Manchester C	33	1		
2004-05	Manchester C	6	0		
2005-06	Manchester C	29	0		
2006-07	Manchester C	13	0		
2007-08	Manchester C	14	0	130	3
2008-09	Sheffield U	12	0	12	0

KENNY, Paddy (G)   409   0
H: 6 1 W: 14 01 b.Halifax 17-5-78
Source: Bradford PA. Honours: Eire 7 full caps.

Season	Club	A	G	A	G
1998-99	Bury	0	0		
1999-2000	Bury	46	0		
2000-01	Bury	46	0		
2001-02	Bury	41	0		
2002-03	Bury	0	0	133	0
2002-03	Sheffield U	45	0		
2003-04	Sheffield U	27	0		
2004-05	Sheffield U	40	0		
2005-06	Sheffield U	46	0		
2006-07	Sheffield U	34	0		
2007-08	Sheffield U	40	0		
2008-09	Sheffield U	44	0	276	0

KILGALLON, Matthew (D)   169   6
H: 6 1 W: 12 10 b.York 8-1-84
Source: Scholar. Honours: England Youth, Under-20, Under-21.

Season	Club	A	G	A	G
2000-01	Leeds U	0	0		
2001-02	Leeds U	0	0		
2002-03	Leeds U	2	0		
2003-04	Leeds U	8	2		
2003-04	*West Ham U*	3	0	3	0
2004-05	Leeds U	26	0		
2005-06	Leeds U	25	1		
2006-07	Leeds U	19	0	80	3
2006-07	Sheffield U	6	0		
2007-08	Sheffield U	40	2		
2008-09	Sheffield U	40	1	86	3

LAW, Nicky (M)   54   5
H: 5 10 W: 11 06 b.Nottingham 29-3-88
Source: Scholar. Honours: England Youth.

Season	Club	A	G	A	G
2005-06	Sheffield U	0	0		
2006-07	Sheffield U	4	0		
2006-07	*Yeovil T*	6	0	6	0
2007-08	Sheffield U	1	0		
2007-08	*Bradford C*	10	2		
2008-09	Sheffield U	0	0	5	0
2008-09	*Bradford C*	33	3	43	5

LOWTON, Matt (M)   0   0
Source: Scholar.

Season	Club	A	G
2008-09	Sheffield U	0	0

LUPOLI, Arturo (F)   79   14
H: 5 7 W: 11 04 b.Brescia 24-6-87
Source: From Parma. Honours: Italy Youth, Under-21.

Season	Club	A	G	A	G
2004-05	Arsenal	0	0		
2005-06	Arsenal	1	0		
2006-07	Arsenal	0	0	1	0
2006-07	*Derby Co*	35	7	35	7
2007-08	Fiorentina	0	0		
2007-08	*Treviso*	17	1	17	1
2008-09	*Norwich C*	17	4	17	4
2008-09	*Sheffield U*	9	2	9	2

On loan from Fiorentina

MONTGOMERY, Nick (M)   255   7
H: 5 9 W: 11 08 b.Leeds 28-10-81
Source: Scholar. Honours: Scotland Under-21, B.

Season	Club	A	G
2000-01	Sheffield U	27	0
2001-02	Sheffield U	31	2
2002-03	Sheffield U	23	0

2003-04	Sheffield U	36	3		
2004-05	Sheffield U	25	1		
2005-06	Sheffield U	39	1		
2006-07	Sheffield U	26	0		
2007-08	Sheffield U	20	0		
2008-09	Sheffield U	28	0	255	7

MORGAN, Chris (D)   387 18
H: 6 1 W: 12 03 b.Barnsley 9-11-77
Source: Trainee.

1996-97	Barnsley	0	0		
1997-98	Barnsley	11	0		
1998-99	Barnsley	19	0		
1999-2000	Barnsley	37	0		
2000-01	Barnsley	40	1		
2001-02	Barnsley	42	4		
2002-03	Barnsley	36	2	185	7
2003-04	Sheffield U	32	1		
2004-05	Sheffield U	41	2		
2005-06	Sheffield U	39	3		
2006-07	Sheffield U	24	1		
2007-08	Sheffield U	25	2		
2008-09	Sheffield U	41	2	202	11

NAUGHTON, Kyle (M)   58 1
H: 5 11 W: 11 07 b.Sheffield 11-11-88
Honours: England Under-21.

2006-07	Sheffield U	0	0		
2007-08	*Gretna*	18	0	18	0
2007-08	Sheffield U	0	0		
2008-09	Sheffield U	40	1	40	1

NAYSMITH, Gary (D)   308 9
H: 5 9 W: 12 01 b.Edinburgh 16-11-78
Source: Whitehill Welfare Colts. *Honours:* Scotland Schools, Under-21, B, 46 full caps, 1 goal.

1995-96	Hearts	1	0		
1996-97	Hearts	10	0		
1997-98	Hearts	16	2		
1998-99	Hearts	26	0		
1999-2000	Hearts	35	1		
2000-01	Hearts	9	0	97	3
2000-01	Everton	20	2		
2001-02	Everton	24	0		
2002-03	Everton	28	1		
2003-04	Everton	29	2		
2004-05	Everton	11	0		
2005-06	Everton	7	0		
2006-07	Everton	15	1	134	6
2007-08	Sheffield U	38	0		
2008-09	Sheffield U	39	0	77	0

QUINN, Keith (M)   0 0
b.Dublin 22-9-88
Source: Scholar. *Honours:* Eire Under-21.

2006-07	Sheffield U	0	0
2007-08	Sheffield U	0	0
2008-09	Sheffield U	0	0

QUINN, Stephen (M)   108 11
H: 5 6 W: 9 08 b.Dublin 4-4-86
Source: Trainee. *Honours:* Eire Under-21.

2005-06	Sheffield U	0	0		
2005-06	*Milton Keynes D*	15	0	15	0
2005-06	*Rotherham U*	16	0	16	0
2006-07	Sheffield U	15	2		
2007-08	Sheffield U	19	2		
2008-09	Sheffield U	43	7	77	11

ROBERTSON, Jordan (F)   53 10
H: 6 0 W: 12 06 b.Sheffield 12-2-88
Source: Scholar.

2006-07	Sheffield U	0	0		
2006-07	*Torquay U*	9	2	9	2
2006-07	*Northampton T*	17	3	17	3
2007-08	Sheffield U	0	0		
2007-08	*Dundee U*	14	3	14	3
2007-08	*Oldham Ath*	3	1	3	1
2008-09	Sheffield U	0	0		
2008-09	*Southampton*	10	1	10	1

On loan to Ferencvaros

S-LATEF, Zeyn (F)   0 0
b.Sweden 22-7-90
Source: Scholar.

2007-08	Sheffield U	0	0
2008-09	Sheffield U	0	0

SHARP, Billy (F)   151 70
H: 5 9 W: 11 00 b.Sheffield 5-2-86
Source: Scholar.

2004-05	Sheffield U	2	0		
2004-05	*Rushden & D*	16	9	16	9
2005-06	Sheffield U	0	0		
2005-06	Scunthorpe U	37	23		
2006-07	Scunthorpe U	45	30	82	53
2007-08	Sheffield U	29	4		
2008-09	Sheffield U	22	4	53	8

SLAVKOVSKI, Goran (F)   0 0
b.Skravlinge 8-4-89
Source: Internazionale.

2007-08	Sheffield U	0	0
2008-09	Sheffield U	0	0

SPEED, Gary (M)   677 104
H: 5 10 W: 12 10 b.Deeside 8-9-69
Source: Trainee. *Honours:* Wales Youth, Under-21, 85 full caps, 7 goals.

1988-89	Leeds U	1	0		
1989-90	Leeds U	25	3		
1990-91	Leeds U	38	7		
1991-92	Leeds U	41	7		
1992-93	Leeds U	39	7		
1993-94	Leeds U	36	10		
1994-95	Leeds U	39	3		
1995-96	Leeds U	29	2	248	39
1996-97	Everton	37	9		
1997-98	Everton	21	7	58	16
1997-98	Newcastle U	13	1		
1998-99	Newcastle U	38	4		
1999-2000	Newcastle U	36	9		
2000-01	Newcastle U	35	5		
2001-02	Newcastle U	29	5		
2002-03	Newcastle U	24	2		
2003-04	Newcastle U	38	3	213	29
2004-05	Bolton W	38	1		
2005-06	Bolton W	31	4		
2006-07	Bolton W	38	8		
2007-08	Bolton W	14	1	121	14
2007-08	Sheffield U	20	3		
2008-09	Sheffield U	17	3	37	6

STAROSTA, Ben (D)   50 0
H: 6 0 W: 12 00 b.Sheffield 7-1-87
Source: Scholar. *Honours:* Poland Youth.

2006-07	Sheffield U	0	0		
2007-08	Sheffield U	0	0		
2007-08	*Brentford*	21	0	21	0
2007-08	*Bradford C*	15	0	15	0
2008-09	Sheffield U	0	0		
2008-09	*Aldershot T*	3	0	3	0
2008-09	*Lech Gdansk*	11	0	11	0

TAHAR, Aymen (M)   0 0
b.Algiers 2-10-89
Source: Scholar. *Honours:* Algeria Youth.

2008-09	Sheffield U	0	0

TRAVIS, Nicky (M)   2 0
H: 6 0 W: 12 01 b.Sheffield 12-3-87
Source: Scholar.

2004-05	Sheffield U	0	0		
2005-06	Sheffield U	0	0		
2006-07	Sheffield U	0	0		
2007-08	Sheffield U	0	0		
2007-08	*Chesterfield*	2	0	2	0
2008-09	Sheffield U	0	0		

WALKER, Kyle (D)   11 0
H: 5 10 W: 11 07 b.Sheffield 28-5-90
Source: Scholar. *Honours:* England Youth.

2008-09	Sheffield U	2	0	2	0
2008-09	*Northampton T*	9	0	9	0

WARD, Jamie (M)   117 41
H: 5 5 W: 9 04 b.Birmingham 12-5-86
Source: Scholar. *Honours:* Northern Ireland Youth, Under-21.

2003-04	Aston Villa	0	0		
2004-05	Aston Villa	0	0		
2005-06	Aston Villa	0	0		
2005-06	*Stockport Co*	9	1	9	1
2006-07	*Torquay U*	25	9	25	9
2006-07	Chesterfield	9	3		
2007-08	Chesterfield	35	12		
2008-09	Chesterfield	23	14	67	29
2008-09	Sheffield U	16	2	16	2

WEBBER, Danny (F)   190 44
H: 5 10 W: 11 04 b.Manchester 28-12-81
Source: Trainee. *Honours:* England Youth, Under-20.

1998-99	Manchester U	0	0		
1999-2000	Manchester U	0	0		
2000-01	Manchester U	0	0		
2001-02	Manchester U	0	0		
2001-02	*Port Vale*	4	0	4	0
2001-02	*Watford*	5	2		
2002-03	Manchester U	0	0		
2002-03	Watford	12	2		
2003-04	Watford	27	5		
2004-05	Watford	28	12	72	21
2004-05	*Sheffield U*	7	3		
2005-06	Sheffield U	35	10		
2006-07	Sheffield U	22	3		
2007-08	Sheffield U	14	3		
2008-09	Sheffield U	36	4	114	23

WEDGBURY, Samuel (M)   0 0
b.Oldbury 26-2-89
Source: Worcester C.

2006-07	Sheffield U	0	0
2007-08	Sheffield U	0	0
2008-09	Sheffield U	0	0

SHEFFIELD W (74)

BEEVERS, Mark (D)   64 0
H: 6 4 W: 13 00 b.Barnsley 21-11-89
Source: Scholar. *Honours:* England Youth.

2006-07	Sheffield W	2	0		
2007-08	Sheffield W	28	0		
2008-09	Sheffield W	34	0	64	0

BODEN, Luke (F)   19 0
H: 6 1 W: 12 00 b.Sheffield 26-11-88
Source: Scholar.

2006-07	Sheffield W	1	0		
2007-08	Sheffield W	2	0		
2008-09	Sheffield W	12	0	15	0
2008-09	*Chesterfield*	4	0	4	0

BUXTON, Lewis (D)   162 2
H: 6 1 W: 13 11 b.Newport (IW) 10-12-83
Source: School.

2000-01	Portsmouth	0	0		
2001-02	Portsmouth	29	0		
2002-03	Portsmouth	1	0		
2002-03	*Exeter C*	4	0	4	0
2002-03	Bournemouth	17	0		
2003-04	Portsmouth	0	0		
2003-04	Bournemouth	26	0	43	0
2004-05	Portsmouth	0	0	30	0
2004-05	Stoke C	16	0		
2005-06	Stoke C	32	1		
2006-07	Stoke C	1	0		
2007-08	Stoke C	4	0		
2008-09	Stoke C	0	0	53	1
2008-09	Sheffield W	32	1	32	1

CLARKE, Leon (F)   152 36
H: 6 2 W: 14 02 b.Birmingham 10-2-85
Source: Scholar.

2003-04	Wolverhampton W	0	0		
2003-04	*Kidderminster H*	4	0	4	0
2004-05	Wolverhampton W	28	7		
2005-06	Wolverhampton W	24	1		
2005-06	*QPR*	1	0	1	0
2005-06	*Plymouth Arg*	5	0	5	0
2006-07	Wolverhampton W	22	5	74	13
2006-07	Sheffield W	10	1		
2006-07	*Oldham Ath*	5	3	5	3
2007-08	Sheffield W	8	3		
2007-08	*Southend U*	16	8	16	8
2008-09	Sheffield W	29	8	47	12

ESAJAS, Etienne (F)   72 6
H: 5 7 W: 10 03 b.Amsterdam 4-11-84
Source: Ajax.

2005-06	Vitesse	11	1		
2006-07	Vitesse	21	2	32	3
2007-08	Sheffield W	18	0		
2008-09	Sheffield W	22	3	40	3

GILBERT, Peter (D)   128 1
H: 5 11 W: 12 00 b.Newcastle 31-7-83
Source: Scholar. *Honours:* Wales Under-21.

2001-02	Birmingham C	0	0		
2002-03	Birmingham C	0	0		
2003-04	Birmingham C	0	0		
2003-04	Plymouth Arg	40	1		
2004-05	Plymouth Arg	38	0	78	1
2005-06	*Leicester C*	5	0	5	0
2005-06	Sheffield W	17	0		
2006-07	Sheffield W	6	0		
2006-07	*Doncaster R*	4	0	4	0
2007-08	Sheffield W	10	0		
2008-09	Sheffield W	8	0	41	0

GRANT, Lee (G)   181   0
H: 6 3   W: 13 01   b.Hemel Hempstead 27-1-83
Source: Scholar. *Honours:* England Youth, Under-21.

2000-01	Derby Co	0	0		
2001-02	Derby Co	0	0		
2002-03	Derby Co	29	0		
2003-04	Derby Co	36	0		
2004-05	Derby Co	2	0		
2005-06	Derby Co	0	0		
2005-06	*Burnley*	1	0	1	0
2005-06	*Oldham Ath*	16	0	16	0
2006-07	Derby Co	7	0	74	0
2007-08	Sheffield W	44	0		
2008-09	Sheffield W	46	0	90	0

GRAY, Michael (D)   504 20
H: 5 8   W: 10 07   b.Sunderland 3-8-74
Source: Trainee. *Honours:* England 3 full caps.

1992-93	Sunderland	27	2		
1993-94	Sunderland	22	1		
1994-95	Sunderland	16	0		
1995-96	Sunderland	46	4		
1996-97	Sunderland	34	3		
1997-98	Sunderland	44	2		
1998-99	Sunderland	37	2		
1999-2000	Sunderland	33	0		
2000-01	Sunderland	36	1		
2001-02	Sunderland	35	0		
2002-03	Sunderland	32	1		
2003-04	Sunderland	1	0	363	16
2003-04	*Celtic*	7	0	7	0
2003-04	Blackburn R	14	0		
2004-05	Blackburn R	9	0		
2004-05	*Leeds U*	10	0		
2005-06	Blackburn R	30	0		
2006-07	Blackburn R	11	0	64	0
2006-07	*Leeds U*	6	0	16	0
2007-08	Wolverhampton W	33	3		
2008-09	Wolverhampton W	8	1	41	4
2008-09	Sheffield W	13	0	13	0

HINDS, Richard (D)   245 11
H: 6 2   W: 12 02   b.Sheffield 22-8-80
Source: Schoolboy.

1998-99	Tranmere R	2	0		
1999-2000	Tranmere R	6	0		
2000-01	Tranmere R	29	0		
2001-02	Tranmere R	10	0		
2002-03	Tranmere R	8	0	55	0
2003-04	Hull C	39	1		
2004-05	Hull C	6	0	45	1
2004-05	*Scunthorpe U*	7	0		
2005-06	Scunthorpe U	42	6		
2006-07	Scunthorpe U	44	2	93	8
2007-08	Sheffield W	38	2		
2008-09	Sheffield W	14	0	52	2

JAMESON, Arron (G)   0   0
H: 6 3   W: 13 01   b. 7-11-89
Source: Scholar.

2008-09	Sheffield W	0	0

JEFFERS, Francis (F)   177 34
H: 5 10   W: 11 02   b.Liverpool 25-1-81
Source: From Trainee. *Honours:* England Schools, Youth, Under-21, 1 full cap, 1 goal.

1997-98	Everton	1	0		
1998-99	Everton	15	6		
1999-2000	Everton	21	6		
2000-01	Everton	12	6		
2001-02	Arsenal	6	2		
2002-03	Arsenal	16	2		
2003-04	Arsenal	0	0	22	4
2003-04	*Everton*	18	0	67	18
2004-05	Charlton Ath	20	3		
2005-06	Charlton Ath	0	0	20	3
2005-06	*Rangers*	8	0	8	0
2006-07	*Blackburn R*	10	0	10	0
2006-07	*Ipswich T*	9	4	9	4
2007-08	Sheffield W	10	2		
2008-09	Sheffield W	31	3	41	5

JOHNSON, Jermaine (M)   157 19
H: 5 11   W: 11 05   b.Kingston, Jamaica 25-6-80
Source: Tivoli Gardens. *Honours:* Jamaica 58 full caps, 9 goals.

2001-02	Bolton W	10	0
2002-03	Bolton W	2	0
2003-04	Bolton W	0	0	12	0
2003-04	Oldham Ath	20	5		
2004-05	Oldham Ath	19	4		
2005-06	Oldham Ath	0	0	39	9
2006-07	Bradford C	27	4	27	4
2006-07	Sheffield W	7	2		
2007-08	Sheffield W	35	1		
2008-09	Sheffield W	37	3	79	6

LEKAJ, Rocky (M)   4   0
H: 5 10   W: 10 05   b.Kosovo 12-10-89
Source: Scholar. *Honours:* Norway Youth.

2006-07	Sheffield W	2	0		
2007-08	Sheffield W	0	0		
2008-09	Sheffield W	2	0	4	0

LIVERSIDGE, Sam (D)   0   0
H: 6 0   W: 11 13   b. 2-11-89
Source: Scholar.

2008-09	Sheffield W	0	0

LUNT, Kenny (M)   431 35
H: 5 10   W: 10 05   b.Runcorn 20-11-79
Source: From Trainee. *Honours:* England Schools, Youth.

1997-98	Crewe Alex	41	2		
1998-99	Crewe Alex	18	1		
1999-2000	Crewe Alex	43	3		
2000-01	Crewe Alex	46	1		
2001-02	Crewe Alex	45	5		
2002-03	Crewe Alex	46	7		
2003-04	Crewe Alex	45	7		
2004-05	Crewe Alex	46	5		
2005-06	Crewe Alex	43	4		
2006-07	Sheffield W	37	0		
2007-08	Sheffield W	4	0		
2007-08	*Crewe Alex*	14	0		
2008-09	Sheffield W	0	0	41	0
2008-09	*Crewe Alex*	3	0	390	35

McALLISTER, Sean (M)   63   4
H: 5 8   W: 10 07   b.Bolton 15-8-87
Source: Scholar.

2005-06	Sheffield W	2	0		
2006-07	Sheffield W	6	1		
2007-08	Sheffield W	8	0		
2007-08	*Mansfield T*	7	0	7	0
2007-08	*Bury*	0	0		
2008-09	Sheffield W	40	3	56	4

McMENAMIN, Liam (D)   0   0
H: 5 11   W: 10 11   b.Derry 10-4-89
Source: Scholar. *Honours:* Northern Ireland Under-21.

2007-08	Sheffield W	0	0
2008-09	Sheffield W	0	0

MODEST, Nathan (F)   4   0
H: 5 9   W: 12 02   b.29-9-91
Source: Scholar.

2008-09	Sheffield W	4	0	4	0

O'CONNOR, James (M)   386 27
H: 5 8   W: 11 00   b.Dublin 1-9-79
Source: From Trainee. *Honours:* Eire Youth, Under-21.

1996-97	Stoke C	0	0		
1997-98	Stoke C	0	0		
1998-99	Stoke C	4	0		
1999-2000	Stoke C	42	6		
2000-01	Stoke C	44	8		
2001-02	Stoke C	43	2		
2002-03	Stoke C	43	0	176	16
2003-04	WBA	30	0		
2004-05	WBA	0	0	30	0
2004-05	Burnley	21	2		
2005-06	Burnley	46	3		
2006-07	Burnley	43	3		
2007-08	Burnley	29	3	139	11
2008-09	Sheffield W	41	0	41	0

O'DONNELL, Richard (G)   4   0
H: 6 2   W: 13 05   b.Sheffield 12-9-88
Source: Scholar.

2007-08	Sheffield W	0	0		
2007-08	*Rotherham U*	0	0		
2007-08	*Oldham Ath*	4	0	4	0
2008-09	Sheffield W	0	0		

SIMEK, Frankie (D)   120   2
H: 6 0   W: 11 06   b.St Louis 13-10-84
Source: Trainee. *Honours:* USA 5 full caps.

2002-03	Arsenal	0	0
2003-04	Arsenal	0	0
2004-05	Arsenal	0	0
2004-05	*QPR*	5	0	5	0
2004-05	*Bournemouth*	8	0	8	0
2005-06	Sheffield W	43	1		
2006-07	Sheffield W	41	1		
2007-08	Sheffield W	17	0		
2008-09	Sheffield W	6	0	107	2

SMALL, Wade (M)   172 20
H: 5 8   W: 11 05   b.Croydon 23-2-84
Source: Scholar.

2003-04	Wimbledon	27	1	27	1
2004-05	Milton Keynes D	44	10		
2005-06	Milton Keynes D	28	1	72	11
2006-07	Sheffield W	20	2		
2007-08	Sheffield W	29	4		
2008-09	Sheffield W	19	1	68	7
2008-09	*Blackpool*	5	1	5	1

SODJE, Akpo (F)   126 32
H: 6 2   W: 12 08   b.Greenwich 31-1-81
Source: QPR, Stevenage B, Margate, Gravesend & N, Erith & Belvedere.

2004-05	Huddersfield T	7	0	7	0
2004-05	*Darlington*	7	1		
2005-06	Darlington	36	8	43	9
2006-07	Port Vale	43	14		
2007-08	Port Vale	3	0	46	14
2008-09	Sheffield W	11	2	30	9

SPURR, Tommy (D)   120   4
H: 6 1   W: 11 05   b.Leeds 13-9-87
Source: Scholar.

2005-06	Sheffield W	2	0		
2006-07	Sheffield W	36	0		
2007-08	Sheffield W	41	2		
2008-09	Sheffield W	41	2	120	4

TUDGAY, Marcus (F)   227 54
H: 5 10   W: 12 04   b.Worthing 3-2-83
Source: Trainee.

2002-03	Derby Co	8	0		
2003-04	Derby Co	29	6		
2004-05	Derby Co	34	9		
2005-06	Derby Co	21	2	92	17
2005-06	Sheffield W	18	5		
2006-07	Sheffield W	40	11		
2007-08	Sheffield W	35	7		
2008-09	Sheffield W	42	14	135	37

WATSON, Steve (D)   473 32
H: 6 0   W: 12 07   b.North Shields 1-4-74
Source: Trainee. *Honours:* England Youth, Under-21, B.

1990-91	Newcastle U	24	0		
1991-92	Newcastle U	28	1		
1992-93	Newcastle U	2	0		
1993-94	Newcastle U	32	2		
1994-95	Newcastle U	27	4		
1995-96	Newcastle U	23	3		
1996-97	Newcastle U	36	1		
1997-98	Newcastle U	29	1		
1998-99	Newcastle U	7	0	208	12
1998-99	Aston Villa	27	0		
1999-2000	Aston Villa	14	0	41	0
2000-01	Everton	34	0		
2001-02	Everton	25	4		
2002-03	Everton	18	5		
2003-04	Everton	24	5		
2004-05	Everton	25	0	126	14
2005-06	WBA	30	1		
2006-07	WBA	12	0	42	1
2006-07	*Sheffield W*	11	0		
2007-08	Sheffield W	23	2		
2008-09	Sheffield W	22	3	56	5

WOOD, Richard (D)   160   5
H: 6 3   W: 12 13   b.Wakefield 5-7-85
Source: Scholar.

2002-03	Sheffield W	3	1		
2003-04	Sheffield W	12	0		
2004-05	Sheffield W	34	1		
2005-06	Sheffield W	30	1		
2006-07	Sheffield W	12	0		
2007-08	Sheffield W	27	2		
2008-09	Sheffield W	42	0	160	5

SHREWSBURY T (75)

ASHIKODI, Moses (M)   44   3
H: 6 0   W: 11 09   b.Lagos 27-6-87
Honours: FA Schools, England Youth.

2002-03	Millwall	5	0		
2003-04	Millwall	0	0	5	0
2004-05	West Ham U	0	0		
2005-06	West Ham U	0	0		
2005-06	*Gillingham*	4	0	4	0
2005-06	Rangers	1	0		
2006-07	Rangers	0	0	1	0
2006-07	Watford	2	0		
2006-07	*Bradford C*	8	2	8	2
2007-08	Watford	0	0		
2007-08	*Swindon T*	10	0	10	0
2008-09	Watford	0	0	2	0
2008-09	*Hereford U*	6	0	6	0
2008-09	Shrewsbury T	8	1	8	1

ASHTON, Neil (M)   177   4
H: 5 8   W: 12 04   b.Liverpool 15-1-85
Source: Scholar.

2002-03	Tranmere R	0	0		
2003-04	Tranmere R	1	0		
2004-05	Tranmere R	0	0	1	0
2004-05	*Shrewsbury T*	24	0		
2005-06	Shrewsbury T	44	1		
2006-07	Shrewsbury T	43	2		
2007-08	Shrewsbury T	15	0		
2007-08	*Macclesfield T*	19	1	19	1
2008-09	Shrewsbury T	31	0	157	3

BEVAN, Scott (G)   57   0
H: 6 6   W: 15 10   b.Southampton 16-9-79
Source: Trainee.

1997-98	Southampton	0	0		
1998-99	Southampton	0	0		
1999-2000	Southampton	0	0		
2000-01	Southampton	0	0		
2001-02	Southampton	0	0		
2001-02	Stoke C	0	0		
2002-03	Southampton	0	0		
2002-03	*Huddersfield T*	30	0	30	0
2003-04	Southampton	0	0		
2003-04	*Wycombe W*	5	0	5	0
2003-04	Wimbledon	10	0	10	0
2004-05	Milton Keynes D	7	0		
2005-06	Milton Keynes D	0	0	7	0

From Kidderminster H.

2007-08	Shrewsbury T	5	0		
2008-09	Shrewsbury T	0	0	5	0

CANSDELL-SHERRIFF, Shane (D) 203 15
H: 5 11   W: 11 08   b.Sydney 10-11-82
Source: NSW Academy. *Honours:* Australia Youth, Under-23.

1999-2000	Leeds U	0	0		
2000-01	Leeds U	0	0		
2001-02	Leeds U	0	0		
2002-03	Leeds U	0	0		
2002-03	*Rochdale*	3	0	3	0
2003-04	Aarhus	29	4		
2004-05	Aarhus	26	2		
2005-06	Aarhus	27	1	82	7
2006-07	Tranmere R	43	3		
2007-08	Tranmere R	44	3	87	6
2008-09	Shrewsbury T	31	2	31	2

CHADWICK, Nick (F)   137   20
H: 6 0   W: 12 08   b.Market Drayton 26-10-82
Source: Scholar.

1999-2000	Everton	0	0		
2000-01	Everton	0	0		
2001-02	Everton	9	3		
2002-03	Everton	1	0		
2002-03	*Derby Co*	6	0	6	0
2003-04	Everton	3	0		
2003-04	*Millwall*	15	4	15	4
2004-05	Everton	1	0	14	3
2004-05	Plymouth Arg	15	1		
2005-06	Plymouth Arg	37	5		
2006-07	Plymouth Arg	16	2		
2007-08	Plymouth Arg	9	2		
2008-09	Plymouth Arg	0	0	77	10
2008-09	Hereford U	10	1	10	1
2008-09	Shrewsbury T	15	2	15	2

CONSTABLE, James (F)   37   7
H: 6 2   W: 12 12   b.Malmesbury 4-10-84
Source: Chippenham T.

2005-06	Walsall	17	3		
2006-07	Walsall	6	0	23	3

From Kidderminster H.

2007-08	Shrewsbury T	14	4		
2008-09	Shrewsbury T	0	0	14	4

COUGHLAN, Graham (D)   376   37
H: 6 2   W: 13 07   b.Dublin 18-11-74
Source: Bray Wanderers.

1995-96	Blackburn R	0	0		
1996-97	Blackburn R	0	0		
1996-97	*Swindon T*	3	0	3	0
1997-98	Blackburn R	0	0		
1998-99	Livingston	6	0		
1999-2000	Livingston	29	0		
2000-01	Livingston	21	2	56	2
2001-02	Plymouth Arg	46	11		
2002-03	Plymouth Arg	42	5		
2003-04	Plymouth Arg	46	7		
2004-05	Plymouth Arg	43	2	177	25
2005-06	Sheffield W	33	4		
2006-07	Sheffield W	18	1	51	5
2006-07	*Burnley*	2	0	2	0
2007-08	Rotherham U	45	1	45	1
2008-09	Shrewsbury T	42	4	42	4

DAVIES, Ben (M)   213   39
H: 5 7   W: 12 03   b.Birmingham 27-5-81
Source: Walsall trainee.

2000-01	Kidderminster H	3	0		
2001-02	Kidderminster H	9	0	12	0
2004-05	Chester C	44	2		
2005-06	Chester C	45	7	89	9
2006-07	Shrewsbury T	43	12		
2007-08	Shrewsbury T	27	6		
2008-09	Shrewsbury T	42	10	112	30

DUNFIELD, Terry (M)   153   7
H: 5 11   W: 12 04   b.Vancouver 20-2-82
Source: Trainee. *Honours:* Canada Under-23, England Youth.

1998-99	Manchester C	0	0		
1999-2000	Manchester C	0	0		
2000-01	Manchester C	1	0		
2001-02	Manchester C	0	0		
2002-03	Manchester C	0	0	1	0
2002-03	Bury	29	2		
2003-04	Bury	30	2		
2004-05	Bury	15	1		
2005-06	Bury	0	0		
2006-07	Bury	0	0	74	5
2007-08	Macclesfield T	41	1		
2008-09	Macclesfield T	20	1	61	2
2008-09	Shrewsbury T	17	0	17	0

GARNER, Glyn (G)   257   0
H: 6 2   W: 13 11   b.Pontypool 9-12-76
Source: Llanelli. *Honours:* Wales 1 full cap.

2000-01	Bury	0	0		
2001-02	Bury	7	0		
2002-03	Bury	46	0		
2003-04	Bury	46	0		
2004-05	Bury	27	0	126	0
2005-06	Leyton Orient	43	0		
2006-07	Leyton Orient	43	0	86	0
2007-08	Shrewsbury T	41	0		
2008-09	Shrewsbury T	4	0	45	0

HERD, Ben (D)   143   3
H: 5 9   W: 10 12   b.Welwyn 21-6-85
Source: Scholar.

2002-03	Watford	0	0		
2003-04	Watford	0	0		
2004-05	Watford	0	0		
2005-06	Shrewsbury T	46	2		
2006-07	Shrewsbury T	31	1		
2007-08	Shrewsbury T	45	0		
2008-09	Shrewsbury T	21	0	143	3

HIBBERT, Dave (F)   115   19
H: 6 2   W: 12 00   b.Eccleshall 28-1-86
Source: Scholar.

2004-05	Port Vale	9	2	9	2
2005-06	Preston NE	10	0		
2006-07	Preston NE	0	0	10	0
2006-07	Rotherham U	21	2	21	2
2006-07	*Bradford C*	8	0	8	0
2007-08	Shrewsbury T	44	12		
2008-09	Shrewsbury T	23	3	67	15

HINDMARCH, Stephen (F)   10   0
H: 5 10   W: 11 11   b.Keswick 16-11-89
Sources: Scholar.

2006-07	Carlisle U	7	0		
2007-08	Carlisle U	0	0	7	0
2008-09	Shrewsbury T	3	0	3	0

HOLT, Grant (F)   248   79
H: 6 1   W: 14 02   b.Carlisle 12-4-81
Source: Workington.

1999-2000	Halifax T	4	0		
2000-01	Halifax T	2	0	6	0

From Sengkang,Barrow

2002-03	Sheffield W	7	1		
2003-04	Sheffield W	17	2	24	3
2003-04	Rochdale	14	4		
2004-05	Rochdale	40	17		
2005-06	Rochdale	21	14	75	35
2005-06	Nottingham F	19	4		
2006-07	Nottingham F	45	14		
2007-08	Nottingham F	32	3	96	21
2007-08	*Blackpool*	4	0	4	0
2008-09	Shrewsbury T	43	20	43	20

HUMPHREY, Chris (M)   74   2
H: 5 10   W: 10 08   b.Walsall 19-9-87
Source: WBA Scholar.

2006-07	Shrewsbury T	12	0		
2007-08	Shrewsbury T	25	0		
2008-09	Shrewsbury T	37	2	74	2

JACKSON, Mike (D)   554   37
H: 6 0   W: 13 08   b.Runcorn 4-12-73
Source: Trainee.

1991-92	Crewe Alex	1	0		
1992-93	Crewe Alex	4	0	5	0
1993-94	Bury	39	0		
1994-95	Bury	24	2		
1995-96	Bury	31	4		
1996-97	Bury	31	3	125	9
1996-97	Preston NE	7	0		
1997-98	Preston NE	40	2		
1998-99	Preston NE	44	8		
1999-2000	Preston NE	46	5		
2000-01	Preston NE	30	1		
2001-02	Preston NE	13	0		
2002-03	Preston NE	22	1		
2002-03	*Tranmere R*	6	0		
2003-04	Preston NE	43	0	245	17
2003-04	Tranmere R	43	5		
2005-06	Tranmere R	41	3	90	8
2006-07	Blackpool	43	1		
2007-08	Blackpool	25	0	68	1
2008-09	Shrewsbury T	21	2	21	2

LANGMEAD, Kelvin (F)   209   18
H: 6 1   W: 12 00   b.Coventry 23-3-85
Source: Scholar.

2003-04	Preston NE	0	0		
2003-04	*Carlisle U*	11	1	11	1
2004-05	Preston NE	1	0	1	0
2004-05	*Kidderminster H*	10	1	10	1
2004-05	Shrewsbury T	28	3		
2005-06	Shrewsbury T	42	9		
2006-07	Shrewsbury T	45	3		
2007-08	Shrewsbury T	39	1		
2008-09	Shrewsbury T	33	0	187	16

LESLIE, Steven (M)   50   1
H: 5 10   W: 11 02   b.Shrewsbury 5-11-87

2005-06	Shrewsbury T	1	0		
2006-07	Shrewsbury T	5	0		
2007-08	Shrewsbury T	17	1		
2008-09	Shrewsbury T	27	0	50	1

MADJO, Guy (F)   25   3
H: 6 0   W: 13 05   b.Cameroon 1-6-84

2005-06	Bristol C	5	0	5	0

From Forest GR, Staff R, Crawley on loan

2007-08	Cheltenham T	5	0	5	0
2007-08	Shrewsbury T	15	3		
2008-09	Shrewsbury T	0	0	15	3

McINTYRE, Kevin (M)   194   18
H: 6 0   W: 11 10   b.Liverpool 23-12-77
Source: Trainee.

1996-97	Tranmere R	0	0		
1997-98	Tranmere R	2	0		
1998-99	Tranmere R	0	0		
1999-2000	Tranmere R	0	0		
2000-01	Tranmere R	0	0		
2001-02	Chester C	0	0	2	0
2004-05	Chester C	10	0	10	0
2004-05	Macclesfield T	23	0		

2005-06	Macclesfield T	44	5		
2006-07	Macclesfield T	44	9		
2007-08	Macclesfield T	23	2	134	16
2007-08	Shrewsbury T	22	2		
2008-09	Shrewsbury T	26	0	48	2

MEREDITH, James (D) 4 0
H: 6 0 W: 11 09 b.Albury 4-4-88
Source: Scholar.

2006-07	Derby Co	0	0		
2006-07	*Chesterfield*	1	0	1	0
2007-08	Sligo R	0	0		
2007-08	Shrewsbury T	3	0		
2008-09	Shrewsbury T	0	0	3	0

MOSS, Darren (D) 258 14
H: 5 10 W: 11 00 b.Wrexham 24-5-81
Source: Trainee. *Honours:* Wales Youth, Under-21.

1998-99	Chester C	7	0		
1999-2000	Chester C	35	0		
2000-01	Chester C	0	0	42	0
2001-02	Shrewsbury T	31	2		
2002-03	Shrewsbury T	40	2		
2003-04	Shrewsbury T	0	0		
2004-05	Shrewsbury T	26	6		
2004-05	Crewe Alex	6	0		
2005-06	Crewe Alex	31	0		
2006-07	Crewe Alex	22	2	59	2
2007-08	Shrewsbury T	31	2		
2008-09	Shrewsbury T	29	0	157	12

MURRAY, Paul (M) 372 29
H: 5 9 W: 10 08 b.Carlisle 31-8-76
Source: Trainee. *Honours:* England Youth, Under-21, B.

1993-94	Carlisle U	8	0		
1994-95	Carlisle U	5	0		
1995-96	Carlisle U	28	1		
1995-96	QPR	1	0		
1996-97	QPR	32	5		
1997-98	QPR	32	1		
1997-98	QPR	0	0		
1998-99	QPR	39	1		
1999-2000	QPR	30	0		
2000-01	QPR	6	0	140	7
2001-02	Southampton	1	0	1	0
2001-02	Oldham Ath	24	5		
2002-03	Oldham Ath	30	1		
2003-04	Oldham Ath	41	9	95	15
2004-05	Beira Mar	17	2	17	2
2005-06	Carlisle U	0	0		
2006-07	Carlisle U	14	1	55	2
2007-08	Gretna	32	1	32	1
2008-09	Shrewsbury T	32	2	32	2

PUGH, Marc (M) 98 9
H: 5 11 W: 11 04 b.Burnley 2-4-87
Source: Scholar.

2005-06	Burnley	0	0		
2005-06	Bury	6	1		
2006-07	Bury	35	3	41	4
2007-08	Shrewsbury T	37	4		
2008-09	Shrewsbury T	7	0	44	4
2008-09	*Luton T*	4	0	4	0
2008-09	Hereford U	9	1	9	1

RIZA, Omer (F) 82 18
H: 5 9 W: 11 00 b.Edmonton 8-11-79
Source: Trainee.

1998-99	Arsenal	0	0		
1999-2000	Arsenal	0	0		
1999-2000	West Ham U	0	0		
2000-01	West Ham U	0	0		
2000-01	*Barnet*	10	4	10	4
2000-01	*Cambridge U*	12	3		
2001-02	West Ham U	0	0		
2002-03	Cambridge U	46	11	58	14
2003-04	Denizli	0	0		
2004-05	Denizli	0	0		
2005-06	Denizli	0	0		
2006-07	Trabzonspor	12	0		
2007-08	Trabzonspor	0	0	12	0
2008-09	Shrewsbury T	2	0	2	0

SINGH, Jasbir (G) 0 0
H: 6 3 W: 12 08 b. 12-3-90
Source: Birmingham C Scholar.

| 2008-09 | Shrewsbury T | 0 | 0 | | |

SYMES, Michael (F) 108 20
H: 6 3 W: 12 04 b.Gt Yarmouth 31-10-83
Source: Scholar.

2001-02	Everton	0	0		
2002-03	Everton	0	0		
2003-04	Everton	0	0		
2003-04	*Crewe Alex*	4	1	4	1
2004-05	Bradford C	12	2		
2004-05	*Darlington*	0	0		
2005-06	Bradford C	3	1		
2005-06	*Stockport Co*	1	0	1	0
2006-07	Bradford C	0	0	15	3
2006-07	Shrewsbury T	33	9		
2007-08	Shrewsbury T	21	3		
2007-08	*Macclesfield T*	14	1	14	1
2008-09	Shrewsbury T	8	2	62	14
2008-09	*Bournemouth*	5	0	5	0
2008-09	*Accrington S*	7	1	7	1

SOUTHAMPTON (76)

ARGENT, Sam (M) 0 0
Source: Scholar.

| 2008-09 | Southampton | 0 | 0 | | |

BIALKOWSKI, Bartosz (G) 21 0
H: 6 3 W: 12 10 b.Braniewo 6-7-87
Honours: Poland Under-10, Under-21.

2004-05	Gornik Zabrze	7	0	7	0
2005-06	Southampton	5	0		
2006-07	Southampton	8	0		
2007-08	Southampton	1	0		
2008-09	Southampton	0	0	14	0

DAVIES, Kyle (D) 0 0
H: 5 11 W: 12 08 b.Oakland 11-4-87

2006-07	Southampton	0	0		
2007-08	Southampton	0	0		
2008-09	Southampton	0	0		

Transferred to Real Salt Lake

DAVIS, Kelvin (G) 463 0
H: 6 1 W: 11 05 b.Bedford 29-9-76
Source: Trainee. *Honours:* England Youth, Under-21.

1993-94	Luton T	1	0		
1994-95	Luton T	9	0		
1994-95	*Torquay U*	2	0	2	0
1995-96	Luton T	6	0		
1996-97	Luton T	0	0		
1997-98	Luton T	32	0		
1997-98	*Hartlepool U*	2	0	2	0
1998-99	Luton T	44	0	92	0
1999-2000	Wimbledon	0	0		
2000-01	Wimbledon	45	0		
2001-02	Wimbledon	40	0		
2002-03	Wimbledon	46	0	131	0
2003-04	Ipswich T	45	0		
2004-05	Ipswich T	39	0	84	0
2005-06	Sunderland	33	0	33	0
2006-07	Southampton	38	0		
2007-08	Southampton	35	0		
2008-09	Southampton	46	0	119	0

DOBIE, Ryan (M) 0 0
Source: Scholar.

| 2008-09 | Southampton | 0 | 0 | | |

DUNFORD, Thomas (M) 0 0
Source: Scholar.

| 2008-09 | Southampton | 0 | 0 | | |

DYER, Nathan (M) 85 6
H: 5 5 W: 9 00 b.Trowbridge 29-11-87
Source: From Scholar. *Honours:* England Youth.

2005-06	Southampton	17	0		
2005-06	*Burnley*	5	2	5	2
2006-07	Southampton	18	0		
2007-08	Southampton	17	1		
2008-09	Southampton	4	0	56	1
2008-09	*Sheffield U*	7	1	7	1
2008-09	*Swansea C*	17	2	17	2

EUELL, Jason (F) 359 80
H: 5 11 W: 11 13 b.Lambeth 6-2-77
Source: Trainee. *Honours:* England Youth, Under-21, Jamaica 3 full caps, 1 goal.

1995-96	Wimbledon	9	2		
1996-97	Wimbledon	7	2		
1997-98	Wimbledon	19	4		
1998-99	Wimbledon	33	10		
1999-2000	Wimbledon	37	4		
2000-01	Wimbledon	36	19	141	41
2001-02	Charlton Ath	36	11		
2002-03	Charlton Ath	36	10		
2003-04	Charlton Ath	31	10		
2004-05	Charlton Ath	26	2		
2005-06	Charlton Ath	10	1		
2006-07	Charlton Ath	0	0	139	34
2006-07	Middlesbrough	17	0		
2007-08	Middlesbrough	0	0	17	0
2007-08	Southampton	38	3		
2008-09	Southampton	24	2	62	5

FORECAST, Tommy (G) 0 0
H: 6 2 W: 11 10 b.Newham 15-10-86
Source: Scholar.

2005-06	Tottenham H	0	0		
2006-07	Tottenham H	0	0		
2007-08	Tottenham H	0	0		
2008-09	Southampton	0	0		

GASMI, Romain (M) 19 1
H: 5 8 W: 11 11 b.Lyon 15-2-87

2006-07	Strasbourg	14	1		
2007-08	Strasbourg	1	0	15	1
2008-09	Southampton	4	0	4	0

GILLETT, Simon (M) 73 2
H: 5 6 W: 11 07 b.Oxford 6-11-85
Source: Trainee. *Honours:* Luxembourg full caps.

2003-04	Southampton	0	0		
2004-05	Southampton	0	0		
2005-06	*Walsall*	2	0	2	0
2006-07	Southampton	0	0		
2006-07	*Blackpool*	31	1	31	1
2006-07	*Bournemouth*	7	1	7	1
2007-08	Southampton	2	0		
2007-08	*Yeovil T*	4	0	4	0
2008-09	Southampton	27	0	29	0

GOBERN, Oscar (M) 6 0
H: 5 11 W: 10 10 b.Birmingham 26-1-91
Source: Scholar.

| 2008-09 | Southampton | 6 | 0 | 6 | 0 |

HATCH, Jamie (M) 0 0
b.Hampshire 21-9-89
Source: Scholar.

2006-07	Southampton	0	0		
2007-08	Southampton	0	0		
2008-09	Southampton	0	0		

HOLMES, Lee (M) 107 7
H: 5 8 W: 10 06 b.Mansfield 2-4-87
Source: Scholar. *Honours:* FA Schools, England Youth.

2002-03	Derby Co	2	0		
2003-04	Derby Co	23	2		
2004-05	Derby Co	3	0		
2004-05	*Swindon T*	15	1	15	1
2005-06	Derby Co	18	0		
2006-07	Derby Co	0	0		
2006-07	*Bradford C*	16	0	16	0
2007-08	Derby Co	0	0	46	2
2007-08	*Walsall*	19	4	19	4
2008-09	Southampton	11	0	11	0

IMUDIA, Jeffrey (D) 0 0
b.Nigeria 29-4-90
Honours: Everton Scholar.

| 2007-08 | Southampton | 0 | 0 | | |
| 2008-09 | Southampton | 0 | 0 | | |

JAMES, Lloyd (M) 41 0
H: 5 11 W: 11 01 b.Bristol 16-2-88
Source: Scholar. *Honours:* Wales Youth, Under-21.

2005-06	Southampton	0	0		
2006-07	Southampton	0	0		
2007-08	Southampton	0	0		
2008-09	Southampton	41	0	41	0

JOHN, Stern (F) 376 130
H: 6 1 W: 12 13 b.Tunapuna 30-10-76
Honours: Trinidad & Tobago 101 full caps, 67 goals.

1998	Columbus Crew	27	26		
1999	Columbus Crew	28	18	55	44
1999-2000	Nottingham F	17	3		
2000-01	Nottingham F	29	2		
2001-02	Nottingham F	26	13	72	18
2001-02	Birmingham C	15	7		
2002-03	Birmingham C	30	5		
2003-04	Birmingham C	29	4		
2004-05	Birmingham C	0	0	77	16
2004-05	Coventry C	30	11		
2005-06	Coventry C	25	10		
2005-06	*Derby Co*	7	0	7	0

2006-07 Coventry C 23 5 78 26
2006-07 Sunderland 15 4
2007-08 Sunderland 1 1 16 5
2007-08 Southampton 40 19
2008-09 Southampton 7 0 47 19
2008-09 *Bristol C* 24 2 24 2

LALLANA, Adam (M) 49 2
H: 5 8 W: 11 06 b.St Albans 10-5-88
Source: Scholar. *Honours:* England Youth, Under-21
2005-06 Southampton 0 0
2006-07 Southampton 1 0
2007-08 Southampton 5 1
2007-08 *Bournemouth* 3 0 3 0
2008-09 Southampton 40 1 46 2

LANCASHIRE, Oliver (D) 11 0
H: 6 1 W: 11 10 b.Basingstoke 13-12-88
Source: Scholar.
2006-07 Southampton 0 0
2007-08 Southampton 0 0
2008-09 Southampton 11 0 11 0

LIPTAK, Zoltan (D) 60 7
H: 6 4 W: 13 00 b.Budapest 10-12-84
Honours: Hungary Under-21.
2005-06 Lombard-Papa 25 3
2006-07 Lombard-Papa 14 4 39 7
2007-08 Southend U 0 0
2008-09 Ujpest 14 0 14 0
2008-09 Southampton 7 0 7 0

McGOLDRICK, David (F) 103 20
H: 6 1 W: 11 10 b.Nottingham 29-11-87
Source: Schoolboy.
2003-04 Notts Co 4 0
2004-05 Notts Co 0 0
2005-06 Southampton 1 0
2005-06 *Notts Co* 6 0 10 0
2006-07 Southampton 9 0
2006-07 *Bournemouth* 12 6 12 6
2007-08 Southampton 8 0
2007-08 *Port Vale* 17 2 17 2
2008-09 Southampton 46 12 64 12

McLAGGON, Kane (F) 7 1
H: 6 2 W: 12 05 b.Barry 21-9-90
Source: Scholar. *Honours:* Wales Youth.
2007-08 Southampton 0 0
2008-09 Southampton 7 1 7 1

McNISH, Callum (M) 0 0
Source: Scholar.
2008-09 Southampton 0 0

MILLS, Joseph (F) 22 0
H: 5 9 W: 11 00 b.Swindon 30-10-89
Source: Scholar.
2006-07 Southampton 0 0
2007-08 Southampton 0 0
2008-09 Southampton 8 0 8 0
2008-09 *Scunthorpe U* 14 0 14 0

MOLYNEUX, Lee (D) 4 0
H: 5 10 W: 11 07 b.Liverpool 24-2-89
Source: Scholar. *Honours:* England Schools, Youth.
2005-06 Everton 0 0
2006-07 Everton 0 0
2007-08 Everton 0 0
2008-09 Everton 0 0
2008-09 Southampton 4 0 4 0

PATERSON, Matthew (F) 11 1
H: 5 10 W: 10 10 b.Glasgow 18-10-89
Source: Scholar. *Honours:* Scotland Youth.
2008-09 Southampton 11 1 11 1

PERRY, Chris (D) 467 11
H: 5 8 W: 11 03 b.Carshalton 26-4-73
Source: Trainee.
1991-92 Wimbledon 0 0
1992-93 Wimbledon 0 0
1993-94 Wimbledon 2 0
1994-95 Wimbledon 22 0
1995-96 Wimbledon 37 0
1996-97 Wimbledon 37 1
1997-98 Wimbledon 35 1
1998-99 Wimbledon 34 0 167 2
1999-2000 Tottenham H 37 1
2000-01 Tottenham H 32 1
2001-02 Tottenham H 33 0
2002-03 Tottenham H 18 1
2003-04 Tottenham H 0 0 120 3
2003-04 Charlton Ath 29 1

2004-05 Charlton Ath 19 1
2005-06 Charlton Ath 28 1 76 3
2006-07 WBA 23 0 23 0
2007-08 Luton T 35 1 35 1
2007-08 *Southampton* 6 0
2008-09 Southampton 40 2 46 2

POKE, Michael (G) 4 0
H: 6 1 W: 13 12 b.Spelthorne 21-11-85
Source: Trainee.
2003-04 Southampton 0 0
2004-05 Southampton 0 0
2005-06 Southampton 0 0
2005-06 *Oldham Ath* 0 0
2005-06 *Northampton T* 0 0
2006-07 Southampton 0 0
2007-08 Southampton 4 0
2008-09 Southampton 0 0 4 0

PULIS, Anthony (M) 20 0
H: 5 10 W: 10 10 b.Bristol 21-7-84
Source: Scholar. *Honours:* Wales Under-21.
2002-03 Portsmouth 0 0
2003-04 Portsmouth 0 0
2004-05 Portsmouth 0 0
2004-05 Stoke C 0 0
2004-05 *Torquay U* 3 0 3 0
2005-06 Stoke C 0 0
2005-06 *Plymouth Arg* 5 0 5 0
2006-07 Stoke C 1 0
2006-07 *Grimsby T* 9 0 9 0
2007-08 Stoke C 1 0
2007-08 *Bristol R* 1 0 1 0
2008-09 Stoke C 0 0 2 0
2008-09 Southampton 0 0

RACINE, Aaron (M) 0 0
Source: Scholar.

RASIAK, Grzegorz (F) 246 97
H: 6 3 W: 13 03 b.Szczecin 12-1-79
Source: From Warta, GKS. *Honours:* Poland 37 full caps, 8 goals.
2000-01 Odra 28 9 28 9
2001-02 Groclin 26 14
2002-03 Groclin 22 10
2003-04 Groclin 18 10 66 34
2003-04 Siena 0 0
2004-05 Derby Co 35 16
2005-06 Derby Co 6 2 41 18
2005-06 Tottenham H 8 0 8 0
2005-06 Southampton 13 4
2006-07 Southampton 39 18
2007-08 Southampton 23 6
2007-08 *Bolton W* 7 0 7 0
2008-09 Southampton 0 0 75 28
2008-09 *Watford* 21 8 21 8

REEVES, Benjamin (M) 0 0
Source: Scholar.
2008-09 Southampton 0 0

SAEIJS, Jan Paul (D) 268 19
H: 6 3 W: 12 08 b.Den Haag 20-6-78
1998-99 Den Haag 5 1
1999-2000 Den Haag 33 1
2000-01 Den Haag 25 1
2001-02 Den Haag 9 0
2002-03 Den Haag 29 3
2003-04 Den Haag 13 2
2004-05 Den Haag 32 1
2005-06 Den Haag 15 3 161 12
2005-06 Roda JC 11 0
2006-07 Roda JC 30 2
2007-08 Roda JC 30 3
2008-09 Roda JC 16 0 87 5
2008-09 Southampton 20 2 20 2

SAGANOWSKI, Marek (F) 338 111
H: 5 10 W: 12 04 b.Lodz 31-10-78
Honours: Poland 32 full caps, 5 goals.
1994-95 Lodz 3 0
1995-96 Lodz 29 11
1996-97 Lodz 2 1
1996-97 Hamburg 3 0 3 0
1996-97 Feyenoord 7 0 7 0
1997-98 Lodz 22 11
1998-99 Lodz 15 1
1999-2000 Lodz 24 6 95 30
2000-01 Plock 23 4 23 4
2001-02 Odra 27 2
2002-03 Odra 3 0 30 2
2002-03 Legia 17 10

2003-04 Legia 24 17
2004-05 Legia 26 14 67 41
2005-06 Guimaraes 32 12 32 12
2006-07 Troyes 6 0 6 0
2006-07 Southampton 13 10
2007-08 Southampton 30 3
2008 Aalborg 13 3 13 3
2008-09 Southampton 19 6 62 19

SCHNEIDERLIN, Morgan (M) 35 0
H: 5 11 W: 11 11 b.Obernai 8-11-89
2007-08 Strasbourg 5 0 5 0
2008-09 Southampton 30 0 30 0

SKACEL, Rudi (M) 218 40
H: 5 10 W: 12 01 b.Trutnov 17-7-79
Honours: Czech Republic Under-21, 4 full caps, 1 goal.
1998-99 Hradec Kralove 0 0
1999-2000 Hradec Kralove 3 0
2000-01 Hradec Kralove 0 0
2001-02 Hradec Kralove 18 6 21 6
2001-02 Slavia Prague 12 3
2002-03 Slavia Prague 28 8 40 11
2003-04 Marseille 20 1 20 1
2004-05 Panathinaikos 16 1 16 1
2005-06 Hearts 35 16 35 16
2006-07 Southampton 37 3
2007-08 *Hertha Berlin* 5 0 5 0
2007-08 Southampton 16 1
2008-09 Southampton 28 1 81 5

SMITH, Ryan (M) 68 1
H: 5 10 W: 11 00 b.Islington 10-11-86
Source: Scholar. *Honours:* England Youth, Under-20.
2004-05 Arsenal 0 0
2005-06 Arsenal 0 0
2005-06 *Leicester C* 17 1 17 1
2006-07 Derby Co 15 0 15 0
2006-07 *Millwall* 6 0
2007-08 Millwall 16 0
2008-09 Millwall 1 0 23 0
2008-09 Southampton 13 0 13 0

SURMAN, Andrew (M) 171 23
H: 5 10 W: 11 06 b.Johannesburg 20-8-86
Source: Trainee. *Honours:* England Under-21.
2003-04 Southampton 0 0
2004-05 Southampton 0 0
2004-05 *Walsall* 14 2 14 2
2005-06 Southampton 12 2
2005-06 *Bournemouth* 24 6 24 6
2006-07 Southampton 37 4
2007-08 Southampton 40 2
2008-09 Southampton 44 7 133 15

SVENSSON, Michael (D) 249 11
H: 6 2 W: 12 02 b.Varnamo 25-11-75
Honours: Sweden 25 full caps.
1992 Skillingaryds 21 0 21 0
1993 Varnamo 20 0
1994 Varnamo 20 0
1995 Varnamo 17 1
1996 Varnamo 0 0 57 1
1997 Halmstad 0 0
1998 Halmstad 14 2
1999 Halmstad 20 0
2000 Halmstad 25 2
2001 Halmstad 18 1 77 5
2001-02 Troyes 23 1 23 1
2002-03 Southampton 34 2
2003-04 Southampton 26 2
2004-05 Southampton 0 0
2005-06 Southampton 7 0
2006-07 Southampton 0 0
2007-08 Southampton 0 0
2008-09 Southampton 4 0 71 4

THOMAS, Wayne (D) 392 13
H: 6 2 W: 14 12 b.Gloucester 17-5-79
Source: Trainee.
1995-96 Torquay U 6 0
1996-97 Torquay U 12 0
1997-98 Torquay U 21 1
1998-99 Torquay U 44 1
1999-2000 Torquay U 40 3 123 5
2000-01 Stoke C 34 0
2001-02 Stoke C 40 2
2002-03 Stoke C 41 0
2003-04 Stoke C 39 3
2004-05 Stoke C 35 2 189 7
2005-06 Burnley 16 1

2006-07	Burnley	33	0		
2007-08	Burnley	1	0	50	1
2007-08	Southampton	30	0		
2008-09	Southampton	0	0	30	0

THOMSON, Jake (M)   16   1
H: 5 11 W: 11 05 b.Southsea 12-5-89
Source: Scholar.

2006-07	Southampton	0	0		
2007-08	Southampton	0	0		
2008-09	Southampton	10	0	10	0
2008-09	*Bournemouth*	6	1	6	1

WHITE, Jamie (F)   12   1
H: 5 8 W: 10 07 b.Southampton 21-9-89
Source: Scholar.

2006-07	Southampton	0	0		
2007-08	Southampton	0	0		
2008-09	Southampton	3	0	3	0
2008-09	*Shrewsbury T*	9	1	9	1

WOTTON, Paul (D)   423   54
H: 5 11 W: 12 00 b.Plymouth 17-8-77
Source: Trainee.

1994-95	Plymouth Arg	7	0		
1995-96	Plymouth Arg	1	0		
1996-97	Plymouth Arg	9	1		
1997-98	Plymouth Arg	34	1		
1998-99	Plymouth Arg	36	1		
1999-2000	Plymouth Arg	23	0		
2000-01	Plymouth Arg	42	4		
2001-02	Plymouth Arg	46	5		
2002-03	Plymouth Arg	43	8		
2003-04	Plymouth Arg	38	9		
2004-05	Plymouth Arg	40	12		
2005-06	Plymouth Arg	45	8		
2006-07	Plymouth Arg	22	4		
2007-08	Plymouth Arg	8	1	394	54
2008-09	Southampton	29	0	29	0

WRIGHT-PHILLIPS, Bradley (M)   143   24
H: 5 10 W: 10 07 b.Lewisham 12-3-85
Source: Scholar. Honours: England Youth, Under-20.

2002-03	Manchester C	0	0		
2003-04	Manchester C	0	0		
2004-05	Manchester C	14	1		
2005-06	Manchester C	18	1	32	2
2006-07	Southampton	39	8		
2007-08	Southampton	39	8		
2008-09	Southampton	33	6	111	22

SOUTHEND U (77)

ADEMENO, Charles (F)   4   0
H: 5 10 W: 11 13 b.Milton Keynes 12-12-88
Source: Scholar.

2005-06	Southend U	1	0		
2006-07	Southend U	1	0		
2007-08	Southend U	0	0		
2008-09	Southend U	2	0	4	0

BARNARD, Lee (F)   79   23
H: 5 10 W: 10 10 b.Romford 18-7-84
Source: Trainee.

2002-03	Tottenham H	0	0		
2002-03	*Exeter C*	3	0	3	0
2003-04	Tottenham H	0	0		
2004-05	Tottenham H	0	0		
2004-05	*Leyton Orient*	8	0	8	0
2004-05	*Northampton T*	5	0	5	0
2005-06	Tottenham H	3	0		
2006-07	Tottenham H	0	0		
2007-08	Tottenham H	0	0	3	0
2007-08	*Crewe Alex*	10	3	10	3
2007-08	Southend U	15	9		
2008-09	Southend U	35	11	50	20

BARRETT, Adam (D)   385   34
H: 5 10 W: 12 00 b.Dagenham 29-11-79
Source: Leyton Orient Trainee.

1998-99	Plymouth Arg	1	0		
1999-2000	Plymouth Arg	42	3		
2000-01	Plymouth Arg	9	0	52	3
2000-01	Mansfield T	8	1		
2001-02	Mansfield T	29	0	37	1
2002-03	Bristol R	45	1		
2003-04	Bristol R	44	4	90	5
2004-05	Southend U	43	11		
2005-06	Southend U	45	3		
2006-07	Southend U	28	3		
2007-08	Southend U	45	6		
2008-09	Southend U	45	2	206	25

BETSY, Kevin (M)   309   42
H: 6 1 W: 12 00 b.Woking 20-3-78
Source: Woking.

1998-99	Fulham	7	1		
1999-2000	Fulham	2	0		
1999-2000	*Bournemouth*	5	0	5	0
1999-2000	*Hull C*	2	0	2	0
2000-01	Fulham	5	0		
2001-02	Fulham	1	0	15	1
2001-02	Barnsley	10	0		
2002-03	Barnsley	39	5		
2003-04	Barnsley	45	10		
2004-05	Barnsley	0	0	94	15
2004-05	*Hartlepool U*	6	1	6	1
2004-05	Oldham Ath	36	5	36	5
2005-06	Wycombe W	42	8		
2006-07	Wycombe W	29	5	71	13
2006-07	Bristol C	17	1		
2007-08	Bristol C	1	0	18	1
2007-08	*Yeovil T*	5	1	5	1
2007-08	Walsall	16	2	16	2
2008-09	Southend U	41	3	41	3

CHRISTOPHE, Jean-Francois (M)   48   5
H: 6 1 W: 13 01 b.Creil 13-6-82
Source: Lens.

2007-08	Portsmouth	0	0		
2007-08	*Bournemouth*	10	1	10	1
2007-08	*Yeovil T*	5	0	5	0
2008-09	Portsmouth	0	0		
2008-09	Southend U	33	4	33	4

CLARKE, Peter (D)   253   25
H: 6 0 W: 12 00 b.Southport 3-1-82
Source: Trainee. Honours: England Schools, Youth, Under-20, Under-21.

1998-99	Everton	0	0		
1999-2000	Everton	0	0		
2000-01	Everton	1	0		
2001-02	Everton	7	0		
2002-03	Everton	0	0		
2002-03	Blackpool	16	3		
2002-03	*Port Vale*	13	1	13	1
2003-04	Everton	1	0		
2003-04	*Coventry C*	5	0	5	0
2004-05	Everton	0	0	9	0
2004-05	Blackpool	38	5		
2005-06	Blackpool	46	6	100	14
2006-07	Southend U	38	2		
2007-08	Southend U	45	4		
2008-09	Southend U	43	4	126	10

FORAN, Richie (F)   255   65
H: 6 1 W: 13 00 b.Dublin 16-6-80
Honours: Eire Under-21.

2000-01	Shelbourne	28	11	28	11
2001-02	Carlisle U	37	14		
2002-03	Carlisle U	31	7		
2003-04	Carlisle U	23	4	91	25
2003-04	*Oxford U*	4	0	4	0
2004-05	Motherwell	35	5		
2005-06	Motherwell	32	11		
2006-07	Motherwell	23	7	90	23
2006-07	Southend U	15	1		
2007-08	Southend U	6	0		
2007-08	*Darlington*	12	2		
2008-09	Southend U	0	0	21	1
2008-09	*Darlington*	9	3	21	5

Transferred to Inverness CT January 2009

FRANCIS, Simon (D)   201   5
H: 6 0 W: 12 06 b.Nottingham 16-2-85
Source: Scholar. Honours: England Youth, Under-20.

2002-03	Bradford C	25	1		
2003-04	Bradford C	30	0	55	1
2003-04	Sheffield U	5	0		
2004-05	Sheffield U	6	0		
2005-06	Sheffield U	1	0	12	0
2005-06	*Grimsby T*	5	0	5	0
2005-06	*Tranmere R*	17	1	17	1
2006-07	Southend U	40	1		
2007-08	Southend U	27	2		
2008-09	Southend U	45	0	112	3

FREEDMAN, Dougie (F)   500   159
H: 5 9 W: 12 05 b.Glasgow 21-1-74
Source: Trainee. Honours: Scotland Schools, Under-21, B, 2 full caps, 1 goal.

1991-92	QPR	0	0		
1992-93	QPR	0	0		
1993-94	QPR	0	0		
1994-95	Barnet	42	24		
1995-96	Barnet	5	3	47	27
1995-96	Crystal Palace	39	20		
1996-97	Crystal Palace	44	11		
1997-98	Crystal Palace	7	0		
1997-98	Wolverhampton W	29	10	29	10
1998-99	Nottingham F	31	9		
1999-2000	Nottingham F	34	9		
2000-01	Nottingham F	5	0	70	18
2000-01	Crystal Palace	26	11		
2001-02	Crystal Palace	40	20		
2002-03	Crystal Palace	29	9		
2003-04	Crystal Palace	35	13		
2004-05	Crystal Palace	20	1		
2005-06	Crystal Palace	34	5		
2006-07	Crystal Palace	34	3		
2007-08	Crystal Palace	19	1		
2007-08	*Leeds U*	11	5	11	5
2008-09	Crystal Palace	0	0	327	94
2008-09	Southend U	16	5	16	5

FURLONG, Paul (F)   542   180
H: 6 0 W: 13 11 b.Wood Green 1-10-68
Source: Enfield.

1991-92	Coventry C	37	4	37	4
1992-93	Watford	41	19		
1993-94	Watford	38	18	79	37
1994-95	Chelsea	36	10		
1995-96	Chelsea	28	3	64	13
1996-97	Birmingham C	43	10		
1997-98	Birmingham C	25	15		
1998-99	Birmingham C	29	13		
1999-2000	Birmingham C	19	11		
2000-01	Birmingham C	4	0		
2000-01	*QPR*	3	1		
2001-02	Birmingham C	11	1		
2001-02	*Sheffield U*	4	2	4	2
2002-03	Birmingham C	0	0	131	50
2002-03	QPR	33	13		
2003-04	QPR	36	16		
2004-05	QPR	40	18		
2005-06	QPR	37	7		
2006-07	QPR	22	2	171	57
2007-08	Luton T	32	8	32	8
2008-09	Southend U	3	0	3	0
2008-09	Barnet	21	9	21	9

GRANT, Anthony (M)   92   1
H: 5 10 W: 11 01 b.Lambeth 4-6-87
Source: Scholar. Honours: England Youth.

2004-05	Chelsea	1	0		
2005-06	Chelsea	0	0		
2005-06	*Oldham Ath*	2	0	2	0
2006-07	Chelsea	0	0		
2006-07	*Wycombe W*	40	0	40	0
2007-08	Chelsea	0	0	1	0
2007-08	*Luton T*	4	0	4	0
2007-08	*Southend U*	10	0		
2008-09	Southend U	35	1	45	1

HAZELL, Justin (M)   0   0
H: 5 9 W: 11 06 b.Leigh-on-Sea 12-1-92

| 2008-09 | Southend U | 0 | 0 | | |

HERD, Johnny (D)   6   0
H: 5 9 W: 12 00 b.Huntingdon 3-10-89
Source: Welling U.

| 2008-09 | Southend U | 6 | 0 | 6 | 0 |

JOYCE, Ian (G)   3   0
H: 6 3 W: 13 07 b.Kinnelon 12-7-85
Source: Watford.

| 2008-09 | Southend U | 3 | 0 | 3 | 0 |

LAURENT, Francis (F)   21   3
H: 6 3 W: 14 00 b.Paris 6-1-86

| 2008-09 | Southend U | 21 | 3 | 21 | 3 |

LOKANDO, Mbive (M)   0   0
H: 5 11 W: 10 12 b.Congo 18-9-89
Source: Scholar. Honours: DR Congo 1 full cap.

| 2007-08 | Southend U | 0 | 0 | | |
| 2008-09 | *Dagenham & R* | 0 | 0 | | |

MASTERS, Clark (G)   12   0
H: 6 3 W: 13 12 b.Hastings 31-5-87
Source: Scholar.

2005-06	Brentford	0	0		
2006-07	Brentford	11	0		
2007-08	Brentford	1	0	12	0
2007-08	Southend U	0	0		
2008-09	Southend U	0	0		

McCORMACK, Alan (M) 150 17
H: 5 8　W: 11 00　b.Dublin 10-1-84
Source: Stella Maris BC.

Season	Club				
2002-03	Preston NE	0	0		
2003-04	Preston NE	5	0		
2003-04	*Leyton Orient*	10	0	10	0
2004-05	Preston NE	3	0		
2004-05	*Southend U*	7	2		
2005-06	Preston NE	0	0		
2005-06	*Motherwell*	24	2	24	2
2006-07	Preston NE	3	0	11	0
2006-07	Southend U	22	3		
2007-08	Southend U	42	8		
2008-09	Southend U	34	2	105	15

MILDENHALL, Steve (G) 270 1
H: 6 4　W: 14 01　b.Swindon 13-5-78
Source: Trainee.

Season	Club				
1996-97	Swindon T	1	0		
1997-98	Swindon T	4	0		
1998-99	Swindon T	0	0		
1999-2000	Swindon T	5	0		
2000-01	Swindon T	23	0	33	0
2001-02	Notts Co	26	0		
2002-03	Notts Co	21	0		
2003-04	Notts Co	28	0		
2004-05	Notts Co	1	0	76	0
2004-05	Oldham Ath	6	0	6	0
2005-06	Grimsby T	46	1	46	1
2006-07	Yeovil T	46	0		
2007-08	Yeovil T	29	0	75	0
2008-09	Southend U	34	0	34	0

MOUSSA, Franck (M) 56 2
H: 5 8　W: 10 08　b.Brussels 24-9-87
Source: Scholar.

Season	Club				
2005-06	Southend U	1	0		
2006-07	Southend U	4	0		
2007-08	Southend U	16	0		
2008-09	Southend U	26	2	47	2
2008-09	*Wycombe W*	9	0	9	0

O'KEEFE, Stuart (M) 3 0
H: 5 8　W: 10 00　b.Eye 4-3-91
Source: Ipswich T Scholar.

Season	Club				
2008-09	Southend U	3	0	3	0

ORENUJA, Femi (M) 0 0
H: 5 6　W: 9 07　b.Greenwich 18-3-93

Season	Club		
2008-09	Southend U	0	0

REVELL, Alex (F) 147 22
H: 6 3　W: 13 00　b.Cambridge 7-7-83
Source: Scholar.

Season	Club				
2000-01	Cambridge U	4	0		
2001-02	Cambridge U	24	2		
2002-03	Cambridge U	9	0		
2003-04	Cambridge U	20	3	57	5
From Braintree T.					
2006-07	Brighton & HA	38	7		
2007-08	Brighton & HA	21	6	59	13
2007-08	Southend U	8	0		
2008-09	Southend U	23	4	31	4

SANKOFA, Osei (D) 61 0
H: 6 0　W: 12 04　b.London 19-3-85
Source: Scholar. *Honours:* England Youth, Under-20.

Season	Club				
2002-03	Charlton Ath	1	0		
2003-04	Charlton Ath	0	0		
2004-05	Charlton Ath	0	0		
2005-06	Charlton Ath	4	0		
2005-06	*Bristol C*	8	0	8	0
2006-07	Charlton Ath	9	0		
2007-08	Charlton Ath	1	0	15	0
2007-08	*Brentford*	11	0	11	0
2008-09	*Southend U*	27	0	27	0

SCANNELL, Damian (M) 30 1
H: 5 10　W: 11 07　b.Croydon 28-4-85
Source: Eastleigh.

Season	Club				
2007-08	Southend U	9	0		
2008-09	Southend U	19	1	28	1
2008-09	*Brentford*	2	0	2	0

THURLBOURNE, Luke (M) 0 0
Source: Scholar.

Season	Club		
2008-09	Southend U	0	0

WALKER, James (F) 75 12
H: 5 10　W: 11 10　b.Hackney 25-11-87
Source: From Scholar. *Honours:* England Youth.

Season	Club		
2004-05	Charlton Ath	0	0
2005-06	Charlton Ath	0	0
2005-06	*Hartlepool U*	4	0	4	0
2006-07	Charlton Ath	0	0		
2006-07	*Bristol R*	4	1	4	1
2006-07	*Leyton Orient*	14	2	14	2
2006-07	*Notts Co*	8	0	8	0
2007-08	Charlton Ath	0	0		
2007-08	*Yeovil T*	13	3	13	3
2007-08	Southend U	15	4		
2008-09	Southend U	17	2	32	6

STOCKPORT CO (78)

BAKER, Carl (M) 64 13
H: 6 2　W: 12 06　b.Prescot 26-12-82
Source: Southport.

Season	Club				
2007-08	Morecambe	42	10	42	10
2008-09	Stockport Co	22	3	22	3

BLIZZARD, Dominic (M) 102 6
H: 6 2　W: 12 04　b.High Wycombe 2-9-83
Source: Scholar.

Season	Club				
2001-02	Watford	0	0		
2002-03	Watford	0	0		
2003-04	Watford	2	1		
2004-05	Watford	17	1		
2005-06	Watford	10	0		
2006-07	Watford	0	0	29	2
2006-07	*Stockport Co*	7	0		
2006-07	*Milton Keynes D*	8	0	8	0
2007-08	Stockport Co	27	1		
2008-09	Stockport Co	31	3	65	4

COWARD, Chris (F) 0 0
H: 6 1　W: 11 07　b.Manchester 23-7-89
Source: Scholar.

Season	Club		
2005-06	Stockport Co	0	0
2006-07	Stockport Co	0	0
2007-08	Stockport Co	0	0
2008-09	Stockport Co	0	0

DICKER, Gary (M) 132 6
H: 6 0　W: 12 00　b.Dublin 31-7-86
Honours: Eire Under-21.

Season	Club				
2004	UCD	9	1		
2005	UCD	31	2		
2006	UCD	28	2	68	5
2006-07	Birmingham C	0	0		
2007-08	Stockport Co	30	0		
2008-09	Stockport Co	25	0	55	0
2008-09	*Brighton & HA*	9	1	9	1

EDWARDS, Declan (M) 0 0
H: 5 10　W: 13 07　b.London 23-12-89

Season	Club		
2008-09	Stockport Co	0	0

Transferred to Galway U March 2009

ENNIS, Paul (M) 2 0
H: 5 6　W: 11 02　b.Cheadle 1-2-90
Source: Scholar.

Season	Club				
2008-09	Stockport Co	2	0	2	0

FISHER, Tom (F) 1 0
H: 5 10　W: 11 07　b.Wythenshawe 28-6-92
Source: Scholar.

Season	Club				
2008-09	Stockport Co	1	0	1	0

GREEN, Darren (M) 0 0
H: 6 0　W: 11 00　b.Preston 15-5-89
Source: Preston NE.

Season	Club		
2008-09	Stockport Co	0	0

HALLS, Andy (D) 5 0
H: 6 0　W: 12 02　b.Altrincham 20-4-92
Source: Scholar.

Season	Club				
2008-09	Stockport Co	5	0	5	0

HAVERN, Gianluca (F) 1 1
H: 6 1　W: 13 00　b.Manchester 24-9-88
Source: Scholar.

Season	Club				
2006-07	Stockport Co	0	0		
2007-08	Stockport Co	1	1		
2008-09	Stockport Co	0	0	1	1

JOHNSON, Oli (F) 24 6
H: 5 11　W: 12 04　b.Wakefield 6-11-87
Source: Nostell MW.

Season	Club				
2008-09	Stockport Co	24	6	24	6

MAINWARING, Matty (M) 21 1
H: 5 11　W: 12 02　b.Salford 28-3-90
Source: Preston NE.

Season	Club				
2008-09	Stockport Co	21	1	21	1

McNEIL, Matthew (F) 83 11
H: 6 5　W: 14 03　b.Macclesfield 14-7-76
Source: Burnley, Curzon Ashton, Altrincham, Woodley Sp, Stalybridge C, Woking, Runcorn, Hyde U.

Season	Club				
2005-06	Macclesfield T	12	1		
2006-07	Macclesfield T	35	5	47	6
2007-08	Stockport Co	17	2		
2008-09	Stockport Co	19	3	36	5

McSWEENEY, Leon (F) 47 5
H: 5 10　W: 10 11　b.Cork 19-2-83
Source: Cork C.

Season	Club				
2001-02	Leicester C	0	0		
2002-03	Leicester C	0	0		
2003-04	Leicester C	0	0		
2004-05	Leicester C	0	0		
2005-06	Leicester C	0	0		
2006-07	Leicester C	0	0		
2007-08	Stockport Co	11	1		
2008-09	Stockport Co	36	4	47	5

MULLINS, John (D) 140 9
H: 5 11　W: 12 07　b.Hampstead 6-11-85
Source: Scholar.

Season	Club				
2004-05	Reading	0	0		
2004-05	*Kidderminster H*	21	2	21	2
2005-06	Reading	0	0		
2006-07	Mansfield T	43	2		
2007-08	Mansfield T	43	2	86	4
2008-09	Stockport Co	33	3	33	3

PILKINGTON, Danny (F) 3 0
H: 5 9　W: 11 10　b.Blackburn 25-5-90

Season	Club				
2008-09	Stockport Co	3	0	3	0

RAYNES, Michael (D) 115 4
H: 6 4　W: 12 00　b.Wythenshawe 15-10-87
Source: Scholar.

Season	Club				
2004-05	Stockport Co	19	0		
2005-06	Stockport Co	25	1		
2006-07	Stockport Co	9	0		
2007-08	Stockport Co	27	0		
2008-09	Stockport Co	35	3	115	4

ROSE, Michael (D) 139 7
H: 5 11　W: 12 04　b.Salford 28-7-82
Source: Trainee.

Season	Club				
1999-2000	Manchester U	0	0		
2000-01	Manchester U	0	0		
2001-02	Manchester U	0	0		
From Hereford U					
2004-05	Yeovil T	40	1		
2005-06	Yeovil T	1	0	41	1
2005-06	*Cheltenham T*	3	0	3	0
2006-07	*Scunthorpe U*	15	0	15	0
2006-07	Stockport Co	25	3		
2007-08	Stockport Co	28	3		
2008-09	Stockport Co	27	0	80	6

ROWE, Daniel (M) 3 0
H: 6 0　W: 11 12　b.Wythenshawe 9-3-92
Source: Bolton W.

Season	Club				
2008-09	Stockport Co	3	0	3	0

SMITH, James (D) 34 0
H: 5 10　W: 11 08　b.Liverpool 17-10-85

Season	Club				
2004-05	Liverpool	0	0		
2005-06	Liverpool	0	0		
2006-07	Liverpool	0	0		
2006-07	*Ross Co*	8	0	8	0
2007-08	Stockport Co	26	0		
2008-09	Stockport Co	0	0	26	0

TANSEY, Greg (M) 28 1
H: 6 1　W: 12 03　b.Huyton 21-11-88
Source: Scholar.

Season	Club				
2006-07	Stockport Co	3	0		
2007-08	Stockport Co	13	0		
2008-09	Stockport Co	12	1	28	1

THOMPSON, Josh (D) 9 0
H: 6 4　W: 12 00　b.Bolton 25-2-91
Source: Scholar.

Season	Club				
2008-09	Stockport Co	9	0	9	0

THOMPSON, Peter (F) 151 92
H: 5 9　W: 13 06　b.Belfast 2-5-84
Source: From Linfield. *Honours:* Northern Ireland 8 full caps.

Season	Club		
2001-02	Linfield	1	0
2002-03	Linfield	11	1
2003-04	Linfield	4	0
2004-05	Linfield	29	14
2005-06	Linfield	29	25

2006-07	Linfield	29	20		
2007-08	Linfield	29	29	132	89
2008-09	Stockport Co	19	3	19	3

TUNNICLIFFE, James (D)   41   0
H: 6 4 W: 12 03 b.Denton 17-1-89
Source: Scholar.

2005-06	Stockport Co	1	0		
2006-07	Stockport Co	5	0		
2007-08	Stockport Co	5	0		
2008-09	Stockport Co	30	0	41	0

TURNBULL, Paul (F)   54   1
H: 6 0 W: 12 07 b.Handforth 23-1-89
Source: Scholar.

2004-05	Stockport Co	1	0		
2005-06	Stockport Co	0	0		
2006-07	Stockport Co	0	0		
2007-08	Stockport Co	19	0		
2008-09	Stockport Co	34	1	54	1

VINCENT, James (M)   17   2
H: 5 11 W: 11 00 b.Glossop 27-9-89
Source: Scholar.

2007-08	Stockport Co	1	0		
2008-09	Stockport Co	16	2	17	2

WILLIAMS, Owain fon (G)   33   0
H: 6 1 W: 12 09 b.Penygroes 17-3-87
Source: Scholar. *Honours:* Wales Youth, Under-21.

2005-06	Crewe Alex	0	0		
2006-07	Crewe Alex	0	0		
2007-08	Crewe Alex	0	0		
2008-09	Stockport Co	33	0	33	0

STOKE C (79)

BEATTIE, James (F)   362   122
H: 6 1 W: 13 06 b.Lancaster 27-2-78
Source: Trainee. *Honours:* England Under-21, 5 full caps.

1994-95	Blackburn R	0	0		
1995-96	Blackburn R	0	0		
1996-97	Blackburn R	1	0		
1997-98	Blackburn R	3	0	4	0
1998-99	Southampton	35	5		
1999-2000	Southampton	18	0		
2000-01	Southampton	37	11		
2001-02	Southampton	28	12		
2002-03	Southampton	38	23		
2003-04	Southampton	37	14		
2004-05	Southampton	11	3	204	68
2004-05	Everton	11	1		
2005-06	Everton	32	10		
2006-07	Everton	33	2	76	13
2007-08	Sheffield U	39	22		
2008-09	Sheffield U	23	12	62	34
2008-09	Stoke C	16	7	16	7

CORT, Leon (D)   316   36
H: 6 3 W: 13 01 b.Bermondsey 11-9-79
Source: Dulwich H.

1997-98	Millwall	0	0		
1998-99	Millwall	0	0		
1999-2000	Millwall	0	0		
2000-01	Millwall	0	0		
2001-02	Southend U	45	4		
2002-03	Southend U	46	6		
2003-04	Southend U	46	1	137	16
2004-05	Hull C	44	6		
2005-06	Hull C	42	4	86	10
2006-07	Crystal Palace	37	7		
2007-08	Crystal Palace	12	0	49	7
2007-08	Stoke C	33	8		
2008-09	Stoke C	11	0	44	8

CRESSWELL, Richard (F)   436   93
H: 6 0 W: 11 08 b.Bridlington 20-9-77
Source: Trainee. *Honours:* England Under-21.

1995-96	York C	16	1		
1996-97	York C	17	0		
1996-97	*Mansfield T*	5	1	5	1
1997-98	York C	26	4		
1998-99	York C	36	16	95	21
1998-99	Sheffield W	7	1		
1999-2000	Sheffield W	20	1		
2000-01	Sheffield W	4	0	31	2
2000-01	Leicester C	8	0	8	0
2000-01	*Preston NE*	11	2		
2001-02	Preston NE	40	13		

2002-03	Preston NE	42	16		
2003-04	Preston NE	45	2		
2004-05	Preston NE	46	16		
2005-06	Preston NE	3	0	187	49
2005-06	Leeds U	16	5		
2006-07	Leeds U	22	4	38	9
2007-08	Stoke C	43	11		
2008-09	Stoke C	29	0	72	11

DAVIES, Andrew (D)   115   3
H: 6 3 W: 14 08 b.Stockton 17-12-84
Source: Scholar. *Honours:* England Youth, Under-20, Under-21.

2002-03	Middlesbrough	1	0		
2003-04	Middlesbrough	10	0		
2004-05	Middlesbrough	3	0		
2004-05	*QPR*	9	0	9	0
2005-06	Middlesbrough	12	0		
2005-06	*Derby Co*	23	3	23	3
2006-07	Middlesbrough	23	0		
2007-08	Middlesbrough	4	0	53	0
2007-08	Southampton	23	0		
2008-09	Southampton	0	0	23	0
2008-09	Stoke C	2	0	2	0
2008-09	*Preston NE*	5	0	5	0

DELAP, Rory (M)   392   28
H: 6 3 W: 13 00 b.Sutton Coldfield 6-7-76
Source: Trainee. *Honours:* Eire Under-21, B, 11 full caps.

1992-93	Carlisle U	1	0		
1993-94	Carlisle U	1	0		
1994-95	Carlisle U	3	0		
1995-96	Carlisle U	19	3		
1996-97	Carlisle U	32	4		
1997-98	Carlisle U	9	0	65	7
1997-98	Derby Co	13	0		
1998-99	Derby Co	23	0		
1999-2000	Derby Co	34	8		
2000-01	Derby Co	33	3	103	11
2001-02	Southampton	28	2		
2002-03	Southampton	24	0		
2003-04	Southampton	27	1		
2004-05	Southampton	37	2		
2005-06	Southampton	16	0	132	5
2005-06	Sunderland	6	1		
2006-07	Sunderland	6	0	12	1
2006-07	Stoke C	2	0		
2007-08	Stoke C	44	2		
2008-09	Stoke C	34	2	80	4

DIAGNE-FAYE, Aboulaye (M)   212   11
H: 6 2 W: 13 10 b.Dakar 26-2-78
Source: Ndiambour Louga. *Honours:* Senegal 34 full caps, 3 goals.

2001-02	Jeanne D'Arc	32	4	32	4
2002-03	Lens	15	0		
2003-04	Lens	19	0	34	0
2004-05	Istres	28	0	28	0
2005-06	Bolton W	27	1		
2006-07	Bolton W	32	2		
2007-08	Bolton W	1	0	60	3
2007-08	Newcastle U	22	1	22	1
2008-09	Stoke C	36	3	36	3

DIAO, Salif (M)   185   1
H: 6 1 W: 12 08 b.Kedougou 10-2-77
Honours: Senegal 39 full caps, 4 goals.

1996-97	Epinal	2	0	2	0
1996-97	Monaco	0	0		
1997-98	Monaco	12	0		
1998-99	Monaco	14	0		
1999-2000	Monaco	1	0	27	0
2000-01	Sedan	26	0		
2001-02	Sedan	22	0	48	0
2002-03	Liverpool	26	1		
2003-04	Liverpool	3	0		
2004-05	Liverpool	8	0		
2004-05	*Birmingham C*	2	0	2	0
2005-06	Liverpool	0	0		
2005-06	*Portsmouth*	11	0	11	0
2006-07	Liverpool	0	0	37	1
2006-07	Stoke C	27	0		
2007-08	Stoke C	11	0		
2008-09	Stoke C	20	0	58	0

DICKINSON, Carl (D)   65   0
H: 6 1 W: 12 04 b.Swadlincote 31-3-87
Source: Scholar.

2004-05	Stoke C	1	0		
2005-06	Stoke C	5	0		
2006-07	Stoke C	13	0		
2006-07	*Blackpool*	7	0	7	0

2007-08	Stoke C	27	0		
2008-09	Stoke C	5	0	51	0
2008-09	*Leeds U*	7	0	7	0

ETHERINGTON, Matthew (M)   288   24
H: 5 10 W: 10 12 b.Truro 14-8-81
Source: School. *Honours:* England Youth, Under-21.

1996-97	Peterborough U	1	0		
1997-98	Peterborough U	2	0		
1998-99	Peterborough U	29	3		
1999-2000	Peterborough U	19	3	51	6
1999-2000	Tottenham H	5	0		
2000-01	Tottenham H	6	0		
2001-02	*Bradford C*	13	1	13	1
2001-02	Tottenham H	11	0		
2002-03	Tottenham H	23	1	45	1
2003-04	West Ham U	35	5		
2004-05	West Ham U	39	4		
2005-06	West Ham U	33	2		
2006-07	West Ham U	27	0		
2007-08	West Ham U	18	3		
2008-09	West Ham U	13	2	165	16
2008-09	Stoke C	14	0	14	0

FAYE, Amdy (M)   212   3
H: 6 1 W: 12 06 b.Dakar 12-3-77
Source: Frejus. *Honours:* Senegal 18 full caps.

1998-99	Auxerre	0	0		
1999-2000	Auxerre	3	0		
2000-01	Auxerre	23	0		
2001-02	Auxerre	20	0		
2002-03	Auxerre	34	2	80	2
2003-04	Portsmouth	27	0		
2004-05	Portsmouth	20	0	47	0
2004-05	Newcastle U	9	0		
2005-06	Newcastle U	22	0	31	0
2006-07	Charlton Ath	28	1		
2007-08	Charlton Ath	1	0	29	1
2007-08	*Rangers*	4	0	4	0
2008-09	Stoke C	21	0	21	0

FULLER, Ricardo (F)   264   83
H: 6 3 W: 12 06 b.Kingston, Jamaica 31-10-79
Source: Tivoli Gardens. *Honours:* Jamaica 33 full caps, 4 goals.

2000-01	Crystal Palace	8	0	8	0
2001-02	Hearts	27	8	27	8

From Tivoli Gardens.

2002-03	Preston NE	18	9		
2003-04	Preston NE	38	17		
2004-05	Preston NE	2	1	58	27
2004-05	Portsmouth	31	1	31	1
2005-06	Southampton	30	9		
2005-06	*Ipswich T*	3	2	3	2
2006-07	Southampton	1	0	31	9
2006-07	Stoke C	30	10		
2007-08	Stoke C	42	15		
2008-09	Stoke C	34	11	106	36

GARRETT, Robert (M)   24   0
H: 5 7 W: 11 05 b.Belfast 5-5-88
Source: Scholar. *Honours:* Northern Ireland Youth, Under-21, 1 full cap.

2005-06	Stoke C	2	0		
2006-07	Stoke C	0	0		
2006-07	*Wrexham*	10	0		
2007-08	Stoke C	0	0		
2007-08	*Wrexham*	12	0	22	0
2008-09	Stoke C	0	0	2	0

GRIFFIN, Andy (D)   260   6
H: 5 9 W: 10 10 b.Billinge 7-3-79
Source: Trainee. *Honours:* England Youth, Under-21.

1996-97	Stoke C	34	1		
1997-98	Stoke C	23	1		
1997-98	Newcastle U	4	0		
1998-99	Newcastle U	14	0		
1999-2000	Newcastle U	3	1		
2000-01	Newcastle U	19	0		
2001-02	Newcastle U	4	0		
2002-03	Newcastle U	27	1		
2003-04	Newcastle U	5	0	76	2
2004-05	Portsmouth	22	0		
2005-06	Portsmouth	22	0		
2006-07	Portsmouth	0	0	44	0
2006-07	*Stoke C*	33	2		
2007-08	*Derby Co*	15	0	15	0
2007-08	Stoke C	15	0		
2008-09	Stoke C	20	0	125	4

GROCUTT, Marc (F)   0   0
Source: Scholar.

2008-09	Stoke C	0	0		

HIGGINBOTHAM, Danny (D)   279   18
H: 6 2   W: 13 01   b.Manchester 29-12-78
Source: Trainee.

1997-98	Manchester U	1	0		
1998-99	Manchester U	0	0		
1999-2000	Manchester U	3	0	4	0
2000-01	Derby Co	26	0		
2001-02	Derby Co	37	1		
2002-03	Derby Co	23	2	86	3
2002-03	Southampton	9	0		
2003-04	Southampton	27	0		
2004-05	Southampton	21	1		
2005-06	Southampton	37	3	94	4
2006-07	Stoke C	44	7		
2007-08	Stoke C	1	0		
2007-08	Sunderland	21	3		
2008-09	Sunderland	1	0	22	3
2008-09	Stoke C	28	1	73	8

KITSON, Dave (F)   263   96
H: 6 3   W: 12 07   b.Hitchin 21-1-80
Source: Arlesey.

2000-01	Cambridge U	8	1		
2001-02	Cambridge U	33	9		
2002-03	Cambridge U	44	20		
2003-04	Cambridge U	17	10	102	40
2003-04	Reading	17	5		
2004-05	Reading	37	19		
2005-06	Reading	34	18		
2006-07	Reading	13	2		
2007-08	Reading	34	10		
2008-09	Stoke C	16	0	16	0
2008-09	*Reading*	10	2	145	56

LAWRENCE, Liam (M)   297   66
H: 5 11   W: 12 06   b.Retford 14-12-81
Source: Trainee. *Honours:* Eire 1 full cap.

1999-2000	Mansfield T	2	0		
2000-01	Mansfield T	18	4		
2001-02	Mansfield T	32	2		
2002-03	Mansfield T	43	10		
2003-04	Mansfield T	41	18	136	34
2004-05	Sunderland	32	7		
2005-06	Sunderland	29	3		
2006-07	Sunderland	12	0	73	10
2006-07	Stoke C	27	5		
2007-08	Stoke C	41	14		
2008-09	Stoke C	20	3	88	22

OLOFINJANA, Seyi (M)   187   29
H: 6 4   W: 11 10   b.Lagos 30-6-80
Source: Kwara United Ilorin. *Honours:*
Nigeria 35 full caps.

2003	Brann	25	9		
2004	Brann	9	2	34	11
2004-05	Wolverhampton W	42	5		
2005-06	Wolverhampton W	13	0		
2006-07	Wolverhampton W	44	8		
2007-08	Wolverhampton W	36	3	135	16
2008-09	Stoke C	18	2	18	2

PERICARD, Vincent de Paul (F)   115   17
H: 6 1   W: 13 08   b.Efok 3-10-82
Source: Juventus.

2002-03	Portsmouth	32	9		
2003-04	Portsmouth	6	0		
2004-05	Portsmouth	0	0		
2005-06	Portsmouth	6	0	44	9
2005-06	*Sheffield U*	11	2	11	2
2005-06	*Plymouth Arg*	15	4	15	4
2006-07	Stoke C	29	2		
2007-08	Stoke C	5	0		
2007-08	*Southampton*	5	0	5	0
2008-09	Stoke C	4	0	38	2
2008-09	*Millwall*	2	0	2	0

PHILLIPS, Demar (M)   2   0
H: 5 6   W: 9 04   b.Kingston 23-9-83
Source: Waterhouse. *Honours:* Jamaica 27 full caps.

2007-08	Stoke C	2	0		
2008-09	Stoke C	0	0	2	0

To Aalesund January 2009

PHILLIPS, Jimmy (M)   0   0
b.Stoke
Source: Scholar.

2008-09	Stoke C	0	0		

PUGH, Danny (M)   150   9
H: 6 0   W: 12 10   b.Manchester 19-10-82
Source: Scholar.

2000-01	Manchester U	0	0		
2001-02	Manchester U	0	0		
2002-03	Manchester U	1	0		
2003-04	Manchester U	0	0	1	0
2004-05	Leeds U	38	5		
2005-06	Leeds U	12	0	50	5
2006-07	Preston NE	45	4		
2007-08	Preston NE	7	0	52	4
2007-08	Stoke C	30	0		
2008-09	Stoke C	17	0	47	0

SHAWCROSS, Ryan (D)   71   10
H: 6 3   W: 13 13   b.Buckley 4-10-87
Source: Scholar. *Honours:* England Under-21.

2006-07	Manchester U	0	0		
2007-08	Manchester U	0	0		
2007-08	Stoke C	41	7		
2008-09	Stoke C	30	3	71	10

SHOTTON, Ryan (D)   33   5
H: 6 3   W: 13 05   b.Stoke 30-9-88
Source: Scholar.

2006-07	Stoke C	0	0		
2007-08	Stoke C	0	0		
2008-09	Stoke C	0	0		
2008-09	*Tranmere R*	33	5	33	5

SIDIBE, Mamady (F)   279   39
H: 6 4   W: 12 02   b.Bamako 18-12-79
Source: CA Paris. *Honours:* Mali 8 full caps, 3 goals.

2001-02	Swansea C	31	7	31	7
2002-03	Gillingham	30	3		
2003-04	Gillingham	41	5		
2004-05	Gillingham	35	2	106	10
2005-06	Stoke C	42	6		
2006-07	Stoke C	43	9		
2007-08	Stoke C	35	4		
2008-09	Stoke C	22	3	142	22

SIMONSEN, Steve (G)   228   0
H: 6 2   W: 12 08   b.South Shields 3-4-79
Source: Trainee. *Honours:* England Youth, Under-21.

1996-97	Tranmere R	0	0		
1997-98	Tranmere R	30	0		
1998-99	Tranmere R	5	0	35	0
1998-99	Everton	0	0		
1999-2000	Everton	1	0		
2000-01	Everton	1	0		
2001-02	Everton	25	0		
2002-03	Everton	2	0		
2003-04	Everton	1	0	30	0
2004-05	Stoke C	31	0		
2005-06	Stoke C	45	0		
2006-07	Stoke C	46	0		
2007-08	Stoke C	36	0		
2008-09	Stoke C	5	0	163	0

SOARES, Tom (M)   167   11
H: 6 0   W: 11 04   b.Reading 10-7-86
Source: Scholar. *Honours:* England Youth, Under-20, Under-21.

2003-04	Crystal Palace	3	0		
2004-05	Crystal Palace	22	0		
2005-06	Crystal Palace	44	0		
2006-07	Crystal Palace	37	3		
2007-08	Crystal Palace	39	6		
2008-09	Crystal Palace	4	0	149	10
2008-09	Stoke C	7	0	7	0
2008-09	*Charlton Ath*	11	1	11	1

SONKO, Ibrahima (D)   221   16
H: 6 3   W: 13 07   b.Bignola 22-1-81
Source: St Etienne, Grenoble. *Honours:*
Senegal Under-21, 5 full caps, 1 goal.

2002-03	Brentford	37	5		
2003-04	Brentford	43	3	80	8
2004-05	Reading	39	1		
2005-06	Reading	46	3		
2006-07	Reading	23	1		
2007-08	Reading	16	0		
2008-09	Reading	3	3	127	8
2008-09	Stoke C	14	0	14	0

SORENSEN, Thomas (G)   346   0
H: 6 4   W: 13 10   b.Fredericia 12-6-76
Source: Odense. *Honours:* Denmark Youth, Under-21, B, 80 full caps.

1998-99	Sunderland	45	0		
1999-2000	Sunderland	37	0		
2000-01	Sunderland	34	0		
2001-02	Sunderland	34	0		
2002-03	Sunderland	21	0	171	0
2003-04	Aston Villa	38	0		
2004-05	Aston Villa	36	0		
2005-06	Aston Villa	36	0		
2006-07	Aston Villa	29	0		
2007-08	Aston Villa	0	0	139	0
2008-09	Stoke C	36	0	36	0

ST LOUIS-HAMILTON, Danzelle (G) 0   0
H: 6 5   W: 14 00   b.Stevenage 7-5-90
Source: Scholar.

2008-09	Stoke C	0	0		
2008-09	*Bristol R*	0	0		

THORLEY, Tom (M)   0   0
H: 5 10   W: 11 00   b.Stafford 5-4-90
Source: Scholar.

2008-09	Stoke C	0	0		

TONGE, Michael (M)   272   21
H: 6 0   W: 11 10   b.Manchester 7-4-83
Source: From Scholar. *Honours:* England
Youth, Under-20, Under-21.

2000-01	Sheffield U	2	0		
2001-02	Sheffield U	30	3		
2002-03	Sheffield U	44	6		
2003-04	Sheffield U	46	4		
2004-05	Sheffield U	34	2		
2005-06	Sheffield U	30	3		
2006-07	Sheffield U	27	2		
2007-08	Sheffield U	45	1		
2008-09	Sheffield U	4	0	262	21
2008-09	Stoke C	10	0	10	0

WEDDERBURN, Nathanial (M)   9   0
H: 6 1   W: 13 05   b.Wolverhampton 30-6-91
Source: Scholar.

2008-09	Stoke C	0	0		
2008-09	*Notts Co*	9	0	9	0

WHELAN, Glenn (M)   195   14
H: 5 11   W: 12 07   b.Dublin 13-1-84
Source: Scholar. *Honours:* Eire Youth,
Under-21, B, 12 full caps, 1 goal.

2000-01	Manchester C	0	0		
2001-02	Manchester C	0	0		
2002-03	Manchester C	0	0		
2003-04	Manchester C	0	0		
2003-04	*Bury*	13	0	13	0
2004-05	Sheffield W	36	2		
2005-06	Sheffield W	43	1		
2006-07	Sheffield W	38	7		
2007-08	Sheffield W	25	2	142	12
2007-08	Stoke C	14	1		
2008-09	Stoke C	26	1	40	2

WILKINSON, Andy (D)   75   0
H: 5 11   W: 11 00   b.Stone 6-8-84
Source: Scholar.

2001-02	Stoke C	0	0		
2002-03	Stoke C	0	0		
2003-04	Stoke C	3	0		
2004-05	Stoke C	1	0		
2004-05	*Shrewsbury T*	9	0	9	0
2005-06	Stoke C	6	0		
2006-07	Stoke C	4	0		
2006-07	*Blackpool*	7	0	7	0
2007-08	Stoke C	23	0		
2008-09	Stoke C	22	0	59	0

Scholars
Alexander, Warwick; Cohen, Matthew;
Connor, Ryan; McDonald, Rodney Troy;
Moult, Louis Elliot; Nicholls, Andrew;
Stockhall, Daniel Mark; Urwin, Thomas
William Robert; Vickers, Adam.

SUNDERLAND (80)

ANDERSON, Russell (D)   293   18
H: 5 11   W: 10 09   b.Aberdeen 25-10-78
Source: Dyce J. *Honours:* Scotland Under-21,
11 full caps.

1996-97	Aberdeen	14	0		
1997-98	Aberdeen	26	0		
1998-99	Aberdeen	16	0		
1999-2000	Aberdeen	34	1		
2000-01	Aberdeen	0	0		
2001-02	Aberdeen	24	1		
2002-03	Aberdeen	33	2		
2003-04	Aberdeen	25	5		

2004-05	Aberdeen	31	1		
2005-06	Aberdeen	36	6		
2006-07	Aberdeen	35	2	274	18
2007-08	Sunderland	1	0		
2007-08	*Plymouth Arg*	14	0	14	0
2008-09	Sunderland	0	0	1	0
2008-09	*Burnley*	4	0	4	0

BARDSLEY, Phillip (D) 87 1
H: 5 11 W: 11 13 b.Salford 28-6-85
Source: Trainee.

2003-04	Manchester U	0	0		
2004-05	Manchester U	0	0		
2005-06	Manchester U	8	0		
2005-06	*Burnley*	6	0	6	0
2006-07	Manchester U	0	0		
2006-07	*Rangers*	5	1	5	1
2006-07	*Aston Villa*	13	0	13	0
2007-08	Manchester U	0	0	8	0
2007-08	*Sheffield U*	16	0	16	0
2007-08	Sunderland	11	0		
2008-09	Sunderland	28	0	39	0

CARSON, Trevor (G) 18 0
H: 6 0 W: 14 11 b.Downpatrick 5-3-88
Source: Honours: Northern Ireland Youth, Under-21, B.

2004-05	Sunderland	0	0		
2005-06	Sunderland	0	0		
2006-07	Sunderland	0	0		
2007-08	Sunderland	0	0		
2008-09	Sunderland	0	0		
2008-09	*Chesterfield*	18	0	18	0

CHANDLER, Jamie (M) 0 0
H: 5 7 W: 11 02 b.South Shields 24-3-89
Source: Scholar. *Honours:* England Youth.

| 2007-08 | Sunderland | 0 | 0 | | |
| 2008-09 | Sunderland | 0 | 0 | | |

CHOPRA, Michael (F) 178 62
H: 5 9 W: 10 10 b.Newcastle 23-12-83
Source: Scholar. *Honours:* England Youth, Under-20, Under-21.

2000-01	Newcastle U	0	0		
2001-02	Newcastle U	0	0		
2002-03	Newcastle U	1	0		
2002-03	*Watford*	5	5	5	5
2003-04	Newcastle U	6	0		
2003-04	*Nottingham F*	5	0	5	0
2004-05	Newcastle U	1	0		
2004-05	*Barnsley*	39	17	39	17
2005-06	Newcastle U	13	1	21	1
2006-07	Cardiff C	42	22		
2007-08	Sunderland	33	6		
2008-09	Sunderland	6	2	39	8
2008-09	*Cardiff C*	27	9	69	31

CISSE, Djibril (F) 268 117
H: 6 0 W: 13 00 b.Arles 12-8-81
Honours: France 37 full caps, 9 goals.

1998-99	Auxerre	1	0		
1999-2000	Auxerre	2	0		
2000-01	Auxerre	25	8		
2001-02	Auxerre	29	22		
2002-03	Auxerre	33	14		
2003-04	Auxerre	38	26	128	70
2004-05	Liverpool	16	4		
2005-06	Liverpool	33	9	49	13
2006-07	Marseille	21	8		
2007-08	Marseille	35	16	56	24
2008-09	Sunderland	35	10	35	10

COLBACK, Jack (M) 0 0
H: 5 9 W: 11 05 b.Newcastle 24-10-89
Source: Scholar. *Honours:* England Youth.

| 2007-08 | Sunderland | 0 | 0 | | |
| 2008-09 | Sunderland | 0 | 0 | | |

COLGAN, Nick (G) 248 0
H: 6 1 W: 12 00 b.Drogheda 19-9-73
Source: Drogheda. *Honours:* Eire Schools, Youth, Under-21, B, 9 full caps.

1992-93	Chelsea	0	0		
1993-94	Chelsea	0	0		
1993-94	*Crewe Alex*	0	0		
1994-95	Chelsea	0	0		
1994-95	*Grimsby T*	0	0		
1995-96	Chelsea	0	0		
1995-96	*Millwall*	0	0		
1996-97	Chelsea	1	0		
1997-98	Chelsea	0	0	1	0
1997-98	*Brentford*	5	0	5	0
1997-98	*Reading*	5	0	5	0

1998-99	Bournemouth	0	0		
1999-2000	Hibernian	24	0		
2000-01	Hibernian	37	0		
2001-02	Hibernian	30	0		
2002-03	Hibernian	30	0		
2003-04	Hibernian	0	0	121	0
2003-04	*Stockport Co*	15	0	15	0
2004-05	Barnsley	13	0		
2005-06	Barnsley	43	0		
2006-07	Barnsley	44	0		
2007-08	Barnsley	1	0	101	0
2007-08	*Ipswich T*	0	0		
2008-09	Sunderland	0	0		

COLLINS, Danny (D) 158 4
H: 6 2 W: 11 13 b.Buckley 6-8-80
Source: Buckley T. *Honours:* Wales 7 full caps.

2004-05	Chester C	12	1	12	1
2004-05	Sunderland	14	0		
2005-06	Sunderland	23	1		
2006-07	Sunderland	38	0		
2007-08	Sunderland	36	1		
2008-09	Sunderland	35	1	146	3

CONNOLLY, David (F) 324 135
H: 5 9 W: 11 00 b.Willesden 6-6-77
Source: Trainee. *Honours:* Eire Under-21, 41 full caps, 9 goals.

1994-95	Watford	2	0		
1995-96	Watford	11	8		
1996-97	Watford	13	2	26	10
1997-98	Feyenoord	10	2		
1998-99	Wolverhampton W	32	6	32	6
1999-2000	Excelsior	32	29	32	29
2000-01	Feyenoord	15	5	25	7
2001-02	Wimbledon	35	18		
2002-03	Wimbledon	28	24	63	42
2003-04	West Ham U	39	10	39	10
2004-05	Leicester C	44	13		
2005-06	Leicester C	5	4	49	17
2005-06	Wigan Ath	17	1		
2006-07	Wigan Ath	2	0	19	1
2006-07	Sunderland	36	13		
2007-08	Sunderland	3	0		
2008-09	Sunderland	0	0	39	13

COOK, Jordan (F) 0 0
b.Hetton-le-Hole 20-3-90
Source: Scholar.

| 2007-08 | Sunderland | 0 | 0 | | |
| 2008-09 | Sunderland | 0 | 0 | | |

DOWSON, David (F) 12 3
H: 5 10 W: 12 00 b.Bishop Auckland 12-9-88
Source: Scholar.

2007-08	Sunderland	0	0		
2007-08	*Chesterfield*	12	3	12	3
2008-09	Sunderland	0	0		

EDWARDS, Carlos (M) 290 36
H: 5 8 W: 11 02 b.Port of Spain 24-10-78
Source: Defence Force. *Honours:* Trinidad & Tobago 72 full caps, 4 goals.

2000-01	Wrexham	36	4		
2001-02	Wrexham	26	5		
2002-03	Wrexham	44	8		
2003-04	Wrexham	42	5		
2004-05	Wrexham	18	1	166	23
2005-06	Luton T	42	2		
2006-07	Luton T	26	6	68	8
2006-07	Sunderland	15	5		
2007-08	Sunderland	13	0		
2008-09	Sunderland	22	0	50	5
2008-09	*Wolverhampton W*	6	0	6	0

FERDINAND, Anton (D) 169 5
H: 6 2 W: 11 00 b.Peckham 18-2-85
Source: Trainee. *Honours:* England Youth, Under-20, Under-21.

2002-03	West Ham U	0	0		
2003-04	West Ham U	20	0		
2004-05	West Ham U	29	1		
2005-06	West Ham U	33	2		
2006-07	West Ham U	31	0		
2007-08	West Ham U	25	2		
2008-09	West Ham U	0	0	138	5
2008-09	Sunderland	31	0	31	0

FULOP, Marton (G) 94 0
H: 6 6 W: 14 07 b.Budapest 3-5-83
Source: MTK, Elore, Bodajk. *Honours:* Hungary Under-21, 19 full caps.

2004-05	Tottenham H	0	0		
2004-05	*Chesterfield*	7	0	7	0
2005-06	Tottenham H	0	0		
2005-06	*Coventry C*	31	0	31	0
2006-07	Tottenham H	0	0		
2006-07	Sunderland	5	0		
2007-08	Sunderland	1	0		
2007-08	*Leicester C*	24	0	24	0
2007-08	*Stoke C*	0	0		
2008-09	Sunderland	26	0	32	0

GORDON, Craig (G) 184 0
H: 6 4 W: 12 02 b.Edinburgh 31-12-82
Honours: Scotland Under-21, 36 full caps.

2000-01	Hearts	0	0		
2001-02	Hearts	0	0		
2002-03	Hearts	1	0		
2003-04	Hearts	29	0		
2004-05	Hearts	38	0		
2005-06	Hearts	36	0		
2006-07	Hearts	34	0	138	0
2007-08	Sunderland	34	0		
2008-09	Sunderland	12	0	46	0

HALFORD, Greg (D) 204 24
H: 6 4 W: 12 10 b.Chelmsford 8-12-84
Source: Scholar. *Honours:* England Youth, Under-20.

2002-03	Colchester U	1	0		
2003-04	Colchester U	18	4		
2004-05	Colchester U	44	4		
2005-06	Colchester U	45	7		
2006-07	Colchester U	28	3	136	18
2006-07	*Reading*	3	0	3	0
2007-08	Sunderland	8	0		
2007-08	*Charlton Ath*	16	2	16	2
2008-09	Sunderland	0	0	8	0
2008-09	*Sheffield U*	41	4	41	4

HARTLEY, Peter (D) 13 0
H: 6 0 W: 12 06 b.Hartlepool 3-4-88
Source: Scholar.

2006-07	Sunderland	1	0		
2007-08	Sunderland	0	0		
2007-08	*Chesterfield*	12	0	12	0
2008-09	Sunderland	0	0	1	0

HEALY, David (F) 320 83
H: 5 8 W: 10 09 b.Downpatrick 5-8-79
Source: Trainee. *Honours:* Northern Ireland Schools, Youth, Under-21, B, 74 full caps, 35 goals.

1997-98	Manchester U	0	0		
1998-99	Manchester U	0	0		
1999-2000	Manchester U	0	0		
1999-2000	*Port Vale*	16	3	16	3
2000-01	Manchester U	1	0	1	0
2000-01	Preston NE	22	9		
2001-02	Preston NE	44	10		
2002-03	Preston NE	24	5		
2002-03	*Norwich C*	13	2	13	2
2003-04	Preston NE	38	15		
2004-05	Preston NE	11	5	139	44
2004-05	Leeds U	28	7		
2005-06	Leeds U	42	12		
2006-07	Leeds U	41	10	111	29
2007-08	Fulham	30	4		
2008-09	Fulham	0	0	30	4
2008-09	Sunderland	10	1	10	1

HENDERSON, Jordan (M) 11 1
H: 6 0 W: 10 07 b.Sunderland 17-6-90
Source: Scholar. *Honours:* England Youth.

| 2008-09 | Sunderland | 1 | 0 | 1 | 0 |
| 2008-09 | *Coventry C* | 10 | 1 | 10 | 1 |

HOURIHANE, Conor (M) 0 0
H: 5 11 W: 9 11 b.Cork 2-2-91
Source: Scholar.

| 2008-09 | Sunderland | 0 | 0 | | |

JONES, Kenwyne (F) 153 46
H: 6 2 W: 13 06 b.Trinidad & Tobago 5-10-84
Source: From W Connection. *Honours:* Trindad & Tobago Youth, Under-23, 39 full caps, 4 goals.

| 2004-05 | Southampton | 2 | 0 | | |
| 2004-05 | *Sheffield W* | 7 | 7 | 7 | 7 |

2004-05	Stoke C	13	3	**13**	**3**
2005-06	Southampton	34	4		
2006-07	Southampton	34	14		
2007-08	Southampton	1	1	**71**	**19**
2007-08	Sunderland	33	7		
2008-09	Sunderland	29	10	**62**	**17**

KAY, Michael (D)   **0 0**
H: 6 0 W: 11 05 b.Consett 12-9-89
Source: Scholar.

2007-08	Sunderland	0	0
2008-09	Sunderland	0	0

LEADBITTER, Grant (M)   **115 12**
H: 5 9 W: 11 06 b.Sunderland 7-1-86
Source: Trainee. *Honours:* FA Schools, England Youth, Under-20, Under-21.

2002-03	Sunderland	0	0		
2003-04	Sunderland	0	0		
2004-05	Sunderland	0	0		
2005-06	Sunderland	12	0		
2005-06	*Rotherham U*	5	1	**5**	**1**
2006-07	Sunderland	44	7		
2007-08	Sunderland	31	2		
2008-09	Sunderland	23	2	**110**	**11**

LIDDLE, Michael (D)   **22 0**
H: 5 6 W: 11 00 b.London 25-12-89
Source: Scholar. *Honours:* Eire Under-21.

2007-08	Sunderland	0	0		
2008-09	Sunderland	0	0		
2008-09	*Carlisle U*	22	0	**22**	**0**

LUSCOMBE, Nathan (M)   **0 0**
H: 5 8 W: 11 07 b.Gateshead 6-11-89
Source: Scholar.

2008-09	Sunderland	0	0

M'VOTO, Jean-Yves (D)   **0 0**
H: 6 4 W: 14 00 b.Paris 6-9-88
Source: From Paris St Germain. *Honours:* France Youth.

2007-08	Sunderland	0	0
2008-09	Sunderland	0	0

MADDEN, Daniel (D)   **0 0**
b. 10-9-90
Source: Scholar.

2008-09	Sunderland	0	0

MALBRANQUE, Steed (M)   **347 44**
H: 5 7 W: 11 07 b.Mouscron 6-1-80
Honours: France Under-21.

1997-98	Lyon	2	0		
1998-99	Lyon	21	0		
1999-2000	Lyon	28	3		
2000-01	Lyon	26	2	**77**	**5**
2001-02	Fulham	37	8		
2002-03	Fulham	37	6		
2003-04	Fulham	38	6		
2004-05	Fulham	26	6		
2005-06	Fulham	34	6	**172**	**32**
2006-07	Tottenham H	25	2		
2007-08	Tottenham H	37	4	**62**	**6**
2008-09	Sunderland	36	1	**36**	**1**

McARDLE, Niall (D)   **0 0**
H: 6 1 W: 11 09 b.Dublin 22-3-90
Source: Scholar. *Honours:* Eire Youth.

2007-08	Sunderland	0	0
2008-09	Sunderland	0	0

McCARTNEY, George (D)   **211 1**
H: 5 11 W: 11 02 b.Belfast 29-4-81
Source: Trainee. *Honours:* Northern Ireland Schools, Youth, Under-21, 31 full caps, 1 goal.

1998-99	Sunderland	0	0		
1999-2000	Sunderland	0	0		
2000-01	Sunderland	2	0		
2001-02	Sunderland	18	0		
2002-03	Sunderland	24	0		
2003-04	Sunderland	41	0		
2004-05	Sunderland	36	0		
2005-06	Sunderland	13	0		
2006-07	West Ham U	22	0		
2007-08	West Ham U	38	1		
2008-09	West Ham U	1	0	**61**	**1**
2008-09	Sunderland	16	0	**150**	**0**

McSHANE, Paul (D)   **115 7**
H: 6 0 W: 11 05 b.Wicklow 6-1-86
Source: Trainee. *Honours:* Eire Youth, Under-21, 17 full caps.

2002-03	Manchester U	0	0		
2003-04	Manchester U	0	0		
2004-05	Manchester U	0	0		
2004-05	*Walsall*	4	1	**4**	**1**
2005-06	Manchester U	0	0		
2005-06	*Brighton & HA*	38	3	**38**	**3**
2006-07	*WBA*	32	2	**32**	**2**
2007-08	Sunderland	21	0		
2008-09	Sunderland	3	0	**24**	**0**
2008-09	*Hull C*	17	1	**17**	**1**

MEYLER, David (M)   **2 0**
H: 6 3 W: 11 09 b.Cork 29-5-89
Honours: Eire Under-21.

2008	Cork C	2	0	**2**	**0**
2008-09	Sunderland	0	0		

MURPHY, Daryl (F)   **111 14**
H: 6 2 W: 13 12 b.Waterford 15-3-83
Honours: Eire Youth, Under-21, 9 full caps.

2000-01	Luton T	0	0		
2001-02	Luton T	0	0		
2005-06	Sunderland	18	1		
2005-06	*Sheffield W*	4	0	**4**	**0**
2006-07	Sunderland	38	10		
2007-08	Sunderland	28	3		
2008-09	Sunderland	23	0	**107**	**14**

NOSWORTHY, Nyron (D)   **278 5**
H: 6 0 W: 12 08 b.Brixton 11-10-80
Source: Trainee.

1998-99	Gillingham	3	0		
1999-2000	Gillingham	29	1		
2000-01	Gillingham	10	0		
2001-02	Gillingham	29	0		
2002-03	Gillingham	39	2		
2003-04	Gillingham	27	2		
2004-05	Gillingham	37	0	**174**	**5**
2005-06	Sunderland	30	0		
2006-07	Sunderland	29	0		
2007-08	Sunderland	29	0		
2008-09	Sunderland	16	0	**104**	**0**

O'DONOVAN, Roy (F)   **114 32**
H: 5 10 W: 11 07 b.Cork 10-8-85
Source: Scholar. *Honours:* Eire Under-21, B.

2002-03	Coventry C	0	0		
2003-04	Coventry C	0	0		
2004-05	Coventry C	0	0		
2005	Cork C	26	6		
2006	Cork C	29	11		
2007	Cork C	19	14	**74**	**31**
2007-08	Sunderland	17	0		
2008-09	Sunderland	0	0	**17**	**0**
2008-09	*Dundee U*	11	1	**11**	**1**
2008-09	*Blackpool*	12	0	**12**	**0**

O'MAHONEY, Liam (M)   **0 0**

2008-09	Sunderland	0	0

PRICA, Rade (F)   **276 91**
H: 6 1 W: 12 08 b.Ljungby 30-6-80
Honours: Sweden Under-21, 14 full caps, 2 goals.

1995	Ljungby	6	1		
1996	Ljungby	20	6		
1997	Ljungby	11	8	**37**	**15**
1997	Helsingborg	0	0		
1998	Helsingborg	1	0		
1999	Helsingborg	17	6		
2000	Helsingborg	24	11		
2001	Helsingborg	25	7		
2002	Helsingborg	6	3	**73**	**27**
2002-03	Hansa Rostock	27	7		
2003-04	Hansa Rostock	27	3		
2004-05	Hansa Rostock	29	6		
2005-06	Hansa Rostock	29	4	**112**	**20**
2006-07	Aalborg	32	19		
2007-08	Aalborg	16	9	**48**	**28**
2007-08	Sunderland	6	1		
2008-09	Sunderland	0	0	**6**	**1**

Transferred to Rosenborg March 2009

REID, Andy (M)   **253 31**
H: 5 9 W: 12 08 b.Dublin 29-7-82
Source: Trainee. *Honours:* Eire Youth, Under-21, 27 full caps, 4 goals.

1999-2000	Nottingham F	0	0		
2000-01	Nottingham F	14	2		
2001-02	Nottingham F	29	0		
2002-03	Nottingham F	30	1		
2003-04	Nottingham F	46	13		
2004-05	Nottingham F	25	5	**144**	**21**
2004-05	Tottenham H	13	1		
2005-06	Tottenham H	13	0	**26**	**1**
2006-07	Charlton Ath	16	2		
2007-08	Charlton Ath	22	5	**38**	**7**
2007-08	Sunderland	13	1		
2008-09	Sunderland	32	1	**45**	**2**

RICHARDSON, Kieran (M)   **102 12**
H: 5 9 W: 11 13 b.Greenwich 21-10-84
Source: Scholar. *Honours:* England Under-21, 8 full caps, 2 goals.

2002-03	Manchester U	2	0		
2003-04	Manchester U	2	0		
2004-05	Manchester U	2	0		
2004-05	*WBA*	12	3	**12**	**3**
2005-06	Manchester U	22	1		
2006-07	Manchester U	15	1	**41**	**2**
2007-08	Sunderland	17	3		
2008-09	Sunderland	32	4	**49**	**7**

STAPLES, Daniel (G)   **0 0**
Source: Scholar.

2007-08	Sunderland	0	0
2008-09	Sunderland	0	0

STOKES, Anthony (F)   **77 18**
H: 5 11 W: 11 06 b.Dublin 25-7-88
Source: Scholar. *Honours:* Eire Youth, B, Under-21, 3 full caps.

2005-06	Arsenal	0	0		
2006-07	Arsenal	0	0		
2006-07	*Falkirk*	16	14	**16**	**14**
2006-07	Sunderland	14	2		
2007-08	Sunderland	20	1		
2008-09	Sunderland	2	0	**36**	**3**
2008-09	*Sheffield U*	12	0	**12**	**0**
2008-09	*Crystal Palace*	13	1	**13**	**1**

TAINIO, Teemu (M)   **226 19**
H: 5 9 W: 11 09 b.Tornio 27-11-79
Honours: Finland Youth, Under-21, 48 full caps, 6 goals.

1996	Haka	20	4	**20**	**4**
1997-98	Auxerre	1	0		
1998-99	Auxerre	13	1		
1999-2000	Auxerre	25	3		
2000-01	Auxerre	10	1		
2001-02	Auxerre	28	3		
2002-03	Auxerre	25	1		
2003-04	Auxerre	22	3		
2004-05	Auxerre	0	0	**124**	**12**
2005-06	Tottenham H	24	1		
2006-07	Tottenham H	21	2		
2007-08	Tottenham H	16	0	**61**	**3**
2008-09	Sunderland	21	0	**21**	**0**

WAGHORN, Martyn (F)   **11 1**
H: 5 9 W: 13 01 b.South Shields 23-1-90
Source: Scholar. *Honours:* England Youth.

2007-08	Sunderland	3	0		
2008-09	Sunderland	1	0	**4**	**0**
2008-09	*Charlton Ath*	7	1	**7**	**1**

WARD, Darren (G)   **489 0**
H: 6 0 W: 13 09 b.Worksop 11-5-74
Source: Trainee. *Honours:* Wales Under-21, B, 5 full caps.

1992-93	Mansfield T	13	0		
1993-94	Mansfield T	33	0		
1994-95	Mansfield T	35	0	**81**	**0**
1995-96	Notts Co	46	0		
1996-97	Notts Co	38	0		
1997-98	Notts Co	44	0		
1998-99	Notts Co	43	0		
1999-2000	Notts Co	45	0		
2000-01	Notts Co	35	0	**251**	**0**
2000-01	Nottingham F	0	0		
2001-02	Nottingham F	46	0		
2002-03	Nottingham F	45	0		
2003-04	Nottingham F	32	0		
2004-05	Nottingham F	0	0	**123**	**0**
2004-05	Norwich C	1	0		
2005-06	Norwich C	0	0	**1**	**0**
2006-07	Sunderland	30	0		
2007-08	Sunderland	3	0		
2008-09	Sunderland	0	0	**33**	**0**
2008-09	*Wolverhampton W*	0	0		

WEIR, Robbie (M)   **0 0**
H: 5 9 W: 11 07 b.Belfast 12-12-88
Source: Scholar. *Honours:* Northern Ireland Under-21, B.

2007-08	Sunderland	0	0
2008-09	Sunderland	0	0

WHITEHEAD, Dean (M)   307   22
H: 5 11   W: 12 06   b.Abingdon 12-1-82
Source: Trainee.

1999-2000	Oxford U	0	0		
2000-01	Oxford U	20	0		
2001-02	Oxford U	40	1		
2002-03	Oxford U	18	1		
2003-04	Oxford U	44	7	122	9
2004-05	Sunderland	42	5		
2005-06	Sunderland	37	3		
2006-07	Sunderland	45	4		
2007-08	Sunderland	27	1		
2008-09	Sunderland	34	0	185	13

YORKE, Dwight (F)   481 148
H: 5 10   W: 12 04   b.Canaan 3-11-71
Source: St Clair's, Tobago. *Honours:* Trinidad & Tobago 59 full caps, 16 goals.

1989-90	Aston Villa	2	0		
1990-91	Aston Villa	18	2		
1991-92	Aston Villa	32	11		
1992-93	Aston Villa	27	6		
1993-94	Aston Villa	12	2		
1994-95	Aston Villa	37	6		
1995-96	Aston Villa	35	17		
1996-97	Aston Villa	37	17		
1997-98	Aston Villa	30	12		
1998-99	Aston Villa	1	0	231	73
1998-99	Manchester U	32	18		
1999-2000	Manchester U	32	20		
2000-01	Manchester U	22	9		
2001-02	Manchester U	10	1	96	48
2002-03	Blackburn R	33	8		
2003-04	Blackburn R	23	4		
2004-05	Blackburn R	4	0	60	12
2004-05	Birmingham C	13	2	13	2
2005-06	Sydney	22	7	22	7
2006-07	Sunderland	32	5		
2007-08	Sunderland	20	1		
2008-09	Sunderland	7	0	59	6

Scholars
Adams, Blair; Bagnall, Liam; Brown, David James; Cornforth, Joe Steven; Fletcher, Matthew; Galer, Andrew Brian; Hubbuck, Liam Keith; Lynch, Craig Thomas; Misiewicz, Michal; Noble, Liam Thomas; Noble, Ryan; Reed, Adam Michael; Slegg, Adam; Wilson, Ben; Wilson, Nathan; Wood, Ben Lewis.

SWANSEA C (81)

ALLEN, Joe (M)   30   1
H: 5 6   W: 9 10   b.Carmarthen 14-3-90
Source: Scholar. *Honours:* Wales Under-21, 1 full cap.

2006-07	Swansea C	1	0		
2007-08	Swansea C	6	0		
2008-09	Swansea C	23	1	30	1

BAUZA, Guillem (F)   43   9
H: 5 11   W: 12 01   b.Palma de Mallorca 25-10-84
Source: Mallorca, Espanyol.

2007-08	Swansea C	28	7		
2008-09	Swansea C	15	2	43	9

BESSONE, Fede (D)   25   0
H: 5 11   W: 11 13   b.Cordoba 23-1-84

2007-08	*Gimnastic*	10	0	10	0
2008-09	Swansea C	15	0	15	0

BODDE, Ferrie (M)   211 24
H: 5 10   W: 12 06   b.Delft 4-5-82

2000-01	Den Haag	4	0		
2001-02	Den Haag	27	3		
2002-03	Den Haag	28	2		
2003-04	Den Haag	27	1		
2004-05	Den Haag	29	2		
2005-06	Den Haag	19	2		
2006-07	Den Haag	27	1	161	11
2007-08	Swansea C	33	6		
2008-09	Swansea C	17	7	50	13

BOND, Chad (F)   0   0
H: 6 0   W: 11 00   b.Neath 20-4-87
Source: Scholar. *Honours:* Wales Youth.

2005-06	Swansea C	0	0		
2006-07	Swansea C	0	0		
2007-08	Swansea C	0	0		
2008-09	Swansea C	0	0		

BRITTON, Leon (M)   259 10
H: 5 6   W: 10 00   b.Merton 16-9-82
Source: Trainee. *Honours:* England Youth.

1999-2000	West Ham U	0	0		
2000-01	West Ham U	0	0		
2001-02	West Ham U	0	0		
2002-03	West Ham U	0	0		
2002-03	*Swansea C*	25	0		
2003-04	Swansea C	42	3		
2004-05	Swansea C	30	1		
2005-06	Swansea C	38	4		
2006-07	Swansea C	41	2		
2007-08	Swansea C	40	0		
2008-09	Swansea C	43	0	259	10

BUTLER, Thomas (M)   189 10
H: 5 7   W: 12 00   b.Dublin 25-4-81
Source: Trainee. *Honours:* Eire Youth, Under-21, 2 full caps.

1998-99	Sunderland	0	0		
1999-2000	Sunderland	1	0		
2000-01	Sunderland	4	0		
2000-01	*Darlington*	8	0	8	0
2001-02	Sunderland	7	0		
2002-03	Sunderland	7	0		
2003-04	Sunderland	12	0	31	0
2004-05	Dunfermline Ath	12	0	12	0
2004-05	Hartlepool U	9	1		
2005-06	Hartlepool U	28	1	37	2
2006-07	Swansea C	30	1		
2007-08	Swansea C	42	6		
2008-09	Swansea C	29	1	101	8

COLLINS, Matty (M)   5   0
H: 5 8   W: 10 10   b.Merthyr 31-3-86
Source: Trainee. *Honours:* Wales Youth, Under-21.

2002-03	Fulham	0	0		
2003-04	Fulham	0	0		
2004-05	Fulham	0	0		
2005-06	Fulham	0	0		
2006-07	Fulham	0	0		
2007-08	Swansea C	0	0		
2007-08	*Wrexham*	2	0	2	0
2008-09	Swansea C	3	0	3	0

DE VRIES, Dorus (G)   244 0
H: 6 1   W: 12 08   b.Beverwijk 29-12-80

1999-2000	Telstar	1	0		
2000-01	Telstar	27	0		
2001-02	Telstar	27	0		
2002-03	Telstar	26	0	81	0
2003-04	Den Haag	18	0		
2004-05	Den Haag	32	0		
2005-06	Den Haag	0	0	50	0
2006-07	Dunfermline Ath	27	0	27	0
2007-08	Swansea C	46	0		
2008-09	Swansea C	40	0	86	0

EVANS, Scott (M)   0   0
H: 6 0   W: 11 07   b.Swansea 6-1-89
Source: Manchester C Scholar.

2006-07	Swansea C	0	0		
2007-08	Swansea C	0	0		
2008-09	Swansea C	0	0		

GOMEZ, Jordi (M)   67 12
H: 5 10   W: 11 09   b.Barcelona 24-5-85

2006-07	Espanyol B	21	0	21	0
2007-08	Espanyol	2	0	2	0
on loan from Espanyol.					
2008-09	Swansea C	44	12	44	12

GOWER, Mark (M)   262 37
H: 5 11   W: 11 12   b.Edmonton 5-10-78
Source: Trainee. *Honours:* England Schools, Youth.

1996-97	Tottenham H	0	0		
1997-98	Tottenham H	0	0		
1998-99	Tottenham H	0	0		
1998-99	*Motherwell*	9	1	9	1
1999-2000	Tottenham H	0	0		
2000-01	Tottenham H	0	0		
2000-01	Barnet	14	1		
2001-02	Barnet	0	0		
2002-03	Barnet	0	0	14	1
2003-04	Southend U	40	6		
2004-05	Southend U	38	6		
2005-06	Southend U	40	6		
2006-07	Southend U	43	8		
2007-08	Southend U	42	9	203	35
2008-09	Swansea C	36	0	36	0

JONES, Chris (F)   7   0
H: 5 7   W: 10 00   b.Swansea 12-9-89
Honours: Wales Youth, Under-21.

2006-07	Swansea C	7	0		
2007-08	Swansea C	0	0		
2008-09	Swansea C	0	0	7	0

MACDONALD, Shaun (M)   25   2
H: 6 1   W: 11 04   b.Swansea 17-6-88
Source: Scholar. *Honours:* Wales Youth, Under-21.

2005-06	Swansea C	7	0		
2006-07	Swansea C	8	0		
2007-08	Swansea C	1	0		
2008-09	Swansea C	5	0	21	0
2008-09	*Yeovil T*	4	2	4	2

MONK, Garry (D)   202 3
H: 6 0   W: 12 01   b.Bedford 6-3-79
Source: Trainee.

1995-96	Torquay U	5	0		
1996-97	Southampton	0	0		
1997-98	Southampton	0	0		
1998-99	Southampton	4	0		
1998-99	*Torquay U*	6	0	11	0
1999-2000	Southampton	2	0		
1999-2000	*Stockport Co*	2	0	2	0
2000-01	Southampton	2	0		
2000-01	*Oxford U*	5	0	5	0
2001-02	Southampton	2	0		
2002-03	Southampton	1	0		
2002-03	*Sheffield W*	15	0	15	0
2003-04	Southampton	0	0	11	0
2003-04	Barnsley	17	0	17	0
2004-05	Swansea C	34	0		
2005-06	Swansea C	33	1		
2006-07	Swansea C	2	0		
2007-08	Swansea C	32	1		
2008-09	Swansea C	40	1	141	3

MORGAN, Kerry (M)   0   0
H: 5 10   W: 11 03   b.Merthyr 31-10-88
Source: Scholar.

2008-09	Swansea C	0	0		

O'LEARY, Kristian (M)   289 11
H: 5 11   W: 12 09   b.Port Talbot 30-8-77
Source: From Trainee. *Honours:* Wales Youth.

1995-96	Swansea C	1	0		
1996-97	Swansea C	12	1		
1997-98	Swansea C	29	0		
1998-99	Swansea C	19	2		
1999-2000	Swansea C	20	0		
2000-01	Swansea C	24	2		
2001-02	Swansea C	31	2		
2002-03	Swansea C	33	0		
2003-04	Swansea C	34	0		
2004-05	Swansea C	32	1		
2005-06	Swansea C	15	1		
2006-07	Swansea C	23	1		
2006-07	*Cheltenham T*	5	1	5	1
2007-08	Swansea C	11	0		
2008-09	Swansea C	0	0	284	10

ORLANDI, Andrea (M)   87   6
H: 6 0   W: 12 01   b.Barcelona 3-8-84

2005-06	Alaves	0	0		
2005-06	*Barcelona*	1	0		
2005-06	Barcelona B	32	4		
2006-07	*Barcelona B*	35	1	1	0
2007-08	Swansea C	8	0		
2008-09	Swansea C	11	1	19	1

PAINTER, Marcos (D)   69   0
H: 5 11   W: 12 04   b.Solihull 17-8-86
Source: Scholar. *Honours:* Eire Youth, Under-21.

2005-06	Birmingham C	4	0		
2006-07	Birmingham C	1	0	5	0
2006-07	Swansea C	23	0		
2007-08	Swansea C	30	0		
2008-09	Swansea C	11	0	64	0

PINTADO, Gorka (F)   267 77
H: 5 11   W: 11 06   b.San Sebastian 24-3-78

2000-01	Union Irun	28	2	28	2
2001-02	Osasuna	35	10	35	10
2002-03	Leganes	12	0		
2003-04	Leganes	4	0	16	0
2003-04	Figures	3	0		
2004-05	Figures	34	7	37	7
2005-06	Gramenet	37	17		
2006-07	Gramenet	36	18	73	35

2007-08	Granada	38	18	**38**	**18**
2008-09	Swansea C	40	5	**40**	**5**

PRATLEY, Darren (M)   **154 15**
H: 6 1   W: 10 12   b.Barking 22-4-85
Source: Scholar.

2001-02	Fulham	0	0		
2002-03	Fulham	0	0		
2003-04	Fulham	1	0		
2004-05	Fulham	0	0		
2004-05	Brentford	14	1		
2005-06	Fulham	0	0	**1**	**0**
2005-06	Brentford	32	4	**46**	**5**
2006-07	Swansea C	28	1		
2007-08	Swansea C	42	5		
2008-09	Swansea C	37	4	**107**	**10**

RANGEL, Angel (D)   **117 5**
H: 5 11   W: 11 09   b.Tortosa 28-10-82
Source: Tortosa, Reus Deportiu, Girona, Sant Andreu.

2006-07	Terrassa	34	2	**34**	**2**
2007-08	Swansea C	43	2		
2008-09	Swansea C	40	1	**83**	**3**

SCOTLAND, Jason (F)   **206 85**
H: 5 8   W: 11 10   b.Morvant 18-2-79
Source: San Juan Jabloteh, Defence Force.
Honours: Trinidad & Tobago 38 full caps, 8 goals.

2003-04	Dundee U	21	4		
2004-05	Dundee U	29	3	**50**	**7**
2005-06	St Johnstone	31	15		
2006-07	St Johnstone	35	18	**66**	**33**
2007-08	Swansea C	45	24		
2008-09	Swansea C	45	21	**90**	**45**

SERRAN, Albert (D)   **16 0**
H: 6 0   W: 12 10   b.Barcelona 17-7-84

2006-07	Espanyol	2	0		
2007-08	Espanyol	1	0	**3**	**0**
2008-09	Swansea C	13	0	**13**	**0**

TATE, Alan (D)   **203 4**
H: 6 1   W: 13 05   b.Easington 2-9-82
Source: Scholar.

2000-01	Manchester U	0	0		
2001-02	Manchester U	0	0		
2002-03	Manchester U	0	0		
2002-03	*Swansea C*	27	0		
2003-04	Manchester U	0	0		
2003-04	Swansea C	26	1		
2004-05	Swansea C	23	0		
2005-06	Swansea C	43	0		
2006-07	Swansea C	38	1		
2007-08	Swansea C	21	1		
2008-09	Swansea C	25	1	**203**	**4**

TUDUR JONES, Owain (M)   **53 4**
H: 6 2   W: 12 00   b.Bangor 15-10-84
Source: Bangor C. *Honours:* Wales Under-21, 4 full caps.

2005-06	Swansea C	21	3		
2006-07	Swansea C	4	0		
2007-08	Swansea C	8	0		
2008-09	Swansea C	9	0	**42**	**3**
2008-09	*Swindon T*	11	1	**11**	**1**

WILLIAMS, Ashley (D)   **211 5**
H: 6 0   W: 11 02   b.Wolverhampton 23-8-84
Source: Hednesford T. *Honours:* Wales 13 full caps.

2003-04	Stockport Co	10	0		
2004-05	Stockport Co	44	1		
2005-06	Stockport Co	36	1		
2006-07	Stockport Co	46	1		
2007-08	Stockport Co	26	0	**162**	**3**
2007-08	*Swansea C*	3	0		
2008-09	Swansea C	46	2	**49**	**2**

SWINDON T (82)

ALJOFREE, Hasney (D)   **248 9**
H: 6 0   W: 12 00   b.Manchester 11-7-78
Source: Trainee.

1996-97	Bolton W	0	0		
1997-98	Bolton W	2	0		
1998-98	Bolton W	4	0		
1999-2000	Bolton W	8	0	**14**	**0**
2000-01	Dundee U	26	2		
2001-02	Dundee U	27	2	**53**	**4**
2002-03	Plymouth Arg	19	1		
2003-04	Plymouth Arg	24	0		

2004-05	Plymouth Arg	12	1		
2004-05	*Sheffield W*	2	0	**2**	**0**
2005-06	Plymouth Arg	37	1		
2006-07	Plymouth Arg	25	0	**117**	**3**
2006-07	*Oldham Ath*	5	0	**5**	**0**
2007-08	Swindon T	39	2		
2008-09	Swindon T	18	0	**57**	**2**

ALLEN, Chris (M)   **12 0**
H: 5 11   W: 11 10   b.Bristol 3-1-89
Source: Scholar.

2007-08	Swindon T	8	0		
2008-09	Swindon T	4	0	**12**	**0**

AMANKWAAH, Kevin (D)   **185 4**
H: 6 1   W: 12 12   b.Harrow 19-5-82
Source: Scholar. *Honours:* England Youth.

1999-2000	Bristol C	5	0		
2000-01	Bristol C	14	0		
2001-02	Bristol C	24	1		
2002-03	Bristol C	1	0		
2002-03	*Torquay U*	6	0	**6**	**0**
2003-04	Bristol C	5	0		
2003-04	*Cheltenham T*	12	0	**12**	**0**
2004-05	Bristol C	5	0	**54**	**1**
2004-05	Yeovil T	15	0		
2005-06	Yeovil T	38	1	**53**	**1**
2006-07	Swansea C	29	0		
2007-08	Swansea C	0	0	**29**	**0**
2008-09	Swindon T	31	2	**31**	**2**

BREZOVAN, Peter (G)   **93 0**
H: 6 6   W: 14 13   b.Bratislava 9-12-79
Source: PS Bratislava, Vinohrady, Devin, Slovan Breclav, Zigma Olomouc. *Honours:* Slovakia Under-21.

2002-03	Brno	10	0		
2003-04	Brno	2	0		
2004-05	Inter Bratislava	8	0	**8**	**0**
2005-06	Brno	7	0	**19**	**0**
2006-07	Swindon T	14	0		
2007-08	Swindon T	31	0		
2008-09	Swindon T	21	0	**66**	**0**

CASAL, Kasali Yinka (D)   **29 0**
H: 6 1   W: 12 08   b.Hendon 21-10-87
Source: Fulham Academy.

2007	DC United	4	0	**4**	**0**
2007-08	Cambuur	20	0	**20**	**0**
2008-09	Swindon T	5	0	**5**	**0**

CORR, Barry (F)   **56 10**
H: 6 3   W: 12 07   b.Co Wicklow 2-4-85
Honours: Eire Youth.

2001-02	Leeds U	0	0		
2002-03	Leeds U	0	0		
2003-04	Leeds U	0	0		
2004-05	Leeds U	0	0		
2005-06	Sheffield W	16	0		
2006-07	Sheffield W	1	0	**17**	**0**
2006-07	*Bristol C*	3	0	**3**	**0**
2006-07	*Swindon T*	8	3		
2007-08	Swindon T	17	5		
2008-09	Swindon T	11	2	**36**	**10**

COX, Simon (M)   **104 47**
H: 5 10   W: 10 12   b.Reading 28-4-87
Source: Scholar.

2005-06	Reading	2	0		
2006-07	Reading	0	0		
2006-07	Brentford	13	0	**13**	**0**
2006-07	*Northampton T*	8	3	**8**	**3**
2007-08	Reading	0	0	**2**	**0**
2007-08	*Swindon T*	36	15		
2008-09	Swindon T	45	29	**81**	**44**

EASTON, Craig (M)   **195 15**
H: 5 11   W: 11 03   b.Bellshill 26-2-79
Source: Dundee U BC. *Honours:* Scotland Youth, Under-21.

1995-96	Dundee U	0	0		
1996-97	Dundee U	2	0		
1997-98	Dundee U	29	1		
1998-99	Dundee U	30	1		
1999-2000	Dundee U	0	0		
2000-01	Dundee U	0	0		
2001-02	Dundee U	0	0	**61**	**2**
2005-06	Leyton Orient	41	4		
2006-07	Leyton Orient	30	1	**71**	**5**
2007-08	Swindon T	40	6		
2008-09	Swindon T	23	2	**63**	**8**

EVANS, Tom (D)   **0 0**
H: 6 1   W: 12 00   b.Surrey 20-6-90
Source: Southampton. *Honours:* Wales Youth.

2008-09	Swindon T	0	0		

HAMMONDS, Kurt (M)   **0 0**
b.Wakefield 6-12-90
Source: Scholar.

2007-08	Swindon T	0	0		
2008-09	Swindon T	0	0		

HYDE, Jake (F)   **0 0**
b.Slough
Source: Scholar.

2007-08	Swindon T	0	0		
2008-09	Swindon T	0	0		

IFIL, Jerel (D)   **219 3**
H: 6 1   W: 12 10   b.Wembley 27-6-82
Source: Academy.

1999-2000	Watford	0	0		
2000-01	Watford	0	0		
2001-02	Watford	0	0		
2001-02	*Huddersfield T*	2	0	**2**	**0**
2002-03	Watford	1	0		
2002-03	*Swindon T*	9	0		
2003-04	Watford	10	0	**11**	**0**
2003-04	*Swindon T*	16	0		
2004-05	Swindon T	35	0		
2005-06	Swindon T	36	0		
2006-07	Swindon T	40	1		
2007-08	Swindon T	40	1		
2008-09	Swindon T	30	1	**206**	**3**

JOYCE, Ben (F)   **4 1**
H: 5 8   W: 11 04   b.Plymouth 9-9-89

2007-08	Swindon T	3	1		
2008-09	Swindon T	1	0	**4**	**1**

KANYUKA, Patrick (D)   **32 1**
H: 6 0   W: 12 06   b.Kinshasa 19-7-87
Source: QPR Juniors.

2004-05	QPR	1	0		
2005-06	QPR	0	0		
2006-07	QPR	11	0		
2007-08	QPR	0	0	**12**	**0**
2007-08	*Swindon T*	4	0		
2008-09	Swindon T	16	1	**20**	**1**

KENNEDY, Callum (M)   **4 0**
H: 6 1   W: 12 10   b.Chertsey 9-11-89
Source: Scholar.

2007-08	Swindon T	0	0		
2008-09	Swindon T	4	0	**4**	**0**

LESCINEL, Jean-Francois (M)   **25 0**
H: 6 2   W: 12 04   b.Cayenne 2-10-86
Source: Paris St Germain, Sedan. *Honours:* Haiti 1 full cap.

2006-07	Falkirk	8	0	**8**	**0**
2006-07	Guingamp	12	0	**12**	**0**
2008-09	Swindon T	5	0	**5**	**0**

MACKLIN, Lloyd (M)   **2 0**
H: 5 9   W: 12 03   b.Camberley 2-8-91

2007-08	Swindon T	0	0		
2008-09	Swindon T	2	0	**2**	**0**

MARSHALL, Mark (M)   **12 0**
H: 5 7   W: 10 07   b.Manchester, Jam 9-5-86
Source: Carshalton Ath, Grays Ath, Eastleigh.

2008-09	Swindon T	12	0	**12**	**0**

McGOVERN, John-Paul (M)   **182 14**
H: 5 10   W: 12 02   b.Glasgow 3-10-80
Source: Celtic BC.

2001-02	Celtic	0	0		
2002-03	Celtic	0	0		
2002-03	*Sheffield U*	15	1	**15**	**1**
2003-04	Celtic	0	0		
2004-05	Sheffield W	46	6		
2005-06	Sheffield W	7	0	**53**	**6**
2006-07	Milton Keynes D	44	3		
2007-08	Milton Keynes D	3	0	**47**	**3**
2007-08	*Swindon T*	41	2		
2008-09	Swindon T	26	2	**67**	**4**

McNAMEE, Anthony (M)   **158 4**
H: 5 6   W: 10 03   b.Kensington 13-7-84
Source: Scholar. *Honours:* England Youth, Under-20.

2001-02	Watford	7	1		
2002-03	Watford	23	0		
2003-04	Watford	2	0		

2004-05	Watford	14	0		
2005-06	Watford	38	1		
2006-07	Watford	7	0		
2006-07	Crewe Alex	5	0	5	0
2007-08	Watford	0	0	91	0
2007-08	Swindon T	19	2		
2008-09	Swindon T	43	0	62	2

MORRIS, Samuel (M)   **0 0**
b.Swindon 17-12-89
Source: Scholar.

2007-08	Swindon T	0	0
2008-09	Swindon T	0	0

MORRISON, Sean (D)   **22 1**
H: 6 4   W: 14 00   b.Plymouth 8-1-91
Source: Plymouth Arg.

2007-08	Swindon T	2	0		
2008-09	Swindon T	20	1	22	1

NALIS, Lilian (M)   **443 33**
H: 6 1   W: 11 00   b.Nogent sur Marne
29-9-71

1992-93	Auxerre	0	0		
1993-94	Caen	16	0		
1994-95	Caen	4	0	20	0
1995-96	Laval	42	4		
1996-97	Laval	39	8	81	12
1997-98	Guingamp	30	0	30	0
1998-99	Le Havre	27	3	27	3
1999-2000	Bastia	28	1		
2000-01	Bastia	28	1		
2001-02	Bastia	26	2	82	4
2002-03	Chievo	8	0	8	0
2003-04	Leicester C	20	1		
2004-05	Leicester C	39	5	59	6
2005-06	Sheffield U	4	0	4	0
2005-06	Coventry C	6	2	6	2
2005-06	Plymouth Arg	20	1		
2006-07	Plymouth Arg	42	4		
2007-08	Plymouth Arg	40	1	102	6
2008-09	Swindon T	24	0	24	0

PAYNTER, Billy (F)   **268 56**
H: 6 1   W: 14 01   b.Liverpool 13-7-84
Source: Schoolboy.

2000-01	Port Vale	1	0		
2001-02	Port Vale	7	0		
2002-03	Port Vale	31	5		
2003-04	Port Vale	44	13		
2004-05	Port Vale	45	10		
2005-06	Port Vale	16	2	144	30
2005-06	Hull C	22	3	22	3
2006-07	Southend U	9	0		
2006-07	Bradford C	15	4	15	4
2007-08	Southend U	0	0	9	0
2007-08	Swindon T	36	8		
2008-09	Swindon T	42	11	78	19

PEACOCK, Lee (F)   **489 120**
H: 6 0   W: 12 07   b.Paisley 9-10-76
Source: Trainee. *Honours:* Scotland Youth,
Under-21.

1993-94	Carlisle U	1	0		
1994-95	Carlisle U	7	0		
1995-96	Carlisle U	22	2		
1996-97	Carlisle U	44	9		
1997-98	Carlisle U	2	0	76	11
1997-98	Mansfield T	32	5		
1998-99	Mansfield T	45	17		
1999-2000	Mansfield T	12	7	89	29
1999-2000	Manchester C	8	0	8	0
2000-01	Bristol C	35	13		
2001-02	Bristol C	31	15		
2002-03	Bristol C	37	12		
2003-04	Bristol C	41	14	144	54
2004-05	Sheffield W	29	4		
2005-06	Sheffield W	22	2	51	6
2005-06	Swindon T	15	2		
2006-07	Swindon T	42	10		
2007-08	Swindon T	37	6		
2008-09	Swindon T	27	2	121	20

POOK, Michael (M)   **109 3**
H: 5 11   W: 11 10   b.Swindon 22-10-85
Source: Scholar.

2003-04	Swindon T	0	0		
2004-05	Swindon T	5	0		
2005-06	Swindon T	30	0		
2006-07	Swindon T	38	2		
2007-08	Swindon T	22	1		
2008-09	Swindon T	14	0	109	3

RAZAK, Hamdi (F)   **3 0**
H: 6 2   W: 13 07   b.Paris 8-10-85
Source: US Chantilly, Les Lilas, Leval, Igny.

2008-09	Swindon T	3	0	3	0

ROBERTS, Chris (F)   **307 63**
H: 5 11   W: 12 08   b.Cardiff 22-10-79
Source: Trainee. *Honours:* Wales Youth,
Under-21.

1997-98	Cardiff C	11	3		
1998-99	Cardiff C	4	0		
1999-2000	Cardiff C	8	0	23	3
2000-01	Exeter C	42	8		
2001-02	Exeter C	37	11	79	19
2001-02	Bristol C	4	0		
2002-03	Bristol C	44	13		
2003-04	Bristol C	38	6		
2004-05	Bristol C	8	1	94	20
2004-05	Swindon T	21	3		
2005-06	Swindon T	21	3		
2006-07	Swindon T	42	10		
2007-08	Swindon T	27	5		
2008-09	Swindon T	0	0	111	21

SCOTT, Mark (G)   **0 0**
b.Fleet 3-1-91
Source: Scholar.

2007-08	Swindon T	0	0
2008-09	Swindon T	0	0

SMITH, Jack (D)   **163 11**
H: 5 11   W: 11 05   b.Hemel Hempstead
14-10-83
Source: Scholar.

2001-02	Watford	0	0		
2002-03	Watford	1	0		
2003-04	Watford	17	2		
2004-05	Watford	7	0	25	2
2005-06	Swindon T	38	0		
2006-07	Swindon T	41	3		
2007-08	Swindon T	21	1		
2008-09	Swindon T	38	5	138	9

SMITH, Phil (G)   **76 0**
H: 6 1   W: 13 11   b.Harrow 14-12-79
Source: Scholar.

1997-98	Millwall	0	0		
1998-99	Millwall	5	0	5	0
From Folkestone, Dover, Margate, Crawley					
2006-07	Swindon T	31	0		
2007-08	Swindon T	15	0		
2008-09	Swindon T	25	0	71	0

STURROCK, Blair (F)   **197 25**
H: 5 10   W: 12 09   b.Dundee 25-8-81
Source: Dundee U.

2000-01	Brechin C	27	6	27	6
2001-02	Plymouth Arg	19	1		
2002-03	Plymouth Arg	20	1		
2003-04	Plymouth Arg	24	0		
2004-05	Plymouth Arg	0	0	63	2
2004-05	Kidderminster H	22	5	22	5
2005-06	Rochdale	31	6		
2006-07	Rochdale	0	0	31	6
2006-07	Swindon T	19	3		
2007-08	Swindon T	21	3		
2008-09	Swindon T	10	0	50	6
2008-09	Bournemouth	4	0	4	0

TIMLIN, Michael (M)   **79 4**
H: 5 8   W: 11 08   b.Lambeth 19-3-85
Source: Trainee. *Honours:* Eire Youth,
Under-21.

2002-03	Fulham	0	0		
2003-04	Fulham	0	0		
2004-05	Fulham	0	0		
2005-06	Fulham	0	0		
2005-06	Scunthorpe U	1	0	1	0
2005-06	Doncaster R	3	0	3	0
2006-07	Fulham	0	0		
2006-07	Swindon T	24	1		
2007-08	Fulham	10	1		
2008-09	Swindon T	41	2	75	4

VINCENT, Jamie (D)   **382 10**
H: 5 10   W: 11 08   b.Wimbledon 18-6-75
Source: Trainee.

1993-94	Crystal Palace	0	0		
1994-95	Crystal Palace	0	0		
1994-95	Bournemouth	8	0		
1995-96	Crystal Palace	25	0		
1996-97	Crystal Palace	0	0	25	0
1996-97	Bournemouth	29	0		

1997-98	Bournemouth	44	3		
1998-99	Bournemouth	32	2	113	5
1998-99	Huddersfield T	7	0		
1999-2000	Huddersfield T	36	2		
2000-01	Huddersfield T	16	0	59	2
2000-01	Portsmouth	14	0		
2001-02	Portsmouth	34	1		
2002-03	Portsmouth	0	0		
2003-04	Portsmouth	0	0	48	1
2003-04	Walsall	12	0	12	0
2003-04	Derby Co	7	1		
2004-05	Derby Co	15	1	22	2
2005-06	Millwall	19	0	19	0
2005-06	Yeovil T	0	0		
2006-07	Swindon T	34	0		
2007-08	Swindon T	32	0		
2008-09	Swindon T	18	0	84	0

WINTER, Jack (D)   **0 0**
b.Hammersmith
Source: Scholar.

2007-08	Swindon T	0	0
2008-09	Swindon T	0	0

TOTTENHAM H (83)

ALNWICK, Ben (G)   **37 0**
H: 6 2   W: 13 12   b.Prudhoe 1-1-87
Source: Scholar. *Honours:* England Youth,
Under-21.

2003-04	Sunderland	0	0		
2004-05	Sunderland	3	0		
2005-06	Sunderland	5	0		
2006-07	Sunderland	11	0	19	0
2006-07	Tottenham H	0	0		
2007-08	Tottenham H	0	0		
2007-08	Luton T	4	0	4	0
2007-08	Leicester C	8	0	8	0
2008-09	Tottenham H	0	0		
2008-09	Carlisle U	6	0	6	0

ARCHIBALD-HENVILLE, Troy (D) 19   0
H: 6 2   W: 13 03   b.Newham 4-11-88
Source: Scholar.

2007-08	Tottenham H	0	0		
2008-09	Tottenham H	0	0		
2008-09	Norwich C	0	0		
2008-09	Exeter C	19	0	19	0

ASSOU-EKOTTO, Benoit (M)   **112 0**
H: 5 10   W: 10 12   b.Arras 24-3-84
Honours: Cameroon B, 2 full caps.

2003-04	Lens	1	0		
2004-05	Lens	29	0		
2005-06	Lens	34	0	66	0
2006-07	Tottenham H	16	0		
2007-08	Tottenham H	1	0		
2008-09	Tottenham H	29	0	46	0

BALE, Gareth (D)   **64 7**
H: 6 0   W: 11 10   b.Cardiff 16-7-89
Source: Scholar. *Honours:* Wales Youth,
Under-21, 20 full caps, 2 goals.

2005-06	Southampton	2	0		
2006-07	Southampton	38	5	40	5
2007-08	Tottenham H	8	2		
2008-09	Tottenham H	16	0	24	2

BENT, Darren (F)   **250 98**
H: 5 11   W: 12 07   b.Wandsworth 6-2-84
Source: Scholar. *Honours:* England Youth,
Under-21, 4 full caps.

2001-02	Ipswich T	5	1		
2002-03	Ipswich T	35	12		
2003-04	Ipswich T	37	16		
2004-05	Ipswich T	45	20	122	49
2005-06	Charlton Ath	36	18		
2006-07	Charlton Ath	32	13	68	31
2007-08	Tottenham H	27	6		
2008-09	Tottenham H	33	12	60	18

BENTLEY, David (F)   **154 16**
H: 5 10   W: 11 03   b.Peterborough 27-8-84
Source: Scholar. *Honours:* England Youth,
Under-20, Under-21, B, 7 full caps.

2001-02	Arsenal	0	0		
2002-03	Arsenal	0	0		
2003-04	Arsenal	1	0		
2004-05	Arsenal	0	0		
2004-05	Norwich C	26	2	26	2
2005-06	Arsenal	0	0	1	0
2005-06	Blackburn R	29	3		

Season	Club	Apps	Gls	Tot A	Tot G
2006-07	Blackburn R	36	4		
2007-08	Blackburn R	37	6	102	13
2008-09	Tottenham H	25	1	25	1

BERCHICHE, Yuri (D)   **7 0**
H: 5 11   W: 12 03   b.Zaroutz 10-2-90
Source: Athletic Bilbao.

Season	Club	Apps	Gls	Tot A	Tot G
2007-08	Tottenham H	0	0		
2008-09	Tottenham H	0	0		
2008-09	*Cheltenham T*	7	0	7	0

BOATENG, Kevin-Prince (M)   **56 4**
H: 6 0   W: 11 09   b.Berlin 6-3-87
Honours: Germany Under-21.

Season	Club	Apps	Gls	Tot A	Tot G
2005-06	Hertha Berlin	21	2		
2006-07	Hertha Berlin	21	2	42	4
2007-08	Tottenham H	13	0		
2008-09	Tottenham H	1	0	14	0

On loan to Borussia Dortmund

BOSTOCK, John (M)   **4 0**
H: 5 10   W: 11 11   b.Romford 13-10-91
Honours: England Youth.

Season	Club	Apps	Gls	Tot A	Tot G
2007-08	Crystal Palace	4	0	4	0
2008-09	Tottenham H	0	0		

BUTCHER, Callum (D)   **0 0**
b.Rochford 26-2-91
Source: Scholar.

Season	Club	Apps	Gls	Tot A	Tot G
2007-08	Tottenham H	0	0		
2008-09	Tottenham H	0	0		

BUTTON, David (G)   **7 0**
H: 6 3   W: 13 00   b.Stevenage 27-2-89
Source: Scholar. *Honours:* England Youth.

Season	Club	Apps	Gls	Tot A	Tot G
2005-06	Tottenham H	0	0		
2006-07	Tottenham H	0	0		
2007-08	*Rochdale*	0	0		
2007-08	Tottenham H	0	0		
2008-09	Tottenham H	0	0		
2008-09	*Bournemouth*	4	0	4	0
2008-09	*Luton T*	0	0		
2008-09	*Dagenham & R*	3	0	3	0

CHIMBONDA, Pascal (D)   **271 14**
H: 5 10   W: 11 05   b.Les Abymes 21-2-79
Honours: France 1 full cap.

Season	Club	Apps	Gls	Tot A	Tot G
1999-2000	Le Havre	2	0		
2000-01	Le Havre	32	1		
2001-02	Le Havre	27	2		
2002-03	Le Havre	24	2	85	5
2003-04	Bastia	31	1		
2004-05	Bastia	36	3	67	4
2005-06	Wigan Ath	37	2		
2006-07	Wigan Ath	1	0	38	2
2006-07	Tottenham H	33	1		
2007-08	Tottenham H	32	2		
2008-09	Sunderland	13	0	13	0
2008-09	Tottenham H	3	0	68	3

CORLUKA, Vedran (D)   **160 12**
H: 6 3   W: 13 03   b.Zagreb 9-2-86
Honours: Croatia 32 full caps.

Season	Club	Apps	Gls	Tot A	Tot G
2003-04	Dynamo Zagreb	0	0		
2004-05	Inter Zapresic	27	4	27	4
2005-06	Dynamo Zagreb	32	3		
2006-07	Dynamo Zagreb	29	4	61	7
2007-08	Manchester C	35	0		
2008-09	Manchester C	3	1	38	1
2008-09	Tottenham H	34	0	34	0

CUDICINI, Carlo (G)   **229 0**
H: 6 1   W: 12 08   b.Milan 6-9-73
Honours: Italy Youth, Under-21.

Season	Club	Apps	Gls	Tot A	Tot G
1991-92	AC Milan	0	0		
1992-93	AC Milan	0	0		
1993-94	Como	6	0		
1994-95	AC Milan	0	0		
1995-96	AC Milan	0	0		
1995-96	Prato	30	0	30	0
1996-97	Lazio	1	0	1	0
1997-98	Castel di Sangro	14	0		
1998-99	Castel di Sangro	32	0	46	0
1999-2000	Chelsea	1	0		
2000-01	Chelsea	24	0		
2001-02	Chelsea	28	0		
2002-03	Chelsea	36	0		
2003-04	Chelsea	26	0		
2004-05	Chelsea	3	0		
2005-06	Chelsea	4	0		
2006-07	Chelsea	8	0		
2007-08	Chelsea	10	0		
2008-09	Chelsea	2	0	142	0
2008-09	Tottenham H	4	0	4	0

DAWKINS, Simon (F)   **11 0**
H: 5 10   W: 11 01   b.Edgware 1-12-87
Source: Scholar.

Season	Club	Apps	Gls	Tot A	Tot G
2005-06	Tottenham H	0	0		
2006-07	Tottenham H	0	0		
2007-08	Tottenham H	0	0		
2008-09	Tottenham H	0	0		
2008-09	*Leyton Orient*	11	0	11	0

DAWSON, Michael (D)   **200 10**
H: 6 2   W: 12 02   b.Northallerton 18-11-83
Source: School. *Honours:* England Youth, Under-21, B.

Season	Club	Apps	Gls	Tot A	Tot G
2000-01	Nottingham F	0	0		
2001-02	Nottingham F	1	0		
2002-03	Nottingham F	38	5		
2003-04	Nottingham F	30	1		
2004-05	Nottingham F	14	1	83	7
2004-05	Tottenham H	5	0		
2005-06	Tottenham H	32	0		
2006-07	Tottenham H	37	1		
2007-08	Tottenham H	27	1		
2008-09	Tottenham H	16	1	117	3

DEFOE, Jermain (F)   **300 109**
H: 5 7   W: 10 04   b.Beckton 7-10-82
Source: Charlton Ath. *Honours:* England Youth, Under-21, B, 34 full caps, 8 goals.

Season	Club	Apps	Gls	Tot A	Tot G
1999-2000	West Ham U	0	0		
2000-01	West Ham U	1	0		
2000-01	*Bournemouth*	29	18	29	18
2001-02	West Ham U	35	10		
2002-03	West Ham U	38	8		
2003-04	West Ham U	19	11	93	29
2003-04	Tottenham H	15	7		
2004-05	Tottenham H	35	13		
2005-06	Tottenham H	36	9		
2006-07	Tottenham H	34	10		
2007-08	Tottenham H	19	4		
2007-08	Portsmouth	12	8		
2008-09	Portsmouth	19	8	31	16
2008-09	Tottenham H	8	3	147	46

DERVITE, Dorian (D)   **18 0**
H: 6 3   W: 14 01   b.Lille 25-7-88
Honours: France Youth.

Season	Club	Apps	Gls	Tot A	Tot G
2006-07	Tottenham H	0	0		
2007-08	Tottenham H	0	0		
2008-09	Tottenham H	0	0		
2008-09	*Southend U*	18	0	18	0

FRASER-ALLEN, Kyle (M)   **2 0**
H: 5 11   W: 11 07   b.Wanstead 12-2-90
Source: Scholar. *Honours:* England Youth.

Season	Club	Apps	Gls	Tot A	Tot G
2008-09	Tottenham H	0	0		
2008-09	*Macclesfield T*	2	0	2	0

GHALY, Hossam (M)   **79 3**
H: 5 11   W: 12 04   b.Cairo 15-12-81
Honours: Egypt 21 full caps, 5 goals.

Season	Club	Apps	Gls	Tot A	Tot G
2003-04	Feyenoord	13	0		
2004-05	Feyenoord	20	1		
2005-06	Feyenoord	10	2	43	3
2005-06	Tottenham H	0	0		
2006-07	Tottenham H	21	0		
2007-08	Tottenham H	0	0		
2007-08	*Derby Co*	15	0	15	0
2008-09	Tottenham H	0	0	21	0

GILBERTO (D)   **277 32**
H: 5 11   W: 12 04   b.Rio de Janeiro 28-2-77
Honours: Brazil 23 full caps, 1 goal.

Season	Club	Apps	Gls	Tot A	Tot G
1995	America	0	0		
1996	Flamengo	17	0		
1997	Flamengo	22	0	39	0
1998	Cruzeiro	28	2	28	2
1998-99	Internazionale	2	0	2	0
1999	Vasco da Gama	16	2		
2000	Vasco da Gama	0	0		
2001	Vasco da Gama	24	4	40	6
2002	Gremio	21	3		
2003	Gremio	33	6	54	9
2004	Sao Caetano	6	0	6	0
2004-05	Hertha Berlin	33	6		
2005-06	Hertha Berlin	23	2		
2006-07	Hertha Berlin	30	5		
2007-08	Hertha Berlin	15	1	101	14
2007-08	Tottenham H	6	1		
2008-09	Tottenham H	1	0	7	1

GIOVANI (F)   **42 7**
H: 5 8   W: 12 03   b.Monterrey 11-5-89
Honours: Mexico Youth, 11 full caps.

Season	Club	Apps	Gls	Tot A	Tot G
2006-07	Barcelona B	0	0		
2007-08	Barcelona	28	3	28	3
2008-09	Tottenham H	6	0	6	0
2008-09	*Ipswich T*	8	4	8	4

GOMES, Heurelho (G)   **221 0**
H: 6 3   W: 12 13   b.Minas Gerais 15-2-81
Source: Democrata. *Honours:* Brazil Under-23, 17 full caps.

Season	Club	Apps	Gls	Tot A	Tot G
2001	Cruzeiro	0	0		
2002	Cruzeiro	14	0		
2003	Cruzeiro	40	0		
2004	Cruzeiro	5	0	59	0
2004-05	PSV Eindhoven	30	0		
2005-06	PSV Eindhoven	32	0		
2006-07	PSV Eindhoven	32	0		
2007-08	PSV Eindhoven	34	0	128	0
2008-09	Tottenham H	34	0	34	0

GUNTER, Chris (D)   **41 0**
H: 5 11   W: 11 02   b.Newport 21-7-89
Source: Scholar. *Honours:* Wales Youth, Under-21, 16 full caps.

Season	Club	Apps	Gls	Tot A	Tot G
2006-07	Cardiff C	15	0		
2007-08	Cardiff C	13	0	28	0
2007-08	Tottenham H	2	0		
2008-09	Tottenham H	3	0	5	0
2008-09	*Nottingham F*	8	0	8	0

HUDDLESTONE, Tom (M)   **176 5**
H: 6 2   W: 11 02   b.Nottingham 28-12-86
Source: Scholar. *Honours:* England Youth, Under-20, Under-21.

Season	Club	Apps	Gls	Tot A	Tot G
2003-04	Derby Co	43	0		
2004-05	Derby Co	45	0	88	0
2005-06	Tottenham H	4	0		
2005-06	*Wolverhampton W*	13	1	13	1
2006-07	Tottenham H	21	1		
2007-08	Tottenham H	28	3		
2008-09	Tottenham H	22	0	75	4

HUGHTON, Cian (D)   **0 0**
b.Enfield 25-1-89
Source: Scholar.

Season	Club	Apps	Gls	Tot A	Tot G
2007-08	Tottenham H	0	0		
2008-09	Tottenham H	0	0		

HUTCHINS, Daniel (D)   **9 0**
H: 6 0   W: 12 00   b.London 23-9-89
Source: Scholar.

Season	Club	Apps	Gls	Tot A	Tot G
2007-08	Tottenham H	0	0		
2008-09	Tottenham H	0	0		
2008-09	*Yeovil T*	9	0	9	0

HUTTON, Alan (D)   **104 1**
H: 6 1   W: 11 05   b.Glasgow 30-11-84
Honours: Scotland Under-21, 10 full caps.

Season	Club	Apps	Gls	Tot A	Tot G
2004-05	Rangers	10	0		
2005-06	Rangers	19	0		
2006-07	Rangers	33	1		
2007-08	Rangers	20	0	82	1
2007-08	Tottenham H	14	0		
2008-09	Tottenham H	8	0	22	0

HUTTON, David (M)   **7 1**
H: 5 5   W: 10 10   b.Enfield 4-12-89
Source: Scholar.

Season	Club	Apps	Gls	Tot A	Tot G
2008-09	Tottenham H	0	0		
2008-09	*Cheltenham T*	7	1	7	1

JANSSON, Oscar (G)   **0 0**
H: 6 0   W: 12 13   b.Orebro 23-12-90
Source: Karlslund.

Season	Club	Apps	Gls	Tot A	Tot G
2007-08	Tottenham H	0	0		
2008-09	Tottenham H	0	0		

JENAS, Jermaine (M)   **255 33**
H: 5 11   W: 11 00   b.Nottingham 18-2-83
Source: Scholar. *Honours:* England Youth, Under-21, B, 20 full caps, 1 goal.

Season	Club	Apps	Gls	Tot A	Tot G
1999-2000	Nottingham F	0	0		
2000-01	Nottingham F	1	0		
2001-02	Nottingham F	28	4	29	4
2001-02	Newcastle U	12	0		
2002-03	Newcastle U	32	6		
2003-04	Newcastle U	31	2		
2004-05	Newcastle U	31	1		
2005-06	Newcastle U	4	0	110	9
2005-06	Tottenham H	30	6		
2006-07	Tottenham H	25	6		
2007-08	Tottenham H	29	4		
2008-09	Tottenham H	32	4	116	20

KEANE, Robbie (F)   **386 139**
H: 5 9   W: 12 02   b.Dublin 8-7-80
Source: Trainee. *Honours:* Eire Youth, B, 90 full caps, 39 goals.

1997-98	Wolverhampton W	38	11		
1998-99	Wolverhampton W	33	11		
1999-2000	Wolverhampton W	2	0	73	24
1999-2000	Coventry C	31	12	31	12
2000-01	Internazionale	6	0	6	0
2000-01	Leeds U	18	9		
2001-02	Leeds U	25	3		
2002-03	Leeds U	3	1	46	13
2002-03	Tottenham H	29	13		
2003-04	Tottenham H	34	14		
2004-05	Tottenham H	35	11		
2005-06	Tottenham H	36	16		
2006-07	Tottenham H	27	11		
2007-08	Tottenham H	36	15		
2008-09	Liverpool	19	5	19	5
2008-09	Tottenham H	14	5	211	85

KING, Ledley (D)   **221 8**
H: 6 2   W: 14 05   b.Bow 12-10-80
Source: Trainee. *Honours:* England Youth, B, Under-21, 19 full caps, 1 goal.

1998-99	Tottenham H	1	0		
1999-2000	Tottenham H	3	0		
2000-01	Tottenham H	18	1		
2001-02	Tottenham H	32	0		
2002-03	Tottenham H	25	0		
2003-04	Tottenham H	29	1		
2004-05	Tottenham H	38	2		
2005-06	Tottenham H	26	3		
2006-07	Tottenham H	21	0		
2007-08	Tottenham H	4	0		
2008-09	Tottenham H	24	1	221	8

LENNON, Aaron (M)   **155 13**
H: 5 6   W: 10 03   b.Leeds 16-4-87
Source: Trainee. *Honours:* England Youth, Under-21, B, 11 full caps.

2003-04	Leeds U	11	0		
2004-05	Leeds U	27	1	38	1
2005-06	Tottenham H	27	2		
2006-07	Tottenham H	26	3		
2007-08	Tottenham H	29	2		
2008-09	Tottenham H	35	5	117	12

LIVERMORE, Jake (M)   **5 0**
b.Enfield 14-11-89
Source: Scholar.

2006-07	Tottenham H	0	0		
2007-08	Tottenham H	0	0		
2007-08	Milton Keynes D	5	0	5	0
2008-09	Tottenham H	0	0		
2008-09	Crewe Alex	0	0		

MAGHOMA, Jacques (M)   **0 0**
H: 5 9   W: 11 06   b.Lubumbashi 23-10-87
Source: Scholar.

2005-06	Tottenham H	0	0		
2006-07	Tottenham H	0	0		
2007-08	Tottenham H	0	0		
2008-09	Tottenham H	0	0		

MASON, Ryan (M)   **0 0**
b.Enfield 13-6-91
Source: Scholar.

| 2007-08 | Tottenham H | 0 | 0 | | |
| 2008-09 | Tottenham H | 0 | 0 | | |

McKENNA, Kieran (M)   **0 0**
H: 5 10   W: 10 07   b.London 14-5-86
Source: Academy. *Honours:* Northern Ireland Under-21.

2003-04	Tottenham H	0	0		
2004-05	Tottenham H	0	0		
2005-06	Tottenham H	0	0		
2006-07	Tottenham H	0	0		
2007-08	Tottenham H	0	0		
2008-09	Tottenham H	0	0		

MILLS, Leigh (D)   **7 1**
H: 6 2   W: 13 00   b.Winchester 8-2-88
Source: Scholar. *Honours:* England Youth.

2005-06	Tottenham H	0	0		
2006-07	Tottenham H	0	0		
2007-08	Tottenham H	0	0		
2008-09	Tottenham H	0	0		
2008-09	Brentford	0	0		
2008-09	Gillingham	7	1	7	1

MODRIC, Luka (M)   **145 34**
H: 5 8   W: 10 03   b.Zadar 9-9-85
Honours: Croatia Youth, Under-21, 35 full caps, 7 goals.

2004-05	Inter Zapresic	18	4	18	4
2004-05	Dinamo Zagreb	6	0		
2005-06	Dinamo Zagreb	32	8		
2006-07	Dinamo Zagreb	30	6		
2007-08	Dinamo Zagreb	25	13	93	27
2008-09	Tottenham H	34	3	34	3

MPUKU, Paul-Jose (M)   **0 0**
b.Kinshasa 19-4-92
Source: Scholar.

| 2008-09 | Tottenham H | 0 | 0 | | |

MTANDARI, Takura (D)   **0 0**
b. 11-10-89
Source: Scholar.

| 2008-09 | Tottenham H | 0 | 0 | | |

O'HARA, Jamie (M)   **65 9**
H: 5 11   W: 12 04   b.South London 25-9-86
Source: From Scholar. *Honours:* England Youth, Under-21.

2004-05	Tottenham H	0	0		
2005-06	Tottenham H	0	0		
2005-06	Chesterfield	19	5	19	5
2006-07	Tottenham H	0	0		
2007-08	Tottenham H	17	1		
2007-08	Millwall	14	2	14	2
2008-09	Tottenham H	15	1	32	2

OBIKA, Jonathan (F)   **10 4**
H: 6 0   W: 12 00   b.Enfield 12-9-90
Source: Scholar. *Honours:* England Youth.

| 2008-09 | Tottenham H | 0 | 0 | | |
| 2008-09 | Yeovil T | 10 | 4 | 10 | 4 |

OLSEN, Alex (F)   **0 0**
b.Gjovik 9-9-89
Source: Gjovik.

2006-07	Tottenham H	0	0		
2007-08	Tottenham H	0	0		
2008-09	Tottenham H	0	0		

PALACIOS, Wilson (D)   **55 0**
H: 5 10   W: 11 11   b.La Ceiba 29-7-84
Source: Olimpia. *Honours:* Honduras 61 full caps, 5 goals.

2007-08	Birmingham C	7	0	7	0
2007-08	Wigan Ath	16	0		
2008-09	Wigan Ath	21	0	37	0
2008-09	Tottenham H	11	0	11	0

PARRETT, Dean (M)   **0 0**
H: 5 10   W: 11 04   b.Hampstead 16-11-91
Source: Scholar. *Honours:* England Youth.

| 2008-09 | Tottenham H | 0 | 0 | | |

PAVLYUCHENKO, Roman (F)   **265 86**
H: 6 2   W: 12 04   b.Mostovskoy 15-12-81
Honours: Russia 27 full caps, 11 goals.

1999	Dinamo Stavropol	31	1	31	1
2000	Rotor Volgograd II	13	3	13	3
2000	Rotor Volgograd	16	5		
2001	Rotor Volgograd	28	5		
2002	Rotor Volgograd	22	4	66	14
2003	Spartak Moscow	27	10		
2004	Spartak Moscow	26	10		
2005	Spartak Moscow	25	11		
2006	Spartak Moscow	27	18		
2007	Spartak Moscow	22	14	127	63
2008-09	Tottenham H	28	5	28	5

PEKHART, Tomas (F)   **9 1**
H: 6 3   W: 14 00   b.Susice 26-5-89
Honours: Czech Republic Youth, Under-21.

2006-07	Tottenham H	0	0		
2007-08	Tottenham H	0	0		
2008-09	Tottenham H	0	0		
2008-09	Southampton	9	1	9	1
On loan to Sparta Prague January 2009

RANIERI, Mirko (G)   **0 0**
b. 8-2-92
Source: Perugia.

| 2008-09 | Tottenham H | 0 | 0 | | |

RICARDO ROCHA (D)   **173 5**
H: 6 0   W: 12 08   b.Santo Tirso 3-10-78
Honours: Portugal 6 full caps.

2000-01	Braga	19	0		
2001-02	Braga	25	2	44	2
2002-03	Benfica	27	0		
2003-04	Benfica	25	0		
2004-05	Benfica	25	0		
2005-06	Benfica	26	0		
2006-07	Benfica	12	3	115	3
2006-07	Tottenham H	9	0		
2007-08	Tottenham H	5	0		
2008-09	Tottenham H	0	0	14	0

ROSE, Danny (M)   **7 0**
H: 5 8   W: 11 11   b.Doncaster 2-6-90
Source: Leeds U. *Honours:* England Youth, Under-21.

2007-08	Tottenham H	0	0		
2008-09	Tottenham H	0	0		
2008-09	Watford	7	0	7	0

SANCHEZ, Cesar (G)   **336 0**
H: 6 1   W: 12 13   b.Caceres 2-9-71
Honours: Spain 1 full cap.

1991-92	Valladolid	1	0		
1992-93	Valladolid	0	0		
1993-94	Valladolid	3	0		
1994-95	Valladolid	10	0		
1995-96	Valladolid	40	0		
1996-97	Valladolid	40	0		
1997-98	Valladolid	38	0		
1998-99	Valladolid	38	0		
1999-2000	Valladolid	36	0	206	0
2000-01	Real Madrid	5	0		
2001-02	Real Madrid	12	0		
2002-03	Real Madrid	0	0		
2003-04	Real Madrid	1	0		
2004-05	Real Madrid	2	0	20	0
2005-06	Zaragoza	35	0		
2006-07	Zaragoza	38	0		
2007-08	Zaragoza	37	0	110	0
2008-09	Tottenham H	0	0		
Transferred to Valencia January 2009

SMITH, Adam (D)   **0 0**
b.London 29-4-91
Source: Scholar.

| 2007-08 | Tottenham H | 0 | 0 | | |
| 2008-09 | Tottenham H | 0 | 0 | | |

STALTERI, Paul (D)   **205 8**
H: 5 11   W: 11 13   b.Etobicoke 18-10-77
Source: Malton Bullets, Toronto Lynx.
Honours: Canada Youth, Under-20, Under-23, 67 full caps, 7 goals.

1999-2000	Werder Bremen	0	0		
2000-01	Werder Bremen	31	1		
2001-02	Werder Bremen	22	3		
2002-03	Werder Bremen	33	0		
2003-04	Werder Bremen	33	2		
2004-05	Werder Bremen	31	0	150	6
2005-06	Tottenham H	33	1		
2006-07	Tottenham H	6	1		
2007-08	Tottenham H	3	0		
2007-08	Fulham	13	0	13	0
2008-09	Tottenham H	0	0	42	2
Transferred to Moenchengladbach Jan 2009

TAARABT, Adel (M)   **17 1**
H: 5 9   W: 10 12   b.Berre-l'Etang 24-5-89
Source: France Youth. Morocco 3 full caps, 1 goal.

2006-07	Lens	1	0	1	0
2006-07	Tottenham H	2	0		
2007-08	Tottenham H	6	0		
2008-09	Tottenham H	1	0	9	0
2008-09	QPR	7	1	7	1

TOWNSEND, Andros (M)   **10 1**
H: 6 0   W: 12 00   b.Chingford 16-7-91
Source: Scholar. *Honours:* England Youth.

| 2008-09 | Tottenham H | 0 | 0 | | |
| 2008-09 | Yeovil T | 10 | 1 | 10 | 1 |

WOODGATE, Jonathan (D)   **233 6**
H: 6 2   W: 12 06   b.Middlesbrough 22-1-80
Source: Trainee. *Honours:* England Youth, Under-21, 8 full caps.

1996-97	Leeds U	0	0		
1997-98	Leeds U	0	0		
1998-99	Leeds U	25	2		
1999-2000	Leeds U	34	1		
2000-01	Leeds U	14	1		
2001-02	Leeds U	13	0		
2002-03	Leeds U	18	0	104	4
2002-03	Newcastle U	10	0		
2003-04	Newcastle U	18	0	28	0
2004-05	Real Madrid	0	0		
2005-06	Real Madrid	9	0	9	0
2006-07	Middlesbrough	30	0		

2007-08	Middlesbrough	16	0	**46** **0**
2007-08	Tottenham H	12	1	
2008-09	Tottenham H	34	1	**46** **2**

ZOKORA, Didier (D)   **278** **1**
H: 5 10   W: 11 00   b.Abidjan 14-12-80
Honours: Ivory Coast 72 full caps, 1 goal.

2000-01	Genk	28	0	
2001-02	Genk	30	0	
2002-03	Genk	33	0	
2003-04	Genk	33	1	**124** **1**
2004-05	St Etienne	35	0	
2005-06	St Etienne	31	0	**66** **0**
2006-07	Tottenham H	31	0	
2007-08	Tottenham H	28	0	
2008-09	Tottenham H	29	0	**88** **0**

Scholars
Butler, Jamie; Byrne, Nathan William;
Carroll, Thomas James; Caulker, Steven Roy;
Cox, Samuel Peter; Ekim, Coskun Josh; Jack,
Anthony Tamundsaki; Kasim, Yaser Safy;
Nicholson, Jake Charlie; O'Neill, Chace
Aaron Paul.

TRANMERE R (84)

ACHTERBERG, John (G)   **298** **0**
H: 6 1   W: 14 03   b.Utrecht 8-7-71
Source: VV RUC, Utrecht.

1993-94	NAC	1	0	
1994-95	NAC	2	0	
1995-96	NAC	6	0	**9** **0**
1996-97	Eindhoven	32	0	**32** **0**
From Utrecht.				
1998-99	Tranmere R	24	0	
1999-2000	Tranmere R	26	0	
2000-01	Tranmere R	25	0	
2001-02	Tranmere R	25	0	
2002-03	Tranmere R	38	0	
2003-04	Tranmere R	45	0	
2004-05	Tranmere R	39	0	
2005-06	Tranmere R	19	0	
2006-07	Tranmere R	4	0	
2007-08	Tranmere R	5	0	
2008-09	Tranmere R	7	0	**257** **0**

AHMED, Adnan (M)   **52** **2**
H: 5 10   W: 11 02   b.Burnley 7-6-84
Source: Scholar. *Honours:* Pakistan 11 full
caps, 2 goals.

2003-04	Huddersfield T	1	0	
2004-05	Huddersfield T	18	1	
2005-06	Huddersfield T	13	0	
2006-07	Huddersfield T	9	0	**41** **1**
2007-08	Tranmere R	6	0	
2008-09	Tranmere R	0	0	**6** **0**
2008-09	*Port Vale*	5	1	**5** **1**

BARNETT, Charlie (M)   **29** **3**
H: 5 7   W: 11 07   b.Liverpool 19-9-88
Source: Scholar.

2006-07	Liverpool	0	0	
2007-08	Liverpool	0	0	
2008-09	Tranmere R	29	3	**29** **3**

CHORLEY, Ben (M)   **230** **8**
H: 6 3   W: 13 02   b.Sidcup 30-9-82
Source: Scholar.

2001-02	Arsenal	0	0	
2002-03	Arsenal	0	0	
2002-03	*Brentford*	2	0	**2** **0**
2002-03	Wimbledon	10	0	
2003-04	Wimbledon	35	2	**45** **2**
2004-05	Milton Keynes D	41	2	
2005-06	Milton Keynes D	26	0	
2006-07	Milton Keynes D	13	1	**80** **3**
2006-07	*Gillingham*	27	1	**27** **1**
2007-08	Tranmere R	31	1	
2008-09	Tranmere R	45	1	**76** **2**

COYNE, Danny (G)   **416** **0**
H: 6 0   W: 13 00   b.Prestatyn 27-8-73
Source: Trainee. *Honours:* Wales Schools,
Youth, Under-21, B, 16 full caps.

1991-92	Tranmere R	0	0	
1992-93	Tranmere R	1	0	
1993-94	Tranmere R	5	0	
1994-95	Tranmere R	5	0	
1995-96	Tranmere R	46	0	
1996-97	Tranmere R	21	0	
1997-98	Tranmere R	16	0	

1998-99	Tranmere R	17	0	
1999-2000	Grimsby T	44	0	
2000-01	Grimsby T	46	0	
2001-02	Grimsby T	45	0	
2002-03	Grimsby T	46	0	**181** **0**
2003-04	Leicester C	4	0	**4** **0**
2004-05	Burnley	20	0	
2005-06	Burnley	8	0	
2006-07	Burnley	12	0	**40** **0**
2007-08	Tranmere R	41	0	
2008-09	Tranmere R	39	0	**191** **0**

CRESSWELL, Aaron (D)   **13** **1**
H: 5 7   W: 10 05   b.Liverpool 15-12-89
Source: Scholar.

2008-09	Tranmere R	13	1	**13** **1**

CURRAN, Craig (F)   **54** **9**
H: 5 11   W: 11 09   b.Liverpool 23-9-89
Source: Scholar.

2006-07	Tranmere R	4	4	
2007-08	Tranmere R	35	2	
2008-09	Tranmere R	15	3	**54** **9**

EDDS, Gareth (D)   **209** **13**
H: 5 11   W: 11 01   b.Sydney 3-2-81
Source: Trainee. *Honours:* Australia
Under-20, Under-23.

1997-98	Nottingham F	0	0	
1998-99	Nottingham F	0	0	
1999-2000	Nottingham F	2	0	
2000-01	Nottingham F	13	1	
2001-02	Nottingham F	1	0	**16** **1**
2002-03	Swindon T	14	0	**14** **0**
2003-04	Bradford C	23	0	**23** **0**
2004-05	Milton Keynes D	39	5	
2005-06	Milton Keynes D	41	3	
2006-07	Milton Keynes D	35	2	
2007-08	Milton Keynes D	7	0	**122** **10**
2008-09	Tranmere R	34	2	**34** **2**

FRAUGHAN, Ryan (M)   **0** **0**
Source: Scholar.

2008-09	Tranmere R	0	0	

GOODISON, Ian (D)   **279** **4**
H: 6 1   W: 13 04   b.St James, Jamaica
21-11-72
Source: From Olympic Gardens. *Honours:*
Jamaica 113 full caps, 9 goals.

1999-2000	Hull C	18	0	
2000-01	Hull C	36	1	
2001-02	Hull C	16	0	
2002-03	Hull C	0	0	**70** **1**
From Seba U.				
2003-04	Tranmere R	12	0	
2004-05	Tranmere R	44	1	
2005-06	Tranmere R	38	1	
2006-07	Tranmere R	40	0	
2007-08	Tranmere R	42	0	
2008-09	Tranmere R	33	1	**209** **3**

GORNELL, Terry (F)   **21** **5**
H: 5 11   W: 12 04   b.Liverpool 16-12-89
Source: Scholar.

2008-09	Tranmere R	10	1	**10** **1**
2008-09	*Accrington S*	11	4	**11** **4**

GREENACRE, Chris (F)   **373** **107**
H: 5 9   W: 12 09   b.Halifax 23-12-77
Source: Trainee.

1995-96	Manchester C	0	0	
1996-97	Manchester C	4	0	
1997-98	Manchester C	3	1	
1997-98	*Cardiff C*	11	2	**11** **2**
1997-98	*Blackpool*	4	0	**4** **0**
1998-99	Manchester C	1	0	
1998-99	*Scarborough*	12	2	**12** **2**
1999-2000	Manchester C	0	0	**8** **1**
1999-2000	Mansfield T	31	9	
2000-01	Mansfield T	46	19	
2001-02	Mansfield T	44	21	**121** **49**
2002-03	Stoke C	30	4	
2003-04	Stoke C	13	2	
2004-05	Stoke C	32	1	**75** **7**
2005-06	Tranmere R	45	16	
2006-07	Tranmere R	44	17	
2007-08	Tranmere R	40	11	
2008-09	Tranmere R	13	2	**142** **46**

HENRY, Paul (M)   **3** **0**
H: 5 8   W: 11 06   b.Liverpool 28-1-88
Source: Scholar.

2005-06	Tranmere R	0	0	
2006-07	Tranmere R	0	0	

2007-08	Tranmere R	2	0	
2008-09	Tranmere R	1	0	**3** **0**

HOLMES, Daniel (D)   **1** **0**
H: 5 10   W: 12 00   b.Wirral 6-1-89
Source: Scholar.

2007-08	Tranmere R	0	0	
2008-09	Tranmere R	1	0	**1** **0**

JENNINGS, Steven (M)   **151** **6**
H: 5 7   W: 11 11   b.Liverpool 28-10-84
Source: Scholar.

2002-03	Tranmere R	0	0	
2003-04	Tranmere R	4	0	
2004-05	Tranmere R	11	0	
2005-06	Tranmere R	38	1	
2006-07	Tranmere R	2	0	
2006-07	*Hereford U*	11	0	**11** **0**
2007-08	Tranmere R	41	2	
2008-09	Tranmere R	44	3	**140** **6**

JOHNSTON, Michael (D)   **0** **0**
H: 5 9   W: 12 03   b.Birkenhead 16-12-87
Source: Scholar.

2005-06	Tranmere R	0	0	
2006-07	Tranmere R	0	0	
2007-08	Tranmere R	0	0	
2008-09	Tranmere R	0	0	

KAY, Antony (D)   **256** **28**
H: 5 11   W: 11 08   b.Barnsley 21-10-82
Source: Trainee. *Honours:* England Youth.

1999-2000	Barnsley	0	0	
2000-01	Barnsley	7	0	
2001-02	Barnsley	1	0	
2002-03	Barnsley	16	0	
2003-04	Barnsley	43	3	
2004-05	Barnsley	39	6	
2005-06	Barnsley	36	1	
2006-07	Barnsley	32	1	**174** **11**
2007-08	Tranmere R	38	6	
2008-09	Tranmere R	44	11	**82** **17**

MACAULEY, Josh (F)   **1** **0**
H: 6 0   W: 12 00   b.Liverpool 2-3-91
Source: Scholar.

2008-09	Tranmere R	1	0	**1** **0**

MOORE, Ian (F)   **507** **91**
H: 5 11   W: 12 00   b.Birkenhead 26-8-76
Source: From Trainee. *Honours:* England
Youth, Under-21.

1994-95	Tranmere R	1	0	
1995-96	Tranmere R	36	9	
1996-97	Tranmere R	21	3	
1996-97	*Bradford C*	6	0	**6** **0**
1996-97	Nottingham F	5	0	
1997-98	Nottingham F	10	1	**15** **1**
1997-98	*West Ham U*	1	0	**1** **0**
1998-99	Stockport Co	38	3	
1999-2000	Stockport Co	38	10	
2000-01	Stockport Co	17	7	**93** **20**
2000-01	Burnley	27	5	
2001-02	Burnley	46	11	
2002-03	Burnley	44	8	
2003-04	Burnley	40	9	
2004-05	Burnley	35	4	**192** **37**
2004-05	Leeds U	6	0	
2005-06	Leeds U	20	0	
2006-07	Leeds U	33	2	**59** **2**
2007-08	*Hartlepool U*	24	6	**24** **6**
2007-08	Tranmere R	17	3	
2008-09	Tranmere R	42	10	**117** **25**

O'CALLAGHAN, George (M)   **159** **20**
H: 6 1   W: 10 11   b.Cork 5-9-79
Source: Trainee. *Honours:* Eire Youth.

1998-99	Port Vale	4	0	
1999-2000	Port Vale	11	0	
2000-01	Port Vale	8	1	
2001-02	Port Vale	11	3	**34** **4**
2002-03	Cork C	26	6	
2003-04	Cork C	0	0	
2004-05	Cork C	35	3	
2005-06	Cork C	32	6	**93** **15**
2006-07	Ipswich T	11	1	
2007-08	Ipswich T	1	0	**12** **1**
2007-08	*Brighton & HA*	14	0	**14** **0**
2008-09	Tranmere R	6	0	**6** **0**
Transferred to Dundalk February 2009				

SAVAGE, Bas (F)   **151** **22**
H: 6 3   W: 12 00   b.London 7-1-82
Source: Walton & Hersham.

2001-02	Reading	1	0	

Season	Club				
2002-03	Reading	0	0		
2003-04	Reading	15	0		
2004-05	Reading	0	0	16	0
2004-05	*Wycombe W*	4	0	4	0
2004-05	*Bury*	5	0	5	0
2005-06	Bristol C	23	1		
2006-07	Bristol C	0	0	23	1
2006-07	Gillingham	14	1	14	1
2006-07	Brighton & HA	15	6		
2007-08	Brighton & HA	21	3	36	9
2007-08	Millwall	11	2	11	2
2008-09	Tranmere R	42	9	42	9

SHUKER, Chris (M)   244 32
H: 5 5 W: 9 03 b.Liverpool 9-5-82
Source: Scholarship.

Season	Club				
1999-2000	Manchester C	0	0		
2000-01	Manchester C	0	0		
2000-01	*Macclesfield T*	9	1	9	1
2001-02	Manchester C	2	0		
2002-03	Manchester C	3	0		
2002-03	*Walsall*	5	0	5	0
2003-04	Manchester C	0	0	5	0
2003-04	*Rochdale*	14	1	14	1
2003-04	*Hartlepool U*	14	1	14	1
2003-04	Barnsley	9	0		
2004-05	Barnsley	45	7		
2005-06	Barnsley	46	10	100	17
2006-07	Tranmere R	46	6		
2007-08	Tranmere R	23	3		
2008-09	Tranmere R	28	3	97	12

SONKO, Edrissa (M)   192 31
H: 5 10 W: 11 05 b.Essau 23-3-80
Honours: Gambia 14 full caps, 7 goals.

Season	Club				
2000-01	Roda JC	16	2		
2001-02	Roda JC	9	2		
2002-03	Roda JC	22	8		
2003-04	Roda JC	18	2		
2004-05	Roda JC	25	1		
2005-06	Roda JC	18	5	108	20
2006-07	Xanthi	9	1	9	1
2007-08	Walsall	37	5	37	5
2008-09	Tranmere R	38	5	38	5

TAYLOR, Andy (D)   87 3
H: 5 11 W: 11 07 b.Blackburn 14-3-86
Source: Scholar. *Honours:* England Youth, Under-20, Under-21.

Season	Club				
2004-05	Blackburn R	0	0		
2005-06	Blackburn R	0	0		
2005-06	*QPR*	3	0	3	0
2005-06	*Blackpool*	3	0	3	0
2006-07	Blackburn R	0	0		
2006-07	*Crewe Alex*	4	0	4	0
2006-07	*Huddersfield T*	8	0	8	0
2007-08	Blackburn R	0	0		
2007-08	Tranmere R	30	2		
2008-09	Tranmere R	39	1	69	3

TAYLOR, Ash (M)   1 0
H: 6 0 W: 12 00 b.Bromborough 2-9-89
Source: Scholar. *Honours:* Wales Youth.

Season	Club				
2008-09	Tranmere R	1	0	1	0

WATERFALL, Luke (D)   0 0
H: 6 1 W: 12 12 b.Sheffield 30-9-90
Source: Barnsley.

Season	Club		
2008-09	Tranmere R	0	0

WALSALL (85)

ADKINS, Sam (M)   1 0
H: 5 10 W: 11 07 b.Birmingham 3-12-91
Source: Scholar.

Season	Club				
2008-09	Walsall	1	0	1	0

BACCHUS, Hassan (D)   0 0
H: 5 11 W: 11 12 b.London 20-1-90

Season	Club		
2008-09	Walsall	0	0

BOERTIEN, Paul (D)   193 3
H: 5 10 W: 11 02 b.Haltwhistle 21-1-79
Source: Trainee.

Season	Club				
1996-97	Carlisle U	0	0		
1997-98	Carlisle U	9	0		
1998-99	Carlisle U	8	1	17	1
1998-99	Derby Co	1	0		
1999-2000	Derby Co	2	0		
1999-2000	*Crewe Alex*	2	0	2	0
2000-01	Derby Co	8	1		
2001-02	Derby Co	32	0		
2002-03	Derby Co	42	1		
2003-04	Derby Co	18	0		
2003-04	*Notts Co*	5	0	5	0
2004-05	Derby Co	0	0		
2005-06	Derby Co	0	0		
2006-07	Derby Co	11	0	114	2
2006-07	*Chesterfield*	4	0	4	0
2007-08	Walsall	20	0		
2008-09	Walsall	31	0	51	0

BRADLEY, Mark (D)   68 5
H: 6 0 W: 11 05 b.Dudley 14-1-88
Source: Scholar. *Honours:* Wales Youth, Under-21.

Season	Club				
2004-05	Walsall	1	0		
2005-06	Walsall	3	0		
2006-07	Walsall	1	0		
2007-08	Walsall	35	3		
2008-09	Walsall	28	2	68	5

CRADDOCK, Josh (M)   3 0
H: 5 11 W: 10 08 b.Wolverhampton 5-3-91
Source: Scholar.

Season	Club				
2007-08	Walsall	1	0		
2008-09	Walsall	2	0	3	0

DAVIES, Charlton (M)   0 0
b.Coleshill 24-1-89
Source: Scholar.

Season	Club		
2007-08	Walsall	0	0
2008-09	Walsall	0	0

DAVIES, Richard (M)   3 0
H: 5 11 W: 11 05 b.Willenhall 15-5-90
Source: Scholar.

Season	Club				
2008-09	Walsall	3	0	3	0

DEENEY, Troy (F)   81 13
H: 5 11 W: 12 00 b.Chelmsley 29-6-88
Source: Chelmsley T.

Season	Club				
2006-07	Walsall	1	0		
2007-08	Walsall	35	1		
2008-09	Walsall	45	12	81	13

DEMONTAGNAC, Ishmel (F)   83 9
H: 5 10 W: 11 05 b.London 15-6-88
Source: Charlton Ath Scholar. *Honours:* England Youth.

Season	Club				
2005-06	Walsall	24	2		
2006-07	Walsall	19	1		
2007-08	Walsall	30	3		
2008-09	Walsall	10	3	83	9

GERRARD, Anthony (D)   163 7
H: 6 2 W: 13 07 b.Liverpool 6-2-86
Source: Scholar. *Honours:* Eire Youth.

Season	Club				
2004-05	Everton	0	0		
2004-05	*Walsall*	8	0		
2005-06	Walsall	34	0		
2006-07	Walsall	35	1		
2007-08	Walsall	44	3		
2008-09	Walsall	42	3	163	7

GILMARTIN, Rene (G)   13 0
H: 6 5 W: 13 06 b.Dublin 31-5-87
Source: St Patrick's BC. *Honours:* Eire Youth, Under-21.

Season	Club				
2005-06	Walsall	2	0		
2006-07	Walsall	0	0		
2007-08	Walsall	0	0		
2008-09	Walsall	11	0	13	0

GRIGG, Will (M)   1 0
H: 5 11 W: 11 00 b.Solihull 3-7-91
Source: Stratford T.

Season	Club				
2008-09	Walsall	1	0	1	0

HARRIS, Harry (F)   0 0
b.Aldridge 9-12-88
Source: Scholar.

Season	Club		
2007-08	Walsall	0	0
2008-09	Walsall	0	0

HUGHES, Stephen (M)   261 13
H: 6 0 W: 12 12 b.Wokingham 18-9-76
Source: Trainee. *Honours:* England Schools, Youth, Under-21.

Season	Club				
1994-95	Arsenal	1	0		
1995-96	Arsenal	1	0		
1996-97	Arsenal	14	1		
1997-98	Arsenal	17	2		
1998-99	Arsenal	14	1		
1999-2000	*Fulham*	3	0	3	0
1999-2000	Arsenal	2	0	49	4
1999-2000	Everton	11	1		
2000-01	Everton	18	0	29	1
2001-02	Watford	15	0		
2002-03	Watford	0	0	15	0
2003-04	Charlton Ath	0	0		
2004-05	Coventry C	40	4		
2005-06	Coventry C	19	0		
2006-07	Coventry C	37	1		
2007-08	Coventry C	37	1	133	6
2008-09	Walsall	32	2	32	2

IBEHRE, Jabo (F)   248 46
H: 6 2 W: 13 13 b.Islington 28-1-83
Source: Trainee.

Season	Club				
1999-2000	Leyton Orient	3	0		
2000-01	Leyton Orient	5	2		
2001-02	Leyton Orient	28	4		
2002-03	Leyton Orient	25	5		
2003-04	Leyton Orient	35	4		
2004-05	Leyton Orient	19	2		
2005-06	Leyton Orient	33	8		
2006-07	Leyton Orient	30	4		
2007-08	Leyton Orient	31	7	209	36
2008-09	Walsall	39	10	39	10

INCE, Clayton (G)   251 0
H: 6 3 W: 13 03 b.Trinidad 13-7-72
Source: Defence Force. *Honours:* Trinidad & Tobago 63 full caps.

Season	Club				
1999-2000	Crewe Alex	1	0		
2000-01	Crewe Alex	1	0		
2001-02	Crewe Alex	19	0		
2002-03	Crewe Alex	43	0		
2003-04	Crewe Alex	36	0		
2004-05	Crewe Alex	23	0	123	0
2005-06	Coventry C	1	0	1	0
2006-07	Walsall	45	0		
2007-08	Walsall	46	0		
2008-09	Walsall	36	0	127	0

MATTIS, Dwayne (M)   211 17
H: 6 1 W: 11 12 b.Huddersfield 31-7-81
Source: Trainee. *Honours:* Eire Youth, Under-21.

Season	Club				
1998-99	Huddersfield T	2	0		
1999-2000	Huddersfield T	0	0		
2000-01	Huddersfield T	0	0		
2001-02	Huddersfield T	29	1		
2002-03	Huddersfield T	33	1		
2003-04	Huddersfield T	5	0	69	2
2004-05	Bury	39	5		
2005-06	Bury	36	5		
2006-07	Bury	22	1	97	11
2006-07	Barnsley	3	0		
2007-08	Barnsley	1	0	4	0
2007-08	*Walsall*				
2008-09	Walsall	37	4	41	4

NICHOLLS, Alex (F)   72 8
H: 5 10 W: 11 00 b.Stourbridge 9-12-87
Source: Scholar.

Season	Club				
2005-06	Walsall	8	0		
2006-07	Walsall	1	0		
2007-08	Walsall	19	2		
2008-09	Walsall	45	6	72	8

PALMER, Chris (M)   135 6
H: 5 7 W: 11 00 b.Derby 16-10-83
Source: Scholar.

Season	Club				
2003-04	Derby Co	0	0		
2004-05	Notts Co	25	4		
2005-06	Notts Co	29	1	54	5
2006-07	Wycombe W	32	0		
2007-08	Wycombe W	1	0	33	0
2007-08	*Darlington*	4	0	4	0
2008-09	Walsall	44	1	44	1

REICH, Marco (M)   256 20
H: 6 0 W: 12 00 b.Meisenheim 30-12-77
Honours: Germany Under-21, 1 full cap.

Season	Club				
1996-97	Kaiserslautern	0	0		
1997-98	Kaiserslautern	31	1		
1998-99	Kaiserslautern	27	3		
1999-2000	Kaiserslautern	28	2		
2000-01	Kaiserslautern	18	2	104	8
2001-02	Cologne	24	0	24	0
2002-03	Werder Bremen	15	0	15	0
2003-04	Derby Co	13	1		
2004-05	Derby Co	37	6	50	7
2005-06	Crystal Palace	21	2		
2006-07	Crystal Palace	6	0	27	2
2007-08	Kickers Offenbach	17	0	17	0
2008-09	Walsall	19	3	19	3

RICKETTS, Michael (F) 337 76
H: 6 2　W: 11 12　b.Birmingham 4-12-78
Source: Trainee. *Honours:* England 1 full cap.

1995-96	Walsall	1	1	
1996-97	Walsall	11	1	
1997-98	Walsall	24	1	
1998-99	Walsall	8	0	
1999-2000	Walsall	32	11	
2000-01	Bolton W	39	19	
2001-02	Bolton W	37	12	
2002-03	Bolton W	22	6	98 37
2002-03	Middlesbrough	9	1	
2003-04	Middlesbrough	23	2	32 3
2004-05	Leeds U	21	0	
2004-05	Stoke C	11	0	11 0
2005-06	Leeds U	4	0	25 0
2005-06	Cardiff C	17	5	17 5
2005-06	Burnley	13	2	13 2
2006-07	Southend U	2	0	2 0
2006-07	Preston NE	14	1	14 1
2007-08	Oldham Ath	9	2	9 2
2007-08	*Walsall*	12	3	
2008-09	Walsall	28	9	116 26

ROBERTS, Steve (D) 238 8
H: 6 1　W: 11 02　b.Wrexham 24-2-80
Source: Trainee. *Honours:* Wales Youth,
Under-21, 1 full cap.

1997-98	Wrexham	0	0	
1998-99	Wrexham	0	0	
1999-2000	Wrexham	19	0	
2000-01	Wrexham	7	0	
2001-02	Wrexham	24	1	
2002-03	Wrexham	39	2	
2003-04	Wrexham	27	0	
2004-05	Wrexham	34	3	150 6
2005-06	Doncaster R	27	1	
2006-07	Doncaster R	21	0	
2007-08	Doncaster R	25	0	73 1
2008-09	Walsall	15	1	15 1

SANSARA, Netan (D) 10 0
H: 6 0　W: 12 00　b.Darlaston 3-8-89
Source: Scholar. *Honours:* England Youth.

2006-07	Walsall	0	0	
2007-08	Walsall	0	0	
2008-09	Walsall	10	0	10 0

SMITH, Manny (D) 33 0
H: 6 2　W: 12 03　b.Birmingham 8-11-87
Source: Scholar.

2005-06	Walsall	0	0	
2006-07	Walsall	3	0	
2007-08	Walsall	4	0	
2008-09	Walsall	26	0	33 0

TAUNDRY, Richard (D) 59 0
H: 5 9　W: 12 10　b.Walsall 15-2-89
Source: Scholar.

2007-08	Walsall	21	0	
2008-09	Walsall	38	0	59 0

WESTON, Rhys (D) 273 3
H: 6 1　W: 12 12　b.Kingston 27-10-80
Source: Trainee. *Honours:* Wales Schools,
Youth, Under-21, 7 full caps.

1999-2000	Arsenal	1	0	
2000-01	Arsenal	0	0	1 0
2000-01	Cardiff C	28	0	
2001-02	Cardiff C	37	0	
2002-03	Cardiff C	38	2	
2003-04	Cardiff C	24	0	
2004-05	Cardiff C	25	0	
2005-06	Cardiff C	30	0	182 2
2006-07	Port Vale	15	0	15 0
2007-08	Walsall	44	0	
2008-09	Walsall	31	1	75 1

ZAABOUB, Sofiane (D) 105 2
H: 5 11　W: 11 09　b.Melun 23-1-83
Source: Montereau, St Etienne, Modena,
Sora, Real Jaen.

2005-06	FC Brussels	20	1	20 1
2006-07	Swindon T	27	1	
2007-08	Swindon T	29	0	56 1
2008-09	Walsall	29	0	29 0

WATFORD (86)

ANTAL, Botond (G) 0 0
b.Budapest 22-8-91
Source: Scholar.

2008-09	Watford	0	0

AVINEL, Cedric (D) 2 0
H: 6 2　W: 13 03　b.Paris 11-9-86

2006-07	Creteil	1	0	1 0
2006-07	Watford	1	0	
2007-08	Watford	0	0	
2008-09	Watford	0	0	1 0

On loan to Gueugnon

BANGURA, Alhassan (M) 68 1
H: 5 11　W: 10 07　b.Freetown 24-1-88
Source: Scholar. *Honours:* Sierra Leone 1 full
cap.

2004-05	Watford	2	0	
2005-06	Watford	35	1	
2006-07	Watford	16	0	
2007-08	Watford	7	0	
2008-09	Watford	2	0	62 1
2008-09	*Brighton & HA*	6	0	6 0

BENNETT, Dale (D) 0 0
b. 6-1-90
Source: Scholar.

2008-09	Watford	0	0

BROMBY, Leigh (D) 274 11
H: 5 11　W: 11 06　b.Dewsbury 2-6-80
Honours: England Schools.

1998-99	Sheffield W	0	0	
1999-2000	Sheffield W	0	0	
1999-2000	*Mansfield T*	10	1	10 1
2000-01	Sheffield W	18	0	
2001-02	Sheffield W	26	1	
2002-03	Sheffield W	27	0	
2002-03	*Norwich C*	5	0	5 0
2003-04	Sheffield W	29	1	100 2
2004-05	Sheffield U	46	5	
2005-06	Sheffield U	35	1	
2006-07	Sheffield U	17	0	
2007-08	Sheffield U	11	0	
2007-08	Watford	16	1	
2008-09	Watford	22	0	38 1
2008-09	*Sheffield U*	12	1	121 7

BRYAN, Michael (F) 0 0
b.Wexford

2008-09	Watford	0	0

CAUNA, Aleksandrs (M) 5 1
H: 5 8　W: 10 05　b.Riga 19-1-88
Honours: Latvia 11 full caps, 1 goal.

2008-09	Watford	5	1	5 1

COWIE, Don (M) 235 32
H: 5 5　W: 8 05　b.Inverness 15-2-83

2000-01	Ross Co	1	0	
2001-02	Ross Co	18	0	
2002-03	Ross Co	30	1	
2003-04	Ross Co	23	0	
2004-05	Ross Co	34	5	
2005-06	Ross Co	32	4	
2006-07	Ross Co	28	7	166 17
2007-08	Inverness CT	37	9	
2008-09	Inverness CT	22	3	59 12
2008-09	Watford	10	3	10 3

DEMERIT, Jay (D) 155 8
H: 6 2　W: 12 13　b.Green Bay 4-12-79
Source: Chicago Fire, Univ of Illinois,
Northwood. *Honours:* USA 15 full caps.

2004-05	Watford	24	3	
2005-06	Watford	32	2	
2006-07	Watford	32	2	
2007-08	Watford	35	1	
2008-09	Watford	32	0	155 8

DOYLEY, Lloyd (D) 218 0
H: 5 10　W: 12 13　b.Whitechapel 1-12-82
Source: Scholar.

2000-01	Watford	0	0	
2001-02	Watford	20	0	
2002-03	Watford	22	0	
2003-04	Watford	9	0	
2004-05	Watford	29	0	
2005-06	Watford	44	0	
2006-07	Watford	21	0	
2007-08	Watford	36	0	
2008-09	Watford	37	0	218 0

ELLINGTON, Nathan (F) 379 115
H: 5 10　W: 13 01　b.Bradford 2-7-81
Source: Walton & Hersham.

1998-99	Bristol R	10	1	
1999-2000	Bristol R	37	4	
2000-01	Bristol R	42	15	
2001-02	Bristol R	27	15	116 35
2001-02	Wigan Ath	3	2	
2002-03	Wigan Ath	42	15	
2003-04	Wigan Ath	44	18	
2004-05	Wigan Ath	45	24	134 59
2005-06	WBA	31	5	
2006-07	WBA	34	9	
2007-08	WBA	3	0	68 14
2007-08	Watford	34	4	
2008-09	Watford	0	0	34 4
2008-09	*Derby Co*	27	3	27 3

EUSTACE, John (M) 219 16
H: 5 11　W: 11 12　b.Solihull 3-11-79
Source: Trainee.

1996-97	Coventry C	0	0	
1997-98	Coventry C	0	0	
1998-99	Coventry C	0	0	
1998-99	Dundee U	11	1	11 1
1999-2000	Coventry C	16	1	
2000-01	Coventry C	32	2	
2001-02	Coventry C	6	0	
2002-03	Coventry C	32	4	86 7
2002-03	*Middlesbrough*	1	0	1 0
2003-04	Stoke C	26	5	
2004-05	Stoke C	7	0	
2005-06	Stoke C	0	0	
2006-07	Stoke C	15	0	
2006-07	*Hereford U*	8	0	8 0
2007-08	Stoke C	26	0	74 5
2007-08	Watford	13	0	
2008-09	Watford	17	2	30 2
2008-09	*Derby Co*	9	1	9 1

FRANCIS, Damien (M) 237 35
H: 6 0　W: 11 10　b.Wandsworth 27-2-79
Source: Trainee. *Honours:* Jamaica 1 full cap.

1996-97	Wimbledon	0	0	
1997-98	Wimbledon	2	0	
1998-99	Wimbledon	9	0	
1999-2000	Wimbledon	9	0	
2000-01	Wimbledon	29	8	
2001-02	Wimbledon	23	1	
2002-03	Wimbledon	34	6	97 15
2003-04	Norwich C	41	7	
2004-05	Norwich C	32	7	73 14
2005-06	Wigan Ath	20	1	20 1
2006-07	Watford	32	3	
2007-08	Watford	11	2	
2008-09	Watford	4	0	47 5

GIBSON, Billy (M) 0 0
H: 6 2　W: 11 07　b.Harrow 30-9-90
Source: Scholar.

2008-09	Watford	0	0

HARLEY, Jon (D) 294 13
H: 5 8　W: 10 03　b.Maidstone 26-9-79
Source: From Trainee. *Honours:* England
Under-21.

1996-97	Chelsea	0	0	
1997-98	Chelsea	3	0	
1998-99	Chelsea	0	0	
1999-2000	Chelsea	17	2	
2000-01	Chelsea	10	0	30 2
2000-01	*Wimbledon*	6	2	6 2
2001-02	Fulham	10	0	
2002-03	Fulham	11	1	
2002-03	*Sheffield U*	9	1	
2003-04	Fulham	4	0	25 1
2003-04	*Sheffield U*	5	0	
2003-04	*West Ham U*	15	1	15 1
2004-05	Sheffield U	44	2	
2005-06	Sheffield U	4	0	62 3
2005-06	Burnley	41	2	
2006-07	Burnley	45	1	
2007-08	Burnley	33	0	119 3
2008-09	Watford	37	1	37 1

HENDERSON, Liam (F) 13 0
H: 5 11　W: 12 02　b.Gateshead 28-12-89
Source: Hartlepool U.

2008-09	Watford	5	0	5 0
2008-09	*Hartlepool U*	8	0	8 0

HODSON, Lee (D)   **1**   **0**
H: 5 11   W: 11 02   b.Boreham Wood
2-10-91
Source: Scholar.

2008-09	Watford	1	0	**1**	**0**

HOSKINS, Will (F)   **127**   **29**
H: 5 11   W: 11 02   b.Nottingham 6-5-86
Source: From Scholar. *Honours:* England
Youth, Under-20.

2003-04	Rotherham U	4	2		
2004-05	Rotherham U	22	2		
2005-06	Rotherham U	23	4		
2006-07	Rotherham U	24	15	**73**	**23**
2006-07	Watford	9	0		
2007-08	Watford	1	0		
2007-08	*Millwall*	10	2	**10**	**2**
2007-08	*Nottingham F*	2	0	**2**	**0**
2008-09	Watford	32	4	**42**	**4**

JENKINS, Ross (M)   **29**   **1**
H: 5 11   W: 12 06   b.Watford 9-11-90
Source: Scholar.

2008-09	Watford	29	1	**29**	**1**

KABBA, Steven (F)   **154**   **28**
H: 5 10   W: 11 03   b.Lambeth 7-3-81
Source: Trainee.

1999-2000	Crystal Palace	1	0		
2000-01	Crystal Palace	1	0		
2001-02	Crystal Palace	4	0		
2001-02	*Luton T*	3	0	**3**	**0**
2002-03	Crystal Palace	4	1	**10**	**1**
2002-03	*Grimsby T*	13	6	**13**	**6**
2002-03	Sheffield U	25	7		
2003-04	Sheffield U	1	0		
2004-05	Sheffield U	11	2		
2005-06	Sheffield U	34	9		
2006-07	Sheffield U	7	0	**78**	**18**
2006-07	Watford	11	0		
2007-08	Watford	14	1		
2008-09	Watford	0	0	**25**	**1**
2008-09	*Blackpool*	17	2	**17**	**2**
2008-09	*Oldham Ath*	8	0	**8**	**0**

KIERNAN, Rob (M)   **0**   **0**
H: 6 1   W: 11 13   b.Rickmansworth 13-1-91
Source: Scholar.

2008-09	Watford	0	0		

LEE, Richard (G)   **92**   **0**
H: 6 0   W: 12 06   b.Oxford 5-10-82
Source: From Scholar. *Honours:* England
Under-20.

2000-01	Watford	0	0		
2001-02	Watford	0	0		
2002-03	Watford	4	0		
2003-04	Watford	0	0		
2004-05	Watford	33	0		
2005-06	Watford	0	0		
2005-06	*Blackburn R*	0	0		
2006-07	Watford	10	0		
2007-08	Watford	35	0		
2008-09	Watford	10	0	**92**	**0**

LOACH, Scott (G)   **53**   **0**
H: 6 1   W: 13 01   b.Nottingham 27-5-88
Source: Lincoln C. *Honours:* England
Under-21.

2006-07	Watford	0	0		
2007-08	Watford	0	0		
2007-08	*Morecambe*	2	0	**2**	**0**
2007-08	*Bradford C*	20	0	**20**	**0**
2008-09	Watford	31	0	**31**	**0**

MARIAPPA, Adrian (D)   **86**   **1**
H: 5 10   W: 11 12   b.Harrow 3-10-86
Source: Scholar.

2005-06	Watford	3	0		
2006-07	Watford	19	0		
2007-08	Watford	25	0		
2008-09	Watford	39	1	**86**	**1**

McANUFF, Jobi (M)   **306**   **34**
H: 5 11   W: 11 05   b.Edmonton 9-11-81
Source: Scholar. *Honours:* Jamaica 1 full cap.

2000-01	Wimbledon	0	0		
2001-02	Wimbledon	38	4		
2002-03	Wimbledon	31	4		
2003-04	Wimbledon	27	5	**96**	**13**
2003-04	West Ham U	12	1		
2004-05	West Ham U	1	0	**13**	**1**
2004-05	Cardiff C	43	2	**43**	**2**
2005-06	Crystal Palace	41	8		
2006-07	Crystal Palace	34	5	**75**	**13**

O'TOOLE, John (M)   **66**   **11**
H: 6 2   W: 13 07   b.Harrow 30-9-88
Honours: Eire Under-21.

2007-08	Watford	35	3		
2008-09	Watford	22	7	**57**	**10**
2008-09	*Sheffield U*	9	1	**9**	**1**

OSHODI, Eddie (D)   **0**   **0**
H: 6 3   W: 12 07   b.Brentford 14-1-92
Source: Scholar.

2008-09	Watford	0	0		

OSHODI, Eddie (D)   **0**   **0**
H: 6 3   W: 12 07   b.Brentford 14-1-92
Source: Scholar.

2008-09	Watford	0	0		

PARKES, Jordan (D)   **12**   **0**
H: 6 0   W: 12 00   b.Hemel Hempstead
26-7-89
Source: From Scholar. *Honours:* England
Youth.

2006-07	Watford	0	0		
2007-08	Watford	0	0		
2007-08	*Brentford*	1	0	**1**	**0**
2007-08	*Barnet*	10	0	**10**	**0**
2008-09	Watford	1	0	**1**	**0**

POOM, Mart (G)   **269**   **1**
H: 6 4   W: 14 02   b.Tallinn 3-2-72
Honours: Estonia 117 full caps.

1992-93	Flora Tallinn	11	0		
1993-94	Flora Tallinn	11	0		
1994-95	Portsmouth	0	0		
1995-96	Portsmouth	4	0		
1995-96	Flora Tallinn	7	0		
1996-97	Portsmouth	0	0	**4**	**0**
1996-97	Flora Tallinn	12	0	**41**	**0**
1996-97	Derby Co	4	0		
1997-98	Derby Co	36	0		
1998-99	Derby Co	17	0		
1999-2000	Derby Co	28	0		
2000-01	Derby Co	33	0		
2001-02	Derby Co	15	0		
2002-03	Derby Co	13	0	**146**	**0**
2002-03	Sunderland	4	0		
2003-04	Sunderland	43	1		
2004-05	Sunderland	11	0		
2005-06	Sunderland	0	0	**58**	**1**
2005-06	Arsenal	0	0		
2006-07	Arsenal	1	0	**1**	**0**
2007-08	Watford	12	0		
2008-09	Watford	7	0	**19**	**0**

PRISKIN, Tamas (F)   **139**   **41**
H: 6 2   W: 13 03   b.Komarno 27-9-86
Honours: Hungary Under-21, 18 full caps, 7
goals.

2002-03	Gyor	3	0		
2003-04	Gyor	17	5		
2004-05	Gyor	23	8		
2005-06	Gyor	25	11	**68**	**24**
2006-07	Watford	16	2		
2007-08	Watford	14	1		
2007-08	*Preston NE*	5	2	**5**	**2**
2008-09	Watford	36	12	**66**	**15**

ROBINSON, Theo (M)   **69**   **20**
H: 5 9   W: 10 03   b.Birmingham 22-1-89
Source: Scholar.

2005-06	Watford	1	0		
2006-07	Watford	1	0		
2007-08	Watford	0	0		
2007-08	*Hereford U*	43	13	**43**	**13**
2008-09	Watford	3	0	**5**	**0**
2008-09	*Southend U*	21	7	**21**	**7**

SADLER, Matthew (D)   **88**   **0**
H: 5 11   W: 11 08   b.Birmingham 26-2-85
Source: Scholar. *Honours:* England Youth.

2001-02	Birmingham C	0	0		
2002-03	Birmingham C	0	0		
2003-04	Birmingham C	0	0		
2003-04	*Northampton T*	7	0	**7**	**0**
2004-05	Birmingham C	0	0		
2005-06	Birmingham C	8	0		
2006-07	Birmingham C	36	0		
2007-08	Birmingham C	5	0	**51**	**0**
2007-08	Watford	15	0		
2008-09	Watford	15	0	**30**	**0**

SEARLE, Stuart (G)   **0**   **0**
H: 6 3   W: 12 04   b.Wimbledon 27-2-79
Source: Basingstoke T.

2008-09	Watford	0	0		

SMITH, Tommy (F)   **394**   **82**
H: 5 8   W: 11 04   b.Hemel Hempstead
22-5-80
Source: From Trainee. *Honours:* England
Youth, Under-21.

1997-98	Watford	1	0		
1998-99	Watford	8	2		
1999-2000	Watford	22	2		
2000-01	Watford	43	11		
2001-02	Watford	40	11		
2002-03	Watford	35	7		
2003-04	Watford	0	0		
2003-04	Sunderland	35	4	**35**	**4**
2004-05	Derby Co	42	11		
2005-06	Derby Co	43	8		
2006-07	Derby Co	5	1	**90**	**20**
2006-07	Watford	32	1		
2007-08	Watford	44	7		
2008-09	Watford	44	17	**269**	**58**

STEPANOV, Andrei (D)   **249**   **9**
H: 6 2   W: 12 00   b.Tallinn 16-3-79
Honours: Estonia 79 full caps, 1 goal.

1995-96	VMK	1	0		
1996-97	VMK	12	0		
1997-98	VMK	3	0	**16**	**0**
1998	Lelle	22	0		
1999	Lelle	21	0	**43**	**0**
2000	Flora	24	0		
2001	Flora	26	1		
2002	Flora	22	2		
2003	Flora	26	3	**98**	**6**
2004	Torpedo Moscow	18	1		
2005	Torpedo Moscow	24	1		
2006	Torpedo Moscow	16	0	**58**	**2**
2007	Khimki	23	0		
2008	Khimki	10	1	**33**	**1**
2008-09	Watford	1	0	**1**	**0**

WILLIAMS, Gareth (M)   **223**   **12**
H: 6 1   W: 12 03   b.Glasgow 16-12-81
Source: Trainee. *Honours:* Scotland Youth, B,
Under-21, 5 full caps.

1998-99	Nottingham F	0	0		
1999-2000	Nottingham F	2	0		
2000-01	Nottingham F	17	0		
2001-02	Nottingham F	44	0		
2002-03	Nottingham F	40	3		
2003-04	Nottingham F	39	6	**142**	**9**
2004-05	Leicester C	33	1		
2005-06	Leicester C	31	1		
2006-07	Leicester C	14	1	**78**	**3**
2006-07	Watford	3	0		
2007-08	Watford	0	0		
2008-09	Watford	0	0	**3**	**0**

WILLIAMSON, Lee (M)   **313**   **17**
H: 5 10   W: 10 04   b.Derby 7-6-82
Source: Trainee.

1999-2000	Mansfield T	4	0		
2000-01	Mansfield T	15	0		
2001-02	Mansfield T	46	3		
2002-03	Mansfield T	40	0		
2003-04	Mansfield T	35	0		
2004-05	Mansfield T	4	0	**144**	**3**
2004-05	Northampton T	37	0	**37**	**0**
2005-06	Rotherham U	37	4		
2006-07	Rotherham U	19	5	**56**	**9**
2006-07	Watford	5	0		
2007-08	Watford	32	2		
2008-09	Watford	34	2	**71**	**4**
2008-09	*Preston NE*	5	1	**5**	**1**

WILLIAMSON, Mike (D)   **174**   **12**
H: 6 4   W: 13 03   b.Stoke 8-11-83
Source: Trainee.

2001-02	Torquay U	3	0		
2001-02	Southampton	0	0		
2002-03	Southampton	0	0		
2003-04	Southampton	0	0		
2003-04	*Torquay U*	11	0	**14**	**0**
2003-04	*Doncaster R*	0	0		
2004-05	Southampton	0	0		
2004-05	*Wycombe W*	37	2		
2005-06	Wycombe W	39	5		
2006-07	Wycombe W	33	1		
2007-08	Wycombe W	12	0		

2008-09	Wycombe W	22	3	143	11
2008-09	Watford	17	1	17	1

YOUNG, Lewis (M)   1   0
H: 5 10   W: 11 02   b.Stevenage 27-9-89
Source: Scholar.

2008-09	Watford	1	0	1	0

WBA (87)

BAKER, Lee (D)   0   0
b.Redditch 20-1-89
Source: Scholar.

2007-08	WBA	0	0		
2008-09	WBA	0	0		

BARNETT, Leon (D)   102   6
H: 6 0   W: 12 04   b.Stevenage 30-11-85
Source: Scholar.

2003-04	Luton T	0	0		
2004-05	Luton T	0	0		
2005-06	Luton T	20	0		
2006-07	Luton T	39	3	59	3
2007-08	WBA	32	3		
2008-09	WBA	11	0	43	3

BEATTIE, Craig (F)   109   23
H: 6 0   W: 11 07   b.Glasgow 16-1-84
Honours: Scotland Under-21, 7 full caps, 1 goal.

2003-04	Celtic	10	1		
2004-05	Celtic	11	4		
2005-06	Celtic	14	6		
2006-07	Celtic	16	2	51	13
2007-08	WBA	21	3		
2007-08	*Preston NE*	2	0	2	0
2008-09	WBA	7	1	28	4
2008-09	*Crystal Palace*	15	5	15	5
2008-09	*Sheffield U*	13	1	13	1

BEDNAR, Roman (F)   120   36
H: 6 3   W: 13 03   b.Prague 26-3-83
Honours: Czech Republic Under-21, 1 full cap.

2001-02	Mlada Boleslav	0	0		
2002-03	Mlada Boleslav	0	0		
2003-04	Mlada Boleslav	0	0		
2004-05	Mlada Boleslav	25	6	25	6
2004-05	Kaunas	0	0		
2005-06	Hearts	22	7		
2006-07	Hearts	18	4	40	11
2007-08	WBA	29	13		
2008-09	WBA	26	6	55	19

BORJA VALERO (M)   140   8
H: 5 9   W: 11 07   b.Madrid 12-1-85
Honours: Spain Youth.

2005-06	R M Castilla	0	0		
2005-06	R M Castilla	39	2		
2006-07	R M Castilla	37	2	76	4
2007-08	Mallorca	34	4	34	4
2008-09	WBA	30	0	30	0

BRUNT, Chris (M)   208   36
H: 6 1   W: 13 04   b.Belfast 14-12-84
Honours: Trainee. *Honours:* Northern Ireland Under-21, Under-23, 23 full caps, 1 goal.

2002-03	Middlesbrough	0	0		
2003-04	Middlesbrough	0	0		
2003-04	Sheffield W	9	2		
2004-05	Sheffield W	42	4		
2005-06	Sheffield W	44	7		
2006-07	Sheffield W	44	11		
2007-08	Sheffield W	1	0	140	24
2007-08	WBA	34	4		
2008-09	WBA	34	8	68	12

CARSON, Scott (G)   122   0
H: 6 3   W: 14 00   b.Whitehaven 3-9-85
Source: Scholar. *Honours:* England Youth, Under-21, B, 3 full caps.

2002-03	Leeds U	0	0		
2003-04	Leeds U	3	0		
2004-05	Leeds U	0	0	3	0
2004-05	Liverpool	4	0		
2005-06	Liverpool	0	0		
2005-06	*Sheffield W*	9	0	9	0
2006-07	Liverpool	0	0		
2006-07	*Charlton Ath*	36	0	36	0
2007-08	Liverpool	0	0	4	0
2007-08	*Aston Villa*	35	0	35	0
2008-09	WBA	35	0	35	0

CECH, Marek (D)   148   3
H: 6 0   W: 11 09   b.Trebisov 26-1-83
Honours: Slovakia 35 full caps, 5 goals.

2000-01	Inter Bratislava	2	0		
2001-02	Inter Bratislava	13	0		
2002-03	Inter Bratislava	30	0		
2003-04	Inter Bratislava	26	1	71	1
2004-05	Sparta Prague	17	0		
2005-06	Sparta Prague	0	0	17	0
2005-06	Porto	14	1		
2006-07	Porto	22	1		
2007-08	Porto	16	0	52	2
2008-09	WBA	8	0	8	0

CLEMENT, Neil (D)   293   22
H: 6 0   W: 12 03   b.Reading 3-10-78
Source: Trainee. *Honours:* England Schools, Youth.

1995-96	Chelsea	0	0		
1996-97	Chelsea	1	0		
1997-98	Chelsea	0	0		
1998-99	Chelsea	0	0		
1998-99	*Reading*	11	1	11	1
1998-99	*Preston NE*	4	0	4	0
1999-2000	Chelsea	0	0	1	0
1999-2000	*Brentford*	8	0	8	0
1999-2000	*WBA*	8	0		
2000-01	WBA	45	5		
2001-02	WBA	45	6		
2002-03	WBA	36	3		
2003-04	WBA	35	2		
2004-05	WBA	35	3		
2005-06	WBA	31	1		
2006-07	WBA	20	1		
2007-08	WBA	9	0		
2007-08	*Hull C*	5	0	5	0
2008-09	WBA	0	0	264	21

DANEK, Michal (G)   0   0
H: 6 5   W: 15 00   b.Czech Republic 6-7-83
Source: Banik Ostrava, Kladno, Chmel Blsany, Banik Ostrava, Viktoria Plzen.
Honours: Czech Republic Youth, Under-20, Under-21.

2007-08	WBA	0	0		
2008-09	WBA	0	0		

To Viktoria Plzen August 2008

DANIELS, Luke (G)   40   0
H: 6 1   W: 12 10   b.Bolton 5-1-88
Source: Manchester U Scholar. *Honours:* England Youth.

2006-07	WBA	0	0		
2007-08	*Motherwell*	2	0	2	0
2007-08	WBA	0	0		
2008-09	WBA	0	0		
2008-09	*Shrewsbury T*	38	0	38	0

DONK, Ryan (D)   65   1
H: 6 3   W: 12 08   b.Amsterdam 30-3-86
Honours: Holland Under-21.

2005-06	RKC Waalwijk	5	0		
2006-07	RKC Waalwijk	2	0	7	0
2006-07	AZ	18	0		
2007-08	AZ	24	1	42	1
2008-09	WBA	16	0	16	0

DORRANS, Graham (F)   99   21
H: 5 9   W: 11 07   b.Glasgow 5-5-87
Honours: Scotland Youth, Under-21.

2006-07	Livingston	8	0		
2006-07	*Partick T*	15	5	15	5
2006-07	Livingston	34	5		
2007-08	Livingston	34	11	76	16
2008-09	WBA	8	0	8	0

FORTUNE, Marc-Antoine (F)   239   59
H: 6 1   W: 11 13   b.Cayenne 2-7-81

2001-02	Angouleme	34	12	34	12
2002-03	Lille	16	0	16	0
2003-04	Rouen	34	10	34	10
2004-05	Brest	33	10	33	10
2005-06	Utrecht	31	6		
2006-07	Utrecht	22	5	53	11
2006-07	Nancy	15	5		
2007-08	Nancy	37	6	52	11
2008-09	WBA	17	5	17	5

GREENING, Jonathan (M)   332   13
H: 5 11   W: 11 00   b.Scarborough 2-1-79
Source: Trainee. *Honours:* England Youth, Under-21.

1996-97	York C	5	0		
1997-98	York C	20	2	25	2
1997-98	Manchester U	0	0		
1998-99	Manchester U	3	0		
1999-2000	Manchester U	4	0		
2000-01	Manchester U	7	0	14	0
2001-02	Middlesbrough	36	1		
2002-03	Middlesbrough	38	2		
2003-04	Middlesbrough	25	1	99	4
2004-05	WBA	34	0		
2005-06	WBA	38	2		
2006-07	WBA	42	2		
2007-08	WBA	46	1		
2008-09	WBA	34	2	194	7

HODGKISS, Jared (M)   15   0
H: 5 6   W: 11 02   b.Stafford 15-11-86
Source: Scholar.

2005-06	WBA	1	0		
2006-07	WBA	5	0		
2007-08	WBA	4	0		
2008-09	WBA	0	0	10	0
2008-09	*Northampton T*	5	0	5	0

HOEFKENS, Carl (D)   367   13
H: 6 1   W: 12 13   b.Lier 6-10-78
Honours: Belgium 23 full caps, 1 goal.

1996-97	Lierse	17	0		
1997-98	Lierse	27	1		
1998-99	Lierse	30	0		
1999-2000	Lierse	31	0		
2000-01	Lierse	27	0	132	1
2001-02	Lommel	33	3		
2002-03	Lommel	22	0	55	3
2002-03	Westerlo	7	0	7	0
2003-04	Beerschot	32	4		
2004-05	Beerschot	0	0	32	4
2005-06	Stoke C	44	3		
2006-07	Stoke C	45	2	89	5
2007-08	WBA	42	0		
2008-09	WBA	10	0	52	0

KIELY, Dean (G)   659   0
H: 6 1   W: 13 10   b.Salford 10-10-70
Source: WBA School. *Honours:* England Schools, FA Schools, Youth, Eire B, 11 full caps.

1987-88	Coventry C	0	0		
1988-89	Coventry C	0	0		
1989-90	Coventry C	0	0		
1989-90	*Ipswich T*	0	0		
1989-90	*York C*	0	0		
1990-91	York C	17	0		
1991-92	York C	21	0		
1992-93	York C	40	0		
1993-94	York C	46	0		
1994-95	York C	46	0		
1995-96	York C	40	0	210	0
1996-97	Bury	46	0		
1997-98	Bury	46	0		
1998-99	Bury	45	0	137	0
1999-2000	Charlton Ath	45	0		
2000-01	Charlton Ath	25	0		
2001-02	Charlton Ath	38	0		
2002-03	Charlton Ath	38	0		
2003-04	Charlton Ath	37	0		
2004-05	Charlton Ath	36	0		
2005-06	Charlton Ath	3	0	222	0
2005-06	Portsmouth	15	0		
2006-07	Portsmouth	0	0	15	0
2006-07	*Luton T*	11	0	11	0
2006-07	WBA	17	0		
2007-08	WBA	44	0		
2008-09	WBA	3	0	64	0

KIM, Do-Heon (M)   179   23
H: 5 9   W: 11 07   b.Incheon 14-7-82
Source: Seongnam. *Honours:* South Korea 50 full caps, 8 goals.

2001	Suwon	15	0		
2002	Suwon	20	2		
2003	Suwon	34	4		
2004	Suwon	19	1		
2005	Suwon	1	0	89	7
2005	Seongnam	20	2		
2006	Seongnam	25	6		
2007	Seongnam	25	7	70	15
2007-08	WBA	4	1		
2008-09	WBA	16	0	20	1

KOREN, Robert (M)   308   63
H: 5 10   W: 11 03   b.Ljubljana 20-9-80
Honours: Slovenia Under-21, 38 full caps, 2 goals.

1999-2000	Dravograd	31	2		

2000-01	Dravograd	31	9	**62 11**
2001-02	Publikum	31	5	
2002-03	Publikum	32	12	
2003-04	Publikum	15	5	**78 22**
2004	Lillestrom	23	1	
2005	Lillestrom	26	8	
2006	Lillestrom	26	10	**75 19**
2006-07	WBA	18	1	
2007-08	WBA	40	9	
2008-09	WBA	35	1	**93 11**

LABADIE, Joss (M)   1   0
H: 5 7   W: 11 02   b.London 31-8-90

2008-09	WBA	0	0	
2008-09	Shrewsbury T	1	0	**1 0**

MACDONALD, Sherjill (F)   117 21
H: 6 0   W: 12 06   b.Amsterdam 20-11-84
Source: Ajax youth. *Honours:* Holland Youth, Under-21.

2001-02	Anderlecht	11	1	
2002-03	Anderlecht	9	0	
2003-04	Anderlecht	6	0	**26 1**
2004-05	Heracles	17	4	**17 4**
2005-06	Hamburg II	22	4	**22 4**
2006-07	Apeldoorn	21	11	**21 11**
2006-07	WBA	9	0	
2007-08	WBA	10	0	
2007-08	Hereford U	7	6	**7 6**
2008-09	WBA	5	0	**24 0**

On loan to Roeselare

MARTIS, Shelton (D)   107 3
H: 6 0   W: 11 11   b.Willemstad 29-11-82
Honours: Netherlands Antilles 1 full cap.

2002-03	Excelsior	12	0	
2003-04	Excelsior	10	0	**22 0**
2005-06	Darlington	40	2	
2006-07	Darlington	2	0	**42 2**
2006-07	Hibernian	26	0	**26 0**
2007-08	WBA	2	0	
2007-08	Scunthorpe U	3	0	**3 0**
2008-09	WBA	7	0	**9 0**
2008-09	Doncaster R	5	1	**5 1**

MEITE, Abdoulaye (D)   194 2
H: 6 1   W: 12 13   b.Paris 6-10-80
Honours: Ivory Coast 43 full caps, 1 goal.

1998-99	Red Star 93	4	1	
1999-2000	Red Star 93	0	0	**4 1**
2000-01	Marseille	1	0	
2001-02	Marseille	10	0	
2002-03	Marseille	28	0	
2003-04	Marseille	30	0	
2004-05	Marseille	34	1	
2005-06	Marseille	13	0	**116 1**
2006-07	Bolton W	35	0	
2007-08	Bolton W	21	0	**56 0**
2008-09	WBA	18	0	**18 0**

MENSEGUEZ, Juan Carlos (M)   144 11
H: 5 8   W: 10 10   b.Cordoba 18-2-84

2003	River Plate	0	0	
2003-04	Wolfsburg	28	0	
2004-05	Wolfsburg	18	1	
2005-06	Wolfsburg	33	2	
2006-07	Wolfsburg	22	1	**101 4**
2007-08	San Lorenzo	20	4	
2008-09	San Lorenzo	16	2	**36 6**
2008-09	WBA	7	1	**7 1**

MILLER, Ishmael (F)   66 12
H: 6 3   W: 14 00   b.Manchester 5-3-87
Source: Scholar.

2005-06	Manchester C	1	0	
2006-07	Manchester C	16	0	
2007-08	Manchester C	0	0	**17 0**
2007-08	WBA	34	9	
2008-09	WBA	15	3	**49 12**

MOORE, Luke (F)   124 19
H: 5 11   W: 11 13   b.Birmingham 13-2-86
Source: Trainee. *Honours:* FA Schools, England Youth, Under-21.

2002-03	Aston Villa	0	0	
2003-04	Aston Villa	7	0	
2003-04	Wycombe W	6	4	**6 4**
2004-05	Aston Villa	25	1	
2005-06	Aston Villa	27	8	
2006-07	Aston Villa	13	4	
2007-08	Aston Villa	15	1	**87 14**
2007-08	WBA	10	0	
2008-09	WBA	21	1	**31 1**

MORRISON, James (M)   132 10
H: 5 10   W: 10 06   b.Darlington 25-5-86
Source: Trainee. *Honours:* England Youth, Under-20. Scotland 5 full caps.

2003-04	Middlesbrough	1	0	
2004-05	Middlesbrough	14	0	
2005-06	Middlesbrough	24	1	
2006-07	Middlesbrough	28	2	**67 3**
2007-08	WBA	35	4	
2008-09	WBA	30	3	**65 7**

MULUMBU, Youssef (M)   42 1
H: 5 9   W: 10 03   b.Kinshasa 25-1-87
Honours: France Youth, Under-21. DR Congo 8 full caps.

2006-07	Paris St Germain	12	0	
2007-08	Paris St Germain	1	0	
2007-08	Amiens	23	1	**23 1**
2008-09	Paris St Germain	0	0	**13 0**
2008-09	WBA	6	0	**6 0**

OLSSON, Jonas (D)   177 8
H: 6 4   W: 12 08   b.Landskrona 10-3-83
Honours: Sweden Under-21.

2002	Landskrona	0	0	
2003	Landskrona	22	0	
2004	Landskrona	22	1	
2005	Landskrona	12	0	**56 1**
2005-06	NEC Nijmegen	34	0	
2006-07	NEC Nijmegen	32	2	
2007-08	NEC Nijmegen	27	3	**93 5**
2008-09	WBA	28	2	**28 2**

PELE (D)   306 12
H: 6 1   W: 13 08   b.Albufeira 2-5-78
Honours: Cape Verde 1 full cap.

1997-98	Imortal	15	0	
1998-99	Imortal	20	0	
1999-2000	Imortal	29	2	
2000-01	Imortal	25	3	
2001-02	Imortal	38	2	**127 7**
2002-03	Farense	28	2	**28 2**
2003-04	Belenenses	25	1	
2004-05	Belenenses	33	1	
2005-06	Belenenses	32	0	**90 2**
2006-07	Southampton	37	1	**37 1**
2007-08	WBA	21	0	
2008-09	WBA	3	0	**24 0**

ROBINSON, Paul (D)   433 12
H: 5 9   W: 11 12   b.Watford 14-12-78
Source: Trainee. *Honours:* England Under-21.

1996-97	Watford	12	0	
1997-98	Watford	22	2	
1998-99	Watford	29	0	
1999-2000	Watford	32	0	
2000-01	Watford	39	0	
2001-02	Watford	38	3	
2002-03	Watford	37	3	
2003-04	Watford	10	0	**219 8**
2003-04	WBA	31	0	
2004-05	WBA	30	1	
2005-06	WBA	33	0	
2006-07	WBA	42	0	
2007-08	WBA	43	1	
2008-09	WBA	35	0	**214 4**

SLUSARSKI, Bartosz (F)   159 44
H: 6 1   W: 12 11   b.Szamocin 11-12-81
Honours: Poland Under-21, 2 full caps.

1999-2000	Lech Poznan	12	2	
2000-01	Lech Poznan	0	0	
2001-02	Lech Poznan	0	0	
2001-02	Widzew Lodz	8	2	**8 2**
2002-03	Lech Poznan	28	8	
2003-04	Lech Poznan	11	2	**51 12**
2003-04	Groclin	12	3	
2004-05	Groclin	21	10	
2005-06	Groclin	22	7	
2006-07	Groclin	0	0	**55 20**
2006-07	Uniao Leiria	24	7	**24 7**
2007-08	WBA	1	0	
2007-08	Blackpool	6	1	**6 1**
2007-08	Sheffield W	7	1	
2008-09	WBA	0	0	**1 0**
2008-09	Sheffield W	7	1	**14 2**

Transferred to Cracovia January 2009

TEIXEIRA, Felipe (M)   233 31
H: 5 9   W: 10 10   b.Paris 2-10-80
Honours: Portugal Under-21.

1998-99	Felgueiras	27	1	
1999-2000	Felgueiras	27	5	
2000-01	Felgueiras	31	9	**85 15**
2001-02	Istres	16	2	**16 2**
2002-03	Paris St Germain	8	2	
2003-04	Paris St Germain	0	0	
2003-04	*Uniao Leiria*	15	3	**15 3**
2004-05	Paris St Germain	10	0	**18 2**
2005-06	Academica	30	3	
2006-07	Academica	29	1	**59 4**
2007-08	WBA	30	5	
2008-09	WBA	10	0	**40 5**

WOOD, Chris (F)   2 0
H: 6 3   W: 12 10   b.Auckland 7-12-91
Honours: New Zealand Youth, 2 full caps.

2008-09	WBA	2	0	**2 0**

WORRALL, David (M)   14 0
H: 6 0   W: 11 03   b.Manchester 12-6-90
Source: Scholar.

2006-07	Bury	1	0	
2007-08	Bury	0	0	**1 0**
2007-08	WBA	0	0	
2008-09	Accrington S	4	0	**4 0**
2008-09	Shrewsbury T	9	0	**9 0**

ZUIVERLOON, Gianni (D)   130 4
H: 5 10   W: 11 00   b.Rotterdam 30-12-86
Honours: Holland Under-21.

2004-05	Feyenoord	9	0	**9 0**
2005-06	RKC Waalwijk	28	1	**28 1**
2006-07	Heerenveen	30	1	
2007-08	Heerenveen	30	2	**60 3**
2008-09	WBA	33	0	**33 0**

Scholars
Allsop, Ryan; Brown, Kayledene; Clarke, Jamal; Downing, Paul; Elford-Alliyu, Lateef; Lovell, Ashley Jon; Lynch, Lee Jordan; Malcolm, Ashley; Mantom, Samuel Stephen; Samuels, Dwayne Andrew; Sawyers, Romaine Theodore; Waghorn, Tom; Wood, Christopher.

WEST HAM U (88)

ABDULLAH, Ahmad (F)   0 0
b.Saudi Arabia 12-11-91
Source: Scholar.

2008-09	West Ham U	0	0	

ASHTON, Dean (F)   249 92
H: 6 2   W: 14 07   b.Crewe 24-11-83
Source: From Schoolboy. *Honours:* England Youth, Under-20, Under-21, 1 full cap.

2000-01	Crewe Alex	21	8	
2001-02	Crewe Alex	31	7	
2002-03	Crewe Alex	39	9	
2003-04	Crewe Alex	44	19	
2004-05	Crewe Alex	24	17	**159 60**
2004-05	Norwich C	16	7	
2005-06	Norwich C	28	10	**44 17**
2005-06	West Ham U	11	3	
2006-07	West Ham U	10	0	
2007-08	West Ham U	31	10	
2008-09	West Ham U	4	2	**46 15**

BAJNER, Balint (F)   0 0
H: 6 0   W: 11 03   b.Szombathely 18-11-90
Honours: Hungary Youth.

2008-09	West Ham U	0	0	

BEHRAMI, Valon (M)   149 8
H: 6 0   W: 11 02   b.Kosovka Mitrovika 19-4-85
Honours: Switzerland 24 full caps, 2 goals.

2002-03	Lugano	2	0	**2 0**
2003-04	Genoa	24	0	**24 0**
2004-05	Verona	33	3	**33 3**
2005-06	Lazio	26	2	
2006-07	Lazio	17	1	
2007-08	Lazio	23	1	**66 4**
2008-09	West Ham U	24	1	**24 1**

BLACKMORE, David (G)   0 0
H: 6 1   W: 13 00   b.Chelmsford 23-3-89
Source: Scholar.

2006-07	West Ham U	0	0	
2007-08	West Ham U	0	0	
2008-09	West Ham U	0	0	

BOA MORTE, Luis (F) 312 46
H: 5 9 W: 12 06 b.Lisbon 4-8-77
Source: Sporting Lisbon, Lourihanense (loan). *Honours:* Portugal Youth, Under-21, 27 full caps, 1 goal.

1997-98	Arsenal	15	0		
1998-99	Arsenal	8	0		
1999-2000	Arsenal	2	0	25	0
1999-2000	Southampton	14	1		
2000-01	Southampton	0	0	14	1
2000-01	Fulham	39	18		
2001-02	Fulham	23	1		
2002-03	Fulham	29	2		
2003-04	Fulham	33	9		
2004-05	Fulham	31	8		
2005-06	Fulham	35	6		
2006-07	Fulham	14	0	205	44
2006-07	West Ham U	14	1		
2007-08	West Ham U	27	0		
2008-09	West Ham U	27	0	68	1

BOWYER, Lee (M) 396 57
H: 5 9 W: 10 12 b.Canning Town 3-1-77
Source: Trainee. *Honours:* England Youth, Under-21, 1 full cap.

1993-94	Charlton Ath	0	0		
1994-95	Charlton Ath	5	0		
1995-96	Charlton Ath	41	8	46	8
1996-97	Leeds U	32	4		
1997-98	Leeds U	25	3		
1998-99	Leeds U	35	9		
1999-2000	Leeds U	33	5		
2000-01	Leeds U	38	9		
2001-02	Leeds U	25	5		
2002-03	Leeds U	15	3	203	38
2002-03	West Ham U	10	0		
2003-04	Newcastle U	24	2		
2004-05	Newcastle U	27	3		
2005-06	Newcastle U	28	1	79	6
2006-07	West Ham U	20	0		
2007-08	West Ham U	15	4		
2008-09	West Ham U	6	0	51	4
2008-09	Birmingham C	17	1	17	1

COLE, Carlton (F) 155 28
H: 6 3 W: 14 02 b.Croydon 12-11-83
Source: Scholar. *Honours:* England Youth, Under-20, Under-21, 2 full caps.

2000-01	Chelsea	0	0		
2001-02	Chelsea	3	1		
2002-03	Chelsea	13	3		
2002-03	Wolverhampton W	7	1	7	1
2003-04	Chelsea	0	0		
2003-04	Charlton Ath	21	4	21	4
2004-05	Chelsea	0	0		
2004-05	Aston Villa	27	3	27	3
2005-06	Chelsea	9	0	25	4
2006-07	West Ham U	17	2		
2007-08	West Ham U	31	4		
2008-09	West Ham U	27	10	75	16

COLLINS, James (D) 117 5
H: 6 2 W: 14 05 b.Newport 23-8-83
Source: Scholar. *Honours:* Wales Youth, Under-21, 29 full caps, 1 goal.

2000-01	Cardiff C	3	0		
2001-02	Cardiff C	7	1		
2002-03	Cardiff C	2	0		
2003-04	Cardiff C	20	1		
2004-05	Cardiff C	34	1	66	3
2005-06	West Ham U	14	2		
2006-07	West Ham U	16	0		
2007-08	West Ham U	3	0		
2008-09	West Ham U	18	0	51	2

COLLISON, Jack (M) 22 3
H: 6 0 W: 13 10 b.Watford 2-10-88
Source: Scholar. *Honours:* Wales Under-21, 5 full caps.

| 2007-08 | West Ham U | 2 | 0 | | |
| 2008-09 | West Ham U | 20 | 3 | 22 | 3 |

DAVENPORT, Calum (D) 144 6
H: 6 4 W: 14 00 b.Bedford 1-1-83
Source: Trainee. *Honours:* England Youth, Under-20, Under-21.

1999-2000	Coventry C	0	0		
2000-01	Coventry C	1	0		
2001-02	Coventry C	3	0		
2002-03	Coventry C	32	3		
2003-04	Coventry C	33	0		
2004-05	Coventry C	6	0	75	3
2004-05	Southampton	7	0	7	0
2004-05	Tottenham H	1	0		
2004-05	West Ham U	10	0		
2005-06	Tottenham H	4	0		
2005-06	Norwich C	15	1	15	1
2006-07	Tottenham H	10	1	15	1
2006-07	West Ham U	6	0		
2007-08	West Ham U	0	0		
2007-08	Watford	1	0	1	0
2008-09	West Ham U	7	1	23	1
2008-09	Sunderland	8	0	8	0

DI MICHELE, David (F) 446 124
H: 5 8 W: 11 00 b.Roma 6-1-76

1993-94	Lodigiani	7	0		
1994-95	Lodigiani	16	0		
1995-96	Lodigiani	20	6	43	6
1996-97	Foggia	36	7		
1997-98	Foggia	32	7	68	14
1998-99	Salernitana	26	3		
1999-2000	Salernitana	36	23		
2000-01	Salernitana	30	14	92	40
2001-02	Udinese	25	5		
2002-03	Reggina	34	7		
2003-04	Reggina	28	8	62	15
2004-05	Udinese	37	15		
2005-06	Udinese	16	3	78	23
2005-06	Palermo	19	7		
2006-07	Palermo	29	9	48	16
2007-08	Torino	25	6	25	6
2008-09	West Ham U	30	4	30	4

DIXON, Terry (F) 0 0
b.Holloway 15-1-90
Honours: Eire Youth, Under-21.

2006-07	Tottenham H	0	0		
2007-08	Tottenham H	0	0		
2008-09	West Ham U	0	0		

DYER, Kieron (M) 290 32
H: 5 8 W: 10 01 b.Ipswich 29-12-78
Source: Trainee. *Honours:* England Youth, Under-21, B, 33 full caps.

1996-97	Ipswich T	13	0		
1997-98	Ipswich T	41	4		
1998-99	Ipswich T	37	5	91	9
1999-2000	Newcastle U	30	3		
2000-01	Newcastle U	26	5		
2001-02	Newcastle U	18	3		
2002-03	Newcastle U	35	2		
2003-04	Newcastle U	25	1		
2004-05	Newcastle U	23	4		
2005-06	Newcastle U	11	0		
2006-07	Newcastle U	22	5		
2007-08	Newcastle U	0	0	190	23
2007-08	West Ham U	2	0		
2008-09	West Ham U	7	0	9	0

EYJOLFSSON, Holmar (D) 0 0
b.Iceland 6-8-90

| 2008-09 | West Ham U | 0 | 0 | | |

FAUBERT, Julien (M) 168 13
H: 5 10 W: 11 08 b.Le Havre 1-8-83
Honours: France 1 full cap, 1 goal.

2002-03	Cannes	26	1		
2003-04	Cannes	19	3	45	4
2004-05	Bordeaux	36	1		
2005-06	Bordeaux	34	5		
2006-07	Bordeaux	26	3	96	9
2007-08	West Ham U	7	0		
2008-09	West Ham U	20	0	27	0

On loan to Real Madrid

GABBIDON, Daniel (D) 277 10
H: 6 0 W: 13 05 b.Cwmbran 8-8-79
Source: Trainee. *Honours:* Wales Youth, Under-21, 40 full caps.

1998-99	WBA	2	0		
1999-2000	WBA	18	0		
2000-01	WBA	0	0	20	0
2000-01	Cardiff C	43	3		
2001-02	Cardiff C	44	3		
2002-03	Cardiff C	24	0		
2003-04	Cardiff C	41	3		
2004-05	Cardiff C	45	1	197	10
2005-06	West Ham U	32	0		
2006-07	West Ham U	18	0		
2007-08	West Ham U	10	0		
2008-09	West Ham U	0	0	60	0

GRASSER, Georg (D) 0 0
b. 3-10-90
Source: Graz.

| 2008-09 | West Ham U | 0 | 0 | | |

GREEN, Rob (G) 325 0
H: 6 3 W: 14 09 b.Chertsey 18-1-80
Source: From Trainee. *Honours:* England Youth, B, 4 full caps.

1997-98	Norwich C	0	0		
1998-99	Norwich C	2	0		
1999-2000	Norwich C	3	0		
2000-01	Norwich C	5	0		
2001-02	Norwich C	41	0		
2002-03	Norwich C	46	0		
2003-04	Norwich C	46	0		
2004-05	Norwich C	38	0		
2005-06	Norwich C	42	0	223	0
2006-07	West Ham U	26	0		
2007-08	West Ham U	38	0		
2008-09	West Ham U	38	0	102	0

HINES, Zavon (F) 7 1
H: 5 10 W: 10 07 b.Jamaica 27-12-88
Source: Scholar.

2007-08	West Ham U	0	0		
2007-08	Coventry C	7	1	7	1
2008-09	West Ham U	0	0		

ILUNGA, Herita (D) 205 2
H: 5 11 W: 11 09 b.Kinshasa 25-2-82
Honours: DR Congo 18 full caps.

2002-03	Espanyol B	0	0		
2003-04	St Etienne	32	0		
2004-05	St Etienne	37	1		
2005-06	St Etienne	30	1		
2006-07	St Etienne	36	0	135	2
2007-08	Toulouse	35	0	35	0
2008-09	West Ham U	35	0	35	0

JEFFERY, Jack (F) 1 0
H: 5 8 W: 11 10 b.Gravesend 13-8-89
Source: Scholar.

2007-08	West Ham U	0	0		
2008-09	West Ham U	0	0		
2008-09	Leyton Orient	1	0	1	0

KOVAC, Radoslav (D) 283 16
H: 6 2 W: 12 04 b.Sumperk 27-11-79
Honours: Czech Republic Under-21, 29 full caps, 2 goals.

1997-98	Olomouc	1	0		
1998-99	Olomouc	20	0		
1999-2000	Olomouc	28	0		
2000-01	Olomouc	27	0		
2001-02	Olomouc	23	1		
2002-03	Olomouc	28	2	127	3
2003-04	Sparta Prague	29	3		
2004-05	Sparta Prague	17	0	46	3
2005	Spartak Moscow	27	4		
2006	Spartak Moscow	27	2		
2007	Spartak Moscow	26	1		
2008	Spartak Moscow	21	2	101	9
2008-09	West Ham U	9	1	9	1

LASTUVKA, Jan (G) 148 0
H: 6 3 W: 13 10 b.Havirov 7-7-82
Honours: Czech Republic Youth, Under-21.

1999-2000	Karvina	3	0	3	0
2000-01	Banik Ostrava	24	0		
2001-02	Banik Ostrava	25	0		
2002-03	Banik Ostrava	30	0	79	0
2003-04	Shakhtar Donetsk	20	0		
2004-05	Shakhtar Donetsk	13	0	33	0
2005-06	Fulham	8	0		
2006-07	Fulham	0	0	8	0
2007-08	Bochum	25	0	25	0
2008-09	West Ham U	0	0		

LOPEZ, Walter (D) 70 6
H: 5 11 W: 12 02 b.Montevideo 15-10-85
Honours: Uruguay 3 full caps.

2003	Racing (Uruguay)	0	0		
2004	Racing (Uruguay)	0	0		
2005	Racing (Uruguay)	5	1	5	1
2005-06	River Plate (Uru)	33	4		
2006-07	River Plate (Uru)	11	1		
2006-07	Xerez	11	0	11	0
2007-08	Tecos UAG	3	0	3	0
2007-08	River Plate (Uru)	2	0	46	5
2008-09	West Ham U	5	0	5	0

MILLER, Ashley (D) 0 0
b. 5-9-89
Source: Scholar.

| 2007-08 | West Ham U | 0 | 0 | | |
| 2008-09 | West Ham U | 0 | 0 | | |

N'GALA, Bondz (D)   **3   0**
H: 6 0   W: 12 03   b.Newham 13-9-89
Source: Scholar.
2007-08	West Ham U	0	0		
2008-09	West Ham U	0	0		
2008-09	*Milton Keynes D*	3	0	**3**	**0**

NEILL, Lucas (D)   **419   19**
H: 6 0   W: 12 03   b.Sydney 9-3-78
Source: NSW Soccer Academy. *Honours:*
Australia Under-20, Under-23, 41 full caps.
1995-96	Millwall	13	0		
1996-97	Millwall	39	3		
1997-98	Millwall	6	0		
1998-99	Millwall	35	6		
1999-2000	Millwall	31	1		
2000-01	Millwall	24	2		
2001-02	Millwall	4	1	152	13
2001-02	Blackburn R	31	1		
2002-03	Blackburn R	34	0		
2003-04	Blackburn R	32	2		
2004-05	Blackburn R	36	1		
2005-06	Blackburn R	35	1		
2006-07	Blackburn R	20	0	188	5
2006-07	West Ham U	11	0		
2007-08	West Ham U	34	0		
2008-09	West Ham U	34	1	79	1

NOBLE, Mark (M)   **106   9**
H: 5 11   W: 12 00   b.West Ham 8-5-87
Source: Scholar. *Honours:* England Youth,
Under-21.
2004-05	West Ham U	13	0		
2005-06	West Ham U	5	0		
2005-06	*Hull C*	5	0	**5**	**0**
2006-07	West Ham U	10	2		
2006-07	*Ipswich T*	13	1	**13**	**1**
2007-08	West Ham U	31	3		
2008-09	West Ham U	29	3	88	8

NSEREKO, Savio (M)   **33   3**
H: 5 9   W: 11 07   b.Kampala 27-7-89
Source: Munich 1860 B, Germany Youth.
2005-06	Brescia	1	0		
2006-07	Brescia	2	0		
2007-08	Brescia	5	0		
2008-09	Brescia	17	3	**23**	**3**
2008-09	West Ham U	10	0	**10**	**0**

O'NEILL, Ryan (D)   **0   0**
b.Dungannon 19-1-90
Source: Scholar.
2007-08	West Ham U	0	0		
2008-09	West Ham U	0	0		

PARKER, Scott (M)   **250   17**
H: 5 9   W: 11 10   b.Lambeth 13-10-80
Source: Trainee. *Honours:* England Schools,
Youth, Under-21, 3 full caps.
1997-98	Charlton Ath	3	0		
1998-99	Charlton Ath	4	0		
1999-2000	Charlton Ath	15	1		
2000-01	Charlton Ath	20	1		
2000-01	*Norwich C*	6	1	**6**	**1**
2001-02	Charlton Ath	38	1		
2002-03	Charlton Ath	28	4		
2003-04	Charlton Ath	20	2	128	9
2003-04	Chelsea	11	1		
2004-05	Chelsea	4	0	15	1
2005-06	Newcastle U	26	1		
2006-07	Newcastle U	29	3	55	4
2007-08	West Ham U	18	1		
2008-09	West Ham U	28	1	46	2

PAYNE, Josh (M)   **13   1**
H: 6 0   W: 11 09   b. 25-11-90
Source: Scholar.
2008-09	West Ham U	2	0	**2**	**0**
2008-09	*Cheltenham T*	11	1	**11**	**1**

QUASHIE, Nigel (M)   **335   24**
H: 6 0   W: 13 10   b.Peckham 20-7-78
Source: Trainee. *Honours:* England Youth,
Under-21, B, Scotland 14 full caps, 1 goal.
1995-96	QPR	11	0		
1996-97	QPR	13	0		
1997-98	QPR	33	3		
1998-99	QPR	0	0	57	3
1998-99	Nottingham F	16	0		
1999-2000	Nottingham F	28	2	44	2
2000-01	Portsmouth	31	5		
2001-02	Portsmouth	35	2		
2002-03	Portsmouth	42	5		
2003-04	Portsmouth	21	1		

2004-05	Portsmouth	19	0	**148**	**13**
2004-05	Southampton	13	1		
2005-06	Southampton	24	4	**37**	**5**
2005-06	WBA	9	1		
2006-07	WBA	20	0	**29**	**1**
2006-07	West Ham U	7	0		
2007-08	West Ham U	0	0		
2008-09	West Ham U	0	0	**7**	**0**
2008-09	*Birmingham C*	10	0	**10**	**0**
2008-09	*Wolverhampton W* 3	0	**3**	**0**	

REID, Kyel (M)   **46   3**
H: 5 10   W: 12 05   b.South London 26-11-87
Source: Scholar. *Honours:* England Youth.
2004-05	West Ham U	0	0		
2005-06	West Ham U	2	0		
2006-07	West Ham U	0	0		
2006-07	*Barnsley*	26	2	**26**	**2**
2007-08	West Ham U	1	0		
2007-08	*Crystal Palace*	2	0	**2**	**0**
2008-09	West Ham U	0	0	**3**	**0**
2008-09	*Blackpool*	7	0	**7**	**0**
2008-09	*Wolverhampton W* 8	1	**8**	**1**	

SEARS, Freddie (F)   **24   1**
H: 5 8   W: 10 01   b.Hornchurch 27-11-89
Source: Scholar. *Honours:* England Youth.
2007-08	West Ham U	7	1		
2008-09	West Ham U	17	0	**24**	**1**

SPECTOR, Jonathan (D)   **83   0**
H: 6 0   W: 12 08   b.Arlington Heights 1-3-86
Source: Chicago Sockers. *Honours:* USA
Youth, 18 full caps.
2003-04	Manchester U	0	0		
2004-05	Manchester U	3	0		
2005-06	Manchester U	0	0	**3**	**0**
2005-06	*Charlton Ath*	20	0	**20**	**0**
2006-07	West Ham U	25	0		
2007-08	West Ham U	26	0		
2008-09	West Ham U	9	0	60	0

SPENCE, Jordan (M)   **20   0**
H: 6 2   W: 12 07   b.Woodford 24-5-90
Source: Scholar. *Honours:* England Youth.
2007-08	West Ham U	0	0		
2008-09	West Ham U	0	0		
2008-09	*Leyton Orient*	20	0	**20**	**0**

STANISLAS, Junior (M)   **15   3**
H: 6 0   W: 12 00   b.Kidbrooke 26-11-89
Source: Scholar. *Honours:* England Youth.
2007-08	West Ham U	0	0		
2008-09	West Ham U	9	2	**9**	**2**
2008-09	*Southend U*	6	1	**6**	**1**

STECH, Marek (G)   **2   0**
H: 6 3   W: 14 00   b.Prague 28-1-90
Source: Sparta Prague, West Ham U Scholar.
Honours: Czech Republic Youth.
2008-09	West Ham U	0	0		
2008-09	*Wycombe W*	2	0	**2**	**0**

STOKES, Tony (M)   **25   0**
H: 5 10   W: 11 10   b.East London 7-1-87
Source: Scholar.
2005-06	West Ham U	0	0		
2005-06	*Rushden & D*	19	0	**19**	**0**
2006-07	West Ham U	0	0		
2006-07	*Brighton & HA*	6	0	**6**	**0**
2007-08	West Ham U	0	0		
2008-09	West Ham U	0	0		
On loan to Ujpest

STREET, Adam (G)   **0   0**
b.Canada 7-7-91
2008-09	West Ham U	0	0		

TOMKINS, James (D)   **25   1**
H: 6 3   W: 11 10   b.Basildon 29-3-89
Source: Scholar. *Honours:* England Schools,
Youth, Under-21.
2005-06	West Ham U	0	0		
2006-07	West Ham U	0	0		
2007-08	West Ham U	6	0		
2008-09	West Ham U	12	1	**18**	**1**
2008-09	*Derby Co*	7	0	**7**	**0**

TRISTAN, Diego (F)   **394 139**
H: 6 1   W: 12 06   b.La Alpabay 5-1-76
Honours: Spain 15 full caps, 4 goals.
1995-96	Betis B	38	11		
1996-97	Betis B	33	1		
1997-98	Betis B	24	11	**95**	**23**
1998-99	Mallorca B	39	15	**39**	**15**
1999-2000	Mallorca	35	19		

2000-01	La Coruna	29	19		
2001-02	La Coruna	33	21		
2002-03	La Coruna	23	9		
2003-04	La Coruna	33	8		
2004-05	La Coruna	23	9		
2005-06	La Coruna	36	12	**177**	**78**
2006-07	Mallorca	13	0	**48**	**19**
2007-08	Livorno	21	1	**21**	**1**
2008-09	West Ham U	14	3	**14**	**3**

UPSON, Matthew (D)   **238   6**
H: 6 1   W: 11 04   b.Stowmarket 18-4-79
Source: Trainee. *Honours:* England Youth,
Under-21, 15 full caps, 1 goal.
1995-96	Luton T	0	0		
1996-97	Luton T	1	0	**1**	**0**
1996-97	Arsenal	0	0		
1997-98	Arsenal	5	0		
1998-99	Arsenal	5	0		
1999-2000	Arsenal	8	0		
2000-01	Arsenal	2	0		
2000-01	*Nottingham F*	1	0	**1**	**0**
2000-01	*Crystal Palace*	7	0	**7**	**0**
2001-02	Arsenal	14	0		
2002-03	Arsenal	0	0	**34**	**0**
2002-03	*Reading*	14	0	**14**	**0**
2002-03	Birmingham C	14	0		
2003-04	Birmingham C	30	0		
2004-05	Birmingham C	36	2		
2005-06	Birmingham C	24	1		
2006-07	Birmingham C	9	2	**113**	**5**
2006-07	West Ham U	2	0		
2007-08	West Ham U	29	1		
2008-09	West Ham U	37	0	68	1

WALKER, Jim (G)   **432   0**
H: 5 11   W: 13 04   b.Sutton-in-Ashfield
9-7-73
Source: Trainee.
1991-92	Notts Co	0	0		
1992-93	Notts Co	0	0		
1993-94	Walsall	31	0		
1994-95	Walsall	4	0		
1995-96	Walsall	26	0		
1996-97	Walsall	36	0		
1997-98	Walsall	46	0		
1998-99	Walsall	46	0		
1999-2000	Walsall	43	0		
2000-01	Walsall	44	0		
2001-02	Walsall	43	0		
2002-03	Walsall	41	0		
2003-04	Walsall	43	0	**403**	**0**
2004-05	West Ham U	10	0		
2005-06	West Ham U	3	0		
2006-07	West Ham U	0	0		
2007-08	West Ham U	0	0		
2008-09	West Ham U	0	0	**13**	**0**
2008-09	*Colchester U*	16	0	**16**	**0**

WIDDOWSON, Joe (D)   **23   1**
H: 6 0   W: 12 00   b.Forest Gate 28-3-89
Source: Scholar.
2007-08	West Ham U	0	0		
2007-08	*Rotherham U*	3	0	**3**	**0**
2008-09	West Ham U	0	0		
2008-09	*Grimsby T*	20	1	**20**	**1**

Scholars
Barrett, Nicholas Paul; Brookes, Antony
Ross; Brown, Jordan; Edgar, Anthony James;
Fry, Matthew; Kearns, Daniel; Lee, Oliver
Robert; Loveday, Peter Charles;
McNaughton, Callum James; Montano,
Cristian; Okus, Conor Ekundayo.

WIGAN ATH (89)

BOUAOUZAN, Rachid (M)   **69   4**
H: 5 6   W: 11 02   b.Rotterdam 20-2-84
2003-04	Sparta Rotterdam	1	0		
2004-05	Sparta Rotterdam	10	1		
2005-06	Sparta Rotterdam	30	1		
2006-07	Sparta Rotterdam	28	2	**69**	**4**
2007-08	Wigan Ath	0	0		
2008-09	Wigan Ath	0	0		
On loan to NEC Nijmegen

BOYCE, Emmerson (D)   **341   11**
H: 6 0   W: 12 03   b.Aylesbury 24-9-79
Source: Trainee. *Honours:* Barbados 2 full
caps.
1997-98	Luton T	0	0		

BIRCHALL (continued)

Season	Club				
1998-99	Luton T	1	0		
1999-2000	Luton T	30	1		
2000-01	Luton T	42	3		
2001-02	Luton T	37	0		
2002-03	Luton T	34	0		
2003-04	Luton T	42	4	**186**	**8**
2004-05	Crystal Palace	27	0		
2005-06	Crystal Palace	42	2	**69**	**2**
2006-07	Wigan Ath	34	0		
2007-08	Wigan Ath	25	0		
2008-09	Wigan Ath	27	1	**86**	**1**

BRAMBLE, Titus (D)   **216 7**
H: 6 2 W: 13 10 b.Ipswich 31-7-81
Source: Trainee. *Honours:* England Under-21.

Season	Club				
1998-99	Ipswich T	4	0		
1999-2000	Ipswich T	0	0		
1999-2000	Colchester U	2	0	**2**	**0**
2000-01	Ipswich T	26	1		
2001-02	Ipswich T	18	0	**48**	**1**
2002-03	Newcastle U	16	0		
2003-04	Newcastle U	29	0		
2004-05	Newcastle U	19	1		
2005-06	Newcastle U	24	2		
2006-07	Newcastle U	17	0	**105**	**3**
2007-08	Wigan Ath	26	2		
2008-09	Wigan Ath	35	1	**61**	**3**

BROWN, Michael (M)   **397 32**
H: 5 9 W: 12 04 b.Hartlepool 25-1-77
Source: Trainee. *Honours:* England Under-21.

Season	Club				
1994-95	Manchester C	0	0		
1995-96	Manchester C	21	0		
1996-97	Manchester C	11	0		
1996-97	Hartlepool U	6	1	**6**	**1**
1997-98	Manchester C	26	0		
1998-99	Manchester C	31	2		
1999-2000	Manchester C	0	0	**89**	**2**
1999-2000	Portsmouth	4	0	**4**	**0**
1999-2000	Sheffield U	24	3		
2000-01	Sheffield U	36	1		
2001-02	Sheffield U	36	5		
2002-03	Sheffield U	40	16		
2003-04	Sheffield U	15	2	**151**	**27**
2003-04	Tottenham H	17	1		
2004-05	Tottenham H	24	1		
2005-06	Tottenham H	9	0	**50**	**2**
2005-06	Fulham	7	0		
2006-07	Fulham	34	0	**41**	**0**
2007-08	Wigan Ath	31	0		
2008-09	Wigan Ath	25	0	**56**	**0**

CAMARA, Henri (F)   **246 81**
H: 5 9 W: 10 08 b.Dakar 10-5-77
Honours: Senegal 65 full caps, 22 goals.

Season	Club				
1999-2000	Neuchatel Xamax	20	12		
2000-01	Neuchatel Xamax	12	5	**32**	**17**
2000-01	Grasshoppers	3		**11**	**3**
2001-02	Sedan	25	8		
2002-03	Sedan	34	14	**59**	**22**
2003-04	Wolverhampton W	30	7		
2004-05	Wolverhampton W	0	0	**30**	**7**
2004-05	Celtic	18	8	**18**	**8**
2004-05	Southampton	13	4	**13**	**4**
2005-06	Wigan Ath	29	12		
2006-07	Wigan Ath	23	6		
2007-08	Wigan Ath	0	0		
2007-08	West Ham U	10	0	**10**	**0**
2008-09	Wigan Ath	17	2	**69**	**20**
2008-09	Stoke C	4	0	**4**	**0**

CATTERMOLE, Lee (M)   **102 4**
H: 5 10 W: 11 13 b.Stockton 21-3-88
Source: Scholar. *Honours:* England Youth, Under-21.

Season	Club				
2005-06	Middlesbrough	14	1		
2006-07	Middlesbrough	31	1		
2007-08	Middlesbrough	24	1	**69**	**3**
2008-09	Wigan Ath	33	1	**33**	**1**

CHO, Won-Hee (M)   **1 0**
H: 5 10 W: 11 07 b.South Korea 17-4-83
Honours: South Korea 30 full caps, 1 goal.

Season	Club				
2008-09	Wigan Ath	1	0	**1**	**0**

CYWKA, Thomasz (M)   **4 0**
H: 5 10 W: 11 09 b.Gliwice 27-6-88
Source: Gwarek Zabrze. *Honours:* Poland Youth, Under-21.

Season	Club				
2006-07	Wigan Ath	0	0		
2006-07	Oldham Ath	4	0	**4**	**0**
2007-08	Wigan Ath	0	0		
2008-09	Wigan Ath	0	0		

DE RIDDER, Daniel (M)   **78 4**
H: 5 11 W: 10 12 b.Amsterdam 6-3-84
Honours: Holland Under-21.

Season	Club				
2003-04	Ajax	15	1		
2004-05	Ajax	15	2	**30**	**3**
2005-06	Celta Vigo	17	1		
2006-07	Celta Vigo	3	0	**20**	**1**
2007-08	Birmingham C	10	0	**10**	**0**
2008-09	Wigan Ath	18	0	**18**	**0**

EDMAN, Erik (D)   **259 3**
H: 5 10 W: 12 04 b.Huskvarna 11-11-78
Source: Habo. *Honours:* Sweden 55 full caps, 1 goal.

Season	Club				
1997	Helsingborg	24	0		
1998	Helsingborg	25	0		
1999	Helsingborg	12	1	**61**	**1**
1999-2000	Torino	0	0		
1999-2000	Karlsruher	8	0	**8**	**0**
2000	AIK Stockholm	8	0		
2001	AIK Stockholm	13	0	**21**	**0**
2001-02	Heerenveen	33	1		
2002-03	Heerenveen	30	0	**63**	**1**
2004-05	Tottenham H	28	1		
2005-06	Tottenham H	3	0	**31**	**1**
2005-06	Rennes	26	0		
2006-07	Rennes	30	0		
2007-08	Rennes	12	0	**68**	**0**
2007-08	Wigan Ath	5	0		
2008-09	Wigan Ath	2	0	**7**	**0**

FIGUEROA, Maynor (D)   **64 3**
H: 5 11 W: 12 02 b.Jutiapa 2-5-83
Honours: Honduras 61 full caps, 2 goals.

Season	Club				
2000-01	Victoria La Ceiba	2	0		
2001-02	Victoria La Ceiba	22	2	**24**	**2**
2007-08	Wigan Ath	2	0		
2008-09	Wigan Ath	38	1	**40**	**1**

HOLT, Joe (M)   **0 0**
H: 5 10 W: 10 05 b.Huyton 1-2-90
Source: Scholar.

Season	Club				
2008-09	Wigan Ath	0	0		

KAPO, Olivier (M)   **233 35**
H: 6 1 W: 12 06 b.Abidjan 27-9-80
Honours: France 9 full caps, 3 goals.

Season	Club				
1999-2000	Auxerre	15	3		
2000-01	Auxerre	29	4		
2001-02	Auxerre	25	4		
2002-03	Auxerre	21	6		
2003-04	Auxerre	29	2	**119**	**19**
2004-05	Juventus	14	0	**14**	**0**
2005-06	Monaco	25	5	**25**	**5**
2006-07	Levante	30	5	**30**	**5**
2007-08	Birmingham C	26	5	**26**	**5**
2008-09	Wigan Ath	19	1	**19**	**1**

KING, Marlon (F)   **342 108**
H: 5 10 W: 12 10 b.Dulwich 26-4-80
Source: Trainee. *Honours:* Jamaica 19 full caps, 12 goals.

Season	Club				
1998-99	Barnet	22	6		
1999-2000	Barnet	31	8	**53**	**14**
2000-01	Gillingham	38	15		
2001-02	Gillingham	42	17		
2002-03	Gillingham	10	4		
2003-04	Gillingham	11	4	**101**	**40**
2003-04	Nottingham F	24	5		
2004-05	Nottingham F	26	5		
2004-05	Leeds U	9	0	**9**	**0**
2005-06	Nottingham F	0	0	**50**	**10**
2005-06	Watford	41	21		
2006-07	Watford	13	4		
2007-08	Watford	27	11	**81**	**36**
2007-08	Wigan Ath	15	1		
2008-09	Wigan Ath	10	0	**15**	**1**
2008-09	Hull C	20	5	**20**	**5**
2008-09	Middlesbrough	13	2	**13**	**2**

KINGSON, Richard (G)   **106 0**
H: 6 3 W: 13 10 b.Accra 13-6-78
Honours: Ghana 58 full caps, 1 goal.

Season	Club				
1998-99	Sakarya	21	0	**21**	**0**
1999-2000	Goztepe	19	0		
2000-01	Goztepe	10	0	**29**	**0**
2001-02	Antalya	15	0	**15**	**0**
2002-03	Elazig	20	0	**20**	**0**
2003-04	Ankara	9	0		
2004-05	Galatasaray	1	0	**1**	**0**
2005-06	Ankara	1	0		
2006-07	Ankara	3	0	**4**	**0**
2007	Hammarby	11	0	**11**	**0**
2007-08	Birmingham C	1	0		
2008-09	Birmingham C	0	0	**1**	**0**
2008-09	Wigan Ath	4	0	**4**	**0**

KIRKLAND, Christopher (G)   **154 0**
H: 6 5 W: 14 08 b.Leicester 2-5-81
Source: Trainee. *Honours:* England Youth, Under-21, 1 full cap.

Season	Club				
1997-98	Coventry C	0	0		
1998-99	Coventry C	0	0		
1999-2000	Coventry C	0	0		
2000-01	Coventry C	23	0		
2001-02	Coventry C	1	0	**24**	**0**
2002-03	Liverpool	8	0		
2003-04	Liverpool	6	0		
2004-05	Liverpool	10	0		
2005-06	Liverpool	0	0		
2005-06	WBA	10	0	**10**	**0**
2006-07	Liverpool	0	0	**25**	**0**
2006-07	Wigan Ath	26	0		
2007-08	Wigan Ath	37	0		
2008-09	Wigan Ath	32	0	**95**	**0**

KOUMAS, Jason (M)   **340 61**
H: 5 10 W: 11 02 b.Wrexham 25-9-79
Source: Trainee. *Honours:* Wales 34 full caps, 10 goals.

Season	Club				
1997-98	Tranmere R	1	0		
1998-99	Tranmere R	23	3		
1999-2000	Tranmere R	23	2		
2000-01	Tranmere R	39	10		
2001-02	Tranmere R	38	8		
2002-03	Tranmere R	4	2	**127**	**25**
2002-03	WBA	32	4		
2003-04	WBA	42	10		
2004-05	WBA	10	0		
2005-06	WBA	0	0		
2005-06	Cardiff C	44	12	**44**	**12**
2006-07	WBA	39	9	**123**	**23**
2007-08	Wigan Ath	30	1		
2008-09	Wigan Ath	16	0	**46**	**1**

KUPISZ, Tomasz (M)   **0 0**
H: 5 11 W: 12 00 b.Radom 2-1-90
Source: Piaseczno.

Season	Club				
2006-07	Wigan Ath	0	0		
2007-08	Wigan Ath	0	0		
2008-09	Wigan Ath	0	0		

MAHON, Craig (F)   **2 0**
H: 5 7 W: 9 10 b.Dublin 21-6-89

Season	Club				
2008-09	Wigan Ath	0	0		
2008-09	Accrington S	2	0	**2**	**0**

McMANAMAN, Callum (F)   **1 0**
H: 5 9 W: 11 03 b.Huyton 25-4-91
Source: Everton.

Season	Club				
2008-09	Wigan Ath	1	0	**1**	**0**

MELCHIOT, Mario (D)   **355 9**
H: 6 2 W: 11 09 b.Amsterdam 4-11-76
Honours: Holland 22 full caps.

Season	Club				
1996-97	Ajax	23	0		
1997-98	Ajax	26	0		
1998-99	Ajax	24	1	**73**	**1**
1999-2000	Chelsea	5	0		
2000-01	Chelsea	31	0		
2001-02	Chelsea	37	2		
2002-03	Chelsea	34	0		
2003-04	Chelsea	23	2	**130**	**4**
2004-05	Birmingham C	34	1		
2005-06	Birmingham C	23	1	**57**	**2**
2006-07	Rennes	30	2	**30**	**2**
2007-08	Wigan Ath	31	0		
2008-09	Wigan Ath	34	0	**65**	**0**

MONTROSE, Lewis (M)   **17 0**
H: 6 0 W: 12 00 b.Manchester 17-11-88
Source: Scholar.

Season	Club				
2006-07	Wigan Ath	0	0		
2007-08	Wigan Ath	0	0		
2008-09	Wigan Ath	0	0		
2008-09	Cheltenham T	5	0	**5**	**0**
2008-09	Chesterfield	12	0	**12**	**0**

N'ZOGBIA, Charles (M)   **130 10**
H: 5 9 W: 11 00 b.Le Havre 28-5-86
Honours: France Youth, Under-21.

Season	Club				
2004-05	Newcastle U	14	0		
2005-06	Newcastle U	32	5		
2006-07	Newcastle U	22	0		
2007-08	Newcastle U	31	3		

2008-09	Newcastle U	18	1	117	9
2008-09	Wigan Ath	13	1	13	1

POLLITT, Mike (G) 498 0
H: 6 4　W: 15 03　b.Farnworth 29-2-72
Source: Trainee.

1990-91	Manchester U	0	0		
1990-91	Oldham Ath	0	0		
1991-92	Bury	0	0		
1992-93	Lincoln C	27	0		
1993-94	Lincoln C	30	0	57	0
1994-95	Darlington	40	0		
1995-96	Darlington	15	0	55	0
1995-96	Notts Co	0	0		
1996-97	Notts Co	8	0		
1997-98	Notts Co	2	0	10	0
1997-98	Oldham Ath	16	0	16	0
1997-98	Gillingham	6	0	6	0
1997-98	Brentford	5	0	5	0
1997-98	Sunderland	0	0		
1998-99	Rotherham U	46	0		
1999-2000	Rotherham U	46	0		
2000-01	Chesterfield	46	0	46	0
2001-02	Rotherham U	46	0		
2002-03	Rotherham U	41	0		
2003-04	Rotherham U	43	0		
2004-05	Rotherham U	45	0	267	0
2005-06	Wigan Ath	24	0		
2006-07	Wigan Ath	3	0		
2006-07	Ipswich T	1	0	1	0
2006-07	Burnley	4	0	4	0
2007-08	Wigan Ath	1	0		
2008-09	Wigan Ath	3	0	31	0

RODALLEGA, Hugo (F) 172 80
H: 5 11　W: 11 05　b.Valle del Cauca 25-7-85
Honours: Colombia 29 full caps, 7 goals.

2004	Quindio	32	31	32	31
2005	Dep Cali	26	12	26	12
2005-06	Monterrey	14	3		
2006-07	Atlas	17	5	17	5
2006-07	Monterrey	15	1	29	4
2007-08	Necaxa	36	16		
2008-09	Necaxa	17	9	53	25
2008-09	Wigan Ath	15	3	15	3

ROUTLEDGE, Jon (M) 1 0
H: 5 7　W: 11 05　b.Liverpool 23-11-89
Source: Liverpool.

2008-09	Wigan Ath	1	0	1	0

SCHARNER, Paul (D) 241 23
H: 6 3　W: 12 09　b.Scheibbs 11-3-80
Source: From St Polten. Honours: Austria 24 full caps.

1998-99	FK Austria	4	0		
1999-2000	FK Austria	12	0		
2000-01	FK Austria	14	0		
2001-02	FK Austria	16	1		
2002-03	FK Austria	29	1		
2003-04	FK Austria	9	1	84	3
2003-04	Salzburg	13	2		
2004-05	Salzburg	5	1	18	3
2004	Brann	7	1		
2005	Brann	25	6	32	7
2005-06	Wigan Ath	16	3		
2006-07	Wigan Ath	25	3		
2007-08	Wigan Ath	37	4		
2008-09	Wigan Ath	29	0	107	10

SIBIERSKI, Antoine (M) 426 81
H: 6 2　W: 12 04　b.Lille 5-8-74
Honours: France Youth, Under-21, Under-23, B.

1992-93	Lille	6	0		
1993-94	Lille	22	1		
1994-95	Lille	36	7		
1995-96	Lille	33	9	97	17
1996-97	Auxerre	30	7		
1997-98	Auxerre	12	1	42	8
1998-99	Nantes	4	0		
1999-2000	Nantes	28	13	32	13
2000-01	Lens	27	5		
2001-02	Lens	25	6		
2002-03	Lens	37	12	89	23
2003-04	Manchester C	33	5		
2004-05	Manchester C	35	4		
2005-06	Manchester C	24	2		
2006-07	Newcastle U	26	3	26	3
2007-08	Wigan Ath	30	4		
2008-09	Wigan Ath	3	0	33	4
2008-09	Norwich C	15	2	15	2

VALENCIA, Luis (M) 146 16
H: 5 10　W: 12 04　b.Lago Agrio 5-8-85
Honours: Ecuador Under-21, Under-23, 38 full caps, 4 goals.

2003	El Nacional	42	5		
2004	El Nacional	14	4	56	9
2004-05	Villarreal	0	0		
2005-06	Villarreal	2	0	2	0
2005-06	Recreativo	4	0	4	0
2006-07	Wigan Ath	22	1		
2007-08	Wigan Ath	31	3		
2008-09	Wigan Ath	31	3	84	7

WATSON, Ben (M) 179 20
H: 5 10　W: 10 11　b.Camberwell 9-7-85
Source: Scholar. Honours: England Under-21.

2002-03	Crystal Palace	5	0		
2003-04	Crystal Palace	16	1		
2004-05	Crystal Palace	21	0		
2005-06	Crystal Palace	42	4		
2006-07	Crystal Palace	25	3		
2007-08	Crystal Palace	42	5		
2008-09	Crystal Palace	18	5	169	18
2008-09	Wigan Ath	10	2	10	2

ZAKI, Amr (F) 29 10
H: 6 1　W: 13 05　b.Mansoura 1-4-83
Source: El Zamalek. Honours: Egypt 51 full caps, 24 goals.

2008-09	Wigan Ath	29	10	29	10

Scholars
Amos, Thomas; Breeze, Jonathan William; Buxton, Adam Mark; Chiocchi, Stephen; Crane, Jonathon Lee; Gracey, Keenan Alexander; Lambert, Daniel Thomas; Langley, Joshua; Mayer, David John; McManaman, Callum Henry; Meace, Nicolas; Mustoe, Jordan David; Rugg, Jordan.

WOLVERHAMPTON W (90)

BAILEY, Matthew (M) 0 0
H: 5 10　W: 9 11　b.Birmingham 24-9-88
Source: Scholar.

2006-07	Wolverhampton W	0	0		
2007-08	Wolverhampton W	0	0		
2008-09	Wolverhampton W	0	0		

BENNETT, Elliott (M) 74 5
H: 5 9　W: 10 11　b.Telford 18-12-88
Source: Scholar.

2006-07	Wolverhampton W	0	0		
2007-08	Wolverhampton W	0	0		
2007-08	Crewe Alex	9	1	9	1
2007-08	Bury	19	1		
2008-09	Wolverhampton W	0	0		
2008-09	Bury	46	3	65	4

BENNETT, Kyle (M) 0 0
b.Telford 9-9-90
Honours: England Youth.

2007-08	Wolverhampton W	0	0		
2008-09	Wolverhampton W	0	0		

BERRA, Christophe (D) 138 4
H: 6 1　W: 12 10　b.Edinburgh 31-1-85
Honours: Scotland Under-21, B, 4 full caps.

2003-04	Hearts	6	0		
2004-05	Hearts	12	0		
2005-06	Hearts	12	1		
2006-07	Hearts	35	1		
2007-08	Hearts	35	2		
2008-09	Hearts	23	0	123	4
2008-09	Wolverhampton W	15	0	15	0

COLLINS, Neill (D) 221 14
H: 6 3　W: 12 07　b.Irvine 2-9-83
Honours: Scoland Under-21, B.

2000-01	Queen's Park	4	0		
2001-02	Queen's Park	28	0	32	0
2002-03	Dumbarton	33	2		
2003-04	Dumbarton	30	2	63	4
2004-05	Sunderland	11	0		
2005-06	Sunderland	0	0		
2005-06	Hartlepool U	22	0	22	0
2005-06	Sheffield U	2	0	2	0
2006-07	Sunderland	7	1	18	1
2007-08	Wolverhampton W	22	2		
2007-08	Wolverhampton W	39	3		
2008-09	Wolverhampton W	23	4	84	9

CRADDOCK, Jody (D) 471 14
H: 6 0　W: 12 04　b.Redditch 25-7-75
Source: Christchurch.

1993-94	Cambridge U	20	0		
1994-95	Cambridge U	38	0		
1995-96	Cambridge U	46	3		
1996-97	Cambridge U	41	1	145	4
1997-98	Sunderland	32	0		
1998-99	Sunderland	6	0		
1999-2000	Sunderland	19	0		
1999-2000	Sheffield U	10	0	10	0
2000-01	Sunderland	34	0		
2001-02	Sunderland	30	1		
2002-03	Sunderland	25	1	146	2
2003-04	Wolverhampton W	32	1		
2004-05	Wolverhampton W	42	1		
2005-06	Wolverhampton W	18	0		
2006-07	Wolverhampton W	34	4		
2007-08	Wolverhampton W	23	1		
2007-08	Stoke C	0	0	4	0
2008-09	Wolverhampton W	17	1	166	8

EBANKS-BLAKE, Sylvan (F) 127 58
H: 5 10　W: 13 04　b.Cambridge 29-3-86
Source: Scholar. Honours: England Under-21.

2004-05	Manchester U	0	0		
2005-06	Manchester U	0	0		
2006-07	Plymouth Arg	41	10		
2007-08	Plymouth Arg	25	11	66	21
2007-08	Wolverhampton W	20	12		
2008-09	Wolverhampton W	41	·25	61	37

EDWARDS, Dave (M) 176 20
H: 5 11　W: 11 04　b.Shrewsbury 3-2-86
Source: Scholar. Honours: Wales Youth, Under-21, 14 full caps, 2 goals.

2002-03	Shrewsbury T	1	0		
2003-04	Shrewsbury T	0	0		
2004-05	Shrewsbury T	27	5		
2005-06	Shrewsbury T	30	2		
2006-07	Shrewsbury T	45	5	103	12
2007-08	Luton T	19	4	19	4
2007-08	Wolverhampton W	10	1		
2008-09	Wolverhampton W	44	3	54	4

ELOKOBI, George (D) 63 2
H: 5 10　W: 13 02　b.Cameroon 31-1-86
Source: Dulwich Hamlet.

2004-05	Colchester U	0	0		
2004-05	Chester C	5	0	5	0
2005-06	Colchester U	12	1		
2006-07	Colchester U	10	0		
2007-08	Colchester U	17	1	39	2
2007-08	Wolverhampton W	15	0		
2008-09	Wolverhampton W	4	0	19	0

FOLEY, Kevin (D) 240 5
H: 5 9　W: 11 11　b.Luton 1-11-84
Source: Scholar. Honours: Eire B, Under-21, 1 full cap.

2002-03	Luton T	2	0		
2003-04	Luton T	33	1		
2004-05	Luton T	39	2		
2005-06	Luton T	38	0		
2006-07	Luton T	39	0		
2007-08	Luton T	0	0	151	3
2007-08	Wolverhampton W	44	1		
2008-09	Wolverhampton W	45	1	89	2

FRIEND, George (D) 10 0
H: 6 2　W: 13 01　b.Dorchester 19-10-87

2008-09	Exeter C	4	0	4	0
2008-09	Wolverhampton W	6	0	6	0

GLEESON, Stephen (M) 53 4
H: 6 2　W: 11 00　b.Dublin 3-8-88
Source: Scholar. Honours: Eire Youth, Under-21, 2 full caps.

2006-07	Wolverhampton W	3	0		
2006-07	Stockport Co	14	2		
2007-08	Wolverhampton W	0	0		
2007-08	Hereford U	4	0	4	0
2007-08	Stockport Co	6	0		
2008-09	Wolverhampton W	0	0	3	0
2008-09	Stockport Co	21	2	41	4
2008-09	Milton Keynes D	5	0	5	0

GOBERN, Lewis (M) 41 4
H: 5 10　W: 11 07　b.Birmingham 28-1-85
Source: Scholar.

2003-04	Wolverhampton W	0	0		
2004-05	Wolverhampton W	0	0		
2004-05	Hartlepool U	1	0	1	0
2005-06	Wolverhampton W	1	0		

2005-06	Blackpool	8	1	8	1
2005-06	Bury	7	1	7	1
2006-07	Wolverhampton W	12	2		
2007-08	Wolverhampton W	0	0		
2008-09	Wolverhampton W	0	0	13	2
2008-09	Colchester U	12	0	12	0

HEMMINGS, Ashley (M) 3 0
H: 5 8 W: 11 06 b.Wolverhampton 3-3-91
Source: Scholar.

2008-09	Wolverhampton W	2	0	2	0
2008-09	Cheltenham T	1	0	1	0

HENNESSEY, Wayne (G) 96 0
H: 6 0 W: 11 06 b.Anglesey 24-1-87
Source: Scholar. *Honours:* Wales Schools, Youth, Under-21, 19 full caps.

2004-05	Wolverhampton W	0	0		
2005-06	Wolverhampton W	0	0		
2006-07	Wolverhampton W	0	0		
2006-07	Bristol C	0	0		
2006-07	Stockport Co	15	0	15	0
2007-08	Wolverhampton W	46	0		
2008-09	Wolverhampton W	35	0	81	0

HENRY, Karl (M) 246 8
H: 6 0 W: 12 00 b.Wolverhampton 26-11-82
Source: Trainee. *Honours:* England Youth, Under-20.

1999-2000	Stoke C	0	0		
2000-01	Stoke C	0	0		
2001-02	Stoke C	24	0		
2002-03	Stoke C	18	1		
2003-04	Stoke C	20	0		
2003-04	Cheltenham T	9	1	9	1
2004-05	Stoke C	34	0		
2005-06	Stoke C	24	0	120	1
2006-07	Wolverhampton W	34	3		
2007-08	Wolverhampton W	40	3		
2008-09	Wolverhampton W	43	0	117	6

HILL, Matt (D) 316 6
H: 5 7 W: 12 06 b.Bristol 26-3-81
Source: Trainee.

1998-99	Bristol C	3	0		
1999-2000	Bristol C	14	0		
2000-01	Bristol C	34	0		
2001-02	Bristol C	40	1		
2002-03	Bristol C	42	3		
2003-04	Bristol C	42	2		
2004-05	Bristol C	23	0	198	6
2004-05	Preston NE	14	0		
2005-06	Preston NE	26	0		
2006-07	Preston NE	38	0		
2007-08	Preston NE	26	0		
2008-09	Preston NE	1	0	105	0
2008-09	Wolverhampton W	13	0	13	0

HUGHES, Liam (F) 4 0
H: 6 2 W: 11 09 b.Stourbridge 11-9-88
Source: Scholar.

2006-07	Wolverhampton W	0	0		
2007-08	Wolverhampton W	0	0		
2007-08	Bury	4	0	4	0
2008-09	Wolverhampton W	0	0		

IKEME, Carl (G) 22 0
H: 6 2 W: 13 09 b.Sutton Coldfield 8-6-86
Source: Scholar.

2005-06	Wolverhampton W	0	0		
2005-06	Stockport Co	9	0	9	0
2006-07	Wolverhampton W	1	0		
2007-08	Wolverhampton W	0	0		
2008-09	Wolverhampton W	12	0	13	0

IWELUMO, Chris (F) 341 86
H: 6 3 W: 15 03 b.Coatbridge 1-8-78
Source: Juniors. *Honours:* Scotland B, 2 full caps.

1996-97	St Mirren	14	0		
1997-98	St Mirren	12	0	26	0
1998-99	Aarhus Fremad	27	4	27	4
1999-2000	Stoke C	3	0		
2000-01	Stoke C	2	1		
2000-01	York C	12	2	12	2
2000-01	Cheltenham T	4	1	4	1
2001-02	Stoke C	38	10		
2002-03	Stoke C	32	5		
2003-04	Stoke C	0	0	84	16
2003-04	Brighton & HA	10	4	10	4
2004-05	Aachen	9	0	9	0
2005-06	Colchester U	46	17		
2006-07	Colchester U	46	18	92	35

2007-08	Charlton Ath	46	10	46	10
2008-09	Wolverhampton W	31	14	31	14

JARVIS, Matthew (M) 164 16
H: 5 8 W: 11 10 b.Middlesbrough 22-5-86
Source: Scholar.

2003-04	Gillingham	10	0		
2004-05	Gillingham	30	3		
2005-06	Gillingham	35	3		
2006-07	Gillingham	35	6	110	12
2007-08	Wolverhampton W	26	1		
2008-09	Wolverhampton W	28	3	54	4

JONES, Daniel (D) 66 4
H: 6 2 W: 13 00 b.Wordsley 14-7-86
Source: Scholar.

2005-06	Wolverhampton W	1	0		
2006-07	Wolverhampton W	8	0		
2007-08	Wolverhampton W	1	0		
2007-08	Northampton T	33	3	33	3
2008-09	Wolverhampton W	0	0	10	0
2008-09	Oldham Ath	23	1	23	1

JONES, David (M) 117 20
H: 5 11 W: 10 10 b.Southport 4-11-84
Source: Trainee. *Honours:* England Youth, Under-21.

2003-04	Manchester U	0	0		
2004-05	Manchester U	0	0		
2005-06	Manchester U	0	0		
2005-06	Preston NE	24	3	24	3
2005-06	NEC Nijmegen	17	6	17	6
2006-07	Manchester U	0	0		
2006-07	Derby Co	28	6		
2007-08	Derby Co	14	1	42	7
2008-09	Wolverhampton W	34	4	34	4

KEOGH, Andy (F) 204 41
H: 6 0 W: 11 00 b.Dublin 16-5-86
Source: Scholar. *Honours:* Eire Youth, B, Under-21, 11 full caps, 1 goal.

2003-04	Leeds U	0	0		
2004-05	Leeds U	0	0		
2004-05	Bury	4	2	4	2
2004-05	Scunthorpe U	25	3		
2005-06	Scunthorpe U	45	11		
2006-07	Scunthorpe U	28	7	98	21
2006-07	Wolverhampton W	17	5		
2007-08	Wolverhampton W	43	8		
2008-09	Wolverhampton W	42	5	102	18

KIGHTLY, Michael (F) 96 20
H: 5 10 W: 10 10 b.Basildon 24-1-86
Source: Scholar. *Honours:* England Under-21.

2002-03	Southend U	1	0		
2003-04	Southend U	11	0		
2004-05	Southend U	1	0	13	0

From Grays Ath.

2006-07	Wolverhampton W	24	8		
2007-08	Wolverhampton W	21	4		
2008-09	Wolverhampton W	38	8	83	20

LITTLE, Mark (D) 53 0
H: 6 1 W: 12 10 b.Worcester 20-8-88
Source: Scholar. *Honours:* England Youth.

2005-06	Wolverhampton W	0	0		
2006-07	Wolverhampton W	26	0		
2007-08	Wolverhampton W	1	0		
2007-08	Northampton T	17	0		
2008-09	Wolverhampton W	0	0	27	0
2008-09	Northampton T	9	0	26	0

LOWE, Keith (D) 79 4
H: 6 2 W: 13 03 b.Wolverhampton 13-9-85
Source: Scholar.

2004-05	Wolverhampton W	11	0		
2005-06	Wolverhampton W	3	0		
2005-06	Burnley	16	0	16	0
2005-06	QPR	1	0	1	0
2005-06	Swansea C	4	0	4	0
2006-07	Wolverhampton W	0	0		
2006-07	Brighton & HA	0	0		
2006-07	Cheltenham T	16	1	16	1
2007-08	Wolverhampton W	0	0		
2007-08	Port Vale	28	3	28	3
2008-09	Wolverhampton W	0	0	14	0

MALONE, Scott (D) 0 0
H: 6 2 W: 11 11 b.Rowley Regis 25-3-91
Source: Scholar.

2008-09	Wolverhampton W	0	0		

On loan to Ujpest

MURRAY, Matt (G) 92 0
H: 6 4 W: 13 10 b.Solihull 2-5-81
Source: From Trainee. *Honours:* England Youth, Under-21.

1997-98	Wolverhampton W	0	0		
1998-99	Wolverhampton W	0	0		
1999-2000	Wolverhampton W	0	0		
2000-01	Wolverhampton W	0	0		
2001-02	Wolverhampton W	0	0		
2002-03	Wolverhampton W	40	0		
2003-04	Wolverhampton W	1	0		
2004-05	Wolverhampton W	1	0		
2005-06	Wolverhampton W	1	0		
2005-06	Tranmere R	2	0	2	0
2006-07	Wolverhampton W	44	0		
2007-08	Wolverhampton W	0	0		
2008-09	Wolverhampton W	0	0	87	0
2008-09	Hereford U	3	0	3	0

POTTER, Darren (M) 85 2
H: 6 0 W: 10 08 b.Liverpool 21-12-84
Source: Scholar. *Honours:* Eire Youth, B, Under-21, 5 full caps.

2001-02	Liverpool	0	0		
2002-03	Liverpool	0	0		
2003-04	Liverpool	0	0		
2004-05	Liverpool	2	0		
2005-06	Liverpool	0	0		
2005-06	Southampton	10	0	10	0
2006-07	Liverpool	0	0	2	0
2007-08	Wolverhampton W	38	0		
2007-08	Wolverhampton W	18	0		
2008-09	Wolverhampton W	0	0	56	0
2008-09	Sheffield W	17	2	17	2

ROSA, Denes (M) 198 29
H: 5 8 W: 11 00 b.Hungary 7-4-77
Honours: Hungary 10 full caps.

1996-97	BVSC	12	0		
1997-98	BVSC	26	5		
1998-99	BVSC	13	4		
1999-2000	BVSC	0	0		
1999-2000	Gyor	8	1		
2000-01	Gyor	25	1		
2001-02	BVSC	0	0	51	9
2001-02	Gyor	12	1	45	3
2002-03	Dunaferr	14	0	14	0
2003-04	Ujpest	9	1	9	1
2003-04	Ferencvaros	25	2		
2004-05	Ferencvaros	27	8		
2005-06	Ferencvaros	14	4	66	14
2005-06	Wolverhampton W	9	2		
2006-07	Wolverhampton W	0	0		
2006-07	Cheltenham T	4	0	4	0
2007-08	Wolverhampton W	0	0		
2008-09	Wolverhampton W	0	0	9	2

SALMON, Mark (M) 9 0
H: 5 10 W: 10 07 b.Dublin 31-10-88
Source: Scholar.

2006-07	Wolverhampton W	0	0		
2007-08	Wolverhampton W	0	0		
2007-08	Port Vale	9	0	9	0
2008-09	Wolverhampton W	0	0		

Transferred to Drogheda U February 2009

SHACKELL, Jason (D) 145 3
H: 6 4 W: 13 06 b.Stevenage 27-9-83
Source: Scholar.

2002-03	Norwich C	2	0		
2003-04	Norwich C	6	0		
2004-05	Norwich C	11	0		
2005-06	Norwich C	17	0		
2006-07	Norwich C	43	3		
2007-08	Norwich C	39	0		
2008-09	Norwich C	15	0	133	3
2008-09	Wolverhampton W	12	0	12	0

SIMON, Kristzian (M) 0 0
H: 6 0 W: 12 00 b.Budapest 6-2-91
Source: Ujpest.

2008-09	Wolverhampton W	0	0		

STEARMAN, Richard (D) 153 8
H: 6 2 W: 10 08 b.Wolverhampton 19-8-87
Source: From Scholar. *Honours:* England Youth, Under-21.

2004-05	Leicester C	8	1		
2005-06	Leicester C	34	3		
2006-07	Leicester C	35	1		
2007-08	Leicester C	39	2	116	7
2008-09	Wolverhampton W	37	1	37	1

VOKES, Sam (F)   90 22
H: 6 1 W: 13 10 b.Southampton 21-10-89
Source: Scholar. Honours: Wales Under-21, 10 full caps, 1 goal.

2006-07	Bournemouth	13	4	
2007-08	Bournemouth	41	12	54 16
2008-09	Wolverhampton W	36	6	36 6

WARD, Darren (D)   334 12
H: 6 3 W: 11 04 b.Kenton 13-9-78
Source: Trainee.

1995-96	Watford	1	0	
1996-97	Watford	7	0	
1997-98	Watford	0	0	
1998-99	Watford	1	0	
1999-2000	Watford	9	1	
1999-2000	QPR	14	0	14 0
2000-01	Watford	40	1	
2001-02	Watford	1	0	
2001-02	Millwall	14	0	
2002-03	Millwall	39	1	
2003-04	Millwall	46	3	
2004-05	Millwall	43	0	142 4
2005-06	Crystal Palace	43	5	
2006-07	Crystal Palace	20	0	63 5
2007-08	Wolverhampton W	30	0	
2008-09	Wolverhampton W	1	0	31 0
2008-09	Watford	9	1	68 3
2008-09	Charlton Ath	16	0	16 0

WARD, Stephen (F)   161 14
H: 5 11 W: 12 02 b.Dublin 20-8-85
Honours: Eire Youth, Under-21, B.

2003	Bohemians	6	0	
2004	Bohemians	16	2	
2005	Bohemians	29	7	
2006	Bohemians	21	2	72 11
2006-07	Wolverhampton W	18	3	
2007-08	Wolverhampton W	29	0	
2008-09	Wolverhampton W	42	0	89 3

WYCOMBE W (91)

ANTWI, Will (D)   46 1
H: 6 2 W: 12 08 b.Epsom 19-10-82
Source: Scholar. Honours: Ghana 1 full cap.

2002-03	Crystal Palace	4	0	
2003-04	Crystal Palace	0	0	4 0
From Aldershot T				
2005-06	Wycombe W	5	0	
2006-07	Wycombe W	25	1	
2007-08	Wycombe W	6	0	
2008-09	Wycombe W	6	0	42 1

ASHTON, Nathan (D)   13 0
H: 5 8 W: 9 07 b.Plaistow 30-1-87
Source: Scholar. Honours: England Youth, Under-20.

2004-05	Charlton Ath	0	0	
2005-06	Charlton Ath	0	0	
2006-07	Charlton Ath	0	0	
2006-07	Millwall	0	0	
2007-08	Fulham	1	0	1 0
2007-08	Crystal Palace	1	0	1 0
2008-09	Wycombe W	11	0	11 0

BEAVON, Stuart (F)   8 0
H: 5 7 W: 10 10 b.Reading 5-5-84
Source: Dicot T, Weymouth.

2008-09	Wycombe W	8	0	8 0

BLOOMFIELD, Matt (M)   173 16
H: 5 9 W: 11 00 b.Felixstowe 8-2-84
Source: Scholar. Honours: England Youth, Under-20.

2001-02	Ipswich T	0	0	
2002-03	Ipswich T	0	0	
2003-04	Ipswich T	0	0	
2003-04	Wycombe W	12	1	
2004-05	Wycombe W	26	2	
2005-06	Wycombe W	39	5	
2006-07	Wycombe W	41	4	
2007-08	Wycombe W	35	4	
2008-09	Wycombe W	20	0	173 16

CHRISTON, Lewis (D)   8 0
H: 6 0 W: 12 02 b.Milton Keynes 24-1-89
Source: Scholar.

2005-06	Wycombe W	0	0	
2006-07	Wycombe W	6	0	
2007-08	Wycombe W	2	0	
2008-09	Wycombe W	0	0	8 0

CROOKS, Leon (M)   65 0
H: 6 0 W: 11 12 b.Greenwich 21-11-85
Source: Scholar.

2004-05	Milton Keynes D	17	0	
2005-06	Milton Keynes D	23	0	
2006-07	Milton Keynes D	12	0	52 0
2006-07	Wycombe W	11	0	
2007-08	Wycombe W	0	0	
2008-09	Wycombe W	2	0	13 0

DALY, George (F)   2 0
H: 5 11 W: 10 11 b.Wycombe 25-10-90
Source: Scholar.

2007-08	Wycombe W	2	0	
2008-09	Wycombe W	0	0	2 0

DOHERTY, Tom (M)   288 9
H: 5 8 W: 10 06 b.Bristol 17-3-79
Source: Trainee. Honours: Northern Ireland 9 full caps.

1997-98	Bristol C	30	2	
1998-99	Bristol C	23	1	
1999-2000	Bristol C	1	0	
2000-01	Bristol C	0	0	
2001-02	Bristol C	34	1	
2002-03	Bristol C	38	0	
2003-04	Bristol C	33	2	
2004-05	Bristol C	29	1	188 7
2005-06	QPR	15	0	
2005-06	Yeovil T	1	0	1 0
2006-07	QPR	0	0	
2006-07	Wycombe W	26	2	
2007-08	QPR	0	0	15 0
2007-08	Wycombe W	24	0	
2008-09	Wycombe W	34	0	84 2

DUNCAN, Derek (M)   20 0
H: 5 10 W: 10 11 b.Newham 23-4-87
Source: Scholar.

2003-04	Leyton Orient	1	0	
2004-05	Leyton Orient	15	0	
2005-06	Leyton Orient	1	0	
2006-07	Leyton Orient	3	0	20 0
2007-08	Wycombe W	0	0	
2008-09	Wycombe W	0	0	

ELLAMS, Darrell (D)   0 0
H: 5 10 W: 10 07 b. 3-11-89
Source: Scholar.

2008-09	Wycombe W	0	0	

GRANT, Gavin (F)   24 1
H: 5 11 W: 11 00 b.Middlesex 27-3-84
Source: Tooting & Mitcham U.

2005-06	Gillingham	10	1	10 1
2005-06	Millwall	0	0	
2006-07	Millwall	4	0	
2007-08	Millwall	0	0	4 0
2008-09	Wycombe W	10	0	10 0

HARROLD, Matt (F)   174 25
H: 6 1 W: 11 10 b.Leyton 25-7-84
Source: Harlow T.

2003-04	Brentford	13	2	
2004-05	Brentford	19	0	32 2
2004-05	Grimsby T	6	2	6 2
2005-06	Yeovil T	42	9	
2006-07	Yeovil T	5	0	47 9
2006-07	Southend U	36	3	
2007-08	Southend U	16	0	
2008-09	Southend U	0	0	52 3
2008-09	Wycombe W	37	9	37 9

HOLT, Gary (M)   461 16
H: 6 0 W: 12 00 b.Irvine 9-3-73
Source: Celtic. Honours: Scotland 10 full caps, 1 goal.

1994-95	Stoke C	0	0	
1995-96	Kilmarnock	26	0	
1996-97	Kilmarnock	12	1	
1997-98	Kilmarnock	27	2	
1998-99	Kilmarnock	33	3	
1999-2000	Kilmarnock	35	0	
2000-01	Kilmarnock	19	3	152 9
2000-01	Norwich C	4	0	
2001-02	Norwich C	46	2	
2002-03	Norwich C	45	0	
2003-04	Norwich C	46	1	
2004-05	Norwich C	27	0	168 3
2005-06	Nottingham F	26	0	
2006-07	Nottingham F	39	1	65 1
2007-08	Wycombe W	43	2	
2008-09	Wycombe W	33	1	76 3

HUNT, Lewis (D)   177 3
H: 5 11 W: 12 09 b.Birmingham 25-8-82
Source: Scholar.

2000-01	Derby Co	0	0	
2001-02	Derby Co	0	0	
2002-03	Derby Co	10	0	
2003-04	Derby Co	1	0	11 0
2003-04	Southend U	26	0	
2004-05	Southend U	31	0	
2005-06	Southend U	30	0	
2006-07	Southend U	35	2	
2007-08	Southend U	24	0	146 2
2008-09	Wycombe W	20	1	20 1

JOHNSON, Leon (D)   220 7
H: 6 1 W: 13 05 b.Shoreditch 10-5-81
Source: Scholarship.

1999-2000	Southend U	0	0	
2000-01	Southend U	20	1	
2001-02	Southend U	28	2	48 3
2002-03	Gillingham	18	0	
2003-04	Gillingham	20	0	
2004-05	Gillingham	8	0	
2005-06	Gillingham	28	1	
2006-07	Gillingham	24	1	98 2
2007-08	Wycombe W	45	0	
2008-09	Wycombe W	29	2	74 2

McCRACKEN, David (D)   254 10
H: 6 2 W: 11 06 b.Glasgow 16-10-81
Source: Dundee U BC. Honours: Scotland Under-21.

1999-2000	Dundee U	2	0	
2000-01	Dundee U	9	1	
2001-02	Dundee U	19	0	
2002-03	Dundee U	25	1	
2003-04	Dundee U	32	1	
2004-05	Dundee U	24	2	
2005-06	Dundee U	34	2	
2006-07	Dundee U	33	1	178 8
2007-08	Wycombe W	37	1	
2008-09	Wycombe W	39	1	76 2

McGLEISH, Scott (F)   575 177
H: 5 9 W: 11 09 b.Barnet 10-2-74
Source: Edgware T.

1994-95	Charlton Ath	6	0	6 0
1994-95	Leyton Orient	6	1	
1995-96	Peterborough U	12	0	
1995-96	Colchester U	15	6	
1996-97	Peterborough U	1	0	13 0
1996-97	Cambridge U	10	7	10 7
1996-97	Leyton Orient	28	7	
1997-98	Leyton Orient	8	0	
1997-98	Barnet	37	13	
1998-99	Barnet	36	8	
1999-2000	Barnet	42	10	
2000-01	Barnet	19	5	134 36
2000-01	Colchester U	21	5	
2001-02	Colchester U	46	15	
2002-03	Colchester U	43	8	
2003-04	Colchester U	34	10	159 44
2004-05	Northampton T	44	13	
2005-06	Northampton T	42	17	
2006-07	Northampton T	25	12	
2006-07	Wycombe W	14	5	
2007-08	Wycombe W	46	25	
2008-09	Wycombe W	15	3	75 33
2008-09	Northampton T	9	1	120 43
2008-09	Leyton Orient	16	6	58 14

MONCUR, T J (D)   23 0
H: 5 10 W: 12 08 b.Hackney 23-9-87
Source: Scholar.

2005-06	Fulham	0	0	
2006-07	Fulham	0	0	
2007-08	Fulham	0	0	
2007-08	Bradford C	7	0	
2008-09	Fulham	0	0	
2008-09	Bradford C	14	0	21 0
2008-09	Wycombe W	2	0	2 0

MOUSINHO, John (D)   98 4
H: 6 1 W: 12 07 b.Buckingham 30-4-86
Source: Univ of Notre Dame.

2005-06	Brentford	7	0	
2006-07	Brentford	34	0	
2007-08	Brentford	23	2	64 2
2008-09	Wycombe W	34	2	34 2

OLIVER, Luke (D)   15 0
H: 6 6 W: 14 05 b.Hammersmith 1-5-84
Source: Brook House.

2002-03	Wycombe W	2	0	

2003-04 Wycombe W 2 0
From Woking
2005-06 Yeovil T 3 0 **3 0**
From Stevenage B.
2008-09 Wycombe W 8 0 **12 0**

PHILLIPS, Matthew (M) 39 3
H: 6 0 W: 12 10 b.Aylesbury 13-3-91
Source: Scholar.
2007-08 Wycombe W 2 0
2008-09 Wycombe W 37 3 **39 3**

PITTMAN, Jon-Paul (F) 29 4
H: 5 9 W: 11 00 b.Oklahoma City 24-10-86
Source: Scholar.
2005-06 Nottingham F 0 0
2005-06 *Hartlepool U* 3 0 **3 0**
2006-07 *Bury* 9 1 **9 1**
2006-07 Doncaster R 0 0
From Crawley T.
2008-09 Wycombe W 17 3 **17 3**

RICE, Robert (D) 2 0
H: 5 8 W: 11 11 b.Hendon 23-2-89
Source: Scholar.
2007-08 Wycombe W 1 0
2008-09 Wycombe W 1 0 **2 0**

RICHARDS, Matt (D) 200 9
H: 5 8 W: 11 00 b.Harlow 26-12-84
Source: Scholar. *Honours:* England Under-21.
2001-02 Ipswich T 0 0
2002-03 Ipswich T 13 0
2003-04 Ipswich T 44 1
2004-05 Ipswich T 24 1
2005-06 Ipswich T 38 4
2006-07 Ipswich T 28 2
2007-08 Ipswich T 0 0
2007-08 *Brighton & HA* 28 0
2008-09 *Brighton & HA* 23 1 **51 1**
2008-09 Wycombe W 0 0
2008-09 *Notts Co* 1 0 **1 0**
2008-09 Ipswich T 1 0 **148 0**

SHEARER, Scott (G) 201 0
H: 6 3 W: 12 00 b.Glasgow 15-2-81
Source: Tower Hearts. *Honours:* Scotland B.
2000-01 Albion R 3 0
2001-02 Albion R 10 0
2002-03 Albion R 36 0 **49 0**
2003-04 Coventry C 30 0
2004-05 Coventry C 8 0 **38 0**
2004-05 *Rushden & D* 13 0 **13 0**
2005-06 Bristol R 45 0
2006-07 Bristol R 2 0 **47 0**
2006-07 *Shrewsbury T* 20 0 **20 0**
2007-08 Wycombe W 5 0
2008-09 Wycombe W 29 0 **34 0**

SPENCE, Lewis (M) 32 2
H: 5 9 W: 11 02 b.Lambeth 29-10-87
Source: Scholar.
2006-07 Crystal Palace 0 0
2007-08 Crystal Palace 0 0 **2 0**
2008-09 Wycombe W 30 2 **30 2**

VIEIRA, Magno (F) 45 7
H: 5 9 W: 11 00 b.Bahia 13-2-85
Source: Juniors.
2003-04 Wigan Ath 0 0
2003-04 *Northampton T* 10 2 **10 2**
2004-05 Wigan Ath 0 0
From Carlisle U (loan).
2006-07 Barnet 21 3 **21 3**
From Crawley T.
2008-09 Wycombe W 14 2 **14 2**

WOODMAN, Craig (D) 197 4
H: 5 9 W: 10 11 b.Tiverton 22-12-82
Source: Trainee.
1999-2000 Bristol C 0 0
2000-01 Bristol C 2 0
2001-02 Bristol C 6 0
2002-03 Bristol C 10 0
2003-04 Bristol C 21 0
2004-05 Bristol C 3 0
2004-05 *Mansfield T* 8 1 **8 1**
2004-05 *Torquay U* 37 1
2005-06 Bristol C 2 0
2005-06 *Torquay U* 2 0 **24 1**
2006-07 Bristol C 11 0 **90 1**
2007-08 Wycombe W 29 0
2008-09 Wycombe W 46 1 **75 1**

YOUNG, Jamie (G) 59 0
H: 5 11 W: 13 00 b.Brisbane 25-8-85
Source: Scholar. *Honours:* England Youth, Under-20.
2003-04 Reading 1 0
2004-05 Reading 0 0
2005-06 Reading 0 0 **1 0**
2005-06 *Rushden & D* 20 0 **20 0**
2006-07 Wycombe W 19 0
2007-08 Wycombe W 4 0
2008-09 Wycombe W 15 0 **38 0**

ZEBROSKI, Chris (F) 62 10
H: 6 1 W: 11 08 b.Swindon 29-10-86
Source: Cirencester T, Scholar.
2005-06 Plymouth Arg 4 0
2006-07 *Plymouth Arg* 0 0 **4 0**
2006-07 Millwall 25 3
2007-08 Millwall 0 0 **25 3**
2008-09 Wycombe W 33 7 **33 7**

YEOVIL T (92)

ALCOCK, Craig (D) 39 1
H: 5 8 W: 11 00 b.Cornwall 8-12-87
Source: Youth.
2006-07 Yeovil T 1 0
2007-08 Yeovil T 8 0
2008-09 Yeovil T 30 1 **39 1**

BIRCHAM, Marc (M) 272 10
H: 5 11 W: 11 06 b.Wembley 11-5-78
Source: Trainee. *Honours:* Canada 17 full caps, 1 goal.
1996-97 Millwall 6 0
1997-98 Millwall 4 0
1998-99 Millwall 28 0
1999-2000 Millwall 22 1
2000-01 Millwall 20 2
2001-02 Millwall 24 0 **104 3**
2002-03 QPR 36 2
2003-04 QPR 38 2
2004-05 QPR 35 1
2005-06 QPR 26 2
2006-07 QPR 17 0 **152 7**
2007-08 Yeovil T 13 0
2008-09 Yeovil T 3 0 **16 0**

BROWN, Aaron (D) 27 3
H: 6 4 W: 14 07 b.Birmingham 23-6-83
Source: Tamworth.
2005-06 Reading 0 0
2005-06 *Bournemouth* 4 0 **4 0**
2006-07 Reading 0 0
2007-08 *Walsall* 0 0
2007-08 Reading 0 0
2008-09 Yeovil T 23 3 **23 3**

DOWNES, Aiden (F) 29 1
H: 5 8 W: 11 07 b.Dublin 24-7-88
Source: Scholar. *Honours:* Eire Youth, Under-21.
2005-06 Everton 0 0
2006-07 Everton 0 0
2007-08 Everton 0 0
2007-08 *Yeovil T* 5 1
2008-09 Yeovil T 24 0 **29 1**

FITZGERALD, Rob (D) 0 0
H: 6 1 W: 12 02 b. 1-10-88
Source: Hillingdon B.
2007-08 Yeovil T 0 0
2008-09 Yeovil T 0 0

FORBES, Terrell (D) 314 0
H: 5 11 W: 12 07 b.Southwark 17-8-81
Source: Trainee.
1999-2000 West Ham U 0 0
1999-2000 *Bournemouth* 3 0 **3 0**
2000-01 West Ham U 0 0
2001-02 QPR 43 0
2002-03 QPR 38 0
2003-04 QPR 30 0
2004-05 QPR 3 0 **114 0**
2004-05 *Grimsby T* 33 0 **33 0**
2005-06 Oldham Ath 39 0 **39 0**
2006-07 Yeovil T 46 0
2007-08 Yeovil T 41 0
2008-09 Yeovil T 38 0 **125 0**

JONES, Nathan (M) 404 11
H: 5 6 W: 10 06 b.Rhondda 28-5-73
Source: Cardiff C Trainee, Maesteg Park, Ton Pentre, Merthyr T.
1995-96 Luton T 0 0
Badajoz, Numaicia
1997-98 Southend U 39 0
1998-99 Southend U 17 0
1998-99 *Scarborough* 9 0 **9 0**
1999-2000 Southend U 43 2 **99 2**
2000-01 Brighton & HA 40 4
2001-02 Brighton & HA 36 2
2002-03 Brighton & HA 28 1
2003-04 Brighton & HA 36 0
2004-05 Brighton & HA 19 0 **159 7**
2005-06 Yeovil T 43 0
2006-07 Yeovil T 42 1
2007-08 Yeovil T 31 1
2008-09 Yeovil T 21 0 **137 2**

McCOLLIN, Andre (F) 11 1
H: 5 7 W: 10 06 b.Lambeth 26-3-85
Source: Fisher Ath.
2008-09 Yeovil T 11 1 **11 1**

MURTAGH, Kieran (M) 26 0
H: 6 0 W: 12 00 b.Wapping 29-10-88
Source: Charlton Ath Academy, Fisher Ath.
2008-09 Yeovil T 26 0 **26 0**

PELTIER, Lee (F) 76 1
H: 5 10 W: 12 00 b.Liverpool 11-12-86
Source: Scholar.
2004-05 Liverpool 0 0
2005-06 Liverpool 0 0
2006-07 Liverpool 0 0
2006-07 *Hull C* 7 0 **7 0**
2007-08 Liverpool 0 0
2007-08 Yeovil T 34 0
2008-09 Yeovil T 35 1 **69 1**

ROBERTS, Gary (M) 152 13
H: 5 8 W: 10 05 b.Chester 4-2-87
Source: Scholar. *Honours:* England Youth.
2003-04 Crewe Alex 2 0
2004-05 Crewe Alex 2 0
2005-06 Crewe Alex 33 2
2006-07 Crewe Alex 43 3
2007-08 Crewe Alex 42 6
2008-09 Crewe Alex 0 0 **122 11**
2008-09 Yeovil T 30 2 **30 2**

RODGERS, Luke (F) 261 79
H: 5 8 W: 11 00 b.Birmingham 1-1-82
Source: Trainee.
1999-2000 Shrewsbury T 6 1
2000-01 Shrewsbury T 26 7
2001-02 Shrewsbury T 38 22
2002-03 Shrewsbury T 36 16
2003-04 Shrewsbury T 0 0
2004-05 Shrewsbury T 36 6 **142 52**
2005-06 Crewe Alex 0 0
2006-07 Crewe Alex 12 3 **38 9**
2006-07 *Port Vale* 8 3
2007-08 Port Vale 36 9
2008-09 Port Vale 15 3 **59 15**
2008-09 Yeovil T 22 3 **22 3**

SCHOFIELD, Danny (F) 287 43
H: 5 10 W: 11 02 b.Doncaster 10-4-80
Source: Brodsworth.
1998-99 Huddersfield T 1 0
1999-2000 Huddersfield T 2 0
2000-01 Huddersfield T 1 0
2001-02 Huddersfield T 40 8
2002-03 Huddersfield T 30 2
2003-04 Huddersfield T 40 8
2004-05 Huddersfield T 33 5
2005-06 Huddersfield T 41 9
2006-07 Huddersfield T 35 5
2007-08 Huddersfield T 25 2 **248 39**
2008-09 Yeovil T 39 4 **39 4**

SKIVERTON, Terry (D) 215 22
H: 6 1 W: 13 06 b.Mile End 26-6-75
Source: Trainee.
1993-94 Chelsea 0 0
1994-95 Chelsea 0 0
1994-95 *Wycombe W* 10 0
1995-96 Chelsea 0 0
1995-96 Wycombe W 4 1
1996-97 Wycombe W 6 0 **20 1**
From Welling U
2003-04 Yeovil T 26 2

2004-05	Yeovil T	38	4		
2005-06	Yeovil T	36	6		
2006-07	Yeovil T	39	2		
2007-08	Yeovil T	31	5		
2008-09	Yeovil T	25	2	195	21

SMITH, Nathan (D)   40 1
H: 5 11 W: 12 00 b.Enfield 11-1-87
Source: Potters Bar T.

2007-08	Yeovil T	7	0		
2008-09	Yeovil T	33	1	40	1

STREET, Jordan (D)   0 0
H: 6 1 W: 12 08 b.Southampton 3-12-89
Source: Scholar.

2007-08	Yeovil T	0	0		
2008-09	Yeovil T	0	0		

TOMLIN, Gavin (F)   54 7
H: 6 0 W: 12 02 b.Brentford 21-8-83
Source: Staines T, Yeading.

2006-07	Brentford	12	0		
2007-08	Brentford	0	0	12	0

From Fisher Ath.

2008-09	Yeovil T	42	7	42	7

WAGENAAR, Josh (G)   30 0
H: 6 0 W: 14 02 b.Ontario 26-2-85
Honours: Canada Under-23, 1 full cap.

2006-07	Den Haag	5	0	5	0
2008	Lyngby	2	0	2	0
2008-09	Yeovil T	23	0	23	0

WARNE, Paul (M)   436 55
H: 5 10 W: 11 07 b.Norwich 8-5-73
Source: Wroxham.

1997-98	Wigan Ath	25	2		
1998-99	Wigan Ath	11	1	36	3
1999-2000	Rotherham U	43	10		
2000-01	Rotherham U	44	7		
2001-02	Rotherham U	25	0		
2002-03	Rotherham U	40	1		
2003-04	Rotherham U	35	1		
2004-05	Rotherham U	24	1	230	28
2004-05	*Mansfield T*	7	1	7	1
2005-06	Oldham Ath	40	9		
2006-07	Oldham Ath	46	9	86	18
2007-08	Yeovil T	33	1		
2008-09	Yeovil T	44	4	77	5

WAY, Darren (M)   137 16
H: 5 7 W: 11 00 b.Plymouth 21-11-79
Source: Norwich C Trainee.

2003-04	Yeovil T	39	5		
2004-05	Yeovil T	45	7		
2005-06	Yeovil T	15	1		
2005-06	Swansea C	5	0		
2006-07	Swansea C	9	0		
2007-08	Swansea C	2	0	16	0
2007-08	*Yeovil T*	7	1		
2008-09	Yeovil T	15	2	121	16

WELSH, Andy (M)   197 8
H: 5 8 W: 10 03 b.Manchester 24-1-83
Source: Scholar. *Honours:* Scotland Youth.

2001-02	Stockport Co	15	0		
2002-03	Stockport Co	13	2		
2002-03	*Macclesfield T*	6	2	6	2
2003-04	Stockport Co	34	1		
2004-05	Stockport Co	13	0	75	3
2004-05	Sunderland	7	1		
2005-06	Sunderland	14	0		
2005-06	*Leicester C*	10	1		
2006-07	Sunderland	0	0	21	1
2006-07	*Leicester C*	7	0	17	1
2007	Toronto Lynx	20	1	20	1
2007-08	Blackpool	21	0		
2008-09	Blackpool	0	0	21	0
2008-09	Yeovil T	37	0	37	0

CONFERENCE ROLL-CALL

BURTON ALBION

Name	Height	Weight	Birthplace	Date of birth	Previous club
Austin Ryan (D)	6 3	13 07	Stoke	15 11 84	Crewe Alex
Banim Jody (F)	5 8	13 01	Manchester	1 4 78	Droylsden
Buxton Jake (D)	5 11	13 01	Sutton-in-Ashfield	4 3 85	Mansfield T
Corbett Andrew (M)	6 0	11 05	Worcester	20 2 82	Nuneaton B
Deeney Saul (G)	6 1	11 07	Derry	23 3 83	Darlington
Gilroy Keith (M)	5 10	10 12	Sligo	8 7 83	Darlington
Goodfellow Marc (M)	5 10	10 01	Swadlincote	20 9 81	Bury
Harrad Shaun (F)	5 10	12 04	Nottingham	11 12 84	Notts Co
Holmes Danny (M)	6 0	11 13	Burton-on-Trent	17 11 86	Port Vale
James Tony (D)	6 3	14 02	Cardiff	9 10 78	Weymouth
McGrath John (M)	5 10	10 03	Limerick	27 3 80	Tamworth
Morris Lee (M)	5 10	11 02	Driffield	30 4 80	Yeovil T
Pearson Greg (F)	6 0	11 00	Birmingham	3 4 85	Bishop's Stortford
Poole Kevin (G)	5 10	11 11	Bromsgrove	21 7 63	Derby Co
Simpson Michael (M)	5 8	11 07	Nottingham	28 7 74	Leyton Orient
Stride Darren (M)	6 0	13 05	Burton-on-Trent	28 9 75	
Webster Aaron (D)	6 2	12 02	Burton-on-Trent	19 12 80	

TORQUAY UNITED

Name	Height	Weight	Birthplace	Date of birth	Previous club
Adams Steve (D)	6 0	12 04	Plymouth	25 9 80	Swindon T
Benyon Elliot (F)	5 9	10 01	High Wycombe	29 8 87	Bristol C
Bevan Scott (G)	6 6	15 04	Southampton	19 9 79	Shrewsbury T
Brough Michael (M)	5 9	11 07	Nottingham	1 8 81	Forest Green R
Carayol Mustapha (M)	5 9	11 11	Banjul	10 6 89	Milton Keynes D
Carlisle Wayne (M)	5 7	11 00	Lisburn	9 9 79	Exeter C
Christie Iyseden (F)	6 0	12 02	Coventry	14 11 76	Stevenage B
D'Sane Roscoe (F)	5 7	10 12	Epsom	16 10 80	Accrington S
Ellis Mark (D)	6 2	12 04	Plymouth	30 9 88	Bolton W
Green Matthew (F)	5 8	10 05	Bath	13 5 87	Cardiff C
Hargreaves Chris (M)	5 11	12 02	Cleethorpes	12 5 72	Oxford U
Hodges Lee (M)	6 0	12 02	Epping	4 9 73	Plymouth Arg
Mansell Lee (M)	5 9	10 10	Gloucester	23 9 82	Oxford U
Nicholson Kevin (M)	5 8	11 05	Derby	2 10 80	Forest Green R
Rice Martin (G)	5 9	12 00	Exeter	7 3 86	Exeter C
Robertson Chris (D)	6 3	11 09	Dundee	11 10 86	Sheffield U
Sills Tim (F)	6 2	12 02	Romsey	10 9 79	Hereford U
Stevens Danny (F)	5 10	11 07	Enfield	26 11 86	Luton T
Thompson Tyrone (M)	5 9	11 02	Sheffield	8 5 81	Crawley T
Todd Chris (D)	6 1	11 09	Swansea	22 8 81	Exeter C
Wroe Nicky (M)	5 11	10 01	Sheffield	28 9 85	York C

ENGLISH LEAGUE PLAYERS – INDEX

REFEREEING AND THE LAWS OF THE GAME

Although the International Football Association Board (IFAB) of FIFA publish their official booklet on the Laws of the Game, usually around August each year, they do however supply the text of their Law amendments prior to that. For the forthcoming season very little has changed and it would appear, thankfully, that the days of widespread changes have passed. It is noticeable that for the most part IFAB are concerned to embrace modern innovations and so artificial turf is something that is becoming acceptable on which to play the game. This has resulted in a change to Law One where the surface must meet FIFA requirements, so that the reference to "Artificial Turf" has now been replaced with the words "Football Turf" to indicate the acceptance of these surfaces.

The biggest alteration comes within arguably the most difficult of the Laws, namely Law Eleven embracing Offside. When a controversial incident takes place IFAB is usually quick to clarify and legislate on it. Thus when in a major tournament a player was left just off the pitch and a goal was scored and the defending side claimed an offside had occurred the decision to award a goal caused some controversy. The decision was upheld but it was felt the situation needed clarifying. So the Law has been altered to cover the position and now states "Any defending player leaving the field of play for any reason without the Referee's permission shall be considered to be on his own goal line or touchline for the purposes of offside until the next stoppage in play. If the player leaves the field of play deliberately he must be cautioned when the ball is next out of play".

It was previously decided at penalty shoot-outs that if one team was not at full strength, the opposition had to lose an equivalent player or players. The player or players excluded had to be named but now a clarification has been made to confirm that any player(s) so excluded may not participate in the shoot-out.

The Technical Area has also produced many problems even though the intention was to allow proper coaching from there. It is now underlined that only one person at a time is authorised to convey tactical instructions from there but he/she no longer has to return to their previous position, usually of course, on the bench. The aim ostensibly is to avoid problems with members of the other bench and to stop teams from "flooding" the Technical Area. Unfortunately, domestically this has been observed more in the breach than the performance and so the Fourth Official at games must in future be prepared to become unpopular in order to make this decree work.

One aspect of the Laws that has not been looked at but should be, relates to the "Drop-Ball". Reference to it comes in Law Eight relating to the Restart of Play after a stoppage. There have been so many problems over this in recent years, especially as the relevant part of the Law gives no clarification of when, where and how the referee should drop the ball or whether to a single player or between two of them, that thought should be given as to whether to create a new Law directly aimed at a defining solution.

FIFA have permitted the extension of an experiment believed to have been formulated by Michele Platini and designated to UEFA to control. The idea is for two extra assistant referees to be able to communicate with the Referee to give opinions on goal line decisions and potential penalties or diving. How this is better than having a referee in each half (the two referee system) or adding an extra "linesman" down each line or better still goal line technology is hard to fathom. However a proposal to increase the maximum number of substitutes in matches requiring extra time will be considered by the relevant FIFA committee. Sins bins were again rejected.

The English FA have published guidelines to the professional game concerning its "Respect" initiative, whilst the other attempt to improve relationships between players, managers and officials known as the "Get on with the Game" campaign seems to be going as well as can be expected. It spawned a special session put on for local school children at Aston Park in the Midlands attended by Aston Villa's Steve Sidwell and referees Chris Foy and Howard Webb. Foy of course refereed last season's League Cup Final and will also be in charge of this season's Community Shield, whilst Webb refereed last season's FA Cup Final as well as officiating in the Confederations Cup with assistants Peter Kirkup and Michael Mullarky. All of these are top of the tree in this season's retained lists of officials. Two, who are again approved as over the specified retirement age, are Alan Wiley and Peter Walton, but there have also been notable changes to that list. Two of those, Mike Riley and Steve Bennett, have moved on in sport whilst a third, Rob Styles has retired from all refereeing. Riley, after 13 seasons on the Premier League, becomes the General Manager of the Professional Game Match Officials (PGMO) and he succeeds Keith Hackett. Bennett changes sports altogether, a former Kent cricketer, he becomes Director of the ECB's new Association of Cricket Officials.

Referees and Assistant Referees are covered by the PGMO and this season Kevin Friend has been promoted to the Select Group of Referees List after six years as a National List Referee. Seven assistant referees have been promoted to their Select Group list and these are: Stuart Burt, David Coote, Paul Thompson, Scott Ledger, Rob Lewis, Simon Long and Bobby Madley. There are also seven referees promoted to the National List of Referees, namely, Geoff Eltringham, Steve Rushton, Darren Sheldrake, Gary Sutton, Peter Quinn, Paul Tierney and Jock Waugh. There are also thirty two people appointed to the National List of Assistant Referees and nine promoted to the Panel List of Referees. One to look out for is Ian Richardson who played for and managed Notts County, a rare case of a crossover involvement in the game, who is working his way up the system.

KEN GOLDMAN

NATIONAL LIST OF REFEREES FOR SEASON 2009–10

Draft

Atkinson, M (Martin) – W. Yorkshire
Attwell, SB (Stuart) – Warwickshire
Bates, A (Tony) – Staffordshire
Bennett, SG (Steve) – Kent
Booth, R (Russell) – Nottinghamshire
Boyeson, C (Carl) – E. Yorkshire
Bratt, SJ (Steve) – West Midlands
Clattenburg, M (Mark) – Tyne & Wear
Cook, SD (Steven) – Surrey
Crossley, PT (Phil) – Kent
Deadman, D (Darren) – Cambs.
Dean, ML (Mike) – Wirral
Dowd, P (Phil) – Staffordshire
D'urso, AP (Andy) – Essex
East, R (Roger) – Wiltshire
Eltringham, G (Geoff) – Tyne & Wear
Evans, KG (Karl) – Lancashire
Foster, D (David) – Tyne & Wear
Foy, CJ (Chris) – Merseyside
Friend, KA (Kevin) – Leicestershire
Gibbs, PN (Phil) – W. Midlands
Graham, F (Fred) – Essex
Haines, A (Andy) – Tyne & Wear
Hall, AR (Andy) – W. Midlands
Halsey, MR (Mark) – Lancashire
Haywood, M (Mark) – W. Yorkshire
Hegley, GK (Grant) – Hertfordshire
Hill, KD (Keith) – Hertfordshire
Hooper, SA (Simon) – Wiltshire
Horwood, GD (Graham) – Bedfordshire
Ilderton, EL (Eddie) – Tyne & Wear
Jones, MJ (Michael) – Cheshire
Kettle, TM (Trevor) – Rutland
Langford, O (Oliver) – W. Midlands
Laws, G (Graham) – Tyne & Wear
Linington, JJ (James) – Isle of Wight
McDermid, D (Danny) – Middlesex
Marriner, AM (Andre) – W. Midlands

Mason, LS (Lee) – Lancashire
Mathieson, SW (Scott) – Cheshire
Miller, NS (Nigel) – Co. Durham
Miller, P (Pat) – Bedfordshire
Moss, J (Jon) – W. Yorkshire
Oliver, CW (Clive) – Northumberland
Oliver, M (Michael) – Northumberland
Pawson, CL (Craig) – S. Yorkshire
Penn, AM (Andy) – W. Midlands
Phillips, DJ (David) – W. Sussex
Probert, LW (Lee) – Wiltshire
Quinn, P (Peter) – Cleveland
Rushton, SJ (Steve) – Staffordshire
Russell, MP (Mike) – Hertfordshire
Salisbury, G (Graham) – Lancashire
Sarginson, CD (Chris) – Staffordshire
Scott, GD (Graham) – Oxfordshire
Sheldrake, D (Darren) – Surrey
Shoebridge, RL (Rob) – Derbyshire
Singh, J (Jarnail) – Middlesex
Stroud, KP (Keith) – Hampshire
Sutton, GJ (Gary) – Lincolnshire
Swarbrick, ND (Neil) – Lancashire
Tanner, SJ (Steve) – Somerset
Taylor, A (Anthony) – Cheshire
Taylor, P (Paul) – Hertfordshire
Thorpe, M (Mike) – Suffolk
Tierney, P (Paul) – Lancashire
Walton, P (Peter) – Northamptonshire
Ward, GL (Gavin) – Surrey
Waugh, J (Jock) – S. Yorkshire
Webb, D (David) – Co. Durham
Webb, HM (Howard) – S. Yorkshire
Webster, CH (Colin) – Tyne & Wear
Whitestone, D (Dean) – Northamptonshire
Wiley, AG (Alan) – Staffordshire
Williamson, IG (Iain) – Berkshire
Woolmer, KA (Andy) – Northamptonshire
Wright, KK (Kevin) – Cambridgeshire

ASSISTANT REFEREES

Draft

Adcock, JG (James) – Nottinghamshire
Akers, C (Chris) – S. Yorkshire
Amey, JR (Justin) – Dorset
Amphlett, MJ (Marvyn) – Worcestershire
Artis, SG (Stephen) – Norfolk
Astley, MA (Mark) – Manchester
Atkin, R (Robert) – Lincolnshire
Atkin, W (Warren) – W. Sussex
Babski, DS (Dave) – Lincolnshire
Bankes, P (Peter) – Merseyside
Bannister, N (Nigel) – E. Yorkshire
Barnes, PW (Paul) – Cambridgeshire
Barratt, W (Wayne) – Worcestershire
Barrow, SJ (Simon) – Staffordshire
Bartlett, R (Richard) – Cheshire
Beck, SP (Simon) – Bedfordshire
Beevor, R (Richard) – Suffolk
Bennett, A (Andrew) – Devon
Bennett, SP (Simon) – Staffordshire
Benton, DK (David) – S. Yorkshire
Berry, CJ (Carl) – Surrey
Beswick, G (Gary) – Co. Durham
Betts, L (Lee) – Norfolk
Blackledge, M (Mike) – Cambridgeshire
Bond, DS (Darren) – Lancashire
Bramley, P (Philip) – W. Yorkshire
Breakspear, CT (Charles) – Surrey
Bristow, M (Matthew) – Manchester
Brown, M (Mark) – E. Yorkshire
Bryan, DS (Dave) – Lincolnshire
Buck, D (David) – Kent
Bull, M (Michael) – Essex
Bull, W (William) – Hampshire
Burt, S (Stuart) – Northamptonshire
Busby, J (John) – Oxfordshire
Bushell, DD (David) – London

Butler, AN (Andrew) – Lancashire
Cairns, MJ (Mike) – Somerset
Cann, DJ (Darren) – Norfolk
Child, SA (Stephen) – Kent
Clark, RM (Richard) – Northumberland
Clayton, S (Simon) – Co. Durham
Collin, J (Jake) – Merseyside
Collins, LM (Lee) – Surrey
Cook, SJ (Steve) – Derbyshire
Cooper, IJ (Ian) – Kent
Coote, DH (David) – Nottinghamshire
Copeland, SJ (Steven) – Merseyside
Cox, JL (James) – Worcestershire
Coy, M (Martin) – Co. Durham
Creighton, SW (Steve) – Berkshire
Crouch, IJ (Ian) – Kent
Curry, PE (Paul) – Northumberland
Daly, SDJ (Stephen) – Middlesex
Davies, A (Andy) – Hampshire
Davies, PP (Peter) – Cheshire
Davison, PA (Paul) – Cleveland
Denton, MJ (Michael) – Lancashire
Dermott, P (Philip) – Cheshire
Dexter, MC (Martin) – Leicestershire
Dicicco, M (Matthew) – Cleveland
Drysdale, D (Darren) – Lincolnshire
Dudley, IA (Ian) – Nottinghamshire
Duncan, SAJ (Scott) – Tyne & Wear
Dunn, C (Carl) – Staffordshire
England, DJH (Darren) – S. Yorkshire
Evetts, GS (Gary) – Hertfordshire
Farries, J (John) – Oxfordshire
Fletcher, R (Russell) – Derbyshire
Flynn, J (John) – Wiltshire
Foley, MJ (Matt) – London
Ford, D (Declan) – Leicestershire
Ganfield, RS (Ron) – Somerset

Garratt, AM (Andy) – West Midlands
George, M (Mike) – Norfolk
Gooch, P (Peter) – Lancashire
Gordon, B (Barry) – Co. Durham
Gosling, IJ (Ian) – Kent
Graham, P (Paul) – Manchester
Gratton, D (Danny) – Staffordshire
Green, RC (Russell) – Lancashire
Greenhalgh, N (Nicholas) – Lancashire
Greenwood, AH (Alf) – Yorkshire
Griffiths, M (Mark) – S. Yorkshire
Grunnill, W (Wayne) – E. Yorkshire
Hair, NA (Neil) – Cambridgeshire
Halliday, A (Andy) – N. Yorkshire
Hambling, GS (Glenn) – Norfolk
Handley, D (Darren) – Lancashire
Harrington, T (Tony) – Cleveland
Hart, G (Glen) – Co. Durham
Harwood, CN (Colin) – Manchester
Haycock, KW (Ken) – W. Yorkshire
Hayward, K (Kevin) – Staffordshire
Hendley, AR (Andy) – W. Midlands
Hewitt, RT (Richard) – N. Yorkshire
Heywood, M (Mark) – Cheshire
Hilton, G (Gary) – Lancashire
Hobbis, N (Nick) – W. Midlands
Hodskinson, P (Paul) – Lancashire
Holderness, BC (Barry) – Essex
Holmes, AR (Adrian) – W. Yorkshire
Hopkins, JD (John) – Essex
Horton, AJ (Tony) – W. Midlands
Hunt, J (Jonathan) – Co. Durham
Hutchinson, AD (Andrew) – Cheshire
Huxtable, B (Brett) – Devon
Ihringova, A (Sasa) – Shropshire
Jerden, GJN (Gary) – Essex
Johnson, KA (Kevin) – Somerset
Johnson, RL (Ryan) – Manchester
Jones, RJ (Robert) – Merseyside
Joyce, R (Ross) – Cleveland
Kavanagh, C (Chris) – Lancashire
Kaye, E (Elliott) – W. Yorkshire
Keane, PJ (Patrick) – W. Midlands
Kendall, R (Richard) – Bedfordshire
Kettlewell, PT (Paul) – Lancashire
Khatib, B (Billy) – Tyne & Wear
Kinseley, N (Nick) – Essex
Kirkup, PJ (Peter) – Northamptonshire
Knapp, SC (Simon) – Gloucestershire
Knight, PJ (Philip) – Kent
Knowles, CJ (Chris) – Northamptonshire
Knowles, J (Jason) – W. Yorkshire
Laver, AA (Andrew) – Hampshire
Law, GC (Geoff) – Leicestershire
Lawson, KD (Keith) – Lincolnshire
Ledger, S (Scott) – S. Yorkshire
Lennard, HW (Harry) – E. Sussex
Lewis, RL (Rob) – Shropshire
Lewis, SD (Sam) – Middlesex
Linden, W (Wes) – Middlesex
Long, SJ (Simon) – Suffolk
Mccallum, DA (Dave) – Tyne & Wear
Mccoy, MT (Michael) – W. Sussex
Mcdonough, M (Mick) – Tyne & Wear
Mclaughlin, M (Mathew) – Bedfordshire
Mackrell, EB (Eric) – Hampshire
Madley, A (Andy) – W. Yorkshire
Madley, RJ (Bobby) – W. Yorkshire
Magill, JP (John) – Essex
Malone, B (Brendan) – Wiltshire
Margetts, DS (David) – Essex
Markham, DR (Danny) – Tyne & Wear
Marsden, PR (Paul) – Lancashire
Martin, PC (Paul) – Northamptonshire
Martin, RJ (Richard) – Somerset
Martin, SJ (Stephen) – Staffordshire
Mason, T (Tony) – Kent
Massey, SL (Sian) – W. Midlands
Massey, T (Trevor) – Cheshire
Matadar, M (Mo) – Lancashire
Maton, A (Tony) – Leicestershire
Matthews, A (Adrian) – Wiltshire
Mattocks, KJ (Kevin) – Lancashire
Meeson, DP (Daniel) – Staffordshire
Melin, PW (Paul) – Surrey
Merchant, R (Rob) – Staffordshire

Metcalfe, RL (Lee) – Lancashire
Mohareb, D (Dean) – Cheshire
Muge, G (Gavin) – Bedfordshire
Mullarkey, M (Mike) – Devon
Murphy, ME (Michael) – W. Midlands
Murphy, N (Nigel) – Nottinghamshire
Naylor, D (Dave) – Nottinghamshire
Naylor, MA (Michael) – Sheffield
Newbold, AM (Andy) – Leicestershire
Newell, AC (Andy) – Lancashire
Newman, RP (Ryan) – S. Yorkshire
Norcott, WG (Wade) – Essex
Norris, P (Paul) – Cheshire
Nunn, AJ (Adam) – Wiltshire
Oldham, SA (Scott) – Lancashire
Parker, AR (Alan) – Derbyshire
Peart, T (Tony) – N. Yorkshire
Perry, MS (Marc) – W. Midlands
Philpott, M (Mark) – Cornwall
Phipps, SJ (Stephen) – Oxfordshire
Plowright, DP (David) – Nottinghamshire
Pollock, RM (Bob) – Merseyside
Porter, W (Wayne) – Lincolnshire
Pottage, M (Mark) – Somerset
Powell, CI (Chris) – Dorset
Procter-Green, SRM (Shaun) – Lincolnshire
Radford, N (Neil) – Worcestershire
Rayner, AE (Amy) – Leicestershire
Richards, DC (Ceri) – Carmarthenshire
Richardson, D (David) – W. Yorkshire
Roberts, B (Bob) – Lancashire
Roberts, DJ (Danny) – Manchester
Robinson, TJ (Tim) – W. Sussex
Rock, DK (David) – Hertfordshire
Rodda, A (Andrew) – Devon
Ross, SJ (Stephen) – Lincolnshire
Rowley, MD (Michael) – Berkshire
Rubery, SP (Steve) – Essex
Russell, GR (Geoff) – Northamptonshire
Russell, M (Mark) – Gloucestershire
Sainsbury, A (Andrew) – Wiltshire
Saliy, O (Oleksandr) – Middlesex
Salt, RA (Richard) – N. Yorkshire
Sannerude, A (Adrian) – Suffolk
Scholes, MS (Mark) – Buckinghamshire
Scregg, AJ (Andrew) – Merseyside
Sharp, PR (Phil) – Hertfordshire
Siddall, I (Iain) – Lancashire
Simpson, J (Jeremy) – Lancashire
Simpson, P (Paul) – Co. Durham
Slaughter, A (Ashley) – Sussex
Smallwood, W (William) – Cheshire
Smedley, I (Ian) – Derbyshire
Smith, AN (Andrew) – W. Yorkshire
Smith, EI (Eamonn) – Surrey
Smith, N (Nigel) – Derbyshire
Smith, S (Stephen) – Co. Durham
Stewart, M (Matt) – Suffolk
Stockbridge, SM (Seb) – Tyne & Wear
Storrie, D (David) – S. Yorkshire
Stott, GT (Gary) – Manchester
Street, DR (Duncan) – W. Yorkshire
Stretton, GS (Guy) – Leicestershire
Sutton, MA (Mark) – Derbyshire
Swabey, L (Lee) – Devon
Thompson, MF (Marvin) – Middlesex
Thompson, PI (Paul) – Derbyshire
Tomlinson, SD (Stephen) – Hampshire
Trott, WL (Wayne) – Merseyside
Turner, A (Andrew) – Devon
Turner, GB (Glenn) – Derbyshire
Tyas, J (Jason) – W. Yorkshire
Unsworth, D (David) – Manchester
Vaughan, RG (Roger) – N. Somerset
Waring, J (Jim) – Lancashire
Watts, AS (Adam) – Worcestershire
Weaver, M (Mark) – W. Midlands
West, RJ (Richard) – E. Yorkshire
Whiteley, J (Jason) – W. Yorkshire
Whitton, RP (Rob) – Essex
Wigglesworth, RJ (Richard) – S. Yorkshire
Wright, P (Peter) – Merseyside
Yates, O (Oliver) – Staffordshire
Yeo, KG (Keith) – Essex
Yerby, MS (Martin) – Kent
Young, GR (Gary) – Bedfordshire

TRANSFERS 2008–09

	From	To	Fee in £
JUNE 2008			
24 Carden, Paul A.	Accrington Stanley	Cambridge United	undisclosed
30 Duguid, Karl	Colchester United	Plymouth Argyle	undisclosed
27 Hoolahan, Wesley	Blackpool	Norwich City	250,000
6 Hughes, Jeffrey	Crystal Palace	Bristol Rovers	120,000
24 Hume, Iain	Leicester City	Barnsley	1,200,000
24 Legzdins, Adam R.	Birmingham City	Crewe Alexandra	undisclosed
3 Lockwood, Matthew D.	Nottingham Forest	Colchester United	undisclosed
18 McAuley, Gareth	Leicester City	Ipswich Town	1,100,000
12 McCarthy, Patrick	Charlton Athletic	Crystal Palace	undisclosed
4 Moore, Luke	Aston Villa	West Bromwich Albion	3,000,000
23 Muamba, Fabrice	Birmingham City	Bolton Wanderers	5,500,000
27 Paterson, Martin	Scunthorpe United	Burnley	1,300,000
24 Perry, Christopher J.	Luton Town	Southampton	undisclosed
10 Ramsey, Aaron J.	Cardiff City	Arsenal	5,000,000
4 Stockdale, David A.	Darlington	Fulham	350,000
28 Vokes, Samuel M.	AFC Bournemouth	Wolverhampton Wanderers	250,000
18 Westwood, Keiren	Carlisle United	Coventry City	750,000
16 Wood, Samuel J.	Bromley	Brentford	undisclosed
30 Zola, Calvin	Tranmere Rovers	Crewe Alexandra	200,000
JULY 2008			
18 Andrew, Calvin H.	Luton Town	Crystal Palace	undisclosed
30 Ashton, Nathan	Fulham	Wycombe Wanderers	undisclosed
25 Baker, Carl P.	Morecambe	Stockport County	175,000
23 Bell, David A.	Luton Town	Norwich City	600,000
18 Bent, Marcus N.	Charlton Athletic	Birmingham City	1,000,000
31 Bentley, David M.	Blackburn Rovers	Tottenham Hotspur	17,000,000
17 Boateng, George	Middlesbrough	Hull City	1,000,000
1 Carle, Nicholas A.	Bristol City	Crystal Palace	undisclosed
18 Carson, Scott P.	Liverpool	West Bromwich Albion	3,250,000
29 Cattermole, Lee B.	Middlesbrough	Wigan Athletic	3,500,000
28 Chimbonda, Pascal	Tottenham Hotspur	Sunderland	4,900,000
31 Cotterill, David	Wigan Athletic	Sheffield United	1,500,000
11 Craig, Tony A.	Crystal Palace	Millwall	250,000
14 Cresswell, Ryan	Sheffield United	Bury	undisclosed
11 Crouch, Peter J.	Liverpool	Portsmouth	11,000,000
3 Davies, Curtis E.	West Bromwich Albion	Aston Villa	8,000,000
25 Diagouraga, Toumani	Watford	Hereford United	undisclosed
1 Dickinson, Liam	Stockport County	Derby County	750,000
29 Diouf, El Hadji O.	Bolton Wanderers	Sunderland	2,500,000
21 Dodds, Louis	Leicester City	Port Vale	undisclosed
11 Duffy, Darryl A.	Swansea City	Bristol Rovers	100,000
12 Eastwood, Freddy	Wolverhampton Wanderers	Coventry City	1,200,000
24 Elding, Anthony L.	Leeds United	Crewe Alexandra	100,000
2 Fagan, Craig	Derby County	Hull City	750,000
18 Forecast, Tommy S.	Tottenham Hotspur	Southampton	undisclosed
28 Friedel, Bradley H.	Blackburn Rovers	Aston Villa	2,500,000
25 Garner, Joseph A.	Carlisle United	Nottingham Forest	1,140,000
11 Gillespie, Steven	Cheltenham Town	Colchester United	400,000
1 Grant, Joel V.	Aldershot Town	Crewe Alexandra	130,000
14 Guthrie, Danny S.	Liverpool	Newcastle United	2,500,000
22 Halmosi, Peter	Plymouth Argyle	Hull City	3,000,000
24 Henderson, Darius A.	Watford	Sheffield United	2,000,000
18 Hooper, Gary	Southend United	Scunthorpe United	175,000
21 Hulse, Robert W.	Sheffield United	Derby County	1,750,000
15 Iwelumo, Chris	Charlton Athletic	Wolverhampton Wanderers	undisclosed
17 Jean–Baptiste, Alex	Mansfield Town	Blackpool	undisclosed
29 Jones, David F.L.	Derby County	Wolverhampton Wanderers	undisclosed
16 Kapo, Narcisse O.	Birmingham City	Wigan Athletic	3,500,000
29 Keane, Robert D.	Tottenham Hotspur	Liverpool	19,000,000
18 Kitson, David	Reading	Stoke City	5,500,000
21 Lisbie, Kevin	Colchester United	Ipswich Town	600,000
9 MacDonald, Charles L.	Southend United	Brentford	undisclosed
7 Martin, Joseph J.	Tottenham Hotspur	Blackpool	undisclosed
4 Martin, Russell K.A.	Wycombe Wanderers	Peterborough United	undisclosed
4 Moore, Darren M.	Derby County	Barnsley	undisclosed
9 Morgan, Marvin	Woking	Aldershot Town	undisclosed
3 Morrison, Michael B.	Cambridge United	Leicester City	undisclosed
29 Olofinjana, Seyi G.	Wolverhampton Wanderers	Stoke City	3,000,000
18 Pantsil, John	West Ham United	Fulham	500,000
11 Perkins, David	Rochdale	Colchester United	150,000
4 Puncheon, Jason D.I.	Barnet	Plymouth Argyle	250,000
29 Roberts, Gary M.	Ipswich Town	Huddersfield Town	250,000
28 Robinson, Paul W.	Tottenham Hotspur	Blackburn Rovers	3,500,000
8 Shaw, Jon S.	FC Halifax Town	Rochdale	undisclosed
10 Sidwell, Steven J.	Chelsea	Aston Villa	5,500,000
2 Stearman, Richard	Leicester City	Wolverhampton Wanderers	1,600,000
18 Stefanovic, Dejan	Fulham	Norwich City	undisclosed
28 Tainio, Teemu	Tottenham Hotspur	Sunderland	3,500,000
22 Thomas, Simon	Boreham Wood	Crystal Palace	nominal
14 Torres, Sergio R.	Wycombe Wanderers	Peterborough United	150,000
17 Warner, Anthony R.	Fulham	Hull City	undisclosed
7 Williams, Gavin J.	Ipswich Town	Bristol City	undisclosed

1 Williams, Marvin T.	Yeovil Town	Brentford	undisclosed
21 Wright, Richard I.	West Ham United	Ipswich Town	500,000
16 Zamora, Robert L.	West Ham United	Fulham	5,800,000

TEMPORARY TRANSFERS

2 Anderson, Paul – Liverpool – Nottingham Forest; 25 Antwi–Birago, Godwin – Liverpool – Tranmere Rovers; 22 Bailey, Matthew – Wolverhampton Wanderers – Burton Albion; 22 Beardsley, Jason C. – Derby County – Notts County; 29 Bennett, Elliott – Wolverhampton Wanderers – Bury; 8 Bertrand, Ryan D. – Chelsea – Norwich City; 24 Brandy, Febian E. – Manchester United – Swansea City; 25 Bridges, Michael – Hull City – Carlisle United; 1 Charles, Wesley D.D. – Brentford – Ebbsfleet United; 28 Clarke, Andre N.J.E. – Blackburn Rovers – Accrington Stanley; 22 Cole, Jake S. – Queens Park Rangers – Oxford United; 18 Constable, James A. – Shrewsbury Town – Oxford United; 23 Davies, Scott – Reading – Aldershot Town; 4 Dawkins, Simon J. – Tottenham Hotspur – Leyton Orient; 28 Gall, Kevin A. – Carlisle United – Lincoln City; 31 Gardner, Anthony – Tottenham Hotspur – Hull City; 10 Gilbert, Kerrea K. – Arsenal – Leicester City; 29 Grocott, Marc D. – Stoke City – Alfreton Town; 26 Guy, Jamie – Colchester United – Oxford United; 17 Haldane, Lewis O. – Bristol Rovers – Oxford United; 3 Halford, Gregory – Sunderland – Sheffield United; 1 Hamer, Ben – Reading – Brentford; 21 Hammill, Adam J. – Liverpool – Blackpool; 25 Hobbs, Jack – Liverpool – Leicester City; 22 Howe, Jermaine R. – Peterborough United – Morecambe; 11 Kabba, Steven – Watford – Blackpool; 14 Livermore, Jake – Tottenham Hotspur – Crewe Alexandra; 5 Mills, Leigh – Tottenham Hotspur – Brentford; 10 Morgan, Paul M.T. – Bury – Macclesfield Town; 18 Omozusi, Elliott – Fulham – Norwich City; 25 Phillips, James P. – Stoke City – Alfreton Town; 31 Poke, Michael H. – Southampton – Torquay United; 19 Randolph, Darren E. – Charlton Athletic – Hereford United; 31 Rehman, Zeshan – Queens Park Rangers – Blackpool; 21 Richards, Matthew – Ipswich Town – Brighton & Hove Albion; 1 Sahar, Ben – Chelsea – Portsmouth; 5 Smith, James D. – Chelsea – Sheffield Wednesday; 24 Starosta, Ben M. – Sheffield United – Aldershot Town; 4 Taylor, Paul T. – Vauxhall Motors – Chester City; 23 Thorley, Thomas R. – Stoke City – Stafford Rangers; 30 Threlfall, Robert R. – Liverpool – Hereford United; 29 Walker, Richard M. – Bristol Rovers – Shrewsbury Town

AUGUST 2008

4 Ameobi, Oluwatomiwo	Leeds United	Doncaster Rovers	undisclosed
28 Andrews, Keith J.	Milton Keynes Dons	Blackburn Rovers	undisclosed
26 Armstrong, Christopher	Sheffield United	Reading	500,000
14 Bailey, Nicholas F.	Southend United	Charlton Athletic	undisclosed
19 Barker, Christopher A.	Queens Park Rangers	Plymouth Argyle	undisclosed
4 Ben–Haim, Tal	Chelsea	Manchester City	6,000,000
8 Betsy, Kevin	Bristol City	Southend United	undisclosed
5 Bothroyd, Jay	Wolverhampton Wanderers	Cardiff City	300,000
8 Canham, Sean	Team Bath	Notts County	undisclosed
5 Chambers, James	Leicester City	Doncaster Rovers	undisclosed
29 Connell, Alan J.	Brentford	AFC Bournemouth	undisclosed
22 Craney, Ian T.W.	Accrington Stanley	Huddersfield Town	undisclosed
19 Davies, Andrew	Southampton	Stoke City	1,300,000
19 Diagne Faye, Abdoulaye	Newcastle United	Stoke City	2,250,000
6 Eagles, Christopher M.	Manchester United	Burnley	1,200,000
7 Edwards, Robert O.	Wolverhampton Wanderers	Blackpool	undisclosed
15 Faye, Amdy M.	Charlton Athletic	Stoke City	2,000,000
8 Fenton, Nicholas L.	Grimsby Town	Rotherham United	undisclosed
27 Ferdinand, Anton J.	West Ham United	Sunderland	8,000,000
21 Gardner, Anthony	Tottenham Hotspur	Hull City	2,500,000
1 Gorkss, Kaspars	Blackpool	Queens Park Rangers	250,000
27 Green, Dominic A.	Dagenham & Redbridge	Peterborough United	undisclosed
8 Guyett, Scott B.	Yeovil Town	Bournemouth	undisclosed
19 Gyepes, Gabor	Northampton Town	Cardiff City	undisclosed
21 Healy, David J.	Fulham	Sunderland	1,500,000
21 Hoyte, Justin R.	Arsenal	Middlesbrough	3,000,000
29 Jalal, Shwan S.	Peterborough United	AFC Bournemouth	undisclosed
7 Johnson, Andrew	Everton	Fulham	10,500,000
12 Kaboul, Younes	Tottenham Hotspur	Portsmouth	5,000,000
22 Keogh, Richard J.	Bristol City	Carlisle United	undisclosed
1 Malbranque, Steed	Tottenham Hotspur	Sunderland	4,000,000
15 Marshall, Mark	Eastleigh	Swindon Town	undisclosed
8 Maynard, Nicholas D.	Crewe Alexandra	Bristol City	2,250,000
10 Meite, Abdoulaye	Bolton Wanderers	West Bromwich Albion	2,000,000
1 Mills, Matthew C.	Manchester City	Doncaster Rovers	300,000
29 Milner, James P.	Newcastle United	Aston Villa	12,000,000
13 Mirfin, David	Huddersfield Town	Scunthorpe United	150,000
14 Noone, Craig	Southport	Plymouth Argyle	undisclosed
20 Osei–Kuffour, Jonathan	AFC Bournemouth	Bristol Rovers	undisclosed
30 Pulis, Anthony J.	Stoke City	Southampton	undisclosed
15 Rigby, Lloyd J.	Vauxhall Motors	Stockport County	undisclosed
8 Shittu, Daniel O.	Watford	Bolton Wanderers	2,000,000
8 Shorey, Nicholas	Reading	Aston Villa	4,000,000
21 Silvestre, Mikael S.	Manchester United	Arsenal	750,000
29 Sonko, Ibrahima	Reading	Stoke City	undisclosed
1 Sorensen, Thomas	Aston Villa	Stoke City	Free
20 Thomas, Jerome W.	Charlton Athletic	Portsmouth	undisclosed
15 Togwell, Samuel J.	Barnsley	Scunthorpe United	undisclosed
7 Walton, Simon W.	Queens Park Rangers	Plymouth Argyle	500,000
29 Weston, Curtis J.	Leeds United	Gillingham	undisclosed
14 Walford, Martyn P.	York City	Scunthorpe United	undisclosed
1 Williams, Ashley E.	Stockport County	Swansea City	300,000
29 Wright–Phillips, Shaun C.	Chelsea	Manchester City	8,500,000
8 Young, Luke P.	Middlesbrough	Aston Villa	5,000,000

TEMPORARY TRANSFERS

8 Aluko, Sone – Birmingham City – Blackpool; 27 Anderson, Russell – Sunderland – Burnley; 15 Araba, Hakeem A.C. – Dagenham & Redbridge – Thurrock – ; 8 Archibald–Henville, Troy – Tottenham Hotspur – Norwich City; 7 Artus, Frankie – Bristol City – Brentford; 5 Ashikodi, Moses – Watford – Hereford United; 22 Ashworth, Luke A. – Wigan Athletic – Leyton Orient; 22 Bailey, Matthew – Wolverhampton Wanderers – Burton Albion; 13 Baker, Lee – West Bromwich Albion – Kidderminster Harriers; 19 Barazite, Nacer – Arsenal – Derby County; 9 Barker, Christopher A. – Queens Park Rangers – Plymouth Argyle; 22 Bayliss, Ashton P. – Blackpool – Fleetwood Town; 21 Beardsley, Jason C. – Derby County – Notts County; 7 Begovic, Asmir – Portsmouth – Yeovil Town; 28 Bellamy, Adrian R. – Bradford City – Salford City; 8 Bennett, Alan J. – Reading – Brentford; 22 Black, Paul – Oldham Athletic – Barrow; 9 Bouazza, Hameur – Fulham – Charlton Athletic; 15 Boyce, Andrew T. – Doncaster Rovers – Worksop Town; 2 Brown, Simon J. – Brentford – Darlington; 5 Camara, Mohamed – Derby County –

Blackpool; 8 Cathcart, Craig G. – Manchester United – Plymouth Argyle; 28 Church, Simon R. – Reading – Wycombe Wanderers; 28 Clarke, William C. – Ipswich Town – Darlington; 15 Clough, Charlie – Bristol Rovers – Mangotsfield United; 1 Collins, Lee H. – Wolverhampton Wanderers – Port Vale; 6 Cook, Lee – Fulham – Queens Park Rangers; 21 Cork, Jack F.P. – Chelsea – Southampton; 4 Cummings, Shaun M. – Chelsea – Milton Keynes Dons; 26 Daniels, Charlie – Tottenham Hotspur – Gillingham; 13 Daniels, Luke – West Bromwich Albion – Shrewsbury Town; 26 Dayton, James F. – Crystal Palace – Yeovil Town; 15 Dean, Harle J. – Dagenham & Redbridge – Redbridge; 19 Dickinson, Liam – Derby County – Huddersfield Town; 15 Erskine, Emmanuel J. – Dagenham & Redbridge – Redbridge; 15 Evans, Scott – Swansea City – Port Talbot Town; 29 Fogden, Wesley K. – Brighton & Hove Albion – Dorchester Town; 5 Fraser, James – Bristol Rovers – Lewes; 29 Gallagher, Paul – Blackburn Rovers – Plymouth Argyle; 11 Gamble, Patrick J. – Nottingham Forest – Mansfield Town; 8 Gargan, Sam J. – Brighton & Hove Albion – Havant & Waterlooville; 8 Gatting, Joe S. – Brighton & Hove Albion – Bognor Regis Town; 8 Gleeson, Stephen M. – Wolverhampton Wanderers – Stockport County; 15 Graves, Kyle N. – Swansea City – Neath; 14 Groves, Matt – Bristol Rovers – Tiverton Town; 8 Harding, Daniel A. – Ipswich Town – Southend United; 12 Hardman, Lewis – Darlington – Sunderland Nissan; 22 Harris, Harry – Walsall – Chasetown; 27 Hatch, Liam M.A. – Peterborough United – Darlington; 14 Hayles, Barrington – Leicester City – Cheltenham Town; 8 Henry, Rhys E. – Southend United – Thurrock; 5 Heslop, Simon – Barnsley – Grimsby Town; 1 Jalal, Shwan S. – Peterborough United – AFC Bournemouth; 26 Johnson, Edward – Fulham – Cardiff City; 20 Jones, Christopher T. – Swansea City – Cambridge United; 8 Kandol, Tresor O. – Leeds United – Millwall; 14 King, Marlon F. – Wigan Athletic – Hull City; 8 Klein-Davies, Joshua – Bristol Rovers – Luton Town; 5 Koroma, Omar A. – Portsmouth – Norwich City; 7 Krysiak, Artur L. – Birmingham City – York City; 29 Lee, Alan D. – Ipswich Town – Crystal Palace; 22 Lindfield, Craig A. – Liverpool – AFC Bournemouth; 22 Little, Mark D. – Wolverhampton Wanderers – Northampton Town; 20 Logan, Conrad – Leicester City – Luton Town; 22 Louis, Kane T. – Brighton & Hove Albion – Burgess Hill Town; 13 Mahdi, Adam – Bristol Rovers – Cirencester Town; 7 Martin, Christopher – Norwich City – Luton Town; 7 Martin, David E. – Liverpool – Leicester City; 27 Martin, Lee R. – Manchester United – Nottingham Forest; 12 Martin, Neil J. – Exeter City – Hayes & Yeading United; 18 McDonald, Clayton – Manchester City – Macclesfield Town; 21 McMahon – Anthony – Middlesbrough – Sheffield Wednesday; 26 Mills, Leigh – Tottenham Hotspur – Gillingham; 29 Mitchell, Paul A. – Milton Keynes Dons – Barnet; 8 Moncur, Thomas J. – Fulham – Bradford City; 29 Moore, Karl – Manchester City – Millwall; 28 Morgan, Dean – Luton Town – Leyton Orient; 15 Morgan, Kerry D. – Swansea City – Neath; 15 Morrison, Stefan – Swansea City – Port Talbot Town; 15 Myrie-Williams, Jennison – Bristol City – Cheltenham Town; 22 Nelthorpe, Craig R. – Doncaster Rovers – Gateshead; 30 Parkin, Jonathan – Stoke City – Preston North End; 19 Pearce, Krystian M.V. – Birmingham City – Scunthorpe United; 27 Pekhart, Tomas – Tottenham Hotspur – Southampton; 21 Pidgeley, Leonard J. – Millwall – Woking; 7 Plummer, Tristan D. – Bristol City – Luton Town; 1 Potter, Alfie – Peterborough United – Kettering Town; 7 Puddy, Willem J.S. – Cheltenham Town – Tamworth; 14 Pugh, Andrew J. – Gillingham – Folkestone Invicta; 15 Rasiak, Grzegorz – Southampton – Watford; 8 Reay, Shaun – Darlington – Harrogate Town; 8 Rigby, Lloyd J. – Vauxhall Motors – Stockport County; 8 Rigters, Maceo – Blackburn Rovers – Barnsley; 22 Roberts, Gary S. – Crewe Alexandra – Yeovil Town; 21 Robson-Kanu, Thomas H. – Reading – Southend United; 12 Sappleton, Reneil – Leicester City – AFC Bournemouth; 18 Sawyer, Lee T. – Chelsea – Southend United; 14 Scott, Mark J. – Swindon Town – Thatcham Town; 29 Shotton, Ryan – Stoke City – Tranmere Rovers; 5 Simpson, Daniel P. – Manchester United – Blackburn Rovers; 21 Sinclair, Dean M. – Charlton Athletic – Cheltenham Town; 7 Spillane, Michael – Norwich City – Luton Town; 1 Spring, Matthew – Luton Town – Sheffield United; 21 Starosta, Ben M. – Sheffield United – Aldershot Town; 29 Taiwo, Thomas – Chelsea – Port Vale; 15 Teale, Gary – Derby County – Barnsley; 15 Thomas, Aswad – Charlton Athletic – Barnet; 15 Thomas, Jerome W. – Charlton Athletic – Portsmouth; 21 Thorley, Thomas R. – Stoke City – Stafford Rangers; 20 Thurgood, Stuart A. – Gillingham – Grays Athletic; 6 Todd, Simon – Darlington – Blyth Spartans; 21 Traore, Armand – Arsenal – Portsmouth; 29 Vipond, Shaun – Carlisle United – Workington; 28 Volz, Moritz – Fulham – Ipswich Town; 21 Wagstaff, Scott A. – Charlton Athletic – AFC Bournemouth; 13 Walker, Lauris D. – Millwall – Tooting & Mitcham United; 1 Wallace, Ross – Sunderland – Preston North End; 21 Ward, Joel E.P. – Portsmouth – AFC Bournemouth; 7 Warlow, Owain J. – Lincoln City – Kettering Town; 6 Weston, Curtis J. – Leeds United – Gillingham; 7 Wilson, James S. – Bristol City – Brentford; 22 Worrall, David – West Bromwich Albion – Accrington Stanley; 28 Yates, Adam P. – Morecambe – Burton Albion

SEPTEMBER 2008

1 Akinde, John	Ebbsfleet United	Bristol City	140,000
1 Berbatov, Dimitar	Tottenham Hotspur	Manchester United	30,750,000
1 Brayford, John R.	Burton Albion	Crewe Alexandra	undisclosed
1 Bunn, Mark	Northampton Town	Blackburn Rovers	undisclosed
1 Corluka, Vedran	Manchester City	Tottenham Hotspur	8,500,000
1 Elliott, Stephen W.	Wolverhampton Wanderers	Preston North End	undisclosed
1 Etuhu, Dixon P.	Sunderland	Fulham	undisclosed
1 Friend, George	Exeter City	Wolverhampton Wanderers	undisclosed
1 Harrold, Matthew	Southend United	Wycombe Wanderers	undisclosed
1 Higginbotham, Daniel J.	Sunderland	Stoke City	undisclosed
1 Hill, Matthew C.	Preston North End	Wolverhampton Wanderers	undisclosed
1 Lee, Alan D.	Ipswich Town	Crystal Palace	undisclosed
1 McCartney, George	West Ham United	Sunderland	undisclosed
1 Nash, Carlo J.	Wigan Athletic	Everton	undisclosed
1 Owusu, Lloyd	Yeovil Town	Cheltenham Town	undisclosed
1 Parkin, Jonathan	Stoke City	Preston North End	undisclosed
1 Saha, Louis	Manchester United	Everton	undisclosed
1 Shackell, Jason	Norwich City	Wolverhampton Wanderers	undisclosed
1 Soares, Thomas J.	Crystal Palace	Stoke City	1,250,000
15 Stead, Jonathan	Sheffield United	Ipswich Town	600,000
1 Thompson, Steven H.	Cardiff City	Burnley	undisclosed
1 Tonge, Michael W.	Sheffield United	Stoke City	2,000,000

TEMPORARY TRANSFERS

1 Alaile, Michael – Dagenham & Redbridge – Fisher Athletic; 25 Ameobi, Oluwatomiwo – Doncaster Rovers – Grimsby Town; 11 Anyinsah, Joseph G. – Preston North End – Brighton & Hove Albion; 12 Arestidou, Andreas J. – Blackburn Rovers – Nantwich Town; 9 Artus, Frankie – Bristol City – Brentford; 27 Ashworth, Luke A. – Wigan Athletic – Leyton Orient; 1 Baker, Lee – West Bromwich Albion – Kidderminster Harriers; 25 Barcham, Andrew – Tottenham Hotspur – Gillingham; 25 Bayliss, Ashton P. – Blackpool – Fleetwood Town; 26 Beattie, Craig – West Bromwich Albion – Crystal Palace; 23 Beavan, George D. – Luton Town – Salisbury City; 1 Bennett, Alan J. – Reading – Brentford; 23 Bevan, David – Aston Villa – Tamworth; 25 Bevan, Scott A. – Shrewsbury Town – Torquay United; 5 Blackmore, David – West Ham United – Thurrock; 18 Boden, Luke – Sheffield Wednesday – Chesterfield; 1 Bore, Peter – Grimsby Town – York City; 25 Borrowdale, Gary I. – Coventry City – Colchester United; 16 Botham, Calum – Wycombe Wanderers – Basingstoke Town; 19 Bradley, Jason – Darlington – Buxton; 18 Brown, Lee J. – Queens Park Rangers – AFCHornchurch; 19 Bryant, Mitchell J. – Reading – Basingstoke Town; 19 Button, David R. – Tottenham Hotspur – Grays Athletic; 9 Camara, Mohamed – Derby County – Blackpool; 1 Campbell, Fraizer L. – Manchester United – Tottenham Hotspur; 1 Carr, Michael A. – Morecambe – Northwich Victoria; 16 Cartman, Nathan – Leeds United – Harrogate Railway; 30 Charge, Daniel – Dagenham & Redbridge – Potters Bar Town; 1 Christophe, Jean F. – Portsmouth – Southend United; 18 Clohessy, Sean D. – Gillingham – Salisbury City; 15 Clough, Charlie – Bristol Rovers – Mangotsfield United; 18 Cook, Anthony L.E. – Dagenham & Redbridge – Concord Rangers; 1 Cranie, Martin J. – Portsmouth – Charlton Athletic; 18 Diallo, Drissa – Milton Keynes Dons – Cheltenham Town; 19 Dickinson, Liam – Derby County – Huddersfield Town; 24 Dixon, Jonathan J. – Brighton & Hove Albion – Grays Athletic; 26 Dyer, Nathan A.J. – Southampton – Sheffield United; 26 Easter, Jermaine – Plymouth Argyle – Millwall; 19 Ennis, Paul – Stockport County – Salford City; 25 Federici, Adam – Reading – Southend United; 12

Fielding, Francis D. – Blackburn Rovers – Northampton Town; 26 Fleetwood, Stuart K. – Charlton Athletic – Cheltenham Town; 4 Fraser, James – Bristol Rovers – Tiverton Town; 1 Gallagher, Paul – Blackburn Rovers – Plymouth Argyle; 19 Gardner, Scott A. – Leeds United – Farsley Celtic; 23 Gargan, Sam J. – Brighton & Hove Albion – Lewes; 19 Gornell, Terence – Tranmere Rovers – Accrington Stanley; 1 Gray, Julian R. – Coventry City – Fulham; 9 Griffiths, Rostyn J. – Blackburn Rovers – Accrington Stanley; 12 Grocott, Marc D. – Stoke City – Solihull Moors; 1 Grounds, Jonathan M. – Middlesbrough – Norwich City; 26 Hardman, Lewis – Darlington – Bishop Auckland; 22 Harris, Harry – Walsall – Chasetown; 12 Hawley, Karl L. – Preston North End – Northampton Town; 11 Hayles, Barrington – Leicester City – Cheltenham Town; 12 Henry, Rhys E. – Southend United – Harlow Town; 22 Holmes, Peter J. – Rotherham United – York City; 11 Hotchkiss, Oliver – Leeds United – Garforth Town; 9 Howard, Charlie S. – Gillingham – Dulwich Hamlet; 1 Illugason, Viktor U. – Reading – Eastbourne Borough; 12 Jeffery, Jack C. – West Ham United – Leyton Orient; 8 Kalipha, Kayan – Dagenham & Redbridge – Hendon; 25 Kamara, Malvin G. – Huddersfield Town – Grimsby Town; 1 Killock, Shane – Huddersfield Town – Harrogate Town; 5 Kite, Alex – Bristol Rovers – Oxford City; 9 Lamplough, Joe – Hull City – North Ferriby United; 30 Lawrence, Dennis W. – Swansea City – Crewe Alexandra; 21 Little, Mark D. – Wolverhampton Wanderers – Northampton Town; 2 Liversedge, Nicholas – Darlington – Whitby Town; 1 Lokando, Peggy – Southend United – Dagenham & Redbridge; 23 Louis, Kane T. – Brighton & Hove Albion – Burgess Hill Town; 25 Lynch, Joel J. – Brighton & Hove Albion – Nottingham Forest; 26 MacKenzie, Neal – Notts County – Kidderminster Harriers; 19 Mahdi, Adam – Bristol Rovers – Clevedon Town; 23 Martin, Alan – Leeds United – Barrow; 11 Mayo, Kerry – Brighton & Hove Albion – Lewes; 11 McDermott, Donal J. – Manchester City – Milton Keynes Dons; 29 McEveley, James – Derby County – Preston North End; 19 McMahon, Anthony – Middlesbrough – Sheffield Wednesday; 1 McShane, Paul D. – Sunderland – Hull City; 19 Minto–St Aimie, Kieron L.J. – Barnet – Grays Athletic; 24 Montrose, Louis – Wigan Athletic – Cheltenham Town; 15 Murray, Scott G. – Bristol City – Cheltenham Town; 19 Myrie–Williams, Jennison – Bristol City – Carlisle United; 25 N'Gotty, Bruno – Leicester City – Hereford United; 1 Osborne, Karleigh A.J. – Brentford – Oxford United; 2 Ovington, Christopher – Leeds United – Guiseley; 19 Panther, Emmanuel – Exeter City – Rushden & Diamonds; 24 Payne, Joshua – West Ham United – Cheltenham Town; 1 Pearce, Krystian M.V. – Birmingham City – Scunthorpe United; 19 Pearson, Andrew C. – Brighton & Hove Albion – Worthing; 11 Phillips, James P. – Stoke City – Stafford Rangers; 22 Pidgeley, Leonard J. – Millwall – Woking; 8 Plummer, Tristan D. – Bristol City – Luton Town; 11 Primus, Linvoy S. – Portsmouth – Charlton Athletic; 12 Pugh, Marc – Shrewsbury Town – Luton Town; 19 Redmond, Shane P. – Nottingham Forest – Eastwood Town; 12 Rhodes, Jordan L. – Ipswich Town – Rochdale; 19 Rigg, Sean M. – Bristol Rovers – Grays Athletic; 25 Ritchie, Matthew T. – Portsmouth – Dagenham & Redbridge; 26 Robertson, Jordan – Sheffield United – Southampton; 23 Robson–Kanu, Thomas H. – Reading – Southend United; 5 Rouse, Domaine – Bury – Droylsden; 3 Sak, Erwin P. – Cardiff City – Newport County; 19 Sharpe, Thomas R. – Nottingham Forest – Stalybridge Celtic; 30 Shotton, Ryan – Stoke City – Tranmere Rovers; 12 Shulton, Scott – Wycombe Wanderers – Basingstoke Town; 1 Sibierski, Antoine – Wigan Athletic – Norwich City; 9 Smith, Daniel – Plymouth Argyle – Morecambe; 26 Sodje, Samuel – Reading – Watford; 9 Southall, Leslie N. – Gillingham – Dover Athletic; 1 Stead, Jonathan – Sheffield United – Ipswich Town; 26 Sturrock, Blair D. – Swindon Town – AFC Bournemouth; 19 Swallow, Ben – Bristol Rovers – Taunton Town; 26 Thomas, Aswad – Charlton Athletic – Lewes; 26 Thornton, Kevin – Coventry City – Brighton & Hove Albion; 12 Thornton, Sean – Leyton Orient – Shrewsbury Town; 19 Thurlbourne, Luke D. – Southend United – St Albans City; 8 Todd, Simon – Darlington – Blyth Spartans; 19 Trotter, Liam – Ipswich Town – Grimsby Town; 30 Tyler, Mark R. – Peterborough United – Watford; 1 Upson, Edward J. – Ipswich Town – Stevenage Borough; 1 Vidal, Javan – Manchester City – Grimsby Town; 18 Vipond, Shaun – Carlisle United – Workington; 30 Ward, Darren P. – Wolverhampton Wanderers – Watford; 22 White, Joe – Bristol Rovers – Chippenham Town; 11 Wilkinson, David M. – Crystal Palace – Truro City; 29 Wilkinson, Ross – Leeds United – Ossett Albion; 1 Williams, Andrew – Bristol Rovers – Hereford United; 5 Wilson, James S. – Bristol City – Brentford; 1 Wordsworth, Daniel – Carlisle United – Kendal Town; 18 Worley, Harry J. – Leicester City – Luton Town; 19 Wright, Joshua W. – Charlton Athletic – Brentford; 11 Zakuani, Gabriel A. – Fulham – Peterborough United

OCTOBER 2008

28 Antonio, Michael	Tooting & Mitcham United	Reading	undisclosed
16 Braham–Barrett, Craig	Welling United	Peterborough United	undisclosed
22 Reay, Shaun	Darlington	Blyth Spartans	undisclosed
30 Roberts, Gary S.	Crewe Alexandra	Yeovil Town	undisclosed

TEMPORARY TRANSFERS

28 Ahmed, Adnan – Tranmere Rovers – Mansfield Town; 21 Alaile, Michael O. – Dagenham & Redbridge – Bishop's Stortford; 16 Alnwick, Ben – Tottenham Hotspur – Carlisle United; 24 Annerson, James – Sheffield United – Rotherham United; 13 Anyinsah, Joseph G. – Preston North End – Brighton & Hove Albion; 31 Atkins, Ross M. – Derby County – Southport; 31 Atkinson, Robert – Barnsley – Grimsby Town; 26 Barcham, Andrew – Tottenham Hotspur – Gillingham; 3 Barker, Richard I. – Hartlepool United – Rotherham United; 29 Beattie, Craig – West Bromwich Albion – Crystal Palace; 27 Bevan, David – Aston Villa – Tamworth; 26 Bevan, Scott A. – Shrewsbury Town – Torquay United; 6 Blackmore, David – West Ham United – Thurrock; 31 Bowditch, Dean – Ipswich Town – Brentford; 17 Bowes, Gary – Millwall – Ebbsfleet United; 31 Brammer, David – Millwall – Port Vale; 27 Brown, Wayne L. – Hull City – Preston North End; 22 Bryant, Mitchell J. – Reading – Basingstoke Town; 24 Button, David R. – Tottenham Hotspur – Grays Athletic; 17 Buxton, Lewis E. – Stoke City – Sheffield Wednesday; 17 Cahill, Thomas – Rotherham United – Ilkeston Town; 17 Camara, Mohamed – Derby County – Blackpool; 20 Camp, Lee M.J. – Queens Park Rangers – Nottingham Forest; 3 Cartman, Nathan – Leeds United – Harrogate Railway; 1 Chadwick, Luke H. – Norwich City – Milton Keynes Dons; 3 Chanot, Maxine – Sheffield United – Mansfield Town; 3 Charles, Elliott G. – Barnet – Farnborough; 17 Charnock, Kieran J. – Peterborough United – Accrington Stanley; 10 Christophe, Jean F. – Portsmouth – Southend United; 20 Church, Simon R. – Reading – Wycombe Wanderers; 23 Clarke, Tom – Huddersfield Town – Bradford City; 20 Clohessy, Sean D. – Gillingham – Salisbury City; 9 Compton, Jack L.P. – Brighton & Hove Albion – Lewes; 27 Cook, Anthony L.E. – Dagenham & Redbridge – Carshalton Athletic; 27 Craddock, Thomas – Middlesbrough – Luton Town; 2 Daniel, Colin – Crewe Alexandra – FC Halifax Town; 31 Davies, Craig M. – Oldham Athletic – Stockport County; 29 Dayton, James F. – Crystal Palace – Crawley Town; 16 Diallo, Drissa – Milton Keynes Dons – Cheltenham Town; 22 Dickinson, Liam – Derby County – Huddersfield Town; 27 Dunne, James W. – Arsenal – Nottingham Forest; 29 Easter, Jermaine – Plymouth Argyle – Millwall; 2 Edwards, Carlos – Sunderland – Wolverhampton Wanderers; 10 Evans, Raphael M. – Rochdale – Bradford Park Avenue; 23 Federici, Adam – Reading – Southend United; 31 Fleetwood, Stuart K. – Charlton Athletic – Brighton & Hove Albion; 17 Fletcher, Carl N. – Crystal Palace – Nottingham Forest; 9 Fojut, Jaroslaw – Bolton Wanderers – Stockport County; 31 Foran, Richard – Southend United – Darlington; 1 Forster, Fraser – Newcastle United – Stockport County; 10 Fraser, James – Bristol Rovers – Tiverton Town; 20 Garner, Scott – Leicester City – Ilkeston Town; 1 Gill, Jeremy M. – Cheltenham Town – Forest Green Rovers; 20 Gornell, Terence – Tranmere Rovers – Accrington Stanley; 8 Griffiths, Rostyn J. – Blackburn Rovers – Accrington Stanley; 24 Grocott, Marc D. – Stoke City – Stafford Rangers; 28 Hardman, Lewis – Darlington – Bishop Auckland; 21 Hart, Daniel – Barnet – Thurrock; 17 Hateley, Thomas N. – Reading – Basingstoke Town; 15 Horley, Karl L. – Preston North End – Northampton Town; 20 Hayes, Jonathan – Leicester City – Cheltenham Town; 17 Higginbotham, Kallum – Rochdale – Accrington Stanley; 31 Hinshelwood, Adam – Brighton & Hove Albion – Lewis; 10 Hotchkiss, Oliver – Leeds United – Garforth Town; 3 Howard, Ryan R.W. – Barnsley – Sheffield United; 30 Howard, Charlie S. – Gillingham – Thurrock; 7 Ireland, Daniel – Coventry City – Nuneaton Town; 24 John, Stern – Southampton – Bristol City; 28 Johnson, Bradley – Leeds United – Brighton & Hove Albion; 3 Jones, Daniel J. – Wolverhampton Wanderers – Oldham Athletic; 17 Jones, Stephen G. – Burnley – Huddersfield Town; 30 Kamudimba Kalala, Jean P. – Oldham Athletic – Grimsby Town; 9 Kane, Anthony M. – Blackburn Rovers – Stockport County; 10 Kavanagh, Graham A. – Sunderland – Carlisle United; 17 Kay, Matthew – Blackpool – Fleetwood Town; 24 Kiely, Christopher M. – Gillingham – Potters Bar Town; Konstantopoulos, Dimitrios – Coventry City – Swansea City; 1 Kyle, Kevin – Coventry City – Hartlepool United; 10 Lambert, Kyle – Rochdale – Bradford Park Avenue; 27 Law, Nicholas – Sheffield United – Bradford City; 10 Ledgister, Aaron T. – Cheltenham Town – Chippenham Town; 2 Lita, Leroy – Reading – Norwich City; 1 Liversedge, Nicholas – Darlington – Whitby Town; 31 Lynch, Joel J. – Brighton & Hove Albion – Nottingham Forest; 27 Mancienne, Michael I. – Chelsea – Wolverhampton Wanderers; 23 Martin, Alan – Leeds United – Barrow; 31 Martis, Shelton – West Bromwich Albion – Doncaster Rovers; 23 McCarthy, Alex S. – Reading – Team Bath; 8 McCrory, Damien P. – Plymouth Argyle – Port Vale; 24 McGivern, Ryan – Manchester City – Morecambe; 28 McGleish, Scott –

Wycombe Wanderers – Northampton Town; 17 Meredith, James G. – Shrewsbury Town – AFC Telford United; 24 Miller, Ashley – West Ham United – Bishop's Stortford; 17 Molesley, Mark C. – Grays Athletic – AFC Bournemouth; 24 Moloney, Brendan A. – Nottingham Forest – Rushden & Diamonds; 17 Montague, Ross P. – Brentford – Basingstoke Town; 28 Montrose, Lewis – Wigan Athletic – Cheltenham Town; 30 Moses-Garvey, Aaron – Birmingham City – Hinckley United; 16 Moussa, Franck N. – Southend United – Wycombe Wanderers; 13 Murray, Scott G. – Bristol City – Cheltenham Town; 20 Myrie–Williams, Jennison – Bristol City – Carlisle United; 31 Neal, Lewis – Preston North End – Notts County; 17 Newsham, Marc – Rotherham United – Gainsborough Trinity; 27 N'Gotty, Bruno – Leicester City – Hereford United; 7 Nolan, Edward W. – Blackburn Rovers – Preston North End; 17 O'Grady, Christopher – Oldham Athletic – Bury; 14 Ormerod, Brett R. – Preston North End – Oldham Athletic; 10 Osborne, Karleigh A.J. – Brentford – Eastbourne Borough; 1 Ovington, Christopher – Leeds United – Guiseley; 17 Owen, Gareth J. – Stockport County – Yeovil Town; 23 Parkin, Sam – Luton Town – Leyton Orient; 28 Payne, Joshua – West Ham United – Cheltenham Town; 30 Pearce, Alex – Reading – Southampton; 23 Pentney, Carl – Leicester City – Woking; 12 Phillips, James P. – Stoke City – Stafford Rangers; 27 Price, Lewis P. – Derby County – Milton Keynes Dons; 17 Primus, Linvoy S. – Portsmouth – Charlton Athletic; 24 Puncheon, Jason D.I. – Plymouth Argyle – Milton Keynes Dons; 21 Quashie, Nigel F. – West Ham United – Birmingham City; 9 Rankine, Michael – Rushden & Diamonds – AFC Bournemouth; 22 Redmond, Shane P. – Nottingham Forest – Eastwood Town; 17 Rendell, Scott – Peterborough United – Yeovil Town; 26 Ritchie, Matthew T. – Portsmouth – Dagenham & Redbridge; 16 Roberts, Dale – Nottingham Forest – Rushden & Diamonds; 27 Robson–Kanu, Thomas H. – Reading – Southend United; 8 Rouse, Domaine – Bury – Droylsden; 17 Rowe–Turner, Lathaniel – Leicester City – Cheltenham Town; 10 Royce, Daniel R. – Brighton & Hove Albion – Havant & Waterlooville; 3 Savage, Robert W. – Derby County – Brighton & Hove Albion; 22 Sharpe, Thomas R. – Nottingham Forest – Stalybridge Celtic; 31 Shotton, Ryan – Stoke City – Tranmere Rovers; 17 Sigurdsson, Gylfi T. – Reading – Shrewsbury Town; 31 Simmons, Paris M. – Derby County – Burton Albion; 17 Sinclair, Emile A. – Nottingham Forest – Mansfield Town; 20 Singh, Jasbir – Shrewsbury Town – Hinckley United; 16 Slater, Christopher J. – Port Vale – Chasetown; 3 Smith, Ryan C.M. – Millwall – Southampton; 17 Spence, Daniel M. – Reading – Woking; 17 Stokes, Anthony – Sunderland – Sheffield United; 31 Tabiri, Joe O. – Barnet – Lewes; 7 Taylforth, Sean J. – Bradford City – Guiseley; 6 Taylor, Lyle – Millwall – Eastbourne Borough; 31 Thomas, Aswad – Charlton Athletic – Lewes; 6 Thomas, Simon – Crystal Palace – Grays Athletic; 27 Thomas, Taylor J. – Gillingham – Folkestone Invicta; 17 Thompson, John – Oldham Athletic – Notts County; 9 Thompson, Joshua J. – Crewe Alexandra – Leek Town; 31 Thorley, Thomas R. – Stoke City – Burscough; 20 Thurlbourne, Luke D. – Southend United – St Albans City; 3 Todd, Andrew J. – Rotherham United – Eastwood Town; 20 Townsend, Michael J. – Cheltenham Town – Barnet; 20 Trotter, Liam – Ipswich Town – Grimsby Town; 29 Tyler, Mark R. – Peterborough United – Watford; 14 Vipond, Shaun – Carlisle United – Workington; 8 Walder, Daniel A.D. – Gillingham – Ramsgate; 29 Ward, Darren P. – Wolverhampton Wanderers – Watford; 13 Waterfall, Luke M. – Tranmere Rovers – Altrincham; 17 Wedgbury, Sam – Sheffield United – Mansfield Town; 28 Welsh, John J. – Hull City – Carlisle United; 2 Wesolowski, James – Leicester City – Cheltenham Town; 24 Westlake, Ian J. – Leeds United – Cheltenham Town; 23 White, Joe – Bristol Rovers – Chippenham Town; 30 Wilkinson, Ross – Leeds United – Garforth Town; 14 Wills, Kane J. – Brighton & Hove Albion – Bognor Regis Town; 13 Winn, Peter H. – Scunthorpe United – Northwich Victoria; 2 Wordsworth, Daniel – Carlisle United – Kendal Town; 20 Worley, Harry J. – Leicester City – Luton Town

NOVEMBER 2008

| 3 Roberts, Gary | Crewe Alexandra | Yeovil Town | undisclosed |

TEMPORARY TRANSFERS

27 Ademeno, Charles – Southend United – Salisbury City; 27 Ahmed, Adnan – Tranmere Rovers – Mansfield Town; 21 Ainsworth, Lionel – Watford – Hereford United; 11 Ambrose, Darren – Charlton Athletic – Ipswich Town; 14 Antwi, William – Wycombe Wanderers – Northwich Victoria; 20 Anyinsah, Joseph G. – Preston North End – Brighton & Hove Albion; 12 Araba, Hakeem A.C. – Dagenham & Redbridge – Redbridge; 21 Armstrong, Steven C. – Cheltenham Town – Burton Albion; 28 Arter, Harry N. – Charlton Athletic – Staines Town; 4 Arthur, Christopher A. – Queens Park Rangers – Kettering Town; 13 Balanta, Angelo – Queens Park Rangers – Wycombe Wanderers; 26 Barcham, Andrew – Tottenham Hotspur – Gillingham; 23 Barnes, Ashley L. – Plymouth Argyle – Eastbourne Borough; 27 Bennett, Dale O. – Watford – Kettering Town; 27 Bevan, Scott A. – Shrewsbury Town – Torquay United; 5 Bignall, Nicholas C. – Reading – Northampton Town; 27 Birchall, Christopher – Coventry City – Carlisle United; 27 Blundell, Gregg – Darlington – Accrington Stanley; 7 Boden, Luke – Sheffield Wednesday – Rushden & Diamonds; 21 Bolasie, Yannick – Plymouth Argyle – Rushden & Diamonds; 8 Bolder, Adam P. – Queens Park Rangers – Millwall; 26 Borrowdale, Gary I. – Coventry City – Queens Park Rangers; 13 Bradley, Jason – Darlington – Blyth Spartans; 27 Bridcutt, Liam R. – Chelsea – Watford; 27 Brooker, Stephen M.L. – Bristol City – Doncaster Rovers; 26 Brown, Jonathan D. – Cardiff City – Wrexham; 21 Brown, Scott – Cheltenham Town – Port Vale; 18 Bryant, Mitchell J. – Reading – Basingstoke Town; 27 Burton, Deon J. – Sheffield Wednesday – Charlton Athletic; 25 Button, David R. – Tottenham Hotspur – Grays Athletic; 14 Byfield, Darren – Doncaster Rovers – Oldham Athletic; 14 Byrne, Michael A. – Southampton – Bognor Regis Town; 7 Cahill, Thomas – Rotherham United – Ilkeston Town; 12 Carlton, Daniel A. – Carlisle United – Morecambe; 4 Chanot, Maxime – Sheffield United – Mansfield Town; 14 Charge, Daniel – Dagenham & Redbridge – Hitchin Town; 16 Charnock, Kieran J. – Peterborough United – Accrington Stanley; 10 Christon, Lewis – Wycombe Wanderers – Oxford City; 11 Christophe, Jean F. – Portsmouth – Southend United; 27 Clarke, Tom – Huddersfield Town – Bradford City; 17 Craddock, Thomas – Middlesbrough – Luton Town; 19 Crofts, Andrew L. – Gillingham – Peterborough United; 27 Cureton, Jamie – Norwich City – Barnsley; 27 Davies, Mark N. – Wolverhampton Wanderers – Leicester City; 14 Dean, Harle J. – Dagenham & Redbridge – Redbridge; 28 Dean, Harle J. – Dagenham & Redbridge – Bishop's Stortford; 14 Dennis, Kristian – Macclesfield Town – Ashton United; 27 Denton, Thomas – Huddersfield Town – Woking; 27 Dickinson, Liam – Derby County – Blackpool; 27 Dobson, Craig G. – Milton Keynes Dons – Wycombe Wanderers; 20 Easter, Jermaine – Plymouth Argyle – Colchester United; 27 Eastwood, Simon – Huddersfield Town – Woking; 25 Erskine, Emmanuel J. – Dagenham & Redbridge – Margate; 28 Evans, Thomas L.J. – Swindon Town – Truro City; 14 Fairhurst, Nathan S. – Preston North End – Wrexham; 26 Feeney, Liam – Salisbury City – Southend United; 27 Flynn, Michael J. – Huddersfield Town – Darlington; 14 Forshaw, Jamie D. – Southend United – Bishop's Stortford; 13 Forte, Jonathan – Scunthorpe United – Notts County; 5 Fortune, Clayton A. – Darlington – Rushden & Diamonds; 10 Fraser, James – Bristol Rovers – Tiverton Town; 14 Gallen, Kevin A. – Milton Keynes Dons – Luton Town; 14 Gargan, Sam J. – Brighton & Hove Albion – Lewes; 21 Gilks, Matthew – Blackpool – Shrewsbury Town; 24 Gillespie, Keith R. – Sheffield United – Charlton Athletic; 17 Gornell, Terence – Tranmere Rovers – Accrington Stanley; 26 Goulding, Jeff – AFC Bournemouth – Eastbourne Borough; 29 Gowling, Joshua – Carlisle United – Hereford United; 14 Green, Stuart – Blackpool – Crewe Alexandra; 10 Griffiths, Rostyn J. – Blackburn Rovers – Accrington Stanley; 24 Hammond, James – Colchester United – Fisher Athletic; 27 Hanson, Mitchell G.B. – Derby County – Notts County; 21 Hart, Daniel – Barnet – Thurrock; 18 Hateley, Thomas N. – Reading – Basingstoke Town; 21 Hayes, Jonathan – Leicester City – Cheltenham Town; 27 Hayles, Barrington – Leicester City – Cheltenham Town; 26 Helguson, Heidar – Bolton Wanderers – Queens Park Rangers; 14 Hendrie, Lee A. – Sheffield United – Blackpool; 27 Higgs, Shane P. – Cheltenham Town – Wolverhampton Wanderers; 20 Hill, Rory D. – Gillingham – Salisbury City; 13 Hills, Lee M. – Crystal Palace – Colchester United; 3 Hirst, Christopher – Macclesfield Town – Mossley; 11 Hotchkiss, Oliver – Leeds United – Garforth Town; 27 Howell, Dean G. – Aldershot Town – Bury; 3 Hunt, Nicholas B. – Bolton Wanderers – Birmingham City; 29 Jameson, Aaron T. – Sheffield Wednesday – Gainsborough Trinity; 25 Johnson, John – Middlesbrough – Tranmere Rovers; 3 Jones, Daniel J. – Wolverhampton Wanderers – Oldham Athletic; 27 Jones, Stephen G. – Burnley – Bradford City; 27 Joyce, Luke – Carlisle United – Barrow; 21 Kalipha, Kayan – Dagenham & Redbridge – Concord Rangers; 28 Kavanagh, Conor M. – Blackburn Rovers – Clitheroe; 7 Kavanagh, Graham A. – Sunderland – Carlisle United; 22 Kay, Matthew – Blackpool – Fleetwood Town; 10 Kite, Alex – Bristol Rovers – Chippenham Town; 21 Krul, Tim – Newcastle United – Carlisle United; 13 Kyle, Kevin – Coventry City – Hartlepool United; 27 Law, Nicholas – Sheffield United – Bradford City; 14 Leitch-Smith, A–Jay – Crewe Alexandra – FC Halifax Town; 14 Liddle, Michael – Sunderland – Carlisle United; 4 Lita, Leroy – Reading – Norwich City; 3 Liversedge, Nicholas – Darlington – Whitby Town; 28 Liversidge, Sam – Sheffield Wednesday – Buxton; 14 Low, Joshua D. – Cheltenham Town – Forest Green Rovers; 20 Lunt, Kenny V. – Sheffield Wednesday – Crewe Alexandra; 27 MacKenzie, Neil – Notts County – Port Vale; 27 Magunda, Joseph – Leicester City – Woking; 27 Mahon, Craig D. – Wigan Athletic – Accrington Stanley; 27 Martin, Alan – Leeds United – Barrow; 21 Masters, Clark J. –

Southend United – Welling United; 5 McCollin, Andre – Yeovil Town – Grays Athletic; 10 McCrory, Damien P. – Plymouth
Argyle – Port Vale; 14 McCubbin, Martin K. – Blackburn Rovers – Vauxhall Motors; 27 McEveley, James – Derby County –
Charlton Athletic; 24 McEvilly, Lee – Cambridge United – Rochdale; 26 McGleish, Scott – Wycombe Wanderers – Northampton
Town; 3 McMahon, Anthony – Middlesbrough – Sheffield Wednesday; 13 Meredith, James G. – Shrewsbury Town – AFC Telford
United; 21 Milsom, Robert S. – Fulham – Southend United; 27 Minto–St Aimie, Kieron L.J. – Barnet – Stevenage Borough; 13
Montague, Ross P. – Brentford – Basingstoke Town; 18 Moussa, Franck N. – Southend United – Wycombe Wanderers; 11 Murray,
Matthew W. – Wolverhampton Wanderers – Hereford United; 13 N'Gala, Bondz – West Ham United – Milton Keynes Dons; 6
Noel–Williams, Gifton R.E. – Millwall – Yeovil Town; 27 Odhiambo, Eric – Leicester City – Brentford; 13 Ogogo, Abumere T. –
Arsenal – Barnet; 25 Owen, Gareth J. – Stockport County – Port Vale; 27 Parkes, Jordan – Watford – Stevenage Borough; 28
Patterson, Marlon – Dagenham & Redbridge – Bishop's Stortford; 24 Payne, Joshua – West Ham United – Cheltenham Town; 6
Proudlock, Adam D. – Darlington – Grimsby Town; 24 Puncheon, Jason D.I. – Plymouth Argyle – Milton Keynes Dons; 24
Quashie, Nigel F. – West Ham United – Birmingham City; 17 Redmond, Shane P. – Nottingham Forest – Eastwood Town; 27 Reid,
Kyel – West Ham United – Blackpool; 18 Rendell, Scott – Peterborough United – Cambridge United; 25 Ritchie, Matthew T. –
Portsmouth – Dagenham & Redbridge; 27 Robinson, Kurt – Ipswich Town – Northampton Town; 24 Rodgers, Luke J. – Port Vale
– Yeovil Town; 14 Rose, Romone A. – Queens Park Rangers – Histon; 10 Rouse, Domaine – Bury – Droylsden; 14 Sandell,
Andrew C. – Salisbury City – Aldershot Town; 27 Scannell, Damian – Southend United – Brentford; 15 Sharpe, Thomas R. –
Nottingham Forest – Stalybridge Celtic; 25 Shulton, Scott – Wycombe Wanderers – Hendon; 19 Sinclair, Emile A. – Nottingham
Forest – Mansfield Town; 27 Slusarski, Bartosz – West Bromwich Albion – Sheffield Wednesday; 21 Smith, Andrew G. –
Accrington Stanley – Clitheroe; 27 Smith, Daniel – Plymouth Argyle – Eastbourne Borough; 17 Spence, Daniel M. – Reading –
Woking; 25 Spence, Jordan J. – West Ham United – Leyton Orient; 27 Stack, Graham – Plymouth Argyle – Blackpool; 27 Stanislas,
Junior – West Ham United – Southend United; 21 Stockdale, David A. – Fulham – Rotherham United; 21 Swallow, Ben – Bristol
Rovers – Bridgwater Town; 14 Symes, Michael – Shrewsbury Town – AFC Bournemouth; 4 Taylor, Lyle – Millwall – Eastbourne
Borough; 28 Thomas, Taylor J. – Gillingham – Folkestone Invicta; 27 Thomas, Wesley – Dagenham & Redbridge – Grays Athletic;
6 Thompson, John – Oldham Athletic – Notts County; 9 Thompson, Joshua J. – Crewe Alexandra – Leek Town; 7 Thornton, Kevin
– Coventry City – Brighton & Hove Albion; 16 Thurlbourne, Luke D. – Southend United – St Albans City; 27 Tierney, Marc –
Shrewsbury Town – Colchester United; 25 Todd, Andrew J.J. – Derby County – Northampton Town; 27 Tomkins, James O.C. –
West Ham United – Derby County; 24 Townsend, Michael J. – Cheltenham Town – Barnet; 27 Trotter, Liam – Ipswich Town –
Grimsby Town; 21 Tubbs, Matthew S. – Salisbury City – AFC Bournemouth; 7 Turley, Jamie – Wycombe Wanderers – Hendon; 27
Varney, Luke I. – Charlton Athletic – Derby County; 17 Waghorn, Martyn – Sunderland – Charlton Athletic; 7 Wagstaff, Scott A. –
Charlton Athletic – Northwich Victoria; 27 Walker, James B. – West Ham United – Colchester United; 13 Walker, Kyle – Sheffield
United – Northampton Town; 27 Weale, Christopher – Bristol City – Hereford United; 27 Wedderburn, Nathaniel C. – Stoke City –
Notts County; 27 Westwood, Ashley R. – Crewe Alexandra – Nantwich Town; 7 Whaley, Simon – Preston North End – Barnsley;
13 White, Jamie A. – Southampton – Shrewsbury Town; 28 White, Joe – Bristol Rovers – Chippenham Town; 28 White, Shane L. –
Plymouth Argyle – Truro City; 7 Wilcox, Joe T. – Scunthorpe United – Rushden & Diamonds; 7 Williams, Peter D. –
Wolverhampton Wanderers – Kettering Town; 3 Williams, Sam – Aston Villa – Colchester United; 20 Wilson, Mark A. – Doncaster
Rovers – Tranmere Rovers; 12 Winn, Peter H. – Scunthorpe United – Northwich Victoria; 5 Wordsworth, Daniel – Carlisle United
– Kendal Town; 14 Wynter, Thomas L. – Gillingham – Ramsgate; 7 Yussuf, Rashid O. – Charlton Athletic – Northwich Victoria; 27
Zieler, Ron R. – Manchester United – Northampton Town

DECEMBER 2008 TEMPORARY TRANSFERS

5 Ademola, Moses – Brentford – Welling United; 22 Ainsworth, Lionel – Watford – Hereford United; 5 Alaile, Michael O. –
Dagenham & Redbridge – Witham Town; 9 Andersen, Mikkel – Reading – Brentford; 9 Annerson, James – Sheffield United –
Mansfield Town; 13 Antwi, William – Wycombe Wanderers – Northwich Victoria; 29 Arter, Harry N. – Charlton Athletic – Staines
Town; 19 Balanta, Angelo – Queens Park Rangers – Wycombe Wanderers; 23 Bateson, Jonathan A. – Blackburn Rovers – Buxton;
7 Bolder, Adam P. – Queens Park Rangers – Millwall; 24 Botham, Calum – Wycombe Wanderers – Hayes & Yeading United; 12
Bowes, Gary – Millwall – Croydon; 1 Brammer, David – Millwall – Port Vale; 31 Bridcutt, Liam R. – Chelsea – Watford; 16 Byfield,
Darren – Doncaster Rovers – Oldham Athletic; 14 Byrne, Michael A. – Southampton – Bognor Regis Town; 8 Cahill, Thomas –
Rotherham United – Ilkeston Town; 12 Campion – Darren – Carlisle United – Workington; 14 Carlton, Daniel A. – Carlisle United
– Morecambe; 19 Cartman, Nathan – Leeds United – Harrogate Town; 5 Clements, Christopher L. – Crewe Alexandra – Leigh
Genesis; 5 Cook, Anthony L.E. – Dagenham & Redbridge – Concord Rangers; 21 Craddock, Thomas – Middlesbrough – Luton
Town; 12 Ellams, Darrell – Wycombe Wanderers – Hitchin Town; 8 Fleetwood, Stuart K. – Charlton Athletic – Brighton & Hove
Albion; 1 Foran, Richard – Southend United – Darlington; 11 Fraser, James – Bristol Rovers – Bognor Regis Town; 18 Garner,
Scott – Leicester City – Ilkeston Town; 12 Groves, Matt – Bristol Rovers – Mangotsfield United; 22 Hammond, James – Colchester
United – Fisher Athletic; 19 Harwood, Liam R. – Bristol Rovers – Margate; 22 Hayes, Jonathan – Leicester City – Cheltenham
Town; 1 Hinshelwood, Adam – Brighton & Hove Albion – Lewes; 5 Hirst, Christopher – Macclesfield Town – Mossley; 4 Howard,
Charlie S. – Gillingham – Thurrock; 8 Hunt, Nicholas B. – Bolton Wanderers – Birmingham City; 11 Ireland, Daniel – Coventry
City – Halesowen Town; 12 Jones, Craig N. – Hereford United – Redditch United; 23 Kalipha, Kayan – Dagenham & Redbridge –
Concord Rangers; 16 Kavanagh, Graham A. – Sunderland – Carlisle United; 11 Kazmierczak, Przemyslaw – Darlington – Whitby
Town; 10 Kite, Alex – Bristol Rovers – Chippenham Town; 23 Krul, Tim – Newcastle United – Carlisle United; 13 Leitch-Smith,
A-Jay – Crewe Alexandra – FC Halifax Town; 8 Lita, Leroy – Reading – Norwich City; 24 Louis, Kane T. – Brighton & Hove
Albion – Whitehawk; 9 Melbourne, Alex J. – Wolverhampton Wanderers – Tamworth; 8 Meredith, James G. – Shrewsbury – AFC
Telford United; 19 Millar, Christian – Macclesfield Town – Stafford Rangers; 5 Newsham, Marc – Rotherham United – Sheffield; 8
Noel–Williams, Gifton R.E. – Millwall – Yeovil Town; 16 Agogo, Abumere T. – Arsenal – Barnet; 12 Parrinello, Tom – Bristol
Rovers – Weston-Super-Mare; 29 Quashie, Nigel F. – West Ham United – Birmingham City; 1 Simmons, Paris M. – Derby County
– Burton Albion; 18 Sinclair, Emile A. – Nottingham Forest – Mansfield Town; 2 Stockdale, David A. – Fulham – Rotherham
United; 3 Tabiri, Joe O. – Barnet – Lewes; 12 Taylor, Lyle – Millwall – Croydon Athletic; 21 Townsend, Michael J. – Cheltenham
Town – Barnet; 12 Turley, Jamie – Wycombe Wanderers – Hendon; 16 Waghorn, Martyn – Sunderland – Charlton Athletic; 22
Walker, Kyle – Sheffield United – Northampton Town; 16 White, Jamie A. – Southampton – Shrewsbury Town; 8 Wilkinson, David
M. – Crystal Palace – Dover Athletic; 1 Wilkinson, Ross – Leeds United – Garforth Town; 17 Wynter, Thomas L. – Gillingham –
Ramsgate; 7 Yussuf, Rashid O. – Charlton Athletic – Northwich Victoria

JANUARY 2009

26 Ainsworth, Lionel	Watford	Huddersfield Town	undisclosed
12 Anyinsah, Joseph G.	Preston North End	Carlisle United	undisclosed
14 Ashworth, Luke A.	Wigan Athletic	Leyton Orient	undisclosed
20 Atkinson, Robert	Barnsley	Grimsby Town	undisclosed
8 Baker, Lee	West Bromwich Albion	Kidderminster Harriers	undisclosed
2 Barcham, Andrew	Tottenham Hotspur	Gillingham	undisclosed
1 Barker, Richard I.	Hartlepool United	Rotherham United	undisclosed
13 Beattie, James S.	Sheffield United	Stoke City	undisclosed
30 Bell, David A.	Norwich City	Coventry City	undisclosed
20 Bellamy, Craig D.	West Ham United	Manchester City	14,000,000
1 Bevan, Scott A.	Shrewsbury Town	Torquay United	undisclosed
12 Blackman, Nicholas	Macclesfield Town	Blackburn Rovers	undisclosed
1 Borrowdale, Gary I.	Coventry City	Queens Park Rangers	undisclosed
7 Bridge, Wayne M.	Chelsea	Manchester City	12,000,000
29 Brooker, Stephen M.L.	Bristol City	Doncaster Rovers	undisclosed
23 Bullard, James R.	Fulham	Hull City	5,000,000
1 Burton, Deon J.	Sheffield Wednesday	Charlton Athletic	undisclosed

26 Buxton, Lewis E.	Stoke City	Sheffield Wednesday	undisclosed
1 Chadwick, Luke H.	Norwich City	Milton Keynes Dons	undisclosed
28 Chimbonda, Pascal	Sunderland	Tottenham Hotspur	3,000,000
1 Christophe, Jean F.	Portsmouth	Southend United	undisclosed
16 Collins, Lee H.	Wolverhampton Wanderers	Port Vale	undisclosed
8 Cook, Lee	Fulham	Queens Park Rangers	750,000
30 Craddock, Thomas	Middlesbrough	Luton Town	80,000
26 Cudicini, Carlo	Chelsea	Tottenham Hotspur	Free
9 Daniels, Charlie	Tottenham Hotspur	Leyton Orient	undisclosed
26 Davies, Mark N.	Wolverhampton Wanderers	Bolton Wanderers	1,000,000
9 De Laet, Ritchie R.A.	Stoke City	Manchester United	3,000,000
9 Defoe, Jermain C.	Portsmouth	Tottenham Hotspur	15,750,000
Fee includes finance owed on Kaboul and Pedro Mendes.			
2 Diallo, Drissa	Milton Keynes Dons	Cheltenham Town	undisclosed
8 Etherington, Matthew	West Ham United	Stoke City	2,000,000
8 Garner, Scott	Leicester City	Mansfield Town	undisclosed
9 Gritton, Martin	Macclesfield Town	Chesterfield	undisclosed
26 Hackney, Simon	Carlisle United	Colchester United	undisclosed
1 Helguson, Heidar	Bolton Wanderers	Queens Park Rangers	750,000
23 Heskey, Emile I.	Wigan Athletic	Aston Villa	3,500,000
2 Howard, Brian R.W.	Barnsley	Sheffield United	undisclosed
16 Kilbane, Kevin	Wigan Athletic	Hull City	500,000
16 Lee, Jason	Mansfield Town	Kettering Town	undisclosed
15 Miller, Liam W.	Sunderland	Queens Park Rangers	undisclosed
2 Moncur, Thomas J.	Fulham	Wycombe Wanderers	undisclosed
1 Montgomery, Graeme	Wealdstone	Dagenham & Redbridge	undisclosed
26 Mullins, Hayden I.	West Ham United	Portsmouth	2,000,000
1 Nolan, Edward W.	Blackburn Rovers	Preston North End	undisclosed
30 Nolan, Kevin A.J.	Bolton Wanderers	Newcastle United	4,000,000
30 Oliver, Luke	Stevenage Borough	Wycombe Wanderers	undisclosed
26 Pilkington, Anthony	Stockport County	Huddersfield Town	undisclosed
8 Proudlock, Adam D.	Darlington	Grimsby Town	undisclosed
2 Roberts, Dale	Nottingham Forest	Rushden & Diamonds	undisclosed
2 Routledge, Wayne N.A.	Aston Villa	Queens Park Rangers	300,000
2 Sandell, Andrew C.	Salisbury City	Aldershot Town	undisclosed
1 Smith, Ryan C.M.	Millwall	Southampton	undisclosed
16 Spring, Matthew	Luton Town	Charlton Athletic	undisclosed
19 Tabb, Jay A.	Coventry City	Reading	undisclosed
2 Tierney, Marc	Shrewsbury Town	Colchester United	undisclosed
1 Varney, Luke I.	Charlton Athletic	Derby County	undisclosed
12 Wallace, Ross	Sunderland	Preston North End	100,000
20 Ward, Jamie J.	Chesterfield	Sheffield United	undisclosed
26 Watson, Ben	Crystal Palace	Wigan Athletic	2,000,000
29 Wright, Ben	Hampton & Richmond Borough	Peterborough United	undisclosed
1 Zakuani, Gabriel A.	Fulham	Peterborough United	undisclosed

TEMPORARY TRANSFERS

19 Adams, Nicholas – Leicester City – Rochdale; 5 Ademola, Moses – Brentford – Welling United; 29 Ahmed, Adnan – Tranmere Rovers – Port Vale; 4 Alaile, Michael O. – Dagenham & Redbridge – Witham Town; 16 Alberto, Mateus C. – Manchester United – Hull City; 15 Ameobi, Oluwatomiwo – Doncaster Rovers – Mansfield Town; 30 Anane, Richard – Bury – Workington; 30 Andrew, Calvin H. – Crystal Palace – Brighton & Hove Albion; 9 Antonio, Michael – Reading – Tooting & Mitcham United; 9 Anyinsah, Joseph G. – Preston North End – Carlisle United; 2 Araba, Hakeem A.C. – Dagenham & Redbridge – Redbridge; 20 Archibald-Henville, Troy – Tottenham Hotspur – Exeter City; 27 Artus, Frankie – Bristol City – Kettering Town; 9 Atkinson, Robert – Barnsley – Grimsby Town; 1 Barazite, Nacer – Arsenal – Derby County; 5 Barnes, Ashley L. – Plymouth Argyle – Eastbourne Borough; 27 Beavan, George D. – Luton Town – Grays Athletic; 2 Bennett, Alan J. – Reading – Brentford; 2 Bennett, Dale O. – Watford – Kettering Town; 27 Bennett, Elliott – Wolverhampton Wanderers – Bury; 1 Bertrand, Ryan D. – Chelsea – Norwich City; 23 Beswick, Ryan – Leicester City – Redditch United; 15 Bignall, Nicholas C. – Reading – Cheltenham Town; 5 Bolasie, Yannick – Plymouth Argyle – Rushden & Diamonds; 22 Bolasie, Yannick – Plymouth Argyle – Barnet; 9 Bouazza, Hameur – Fulham – Birmingham City; 26 Bower, Mark – Bradford City – Luton Town; 9 Bowyer, Lee D. – West Ham United – Birmingham City; 1 Boyce, Andrew T. – Doncaster Rovers – Worksop Town; 23 Bozanic, Oliver J. – Reading – Woking; 9 Braham-Barrett, Craig – Peterborough United – Kettering Town; 16 Broadbent, Daniel – Huddersfield Town – Rushden & Diamonds; 13 Bromby, Leigh – Watford – Sheffield United; 26 Broomes, Marlon C. – Blackpool – Crewe Alexandra; 29 Brown, Wayne L. – Hull City – Leicester City; 1 Butcher, Lee A. – Tottenham Hotspur – Grays Athletic; 16 Button, David R. – Tottenham Hotspur – AFC Bournemouth; 11 Cahill, Thomas – Rotherham United – Ilkeston Town; 8 Campbell, Dudley J. – Leicester City – Blackpool; 23 Carew, Ashley – Barnet – Eastleigh; 14 Carlton, David A. – Carlisle United – Darlington; 28 Carney, David – Sheffield United – Norwich City; 8 Casement, Christopher – Ipswich Town – Wycombe Wanderers; 1 Cathcart, Craig G. – Manchester United – Plymouth Argyle; 8 Chalmers, Lewis – Aldershot Town – Crawley Town; 2 Chapman, Adam – Sheffield United – Oxford United; 16 Charge, Daniel – Dagenham & Redbridge – St Albans City; 9 Charles, Elliott G. – Barnet – Lewes; 5 Charnock, Kieran J. – Peterborough United – Accrington Stanley; 23 Clarke, William C. – Ipswich Town – Northampton Town; 16 Cleverley, Thomas W. – Manchester United – Leicester City; 1 Clohessy, Sean D. – Gillingham – Salisbury City; 16 Convey, Matthew T. – Bradford City – Salford City; 2 Cork, Jack F.P. – Chelsea – Watford; 22 Cox, Lee – Leicester City – Yeovil Town; 16 Crooks, Leon E.G. – Wycombe Wanderers – Ebbsfleet United; 5 Cummings, Shaun M. – Chelsea – Milton Keynes Dons; 1 Curtis, Wayne J. – Morecambe – Barrow; 4 Daniels, Luke – West Bromwich Albion – Shrewsbury Town; 9 Davies, Mark N. – Wolverhampton Wanderers – Leicester City; 30 Dean, Harle J. – Dagenham & Redbridge – Bishop's Stortford; 5 Denton, Thomas – Huddersfield Town – Woking; 29 Dervite, Dorian – Tottenham Hotspur – Southend United; 15 Dickinson, Carl – Stoke City – Leeds United; 30 Diouf, El Hadji O. – Sunderland – Blackburn Rovers; 9 Dixon, Jonathan J. – Brighton & Hove Albion – Eastleigh; 30 Dorney, Jack – Bury – Workington; 5 Eastwood, Simon – Huddersfield Town – Woking; 29 Edwards, Preston M. – Millwall – Dover Athletic; 5 Elding, Anthony L. – Crewe Alexandra – Lincoln City; 13 Ellams, Darrell – Wycombe Wanderers – Hitchin Town; 8 Elliott, Stuart – Doncaster Rovers – Grimsby Town; 27 Elliott, Thomas J. – Leeds United – Macclesfield Town; 8 Erskine, Emmanuel J. – Dagenham & Redbridge – Sutton United; 30 Fairhurst, Waide S. – Doncaster Rovers – Solihull Moors; 6 Fielding, Francis D. – Blackburn Rovers – Rochdale; 11 Fleetwood, Stuart K. – Charlton Athletic – Brighton & Hove Albion; 30 Fonte, Rui D. – Arsenal – Crystal Palace; 15 Fraser, James – Bristol Rovers – Bognor Regis Town; 2 Furlong, Paul A. – Southend United – Barnet; 2 Gallen, Kevin A. – Milton Keynes Dons – Luton Town; 30 Gargan, Sam J. – Brighton & Hove Albion – Eastbourne Borough; 15 Gerken, Dean J. – Colchester United – Darlington; 2 Gill, Jeremy M. – Cheltenham Town – Forest Green Rovers; 15 Gobern, Lewis T. – Wolverhampton Wanderers – Colchester United; 19 Golbourne, Julio S. – Reading – Oldham Athletic; 25 Gowling, Joshua – Carlisle United – Hereford United; 1 Graham, Richard S. – Dagenham & Redbridge – Kettering Town; 1 Gray, David P. – Manchester United – Plymouth Argyle; 9 Gray, Michael – Wolverhampton Wanderers – Sheffield Wednesday; 26 Greer, Gordon – Doncaster Rovers – Swindon Town; 7 Grounds, Jonathan M. – Middlesbrough – Norwich City; 16 Groves, Matt – Bristol Rovers – Mangotsfield United; 23 Hadfield, Jordan – Macclesfield Town – Altricham; 30 Harding, Daniel A.

– Ipswich Town – Reading; 30 Hart, Daniel – Barnet – Thurrock; 18 Harwood, Liam R. – Bristol Rovers – Margate; 8 Hatch, Liam M.A. – Peterborough United – Darlington; 2 Hateley, Thomas N. – Reading – Basingstoke Town; 28 Henderson, Jordan – Sunderland – Coventry City; 16 Henderson, Liam – Watford – Hartlepool United; 5 Hewson, Sam – Manchester United – Hereford United; 23 Higginbotham, Kallum – Rochdale – Accrington Stanley; 29 Higgs, Shane P. – Cheltenham Town – Wolverhampton Wanderers; 5 Hines, Sebastian T. – Middlesbrough – Derby County; 9 Hirst, Christopher – Macclesfield Town – Mossley; 6 Holness, Marcus L. – Rochdale – Barrow; 30 Howard, Charlie S. – Gillingham – Thurrock; 1 Hoyte, Gavin A. – Arsenal – Watford; 2 John, Stern – Southampton – Bristol City; 8 Jones, Stephen G. – Burnley – Bradford City; 29 Judge, Alan C. – Blackburn Rovers – Plymouth Argyle; 30 Kalipha, Kayan – Dagenham & Redbridge – Boreham Wood; 9 Kamudimba Kalala, Jean P. – Oldham Athletic – Grimsby Town; 30 Kandol, Tresor O. – Leeds United – Charlton Athletic; 30 Kiely, Christopher M. – Gillingham – Bromsgrove Rovers; 2 Killock, Shane – Huddersfield Town – Oxford United; 8 King, Gary I. – Lincoln City – Boston United; 26 King, Marlon F. – Wigan Athletic – Middlesbrough; 29 Kissock, John P. – Everton – Accrington Stanley; 11 Kite, Alex – Bristol Rovers – Chippenham Town; 1 Klein–Davies, Joshua – Bristol Rovers – Lewes; 2 Labadie, Joss – West Bromwich Albion – Shrewsbury Town; 31 Lansbury, Henri G. – Arsenal – Scunthorpe United; 6 Law, Nicholas – Sheffield United – Bradford City; 27 Letheren, Kyle – Barnsley – Doncaster Rovers; 6 Liddle, Michael – Sunderland – Carlisle United; 20 Lillis, Joshua M. – Scunthorpe United – Notts County; 27 Lindfield, Craig A. – Liverpool – Accrington Stanley; 16 Liversedge, Nicholas – Darlington – Whitby Town; 13 Logan, Conrad – Leicester City – Luton Town; 4 Lunt, Kenny V. – Sheffield Wednesday – Crewe Alexandra; 1 Lynch, Joel J. – Brighton & Hove Albion – Nottingham Forest; 29 Magnay, Carl R.J. – Chelsea – Milton Keynes Dons; 9 Mahdi, Adam – Bristol Rovers – Godalming Town; 29 Marshall, Paul A. – Manchester City – Blackpool; 1 Martin, Alan – Leeds United – Barrow; 12 Martin, David E. – Liverpool – Leicester City; 23 McKerr, Michael – Birmingham City – Redditch United; 15 McLeod, Izale M. – Charlton Athletic – Millwall; 13 McPike, James – Birmingham City – Solihull Moors; 9 Meredith, James G. – Shrewsbury Town – AFC Telford United; 23 Mido, Middlesbrough – Wigan Athletic; 19 Millar, Christian – Macclesfield Town – Stafford Rangers; 9 Minto–St Aimie, Kieron L.J. – Barnet – Lewes; 5 Montrose, Lewis – Wigan Athletic – Cheltenham Town; 6 Mooney, David – Liverpool – Stockport County; 6 Murty, Graeme S. – Reading – Charlton Athletic; 23 Myrie–Williams, Jennison – Bristol City – Hereford United; 30 Nardiello, Daniel A. – Blackpool – Hartlepool United; 14 Naylor, Richard A. – Ipswich Town – Leeds United; 26 Nemeth, Krisztian – Liverpool – Blackpool; 7 Newsham, Marc – Rotherham United – Ilkeston Town; 13 O'Brien, James – Birmingham City – Solihull Moors; 9 O'Donovan, Roy – Sunderland – Blackpool; 21 Ogogo, Abumere T. – Arsenal – Barnet; 2 O'Grady, Christopher – Oldham Athletic – Bradford City; 8 Owens, Graeme A. – Middlesbrough – Blackpool; 23 Palacios, Wilson R.S. – Wigan Athletic – Tottenham Hotspur; 27 Palmer, Aiden – Leighton Orient – Dagenham & Redbridge; 15 Parinello, Tomasso – Bristol Rovers – Weston–Super–Mare; 12 Parkin, Sam – Luton Town – Leyton Orient; 5 Pearce, Krystian M.V. – Birmingham City – Scunthorpe United; 2 Pearson, Andrew C. – Brighton & Hove Albion – Lewes; 21 Pennant, Jermaine – Liverpool – Portsmouth; 23 Peters, Jaime B. – Ipswich Town – Gillingham; 8 Picken, Philip J. – Chesterfield – Notts County; 2 Plummer, Tristan D. – Bristol City – Torquay United; 1 Potter, Alfie – Peterborough United – Kettering Town; 15 Potter, Darren M. – Wolverhampton Wanderers – Sheffield Wednesday; 27 Prijovic, Aleksander – Derby County – Yeovil Town; 23 Pugh, Andrew J. – Gillingham – Grays Athletic; 12 Puncheon, Jason D.I. – Plymouth Argyle – Milton Keynes Dons; 22 Quashie, Nigel F. – West Ham United – Wolverhampton Wanderers; 2 Redmond, Shane P. – Nottingham Forest – Eastwood Town; 12 Reece, Charlie – Bristol Rovers – Solihull Moors; 15 Reid, Kyel – West Ham United – Wolverhampton Wanderers; 19 Rendell, Scott – Peterborough United – Cambridge United; 23 Rhodes, Jordan L. – Ipswich Town – Brentford; 2 Ritchie, Matthew T. – Portsmouth – Dagenham & Redbridge; 8 Robinson, Kurt – Ipswich Town – Rushden & Diamonds; 29 Robinson, Theo – Watford – Southend United; 26 Robson–Kanu, Thomas H. – Reading – Swindon Town; 30 Rochester, Kraig – Dagenham & Redbridge – Dulwich Hamlet; 23 Rodgers, Paul L.H. – Arsenal – Northampton Town; 29 Ruddy, John T.G. – Everton – Crewe Alexandra; 1 Sappleton, Reneil – Leicester City – Oxford United; 26 Sawyer, Lee T. – Chelsea – Coventry City; 6 Sharry, Luke I. – Bradford City – Barrow; 8 Shaw, Jon S. – Rochdale – Crawley Town; 16 Shotton, Ryan – Stoke City – Tranmere Rovers; 1 Simpson, Jay–Alistaire F. – Arsenal – West Bromwich Albion; 8 Sinclair, Dean M. – Charlton Athletic – Grimsby Town; 15 Sinclair, Emile A. – Nottingham Forest – Macclesfield Town; 6 Sinclair, Scott A. – Chelsea – Birmingham City; 23 Singh, Jasbir – Shrewsbury Town – Sutton Coldfield Town; 30 Smith, Andrew G. – Accrington Stanley – Clitheroe; 5 Smith, Daniel – Plymouth Argyle – Eastbourne Borough; 15 Soares, Thomas J. – Stoke City – Charlton Athletic; 24 Spence, Daniel M. – Reading – Salisbury City; 23 Spence, Jordan J. – West Ham United – Leyton Orient; 9 Spring, Matthew – Luton Town – Charlton Athletic; 23 Steer, Rene A. – Arsenal – Gillingham; 30 Tabiri, Joe O. – Barnet – Grays Athletic; 27 Talbot, Andrew – Luton Town – Chesterfield; 9 Taylor, Lyle – Millwall – Croydon Athletic; 26 Thomas, Wesley – Dagenham & Redbridge – Grays Athletic; 15 Thomson, Jake S. – Southampton – AFC Bournemouth; 30 Thorley, Thomas R. – Stoke City – Stafford Rangers; 3 Threlfall, Robert R. – Liverpool – Stockport County; 16 Till, Peter – Grimsby Town – Chesterfield; 3 Todd, Andrew J. – Rotherham United – Eastwood Town; 2 Todd, Simon – Darlington – Blyth Spartans; 9 Trundle, Lee C. – Bristol City – Leeds United; 9 Tyler, Mark R. – Peterborough United – Bury; 10 Walker, James B. – West Ham United – Colchester United; 23 Walker, Lauris D. – Millwall – Harrow Borough; 30 Ward, Darren P. – Wolverhampton Wanderers – Charlton Athletic; 15 Wasiu, Sunday A. – Colchester United – Luton Town; 9 Wedderburn, Nathaniel C. – Stoke City – Notts County; 5 Westwood, Christopher J. – Peterborough United – Cheltenham Town; 16 White, Joe – Bristol Rovers – Yate Town; 29 Widdowson, Joseph – West Ham United – Grimsby Town; 16 Wiggins, Rhoys – Crystal Palace – AFC Bournemouth; 27 Wilkinson, David M. – Crystal Palace – Welling United; 6 Williams, Andrew – Bristol Rovers – Hereford United; 30 Williams, Rhys – Middlesbrough – Burnley; 30 Williams, Sam – Aston Villa – Walsall; 9 Wills, Kane J. – Brighton & Hove Albion – Bognor Regis Town; 21 Windass, Dean – Hull City – Oldham Athletic; 2 Winfield, David – Aldershot Town – Salisbury City; 30 Worthington, Jonathan – Huddersfield Town – Yeovil Town; 15 Wynter, Thomas L. – Gillingham – Ramsgate; 6 Yates, Jamie – Rotherham United – Burton Albion; 5 Zieler, Ron R. – Manchester United – Northampton Town

FEBRUARY 2009

2 Clarke, Andre N.J.E.(Jamie)	Blackburn Rovers	Rotherham United	Free
2 Davies, Craig M.	Oldham Athletic	Brighton & Hove Albion	undisclosed
23 Dawson, Craig	Radcliffe Borough	Rochdale	undisclosed
2 Dunfield, Terry B.	Macclesfield Town	Shrewsbury Town	undisclosed
2 Given, Shay J.J.	Newcastle United	Manchester City	undisclosed
2 Gray, Julian R.	Coventry City	Fulham	undisclosed
2 Gray, Michael	Wolverhampton Wanderers	Sheffield Wednesday	Free
2 Keane, Robert D.	Liverpool	Tottenham Hotspur	12,000,000
2 McConville, Sean	Skelmersdale United	Accrington Stanley	undisclosed
2 McDonald, Cody D.J.	Dartford	Norwich City	undisclosed
2 McNulty, Jimmy	Stockport County	Brighton & Hove Albion	150,000
2 N'Zogbia, Charles	Newcastle United	Wigan Athletic	undisclosed
2 Pittman, Jon P.	Crawley Town	Wycombe Wanderers	undisclosed
2 Taylor, Ryan A.	Wigan Athletic	Newcastle United	undisclosed

TEMPORARY TRANSFERS

19 Adams, Nicholas – Leicester City – Rochdale; 2 Ademeno, Charles – Southend United – Salisbury City; 17 Ademola, Moses – Brentford – Welling United; 6 Alaile, Michael O. – Dagenham & Redbridge – Billericay Town; 2 Alves, de Assis Silva Joao (Joe) – Manchester City – Everton; 20 Anderson, Joe – Fulham – Woking; 19 Antonio, Michael – Reading – Tooting & Mitcham United; 19 Antonio, Michael – Reading – Cheltenham Town; 17 Antwi–Birago, Godwin – Liverpool – Hereford United; 27 Appiah, Kwesi – Peterborough United – Weymouth; 2 Archibald–Henville, Troy – Tottenham Hotspur – Exeter City; 27 Arthur, Christopher A. – Queens Park Rangers – Rushden & Diamonds; 2 Barnes, Giles G. – Derby County – Fulham; 20 Beattie, Craig – West Bromwich Albion – Sheffield United; 19 Beavon, Stuart – Weymouth – Wycombe Wanderers; 2 Ben–Haim, Tal – Manchester City – Sunderland; 2 Bennett, Elliott – Wolverhampton Wanderers – Bury; 24 Beswick, Ryan – Leicester City – Redditch United; 19 Bignall, Nicholas C. – Reading – Cheltenham Town; 27 Bozanic, Oliver J. – Reading – Woking; 2 Brandy, Febian E. – Manchester United – Hereford United; 19 Broadbent, Daniel – Huddersfield Town – Gateshead; 13 Budtz, Jan – Hartlepool United – Oldham

Athletic; 2 Camara, Henri – Wigan Athletic – Stoke City; 23 Carew, Ashley – Barnet – Eastleigh; 28 Cartman, Nathan – Leeds United – Curzon Ashton; 12 Casement, Christopher – Ipswich Town – Wycombe Wanderers; 8 Chalmers, Lewis – Aldershot Town – Crawley Town; 2 Chester, James G. – Manchester United – Peterborough United; 17 Church, Simon R. – Reading – Leyton Orient; 17 Cook, Andrew E. – Carlisle United – Workington; 19 Crooks, Leon E.G. – Wycombe Wanderers – Ebbsfleet United; 2 Davenport, Callum R.P. – West Ham United – Sunderland; 13 Davies, Andrew – Stoke City – Preston North End; 2 Davis, Claude – Derby County – Crystal Palace; 23 Dinning, Anthony – Chester City – Grays Athletic; 18 Dixon, Jonathan J. – Brighton & Hove Albion – Eastleigh; 20 D'Laryea, Nathan A. – Rochdale – Farsley Celtic; 23 Duffy, Mark – Southport – Morecambe; 2 Eastwood, Simon – Huddersfield Town – Woking; 19 Ebsworth, Darren – Millwall – Sutton United; 9 Elliott, Stuart – Doncaster Rovers – Grimsby Town; 10 Elvins, Robert – Aldershot Town – Woking; 2 Fielding, Francis D. – Blackburn Rovers – Rochdale; 14 Fitzgerald, Robert O. – Yeovil Town – Enfield Town; 20 Fletcher, Carl N. – Crystal Palace – Plymouth Argyle; 2 Forbes, Adrian E. – Millwall – Grimsby Town; 16 Forte, Jonathan – Scunthorpe United – Notts County; 25 Fraser–Allen, Kyle – Tottenham Hotspur – Macclesfield Town; 10 Frecklington, Lee – Lincoln City – Peterborough United; 2 Furlong, Paul A. – Southend United – Barnet; 24 Gall, Kevin A. – Carlisle United – Port Vale; 15 Gerken, Dean J. – Colchester United – Darlington; 2 Gobern, Lewis T. – Wolverhampton Wanderers – Colchester United; 15 Groves, Matt – Bristol Rovers – Mangotsfield United; 2 Gulacsi, Peter – Liverpool – Hereford United; 19 Guy, Lewis B. – Doncaster Rovers – Hartlepool United; 2 Hammill, Adam J. – Liverpool – Barnsley; 13 Harvey, Neil – Macclesfield Town – Retford United; 23 Hemmings, Ashley J. – Wolverhampton Wanderers – Cheltenham Town; 27 Henderson, Wayne – Preston North End – Grimsby Town; 12 Henry, James – Reading – Millwall; 20 Henry, Rhys E. – Southend United – Lewes; 13 Hines, Sebastian T. – Middlesbrough – Oldham Athletic; 6 Holness, Marcus L. – Rochdale – Barrow; 20 Hotchkiss, Oliver – Leeds United – Farsley Celtic; 23 Jameson, Arron T. – Sheffield Wednesday – Ilkeston Town; 2 Jones, Daniel J. – Wolverhampton Wanderers – Oldham Athletic; 2 Jones, Stephen G. – Burnley – Bradford City; 13 Jutkiewicz, Lukas I.P. – Everton – Huddersfield Town; 26 Kabba, Steven – Watford – Oldham Athletic; 10 Kane, Anthony M. – Blackburn Rovers – Carlisle United; 2 Kelly, Stephen M. – Birmingham City – Stoke City; 13 King, Gary I. – Lincoln City – Boston United; 27 Kite, Alexandrous – Bristol Rovers – Weston–Super–Mare; 3 Klein–Davies, Joshua – Bristol Rovers – Lewes; 2 Leijer, Adrian – Fulham – Norwich City; 27 Letheren, Kyle – Barnsley – Doncaster Rovers; 2 Liddle, Michael – Sunderland – Carlisle United; 2 Lindegaard, Andrew R. – Cheltenham Town – Aldershot Town; 13 Lindie, James – Southend United – Grays Athletic; 2 Lockwood, Matthew D. – Colchester United – Barnet; 2 Loft, Douglas J. – Brighton & Hove Albion – Dagenham & Redbridge; 2 McCarthy, Alex S. – Reading – Aldershot Town; 2 McDonald, Clayton – Manchester City – Chesterfield; 12 McGleish, Scott – Wycombe Wanderers – Leyton Orient; 18 McPike, James – Birmingham City – Solihull Moors; 19 Millar, Christian – Macclesfield Town – Stafford Rangers; 23 Mills, Joseph N. – Southampton – Scunthorpe United; 2 Mifsud, Michael – Coventry City – Barnsley; 26 Montrose, Lewis – Wigan Athletic – Chesterfield; 1 Morgan, Dean – Luton Town – Leyton Orient; 3 Murty, Graeme S. – Reading – Charlton Athletic; 2 Novak, Lee – Huddersfield Town – Gateshead; 26 Odejayi, Olukayode – Barnsley – Scunthorpe United; 2 O'Grady, Christopher – Oldham Athletic – Stockport County; 24 O'Toole, John–Joe – Watford – Sheffield United; 20 Ovington, Christopher – Leeds United – Farsley Celtic; 11 Owens, Graeme A. – Middlesbrough – Blackpool; 13 Pearson, Andrew C. – Brighton & Hove Albion – Bognor Regis Town; 20 Pericard, Vincent D.P. – Stoke City – Millwall; 2 Picken, Philip J. – Chesterfield – Notts County; 2 Potter, Luke A. – Barnsley – Kettering Town; 2 Price, Lewis P. – Derby County – Luton Town; 23 Pugh, Andrew J. – Gillingham – Grays Athletic; 9 Reason, Jai M. – Ipswich Town – Cambridge United; 10 Robinson, Jake D. – Brighton & Hove Albion – Aldershot Town; 2 Robinson, Kurt – Ipswich Town – Rushden & Diamonds; 26 Robson–Kanu, Thomas H. – Reading – Swindon Town; 2 Rodgers, Paul L.H. – Arsenal – Northampton Town; 23 Rowe–Turner, Lathaniel – Leicester City – Redditch United; 26 Russell, Alexander J. – Cheltenham Town – Exeter City; 10 Shackell, Jason – Wolverhampton Wanderers – Norwich City; 12 Sharry, Luke I. – Bradford City – Barrow; 6 Shields, Solomon – Leyton Orient – St Albans City; 27 Sigurdsson, Gylfi T. – Reading – Crewe Alexandra; 9 Sinclair, Dean M. – Charlton Athletic – Grimsby Town; 27 Sinclair, Emile A. – Nottingham Forest – Macclesfield Town; 2 Sinclair, Scott A. – Chelsea – Birmingham City; 2 Smith, Daniel – Plymouth Argyle – Eastbourne Borough; 2 Smith, James D. – Chelsea – Leyton Orient; 20 Soares, Thomas J. – Stoke City – Charlton Athletic; 16 St Louis–Hamilton, Danzelle D. – Stoke City – Bristol Rovers; 23 Steer, Rene A. – Arsenal – Gillingham; 20 Swallow, Ben – Bristol Rovers – Chippenham Town; 21 Taylor, Lyle – Millwall – Croydon Athletic; 13 Thomas, Simon – Crystal Palace – Rotherham United; 20 Thomas, Taylor J. – Gillingham – Halesowen Town; 2 Till, Peter – Grimsby Town – Chesterfield; 2 Timotian–Samarani, Andranik – Fulham – Barnsley; 13 Traore, Djimi – Portsmouth – Birmingham City; 23 Trotter, Liam – Ipswich Town – Scunthorpe United; 10 Trundle, Lee C. – Bristol City – Leeds United; 8 Tyler, Mark R. – Peterborough United – Bury; 6 Tymon, Matthew R. – Hartlepool United – Newcastle Blue Star; 8 Walker, James B. – West Ham United – Colchester United; 27 Webb, Jonathan – Leeds United – Newcastle Blue Star; 9 Wedderburn, Nathaniel C. – Stoke City – Notts County; 2 Westwood, Christopher J. – Peterborough United – Cheltenham Town; 15 White, Joe – Bristol Rovers – Yate Town; 2 Wiggins, Rhys – Crystal Palace – AFC Bournemouth; 2 Wilson, Jared A. – Birmingham City – Chesterfield; 26 Winn, Peter H. – Scunthorpe United – Barrow; 2 Yates, Jamie – Rotherham United – Burton Albion; 1 Zieler, Ron R. – Manchester United – Northampton Town

MARCH 2009

2 Diouf, El Hadji	Sunderland	Blackburn Rovers	£2,000,000
10 Palacios, Wilson	Wigan Athletic	Tottenham Hotspur	£12,000,000

Both players transferred in January, not registered until March.

TEMPORARY TRANSFERS

2 Ahmed, Adnan – Tranmere Rovers – Port Vale; 26 Ainge, Simon – Bradford City – Cambridge City; 26 Ajdarevic, Astrit – Liverpool – Leicester City; 12 Akinde, John – Bristol City – Wycombe Wanderers; 26 Akurang, Cliff – Barnet – Weymouth; 9 Alaile, Michael – Dagenham & Redbridge – Billericay Town; 26 Anane, Richard – Bury – Fleetwood Town; 6 Andersen, Mikkel – Reading – Brighton & Hove Albion; 26 Anderson, Joe – Fulham – Woking; 19 Antonio, Michael – Reading – Cheltenham Town; 6 Arter, Harry – Charlton Athletic – Welling United; 23 Artus, Frankie – Bristol City – Cheltenham Town; 20 Askham, Lee – Chesterfield – Garforth Town; 26 Atkins, Ross M. – Derby County – Southport; 3 Bangura, Alhassan – Watford – Brighton & Hove Albion; 13 Bannan, Barry – Aston Villa – Derby County; 24 Bayliss, Ashton P. – Blackpool – Burscough; 26 Beattie, Craig – West Bromwich Albion – Sheffield United; 2 Beavan, George D. – Luton Town – Grays Athletic; 26 Bennett, James R. – Hull City – Lincoln City; 26 Berchiche, Yuri – Tottenham Hotspur – Cheltenham Town; 27 Beswick, Ryan – Leicester City – Redditch United; 17 Bialkowski, Bartosz – Southampton – Ipswich Town; 16 Bignall, Nicholas C. – Reading – Cheltenham Town; 2 Blackman, Nicholas – Blackburn Rovers – Blackpool; 26 Blackstock, Dexter A.T. – Queens Park Rangers – Nottingham Forest; 30 Bolasie, Yannick – Plymouth Argyle – Barnet; 6 Borrowdale, Gary I. – Queens Park Rangers – Brighton & Hove Albion; 2 Bower, Mark – Bradford City – Luton Town; 8 Brandy, Febian E. – Manchester United – Hereford United; 24 Broadbent, Daniel – Huddersfield Town – Harrogate Town; 13 Broomes, Marlon C. – Blackpool – Crewe Alexandra; 20 Burns, Robbie L. – Leicester City – Tranmere Rovers; 10 Butcher, Lee A. – Tottenham Hotspur – St Albans City; 2 Butterfield, Daniel – Crystal Palace – Charlton Athletic; 6 Button, David R. – Tottenham Hotspur – Luton Town; 13 Byrne, Mark – Nottingham Forest – Burton Albion; 26 Cartman, Nathan – Leeds United – Curzon Ashton; 12 Casement, Christopher – Ipswich Town – Wycombe Wanderers; 9 Charles, Elliott G. – Barnet – Hemel Hempstead Town; 26 Charles, Ryan A. – Lutonn Town – Kettering Town; 22 Church, Simon R. – Reading – Leyton Orient; 21 Clarke, William C. – Ipswich Town – Brentford; 9 Clements, Christopher L. – Crewe Alexandra – Stafford Rangers; 10 Codman, Daniel – Huddersfield Town – Wakefield; 6 Cole, Jake S. – Queens Park Rangers – Barnet; 20 Conlon, Barry J. – Bradford City – Grimsby Town; 20 Constantine, Leon – Northampton Town – Cheltenham Town; 23 Cook, Andrew E. – Carlisle United – Workington; 20 Crooks, Leon E.G. – Wycombe Wanderers – Ebbsfleet United; 13 Cumbers, Luis C. – Gillingham – Ebbsfleet United; 24 Daniel, Colin – Crewe Alexandra – Macclesfield Town; 8 Danville, Luke A. – Crewe Alexandra – Curzon Ashton; 4 Davis, Claude – Derby County – Crystal Palace; 5 Dawson, Craig – Radcliffe Borough; 19 Dean, Harle J. – Dagenham & Redbridge – Thurrock; 6 Denton, Thomas – Huddersfield Town – Wakefield; 26 Dicker, Gary – Stockport County – Brighton & Hove Albion; 13 Dickinson, Liam – Derby County – Leeds United; 26 Dinning, Anthony – Chester City – Gateshead; 26 Dixon, Jonathan J. – Brighton & Hove Albion – Eastleigh; 24 D'Laryea, Nathan A. – Rochdale – Farsley Celtic; 13 Doe, Scott M. – Kettering Town – Dagenham & Redbridge; 26 Dorney, Jack – Bury – Leigh Genesis; 13 Giovani – Tottenham Hotspur – Ipswich Town; 26 Dudley, Mark – Derby County – Tamworth; 23 Ebbsworth, Darren – Millwall – Sutton

United; 1 Edwards, Preston M. – Millwall – Dover Athletic; 17 Erskine, Emmanuel J. – Dagenham & Redbridge – Dorchester Town; 9 Eustace, John M. – Watford – Derby County; 27 Evans, Thomas L.J. – Swindon Town – Weston–Super–Mare; 23 Ferreira, Fabio M. – Chelsea – Oldham Athletic; 26 Flahavan, Darryl J. – Crystal Palace – Leeds United; 18 Fleetwood, Stuart K. – Charlton Athletic – Exeter City; 23 Fletcher, Carl N. – Crystal Palace – Plymouth Argyle; 24 Forte, Jonathan – Scunthorpe United – Notts County; 13 Gargan, Sam J. – Brighton & Hove Albion – Eastbourne Borough; 6 Gazet Du Chattelier, Ryan – Portsmouth – Bognor Regis Town; 25 Gleeson, Stephen M. – Wolverhampton Wanderers – Milton Keynes Dons; 27 Green, Darren – Stockport County – Farsley Celtic; 30 Green, Michael J. – Bristol Rovers – Clevedon Town; 12 Gunter, Christopher R. – Tottenham Hotspur – Nottingham Forest; 3 Guy, Jamie – Colchester United – Dagenham & Redbridge; 23 Harewood, Marlon A. – Aston Villa – Wolverhampton Wanderers; 9 Harvey, Daniel J. – Southend United – Tiptree United; 20 Harwood, Liam R. – Bristol Rovers – Carshalton Athletic; 20 Hawley, Karl L. – Preston North End – Colchester United; 3 Heath, Matthew P. – Colchester United – Brighton & Hove Albion; 28 Henderson, Wayne – Preston North End – Grimsby Town; 15 Henry, James – Reading – Millwall; 26 Hodgkiss, Jared – West Bromwich Albion – Northampton Town; 25 Hotchkiss, Oliver – Leeds United – Mansfield Town; 6 Hudson–Odoi, Bradley – Hereford United – Grays Athletic; 26 Hughes, Lee – Oldham Athletic – Blackpool; 3 Hutchins, Daniel – Tottenham Hotspur – Yeovil Town; 26 Hutton, David – Tottenham Hotspur – Cheltenham Town; 4 Hyde, Jake M. – Swindon Town – Weymouth; 3 Jeffery, Jack C. – West Ham United – Eastbourne Borough; 23 Jevons, Phillip – Huddersfield Town – Bury; 12 Joyce, Luke – Carlisle United – Northwich Victoria; 19 Kalipha, Kayan – Dagenham & Redbridge – Boreham Wood; 20 Kay, Adam B. – Burnley – Accrington Stanley; 26 Kelly, Martin R. – Liverpool – Huddersfield Town; 10 Kitson, David – Stoke City – Reading; 13 Klein–Davies, Joshua – Bristol Rovers – Bath City; 26 Lansbury, Henri G. – Arsenal – Scunthorpe United; 19 Lee, Alan D. – Crystal Palace – Norwich City; 26 Legzdins, Adam R. – Crewe Alexandra – Weymouth; 5 Leitch–Smith, A–Jay – Crewe Alexandra – Newcastle Town; 3 Lindgaard, Andrew R. – Cheltenham Town – Aldershot Town; 9 Little, Glen M. – Portsmouth – Reading; 26 Livermore, David – Brighton & Hove Albion – Luton Town; 6 Lockwood, Matthew D. – Colchester United – Barnet; 28 Logan, Conrad – Leicester City – Stockport County; 26 Lua Lua, Kazenga – Newcastle United – Doncaster Rovers; 20 Madine, Gary L. – Carlisle United – Rochdale; 9 Magnay, Carl R. J. – Chelsea – Northampton Town; 25 Maguire, Danny – Queens Park Rangers – Yeovil Town; 17 Mahon, Alan – Burnley – Blackpool; 6 Marshall, Paul A. – Manchester City – Port Vale; 5 Mayor, Danny – Preston North End – Tranmere Rovers; 19 McEvilly, Lee – Rochdale – Barrow; 20 McPike, James – Birmingham City – Solihull Moors; 5 McSheffrey, Gary – Birmingham City – Nottingham Forest; 23 Medley, Luke – Barnet – Havant & Waterlooville; 26 Mendes, Junior A. – Aldershot Town – Stevenage Borough; 24 Mills, Joseph N. – Southampton – Scunthorpe United; 27 Mitchley, Daniel – Blackpool – Southport; 6 Mooney, David – Reading – Norwich City; 26 Morris, Ian – Scunthorpe United – Carlisle United; 20 Morris, Samuel P. – Swindon Town – Swindon Supermarine; 20 Mullin, Paul – Accrington Stanley – Bradford City; 26 Myrie–Williams, Jennison – Bristol City – Hereford United; 26 Newbold, Adam C. – Nottingham Forest – Stalybridge Celtic; 25 Newey, Thomas – Grimsby Town – Rochdale; 25 Noble, David J. – Bristol City – Yeovil Town; 19 Obika, Jonathan – Tottenham Hotspur – Yeovil Town; 6 O'Connor, Michael – Crewe Alexandra – Lincoln City; 2 Osbourne, Isaiah – Aston Villa – Nottingham Forest; 26 Osman, Ben F. – Exeter City – Salisbury City; 26 Osman, Toby – Exeter City – Salisbury City; 12 Owens, Graeme A. – Middlesbrough – Blackpool; 2 Owusu, Lloyd – Cheltenham Town – Brighton & Hove Albion; 2 Parker, Keigan – Huddersfield Town – Hartlepool United; 16 Pearson, Andrew C. – Brighton & Hove Albion – Bognor Regis Town; 6 Pembleton, Martin J. – Lincoln City – Lincoln United; 6 Perry, Kyle – Port Vale – Northwich Victoria; 26 Price, Jason – Doncaster Rovers – Millwall; 28 Priest, Richard M. – Dagenham & Redbridge – Witham Town; 20 Prijovic, Aleksander – Derby County – Northampton Town; 24 Pugh, Andrew J. – Gillingham – Grays Athletic; 25 Pugh, Marc – Shrewsbury Town – Hereford United; 10 Reason, Jai M. – Ipswich Town – Cambridge United; 5 Renton, Kris – Norwich City – Kings Lynn; 13 Reynolds, Callum F. – Portsmouth – Basingstoke Town; 12 Rhodes, Alexander – Rotherham United – Woking; 26 Richards, Matthew W. – Wycombe Wanderers – Notts County; 26 Robson–Kanu, Thomas H. – Reading – Swindon Town; 6 Rocha Fonte, Rui – Arsenal – Crystal Palace; 24 Rose, Daniel – Tottenham Hotspur – Watford; 26 Rouse, Domaine – Bury – Fleetwood Town; 27 Rowe–Turner, Lathaniel – Leicester City – Redditch United; 1 Ruddy, John T.G. – Everton – Crewe Alexandra; 19 Sappleton, Reneil – Leicester City – AFC Telford United; 19 Sawyer, Lee T. – Chelsea – Wycombe Wanderers; 23 Sheehan, Alan – Leeds United – Crewe Alexandra; 6 Shields, Solomon – Leyton Orient – St Albans City; 6 Shroot, Robin – Birmingham City – Walsall; 25 Sigurdsson, Gylfi T. – Reading – Crewe Alexandra; 9 Simmons, Paris M. – Derby County – Lincoln City; 26 Sinclair, Frank M. – Lincoln City – Wycombe Wanderers; 26 Skarz, Joe – Huddersfield Town – Hartlepool United; 13 Small, Wade K. – Sheffield Wednesday – Blackpool; 3 Smith, Andrew G. – Accrington Stanley – Clitheroe; 26 Sodje, Samuel – Reading – Leeds United; 20 Spencer, Damian M. – Cheltenham Town – Brentford; 18 St Louis–Hamilton, Danzelle D. – Stoke City – Bristol Rovers; 26 Stack, Graham – Plymouth Argyle – Wolverhampton Wanderers; 11 Stech, Marek – West Ham United – Wycombe Wanderers; 23 Steer, Rene A. – Arsenal – Gillingham; 2 Stockdale, David A. – Fulham – Leicester City; 2 Stokes, Anthony – Sunderland – Crystal Palace; 26 Sturrock, Blair D. – Swindon Town – Torquay United; 18 Supple, Shane – Ipswich Town – Oldham Athletic; 27 Swallow, Ben – Bristol Rovers – Mangotsfield United; 20 Sweeney, Peter – Leeds United – Grimsby Town; 20 Symes, Michael – Shrewsbury Town – Accrington Stanley; 13 Taarabt, Adel – Tottenham Hotspur – Queens Park Rangers; 26 Tait, Richard – Nottingham Forest – Tamworth; 2 Taylor, Gareth K. – Doncaster Rovers – Carlisle United; 13 Taylor, Stuart J. – Aston Villa – Cardiff City; 26 Thompson, Joshua J. – Crewe Alexandra – Cammell Laird; 19 Townsend, Andros – Tottenham Hotspur – Yeovil Town; 19 Trotman, Neal – Preston North End – Colchester United; 24 Trotter, Liam – Ipswich Town – Scunthorpe United; 19 Turner, Iain R. – Everton – Nottingham Forest; 8 Tymon, Matthew R. – Hartlepool United – Newcastle Blue Star; 20 Varney, Luke I. – Derby County – Sheffield Wednesday; 20 Vernon, Scott M. – Colchester United – Northampton Town; 19 Vincent, Ashley D. – Cheltenham Town – Colchester United; 26 Walton, Simon W. – Plymouth Argyle – Blackpool; 2 Ward, Darren – Sunderland – Wolverhampton Wanderers; 13 Warner, Anthony R. – Hull City – Leicester City; 26 Watts, Adam – Fulham – Northampton Town; 16 Weale, Christopher – Bristol City – Yeovil Town; 25 Webb, Jonathan – Leeds United – Newcastle Blue Star; 26 Welsh, John J. – Hull City – Bury; 19 Westlake, Ian J. – Cheltenham Town – Oldham Athletic; 18 White, Joe – Bristol Rovers – Yate Town; 26 Wilkinson, Alistair B. – York City – Altrincham; 9 Williams, Sam – Aston Villa – Brentford; 26 Williamson, Lee – Watford – Preston North End; 4 Worrall, David – West Bromwich Albion – Shrewsbury Town; 6 Worthington, Jonathan – Huddersfield Town – Yeovil Town; 20 Wright, Ben – Peterborough United – Kettering Town; 24 Wright, Joshua W. – Charlton Atletic – Gillingham; 26 Young, Martin – Hartlepool United – Kendal Town; 26 Yussuf, Rashid O. – Charlton Athletic – Ebbsfleet United

APRIL 2009

28 Constable, James A.	Shrewsbury Town	Oxford United	undisclosed

TEMPORARY TRANSFERS

17 Butcher, Lee A. – Tottenham Hotspur – Grays Athletic; 17 Button, David R. – Tottenham Hotspur – Dagenham & Redbridge; 9 Convey, Matthew T. – Bradford City – Guiseley; 2 Elding, Anthony L. – Crewe Alexandra – Lincoln City; 4 Kite, Alexandrous – Bristol Rovers – Weston–Super–Mare; 17 Martin, Richard W. – Manchester City – Burton Albion; 23 Spencer, James M. – Rochdale – Chester City

MAY 2009

14 Duffy, Mark	Southport	Morecambe	undisclosed
14 Frecklington, Lee	Lincoln City	Peterborough United	undisclosed
1 Hobbs, Jack	Liverpool	Leicester City	Free
16 Morison, Steve	Stevenage Borough	Millwall	130,000
12 Rowe, Thomas	Stockport County	Peterborough United	undisclosed
29 Vincent, Ashley D.	Cheltenham Town	Colchester United	Free

TEMPORARY TRANSFERS

4 Fielding, Francis C. – Blackburn Rovers – Rochdale; 4 Newey, Thomas – Grimsby Town – Rochdale; 1 Price, Jason – Doncaster Rovers – Millwall; 6 Williamson, Lee – Watford – Preston North End; 6 Worrall, David – West Bromwich Albion – Shrewsbury Town; 5 Wright, Joshua W. – Charlton Athletic – Gillingham

THE NEW FOREIGN LEGION 2008-09

JUNE 2008	From	To	Fee in £
5 Bednar, Roman	Hearts	West Bromwich Albion	2,300,000
9 Bosingwa, Jose	Porto	Chelsea	16,200,000
30 Deco	Barcelona	Chelsea	7,900,000
10 Giovani	Barcelona	Tottenham Hotspur	4,700,000
JULY 2008			
1 Bassong, Sebastien	Metz	Newcastle United	1,800,000
31 Behrami, Valon	Lazio	West Ham United	5,000,000
30 Bischoff, Amaury	Werder Bremen	Arsenal	undisclosed
28 Cavalieri, Diego	Palmeiras	Liverpool	3,000,000
21 Cech, Marek	Porto	West Bromwich Albion	2,000,000
18 Digard, Didier	Paris St Germain	Middlesbrough	4,000,000
21 Dossena, Andrea	Udinese	Liverpool	7,000,000
11 Elmander, Johan	Toulouse	Bolton Wanderers	10,000,000+exch.
21 Emnes, Marvin	Sparta Rotterdam	Middlesbrough	3,200,000
22 Gomes, Heurelho	PSV Eindhoven	Tottenham Hotspur	8,000,000
2 Gutierrez, Jonas	Mallorca	Newcastle United	9,000,000
11 Jo	CSKA Moscow	Manchester City	19,000,000
4 Kallio, Toni	Young Boys	Fulham	Free
14 Kim	Seongnam	West Bromwich Albion	500,000
3 Modric, Luka	Dinamo Zagreb	Tottenham Hotspur	16,800,000
28 Mustapha, Riga	Levante	Bolton Wanderers	undisclosed
24 Nasri, Samir	Marseille	Arsenal	12,800,000
30 N'Gog, David	Paris St Germain	Liverpool	1,500,000
30 Stoor, Fredrik	Rosenborg	Fulham	2,000,000
22 Zaki, Amr	Zamalek	Wigan Athletic	Loan
3 Zuiverloon, Gianni	Heerenveen	West Bromwich Albion	3,200,000
AUGUST 2008			
22 Borja Valero	Mallorca	West Bromwich Albion	4,700,000
29 Castillo, Segundo	Red Star Belgrade	Everton	Loan
30 Coloccini, Fabricio	La Coruna	Newcastle United	10,000,000
12 Cuellar, Carlos	Rangers	Aston Villa	7,800,000
31 Donk, Ryan	AZ	West Bromwich Albion	Loan
1 Guzan, Brad	Chivas USA	Aston Villa	600,000
28 Jacobsen, Lars	Nuremberg	Everton	Free
22 Kompany, Vincent	Hamburg	Manchester City	6,000,000
31 Olsson, Jonas	NEC Nijmegen	West Bromwich Albion	800,000
29 Smolarek, Ebi	Santander	Bolton Wanderers	Loan
2 Villaneuva, Carlos	Audax Italiano	Blackburn Rovers	Loan
31 Zabaleta, Pablo	Espanyol	Manchester City	undisclosed
31 Zayatte, Kamil	Young Boys	Hull City	Loan

(Then signed for £3,360,000).

SEPTEMBER 2008			
1 Belhadj, Nadir	Lens	Portsmouth	Loan
1 Cousin, Daniel	Rangers	Hull City	4,000,000
1 Fellaini, Marouane	Standard Liege	Everton	15,000,000
1 Gonzalez, Ignacio	Valencia	Newcastle United	Loan
2 Ilunga, Herita	Toulouse	West Ham United	Loan
1 Pavlyuchenko, Roman	Spartak Moscow	Tottenham Hotspur	14,000,000
1 Riera, Albert	Espanyol	Liverpool	8,000,000
1 Robinho	Real Madrid	Manchester City	32,500,000
1 Xisco	La Coruna	Newcastle United	8,200,000
JANUARY 2009			
21 De Jong, Nigel	Hamburg	Manchester City	17,000,000
8 De Laet, Ritchie	Stoke City	Manchester United	3,000,000

(Loan spell with Wrexham (Blue Square Premier)).

15 Fortune, Marc-Antoine	Nancy	West Bromwich Albion	Loan
14 Givet, Gael	Marseille	Blackburn Rovers	Loan
30 Kovac, Radoslav	Spartak Moscow	West Ham United	Loan
23 Lovenkrands, Peter	Schalke	Newcastle United	Free
16 Makukla, Ariza	Benfica	Bolton Wanderers	Loan
26 Nsereko, Savio	Brescia	West Ham United	9,000,000
5 Puygrenier, Sebastien	Zenit	Bolton Wanderers	Loan
6 Rodallega, Hugo	Necaxa	Wigan Athletic	4,500,000
2 Tosic, Zoran	Partizan Belgrade	Manchester United	16,300,000

(Combined fee with Adem Ljajic).

FEBRUARY 2009			
3 Arshavin, Andrei	Zenit	Arsenal	15,000,000
2 Basinas, Angelos	AEK Athens	Portsmouth	undisclosed
2 Berra, Christophe	Hearts	Wolverhampton Wanderers	2,500,000
2 Gekas, Theofanis	Leverkusen	Portsmouth	Loan
2 Menseguez, Juan Carlos	San Lorenzo	West Bromwich Albion	Loan
2 Mulumbu, Youssouf	Paris St Germain	West Bromwich Albion	Loan
2 Quaresma, Ricardo	Internazionale	Chelsea	Loan
MARCH 2009			
9 Cho, Won Hee	Monaco	Wigan Athletic	Free

THE THINGS THEY SAID . . .

Pre-season thoughts of Internazionale manager Jose Mourinho on the likely champions of the Premier League:
"I expect a two-horse race between Manchester United and Chelsea. I saw Arsenal play in the Amsterdam tournament. They have a good squad but there are too few experienced players. One day Liverpool will be there with them. Maybe even this year."

Amr Zaki, the one-time zenith of Zamalek, with his view on life with Wigan Athletic:
"If any other club came in for me I would still want to stay at Wigan. I feel at home here. Yes, even if it was Manchester United even though Steve Bruce used to play there."

In the wake of losing 2-1 to Hull City at the Emirates, Arsenal manager Arsène Wenger was so shell shocked by the outcome that he had a total loss of memory:
"After going 1-0 up, instead of pressing on, we gave too much room to West Brom!"

In the wake of Tottenham Hotspur's worst start to a season in their history, Jonathan Woodgate put the situation into perspective:
"Spurs are worse than Leeds when they were relegated."

When an assistant referee erroneously awarded a goal after the ball went off for a corner and the score was allowed to stand, Watford manager Aidy Boothroyd's thoughts were out of this world:
"It was like a UFO had landed. I just could not believe it. I spoke to the referee afterwards and he told me he works as a team with his assistants. If one of them tells him it's a goal he has to go with it."

Gianfranco Zola yearning for the good old days of the UEFA Cup before it disappeared to become the Europa League:
"Years ago, this competition was more attractive and that is something that maybe should be thought about for the future. For me it became nonsense. I have the same idea about the Champions League. To take part you had to come first."

The reality of the contemporary Champions League is an entirely different ball game according to Arsène Wenger:
"You sit here, you are in the last four in Europe and every day you feel you have killed someone."

Guus Hiddink had a brief but successful stint as interim first-team coach of Chelsea last season and was rewarded in the FA Cup final with success over Everton:
"Winning in the mecca of world football, the FA Cup, that's something I cannot believe."

David Moyes at Everton recalled his club's recent record and then pinpointed what was necessary to improve upon it:
"We've had fourth, fifth, sixth and seventh places in six seasons and got close to establishing ourselves alongside the big four. I think £30 million to £40 million would have given us a realistic chance."

When Aston Villa were riding high and had hopes of finishing in fourth place, the fixture pile-up concerned manager Martin O'Neill and though he had one of the smallest first-team squads of the Premier League he was prepared for changes:
"We will have to do a bit of rotating because we are looking tired and have to play Monday, Thursday in Europe and on back here for Sunday."

Before he eventually moved to Real Madrid, Kaka was linked with a January transfer window move to Manchester City:
"As long as the club keeps high objectives my desire will always be to play at Milan."

One who did arrive at Eastlands was Robinho the Brazilian who cost a British record fee at the time. His ambition seemed to be modest enough:
"Today I am at Manchester City and I have a dream of becoming the best player in the world."

When Liverpool ended Chelsea's 86-game unbeaten home League record, the Reds manager Rafa Benitez was on a high:
"We have belief, we have quality and we have shown by coming from behind in other games this season, that we have character."

Man of few words – that was Roy Keane when in charge of Sunderland. Following reports he was about to quit the post on 15 November:
"Complete nonsense."

The same manager leaving the job on 4 December:
"Niall, I'm off."

Mark Hughes as Manchester City manager was under pressure for much of the season but had a realistic view of his position:
"At this moment in time we're trying to build for the future. There will be a little bit of pain along the way and we have to accept that."

Difference of opinion between Cristiano Ronaldo and Newcastle United's Steven Taylor where it was alleged the conversation went as follows:
Ronaldo: *"You're a rubbish footballer"*
Taylor: *"At least I'm not ugly"*

Arsène Wenger on the caution which he claimed had been edging into the Premiership:
"The Premier League has definitely lost something. When I arrived here in 1996 everybody had a go at you and there was space up and down the flanks. Sometimes you lost the game, but you could see more chances than today.

"You go back 10 years and everybody played a strict 4-4-2. This year I cannot remember any team coming here with two strikers – except Hull at first against us." (Or was that West Brom!)

Liverpool manager Rafa Benitez on how he views Sir Alex Ferguson's version of the Respect campaign:
"Mr Ferguson is killing the referees. He is the only manager in English league that cannot be punished for these things."

Wayne Rooney, clearly with a keen eye on entering the diplomatic corps once he retires from football, with a passing reference to Manchester City:
"If they were winning trophies it would irritate me, but while they are still mid-table I am not really too bothered about it."

Former Scotland manager Craig Brown on FIFA's decision to allow a combined British Olympic team in the next Games with possible sinister implications later on:
"Although we've got assurances now from FIFA, the Scottish national team could easily disappear altogether and that is horrendous."

When Harry Redknapp was appointed manager at Tottenham Hotspur he recommended successors to his previous role at Portsmouth. Sadly a few months proved a short time in football management for them:
"I spoke to Peter (Storrie) about it and told him that he had Joe (Jordan) and Tony (Adams) and they are both terrific guys."

League Managers Association chief executive Richard Bevan on how refereeing standards could be improved:
"Managers have sympathy for match officials who are doing a tough job in often difficult circumstances and they genuinely want to explore ideas that will improve everything."

Seven days to be remembered for Ryan Giggs which began by being voted Player of the Year by the Professional Footballers Association:
"It's been a great week – winning the award, making my 800th appearance and now scoring a goal. It couldn't get better than that."

Once clear of the possibility of relegation from the Premier League, Tony Pulis the Stoke City manager explained his feelings:
"I'm absolutely delighted. It has been a tough season for us. We had a bad start and had to bounce back. The players have always believed it."

Those other escapees from Blackburn Rovers produced this statement from manager Sam Allardyce, who took over mid-season at Ewood Park:
"What we have done in the quest to survive has been magnificent and the players have always got a result when they needed one."

On 9 May after beating Celtic in the final Auld Firm derby of the season, Rangers manager Walter Smith said:
"We were in a good position last year but had a fixture pile-up. We don't have that this year so we have to show the ability to go on and take the championship."

Lionel Messi of Barcelona fame on the prospects for the Champions League confrontation with Manchester United:
"There are no favourites, but they are the ones who are defending the title so perhaps they are just ahead. For us, it has been a magnificent year but we still have one big test left. Being so close to history gives us great motivation."

Five days before the Champions League final, Cristiano Ronaldo aired his views on the continual rumour about him moving to Real Madrid:
"At the moment I'm only thinking of the final, independently of what will happen to me or my teammates next season. I'm at United and only care about what happens next season at Manchester United."

Cristiano Ronaldo with his remarks following the disappointment of losing to Barcelona, in what proved to be his swansong at Old Trafford:
"We started well in the game but after they scored we did nothing. We didn't control the game and we lost. I think Barcelona played better than us and they deserved to win."

A different Ronaldo after being named FIFA World Player of the Year, praising Sir Alex Ferguson:
"It's true that the manager always has an important role to play. It was a great season for me and for my club. It's a privilege to have such a great club manager."

George Burley the Scotland manager on the hazards presented by such a position:
"You are given the job because people thought you were the best man and you have got to have that belief in your own ability. Nothing changes there and you cannot get derailed with criticism."

When Manchester United goalkeeper Edwin Van der Sar set a new individual record for the most minutes without conceding a goal, there was understandable praise from colleagues:
"He is the best keeper I've played with. It's as simple as that (Rio Ferdinand)."

"Edwin just gives that calming influence right throughout the team (Ryan Giggs)."

Alan Shearer in the wake of Newcastle United losing their Premier League status:
"There are huge problems at the club, which are clear for everyone to see. It has not just gone on this season, but last season, the season before and four seasons before that. The fact is that inside the dressing-room hasn't been good enough. I include myself. I include Joe (Kinnear), Chris (Hughton), Kevin (Keegan), Mike (Ashley). Newcastle have got what they deserved."

On achieving safety at the end of the season, Ricky Sbragia gave his thoughts on his decision to resign as manager of Sunderland:
"My biggest concern was keeping us in the League. My brief was to keep us up. I am not sad I made the right choice. I could have been selfish and kept it, but Sunderland need a new mentality and someone with fresh ideas. I am doing the right thing."

Relegation for Middlesbrough but manager Gareth Southgate had words of praise for his team:
"We ended up with an extremely young team, but I was proud of the way they performed on the day. Today wasn't the reason we went down, but it did highlight the lack of depth to our squad."

Roy Hodgson earned much credit for helping guide Fulham to a position which ensured participation in European football for 2009–10:
"I don't like ranking achievements but this will always be my finest moment. I will probably forget the game pretty quickly, but I will never forget what we have done and that's what I told the players."

Andrei Arshavin with his thoughts on joining Arsenal at the end of the transfer window in January:
"They are one of the leading football clubs in the world with a group of fantastic young players and a great manager."

On the eve of England's bid to win the European Under-21 Championship in Sweden, Stuart Pearce made this statement:
"Success is not coming away as a gallant loser."

Following defeat by Germany in the final he had a different view of events:
"As a learning curve for young players this has been a fantastic tournament, win or lose it was irrelevant."

ENGLISH LEAGUE HONOURS 1888 TO 2009

FA PREMIER LEAGUE

MAXIMUM POINTS: *a* 126; *b* 114.
Won or placed on goal average (ratio), goal difference or most goals scored. ††Not promoted after play-offs.

	First	Pts	Second	Pts	Third	Pts
1992–93*a*	Manchester U	84	Aston Villa	74	Norwich C	72
1993–94*a*	Manchester U	92	Blackburn R	84	Newcastle U	77
1994–95*a*	Blackburn R	89	Manchester U	88	Nottingham F	77
1995–96*b*	Manchester U	82	Newcastle U	78	Liverpool	71
1996–97*b*	Manchester U	75	Newcastle U*	68	Arsenal*	68
1997–98*b*	Arsenal	78	Manchester U	77	Liverpool	65
1998–99*b*	Manchester U	79	Arsenal	78	Chelsea	75
1999–2000*b*	Manchester U	91	Arsenal	73	Leeds U	69
2000–01	Manchester U	80	Arsenal	70	Liverpool	69
2001–02	Arsenal	87	Liverpool	80	Manchester U	77
2002–03	Manchester U	83	Arsenal	78	Newcastle U	69
2003–04	Arsenal	90	Chelsea	79	Manchester U	75
2004–05	Chelsea	95	Arsenal	83	Manchester U	77
2005–06	Chelsea	91	Manchester U	83	Liverpool	82
2006–07	Manchester U	89	Chelsea	83	Liverpool*	68
2007–08	Manchester U	87	Chelsea	85	Arsenal	83
2008–09	Manchester U	90	Liverpool	86	Chelsea	83

FOOTBALL LEAGUE CHAMPIONSHIP

MAXIMUM POINTS: 138

2004–05	Sunderland	94	Wigan Ath	87	Ipswich T††	85
2005–06	Reading	106	Sheffield U	90	Watford	81
2006–07	Sunderland	88	Birmingham C	86	Derby Co	84
2007–08	WBA	81	Stoke C	79	Hull C	75
2008–09	Wolverhampton W	90	Birmingham C	83	Sheffield U††	80

FIRST DIVISION

MAXIMUM POINTS: 138

1992–93	Newcastle U	96	West Ham U*	88	Portsmouth††	88
1993–94	Crystal Palace	90	Nottingham F	83	Millwall††	74
1994–95	Middlesbrough	82	Reading††	79	Bolton W	77
1995–96	Sunderland	83	Derby Co	79	Crystal Palace††	75
1996–97	Bolton W	98	Barnsley	80	Wolverhampton W††	76
1997–98	Nottingham F	94	Middlesbrough	91	Sunderland††	90
1998–99	Sunderland	105	Bradford C	87	Ipswich T††	86
1999–2000	Charlton Ath	91	Manchester C	89	Ipswich T	87
2000–01	Fulham	101	Blackburn R	91	Bolton W	87
2001–02	Manchester C	99	WBA	89	Wolverhampton W††	86
2002–03	Portsmouth	98	Leicester C	92	Sheffield U††	80
2003–04	Norwich C	94	WBA	86	Sunderland††	79

FOOTBALL LEAGUE CHAMPIONSHIP 1

MAXIMUM POINTS: 138

2004–05	Luton T	98	Hull C	86	Tranmere R††	79
2005–06	Southend U	82	Colchester U	79	Brentford††	76
2006–07	Scunthorpe U	91	Bristol C	85	Blackpool	83
2007–08	Swansea C	92	Nottingham F	82	Doncaster R	80
2008–09	Leicester C	96	Peterborough U	89	Milton Keynes D††	87

SECOND DIVISION

MAXIMUM POINTS: 138

1992–93	Stoke C	93	Bolton W	90	Port Vale††	89
1993–94	Reading	89	Port Vale	88	Plymouth Arg*††	85
1994–95	Birmingham C	89	Brentford††	85	Crewe Alex††	83
1995–96	Swindon T	92	Oxford U	83	Blackpool††	82
1996–97	Bury	84	Stockport Co	82	Luton T††	78
1997–98	Watford	88	Bristol C	85	Grimsby T	72
1998–99	Fulham	101	Walsall	87	Manchester C	82
1999–2000	Preston NE	95	Burnley	88	Gillingham	85
2000–01	Millwall	93	Rotherham U	91	Reading††	86
2001–02	Brighton & HA	90	Reading	84	Brentford*††	83
2002–03	Wigan Ath	100	Crewe Alex	86	Bristol C††	83
2003–04	Plymouth Arg	90	QPR	83	Bristol C††	82

FOOTBALL LEAGUE CHAMPIONSHIP 2

MAXIMUM POINTS: 138

2004–05	Yeovil T	83	Scunthorpe U*	80	Swansea C	80
2005–06	Carlisle U	86	Northampton T	83	Leyton Orient	81
2006–07	Walsall	89	Hartlepool U	88	Swindon T	85
2007–08	Milton Keynes D	97	Peterborough U	92	Hereford U	88
2008–09	Brentford	85	Exeter C	79	Wycombe W*	78

THIRD DIVISION

MAXIMUM POINTS: *a* 126; *b* 138.

1992–93*a*	Cardiff C	83	Wrexham	80	Barnet	79
1993–94*a*	Shrewsbury T	79	Chester C	74	Crewe Alex	73
1994–95*a*	Carlisle U	91	Walsall	83	Chesterfield	81
1995–96*b*	Preston NE	86	Gillingham	83	Bury	79
1996–97*b*	Wigan Ath*	87	Fulham	87	Carlisle U	84

	First	Pts	Second	Pts	Third	Pts
1997–98*b*	Notts Co	99	Macclesfield T	82	Lincoln C	72
1998–99*b*	Brentford	85	Cambridge U	81	Cardiff C	80
1999–2000*b*	Swansea C	85	Rotherham U	84	Northampton T	82
2000–01	Brighton & HA	92	Cardiff C	82	Chesterfield¶	80
2001–02	Plymouth Arg	102	Luton T	97	Mansfield T	79
2002–03	Rushden & D	87	Hartlepool U	85	Wrexham	84
2003–04	Doncaster R	92	Hull C	88	Torquay U*	81

¶9pts deducted for irregularities.

FOOTBALL LEAGUE

MAXIMUM POINTS: *a* 44; *b* 60

	First	Pts	Second	Pts	Third	Pts
1888–89*a*	Preston NE	40	Aston Villa	29	Wolverhampton W	28
1889–90*a*	Preston NE	33	Everton	31	Blackburn R	27
1890–91*a*	Everton	29	Preston NE	27	Notts Co	26
1891–92*b*	Sunderland	42	Preston NE	37	Bolton W	36

FIRST DIVISION to 1991–92

MAXIMUM POINTS: *a* 44; *b* 52; *c* 60; *d* 68; *e* 76; *f* 84; *g* 126; *h* 120; *k* 114.

	First	Pts	Second	Pts	Third	Pts
1892–93*c*	Sunderland	48	Preston NE	37	Everton	36
1893–94*c*	Aston Villa	44	Sunderland	38	Derby Co	36
1894–95*c*	Sunderland	47	Everton	42	Aston Villa	39
1895–96*c*	Aston Villa	45	Derby Co	41	Everton	39
1896–97*c*	Aston Villa	47	Sheffield U*	36	Derby Co	36
1897–98*c*	Sheffield U	42	Sunderland	37	Wolverhampton W*	35
1898–99*d*	Aston Villa	45	Liverpool	43	Burnley	39
1899–1900*d*	Aston Villa	50	Sheffield U	48	Sunderland	41
1900–01*d*	Liverpool	45	Sunderland	43	Notts Co	40
1901–02*d*	Sunderland	44	Everton	41	Newcastle U	37
1902–03*d*	The Wednesday	42	Aston Villa*	41	Sunderland	41
1903–04*d*	The Wednesday	47	Manchester C	44	Everton	43
1904–05*d*	Newcastle U	48	Everton	47	Manchester C	46
1905–06*e*	Liverpool	51	Preston NE	47	The Wednesday	44
1906–07*e*	Newcastle U	51	Bristol C	48	Everton*	45
1907–08*e*	Manchester U	52	Aston Villa*	43	Manchester C	43
1908–09*e*	Newcastle U	53	Everton	46	Sunderland	44
1909–10*e*	Aston Villa	53	Liverpool	48	Blackburn R*	45
1910–11*e*	Manchester U	52	Aston Villa	51	Sunderland*	45
1911–12*e*	Blackburn R	49	Everton	46	Newcastle U	44
1912–13*e*	Sunderland	54	Aston Villa	50	Sheffield W	49
1913–14*e*	Blackburn R	51	Aston Villa	44	Middlesbrough*	43
1914–15*e*	Everton	46	Oldham Ath	45	Blackburn R*	43
1919–20*f*	WBA	60	Burnley	51	Chelsea	49
1920–21*f*	Burnley	59	Manchester C	54	Bolton W	52
1921–22*f*	Liverpool	57	Tottenham H	51	Burnley	49
1922–23*f*	Liverpool	60	Sunderland	54	Huddersfield T	53
1923–24*f*	Huddersfield T*	57	Cardiff C	57	Sunderland	53
1924–25*f*	Huddersfield T	58	WBA	56	Bolton W	55
1925–26*f*	Huddersfield T	57	Arsenal	52	Sunderland	48
1926–27*f*	Newcastle U	56	Huddersfield T	51	Sunderland	49
1927–28*f*	Everton	53	Huddersfield T	51	Leicester C	48
1928–29*f*	Sheffield W	52	Leicester C	51	Aston Villa	50
1929–30*f*	Sheffield W	60	Derby Co	50	Manchester C*	47
1930–31*f*	Arsenal	66	Aston Villa	59	Sheffield W	52
1931–32*f*	Everton	56	Arsenal	54	Sheffield W	50
1932–33*f*	Arsenal	58	Aston Villa	54	Sheffield W	51
1933–34*f*	Arsenal	59	Huddersfield T	56	Tottenham H	49
1934–35*f*	Arsenal	58	Sunderland	54	Sheffield W	49
1935–36*f*	Sunderland	56	Derby Co*	48	Huddersfield T	48
1936–37*f*	Manchester C	57	Charlton Ath	54	Arsenal	52
1937–38*f*	Arsenal	52	Wolverhampton W	51	Preston NE	49
1938–39*f*	Everton	59	Wolverhampton W	55	Charlton Ath	50
1946–47*f*	Liverpool	57	Manchester U*	56	Wolverhampton W	56
1947–48*f*	Arsenal	59	Manchester U*	52	Burnley	52
1948–49*f*	Portsmouth	58	Manchester U*	53	Derby Co	53
1949–50*f*	Portsmouth*	53	Wolverhampton W	53	Sunderland	52
1950–51*f*	Tottenham H	60	Manchester U	56	Blackpool	50
1951–52*f*	Manchester U	57	Tottenham H*	53	Arsenal	53
1952–53*f*	Arsenal*	54	Preston NE	54	Wolverhampton W	51
1953–54*f*	Wolverhampton W	57	WBA	53	Huddersfield T	51
1954–55*f*	Chelsea	52	Wolverhampton W*	48	Portsmouth*	48
1955–56*f*	Manchester U	60	Blackpool*	49	Wolverhampton W	49
1956–57*f*	Manchester U	64	Tottenham H*	56	Preston NE	56
1957–58*f*	Wolverhampton W	64	Preston NE	59	Tottenham H	51
1958–59*f*	Wolverhampton W	61	Manchester U	55	Arsenal*	50
1959–60*f*	Burnley	55	Wolverhampton W	54	Tottenham H	53
1960–61*f*	Tottenham H	66	Sheffield W	58	Wolverhampton W	57
1961–62*f*	Ipswich T	56	Burnley	53	Tottenham H	52
1962–63*f*	Everton	61	Tottenham H	55	Burnley	54
1963–64*f*	Liverpool	57	Manchester U	53	Everton	52
1964–65*f*	Manchester U*	61	Leeds U	61	Chelsea	56
1965–66*f*	Liverpool	61	Leeds U*	55	Burnley	55
1966–67*f*	Manchester U	60	Nottingham F*	56	Tottenham H	56
1967–68*f*	Manchester C	58	Manchester U	56	Liverpool	55

	First	Pts	Second	Pts	Third	Pts
1968–69f	Leeds U	67	Liverpool	61	Everton	57
1969–70f	Everton	66	Leeds U	57	Chelsea	55
1970–71f	Arsenal	65	Leeds U	64	Tottenham H*	52
1971–72f	Derby Co	58	Leeds U*	57	Liverpool*	57
1972–73f	Liverpool	60	Arsenal	57	Leeds U	53
1973–74f	Leeds U	62	Liverpool	57	Derby Co	48
1974–75f	Derby Co	53	Liverpool*	51	Ipswich T	51
1975–76f	Liverpool	60	QPR	59	Manchester U	56
1976–77f	Liverpool	57	Manchester C	56	Ipswich T	52
1977–78f	Nottingham F	64	Liverpool	57	Everton	55
1978–79f	Liverpool	68	Nottingham F	60	WBA	59
1979–80f	Liverpool	60	Manchester U	58	Ipswich T	52
1980–81f	Aston Villa	60	Ipswich T	56	Arsenal	53
1981–82g	Liverpool	87	Ipswich T	83	Manchester U	78
1982–83g	Liverpool	82	Watford	71	Manchester U	70
1983–84g	Liverpool	80	Southampton	77	Nottingham F*	74
1984–85g	Everton	90	Liverpool*	77	Tottenham H	77
1985–86g	Liverpool	88	Everton	86	West Ham U	84
1986–87g	Everton	86	Liverpool	77	Tottenham H	71
1987–88h	Liverpool	90	Manchester U	81	Nottingham F	73
1988–89k	Arsenal*	76	Liverpool	76	Nottingham F	64
1989–90k	Liverpool	79	Aston Villa	70	Tottenham H	63
1990–91k	Arsenal†	83	Liverpool	76	Crystal Palace	69
1991–92g	Leeds U	82	Manchester U	78	Sheffield W	75

No official competition during 1915–19 and 1939–46; Regional Leagues operated. †2 pts deducted.

SECOND DIVISION to 1991–92

MAXIMUM POINTS: *a* 44; *b* 56; *c* 60; *d* 68; *e* 76; *f* 84; *g* 126; *h* 132; *k* 138.

	First	Pts	Second	Pts	Third	Pts
1892–93a	Small Heath	36	Sheffield U	35	Darwen	30
1893–94b	Liverpool	50	Small Heath	42	Notts Co	39
1894–95c	Bury	48	Notts Co	39	Newton Heath*	38
1895–96c	Liverpool*	46	Manchester C	46	Grimsby T*	42
1896–97c	Notts Co	42	Newton Heath	39	Grimsby T	38
1897–98c	Burnley	48	Newcastle U	45	Manchester C	39
1898–99d	Manchester C	52	Glossop NE	46	Leicester Fosse	45
1899–1900d	The Wednesday	54	Bolton W	52	Small Heath	46
1900–01d	Grimsby T	49	Small Heath	48	Burnley	44
1901–02d	WBA	55	Middlesbrough	51	Preston NE*	42
1902–03d	Manchester C	54	Small Heath	51	Woolwich A	48
1903–04d	Preston NE	50	Woolwich A	49	Manchester U	48
1904–05d	Liverpool	58	Bolton W	56	Manchester U	53
1905–06e	Bristol C	66	Manchester U	62	Chelsea	53
1906–07e	Nottingham F	60	Chelsea	57	Leicester Fosse	48
1907–08e	Bradford C	54	Leicester Fosse	52	Oldham Ath	50
1908–09e	Bolton W	52	Tottenham H*	51	WBA	51
1909–10e	Manchester C	54	Oldham Ath*	53	Hull C*	53
1910–11e	WBA	53	Bolton W	51	Chelsea	49
1911–12e	Derby Co*	54	Chelsea	54	Burnley	52
1912–13e	Preston NE	53	Burnley	50	Birmingham	46
1913–14e	Notts Co	53	Bradford PA*	49	Woolwich A	49
1914–15e	Derby Co	53	Preston NE	50	Barnsley	47
1919–20f	Tottenham H	70	Huddersfield T	64	Birmingham	56
1920–21f	Birmingham*	58	Cardiff C	58	Bristol C	51
1921–22f	Nottingham F	56	Stoke C*	52	Barnsley	52
1922–23f	Notts Co	53	West Ham U*	51	Leicester C	51
1923–24f	Leeds U	54	Bury*	51	Derby Co	51
1924–25f	Leicester C	59	Manchester U	57	Derby Co	55
1925–26f	Sheffield W	60	Derby Co	57	Chelsea	52
1926–27f	Middlesbrough	62	Portsmouth*	54	Manchester C	54
1927–28f	Manchester C	59	Leeds U	57	Chelsea	54
1928–29f	Middlesbrough	55	Grimsby T	53	Bradford PA*	48
1929–30f	Blackpool	58	Chelsea	55	Oldham Ath	53
1930–31f	Everton	61	WBA	54	Tottenham H	51
1931–32f	Wolverhampton W	56	Leeds U	54	Stoke C	52
1932–33f	Stoke C	56	Tottenham H	55	Fulham	50
1933–34f	Grimsby T	59	Preston NE	52	Bolton W*	51
1934–35f	Brentford	61	Bolton W*	56	West Ham U	56
1935–36f	Manchester U	56	Charlton Ath	55	Sheffield U*	52
1936–37f	Leicester C	56	Blackpool	55	Bury	52
1937–38f	Aston Villa	57	Manchester U*	53	Sheffield U	53
1938–39f	Blackburn R	55	Sheffield U	54	Sheffield W	53
1946–47f	Manchester C	62	Burnley	58	Birmingham C	55
1947–48f	Birmingham C	59	Newcastle U	56	Southampton	52
1948–49f	Fulham	57	WBA	56	Southampton	55
1949–50f	Tottenham H	61	Sheffield W*	52	Sheffield U*	52
1950–51f	Preston NE	57	Manchester C	52	Cardiff C	50
1951–52f	Sheffield W	53	Cardiff C*	51	Birmingham C	51
1952–53f	Sheffield U	60	Huddersfield T	58	Luton T	52
1953–54f	Leicester C*	56	Everton	56	Blackburn R	55
1954–55f	Birmingham C*	54	Luton T*	54	Rotherham U	54
1955–56f	Sheffield W	55	Leeds U	52	Liverpool*	48
1956–57f	Leicester C	61	Nottingham F	54	Liverpool	53
1957–58f	West Ham U	57	Blackburn R	56	Charlton Ath	55

	First	Pts	Second	Pts	Third	Pts
1958–59f	Sheffield W	62	Fulham	60	Sheffield U*	53
1959–60f	Aston Villa	59	Cardiff C	58	Liverpool*	50
1960–61f	Ipswich T	59	Sheffield U	58	Liverpool	52
1961–62f	Liverpool	62	Leyton Orient	54	Sunderland	53
1962–63f	Stoke C	53	Chelsea*	52	Sunderland	52
1963–64f	Leeds U	63	Sunderland	61	Preston NE	56
1964–65f	Newcastle U	57	Northampton T	56	Bolton W	50
1965–66f	Manchester C	59	Southampton	54	Coventry C	53
1966–67f	Coventry C	59	Wolverhampton W	58	Carlisle U	52
1967–68f	Ipswich T	59	QPR*	58	Blackpool	58
1968–69f	Derby Co	63	Crystal Palace	56	Charlton Ath	50
1969–70f	Huddersfield T	60	Blackpool	53	Leicester C	51
1970–71f	Leicester C	59	Sheffield U	56	Cardiff C*	53
1971–72f	Norwich C	57	Birmingham C	56	Millwall	55
1972–73f	Burnley	62	QPR	61	Aston Villa	50
1973–74f	Middlesbrough	65	Luton T	50	Carlisle U	49
1974–75f	Manchester U	61	Aston Villa	58	Norwich C	53
1975–76f	Sunderland	56	Bristol C*	53	WBA	53
1976–77f	Wolverhampton W	57	Chelsea	55	Nottingham F	52
1977–78f	Bolton W	58	Southampton	57	Tottenham H*	56
1978–79f	Crystal Palace	57	Brighton & HA*	56	Stoke C	56
1979–80f	Leicester C	55	Sunderland	54	Birmingham C*	53
1980–81f	West Ham U	66	Notts Co	53	Swansea C*	50
1981–82g	Luton T	88	Watford	80	Norwich C	71
1982–83g	QPR	85	Wolverhampton W	75	Leicester C	70
1983–84g	Chelsea*	88	Sheffield W	88	Newcastle U	80
1984–85g	Oxford U	84	Birmingham C	82	Manchester C	74
1985–86g	Norwich C	84	Charlton Ath	77	Wimbledon	76
1986–87g	Derby Co	84	Portsmouth	78	Oldham Ath††	75
1987–88h	Millwall	82	Aston Villa*	78	Middlesbrough	78
1988–89k	Chelsea	99	Manchester C	82	Crystal Palace	81
1989–90k	Leeds U*	85	Sheffield U	85	Newcastle U††	80
1990–91k	Oldham Ath	88	West Ham U	87	Sheffield W	82
1991–92k	Ipswich T	84	Middlesbrough	80	Derby Co	78

No official competition during 1915–19 and 1939–46; Regional Leagues operated.

THIRD DIVISION to 1991–92

MAXIMUM POINTS: 92; 138 FROM 1981–82.

	First	Pts	Second	Pts	Third	Pts
1958–59	Plymouth Arg	62	Hull C	61	Brentford*	57
1959–60	Southampton	61	Norwich C	59	Shrewsbury T*	52
1960–61	Bury	68	Walsall	62	QPR	60
1961–62	Portsmouth	65	Grimsby T	62	Bournemouth*	59
1962–63	Northampton T	62	Swindon T	58	Port Vale	54
1963–64	Coventry C*	60	Crystal Palace	60	Watford	58
1964–65	Carlisle U	60	Bristol C*	59	Mansfield T	59
1965–66	Hull C	69	Millwall	65	QPR	57
1966–67	QPR	67	Middlesbrough	55	Watford	54
1967–68	Oxford U	57	Bury	56	Shrewsbury T	55
1968–69	Watford*	64	Swindon T	64	Luton T	61
1969–70	Orient	62	Luton T	60	Bristol R	56
1970–71	Preston NE	61	Fulham	60	Halifax T	56
1971–72	Aston Villa	70	Brighton & HA	65	Bournemouth*	62
1972–73	Bolton W	61	Notts Co	57	Blackburn R	55
1973–74	Oldham Ath	62	Bristol R*	61	York C	61
1974–75	Blackburn R	60	Plymouth Arg	59	Charlton Ath	55
1975–76	Hereford U	63	Cardiff C	57	Millwall	56
1976–77	Mansfield T	64	Brighton & HA	61	Crystal Palace*	59
1977–78	Wrexham	61	Cambridge U	58	Preston NE*	56
1978–79	Shrewsbury T	61	Watford*	60	Swansea C	60
1979–80	Grimsby T	62	Blackburn R	59	Sheffield W	58
1980–81	Rotherham U	61	Barnsley*	59	Charlton Ath	59
1981–82	Burnley*	80	Carlisle U	80	Fulham	78
1982–83	Portsmouth	91	Cardiff C	86	Huddersfield T	82
1983–84	Oxford U	95	Wimbledon	87	Sheffield U*	83
1984–85	Bradford C	94	Millwall	90	Hull C	87
1985–86	Reading	94	Plymouth Arg	87	Derby Co	84
1986–87	Bournemouth	97	Middlesbrough	94	Swindon T	87
1987–88	Sunderland	93	Brighton & HA	84	Walsall	82
1988–89	Wolverhampton W	92	Sheffield U*	84	Port Vale	84
1989–90	Bristol R	93	Bristol C	91	Notts Co	87
1990–91	Cambridge U	86	Southend U	85	Grimsby T*	83
1991–92	Brentford	82	Birmingham C	81	Huddersfield T	78

FOURTH DIVISION (1958–1992)

MAXIMUM POINTS: 92; 138 FROM 1981–82.

	First	Pts	Second	Pts	Third	Pts	Fourth	Pts
1958–59	Port Vale	64	Coventry C*	60	York C	60	Shrewsbury T	58
1959–60	Walsall	65	Notts Co*	60	Torquay U	60	Watford	57
1960–61	Peterborough U	66	Crystal Palace	64	Northampton T*	60	Bradford PA	60
1961–62†	Millwall	56	Colchester U	55	Wrexham	53	Carlisle U	52
1962–63	Brentford	62	Oldham Ath*	59	Crewe Alex	59	Mansfield T*	57
1963–64	Gillingham*	60	Carlisle U	60	Workington	59	Exeter C	58

	First	Pts	Second	Pts	Third	Pts	Fourth	Pts
1964–65	Brighton & HA	63	Millwall*	62	York C	62	Oxford U	61
1965–66	Doncaster R*	59	Darlington	59	Torquay U	58	Colchester U*	56
1966–67	Stockport Co	64	Southport*	59	Barrow	59	Tranmere R	58
1967–68	Luton T	66	Barnsley	61	Hartlepools U	60	Crewe Alex	58
1968–69	Doncaster R	59	Halifax T	57	Rochdale*	56	Bradford C	56
1969–70	Chesterfield	64	Wrexham	61	Swansea C	60	Port Vale	59
1970–71	Notts Co	69	Bournemouth	60	Oldham Ath	59	York C	56
1971–72	Grimsby T	63	Southend U	60	Brentford	59	Scunthorpe U	57
1972–73	Southport	62	Hereford U	58	Cambridge U	57	Aldershot*	56
1973–74	Peterborough U	65	Gillingham	62	Colchester U	60	Bury	59
1974–75	Mansfield T	68	Shrewsbury T	62	Rotherham U	59	Chester*	57
1975–76	Lincoln C	74	Northampton T	68	Reading	60	Tranmere R	58
1976–77	Cambridge U	65	Exeter C	62	Colchester U*	59	Bradford C	59
1977–78	Watford	71	Southend U	60	Swansea C*	56	Brentford	56
1978–79	Reading	65	Grimsby T*	61	Wimbledon*	61	Barnsley	61
1979–80	Huddersfield T	66	Walsall	64	Newport Co	61	Portsmouth*	60
1980–81	Southend U	67	Lincoln C	65	Doncaster R	56	Wimbledon	55
1981–82	Sheffield U	96	Bradford C*	91	Wigan Ath	91	Bournemouth	88
1982–83	Wimbledon	98	Hull C	90	Port Vale	88	Scunthorpe U	83
1983–84	York C	101	Doncaster R	85	Reading*	82	Bristol C	82
1984–85	Chesterfield	91	Blackpool	86	Darlington	85	Bury	84
1985–86	Swindon T	102	Chester C	84	Mansfield T	81	Port Vale	79
1986–87	Northampton T	99	Preston NE	90	Southend U	80	Wolverhampton W††	79
1987–88	Wolverhampton W	90	Cardiff C	85	Bolton W	78	Scunthorpe U††	77
1988–89	Rotherham U	82	Tranmere R	80	Crewe Alex	78	Scunthorpe U††	77
1989–90	Exeter C	89	Grimsby T	79	Southend U	75	Stockport Co††	74
1990–91	Darlington	83	Stockport Co*	82	Hartlepool U	82	Peterborough U	80
1991–92†*	Burnley	83	Rotherham U*	77	Mansfield T	77	Blackpool	76

†*Maximum points:* 88 owing to Accrington Stanley's resignation.

†**Maximum points:* 126 owing to Aldershot being expelled (and only 23 teams started the competition).

THIRD DIVISION—SOUTH (1920–1958)

1920–21 SEASON AS THIRD DIVISION. MAXIMUM POINTS: *a* 84; *b* 92.

	First	Pts	Second	Pts	Third	Pts
1920–21*a*	Crystal Palace	59	Southampton	54	QPR	53
1921–22*a*	Southampton*	61	Plymouth Arg	61	Portsmouth	53
1922–23*a*	Bristol C	59	Plymouth Arg*	53	Swansea T	53
1923–24*a*	Portsmouth	59	Plymouth Arg	55	Millwall	54
1924–25*a*	Swansea T	57	Plymouth Arg	56	Bristol C	53
1925–26*a*	Reading	57	Plymouth Arg	56	Millwall	53
1926–27*a*	Bristol C	62	Plymouth Arg	60	Millwall	56
1927–28*a*	Millwall	65	Northampton T	55	Plymouth Arg	53
1928–29*a*	Charlton Ath*	54	Crystal Palace	54	Northampton T*	52
1929–30*a*	Plymouth Arg	68	Brentford	61	QPR	51
1930–31*a*	Notts Co	59	Crystal Palace	51	Brentford	50
1931–32*a*	Fulham	57	Reading	55	Southend U	53
1932–33*a*	Brentford	62	Exeter C	58	Norwich C	57
1933–34*a*	Norwich C	61	Coventry C*	54	Reading*	54
1934–35*a*	Charlton Ath	61	Reading	53	Coventry C	51
1935–36*a*	Coventry C	57	Luton T	56	Reading	54
1936–37*a*	Luton T	58	Notts Co	56	Brighton & HA	53
1937–38*a*	Millwall	56	Bristol C	55	QPR*	53
1938–39*a*	Newport Co	55	Crystal Palace	52	Brighton & HA	49
1939–46	Competition cancelled owing to war. Regional Leagues operated.					
1946–47*a*	Cardiff C	66	QPR	57	Bristol C	51
1947–48*a*	QPR	61	Bournemouth	57	Walsall	51
1948–49*a*	Swansea T	62	Reading	55	Bournemouth	52
1949–50*a*	Notts Co	58	Northampton T*	51	Southend U	51
1950–51*b*	Nottingham F	70	Norwich C	64	Reading*	57
1951–52*b*	Plymouth Arg	66	Reading*	61	Norwich C	61
1952–53*b*	Bristol R	64	Millwall*	62	Northampton T	62
1953–54*b*	Ipswich T	64	Brighton & HA	61	Bristol C	56
1954–55*b*	Bristol C	70	Leyton Orient	61	Southampton	59
1955–56*b*	Leyton Orient	66	Brighton & HA	65	Ipswich T	64
1956–57*b*	Ipswich T*	59	Torquay U	59	Colchester U	58
1957–58*b*	Brighton & HA	60	Brentford*	58	Plymouth Arg	58

THIRD DIVISION—NORTH (1921–1958)

MAXIMUM POINTS: *a* 76; *b* 84; *c* 80; *d* 92.

	First	Pts	Second	Pts	Third	Pts
1921–22*a*	Stockport Co	56	Darlington*	50	Grimsby T	50
1922–23*a*	Nelson	51	Bradford PA	47	Walsall	46
1923–24*b*	Wolverhampton W	63	Rochdale	62	Chesterfield	54
1924–25*b*	Darlington	58	Nelson*	53	New Brighton	53
1925–26*b*	Grimsby T	61	Bradford PA	60	Rochdale	59
1926–27*b*	Stoke C	63	Rochdale	58	Bradford PA	55
1927–28*b*	Bradford PA	63	Lincoln C	55	Stockport Co	54
1928–29*b*	Bradford C	63	Stockport Co	62	Wrexham	52
1929–30*b*	Port Vale	67	Stockport Co	63	Darlington*	50
1930–31*b*	Chesterfield	58	Lincoln C	57	Wrexham*	54
1931–32*c*	Lincoln C*	57	Gateshead	57	Chester	50
1932–33*b*	Hull C	59	Wrexham	57	Stockport Co	54
1933–34*b*	Barnsley	62	Chesterfield	61	Stockport Co	59
1934–35*b*	Doncaster R	57	Halifax T	55	Chester	54

	First	Pts	Second	Pts	Third	Pts
1935–36*b*	Chesterfield	60	Chester*	55	Tranmere R	55
1936–37*b*	Stockport Co	60	Lincoln C	57	Chester	53
1937–38*b*	Tranmere R	56	Doncaster R	54	Hull C	53
1938–39*b*	Barnsley	67	Doncaster R	56	Bradford C	52
1939–46	Competition cancelled owing to war. Regional Leagues operated.					
1946–47*b*	Doncaster R	72	Rotherham U	60	Chester	56
1947–48*b*	Lincoln C	60	Rotherham U	59	Wrexham	50
1948–49*b*	Hull C	65	Rotherham U	62	Doncaster R	50
1949–50*b*	Doncaster R	55	Gateshead	53	Rochdale*	51
1950–51*d*	Rotherham U	71	Mansfield T	64	Carlisle U	62
1951–52*d*	Lincoln C	69	Grimsby T	66	Stockport Co	59
1952–53*d*	Oldham Ath	59	Port Vale	58	Wrexham	56
1953–54*d*	Port Vale	69	Barnsley	58	Scunthorpe U	57
1954–55*d*	Barnsley	65	Accrington S	61	Scunthorpe U*	58
1955–56*d*	Grimsby T	68	Derby Co	63	Accrington S	59
1956–57*d*	Derby Co	63	Hartlepools U	59	Accrington S*	58
1957–58*d*	Scunthorpe U	66	Accrington S	59	Bradford C	57

PROMOTED AFTER PLAY-OFFS

(NOT ACCOUNTED FOR IN PREVIOUS SECTION)

1986–87	Aldershot to Division 3.
1987–88	Swansea C to Division 3.
1988–89	Leyton Orient to Division 3.
1989–90	Sunderland to Division 1; Notts Co to Division 2; Cambridge U to Division 3.
1990–91	Notts Co to Division 1; Tranmere R to Division 2; Torquay U to Division 3.
1991–92	Blackburn R to Premier League; Peterborough U to Division 1.
1992–93	Swindon T to Premier League; WBA to Division 1; York C to Division 2.
1993–94	Leicester C to Premier League; Burnley to Division 1; Wycombe W to Division 2.
1994–95	Huddersfield T to Division 1.
1995–96	Leicester C to Premier League; Bradford C to Division 1; Plymouth Arg to Division 2.
1996–97	Crystal Palace to Premier League; Crewe Alex to Division 1; Northampton T to Division 2.
1997–98	Charlton Ath to Premier League; Colchester U to Division 2.
1998–99	Watford to Premier League; Scunthorpe U to Division 2.
1999–2000	Peterborough U to Division 2
2000–01	Walsall to Division 1; Blackpool to Division 2
2001–02	Birmingham C to Premier League; Stoke C to Division 1; Cheltenham T to Division 2
2002–03	Wolverhampton W to Premier League; Cardiff C to Division 1; Bournemouth to Division 2
2003–04	Crystal Palace to Premier League; Brighton & HA to Division 1; Huddersfield T to Division 2
2004–05	West Ham U to Premier League; Sheffield W to Championship; Southend U to Championship 1
2005–06	Watford to Premier League; Barnsley to Championship; Cheltenham T to Championship 1
2006–07	Derby Co to Premier League; Blackpool to Championship; Bristol R to Championship 1
2007–08	Hull C to Premier League; Doncaster R to Championship; Stockport Co to Championship 1
2008–09	Burnley to Premier League; Scunthorpe U to Championship; Gillingham to Championship 1

LEAGUE TITLE WINS

FA PREMIER LEAGUE – Manchester U 11, Arsenal 3, Chelsea 2, Blackburn R 1.

FOOTBALL LEAGUE CHAMPIONSHIP – Sunderland 2, Reading 1, WBA 1, Wolverhampton W 1.

LEAGUE DIVISION 1 – Liverpool 18, Arsenal 10, Everton 9, Sunderland 8, Aston Villa 7, Manchester U 7, Newcastle U 5, Sheffield W 4, Huddersfield T 3, Leeds U 3, Manchester C 3, Portsmouth 3, Wolverhampton W 3, Blackburn R 2, Burnley 2, Derby Co 2, Nottingham F 2, Preston NE 2, Tottenham H 2; Bolton W, Charlton Ath, Chelsea, Crystal Palace, Fulham, Ipswich T, Middlesbrough, Norwich C, Sheffield U, WBA 1 each.

FOOTBALL LEAGUE CHAMPIONSHIP 1 – Leicester C 1, Luton T 1, Scunthorpe U 1, Southend U 1, Swansea C 1.

LEAGUE DIVISION 2 – Leicester C 6, Manchester C 6, Birmingham C (one as Small Heath) 5, Sheffield W 5, Derby Co 4, Liverpool 4, Preston NE 4, Ipswich T 3, Leeds U 3, Middlesbrough 3, Notts Co 3, Stoke C 3, Aston Villa 2, Bolton W 2, Burnley 2, Bury 2, Chelsea 2, Fulham 2, Grimsby T 2, Manchester U 2, Millwall 2, Norwich C 2, Nottingham F 2, Tottenham H 2, WBA 2, West Ham U 2, Wolverhampton W 2; Blackburn R, Blackpool, Bradford C, Brentford, Brighton & HA, Bristol C, Coventry C, Crystal Palace, Everton, Huddersfield T, Luton T, Newcastle U, QPR, Oldham Ath, Oxford U, Plymouth Arg, Reading, Sheffield U, Sunderland, Swindon T, Watford, Wigan Ath 1 each.

FOOTBALL LEAGUE CHAMPIONSHIP 2 – Brentford 1, Carlisle U 1, Milton Keynes D 1, Walsall 1, Yeovil T 1.

LEAGUE DIVISION 3 – Brentford 2, Carlisle U 2, Oxford U 2, Plymouth Arg 2, Portsmouth 2, Preston NE 2, Shrewsbury T 2; Aston Villa, Blackburn R, Bolton W, Bournemouth, Bradford C, Brighton & HA, Bristol R, Burnley, Bury, Cambridge U, Cardiff C, Coventry C, Doncaster R, Grimsby T, Hereford U, Hull C, Leyton Orient, Mansfield T, Northampton T, Notts Co, Oldham Ath, QPR, Reading, Rotherham U, Rushden & D Southampton, Sunderland, Swansea C, Watford, Wigan Ath, Wolverhampton W, Wrexham 1 each.

LEAGUE DIVISION 4 – Chesterfield 2, Doncaster R 2, Peterborough U 2; Brentford, Brighton & HA, Burnley, Cambridge U, Darlington, Exeter C, Gillingham, Grimsby T, Huddersfield T, Lincoln C, Luton T, Mansfield T, Millwall, Northampton T, Notts Co, Port Vale, Reading, Rotherham U, Sheffield U, Southend U, Southport, Stockport Co, Swindon T, Walsall, Watford, Wimbledon, Wolverhampton W, York C 1 each.

TO 1957–58

DIVISION 3 (South) – Bristol C 3, Charlton Ath 2, Ipswich T 2, Millwall 2, Notts Co 2, Plymouth Arg 2, Swansea T 2; Brentford, Brighton & HA, Bristol R, Cardiff C, Coventry C, Crystal Palace, Fulham, Leyton Orient, Luton T, Newport Co, Norwich C, Nottingham F, Portsmouth, QPR, Reading, Southampton 1 each.

DIVISION 3 (North) – Barnsley 3, Doncaster R 3, Lincoln C 3, Chesterfield 2, Grimsby T 2, Hull C 2, Port Vale 2, Stockport Co 2; Bradford C, Bradford PA, Darlington, Derby Co, Nelson, Oldham Ath, Rotherham U, Scunthorpe U, Stoke C, Tranmere R, Wolverhampton W 1 each.

RELEGATED CLUBS

1891–92 League extended. Newton Heath, Sheffield W and Nottingham F admitted. *Second Division formed* including Darwen.
1892–93 In Test matches, Sheffield U and Darwen won promotion in place of Notts Co and Accrington S.
1893–94 In Tests, Liverpool and Small Heath won promotion. Newton Heath and Darwen relegated.
1894–95 After Tests, Bury promoted, Liverpool relegated.
1895–96 After Tests, Liverpool promoted, Small Heath relegated.
1896–97 After Tests, Notts Co promoted, Burnley relegated.
1897–98 Test system abolished after success of Stoke C and Burnley. League extended. Blackburn R and Newcastle U elected to First Division. *Automatic promotion and relegation introduced.*

FA PREMIER LEAGUE TO DIVISION 1

1992–93 Crystal Palace, Middlesbrough, Nottingham F
1993–94 Sheffield U, Oldham Ath, Swindon T
1994–95 Crystal Palace, Norwich C, Leicester C, Ipswich T
1995–96 Manchester C, QPR, Bolton W
1996–97 Sunderland, Middlesbrough, Nottingham F
1997–98 Bolton W, Barnsley, Crystal Palace

1998–99 Charlton Ath, Blackburn R, Nottingham F
1999–2000 Wimbledon, Sheffield W, Watford
2000–01 Manchester C, Coventry C, Bradford C
2001–02 Ipswich T, Derby Co, Leicester C
2002–03 West Ham U, WBA, Sunderland
2003–04 Leicester C, Leeds U, Wolverhampton W.

FA PREMIER LEAGUE TO CHAMPIONSHIP

2004–05 Crystal Palace, Norwich C, Southampton
2005–06 Birmingham C, WBA, Sunderland

2006–07 Sheffield U, Charlton Ath, Watford
2007–08 Reading, Birmingham C, Derby Co
2008–09 Newcastle U, Middlesbrough, WBA

DIVISION 1 TO DIVISION 2

1898–99 Bolton W and Sheffield W
1899–1900 Burnley and Glossop
1900–01 Preston NE and WBA
1901–02 Small Heath and Manchester C
1902–03 Grimsby T and Bolton W
1903–04 Liverpool and WBA
1904–05 League extended. Bury and Notts Co, two bottom clubs in First Division, re-elected.
1905–06 Nottingham F and Wolverhampton W
1906–07 Derby Co and Stoke C
1907–08 Bolton W and Birmingham C
1908–09 Manchester C and Leicester Fosse
1909–10 Bolton W and Chelsea
1910–11 Bristol C and Nottingham F
1911–12 Preston NE and Bury
1912–13 Notts Co and Woolwich Arsenal
1913–14 Preston NE and Derby Co
1914–15 Tottenham H and Chelsea*
1919–20 Notts Co and Sheffield W
1920–21 Derby Co and Bradford PA
1921–22 Bradford C and Manchester U
1922–23 Stoke C and Oldham Ath
1923–24 Chelsea and Middlesbrough
1924–25 Preston NE and Nottingham F
1925–26 Manchester C and Notts Co
1926–27 Leeds U and WBA
1927–28 Tottenham H and Middlesbrough
1928–29 Bury and Cardiff C
1929–30 Burnley and Everton
1930–31 Leeds U and Manchester U
1931–32 Grimsby T and West Ham U
1932–33 Bolton W and Blackpool
1933–34 Newcastle U and Sheffield U
1934–35 Leicester C and Tottenham H
1935–36 Aston Villa and Blackburn R
1936–37 Manchester U and Sheffield W
1937–38 Manchester C and WBA
1938–39 Birmingham C and Leicester C
1946–47 Brentford and Leeds U
1947–48 Blackburn R and Grimsby T
1948–49 Preston NE and Sheffield U
1949–50 Manchester C and Birmingham C
1950–51 Sheffield W and Everton
1951–52 Huddersfield T and Fulham
1952–53 Stoke C and Derby Co
1953–54 Middlesbrough and Liverpool
1954–55 Leicester C and Sheffield W
1955–56 Huddersfield T and Sheffield U
1956–57 Charlton Ath and Cardiff C

1957–58 Sheffield W and Sunderland
1958–59 Portsmouth and Aston Villa
1959–60 Luton T and Leeds U
1960–61 Preston NE and Newcastle U
1961–62 Chelsea and Cardiff C
1962–63 Manchester C and Leyton Orient
1963–64 Bolton W and Ipswich T
1964–65 Wolverhampton W and Birmingham C
1965–66 Northampton T and Blackburn R
1966–67 Aston Villa and Blackpool
1967–68 Fulham and Sheffield U
1968–69 Leicester C and QPR
1969–70 Sunderland and Sheffield W
1970–71 Burnley and Blackpool
1971–72 Huddersfield T and Nottingham F
1972–73 Crystal Palace and WBA
1973–74 Southampton, Manchester U, Norwich C
1974–75 Luton T, Chelsea, Carlisle U
1975–76 Wolverhampton W, Burnley, Sheffield U
1976–77 Sunderland, Stoke C, Tottenham H
1977–78 West Ham U, Newcastle U, Leicester C
1978–79 QPR, Birmingham C, Chelsea
1979–80 Bristol C, Derby Co, Bolton W
1980–81 Norwich C, Leicester C, Crystal Palace
1981–82 Leeds U, Wolverhampton W, Middlesbrough
1982–83 Manchester C, Swansea C, Brighton & HA
1983–84 Birmingham C, Notts Co, Wolverhampton W
1984–85 Norwich C, Sunderland, Stoke C
1985–86 Ipswich T, Birmingham C, WBA
1986–87 Leicester C, Manchester C, Aston Villa
1987–88 Chelsea**, Portsmouth, Watford, Oxford U
1988–89 Middlesbrough, West Ham U, Newcastle U
1989–90 Sheffield W, Charlton Ath, Millwall
1990–91 Sunderland and Derby Co
1991–92 Luton T, Notts Co, West Ham U
1992–93 Brentford, Cambridge U, Bristol R
1993–94 Birmingham C, Oxford U, Peterborough U
1994–95 Swindon T, Burnley, Bristol C, Notts Co
1995–96 Millwall, Watford, Luton T
1996–97 Grimsby T, Oldham Ath, Southend U
1997–98 Manchester C, Stoke C, Reading
1998–99 Bury, Oxford U, Bristol C
1999–2000 Walsall, Port Vale, Swindon T
2000–01 Huddersfield T, QPR, Tranmere R
2001–02 Crewe Alex, Barnsley, Stockport Co
2002–03 Sheffield W, Brighton & HA, Grimsby T
2003–04 Walsall, Bradford C, Wimbledon
**Relegated after play-offs.*
**Subsequently re-elected to Division 1 when League was extended after the War.*

FOOTBALL LEAGUE CHAMPIONSHIP TO FOOTBALL LEAGUE CHAMPIONSHIP 1

2004–05 Gillingham, Nottingham F, Rotherham U
2005–06 Crewe Alex, Millwall, Brighton & HA
2006–07 Southend U, Luton T, Leeds U

2007–08 Leicester C, Scunthorpe U, Colchester U
2008–09 Norwich C, Southampton, Charlton Ath

DIVISION 2 TO DIVISION 3

1920–21 Stockport Co
1921–22 Bradford PA and Bristol C
1922–23 Rotherham Co and Wolverhampton W
1923–24 Nelson and Bristol C
1924–25 Crystal Palace and Coventry C
1925–26 Stoke C and Stockport Co
1926–27 Darlington and Bradford C
1927–28 Fulham and South Shields
1928–29 Port Vale and Clapton Orient
1929–30 Hull C and Notts Co
1930–31 Reading and Cardiff C
1931–32 Barnsley and Bristol C
1932–33 Chesterfield and Charlton Ath
1933–34 Millwall and Lincoln C
1934–35 Oldham Ath and Notts Co
1935–36 Port Vale and Hull C
1936–37 Doncaster R and Bradford C
1937–38 Barnsley and Stockport Co
1938–39 Norwich C and Tranmere R
1946–47 Swansea T and Newport Co
1947–48 Doncaster R and Millwall
1948–49 Nottingham F and Lincoln C
1949–50 Plymouth Arg and Bradford PA
1950–51 Grimsby T and Chesterfield
1951–52 Coventry C and QPR
1952–53 Southampton and Barnsley
1953–54 Brentford and Oldham Ath
1954–55 Ipswich T and Derby Co
1955–56 Plymouth Arg and Hull C
1956–57 Port Vale and Bury
1957–58 Doncaster R and Notts Co
1958–59 Barnsley and Grimsby T
1959–60 Bristol C and Hull C
1960–61 Lincoln C and Portsmouth
1961–62 Brighton & HA and Bristol R
1962–63 Walsall and Luton T
1963–64 Grimsby T and Scunthorpe U
1964–65 Swindon T and Swansea T
1965–66 Middlesbrough and Leyton Orient
1966–67 Northampton T and Bury
1967–68 Plymouth Arg and Rotherham U

1968–69 Fulham and Bury
1969–70 Preston NE and Aston Villa
1970–71 Blackburn R and Bolton W
1971–72 Charlton Ath and Watford
1972–73 Huddersfield T and Brighton & HA
1973–74 Crystal Palace, Preston NE, Swindon T
1974–75 Millwall, Cardiff C, Sheffield W
1975–76 Oxford U, York C, Portsmouth
1976–77 Carlisle U, Plymouth Arg, Hereford U
1977–78 Blackpool, Mansfield T, Hull C
1978–79 Sheffield U, Millwall, Blackburn R
1979–80 Fulham, Burnley, Charlton Ath
1980–81 Preston NE, Bristol C, Bristol R
1981–82 Cardiff C, Wrexham, Orient
1982–83 Rotherham U, Burnley, Bolton W
1983–84 Derby Co, Swansea C, Cambridge U
1984–85 Notts Co, Cardiff C, Wolverhampton W
1985–86 Carlisle U, Middlesbrough, Fulham
1986–87 Sunderland**, Grimsby T, Brighton & HA
1987–88 Huddersfield T, Reading, Sheffield U**
1988–89 Shrewsbury T, Birmingham C, Walsall
1989–90 Bournemouth, Bradford C, Stoke C
1990–91 WBA and Hull C
1991–92 Plymouth Arg, Brighton & HA, Port Vale
1992–93 Preston NE, Mansfield T, Wigan Ath, Chester C
1993–94 Fulham, Exeter C, Hartlepool U, Barnet
1994–95 Cambridge U, Plymouth Arg, Cardiff C,
          Chester C, Leyton Orient
1995–96 Carlisle U, Swansea C, Brighton & HA, Hull C
1996–97 Peterborough U, Shrewsbury T, Rotherham U,
          Notts Co
1997–98 Brentford, Plymouth Arg, Carlisle U, Southend U
1998–99 York C, Northampton T, Lincoln C,
          Macclesfield T
1999–2000 Cardiff C, Blackpool, Scunthorpe U,
          Chesterfield
2000–01 Bristol R, Luton T, Swansea C, Oxford U
2001–02 Bournemouth, Bury, Wrexham, Cambridge U
2002–03 Cheltenham T, Huddersfield T, Mansfield T
          Northampton T
2003–04 Grimsby T, Rushden & D, Notts Co, Wycombe W

FOOTBALL LEAGUE CHAMPIONSHIP 1 TO FOOTBALL LEAGUE CHAMPIONSHIP 2

2004–05 Torquay U, Wrexham, Peterborough U,
          Stockport Co
2005–06 Hartlepool U, Milton Keynes D, Swindon T,
          Walsall
2006–07 Chesterfield, Bradford C, Rotherham U,
          Brentford

2007–08 Bournemouth, Gillingham, Port Vale, Luton T
2008–09 Northampton T, Crewe Alex, Cheltenham T,
          Hereford U

DIVISION 3 TO DIVISION 4

1958–59 Stockport Co, Doncaster R, Notts Co, Rochdale
1959–60 York C, Mansfield T, Wrexham, Accrington S
1960–61 Tranmere R, Bradford C, Colchester U,
          Chesterfield
1961–62 Torquay U, Lincoln C, Brentford, Newport Co
1962–63 Bradford PA, Brighton & HA, Carlisle U,
          Halifax T
1963–64 Millwall, Crewe Alex, Wrexham, Notts Co
1964–65 Luton T, Port Vale, Colchester U, Barnsley
1965–66 Southend U, Exeter C, Brentford, York C
1966–67 Swansea T, Darlington, Doncaster R, Workington
1967–68 Grimsby T, Colchester U, Scunthorpe U,
          Peterborough U (demoted)
1968–69 Northampton T, Hartlepool, Crewe Alex,
          Oldham Ath
1969–70 Bournemouth, Southport, Barrow, Stockport Co
1970–71 Reading, Bury, Doncaster R, Gillingham
1971–72 Mansfield T, Barnsley, Torquay U, Bradford C
1972–73 Rotherham U, Brentford, Swansea C,
          Scunthorpe U
1973–74 Cambridge U, Shrewsbury T, Southport,
          Rochdale

1974–75 Bournemouth, Tranmere R, Watford,
          Huddersfield T
1975–76 Aldershot, Colchester U, Southend U, Halifax T
1976–77 Reading, Northampton T, Grimsby T, York C
1977–78 Port Vale, Bradford C, Hereford U, Portsmouth
1978–79 Peterborough U, Walsall, Tranmere R, Lincoln C
1979–80 Bury, Southend U, Mansfield T, Wimbledon
1980–81 Sheffield U, Colchester U, Blackpool, Hull C
1981–82 Wimbledon, Swindon T, Bristol C, Chester
1982–83 Reading, Wrexham, Doncaster R, Chesterfield
1983–84 Scunthorpe U, Southend U, Port Vale, Exeter C
1984–85 Burnley, Orient, Preston NE, Cambridge U
1985–86 Lincoln C, Cardiff C, Wolverhampton W,
          Swansea C
1986–87 Bolton W**, Carlisle U, Darlington, Newport Co
1987–88 Rotherham U**, Grimsby T, York C, Doncaster R
1988–89 Southend U, Chesterfield, Gillingham, Aldershot
1989–90 Cardiff C, Northampton T, Blackpool, Walsall
1990–91 Crewe Alex, Rotherham U, Mansfield T
1991–92 Bury, Shrewsbury T, Torquay U, Darlington

** *Relegated after play-offs.*

APPLICATIONS FOR RE-ELECTION

FOURTH DIVISION
Eleven: Hartlepool U.
Seven: Crewe Alex.
Six: Barrow (lost League place to Hereford U 1972), Halifax T, Rochdale, Southport (lost League place to Wigan Ath 1978), York C.
Five: Chester C, Darlington, Lincoln C, Stockport Co, Workington (lost League place to Wimbledon 1977).
Four: Bradford PA (lost League place to Cambridge U 1970), Newport Co, Northampton T.
Three: Doncaster R, Hereford U.
Two: Bradford C, Exeter C, Oldham Ath, Scunthorpe U, Torquay U.
One: Aldershot, Colchester U, Gateshead (lost League place to Peterborough U 1960), Grimsby T, Swansea C, Tranmere R, Wrexham, Blackpool, Cambridge U, Preston NE.
Accrington S resigned and Oxford U were elected 1962.
Port Vale were forced to re-apply following expulsion in 1968.
Aldershot expelled March 1992. Maidstone U resigned August 1992.

THIRD DIVISIONS NORTH & SOUTH
Seven: Walsall.
Six: Exeter C, Halifax T, Newport Co.
Five: Accrington S, Barrow, Gillingham, New Brighton, Southport.
Four: Rochdale, Norwich C.
Three: Crystal Palace, Crewe Alex, Darlington, Hartlepool U, Merthyr T, Swindon T.
Two: Aberdare Ath, Aldershot, Ashington, Bournemouth, Brentford, Chester, Colchester U, Durham C, Millwall, Nelson, QPR, Rotherham U, Southend U, Tranmere R, Watford, Workington.
One: Bradford C, Bradford PA, Brighton & HA, Bristol R, Cardiff C, Carlisle U, Charlton Ath, Gateshead, Grimsby T, Mansfield T, Shrewsbury T, Torquay U, York C.

LEAGUE STATUS FROM 1986–87

RELEGATED FROM LEAGUE

1986–87 Lincoln C	1987–88 Newport Co
1988–89 Darlington	1989–90 Colchester U
1990–91 —	1991–92 —
1992–93 Halifax T	1993–94 —
1994–95 —	1995–96 —
1996–97 Hereford U	1997–98 Doncaster R
1998–99 Scarborough	1999–2000 Chester C
2000–01 Barnet	2001–02 Halifax T
2002–03 Shrewsbury T, Exeter C	
2003–04 Carlisle U, York C	
2004–05 Kidderminster H, Cambridge U	
2005–06 Oxford U, Rushden & D	
2006–07 Boston U, Torquay U	
2007–08 Mansfield T, Wrexham	
2008–09 Chester C, Luton T	

PROMOTED TO LEAGUE

1986–87 Scarborough	1987–88 Lincoln C
1988–89 Maidstone U	1989–90 Darlington
1990–91 Barnet	1991–92 Colchester U
1992–93 Wycombe W	1993–94 —
1994–95 —	1995–96 —
1996–97 Macclesfield T	1997–98 Halifax T
1998–99 Cheltenham T	1999–2000 Kidderminster H
2000–01 Rushden & D	2001–02 Boston U
2002–03 Yeovil T, Doncaster R	
2003–04 Chester C, Shrewsbury T	
2004–05 Barnet, Carlisle U	
2005–06 Accrington S, Hereford U	
2006–07 Dagenham & R, Morecambe	
2007–08 Aldershot T, Exeter C	
2008–09 Burton Alb, Torquay U	

Wayne Rooney of Manchester United and Javier Mascherano fight for possession during Liverpool's 4-1 thumping of their north-west rivals in the Premier League fixture at Old Trafford. Despite the heavy reverse United still went on to record their 11th Premier League title. (PA Photos)

LEAGUE ATTENDANCES SINCE 1946–47

Season	Matches	Total	Div. 1	Div. 2	Div. 3 (S)	Div. 3 (N)
1946–47	1848	35,604,606	15,005,316	11,071,572	5,664,004	3,863,714
1947–48	1848	40,259,130	16,732,341	12,286,350	6,653,610	4,586,829
1948–49	1848	41,271,414	17,914,667	11,353,237	6,998,429	5,005,081
1949–50	1848	40,517,865	17,278,625	11,694,158	7,104,155	4,440,927
1950–51	2028	39,584,967	16,679,454	10,780,580	7,367,884	4,757,109
1951–52	2028	39,015,866	16,110,322	11,066,189	6,958,927	4,880,428
1952–53	2028	37,149,966	16,050,278	9,686,654	6,704,299	4,708,735
1953–54	2028	36,174,590	16,154,915	9,510,053	6,311,508	4,198,114
1954–55	2028	34,133,103	15,087,221	8,988,794	5,996,017	4,051,071
1955–56	2028	33,150,809	14,108,961	9,080,002	5,692,479	4,269,367
1956–57	2028	32,744,405	13,803,037	8,718,162	5,622,189	4,601,017
1957–58	2028	33,562,208	14,468,652	8,663,712	6,097,183	4,332,661

		Total	Div. 1	Div. 2	Div. 3	Div. 4
1958–59	2028	33,610,985	14,727,691	8,641,997	5,946,600	4,276,697
1959–60	2028	32,538,611	14,391,227	8,399,627	5,739,707	4,008,050
1960–61	2028	28,619,754	12,926,948	7,033,936	4,784,256	3,874,614
1961–62	2015	27,979,902	12,061,194	7,453,089	5,199,106	3,266,513
1962–63	2028	28,885,852	12,490,239	7,792,770	5,341,362	3,261,481
1963–64	2028	28,535,022	12,486,626	7,594,158	5,419,157	3,035,081
1964–65	2028	27,641,168	12,708,752	6,984,104	4,436,245	3,512,067
1965–66	2028	27,206,980	12,480,644	6,914,757	4,779,150	3,032,429
1966–67	2028	28,902,596	14,242,957	7,253,819	4,421,172	2,984,648
1967–68	2028	30,107,298	15,289,410	7,450,410	4,013,087	3,354,391
1968–69	2028	29,382,172	14,584,851	7,382,390	4,339,656	3,075,275
1969–70	2028	29,600,972	14,868,754	7,581,728	4,223,761	2,926,729
1970–71	2028	28,194,146	13,954,337	7,098,265	4,377,213	2,764,331
1971–72	2028	28,700,729	14,484,603	6,769,308	4,697,392	2,749,426
1972–73	2028	25,448,642	13,998,154	5,631,730	3,737,252	2,081,506
1973–74	2027	24,982,203	13,070,991	6,326,108	3,421,624	2,163,480
1974–75	2028	25,577,977	12,613,178	6,955,970	4,086,145	1,992,684
1975–76	2028	24,896,053	13,089,861	5,798,405	3,948,449	2,059,338
1976–77	2028	26,182,800	13,647,585	6,250,597	4,152,218	2,132,400
1977–78	2028	25,392,872	13,255,677	6,474,763	3,332,042	2,330,390
1978–79	2028	24,540,627	12,704,549	6,153,223	3,374,558	2,308,297
1979–80	2028	24,623,975	12,163,002	6,112,025	3,999,328	2,349,620
1980–81	2028	21,907,569	11,392,894	5,175,442	3,637,854	1,701,379
1981–82	2028	20,006,961	10,420,793	4,750,463	2,836,915	1,998,790
1982–83	2028	18,766,158	9,295,613	4,974,937	2,943,568	1,552,040
1983–84	2028	18,358,631	8,711,448	5,359,757	2,729,942	1,557,484
1984–85	2028	17,849,835	9,761,404	4,030,823	2,667,008	1,390,600
1985–86	2028	16,488,577	9,037,854	3,551,968	2,490,481	1,408,274
1986–87	2028	17,379,218	9,144,676	4,168,131	2,350,970	1,715,441
1987–88	2030	17,959,732	8,094,571	5,341,599	2,751,275	1,772,287
1988–89	2036	18,464,192	7,809,993	5,887,805	3,035,327	1,791,067
1989–90	2036	19,445,442	7,883,039	6,867,674	2,803,551	1,891,178
1990–91	2036	19,508,202	8,618,709	6,285,068	2,835,759	1,768,666
1991–92	2064*	20,487,273	9,989,160	5,809,787	2,993,352	1,694,974

		Total	FA Premier	Div. 1	Div. 2	Div. 3
1992–93	2028	20,657,327	9,759,809	5,874,017	3,483,073	1,540,428
1993–94	2028	21,683,381	10,644,551	6,487,104	2,972,702	1,579,024
1994–95	2028	21,856,020	11,213,168	6,044,293	3,037,752	1,560,807
1995–96	2036	21,844,416	10,469,107	6,566,349	2,843,652	1,965,308
1996–97	2036	22,783,163	10,804,762	6,931,539	3,195,223	1,851,639
1997–98	2036	24,692,608	11,092,106	8,330,018	3,503,264	1,767,220
1998–99	2036	25,435,542	11,620,326	7,543,369	4,169,697	2,102,150
1999–2000	2036	25,341,090	11,668,497	7,810,208	3,700,433	2,161,952
2000–01	2036	26,030,167	12,472,094	7,909,512	3,488,166	2,160,395
2001–02	2036	27,756,977	13,043,118	8,352,128	3,963,153	2,398,578
2002–03	2036	28,343,386	13,468,965	8,521,017	3,892,469	2,460,935
2003–04	2036	29,197,510	13,303,136	8,772,780	4,146,495	2,975,099

		Total	FA Premier	Championship	Championship 1	Championship 2
2004–05	2036	29,245,870	12,878,791	9,612,761	4,270,674	2,483,644
2005–06	2036	29,089,084	12,871,643	9,719,204	4,183,011	2,315,226
2006–07	2036	29,541,949	13,058,115	10,057,813	4,135,599	2,290,422
2007–08	2036	29,914,212	13,708,875	9,397,036	4,412,023	2,396,278
2008–09	2036	29,881,966	13,527,815	9,877,552	4,171,834	2,304,765

*Figures include matches played by Aldershot.
Football League official total for their three divisions in 2001–02 was 14,716,162.

ENGLISH LEAGUE ATTENDANCES 2008–09

FA BARCLAYCARD PREMIERSHIP ATTENDANCES

	Average Gate			Season 2008–09	
	2007–08	2008–09	+/–%	Highest	Lowest
Arsenal	60,070	60,040	–0.05	60,109	59,317
Aston Villa	40,029	39,812	–0.54	42,585	35,134
Blackburn Rovers	23,944	23,479	–1.94	28,389	17,606
Bolton Wanderers	20,901	22,486	+7.58	26,021	19,884
Chelsea	41,397	41,589	+0.46	43,417	40,290
Everton	36,955	35,667	–3.49	39,574	31,063
Fulham	23,774	24,344	+2.40	25,661	22,259
Hull City	18,025	24,816	+37.68	24,945	24,282
Liverpool	43,532	43,611	+0.18	44,424	41,169
Manchester City	42,126	42,899	+1.83	47,331	36,635
Manchester United	75,691	75,304	–0.51	75,569	73,917
Middlesbrough	26,708	28,429	+6.44	33,767	24,020
Newcastle United	51,321	48,750	–5.01	52,114	44,567
Portsmouth	19,914	19,830	–0.42	20,540	18,111
Stoke City	16,823	26,960	+60.26	27,500	25,287
Sunderland	43,344	40,168	–7.33	47,936	35,222
Tottenham Hotspur	35,967	35,929	–0.11	36,183	35,507
West Bromwich Albion	22,311	25,828	+15.76	26,344	24,741
West Ham United	34,601	33,701	–2.60	34,958	30,842
Wigan Athletic	19,046	18,350	–3.65	22,954	14,169

TOTAL ATTENDANCES: 13,527,815 (380 games)
Average 35,600 (–1.32%)
HIGHEST: 75,569 Manchester United v Liverpool
LOWEST: 14,169 Wigan Athletic v West Ham United
HIGHEST AVERAGE: 75,304 Manchester United
LOWEST AVERAGE: 18,350 Wigan Athletic

FOOTBALL LEAGUE: CHAMPIONSHIP ATTENDANCES

	Average Gate			Season 2008–09	
	2007–08	2008–09	+/–%	Highest	Lowest
Barnsley	11,425	13,189	+15.4	19,681	10,678
Birmingham City	26,181	19,090	–27.1	25,935	15,330
Blackpool	8,861	7,843	–11.5	9,643	6,648
Bristol City	16,276	16,816	+3.3	18,456	15,304
Burnley	12,365	13,082	+5.8	18,005	10,032
Cardiff City	13,939	18,044	+29.4	20,156	15,902
Charlton Athletic	23,191	20,894	–9.9	24,553	19,215
Coventry City	19,123	17,451	–8.7	22,637	14,621
Crystal Palace	16,031	15,220	–5.1	22,824	12,847
Derby County	32,432	29,440	–9.2	33,079	25,534
Doncaster Rovers	7,978	11,964	+50.0	14,823	9,534
Ipswich Town	21,935	20,961	–4.4	28,274	17,749
Norwich City	24,527	24,543	+0.1	25,487	23,225
Nottingham Forest	19,964	22,299	+11.7	29,140	17,568
Plymouth Argyle	13,000	11,533	–11.3	15,197	9,203
Preston North End	12,647	13,426	+6.2	21,273	10,558
Queens Park Rangers	13,959	14,090	+0.9	17,120	12,286
Reading	23,585	19,942	–15.4	24,011	16,514
Sheffield United	25,631	26,023	+1.5	30,786	23,045
Sheffield Wednesday	21,418	21,542	+0.6	30,658	14,792
Southampton	21,254	17,858	–16.0	27,228	13,257
Swansea City	13,520	15,195	+12.4	18,053	11,442
Watford	16,876	14,858	–12.0	16,386	13,193
Wolverhampton Wanderers	23,499	24,153	+2.8	28,252	21,326

TOTAL ATTENDANCES: 9,877,552 (552 games)
Average 17,894 (+5.1%)
HIGHEST: 33,079 Derby County v Wolverhampton Wanderers
LOWEST: 6,648 Blackpool v Charlton Athletic
HIGHEST AVERAGE: 29,440 Derby County
LOWEST AVERAGE: 7,843 Blackpool

Premiership and Football League attendance averages and highest crowd figures for 2008–09 are unofficial.

FOOTBALL LEAGUE: DIVISION 1 ATTENDANCES

	Average Gate			Season 2008–09	
	2007–08	2008–09	+/–%	Highest	Lowest
Brighton & Hove Albion	5,937	6,092	+2.6	8,618	5,035
Bristol Rovers	6,850	7,171	+4.7	10,293	5,870
Carlisle United	7,835	6,268	–20.0	12,148	4,223
Cheltenham Town	4,310	3,854	–10.6	5,726	2,845
Colchester United	5,509	5,084	–7.7	9,559	3,179
Crewe Alexandra	4,932	4,537	–8.0	7,138	3,432
Hartlepool United	4,507	3,835	–14.9	6,402	3,033
Hereford United	3,421	3,270	–4.4	6,120	2,033
Huddersfield Town	9,391	13,298	+41.6	20,928	9,294
Leeds United	26,543	23,815	–10.3	34,214	18,847
Leicester City	23,509	20,253	–13.9	30,542	16,378
Leyton Orient	5,210	4,692	–9.9	6,951	3,381
Millwall	8,691	8,940	+2.9	13,261	6,685
Milton Keynes Dons	9,456	10,551	+11.6	17,717	6,931
Northampton Town	5,409	5,200	–3.9	7,028	4,402
Oldham Athletic	5,326	5,636	+5.8	8,901	3,745
Peterborough United	5,995	7,599	+26.8	14,110	4,876
Scunthorpe United	6,434	4,998	–22.3	8,315	3,423
Southend United	8,173	7,850	–4.0	10,241	6,028
Stockport County	5,643	6,130	+8.6	10,273	4,790
Swindon Town	7,170	7,499	+4.6	13,001	6,002
Tranmere Rovers	6,504	5,820	–10.5	8,700	4,535
Walsall	5,620	4,572	–18.6	8,920	3,549
Yeovil Town	5,468	4,423	–19.1	6,580	3,275

TOTAL ATTENDANCES: 4,171,834 (552 games)
                                Average 7,558 (–5.4%)
HIGHEST: 34,214 Leeds United v Northampton Town
LOWEST: 2,033 Hereford United v Brighton & Hove Albion
HIGHEST AVERAGE: 23,815 Leeds United
LOWEST AVERAGE: 3,270 Hereford United

FOOTBALL LEAGUE: DIVISION 2 ATTENDANCES

	Average Gate			Season 2008–09	
	2007–08	2008–09	+/–%	Highest	Lowest
Accrington Stanley	1,634	1,414	–13.5	3,012	1,033
Aldershot Town	3,031	3,276	+8.1	5,023	2,090
Barnet	2,147	2,153	+0.3	3,133	1,332
AFC Bournemouth	5,504	4,931	–10.4	9,008	3,068
Bradford City	13,659	12,704	–7.0	14,038	11,908
Brentford	4,469	5,707	+27.7	10,642	3,733
Bury	2,601	3,342	+28.5	7,589	2,068
Chester City	2,479	1,972	–20.5	3,349	1,235
Chesterfield	4,103	3,449	–15.9	4,951	2,451
Dagenham & Redbridge	2,007	2,048	+2.0	4,791	1,302
Darlington	3,818	2,932	–23.2	3,868	2,180
Exeter City	3,705	4,939	+33.3	8,544	2,839
Gillingham	6,077	5,307	–12.7	8,360	4,029
Grimsby Town	4,115	4,475	+8.7	7,095	2,644
Lincoln City	4,078	3,940	–3.4	6,156	2,478
Luton Town	6,492	6,019	–7.3	7,149	5,248
Macclesfield Town	2,298	1,898	–17.4	2,556	1,182
Morecambe	2,812	2,153	–23.4	4,546	1,253
Notts County	4,732	4,446	–6.0	6,686	2,886
Port Vale	4,417	5,522	+25.0	7,273	4,090
Rochdale	3,057	3,222	+5.4	5,500	2,162
Rotherham United	4,201	3,587	–14.6	6,184	2,078
Shrewsbury Town	5,659	5,664	+0.1	7,162	4,134
Wycombe Wanderers	4,747	5,109	+7.6	9,625	3,713

TOTAL ATTENDANCES: 2,304,765 (552 games)
                                Average 4,175 (–3.8%)
HIGHEST: 14,038 Bradford City v Notts County
LOWEST: 1,033 Accrington Stanley v Luton Town
HIGHEST AVERAGE: 12,704 Bradford City
LOWEST AVERAGE: 1,414 Accrington Stanley

LEAGUE CUP FINALISTS 1961–2009

Played as a two-leg final until 1966. All subsequent finals at Wembley until 2000, then at Millennium Stadium, Cardiff.

Year	Winners	Runners-up	Score
1961	Aston Villa	Rotherham U	0-2, 3-0 (aet)
1962	Norwich C	Rochdale	3-0, 1-0
1963	Birmingham C	Aston Villa	3-1, 0-0
1964	Leicester C	Stoke C	1-1, 3-2
1965	Chelsea	Leicester C	3-2, 0-0
1966	WBA	West Ham U	1-2, 4-1
1967	QPR	WBA	3-2
1968	Leeds U	Arsenal	1-0
1969	Swindon T	Arsenal	3-1 (aet)
1970	Manchester C	WBA	2-1 (aet)
1971	Tottenham H	Aston Villa	2-0
1972	Stoke C	Chelsea	2-1
1973	Tottenham H	Norwich C	1-0
1974	Wolverhampton W	Manchester C	2-1
1975	Aston Villa	Norwich C	1-0
1976	Manchester C	Newcastle U	2-1
1977	Aston Villa	Everton	0-0, 1-1 (aet), 3-2 (aet)
1978	Nottingham F	Liverpool	0-0 (aet), 1-0
1979	Nottingham F	Southampton	3-2
1980	Wolverhampton W	Nottingham F	1-0
1981	Liverpool	West Ham U	1-1 (aet), 2-1

MILK CUP

Year	Winners	Runners-up	Score
1982	Liverpool	Tottenham H	3-1 (aet)
1983	Liverpool	Manchester U	2-1 (aet)
1984	Liverpool	Everton	0-0 (aet), 1-0
1985	Norwich C	Sunderland	1-0
1986	Oxford U	QPR	3-0

LITTLEWOODS CUP

Year	Winners	Runners-up	Score
1987	Arsenal	Liverpool	2-1
1988	Luton T	Arsenal	3-2
1989	Nottingham F	Luton T	3-1
1990	Nottingham F	Oldham Ath	1-0

RUMBELOWS LEAGUE CUP

Year	Winners	Runners-up	Score
1991	Sheffield W	Manchester U	1-0
1992	Manchester U	Nottingham F	1-0

COCA-COLA CUP

Year	Winners	Runners-up	Score
1993	Arsenal	Sheffield W	2-1
1994	Aston Villa	Manchester U	3-1
1995	Liverpool	Bolton W	2-1
1996	Aston Villa	Leeds U	3-0
1997	Leicester C	Middlesbrough	1-1 (aet), 1-0 (aet)
1998	Chelsea	Middlesbrough	2-0 (aet)

WORTHINGTON CUP

Year	Winners	Runners-up	Score
1999	Tottenham H	Leicester C	1-0
2000	Leicester C	Tranmere R	2-1
2001	Liverpool	Birmingham C	1-1 (aet)
Liverpool won 5-4 on penalties			
2002	Blackburn R	Tottenham H	2-1
2003	Liverpool	Manchester U	2-0

CARLING CUP

Year	Winners	Runners-up	Score
2004	Middlesbrough	Bolton W	2-1
2005	Chelsea	Liverpool	3-2 (aet)
2006	Manchester U	Wigan Ath	4-0
2007	Chelsea	Arsenal	2-1
2008	Tottenham H	Chelsea	2-1 (aet)
2009	Manchester U	Tottenham H	0-0 (aet)

Manchester U won 4-1 on penalties

LEAGUE CUP WINS
Liverpool 7, Aston Villa 5, Chelsea 4, Nottingham F 4, Tottenham H 4, Leicester C 3, Manchester U 3, Arsenal 2, Manchester C 2, Norwich C 2, Wolverhampton W 2, Birmingham C 1, Blackburn R 1, Leeds U 1, Luton T 1, Middlesbrough 1, Oxford U 1, QPR 1, Sheffield W 1, Stoke C 1, Swindon T 1, WBA 1.

APPEARANCES IN FINALS
Liverpool 10, Aston Villa 7, Manchester U 7, Tottenham H 7, Arsenal 6, Chelsea 6, Nottingham F 6, Leicester C 5, Norwich C 4, Manchester C 3, Middlesbrough 3, WBA 3, Birmingham C 2, Bolton W 2, Everton 2, Leeds U 2, Luton T 2, QPR 2, Sheffield W 2, Stoke C 2, West Ham U 2, Wolverhampton W 2, Blackburn R 1, Newcastle U 1, Oldham Ath 1, Oxford U 1, Rochdale 1, Rotherham U 1, Southampton 1, Sunderland 1, Swindon T 1, Tranmere R 1, Wigan Ath 1.

APPEARANCES IN SEMI-FINALS
Arsenal 13, Liverpool 13, Tottenham H 13, Aston Villa 12, Manchester U 11, Chelsea 10, West Ham U 7, Nottingham F 6, Blackburn R 5, Leeds U 5, Leicester C 5, Manchester C 5, Middlesbrough 5, Norwich C 5, Birmingham C 4, Bolton W 4, Burnley 4, Everton 4, Sheffield W 4, WBA 4, Crystal Palace 3, Ipswich T 3, QPR 3, Sunderland 3, Swindon T 3, Wolverhampton W 3, Bristol C 2, Coventry C 2, Derby Co 2, Luton T 2, Oxford U 2, Plymouth Arg 2, Southampton 2, Stoke C 2, Tranmere R 2, Watford 2, Wimbledon 2, Blackpool 1, Bury 1, Cardiff C 1, Carlisle U 1, Chester C 1, Huddersfield T 1, Newcastle U 1, Oldham Ath 1, Peterborough U 1, Rochdale 1, Rotherham U 1, Sheffield U 1, Shrewsbury T 1, Stockport Co 1, Walsall 1, Wigan Ath 1, Wycombe W 1.

CARLING CUP 2008–09

■ Denotes player sent off.

FIRST ROUND

Tuesday, 12 August 2008

Bournemouth (1) 1 *(Osei-Kuffour 28)*
Cardiff C (2) 2 *(Parry 7, 12)*   3399
Bournemouth: Jalal; Cummings, Ward, Cooper, Pearce, Guyett, Igoe, Anderton, Bradbury (Sappleton), Osei-Kuffour (McQuoid), Bartley (Pettefer).
Cardiff C: Heaton; McNaughton, Kennedy, Rae, Johnson R, Loovens, Whittingham (McCormack), McPhail, Parry (Comminges), Bothroyd (Thompson), Ledley.

Brighton & HA (4) 4 *(Virgo 2, 35, Forster 28, Richards 43)*
Barnet (0) 0   2571
Brighton & HA: Kuipers; Whing (Fraser), Richards, Thomson, Elphick, Hawkins, Cox, Virgo, Murray■, Forster (Robinson), McLeod (Livermore).
Barnet: Beckwith; Devera, Gillet■, Porter, Yakubu, Carew, Adomah, Bishop, Birchall (St Aimie), Medley (Hart), Tabiri (Leary).

Bristol C (0) 2 *(Carey 53, Brooker 85)*
Peterborough U (1) 1 *(Boyd 17)*   5684
Bristol C: Weale; Ribeiro (Wilson B), McAllister, Skuse, Carey, Fontaine, Sproule (Williams), Johnson, Brooker, Maynard (Trundle), McIndoe.
Peterborough U: Lewis; Martin, Williams, Lee, Morgan, Westwood, Torres (Hatch), Keates, Mackail-Smith, McLean (Rendell), Boyd.

Bury (0) 0
Burnley (1) 2 *(Paterson 40, 90)*   4276
Bury: Brown; Scott, Buchanan, Dawson (Baker), Sodje, Futcher, Bennett, Barry-Murphy, Hurst (Morrell), Bishop, Jones.
Burnley: Jensen; Jordan, Kalvenes (Duff), McCann, Alexander, Caldwell, Elliott, Gudjonsson (McDonald), Blake (Mahon), Paterson, Eagles.

Charlton Ath (0) 0
Yeovil T (1) 1 *(Warne 28)*   6239
Charlton Ath: Elliot; Moutaouakil, Youga, Holland, Fortune (Semedo), Basey, Wagstaff (Sam), Shelvey, Varney L, Bouazza, Thomas (Dickson).
Yeovil T: Wagenaar; Peltier, Smith, Murtagh, Skiverton, Forbes, Downes, Way, Tomlin (Alcock), Warne (Owusu), Schofield.

Chester C (1) 2 *(Lowe 15, 75 (pen))*
Leeds U (5) 5 *(Beckford 3, 25, 35, Snodgrass 10, Robinson 31)*   3644
Chester C: Danby; Vaughan J, Wilson, Barry, Linwood, Butler (Kelly), Partridge (Harris), Lowe, Mozika, Mannix, Ellison.
Leeds U: Ankergren; Richardson, Sheehan, Howson (Douglas), Huntington, Rui Marques, Delph, Snodgrass, Beckford (Showunmi), Becchio, Robinson (Johnson).

Crewe Alex (2) 2 *(O'Connor 14 (pen), Elding 36 (pen))*
Barnsley (0) 0   2492
Crewe Alex: Collis; Woodards, McCready, Bailey, Jones, Baudet, Moore, O'Connor, Elding, Pope, Grant (Schumacher).
Barnsley: Steele; Souza, Kozluk (Mostto), Foster, Moore, Howard, Hassell (Macken), Leon, Hume, Rigters (Odejayi), Devaney.

Crystal Palace (1) 2 *(Carle 45, Oster 49)*
Hereford U (1) 1 *(Ashikodi 41)*   3094
Crystal Palace: Flahavan; Butterfield, Hill, Carle, McCarthy, Fonte J, Ifil (Fletcher), Derry, Moses (Djilali), Andrew, Oster (Scannell).
Hereford U: Randolph; Rose, Threlfall, Diagouraga, Beckwith, Oji, Johnson (Guinan), Smith, Ashikodi, Done (Hudson-Odoi), Taylor (Easton).

Dagenham & R (0) 1 *(Taiwo 68)*
Reading (1) 2 *(Henry 26, Hunt N 89)*   2360
Dagenham & R: Roberts; Okuonghae, Griffiths, Arber, Uddin, Taiwo, Saunders, Green, Benson, Strevens, Gain.
Reading: Hahnemann; Kelly, Hunt S, Ingimarsson, Pearce, Harper, Henry, Cisse, Hunt N, Long, Convey.

Derby Co (0) 3 *(Ellington 83, 100, 105)*
Lincoln C (0) 1 *(Wright 48)*   10,091
Derby Co: Carroll; Mears, McEveley, Green, Albrechtsen, Davis, Davies (Pereplotkins), Savage (Kazmierczak), Hulse (Villa), Ellington, Commons.
Lincoln C: Burch; Green, Brown A, Kovacs, Beevers, Kerr, John-Lewis (Frecklington), Oakes (Clarke), Wright, Gall, N'Guessan (King).
aet.

Exeter C (0) 1 *(Moxey 85)*
Southampton (1) 3 *(Holmes 29, McGoldrick 77, 90 (pen))*   6471
Exeter C: Jones; Tully, Friend, Edwards (Moxey), Seaborne, Taylor, Gill, Stewart, Stansfield (Logan), McAllister (Basham), Harley.
Southampton: Bialkowski; James, Surman, Thomson (John), Perry, Wotton, Holmes, Schneiderlin, Lallana, McGoldrick, Gillett.

Gillingham (0) 0
Colchester U (1) 1 *(Heath 11)*   2566
Gillingham: Julian; Fuller, Nutter, Crofts, Richards, King, Southall (Berry), Bentley, Jackson, McCammon (Mulligan), Miller (Oli).
Colchester U: Gerken; White, Ifil, Hammond, Heath, Reid, Yeates (Elito), Izzet, Platt, Vernon, Wordsworth.

Grimsby T (1) 2 *(Hunt 20, Chorley 54 (og))*
Tranmere R (0) 0   1858
Grimsby T: Barnes; Stockdale, Newey, Hunt, Heywood, Hope, Till, Heslop (Clarke), Taylor (North), Butler (Bore), Llewellyn.
Tranmere R: Achterberg; Antwi (Waterfall), Andy Taylor, O'Callaghan, Chorley, Kay, Jennings, Barnett (Greenacre), Moore (Gornell), Sonko, Curran.

Hartlepool U (0) 3 *(Porter 51, Foley 58, Brown 76)*
Scunthorpe U (0) 0   2076
Hartlepool U: Lee-Barrett; Sweeney, Humphreys, Liddle, Nelson, Collins, Foley, Power (Boland), Porter (Barker), Brown (Mackay), Robson.
Scunthorpe U: Lillis; Byrne, Williams, Morris (Sparrow), Milne (Wright), Iriekpen, Thompson, McCann, Forte (May), Hooper, Hurst.

Huddersfield T (0) 4 *(Worthington 48, Roberts 62, 80, Williams 75)*
Bradford C (0) 0   8932
Huddersfield T: Glennon; Holdsworth, Williams, Goodwin (Collins), Butler, Lucketti, Worthington, Flynn, Cadamarteri, Beckett (Parker), Roberts (Kamara).
Bradford C: Evans; Arnison, Heckingbottom, Bullock, Lee, Clarke M, Daley, McLaren, Conlon (Moncur), Boulding M (Thorne), Nix (Taylforth).

Ipswich T (3) 4 *(Haynes 20, 44, Miller 22, Lee 48)*
Leyton Orient (0) 1 *(Boyd 49)*   10,477
Ipswich T: Supple; Casement, Balkestein, Miller, Bruce, Naylor, Walters (Lisbie), Trotter (Garvan), Lee, Haynes, Quinn (Norris).
Leyton Orient: Morris; Purches, Granville (Palmer), Chambers, Mkandawire (Thelwell), Saah, Melligan, Terry (Thornton), Boyd, Jarvis, Demetriou.

Leicester C (1) 1 *(Howard 36)*
Stockport Co (0) 0   7386
Leicester C: Martin; Gilbert, Mattock, Kishishev (King A), Morrison, Hobbs, Gradel, Wesolowski, Howard, Campbell (Dickov), Adams (Porter).
Stockport Co: fon Williams; McSweeney, McNulty, Gleeson, Owen, McNeil■, Turnbull (Blizzard), Dicker (Mullins), Rowe T, Baker (Thompson P), Pilkington A.

Luton T (1) 2 *(Jarvis 16, Plummer 77)*
Plymouth Arg (0) 0   2682
Luton T: Brill; Gnakpa, Davis (Keane), Nicholls, Spillane, Pilkington, Hall, Jarvis, Martin (Watson), Parkin, Emanuel (Plummer).
Plymouth Arg: Stack; Duguid, Barker, Walton, Timar, Cathcart, Folly (Summerfield), Paterson (Mackie), MacLean, Easter (Fallon), Puncheon.

Macclesfield T (1) 2 *(Brisley 25, Gritton 59)*
Blackpool (0) 0   1631
Macclesfield T: Brain; Deen, Brisley, Hessey, Walker, Dunfield∎, Tolley, Morgan, Gritton (Green), Evans (Bell), Thomas (Reid I).
Blackpool: Gilks; Coid (Vaughan), Martin, Hammill, Edwards, Evatt, Wright (Rehman), Southern∎, Burgess, Taylor-Fletcher, Aluko (Green).

Millwall (0) 0
Northampton T (1) 1 *(Crowe 16)*   3525
Millwall: Forde; Frampton, Craig, Laird, Whitbread, Abdou, Hackett, Fuseini (Brkovic), Alexander (Kandol), Grabban, Martin.
Northampton T: Bunn; Crowe, Jackman, Hughes, Gyepes, Doig, Davis, Guttridge (Coke), Constantine (Holt), Akinfenwa, Gilligan (Osman).

Milton Keynes D (1) 1 *(Baldock 34)*
Norwich C (0) 0   6261
Milton Keynes D: Gueret; Howell, Lewington, Andrews, Stirling, Swailes (O'Hanlon), Wright (Regan), Leven, Baldock, Wilbraham, Johnson (Sturm).
Norwich C: Marshall; Otsemobor, Drury, Shackell, Omozusi, Clingan, Russell, Fotheringham, Koroma (Cureton), Lupoli (Pattison), Hoolahan (Croft).

Notts Co (0) 1 *(Weston 106)*
Doncaster R (0) 0   3272
Notts Co: Pilkington; Beardsley, Mayo, MacKenzie, Edwards, Tann, Fairclough (Hamshaw), Smith, Facey (Canham), Weir-Daley (Weston), Butcher.
Doncaster R: Sullivan; Chambers, Roberts, Hird, Van Nieuwstadt, Wilson, Wellens (Woods M), Hayter (Elliott), Heffernan, Guy, Spicer (Coppinger).
aet.

Preston NE (1) 2 *(Mellor 37, 90)*
Chesterfield (0) 0   5150
Preston NE: Lonergan; Hart, Davidson, Carter, St Ledger-Hall, Jones, McKenna, Nicholson, Mellor, Hawley, Wallace.
Chesterfield: Lee; Picken, Goodall, Kerry (Niven), Page, Austin, Lowry, Harsley, Lester, Ward, Robertson (Currie).

Rochdale (0) 0
Oldham Ath (0) 0   5786
Rochdale: Russell; Ramsden, Kennedy, Keltie, Stanton, McArdle, Higginbotham (Toner), Jones G, Dagnall, Shaw (Le Fondre), Rundle (Thorpe).
Oldham Ath: Crossley; Eardley, O'Grady (Alessandra), Whitaker, Hazell, Gregan, Smalley (Stam), Allott (Liddell), Hughes, Davies∎, Taylor.
aet; Oldham Ath won 4-1 on penalties.

Sheffield W (1) 2 *(Esajas 14, 117)*
Rotherham U (1) 2 *(Rhodes 15, Reid 119)*   16,298
Sheffield W: Grant; Gilbert, Spurr, O'Connor, Beevers, Wood, Watson (Boden L), Smith (Lekaj), Clarke, Burton (McAllister), Esajas.
Rotherham U: Warrington; Lynch, Joseph∎, Harrison, Sharps, Fenton (Todd), Mills, Hudson, Taylor R (Yates), Rhodes (Green), Reid.
aet; Rotherham U won 5-3 on penalties.

Shrewsbury T (0) 0
Carlisle U (1) 1 *(Murphy 41)*   3337
Shrewsbury T: Daniels; Herd, Tierney, Moss (Humphrey), Jackson, Coughlan (Langmead), Cansdell-Sherriff, Davies, Walker (Hibbert), Holt, McIntyre.
Carlisle U: Williams; Raven, Horwood, Thirlwell, Livesey, Murphy, Dobie (Bridges), Bridge-Wilkinson, Graham (Joyce), Carlton (Madine), Hackney.

Southend U (0) 0
Cheltenham T (0) 1 *(Gill B 115)*   2998
Southend U: Mildenhall; Francis, Harding, Grant (Sankofa), Clarke, Barrett, Moussa, Betsy, Furlong (Revell), Barnard, Scannell (Ademeno).
Cheltenham T: Higgs; Gill J, Wright, Bird, Townsend, Duff (Gallinagh), Lindegaard (Gill B), Russell, Connor (Ledgister), Vincent, Armstrong.
aet.

Swansea C (1) 2 *(MacDonald 31, 69)*
Brentford (0) 0   5366
Swansea C: De Vries; Serran, Bessone (Rangel), Tudur-Jones, Tate, Lawrence, Gomez, MacDonald, Brandy (Pratley), Scotland (Bauza), Orlandi.
Brentford: Hamer; Newton, Pead, O'Connor, Bennett, Wilson, Poole, Bean∎, Marvin Williams, Elder (Ademola), Johnson.

Swindon T (2) 2 *(Cox 34, Paynter 41)*
QPR (1) 3 *(Balanta 32, Blackstock 46, Delaney 54)* 7230
Swindon T: Brezovan; Smith J, Casal, Nalis, Morrison, Aljofree, McGovern (Peacock), Timlin (Easton), Paynter, Cox, McNamee.
QPR: Camp; Connolly, Delaney, Parejo, Stewart, Gorkss, Ledesma (Alberti), Leigertwood, Balanta, Blackstock (Di Carmine), Cook.

Walsall (1) 1 *(Ricketts 11)*
Darlington (1) 2 *(Kennedy 31, Clarke B 67)*   2702
Walsall: Ince; Palmer, Sansara (Deeney), Taundry, Gerrard, Roberts (Smith), Nicholls, Hughes, Ricketts∎, Ibehre, Zaaboub (Reich).
Darlington: Brown; Purdie, Austin, Ravenhill (Hulbert), Miller, Foster, Poole, Kennedy, Clarke B (Main), Proudlock (Blundell), Griffin.

Watford (0) 1 *(Hoskins 88)*
Bristol R (0) 0   5574
Watford: Loach; Doyley, Sadler, Francis (Bangura), Bromby, Mariappa, Ainsworth (Young), Jenkins, Robinson, Hoskins, Harley (Gibson).
Bristol R: Phillips; Pipe, Lescott, Campbell, Anthony, Elliott, Lines, Disley, Lambert, Duffy (Williams), Hughes (Rigg).

Wolverhampton W (0) 3 *(Iwelumo 73, 102, Davies 106)*
Accrington S (1) 2 *(Mullin P 40, Craney 104)*   9424
Wolverhampton W: Hennessey; Foley, Elokobi, Edwards D, Collins, Stearman, Gray (Davies), Henry, Iwelumo, Vokes (Ebanks-Blake), Daniel Jones (Keogh).
Accrington S: Arthur; Cavanagh, King, Richardson, Williams∎, Edwards, Mullin J (Murphy), Craney, Clarke (Ryan), Mullin P, Grant (Miles).
aet.

Wednesday, 13 August 2008

Coventry C (1) 3 *(Morrison 31, Simpson 58, 65)*
Aldershot T (1) 1 *(Morgan 37)*   9293
Coventry C: Ireland; Wright, Fox, Gunnarsson (Doyle), Turner, Dann, Simpson (McKenzie), Beuzelin, Morrison, Eastwood, Mifsud.
Aldershot T: Bull; Starosta, Howell, Harding, Blackburn, Charles, Soares (Mendes), Donnelly (Chalmers), Grant, Morgan (Hylton), Hudson.

Nottingham F (1) 4 *(Cohen 14, Earnshaw 62, 89,*
Newbold 81)
Morecambe (0) 0   4030
Nottingham F: Smith; Chambers (Thornhill), Heath, Perch (Newbold), Morgan, Breckin, Moussi, Cohen, Earnshaw, Martin, Davies (McCleary).
Morecambe: Roche; Parrish, Adams, Carr, Artell, Bentley, Wainwright (Blinkhorn), Hunter, Howe (O'Carroll), Curtis, McLachlan (Drummond).

Sheffield U (1) 3 *(Hendrie 41, Quinn S 71, Webber 90 (pen))*
Port Vale (0) 1 *(Rodgers 53)*   7694
Sheffield U: Bennett; Geary, Armstrong, Spring, Ehiogu, Kilgallon, Cotterill, Hendrie (Naughton), Henderson, Webber, Quinn S.

Port Vale: Anyon; Stockley, Collins, Griffith, McCombe, Slater (Tudor), Taylor (Rodgers), Davidson, Richards, Perry, Dodds (Richman).

Wycombe W (0) 0

Birmingham C (1) 4 *(Nafti 14, O'Connor 64, Jerome 73, Owusu-Abeyie 86)*   2735

Wycombe W: Young; Crooks (Ashton), Woodman, Doherty (Rice), Johnson, Antwi, Spence, Grant, Zebroski, McGleish (Vieira), Mousinho.
Birmingham C: Doyle; Parnaby, Murphy (Queudrue), Carsley, Martin Taylor, Ridgewell, Larsson, Nafti, Phillips (Jerome), O'Connor, McSheffrey (Owusu-Abeyie).

SECOND ROUND

Tuesday, 26 August 2008

Bolton W (0) 1 *(Nolan 82)*

Northampton T (2) 2 *(Akinfenwa 22 (pen), 28)*   7136

Bolton W: Jaaskalainen; Steinsson, Samuel (Nolan), McCann (O'Brien A), Shittu, Cahill■, O'Brien J, Muamba, Helguson, Mustapha (Davies K), Gardner.
Northampton T: Bunn; Crowe, Jackman, Gilligan (Dolman), Hughes, Doig, Little, Osman, Coke (Taylor), Akinfenwa (Henderson), Holt.

Burnley (1) 3 *(McCann 12, Paterson 63, 79)*

Oldham Ath (0) 0   5528

Burnley: Jensen; Alexander, Kalvenes, Duff (Blake), Caldwell, Carlisle, Elliott, McCann (Mahon), Eagles, Paterson, McDonald (Gudjonsson).
Oldham Ath: Fleming; Eardley, Lomax, Maher (Lee), Hazell, Stam, Taylor, Allott, Smalley (Alessandra), O'Grady (Hughes), Whitaker.

Cardiff C (1) 2 *(McCormack 45 (pen), Whittingham)*

Milton Keynes D (0) 1 *(O'Hanlon 75)*   6334

Cardiff C: Heaton; Blake (Parry), Capaldi (Comminges), Scimeca (Morris), Johnson R, Purse, Whittingham, McPhail, Johnson E, McCormack, Ledley.
Milton Keynes D: Gueret; Stirling (O'Hanlon), Lewington (King), Mitchell, Diallo, Cummings, Navarro, Chicksen, Baldock, Dobson, Johnson.

Cheltenham T (0) 2 *(Vincent 57, Russell 90)*

Stoke C (0) 3 *(Whelan 51, Cresswell 54, Parkin 78)*   3600

Cheltenham T: Higgs; Gill J, Wright, Gill B (Caines), Townsend, Duff (Gallinagh), Lindegaard, Russell, Connor, Vincent (Ledgister), Armstrong.
Stoke C: Simonsen; Wilkinson (Shotton), Dickinson (Phillips D), Whelan, Buxton, Shawcross, Cresswell, Diao (Matteo), Pericard, Parkin, Pugh.

Coventry C (1) 2 *(Morrison 45, Dann 90)*

Newcastle U (2) 3 *(Dann 21 (og), Milner 38, Owen 97)*   19,249

Coventry C: Marshall; Hall, Fox, Gunnarsson, Ward, Dann, Beuzelin (Doyle), Mifsud, Morrison, McKenzie (Gray), Tabb (Simpson).
Newcastle U: Given; Beye, Jose Enrique, Butt, Coloccini, Bassong, Milner, Geremi (Owen) Guthrie, Gutierrez, N'Zogbia.
aet.

Crewe Alex (1) 2 *(Elding 24, Moore 76)*

Bristol C (0) 1 *(Wilson B 79)*   3227

Crewe Alex: Collis; Woodards, Bailey, O'Connor, O'Donnell, Baudet, Moore, Rix (Schumacher), Pope, Elding (Carrington), Grant (Donaldson 87).
Bristol C: Weale; Orr, McAllister (Webster), Skuse (Trundle), Carey, Fontaine, Wilson B, Johnson, Adebola (Brooker), Maynard, McIndoe.

Hartlepool U (0) 3 *(Porter 61, Foley 102, Barker 105)*

WBA (0) 1 *(Koren 90)*   3387

Hartlepool U: Lee-Barrett; Sweeney, Humphreys, Liddle, Nelson, Collins, McCunnie, Jones, Porter (Barker), Brown (Foley), Monkhouse (Robson).
WBA: Kiely; Hoefkens, Cech, Koren (Pele), Barnett, Meite, Borja Valero, Brunt (MacDonald), Bednar (Beattie), Moore, Greening.
aet.

Ipswich T (1) 2 *(Counago 28, Lisbie 56)*

Colchester U (0) 1 *(Gillespie 87)*   17,084

Ipswich T: Wright R; Casement, Thatcher, Campo (Miller), McAuley, Naylor, Walters, Trotter, Lisbie (Haynes), Counago, Quinn.
Colchester U: Gerken; Reid, Ifil, Hammond (Izzet), Coyne, Heath, Yeates, Jackson, Vernon, Platt (Gillespie), Wordsworth (Perkins).

Leeds U (2) 4 *(Douglas 11, Beckford 32, Becchio 52, Showunmi 76)*

Crystal Palace (0) 0   10,765

Leeds U: Lucas; Richardson, White (Johnson), Kilkenny, Telfer, Michalik, Douglas, Hughes, Beckford (Howson), Becchio (Showunmi), Delph.
Crystal Palace: Flahavan; Ertl, Hill, Watson (Fletcher), McCarthy, Lawrence, Soares, Djilali, Andrew, Moses (Ifill), Carle (Hills).

Middlesbrough (3) 5 *(Mido 11, Digard 23, Aliadiere 32, Emnes 47, Johnson A 66)*

Yeovil T (1) 1 *(Tomlin 45)*   15,651

Middlesbrough: Turnbull; Hoyte, Grounds, Digard, Pogatetz (Williams), Riggott, Aliadiere (O'Neil), Shawky (Walker), Mido, Emnes, Johnson A.
Yeovil T: Wagenaar; Peltier (Alcock), Jones, Murtagh, Skiverton, Forbes, Roberts, Way (Bircham), Tomlin, Warne (McCollin), Dayton.

Preston NE (0) 0

Derby Co (1) 1 *(Green 40)*   8037

Preston NE: Lonergan; Hart, Hill, Carter (Chaplow), St Ledger-Hall, Jones, Sedgwick (Whaley), McKenna, Mellor, Hawley, Wallace.
Derby Co: Carroll; Connolly, Stewart, Green, Albrechtsen, Leacock, Kazmierczak (Mears), Addison, Hulse (Davies), Villa, Commons.

QPR (0) 4 *(Stewart 48, Ledesma 56, 63, 85)*

Carlisle U (0) 0   8021

QPR: Cerny; Connolly, Delaney (Gorkss), Mahon (Bolder), Stewart, Ramage, Ledesma, Rowlands, Di Carmine (Balanta), Parejo, Cook.
Carlisle U: Williams; Raven, Horwood, Thirlwell, Livesey, Murphy, Taylor C, Bridge-Wilkinson, Bridges (Smith G), Madine, Hackney (Smith J).

Reading (2) 5 *(Hunt N 11, Hunt S 15, Pearce 54, Karacan 55, Henry 75)*

Luton T (0) 1 *(Charles 80)*   7498

Reading: Federici; Kelly, Golbourne, Pearce, Duberry (Ingimarsson), Harper (Sigurdsson), Henry, Karacan, Hunt N, Long (Mooney), Hunt S.
Luton T: Logan; Gnakpa, Davis (Jarvis), Nicholls, Pilkington, Keane, Plummer, Watson, Martin (Hall), Parkin (Charles), Emanuel.

Rotherham U (0) 0

Wolverhampton W (0) 0   5404

Rotherham U: Warrington; Lynch, Nicholas, Harrison, Sharps, Fenton, Cummins (Mills), Hudson, Broughton (Taylor R), Rhodes (Burchill), Reid.
Wolverhampton W: Ikeme; Foley, Gray (Elliott), Edwards D (David Jones), Collins, Stearman, Kightly, Henry, Keogh (Iwelumo), Ward S, Ward D.
aet; Rotherham U won 4-3 on penalties.

Southampton (1) 2 *(Holmes 17, Lallana 86)*

Birmingham C (0) 0   11,331

Southampton: Bialkowski; James, Surman, Wotton, Thomas, Cork, Gillett (Mills), Schneiderlin (John), Lallana, McGoldrick, Holmes.
Birmingham C: Doyle; Parnaby, Murphy, Carsley, Kelly, Ridgewell, Agustien, O'Connor (Phillips), Bent, McSheffrey (Mutch), Owusu-Abeyie.

Swansea C (0) 2 *(Pintado 63, Gomez 105 (pen))*
Hull C (1) 1 *(Windass 11)*   8622
Swansea C: De Vries; Serran, Painter, Tudur-Jones, Monk, Collins (Rangel), Orlandi, MacDonald, Gomez, Bauza (Brandy), Allen (Pintado).
Hull C: Duke; Brown, Cooper (Turner), Hughes, Mendy, Doyle, France, Barmby (Featherstone), Folan, Windass (King), Halmosi.
aet.

Watford (1) 2 *(Francis 37, O'Toole 116)*
Darlington (0) 1 *(Blundell 90)*   5236
Watford: Loach; Doyley, Sadler, Jenkins, Bromby, Mariappa, Ainsworth, Francis (Bangura), Priskin (Henderson), Hoskins (O'Toole), Young.
Darlington: Brown; Austin, Valentine (Purdie), Ravenhill, Foster, Miller, Hulbert (Griffin), Kennedy, Blundell, Clarke B, Burgmeier (Poole).
aet.

Wigan Ath (1) 4 *(Camara 32, 62, Zaki 60, Kupisz 90)*
Notts Co (0) 0   4100
Wigan Ath: Nash; Montrose, Figueroa, Brown, Boyce, Bramble, Valencia (Kupisz), De Ridder, Heskey (Zaki), Camara, Kilbane (Bouaouzari).
Notts Co: Hoult; Beardsley, Mayo, Smith, Tann, Edwards, Fairclough, MacKenzie (Hamshaw), Facey (Canham), Weir-Daley (Weston), Butcher.

Wednesday, 27 August 2008

Blackburn R (3) 4 *(Villanueva 18, Derbyshire 32, 55, Emerton 39)*
Grimsby T (1) 1 *(Newey 7)*   8379
Blackburn R: Brown; Simpson, Treacy, Mokoena, Nelsen (Judge), Khizanishvili, Emerton (Gallagher), Tugay, Derbyshire, Villanueva, Pedersen (Marshall).
Grimsby T: Barnes; Bennett, Newey, Hunt, Heywood, Hegarty, Till (Taylor), Clarke, Jarman (Butler), Heslop, Boshell.

Fulham (1) 3 *(Gera 31, Bullard 83, Murphy 90)*
Leicester C (0) 2 *(Dickov 46, King A 48)*   7584
Fulham: Schwarzer; Stoor, Kallio, Murphy, Hughes, Hangeland, Davies, Bullard, Gera, Zamora, Seol (Nevland).
Leicester C: Martin; Gilbert, Powell, King A, Morrison, Tunchev, Dickov (Campbell), Wesolowski, Howard, Fryatt (Gradel), Dyer.

Huddersfield T (1) 1 *(Flynn 34)*
Sheffield U (0) 2 *(Henderson 82, Naughton 83)*   15,189
Huddersfield T: Glennon; Holdsworth, Williams (Kamara), Clarke N, Lucketti, Flynn, Roberts, Worthington (Jevons), Cadamarteri, Beckett (Goodwin), Parker.
Sheffield U: Bennett; Geary (Sharp), Jihai, Spring, Morgan, Kilgallon, Carney (Naughton), Tonge, Henderson, Stead (Webber), Cotterill.

Nottingham F (0) 1 *(Earnshaw 60)*
Sunderland (0) 2 *(Bardsley 86, Healy 93)*   9198
Nottingham F: Smith; Chambers, Bennett, Perch, Morgan, Breckin, Moussi (Sinclair), Thornhill (Cole), Earnshaw, Cohen, McCleary (Tyson).
Sunderland: Gordon; Chimbonda, Bardsley, Whitehead (Leadbitter), Nosworthy, Collins, Malbranque (Miller), Reid, Murphy (Healy), Diouf, Cisse.
aet.

West Ham U (0) 4 *(Bowyer 74, Cole 100, Hines 105, Reid 117)*
Macclesfield T (1) 1 *(Evans 5)*   10,055
West Ham U: Green; Behrami (Hines), McCartney (Reid), Davenport, Upson, Mullins, Faubert, Bowyer, Sears (Cole), Ashton, Boa Morte.
Macclesfield T: Brain; Reid I■, Brisley, Hessey, Walker, Tolley, Deen, Bell, Evans (Rooney), Green (Hadfield), Thomas (Yeo).
aet.

THIRD ROUND

Tuesday, 23 September 2008

Arsenal (3) 6 *(Bendtner 31, 42, Vela 44, 50, 87, Wilshere 57)*
Sheffield U (0) 0   56,632
Arsenal: Fabianski; Hoyte, Gibbs, Merida (Coquelin), Djourou, Song-Billong (Lansbury), Randall, Ramsey, Vela, Bendtner (Simpson), Wilshere.
Sheffield U: Kenny; Halford, Naysmith, Speed (Hendrie), Morgan, Kilgallon, Cotterill (Naughton), Montgomery, Beattie J (Robertson), Webber, Quinn S.

Burnley (0) 1 *(Rodriguez 88)*
Fulham (0) 0   7119
Burnley: Jensen; Anderson (Duff), Jordan, McCann, Caldwell, Carlisle, Alexander, Gudjonsson, Blake (Eagles), Paterson (Rodriguez), Elliott.
Fulham: Zuberbuhler; Baird, Konchesky, Teimourian, Stoor, Andreasen, Seol (Milsom), Dempsey, Gera (Pantsil), Johnson (Nevland), Kallio.

Leeds U (1) 3 *(Snodgrass 14, Showunmi 58, Robinson 90)*
Hartlepool U (2) 2 *(Monkhouse 2, Porter 33)*   14,599
Leeds U: Ankergren; Hughes, Parker, Kilkenny, Huntington, Michalik, Prutton (Delph), Howson, Snodgrass (Beckford), Showunmi (Becchio), Robinson.
Hartlepool U: Lee-Barrett; McCunnie, Humphreys, Liddle, Nelson, Collins, Sweeney (Barker), Jones, Porter, Brown (Mackay), Monkhouse (Robson).

Liverpool (1) 2 *(Agger 15, Lucas 58)*
Crewe Alex (1) 1 *(O'Connor 25)*   28,591
Liverpool: Cavallieri; Degen (Carragher), Insua, Plessis, Agger, Hyypia, Pennant, Lucas, Babel, N'Gog (Torres), El Zhar (Keane).
Crewe Alex: Collis; Woodards, Jones, Bailey, O'Donnell, Baudet, Moore, O'Connor, Pope (Elding), Zola (Miller), Carrington (Grant).

Manchester U (1) 3 *(Ronaldo 25, Giggs 79, Nani 90)*
Middlesbrough (0) 1 *(Johnson A 56)*   53,729
Manchester U: Amos; Rafael, O'Shea, Anderson, Brown, Vidic, Nani, Possebon (Gibson), Welbeck, Ronaldo (Tevez), Giggs (Manucho).
Middlesbrough: Jones; Hoyte, Taylor, O'Neil, Wheater, Pogatetz■, Digard (Riggott), Shawky (Johnson A), Alves (Emnes), Aladiere, Downing.

Rotherham U (1) 3 *(Fenton 20, Harrison 56, Broughton 69)*
Southampton (0) 1 *(John 61)*   5147
Rotherham U: Warrington; Tonge, Nicholas, Harrison, Sharps, Fenton, Mills, Cummins, Broughton, Rhodes, Reid.
Southampton: Bialkowski; James, Mills (John), Cork, Perry (Pekhart), Svensson, Wright-Phillips (Dyer), Wotton, McGoldrick, Lallana, Surman.

Stoke C (1) 2 *(Pericard 9, Sidibe 50)*
Reading (1) 2 *(Henry 45 (pen), 75)*   9141
Stoke C: Simonsen; Wilkinson, Dickinson, Buxton, Shawcross, Higginbotham (Cort), Lawrence, Whelan, Sidibe (Phillips D), Pericard, Cresswell (Fuller).
Reading: Federici; Kelly, Golbourne, Gunnarsson (Sigurdsson), Bikey, Ingimarsson, Henry, Cisse (Pearce), Lita, Long, Convey (Mooney).
aet; Stoke C won 4-3 on penalties.

Sunderland (0) 2 *(Stokes 86, 90)*
Northampton T (1) 2 *(Larkin 20, Guttridge 81)*   21,082
Sunderland: Fulop; Bardsley, Collins, Whitehead, Nosworthy, Ferdinand, Edwards (Richardson), Leadbitter (Stokes), Murphy, Healy (Chopra), Reid.
Northampton T: Fielding; Little, Crowe, Davis, Hughes, Coke (Gilligan), Osman, Guttridge, Constantine, Larkin (Akinfenwa), Holt (Jackman).
aet; Sunderland won 4-3 on penalties.

Swansea C (0) 1 *(Gomez 57)*
Cardiff C (0) 0 17,411
Swansea C: De Vries; Rangel, Bessone, Britton, Monk, Williams, Gower (Pintado), Bodde, Butler, Scotland (Brandy), Gomez.
Cardiff C: Enckelman; McNaughton, Comminges, Rae, Johnson R, Purse, Ledley (Whittingham), McPhail■, Johnson E (McCormack), Bothroyd, Parry.

Watford (0) 1 *(Mullins 70 (og))*
West Ham U (0) 0 12,914
Watford: Loach; Mariappa, Parkes, Bangura, Bromby, DeMerit, Ainsworth, Jenkins, Hoskins (Young), Smith (Harley), Williamson L (Bennett).
West Ham U: Lastuvka; Neill, Lopez, Noble, Upson, Mullins, Faubert, Di Michele (Reid), Sears, Boa Morte (Parker), Etherington.

SECOND ROUND

Wednesday, 24 September 2008

Brighton & HA (0) 2 *(Murray 89, Anyinsah 95)*
Manchester C (0) 2 *(Gelson 64, Ireland 108)* 8729
Brighton & HA: Kuipers; Whing (Cook), Richards, Thomson, Elphick, El-Abd, Fraser (Cox), Virgo, Murray, Loft (Anyinsah), Livermore.
Manchester C: Schmeichel; Zabaleta, Ball, Kompany, Ben-Haim, Dunne, Ireland, Gelson, Jo (Caicedo), Sturridge (Evans), Johnson (Elano).
aet; Brighton & HA won 5-3 on penalties.

THIRD ROUND

Wednesday, 24 September 2008

Aston Villa (0) 0
QPR (0) 1 *(Stewart 58)* 21,541
Aston Villa: Guzan; Gardner, Shorey, Cuellar, Knight, Osbourne (Routledge), Petrov, Young A, Harewood (Agbonlahor), Carew, Barry.
QPR: Cerny; Connolly, Delaney, Mahon, Hall, Stewart, Rowlands, Parejo, Ledesma (Balanta), Agyemang (Di Carmine), Buzsaky (Leigertwood).

Blackburn R (1) 1 *(Olsson 10)*
Everton (0) 0 14,366
Blackburn R: Robinson (Brown); Simpson, Olsson, Tugay, Khizanishvili, Ooijer, Villanueva (Santa Cruz), Treacy (Pedersen), Derbyshire, Fowler, Warnock.
Everton: Howard; Neville, Lescott, Yobo, Jagielka, Castillo (Cahill), Rodwell, Fellaini (Yakubu), Saha, Vaughan (Baxter), Osman.

Ipswich T (0) 1 *(Walters 61)*
Wigan Ath (0) 4 *(Cattermole 52, Kapo 64, Scharner 70, Camara 90)* 13,803
Ipswich T: Wright R; Volz, Thatcher (Balkestein), Campo, McAuley, Bruce, Norris, Miller, Lisbie (Bowditch), Walters, Quinn (Haynes).
Wigan Ath: Kirkland; Cattermole, Kilbane, Scharner, Boyce, Bramble, Valencia, Palacios (De Ridder), Heskey (Camara), Kapo, Zaki (Koumas).

Newcastle U (0) 1 *(Owen 90)*
Tottenham H (1) 2 *(Pavlyuchenko 62, O'Hara 66)* 20,577
Newcastle U: Given; Geremi, Bassong, Butt, Coloccini, Taylor S, Cacapa (Edgar), Duff (Xisco), Owen, Martins, N'Zogbia.
Tottenham H: Gomes; Corluka, Assou-Ekotto, Zokora, Woodgate, King, Lennon (Campbell), Jenas, Pavlyuchenko (Modric), Bale (Giovani), O'Hara.

Portsmouth (0) 0
Chelsea (2) 4 *(Lampard 36 (pen), 49, Malouda 45, Kalou 64)* 15,339
Portsmouth: James; Johnson, Hreidarsson, Kaboul, Pamarot, Distin, Utaka, Mvuemba, Crouch (Kanu), Belhadj (Traore A), Hughes (Wilson).
Chelsea: Cech; Ivanovic, Bridge, Ballack (Paulo Ferreira), Terry, Alex, Belletti, Lampard (Sinclair), Drogba (Di Santo), Kalou, Malouda.

Tuesday, 4 November 2008

Brighton & HA (1) 1 *(Elphick 36)*
Derby Co (2) 4 *(Villa 28, 73, 87, Ellington 34)* 6625
Brighton & HA: Sullivan; Whing, Richards, Thomson, Elphick, Hawkins (El-Abd), Cox (McLeod), Thornton, Murray (Livermore), Fleetwood, Anyinsah.
Derby Co: Carroll; Connolly, Stewart, Green, Nyatanga, Leacock (Zadkovich), Kazmierczak (Teale), Addison, Ellington, Villa (Hanson), Commons.

FOURTH ROUND

Tuesday, 11 November 2008

Arsenal (1) 3 *(Simpson 42, 66, Vela 70)*
Wigan Ath (0) 0 59,665
Arsenal: Fabianski; Hoyte, Gibbs, Song Billong, Djourou, Randall, Wilshere (Bischoff), Ramsey, Simpson (Lansbury), Vela (Fonte), Merida.
Wigan Ath: Kirkland; Melchiot, Figueroa, Palacios, Boyce, Bramble, Valencia, Cattermole (Brown), De Ridder, Zaki, Koumas (Camara).

Derby Co (2) 2 *(Villa 6, Ellington 18)*
Leeds U (1) 1 *(Becchio 40)* 18,540
Derby Co: Carroll; Connolly, Stewart, Green, Nyatanga, Davis, Teale (Zadkovich), Kazmierczak, Ellington (Sterjovski), Villa (Hulse), Commons.
Leeds U: Ankergren; Richardson, Parker (White), Kilkenny (Howson), Telfer, Michalik, Douglas, Robinson (Beckford), Snodgrass, Becchio, Delph.

Manchester U (0) 1 *(Tevez 76 (pen))*
QPR (0) 0 62,539
Manchester U: Kuszczak; Rafael, O'Shea, Anderson, Evans, Neville (Vidic), Gibson, Posssebon (Welbeck), Park, Tevez, Nani.
QPR: Cerny; Ramage, Connolly, Mahon, Hall, Stewart, Rowlands, Buzsaky (Agyemang), Parejo (Ledesma), Blackstock, Cook (Di Carmine).

Stoke C (1) 2 *(Whelan 21, Pugh 59)*
Rotherham U (0) 0 15,458
Stoke C: Simonsen; Wilkinson, Dickinson, Olofinjana (Amdy Faye), Cort, Shawcross, Pugh, Whelan, Kitson, Pericard (Fuller), Cresswell.
Rotherham U: Warrington; Mills, Nicholas, Harrison (Taylor R), Sharps, Fenton, Tonge, Cummins, Broughton (Yates), Rhodes, Reid.

Swansea C (0) 0
Watford (1) 1 *(Williamson L 21)* 9549
Swansea C: Konstantopoulos; Tate, Serran, Tudur-Jones (Gomez), Monk, O'Halloran, MacDonald, Bodde, Pintado, Bauza (Gower), Brandy (Scotland).
Watford: Lee; Doyley, Harley, Mariappa, Bromby, DeMerit, McAnuff (Hoskins), Williamson L (O'Toole), Priskin (Rasiak), Smith, Jenkins.

Wednesday, 12 November 2008

Chelsea (1) 1 *(Drogba 27)*
Burnley (0) 1 *(Akinbiyi 69)* 41,369
Chelsea: Cudicini; Paulo Ferreira, Bridge, Belletti (Lampard), Ivanovic, Alex, Deco (Mikel), Mineiro, Drogba (Di Santo), Kalou, Malouda.
Burnley: Jensen; Alexander, Jordan, McCann, Duff, Caldwell■, Eagles, Gudjonsson (McDonald), Blake (Mahon), Paterson (Akinbiyi), Elliott.
aet; Burnley won 5-4 on penalties.

Sunderland (0) 1 *(Jones 71)*
Blackburn R (0) 2 *(Santa Cruz 65, Bardsley 70 (og))* 18,555
Sunderland: Fulop; Bardsley, Collins, Whitehead, Nosworthy, Ferdinand, Malbranque (Reid), Henderson (Leadbitter), Cisse, Jones (Murphy), Richardson.
Blackburn R: Robinson; Simpson, Olsson, Tugay, Khizanishvili, Samba, Derbyshire, Mokoena, Fowler (Villaneuva), Haworth (Santa Cruz), Treacy (Warnock).

Tottenham H (3) 4 *(Pavlyuchenko 38, 52, Campbell 42, 45)*
Liverpool (0) 2 *(Plessis 49, Hyppia 63)* 33,242
Tottenham H: Gomes (Cesar); Hutton, Bale, Zokora, Corluka, Dawson, Lennon, Huddlestone, Pavlyuchenko (Boateng), Campbell (Bent), O'Hara.
Liverpool: Cavalieri; Dossena, Degen (Darby), N'Gog, Agger, Hyypia, Lucas, Plessis (Xabi Alonso), Torres (Insua), El Zhar, Babel.

QUARTER-FINALS

Tuesday, 2 December 2008
Burnley (1) 2 *(McDonald 6, 57)*
Arsenal (0) 0 19,045
Burnley: Jensen; Duff, Jordan, McCann, Caldwell, Carlisle, Alexander, McDonald (Gudjonsson), Blake (Elliott), Paterson (Akinbiyi 74), Eagles.
Arsenal: Fabianski; Hoyte, Gibbs, Randall (Bischoff), Silvestre, Ramsey, Rodgers (Lansbury), Merida, Bendtner, Vela, Wilshere (Simpson).

Stoke C (0) 0
Derby Co (0) 1 *(Ellington 90 (pen))* 22,034
Stoke C: Simonsen; Griffin, Higginbotham, Olofinjana (Pugh), Cort, Sonko, Delap, Whelan, Sidibe, Fuller, Cresswell.
Derby Co: Carroll; Connolly, Stewart, Green (Teale), Tomkins, Powell, Kazmierczak, Addison, Hulse (Villa), Ellington, Commons.

Wednesday, 3 December 2008
Manchester United (2) 5 *(Tevez 36, 51 (pen), 54, 90, Nani 40)*
Blackburn R (0) 3 *(McCarthy 48, 89, Derbyshire 84)*
53,997
Manchester United: Foster; Rafael, O'Shea (Evra), Anderson, Neville, Evans, Nani, Gibson, Possebon (Scholes), Tevez, Giggs (Manucho).
Blackburn R: Robinson; Ooijer, Warnock, Tugay (Pedersen), Nelsen, Olsson, Emerton (McCarthy), Mokoena, Santa Cruz (Fowler), Derbyshire, Treacy.

Watford (1) 1 *(Priskin 13)*
Tottenham H (1) 2 *(Pavlyuchenko 45 (pen), Bent 76)*
16,501
Watford: Loach; Mariappa, Harley, Bridcutt, Bromby, DeMerit (Doyley), McAnuff (Hoskins), Williamson L, Priskin, Smith, Jenkins (O'Toole).
Tottenham H: Gomes; Corluka, Assou-Ekotto, Zokora, Woodgate, Dawson, Lennon, Jenas, Pavlyuchenko, Campbell (Bent), O'Hara.

SEMI-FINAL FIRST LEG

Tuesday, 6 January 2009
Tottenham H (0) 4 *(Dawson 47, O'Hara 52, Pavlyuchenko 65, Duff 68 (og))*
Burnley (1) 1 *(Paterson 15)* 31,377
Tottenham H: Gomes; Corluka, Bale, Zokora, Woodgate, Dawson, Lennon, Modric, Pavlyuchenko, Campbell, Bentley (O'Hara).
Burnley: Jensen; Alexander, Jordan, Gudjonsson (McDonald), Duff, Carlisle, Eagles, McCann, Blake (Rodriguez), Paterson (Akinbiyi), Elliott.

Wednesday, 7 January 2009
Derby Co (1) 1 *(Commons 30)*
Manchester U (0) 0 30,194
Derby Co: Carroll; Connolly, Camara, Green, Nyatanga, Todd (Savage), Sterjovski (Teale), Addison, Hulse, Davies (Barazite), Commons.
Manchester U: Kuszczak; Rafael, O'Shea, Anderson (Carrick), Evans, Vidic, Gibson, Scholes (Rooney), Welbeck (Ronaldo), Tevez, Nani.

SEMI-FINAL SECOND LEG

Tuesday, 20 January 2009
Manchester U (3) 4 *(Nani 16, O'Shea 22, Tevez 34, Ronaldo 89 (pen))*
Derby Co (0) 2 *(Barnes 80 (pen), 90)* 73,374
Manchester U: Foster; Rafael (Fletcher), O'Shea, Gibson, Evans, Neville (Chester), Nani, Anderson, Welbeck, Tevez, Giggs (Ronaldo).
Derby Co: Carroll; Connolly, Stewart, Green, Albrechtsen, Todd (Barazite), Teale, Addison, Hulse, Commons (Barnes), Davies (Savage).

Wednesday, 21 January 2009
Burnley (1) 3 *(Blake 34, McCann 73, Rodriguez 88)*
Tottenham H (0) 2 *(Pavlyuchenko 118, Defoe 120)* 19,533
Burnley: Jensen; Alexander, Jordan (Kalvenes), McCann, Duff, Carlisle, Eagles, Gudjonsson (Rodriguez), Blake, Paterson (Akinbiyi), Elliott.
Tottenham H: Alnwick; Gunter (Taarabt), Assou-Ekotto, Zokora, Woodgate, Dawson, Bentley, Huddlestone, Modric (Pavlyuchenko), Defoe, O'Hara (Bale).
aet.

CARLING CUP FINAL

Sunday, 1 March 2009

Manchester U (0) 0   Tottenham H (0) 0

(at Wembley Stadium, attendance 88,217)

Manchester U: Foster; O'Shea (Vidic), Evra, Gibson (Giggs), Ferdinand, Evans, Ronaldo, Scholes, Welbeck (Anderson), Tevez, Nani.

Tottenham H: Gomes; Corluka, Assou-Ekotto, Zokora, Dawson, King, Lennon (Bentley), Jenas (Bale), Pavlyuchenko (O'Hara), Bent, Modric.

aet; Manchester U won 4-1 on penalties: Giggs scored; O'Hara saved; Tevez scored; Corluka scored; Ronaldo scored; Bentley missed; Anderson scored.

Referee: C. Foy (Merseyside).

JOHNSTONE'S PAINT TROPHY 2008-09

■ *Denotes player sent off.*

NORTHERN SECTION FIRST ROUND
Tuesday, 2 September 2008
Crewe Alex (3) 3 *(Schumacher 5, Jones 27, O'Donnell 42)*
Macclesfield T (0) 0   2463
Crewe Alex: Collis; Woodards, Jones, Schumacher, O'Donnell, Baudet, Bopp, Rix, Elding (Donaldson), Zola (Miller), Moore.
Macclesfield T: Brain; Flynn, Brisley, Jennings (Hadfield), Morgan, Dunfield, Reid I, Bell, Gritton■, Yeo (Dennis), Thomas.

Hartlepool U (0) 0
Leicester C (0) 3 *(Howard 52, Adams 66, Fryatt 87)* 2807
Hartlepool U: Lee-Barrett; McCunnie, Humphreys, Liddle, Nelson, Collins, Foley (Sweeney), Power (Rowell), Barker, Brown (Porter), Robson.
Leicester C: Henderson; O'Neill, Powell, King A, Morrison, Gilbert, Adams, Wesolowski, Howard (Fryatt), Dickov (Campbell), Dyer.

Leeds U (2) 2 *(Robinson 8 (pen), Becchio 42)*
Bradford C (0) 1 *(Conlon 71)*   20,128
Leeds U: Lucas; Richardson, White (Delph), Kilkenny (Johnson), Huntington, Rui Marques, Prutton, Howson, Snodgrass, Showunmi (Becchio), Robinson.
Bradford C: Evans; Moncur, Heckingbottom, Furman (Bullock), Lee, Bower, Daley, McLaren, Conlon, Nix (Boulding M), Colbeck.

Oldham Ath (0) 1 *(Whitaker 56)*
Morecambe (0) 1 *(Drummond 65)*   2016
Oldham Ath: Fleming; Eardley, Lomax, Maher, Hazell, Stam (O'Grady), Smalley (Lee), Allott, Hughes (Alessandra), Davies, Whitaker.
Morecambe: Roche; Parrish, Howard (McCann), Drummond, Artell, Bentley, Wainwright, Hunter, Howe, O'Carroll, Curtis (Lloyd).
Morecambe won 5-4 on penalties.

Scunthorpe U (0) 2 *(Hayes 89, 90)*
Notts Co (1) 1 *(Butcher 9)*   1755
Scunthorpe U: Lillis; Byrne, Williams (Lea), McCann (Forte), Mirfin (Hooper), Pearce, Sparrow, Morris, Hayes, May, Woolford.
Notts Co: Hoult; Beardsley, Mayo, Smith, Edwards, Tann (Johnson), Hamshaw, Butcher, Facey, Canham (Weston), Fairclough (MacKenzie).

Stockport Co (1) 1 *(McSweeney 4)*
Port Vale (0) 0   2290
Stockport Co: Williams; McSweeney, Rose, Turnbull, McNulty, Raynes, Tunnicliffe, Dicker, Baker (Owen), Vincent, Mainwaring.
Port Vale: Martin; Stockley, Prosser, Taiwo (Griffith), McCombe, Taylor, Glover (Richman), Howland, Richards, Perry, Dodds (Rodgers).

Tranmere R (0) 1 *(Sonko 49)*
Accrington S (0) 0   2410
Tranmere R: Coyne; Shotton, Andy Taylor, O'Callaghan, Waterfall, Kay (Barnett), Jennings, Shuker (Moore), Sonko (Greenacre), Savage, Curran.
Accrington S: Dunbavin (Arthur); Cavanagh, King, Williams, Edwards, Murphy (Mullin P), Worrall, Mullin J, Onibuje, Clarke, Miles.

SOUTHERN SECTION FIRST ROUND
Tuesday, 2 September 2008
Aldershot T (1) 2 *(Elvins 45, Davies 48 (pen))*
Swindon T (1) 2 *(Cox 32, Ifil 83)*   1814
Aldershot T: Bull; Osborne, Charles, Donnelly, Blackburn, Newman, Soares, Chalmers, Hylton (Morgan), Elvins (Grant), Davies (Hudson).
Swindon T: Smith P; Amankwaah, Smith J, Easton, Ifil, Kanyuka, McGovern (Marshall), Timlin (Allen), Cox, Peacock, McNamee (Paynter).
Swindon T won 7-6 on penalties.

Bournemouth (1) 3 *(Goulding 38, Igoe 67, Hollands 76)*
Bristol R (0) 0   2220
Bournemouth: Jalal; Bradbury, Cummings, Cooper, Pearce, Hollands, Igoe (Partington), Anderton (Bartley), Pitman, Goulding (McQuoid), Wagstaff.
Bristol R: Phillips; Green R (Hinton), Lescott, Campbell, Anthony, Elliott, Lines, Disley, Lambert, Duffy (Hunt), Hughes (Rigg).

Brentford (2) 2 *(Poole 28 (pen), O'Connor 37)*
Yeovil T (1) 2 *(Bircham 39, Tomlin 37 (pen))*   1339
Brentford: Brown; Newton, Johnson, O'Connor, Phillips, Wilson, Artus (Ochoa), Bean, MacDonald (Montague), Ademola, Poole (Dickson).
Yeovil T: Wagenaar; Alcock, Jones, Bircham (Way), Brown, Forbes, Roberts, Murtagh, Dayton, Warne (McCollin), Tomlin.
Brentford won 4-2 on penalties.

Dagenham & R (3) 4 *(Benson 4, 34, Nwokeji 28, Southam 75 (pen))*
Barnet (2) 2 *(Birchall 6, 18)*   1412
Dagenham & R: Thompson; Okuonghae, Griffiths, Graham, Uddin, Boardman, Southam, Patterson (Lokando), Benson (Strevens), Nwokeji (Nurse), Taiwo.
Barnet: Kadoch; Carew, Thomas, Porter (Medley), Leary, Gillet, Adomah, Mitchell, Birchall, Akurang (Charles), Bishop.

Exeter C (1) 1 *(Harley 22)*
Shrewsbury T (1) 2 *(McIntyre 9, Davies 90)*   1530
Exeter C: Jones; Tully, Moxey, Edwards (Panther), Seaborne, Taylor, Gill, Stewart, Stansfield (Logan), Watson (McAllister), Harley.
Shrewsbury T: Daniels; Herd, Ashton, Hindmarch (Leslie), Cansdell-Sherriff, Moss (Pugh), Davies, Humphrey, Symes, Langmead, McIntyre.

Millwall (0) 0
Colchester U (1) 1 *(Perkins 8)*   2456
Millwall: Forde; Hackett, Frampton (Fuseini), Abdou, Robinson, Whitbread, Brkovic, Moore, Kandol, Grimes (Bowes) (Martin), Craig.
Colchester U: Cousins; White, Ifil, Hammond, Coyne, Heath, Elito, Perkins, Vernon (Platt), Wasiu (Yeates), Wordsworth.

Northampton T (0) 0
Brighton & HA (0) 1 *(McLeod 68)*   2047
Northampton T: Dunn; Little, Jackman (Henderson), Coke (Davis), Hughes, Doig, Dyer (Osman), Guttridge, Constantine, Larkin, Holt.
Brighton & HA: Kuipers; Whing, Richards, Loft, Lynch, Hawkins, Livermore, Virgo (Cox), Murray, Forster, McLeod.

Southend U (2) 2 *(Sawyer 13, 34)*
Leyton Orient (2) 4 *(Jarvis 20, Chambers 25, Melligan 48, Boyd 86 (pen))*   3499
Southend U: Mildenhall; Francis, Sankofa, Grant (Christophe), Clarke, Barrett, Sawyer, Betsy, Walker (Laurent), Barnard, Robson-Kanu (Scannell).
Leyton Orient: Jones; Cave-Brown, Palmer, Chambers, Ashworth, Saah, Melligan, Pires (Terry), Dawkins (Boyd), Jarvis, Demetriou (Gray B).

NORTHERN SECTION FIRST ROUND
Wednesday, 3 September 2008
Chesterfield (1) 2 *(Lester 18, Kerry 52)*
Grimsby T (1) 2 *(Jarman 32, North 78)*   1665
Chesterfield: Lee; Picken, Goodall, Kerry, Page, Downes, Lowry, Winter (Niven), Lester, Ward, Currie (Robertson).
Grimsby T: Barnes; Clarke, Newey, Bennett, Heywood, Hegarty, Hunt, Boshell (Llewellyn), Jarman, Till (North), Heslop (Vidal).
Grimsby T won 4-1 on penalties.

NORTHERN SECTION SECOND ROUND

Tuesday, 23 September 2008

Leicester C (0) 0

Lincoln C (0) 0   8046

Leicester C: Henderson; Hobbs, Berner, King A, Morrison, Tunchev, Adams, Wesolowski, Howard (King C), Fryatt, Dyer (Gradel) (Powell).
Lincoln C: Duffy; Sinclair, Beevers, Kovacs, Hone, Kerr, Clarke, Frecklington, John-Lewis (Wright), Patulea (Gall), N'Guessan.
Leicester C won 3-1 on penalties.

NORTHERN SECTION SECOND ROUND

Monday, 6 October 2008

Tranmere R (0) 1 *(Shuker 86)*

Crewe Alex (0) 0   2626

Tranmere R: Coyne; Shotton, Andy Taylor, Goodison, Chorley, Kay, Moore, Jennings (Edds), Savage, Greenacre, Sonko (Shuker).
Crewe Alex: Collis; Woodards, Jones, Schumacher, O'Donnell (Donaldson), Lawrence, Carrington (Bopp), Pope, Miller, Zola (Elding), O'Connor.

Tuesday, 7 October 2008

Bury (0) 1 *(Bishop 77)*

Stockport Co (0) 0   2384

Bury: Brown; Scott, Buchanan, Baker, Cresswell, Futcher, Bennett, Barry-Murphy, Morrell (Hurst), Bishop, Jones.
Stockport Co: Forster; Mullins, Rose, Tunnicliffe, McNulty, Turnbull, McSweeney (Vincent), Dicker, Rowe T, Pilkington A (Baker), Gleeson.

Chester C (0) 1 *(Ellison 82)*

Morecambe (1) 1 *(Howe 42)*   926

Chester C: Danby; Vaughan J, Wilson, Roberts, Linwood, Hughes, Mozike, Barry, McManus (Taylor), Partridge (Lowe), Ellison.
Morecambe: Roche; McCann, Parrish, Stanley, Artell, Bentley, Hunter, Drummond, Howe (O'Carroll), Curtis (Taylor), Twiss (Wainwright).
Morecambe won 3-1 on penalties.

Darlington (1) 1 *(White 45)*

Huddersfield T (0) 0   1791

Darlington: Kazimierczak; Austin, Purdie, Ravenhill (Kennedy), Foster, White, Poole (Clarke B), Hulbert, Blundell, Proudlock (Hatch), Burgmeier.
Huddersfield T: Smithies; Holdsworth, Williams, Unsworth (Butler), Lucketti, Clarke T (Skarz), Roberts■, Collins, Cadamarteri, Berrett (Worthington), Parker.

Rochdale (2) 2 *(Thorpe 10, Dagnall 16)*

Carlisle U (1) 2 *(Bridges 4, Madine 71)*   1608

Rochdale: Russell; Holness (Keltie), Kennedy (Wiseman), Toner, Stanton, McArdle, Thompson, Jones G, Dagnall (Le Fondre), Thorpe, Rundle.
Carlisle U: Williams; Gowling, Horwood, Thirwell (Smith G), Livesey, Keogh, Carlton, Joyce, Graham (Madine), Bridges, Myrie-Williams (Hackney).
Rochdale won 4-3 on penalties.

Scunthorpe U (2) 2 *(Togwell 38, Morris 42)*

Grimsby T (0) 1 *(Hegarty 48)*   4844

Scunthorpe U: Lillis; Byrne, Williams, Morris, Mirfin, Crosby, Sparrow, Togwell, Hayes, Hooper (May), Woolford (Forte).
Grimsby T: Barnes; Bennett, Newey, Hunt (Llewellyn), Heywood, Clarke, Hegarty, Trotter, Jarman (Ameobi), Till (Taylor), Boshell.

SOUTHERN SECTION SECOND ROUND

Tuesday, 7 October 2008

Brighton & HA (2) 2 *(Virgo 5 (pen), Anyinsah 14)*

Leyton Orient (1) 2 *(Jarvis 21, Boyd 72 (pen))*   2157

Brighton & HA: Kuipers; Whing, Richards, El-Abd, Elphick, Hawkins, Cox, Thornton, Anyinsah (Robinson), Savage, Virgo.

Leyton Orient: Jones; Saah, Cave-Brown (Purches), Chambers, Dawkins (Boyd), Palmer, Ashworth, Terry, Baker, Jarvis, Demetriou.
Brighton & HA won 5-4 on penalties.

Cheltenham T (1) 1 *(Low 4)*

Walsall (0) 2 *(Ibehre 61, Ricketts 74)*   1741

Cheltenham T: Brown SP; Lindegaard, Ridley, Montrose, Gallinagh, Caines, Armstrong, Low (Brown S), Connor, Fleetwood (Vincent), Gill B.
Walsall: Gilmartin; Palmer, Boertien, Taundry, Gerrard, Roberts, Hughes (Deeney), Mattis, Ricketts, Ibehre (Reich), Nicholls (Demontagnac).

Gillingham (0) 0

Colchester U (0) 1 *(Yeates 60)*   1557

Gillingham: Royce; Fuller, Nutter, Weston, Mills, King, Southall, Bentley, Jackson (Pugh), Barcham (Murphy), Jarrett (Richards).
Colchester U: Cousins; White, Borrowdale, Hammond, Heath, Reid, Yeates, Jackson, Platt, Gillespie (Vernon), Perkins.

Hereford U (1) 1 *(Done 30)*

Swindon T (1) 2 *(Cox 45, Peacock 84)*   1458

Hereford U: Samson; Jackson, Taylor, Easton, Beckwith, Broadhurst, Johnson, O'Leary, Ashikodi (Williams), Chadwick, Done (Hudson-Odoi).
Swindon T: Brezovan; Amankwaah, Smith J, Nalis (McNamee), Ifil, Morrison, Easton, Timlin, Paynter (Corr), Cox, Peacock (McGovern).

Luton T (1) 2 *(Hall 39, Martin 55)*

Brentford (2) 2 *(Poole 18, Marvin Williams 37)*   2029

Luton T: Logan; Asafu-Adjaye (Plummer), Howells, Gnakpa, Spillane, Worley, Hall, O'Connor (McVeigh), Martin, Charles (Sinclair), Jarvis.
Brentford: Hamer; Newton, Osborne, Pead, Dickson (Wood), Phillips, O'Connor, Montague, Marvin Williams, Wright, Poole (Ademola).
Luton T won 4-3 on penalties.

Milton Keynes D (0) 0

Bournemouth (0) 1 *(Anderton 77)*   4329

Milton Keynes D: Abbey; Regan, Lewington, Belson■, O'Hanlon (Liera), Stirling, Wright (Chadwick), Navarro, Johnson, Gallen, Sturm (Chicksen).
Bournemouth: Jalal; Guyett, Bradbury, Hollands, Pearce, Cooper, Bartley, Anderton, Goulding (Pitman), Sturrock (McQuoid), Cummings.

Peterborough U (0) 0

Dagenham & R (0) 1 *(Nwokeji 65)*   2644

Peterborough U: Lewis; Martin, Williams, Hyde, Morgan, Lee, Green (Whelpdale), Coutts (Rendell), Mackail-Smith, Batt, Boyd.
Dagenham & R: Roberts; Foster, Griffiths, Okuonghae, Uddin, Graham (Huke), Nurse, Southam, Benson (Strevens), Nwokeji (Tejan-Sie), Gain.

Wycombe W (0) 0

Shrewsbury T (3) 7 *(Holt 12, 27, 80, 81, 86, McIntyre 39, Cansdell-Sherriff 74)*   1730

Wycombe W: Young; Rice, Woodman, Ashton (Zebroski), Johnson, McCracken, Spence (Duncan), Phillips, Vieira (Grant), McGleish, Mousinho.
Shrewsbury T: Garner; Herd, Tierney, Davies, Coughlan, Langmead, Cansdell-Sherriff (Ashton), Thornton, Hibbert (Walker), Holt, McIntyre (Leslie).

NORTHERN SECTION SECOND ROUND

Wednesday, 8 October 2008

Rotherham U (2) 4 *(Sharps 17, Hudson 44, Broughton 48, Fenton 53)*

Leeds U (1) 2 *(Howson 31, Showunmi 56)*   4658

Rotherham U: Warrington; Tonge, Nicholas, Cummins, Sharps, Fenton, Mills, Hudson, Broughton, Rhodes, Reid.
Leeds U: Lucas; Hughes, Parker (Sheehan), Kilkenny, Michalik, Rui Marques, Prutton, Howson, Snodgrass, Showunmi (Beckford), Robinson (Becchio).

NORTHERN QUARTER-FINAL

Tuesday, 4 November 2008

Tranmere R (1) 1 *(Shotton 45)*
Morecambe (0) 0 2110

Tranmere R: Coyne; Shotton, Andy Taylor, Jennings (Sonko), Chorley, Kay, Barnett, Greenacre, Moore (Henry), Shuker, Edds.
Morecambe: Roche; Yates, Adams, Stanley (McCann), McStay, Bentley, McGivern (Wainwright), Drummond, Taylor (Artell), O'Carroll, McLachlan.

NORTHERN QUARTER-FINALS

Tuesday, 4 November 2008

Darlington (0) 1 *(White 53)*
Bury (0) 0 1651

Darlington: Kazmierczak; Austin, Ryan, Ravenhill, Foster, White, Poole (Griffin), Hulbert, Proudlock (Blundell), Foran, Burgmeier (Kennedy).
Bury: Brown; Scott, Buchanan, Bennett, Cresswell, Futcher, Baker, Barry-Murphy (Haslam), Morrell (Hurst), Bishop, Jones (Racchi).

Rotherham U (1) 2 *(Broughton 45, Tonge 58)*
Leicester C (0) 0 4255

Rotherham U: Warrington; Tonge, Nicholas, Harrison, Sharps, Fenton, Mills, Cummins (Hudson), Broughton, Rhodes, Garcia.
Leicester C: Henderson; Hobbs, Powell, King A, Kisnorbo, Morrison, Adams (Berner), Oakley, Howard, Hayles (Fryatt), Dyer (Chambers).

Scunthorpe U (0) 1 *(Mirfin 90)*
Rochdale (0) 0 2474

Scunthorpe U: Murphy; Byrne, Lea, McCann, Mirfin, Iriekpen, Sparrow, Togwell (Morris), Hayes (May), Forte (Hurst), Woolford.
Rochdale: Russell; Wiseman, Kennedy, Toner, Stanton, McArdle, Thompson (Rundle), Keltie, Jones M (Dagnall), Le Fondre (Thorpe), Buckley.

SOUTHERN QUARTER-FINALS

Tuesday, 4 November 2008

Bournemouth (0) 0
Colchester U (1) 1 *(Williams 17)* 2275

Bournemouth: Pryce; Pearce, Bradbury, Hollands (McQuoid), Ward, Cooper, Cummings, Molesley (Anderton), Pitman, Rankine (Lindfield), Bartley.
Colchester U: Cousins; White, Ifil, Izzet (Perkins), Heath, Baldwin, Jackson, Hammond, Vernon (Wasiu), Williams (Yeates), Wordsworth.

Shrewsbury T (3) 5 *(Holt 13, 45, Leslie 22, Walker 69, Coughlin 81)*
Dagenham & R (0) 0 2747

Shrewsbury T: Garner; Herd, Tierney, Sigurdsson, Coughlin, Langmead, Humphrey (Hindmarch), Leslie, Walker, Holt (Symes), McIntyre (Ashton).
Dagenham & R: Roberts; Huke, Griffiths, Okuonghae, Uddin, Taiwo (Tejan-Sie), Saunders (Ritchie), Southam, Benson, Nurse (Nwokeji), Graham.

Walsall (0) 0
Luton T (0) 1 *(Jarvis 90)* 1844

Walsall: Ince; Roberts, Boertien (Nicholls), Mattis, Gerrard, Taundry, Palmer, Hughes, Ricketts, Ibehre, Deeney (Zaaboub).
Luton T: Logan; Gnakpa, Howells (O'Connor), Keane, Roper (Worley), Beavan, McVeigh, Jarvis, Martin, Craddock (Watson), Spillane.

SOUTHERN QUARTER-FINAL

Wednesday, 12 November 2008

Brighton & HA (1) 2 *(Forster 24 (pen), Livermore 75)*
Swindon T (0) 0 2234

Brighton & HA: Kuipers; Whing, Richards, El-Abd, Elphick, Virgo (Fraser), Cox, Anyinsah, Forster, McLeod (Loft), Livermore.
Swindon T: Smith P; Smith J (Paynter), Timlin, Easton (Nalis), Morrison, Kanyuka, McGovern, Pook, Corr, Cox, Marshall.

NORTHERN SEMI-FINALS

Tuesday, 16 December 2008

Rotherham U (0) 1 *(Harrison 74)*
Darlington (1) 1 *(Foster 35)* 2706

Rotherham U: Cann; Green, Tonge, Harrison, Sharps, Fenton, Cummins, Holmes (Joseph), Rhodes (Hudson), Reid (Burchill), Taylor R.
Darlington: Brown; Austin, Ryan, Kennedy, White, Foster, Carole, Flynn, Foran, Hatch, Clarke B.
Rotherham U won 4-2 on penalties.

Scunthorpe U (1) 2 *(May 26, Hayes 90)*
Tranmere R (0) 1 *(Moore 53)* 2669

Scunthorpe U: Murphy; Wright, Williams, Morris, Crosby (Pearce), Byrne, Sparrow, Thompson, May, Togwell (Hayes), Woolford.
Tranmere R: Coyne; Johnson, Andy Taylor, Goodison, Chorley, Kay, Jennings, Greenacre, Moore, Savage, Sonko (Shuker).

SOUTHERN SEMI-FINALS

Tuesday, 16 December 2008

Luton T (1) 1 *(Gnakpa 29)*
Colchester U (0) 0 2638

Luton T: Logan; Asafu-Adjaye, Howells, Keane (Beavan), Roper, Spillane, Gnakpa, Hall, Talbot (Martin), Andrews (McVeigh), Jarvis.
Colchester U: Gerken; Maybury, White, Izzet, Heath (Coyne), Baldwin, Jackson, Hammond (Gillespie), Vernon, Wasiu (Yeates), Wordsworth.

Shrewsbury T (0) 0
Brighton & HA (0) 0 4052

Shrewsbury T: Daniels; Moss, Cansdell-Sherriff, Hunt (Leslie), Davies, Coughlan, Langmead, Walker (Hibbert), White, Holt, McIntyre.
Brighton & HA: Sullivan; Whing, Richards, El-Abd, Elphick, Hawkins (Hinshelwood), Cox, Virgo, Forster, McLeod (Robinson), Thornton (Fraser).
Brighton & HA won 5-4 on penalties.

NORTHERN FINAL FIRST LEG

Tuesday, 20 January 2009

Scunthorpe U (0) 2 *(Woolford 60, Pearce 67)*
Rotherham U (0) 0 6038

Scunthorpe U: Murphy; Byrne, Williams, Wright, Mirfin, Pearce, Thompson, Sparrow, Hayes (Morris), Hooper (Forte), Woolford.
Rotherham U: Warrington; Tonge, Nicholas, Green, Sharps, Fenton, Taylor J (Harrison), Hudson, Broughton, Reid (Burchill), Cummins.

SOUTHERN FINAL FIRST LEG

Tuesday, 20 January 2009

Brighton & HA (0) 0
Luton T (0) 0 6127

Brighton & HA: Sullivan; Whing, Hinshelwood, Virgo, Elphick, El-Abd, Cox (Loft), Fraser, Robinson (Mayo), Forster, McLeod (Livermore).
Luton T: Logan; Gnakpa, Davis, Keane, Asafu-Adjaye, Spillane, Hall, Jarvis, Martin, Talbot (Parkin), McVeigh (Howells).

NORTHERN FINAL SECOND LEG

Tuesday, 17 February 2009

Rotherham U (0) 0

Scunthorpe U (0) 1 *(Hooper 74)*   6555

Rotherham U: Warrington; Tonge, Green, Hudson, Sharps, Fenton, Reid (Taylor R), Mills, Broughton (Thomas), Joseph, Taylor J (Cummins).
Scunthorpe U: Murphy; Byrne, Wright, McCann, Mirfin, Pearce, Thompson (Sparrow), Togwell, Hayes (Morris), Hooper (Lansbury), Woolford.

SOUTHERN FINAL SECOND LEG

Tuesday, 17 February 2009

Luton T (1) 1 *(Craddock 2)*

Brighton & HA (1) 1 *(Forster 20)*   8711

Luton T: Price; Gnakpa, Davis (Charles), Keane, Roper (Hall), Spillane (Howells), Jarvis, Martin, Craddock, Parkin, Asafu-Adjaye.
Brighton & HA: Kuipers; Whing, Virgo, Jarrett, Fraser, El-Abd, Cox (Elphick), Birchall, Andrew (Cook), Forster, Livermore■.
Luton T won 4-3 on penalties.

JOHNSTONE'S PAINT TROPHY FINAL

Sunday, 5 April 2009

(at Wembley Stadium, attendance 55,378)

Luton T (1) 3   **Scunthorpe U (1) 2 (aet)**

Luton T: Brill; Asafu-Adjaye, Emanuel, Keane, Pilkington, Spillane, Nicholls, Hall, Martin, Craddock (Gnakpa), Jarvis (Parkin).

Scorers: Martin 32, Craddock 70, Gnakpa 95.

Scunthorpe U: Murphy; Byrne, Williams, McCann, Mirfin, Pearce (Wright), Lansbury, Sparrow (Woolford), Hayes, Hooper, Hurst (Togwell).

Scorers: Hooper 14, McCann 88.

Referee: P. Crossley.

FOOTBALL LEAGUE COMPETITION ATTENDANCES

LEAGUE CUP ATTENDANCES

Season	Attendances	Games	Average
1960–61	1,204,580	112	10,755
1961–62	1,030,534	104	9,909
1962–63	1,029,893	102	10,097
1963–64	945,265	104	9,089
1964–65	962,802	98	9,825
1965–66	1,205,876	106	11,376
1966–67	1,394,553	118	11,818
1967–68	1,671,326	110	15,194
1968–69	2,064,647	118	17,497
1969–70	2,299,819	122	18,851
1970–71	2,035,315	116	17,546
1971–72	2,397,154	123	19,489
1972–73	1,935,474	120	16,129
1973–74	1,722,629	132	13,050
1974–75	1,901,094	127	14,969
1975–76	1,841,735	140	13,155
1976–77	2,236,636	147	15,215
1977–78	2,038,295	148	13,772
1978–79	1,825,643	139	13,134
1979–80	2,322,866	169	13,745
1980–81	2,051,576	161	12,743
1981–82	1,880,682	161	11,681
1982–83	1,679,756	160	10,498
1983–84	1,900,491	168	11,312
1984–85	1,876,429	167	11,236
1985–86	1,579,916	163	9,693
1986–87	1,531,498	157	9,755
1987–88	1,539,253	158	9,742
1988–89	1,552,780	162	9,585
1989–90	1,836,916	168	10,934
1990–91	1,675,496	159	10,538
1991–92	1,622,337	164	9,892
1992–93	1,558,031	161	9,677
1993–94	1,744,120	163	10,700
1994–95	1,530,478	157	9,748
1995–96	1,776,060	162	10,963
1996–97	1,529,321	163	9,382
1997–98	1,484,297	153	9,701
1998–99	1,555,856	153	10,169
1999–2000	1,354,233	153	8,851
2000–01	1,501,304	154	9,749
2001–02	1,076,390	93	11,574
2002–03	1,242,478	92	13,505
2003–04	1,267,729	93	13,631
2004–05	1,313,693	93	14,216
2005–06	1,072,362	93	11,531
2006–07	1,098,403	93	11,811
2007–08	1,332,841	94	14,179
2008–09	1,329,753	93	14,298

CARLING CUP 2008–09

Round	Aggregate	Games	Average
One	188,604	36	5,239
Two	209,344	24	8,723
Three	318,616	16	19,914
Four	258,917	8	32,365
Quarter-finals	111,577	4	27,894
Semi-finals	154,478	4	38,620
Final	88,217	1	88,217
Total	1,329,753	93	14,298

JOHNSTONE'S PAINT TROPHY 2008–09

Round	Aggregate	Games	Average
One	51,851	16	3,241
Two	44,528	16	2,783
Area Quarter-finals	19,590	8	2,449
Area Semi-finals	12,065	4	3,016
Area finals	27,431	4	6,858
Final	55,378	1	55,378
Total	210,843	49	4,303

FA CUP FINALS 1872–2009

1872 and 1874–92	Kennington Oval	1911	Replay at Old Trafford
1873	Lillie Bridge	1912	Replay at Bramall Lane
1886	Replay at Derby (Racecourse Ground)	1915	Old Trafford, Manchester
1893	Fallowfield, Manchester	1920–22	Stamford Bridge
1894	Everton	1923–2000	Wembley
1895–1914	Crystal Palace	1970	Replay at Old Trafford
1901	Replay at Bolton	2001–2006	Millennium Stadium, Cardiff
1910	Replay at Everton	2007 to date	Wembley

Year	Winners	Runners-up	Score
1872	Wanderers	Royal Engineers	1-0
1873	Wanderers	Oxford University	2-0
1874	Oxford University	Royal Engineers	2-0
1875	Royal Engineers	Old Etonians	2-0 (after 1-1 draw aet)
1876	Wanderers	Old Etonians	3-0 (after 1-1 draw aet)
1877	Wanderers	Oxford University	2-1 (aet)
1878	Wanderers*	Royal Engineers	3-1
1879	Old Etonians	Clapham R	1-0
1880	Clapham R	Oxford University	1-0
1881	Old Carthusians	Old Etonians	3-0
1882	Old Etonians	Blackburn R	1-0
1883	Blackburn Olympic	Old Etonians	2-1 (aet)
1884	Blackburn R	Queen's Park, Glasgow	2-1
1885	Blackburn R	Queen's Park, Glasgow	2-0
1886	Blackburn R†	WBA	2-0 (after 0-0 draw)
1887	Aston Villa	WBA	2-0
1888	WBA	Preston NE	2-1
1889	Preston NE	Wolverhampton W	3-0
1890	Blackburn R	The Wednesday	6-1
1891	Blackburn R	Notts Co	3-1
1892	WBA	Aston Villa	3-0
1893	Wolverhampton W	Everton	1-0
1894	Notts Co	Bolton W	4-1
1895	Aston Villa	WBA	1-0
1896	The Wednesday	Wolverhampton W	2-1
1897	Aston Villa	Everton	3-2
1898	Nottingham F	Derby Co	3-1
1899	Sheffield U	Derby Co	4-1
1900	Bury	Southampton	4-0
1901	Tottenham H	Sheffield U	3-1 (after 2-2 draw)
1902	Sheffield U	Southampton	2-1 (after 1-1 draw)
1903	Bury	Derby Co	6-0
1904	Manchester C	Bolton W	1-0
1905	Aston Villa	Newcastle U	2-0
1906	Everton	Newcastle U	1-0
1907	The Wednesday	Everton	2-1
1908	Wolverhampton W	Newcastle U	3-1
1909	Manchester U	Bristol C	1-0
1910	Newcastle U	Barnsley	2-0 (after 1-1 draw)
1911	Bradford C	Newcastle U	1-0 (after 0-0 draw)
1912	Barnsley	WBA	1-0 (aet, after 0-0 draw)
1913	Aston Villa	Sunderland	1-0
1914	Burnley	Liverpool	1-0
1915	Sheffield U	Chelsea	3-0
1920	Aston Villa	Huddersfield T	1-0 (aet)
1921	Tottenham H	Wolverhampton W	1-0
1922	Huddersfield T	Preston NE	1-0
1923	Bolton W	West Ham U	2-0
1924	Newcastle U	Aston Villa	2-0
1925	Sheffield U	Cardiff C	1-0
1926	Bolton W	Manchester C	1-0
1927	Cardiff C	Arsenal	1-0
1928	Blackburn R	Huddersfield T	3-1
1929	Bolton W	Portsmouth	2-0
1930	Arsenal	Huddersfield T	2-0
1931	WBA	Birmingham	2-1
1932	Newcastle U	Arsenal	2-1
1933	Everton	Manchester C	3-0
1934	Manchester C	Portsmouth	2-1
1935	Sheffield W	WBA	4-2

Year	Winners	Runners-up	Score
1936	Arsenal	Sheffield U	1-0
1937	Sunderland	Preston NE	3-1
1938	Preston NE	Huddersfield T	1-0 (aet)
1939	Portsmouth	Wolverhampton W	4-1
1946	Derby Co	Charlton Ath	4-1 (aet)
1947	Charlton Ath	Burnley	1-0 (aet)
1948	Manchester U	Blackpool	4-2
1949	Wolverhampton W	Leicester C	3-1
1950	Arsenal	Liverpool	2-0
1951	Newcastle U	Blackpool	2-0
1952	Newcastle U	Arsenal	1-0
1953	Blackpool	Bolton W	4-3
1954	WBA	Preston NE	3-2
1955	Newcastle U	Manchester C	3-1
1956	Manchester C	Birmingham C	3-1
1957	Aston Villa	Manchester U	2-1
1958	Bolton W	Manchester U	2-0
1959	Nottingham F	Luton T	2-1
1960	Wolverhampton W	Blackburn R	3-0
1961	Tottenham H	Leicester C	2-0
1962	Tottenham H	Burnley	3-1
1963	Manchester U	Leicester C	3-1
1964	West Ham U	Preston NE	3-2
1965	Liverpool	Leeds U	2-1 (aet)
1966	Everton	Sheffield W	3-2
1967	Tottenham H	Chelsea	2-1
1968	WBA	Everton	1-0 (aet)
1969	Manchester C	Leicester C	1-0
1970	Chelsea	Leeds U	2-1 (aet)
	(after 2-2 draw, after extra time)		
1971	Arsenal	Liverpool	2-1 (aet)
1972	Leeds U	Arsenal	1-0
1973	Sunderland	Leeds U	1-0
1974	Liverpool	Newcastle U	3-0
1975	West Ham U	Fulham	2-0
1976	Southampton	Manchester U	1-0
1977	Manchester U	Liverpool	2-1
1978	Ipswich T	Arsenal	1-0
1979	Arsenal	Manchester U	3-2
1980	West Ham U	Arsenal	1-0
1981	Tottenham H	Manchester C	3-2
	(after 1-1 draw, after extra time)		
1982	Tottenham H	QPR	1-0
	(after 1-1 draw, after extra time)		
1983	Manchester U	Brighton & HA	4-0
	(after 2-2 draw, after extra time)		
1984	Everton	Watford	2-0
1985	Manchester U	Everton	1-0 (aet)
1986	Liverpool	Everton	3-1
1987	Coventry C	Tottenham H	3-2 (aet)
1988	Wimbledon	Liverpool	1-0
1989	Liverpool	Everton	3-2 (aet)
1990	Manchester U	Crystal Palace	1-0
	(after 3-3 draw, after extra time)		
1991	Tottenham H	Nottingham F	2-1 (aet)
1992	Liverpool	Sunderland	2-0
1993	Arsenal	Sheffield W	2-1 (aet)
	(after 1-1 draw, after extra time)		
1994	Manchester U	Chelsea	4-0
1995	Everton	Manchester U	1-0
1996	Manchester U	Liverpool	1-0
1997	Chelsea	Middlesbrough	2-0
1998	Arsenal	Newcastle U	2-0
1999	Manchester U	Newcastle U	2-0
2000	Chelsea	Aston Villa	1-0
2001	Liverpool	Arsenal	2-1
2002	Arsenal	Chelsea	2-0
2003	Arsenal	Southampton	1-0
2004	Manchester U	Millwall	3-0
2005	Arsenal	Manchester U	0-0 (aet)
	(Arsenal won 5-4 on penalties)		
2006	Liverpool	West Ham U	3-3 (aet)
	(Liverpool won 3-1 on penalties)		
2007	Chelsea	Manchester U	1-0 (aet)
2008	Portsmouth	Cardiff C	1-0
2009	Chelsea	Everton	2-1

* Won outright, but restored to the Football Association. † A special trophy was awarded for third consecutive win.

FA CUP WINS

Manchester U 11, Arsenal 10, Tottenham H 8, Aston Villa 7, Liverpool 7, Blackburn R 6, Newcastle U 6, Chelsea 5, Everton 5, The Wanderers 5, WBA 5, Bolton W 4, Manchester C 4, Sheffield U 4, Wolverhampton W 4, Sheffield W 3, West Ham U 3, Bury 2, Nottingham F 2, Old Etonians 2, Portsmouth 2, Preston NE 2, Sunderland 2, Barnsley 1, Blackburn Olympic 1, Blackpool 1, Bradford C 1, Burnley 1, Cardiff C 1, Charlton Ath 1, Clapham R 1, Coventry C 1, Derby Co 1, Huddersfield T 1, Ipswich T 1, Leeds U 1, Notts Co 1, Old Carthusians 1, Oxford University 1, Royal Engineers 1, Southampton 1, Wimbledon 1.

APPEARANCES IN FINALS

Manchester U 18, Arsenal 17, Everton 13, Liverpool 13, Newcastle U 13, Aston Villa 10, WBA 10, Chelsea 9, Tottenham H 9, Blackburn R 8, Manchester C 8, Wolverhampton W 8, Bolton W 7, Preston NE 7, Old Etonians 6, Sheffield U 6, Sheffield W 6, Huddersfield T 5, *The Wanderers 5, West Ham U 5, Derby Co 4, Leeds U 4, Leicester C 4, Oxford University 4, Portsmouth 4, Royal Engineers 4, Southampton 4, Sunderland 4, Blackpool 3, Burnley 3, Cardiff C 3, Nottingham F 3, Barnsley 2, Birmingham C 2, *Bury 2, Charlton Ath 2, Clapham R 2, Notts Co 2, Queen's Park (Glasgow) 2, *Blackburn Olympic 1, *Bradford C 1, Brighton & HA 1, Bristol C 1, *Coventry C 1, Crystal Palace 1, Fulham 1, *Ipswich T 1, Luton T 4, Middlesbrough 1, Millwall 1, *Old Carthusians 1, QPR 1, Watford 1, *Wimbledon 1.
Denotes undefeated.

APPEARANCES IN SEMI-FINALS

Arsenal 26, Manchester U 26, Everton 24, Liverpool 22, WBA 20, Aston Villa 19, Blackburn R 18, Chelsea 18, Newcastle U 17, Tottenham H 17, Sheffield W 16, Wolverhampton W 14, Bolton W 13, Derby Co 13, Sheffield U 13, Nottingham F 12, Sunderland 12, Southampton 11, Manchester C 10, Preston NE 10, Birmingham C 9, Burnley 8, Leeds U 8, Leicester C 8, Huddersfield T 7, West Ham U 7, Old Etonians 6, Fulham 6, Oxford University 6, Portsmouth 6, Notts Co 5, The Wanderers 5, Watford 5, Cardiff C 4, Luton T 4, Millwall 4, Queen's Park (Glasgow) 4, Royal Engineers 4, Barnsley 3, Blackpool 3, Clapham R 3, Crystal Palace (professional club) 3, Ipswich T 3, Middlesbrough 3, Norwich C 3, Old Carthusians 3, Oldham Ath 3, Stoke C 3, The Swifts 3, Blackburn Olympic 2, Bristol C 2, Bury 2, Charlton Ath 2, Grimsby T 2, Swansea T 2, Swindon T 2, Wimbledon 2, Bradford C 1, Brighton & HA 1, Cambridge University 1, Chesterfield 1, Coventry C 1, Crewe Alex 1, Crystal Palace (amateur club) 1, Darwen 1, Derby Junction 1, Glasgow R 1, Hull C 1, Marlow 1, Old Harrovians 1, Orient 1, Plymouth Arg 1, Port Vale 1, QPR 1, Reading 1, Shropshire W 1, Wycombe W 1, York C 1.

FA CUP ATTENDANCES 1969–2009

	1st Round	2nd Round	3rd Round	4th Round	5th Round	6th Round	Semi-finals & Final	Total	No. of matches	Average per match
2008–09	161,526	96,923	631,070	529,585	297,364	149,566	264,635	2,131,669	163	13,078
2007–08	175,195	99,528	704,300	356,404	276,903	142,780	256,210	2,011,320	152	13,232
2006–07	168,884	113,924	708,628	478,924	340,612	230,064	177,810	2,218,846	158	14,043
2005–06	188,876	107,456	654,570	388,339	286,225	163,449	177,723	1,966,638	160	12,291
2004–05	161,197	98,702	602,152	477,472	339,082	127,914	193,233	1,999,752	146	13,697
2003–04	162,738	117,967	624,732	347,964	292,521	156,780	167,401	1,870,103	149	12,551
2002–03	189,905	104,103	577,494	404,599	242,483	156,244	175,498	1,850,326	150	12,336
2001–02	198,369	119,781	566,284	330,434	249,190	173,757	171,278	1,809,093	148	12,224
2000–01	171,689	122,061	577,204	398,241	256,899	100,663	177,778	1,804,535	151	11,951
1999–2000	181,485	127,728	514,030	374,795	182,511	105,443	214,921	1,700,913	158	10,765
1998–99	191,954	132,341	609,486	431,613	359,398	181,005	202,150	2,107,947	155	13,599
1997–98	204,803	130,261	629,127	455,557	341,290	192,651	172,007	2,125,696	165	12,883
1996–97	209,521	122,324	651,139	402,293	199,873	67,035	191,813	1,843,998	151	12,211
1995–96	185,538	115,669	748,997	391,218	274,055	174,142	156,500	2,046,199	167	12,252
1994–95	219,511	125,629	640,017	438,596	257,650	159,787	174,059	2,015,249	161	12,517
1993–94	190,683	118,031	691,064	430,234	172,196	134,705	228,233	1,965,146	159	12,359
1992–93	241,968	174,702	612,494	377,211	198,379	149,675	293,241	2,047,670	161	12,718
1991–92	231,940	117,078	586,014	372,576	270,537	155,603	201,592	1,935,340	160	12,095
1990–91	194,195	121,450	594,592	530,279	276,112	124,826	196,434	2,038,518	162	12,583
1989–90	209,542	133,483	683,047	412,483	351,423	123,065	277,420	2,190,463	170	12,885
1988–89	212,775	121,326	690,199	421,255	206,781	176,629	167,353	1,966,318	164	12,173
1987–88	204,411	104,561	720,121	443,133	281,461	119,313	177,585	2,050,585	155	13,229
1986–87	209,290	146,761	593,520	349,342	263,550	119,396	195,533	1,877,400	165	11,378
1985–86	171,142	130,034	486,838	495,526	311,833	184,262	192,316	1,971,951	168	11,738
1984–85	174,604	137,078	616,229	320,772	269,232	148,690	242,754	1,909,359	157	12,162
1983–84	192,276	151,647	625,965	417,298	181,832	185,282	187,000	1,941,400	166	11,695
1982–83	191,312	150,046	670,503	452,688	260,069	193,845	291,162	2,209,625	154	14,348
1981–82	236,220	127,300	513,185	356,987	203,334	124,308	279,621	1,840,955	160	11,506
1980–81	246,824	194,502	832,578	534,402	320,530	288,714	339,250	2,756,800	169	16,312
1979–80	267,121	204,759	804,701	507,725	364,039	157,530	355,541	2,661,416	163	16,328
1978–79	243,773	185,343	880,345	537,748	243,683	263,213	249,897	2,604,002	166	15,687
1977–78	258,248	178,930	881,406	540,164	400,751	137,059	198,020	2,594,578	160	16,216
1976–77	379,230	192,159	942,523	631,265	373,330	205,379	258,216	2,982,102	174	17,139
1975–76	255,533	178,099	867,880	573,843	471,925	206,851	205,810	2,759,941	161	17,142
1974–75	283,956	170,466	914,994	646,434	393,323	268,361	291,368	2,968,903	172	17,261
1973–74	214,236	125,295	840,142	747,909	346,012	233,307	273,051	2,779,952	167	16,646
1972–73	259,432	169,114	938,741	735,825	357,386	241,934	226,543	2,928,975	160	18,306
1971–72	277,726	236,127	986,094	711,399	486,378	230,292	248,546	3,158,562	160	19,741
1970–71	329,687	230,942	956,683	757,852	360,612	304,937	279,644	3,220,432	162	19,879
1969–70	345,229	195,102	925,930	651,374	319,893	198,537	390,700	3,026,765	170	17,805

THE FA CUP 2008–09
PRELIMINARY AND QUALIFYING ROUNDS

EXTRA PRELIMINARY ROUND

Bedlington Terriers v Chester-Le-Street Town	1-0
Consett v Pontefract Collieries	5-1
South Shields v Hebburn Town	5-1
Horden CW v Sunderland Nissan	1-3
Northallerton Town v Whitley Bay	1-3
Glasshoughton Welfare v Billingham Synthonia	2-2, 1-5
Crook Town v North Shields	6-1
Pickering Town v Liversedge	4-1
West Auckland Town v Hall Road Rangers	2-1
Jarrow Roofing Boldon CA v Spennymoor Town	2-1
Team Northumbria v Esh Winning	4-1
West Allotment Celtic v Sunderland RCA	2-1
Shildon v Leeds Carnegie	3-0
Armthorpe Welfare v Yorkshire Amateur	5-0
Marske United v Whickham	0-1
Billingham Town v Brandon United	2-2, 2-1
Morpeth Town v Ryton	0-2
Washington v Stokesley SC	0-0, 0-2
Seaham Red Star v Selby Town	1-3
Bridlington Town v Guisborough Town	3-2
Norton & Stockton Ancients v Newcastle Benfield	0-1
Silsden v Eccleshill United	4-1
Ashington v Thackley	1-0
Thornaby v Tow Law Town	0-3
Dunston Federation v Tadcaster Albion	4-0
Cheadle Town v Newcastle Town	1-2
Leek CSOB v AFC Fylde	1-4
Maltby Main v Bottesford Town	3-4
Dinnington Town v Atherton LR	1-2
Parkgate v Norton United	1-2
Darwen v Penrith	4-7
Holker Old Boys v St Helens Town	2-2, 0-1
Formby v AFC Emley	3-1
Winsford United v Nostell MW	3-3, 0-3
Bootle v Eccleshall	5-1
Abbey Hey v Flixton	1-1, 1-3
Barton Town Old Boys v Winterton Rangers	1-3
Maine Road v Chadderton	2-1
Brodsworth MW v Ashton Town	2-1
Oldham Town v Ashton Athletic	2-0
Congleton Town v AFC Blackpool	2-2, 4-1
Ramsbottom United v Hallam	2-0
Alsager Town v Padiham	0-1
Runcorn Linnets v Rossington Main	3-2
Colne v Daisy Hill	4-1
Atherton Collieries v Bacup Borough	1-2
Squires Gate v Biddulph Victoria	3-1
AFC Wulfrunians v Pilkington XXX	1-1, 1-2
Arnold Town v Long Eaton United	1-2
Tipton Town v Teversall	2-0
Highgate United w.o. v Brierley Hill & Withymoor withdrew.	
Racing Club Warwick v Cadbury Athletic	6-2
Westfields v Gedling MW	7-1
Stratford Town v Pershore Town	2-0
Shirebrook Town v Causeway United	3-2
Gedling Town w.o. v Stapenhill withdrew.	
New Mills v Friar Lane & Epworth	1-2
Barrowash Victoria v Market Drayton Town	2-4
Coventry Sphinx v Barwell	1-2
Tividale v Coleshill Town	1-3
Wellington v Mickleover Sports	1-4
Dunkirk v Alvechurch	1-4
Heather St Johns v Cradley Town	0-3
Ledbury Town v Bromyard Town	2-3
Staveley MW v Bridgnorth Town	3-1
Goodrich v Meir KA	1-1, 4-4
Meir KA won 5-4 on penalties.	
Pegasus Juniors v Glossop North End	1-4
Rocester v Nuneaton Griff	0-1
Southam United v Boldmere St Michaels	3-1
Hinckley Downes v Shawbury United	4-2
Heath Hayes v Shifnal Town	1-3
Oadby Town v Oldbury United	0-3
Ellesmere Rangers v Dudley Sports	4-0
Dudley Town v Rainworth MW	1-2
Brocton v Lye Town	1-1, 1-5
Gornal Athletic v Pelsall Victoria	3-1

GSA Sports v Coalville Town	1-3
Stone Dominoes v Walsall Wood	3-2
Bolehall Swifts v Studley	1-3
Castle Vale v Barrow Town	0-2
Yaxley v Lincoln Moorlands Railway	4-3
Sleaford Town v Ely City	3-2
Haverhill Rovers v March Town United	2-2, 0-2
Stowmarket Town v Ipswich Wanderers	2-2, 0-2
St Neots Town v Holbeach United	7-1
Mildenhall Town v Felixstowe & Walton United	8-0
Gorleston v Fakenham Town	3-5
Woodbridge Town v Newmarket Town	1-0
Diss Town v Walsham Le Willows	1-2
Hadleigh United v Great Yarmouth Town	0-1
Whitton United v Cornard United	1-1, 3-3
Cornard United won 4-2 on penalties.	
Leiston v Blackstones	2-1
Long Melford v Boston Town	2-5
Thetford Town v Needham Market	0-1
Debenham LC v Dereham Town	0-1
Lowestoft Town v St Ives Town	2-1
Wisbech Town v Norwich United	1-1, 3-1
Deeping Rangers v Bourne Town	3-0
Wroxham v Kirklee & Pakefield	1-0
Raunds Town v Harwich & Parkeston	2-2, 3-0
FC Clacton v St Margaretsbury	2-0
Rothwell Corinthians v Langford	2-3
Erith Town v Potton United	7-1
Clapton v Stewarts & Lloyds	0-3
Cockfosters v Ampthill Town	0-1
Tring Athletic v Berkhamsted Town	5-3
Desborough Town v Saffron Walden Town	4-4, 1-2
Southend Manor v AFC Kempston Rovers	2-1
North Greenford United v Tiptree United	0-1
Tokyngton Manor v Biggleswade United	2-3
Kentish Town v Wellingborough Town	1-1, 0-2
Cogenhoe United v Northampton Spencer	0-1
Stotfold v Colney Heath	3-1
Kingsbury London Tigers v Eton Manor	1-0
Long Buckby v Broxbourne Borough V&E	0-2
Hanwell Town v Wootton Blue Cross	3-2
London Colney v Sporting Bengal United	1-1, 0-1
Stanway Rovers v Welwyn Garden City	4-0
Halstead Town v London APSA	4-1
Haringey Borough v Bedfont	1-3
Wivenhoe Town v Barkingside	1-4
Hullbridge Sports v Leverstock Green	2-1
Oxhey Jets v Hertford Town	5-0
Hoddesdon Town v Stansted	2-3
Wembley v Royston Town	1-1, 0-4
Bedfont Green v Barking	4-0
Bowers & Pitsea v Harefield United	1-2
Brimsdown Rovers v Hatfield Town	0-2
Romford v Biggleswade Town	3-0
Daventry United v Burnham Ramblers	0-0, 3-5
Selsey v Egham Town	1-0
Three Bridges v VCD Athletic	2-3
Mile Oak v Bookham	3-0
Hailsham Town v Worthing United	1-0
Ash United v Sevenoaks Town	0-4
Westfield v East Preston	0-3
Banstead Athletic v Colliers Wood United	0-2
Hassocks v Shoreham	0-5
Slade Green v Tunbridge Wells	1-1, 1-2
Ringmer v Rye United	4-3
Pagham v Hythe Town	1-5
Dorking v Chessington & Hook United	2-1
Littlehampton Town v Peacehaven & Telscombe	2-5
Whitehawk v Croydon	0-0, 3-4
Eastbourne United v Epsom & Ewell	2-4
Crawley Down v Chichester City United	2-2
abandoned 45 minutes; floodlit failure.	
Cobham v Southwick	1-1, 3-1
Erith & Belvedere v Lancing	4-2
Wick v Molesey	0-3
Wealden v East Grinstead Town	3-4
Frimley Green v Guildford City	1-0
Faversham Town v Horsham YMCA	0-2
Redhill v Herne Bay	1-2

Camberley Town v Lordswood	1-1, 4-2
Sidley United v Farnham Town	4-2
Chertsey Town v Deal Town	2-2, 2-1
Lingfield v Arundel	0-3
Horley Town v Raynes Park Vale	2-2, 1-3
Bournemouth v Fareham Town	2-1
New Milton Town v Amesbury Town	5-0
Westbury United v Hamble ASSC	0-0, 2-2
Westbury United won 4-2 on penalties.	
Brockenhurst v Reading Town	2-1
Aylesbury Vale v Highworth Town	4-2
Kidlington v Sandhurst Town	4-1
Christchurch v Melksham Town	2-1
Witney United v Buckingham Town	2-0
Milton United v Lymington Town	1-2
Hartley Wintney v Cove	3-1
VT v Newport Pagnell Town	0-2
Hungerford Town v Marlow United	0-0, 2-2
Marlow United won 4-2 on penalties.	
Devizes Town v Calne Town	2-2, 0-3
Downton v Abingdon Town	2-0
Chalfont St Peter v Ardleigh United	4-3
Bicester Town v Bristol Manor Farm	1-0
Thame United v Bitton	0-0, 0-3
Bemerton Heath Harlequins v Almondsbury Town	1-4
Corsham Town v Moneyfields	0-2
Shortwood United v Henley Town	5-0
Harrow Hill v Alresford Town	4-1
Cowes Sports v Alton Town	4-3
Ringwood v Hallen	1-0
Carterton v Newport (IW)	2-1
Flackwell Heath v Wootton Bassett Town	1-1, 6-1
Wantage Town v Brading Town	1-3
Fairford Town v Shrivenham	4-1
Chard Town v Street	2-2, 1-5
Elmore v Bodmin Town	0-4
Willand Rovers v Wadebridge Town	6-0
Welton Rovers v Poole Town	0-1
Launceston v Sherborne Town	3-0
Liskeard Athletic v Larkhall Athletic	0-5
Ilfracombe Town v Tavistock	1-4
Bideford v Keynsham Town	4-2
Shaftesbury v Falmouth Town	2-2, 2-4
Odd Down v Bishop Sutton	2-1
Gillingham Town v Saltash United	2-2, 4-2
Radstock Town v Brislington	1-2
Bridport v Barnstaple Town	2-1
Dawlish Town v Wimborne Town	0-0, 2-3
Minehead v Clevedon United	0-3
St Blazey v Hamworthy United	0-2
Frome Town v Shepton Mallet	3-1

PRELIMINARY ROUND

Ashington v Ossett Albion	2-1
Team Northumbria v Bedlington Terriers	0-3
Armthorpe Welfare v Crook Town	1-1, 0-3
Wakefield v Stokesley SC	2-0
South Shields v Selby Town	0-4
Sunderland Nissan v Newcastle Blue Star	1-2
West Allotment Celtic v Shildon	1-3
West Auckland Town v Durham City	0-5
Bishop Auckland v Consett	3-3, 1-4
Goole v Newcastle Benfield	0-4
Billingham Town v Whitley Bay	0-4
FC Halifax Town v Silsden	0-0, 3-1
Whickham v Pickering Town	0-2
Jarrow Roofing Boldon CA v Bridlington Town	2-2, 1-2
Garforth Town v Tow Law Town	1-0
Billingham Synthonia v Harrogate Railway	0-2
Dunston Federation v Harrogate Railway	1-0
Newcastle Town v Skelmersdale United	0-1
Oldham United v Rossendale United	1-1, 0-3
Bootle v Padiham	1-0
Trafford v Stocksbridge Park Steels	2-4
Congleton Town v Squires Gate	1-1, 3-0
Penrith v Clitheroe	1-3
Bottesford Town v Flixton	2-2, 5-7
Lancaster City v Salford City	1-2
Norton United v Leek Town	1-3
Mossley v Ramsbottom United	3-1
Formby v Colne	0-5
Brigg Town v Maine Road	2-2, 2-1
Radcliffe Borough v Winterton Rangers	1-2
Warrington Town v Nostell MW	0-0, 2-1
Bacup Borough v St Helens Town	3-1

Chorley v Atherton LR	0-1
AFC Fylde v Sheffield	1-1, 0-4
Woodley Sports v Brodsworth MW	0-0, 2-0
Curzon Ashton v Runcorn Linnets	4-0
Bamber Bridge v Colwyn Bay	4-3
Hinckley Downes v Gornal Athletic	0-4
Atherstone Town v Quorn	1-0
Malvern Town v Coalville Town	1-3
Oldbury United v Friar Lane & Epworth	0-1
Long Eaton United v Rushall Olympic	1-0
Glapwell v Market Drayton Town	2-1
Ellesmere Rangers v Bromsgrove Rovers	2-1
Loughborough Dynamo v Tipton Town	0-1
Shirebrook Town v Studley	1-3
Stone Dominoes v Rainworth MW	1-2
Nuneaton Town v Gedling Town	1-0
Westfields v Stratford Town	2-4
Chasetown v Carlton Town	5-0
Kidsgrove Athletic v Pilkington XXX	3-0
Highgate United v Romulus	1-4
Sutton Coldfield Town v Cradley Town	2-3
Gresley Rovers v Alvechurch	4-1
Shepshed Dynamo v Mickleover Sports	3-2
Retford United v Barrow Town	3-1
Glossop North End v Belper Town	1-2
Meir KA v Nuneaton Griff	1-0
Lye Town v Southam United	1-2
Leamington v Staveley MW	4-0
Willenhall Town v Bedworth United	0-0, 3-2
Racing Club Warwick v Stourport Swifts	0-2
Coleshill United v Shifnal Town	2-3
Bromyard Town v Barwell	1-5
Spalding United v Yaxley	2-3
Soham Town Rangers v Needham Market	0-2
Leiston v March Town United	3-1
Wisbech Town v Mildenhall Town	2-2, 0-4
Fakenham Town v Boston Town	0-4
Grantham Town v Woodbridge Town	4-1
Walsham Le Willows v Sleaford Town	1-2
Dereham Town v Stamford	2-2, 0-1
AFC Sudbury v Lowestoft Town	1-1, 2-2
Lowestoft Town won 4-1 on penalties.	
Ipswich Wanderers v Cornard United	1-1, 0-3
Great Yarmouth Town v Wroxham	2-2, 0-3
St Neots Town v Lincoln United	2-3
Deeping Rangers v Bury Town	0-4
Brentwood Town v Erith Town	2-1
Dulwich Hamlet v Broxbourne Borough V&E	1-1, 2-1
Great Wakering Rovers v Bedfont Green	4-0
Langford v Arlesey Town	0-1
Oxhey Jets v Ilford	5-2
Northwood v Metropolitan Police	0-2
Northampton Spencer v Wingate & Finchley	2-2, 0-4
Bedfont v Tiptree United	2-4
Barton Rovers v Burnham Ramblers	2-1
Leyton v Romford	2-1
Ampthill Town v Dunstable Town	0-4
Halstead Town v Stotfold	1-2
East Thurrock United v Hatfield Town	4-2
FC Clacton v Stansted	4-0
Barkingside v Stanway Rovers	0-4
Cheshunt v Southend Manor	2-1
Tilbury v Leighton Town	0-2
Stewarts & Lloyds v Corinthian Casuals	3-2
Hanwell Town v Aveley	0-5
Witham Town v Maldon Town	3-3, 4-1
Waltham Forest v Thamesmead Town	0-1
Harefield United v Saffron Walden Town	1-1, 0-2
Ware v Sporting Bengal United	4-0
Concord Rangers v Kingsbury London Tigers	2-0
Rothwell Town v Hullbridge Sports	2-0
Hillingdon Borough v Enfield Town	3-1
Redbridge v Uxbridge	1-3
Croydon Athletic v Wellingborough Town	3-1
Tring Athletic v Biggleswade United	1-2
AFC Hayes v Royston Town	1-3
Woodford United v Raunds Town	1-1, 0-0
Raunds Town won 4-3 on penalties.	
Potters Bar Town v Waltham Abbey	1-1, 0-1
Walton Casuals v Molesey	2-0
Mile Oak v Arundel	0-2
Horsham YMCA v Tunbridge Wells	3-1
Sevenoaks Town v Folkestone Invicta	4-4, 1-4
Ashford Town v Leatherhead	3-2
Herne Bay v Chipstead	2-2, 0-2
Epsom & Ewell v Frimley Green	2-1

Whitstable Town v Selsey	1-0
Camberley Town v Worthing	0-6
Hythe Town v Walton & Hersham	2-1
Crowborough Athletic v Ringmer	3-1
East Preston v Erith & Belvedere	1-2
Sittingbourne v Chertsey Town	2-1
Burgess Hill Town v Hailsham Town	2-0
Cobham v Merstham	0-2
Shoreham v Kingstonian	1-3
Chatham Town v Dorking	2-2, 1-0
East Grinstead Town v Colliers Wood United	0-3
Raynes Park Vale v Godalming Town	1-2
Whyteleafe v Peacehaven & Telscombe	0-0, 3-1
VCD Athletic v Croydon	3-1
Sidley United v Eastbourne Town	1-2
Cray Wanderers v Chichester City United	4-1
AFC Totton v Moneyfields	2-1
Westbury United v Fairford Town	0-6
Cowes Sports v Lymington Town	4-0
Aylesbury Vale v Burnham	1-1, 2-1
Aylesbury United v Windsor & Eton	2-0
Ringwood Town v Marlow	2-2, 0-4
Chalfont St Peter v Harrow Hill	2-1
Didcot Town v Bournemouth	5-0
Carterton v North Leigh	0-1
Newport Pagnell Town v Cirencester Town	1-0
Gosport Borough v Hartley Wintney	5-0
Kidlington v Almondsbury Town	2-3
Chesham United v Brading Town	5-1
Fleet Town v Brockenhurst	1-1, 1-0
Bitton v Bishop's Cleeve	2-1
Witney United v Thatcham Town	2-2, 1-3
Beaconsfield SYCOB v Marlow United	1-0
Shortwood United v Christchurch	2-0
Abingdon United v Slough Town	1-1, 2-5
Andover v Calne Town	1-3
New Milton Town v Downton	1-2
Flackwell Heath v Winchester City	3-4
Bracknell Town v Bicester Town	3-0
Bodmin Town v Bridgwater Town	0-3
Launceston v Paulton Rovers	0-2
Clevedon United v Taunton Town	0-3
Odd Down v Wimborne Town	0-2
Street v Bideford	3-3, 1-2
Cinderford Town v Frome Town	0-1
Falmouth Town v Truro City	0-4
Poole Town v Willand Rovers	2-1
Hamworthy United v Brislington	3-2
Larkhall Athletic v Tavistock	6-2
Bridport v Gillingham Town	3-0

FIRST QUALIFYING ROUND

Bedlington Terriers v Bradford Park Avenue	0-1
Selby Town v Guiseley	2-4
Garforth Town v Ossett Town	1-0
Newcastle Benfield v Bridlington Town	1-1, 2-1
Ashington v Durham City	0-6
Whitby Town v Dunston Federation	3-2
Consett v North Ferriby United	4-4, 1-6
Wakefield v Crook Town	4-3
Ryton v FC Halifax Town	0-4
Newcastle Blue Star v Shildon	2-0
Pickering Town v Whitley Bay	0-1
Congleton Town v Prescot Cables	0-2
Sheffield v Colne	3-2
Woodley Sports v Rossendale United	1-3
Bacup Borough v Cammell Laird	3-0
Brigg Town v Stocksbridge Park Steels	0-4
Clitheroe v Leek Town	1-1, 1-0
Buxton v Bootle	3-1
Frickley Athletic v Skelmersdale United	1-0
Nantwich Town v FC United of Manchester	0-0, 4-3
Flixton v Mossley	1-4
Bamber Bridge v Witton Albion	1-2
Salford City v Atherton LR	5-0
Curzon Ashton v Leigh Genesis	1-0
Winterton Rangers v Warrington Town	4-2
Ashton United v Kendal Town	2-3
Marine v Worksop Town	1-5
Hednesford Town v Atherstone Town	1-2
Shepshed Dynamo v Stourport Swifts	7-0
Friar Lane & Epworth v Rugby Town	0-0, 3-5
Cradley Town v Ellesmere Rangers	2-2, 3-1
Stourbridge v Rainworth MW	0-0, 3-1
Gresley Rovers v Chasetown	2-4

Meir KA v Halesowen Town	1-1, 1-8
Shifnal Town v Long Eaton United	0-1
Gornal Athletic v Southam United	0-0, 1-2
Retford United v Willenhall Town	1-1, 3-1
Ilkeston Town v Matlock Town	4-1
Coalville Town v Studley	2-1
Romulus v Stratford Town	2-1
Eastwood Town v Kidsgrove Athletic	4-0
Leamington v Evesham United	0-3
Belper Town v Barwell	3-2
Boston United v Glapwell	6-1
Nuneaton Town v Tipton Town	3-1
Cambridge City v Lowestoft Town	2-0
Cornard United v Leiston	0-5
Grantham Town v Wroxham	3-4
Lincoln United v Mildenhall Town	3-2
Bury Town v Boston Town	3-1
Sleaford Town v Stamford	2-6
Needham Market v Yaxley	2-2, 3-0
Boreham Wood v Biggleswade United	3-0
Hillingdon Borough v East Thurrock United	0-6
Royston Town v Hendon	2-4
Ware v Barton Rovers	1-1, 2-1
Stewarts & Lloyds v Croydon Athletic	5-1
Tiptree United v Stanway Rovers	1-3
Billericay Town v FC Clacton	4-1
Oxhey Jets v Dulwich Hamlet	1-5
Hemel Hempstead Town v Harrow Borough	1-1, 2-1
Thamesmead Town v Great Wakering Rovers	2-1
Metropolitan Police v Corby Town	0-3
Wingate & Finchley v Witham Town	2-0
Stotfold v Leighton Town	0-3
Hitchin Town v Concord Rangers	5-0
Leyton v Brackley Town	2-4
Canvey Island v Dunstable Town	1-5
Raunds Town v Ashford Town (Middlesex)	0-3
Heybridge Swifts v Uxbridge	1-1, 3-1
Cheshunt v Staines Town	0-3
Saffron Walden Town v AFC Hornchurch	0-2
Harlow Town v Aveley	5-1
Brentwood Town v Arlesey Town	1-1, 0-1
Waltham Abbey v Rothwell Town	0-1
Wealdstone v Bedford Town	2-2, 1-1
Bedford Town won 4-2 on penalties.	
Dartford v Hastings United	3-2
Crowborough Athletic v Walton Casuals	1-0
Burgess Hill Town v Epsom & Ewell	5-2
Horsham v Colliers Wood United	1-0
Horsham YMCA v Whyteleafe	1-1, 0-2
Folkestone Invicta v Ramsgate	1-0
Erith & Belvedere v Sittingbourne	2-0
Worthing v Margate	5-1
Godalming Town v Arundel	1-1, 2-1
Carshalton Athletic v Eastbourne Town	4-1
Kingstonian v Ashford Town	3-0
Sutton United v Cray Wanderers	3-1
Merstham v Whitstable Town	3-1
Hythe Town v VCD Athletic	0-0, 0-3
Tonbridge Angels v Dover Athletic	1-2
Chipstead v Chatham Town	1-0
Maidstone United v Tooting & Mitcham United	2-1
Bracknell Town v Oxford City	2-0
Tie awarded to Oxford City – Bracknell Town removed.	
Aylesbury Vale v Downton	2-0
Shortwood United v Didcot Town	3-2
Farnborough v Slough Town	1-0
Fleet Town v Cowes Sports	3-0
Newport Pagnell Town v Marlow	2-1
Aylesbury United v Almondsbury Town	2-0
Chalfont St Peter v Gloucester City	5-3
Chippenham Town v Banbury United	2-0
Calne Town v Bashley	0-5
Bitton v Beaconsfield SYCOB	3-2
Fairford Town v Gosport Borough	1-2
Winchester City v AFC Totton	0-3
North Leigh v Chesham United	2-3
Thatcham Town v Swindon Supermarine	1-0
Frome Town v Bideford	1-1, 3-1
Paulton Rovers v Larkhall Athletic	3-0
Bridgwater Town v Mangotsfield United	1-3
Hamworthy United v Taunton Town	2-1
Truro City v Yate Town	3-1
Clevedon Town v Bridport	4-1
Wimborne Town v Tiverton Town	0-1
Poole Town v Merthyr Tydfil	3-0

SECOND QUALIFYING ROUND

Nantwich Town v FC Halifax Town	4-1
Kendal Town v Mossley	1-2
Southport v Vauxhall Motors	3-2
Frickley Athletic v Clitheroe	1-0
North Ferriby United v Newcastle Blue Star	1-4
Whitby Town v Blyth Spartans	2-2, 2-5
Stocksbridge Park Steels v Curzon Ashton	1-2
Wakefield v Fleetwood Town	0-3
Droylsden v Bradford Park Avenue	2-1
Winterton Rangers v Newcastle Benfield	1-1, 1-2
Durham City v Rossendale United	4-0
Whitley Bay v Hyde United	3-1
Guiseley v Garforth Town	2-2, 3-1
Buxton v Burscough	1-0
Prescot Cables v Salford City	2-1
Workington v Harrogate Town	0-0, 0-0
Harrogate Town won 5-4 on penalties.	
Gateshead v Witton Albion	1-1, 3-1
Stalybridge Celtic v Farsley Celtic	4-0
Sheffield v Bacup Borough	4-1
Coalville Town v Stafford Rangers	2-1
Evesham United v Nuneaton Town	2-2, 2-1
Lincoln United v Eastwood Town	0-1
Rugby Town v Long Eaton United	5-1
Shepshed Dynamo v Alfreton Town	1-2
Chasetown v Rothwell Town	1-1, 5-2
Hucknall Town v Cradley Town	3-0
Belper Town v Redditch United	4-1
Boston United v Stamford	2-1
Retford United v Romulus	3-1
Stourbridge v Brackley Town	1-1, 0-1
Halesowen Town v Gainsborough Trinity	3-0
Southam United v Atherstone Town	1-1, 1-3
Stewarts & Lloyds v Ilkeston Town	2-3
King's Lynn v Worksop Town	2-1
AFC Telford United v Corby Town	3-2
Worcester City v Tamworth	0-1
Hinckley United v Solihull Moors	4-1
Bromley v AFC Hornchurch	0-1
Thurrock v Boreham Wood	0-5
Dunstable Town v Chipstead	2-3
Folkestone Invicta v Thamesmead Town	1-2
Wroxham v Heybridge Swifts	2-1
Burgess Hill Town v Bognor Regis Town	0-0, 2-0
Bedford Town v AFC Wimbledon	2-2, 0-3
Welling United v Whyteleafe	1-1, 0-2
Bishop's Stortford v Wingate & Finchley	3-2
Hitchin Town v Stanway Rovers	0-0, 2-0
St Albans City v Harlow Town	0-0, 2-3
Erith & Belvedere v Godalming Town	0-2
Dulwich Hamlet v Hendon	2-2, 1-2
Merstham v Thamesmead Town	1-1, 5-1
Leighton Town v Crowborough Athletic	0-1
Dartford v Hampton & Richmond Borough	0-1
Staines Town v Hayes & Yeading United	0-0, 3-5
Maidstone United v Fisher Athletic	3-2
Bury Town v Chelmsford City	2-1
Hemel Hempstead Town v Ware	1-2
Carshalton Athletic v Leiston	1-2
Sutton United v Billericay Town	3-1
Cambridge City v Worthing	1-1, 1-2
Kingstonian v Braintree Town	4-0
Dover Athletic v Needham Market	3-1
East Thurrock United v VCD Athletic	3-0
Arlesey Town v Ashford Town (Middlesex)	1-4
Paulton Rovers v Bitton	1-0
Fleet Town v Newport Pagnell Town	5-0
Poole Town v Frome Town	1-3
Bath City v Clevedon Town	2-0
Aylesbury United v Mangotsfield United	4-1
Weston-Super-Mare v Chesham United	2-4
Eastleigh v Farnborough	1-0
AFC Totton v Thatcham Town	2-1
Havant & Waterlooville v Shortwood United	2-2, 1-0
Bashley v Maidenhead United	2-1
Basingstoke Town v Hamworthy United	3-1
Oxford City v Tiverton Town	2-1
Aylesbury Vale v Gosport Borough	1-1, 0-4
Dorchester Town v Newport County	2-2, 2-1
Chalfont St Peter v Team Bath	0-1
Truro City v Chippenham Town	1-1, 2-4

THIRD QUALIFYING ROUND

Belper Town v Prescot Cables	4-1
Guiseley v Sheffield	3-3, 1-2
Buxton v Blyth Spartans	0-1
Curzon Ashton v Mossley	4-3
Retford United v Newcastle Benfield	1-0
Droylsden v Gateshead	3-2
Eastwood Town v Harrogate Town	2-2, 2-0
Alfreton Town v Ilkeston Town	0-0, 3-1
Stalybridge Celtic v Durham City	1-6
Fleetwood Town v Frickley Athletic	2-0
Whitley Bay v Nantwich Town	1-5
Newcastle Blue Star v Hucknall Town	4-0
Southport v Boston United	0-2
AFC Hornchurch v Merstham	2-0
Boreham Wood v Brackley Town	0-1
Hendon v AFC Telford United	1-2
Hitchin Town v Hinckley United	1-2
Kingstonian v Hayes & Yeading United	1-3
Hampton & Richmond Borough v Whyteleafe	2-0
Tamworth v East Thurrock United	3-1
Wroxham v King's Lynn	0-2
Leiston v Coalville Town	1-0
Dover Athletic v AFC Wimbledon	0-0, 0-2
Evesham United v Chasetown	2-0
Halesowen Town v Maidstone United	1-4
Bishop's Stortford v Rugby Town	2-1
Harlow Town v Crowborough Athletic	1-1, 2-0
Bury Town v Worthing	1-0
Atherstone Town v Chipstead	1-1, 0-3
Ware v Sutton United	1-2
Havant & Waterlooville v Godalming Town	2-1
Horsham v Paulton Rovers	2-1
Basingstoke Town v Bashley	2-2, 3-0
Oxford City v Chesham United	2-1
AFC Totton v Fleet Town	5-2
Ashford Town (Middlesex) v Chippenham Town	1-0
Frome Town v Team Bath	2-2, 0-4
Burgess Hill Town v Eastleigh	2-1
Dorchester Town v Gosport Borough	1-0
Bath City v Aylesbury United	0-1

FOURTH QUALIFYING ROUND

Hinckley United v Curzon Ashton	1-1, 1-1
Curzon Ashton won 3-2 on penalties.	
Kettering Town v Burton Albion	3-0
Tamworth v Barrow	0-4
King's Lynn v Kidderminster Harriers	1-5
Boston United v Cambridge United	2-3
Newcastle Blue Star v Altrincham	1-2
Droylsden v Belper Town	0-0, 2-1
Durham City v Histon	2-2, 2-5
Retford United v Alfreton Town	1-3
Northwich Victoria v AFC Telford United	0-3
Blyth Spartans v Sheffield	3-1
York City v Mansfield Town	0-0, 0-1
Fleetwood Town v Nantwich Town	4-3
Wrexham v Eastwood Town	0-0, 0-2
Stevenage Borough v Horsham	2-2, 4-1
Woking v Ebbsfleet United	2-2, 0-1
Hampton & Richmond Borough v Brackley Town	0-1
Oxford United v Hayes & Yeading United	2-0
Maidstone United v AFC Wimbledon	0-1
Team Bath v Salisbury City	1-0
Dorchester Town v Bishop's Stortford	1-0
Oxford City v Eastbourne Borough	0-1
Ashford Town (Middlesex) v Forest Green Rovers	0-0, 0-4
Evesham United v Rushden & Diamonds	2-0
Bury Town v Basingstoke Town	4-1
Burgess Hill Town v Harlow Town	0-3
Grays Athletic v AFC Totton	2-0
Aylesbury United v Sutton United	0-1
Torquay United v Chipstead	4-1
Leiston v Lewes	1-1, 3-1
Crawley Town v Havant & Waterlooville	0-3
Weymouth v AFC Hornchurch	1-2

THE E.ON FA CUP 2008–09
COMPETITION PROPER

■ *Denotes player sent off.*

FIRST ROUND

Friday, 7 November 2008

Leeds U (1) 1 *(Robinson 37 (pen))*
Northampton T (1) 1 *(McGleish 9)*   9531
Leeds U: Ankergren; Richardson, Parker (White), Howson (Showunmi), Telfer, Michalik, Douglas, Snodgrass, Robinson, Becchio, Delph.
Northampton T: Fielding; Dolman, Jackman, Gilligan, Hughes, Doig (Dyer), Coke■, Crowe, McGleish (Bignall), Constantine (Davis), Holt.

Saturday, 8 November 2008

AFC Telford (0) 2 *(Adams 70, 83)*
Southend U (1) 2 *(Laurent 34, Christophe 90)*   3631
AFC Telford: Young; Vaughan, Meredith, Adams, Whitehead, Cowan, Naylor (Fearns), Bermiglio, Moore (Jagielka), Brown, Blakeman (Rodgers).
Southend U: Mildenhall; Francis, Herd, Christophe, Clarke, Barrett, Betsy (Scannell), McCormack, Revell, Laurent, Grant (Walker).

Accrington S (0) 0
Tranmere R (0) 0   2126
Accrington S: Arthur; Edwards, King, Griffiths, Williams, Charnock, Ryan (Richardson), Mullin J, Mullin P, Procter, Miles.
Tranmere R: Coyne; Edds (Greenacre), Andy Taylor, Shotton, Chorley, Kay, Barnett, Shuker, Moore, Savage, Jennings.

Aldershot T (0) 1 *(Grant 90 (pen))*
Rotherham U (0) 1 *(Cummins 54)*   2632
Aldershot T: Bull; Blackburn, Straker, Harding, Day, Charles, Soares (Morgan), Davies, Grant, Hylton (Elvins), Hudson.
Rotherham U: Warrington; Tonge, Nicholas, Harrison, Sharps, Fenton, Mills, Cummins, Broughton (Barker), Rhodes (Reid), Garcia (Joseph).

Alfreton T (1) 4 *(McIntosh 4, Fortune-West 61, Law 65 (pen), Clayton 90)*
Bury T (2) 2 *(Johnson 23, Reed L 34)*   1060
Alfreton T: Evans; Hall (Marples), McIntosh, Butler, Brown, Muirhead, Mayman, Curtis, Law (Bowler), Fortune-West, Clayton.
Bury T: Garnham; Walker, Bullard, Nunn, Sloots, Smith, Steward, Johnson (Bugg), Reed L, Reed S, Barrett.

Barnet (0) 1 *(Yakubu 67)*
Rochdale (0) 1 *(Dagnall 49)*   1782
Barnet: Harrison; Devera (Deverdics) (Birchall), Gillet, Townsend, Yakubu, Leary, Adomah, Bishop, O'Flynn, Porter, Nicolau (St Aimie).
Rochdale: Russell; Wiseman, Kennedy, Jones G, Stanton (Holness), McArdle, Buckley, Toner, Dagnall, Thorpe (Shaw), Rundle (Jones M).

Blyth Spartans (2) 3 *(Reay 1, 29, Todd 53)*
Shrewsbury T (0) 1 *(Holt 68)*   2742
Blyth Spartans: Bell; Leeson, Boyle, Williams, Pell, Gildea, Todd, McCabe (Watson), Dale, Reay (Dalton), Wright (Poole).
Shrewsbury T: Garner; Herd, Tierney, Leslie (Hunt), Jackson (Symes), Coughlan, Humphrey (Hindmarch), Murray, Walker, Holt, McIntyre.

Bournemouth (0) 1 *(Pearce 76)*
Bristol R (0) 0   3935
Bournemouth: Jalal; Guyett, Ward, Bartley (Hollands), Pearce, Cooper, Cummings, Anderton, Pitman (Goulding), Bradbury■, Igoe.
Bristol R: Phillips; Green R, Lescott, Campbell, Anthony■, Hinton, Lines (Hunt), Disley, Lambert, Osei-Kuffour (Duffy), Hughes.

Brighton & HA (2) 3 *(McLeod 19, Cox 38, Fraser 78)*
Hartlepool U (0) 3 *(Hawkins 53 (og), Brown 55, Monkhouse 69)*   2545
Brighton & HA: Sullivan; Whing, Richards, Thomson (Fraser), Elphick, Hawkins (Forster), Cox (Robinson), El-Abd, Fleetwood, Virgo, McLeod.
Hartlepool U: Lee-Barrett; Sweeney, Humphreys (Robson), Clark, Nelson, Collins, Jones, Mackay (Foley), Porter, Brown (Liddle), Monkhouse.

Bury (0) 0
Gillingham (0) 1 *(Barcham 71)*   2161
Bury: Brown; Scott, Buchanan, Dawson (Baker), Sodje, Cresswell, Bennett, Barry-Murphy, Morrell (Hurst), Bishop, Jones (Racchi).
Gillingham: Julian; Fuller, Nutter, Weston, Richards, King, Bentley, Jarrett (Crofts), Mulligan, Barcham, Miller.

Carlisle U (0) 1 *(Madine 84)*
Grays Ath (0) 1 *(Stuart 52)*   3921
Carlisle U: Williams; Raven, Horwood (Smith J), Kavanagh, Livesey, Gowling, Welsh (Madine), Bridge-Wilkinson, Graham, Hackney, Myrie-Williams (Taylor C).
Grays Ath: Button; Gier, Dayes (Elliott), Wilnis (Davis), Stuart, Ashton, Thurgood, Cogan, McCollin, Welsh (Hickie), Sloma.

Cheltenham T (2) 2 *(Murray 5, Owusu 45 (pen))*
Oldham Ath (0) 2 *(Taylor 49, Whitaker 76)*   2585
Cheltenham T: Higgs; Gallinagh, Wright, Westlake, Kenton, Diallo, Payne (Ridley), Montrose (Spencer), Connor (Hayes), Owusu, Murray.
Oldham Ath: Crossley; Hazell, Lomax, Whitaker, Stam, Gregan (Maher), Jones D, Allott, Alessandra, Smalley, Taylor.

Chester C (0) 0
Millwall (0) 3 *(Grabban 76, Harris 79, Grimes 90)*   1932
Chester C: Danby; Vaughan J, Barry, Harris, Linwood, Roberts (Rutherford), Mozika (Wilson), Hughes, Johnson, Lowe, Ellison.
Millwall: Forde; Dunne, Frampton, Bolder, Robinson, Craig, Grabban (Grimes), Fuseini (Spiller), Easter (Hackett), Harris, Martin.

Chesterfield (1) 3 *(Winter 32, 58, Ward 51)*
Mansfield T (0) 1 *(Arnold 78)*   6612
Chesterfield: Carson; Gray, Austin, Kerry, Page, Downes, Lowry (Niven), Winter, Lester, Ward, Goodall (Robertson).
Mansfield T: Gamble; Silk, Jeannin, D'Laryea, Moses, O'Hare, Arnold, Somner (O'Connor), Lee (Stallard), Sinclair, Ahmed.

Colchester U (0) 0
Leyton Orient (0) 1 *(Demetriou 80)*   4600
Colchester U: Cousins; White, Wordsworth (Elito), Izzet (Wasiu), Heath, Baldwin, Yeates, Jackson, Platt, Williams (Vernon), Perkins.
Leyton Orient: Morris; Purches, Granville, Chambers (Jarvis), Mkandawire, Saah, Melligan (Morgan D), Thornton, Boyd (Terry), Parkin, Demetriou.

Crewe Alex (1) 1 *(Donaldson 34)*
Ebbsfleet U (0) 0   2593
Crewe Alex: Collis; Brayford, Jones, Bailey, O'Donnell, Baudet, Miller (Zola), O'Connor, Moore, Donaldson, Grant (Carrington).
Ebbsfleet U: Cronin; Ricketts, Opinel, Purcell, Smith, Charles, Hand (Long), Barrett, Ibe (Shakes), Gash, Stone.

Curzon Ashton (1) 3 *(Worsley 26, Ogoo 56, Norton 79)*
Exeter C (0) 2 *(Basham 84, Moxey 90)* 1259
Curzon Ashton: Carnell; Russell, Whelan, Birch, Jones, Curley, Ogoo (Byrne), Worsley, Elliot (O'Connor), Norton, Edghill.
Exeter C: Jones; Tully, Moxey, Edwards, Seaborne, Taylor, Gill■, Cozic (Basham), Stansfield (Watson), Stewart, Logan (Harley).

Darlington (0) 0
Droylsden (0) 0 2479
Darlington: Brown; Austin, Valentine, Hulbert (Ravenhill), Foster, Miller, Purdie, Kennedy, Clarke B (Foran), Blundell, Griffin (Gray).
Droylsden: Mawson (Clancy); Brownhill, Byron, Cryan, Newton, McGuire, Pickford (Brown), Sorvel, Lamb, Tipton, Townson (Prince).

Eastbourne B (0) 0
Barrow (0) 0 1216
Eastbourne B: Hook; Lovett, Jenkins, Baker, Pullan, Harding, Crabb M (Harkin), Smart, Brown, Atkin, Tait (Crabb N).
Barrow: Martin; Pearson, Logan, Bond (Jones), McNulty, Henney, Winn, Boyd, Brodie (Tait), Brown D (Walker), Brown P.

Eastwood T (0) 2 *(Cooke 54, Meikle 65)*
Brackley (1) 1 *(Winters 20)* 960
Eastwood T: Redmond; Asher, Cooke, Sturdy, Robinson, Meikle (Diuk), Foster, Dunning, Todd, Gardner (Rhead), Holmes.
Brackley: Knight; Fontanelle, Perpetunia (Patterson), Green, Blossom, Farley (Harper), Pierson, Cracknell, Thorpe (Spencer), Mackey, Winters.

Harlow T (0) 0
Macclesfield T (0) 2 *(Brisley 65, Dunfield 86)* 2149
Harlow T: Hasell; Taylor, Chapman, Kear, Kirby, Fowler, Hollenbach (Allen), Lalite, Green, Adeyinka (Charles), Bunn.
Macclesfield T: Brain; Brisley, Deen, Hessey, Brown (Harvey), Dunfield, Reid I, Flynn, Green (Bell), Yeo, Thomas (Gritton).

Hereford U (0) 0
Dagenham & R (0) 0 1825
Hereford U: Samson; Rose, Taylor, Diagouraga, Beckwith, Broadhurst, Hudson-Odoi (Johnson), Smith (Done), Williams, Guinan (Chadwick), Easton.
Dagenham & R: Roberts; Foster, Griffiths, Arber, Okuonghae, Taiwo, Saunders, Ritchie (Nurse), Benson, Strevens, Gain.

Histon (0) 1 *(Wright 66)*
Swindon T (0) 0 1541
Histon: Naisbitt; Oyebanjo, Gwillam, Simpson, Ada, Langston, Midson, Murray (Knight-Percival), Wright (Reeves), Barker, Mitchell-King.
Swindon T: Smith P (Brezovan); Smith J, Timlin, Pook, Kanyuka, Aljofree, McGovern, Peacock, Paynter (Corr), Cox, McNamee (Marshall).

Huddersfield T (1) 3 *(Collins 45, Craney 51, Williams 65)*
Port Vale (1) 4 *(Dodds 27, 85, Howland 79, Richards 90)* 6942
Huddersfield T: Glennon; Goodwin, Williams, Craney, Butler, Clarke N, Roberts, Collins, Jevons (Cadamarteri), Holdsworth, Skarz.
Port Vale: Anyon; Griffith, McCrory (Stockley), Howland, McCombe, Collins, Dodds, Brammer, Richards, Richman (Davidson), Edwards (Glover).

Kettering T (0) 1 *(Geohaghan 85)*
Lincoln C (0) 1 *(N'Guessan 86)* 3314
Kettering T: Harper; Eaden, Jaszczun, Wrack, Dempster, Geohaghan, Potter A, Boucaud (Solkhon), Christie (Beardsley), Seddon, Arther (Marna).
Lincoln C: Burch; Green, Beevers, Kovacs, Hone, Kerr, John-Lewis, Frecklington, Patulea (Wright), Clarke, N'Guessan.

Kidderminster H (1) 1 *(Richards 17 (pen))*
Cambridge U (0) 0 1717
Kidderminster H: Bartlett; Baker, Lowe, Ferrell, Creighton, Riley, Smikle, Penn (Bennett), Barnes-Homer (Moore), Richards, Brittain.
Cambridge U: Potter; Gleeson, Tonkin, Bolland, Hatswell, Willmott (Jardim), Challinor, Carden, Holroyd (Farrell), McEvilly, Crow (Beasley).

Leicester C (1) 3 *(Dyer 37, Fryatt 57, King A 69)*
Stevenage B (0) 0 7586
Leicester C: Henderson; Edworthy, Mattock, King A, Kisnorbo (Morrison), Tunchev, Dyer, Oakley, Howard (Campbell), Fryatt (Dickov), Berner.
Stevenage B: Day; Bostwick, Anaclet, Wilson, Henry, Albrighton, McMahon (Oliver), Drury (Cole), Morison, Mills, Vincenti (Willock).

Leiston (0) 0
Fleetwood T (0) 0 1250
Leiston: Stannard; Girling, Goldfinch, Wardley, Lowe, Eagle (Sillett), Head D, Saker, Chenery (Trotter), McClone, Head S.
Fleetwood T: Hurst; Walmsley, Mercer, Hills, Potts (Robinson), Pond■, Milligan, Leadbitter (Beattie), Kay, Bell (Foster), Warlow.

Luton T (0) 0
Altrincham (0) 0 3200
Luton T: Logan; Gnakpa, Beavan, Nicholls (Watson), Keane, Spillane, McVeigh (Talbot), Howells, Martin, Andrews (O'Connor), Jarvis.
Altrincham: Ralph; Lane, Doughty, McGregor, Young, Densmore (Meechan), Lawton, Danylyk, Little (Elam), Senior (Johnson), Peyton.

Milton Keynes D (1) 1 *(Johnson 43)*
Bradford C (1) 2 *(Daley 2, Lee 82)* 5542
Milton Keynes D: Price; Cummings, Lewington, Leven, O'Hanlon, Stirling (Llera), Wright, Navarro, Johnson, Gerba, Belson (Gallen),.
Bradford C: Evans; Moncur, O'Brien, Osborne, Lee, Clarke M, Daley, McLaren, Conlon, Boulding M (Heckingbottom), Law.

Morecambe (1) 2 *(Taylor 45, 77)*
Grimsby T (0) 1 *(Stockdale 88)* 1713
Morecambe: Roche; Yates (McCann), Adams, Stanley, McStay, Bentley, Wainwright, Drummond, O'Carroll, Taylor (Artell), McLachlan.
Grimsby T: Barnes; Stockdale, Newey, Hunt (Boshell), Atkinson, Bennett, Till (Bore), Kalala, Jarman, Proudlock, Llewellyn (North).

Oxford U (0) 0
Dorchester T (0) 0 3196
Oxford U: Turley; Day, Carruthers, Burnell, Willmott, Hutchinson, Trainer (Odubade), Murray, Constable (Guy), Deering, Haldane (Dobson).
Dorchester T: Stewart; Jemyn, Hill, Bowles, Marsh-Brown, Crittenden, Clay, Gleeson (Nicholson), Mudge, Moss, Fogdon.

Sutton U (0) 0
Notts Co (0) 1 *(Butcher 75)* 2041
Sutton U: Nicholls; Jackson, El-Salahi, Bray, Heeroo, Collins, Palmer (Hughes), McKimm (Dunn), West (Hann), Dundas, McCallum.
Notts Co: Hoult; Clapham, Mayo, Neal, Edwards, Thompson, Hamshaw, Butcher, Facey, Canham (Weir-Daley), Weston (Nowland).

Torquay U (1) 2 *(Sills 28, 75)*
Evesham U (0) 0 2275
Torquay U: Bevan; Mansell, Nicholson, Hargreaves, Woods, Hodges, Carayol (Stevens), Wroe, Thompson (Benyon), Sills, D'Sane.
Evesham U: Vaughan; Watson, Luckett, Hands S, Fitter (Lennon), Sheppell, Hands M (Davis), Luiz, Hayden, Owen (Batchelor), Hay.

Walsall (1) 1 *(Ricketts 25)*
Scunthorpe U (1) 3 *(Hooper 42, 58, Hurst 90)*   2318
Walsall: Ince; Palmer, Roberts, Taundry, Gerrard, Mattis, Deeney (Nicholls), Hughes (Bradley), Ricketts, Ibehre, Zaaboub (Demontagnac■).
Scunthorpe U: Murphy; Byrne, Lea, McCann, Mirfin, Iriekpen, Sparrow, Togwell, Hayes (Morris), Hooper (Thompson), Woolford (Hurst).

Yeovil T (0) 1 *(Skiverton 60)*
Stockport Co (1) 1 *(Davies 44)*   3582
Yeovil T: Wagenaar; Alcock (Welsh), Jones, Roberts, Skiverton, Forbes, Peltier, Way, Noel-Williams (Rendell), Warne (Tomlin), Schofield.
Stockport Co: fon Williams; Mullins, McNulty, Dicker, Raynes, Tunnicliffe, McSweeney, Baker (Turnbull), Rowe T, Davies (Pilkington A), Gleeson■.

Sunday, 9 November 2008

AFC Hornchurch (0) 0
Peterborough U (0) 1 *(Mackail-Smith 90)*   3000
AFC Hornchurch: Brightly; Barnard, Goodfellow, Purdie (McFarlane), Brown (Hodges), Janney, Curley, Styles, Tomlinson, Lee (Parker), Green.
Peterborough U: Lewis; Martin, Williams, Keates, Morgan, Zakuani, Torres (Mackail-Smith), Coutts, Green (Batt), McLean, Boyd.

Havant & W (0) 1 *(Simpemba 73)*
Brentford (1) 3 *(Marvin Williams 42, MacDonald 66, Elder 83)*   1631
Havant & W: Scriven; Conroy, Gasson, Collins, Elphick, Simpemba, Gray (Henry), Holloway, Nightingale (Booth), Watkins, Wilkinson (Poate).
Brentford: Hamer; Halls (Osborne), Dickson, O'Connor, Bennett, Phillips, Marvin Williams (Newton), Bean, MacDonald, Elder, Poole (Wood).

Team Bath (0) 0
Forest Green R (0) 1 *(Mohamed 75)*   906
Team Bath: McCarthy; Lock, Caton, Smith (Hobbs), El-Abd, Warren, Perrott, Canham (Cooper), Llewellyn, Abbott (Dillon), Bell.
Forest Green R: Burton; Gill, Hardiker (Afful), Clist, Jones, Kempson, Fowler (Rigoglioso) (Platt), Smith, Mangan, Mohamed, Stonehouse.

Monday, 10 November 2008

AFC Wimbledon (0) 1 *(Hatton 56)*
Wycombe W (2) 4 *(Harrold 9, 36, 74, Phillips 62)*   4528
AFC Wimbledon: Little; Garrard, Haswell (Hussey), Adjei, Inns, Leberl, Hatton, Davis, Kedwell, Main (Mason), Godfrey (Finn).
Wycombe W: Shearer; Hunt, Woodman, Spence, McCracken, Williamson, Mousinho, Phillips (Vieira), Harrold (Bloomfield), Zebroski, Holt (Duncan).

FIRST ROUND REPLAYS

Thursday, 13 November 2008

Tranmere R (0) 1 *(Shuker 69)*
Accrington S (0) 0   2560
Tranmere R: Coyne; Shotton, Andy Taylor, Barnett, Chorley, Kay, Jennings, Shuker (Greenacre), Moore, Savage, Edds (Sonko).
Accrington S: Arthur; Williams (Murdock) (Smith), King, Procter, Edwards, Charnock, Ryan, Mullin J, Miles (Richardson), Mullin P, Griffiths.

Monday, 17 November 2008

Northampton T (1) 2 *(Crowe 44, 90)*
Leeds U (4) 5 *(Beckford 13, 45, 55, Hughes 28 (og), Parker 41)*   3960
Northampton T: Fielding; Crowe, Jackman, Hughes, Dolman, Davis, Gilligan, Guttridge, Constantine (Henderson), McGleish, Holt (Bignall).
Leeds U: Lucas; Hughes, Parker, Kilkenny, Telfer (Webb), Michalik, Prutton, Howson, Beckford (Becchio), Christie (Showunmi), Douglas.

Tuesday, 18 November 2008

Altrincham (0) 0
Luton T (0) 0   2397
Altrincham: Ralph; Smith, Doughty, McGregor, Young, Danylyk, Lawton, Johnson (Lane), Little (Elam), Senior (Meechan), Peyton.
Luton T: Logan; Gnakpa, Howells (Davis■), Nicholls (Talbot), Roper, Spillane, O'Connor (Jarvis), Keane, Martin, McVeigh, Hall.
aet; Luton T won 4-2 on penalties.

Barrow (1) 4 *(Brodie 45, Brown P 47, Henney 57, Logan 76)*
Eastbourne B (0) 0   2031
Barrow: Deasy; Pearson, Logan, Jones, McNulty, Henney, Winn, Boyd, Brown D (Tait), Brodie (Walker), Brown P.
Eastbourne B: Hook; Baker, Jenkins, Smart, Pullan, Lovett (Austin), Crabb M, Harding (Harkin), Atkin, Brown, Crabb N (Taylor).

Dagenham & R (2) 2 *(Benson 17, Taiwo 33)*
Hereford U (1) 1 *(Taylor 34)*   1409
Dagenham & R: Roberts; Foster, Griffiths, Arber, Okuonghae, Taiwo, Saunders (Southam), Ritchie (Nurse), Benson (Nwokeji), Strevens, Gain.
Hereford U: Samson; Gwynne (Johnson), Taylor, Diagouraga, Beckwith, Broadhurst, O'Leary (Hudson-Odoi), Smith, Williams (Rose), Guinan, Easton.

Dorchester T (1) 1 *(Mudge 22)*
Oxford U (0) 3 *(Constable 78, Trainer 110, Odubade 120)*   1474
Dorchester T: Stewart; Jermyn, Marsh-Brown (Mitchell), Clay, Liburd, Hill, Crittenden, Mudge, Moss, Nicholson (Watts), Gleeson■.
Oxford U: Turley; Clarke, Carruthers, Hutchinson, Foster, Day, Deering, Murray, Constable, Guy (Odubade),·Haldane (Trainer).
aet.

Droylsden (1) 1 *(Tipton 26)*
Darlington (0) 0   1672
Droylsden: Clancy; Brownhill, Newton, Byron (Halford), Cryan, Brown, Beck (Burbeary), McGuire, Tipton, Lamb, Prince (Rouse).
Darlington: Oakes; Austin, Valentine, Ravenhill (Ryan), Miller (Griffin), White, Purdie, Kennedy (Hulbert), Blundell, Hatch, Foran.

Fleetwood T (0) 2 *(Bell 48, Warlow 79)*
Leiston (0) 0   2010
Fleetwood T: Hurst; Walmsley, Hills, Pond (Robinson), Mercer (Kilbane), Penswick, Kay, Milligan, Bell, Foster (Warlow), Beattie.
Leiston: Stannard; Girling (Sillett), Wardley, Head D, Goldfinch, Lowe, Boardley, Head S (Eagle), Chenery (Bramble), McClone, Saker.

Hartlepool U (0) 2 *(Porter 67 (pen), Liddle 70)*
Brighton & HA (1) 1 *(Forster 23)*   3288
Hartlepool U: Lee-Barrett; Sweeney, Humphreys (Monkhouse), Clark, Nelson, Liddle, Foley (Mackay), Jones, Porter, Brown, Robson.
Brighton & HA: Kuipers; Whing (Robinson), Richards, El-Abd (Fleetwood), Elphick, Hawkins, Cox, Fraser, Forster, Murray, Livermore (Cook).

Lincoln C (0) 1 *(John-Lewis 54)*
Kettering T (0) 2 *(Westcarr 68, Christie 90)*   3953
Lincoln C: Burch; Green, Beevers, Kovacs (Brown A), Hone, Kerr, Oakes, Frecklington (Graham), Wright, John-Lewis, N'Guessan.
Kettering T: Harper; Dempster, Jaszczun, Boucaud, Branston, Geohaghan, Potter A (Wrack), Solkhon, Beardsley (Seddon), Marna (Christie), Westcarr.

Oldham Ath (0) 0
Cheltenham T (1) 1 *(Montrose 22)* 2552
Oldham Ath: Crossley; Lomax, Jones D, Maher (Lee), Hazell, Stam (Liddell), Gregan, Allott, Alessandra, Smalley (Wolfenden), Taylor.
Cheltenham T: Brown SP; Gallinagh, Wright, Montrose, Diallo, Westlake, Murray, Bird, Spencer (Owusu), Vincent (Connor), Ridley.

Rochdale (0) 3 *(Le Fondre 56, 73, 105)*
Barnet (2) 2 *(O'Flynn 10, Adomah 19)* 2339
Rochdale: Russell; Wiseman, Kennedy, Keltie, Stanton, McArdle, Buckley, Jones G, Shaw (Thompson), Le Fondre (Rundle), Jones M (Thorpe).
Barnet: Harrison; Porter, Gillet, Bishop, Yakubu, Townsend, Adomah, Leary, O'Flynn (Carew), Medley (Nicolau), Deverdics (Birchall).
aet.

Rotherham U (0) 0
Aldershot T (1) 3 *(Hudson 15, 81, Morgan 55)* 2431
Rotherham U: Cann; Tonge, Nicholas, Hudson, Sharps, Fenton, Mills (Burchill), Cummins, Barker (Broughton), Rhodes, Reid (Yates).
Aldershot T: Bull; Blackburn, Straker, Harding, Day, Charles, Soares, Davies, Grant, Morgan (Elvins), Hudson.

Southend U (0) 2 *(Francis 74, Walker 79)*
AFC Telford U (0) 0 4415
Southend U: Mildenhall; Francis, Herd, Christophe, Clarke, Barrett, Grant (Hazell), McCormack (O'Keefe), Walker, Betsy, Scannell (Ademeno).
AFC Telford U: Young; Vaughan, Meredith, Cowan, Whitehead, Naylor (Jagielka), Adams, Rodgers, Blakeman (Fearns), Brown, Moore.

Stockport Co (3) 5 *(Dicker 6, Rose 16, McNeil 42, Pilkington A 48, Vincent 90)*
Yeovil T (0) 0 3260
Stockport Co: fon Williams; Mullins, Rose, Raynes, Tunnicliffe (McSweeney), McNeil, Taylor, Dicker, Rowe T (Tansey), Davies, Pilkington A (Vincent).
Yeovil T: Wagenaar; Alcock, Jones, Roberts (Tomlin), Skiverton, Brown■, Peltier, Murtagh, Noel-Williams (Warne), Downes (Forbes), Schofield.

Saturday, 29 November 2008
Grays Ath (0) 0
Carlisle U (1) 2 *(Graham 27, Kavanagh 52)* 1217
Grays Ath: Button; Gier (Olima), Dayes, Thurgood, Stuart, Wilnis, Welsh, Cogan, McCollin, Ashton, Sloma.
Carlisle U: Williams; Raven, Horwood, Kavanagh (Lumsdon), Livesey, Keogh, Taylor C, Bridge-Wilkinson (Dobie), Graham, Madine (Welsh), Smith J.

SECOND ROUND

Friday, 28 November 2008
Barrow (1) 2 *(Brown D 39 (pen), Henney 71)*
Brentford (0) 1 *(MacDonald 50)* 3120
Barrow: Martin; Pearson, Logan, Jones, McNulty, Henney, Joyce, Boyd, Walker, Brown D (Tait), Brown P.
Brentford: Hamer■; Osborne, Dickson, O'Connor, Bennett (Odhiambo), Phillips, Pead (Anderson), Bean, MacDonald, Elder, Wood.

Port Vale (0) 1 *(Dodds 71)*
Macclesfield T (1) 3 *(Green 9, 73, Gritton 90)* 4684
Port Vale: Anyon; Griffith, McCrory, MacKenzie, Collins (Prosser), Owen, Richman (Glover), Brown S, Richards, Dodds, Edwards (Lawrie).
Macclesfield T: Brain; Flynn, Brisley, Hessey, Morgan, Dunfield, Brown, Bell (Deen), Gritton, Green, Thomas (Evans).

Saturday, 29 November 2008
Bournemouth (0) 0
Blyth Spartans (0) 0 4165
Bournemouth: Jalal; Guyett, Garry (McQuoid), Hollands, Pearce, Cooper, Bartley, Anderton, Bradbury (Lindfield), Molesley, Igoe (Pitman).
Blyth Spartans: Bell; Leeson, Pell, Brown, Boyle, Gildea (Watson), Williams, McCabe, Dale, Hume (Poole), Reay (Dalton).

Bradford C (0) 1 *(Boulding M 58)*
Leyton Orient (1) 2 *(Demetriou 14, Granville 65)* 5065
Bradford C: Evans; Moncur, O'Brien, Clarke T, Lee, Clarke M, Jones, Law, Conlon (Thorne), Boulding M, Nix (Osborne).
Leyton Orient: Morris; Purches, Granville, Chambers, Spence, Thelwell, Melligan, Thornton, Boyd (Jarvis), Morgan D (Dawkins), Demetriou.

Chesterfield (0) 0
Droylsden (1) 1
Abandoned half time; fog.

Eastwood T (1) 2 *(Meikle 34, Knox 90)*
Wycombe W (0) 0 1955
Eastwood T: Redmond; Asher, Hume, Sturdy, Cooke, Meikle, Dunning, Foster, Gardner, Todd, Holmes (Knox).
Wycombe W: Shearer; Hunt, Woodman, Spence, McCracken, Johnson, Mousinho (Doherty), Phillips (Crooks), Harrold, Zebroski (Vieira), Holt.

Fleetwood T (1) 2 *(Bell 14, Warlow 66)*
Hartlepool U (1) 3 *(Mackay 17, 47, Porter 56)* 3280
Fleetwood T: Hurst; Walmsley, Robinson, Mercer, Hills, Maylett (Hunt), Beattie, Kay, Milligan, Warlow, Bell.
Hartlepool U: Lee-Barrett; McCunnie, Robson, Liddle, Nelson, Clark, Sweeney, Humphreys, Mackay, Porter, Monkhouse.

Forest Green R (1) 2 *(Smith 27, Low 56)*
Rochdale (0) 0 1715
Forest Green R: Burton; Gill, Stonehouse, Fowler, Jones, Kempson, Low (Thomas), Smith (Rigoglioso), Platt, Mangan (Mohamed), Clist.
Rochdale: Russell; Ramsden, Kennedy, Keltie, Holness, McArdle, Buckley (Jones M), Toner, Le Fondre, Thorpe, Higginbotham (Shaw).

Gillingham (0) 0
Stockport Co (0) 0 4419
Gillingham: Royce; Fuller, Nutter, Weston, Richards, King, Barcham (McCammon) (Pugh), Bentley, Jackson, Jarrett, Miller (Mulligan).
Stockport Co: fon Williams; McSweeney, McNulty, Blizzard, Mullins, Tunnicliffe, Pilkington A, Taylor (Dicker), Davies (Rowe T), McNeil (Thompson P), Gleeson.

Kidderminster H (1) 2 *(Moore 38, Creighton 65)*
Curzon Ashton (0) 0 2070
Kidderminster H: Bartlett; Lowe, Baker, Ferrell, Creighton, Riley, Smikle (McDermott), Penn (Jones), Moore, Barnes-Homer, Brittain (Knights).
Curzon Ashton: Carnell■; Russell, Birch, Jones, Whelan, Worsley, Curley (Byrne), Ogoo (Barlow), Edghill (Barker), Norton, Elliot.

Leicester C (2) 3 *(Fryatt 11, 30 (pen), 55)*
Dagenham & R (2) 2 *(Ritchie 9, Strevens 25)* 7791
Leicester C: Martin; Edworthy, Mattock (Powell), King A, Morrison, Tunchev, Adams, Berner (Davies), Howard, Fryatt, Dyer.
Dagenham & R: Roberts; Foster, Griffiths, Arber, Okuonghae, Taiwo (Southam), Saunders, Ritchie, Benson, Strevens, Gain.

Millwall (1) 3 *(Alexander 30, 77, Grimes 88)*
Aldershot T (0) 0   6159
Millwall: Forde; Hackett, Frampton, Laird (Abdou),
Robinson, Craig, Grabban (Dunne), Bolder, Alexander,
Harris (Grimes), Martin.
Aldershot T: Bull; Blackburn, Straker, Harding,
Newman, Charles, Hudson, Davies, Grant (Soares),
Morgan, Hylton.

Morecambe (1) 1
Cheltenham T (0) 1   1984
Abandoned 65 minutes; fog.

Peterborough U (0) 0
Tranmere R (0) 0   5980
Peterborough U: Lewis; Martin, Williams, Coutts,
Morgan, Zakuani, Lee (Batt), Keates, Mackail-Smith,
McLean, Boyd.
Tranmere R: Coyne; Shotton, Andy Taylor, Goodison,
Chorley, Kay, Moore, Jennings, Sonko, Savage, Edds
(Gornell).

Scunthorpe U (1) 4 *(May 30, Hooper 62, 83, Togwell 90)*
Alfreton T (0) 0   4249
Scunthorpe U: Murphy; Byrne, Williams, McCann
(Morris), Mirfin, Pearce, Sparrow, Togwell, Hayes (May),
Hooper, Woolford (Hurst).
Alfreton T: Evans; McFadzean, Butler, McIntosh, Brown
(Marples), Hall, Bowler (Davidson), Curtis, Law,
Clayton■, Muirhead (Cusworth).

Southend U (1) 3 *(Stanislas 34, 84, Walker 90)*
Luton T (0) 1 *(Spillane 80)*   4111
Southend U: Mildenhall; Francis, Herd, Christophe
(Grant), Clarke, Barrett, Betsy, McCormack, Revell
(Walker), Laurent, Stanislas (Orenuja).
Luton T: Logan; Gnakpa, Davis (Emanuel), Watson,
Roper (Pilkington), Spillane, Hall, Howells, Martin,
Jarvis (Andrews), McVeigh.

Torquay U (1) 2 *(Benyon 41, 83)*
Oxford U (0) 0   2647
Torquay U: Bevan; Mansell, Nicholson, Hargreaves,
Woods, Hodges, Carayol, Wroe, D'Sane■, Sills,
Thompson (Benyon) (Green).
Oxford U: Turley; Clarke (Groves), Carruthers,
Hutchinson, Day, Foster, Deering, Murray, Constable,
Odubade, Haldane (Taylor).

Sunday, 30 November 2008

Histon (1) 1 *(Langston 39)*
Leeds U (0) 0   4500
Histon: Naisbitt; Oyebanjo, Gwillim, Simpson, Ada,
Langston, Barker (Murray), Mitchell-King, Midson,
Wright, Knight-Percival.
Leeds U: Lucas; Richardson, Sheehan, Delph, Rui
Marques, Michalik, Douglas, Snodgrass, Hughes
(Howson), Becchio, Robinson (Showunmi).

Notts Co (1) 1 *(Canham 34)*
Kettering T (1) 1 *(Solkhon 18)*   4451
Notts Co: Hoult; Hunt, Clapham, Neal (Weston),
Edwards, Thompson, Wedderburn, Butcher (Smith)
(Strachan), Facey, Forrester, Canham.
Kettering T: Harper; Dempster, Jaszczun, Boucaud,
Branston, Geohaghan, Potter A (Arthur), Solkhon,
Christie (Marna), Rawle (Seddon), Westcarr.

Tuesday, 2 December 2008

Morecambe (2) 2 *(McStay 5, Howe 27 (pen))*
Cheltenham T (2) 3 *(Vincent 23, 54, Finnigan 36 (pen))*
                                                       1758
Morecambe: Roche; McCann, Adams, Stanley, Artell,
McStay, Yates (O'Carroll), Drummond, Howe, Carlton,
McLachlan (Carr).
Cheltenham T: Brown SP; Kenton, Ridley, Westlake,
Diallo, Bird (Gallinagh), Finnigan, Payne, Vincent
(Spencer), Hayles (Connor), Murray.

Wednesday, 3 December 2008

Carlisle U (0) 0
Crewe Alex (2) 2 *(Miller 3, 12)*   2755
Carlisle U: Howarth; Raven, Liddle, Kavanagh, Livesey
(Dobie), Keogh, Taylor C, Bridge-Wilkinson, Graham
(Bridges), Madine, Smith J.
Crewe Alex: Tomlinson; Brayford, Jones, Bailey,
O'Donnell, Baudet, Miller (Rix), O'Connor (Woodards),
Daniel, Zola (Pope), Lunt.

Tuesday, 9 December 2008

Chesterfield (1) 2 *(Ward 31, Lester 79)*
Droylsden (0) 2 *(Brown 50, Halford 82)*   5698
Chesterfield: Carson; Gray, Goodall, Kerry, Austin,
Downes, Currie (Boden S), Winter, Lester, Ward,
Robertson.
Droylsden: Mawson; Brownhill, Newton, Cryan, Halford
(Byron), Sorvel (Pickford), Beck, Brown, Tipton, Lamb,
Prince (Townson).

SECOND ROUND REPLAYS

Tuesday, 9 December 2008

Stockport Co (1) 1 *(Gleeson 17)*
Gillingham (2) 2 *(Barcham 25, 34)*   3329
Stockport Co: Ion Williams; McSweeney, Mullins, Taylor,
McNulty, Tunnicliffe, Pilkington A, Dicker (Rowe T),
Davies (Baker), Raynes (Thompson P), Gleeson.
Gillingham: Royce; Fuller, Nutter, Weston, Richards,
King, Bentley, Barcham, Jackson, Jarrett (Lewis), Miller
(Mulligan).

Tranmere R (0) 1 *(Kay 47)*
Peterborough U (0) 2 *(McLean 90, Mackail-Smith 114)*
                                                       3139
Tranmere R: Coyne; Antwi, Andy Taylor, Goodison,
Chorley, Kay, Jennings, Sonko (Cresswell), Moore
(Gornell), Savage, Edds (Shuker).
Peterborough U: Lewis; Lee, Batt (Green), Blanchett
(Whelpdale), Morgan, Zakuani (Westwood), Coutts,
Keates, Mackail-Smith, McLean, Boyd.
aet.

Wednesday, 10 December 2008

Kettering T (0) 2 *(Solkhon 53, Seddon 54)*
Notts Co (1) 1 *(Smith 43)*   3019
Kettering T: Harper; Dempster, Jaszczun, Boucaud,
Branston, Geohaghan, Potter A (Marna), Solkhon,
Westcarr, Seddon (Christie), Wrack.
Notts Co: Hoult; Thompson, Clapham, Smith, Edwards,
Hunt, Hamshaw (Weir-Daley), Wedderburn, Facey,
Canham (Forrester), Weston.

Tuesday, 16 December 2008

Blyth Spartans (0) 1 *(Dalton 90)*
Bournemouth (0) 0   4040
Blyth Spartans: Bell; Leeson, Boyle, Williams, Pell, Poole
(Wright), Watson, Gildea, Dale, Reay, Hume (Dalton).
Bournemouth: Jalal; Cummings, Ward, Guyett, Pearce,
Hollands, Cooper (Partington), Bartley, Molesley
(Connell), Bradbury, McQuoid (Pitman■).

Droylsden (0) 0
Chesterfield (1) 2   2251
abandoned 72 minutes; floodlight failure.

Tuesday, 23 December 2008

Droylsden (1) 2 *(Newton 31, 55 (pen))*
Chesterfield (1) 1 *(Lester 35)*   2824
Droylsden: Mawson; Brownhill, Newton, Byron, Cryan,
McGuire, Beck, Pickford, Tipton (Townson), Lamb,
Brown.
Chesterfield: Lee; Gray, Picken (Bowery), Downes, Hall,
Harsley, Lowry, Kerry (Currie), Lester■, Ward,
Robertson.
*Droylsden removed from the Cup for fielding a suspended
player.*

THIRD ROUND

Friday, 2 January 2009

Tottenham H (0) 3 *(Pavlyuchenko 52 (pen), 90, Modric 76)*
Wigan Ath (0) 1 *(Camara 88)*   34,040

Tottenham H: Gomes; Corluka, Bale, Zokora, Woodgate, Dawson, Bentley, Modric (Lennon), Pavlyuchenko, Bent (Campbell), O'Hara.
Wigan Ath: Kingson; Boyce, Kilbane, Palacios, Bramble, Scharner (Figueroa), Valencia, De Ridder (Cywka), Camara, Kapo (Edman), Brown.

Saturday, 3 January 2009

Arsenal (0) 3 *(Van Persie 47, 85, Gray 50 (og))*
Plymouth Arg (0) 1 *(Duguid 53)*   59,424

Arsenal: Fabianski; Sagna, Silvestre (Gibbs), Nasri, Djourou, Gallas, Eboue (Vela), Diaby, Bendtner (Wilshere), Van Persie, Ramsey.
Plymouth Arg: Larrieu; Duguid, Barker, Gray, Cathcart, Seip, Clark (Noone), Summerfield, Fallon, Gallagher (MacLean), Mackie.

Cardiff C (0) 2 *(McCormack 57, Ledley 83)*
Reading (0) 0   12,448

Cardiff C: Enckelman; McNaughton, Kennedy, Rae, Johnson R, Gyepes, Whittingham, Parry, Bothroyd (McPhail), McCormack, Ledley.
Reading: Federici; Murty, Kelly, Karacan (Sigurdsson), Bikey, Pearce, Convey (Church), Matejovsky, Lita, Long, Henry (Kebe).

Charlton Ath (1) 1 *(Shelvey 20)*
Norwich C (0) 1 *(Lupoli 71)*   12,615

Charlton Ath: Elliot; Moutaouakil, Basey, Semedo, Fortune, Holland, Sam, Shelvey (Dickson), Burton (Youga), Bouazza, Bailey.
Norwich C: Marshall; Omozusi (Otsemobor), Bertrand, Doherty, Drury, Clingan, Croft, Fotheringham, Sibierski, Russell (Lupoli), Pattison (Hoolahan).

Chelsea (1) 1 *(Kalou 31)*
Southend U (0) 1 *(Clarke 90)*   41,090

Chelsea: Cudicini; Paulo Ferreira, Cole A, Mikel, Ivanovic, Ricardo Carvalho, Belletti, Lampard, Drogba, Kalou (Sinclair), Cole J (Di Santo).
Southend U: Mildenhall; Sankofa, Herd, Christophe (Moussa), Clarke, Barrett, Grant, McCormack, Revell (Laurent), Barnard (Freedman), Stanislas.

Coventry C (0) 2 *(McKenzie 52, Best 82)*
Kidderminster H (0) 0   13,652

Coventry C: Marshall; Wright, Hall, Doyle, Wynter, Turner, Simpson (Morrison), Gunnarsson, Best, Eastwood, McKenzie (Fox).
Kidderminster H: Bartlett; Lowe, Baker, Bennett, Creighton, Robertson, Ferrell (Smikle), Penn, Barnes-Homer (Moore), Richards, Brittain (Knights).

Forest Green R (2) 3 *(Smith 14, Lawless 20, Stonehouse 72)*
Derby Co (2) 4 *(Hulse 40, Albrechtsen 45, Green 76, Davies 87 (pen))*   4836

Forest Green R: Burton; Gill, Stonehouse, Clist, Jones■, Kempson, Lawless■, Smith (Afful), Mangan (Mohamed), Rigoglioso, Fowler.
Derby Co: Carroll; Beardsley, Camara, Green, Nyatanga, Albrechtsen (Powell), Teale (Barazite), Addison, Hulse, Varney (Davies), Commons.

Hartlepool U (0) 2 *(Nelson 49, Foley 76)*
Stoke C (0) 0   5367

Hartlepool U: Lee-Barrett; Sweeney (McCunnie), Humphreys, Liddle, Nelson, Collins, Jones (Monkhouse), Clark, Porter, Mackay (Foley), Robson.
Stoke C: Simonsen; Davies (Wilkinson), Dickinson, Olofinjana (Lawrence), Shawcross, Sonko, Soares (Kitson), Whelan, Pericard, Delap, Tonge.

Hull C (0) 0
Newcastle U (0) 0   20,557

Hull C: Duke; Doyle, Ricketts, Boateng, Turner, McShane, Marney, Fagan (Halmosi), Geovanni, Cousin (King), Giannakopoulos.
Newcastle U: Given; Bassong, Jose Enrique, Butt, Coloccini, Taylor S, Duff, Guthrie, Owen, Carroll, N'Zogbia (Gutierrez).

Ipswich T (0) 3 *(Walters 50 (pen), Counago 53, Stead 88)*
Chesterfield (0) 0   12,524

Ipswich T: Wright R; Wright D (Bruce), Thatcher, Miller (Haynes), McAuley, Campo, Norris, Sumulikoski, Walters, Counago (Stead).
Chesterfield: Lee; Picken, Austin, Kerry, Hall (Currie), Downes, Lowry, Winter, Ward, Boden S (Bowery), Robertson.

Kettering T (1) 2 *(Westcarr 24, Seddon 58)*
Eastwood T (0) 1 *(Robinson 60)*   5090

Kettering T: Harper; Bennett, Jaszczun (Dempster), Wrack, Branston, Geohaghan, Graham, Boucaud (Solkhon), Christie, Seddon, Westcarr.
Eastwood T: Redmond; Asher (Rhead), Cooke, Robinson, Hume, Sturdy, Meikle (Shaw), Dunning, Holmes (Knox), Gardner, Todd.

Leicester C (0) 0
Crystal Palace (0) 0   15,976

Leicester C: Martin; Gilbert, Mattock, King A, Hobbs, Tunchev, Gradel, Davies, Howard, Dyer (Adams), Berner (Dickov).
Crystal Palace: Speroni; Clyne, Hill, Carle, Lawrence, Fonte J, Butterfield, Danns, Lee, Griffit (Moses), Ifill.

Macclesfield T (0) 0
Everton (1) 1 *(Osman 43)*   6008

Macclesfield T: Brain; Reid I, Hessey, Walker, Morgan, Dunfield, Brown, Bell (Yeo), Gritton, Evans (Rooney), Jennings (Thomas).
Everton: Howard; Hibbert, Baines, Neville, Jagielka, Lescott, Osman, Pienaar (Gosling), Anichebe, Cahill, Arteta.

Manchester C (0) 0
Nottingham F (2) 3 *(Tyson 38, Earnshaw 42, Garner 75)*   31,869

Manchester C: Hart; Zabaleta, Ball, Kompany, Richards, Dunne, Wright-Phillips (Vassell), Gelson (Hamann), Caicedo (Jo), Elano, Sturridge.
Nottingham F: Smith; Chambers, Thornhill, Perch (Wilson), Morgan, Breckin, Anderson, McGugan, Tyson (Davies), Earnshaw (Garner), Cohen.

Middlesbrough (1) 2 *(Alves 23, 62)*
Barrow (0) 1 *(Walker 80)*   25,132

Middlesbrough: Jones; McMahon, Pogatetz, Walker, Huth, Wheater, Johnson A, Digard, Alves, Aliadiere (Emnes) (Mido), Downing.
Barrow: Martin; Pearson (Bond), Logan, Jones, McNulty, Henney, Joyce, Boyd, Walker, Brown D (Curtis), Brown P.

Millwall (2) 2 *(Laird 40, Frampton 45)*
Crewe Alex (1) 2 *(Lawrence 12, Shelley 58)*   5754

Millwall: Forde; Dunne, Frampton, Barron, Robinson, Laird, Fuseini, Bolder (Harris), Kandol (Moore), Alexander, Grabban.
Crewe Alex: Tomlinson; Brayford, Daniel, Carrington, O'Donnell, Lawrence, Shelley (Zola), Bailey, Miller, Donaldson, Murphy.

Portsmouth (0) 0
Bristol C (0) 0   14,446

Portsmouth: James; Wilson, Belhadj, Davis, Campbell, Distin, Cranie (Pamarot), Mvuemba, Crouch, Nugent, Kranjcar.
Bristol C: Basso; Orr, Fontaine, Skuse, Carey, McCombe, Elliott, Johnson, John (Adebola), Styvar (McAllister), Sproule (Williams).

Preston NE (0) 0
Liverpool (1) 2 *(Riera 25, Torres 90)* 23,046
Preston NE: Lonergan; Jones, Davidson (Nolan), Chaplow (Nicholson), St Ledger-Hall, Mawene, Sedgwick, McKenna, Mellor (Elliott), Parkin, Wallace.
Liverpool: Cavalieri; Carragher, Insua, Xabi Alonso (Lucas), Agger, Hyypia, Babel, Mascherano (Fabio Aurelio), Gerrard, Keane (Torres), Riera.

QPR (0) 0
Burnley (0) 0 8896
QPR: Cerny; Delaney, Stewart, Mahon (Ephraim), Ramage, Gorkss, Rowlands, Leigertwood, Di Carmine (Agyemang), Blackstock, Cook (Ledesma).
Burnley: Jensen; Alexander, Kalvenes, Gudjonsson, Duff, Carlisle, Eagles, Thompson (Rodriguez), Blake (Mahon), Paterson, Elliott.

Sheffield W (1) 1 *(Spurr 21)*
Fulham (1) 2 *(Johnson 12, 88)* 18,377
Sheffield W: Grant; Buxton, Spurr, McAllister, Beevers, Wood, Small (Modest), O'Connor, Jeffers, Johnson (Lekaj), Boden.
Fulham: Schwarzer; Stoor, Konchesky, Murphy, Hughes, Hangeland, Gray (Davies), Etuhu, Johnson, Zamora (Nevland), Dempsey.

Sunderland (0) 2 *(Jones 57, Cisse 67)*
Bolton W (0) 1 *(Smolarek 79)* 20,685
Sunderland: Fulop; Chimbonda, Collins, Whitehead, Nosworthy, Ferdinand, Edwards (Reid), Cisse, Jones, Diouf, Richardson (Tainio).
Bolton W: Jaaskelainen; Steinsson, Samuel (Mustapha), Muamba, O'Brien A, Shittu, Nolan, Gardner, Elmander, Davies K (Smolarek), Taylor.

Torquay U (1) 1 *(Green 32)*
Blackpool (0) 0 3654
Torquay U: Bevan; Mansell, Nicholson, Hargreaves, Woods, Hodges, Carlisle, Wroe, Green (Thompson), Sills, D'Sane (Benyon).
Blackpool: Rachubka; Coid, Harte, Fox, Barker, Evatt, Vaughan, Southern, Burgess, Nardiello (Merella), Green (Jorgensen).

WBA (0) 1 *(Olsson 64)*
Peterborough U (0) 1 *(Mackail-Smith 87)* 18,659
WBA: Carson; Hoefkens, Cech, Koren (Simpson), Barnett, Olsson, Borja Valero, Moore (Dorrans), Bednar (Beattie), Brunt, Greening.
Peterborough U: Lewis; Martin, Lee, Coutts, Morgan, Zakuani, Whelpdale (Batt), Keates, Mackail-Smith, McLean (Torres), Boyd.

Watford (0) 1 *(Rasiak 67)*
Scunthorpe U (0) 0 8690
Watford: Loach; Hoyte (Bridcutt), Cork, Jenkins, Mariappa, DeMerit, McAnuff, O'Toole (Rasiak), Priskin (Bromby), Smith, Harley.
Scunthorpe U: Murphy; Wright, Williams, McCann, Byrne, Pearce, Thompson (Sparrow), Togwell (Forte), Hayes, Hooper, Woolford (Hurst).

West Ham U (2) 3 *(Ilunga 10, Noble 39 (pen), Cole 68)*
Barnsley (0) 0 28,869
West Ham U: Green; Faubert, Ilunga, Noble, Collins, Tomkins, Collison (Dyer), Mullins, Cole (Tristan), Bellamy, Boa Morte (Etherington).
Barnsley: Muller; Souza, Van Homoet, Foster, Hassell, Colace, Campbell-Ryce, Leon (Butterfield), Odejayi (Coulson), Rigters (Adam), El Haimour.

Sunday, 4 January 2009

Gillingham (0) 1 *(Jackson 57)*
Aston Villa (1) 2 *(Milner 13, 79 (pen))* 10,107
Gillingham: Royce; Lewis, Nutter, Weston, King, Bentley, Oli, Barcham, Mulligan, Jackson, Miller.
Aston Villa: Friedel; Reo-Coker, Shorey, Sidwell, Davies, Knight, Petrov, Young A, Delfouneso (Harewood), Milner, Gardner.

Southampton (0) 0
Manchester U (1) 3 *(Welbeck 20, Nani 48 (pen), Gibson 81)* 31,901
Southampton: Davis; James, Skacel, Gillett (Schneiderlin), Perry, Lancashire, Smith (Holmes), Gobern (McLaggon), McGoldrick, Paterson■, Surman.
Manchester U: Van der Sar; Neville, O'Shea, Carrick (Gibson), Evans, Vidic, Nani, Anderson, Berbatov, Welbeck (Rooney), Giggs (Possebon).

Monday, 5 January 2009

Blyth Spartans (0) 0
Blackburn R (0) 1 *(Villanueva 58)* 3445
Blyth Spartans: Bell; Boyle, White (Todd), Williams, Pell, Leeson, Dalton (Wright), McCabe, Dale, Reay, Gildea.
Blackburn R: Bunn; Simpson, Olsson, Grella (Andrews), Khizanishvili, Mokoena, Vogel, Treacy, Derbyshire (Hodge), Villanueva (Roberts), Judge.

Tuesday, 13 January 2009

Birmingham C (0) 0
Wolverhampton W (1) 2 *(Keogh 38, Vokes 51)* 22,232
Birmingham C: Maik Taylor; Parnaby, Queudrue, Carsley, Jaidi, Ridgewell, Quashie, Agustien (Kelly), Jerome, Bent (Johnson), Shroot.
Wolverhampton W: Hennessey; Friend, Ward S, Edwards D, Collins, Stearman, Kightly (Ebanks-Blake), Henry, Keogh, Vokes (Iwelumo), David Jones.

Cheltenham T (0) 0
Doncaster R (0) 0 4417
Cheltenham T: Brown SP; Lindegaard, Wright, Westlake, Gallinagh, Ridley, Russell, Bird, Hayes (Connor), Owusu, Hammond (Finnigan).
Doncaster R: Sullivan; O'Connor, Chambers, Hird, Mills, Stock (Taylor), Coppinger (Wilson), Wellens, Heffernan (Lockwood), Woods M, Spicer.

Histon (0) 1 *(Simpson 84)*
Swansea C (2) 2 *(Pintado 22, Bauza 38)* 2821
Histon: Naisbitt; Oyebanjo, Patterson (Bygrave), Simpson, Ada, Langston, Mitchell-King, Murray, Wright, Reeves (Andrews), Knight-Percival.
Swansea C: De Vries; Serran, Tate, Britton, Monk, Williams, Orlandi (MacDonald), Tudur-Jones (O'Leary), Pintado, Bauza, Butler (Dyer).

Leyton Orient (1) 1 *(Melligan 38 (pen))*
Sheffield U (0) 4 *(Halford 59, 78, Sharp 62, Naughton 69)* 4527
Leyton Orient: Morris; Purches, Cave-Brown, Chambers, Mkandawire, Saah, Melligan, Thornton, Boyd, Parkin, Demetriou.
Sheffield U: Bennett; Walker, Jihai, Montgomery, Morgan, Kilgallon, Halford, Naughton, Henderson (Hendrie), Sharp, Cotterill.

THIRD ROUND REPLAYS

Tuesday, 13 January 2009

Bristol C (0) 0
Portsmouth (1) 2 *(Crouch 38, Kranjcar 88)* 14,302
Bristol C: Basso; Orr, Fontaine (Adebola), Elliott, Carey, McCombe, Skuse (McIndoe), Johnson, Styvar (John), Maynard, Sproule.
Portsmouth: James; Johnson, Kaboul, Wilson, Campbell, Distin, Belhadj, Nugent (Utaka), Crouch (Kanu), Kranjcar, Traore A (Hreidarsson).

Burnley (0) 2 *(Thompson 60, Rodriguez 120)*
QPR (0) 1 *(Di Carmine 54)* 3760
Burnley: Jensen; Alexander, Jordan, McCann (Mahon), Caldwell, Carlisle, Eagles, Gudjonsson (MacDonald), Blake (Rodriguez), Thompson, Elliott.
QPR: Cerny; Delaney, Stewart, Mahon (Rose), Hall, Gorkss, Rowlands, Leigertwood, Di Carmine (Helguson), Ledesma (Ephraim), Alberti.
aet.

Crewe Alex (1) 2 *(Murphy 7, Miller 58)*
Millwall (1) 3 *(Barron 8, Harris 54, Whitbread 86)*   3060
Crewe Alex: Collis; Brayford, Jones (Zola), Bailey, Lawrence, Baudet, Murphy, O'Connor (Carrington), Miller (Pope), Donaldson, Daniel.
Millwall: Forde; Dunne, Barron, Laird, Whitbread, Frampton, Grabban, Fuseini, Kandol (Alexander), Harris, Martin.

Norwich C (0) 0
Charlton Ath (1) 1 *(Ambrose 6)*   13,997
Norwich C: Marshall; Otsemobor, Drury (Bertrand), Doherty, Omozusi, Clingan, Croft, Fotheringham (Russell), Cort (Hoolahan), Lupoli, Bell.
Charlton Ath: Randolph; Moutaouakil, Basey, Wagstaff (Shelvey), Fortune, Hudson, Wright, Bailey, Burton, Sam (Yussuff), Ambrose (Holland).

Peterborough U (0) 0
WBA (2) 2 *(Simpson 18, Robinson 37)*   10,735
Peterborough U: Lewis; Martin, Williams, Lee (Batt), Morgan, Zakuani, Whelpdale, Keates, Mackail-Smith, McLean, Boyd.
WBA: Carson; Hoefkens, Robinson, Koren, Barnett, Donk, Teixeira (Dorrans), Kim (Borja Valero), Bednar, Simpson (Beattie), Greening.

Wednesday, 14 January 2009

Crystal Palace (1) 2 *(Ifill 38, Scannell 55)*
Leicester C (0) 1 *(Gradel 90)*   6023
Crystal Palace: Speroni; Clyne, Hill, Carle, Butterfield, Lawrence, Danns, Derry, Moses (Scannell), Lee (Kuqi), Ifill (Andrew).
Leicester C: Martin; Edworthy (Gilbert), Mattock, King A, Hobbs, Tunchev (Morrison), Berner, Oakley, Howard, Dickov (Chambers), Gradel.

Newcastle U (0) 0
Hull C (0) 1 *(Cousin 81)*   31,380
Newcastle U: Given; Edgar, N'Zogbia, Butt, Coloccini, Bassong, Gutierrez (LuaLua), Guthrie, Owen, Xisco (Carroll), Duff.
Hull C: Duke; Doyle, Ricketts, Boateng (Ashbee), McShane, Zayatte, Garcia, France, Fagan (Mendy), Cousin (Folan), Halmosi.

Southend U (1) 1 *(Barrett 15)*
Chelsea (1) 4 *(Ballack 45, Kalou 60, Anelka 78, Lampard 90)*   11,314
Southend U: Mildenhall; Sankofa, Herd, Grant (Francis), Clarke, Barrett, Moussa, Christophe, Revell (Betsy), Barnard (Freedman), Stanislas.
Chelsea: Cech; Bosingwa, Cole A, Mikel (Belletti), Terry, Alex, Ballack, Lampard, Anelka, Kalou, Cole J (Di Santo).

Tuesday, 20 January 2009

Doncaster R (2) 3 *(Stock 26, 58, Hird 36)*
Cheltenham T (0) 0   5345
Doncaster R: Sullivan; O'Connor, Chambers (Roberts), Hird, Mills (Lockwood), Stock, Woods M, Wellens, Coppinger (Heffernan), Guy, Spicer.
Cheltenham T: Brown SP; Lindegaard, Ridley, Bird (Durrant), Gallinagh, Duff, Wright (Hayes), Russell, Owusu, Hammond, Vincent (Watkins).

FOURTH ROUND

Friday, 23 January 2009

Derby Co (1) 1 *(Hulse 36)*
Nottingham F (0) 1 *(Earnshaw 64)*   32,035
Derby Co: Bywater; Connolly, Stewart, Green, Albrechtsen, Addison, Barazite (Villa), Savage, Hulse, Barnes (Varney), Teale (Commons).
Nottingham F: Smith; Chambers, Lynch (McCleary), Perch, Wilson, Breckin, Anderson (Davies), McGugan, Tyson, Earnshaw (Garner), Cohen.

Saturday, 24 January 2009

Chelsea (1) 3 *(Ballack 16, 59, Lampard 85)*
Ipswich T (1) 1 *(Bruce 34)*   41,137
Chelsea: Cech; Bosingwa, Cole A, Belletti, Alex, Ricardo Carvalho (Ivanovic), Ballack (Deco), Lampard, Anelka, Kalou, Malouda (Drogba).
Ipswich T: Wright T; Wright D, Bruce, Garvan, McAuley, Balkestein, Norris, Miller (Quinn), Walters (Stead), Counago, Haynes (Lisbie).

Doncaster R (0) 0
Aston Villa (0) 0   13,517
Doncaster R: Sullivan; O'Connor, Roberts, Hird, Mills, Stock, Woods M, Wellens, Coppinger (Price), Guy (Heffernan), Spicer (Lockwood).
Aston Villa: Friedel; Reo-Coker (Gardner), Shorey, Cuellar, Davies, Knight, Petrov, Sidwell, Agbonlahor, Milner, Barry.

Hartlepool U (0) 0
West Ham U (2) 2 *(Behrami 44, Noble 45 (pen))*   6849
Hartlepool U: Lee-Barratt; Sweeney, Humphreys, Liddle, Nelson, Clark, Robson, Jones (Foley), Porter, Mackay (Henderson), Monkhouse.
West Ham U: Green; Faubert, Ilunga, Noble, Collins, Tomkins, Behrami, Parker, Cole (Sears), Di Michele (Mullins), Collison (Boa Morte).

Hull C (1) 2 *(Turner 15, Ashbee 84)*
Millwall (0) 0   18,639
Hull C: Warner; Ricketts, Dawson, Ashbee, Turner, Zayatte, Garcia, Marney, Cousin, Manucho (Folan), Halmosi (Featherstone).
Millwall: Forde; Dunne, Craig, Laird, Robinson, Frampton, Grabban (Hackett), Abdou, McLeod (Alexander), Harris, Martin (Grimes).

Kettering T (1) 2 *(Westcarr 36, 83 (pen))*
Fulham (1) 4 *(Davies 12, Murphy 77, Johnson 88, Zamora 89)*   5406
Kettering T: Harper; Eaden, Jaszczun (Potter A), Boucaud, Dempster, Geohaghan, Bennett, Solkhon, Westcarr, Seddon (Beardsley), Graham (Marna).
Fulham: Schwarzer; Stoor, Konchesky, Andreasen, Hughes, Hangeland, Davies, Etuhu (Zamora), Johnson, Dempsey, Gera (Murphy).

Manchester U (2) 2 *(Scholes 35, Berbatov 36)*
Tottenham H (1) 1 *(Pavlyuchenko 5)*   75,014
Manchester U: Foster; Fabio (Eckersley), O'Shea, Carrick, Neville, Vidic, Ronaldo (Tosic), Scholes, Berbatov, Tevez, Welbeck (Fletcher).
Tottenham H: Alnwick; Gunter, Assou-Ekotto, Zokora, Corluka, Dawson, Bentley (Defoe), Huddlestone, Pavlyuchenko, Modric (Giovani), Bale (Taarabt).

Portsmouth (0) 0
Swansea C (2) 2 *(Dyer 26, Scotland 45 (pen))*   17,357
Portsmouth: James; Cranie, Belhadj, Davis, Campbell, Distin, Pennant, Hughes (Kaboul), Crouch, Nugent (Kanu), Traore A (Hreidarsson).
Swansea C: Konstantopoulos; Rangel, Tate, Britton, Monk, Williams, Dyer (Gower), Allen (Pintado), Gomez, Scotland, Pratley.

Sheffield U (1) 2 *(Webber 26, Hendrie 62)*
Charlton Ath (0) 1 *(Dickson 69)*   15,957
Sheffield U: Bennett; Jihai (Howard), Naysmith, Montgomery, Morgan, Kilgallon, Halford, Henderson, Webber (Hendrie), Sharp, Naughton.
Charlton Ath: Elliot; Moutaouakil, Youga, Bailey, Fortune, Hudson, Holland (Racon), Shelvey (Dickson), Burton (Gray), Sam, Ambrose.

Sunderland (0) 0
Blackburn R (0) 0   22,634
Sunderland: Fulop; Chimbonda, Bardsley (McCartney), Leadbitter, Collins, Ferdinand, Edwards, Reid, Healy (Jones), Chopra, Malbranque.
Blackburn R: Robinson; Simpson, Warnock (Givet), Mokoena, Nelsen, Samba, Olsson (Haworth), Grella, Santa Cruz (Villanueva), McCarthy, Pedersen.

Torquay U (0) 0
Coventry C (0) 1 *(Ward 87)*   6018
Torquay U: Bevan; Mansell, Nicholson, Hargreaves, Woods, Hodges, Carlisle (Carayol), Wroe, Green (Benyon), Sills, D'Sane (Stevens).
Coventry C: Westwood; Gunnarsson (Ward), Fox, Doyle, Hall, Turner, Beuzelin (Thornton), McKenzie, Morrison, Eastwood, Mifsud.

WBA (2) 2 *(Koren 31, Kim 45)*
Burnley (1) 2 *(Alexander 25 (pen), Paterson 89)*   18,294
WBA: Carson; Hoefkens, Robinson, Koren, Donk (Zuiverloon), Pele, Teixeira (Brunt), Kim, Bednar, Simpson, Greening (Borja Valero).
Burnley: Jensen; Duff (Thompson), Kalvenes (Rodriguez), McCann, Caldwell, Carlisle, Alexander, Eagles (Gudjonsson), Blake, Paterson, Elliott.

Watford (2) 4 *(DeMerit 17, Cork 27, Hoskins 67, Rasiak 70)*
Crystal Palace (0) 3 *(Hill 48, Danns 83, Ifill 90)*   10,006
Watford: Loach; Hoyte (Kiernan), Doyley, Cork, Mariappa, DeMerit, McAnuff, Jenkins, Rasiak (O'Toole), Hoskins (Bridcutt), Harley.
Crystal Palace: Speroni; Clyne (Butterfield), Hill, Danns, Lawrence, Fonte J, Oster, Derry (Fletcher), Moses, Lee (Kuqi), Ifill.

Wolverhampton W (0) 1 *(Vokes 63)*
Middlesbrough (1) 2 *(Alves 44, Emnes 83)*   18,013
Wolverhampton W: Hennessey; Edwards D, Hill, David Jones, Collins, Shackell, Jarvis (Ebanks-Blake), Henry, Iwelumo (Keogh), Vokes, Reid (Kightly).
Middlesbrough: Jones; Bates, Taylor (McMahon), O'Neil, Wheater, Riggott, Johnson A, Shawky (Hoyte), Alves (Emnes), Tuncay, Downing.

Sunday, 25 January 2009

Cardiff C (0) 0
Arsenal (0) 0   20,079
Cardiff C: Enckelman; McNaughton, Kennedy, Rae, Johnson R, Gyepes, Burke (Capaldi), Parry, Bothroyd (Johnson E), McCormack, Ledley.
Arsenal: Fabianski; Sagna, Gibbs, Song Billong, Djourou, Toure, Eboue (Adebayor), Ramsey (Diaby), Bendtner (Wilshere), Van Persie, Nasri.

Liverpool (0) 1 *(Gerrard 54)*
Everton (1) 1 *(Lescott 27)*   43,524
Liverpool: Reina; Arbeloa, Dossena, Xabi Alonso, Carragher, Skrtel, Kuyt, Mascherano, Torres, Gerrard, Babel (Riera).
Everton: Howard; Hibbert, Baines, Neville, Jagielka, Lescott, Osman, Castillo (Rodwell), Anichebe (Gosling), Cahill, Pienaar.

FOURTH ROUND REPLAYS

Tuesday, 3 February 2009

Burnley (1) 3 *(Elliott 45, Thompson 52, 88)*
WBA (0) 1 *(Zuiverloon 60)*   6635
Burnley: Jensen; Alexander, Kalvenes, McCann, Caldwell, Duff, McDonald (Gudjonsson), Thompson (MacDonald), Blake, Paterson (Rodriguez), Elliott.
WBA: Carson; Zuiverloon, Cech, Dorrans, Donk, Pele, Kim, Simpson (Brunt), Fortune, Bednar, Teixeira (Hoefkens).

Wednesday, 4 February 2009

Aston Villa (2) 3 *(Sidwell 15, Carew 19, Delfouneso 61)*
Doncaster R (1) 1 *(Price 45)*   24,203
Aston Villa: Guzan; Young L, Shorey, Salifou, Davies, Cuellar, Gardner, Sidwell, Delfouneso, Carew, Young A (Osbourne).
Doncaster R: Sullivan; O'Connor, Chambers, Hird, Mills, Stock, Coppinger (Byfield), Wellens, Price (Heffernan), Woods M, Spicer (Guy).

Blackburn R (1) 2 *(Mokoena 37, McCarthy 118)*
Sunderland (1) 1 *(Healy 7)*   10,112
Blackburn R: Robinson; Simpson, Givet, Mokoena, Nelsen (Ooijer), Khizanishvili, Villanueva, Dunn (Tugay), Santa Cruz (McCarthy), Roberts, Treacy.

Sunderland: Gordon; Kay (Bardsley), McCartney (Luscombe), Leadbitter, Ferdinand, Collins, Edwards, Reid, Murphy, Healy, Malbranque (Yorke).
aet.

Everton (0) 1 *(Gosling 118)*
Liverpool (0) 0   37,918
Everton: Howard; Hibbert, Baines, Neville (Van der Meyde), Jagielka, Lescott, Osman, Fellaini (Gosling), Pienaar (Rodwell), Cahill, Arteta.
Liverpool: Reina; Arbeloa, Dossena, Xabi Alonso, Carragher, Skrtel, Kuyt, Lucas*, Torres (Babel), Gerrard (Benayoun), Riera (Mascherano).
aet.

Nottingham F (2) 2 *(Cohen 2, Tyson 14 (pen))*
Derby Co (1) 3 *(Hulse 27, Green 60, Commons 74)*   29,001
Nottingham F: Smith; Chambers, Wilson, Perch (Byrne), Morgan, Breckin, McCleary (Heath), McGugan, Tyson (Newbold), Cohen, Thornhill.
Derby Co: Bywater; Connolly, McEveley, Green, Albrechtsen, Nyatanga, Barazite, Savage, Hulse (Ellington), Commons, Teale.

Monday, 16 February 2009

Arsenal (2) 4 *(Eduardo 20, 60 (pen), Bendtner 34, Van Persie 89)*
Cardiff C (0) 0   57,237
Arsenal: Fabianski; Sagna, Gibbs, Denilson, Toure, Gallas, Song Billong, Vela (Bischoff), Eduardo (Van Persie), Bendtner, Nasri (Ramsey).
Cardiff C: Heaton; McNaughton, Kennedy, Rae (Scimeca), Johnson R, Purse (Whittingham), Burke, Parry (Blake), Bothroyd, McCormack, Ledley.

FIFTH ROUND

Saturday, 14 February 2009

Blackburn R (1) 2 *(Santa Cruz 2, Samba 90)*
Coventry C (0) 2 *(Gunnarsson 61, Doyle 76)*   15,053
Blackburn R: Robinson; Simpson, Givet, Tugay (Andrews), Khizanishvili, Samba, Villanueva, Dunn (Treacy), Santa Cruz, Roberts (McCarthy), Warnock.
Coventry C: Marshall; Osbourne, Fox, Doyle, Ward, McPake (Dann), Henderson, Beuzelin (Best), Morrison, Eastwood, Gunnarsson.

Sheffield U (1) 1 *(Halford 7)*
Hull C (1) 1 *(Zayatte 34)*   22,283
Sheffield U: Kenny; Jihai (Naughton), Naysmith, Montgomery, Morgan (Webber), Kilgallon, Cotterill, Hendrie (Howard), Halford, Sharp, Quinn S.
Hull C: Myhill; Ricketts, Dawson, Gardner, Turner, Zayatte, Mendy (France), Marney, Folan, Geovanni (Barmby), Garcia (Manucho).

Swansea C (0) 1 *(Scotland 52)*
Fulham (1) 1 *(Monk 44 (og))*   16,573
Swansea C: De Vries; Rangel, Tate, Britton, Monk, Williams, Gower (Orlandi), Allen (Bauza), Gomez, Scotland, Dyer.
Fulham: Schwarzer; Stoor, Konchesky, Murphy, Hughes, Hangeland, Davies, Dacourt (Dempsey), Johnson (Gray), Nevland (Zamora), Gera.

Watford (0) 1 *(Priskin 69)*
Chelsea (0) 3 *(Anelka 75, 77, 90)*   16,851
Watford: Loach; Hoyte, Doyley, Jenkins, Mariappa, DeMerit, McAnuff, Williamson L (Cowie), Rasiak (Priskin), Smith, Hoskins (O'Toole).
Chelsea: Cech; Mancienne, Cole A, Mikel (Stoch), Ivanovic, Alex, Ballack (Belletti), Lampard, Anelka, Drogba, Kalou.

West Ham U (0) 1 *(Ilunga 83)*
Middlesbrough (1) 1 *(Downing 22)*   33,658
West Ham U: Green; Neill, Ilunga, Noble (Nsereko), Upson, Collins, Collison, Parker, Cole (Tristan), Di Michele, Boa Morte (Sears).
Middlesbrough: Jones; Hoyte, Pogatetz, O'Neil, Huth, Wheater, Johnson A, Digard, Alves (Tuncay), Arca (Walker), Downing.

Sunday, 15 February 2009
Derby Co (0) 1 *(Addison 56)*
Manchester U (2) 4 *(Nani 29, Gibson 44, Ronaldo 48, Welbeck 81)* 32,103
Derby Co: Bywater; Connolly, Stewart, Green, Albrechtsen, Addison, Barazite (Sterjovski), Savage (Pearson), Hulse (Porter), Commons, Teale.
Manchester U: Foster; Rafael, Evra (Welbeck), Park (O'Shea), Ferdinand, Evans, Gibson, Fletcher, Ronaldo (Possebon), Giggs, Nani.

Everton (2) 3 *(Rodwell 4, Arteta 24 (pen), Cahill 76)*
Aston Villa (1) 1 *(Milner 8 (pen))* 35,439
Everton: Howard; Hibbert, Baines, Neville, Jagielka, Lescott, Gosling, Rodwell, Anichebe (Yobo), Cahill, Arteta (Castillo).
Aston Villa: Friedel; Gardner, Young L, Sidwell (Delfouneso), Davies, Knight, Petrov, Young A, Agbonlahor, Carew, Milner.

Sunday, 8 March 2009
Arsenal (1) 3 *(Vela 25, Eduardo 51, Eboue 84)*
Burnley (0) 0 57,454
Arsenal: Fabianski; Sagna, Gibbs, Diaby (Ramsey), Djourou, Gallas, Eboue, Song Billong, Eduardo (Walcott), Arshavin, Vela (Van Persie).
Burnley: Jensen; Alexander, Kalvenes, McCann, Caldwell, Carlisle, McDonald (MacDonald), Gudjonsson (Thompson), Blake, Paterson, Eagles (Elliott).

FIFTH ROUND REPLAYS

Tuesday, 24 February 2009
Coventry City (0) 1 *(Best 59)*
Blackburn R (0) 0 22,793
Coventry City: Westwood; Wright, Fox, Doyle, Turner, Ward, Henderson, Gunnarsson, Morrison, Best, Eastwood (Simpson).
Blackburn R: Brown; Simpson, Olsson, Tugay, Khizanishvili (Givet), Samba, Villanueva (Warnock), Mokoena, Roberts, McCarthy, Treacy (Santa Cruz).

Fulham (0) 2 *(Dempsey 77, Zamora 81)*
Swansea C (0) 1 *(Scotland 47)* 12,316
Fulham: Schwarzer; Pantsil, Konchesky, Dacourt (Murphy), Hughes, Hangeland, Davies, Etuhu, Nevland (Gera), Zamora, Dempsey (Kamara).
Swansea C: De Vries; Rangel, Tate, Britton, Serran, Williams (Bessone), Gower (Tudur-Jones), Gomez, Dyer, Scotland, Bauza (Butler).

Wednesday, 25 February 2009
Middlesbrough (2) 2 *(Downing 5, Tuncay 20)*
West Ham U (0) 0 15,602
Middlesbrough: Jones; Hoyte, Pogatetz, O'Neil, Huth, Wheater, Bates, Arca (Walker), Aliadiere (Emnes), Tuncay (Johnson A), Downing.
West Ham U: Green; Neill, Ilunga, Noble (Collison), Upson, Tomkins, Behrami, Parker, Cole, Sears (Di Michele), Kovac (Tristan).

Thursday, 26 February 2009
Hull C (1) 2 *(Naughton 24 (og), Halmosi 56)*
Sheffield U (1) 1 *(Sharp 32)* 17,239
Hull C: Myhill; Doyle, Ricketts, Marney, Turner, Zayatte, Mendy, France, Folan (Manucho), Barmby (Garcia), Halmosi.
Sheffield U: Kenny; Naughton, Naysmith (Jihai), Hendrie (Tahar), Morgan, Walker, Cotterill, Howard, Halford, Sharp, Quinn S.

SIXTH ROUND

Saturday, 7 March 2009
Coventry C (0) 0
Chelsea (1) 2 *(Drogba 15, Alex 72)* 31,407
Coventry C: Westwood; Wright, Hall, Doyle (Beuzelin), Turner, Dann, Henderson, Gunnarsson, Morrison, Eastwood, Best.
Chelsea: Cech; Bosingwa, Cole A, Mikel (Essien), Terry, Alex, Ballack, Lampard, Drogba (Di Santo), Kalou (Quaresma), Malouda.

Fulham (0) 0
Manchester U (2) 4 *(Tevez 20, 35, Rooney 50, Park 81)* 24,662
Fulham: Schwarzer; Pantsil, Konchesky, Murphy (Dacourt), Hughes, Hangeland, Davies, Etuhu, Johnson (Kamara), Zamora (Gera), Dempsey.
Manchester U: Van der Sar; O'Shea (Eckersley), Evra, Carrick, Ferdinand (Evans), Vidic, Fletcher, Anderson, Rooney (Welbeck), Tevez, Park.

Sunday, 8 March 2009
Everton (0) 2 *(Fellaini 50, Saha 56)*
Middlesbrough (1) 1 *(Wheater 44)* 37,856
Everton: Howard; Neville, Baines, Yobo, Jagielka, Lescott, Osman, Rodwell (Saha), Cahill, Fellaini, Pienaar (Gosling).
Middlesbrough: Jones; Hoyte, Pogatetz, O'Neil, Huth, Wheater, Bates (Johnson A), Arca, Aliadiere (Emnes), Tuncay, Downing.

Tuesday, 17 March 2009
Arsenal (0) 2 *(Van Persie 74, Gallas 84)*
Hull C (1) 1 *(Barmby 13)* 55,641
Arsenal: Fabianski; Sagna, Gibbs, Diaby, Djourou, Gallas, Walcott (Eboue), Song Billong (Bendtner), Arshavin, Van Persie, Vela (Nasri).
Hull C: Myhill; Ricketts, Dawson, Ashbee (Hughes), Gardner, Zayatte, Barmby (France), Manucho, Fagan, Geovanni, Halmosi (Mendy).

SEMI-FINALS (AT WEMBLEY)

Saturday, 18 April 2009
Arsenal (1) 1 *(Walcott 18)*
Chelsea (1) 2 *(Malouda 33, Drogba 84)* 88,103
Arsenal: Fabianski; Eboue, Gibbs, Denilson (Nasri), Toure, Silvestre, Walcott, Fabregas, Adebayor (Bendtner), Van Persie (Arshavin), Diaby.
Chelsea: Cech; Ivanovic, Cole A, Essien, Terry, Alex, Ballack, Lampard, Anelka (Kalou), Drogba, Malouda.

Sunday, 19 April 2009
Manchester U (0) 0
Everton (0) 0 88,141
Manchester U: Foster; Rafael, Fabio (Evra), Anderson, Ferdinand, Vidic, Welbeck, Gibson, Macheda (Berbatov), Tevez, Park (Scholes).
Everton: Howard; Hibbert, Baines, Neville, Jagielka, Lescott, Osman, Fellaini (Vaughan), Saha (Rodwell), Cahill, Pienaar.
aet; Everton won 4-2 on penalties: Cahill missed; Berbatov saved; Baines scored; Ferdinand saved; Neville scored; Vidic scored; Vaughan scored; Anderson scored; Jagielka scored.

THE FA CUP FINAL

(Saturday, 30 May 2009 at Wembley Stadium, attendance 89,391)

Chelsea (1) 2   **Everton (1) 1**

Chelsea: Cech; Bosingwa, Cole A, Mikel, Terry, Alex, Essien (Ballack), Lampard, Anelka, Drogba, Malouda.
Scorers: Drogba 21, Lampard 72.

Everton: Howard; Hibbert (Jacobsen), Baines, Yobo, Lescott, Neville, Osman (Gosling), Fellani, Saha (Vaughan), Cahill, Pienaar.
Scorer: Saha 1.

Referee: H. Webb (South Yorkshire).

BLUE SQUARE 2008–09

Burton Albion just made it, limping over the line with scarcely anything to spare, having at one time threatened to overhaul the records created the previous year by Aldershot Town. How much of the collapse was due to the earlier departure of Nigel Clough to become manager of his father's old Derby County cannot easily be explained. Roy McFarland stood in as caretaker but clearly had no intention of making it a permanent move.

From not the best opening to a championship season Burton after five matches were eleventh. Defeat by 2-1 at Oxford United on 18 October changed matters dramatically. A run of 17 unbeaten games in which just two matches were drawn put them in an almost unassailable position at the top – at least this was the theory.

In practice it was an extremely close run affair and almost an unlucky thirteen for them and but for a three match revival they won only four of these last fixtures. It went down to the wire on the last day with Cambridge United needing to beat Altrincham at home and hoping Torquay United would take care of Burton down in Devon. Of course Cambridge could only draw and it was of no consequence after all that the Brewers were beaten, with Torquay completing a double over Albion. In that respect gaining promotion back to the Football League you might say that Torquay deserved to come through the play-offs.

Oddly enough successes over Burton represented Torquay's only wins in the six games. Disappointment then for Cambridge but also Stevenage Borough who lost to them in the semi-final having run into top form from early December and losing only twice from then on. Histon the other play-off candidates pushed Torquay all the way after an encouraging season which at one stage had produced eight successive wins.

Oxford United expected to be among the pack but left their surge far too late and suffered from their points penalty. When you realise that they lost just two matches from the end of December their early efforts were meagre indeed. Kettering Town and Kidderminster Harriers were always on the fringe of it all, but the Poppies lacked consistency in the second half of the season and the Harriers, second at the end of September, failed to sustain this form until it was too late and fourteen matches without defeat was followed by losing the last two games.

Rushden & Diamonds, another fancied outfit, was unable to shake off a middle of the table look and the relegated pair Mansfield Town and Wrexham both disappointed: Mansfield with a points deduction which helped their cause not at all and Wrexham hit by injuries scored just eight goals in their last eleven matches.

Of course after six matches the League leaders were Forest Green Rovers and only six points separated the first eleven clubs. But half a dozen games later, FGR had slumped to the bottom half and Crawley Town were in front. Crawley was just one of several clubs with points deducted from them. In their case it was one, but Mansfield had four and Oxford five as previously mentioned.

Eastbourne Borough could be satisfied with a mid-table berth but Ebbsfleet United had two bad spells of defeats which prevented any real movement upwards. Altrincham acquitted themselves well compared with previous seasons of trauma, Salisbury City tailed off after a useful start and York City was another disappointing outfit after much had been hoped for in that quarter.

Grays Athletic – 51 different players – wrenched away from the relegation zone towards the close and Barrow again after a fine opening steered out of danger late on. But it was relegation for Woking, Northwich Victoria, Weymouth and Lewes. Nineteenth was the highest Woking achieved, Northwich one place lower at their best and Weymouth beset by financial problems faced the inevitable. Both used 51 players. Lewes, one better with 52 called upon, were game but out of their depth at times.

BLUE SQUARE PREMIER ATTENDANCES BY CLUB 2008–09

	Aggregate 2008–09	Average 2008–09	Highest Attendance 2008–09
Oxford United	112,228	4,879	10,298 v Northwich Victoria
Cambridge United	82,117	3,570	7,090 v Altrincham
Wrexham	75,730	3,293	5,173 v York City
Mansfield Town	55,721	2,423	3,614 v Stevenage Borough
Burton Albion	55,229	2,401	6,192 v Oxford United
York City	52,794	2,295	2,703 v Burton Albion
Torquay United	51,578	2,243	4,528 v Burton Albion
Stevenage Borough	45,756	1,989	3,700 v Oxford United
Woking	39,739	1,728	3,791 v Oxford United
Kidderminster Harriers	38,835	1,688	3,025 v Burton Albion
Kettering Town	37,150	1,615	2,897 v Rushden & Diamonds
Barrow	35,900	1,561	2,790 v Oxford United
Rushden & Diamonds	34,715	1,509	3,406 v Kettering Town
Eastbourne Borough	31,905	1,387	3,105 v Cambridge United
Ebbsfleet United	27,667	1,203	1,872 v Mansfield Town
Crawley Town	27,467	1,194	2,207 v Kettering Town
Salisbury City	26,306	1,144	2,418 v Oxford United
Histon	25,763	1,120	2,716 v Kettering Town
Weymouth	25,096	1,091	2,323 v Torquay United
Altrincham	24,863	1,081	2,619 v Wrexham
Forest Green Rovers	21,970	955	2,027 v Oxford United
Northwich Victoria	18,112	787	1,709 v Wrexham
Lewes	16,537	719	2,232 v Eastbourne Borough
Grays Athletic	15,793	687	1,246 v Forest Green Rovers

BLUE SQUARE PREMIER FINAL LEAGUE TABLE

		Home					Away					Total						
		P	W	D	L	F	A	W	D	L	F	A	W	D	L	F	A	GD	Pts
1	Burton Alb	46	15	5	3	48	23	12	2	9	33	29	27	7	12	81	52	29	88
2	Cambridge U	46	14	6	3	34	15	10	8	5	31	24	24	14	8	65	39	26	86
3	Histon	46	14	8	1	41	18	9	6	8	37	30	23	14	9	78	48	30	83
4	Torquay U	46	11	7	5	38	23	12	7	4	34	24	23	14	9	72	47	25	83
5	Stevenage B	46	12	8	3	41	23	11	4	8	32	31	23	12	11	73	54	19	81
6	Kidderminster H	46	16	2	5	40	18	7	8	8	29	30	23	10	13	69	48	21	79
7	Oxford U*	46	16	3	4	42	20	8	7	8	30	31	24	10	12	72	51	21	77
8	Kettering T	46	12	5	6	26	19	9	8	6	24	18	21	13	12	50	37	13	76
9	Crawley T*	46	13	5	5	48	26	6	9	8	29	29	19	14	13	77	55	22	70
10	Wrexham	46	11	7	5	39	22	7	5	11	25	26	18	12	16	64	48	16	66
11	Rushden & D	46	11	5	7	30	24	5	10	8	31	26	16	15	15	61	50	11	63
12	Mansfield T*	46	14	5	4	35	19	5	4	14	22	36	19	9	18	57	55	2	62
13	Eastbourne B	46	11	3	9	29	27	7	3	13	29	43	18	6	22	58	70	–12	60
14	Ebbsfleet U	46	10	9	4	28	19	6	1	16	24	41	16	10	20	52	60	–8	58
15	Altrincham	46	9	7	7	30	29	6	4	13	19	37	15	11	20	49	66	–17	56
16	Salisbury C	46	8	6	9	29	33	6	7	10	25	31	14	13	19	54	64	–10	55
17	York C	46	8	9	6	26	20	3	10	10	21	31	11	19	16	47	51	–4	52
18	Forest Green R	46	7	6	10	39	40	5	10	8	31	36	12	16	18	70	76	–6	52
19	Grays Ath	46	12	5	6	31	24	2	5	16	13	40	14	10	22	44	64	–20	52
20	Barrow	46	7	10	6	27	26	5	5	13	24	39	12	15	19	51	65	–14	51
21	Woking	46	6	8	9	21	29	4	6	13	16	31	10	14	22	37	60	–23	44
22	Northwich Vic	46	7	5	11	29	26	4	5	14	27	49	11	10	25	56	75	–19	43
23	Weymouth	46	5	6	12	27	53	6	4	13	18	33	11	10	25	45	86	–41	43
24	Lewes	46	5	2	16	15	41	1	4	18	13	48	6	6	34	28	89	–61	24

*Oxford U deducted 5 points, Crawley T deducted 1 point, Mansfield T deducted 4 points.

BLUE SQUARE PREMIER LEADING GOALSCORERS 2008–09

League Goals only

Andrew Mangan	(Forest Green Rovers)	26
James Constable	(Oxford United)	23
Steve Morison	(Stevenage Borough)	22
Charlie Griffin	(Salisbury City)	21
Matthew Barnes-Homer	(Kidderminster Harriers)	20
Justin Richards	(Kidderminster Harriers)	20
Greg Pearson	(Burton Albion)	18
Richard Brodie	(York City)	15
Shaun Harrad	(Burton Albion)	15
Jefferson Louis	(Wrexham)	15
Gareth Seddon	(Kettering Town)	15
Stuart Beavon	(Weymouth)	14
Tim Sills	(Torquay United)	14

BLUE SQUARE PREMIER LEAGUE PLAY-OFFS

SEMI-FINALS FIRST LEG

Thursday, 30 April 2009

Stevenage B (0) 3 *(Roberts 47, Morison 61, 84)*

Cambridge U (0) 1 *(Phillips 49)* 4446

Stevenage B: Day; Bostwick, Laird, Murphy■, Henry, Roberts, Ashton, Drury (Willock), Morison, Boylan (Wilson), Mendes (Mills).
Cambridge U: Potter; Gleeson, Tonkin, Bolland, Hatswell, Coulson (Pitt), Reason, Carden, Phillips, Crow (Holroyd), Challinor (Willmott).

Friday, 1 May 2009

Torquay U (1) 2 *(Wroe 36, Sills 74)*

Histon (0) 0 3737

Torquay U: Poke; Mansell, Nicholson, Hargreaves, Tod, Robertson, Carlisle, Wroe, Sturrock (Christie), Sills, Stevens.
Histon: Welch; Pope (Andrews), Gwillim, Mitchell-King, Ada, Oyebanjo, Langston, Murray, Barker, Midson, Knight-Percival.

SEMI-FINALS SECOND LEG

Monday, 4 May 2009

Cambridge U (0) 3 *(Willmott 55, Rendell 72, 119)*

Stevenage B (0) 0 6507

Cambridge U: Potter; Gleeson, Tonkin, Bolland, Hatswell, Willmott, Reason, Carden, Rendell, Phillips (Holroyd), Pitt (Parkinson).
Stevenage B: Day; Henry, Laird■, Bostock, Ashton, Roberts, Drury (Mendes), Mills, Morison, Boylan (Willock), Murphy (Wilson).

Histon (1) 1 *(Andrews 16)*

Torquay U (0) 0 2481

Histon: Naisbitt; Oyebanjo, Gwillim, Mitchell-King, Ada, Langston, Midson, Murray, Barker (Simpson), Andrews, Knight-Percival.
Torquay U: Poke; Mansell, Nicholson, Hargreaves, Todd, Robertson, Carlisle, Wroe, Sturrock (Benyon), Sills, Stevens (Hodges).

FINAL (at Wembley)

Sunday, 17 May 2009

Cambridge U (0) 0 **Torquay U (1) 2** *(Hargreaves 35, Sills 75)* 35,089

Cambridge U: Bartlett; Gleeson, Tonkin, Bolland■, Hatswell, Wilmott (Holroyd), Reason, Carden (Challinor), Rendell, Phillips, Pitt (Parkinson).
Torquay U: Poke; Mansell, Nicholson, Hargreaves, Todd, Robertson, Carlisle (Carayol), Wroe, Benyon (Thompson), Sills, Stevens (Hodges).
Referee: G. Sutton (Lincolnshire).

BLUE SQUARE SETANTA SHIELD 2008–09

NORTHERN Section

FIRST ROUND
AFC Telford United v Gainsborough Trinity	3-2
Alfreton Town v Stafford Rangers	2-3
Burscough v Blyth Spartans	1-4
Droylsden v Gateshead	1-2
Farsley Celtic v Workington	3-1
Harrogate Town v Fleetwood Town	1-1

Fleetwood Town won 5-4 on penalties.

Hucknall Town v Hinckley United	1-3
Hyde United v Vauxhall Motors	1-2
Kings Lynn v Tamworth	1-2
Redditch United v Solihull Moors	0-1
Stalybridge Celtic v Southport	1-4

SECOND ROUND
AFC Telford United v Solihull Moors	2-1
Altrincham v Farsley Celtic	1-1

Altrincham won 4-2 on penalties.

Barrow v Fleetwood Town	3-2
Blyth Spartans v Gateshead	1-2
Hinckley United v Tamworth	2-1
Stafford Rangers v Northwich Victoria	3-1
Vauxhall Motors v Southport	0-3

THIRD ROUND
AFC Telford United v Cambridge United	4-3
Altrincham v Wrexham	1-2
Barrow v Gateshead	3-1
Burton Albion v Kidderminster Harriers	3-2
Hinckley United v Histon	2-1
Kettering Town v Thurrock	4-1
Stafford Rangers v Southport	1-2
York City v Mansfield Town	1-1

York City won 4-2 on penalties.

FOURTH ROUND
AFC Telford United v Burton Albion	3-0
Barrow v York City	3-1
Hinckley United v Kettering Town	2-3
Wrexham v Southport	1-2

QUARTER-FINALS
AFC Telford United v Kettering Town	3-2
Barrow v Southport	3-1

SEMI-FINAL
Barrow v AFC Telford United	0-0, 0-1

First game abandoned; high winds.

SOUTHERN Section

FIRST ROUND
Basingstoke Town v Fisher Athletic	1-3
Bishop's Stortford v Bromley	2-1
Bognor Regis Town v Worcester City	2-0
Braintree Town v Hampton & Richmond Borough	3-0
Chelmsford City v AFC Wimbledon	1-0
Dorchester Town v Newport County	4-5
Eastleigh v Weston-Super-Mare	4-4

Eastleigh won 5-4 on penalties.

Maidenhead United v Havant & Waterlooville	1-2
St Albans City v Hayes & Yeading	0-1
Team Bath v Bath City	1-2
Thurrock v Welling United	2-0

SECOND ROUND
Bath City v Newport County	4-1
Chelmsford City v Braintree Town	3-1
Eastleigh v Havant & Waterlooville	2-3
Fisher Athletic v Eastbourne Borough	2-3
Kettering Town v Bishop's Stortford	4-2
Lewes v Bognor Regis Town	0-2
Thurrock v Hayes & Yeading	3-3

Thurrock won 5-4 on penalties.
Kettering Town and Thurrock transferred to Northern Section Third Round.

THIRD ROUND
Bath City v Salisbury City	0-1
Crawley Town v Havant & Waterlooville	3-0
Eastbourne Borough v Ebbsfleet United	1-3
Forest Green Rovers v Oxford United	2-1
Grays Athletic v Chelmsford City	2-4
Rushden & Diamonds v Stevenage Borough	0-3
Weymouth v Torquay United	0-3
Woking v Bognor Regis Town	3-0

FOURTH ROUND
Crawley Town v Chelmsford City	2-1
Ebbsfleet United v Stevenage Borough	3-0
Forest Green Rovers v Torquay United	1-0
Salisbury City v Woking	0-3

QUARTER-FINALS
Woking v Forest Green Rovers	2-2

Forest Green Rovers won 5-4 on penalties.

Crawley Town v Ebbsfleet United	1-2

SEMI-FINAL
Ebbsfleet v Forest Green Rovers	0-1

BLUE SQUARE SETANTA SHIELD 2008–09 FINAL

at Forest Green
Attendance 2323

Forest Green Rovers (0) 0
AFC Telford United (0) 0

aet; AFC Telford United won 3-0 on penalties.

Forest Green Rovers: Burton; Smith, Stonehouse (McDonald), Preece, Jones, Fowler, Lawless (Baldwin), Rigoglioso, Mangan, Platt, Mohamed (Lloyd).

AFC Telford United: Young; Vaughan, Khela, Cowan, Whitehead, Nwadike, Jagielka (Blakeman), Rodgers, Danks, Brown (Lewis), Moore (Adams).

Penalties: Mangan saved; Adams scored; Platt saved; Danks scored; Lloyd saved; Cowan scored.

Referee: S. Creighton (Berkshire).

BLUE SQUARE NORTH & SOUTH 2008–09

BLUE SQUARE NORTH FINAL LEAGUE TABLE

		P	W	D	L	F	A	W	D	L	F	A	W	D	L	F	A	GD	Pts
				Home						Away					Total				
1	Tamworth	42	12	5	4	32	18	12	8	1	38	23	24	13	5	70	41	29	85
2	Gateshead	42	14	5	2	50	19	10	3	8	31	29	24	8	10	81	48	33	80
3	Alfreton T	42	12	6	3	46	25	8	11	2	35	23	20	17	5	81	48	33	77
4	AFC Telford U	42	13	6	2	36	13	9	4	8	29	21	22	10	10	65	34	31	76
5	Southport	42	13	4	4	41	20	8	9	4	22	16	21	13	8	63	36	27	76
6	Stalybridge Celtic	42	8	6	7	42	33	12	4	5	29	17	20	10	12	71	50	21	70
7	Droylsden	42	12	6	3	35	18	6	8	7	29	26	18	14	10	64	44	20	68
8	Fleetwood T	42	12	4	5	32	23	5	7	9	38	43	17	11	14	70	66	4	62
9	Harrogate T	42	11	6	4	39	23	6	4	11	27	34	17	10	15	66	57	9	61
10	Hinckley U	42	10	3	8	29	21	6	6	9	27	38	16	9	17	56	59	-3	57
11	Vauxhall Motors	42	7	8	6	28	29	7	3	11	23	38	14	11	17	51	67	-16	53
12	Workington	42	8	5	8	31	30	5	7	9	23	25	13	12	17	54	55	-1	51
13	Gainsborough Trinity	42	5	7	9	25	31	7	7	7	32	32	12	14	16	57	63	-6	50
14	Redditch U	42	6	7	8	23	28	6	7	8	26	33	12	14	16	49	61	-12	50
15	Blyth Spartans	42	11	3	7	35	23	3	4	14	15	35	14	7	21	50	58	-8	49
16	Solihull Moors	42	9	6	6	34	31	4	4	13	15	42	13	10	19	49	73	-24	49
17	King's Lynn	42	5	10	6	28	30	5	8	8	22	30	10	18	14	50	60	-10	48
18	Stafford R	42	6	5	10	15	20	6	7	8	26	36	12	12	18	41	56	-15	48
19	Farsley Celtic	42	10	3	8	42	29	4	2	15	16	36	14	5	23	58	65	-7	47
20	Hyde U	42	6	6	9	31	36	5	3	13	26	44	11	9	22	57	80	-23	42
21	Burscough	42	3	5	13	20	35	7	1	13	23	45	10	6	26	43	80	-37	36
22	Hucknall T	42	2	7	12	20	36	3	6	12	19	48	5	13	24	39	84	-45	28

BLUE SQUARE SOUTH FINAL LEAGUE TABLE

		P	W	D	L	F	A	W	D	L	F	A	W	D	L	F	A	GD	Pts
				Home						Away					Total				
1	AFC Wimbledon	42	17	2	2	49	14	9	8	4	37	22	26	10	6	86	36	50	88
2	Hampton & Richmond B	42	13	5	3	38	16	12	5	4	36	21	25	10	7	74	37	37	85
3	Eastleigh	42	15	4	2	37	18	10	4	7	32	31	25	8	9	69	49	20	83
4	Hayes & Yeading U	42	14	3	4	39	19	10	6	5	35	24	24	9	9	74	43	31	81
5	Chelmsford C	42	12	6	3	42	24	11	2	8	30	28	23	8	11	72	52	20	77
6	Maidenhead U	42	11	3	7	28	23	10	5	6	29	23	21	8	13	57	46	11	71
7	Welling U	42	9	6	6	32	25	10	5	6	29	19	19	11	12	61	44	17	68
8	Bath C	42	11	4	6	28	24	9	4	8	28	21	20	8	14	56	45	11	68
9	Bishop's Stortford	42	9	4	8	28	28	8	4	9	32	32	17	8	17	60	60	0	59
10	Newport Co	42	10	3	8	31	29	6	8	7	19	22	16	11	15	50	51	-1	59
11	Team Bath	42	9	1	11	30	29	7	6	8	32	35	16	7	19	62	64	-2	55
12	St Albans C	42	8	6	7	35	26	6	6	9	21	24	14	12	16	56	50	6	54
13	Bromley	42	9	5	7	36	30	6	4	11	24	34	15	9	18	60	64	-4	54
14	Braintree T	42	7	5	9	23	24	7	5	9	34	30	14	10	18	57	54	3	52
15	Havant & Waterlooville	42	6	10	5	34	28	5	5	11	25	30	11	15	16	59	58	1	48
16	Worcester C	42	8	6	7	18	25	8	3	10	20	28	12	11	19	38	53	-15	47
17	Weston Super Mare	42	5	7	9	24	34	7	4	10	19	34	12	11	19	43	68	-25	47
18	Basingstoke T	42	4	11	6	17	19	6	5	10	19	36	10	16	16	36	55	-19	46
19	Dorchester T	42	6	6	9	23	30	4	6	11	16	31	10	12	20	39	61	-22	42
20	Thurrock	42	6	6	10	25	23	3	8	10	29	37	9	13	20	54	60	-6	40
21	Bognor Regis T	42	4	6	11	19	38	3	6	12	14	30	7	12	23	33	68	-35	26
22	Fisher Ath	42	3	1	17	9	47	2	2	17	13	53	5	3	34	22	100	-78	18

BLUE SQUARE NORTH & SOUTH PLAY-OFFS

BLUE SQUARE NORTH

SEMI-FINALS FIRST LEG

AFC Telford U 2 *(Nwadike 48, Carey-Bertram 78)*
Alfreton T 0

Southport 0   Gateshead 1 *(Armstrong 15)*

SEMI-FINALS SECOND LEG

Alfreton T 4 *(Butler 9, Brown 16, Clayton 49, Howell 73)*
AFC Telford U 3 *(Edwards 19, Carey-Bertram 42, Rodgers 52)*

Gateshead 1 *(Novak 24)*   Southport 1 *(Booth 52)*

FINAL

Gateshead 1 *(Phillips 82)*   AFC Telford U 0

BLUE SQUARE SOUTH

SEMI-FINALS FIRST LEG

Hayes & Yeading U 2 *(Hendry 72 (pen), Ruby 89)*
Eastleigh 4 *(Taggart 5, Williams 26, Riviere 45, Mulley 50 (og))*

Chelmsford C 1 *(Rainford 60)*
Hampton & Richmond B 3 *(Yaku 44, 50, Hodges 82)*

SEMI-FINALS SECOND LEG

Eastleigh 0   Hayes & Yeading U 4 *(Perkins 45, Hendry 81 (pen), Fitzgerald 93, 97)*

Hampton & Richmond B 0   Chelmsford C 0

FINAL

Hampton & Richmond B 2 *(McAuley 49, Hodges 69)*
Hayes & Yeading U 3 *(Gregory 8, 71, 73)*

BLUE SQUARE NORTH RESULTS 2008–09

	AFC Telford U	Alfreton T	Blyth Spartans	Burscough	Droylsden	Farsley Celtic	Fleetwood T	Gainsborough T	Gateshead	Harrogate T	Hinckley U	Hucknall T	Hyde U	King's Lynn	Redditch U	Solihull Moors	Southport	Stafford Rangers	Stalybridge C	Tamworth	Vauxhall Motors	Workington
AFC Telford U	—	0-0	2-1	3-0	2-0	2-0	0-0	2-1	1-0	3-1	4-2	3-1	2-3	1-1	1-1	3-0	1-0	0-1	1-0	0-0	5-1	0-0
Alfreton T	3-1	—	1-1	2-0	2-3	3-1	3-3	1-4	1-3	4-1	1-1	5-0	3-2	1-1	2-0	4-1	2-0	2-0	2-1	1-1	3-1	0-0
Blyth Spartans	2-0	2-2	—	0-2	0-2	5-0	3-0	1-1	0-1	3-4	1-0	3-0	3-0	2-4	1-0	3-0	1-0	2-1	0-0	0-4	0-1	3-1
Burscough	0-2	1-3	2-3	—	0-1	2-0	1-1	0-2	2-4	0-2	1-1	2-3	2-1	1-0	1-0	1-2	2-3	2-0	0-2	0-4	0-1	3-1
Droylsden	1-0	2-0	2-0	3-1	—	2-0	1-3	3-2	0-0	2-1	3-0	5-1	2-1	1-1	2-2	2-1	0-0	0-1	0-2	1-3	0-1	2-1
Farsley Celtic	1-0	3-3	5-0	5-1	1-1	—	4-1	2-1	0-1	1-0	2-3	4-0	2-1	1-1	1-2	0-1	5-1	4-0	2-3	1-3	1-2	1-1
Fleetwood T	1-0	1-1	1-0	3-1	2-1	2-1	—	2-2	0-2	1-0	1-0	1-3	1-3	3-0	3-1	2-1	1-1	2-2	1-2	1-2	2-0	0-5
Gainsborough T	1-2	0-2	0-0	0-4	1-0	0-0	3-4	—	0-0	3-2	1-0	2-2	0-1	2-0	4-1	1-1	0-1	0-3	3-3	1-2	1-1	1-0
Gateshead	1-1	3-0	3-0	4-1	1-1	1-0	2-2	1-0	—	1-3	3-1	1-0	6-3	3-2	2-0	3-0	1-1	0-1	1-0	5-1	2-2	1-2
Harrogate T	2-0	1-1	3-1	2-0	1-1	1-0	5-2	0-3	1-3	—	5-0	1-3	2-1	4-0	1-1	4-0	0-3	3-3	0-1	1-3	2-0	2-1
Hinckley U	0-2	1-1	2-1	0-1	1-0	1-2	3-2	0-2	1-0	2-0	—	4-0	0-1	1-0	4-2	0-0	1-1	4-0	0-1	2-3	2-3	0-1
Hucknall T	0-5	1-1	1-1	0-2	1-1	1-2	5-3	1-2	2-0	2-0	4-0	—	2-0	1-2	0-2	0-2	0-0	3-1	2-3	1-2	0-1	1-0
Hyde U	0-4	1-1	1-0	0-1	1-3	3-1	5-3	0-0	2-5	2-3	0-1	2-0	—	0-1	1-2	3-1	1-1	1-1	0-2	1-2	3-1	0-0
King's Lynn	1-1	1-1	2-3	0-0	2-2	1-4	1-0	2-2	0-2	2-3	0-0	0-0	4-1	—	1-1	3-0	0-0	2-2	1-0	1-1	1-1	4-4
Redditch U	0-1	1-2	2-0	1-2	0-4	3-1	1-1	1-1	0-2	2-3	1-1	3-1	1-0	1-2	—	0-0	0-0	2-2	0-1	1-1	2-1	1-3
Solihull Moors	1-3	2-2	2-0	3-2	2-1	1-0	2-2	2-3	2-0	1-1	0-2	3-0	2-0	1-2	2-1	—	3-0	0-1	0-2	1-3	3-2	2-0
Southport	1-1	0-1	2-1	3-0	3-1	1-0	1-1	2-0	2-3	1-1	1-3	3-0	2-0	2-1	2-3	3-0	—	3-2	2-0	0-1	5-2	0-0
Stafford Rangers	1-3	0-2	2-0	0-2	0-0	1-0	1-2	2-0	4-1	0-0	0-0	0-0	4-1	0-0	0-1	0-2	0-3	—	0-1	0-1	0-1	0-0
Stalybridge C	2-2	0-2	2-0	4-0	2-2	1-0	0-5	1-2	1-2	1-3	3-1	2-2	2-0	1-1	3-3	5-0	0-1	2-0	—	2-2	1-0	1-4
Tamworth	0-1	1-2	1-1	6-2	1-1	2-1	2-1	0-0	2-1	3-1	7-1	1-1	2-1	2-0	1-1	1-0	1-1	1-2	0-3	—	2-0	1-0
Vauxhall Motors	2-0	1-1	1-1	2-0	1-4	2-0	0-2	1-1	1-2	1-0	1-0	2-3	2-2	1-3	1-3	2-2	0-0	1-1	1-1	2-0	—	3-0
Workington	1-0	0-3	0-1	4-1	1-1	0-2	3-2	5-0	4-2	0-0	1-3	1-0	0-1	1-1	0-1	2-1	0-1	2-2	0-2	1-4	3-1	—

BLUE SQUARE SOUTH RESULTS 2008–09

Home \ Away	AFC Wimbledon	Basingstoke T	Bath C	Bishop's Stortford	Bognor Regis T	Braintree T	Bromley	Chelmsford C	Dorchester T	Eastleigh	Fisher Ath	Hampton & Richmond B	Havant & Waterlooville	Hayes & Yeading U	Maidenhead U	Newport Co	St Albans C	Team Bath	Thurrock	Welling U	Weston Super Mare	Worcester C
AFC Wimbledon	—	1-0	3-2	4-1	3-1	5-1	3-1	3-1	3-1	0-2	3-0	1-1	3-0	2-0	3-1	3-0	3-0	2-0	2-1	0-1	1-1	2-0
Basingstoke T	0-1	—	1-0	1-1	3-2	2-3	2-0	1-2	0-0	1-0	2-2	1-1	2-2	1-1	0-1	0-0	0-0	1-3	1-0	0-4	0-1	0-0
Bath C	2-2	1-0	—	1-0	0-2	1-1	1-1	2-1	2-0	1-1	1-0	0-1	1-0	0-0	1-0	2-1	1-0	1-1	2-2	3-0	3-0	1-0
Bishop's Stortford	0-1	2-3	0-2	—	2-0	2-0	2-0	2-1	0-2	3-4	0-1	1-3	1-0	0-0	2-0	1-1	1-1	4-3	2-1	0-1	2-1	3-0
Bognor Regis T	1-5	3-2	0-2	0-1	—	1-1	1-4	2-1	0-0	1-0	2-1	0-1	1-5	0-1	0-2	0-1	0-5	3-0	1-1	0-0	1-1	1-2
Braintree T	0-1	2-3	0-4	3-2	0-2	—	1-1	1-2	0-1	1-1	3-0	1-2	1-0	1-0	0-2	3-2	1-0	4-1	1-2	1-3	1-1	1-1
Bromley	2-2	0-2	1-1	1-3	1-1	2-0	—	2-0	1-0	5-1	3-0	0-2	2-2	1-0	1-2	0-0	2-3	4-0	3-3	1-1	3-0	1-1
Chelmsford C	3-2	0-2	0-2	2-1	2-1	1-2	2-2	—	2-1	3-0	3-0	0-2	1-0	0-1	0-2	0-1	1-1	1-1	3-2	1-3	4-1	0-2
Dorchester T	1-1	1-0	2-3	2-0	0-2	1-0	2-1	2-2	—	0-4	3-0	0-2	1-0	1-2	0-3	3-2	3-0	1-1	4-3	1-1	1-1	3-1
Eastleigh	2-1	1-0	2-0	3-4	3-4	1-1	2-1	0-1	0-1	—	3-0	0-2	2-0	3-3	0-0	1-3	0-4	2-2	1-1	4-2	1-0	1-0
Fisher Ath	0-3	1-0	1-0	0-1	2-1	2-0	3-0	2-1	4-0	1-2	—	0-2	1-1	0-5	0-1	0-1	0-0	1-3	0-3	0-5	0-2	0-1
Hampton & Richmond B	1-1	0-0	3-1	1-3	0-1	1-2	0-1	4-1	2-0	2-1	3-0	—	2-1	2-3	1-0	1-0	2-0	0-6	3-1	2-0	4-1	1-2
Havant & Waterlooville	0-0	5-1	0-0	3-0	1-5	1-0	2-1	1-1	1-2	2-2	3-0	1-4	—	2-2	3-3	2-0	2-1	3-0	2-2	1-0	1-0	0-2
Hayes & Yeading U	2-1	5-0	2-2	0-0	1-1	0-1	1-2	0-1	2-1	0-1	3-4	0-0	2-0	—	2-0	2-0	1-0	2-1	2-1	2-0	2-3	3-1
Maidenhead U	0-4	3-0	0-0	2-0	0-2	0-2	2-1	0-2	4-4	1-4	1-0	0-3	1-0	2-0	—	0-1	1-0	1-1	1-1	0-0	3-0	5-0
Newport Co	1-4	3-0	0-4	1-1	3-2	0-1	2-1	3-1	2-0	0-1	4-0	1-0	1-1	2-0	0-1	—	0-1	0-2	0-2	2-3	0-0	1-0
St Albans C	0-0	3-0	2-1	1-1	1-0	2-3	1-1	1-2	4-1	5-0	4-1	2-2	1-1	2-1	0-1	1-1	—	4-2	4-1	0-1	3-0	0-2
Team Bath	1-2	1-2	0-1	4-3	4-1	4-0	1-1	2-0	0-0	1-3	4-1	0-2	1-0	1-1	0-2	2-0	2-0	—	1-2	1-2	1-2	0-2
Thurrock	0-1	6-0	2-0	2-1	1-2	3-3	4-3	0-1	4-1	0-1	2-1	3-3	2-3	0-1	1-2	0-0	0-0	1-2	—	0-3	0-1	2-0
Welling U	2-2	1-1	2-1	0-4	0-0	1-3	1-1	1-3	0-0	3-2	3-0	4-0	0-1	1-2	1-1	0-2	0-1	1-1	0-0	—	2-0	1-3
Weston Super Mare	1-1	0-3	0-1	2-1	1-1	3-0	3-0	1-4	2-2	1-1	3-1	0-3	0-1	3-0	2-2	1-1	1-1	0-1	2-1	2-0	—	1-1
Worcester C	3-2	0-0	0-1	3-0	1-2	1-1	1-1	0-1	0-0	0-1	1-1	1-2	2-2	3-1	1-1	0-0	2-0	0-2	2-0	1-3	1-2	—

ALTRINCHAM

Blue Square Premier

Ground: Moss Lane, Altrincham WA15 8AP.   *Tel:* (0161) 928 1045.   *Year Formed:* 1903.   *Record Gate:* 10,275
(1991 Altrincham Boys v Sunderland Boys, ESFA Shield).   *Nickname:* The Robins.   *Manager:* Graham Heathcote.
Secretary: Graham Heathcote.   *Colours:* Red and white striped shirts, black shorts, red stockings.

ALTRINCHAM 2008–09 LEAGUE RECORD

Match No.	Date	Venue	Opponents	Result	H/T Score	Lg. Pos.	Goalscorers	Attendance
1	Aug 9	A	Woking	W 2-1	1-0	—	Meechan [45], Little [90]	1645
2	12	H	Barrow	L 3-4	0-1	—	Little 2 [64, 77], Denham [73]	1312
3	16	H	Kettering T	D 1-1	0-1	10	McGregor [83]	1045
4	23	A	Kidderminster H	L 0-4	0-2	18		1335
5	25	H	Wrexham	D 1-1	1-1	17	Senior [5]	2619
6	30	A	Eastbourne Bor	L 0-1	0-1	19		1170
7	Sept 2	A	Histon	L 0-1	0-0	—		692
8	6	H	Salisbury C	D 0-0	0-0	21		1002
9	13	A	Stevenage Bor	L 0-3	0-2	21		1804
10	20	H	Lewes	W 1-0	0-0	21	Peyton [88]	827
11	23	H	Mansfield T	W 1-0	1-0	—	Senior [1]	1005
12	29	A	Rushden & D	D 1-1	1-0	—	Little [44]	1341
13	Oct 4	H	Ebbsfleet U	W 2-0	2-0	17	Little [28], Senior [45]	967
14	7	A	Salisbury C	W 3-1	0-0	—	Little [46], Johnson [85], O'Neill (pen) [90]	950
15	12	H	Oxford U	W 1-0	0-0	9	Little [64]	1806
16	18	A	Weymouth	L 0-2	0-1	13		926
17	Nov 1	H	Histon	L 0-1	0-0	16		953
18	15	A	Forest Green R	W 3-1	3-1	12	Little [4], Senior 2 [29, 32]	851
19	22	H	Cambridge U	W 1-0	1-0	11	Lawton [45]	1123
20	29	H	Rushden & D	L 0-4	0-2	12		924
21	Dec 6	A	Crawley T	L 0-4	0-3	14		978
22	9	A	Barrow	D 2-2	2-1	—	Meechan [31], Little [36]	1175
23	20	H	Burton Alb	L 1-3	0-1	15	Johnson [56]	931
24	26	H	Northwich Vic	W 1-0	0-0	12	Young [74]	1400
25	28	A	York C	W 2-1	0-1	11	Senior [52], Johnson [89]	2389
26	Jan 17	A	Oxford U	L 0-1	0-0	14		4249
27	24	A	Burton Alb	D 1-1	1-0	14	O'Neill [24]	2124
28	27	H	York C	D 1-1	1-0	—	Densmore [14]	1027
29	Feb 3	H	Northwich Vic	W 1-0	1-0	—	Banim [28]	1209
30	14	A	Torquay U	L 1-3	0-1	—	Doughty [87]	1760
31	21	H	Woking	W 1-0	1-0	13	Senior [27]	943
32	28	H	Stevenage Bor	L 1-2	1-0	14	Little (pen) [22]	958
33	Mar 3	A	Kettering T	L 1-3	0-1	—	Densmore [63]	1036
34	7	A	Grays Ath	L 1-2	0-1	14	Doughty (pen) [90]	710
35	10	H	Torquay U	L 0-1	0-0	—		735
36	14	H	Weymouth	W 4-0	3-0	14	Welch [2], Little [8], Johnson [14], O'Neill [53]	770
37	21	H	Forest Green R	L 2-5	2-0	15	Little 2 [2, 21]	852
38	28	H	Crawley T	D 2-2	1-1	15	Welch [27], Densmore [57]	960
39	31	A	Ebbsfleet U	L 0-1	0-1	—		774
40	Apr 4	A	Lewes	L 0-2	0-2	17		337
41	7	H	Eastbourne Bor	D 2-2	1-2	—	Little [44], Densmore [70]	605
42	11	H	Kidderminster H	D 2-2	1-0	15	Welch [38], Little (pen) [90]	1142
43	13	A	Wrexham	W 1-0	0-0	15	Young [52]	2554
44	18	H	Grays Ath	W 2-0	1-0	14	Little [23], Denham [80]	1148
45	21	A	Mansfield T	L 0-2	0-1	—		1682
46	26	A	Cambridge U	D 0-0	0-0	15		7090

Final League Position: 15

GOALSCORERS

League (49): Little 16 (2 pens), Senior 7, Densmore 4, Johnson 4, O'Neill 3 (1 pen), Welch 3, Denham 2, Doughty 2 (1 pen), Meechan 2, Young 2, Banim 1, Lawton 1, McGregor 1, Peyton 1.
FA Cup (2): Lane 1, Little 1.

Coburn 40	Lane 30 + 4	Doughty 42 + 1	McGregor 41 + 1	Young 44 + 1	Street 3 + 2	Lawton 35 + 1	Johnson 31 + 13	Little 41 + 2	Denham 10 + 8	Meechan 7 + 13	Elam 11 + 10	O'Neill 4 + 24	Senior 23 + 7	Peyton 19 + 21	Battersby 5	Tierney — + 3	Densmore 33	Waterfall — + 1	Ralph 4 + 1	Smith 24	Hadfield 1 + 3	Banim 2 + 1	Acton 2	Welch 9 + 4	Wilkinson 6 + 3	Thornley — + 3	Match No.
1	2	3	4	5	6^2	7	8^3	9	10^1	11	12	13	14														1
1	2	3	4	5	6^2	7	8^3	9	10	11^1	12	13		14													2
1	2	3	4	5	6^1	7	8^3	9	10		11^2	12	13	14													3
1	2	3	4	5		7	8^3	9^2	10^1	12		6	14	13	11												4
1		3	4	5	13	2	14	9^1	12	7		6		10^3	11	8^2											5
1		3^2	4	5		7	14	13	10	8^1	12	6		9^3	11	2											6
1	2		4	5		7	8^3	9	10^1		12	6^2	14		11	3	13										7
1	2		4	5	13	7	8^3	9	10	14		6^2			11	3^1	12										8
1	2^1		4	5		7	13	9	10^2		8^3	6		12	11	3	14										9
1	2	14	4	13		7		9^2			8^1	3	6	10^3	12	11	5										10
1	2	3^1	4	5		7		9^3		14	11	6	12	10^2	13		8										11
1	2	3	4	5		7	14	9^3	12		11^2	6		10^1	13		8										12
1	2	3	4	5		7	12	9^2			11^3	6	14	10^1	13		8										13
1	2	3	4	5		7	12	9^2		14	11^3	6	13	10^1			8										14
1	2	3	4	5		7	14	9^2			11	6	13	10^3	12		8										15
1	2^2	3^3	4	5		7	12	9			11	6		10^1	13	14	8										16
1^6	2	3	4	5		7	13	9			12	11^2	6	10^1			8	15									17
		3	4	5		7	8^1	9^3		14	12	6		10	13		11^2		1	2							18
	14	3	4	5		7	8^3	9			12	6		10^1	13		11^2		1	2							19
		3	4	5		7^1	8	9^3		14	13	6		10^2	12		11		1	2							20
	2	3	4^1	5			13	9^3	12	7^2		6	14	10	11					1	8						21
1	2	3^2	4	5			8	9^1			7	6	13	12	11					10							22
1		3	4	5			12	9			7^1	13	6	14	10^2	11	8^3			2							23
1		3	4	5			8^3	9^1		14	12	6	13	10^2	11		7			2							24
1	7	3	4	5			8	12		14	13	6^3		10^2	11	9				2^1							25
1	2	3	4	5			12	8	9^1	13		$6^●$	14	10^2	11^3		7										26
1	2^2	3	4	5		7	8^3	9^1	14				12	11			10				6	13					27
1		3	4	5		7	8		10^1			6^3	9^2		12		11				2			14	13		28
1	2	3	4	5		7	8^1					13	10	12			11							6	9^2		29
1	2	3	4	5		7	12					6^1		13	11^2		10							8	14	9^3	30
		3	4	5		7	8^1	9^3				6	12	10	13		11^2			2				1	14		31
1		3^3	4	5		7	8^2	9				6	13	10^1	14		11			2				12			32
1		3	4	5		7	8	9	12			6^2		10^1	13		11			2							33
1		3	4	5		7^2	8^1	9^3				6	12	10^1			11			2				14			34
1		3	4^2	5		7	8	9				6^3	12	10^1			11			2				13			35
1	12	3		5		7^3	8^1	9	13			6	10^2		14		11			2				4			36
1	12	3	4	5		7	8	9	13			6^1		11^2			10			$2^●$				11^1	13		37
1	2	3	4	5		7	8^2	9				6	12				10							11^1	13		38
1	2	3	4	5			8^1	9				6	12				10								7		39
1	2	3	4^1	5			8	9				$6^●$	10^2	13			11							7	12		40
1	2	3	14	5			8^2	9					12	11^1			10				6			4^3	7	13	41
1	2^3	3	4^1	5		7	12	9	14					10			11							8	6^2	13	42
1	2	3		5		7	8^1	9^2	12			6	14								4			10	11	13^3	43
1	2	3					8^3	9^2	13			6	14				10				4			11	7^1		44
	2	3		5			8^3	9^2	12			6	14	13			11				4		1	10	7^1		45
1	13	3	4			7	8^3	9^2	10^1			6	12				11			2				5	14		46

FA Cup
Fourth Qualifying Round

	Newcastle Blue Star	(a)	2-1
First Round	Luton T	(a)	0-0
		(h)	0-0

BARROW

Blue Square Premier

Ground: Holker Street, Wilkie Road, Barrow-in-Furness LA14 5UH. *Tel:* (01229) 828 227.   *Year Formed:* 1901.
Record Gate: 16,854 v Swansea T, FA Cup 3rd rd, 1954.   *Nickname:* Bluebirds.   *Managers:* Dave Bayliss and Darren Sheridan.   *Colours:* White shirts, blue shorts, white stockings.

BARROW 2008–09 LEAGUE RECORD

Match No.	Date	Venue	Opponents	Result	H/T Score	Lg. Pos.	Goalscorers	Atten- dance
1	Aug 8	H	Oxford U	W 3-0	0-0	—	Boyd [71], McNulty (pen) [76], Brown B [82]	2790
2	12	A	Altrincham	W 4-3	1-0	—	Walker 2 [21, 74], Logan [54], Brown B [80]	1312
3	16	A	Cambridge U	L 1-2	1-2	6	Tait [36]	2663
4	23	H	Mansfield T	W 2-1	1-1	3	O'Hare (og) [44], Walker [88]	2063
5	25	A	York C	D 1-1	1-1	3	Hunt [10]	2664
6	30	H	Stevenage Bor	L 1-3	1-2	10	McNulty (pen) [12]	1764
7	Sept 2	H	Rushden & D	D 1-1	0-1	—	Brown B [90]	1663
8	6	A	Lewes	W 3-0	1-0	5	Brown B [39], McNulty (pen) [45], Rogan [71]	679
9	13	A	Salisbury C	L 0-3	0-1	10		1116
10	20	H	Kettering T	L 2-4	0-1	13	Henney [65], Tait [75]	1596
11	23	A	Northwich Vic	L 1-2	1-0	—	Henney [2]	906
12	27	H	Ebbsfleet U	L 0-1	0-0	16		1378
13	Oct 4	A	Kidderminster H	W 1-0	1-0	16	Boyd [5]	1686
14	7	H	Burton Alb	D 0-0	0-0	—		1466
15	11	A	Crawley T	L 0-4	0-2	17		1601
16	18	H	Eastbourne Bor	W 3-1	2-0	15	Brown D [4], Logan [31], Henney [90]	1206
17	Nov 1	H	Forest Green R	W 3-1	1-0	11	Brown D (pen) [2], Henney [63], Walker [88]	1440
18	15	A	Ebbsfleet U	L 0-1	0-0	13		1187
19	22	H	Weymouth	L 0-1	0-0	16		1350
20	Dec 6	A	Rushden & D	D 1-1	0-0	16	Walker [11]	1120
21	9	H	Altrincham	D 2-2	1-2	—	Walker [9], Jones [69]	1175
22	20	A	Grays Ath	L 1-2	1-1	17	Walker [26]	502
23	26	H	Wrexham	D 1-1	1-0	19	Walker [30]	1250
24	28	A	Forest Green R	L 1-2	1-2	19	Brown D [45]	747
25	Jan 17	A	Stevenage Bor	L 0-3	0-1	20		2205
26	24	H	Kidderminster H	W 1-0	0-0	18	Walker [87]	1532
27	26	A	Burton Alb	L 1-2	0-0	—	Walker [70]	1939
28	31	H	Salisbury C	D 0-0	0-0	—		1613
29	Feb 14	A	Oxford U	L 0-3	0-0	—		4532
30	21	H	Grays Ath	D 1-1	1-1	21	Walker [59]	1515
31	24	A	Histon	L 0-2	0-0	—		541
32	28	H	Northwich Vic	D 0-0	0-0	21		1437
33	Mar 7	A	Woking	L 0-1	0-1	22		1529
34	10	A	Histon	W 1-0	0-0	—	Boyd [88]	965
35	14	A	Torquay U	L 1-4	1-2	21	Brown P [12]	2269
36	17	H	Cambridge U	L 0-2	0-0	—		1341
37	21	H	Lewes	W 2-0	1-0	18	McEvilly [7], Hunt [64]	1390
38	29	A	Weymouth	W 3-0	0-0	17	Boyd [51], Jones 2 [54, 81]	1264
39	Apr 2	A	Wrexham	D 1-1	0-0	—	Rogan [90]	2272
40	4	H	Woking	L 0-1	0-0	18		1424
41	7	H	Kettering T	D 0-0	0-0	—		976
42	11	A	Mansfield T	D 2-2	0-0	19	Bond (pen) [52], Rogan [90]	2122
43	13	H	York C	D 0-0	0-0	18		2168
44	18	H	Crawley T	D 3-3	0-2	18	Rogan 2 [53, 90], McNulty [65]	1456
45	21	H	Torquay U	D 1-1	1-0	—	Walker [12]	1918
46	26	A	Eastbourne Bor	W 2-0	0-0	20	Boyd [70], Bond [87]	1584

Final League Position: 20

GOALSCORERS

League (51): Walker 12, Boyd 5, Brown P 5, Henney 4, McNulty 4 (3 pens), Brown D 3 (1 pen), Jones 3, Bond 2 (1 pen), Hunt 2, Logan 2, Tait 2, McEvilly 1, own goal 1.
FA Cup (11): Brodie 3, Brown D 2 (2 pens), Henney 2, Brown P 1, Logan 1, McNulty 1, Walker 1.

Deasy 26 + 1	Pearson 21 + 1	Elderton 3	Jones 44	McNulty 36 + 1	Henney 28 + 2	Boyd 34 + 5	Walker 35 + 6	Logan 43 + 1	Hunt 18 + 8	Brown P 21 + 12	Tait 6 + 19	Rogan 8 + 24	Black 5 + 2	Winn 13 + 5	Martin 20 + 1	Brown D 11	Kerr 12 + 7	Brodie 3	Sheridan 8	Joyce 5	Holness 11 + 1	Curtis 2	Sharry 4	McGill 17 + 1	Thompson — + 1	Horne 1	Steele 4 + 3	Spender 12	McEvilly 6	Jelleyman 9	Woodyatt 1	Match No.
1	2	3	4	5	6	7	8	9	10¹	11²	12	13																				1
1	2	3	4	5	6	7	8	9	10¹	11²	12	13																				2
1	2	3	4	5	6	7	8		10¹	11²	12	9	13																			3
1			4	5	6	7	8		10¹	11²	12		13	2	3																	4
1			4	5	6	7	8	9	10	11¹			12	2	3																	5
1	12		4²	5	6	7	8	9	10	11³	13	14		2¹	3																	6
1	2		4	5	6	7	8¹	9³	10	11²	3	13	14			12																7
1	2		4	5	6	7	8¹	9²	10	11³	3	13	14			12																8
1	2		4	5	6¹	7	8²	9	10	12	3³	14	11			13																9
1	2		4	5	6	7¹	8	9³	3	11²	14	10	13			12																10
	2		4	5	6	7	8	12	10	11¹	13	9²	3		1																	11
	2		4	5	6	7	8²	9	10	12	11³	14	3¹	13	1																	12
	2		4	5	6	7	8		10	11¹	13	12	3			1	9²															13
	2		4	5	6	7	8	12	10	11¹	13		3			1	9²															14
	2		4¹	5	6	7	8	13	10	11²	12		3			1	9															15
	2		4	5	6	7	8	9³	10	14	12	13			3	1	11²															16
			4²	5	6¹	7	8	13	10	11	14		3			1	9³	12														17
15	2		4	5	6			12	10			9	3			1⁶	7		8¹	11												18
1	2		4³	5	6		8	12	10	11²	14		3				9¹		13	7												19
	2		4	5	6		8	9²	10	11	13	12				1	7¹		3													20
	2		4	5	6		8	9	3	11¹	14	13³				1	10²		12	7												21
	2		4	5	6¹	13	8	9	3	14	11	10³				1			12	7²												22
	2		4	5		13	8¹	9²	10	7	12					1	11¹	3	6													23
	2		4	5		12	8¹	9	10	7	13					1	11¹	3	6													24
1			4	5⁸	6	7	8²	9³	3	12	14	11	13								2			10¹								25
			4		6¹		8	9²	3	11		13				1				5	2			10			7	12				26
			4				8	9	3	11²	10¹	12				1				2	5		6				7	13				27
1			4				12	8¹	9	3		11								10¹	2			5			7	6				28
			4		6	7		9	12	10¹						1	3		8		2			11			5					29
			4	5	12	7		9³		11	14	13				1	3		8		2			6¹					10²			30
			4	12	6	7¹		9	3	11	13					1			8		2			5					10²			31
			4	5♦	6		8	9²	3	10¹	13	11				1					2						7	12				32
			4	12	6		8	9	3	10²	13³	11				1			14		2			5			7¹					33
1			4			7	8	9	3	10		11									5			6			2					34
1			4			7	8	9♦	3	10¹	11²	13									5			6			2	12				35
1			4			7	8		3	10	11										5			6			2		9			36
1			4	5		7	8		3	10¹	13			11										6			2	12	9²			37
1			4	5		7	8		3¹		12	13		11										6			2		9²	10		38
1			4	5		7	8	9	10¹	11²	13				2									6				12		3		39
1			4	5		7		9	10²	11¹	13			14			8³							6			2	12		3		40
1			4	5		7		9		11									8					6			2		10	3		41
1			4	5		7		9²	12	11	14								8					6			2		10³	3¹		42
1			4	5		7	8	9²		11³	13	14												6			2	12	10¹	3		43
1			4	5		7	8	9		11³	13	14												6¹			2	12	10²	3		44
1			4	5		7	8	9	10¹	11	12													6			2			3		45
1⁶			4¹	5	12	7	8	9		11		13		15										6²					10	3	2	46

FA Cup
Fourth Qualifying Round

	Tamworth	(a)	4-0
First Round	Eastbourne B	(a)	0-0
		(h)	4-0
Second Round	Brentford	(h)	2-1
Third Round	Middlesbrough	(a)	1-2

BURTON ALBION

FL Championship 2

Ground: Pirelli Stadium, Princess Way, Burton-on-Trent, Staffordshire DE13 0AR. *Tel:* (01283) 565 938.
Year Formed: 1950. *Record Gate:* 6,191 (2006 v Manchester U, FA Cup 3rd rd). *Nickname:* Brewers.
Manager: Paul Peschisolido. *Secretary:* Tony Kirkland. *Colours:* All yellow with black trim.

BURTON ALBION 2008–09 LEAGUE RECORD

Match No.	Date	Venue	Opponents	Result	H/T Score	Lg. Pos.	Goalscorers	Attendance
1	Aug 9	A	Salisbury C	W 1-0	1-0	—	Pearson [2]	1122
2	12	H	Northwich Vic	D 1-1	0-1	—	Webster [83]	1701
3	16	H	Woking	W 3-2	0-2	4	Goodfellow 2 [58, 84], Pearson (pen) [65]	1456
4	23	A	Histon	L 3-4	2-3	10	Stride [40], Pearson (pen) [45], McGrath [85]	910
5	25	H	Kidderminster H	D 2-2	1-0	11	Pearson [31], Brayford [78]	1798
6	30	H	Lewes	W 5-2	2-2	6	Pearson [10], Gilroy [23], Webster 2 [60, 89], Harrad [71]	1432
7	Sept 2	A	Wrexham	W 1-0	1-0	—	Harrad [15]	4104
8	6	A	Stevenage Bor	L 1-4	0-2	9	Corbett [75]	1717
9	13	H	Weymouth	D 1-1	1-1	7	Pearson [38]	1435
10	20	A	Rushden & D	L 1-2	0-1	11	Harrad (pen) [66]	1448
11	22	A	Kettering T	W 1-0	0-0	—	Pearson [79]	1616
12	27	A	Forest Green R	W 4-2	0-1	4	Gilroy [58], Goodfellow [71], Harrad 2 (1 pen) [75 (p), 90]	1545
13	Oct 4	H	Crawley T	W 2-1	1-1	2	Pearson 2 (1 pen) [37, 90 (p)]	1915
14	7	A	Barrow	D 0-0	0-0	—		1466
15	13	H	Mansfield T	W 1-0	1-0	—	McGrath [43]	2871
16	18	A	Oxford U	L 1-2	0-1	6	Webster [89]	4494
17	Nov 1	H	Ebbsfleet U	W 3-1	1-0	4	Webster 2 [3, 81], Gilroy [55]	1584
18	8	A	Northwich Vic	W 1-0	1-0	—	Harrad [19]	932
19	15	A	Lewes	W 1-0	1-0	1	Pearson (pen) [45]	630
20	22	H	Stevenage Bor	W 2-0	1-0	2	Simpson 2 [32, 70]	1944
21	29	H	Eastbourne Bor	W 2-0	0-0	1	Pearson (pen) [56], Armstrong [61]	1870
22	Dec 6	A	Forest Green R	W 3-2	2-1	1	Harrad 2 [21, 27], Pearson (pen) [58]	812
23	9	H	Cambridge U	W 3-1	2-0	1	McGrath [5], Harrad (pen) [42], Pearson [84]	1804
24	20	A	Altrincham	W 3-1	1-0	1	Pearson 2 (1 pen) [40, 65 (p)], McGrath [86]	931
25	26	H	York C	W 2-1	0-0	1	Harrad [62], Greaves (og) [70]	3578
26	29	H	Mansfield T	W 2-0	2-0	1	Pearson [26], Goodfellow [38]	3612
27	Jan 1	A	York C	W 3-1	1-1	1	Simpson [34], Harrad [62], Goodfellow [83]	2703
28	17	A	Grays Ath	W 1-0	1-0	1	Yates [31]	651
29	24	H	Altrincham	D 1-1	0-1	1	Harrad [52]	2124
30	26	H	Barrow	W 2-1	0-0	1	Harrad [52], Buxton [59]	1939
31	Feb 9	H	Rushden & D	W 3-0	1-0	1	McGrath [41], Austin [46], Harrad [65]	1291
32	17	H	Wrexham	W 2-1	0-1	—	Butler [57], Morris [79]	3262
33	28	A	Woking	D 0-0	0-0	1		1813
34	Mar 7	A	Cambridge U	L 0-2	0-1	1		4377
35	11	A	Ebbsfleet U	L 1-2	0-1	1	Pearson [49]	711
36	14	H	Salisbury C	L 1-2	0-2	1	Morris [82]	2274
37	17	A	Weymouth	W 5-0	3-0	1	Morris 2 [24, 52], Harrad [37], Gilroy [44], Hoyte (og) [86]	848
38	21	A	Eastbourne Bor	W 2-1	0-1	1	Butler [63], Pearson [90]	1521
39	28	H	Grays Ath	W 4-0	3-0	1	Morris 2 [2, 22], McGrath [16], Gilroy [84]	2388
40	31	H	Kettering T	D 1-1	1-1	—	Stride [8]	2624
41	Apr 4	A	Crawley T	L 0-4	0-2	1		1131
42	6	H	Torquay U	L 0-1	0-1	—		4891
43	11	H	Histon	W 3-1	1-0	1	Webster [13], Corbett [53], Austin [84]	3311
44	13	A	Kidderminster H	L 1-2	1-0	1	Morris [45]	3025
45	17	H	Oxford U	L 0-1	0-0	—		6192
46	26	A	Torquay U	L 1-2	1-1	1	Goodfellow [8]	4528

Final League Position: 1

GOALSCORERS

League (81): Pearson 18 (7 pens), Harrad 15 (3 pens), Morris 7, Webster 7, Goodfellow 6, McGrath 6, Gilroy 5, Simpson 3, Austin 2, Butler 2, Corbett 2, Stride 2, Armstrong 1, Brayford 1, Buxton 1, Yates 1, own goals 2.
FA Cup (0).

Poole 38	Brayford 6	Webster 36 + 2	Austin 19 + 15	James 29	McGrath 46	Corbett 45	Holmes 6 + 10	Pearson 34 + 6	Banim 8 + 7	Bailey 6 + 4	Harrad 28 + 13	Stride 17 + 12	Gilroy 38 + 1	Simpson 40 + 1	Goodfellow 18 + 12	Buxton 41	Morris 16 + 13	Yates 9 + 1	Newby 10 + 12	Deeney 8	Simmons 1 + 1	Armstrong 1 + 2	Butler 3 + 9	Byrne 3 + 4	Match No.
1	2	3	4	5	6	7	8	9^2	10^1	11	12	13													1
1	2	12	4	5	6	7	8	9^3	10	3^1	14	13	11^2												2
1	2	3	4	5	6	7		9^3	10^2		13	14	11^1	8	12										3
1	2	3			6	7		9^2	13	11^1	10	4		8	12	5									4
1	2	5	4		6	7		9^3	10^2	3^1	13	12		8	11		14								5
1	2^1	3	12		6	7		9^3	10		14	4	11^2	8	13	5									6
1	3^1	4			6	7		9^2			10	12	11^3	8	14	5		2	13						7
1		4			6	7	12	9^3	14		10^2	3	11	8^1	5			2	13						8
1		4			6	7		9^3	10^2		14	3	11^1	8	12	5		2	13						9
1		4			6	7		9^2	13		14	3	11	8^4	12	5^1		2	10^3						10
	4^2				6	7	8	9	14	13		12	11		3	5		2^1	10^3	1					11
	3				6	7	8	9^3	10^2		14	4	11^1		2	5	13		12	1					12
	3^1				6	7	8	9			12	10^3	4	11^2	2	5	14		13	1					13
	3				6	7	8^2	9^3	4	10	11	13	2^1	5	14				12	1					14
1	3				6	7	13	9^2			14	12	4^3	11	8	2	5		10^1						15
1	3	13			6	7		9			4^1	12		11^3	8	2	5	10^2	14						16
1	3	13	5		6	7		9^2			14	12		11	2				8^3			10^1			17
1	3	12	5		6	7		9^2			10			11	2	4	13		8						18
1	3	14	5^3		6	7		9^2	13		12			11	4	2	8^1		10						19
1	3	14	5		6	7		9^2			10			11^1	4	2			8^3				12	13	20
1		13	5		6	7		9^2	12		10^1			11^3	2	4	14		8			3			21
1	3	13	5		6	7	14	9^3			10			11^1	4	2	12		8^2						22
1	3	14	5		6	7	13	12			10			11^3	4	2	9^1		8^2						23
1	3	12	5		6	7	14	9^2			10			11^3	2	4	8^1		13						24
1	3	4			6	7	13	9			10			11^2	2	12	5	8^1							25
1	3	4			6	7	14	9^2	13		10			11^1	2	12	5	8^3							26
1	3	4			6	7	13	9^1			10^3		2	11	5	12			8^2				14		27
1	3	4	5	6				9^1			10			8	11	2	12	7^2	13						28
1	3^3	14	5	6	7			9^2			10	13	12	2	11	4			8^1						29
1	2		5	6	7			9^1			10^2	13	11	3	8	4	12								30
1	3		5	6^2	7	13		9^1			10			11	4	8	2	12							31
1	3		5	6	7			9^2			10	14	11^1	4	8^3	2	13						12		32
	13	3	5	6	7			9^3			10	14	11^2	4	8^1	2							12		33
1	3	4	5	6	7^1		12				10			11^2	8	13	2						9		34
1	3		5	6	7	12		9^1			10^3	13		8		11^2	2	4	14						35
1	3	12	5^1	6	7			9^3			10	14	11	4	8^2	2	13								36
1	3		5	6	7		12				10	4^1	11^3	8		2	9^2	14						13	37
1	3		5	6	7		14				10^3	4^2	11	8		2	9^1						12	13	38
1	3		5	6	7		14				10^2	4^1	11	8		2	9^3						12	13	39
1	3		5	6	7						8	11	4	12		2	9^2						13	10^1	40
1	3		5	6	7		12				8	11^1	4	14		2	9^2						13	10	41
1	3	13	5	6	7			9				11^1	4	12		2							10^2	8	42
	3	13	5	6	7						10^2	8^3	11	4		2	9^1		14	1			12		43
	3	12	5	6	7						10^3	8^1	11	4		2	9^2		14	1			13		44
	3		5	6	7^2						12	8	11	4	10	2	9^1			1			13		45
	3		5	6	7						8			4	11	2	9^1			1			10	12	46

FA Cup
Fourth Qualifying Round
              Kettering T   (a)   0-3

CAMBRIDGE UNITED · Blue Square Premier

Ground: Abbey Stadium, Newmarket Road, Cambridge CB5 8LN. *Tel:* (01223) 566 500. *Year Formed:* 1912.
Record Gate: 14,000 (1970 v Chelsea, Friendly). *Nickname:* The U's. *Manager:* TBC. *Secretary:* Andrew Pincher.
Colours: Navy and sky blue shirts, sky blue shorts, sky blue stockings.

CAMBRIDGE UNITED 2008–09 LEAGUE RECORD

Match No.	Date	Venue	Opponents	Result	H/T Score	Lg. Pos.	Goalscorers	Attendance
1	Aug 9	A	Northwich Vic	W	1-0	1-0	—	Jardim [28]	1445
2	12	H	Kidderminster H	W	2-1	1-0	—	McEvilly 2 [27, 61]	3008
3	16	H	Barrow	W	2-1	2-1	1	McEvilly [29], Hatswell [40]	2663
4	23	A	Eastbourne Bor	W	3-0	2-0	1	McEvilly [22], Farrell [39], Holroyd [84]	3105
5	25	H	Kettering T	L	0-2	0-0	2		3489
6	30	A	Weymouth	D	2-2	2-0	3	McEvilly [42], Beesley [45]	1367
7	Sept 2	A	Ebbsfleet U	D	1-1	1-0	—	McEvilly [45]	1832
8	6	H	Wrexham	W	2-0	1-0	2	Beesley 2 [28, 64]	3076
9	13	H	Torquay U	L	0-1	0-0	5		4041
10	20	A	Mansfield T	D	1-1	1-0	6	Brown [33]	3171
11	23	A	Oxford U	L	1-3	0-1	—	Jardim [57]	4170
12	28	H	Grays Ath	W	1-0	0-0	10	McEvilly (pen) [90]	2971
13	Oct 4	A	York C	D	0-0	0-0	6		2608
14	7	H	Lewes	W	1-0	0-0	—	Challinor [90]	3194
15	11	H	Weymouth	W	1-0	1-0	3	Challinor [11]	3981
16	16	A	Forest Green R	D	2-2	1-1	—	Hatswell [34], Crow [66]	789
17	Nov 1	H	Rushden & D	D	0-0	0-0	7		3547
18	15	A	Crawley T	D	2-2	0-1	7	McEvilly (pen) [54], Convery [90]	1578
19	18	H	York C	W	1-0	0-0	—	Purkiss (og) [51]	2914
20	22	A	Altrincham	L	0-1	0-1	5		1123
21	29	H	Ebbsfleet U	W	1-0	1-0	4	Rendell [45]	2807
22	Dec 6	A	Torquay U	D	0-0	0-0	6		2310
23	9	A	Burton Alb	L	1-3	0-2	—	Rendell [63]	1804
24	20	H	Salisbury C	W	4-0	1-0	6	Willmott [24], Rendell [50], Holroyd [62], Pitt [63]	3340
25	26	H	Histon	D	2-2	2-0	6	Hatswell [15], Rendell [41]	6488
26	28	H	Stevenage Bor	D	1-1	1-0	6	Rendell [3]	3351
27	Jan 17	H	Woking	W	4-1	2-0	5	Crow 2 [3, 21], Beesley [66], Willmott [83]	2696
28	22	A	Wrexham	L	0-2	0-1	—		3103
29	24	H	Oxford U	D	1-1	0-0	—	Carden [72]	3774
30	Feb 1	A	Rushden & D	W	2-1	1-1	—	Holroyd (pen) [22], Bolland [89]	2058
31	17	A	Kidderminster H	W	3-1	2-1	—	Rendell (pen) [20], Holroyd 2 [30, 56]	1361
32	21	A	Lewes	W	2-0	0-0	3	Rendell (pen) [83], Willmott [87]	962
33	24	A	Grays Ath	W	1-0	1-0	—	Rendell [42]	754
34	28	H	Crawley T	D	1-1	0-1	3	Pitt [82]	3231
35	Mar 2	A	Histon	D	1-1	0-0	—	Hatswell [74]	2579
36	7	H	Burton Alb	W	2-0	0-0	2	Rendell [55], Willmott [76]	4377
37	10	H	Mansfield T	W	2-1	0-1	—	Rendell [49], Reason [90]	2781
38	14	H	Northwich Vic	W	4-1	3-1	2	Holroyd [24], Rendell 2 [31, 37], Parkinson [80]	2662
39	17	A	Barrow	W	2-0	0-0	—	Holroyd 2 [62, 83]	1341
40	30	A	Woking	W	1-0	0-0	—	Reason [82]	1775
41	Apr 4	H	Forest Green R	L	0-1	0-1	2		3245
42	7	A	Stevenage Bor	L	1-2	1-2	—	Willmott [16]	3408
43	11	H	Eastbourne Bor	W	2-1	0-0	2	Phillips [65], Holroyd (pen) [71]	3391
44	13	A	Kettering T	W	2-1	1-0	2	Holroyd (pen) [14], Willmott [74]	2340
45	18	A	Salisbury C	W	2-1	2-1	2	Rendell [20], Martin (og) [45]	1031
46	26	H	Altrincham	D	0-0	0-0	2		7090

Final League Position: 2

GOALSCORERS

League (65): Rendell 13 (2 pens), Holroyd 10 (3 pens), McEvilly 8 (2 pens), Willmott 6, Beesley 4, Hatswell 4, Crow 3, Challinor 2, Jardim 2, Pitt 2, Reason 2, Bolland 1, Brown 1, Carden 1, Convery 1, Farrell 1, Parkinson 1, Phillips 1, own goals 2.
FA Cup (3): Crow 1, Willmott 1, own goal 1.
Play-Offs (4): Rendell 2, Phillips 1, Willmott 1.

Potter 46	Gleeson 37	Tonkin 42	Bolland 40	Hatswell 44	Parkinson 5 + 6	Challinor 26 + 7	Carden 40	Beesley 23 + 5	McEvilly 17 + 1	Jardim 14 + 8	Farrell 10 + 4	Jones 2 + 6	Willmott 30 + 7	Holroyd 24 + 11	Coulson 10 + 2	Convery 10 + 2	McAuley 3	Brown 6	Crow 13 + 9	Collins 1	Rendell 24 + 2	Pitt 13 + 7	McMahon 8 + 1	Ives — + 1	Reason 15	Phillips 2 + 3	Ainge 1 + 1	Match No.
1	2	3	4	5	6	7	8	9^2	10	11^1	13	12																1
1	2	3	4	5		7	8	9	10	11			12	6^1														2
1	2	3	4	5		7	8^2	9	10	11	13	12	6^1															3
1	2	3	4	5		7		9	10^2	11	8	12	6^1	13														4
1	2	3	4	5		7		9^2	10	11	8^4	6^1	12	13														5
1	2^1	3	4	5		7	8	9	10	11^3	13	6^2	12	14														6
1		3	4	5		7	8	9	10	11^1		6	12				2^8											7
1		3	4	5		7	8	9	10	11							2	6										8
1		3	4	5	2	8		9^2	10	12		11^1	7		6	13												9
1	2	3	4	5		7	8			10	11		9	6^1	12													10
1	2		4	5		7	8		10	11^2		6^1	13		12	3		9										11
1	2		4	5		7	8		12	11^1		13	10		6	3		9^2										12
1	2	3	4	5		7	8		10	12			11		6^1			9										13
1	2	3	4	5		7	8	9	10	11^2	13		6^1	12														14
1	2		4	5		7	8	9	10^4		11		6^1	12		3												15
1	2	3	4	5		7		9		11			6	12			8		10^1									16
1	2	3	4	5		7	8	9^1		11			6	12					10									17
1	2	3		5		7^2		9	10	13	11^4		6^1		4	8			12									18
1	2^3	3	4	5		8		9^1	10^2	11			6		14	7			13	12								19
1	2	3	4	5		7	8	9^1	10^2	12			14		6^3				13	11								20
1	2	3	4	5			8	13		11			6^1		7				10^2		9	12						21
1		3	4			7		6	13	11^1	14		5	8^3	2				10^2		9	12						22
1	2	3	4	5	12		8			13			6		7^1				10		9	11^2						23
1		3		5		7	8	13			12	2	6	10^2	4						9	11^1						24
1		3		5			2	8	13		12	7	6	10^2	4						9	11^1						25
1	2^8	3	4	5			13	8			12	7^2	6	10							9	11^1						26
1	3^2	4	5					11^3			7		12	9^1	2		6		10			13	8	14				27
1	2	3	4	5				7^2			12	11	6	13					10^1		9		8					28
1	2	3	4			12	8	13					6		5				10^2		9	11^1	7					29
1	2		4	5		7	8	11^1			12		9	6					10		3							30
1	2	3		5	6	12	8	11^1					10						9			4			7			31
1	2	3		5	6		8	11^1			12		10						9		13	4^2			7			32
1	2	3		5	6	7	8	11^1			12		10						9		13	4^1			7			33
1	2	3		5	6		8	11^2			12		10						9		13	4^1			7			34
1	2	3	4	5			8						6						9		11				7	10		35
1	2	3	4	5		12	8						6^1	10					9		11				7			36
1	2	3	4	5		12	8						6	10^1					9		11^2				7			37
1	2	3	4	5		12	13	8					6	10^3					9		11^1	14			7^2			38
1	2	3	4	5			12	8					6	10					9		11				7^1			39
1		3	4	5		12	2	8					6	10					9			14			7^3	13		40
1		3	4^1	5		11^2	12	8					6	10		13			9		14				7^3		2	41
1	2	3		5		12	8						11^2	10	6				9			4^1			7	13		42
1	2	3		5		11	7^1	8			13		6	10	4				10^2		14	12	4			9^3		43
1	2	3		5		12	8						6^1	10	4				9			11^2			7	13		44
1	2	3	4	5		11	8						6	10					9						7			45
1	2	3	4	5^2		11^1	8						6	10					13		9	12			7^3	14		46

FA Cup
Fourth Qualifying Round   Boston U   (a)   3-2
First Round   Kidderminster H   (a)   0-1

Play-Offs
Semi-Final   Stevenage B   (a)   1-3
      (h)   3-0
Final   Torquay U   0-2
(at Wembley)

CRAWLEY TOWN — Blue Square Premier

Ground: Broadfield Ground, Broadfield Stadium, Brighton Road, West Sussex RH11 9RX. *Tel:* (01293) 410 000.
Year Formed: 1896. *Record Gate:* 4,522 (2004 v Weymouth, Dr Martens League). *Nickname:* The Reds.
Manager: Steve Evans. *Secretary:* Barry Munn. *Colours:* All red.

CRAWLEY TOWN 2008–09 LEAGUE RECORD

Match No.	Date	Venue	Opponents	Result	H/T Score	Lg. Pos.	Goalscorers	Attendance
1	Aug 9	H	York C	L	0-1	0-0	—		1372
2	12	A	Lewes	W	3-0	2-0	—	Pittman [41], Forrest [42], Weatherstone [74]	1280
3	16	A	Forest Green R	L	0-1	0-0	14		732
4	23	H	Torquay U	W	3-1	2-0	12	Pittman [9], Pinault (pen) [32], Cook (pen) [77]	1154
5	25	A	Stevenage Bor	D	1-1	0-1	13	Wilson [74]	1492
6	30	H	Northwich Vic	W	5-2	4-0	8	Roberts (og) [17], Cook 2 [24, 58], Rents [27], Weatherstone [45]	776
7	Sept 2	H	Grays Ath	W	2-1	2-1	—	Killeen [21], Weatherstone [40]	1189
8	6	A	Rushden & D	W	1-0	0-0	3	Fletcher [90]	1376
9	13	H	Mansfield T	W	2-1	1-0	1	Quinn [16], Cook [46]	2013
10	20	A	Oxford U	W	2-1	2-1	1	Pittman [36], Cook [41]	3992
11	23	A	Weymouth	D	2-2	1-1	—	Weatherstone [1], Quinn [81]	1005
12	27	H	Kettering T	W	1-0	1-0	1	Pittman [12]	2207
13	Oct 4	A	Burton Alb	L	1-2	1-1	1	Wilson [15]	1915
14	7	H	Forest Green R	D	2-2	2-0	—	Quinn [3], Cook [36]	876
15	11	H	Barrow	W	4-0	2-0	1	Wilson [36], Cook 2 (1 pen) [43, 58 (p)], Pittman [64]	1601
16	18	A	Histon	L	0-1	0-0	2		1256
17	30	A	Salisbury C	L	0-2	0-0	—		884
18	Nov 15	H	Cambridge U	D	2-2	1-0	6	Pittman [30], Pinault (pen) [61]	1578
19	20	H	Ebbsfleet U	L	1-2	1-0	—	Pittman [33]	922
20	23	A	York C	D	2-2	0-1	7	Quinn [54], Killeen [90]	1935
21	29	A	Northwich Vic	W	1-0	0-0	6	Fletcher [84]	610
22	Dec 6	H	Altrincham	W	4-0	3-0	5	Killeen [3], Cook [28], Pinault [43], Pittman [90]	978
23	20	H	Kidderminster H	W	2-0	1-0	5	Malcolm 2 [30, 71]	1022
24	26	A	Woking	D	0-0	0-0	5		1910
25	28	H	Eastbourne Bor	W	1-0	0-0	4	Pittman [60]	1479
26	Jan 1	H	Woking	D	2-2	0-1	3	Quinn [47], Malcolm [52]	1525
27	17	A	Mansfield T	L	0-1	0-1	3		2414
28	24	H	Oxford U	L	0-1	0-1	4		1603
29	27	A	Ebbsfleet U	D	4-4	1-2	—	Matthews [4], Quinn [50], Pittman [84], Shaw [90]	795
30	Feb 21	H	Salisbury C	L	0-3	0-1	9		964
31	24	H	Lewes	W	5-1	4-0	—	Shaw 2 [2, 45], Rents (pen) [4], Weatherstone [38], Quinn [85]	600
32	28	A	Cambridge U	D	1-1	1-0	8	Shaw [34]	3231
33	Mar 3	H	Wrexham	W	1-0	0-0	—	Weatherstone [75]	737
34	8	H	Weymouth	W	4-2	3-2	6	Gaia [6], Bulman [26], Rents [29], Killeen [79]	901
35	10	A	Kidderminster H	L	0-2	0-1	—		1211
36	14	H	Rushden & D	D	0-0	0-0	7		777
37	21	A	Wrexham	W	2-0	2-0	7	Rankin [10], Matthews [34]	3303
38	28	A	Altrincham	D	2-2	1-1	9	Rankin [31], Wilson [88]	960
39	31	A	Eastbourne Bor	L	1-2	0-0	—	Jenkins (og) [68]	1268
40	Apr 4	H	Burton Alb	W	4-0	2-0	9	Giles [5], Cook (pen) [15], Forrest [68], Killeen [79]	1131
41	11	A	Torquay U	W	2-0	1-0	8	Bulman [38], Matthews [90]	3031
42	13	A	Stevenage Bor	L	0-2	0-1	8		1161
43	15	A	Kettering T	D	1-1	1-0	—	Bulman [20]	961
44	18	A	Barrow	D	3-3	2-0	9	Cook 2 (1 pen) [19, 45 (p)], Rankin [76]	1456
45	21	A	Grays Ath	L	0-1	0-1	—		630
46	26	H	Histon	D	3-3	0-3	9	Cook (pen) [52], Malcolm [66], Shaw [82]	901

Final League Position: 9

GOALSCORERS

League (77): Cook 13 (5 pens), Pittman 10, Quinn 7, Weatherstone 6, Killeen 5, Shaw 5, Malcolm 4, Wilson 4, Bulman 3, Matthews 3, Pinault 3 (2 pens), Rankin 3, Rents 3 (1 pen), Fletcher 2, Forrest 2, Gaia 1, Giles 1, own goals 2.
FA Cup (0).

Rayner 46	Stevens 4+2	Forrest 31+7	Pinault 26+2	Giles 18+8	Wright 41	Bulman 44+1	Wilson 36+4	Pittman 22+3	Killeen 19+10	Cook 27+5	Thomas 3+6	Weatherstone 34+5	Anton —+9	Rents 36+3	Quinn 37	Rankin 6+12	Fletcher 4+16	Dark —+1	Dayton 1+2	Malcolm 25+3	Mills —+2	Douglas —+1	Raynor —+1	Chalmers 4	Matthews 15+4	Gill 1+1	Shaw 12+5	Nayee —+1	Gaia 9+1	Hurren 3+2	Napper 1+1	Lake-Edwards 1	Nayee —+1	Match No.
1	2	3^2	4	5^1	6	7	8	9	10	11^3	12	13	14																					1
1		3	4		6	7	2	9^1	10					5	8	12	11																	2
1		3	4		6	7	8^1	9^3	10	13	12	11			2^2	5	14																	3
1		3^1	4		6	7	13	9^3	10	12	8^2	5			2	11	14																	4
1	13	4^2			6	7	2^1	9	14	11	12	8			3	5	10^3																	5
1		3	4	12	6	7	8					10^2	9^3	11	14	2	5^1			13														6
1		3^1	4		6	7	8					10^2	9^3	12	11	14	2	5		13														7
1		3	4		9	7	8					10^2	11^1	2	12	6			5	13														8
1		3	4		6	7	8					10^2	9^1	14	11^3	12	2	5		13														9
1	12	3	4^2	13	6	7	8^1	9^3	10					2	11	5	14																	10
1	2	3^1	4^2		6	7		9				11		10	13	8	5			12														11
1		3^2	4	12	6	7	8	9^3				10	11^1		2	5	13			14														12
1		3	4^2	13	6	7	8	9^3				11	12	10^1	2	5	14																	13
1		3	4	5^1	6	7	8	9^2				10		11	12		2			13														14
1		3^2	4		6	7	8^1	9				11^3		10	14	2	5			13	12													15
1		3^1	4		6	7	8	9				11	5	10	13	2^2				12														16
1	2	3			5	6^1	7					14	10^2	11	8	12	4			13		9^3												17
1	12	3	4	5	6	7	8	9^2					14	2						10	11^1	13^3												18
1	2^1		4	5	6	7		9^3				10^2	14	12	3	11			13	8														19
1	14		4	5	6	7	2	9^2				13	11^3	8	3	12				10^1														20
1		3^1		5	6	7	8	9				13	11^3	2	4	12			14	10^2														21
1		4	5		6^3	7	8	12				10^2	11^1	2	3	14			13	9														22
1	14	4	5		6^1	7	8	12				10^3	11^2	2	13				3	9														23
1	3	4			6	7		9^1				11^2	5	2	8				12	10	13													24
1		3	4		8	9^1						11	5	2	6	7				10^2		13	12											25
1		4			6	7	8	9				11	5	2	3					10														26
1					6	7	8	9					5	2	3					10				4	11									27
1	13				6	7	8	9					4	2	5					11^1					10		3^2	12						28
1					5	7	6	9					4	2^2	3					11^1					8		10		12	13				29
1	12				6	7	8		11^1				14	2	5					9^2				3^3	4	13	10							30
1		3		12	6^1	7	13						4	2	5^2					11					8	9	14		10^3					31
1	3^1	14			6	7	4^3	13					8	2						11					9		10^2		5	12				32
1	8	13			6	7	3						4	2	12					11					9^2		10^1		5					33
1	8	4^1			6	7	3^3	12						2	13					11					9		10^2		5	14				34
1	12	4^1			6	7	3^3	14					8	2	13					11					9		10^2		5					35
1	2	4		12	6^1	7		9					8^2	3	14					11					13		10^3		5					36
1	14		5		6	7	3	13					8^3	2	4					10^1					11^2		9		12					37
1	12		5		6	7	3	13					8^2	2^1	4					10					11		9							38
1	2		5		6	7	3					10^2	11	4^1	8					13					12		9							39
1	8		4		6	7	3	12				11^2		2	5					13					10^1		9^3		14					40
1	8^1		4		6	7	3	9^3				11		2	5					12					13		10^2			14				41
1	8^2		4		6	7	3	14				11		2	5					10^1					9^3		12		13					42
1		4				7		11	12					2^1	3					8^2					13		9		10	5	6^3		14	43
1		4				7		12	14			11^2		2	3					13					8^3		9		10	5	6^1			44
1	2								13	12		11^3			3^2					8					9		10		5	4	7^1	6	14	45
1	2^1	14			6	7		8^2				11	12		3	4				13					9		10^3		5					46

FA Cup
Fourth Qualifying Round
Havant & W　(h)　0-3

EASTBOURNE BOROUGH Blue Square Premier

Ground: Langney Sports Club, Priory Lane, Eastbourne, Sussex BN23 7QH.   *Tel:* (01323) 766 265.
Year Formed: 1964.   *Record Gate:* 3,770 (2005 v Oxford U, FA Cup 1st rd).   *Nickname:* The Sports.
Manager: Garry Wilson.   *Secretary:* Myra Stephens.   *Colours:* Red shirts, black shorts, red stockings.

EASTBOURNE BOROUGH 2008–09 LEAGUE RECORD

Match No.	Date	Venue	Opponents	Result	H/T Score	Lg. Pos.	Goalscorers	Atten- dance
1	Aug 9	H	Rushden & D	L 0-1	0-1	—		1605
2	12	A	Stevenage Bor	W 3-1	2-1	—	Harding [12], Atkin 2 [14, 55]	1681
3	16	A	Oxford U	L 3-6	2-3	17	Harding [11], Tait [17], Armstrong [65]	3969
4	23	H	Cambridge U	L 0-3	0-2	20		3105
5	25	A	Grays Ath	W 1-0	0-0	15	Smart [90]	641
6	30	H	Altrincham	W 1-0	1-0	13	Armstrong [28]	1170
7	Sept 2	H	Forest Green R	W 1-0	0-0	—	Crabb N [64]	1065
8	6	A	Mansfield T	L 1-3	0-2	12	Crabb N [50]	2536
9	13	H	Histon	D 1-1	1-0	14	Austin [44]	1045
10	20	A	Torquay U	L 0-2	0-1	17		1921
11	23	A	Ebbsfleet U	D 1-1	1-0	—	Atkin [22]	1120
12	27	H	Kidderminster H	L 2-3	0-2	18	Armstrong [59], Crabb M [69]	1248
13	Oct 4	A	Weymouth	L 2-3	1-2	21	Crabb M [8], Smart [58]	931
14	7	H	Kettering T	L 1-2	0-1	—	Armstrong [56]	1035
15	12	H	Stevenage Bor	W 2-1	0-0	18	Wormull [56], Taylor [90]	1618
16	18	A	Barrow	L 1-3	0-2	19	Osborne [90]	1206
17	Nov 1	A	Northwich Vic	W 2-1	1-0	18	Armstrong [27], Tait [83]	564
18	15	H	Woking	D 0-0	0-0	14		1105
19	22	A	Rushden & D	L 0-2	0-1	18		1037
20	29	A	Burton Alb	L 0-2	0-0	19		1870
21	Dec 6	H	Northwich Vic	W 4-1	2-1	18	Barnes 2 [13, 70], Armstrong (pen) [32], Wormull [67]	1086
22	9	H	Torquay U	W 4-2	1-1	—	Barnes [8], Crabb M 2 [51, 56], Smith [71]	1204
23	20	A	Wrexham	L 0-5	0-1	16		3463
24	26	H	Lewes	W 1-0	1-0	15	Armstrong [30]	2216
25	28	A	Crawley T	L 0-1	0-0	15		1479
26	Jan 1	A	Lewes	W 2-0	0-0	13	Barnes [61], Crabb N [90]	2232
27	17	A	Forest Green R	W 2-1	0-1	12	Smith [62], Smart [88]	854
28	24	H	York C	W 2-1	1-0	12	Barnes [15], Austin [55]	1668
29	27	A	Woking	W 4-0	3-0	—	Atkin 3 [2, 31, 41], Smith [65]	1101
30	31	H	Mansfield T	L 1-2	1-1	—	Atkin [7]	1420
31	Feb 21	A	Histon	D 3-3	2-2	12	Atkin [34], Crabb M [45], Gargan [79]	821
32	28	A	Kidderminster H	L 0-2	0-2	13		1430
33	Mar 3	H	Oxford U	L 0-3	0-1	—		1168
34	7	H	Wrexham	W 1-0	0-0	13	Smart [85]	1428
35	14	A	Kettering T	W 1-0	0-0	13	Crabb N [78]	1415
36	17	H	Salisbury C	D 0-0	0-0	—		1047
37	21	H	Burton Alb	L 1-2	1-0	13	Brown [25]	1521
38	28	A	Salisbury C	L 0-2	0-0	14		1011
39	31	H	Crawley T	W 2-1	0-0	—	Pullan [47], Crabb N [60]	1268
40	Apr 2	H	Ebbsfleet U	L 0-1	0-0	12		919
41	4	H	Weymouth	W 3-0	1-0	12	Crabb M [45], Jeffery 2 [83, 90]	1075
42	7	A	Altrincham	D 2-2	2-1	—	Jeffery [8], Austin [40]	605
43	11	A	Cambridge U	L 1-2	0-0	12	Armstrong (pen) [59]	3391
44	13	H	Grays Ath	W 2-1	1-1	12	Lovett [13], Armstrong (pen) [50]	1305
45	18	A	York C	L 0-1	0-1	12		2487
46	26	H	Barrow	L 0-2	0-0	13		1584

Final League Position: 13

GOALSCORERS
League (58): Armstrong 9 (3 pens), Atkin 8, Crabb M 6, Barnes 5, Crabb N 5, Smart 4, Austin 3, Jeffery 3, Smith 3, Harding 2, Tait 2, Wormull 2, Brown 1, Gargan 1, Lovett 1, Osborne 1, Pullan 1, Taylor 1.
FA Cup (1): Baker 1.

Hook 44	Baker 42	Jenkins 43	Smart 37+3	Austin 42+2	Pullan 44	Harding 14+18	Armstrong 38	Atkin 21+10	Sigere 3+2	Crabb M 36+3	Wormull 11+18	Tait 21+5	Crabb N 14+21	Harkin 6+5	Lovett 28+12	Budd —+6	Illugason —+3	Taylor 1+3	Osborne 3	Brown 23+1	Smith 13	Barnes 8	Goulding 1+2	Johnson —+1	Gargan 3+3	Jeffery 7+6	Mingle 1+2	Jordan 2	Match No.
1	2	3	4	5	6	7	8	9³	10²	11¹	12	13	14																1
1	2	3	4	5	6	7	8	9³	14		13	10²		11¹	12														2
1	2	3	4	5	6¹	7²	8	9			13	10³	14	11	12														3
1	2	3	4	5	6	7¹	8	9²	13	12		10³		11		14													4
1	2	3¹	4	5	6	7	8	9³	10²	12⁴		13	14		11														5
1	2	3¹	4	5	6	7¹	8		10²			9³	13	12	11	14													6
1	2	3	4	5	6		12	8		11¹		9	10²		7		13												7
1	2	3¹	4	5	6		8			11²		9	10³	13	7	12	14												8
1	2	3	4	5	6	13	8			9³	7¹	10²	11	14	12														9
1	2	3	4	5	6	13	8	14		12	9³	10	11²	7¹															10
1	2	3	4	5	6	12	8	9		11¹	14	10²	13³		7														11
1	2	3	4²	5	6	14	8	9		11	12	10³	13		7¹														12
1	2	3	4	5	6	7¹	8	9²		11		10	13			12													13
1	2	3	4	5	6¹		8	9³		11	10²	14	7		12		13												14
1	2		4	5		12	8	9²		11	6	10³	14		7		13	3											15
1		3	4	5	6	12	8	9		11²	7³	14		13			10¹	2											16
1	2	3	4	5		7¹	8²	9		11	13	14	10³	12					6										17
1	2	3	4		6	7²		9		11		8	12	5¹		13	10												18
1	2	3	4	5	6	14		9³		11²	13	10		7¹	12					8									19
1	2	3	4	5	6		8			12	13			10						11²	7¹	9							20
1	2	3	4¹	5	6	14	8	13		11³	12			7						10	9²								21
1	2	3		5	6	12	8	13		11¹	7			4						10²	9								22
1	2⁴	3	12	5	6		8	14		7¹				13	4					11	9³	10²							23
1		3	4	5	6	7	8	12		11				2						10²	9¹	13							24
1		3	4	5	6		8	13		11	7¹			2						10²	9	12							25
1		3	4		6	7		13		11	5		12	2	2				8	10¹	9²								26
1	2	3	4	12	6	14		9		11³	7²		13	8						5	10¹								27
1	2	3	4	5	6	13		14		11¹			12	7						10	9²	8³							28
1	2	3	4	5	6		9¹			11	8²		12	13						10	7³		14						29
1	2		4	5	6	7¹		9²		11	12		13	3						8	10³			14					30
1	2		4	5	6	14	8	9²		11³			12	3						10	7¹		13						31
1	2	3	4²	5¹	6		8	9		11³	14		13	12						10	7								32
1	2	3	4	5	6²	13	8	9¹		11³	14		12							7						10			33
1	2	3	4	5	6	13	8			11			9²	12						7						10¹			34
1	2	3	4	5	6		8²			11	13		12	7						10			9¹						35
1	2	3	4¹	5	6		8	9²		11			7³	14						10					13	12			36
1	2	3³		5	6	14	8	12		11			13	4						7					10²	9¹			37
1	2	3		5	6	7	8			12	10		4²							11³					9¹	13	14		38
1	2	3	4²	5	6		8			11	10	9¹	13							7						12			39
	2	3		14	6	7³		11	8	10¹	12		4							13					9²	5	1		40
1	2	3	4	5	6		8			11³	12	10¹	9²	13						7						14			41
1	2	3		5	6	12	8			11³	10²		7	13						4					9¹	14			42
1	2	3	4¹	5	6		8			11		10	9²	12						7					13				43
	2	3	13	5	6	14	8²			11³		10¹	12	4						7					9		1		44
1	2	3	12	5	6¹		8			11³	14	10	13	4						7					9²				45
1	2	3		5	6		8	12		11²	13	10¹	9³	4						7					14				46

FA Cup
Fourth Qualifying Round
	Oxford C	(a)	1-0
First Round	Barrow	(h)	0-0
		(a)	0-4

EBBSFLEET UNITED   Blue Square Premier

Ground : Stonebridge Road, Northfleet, Kent DA11 9BA.   *Tel:* (01474) 533 796.   *Year Formed:* 1946.
Record Gate: 12,036 (1963 v Sunderland, FA Cup 4th rd).   *Nickname:* The Fleet.   *Manager:* Liam Daish.
Secretary: Roly Edwards.   *Colours:* Red shirts, white shorts, red stockings.

EBBSFLEET UNITED 2008–09 LEAGUE RECORD

Match No.	Date	Venue	Opponents	Result	H/T Score	Lg. Pos.	Goalscorers	Attendance
1	Aug 9	H	Mansfield T	D	2-2	2-0	—	Gash [8], Long [26]	1872
2	12	A	Rushden & D	L	0-2	0-0	—		1467
3	18	A	Torquay U	W	2-0	1-0	—	Moore [26], Akinde [78]	2372
4	23	H	Stevenage Bor	W	4-0	2-0	8	Barrett [19], Akinde [45], Moore (pen) [69], Ibe [84]	1420
5	25	A	Lewes	D	0-0	0-0	9		851
6	30	H	Oxford U	D	1-1	0-0	12	Gash [56]	1842
7	Sept 2	H	Cambridge U	D	1-1	0-1	—	Moore [52]	1832
8	6	A	Forest Green R	W	4-1	2-1	10	Barrett [3], Moore [42], Gash [66], Ibe [83]	1272
9	13	A	Wrexham	L	2-3	1-1	13	Barrett [27], Gash [90]	3132
10	20	H	Woking	W	2-0	0-0	8	Appiah [57], Barrett [58]	1498
11	23	H	Eastbourne Bor	D	1-1	0-1	—	Gash [65]	1120
12	27	A	Barrow	W	3-0	1-0	5	Moore [32], Gash 2 [63, 87]	1378
13	Oct 4	A	Altrincham	L	0-2	0-2	9		967
14	6	H	Histon	L	0-1	0-1	—		1226
15	11	A	Kidderminster H	L	1-3	1-0	13	Shakes [15]	1512
16	18	H	Torquay U	L	0-2	0-1	16		1781
17	Nov 1	A	Burton Alb	L	1-3	0-1	17	Ibe [59]	1584
18	15	H	Barrow	W	1-0	0-0	14	Barrett [90]	1187
19	20	A	Crawley T	W	2-1	0-1	—	Gash [83], Moore [90]	922
20	23	H	Kettering T	D	0-0	0-0	15		1018
21	29	A	Cambridge U	L	0-1	0-1	13		2807
22	Dec 6	H	Weymouth	W	1-0	1-0	12	Purcell [24]	1005
23	9	H	Forest Green R	L	0-1	0-1	—		728
24	20	A	York C	L	1-3	1-0	12	Gash [26]	1997
25	26	H	Grays Ath	L	0-1	0-0	13		1143
26	28	A	Oxford U	L	1-5	0-2	14	Long [77]	5120
27	Jan 1	A	Grays Ath	L	1-3	0-1	15	Ibe [73]	748
28	17	H	Rushden & D	W	1-0	1-0	15	Barrett [41]	1121
29	24	A	Woking	L	0-1	0-0	16		1471
30	27	H	Crawley T	D	4-4	2-1	—	Long [13], Gash [17], Sole [47], Shakes [65]	795
31	Mar 8	A	York C	D	0-0	0-0	20		1244
32	11	H	Burton Alb	W	2-1	1-0	—	Sole 2 (1 pen) [34, 69 (p)]	711
33	24	A	Salisbury C	L	0-1	0-1	—		939
34	28	A	Kettering T	L	1-2	1-1	21	Cumbers [6]	1533
35	31	H	Altrincham	W	1-0	1-0	—	Shakes [6]	774
36	Apr 2	A	Eastbourne Bor	W	1-0	0-0	—	Gash [56]	919
37	4	H	Northwich Vic	W	1-0	0-0	15	Smith [69]	1003
38	7	A	Mansfield T	L	0-2	0-1	—		1630
39	9	H	Kidderminster H	D	1-1	0-0	—	Long (pen) [27]	979
40	11	A	Stevenage Bor	L	0-1	0-1	16		1913
41	13	H	Lewes	W	2-1	1-1	16	Yussuff [45], Sole (pen) [71]	1098
42	16	A	Histon	L	2-5	2-2	—	Pooley [4], Sole [13]	1015
43	18	A	Weymouth	W	2-0	2-0	15	Shakes [5], Ibe [11]	1007
44	21	H	Wrexham	W	1-0	0-0	—	Ricketts [65]	880
45	23	A	Northwich Vic	L	0-2	0-0	—		474
46	26	H	Salisbury C	D	2-2	0-1	14	McCarthy [52], Smith [90]	1390

Final League Position: 14

GOALSCORERS

League (52): Gash 11, Barrett 6, Moore 6 (1 pen), Ibe 5, Sole 5 (2 pens), Long 4 (1 pen), Shakes 4, Akinde 2, Smith 2, Appiah 1, Cumbers 1, McCarthy 1, Pooley 1, Purcell 1, Ricketts 1, Yussuff 1.
FA Cup (3): Moore 2 (2 pens), Ibe 1.

Cronin 46	Hawkins 9+2	Opinel 31+2	Shakes 23+11	Smith 18+2	Charles 35+1	Stone 16+7	Barrett 29	Moore 34+2	Gash 40	Long 43+2	Akinde 1+4	Purcell 12+17	Appiah 1+2	Ricketts 34+2	McCarthy 19	Hand 17+6	Ibe 7+19	Slatter 10+11	Pooley 12+5	Bowes —+2	Murray 5+3	Delicate 3	Duncan 6+2	Crooks 16	Judge 1	Sole 8+5	Martin 7	Stevens 8+1	Cumbers 2	Yussuff 4+4	West 8+2	Henry 1+1	Match No.
1	2	3	4¹	5	6	7	8	9	10	11	12																						1
1	2¹	3	4	5	6	7	8²	9	10³	11	12	13	14																				2
1		3	4²		6	7	8	9	10³	11¹		13	14	2	5	12																	3
1		3	4¹		6	7	8	9	10³	11²	12			2	5	13	14																4
1		3			6	7	4¹	9	10³	11	8²	13		2	5	12	14																5
1	12	3			6	7²	8	9	10	11	4²			2¹	5	14	13																6
1		3			6		8	9	10	11	4¹			2	5	7	12																7
1		3	13		6	12	8	9	10³	11¹	4²			2	5	7	14																8
1	3¹	4²	5		6		8	9	10	11				2		7	13	12															9
1		3	4¹		6	13	8²		10	11	12			2	5	7	9³	14															10
1		3¹			6		8	9	10	11		7²		2	5	4	12	13															11
1		3¹	14		6	13	8	9	10	11²				2	5	4			7³		12												12
1	2		12		6		8	9	10	11²				3		4	13	7¹	5														13
1			4²		6■	14	8³	9	10	11				2¹	5	7	13	12	3														14
1	2		4			7	8	9	10²		12			3	5	11¹	13		6														15
1		3	4¹		6	13	8	9	10	11					5	7²		2	12														16
1		3	4	5¹	6	7	8		10	11²	13			2■		12	9³		14														17
1		3		5	6	7²	8	9	10³	13	4			2¹		14	12				11												18
1		3		5	6	7	8	9	10	11²	12			2		13							4¹										19
1		3		5	6	7²	8	9	10	11	12			2³		14							13	4¹									20
1		3	14	5	6	7²	8	9	10	11³	12			2									13	4¹									21
1		3			6¹	13	8²	9	10	11	4			12		7		2	5														22
1	2	3					8²	9³	10	11	4			12		7	14	6	5¹		13												23
1		3	12	5		7²		9¹	10	11	4						13	8	2		6												24
1	12	3¹	13	5				9²	10	11	4					7	14	2¹	6		8												25
1	2	3	13	5¹	12			9		11	6			4		7²	10				8												26
1	2	3	4				8	9²	10	11³	12					13	14	6	5		7¹												27
1			12	5	2		8	9	10	11¹	4					7										3	6						28
1			12	5	2		8²		10	11	4¹					7	13									3	6	9					29
1			4¹	5	2		8		10	11						7	12									3	6				9		30
1		3	12	5			11	7	10	8²				2									13	4		6		9¹					31
1		3		5		7	11	10	8¹					2		13							12	4		6		9²					32
1		4³	12	5				9	8					2²		14							3			6	13			7¹	11	10	33
1	3²	14	13	5					10	8	12			2		7								4		6		9³			11¹		34
1	12	4	3					9³	10	11²	14			2¹	5	7										6		8			13		35
1	13	8³	5					9¹	10	11³	12			2	6	14								4			7				13		36
1		8	5	3					10	11²				2	6¹	7								4		12	9				13		37
1	3¹	7	5³	6					10	8	12			2		13								4		9²					11		38
1	3²	9	5						10	8	13			2		7¹								4		12	6				11		39
1	3¹	9	5						10²	8	14			2	13	12								4			6			7	11³		40
1	3¹	9	5						10³	8				2	14	12								4		13	6			7	11²		41
1	3		12				13			8				2	10	5								4		9¹	6²			7³	14	11	42
1	3	7²	5				13			8	14			2	6	10³								4		9¹					12	11	43
1				5					7	10¹	8			2	6	12	13						3²			9³	4				14	11	44
1		7					9³			8	14			2	6	10	5¹									13		4²		11	3	12	45
1		7	5	3			9¹			8	13			2	6	10	4²													12	11		46

FA Cup
Fourth Qualifying Round   Woking   (a) 2-2
    (h) 1-0
First Round   Crewe Alex   (a) 0-1

FOREST GREEN ROVERS   Blue Square Premier

Ground: The Lawn, Nympsfield Road, Forest Green, Nailsworth GL6 0ET.   *Tel:* (01453) 834 860.
Year Formed: 1890.   *Record Gate:* 3,021 (2006 v Oxford U, Conference).   *Nickname:* Rovers.   *Manager:* Jim Harvey.
Secretary: David Honeybill.   *Colours:* Black and white striped shirts, black shorts, red stockings.

FOREST GREEN ROVERS 2008–09 LEAGUE RECORD

Match No.	Date	Venue	Opponents	Result		H/T Score	Lg. Pos.	Goalscorers	Attendance
1	Aug 9	A	Kettering T	D	1-1	0-1	—	Lawless [78]	1346
2	12	H	Salisbury C	L	1-2	0-1	—	Mangan [57]	927
3	16	H	Crawley T	W	1-0	0-0	11	Mangan [82]	732
4	23	A	Woking	W	1-0	0-0	11	Mohamed [48]	1617
5	25	H	Weymouth	W	4-1	1-0	4	Smith [35], Rigoglioso 2 [75, 82], Fowler [90]	1132
6	30	A	Histon	W	1-0	1-0	1	Hardiker [20]	740
7	Sept 2	A	Eastbourne Bor	L	0-1	0-0	—		1065
8	6	H	Ebbsfleet U	L	1-4	1-2	11	Rigoglioso [5]	1272
9	13	A	Northwich Vic	D	0-0	0-0	12		603
10	20	H	Stevenage Bor	L	0-3	0-2	16		751
11	23	H	Torquay U	L	1-2	1-0	—	Smith [45]	1022
12	27	A	Burton Alb	L	2-4	1-0	17	Jones [7], Mangan [89]	1545
13	Oct 4	H	Wrexham	L	2-3	1-1	20	Mangan 2 [4, 52]	1216
14	7	A	Crawley T	D	2-2	0-2	—	Smith [48], Mohamed [88]	876
15	11	A	Lewes	L	2-3	0-3	21	Platt [64], Smith [67]	666
16	16	H	Cambridge U	D	2-2	1-1	—	Symonds [20], Preece [73]	789
17	Nov 1	A	Barrow	L	1-3	0-1	21	Mangan [68]	1440
18	15	H	Altrincham	L	1-3	1-3	21	Mangan [39]	851
19	22	H	Mansfield T	W	1-0	1-0	21	Lawless [11]	872
20	Dec 6	A	Burton Alb	L	2-3	1-2	21	Mangan [7], Smith [69]	812
21	9	A	Ebbsfleet U	W	1-0	1-0	—	Smith [42]	728
22	20	H	Kettering T	L	0-2	0-2	22		923
23	26	A	Kidderminster H	D	1-1	1-1	22	Bartlett (og) [44]	2102
24	28	H	Barrow	W	2-1	2-1	20	Rigoglioso [19], Mangan [34]	747
25	Jan 17	H	Eastbourne Bor	L	1-2	1-0	22	Preece [45]	854
26	20	A	Oxford U	L	1-2	0-0	—	Brown [89]	3728
27	23	A	Rushden & D	D	2-2	1-2	—	Lawless [11], Ayres [67]	1066
28	27	A	Salisbury C	D	2-2	2-1	—	Clist [22], Brown [42]	771
29	Feb 3	H	Histon	D	2-2	1-0	—	Mangan [45], Platt (pen) [57]	464
30	18	H	Northwich Vic	W	3-0	2-0	—	Hardiker 2 [12, 16], Lawless [87]	744
31	24	A	Torquay U	D	3-3	3-2	—	Mangan 3 (1 pen) [28 (p), 36, 42]	1554
32	28	H	Grays Ath	D	1-1	1-0	19	Mangan [28]	992
33	Mar 3	A	Stevenage Bor	D	1-1	1-1	—	Mangan [27]	1242
34	7	H	Oxford U	D	3-3	2-2	18	Jones [28], Platt 2 [33, 70]	2027
35	10	A	Wrexham	D	1-1	0-0	—	Mangan [76]	2405
36	14	A	Mansfield T	L	0-3	0-1	20		2174
37	17	H	York C	D	1-1	1-0	—	Mohamed [41]	681
38	21	A	Altrincham	W	5-2	0-2	17	Lloyd [47], Brown [54], Lawless [72], Platt (pen) [76], Palmer [90]	852
39	28	H	Lewes	W	4-1	2-1	16	Mangan 3 (1 pen) [31 (p), 64, 86], Ayres [35]	898
40	Apr 4	A	Cambridge U	W	1-0	1-0	16	Mangan [14]	3245
41	7	A	Kidderminster H	D	2-2	1-1	—	Platt [40], Mangan [77]	970
42	11	H	Woking	L	0-2	0-1	17		1109
43	13	A	Weymouth	D	1-1	0-1	17	Mangan [51]	1183
44	18	H	Rushden & D	W	4-0	2-0	17	Mangan 3 (1 pen) [6, 71, 85 (p)], Rigoglioso [37]	1185
45	21	A	York C	L	1-2	0-0	—	Palmer [89]	2164
46	26	A	Grays Ath	L	1-2	1-0	18	Mangan (pen) [26]	1246

Final League Position: 18

GOALSCORERS

League (70): Mangan 26 (4 pens), Platt 6 (2 pens), Smith 6, Lawless 5, Rigoglioso 5, Brown 3, Hardiker 3, Mohamed 3, Ayres 2, Jones 2, Palmer 2, Preece 2, Clist 1, Fowler 1, Lloyd 1, Symonds 1, own goal 1.
FA Cup (10): Mohamed 3, Afful 2, Smith 2, Lawless 1, Low 1, Stonehouse 1.

Robinson 19 + 1	Lawless 32	Hardiker 11	Clist 21	Jones 39	Fowler 38 + 2	Afful 8 + 16	Pitman 2	Mangan 38 + 3	Mohamed 17 + 10	Stonehouse 37 + 3	McDonald 17 + 7	Platt 27 + 12	Smith 33 + 9	Preece 32 + 3	Thomas 7 + 2	Rigoglioso 14 + 11	Simpson — + 3	Molyneux 2 + 2	Symonds 7 + 10	Gill 20	Burton 27	Kempson 5	Low 3 + 1	Ayres 19 + 1	Brown 16 + 2	Lloyd 11 + 5	Ashford — + 2	Baldwin 1 + 3	Palmer — + 4	Else 1 + 3	Casey 1 + 1	Pugh 1	Courtney — + 1	Match No.
1	2	3	4	5	6^3	7	8^2	9	10	11^1	12	13	14																					1
1	2	3	4	5	6^3	12	8^2	9	10	14	11		13		7^1																			2
1	2	3	4	5	6^1	12		9^2	10	13	11			8		7																		3
1	2	3	4	5	6^2	7		12	9^3	13	11^1	14	10			8																		4
1	2	3	4	5	6	14		9^3	12	11			10^2	8^1	7	13																		5
1	2	3		5	6	12		9^2	8	11			10^1	4	7	13																		6
1	2	3		5	6	14		9	7	11			10^3	13	12	4^1	8^2																	7
1	2	3	4	5	6^1	14		9^3	7	11		13	8	12		10^2																		8
1			4	5	6^4	7^3		8	11			9^1	2	3	14	10^2	12	13																9
1	2		4^2	5		14		12	10	11		13	7	6		8^1		3	9^3															10
1	2			5		7		9^2	10^1	3		12	4	6		8			13															11
1				5		7		9		11	3	10	4	6		8^1	12		2															12
1			4^1	5	6	14		9^2	10	11	12	13	8	3					7^3	2														13
1				5	6^2	7^1		9	12	11	4	10^8	8	3	13				14	2														14
1				5	6	14		9^3	10	11	4^2	13	8	7^1			12	3	2															15
1	2		4	5	6	13		9^2	12	11	14		8^1	3					10^3	7														16
1		3	4	5	6	7^2		12	10			13	8			11^1			9^3	14	2													17
			4	5		12		9	10^2	11		13	8		14				7^1	2^3	1	6	3											18
	2^1		4	5	12	13		14	11	9	8								10^3	7^2	1	6												19
			4	5	6	13		10^2		11		9^3	8		14				12	2	1	3		7^1										20
			4	5	6			9^3		11		10^2	8		7^1	13			12	2	1	3		14										21
			4	5	3			9^3	13	11	8	10^2	14		7^1				12	2	1	6												22
7^1			4	5	6	13		9^2	12	11	10		8	3						2	1													23
7			4	5^1	6			9^3		11		14	8	3		10^2				13	2	1		12										24
7^1			4		6^2	14		9^3		11	13		8	5		10				2	1			3	12									25
7			4		6^1			9		11	10^2	12	8	5						14	2^3	1		3	13									26
7			4					9		3		10	8	5						2	1			6	11									27
7			4		10			9		3	6		8	5						2	1				11									28
1					4	12		9^2		3	13	10	8	6		7^1				14	2			5	11^3									29
1	2	7			4^3			9^2		3	14	10	12	6		8^1								5	11	13								30
	7	2		5				9^3		3	11^2	13	8	4						14	1			6^1		10	12							31
	7			5	12			9	14	3	8	10			13					2^2	1			6	11^3	4^1								32
	7			5	8			9		3	10			6						2	1			4	11									33
15	7			5	8			9		3	10			4		12^2				2^1	1^6			6	11	13								34
	2			5	8			9^2	13	3	10	12	4								1			6	11	7^1								35
	2			5	8^3			9^4		3	10	12	4			14					1			6	11^2	7^1	13							36
	2			5	8			9^2		3	10	13	4		12						1			6	11	7^1								37
	2				6			9		3	10	8^3	4		12						1			5	11^2	7^1		14	13					38
	2			5^3	8			9	7^2	3	10^1	12	4								1			6	11	13	14							39
				5	7			9	12	3	14	10^8	8	4	13						1			6	11^3	2^1								40
				5	8			9	12	3		10	2	4	13						1			6	11^2	7^1								41
	2			5	7^3			9		3		10^2	8	4							1			6	11^1	12			13	14				42
	2			5	11			9		3		10	8	4							1			6		7								43
	2			5^3	11			9		3		10	12	4		8^1					1			6		7^2			14		13			44
	2^1			5	6^3			9				10	8	4		11					1					7			12	14	13	3^2		45
				5^3				9				10	8	4		11^2					1					7	2	13	6	12	3^1		14	46

FA Cup
Fourth Qualifying Round

	Ashford Town (M)	(a)	0-0
		(h)	4-0
First Round	Team Bath	(a)	1-0
Second Round	Rochdale	(h)	2-0
Third Round	Derby Co	(h)	3-4

GRAYS ATHLETIC

Blue Square Premier

Ground: Recreation Ground, Bridge Road, Grays RM17 6BZ. *Tel:* (01375) 391 649. *Year Formed:* 1890.
Record Gate: 9,500 (1959 v Chelmsford City, FA Cup). *Nickname:* The Blues. *Manager:* Craig Edwards.
Secretary: Phil O'Reilly. *Colours:* All sky blue.

GRAYS ATHLETIC 2008–09 LEAGUE RECORD

Match No.	Date		Venue	Opponents	Result		H/T Score	Lg. Pos.	Goalscorers	Atten- dance
1	Aug	9	A	Weymouth	L	1-3	1-2	—	Molesley [6]	1059
2		12	H	Kettering T	D	1-1	0-0	—	Branston (og) [72]	696
3		16	H	Northwich Vic	W	2-1	1-0	12	Elliott [44], Sloma [67]	523
4		23	A	Salisbury C	L	0-1	0-0	16		987
5		25	H	Eastbourne Bor	L	0-1	0-0	19		641
6		30	A	Mansfield T	L	0-1	0-1	21		2378
7	Sept	2	A	Crawley T	L	1-2	1-2	—	Taylor [9]	1189
8		7	H	Kidderminster H	W	3-2	0-0	20	Thurgood [54], Sloma [68], Cogan [72]	525
9		13	A	Woking	L	1-3	1-0	20	Molesley [10]	1619
10		20	H	Wrexham	W	2-1	2-0	19	St Aimie 2 [40, 45]	746
11		25	H	Stevenage Bor	L	1-2	0-0	—	Stuart [50]	791
12		28	A	Cambridge U	L	0-1	0-0	22		2971
13	Oct	4	H	Lewes	D	0-0	0-0	22		729
14		7	A	Rushden & D	L	0-1	0-0	—		1124
15		11	A	Northwich Vic	L	0-2	0-0	22		579
16		18	H	Woking	D	1-1	0-0	23	Cogan [47]	581
17	Nov	1	A	Kidderminster H	L	0-2	0-1	23		1400
18		15	H	Oxford U	W	2-0	1-0	22	Forrester [43], Sloma [87]	892
19		22	H	Lewes	L	0-2	0-2	23		519
20	Dec	6	A	York C	W	1-0	1-0	22	Thomas [26]	2154
21		9	A	Stevenage Bor	D	0-0	0-0	—		1289
22		20	H	Barrow	W	2-1	1-1	21	Cogan 2 [41, 56]	502
23		26	A	Ebbsfleet U	W	1-0	0-0	20	Slabber [78]	1143
24		28	H	Histon	L	1-4	1-0	22	Welsh [37]	525
25	Jan	1	H	Ebbsfleet U	W	3-1	1-0	17	Thurgood [31], Welsh [50], Stuart [79]	748
26		17	H	Burton Alb	L	0-1	0-1	18		651
27		27	H	Weymouth	D	1-1	0-1	—	Thomas [69]	415
28	Feb	14	A	Wrexham	L	2-3	1-1	—	Cogan [30], Pugh [90]	3419
29		21	A	Barrow	D	1-1	1-1	22	Pugh [65]	1515
30		24	H	Cambridge U	L	0-1	0-1	—		754
31		28	A	Forest Green R	D	1-1	0-1	22	Welsh [70]	992
32	Mar	3	H	Torquay U	L	1-2	1-1	—	Dinning [26]	510
33		7	H	Altrincham	W	2-1	1-0	21	Cogan [45], Slabber [52]	710
34		10	A	Kettering T	D	0-0	0-0	—		1117
35		14	A	Oxford U	L	1-4	0-3	22	Dinning [62]	4764
36		17	A	Histon	L	1-4	1-4	—	Pugh [42]	641
37		21	H	Mansfield T	W	2-1	0-0	21	Slabber [82], Pugh [90]	802
38		24	A	Torquay U	D	1-1	1-0	—	Taylor [39]	1996
39		28	H	Burton Alb	L	0-4	0-3	20		2388
40		31	H	Rushden & D	D	0-0	0-0	—		695
41	Apr	4	H	York C	W	1-0	1-0	19	Pugh [38]	720
42		11	H	Salisbury C	W	3-1	2-0	18	Pugh 2 [12, 43], Taylor [52]	761
43		13	A	Eastbourne Bor	L	1-2	1-1	19	Black [45]	1305
44		18	A	Altrincham	L	0-2	0-1	19		1148
45		21	H	Crawley T	W	1-0	1-0	—	Beavan [32]	630
46		26	H	Forest Green R	W	2-1	0-1	19	Thurgood [69], Berry [70]	1246

Final League Position: 19

GOALSCORERS

League (44): Pugh 7, Cogan 6, Slabber 3, Sloma 3, Taylor 3, Thurgood 3, Welsh 3, Dinning 2, Molesley 2, St Aimie 2, Stuart 2, Thomas 2, Beavan 1, Berry 1, Black 1, Elliott 1, Forrester 1, own goal 1.
FA Cup (3): Cogan 1 (pen), Elliott 1, Stuart 1.

Arnold 17+1	Gier 16+2	Pugh 16+1	Gross 6	Elliott 22+4	Stuart 46	Ashton 15+2	Tabiri 3	Bodkin 2	Molesley 6+4	Lindie 1+4	Taylor 15+2	Kedwell 7+1	Welsh 33+7	Candrain 1+1	Cogan 38+5	Dinning 8+1	Ide 4+3	Sloma 19+3	Beckwith 7	Flitney 6	Campana 2+3	Thurgood 35+2	Wilnis 31+2	Hudson-Odoi 8+2	Bailey 9+6	Reid —+3	Quistin 1+1	Button 13	St Aimie 4+2	Batchelor —+1	Rigg 6	Davis 17+8	Black 7+1	Dayes 5	Dixon 1+3	Hickie 6+4	Long 3+3	Thomas 10	Batt 9+1	Jones 2	Deany 1	Forrester 6+2	Gray —+1	Butcher 3	McCollin 3	Slabber 15+10	McKenzie 1	Sweeney —+1	Beavan 18+1	Berry 2+7	Match No.
2	3	4[2]	5	6	7[1]	8	9	10[3]	11	12	13	14																																							1
1	2	3	4	5	6	12	9	13	11	7[1]	8	10[2]																																							2
1	2	3	4	5	6	7[1]	9[2]	10	12	8[3]	13	11			14																																				3
2	3	4[2]	5	6[8]	10	12	8	9[3]	11	1	7[1]	13	14																																						4
2	3	5	12	9[2]	10	7	8	1	4	6	11[1]	13																																							5
4	5	6	13	9[3]	10	7	8[1]	11	1	12	4	3[2]	14																																						6
13	3[2]	4	5	6	12	9	10	11[1]	8	1	14	2	7[3]																																						7
4	5	6	8[2]	12	10	14	13	7[1]	11	1	9[3]	3	2																																						8
5	6	8[1]	9[3]	12	7	10	11	1	13	4	2	3[2]	14																																						9
2	4	5	8[1]	11[3]	12	13	7	6	3	14	1	9[2]	10																																						10
2[1]	4[3]	5	8	11	12	3	7	6[2]	14	1	9	10	13																																						11
4	5	8[2]	11	13	3	7	12	1	9[3]	10	2	6[1]	14																																						12
12	5	11	8	3	14	4	7	1	9[2]	2	6[1]	10[3]	13																																						13
4	5	11	3	6	8	1	13	10	2	12	7[1]	9[2]																																							14
5	12	11	6	6[1]	8[2]	1	13	10	2	3	7	9																																							15
2[1]	14	5	11	8	3	4	12	1	10[3]	6	13	7	9[2]																																						16
2	4	5	11	8	7	1	6	3	9[1]	10	12																																							17
2	13	5	12	7	8	11	4[2]	1	6[1]	3	10[3]	9	14																																						18
2	5	14	11	8	3	4	7[2]	1	6	13	9[1]	12																																							19
5	6	8	11[2]	4	2	1	13	9	3	12	7	10[1]																																							20
14	5	6	7[2]	8	11	4	1	2[3]	13	9	3	12	10[1]																																						21
5	6	11	8	12	4	2	1	7	3	9	10[1]																																							22
1	5	6	11	12	4	3	7	9	2	10[2]	13	8[1]																																						23
1	5	6	11	8	13	4	3[2]	7	9	2	10[1]	12																																						24
1	5	6	7	8	11	4	3	12	9	2	10[1]																																							25
1	5	7	8	11[1]	4	6	3	12	9	2	10																																							26
1	5	6	7[2]	8	11[1]	4	2	9	3	13																																								27
1	2	9	5	7	13	11	8	4[1]	6	12	14	10[2]	3[3]																																						28
1	2	9	5	7	13	11[3]	8	6	3[1]	12	10[2]	4	14																																						29
1	2	9	5	7[1]	13	11	8	6	4	12	10[2]	3[8]																																							30
1	2	9	5	11	8	7	4	6	3	10																																								31
1	9	5	12	11	8	7	4	6	2[1]	3	10																																							32
9	12	5	7[1]	8	6	1	4	2	11[8]	14	10[2]	3	13																																						33
12	7	5	9[1]	8	6	1	4	2	11	10	3																																							34
15	2	9	7[8]	5	8	6	1[6]	4	3	11[1]	13	12	10	3[2]																																						35
9	5	8	6	1	4	3	7[1]	12	2	10	11																																							36
9	2	5	10[5]	8	13	1	4[3]	6	11	12	7[1]	14	3																																						37
9	2	5	10[2]	8	4[1]	1	6	11	3	7	13	12																																							38
9	2	5	10	12	8	1	6	11[1]	4[3]	7[2]	13	14	3																																						39
1	9	2	5	13	11	8[3]	4	7[1]	12	6	10[2]	3	14																																						40
1	9	7	5	10[1]	11	8	4	6	2	12	3																																							41
1	9	5	10	11[1]	8	4	6	7	2	3	12																																							42
1	9[8]	5	10	11	8	4	6	7[1]	12	2[2]	13	3																																							43
11[2]	5	10	12	8	4	13	2	7[1]	6	1	9[3]	14[3]	3																																						44
11	5	10[2]	9[1]	8	4	6	2	7	1	13	3	12																																							45
7	5	11[1]	8	4	6	14	2[2]	9	12	1	10	3	13[3]																																						46

FA Cup
Fourth Qualifying Round

	AFC Totton	(h)	2-0
First Round	Carlisle U	(a)	1-1
		(h)	0-2

HISTON
Blue Square Premier

Ground: Glassworld Stadium, Bridge Road, Impington, Cambridge CB24 9PH.   *Tel:* (01223) 237 373.   *Year Formed:* 1904.   *Record Gate:* 3,800.   *Nickname:* The Stutes.   *Manager:* Steve Fallon.   *Secretary:* Lisa Baldwin.   *Colours:* Red shirts, black shorts, black stockings.

HISTON 2008–09 LEAGUE RECORD

Match No.	Date	Venue	Opponents	Result	H/T Score	Lg. Pos.	Goalscorers	Attendance
1	Aug 9	H	Torquay U	D 1-1	0-0	—	Knight-Percival [89]	928
2	12	A	Mansfield T	L 0-1	0-1	—		2703
3	16	A	York C	D 1-1	1-0	18	Wright (pen) [38]	2125
4	23	H	Burton Alb	W 4-3	3-2	13	Wright 3 (2 pens) [18 (p), 27, 31 (p)], Midson [87]	910
5	25	A	Rushden & D	W 2-1	1-0	—	Murray [16], Midson [54]	1613
6	30	H	Forest Green R	L 0-1	0-1	16		740
7	Sept 2	H	Altrincham	W 1-0	0-0	—	Gwillim [74]	692
8	6	A	Weymouth	W 5-2	2-1	6	Midson [31], Bygrave (og) [33], Reeves 2 [63, 72], Wright [90]	1003
9	13	A	Eastbourne Bor	D 1-1	0-1	6	Midson [58]	1045
10	20	H	Northwich Vic	W 2-1	1-1	5	Reeves [6], Barker [77]	829
11	23	H	Lewes	D 1-1	0-1	—	Midson [90]	592
12	27	A	Woking	L 0-1	0-0	8		1797
13	Oct 4	H	Salisbury C	W 2-0	0-0	5	Simpson [53], Bass (og) [76]	961
14	6	A	Ebbsfleet U	W 1-0	1-0	—	Reeves [45]	1226
15	18	H	Crawley T	W 1-0	0-0	4	Murray [75]	1256
16	Nov 1	A	Altrincham	W 1-0	0-0	3	Midson [72]	953
17	15	H	Kettering T	W 1-0	0-0	3	Midson [52]	2716
18	18	A	Stevenage Bor	W 3-1	2-1	—	Mitchell-King [2], Knight-Percival [35], Gwillim [72]	1623
19	22	H	Oxford U	W 5-2	3-1	1	Knight-Percival 2 [5, 31], Midson [18], Wright [72], Mitchell-King [74]	1242
20	Dec 6	H	Woking	W 1-0	0-0	2	Oyebanjo [90]	1249
21	9	H	York C	D 1-1	0-1	—	Parslow (og) [59]	901
22	20	A	Torquay U	L 1-4	0-2	2	Wright [49]	2201
23	26	A	Cambridge U	D 2-2	0-2	3	Midson [49], Murray [59]	6488
24	28	A	Grays Ath	W 4-1	0-1	2	Langston [69], Midson [71], Knight-Percival [74], Reeves [89]	525
25	Jan 17	A	Northwich Vic	W 2-1	0-1	2	Knight-Percival [89], Simpson [90]	428
26	27	A	Kidderminster H	L 0-2	0-1	—		1277
27	Feb 3	A	Forest Green R	D 2-2	2-1	—	Knight-Percival [78], Simpson [87]	464
28	14	A	Salisbury C	W 4-0	1-0	—	Midson 2 [30, 76], Wright (pen) [54], Murray [77]	908
29	21	H	Eastbourne Bor	D 3-3	2-2	2	Midson [8], Murray 2 [24, 90]	821
30	24	H	Barrow	W 2-0	0-0	—	Murray [84], Wright [86]	541
31	28	A	Lewes	W 3-0	1-0	2	Simpson [25], Barker 2 [53, 71]	345
32	Mar 2	H	Cambridge U	D 1-1	0-0	—	Midson [85]	2579
33	7	A	Kettering T	L 0-1	0-0	3		1870
34	10	A	Barrow	L 0-1	0-0	—		965
35	17	H	Grays Ath	W 4-1	4-1	—	Barker 3 [11, 24, 30], Murray [18]	641
36	24	H	Stevenage Bor	D 0-0	0-0	—		1133
37	28	H	Wrexham	W 1-0	1-0	4	Simpson [30]	1106
38	31	H	Mansfield T	W 3-0	2-0	—	Murray [41], Knight-Percival 2 [45, 86]	914
39	Apr 4	A	Oxford U	L 1-2	1-0	4	Midson [17]	6231
40	7	A	Wrexham	D 0-0	0-0	—		2234
41	11	A	Burton Alb	L 1-3	0-1	5	Andrews [90]	3311
42	13	H	Rushden & D	D 0-0	0-0	6		1263
43	16	H	Ebbsfleet U	W 5-2	2-2	—	Midson 2 [14, 72], Barker [42], Langston [60], Wright [90]	1015
44	18	A	Kidderminster H	D 1-1	1-1	3	Midson [4]	1718
45	21	H	Weymouth	W 1-0	1-0	—	Langston [5]	1016
46	26	A	Crawley T	D 3-3	3-0	3	Midson 2 [11, 39], Barker [35]	901

Final League Position: 3

GOALSCORERS

League (78): Midson 20, Wright 10 (4 pens), Knight-Percival 9, Murray 9, Barker 8, Reeves 5, Simpson 5, Langston 3, Gwillim 2, Mitchell-King 2, Andrews 1, Oyebanjo 1, own goals 3.
FA Cup (10): Simpson 4, Wright 3, Midson 2, Langston 1.
Play-Offs (1): Andrews 1.

Naisbitt 43	Pope 12 + 4	Gwillim 41	Kennedy 4 + 3	Mitchell-King 38 + 1	Langston 45	Midson 46	Wright 34 + 3	Reeves 12 + 8	Murray 39 + 2	Knight-Percival 36 + 5	Okay 5 + 3	Nightingale 1 + 4	Andrews 8 + 24	Oyebanjo 37 + 3	Ada 41	Barker 25 + 5	Coker — + 1	Campbell — + 1	Simpson 32	Rose — + 1	Welch 3 + 1	Patterson 1	Bygrave 2	Roache — + 12	Pacquette 1 + 2	Match No.
1	2	3^1	4^3	5	6	7^2	8	9	10	11	12	13	14													1
1	2^1		4^2	5	6	7	8	9	10	11	3		13	12												2
1			4^2	5	6	7	8^3	14	10	11	3^1		13	9	2	12										3
1		12		5	6	7^2	9		10	11	3^1	13	4	8	2											4
1				5	6	7	9^3	13	10^2				8	4	2	3	11^1	12	14							5
1		3	14	5	6^1	7^2	9	13	10	11			12	4^3	8	2										6
1		3		5	6	7	9	12	10	13			4^1	2	8	11^2										7
1		3		5^1	6	7	9	8	10	11			12	2	4											8
1	12	3			6	7	9^2	10	8	11	13			2^1	5				4							9
1	12	3			6	7	9		10	11^2			4^1	2	5	13			8							10
1		3	13		6^1	7	9		10	11^3	12		4^2	2	5	14			8							11
1		3		5	6^1	7	9^3		10	11^2	14		12	2	4	13			8							12
1	2	3		5	6	7	13	9^2	10	12			11		4				8^1							13
1		3		5	6	7	13	9^2	10	12				2	4	11			8^1							14
1		3		5	6	7^3	12	9^1	10	14	13			2	4	11^2			8							15
1		3		5	6	7	8		10	12				2	4	11			9^1							16
1		3		5	6	7	8	13		11	12			2	4	9^2			10^1							17
1	2	3		5	6	7	9			11				4		10^1	12		8							18
1	2	3		5^2	6	7^1	9	12		11	13			4		10^1			8							19
1		3		5	6	7	9^1	12	10	11				2	4				8							20
1		3		5	6	7	9^1	12	10	11				2	4				8							21
1	2	3	12			7	9		10	11			8^1	5	4				6							22
		3			6	7	9	10	8	11			12	2		5			4^1		1					23
		3^1	4		6	7	9	10	8	11	13		12^2	2		5					1					24
1	13			4	6	7	9		10^1	11	12			2		5			8				3^2			25
1		3		4	6	7	9	8		11				2					10			5				26
1		3		4	6	7	9		10	11				2					8			5^1	12			27
1	2	3		4^1	6	7	9^2		10		12		11			5			8					13		28
1	2^3	3			6	7	9^2		10	11^1	12		14		4	5			8					13		29
1		3			6	7	9	8			12			2	4	5			10^2					13	11^1	30
1		3		4^1	6	7^3	9^2		10	11	12			2		5			8					13	14	31
1		3		4	6	7	9			11				2	8	5			10^1					12		32
1		3		4	6	7	9^1		10	11	13			2		5			8^2					12		33
1		3		4	6	7			10	11				2	9	5			8							34
1		3		4	6	7			10	11	12			2	9^2	5			8^1					13		35
1		3		4	6	7			10	11				2	9^1	5			8					12		36
1		3		4	6	7			10	11	12			2	9^1	5			8							37
1		3		4	6	7^2			10	11	12			2	9	5			8^1					13		38
1	14	3		4	6	7			10	11			13^3	2	9^1	5			8^2					12		39
1		3		4	6	7	9	8		11				2		5			10							40
1		3		4	6	7	9		10	11^2	12			2		5			8^1					13		41
1		3		4	6	7^2	9		10	11	12			2		5			8^1					13		42
1	2	3		4	6	7^1	9			11			8			5			10					12		43
	2	3		4	6	7	9^1	12		11			8			5			10		1					44
1	2	3		4	6	7	9	12		11	13		8^2			5			10^1							45
1	11^1	2		4	6	7	10	9			12			3		5			8		15					46

FA Cup

Fourth Qualifying Round				
	Durham C	(a)	2-2	
		(h)	5-2	
First Round	Swindon T	(h)	1-0	
Second Round	Leeds U	(h)	1-0	
Third Round	Swansea C	(h)	1-2	

Play-Offs

Semi-Final	Torquay U	(a)	0-2
		(h)	1-0

KETTERING TOWN   Blue Square Premier

Ground: Rockingham Road, Kettering, Northants NN16 9AW.   *Tel:* (01536) 483 028.   *Year Formed:* 1872.
Record Gate: 11,536 v Peterborough U.   *Nickname:* Poppies.   *Manager:* Mark Cooper.   *Colours:* Red shirts, black and white trim, red shorts, black stockings.

KETTERING TOWN 2008–09 LEAGUE RECORD

Match No.	Date	Venue	Opponents	Result	H/T Score	Lg. Pos.	Goalscorers	Attendance
1	Aug 9	H	Forest Green R	D	1-1	1-0	—	Dempster [14]	1346
2	12	A	Grays Ath	D	1-1	0-0	—	Dempster [78]	696
3	16	A	Altrincham	D	1-1	1-0	15	Seddon (pen) [5]	1045
4	23	H	Rushden & D	D	1-1	1-0	15	Seddon [9]	2897
5	25	A	Cambridge U	W	2-0	0-0	14	Westcarr [51], Beardsley [82]	3489
6	30	H	Woking	W	1-0	0-0	9	Marna [81]	1493
7	Sept 2	H	Stevenage Bor	W	1-0	1-0	—	Beardsley [15]	1592
8	6	A	Oxford U	D	1-1	0-0	8	Seddon [90]	4499
9	13	H	York C	W	4-2	2-1	3	Christie 2 [20, 65], Seddon 2 (1 pen) [43, 54 (p)]	2017
10	20	A	Barrow	W	4-2	1-0	2	Westcarr [12], Seddon 2 [56, 63], Marna [86]	1596
11	22	H	Burton Alb	L	0-1	0-0	—		1616
12	27	A	Crawley T	L	0-1	0-1	6		2207
13	Oct 4	H	Northwich Vic	W	2-1	0-0	3	Beardsley [72], Westcarr [81]	1401
14	7	A	Eastbourne Bor	W	2-1	1-0	—	Marna [39], Westcarr [50]	1035
15	11	A	Salisbury C	W	2-1	0-1	2	Dempster [76], Christie [90]	1191
16	18	H	Kidderminster H	W	1-0	0-0	1	Dempster [83]	2010
17	Nov 1	H	Weymouth	L	0-1	0-0	1		1607
18	15	A	Histon	L	0-1	0-0	5		2716
19	23	A	Ebbsfleet U	D	0-0	0-0	6		1018
20	Dec 6	A	Wrexham	L	1-2	1-0	9	Christie [42]	3687
21	20	A	Forest Green R	W	2-0	2-0	9	Potter A [29], Seddon (pen) [32]	923
22	26	H	Mansfield T	L	1-3	1-1	9	Christie (pen) [33]	2433
23	Jan 1	H	Salisbury C	W	1-0	0-0	9	Dempster [90]	1541
24	27	A	Stevenage Bor	L	1-2	1-0	—	Lee [45]	1880
25	Feb 14	A	Woking	W	1-0	1-0	—	Marna [20]	1414
26	17	A	Mansfield T	D	0-0	0-0	—		2355
27	21	H	Torquay U	W	2-1	2-1	10	Marna [9], Seddon (pen) [12]	1869
28	24	A	Northwich Vic	D	0-0	0-0	—		479
29	Mar 3	H	Altrincham	W	3-1	1-0	—	Marna 2 [10, 75], Solkhon [90]	1036
30	7	H	Histon	W	1-0	0-0	9	Seddon [54]	1870
31	10	H	Grays Ath	D	0-0	0-0	—		1117
32	14	H	Eastbourne Bor	L	0-1	0-0	10		1415
33	17	H	Lewes	W	1-0	1-0	—	Marna [24]	867
34	19	H	Oxford U	L	1-2	0-2	—	Marna [77]	1716
35	21	A	Weymouth	W	2-0	0-0	9	Seddon [53], Lorougnon [81]	913
36	24	A	York C	D	0-0	0-0	—		1714
37	28	H	Ebbsfleet U	W	2-1	1-1	8	Wright 2 [22, 55]	1533
38	31	A	Burton Alb	D	1-1	1-1	—	Seddon [20]	2624
39	Apr 4	A	Torquay U	L	0-2	0-1	8		2503
40	7	H	Barrow	D	0-0	0-0	—		976
41	11	A	Rushden & D	L	0-1	0-0	9		3406
42	13	H	Cambridge U	L	1-2	0-1	9	Seddon [90]	2340
43	15	H	Crawley T	D	1-1	0-1	—	Marna [64]	961
44	18	H	Wrexham	W	1-0	1-0	8	Charles [3]	1497
45	21	A	Lewes	W	2-1	1-0	—	Seddon 2 [6, 64]	343
46	26	A	Kidderminster H	W	1-0	0-0	8	Wright [90]	2896

Final League Position: 8

GOALSCORERS

League (50): Seddon 15 (4 pens), Marna 9, Christie 5 (1 pen), Dempster 5, Beardsley 4, Westcarr 4, Wright 3, Charles 1, Lee 1, Lorougnon 1, Potter A 1, Solkhon 1.
FA Cup (13): Westcarr 4 (1 pen), Seddon 3, Solkhon 2, Christie 1, Dempster 1, Geohaghan 1, Potter A 1.

Harper 46	Dempster 27 + 9	Jaszczun 22	Wrack 31 + 5	Branston 39	Geohaghan 44	Potter A 29 + 9	Solkhon 21 + 16	Beardsley 14 + 23	Seddon 34 + 6	Warlow 3 + 1	Taylor — + 2	Marna 20 + 19	Boucaud 40 + 2	Graham 11 + 6	Eaden 20	Westcarr 33 + 6	Christie 11 + 2	Lee 2 + 6	Arther 1 + 3	Smith — + 1	Rawle 1	Bennett 16 + 1	Branam-Barrett 2	Artus 5	Potter L 22	Lorougnon — + 4	Wright 6 + 5	Charles 6 + 3	Match No.
1	2	3	4	5	6	7^1	8	9^2	10^3	11	12	13	14																1
1	2	3	4	5	6	7	8^1		10	11^2	13	9	12																2
1	2	3^1	4	5	6	7	8	14	10^3	13		9	11^2	12															3
1	12	3	4	5	6^1	7	8	9^3	10			14	11^2				2	13											4
1	2	3	4	5	6	7		13	10^2	11^1		12	8^3	14		9													5
1	12	3	4	5	6	7^1	13	9	10^3			14	8^2		2	11													6
1	12	3	4	5	6	7^1	13	9^3	10			14	8^2		2	11													7
1		3	4	5	6	7^2	13	12	10			14	8^3		2	9	11^1												8
1	12	3	4	5	6^1	7^2	13	14	10				8		2	11	9^3												9
1	12	3	4	5	6		8	13	10^3			14	7^1		2	11	9^2												10
1		3	4	5	6	12	8	14	10^3			13	7^1		2	11^2	9■												11
1	12	3	4	5	6■	13	8	14	10^3			9	7		2^1	11^2													12
1	6	3	4	5		7^1	12	9	10^2			13	8^3		2	11		14											13
1	7	3	4	5	6		13	9^3	10			14	8^2		2^1	11		12											14
1	2	3■	4	5	6	12		9^3	13			14	8			7^1	11^2	10											15
1	2	3	4	5	6	7	14	9^1	12			13	8^3			11^2	10												16
1	2	3	4	5■	6	7^1	13		10			11	8^2			12	9												17
1	2	3	4		6	7	12		10			13	8	5^1		14	9^2		11^3										18
1	2	3	4	5	6	7^2	8	9^1	12							11	10^3	13	14										19
1	2^3	3	13	5	6	7	8		12				4			11	9^2		10^1	14									20
1		3	4	5	6	7^3	8		10^1			13			2^2	11	12		14		9								21
1	14	3	4	5	6	7^1	8					12	11^2		10	9		13				2^3							22
1	6		4	5			8					7	11		2	10^1	12	9							3				23
1	5			6	14	13	12	10^1				4	11^3			7	9					2			3		8^2		24
1		12	5	6		7	14	13				9^2	4^1	11		10						2		8^3	3				25
1		12	5	6		7	14	13				9^2	4	11		10						2		8^3	3				26
1	12	13	5	6		14		8				9^2	4	11		10						2^1		7^3	3				27
1	2		4	5	6	7^1	8		10^3			12		13	9		14								3	11^2			28
1	2	14	5	6		12	8	13	10^2			7^3	4	11^1		9									3				29
1	2	7^1	5	6		14	8	13	10^2			9^3	4			11	12								3				30
1	5	7^2		6			8	14	10^3			9^1	4	12		11	13					2			3				31
1	5			6		13	8	9^2	10^3			4	7^1			11	14					2			3	12			32
1	5	4		6	7			12	10^1			9^2	8	11^3		13						2			3	14			33
1	5	4^1		6	7	8	13	12				9^2	11			10■						2			3				34
1	5	4		6	7	8	13	10^2								11^1						2			3	12	9		35
1	12	4		5	6	7^1			14			10^2	11									2			3		13	9^3	36
1			4	5	6	7^3	13	14	10			11	8^2									2			3		9^1	12	37
1			4^1	5	6	7^3	12	14	10			13	8									2			3		9	11^2	38
1	4			5	6		8^1	14	10			12	7				13					2			3		9^2	11^3	39
1	4			5	6	7^3		13	10^2			11	8		2	9									3		12	14	40
1	4			5	6	7^3		9^2	12			10	8		2	11									3		13	14	41
1				5	6		8	13	7			14	4	11^2		12						2			3		9^1	10^3	42
1	4			5	6	7^1	12	13	10^2			9	8		2	11									3				43
1	4^1			5	6				10			8	12		2	7									3		13	11^2	44
1				5	6	13		9	8			10^1	4		2	11^2									3		12	7	45
1				5	6	12		9	8			10^1	4	14	2	11^3									3		13	7^2	46

FA Cup

Fourth Qualifying Round		Burton Alb	(h)	3-0	Third Round	Eastwood T	(h)	2-1
First Round	Lincoln C	(h)	1-1		Fourth Round	Fulham	(h)	2-4
		(a)	2-1			
Second Round	Notts Co	(a)	1-1			
		(h)	2-1			

KIDDERMINSTER HARRIERS Blue Square Premier

Ground: Aggborough Stadium, Hoo Road, Kidderminster DY10 1NB. *Tel:* (01562) 823 951. *Year Formed:* 1886.
Record Gate: 9,155 (1948 v Hereford U). *Nickname:* Harriers. *Manager:* Mark Yates. *Secretary:* Roger Barlow.
Colours: Red shirts, white shorts, red stockings.

KIDDERMINSTER HARRIERS 2008–09 LEAGUE RECORD

Match No.	Date	Venue	Opponents	Result		H/T Score	Lg. Pos.	Goalscorers	Atten- dance
1	Aug 9	H	Lewes	D	1-1	1-1	—	Richards [22]	1503
2	12	A	Cambridge U	L	1-2	0-1	—	Richards [90]	3008
3	16	A	Mansfield T	L	2-4	0-3	21	Barnes-Homer [69], Richards [80]	2479
4	23	H	Altrincham	W	4-0	2-0	14	Creighton [6], Richards (pen) [34], Brittain [70], Smikle [84]	1335
5	25	A	Burton Alb	D	2-2	0-1	16	Barnes-Homer [76], Jones [81]	1798
6	30	H	Rushden & D	W	2-1	1-1	14	Penn 2 [14, 79]	1524
7	Sept 4	H	Torquay U	W	1-0	1-0	—	Barnes-Homer [44]	1345
8	7	A	Grays Ath	L	2-3	0-0	14	Richards [59], Barnes-Homer [89]	525
9	13	A	Oxford U	W	1-0	1-0	9	Barnes-Homer [22]	2065
10	20	A	Weymouth	W	2-1	1-1	7	Richards [22], Knights [90]	1014
11	23	H	York C	W	2-0	0-0	—	Smikle [63], Richards [90]	1481
12	27	A	Eastbourne Bor	W	3-2	2-0	2	Richards [14], Smikle [37], Ferrell [62]	1248
13	Oct 4	H	Barrow	L	0-1	0-1	4		1686
14	7	A	Northwich Vic	D	1-1	0-0	—	Smikle [47]	725
15	11	H	Ebbsfleet U	W	3-1	1-0	4	MacKenzie [63], Smikle [68], Barnes-Homer [74]	1512
16	18	A	Kettering T	L	0-1	0-0	7		2010
17	Nov 1	H	Grays Ath	W	2-0	1-0	6	Richards [40], Barnes-Homer [59]	1400
18	15	A	Rushden & D	W	1-0	1-0	4	Richards (pen) [42]	1391
19	22	H	Wrexham	W	1-0	1-0	—	Smikle [26]	2403
20	25	A	Oxford U	L	0-1	0-1	—		3690
21	Dec 6	H	Salisbury C	W	3-2	2-1	4	Bass (og) [10], Barnes-Homer [30], Bartlett (og) [54]	1325
22	9	H	Mansfield T	W	2-0	0-0	—	Lowe [73], Richards [85]	1266
23	20	A	Crawley T	L	0-2	0-1	4		1022
24	26	H	Forest Green R	D	1-1	0-1	4	Reilly [45]	2102
25	28	A	Torquay U	W	1-0	0-0	3	Reilly [73]	2749
26	Jan 17	H	Weymouth	L	0-2	0-1	6		1569
27	24	A	Barrow	L	0-1	0-0	7		1532
28	27	H	Histon	W	2-0	1-0	—	Barnes-Homer 2 [18, 90]	1277
29	Feb 15	A	Northwich Vic	L	1-2	1-1	—	Barnes-Homer [10]	1410
30	17	H	Cambridge U	L	1-3	1-2	—	Barnes-Homer [38]	1361
31	28	H	Eastbourne Bor	W	2-0	2-0	7	Barnes-Homer 2 [21, 24]	1430
32	Mar 7	H	Salisbury C	D	0-0	0-0	10		1105
33	10	H	Crawley T	W	2-0	1-0	—	Lowe [28], Richards [63]	1211
34	14	A	Lewes	W	1-0	1-0	6	Richards [19]	385
35	21	H	Woking	W	3-0	1-0	6	Reilly [45], Richards [68], McPhee [90]	1594
36	23	A	Wrexham	W	1-0	0-0	—	McPhee [90]	2674
37	28	A	York C	D	0-0	0-0	5		2384
38	Apr 1	A	Woking	W	5-1	4-0	—	Lowe [18], Barnes-Homer 2 [28, 39], McPhee [45], Smikle [72]	751
39	4	H	Stevenage Bor	W	4-2	1-2	5	Barnes-Homer [44], Penn [49], Richards [58], Brittain [61]	2115
40	7	A	Forest Green R	D	2-2	1-1	—	Brittain [30], Moore [88]	970
41	9	A	Ebbsfleet U	D	1-1	0-1	—	Barnes-Homer [83]	979
42	11	A	Altrincham	D	2-2	0-1	4	Brittain [49], Barnes-Homer [73]	1142
43	13	H	Burton Alb	W	2-1	0-1	4	Barnes-Homer [68], Smikle [80]	3025
44	18	H	Histon	D	1-1	1-1	5	Lowe [29]	1718
45	21	A	Stevenage Bor	L	1-3	1-1	—	Richards [45]	2530
46	26	H	Kettering T	L	0-1	0-0	6		2896

Final League Position: 6

GOALSCORERS

League (69): Barnes-Homer 20, Richards 16 (2 pens), Smikle 8, Brittain 4, Lowe 4, McPhee 3, Penn 3, Reilly 3, Creighton 1, Ferrell 1, Jones 1, Knights 1, MacKenzie 1, Moore 1, own goals 2.
FA Cup (8): Richards 2 (1 pen), Barnes-Homer 1, Brittain 1, Creighton 1, Moore 1, Penn 1, Smikle 1.

Bartlett 46	Bowler 3	Baker 36 + 1	Ferrell 28 + 3	Creighton 43 + 1	Jones 23 + 8	Bennett 25 + 12	Penn 38 + 4	Russell 3	Knights 21 + 16	Richards 38 + 1	Brittain 30 + 12	McDermott 6 + 17	Barnes-Homer 41 + 5	Bignot 2 + 1	Lowe 43	Smikle 22 + 19	McGrath — + 1	MacKenzie 2 + 2	Moore 5 + 12	Reilly 26	Beardsley — + 3	Armstrong 7	Carr 2 + 6	McPhee 16	Match No.
1	2[1]	3	4	5	6	7	8	9[3]	10[2]	11	12	13	14												1
1	2		4	5	6	14	8[3]	7[1]	11[2]	9	13	12	10	3											2
1	2[1]		4	5	6	7	8	9[2]	11[3]	10	13	14	12	3											3
1		3	4	5	6		8		14	9	7[1]	11[2]	10[3]		2	12	13								4
1		3[1]	4	5	6	13	8		12	9	7[2]	11[3]	10		2	14									5
1		3	4	5	6	12	8		10		11[2]	13	9[1]		2	7									6
1		3	4[1]	5	6	12	8		10		11[2]	13	9		2	7									7
1		3[1]	4	5	6	12	8		13	9	11[2]		10		2	7									8
1		3	4	5	6	12	8		13	10	11[1]		9[2]		2	7									9
1		3	4	5	6		8		13	10	11[1]	12	9		2	7[2]									10
1		3	4	5	6		8			10	11[1]	12	9		2	7									11
1		3	4	5	6	13	8		12	10	11[3]		9[1]		2	7[2]			14						12
1		3[1]	4	5	6		8		13	10	11[2]	12	9		2	7[3]			14						13
1		3	4	5	6	12	8		13	10[2]	11[1]		9		2	7									14
1		3	13	5	6	12	8[1]		10[3]		11		9		2	7		4[2]	14						15
1		3	12	5	6		8		14		11[2]	13	9		2	7		4[3]	10[1]						16
1		3[1]	4	5		12	8		14	10[2]	11		9[3]		2	7			13	6					17
1		3	4	5	12	14	8[2]		13	10	11[3]		9[1]		2	7				6					18
1		3	4	5		13	8		12	10[1]	11[2]		9		2	7				6					19
1		3	4	5			8		13	10[2]	11	12			2	7[1]			9	6					20
1		3	4	5	14		8			10[2]	11[1]	12	9		2	7[3]				6	13				21
1		3	12	5	4[1]		8		13	10	11		9[3]		2	7[2]				6	14				22
1			4	5[6]	6	12	8		13	10	11		9[3]		2	7[2]			14	3					23
1		3[3]	4		6		8		14	10	11[2]	12	9		2	7[1]			13	5					24
1		3	7	5	13	4	8			10[2]	11[1]		9[3]		2	12				6	14				25
1		3[2]	4	5			8		14	10	11	13	12		2	7[1]			9[3]	6					26
1			4	5	7		8[1]		13	10	11	12	9[2]		2					6		3			27
1			4	5	7		8[2]		13	10	11		9[1]		2	12				6		3			28
1			4[3]	5	6	12			11	10	7		9[2]		2	13			14			3	8[1]		29
1		14	4	5	6		8		13	10	11[1]	12	9		2	7[2]						3[3]			30
1				5	4	12				10[1]	11[2]	8[3]	9		2	14				6	3[1]		13	7	31
1		3		5	4	14			11[1]	10[2]	7[3]	12	9		2	13				6				8	32
1		3		5	4	8[2]			11[1]	10[3]			9		2	12			13	6			14	7	33
1		3		5	4	8[3]			11[2]	10	14		9[1]		2	13			12	6				7	34
1		3		5	4[2]	8			11[1]	10[3]	13		9		2	12			14	6				7	35
1		3		5	4	8[3]			11[1]	10	12		9[2]		2	13				6			14	7	36
1				5	4	8[2]			11[1]	10	12		9		2	13				6		3		7	37
1		3	4	5	6	8[2]			11	10[1]			9[3]		2	14			12				13	7	38
1		3		5	4[3]	8			11[1]	10	12		9[2]		2	13				6			14	7	39
1		3[3]	13	5	4	8[2]			10[4]		11[1]		9		2	12			14	6				7	40
1		3[8]	4[2]	5	6	12			11[1]		14		9		2	13			10				8[3]	7	41
1			4	13	6		8			10[3]	11	12			2				9[1]	5[2]	3		14	7	42
1		3	4[1]	5	14	11	8[3]			10[2]		12	9		2	13				6				7	43
1		3	4	5[1]	12		8				11[2]		9		2	13				6				7	44
1		3		5	4	8[1]			13	10	11		9[3]		2[2]	12			14	6				7	45
1		3[3]		5	4	12			11[2]	10	13	8[1]	9		2	14				6				7	46

FA Cup
Fourth Qualifying Round

Fourth Qualifying Round	Kings Lynn	(a)	5-1
First Round	Cambridge U	(h)	1-0
Second Round	Curzon Ashton	(h)	2-0
Third Round	Coventry C	(a)	0-2

LEWES

Blue Square South

Ground: The Dripping Pan, Mountfield Road, Lewes, East Sussex BN7 2XD. *Tel:* (01273) 472 100.
Year Formed: 1885. *Record Gate:* 2,500 (1947 v Newhaven, Sussex County League). *Nickname:* The Rooks.
Manager: Steve Ibbitson. *Secretary:* Carole Bailey. *Colours:* Red and black striped shirts, black shorts, black stockings.

LEWES 2008–09 LEAGUE RECORD

Match No.	Date	Venue	Opponents	Result		H/T Score	Lg. Pos.	Goalscorers	Attendance
1	Aug 9	A	Kidderminster H	D	1-1	1-1	—	Bennett (og) [43]	1503
2	12	H	Crawley T	L	0-3	0-2	—		1280
3	16	H	Salisbury C	L	1-4	1-2	22	Fenelon [24]	564
4	23	A	Weymouth	L	0-2	0-1	22		1172
5	25	H	Ebbsfleet U	D	0-0	0-0	22		851
6	30	A	Burton Alb	L	2-5	2-2	23	Taylor [16], Standing (pen) [19]	1432
7	Sept 2	A	Woking	D	1-1	1-0	—	Taylor [23]	1604
8	6	H	Barrow	L	0-3	0-2	22		679
9	11	H	Rushden & D	L	0-4	0-0	—		636
10	20	A	Altrincham	L	0-1	0-0	24		827
11	23	A	Histon	D	1-1	1-0	—	Gargan [2]	592
12	27	H	Oxford U	W	2-1	0-0	23	Standing [79], Gargan [88]	1156
13	Oct 4	A	Grays Ath	D	0-0	0-0	23		729
14	7	A	Cambridge U	L	0-1	0-0	—		3194
15	11	H	Forest Green R	W	3-2	3-0	23	Keehan 2 [35, 38], Gargan [43]	666
16	18	H	Northwich Vic	L	2-3	1-2	24	Taylor [36], Roberts (og) [90]	669
17	Nov 1	A	Wrexham	L	0-2	0-1	24		3201
18	15	H	Burton Alb	L	0-1	0-1	24		630
19	18	A	Torquay U	L	1-4	0-3	—	Taylor [52]	2118
20	22	H	Grays Ath	W	2-0	2-0	24	Taylor [4], Standing (pen) [35]	519
21	Dec 6	H	Stevenage Bor	L	0-2	0-0	24		486
22	9	A	Salisbury C	W	2-1	2-0	—	Fenelon [32], Tabiri [42]	579
23	20	H	Woking	L	0-2	0-1	23		694
24	26	A	Eastbourne Bor	L	0-1	0-1	23		2216
25	Jan 1	H	Eastbourne Bor	L	0-2	0-0	23		2232
26	3	A	Stevenage Bor	L	0-3	0-2	—		1764
27	17	A	York C	L	0-3	0-0	23		2073
28	24	H	Mansfield T	L	0-1	0-1	23		598
29	27	H	Torquay U	L	0-2	0-1	—		558
30	Feb 1	A	Oxford U	L	1-2	1-1	—	Keehan [11]	4595
31	7	H	Wrexham	L	0-2	0-0	—		689
32	21	H	Cambridge U	L	0-2	0-0	24		962
33	24	A	Crawley T	L	1-5	0-4	—	Keehan [51]	600
34	28	H	Histon	L	0-3	0-1	24		345
35	Mar 7	A	Mansfield T	L	0-1	0-0	24		2434
36	10	A	Rushden & D	L	1-2	1-1	—	Henry [6]	918
37	14	H	Kidderminster H	L	0-1	0-1	24		385
38	17	A	Kettering T	L	0-1	0-1	—		867
39	21	A	Barrow	L	0-2	0-1	24		1390
40	28	A	Forest Green R	L	1-4	1-2	24	Keehan [5]	898
41	Apr 4	H	Altrincham	W	2-0	2-0	24	Wheeler [25], Keehan [41]	337
42	11	H	Weymouth	W	1-0	0-0	24	Breach [70]	456
43	13	A	Ebbsfleet U	L	1-2	1-1	24	Jirbandey [41]	1098
44	18	A	Northwich Vic	L	0-3	0-1	24		487
45	21	H	Kettering T	L	1-2	0-1	—	Keehan (pen) [71]	343
46	26	H	York C	D	1-1	0-0	24	Keehan [87]	802

Final League Position: 24

GOALSCORERS

League (28): Keehan 8 (1 pen), Taylor 5, Gargan 3, Standing 3 (2 pens), Fenelon 2, Breach 1, Henry 1, Jirbandey 1, Tabiri 1, Wheeler 1, own goals 2.
FA Cup (2): Cox 1, Wheeler 1.

Banks 44	Breach 38	Richards 6+1	Charles 5	Geard 4+2	Barness 43	Fisk 16	Graves 4+1	Keehan 44	Wilkinson S 8	Standing 35+1	Taylor 19	Fraser 4	Wallis-Taylor 22+2	Fenelon 8+9	Hall 4+1	Rowland 9+4	Cullip 33	Cox 18+17	Butters 7	Davis 2	Elliott 4+5	Henry 4+3	Beda 1	Baidoo 2+3	Sutton —+8	Lyons 1+2	Mayo 6	Storrie 6+3	Sackey 1+3	Wheeler 15+4	Jirhandy 5	Gargan 8	Wilkinson A 4+2	Thomas 14	Ruddy 2+1	Compton 3	Rooney 6	Hinshelwood 4	Tabiri 9	Osborne —+2	Bell —+3	Clark —+1	Rivers 10+6	Foreman 10+9	Klein-Davies 8+1	Pearson 2	Liburd —+2	Banks-Smith 1	Greaves —+1	Timms 2	St Aimie 5	Match No.
1	2	3	4	5	6	7	8	9	10^1	11	12																																									1
1	2	3	4^1	5	6	7	8	9	10^2	11	13		12																																						2
1	2	3		5	6	7	8	9	10	11			4																																						3
1	2	3		5		7	8	9	10^1	11	6		4	12																																					4
1	2		4^1	5		7	8	9^2	3	10	12		6	13	11																																				5
1	2^1		4^2	5	12	7	8	9	11	10	13		6	14	3^3																																				6
1		3		5	6	7	8	9		11			2		10		4																																		7
1		3^1		5		7	8	9		11			2	6	12		4	10^2						13																											8
1	2		12	5		7	8	9						6^1	11	4	13	10^2			3																														9
1	2			5		7	8	9		11				6^1	12	4	13	10^2			3																														10
1	2		12	5		7	8	9	3	11			$4^\bullet$			6		10^1																																	11
1	2			5		7^2	8	9^3		11^1	6			12	14	13	4	10																																	12
1^G	2			5		7	8	9^2		11^1	4			12	13	3	10	6	15																																13
1	2			5		7	8^1	14	12	13	4		11^3	6		3^2	10	9																																	14
1	2			5		7		9^1	13	12	3		11^3	14		10	6	1	8^2																																15
1	2^2			5		7	8^1	9			12		6	4		13	10	3	11																																16
1	2^1	13		5		7			10		9		11^3	14		3^2	8	4	$6^\bullet$	12																															17
1	2			5		7	8	9	11	12	10^2		4	13		6^1	3																																	18
1	2			5		7	8	9	11	12	4		13			6^1	3	10^2																																	19
1				5		7	8^1	9^3	11	13	4		14			12	6						2	10																											20
1	2^3			5		7	8	11^2	12	4	13		14			10^1	3	6	9																																21
1	2			5		7	8	11	10^2	4	12						3	6	9^1	13																																22
1	2			5		7	8	11	9	4	13		12				3	10^1	6^2																																23
1	2			5		7	8^1	11	9^2	4	12					6	3	10	13																																24
1	2			5		7		11	4	12						6	3	10			8^1	9																														25
1	2			5		7^3		3	10^1	4^2	11		13			8	$9^\bullet$	6	12	14																																26
1	2		9^2	5		7		11^1		4	12					6	10	3																							13			8								27
1	2	11		5	3		8	6	9^2	12	4															13														10									7^1		28
1	2	11		5	6	7	8^2	3		4	12															13														10									9^1		29
1	8^1	10		5	2	7		$3^\bullet$		4	11					6																							12										9		30
1	2	10		5	11	7	8^2			4	3^1					6											13												12										9		31
1	2			5	11	7	8^1			4	6	3									12																			10	9										32
1	2			5		7	12		11	4	3	6																		10										13	8^1	9^2									33
1	2				11	7	8^2	3		4	10^1	5										12											6								13		9								34
1				2	11	7	8	3		4	12	5								9												6^2								13	10^1										35
1	2^1			6	3	7	8	11		4	12	5								10																					9											36
1	2^1			5	3	7		11		4	9^3	6								10^2	13									8										14	12										37
1	2			5	7^3	8		3		4	9^2									10^1					13	12							14								11	6									38
1	2			5	3^2	7		11		4	9^1									13					14	6							12								10^3	8									39
1				$5^\bullet$		7	8	11			$9^\bullet$									12	4		2		3^1			10^2							13	6^3	14													40
1	5				3	7	8^2			4									12	9	6	2				10							11^{11}	13																	41
1	2			5	3	7	8			11									12	13	6				10							9^2							4^1											42
1	4^2			5	3	7^1	8			13									14	11	6	2				10							12	9^3																43
1					3		8	4		10								12	6	2	7					13							11^1	9^2									5							44
1				5		7	8^2			4									12	6^3	2	3				9		14					11	13																45
1				5	2	7	8^1			4									14	11^2	13					3^3		10					9	12									6							46

FA Cup
Fourth Qualifying Round
        Leiston   (a)   1-1
                             (h)   1-3

MANSFIELD TOWN

Blue Square Premier

Ground: Field Mill Ground, Quarry Lane, Mansfield, Notts NG18 5DA. *Tel:* (01623) 482 482. *Year Formed:* 1897.
Record Gate: 24,467 (1953 v Nottingham F, FA Cup 3rd rd). *Nickname:* The Stags. *Manager:* David Holdsworth.
Colours: Yellow shirts, blue shorts, blue stockings.

MANSFIELD TOWN 2008–09 LEAGUE RECORD

Match No.	Date	Venue	Opponents	Result	H/T Score	Lg. Pos.	Goalscorers	Atten- dance
1	Aug 9	A	Ebbsfleet U	D	2-2	0-2	—	Blackwood [63], Lee [89]	1872
2	12	H	Histon	W	1-0	1-0	—	Lee [16]	2703
3	16	H	Kidderminster H	W	4-2	3-0	2	Stallard 2 (1 pen) [20 (p), 45], Blackwood [32], O'Connor [90]	2479
4	23	A	Barrow	L	1-2	1-1	9	Lee [41]	2063
5	25	H	Northwich Vic	W	3-2	2-0	5	O'Connor 2 [25, 29], Stallard [90]	2741
6	30	H	Grays Ath	W	1-0	1-0	2	Stallard (pen) [25]	2378
7	Sept 2	A	York C	D	1-1	0-1	—	Blackwood [52]	2520
8	6	H	Eastbourne Bor	W	3-1	2-0	1	Stallard [13], Arnold [41], Somner [88]	2536
9	13	A	Crawley T	L	1-2	0-1	4	Silk [79]	2013
10	20	H	Cambridge U	D	1-1	0-1	4	O'Hare [51]	3171
11	23	A	Altrincham	L	0-1	0-1	—		1005
12	27	A	Salisbury C	W	3-2	0-1	3	Bass (og) [60], Stallard [63], O'Connor [70]	1494
13	Oct 4	H	Woking	L	0-1	0-0	7		2563
14	7	A	Stevenage Bor	L	2-3	0-1	—	Hurren [56], O'Connor [59]	1517
15	13	A	Burton Alb	L	0-1	0-1	—		2871
16	18	H	Wrexham	L	1-2	1-1	14	Sinclair [29]	2757
17	Nov 1	A	Torquay U	L	0-2	0-0	19		2267
18	15	H	Salisbury C	W	3-0	2-0	19	Sinclair [19], Ahmed (pen) [36], Stallard [89]	1921
19	22	A	Forest Green R	L	0-1	0-1	19		872
20	29	A	Weymouth	D	1-1	1-1	18	Sinclair [42]	931
21	Dec 4	H	Oxford U	L	1-3	1-1	—	Arnold [21]	1553
22	9	H	Kidderminster H	L	0-2	0-0	—		1266
23	20	H	Weymouth	W	2-1	0-1	19	Ahmed [58], D'Laryea [90]	1841
24	26	A	Kettering T	W	3-1	1-1	18	Sinclair [26], O'Connor [80], Arnold [86]	2433
25	29	H	Burton Alb	L	0-2	0-2	—		3612
26	Jan 17	H	Crawley T	W	1-0	1-0	17	Duffy [29]	2414
27	24	A	Lewes	W	1-0	1-0	15	Mayo [22]	598
28	27	H	Rushden & D	D	0-0	0-0	—		2028
29	31	A	Eastbourne Bor	W	2-1	1-1	—	D'Laryea [45], Garner [79]	1420
30	Feb 7	H	York C	W	1-0	1-0	—	Duffy (pen) [42]	2576
31	17	H	Kettering T	D	0-0	0-0	—		2355
32	21	A	Oxford U	L	0-1	0-1	15		4618
33	28	A	Rushden & D	W	1-0	0-0	12	Duffy (pen) [90]	1774
34	Mar 7	H	Lewes	W	1-0	0-0	12	Arnold [70]	2434
35	10	A	Cambridge U	L	1-2	1-0	12	Duffy [34]	2781
36	14	H	Forest Green R	W	3-0	1-0	12	Stallard [10], Duffy (pen) [63], Garner [80]	2174
37	21	A	Grays Ath	L	1-2	0-0	12	Clare [73]	802
38	28	H	Torquay U	D	1-1	1-0	13	Duffy [36]	2437
39	31	A	Histon	L	0-3	0-2	—		914
40	Apr 4	A	Wrexham	L	0-2	0-2	14		2401
41	7	H	Ebbsfleet U	W	2-0	1-0	—	Briscoe [22], Duffy [47]	1630
42	11	H	Barrow	D	2-2	0-0	13	Williams [47], O'Connor [79]	2122
43	13	A	Northwich Vic	L	0-2	0-1	13		858
44	18	A	Woking	D	2-2	1-1	13	Duffy 2 [41, 80]	2096
45	21	H	Altrincham	W	2-0	1-0	—	Garner [29], Arnold [52]	1682
46	26	H	Stevenage Bor	W	2-1	0-0	12	Garner [71], O'Connor [88]	3614

Final League Position: 12

GOALSCORERS

League (57): Duffy 9 (3 pens), O'Connor 8, Stallard 8 (2 pens), Arnold 5, Garner 4, Sinclair 4, Blackwood 3, Lee 3, Ahmed 2 (1 pen), D'Laryea 2, Briscoe 1, Clare 1, Hurren 1, Mayo 1, O'Hare 1, Silk 1, Somner 1, Williams 1, own goal 1.
FA Cup (2): Arnold 1, Hurren 1.

Gamble 24	Silk 40+1	Jeannin 25+1	D'Laryea 39+2	Moses 42	O'Hare 24+1	O'Connor 21+18	Somner 33+2	Stallard 18+10	Blackwood 20+5	Arnold 38+4	Lee 13+8	Hurren 9+5	Ryan —+1	Robinson 1+12	Chanot 5	Wedgbury 1	Sinclair 9+1	Ahmed 9	Annerson 1	Kay 4+1	Marriott 18	Garner 12	Duffy 20+1	Briscoe 10+8	Aneobi 1+4	Mayo 12	Woodhouse 11+1	Howell —+2	MacKenzie 3+5	Gardner 11+3	Williams 12+2	Clare 4+5	Havern 4	Hotchkiss 6	White 3+1	Higginson —+1	Shaw 2+1	Naylor 1	Match No.
1	2	3	4	5	6	7^1	8	9	10	11	12																												1
1	2	3	4	5	6	12	8	9^1	11	7	10																												2
1	2	3	4	5	6	12	8	9^1	11	7	10^2			13																									3
1	2	3	4	5	6	13	8	9^2	11^1	7	10^3	12		14																									4
1	2	3	4	5	6	7^1	8	9		10		11		12																									5
1	2	3	4	5	6		8	9	11	7	10^1	12																											6
1	2	3	4	5	6	7^1	8	9	10	11		12																											7
1	2	3	4	5	6	7^1	8	9^2	10^1	11		12		13																									8
1	2	3	4	5	6	12	8	9	10	11				7^1																									9
1	2	3	4	5	6		8	9	7	11^1	10																												10
1	2	3^1	4	5	6		8	9	11	7	10^2	12		13																									11
1	2	3	12	5^1	6	7^3	8	9^2	10	11	13	4		14																									12
1	2	3^1	13		6	7^3	8	9	10	11	12	4^2		14	5																								13
1	2	3^1	4		6	7	12	9^2	10	11^3	13	8		14	5^1																								14
1	2	12	4	5	6	7^3	8^1	13	3	11	9^2	10		14																									15
1	2	3	4	5				9^2	10	11	13	12		14	6^3	7^1	8																						16
1	2	3	4	5		7	8	13		11	9^2				6		12	10^1																					17
1	2	3	4	5	6	14	8	12	7	9^1	13						10^3	11^2																					18
1	2	3	4	5	6	13	8^1	12	11	9^2							10	7																					19
1	2	3	4	5	6	12	8	13	9^2	10							11^1	7																					20
1	2	3	4	5	6	12	8	13	11	9^2							10	7^1																					21
	2	3	4	5^1	6	13	12		10^2					9	8		11	7	1																				22
1	2	11	4		6		9^2		12	8	13	5					10	7			3^1																		23
1	2	11	4	5			9			8	12	6					10^1	7			3																		24
1	2	11	4	5			9		13	8	12	6					10^1	7			3^2																		25
	2	3^1	4	5			10	8	14		7^2									12	1	6	9^3	11		13													26
	2		4	5			10^2	8	13	11											1	6	9	11^1		12	3	7											27
	2		4	5			10^2	8		11											1	6	9	7^3	12	3^1			14	13									28
	2		4	5			12	8		11										3^1	1	7	9^3	13	10	10^2	6	14											29
			4	5			7^2	8		11^1											1	2^1	9	12	14	3	10		13	6^3									30
	12		4	5	6		8	13	14	7^2											1		9	11		3	10^3	2^1											31
	2		4	5			12	8		13	7										1		9^2	11^1		3	10^2	14	6										32
	2		4	5			10^2	8	13	11^1	7^3										1		9			3	14	6	12										33
	2		4	5			10^2			11^1	7										1		9	13		3	8	6	12										34
	2		4	5			12	8	10^1	7^3											1	6	9^2	13		3	14	11											35
	2		4	5			14	8^1	10^2	7^1											1	6	9^3	12		3	13	11											36
	2		4	5					10^2	7^1											1		9	12	3	8	14	6	11^3	13									37
	2		4	5				13		7^1											1		9^2	10	3	8	6	11	12										38
	2		4	5	3		10^1			7											1	6	9^2	12	8		11	13											39
		4	5				14^8			7											1		9^3	13	3	10^1	6	11^2	12	2									40
		5					12	8		13											1		9	7^2	4	6	11	10^1	2	3									41
		5					12	8		13											1^1		9^1	7	4	6	11^6	10^2	2	3	15								42
		5					9^2	8		13												6	12	7^1	4		11	10^3	2	3	1	14							43
	2		5	13	12					7												6	9^3	10^1		4^2	14	11			3	1					8		44
	2^2		6	10^1						7			14									4	9^3				13	11	12	3	1					8	5		45
	2	8^1	5				13		14	7											1	6	9^2				3	11	10^3	4						12			46

FA Cup

Fourth Qualifying Round   York C   (a)   0-0

                                          (h)   1-0

First Round   Chesterfield   (a)   1-3

NORTHWICH VICTORIA   Blue Square North

Ground: Victoria Stadium, Wincham Avenue, Northwich, Cheshire CW9 6GB.   *Tel:* (01606) 815 200.
Year Formed: 1874. *Record Gate:* 12,000 (1977 v Watford, FA Cup 4th rd).   *Nickname:* The Vics.
Manager: Andy Preece.   *Secretary:* Derek Nuttall.   *Colours:* Green and white hooped shirts, white shorts, white stockings.

NORTHWICH VICTORIA 2008–09 LEAGUE RECORD

Match No.	Date	Venue	Opponents	Result	H/T Score	Lg. Pos.	Goalscorers	Attendance
1	Aug 9	H	Cambridge U	L	0-1	0-1	—	1445
2	12	A	Burton Alb	D	1-1	1-0	—	Stamp [29]	1701
3	16	A	Grays Ath	L	1-2	0-1	20	Flynn [85]	523
4	23	H	York C	D	2-2	2-1	21	McGurk (og) [15], Allan [42]	1065
5	25	A	Mansfield T	L	2-3	0-2	21	Stamp [60], Steele [86]	2741
6	30	A	Crawley T	L	2-5	0-4	22	Steele [50], Mullan [54]	776
7	Sept 2	H	Oxford U	L	1-2	0-0	—	Stamp [50]	973
8	7	A	Torquay U	L	1-2	0-1	24	Steele [53]	1752
9	13	H	Forest Green R	D	0-0	0-0	23		603
10	20	A	Histon	L	1-2	1-1	23	Grand [19]	829
11	23	H	Barrow	W	2-1	0-1	—	Welch [47], Burns [85]	906
12	27	H	Weymouth	L	2-3	0-0	24	Roberts [60], Burns [74]	700
13	Oct 4	A	Kettering T	L	1-2	0-0	24	Byrom [53]	1401
14	7	H	Kidderminster H	D	1-1	0-0	—	Brown [90]	725
15	11	H	Grays Ath	W	2-0	0-0	24	Crowell [70], Stamp [85]	579
16	18	A	Lewes	W	3-2	2-1	22	Allan [8], Stamp [11], Williams (pen) [52]	669
17	Nov 1	H	Eastbourne Bor	L	1-2	0-1	22	Burns [54]	564
18	8	H	Burton Alb	L	0-1	0-1	—		932
19	15	A	Stevenage Bor	D	1-1	1-0	23	Stamp [28]	2536
20	22	A	Salisbury C	D	1-1	0-1	22	Winn [56]	999
21	29	H	Crawley T	L	0-1	0-0	22		610
22	Dec 6	A	Eastbourne Bor	L	1-4	1-2	23	Wagstaff [26]	1086
23	20	A	Rushden & D	L	1-2	1-0	24	Crowell [15]	1134
24	26	H	Altrincham	L	0-1	0-0	24		1400
25	Jan 17	H	Histon	L	1-2	1-0	24	Crowell [14]	428
26	24	A	Weymouth	L	0-3	0-3	24		1105
27	27	A	Wrexham	D	3-3	0-0	—	Bailey 2 [60, 86], Robinson [83]	3722
28	31	H	Woking	L	1-4	0-2	—	Bailey [56]	1092
29	Feb 3	A	Altrincham	L	0-1	0-1	—		1209
30	15	A	Kidderminster H	W	2-1	1-1	—	Reeves [30], McDonald [82]	1410
31	18	A	Forest Green R	L	0-3	0-2	—		744
32	24	H	Kettering T	D	0-0	0-0	—		479
33	28	A	Barrow	D	0-0	0-0	23		1437
34	Mar 7	H	Stevenage Bor	L	0-1	0-0	23		801
35	14	A	Cambridge U	L	1-4	1-3	23	Joyce [35]	2662
36	17	H	Wrexham	L	1-2	1-1	—	Perry [13]	1709
37	21	H	Torquay U	L	2-3	1-0	23	Perry [34], Allan [56]	705
38	28	H	Rushden & D	W	4-2	1-0	23	Byrom 3 [13, 57, 68], Joyce [71]	687
39	31	H	Salisbury C	D	1-1	1-0	—	Grand [23]	532
40	Apr 4	A	Ebbsfleet U	L	0-1	0-0	23		1003
41	7	H	Woking	W	2-0	1-0	—	Grand [25], Horrocks [78]	450
42	11	A	York C	W	2-1	1-0	23	Allan 2 [26, 90]	2421
43	13	H	Mansfield T	W	2-0	1-0	23	Grand [31], Elam [76]	858
44	18	H	Lewes	W	3-0	1-0	23	Grand [32], Allan 2 [78, 83]	487
45	23	H	Ebbsfleet U	W	2-0	0-0	—	Burns [61], Allan [83]	474
46	26	A	Oxford U	W	2-1	1-0	22	Mullan [45], Crowell [90]	10,298

Final League Position: 22

GOALSCORERS

League (56): Allan 8, Stamp 6, Grand 5, Burns 4, Byrom 4, Crowell 4, Bailey 3, Steele 3, Joyce 2, Mullan 2, Perry 2, Brown 1, Elam 1, Flynn 1, Horrocks 1, McDonald 1, Reeves 1, Roberts 1, Robinson 1, Wagstaff 1, Welch 1, Williams 1 (pen), Winn 1, own goal 1.
FA Cup (0).

Tynan 19	Clarke 22+1	Sutton 4	Brown 30+2	Welch 12+2	Roberts 20	Birch 1	Crowell 38+3	Mullan 18+14	Byrom 23+5	Steele 12+6	Stamp 15+11	Barrett 2+5	Allan 31+3	Price 2	Byrne 5+6	Flynn 11+6	Murray 5	Barnes —+1	Williams 8	Aspin 30+2	Bailey 20+6	Connett 1	Elam 21+1	Marsh M 1	Conroy 1+1	Marsh P —+5	Stevens 6+1	Carr 3+1	Almeida —+1	Grand 34	Reeves 7+2	King 1	Burns 18+6	McDonald 2	Benjamin —+2	Winn 9	Riley 1+5	Farran —+2	Whitley 2	Jones 4	Horrocks 8+4	Richards —+4	Perry 7	Yussuff 7	Wagstaff 5	Joyce 12	Antwi 5	Lodge 6+4	Meadowcroft 8+1	Robinson 9	Match No.
1	2	3	4	5	6¹	7	8	9³	10	11²	14	13	12																																						1
1	2	3	4	5	6²	7¹	8	9	10		13	12	11																																						2
1		3	4¹	5	6³	7	8	9	10		13	14				11²	2	12																																	3
1	2¹	3	4	5	6	7²	8³	13	10	9	14	11	12																																					4
1	2¹	3	4	5	6²	13		14	10	9	7	8	11³	12																																				5
	3		5	12	13		9	10³		8	11²	7		2	4	1	6¹	14																																6
1		3		5	14	7¹	9	10²	11	12	8		2	4	6³	13																																		7
1		4	5	6	12	9³	10²	13	11		8	2	14	3	7¹																																		8
1		3	5	6	10	13	9³	12	11	7¹	2	14	8²	4																																			9
1		3	5	6	10³	13	9	11	7¹	2	14	12	8²	4																																			10
1		4	5	6¹	7³	13	9	8²	11	2	14	12	3	10																																			11
1	12	4¹	5	6	7	8²	14	9³	13	11	2	3	10																																				12
1		4¹	5	6	7	8	12	9	11	2	3	10																																					13
1		3	5	6	7²	8¹	12	9	11	13	2	4	10																																				14
1		3	5	6	7¹	8	12	9	11²	13	2	4	10³	14																																			15
1		3	4	5			10¹	9			7	2	6	11²	12	8³	14	13																																16
		4	5	6⁸	13		9	8	2¹	3	10³	11	7²	1	12	14																																	17
		4	5	14	12	9¹	8	2²	13	6	10	11	1	3	7³																																		18
	14		5	6¹	13	10⁸	12	2	4	9²	8³	1	7	11	3																																		19
	3		5	6	12		8	2		9²	10	1	7	11¹	4	13																																	20
1	3		6	8¹	13	12	2	4	9²	10	11	7³	14	5																																			21
1	14	6²	13	9¹	10	2³	4	12	11	8	7⁸	3	5⁸																																			22
1	3	6	10	12	9¹	2	4	11	7	5	8																																						23
1	3	6	14	10²	12	7¹	2	4	13	11	8	5	9³																																				24
1⁶	15	3⁸	6	10	9	8	2	12	11	4	7¹	5																																						25
1	6	9	10¹	7	11	2	4	3	12	8	5																																							26
1	6	9²	13	8	2	12	11	4	3¹	10	7	5																																						27
1	12	6	9	8	2¹	3	11	4	10	7	5																																							28
1	6	8	9	13	7²	2¹	4	11	12	3	10	5																																						29
1	6	7¹	8	13	4	11	2	3	9	10²	12	5																																						30
1	6	7³	8	13	14⁸	4	11	2	3	9¹	10²	12	5																																					31
1	3	6	7²	8	13	9³	2	4	11	12	10¹	14	5																																					32
1	3	6	12	8	7¹	9	2	4	11²	5	10	13																																						33
1	3	6	7	13	2	4	11	5	9²	12	8¹	10																																						34
1	3	6¹	13	12	9	2	4	11³	7²	14	10	8	5																																					35
1	3	6	12	14	13	9²	2	4	11	8¹	10	7³	5																																					36
1	3	6	12	13	9	2	4	11²	5	8¹	10	7																																						37
1	3	6	8	9²	12	4	11¹	5	13	7	10	2																																						38
1	3	6	7	8	9	4	12	5	11¹	10	2																																							39
1	3³	6	7²	8	9	4	11	5	13	14	10	2	12																																					40
1	3	6³	13	8	9	4	11²	5	10¹	12	14	7	2																																					41
1	3	6	13	8	9	4	11¹	5	10²	12	7	2																																						42
1	3	6	12	8²	9	11	5	10¹	14	7³	13	2	4																																					43
1	3¹	12	8³	9	4	11	5	10²	13	14	7	2	6																																					44
1	7	8	9	4	11	5	10	12	6	2	3¹																																						45
1	12	7	8	9	4²	11	5	10¹	13	3	2	6																																					46

FA Cup
Fourth Qualifying Round
AFC Telford U   (h)   0-3

OXFORD UNITED · Blue Square Premier

Ground: The Kassam Stadium, Grenoble Road, Oxford OX4 4XP. *Tel:* (01865) 337 500. *Year Formed:* 1893.
Record Gate: 22,730 (1964 v Preston NE, FA Cup 6th rd). *Nickname:* The U's. *Manager:* Chris Wilder.
Secretary: Mick Brown. *Colours:* Yellow with navy trim shirts, navy shorts, navy stockings.

OXFORD UNITED 2008–09 LEAGUE RECORD

Match No.	Date	Venue	Opponents	Result	H/T Score	Lg. Pos.	Goalscorers	Attendance
1	Aug 8	A	Barrow	L	0-3	0-0	—	2790
2	12	H	Weymouth	L	0-1	0-1	—	4547
3	16	H	Eastbourne Bor	W	6-3	3-2	16	Constable 2 [5, 79], Reid [7], Pullan (og) [41], Hutchinson [69], Quinn [88]	3969
4	21	A	Wrexham	L	0-2	0-1	—	3515
5	25	H	Woking	D	0-0	0-0	18		4314
6	30	A	Ebbsfleet U	D	1-1	0-0	17	Reid [90]	1842
7	Sept 2	A	Northwich Vic	W	2-1	0-0	—	Constable 2 [54, 68]	973
8	6	H	Kettering T	D	1-1	0-0	17	Odubade [72]	4499
9	13	A	Kidderminster H	L	0-1	0-1	19		2065
10	20	H	Crawley T	L	1-2	1-2	20	Odubade (pen) [17]	3992
11	23	H	Cambridge U	W	3-1	1-0	—	Guy [4], Murray [72], Haldane [90]	4170
12	27	A	Lewes	L	1-2	0-0	19	Burnell [63]	1156
13	Oct 4	H	Rushden & D	W	2-1	1-0	18	Quinn [42], Trainer [55]	4645
14	9	A	Torquay U	D	1-1	0-1	—	Trainer [89]	1955
15	12	A	Altrincham	L	0-1	0-0	19		1806
16	18	H	Burton Alb	W	2-1	1-0	18	Trainer [8], Constable (pen) [50]	4494
17	Nov 1	H	York C	W	1-0	0-0	15	Odubade (pen) [87]	4449
18	15	A	Grays Ath	L	0-2	0-1	17		892
19	22	A	Histon	L	2-5	1-3	17	Willmott [27], Hutchinson [80]	1242
20	25	H	Kidderminster H	W	1-0	1-0	—	Constable (pen) [25]	3690
21	Dec 4	A	Mansfield T	W	3-1	1-1	—	Constable [9], Guy [58], Deering [72]	1553
22	9	A	Weymouth	D	2-2	1-1	—	Day [42], Bygrave (og) [82]	822
23	20	H	Stevenage Bor	D	1-1	1-1	14	Constable [43]	4343
24	26	A	Salisbury C	L	1-2	0-2	14	Deering [55]	2418
25	28	H	Ebbsfleet U	W	5-1	2-0	12	Haldane [16], Constable [20], Odubade [51], Trainer [81], Fisher [85]	5120
26	Jan 1	H	Salisbury C	W	2-0	0-0	15	Constable [71], Sappleton [84]	5312
27	17	H	Altrincham	W	1-0	0-0	10	Constable [68]	4249
28	20	H	Forest Green R	W	2-1	0-0	—	Odubade [70], Constable [73]	3728
29	24	A	Crawley T	W	1-0	0-0	9	Murray [61]	1603
30	29	A	Cambridge U	D	1-1	1-0	—	Murray [9]	3774
31	Feb 1	H	Lewes	W	2-1	1-1	—	Murray [17], Foster [82]	4595
32	14	H	Barrow	W	3-0	0-0	—	Farrell [62], Haldane [79], Odubade [86]	4532
33	21	H	Mansfield T	W	1-0	0-0	7	Nelthorpe [60]	4618
34	28	H	Torquay U	L	0-2	0-0	9		5837
35	Mar 3	A	Eastbourne Bor	W	3-0	1-0	—	Murray [44], Clist [71], Farrell [90]	1168
36	7	A	Forest Green R	D	3-3	2-2	7	Constable 2 (2 pens) [21, 26], Murray [65]	2027
37	14	H	Grays Ath	W	4-1	3-0	8	Sandwith [8], Constable 2 [26, 45], Chapman [69]	4764
38	19	A	Kettering T	W	2-1	2-0	—	Nelthorpe [6], Willmott [8]	1716
39	24	A	Rushden & D	W	3-1	1-0	—	Constable 2 (1 pen) [26, 70 (p)], Clist [90]	2085
40	28	A	Stevenage Bor	D	1-1	0-0	7	Constable (pen) [68]	3700
41	Apr 4	H	Histon	W	2-1	0-1	7	Constable 2 [66, 84]	6231
42	7	A	York C	D	0-0	0-0	—		2268
43	11	H	Wrexham	W	1-0	0-0	7	Constable [90]	5832
44	13	A	Woking	W	2-0	2-0	7	Murray [5], Clist [18]	3791
45	17	A	Burton Alb	W	1-0	0-0	7	Chapman [70]	6192
46	26	H	Northwich Vic	L	1-2	0-1	7	Constable [84]	10,298

Final League Position: 7

GOALSCORERS

League (72): Constable 23 (6 pens), Murray 7, Odubade 6 (2 pens), Trainer 4, Clist 3, Haldane 3, Chapman 2, Deering 2, Farrell 2, Guy 2, Hutchinson 2, Nelthorpe 2, Quinn 2, Reid 2, Willmott 2, Burnell 1, Day 1, Fisher 1, Foster 1, Sandwith 1, Sappleton 1, own goals 2.
FA Cup (5): Constable 2, Guy 1, Odubade 1, Trainer 1.

Hinchliffe 5+2	Clarke 12+2	Carruthers 31+4	Burnell 21	Foster 39	Quinn 15	Davies 1	Murray 45+1	Constable 41+1	Odubade 20+23	Haldane 34+9	Husbands 1+1	Reid 5+5	Willmott 34+3	Cole 4	Day 15+3	Deering 8+11	Fisher —+4	Hutchinson 12+16	Guy 18+3	Osbourne 6	Evans 2+1	Turley 37	Trainer 16+1	Taylor —+4	Groves —+1	Sappleton 1+3	Chapman 20	Killock 3	Nelthorpe 14+2	Batt 16	Farrell 7+7	Clist 14	Sandwith 9+3	Match No.
1	2⁸	3	4	5	6	7¹	8	9	10³	11²	13	14	12																					1
		3	4	5	6		8	9³	10¹	11	7²	13			1	2		12	14															2
		3	4¹	5	6		8	9	10	11	7²		1	2	13	12																		3
		3¹		5⁸	6		8	9³	10	11	7²	13	1	2	14	12	4																	4
1	12	3			6		8	9	10	11²	14	5	2¹	13	4	7³																		5
2	3	4¹	5⁸	6			8	13	10²	14	12	7	1	11	9³																			6
1		3	4		6		8	9		12		7	5		11	10¹	2																	7
1		3¹	4		6		8	9²	13	11	7	5		12	10	2																		8
1	13	4		6			8	9²	14	11	3	2	12	10³	5	7¹																		9
15	2	4		6			8		10	11²	5	13	12	3	7¹	1⁹	9																	10
2	3	4	5				8	9	10¹	13	12	11	6	1	7²																			11
2	3	4	5				8	9³	10¹	13	14	12	11	6	1	7²																		12
2	3	4	5	6¹			8		10	11	12	9		1	7																			13
2	3	4	5	6			8	9¹	12	11	13	10²		1	7																			14
2	3	4	5	6			8	10²	11¹	13	12	9³		1	7	14																		15
2	3		5	6			8	9	12	11²	4	10¹		1	7	13																		16
	3		5				8	9	13	11¹	4	2	6	12	10²	1	7																	17
	3	4¹		6			8	9²	12	11³	5	2	10	13	14	1	7																	18
15	3		5				8	9	12		4	2	6	11	10¹	1⁹	7																	19
2	3		5				8	9	10²	11¹	4	7	6	13	1	12																		20
3¹		4	5				8	9	13		6	2	12	11	10²	1	7																	21
		4	5				8	9	12	13	3	2	11	6¹	10	1	7²																	22
		4	5				8	9	12	11	6	2	3	13	10¹	1	7²																	23
12		4	5				8	9	13	11	3³	2	6²	14	10	1	7¹																	24
3			5				8	9²	10¹	11³	6	2	12	4		1	7	13	14															25
3			5				8	9		11²	6	2	4	10³	13	1	7¹	14	•12															26
	12	4	5				8	9	10³	11²	6¹	14			1			13	2	3	7													27
	4³	5					8	9	12	11¹	6	14		13		1		10²	2	3	7													28
	3	4¹	5				8	9	13	11²	6			12		1		14	2	6¹	11³ 7													29
	3	4¹	5				8		13	11²	6			12		1		10	7	2														30
	3		5				8		12	11	6	13		4¹		1		9	7	2	10²													31
	3		5				8	9	13	11	6					1		7	10¹	2²	12 4													32
	3		5				8	9	12		6					1		7	11¹	2	10 4													33
	3³		5				8	9	12	13	6²					1		7	11⁸	2	10¹ 4	14												34
	3²		5				8	9	10³	11	6			12		1		7	2¹	14	4	13												35
		5					8	9	12	11	6	2		4¹		1		7		10	3													36
	13		5				8¹	9	10	11²	6					1		7	2	12	4 3													37
	13		5				12	9		11²	6		14			1		7	10³	2	8¹ 4 3⁸													38
	3		5				8²	9³	10¹	12	6	13				1		7	11	2	14 4													39
	3²		5				8	9	14	11³	6	13				1		7	10¹	2⁸	13 4 12													40
		5					8	9	12	11²	6	13				1		2	7¹	10	4 3													41
		5					8	9	12	11	6	13				1		7	10¹	2	4² 3													42
		5					8	9	10¹	11	6²					1		7	13	2	12 4 3													43
	11²	5					8	9³	14	13	6			12		1		7¹		2	10 4 3													44
		5					8	9	12	11²	6⁸	13				1		7	10	2¹	4 3													45
	3²	5					8	9	10	11¹						1		7	13	2	12 4 6													46

FA Cup

Fourth Qualifying Round

	Hayes & Yeading U	(h)	2-0
First Round	Dorchester T	(h)	0-0
		(a)	3-1
Second Round	Torquay U	(a)	0-2

RUSHDEN & DIAMONDS Blue Square Premier

Ground: Nene Park, Irthlingborough, Northants NN9 5QF. *Tel:* (01933) 652 000. *Year Formed:* 1992.
Record Gate: 6,431 (1999 v Leeds U, FA Cup 3rd rd). *Nickname:* The Diamonds. *Manager:* Justin Edinburgh.
Secretary: Matt Wild. *Colours:* White shirts, white shorts, white stockings.

RUSHDEN & DIAMONDS 2008–09 LEAGUE RECORD

Match No.	Date	Venue	Opponents	Result	H/T Score	Lg. Pos.	Goalscorers	Attendance
1	Aug 9	A	Eastbourne Bor	W 1-0	1-0	—	Woodhouse (pen) [26]	1605
2	12	H	Ebbsfleet U	W 2-0	0-0	—	Smith [64], Phillips [77]	1467
3	17	H	Wrexham	D 1-1	0-0	—	Smith [61]	1805
4	23	A	Kettering T	D 1-1	0-1	5	Smith [83]	2897
5	25	H	Histon	L 1-2	0-1	10	Corcoran [64]	1613
6	30	A	Kidderminster H	L 1-2	1-1	15	McDonald [11]	1524
7	Sept 2	A	Barrow	D 1-1	1-0	—	Knight [27]	1663
8	6	H	Crawley T	L 0-1	0-0	16		1376
9	11	A	Lewes	W 4-0	0-0	—	Clare [54], Knight 2 [67, 73], Hope [69]	636
10	20	H	Burton Alb	W 2-1	1-0	9	Clare [45], Wolleaston [63]	1448
11	23	A	Wrexham	W 3-0	2-0	—	Clare [11], Hope 2 [32, 83]	2805
12	29	H	Altrincham	D 1-1	0-1	—	Knight [77]	1341
13	Oct 4	A	Oxford U	L 1-2	0-1	11	Clare [57]	4645
14	7	H	Grays Ath	W 1-0	0-0	—	Kelly [24]	1124
15	12	H	Torquay U	L 1-3	0-2	8	Smith [68]	1649
16	18	A	York C	L 0-2	0-1	12		2313
17	Nov 1	A	Cambridge U	D 0-0	0-0	12		3547
18	8	H	Weymouth	W 1-0	0-0	—	Clare [54]	1002
19	15	H	Kidderminster H	L 0-1	0-1	10		1391
20	22	H	Eastbourne Bor	W 2-0	1-0	10	Tomlin [34], Rankine [56]	1037
21	29	A	Altrincham	W 4-0	2-0	9	Burgess 2 [30, 88], Tomlin [41], Osano [65]	924
22	Dec 6	A	Barrow	D 1-1	0-1	8	Phillips [72]	1120
23	9	A	Woking	D 1-1	1-1	—	Rankine [41]	1119
24	20	H	Northwich Vic	W 2-1	0-1	8	Smith [67], Tomlin [70]	1134
25	26	A	Stevenage Bor	L 1-3	0-1	8	Tomlin [77]	2012
26	Jan 1	H	Stevenage Bor	D 1-1	0-1	8	Smith [90]	1853
27	17	A	Ebbsfleet U	L 0-1	0-1	11		1121
28	23	H	Forest Green R	D 2-2	2-1	—	Tomlin [12], Corcoran [29]	1066
29	27	A	Mansfield T	D 0-0	0-0	—		2028
30	Feb 1	H	Cambridge U	L 1-2	1-1	—	Smith [42]	2058
31	9	A	Burton Alb	L 0-3	0-1	—		1291
32	21	A	Weymouth	W 9-0	4-0	11	Rankine 2 [8, 49], Tomlin 2 [12, 18], Hope [33], Wolleaston [59], Kelly 2 [66, 75], Robinson [88]	967
33	24	H	York C	W 2-0	0-0	—	Burgess [58], Wolleaston [72]	1020
34	28	H	Mansfield T	L 0-1	0-0	11		1774
35	Mar 7	A	Torquay U	D 1-1	0-1	11	Tomlin [65]	2161
36	10	H	Lewes	W 2-1	1-1	—	Wolleaston [2], Rankine (pen) [51]	918
37	14	A	Crawley T	D 0-0	0-0	11		777
38	21	A	Salisbury C	D 1-1	1-0	11	Wolleaston [18]	924
39	24	H	Oxford U	L 1-3	0-1	—	Wolleaston [59]	2085
40	28	A	Northwich Vic	L 2-4	0-1	11	Rankine (pen) [61], Wolleaston [62]	687
41	31	A	Grays Ath	D 0-0	0-0	—		695
42	Apr 4	H	Salisbury C	W 2-1	2-0	11	Hope [31], Cousins [42]	1352
43	11	H	Kettering T	W 1-0	0-0	11	Smith [82]	3406
44	13	A	Histon	D 0-0	0-0	11		1263
45	18	A	Forest Green R	L 0-4	0-2	11		1185
46	26	H	Woking	W 3-1	2-1	11	Wolleaston [6], Rankine [35], Beecroft [50]	1676

Final League Position: 11

GOALSCORERS

League (61): Smith 8, Tomlin 8, Wolleaston 8, Rankine 7 (2 pens), Clare 5, Hope 5, Knight 4, Burgess 3, Kelly 3, Corcoran 2, Phillips 2, Beecroft 1, Cousins 1, McDonald 1, Osano 1, Robinson 1, Woodhouse 1 (pen).
FA Cup (0).

Marriott 12	Osano 39	Jelleyman 14 + 3	Burton 8 + 3	Hope 46	McDonald 3	Kelly 28 + 11	Woodhouse 20	Phillips 13 + 7	Tomlin 36 + 5	Burgess 38 + 2	Gulliver 6 + 2	Corcoran 30 + 7	Wolleaston 36 + 5	Smith 7 + 26	Beecroft 15 + 10	Rankine 24 + 11	Knight 10 + 2	Roberts 37	Clare 10 + 2	Panther 3	Moloney 4	Fortune 1	Boden 2 + 2	Bolasie 5 + 2	Brown 2 + 1	Cochrane 4	Roget 1	Cousins 11 + 9	Downer 16 + 1	Robinson 20	Broadbent 2 + 1	McGuinness — + 5	Arthur 1 + 1	McNamara 2 + 3	Hilliard — + 1	Match No.
1	2	3	4	5	6[3]	7[1]	8	9	10	11[2]	12	13	14																							1
1	2	3	12	5	8[3]	7[2]	4	9	10	11	6[1]	13		14																						2
1	2	3	4	5			8	9	10	11	6[2]	7[1]	12	13																						3
1	2	3	4[1]	5	12		8	9	10	11	6[2]	13	14				7[3]																			4
1	2	3	4[1]	5	12[2]		8[s]	9	10[s]	11	13	6	14				7[3]																			5
1	2	3[1]	13	5	6[2]			9[3]		11				8	14	7	12	10	4																	6
1	2	3[1]	12	5			4	9[3]		11				7	8[2]	14	13	10	6																	7
1	2		4	5	13	6		9[3]		11[2]	3	8[1]		12	14	10	7																			8
1	2	3	4	5[1]	8[2]			10	11	12	13	6		14	7				9[3]																	9
1	2		4	5		14	10[1]	11		3	8		12	13	7[3]				9[2]	6[s]																10
1	2	12		5	8	13	10[1]	11	6	3	4		14	7[2]					9[3]																	11
1	2			5	14	8	12	10	11[2]	6	3	4[1]		13	7				9[3]																	12
	2	3[s]	4[1]	5	7	8	12	10[2]	13		6		14	11	1			1	9[3]																	13
	2			5	7[2]	8[1]	10	13	11	6	3	12		14				1	9[3]	4																14
	2			5	7	8	10[2]	14	11	6	3[1]		13		12			1	9[3]	4[s]																15
	2	3		5		8	9[3]	10[1]	11	4	6[2]	13	14		7			1	12																	16
	2			5	7	8			11		3	4	10	12				1	9[1]		6															17
	2			5	7[2]	8	14	13		12	4			10				1	9[1]	3[3]	6	11														18
	2			5	7[3]	8	12	14	13		3[1]	4			10			1	9	6		11[2]														19
	2	3		5	13		9[1]	10[2]		6	8[3]	12		7			1		4		14	11														20
	2	3		5	12		10	11		6	4[3]		8			1		13		14	7[1]	9[2]														21
	2	3[2]		5	13		12	10	11	4	6	14	8[3]			1					7	9[1]														22
	2			5	12	8	9[2]	10	11	3	4	13	7			1		6[1]																		23
	2	13		5	7[2]	8		10		3	4	9[3]	11			1				12	14	6[1]														24
	2	3		5	7	8		10		4[1]	11[3]	13	9			1			12		6[2]	14														25
	2[3]			5	13		10		4	12	14	7	9			1		8[2]		6[1]	11	3														26
	2			5	7		10	11	14	13	4[1]	9[2]			1			12	6[s]	3	8[3]															27
	2			5	7		10	11	6[2]	12	9[1]			1			4	14	3	8[3]	13															28
	2			5	7		11	3	4[1]	12	8	10		1			9[2]	6	13																	29
	2			5	7[2]		10	6	4	11	8			1			9[1]	3	13	12																30
	2			5	7[1]		10[3]	11	4	8[2]	9	13	14			1		12	6	3																31
	2[2]			5	7		10[1]	11	4	8	14	9[3]			1			12	6	3	13															32
	2			5	7		10[3]	11	8	12	13	14		1				4							9[1]	6[2]	3									33
	2			5	7[3]		10	11	4[2]	8	12	13		1										9[1]	6	3			14			34
	2	12		5	13		10	11	4	14	7	9[3]		1										6	3[1]		8[2]				35
	2			5	7		10	11	4	12	8	9[1]		1										6	3						36
	2			5	7		10	11	13	4[3]	12	8	9[1]		1										14	6[2]	3					37
	2			5	7		10	11	6	4	8[1]	9		1										12	3						38
	2[1]			5	7		10	11	6	4	14	8[2]	9[3]		1										13	12	3					39
				5	7		10	11	6[s]	4	13	8[1]	12		1										9[2]	2	3					40
				5	7		10[1]	11	4[2]	12	6	9		1										8	2	3		13			41
				5	7		10	11	4[1]	8	9		1										6	2	3		12				42
				5	7		10	11	4[2]	12	6	9		1										8[1]	2	3[3]		13		14	43
				5	12		10[1]	11	6	8	9		1										7	2	3			4		44
				5	7[1]		14	11	6	8[2]	10	13	12		1									9[3]	2	3			4		45
				5	7		10[1]	11	6	4	12	8[3]	9[2]		1									13	2	3				14	46

FA Cup
Fourth Qualifying Round
      Evesham U   (a)   0-2

SALISBURY CITY

Blue Square Premier

Ground: The Raymond McEnhill Stadium, Partridge Way, Old Sarum, Salisbury SP4 6PU. *Tel:* (01722) 326 454.
Year Formed: 1947. *Record Gate:* 8,902 (1948 v Weymouth, Western League). *Nickname:* The Whites. *Manager:*
Nick Holmes. *Secretary:* Alec Hayter. *Colours:* White shirts, black shorts, white stockings.

SALISBURY CITY 2008–09 LEAGUE RECORD

Match No.	Date		Venue	Opponents	Result		H/T Score	Lg. Pos.	Goalscorers	Attendance
1	Aug	9	H	Burton Alb	L	0-1	0-1	—		1122
2		12	A	Forest Green R	W	2-1	1-0	—	Clarke D 2 [18, 47]	927
3		16	A	Lewes	W	4-1	2-1	7	Sandell 2 [19, 30], Griffin 2 [87, 90]	564
4		23	H	Grays Ath	W	1-0	0-0	4	Tubbs (pen) [55]	987
5		25	A	Torquay U	W	1-0	0-0	1	Griffin [90]	2001
6		30	H	Wrexham	L	1-4	1-1	4	Sandell [10]	1532
7	Sept	2	H	Weymouth	W	1-0	0-0	—	Feeney [55]	1382
8		6	A	Altrincham	D	0-0	0-0	4		1002
9		13	H	Barrow	W	3-0	1-0	2	Fowler [44], Sandell (pen) [68], Griffin [83]	1116
10		20	A	York C	D	1-1	0-0	3	Clohessy [72]	2280
11		23	A	Woking	L	0-1	0-0	—		1369
12		27	H	Mansfield T	L	2-3	1-0	7	Sandell [11], Feeney [61]	1494
13	Oct	4	A	Histon	L	0-2	0-0	10		961
14		7	H	Altrincham	L	1-3	0-0	—	Griffin [90]	950
15		11	H	Kettering T	L	1-2	1-0	15	Griffin [5]	1191
16		18	A	Stevenage Bor	L	0-2	0-0	17		1712
17		30	H	Crawley T	W	2-0	0-0	—	Rayner (og) [50], Clohessy [75]	884
18	Nov	15	A	Mansfield T	L	0-3	0-2	16		1921
19		22	H	Northwich Vic	D	1-1	1-0	15	Robinson [2]	999
20		29	H	York C	D	1-1	1-0	15	Griffin [40]	986
21	Dec	6	A	Kidderminster H	L	1-2	1-2	17	Griffin [45], Dutton [65]	1325
22		9	H	Lewes	L	1-2	0-2	—	Griffin (pen) [55]	579
23		20	A	Cambridge U	L	0-4	0-1	18		3340
24		26	H	Oxford U	W	2-1	2-0	17	Griffin [4], Ademeno [17]	2418
25	Jan	1	A	Oxford U	L	0-2	0-0	18		5312
26		17	A	Kettering T	L	0-1	0-1	19		1541
27		24	H	Stevenage Bor	L	2-4	0-1	21	Griffin 2 [70, 83]	1015
28		27	H	Forest Green R	D	2-2	1-2	—	Griffin 2 [7, 81]	771
29		31	A	Barrow	D	0-0	0-0	—		1613
30	Feb	14	H	Histon	L	0-4	0-1	—		908
31		17	H	Woking	W	1-0	0-0	—	Griffin [49]	923
32		21	A	Crawley T	W	3-0	1-0	16	Clarke D [43], Griffin [48], Webb [90]	964
33		28	A	Wrexham	D	1-1	0-1	16	Ademeno [73]	3206
34	Mar	7	H	Kidderminster H	D	0-0	0-0	16		1105
35		10	A	Weymouth	W	4-0	1-0	—	Todd [31], Tubbs [55], Griffin [68], Clarke D [72]	1005
36		14	A	Burton Alb	W	2-1	2-0	15	Griffin [34], Ademeno [45]	2274
37		17	A	Eastbourne Bor	D	0-0	0-0	—		1047
38		21	H	Rushden & D	D	1-1	0-1	14	Sangare [78]	924
39		24	H	Ebbsfleet U	W	1-0	1-0	—	Clohessy [4]	939
40		28	H	Eastbourne Bor	W	2-0	0-0	12	Dutton [70], Ademeno [89]	1011
41		31	A	Northwich Vic	D	1-1	0-1	—	Griffin [55]	532
42	Apr	4	A	Rushden & D	L	1-2	0-2	13	Sangare [86]	1352
43		11	A	Grays Ath	L	1-3	0-2	14	Ademeno [70]	761
44		13	H	Torquay U	D	2-2	1-1	14	Griffin [45], Ademeno [81]	2039
45		18	H	Cambridge U	L	1-2	1-2	16	Griffin [32]	1031
46		26	A	Ebbsfleet U	D	2-2	1-0	16	Sinclair [32], Tubbs [84]	1390

Final League Position: 16

GOALSCORERS
League (54): Griffin 21 (1 pen), Ademeno 6, Sandell 5 (1 pen), Clarke D 4, Clohessy 3, Tubbs 3 (1 pen), Dutton 2,
Feeney 2, Sangare 2, Fowler 1, Robinson 1, Sinclair 1, Todd 1, Webb 1, own goal 1.
FA Cup (0).

Bittner 46	Bass 32+4	Robinson 12+1	Cook 17+2	Bond 10+2	Clarke D 28+11	Turk 15+3	Bartlett 19+3	Feeney 20+3	Tubbs 27+5	Sandell 16	Matthews 2+11	Herring 35+2	Griffin 32+13	Fowler 25+3	Sangare 16+1	Dutton 18+9	Davies 3+4	Clohessy 35+1	Beavan 2+1	Sinclair 10+4	Maher 1+2	Ruddick 20+4	Hill 2+3	Ademeno 17+3	Webb 11+9	Winfield 4	Spence 4	Todd 8	Brough 13	Martin 1+1	Pearce 5+1	Osman —+2	Cox —+1	Match No.
1	2	3	4	5	6²	7	8¹	9	10	11	12	13																						1
1	2		4	5	8¹	7	3	9	10²	11	13	6	12																					2
1	2		4	5	8¹	7	3	9²	10³	11	13	6¹	14	12																				3
1	2		4	5	8	7	3	9²	10³	11	13	6¹	14	12																				4
1		3	12	5	8	13	2	9		11	10³	6²	14	7	4¹																			5
1	2¹	3	4	5	8²	7	13	9	10	11³	14	12	6																					6
1	2	3	4	5		7	6	9	10¹	11	12	8																						7
1	2		4		12	7	3¹	9	10²	11³	14	6	13	8	5																			8
1	2	3¹	4		12	7		9		11		6²	10³	8	5	13	14																	9
1	2		4		12	7		9	13	11	14	6	10³	8²	5¹			3																10
1	2		4		8¹	7		9	10³	11	14	6²	12		13	5		3																11
1	2		4		12	7	8	9²	10³	11	14	6	13		5	3¹																		12
1	2	3	4		13	7	8³	14	10	11	9²	12	5		6¹																			13
1	2²	3	4			7	8¹	9³	10	11²	14	6²	12		13	5																		14
1		3	4		8	7²		9³	10	14	11		6¹		2	13		5		12														15
1	2	3	4		13	7	8¹	9	12	11	14		10³		5	6²																		16
1	2	12	4		13	7¹	14		10³	11		6	9	8²				5		3														17
1	2		12		8²		4³					6	9		5	7	10¹	3		11	13	14												18
1	2	3	4		12		13					6¹	9	7	10³	5		11		14		8²												19
1	2	3			12							6	9²		5	8		4		7		11¹		10	13									20
1	2	3¹	14		12							6³	9		4	8		5		7		13		11²	10									21
1	2²			13	8							6³	9		3	7¹		5		4		14		12	11	10								22
1	2	5				6		12	8			4		7	11¹			3		13				9	10²									23
1	2	5			8				11		10	4	9		6¹			12		3				7²	13									24
1	2	5			8³	7²					12			4	9	11		13		6		3		14	10¹									25
1		8¹		12			10						9	13	6	5	7	2		3		11²			4									26
1	2²				13		8			11				10¹	9	6	7	5		3		12			4									27
1		5		12			3			11				10	9	6	7	2		4					8¹									28
1		5		12			3			11				10²	9	6	8	2		13		4			7¹									29
1	2¹		13		3		10						9	6	7²		12			14		11³		8				4	5					30
1			8				10					7²	9¹	6		13		2				3		11	12			4	5					31
1			8				10					7	9¹	6²		13		2				3		11	12			4	5					32
1	13		8				10					9	7	6¹				2				12		3	11			4	5²					33
1			8				10					7¹	9²	6				2				12		3	11	13		4	5					34
1			8				10					7³	9²	6	14			2				12		3	11¹	13		4	5					35
1			8				10					7¹	9	6	12			2				10		3	11			4	5					36
1	12		8									7	9	6¹	10			2				3			11			4	5					37
1	12		8									6	9		4	11¹	7²	2				3			10			5		13			38
1	2		8									6	9			11		12	4			3			10¹			5		7			39
1	2²		8									6	9			11		13	4			3			12	10¹		5		7			40
1	2		8²				13					6	9			11		4				3			12	10¹		5		7			41
1	2³		8				13					7	9²	12	6	11¹		4				3			14	10		5					42
1	2		8³				10²					7	9¹	6	5			4				3			11	13		12	14					43
1			8				10					4	9¹	6	5	12		2				3			11	7								44
1			8				10					7	9	6		2		12				3			11					4¹	5²	13		45
1	12		8				10²					7	9	6		2		11				3¹			4					5	13		46

FA Cup
Fourth Qualifying Round
        Team Bath   (a)   0-1

STEVENAGE BOROUGH   Blue Square Premier

Ground: Broadhall Way Stadium, Broadhall Way, Stevenage, Hertfordshire SG2 8RH.   *Tel:* (01438) 223 223.
Year Formed: 1976.   *Record Gate:* 6,489 (1997 v Kidderminster Harriers, Conference).   *Nickname:* The Boro.
Manager: Graham Westley.   *Secretary:* Roger Austin.   *Colours:* Red and white shirts, black shorts, white stockings.

STEVENAGE BOROUGH 2008–09 LEAGUE RECORD

Match No.	Date	Venue	Opponents	Result	H/T Score	Lg. Pos.	Goalscorers	Attendance
1	Aug 9	A	Wrexham	L	0-5	0-1	—		4901
2	12	H	Eastbourne Bor	L	1-3	1-2	—	Drury [44]	1681
3	16	H	Weymouth	D	1-1	1-1	23	Willock [26]	1357
4	23	A	Ebbsfleet U	L	0-4	0-2	23		1420
5	25	H	Crawley T	D	1-1	1-0	23	Cole [16]	1492
6	30	A	Barrow	W	3-1	2-1	20	Vincenti [30], Murray [45], Wilson [75]	1764
7	Sept 2	A	Kettering T	L	0-1	0-1	—		1592
8	6	H	Burton Alb	W	4-1	2-0	19	Boylan [3], Morison 3 [19, 55, 56]	1717
9	13	H	Altrincham	W	3-0	2-0	18	Morison 2 (1 pen) [16, 74 (p)], Cole [36]	1804
10	20	A	Forest Green R	W	3-0	2-0	14	Boylan [2], Morison [23], Willock [90]	751
11	25	A	Grays Ath	W	2-1	0-0	—	Cole 2 [48, 53]	791
12	28	H	York C	D	3-3	2-2	12	Robinson (og) [3], Morison 2 [19, 57]	1917
13	Oct 4	A	Torquay U	L	0-3	0-0	14		2066
14	7	H	Mansfield T	W	3-2	1-0	—	Morison (pen) [45], Cole [64], Bostwick [80]	1517
15	12	A	Eastbourne Bor	L	1-2	0-0	12	Anaclet [66]	1618
16	18	H	Salisbury C	W	2-0	0-0	9	Albrighton [58], Morison [86]	1712
17	Nov 1	A	Woking	W	1-0	1-0	9	Vincenti [11]	1955
18	15	A	Northwich Vic	D	1-1	0-1	9	Drury [84]	2536
19	18	H	Histon	L	1-3	1-2	—	Morison [21]	1623
20	22	A	Burton Alb	L	0-2	0-1	12		1944
21	29	H	Wrexham	L	1-2	0-0	11	Willock [64]	1673
22	Dec 6	A	Lewes	W	2-0	0-0	11	Morison (pen) [74], Vincenti [90]	486
23	9	H	Grays Ath	D	0-0	0-0	—		1289
24	20	A	Oxford U	D	1-1	1-1	12	Bridges [27]	4343
25	26	H	Rushden & D	W	3-1	1-0	10	Morison 2 [41, 59], Boylan [47]	2012
26	28	A	Cambridge U	D	1-1	0-1	9	Cole (pen) [90]	3351
27	Jan 1	A	Rushden & D	D	1-1	1-0	9	Morison [32]	1853
28	3	H	Lewes	W	3-0	2-0	—	Boylan [33], Morison 2 [36, 87]	1764
29	17	H	Barrow	W	3-0	1-0	7	Bridges [39], Morison 2 [50, 53]	2205
30	24	A	Salisbury C	W	4-2	1-0	3	Cole 3 [38, 87, 90], Drury [66]	1015
31	27	H	Kettering T	W	2-1	0-1	—	Murphy [50], Vincenti [84]	1880
32	Feb 14	A	Weymouth	W	3-0	1-0	—	Drury [43], Morison [86], Bostwick [88]	1226
33	24	H	Woking	W	1-0	0-0	—	Boylan [59]	1965
34	28	A	Altrincham	W	2-1	0-0	4	Drury [72], Roberts [90]	958
35	Mar 3	H	Forest Green R	D	1-1	1-1	—	Cole (pen) [33]	1242
36	7	A	Northwich Vic	W	1-0	0-0	4	Roberts [54]	801
37	24	A	Histon	D	0-0	0-0	—		1133
38	28	H	Oxford U	D	1-1	0-0	6	Bridges [51]	3700
39	31	A	York C	W	2-0	0-0	—	Boylan [48], Morison [67]	1924
40	Apr 4	A	Kidderminster H	L	2-4	2-1	6	Boylan [7], Cole [22]	2115
41	7	H	Cambridge U	W	2-1	2-1	—	Mendes [4], Boylan [31]	3408
42	11	H	Ebbsfleet U	W	1-0	1-0	6	Cole [32]	1913
43	13	A	Crawley T	W	2-0	1-0	5	Bostwick [40], Willock [89]	1161
44	18	H	Torquay U	D	0-0	0-0	6		2819
45	21	H	Kidderminster H	W	3-1	1-1	—	Morison [4], Boylan 2 [48, 65]	2530
46	26	A	Mansfield T	L	1-2	0-0	5	Laird [86]	3614

Final League Position: 5

GOALSCORERS

League (73): Morison 22 (3 pens), Cole 12 (2 pens), Boylan 10, Drury 5, Vincenti 4, Willock 4, Bostwick 3, Bridges 3, Roberts 2, Albrighton 1, Anaclet 1, Laird 1, Mendes 1, Murphy 1, Murray 1, Wilson 1, own goal 1.
FA Cup (6): Willock 2, Cole 1, Laird 1, McMahon 1, Morison 1.
Play-Offs (3): Morison 2, Roberts 1.

Bayes 5 + 1	Bostwick 39	Laird 42	Anaclet 9 + 8	Henry 40 + 1	Albrighton 25 + 4	McMahon 11 + 2	Mills 21 + 9	Morison 40 + 1	Cole 36 + 6	Drury 23 + 2	Wilson 24 + 11	Thomas 5 + 6	Boylan 25 + 7	Willock 12 + 17	Oliver 18 + 4	Christie 2 + 1	Nurse — + 2	Anderson — + 7	Day 41	Vincenti 10 + 16	Murray 1'	Upson — + 1	Martin 11	Black 3 + 3	Roberts 25	St Aimie — + 1	Bridges 15	Murphy 10 + 2	Ashton 10 + 1	Mendes 3 + 3	Maamria — + 1	Match No.
1	2	3	4	5	6	7	8¹	9⁴	10³	11²	12	13	14																			1
1	2	3	4	5	6¹	14	8			11²		7	10	12	13	9³																2
1	2	3	4¹	5		7²	8			11	12	9	13	10³	6	14																3
1	2	3		5	6		8		10¹		7	11²		4	9	12	13															4
	3		5	6		8	9	11¹		2	12		10	4		1	7															5
	2		4¹		7	8	9		3	14	12	10¹	5		13	1	11²	6														6
	2	3		5		4	8¹	9		7	12²	14	10³	6		1	11		13													7
	2	3	12	5	6¹	7²		9	13		8		10			4			1			11										8
	2¹	3	12	5	6	7²		9	13		8	14	10³			4			1			11										9
	2³	3	13	5	6			9	11¹		7		10²	12	4				1	14				8								10
	2¹	3	12	5	6		13	9	11³		7	14	10²		4				1					8								11
	2	3	12	5	6¹			9	11		8	10²	13			1	7					4										12
	2	3	12	5	6¹		13	9	10		11³			4		14	1	7	8²													13
	2	3	12	5		8	6	9	11		7¹			4		1										10						14
	2	3	4¹	5		7	8²	9	11		13		14	6		1				10³	12											15
	2		4	13	6	7³		9	12	11²	3		14	5		1				8	10¹											16
	2		4	5	6	7²	8	9	13		3			10	12	1	11¹															17
		4	5	6	14	8²	9¹	11	7³	2		10		12		1	3						13									18
11	3		6	4	7²		9	12		2⁴		10³	14	5		1				8¹	13											19
	2	3		5		8	12	13	4		10¹	9	6			1	7			11²												20
	3		5		8		11	6		9¹	13	10	4²			1	2					7	12									21
	3		5		8	9	11¹	7	2		12	10²	4			1	13			6												22
	3		5		8	9	11¹	7	6			10	4			1	12			2												23
	2	3	5	6		9	11	12	7¹		10²	13				1	14			4		8³										24
	2	3	5	6		14	9	11¹	7³		10²	13		12	1					4		8										25
	2	3	4¹	5	6			11	7²			10		12	1	13				8	9											26
	2	3	5	6		13	9	11²	7		10¹	12			1					4	8											27
	2	3	5	6		9	11	7		10³	14		13	1					4	8¹	12											28
15	2	3	5	6		9	11	7		10¹	12²		13	1⁶					4	8												29
	2	3	5	6¹		14	9	11	10³	13		12		1					4	8	7²											30
	2	3	5		13	9	11	7²	4¹					1	12				6	8	10											31
	2	3	5	13		9	11	7	12	10³				1	14				6	8¹	4²											32
1	2	3	5¹			9	11³	7	12	10				14					6	8	4²	13										33
	2	3		4²		9	11	7	12	10³	14			1	13				6	8	5¹											34
	2	3	5			14	9	11¹	7	12				13	1	10²			6	8	4³											35
	2	3	5⁸			9	11²	7	12	10¹				1	13				6	8	4											36
	2	3			12	9	11²	4		13	10¹			1					6	8	7	5										37
	2	3	5		13	9	11		10					1	14				6	8¹	12	4²	7³									38
	2	3	5	13		9	11³		10¹					1	12				6		7²	4	14									39
	2	3²	5¹	12		9	11		10³	14				1	13				6		7⁸	4										40
	3		12		8	9	11	2	10²					1	13	6	5⁸					4	7¹									41
	3	12	4		8	9³	11¹	2		10²				1	13	6					5	7	14									42
	2	3	5			8	9	11	7		10¹	12		1	13				6			4²										43
	2	3	5			8	9	11	12	4¹				1					6		7											44
	2	3	5	4		9	11²	8¹	12		10³	14		1					6		7		13									45
	2	3	5	4¹		9	11⁸	8²	12		10³	14		1					6		7		13									46

FA Cup

Fourth Qualifying Round	Horsham	(h)	2-2
		(a)	4-1
First Round	Leicester C	(a)	0-3

Play-Offs

Semi-Final	Cambridge U	(h)	3-1
		(a)	0-3

TORQUAY UNITED   FL Championship 2

Ground: Plainmoor Ground, Torquay, Devon TQ1 3PS.   *Tel:* (01803) 328 666.   *Year Formed:* 1899.
Record Gate: 21,908 (2005 v Huddersfield T, FA Cup 4th rd).   *Nickname:* The Gulls.   *Manager:* Paul Buckle.
Secretary: Deborah Hancox.   *Colours:* Yellow shirts, yellow shorts, yellow stockings.

TORQUAY UNITED 2008–09 LEAGUE RECORD

Match No.	Date	Venue	Opponents	Result	H/T Score	Lg. Pos.	Goalscorers	Attendance
1	Aug 9	A	Histon	D 1-1	0-0	—	Sills (pen) [55]	928
2	12	H	Woking	W 2-1	0-1	—	Benyon [60], Carlisle [82]	2881
3	18	H	Ebbsfleet U	L 0-2	0-1	—		2372
4	23	A	Crawley T	L 1-3	0-2	17	D'Sane [49]	1154
5	25	H	Salisbury C	L 0-1	0-0	20		2001
6	28	H	York C	D 1-1	0-0	—	Stevens [65]	1598
7	Sept 4	A	Kidderminster H	L 0-1	0-1	—		1345
8	7	H	Northwich Vic	W 2-1	1-0	18	Carlisle [10], Sills (pen) [90]	1752
9	13	A	Cambridge U	W 1-0	0-0	17	Carlisle [90]	4041
10	20	H	Eastbourne Bor	W 2-0	1-0	15	Thompson [23], Hargreaves [73]	1921
11	23	A	Forest Green R	W 2-1	0-1	—	Benyon [69], Green [90]	1022
12	27	A	Wrexham	D 1-1	1-1	11	Sills [35]	2897
13	Oct 4	H	Stevenage Bor	W 3-0	0-0	8	Robertson [67], Sills [71], Wroe [87]	2066
14	9	H	Oxford U	D 1-1	1-0	—	Robertson [21]	1955
15	12	A	Rushden & D	W 3-1	2-0	7	Carlisle [7], Sills [15], Wroe [51]	1649
16	18	A	Ebbsfleet U	W 2-0	1-0	5	Wroe [42], Carlisle [55]	1781
17	Nov 1	H	Mansfield T	W 2-0	0-0	2	D'Sane [54], Woods [69]	2267
18	15	A	York C	W 2-1	0-0	2	D'Sane [66], Ellis [90]	2412
19	18	H	Lewes	W 4-1	3-0	—	Sills 2 [2, 45], Stevens 2 [28, 48]	2118
20	22	A	Woking	D 2-2	0-2	3	Benyon [55], Stevens [65]	2452
21	Dec 6	H	Cambridge U	D 0-0	0-0	3		2310
22	9	A	Eastbourne Bor	L 2-4	1-1	—	Benyon [34], Sills [90]	1204
23	20	H	Histon	W 4-1	2-0	3	D'Sane 2 [7, 22], Wroe [62], Sills [85]	2201
24	26	A	Weymouth	W 1-0	1-0	2	Green [24]	2323
25	28	H	Kidderminster H	L 0-1	0-0	5		2749
26	Jan 16	A	Wrexham	D 1-1	0-1	—	D'Sane [61]	1842
27	27	A	Lewes	W 2-0	1-0	—	Nicholson [44], D'Sane [84]	558
28	Feb 10	H	Weymouth	L 0-2	0-1	—		1743
29	14	A	Altrincham	W 3-1	1-0	—	Sills 2 (1 pen) [19, 55 (p)], Benyon [76]	1760
30	21	A	Kettering T	L 1-2	1-2	6	Nicholson [45]	1869
31	24	H	Forest Green R	D 3-3	2-3	—	Green [18], Hargreaves [45], Christie [80]	1554
32	28	A	Oxford U	W 2-0	0-0	5	Benyon 2 [64, 70]	5837
33	Mar 3	A	Grays Ath	W 2-1	1-1	—	Nicholson [13], Carlisle [87]	510
34	7	H	Rushden & D	D 1-1	1-0	5	Sills [41]	2161
35	10	A	Altrincham	W 1-0	0-0	—	Carlisle [90]	735
36	14	H	Barrow	W 4-1	2-1	3	Wroe [4], Benyon [39], Sills [68], Green [90]	2269
37	21	A	Northwich Vic	W 3-2	0-1	3	Todd [49], Sills [68], D'Sane [76]	705
38	24	H	Grays Ath	D 1-1	0-1	—	D'Sane [48]	1996
39	28	A	Mansfield T	D 1-1	0-1	3	Sturrock [64]	2437
40	Apr 4	H	Kettering T	W 2-0	1-0	3	Robertson [20], Sturrock [65]	2503
41	6	A	Burton Alb	W 1-0	1-0	—	Stevens [10]	4891
42	11	A	Crawley T	L 0-2	0-1	3		3031
43	13	A	Salisbury C	D 2-2	1-1	3	Carlisle (pen) [20], Wroe [90]	2039
44	18	A	Stevenage Bor	D 0-0	0-0	4		2819
45	21	A	Barrow	D 1-1	0-1	—	Hargreaves [49]	1918
46	26	H	Burton Alb	W 2-1	1-1	4	Hargreaves [13], Benyon [46]	4528

Final League Position: 4

GOALSCORERS

League (72): Sills 14 (3 pens), Benyon 9, D'Sane 9, Carlisle 8 (1 pen), Wroe 6, Stevens 5, Green 4, Hargreaves 4, Nicholson 3, Robertson 3, Sturrock 2, Christie 1, Ellis 1, Thompson 1, Todd 1, Woods 1.
FA Cup (9): Sills 4, Benyon 2, Thompson 2, Green 1.
Play-Offs (4): Sills 2, Hargreaves 1, Wroe 1.

Poke 12 + 1	Mansell 41 + 1	Hodges 31 + 4	Thompson 17 + 6	Todd 16	Hargreaves 44	Carlisle 34 + 3	Wroe 40	Benyon 17 + 17	Sills 43 + 2	Stevens 15 + 14	D'Sane 22 + 5	Carayol 14 + 16	Nicholson 38 + 2	Robertson 27 + 3	Green 15 + 14	Brough 2 + 1	Adams 1 + 2	Woods 27	Ellis 8 + 1	Bevan 34	Yeoman — + 1	Charran — + 1	Christie 2 + 4	Sturrock 6 + 1	Match No.
1	2	3	4	5	6	7	8	9[1]	10	11[2]	12	13													1
1	2	3[1]	4	5	6	7	8	9[3]	10	11[2]		13	12		14										2
1	2		4	5[1]	6	7	8	9[3]	10	11[2]		13	3	12	14										3
1	2	8	4		6[1]	7		14	13		9[3]	10	3		11[2]		12	5							4
1	4	3			8	7		10	12	9[2]	11[1]		2	13				5	6						5
1	4	3			8	7		10[1]	12	9[2]	11		2	13				5	6						6
1	4	11[1]			8	7		13	10[2]	9[3]	12		3	2	14			5	6						7
1	4	3		12	8	7		9	14	13	11[2]		2	10[3]				5[1]	6						8
1	2	3	4	5	11	7[3]	8		10	13	9[2]		12		14				6[1]						9
1	2	3	4[3]	5	8	7	11	14	10[2]	12	9[1]	13							6						10
1[6]	2	3	4[2]	5[1]	8		11	13	10	7	9	12			15				6						11
	2	3		12	8			11	9[2]	10	13		4	6	7[1]			5		1					12
	2	13			6	7	8	10	11[1]	12	3		4		9[2]			5		1					13
	2	12			6	7[3]	8	10	11[1]	14	3		4		9[2]			5		1	13				14
	2	12		14	6	7	8	10[3]	11[2]	13	3		4		9[4]			5[1]		1					15
	2	11[1]			6	7	8	12	10	9	3		4					5		1					16
	2	3	4		6		8	10[2]	12	9[1]	7	11						5		1		13			17
	2	3	4				11	8	10[1]	9	7	12						5	6	1					18
	2				6		4[1]	11	8	12	10	7[2]	9	13	3			5		1					19
	2		4	9	6	8[1]	12	10	7	11	3							5		1					20
	2				6		4	11	8	9[2]	10	7[1]	12		3	13		5		1					21
	2				6		4	11	8[2]	9	10	7[1]	12		3	13		5		1					22
	2				6		4	7	8	13	10	9[1]	12		3	11[2]		5		1					23
	2				6		4	7	8	12	10	13		11[2]	3	9[1]		5		1					24
	2				6	13	4	7	8	12	10			11[2]	3	9[1]		5		1					25
	2				6		4	7	8	12	10		11		3	9[1]		5		1					26
	2				8[1]		4	7		12	10		9		3	6	11	5		1					27
	2				6		4	7[1]	8		10	13		11[2]	12	3		5		1			9		28
	2						4	7	8	9[1]	10		11		3	6		5		1				12	29
	2				6		4	7[1]	8	9[2]	10	11[3]	13		3			5	12	1		14			30
	2				6		4		8	9[1]	10	13	7		3	11[2]		5		1				12	31
	2				6[2]		4		8	12	10	14[4]	7		3	13	11[3]	5		1			9[1]		32
	2				12		4	13	8	9	10[3]	7[1]	3	6	11[2]		14	5		1					33
	2						4		8	9	10[1]	12	7		3	6	11	5		1					34
	2				6			7	11	12	8		9		3		10[1]	5	4	1					35
					6		11[1]	4	12	8	9[2]	10	7		3	2	13	5		1					36
14	6	9[1]		5			4	11	8	12	10	7[2]	13		3[3]	2				1					37
	6			5			4	7	8	9	10[1]	13		11[2]	3	2			12	1					38
	6			5			4	7	8		10	12		11[1]	3	2				1			9		39
	2			5			4	7	8	13	10	12		11[1]	3	6				1			9[2]		40
	2	13		5			4	7	8	12	10			11[2]	3	6				1			9[1]		41
	2			5			4	11[2]	8	14	10	7[1]	13	12	3	6				1			9[3]		42
			4	5				7	8	9[3]	10[2]	11[1]	12		3	6	13		2[4]	1		14			43
	2[4]	12		5			4	7	8		10	11[1]	13		3	6				1			9[2]		44
15		3[2]		5			4	7	8		10	12		11[1]	2	6	13			1[6]			9		45
1	2			5			4	7	8	9[1]	10		11		3	6								12	46

FA Cup

Fourth Qualifying Round	Chipstead	(h)	4-1
First Round	Evesham U	(h)	2-0
Second Round	Oxford U	(h)	2-0
Third Round	Blackpool	(h)	1-0
Fourth Round	Coventry C	(h)	0-1

Play-Offs

Semi-Final	Histon	(h)	2-0
		(a)	0-1
Final	Cambridge U	(h)	2-0
(at Wembley)			

WEYMOUTH

Blue Square South

Ground: Wessex Stadium, Radipole Road, Weymouth, Dorset DT4 9XJ.   *Tel:* (01305) 785 558.   *Year formed:* 1890.
Record gate: 6,680 (2005 v Nottingham F, FA Cup 1st rd replay).   *Nickname:* The Terras.   *Manager:* Matty Hale.
Secretary: Pete Saxby.   *Colours:* Claret and sky blue.

WEYMOUTH 2008–09 LEAGUE RECORD

Match No.	Date	Venue	Opponents	Result		H/T Score	Lg. Pos.	Goalscorers	Attendance
1	Aug 9	H	Grays Ath	W	3-1	2-1	—	Robinson [17], Reed [36], McPhee [78]	1059
2	12	A	Oxford U	W	1-0	1-0	—	Beavon [17]	4547
3	16	A	Stevenage Bor	D	1-1	1-1	3	Malcolm [28]	1357
4	23	H	Lewes	W	2-0	1-0	2	Malcolm [42], McPhee [69]	1172
5	25	A	Forest Green R	L	1-4	0-1	—	Doe [71]	1132
6	30	H	Cambridge U	D	2-2	0-2	7	McPhee [71], Malcolm [83]	1367
7	Sept 2	A	Salisbury C	L	0-1	0-0	—		1382
8	6	H	Histon	L	2-5	1-2	15	Malcolm [24], Bygrave [49]	1003
9	13	A	Burton Alb	D	1-1	1-1	16	Malcolm [34]	1435
10	20	H	Kidderminster H	L	1-2	1-1	18	Joseph-Dubois [15]	1014
11	23	H	Crawley T	D	2-2	1-1	—	McPhee [22], Malcolm [54]	1005
12	27	A	Northwich Vic	W	3-2	0-0	13	Welch (og) [52], Beavon (pen) [81], Coutts [90]	700
13	Oct 4	H	Eastbourne Bor	W	3-2	2-1	12	Beavon (pen) [17], McPhee [29], Joseph-Dubois [90]	931
14	7	A	Woking	D	1-1	0-0	—	Beavon [58]	1802
15	11	H	Cambridge U	L	0-1	0-1	16		3981
16	18	H	Altrincham	W	2-0	1-0	17	McPhee [34], Williams [83]	926
17	Nov 1	A	Kettering T	W	1-0	0-0	10	Coutts [87]	1607
18	8	A	Rushden & D	L	0-1	0-0	—		1002
19	15	H	Wrexham	L	1-3	0-1	11	Beavon [90]	1207
20	18	H	Woking	D	1-1	0-0	—	Coutts [50]	696
21	22	A	Barrow	W	1-0	0-0	9	Joseph-Dubois [52]	1350
22	29	H	Mansfield T	D	1-1	1-1	10	McPhee [21]	931
23	Dec 6	A	Ebbsfleet U	L	0-1	0-1	10		1005
24	9	H	Oxford U	D	2-2	1-1	—	Beavon 2 [39, 51]	822
25	20	A	Mansfield T	L	1-2	1-0	11	Beavon (pen) [20]	1841
26	26	H	Torquay U	L	0-1	0-1	11		2323
27	Jan 17	A	Kidderminster H	W	2-0	1-0	13	Beavon 2 [43, 56]	1569
28	24	H	Northwich Vic	W	3-0	3-0	13	Beavon 2 (1 pen) [5 (p), 10], Phillips [32]	1105
29	27	A	Grays Ath	D	1-1	0-0	—	Beavon [9]	415
30	Feb 10	A	Torquay U	W	2-0	1-0	—	Williams [45], Beavon [88]	1743
31	14	H	Stevenage Bor	L	0-3	0-1	—		1226
32	21	H	Rushden & D	L	0-9	0-4	14		967
33	28	A	York C	L	0-2	0-1	15		2349
34	Mar 8	A	Crawley T	L	2-4	2-3	15	Vincent [18], Rayner (og) [38]	901
35	10	H	Salisbury C	L	0-4	0-1	—		1005
36	14	A	Altrincham	L	0-4	0-3	16		770
37	17	H	Burton Alb	L	0-5	0-3	—		848
38	21	A	Kettering T	L	0-2	0-0	16		913
39	29	H	Barrow	L	0-3	0-0	18		1264
40	Apr 4	A	Eastbourne Bor	L	0-3	0-1	20		1075
41	11	A	Lewes	L	0-1	0-0	21		456
42	13	H	Forest Green R	D	1-1	1-0	21	Akurang [33]	1183
43	18	H	Ebbsfleet U	L	0-2	0-2	22		1007
44	21	A	Histon	L	0-1	0-1	—		1016
45	24	H	York C	L	1-2	1-1	—	Akurang [46]	1122
46	26	A	Wrexham	L	0-2	0-2	23		2756

Final League Position: 23

GOALSCORERS

League (45): Beavon 14 (4 pens), McPhee 7, Malcolm 6, Coutts 3, Joseph-Dubois 3, Akurang 2, Williams 2, Bygrave 1, Doe 1, Phillips 1, Reed 1, Robinson 1, Vincent 1, own goals 2.
FA Cup (1): Beavon 1.

Bernard 14	Mawer 34 + 2	Hart 5 + 3	Sandwith 30	Malcolm 14 + 3	Hyde 6	Doe 29	Gaia 24 + 1	Palmer 4 + 4	Williams 28 + 3	Robinson 28 + 1	McPhee 30	Ryan 3	Beavon 26 + 1	Reed 31 + 1	Coutts 23 + 10	Joseph-Dubois 10 + 11	Critchell 8	Webb 1 + 3	Cutler 22 + 7	Gill 9	Bygrave 13 + 3	Knowles 17	Collins 8 + 3	Onibuje 5 + 4	Phillips 5	Browning 3 + 2	Prodomo 1	Vincent 6	Legzdins 8	Robins 1	Dickson 3 + 1	Merella 6 + 1	Babson 1	Akurang 8	Richardson 1 + 7	Frampton 1 + 1	Poole — + 1	Tribe 1 + 2	Gwinnett 2 + 2	Luther 1	Tubbs — + 1	Bansenbe 1	Cooke 2 + 2	McKechnie 1 + 3	Agera 1 + 1	Evans 6	Strickland 1	Hoyte 14	Crook 6	Appiah 4	Match No.
1	2	3	4	5	6	7	8	9	10	11																																									1
1	2	3	4^2	5	6	7^1	8	9	10	11	12	13																																							2
1	2	3	4	5	6	7^1	8	9	10	11	12																																							3
1	2	3	4^3	5	6	7	8^2	9	10	11^1	14				12	13																																		4
1	2^1	3	4^3	5	6	7	8	9	10	11^2	14				13	12																																		5
1	2*	3	4	5	6	7^1	8	9	10^2	11					12	13																																		6
1			4	5	6	7	8	9	10	11					2		3																																	7
1		3	4^3	5	6	7^1	8	9	10	11^2	12	13			14				2																															8
1		3	4	5	6	7	8	9					11		13	10^2	12		2^1																															9
1	2	3	4	5	6^1	7	8	9					11			10			12																															10
1	2	3	4	5		7	8	9					11		12	10^1			6																															11
1	2	3	4^1	5		7	8	9	13	11	12	10^2			6																																			12
	2	3	4^2	5	12	7^3	8	9	10	11^1					14				6	13	1																												13
1	2	3	12		6	7^1	8	9	10^2	11					13						4	5																												14
1	2^1	3	13	5	6	12	8	7	10	11					9				4^2																															15
	2	3	13	5	6	7^3	12	9	10	11					8^2				4^1	14	1																												16
13	3	4	5		6^1	7^2	8	9	10	11	12								2	1																														17
	2	3		5		7	8	9	10	11					4							6							1																					18
	2^1	3		5	6	12	8	9	10	11					7							4							1																					19
		3		5	6	7	8	9	10	11					2^1	12						2							1																					20
	2	3		5		7^1	8		10	11			9		4	6	1	12																																21
	2	3		5		7^1	8	9					11		12	10	13		4^2	6	1																												22
	2	3		5		12	8	7					10		11^1	9			4	6	1																												23
12		3		5	6*	7^2	8	9	10						13	2			4		1	11^1																												24
		3		5	6	11^1	8	7	10						12	9			4	2	1																												25
	2	3			6	11	8	7	10						5	9			4		1																												26
	2	3		5	6	11^1	8	7	10^2							4	13				1	9	12																										27
	2^3	3		5	6	11^2	8	7	10	14						4^1	12				1	13	9																										28
	2	3		5	6	11^1	8	7	10							4					1	12	9																										29
	2	3		5	6	7				8					10	11	4				1		9																											30
	2	3		5	6	7				8					10	11	4				1		9																											31
																	3								1	2	4^1	5	7^2	13	12	6	8^3	14	11	9	10														32
	2														11										4^1			6	7	9^2	13	12		13				12		1	3		5	8	10						33
		6		3			12								11	2			4^2										10		9		13							1				5	7	8^1		34
	2	3		7^2			12								11^*	8			4									6^3		14				13							1			5	10	9^1		35
	2^3	3		9			8		7							4						11^1						6					12		14				13		1			5^2	10			36
	3			10			11		6						8^1				4								2					12						13		1			5	7	9^2		37
	2			10^2			9		6^1						8		3	4		7		12									13							13		1			5	11			38
	2			9^1			12								8	6		4		7		13	1		3			10						11^2						5								39
	2	14					13										11^1	3	4		9	8^3	12	6	1		7^2		10											5								40
	12						9								11	8		3	4^1		7	2^2	13	6^*	1				10											5								41
	2	14													11	4		3			7	6	9^1		1			8^2		10^3	13						12			5								42
	2	6^3													11	4		3			7^2		9	12	1			14		10				13			8^1			5								43
	2														11^2	4	13	3			7^1	6^1	9		1			8		10				12						5								44
	2^2														8	12	3	4			7^1		9		1			11		10		13		6				3		13	14		5					45
															8	12^2		4			7^3		9^1	6	1			11		10		2		3				13		14			5					46

FA Cup
Fourth Qualifying Round
AFC Hornchurch   (h)   1-2

WOKING   Blue Square South

Ground: Kingfield Sports Ground, Kingfield, Woking, Surrey GU22 9AA.   *Tel:* (01483) 772 470.   *Year Formed:* 1889.
Record Gate: 6,084 (1997 v Coventry City, FA Cup 3rd rd).   *Nickname:* The Cards.   *Manager:* Graham Baker.
Secretary: Phil Ledger.   *Colours:* Red and white shirts, black shorts, red stockings.

WOKING 2008–09 LEAGUE RECORD

Match No.	Date	Venue	Opponents	Result	H/T Score	Lg. Pos.	Goalscorers	Atten- dance
1	Aug 9	H	Altrincham	L 1-2	0-1	—	Ledgister 66	1645
2	12	A	Torquay U	L 1-2	1-0	—	Sole 35	2881
3	16	A	Burton Alb	L 2-3	2-0	24	Pattison 19, Sole 21	1456
4	23	H	Forest Green R	L 0-1	0-0	24		1617
5	25	A	Oxford U	D 0-0	0-0	24		4314
6	30	A	Kettering T	L 0-1	0-0	24		1493
7	Sept 2	H	Lewes	D 1-1	0-1	—	Sole 85	1604
8	6	A	York C	L 0-2	0-0	23		2307
9	13	H	Grays Ath	W 3-1	0-1	22	Domoraud 48, Lorraine 56, Ledgister 90	1619
10	20	A	Ebbsfleet U	L 0-2	0-0	22		1498
11	23	H	Salisbury C	W 1-0	0-0	—	Marum 58	1369
12	27	H	Histon	W 1-0	0-0	21	Domoraud 56	1797
13	Oct 4	A	Mansfield T	W 1-0	0-0	19	Sole (pen) 58	2563
14	7	H	Weymouth	D 1-1	0-0	—	Ledgister 80	1802
15	11	H	York C	L 0-2	0-0	20		2341
16	18	A	Grays Ath	D 1-1	0-0	20	Lorraine 67	581
17	Nov 1	H	Stevenage Bor	L 0-1	0-1	20		1955
18	15	A	Eastbourne Bor	D 0-0	0-0	20		1105
19	18	A	Weymouth	D 1-1	0-0	—	Lorraine 51	696
20	22	H	Torquay U	D 2-2	2-0	20	Marum 6, Vernazza 22	2452
21	Dec 6	A	Histon	L 0-1	0-0	20		1249
22	9	H	Rushden & D	D 1-1	1-1	—	Denton 17	1119
23	20	A	Lewes	W 2-0	1-0	20	Domoraud 2 42, 71	694
24	26	H	Crawley T	D 0-0	0-0	21		1910
25	28	A	Wrexham	D 1-1	0-1	21	Denton 72	4803
26	Jan 1	A	Crawley T	D 2-2	1-0	21	Domoraud 26, Spence 57	1525
27	17	A	Cambridge U	L 1-4	0-2	21	Sole 90	2696
28	24	H	Ebbsfleet U	W 1-0	0-0	19	Ledgister 70	1471
29	27	H	Eastbourne Bor	L 0-4	0-3	—		1101
30	31	H	Northwich Vic	W 4-1	2-0	—	Domoraud 3 17, 30, 79, Lambu 88	1092
31	Feb 14	H	Kettering T	L 0-1	0-1	—		1414
32	17	A	Salisbury C	L 0-1	0-0	—		923
33	21	A	Altrincham	L 0-1	0-1	20		943
34	24	A	Stevenage Bor	L 0-1	0-0	—		1965
35	28	H	Burton Alb	D 0-0	0-0	20		1813
36	Mar 7	H	Barrow	W 1-0	1-0	19	Bozanic 22	1529
37	14	H	Wrexham	D 1-1	0-1	19	Elvins 53	1676
38	21	A	Kidderminster H	L 0-3	0-1	22		1594
39	30	H	Cambridge U	L 0-1	0-0	—		1775
40	Apr 1	H	Kidderminster H	L 1-5	0-4	—	Bozanic 66	751
41	4	A	Barrow	W 1-0	0-0	22	Marum 88	1424
42	7	A	Northwich Vic	L 0-2	0-1	—		450
43	11	A	Forest Green R	W 2-0	1-0	20	Rhodes 18, Marum 90	1109
44	13	H	Oxford U	L 0-2	0-2	20		3791
45	18	H	Mansfield T	D 2-2	1-1	21	Miles 44, Anderson 67	2096
46	26	A	Rushden & D	L 1-3	1-2	21	Kamara 10	1676

Final League Position: 21

GOALSCORERS

League (37): Domoraud 8, Sole 5 (1 pen), Ledgister 4, Marum 4, Lorraine 3, Bozanic 2, Denton 2, Anderson 1, Elvins 1, Kamara 1, Lambu 1, Miles 1, Pattison 1, Rhodes 1, Spence 1, Vernazza 1.
FA Cup (2): Domoraud 1, Marum 1.

Worner 4	Mondon-Konan 37 + 4	Bunce 22 + 3	Vernazza 21 + 4	Hutchinson 17 + 1	Miles 30	Salau 1 + 1	Pattison 34 + 7	Williams 4 + 8	Marum 26 + 14	El Kholti 15	Lorraine 33 + 3	San-Yorke 5 + 12	Ledgister 19 + 12	Sole 17 + 4	Ouamina 28 + 4	Lambu 19 + 10	Pidgeley 16	Domoraud 35 + 2	Thorpe 1	Moone 2 + 10	Spence 11	Gindre 2	Magunda 8 + 2	Denton 3 + 2	Kamara 14 + 1	Eastwood 12	Bozanic 18	Elvins 7 + 2	Anderson 14	Bossman 7 + 1	McNerney — + 3	Knowles 12	Sintin 6 + 4	Hyde 4	Rhodes 2 + 1	Match No.
1	2	3	4	5	6¹	7²	8	9³	10	11	12	13	14																							1
1	2	3	4	5	6		8		10²	11		13	7	9¹	12																					2
1	2	3	4	5	6¹	13	8²	14	10³	11	12	9	7																							3
	2	3¹	4	5	6		8²	14	10³	11	12	9	13	7	1																					4
	2		4	5	3		12	10²		11	6	7		9¹	8	13	1																			5
	2	12	4	5	6¹		13	9	14	11²	3	7³		10	8		1																			6
	2	3	4²	5			8	12			13	9	6	7¹	1	11	10																			7
	2	3¹		5	6		8²	14	13		10³	9	4	7	1	11	12																			8
	12	3		5	6		14	9²	10³		2	13	11	8	7¹	1	4																			9
	12	3²		5	6		14	10¹		2	13	9³	11	8	7	1	4																			10
	2			5	6		8²	10		3		12	9	4	7¹	1	11	13																		11
	2	12		5	6¹		8²	10		3	14	13	9	4	7³	1	11																			12
	2	12		5	6¹			10		3	13	11	9	4	7	1	8²																			13
	2	3		5			14	13	10³	6	11¹	8	9²	4	7	1		12																		14
	2	3		5¹	6		12		10³		4¹	13	11	9²	8¹	7	1	14																		15
	2		4		6		8¹	13	10	3³	5	11	9²		1	12	14	7																		16
	2¹	3		5	6			10	11		13	12	4	7²¹	9		8																			17
	2	3	4	5	6¹		8¹	10	11			12		1	9		7																			18
	2	3	4		8		10¹	11	5			12	6		1	9		7																		19
	2	3	4		8		10²	11	5	13			12		9		7	1																		20
	3			6			8	12	11	5			4		9¹		7	1	2²	10	13															21
	3	4		6			8	10²	11¹	5		13	7		12				2	9		1														22
	2	3			6		8	10				12	7	9¹		11				4		5		1												23
	2	3			6		8	10¹				7	9¹	12		11				4		5		1												24
	2	3					8					9²	7¹		11	12		10		4		5	13	6	1											25
	2¹	3					8					12	14	7²	4	13		10		11		5	9³	6	1											26
	13	3¹	12				8	10		6		7	14		11³	9				4		5²	2	1												27
	2²	4¹	6					10³		3		7		8	12	9		14		13		5	1	11												28
	2²		6		8			10¹		3		7³		4	12	9				14	13	5	1	11												29
	14		6		8		13			3		7¹		4	12	9		10²		2		5³	1	11												30
	2		6		8¹			12	3			7		4	9							5	1	11	10											31
	2	12			8			10¹	3¹	6		7		4²	9	13						5	1	11												32
	2	4²			8			13	6			7¹			9	10³						5	1	11		3	12	14								33
		4					8²	12	5						9	13						2			11	10	3³	7¹	14	1	6					34
	2	4					8²	12	5	13					9	13									11	10	3	9¹		1	6	7				35
	2		6		8		12	5				13			9										11	10³	3	7²		1	14	4¹				36
	2	6¹			8		5	14				13			9										11	10	3	7²		1	12			4³		37
	2	4	6¹		8³		13	5				14			9										11	10²	3	7		1	12					38
					8		10	6				13		4	7¹	9						5			11	12	3²			1	2					39
		14			8²		10	6				13		4	7¹	9³						5			11	12	3			1	2					40
	2	4³	6⁴		8		13	5				7		9²	12										11		3	10¹		1	14					41
1	2	4³			8		12	6				14		7	9							5²			11		3	10¹						13		42
	2	13					12	14	6					4³	7	9									11		3			1	5	8²	10¹			43
	2						8³	12	13	6		14		4²	7	9									11		3			1	5¹	10				44
	2	8¹	14	6			12		10³	5		7		4	13	9									11²		3			1						45
	2	3	8							6	13	7		4²		9		14						5¹	11		10³		12	1						46

FA Cup
Fourth Qualifying Round

	Ebbsfleet U	(h)	2-2
		(a)	0-1

WREXHAM
Blue Square Premier

Ground: Recreation Ground, Mold Road, Wrexham LL11 2AH. Tel: (01978) 262 129. *Year Formed:* 1872.
Record Gate: 34,445 v Manchester U, FA Cup 4th rd, 1957. *Nickname:* Red Dragons. *Manager:* Dean Saunders.
Secretary: Geraint Parry. *Colours:* Red shirts, white shorts, red stockings.

WREXHAM 2008–09 LEAGUE RECORD

Match No.	Date	Venue	Opponents	Result	H/T Score	Lg. Pos.	Goalscorers	Attendance
1	Aug 9	H	Stevenage Bor	W 5-0	1-0	—	Kearney [18], Louis [66], Whalley [71], Smith [85], Williams Marc [87]	4901
2	14	A	York C	L 0-1	0-0	—		2603
3	17	A	Rushden & D	D 1-1	0-0	—	Whalley [75]	1805
4	21	H	Oxford U	W 2-0	1-0	—	Evans S [29], Louis [90]	3515
5	25	A	Altrincham	D 1-1	1-1	8	Louis [39]	2619
6	30	A	Salisbury C	W 4-1	1-1	5	Whalley 2 [43, 90], Louis 2 [54, 76]	1532
7	Sept 2	H	Burton Alb	L 0-1	0-1	—		4104
8	6	A	Cambridge U	L 0-2	0-1	13		3076
9	13	H	Ebbsfleet U	W 3-2	1-1	8	Louis 2 [37, 51], Brown S (pen) [77]	3132
10	20	A	Grays Ath	L 1-2	0-2	12	Mackin [51]	746
11	23	H	Rushden & D	L 0-3	0-2			2805
12	27	H	Torquay U	D 1-1	1-1	14	Brown S [44]	2897
13	Oct 4	A	Forest Green R	W 3-2	1-1	13	Williams Marc 2 [29, 65], Louis [90]	1216
14	7	H	York C	W 3-1	0-0	—	Allen [65], Taylor [85], Williams Marc [90]	5173
15	18	A	Mansfield T	W 2-1	1-1	8	Williams Mike [32], Williams Marc [57]	2757
16	Nov 1	H	Lewes	W 2-0	1-0	8	Westwood [18], Williams Mike [69]	3201
17	15	A	Weymouth	W 3-1	1-0	8	Woolfe [15], Louis [83], Williams Marc [84]	1207
18	22	A	Kidderminster H	L 0-1	0-1	8		2403
19	29	A	Stevenage Bor	W 2-1	0-0	7	Louis [56], Williams Marc [81]	1673
20	Dec 6	H	Kettering T	W 2-1	0-1	7	Suffo (pen) [88], Brown J [90]	3687
21	20	H	Eastbourne Bor	W 5-0	1-0	7	Williams Marc 3 [44, 65, 90], Louis [47], Taylor [89]	3463
22	26	A	Barrow	D 1-1	0-1	7	Louis [90]	1250
23	28	H	Woking	D 1-1	1-0	7	Williams Marc [24]	4803
24	Jan 16	A	Torquay U	D 1-1	1-0	—	Flynn [31]	1842
25	22	H	Cambridge U	W 2-0	1-0	—	Brown J [26], Louis [59]	3103
26	27	H	Northwich Vic	D 3-3	0-0	—	Evans S [64], Williams Marc [79], Suffo (pen) [90]	3722
27	Feb 7	A	Lewes	W 2-0	0-0	—	Williams Marc [68], Baynes [83]	689
28	14	H	Grays Ath	W 3-2	1-1	—	Fairhurst [6], Brown J [55], Flynn [57]	3419
29	17	H	Burton Alb	L 1-2	1-0	—	Louis [23]	3262
30	28	H	Salisbury C	D 1-1	1-0	6	Flynn [6]	3206
31	Mar 3	A	Crawley T	L 0-1	0-0	—		737
32	7	A	Eastbourne Bor	L 0-1	0-0	8		1428
33	10	A	Forest Green R	D 1-1	0-0	—	Louis [86]	2405
34	14	A	Woking	D 1-1	1-0	9	Baynes [11]	1676
35	17	A	Northwich Vic	W 2-1	1-1	—	Jansen [15], Fairhurst [74]	1709
36	21	H	Crawley T	L 0-2	0-2	10		3303
37	23	H	Kidderminster H	L 0-1	0-0	—		2674
38	28	A	Histon	L 0-1	0-1	10		1106
39	Apr 2	H	Barrow	D 1-1	0-0	—	Anoruo [76]	2272
40	4	H	Mansfield T	W 2-0	2-0	10	Anoruo (pen) [10], Crofts [25]	2401
41	7	H	Histon	D 0-0	0-0	—		2234
42	11	A	Oxford U	L 0-1	0-0	10		5832
43	13	H	Altrincham	L 0-1	0-0	10		2554
44	18	A	Kettering T	L 0-1	0-1	10		1497
45	21	A	Ebbsfleet U	L 0-1	0-0	10		880
46	26	H	Weymouth	W 2-0	2-0	10	Proctor [30], Flynn [33]	2756

Final League Position: 10

GOALSCORERS
League (64): Louis 15, Marc Williams 13, Flynn 4, Whalley 4, Brown J 3, Anoruo 2 (1 pen), Baynes 2, Brown S 2 (1 pen), Evans S 2, Fairhurst 2, Suffo 2 (2 pens), Taylor 2, Mike Williams 2, Allen 1, Crofts 1, Jansen 1, Kearney 1, Mackin 1, Proctor 1, Smith 1, Westwood 1, Woolfe 1.
FA Cup (0).

Ward 32	Spender 12+1	Tremarco 17	Kempson 15	Brown N 6+1	Williams A 5	Mackin 13+3	Anoruo 4+7	Kearney 13+2	Brown S 10+3	Louis 38+4	Whalley 14+2	Jansen 3	Aiston 11+8	Evans S 11+3	Williams Marc 19+3	Neilsen 5	Smith 2+6	Baynes 15+13	Taylor 18+8	Critchell 2	Assoumani 3	Evans G —+1	Proctor 8+10	Maxwell 4	Pejic 1	Williams Mike 25+2	Fleming 24	Spann 7+6	Edwards —+1	Allen 2	Westwood 31	De Laet 3	Tsiaklis 6	Woolfe 8+2	Fairhurst 15+5	Suffo 1+13	Williamson 23+3	Brown J 16+5	Abbott 1+1	Flynn 21+4	McCluskey 3+5	Crofts 16	Curtis 13	Collin 10+2	Match No.
1	2	3	4^1	5	6^1	7	8	9^2	10^3	11	12	13	14																																1
1	2	3	4	5^1		7	8^2	9^3	10	11	12	14	6	13																															2
1	2	3	6		4	7	8	9^2	10	11^1	5							12	13																										3
1	2	3	4		6	7	14	9^3	10	11^2	5							12	13	8^1																									4
1	2^2	3	4		6	7	14	9	10^1	11^3	5							13	12	8																									5
1	2	3	4	5^2	13	7	8	9^3	10	14	6							11^1			12																								6
1	2	3	4	6^2	7	8	9^3	10	13	5					12^{1}			11			14																								7
1	2	3	4	6	7	8^2	9	10	13						11^1			12	5																									8
1	2	3	4	6^1	7	8	9^3	10		5			14					12	11^2		13																								9
1	2^1	3	4	13	6	7^2	8	9	10	5								14	11^3		12																								10
1		3	4	2	6^1	7	13	9^3	10	11^2	5		14	12					8																										11
1	2^3	3	4	5	6		8	12	10^1					9^2	11	13	14					7																							12
1			4	6				9	10^1				5	11				2	8				12			3	7																		13
1		3				12			9					5	10			2	11				6	4		7^1	8																		14
1	3^1			6			8^2				14	13	9				2	7					10	4^3		12	11	5																	15
1				6				9	10					8^1			2	7	11				4			12	5	3	7																16
1		3						9	13					10	14	2							6			12	5	7^1	8	4^3	11^2														17
1		3^2				14		9						10			7	12					6				5	2^1	4	11	8^3	13													18
1								9	14						10	13	2^1	12					6				5	4	7^2	8		11^3		3	11^3									19
1								9		12		9^3	13		10			2					6				5	4^1	11^2	8	14	3	7												20
1								9							10			2					6	8^1			5	4^2	11^3	12	14	3	7	13											21
1	12							9							10			2					6	4			5		11^3	8^2	14	3	7			13									22
1	2							9		14					10		2						6	4			5		11		3	7		8^1											23
1	2							9^3	12						10			2^2					6	4	13		5		14	11		3	7	8^1											24
1								9							10	5		2					6	4			5		11^1	8^2	13	12	3	7^3											25
1								9^2							10								6	4			5		11^1	8^2	13	3	7	12											26
1								9				10^3			10			12	2				6	4			5		14	7	13	3	11^1	8^3											27
1								9							10			12	2				6	4			5		11	14	3	7^1	8^2	13											28
1								9							10^1			12	2				6	4			5		13	3	7^1	11^3	14	8^2											29
1								9							10^1								6	4			5		12	3	7	11^2	13	8	2										30
1								9							14								6	4^1			5		12	13	3	7	11^3	10^2	8	2									31
1								9^1	7						13								10^3				5		4	12	3	14	11^2	8	2	6									32
				1		13	9^3												10								5		4^2	12			3	7^1	11		8	2	6					33
				1		13	9^3					10^1						2					14				5		4	12			3	7		11^2	8	7	6					34
		3		1		13						10^5							7^1				9^2	14			5		4					12	11		8	2	6					35
				1		13						10^2											9	12			5					4^3	14	3	7	11		8	2	6				36
				1		10	9	7^2											2				13				5		4					3	12		11^1	8		6				37
		3				13	12	7					1						6	4							2			10^1			14		9^2	11^3	8	5						38
						12	13						1	7			1	7					10^2				6	4	11^3		5		9^1	3		14		8	2					39
						10^5	9						1	13	3			1	13	3			6	4		7^2	5		14	12		13^3	10^3		14	8		4						40
						9							1	12	2^2	3		6	11				7^1				5		13	10^3		14			8		4							41
						13	9^2						1^6	12		4		6	11	7							5		3^1			10		3^1		10	8	2	15					42
						9									7^2	14			3	2^8	12	1	4	11^1			5		4	11^1		3^3		10	13	8		6						43
						14	13	9							3				1			1					5		7^1			4^3		12		11^2	10	8	2	6				44
				6			8^2	10^1	9^3	11								12^1				1	4				5		3			4^3		3		7	13	2	14					45
				6			8			11								9^3	1				4^2		12	5					13		3	14	10	7		2^1						46

FA Cup
Fourth Qualifying Round

Eastwood T	(h)	0-0
	(a)	0-2

YORK CITY

Blue Square Premier

Ground: KitKat Crescent, York YO30 7AQ. *Tel:* (01904) 624 447. *Year Formed:* 1922.
Record Gate: 28,123 (1938 v Huddersfield T, FA Cup 6th rd). *Nickname:* Minster Men.
Manager: Martin Foyle. *Secretary:* Nick Barrett. *Colours:* Red shirts, navy shorts, navy stockings.

YORK CITY 2008–09 LEAGUE RECORD

Match No.	Date	Venue	Opponents	Result		H/T Score	Lg. Pos.	Goalscorers	Attendance
1	Aug 9	A	Crawley T	W	1-0	0-0	—	Farrell [71]	1372
2	14	H	Wrexham	W	1-0	0-0	—	Greaves [74]	2603
3	16	H	Histon	D	1-1	0-1	5	McBreen [69]	2125
4	23	A	Northwich Vic	D	2-2	1-2	6	Brodie [26], Crowell (og) [57]	1065
5	25	H	Barrow	D	1-1	1-1	7	Brodie [3]	2664
6	28	A	Torquay U	D	1-1	0-0	—	Sodje [87]	1598
7	Sept 2	H	Mansfield T	D	1-1	1-0	—	Sodje [35]	2520
8	6	H	Woking	W	2-0	1-0	7	McBreen [38], Bunce (og) [49]	2307
9	13	A	Kettering T	L	2-4	1-2	11	Brodie [23], Purkiss [49]	2017
10	20	H	Salisbury C	D	1-1	0-0	10	McBreen [86]	2280
11	23	A	Kidderminster H	L	0-2	0-0	—		1481
12	28	A	Stevenage Bor	D	3-3	2-2	15	Sodje [25], Holmes [45], Farrell [49]	1917
13	Oct 4	H	Cambridge U	D	0-0	0-0	15		2608
14	7	A	Wrexham	L	1-3	0-0	—	Wilkinson [89]	5173
15	11	A	Woking	W	2-0	0-0	14	Wilkinson [66], McBreen [72]	2341
16	18	H	Rushden & D	W	2-0	1-0	10	Robinson [18], Farrell [50]	2313
17	Nov 1	A	Oxford U	L	0-1	0-0	13		4449
18	15	H	Torquay U	L	1-2	0-0	15	Greaves [85]	2412
19	18	A	Cambridge U	L	0-1	0-0	—		2914
20	23	H	Crawley T	D	2-2	1-0	14	Sodje 2 [7, 48]	1935
21	29	A	Salisbury C	D	1-1	0-1	14	Brodie [83]	986
22	Dec 6	H	Grays Ath	L	0-1	0-1	15		2154
23	9	A	Histon	D	1-1	1-0	—	Brodie [14]	901
24	20	H	Ebbsfleet U	W	3-1	0-1	14	Smith A [60], Brodie [67], Sodje [77]	1997
25	26	A	Burton Alb	L	1-2	0-0	16	Smith A [53]	3578
26	28	H	Altrincham	L	1-2	1-0	16	Brodie [32]	2389
27	Jan 1	H	Burton Alb	L	1-3	1-1	16	Brodie [39]	2703
28	17	H	Lewes	W	3-0	0-0	16	Brodie 2 [56, 78], Smith C [68]	2073
29	24	A	Eastbourne Bor	L	1-2	0-1	17	Smith C [63]	1668
30	27	A	Altrincham	D	1-1	0-1	—	Brodie [46]	1027
31	Feb 7	A	Mansfield T	L	0-1	0-1	—		2576
32	24	A	Rushden & D	L	0-2	0-0	—		1020
33	28	H	Weymouth	W	2-0	1-0	17	Brodie 2 [23, 90]	2349
34	Mar 8	A	Ebbsfleet U	D	0-0	0-0	17		1244
35	17	A	Forest Green R	D	1-1	0-1	—	Sodje [86]	681
36	24	H	Kettering T	D	0-0	0-0	—		1714
37	28	H	Kidderminster H	D	0-0	0-0	19		2384
38	31	H	Stevenage Bor	L	0-2	0-0	—		1924
39	Apr 4	A	Grays Ath	L	0-1	0-1	21		720
40	7	H	Oxford U	D	0-0	0-0	—		2268
41	11	A	Northwich Vic	L	1-2	0-1	22	Robinson (pen) [68]	2421
42	13	A	Barrow	D	0-0	0-0	22		2168
43	18	H	Eastbourne Bor	W	1-0	1-0	20	McBreen [35]	2487
44	21	H	Forest Green R	W	2-1	0-0	—	Boyes [59], Brodie [63]	2164
45	24	H	Weymouth	W	2-1	1-1	—	Brodie [14], Boyes [77]	1122
46	26	A	Lewes	D	1-1	0-0	17	Greaves [80]	802

Final League Position: 17

GOALSCORERS

League (47): Brodie 15, Sodje 7, McBreen 5, Farrell 3, Greaves 3, Boyes 2, Robinson 2 (1 pen), Smith A 2, Smith C 2, Wilkinson 2, Holmes 1, Purkiss 1, own goals 2.
FA Cup (0).

Krysiak 2	Purkiss 38 + 1	Robinson 37	Wilkinson 11 + 10	McGurk 35 + 2	Parslow 45	Rusk 35 + 2	Greaves 27 + 8	McBreen 31 + 7	Brodie 29 + 9	Farrell 15 + 10	Mimms 4 + 2	Sodje 17 + 19	Henderson 4 + 2	Shepherd 1 + 7	Kelly 8 + 2	Russell 15 + 8	Ingham 40	Bore 2 + 2	Boyes 10 + 13	Holmes 5	Rothery — + 1	Hogg 8 + 1	Dyer 2	McWilliams 14 + 2	Smith A 9 + 8	Critchell 6	Brown 11 + 6	Mackin 15	Smith C 14 + 1	Pejic 15	Torpey 1 + 1	Match No.
1	2	3	4	5	6	7	8	9	10	11																						1
1[6]	2	3	4	5	6	7	8	9[1]	10[2]	11	15	12	13																			2
	2	3	4[1]	5	6	7	8	9[3]	13	10	1	12	11[2]	14																		3
	2[1]	3	4[2]	5	6	7		9	10[3]	11	1	13	8		12	14																4
	2	3	12	5	6	7	8	10	9[3]	13		4[1]	14		11[2]		1															5
	2	3	4[2]	5	6	7[1]	8	9	10	11[3]		14	12		13		1															6
	2	3	4	5	6		8	9	10	12		11[2]			7[1]	13	1															7
	2	3	4	5	6		8	9[3]	10[2]	14		12			7	11[1]	1	13														8
	2	3	13	5	6		8	9[3]	10	14		12	4		11[2]		1	7[1]														9
	2	3	12	5	6	7[1]	8	14	10	11[3]		9[2]			4		1	13														10
	2	3	4	5	6	7		9	10[2]			12			13	11[1]	1		8													11
	2[1]	3	13	5	6	7	8	14	12	10		9[3]			11[2]	4	1															12
	2	3	12	5	6	7	8	9[2]	13	11[3]		10[1]			14	4	1															13
	2	3	4	5	6	7	8[1]	9	12[4]	10[3]		14	13		11[2]		1															14
	2	3	4	5	6	7	12	9[2]	10	11		13			8[1]																	15
	2	3	4[2]	5	6	7	12	9	14	11[3]		8[1]	13		10		1															16
	2	3		5	6	7	8	9	12			10[1]			4[2]	11[3]	1		14		13											17
	2	3		5	6	7	8		12	13		9			4[2]		1		14						11[3]							18
	2	3[1]	14	5	6	7	8	9[2]	10	13		12			4		1								11[3]							19
	2			5	6	7	8		12	13		9		11[1]	4		1		10[2]				3									20
	2	3	14	5	6	7[3]	8	9	13			11[1]			4[2]		1		10						12							21
	2	3[2]	14	5	6	7	8[3]	9	10						4[1]		1		13						11	12						22
	2			5	6	7	8	13	10			12	15		9[2]		1[6]					4			11[1]		3					23
	2	3[1]		5	6	7	8[2]	10	9			12					1		13			4			11							24
	2			5	6	7	8	10[3]	13			9[2]			12		1		14			4[1]			11		3					25
	2		13	5	6	7[3]	8	9[1]	12			10			11[2]		1		14			4					3					26
		3	12	5	6	7		9[2]	10	14		8[3]	13			2	1					4[1]			11							27
		3			6			9[2]	10								1		14			8		12	11[1]		4	13	5	7	2[3]	28
	2[2]	3			6	7	8[1]	9[3]	10								1		14					12	11		4	13	5			29
	2	3			6	7[2]		9	10			13					1							12	11[1]		4		5	8		30
	2	3[2]			6	7	2	9[1]	10			13					1							12	11		4		5	8		31
	2	3			6	7[1]		9[3]	10[2]			13					1		14					12	11		4		5	8		32
		3			6		13	9[1]	10	14							1		12						11		7[3]	2	5	4	8[2]	33
	2	3	14		6	7[3]		9				13					1		10[2]						12		4	8	5	11[1]		34
	2	3		5	6	7		9[1]				13					1		12					14	10	11	8[3]	4[2]	5			35
	2	3			6	7[1]	12	9[3]	10	14							1		11[2]					8	13	4	5					36
	2	3	14		6	7[1]	12	9[2]	10	11							1							8	13	4[3]	5					37
	2	3			6	7		9[1]	10	11							1		12					8[2]	13	4	5					38
	2[2]	3		5	6	7[4]	14	9				12					1		13					11[1]	10	8[3]	4					39
		3		5	6		8[2]	9	10[1]								1		11	13				12	7	4	2					40
	12	3		5	6	4		9[2]	13	7							1		11					14	10[3]	8	2[1]					41
	2			5	6		14	13	10			12					1		11					7[2]	9[1]	4	8	3[3]				42
	2			5	6		9[2]	10[3]	14								1		11					7[1]	12	4	8	3	13			43
	2			5	6		9[1]	10	12								1		11					7[2]	13	4	8	3				44
	2			5	6		12	9[2]	10	13							1		11					7[1]		4	8	3				45
	2	3				7	8	12		1		9[3]	11[1]	13								4			6		14	5	10[2]			46

FA Cup
Fourth Qualifying Round

Mansfield T	(h)	0-0
	(a)	0-1

REVIEW OF THE SCOTTISH SEASON 2008–09

Odd how a season can start with something of a nightmare and finish with daydreams simply coming true. That might well be how Walter Smith regarded Rangers in 2008–09, suffering the ignominy of being knocked out of the Champions League at the first instance by FBK Kaunas from Lithuania, yet finishing as champions of the Scottish Premier League on the final day of the competition, then getting the added bonus of the Homecoming Scottish Cup.

Much of course in between these two events but in respect of Scottish clubs' success in Europe it was a poor season indeed. Celtic as champions were little better than their Auld Firm rivals. In Group E they scraped just four goals in six matches only one of which they managed to win, the last fixture when they were already eliminated.

Motherwell was also knocked out in their first tie against Nancy. But flying the Scottish League flag Queen of the South was in no way disgraced against Nordsjaelland despite losing the home leg – played at Airdrie's Excelsior Stadium – they were level on aggregate away with five minutes remaining.

Thoughts naturally turned inwards to domestic issues after such events and it is some time since the Scottish Premier League climaxed in such an exciting way following the split after 33 matches. Not only was the title still open to Rangers trailing Celtic by a point, but European places were still up for grabs, three of the other top six in with a chance and only one club who missed the cut could consider itself safe from relegation and just six points separated the bottom five!

After the Scottish Cup semi-finals in which Rangers beat St Mirren 3-0 and Falkirk defeated Dunfermline Athletic 2-0, the SPL resumed. Celtic improved their position at Aberdeen but Rangers kept in touch. Falkirk improved their plight. Dundee United continued to menace Hearts in third place. Then came the last Auld Firm clash of the season at Ibrox and a single goal victory for Rangers leaving them two points ahead, a situation not really enjoyed for any appreciable time since September.

Falkirk continued to do better than St Mirren, Dundee United again failed to make ground on Hearts and into the overall situation came Hibernian, unable to improve their own position but likely to have an effect on the title race. They took a point off Rangers. Falkirk swapped places with St Mirren only to follow it up by losing to the Buddies at home!

Meanwhile Inverness Caley and newcomers Hamilton Academical were toiling – ironically both had been early SPL leaders! Rangers led by three points, Celtic with a game in hand. Hearts finally finished off Dundee United for third place and Hibernian held Celtic. With a game to go Rangers led by two points.

Depending on individual results four teams were threatened by relegation. Hamilton was safe with a win at St Mirren, who in turn survived because Falkirk not only won at Caley but the result relegated them! On the Sunday Rangers won at Dundee United to win the title, depriving the losers of a place in Europe as Aberdeen beat Hibs and Celtic's draw with Hearts was not enough. Kilmarnock, at one stage drawn into the relegation mix, won their last three – their best run of the season. In the wake of it manager Gordon Strachan resigned. Yet Celtic had beaten Rangers in the CIS Cup. Rangers won the Scottish Cup, runners-up Falkirk earning a place in Europe as a result.

St Johnstone thanks chiefly to a run of 22 unbeaten matches were promoted to the SPL. Airdrie who had won the League Challenge Cup against Ross County on penalties, were beaten by Ayr United in the play-offs following Raith Rovers' promotion as champions of Division Two. Clyde were relegated from Division One. In Division Three Dumbarton lasted longer to head off Cowdenbeath, who then lost in the play-off on penalties to Stenhousemuir. Queen's Park and Stranraer, the latter saved from extinction by a rescue from a local housing association, were both demoted from Division Two.

One unfortunate incident involving two Rangers players affected the national team. Allan McGregor and Barry Ferguson were informed that they were not to be considered for future international selection following unacceptable behaviour while on duty abroad. Scottish Football Association chief executive Gordon Smith ruled out any change in the situation under the current regime.

Internationally in terms of the World Cup qualifying stage, the table looks fine as it stands, but underlying it all is the fact that Scotland's two victories to date have been achieved against Iceland. The difficult fixtures which will determine whether a place will be secured in the play-offs are yet to come, because automatic qualification is now not on the table for Scotland, since Holland became the first European country to reach South Africa.

Group Nine is a five country affair and the eight best performing runners-up from the nine groups are determined by results against all others except the last finishing country in the eight groups with six teams, whereas Scotland's group has the other five in the equation.

Currently Scotland is standing in eighth position chiefly because Iceland is third and Norway bottom. Moreover for Manager George Burley and the Scots, their next game is in Oslo! They conclude the programme with home games against Macedonia and Holland who may well have relaxed by then – or that is at least the hope!

On a cautionary note, the goals scored against Iceland were the only ones Scotland registered during the season.

SCOTTISH LEAGUE TABLES 2008–09

CLYDESDALE BANK SCOTTISH PREMIER LEAGUE

			Home				Away				Total					
		P	W	D	L	F	A	W	D	L	F	A	W	D	L	F	A	GD	Pts
1	Rangers	38	15	2	2	44	15	11	6	2	33	13	26	8	4	77	28	49	86
2	Celtic	38	14	4	1	48	13	10	6	3	32	20	24	10	4	80	33	47	82
3	Hearts	38	11	5	3	28	18	5	6	8	12	19	16	11	11	40	37	3	59
4	Aberdeen	38	9	5	5	22	17	5	6	8	19	23	14	11	13	41	40	1	53
5	Dundee U	38	7	8	4	25	24	6	6	7	22	26	13	14	11	47	50	–3	53
6	Hibernian	38	6	7	6	23	23	5	7	7	19	23	11	14	13	42	46	–4	47
7	Motherwell	38	7	6	6	24	27	6	3	10	22	24	13	9	16	46	51	–5	48
8	Kilmarnock	38	7	3	9	18	22	5	5	9	20	26	12	8	18	38	48	–10	44
9	Hamilton A	38	7	2	10	18	20	5	3	11	12	33	12	5	21	30	53	–23	41
10	Falkirk	38	6	4	9	19	20	3	7	9	18	32	9	11	18	37	52	–15	38
11	St Mirren	38	3	8	8	14	21	6	2	11	19	31	9	10	19	33	52	–19	37
12	Inverness CT	38	4	5	10	18	27	6	2	11	19	31	10	7	21	37	58	–21	37

IRN-BRU SCOTTISH FOOTBALL LEAGUE FIRST DIVISION

			Home				Away				Total					
		P	W	D	L	F	A	W	D	L	F	A	W	D	L	F	A	GD	Pts
1	St Johnstone	36	10	5	3	26	13	7	9	2	29	22	17	14	5	55	35	20	65
2	Partick Th	36	9	3	6	20	14	7	4	7	19	24	16	7	13	39	38	1	55
3	Dunfermline Ath	36	5	5	8	20	24	9	4	5	32	20	14	9	13	52	44	8	51
4	Dundee	36	8	5	5	22	14	5	6	7	11	18	13	11	12	33	32	1	50
5	Queen of the S	36	6	6	6	37	28	6	5	7	20	22	12	11	13	57	50	7	47
6	Morton	36	8	7	3	23	14	4	4	10	17	26	12	11	13	40	40	0	47
7	Livingston	36	8	3	7	29	25	5	5	8	27	33	13	8	15	56	58	–2	47
8	Ross Co	36	6	6	6	22	22	7	2	9	20	24	13	8	15	42	46	–4	47
9	Airdrie U	36	7	5	6	20	19	3	7	8	9	24	10	12	14	29	43	–14	42
10	Clyde	36	6	5	7	24	28	4	4	10	17	30	10	9	17	41	58	–17	39

IRN-BRU SCOTTISH FOOTBALL LEAGUE SECOND DIVISION

			Home				Away				Total					
		P	W	D	L	F	A	W	D	L	F	A	W	D	L	F	A	GD	Pts
1	Raith R	36	11	6	1	33	16	11	4	3	27	11	22	10	4	60	27	33	76
2	Ayr U	36	11	7	0	38	16	11	1	6	33	22	22	8	6	71	38	33	74
3	Brechin C	36	12	2	4	27	18	6	6	6	24	27	18	8	10	51	45	6	62
4	Peterhead	36	9	4	4	32	16	6	6	6	22	23	15	11	10	54	39	15	56
5	Stirling Alb	36	7	5	6	26	23	7	6	5	33	26	14	11	11	59	49	10	53
6	East Fife	36	6	2	10	19	24	7	3	8	20	20	13	5	18	39	44	–5	44
7	Arbroath	36	6	3	9	22	23	5	5	8	22	23	11	8	17	44	46	–2	41
8	Alloa Ath	36	8	4	6	29	27	3	4	11	18	32	11	8	17	47	59	–12	41
9	Queen's Park	36	4	6	8	17	23	3	6	9	18	31	7	12	17	35	54	–19	33
10	Stranraer	36	1	4	13	14	48	2	3	13	17	42	3	7	26	31	90	–59	16

IRN-BRU SCOTTISH FOOTBALL LEAGUE THIRD DIVISION

			Home				Away				Total					
		P	W	D	L	F	A	W	D	L	F	A	W	D	L	F	A	GD	Pts
1	Dumbarton	36	11	5	2	38	13	8	5	5	27	23	19	10	7	65	36	29	67
2	Cowdenbeath	36	11	5	2	27	15	7	4	7	21	19	18	9	9	48	34	14	63
3	East Stirling	36	10	1	7	30	29	9	3	6	27	21	19	4	13	57	50	7	61
4	Stenhousemuir	36	8	5	5	23	19	8	3	7	32	27	16	8	12	55	46	9	56
5	Montrose	36	8	3	7	28	24	8	3	7	24	24	16	6	14	47	48	–1	54
6	Forfar Ath	36	6	5	7	26	28	8	4	6	27	23	14	9	13	53	51	2	51
7	Annan Ath	36	8	4	6	35	23	6	4	8	21	22	14	8	14	56	45	11	50
8	Albion R	36	6	2	10	18	25	5	4	9	21	22	11	6	19	39	47	–8	39
9	Berwick R	36	6	4	8	24	29	4	3	11	22	32	10	7	19	46	61	–15	37
10	Elgin C	36	5	2	11	16	32	2	3	13	15	47	7	5	24	31	79	–48	26

ABERDEEN   Premier League

Year Formed: 1903. *Ground & Address:* Pittodrie Stadium, Pittodrie St, Aberdeen AB24 5QH. *Telephone:* 01224 650400. *Fax:* 01224 644173. *E-mail:* davidj@afc.co.uk *Website:* www.afc.co.uk
Ground Capacity: all seated: 21,421. *Size of Pitch:* 115yd × 72yd.
Chairman: Stewart Milne. *Executive Director:* Duncan Fraser. *Director of Football:* Willie Miller. *Secretary:* David Johnston. *Operations Manager:* John Morgan.
Manager: Mark McGhee. *Assistant Manager:* Jimmy Nicholl. *U-19 Manager:* Neil Cooper. *Physios:* David Wylie, John Sharp. *Reserve Team Coach:* Sandy Clark.
Previous Grounds: None.
Record Attendance: 45,061 v Hearts, Scottish Cup 4th rd, 13 Mar 1954.
Record Transfer Fee received: £1.75 million for Eoin Jess to Coventry City (February 1996).
Record Transfer Fee paid: £1m+ for Paul Bernard from Oldham Athletic (September 1995).
Record Victory: 13-0 v Peterhead, Scottish Cup, 9 Feb 1923.
Record Defeat: 0-8 v Celtic, Division 1, 30 Jan 1965.
Most Capped Player: Alex McLeish, 77 (Scotland).
Most League Appearances: 556: Willie Miller, 1973-90.
Most League Goals in Season (Individual): 38: Benny Yorston, Division I, 1929-30.
Most Goals Overall (Individual): 199: Joe Harper, 1969-72; 1976-81.

ABERDEEN 2008–09 LEAGUE RECORD

Match No.	Date	Venue	Opponents	Result	H/T Score	Lg. Pos.	Goalscorers	Atten- dance
1	Aug 9	H	Inverness CT	L	0-2	0-1	—	12,659
2	16	A	Motherwell	W	1-0	0-0	8	Mulgrew 86	5872
3	23	H	Rangers	D	1-1	1-1	8	Young 46	16,489
4	30	A	St Mirren	W	1-0	1-0	6	Mackie 43	4680
5	Sept 13	H	Hamilton A	L	1-2	1-1	8	McDonald 7	10,865
6	20	H	Dundee U	L	0-1	0-0	8		11,041
7	27	A	Celtic	L	2-3	0-1	11	Mulgrew 2 57, 65	58,565
8	Oct 4	H	Hibernian	L	1-2	1-1	12	Miller (pen) 42	10,793
9	18	A	Falkirk	W	1-0	0-0	10	Miller 48	5662
10	25	A	Hearts	D	1-1	1-1	8	Mackie 13	14,265
11	Nov 1	H	Kilmarnock	W	1-0	0-0	7	Aluko 51	10,599
12	8	A	Dundee U	L	1-2	0-2	8	Mackie 66	9490
13	11	H	St Mirren	W	2-0	0-0	—	Considine 80, Aluko 89	9452
14	15	A	Hibernian	D	2-2	1-0	6	Mackie 40, Diamond 53	11,640
15	22	A	Rangers	L	0-2	0-0	7		50,166
16	29	H	Motherwell	W	2-0	0-0	5	McDonald 61, Miller (pen) 67	10,302
17	Dec 13	H	Falkirk	W	2-1	2-0	6	Miller 2 (1 pen) 16, 42 (p)	8909
18	20	A	Inverness CT	W	3-0	1-0	5	Mulgrew 6, McDonald 51, Mackie 56	5862
19	27	H	Hearts	W	1-0	1-0	5	Miller 36	18,021
20	Jan 3	A	Hamilton A	L	0-2	0-0	5		4334
21	13	A	Kilmarnock	W	2-1	1-1	—	Miller 2 30, 59	4354
22	18	H	Celtic	W	4-2	2-1	3	McDonald 24, Duff 31, Diamond 2 75, 78	18,100
23	24	H	Rangers	D	0-0	0-0	5		20,441
24	31	A	Falkirk	L	0-1	0-0	5		5605
25	Feb 14	A	Hearts	L	1-2	1-1	5	Mackie 20	15,049
26	21	H	Dundee U	D	2-2	0-1	5	Severin 46, Diamond 72	14,673
27	28	H	Kilmarnock	D	0-0	0-0	5		11,457
28	Mar 3	A	St Mirren	D	1-1	0-0	—	Wright 90	4383
29	14	H	Hamilton A	W	1-0	1-0	4	Maguire 28	10,312
30	21	A	Hibernian	D	0-0	0-0	4		11,754
31	Apr 4	A	Motherwell	D	1-1	0-1	4	Maguire 67	4686
32	11	A	Inverness CT	W	1-0	0-0	4	McDonald 79	11,114
33	18	A	Celtic	L	0-2	0-1	5		58,581
34	May 2	H	Celtic	L	1-3	1-1	5	Maguire 22	14,752
35	7	A	Dundee U	D	1-1	1-1	—	Miller 33	10,407
36	12	H	Hearts	D	0-0	0-0	—		11,588
37	16	A	Rangers	L	1-2	0-0	5	Paton 77	50,295
38	24	H	Hibernian	W	2-1	2-1	4	Miller 13, Mulgrew 45	14,083

Final League Position: 4

Honours
League Champions: Division I 1954-55. Premier Division 1979-80, 1983-84, 1984-85; *Runners-up:* Division I 1910-11, 1936-37, 1955-56, 1970-71, 1971-72. Premier Division 1977-78, 1980-81, 1981-82, 1988-89, 1989-90, 1990-91, 1992-93, 1993-94.
Scottish Cup Winners: 1947, 1970, 1982, 1983, 1984, 1986, 1990; *Runners-up:* 1937, 1953, 1954, 1959, 1967, 1978, 1993, 2000.
League Cup Winners: 1955-56, 1976-77, 1985-86, 1989-90, 1995-96; *Runners-up:* 1946-47, 1978-79, 1979-80, 1987-88, 1988-89, 1992-93, 1999-2000.
Drybrough Cup Winners: 1971, 1980.

European: *European Cup:* 12 matches (1980-81, 1984-85, 1985-86); *Cup Winners' Cup:* 39 matches (1967-68, 1970-71, 1978-79, 1982-83 winners, 1983-84 semi-finals, 1986-87, 1990-91, 1993-94); *UEFA Cup:* 56 matches (*Fairs Cup:* 1968-69. *UEFA Cup:* 1971-72, 1972-73, 1973-74, 1977-78, 1979-80, 1981-82, 1987-88, 1988-89, 1989-90, 1991-92, 1994-95, 1996-97, 2000-01, 2002-03, 2007-08).

Club colours: Shirt, Shorts, Stockings: Red.

Goalscorers: *League* (41): Miller 10 (3 pens), Mackie 6, McDonald 5, Mulgrew 5, Diamond 4, Maguire 3, Aluko 2, Considine 1, Duff 1, Paton 1, Severin 1, Wright 1, Young 1.
Scottish Cup (8): Aluko 2, Maguire 2, Miller 1, Vidal 1, Wright 1, own goal 1.
CIS Cup (3): McDonald 1, Maguire 1, Miller 1 (pen).

Langfield J 38	Foster R 30+4	Mulgrew C 32+3	McDonald G 24+4	Considine A 17+3	Severin S 37	De Visscher J 6+5	Kerr M 31+1	Miller L 34	Maguire C 13+18	Smith J 9+3	Mackie D 25+4	Young D 17+5	Diamond Z 26+2	Duff S 9+10	Wright T 4+11	Mair L 21+3	Aluko S 28+4	Hodgkiss J 6+1	Paton M —+4	Bossu B —+1	Vidal J 9+4	Pawlett P 2+3	Stewart S —+1	Match No.
1	2	3	4	5	6	7[1]	8[3]	9	10[2]	11	12	13	14											1
1	2	3	11	5	6	12	8	9[2]			10	7	4[1]			13								2
1	2	3	4	5	6		8	9	7[2]		10[1]	11	12	13										3
1	2	3	4	5		12	8	9[2]	14	7	10[3]	11[1]		13		6								4
1	2	3	4	5[3]	6	14	8	9	12	10[1]	7[2]	13	11											5
1	2	3	4		6	13	8	9	7[3]	12	14	5	10[1]	11[2]										6
1	2	12			6[1]		8	9[2]	10	7	5	11	13	4	14	3[3]								7
1	7	3[4]			6		8	9	12	10[1]	13	5	4	11		2[2]								8
1	2	13		5	6		8[2]	9[3]	14	10	11	4	7[1]	3	12									9
1	2	12		5	6			9[1]	10	7	4	3	11	8										10
1	7	3[1]		5	6	12	9	14	10	8[2]	4	13	11[3]	2										11
1	2	12	13		6	7[3]	8	9	14	10	4[1]	5	11	3[2]										12
1	2	3[2]		5	6		8	9	12	10	7[1]	4	11	13										13
1	2	14		5	6		8	9	12	10[1]	7[3]	4	13	11	3[2]									14
1	12	3	4	5	6		8	9	13	10[2]	2	7[1]	11											15
1		3	12	5[1]	6	13	8	9	14	10	7[2]	4	2	11[3]										16
1	12	3	4		6	7[1]	8	9	11[2]	10	13	5	2											17
1	12	3	4		6	7[1]	8	9[3]	13	10	5	2	11[2]	14										18
1	2	3[1]	4[3]	12	6	7	8	9	13	10	5	14	11[2]											19
1	2		4		6	7	8[1]	9	12	10	5	3	11											20
1	2	3	4	5	6[1]		8	9	10	7	12	11												21
1	2	3	4		6		8	9	12	10	5	7				11[1]								22
1	2	3	4		6		8	9	13	10	5	7[1]	11[2]								15	12		23
1	2	3	4		6		8	9	13	10[2]	11[1]	14	5			12	7[3]							24
1	2	3	12		6		8	9	13	10[3]	7[1]	5	4[2]			14	11							25
1		3			6		8	9	10[1]	7	5	12	4				11				2			26
1		3			6		8	9	7[1]	13	10[2]	5	12	4			11				2			27
1		3			6		9[1]	7	14	10[3]	5	13	12	4			11				2[2]			28
1	12	3	14		6		8		10[3]	7	13	5	9[2]	4			11				2[1]			29
1	2	3	4		6		10	8[4]	12	7	13	5	9[1]				11[2]							30
1		3	11	4	5[4]	6	9	10[3]	7	8[2]	14	2[1]	12	13										31
1	2	3	4		6		9[1]	10[2]	7[3]	13	8	14	12	5			11							32
1	2	3	11	5	6		10	7[2]	8[1]	4[3]	12	13	9	14										33
1	2	3	4	5	6		8	10	7[2]	9[1]							11		12		13			34
1	2	3	4		6		8[4]	9[3]	10[2]	7	14	5[1]					11		12		13			35
1	2	3	4		6			9	10[1]	7[2]	13	5					11	8	12					36
1	2	3[4]	4		6		8	9[2]	14	12	5			13		11					7[3]	10[1]		37
1	2	3	4		6			9[2]	8	13	5	11[3]	12								7	10[1]	14	38

AIRDRIE UNITED $\qquad$ Second Division

Year Formed: 2002. *Ground & Address:* Shyberry Excelsior Stadium, Broomfield Park, Craigneuk Avenue, Airdrie ML6 8QZ. *Telephone:* (Stadium) 01236 622000. *Fax:* 01412 11497. *Postal Address:* 60 St Enoch Square, Glasgow G1 4AG.
E-mail: annmarie@airdrieunitedfc.com *Website:* www.airdrieunited.com
Ground Capacity: all seated: 10,000. *Size of Pitch:* 112yd × 76yd.
Chairman: James Ballantyne. *Secretary:* Ann Marie Ballantyne. *Commercial Manager:* Nicola Dickson (tel: 07956 632296; fax: 01236 626002).
Manager: Kenny Black. *Management team:* Jimmy Boyle, Michael McLaughlin, John Donnelly.
Record Attendance: 5924 v Motherwell, Scottish Cup 3rd rd, 6 Jan 2007.
Record Victory: 7-0 v Dundee, First Division, 11 March 2006.
Record Defeat: 1-6 v Morton, Second Division, 1 Nov 2003.
Most League Appearances: 101: Mark McGeown, 2002-05.
Most League Goals in Season (Individual): 18: Jerome Vareille, 2002-03.
Most Goals Overall (Individual): 28: Jerome Vareille, 2002-04.

AIRDRIE UNITED 2008–09 LEAGUE RECORD

Match No.	Date		Venue	Opponents	Result		H/T Score	Lg. Pos.	Goalscorers	Attendance
1	Aug	2	A	Queen of the S	D	0-0	0-0	—		2914
2		9	H	Partick Th	L	0-1	0-0	9		2165
3		16	H	Dundee	D	0-0	0-0	9		1787
4		23	A	Dunfermline Ath	D	0-0	0-0	7		3334
5		30	H	Morton	W	5-0	3-0	6	McLaughlin 2 [13, 26], Di Giacomo [36], Nixon [59], Lynch [63]	1793
6	Sept	13	A	Livingston	W	2-1	1-0	5	Lynch [34], McLaughlin [64]	1710
7		20	H	Clyde	L	0-2	0-1	6		1489
8		27	A	Ross Co	L	0-2	0-1	7		2259
9	Oct	4	A	St Johnstone	L	1-3	0-1	8	Nixon [48]	2259
10		18	H	Queen of the S	W	2-0	2-0	7	Cardle [7], Lynch [44]	1524
11	Nov	1	A	Dundee	D	1-1	1-0	7	Lynch [11]	3456
12		4	H	Dunfermline Ath	L	1-3	1-2	—	Di Giacomo [10]	1099
13		8	H	Livingston	D	0-0	0-0	8		1201
14		22	H	Ross Co	L	0-2	0-1	10		939
15		25	A	Morton	L	0-2	0-1	—		1642
16	Dec	13	A	Partick Th	L	1-2	1-1	10	Lynch [14]	2296
17		16	A	Clyde	L	0-1	0-0	—		864
18		20	H	St Johnstone	D	1-1	0-0	10	Maguire [89]	1175
19		27	H	Morton	W	1-0	1-0	10	Lynch (pen) [45]	1663
20	Jan	3	A	Livingston	D	1-1	0-0	10	Lynch [68]	1462
21		17	A	Dunfermline Ath	D	1-1	1-0	10	Lynch [15]	2915
22		24	H	Dundee	W	1-0	0-0	10	Di Giacomo [69]	1303
23		31	H	Partick Th	L	0-1	0-1	10		1988
24	Feb	14	A	Queen of the S	L	0-4	0-1	—		2443
25		22	H	Clyde	W	1-0	1-0	10	Di Giacomo [5]	1189
26		28	A	Ross Co	D	0-0	0-0	10		2290
27	Mar	7	H	Livingston	D	4-4	1-2	10	Baird 2 [8, 64], Di Giacomo [54], Smyth [66]	1100
28		10	A	Morton	D	0-0	0-0	—		1865
29		14	H	Queen of the S	W	2-0	0-0	9	Smyth [50], McLaughlin [58]	1320
30		21	A	St Johnstone	L	0-3	0-2	9		2561
31	Apr	4	H	Dunfermline Ath	D	1-1	0-0	9	Smith Darren [83]	1136
32		11	A	Dundee	W	1-0	1-0	9	Lynch [18]	2870
33		18	A	Clyde	L	0-3	0-1	9		1614
34		25	H	Ross Co	W	1-0	0-0	9	McKenna [65]	927
35	May	2	A	Partick Th	W	1-0	0-0	9	Lynch [89]	3242
36		11	H	St Johnstone	L	0-4	0-0	9		633

Final League Position: 9

Honours
League Champions: Second Division 2003-04; *Runners-up:* Second Division 2007-08.
League Challenge Cup Winners: 2008-09; *Runners-up:* 2003-04.

Club colours: Shirt: White with red diamond. Shorts: Red. Stockings: Red.

Goalscorers: *League* (29): Lynch 10 (1 pen), Di Giacomo 5, McLaughlin 4, Baird 2, Nixon 2, Smyth 2, Cardle 1, Maguire 1, McKenna 1, Smith Darren 1.
Scottish Cup (6): Lynch 3, Cardle 1, Di Giacomo 1, McLaughlin 1 (pen).
CIS Cup (0).
Challenge Cup (10): Di Giacomo 4, Cardle 1, Lynch 1, McKenna 1, Noble 1, Smith 1, own goal 1.
Play-Offs (6): Baird 3, Di Giacomo 1, McLaughlin 1, Smyth 1.

Robertson S 33	Smyth M 32	Donnelly B 31+1	Nixon D 28+4	Hazley M 17+2	McDougall S 20+10	McKenna S 35	McDonald K 27+5	McLaughlin S 28+6	Cardle J 21+3	Di Giacomo P 30+3	Smith Darren 14+7	Lynch S 24+9	Noble S 3+13	Maguire S 3+8	Brown M 2+9	Lovering P 10+1	Smith L 1	Watt K 1+5	McLachlan W 18	Hollis L 3	Baird J 9+3	Smith Darran 1	Bain J 1	McCabe P 1	Floan L 1	Taylor D 1	Keast F 1	Donnaghy K -+1	McCluskey S -+1	Match No.
1	2¹	3	4	5	6	7	8	9	10	11²	12	13																		1
1	2	5	6	3	7¹	8	4²	13	11³	9		10	12	14																2
1	2	5	6¹	3	7³	8	4	12	11	9	14	10²	13																	3
1	2	3	4³	5	6¹	7	8	13	10	9	12	11²	14																	4
1	2	5	6	3	7¹	8	4³	10	12²	9	13	11				14														5
1	2	5	6			7²	4	11		9¹	12	10³	14					13	3											6
1	2	5	6			7²	8	4³	11	9	14	10¹	13	12				3												7
1	2	5	6			7	8	4	11	13	9	10¹	12					3²												8
1	2	5	6			7	8	4	10	11	9	12						3¹												9
1	2	5	6	13			4	12	7	11²	9	8¹	10³	14																10
1			6		12	8	4²	11	7	9³	2¹	10	14					13	3	5										11
1	2			6	13	5	4	8	11	9	7²	10	12					3¹												12
1	2			6	12	5	4³	8	11	9	7¹	10²	13					14	3											13
1		5	6	3	14	2	4	8	11	9¹	7³	10²	12						13											14
1	2	3	4	5		8	7	9	6	10	11¹	12																		15
1	2	5		3²	7	6	4¹	8	11	9	10	13		12			12													16
1	2	5	6	3²	13	4		7	11	12	9³	10¹	14	8					8											17
1	2	5	6¹		7²	8	4	10	11	9		12						13	3		13	3								18
1	6	5	3		7³	8	4	10	11²	12	13	9¹	14						2											19
1	6	5	3		7²	8	4	10	11¹	12	9							13	2											20
	6	5²12	3	7	8	4		11	9	10									2		1									21
1	6	5²12	3	7	8	4	13	11	9³	10¹	14								2											22
1	6	5		3³	7	8	4²	13	11	9	10¹	12							2			14								23
1	4		5	3	7²	8	6¹	12	9¹	10	11	13							2											24
1	4	5	6	3		8	10	11	9²	13	7¹								2		12									25
1		5	3	11		8		6	9¹	4³	12	10²	14						2		13	7								26
1	4	5	14	3³12	8		6	11■	9²	7¹	13								2		10									27
1	4	5	3²		8	11¹	6	9	7	12		13							2		10									28
1	4	5	3	11²	8	13	6	9¹	7	12				14					2		10³									29
1	4	5	3³	11	8	12	6	7¹	9²	14				13					2		10									30
1	2	5	6	7¹	8	4	11	9²	12	13				14					3		10³									31
	2	5	6	13	12	8	14	7	9³	4¹	10²								3		1	11								32
1	3	4	5²	13	7	12	8	10	6	11¹									2		9									33
1	6	5		13	8	4	11	9¹	7²	12								3	2		10									34
1	6	5	14	12	8	4	11	9¹	7³13									3	2		10²									35
	14		3					11	9³	10								8²				1	2	4	5	6	7¹	13	12	36

ALBION ROVERS   Third Division

Year Formed: 1882. *Ground & Address:* Cliftonhill Stadium, Main St, Coatbridge ML5 3RB. *Telephone/Fax:* 01236 606334.
E-mail: general@albionrovers.co.uk *Website:* albionrovers.co.uk
Ground capacity: 1249 (seated 489). *Size of Pitch:* 110yd × 72yd.
Chairman and Secretary: Frank Meade ACMA. *General Manager:* John Reynolds. *Commercial Manager:* Patrick Rollink.
Manager: Paul Martin. *Assistant Manager:* Graham Diamond. *Physio:* Derek Kelly.
Club Nickname(s): The Wee Rovers. *Previous Grounds:* Cowheath Park, Meadow Park, Whifflet.
Record Attendance: 27,381 v Rangers, Scottish Cup 2nd rd, 8 Feb 1936.
Record Transfer Fee received: £40,000 from Motherwell for Bruce Cleland.
Record Transfer Fee paid: £7000 for Gerry McTeague to Stirling Albion, September 1989.
Record Victory: 12-0 v Airdriehill, Scottish Cup, 3 Sept 1887.
Record Defeat: 1-11 v Partick Th, League Cup, 11 Aug 1993.
Most Capped Player: Jock White, 1 (2), Scotland.
Most League Appearances: 399: Murdy Walls, 1921-36.
Most League Goals in Season (Individual): 41: Jim Renwick, Division II, 1932-33.
Most Goals Overall (Individual): 105: Bunty Weir, 1928-31.

ALBION ROVERS 2008–09 LEAGUE RECORD

Match No.	Date	Venue	Opponents	Result	H/T Score	Lg. Pos.	Goalscorers	Attendance
1	Aug 2	H	Forfar Ath	L 1-3	1-1	—	Barr [44]	289
2	9	A	East Stirling	L 0-1	0-1	10		348
3	16	A	Cowdenbeath	L 1-2	0-1	10	Walker P [58]	302
4	23	H	Berwick R	W 2-0	1-0	9	Walker P 2 [25, 47]	269
5	30	A	Annan Ath	W 4-2	2-1	6	Walker P 2 [25, 72], Barr [27], Pollock [89]	937
6	Sept 13	H	Dumbarton	L 1-3	0-2	7	Walker P (pen) [61]	327
7	20	A	Elgin C	W 6-1	2-0	7	Watt 3 [7, 56, 90], Barr 3 [30, 50, 83]	407
8	27	H	Stenhousemuir	L 1-2	0-1	7	Adam [66]	279
9	Oct 4	H	Montrose	L 0-1	0-0	7		237
10	18	A	Forfar Ath	D 0-0	0-0	8		426
11	Nov 1	H	Cowdenbeath	W 3-1	1-0	6	Barr [16], Benton [74], Harris [90]	259
12	8	A	Berwick R	W 3-0	1-0	5	Harris 2 [18, 74], Barr [72]	288
13	15	H	Annan Ath	L 0-1	0-1	7		310
14	22	A	Dumbarton	D 1-1	0-0	7	Donnelly [37]	646
15	Dec 13	A	Stenhousemuir	L 0-1	0-0	7		508
16	20	A	Montrose	W 2-1	0-1	7	Adreoni [56], Barr [60]	321
17	Jan 17	H	Berwick R	W 2-1	1-1	7	Harty [12], McCusker [53]	264
18	24	A	Cowdenbeath	L 1-2	1-2	7	Harty (pen) [41]	409
19	31	H	Forfar Ath	W 2-0	1-0	7	Harty [27], Barr [48]	284
20	Feb 7	A	East Stirling	W 1-0	1-0	—	Barr [29]	453
21	21	A	Elgin C	L 0-1	0-1	7		357
22	28	H	Annan Ath	W 2-1	1-1	6	Donnelly [42], McKeown [49]	427
23	Mar 3	H	Elgin C	W 2-1	1-1	—	Crozier [3], Harty (pen) [65]	237
24	7	A	Dumbarton	L 0-1	0-0	6		692
25	10	H	East Stirling	L 0-2	0-2	—		420
26	14	A	Forfar Ath	L 0-4	0-1	8		319
27	17	H	Dumbarton	D 1-1	1-0	—	Barr [11]	535
28	21	H	Montrose	L 0-1	0-0	8		263
29	25	A	Annan Ath	D 1-1	0-1	—	Adam [88]	864
30	31	H	Stenhousemuir	L 1-2	1-1	—	Donnelly [27]	342
31	Apr 4	A	Berwick R	D 1-1	1-0	8	Harty [9]	323
32	11	H	Cowdenbeath	D 0-0	0-0	8		452
33	18	H	Elgin C	L 0-3	0-1	8		275
34	25	A	Stenhousemuir	L 0-2	0-0	8		428
35	May 2	H	East Stirling	L 0-2	0-1	8		346
36	9	A	Montrose	L 0-1	0-1	8		324

Final League Position: 8

Honours
League Champions: Division II 1933-34, Second Division 1988-89; *Runners-up:* Division II 1913-14, 1937-38, 1947-48.
Scottish Cup Runners-up: 1920.

Club colours: Shirt: Red and yellow stripes. Shorts: Red with yellow flashes. Stockings: Yellow.

Goalscorers: *League* (39): Barr 11, Walker P 6 (1 pen), Harty 5 (2 pens), Donnelly 3, Harris 3, Watt 3, Adam 2, Adreoni 1, Benton 1, Crozier 1, McCusker 1, McKeown 1, Pollock 1.
Scottish Cup (3): Barr 1, Coyne 1, Harris 1.
Challenge Cup (3): Barr 1, Donnelly 1 (pen), Martin 1.

Scott D 10+1	Hughes C 3+1	McGowan M 33	Walker R 24+3	Benton A 20	Donnelly C 31	Ferry D 17+8	Wright B 2+2	Pollock M 19+14	Barr B 31+1	Walker P 5+1	Coyne T 7+6	McGoldrick M 6+3	McKenna G —+3	Reid A 32	Martin W 2+1	Smith B 2+1	Casey M 1	Harris R 17+5	Lumsden T 9	Adam C 18+1	Watt K 3+1	Canning S 7	Crozier B 8+13	McCluskey C 7	Eaglesham G 1+5	Adreoni M 8+8	McCusker M 3	Ewings J 19	Harty I 15	Fleming S 16+1	McKeown S 17	Archdeacon M 3+7	Match No.
1	2	3	4	5	6	7¹	8²	9³	10	11	12	13	14																				1
1	5	3	4		6	8		14	7	13	9³		12	2	10¹	11²																	2
1	5	3			7	8²	13	6	10	12	4		14	2	11¹	9³																	3
1	5	3			6	12	13	7	10³	9²	4			2	14			8¹	11														4
1		3	4		6¹	8	13	7	11	9²	5			2				10		12													5
1		3			6		12	7	10²	9¹	4			2				8		5	11	13											6
1		3	12		6¹			4³	14	11²	7	13		2						10	5	8	9										7
1		3			6	4	7		10²			13		2						5	8	9	11¹	12									8
1		3			6	4			10			13		2				12		5	11	9²	8	7¹									9
		3	4	5		14		10¹		9³				2				7		6	11²		8	13	1	12							10
		3	4	5		13		12	10	8¹				2				7		6	11²		9		1								11
		3³	4	5		14		12	10²	8¹				2				7		6	11		9		1	13							12
	12	3	4	5				10		14				2				7		6¹	11²		9	8³	1	13							13
	14	5	4	3		12		9	10					2³				6¹		8	11		7²		1	13							14
	6	3³	4	5		7		12	11			14		2						13				1		10¹	8²	9					15
	7	5³	4	3		9		11²	6			14		2¹						12				1		13	8	10					16
	6	3	4	5		12		13	11					2				7						8¹		9³	1	10²	14				17
14	5	8	4	3		12		11						2				13		7²							1	10³	9¹	6			18
	8	5	4			11								2				7²		13					10¹		1	9	3	6	12		19
	8	5	4			10¹		11						2				7²	14	13					12		1	3	6	9¹			20
	8	5	6			10¹		11						2				7²	4³	13					14		1	9	3	12			21
	4	8			6²	13		10³	11					2				7¹		12							1	9	3	5	14		22
	6	8			5²	10		12						2				7¹		11					13		1	9	3	4			23
	7	8	4			11²		9▪						2				6¹		13							1	10	5	3	12		24
1		5	6		8	12		11						2¹				7³	4²	13					10			9	3			14	25
		6	5			2		10	11					12				7¹		8							1	9²	3	4	13		26
		6	4		5			10	7					2				11¹		12							1	9²	3	8	13		27
		6	5		8			10	11					2				7		12							1	9	3	4¹			28
		3	6		8			12	10				5	2²				13	7						11¹		1		4	9			29
		3	2	5	8	11		9	7				6¹					13		12						11¹	1		4	10²			30
		3	11	5	2¹			12	7					6				8										1	9	10	4		31
		4	5	6	8¹			12	10				2					11										1	9	3	7		32
		4	7	3	8³			12	11				2					9¹		13			14			1		10²	5	6			33
		5	4	6				9	10				2					12	11						7¹		1		3	8			34
		3	6	5▪	10	8		7¹	11				2					12		9							1		4				35
		14	7	4		8	6²		12	11			2					9		13³							1▪	10¹	5	3		36

ALLOA ATHLETIC Second Division

Year Formed: 1878. *Ground & Address:* Recreation Park, Clackmannan Rd, Alloa FK10 1RY. *Telephone:* 01259 722695. *Fax:* 01259 210886. *E-mail:* fcadmin@alloaathletic.co.uk *Website:* www.alloaathletic.co.uk
Ground Capacity: total: 3100, seated: 400. *Size of Pitch:* 110yd × 75yd.
Honorary President: George Ormiston. *Chairman:* Robert Hopkins. *Secretary:* Ewen G. Cameron.
Manager: Allan Maitland. *Assistant Manager:* James Ward. *Head of Youth Development:* Hugh McCann. *Sports Therapist:* Vanessa Smith. *Physios:* Vanessa Smith & Stuart Murphy.
Club Nickname(s): The Wasps. *Previous Grounds:* West End Public Park, Gabberston Park, Belleview Park.
Record Attendance: 13,000 v Dunfermline Athletic, Scottish Cup 3rd rd replay, 26 Feb 1939.
Record Transfer Fee received: £100,000 for Martin Cameron to Bristol Rovers.
Record Transfer Fee paid: £26,000 for Ross Hamilton from Stenhousemuir.
Record Victory: 9-0 v Selkirk, Scottish Cup First Round, 28 November 2005.
Record Defeat: 0-10 v Dundee, Division II, 8 Mar 1947 v Third Lanark, League Cup, 8 Aug 1953.
Most Capped Player: Jock Hepburn, 1, Scotland.
Most League Goals in Season (Individual): 49: 'Wee' Willie Crilley, Division II, 1921-22.

ALLOA ATHLETIC 2008–09 LEAGUE RECORD

Match No.	Date		Venue	Opponents	Result		H/T Score	Lg. Pos.	Goalscorers	Atten- dance
1	Aug	2	A	Arbroath	L	1-4	0-3	—	Ferguson A [51]	611
2		9	H	Ayr U	L	0-2	0-2	10		569
3		16	H	Raith R	D	1-1	1-1	10	Brown [27]	899
4		23	A	Peterhead	L	0-1	0-1	10		670
5		30	H	Stranraer	W	5-1	0-0	9	MacAulay 2 [57, 65], Buist [62], Brown [63], Scott [80]	408
6	Sept	13	A	Stirling A	L	2-3	2-3	9	Wilson [5], Ferguson A [44]	906
7		20	H	East Fife	L	0-3	0-1	9		776
8		27	A	Queen's Park	L	0-1	0-0	10		518
9	Oct	4	A	Brechin C	L	1-3	0-2	10	Townsley [75]	412
10		18	H	Arbroath	W	2-1	0-1	9	MacAulay [56], Forrest [83]	508
11		25	H	Peterhead	W	1-0	0-0	8	Grant [68]	331
12	Nov	1	A	Raith R	L	1-4	1-1	8	Scott [6]	1669
13		8	H	Stirling A	W	4-3	1-0	7	Stevenson [21], MacAulay [46], Forrest [51], Ferguson B (pen) [75]	1001
14		15	A	Stranraer	D	2-2	0-1	7	Scott [55], Hill [72]	280
15		22	H	Queen's Park	L	1-3	0-2	8	MacAulay [51]	557
16	Dec	6	A	East Fife	L	0-1	0-0	—		653
17		13	A	Ayr U	L	0-3	0-1	9		1079
18		20	H	Brechin C	W	2-1	2-1	9	Ferguson A [24], Stevenson [29]	405
19		27	H	Stranraer	D	2-2	1-1	9	Scott [30], Ferguson B [57]	463
20	Jan	17	A	Peterhead	D	2-2	1-1	8	Wilson [21], Scott (pen) [80]	601
21		24	H	Raith R	D	0-0	0-0	8		953
22		31	A	Arbroath	L	0-1	0-0	9		478
23	Feb	7	H	Ayr U	W	3-2	2-0	—	Carrigan 2 (2 pens) [20, 88], Grant [34]	752
24		14	A	Queen's Park	W	2-1	0-1	—	Spence [47], Noble [88]	606
25		21	H	East Fife	L	0-1	0-0	8		695
26		28	A	Stranraer	W	3-1	2-1	7	Ferguson B [2], Noble [4], Campbell [63]	286
27	Mar	3	A	Stirling A	D	0-0	0-0	—		768
28		7	H	Stirling A	L	2-3	1-0	7	Noble [5], Scullion [62]	1057
29		14	H	Arbroath	W	2-0	1-0	7	Campbell [11], McClune [46]	505
30		21	A	Brechin C	L	0-1	0-0	7		421
31	Apr	4	H	Peterhead	L	1-2	1-0	8	Wilson [27]	479
32		11	A	Raith R	L	1-3	0-1	8	Ferguson B [65]	1770
33		18	A	East Fife	W	2-0	2-0	8	Noble [20], Scott (pen) [30]	623
34		25	H	Queen's Park	D	0-0	0-0	8		704
35	May	2	A	Ayr U	D	1-1	0-1	8	Spence [75]	2195
36		9	H	Brechin C	W	3-2	2-0	8	Spence 2 [3, 27], Scott [85]	401

Final League Position: 8

Honours
League Champions: Division II 1921-22; Third Division 1997-98. *Runners-up:* Division II 1938-39. Second Division 1976-77, 1981-82, 1984-85, 1988-89, 1999-2000, 2001-02.
League Challenge Cup Winners: 1999-2000; *Runners-up:* 2001-02.

Club colours: Shirt: Black with gold hoops on front. Shorts: Black. Stockings: Black.

Goalscorers: *League* (47): Scott 7 (2 pens), MacAulay 5, Ferguson B 4 (1 pen), Noble 4, Spence 4, Ferguson A 3, Wilson 3, Brown 2, Campbell 2, Carrigan 2 (2 pens), Forrest 2, Grant 2, Stevenson 2, Buist 1, Hill 1, McClune 1, Scullion 1, Townsley 1.
Scottish Cup (3): Ferguson B 2, Scott 1 (pen).
CIS Cup (0).
Challenge Cup (2): Stevenson 1, Townsley 1.

Jellema R 35	Buist S 27	Hill D 30+2	Scullion P 21+9	Townsley C 31	McClune D 23+3	Stevenson J 13+3	McKeown S 9+4	Ferguson A 8+4	Grant J 24+4	Brown G 8+3	Kelly F —+6	Scott A 24+6	MacAulay K 21+9	Campbell 30	Hay J 1+3	Wilson D 16+5	Spence G 6+12	Ferguson B 30+1	Forrest F 9+1	O'Neill M —+1	Barker S —+4	White M 1	Noble S 14	Carrigan B 6+3	Ferguson M 1	Carroll G 4+2	McCafferty M 4	Kerr H —+2	Match No.
1	2	3	4	5	6	7	8^1	9^3	10	11^2	12	13	14																1
1	2	6	4	5^2	7	8	14	10	12	11^1	9	3^3	13																2
1	2	6	4^1	5		10	8	7	9^2			13	11	3		12													3
1	2	5	6	4	11	7^1	8^2	9	10^3	3		12	14	13															4
1	2	5	4	12	6	9^2	14	11	10	3						7^3	13	8^1											5
1	5	4	2	11	10	6					9^1	12		3		7		8											6
1	5	12	4	2	10	6		9		11^1		13	14	3^3		7^2		8											7
1	4^3	3	2	9	7^2	10	13	12	11^1				14	5		6		8											8
1	5	14	3	2	6	12	10^1	7	9			13	11^2					8^3	4										9
1	5	6	4	9^2	7	14	13^3	11	10	3				2^1		8	12												10
1	5	6^1	4	12	7	9^2	11^3	10	3			13				8^1	2	14											11
1	4	8^3	3	13	12	14	6^2	10^1	9	11				5		7	2												12
1	6	7^2	2	9	4	12		11^1	10	3						8	5		13										13
1	6	7	2	9	4			11	10	3						8	5												14
1	6	4	2	9^1	7	12		10	11	3^2		13				8	5												15
	2	4^1	7	6	13	12	11	10	9^2	5		8	3									1							16
1	3	8^3	9^1	2	12	13	6	10	11^2	5		14	7	4															17
1	4	5	2	10	13	9^2	12	11^3	14	3		7				8^1	6												18
1	2	6	4^1	5	10	9		11	12	3		7				8													19
1	5	6	10	4	2	12		9	13	3		7^1		8										11^2					20
1	5	6	10	4	2	9^1	12	3	7			8												11					21
1	2	5^1	6	4	10	9^2	12	3	7			8												11	13				22
1	5	6	12	4	2			11^1	3			7^3	14	8^2							13		10	9					23
1	4	7	3	2				12	9^1	5		6	10	8										11					24
1	5	12	4	3	2			13	11			7^2	14	8										10		9^3	6^1		25
1	5	6	13	2	12		4	7^3	11	3^2		14	9^1	8										10					26
1	5	6	12	4	7	2		9^2	11^1	3		13	8											10					27
1	5	6	11^3	4	12	2		13	7^1	9^2		8												10	14				28
1	5	6	13	4	2	10		9^2	3			14	12	8										11^3	7^1				29
1	7	4	10	3	2			5		6^1	11	8				9	12												30
1	4^2	6	10^3	5	2			11^1	12	3		7	14	8										9		13			31
1	4	6	10^3	5	2			11	13	3^2		7^1	12	8										9		14			32
1	5	14	4	2	6			7^1	11			12	8		13									9^3		10^2	3		33
1	5	14	13	4	2	6		7	11			12	8^2											9^3		10^1	3		34
1	4	7^1	12	3	2			8		9		11				10^2											6	5	13
1	5^1	8	4	2	6			11		12		10^3		14		9										7^2	3	13

ANNAN ATHLETIC   Third Division

Year Formed: 1942. *Ground & Address:* Galabank, North Street, Annan DG12 5DQ. *Telephone:* 01461 204108.
E-mail: annanathleticfc@aol.com *Website:* www.annanathleticfc.com
Ground capacity: 3000 (426 seated). *Size of Pitch:* 110yd × 67yd.
President: Simon H. King.
Chairman: Henry McClelland.
Secretary: Alan Irving.
Manager: Harry Cairney.
Club Nickname: Galabankies.

ANNAN ATHLETIC 2008–09 LEAGUE RECORD

Match No.	Date	Venue	Opponents	Result	H/T Score	Lg. Pos.	Goalscorers	Attendance
1	Aug 2	A	Cowdenbeath	W 4-1	1-1	—	Jack 2 (1 pen) [29 (p), 48], Archibald [57], Johnstone [90]	596
2	9	H	Stenhousemuir	D 1-1	1-1	1	Jack [6]	1152
3	16	H	East Stirling	W 2-1	0-1	1	Jack (pen) [49], Sloan [89]	968
4	23	A	Montrose	D 1-1	0-1	2	Bell [73]	427
5	30	H	Albion R	L 2-4	1-2	3	Townsley [33], Neilson [60]	937
6	Sept 13	A	Elgin C	W 2-1	1-0	3	Jack 2 [9, 68]	468
7	20	H	Forfar Ath	L 1-3	1-1	5	Dunbar [17]	690
8	27	A	Berwick R	L 0-3	0-1	6		502
9	Oct 4	A	Dumbarton	L 1-4	0-4	6	Inglis [59]	574
10	18	H	Cowdenbeath	L 0-1	0-1	7		578
11	Nov 8	H	Montrose	L 1-2	1-1	8	Hoolickin [25]	506
12	12	A	East Stirling	L 1-2	1-0	—	Hoolickin [40]	343
13	15	A	Albion R	W 1-0	1-0	8	Jack [2]	310
14	22	H	Elgin C	W 5-0	1-0	8	Neilson [25], Bell [47], Jack 2 (1 pen) [49, 86 (p)], Johnstone [79]	422
15	Dec 13	H	Berwick R	L 1-2	1-1	8	Neilson [13]	447
16	20	H	Dumbarton	W 2-1	1-1	8	Neilson 2 [42, 90]	634
17	27	A	Stenhousemuir	D 0-0	0-0	7		524
18	Jan 17	A	Montrose	W 3-0	1-0	6	Bell [16], Anson [65], Gibson (og) [90]	329
19	24	A	East Stirling	W 4-0	2-0	6	Bell [27], Jack 2 (1 pen) [43 (p), 90], Anson [83]	714
20	31	A	Cowdenbeath	L 0-1	0-1	6		326
21	Feb 7	H	Stenhousemuir	D 1-1	1-0	—	McBeth [32]	805
22	21	H	Forfar Ath	W 1-0	1-0	6	Bell [28]	542
23	24	A	Berwick R	D 1-1	1-1	—	Hoolickin [39]	306
24	28	A	Albion R	L 1-2	1-1	7	Jack (pen) [28]	427
25	Mar 3	A	Forfar Ath	L 1-2	0-0	—	Adamson [83]	366
26	7	H	Elgin C	W 6-0	3-0	5	Bell 2 [4, 32], Jack (pen) [29], Dunbar 2 [67, 80], Storey [69]	487
27	14	H	Cowdenbeath	W 3-1	1-1	5	Sloan [12], Dunbar [87], Storey [90]	629
28	21	A	Dumbarton	W 2-0	2-0	5	Neilson [20], Jack (pen) [39]	815
29	25	H	Albion R	D 1-1	1-0	—	Bell [32]	864
30	28	A	Elgin C	W 1-0	1-0	3	Storey [20]	321
31	Apr 4	H	Montrose	W 2-1	1-1	4	Dunbar [39], Jack (pen) [62]	617
32	11	A	East Stirling	D 1-1	1-1	4	Storey [18]	503
33	18	A	Forfar Ath	L 1-2	1-0	4	Storey [10]	463
34	25	H	Berwick R	D 1-1	0-0	5	Storey [59]	786
35	May 2	A	Stenhousemuir	L 0-1	0-1	6		581
36	9	H	Dumbarton	L 1-3	0-1	7	Watson [86]	1343

Final League Position: 7

Club colours: Shirt: Black and gold stripes. Shorts: Black. Stockings: Black with gold trim.

Goalscorers: *League* (56): Jack 15 (8 pens), Bell 8, Neilson 6, Storey 6, Dunbar 5, Hoolickin 3, Anson 2, Johnstone 2, Sloan 2, Adamson 1, Archibald 1, Inglis 1, McBeth 1, Townsley 1, Watson 1, own goal 1.
Scottish Cup (1): Neilson 1.
Challenge Cup (0).

Summersgill C 34	Brown G 13	Inglis A 18 + 2	Townsley D 27	Neilson K 32	Jack M 33	Sloan S 34	Jardine C 14 + 3	Archibald S 7 + 4	Johnstone D 12 + 4	Hoolickin L 26	Adamson R 10 + 18	Hill S 7	Grainger I 3 + 1	Bell G 26 + 3	Dunbar J 24 + 4	Walker L — + 5	Watson P 23 + 2	Cameron H 2 + 2	Calder D 2 + 1	Kassim A — + 1	Parker G — + 1	Gilfillan B 6	Storey P 7 + 11	Muirhead A 9 + 2	Anson S 3	Cuseck L 2 + 1	McBeth J 15 + 1	Campbell R 7 + 4	Batey J — + 1	Match No.
1	2	3	4	5	6	7	8	9	10	11¹	12																			1
1	2	3		5	6	7	8	9	10	11¹			4	12																2
1	2	3	11	5	6	7	8	9¹	10				12	4																3
1			5	9	4	7	6	8	10²	11			12	3	2¹	13														4
1	2	3	11	5	6	7	8	9²	10				12	4¹	13															5
1	2	3	5		6	7	8	9¹	10²					4³	11⁴	13	12	14												6
1	2	3		5	6	7	8	12	10¹					4²	11³	9	13	14												7
	2⁴	3	4	5	6	7	8	13	12					11²	10³	9¹	14		1											8
		5	4		7	6	8	12		9²	3	11¹	10	13	2				1											9
1	2	3	4	5⁴	6⁴	7	8		10²	13				9¹	11³	12	14													10
1	2	3	4			7	8²	13	6	12				9	10	5	11¹													11
1	2	3	4	5	6	7	8²	14	11³	9	10¹			12	13															12
1	2		4	5	6	7		8	11	9	10¹			12	3															13
1	2	13	4	5²	6	7	12	8	11	9¹	10			3																14
1	5¹	3	4		7	12	10⁴	8		9	11			2									6²	13						15
1				5	6	7	8²	11	13					9¹	10	3							4	12	2					16
1		6	5		7	8¹	11	12	9	10	3			13		4							2²							17
1		3	4	7	6		5	12	11¹	8	2			9	10															18
1		4	5	6	7	13		3	12					9¹	10		2						11²	8						19
1		3	4	7²	6	5	13		11³					2	9	14							8	10¹	12					20
1	14	3	4	6	7	5³	13							9	10		2						12				8²	11¹		21
1			4	5	6	7		3	13					9¹	10		2						12				8	11²		22
1			4	5	6	7		3	13					9²	10¹		2						12				8	11		23
1				5	6	7		3	13					9¹	10²		2						12	4			8	11		24
1			4	5	6	7		13	3	10				9¹			2						12	2			8⁴	11²		25
1		4³	5	6	7	14		3	10					9¹		12	2						13	8				11²		26
1			4	5	6	7		3	10²					9		13	2						12				8	11¹		27
1		3	4		6¹	7				11				10²	13		2						12	5			8	9		28
1		3		5	6	7			10	11				9¹			2						12	4			8			29
1				5	6	7		3	10¹	11				9			2						9	4			8		12	30
1		3		5	6	7			10	11				9			2						9	4			8			31
1	2		4	5	6	7		3	10¹	11²				9									12				8	13		32
1	2¹		4	5	6	7		3	13	10	11			9²									9²				8	12		33
1			4	5	6	7		3	12	10	11¹			2									9				8			34
1			4	5	6	7		3³	12	10²	11¹			2									9	14			8	13		35
1			4	5	6	7		3¹	11²	10	12			2									9				8	13		36

ARBROATH   Second Division

Year Formed: 1878. *Ground & Address:* Gayfield Park, Arbroath DD11 1QB. *Telephone:* 01241 872157. *Fax:* 01241 431125. *E-mail:* afc@gayfield.fsnet.co.uk *Website:* www.arbroathfc.co.uk
Ground Capacity: 8488. *Size of Pitch:* 115yd × 71yd.
President: John D. Christison. *Secretary:* Dr Gary Callon. *Administrator:* Mike Cargill.
Manager: John McGlashan. *Assistant Manager:* Robbie Raeside. *Physio:* Jim Crosby.
Club Nickname(s): The Red Lichties. *Previous Grounds:* None.
Record Attendance: 13,510 v Rangers, Scottish Cup 3rd rd, 23 Feb 1952.
Record Transfer Fee received: £120,000 for Paul Tosh to Dundee (Aug 1993).
Record Transfer Fee paid: £20,000 for Douglas Robb from Montrose (1981).
Record Victory: 36-0 v Bon Accord, Scottish Cup 1st rd, 12 Sept 1885.
Record Defeat: 1-9 v Celtic, League Cup 3rd rd, 25 Aug 1993.
Most Capped Player: Ned Doig, 2 (5), Scotland.
Most League Appearances: 445: Tom Cargill, 1966-81.
Most League Goals in Season (Individual): 45: Dave Easson, Division II, 1958-59.
Most Goals Overall (Individual): 120: Jimmy Jack, 1966-71.

ARBROATH 2008–09 LEAGUE RECORD

Match No.	Date	Venue	Opponents	Result	H/T Score	Lg. Pos.	Goalscorers	Atten-dance
1	Aug 2	H	Alloa Ath	W 4-1	3-0	—	Rattray [7], Sellars [24], Scott [37], Reilly [79]	611
2	9	A	Peterhead	D 1-1	0-0	2	Masson [64]	630
3	16	A	Ayr U	L 1-2	1-0	5	McMullan [26]	1304
4	23	H	East Fife	L 0-1	0-0	6		766
5	30	H	Stirling A	L 1-2	1-1	8	Gates [20]	631
6	Sept 13	A	Brechin C	L 1-3	0-1	8	Gates [57]	615
7	20	H	Queen's Park	D 1-1	1-1	8	Sellars [26]	523
8	27	A	Stranraer	D 2-2	0-1	8	Sellars 2 [52, 83]	228
9	Oct 4	H	Raith R	L 0-2	0-2	9		855
10	18	A	Alloa Ath	L 1-2	1-0	10	McGowan [22]	508
11	25	H	East Fife	L 2-3	2-2	10	McGowan [8], Weir [37]	677
12	Nov 1	H	Ayr U	L 0-3	0-3	10		535
13	8	H	Brechin C	L 1-2	1-1	10	Scott [20]	702
14	15	A	Stirling A	W 2-0	0-0	10	Scott [52], Sellars [53]	509
15	22	H	Stranraer	W 1-0	1-0	9	Scott [20]	411
16	Dec 6	A	Queen's Park	W 2-1	2-1	—	Scott [3], Little (og) [28]	637
17	13	H	Peterhead	W 4-0	2-0	7	Dorris [24], Scott [36], Weir 2 [52, 60]	451
18	20	A	Raith R	L 1-2	0-0	7	Dorris [90]	1477
19	27	A	Stirling A	L 1-2	1-2	7	Gibb (og) [39]	635
20	Jan 17	H	East Fife	L 0-2	0-1	9		740
21	25	A	Ayr U	L 1-2	1-1	9	Weir (pen) [35]	1256
22	31	H	Alloa Ath	W 1-0	0-0	8	Weir (pen) [66]	478
23	Feb 14	A	Stranraer	W 5-1	3-1	—	Ross 2 [5, 68], Raeside (pen) [8], McGowan [37], McMullan [77]	277
24	21	H	Queen's Park	W 3-0	2-0	7	Sellars [28], Raeside (pen) [44], Dobbins [76]	568
25	28	A	Stirling A	D 1-1	1-0	8	Raeside [24]	576
26	Mar 7	H	Brechin C	D 0-0	0-0	8		749
27	10	A	Peterhead	L 0-1	0-1	—		470
28	14	A	Alloa Ath	L 0-2	0-1	8		505
29	21	H	Raith R	L 0-2	0-1	8		921
30	28	A	Brechin C	W 1-0	1-0	8	Forsyth [43]	580
31	Apr 4	A	East Fife	D 0-0	0-0	7		629
32	11	H	Ayr U	L 1-3	0-0	7	Bishop [66]	820
33	18	A	Queen's Park	W 1-0	0-0	7	Ross [81]	722
34	25	H	Stranraer	W 2-0	1-0	7	Forsyth [23], Ross [55]	506
35	May 2	H	Peterhead	D 2-2	1-1	7	Rennie [34], Ross [59]	599
36	9	A	Raith R	D 0-0	0-0	7		4426

Final League Position: 7

Honours
League Runners-up: Division II 1934-35, 1958-59, 1967-68, 1971-72; Second Division 2000-01; Third Division 1997-98, 2007-08.
Scottish Cup: Quarter-finals 1993.

Club colours: Shirt: Maroon with white trim. Shorts: Maroon. Stockings: Maroon.

Goalscorers: *League* (44): Scott 6, Sellars 6, Ross 5, Weir 5 (2 pens), McGowan 3, Raeside 3 (2 pens), Dorris 2, Forsyth 2, Gates 2, McMullan 2, Bishop 1, Dobbins 1, Masson 1, Rattray 1, Reilly 1, Rennie 1, own goals 2.
Scottish Cup (0).
CIS Cup (2): Sellars 1 (pen), Tosh 1.
Challenge Cup (1): Scott 1.

Hill D 35	Rennie S 30+4	Black R 18+4	Rattray A 15	Bishop J 24+1	Fraser J 10+2	McMullan K 26+5	Lunan P 25	Scott B 16+5	Sellars B 31	Gates S 12+11	Masson T 1+11	Reilly A 1+7	Wright K —+3	Raeside R 31	Tosh P 3+9	Weir S 15+9	Simpson S 1+3	Forsyth C 26	Smith N 1+3	McGowan D 10+4	Morrison S 1	Campbell A 8	Dorris S 6	Watson P 4+3	Cameron C 3	McCulloch M 11	Ross R 9+6	Dobbins I 15	Gibson K 8	Match No.
1	2	3	4	5	6^1	7	8	9^3	10	11^2	12	13	14																	1
1	2	3		5	6^2	7	8	9^1	10	11		13	12	4																2
1	2	5	4	8^1	6	7	11	9^3	12	10^2	13			3	14															3
1	2	3		5	6	7	8^1		10	11	12			4	13	9^2														4
1	2	3		5	6^2	7^3	8		10	11	13			4		9^1	12	14												5
1	2	5	4	7^1	6^2	10	8	9	12	3	11^8	13																		6
1	3	2		5	6	7	8		10	11	12			4		9^1														7
1	2			5	6	7^1	8		10	11		13		4	12	9^2		3												8
1	2			5	6	7^2			10	11	12			4		9	8^1	3	13											9
1	13	7^1		5	6^3	2	8		10	11	14			4^2		12		3		9										10
	2	3			6		8		12	11	13			4		9	14	5^2		10^1	1	7^3								11
1	2	3^3			6		8		10^8	13	12			4	7^1	11^2	14	9	5											12
1	2	6		5		7	8^1	10^3	11^2	13				4		14	12	3		9										13
1	13	5	2			12	8	9^3	10^2					4		14		3		11				6	7^1					14
1	2	4^1		5		12	8	9^1	10	11^2	13			14				3						6	7					15
1	2	11		5		7^1		9	10	13				4		12		3						6		8^2				16
1	2	10		5		7		9^2	14	12				4		13		3		11^1				6		8^3				17
1	2	3		5		7^3		9	10	12^2	13			4		14				11^1				6		8				18
1	2^2	5	3			7		9^1	10		14			4		12				11^3				6		8	13			19
1	6	14	5^8	2				9^1	10	13				4				3		8^3				7^2		11	12			20
1	2		4				8			11	12					3		9	5	10				6^1	7					21
1	12	5	2^1			7			13	10				4		9^2		3								8	11	6		22
1	13	12		5		2	7^1		10	14				4^2		3^3		9								11	8	6		23
1	13	7		5		12	2		14	10				4^2		3		9								11^1	8^3	6		24
1	2	7		5				13	10^8					4		9^2		3		12				11		8^1	6			25
1	2	4	5^2			14	7							9^1		11	13	12		10				3		8^3	6			26
1	5	3^2		2				12	10	13				14		11		9^1						7		8^3	6	4		27
1	5		2			13	8			14				4		9^3		3	7^2					10^1		11	12	6		28
1	2	3		5		7^1		9								12^2		11	13					10		8	6	4		29
1	2	4				12		6^1	10^2	11^3				3		14		5						9		13	7	8		30
1	2^1	4				12		6	10^2	11				3				5						9		13	7	8		31
1	2	4^1		12			7	9	10					5		11^2		3					13			14	6	8^3		32
1	2		4			6	7	11^1	8					3				9								12	5	10		33
1	2		5	3		7			10^2	13				4		12		11								9^1	6	8		34
1	2		5^1	3		7			10					4				11	13					12		9^2	6	8		35
1	2	12		4		6^1	8	9^3	14					3				10	13					7		11^2	5			36

AYR UNITED
First Division

Year Formed: 1910. *Ground & Address:* Somerset Park, Tryfield Place, Ayr KA8 9NB. *Telephone:* 01292 263435.
Fax: 01292 281314. *E-mail:* lachlan@ayrunitedfc.co.uk *Website:* ayrunitedfc.co.uk
Ground Capacity: 10,185, seated: 1549. *Size of Pitch:* 110yd × 72yd.
Chairman and Managing Director: Lachlan Cameron.
Manager: Brian Reid. *Assistant Manager:* Scott MacKenzie. *Physio:* Karen MacLellan.
Club Nickname(s): The Honest Men. *Previous Grounds:* None.
Record Attendance: 25,225 v Rangers, Division I, 13 Sept 1969.
Record Transfer Fee received: £300,000 for Steven Nicol to Liverpool (Oct 1981).
Record Transfer Fee paid: £90,000 for Mark Campbell from Stranraer (March 1999).
Record Victory: 11-1 v Dumbarton, League Cup, 13 Aug 1952.
Record Defeat: 0-9 in Division I v Rangers (1929); v Hearts (1931); B Division v Third Lanark (1954).
Most Capped Player: Jim Nisbet, 3, Scotland.
Most League Appearances: 459: John Murphy, 1963-78.
Most League League and Cup Goals in Season (Individual): 66: Jimmy Smith, 1927-28.
Most League and Cup Goals Overall (Individual): 213: Peter Price, 1955-61.

AYR UNITED 2008–09 LEAGUE RECORD

Match No.	Date	Venue	Opponents	Result	H/T Score	Lg. Pos.	Goalscorers	Attendance
1	Aug 2	H	Raith R	D 0-0	0-0	—		1391
2	9	A	Alloa Ath	W 2-0	2-0	4	Williams [4], Prunty [38]	569
3	16	H	Arbroath	W 2-1	0-1	1	Stevenson [62], Prunty [84]	1304
4	23	A	Stirling A	D 2-2	2-1	1	Prunty 2 [9, 11]	876
5	30	H	Queen's Park	W 2-1	2-0	1	Prunty 2 [2, 26]	1426
6	Sept 13	A	Stranraer	W 3-1	1-0	1	Aitken [32], Borris [60], Prunty [85]	1003
7	21	H	Brechin C	D 1-1	1-1	1	Stevenson [41]	1317
8	27	A	East Fife	L 0-3	0-1	3		1010
9	Oct 4	H	Peterhead	W 2-0	1-0	2	Stevenson (pen) [44], Williams [88]	1104
10	18	A	Raith R	L 2-3	1-1	3	Gormley [29], Walker [88]	1746
11	25	H	Stirling A	D 1-1	1-0	3	Aitken [30]	1070
12	Nov 1	A	Arbroath	W 3-0	3-0	3	Campbell [9], Easton [11], Prunty [22]	535
13	8	H	Stranraer	W 3-2	2-1	3	Gormley [2], Prunty [25], Easton [47]	1357
14	15	A	Queen's Park	W 3-0	1-0	3	Prunty 3 [9, 47, 67]	1009
15	22	H	East Fife	W 4-2	3-0	3	Stevenson [14], Gormley [17], Easton [23], Keenan [81]	1254
16	Dec 13	A	Alloa Ath	W 3-0	1-0	2	Agnew [13], Williams 2 [79, 90]	1079
17	20	A	Peterhead	L 0-3	0-1	2		631
18	30	A	Brechin C	W 1-0	0-0	—	Prunty [60]	548
19	Jan 17	A	Stirling A	L 0-2	0-0	2		779
20	25	H	Arbroath	W 2-1	1-1	2	Williams [44], Stevenson [63]	1256
21	31	H	Raith R	D 2-2	1-2	2	Davidson (og) [30], Agnew [71]	2368
22	Feb 7	A	Alloa Ath	L 2-3	0-2	—	Gormley 2 [64, 80]	752
23	21	H	Brechin C	W 4-2	1-2	2	Aitken (pen) [40], Stevenson [47], Roberts 2 [71, 77]	1404
24	28	A	Queen's Park	W 3-0	2-0	2	Roberts [12], Connolly [24], Stevenson [81]	1139
25	Mar 4	H	Queen's Park	D 1-1	0-1	—	Borris [52]	1363
26	7	H	Stranraer	W 5-0	3-0	1	Prunty [24], Stevenson [40], McGowan [42], Aitken [49], Williams [81]	1580
27	14	A	Raith R	W 1-0	0-0	1	Gormley [78]	3438
28	18	A	East Fife	W 1-0	1-0	—	Prunty [12]	832
29	21	H	Peterhead	D 0-0	0-0	1		1605
30	28	A	Stranraer	W 4-1	2-0	1	Nicoll (og) [17], Connolly [31], Easton [62], Borris [82]	1019
31	Apr 4	H	Stirling A	W 3-1	2-1	1	Gormley 2 [29, 45], Williams [89]	1583
32	11	A	Arbroath	W 3-1	0-0	1	Aitken (pen) [50], Stevenson 2 [72, 74]	820
33	18	A	Brechin C	L 0-1	0-0	2		712
34	25	H	East Fife	W 2-0	0-0	2	Roberts [52], Connolly [53]	1849
35	May 2	H	Alloa Ath	D 1-1	1-0	2	Roberts [38]	2195
36	9	A	Peterhead	W 3-2	0-0	2	Gormley [51], Connolly [56], Agnew [85]	602

Final League Position: 2

Honours

League Champions: Division II 1911-12, 1912-13, 1927-28, 1936-37, 1958-59, 1965-66. Second Division 1987-88, 1996-97;
Runners-up: Division II 1910-11, 1955-56, 1968-69. Second Divison 2008-09.
Scottish Cup: Semi-finals 2002.
League Cup: Runners-up: 2001-02.
B&Q Cup Runners-up: 1990-91, 1991-92.

Club colours: Shirt: White with black hoops. Shorts: White with black flashes. Stockings: Black.

Goalscorers: *League* (71): Prunty 15, Stevenson 10 (1 pen), Gormley 9, Williams 7, Aitken 5 (2 pens), Roberts 5, Connolly 4, Easton 4, Agnew 3, Borris 3, Campbell 1, Keenan 1, McGowan 1, Walker 1, own goals 2.
Scottish Cup (7): Prunty 2, Williams 2, Gormley 1, Keenan 1, McGowan 1.
CIS Cup (0).
Play-Offs (8): Aitken 3 (1 pen), Baird 2, Connelly 1, Prunty 1, Stevenson 1.

Grindlay S 36	Dempsie A 31 + 1	Walker S 33 + 1	Campbell M 28	Easton W 25 + 4	Borris R 25 + 3	Aitken C 27 + 2	Keenan D 33 + 1	Stevenson R 32 + 2	Prunty B 29 + 2	Williams A 16 + 17	Gormley D 17 + 19	Agnew S 7 + 10	McGowan N 24 + 3	Gillies D — + 1	Weaver P 1 + 4	Woodburn A 1 + 5	Connolly K 13 + 5	Henderson M 1 + 1	Roberts M 12 + 2	James K 5	Fisher I — + 1	Match No.
1	2	3	4	5	6	7	8	9	10	11^1	12											1
1	2	4	5	3	7	8	11	6^1	9^2	10	13	12										2
1	2	3	4	5	6^1	8	7	9	10	11^2	13	12										3
1	2	4	5	3	13	8	11	6	9	10^2	12	7^1										4
1	2	3	4^1	5	6^3	7	8	9	10	11^2	13	14	12									5
1	2	4	5^1	3^3	7	8	11	6	9	10^2	13	14	12									6
1	2	3	4	5^1	6		7	8	10	11^2	13	9	12									7
1	2	3^2	4	13	6	$8^•$	9	7	10	11^1	12		5									8
1	2	3	4	9	6	7	8	10^2	12	11^1			5	13								9
1	2	3	4	8^1	6	7	9	10	12	11			5									10
1	11	4	5		7	8	2	$6^•$	9		10	12	3^1									11
1	2	4	5	11^3	7	8^1	6	9^2	13	10	14	3			12							12
1	2	3	4	9	6	7^1	8	12	10	13	11^2		5									13
1	5^2	2	3	8	6	7^1	4	12	10^3	14	11	13	9									14
1	2	3	4	9	6	8	7	10	12	11^3			$5^•$									15
1	2^1	3	4	5	6^2	12	8	7	10	13	11^3	9		14								16
1	2	4	5	3^1	8	7^3	6	10	11^2	12	9			13	14							17
1	5	3	4	9^1	6^2	8	2	7	10^3	14	11	12	13									18
1	2^2	4	5^1	11		8	6	9	13	10	3				7^3	14	12					19
1	2	3	4^1	9^2	6	7	8	10	11	13	5				12							20
1	5	3			6	7	8		10	12	9	4			2		11^1					21
1	3	4	14	7	13	8	6	9^1	12	11^3			5			2^2	10					22
1	3	4	9^1	6	8	2	7	10	11^2				5				12	13				23
1	13	3	4	6^1	8	2	7	10^3	14	12			5^2				9		11			24
1	3	4	9	7^2	2	8	10^1	12	13				5				6		11			25
1	2	4	9^3	7	6	8	10^1	13	12				5				14		11^2	3		26
1	2	13	5^2	8	7	6	9^1	12	14	3							11		10^3	4		27
1	2	4		8	6	7	10^2	13	12				5				9		11^1	3		28
1		4	12	6	7	2	8	10^2	14	13			5				9^1		11^3	3		29
1	5	11	14	8	2^3	6	9^2	13	12	3							7		10^1	4		30
1	2	3	4	9	7	8	10	11					5		12	6^1						31
1	2	4	5^1	11	3	8	6	14	9^3	10^2					12	7	13					32
1	2^1	3	9	8	4	6	12	10^2	13	5					14	7^3	11					33
1	2	3	8	7	4	6^3	10^2	13	9	5^1					14	12	11					34
1	2	3	5^1	13	8	4	7	9^2	12	11						6	10					35
1	2^3	5^2	12	7	13			10	9	11			3^1			8	6	4			14	36

BERWICK RANGERS   Third Division

Year Formed: 1881. *Ground & Address:* Shielfield Park, Tweedmouth, Berwick-upon-Tweed TD15 2EF. *Telephone:* 01289 307424. *Fax:* 01289 309424. *Email:* club@berwickrangers.net *Website:* berwickrangers.net
Ground Capacity: 4131, seated: 1366. *Size of Pitch:* 110yd × 70yd.
Chairman: Brian Porteous. *Vice-Chairman:* Moray McLaren. *Company Secretary:* Ross Hood. *Football Secretary:* Dennis McCleary. *Treasurer:* Lyndsay Flannigan.
Manager: Alan McGonigal. *Coach:* Ian Smith. *Physios:* Ian Smith, Ian Oliver. *Ground/Kit:* Ian Oliver.
Club Nickname(s): The Borderers, The Wee Gers. *Previous Grounds:* Bull Stob Close, Pier Field, Meadow Field, Union Park, Old Shielfield.
Record Attendance: 13,283 v Rangers, Scottish Cup 1st rd, 28 Jan 1967.
Record Victory: 8-1 v Forfar Ath, Division II, 25 Dec 1965; v Vale of Leithen, Scottish Cup, Dec 1966.
Record Defeat: 1-9 v Hamilton A, First Division, 9 Aug 1980.
Most League Appearances: 435: Eric Tait, 1970-87.
Most League Goals in Season (Individual): 33: Ken Bowron, Division II, 1963-64.
Most Goals Overall (Individual): 115: Eric Tait, 1970-87.

BERWICK RANGERS 2008–09 LEAGUE RECORD

Match No.	Date	Venue	Opponents	Result	H/T Score	Lg. Pos.	Goalscorers	Attendance
1	Aug 2	H	East Stirling	W 2-1	2-1	—	Gribben [14], Dillon [28]	570
2	9	A	Montrose	D 1-1	0-1	3	Howat [83]	344
3	16	H	Dumbarton	L 1-2	1-0	5	Gribben [40]	516
4	23	A	Albion R	L 0-2	0-1	7		269
5	30	H	Forfar Ath	D 2-2	1-1	8	Gribben 2 (2 pens) [42, 60]	390
6	Sept 13	A	Cowdenbeath	L 1-2	0-2	8	Ewart [60]	375
7	20	A	Stenhousemuir	L 0-2	0-1	8		446
8	27	H	Annan Ath	W 3-0	1-0	8	Ewart [20], Dillon 2 (2 pens) [67, 79]	502
9	Oct 4	H	Elgin C	D 1-1	1-0	8	Lister [21]	367
10	18	A	East Stirling	L 0-1	0-1	9		387
11	Nov 1	A	Dumbarton	L 2-5	1-3	9	Anderson Craig [32], Ewart [83]	673
12	8	H	Albion R	L 0-3	0-1	9		288
13	15	A	Forfar Ath	L 1-2	1-1	9	Ewart [32]	327
14	22	H	Cowdenbeath	L 2-3	1-1	9	Gribben 2 [11, 59]	389
15	Dec 6	H	Stenhousemuir	W 3-2	2-1	—	McLaren [18], Thom (og) [30], McMenamin [76]	367
16	13	A	Annan Ath	W 2-1	1-1	9	Horn [30], McMenamin [73]	447
17	20	A	Elgin C	W 2-0	1-0	9	Gribben 2 [12, 59]	304
18	27	H	Montrose	W 3-2	0-2	8	Callaghan [66], McMenamin [70], Gribben [86]	510
19	Jan 13	A	Cowdenbeath	L 0-2	0-1	—		282
20	17	A	Albion R	L 1-2	1-1	9	Andreoni (og) [33]	264
21	24	H	Dumbarton	L 1-2	1-2	9	Callaghan [28]	425
22	Feb 7	A	Montrose	D 1-1	0-1	—	Guy [80]	318
23	21	A	Stenhousemuir	W 2-1	0-1	8	Callaghan [67], McLaren [81]	439
24	24	H	Annan Ath	D 1-1	1-1	—	Forrest [35]	306
25	28	A	Forfar Ath	L 4-5	0-1	8	McLaren 3 [49, 79, 89], Tod (og) [69]	382
26	Mar 7	H	Cowdenbeath	W 1-0	0-0	9	Bonar [51]	523
27	14	A	East Stirling	W 4-0	1-0	9	Gribben 3 [28, 67, 84], McLaren [85]	438
28	17	H	Forfar Ath	L 0-2	0-0	—		382
29	21	H	Elgin C	W 2-1	1-1	9	McLaren [14], Callaghan [89]	348
30	28	H	East Stirling	L 1-2	1-1	9	Gribben [14]	431
31	Apr 4	H	Albion R	D 1-1	0-1	9	McLaren [65]	323
32	11	A	Dumbarton	L 0-2	0-1	9		702
33	18	H	Stenhousemuir	L 0-3	0-1	9		390
34	25	A	Annan Ath	D 1-1	0-0	9	Gribben [57]	786
35	May 2	H	Montrose	L 0-1	0-0	9		418
36	9	A	Elgin C	L 0-2	0-1	9		429

Final League Position: 9

Honours
League Champions: Second Division 1978-79. Third Division 2006-07; *Runners-up:* Second Division 1993-94. Third Division 1999-2000.
Scottish Cup: Quarter-finals 1953-54, 1979-80.
League Cup: Semi-finals 1963-64.
League Challenge Cup: Quarter-finals 2004-05.

Club colours: Shirt: Black with gold vertical stripes. Shorts: Black. Stockings: Black.

Goalscorers: *League* (46): Gribben 14 (2 pens), McLaren 8, Callaghan 4, Ewart 4, Dillon 3 (2 pens), McMenamin 3, Anderson Craig 1, Bonar 1, Forrest 1, Guy 1, Horn 1, Howat 1, Lister 1, own goals 3.
Scottish Cup (1): Gribben 1.
Challenge Cup (1): Little 1.

McGurk R 21	Guy G 20 + 1	McMahon P 13 + 3	Ewart J 35	Horn R 24 + 3	Bonar S 24 + 3	McLaren F 34	Callaghan S 28 + 3	Lister J 9	Gribben D 31 + 3	Dillon J 28	Little I 6 + 11	Greenhill D 23 + 10	Grant D — + 7	Kiczynski S 3	Anderson Craig 6 + 5	Anderson Chris 1 + 14	Howat A 1 + 2	McLean A 2 + 1	Lennox T 13 + 3	Greenhill G 8 + 1	Fraser S 5 + 2	Lunn M 2	McMenamin C 22 + 2	Robertson D 2	Forrest F 10 + 2	Mearns E 6 + 4	Hampshire S 6 + 1	Barclay J 13	*Match No.*
1	2	3	4	5	6^1	7	8	9^2	10^3	11	12	13	14																1
1	2	5	3				8	10^3	11	9		6^2	13	4	7^1	12	14												2
1	2	3^2	4		6	7	8^3	9	10^1	11			13	5	14		12												3
1	2^1		4^3	3	6	7	8		10			11	13	5		14	9^2	12											4
1	2		4		6	7	12	10^2	9			11	13		8^1			5	3										5
1	2		3		6	9		11	10			12			8^1	13		4	5	7^2									6
1	2^1		4	5	6	7		10	9^3	11		12			14	13			3	8^2									7
1			4	5	2	7	6	10	9^2	11		13				14			3^3	8^1	12								8
1			4	5	2	9	8^1	10	14	11		12				13			3	7^3	6^2								9
1	12		4	5	2^1	10	8	9	14	11		13							3^2	7^3	6								10
		9^3	3	4		10	14		11^2	5		12			8	13			2^1	7■		1	6						11
1	2^1	11^3	4	5		9	6^2			3		13	12		8				14				7	10					12
1			4	5		10	6		9^1	3		11				12			2				8	7					13
1	2		4	5		10	6		9	3		11	12			7^1							8						14
1	2		4	5		10	6		9	3		11								8^1	12		7						15
1	2		4	5		10	6		9	3	12	11									8^1		7						16
1	2		4	5	13	10	6		9	3	12	11^1									8		7^2						17
1	2		4	5	13		6		9^3	3	10■	11^2			14					12	8^1		7						18
1	2		3	4	12	11	7■		10	5		9^2				13				8^1			6						19
1	2^1		4	5	6	10			9	3	8	11				13							7^2		12				20
1	2		4	5^1	8^3	10	6		9	3	11^2	13				14							7		12■				21
1	3	12		4	2^2	11	7			5	9					13							6^1			8■	10		22
	2		4			10	6		9	3	12	11^1											7		5	8		1	23
	2^1	14	4			10	6		9	3	13	11^3							12				7		5	8^2		1	24
		14	4^1	12	8	10	6		9	3		11^2				13			2^3				7		5			1	25
	2		4	14	8^1	10	6		9^3	3		13			11								7^2		5	12		1	26
		2	4	13	8	10^2			9	3		11				12							7^1		5	6		1	27
		3	4		8	10			9	2^2	12	11			13								7		5	6^1		1	28
		3	4		8^1	10	6		9	2	11	7^2							13						5	12		1	29
		3	4	2	8^1	10	6		9		12	11										1	7^2		5	13			30
		3	4	2	8	10	6		9^1	11	7^2														5	13	12	1	31
		5^2	3		8	6^1	7		10	2■	13	9											12		4		11	1	32
			4	5	3	10^2	6		13		14	11			12				2				8			7^1	9^3	1	33
			4	5	8	10	3		9			11							2				7				6	1	34
		3	4	5	7^2	10	6		9		12	11							2				13				8^1	1	35
		3	4■	5	8	10	13		9		12	11							2^1				7^2				6	1	36

BRECHIN CITY

Second Division

Year Formed: 1906. *Ground & Address:* Glebe Park, Trinity Rd, Brechin, Angus DD9 6BJ. *Telephone:* 01356 622856.
Fax: 01382 206331. *E-mail:* secretary@brechincityfc.com *Website:* www.brechincity.com
Ground Capacity: total: 3960, seated: 1519. *Size of Pitch:* 110yd × 67yd.
Chairman: Kenneth Ferguson. *Vice-Chairman:* Hugh Campbell Adamson. *Secretary:* Angus Fairlie.
Manager: Jim Duffy. *Physio:* Tom Gilmartin.
Club Nickname(s): The City. *Previous Grounds:* Nursery Park.
Record Attendance: 8122 v Aberdeen, Scottish Cup 3rd rd, 3 Feb 1973.
Record Transfer Fee received: £100,000 for Scott Thomson to Aberdeen (1991) and Chris Templeman to Morton (2004).
Record Transfer Fee paid: £16,000 for Sandy Ross from Berwick Rangers (1991).
Record Victory: 12-1 v Thornhill, Scottish Cup 1st rd, 28 Jan 1926.
Record Defeat: 0-10 v Airdrieonians, Albion R and Cowdenbeath, all in Division II, 1937-38.
Most League Appearances: 459: David Watt, 1975-89.
Most League Goals in Season (Individual): 26: Ronald McIntosh, Division II, 1959-60.
Most Goals Overall (Individual): 131: Ian Campbell, 1977-85.

BRECHIN CITY 2008–09 LEAGUE RECORD

Match No.	Date	Venue	Opponents	Result	H/T Score	Lg. Pos.	Goalscorers	Atten-dance
1	Aug 2	H	Stirling A	W 2-1	1-0	—	Twigg [39], Smith D [85]	535
2	9	A	Stranraer	W 2-1	1-1	1	Diack 2 [21, 83]	279
3	16	H	Peterhead	D 2-2	2-0	2	Nimmo 2 [9, 16]	525
4	23	A	Queen's Park	D 1-1	0-0	4	Twigg [58]	613
5	30	A	East Fife	D 0-0	0-0	3		726
6	Sept 13	H	Arbroath	W 3-1	1-0	2	Byers [24], Smith C 2 [67, 74]	615
7	21	A	Ayr U	D 1-1	1-1	3	Twigg [30]	1317
8	27	H	Raith R	W 2-0	2-0	1	White [12], Paton [43]	769
9	Oct 4	H	Alloa Ath	W 3-1	2-0	1	Twigg [29], King 2 [43, 73]	412
10	18	A	Stirling A	W 2-1	1-0	1	Twigg [40], Byers [52]	577
11	25	H	Queen's Park	W 2-1	1-0	1	Byers [41], Smith D [79]	483
12	Nov 1	A	Peterhead	L 1-5	1-4	2	Smith D [8]	602
13	8	A	Arbroath	W 2-1	1-1	2	Twigg 2 [34, 80]	702
14	15	H	East Fife	W 2-1	1-0	2	Byers [7], Diack [90]	691
15	22	A	Raith R	D 2-2	0-1	2	Diack [55], Twigg [82]	2229
16	Dec 20	A	Alloa Ath	L 1-2	1-2	3	Twigg [7]	405
17	27	A	East Fife	L 1-2	0-1	3	Dyer [90]	857
18	30	H	Ayr U	L 0-1	0-0	—		548
19	Jan 17	A	Queen's Park	D 0-0	0-0	3		466
20	24	H	Peterhead	D 1-1	0-0	4	Twigg [75]	517
21	31	H	Stirling A	L 1-2	1-1	5	Walker [8]	565
22	Feb 7	A	Stranraer	W 3-0	2-0	—	Twigg 2 (1 pen) [5 (p), 35], Byers [79]	283
23	21	A	Ayr U	L 2-4	2-1	4	Byers [15], McAllister [28]	1404
24	28	H	East Fife	W 2-1	1-1	3	Byers [19], Janczyk [90]	595
25	Mar 7	A	Arbroath	D 0-0	0-0	4		749
26	10	H	Stranraer	W 1-0	0-0	—	McAllister [63]	315
27	14	A	Stirling A	W 3-2	2-2	4	Ettien 2 [13, 68], McAllister [45]	544
28	21	H	Alloa Ath	W 1-0	0-0	3	McAllister [59]	421
29	24	H	Raith R	L 0-4	0-2	—		780
30	28	A	Arbroath	L 0-1	0-1	3		580
31	Apr 4	H	Queen's Park	W 2-0	1-0	3	King 2 [30, 60]	467
32	11	A	Peterhead	W 1-0	0-0	3	Smith D [66]	739
33	18	H	Ayr U	W 1-0	0-0	3	McAllister [64]	712
34	25	A	Raith R	L 0-2	0-0	3		2529
35	May 2	H	Stranraer	W 2-1	2-1	3	Ettien [2], Nimmo [22]	418
36	9	A	Alloa Ath	L 2-3	0-2	3	Ettien [70], Townsley (og) [72]	401

Final League Position: 3

Honours
League Champions: C Division 1953-54. Second Division 1982-83, 1989-90, 2004-05. Third Division 2001-02. *Runners-up:* Second Division 1992-93, 2002-03. Third Division 1995-96. Second Division 2004-05.
League Challenge Cup: Runners-up 2002-03. Semi-finals 2001-02.

Club colours: Shirt, Shorts, Stockings: Red with white trim.

Goalscorers: *League* (51): Twigg 12 (1 pen), Byers 7, McAllister 5, Diack 4, Ettien 4, King 4, Smith D 4, Nimmo 3, Smith C 2, Dyer 1, Janczyk 1, Paton 1, Walker 1, White 1, own goal 1.
Scottish Cup (4): Diack 3 (1 pen), Janczyk 1.
Challenge Cup (0).
Play-Offs (2): McAllister 2 (1 pen).

Nelson C 36	Murie D 12+6	Ward J 20+1	White D 18	Dyer W 35	Byers K 27+3	Janczyk N 30+1	King C 26+9	Smith D 21+6	Diack J 18+4	Twigg G 23	Walker R 28+7	Canning S 5+7	Nelson A 1+6	Nimmo I 27+6	Smith C —+5	Seeley J 17+1	Paton M 7+1	Fusco G 15+4	Baird J 5+5	Ettien S 8+6	McAllister R 13+2	Smith B 14	Harvey R —+3	Match No.
1	2	3¹	4	5	6	7³	8²	9	10	11	12	13	14											1
1	2		4	5	3	7¹	8²	12	11	10³	9	14	13		6									2
1	2	3¹	4	5	6	7²	12	9	11¹	10	14	13			8									3
1	2³		4	5	6¹	7	13	9	10	11²	12				8	14	3							4
1			4	5	6	7	12	9	11	10	2				8¹		3							5
1	2		4	5	6	7	12	9¹	11²	10	3		14		8³	13								6
1		3		5	6	8		9¹		10	2			7	12	4	11							7
1		3		5	6	7		9²	14	10³	2			12	8¹	13	4	11						8
1		3		5	6¹	7		9	12	10	2				8	4	11							9
1			4		3	7	6²	11¹	12	9³	2	13		8	14	5	10							10
1	5		4		3	7	6	11¹	14	9²	2				8³			10	12	13				11
1	5		3		7³		6¹	8²	11	9	2		14	13	4	10	12							12
1			4	5	3		6	12	11	9	2			7	10¹		8							13
1	2	3	4	5	6²	7		9	13	10¹					8	12	11							14
1	2¹		4	5	3	7	6³	10²	11	12	9	13	14		8									15
1	2³		4	5	3	7	12	11¹	10	9	14	6²			8	13								16
1	2¹	3	4	5	10	7	8²	9	11	12	6³	13	14											17
1	12	3	4¹	5	14	7	6³	9	13	10	2				8²		11							18
1		3		5	7²	6		9	11¹	10	2				8			4	13	12				19
1		3		5	12	7		9		10	2				8			4	6¹	11				20
1		3		5	9	7		11		10	2	13			8²			4	6¹		12			21
1			4		3	7	6²	11	13	9	2							8		10¹	12	5		22
1		3		5	6	8		11¹	14	10	2				12			7²	13	9³	4			23
1	14	3		5	6		12	11		9²	2				8¹			7	13	10³	4			24
1			4		3	7	6	10		11¹	2				12			8			9	5		25
1		3		5	6	7		9			2				8			12		11	10¹	4		26
1		3	11				6¹		12		2		13	7²			4	8		10	9	5		27
1	14		5			8¹		9	12		2		6³		3	7		11		10²	4		13	28
1	13		5		6¹			9			2²		14	7³	3			8		11	10	4	12	29
1	13	3¹		5		7	6			9³	2				8²		14			11	10	4	12¹	30
1			5			7		11		9¹	2			6²	12	3		8		13	10	4		31
1	12			3		6		10		11²	2		13	7¹		5		8			9	4		32
1	6		3	5		7		11		9	2				12			8¹	13	10²	4			33
1	4			5				7¹	11		2		10	6				5		8	12	9		34
1			5				12		13	9	2			7¹	6	3		8		11	10²	4		35
1	13	4			3	7			11²		2		10	6³		12		8			9	14	5¹	36

CELTIC   Premier League

Year Formed: 1888. *Ground & Address:* Celtic Park, Glasgow G40 3RE. *Telephone:* 0871 226 1888. *Fax:* 0141 551 8106.
E-mail: customerservices@celticfc.co.uk. *Website:* www.celticfc.net
Ground Capacity: all seated: 60,355. *Size of Pitch:* 105m × 68m.
Chairman: Brian Quinn. *Chief Executive:* Peter Lawwell. *Commercial Manager:* Adrian Filby. *Secretary:* Robert Howat.
Manager: Tony Mowbray. *Assistant Manager:* Mark Venus. *First Team Coach:* Peter Grant. *Physio:* Tim Williamson. *Club
Doctor:* Derek McCormack. *Kit Manager:* John Clark.
Club Nickname(s): The Bhoys. *Previous Grounds:* None.
Record Attendance: 92,000 v Rangers, Division I, 1 Jan 1938.
Record Transfer Fee received: £6,500,000 for Stilian Petrov to Aston Villa (August 2007).
Record Transfer Fee paid: £6,000,000 for Chris Sutton from Chelsea (July 2000).
Record Victory: 11-0 Dundee, Division I, 26 Oct 1895.
Record Defeat: 0-8 v Motherwell, Division I, 30 Apr 1937.
Most Capped Player: Pat Bonner 80, Republic of Ireland.
Most League Appearances: 486: Billy McNeill, 1957-75.
Most League Goals in Season (Individual): 50: James McGrory, Division I, 1935-36.
Most Goals Overall (Individual): 397: James McGrory, 1922-39.

Honours
League Champions: (42 times) Division I 1892-93, 1893-94, 1895-96, 1897-98, 1904-05, 1905-06, 1906-07, 1907-08, 1908-09,
1909-10, 1913-14, 1914-15, 1915-16, 1916-17, 1918-19, 1921-22, 1925-26, 1935-36, 1937-38, 1953-54, 1965-66, 1966-67,
1967-68, 1968-69, 1969-70, 1970-71, 1971-72, 1972-73, 1973-74. Premier Division 1976-77, 1978-79, 1980-81, 1981-82,
1985-86, 1987-88, 1997-98, 2000-01, 2001-02, 2003-04, 2005-06, 2006-07, 2007-08. *Runners-up:* 28 times.

CELTIC 2008–09 LEAGUE RECORD

Match No.	Date	Venue	Opponents	Result	H/T Score	Lg. Pos.	Goalscorers	Attendance
1	Aug 10	H	St Mirren	W 1-0	0-0	—	Robson (pen) 62	57,441
2	17	A	Dundee U	D 1-1	0-0	3	Hartley 51	11,648
3	23	H	Falkirk	W 3-0	2-0	1	McManus 32, Samaras 2 44, 68	56,031
4	31	H	Rangers	L 2-4	1-1	4	Samaras 39, Nakamura 90	58,595
5	Sept 13	A	Motherwell	W 4-2	4-0	2	Maloney 5, Samaras 2 9, 42, McDonald 24	8407
6	21	A	Kilmarnock	W 3-1	1-0	2	Maloney 26, Samaras 2 (1 pen) 56, 82 (p)	8111
7	27	H	Aberdeen	W 3-2	1-0	2	Vennegoor 2 14, 90, McDonald 78	58,565
8	Oct 4	H	Hamilton A	W 4-0	2-0	1	Nakamura 25, Samaras 37, McDonald 76, McGeady 83	55,881
9	18	A	Inverness CT	W 2-1	0-0	1	Brown S 48, Loovens 65	7143
10	25	H	Hibernian	W 4-2	2-1	1	McManus 32, Sheridan 36, Loovens 76, Brown S 82	58,337
11	Nov 2	A	Hearts	W 2-0	2-0	1	Maloney 7, Caldwell 20	15,460
12	8	H	Motherwell	W 2-0	1-0	1	Hartley 45, McDonald 71	56,504
13	12	H	Kilmarnock	W 3-0	1-0	—	Sheridan 2 18, 75, Nakamura 84	55,347
14	16	A	Hamilton A	W 2-1	1-1	1	Nakamura (pen) 39, Hartley 86	5550
15	22	A	St Mirren	W 3-1	0-0	1	Samaras 64, Nakamura 66, Sheridan 80	7433
16	29	H	Inverness CT	W 1-0	1-0	1	Maloney 29	55,117
17	Dec 7	A	Hibernian	L 0-2	0-0	1		14,289
18	13	H	Hearts	D 1-1	0-1	1	McManus 79	56,079
19	21	A	Falkirk	W 3-0	0-0	1	Samaras 48, Mizuno 89, McDonald 90	6543
20	27	A	Rangers	W 1-0	0-0	1	McDonald 58	50,403
21	Jan 3	H	Dundee U	D 2-2	1-0	1	Samaras 2 12, 58	59,558
22	18	A	Aberdeen	L 2-4	1-2	1	Brown S 25, McDonald 73	18,100
23	24	H	Hibernian	W 3-1	2-1	1	McDonald 2 3, 76, McManus 9	58,930
24	Feb 1	A	Inverness CT	D 0-0	0-0	1		7007
25	15	H	Rangers	D 0-0	0-0	1		58,766
26	22	A	Motherwell	D 1-1	0-0	2	McDonald 60	8593
27	28	H	St Mirren	W 7-0	2-0	2	Nakamura 3 16, 35, 58, Crosas 51, Brown S 2 55, 66, Potter (og) 76	58,286
28	Mar 4	A	Kilmarnock	W 2-1	1-1	—	McDonald 2 27, 81	6712
29	22	A	Dundee U	D 2-2	1-0	1	McDonald 24, Naylor 81	12,043
30	Apr 4	H	Hamilton A	W 4-0	2-0	1	Samaras 2 5, 66, McGeady 22, Vennegoor 83	58,961
31	8	H	Falkirk	W 4-0	1-0	—	Caldwell 29, Vennegoor 62, McGeady 78, O'Dea 90	57,669
32	11	A	Hearts	D 1-1	1-1	1	Vennegoor 1	16,514
33	18	H	Aberdeen	W 2-0	1-0	1	Vennegoor 43, McDonald 55	58,581
34	May 2	A	Aberdeen	W 3-1	1-1	1	Considine (og) 44, McDonald 2 72, 90	14,752
35	9	A	Rangers	L 0-1	0-1	2		50,321
36	12	H	Dundee U	W 2-1	1-0	—	Loovens 22, Samaras 52	57,407
37	17	A	Hibernian	D 0-0	0-0	2		14,074
38	24	H	Hearts	D 0-0	0-0	2		59,685

Final League Position: 2

Scottish Cup Winners: (34 times) 1892, 1899, 1900, 1904, 1907, 1908, 1911, 1912, 1914, 1923, 1925, 1927, 1931, 1933, 1937, 1951, 1954, 1965, 1967, 1969, 1971, 1972, 1974, 1975, 1977, 1980, 1985, 1988, 1989, 1995, 2001, 2004, 2005, 2007. *Runners-up:* 18 times.
League Cup Winners: (14 times) 1956-57, 1957-58, 1965-66, 1966-67, 1967-68, 1968-69, 1969-70, 1974-75, 1982-83, 1997-98, 1999-2000, 2000-01, 2005-06, 2008-09; *Runners-up:* 14 times.

European: *European Cup:* 128 matches (1966-67 winners, 1967-68, 1968-69, 1969-70 runners-up, 1970-71, 1971-72, 1972-73, 1973-74 semi-finals, 1974-75, 1977-78, 1979-80, 1981-82, 1982-83, 1986-87, 1988-89, 1998-99, 2001-02, 2002-03, 2003-04, 2005-06, 2006-07, 2007-08, 2008-09). *Cup Winners' Cup:* 39 matches (1963-64 semi-finals, 1965-66 semi-finals, 1975-76, 1980-81, 1984-85, 1985-86, 1989-90, 1995-96). *UEFA Cup:* 73 matches (*Fairs Cup:* 1962-63, 1964-65. *UEFA Cup:* 1976-77, 1983-84, 1987-88, 1991-92, 1992-93, 1993-94, 1996-97, 1997-98, 1998-99, 1999-2000, 2000-01, 2001-02, 2002-03 runners-up, 2003-04 quarter-finals).

Club colours: Shirt: Emerald green and white hoops. Shorts: White with emerald green trim. Stockings: White.

Goalscorers: *League* (80): McDonald 16, Samaras 15 (1 pen), Nakamura 8 (1 pen), Vennegoor 6, Brown S 5, Maloney 4, McManus 4, Sheridan 4, Hartley 3, Loovens 3, McGeady 3, Caldwell 2, Crosas 1, Mizuno 1, Naylor 1, O'Dea 1, Robson 1 (pen), own goals 2.
Scottish Cup (4): Brown S 1, Caldwell 1, McDonald 1, McGeady 1.
CIS Cup (9): McGeady 2 (1 pen), Samaras 2 (1 pen), Brown S 1, Loovens 1, McDonald 1, Nakamura 1, O'Dea 1.
Champions League (4): Maloney 1, McDonald 1, McGeady 1, Robson 1.

Boruc A 34	Hinkel A 32	Naylor L 19 + 4	Hartley P 20 + 5	Caldwell G 36	McManus S 31	Robson B 13 + 4	Brown S 36	McDonald S 33 + 1	Vennegoor J 15 + 10	McGeady A 21 + 8	Wilson M 15 + 3	Samaras G 19 + 12	Caddis P — + 5	Nakamura S 30 + 2	Loovens G 13 + 4	Crosas M 14 + 4	Maloney S 14 + 6	Killen C — + 1	Hutchinson B — + 3	Sheridan C 6 + 6	O'Dea D 7 + 3	McCourt P — + 4	Donati M 2 + 2	Brown M 4	Mizuno K 2 + 8	Flood W 2 + 3	Conroy R — + 1	Match No.
1	2	3[1]	4	5	6	7[3]	8	9[2]	10	11	12	13	14															1
1	2		4	5	6	12	8	9[2]	10	11	3	13		7[1]														2
1	2		4		6		8[2]		10[1]	11	3	9[3]		7	5	13	12	14										3
1	2	4[1]		5	6	12	8	13		11	3[3]	9[2]		7	10				14									4
1		3		5	6	7	8	9[2]						2	10		12		4[1]	11	13							5
1		3	13	5[4]	6		8	10[3]	12					2	9	7	14		4[2]	11[1]								6
1		3	14		6		8	13	10		12			2	9[3]	7	5		4[2]	11[1]								7
1				5	6	3	8[3]	9	10[1]	11				2	12[2]	7	4			13	14							8
1		3	14	2[1]	6	7	8	9[2]		11	12			5	4[3]		10			13								9
1	2		4	5	6[1]	3	8	9[3]	13					7[2]	12		11		10	14								10
1	2		4	5	6	7[2]	8	9[3]	12		3			11[1]	10	14	13											11
	2		4	5	6	7[2]	8	9[3]	3		12			11[1]	10						13			1	14			12
	2			5	6		8	9[1]	3			12	14	7	11[2]	10[3]	4							1	13			13
	2	11		5	6		8		3[1]		12	13	14	7[2]	9	10			4[3]					1				14
1	2	14		5[3]	6	11[1]	8	9	3					10[2]	7		4			12	13							15
1	2	12	4	5	6	3[1]	8	9						10[2]	7		11		13[3]	14								16
1	2	7[2]		5	6		8	9	13		3			12	4		11		10[1]									17
1	2	13	4	5	6		8	9		11	3[2]			12	7				10[1]									18
1	2	3		5			8	9	10[1]					7	4					12	6	11						19
1	2[1]	3	4	5	6	11	8	9[3]	14					12	10						13	7[2]						20
1		3	4	5	6	11	8	9	13					2[1]	10[2]		12				7[3]	14						21
	2		4	5	6		8	9	3	11	12			10[1]							7			1				22
1	2	3		5	6[1]	13	8	9	10[3]	11				14	7		12				4[2]							23
1	2	3		5	6	4	8	9[3]	12	11				10[1]	7[2]					13	14							24
1	2	3	11	5	6		8[3]	9	10[2]					12	13		7						14		4[1]			25
1	2	3		5	6		8	9	10[1]					12	7		11				4							26
1	2	3[1]		5	6		8	9[2]	10[3]	11				13	7		4			14	12							27
1	2			5	6		8	9		11				10[1]	7		4			12	3							28
1	2	3	4	5			8	9	10[2]	11				13	7[1]					6	12							29
1	2			5	6		8	9[2]	13	11[3]				10	7[1]		4				3	14	12					30
1	2			5	6		8	9	12	11[3]				10[1]	7[1]		4				3	13	14					31
1	2	3		5	6[1]		8	9	10	11[3]				13	4		12						14		7[2]			32
1	2	3	12	5			8	9[3]	10	11[2]				7	6		4[1]						14		13			33
1	2	3	8	5	6[1]			9	10	11[2]				7	12		4								13			34
1	2	14	8	5				9	10[2]	12				7	6		4			11[1]	3[3]							35
1	2	3	12	5			8	9	13	11				10[2]	7[3]		6				4[1]	14						36
1	2	3	4	5			8[2]	9	12	11				10[1]	7		6				13	14						37
1	2		4	5			8[3]	9[2]	12	11				10[1]	7		6				3	14						38

CLYDE

Second Division

Year Formed: 1877. *Ground & Address:* Broadwood Stadium, Cumbernauld, G68 9NE. *Telephone:* 01236 451511.
Fax: 01236 733490. *E-mail:* info@clydefc.co.uk *Website:* www.clydefc.co.uk
Ground Capacity: all seated: 8200. *Size of Pitch:* 112yd × 76yd.
Chairman: Ian Letham. *Secretary:* John D. Taylor.
Manager: John Brown. *Physio:* Ian McKinlay.
Club Nickname(s): The Bully Wee. *Previous Grounds:* Barrowfield Park 1877-97, Shawfield Stadium 1897-1986.
Record Attendance: 52,000 v Rangers, Division I, 21 Nov 1908.
Record Transfer Fee received: £175,000 for Scott Howie to Norwich City (Aug 1993).
Record Transfer Fee paid: £14,000 for Harry Hood from Sunderland (1966).
Record Victory: 11-1 v Cowdenbeath, Division II, 6 Oct 1951.
Record Defeat: 0-11 v Dumbarton, Scottish Cup 4th rd, 22 Nov, 1879; v Rangers, Scottish Cup 4th rd, 13 Nov 1880.
Most Capped Player: Tommy Ring, 12, Scotland.
Most League Appearances: 420: Brian Ahern, 1971-81; 1987-88.
Most League Goals in Season (Individual): 32: Bill Boyd, 1932-33.

CLYDE 2008–09 LEAGUE RECORD

Match No.	Date		Venue	Opponents	Result	H/T Score	Lg. Pos.	Goalscorers	Attendance
1	Aug	2	H	Morton	D 1-1	0-1	—	Brown [90]	1638
2		9	A	Dundee	L 0-1	0-1	7		4042
3		16	H	Ross Co	D 2-2	0-2	8	MacLennan Ruari [68], Clarke [82]	966
4		23	A	Livingston	L 1-2	1-1	8	Clarke [29]	1725
5		30	A	St Johnstone	W 3-2	2-1	7	McKay [2], Gemmill [37], Waddell [81]	2412
6	Sept	13	H	Partick Th	D 1-1	0-1	8	Clarke (pen) [69]	2191
7		20	A	Airdrie U	W 2-0	1-0	7	Waddell [27], MacLennan Ruari [59]	1489
8		27	H	Queen of the S	L 0-2	0-0	8		1096
9	Oct	4	H	Dunfermline Ath	L 0-2	0-2	9		1273
10		18	A	Morton	L 0-1	0-1	9		2041
11		25	H	Livingston	W 2-1	0-1	8	Trouten [63], McSwegan [90]	820
12	Nov	1	A	Ross Co	L 0-3	0-0	9		2205
13		8	A	Partick Th	L 0-2	0-1	10		3003
14		15	H	St Johnstone	D 2-2	1-1	10	Clarke 2 [17, 85]	1419
15		22	A	Queen of the S	W 2-0	0-0	9	Clarke 2 [55, 83]	2324
16	Dec	13	H	Dundee	W 1-0	0-0	9	McLaren [66]	1176
17		16	H	Airdrie U	W 1-0	0-0	—	Trouten [74]	864
18		20	A	Dunfermline Ath	D 4-4	1-1	5	Trouten [1], Higgins [50], Clarke 2 [65, 70]	3279
19		27	A	St Johnstone	L 0-1	0-1	7		3491
20	Jan	3	H	Partick Th	L 2-4	1-3	9	Clarke 2 (1 pen) [20, 53 (p)]	2016
21		17	A	Livingston	D 1-1	1-1	8	McLaren [41]	1354
22		24	H	Ross Co	W 2-0	1-0	8	McLaren [44], Waddell [66]	776
23		31	A	Dundee	L 1-2	1-2	9	McLaren [12]	3217
24	Feb	22	A	Airdrie U	L 0-1	0-1	9		1189
25		28	H	Queen of the S	D 1-1	1-0	9	Trouten (pen) [9]	1142
26	Mar	3	H	Morton	L 2-4	2-1	—	MacLennan Ruari [44], Gemmill [45]	1165
27		7	A	Partick Th	W 1-0	0-0	9	Maxwell (og) [54]	3579
28		10	H	St Johnstone	L 1-3	0-1	—	Lithgow [63]	1093
29		14	A	Morton	L 0-2	0-1	10		2168
30		21	H	Dunfermline Ath	L 1-4	1-2	10	MacLennan Ruari [38]	1109
31	Apr	4	H	Livingston	L 0-1	0-1	10		957
32		11	A	Ross Co	D 0-0	0-0	10		2078
33		18	H	Airdrie U	W 3-0	1-0	10	Waddell [5], MacLennan Ruari 2 [61, 74]	1614
34		25	A	Queen of the S	L 1-7	1-3	10	McLaren [24]	2601
35	May	2	H	Dundee	W 2-0	0-0	10	Shinnie (og) [53], McLaren [77]	944
36		9	A	Dunfermline Ath	D 1-1	1-1	10	Higgins [27]	2418

Final League Position: 10

Honours
League Champions: Division II 1904-05, 1951-52, 1956-57, 1961-62, 1972-73. Second Division 1977-78, 1981-82, 1992-93, 1999-2000.
Runners-up: Division II 1903-04, 1905-06, 1925-26, 1963-64. Second Division 2003-04.
Scottish Cup Winners: 1939, 1955, 1958; *Runners-up:* 1910, 1912, 1949.
League Challenge Cup Runners-up: 2006-07.

Club colours: Shirt: White with red flashes. Shorts: Black with red flashes. Stockings: Red with white hoops.

Goalscorers: *League* (41): Clarke 11 (2 pens), MacLennan Ruari 6, McLaren 6, Trouten 4 (1 pen), Waddell 4, Gemmill 2, Higgins 2, Brown 1, Lithgow 1, McKay 1, McSwegan 1, own goals 2.
Scottish Cup (2): Clarke 1 (pen), McKay 1.
CIS Cup (1): Clarke 1.
Challenge Cup (4): Trouten 2 (1 pen), Clarke 1, Gibson 1.

Hutton D 31	McGregor N 7	Ohnesorge M 10	Higgins C 30 + 2	Brown M 24 + 2	Kettlewell S 26	Gibson B 30	Trouten A 15 + 12	Gemmill S 23 + 7	McKay D 14 + 16	McLaren W 24	Clarke P 28 + 1	McSwegan G 2 + 14	MacLennan Ruari 16 + 13	MacLennan Roddy 1 + 2	Waddell R 24 + 4	McGowan D — + 1	Wilson M 14 + 5	Winters R 4 + 2	McLaughlin G —	Cherrie P 5 + 1	Lowing A 17	Emslie P 9	McCusker M — + 1	Murch J — + 1	Lithgow A 22	Stevenson T 9 + 2	O'Reilly C — + 3	Tade G 11 + 2	Match No.
1	2	3³	4	5	6	7	8	9¹	10²	11	12	13	14																1
1		3	4	5	6³	2	7	10²	14	11¹	9	13	8	12															2
1		5	3³	4	7	2		6²	11	13	10		8		9¹	12	14												3
1		3¹	4	5	6	2		9	12		11		8		10	7													4
	3	12	5¹	6	4	13	10	7		9		8²		11						1	2								5
	4	5		8²	3		11	6		10	12	13		9¹						1	2	7							6
	5	3	4¹	6	8	14	10²	7³		9	12	13		11						1	2	7							7
1	4	5	12²	8	3¹	13	11	6		10¹	14		9							1	2	7							8
1	4	5¹	13	3	8		11	6		10	12	14		9²							2³	7							9
1	4	3		5	13	10¹	7		9	14	11	12		6²							2³	8							10
1	2¹	4	12		3	8	11	5³		10²	13	6		9	14						7								11
1		4	8³	5	7	10²		9	11¹	12	3		6							2	13	14							12
1		4	7	6	5	12	10²	13	11	9	8		3	2¹															13
1	5³	3		7	4	13	14	6¹	8	10	12	9								2			11²						14
1		4	3	7	5		10	9¹	11	12			2	8						6									15
1		4	5	3	13	12⁴	10¹	8²	11		9		2	7						6									16
1		4	3¹	5	12		7	11³	9	14	13⁴	8²		2	10					6									17
1		4	3	5	7	10¹		11	9		12	8		2						6									18
1		4	3¹	5	7		13	11³	9	14⁴	12	10²		2	8					6									19
1			5	8	3	6		12	11	10		14		7³						2¹					4	9²	13		20
1			8	5	10	12	7¹	11	9			3	4							2					4				21
1		3		8	4		13	12	9³	10²			6	7						2					5		14	11¹	22
1		4	8	5	12			11	9		13	3	10¹							2					6			7²	23
1		4	2		5	7	12	10¹	11		9⁴	14	13		3²		8³								6				24
1		5	2		3		6¹	10	12	11		7													4	9		8	25
1		4	2	7¹	5⁴	12	9²		11		3				13										6	10³	14	8	26
1		4	5	7¹		9	13	11²		8	3	12			3	14									6	2		10	27
1		4		7³	5	12	9¹	13	11		8			3	14										6	2		10²	28
1⁴		4		10²	5	7¹	9		11⁶		12			3	8			15							6	2		13	29
		4	6		5	7	11¹	12		9		8		3	13			1								2		10²	30
1		4	2¹	8	5		7²	12	11⁴	9		14			3³	10									6			13	31
1		4	2	8¹	5		13	14		9		12			3	10²									6	11³			32
1		3	4	8		7	13	14	11		12		6³			10²									5	2¹	9		33
1		2	3	8³		7		13	9	11²	12	6		5		10¹									4	14			34
1		4	5	8²			2	14	11³	9¹		7		3		12									6	13		10	35
1		4	5			12	2³		11	9²	13	8¹		3		7	14								6			10	36

COWDENBEATH
Third Division

Year Formed: 1881. *Ground & Address:* Central Park, Cowdenbeath KY4 9EY. *Telephone:* 01383 610166. *Fax:* 01383 512132.
E-mail: secretary@cowdenbeathfc.com *Website:* www.cowdenbeathfc.com
Ground Capacity: total: 5268, seated: 1622. *Size of Pitch:* 107yd × 66yd.
Commercial Managers: Joe MacNamara and Susan Welsh.
Manager: Brian Welsh. *Assistant Manager:* Danny Lennon. *First Team Coaches:* S. McLeish, M. Renwick. *Physio:* Neil Bryson.
Previous Grounds: North End Park, Cowdenbeath.
Record Attendance: 25,586 v Rangers, League Cup quarter-final, 21 Sept 1949.
Record Transfer Fee received: £30,000 for Nicky Henderson to Falkirk (March 1994).
Record Victory: 12-0 v Johnstone, Scottish Cup 1st rd, 21 Jan 1928.
Record Defeat: 1-11 v Clyde, Division II, 6 Oct 1951.
Most Capped Player: Jim Paterson, 3, Scotland.
Most League and Cup Appearances: 491 Ray Allan 1972-75, 1979-89.
Most League Goals in Season (Individual): 54, Rab Walls, Division II, 1938-39.
Most Goals Overall (Individual): 127, Willie Devlin, 1922-26, 1929-30.

COWDENBEATH 2008–09 LEAGUE RECORD

Match No.	Date	Venue	Opponents	Result	H/T Score	Lg. Pos.	Goalscorers	Atten- dance
1	Aug 2	H	Annan Ath	L 1-4	1-1	—	McQuade [16]	596
2	9	A	Forfar Ath	W 1-0	0-0	6	Ramsay [69]	412
3	16	H	Albion R	W 2-1	1-0	2	Fairbairn [22], Gemmell [81]	302
4	23	A	Elgin C	W 2-0	0-0	1	McGregor [59], Gemmell [60]	537
5	30	A	Stenhousemuir	L 0-1	0-0	2		456
6	Sept 13	H	Berwick R	W 2-1	2-0	2	Gemmell [2], Fairbairn [9]	375
7	20	A	Dumbarton	L 1-2	0-1	4	McQuade [90]	801
8	27	H	Montrose	W 2-1	1-1	2	Gemmell [32], McQuade [71]	296
9	Oct 4	H	East Stirling	D 0-0	0-0	4		431
10	18	A	Annan Ath	W 1-0	0-0	3	McQuade [22]	578
11	Nov 1	A	Albion R	L 1-3	0-1	3	Armstrong [58]	259
12	8	H	Elgin C	W 4-1	3-1	3	McQuade 2 [8, 30], Armstrong 2 [10, 74]	193
13	15	H	Stenhousemuir	L 1-2	0-2	4	Dempster [83]	406
14	22	A	Berwick R	W 3-2	1-1	3	Armstrong [19], Dempster [63], McQuade [75]	389
15	Dec 13	A	Montrose	W 1-0	1-0	2	Dempster [38]	334
16	20	A	East Stirling	W 4-1	1-1	2	Fairbairn 2 [9, 87], Adamson [57], McQuade [73]	457
17	Jan 10	H	Dumbarton	W 2-0	1-0	—	Adamson [13], McQuade [80]	416
18	13	H	Berwick R	W 2-0	1-0	—	Dempster [30], Tomana [90]	282
19	17	A	Elgin C	D 1-1	1-0	1	Brown [60]	380
20	24	A	Albion R	W 2-1	2-1	1	Gemmell 2 [21, 38]	409
21	31	H	Annan Ath	W 1-0	1-0	1	Gemmell [37]	326
22	Feb 21	A	Dumbarton	D 1-1	0-1	1	Dempster [57]	846
23	28	H	Stenhousemuir	W 1-0	0-0	1	Dempster [86]	459
24	Mar 3	A	Stenhousemuir	L 0-1	0-1	—		423
25	7	A	Berwick R	L 0-1	0-0	1		523
26	10	H	Forfar Ath	D 0-0	0-0	—		317
27	14	A	Annan Ath	L 1-3	1-1	1	MacKay [21]	629
28	17	H	Montrose	W 2-1	2-1	—	Gemmell 2 [4, 18]	303
29	21	H	East Stirling	W 2-0	1-0	1	Fairbairn [36], Armstrong [73]	430
30	31	A	Forfar Ath	D 1-1	1-1	—	Gemmell [7]	621
31	Apr 4	H	Elgin C	D 1-1	0-0	1	Gemmell [84]	331
32	11	A	Albion R	D 0-0	0-0	1		452
33	18	H	Dumbarton	D 0-0	0-0	1		1181
34	25	A	Montrose	L 1-2	1-0	2	Gemmell [8]	403
35	May 2	H	Forfar Ath	D 2-2	2-2	3	Stein 2 [30, 40]	527
36	9	A	East Stirling	W 2-0	0-0	2	Ferguson 2 [76, 90]	434

Final League Position: 2

Honours
League Champions: Division II 1913-14, 1914-15, 1938-39; *Champions:* Third Division 2005-06. *Runners-up:* Division II 1921-22, 1923-24, 1969-70. Second Division 1991-92. *Runners-up:* Third Division 2000-01, 2008-09.
Scottish Cup: Quarter-finals 1931.
League Cup: Semi-finals 1959-60, 1970-71.

Club colours: Shirt: Royal blue. Shorts: Royal blue. Stockings: Royal blue.

Goalscorers: *League* (48): Gemmell 12, McQuade 9, Dempster 6, Armstrong 5, Fairbairn 5, Adamson 2, Ferguson 2, Stein 2, Brown 1, MacKay 1, McGregor 1, Ramsay 1, Tomana 1.
Scottish Cup (1): McQuade 1.
CIS Cup (1): Dempster 1.
Challenge Cup (6): Fairbairn 2, McQuade 2, Gemmell 1, McGregor 1.
Play-Offs (3): Dempster 1, Gemmell 1, Stein 1.

Hay D 29	Cennerazzo G 1	Adamson K 21+4	McGregor D 34	Mbu J 18+1	Hodge S 12	Fairbairn B 20+8	Shields J 20+2	McQuade P 20+3	Ramsay M 26+6	Tomana M 18+9	Gemmell J 25+6	Linton S 5+4	Droudge D 3+1	Fleming D 19+5	Robertson J 3+6	Dempster J 17+9	MacKay D 21+1	Baxter M 24+2	Stein J 10+9	Ross G 2+2	Armstrong J 31	Gallacher S 7	O'Neil J —+1	Ferguson J 1+1	Brown G 8+9	Lennon D —+1	Reid J 1	Forbes M —+1	Young C —+1	Wallace D —+1	Match No.
1	2	3	4	5	6	7	8	9	10[2]	11[1]	12	13																			1
1		3	4	5	6	7[1]	8[3]	11	10[2]		9	13		2	12	14															2
1		5	8		4	6	2[3]	10[1]		9[2]	11	12	3	7			13	14													3
1		4	5[1]	6	7			12	11	10	9[2]			14	8		13	3	2[3]												4
1		3	4		6	7[2]			11	12	10[1]	9		8			14	5	2[3]	13											5
1		7	6		4[1]	9	13		11[2]	8	10[3]			5		14			12	2	3										6
1		13	3	4	6[3]			9	14	11[1]	10			8			2	12	5[2]	7											7
		7	6		4	13		9[3]		8	10[1]			5		12	2	11[2]	14		3	1									8
		8	7		4[2]	14		9		6[3]	10[1]			5		12	2	11	13		3	1									9
			4		6	14		3[2]	11[3]	7	10	9[1]		8		12	2		5		1	13									10
		12	4		6	7[1]			11	13	8	10		2[2]	3	9					5	1									11
		8	6		4			2	11	9	7[1]	13		5		10[2]			12		3	1									12
		3	4		6[1]			2	11	9	7[2]	13		8		10			12		5	1									13
		3	4			13			10	7[3]	12	11	8[1]			9[2]	6	2	14		5	1									14
1		3				13	12	11	6[1]	8[2]		5		14	10	7	2	9[3]			4										15
1		3	4			7		8	10	11		13				12	9[2]	6[1]	2		5										16
1		5	3					9	7	11	6[1]					10	8	2			4				12						17
1		5	3					9[3]	8	11	6	14		13		10	7[2]	2			4				12						18
1		3[2]	4					12	8	10	7	14		13		9	6[3]	2			5				11						19
1		3						9[3]	7		13	12	6[2]	5	11	8	2	14			4				10[1]						20
1		3						7	12	9	13		6[2]	5	10	8	2				4				11[1]						21
1		3	12					6	8	11[2]	13	9		5	10	7[1]	2				4				12						22
1		14	8	4	6[2]	7		13	12	9[3]				5	10		2				3				11[1]						23
1		12	4	6		7[3]	8	11	10[2]	13				3	9	2[1]					5				14						24
1		3	4	6		13			12	7[2]		11[1]				9	8	2	14		5				10[3]						25
1		5	7	4		9			11[2]	6		12					10[1]	8	2		3				13						26
1		3	4	6				2[1]	10	7	13	11		8		12					5				9[2]						27
1		5	7	4		9				6	11[3]	10				12	8[2]	2[1]	13		3				14						28
1		8	2	4		9			10[2]	7[1]	11[3]			14	13	5	6				3				12						29
1		3	4	6		11[2]	10[1]	8				9					2	13	7		5				12						30
1		7	2	4		14			11[2]	9[1]	10			8	13		5[3]	6			3				12						31
1		4	6			7[1]		8				9		3	12	2	11				5				13	10[2]					32
1		4				7		6	10		12			5[1]	11[2]	13	8	2	9[3]		3		14								33
1		3	4					6	10[2]		5				11[1]	13	8	2	9		7				12						34
1		2	3[1]					6[2]	13	12	10	9			11	8	5	7			4										35
1		4						6[1]	7	10[3]		3		8							5				11	9[2]	2	12	13	14	36

DUMBARTON
Second Division

Year Formed: 1872. *Ground:* Strathclyde Homes Stadium, Dumbarton G82 1JJ. *Telephone:* 01389 762569. *Fax:* 01389 762629. *E-mail:* david_prophet58@hotmail.com *Website:* www.dumbartonfootballclub.com
Ground Capacity: total: 2050. *Size of Pitch:* 110yd × 75yd.
Chairman: Alan Jardine. *Club Secretary:* David Prophet. *Company Secretary:* Gilbert Lawrie.
Manager: Jim Chapman. *Assistant Manager:* Jim Clark. *Physio:* Lindsay Smart.
Club Nickname(s): The Sons. *Previous Grounds:* Broadmeadow, Ropework Lane, Townend Ground, Boghead Park.
Record Attendance: 18,000 v Raith Rovers, Scottish Cup, 2 Mar 1957.
Record Transfer Fee received: £125,000 for Graeme Sharp to Everton (March 1982).
Record Transfer Fee paid: £50,000 for Charlie Gibson from Stirling Albion (1989).
Record Victory: 13-1 v Kirkintilloch Central. 1st rd, 1 Sept 1888.
Record Defeat: 1-11 v Albion Rovers, Division II; 30 Jan, 1926: v Ayr United, League Cup, 13 Aug 1952.
Most Capped Player: James McAulay, 9, Scotland.
Most League Appearances: 297: Andy Jardine, 1957-67.
Most Goals in Season (Individual): 38: Kenny Wilson, Division II, 1971-72. *(League and Cup):* 46 Hughie Gallacher, 1955-56.
Most Goals Overall (Individual): 169: Hughie Gallacher, 1954-62 (including C Division 1954-55). *(League and Cup):* 202 Hughie Gallacher, 1954-62

DUMBARTON 2008–09 LEAGUE RECORD

Match No.	Date	Venue	Opponents	Result	H/T Score	Lg. Pos.	Goalscorers	Atten-dance
1	Aug 2	H	Montrose	D 1-1	0-1	—	Clark (pen) [83]	580
2	9	A	Elgin C	D 1-1	0-1	7	Logan [75]	462
3	16	A	Berwick R	W 2-1	0-1	4	Lennon [55], Tiernan [61]	516
4	23	H	Stenhousemuir	L 1-2	0-1	5	Keegan [71]	660
5	30	H	East Stirling	D 1-1	1-0	7	Murray [25]	592
6	Sept13	A	Albion R	W 3-1	2-0	5	Clark [8], Gordon [18], McLeod (pen) [60]	327
7	20	A	Cowdenbeath	W 2-1	1-0	3	Carcary [36], Gordon [90]	801
8	27	A	Forfar Ath	D 2-2	1-0	4	Tulloch (og) [7], McLeod [52]	431
9	Oct 4	H	Annan Ath	W 4-1	4-0	2	Watson (og) [6], Keegan [30], Clark (pen) [34], Hill (og) [45]	574
10	18	A	Montrose	W 2-1	1-0	2	Clark [32], McLeod [61]	570
11	Nov 1	H	Berwick R	W 5-2	3-1	2	McLeod [9], Clark 2 (1 pen) [19 (p), 52], Murray [34], Cusack [75]	673
12	8	A	Stenhousemuir	D 1-1	0-0	2	Murray [82]	723
13	15	A	East Stirling	L 2-5	0-2	2	Carcary [87], Moore [90]	516
14	22	H	Albion R	D 1-1	1-1	4	Clark [42]	646
15	Dec 13	H	Forfar Ath	W 3-0	1-0	3	Chisholm [24], McLeod [67], Keegan [88]	539
16	20	A	Annan Ath	L 1-2	1-1	3	Clark (pen) [45]	634
17	Jan 10	A	Cowdenbeath	L 0-2	0-1	—		416
18	17	H	Stenhousemuir	W 1-0	1-0	3	Chisholm [42]	737
19	24	A	Berwick R	W 2-1	2-1	3	McLeod [21], Carcary [43]	425
20	31	H	Montrose	D 1-1	1-0	3	Carcary [5]	652
21	Feb 21	H	Cowdenbeath	D 1-1	1-0	4	Boyle [33]	846
22	28	A	East Stirling	L 1-3	1-1	4	Clark [39]	526
23	Mar 3	A	East Stirling	W 2-0	2-0	—	McLaughlin [22], Craig [32]	462
24	7	H	Albion R	W 1-0	0-0	4	Boyle [68]	692
25	10	H	Elgin C	W 2-0	1-0	—	McLaughlin [35], Carcary [67]	474
26	14	A	Montrose	L 0-1	0-0	3		343
27	17	A	Albion R	D 1-1	0-1	—	Clark [90]	535
28	21	H	Annan Ath	L 0-2	0-2	2		815
29	31	A	Elgin C	W 2-0	1-0	—	Edwards (og) [39], McLaughlin [80]	271
30	Apr 4	A	Stenhousemuir	W 2-0	1-0	2	Gordon [44], Clark [75]	588
31	7	A	Forfar Ath	W 2-0	0-0	—	Clark 2 [55, 73]	513
32	11	H	Berwick R	W 2-0	1-0	2	Forbes [15], Boyle [64]	702
33	18	A	Cowdenbeath	D 0-0	0-0	2		1181
34	25	H	Forfar Ath	W 4-0	3-0	1	Smith E (og) [4], McLaughlin [25], Carcary [33], Brannan [80]	917
35	May 2	H	Elgin C	W 6-0	4-0	1	Carcary 4 [19, 39, 43, 66], McLaughlin [28], Murray [84]	1396
36	9	A	Annan Ath	W 3-1	1-0	1	Clark [23], McLaughlin [48], Carcary [88]	1343

Final League Position: 1

Honours
League Champions: Division I 1890-91 (shared with Rangers), 1891-92. Division II 1910-11, 1971-72. Second Division 1991-92. Third Division 2008-09; *Runners-up:* First Division 1983-84. Division II 1907-08. Third Division 2001-02.
Scottish Cup Winners: 1883; *Runners-up:* 1881, 1882, 1887, 1891, 1897.

Club colours: Shirt: White with black and amber. Shorts: White. Stockings: White.

Goalscorers: *League* (65): Clark 14 (4 pens), Carcary 11, McLaughlin 6, McLeod 6 (1 pen), Murray 4, Boyle 3, Gordon 3, Keegan 3, Chisholm 2, Brannan 1, Craig 1, Cusack 1, Forbes 1, Lennon 1, Logan 1, Moore 1, Tiernan 1, own goals 5.
Scottish Cup (4): Carcary 2, Chisholm 1, Gordon 1.
CIS Cup (0).
Challenge Cup (2): Carcary 1, Clark 1.

McEwan D 22	Geggan A 23 + 2	Lennon G 32 + 2	Gordon B 36	Brittain C 3	Gray D 2 + 5	Canning M 10 + 10	Clark R 30 + 1	Murray S 34 + 1	Keegan P 12 + 9	Carcary D 25 + 8	Logan R 4 + 2	Gourlay A — + 3	O'Byrne M 13	Weir S 1	Chisholm I 15 + 12	Tiernan F 2 + 2	Brannan K — + 6	Wilson G 8	Cusack L 1 + 8	McLeod P 19 + 5	McNiff M — + 1	Moore M — + 6	McGeown M 14 + 1	Dunlop M 21	White M 1	Boyle P 20	McAnespie K 2 + 2	McKillen R 2	Taylor N — + 1	Forbes R 15 + 3	McStay R 10 + 2	McLaughlin D 16	Craig P 3	Match No.
1	2	3	4	5	6^2	7^1	8	9	10	11	12	13																						1
1	2^1		4	5	13		6	11	10	8	12	3	7^2	9																				2
1		2	5	3	12		6	11^2		10^1	8		4		9	7	13																	3
1		2	4	5	6^1		7	9	13		8	12	3		10	11^2																		4
1	6^3	2	4		14		7	9		11	8^1		3		10^2	12		5	13															5
1	8	2	5				6^1	11	10^2	7^3			4			12		3	14	9	13													6
1	8	2	4		12	13	7	9	11^3	6^1			3			5			10^2		14													7
1^6	8	2	5				12	6	11	10^1	7		4			3			9			15												8
	8	2	4				7	9^1	11^2	6			3			5	12	10		13	1													9
	8	2	4		14		7		11^1	12			3		5	13	6		9^2	10^3	1													10
	8	2	4			14	7^3	9	11^2	6^1			3		12		5	13	10		1													11
	8	2	5				6	11	10^1	7^2			4		12		3^4	14	9^3		13	1												12
	8	2^1	5				13	6^2	11		7		4		10			9	12	1	3													13
1	7	2	4			3^3	8	9^2	11^1	6					13			14	10		12	5												14
1	8	13	5			2^3	7	9	12	6^2			4		11			14	10^1		3													15
1	8		5			2	6	11^3	14	7^1					10			13	9^2	12	3	4												16
1	8	13	4			2	7	9	11^1	12								10			3^4		5	6^2										17
1	8	3	4			2^3	7^1	9	14	6					12			10^2				5			11	13								18
1	8	4	5			2^1	6	11^2		7					12			9				3		10	13									19
1	8	3	4			2	7	9	13	6^2								10				5			11^1	12								20
	2	4	5		13			9^3	14	12								10^1		1	6		3			8			7^2	11				21
1	2	4	5^1		12		8^2	11^3	14	7					13						6		3			10			9					22
	2	3	4				9^2	14	12						6						1	7		5	13			11			10^3	8^1		23
	2	3	4				8^1	9		6					12						1	7		5				11			10			24
	2	3	4				9^2		12	6					14						1	7		5			11	13			10^3	8^1		25
		3	4				8	13		12					2					9^2	1	7		5	14			11^3	6^1	10				26
		4	5			14	11		13						2					12	1	6	3	7			10^3			9^2	8^1		27
		3	4^2			8	9^1	6	11						2					12	1	7	5			13	10			9^2	8^1		28
			5				2	6	11^3						10^1	12	14			13	1	4	3			8	7			9^2				29
		2	5				6	11							13	12				10	1	4	3			8^1	7			9^2				30
1		2	5			13	6^2	11		12					8					10^1		4	3			14	7			9^3				31
1		2	4			12		9	13	11^1					8							3	5			7	6			10^2				32
1		2	4			7		9	11^1	12			13									3	5			8^2	6			10				33
1		2	4^1			14	7^3	9		11^2			12	13								3	5			8	6			10				34
1	14	2	4			13	7^2	9		11^1			12									3	5			8	6^3			10				35
1	12	2	5				6^2	11^1		10^3					13							14				4	3			8	7	9		36

DUNDEE

First Division

Year Formed: 1893. *Ground & Address:* Dens Park Stadium, Sandeman St, Dundee DD3 7JY. *Telephone:* 01382 889966. *Fax:* 01382 832284. *E-mail:* laura@dundeefc.co.uk *Website:* www.thedees.co.uk
Ground Capacity: all seated: 11,760. *Size of Pitch:* 101m × 66m.
Chairman: Bob Brannan. *Chief Executive:* David MacKinnon. *Club Secretary:* Laura Hayes (tel: 01382 826104; mob: 07855 410 929). *Email:* laura@dundeefc.co.uk
Manager: Jocky Scott. *Assistant Manager:* Davie Farrell. *Youth Development Coach:* Gordon Wallace. *Community Coach:* Gavin Timley. *Physio:* Karen Gibson.
Club Nickname(s): The Dark Blues or The Dee. *Previous Grounds:* Carolina Port 1893-98.
Record Attendance: 43,024 v Rangers, Scottish Cup, 1953.
Record Transfer Fee received: £500,000 for Tommy Coyne to Celtic (March 1989).
Record Transfer Fee paid: £200,000 for Jim Leighton (Feb 1992).
Record Victory: 10-0 Division II v Alloa, 9 Mar 1947 and v Dunfermline Ath, 22 Mar 1947.
Record Defeat: 0-11 v Celtic, Division I, 26 Oct 1895.
Most Capped Player: Alex Hamilton, 24, Scotland.
Most League Appearances: 341: Doug Cowie, 1945-61.
Most League Goals in Season (Individual): 52: Alan Gilzean, 1960-64.
Most Goals Overall (Individual): 113: Alan Gilzean 1960-64.

DUNDEE 2008–09 LEAGUE RECORD

Match No.	Date	Venue	Opponents	Result	H/T Score	Lg. Pos.	Goalscorers	Atten-dance
1	Aug 2	A	Ross Co	W 2-1	1-0	—	Antoine-Curier (pen) [34], Paton [50]	3444
2	9	H	Clyde	W 1-0	1-0	1	Antoine-Curier [44]	4042
3	16	A	Airdrie U	D 0-0	0-0	1		1787
4	23	H	Morton	W 1-0	1-0	1	Paton [28]	4032
5	30	A	Queen of the S	L 1-3	1-2	2	Pozniak [14]	2646
6	Sept 13	H	Dunfermline Ath	D 0-0	0-0	3		4259
7	20	H	Livingston	L 0-3	0-1	5		3631
8	27	A	St Johnstone	L 0-2	0-0	6		4307
9	Oct 4	A	Partick Th	D 0-0	0-0	6		2556
10	18	H	Ross Co	L 1-2	0-2	8	Antoine-Curier [58]	3228
11	25	A	Morton	L 0-2	0-1	9		1741
12	Nov 1	H	Airdrie U	D 1-1	0-1	8	Antoine-Curier [66]	3456
13	8	A	Dunfermline Ath	W 1-0	0-0	7	Antoine-Curier [68]	3506
14	15	H	Queen of the S	W 2-0	0-0	6	Paton [64], Deasley [79]	3630
15	29	H	St Johnstone	D 1-1	0-1	—	Antoine-Curier [74]	6537
16	Dec 13	A	Clyde	L 0-1	0-0	7		1176
17	20	H	Partick Th	D 0-0	0-0	9		3569
18	27	A	Queen of the S	W 1-0	1-0	6	McMenamin [30]	2616
19	Jan 3	H	Dunfermline Ath	W 1-0	0-0	5	Paton [67]	5033
20	17	H	Morton	D 0-0	0-0	6		3736
21	24	A	Airdrie U	L 0-1	0-0	7		1303
22	31	H	Clyde	W 2-1	2-1	5	McMenamin [39], Antoine-Curier [42]	3217
23	Feb 7	A	Livingston	W 2-1	2-0	—	Antoine-Curier [1], Efrem [33]	1535
24	21	H	Livingston	W 4-1	0-0	3	Shinnie [48], Efrem [55], Antoine-Curier 2 [68, 79]	3679
25	28	A	St Johnstone	D 0-0	0-0	3		7238
26	Mar 10	H	Queen of the S	L 2-3	0-1	—	Antoine-Curier 2 [55, 69]	3757
27	14	H	Ross Co	W 2-0	2-0	3	McMenamin [32], Antoine-Curier (pen) [45]	3381
28	22	A	Partick Th	D 1-1	1-0	3	McMenamin [37]	3303
29	28	A	Ross Co	D 1-1	0-0	—	Antoine-Curier [66]	2296
30	31	A	Dunfermline Ath	D 1-1	0-0	—	Malone [61]	2382
31	Apr 4	A	Morton	L 0-2	0-1	5		2133
32	11	H	Airdrie U	L 0-1	0-1	5		2870
33	18	A	Livingston	W 1-0	0-0	4	Young [61]	1988
34	25	H	St Johnstone	L 0-1	0-1	4		6305
35	May 2	A	Clyde	L 0-2	0-0	5		944
36	9	H	Partick Th	W 4-0	2-0	4	Young [1], McMenamin 3 [34, 69, 74]	2831

Final League Position: 4

Honours
League Champions: Division I 1961-62. First Division 1978-79, 1991-92, 1997-98. Division II 1946-47; *Runners-up:* Division I 1902-03, 1906-07, 1908-09, 1948-49, 1980-81. First Division 2007-08.
Scottish Cup Winners: 1910; *Runners-up:* 1925, 1952, 1964, 2003.
League Cup Winners: 1951-52, 1952-53, 1973-74; *Runners-up:* 1967-68, 1980-81, 1995-96.
B&Q (Centenary) Cup Winners: 1990-91; *Runners-up:* 1994-95.

European: *European Cup:* 8 matches (1962-63 semi-finals). *Cup Winners' Cup:* 2 matches: (1964-65).
UEFA Cup: 22 matches: (*Fairs Cup:* 1967-68 semi-finals. *UEFA Cup:* 1971-72, 1973-74, 1974-75, 2003-04).

Club colours: Shirt: Navy blue. Shorts: White. Stockings: Navy blue.

Goalscorers: *League* (33): Antoine-Curier 14 (2 pens), McMenamin 7, Paton 4, Efrem 2, Young 2, Deasley 1, Malone 1, Pozniak 1, Shinnie 1.
Scottish Cup (1): McMenamin 1.
CIS Cup (1): McHale 1.
Challenge Cup (1): Antoine-Curier 1.

Douglas R 36	Paton E 31	Malone P 21+2	McHale P 21+2	Cowan D 15+3	Williams D 16+4	Daquin F 16+3	Pozniak C 23+3	McMenamin C 24+5	Antoine-Curier M 29+3	Gilhaney M 13+6	O'Brien D 18+6	MacKenzie G 17+2	Davidson R 6+6	Deasley B 9+4	McKeown C 19+2	Cameron C 7+2	Dodds R 4	Mearns E 1+2	Benedictus K 10+1	Lauchlan J 15+1	Shinnie A 19+1	Young D 4+3	Forsyth C —+1	Efrem G 8	Roy L —+1	Match No.
1	2	3	4	5	6	7	8	9	10	11^1	12															1
1	2	3	4	5^1	6	7	8	9^2	10	11^3	14	12	13													2
1	2	3	4		6	7^2	8	9	10	11^1	12	5	13													3
1	2	3	4		6	7	8	9	10^2	12	11	5		13												4
1	7	3	6	2	5^1		8^2	10^3	11	13	9	4	14		12											5
1	2	3	4				8^1	13	10	11	7^2	5	9		6	12										6
1	2	3	4				8^1	12	10^2	11	7	5	9		6	13										7
1	8	3		2		7^1	10^9	12^2	9	11	13	5	14		6		4									8
1	2	3		6		7	8		9^1	11		10	12	5		4										9
1	2	3	4^3		6^1	12	8		13	11		10	9^2	5		7		14								10
1	2	3		6	7^1	8		10	12	11^2		9		5	4	13										11
1		3		6	7^1	2		9	13	11		12	10^2	4		8	5									12
1	2	3		4	7	8		9		11		12	10^1	6		5										13
1	2	3		4	7	8		9		11		10	6		5^1	12										14
1	2	3	13		4^2	7^1	8		9		11	5	10	6		12										15
1	2^2	5	8	13		7	12		9^3	3	10^1	11	4		6	14										16
1	3^3	4		2^1	12	8	13	9		11		10^2	5		6	7		14								17
1	6	2	12	3		9^1	8	11^2		13	10		4		5	7										18
1	9	5		2		6	7^1	11	12		10		4		3	8										19
1	2^3	3	4	12		7	13	9	10		11		5		6^1	8										20
1	2	3	4	12	10^1	7^3		9	13		11		5		6	8^2		14								21
1	2	3	4^2		8	9	10	11^1	12	13		5		6	7											22
1	2	3	4^1		12		9	10							5	8			6	7				11		23
1	2		4	3			9	11							5	8			6			7		10		24
1	2	3	4	6			9	10							5	8					7			11		25
1	2	3	4	6	8		9	10							5^1	12					7			11		26
1	2	3	4	6	8		9	10							5						7			11		27
1	8	3	4	2			9	10							5						6^1	7		11		28
1	2	3	4^4	12	13		9	10	7^1	11^2	5^4		8		6											29
1	2	3		4			9	10	7	11					8				5	6						30
1	2	5	7	12			10	11	9		3				8				4	6^1						31
1	2	3	4^1				9	10	11^2						5	13			8		6	7		12		32
1	3	2	12		8		9	10^1	5^4						4				6	7	11					33
1	2	3	4^1				9	10^8	12		13				5	6			7	8			11^2			34
1	3	2	13				9	12	11^1		10				5	6^2	8	4		7						35
1^6	3	2		12	8	9		5	10						4	6			7^1	11					15	36

DUNDEE UNITED   Premier League

Year Formed: 1909 (1923). *Ground & Address:* Tannadice Park, Tannadice St, Dundee DD3 7JW. *Telephone:* 01382 833166. *Fax:* 01382 889398. *E-mail:* enquiries@dundeeunited.co.uk *Website:* www.dundeeunitedfc.co.uk
Ground Capacity: total: 14,223 all seated: stands: east 2868, west 2096, south 2201, Fair Play 1601, George Fox 5151, executive boxes 292. *Size of Pitch:* 110yd × 72yd.
Chairman: Stephen Thompson, OBE. *Secretary:* Spence Anderson. *Commercial Manager:* Bill Campbell.
Manager: Craig Levein. *Assistant Manager:* Peter Houston. *First Team Coach:* Tony Docherty. *Coach:* Graeme Liveston.
Goalkeeping Coach: Scott Thomson. *Youth Coach:* Stevie Campbell. *Youth Development:* Graeme Liveston. *Physio:* Jeff Clarke. *Stadium Manager:* Ron West.
Club Nickname(s): The Terrors. *Previous Grounds:* None.
Record Attendance: 28,000 v Barcelona, Fairs Cup, 16 Nov 1966.
Record Transfer Fee received: £4,000,000 for Duncan Ferguson from Rangers (July 1993).
Record Transfer Fee paid: £750,000 for Steven Pressley from Coventry C (July 1995).
Record Victory: 14-0 v Nithsdale Wanderers, Scottish Cup 1st rd, 17 Jan 1931.
Record Defeat: 1-12 v Motherwell, Division II, 23 Jan 1954.
Most Capped Player: Maurice Malpas, 55, Scotland.
Most League Appearances: 618, Maurice Malpas, 1980-2000.
Most Appearances in European Matches: 76, Dave Narey (record for Scottish player).
Most League Goals in Season (Individual): 41: John Coyle, Division II, 1955-56.
Most Goals Overall (Individual): 158: Peter McKay, 1947-54.

DUNDEE UNITED 2008–09 LEAGUE RECORD

Match No.	Date	Venue	Opponents	Result	H/T Score	Lg. Pos.	Goalscorers	Atten- dance
1	Aug 11	A	Hamilton A	L	1-3	1-2	—	McLaughlin (og) [23]	4385
2	17	H	Celtic	D	1-1	0-0	10	Sandaza [79]	11,648
3	23	A	Motherwell	D	1-1	1-1	9	Wilkie [40]	5149
4	30	H	Kilmarnock	L	0-2	0-1	10		6823
5	Sept 13	A	Hibernian	L	1-2	1-1	12	Wilkie [45]	13,390
6	20	A	Aberdeen	W	1-0	0-0	10	Sandaza (pen) [47]	11,041
7	27	H	Hearts	W	3-0	1-0	8	Conway [39], Daly [50], Robertson S [61]	8004
8	Oct 4	A	Inverness CT	W	2-1	1-0	6	Daly [40], Wilkie [65]	6279
9	25	H	St Mirren	W	2-0	0-0	4	O'Donovan [85], Conway [90]	11,378
10	Nov 1	A	Falkirk	D	0-0	0-0	5		5608
11	4	A	Rangers	D	3-3	2-2	—	Sandaza 2 [17, 28], Robertson S [59]	48,686
12	8	H	Aberdeen	W	2-1	2-0	3	Sandaza [8], Feeney [14]	9490
13	12	H	Hibernian	W	2-0	0-0	—	Dods [54], Sandaza [60]	7490
14	15	A	Kilmarnock	L	0-2	0-1	4		4652
15	22	H	Hamilton A	D	1-1	0-1	4	Easton (og) [90]	6108
16	29	A	St Mirren	W	2-0	1-0	4	Daly 2 (1 pen) [37, 89 (p)]	4013
17	Dec 6	A	Inverness CT	W	3-1	0-0	3	Daly [51], Conway [64], Robertson D [71]	3560
18	13	H	Rangers	D	2-2	0-1	3	Wilkie [50], Feeney [54]	11,362
19	20	A	Hearts	D	0-0	0-0	3		16,442
20	27	H	Falkirk	W	1-0	0-0	3	Robertson S [21]	7972
21	Jan 3	A	Celtic	D	2-2	0-1	3	Dixon [60], Feeney [77]	59,558
22	18	H	Motherwell	L	0-4	0-3	4		7090
23	24	H	St Mirren	W	3-2	0-1	3	Feeney 2 (1 pen) [72 (p), 86], Buaben [84]	6556
24	31	A	Rangers	L	0-2	0-0	3		49,918
25	Feb 14	H	Inverness CT	D	1-1	0-1	4	Wilkie [79]	5926
26	21	A	Aberdeen	D	2-2	1-0	4	Sandaza (pen) [11], Robertson D [56]	14,673
27	28	H	Hearts	L	0-1	0-0	4		8529
28	Mar 3	A	Falkirk	W	1-0	1-0	—	Conway (pen) [27]	4385
29	14	A	Motherwell	L	1-2	0-1	5	Sandaza [51]	4798
30	22	H	Celtic	D	2-2	0-1	5	Sandaza 2 [47, 58]	12,043
31	Apr 4	H	Hibernian	D	2-2	0-2	5	Kenneth [53], Goodwillie [90]	6623
32	11	A	Hamilton A	W	1-0	1-0	5	Conway [4]	3025
33	18	H	Kilmarnock	D	0-0	0-0	4		6627
34	May 2	H	Hibernian	W	2-1	1-1	4	Feeney [28], Goodwillie [89]	10,591
35	7	H	Aberdeen	D	1-1	1-1	—	Goodwillie [38]	10,407
36	12	A	Celtic	L	1-2	0-1	—	Robertson D [57]	57,407
37	16	A	Hearts	L	0-3	0-2	4		15,664
38	24	H	Rangers	L	0-3	0-2	5		14,077

Final League Position: 5

Honours
League Champions: Premier Division 1982-83. Division II 1924-25, 1928-29; *Runners-up:* Division II 1930-31, 1959-60. First Division Runners-up 1995-96.
Scottish Cup Winners: 1994; *Runners-up:* 1974, 1981, 1985, 1987, 1988, 1991, 2005.
League Cup Winners: 1979-80, 1980-81; *Runners-up:* 1981-82, 1984-85, 1997-98, 2007-08.
Summer Cup Runners-up: 1964-65. *Scottish War Cup Runners-up:* 1939-40.

European: *European Cup:* 8 matches (1983-84, semi-finals). *Cup Winners' Cup:* 10 matches (1974-75, 1988-89, 1994-95). *UEFA Cup:* 86 matches (*Fairs Cup*): 1966-67, 1969-70, 1970-71. *UEFA Cup:* 1975-76, 1977-78, 1978-79, 1979-80, 1980-81, 1981-82, 1982-83, 1984-85, 1985-86, 1986-87 runners-up, 1987-88, 1989-90, 1990-91, 1993-94, 1997-98, 2005-06).

Club colours: Shirts: Tangerine. Shorts: Tangerine. Stockings: Tangerine.

Goalscorers: *League* (47): Sandaza 10 (2 pens), Feeney 6 (1 pen), Conway 5 (1 pen), Daly 5 (1 pen), Wilkie 5, Goodwillie 3, Robertson D 3, Robertson S 3, Buaben 1, Dixon 1, Dods 1, Kenneth 1, O'Donovan 1, own goals 2.
Scottish Cup (5): Buaben 1, Daly 1, Dods 1, Grainger 1, Russell 1 (pen).
CIS Cup (8): Daly 3, Goodwillie 3, Robertson S 2.

Zaluska L 38	Dillon S 18+1	Grainger D 9	Wilkie L 35	Dods D 19	Flood W 20	Robertson S 22+1	O'Donovan R 7+4	Gomis M 36+1	Feeney W 18+5	Buaben P 20+2	Swanson D 7+23	Sandaza F 23+8	Kovacevic M 17	Kenneth G 22+3	Conway C 28+8	Robertson D 12+7	Daly J 16+7	Goodwillie D 3+13	Dixon P 28+1	Caddis P 10+1	Shala A 3+5	Wesolowski J 7+1	Match No.
1	2	3	4	5	6	7	8^2	9	10	11^1	12	13											1
1		3	4			6^3	7	8	9	10^2	13	12	2	5	14	11^1							2
1		3	4		6	7	8^2	9	10^1	11	12	13	2	5									3
1	2	3	4		6^1	7		11	10^2		8	9^3		5	12		13	14					4
1		3	4	5		7	8^1	9		11^2	13	10^3	2		6		12	14					5
1		3	4	5		7		8		6	12	10^2	2^3	14	11^1		9	13					6
1	2		4	5	6^2	7	12	8		13	9^1			11	10				3				7
1	2		4	5	6	7	12	8		13	9^1			11^2	10				3				8
1	2		4	5^3	6^1	7	12	8		13	9		14	11	10^2				3				9
1	2		4	5	6	7	8^4	9	10	12				11^1					3				10
1	2		4	5	6	7		8	9			10^1		11			12		3				11
1	2		4	5	6	7	12	8	9^1			10^2		11^3	14		13		3				12
1	2		4	5	6	7	10^1	8			9		11				12		3				13
1	2		4	5	6^1	7	10^2	8		12	9		11		13				3				14
1	2		4	5	6	7^2	8^1		12	9^3		11	13	10	14				3				15
1			4		6	7	8		11^2	9^1	2	5	12	13	10				3				16
1			4			7	9		11		2	5	8	6	10				3				17
1			4		6	7	8^2	9^1	13		2	5	11	12	10				3				18
1			4		6	7	8		12		2	5	11	9^1	10				3				19
1	2		4		6	7	8	9^1		12		5	11		10				3				20
1	2		4		6	7	8	12		9^1		5	11		10				3				21
1	2		4		6^3	7^1	8	9		12	13		5	11	14	10^2			3				22
1	2		4		6^3		8	9	7	13	12		5	11^2	14	10^1			3				23
1		3		5			8	9	4	12	10^2	2	6	11^1	7^3	14	13						24
1			4			8	13	6	12	9^2	2^1	5	11		10^3			3	7	14			25
1		3	4	5		8	10	7	13	9^1	2		12	11^2			6^3	14					26
1		3^2	4	5		8	10^3	6		9	2		12		14	13	7	11^1					27
1			4	5		8	12	6		9^1	2		11	10^3	14		3	7^2	13				28
1			4			8	9	6^1	13	12	2		5	14	10^2		3	7^3	11				29
1			4			8	10^2	6	12	9	2		5	11^1	14	13	3		7^3				30
1	2		4			8	12^2	6	14	9	2		5	11		10^1	13	3	7^3				31
1			4				6	13	9^1		5	11^2	7	12	3	2	8	10					32
1			4				8^1	9^2	6	12	10^3		5	11		14	3^4	2	13	7			33
1		3		5			12	10	6	9^3		4	14	7	13		2	11^2	8^1				34
1			5		13		8^2	14	6	7^1		4	12	11		9	3	2	10^3				35
1	14		4				8		6	10^1	9^2	2^3	5	11	7		13		12				36
1	2^1		4				8		6	14	10^2		5	11	7^3		9	3	12	13			37
1		4^2	5				8		6	14	12	2	13	11^3	10^1		9	3	7				38

DUNFERMLINE ATHLETIC First Division

Year Formed: 1885. *Ground & Address:* East End Park, Halbeath Rd, Dunfermline KY12 7RB.
Telephone: 01383 724295. *Fax:* 01383 723468. *Ticket office telephone:* 0870 300 1201. *E-mail:* shirley@dafc.co.uk
Website: www.dafc.co.uk
Ground Capacity: all seated: 11,780. *Size of Pitch:* 115yd × 71yd.
Chairman: John Yorkston. *Chief Executive:* William Hodgins. *Commercial Director:* Wilma Cameron. *Commercial Manager:* Karen Brown.
Manager: Jim McIntyre. *Assistant Manager:* Gerry McCabe. *Physio:* Gerry Docherty. *First Team Coach:* Steven Wright.
Head of Youth: Hamish French.
Club Nickname(s): The Pars. *Previous Grounds:* None.
Record Attendance: 27,816 v Celtic, Division I, 30 Apr 1968.
Record Transfer Fee received: £650,000 for Jackie McNamara to Celtic (Oct 1995).
Record Transfer Fee paid: £540,000 for Istvan Kozma from Bordeaux (Sept 1989).
Record Victory: 11-2 v Stenhousemuir, Division II, 27 Sept 1930.
Record Defeat: 1-11 v Hibernian, Scottish Cup, 3rd rd replay, 26 Oct 1889.
Most Capped Player: Colin Miller 16 (61), Canada.
Most League Appearances: 497: Norrie McCathie, 1981-96.
Most League Goals in Season (Individual): 53: Bobby Skinner, Division II, 1925-26.
Most Goals Overall (Individual): 154: Charles Dickson, 1954-64.

DUNFERMLINE ATHLETIC 2008–09 LEAGUE RECORD

Match No.	Date		Venue	Opponents		Result	H/T Score	Lg. Pos.	Goalscorers	Atten-dance
1	Aug	2	A	Partick Th	L	0-1	0-0	—		3092
2		9	H	Queen of the S	W	2-1	0-1	4	Kirk 2 [54, 69]	2930
3		16	A	St Johnstone	W	3-0	1-0	2	Williamson [43], Phinn [56], Bayne [89]	3797
4		23	H	Airdrie U	D	0-0	0-0	4		3334
5		30	H	Livingston	L	1-2	0-1	5	Kirk [53]	3414
6	Sept	13	A	Dundee	D	0-0	0-0	6		4259
7		20	A	Ross Co	W	3-1	2-0	4	Thomson [5], Phinn [44], Bell [71]	2631
8		27	A	Morton	D	1-1	0-0	4	Campbell [89]	2156
9	Oct	4	A	Clyde	W	2-0	2-0	3	Kirk [37], Harper [43]	1273
10		18	H	Partick Th	W	1-0	1-0	2	Kirk [36]	3242
11	Nov	1	H	St Johnstone	L	1-2	1-1	4	Wilson [24]	4653
12		4	A	Airdrie U	W	3-1	2-1	—	Woods [4], Glass [28], Phinn [55]	1099
13		8	H	Dundee	L	0-1	0-0	3		3506
14		15	A	Livingston	W	3-2	1-1	2	Kirk 2 [19, 89], Bayne [59]	2326
15		22	H	Morton	L	0-1	0-1	2		4400
16	Dec	13	A	Queen of the S	W	2-1	1-1	2	Phinn [4], Bayne [89]	2312
17		20	H	Clyde	D	4-4	1-1	2	Glass (pen) [10], Kirk 2 [47, 72], Phinn [79]	3279
18		30	H	Livingston	W	1-0	0-0	—	Shields [65]	3036
19	Jan	3	A	Dundee	L	0-1	0-0	2		5033
20		17	A	Airdrie U	D	1-1	0-1	2	Loy [49]	2915
21		31	H	Queen of the S	L	0-2	0-1	4		2770
22	Feb	14	A	Partick Th	W	3-2	2-2	—	Bell [13], Kirk [50], Loy [88]	2957
23		21	H	Ross Co	L	1-2	0-1	4	Bayne [60]	3331
24		28	A	Morton	L	1-2	0-1	4	Kirk (pen) [83]	2092
25	Mar	10	A	Livingston	L	2-4	0-1	—	Bell [56], Graham [66]	1859
26		14	H	Partick Th	L	0-1	0-1	7		2736
27		21	A	Clyde	W	4-1	2-1	6	Phinn 2 [4, 62], Woods [37], Burke [51]	1109
28		24	A	Ross Co	L	1-2	0-0	—	Bayne [87]	1782
29		31	H	Dundee	D	1-1	0-0	—	Woods [90]	2382
30	Apr	4	A	Airdrie U	D	1-1	0-0	7	Ross [90]	1136
31		7	A	St Johnstone	D	0-0	0-0	—		3199
32		11	H	St Johnstone	L	1-3	1-2	7	Kirk (pen) [29]	3595
33		18	A	Ross Co	W	3-1	1-0	6	Woods [35], Kirk [73], Bayne [77]	2413
34	May	2	A	Queen of the S	W	3-0	3-0	3	Kirk [21], Woods [26], Phinn [34]	2750
35		5	H	Morton	W	2-1	0-0	—	Loy [56], Kirk [86]	1438
36		9	H	Clyde	D	1-1	1-1	3	Graham [43]	2418

Final League Position: 3

Honours
League Champions: First Division 1988-89, 1995-96. Division II 1925-26. Second Division 1985-86; *Runners-up:* First Division 1986-87, 1993-94, 1994-95, 1999-2000. Division II 1912-13, 1933-34, 1954-55, 1957-58, 1972-73. Second Division 1978-79.
Scottish Cup Winners: 1961, 1968; *Runners-up:* 1965, 2004, 2007.
League Cup Runners-up: 1949-50, 1991-92, 2005-06.
League Challenge Cup Runners-up: 2007-08.

European: *Cup Winners' Cup:* 14 matches (1961-62, 1968-69 semi-finals). *UEFA Cup:* 32 matches (*Fairs Cup:* 1962-63, 1964-65, 1965-66, 1966-67, 1969-70. *UEFA Cup:* 2004-05, 2007-08).

Club colours: Shirt: White and black stripes. Shorts: White. Stockings: Black.

Goalscorers: *League* (52): Kirk 15 (2 pens), Phinn 8, Bayne 6, Woods 5, Bell 3, Loy 3, Glass 2 (1 pen), Graham 2, Burke 1, Campbell 1, Harper 1, Ross 1, Shields 1, Thomson 1, Williamson 1, Wilson 1.
Scottish Cup (5): Bayne 2, Phinn 2, Holmes 1.
CIS Cup (3): Bayne 1, Kirk 1, Wiles 1.
Challenge Cup (3): Burke 1, Phinn 1, Williamson 1.

Gallacher P 36	Shields G 27+1	Thomson S 21+6	Wilson S 29	McCann A 30+2	Phinn N 33+2	Burke A 29+3	Glass S 26	Williamson 12+7	Harper K 12+2	Bayne G 32	Kirk A 27+5	Muirhead S 8+11	Woods C 25+5	Bell S 19+5	Willis P —+3	Bamba S 1	Wiles S 2+7	Campbell R —+3	Ross G 10+6	McIntyre J —+2	Holmes G 4+3	Loy R 6+12	Mole J 3+7	Graham D 14+1	Match No.
1	2	3	4	5[1]	6[3]	7	8	9[2]	10	11	13	12	14												1
1	2	5[1]	3	6	4	11[3]	8	13		7[2]	9	10	14	12											2
1	5		3	6	4	11	8	12		7[1]	9	10[2]	13	2											3
1	3	14	4	5	6	7	8[3]	9[1]		11[2]	10		2	12	13										4
1		5[2]	3	6		11		12			9	10	13	2	8			4	7[1]						5
1	5	13	3	6	4	11	8[1]		9	10		2[5]	12				7[2]								6
1	5	2	3	6	4	11		7[1]	9	10[2]		8					12	13							7
1	5	2	3[1]	6	4[3]	11	8	7[2]	9	10		12					13	14							8
1		2[1]	3	5	7	9[2]	8	6	11	10[3]	4	12					13	14							9
1	5			6	4	11	8	13	7[1]	9[2]	10	3					12	2							10
1	5	14	3	6[3]	4	11[1]	8	12	7	9	10[2]	2					13								11
1	5	12	3	6	4	11	8	14	7[2]	9	10	2[1]					13[3]								12
1	5	14	3	6[1]	4	11[3]	8	7[2]	9	10	12	2					13								13
1		5	3	12	4[3]	11	8	9	10	6[1]	2[2]	13							7	14					14
1	5	6		3	13	11[1]	8	9	10	7	4						2[2]	12							15
1	4	5		3	9	13	8	7[2]	10	11[1]		2	6[3]				14	12							16
1	5	6		3	4	11	8	12	9	10[2]		2					13	7[1]							17
1	5		3		4		8	7[1]	9	10[2]	6	2	11				12		13						18
1	3		4	7[3]	14	9	12			11	5	2	8	13			6[2]		10[1]						19
1	5	12	3		4	8		9[1]	10[2]	6	2[1]	11	13						7	14					20
1	5	2	3[3]	6	4	8[1]		9	13	14	11						12	10			7[2]				21
1	3	2	4	5	8[3]			9	13	6						7[1]	11	12	14	10[2]					22
1	5		3	6	11			9	13	2[3]	8					7[2]	4	10[1]	14	12					23
1	5	2[2]	3	6	4		8[3]			9	10	14[7]					11[1]	12	13						24
1	5	2	3	6[3]	4	11	8	13		14	7[1]						12	9	10[2]						25
1	5	2	3	6	4	11[2]	8			13	7[1]						9	12	10						26
1		5	3	6	4	11[2]	8[1]		9	12	2	7[3]					14		13	10					27
1		5	3	6	4	11[2]	8		9	13	2	7[1]							12	10					28
1	12	5	3[1]	6	4	11[3]	8		9	13	2	14							10[2]	7					29
1	3	5		6	4	11[1]	8		9	12	2	7[2]					13		14	10[3]					30
1	5	4[2]	3		6[3]	13			9	10	12	2	7				14		11[1]	8					31
1	5			3[4]	12	4[3]	8		9	10	6[1]	2	7				13		14	11[2]					32
1	5[1]	6		3	12	11			9	10		2	8				4		13	7[2]					33
1			3	5	7	9		8[2]	11[1]	6	2						4		12	13	10				34
1		3[1]	6	4	11	8		9	10	5							2		12	7					35
1		6	4	11	8			9	10	3		12					2		5[2]	13	7[1]				36

EAST FIFE   Second Division

Year Formed: 1903. *Ground & Address:* Bayview Stadium, Harbour View, Methil, Fife KY8 3RW. *Telephone:* 01333
426323. *Fax:* 01333 426376. *E-mail:* office@eastfife.org. *Website:* www.eastfife.org
Ground Capacity: all seated: 2000. *Size of Pitch:* 115yd × 75yd.
Chairman: Sidney Columbine. *Secretary:* Stevie Crawford.
Manager: Stevie Crawford. *Assistant Manager:* Graeme Irons. *Physio:* Brian McNeil.
Club Nickname(s): The Fifers. *Previous Ground:* Bayview Park.
Record Attendance: 22,515 v Raith Rovers, Division I, 2 Jan 1950.
Record Transfer Fee received: £150,000 for Paul Hunter from Hull C (March 1990).
Record Transfer Fee paid: £70,000 for John Sludden from Kilmarnock (July 1991).
Record Victory: 13-2 v Edinburgh City, Division II, 11 Dec 1937.
Record Defeat: 0-9 v Hearts, Division I, 5 Oct 1957.
Most Capped Player: George Aitken, 5 (8), Scotland.
Most League Appearances: 517: David Clarke, 1968-86.
Most League Goals in Season (Individual): 41: Jock Wood, Division II; 1926-27 and Henry Morris, Division II, 1947-48.
Most Goals Overall (Individual): 225: Phil Weir, 1922-35.

EAST FIFE 2008–09 LEAGUE RECORD

Match No.	Date	Venue	Opponents	Result	H/T Score	Lg. Pos.	Goalscorers	Atten- dance
1	Aug 2	H	Peterhead	L 0-2	0-2	—		888
2	9	A	Stirling A	D 1-1	0-0	9	Cameron [67]	686
3	16	H	Queen's Park	L 1-2	1-2	9	Templeman [13]	789
4	23	A	Arbroath	W 1-0	0-0	8	Fotheringham [88]	766
5	30	H	Brechin C	D 0-0	0-0	7		726
6	Sept 13	A	Raith R	D 1-1	0-0	6	Fotheringham [63]	3637
7	20	A	Alloa Ath	W 3-0	1-0	5	McManus 3 (2 pens) [29 (p), 48 (p), 66]	776
8	27	H	Ayr U	W 3-0	1-0	5	McManus 2 (1 pen) [35, 83 (p)], Young [48]	1010
9	Oct 4	H	Stranraer	L 1-2	1-2	5	Templeman [43]	730
10	18	A	Peterhead	W 1-0	0-0	4	McManus [74]	715
11	25	H	Arbroath	W 3-2	2-2	4	Cameron [5], McManus [36], Tweed [86]	677
12	Nov 1	A	Queen's Park	D 0-0	0-0	4		752
13	8	H	Raith R	L 0-2	0-1	5		1980
14	15	A	Brechin C	L 1-2	0-1	5	McDonald [50]	691
15	22	A	Ayr U	L 2-4	0-3	5	Linn [62], Fotheringham [86]	1254
16	Dec 6	H	Alloa Ath	W 1-0	0-0	—	McManus (pen) [66]	653
17	13	H	Stirling A	L 0-1	0-1	5		593
18	20	A	Stranraer	W 4-0	2-0	5	Crawford [41], McDonald 2 [44, 51], McManus [71]	200
19	27	H	Brechin C	W 2-1	1-0	5	Linn [28], McManus [80]	857
20	Jan 3	A	Raith R	L 0-1	0-0	5		4812
21	17	A	Arbroath	W 2-0	1-0	4	Linn 2 (2 pens) [32, 61]	740
22	24	H	Queen's Park	W 4-2	0-1	3	Crawford 2 [60, 63], McDonald [69], Templeman [75]	785
23	31	H	Peterhead	L 0-3	0-2	4		698
24	Feb 21	A	Alloa Ath	W 1-0	0-0	3	McDonald [48]	695
25	28	A	Brechin C	L 1-2	1-1	5	McManus (pen) [27]	595
26	Mar 7	H	Raith R	L 0-1	0-0	6		1957
27	14	A	Peterhead	L 0-2	0-1	6		607
28	18	H	Ayr U	L 0-1	0-1	—		832
29	21	H	Stranraer	W 4-0	1-0	6	Templeman [3], Makel [59], Linn 2 [62, 72]	533
30	28	A	Stirling A	L 0-2	0-0	6		636
31	Apr 4	H	Arbroath	D 0-0	0-0	6		629
32	11	A	Queen's Park	L 1-3	1-2	6	McManus [1]	601
33	18	H	Alloa Ath	L 0-2	0-2	6		623
34	25	A	Ayr U	L 0-2	0-0	6		1849
35	May 2	H	Stirling A	L 0-3	0-1	6		569
36	9	A	Stranraer	W 1-0	1-0	6	Kane (og) [20]	249

Final League Position: 6

Honours
League Champions: Division II 1947-48. Third Division 2007-08. *Runners-up:* Division II 1929-30, 1970-71. Second Division 1983-84, 1995-96. Third Division 2002-03.
Scottish Cup Winners: 1938; *Runners-up:* 1927, 1950.
League Cup Winners: 1947-48, 1949-50, 1953-54.

Club colours: Shirt: Gold and black. Shorts: Black. Stockings: Black.

Goalscorers: *League* (39): McManus 12 (5 pens), Linn 6 (2 pens), McDonald 5, Templeman 4, Crawford 3, Fotheringham 3, Cameron 2, Makel 1, Tweed 1, Young 1, own goal 1.
Scottish Cup (3): Crawford 1, Linn 1, O'Reilly 1.
Challenge Cup (1): Templeman 1.

McCulloch W 23	Nugent P 19+2	Smart J 28	Tweed S 16	Cameron D 36	Young L 22+10	Fotheringham K 23+1	Stanik G 11+2	Linn B 32+2	Crawford S 22+5	Templeman C 25+8	Stewart P 21+9	Campbell R 5+5	McManus P 30+3	McDonald G 23+1	O'Reilly C —+11	Gordon K —+2	Shields D 7+2	Fagan S 18+5	Brown M 13	Muir D 14+5	Walker P —+1	Blackadder R —+1	Makel L 7+1	Sheerin J 1+4	Cargill S —+4	Thomson D —+1	McRae J —+1	Match No.
1	2	3	4	5	6	7	8¹	9³	10	11²	12	13	14															1
1	2	4	5¹	11	8	3	7	9²	13	6			10³	12	14													2
1	2	3		9	6	4	5	7	10¹	8²	12			13														3
1	2	4		11³	8	5	3	7¹	13	10²	12		9	6			14											4
1	2	3		5	8	4	6³	14	11¹	9²	10	7	12	13														5
1	2¹	4	5	3		6	12	10	11²	9³	8	14	7	13														6
1		4	5	3	13	6¹	11	10²	12	9³	2	14	7	8														7
1		3²	4	5	12	7	9³	11	13	14	10	2¹	6	8														8
1	2¹	4	5	7	3	9	8	11²	12	13	10	6																9
1		5	3	12	4	11	8	10	2	9²	13	7¹	6															10
1		4	5	12	3	9	8	11	2	10²	13	6¹	7															11
		4	5	6		10	11¹	3	8	9²	13	7	1	2	12													12
		4³	5	6	7	9²	11	3¹	8	10	2	13	12	1	14													13
		3	5	6²	4	13	11	14	8³	9	10¹	2	12	7	1													14
		3	7	5		10	8	9	2	11²	4	12	6¹	1	13													15
1		3	4	5	13	7³	9	11²	10¹	6	12	2	14	8														16
1		3	4	5	14	7¹	6	11³	13	8	9²	10	2	12														17
1	2	4³	5	3	13	11¹	10	8	12	9	6	7²	14															18
1	2	3	4	5	9	8	10	11	7	6																		19
1	2	4¹	5	3	12	11	10	8	7	9	6																	20
1	2	4	3	7	11	10	9¹	8	12	5							6											21
1	5	2¹	9	6	11	10	8	7	3				12	4				6										22
1	2¹	5	6	13	11	9²	12	8	10	4			7	3														23
1		4	3	7	6	11	13	10¹	12	9²	5		8	2														24
1		3	5	6	14	7³	9¹	12	11	13	10²	4	8	2														25
1		4	3	7	6²	11	8	10³	14	9¹	5		13	2						12								26
1	13	4	3	2¹	11	7	10	12	9	5²	6		14	8³														27
	3	9²	7¹	5	11	13	6	10	4	12	1	2	8															28
13	3	9	8	5	6	11	2	10	4¹	1	12	7²																29
2	4¹	3	11	6	13	7³	10	14	9	5²	1	12	8															30
2	3	8	13	5	9	12²	10¹	6	11		7	1	4															31
2²	3	9¹	12	5	11	6	10	7	1	4	8	13																32
	5	3	7¹	6	11²	2	9	8	1	4	10	12	13															33
2	4	5	8	11⁴	9²	12	10³	6¹	1	3	7	13	14															34
2	4	5	9¹	7	12	11	10	8³	1	3	6²	13	14															35
2	5	11	8	6	3³	10²	7	9	1	4¹	13	12		14														36

EAST STIRLINGSHIRE   Third Division

Year Formed: 1880. *Ground & Address:* Firs Park, Firs St, Falkirk FK2 7AY. *Telephone:* 01324 623583. *Fax:* 01324 637 862.
E-mail: lestshire@aol.com *Website:* www.eaststirlingfc.com
Ground Capacity: total: 1880, seated: 200. *Size of Pitch:* 112yd × 72yd.
Chairman: Les Thomson. *Vice Chairman:* Douglas Morrison. *Chief Executive/Secretary:* Leslie G. Thomson.
Manager: Jim McInally. *Physio:* David Jenkins.
Club Nickname(s): The Shire. *Previous Grounds:* Burnhouse, Randyford Park, Merchiston Park, New Kilbowie Park.
Record Attendance: 12,000 v Partick Th, *Scottish Cup* 3rd rd, 21 Feb 1921.
Record Transfer Fee received: £35,000 for Jim Docherty to Chelsea (1978).
Record Transfer Fee paid: £6,000 for Colin McKinnon from Falkirk (March 1991).
Record Victory: 11-2 v Vale of Bannock, *Scottish Cup* 2nd rd, 22 Sept 1888.
Record Defeat: 1-12 v Dundee United, Division II, 13 Apr 1936.
Most Capped Player: Humphrey Jones, 5 (14), Wales.
Most League Appearances: 415: Gordon Russell, 1983-2001.
Most League Goals in Season (Individual): 36: Malcolm Morrison, Division II, 1938-39.

EAST STIRLINGSHIRE 2008–09 LEAGUE RECORD

Match No.	Date		Venue	Opponents	Result	H/T Score	Lg. Pos.	Goalscorers	Attendance
1	Aug	2	A	Berwick R	L 1-2	1-2	—	Rodgers [44]	570
2		9	H	Albion R	W 1-0	1-0	5	Forrest [31]	348
3		16	A	Annan Ath	L 1-2	1-0	9	Cramb [1]	968
4		23	H	Forfar Ath	L 0-3	0-1	10		386
5		30	A	Dumbarton	D 1-1	0-1	9	McKenzie [69]	592
6	Sept	13	H	Stenhousemuir	L 0-2	0-1	9		511
7		20	A	Montrose	L 0-3	0-1	9		364
8		27	H	Elgin C	W 5-2	3-1	9	Cramb (pen) [10], Richardson [22], Kaczan (og) [24], Rodgers [57], Donaldson [86]	352
9	Oct	4	A	Cowdenbeath	D 0-0	0-0	9		431
10		18	H	Berwick R	W 1-0	1-0	6	Bolochoweckyj [10]	387
11	Nov	8	A	Forfar Ath	W 3-2	2-2	7	Cramb (pen) [5], Bolochoweckyj [35], Rodgers (pen) [47]	427
12		12	H	Annan Ath	W 2-1	0-1	—	Cramb [57], Graham [71]	343
13		15	H	Dumbarton	W 5-2	2-0	5	Graham 2 [22, 60], Rodgers (pen) [44], Donaldson [46], Dunn [64]	516
14		22	A	Stenhousemuir	D 1-1	1-0	5	Graham [26]	737
15	Dec	6	H	Montrose	W 5-0	1-0	—	Cramb 2 [40, 47], Graham 2 [53, 54], Bolochoweckyj [64]	427
16		13	A	Elgin C	W 4-0	1-0	4	Rodgers 3 [7, 63, 82], Graham [87]	366
17		20	H	Cowdenbeath	L 1-4	1-1	4	Graham [18]	457
18	Jan	3	H	Stenhousemuir	L 0-3	0-2	4		814
19		17	H	Forfar Ath	W 3-2	2-0	4	Dunn [18], Rodgers [21], Cramb [90]	405
20		24	A	Annan Ath	L 0-4	0-2	5		714
21	Feb	7	H	Albion R	L 0-1	0-1	—		453
22		14	H	Elgin C	W 1-0	1-0	—	Rodgers [45]	489
23		21	A	Montrose	W 2-0	0-0	3	Stevenson [51], Cramb [90]	400
24		28	H	Dumbarton	W 3-1	1-1	3	Stevenson [5], Cramb (pen) [67], Rodgers [87]	526
25	Mar	3	A	Dumbarton	L 0-2	0-2	—		462
26		7	A	Stenhousemuir	W 4-1	3-1	3	Donaldson [4], Graham 2 [31, 41], Stevenson [62]	805
27		10	A	Albion R	W 2-0	2-0	3	Graham [25], Hay [45]	420
28		14	H	Berwick R	L 0-4	0-1	2		438
29		21	A	Cowdenbeath	L 0-2	0-1	3		430
30		28	A	Berwick R	W 2-1	1-1	2	Rodgers 2 [11, 90]	431
31	Apr	4	A	Forfar Ath	W 2-0	1-0	3	Bolochoweckyj [25], McKenzie [71]	491
32		11	A	Annan Ath	D 1-1	1-1	3	Rodgers [25]	503
33		18	H	Montrose	W 2-1	1-0	3	Graham 2 [22, 75]	401
34		25	A	Elgin C	W 2-0	1-0	3	Graham 2 [22, 60]	381
35	May	2	A	Albion R	W 2-0	1-0	2	Rodgers [30], Stevenson [51]	346
36		9	H	Cowdenbeath	L 0-2	0-0	3		434

Final League Position: 3

Honours

League Champions: Division II 1931-32; C Division 1947-48. *Runners-up:* Division II 1962-63. Second Division 1979-80. Division Three 1923-24.

Club colours: Shirt: Black. Shorts: Black. Stockings: Black.

Goalscorers: *League* (57): Graham 15, Rodgers 14 (2 pens), Cramb 9 (3 pens), Bolochoweckyj 4, Stevenson 4, Donaldson 3, Dunn 2, McKenzie 2, Forrest 1, Hay 1, Richardson 1, own goal 1.
Scottish Cup (2): Forrest 1, Graham 1.
Challenge Cup (0).
Play-Offs (2): Graham 1, Rodgers 1.

Hillcoat J 3	Anderson S 16+10	Richardson D 19+6	Oates S 2	Bolochoweckyj M 33	Ure D 31+1	Dunn D 18+15	Nicholls D 4	Cramb C 15+6	Graham B 29+4	Rodgers A 28+2	Donaldson C 26+4	Gibson J 2+1	McKenzie M 1+33	Forrest E 25+1	Tully C 27	Moffat G —+1	Hay P 31+1	Kelly G 14+11	Mitchell G 2	Barclay J 11	Thornton D 1+2	Peat M 16	Krivokapic B 1+1	Camara K 1	Corr B 1	Peters M 2	O'Neill J 1+1	Weaver P 15	Stevenson J 13	King D 7	Newman J —+1	O'Hara G 1	Paige S —+1	Elliot J —+1	Match No.
1	2^3	3^1	4	5	6	7^2	8	9	10	11	12	13	14																						1
1	13			5^1	3	7^3	10^2	11	9	2	8			14	4		6	12																	2
1	12			4	3	7^2	10^3	9	11		13	8	14	6	5		2^1																		3
	13	12			3			6^1	9	11^3	10	7		14	4		5									2	8^2	1							4
		5			3	9	8^2		10^1	11^3	12	6		13	7		4								2	14	1								5
8	3	4^2	5	10	13			11^3	9^1	7		12	6				2						1	14											6
12	5^1		4	10	8^2			11	13	6		9	3				2	7					1												7
13	3		5	8	10^2			9^1		11	7		12	4			2	6					1												8
	5				4	8		10^1	12	9^2	6		13	3	7		2	11					1												9
14				5^3	10			9^1	12	11	7		13	4	6		2	8^2					1												10
13	10			5		3^2		9^1	12	11^3	7		14	4	6		2	8^2					1												11
10				5	12	3^1		9	13	11	8		14	4	6		2^2	7^3					1												12
8	3^2			5	10	13		9^3	11	7^1			14	4	6		2	12					1												13
8^1	3^2			5	10	13		12	9^3	11			14	4	6		2	7					1												14
13	3			5	10^2	8		9^3	7	11^1			12	4	6		2						1	14											15
	3^2			5	10	8		9^3	7	11	12		14	4	6		13	2^1					1												16
14	3^3			5		8^2		9	7	11	10^1		13	4	6		2	12					1												17
7^3	10^2			5	8	3		12	9	11	4		13		6		2^1	14			1														18
7^2	10			5	8	3		12	9^1	11^3	4		13		6		2	14									1								19
	10^2			5		3		12	9^1	11	7		13	4^3	6		2	8					1	14											20
10				5	3	14		12	9^1	11^2	7		13		6^3		2										1		4	8					21
4				5	3	13		9^2	10	11^1	7		12				2	14									1		6^2	8					22
				4	5	14		10	9^3	11^2	6		12	3			2	13									1		7	8^1					23
				5	3	14		9^2	10	11	7		13	12	4		2^1										1		6	8^3					24
14				4	11	8^3		12	10	9	6^2		13	5	3		2^1										1		7						25
11^3	13			5	10	14		9		7			12	3			2^2	4									1		6	8^1					26
11^3	13			5	10	14		9		7^2			12	3	4		2										1		6	8^1					27
11	12			5^1	10	14		9		7^3			13	3	4		2										1		6	8^2					28
3	9			5	8^1			10		6^2			12				2	11					13				1		7		4				29
7^1				5	10	14		9	11				12	3			2^3	13									1		6	8^3	4				30
7^1	14			5	10			9	11^3				12	3			2	13									1		6	8^2	4				31
7^1				5	10^3	14		9^2	11				12				3						2	13			1		6	8	4				32
	7^1			5	10	13		9	11	12				3			2										1		6	8^2	4				33
	14			5	10	13		9^1	11^3	7^2			12				3						2				1		6	8^2	4				34
				5	10	13		11	7				12	8^1	3^2		2	14					1						6	9^3	4				35
	6	3		10				5	4					8			9	1^9	7^2								11^1			15	2	13	12	36

ELGIN CITY   Third Division

Year Formed: 1893. *Ground and Address:* Borough Briggs, Borough Briggs Road, Elgin IV30 1AP.
Telephone: 01343 551114. *Fax:* 01343 547921. *E-mail:* elgincityfc@ukonline.co.uk *Website:* www.elgincity.com
Ground Capacity: 3927, seated 478, standing 3449. *Size of pitch:* 111yd × 72yd.
Chairman: Graham Tatters. *Secretary:* Ian A. Allan. *Administrator:* Audrey Fanning.
Manager: Ross Jack. *Assistant Manager:* Kenny Gilbert. *Director of Football:* Graham Tatters. *Physios:* Billy Belcher
and Leigh Thomas.
Previous names: 1893-1900 Elgin City, 1900–03 Elgin City United, 1903– Elgin City.
Club Nickname(s): City or Black & Whites. *Previous Grounds:* Association Park 1893-95; Milnfield Park 1895-1909;
Station Park 1909-19; Cooper Park 1919-21.
Record Attendance: 12,608 v Arbroath, Scottish Cup, 17 Feb 1968.
Record Transfer Fee received: £32,000 for Michael Teasdale to Dundee (Jan 1994).
Record Transfer Fee paid: £10,000 to Fraserburgh for Russell McBride (July 2001).
Record Victory: 18-1 v Brora Rangers, North of Scotland Cup, 6 Feb 1960.
Record Defeat: 1-14 v Hearts, Scottish Cup, 4 Feb 1939.
Most League Appearances: 224: David Hind, 2001-09.
Most League Goals in Season (Individual): 20: Martin Johnston, 2005-06.
Most Goals Overall (Individual): 39: Martin Johnston, 2005-07.

ELGIN CITY 2008–09 LEAGUE RECORD

Match No.	Date	Venue	Opponents	Result	H/T Score	Lg. Pos.	Goalscorers	Attendance
1	Aug 2	A	Stenhousemuir	L 0-3	0-1	—		320
2	9	H	Dumbarton	D 1-1	1-0	9	McKay [24]	462
3	16	A	Forfar Ath	W 1-0	0-0	6	McKay [60]	377
4	23	H	Cowdenbeath	L 0-2	0-0	8		537
5	30	A	Montrose	L 0-1	0-0	10		304
6	Sept 13	H	Annan Ath	L 1-2	0-1	10	Shallicker (pen) [73]	468
7	20	H	Albion R	L 1-6	0-2	10	Shallicker [88]	407
8	27	A	East Stirling	L 2-5	1-3	10	Kerr [39], Wright [63]	352
9	Oct 4	A	Berwick R	D 1-1	0-1	10	Shallicker (pen) [76]	367
10	18	H	Stenhousemuir	W 4-2	1-2	10	Campbell [21], Shallicker [62], Kerr [76], Kaczan [90]	359
11	Nov 1	H	Forfar Ath	L 0-1	0-1	10		491
12	8	A	Cowdenbeath	L 1-4	1-3	10	Shallicker [7]	193
13	15	H	Montrose	L 1-2	0-0	10	O'Donoghue [78]	376
14	22	A	Annan Ath	L 0-5	0-1	10		422
15	Dec 13	H	East Stirling	L 0-4	0-1	10		366
16	20	H	Berwick R	L 0-2	0-1	10		304
17	Jan 10	A	Montrose	L 1-3	1-1	—	Wright [6]	306
18	17	H	Cowdenbeath	D 1-1	0-0	10	Wright [75]	380
19	31	A	Stenhousemuir	L 2-4	0-2	10	Wright 2 [47, 52]	311
20	Feb 14	A	East Stirling	L 0-1	0-1	—		489
21	21	H	Albion R	W 1-0	1-0	10	MacKay (pen) [19]	357
22	28	H	Montrose	W 1-0	0-0	10	Crooks [71]	364
23	Mar 3	A	Albion R	L 1-2	1-1	—	Crooks [39]	237
24	7	A	Annan Ath	L 0-6	0-3	10		487
25	10	A	Dumbarton	L 0-2	0-1	—		474
26	14	H	Stenhousemuir	W 2-0	0-0	10	MacKay [52], Campbell [58]	318
27	21	A	Berwick R	L 1-2	1-1	10	Wright [34]	348
28	24	A	Forfar Ath	D 1-1	1-1	—	Brown (og) [21]	578
29	28	H	Annan Ath	L 0-1	0-1	10		321
30	31	H	Dumbarton	L 0-2	0-1	—		271
31	Apr 4	A	Cowdenbeath	D 1-1	0-0	10	Shallicker (pen) [70]	331
32	11	H	Forfar Ath	L 1-4	0-2	10	Shallicker [90]	452
33	18	A	Albion R	W 3-0	1-0	10	Nicolson [15], Campbell 2 [85, 90]	275
34	25	H	East Stirling	L 0-2	0-1	10		381
35	May 2	A	Dumbarton	L 0-6	0-4	10		1396
36	9	H	Berwick R	W 2-0	1-0	10	Nicolson [13], MacDonald [56]	429

Final League Position: 10

Honours
Scottish Cup: Quarter-finals 1968.
Highland League Champions: winners 15 times.
Scottish Qualifying Cup (North): winners 7 times.
North of Scotland Cup: winners 17 times.
Highland League Cup: winners 5 times.
Inverness Cup: winners twice.

Club colours: Shirt: Black and white stripes. Shorts: Black. Stockings: White.

Goalscorers: *League* (31): Shallicker 7 (3 pens), Wright 6, Campbell 4, MacKay 4 (1 pen), Crooks 2, Kerr 2, Nicolson 2, Kaczan 1, MacDonald 1, O'Donoghue 1, own goal 1.
Scottish Cup (5): Wright 2, Kaczan 1, Mackay 1 (pen), Nicolson 1.
Challenge Cup (0).

Ridgers A 15+3	Gilbert K 9	MacKay S 23+3	Nicolson M 33	Kaczan P 27+1	Hind D 10+3	Campbell C 29	O'Donoghue R 33	Shallicker D 22+7	Crooks J 26+7	Low T 2+4	MacDonald A 30+1	Lindsay A —+1	McNulty A 19	Kerr G 13+1	Allan D 1+7	Niven D 17+2	Wright K 20+3	Nixon D 1	Keogh L 5	Malin J 2	Ramsay D —+3	Charlesworth C —+1	McKenzie G 2+7	McPhee D 2+2	Cameron B 4+10	Jack Z 6+5	Craig D 9+6	Archibald L —+1	Gillespie D 16+1	Munro G 7	Smith D —+1	Tweegie G —+1	Craig D 8	Edwards S 5+2	Match No.
1	2*	3	4	5	6	7	8	9	10	11¹	12																								1
1	11	5	4	6	2	8	9¹	10	7	3	12																								2
	11	2	4	6	7	8*	10	9	3					1		5																			3
8	11*	2	4	6³	7		10	9¹	13	3²				1	5	14	12																		4
		3	4	7²	6	8	11³	12	14	9				1	5¹	13	2	10																	5
	11¹	6	4		7	8	13	10²	12	3				1	5	14	2	9³																	6
1	3*	4	5	8¹	7*	6	9	13	11²	12			14	2*	10³																				7
1	12	2	5	4		8	9	10	6	3	11¹		7																						8
15	2		4	12	6¹	11	8	9	10	3			1⁶	5		7*																			9
	2		4	10	11	6	8	9	7	3			1	5																					10
	2		4	10	12	7	8	9¹	11²	3¹			1	5	14	6	13																		11
8		3	11	6		7	10		5				1	4	12	9¹	2																		12
1	6³	13	4	10¹		7	8	9		3			5	14	2	12	11²																		13
1	11		4	10¹	14	7	8	9²	13	3			5	2	12	6³																			14
	2	6		5	12	7	8	9³	11	3	4²		10¹	1	13	14																			15
	11		6³	7	8	9²	10	3	5	4			1	14	2¹	12	13																		16
1	5	4		7	11	6	8	3	9		10¹	12²	2	13																					17
		5		8		7	6	1	4	9	3	2	12	10²	11¹	13																			18
	10	4	5¹	7*	8	13	3	1	9³	6	14	2	11²	12																					19
15	10	4		8	12	6	3²	1⁶	9	2	11¹	7	5	13																					20
	10	2		7	8	12	11¹	3	1	4	9²	13	6	5																					21
	10	2		7	8	11	3	1	4	9¹	12	6	5																						22
	10²	2		7	8	11	3¹	1	4	9	13	12	6	5³	14																				23
15	10	2		7	8	12	11¹	3⁶	1*	4	9	13	6	5																					24
1	11³	2	9	6²	8	13	12	5	3	10	14	7	4¹																						25
1	10	2	6	7	8	12	11³	3	4¹	9²	14	13	5																						26
1	10	6	4	7	8	11²	3	9¹	12	13	5	2																							27
1	10	6	4	7	8	12	11¹	3	9²	13	5	2																							28
1	10	3	4	7¹		9	11³	5²	14	13	8	6	2	12																					29
1	2	4	10	7¹	9	13	12	3²	5*	8	11	6	2																						30
1	3	4	8	11	9	10²	13	12	6¹	5	7	2																							31
1	13	3	4	8	10	11³	9¹	12	7²	14	6	5	2																						32
	10	2	11	8	6¹	12	5	1	13	9²	3	7	4																						33
1	10	2	4	9	8	11	12	3¹	1	7²	13	5	6³	14																					34
	11	5	3	10	8	12	1	13	14	6¹	9	7³	4	2²																					35
	11	4		8¹	10	3	1	6	13	9	14	12²	7³	5	2																				36

FALKIRK   Premier League

Year Formed: 1876. *Ground & Address:* The Falkirk Stadium, Westfield, Falkirk FK2 9DX. *Telephone:* 01324 624121.
Fax: 01324 612418. *Website:* www.falkirkfc.co.uk
Ground Capacity: seated: 6123. *Size of Pitch:* 110yd × 72yd.
Chairman: Campbell Christie. *Managing Director:* George Craig. *Head of Development:* Eddie May. *Secretary:* Alex
Blackwood.
Manager: Eddie May. *Assistant Manager:* Steven Pressley. *Director of Football:* Alex Totten. *Youth Co-ordinator:* Ian
McIntyre.
Club Nickname(s): The Bairns. *Previous Grounds:* Randyford 1876-81; Blinkbonny Grounds 1881-83; Brockville Park
1883-2003.
Record Attendance: 23,100 v Celtic, Scottish Cup 3rd rd, 21 Feb 1953.
Record Transfer Fee received: £380,000 for John Hughes to Celtic (Aug 1995).
Record Transfer Fee paid: £225,000 to Chelsea for Kevin McAllister (Aug 1991).
Record Victory: 12-1 v Laurieston, Scottish Cup 2nd rd, 23 Sept 1893.
Record Defeat: 1-11 v Airdrieonians, Division I, 28 Apr 1951.
Most Capped Player: Alex Parker, 14 (15), Scotland.
Most League Appearances: (post-war): 353: George Watson, 1975-87.
Most League Goals in Season (Individual): 43: Evelyn Morrison, Division I, 1928-29.
Most Goals Overall (Individual): 86: Dougie Moran, 1957-61 and 1964-67.

FALKIRK 2008–09 LEAGUE RECORD

Match No.	Date	Venue	Opponents	Result	H/T Score	Lg. Pos.	Goalscorers	Atten- dance
1	Aug 9	H	Rangers	L 0-1	0-0	—		6669
2	16	A	Hibernian	L 2-3	1-2	11	Higdon 2 [30, 53]	12,445
3	23	A	Celtic	L 0-3	0-2	12		56,031
4	30	H	Inverness CT	L 1-2	0-0	12	Stewart M [60]	4730
5	Sept 13	H	Hearts	W 2-1	1-0	11	McCann [3], Arfield [90]	5960
6	20	A	St Mirren	D 1-1	0-0	12	Barrett [47]	4134
7	27	H	Hamilton A	W 4-1	1-0	9	Lovell [44], Arfield 2 (1 pen) [69, 87 (p)], O'Brien [72]	4734
8	Oct 5	A	Motherwell	L 2-3	1-2	11	Lovell [22], Barrett [48]	4509
9	18	H	Aberdeen	L 0-1	0-0	12		5662
10	25	A	Kilmarnock	W 2-1	1-0	11	Lovell [28], Arfield (pen) [66]	4267
11	Nov 1	H	Dundee U	D 0-0	0-0	10		5608
12	8	A	Hamilton A	D 1-1	0-1	10	Higdon [49]	2600
13	12	A	Inverness CT	D 1-1	1-0	—	Higdon [19]	3111
14	15	H	Motherwell	W 1-0	1-0	8	Higdon [37]	5279
15	22	A	Hearts	L 1-2	1-1	10	Lovell [16]	13,009
16	29	H	Hibernian	D 1-1	0-0	8	Barr [69]	6260
17	Dec 6	H	St Mirren	L 1-2	0-1	8	Lovell [62]	4828
18	13	A	Aberdeen	L 1-2	0-2	9	Lovell [89]	8909
19	21	H	Celtic	L 0-3	0-0	9		6543
20	27	A	Dundee U	L 0-1	0-1	10		7972
21	Jan 3	H	Kilmarnock	D 1-1	1-0	11	Lovell [41]	5375
22	17	A	Rangers	L 1-3	1-1	11	Lovell [12]	48,811
23	24	A	Motherwell	D 1-1	0-1	11	Holden [53]	5018
24	31	H	Aberdeen	W 1-0	0-0	11	Higdon [55]	5605
25	Feb 14	A	St Mirren	D 2-2	1-1	11	Finnigan [35], Arfield (pen) [85]	5504
26	21	H	Hamilton A	L 1-2	1-1	11	Swailes (og) [7]	5307
27	28	A	Hibernian	D 0-0	0-0	11		10,682
28	Mar 3	H	Dundee U	L 0-1	0-1	—		4385
29	21	H	Inverness CT	W 4-0	1-0	12	Finnigan 2 [37, 90], Stewart M [65], Arfield (pen) [82]	5523
30	Apr 5	H	Rangers	L 0-1	0-1	12		6853
31	8	A	Celtic	L 0-4	0-1	—		57,669
32	11	A	Kilmarnock	L 0-3	0-2	12		5835
33	18	H	Hearts	D 0-0	0-0	12		6156
34	May 2	H	Motherwell	W 2-1	1-0	12	Finnigan [9], Scobbie [56]	4937
35	9	A	Kilmarnock	D 1-1	0-0	12	Barr [56]	5955
36	13	A	Hamilton A	W 1-0	0-0	—	Arfield [60]	3710
37	16	H	St Mirren	L 0-2	0-1	12		6744
38	23	A	Inverness CT	W 1-0	0-0	10	Higdon [68]	6489

Final League Position: 10

Honours

League Champions: Division II 1935-36, 1969-70, 1974-75. First Division 1990-91, 1993-94, 2002-03, 2004-05. Second Division 1979-80; *Runners-up:* Division I 1907-08, 1909-10. First Division 1985-86, 1988-89. Division II 1904-05, 1951-52, 1960-61.
Scottish Cup Winners: 1913, 1957; *Runners-up:* 1997, 2009. *League Cup Runners-up:* 1947-48. *B&Q Cup Winners:* 1993-94. *League Challenge Cup Winners:* 1997-98, 2004-05.

Club colours: Shirt: Navy blue with white seams. Shorts: Navy. Stockings: Navy with two white hoops.

Goalscorers: *League* (37): Lovell 8, Arfield 7 (4 pens), Higdon 7, Finnigan 4, Barr 2, Barrett 2, Stewart M 2, Holden 1, McCann 1, O'Brien 1, Scobbie 1, own goal 1.
Scottish Cup (8): Arfield 3 (2 pens), Barrett 2, Finnigan 1 (pen), Lovell 1, Scobbie 1.
CIS Cup (6): McCann 2, Higdon 1, Lovell 1, Stewart M 1, Stewart J 1 (pen).

Olejnik R 15	McNamara J 29	Aafjes G 10+7	Cregg P 16+7	Barr D 35	Bullen L 29+3	Latapy R 2+1	McBride K 25+3	Higdon M 27+7	Stewart J 4	Arfield S 35+2	Robertson D —+4	Stewart M 5+15	Mitchell C 3+6	McCaffrey D 1+1	Barrett G 9+6	O'Brien B 30+2	Lovell S 25+3	Scobbie T 18+2	McCann N 22+2	Lynch S —+2	Flinders S 8	Holden D 16+3	Arnau 14+3	Finnigan C 10+4	Pressley S 15+1	Dani Mallo 15	Moffat K —+4	Match No.
1	2	3	4	5	6	7^1	8^3	9^2	10	11	12	13	14															1
1	2	3	4	5	6	7^1	8	9	10^2	11	12	13																2
1	2	3^1	4	5	6		8	9	7^2	11	14	10^3	12	13														3
1	2	3	4	5	6		8		10^1	11		7			9^2	13	12											4
1	2	13		5	6		8	9		11			14		10^3	4^2	12	3	7^1									5
1	2			5	6		8	9		11					10^1	7	12	3	4									6
1	2^1	13	12	5	6		8^1	9		11					10^3	7	4	3		14								7
1	2^1	12		5	6	14	8	9		11					10^3	4^2	7	3	13									8
	2	13		5	6^8		8^3	9^1		11^2		14			12	7	10		4		1	3						9
	2	3		5			8	12		11					9^1	7^2	10^8		6		1	4	13					10
	2^1	3	4	5	12		8			11					13	10	9		7		1	6^2						11
	2	3	4^1	5	6		8	12		11						7	9	10			1	6						12
	2			5	6		8	9		11					12	4	10		7^1		1	3						13
	2			5	6		8	9		11			13	12	7^2	4	10				1	3^1						14
		4^1		5	6		8	9				13	3	2	12	7	10				1			11^2				15
	2	4		5	6		8	9		12						7	10				1	3		11^1				16
1	2^8	4^1		5	6		8	9		12		14			13	7	10					3^3		11^2				17
1	2^2			5	6		8^1	9		11			12	13	4	7	10					3						18
1				5	6					7		13	2		9^2	8	10		4			3		11^1	12			19
1	2	13		5^8	6		12	9		7					4^1	10	14		8			3^3		11^{12}				20
1	2				6		8	9		7					12	10	3	4				5		11^1				21
1	2^1	4^8		5	6		8	14		11		13			9^2	10	7					12			3^3			22
1				5^2	6		8^3	12		11			13		7^1	9	3	10				2	14		4			23
	2			5	6			9		7			12				10^2		8			3^1	11	13	4	1		24
				5	6			9		7			12		11^2	4	10^1	3	8						2	1	13	25
	2^2	12		5				9^1		11			13			8	10		6^3			3	7	4		1	14	26
		4		5	6			9		7			13			8	10^2	3				12		11^1	2	1		27
		14	4^3	5	6^2			9		7					12	8	10	3					11^1	13	2	1		28
	2	14	4		6		12	9^1		11					8^2	7		3	13				10	5^3		1		29
	2	13	4^1		6^2		8^3	12		11						10		3	7				9	5		1	14	30
	2			5	12		8	9		11						4		3^2	7^3			13	10	6^1		1	14	31
	2^2	12		5	6		8	9		11						7	13		4^1			14	10	3^3		1		32
	2	4^1		5				9		7	12					8		3	10				11	6		1		33
	2	4^8	14	5											13	7	10^3		8			3	6^1	11^2	9	12	1	34
	2^2			5	13										12	7	8^1		10			3	4	11	9	6	1	35
				5	6		8^1	9		11					12	10^2	3	4				13	7		2	1		36
		14	13	5	6^3			9		7					8	10		3	4^1				11^2	12	2^8	1		37
	2	6	4	5						7			13		12	8	10^2	3						11^1	9	1		38

FORFAR ATHLETIC   Third Division

Year Formed: 1885. *Ground & Address:* Station Park, Carseview Road, Forfar. *Telephone:* 01307 463576/462259.
Fax: 01307 466956. *E-mail:* pat@ramsayladders.co.uk *Website:* www.forfarathletic.co.uk
Ground Capacity: total: 4602, seated: 739. *Size of Pitch:* 115yd × 69yd.
Chairman: Neill Wilson. *Secretary:* David McGregor.
Manager: Dick Campbell.
Club Nickname(s): Loons. *Previous Grounds:* None.
Record Attendance: 10,780 v Rangers, Scottish Cup 2nd rd, 2 Feb 1970.
Record Transfer Fee received: £65,000 for David Bingham to Dunfermline Ath (September 1995).
Record Transfer Fee paid: £50,000 for Ian McPhee from Airdrieonians (1991).
Record Victory: 14-1 v Lindertis, Scottish Cup 1st rd, 1 Sept 1988.
Record Defeat: 2-12 v King's Park, Division II, 2 Jan 1930.
Most League Appearances: 484: Ian McPhee, 1978-88 and 1991-98.
Most League Goals in Season (Individual): 45: Dave Kilgour, Division II, 1929-30.
Most Goals Overall: 124: John Clark, 1978-91.

FORFAR ATHLETIC 2008–09 LEAGUE RECORD

Match No.	Date	Venue	Opponents	Result	H/T Score	Lg. Pos.	Goalscorers	Attendance
1	Aug 2	A	Albion R	W 3-1	1-1	—	McLeish (pen) [17], Winter [69], Manson [84]	289
2	9	H	Cowdenbeath	L 0-1	0-0	4		412
3	16	H	Elgin C	L 0-1	0-0	8		377
4	23	A	East Stirling	W 3-0	1-0	4	Russell 2 [20, 55], Lilley [58]	386
5	30	A	Berwick R	D 2-2	1-1	4	McLeish (pen) [21], Gibson G [79]	390
6	Sept 13	H	Montrose	L 0-1	0-0	6		518
7	20	A	Annan Ath	W 3-1	1-1	6	Gibson G [5], Fotheringham [46], Russell [58]	690
8	27	H	Dumbarton	D 2-2	0-1	5	Russell [57], Gibson G [88]	431
9	Oct 4	A	Stenhousemuir	D 1-1	0-0	5	Kilgannon [90]	429
10	18	H	Albion R	D 0-0	0-0	5		426
11	Nov 1	A	Elgin C	W 1-0	1-0	4	Campbell [19]	491
12	8	H	East Stirling	L 2-3	2-2	6	Campbell [13], Gibson G [22]	427
13	15	H	Berwick R	W 2-1	1-1	6	Lilley (pen) [30], McLeish [88]	327
14	22	A	Montrose	L 0-1	0-1	6		465
15	Dec 13	A	Dumbarton	L 0-3	0-1	6		539
16	20	H	Stenhousemuir	W 1-0	0-0	6	Kilgannon (pen) [90]	468
17	Jan 17	A	East Stirling	L 2-3	0-2	8	Fotheringham [68], Tulloch [87]	405
18	31	A	Albion R	L 0-2	0-1	8		284
19	Feb 21	A	Annan Ath	L 0-1	0-1	9		542
20	28	H	Berwick R	W 5-4	1-0	9	Gibson G [41], Campbell [60], Tulloch [64], Gordon [77], Russell [84]	382
21	Mar 3	H	Annan Ath	W 2-1	0-0	—	Campbell 2 (1 pen) [47 (p), 70]	366
22	7	A	Montrose	W 3-1	1-0	8	Campbell 2 (1 pen) [43 (p), 55], McNally [46]	530
23	10	A	Cowdenbeath	D 0-0	0-0	—		317
24	14	H	Albion R	W 4-0	1-0	7	Gordon [36], Brady [70], Fotheringham [77], Divine [89]	319
25	17	A	Berwick R	W 2-0	0-0	—	Russell [68], Campbell [84]	382
26	21	A	Stenhousemuir	W 1-0	1-0	6	Gibson G [36]	399
27	24	H	Elgin C	D 1-1	1-1	—	Campbell [7]	578
28	28	H	Montrose	L 0-3	0-1	6		621
29	31	H	Cowdenbeath	D 1-1	1-1	—	Campbell [14]	621
30	Apr 4	H	East Stirling	L 0-2	0-1	6		491
31	7	H	Dumbarton	L 0-2	0-0	—		513
32	11	A	Elgin C	W 4-1	2-0	5	Kaczan (og) [11], Tulloch [26], Campbell [82], Russell [89]	452
33	18	H	Annan Ath	W 2-1	0-1	6	Fotheringham [60], Campbell (pen) [71]	463
34	25	A	Dumbarton	L 0-4	0-3	6		917
35	May 2	A	Cowdenbeath	D 2-2	2-2	7	Gordon [3], Russell [4]	527
36	9	H	Stenhousemuir	D 4-4	2-2	6	Gordon 2 [21, 37], Campbell [64], Gibson G [81]	392

Final League Position: 6

Honours
League Champions: Second Division 1983-84. Third Division 1994-95; *Runners-up:* 1996-97. C Division 1948-49.
Scottish Cup: Semi-finals 1982.
League Cup: Semi-finals 1977-78.
League Challenge Cup: Semi-finals 2004-05.

Club colours: Shirt: Sky blue with navy stripes. Shorts: Navy bue. Stockings: Navy blue.

Goalscorers: *League* (53): Campbell 13 (3 pens), Russell 8, Gibson G 7, Gordon 5, Fotheringham 4, McLeish 3 (2 pens), Tulloch 3, Kilgannon 2 (1 pen), Lilley 2 (1 pen), Brady 1, Divine 1, Manson 1, McNally 1, Winter 1, own goal 1.
Scottish Cup (11): Gordon 3, Campbell 2, Gibson G 2, Dunn 1, Kilgannon 1, Tulloch 1, own goal 1.
Challenge Cup (2): Kilgannon 1 (pen), McLeish 1.

Brown A 32	McNally S 20 + 7	Ferguson S 4	Tulloch S 33	Dunn D 10 + 1	Smith E 14 + 5	McLeish K 11 + 7	Winter C 21 + 12	Lilley D 23 + 3	Brady D 30	Campbell R 24 + 7	Duell B — + 3	Fotheringham M 22 + 10	Manson S — + 4	Donachie B 6 + 6	Kilgannon S 7 + 9	Russell J 25 + 1	Gibson G 26 + 3	Gordon K 24 + 5	Keogh P 2	Tod A 23	Tosh S 2	Simpson S 3 + 7	McGuigan M — + 1	Smith C 3 + 12	Divine A 14 + 1	Cairns S 12	Derden S 1	Gibson J 4	Match No.
1	2^1	3	4	5	6^3	7	8	9	10	11^2	12	13	14																1
1	2	3^1	6	5	11^2	7	4^3	9	8	10	12	14	13																2
1	12	3^1	6	5	2	7	11^3	9	8	10^1		13			4^1	14													3
1	2		4	5	3	8	6	9^2	10^1	14	12	13				11	7^2												4
1	2		5	4	3	7	6^1	9	8	13		12				11^{12}	10^3	14											5
1	2		6	5	3	11^1	13	9	8					4^2	14	12	10^3	7											6
1	4		5	3	2	10	9^2	6	13	7					14	8^3	11^1	12											7
1	4		5	13	3	2^1	10^3	9	6	14		7^2				8	11	12											8
1	3^3		4	5	2	14	9	6	12	10^1		13				8	11	7^2											9
1	2^1		6	5	3	4	12	9^2	10	14		13				11^3	8	7											10
1	2	6				13	4	9^1	8	10^2				12	3	11	7	5											11
1	2^2				14	13	4^1	9^3	8	10					3^1	12	11	7	5	6									12
1	13		6	4^3		14	8^1	9	10	7		12	3			11	2^2		5										13
1	11		7	3		12	8	10^3	9	6^2		13		5	14		2^1	4											14
1	2	5					14		10	8^3		12			3^1	11	9	6^2	4	7		13							15
1	2		3				4	9^1	8^2			13			12	10	11	7^1		5		6	14						16
1		6			3		4^1	9^3	8	10^2				11	14	2	12	7		5		13							17
1	2	6			3^2		8^3		4	10			14			11	7^1			5			12	13	9				18
1	2	3							12	8						11	10^3	14	7^2	5		13		9	4^1	6			19
1		3						9^1	6	8			4			10	11	12		5		7		2					20
1		3				12		6	8^2				4			13	11	9^3	10	5		7^1		14	2				21
1	2		5			12		7	10	8^1			14				9	11^2	6^3	4		13		3					22
1	2		5			13		7	8^2	11^3							9	10	6	3				14	12	4^1			23
1		3			14	13	6		10	8							11	9^1	7^3	5^2				12	2	4			24
1	14	3				13	4		10	8^2							11^3	9^1	7	5				12	2	6			25
1	14	3				13	4		10^1	8^3							11	9	7^2	5				12	2	6			26
1	12	3				14	4		10	8							11	9^2	7^3	5^1				13	2	6			27
1	2*	6	13			12	4			8^2			14				11	10	7					9^3	3^1	5			28
1		3					6	4	8^1	7						13	10^2	9^3	11	5				12	14	2			29
1		3	14					8	13	6			11^3				10	9	7^2	5				12	2^1	4			30
	12	3					6	9	8								10^2	11	7^1					13	2	4		1	31
	6	3				12		8	9^2	4^1		10		7		13	11	14		5				2^3				1	32
		3			14	13	6	9^1	8^3	10			4				11	7	12	5				2^2				1	33
	2		7	5^1	6^2	3	10^3			11							9	13	4		14	12	8					1	34
1	5	14						8	13	10^3		7		12			9^2	11	6	3^1					4	2			35
1	14	5						12	4	8		10^2	3				7^3	9	11	6^1				13	2				36

HAMILTON ACADEMICAL   Premier League

Year Formed: 1874. *Ground:* New Douglas Park, Cadzow Avenue, Hamilton ML3 0FT. *Telephone:* 01698 368652.
Fax: 01698 285422. *E-mail:* scott@acciesfc.co.uk *Website:* www.acciesfc.co.uk
Ground Capacity: 6078. *Size of Pitch:* 115yd × 75yd.
Chairman: Ronnie MacDonald. *Vice-Chairman:* Les Gray. *Chief Executive:* George W. Fairley. *Commercial:* Arthur
Lynch/John Vint. *Secretary:* Scott A. Struthers BA. *Commercial Manager:* Derek McQuade.
Manager: Billy Reid. *Assistant Manager:* John McCormack. *First Team Coach:* Stuart Taylor. *Goalkeeper Coach:* Brian
Potter. *Physio:* Alan Rankin. *Sports Science Coach:* Ross Hughes. *Sports Therapist:* Avril Downs.
Club Nickname(s): The Accies. *Previous Grounds:* Bent Farm, South Avenue, South Haugh, Douglas Park, Cliftonhill
Stadium, Firhill Stadium.
Record Attendance: 28,690 v Hearts, Scottish Cup 3rd rd, 3 Mar 1937.
Record Transfer Fee received: £380,000 for Paul Hartley to Millwall (July 1996).
Record Transfer Fee paid: £60,000 for Paul Martin from Kilmarnock (Oct 1988) and for John McQuade from Dumbarton
(Aug 1993).
Record Victory: 11-1 v Chryston, Lanarkshire Cup, 28 Nov 1885.
Record Defeat: 1-11 v Hibernian, Division I, 6 Nov 1965.
Most Capped Player: Colin Miller, 29, Canada, 1988-94.
Most League Appearances: 452: Rikki Ferguson, 1974-88.
Most League Goals in Season (Individual): 35: David Wilson, Division I; 1936-37.
Most Goals Overall (Individual): 246: David Wilson, 1928-39.

HAMILTON ACADEMICAL 2008–09 LEAGUE RECORD

Match No.	Date	Venue	Opponents	Result	H/T Score	Lg. Pos.	Goalscorers	Atten- dance
1	Aug 11	H	Dundee U	W 3-1	2-1	—	Stevenson [29], McArthur [39], Graham [63]	4385
2	16	A	Inverness CT	W 1-0	1-0	1	Offiong [45]	3595
3	23	A	Kilmarnock	L 0-1	0-1	4		5339
4	30	H	Hearts	L 1-2	0-1	7	Lyle [80]	4210
5	Sept 13	A	Aberdeen	W 2-1	1-1	4	Graham [34], McCarthy [58]	10,865
6	20	H	Hibernian	L 0-1	0-1	6		4058
7	27	A	Falkirk	L 1-4	0-1	7	Olejnik (og) [90]	4734
8	Oct 4	A	Celtic	L 0-4	0-2	9		55,881
9	18	H	St Mirren	L 1-2	1-2	11	Corcoran [27]	3397
10	25	H	Rangers	L 1-3	1-1	12	Easton [26]	4613
11	Nov 1	A	Motherwell	L 0-2	0-1	12		6205
12	8	H	Falkirk	D 1-1	1-0	12	McCarthy [36]	2600
13	12	A	Hearts	L 0-1	0-1	—		12,030
14	16	H	Celtic	L 1-2	1-1	12	Offiong [15]	5550
15	22	A	Dundee U	D 1-1	1-0	12	Offiong [8]	6108
16	29	H	Kilmarnock	W 1-0	0-0	11	Offiong [52]	2903
17	Dec 6	A	Rangers	L 1-7	1-2	12	McArthur [2]	48,282
18	13	A	Hibernian	L 0-2	0-1	12		10,437
19	20	H	Motherwell	W 2-0	1-0	12	McCarthy 2 [45, 67]	3527
20	27	A	St Mirren	L 0-1	0-0	12		4794
21	Jan 3	H	Aberdeen	W 2-0	0-0	10	Mensing (pen) [52], Offiong [78]	4334
22	17	H	Inverness CT	W 1-0	1-0	10	Mensing (pen) [39]	3070
23	25	A	Kilmarnock	W 1-0	0-0	9	Offiong [46]	5063
24	31	A	Hearts	W 2-0	1-0	8	Mensing 2 (1 pen) [12, 52 (p)]	3567
25	Feb 14	A	Motherwell	L 0-1	0-1	8		5917
26	21	A	Falkirk	W 2-1	1-1	8	Mensing [17], McGowan [76]	5307
27	28	H	Rangers	L 0-1	0-1	8		5895
28	Mar 4	H	Hibernian	L 0-1	0-0	—		4046
29	14	A	Aberdeen	L 0-1	0-1	8		10,312
30	21	H	St Mirren	D 0-0	0-0	8		3072
31	Apr 4	A	Celtic	L 0-4	0-2	8		58,961
32	11	H	Dundee U	L 0-1	0-1	9		3025
33	18	A	Inverness CT	D 1-1	1-0	10	Gibson [17]	3646
34	May 2	H	Kilmarnock	W 2-1	1-0	8	McCarthy 2 [5, 55]	3289
35	10	A	Inverness CT	D 1-1	0-0	8	Canning [63]	3623
36	13	H	Falkirk	L 0-1	0-0	—		3710
37	16	A	Motherwell	L 0-3	0-1	9		3383
38	23	A	St Mirren	W 1-0	1-0	9	Mensing [28]	6747

Final League Position: 9

Honours
League Champions: First Division 1903-04, 1985-86, 1987-88, 2007-08; Third Division 2000-01. *Runners-up:* Division II 1903-04, 1952-53, 1964-65; Second Division 1996-97, 2003-04.
Scottish Cup Runners-up: 1911, 1935. *League Cup:* Semi-finalists three times. *League Challenge Cup*: Runners-up 2006.
B&Q Cup Winners: 1991-92, 1992-93.

Club colours: Shirt: Red and white hoops. Shorts: White. Stockings: White.

Goalscorers: *League* (30): McCarthy 6, Mensing 6 (3 pens), Offiong 6, Graham 2, McArthur 2, Canning 1, Corcoran 1, Easton 1, Gibson 1, Lyle 1, McGowan 1, Stevenson 1, own goal 1.
Scottish Cup (4): Swailes 3, Quinn 1.
CIS Cup (5): Ettien 1, Grady 1, Graham 1, Stevenson 1 (pen), Thomas 1.

Cerny T 36	Stevenson T 7	Easton B 35	McLaughlin M 27	Swailes C 22 + 3	Mensing S 33	McArthur J 36	McCarthy J 34 + 4	Graham D 11 + 5	Offiong R 24 + 6	Neil A 33	Corcoran M 3 + 10	Akins L 4 + 7	Lyle D 8 + 13	Elebert D 14 + 3	Thomas J 10 + 16	Canning M 29 + 1	Sorsa S 2	Ettien S — + 6	McClenahan T 20 + 3	Casement C — + 1	Gibson J 7 + 10	Murdoch S 2 + 2	McGowan P 11 + 3	McMillan J 3 + 1	Deuchar K 3 + 6	Quinn R — + 2	Evans G 2 + 1	Mills S 1	Asamoah D 1 + 2	Taylor S — + 2	Match No.
1	2	3	4	5	6	7	8	9^1	10^2	11	12	13																			1
1	2	3	4	5	6	7	8^3	9^1	10^2	11	12	13	14																		2
1	2	3	4^2	5	6^3	7	8	9	10	11^1			14		13	12															3
1	2	3		5^1	6	7	12		10	11			14	8^2	13	4	9^3														4
1	2^1	3			6	7	12	9^3	10^2	11		13	14			4	5	8													5
1		3			2	7	8	9^1	10^2	11	12			6	13	5	4^3	14													6
1	2^3	3			11	7	8	9	12	10^2	6	4^1	5	13	14																7
1		3		5^1	2	7	8	9^3	11	12	10^2	6	14	4	13																8
1		3		5	2^1	7	8	9^2	10	11	4^3	14	6	13	12																9
1		3		5	2^3	7	8	12	14	4	13	9^2	6	11	10^1																10
1		3			7	6	12	10^3	8^1	11	9^2	4	14	5	13	2															11
1		3	4	5		7	8	13	10^1	11	6^2	9^3	14	12	2																12
1		3	4		6	7^2	8	9	12	11	10^1	14	5	2^3	13																13
1		3	4	5^3	9	7	8	13	10^2	11^1	12	14	6^4	2																	14
1	11	4	5	6^4	7	8		10^1	9	12	$2^?$	3	13	2																	15
1		3	4	5		7	8^3	9^1	10^2	11	13	12	6	2	14																16
1		3	4	5	10	7	8^2	12		11	14	9^3	6^4	2^1	13																17
1	11	4	5^2	6	7	8		10			9^1	3	12	13	2																18
1^6		3	4^1	5	9	7	8		10^2	11	6	13	12	2						15											19
1	2^1	11^3		5^2	9	7	8	14	10		12	4	13	6		3															20
1		3	4^3	14	11	7	8	9^2	10^4		13	2^1	5	6	12																21
1		3	4	12	11	7	8^3		13	14	6^1	10^2	5	2		9															22
1		3	4		6	7	8^3	10^2	11	14	13	5	12			9	2^1														23
1		3	4		11	7	8	10^2	6		12	13	5	2		9^1															24
1		3	4	5^2	9^3	7	8		12	11	14	6	2	13		10^1															25
1		3	4^2	5	9	7	8	10^1	11		2	13	6	12																	26
1		3		5^1	9	7	8	10	6		13	4^3	2^2	12	11	14															27
1		3	5		9	7^3	12	8	14	4	6	11^2	2	10^1	13																28
1		4				7^3	8	14	11	10^2	9	5	3	6^1	2	12	13														29
1^4		4	5		7	8^6	11		9		6	3	15	12	13	10^1	2^2														30
	3	2		7	8		11		9	5	13	4	1							6^2	10^1	12									31
1	3^1	4	5^3	9	7	8	11		13	6	2	12	10^2			14															32
1		4	11^3	7	8		6	12	9^1	5	2	3	10^2	13	14																33
1	3	4	11	7	8^3		10	6	14	12	5	2^2	13	9^1																	34
1	3	4^1	13	6	7^4	12	10	11	9	5^2	2	14															8^3				35
1	3	4		7	8	10^1	11	12	5	2	6^3	9^2	13															14			36
1	3	4	5^1	11	7^3	8	2	10	9^2	6	13	12																14			37
	3	4	2	7	8^2	10^1	11	12	6	9	5	13	1																		38

HEART OF MIDLOTHIAN   Premier League

Year Formed: 1874. *Ground & Address:* Tynecastle Stadium, Gorgie Rd, Edinburgh EH11 2NL. *Telephone:* 0871 663 1874. *Fax:* 0131 200 7222. *E-mail:* hearts@homplc.co.uk *Website:* www.heartsfc.co.uk
Ground Capacity: 17,402. *Size of Pitch:* 100m × 64m.
Chairman: Roman Romanov. *Managing Director:* Campbell Ogilvie.
Manager: Csaba Laszlo. *Coach:* Stephen Frail. *Physio:* Alan Rae.
Club Nickname(s): Hearts, Jambos. *Previous Grounds:* The Meadows 1874, Powderhall 1878, Old Tynecastle 1881, (Tynecastle Park, 1886).
Record Attendance: 53,396 v Rangers, Scottish Cup 3rd rd, 13 Feb 1932 (57,857 v Barcelona, 28 July 2007 at Murrayfield).
Record Transfer Fee received: £9,000,000 for Craig Gordon to Sunderland (August 2008).
Record of Transfer paid: £850,000 for Mirsad Beslija to Celtic (January 2006).
Record Victory: 21-0 v Anchor, EFA Cup, 30 Oct 1880.
Record Defeat: 1-8 v Vale of Leven, Scottish Cup, 1888.
Most Capped Player: Bobby Walker, 29, Scotland.
Most League Appearances: 515: Gary Mackay, 1980-97.
Most League Goals in Season (Individual): 44: Barney Battles, 1930-31.
Most Goals Overall (Individual): 214: John Robertson, 1983-98.

HEART OF MIDLOTHIAN 2008–09 LEAGUE RECORD

Match No.	Date	Venue	Opponents	Result	H/T Score	Lg. Pos.	Goalscorers	Attendance
1	Aug 9	H	Motherwell	W 3-2	2-1	—	Stewart M [25], Ksanavicius [40], Mikoliunas [82]	14,219
2	16	A	Rangers	L 0-2	0-1	7		48,191
3	23	H	St Mirren	W 2-1	1-0	5	Mole [45], Stewart M (pen) [75]	13,357
4	30	A	Hamilton A	W 2-1	1-0	3	Zaliukas [18], Driver [59]	4210
5	Sept 13	A	Falkirk	L 1-2	0-1	5	Stewart M [71]	5960
6	20	H	Inverness CT	W 1-0	1-0	3	Mikoliunas [8]	12,890
7	27	H	Dundee U	L 0-3	0-1	3		8004
8	Oct 4	H	Kilmarnock	L 1-2	1-1	5	Kingston [34]	13,189
9	19	A	Hibernian	D 1-1	1-1	5	Aguair [42]	17,223
10	25	H	Aberdeen	D 1-1	1-1	5	Wallace [21]	14,265
11	Nov 2	H	Celtic	L 0-2	0-2	8		15,460
12	8	A	St Mirren	W 1-0	0-0	4	Jonsson [79]	4192
13	12	H	Hamilton A	W 1-0	1-0	—	Nade [6]	12,030
14	15	A	Inverness CT	W 1-0	1-0	3	Aguair [22]	4011
15	22	H	Falkirk	W 2-1	1-1	3	Aguair [18], Driver [59]	13,009
16	29	H	Rangers	W 2-1	2-1	3	Zaliukas [20], Kingston [23]	15,710
17	Dec 13	A	Celtic	D 1-1	1-0	4	Driver [23]	56,079
18	20	H	Dundee U	D 0-0	0-0	4		16,442
19	27	A	Aberdeen	L 0-1	0-1	4		18,021
20	Jan 3	H	Hibernian	D 0-0	0-0	4		17,244
21	7	A	Motherwell	L 0-1	0-1	—		4928
22	17	A	Kilmarnock	W 2-0	0-0	5	Aguair [61], Karipidis [80]	5469
23	24	H	Inverness CT	W 3-2	1-0	4	Obua 2 [39, 79], Kingston [90]	13,224
24	31	A	Hamilton A	L 0-2	0-1	4		3567
25	Feb 14	H	Aberdeen	W 2-1	1-1	3	Nade [45], Driver [66]	15,049
26	21	H	St Mirren	D 1-1	0-0	3	Jonsson [78]	13,609
27	28	A	Dundee U	W 1-0	0-0	3	Stewart M [62]	8529
28	Mar 4	H	Motherwell	W 2-1	0-0	—	Driver [50], Palazuelos [90]	13,306
29	14	A	Hibernian	L 0-1	0-1	3		15,091
30	21	A	Rangers	D 2-2	0-2	3	Karipidis [64], Palazuelos [67]	50,310
31	Apr 4	H	Kilmarnock	W 3-1	2-1	3	Elliot 2 [22, 29], Aguair [49]	13,659
32	11	H	Celtic	D 1-1	1-1	3	Aguair [32]	16,514
33	18	A	Falkirk	D 0-0	0-0	3		6156
34	May 3	A	Rangers	L 0-2	0-1	3		49,663
35	7	H	Hibernian	L 0-1	0-0	—		14,714
36	12	A	Aberdeen	D 0-0	0-0	—		11,588
37	16	H	Dundee U	W 3-0	2-0	3	Wallace [11], Aguair [26], Jonsson (pen) [79]	15,664
38	24	A	Celtic	D 0-0	0-0	3		59,685

Final League Position: 3

Honours
League Champions: Division I 1894-95, 1896-97, 1957-58, 1959-60. First Division 1979-80; *Runners-up:* Division I 1893-94, 1898-99, 1903-04, 1905-06, 1914-15, 1937-38, 1953-54, 1956-57, 1958-59, 1964-65. Premier Division 1985-86, 1987-88, 1991-92; *Runners-up:* 2005-06. First Division 1977-78, 1982-83.
Scottish Cup Winners: 1891, 1896, 1901, 1906, 1956, 1998, 2006; *Runners-up:* 1903, 1907, 1968, 1976, 1986, 1996.
League Cup Winners: 1954-55, 1958-59, 1959-60, 1962-63; *Runners-up:* 1961-62, 1996-97.

European: *European Cup:* 8 matches (1958-59, 1960-61, 2006-07). *Cup Winners' Cup:* 10 matches (1976-77, 1996-97, 1998-99). *UEFA Cup:* 47 matches (*Fairs Cup:* 1961-62, 1963-64, 1965-66. *UEFA Cup:* 1984-85, 1986-87, 1988-89, 1990-91, 1992-93, 1993-94, 2000-01, 2003-04, 2004-05, 2006-07).

Club colours: Shirt: Maroon. Shorts: White. Stockings: Maroon.

Goalscorers: *League* (40): Aguair 7, Driver 5, Stewart M 4 (1 pen), Jonsson 3 (1 pen), Kingston 3, Elliot 2, Karipidis 2, Mikoliunas 2, Nade 2, Obua 2, Palazuelos 2, Wallace 2, Zaliukas 2, Ksanavicius 1, Mole 1.
Scottish Cup (2): Glen 1, Nade 1.
CIS Cup (0).

Banks S 1	Thomson J 8+3	Wallace L 34	Berra C 23	Karipidis C 34	Zaliukas M 28	Kingston L 15+4	Stewart M 33+1	Ksanavicius A 4+5	Mole J 8+6	Driver A 29	Cesnauskis D 2+11	Makela J —+4	Mikoliunas S 6+6	MacDonald J 6+1	Nade C 20+16	Kello M 13	Obua D 21+6	Palazuelos R 18+7	Jonsson E 27+3	Mrowiec A 6+4	Tullberg M 2+5	Balogh J 18+1	Aguair B 26	Nielson R 25+2	Glen G 2+6	Elliot C 8+4	Templeton D 1+2	Stewart J —+1	Novikovas A —+1	Match No.
1	2	3	4	5	6	7^3	8	9^2	10	11^1	12	13	14																	1
	2	3	4	5	6	7^2	8	9^1	10^3	11			14	13■		1	12													2
	2	3^1	4	5	6	9^3	8	14	10^2	11	12			13		1	7													3
		3	4	5	6	7^3	8	13	10^1	11					12	1	9^2	14	2											4
		3	4	5^3	6	7	8	12	10^2				11^1	13		1		14	2	9										5
		3	4	5	6	7	8^3	9^1	10				11^2		12	1	13		2	14										6
		3	4	5	6	11	8^3	9^1	10^2				7		12	1	13	14	2■											7
	2	3	4	5	6	7	8	12	10^1			14	11^3		13	1				9^2										8
13		3	4	5	6	9^1	8				12		11		10^2	1^6			2					15	7					9
		3	4	5	6		8	14		11^3	12	13	7^2		10^1	1	9		2											10
		3	4	5	6■		8					13	11	7^1	12	1	10^2	14	2	9^1										11
	2	3	4				8■					13	11^3		9^1		10^2	14	5	6		1		7	12					12
		3	4	5	6							13	11		10^2			9^1	8	2		1		7	12					13
		3	4	5	6		8					13	11^1		10^2			12	2			1		7	9					14
		3	4	5	6							13	11		10^2		12	7^1	8			1		9	2					15
		3^1	4	5	6	7^1						13	11		10^3	1		14	8	12				9^2	2					16
		3	4	5	6	7^1		14				13	11		10^3		12		8	2		1		9^2	3					17
		3	4	5	6	7		14				13	11		10^1		12^2		8			1		9^3	2					18
		3	4	5	6■	7^1	9						11		10^2		8	12				1		2	13					19
3^1			4	5		7^2	8						11	13	9		10	6				1		2	12					20
3^3			4		6	8		14					11		10^1		9^2	5	7			1		2	13	12				21
3			4	5		8							11^1	12	12	1	10	9	6					7^2	2	13				22
		3	4	5		13	8						11		10^2	1		9	6					7^1	2	12				23
3				5	6	12	8						11		10^2	1		9	4					7^1	2^3	13	14			24
		3		5		8							11		10^2		7	12	6	13		1	4	2	9^1					25
	2	3				12^2	8^3						11	14	10		7	13	5			1	4	6	9^1					26
		3		5		8							11	12			7	6	4	9^1		1	10	2						27
		3		5		10							11^3	14	12		9	8	6	4^1		1		7^2	2	13				28
		3		5		8^2							11^1	12	15	10	7	4	6	13		1■	9^6	2						29
		3		5	6		8						7^1		10^2	1	9	4				13		11	2	12				30
		3		5	6	8^1							11	13	12		7	4		14		1	10^3	2	9^2					31
		3		5	6	8							11	12			7	4	13			1	10^2	2	9^1					32
		3		5	6	8^1							11	12	1	9	4		13			7	2	10^2						33
				5	6	13	8						11	12	1	7^2	3		10^1			4	2	9						34
		3		5■	6	8							11	12	1	7	4^1	13				10	2	9^2						35
13		3			6■	10^1	8						14	1	7	5	4^4				11	2		9^3	12^2					36
14		3		5^3		10^1							12	1	7	6	4	11		8^2	2		9	13						37
		3		5	6^3	8						13	1	11	7	4				2				9^2	10^1	14	12			38

HIBERNIAN   Premier League

Year Formed: 1875. *Ground & Address:* Easter Road Stadium, Albion Rd, Edinburgh EH7 5QG. *Telephone:* 0131 661 2159. *Fax:* 0131 659 6488. *E-mail:* club@hibernianfc.co.uk *Website:* www.hibernianfc.co.uk
Ground Capacity: total: 17,400. *Size of Pitch:* 112yd × 74yd.
Chairman: Rod Petrie. *Chief Executive:* Scott Lindsay. *Club Secretary:* Garry O'Hagan. *Commercial and Communications Director:* Fife Hyland.
Manager: John Hughes. *Assistant Manager:* Brian Rice. *Goalkeeping Coach:* Gordon Marshall. *Reserve Team Coach:* Gareth Evans. *Physio:* Colin McLelland.
Club Nickname(s): Hibees. *Previous Grounds:* Meadows 1875-78, Powderhall 1878-79, Mayfield 1879-80, First Easter Road 1880-92, Second Easter Road 1892-.
Record Attendance: 65,860 v Hearts, Division I, 2 Jan 1950.
Record Victory: 22-1 v 42nd Highlanders, 3 Sept 1881.
Record Defeat: 0-10 v Rangers, 24 Dec 1898.
Most Capped Player: Lawrie Reilly, 38, Scotland.
Most League Appearances: 446: Arthur Duncan.
Most League Goals in Season (Individual): 42: Joe Baker, 1959-60.
Most Goals Overall (Individual): 364: Gordon Smith, 1941-1959.

HIBERNIAN 2008–09 LEAGUE RECORD

Match No.	Date		Venue	Opponents		Result	H/T Score	Lg. Pos.	Goalscorers	Atten- dance
1	Aug	9	A	Kilmarnock	L	0-1	0-0	—		6168
2		16	H	Falkirk	W	3-2	2-1	6	Nish 2 [1, 25], Hanlon [47]	12,445
3		23	A	Inverness CT	D	1-1	0-1	7	Nish [46]	4022
4		30	H	Motherwell	L	0-1	0-0	8		11,285
5	Sept	13	H	Dundee U	W	2-1	1-1	7	Fletcher 2 [22, 63]	13,390
6		20	A	Hamilton A	W	1-0	1-0	4	Riordan [39]	4058
7		28	H	Rangers	L	0-3	0-2	6		15,292
8	Oct	4	A	Aberdeen	W	2-1	1-1	4	Riordan 2 (1 pen) [33, 80 (p)]	10,793
9		19	H	Hearts	D	1-1	1-1	4	Fletcher [2]	17,223
10		25	A	Celtic	L	2-4	1-2	6	Fletcher 2 [41, 50]	58,337
11	Nov	1	A	St Mirren	D	0-0	0-0	6		4588
12		8	H	Inverness CT	L	1-2	0-1	7	Riordan [90]	11,688
13		12	A	Dundee U	L	0-2	0-0	—		7490
14		15	H	Aberdeen	D	2-2	0-1	9	Jones [62], Fletcher [90]	11,640
15		22	A	Motherwell	W	4-1	1-1	5	Rankin [6], Shiels [50], Fletcher [61], Riordan [90]	4957
16		29	A	Falkirk	D	1-1	0-0	6	Nish [82]	6260
17	Dec	7	H	Celtic	W	2-0	0-0	5	Rankin [55], Nish [69]	14,289
18		13	H	Hamilton A	W	2-0	1-0	5	Riordan [42], Jones [88]	10,437
19		20	A	Rangers	L	0-1	0-0	6		49,538
20		27	H	Kilmarnock	L	2-4	2-2	6	Shiels 2 (2 pens) [36, 40]	12,117
21	Jan	3	A	Hearts	D	0-0	0-0	6		17,244
22		17	H	St Mirren	W	2-0	1-0	6	Jones [14], Riordan [84]	10,317
23		24	A	Celtic	L	1-3	1-2	6	Jones [17]	58,930
24		31	H	Motherwell	D	1-1	1-0	6	Riordan [7]	10,903
25	Feb	14	A	Kilmarnock	D	1-1	1-0	6	Riordan [45]	4649
26		21	A	Inverness CT	L	0-2	0-1	7		4116
27		28	H	Falkirk	D	0-0	0-0	7		10,682
28	Mar	4	A	Hamilton A	W	1-0	0-0	—	Fletcher [80]	4046
29		14	H	Hearts	W	1-0	1-0	6	Fletcher [14]	15,091
30		21	H	Aberdeen	D	0-0	0-0	6		11,754
31	Apr	4	A	Dundee U	D	2-2	2-0	6	Nish 2 [6, 10]	6623
32		13	A	St Mirren	D	1-1	1-1	—	Fletcher [45]	5151
33		19	H	Rangers	L	2-3	1-1	6	Fletcher [34], Rankin [84]	14,014
34	May	2	H	Dundee U	L	1-2	1-1	6	Fletcher [40]	10,591
35		7	A	Hearts	W	1-0	0-0	—	Riordan (pen) [79]	14,714
36		13	H	Rangers	D	1-1	1-0	—	Riordan [41]	13,765
37		17	H	Celtic	D	0-0	0-0	6		14,074
38		24	A	Aberdeen	L	1-2	1-2	6	Riordan [45]	14,083

Final League Position: 6

Honours
League Champions: Division I 1902-03, 1947-48, 1950-51, 1951-52. First Division 1980-81, 1998-99. Division II 1893-94, 1894-95, 1932-33; *Runners-up:* Division I 1896-97, 1946-47, 1949-50, 1952-53, 1973-74, 1974-75.
Scottish Cup Winners: 1887, 1902; *Runners-up:* 1896, 1914, 1923, 1924, 1947, 1958, 1972, 1979, 2001.
League Cup Winners: 1972-73, 1991-92, 2006-07; *Runners-up:* 1950-51, 1968-69, 1974-75, 1993-94, 2003-04.

European: *European Cup:* 6 matches (1955-56 semi-finals). *Cup Winners' Cup:* 6 matches (1972-73). *UEFA Cup:* 63 matches (*Fairs Cup:* 1960-61 semi-finals, 1961-62, 1962-63, 1965-66, 1967-68, 1968-69, 1970-71. *UEFA Cup:* 1973-74, 1974-75, 1975-76, 1976-77, 1978-79, 1989-90, 1992-93, 2001-02, 2005-06).

Club colours: Shirt: Green with white sleeves and collar. Shorts: White with green stripe. Stockings: White with green trim.

Goalscorers: *League* (42): Fletcher 12, Riordan 12 (2 pens), Nish 7, Jones 4, Rankin 3, Shiels 3 (2 pens), Hanlon 1.
Scottish Cup (0).
CIS Cup (3): Keenan 1, Pinao 1, Shiels 1.

McNeil A 5+1	Van Zanten D 26+3	Hanlon P 6+1	Thicot S 15+5	Jones R 32	Hogg C 31	O'Brien A 14+10	Nish C 27+4	Fletcher S 34	Shiels D 16+3	Keenan J 9+6	Chisholm R 10+9	Morais F —+2	Yantorno F 1+6	Murray I 23+5	Rankin J 30+3	Campbell R —+2	Stevenson L 26+3	Pinau S —+8	Ma-Kalambay Y 21	Canning M 1	Zemmmama M —+1	Riordan D 28+4	Bamba S 29	Johansson J 5+4	Szamotulski G 12	McCormack D 7+1	Rosa D 10+2	Match No.
1	2	3	4¹	5	6	7²	8	9	10	11³	12	13	14															1
1	2	3		5	6	7²	8	9	10³	11¹			14	12	4	13												2
1	2	3²		5	6	7¹	8	9	10	11³				12	4	13	14											3
	2				6		8	9	10	11				4²	7¹		3	13	1			5	12					4
	2			5	6		8³	9	10²	7¹	13			4	14		3		1			12	11■					5
	2			5	6		8²	9¹	10³	11			14	4	7		3	13	1			12						6
	2			5	6			9	10²	11¹				13	7	14	3	12	1			8³	4					7
	2		4¹	5			8	9			12				3		7	11	1			10	6					8
	2		4¹	5			8	9		7				12	11		3		1			10	6					9
	2			5			8	9		7				4	11		3		1			10	6					10
	2			5			8²	9		7³			14	12	4	11¹	3	13	1			10	6					11
15	2			5	6²		8	9¹		7				11	3		13	12	1⁶			10	4					12
1			4	5		7	8¹	9²		11³	12			3	2	14			13			10	6					13
1			4¹	5	6		8	9		11²	12	13			7		3					10	2					14
	2			5	6		8²	9¹		11	12		14		7		3	13	1			10	4³					15
	2			5	6		8¹	9		7	12	13		4	11				1			10²	3					16
	2		4²	5	6	7¹	8	9				13		3	10	12			1			11						17
	2		4	5	6	7	8	9¹							10		3		1			12	11					18
	2		4²	5	6	7	8¹	9						13	3		11	12	1			10						19
	2²			5¹	6	7	8	9		11	12			14	3	10³			1			13	4					20
	2		4		6	7¹		9			12			5			3		1			10	11	8				21
			4¹	5	6		8		13		12				10		3					9	11	7²	1	2		22
			4	5	6		8¹	9³					14		7		3					10²	11	12	1	2	13	23
	14	3		5	6	7¹	8²		13		12			9	11							10			1	2³	4	24
		3		5¹	6		8				12			9	7							10	4		1	2	11	25
				5	6			9	13	11¹	12		14				3					10	4	8	1	2³	7²	26
				5	6		8	9		11²	12						3					10	4	7¹	1	2	13	27
				5			8	9	13	11²	12				7		3					10	4		1	2¹	6	28
				5	6	7²	8¹	9	13		12			14	11		3					10³		2■	1	4		29
	2			5	6	7	8	9			12				11		3¹					10			1	4		30
				5	6		8	9		11	12			13	7		3					10²		2¹	1	4		31
				5	6	7¹	8	9²					14	13	11		3					10	4	12	1	2³		32
	2²			5	6		8¹	9	13						11		3					10	4	12	1	7		33
	2²		4		6			9			12			5	11		3		1			10		8		13	7¹	34
	2		4		6	7		9		11¹	12			5	8		3		1			10						35
	2			5	6	7		9¹	13		12			8	11		3		1			10	4²					36
	2		4	5		7		9	13		12			11	8		3		1			10²	6¹					37
	2		4	5¹		7		9²			12			6■	11		3		1			10	8	13				38

INVERNESS CALEDONIAN THISTLE
First Division

Year Formed: 1994. *Ground & Address:* Tulloch Caledonian Stadium, East Longman, Inverness IV1 1FF. *Telephone:* 01463 222880. *Fax:* 01463 227479. *E-mail:* jim.falconer@ictfc.co.uk *Website:* www.ictfc.co.uk
Ground Capacity (seated): 7780. *Size of Pitch:* 115yd × 75yd.
Chairman: George Fraser. *President:* John MacDonald. *Chief Executive:* Mike Smith. *Secretary:* Jim Falconer.
Commercial Manager: Darren Mackintosh. *Football and Community Development Manager:* Danny MacDonald.
Director of Football: Graeme Bennett.
Manager: Terry Butcher. *Assistant Manager:* Maurice Malpas. *First Team Coach:* John Docherty. *Physio:* David Brandie.
Record Attendance: 7753 v Rangers, SPL, 20 January 2008.
Record Victory: 8-1, v Annan Ath, Scottish Cup 3rd rd, 24 January 1998.
Record Defeat: 1-5, v Morton, First Division, 12 November 1999 and v Airdrieonians, First Division, 15 April 2000.
Most League Appearances: 476: Ross Tokely, 1995-2009.
Most League Goals in Season: 27: Iain Stewart, 1996-97; Denis Wyness, 2002-03.
Most Goals Overall (Individual): 118: Denis Wyness, 2000-03, 2005-08.

INVERNESS CALEDONIAN TH 2008–09 LEAGUE RECORD

Match No.	Date		Venue	Opponents	Result	H/T Score	Lg. Pos.	Goalscorers	Attendance
1	Aug	9	A	Aberdeen	W 2-0	1-0	—	Barrowman 27, McBain 90	12,659
2		16	H	Hamilton A	L 0-1	0-1	5		3595
3		23	H	Hibernian	D 1-1	1-0	6	Cowie 21	4022
4		30	A	Falkirk	W 2-1	0-0	5	Cowie 68, Imrie 85	4730
5	Sept	13	H	St Mirren	L 1-2	1-0	6	Rooney (pen) 43	3501
6		20	A	Hearts	L 0-1	0-1	7		12,890
7		27	H	Kilmarnock	W 3-1	2-1	4	McGuire 21, Barrowman (pen) 43, Black 81	3426
8	Oct	4	A	Dundee U	L 1-2	0-1	7	Wilkie (og) 90	6279
9		18	H	Celtic	L 1-2	0-0	8	Wood 69	7143
10		25	H	Motherwell	L 1-2	0-0	10	Rooney 47	3110
11	Nov	1	A	Rangers	L 0-5	0-5	11		49,255
12		8	A	Hibernian	W 2-1	1-0	9	Cowie 30, Black 47	11,688
13		12	H	Falkirk	D 1-1	0-1	—	Rooney 80	3111
14		15	H	Hearts	L 0-1	0-1	10		4011
15		22	A	Kilmarnock	W 2-1	2-0	8	Imrie 14, Wood 38	4328
16		29	A	Celtic	L 0-1	0-1	9		55,117
17	Dec	6	H	Dundee U	L 1-3	0-0	9	Rooney 73	3560
18		13	A	St Mirren	L 0-2	0-1	11		3364
19		20	H	Aberdeen	L 0-3	0-1	11		5862
20		27	A	Motherwell	L 2-3	1-2	11	Tokely 44, Rooney 90	4521
21	Jan	4	H	Rangers	L 0-3	0-0	12		7056
22		17	A	Hamilton A	L 0-1	0-1	12		3070
23		24	A	Hearts	L 2-3	0-1	12	Mihadjuks 56, Imrie 88	13,224
24	Feb	1	H	Celtic	D 0-0	0-0	12		7007
25		14	A	Dundee U	D 1-1	1-0	12	Odhiambo 16	5926
26		21	H	Hibernian	W 2-0	1-0	12	Proctor 15, Foran 65	4116
27		28	H	Motherwell	L 1-2	1-1	12	Munro 39	3611
28	Mar	4	A	Rangers	W 1-0	0-0	—	Black (pen) 90	48,129
29		14	H	Kilmarnock	W 2-1	2-1	11	Foran 19, Black 21	4005
30		21	A	Falkirk	L 0-4	0-1	11		5523
31	Apr	4	H	St Mirren	W 2-1	1-1	—	Morais 2 40, 47	3794
32		11	A	Aberdeen	L 0-1	0-0	11		11,114
33		18	H	Hamilton A	D 1-1	0-1	11	Kerr 88	3646
34	May	2	A	St Mirren	W 2-1	1-0	9	Munro 12, Tokely 84	4171
35		10	H	Hamilton A	D 1-1	0-0	9	Foran 47	3623
36		13	A	Motherwell	D 2-2	1-1	—	Morais 40, Imrie 56	2818
37		16	A	Kilmarnock	L 0-1	0-0	11		6096
38		23	H	Falkirk	L 0-1	0-0	12		6489

Final League Position: 12

Honours
Scottish Cup: Semi-finals 2003, 2004; Quarter-finals 1996.
League Champions: First Division 2003-04. Third Division 1996-97; *Runners-up:* Second Division 1998-99.
League Challenge Cup Winners: 2003-04. *Runners-up:* 1999-2000.

Club colours: Shirts: Royal blue with red. Shorts: Royal blue with red. Stockings: Royal blue.

Goalscorers: *League* (37): Rooney 5 (1 pen), Black 4 (1 pen), Imrie 4, Cowie 3, Foran 3, Morais 3, Barrowman 2 (1 pen), Munro 2, Tokely 2, Wood 2, Kerr 1, McBain 1, McGuire 1, Mihadjuks 1, Odhiambo 1, Proctor 1, own goal 1.
Scottish Cup (5): Morais 2, Mihadjuks 1, Rooney 1, Vigurs 1.
CIS Cup (4): Hastings 1, Imrie 1, Vigurs 1, Wood 1.

Fraser M 17 + 1	Tokely R 36	Hastings R 22 + 3	Duncan R 24 + 3	McGuire P 10 + 1	Munro G 34	Cowie D 21 + 1	Black I 34	Barrowman A 14 + 16	Imrie D 33 + 5	McBain R 21 + 6	Wilson B 1 + 11	McAllister R — + 3	Rooney A 10 + 20	Duff J 7 + 5	Djebi-Zadi L 15 + 1	Vigurs I 12 + 5	Wood G 11 + 7	Proctor D 25 + 1	Esson R 21	Sutherland Z — + 3	Mihadjuks P 12	Morais F 9 + 3	Gathuessi T 1	Foran R 15	Odhiambo E 3 + 5	Kerr G 10	Match No.
1	2	3	4	5	6	7	8[1]	9[2]	10	11	12	13															1
1	2	3	4[1]	5		7[2]	8	9	10	11	13	14	12	6[3]													2
1	2	3		5		7	8	9[3]	4[1]	11[2]	14		10	6	12	13											3
1	2	3		5		7	8	12	14	11[2]	13		9	4[1]		10[3]	6										4
1	2	3		5		7	8	13	12	11[3]	14		9[2]	6		4[1]	10										5
1	2	3		5	6	7	8[2]	9	11		4[3]	13	10[1]			14	12										6
1	2	3	4	5	6	12	8	9[3]	10	11[3]	13		14			7[2]											7
1	2	3			6	7	8[1]	9[3]	10	11[2]	12		13	5		4	14										8
1	2	3	4	5[1]	6	7	8[2]		10	11[3]	14		13	12		9											9
1	2	3	4[3]		6	7	8[1]	14	11		12		9[2]	5		13	10										10
1	2	3	4		6	7	8	9[2]	10	11[1]			13			12	5										11
	2	3	4		6	7	8[1]	13	10[3]	12	14		11			9[2]		5	1								12
	2	3	4		6	7[3]	8	13	10	14	12		11[1]			9[2]		5	1								13
	2	3	4		6		8[1]	9[3]	11	12	7[2]		10		13	14		5	1								14
	2	3	4		6	7	8[2]	12	10[3]	13	11		9[1]			5		1		14							15
	2	3	4		6	7	8[3]	12	10	14	13		11[2]		9[1]	5		1									16
		3	4		6	7	8	9[3]	10[1]		12		2		11[2]	14		5	1	13							17
		3	4	5	6	7	8[1]	9[2]	11[3]	12	13	10				2		1		14							18
	2	3	4[1]		6	7	8		10	11					12	9		5	1								19
	2	3	4	5	6	7		13	10[1]	11					12	9[2]		8	1								20
	2[3]	3	4		6	7	8[1]	9	12	11			13	14		10[2]		5	1								21
	2	3	4[2]		6	7[3]		9[1]	13	11			14			8	12		1		5	10					22
	2		4	13	6	7		8[1]			8	14			9[2]	10[3]	12		1		5	3[1]					23
	2		4		6		8	9[1]	11[3]						12	3	13	7	1		5			10[2]	14		24
	2		4		6		8	11[2]	13						12	3	14	7	1		5			10[3]	9[1]		25
	2				6			10[2]	11						12	3		7	1		5	13	8		9[1]	4	26
	2		4		6		8		11						13	3		7[2]	1		5	12			10	9[1]	27
	2	14	4		6		8		12						9[2]	3		7	1		5	11[1]			10[3]	13	28
	2	12			6		8		11						9[2]	13	3	4	1		5	10[1]				7	29
15	2		4[1]		6		8		12	11					9[2]	3		7	1		5[6]	13			10		30
1	2				6		8		12	11[2]					13	3	3	4			5	9[1]		10		7	31
	2	12			6		8[1]	13	10	14					3		11	1			5	7[2]	9[3]			4	32
	2		4[1]		6		8	13	10						12	3		5	1			11[2]	9			7	33
1	2	14	13		6		8[2]	9[1]	11	5					12	3		4							10[3]	7	34
1	2				6		8	12	11	7[1]					3			5			9[2]			10	13	4	35
1	2				6		8	12	11	4					3		5				9[1]			10		7	36
1	2				6		8	12	11[2]	4[1]					3		5				9			10	13	7	37
1	2[8]	12			6		8[3]	14	11	4[1]					3		5				9[2]			10	13	7	38

KILMARNOCK — Premier League

Year Formed: 1869. *Ground & Address:* Rugby Park, Kilmarnock KA1 2DP. *Telephone:* 01563 545300. *Fax:* 01563 522181. *Website:* www.kilmarnockfc.co.uk
Ground Capacity: all seated: 18,128. *Size of Pitch:* 115yd × 74yd.
Chairman: Michael Johnston. *Secretary:* Kirsten Callaghan..
Manager: Jim Jefferies. *Assistant Manager:* Billy Brown. *Physio:* A. MacQueen.
Club Nickname(s): Killie. *Previous Grounds:* Rugby Park (Dundonald Road); The Grange; Holm Quarry; Present ground since 1899.
Record Attendance: 35,995 v Rangers, Scottish Cup, 10 Mar 1962.
Record Transfer Fee received: £2,000,000 for Stephen Naismith to Rangers (2007).
Record Transfer Fee paid: £300,000 for Paul Wright from St Johnstone (1995).
Record Victory: 11-1 v Paisley Academical, Scottish Cup, 18 Jan 1930 (15-0 v Lanemark, Ayrshire Cup, 15 Nov 1890).
Record Defeat: 1-9 v Celtic, Division I, 13 Aug 1938.
Most Capped Player: Joe Nibloe, 11, Scotland.
Most League Appearances: 481: Alan Robertson, 1972-88.
Most League Goals in Season (Individual): 34: Harry 'Peerie' Cunningham 1927-28; Andy Kerr 1960-61.
Most Goals Overall (Individual): 148: Willy Culley, 1912-23.

KILMARNOCK 2008–09 LEAGUE RECORD

Match No.	Date	Venue	Opponents	Result	H/T Score	Lg. Pos.	Goalscorers	Atten- dance
1	Aug 9	H	Hibernian	W 1-0	0-0	—	Hamill [80]	6168
2	16	A	St Mirren	D 0-0	0-0	4		4176
3	23	H	Hamilton A	W 1-0	1-0	3	Pascali [45]	5339
4	30	A	Dundee U	W 2-0	1-0	2	Skelton [40], Invincibile [59]	6823
5	Sept 13	A	Rangers	L 1-2	1-0	3	Wright [9]	50,019
6	21	H	Celtic	L 1-3	0-1	5	Taouil (pen) [89]	8111
7	27	A	Inverness CT	L 1-3	1-2	5	Sammon [4]	3426
8	Oct 4	A	Hearts	W 2-1	1-1	3	Taouil [19], Bryson [82]	13,189
9	18	H	Motherwell	W 1-0	0-0	3	Bryson [89]	5113
10	25	H	Falkirk	L 1-2	0-1	3	Simmonds [90]	4267
11	Nov 1	A	Aberdeen	L 0-1	0-0	4		10,599
12	9	H	Rangers	L 0-4	0-0	6		10,153
13	12	A	Celtic	L 0-3	0-1	—		55,347
14	15	H	Dundee U	W 2-0	1-0	5	Hamill (pen) [45], Fernandez [61]	4652
15	22	H	Inverness CT	L 1-2	0-2	6	Gibson [85]	4328
16	29	A	Hamilton A	L 0-1	0-0	7		2903
17	Dec 15	A	Motherwell	W 2-0	1-0	—	Pascali [35], Russell [77]	3339
18	20	H	St Mirren	L 0-1	0-1	7		5183
19	27	A	Hibernian	W 4-2	2-2	7	Invincibile 2 [5, 47], Russell [12], Hay [76]	12,117
20	Jan 3	A	Falkirk	D 1-1	0-1	7	Fernandez [68]	5375
21	13	H	Aberdeen	L 1-2	1-1	—	Russell [10]	4354
22	17	H	Hearts	L 0-2	0-0	8		5469
23	25	A	Hamilton A	L 0-1	0-0	8		5063
24	31	A	St Mirren	D 1-1	1-0	9	Kyle [29]	7542
25	Feb 14	H	Hibernian	D 1-1	0-1	9	Hamill [76]	4649
26	21	A	Rangers	L 1-3	1-3	10	Hamill [17]	50,301
27	28	A	Aberdeen	D 0-0	0-0	9		11,457
28	Mar 4	H	Celtic	L 1-2	1-1	—	Invincibile [36]	6712
29	14	A	Inverness CT	L 1-2	1-2	9	Ford [45]	4005
30	21	H	Motherwell	D 0-0	0-0	9		5434
31	Apr 4	A	Hearts	L 1-3	1-2	10	Invincibile [8]	13,659
32	11	H	Falkirk	W 3-0	2-0	8	Kyle 3 [11, 36, 84]	5835
33	18	A	Dundee U	D 0-0	0-0	8		6627
34	May 2	A	Hamilton A	L 1-2	0-1	10	Hamill (pen) [90]	3289
35	9	H	Falkirk	D 1-1	0-0	10	Kyle [67]	5955
36	13	H	St Mirren	W 2-1	1-0	—	Kyle 2 [23, 49]	5927
37	16	A	Inverness CT	W 1-0	0-0	8	Kyle [79]	6096
38	23	A	Motherwell	W 2-1	1-0	8	Invincibile [27], Taouil [90]	4186

Final League Position: 8

Honours

League Champions: Division I 1964-65. Division II 1897-98, 1898-99; *Runners-up:* Division I 1959-60, 1960-61, 1962-63, 1963-64. First Division 1975-76, 1978-79, 1981-82, 1992-93. Division II 1953-54, 1973-74. Second Division 1989-90.
Scottish Cup Winners: 1920, 1929, 1997; *Runners-up:* 1898, 1932, 1938, 1957, 1960.
League Cup Runners-up: 1952-53, 1960-61, 1962-63, 2000-01, 2006-07.

European: *European Cup:* 4 matches (1965-66). *Cup Winners' Cup:* 4 matches (1997-98). *UEFA Cup:* 24 matches (*Fairs Cup:* 1964-65, 1966-67, 1969-70, 1970-71. *UEFA Cup:* 1998-99, 1999-2000, 2001-02).

Club colours: Shirt: Blue and white vertical stripes. Shorts: White. Stockings: White.

Goalscorers: *League* (38): Kyle 8, Invincibile 6, Hamill 5 (2 pens), Russell 3, Taouil 3 (1 pen), Bryson 2, Fernandez 2, Pascali 2, Ford 1, Gibson 1, Hay 1, Sammon 1, Simmonds 1, Skelton 1, Wright 1.
Scottish Cup (5): Ford 2, Bryson 1, Pascali 1, Taouil 1.
CIS Cup (7): Sammon 2, Bryson 1, Fernandez 1, Invincibile 1, Taouil 1 (pen), Wright 1.

Combe A 34	Fowler J 23 + 3	Hay G 30	Pascali M 31 + 1	O'Leary R 1 + 2	Ford S 27	Invincibile D 21 + 4	Bryson C 31 + 2	Fernandez D 28 + 4	Sammon C 10 + 9	Taouil M 30 + 4	Wright F 23 + 4	Hamill J 28 + 5	Skelton G 20 + 7	Simmonds D 4 + 15	Lilley D 20	Murray G 10	Flannigan I 1 + 6	Gibson W 10 + 12	Cox D — + 2	Clancy T 12 + 1	Corrigan M 1	Russell A 8 + 3	Rascle D 3 + 2	Kyle K 11	Anson S — + 1	Bell C 1	Match No.
1	2	3	4	5[1]	6[2]	7	8[3]	9	10	11	12	13	14														1
1	2	3	4		6	7	8	9	10	11[1]	5	12															2
1	2	3	4		6	7	8	9	10[1]	11	5				12												3
1	2	3	4			7	8	9		10		6			11[1]	5		12									4
1	2	3	4[3]		6	7	8	9[2]	12	10	5	14	11[1]	13													5
1	2	3[2]	4		6	7	8	9[3]	12	10	5	13	11[1]	14													6
1	2[4]		4		6[1]	12	8[2]	9	10[3]	11	3	7	14	13	5												7
1			4		6	7	8	9	10[1]	11[2]	5	3	13	12	2												8
1	12		4		6[1]	7[3]	8	9	10[2]	11	5	3		13	2	14											9
1	2[1]		4			7	8	9[2]	10	11	6	3	13	5		12											10
1	2		4				8	9[2]	10[1]	7[3]		11	3	12	5	6	13	14									11
1	2						8	9	13	11	6	4[1]	3	10[2]	5		7	12									12
1	2		4				8[3]		9[1]	5		3	7[2]	14	10	13	11	6	12								13
1	2	3	4		6		8[1]	9[3]	10[2]	11	5	7	14			12			13								14
1[0]	2	3	4		6[2]		8	9		11	5	7		12				10[1]	15								15
	2	3[1]	4		6		8	9[2]		11	5	7		12				10		13	1						16
1	2	3	4			7[1]		13		5	6	11	10		8	12		9[2]									17
1	2	3	4				12	9	14	5[1]	7[2]	11	8		6	13		10[3]									18
1[4]	2	3	4			7		9[2]		8[6]		6	11	13	5		12	10[1]	15								19
	2	3	4			7		12	9		5	6[1]	11	13		8		7		10[2]	1						20
	2	3	4			7	8	9		12	5	6[1]	13			11				10[2]	1						21
1	2	3	4		6	7[2]	8	9		11	5			12				13		10[1]							22
1	2[1]	3[2]	4		6	9	8			11	5	14	13	12		7				10[3]							23
1	2	3	4		6	12	8	9		7[1]	5		11											10			24
1		3	4		6		8		10			9	11		5	2		7									25
1		3[2]	4		6		8			12	5	7	11[1]		10	2		13							9		26
1		3	4		6	13	8	9[3]	14	7[1]		11			5			12[2]		2				10			27
1		3	4		6	7[2]	8	9[1]	12	13		11			5					2				10			28
1		3	4[2]		6[3]	9	8	13		12		7	11[1]		5	14				2				10			29
1		3	4		6	12	8	9[3]	14	11[2]		7[1]	13		5					2				10			30
1		3	4[2]	13	6	7		9[3]		11		8			5	2[1]		12						10	14		31
1		3			6	9	8	12		7		4	11		5					2				10[1]			32
1		3			6[1]	10	8	9[2]		4	12	7	11		5			13		2							33
1		3			6	10[2]	8	9	14	7	12	4	11		5[1]			13		2[3]							34
1		3			6		8			10[1]		4	11		5		12	7		2				9			35
1	13	3			6[1]		8[2]	14		10[3]	12	7	11		5			4		2				9			36
1	2[2]	3	13					12		10	5	8	11		4			7[1]		6				9			37
	13		4[2]	14	6	7		9		10		11	12		5[3]	3[1]	8			2						1	38

LIVINGSTON   First Division

Year Formed: 1974. *Ground:* Almondvale Stadium, Alderton Road, Livingston EH54 7DN. *Telephone:* 01506 417000.
Fax: 01506 418888. *Email:* info@livingstonfc.co.uk *Website:* www.livingstonfc.co.uk
Ground Capacity: 10,005 (all seated). *Size of Pitch:* 107yd × 75yd.
Chairman: Angelo Massone. *Chief Executive:* Vivien Kyles. *General Manager:* David Hay. *Secretary:* M. Kaplan.
Head Coach: John Murphy. *Physios:* Arthur Duncan, Marie McPhail.
Club Nickname: Livi Lions. *Previous Grounds:* None.
Record Attendance: 10,024 v Celtic, Premier League, 18 Aug 2001.
Record Transfer Fee received: £1,000,000 for D. Fernandez to Celtic (June 2002).
Record Transfer Fee paid: £120,000 for Wes Hoolahan from Shelbourne (December 2005).
Record Victory: 7-0 v Queen of the South, Scottish Cup, 29 Jan 2000.
Record Defeat: 0-8 v Hamilton A. Division II, 14 Dec 1974.
Most Capped Player (under 18): I. Little.
Most League Appearances: 446: Walter Boyd, 1979-89.
Most League Goals in Season (Individual): 21: John McGachie, 1986-87. *(Team):* 69; Second Division, 1986-87.
Most Goals Overall (Individual): 64: David Roseburgh, 1986-93.

LIVINGSTON 2008–09 LEAGUE RECORD

Match No.	Date		Venue	Opponents	Result	H/T Score	Lg. Pos.	Goalscorers	Atten- dance
1	Aug	2	A	St Johnstone	L 0-2	0-0	—		2692
2		9	H	Ross Co	W 2-0	1-0	5	Griffiths 12, Talbot 66	1068
3		16	A	Morton	W 2-1	2-1	3	Davidson 10, Griffiths 12	2502
4		23	H	Clyde	W 2-1	1-1	3	McPartland 39, Griffiths 86	1725
5		30	A	Dunfermline Ath	W 2-1	1-0	1	Griffiths 2 41, 74	3414
6	Sept	13	H	Airdrie U	L 1-2	0-1	1	Elliot 90	1710
7		20	A	Dundee	W 3-0	1-0	1	Innes 40, Elliot 2 84, 90	3631
8		27	H	Partick Th	W 3-1	2-1	1	Davidson 6, Elliot 2 18, 82	2150
9	Oct	4	A	Queen of the S	L 1-6	1-3	2	MacKay 25	3266
10		18	H	St Johnstone	L 0-1	0-1	3		2542
11		25	A	Clyde	L 1-2	1-0	4	Elliot 15	820
12	Nov	1	H	Morton	W 1-0	0-0	3	Elliot 76	1733
13		8	A	Airdrie U	D 0-0	0-0	2		1201
14		15	H	Dunfermline Ath	L 2-3	1-1	3	McPake 5, Elliot 61	2326
15		22	A	Partick Th	L 1-2	1-2	4	MacKay (pen) 27	2416
16	Dec	13	A	Ross Co	W 4-1	1-1	4	Davidson 34, Elliot 47, Griffiths 70, Quinn 90	2180
17		20	H	Queen of the S	W 2-0	0-0	3	McPake 51, Elliot 55	1874
18		30	A	Dunfermline Ath	L 0-1	0-0	—		3036
19	Jan	3	H	Airdrie U	D 1-1	0-0	4	Elliot 86	1462
20		17	H	Clyde	D 1-1	1-1	4	Winters 31	1354
21		24	A	Morton	D 2-2	0-2	4	Griffiths 81, Smith (og) 87	2307
22		31	H	Ross Co	W 4-2	3-0	3	One 10, Davidson 18, MacKay (pen) 45, Griffiths 90	1378
23	Feb	7	H	Dundee	L 1-2	0-2	—	McPartland 73	1535
24		14	A	St Johnstone	L 0-1	0-0	—		2752
25		21	A	Dundee	L 1-4	0-0	5	De Vita 90	3679
26		28	H	Partick Th	L 2-4	0-2	5	Griffiths 2 52, 73	2876
27	Mar	7	A	Airdrie U	D 4-4	2-1	6	Griffiths 2 42, 57, One 2 43, 51	1100
28		10	H	Dunfermline Ath	W 4-2	1-0	—	McPartland 22, Davidson 2 65, 68, Griffin 77	1859
29		14	H	St Johnstone	W 1-0	1-0	4	Griffiths 33	1882
30		21	A	Queen of the S	D 3-3	0-1	4	Griffiths 2 (1 pen) 57, 90 (p), Winters 88	2487
31	Apr	4	A	Clyde	W 1-0	1-0	3	Hamill 22	957
32		11	H	Morton	L 0-2	0-0	4		1815
33		18	H	Dundee	L 0-1	0-0	5		1988
34		25	A	Partick Th	L 0-1	0-0	6		2803
35	May	2	A	Ross Co	D 2-2	1-0	7	Griffiths 17, Halliday 51	2567
36		9	H	Queen of the S	D 2-2	2-0	7	Winters 7, Griffiths (pen) 8	1652

Final League Position: 7

Honours
League Champions: First Division 2000-01. Second Division 1986-87, 1998-99. Third Division 1995-96; *Runners-up:* Second Division 1982-83. First Division 1987-88.
Scottish Cup: Semi-finals 2004.
League Cup Winners: 2003-04. Semi-finals 1984-85. *B&Q Cup:* Semi-finals 1992-93, 1993-94, 2001.
League Challenge Cup Runners-up: 2000-01.

European: *UEFA Cup:* 4 matches (2002-03).

Club colours: Shirt: Yellow. Shorts: Black. Stockings: Yellow.

Goalscorers: *League* (56): Griffiths 17 (2 pens), Elliot 11, Davidson 6, MacKay 3 (2 pens), McPartland 3, One 3, Winters 3, McPake 2, De Vita 1, Griffin 1, Halliday 1, Hamill 1, Innes 1, Quinn 1, Talbot 1, own goal 1.
Scottish Cup (1): Fox 1.
CIS Cup (2): Cuenca 1, Griffiths 1.
Challenge Cup (5): Griffiths 3, Hamil 1, McParland 1.

Martini P 12+1	MacKay D 28	Talbot J 24+4	McPake J 18	Fox L 18+2	Innes C 30	McPartland A 36	Davidson M 29	Cuenca J 2+6	Griffiths L 25+2	Hamill J 32+1	Jacobs K 2+14	Smith G 1+3	Millar G 13+10	Quinn R 14+1	Cave P 2+1	McDonald C 12+5	Elliot C 13	Giarrizzo F 2+2	McKenzie R 24	Thomas M 1+1	Halliday A 7+6	Griffin D 17	Sinclair D —+1	Winters D 10+4	One A 12+3	De Vita R 2+5	Torrance M 2+2	Malone C 8	Match No.
1	2	3	4	5	6	7^1	8	9	10	11	12																		1
1	2	3	4	5^3	6	7	8^1	9^2	10	11	12	13	14																2
1	2	3	4	5	6	7	8^1		10	11		12	9																3
1	2	3^2	4	5	6	7^1	8	12	10	11			9		13														4
1	2^2	12	4	5	6	7	8	14	9^3	11			13	10		3^1													5
1	2	3		5^2	6	7^1	8	12		11			10			4	9	13											6
1	2	3	4	12	6	7^2	8^1			11			13	10		9	5												7
1	2	3	4	5	6	7^1	8			11			10			9	12												8
1	2	3	6	5		7^2	8	13	9				11			12	10^8	4^1											9
1	2	3	4	5	6	7^1	8	12		11		9	10																10
1	2		3	8	4	6	7		9				11	5		10													11
	2	3	4	5	6	7^1	8		12	11			10^2	13			9		1										12
	2	3	4	5	6	7	8			11			12	10^1			9		1										13
15	2	3	4	5	6	7	8^1			11			10				9		1^6	12									14
1	2	3	4	5	6	7^1		12		13	14		11^3	10			9		8^2										15
	3	4		6	7^3	5^1	14	10	11	12			2^2	8		13	9		1										16
	2	3	4		6	7	5		10^1	11		12		8			9		1										17
	2	3	4		6	7			10	11	12		5^1	8			9		1										18
	2	3	4		6^3	7	8		10	11^1	5^2		13			14	9		1	12									19
	2	3		6	7	5		9	11^1	8									1	12	4	10							20
	2	3^1	4		7	5	9			13		12		6^2					1		8	10	11						21
	2	12		6	7	5	9			8^1			3						1		4	10	11						22
	2	12		6	7^3	5	9^8		14	8^1			3						1		13	4	10^2	11					23
	2	8^2		6	7	5			9	13			3						1		10	11^1	12						24
	2	3		6	7	5^2	9		8	13									1		14	4	10^3	11^1	12				25
	5	3		7			9	8				2							1		11	4	13	12	10^1	6^2			26
	2^1	10		7	5		9	8	13				6^2					3	1		4			11		12			27
		3^1		6	7	5	9	8	12				2						1		10^3	4		11^2	13	14			28
				6	7	5	9	8					2						1		13	4		11^1	12	10^2	3		29
				5	7^2	6	10	8		13			2^3						1		9^1	4		14	11	12	3		30
2		14	6^1	7^3	5		9	8		12									1		4			10^2	11	13	3		31
2^1		10^2		6	5		9	8		6			12						1		14	4		13	11^3		3		32
			6	7			9	8	12	2			5						1		10^1	4		11			3		33
		5	6	7^3			9^1	8	14				13						2		1			10^2	4	12	11	3	34
		5	6	7			9	8	14				2^3						12		1			11^2	4	10	13	3^1	35
	13			7			9	8	12				2^2						5		1			11^1	4	14	10		36

MONTROSE Third Division

Year Formed: 1879. *Ground & Address:* Links Park, Wellington St, Montrose DD10 8QD. *Telephone:* 01674 673200.
Fax: 01674 677311. *E-mail:* malcolmwatters@btconnect.com *Website:* www.montrosefc.co.uk
Ground Capacity: total: 3292, seated: 1338. *Size of Pitch:* 113yd × 70yd.
Chairman: Brian Winton. *Secretary:* Malcolm J. Watters.
Manager: Steven Tweed. *Physio:* Brian Duncan.
Club Nickname(s): The Gable Endies. *Previous Grounds:* None.
Record Attendance: 8983 v Dundee, Scottish Cup 3rd rd, 17 Mar 1973.
Record Transfer Fee received: £50,000 for Gary Murray to Hibernian (Dec 1980).
Record Transfer Fee paid: £17,500 for Jim Smith from Airdrieonians (Feb 1992).
Record Victory: 12-0 v Vale of Leithen, Scottish Cup 2nd rd, 4 Jan 1975.
Record Defeat: 0-13 v Aberdeen, 17 Mar 1951.
Most Capped Player: Alexander Keillor, 2 (6), Scotland.
Most League Appearances: 432: David Larter, 1987-98.
Most League Goals in Season (Individual): 28: Brian Third, Division II, 1972-73.

MONTROSE 2008–09 LEAGUE RECORD

Match No.	Date	Venue	Opponents	Result	H/T Score	Lg. Pos.	Goalscorers	Attendance
1	Aug 2	A	Dumbarton	D	1-1	1-0	—	Stewart 28	580
2	9	H	Berwick R	D	1-1	1-0	8	McLeod 6	344
3	16	A	Stenhousemuir	D	2-2	2-0	7	Bradley 10, Baird 21	352
4	23	H	Annan Ath	D	1-1	1-0	6	Anson 28	427
5	30	H	Elgin C	W	1-0	0-0	5	Buchan 55	304
6	Sept 13	A	Forfar Ath	W	1-0	0-0	4	Anson 89	518
7	20	H	East Stirling	W	3-0	1-0	2	Anson 11, Buchan 58, Bradley 73	364
8	27	A	Cowdenbeath	L	1-2	1-1	3	Baird 44	296
9	Oct 4	A	Albion R	W	1-0	0-0	3	Bradley 78	237
10	18	H	Dumbarton	L	1-2	0-1	4	Black 90	570
11	Nov 1	H	Stenhousemuir	L	0-3	0-2	5		419
12	8	A	Annan Ath	W	2-1	1-1	4	Bradley 2 13, 71	506
13	15	A	Elgin C	W	2-1	0-0	3	Hunter 2 56, 65	376
14	22	H	Forfar Ath	W	1-0	1-0	2	Davidson 2	465
15	Dec 6	A	East Stirling	L	0-5	0-1	—		427
16	13	H	Cowdenbeath	L	0-1	0-1	5		334
17	20	H	Albion R	L	1-2	1-0	5	Smith 7	321
18	27	A	Berwick R	L	2-3	2-0	5	Black 13, Davidson 43	510
19	Jan 10	H	Elgin C	W	3-1	1-1	—	Hunter 9, Hegarty (pen) 46, Gibson 73	306
20	17	H	Annan Ath	L	0-3	0-1	5		329
21	24	A	Stenhousemuir	W	3-1	1-1	4	Ovenstone (og) 21, Hunter 2 47, 75	447
22	31	A	Dumbarton	D	1-1	0-1	3	Hunter 54	652
23	Feb 7	H	Berwick R	D	1-1	1-0	—	Gibson 15	318
24	21	A	East Stirling	L	0-2	0-0	5		400
25	28	A	Elgin C	L	0-1	0-0	5		364
26	Mar 7	H	Forfar Ath	L	1-3	0-1	7	Cox 86	530
27	14	H	Dumbarton	W	1-0	0-0	6	McKenzie 55	343
28	17	A	Cowdenbeath	L	1-2	1-2	—	McKenzie 27	303
29	21	A	Albion R	W	1-0	0-0	7	Nicol 79	263
30	28	A	Forfar Ath	W	3-0	1-0	7	Cox 26, Davidson 57, Stewart 90	621
31	Apr 4	A	Annan Ath	L	1-2	1-1	7	O'Reilly 25	617
32	11	H	Stenhousemuir	W	5-3	2-0	7	Tweed 4, O'Reilly 2 13, 71, Hunter 2 80, 81	358
33	18	A	East Stirling	L	1-2	0-1	7	Hunter 65	401
34	25	H	Cowdenbeath	W	2-1	0-1	7	Tweed 65, Hegarty (pen) 72	403
35	May 2	A	Berwick R	W	1-0	0-0	5	Bradley 52	418
36	9	H	Albion R	W	1-0	1-0	5	Pope 14	324

Final League Position: 5

Honours
League Champions: Second Division 1984-85; *Runners-up:* Second Division 1990-91. Third Division 1994-95.
Scottish Cup: Quarter-finals 1973, 1976.
League Cup: Semi-finals 1975-76.
B&Q Cup: Semi-finals 1992-93.
League Challenge Cup: Semi-finals 1996-97.

Club colours: Shirt: Royal blue. Shorts: Royal blue. Stockings: Royal blue.

Goalscorers: *League* (47): Hunter 9, Bradley 6, Anson 3, Davidson 3, O'Reilly 3, Baird 2, Black 2, Buchan 2, Cox 2, Gibson 2, Hegarty 2 (2 pens), McKenzie 2, Stewart 2, Tweed 2, McLeod 1, Nicol 1, Pope 1, Smith 1, own goal 1.
Scottish Cup (2): Davidson 1, Smith 1.
Challenge Cup (0).

Peat M 3	Worrall D 12+1	McLeod C 13+1	O'Reilly C 8	Buchan J 28	Wright K —+1	Thomson S 11	Maitland J 3+6	Hegarty C 24+4	Davidson H 30	Sinclair A 1	Stein J 1+2	Stewart P 14+17	Black S 30+2	Bradley K 23+9	Nicol D 2+14	Kelly G 16	McLaughlan G 12+1	Anson S 9+1	Hunter R 18+7	Cumming S 1+1	Leyden J —+1	Doris S 5	Baird J 8	Gardiner R —+1	Gibson K 18+2	Hannah D 1	Smith C 7+3	Craig D 4	Stark F 1	Russell M —+2	Adams K —+1	Gray N 1+1	McCay R 2	Crighton S 18	Cox D 10+1	Winton J —+1	Tweed S 15+1	Bullock T 16	Pope G 16	Milligan F 8+1	McKenzie J 7	Match No.
1	2	3		4		5	6¹	7	8		9	10	11²	12	13																											1
	2	3	4	5		7²	8¹	12	9		6	14					1	10	11³	13																						2
	2	4¹	5	3		8	13	14	11³		7						1	9		6	10	12²																					3
	5		4	13	3	8⁴	12	14	9¹		6²						1	10		2	7	11³																					4
	2		4	5	8	7	13	12	9¹		1	3	10				6²	11																								5
	2	5⁴	6	3		8	13	11¹	7²		1	4	12	9	10																											6
	2		4	5	13	8	6		9		14	1	3	10²	7³	11¹	12																									7
	2	13⁴	4	5		7¹	8	6²	9		1	3	10	14	11³	12																										8
	2		5	3	12	8		7			11	1	4	9¹	13	10²	6																									9
	2		5¹	13	12	7	9	6	1		4	10²	11	8																												10
	2	7¹				8	12	9	5		1	4	10	13									6	3	11²																		11
1		5	2	11¹		13	8	12	10³	7		6		14									4²		9	3																12
1	12	5	2	6¹		13	8	14	11²	7		10³										4		9	3																	13
	5	3	2			13	8	12	9	6²		4		11								7		10¹	1																	14
	5	3¹				4	12	11²	7		1	2	10									8	9	6³	14	13																15
	3	2		5	7	6			12	1	4	11⁸									8	10			9¹																	16
	3	5	2	7		11	9	6⁸	12	1	4										8	10¹																				17
	6	2	7³	4		11²	10				1	12	9					8	13				14	3¹	5																	18
	3	5	2	7		6³	11	1			10²	8	13					9¹	4	12	14																					19
	4	5	2	7		6²	9	12	1		11¹	8	13						10	3																						20
		8	2	4		11	12	10¹	7		6	9	5	1	3																			21
		9	2	3		10	12	11¹	7	8	4	5	1	6																			22
		8	6¹	2	7	9	12	11	7	4	10⁸	3	1	5																			23
		8	2	7	13	10²	9¹	12	11	6	4	3	1	5																			24
		5	2³	4	14	11²	7	12	10¹	8	6	9	13	1	3																		25
		8	2	7	12	9³	14	10²	6¹	4	11	3	1	5	13																		26
		8	2¹	12	9²	13	10	4	11	3	1	5	6	7																			27
		8¹	2³	12	9	14	13	11	7	10	4	1	5	6²	3																		28
		9	14	2	8¹	11	12	13	6	10	5³	3	7²	4																			29
		9	2	8	13	11	12	6	10¹	5	1	3	7²	4																			30
		9²	8	2²	9	11	12	13	14	6	10	5	1	3	7¹	4																	31
		10	8	14	4	3	1	5	6¹	7²																							32
		9	2¹	8	12	11	10	7	6	5	1	3	4²																				33
		10	12	2	7	8¹	9	6	11	4	3	1	5																				34
		9¹	2	8	11	7	12	10	6	5	1	3	4																				35
		10⁵	14	2	7	5	12	9	6	11³	13	4	1	3	8¹																		36

MORTON

First Division

Year Formed: 1874. *Ground & Address:* Cappielow Park, Sinclair St, Greenock. *Telephone:* 01475 723571. *Fax:* 01475 781084. *E-mail:* info@gmfc.net *Website:* www.gmfc.net
Ground Capacity: total: 11,612, seated: 6062. *Size of Pitch:* 110yd × 71yd.
Chairman: Douglas Rae. *Chief Executive:* Gillian Donaldson. *Company Secretary:* Mary Davidson. *Commercial Manager:* Susan Gregory.
Manager: Davie Irons. *Assistant Manager:* Martin Clark. *Physios:* Paul Kelly, Bruce Coyle.
Club Nickname(s): The Ton. *Previous Grounds:* Grant Street 1874, Garvel Park 1875, Cappielow Park 1879, Ladyburn Park 1882, (Cappielow Park 1883).
Record Attendance: 23,500 v Celtic, 29 April 1922.
Record Transfer Fee received: £350,000 for Neil Orr to West Ham U.
Record Transfer Fee paid: £150,000 for Alan Mahood from Nottingham Forest (August 1998).
Record Victory: 11-0 v Carfin Shamrock, Scottish Cup 1st rd, 13 Nov 1886.
Record Defeat: 1-10 v Port Glasgow Ath, Division II, 5 May, 1894 and v St Bernards, Division II, 14 Oct 1933.
Most Capped Player: Jimmy Cowan, 25, Scotland.
Most League Appearances: 358: David Hayes, 1969-84.
Most League Goals in Season (Individual): 58: Allan McGraw, Division II, 1963-64.

MORTON 2008–09 LEAGUE RECORD

Match No.	Date	Venue	Opponents	Result	H/T Score	Lg. Pos.	Goalscorers	Atten-dance
1	Aug 2	A	Clyde	D	1-1	1-0	—	Newby [40]	1638
2	9	H	St Johnstone	D	2-2	1-2	6	McGuffie [5], Paartalu [82]	2649
3	16	H	Livingston	L	1-2	1-2	7	Wake [31]	2502
4	23	A	Dundee	L	0-1	0-1	9		4032
5	30	A	Airdrie U	L	0-5	0-3	10		1793
6	Sept 13	H	Queen of the S	D	0-0	0-0	10		2235
7	20	A	Partick Th	L	1-2	1-1	10	Russell [44]	3368
8	27	H	Dunfermline Ath	D	1-1	0-0	10	Wake [60]	2156
9	Oct 4	A	Ross Co	L	0-3	0-0	10		2290
10	18	H	Clyde	W	1-0	1-0	10	Grady [37]	2041
11	25	H	Dundee	W	2-0	1-0	10	Weatherson [26], McGuffie (pen) [59]	1741
12	Nov 1	A	Livingston	L	0-1	0-0	10		1733
13	8	A	Queen of the S	W	4-1	3-0	9	Weatherson 2 [19, 28], Jenkins [37], Greacen [74]	2944
14	22	A	Dunfermline Ath	W	1-0	1-0	8	Paartalu [24]	4400
15	25	H	Airdrie U	W	2-0	1-0	—	Wake [34], Jenkins [90]	1642
16	Dec 13	A	St Johnstone	L	0-1	0-0	8		2749
17	20	H	Ross Co	W	2-1	1-1	8	Masterson [35], Wake [64]	1853
18	27	A	Airdrie U	L	0-1	0-1	9		1663
19	30	H	Partick Th	W	2-0	1-0	—	Masterson [17], Weatherson [65]	2385
20	Jan 3	H	Queen of the S	D	2-2	1-2	6	Weatherson 2 [33, 90]	2647
21	17	A	Dundee	D	0-0	0-0	7		3736
22	24	H	Livingston	D	2-2	2-0	6	Wake [13], McGuffie [16]	2307
23	31	A	St Johnstone	D	0-0	0-0	6		2810
24	Feb 21	A	Partick Th	L	0-1	0-0	8		3348
25	28	H	Dunfermline Ath	W	2-1	1-0	8	Weatherson [28], Greacen [48]	2092
26	Mar 3	A	Clyde	W	4-2	1-2	—	Paartalu [31], Russell [70], Wake 2 [86, 90]	1165
27	7	A	Queen of the S	D	1-1	1-0	4	Grady [41]	2643
28	10	A	Airdrie U	D	0-0	0-0	—		1865
29	14	H	Clyde	W	2-0	1-0	5	Jenkins [18], Masterson (pen) [68]	2168
30	21	A	Ross Co	D	1-1	0-1	5	Russell [90]	2236
31	Apr 4	H	Dundee	W	2-0	1-0	4	Weatherson 2 [29, 79]	2133
32	11	A	Livingston	W	2-0	1-0	3	Wake 2 [19, 83]	1815
33	18	H	Partick Th	L	0-1	0-1	3		3323
34	May 2	A	St Johnstone	L	1-3	1-1	4	McGuffie (pen) [25]	6453
35	5	A	Dunfermline Ath	L	1-2	0-0	—	Monti [62]	1438
36	9	H	Ross Co	L	0-2	0-0	6		1956

Final League Position: 6

Honours
League Champions: First Division 1977-78, 1983-84, 1986-87. Division II 1949-50, 1963-64, 1966-67. Second Division 1994-95, 2006-07. Third Division 2002-03. *Runners-up:* Division 1 1916-17, Division II 1899-1900, 1928-29, 1936-37. *Scottish Cup Winners:* 1922; *Runners-up:* 1948. *League Cup Runners-up:* 1963-64. *B&Q Cup Runners-up:* 1992-93.

European: *UEFA Cup:* 2 matches (*Fairs Cup:* 1968-69).

Club colours: Shirt: Canary yellow. Shorts: Canary yellow. Stockings: Canary yellow.

Goalscorers: *League* (40): Wake 9, Weatherson 9, McGuffie 4 (2 pens), Jenkins 3, Masterton 3 (1 pen), Paartalu 3, Russell 3, Grady 2, Greacen 2, Monti 1, Newby 1.
Scottish Cup (1): Masterton 1.
CIS Cup (5): Russell 2 (1 pen), Harding 1, McAlister 1, Masterton 1.
Challenge Cup (6): McGuffie 3, Masterton 1, Wake 1, Weatherson 1.

Stewart C 2+2	Weatherson P 31+3	Walker A 23+1	Greacen S 28	Paartalu E 19+8	McGuffie R 31+1	McAlister J 35	Finlayson K 27+5	Wake B 18+14	Newby J 3+1	Russell I 11+14	Reid A —+1	Cuthbert K 34	Shimmin D 21	Masterton S 21+7	McManus A 18+1	Harding R 7+1	Jenkins A 20+9	Smith C 18+3	MacGregor D 10	Grady J 16+6	Monti C 3+1	Match No.
1	2	3	4	5	6	7	8	9¹	10¹	11	12											1
2	5¹	3²	8	7³	9	14			10	11		1	4	6	12	13						2
14			5	7³	11	12	9	10¹	8			1	2	6²	4	3	13					3
2²	3		5¹	8	11	7¹	9	14	10			1	4	13			6	12				4
15	3¹		5	7	11		9		10			1⁶	2²	8	4		6	13	12			5
13	2		5	7	11	12	9		10			1	4				6	8¹	3²			6
14	2²		5³	8	11	7¹	9		10			1	4	12			6	13	3			7
10	2		5		11		9		7¹			1	4	8			6	12	3			8
10	2		5¹	7	11	15	9		12			1⁶	4	8²			6	13	3			9
9		5	12	8¹	11	7						1	4	6					3	2	10	10
9¹		5		8	11	7	12					1	4				6	3	2	10		11
9		5	13	8²	11	7¹		12				1		4			6	3	2	10		12
10¹		5	6	7	9		13					1		12	4	8		3	2	11²		13
9				8	6	11		12				1	4		5	7		3	2	10¹		14
10		4	8	6¹	9²	12	11					1	3	13			7	5	2			15
		5	8	7²	11		9	12			13	1	4				6	3	2	10¹		16
		5	13		11		7	9		10¹		1	4	8²			6	3	2	12		17
15	9		5		11		7	12				1	4	8			6	3	2	10¹		18
1	11	5	4			9		6	12			3	7		8				2	10¹		19
9	3	5	13		2	11	7	12				1	4	8		6²				10¹		20
9	2	5		8	11	7	10					1		6¹	4		12	3				21
9	2	5		8¹	11	7	10					1	4	6			12	3				22
9	2	5		8	11²	7	10¹		12			1	4	6			13	3				23
10	2	4	13	8²	9	6	11³		14			1	3	7				5¹	12			24
9³	3	5	4¹	8	11	7	13		14			1			2	6	12		10²			25
9	3	5	4³	8²	11	7	12		13			1		14	2	6			10¹			26
10³		4	5²	8	9	7	14		12		1		13	2	6		3	11¹				27
9	14	5	4¹	8	11	7			13		1	3³	12	2	6			10²				28
9	3	5	12	8¹	11	7	13				1	4	2	6			10²					29
9³	3	5	4²	14	11	7	12	13			1	8	2	6			10¹					30
10³	3	4		8²	9	5	11¹	12		1	6	2	7				13	14				31
9¹	3	5		4	11	7	10²	12		1	6	2	8				13					32
9	3	5	14	4¹	11	7	10²	12		1	6	2	8³		13							33
9	3	5	4²	8		7	11	12			1	2		13	10¹	6						34
9¹	3	5	13	4²	11	7	12	10		1	6	2			8							35
10²	3	4		5	9	7¹	12	11		1	6	2			13	8						36

MOTHERWELL

Premier League

Year Formed: 1886. *Ground & Address:* Fir Park Stadium, Motherwell ML1 2QN. *Telephone:* 01698 333333. *Fax:* 01698 338001.
E-mail: info@motherwellfc.co.uk *Website:* www.motherwellfc.co.uk
Ground Capacity: all seated: 13,742. *Size of Pitch:* 110yd × 75yd.
Chairman: William Dickie. *Chief Executive:* Ian Stillie. *Secretary:* Stewart Robertson.
Manager: Jim Gannon. *Assistant Manager:* Peter Ward. *Physios:* John Porteous, R. Mayberry.
Club Nickname(s): The Well. *Previous Grounds:* Roman Road, Dalziel Park.
Record Attendance: 35,632 v Rangers, Scottish Cup 4th rd replay, 12 Mar 1952.
Record Transfer Fee received: £1,750,000 for Phil O'Donnell to Celtic (September 1994).
Record Transfer Fee paid: £500,000 for John Spencer from Everton (Jan 1999).
Record Victory: 12-1 v Dundee U, Division II, 23 Jan 1954.
Record Defeat: 0-8 v Aberdeen, Premier Division, 26 Mar 1979.
Most Capped Player: Tommy Coyne, 13, Republic of Ireland.
Most League Appearances: 626: Bobby Ferrier, 1918-37.
Most League Goals in Season (Individual): 52: Willie McFadyen, Division I, 1931-32.
Most Goals Overall (Individual): 283: Hugh Ferguson, 1916-25.

MOTHERWELL 2008–09 LEAGUE RECORD

Match No.	Date		Venue	Opponents	Result		H/T Score	Lg. Pos.	Goalscorers	Atten- dance
1	Aug	9	A	Hearts	L	2-3	1-2	—	Clarkson 2 [33, 81]	14,219
2		16	H	Aberdeen	L	0-1	0-0	12		5872
3		23	H	Dundee U	D	1-1	1-1	1	Sutton [34]	5149
4		30	A	Hibernian	W	1-0	0-0	9	Sutton [79]	11,285
5	Sept	13	H	Celtic	L	2-4	0-4	10	Sutton [55], Clarkson [57]	8407
6		21	A	Rangers	L	1-2	0-0	11	Clarkson [87]	49,448
7		27	H	St Mirren	W	2-1	0-1	10	Sutton [48], Malcolm [62]	4786
8	Oct	5	H	Falkirk	W	3-2	2-1	8	Murphy [12], Porter [23], Sutton [55]	4509
9		18	A	Kilmarnock	L	0-1	0-0	9		5113
10		25	A	Inverness CT	W	2-1	0-0	7	Porter [69], Malcolm [83]	3110
11	Nov	1	H	Hamilton A	W	2-0	1-0	3	Porter [37], Clarkson [66]	6205
12		8	A	Celtic	L	0-2	0-1	5		56,504
13		12	H	Rangers	D	0-0	0-0	—		9600
14		15	A	Falkirk	L	0-1	0-1	7		5279
15		22	H	Hibernian	L	1-4	1-1	9	Malcolm [42]	4957
16		29	A	Aberdeen	L	0-2	0-0	10		10,302
17	Dec	15	H	Kilmarnock	L	0-2	0-1	—		3339
18		20	A	Hamilton A	L	0-2	0-1	10		3527
19		27	H	Inverness CT	W	3-2	2-1	9	Porter 3 [8, 39, 78]	4521
20	Jan	3	A	St Mirren	D	0-0	0-0	9		10,189
21		7	H	Hearts	W	1-0	1-0	—	Porter [11]	4928
22		18	A	Dundee U	W	4-0	3-0	7	Fitzpatrick [23], Klimpl [27], Clarkson [33], Porter [63]	7090
23		24	H	Falkirk	D	1-1	1-0	7	Clarkson [43]	5018
24		31	A	Hibernian	D	1-1	0-1	7	Clarkson (pen) [77]	10,903
25	Feb	14	H	Hamilton A	W	1-0	1-0	7	Clarkson [45]	5917
26		22	H	Celtic	D	1-1	0-0	6	Quinn [81]	8593
27		28	A	Inverness CT	W	2-1	1-1	6	Sutton [26], Sheridan [53]	3611
28	Mar	4	A	Hearts	L	1-2	0-0	—	Hughes [76]	13,306
29		14	A	Dundee U	W	2-1	1-0	7	Sutton [27], Clarkson [75]	4798
30		21	A	Kilmarnock	D	0-0	0-0	7		5434
31	Apr	4	A	Aberdeen	D	1-1	1-0	7	O'Brien [9]	4686
32		11	A	Rangers	L	1-3	1-2	7	Sutton [37]	50,080
33		18	H	St Mirren	L	0-2	0-0	7		6626
34	May	2	A	Falkirk	L	1-2	0-1	7	Clarkson (pen) [70]	4937
35		9	A	St Mirren	W	3-1	2-0	7	Murphy [18], Clarkson 2 [32, 60]	4002
36		13	H	Inverness CT	D	2-2	1-1	—	McLean [26], Sutton [79]	2818
37		16	A	Hamilton A	W	3-0	1-0	7	Clarkson [22], Sheridan [58], Sutton [86]	3383
38		23	H	Kilmarnock	L	1-2	0-1	7	McLean [80]	4186

Final League Position: 7

Honours
League Champions: Division I 1931-32. First Division 1981-82, 1984-85. Division II 1953-54, 1968-69; *Runners-up:* Premier Division 1994-95. Division I 1926-27, 1929-30, 1932-33, 1933-34. Division II 1894-95, 1902-03. *Scottish Cup:* 1952, 1991; *Runners-up:* 1931, 1933, 1939, 1951.
League Cup Winners: 1950-51; *Runners-up:* 1954-55, 2004-05. *Scottish Summer Cup:* 1944, 1965.

European: *Cup Winners' Cup:* 2 matches (1991-92). *UEFA Cup:* 8 matches (1994-95, 1995-96, 2008-09).

Club colours: Shirt: Amber with claret hoop and trimmings. Shorts: Amber. Stockings: Amber with claret trim.

Goalscorers: *League* (46): Clarkson 14 (2 pens), Sutton 10, Porter 8, Malcolm 3, McLean 2, Murphy 2, Sheridan 2, Fitzpatrick 1, Hughes 1, Klimpl 1, O'Brien 1, Quinn 1.
Scottish Cup (4): Sutton 2, Clarkson 1, Hughes 1.
CIS Cup (1): Murphy 1.
UEFA Cup (0).

Smith G 37	Quinn P 33	Hammell S 37	Reynolds M 36	Craigan S 22	Malcolm R 11 + 2	McGarry S 16 + 7	Hughes S 35	Porter C 21 + 1	Clarkson D 30 + 3	Lasley K 24 + 4	Fitzpatrick M 14 + 9	Smith D 1 + 15	O'Brien J 19 + 10	Murphy J 11 + 19	Sutton J 26 + 2	Klimpl M 20 + 1	Saunders S 2 + 1	McHugh R — + 2	Sheridan C 9 + 4	McLean B 12	Hutchinson S 1	Slane P — + 1	Krysiak A 1	Match No.
1	2	3	4	5	6^1	7^2	8	9	10	11^3	12	13	14											1
1	2	3	4	5			8	9	10	11	6^2	12	13	7^1										2
1	2	3	4	5		7		9	8	11	6				10									3
1	2	3	4	5		7^3	6^2	9	8	11	13		14	12	10^1									4
1	2	3	4	5		7^1	8	9	10^2	6		12	13	11										5
1	2	3	4	5	6		8^2	9	10	11		13		12	7^1									6
1	2	3	4		6	7			10^1	5	11	12		8	9									7
1	2	3	4	5		7^1	8	9	13	11	12			6^2	10									8
1	2^4	3	4		12	7	5	9	10^2	11	13		14	6^3	8^1									9
1		3	4		5	7^3	8	9	10^1	2	14	12	13	6^2	11									10
1	2^2	3	4		6	13	8	9	10	11	5			12	7^1									11
1	2	3	4		6		8	9^1	10^4	11^2	5		13	12	7									12
1	2	3	4		6	7	8	9		11	5				10									13
1	2	3	4		6	7^2	8	12	10^3	11^1	5	14	13	9										14
1	2	3	4		6	7^1	5	9		11		13	12	8^2	10									15
1	2^4	3	4		6		8	9		11	7		10^1			5	12							16
1		3	4		6^2	7^3	8	9		11			14	13	12	10^1	5	2						17
1	2	3	4			7^2		9		11		13	12	8^1	10	5	6							18
1	2	3	4	5			8	9	10^2	11	12				7^1	6				13				19
1	2	3	4	5			8	9	10	11				7^1	12	6								20
1	2	3	4	5			8	9^1	10	11	12	13			7^2	6								21
1	2	3	4	5			8	9^3	10^2	11	12	13	14		7^1	6								22
1	2	3^1	4	5			8	9^2	10	11	12	13			7	6								23
1	2	3	4	5			8		10	11^1		13	12	9^2	7	6								24
1	2	3	4	5			8		10^3	11	12	13	14		7^1	6^2			9					25
1	2	3	4	5			8		10	11^1			7	12	9	6								26
1		3	4				8		10^1		12^2	13	14	11^3	9	6			7	2				27
1		3	4	5^2	12		8		10^1			13	7		9	6			11	2				28
1	2	3	4	5			8	12				13	7	9		6			10^1	11^2				29
1	2	3	4	5	13		8	12		11			14	9		6^3			10^2	7^1				30
1	2	3	4			7^2	8		10^1	11		13		9		6			12	5				31
1	2	3	4			7^1	8		10	11		13		9		6^1			12	5				32
1	11	3	4	5^2			8		10				7	12	9	6^1			13	2				33
1		3	4				8		10	11^1		2	7	12	9^2	6			13	5				34
1	2	3	4		12			10		11		13	7	8^1		6			9^2	5				35
1	2	3	4				8		10		12	13	7^1	11^3	14	6			9^2	5				36
1	2			5	12	8			10^2	7^3	11^1	13				6			9	4	3	14		37
	2	3		5	12^2	13	8		10	7			14	9^3		6^1			11	4			1	38

PARTICK THISTLE — First Division

Year Formed: 1876. *Ground & Address:* Firhill Stadium, 80 Firhill Rd, Glasgow G20 7AL. *Telephone:* 0141 579 1971. *Fax:* 0141 945 1525. *E-mail:* mail@ptfc.co.uk *Website:* www.ptfc.co.uk
Ground Capacity: total: 13,141, seated: 10,921. *Size of Pitch:* 105yd × 68yd.
Chairman: Allan Cowan. *Secretary:* Antonia Kerr. *Chief Executive:* Eddie Prentice.
Manager: Ian McCall. *Assistant Manager:* Gerry Britton. *Coach:* John Henry. *Physio:* George Hannah.
Club Nickname(s): The Jags. *Previous Grounds:* Jordanvale Park; Muirpark; Inchview; Meadowside Park.
Record Attendance: 49,838 v Rangers, Division I, 18 Feb 1922. *Ground Record:* 54,728, Scotland v Ireland, 25 Feb 1928.
Record Transfer Fee received: £200,000 for Mo Johnston to Watford.
Record Transfer Fee paid: £85,000 for Andy Murdoch from Celtic (Feb 1991).
Record Victory: 16-0 v Royal Albert, Scottish Cup 1st rd, 17 Jan 1931.
Record Defeat: 0-10 v Queen's Park, Scottish Cup, 3 Dec 1881.
Most Capped Player: Alan Rough, 51 (53), Scotland.
Most League Appearances: 410: Alan Rough, 1969-82.
Most League Goals in Season (Individual): 41: Alex Hair, Division I, 1926-27.

PARTICK THISTLE 2008–09 LEAGUE RECORD

Match No.	Date	Venue	Opponents	Result	H/T Score	Lg. Pos.	Goalscorers	Attendance
1	Aug 2	H	Dunfermline Ath	W 1-0	0-0	—	McKeown [87]	3092
2	9	A	Airdrie U	W 1-0	0-0	2	Gray [74]	2165
3	17	H	Queen of the S	L 0-2	0-2	4		3272
4	23	H	St Johnstone	W 4-0	1-0	2	Robertson J [6], Maxwell [48], Paton [67], Harkins [74]	2861
5	30	H	Ross Co	L 0-1	0-1	3		2945
6	Sept 13	A	Clyde	D 1-1	1-0	4	Chaplain [27]	2191
7	20	H	Morton	W 2-1	1-1	2	Harkins [37], Maxwell [66]	3368
8	27	A	Livingston	L 1-3	1-2	3	Maxwell [28]	2150
9	Oct 4	H	Dundee	D 0-0	0-0	4		2556
10	18	A	Dunfermline Ath	L 0-1	0-1	5		3242
11	25	A	St Johnstone	L 0-3	0-1	5		2772
12	Nov 1	H	Queen of the S	W 2-0	1-0	5	McKinlay [45], Harkins (pen) [87]	2971
13	8	H	Clyde	W 2-0	1-0	5	Buchanan [9], McKeown [73]	3003
14	22	H	Livingston	W 2-1	2-1	3	Buchanan [11], McKeown [43]	2416
15	25	A	Ross Co	L 0-2	0-0	—		1625
16	Dec 13	H	Airdrie U	W 2-1	1-1	3	Harkins [19], McLaughlin (og) [62]	2296
17	20	A	Dundee	D 0-0	0-0	4		3569
18	27	H	Ross Co	L 0-2	0-1	4		2465
19	30	A	Morton	L 0-2	0-1	—		2385
20	Jan 3	A	Clyde	W 4-2	3-1	3	Donnelly [29], Harkins (pen) [32], Paton [41], Buchanan [86]	2016
21	17	H	St Johnstone	D 0-0	0-0	3		3353
22	24	A	Queen of the S	D 2-2	1-1	3	Doohlan [17], Chaplain [76]	2811
23	31	A	Airdrie U	W 1-0	1-0	2	Buchanan [44]	1988
24	Feb 14	A	Dunfermline Ath	L 2-3	2-2	—	Buchanan [9], Doohlan [34]	2957
25	21	H	Morton	W 1-0	0-0	2	Doohlan [49]	3348
26	28	A	Livingston	W 4-2	2-0	2	Harkins 2 (1 pen) [18 (pl), 90], Paton [34], Rowson [47]	2876
27	Mar 7	H	Clyde	L 0-1	0-0	2		3579
28	10	A	Ross Co	W 2-0	0-0	—	Doohlan 2 [67, 69]	2017
29	14	A	Dunfermline Ath	W 1-0	1-0	2	Harkins (pen) [19]	2736
30	22	H	Dundee	D 1-1	0-1	2	McKinlay [81]	3303
31	Apr 4	A	St Johnstone	D 1-1	0-0	2	Harkins [87]	4909
32	11	H	Queen of the S	L 0-2	0-1	2		2830
33	18	A	Morton	W 1-0	1-0	2	Akins [20]	3323
34	25	H	Livingston	W 1-0	0-0	2	Buchanan (pen) [90]	2803
35	May 2	H	Airdrie U	L 0-1	0-0	2		3242
36	9	A	Dundee	L 0-4	0-2	2		2831

Final League Position: 2

Honours
League Champions: First Division 1975-76, 2001-02; *Runners-up:* 2008-09. Division II 1896-97, 1899-1900, 1970-71; Second Division 2000-01; *Runners-up:* First Division 1991-92. Division II 1901-02.
Scottish Cup Winners: 1921; *Runners-up:* 1930; *Semi-finals:* 2002.
League Cup Winners: 1971-72; *Runners-up:* 1953-54, 1956-57, 1958-59.
League Challenge Cup: Quarter-finals 2004-05.

European: *Fairs Cup:* 4 matches (1963-64). *UEFA Cup:* 2 matches (1972-73). *Intertoto Cup:* 4 matches 1995-96.

Club colours: Shirt: Red and yellow halves with black sleeves. Shorts: Black. Stockings: Black.

Goalscorers: *League* (39): Harkins 9 (4 pens), Buchanan 6 (1 pen), Doohan 5, Maxwell 3, McKeown 3, Paton 3, Chaplain 2, McKinlay 2, Akins 1, Donnelly 1, Gray 1, Robertson J 1, Rowson 1, own goal 1.
Scottish Cup (3): Buchanan 1, Chaplain 1, Harkins 1 (pen).
CIS Cup (3): Harkins 1 (pen), Maxwell 1, McKeown 1.
Challenge Cup (8): McKeown 2, Donnelly 1, Gray 1, Harkins 1, Roberts 1, Turner 1, Twaddle 1.

Tuffey J 36	Paton P 32+3	Robertson J 28	Maxwell I 21+3	Twaddle M 28+2	Storey S 31+1	Chaplain S 13+17	Harkins G 34	Rowson D 35	Roberts M 6+9	Gray D 5+5	Donnelly S 19+12	McKinlay K 12+17	McKeown S 18+7	Lennon S 5+4	McStay R 1+2	Kinniburgh W 14+4	Turner C 1+1	Buchanan L 17+2	Archibald A 19+1	Doohan K 15+1	Akins L 6+3	Little R —+1	Match No.
1	2	3	4	5	6	7[3]	8	9	10[1]	11[2]	12	13	14										1
1	2	5	6	3	4	7[1]	11	8			9	10[2]	13	12									2
1	13	4	5	3	2	12	6	9[1]	14	10[3]	8		7[3]	11									3
1	2	3	4	5	6	7	9	13	12	10[2]		8	11[1]										4
1	5	3[9]	4	9	2[1]	12	7	6			14	11			10[3]	8[2]	13						5
1	2	3	4	5[3]	6	7[2]	9	8	12	11[1]		10	14	13									6
1	2	6	3	4	13	11[2]	8	10[3]	9[1]	12	14	7				5							7
1	2[1]	4	6	13	7	11	8	14	9	12	3[3]		10[2]			5							8
1	2[3]	5	6	3	4	13	11	8	10[1]		9	14	7[2]	12									9
1	2	5	6	3	4	7[1]	11[3]	8		10[2]	9	13	14		12								10
1	2	5	6		4[4]	13	11[2]	8		12		10	7		3		9[1]						11
1	5	2	4		12	8	7			13	10	9	6		3[1]		11[2]						12
1	2	4	6		13	11[3]	8			12	10[1]	3	7		14	5			9[2]				13
1	2		6		4	12	11	8	14		10[3]	3	7[1]	13		5			9[2]				14
1	2		6		4	12	11	8[3]	13		10[2]	3	7[1]		14	5			9				15
1	2		6[1]	13	4		11	8	10[5]		14	3			5	7[2]		9	12				16
1	2	6		3	4		11	8	10		12	7				5[1]		9					17
1	2	5		3[8]	4[1]	14	11	8[3]	13		10[2]	7	12					9	6				18
1	2	3			12	13	9[2]	8	11		6[1]	7	14			4		10[3]	5				19
1	2	4		6[1]	3	7	9	8	12		10[2]		13					11	5				20
1	2		3	4	7[1]	11	8	14			10[3]	13	12			5		6	9[2]				21
1	2		3	4	13	9	8				7[2]					5		10[1]	6	11	12		22
1	2		3	4	14	11[1]	8				10[2]	13	12			5		9[3]	6	7			23
1	2	13[8]	6[2]	3[1]	8	9	7				14	12				4		10[3]	5	11			24
1	2	4		6	3	13	9	8			14	12	7[2]					10[1]	5	11[3]			25
1	2	5[1]	12	3	4		11	8			13	14	7					9[2]	6	10[3]			26
1	2		5	3	4	12	11	8			10[3]	13	7[1]					6	9[2]	14			27
1	12	5		3	2	4[1]	11	8			13	7						6	10	9[2]			28
1	4	5		3	2	11[1]	8				12	13	7[2]					6	10	9			29
1	4	5		3	2	12	11	8			12	7				13		6	10	9[1]			30
1	4	5		3	2	12	11	8			13	14	7[1]					6	10[3]	9[2]			31
1	4	5	14	3	2	12	11	8[3]			10[1]	7[2]						6	9	13			32
1	2	5	4	3		7	11	8			12	13						6	10[1]	9[2]			33
1	2	5	4	3	11[2]	7		8			13	14					12	6	10[3]	9[1]			34
1	12	5	4	3	2	7[1]		8			10	13				14		9[3]	6	11[2]			35
1	7[2]	5	4	3	2		11	8			10							9[1]	6	12		13	36

PETERHEAD

Second Division

Year Formed: 1891. *Ground and Address:* Balmoor Stadium, Lord Catto Park, Peterhead AB42 1EU.
Telephone: 01779 478256. *Fax:* 01779 490682. *E-mail:* office@peterheadfc.org.uk *Website:* www.peterheadfc.co.uk
Ground Capacity: 3250, seated 1000.
Chairman: Rodger Morrison. *General Manager:* Dave Watson. *Secretary:* George Moore.
Manager: Neil Cooper. *First Team Coach:* Dave McGinlay.
Club Nickname(s): Blue Toon. *Previous Ground:* Recreation Park.
Record Attendance: 6310 friendly v Celtic, 1948.
Record Victory: 17-0 v Fort William, 1998-99 (in Highland League).
Record Defeat: 0-13 v Aberdeen, Scottish Cup, 1923-24.
Most League Appearances: 135: Martin Johnston, 2000-05.
Most League Goals in Season (Individual): 21: Iain Stewart, 2002-03; 21, Scott Michie, 2004-05.
Most Goals Overall (Individual): 58: Iain Stewart, 2000-05.

PETERHEAD 2008–09 LEAGUE RECORD

Match No.	Date	Venue	Opponents	Result	H/T Score	Lg. Pos.	Goalscorers	Attendance
1	Aug 2	A	East Fife	W 2-0	2-0	—	Sharp [30], Gunn [45]	888
2	9	H	Arbroath	D 1-1	0-0	3	McKay [88]	630
3	16	A	Brechin C	D 2-2	0-2	3	Gunn [55], Bavidge [80]	525
4	23	H	Alloa Ath	W 1-0	1-0	2	Anderson [6]	670
5	30	H	Raith R	L 1-2	0-1	4	Anderson [57]	837
6	Sept 13	A	Queen's Park	W 1-0	0-0	4	Anderson [69]	578
7	20	H	Stranraer	W 4-0	2-0	2	Gunn [16], MacDonald [18], Ross 2 [55, 88]	495
8	27	A	Stirling A	D 0-0	0-0	2		527
9	Oct 4	A	Ayr U	L 0-2	0-1	4		1104
10	18	H	East Fife	L 0-1	0-0	5		715
11	25	A	Alloa Ath	L 0-1	0-0	5		331
12	Nov 1	H	Brechin C	W 5-1	4-1	5	Ross [19], Bavidge 2 [21, 39], Sharp [44], Cowie [90]	602
13	8	H	Queen's Park	W 4-1	1-1	4	Sharp [19], Bavidge 3 (1 pen) [54, 72, 75 (p)]	697
14	15	A	Raith R	L 0-3	0-0	4		1762
15	22	H	Stirling A	D 1-1	1-0	4	Sharp [24]	461
16	Dec 13	A	Arbroath	L 0-4	0-2	4		451
17	20	H	Ayr U	W 3-0	1-0	4	Sharp [13], Bavidge [72], Gunn [86]	631
18	27	H	Raith R	W 2-1	0-0	4	Ross 2 [48, 73]	820
19	Jan 3	A	Queen's Park	L 1-2	1-2	4	McKay [31]	617
20	17	A	Alloa Ath	D 2-2	1-1	5	McKay [30], Ross [90]	601
21	24	A	Brechin C	D 1-1	0-0	6	Bavidge [86]	517
22	31	A	East Fife	W 3-0	2-0	6	McKay 2 [8, 36], Sharp [54]	698
23	Feb 21	H	Stranraer	W 1-0	0-0	5	Bavidge [79]	531
24	28	A	Raith R	D 3-3	3-3	4	McKay [12], MacDonald 2 [22, 45]	1564
25	Mar 4	A	Stranraer	W 3-0	1-0	—	Moore 2 [27, 52], McVitie [71]	154
26	7	H	Queen's Park	D 1-1	0-0	3	Anderson [57]	695
27	10	H	Arbroath	W 1-0	1-0	—	Anderson [36]	470
28	14	H	East Fife	W 2-0	1-0	3	Sharp [15], MacDonald [62]	607
29	17	A	Stirling A	L 1-2	0-0	—	MacDonald [70]	404
30	21	A	Ayr U	D 0-0	0-0	4		1605
31	Apr 4	A	Alloa Ath	W 2-1	0-1	4	Kozminski [72], MacDonald [86]	479
32	11	H	Brechin C	L 0-1	0-0	4		739
33	18	A	Stranraer	W 1-0	0-0	4	Mann (pen) [83]	252
34	25	H	Stirling A	D 1-1	0-0	4	Mann [53]	855
35	May 2	A	Arbroath	D 2-2	1-1	4	Anderson 2 (1 pen) [11, 54 (p)]	599
36	9	H	Ayr U	L 2-3	0-0	4	Sharp 2 [56, 82]	602

Final League Position: 4

Honours
Third Division Runners up: 2004-05.
Scottish Cup: Quarter-finals 2001.
Highland League Champions: winners 5 times.
Scottish Qualifying Cup (North): winners 6 times.
North of Scotland Cup: winners 5 times.
Aberdeenshire Cup: winners: 20 times.

Club colours: Shirt: Royal blue with navy sleeves; Shorts: Royal blue; Stockings: Royal blue.

Goalscorers: *League* (54): Bavidge 9 (1 pen), Sharp 9, Anderson 7 (1 pen), MacDonald 6, McKay 6, Ross 6, Gunn 4, Mann 2 (1 pen), Moore 2, Cowie 1, Kozminski 1, McVitie 1.
Scottish Cup (4): Bavidge 2, Anderson 1, Ross 1.
Challenge Cup (8): Gunn 4 (1 pen), Bavidge 2, Kozminski 1, own goal 1.
Play-Offs (1): McKay 1.

Kula M 25+1	Donald D 36	Mann B 17+4	Skinner M 13+1	Moore D 32+1	Sharp G 29+1	McVitie N 24	Gunn C 26+10	McKay S 32+3	Bavidge M 32+1	Anderson S 35+1	Ross D 16+14	MacDonald C 34	Cowie D 2+5	Flemming S 5+2	Bagshaw A 4+2	Kozminski K 1+16	Smith S 22	Jarvie P 11	Duncan R —+2	Davidson L —+1	Match No.
1	2	3	4	5	6	7	8^1	9	10	11	12										1
1	2	4		3	7	6	10^1	9	11	8^2	12	5	13								2
1	2	3		5	6	7	10	9	11	8		4									3
1	2	4		3	7	6	10^1	9	11	8	12	5									4
1	2	4		3	7	6	8	11	9	10^1		5		12							5
1	2	3			6	7	10^2	9	11	8	12	4		5		13					6
1	2^2	14	4	7	6^1		8	11^3	9	10	12	5	13			3					7
1	2	4		7	12	6	8	11^2	9	10	13	5			3^1						8
1	2	12^2	3^1	5	6		7	9	10	11	13	4	8								9
1	2	4	3	7	8^1	6	10	9	11	5					12						10
1	2	4	6	7	8^2	13	9^1	10	11	5	3^3	14	12								11
1	2	4	3	7^1	6^3	12	9	11	8	10^2	5	14	13								12
1	2	4	3^3	7^1	6	12	9	11^2	8	10	5	14	13								13
1	2	4		7^1	6^4	12	11	9^2	10	8	5	3	13								14
1	2	4		7	11^1	6	9	10	8	5	12						3				15
1	2	4		7	11	12	9^2	10	8	5	6^1	13					3				16
1	2	3		7	6	12	9	11	8	10^1	5						4				17
1	2	3		7	13	9	11	8	10^2	5	12	6^1					4				18
1	2	14	5	3	7^3	12	11	9	10	8^1	6^2	13					4				19
1	2	14	3	7	6^2	8	11	9^1	10^3	13	5	12					4				20
	2	3	9^2	7	12	6	10	14	8^1	4	11^3	13	5					1			21
	2	3	9	6^1	7	12	8^2	10	11	13	4	5						1			22
	2	4	9^1	7	6	12	10^2	11	8	5	13						3	1			23
	2	3	9	6^1	7	10	8	11	4	12	5							1			24
	2	4	11	7	6	10	8^1	9	12	5							3	1			25
	2	4	11	7	6	8	9^1	12	10								3	1			26
15	2	3		7	6	10	9^1	11	8	12	5						4		1^6		27
1	2	4	9	7	6	10^1	13	11^2	8	12	5						3				28
1	2	3	7	6	8	11^1	9	10	12	5							4				29
1	2	5	6^4	8	10	9^4	11	7	4	12							3				30
1	2	4	11	8	9	10	7	5		6^1	12						3				31
1	2	4	11^1	7	6	8	9	10^2	5	12						13	3				32
	2	4	11	8^1	6	10	7	5	9							12	3	1			33
	2	4	6	7^2	10^1	9	11	8	12	5	13						3	1			34
	2	3	7	8^1	6	9^2	10	11	5	13						12	4	1			35
	2	4^3	14	12	7	5^1	13	10	11	9^2	8	6	3	1							36

QUEEN OF THE SOUTH First Division

Year Formed: 1919. *Ground & Address:* Palmerston Park, Dumfries DG2 9BA. *Telephone:* 01387 254853.
Fax: 01387 240470. *E-mail:* admin@qosfc.com *Website:* www.qosfc.com
Ground Capacity: total: 7412, seated: 3509. *Size of Pitch:* 112yd × 73yd.
Chairman: David Rae. *Vice-Chairman:* Thomas Harkness. *Club Secretary:* Eric Moffat. *Commercial Manager:* Margaret Heuchan.
Manager: Gordon Chisholm. *First Team Coach:* Stevie Morrison. *Physio:* John Kerr.
Club Nickname(s): The Doonhamers. *Previous Grounds:* None.
Record Attendance: 26,552 v Hearts, Scottish Cup 3rd rd, 23 Feb 1952.
Record Transfer Fee received: £250,000 for Andy Thomson to Southend U (1994).
Record Transfer Fee paid: £30,000 for Jim Butter from Alloa Athletic (1995).
Record Victory: 11-1 v Stranraer, Scottish Cup 1st rd, 16 Jan 1932.
Record Defeat: 2-10 v Dundee, Division I, 1 Dec 1962.
Most Capped Player: Billy Houliston, 3, Scotland.
Most League Appearances: 731: Allan Ball, 1963-82.
Most League Goals in Season (Individual): 37: Jimmy Gray, Division II, 1927-28.
Most Goals in Season: 41: Jimmy Rutherford, 1931-32.
Most Goals Overall (Individual): 250: Jim Patterson, 1949-63.

QUEEN OF THE SOUTH 2008–09 LEAGUE RECORD

Match No.	Date		Venue	Opponents	Result	H/T Score	Lg. Pos.	Goalscorers	Atten- dance
1	Aug	2	H	Airdrie U	D 0-0	0-0	—		2914
2		9	A	Dunfermline Ath	L 1-2	1-0	8	Kean [26]	2930
3		17	H	Partick Th	W 2-0	2-0	5	Tosh (pen) [25], Dobbie [34]	3272
4		30	H	Dundee	W 3-1	2-1	4	Barr [27], Dobbie 2 [44, 68]	2646
5	Sept	3	H	Ross Co	W 1-0	0-0	—	Weatherston [87]	2525
6		13	A	Morton	D 0-0	0-0	2		2235
7		20	H	St Johnstone	D 2-2	0-0	3	Dobbie (pen) [53], Thomson [82]	2831
8		27	A	Clyde	W 2-0	0-0	2	Arbuckle [54], Dobbie [58]	1096
9	Oct	4	H	Livingston	W 6-1	3-1	1	Dobbie 2 [3, 12], Weatherston 2 [45, 58], McQuilken [75], Burns [83]	3266
10		18	A	Airdrie U	L 0-2	0-2	1		1524
11		25	A	Ross Co	W 2-0	1-0	1	Dobbie [36], McGowan [90]	232
12	Nov	1	A	Partick Th	L 0-2	0-1	2		2971
13		8	H	Morton	L 1-4	0-3	4	O'Connor [49]	2944
14		15	A	Dundee	L 0-2	0-0	4		3630
15		22	H	Clyde	L 0-2	0-0	5		2324
16	Dec	6	A	St Johnstone	D 0-0	0-0	—		3068
17		13	H	Dunfermline Ath	L 1-2	1-1	5	McQuilken [20]	2312
18		20	A	Livingston	L 0-2	0-0	7		1874
19		27	H	Dundee	L 0-1	0-1	8		2616
20	Jan	3	A	Morton	D 2-2	2-1	8	Wilson [7], Arbuckle [19]	2647
21		17	A	Ross Co	L 0-1	0-0	9		2323
22		24	H	Partick Th	D 2-2	1-1	9	Dobbie [10], Tosh (pen) [55]	2811
23		31	A	Dunfermline Ath	W 2-0	1-0	8	Burns [29], Dobbie [67]	2770
24	Feb	14	H	Airdrie U	W 4-0	1-0	—	Burns (pen) [35], Harris [52], Dobbie [67], Weatherston [84]	2443
25		21	H	St Johnstone	D 3-3	1-0	7	Wilson [17], Dobbie [52], Burns [65]	2857
26		28	A	Clyde	D 1-1	0-1	7	Tosh [79]	1142
27	Mar	7	H	Morton	D 1-1	0-1	8	Lancaster [72]	2643
28		10	A	Dundee	W 3-2	1-0	—	Wilson [43], Dobbie [65], Lancaster [77]	3757
29		14	A	Airdrie U	L 0-2	0-0	6		1320
30		21	H	Livingston	D 3-3	1-0	7	Wilson [35], Dobbie 2 [54, 84]	2487
31	Apr	4	H	Ross Co	L 1-2	0-2	8	Dobbie [46]	2029
32		11	A	Partick Th	W 2-0	1-0	8	Dobbie [12], Tosh [53]	2830
33		19	A	St Johnstone	W 3-2	1-0	7	Dobbie 2 [11, 55], Kean [90]	3294
34		25	H	Clyde	W 7-1	3-1	5	Dobbie 4 [4, 47, 56, 61], Kean [9], Tosh [21], Harris [55]	2601
35	May	2	H	Dunfermline Ath	L 0-3	0-3	6		2750
36		9	A	Livingston	D 2-2	0-2	5	Tosh (pen) [60], McCann [67]	1652

Final League Position: 5

Honours
League Champions: Division II 1950-51. Second Division 2001-02. *Runners-up:* Division II 1932-33, 1961-62, 1974-75. Second Division 1980-81, 1985-86.
Scottish Cup Runners-up: 2007-08.
League Cup: semi-finals 1950-51, 1960-61.
B&Q Cup: semi-finals 1991-92. *League Challenge Cup Winners:* 2002-03; *Runners-up:* 1997-98.

European: *UEFA Cup:* 2 matches (2008-09).

Club colours: Shirt: Royal blue with white flashes. Shorts: White. Stockings: Royal blue.

Goalscorers: *League* (57): Dobbie 23 (1 pen), Tosh 6 (3 pens), Burns 4 (1 pen), Weatherston 4, Wilson 4, Kean 3, Arbuckle 2, Harris 2, Lancaster 2, McQuilken 2, Barr 1, McCann 1, McGowan 1, O'Connor 1, Thomson 1.
Scottish Cup (2): Harris 1, Wilson 1.
CIS Cup (1): Kean 1.
Challenge Cup (7): Kean 3, O'Connor 3, Barr 1.
UEFA Cup (2): Harris 1, O'Connor 1.

Halliwell B 4	Barr C 22+2	McQuilken J 24+10	Thomson J 22+2	Reid C 12+3	MacFarlane N 26+7	Burns P 28+1	Tosh S 26+3	Dobbie S 30+3	O'Connor S 22+6	Kean S 19+12	McGowan M 8+5	Aitken A 9+4	Arbuckle G 5+3	Adams J 2+1	Bell C 15	Harris R 21	Parratt T 9	Weatherston D 4+16	Robertson S 5+5	Sives C 10	Simmons S 6+4	Kinniburgh S 2	Robinson L 17	Wilson B 14+2	Scally N 10+1	Lancaster M 15	McCann R 8+4	McLaughlin G 1	Match No.
1	2	3	4^{8}	5	6^{1}	7	8	9^{2}	10	11	12	13																	1
1	2	3		6	4^{2}	11	8	12	9^{1}	7					5^{8}	10	13												2
	5	14	12	2^{1}	4	9	8	11^{2}	10	13		7^{3}		6	1	3													3
	4	3		5	6	9	8	11^{3}	10	14					1	7^{1}		2			12^{2}	13							4
	4	3			6	9	8	11	10^{3}	14		7^{1}			1			2			12	13	5^{2}						5
	5	7	3		4	11	8^{8}	10	9	12					1			2^{1}			6								6
	4	7^{1}	2		6		11	10		9^{3}		14			1	3		12	8^{2}		5	13							7
	4		14	12	13	7	11^{2}		10	9			6		1	5^{3}		2	3	8^{1}									8
	13			5	6^{1}	7	8	11	14	10^{3}		2			1	3^{2}		9	4	12									9
	13			6	4	7	8	10	12	9^{1}		2			1	3^{2}		11	5										10
	4	3^{3}		6	14	7	8	10^{1}	9	12	13				1	2		5		11^{2}									11
	2^{2}	5	4^{8}	13	8	6	7	11	10	12	9^{1}				1	3													12
		3			6^{3}	7	8	11	10	12		5		13	1	2^{1}		9^{2}	4	14									13
		3	4		6	7	8	10	9			5		11^{1}	1	2	12												14
		3	5		6	7^{1}	8^{3}	11	12	10				13	1	2		9^{2}	4	14									15
	2	3	4		6	7	8	9^{1}	11			5			1	12		10											16
	2	5	4^{1}		6	7^{2}	8	10^{3}	11			14			1	3		12	13		9								17
1	6^{8}	3	12	2	4	7		10^{1}	9			5						14	13		8^{2}	11^{3}							18
1	3	5	4		6	7^{1}		10^{3}	11	12								2	14	13	8	9^{2}							19
	5	11	6	2	4	8^{1}		9^{2}		12								3	13	10			1	7^{3}	14				20
	5	12		2	4	11	8^{2}	9^{3}		14		13						3^{1}		10			1	7	6				21
	4				9	11	8	10										3		12			1	7^{1}	6	5	2		22
	5	12				11	8	10^{3}		9^{2}		13						3		14			1	7^{1}	4	6	2		23
	4	7^{2}			9	11	8	10^{1}		14								3^{3}	13	12			1		6	5	2		24
	4	13			9	11^{2}	8	10		14								3^{2}		12			1	7^{1}	6	5	2		25
	3	14		13	7	6		10	11^{1}	12										5			1	9^{3}	8^{2}	4	2		26
		14	4	12	9^{1}	11	8	10										3			6		1	7^{3}	13	5	2		27
	2	6^{1}		13		11	8	10	9									3		5			1	7^{2}		4	12		28
		12		14		11	8	10	9^{2}									3	13	5	4^{3}		1	7^{1}	6		2		29
	3	7		14	9	11	8^{3}	10^{2}		13								4^{1}		2			1		12	5	6		30
	4^{1}	6^{2}	5	14	9	11	8^{3}	10										3	13				1	7	12		2		31
		12	13	2	6^{2}	4	11	10	9^{3}	14								3					1	7	8	5^{1}			32
		13	3	2	6	4^{3}	11	10	9^{1}	14										12			1	7	8	5^{2}			33
		5		2	9		8^{3}	10		14								3		12			1	7^{2}	6	4	13	11^{1}	34
	5^{8}		2		9^{2}	11^{3}	8^{1}	10		14								3	13	12			1	7	6	4			35
	6	11^{1}	2^{8}	4		8			9									3		12			1	7	10	13		5	36

QUEEN'S PARK　　　　　　　　　　　Third Division

Year Formed: 1867. *Ground & Address:* Hampden Park, Mount Florida, Glasgow G42 9BA. *Telephone:* 0141 632 1275.
Fax: 0141 636 1612. *E-mail:* secretary@queensparkfc.co.uk *Website:* queensparkfc.co.uk
Ground Capacity: all seated: 52,000. *Size of Pitch:* 115yd × 75yd.
President: James M. Hastie. *Secretary:* Alistair MacKay. *Treasurer:* David Gordon.
Coach: Gardner Spiers. *Physio:* R. C. Findlay.
Club Nickname(s): The Spiders. *Previous Grounds:* 1st Hampden (Recreation Ground); (Titwood Park was used as an
interim measure between 1st & 2nd Hampdens); 2nd Hampden (Cathkin); 3rd Hampden.
Record Attendance: 95,772 v Rangers, Scottish Cup, 18 Jan 1930.
Record for Ground: 149,547 Scotland v England, 1937.
Record Transfer Fee received: Not applicable due to amateur status.
Record Transfer Fee paid: Not applicable due to amateur status.
Record Victory: 16-0 v St. Peters, Scottish Cup 1st rd, 29 Aug 1885.
Record Defeat: 0-9 v Motherwell, Division I, 26 Apr 1930.
Most Capped Player: Walter Arnott, 14, Scotland.
Most League Appearances: 532: Ross Caven, 1982-2002.
Most League Goals in Season (Individual): 30: William Martin, Division I, 1937-38.
Most Goals Overall (Individual): 163: James B. McAlpine, 1919-33.

QUEEN'S PARK 2008–09 LEAGUE RECORD

Match No.	Date	Venue	Opponents	Result	H/T Score	Lg. Pos.	Goalscorers	Atten- dance
1	Aug 2	H	Stranraer	D 2-2	0-2	—	Dunn [60], Cairney (pen) [82]	611
2	9	A	Raith R	L 0-2	0-1	8		1507
3	16	A	East Fife	W 2-1	2-1	7	Dunlop [12], Coakley [38]	789
4	23	H	Brechin C	D 1-1	0-0	5	Douglas [82]	613
5	30	A	Ayr U	L 1-2	0-2	6	Quinn [50]	1426
6	Sept 13	H	Peterhead	L 0-1	0-0	7		578
7	20	A	Arbroath	D 1-1	1-1	7	Brough [39]	523
8	27	H	Alloa Ath	W 1-0	0-0	7	Harkins [75]	518
9	Oct 4	H	Stirling A	D 1-1	0-1	7	Watt [85]	713
10	18	A	Stranraer	D 0-0	0-0	7		427
11	25	A	Brechin C	L 1-2	0-1	7	Watt [78]	483
12	Nov 1	H	East Fife	D 0-0	0-0	7		752
13	8	A	Peterhead	L 1-4	1-1	8	Coakley [8]	697
14	15	H	Ayr U	L 0-3	0-1	8		1009
15	22	A	Alloa Ath	W 3-1	2-0	7	Cairney (pen) [42], Watt [45], Harkins [88]	557
16	Dec 6	H	Arbroath	L 1-2	1-2	—	Cairney (pen) [38]	637
17	13	H	Raith R	L 1-2	1-1	8	Nicholas [22]	735
18	20	A	Stirling A	W 3-0	2-0	8	Brough [25], Holmes [30], Coakley [90]	530
19	Jan 3	H	Peterhead	W 2-1	2-1	7	Watt [13], Cairney [40]	617
20	17	H	Brechin C	D 0-0	0-0	7		466
21	24	A	East Fife	L 2-4	1-0	7	Watt [31], Cairney (pen) [85]	785
22	31	H	Stranraer	D 1-1	0-1	7	Douglas [90]	474
23	Feb 14	A	Alloa Ath	L 1-2	1-0	—	Harkins [12]	606
24	21	A	Arbroath	L 0-3	0-2	9		568
25	28	H	Ayr U	L 0-3	0-2	9		1139
26	Mar 4	A	Ayr U	D 1-1	1-0	—	Odenewo [34]	1363
27	7	A	Peterhead	D 1-1	0-0	9	Watt [54]	695
28	14	A	Stranraer	D 2-2	1-1	9	Cairney [28], Barry [61]	323
29	17	A	Raith R	L 0-1	0-1	—		1294
30	21	H	Stirling A	W 3-1	0-0	9	Odenewo [48], Harkins [77], Cairney [90]	594
31	Apr 4	A	Brechin C	L 0-2	0-1	9		467
32	11	H	East Fife	W 3-1	2-1	9	Holmes [41], Cairney [43], Harkins [53]	601
33	18	H	Arbroath	L 0-1	0-0	9		722
34	25	A	Alloa Ath	D 0-0	0-0	9		704
35	May 2	H	Raith R	L 0-1	0-1	9		1763
36	11	A	Stirling A	L 0-4	0-3	9		284

Final League Position: 9

Honours
League Champions: Division II 1922-23. B Division 1955-56. Second Division 1980-81. Third Division 1999-2000.
Scottish Cup Winners: 1874, 1875, 1876, 1880, 1881, 1882, 1884, 1886, 1890, 1893; *Runners-up:* 1892, 1900.
FA Cup runners-up: 1884, 1885.

Club colours: Shirt: Black and white. Shorts: White. Stockings: White with black tops.

Goalscorers: *League* (35): Cairney 8 (4 pens), Watt 6, Harkins 5, Coakley 3, Brough 2, Douglas 2, Holmes 2, Odenewo 2, Barry 1, Dunlop 1, Dunn 1, Nicholas 1, Quinn 1.
Scottish Cup (6): Cairney 2 (1 pen), Brough 1, Coakley 1, Holmes 1, Watt 1.
Challenge Cup (1): Henry 1.
Play-Offs (1): Harkins 1.

Cowie A 13	Ure M 24	Sinclair R 17	Brough J 32+1	Douglas B 30	Henry J 3+1	Harkins P 27+3	Cairney P 33	Neill J 20	Coakley A 12+9	Holmes R 25+6	Dunlop R 17+10	Quinn T 22+1	Dunn R 2+5	Crawford D 23	McGrady S 5+5	Agostini D 14+2	Murray D 5+8	Boslem A 3+4	Ronald P 4+7	Little R 11	Watt I 16+13	McGrogan A —+7	Nicholas S 16+1	Waters D 5	Odenewo S 10	Reilly S 6+1	Barry D 1	McGinn P —+1	Baillie S —+1	Capuano G —+1	Match No.
	2[1]	3	4	5	6[2]	7	8	9[3]	10	11	12	13	14																		1
	2		4	5	3	13	6[3]	8[4]	10	9	11[2]	14		7[1]	1	12															2
	2	3[2]	4	5		7				11	10[3]	12	9	8	14	1		6[1]	13												3
	2		4	5		6[1]	7	8	11[2]	9	10	13		1				3	12												4
	2	3		5		8	10	9[2]	13	11	6	7[1]		1		4[3]	12	14													5
		2[2]	4	5		6	7	8[4]	11[1]	12	9	10		13	1			3	14												6
		3		5		8	10	13	6[1]	11	9		1	4	7[2]						2		12								7
			4	5	7	8	9	6	11			1	3							2		10[1]	12								8
		3		5	6	8	10	7[1]	9[2]	12		1	4				11[3]		13	2	14									9
		3		5	6[1]	8	10[2]	14	11	9[3]		1	4	7			13[4]		13	2	12									10
		3	7[1]	5	8	10	6[2]	11	9			1	4				13		2	11	12									11
			4	5	7	8	11[3]	6[1]	9[2]	10		1	3				13	2	14	12										12
		3		5	8[1]	10	9	6[3]	14	11	7[2]	1	4				13	2	12	13										13
			4	5	7	8[1]	10[3]	14	12	11	6[2]	1	3				13	2	14	9										14
		3		5	10	8	12	7	13	6		1	4					2	11[1]	9[2]										15
		3		5	10[1]	8	13	7	12	6		1	4					2	11	9[2]										16
			4	5	9[1]	8	6	12	7			1	3					2	11	10										17
	2	3	4	5	10	8	12	7	6			1					13	11[2]	9[1]											18
	2	3	4	5	10	8	7	6				1					12	11	9[1]											19
	2	3[1]	4	5	9	8	13	6	7			1					12	11	10[2]											20
	2	3[1]	4	5	11	8	13	6[2]	7			1					12	9	14	10[3]									21
	2	3	4	5	9[3]	8	14	6[2]	7			1	12				13	11	10[1]										22
	2	3[2]	4	5[5]	9	8[1]	6	12	7			1	14				13	11	10[3]										23
	2		4	5	10	8	12	7[1]	6			1					11	13	9[2]	3									24
1	2	3	4		8	9	10[1]	6	11	7[2]							12	13		5										25
1	2		4	5[5]	13	8	6	7[2]	10	14							11[1]		3	9[3]	12								26
1	2		4		12	8	6	7[1]	10								13	11	3	9[2]	5							27
1	2		4		7[1]	8	6	12	10								13	11		9[2]	5	3						28
1	2		4	3	12	8	6[1]	7[2]	10[3]	14							13	11		9	5								29
1	2			5	9	8	7	13	6[2]	14						3	11[3]	12	10[1]	4									30
1	2	3	14	5	6	8	7		13	9[1]							11[2]	12	10	4[3]									31
1	4	2	3	8	9	7	5	6	12	10[1]	11																				32
1	2	3	4	5	9	7	6	8	12	11	10[3]																				33
1	2	4[1]	5	3	11	8	7	14	12	6[3]	13	10	9[2]																		34
1	2	4[2]	5	9[1]	8	6	14	3	7	12	11[3]	10	13[5]																		35
1	2[5]		6	7[2]	11	8	12	10	4	3	9[1]	5															14	13		36

RAITH ROVERS

First Division

Year Formed: 1883. *Ground & Address:* Stark's Park, Pratt St, Kirkcaldy KY1 1SA. *Telephone:* 01592 263514. *Fax:* 01592 642833. *E-mail:* office@raithroversfc.com *Website:* www.raithroversfc.com
Ground Capacity: all seated: 10,104. *Size of Pitch:* 113yd × 70yd.
Chairman: David Somerville. *General Manager:* Bob Mullen. *Commercial Manager:* John Drysdale.
Manager: John McGlynn. *Assistant Manager:* Gary Kirk. *Coach:* Shaun Dennis. *Physio:* Lesley Mackie
Club Nickname: Rovers. *Previous Grounds:* Robbie's Park.
Record Attendance: 31,306 v Hearts, Scottish Cup 2nd rd, 7 Feb 1953.
Record Transfer Fee received: £900,000 for S. McAnespie to Bolton Wanderers (Sept 1995).
Record Transfer Fee paid: £225,000 for Paul Harvey from Airdrieonians (1996).
Record Victory: 10-1 v Coldstream, Scottish Cup 2nd rd, 13 Feb 1954.
Record Defeat: 2-11 v Morton, Division II, 18 Mar 1936.
Most Capped Player: David Morris, 6, Scotland.
Most League Appearances: 430: Willie McNaught, 1946-51.
Most League Goals in Season (Individual): 38: Norman Haywood, Division II, 1937-38.
Most Goals Overall (Individual): 154: Gordon Dalziel (League), 1987-94.

RAITH ROVERS 2008–09 LEAGUE RECORD

Match No.	Date	Venue	Opponents	Result	H/T Score	Lg. Pos.	Goalscorers	Attendance
1	Aug 2	A	Ayr U	D 0-0	0-0	—		1391
2	9	H	Queen's Park	W 2-0	1-0	5	Smith [10], Walker [54]	1507
3	16	A	Alloa Ath	D 1-1	1-1	4	Smith [34]	899
4	23	H	Stranraer	W 2-1	1-1	3	Campbell [7], Smith [90]	1483
5	30	A	Peterhead	W 2-1	1-0	2	Wardlaw [8], Smith [72]	837
6	Sept 13	H	East Fife	D 1-1	0-0	3	Ellis [68]	3637
7	20	H	Stirling A	D 1-1	0-1	4	Smith (pen) [90]	1648
8	27	A	Brechin C	L 0-2	0-2	4		769
9	Oct 4	A	Arbroath	W 2-0	2-0	3	Walker [20], Ferry [22]	855
10	18	A	Ayr U	W 3-2	1-1	2	Wales (pen) [36], Smith [71], Weir [90]	1746
11	25	A	Stranraer	W 2-0	1-0	2	Wales [38], Smith [64]	338
12	Nov 1	H	Alloa Ath	W 4-1	1-1	1	Wales (pen) [7], Ferry [58], Smith 2 [62, 70]	1669
13	8	A	East Fife	W 2-0	1-0	1	Smith [27], Sloan [48]	1980
14	15	H	Peterhead	W 3-0	0-0	1	Wales 2 [62, 70], Weir [65]	1762
15	22	H	Brechin C	D 2-2	1-0	1	Wales [37], Wardlaw [50]	2229
16	Dec 13	A	Queen's Park	W 2-1	1-1	1	Smith 2 [11, 89]	735
17	20	H	Arbroath	W 2-1	0-0	1	Davidson [82], Ferry [90]	1477
18	27	A	Peterhead	L 1-2	0-0	1	Wales [80]	820
19	Jan 3	H	East Fife	W 1-0	0-0	1	Ferry [69]	4812
20	10	A	Stirling A	L 1-2	0-1	—	Sloan [61]	906
21	17	H	Stranraer	W 2-1	1-0	1	Weir [1], Wilson [46]	1455
22	24	A	Alloa Ath	D 0-0	0-0	1		953
23	31	A	Ayr U	D 2-2	2-1	1	Campbell [6], Ferry [9]	2368
24	Feb 21	H	Stirling A	D 1-1	1-1	1	Smith [21]	1770
25	28	H	Peterhead	D 3-3	3-3	1	Campbell [6], Smith [10], Weir [27]	1564
26	Mar 7	A	East Fife	W 1-0	0-0	2	Weir [76]	1957
27	14	H	Ayr U	L 0-1	0-0	2		3438
28	17	H	Queen's Park	W 1-0	1-0	—	Weir [24]	1294
29	21	A	Arbroath	W 2-0	1-0	2	Sloan [26], Campbell [55]	921
30	24	A	Brechin C	W 4-0	2-0	—	Smith 2 [18, 26], Campbell [49], Wales [83]	780
31	Apr 4	A	Stranraer	W 3-0	2-0	2	Williamson [18], Sloan [36], Hislop [85]	398
32	11	H	Alloa Ath	W 3-1	1-0	2	Smith 2 [26, 70], Weir [90]	1770
33	18	A	Stirling A	W 1-0	0-0	1	Hislop [52]	1125
34	25	H	Brechin C	W 2-0	0-0	1	Sloan [75], Weir [85]	2529
35	May 2	A	Queen's Park	W 1-0	1-0	1	Weir [1]	1763
36	9	H	Arbroath	D 0-0	0-0	1		4426

Final League Position: 1

Honours
League Champions: First Division: 1992-93, 1994-95. Second Division: 2008-09. Division II 1907-08, 1909-10 (shared), 1937-38, 1948-49; *Runners-up:* Division II 1908-09, 1926-27, 1966-67. Second Division 1975-76, 1977-78, 1986-87. *Scottish Cup Runners-up:* 1913. *League Cup Winners:* 1994-95. *Runners-up:* 1948-49.

European: *UEFA Cup:* 6 matches (1995-96).

Club colours: Shirt: Navy with white. Shorts: Navy. Stockings: Navy with white tops.

Goalscorers: *League* (60): Smith 18 (1 pen), Weir 9, Wales 8 (2 pens), Campbell 5, Ferry 5, Sloan 5, Hislop 2, Walker 2, Wardlaw 2, Davidson 1, Ellis 1, Williamson 1, Wilson 1.
Scottish Cup (1): Wales 1.
CIS Cup (1): Campbell 1.
Challenge Cup (1): Weir 1.

McGurn D 30	Wilson C 36	Campbell M 31	Ellis L 28	Cook A 13+5	Sloan R 31+2	Davidson I 33	Walker A 24+8	Ferry M 27+8	Weir G 34+2	Smith K 25+3	Dunbar J —+3	Graham T —+2	Silvestro C 8+3	Wardlaw G 4+16	Bryce L —+12	O'Connor G 6+1	Simmons S 13+1	Armstrong D —+1	Wales G 20+3	Guerrero J —+1	Lumsden T 10+1	Williamson 19+3	Andrews M 11	Hislop S 3+8	Match No.
1	2	3	4	5	6	7	8	9^1	10	11^2	12	13													1
1	2	4	5	3^9	7	8	6	11	10	9															2
1	2	4			7	5	8	3	10	9						6	11^1	12							3
1	2	4	3		7	5	8	11^1	10	9						6^2	12	13							4
1^0	2	4	5	3		8		11	10^2	9						6	7^1	13	15	12					5
	2	4	5	3		8	7	11	10^2			13				6	9^1	12	1						6
	2	4^1	5	3	13	8	7	11^2	10	9			6^3				14	1	12						7
	2	3	4	5	9^1	8	6	12	13	10^2			7^3				14	1	11						8
1	2	4	5	3	6^2	7	8	11	10^3	12			13	14			9^1								9
1	6	4^1	5	2	8	3	7	9	11	13						10	12^2								10
1	2	4	3		7	5	6	11	10	8^1	12					9									11
1	2	3	5		6	4	7^3	8	11^1	9^2	13		14	12			10								12
	2	3	5^2	13	6	4	7	9	11	8^1			12				1		10						13
	2	4^2	3	14	7	5	6^3	11	10	8^1	13		12				1		9						14
	2	4	3		7	5	6	11	10	8^1	12						1		9						15
1	2	3	5		8^3	7	12	14	11^2	9			6^1	13					10		4				16
1	2	4^1	3	12	11	7	8	13	10^3				6^2	14					9		5				17
1	2		3		7	4	6	11	10^2	8^1			12	13					9		5				18
1	2	4^1	3		11	7	6	12	10	8^2			13						9		5				19
1	2		5	3	11	8	6^1	12	10				7						9		4				20
1	2	3	13	7^1	5	6	11	10				12					8		9		4^2				21
1	2	4	3		7	6	12	11	10	9^2			13			8^1					5				22
1	2	3	5^1	12	6	8		9	11^3	10^1			13	14			7				4				23
1	2	3		5	6	4	12	8^1	11	9							7		10^2			13			24
1	2	3	5^1	8	4	6	12	11^3	9				14				7		10^2			13			25
1	2	4		3		6	7	13	10^3	8^1			11				9				12^2		5	14	26
1	2	4		3	12	6	7		10^2	8							9^1				11		5	13	27
1	2	4^1		3	7	6	8	12	10^3	9							13				11^2		5	14	28
1	2	4	3		8	6^4		11	10^2	12							9^1				7		5	13	29
1	2	3	5		8			9	11^2	10^1			14				7		13		6^3	4		12	30
1	2		3		6		13	11	10^3	9^1						8			12		4	7^2	5	14	31
1	2		3		6		12	11	10^3	9^2			14				8^4	7^1		4		5	13		32
1	2	4	3^3		6	8	13	11	10	9^1			14						7^2	5		12			33
1	2	4		11	6	13	3		10^2	12						8			7		5	9^1			34
1	2	3		6	8	12	5	11	13				9						7^1		4	10^2			35
1	2	3		9	7	6^2	5	13	12	8			14						11		4^3	10^1			36

RANGERS   Premier League

Year Formed: 1873. *Ground & Address:* Ibrox Stadium, 150 Edmiston Drive, Glasgow G51 2XD.
Telephone: 0871 702 1972. *Fax:* 0870 600 1978. *Website:* www.rangers.co.uk
Ground Capacity: all seated: 51,082. *Size of Pitch:* 105m × 68m.
Executive Chairman: Sir David Murray. *Chief Executive:* Martin Bain. *Head of Football Administration:* Andrew Dickson.
Manager: Walter Smith. *Assistant Manager:* Ally McCoist. *Physio:* David Henderson.
Club Nickname(s): The Gers. *Previous Grounds:* Flesher's Haugh, Burnbank, Kinning Park, Old Ibrox.
Record Attendance: 118,567 v Celtic, Division I, 2 Jan 1939.
Record Transfer Fee received: £9,000,000 for Alan Hutton to Tottenham H (January 2008).
Record Transfer Fee paid: £12,000,000 for Tore Andre Flo from Chelsea (November 2000).
Record Victory: 14-2 v Blairgowrie, Scottish Cup 1st rd, 20 Jan, 1934. *Record Defeat:* 2-10 v Airdrieonians; 1886.
Most Capped Player: Ally McCoist, 60, Scotland.
Most League Appearances: 496: John Greig, 1962-78.
Most League Goals in Season (Individual): 44: Sam English, Division I, 1931-32.
Most Goals Overall (Individual): 355: Ally McCoist; 1985-98.

Honours

League Champions: (52 times) Division I 1890-91 (shared), 1898-99, 1899-1900, 1900-01, 1901-02, 1910-11, 1911-12, 1912-13, 1917-18, 1919-20, 1920-21, 1922-23, 1923-24, 1924-25, 1926-27, 1927-28, 1928-29, 1929-30, 1930-31, 1932-33, 1933-34, 1934-35, 1936-37, 1938-39, 1946-47, 1948-49, 1949-50, 1952-53, 1955-56, 1956-57, 1958-59, 1960-61, 1962-63, 1963-64, 1974-75. Premier Division: 1975-76, 1977-78, 1986-87, 1988-89, 1989-90, 1990-91, 1991-92, 1992-93, 1993-94, 1994-95, 1995-96, 1996-97, 1998-99, 1999-2000, 2002-03, 2004-05, 2008-09; *Runners-up:* 26 times.

RANGERS 2008–09 LEAGUE RECORD

Match No.	Date	Venue	Opponents	Result	H/T Score	Lg. Pos.	Goalscorers	Atten-dance
1	Aug 9	A	Falkirk	W 1-0	0-0	—	Velicka [64]	6669
2	16	H	Hearts	W 2-0	1-0	2	Lafferty [37], Boyd (pen) [90]	48,191
3	23	A	Aberdeen	D 1-1	1-1	2	Weir [24]	16,489
4	31	A	Celtic	W 4-2	1-1	1	Cousin [37], Miller 2 [52, 79], Pedro Mendes [62]	58,595
5	Sept 13	H	Kilmarnock	W 2-1	0-1	1	Boyd 2 (1 pen) [58 (p), 62]	50,019
6	21	H	Motherwell	W 2-1	0-0	1	Davis [57], Novo [76]	49,448
7	28	A	Hibernian	W 3-0	2-0	1	Miller 2 [31, 40], Bougherra [73]	15,292
8	Oct 4	A	St Mirren	L 0-1	0-0	2		7520
9	25	A	Hamilton A	W 3-1	1-1	2	Boyd 2 (1 pen) [42 (p), 50], Novo [80]	4613
10	Nov 1	H	Inverness CT	W 5-0	5-0	2	Novo [7], Boyd 3 (1 pen) [14, 19, 28 (p)], Miller [45]	49,255
11	4	H	Dundee U	D 3-3	2-2	—	Davis [11], Papac [37], Thomson [90]	48,686
12	9	A	Kilmarnock	W 4-0	0-0	2	Weir [50], Boyd [54], Miller [87], Whittaker [90]	10,153
13	12	A	Motherwell	D 0-0	0-0	—		9600
14	15	H	St Mirren	W 2-1	2-0	2	Boyd [5], Davis [10]	49,321
15	22	A	Aberdeen	W 2-0	0-0	2	Darcheville [52], Boyd [68]	50,166
16	29	A	Hearts	L 1-2	1-2	2	Karipidis (og) [26]	15,710
17	Dec 6	H	Hamilton A	W 7-1	2-1	2	Miller [11], Boyd 3 (1 pen) [28, 52 (p), 62], Lafferty [80], Novo [88], Davis [90]	48,282
18	13	A	Dundee U	D 2-2	1-0	2	Boyd [11], Lafferty [76]	11,362
19	20	A	Hibernian	W 1-0	0-0	2	Boyd [61]	49,538
20	27	H	Celtic	L 0-1	0-0	2		50,403
21	Jan 4	A	Inverness CT	W 3-0	0-0	2	Pedro Mendes [46], Boyd 2 [81, 87]	7056
22	17	H	Falkirk	W 3-1	1-1	2	Boyd 2 (1 pen) [45 (p), 80], Davis [90]	48,811
23	24	A	Aberdeen	D 0-0	0-0	2		20,441
24	31	H	Dundee U	W 2-0	0-0	2	Fleck (pen) [78], Lafferty [90]	49,918
25	Feb 15	A	Celtic	D 0-0	0-0	2		58,766
26	21	H	Kilmarnock	W 3-1	3-1	1	Boyd [29], Miller 2 [33, 35]	50,301
27	28	A	Hamilton A	W 1-0	1-0	1	Ferguson [35]	5895
28	Mar 4	H	Inverness CT	L 0-1	0-0	—		48,129
29	21	H	Hearts	D 2-2	2-0	2	Lafferty [9], Ferguson [45]	50,310
30	Apr 5	A	Falkirk	W 1-0	1-0	2	Boyd [9]	6853
31	8	A	St Mirren	W 2-1	2-0	—	Boyd [12], Edu [19]	6231
32	11	H	Motherwell	W 3-1	2-1	2	Velicka [2], Boyd 2 (1 pen) [10, 65 (p)]	50,080
33	19	A	Hibernian	W 3-2	1-1	2	Whittaker [2], Velicka [52], Edu [73]	14,014
34	May 3	H	Hearts	W 2-0	1-0	2	Velicka [45], Boyd [89]	49,663
35	9	H	Celtic	W 1-0	1-0	1	Davis [37]	50,321
36	13	A	Hibernian	D 1-1	0-1	—	Novo [80]	13,765
37	16	H	Aberdeen	W 2-1	0-0	1	Foster (og) [66], Miller [68]	50,295
38	24	A	Dundee U	W 3-0	2-0	1	Lafferty [6], Pedro Mendes [46], Boyd [52]	14,077

Final League Position: 1

Scottish Cup Winners: (33 times) 1894, 1897, 1898, 1903, 1928, 1930, 1932, 1934, 1935, 1936, 1948, 1949, 1950, 1953, 1960, 1962, 1963, 1964, 1966, 1973, 1976, 1978, 1979, 1981, 1992, 1993, 1996, 1999, 2000, 2002, 2003, 2008, 2009; *Runners-up:* 17 times.

League Cup Winners: (25 times) 1946-47, 1948-49, 1960-61, 1961-62, 1963-64, 1964-65, 1970-71, 1975-76, 1977-78, 1978-79, 1981-82, 1983-84, 1984-85, 1986-87, 1987-88, 1988-89, 1990-91, 1992-93, 1993-94, 1996-97, 1998-99, 2001-02, 2002-03, 2004-05, 2007-08; *Runners-up:* 7 times.

European: *European Cup:* 139 matches (1956-57, 1957-58, 1959-60 semi-finals, 1961-62, 1963-64, 1964-65, 1975-76, 1976-77, 1978-79, 1987-88, 1989-90, 1990-91, 1991-92, 1992-93 final pool, 1993-94, 1994-95, 1995-96; 1996-97, 1997-98, 1999-2000, 2000-01, 2003-04, 2005-06, 2007-08, 2008-09). *Cup Winners' Cup:* 54 matches (1960-61, 1962-63, 1966-67 runners-up, 1969-70, 1971-72 winners, 1973-74, 1977-78, 1979-80, 1981-82, 1983-84). *UEFA Cup:* 77 matches (*Fairs Cup:* 1967-68, 1968-69 semi-finals, 1970-71. *UEFA Cup:* 1982-83, 1984-85, 1985-86, 1986-87, 1988-89, 1997-98, 1998-99, 1999-2000, 2000-01, 2002-03, 2004-05, 2006-07, 2007-08 runners-up).

Club colours: Shirt: Royal blue with red and white trim. Shorts: White with red and blue trim. Stockings: Black with red tops.

Goalscorers: *League* (77): Boyd 27 (7 pens), Miller 10, Davis 6, Lafferty 6, Novo 5, Velicka 4, Pedro Mendes 3, Edu 2, Ferguson 2, Weir 2, Whittaker 2, Bougherra 1, Cousin 1, Darcheville 1, Fleck 1 (pen), Papac 1, Thomson 1, own goals 2. *Scottish Cup* (15): Miller 3, Lafferty 2, Niguez 2 (1 pen), Novo 2, Boyd 1, Davis 1, Papac 1, Velicka 1, Whittaker 1, own goal 1. *CIS Cup* (7): Boyd 3, Novo 2, Lafferty 1, Pedro Mendes 1. *Champions League* (1): Thomson 1.

McGregor A 27	Dailly C 7+2	Papac S 29	Broadfoot K 27	Bougherra M 31	Thomson K 11	Whittaker S 19+5	McCulloch L 10+2	Boyd K 33+2	Velicka A 6+2	Lafferty K 11+14	Darcheville J 4+4	Adam C 7+2	Cousin D 1+1	Weir D 36	Pedro Mendes 35	Beasley D 6+4	Miller K 25+5	Novo N 7+22	Davis S 34	Edu M 11+1	Alexander N 11	Ferguson B 17+5	Loy R —+1	Burke C —+2	Niguez A —+3	Fleck J 7+1	Naismith S 1+6	Smith S 5	Match No.
1	2	3	4	5	6²	7	8	9³	10¹	11	12	13	14																1
1		3	2	6	4	7¹		9	10³	11²	14			5	8	13	12												2
1		3	2	6	4			9			12			5	8	13	10²	7¹	11										3
1		3	2	4	6	7¹		9						5	8		10	12	11										4
1		3	2	6				9³		14	13			5	8	11¹	10	12	7	4²									5
		3	2	6	4			9						5	8	11¹	10	12	7		1								6
		3	2	6	4				13	9¹	11²			5	8		10	12	7		1								7
1		3	2	6	4¹		13		12	9²	7			5	8		10		11										8
1		3	2	6	4			9	13					5	8	11¹	10²	12	7										9
1		3	2	6	4¹			9³						5	8	14	10²	11	7				12	13					10
1		3²	2	6	4			9	13					5	8		10	11¹	7				12						11
1		3	2	6	4³	14		9	12					5	8²		10	7¹	11					13					12
1		3²	2	6			13	9		11¹				5	8		10	12	7	4									13
1	2	3		6				9		11¹				5	8		10	12	7	4									14
1	2	3	4					9¹		11	10²	7		5	8		12	13				6							15
1	2	6	3					9	11					5	8	13	10²	7¹		4			12						16
1		3	2	6				9²	13					5	8	11³	10¹	7				4		14					17
1		3	2	4				9	12	11¹				5	8		10²	13	7			6							18
1		3	2	4				9		11				5	8		10¹	12	7			6							19
1		3	2²	4				9		11¹				5	8		10	13	7			6							20
1		3	2	4				9	13					5	8²		10¹	7	11			6		12					21
1		3ᵃ	2	4				9²	13					5	8		10¹	12	7			6				11			22
1		3	2	4			11		12					5	8		10¹	13	7			6				9²			23
1			2	4	3			9¹	12					5	8	13	10²		7			6				11			24
1		3	2	4			11							5	8		10²	12	7			6			9¹	13			25
1		3	2	4				9²	13					5	8		10		7			6		12		11¹			26
1		3	2	4		12		9		11¹				5	8		10²		7			6				13			27
1		3	2	4				9	12					5ᵃ	8¹		10³		7			6		14	11²	13			28
1	5	3	2	4				9							8	11²	10¹	12	7			6				13			29
		3	2	6	4²	14		9³						5	8	13	10		7		1				11¹	12			30
14		3³	2	6				9	13					5	8		10¹	12²	7	4	1						11		31
11			2	6				9						5	8		10¹	12	7	4	1					13		3²	32
13		3²	2	6				9³						5	8		10¹	12	7	4	1			14			11		33
	2	3		6				9	13					5	8		10¹	12	7	4	1						11²		34
	2	3		6				9²	13					5	8		10	12	7	4	1						11¹		35
	2	3		6				9	13					5	8		10²	12	7	4	1						11¹		36
		3	2	6ᵃ				9²		11³				5	8¹	13	10		7	4	1		12	14					37
		3	2	6		14		9¹		11³				5	8		10²	12	7	4	1					13			38

ROSS COUNTY
First Division

Year Formed: 1929. *Ground & Address:* Victoria Park, Dingwall IV15 9QW. *Telephone:* 01349 860860. *Fax:* 01349 866277.
E-mail: donnie@rosscountyfootballclub.co.uk *Website:* www.rosscountyfootballclub.co.uk
Ground Capacity: 6700. *Size of Ground:* 105×68m.
Chairman: David Siegel. *Secretary:* Donnie MacBean.
Manager: Derek Adams. *Director of Football:* George Adams. *Coaches:* Derek Adams and (*Head of Youth*) David
Kirkwood. *Physio:* Douglas Sim.
Club Nickname(s): The Staggies.
Record Attendance: 6600, benefit match v Celtic, 31 August 1970.
Record Transfer Fee Received: £200,000 for Neil Tarrant to Aston Villa (April 1999).
Record Transfer Fee Paid: £25,000 for Barry Wilson from Southampton (Oct. 1992).
Record Victory: 11-0 v St Cuthbert Wanderers, Scottish Cup, 11 Dec 1993.
Record Defeat: 1-10 v Inverness Thistle, Highland League.
Most League Appearances: 230: Mark McCulloch, 2002-2009.
Most League Goals in Season: 24: Andrew Barrowman, 2007-08.
Most League Goals (Overall): 44: Steven Ferguson, 1996-2002.

ROSS COUNTY 2008–09 LEAGUE RECORD

Match No.	Date		Venue	Opponents	Result	H/T Score	Lg. Pos.	Goalscorers	Atten-dance
1	Aug	2	H	Dundee	L 1-2	0-1	—	Daal [90]	3444
2		9	A	Livingston	L 0-2	0-1	10		1068
3		16	A	Clyde	D 2-2	2-0	10	Craig [17], Morrison [19]	966
4		30	A	Partick Th	W 1-0	1-0	8	Craig [7]	2945
5	Sept	3	A	Queen of the S	L 0-1	0-0	—		2525
6		13	H	St Johnstone	L 1-2	0-0	9	Brittain [70]	2474
7		20	A	Dunfermline Ath	L 1-3	0-2	9	Craig [57]	2631
8		27	H	Airdrie U	W 2-0	1-0	9	Smyth (og) [10], Craig [77]	2259
9	Oct	4	H	Morton	W 3-0	0-0	7	Hart [76], Craig [76], Higgins [84]	2290
10		18	A	Dundee	W 2-1	2-0	6	Dowie [23], Craig [41]	3228
11		25	H	Queen of the S	L 0-2	0-1	6		232
12	Nov	1	H	Clyde	W 3-0	0-0	6	Higgins [82], Gardyne [84], Hart [90]	2205
13		8	A	St Johnstone	L 1-2	0-1	6	McCulloch [63]	2714
14		22	A	Airdrie U	W 2-0	1-0	6	Higgins [33], Brittain [66]	939
15		25	H	Partick Th	W 1-0	0-0	—	Daal [68]	1625
16	Dec	13	H	Livingston	L 1-4	1-1	6	McCulloch [45]	2180
17		20	A	Morton	L 1-2	1-1	6	Morrison [24]	1853
18		27	A	Partick Th	W 2-0	1-0	5	Higgins 2 [24, 84]	2465
19	Jan	17	H	Queen of the S	W 1-0	0-0	5	Daal [73]	2323
20		24	A	Clyde	L 0-2	0-1	5		776
21		31	A	Livingston	L 2-4	0-3	7	Hart [50], Higgins [86]	1378
22	Feb	7	H	St Johnstone	D 2-2	2-0	—	McCulloch [33], Craig [45]	2240
23		21	A	Dunfermline Ath	W 2-1	1-0	6	Brewster [45], Higgins [67]	3331
24		28	H	Airdrie U	D 0-0	0-0	6		2290
25	Mar	7	A	St Johnstone	D 0-0	0-0	7		2727
26		10	H	Partick Th	L 0-2	0-0	—		2017
27		14	A	Dundee	L 0-2	0-2	8		3381
28		21	H	Morton	D 1-1	1-0	8	Keddie [44]	2236
29		24	H	Dunfermline Ath	W 2-1	0-0	—	Brittain [62], Brewster [90]	1782
30		28	H	Dundee	D 1-1	0-0	—	Higgins [90]	2296
31	Apr	4	A	Queen of the S	W 2-1	2-0	6	Higgins [5], Brewster [19]	2029
32		11	H	Clyde	D 0-0	0-0	6		2078
33		18	H	Dunfermline Ath	L 1-3	0-1	8	Craig [47]	2413
34		25	A	Airdrie U	L 0-1	0-0	8		927
35	May	2	A	Livingston	D 2-2	0-1	8	Craig 2 (1 pen) [53, 59 (p)]	2567
36		9	A	Morton	W 2-0	0-0	8	Brittain [55], Higgins [67]	1956

Final League Position: 8

Honours
League Champions: Second Division 2007-08. Third Division 1998-99.
League Challenge Cup Winners: 2006-07; *Runners up:* 2004-05, 2008-09.

Club colours: Shirt: Navy blue with white trim. Shorts: Navy with white flashes. Stockings: White.

Goalscorers: *League* (42): Craig 10 (1 pen), Higgins 10, Brittain 4, Brewster 3, Daal 3, Hart 3, McCulloch 3, Morrison 2, Dowie 1, Gardyne 1, Keddie 1, own goal 1.
Scottish Cup (4): Higgins 2, Brittain 1 (pen), Hart 1.
Challenge Cup (11): Craig 2, Daal 2, Higgins 2, Keddie 2, Dowie 1, Winters 1, own goal 1.

Bullock T 16	McCulloch M 35	Golabek S 14 + 1	Dowie A 28 + 1	Boyd S 28	Lawson P 18 + 2	Hart R 24 + 9	Brittain R 30	Higgins S 23 + 8	Winters D 3 + 3	Strachan A 12 + 12	Daal D 16 + 12	Craig S 26 + 5	Scott M 16 + 8	Morrison S 7 + 8	Watt S 23 + 1	Keddie A 25 + 4	Shields D — + 1	Gardyne M 9 + 18	Soutar D 13	Stewart J 3 + 6	Corrigan M 10	Brewster C 10	Malin J 7 + 1	Match No.
1	2	3	4	5	6^1	7	8	9	10^2	11^3	12	13	14											1
1			4		6	7^2	8	11^4	12	13	10^1	9	2	3	5^3	14								2
1	2		3	4	6^3	7	8			10^1		12	11^{12}	14	9				5	13				3
1	2		3	4	6^1	7	8	13	10^2				14	11^3	9			5	12					4
1	2			4	5	6	7^1	8		9	13	11^2	10		3			12						5
1	2			4	5	6^1	7^3	8		9	12	14	10	13	11^2	3								6
1	2			4	5	7^4	8			12	9	10	11	3		6^1								7
1	2			4	5	7	8	12		13	9^1	10^3	11	14	3	6^2								8
1	2			4	5	7^1	13	8		14	12	9^3	10	11^2	3	6								9
1	2			4	5	14	7	8	13	6	9^2	10^3	11^1	3	12									10
1	2			4	5		7	8	13	6^3	9^2	10	11	14	3^1	12								11
1	2			4	5	14	7	8^3	13	6	9^1	10	11^2	3	12									12
	2			4	5		7	8	9^3	6^1	14	10	13	11^2	3	12	1							13
1	2	13		5	4		8	10^1	12	11	9		7^3	14	6	3^2								14
1	2			4	5	12	8	10^2		11^3	9		7^1	14	6	3	13							15
1	2			4	5	12	8	10^3		11		9	7^2	14	6^1	3	13							16
1	2			4	5	7^2	8	13		12		9	10	11^1	6^3	3	14							17
	2	3	12^2	5		7	8^1	9	14	6		10^3		11	4			13	1					18
	2	3		5			8	11^3		13	10		6	14	4^1	12				1		9^2		19
	2	5	4			7	6	9^2		13	11	14	8^3		3^1	12				1		10		20
	2	3	4^1	5		7^2	8	11		12	10^3	14	9			6		13		1				21
		4	3	5		7^2	8	11^1		10^3	9	12	13		6			1		14	2			22
		4	3	5		7	8	11^1		9	6	12						1		13	2	10^2		23
		4	3	5		7^3		11^2		12	9	8^1	14		6			1		2	10			24
		4	3	5		8^2	7	11^1		12	9	13			6	14		1		2	10^3			25
		4	3	5			11	8^2	12	9	7^1		6			13	1^6			2	10	15		26
		4	3	5		7	11	8	12	9^2		6				13				2	10^1	1		27
		4		5	8	12	7^2	13	10^3	9	14				6	3		11^1		2		1		28
		4		5	8^1	12	7			10	13				6	3		11^2		2	9	1		29
		4		5	8^2	13	7	12		10^3	9				6	3		11^1	14	2		1		30
		4	2	5	8	13	7^2	10^3		14	12				6	3		9		11^1		1		31
		4	2	5	8^1	12	7	9^3		13	14				6	3		11		10^2		1		32
		4	3		8^2	7		9	12		10				6	5		11		13	2^1	1		33
		4	3	2	8	7^2		9			10^3		14	6	5			13	1	12		11^1		34
		4	2	5	8	11	7	9^1			10^2			6	$3^{■}$			12	1	13				35
	2	8	5	3	7	12	6	10^3		13			4		14			1		9^1		11^2		36

ST JOHNSTONE   Premier League

Year Formed: 1884. *Ground & Address:* McDiarmid Park, Crieff Road, Perth PH1 2SJ. *Telephone:* 01738 459090. *Fax:* 01738 625 771. *Clubcall:* 0898 121559. *Email:* karin@perthsaints.co.uk *Website:* www.perthstjohnstonefc.co.uk
Ground Capacity: all seated: 10,673. *Size of Pitch:* 115yd × 75yd.
Chairman: G.S. Brown. *Secretary and Managing Director:* Stewart Duff. *Sales Executives:* Paul Smith and Susan Weir.
Manager: Derek McInnes. *Assistant Manager:* Tony Docherty. *Youth Coach:* Tommy Campbell.
Club Nickname(s): Saints. *Previous Grounds:* Recreation Grounds, Muirton Park.
Record Attendance: (McDiarmid Park): 10,545 v Dundee, Premier Division, 23 May 1999.
Record Transfer Fee received: £1,750,000 for Calum Davidson to Blackburn R (March 1998).
Record Transfer Fee paid: £400,000 for Billy Dodds from Dundee (1994).
Record Victory: 9-0 v Albion R, League Cup, 9 Mar 1946.
Record Defeat: 1-10 v Third Lanark, Scottish Cup, 24 Jan 1903.
Most Capped Player: Nick Dasovic, 26, Canada.
Most League Appearances: 298: Drew Rutherford, 1976-85.
Most League Goals in Season (Individual): 36: Jimmy Benson, Division II, 1931-32.
Most Goals Overall (Individual): 140: John Brogan, 1977-83.

ST JOHNSTONE 2008–09 LEAGUE RECORD

Match No.	Date	Venue	Opponents	Result	H/T Score	Lg. Pos.	Goalscorers	Attendance
1	Aug 2	H	Livingston	W 2-0	0-0	—	MacDonald [55], Sheerin (pen) [90]	2692
2	9	A	Morton	D 2-2	2-1	3	Milne [3], Swankie [41]	2649
3	16	H	Dunfermline Ath	L 0-3	0-1	6		3797
4	23	A	Partick Th	L 0-4	0-1	6		2861
5	30	H	Clyde	L 2-3	1-2	9	McCaffrey [43], Holmes [67]	2412
6	Sept 13	A	Ross Co	W 2-1	0-0	7	Samuel 2 [29, 47]	2474
7	20	A	Queen of the S	D 2-2	0-0	8	Thomson (og) [64], Holmes [76]	2831
8	27	H	Dundee	W 2-0	0-0	5	Sheerin [53], Milne [86]	4307
9	Oct 4	H	Airdrie U	W 3-1	1-0	5	Swankie [4], Milne 2 [56, 90]	2259
10	18	A	Livingston	W 1-0	0-0	4	Milne [30]	2542
11	25	H	Partick Th	W 3-0	1-0	2	McCaffrey [14], Craig (pen) [62], Milne [69]	2772
12	Nov 1	A	Dunfermline Ath	W 2-1	1-1	1	Hardie [5], Craig [66]	4653
13	8	H	Ross Co	W 2-1	1-0	1	Hardie [45], Samuel [81]	2714
14	15	A	Clyde	D 2-2	1-1	1	Craig (pen) [19], Rutkiewicz [62]	1419
15	29	A	Dundee	D 1-1	1-0	—	Milne [28]	6537
16	Dec 6	H	Queen of the S	D 0-0	0-0	—		3068
17	13	H	Morton	W 1-0	0-0	1	Rutkiewicz [88]	2749
18	20	A	Airdrie U	D 1-1	0-0	1	Craig (pen) [90]	1175
19	27	H	Clyde	W 1-0	1-0	1	Milne [28]	3491
20	Jan 17	A	Partick Th	D 0-0	0-0	1		3353
21	31	A	Morton	D 0-0	0-0	1		2810
22	Feb 7	A	Ross Co	D 2-2	0-2	—	McCaffrey [53], Holmes [77]	2240
23	14	H	Livingston	W 1-0	0-0	—	Samuel [70]	2752
24	21	A	Queen of the S	D 3-3	0-1	1	Rutkiewicz [56], Millar [64], Holmes [87]	2857
25	28	H	Dundee	D 0-0	0-0	1		7238
26	Mar 7	H	Ross Co	D 0-0	0-0	1		2727
27	10	A	Clyde	W 3-1	1-0	—	Milne 2 [38, 90], Swankie [47]	1093
28	14	A	Livingston	L 0-1	0-1	1		1882
29	21	H	Airdrie U	W 3-0	2-0	1	Samuel 2 [13, 36], Sheerin [90]	2561
30	Apr 4	H	Partick Th	D 1-1	0-0	1	Milne [65]	4909
31	7	H	Dunfermline Ath	D 0-0	0-0	—		3199
32	11	A	Dunfermline Ath	W 3-1	2-1	1	Hardie [18], Irvine [41], Craig (pen) [48]	3595
33	19	H	Queen of the S	L 2-3	0-1	1	Holmes [83], Millar [88]	3294
34	25	A	Dundee	W 1-0	1-0	1	Milne [2]	6305
35	May 2	H	Morton	W 3-1	1-1	1	Hardie [29], Milne 2 [51, 79]	6453
36	11	A	Airdrie U	W 4-0	0-0	1	Swankie [49], Anderson [80], May [86], Barrett [90]	633

Final League Position: 1

Honours
League Champions: First Division 1982-83, 1989-90, 1996-97, 2008-09. Division II 1923-24, 1959-60, 1962-63; *Runners-up:* Division II 1931-32. First Division 2005-06, 2006-07. Second Division 1987-88.
Scottish Cup: Semi-finals 1934, 1968, 1989, 1991, 2007, 2008.
League Cup: Runners-up: 1969-70, 1998-99.
League Challenge Cup Winners: 2007-08; *Runners-up:* 1996-97.

European: *UEFA Cup:* 10 matches (1971-72, 1999-2000).

Club colours: Shirt: Royal blue with white trim. Shorts: White. Stockings: Royal blue with white hoops.

Goalscorers: *League* (55): Milne 14, Samuel 6, Craig 5 (4 pens), Holmes 5, Hardie 4, Swankie 4, McCaffrey 3, Rutkiewicz 3, Sheerin 3 (1 pen), Millar 2, Anderson 1, Barrett 1, Irvine 1, MacDonald 1, May 1, own goal 1.
Scottish Cup (0).
CIS Cup (1): Craig 1.
Challenge Cup (1): Samuel 1.

McLean E 4	Irvine G 34 + 1	Craig L 31 + 3	Millar C 30 + 4	Rutkiewicz K 34	James K 4	MacDonald P 2 + 10	Hardie M 20 + 4	Jackson A 5 + 5	Samuel C 20 + 8	Sheerin P 29 + 5	Swankie G 17 + 10	McCaffrey S 25 + 1	Holmes D 22 + 13	Smith D 3	Milne S 26 + 6	Weatherston D — + 1	Main A 32	Anderson S 11 + 4	McKoy N 2 + 3	Morgan A 2 + 2	Moon K 12 + 10	Morris J 10 + 4	Hanlon P 2	Gartland G 7	Byrne R 5	Barrett G 4 + 5	Doris S 1 + 1	Lindsay J 1	Reynolds S 1	May S — + 1	*Match No.*
1	2	3	4	5	6	7^{2}	8	9^{3}	10^{1}	11	12	13	14																		1
1	2		8	3	4	14	7	12		9^{3}	6^{1}		10	5	11^{2}	13															2
1	2	8	4	5	6	14		12	13	11^{3}	7^{1}		9^{2}	3	10																3
	13	7^{3}	9	4^{2}		10^{1}	8		6			2	12	5	11		1	3	14												4
	2	11	7				8	9^{2}	10	12		6	13		14		1	5	4^{3}	3^{1}											5
	2	10	4	5			8^{2}		9^{1}	11	7^{3}	6	14		12		1	3	13												6
	2	8	6	4			7^{2}	10^{1}	11	9		5	12				1	3	13												7
	2	3	4	5			8^{3}		9^{2}	11	7^{1}	6	12		10		1			14	13										8
	2	3	4	5		14				11	7^{2}	6	9^{3}		10		1		8^{1}	13	12										9
	2	3	4	5			8			7^{2}		6	9		10		1	13		11^{1}	12										10
	2	3	4	5		12	8			11	7^{2}	6	9^{1}		10		1				13										11
	2	3	4	5			8		14	11^{2}	12	6	9^{3}		10		1	13			7^{1}										12
	2	3	4	5			8		14	11	7^{2}	6^{1}	9^{3}		10		1	12				13									13
	2	5	7	3		14	8		12	9	6^{2}		10^{1}		11^{3}		1	4				13									14
	2	3	7	5	6				13	12			9^{2}		10		1	8			11	4^{1}									15
	2	3	7^{2}	5		12	8		11			6	9^{1}		10		1				13	4									16
	2	3	7^{1}	5		13	8^{3}		9	11		6	12		10^{2}		1				14	4									17
	2	3	7	5			8^{3}	13	11^{1}	14	12	6	9		10^{2}		1					4									18
	2	8	12	5				14		11	7^{2}		9		10^{3}		1	6^{1}			13	4	3								19
	2	8^{3}	12	5				10^{2}	13	11	7^{1}	6	9				1				14	4	3								20
	2	8	7	5					12	11		6	9		10^{1}		1					4		3							21
	2	8	7^{3}	5				12	10	11^{2}	13	6	9				1				14	4		3^{1}							22
	2	3	8	5			14	10^{1}	13	11^{3}	7^{2}	6	9		12		1					4									23
	2	8	7	4		14			11^{1}	9	13		10		12		1					6^{2}		5	3^{3}						24
	2	8	7	5			13			12	11^{1}	6	9		10^{3}		1				4^{2}				3	14					25
	2	3	7^{1}	5			14		8	11	12	6	9		13		1				4^{3}					10^{2}					26
	2	13	8	5		14				11	7^{2}	6	12		9^{3}		1				4				3	10^{1}					27
	2	13	8	5		14				11^{3}	7	6	12		9		1				4				3^{2}	10^{1}					28
	2	8^{3}		5			14		7^{1}	11	12	6	9^{2}		10		1				4				3	13					29
	2	3		5			8^{2}		7^{1}	11	13	6	9		10^{3}		1	12			4					14					30
	2	13	8^{3}	5					7	11	14		9^{1}		10		1	3^{2}			4			6		12					31
	2	11	4	5			8^{2}		10^{3}	12	7^{1}		14		9		1	3						6			13				32
	2	4	13	5			8^{3}		10	11	7^{2}		14		9		1	3			12			6^{1}							33
	2	3	7	5			8^{2}		10^{3}	11		6	12		9^{1}		1				4	13				14					34
	2	3	7	5			8^{3}		10^{1}	11	14	6	12		9		1				4^{2}	13									35
1			13						10^{2}	11	7^{3}				12			5			4			6		9	2	3	8^{1}	14	36

ST MIRREN

Premier League

Year Formed: 1877. *Ground & Address:* St Mirren Park, Love St, Paisley PA3 2EA. *Telephone:* 0141 889 2558.
Fax: 0141 848 6444. *E-mail:* commercial@saintmirren.net *Website:* www.saintmirren.net
Ground Capacity: 10,476 (all seated). *Size of Pitch:* 105yd × 68yd.
Chairman: Stewart Gilmour. *Vice-Chairman:* George Campbell. *General Manager:* Brian Caldwell (tel: 0141 8892558;
fax: 0141 8406139). *Commercial Manager:* Campbell Kennedy. *Secretary:* Allan Marshall.
Manager: Gus MacPherson. *Assistant Manager:* Andy Millen. *Youth Development Officer:* David Longwell.
Club Nickname(s): The Buddies. *Previous Grounds:* Short Roods 1877-79, Thistle Park Greenhill 1879-83, Westmarch
1883-94.
Record Attendance: 47,438 v Celtic, League Cup, 20 Aug 1949.
Record Transfer Fee received: £850,000 for Ian Ferguson to Rangers (1988).
Record Transfer Fee paid: £400,000 for Thomas Stickroth from Bayer Uerdingen (1990).
Record Victory: 15-0 v Glasgow University, Scottish Cup 1st rd, 30 Jan 1960.
Record Defeat: 0-9 v Rangers, Division I, 4 Dec 1897.
Most Capped Player: Godmundor Torfason, 29, Iceland.
Most League Appearances: 351: Tony Fitzpatrick, 1973-88.
Most League Goals in Season (Individual): 45: Dunky Walker, Division I, 1921-22.
Most Goals Overall (Individual): 221: David McCrae, 1923-34.

ST MIRREN 2008–09 LEAGUE RECORD

Match No.	Date	Venue	Opponents	Result	H/T Score	Lg. Pos.	Goalscorers	Attendance
1	Aug 10	A	Celtic	L 0-1	0-0	—		57,441
2	16	H	Kilmarnock	D 0-0	0-0	9		4176
3	23	A	Hearts	L 1-2	0-1	11	Mehmet [70]	13,357
4	30	H	Aberdeen	L 0-1	0-1	—		4680
5	Sept 13	A	Inverness CT	W 2-1	0-1	9	Mehmet [61], Brady [80]	3501
6	20	H	Falkirk	D 1-1	0-0	9	Mehmet (pen) [50]	4134
7	27	A	Motherwell	L 1-2	1-0	12	Mehmet [30]	4786
8	Oct 4	H	Rangers	W 1-0	0-0	10	McGinn [77]	7520
9	18	A	Hamilton A	W 2-1	2-1	7	Miranda [17], Mehmet [41]	3397
10	25	A	Dundee U	L 0-2	0-0	9		11,378
11	Nov 1	H	Hibernian	D 0-0	0-0	9		4588
12	8	H	Hearts	L 0-1	0-0	11		4192
13	11	A	Aberdeen	L 0-2	0-0	—		9452
14	15	A	Rangers	L 1-2	0-2	11	Miranda [81]	49,321
15	22	H	Celtic	L 1-3	0-0	11	Hamilton [89]	7433
16	29	H	Dundee U	L 0-2	0-1	12		4013
17	Dec 6	A	Falkirk	W 2-1	1-0	11	Hamilton [41], Wyness [73]	4828
18	13	H	Inverness CT	W 2-0	1-0	8	Dorman [17], Brady [46]	3364
19	20	A	Kilmarnock	W 1-0	1-0	8	Dorman [38]	5183
20	27	A	Hamilton A	W 1-0	0-0	7	Dargo [79]	4794
21	Jan 3	H	Motherwell	D 0-0	0-0	8		10,189
22	17	A	Hibernian	L 0-2	0-1	9		10,317
23	24	A	Dundee U	L 2-3	1-0	10	Ross [17], Mehmet (pen) [73]	6556
24	31	H	Kilmarnock	D 1-1	1-0	10	Wyness [83]	7542
25	Feb 14	H	Falkirk	D 2-2	1-1	10	Dorman 2 [20, 79]	5504
26	21	A	Hearts	D 1-1	0-0	9	Dorman [90]	13,609
27	28	A	Celtic	L 0-7	0-2	10		58,286
28	Mar 3	H	Aberdeen	D 1-1	0-0	—	Dargo [78]	4383
29	21	A	Hamilton A	D 0-0	0-0	10		3072
30	Apr 4	A	Inverness CT	L 1-2	1-1	11	Dorman [7]	3794
31	8	H	Rangers	L 1-2	0-2	—	Dorman [56]	6231
32	13	H	Hibernian	D 1-1	1-1	—	Dorman [28]	5151
33	18	A	Motherwell	W 2-0	0-0	9	Thomson [77], Dorman [87]	6626
34	May 2	H	Inverness CT	L 1-2	0-1	11	Hamilton [70]	4171
35	9	H	Motherwell	L 1-3	0-2	11	O'Donnell [72]	4002
36	13	A	Kilmarnock	L 1-2	0-1	—	Wyness [90]	5927
37	16	A	Falkirk	W 2-0	1-0	10	Mehmet [37], Dorman [72]	6744
38	23	H	Hamilton A	L 0-1	0-1	11		6747

Final League Position: 11

Honours
League Champions: First Division 1976-77, 1999-2000, 2005-06; *Runners-up:* 2004-05. Division II 1967-68; *Runners-up:* 1935-36.
Scottish Cup Winners: 1926, 1959, 1987; *Runners-up:* 1908, 1934, 1962.
League Cup Runners-up: 1955-56.
League Challenge Cup Winners: 2005-06.
B&Q Cup Runners-up: 1993-94. *Anglo-Scottish Cup:* 1979-80.

European: *Cup Winners' Cup:* 4 matches (1987-88). *UEFA Cup:* 10 matches (1980-81, 1983-84, 1985-86).

Club colours: Shirt: Black and white vertical stripes. Shorts: White with black trim. Stockings: White with two black hoops. Change colours: Predominantly red.

Goalscorers: *League* (33): Dorman 10, Mehmet 7 (2 pens), Hamilton 3, Wyness 3, Brady 2, Dargo 2, Miranda 2, McGinn 1, O'Donnell 1, Ross 1, Thomson 1.
Scottish Cup (6): Hamilton 2 (1 pen), Mehmet 2 (1 pen), Dorman 1, Wyness 1.
CIS Cup (7): Mehmet 3, Dargo 1, Dorman 1, Mason 1, Robb 1.

Howard M 34	Ross J 36	Miranda F 22	O'Donnell S 3 + 5	Haining W 17 + 2	Potter J 35	Murray H 28 + 2	Brady G 31 + 3	Mehmet B 28 + 6	Brighton T 1 + 4	McGinn S 17 + 12	Guerao T 2 + 1	McAusland M — + 4	Wyness D 17 + 14	Mason G 20 + 3	Cuthbert S 28 + 1	Dorman A 32 + 4	Hamilton J 13 + 11	Robb S 11 + 4	Dargo C 12 + 15	Thomson S 12 + 2	Smith C 4	Camara M 10	Burns S — + 2	Barron D 5 + 5	Match No.
1	2	3	4³	5⁴	6	7	8¹	9	10²	11	12	13	14												1
1	2	3	4		6		8	9²					7¹	13	11	5	12	10							2
1	2	3	4¹	5	6	12	8³	9		11			13	10⁴		7²	14								3
1	2	5	14	3¹	6		8	9					13	7	12	4	11²	10³							4
1	2	3		5	6		8	9²	12				13	7		4	11¹		10						5
1	2	3		5	6		8	9³	12		14		13	7		4	11¹		10²						6
1	2¹	3⁴			6		8	9	12	11			13	7	5	4²	14		10³						7
1	2	3		5	6		8³	9	12	11	14		13	7¹		4			10²						8
1	2	3		5	6	7³	8	9	12	11¹	14		13			4			10²						9
1	11	3		5	6	7	8²	9	12		14	2³	13			4			10¹						10
1	2	3			6	7	8²	9	12	11			13		5	4			10¹						11
1	2	3		5	6	7	8¹	9³	12	11	14		13			4			10²						12
1	2	3		5	6	7	8	9	12	11			13			4²			10¹						13
1	2	3		5	6	7	8	9³	12	11¹	14		13			4			10²						14
1	2	3		5²	6	7¹	8	9³	12	11	14		13			4			10						15
1	2	3			6	7	8¹	9²	12	11	14		13		5	4³			10						16
1	2	3			6	7	8	9¹	12	11					5	4			10						17
1	2	3			6	7	8	9	12	11			13		5	4²			10¹						18
1	2	3			6	7	8	9²	12	11	14		13		5	4³			10¹						19
1	2	3			6	7	8³	9¹	12	11	14		13		5	4			10²						20
1	2	3³			6	7	8²	9	12	11	14		13		5	4			10¹						21
1	2	3			6	7	8¹	9³	12	11²	14		13		5	4			10						22
1	2	3			6	7	8³	9	12	11²	14		13		5	4			10¹						23
1	2	3			6	7	8	9³	12	11²	14		13		5	4			10¹						24
	2	3			6	7	8	9	12	11¹			13		5	4			10²		1				25
	2	3			6³	7¹	8	9	12	11²	14		13		5	4			10		1				26
	2⁴	3			6	7²	8	9³	12	11¹	14		13		5	4			10		1				27
	2	3			6	7	8¹	9²		11	14		13		5	4			10³		1				28
1	2	3¹			6	7	8	9	12	11²	14		13		5	4			10³						29
1	2	3³			6	7	8²	9	12	11¹	14		13		5	4			10						30
1	2	3			6²	7	8	9	12	11			13		5	4¹			10						31
1	2	3			6	7²	8	9¹	12	11			13		5	4			10						32
1	2²	3		5	6	7	8	9¹	10	11	12		13			4									33
1	2	3¹			6	7	8²	9	10³	11	14		13		5	4			12						34
1	2¹	3			6	7	8	9	10³	11²	14		13		5	4			12						35
1	2	3		5	6¹	7	8³	9	10	11²	14		13			4			12						36
1	2	3		5	6	7	8	9²	10¹	11			13			4			12						37
1	2	3		5	6	7	8¹	9	10	11						4			12						38

STENHOUSEMUIR   Second Division

Year Formed: 1884. *Ground & Address:* Ochilview Park, Gladstone Rd, Stenhousemuir FK5 4QL. *Telephone:* 01324
562992. *Fax:* 01324 562980. *E-mail:* stenhousemuirfc@talk21.com *Website:* www.stenhousemuirfc.com
Ground Capacity (total): 3746. *Size of Pitch:* 110yd × 72yd.
Chairman: David O. Reid. *Secretary:* Margaret Kilpatrick. *Commercial Manager:* Brian McGinlay.
Manager: John Coughlin. *Assistant Manager:* Matt Kerr. *Community Coach:* Steven Ferguson. *Physio:* Alain Davidson.
Club Nickname(s): The Warriors. *Previous Grounds:* Tryst Ground 1884-86, Goschen Park 1886-90.
Record Attendance: 12,500 v East Fife, Scottish Cup 4th rd, 11 Mar 1950.
Record Transfer Fee received: £70,000 for Euan Donaldson to St Johnstone (May 1995).
Record Transfer Fee paid: £20,000 to Livingston for Ian Little (June 1995).
Record Victory: 9-2 v Dundee U, Division II, 16 Apr 1937.
Record Defeat: 2-11 v Dunfermline Ath, Division II, 27 Sept 1930.
Most League Appearances: 434: Jimmy Richardson, 1957-73.
Most League Goals in Season (Individual): 32: Robert Taylor, Division II, 1925-26.

STENHOUSEMUIR 2008–09 LEAGUE RECORD

Match No.	Date	Venue	Opponents	Result	H/T Score	Lg. Pos.	Goalscorers	Atten-dance
1	Aug 2	H	Elgin C	W 3-0	1-0	—	Brand 2 [33, 89], Hampshire [76]	320
2	9	A	Annan Ath	D 1-1	1-1	2	Brand [4]	1152
3	16	H	Montrose	D 2-2	0-2	3	Dalziel 2 [66, 69]	352
4	23	A	Dumbarton	W 2-1	1-0	3	Motion [23], Shirra [90]	660
5	30	H	Cowdenbeath	W 1-0	0-0	1	Motion [85]	456
6	Sept 13	A	East Stirling	W 2-0	1-0	1	Motion 2 [45, 65]	511
7	20	H	Berwick R	W 2-0	1-0	1	Ovenstone [20], Dalziel (pen) [76]	446
8	27	A	Albion R	W 2-1	1-0	1	Motion [36], McGowan (og) [71]	279
9	Oct 4	H	Forfar Ath	D 1-1	0-0	1	Dalziel [60]	429
10	18	A	Elgin C	L 2-4	2-1	1	Motion [17], Brand [44]	359
11	Nov 1	A	Montrose	W 3-0	2-0	1	Motion [3], Thom [44], Dalziel [57]	419
12	8	H	Dumbarton	D 1-1	0-0	1	Brand [61]	723
13	15	A	Cowdenbeath	W 2-1	2-0	1	Thom [15], Dalziel [26]	406
14	22	H	East Stirling	D 1-1	0-1	1	Dalziel [51]	737
15	Dec 6	A	Berwick R	L 2-3	1-2	—	Hampshire [2], Love [67]	367
16	13	H	Albion R	W 1-0	0-0	1	Thomson [54]	508
17	20	A	Forfar Ath	L 0-1	0-0	1		468
18	27	H	Annan Ath	D 0-0	0-0	1		524
19	Jan 3	A	East Stirling	W 3-0	2-0	1	Dalziel 2 [36, 69], Motion [37]	814
20	17	A	Dumbarton	L 0-1	0-0	2		737
21	24	H	Montrose	L 1-3	1-1	2	Motion [36]	447
22	31	H	Elgin C	W 4-2	2-0	2	Smith [1], Dalziel [31], Love [56], McLeod [71]	311
23	Feb 7	A	Annan Ath	D 1-1	0-1	—	McLeod [48]	805
24	21	H	Berwick R	L 1-2	1-0	2	Dalziel [28]	439
25	28	A	Cowdenbeath	L 0-1	0-0	2		459
26	Mar 3	H	Cowdenbeath	W 1-0	1-0	—	Diack [33]	423
27	7	H	East Stirling	L 1-4	1-3	2	Motion [13]	805
28	14	A	Elgin C	L 0-2	0-0	4		318
29	21	H	Forfar Ath	L 0-1	0-1	4		399
30	31	A	Albion R	W 2-1	1-1	—	Ovenstone [36], Motion [88]	342
31	Apr 4	H	Dumbarton	L 0-2	0-1	5		588
32	11	A	Montrose	L 3-5	0-2	6	Love 2 [57, 88], Ovenstone [86]	358
33	18	A	Berwick R	W 3-0	1-0	5	Thom [23], Diack [55], Dalziel [84]	390
34	25	H	Albion R	W 2-0	0-0	4	Motion [48], Diack [76]	428
35	May 2	H	Annan Ath	W 1-0	1-0	4	Smith [44]	581
36	9	A	Forfar Ath	D 4-4	2-2	4	Thomson [16], Dalziel 2 [23, 85], Stirling [87]	392

Final League Position: 4

Honours
League Champions: Third Division runners-up: 1998-99.
Scottish Cup: Semi-finals 1902-03. Quarter-finals 1948-49, 1949-50, 1994-95.
League Cup: Quarter-finals 1947-48, 1960-61, 1975-76.
League Challenge Cup Winners: 1995-96.

Club colours: Shirt: Maroon with white flashes. Shorts: White. Stockings: White.

Goalscorers: *League* (55): Dalziel 14 (1 pen), Motion 12, Brand 5, Love 4, Diack 3, Ovenstone 3, Thom 3, Hampshire 2, McLeod 2, Smith 2, Thomson 2, Shirra 1, Stirling 1, own goal 1.
Scottish Cup (10): Dalziel 3, Motion 2, Desmond 1, Hampshire 1, Shirra 1, Thom 1, Thomson 1.
Challenge Cup (0).
Play-Offs (2): Dalziel 1 (pen), Love 1.

Renton K 11	Lyle W 28	McGroarty C 30	Smith J 24 + 1	Ovenstone J 31	Tyrrell P 13 + 4	Thomson I 26 + 3	Ferguson S 16 + 1	Dalziel S 28 + 7	Brand A 25 + 5	Hampshire S 8 + 6	Motion K 28 + 4	Gibson G — + 2	Love R 12 + 11	Brazil A 8 + 2	Shirra A 11 + 12	Desmond S 2 + 5	Thom G 15 + 1	Rankin C 1	Bennett S 24	McEwan C 3 + 3	McManus S — + 1	Jack M — + 1	Forde R 1	Connolly S 1 + 2	Diack I 13 + 1	McLeod C 11	Molloy C 12 + 1	Morgan A 4 + 3	Ferguson A 2 + 1	Reid A 7	Stirling A 1 + 3		Match No.
1	2	3[1]	4	5	6	7	8	9[2]	10	11[3]	12	13	14																				1
1	2	3	4	5	6[1]	7[3]	8	9[1]	10	12	14	13		11[2]																			2
1	2	3	4	5		7[1]	8	9	10		6			11[2]	12	13																	3
1	2	5	4	3	13		7	10	11[1]	12	9				8	6[2]																4
1	2	3	4	5		12	8	9[2]	10	11	6			13	7[1]																	5
1	2	3	4	5		6	8	9	10[1]		11			7[2]	13	12																6
1	2	3	4	5	13	6[2]	8	9	10[1]	14	11		12	7[3]																		7
1	2	3		5	7	6	8		9	10[1]	11				12	4																8
	2	3	4	5	14	6[3]	8	9	10	7[1]	11		12[2]		13			1														9
1	2	3	4[1]	5	12	6	8[3]	9	10		11		13		14	7[2]																10
	2	5		4		7		10	11		9		6[1]		8		3		1	12												11
	2	3	12[2]	5		6		9	10		11[■]		7[1]		8		4		1	13												12
	2[■]	5		3		8	7	10[1]	11	12			9[2]		6		4		1	13												13
		3		5		6	8[1]	9	10	12			11[2]		7	13	4		1	2												14
		3		5	8	6		9		10[2]			11		7[1]	12	4		1	2[3]	14	13										15
		3		5	7	6	8[■]	13		9[1]	11		10[2]		12		4		1	2												16
		3	4	5	6	8		9[2]		10	11			13[■]			2		1					7[1]	12							17
	2		5	6	8	7		9	12	10[2]	3		13				4[1]		1						11							18
	2		5	6		7	8	9	10[1]		3			11			4		1						12							19
	2	5[3]	3	4	7	6	8	10[1]	11[2]	12	9		13				14		1													20
	2	3	4	5	6		8	9[1]	12		11		13		7[2]				1							10						21
	2	3	5	6		7		9	8[2]		11[3]		12		14				1							10[1]	4	13				22
	2	3	4			7		10	8		9[1]		13						1							11[2]	5	6	12				23
1	2	3	5	6	8		9			13			7[2]						1							10	4	11[1]	12			24
	2	5	3		8[2]	7		10			12		·13						1							11	4	6	9[1]			25
	2	3		5		14	9	8		6			12[2]		13				1							10[1]	4	7	11[3]			26
	2	3[1]	4	5	6[3]	8[2]		14	10		11				13				1							9		7		12		27
	2	3	4	5		14		9	8[2]		6			12				1	1							13		7[1]	11[3]	10		28
		4	5	6			9[1]	12		11						2			1							8[2]		7[3]	13	10	3	14	29
		3		5	6[1]		12	10		11			7		13				1							9[2]	4	8		2		30
		3		5		6		12	10[2]		11		7[1]	13					1							9	4	8		2		31
		5		4				10	11[2]		7		6	9[1]	13				1							3	8			2	12	32
	2		5			12		13	11		7[1]		10[2]				4		1							9[3]	6	8		3	14	33
	2		5					13	12		11		7[1]	10			4		1							9[2]	6	8		3		34
	2		5		8			12	13		11		7[2]	10			4		1							9[1]	6			3		35
1	2	3		5		6		9	10					8	4												11			7		36

STIRLING ALBION — Second Division

Year Formed: 1945. *Ground & Address:* Forthbank Stadium, Springkerse Industrial Estate, Stirling FK7 7UJ. *Telephone:* 01786 450399. *Fax:* 01786 448400. *Email:* stirlingalbion@btconnect.com *Website:* www.stirlingalbionfc.co.uk
Ground Capacity: 3808, seated: 2508. *Size of Pitch:* 110yd × 74yd.
Chairman: Peter McKenzie. *Secretary:* Mrs Marlyn Hallam.
Manager: Allan Moore. *Assistant Manager:* John O'Neill. *Physio:* Andy Myles.
Club Nickname(s): The Binos. *Previous Grounds:* Annfield 1945-92.
Record Attendance: 26,400 (at Annfield) v Celtic, Scottish Cup 4th rd, 14 Mar 1959; 3808 v Aberdeen, Scottish Cup 4th rd, 15 February 1996 (Forthbank).
Record Transfer Fee received: £90,000 for Stephen Nicholas to Motherwell (Mar 1999).
Record Transfer Fee paid: £25,000 for Craig Taggart from Falkirk (Aug 1994).
Record Victory: 20-0 v Selkirk, Scottish Cup 1st rd, 8 Dec 1984.
Record Defeat: 0-9 v Dundee U, Division I, 30 Dec 1967.
Most League Appearances: 504: Matt McPhee, 1967-81.
Most League Goals in Season (Individual): 27: Joe Hughes, Division II, 1969-70.
Most Goals Overall (Individual): 129: Billy Steele, 1971-83.

STIRLING ALBION 2008–09 LEAGUE RECORD

Match No.	Date	Venue	Opponents	Result	H/T Score	Lg. Pos.	Goalscorers	Attendance
1	Aug 2	A	Brechin C	L 1-2	0-1	—	White (og) [50]	535
2	9	H	East Fife	D 1-1	0-0	7	O'Neil [53]	686
3	16	A	Stranraer	L 0-1	0-0	8		304
4	23	H	Ayr U	D 2-2	1-2	9	Taggart [19], Harty (pen) [65]	876
5	30	A	Arbroath	W 2-1	1-1	5	O'Neil [25], McKenna [48]	631
6	Sept 13	H	Alloa Ath	W 3-2	3-2	5	Graham [12], Harty [21], Corr [39]	906
7	20	A	Raith R	D 1-1	1-0	6	Taggart [15]	1648
8	27	H	Peterhead	D 0-0	0-0	6		527
9	Oct 4	A	Queen's Park	D 1-1	1-0	6	Harty [23]	713
10	18	H	Brechin C	L 1-2	0-1	6	Grehan [55]	577
11	25	A	Ayr U	D 1-1	0-1	6	O'Neil [54]	1070
12	Nov 1	H	Stranraer	W 3-2	0-0	6	Grehan [51], Molloy 2 [70, 78]	509
13	8	A	Alloa Ath	L 3-4	0-1	6	Grehan [63], Hill (og) [78], Murphy [86]	1001
14	15	H	Arbroath	L 0-2	0-0	6		509
15	22	A	Peterhead	D 1-1	0-1	6	O'Neil [53]	461
16	Dec 13	A	East Fife	W 1-0	1-0	6	Fotheringham (og) [42]	593
17	20	H	Queen's Park	L 0-3	0-2	6		530
18	27	A	Arbroath	W 2-1	2-1	6	McKenna 2 [2, 30]	635
19	Jan 10	H	Raith R	W 2-1	1-0	—	O'Neil [31], McKenna [50]	906
20	17	H	Ayr U	W 2-0	0-0	6	Grehan [55], McCord [75]	779
21	24	A	Stranraer	W 8-2	1-1	6	Hamilton 3 [6, 55, 67], McKinstry (og) [54], Grehan 3 [70, 76, 88], O'Neil [82]	305
22	31	A	Brechin C	W 2-1	1-1	3	Grehan [6], Graham [61]	565
23	Feb 21	A	Raith R	D 1-1	1-1	6	McKenna [2]	1770
24	28	A	Arbroath	D 1-1	0-1	6	Docherty [90]	576
25	Mar 3	H	Alloa Ath	D 0-0	0-0	—		768
26	7	A	Alloa Ath	W 3-2	0-1	5	McKenna 2 (1 pen) [54 (p), 73], Grehan [58]	1057
27	14	H	Brechin C	L 2-3	2-2	6	Roycroft [16], O'Neil [35]	544
28	17	H	Peterhead	W 2-1	0-0	—	Grehan [65], McKenna [65]	404
29	21	A	Queen's Park	L 1-3	0-0	5	Docherty [70]	594
30	28	H	East Fife	W 2-0	0-0	5	McKenna 2 [49, 60]	636
31	Apr 4	A	Ayr U	L 1-3	1-2	5	Grehan [14]	1583
32	11	A	Stranraer	L 1-2	1-1	5	McKenna [16]	459
33	18	H	Raith R	L 0-1	0-0	5		1125
34	25	A	Peterhead	D 1-1	0-0	5	Murphy [58]	855
35	May 2	A	East Fife	W 3-0	1-0	5	McKenna [28], Mullen 2 [68, 89]	569
36	11	H	Queen's Park	W 4-0	3-0	5	Mullen [14], Grehan [34], Hamilton [40], Docherty [68]	284

Final League Position: 5

Scottish League Clubs – Stirling Albion 761

Honours

League Champions: Division II 1952-53, 1957-58, 1960-61, 1964-65. Second Division 1976-77, 1990-91, 1995-96; *Runners-up:* Division II 1948-49, 1950-51. Second Division 2006-07. Third Division 2003-04.
League Cup: Semi-finals 1961-62.

Club colours: All red.

Goalscorers: *League* (59): Grehan 12, McKenna 12 (1 pen), O'Neil 7, Hamilton 4, Docherty 3, Harty 3 (1 pen), Mullen 3, Graham 2, Molloy 2, Murphy 2, Taggart 2, Corr 1, McCord 1, Roycroft 1, own goals 4.
Scottish Cup (2): Molloy 1, Murphy 1.
Challenge Cup (0).

Hogarth M 17+1	Graham A 24+1	Lawrie A 25+1	Forsyth R 26+1	Lowing D 20+1	Corr L 12+12	O'Neil J 30+1	Murphy P 26+6	Devine S 20+3	Harty I 12+1	Grehan M 30+3	Taggart N 11+2	McKenna D 26+8	Waddell S —+8	Andrew G 1	Hamilton C 12+9	Fagan S —+1	Docherty M 22+7	Molloy C 11	Roycroft S 20	Gibb S 20	Christie S 19	Boyle J 2+9	McCord R 3+4	Mullen M 5+7	Dunn R —+5	Feaks K 2+1	Match No.
1	2	3	4	5	6^1	7	8	9	10^3	11^1	12	13	14														1
1		4	5	3	7^2	6	8		9^3	10^1	11	12	14	2	13												2
1	2	4	5	3	7^2	6	8^3	13	9	10^1	11	12		14													3
1	2	4	5	3	13	6		9	11^3	7	10^1	12		14	8^2												4
1	2	4	5	3		6	12		9^2	11	7	10^1	13		8^8												5
1	2	4	5	3	8^1	6	12		9^2	11	7	10	13														6
1	2^3	4	5	3	13	6	14		9		7^2	10^1		12		11	8										7
1	2	4	5	3	14	6^3		9	12	7^2	10^1		13		11	8											8
1	2	4	5	3	13		14		9	10^1	11		12	7^3		6	8^2										9
1	2	4	5	3^3	13	6		9	11	7^1	14		12		10^2	8											10
1	2	4	5	3^3	10	6		14	13	12	7^1	9^2															11
1	2	4		3	10^3	6	14	5	9	13	12		7^1		11^2	8											12
1	2	5		4^1	7	6	14	3	9^2	11		12		13	10^3	8											13
1		5		11^2	6^3	10	3		9	7^1	13		12		14	8	2	4									14
	5	2		3	12	6^1	8		9^2		10	13			11	7		4	1								15
15		3		5	13	12	8	9^2		11		10			6^1	7	2	4	1^6								16
	2			3	12	10^3	8	11			9	14	13		7^2	6^1	5	4	1								17
		2	13	3^2		6	8	11		10^1	9		7				5	4	1	12							18
	2		3			6	8	11		9	10^2		7^1				4	5	1	13	12						19
	2		3^4			6	8	11		10	9^2		7^1				4	5	1	13	12						20
	2	13		3		6	8	11^3		10	9		7^1		14		5^2	4	1		12						21
	2		5			7	8	9^3		11^2	10		6^1		14		4	3	1	13	12						22
	2^3					8	9	11		10		6^1		5	4	1	7^4	12									23
	2	3^2				8	11	10		9^1	13			5	4	1	6	7^4	12								24
	2	3		13	6	8^2	11^3	9		12			7		5	4	1	14		10^1							25
	2	3			6	8		9		10^1			11		5	4	1		7	12							26
	2	4		7^1	6	8	3^3	10^2		9			11		5		1	14		13	12						27
	2	3		7^1	6	8	13	10		9			11		5^2	4	1			12							28
	2	5			7	8	4	11		9					3	1	12			6^1							29
2^2		3			6	8		10^3		9					11	4	5	1	14		7^1	12	13				30
1	2		5	13	14	8	7			11^2		10^3			9	4^4	3^1			6	12						31
	2	5	3^2		6	8		10		9			7^1		11^2		4	1	14		12	13					32
	2	11		12	6^2	8	3	10		9			7^1		13		5	4	1		12						33
	2	3		13	6	7	11	10		9			12		8^2		5^1	4	1								34
1		4	5		8		7	9					10^3		6^2	13	3			11		11^1		12	14	2	35
1	14		3		6		8	11^2		9^1	12		7		13		5^3	4					10			2	36

STRANRAER Third Division

Year Formed: 1870. *Ground & Address:* Stair Park, London Rd, Stranraer DG9 8BS. *Telephone and Fax:* 01776 703271.
E-mail: secretary@yahoo.co.uk *Website:* www.stranraerfc.org
Ground Capacity: 5600, seated: 1830. *Size of Pitch:* 110yd × 70yd.
Chairman: Nigel Redhead. *Secretary:* Hilde Law. *Commercial Manager:* Ian Alldred.
Manager: Keith Knox. *Physio:* Walter Cannon.
Club Nickname(s): The Blues. *Previous Grounds:* None.
Record Attendance: 6500 v Rangers, Scottish Cup 1st rd, 24 Jan 1948.
Record Transfer Fee received: £90,000 for Mark Campbell to Ayr U (1999).
Record Transfer Fee paid: £15,000 for Colin Harkness from Kilmarnock (Aug 1989).
Record Victory: 7-0 v Brechin C, Division II, 6 Feb 1965.
Record Defeat: 1-11 v Queen of the South, Scottish Cup 1st rd, 16 Jan 1932.
Most League Appearances: 301: Keith Knox, 1986-90; 1999-2001.
Most League Goals in Season (Individual): 59: Tommy Sloan.

STRANRAER 2008–09 LEAGUE RECORD

Match No.	Date	Venue	Opponents	Result	H/T Score	Lg. Pos.	Goalscorers	Atten- dance
1	Aug 2	A	Queen's Park	D 2-2	2-0	—	Tade [15], McBride [20]	611
2	9	H	Brechin C	L 1-2	1-1	6	Frizzel [37]	279
3	16	H	Stirling A	W 1-0	0-0	6	Tade [86]	304
4	23	A	Raith R	L 1-2	1-1	7	Tade [23]	1483
5	30	A	Alloa Ath	L 1-5	0-0	10	Tade [49]	408
6	Sept 13	H	Ayr U	L 1-3	0-1	10	McConalogue [70]	1003
7	20	A	Peterhead	L 0-4	0-2	10		495
8	27	H	Arbroath	D 2-2	1-0	9	Mitchell 2 [17, 46]	228
9	Oct 4	A	East Fife	W 2-1	2-1	8	Nicoll [30], McConalogue [38]	730
10	18	H	Queen's Park	D 0-0	0-0	8		427
11	25	H	Raith R	L 0-2	0-1	9		338
12	Nov 1	A	Stirling A	L 2-3	1-0	9	Tade [44], Dobbins [66]	509
13	8	A	Ayr U	L 2-3	1-2	9	Tade (pen) [37], White [76]	1357
14	15	H	Alloa Ath	D 2-2	1-0	9	Tade (pen) [38], Kane [86]	280
15	22	A	Arbroath	L 0-1	0-1	10		411
16	Dec 20	A	East Fife	L 0-4	0-2	10		200
17	27	A	Alloa Ath	D 2-2	1-1	10	Mullen [4], McConalogue [73]	463
18	Jan 17	A	Raith R	L 1-2	0-1	10	Mullen [52]	1455
19	24	H	Stirling A	L 2-8	1-1	10	Mullen [40], McConalogue [77]	305
20	31	A	Queen's Park	D 1-1	1-0	10	Frizzel [16]	474
21	Feb 7	H	Brechin C	L 0-3	0-2	—		283
22	14	H	Arbroath	L 1-5	1-3	—	McConalogue [23]	277
23	21	A	Peterhead	L 0-1	0-0	10		531
24	28	H	Alloa Ath	L 1-3	1-2	10	McBride (pen) [18]	286
25	Mar 4	H	Peterhead	L 0-3	0-1	—		154
26	7	A	Ayr U	L 0-5	0-3	10		1580
27	10	A	Brechin C	L 0-1	0-0	—		315
28	14	H	Queen's Park	D 2-2	1-1	10	Mitchell 2 [18, 88]	323
29	21	A	East Fife	L 0-4	0-1	10		533
30	28	H	Ayr U	L 1-4	0-2	10	McConalogue [49]	1019
31	Apr 4	H	Raith R	L 0-3	0-2	10		398
32	11	A	Stirling A	W 2-1	1-1	10	McColm [34], Moore [90]	459
33	18	H	Peterhead	L 0-1	0-0	10		252
34	25	A	Arbroath	L 0-2	0-1	10		506
35	May 2	A	Brechin C	L 1-2	1-2	10	Mitchell [27]	418
36	9	H	East Fife	L 0-1	0-1	10		249

Final League Position: 10

Honours
League Champions: Second Division 1993-94, 1997-98; *Runners-up:* 2004-05, 2007-08. Third Division 2003-04.
Qualifying Cup Winners: 1937.
Scottish Cup: Quarter-finals 2003
League Challenge Cup Winners: 1996-97.

Club colours: Shirt: Royal blue with white design. Shorts: White. Stockings: Royal blue.

Goalscorers: *League* (31): Tade 7 (2 pens), McConalogue 6, Mitchell 5, Mullen 3, Frizzel 2, McBride 2 (1 pen), Dobbins 1, Kane 1, McColm 1, Moore 1, Nicoll 1, White 1.
Scottish Cup (0).
Challenge Cup (0).

Black S 26	Kane J 36	Jones R 3+1	Dobbins I 16	White A 10+2	Creaney J 13+7	Mitchell D 27+6	Gibson A 26+2	McBride M 23+2	Frizzel C 26+6	Mullen M 11+7	Tade G 16	McConalogue S 28+6	Noble S 27+4	McKinstry J 26+3	Nicoll K 21+1	McColm S 11+10	Bradley C —+7	Dougan D 1	Cantley F 1+1	Mutch J 1+1	Connolly S 1+2	Anglade A —+1	Cooksley R —+4	Wilson M 10+1	Murdoch A —+4	McGrath P 5+2	Crossthwaite D 9	Campbell M —+1	Aitken S 9+1	Moore M 6+2	Craig D 3	Paisley R 1+3	McGregor S 1	Ritchie J —+1	Hogan D —+1	Kiltie J —+1	Miller I —+1	Whorlow M 2+2	Match No.
1	2	3	4[4]	5	6	7	8[3]	9[2]	10[1]	11	12	13	14																										1
1	2		4	5	3	13	7[1]	8	11	9[3]	10	14			12[2]	6																							2
1	2		4	5	3[1]	13	7	8	9[3]	14	11	10[2]	12			6																							3
1	2		4			3	14	7	8[3]	10[2]	12	11	9[1]	5		6	13																						4
1	2		4	13	3	12	7	8	11[2]	14	10	9[1]	5			6[6]																							5
1	2		4	6	3	13	7	8[2]	11	9[1]	10[6]	12	5																										6
1	6		4	5	3	11	7	8[1]	9[2]	12	10[3]		2		13	14																							7
1	5		4		13	6[6]	7		10[2]	12	8	9[1]	3	2	11																								8
1	4	3	8	12		6		9[2]	10[6]	11[1]	5	2	7		13																								9
1	5	4	8[2]	13	9	7		11[1]	12		10	3	2	6[3]	14																								10
1	5	4	8[1]	12	13	7		14	9[3]	11	10[2]	3	2	6																									11
1	5	4			8	7		11	9	10		3[1]	2	6	12																								12
1	4	3	13		7	6		9	10[1]	11	12	5	2[2]	8																									13
1	5	4[2]	6		8	7		11[1]	9	10	12	3	2		13																								14
1	5	4	6		8	7		12	10	9[1]	3	2		11																									15
1	3		5	7	12	11[3]	9[2]	10	8[1]	4	2	6	13	14																									16
1	5	4		6		8	7[1]	9	11	10	3	2		12																									17
1[6]	4			8	12	6	7[1]	9	11	10[2]	3	2	5[6]			13		15																					18
	4			5	7[3]	6		9		10	3	2		12	13			1	8[2]	11[1]	14																		19
1	3			6	7[3]	8	9[2]		11	5	2	4	10[1]							12	13	14																	20
1	4			7		8	11		10	3[2]	2	6[1]	9								13			14	5[3]	12													21
1	4	12	7		8[1]	11		10[3]	3		6[2]	9												14	5	13	2[1]												22
	4		3	6		10		9	11[3]	7[2]	8[1]		13											14	5		2	1	12										23
1	4		3	7		8	11		10		12															5	13	2		6[1]	9[2]								24
1	4		3	7	13		8[1]	11[3]		10[2]	14	2		12												5				6	9								25
1	2		5	11		7	6[1]		13		14	9															4			8[2]	10	3[3]	12						26
1	5[3]		14	7	6	8		11	9	2		12														13			10[1]	3		4[2]							27
1	3		14	6	7	8	12		10[2]	11[1]	2	4	9													13				5[3]									28
11			5		6	8[3]	12		2	4	10[2]			3										9[1]	1		7							14	13				29
	4			7[1]	8	11		10	3	2	5	9		1			6[2]							12							13								30
	4		6		8	11		10	3	2		9[2]		5		1						7[1]											13	12				31
	4		3	8	7	12		10	11[1]	2	5	9[2]										14	1		6[3]	13												32
	4	11[1]		8	7	12		10[3]	3	2[5]	5	9									13	1		6	14													33
	4	14		8		11	12		10[3]	3	2	9[1]								5[2]	1		6	7						13								34
	3	9		8	6[3]	13		11	12	2		14							4[2]		1	7	10						5[1]									35
	4	2[1]		6	7	8	9		10	11									5	13	1			12					3[2]									36

SCOTTISH LEAGUE PLAY-OFFS 2008-09

DIV 1 SEMI-FINALS FIRST LEG

Wednesday, 13 May 2009

Brechin C (0) 0

Ayr U (2) 2 *(Aitken 8, 36 (pen))*   902

Brechin C: Nelson C; Walker, Seeley, Smith B, Dyer, Nimmo (Smith D), Murie (King), Fusco, Canning, McAllister, Ettien (Byers).
Ayr U: Grindlay; Dempsie, Walker, Campbell, McGowan, Stevenson, Keenan, Aitken, Easton (Connolly), Prunty (Gormley), Roberts.

Thursday, 14 May 2009

Peterhead (0) 0

Airdrie U (1) 2 *(Baird 9, McLaughlin 47)*   1364

Peterhead: Jarvie; Donald, Smith, Mann, MacDonald, Moore, Sharp (McVitie), Anderson, McKay, Ross (Gunn), Bavidge.
Airdrie U: Robertson; McLachlan, Lovering, McDonald, Donnelly, Smyth, Smith (Brown), McKenna, McLaughlin, Di Giacomo (McDougall), Baird (Lynch).

DIV 1 SEMI-FINALS SECOND LEG

Saturday, 16 May 2009

Ayr U (1) 3 *(Prunty 15, Connolly 70, Aitken 72)*

Brechin C (1) 2 *(McAllister 38, 53 (pen))*   1974

Ayr U: Grindlay; Dempsie, Walker, Campbell (Henderson), McGowan, Connolly, Keenan (Woodburn), Aitken, Easton, Prunty, Roberts (Gormley).
Brechin C: Nelson C; Walker, Seeley, Smith B, Dyer, Smith D, Fusco, Canning, Byers (Ettien), McAllister, King.

Sunday, 17 May 2009

Airdrie U (0) 2 *(Smyth 61, Baird 85)*

Peterhead (1) 1 *(McKay 45)*   1008

Airdrie U: Robertson; McLachlan, Lovering, McDonald, Donnelly (Nixon), Smyth, McDougall, McKenna, Di Giacomo (Smith), Lynch (Baird), McLaughlin.
Peterhead: Jarvie; Donald, Smith, Mann, MacDonald, Moore, Sharp (Gunn), McVitie, Bavidge, Anderson, McKay.

DIV 1 FINAL FIRST LEG

Wednesday, 20 May 2009

Ayr U (0) 2 *(Roberts 48, 67)*

Airdrie U (2) 2 *(Di Giacomo 30, Baird 43)*   3378

Ayr U: Grindlay; Dempsie, Walker, Campbell, McGowan■, Connolly, Keenan, Aitken, Easton, Prunty (Gormley), Roberts.
Airdrie U: Robertson; McLachlan, Donnelly, Smyth, Lovering, Smith, McDonald (McDougall), McKenna, McLaughlin, Di Giacomo (Lynch), Baird.

DIV 1 FINAL SECOND LEG

Sunday, 24 May 2009

Airdrie U (0) 0

Ayr U (1) 1 *(Stevenson 29)*   3303

Airdrie U: Robertson; McLachlan (Watt), Lovering, McDonald (McDougall), Donnelly, Smyth, Smith, McKenna, Di Giacomo (Lynch), Baird, McLaughlin.
Ayr U: Grindlay; Keenan, Easton, Walker, Campbell, Stevenson, Borris, Aitken, Prunty (Gormley), Roberts, Connolly.

DIV 2 SEMI-FINALS FIRST LEG

Wednesday, 13 May 2009

East Stirling (0) 1 *(Rodgers 62)*

Cowdenbeath (2) 2 *(Gemmell 12, Stein 30)*   605

East Stirling: Peat; Hay, Tully, King (Forrest), Bolochoweckyi, Weaver, Donaldson (McKenzie), Stevenson, Graham, Ure (Richardson), Rodgers.
Cowdenbeath: Hay; Baxter, Linton, McGregor, Armstrong, Shields, Ramsay, MacKay (Fleming), Gemmell (Dempster), Ferguson, Stein.

Thursday, 14 May 2009

Stenhousemuir (2) 2 *(Dalziel 6 (pen), Love 32)*

Queen's Park (1) 1 *(Harkins 33)*   617

Stenhousemuir: Bennett; Lyle, Reid, Thom, Smith, McLeod, Love (Brand), Molloy, Dalziel, Diack (Brazil), Motion.
Queen's Park: Cowie; Ure, Douglas, Reilly, Brough, Ronald (McGrady), Holmes, Cairney, Nicholas, Harkins, Watt (Murray).

DIV 2 SEMI-FINALS SECOND LEG

Saturday, 16 May 2009

Cowdenbeath (0) 1 *(Dempster 84)*

East Stirling (1) 1 *(Graham 3)*   633

Cowdenbeath: Hay; Baxter, Linton, McGregor, Armstrong, Ramsay, Robertson (Tomana), Shields, Stein, Gemmell (McQuade), Ferguson (Dempster).
East Stirling: Peat; Hay, Tully, Bolochoweckyi■, Forrest, Donaldson (Anderson■), Weaver (McKenzie), Stevenson, Richardson, Graham, Rodgers.

Sunday, 17 May 2009

Queen's Park (0) 0

Stenhousemuir (0) 0   854

Queen's Park: Crawford; Ure (Dunlop), Reilly, Brough, Douglas, Holmes, Ronald (Murray), Cairney, Harkins, Nicholas (McGrady), Watt.
Stenhousemuir: Bennett; Lyle, Thom, Smith, McLeod, Reid, Molloy, Motion, Love (Brand), Dalziel (Diack), Brazil (Thomson).

DIV 2 FINAL FIRST LEG

Wednesday, 20 May 2009

Cowdenbeath (0) 0

Stenhousemuir (0) 0   775

Cowdenbeath: Hay; Baxter, McGregor■, Armstrong, Linton, Gemmell, Ramsay, Shields, Stein (Ferguson), Dempster, McQuade (Robertson).
Stenhousemuir: Bennett; Lyle, Thom, Smith, Reid, Brazil (Tyrrell), McLeod■, Molloy (Thomson), Motion, Dalziel, Diack (Brand).

DIV 2 FINAL SECOND LEG

Saturday, 23 May 2009

Stenhousemuir (0) 0

Cowdenbeath (0) 0   1530

Stenhousemuir: Bennett; Lyle, Ovenstone, Thom, Smith, Reid, Love (Thomson), Molloy, Dalziel (Brand), Diack, Motion (Brazil).
Cowdenbeath: Hay; Baxter, Mbu, Robertson, Armstrong, Shields (Fleming), Ramsay, McQuade (Ferguson), Gemmell, Dempster (Tomana), Stein.
(aet; Stenhousemuir won 5-4 on penalties.)

SCOTTISH LEAGUE HONOURS 1890 to 2009

*On goal average (ratio)/difference. †Held jointly after indecisive play-off. ‡Won on deciding match.
††Held jointly. ¶Two points deducted for fielding ineligible player.
Competition suspended 1940–45 during war; Regional Leagues operating. ‡‡Two points deducted for registration
irregularities. §Not promoted after play-offs.

PREMIER LEAGUE

Maximum points: 108

	First	Pts	Second	Pts	Third	Pts
1998–99	Rangers	77	Celtic	71	St Johnstone	57
1999–2000	Rangers	90	Celtic	69	Hearts	54

Maximum points: 114

2000–01	Celtic	97	Rangers	82	Hibernian	66
2001–02	Celtic	103	Rangers	85	Livingston	58
2002–03	Rangers*	97	Celtic	97	Hearts	63
2003–04	Celtic	98	Rangers	81	Hearts	68
2004–05	Rangers	93	Celtic	92	Hibernian*	61
2005–06	Celtic	91	Hearts	74	Rangers	73
2006–07	Celtic	84	Rangers	72	Aberdeen	65
2007–08	Celtic	89	Rangers	86	Motherwell	60
2008–09	Rangers	86	Celtic	82	Hearts	59

PREMIER DIVISION

Maximum points: 72

1975–76	Rangers	54	Celtic	48	Hibernian	43
1976–77	Celtic	55	Rangers	46	Aberdeen	43
1977–78	Rangers	55	Aberdeen	53	Dundee U	40
1978–79	Celtic	48	Rangers	45	Dundee U	44
1979–80	Aberdeen	48	Celtic	47	St Mirren	42
1980–81	Celtic	56	Aberdeen	49	Rangers*	44
1981–82	Celtic	55	Aberdeen	53	Rangers	43
1982–83	Dundee U	56	Celtic*	55	Aberdeen	55
1983–84	Aberdeen	57	Celtic	50	Dundee U	47
1984–85	Aberdeen	59	Celtic	52	Dundee U	47
1985–86	Celtic*	50	Hearts	50	Dundee U	47

Maximum points: 88

1986–87	Rangers	69	Celtic	63	Dundee U	60
1987–88	Celtic	72	Hearts	62	Rangers	60

Maximum points: 72

1988–89	Rangers	56	Aberdeen	50	Celtic	46
1989–90	Rangers	51	Aberdeen*	44	Hearts	44
1990–91	Rangers	55	Aberdeen	53	Celtic*	41

Maximum points: 88

1991–92	Rangers	72	Hearts	63	Celtic	62
1992–93	Rangers	73	Aberdeen	64	Celtic	60
1993–94	Rangers	58	Aberdeen	55	Motherwell	54

Maximum points: 108

1994–95	Rangers	69	Motherwell	54	Hibernian	53
1995–96	Rangers	87	Celtic	83	Aberdeen*	55
1996–97	Rangers	80	Celtic	75	Dundee U	60
1997–98	Celtic	74	Rangers	72	Hearts	67

FIRST DIVISION

Maximum points: 52

1975–76	Partick Th	41	Kilmarnock	35	Montrose	30

Maximum points: 78

1976–77	St Mirren	62	Clydebank	58	Dundee	51
1977–78	Morton*	58	Hearts	58	Dundee	57
1978–79	Dundee	55	Kilmarnock*	54	Clydebank	54
1979–80	Hearts	53	Airdrieonians	51	Ayr U*	44
1980–81	Hibernian	57	Dundee	52	St Johnstone	51
1981–82	Motherwell	61	Kilmarnock	51	Hearts	50
1982–83	St Johnstone	55	Hearts	54	Clydebank	50
1983–84	Morton	54	Dumbarton	51	Partick Th	46
1984–85	Motherwell	50	Clydebank	48	Falkirk	45
1985–86	Hamilton A	56	Falkirk	45	Kilmarnock	44

Maximum points: 88

1986–87	Morton	57	Dunfermline Ath	56	Dumbarton	53
1987–88	Hamilton A	56	Meadowbank Th	52	Clydebank	49

Maximum points: 78

1988–89	Dunfermline Ath	54	Falkirk	52	Clydebank	48
1989–90	St Johnstone	58	Airdrieonians	54	Clydebank	44
1990–91	Falkirk	54	Airdrieonians	53	Dundee	52

Maximum points: 88

1991–92	Dundee	58	Partick Th*	57	Hamilton A	57
1992–93	Raith R	65	Kilmarnock	54	Dunfermline Ath	52
1993–94	Falkirk	66	Dunfermline Ath	65	Airdrieonians	54

Maximum points: 108

1994–95	Raith R	69	Dunfermline Ath*	68	Dundee	68
1995–96	Dunfermline Ath	71	Dundee U*	67	Morton	67
1996–97	St Johnstone	80	Airdieonians	60	Dundee*	58

	First	*Pts*	*Second*	*Pts*	*Third*	*Pts*
1997–98	Dundee	70	Falkirk	65	Raith R*	60
1998–99	Hibernian	89	Falkirk	66	Ayr U	62
1999–2000	St Mirren	76	Dunfermline Ath	71	Falkirk	68
2000–01	Livingston	76	Ayr U	69	Falkirk	56
2001–02	Partick Th	66	Airdrieonians	56	Ayr U	52
2002–03	Falkirk	81	Clyde	72	St Johnstone	67
2003–04	Inverness CT	70	Clyde	69	St Johnstone	57
2004–05	Falkirk	75	St Mirren*	60	Clyde	60
2005–06	St Mirren	76	St Johnstone	66	Hamilton A	59
2006–07	Gretna	66	St Johnstone	65	Dundee*	53
2007–08	Hamilton A	76	Dundee	69	St Johnstone	58
2008–09	St Johnstone	65	Partick Th	55	Dunfermline Ath	51

SECOND DIVISION

	First	*Pts*	*Second*	*Pts*	*Third*	*Pts*
	Maximum points: 52					
1975–76	Clydebank*	40	Raith R	40	Alloa Ath	35
	Maximum points: 78					
1976–77	Stirling A	55	Alloa Ath	51	Dunfermline Ath	50
1977–78	Clyde*	53	Raith R	53	Dunfermline Ath	48
1978–79	Berwick R	54	Dunfermline Ath	52	Falkirk	50
1979–80	Falkirk	50	East Stirling	49	Forfar Ath	46
1980–81	Queen's Park	50	Queen of the S	46	Cowdenbeath	45
1981–82	Clyde	59	Alloa Ath*	50	Arbroath	50
1982–83	Brechin C	55	Meadowbank Th	54	Arbroath	49
1983–84	Forfar Ath	63	East Fife	47	Berwick R	43
1984–85	Montrose	53	Alloa Ath	50	Dunfermline Ath	49
1985–86	Dunfermline Ath	57	Queen of the S	55	Meadowbank Th	49
1986–87	Meadowbank Th	55	Raith R*	52	Stirling A*	52
1987–88	Ayr U	61	St Johnstone	59	Queen's Park	51
1988–89	Albion R	50	Alloa Ath	45	Brechin C	43
1989–90	Brechin C	49	Kilmarnock	48	Stirling A	47
1990–91	Stirling A	54	Montrose	46	Cowdenbeath	45
1991–92	Dumbarton	52	Cowdenbeath	51	Alloa Ath	50
1992–93	Clyde	54	Brechin C*	53	Stranraer	53
1993–94	Stranraer	56	Berwick R	48	Stenhousemuir*	47
	Maximum points: 108					
1994–95	Morton	64	Dumbarton	60	Stirling A	58
1995–96	Stirling A	81	East Fife	67	Berwick R	60
1996–97	Ayr U	77	Hamilton A	74	Livingston	64
1997–98	Stranraer	61	Clydebank	60	Livingston	59
1998–99	Livingston	77	Inverness CT	72	Clyde	53
1999–2000	Clyde	65	Alloa Ath	64	Ross Co	62
2000–01	Partick Th	75	Arbroath	58	Berwick R*	54
2001–02	Queen of the S	67	Alloa Ath	59	Forfar Ath	53
2002–03	Raith R	59	Brechin C	55	Airdrie U	54
2003–04	Airdrie U	70	Hamilton A	62	Dumbarton	60
2004–05	Brechin C	72	Stranraer	63	Morton	62
2005–06	Gretna	88	Morton§	70	Peterhead*§	57
2006–07	Morton	77	Stirling A	69	Raith R§	62
2007–08	Ross Co	73	Airdrie U	66	Raith R§	60
2008–09	Raith R	76	Ayr U	74	Brechin C§	62

THIRD DIVISION

	First	*Pts*	*Second*	*Pts*	*Third*	*Pts*
	Maximum points: 108					
1994–95	Forfar Ath	80	Montrose	67	Ross Co	60
1995–96	Livingston	72	Brechin C	63	Inverness CT	57
1996–97	Inverness CT	76	Forfar Ath*	67	Ross Co	67
1997–98	Alloa Ath	76	Arbroath	68	Ross Co*	67
1998–99	Ross Co	77	Stenhousemuir	64	Brechin C	59
1999–2000	Queen's Park	69	Berwick R	66	Forfar Ath	61
2000–01	Hamilton A*	76	Cowdenbeath	76	Brechin C	72
2001–02	Brechin C	73	Dumbarton	61	Albion R	59
2002–03	Morton	72	East Fife	71	Albion R	70
2003–04	Stranraer	79	Stirling A	77	Gretna	68
2004–05	Gretna	98	Peterhead	78	Cowdenbeath	51
2005–06	Cowdenbeath*	76	Berwick R§	76	Stenhousemuir§	73
2006–07	Berwick R	75	Arbroath§	70	Queen's Park	68
2007–08	East Fife	88	Stranraer	65	Montrose§	59
2008–09	Dumbarton	67	Cowdenbeath§	63	East Stirling§	61

FIRST DIVISION to 1974–75

	First	*Pts*	*Second*	*Pts*	*Third*	*Pts*
	Maximum points: a 36; b 44; c 40; d 52; e 60; f 68; g 76; h 84.					
1890–91*a*	Dumbarton††	29	Rangers††	29	Celtic	21
1891–92*b*	Dumbarton	37	Celtic	35	Hearts	34
1892–93*a*	Celtic	29	Rangers	28	St Mirren	20
1893–94*a*	Celtic	29	Hearts	26	St Bernard's	23
1894–95*a*	Hearts	31	Celtic	26	Rangers	22
1895–96*a*	Celtic	30	Rangers	26	Hibernian	24
1896–97*a*	Hearts	28	Hibernian	26	Rangers	25
1897–98*a*	Celtic	33	Rangers	29	Hibernian	22
1898–99*a*	Rangers	36	Hearts	26	Celtic	24
1899–1900*a*	Rangers	32	Celtic	25	Hibernian	24
1900–01*c*	Rangers	35	Celtic	29	Hibernian	25

	First	Pts	Second	Pts	Third	Pts
1901–02a	Rangers	28	Celtic	26	Hearts	22
1902–03b	Hibernian	37	Dundee	31	Rangers	29
1903–04d	Third Lanark	43	Hearts	39	Celtic*	38
1904–05d	Celtic‡	41	Rangers	41	Third Lanark	35
1905–06e	Celtic	49	Hearts	43	Airdrieonians	38
1906–07f	Celtic	55	Dundee	48	Rangers	45
1907–08f	Celtic	55	Falkirk	51	Rangers	50
1908–09f	Celtic	51	Dundee	50	Clyde	48
1909–10f	Celtic	54	Falkirk	52	Rangers	46
1910–11f	Rangers	52	Aberdeen	48	Falkirk	44
1911–12f	Rangers	51	Celtic	45	Clyde	42
1912–13f	Rangers	53	Celtic	49	Hearts*	41
1913–14g	Celtic	65	Rangers	59	Hearts*	54
1914–15g	Celtic	65	Hearts	61	Rangers	50
1915–16g	Celtic	67	Rangers	56	Morton	51
1916–17g	Celtic	64	Morton	54	Rangers	53
1917–18f	Rangers	56	Celtic	55	Kilmarnock*	43
1918–19f	Celtic	58	Rangers	57	Morton	47
1919–20h	Rangers	71	Celtic	68	Motherwell	57
1920–21h	Rangers	76	Celtic	66	Hearts	50
1921–22h	Celtic	67	Rangers	66	Raith R	51
1922–23g	Rangers	55	Airdrieonians	50	Celtic	46
1923–24g	Rangers	59	Airdrieonians	50	Celtic	46
1924–25g	Rangers	60	Airdrieonians	57	Hibernian	52
1925–26g	Celtic	58	Airdrieonians*	50	Hearts	50
1926–27g	Rangers	56	Motherwell	51	Celtic	49
1927–28g	Rangers	60	Celtic*	55	Motherwell	55
1928–29g	Rangers	67	Celtic	51	Motherwell	50
1929–30g	Rangers	60	Motherwell	55	Aberdeen	53
1930–31g	Rangers	60	Celtic	58	Motherwell	56
1931–32g	Motherwell	66	Rangers	61	Celtic	48
1932–33g	Rangers	62	Motherwell	59	Hearts	50
1933–34g	Rangers	66	Motherwell	62	Celtic	47
1934–35g	Rangers	55	Celtic	52	Hearts	50
1935–36g	Celtic	66	Rangers*	61	Aberdeen	61
1936–37g	Rangers	61	Aberdeen	54	Celtic	52
1937–38g	Celtic	61	Hearts	58	Rangers	49
1938–39g	Rangers	59	Celtic	48	Aberdeen	46
1946–47e	Rangers	46	Hibernian	44	Aberdeen	39
1947–48e	Hibernian	48	Rangers	46	Partick Th	36
1948–49e	Rangers	46	Dundee	45	Hibernian	39
1949–50e	Rangers	50	Hibernian	49	Hearts	43
1950–51e	Hibernian	48	Rangers*	38	Dundee	38
1951–52e	Hibernian	45	Rangers	41	East Fife	37
1952–53e	Rangers*	43	Hibernian	43	East Fife	39
1953–54e	Celtic	43	Hearts	38	Partick Th	35
1954–55e	Aberdeen	49	Celtic	46	Rangers	41
1955–56f	Rangers	52	Aberdeen	46	Hearts*	45
1956–57f	Rangers	55	Hearts	53	Kilmarnock	42
1957–58f	Hearts	62	Rangers	49	Celtic	46
1958–59f	Rangers	50	Hearts	48	Motherwell	44
1959–60f	Hearts	54	Kilmarnock	50	Rangers*	42
1960–61f	Rangers	51	Kilmarnock	50	Third Lanark	42
1961–62f	Dundee	54	Rangers	51	Celtic	46
1962–63f	Rangers	57	Kilmarnock	48	Partick Th	46
1963–64f	Rangers	55	Kilmarnock	49	Celtic*	47
1964–65f	Kilmarnock*	50	Hearts	50	Dunfermline Ath	49
1965–66f	Celtic	57	Rangers	55	Kilmarnock	45
1966–67f	Celtic	58	Rangers	55	Clyde	46
1967–68f	Celtic	63	Rangers	61	Hibernian	45
1968–69f	Celtic	54	Rangers	49	Dunfermline Ath	45
1969–70f	Celtic	57	Rangers	45	Hibernian	44
1970–71f	Celtic	56	Aberdeen	54	St Johnstone	44
1971–72f	Celtic	60	Aberdeen	50	Rangers	44
1972–73f	Celtic	57	Rangers	56	Hibernian	45
1973–74f	Celtic	53	Hibernian	49	Rangers	48
1974–75f	Rangers	56	Hibernian	49	Celtic	45

SECOND DIVISION to 1974–75

Maximum points: a 76; b 72; c 68; d 52; e 60; f 36; g 44.

	First	Pts	Second	Pts	Third	Pts
1893–94f	Hibernian	29	Cowlairs	27	Clyde	24
1894–95f	Hibernian	30	Motherwell	22	Port Glasgow	20
1895–96f	Abercorn	27	Leith Ath	23	Renton	21
1896–97f	Partick Th	31	Leith Ath	27	Kilmarnock*.	21
1897–98f	Kilmarnock	29	Port Glasgow	25	Morton	22
1898–99f	Kilmarnock	32	Leith Ath	27	Port Glasgow	25
1899–1900f	Partick Th	29	Morton	28	Port Glasgow	20
1900–01f	St Bernard's	25	Airdrieonians	23	Abercorn	21
1901–02g	Port Glasgow	32	Partick Th	31	Motherwell	26
1902–03g	Airdrieonians	35	Motherwell	28	Ayr U*	27
1903–04g	Hamilton A	37	Clyde	29	Ayr U	28
1904–05g	Clyde	32	Falkirk	28	Hamilton A	27
1905–06g	Leith Ath	34	Clyde	31	Albion R	27
1906–07g	St Bernard's	32	Vale of Leven*	27	Arthurlie	27
1907–08g	Raith R	30	Dumbarton*‡‡	27	Ayr U	27

	First	Pts	Second	Pts	Third	Pts
1908–09g	Abercorn	31	Raith R*	28	Vale of Leven	28
1909–10g	Leith Ath‡	33	Raith R	33	St Bernard's	27
1910–11g	Dumbarton	31	Ayr U	27	Albion R	25
1911–12g	Ayr U	35	Abercorn	30	Dumbarton	27
1912–13d	Ayr U	34	Dunfermline Ath	33	East Stirling	32
1913–14g	Cowdenbeath	31	Albion R	27	Dunfermline Ath*	26
1914–15d	Cowdenbeath*	37	St Bernard's*	37	Leith Ath	37
1921–22a	Alloa Ath	60	Cowdenbeath	47	Armadale	45
1922–23a	Queen's Park	57	Clydebank¶	50	St Johnstone¶	45
1923–24a	St Johnstone	56	Cowdenbeath	55	Bathgate	44
1924–25a	Dundee U	50	Clydebank	48	Clyde	47
1925–26a	Dunfermline Ath	59	Clyde	53	Ayr U	52
1926–27a	Bo'ness	56	Raith R	49	Clydebank	45
1927–28a	Ayr U	54	Third Lanark	45	King's Park	44
1928–29b	Dundee U	51	Morton	50	Arbroath	47
1929–30a	Leith Ath*	57	East Fife	57	Albion R	54
1930–31a	Third Lanark	61	Dundee U	50	Dunfermline Ath	47
1931–32a	East Stirling*	55	St Johnstone	55	Raith R*	46
1932–33c	Hibernian	54	Queen of the S	49	Dunfermline Ath	47
1933–34c	Albion R	45	Dunfermline Ath*	44	Arbroath	44
1934–35c	Third Lanark	52	Arbroath	50	St Bernard's	47
1935–36c	Falkirk	59	St Mirren	52	Morton	48
1936–37c	Ayr U	54	Morton	51	St Bernard's	48
1937–38c	Raith R	59	Albion R	48	Airdrieonians	47
1938–39c	Cowdenbeath	60	Alloa Ath*	48	East Fife	48
1946–47d	Dundee	45	Airdrieonians	42	East Fife	31
1947–48e	East Fife	53	Albion R	42	Hamilton A	40
1948–49e	Raith R*	42	Stirling A	42	Airdrieonians*	41
1949–50e	Morton	47	Airdrieonians	44	Dunfermline Ath*	36
1950–51e	Queen of the S*	45	Stirling A	45	Ayr U*	36
1951–52e	Clyde	44	Falkirk	43	Ayr U	39
1952–53e	Stirling A	44	Hamilton A	43	Queen's Park	37
1953–54e	Motherwell	45	Kilmarnock	42	Third Lanark*	36
1954–55e	Airdrieonians	46	Dunfermline Ath	42	Hamilton A	39
1955–56b	Queen's Park	54	Ayr U	51	St Johnstone	49
1956–57b	Clyde	64	Third Lanark	51	Cowdenbeath	45
1957–58b	Stirling A	55	Dunfermline Ath	53	Arbroath	47
1958–59b	Ayr U	60	Arbroath	51	Stenhousemuir	46
1959–60b	St Johnstone	53	Dundee U	50	Queen of the S	49
1960–61b	Stirling A	55	Falkirk	54	Stenhousemuir	50
1961–62b	Clyde	54	Queen of the S	53	Morton	44
1962–63b	St Johnstone	55	East Stirling	49	Morton	48
1963–64b	Morton	67	Clyde	53	Arbroath	46
1964–65b	Stirling A	59	Hamilton A	50	Queen of the S	45
1965–66b	Ayr U	53	Airdrieonians	50	Queen of the S	47
1966–67a	Morton	69	Raith R	58	Arbroath	57
1967–68b	St Mirren	62	Arbroath	53	East Fife	49
1968–69b	Motherwell	64	Ayr U	53	East Fife*	48
1969–70b	Falkirk	56	Cowdenbeath	55	Queen of the S	50
1970–71b	Partick Th	56	East Fife	51	Arbroath	46
1971–72b	Dumbarton*	52	Arbroath	52	Stirling A	50
1972–73b	Clyde	56	Dunfermline Ath	52	Raith R*	47
1973–74b	Airdrieonians	60	Kilmarnock	58	Hamilton A	55
1974–75a	Falkirk	54	Queen of the S*	53	Montrose	53

Elected to First Division: 1894 Clyde; 1895 Hibernian; 1896 Abercorn; 1897 Partick Th; 1899 Kilmarnock; 1900 Morton and Partick Th; 1902 Port Glasgow and Partick Th; 1903 Airdrieonians and Motherwell; 1905 Falkirk and Aberdeen; 1906 Clyde and Hamilton A; 1910 Raith R; 1913 Ayr U and Dumbarton.

RELEGATED FROM PREMIER LEAGUE

1998–99 Dunfermline Ath
1999–2000 *No relegation due to League reorganization*
2000–01 St Mirren
2001–02 St Johnstone
2002–03 *No relegated team*
2003–04 Partick Th

2004–05 Dundee
2005–06 Livingston
2006–07 Dunfermline Ath
2007–08 Gretna
2008–09 Inverness CT

RELEGATED FROM PREMIER DIVISION

1974–75 *No relegation due to League reorganization*
1975–76 Dundee, St Johnstone
1976–77 Hearts, Kilmarnock
1977–78 Ayr U, Clydebank
1978–79 Hearts, Motherwell
1979–80 Dundee, Hibernian
1980–81 Kilmarnock, Hearts
1981–82 Partick Th, Airdrieonians
1982–83 Morton, Kilmarnock
1983–84 St Johnstone, Motherwell
1984–85 Dumbarton, Morton
1985–86 *No relegation due to League reorganization*

1986–87 Clydebank, Hamilton A
1987–88 Falkirk, Dunfermline Ath, Morton
1988–89 Hamilton A
1989–90 Dundee
1990–91 *None*
1991–92 St Mirren, Dunfermline Ath
1992–93 Falkirk, Airdrieonians
1993–94 *See footnote*
1994–95 Dundee U
1995–96 Partick Th, Falkirk
1996–97 Raith R
1997–98 Hibernian

RELEGATED FROM DIVISION 1

1975–76 Dunfermline Ath, Clyde
1976–77 Raith R, Falkirk
1977–78 Alloa Ath, East Fife

1978–79 Montrose, Queen of the S
1979–80 Arbroath, Clyde
1980–81 Stirling A, Berwick R

1981–82 East Stirling, Queen of the S	1996–97 Clydebank, East Fife
1982–83 Dunfermline Ath, Queen's Park	1997–98 Partick Th, Stirling A
1983–84 Raith R, Alloa Ath	1998–99 Hamilton A, Stranraer
1984–85 Meadowbank Th, St Johnstone	1999–2000 Clydebank
1985–86 Ayr U, Alloa Ath	2000–01 Morton, Alloa Ath
1986–87 Brechin C, Montrose	2001–02 Raith R
1987–88 East Fife, Dumbarton	2002–03 Alloa Ath, Arbroath
1988–89 Kilmarnock, Queen of the S	2003–04 Ayr U, Brechin C
1989–90 Albion R, Alloa Ath	2004–05 Partick Th, Raith R
1990–91 Clyde, Brechin C	2005–06 Stranraer, Brechin C
1992–93 Meadowbank Th, Cowdenbeath	2006–07 Airdrie U, Ross Co
1993–94 *See footnote*	2007–08 Stirling A
1994–95 Ayr U, Stranraer	2008–09 Clyde, Airdrie U
1995–96 Hamilton A, Dumbarton	

RELEGATED FROM DIVISION 2

1994–95 Meadowbank Th, Brechin C	1998–99 East Fife, Forfar Ath
2000–01 Queen's Park, Stirling A	2004–05 Arbroath, Berwick R
1995–96 Forfar Ath, Montrose	1999–2000 Hamilton A**
2001–02 Morton	2005–06 Dumbarton
1996–97 Dumbarton, Berwick R	2006–07 Stranraer, Forfar Ath
2002–03 Stranraer, Cowdenbeath	2007–08 Cowdenbeath, Berwick R
1997–98 Stenhousemuir, Brechin C	2008–09 Stranraer, Queen's Park
2003–04 East Fife, Stenhousemuir	

RELEGATED FROM DIVISION 1 (TO 1973–74)

1921–22 *Queen's Park, Dumbarton, Clydebank	1951–52 Morton, Stirling A
1922–23 Albion R, Alloa Ath	1952–53 Motherwell, Third Lanark
1923–24 Clyde, Clydebank	1953–54 Airdrieonians, Hamilton A
1924–25 Third Lanark, Ayr U	1954–55 *No clubs relegated*
1925–26 Raith R, Clydebank	1955–56 Stirling A, Clyde
1926–27 Morton, Dundee U	1956–57 Dunfermline Ath, Ayr U
1927–28 Dunfermline Ath, Bo'ness	1957–58 East Fife, Queen's Park
1928–29 Third Lanark, Raith R	1958–59 Queen of the S, Falkirk
1929–30 St Johnstone, Dundee U	1959–60 Arbroath, Stirling A
1930–31 Hibernian, East Fife	1960–61 Ayr U, Clyde
1931–32 Dundee U, Leith Ath	1961–62 St Johnstone, Stirling A
1932–33 Morton, East Stirling	1962–63 Clyde, Raith R
1933–34 Third Lanark, Cowdenbeath	1963–64 Queen of the S, East Stirling
1934–35 St Mirren, Falkirk	1964–65 Airdrieonians, Third Lanark
1935–36 Airdrieonians, Ayr U	1965–66 Morton, Hamilton A
1936–37 Dunfermline Ath, Albion R	1966–67 St Mirren, Ayr U
1937–38 Dundee, Morton	1967–68 Motherwell, Stirling A
1938–39 Queen's Park, Raith R	1968–69 Falkirk, Arbroath
1946–47 Kilmarnock, Hamilton A	1969–70 Raith R, Partick Th
1947–48 Airdrieonians, Queen's Park	1970–71 St Mirren, Cowdenbeath
1948–49 Morton, Albion R	1971–72 Clyde, Dunfermline Ath
1949–50 Queen of the S, Stirling A	1972–73 Kilmarnock, Airdrieonians
1950–51 Clyde, Falkirk	1973–74 East Fife, Falkirk

*Season 1921–22 – only 1 club promoted, 3 clubs relegated. **15pts deducted for failing to field a team.*

Scottish League Championship wins: Rangers 52, Celtic 42, Aberdeen 4, Hearts 4, Hibernian 4, Dumbarton 2, Dundee 1, Dundee U 1, Kilmarnock 1, Motherwell 1, Third Lanark 1.

At the end of the 1993–94 season four divisions were created assisted by the admission of two new clubs Ross County and Caledonian Thistle. Only one club was promoted from Division 1 and Division 2. The three relegated from the Premier joined with teams finishing second to seventh in Division 1 to form the new Division 1. Five relegated from Division 1 combined with those who finished second to sixth to form a new Division 2 and the bottom eight in Division 2 linked with the two newcomers to form a new Division 3. At the end of the 1997–98 season the nine clubs remaining in the Premier Division plus the promoted team from Division 1 formed a breakaway Premier League. At the end of the 1999–2000 season two teams were added to the Scottish League. There was no relegation from the Premier League but two promoted from the First Division and three from each of the Second and Third Divisions. One team was relegated from the First Division and one from the Second Division, leaving 12 teams in each division. In season 2002–03, Falkirk were not promoted to the Premier League due to the failure of their ground to meet League rules. Inverness CT were promoted after a previous refusal in 2003–04 because of ground sharing. At the end of 2005–06 the Scottish League introduced play-offs for the team finishing second from the bottom of Division 1 against the winners of the second, third and fourth finishing teams in Division 2 and with a similar procedure for Division 2 and Division 3.

LEAGUE CHALLENGE FINALS 1991–2009

Year	Winners	Runners-up	Score	Year	Winners	Runners-up	Score
1990–91	Dundee	Ayr U	3-2	2000–01	Airdrieonians	Livingston	2-2
1991–92	Hamilton A	Ayr U	1-0		*(aet; Airdrieonians won 3-2 on penalties)*		
1992–93	Hamilton A	Morton	3-2	2001–02	Airdrieonians	Alloa Ath	2-1
1993–94	Falkirk	St Mirren	3-0	2002–03	Queen of the S	Brechin C	2-0
1994–95	Airdrieonians	Dundee	3-2	2003–04	Inverness CT	Airdrie U	2-0
1995–96	Stenhousemuir	Dundee U	0-0	2004–05	Falkirk	Ross Co	2-1
	(aet; Stenhousemuir won 5-4 on penalties)			2005–06	St Mirren	Hamilton A	2-1
1996–97	Stranraer	St Johnstone	1-0	2006–07	Ross Co	Clyde	1-1
1997–98	Falkirk	Queen of the South	1-0		*(aet; Ross Co won 5-4 on penalties)*		
1998–99	no competition			2007–08	St Johnstone	Dunfermline Ath	3-2
1999–2000	Alloa Ath	Inverness CT	4-4	2008–09	Airdrie U	Ross Co	2-2
	(aet; Alloa Ath won 5-4 on penalties)				*(aet; Airdrie U won 3-2 on penalties)*		

SCOTTISH LEAGUE CUP FINALS 1946–2009

Season	Winners	Runners-up	Score
1946–47	Rangers	Aberdeen	4-0
1947–48	East Fife	Falkirk	4-1 after 0-0 draw (*aet.*)
1948–49	Rangers	Raith R	2-0
1949–50	East Fife	Dunfermline Ath	3-0
1950–51	Motherwell	Hibernian	3-0
1951–52	Dundee	Rangers	3-2
1952–53	Dundee	Kilmarnock	2-0
1953–54	East Fife	Partick Th	3-2
1954–55	Hearts	Motherwell	4-2
1955–56	Aberdeen	St Mirren	2-1
1956–57	Celtic	Partick Th	3-0 after 0-0 draw
1957–58	Celtic	Rangers	7-1
1958–59	Hearts	Partick Th	5-1
1959–60	Hearts	Third Lanark	2-1
1960–61	Rangers	Kilmarnock	2-0
1961–62	Rangers	Hearts	3-1 after 1-1 draw
1962–63	Hearts	Kilmarnock	1-0
1963–64	Rangers	Morton	5-0
1964–65	Rangers	Celtic	2-1
1965–66	Celtic	Rangers	2-1
1966–67	Celtic	Rangers	1-0
1967–68	Celtic	Dundee	5-3
1968–69	Celtic	Hibernian	6-2
1969–70	Celtic	St Johnstone	1-0
1970–71	Rangers	Celtic	1-0
1971–72	Partick Th	Celtic	4-1
1972–73	Hibernian	Celtic	2-1
1973–74	Dundee	Celtic	1-0
1974–75	Celtic	Hibernian	6-3
1975–76	Rangers	Celtic	1-0
1976–77	Aberdeen	Celtic	2-1
1977–78	Rangers	Celtic	2-1 (*aet.*)
1978–79	Rangers	Aberdeen	2-1
1979–80	Dundee U	Aberdeen	3-0 after 0-0 draw (*aet.*)
1980–81	Dundee U	Dundee	3-0
1981–82	Rangers	Dundee U	2-1
1982–83	Celtic	Rangers	2-1
1983–84	Rangers	Celtic	3-2
1984–85	Rangers	Dundee U	1-0
1985–86	Aberdeen	Hibernian	3-0
1986–87	Rangers	Celtic	2-1
1987–88	Rangers	Aberdeen	3-3
		(aet; Rangers won 5-3 on penalties)	
1988–89	Rangers	Aberdeen	3-2 (*aet.*)
1989–90	Aberdeen	Rangers	2-1
1990–91	Rangers	Celtic	2-1
1991–92	Hibernian	Dunfermline Ath	2-0
1992–93	Rangers	Aberdeen	2-1 (*aet.*)
1993–94	Rangers	Hibernian	2-1
1994–95	Raith R	Celtic	2-2
		(aet; Raith R won 6-5 on penalties)	
1995–96	Aberdeen	Dundee	2-0
1996–97	Rangers	Hearts	4-3
1997–98	Celtic	Dundee U	3-0
1998–99	Rangers	St Johnstone	2-1
1999–2000	Celtic	Aberdeen	2-0
2000–01	Celtic	Kilmarnock	3-0
2001–02	Rangers	Ayr U	4-0
2002–03	Rangers	Celtic	2-1
2003–04	Livingston	Hibernian	2-0
2004–05	Rangers	Motherwell	5-1
2005–06	Celtic	Dunfermline Ath	3-0
2005–06	Celtic	Dunfermline Ath	3-0
2006–07	Hibernian	Kilmarnock	5-1
2007–08	Rangers	Dundee U	2-2
		(aet; Rangers won 3-2 on penalties)	
2008–09	Celtic	Rangers	2-0 (*aet.*)

SCOTTISH LEAGUE CUP WINS

Rangers 25, Celtic 14, Aberdeen 5, Hearts 4, Dundee 3, East Fife 3, Hibernian 3, Dundee U 2, Livingston 1, Motherwell 1, Partick Th 1, Raith R 1.

APPEARANCES IN FINALS

Rangers 32, Celtic 27, Aberdeen 12, Hibernian 9, Dundee 6, Dundee U 6, Hearts 6, Kilmarnock 5, Partick Th 4, Dunfermline Ath 3, East Fife 3, Motherwell 3, Raith R 2, St Johnstone 2, Ayr U 1, Falkirk 1, Livingston 1, Morton 1, St Mirren 1, Third Lanark 1.

CIS SCOTTISH LEAGUE CUP 2008–09

■ *Denotes player sent off.*

FIRST ROUND

Tuesday, 5 August 2008

Albion R (0) 0

Raith R (0) 0   415

Albion R: Scott; Reid, McGowan, Walker R, Hughes, Ferry, Barr, Donnelly, Martin (McKenna), Coyne (Pollock), Smith (Walker P).
Raith R: McGurn; Wilson, Cook, Campbell, Ellis, Walker (Dunbar), Sloan, Davidson■, Weir (Graham), Wardlaw, Ferry (Silvestro).
aet; Raith R won 4-3 on penalties.

Alloa Ath (0) 2 *(Scott 71, Kelly 78)*

Elgin C (0) 0   269

Alloa Ath: Jellema; Buist, McClune (Ferguson M), Scullion (MacAulay), Townsley, Hill, Stevenson, McKeown, Brown (Scott), Grant, Kelly.
Elgin C: Ridgers; Gilbert, MacDonald, Kaczan, Nicolson, Hind, Campbell, O'Donoghue, Shallicker, Crooks, McKay.

Clyde (1) 4 *(Roddy MacLennan 15, Gibson 63, McSwegan 86, 88)*

Queen's Park (0) 1 *(Harkins 82)*   690

Clyde: Cherrie; Gibson, Ruari MacLennan (McSwegan), Higgins, Brown, Kettlewell, Trouten, Wilson (McLaren), Clarke (Ohnesorge), Gemmill, Roddy MacLennan.
Queen's Park: Crawford; Ure, Douglas, Sinclair, Brough, Harkins, Dunn (Quinn), Cairney, Coakley (McGrady), Neill, Holmes.

Dumbarton (0) 1 *(Logan 115)*

Annan Ath (0) 1 *(Jack 103 (pen))*   462

Dumbarton: McEwan; Geggan■, O'Byrne, Gordon, Brittain (Lennon), Gourlay (Tiernan), Clark, Logan, Murray, Keegan (Chisholm), Carcary.
Annan Ath: Calder; Brown, Hill, Neilson, Inglis, Sloan, Jack (Parker), Jardine, Hoolickin (Watson), Archibald (Adamson), Johnstone.
aet; Dumbarton won 5-4 on penalties.

Montrose (0) 0

Cowdenbeath (1) 2 *(McGregor 6, Fairbairn 81)* 382

Montrose: Peat (Butter); Worrell, McLeod, Buchan, Thomson, Hegarty, Gibson, Davidson (Hunter), Stein (Black), Stewart, Baird.
Cowdenbeath: Hay; Droudge, McGregor, Mbu, Adamson, Fairbairn (Fleming), Hodge, Ramsay (Tomana), McQuade, Shields (Robertson), Gemmell.

Partick Th (1) 4 *(McKeown 39, Gray 70, 97, Chaplain 112)*

Forfar Ath (1) 3 *(Fotheringham 13, Lilley 65, Smith 103)*   1192

Partick Th: Tuffey; Paton, Storey, Robertson, Twaddle, Rowson, McStay (Harkins), McKeown (Chaplain), McKinlay (Maxwell), Gray, Donnelly.
Forfar Ath: Brown; McNally, Tulloch, Dunn, Ferguson, McLeish, Brady (Fraser), Fotheringham, Smith E, Lilley (Duell), Winter.
aet.

Peterhead (0) 0

Dunfermline Ath (0) 2 *(Phinn 46, Kirk 50)* 1291

Peterhead: Kula; Donald, Moore, Mann, Skinner (Munro), McVitie, Sharp, Anderson (MacDonald), McKay, Gunn (Ross), Bavidge.
Dunfermline Ath: Gallacher; Shields, Wilson (Woods), Phinn (Holmes), Thomson S, McCann, Harper, Glass, Bayne, Kirk (Williamson), Burke.

Ross Co (1) 2 *(Daal 43, Hart 76)*

Airdrie U (1) 3 *(Di Giacomo 23, 112, Noble 86)* 869

Ross Co: Bullock; McCulloch, Golabek, Dowie, Watt, Lawson, Hart, Brittain, Craig (Higgins), Daal (Winters), Strachan.
Airdrie U: Robertson; McKenna, Hazley (Maguire), McDonald, Donnelly, Nixon, Smith (Cardle), McLaughlin, Di Giacomo, Lynch (Noble), McDougall.
aet.

Stenhousemuir (1) 1 *(Love 12)*

St Johnstone (1) 5 *(Sheerin 23 (pen), Milne 78, Holmes 79, 83, Hardie 88)*   687

Stenhousemuir: Bennett; McEwan, Motion, Thom, Ovenstone, Desmond (Brazil), Love (Tyrrell), Shirra, Dalziel (Hampshire), Brand, Gibson.
St Johnstone: McLean; Irvine, Craig, Millar, Rutkiewicz (Weatherston), James, Swankie, Hardie, Jackson (Milne), MacDonald (Holmes), Sheerin.

Stranraer (1) 3 *(Frizzel 37, McColm 72, Gibson 84)*

Morton (5) 6 *(McGuffie 5, Wake 12, 85, Russell 23, 32, Paartalu 40)*   317

Stranraer: Black; Kane, Creaney, Dobbins, Nicoll (McColm), Mitchell, Gibson, McBride, Osbourne, Noble (Murdoch), Frizzel (Paisley).
Morton: Cuthbert; Weatherson, Walker (McManus), Shimmin, Paartalu, McGuffie (Finlayson), McAlister, Masterton, Wake, Newby, Russell (Harding).

Wednesday, 6 August 2008

Arbroath (0) 3 *(McMullan 48, Wright 64, Bishop 80)*

Stirling Alb (1) 2 *(Graham 5, Harty 63)*   448

Arbroath: Hill; Rennie, Black, Rattray (Dingwall), Bishop, Masson; McMullan, Lunan, Scott (Wright), Sellars, Gates (Fraser).
Stirling Alb: Christie; Graham, Lowing (Corr), Lawrie, Forsyth, O'Neil, Taggart, Murphy, Harty, Grehan (McKenna), Devine (Waddell).

Ayr U (2) 2 *(Aitken 40, Williams 45)*

Berwick R (1) 1 *(Greenhill D 12)*   745

Ayr U: Grindlay; Keenan, Walker, Campbell, Easton, Borris, Aitken, Stevenson, Agnew, Prunty (Gormley), Williams.
Berwick R: McGurk; Guy, Ewart, Kiczynski, McMahon, Little, Greenhill D, Craig Anderson (Callaghan), Dillon (Howat), Lister, Gribben (Grant).

East Fife (0) 0

Brechin C (1) 3 *(Twigg 44, White 65, Ward 74)* 523

East Fife: McCulloch; Nugent, Smart, McDonald, Cameron, Young, Fotheringham, Stewart, Stanik (Gordon), McManus (Templeman), Crawford (O'Reilly).
Brechin C: Nelson C; Murie, Ward, White, Dyer, Janczyk, Nimmo (Canning), Twigg (Walker R), Smith D, Byers (King), Diack.

East Stirling (0) 0 *(Graham 90)*

Livingston (0) 2 *(Fox 80, Smith 113)*   360

East Stirling: Hillcoat; Moffat, Ure, Anderson, Tully, Gibson, Donaldson, Kelly, Cramb (Forrest), McKenzie (Rodgers), Dunn (Graham).
Livingston: Martini; Miller, Talbot, McDonald, Fox, Innes, Jacobs, Davidson, Cuenca (Sinclair), Griffiths (Smith), Hamill.
aet.

SECOND ROUND

Tuesday, 26 August 2008

Cowdenbeath (0) 1 *(Dempster 74)*

Dundee U (2) 5 *(Daly 30, 47, 80, Goodwillie 41, 60)* 1423

Cowdenbeath: Hay; McKay, Mbu, Hodge, Fleming, McGregor, Fairbairn (Tomana), Shields (Baxter), McQuade, Gemmell (Dempster), Ramsay.
Dundee U: Zaluska; Dillon, Grainger, Kenneth, Dods, Flood, Robertson S, Gomis, Goodwillie, Daly (Shala), Conway (Swanson).

Dundee (0) 1 *(McHale 80)*

Partick Th (0) 2 *(Maxwell 78, Harkins 87 (pen))* 2507

Dundee: Douglas; Paton, Malone, McHale, MacKenzie, Williams, Daquin (Gilhaney), Pozniak (Cowan), McMenamin, Antoine-Curier (Deasley), O'Brien.
Partick Th: Tuffey; Paton, Twaddle, Storey, Robertson J, Maxwell, Chaplain (McKinlay), McStay, Gray (Lennon), Roberts (Donnelly), Harkins.

Dunfermline Ath (1) 1 *(Kirk 8)*
Alloa Ath (0) 0   1326
Dunfermline Ath: Gallacher; Woods, Wilson, Phinn, Shields (Muirhead), McCann, Harper (Wiles), Glass (Bell), Bayne, Kirk, Burke.
Alloa Ath: Jellema; Buist, Campbell, Townsley, Hill, Scullion (McKeown■), Wilson, Ferguson B (Spence), Grant, Stevenson (Scott), MacAulay.

Hamilton A (1) 3 *(Grady 17, Thomas 81,*
Stevenson 90 (pen))
Clyde (1) 1 *(Clarke 19)*   1146
Hamilton A: Cerny; Stevenson, Elebert, Swailes, Easton (Corcoran), Akins, McCarthy, Mensing, McArthur, Grady (Thomas), Sorsa (Lyle).
Clyde: Cherrie; Gibson, Higgins, Brown, Ohnesorge■, Ruari MacLennan, Kettlewell, Wilson (Trouten), Waddell, Clarke (McKay), Gemmill (McGowan).

Hibernian (0) 3 *(Keenan 80, Shiels 85, Pinau 91)*
Morton (1) 4 *(Russell 29, 115 (pen), Masterton 66,*
Harding 118)   14,874
Hibernian: McNeil (Grof); Van Zanten, Stevenson, Murray, Hogg, Rankin, Morais (Zemmama), Nish (Pinau), Fletcher, Shiels, Keenan.
Morton: Cuthbert; Shimmin, McManus, Harding, Walker (Weatherson), McGuffie, Paartalu, Masterton (Jenkins), McAlister, Wake (Newby), Russell.
aet.

Livingston (0) 2 *(Griffiths 58, Cuenca 95)*
St Johnstone (0) 1 *(Craig 46)*   979
Livingston: McKenzie; MacKay, Hamill, McPake, Fox (Millar), Innes, Quinn, Davidson, Griffiths, Cuenca (Smith), McPartland (Cave).
St Johnstone: Main; Irvine, Morgan, McKoy (Swankie), Anderson, McCaffrey, Millar, Hardie, Jackson, Holmes (Samuel), Sheerin (Craig).

Raith R (0) 1 *(Campbell 74)*
Falkirk (2) 3 *(Higdon 16, Stewart J 35 (pen), Stewart M 84)*
                                                               2090
Raith R: McGurn; Wilson, Ellis, Silvestro (Guerrero), Cook, Sloan (Ferry), Walker■, Campbell, Wardlaw (Bryce), Smith, Weir.
Falkirk: Olejnik; McNamara (Scobbie), Barr, Bullen, Aafjes, McBride, Cregg (Mitchell), Arfield, Stewart J (Barrett), Higdon, Stewart M.

St Mirren (3) 7 *(Robb 18, Mehmet 33, 50, 52, Dorman 39,*
Dargo 75, Mason 77)
Dumbarton (0) 0   1747
St Mirren: Howard; Moss, Miranda, Mason, Haining, Potter, Dorman (Murray), Brady, Mehmet (Wyness), Hamilton (Dargo), Robb.
Dumbarton: McEwan; Lennon, Wilson, O'Byrne, Gordon, Clark, Chisholm, Logan (Gray), Keegan (Tiernan), Gourlay (Brannan), Murray.

Wednesday, 27 August 2008

Arbroath (1) 2 *(Tosh 21, Sellars 67 (pen))*
Inverness CT (1) 2 *(Vigurs 18, Wood 64)*   596
Arbroath: Morrison; Rennie, Raeside, Bishop, Campbell, Masson (McMullan), Fraser (Simpson), Lunan, Weir (Gates), Tosh, Sellars.
Inverness CT: Esson; Tokely, Djebi-Zadi, Black, Cowie, McGuire, Wilson (Rooney), Duff, Vigurs, McAllister (Imrie), Wood (Barrowman■).
aet; Inverness CT won 4-2 on penalties.

Ayr U (0) 0
Aberdeen (1) 1 *(Maguire 40)*   2979
Ayr U: Grindlay; Dempsie, Easton, Walker, Campbell, Stevenson, Borris, Aitken, Prunty, Williams (Gormley), Keenan.
Aberdeen: Bossu; Foster, Mulgrew, McDonald, Considine, Mair, Smith J, Kerr, Maguire (Wright), Mackie (De Visscher), Young.

Brechin C (0) 0
Kilmarnock (0) 2 *(Wright 58, Bryson 65)*   802
Brechin C: Nelson C; Murie (Walker R), White, Dyer, Feeley, Byers, Nimmo, Janczyk (Nelson A), Smith D, Twigg, Diack (King).
Kilmarnock: Combe; Fowler, Hay, Pascali, Wright, Ford (Murray), Invincibile, Bryson, Russell (Gibson), Sammon (Simmonds), Taouil.

Hearts (0) 0
Airdrie U (0) 0   6844
Hearts: Kello; Karipidis, Wallace, Jonsson, Zaliukas, Berra, Mikoliunas (Cesnauskis), Stewart, Kingston (Ksanavicius), Mole (Nade), Obua.
Airdrie U: Robertson; Smyth, Donnelly, Nixon, Hazley, McDougall (Smith D), McKenna, McDonald■, Cardle (Brown), Di Giacomo (Lynch), McLaughlin.
aet; Airdrie U won 4-3 on penalties.

THIRD ROUND

Tuesday, 23 September 2008

Celtic (1) 4 *(Loovens 24, Samaras 64, 85 (pen), Brown S 81)*
Livingston (0) 0   23,569
Celtic: Boruc; Hinkel, Naylor, Donati (Brown S), Loovens, McManus, Caddis, Hartley, McDonald (Maloney), Samaras, McGeady.
Livingston: McKenzie; MacKay, Talbot (Miller), McPake, Fox (Giarrizzo), Innes, Davidson, McParland, Elliot (Cuenca), Hamill, Quinn.

Dundee U (2) 2 *(Goodwillie 33, Robertson S 42)*
Airdrie U (0) 0   3444
Dundee U: Zaluska; Dillon, Dixon, Wilkie, Dods, Gomis, Robertson S, Conway (Swanson), Goodwillie, Sandaza (O'Donovan), Robertson D (McCord).
Airdrie U: Robertson; Smyth, Donnelly, Nixon, Smith D (Noble), Cardle (Maguire), McLaughlin, McKenna, Brown, McDougall, Di Giacomo.

Dunfermline Ath (0) 2 *(Bayne 69, Wiles 74)*
St Mirren (0) 0   2186
Dunfermline Ath: Gallacher; Thomson S, McCann, Wilson, Phinn, Shields, Bell (Wiles), Harper (Woods), Kirk, Bayne, Burke.
St Mirren: Howard; Ross, Miranda, Mason (Wyness), Haining (Cuthbert), Potter, Murray (Robb), Brady, Mehmet, Hamilton, McGinn.

Falkirk (1) 2 *(McCann 29, Lovell 73)*
Queen of the S (0) 1 *(Kean 58)*   2058
Falkirk: Olejnik; McNamara, Scobbie, McCann, Barr, McBride, Aafjes, Lovell, Higdon (O'Brien), Barrett (Stewart M), Arfield (Cregg).
Queen of the S: Bell; Barr, Sives, Thomson, Harris, MacFarlane, Robertson (Simmons), Tosh, Arbuckle (McGowan), Dobbie, Kean.

Morton (1) 1 *(McAlister 34)*
Inverness CT (0) 2 *(Hastings 79, Imrie 111)*   2023
Morton: Cuthbert; Walker, Smith, Harding, Shimmin, Paartalu, McGuffie (Finlayson), Masterton (Jenkins), Russell (Weatherson), Wake, McAlister.
Inverness CT: Esson; Tokely, Hastings, Black (Rooney), Cowie (Vigurs), Munro, McAllister (Wilson), Duncan, Wood, Imrie, Duff.
aet.

Wednesday, 24 September 2008

Kilmarnock (4) 4 *(Sammon 2, 33, Fernandez 12,*
Taouil 17 (pen))
Aberdeen (2) 2 *(McDonald 6, Miller 26 (pen))*   4339
Kilmarnock: Combe; Fowler, Lilley, Wright, Ford, Hamill, Sammon (Simmonds), Bryson, Fernandez, Taouil, Pascali.
Aberdeen: Bossu; Foster, Hodgkiss, Mulgrew (Young), Diamond, Severin, McDonald, Kerr (Mair), Miller, Mackie, Aluko.

Motherwell (0) 1 *(Murphy 66)*
Hamilton A (0) 2 *(Graham 53, Ettien 95)*   5590
Motherwell: Smith G; Quinn, Hammell, Craigan (Fitzpatrick), Reynolds, Malcolm, Lasley, Hughes (Sutton), Porter■, Clarkson, Murphy (Smith D).
Hamilton A: Murdoch; Mensing■, Easton, Swailes, Casement, Elebert, McArthur, Neil, Graham, Lyle (Thomas), Corcoran (Ettien).
aet.

Partick Th (1) 1 *(McKeown 33)*
Rangers (1) 2 *(Boyd 25, Pedro Mendes 116)*   6497
Partick Th: Tuffey; Storey, Twaddle, Robertson J, McKinlay, Rowson, McKeown (Chaplain), Maxwell, Harkins, Donnelly (Gray), Roberts (Turner).
Rangers: Alexander; Broadfoot, Papac, Thomson, Weir, Bougherra, Davis, Pedro Mendes, Darcheville (Beasley), Boyd, Novo (Lafferty).
aet.

QUARTER-FINALS

Tuesday, 28 October 2008

Dundee U (1) 1 *(Robertson S 16)*
Dunfermline Ath (0) 0   5350
Dundee U: Zaluska; Dillon, Dixon, Wilkie, Dods, Flood, Robertson S, Gomis, Sandaza (Feeney), O'Donovan, Conway.
Dunfermline Ath: Gallacher; Woods, Shields, Wilson, McCann, Harper (Bell), Phinn, Burke (Wiles), Glass, Bayne, Kirk (Williamson).

Falkirk (1) 1 *(McCann 36)*
Inverness CT (0) 0   3007
Falkirk: Flinders; McNamara, Holden, McCann (Cregg), Aafjes, Barr, O'Brien, McBride, Higdon, Barrett (Latapy), Arfield.
Inverness CT: Esson; Tokely, Hastings, Duncan, Duff, Munro, Cowie, McBain (Wilson), Rooney, Wood (Barrowman), Imrie (Vigurs).

Rangers (1) 2 *(Boyd 25, Lafferty 50)*
Hamilton A (0) 0   32,083
Rangers: McGregor; Broadfoot, Papac, Bougherra, Weir, Edu, Davis, Pedro Mendes, Boyd, Darcheville (Novo), Lafferty.
Hamilton A: Cerny; McClenahan, Easton, Graham, Swailes (Corcoran), Elebert, McArthur, McCarthy (Ettien), Akins (Offiong), Gibson, Neil.

Wednesday, 29 October 2008
Kilmarnock (0) 1 *(Invincibile 68)*
Celtic (2) 3 *(McDonald 11, Nakamura 45, McGeady 71)*   6319
Kilmarnock: Combe; Murray, Hamill, Pascali, Lilley, Wright (Skelton), Invincibile (Sammon), Bryson, Fernandez, Taouil (Simmonds), Fowler.
Celtic: Boruc; Hinkel, Wilson, Donati, Caldwell, O'Dea, Nakamura (Hartley), Brown S, McDonald (Sheridan), Maloney, McGeady.

SEMI-FINALS

Tuesday, 27 January 2009
Rangers (2) 3 *(Novo 8, 40, Boyd 88)*
Falkirk (0) 0   24,507
Rangers: McGregor; Broadfoot, Papac, Bougherra, Weir, Ferguson (McCulloch), Davis, Pedro Mendes, Boyd, Novo, Naismith (Fleck).
Falkirk: Dani Mallo; McNamara, Scobbie, Cregg (Stewart M), Barr, Bullen (Higdon), Pressley, McBride, Lovell, McCann, Arfield.

Wednesday, 28 January 2009
Celtic (0) 0
Dundee U (0) 0   19,258
Celtic: Boruc; Hinkel, Naylor, Crosas, Caldwell, Loovens, Nakamura, Brown S, McDonald, Vennegoor (Samaras), McGeady (Robson).
Dundee U: Zaluska; Kovacevic, Dixon, Wilkie, Kenneth, Flood, Buaben (Robertson D), Gomis, Feeney, Sandaza (Daly), Conway.
aet; Celtic won 11-10 on penalties.

FINAL (at Hampden Park)

Sunday, 15 March 2009
Rangers (0) 0
Celtic (0) 2 *(O'Dea 91, McGeady 120 (pen))*   51,193
Rangers: McGregor; Whittaker, Papac, Broadfoot■, Weir, Ferguson, Davis, Pedro Mendes, Lafferty (Boyd), Miller (Novo), McCulloch (Dailly).
Celtic: Boruc; Hinkel, O'Dea (Wilson), Loovens, Caldwell, McManus, Nakamura, Brown S, McDonald, Hartley (Samaras), McGeady.
aet.
Referee: D. McDonald.

SCOTTISH LEAGUE ATTENDANCES 2008–09

PREMIER LEAGUE

	Average	Highest	Lowest
Aberdeen	12,929	20,441	8,909
Celtic	57,671	59,685	55,117
Dundee U	8,654	14,077	5,926
Falkirk	5,640	6,853	4,385
Hamilton A	3,823	5,895	2,600
Hearts	14,398	17,244	12,030
Hibernian	12,684	17,223	10,317
Inverness CT	4,457	7,143	3,110
Kilmarnock	5,727	10,153	4,267
Motherwell	5,522	9,600	2,818
Rangers	49,534	50,403	48,129
St Mirren	5,411	10,189	3,364

FIRST DIVISION

	Average	Highest	Lowest
Airdrie U	1,357	2,165	633
Clyde	1,237	2,191	776
Dundee	3,955	6,537	2,831
Dunfermline Ath	3,112	4,653	1,438
Livingston	1,829	2,876	1,068
Morton	2,250	3,323	1,642
Partick Th	2,966	3,579	2,296
Queen of the S	2,682	3,272	2,029
Ross Co	2,164	3,444	232
St Johnstone	3,522	7,238	2,259

SECOND DIVISION

	Average	Highest	Lowest
Alloa Ath	637	1,057	331
Arbroath	639	921	411
Ayr U	1,473	2,368	1,070
Brechin C	553	780	315
East Fife	863	1,980	533
Peterhead	648	855	461
Queen's Park	730	1,763	466
Raith R	2,234	4,812	1,294
Stirling A	645	1,125	284
Stranraer	367	1,019	154

THIRD DIVISION

	Average	Highest	Lowest
Albion R	323	535	237
Annan Ath	729	1,343	422
Berwick R	414	570	288
Cowdenbeath	421	1,181	193
Dumbarton	709	1,396	462
East Stirling	455	814	343
Elgin C	391	537	271
Forfar Ath	452	621	319
Montrose	381	570	304
Stenhousemuir	495	805	311

ALBA LEAGUE CHALLENGE CUP 2008–09

■ *Denotes player sent off.*

FIRST ROUND NORTH EAST

Saturday, 26 July 2008

Alloa Ath (0) 2 *(Townsley 59, Stevenson 83)*
Dundee (0) 1 *(Antoine-Curier 88)*   793
Alloa Ath: Jellema; McClune, Campbell, Scullion, Townsley, Hall, Stevenson (Kelly), McKeown, Brown (Ferguson A), Grant, MacAulay (Scott).
Dundee: Roy; Paton, Malone, Mearns, MacKenzie (Forsyth), Cowan, Daquin (Deasley), McHale, McMenamin, Antoine-Curier, Gilhaney.

Arbroath (1) 1 *(Scott 44)*
Forfar Ath (0) 2 *(Kilgannon 62 (pen), McLeish 71 (pen))*   563
Arbroath: Hill; Rennie, Black, Rattray, Bishop, Masson (Reilly), McMullan (Wright), Lunan, Scott, Sellars, Gates.
Forfar Ath: Brown; Donachie, Smith E, McNally, Dunn, Kilgannon, McLeish, Winter, Lilley (Fotheringham), Brady (Duell), Campbell.

Brechin C (0) 0
East Fife (0) 1 *(Templeman 69)*   446
Brechin C: Nelson C; Murie (Walker R), Dyer, Ward, White, Nimmo■, Byers, Janczyk, Twigg (Smith C), King, Smith D (Diack).
East Fife: McCulloch; Nugent, Cameron, Smart, Tweed, Fotheringham, Young, Stanik (Campbell), Crawford, O'Reilly (Templeman), Linn (Stewart).

Dunfermline Ath (1) 3 *(Burke 4, Phinn 61, Williamson 74)*
Stirling Alb (0) 0   1340
Dunfermline Ath: Gallacher; Shields, Wilson, Woods (Williamson), Thomson, McCann, Harper (Willis), Glass, Bayne, Burke, Phinn.
Stirling Alb: Christie; Andrew, Lowing, Lawrie, Forsyth, O'Neil, Corr, Murphy (Taggart), Harty (Grehan), Waddell (McKenna), Devine.

Elgin C (0) 0
Cowdenbeath (1) 2 *(McGregor 13, McQuade 80)*   379
Elgin C: Ridgers; Niven (Shallicker), McKay, Nicolson, Kaczan, Gilbert, Low, Hind, Crooks, Charlesworth (Allan), Campbell.
Cowdenbeath: Hay; Cennerazzo, Adamson, McGregor, Mbu, Hodge, Fairbairn (Tomana), Shields, Gemmill (Ferguson), Ramsay, McQuade (McKay).

Peterhead (2) 6 *(Bavidge 24, 78, Cumming 45 (og), Gunn 52, 58, 68 (pen))*
Montrose (0) 0   503
Peterhead: Kula; Donald, Moore, Mann (MacDonald), Skinner, McVitie, Sharp, Anderson, McKay, Gunn (Munro), Bavidge (Bagshaw).
Montrose: Peat; Worrell, Gardiner, McLeod, Cumming, Buchan, Gibson, Davidson (Maitland), Hunter, Stewart (Nicol), Stein (Black).

Ross Co (0) 2 *(Winters 53, Higgins 65)*
St Johnstone (0) 1 *(Samuel 84)*   2365
Ross Co: Bullock; McCulloch, Golabek, Dowie, Boyd, Lawson (Scott), Hart, Griffin, Higgins, Winters, Strachan (Morrison).
St Johnstone: McLean; Irvine, Anderson (Swankie), Millar, Rutkiewicz, McCaffrey, Craig, Hardie, Holmes, Milne (Samuel), Sheerin (Jackson).

FIRST ROUND SOUTH-WEST

Saturday, 26 July 2008

Airdrie U (0) 3 *(Noble 53, Cardle 58, Di Giacomo 75)*
Dumbarton (2) 2 *(Clark 25, Carcary 43)*   808
Airdrie U: Robertson; Smyth, Hazley, McDonald, Donnelly (Smith D), Nixon, McDougall (McLaughlin), McKenna, Di Giacomo, Noble (Maguire), Cardle.
Dumbarton: McEwan; Geggan, Wilson, O'Byrne (Lennon), Gordon, Canning, Gray, Clark (Logan), Keegan, Carcary (Tiernan), Murray.

Berwick R (0) 1 *(Little 47)*
Queen of the S (2) 5 *(O'Connor 12, 58, Kean 31, 65, Barr 80)*   655
Berwick R: McGurk; Guy, Kiczynski (McMahon), Ewart, McLean, Bonar, Chris Anderson (Little), Callaghan, Lister, McLaren, Howat (Gribben).
Queen of the S: Halliwell; Barr, McQuilken, MacFarlane, Thomson, Reid, Kean, Tosh (Robertson), O'Connor (Arbuckle), Dobbie (McGowan), Burns.

Clyde (0) 2 *(Trouten 61 (pen), 74)*
Annan Ath (0) 0   700
Clyde: Hutton; McGregor, Higgins, Brown, Gibson, Trouten, Kettlewell, Roddy MacLennan (Connelly), Clarke, McSwegan (Gemmill), McKay (McLaren).
Annan Ath: Summersgill; Brown, Townsley, Neilson, Inglis, Jack, Grainger (Sloan), Jardine, Hoolickin (Adamson), Archibald, Hill (Watson).

Livingston (1) 4 *(Griffiths 33, 72, Hamill 67, McParland 70)*
Stranraer (0) 0   642
Livingston: Martini; MacKay, Talbot, McPake, McParland, Innes (MacDonald), Fox, Davidson (Jacobs), Cuenca, Griffiths (Smith), Hamill.
Stranraer: Black; Kane, Creaney, Dobbins, Nicoll■, White (Mitchell), Gibson, McBride, Tade, McConalogue, Frizzell (Mullen).

Partick Th (2) 2 *(Gray 7, Roberts 9)*
Queen's Park (1) 1 *(Henry 17)*   1386
Partick Th: Tuffey; Paton, Twaddle, Storey, Robertson, Maxwell, Chaplain (McStay), Rowson, Gray (McKinlay), Roberts (Donnelly), Harkins.
Queen's Park: Cowie; Ure, Douglas, Sinclair■, Brough, Neill, Henry (Dunn), Harkins (Quinn), Coakley, Dunlop (Boslem), Holmes.

Stenhousemuir (0) 0
Albion R (0) 1 *(Donnelly 87 (pen))*   323
Stenhousemuir: Bennett; Lyle, McGroarty, Thom, Smith, Tyrrell, Shirra, Hampshire (Ferguson), Dalziel, Gibson (Love), Thompson.
Albion R: Scott; Reid, McGowan, Walker R, Benton, Hughes, Ferry (Martin), Donnelly, Pollock, Barr, Walker P.

Sunday, 27 July 2008

East Stirling (0) 2 *(Richardson 86, Rodgers 89)*
Ayr U (1) 1 *(Wiliams 15)*   761
East Stirling: Hillcoat; Ure, Richardson, Oates, Bolochoweckyj, Nicholls, Dunn (McKenzie), Gibson (Donaldson), Cramb (Graham), Rodgers, Anderson.
Ayr U: Grindlay; Dempsie, Easton, Walker, Campbell, Stevenson, Borris, Aitken, Prunty, Williams (Agnew), Keegan.

SECOND ROUND

Tuesday, 12 August 2008

Alloa Ath (0) 0

Clyde (0) 2 *(Clarke 58, Gibson 76)*   414

Alloa Ath: Jellema; McKeown, Campbell, Scullion, Townsley, Hill, Stevenson, Grant, Brown (Scott), MacAulay (Buist), Kelly (Hay).
Clyde: Cherrie; Gibson, Ohnesorge, Higgins, Brown, Wilson, Roddy MacLennan, Ruari MacLennan (Kettlewell), Clarke (Gemmill), McKay, Waddell (Trouten).

Cowdenbeath (1) 3 *(McQuade 8, Gemmell 54, Fairbairn 89)*

Albion R (1) 2 *(Barr 30, Martin 75)*   204

Cowdenbeath: Hay; Cennerazzo, Adamson, Mbu, Hodge, Linton (Ferguson), Robertson (McGregor), Shields, Fleming, Gemmell, McQuade (Fairbairn).
Albion R: Mitchell; Reid, Walker R, McGoldrick, McGowan, Barr, Donnelly, Ferry, Smith (Walker P), Coyne (Martin), McKenna (Pollock).

Livingston (0) 1 *(Griffiths 51)*

Forfar Ath (0) 0   800

Livingston: Martini; MacKay, Talbot, McPake, Fox, Innes, McPartland, Davidson (Millar), Cuenca, Griffiths, Jacobs (Quinn).
Forfar Ath: Brown; Donachie (McNally), Smith E, Winter, Dunn, Tulloch, Fotheringham (Fraser), Campbell, Lilley, Brady, Kilgannon (McLeish).

Partick Th (0) 4 *(Donnelly 52, McKeown 92, 115, Harkins 112)*

Peterhead (1) 2 *(Gunn 23, Kozminski 103)*   1133

Partick Th: Hinchcliffe; Taton (Donnelly), Storey, Kinniburgh, Maxwell, Robertson J, Chaplain (McStay), Rowson, Harkins, Gray (McKeown), McKinlay.
Peterhead: Kula; MacDonald, McVitie, Moore, Sharp, Skinner (Anderson), Cowie, McKay, Gunn, Bavidge (Kozminski).
aet.

Raith R (0) 1 *(Weir 74)*

Ross Co (0) 2 *(Keddie 52, 54)*   1080

Raith R: McGurn; Wilson, Ellis (Wardlaw), Campbell, Davidson, Walker, Dunbar (Whatley), Sloan (Mackie), Smith, Weir, Ferry.
Ross Co: Bullock; McCulloch, Keddie, Dowie, Boyd, Lawson (Scott), Hart, Brittain, Winters, Higgins (Daal), Morrison (Strachan).

Wednesday, 13 August 2008

East Fife (0) 0

Airdrie U (1) 2 *(Lynch 10, Smith 84)*   606

East Fife: Brown; Nugent, Smart, Fotheringham, Stanik, Gordon (Campbell), Young, Stewart, Cameron (McManus), Templeman, O'Reilly.
Airdrie U: Robertson; Smyth, McDonald, Donnelly, Hazley, McDougall (Smith), Nixon, McKenna, Cardle (McLaughlin), Di Giacomo, Lynch (Noble).

East Stirling (0) 0

Morton (2) 3 *(Masterton 22, McGuffie 32, 53)*   753

East Stirling: Hillcoat; Hay (Moffat), Richardson, Anderson, Tully, Forrest, McKenzie, Gibson (Donaldson), Cramb (Dunn), Kelly, Ure.
Morton: Cuthbert; Shimmin (Weatherson), Harding, McManus, Paartalu (Jenkins), Masterton (Finlayson), McGuffie, Russell, Wake, Newby, McAlister.

Wednesday, 20 August 2008

Dunfermline Ath (0) 0

Queen of the S (1) 2 *(Kean 3, O'Connor 75)*   1373

Dunfermline Ath: Reidford (Gallacher), Shields (Dearden), Muirhead, Phinn (McCann), Thomson S, Bamba, Willis, Thomson R, Williamson, Kirk, McBride.
Queen of the S: Bell; Reid, Harris, Adams, Barr, Thomson, Arbuckle (McQuilken), Tosh (MacFarlane), Kean, Dobbie (O'Connor), Burns.

QUARTER-FINALS

Sunday, 7 September 2008

Clyde (0) 0

Ross Co (1) 1 *(Craig 25)*   756

Clyde: Cherrie; Higgins (Ruari MacLennan), McGregor[■], Ohnesorge (Trouten), Gibson, Lowing, Emslie, Kettlewell, Waddell (McSweegan), McKay, Gemmill.
Ross Co: Bullock; McCulloch, Boyd, Dowie, Keddie, Hart, Brittain, Lawson, Morrison (Strachan), Higgins (Scott), Craig.

Cowdenbeath (0) 1 *(Fairbairn 79)*

Airdrie U (0) 2 *(Di Giacomo 53, 75)*   643

Cowdenbeath: Hay; McGregor, Armstrong, Hodge, Baxter[■], Fleming, Fairbairn, MacKay, Adamson, McQuade (Dempster), Ramsay (Linton).
Airdrie U: Robertson; Smyth, McDonald (Brown), Donnelly, Lovering, McDougall (Smith), McKenna, Nixon, Lynch (Noble), Di Giacomo, McLaughlin.

Livingston (0) 0

Partick Th (0) 2 *(Turner 75, Twaddle 78)*   1339

Livingston: McKenzie; Millar, Talbot, McDonald, Fox (Smith), Innes (Cave), McPartland, Davidson, Cuenca (Giarrizzo), Quinn, Hamill.
Partick Th: Hinchcliffe; Paton, Twaddle, Storey, Kinniburgh, Maxwell, Chaplain (Turner), Rowson, Gray (McKinlay), Donnelly (Roberts), Harkins.

Queen of the S (0) 0

Morton (0) 2 *(Wake 48, McGuffie 77)*   2991

Queen of the S: Bell; Parratt, Barr, Sives, Aitken (Weatherston), McQuilken, MacFarlane (Robertson), Tosh, Burns (Simmons), Kean, Dobbie.
Morton: Cuthbert; Walker, Smith, Shimmin, Harding, Paartalu, McGuffie, Masterton (Jenkins), McAlister, Wake (Finlayson), Russell (Weatherson).

SEMI-FINALS

Sunday, 12 October 2008

Partick Th (0) 0

Airdrie U (1) 1 *(Di Giacomo 4)*   2761

Partick Th: Hinchcliffe; Storey, Twaddle, Robertson J, Turner, Maxwell, Rowson (Chaplain), McKeown (Paton), Roberts (Buchanan), Donnelly, McKinlay.
Airdrie U: Robertson; Donnelly, Lovering, McDougall (Brown), McKenna, Nixon, Smith D, McLaughlin, Di Giacomo, Lynch (Noble), Cardle.

Ross Co (2) 4 *(Craig 6, Daal 42, 62, Dowie 84)*

Morton (0) 1 *(Weatherson 77)*   1396

Ross Co: Bullock; McCulloch, Keddie, Dowie, Boyd (Watt), Strachan, Hart (Gardyne), Brittain, Scott, Daal (Higgins), Craig.
Morton: Cuthbert; Harding (Paartalu), Smith, Shimmin, McManus[■], Masterton (Weatherson), McGuffie, Jenkins, Wake (Finlayson), Russell, McAlister.

FINAL (at St Johnstone)

Sunday, 16 November 2008

Airdrie U (0) 2 *(McKenna 80, Dowie 103 (og))*

Ross Co (0) 2 *(Nixon 59 (og), Higgins 113)*   4091

Airdrie U: Robertson; Smyth, Lovering (Hazley), McDonald, Donnelly, Nixon (Smith D), McDougall (Lynch), McKenna, Di Giacomo, McLaughlin, Cardle.
Ross Co: Bullock; McCulloch, Keddie, Dowie, Boyd, Gardyne (Scott), Hart, Brittain (Winters), Daal, Higgins, Strachan (Morrison).
aet; Airdrie U won 3-2 on penalties.
Referee: C. Murray.

SCOTTISH CUP FINALS 1874–2009

Year	Winners	Runners-up	Score
1874	Queen's Park	Clydesdale	2-0
1875	Queen's Park	Renton	3-0
1876	Queen's Park	Third Lanark	2-0 after 1-1 draw
1877	Vale of Leven	Rangers	3-2 after 0-0 and 1-1 draws
1878	Vale of Leven	Third Lanark	1-0
1879	Vale of Leven*	Rangers	
1880	Queen's Park	Thornlibank	3-0
1881	Queen's Park†	Dumbarton	3-1
1882	Queen's Park	Dumbarton	4-1 after 2-2 draw
1883	Dumbarton	Vale of Leven	2-1 after 2-2 draw
1884	Queen's Park‡	Vale of Leven	
1885	Renton	Vale of Leven	3-1 after 0-0 draw
1886	Queen's Park	Renton	3-1
1887	Hibernian	Dumbarton	2-1
1888	Renton	Cambuslang	6-1
1889	Third Lanark§	Celtic	2-1
1890	Queen's Park	Vale of Leven	2-1 after 1-1 draw
1891	Hearts	Dumbarton	1-0
1892	Celtic¶	Queen's Park	5-1
1893	Queen's Park	Celtic	2-1
1894	Rangers	Celtic	3-1
1895	St Bernard's	Renton	2-1
1896	Hearts	Hibernian	3-1
1897	Rangers	Dumbarton	5-1
1898	Rangers	Kilmarnock	2-0
1899	Celtic	Rangers	2-0
1900	Celtic	Queen's Park	4-3
1901	Hearts	Celtic	4-3
1902	Hibernian	Celtic	1-0
1903	Rangers	Hearts	2-0 after 1-1 and 0-0 draws
1904	Celtic	Rangers	3-2
1905	Third Lanark	Rangers	3-1 after 0-0 draw
1906	Hearts	Third Lanark	1-0
1907	Celtic	Hearts	3-0
1908	Celtic	St Mirren	5-1
1909	••		
1910	Dundee	Clyde	2-1 after 2-2 and 0-0 draws
1911	Celtic	Hamilton A	2-0 after 0-0 draw
1912	Celtic	Clyde	2-0
1913	Falkirk	Raith R	2-0
1914	Celtic	Hibernian	4-1 after 0-0 draw
1920	Kilmarnock	Albion R	3-2
1921	Partick Th	Rangers	1-0
1922	Morton	Rangers	1-0
1923	Celtic	Hibernian	1-0
1924	Airdrieonians	Hibernian	2-0
1925	Celtic	Dundee	2-1
1926	St Mirren	Celtic	2-0
1927	Celtic	East Fife	3-1
1928	Rangers	Celtic	4-0
1929	Kilmarnock	Rangers	2-0
1930	Rangers	Partick Th	2-1 after 0-0 draw
1931	Celtic	Motherwell	4-2 after 2-2 draw
1932	Rangers	Kilmarnock	3-0 after 1-1 draw
1933	Celtic	Motherwell	1-0
1934	Rangers	St Mirren	5-0
1935	Rangers	Hamilton A	2-1
1936	Rangers	Third Lanark	1-0
1937	Celtic	Aberdeen	2-1
1938	East Fife	Kilmarnock	4-2 after 1-1 draw
1939	Clyde	Motherwell	4-0
1947	Aberdeen	Hibernian	2-1
1948	Rangers	Morton	1-0 after 1-1 draw
1949	Rangers	Clyde	4-1
1950	Rangers	East Fife	3-0
1951	Celtic	Motherwell	1-0
1952	Motherwell	Dundee	4-0
1953	Rangers	Aberdeen	1-0 after 1-1 draw
1954	Celtic	Aberdeen	2-1
1955	Clyde	Celtic	1-0 after 1-1 draw
1956	Hearts	Celtic	3-1
1957	Falkirk	Kilmarnock	2-1 after 1-1 draw
1958	Clyde	Hibernian	1-0
1959	St Mirren	Aberdeen	3-1
1960	Rangers	Kilmarnock	2-0
1961	Dunfermline Ath	Celtic	2-0 after 0-0 draw
1962	Rangers	St Mirren	2-0
1963	Rangers	Celtic	3-0 after 1-1 draw

Year	Winners	Runners-up	Score
1964	Rangers	Dundee	3-1
1965	Celtic	Dunfermline Ath	3-2
1966	Rangers	Celtic	1-0 after 0-0 draw
1967	Celtic	Aberdeen	2-0
1968	Dunfermline Ath	Hearts	3-1
1969	Celtic	Rangers	4-0
1970	Aberdeen	Celtic	3-1
1971	Celtic	Rangers	2-1 after 1-1 draw
1972	Celtic	Hibernian	6-1
1973	Rangers	Celtic	3-2
1974	Celtic	Dundee U	3-0
1975	Celtic	Airdrieonians	3-1
1976	Rangers	Hearts	3-1
1977	Celtic	Rangers	1-0
1978	Rangers	Aberdeen	2-1
1979	Rangers	Hibernian	3-2 after 0-0 and 0-0 draws
1980	Celtic	Rangers	1-0
1981	Rangers	Dundee U	4-1 after 0-0 draw
1982	Aberdeen	Rangers	4-1 (aet)
1983	Aberdeen	Rangers	1-0 (aet)
1984	Aberdeen	Celtic	2-1 (aet)
1985	Celtic	Dundee U	2-1
1986	Aberdeen	Hearts	3-0
1987	St Mirren	Dundee U	1-0 (aet)
1988	Celtic	Dundee U	2-1
1989	Celtic	Rangers	1-0
1990	Aberdeen	Celtic	0-0 (aet)
		(Aberdeen won 9-8 on penalties)	
1991	Motherwell	Dundee U	4-3 (aet)
1992	Rangers	Airdrieonians	2-1
1993	Rangers	Aberdeen	2-1
1994	Dundee U	Rangers	1-0
1995	Celtic	Airdrieonians	1-0
1996	Rangers	Hearts	5-1
1997	Kilmarnock	Falkirk	1-0
1998	Hearts	Rangers	2-1
1999	Rangers	Celtic	1-0
2000	Rangers	Aberdeen	4-0
2001	Celtic	Hibernian	3-0
2002	Rangers	Celtic	3-2
2003	Rangers	Dundee	1-0
2004	Celtic	Dunfermline Ath	3-1
2005	Celtic	Dundee U	1-0
2006	Hearts	Gretna	1-1 (aet)
		(Hearts won 4-2 on penalties)	
2007	Celtic	Dunfermline Ath	1-0
2008	Rangers	Queen of the S	3-2
2009	Rangers	Falkirk	1-0

*Vale of Leven awarded cup, Rangers failing to appear for replay after 1-1 draw.
†After Dumbarton protested the first game, which Queen's Park won 2-1.
‡Queen's Park awarded cup, Vale of Leven failing to appear.
§Replay by order of Scottish FA because of playing conditions in first match, won 3-0 by Third Lanark.
¶After mutually protested game which Celtic won 1-0.
••Owing to riot, the cup was withheld after two drawn games – between Celtic and Rangers 2-2 and 1-1.

SCOTTISH CUP WINS

Celtic 34, Rangers 33, Queen's Park 10, Aberdeen 7, Hearts 7, Clyde 3, Kilmarnock 3, St Mirren 3, Vale of Leven 3, Dunfermline Ath 2, Falkirk 2, Hibernian 2, Motherwell 2, Renton 2, Third Lanark 2, Airdrieonians 1, Dumbarton 1, Dundee 1, Dundee U 1, East Fife 1, Morton 1, Partick Th 1, St Bernard's 1.

APPEARANCES IN FINAL

Celtic 53, Rangers 50, Aberdeen 15, Hearts 13, Queen's Park 12, Hibernian 11, Dundee U 8, Kilmarnock 8, Vale of Leven 7, Clyde 6, Dumbarton 6, Motherwell 6, St Mirren 6, Third Lanark 6, Dundee 5, Dunfermline Ath 5, Renton 5, Airdrieonians 4, Falkirk 4, East Fife 3, Hamilton A 2, Morton 2, Partick Th 2, Albion R 1, Cambuslang 1, Clydesdale 1, Gretna 1, Queen of the S 1, Raith R 1, St Bernard's 1, Thornlibank 1.

HOMECOMING SCOTTISH CUP 2008–09

■ *Denotes player sent off.*

FIRST ROUND

Banks o'Dee v Fort William	10-0
Clachnacuddin v Burntisland Shipyard	4-0
Dalbeattie Star v Lossiemouth	5-1
Edinburgh City v Nairn County	2-0
Edinburgh Univ v Civil Service Strollers	1-2
Fraserburgh v Hawick Royal Albert	6-3
Glasgow Univ v Vale of Leithen	0-1
Golspie v Threave Rovers	0-3
Huntly v Girvan	1-0
Inverurie Loco Works v Deveronvale	5-2
Lochee United v Bathgate Thistle	3-1
Newton Stewart v Brora Rangers	1-1, 1-2
Pollok v Spartans	1-1, 0-1
Preston Ath v Gala Fairydean	3-1
Rothes v Buckie Thistle	1-3
Selkirk v Coldstream	1-1, 2-2
Selkirk won 3-2 on penalties.	
St Cuthbert's v Wick Academy	0-3
Wigtown & B v Forres Mechanics	2-2, 0-2

SECOND ROUND

East Stirling v Preston Ath	4-2
Berwick R v Albion R	1-2
Brora Rangers v Forfar Ath	1-2
Clachnacuddin v Crichton	1-0
Cove Rangers v Whitehill Welfare	1-0
Cowdenbeath v Elgin City	1-2
Dalbeattie Star v Selkirk	6-0
Edinburgh City v Wick Academy	0-0, 4-1
Forres Mechanics v Keith	1-1, 1-1
Forres Mechanics won on penalties.	
Fraserburgh v Dumbarton	0-1
Inverurie Loco Works v Banks o'Dee	5-1
Lochee United v Buckie Thistle	3-0
Montrose v Huntly	2-0
Stenhousemuir v Threave Rovers	5-0
Annan Athletic v Spartans	1-2
Civil Service Strollers v Vale of Leithen	0-1

THIRD ROUND

Saturday, 29 November 2008

Airdrie U (3) 3 *(Cardle 20, Lynch 38, 41)*
Cove R (0) 0   821
Airdrie U: Robertson; McKenna, Hazley, McDonald (Brown), Donnelly (Watt), Smyth, McDougall, McLaughlin, Di Giacomo (Noble), Lynch, Cardle.
Cove R: McKenzie; Cruickshank, Lawrie, McCulloch (Smith), Watson, Tindal, Stephen, Bain (Henderson), Watt, Johnston, Livingstone (McKibben).

Albion R (0) 1 *(Barr 63)*
Queen's Park (1) 2 *(Watt 11, Cairney 52 (pen))*   619
Albion R: Mitchell; Reid, McGowan, Donnelly, Benton, Walker R, Barr, Ferry, Eaglesham (Coyne), Pollock, Adam (Crozier).
Queen's Park: Crawford; Little, Douglas, Agostini, Brough, Quinn, Holmes (Dunlop), Cairney, Nicholas (Coakley), Harkins (Neill), Watt.

Clachnacuddin (0) 0
Stenhousemuir (2) 5 *(Dalziel 13, 28, 78, Desmond 53, Hampshire 90)*   350
Clachnacuddin: Harrison; MacCuish, MacKenzie (Lawrie), MacDonald, Williamson, Lewis, Watson, Ross D, Morrison, Rutherford (Kellacher), Ross C.
Stenhousemuir: Bennett; McEwan (Lyle), McGroarty, Thom, Ovenstone, Thomson, Love, Brand (Desmond), Dalziel (Hampshire), Tyrrell, Motion.

Clyde (1) 2 *(McKay 38, Clarke 87 (pen))*
Montrose (0) 0   677
Clyde: Hutton; Lowing, Brown, Higgins, Gibson, Lithgow, McKay (Trouten), Kettlewell (Ruari MacLennan), Clarke, Emslie, McLaren (McSweegan).
Montrose: Kelly; Worrell, Buchan, Gibson, McLeod, Craig, Bradley (Stewart), Davidson, Hegarty (Smith), Hunter, Black.

East Fife (0) 2 *(Crawford 70, O'Reilly 90)*
Arbroath (0) 0   729
East Fife: McCulloch; McDonald, Smart, Fotheringham, Cameron, Shields (Young), Fagan, Stewart, Linn, Templeman (O'Reilly), Crawford.
Arbroath: Hill; Rennie, Raeside, Bishop, Forsyth, McMullan (Gates), Campbell, Reilly (Weir), Black (Masson), Scott, Sellars.

East Stirling (1) 2 *(Forrest 9, Graham 55)*
Livingston (1) 1 *(Fox 39)*   563
East Stirling: Barclay; Hay, Richardson (Kelly), Forrest, Bolochoweckyj, Tully, Graham (Anderson), Dunn, Cramb (McKenzie), Ure, Rodgers.
Livingston: Martini; MacKay, Talbot, McPake, Fox, Miller, McParland, Thomas, Smith, Cuenca (Jacobs), Hamill.

Peterhead (0) 2 *(Ross 74, Bavidge 90)*
Morton (1) 1 *(Masterton 24)*   817
Peterhead: Kula; Donald, Smith, Skinner, MacDonald, McVitie (Cowie), Sharp, Anderson, Gunn, Ross, Bavidge.
Morton: Cuthbert; MacGregor, Smith, Shimmin, Greacen, Masterton (Finlayson), McGuffie, Jenkins, Weatherson■, Wake (Russell), McAlister.

Raith R (0) 0
Alloa A (0) 0   1493
Raith R: O'Connor; Wilson, Ellis, Campbell, Davidson, Walker, Sloan, Wardlaw (Bryce), Wales, Weir, Ferry.
Alloa A: Jellema; Buist, Campbell, Scullion■, Forrest, Hill (Ferguson A), McClune, Ferguson B, Scott (Stevenson), Grant, MacAulay.

Ross Co (1) 2 *(Higgins 23, 57)*
Dumbarton (0) 2 *(Carcary 80, 83)*   1200
Ross Co: Bullock; McCulloch, Keddie, Dowie, Boyd (Morrison), Watt (Hart), Scott, Brittain, Daal■, Higgins, Strachan (Gardyne).
Dumbarton: McEwan; Canning, Dunlop (Cusack), O'Byrne, Gordon, Clark, Chisholm (Carcary), Geggan, McLeod, Moore (Keegan), Murray.

Stirling Alb (0) 2 *(Molloy 55, Murphy 89)*
Partick Th (2) 3 *(Chaplain 28, Harkins 33 (pen), Buchanan 83)*   1472
Stirling Alb: Christie; Lawrie, Lowing (Waddell), Graham (Ross), Gibb, Molloy, Corr (Hamilton), Murphy, Grehan, McKenna, Docherty.
Partick Th: Tuffey; Paton, McKinlay, McStay (Turner), Archibald (MacBeth), Maxwell, Chaplain, Rowson, Buchanan, Donnelly (Roberts), Harkins.

Saturday, 6 December 2008

Elgin C (0) 2 *(Wright 52, Nicolson 63)*
Spartans (0) 1 *(Henretty 83)*   519
Elgin C: Malin; Nicolson, Kerr, Niven, Kaczan, Gilbert (MacDonald), Campbell, O'Donoghue, Wright■, Crooks (Shallicker), Keogh.
Spartans: Flockhart; O'Donnell, Fowlie, Archibald, Gerrard, Manson, King■, Kader (Malin), Walker (Hoskins), McLeod (Devil), Henretty.
Tie replayed; Elgin C fielded ineligible player.

Forres Mechanics (1) 2 *(Sharp 30, Collins 77)*
Dalbeattie Star (1) 2 *(Steele 85, Sloan 89 (pen))*   378
Forres Mechanics: Knight; Allan, Main, Grant, Sharp, Bremner, Whyte, Calder, Hendry (Wardrop), Green, Moore (Collins).
Dalbeattie Star: Wright; MacBeth, Robinson (Kerr R), McMinn, Laurie (Harkness), McQuade, Sloan, Redpath, Kerr D (Steele), Milligan, Kerr G.

Monday, 8 December 2008
Edinburgh C (0) 0
Brechin C (3) 3 *(Diack 5, 16, 43 (pen))*   333
Edinburgh C: Montieth; John Hall, Ross K, MacNamara, Bruce, Jordan Hall, Caddow, Morrison (Munro), Ross R, Clee (Callandine), Gair (Taylor).
Brechin C: Nelson C; Murie, Dyer, Ward, White, Nelson A, Byers (King), Nimmo (Fusco), Twigg (Baird), Diack, Smith D.

Saturday, 13 December 2008
Inverurie Loco Works (2) 4 *(Tan 1, Milne 22, Smith 55, 62)*
Vale of Leithen (0) 0   608
Inverurie Loco Works: Reid A; Stewart (Pirie), Buchan, Wilson, Park, Simpson, Tan (Bisset), Ross, Smith (Singer), Milne, McLean.
Vale of Leithen: Gordon; Ryan McManus, Ross McManus, Tainish, Forsyth, Raymond Fleming (Osbourne), Shortreed (Dewar), Notman, Graham, Rossi, Martin (Ronald Fleming).

Monday, 15 December 2008
Elgin C (1) 1 *(MacKay 5 (pen))*
Spartans (1) 2 *(Kader 36, Malin 72)*   551
Elgin C: Ridgers; Nicolson■, MacDonald (Gilbert), Niven, Kaczan (Kerr), Hind (Crooks), Campbell, O'Donoghue, Wright, Shallicker, MacKay.
Spartans: Flockhart; O'Donnell, Fowlie, Archibald, Gerrard, Manson, Malin, Kader (Devil), Walker, McLeod, Henretty.

Forfar Ath (0) 2 *(Gibson G 83, Kilgannon 90)*
Stranraer (0) 0   305
Forfar Ath: Brown; McNally, Smith E, Brady (Kilgannon), Tod, Tosh, Gordon, Campbell, Lilley (McLeish), Winter (Donachie), Gibson G.
Stranraer: Black; McKinstry■, Noble (McColm) (Bradley), Dobbins■, Kane, Nicoll, Gibson, Mitchell, McConalogue, Tade, Frizzel.

Wednesday, 17 December 2008
Lochee U (0) 1 *(Hagan 86)*
Ayr U (0) 1 *(Williams 60)*   1223
Lochee U: Ross; Krobot, Kirk, Hay, McMillan, Dailly, Hagan (Abbot), Cargill, Middleton, Thomson, Robertson (Blackwood).
Ayr U: Grindlay; Keenan, McGowan, Walker, Henderson, Stevenson, Borris (Weaver), Aitken, Williams, Gormley (Prunty), Agnew.

THIRD ROUND REPLAYS
Tuesday, 9 December 2008
Alloa Ath (0) 2 *(Ferguson B 79, 81)*
Raith R (0) 1 *(Wales 57)*   860
Alloa Ath: Jellema; McClune, Campbell, Buist, Forrest (Wilson), Hill, Stevenson (McKeown), Ferguson B, Scott (Ferguson A), Grant, MacAulay.
Raith R: O'Connor; Wilson, Ellis, Campbell, Davidson, Walker, Sloan, Wardlaw, Wales, Weir (Silvestro), Ferry.

Monday, 15 December 2008
Dalbeattie Star (1) 2 *(MacBeth 22, Redpath 94)*
Forres Mechanics (0) 4 *(Allen 66 (pen), Green 92, Whyte 101, 112)*   378
Dalbeattie Star: Wright; MacBeth, Kerr D (Robinson), McMinn, Laurie, McQuade (Kerr R), Sloan, Redpath, Harkness (Steele), Milligan, Kerr G.
Forres Mechanics: Knight; Allan, Main (Dugiud), Milne, Sharp, Whyte, Calder, Hendry (Bremner), Green, Collins (Penwright), Wardrop.
aet.

Dumbarton (0) 1 *(Gordon 46)*
Ross Co (2) 2 *(Brittain 24 (pen), Hart 37)*   557
Dumbarton: McEwan; Lennon, O'Byrne (McLeod), Gordon, Dunlop, Carcary, Clark (Chisholm), Geggan, Murray, Moore (Keegan), Canning.
Ross Co: Bullock; McCulloch, Dowie, Boyd, Keddie, Hart (Strachan), Watt, Brittain, Morrison, Craig (Winters), Daal (Scott).

Tuesday, 23 December 2008
Ayr U (1) 3 *(McGowan 36, Gormley 53, Prunty 58)*
Lochee U (0) 1 *(Blackwood 76)*   2049
Ayr U: Grindlay; Keenan, Walker, Henderson, McGowan (Dempsie), Borris, Stevenson, Aitken, Easton (Agnew), Prunty, Gormley (Williams).
Lochee U: Ross; Krobot, Kirk, Hay, McMillan, Dailly (Abbot), Thomson (Blackwood), Cargill■, Middleton, Hagan (Watson), Robertson.

FOURTH ROUND
Saturday, 10 January 2009
Airdrie U (2) 2 *(Di Giacomo 26, Lynch 43)*
Spartans (0) 1 *(Malin 54)*   1460
Airdrie U: Robertson; McLachlan, Hazley, McDonald, Donnelly (Brown), Smyth, McDougall, McKenna, Di Giacomo, Lynch (Maguire), Cardle (Smith D).
Spartans: Flockhart; Gerrard, Fowlie (Hoskins), Archibald, O'Donnell, Malin, King, Manson (Devil), Walker (Kader), McLeod, Henretty.

Alloa Ath (1) 1 *(Scott 42 (pen))*
Aberdeen (1) 2 *(Miller 9, Aluko 57)*   3012
Alloa Ath: Jellema; McClune, Campbell, Buist, Townsley, Hill, Wilson, Ferguson B, MacAulay (Ferguson A), Grant (Scullion), Scott.
Aberdeen: Langfield; McDonald, Foster, Mulgrew, Diamond, Severin, De Visscher (Mackie), Kerr, Miller, Maguire, Aluko.

Ayr U (1) 2 *(Keenan 15, Williams 90)*
Kilmarnock (1) 2 *(Pascali 9, Bryson 54)*   9280
Ayr U: Grindlay; Dempsie (Williams), Campbell, Walker, McGowan, Keenan, Stevenson, Aitken, Gormley, Prunty, Easton.
Kilmarnock: Rascle; Murray, Wright, Pascali, Hay, Gibson, Fowler, Bryson, Invicibile, Russell, Fernandez.

Celtic (2) 2 *(Brown S 37, McGeady 44)*
Dundee (1) 1 *(McMenamin 14)*   23,070
Celtic: Boruc; Caddis, Naylor, Crosas (Robson), Loovens, McManus, Nakamura, Brown S, McDonald, Vennegoor (Samaras), McGeady.
Dundee: Douglas; Paton, Lauchlan, McKeown, Malone, Shinnie (Antoine-Curier), Cowan (Benedictus), Posniak (McHale), O'Brien, Daquin, McMenamin.

Dunfermline Ath (1) 2 *(Phinn 20, Bayne 66)*
Clyde (0) 0   2871
Dunfermline Ath: Gallacher; Woods (Thomson S), Wilson, Phinn, Shields, Muirhead, Loy, Glass, Bayne (Burke), Kirk (Mole), Bell.
Clyde: Hutton; Wilson, Kettlewell, Higgins, Gibson, Lithgow, Trouten, Ruari MacLennan (McSwegan), Clarke, McKay, McLaren.

Falkirk (1) 4 *(Arfield 37 (pen), 48, Barrett 68, 81)*
Queen of the S (1) 2 *(Wilson 41, Harris 48)*   3423
Falkirk: Olejnik; McNamara, Scobbie, McCann, Barr, Bullen (Holden), O'Brien (Stewart M), McBride, Higdon (Finnigan), Barrett, Arfield.
Queen of the S: Robinson; McLaughlan, Harris, MacFarlane, Barr, Lancaster, Wilson (Burns), Tosh (Dobbie), Kean, Robertson (O'Connor), McQuilken.

Inverness CT (1) 3 *(Morais 28, 56, Vigurs 46)*
Partick Th (0) 0 1803
Inverness CT: Fraser; Tokely, Djebi-Zadi (Hastings), Duncan (Gathuessi), Munro, Mihadjuks, Morais (Rooney), Cowie, Barrowman, Vigurs, McBain.
Partick Th: Tuffey; Archibald, Harkins, Storey, Robertson (Roberts), Paton, McKinlay (Doohlan), Rowson, Twaddle, Donnelly, Buchanan (Chaplain).

Peterhead (1) 2 *(Bavidge 17, Anderson 73)*
Queen's Park (2) 2 *(Brough 35, Cairney 43)* 842
Peterhead: Kula; Donald, Moore, Smith, MacDonald, McKay, Sharp, Ross (Kozminski), Bavidge, Anderson, Gunn (Mann).
Queen's Park: Crawford; Ure, Douglas, Sinclair, Brough, Quinn, Holmes, Cairney, Nicholas, Harkins, Watt.

Ross Co (0) 0
Hamilton A (1) 1 *(Swailes 22)* 1503
Ross Co: Soutar; McCulloch, Watt, Boyd, Golabek, Strachan (Scott), Hart (Stewart), Brittain, Morrison (Daal), Higgins, Craig.
Hamilton A: Cerny; McMillan (Lyle), Easton, McLaughlin, Canning, Swailes, McCarthy, McArthur■, Elebert, Offiong (Thomas), McGowan.

Stenhousemuir (0) 0
East Fife (0) 1 *(Linn 84)* 784
Stenhousemuir: Bennett; Thom, Lyle (Connolly), Smith, Ovenstone, Tyrrell, Shirra (Love), Ferguson, Thomson (Hampshire), Brand, Motion.
East Fife: McCulloch; Nugent (Young), Cameron, Smart, McDonald, Muir, Fagan, Templeman, McManus, Crawford (Stewart), Linn.

Sunday, 11 January 2009

East Stirling (0) 0
Dundee U (3) 4 *(Buaben 15, Dods 40, Daly 43, Russell 55 (pen))* 2153
East Stirling: Newman; Hay, Bolochoweckyj, Forrest, Dunn, Graham, Donaldson, Tully, Rodgers (Anderson), Cramb (McKenzie), Ure (Richardson).
Dundee U: Zaluska; Dillon, Dixon, Kenneth, Dods (Grainger), Flood (Robertson D), Buaben, Gomis, Russell, Daly, Conway (Swanson).

Hibernian (0) 0
Hearts (1) 2 *(Nade 38, Glen 90)* 14,837
Hibernian: Ma-Kalambay (Szamotulski); Van Zanten, Murray, Bamba, Jones, Hogg, Johansson (Nish), Rankin, Fletcher■, Riordan (O'Brien), Stevenson.
Hearts: Balogh; Jonsson, Wallace, Berra, Karipidis, Zaliukas, Cesnauskis, Palazuelos, Nade (Stewart), Obua (Glen), Driver.

Tuesday, 13 January 2009

Brechin C (0) 1 *(Janczyk 46)*
St Mirren (1) 3 *(Hamilton 25 (pen), 70, Wyness 56)* 1026
Brechin C: McCluskey; Walker R, Ward, Seeley, Dyer, Byers (King), Nimmo, Janczyk, Smith D, Twigg (Fusco), Baird (Diack).
St Mirren: Howard; Ross, Miranda, Dorman, Cuthbert, Potter, Murray, Thomson (Brighton), Wyness, Hamilton (Robb), McGinn.

Forfar Ath (5) 6 *(Gibson G 2, Milne 4 (og), Tulloch 24, Campbell 31, Gordon 43, 54)*
Forres Mechanics (1) 1 *(Green 23)* 775
Forfar Ath: Gibson J; Watson, McNally (Donachie), Winter (Kilgannon), Tod, Tulloch, Gordon, Brady, Lilley, Campbell, Gibson G (Simpson).
Forres Mechanics: Knight (Watt); Milne, Munro, Grant, Sharp, Bremner, Collins (Wardrop), Calder, Green (Penwright), Dugiud, Moore.

St Johnstone (0) 0
Rangers (1) 2 *(McCaffrey 43 (og), Novo 79)* 7746
St Johnstone: Main; Irvine, Hanlon (Sheerin), Morris, Rutkiewicz, McCaffrey, Millar, Craig, Jackson (Samuel), Holmes, Swankie (Milne).
Rangers: McGregor; Broadfoot, Papac, Bougherra, Weir, Ferguson, Davis, Pedro Mendes, Boyd (McCulloch), Miller (Fleck), Naismith (Novo).

Monday, 2 February 2009

Inverurie Loco Works (0) 0
Motherwell (1) 3 *(Sutton 2, Clarkson 57, Sutton 69)* 2500
Inverurie Loco Works: Reid A; Park, Simpson, Buchan, Pirie, Ross (Tan), Wilson, Stewart, Smith, McLean (Graham), Gauld (Milne).
Motherwell: Smith G; Quinn, Hammell, Reynolds, Craigan, Klimpl (Smith D), Lasley, O'Brien (McGarry), Sutton, Clarkson (Murphy), Fitzpatrick.

FOURTH ROUND REPLAYS

Tuesday, 20 January 2009

Queen's Park (0) 1 *(Holmes 51)*
Peterhead (0) 0 782
Queen's Park: Crawford; Ure, Douglas, Sinclair, Brough, Quinn, Holmes, Gallacher, Nicholas, Harkins, Watt.
Peterhead: Kula; Donald, Moore (Mann), Smith, MacDonald, McVitie, Sharp, Ross (Gunn), Bavidge (Kozminski), Anderson, McKay.

Thursday, 22 January 2009

Kilmarnock (0) 3 *(Ford 50, 80, Taouil 76)*
Ayr U (1) 1 *(Prunty 10)* 11,563
Kilmarnock: Combe; Fowler, Hay, Pascali, Wright, Ford, Gibson, Bryson (Flannigan), Fernandez■, Russell (Invincible), Taouil (Skelton).
Ayr U: Grindlay; Dempsie, McGowan, Walker, Campbell, Stevenson, Keenan, Aitken, Prunty, Gormley (Borris), Easton (Agnew).

FIFTH ROUND

Saturday, 7 February 2009

Celtic (2) 2 *(Caldwell 19, McDonald 45)*
Queen's Park (0) 1 *(Coakley 66)* 22,223
Celtic: Boruc; Hinkel, Naylor, Crosas (Donati), Caldwell, O'Dea, Maloney (McCourt), Hartley, McDonald, Vennegoor (Samaras), McGeady.
Queen's Park: Crawford; Ure (Ronald), Sinclair, Brough, Douglas, Holmes, Cairney, Quinn, Watt (Coakley■), Harkins (Dunlop), Nicholas.

Hamilton A (0) 2 *(Swailes 47, 55)*
Dundee U (1) 1 *(Grainger 35)* 3058
Hamilton A: Cerny; McClenahan, Gibson, Neil, Swailes, Canning, Quinn (Lyle), McCarthy, Deuchar (Offiong), Easton, Mensing.
Dundee U: Zaluska; Dillon (Swanson), Grainger, Wilkie, Kenneth, Buaben, Kovacevic, Gomis (Robertson D), Feeney (Sandaza), Daly, Conway.

Hearts (0) 0
Falkirk (0) 1 *(Lovell 59)* 14,569
Hearts: Balogh; Neilson, Wallace, Stewart, Zaliukas■, Karipidis, Jonsson (Kingston), Aguiar, Obua, Glen (Elliot), Driver.
Falkirk: Dani Mallo; McNamara (O'Brien), Holden, Pressley, Barr, Bullen, Arfield■, McCann (Cregg), Higdon, Lovell, Arnau (Finnigan).

Inverness CT (1) 2 *(Mihadjuks 36, Rooney 90)*
Kilmarnock (0) 0 2578
Inverness CT: Esson; Tokely, Djebi-Zadi, Proctor, Mihadjuks, Munro, Duncan (Kerr), Black, Odhiambo (Rooney), Foran, Imrie (McBain).
Kilmarnock: Combe; Fowler (Hamill), Hay, Pascali, Wright, Ford, Gibson (Flannigan), Bryson, Fernandez (Russell), Kyle■, Skelton.

Motherwell (0) 1 *(Hughes 65)*
St Mirren (1) 1 *(Dorman 12)*   5695
Motherwell: Smith G; Quinn, Hammell, Reynolds, Craigan, Klimpl, Lasley (Sheridan), Hughes, Fitzpatrick (Smith D), Clarkson, O'Brien.
St Mirren: Howard; Ross, Robb, Dorman, Cuthbert, Potter, Murray, Brady, Mehmet (Brighton), Hamilton, McGinn (Thomson).

Tuesday, 17 February 2009

Aberdeen (3) 5 *(Wright 11, Vidal 16, McDonald 29 (og), Maguire 82, 84)*
East Fife (0) 0   8960
Aberdeen: Langfield; Foster, Mulgrew, Maguire, Mair, Severin, Vidal (Pawlett), Kerr, Miller (Paton), Wright, Aluko (Young).
East Fife: McCulloch■; Smart, McDonald, Stanik (Brown), Nugent (Muir), Young, Linn, Fagan (Stewart), Cameron, Crawford, Templeman.

Airdrie U (1) 1 *(McLaughlin 14 (pen))*
Dunfermline Ath (1) 2 *(Holmes 2, Bayne 73)*   1772
Airdrie U: Robertson; McLachlan, Hazley, McLaughlin, Smyth, Nixon, McDougall (McGuire), McKenna, Di Giacomo, Lynch (Watt), Cardle.
Dunfermline Ath: Gallacher; Thomson S (Bayne), Wilson, Phinn, Shields, McCann, Ross (Woods), Holmes, Loy, Kirk (Mole), Bell.

Wednesday, 18 February 2009

Forfar Ath (0) 0
Rangers (1) 4 *(Papac 8, Miller 54, 90, Niguez 84)*   4718
Forfar Ath: Brown; McNally, Tod, Tulloch, Smith E■, Gordon (Donachie), Winter (Fotheringham), Brady (McGuigan), Gibson G, Lilley, Campbell.
Rangers: McGregor; Whittaker, Papac, Bougherra, Weir, Edu, Beasley (Niguez), McCulloch (Davis), Boyd (Lafferty), Miller, Naismith.

FIFTH ROUND REPLAY

Thursday, 19 February 2009

St Mirren (0) 1 *(Mehmet 85)*
Motherwell (0) 0   4555
St Mirren: Smith; Ross, Barron, Dorman, Cuthbert, Potter, Murray, Brady, Mehmet, Wyness (Dargo), Thomson.
Motherwell: Smith G; Quinn, Hammell, Craigan, Reynolds, Klimpl, O'Brien, Hughes, Sheridan (Sutton), Clarkson, Fitzpatrick (Smith D).

SIXTH ROUND

Saturday, 7 March 2009

Dunfermline Ath (0) 1 *(Phinn 82)*
Aberdeen (0) 1 *(Aluko 61)*   9696
Dunfermline Ath: Gallacher; Wiles, Wilson, Phinn, Shields, McCann (Loy), Bell, Glass, Bayne (Kirk), Mole, Burke (Muirhead).
Aberdeen: Langfield; Duff, Mulgrew (Considine), Mair, Diamond, Severin, Smith J, Kerr, Wright (Mackie), Young (Foster), Aluko.

Inverness CT (0) 0
Falkirk (1) 1 *(Finnigan 31 (pen))*   3024
Inverness CT: Esson; Tokely, Djebi-Zadi■, Duncan, Mihadjuks, Munro, Morais (Rooney), Black (Kerr), Odhiambo (Hastings), Foran, Imrie.
Falkirk: Dani Mallo; Pressley, Scobbie, Cregg, Bullen, Barr, Finnigan (Aafjes), O'Brien, Lovell, Stewart M, Arnau.

St Mirren (0) 1 *(Mehmet 55 (pen))*
Celtic (0) 0   5925
St Mirren: Smith; Ross, Camara, Dorman, Haining, Potter, Murray, Brady, Mehmet, Dargo (Wyness), Thomson.
Celtic: Boruc; Hinkel, O'Dea (Conroy), Crosas (Samaras), Caldwell, McManus, Nakamura, Brown S, McDonald, Vennegoor, McGeady.

Sunday, 8 March 2009

Rangers (3) 5 *(Whittaker 15, Lafferty 35, 81, Niguez 45 (pen), Davis 53)*
Hamilton A (1) 1 *(Quinn 26)*   27,588
Rangers: McGregor; Whittaker, Papac, Bougherra (Edu), Weir, Ferguson, Davis, Pedro Mendes (McCulloch), Lafferty, Miller (Boyd), Niguez.
Hamilton A: Cerny; Elebert (Lyle), Easton (Evans), McLaughlin (Swailes), Gibson, Quinn, McGowan, McCarthy, Mensing, Offiong, Neil.

SIXTH ROUND REPLAY

Wednesday, 18 March 2009

Aberdeen (0) 0
Dunfermline Ath (0) 0   13,567
Aberdeen: Langfield; Foster, Mulgrew, Mair (Considine), Diamond, Severin, Smith J, Kerr, Maguire (Duff), Mackie, Aluko (Wright).
Dunfermline Ath: Gallacher; Woods, Thomson S, Wilson, McCann, Burke, Glass, Bell (Ross), Phinn (Loy), Mole (Muirhead), Bayne.
aet; Dunfermline Ath won 4-2 on penalties.

SEMI-FINALS

Saturday, 25 April 2009

Rangers (1) 3 *(Velicka 2, Boyd 66, Miller 70)*
St Mirren (0) 0   32,431
Rangers: Alexander; Dailly, Whittaker, Edu, Weir, Bougherra, Davis, Pedro Mendes (Novo), Boyd (Little), Velicka (Miller), Smith.
St Mirren: Howard; Ross, Camara, Dorman, Haining, Cuthbert, Thomson (Burns), Murray, Mehmet, Wyness (Brady), McGinn (Hamilton).

Sunday, 26 April 2009

Falkirk (0) 2 *(Scobbie 54, Arfield 89 (pen))*
Dunfermline Ath (0) 0   17,124
Falkirk: Dani Mallo; McNamara, Scobbie, Aafjes, Barr, McCann (Cregg), Arfield, O'Brien, Higdon, Finnigan (Stewart M), Arnau (McBride).
Dunfermline Ath: Gallacher; Woods, Wilson, Thomson S (Ross), McCann, Phinn, Bell (Kirk), Glass, Bayne, Mole (Loy), Burke.

SCOTTISH FA CUP FINAL

(Saturday, 30 May 2009 at Hampden Park, attendance 50,956)

Rangers (0) 1   Falkirk (0) 0

Rangers: Alexander; Whittaker, Papac, Bougherra, Weir, Ferguson, Davis, McCulloch, Boyd (Novo), Miller (Naismith), Lafferty (Dailly).
Scorers: Novo 46.

Falkirk: Dani Mallo; McNamara, Scobbie, Cregg (Stewart M), Barr, Aafjes, Arfield, McBride (Finnigan), Lovell, McCann (Higdon), O'Brien.

Referee: C. Thompson.

WELSH FOOTBALL 2008–09

There can hardly have been a more anti-climactic season for Welsh football. It promised so much but, in the end, delivered depressingly little. The national team's hopes of reaching the 2010 World Cup finals disappeared in the wake of a woeful home performance against Finland, a single goal prevented Cardiff City from reaching the Championship's play-offs and Wrexham flattered to deceive as they tried to regain their Football League status at the first attempt. It was left to Swansea City to buck the trend by finishing a very creditable eighth on their return to the second tier of English football after 24 years – an achievement which would cost them the services of their manager come the close season.

With Germany and Russia in their qualifying group, it was always going to be difficult for Wales to reach South Africa but they made a decent enough start to their campaign. After beating Azerbaijan in Cardiff thanks to a late goal from substitute Sam Vokes of Wolves, they nearly picked up an unexpected point in a 2-1 defeat in Russia and then recorded their second win by finally overcoming Leichtenstein 2-0 at the Millennium Stadium. So far, so good but a 1-0 defeat in Germany was followed by a catastrophic display against the Finns in their next game. Needing to win to keep alive any hopes of qualification, Wales meekly succumbed to a moderate Finnish team who scored just before the end of a first half dominated by the home side. A second stoppage-time goal at the conclusion of a lacklustre and clueless performance merely rubbed salt into an already gaping wound which effectively ended the Welsh campaign. Manager John Toshack, having been given a two-year contract extension in February, received some serious criticism for his tactics – particularly the use of a lone striker – and the first "Toshack Out" banner was seen at the next game when some pride was restored in a 2-0 defeat by Germany in Cardiff. But a few of his underperforming senior players need to shoulder some of the blame – as does the FAW for continuing to stage qualifiers in a near-deserted Millennium Stadium rather than in Swansea or Wrexham. The season ended on a positive note when the youngest side in Welsh football history secured a 1-0 win against Estonia at Llanelli in a warm-up match for the last qualifier of the season in Azerbaijan in June. A severely depleted team, missing 10 Premier League and Championship players and with an average age of just 21.7 years, produced a very impressive result – with David Edwards of Wolves scoring the only goal just before half time and Reading striker Simon Church providing some much needed mobility alongside Nottingham Forest's Robert Earnshaw as Toshack's youngsters came of age in Baku.

For the second successive season, Cardiff's fortunes hinged on a solitary goal. As they prepared to move to a new stadium opposite Ninian Park and twelve months after losing 1-0 to Portsmouth in the FA Cup Final, they amazingly blew their chances of reaching The Championship's play-offs. For months, The Bluebirds had, indeed, been flying high. After appearing to be shoo-ins as the season reached its climax, they collected just one point from their last four games and failed to qualify by a single goal – losing out to Preston who had hammered them 6-0 a fortnight earlier. For much of the season, Swansea's attractive and effective brand of passing football, coupled with Jason Scotland's lethal eye for goal, threatened to propel them into the top six before their challenge eventually petered out. But The Swans became victims of their own success when manager Roberto Martinez, having been approached by Celtic, was lured back to his former club, Wigan, as the Premier League side chose him to replace the Sunderland-bound Steve Bruce. He was succeeded by the former Portuguese international and Queens Park Rangers coach Paulo Sousa, who became the club's 12th manager in 14 years.

Of the four clubs competing in the English pyramid, much was expected of Wrexham when Toshack's assistant, Dean Saunders, took over from Brian Little as manager in October. But after a complete personnel overhaul had raised hopes of reversing the previous season's relegation, crucial injuries and a disastrous run of poor form led to a disappointing mid-table finish in the Blue Square Premier. In-fighting over a student housing project on land surrounding The Racecourse – considered vital to the club's financial future – didn't help. Colwyn Bay lost a penalty shoot-out to Newcastle Blue Star in the semi-finals of the Unibond First Division North's play-offs, Newport finished 10th in the Blue Square South while debt-ridden Merthyr somehow managed to survive the season and maintain a promotion challenge right up to the final week of the campaign before finishing seventh in the Southern League Premier Division.

It was another barren European experience for the four Welsh Premier League clubs. In the first qualifying round of the Champions League, Llanelli couldn't hold on to a 1-0 first-leg lead against Ventspils as the Latvians scored four goals without reply in the second leg. In the UEFA Cup, Bangor were on the receiving end of a 10-1 thumping by Midtjylland of Denmark, having lost the home tie at The Racecourse while The New Saints failed to break their European duck at the 10th attempt by going down 2-0 on aggregate to Lithuania's Suduva. Rhyl came unstuck by losing 9-3 on aggregate to the Dublin side, Bohemians, in the Intertoto Cup.

As the debate continues over plans to reduce the Welsh Premier League to 10 teams in 2010, Rhyl won the title by seven points while runners-up Llanelli, who replaced manager Peter Nicholas with Andy Legg, were joined by The New Saints in the first qualifying round of the Europa League. After beating Aberystwyth 2-0 in the Welsh Cup Final, Bangor City went straight into the second qualifying round of the new competition.

Their attempt to reach the 2010 Word Cup finals may be over but Wales must now target third place in their remaining group games to boost their seedings for future qualification campaigns – starting with a home match against Russia in September. Since becoming national coach four years ago, Toshack has had to deal with a series of retirements and injuries and there is now no alternative but to continue with his youth policy, via the outstanding Under-21 side, as he prepares for the next European Championships. His fledgling team should take heart from their performance – and especially the clean sheet – in Baku and if Arsenal's Aaron Ramsey maintains his development at the heart of the Welsh midfield, then there is some hope that a trip to Poland and Ukraine in 2012 might turn out to be more than just a pipedream.

GRAHAME LLOYD

PRINCIPALITY BUILDING SOCIETY WELSH PREMIER LEAGUE 2008–09

				Home					Away					Total					
		P	W	D	L	F	A	W	D	L	F	A	W	D	L	F	A	GD	Pts
1	Rhyl	34	14	1	2	54	16	15	2	0	41	13	29	3	2	95	29	66	90
2	Llanelli	34	14	2	1	51	18	12	3	2	47	20	26	5	3	98	38	60	83
3	The New Saints	34	12	4	1	44	10	8	7	2	35	17	20	11	3	79	27	52	71
4	Carmarthen Town	34	10	3	4	27	17	9	2	6	25	30	19	5	10	52	47	5	62
5	Port Talbot Town	34	8	4	5	29	23	8	4	5	28	25	16	8	10	57	48	9	56
6	Bangor City	34	7	5	5	25	16	9	2	6	33	24	16	7	11	58	40	18	55
7	Haverfordwest County	34	9	4	4	31	17	7	3	7	22	22	16	7	11	53	39	14	55
8	Aberystwyth Town	34	6	6	5	28	25	6	4	7	23	25	12	10	12	51	50	1	46
9	Connah's Quay Nomads	34	7	2	8	31	29	5	3	9	18	36	12	5	17	49	65	-16	41
10	Newtown	34	7	4	6	29	24	3	6	8	17	30	10	10	14	46	54	-8	40
11	Welshpool Town	34	6	5	6	26	27	5	2	10	22	43	11	7	16	48	70	-22	40
12	Airbus UK	34	6	3	8	26	31	6	0	11	21	26	12	3	19	47	57	-10	39
13	NEWI Cefn Druids	34	5	2	10	29	35	4	5	8	28	39	9	7	18	57	74	-17	34
14	Neath Athletic	34	8	3	6	25	23	2	1	14	18	42	10	4	20	43	65	-22	34
15	Prestatyn Town	34	7	4	6	29	28	1	5	11	19	42	8	9	17	48	70	-22	33
16	Porthmadog	34	6	2	9	34	45	4	0	13	23	46	10	2	22	57	91	-34	32
17	Caersws	34	4	2	11	16	31	2	5	10	12	30	6	7	21	28	61	-33	25
18	Caernarfon Town*	34	3	3	11	14	35	2	5	10	18	38	5	8	21	32	73	-41	20

*3 points deducted.

PREVIOUS WELSH LEAGUE WINNERS

1993	Cwmbran Town	1998	Barry Town	2003	Barry Town	2008	Llanelli
1994	Bangor City	1999	Barry Town	2004	Rhyl	2009	Rhyl
1995	Bangor City	2000	TNS	2005	TNS		
1996	Barry Town	2001	Barry Town	2006	TNS		
1997	Barry Town	2002	Barry Town	2007	TNS		

MACWHIRTER WELSH LEAGUE 2008–09

DIVISION ONE	P	W	D	L	F	A	GD	Pts
ENTO Aberaman Ath	34	24	5	5	73	33	40	77
Goytre United	34	24	4	6	90	39	51	76
Barry Town*	34	22	7	5	63	26	37	70
Bettws	34	18	8	8	64	32	32	62
Bridgend Town	34	18	6	10	65	49	16	60
Cambrian & Clydach	34	16	9	9	62	48	14	57
Afan Lido	34	15	9	10	70	49	21	54
Pontardawe Town	34	14	10	10	48	32	16	52
Ton Pentre	34	14	7	13	59	51	8	49
Cardiff Corinthians	34	13	7	14	51	53	-2	46
Bryntirion Athletic	34	12	9	13	54	54	0	45
Dinas Powys	34	10	5	19	43	73	-30	35
Caldicot Town	34	9	7	18	41	67	-26	34
Caerleon	34	9	7	18	36	64	-28	34
Taffs Well	34	7	10	17	39	58	-19	31
Newport YMCA	34	8	4	22	41	76	-35	28
Croesyceiliog	34	7	5	22	45	82	-37	26
Cwmbran Town	34	3	7	24	32	90	-58	16

*3 points deducted.

HUWS GRAY-FITLOCK CYMRU ALLIANCE LEAGUE 2008–09

	P	W	D	L	F	A	GD	Pts
Bala Town	32	23	6	3	81	23	58	75
Holyhead Hotspur	32	23	3	6	71	36	35	72
Llangefni Town	32	20	7	5	74	27	47	67
Mynydd Isa	32	19	4	9	73	50	23	61
Llandudno Town	32	16	9	7	65	33	32	57
Ruthin Town	32	18	3	11	56	50	6	57
Flint Town United*	32	16	9	7	81	52	29	54
Buckley Town	32	12	5	15	46	64	-18	41
Lex XI*	32	12	7	13	58	63	-5	40
Mold Alexandra	32	10	9	13	62	71	-9	39
Denbigh Town	32	10	8	14	41	48	-7	38
Llanfairpwll	32	9	9	14	47	67	-20	36
Guilsfield	32	11	1	20	52	67	-15	34
Penrhyncoch*	32	10	5	17	41	72	-31	32
Gresford Athletic	32	7	6	19	32	63	-31	27
Glantraeth	32	4	6	22	39	82	-43	18
Llandyrnog United	32	2	3	27	32	83	-51	9

*3 points deducted.

PRINCIPALITY BUILDING SOCIETY WELSH PREMIER LEAGUE RESULTS 2008–09

	Aberystwyth Town	Airbus UK	Bangor City	Caernarfon Town	Caersws	Carmarthen Town	Connah's Quay Nomads	Haverfordwest County	Llanelli	NEWI Cefn Druids	Neath Athletic	Newtown	Port Talbot Town	Porthmadog	Prestatyn Town	Rhyl	The New Saints	Welshpool Town
Aberystwyth Town	—	1-0	1-2	3-1	2-2	0-3	1-1	0-3	1-1	1-1	6-2	2-0	1-1	5-2	2-1	0-1	2-2	0-2
Airbus UK	1-2	—	2-3	4-3	0-2	0-1	0-0	2-4	0-4	1-0	4-3	3-1	1-1	0-3	1-1	1-3	1-0	5-0
Bangor City	0-0	1-0	—	1-1	3-0	2-0	6-0	1-1	0-2	4-2	0-1	1-2	4-2	1-0	1-1	0-2	0-0	0-2
Caernarfon Town	1-0	0-2	0-2	—	2-2	1-3	0-2	0-1	0-5	4-2	1-0	0-0	2-4	0-2	1-1	0-1	0-5	2-3
Caersws	1-3	1-3	0-1	1-0	—	0-2	0-1	1-0	0-2	1-2	0-0	1-1	4-2	3-2	1-2	0-3	2-6	0-1
Carmarthen Town	2-1	1-0	3-1	2-1	1-1	—	2-0	3-0	1-4	1-0	5-2	0-0	1-1	1-0	1-0	1-2	2-3	0-1
Connah's Quay Nomads	1-2	2-3	1-3	1-1	1-0	1-3	—	2-1	3-1	2-3	5-0	3-3	0-2	3-1	3-1	2-3	0-2	1-0
Haverfordwest County	5-1	3-0	0-2	2-0	2-0	1-1	2-0	—	0-1	1-1	2-1	1-0	0-1	4-2	3-1	1-3	2-2	3-1
Llanelli	3-0	3-2	4-3	3-2	3-0	5-2	4-1	2-1	—	1-1	2-1	3-1	2-0	5-0	2-0	0-1	0-2	4-1
NEWI Cefn Druids	2-5	0-2	1-0	0-1	3-1	1-2	6-0	0-1	0-4	—	3-1	2-3	1-1	2-4	3-2	2-4	0-1	3-3
Neath Athletic	0-4	3-1	0-1	2-1	0-0	2-0	0-1	1-1	0-3	3-1	—	3-0	2-3	3-0	2-0	2-2	1-4	3-2
Newtown	2-1	0-1	1-3	2-2	0-0	2-3	1-2	4-2	2-6	4-0	2-0	—	1-0	2-0	1-1	1-2	0-0	4-1
Port Talbot Town	1-1	2-1	2-1	1-3	2-0	0-0	0-2	1-2	4-6	3-2	2-0	1-2	—	1-3	3-1	2-2	0-0	4-0
Porthmadog	4-1	3-4	0-6	5-0	0-1	1-3	6-5	2-1	3-3	2-3	1-4	3-1	1-2	—	3-2	0-3	2-2	2-1
Prestatyn Town	1-0	2-1	2-2	3-2	3-2	1-2	1-1	0-1	0-1	3-3	1-0	3-0	0-3	5-2	—	1-4	1-4	2-2
Rhyl	0-0	1-0	4-1	4-0	3-1	3-0	2-0	2-0	5-1	3-4	4-2	1-1	2-3	2-0	7-2	—	2-1	7-1
The New Saints	1-1	1-0	2-1	6-0	4-0	8-0	2-1	0-0	0-0	4-1	2-1	2-2	2-0	6-0	2-0	0-3	—	3-1
Welshpool Town	0-1	2-1	1-1	1-1	1-0	2-0	3-1	1-3	1-3	3-3	2-1	2-2	1-2	3-2	2-2	0-2	1-2	—

WELSH CUP 2008–09

PRELIMINARY ROUND

Aberbargoed Buds v Cwmaman Institute	3-4
AFC Llwydcoed v Ystradgynlais	4-0
Bethesda Athletic v Corwen	7-0
Borras Park Albion v Brickfield Rangers	2-3
Bow Street v Overton Recreational	4-2
Briton Ferry Athletic v Troedyrhiw	2-1
Castell Alun Colts v Presteigne St Andrews	4-0
Cwmamman United v Llansawel	4-2
Glyn Ceiriog v Coedpoeth United	0-6
Goytre v Newport Civil Service	1-3
Holywell Town v Nefyn United	1-2
Kerry v Llanberis	0-2
Llanllyfni v Llanfyllin Town	4-2
Llanrug United v Llanhaedr ym Mochnant	5-1
Llantwit Fadre v AFC Porth	0-2
Merthyr Saints v Pontyclun	0-9
Porthcawl Town v Monmouth Town	2-1
Rhayader Town v Pwllheli	2-4
Risca United v Seven Sisters	2-2
aet; Risca United won 3-2 on penalties.	
Tredegar Town v Carno	3-1
Tywyn Bryncrug v Newbridge on Wye	2-0
Venture Community v Dyffryn Banw	2-1

FIRST ROUND

Afan Lido v Cwmamman United	3-0
AFC Llwydcoed v Porthcawl Town	3-0
Berriew v Llangollen United	0-1
Bettws v Taffs Well	3-4
aet; Taffs Well won 4-3 on penalties.	
Brickfield Rangers v Nefyn United	4-3
Briton Ferry Athletic v AFC Porth	3-1
Brymbo v Mold Alexandra	0-8
Buckley Town v Penycae	6-3
Caerau Ely v Pentwyn Dynamos	1-2
Caerleon v Goytre United	1-4
Caldicot Town v Ammanford Town	0-1
Cambrian & Clydach Vale v Newcastle Emlyn	4-1
Cardiff Corinthians v Ely Rangers	3-0
Castell Alun Colts v Llandymog United	1-0
Conwy United v Penrhyncoch	2-3
Croesyceiliog v Maesteg Park Athletic	0-3
Cwmbran Celtic v Garw SBGC	3-1
Denbigh Town v Llanllyfni	4-1
Ento Aberaman Athletic v Barry Town	2-1
Flint Town United v Rhos Aelwyd	4-3
Glan Conwy v Llanrwst United	2-1
Glantraeth v Bala Town	1-6
Grange Harlequins v Newport Civil Service	1-5
Gullsfield Athletic v Ruthin Town	2-0
Halkyn United v Coedpoeth United	4-2
Hawarden Rangers v Llanfairpwll	0-2
Llanberis v Bow Street	2-3
Llandudno Junction v Penparcau	4-2
Llangefni Town v Llandudno	3-1
Llangelnor v Dinas Powys	0-2
Llanrug United v Pwllheli	0-2
Llanwern v Ton Pentre	3-0
Llay Welfare v Amlwch Town	8-1
Mynydd Isa v Holyhead Hotspurs	3-3
aet; Holyhead Hotspurs won 6-5 on penalties.	
Nantlle Vale v Chirk AAA	1-4
Newport YMCA v Cwmaman Institute	3-2
Penrhiwceiber Rangers v Pontypridd Town	3-4
Pontyclun v Bridgend Town	1-3
aet; Bridgend Town won 3-1 on penalties.	
Risca United v Pontardawe Town	2-0
Tredegar Town v Gresford Athletic	0-1
Treharris Athletic v Bryntirion Athletic	1-9
Tywyn Bryncrug v Bethesda Athletic	4-1
UWIC v Cwmbran Town	1-3
Venture Community v Lex XI	1-2
West End v Garden Village	2-3
Rhydymwyn w.o. v Cefn United withdrew	

SECOND ROUND

Aberystwyth Town v Afan Lido	2-2
aet; Aberystwyth Town won 3-2 on penalties.	
Airbus UK v Welshpool Town	2-1
Bala Town v Prestatyn Town	3-3
aet; Prestatyn Town won 5-4 on penalties.	
Bangor City v Connah's Quay	1-0
Brickfield Rangers v Buckley Town	3-4

Bridgend Town v Cwmbran Town	3-1
Bryntirion Athletic v Cardiff Corinthians	1-2
Cambrian & Clydach Vale v Newtown	0-1
Carmarthen Town v Bow Street	6-1
Penrhyncoch v Maesteg Park Athletic	3-2
Porthmadog v Caernarfon Town	5-3
Denbigh Town v Chirk AAA	4-1
Dinas Powys v Briton Ferry Athletic	0-1
Flint Town United v Mold Alexandra	4-0
Garden Village v Risca United	2-0
Gresford Athletic v Rhydymwyn	4-1
Holyhead Hotspurs v Llay Welfare	2-1
Lex XI v Glan Conwy	2-1
Llandudno Junction v Pwllheli	0-2
Llanelli v Neath	4-0
Llangefni Town v Llanfairpwll	3-0
Llangollen United v Tywyn Bryncrug	1-2
Llanwern v AFC Llwydcoed	1-6
NEWI Cefn Druids v Halkyn United	4-2
Newport Civil Service v Caersws	0-1
Newport YMCA v Cwmbran Celtic	3-2
Pentwyn Dynamos v Ammanford Town	1-0
Pontypridd Town v Haverfordwest County	1-4
Port Talbot Town v Ento Aberaman Athletic	1-0
Rhyl v Castell Alun Colts	8-0
Taffs Well v Goytre United	0-2
The New Saints v Gullsfield Athletic	4-2

THIRD ROUND

Bangor City v Garden Village	4-0
Bridgend Town v Llangefni Town	1-0
Buckley Town v Airbus UK	1-5
Caersws v Aberystwyth Town	0-3
Cardiff Corinthians v Goytre United	0-6
Gresford Athletic v Prestatyn Town	2-3
Holyhead Hotspur v Pentwyn Dynamos	2-1
Lex XI v Porthmadog	2-0
AFC Llwydcoed v Flint Town United	1-0
NEWI Cefn Druids v Newtown	1-0
Newport YMCA v Briton Ferry Athletic	1-0
Port Talbot Town v Denbigh Town	7-0
Pwllheli v Carmarthen Town	0-6
Rhyl v Haverfordwest County	4-0
The New Saints v Penrhyncoch	7-1
Tywyn Bryncrug v Llanelli	0-3

FOURTH ROUND

AFC Llwydcoed v Aberystwyth Town	0-3
Airbus UK v NEWI Cefn Druids	2-1
Bangor City v Rhyl	1-1
aet; Bangor City won 4-2 on penalties.	
Bridgend Town v Lex XI	4-0
Holyhead Hotspur v Newport YMCA	1-1
aet; Newport YMCA won 6-5 on penalties.	
Port Talbot Town v Llanelli	2-1
Prestatyn Town v Goytre United	5-3
The New Saints v Carmarthen Town	2-3

QUARTER-FINALS

Aberystwyth Town v Prestatyn Town	5-1
Airbus UK v Bangor City	0-5
Carmarthen Town v Port Talbot Town	1-1
aet; Carmarthen Town won 4-1 on penalties.	
Newport YMCA v Bridgend Town	0-1

SEMI-FINALS

Aberystwyth Town v Carmarthen Town	2-3
Bangor City v Bridgend Town	2-1

FINAL (at Llanelli)   1044
4 May 2009

Bangor C (1) 2   Aberystwyth T (0) 0
Bangor C: Smith; Swanick, Hoy, Johnston, Brewerton, Killackey (McManus 88), Limbert, Walsh, Davies (Williams 81), Seargeant, Edwards (Beattie 72).
Scorers: Davies 43, Seargeant 49.
Aberystwyth T: Roberts; James S, James K (Reynolds 86), Thomas, Edwards, Evans R (Evans A 79), Venables, Morgan, Evans G (Bradshaw 54), Hughes, Kellaway.
Referee: H. Jones (Llanrhaedr).

PREVIOUS WELSH CUP WINNERS

1878	Wrexham Town	1909	Wrexham	1950	Swansea Town	1981	Swansea City
1879	White Star Newtown	1910	Wrexham	1951	Merthyr Tydfil	1982	Swansea City
1880	Druids	1911	Wrexham	1952	Rhyl	1983	Swansea City
1881	Druids	1912	Cardiff City	1953	Rhyl	1984	Shrewsbury Town
1882	Druids	1913	Swansea Town	1954	Flint Town United	1985	Shrewsbury Town
1883	Wrexham	1914	Wrexham	1955	Barry Town	1986	Wrexham
1884	Oswestry United	1915	Wrexham	1956	Cardiff City	1987	Merthyr Tydfil
1885	Druids	1920	Cardiff City	1957	Wrexham	1988	Cardiff City
1886	Druids	1921	Wrexham	1958	Wrexham	1989	Swansea City
1887	Chirk	1922	Cardiff City	1959	Cardiff City	1990	Hereford United
1888	Chirk	1923	Cardiff City	1960	Wrexham	1991	Swansea City
1889	Bangor	1924	Wrexham	1961	Swansea Town	1992	Cardiff City
1890	Druids	1925	Wrexham	1962	Bangor City	1993	Cardiff City
1891	Shrewsbury Town	1926	Ebbw Vale	1963	Borough United	1994	Barry Town
1892	Chirk	1927	Cardiff City	1964	Cardiff City	1995	Wrexham
1893	Wrexham	1928	Cardiff City	1965	Cardiff City	1996	TNS
1894	Chirk	1929	Connah's Quay	1966	Swansea Town	1997	Barry Town
1895	Newtown	1930	Cardiff City	1967	Cardiff City	1998	Bangor City
1896	Bangor	1931	Wrexham	1968	Cardiff City	1999	Inter Cable-Tel
1897	Wrexham	1932	Swansea Town	1969	Cardiff City	2000	Bangor City
1898	Druids	1933	Chester	1970	Cardiff City	2001	Barry Town
1899	Druids	1934	Bristol City	1971	Cardiff City	2002	Barry Town
1900	Aberystwyth	1935	Tranmere Rovers	1972	Wrexham	2003	Barry Town
1901	Oswestry United	1936	Crewe Alexandra	1973	Cardiff City	2004	Rhyl
1902	Wellington Town	1937	Crewe Alexandra	1974	Cardiff City	2005	Rhyl
1903	Wrexham	1938	Shrewsbury Town	1975	Wrexham	2006	Rhyl
1904	Druids	1939	South Liverpool	1976	Cardiff City	2007	Carmarthen Town
1905	Wrexham	1940	Wellington Town	1977	Shrewsbury Town	2008	Bangor C
1906	Wellington Town	1947	Chester	1978	Wrexham	2009	Bangor C
1907	Oswestry United	1948	Lovell's Athletic	1979	Shrewsbury Town		
1908	Chester	1949	Merthyr Tydfil	1980	Newport County		

THE LOOSEMORES OF CARDIFF CHALLENGE CUP 2008–09

GROUP 1	P	W	D	L	F	A	GD	Pts
Aberystwyth Town	4	1	3	0	7	3	4	6
Carmarthen Town	4	1	2	1	4	4	0	5
Haverfordwest County	4	1	1	2	3	7	–4	4

GROUP 2	P	W	D	L	F	A	GD	Pts
Neath	4	2	1	1	13	12	1	7
Llanelli	4	2	0	2	12	10	2	6
Port Talbot Town	4	1	1	2	11	14	–3	4

GROUP 3	P	W	D	L	F	A	GD	Pts
Newtown	4	2	1	1	11	4	7	7
NEWI Cefn Druids	4	2	1	1	7	7	0	5
Caernarfon Town	4	0	2	2	4	11	–7	2

GROUP 4	P	W	D	L	F	A	GD	Pts
Caersws	4	2	2	0	13	7	6	8
Bangor City	4	2	1	1	10	11	–1	7
Porthmadog	4	0	1	3	5	10	–5	1

GROUP 5	P	W	D	L	F	A	GD	Pts
Rhyl	4	3	0	1	13	3	10	9
Technogroup Welshpool	4	2	0	2	7	7	0	6
Airbus UK	4	1	0	3	5	15	–10	3

GROUP 6	P	W	D	L	F	A	GD	Pts
The New Saints	4	3	1	0	12	6	6	10
Connah's Quay	4	2	0	2	3	6	–3	6
Prestatyn Town	4	0	1	3	7	10	–3	1

QUARTER-FINALS

Aberystwyth Town v Caersws	4-1
Bangor City v Rhyl	3-1
NEWI Cefn Druids v The New Saints	0-2
Newtown v Neath	1-1

Neath won 4-2 on penalties.

SEMI-FINALS FIRST LEG

Neath v The New Saints	2-0
Bangor City v Aberystwyth Town	1-2

SEMI-FINALS SECOND LEG

The New Saints v Neath	3-0
Aberystwyth Town v Bangor City	2-4

FINAL (at Newtown)

4 April 2009

Bangor City (0) 0

The New Saints (1) 2 *(Leah 11 (pen), Murtagh 75)* 555

Bangor City: Smith; Swanick (Lloyd 73), Hoy, Johnston (Mitchell 82), Brewerton, Killackey, Limbert, Walsh, Davies, Seargeant, Edwards (McManus 73).

The New Saints: Harrison; Hogan, Holmes, Baker, Evans, Leah (Whitfield 90), Ruscoe, Darlington (Courtney 90), Berkeley■, McKenna, Murtagh.

Referee: P. Southall.

NORTHERN IRISH FOOTBALL 2008–09

Northern Ireland football experienced a year of highs and lows at virtually every level – and a degree of prosperity due primarily to the multi-million pound cash injection by Sky TV for live televising of internationals and selected Irish Premiership games.

With the current financial crisis showing no signs of diminishing, the prospects of obtaining sponsorship for several competitions remain difficult. All stops are being pulled out by the Irish FA to overcome the situation.

The reality of the hardship was pinpointed by the shock announcement in February that Bangor could not continue in the Premiership "due to the current economic climate, resulting in lack of sponsorship, poor attendances and spiralling costs".

They took the step with reluctance after only a year back in senior football and having spent huge amounts on upgrading their compact Clandeboye Road Stadium to meet the regulations.

This development meant no club was relegated while Portadown as Championship winners automatically regained senior status. Dungannon Swifts did the same after a play-off with Donegal Celtic, who were unhappy with the selection method. The problem was exacerbated by the referees going on strike on the first Saturday of the season over a new pay structure followed by torrential rain seven days later, virtually wiping out all football, necessitating clubs playing fixture catch-up until the end of the season. Budgets were trimmed, with some clubs requesting players take voluntary wage reduction.

On the international front, manager Nigel Worthington, who has established excellent rapport with players, supporters and media, still hopes to qualify for the World Cup Finals in South Africa 2010, despite early defeats by Slovakia and Slovenia, followed by back-to-back wins against San Marino and Windsor Park triumphs against Poland and Slovenia. Tough away challenges remain and reaching South Africa will be hard but not mission impossible if they can obtain maximum points from the September game with the Poles.

When Linfield, Ireland's best supported club, fails to win a major trophy, as it did this season, then it is considered nothing short of a disaster by fans accustomed to constant success. They were going for an incredible fourth League and Cup double but it was not to be. They lost the Premiership by one point to Glentoran with the series going to the wire, while Cliftonville eliminated them from the Irish Cup in the semi-finals. Manager David Jeffrey's approach is calm and collected without a knee-jerk reaction. In fact, he paraphrased the immortal words of US General Douglas MacArthur as the Japanese conquered the Philippines ... "We shall return".

Linfield are determined to be the pace-setters again. Newcomers will be recruited to replace departed stars – among them ex-Northern Ireland striker Glenn Ferguson, 40, whose contract was not extended after 11 seasons and who hit 536 goals in a distinguished career; last season alone he scored 25 in 48 fixtures.

Crusaders, led by inspirational manager Stephen Baxter, won the JJB Sports Irish Cup, Cliftonville the County Antrim Shield and Portadown the Co-operative Sports Cup and two teams dominated the junior scene – Knockbreda and Immaculata.

Excellent progress is being made in coaching, grassroots, women and schools football and community relations. It is, therefore, not all doom and gloom but simply being pragmatic in outlook ensuring ends meet.

DR MALCOLM BRODIE MBE

JJB PREMIERSHIP 2008-09

	P	W	D	L	F	A	GD	Pts
Glentoran	38	24	9	5	63	36	27	81
Linfield	38	24	8	6	69	28	41	80
Crusaders	38	16	14	8	63	45	18	62
Lisburn Distillery	38	15	11	12	53	41	12	56
Coleraine	38	15	6	17	46	51	–5	51
Cliftonville	38	12	14	12	52	48	4	50
Institute	38	13	9	16	47	55	–8	48
Newry City	38	11	11	16	47	57	–10	44
Glenavon	38	11	8	19	49	63	–14	41
Ballymena United	38	11	8	19	39	57	–18	41
Bangor	38	9	9	20	42	67	–25	36
Dungannon Swifts	38	8	11	19	49	71	–22	35

PROMOTION/RELEGATION PLAY-OFF
Donegal Celtic 2, Dungannon Swifts 1 (at Suffolk), Dungannon Swifts 1, Donegal Celtic 0 (at Stangmore Park). Dungannon Swifts qualified on away goals.

LADBROKES.COM CHAMPIONSHIP 2008-09

	P	W	D	L	F	A	GD	Pts
Portadown	32	25	2	5	88	23	65	77
Donegal Celtic	32	24	1	7	65	27	38	73
Loughgall	32	22	4	6	77	29	48	70
Ards	32	20	5	7	53	26	27	65
Ballinamallard United	32	19	6	7	73	47	26	63
Coagh United	32	19	4	9	60	43	17	61
Banbridge Town	32	15	5	12	66	67	–1	50
Ballymoney United	32	12	7	13	41	35	6	43
Larne	32	12	7	13	53	56	–3	43
Carrick Rangers	32	12	6	14	56	53	3	42
Glebe Rangers	32	9	7	16	37	56	–19	34
Armagh City	32	8	8	16	39	61	–22	32
Limavady United	32	9	3	20	46	72	–26	30
Ballyclare Comrades	32	8	6	18	34	62	–28	30
Tobermore United	32	7	5	20	34	64	–30	26
Dergview	32	6	1	25	31	84	–53	19
Killymoon Rangers	32	4	5	23	33	81	–48	17

IFA INTERIM INTERMEDIATE LEAGUE

	P	W	D	L	F	A	GD	Pts
H&W Welders	22	19	2	1	55	18	37	59
Dundela	22	18	2	2	70	19	51	56
PSNI	22	12	4	6	38	27	11	40
Queens University	22	10	5	7	36	24	12	35
Lurgan Celtic	22	11	2	9	44	36	8	35
Annagh United	22	9	3	10	33	30	3	30
Oxford United Stars	22	9	2	11	26	31	–5	29
Portstewart	22	7	4	11	23	38	–15	25
Moyola Park	22	6	6	10	24	37	–13	24
Wakehurst	22	4	5	13	22	36	–14	17
Brantwood	22	3	5	14	23	56	–33	14
Chimney Corner	22	3	2	17	19	61	–42	11

IFA YOUTH LEAGUE (SECTION A)

	P	W	D	L	F	A	GD	Pts
Linfield Rangers	22	16	5	1	62	18	44	53
Cliftonville Strollers	22	14	3	5	58	37	21	45
Glenavon U-18	22	12	8	2	44	26	18	44
Donegal Celtic Youth	22	12	4	6	58	35	23	40
Ballymena United Youth	22	9	6	7	40	37	3	33
Glentoran Colts	22	7	4	11	55	50	5	25
Newry City Wanderers	22	6	7	9	35	40	–5	25
Dungannon Swifts Youth	22	7	4	11	32	43	–11	25
Ballymoney United Colts	22	7	3	12	41	60	–19	24
Lisburn Distillery Youth	22	5	6	11	33	52	–19	21
Coleraine Colts	22	4	5	13	27	57	–30	17
Crusaders Colts	22	4	3	15	35	65	–30	15

IFA YOUTH LEAGUE (SECTION B)

	P	W	D	L	F	A	GD	Pts
Ballinamallard United Youth	21	15	4	2	44	19	25	49
Portadown III	21	10	4	7	52	41	11	34
Ballyclare Comrades Colts	21	10	4	7	49	46	3	34
Limavady United Youth	21	9	3	9	43	46	–3	30
Loughgall Colts	21	9	2	10	44	35	9	29
Carrick Rangers Colts	21	8	4	9	48	43	5	29
Larne U-18	21	5	3	13	45	62	–17	18
Cookstown Youth	21	4	3	14	26	59	–33	15

IRISH LEAGUE CHAMPIONSHIP WINNERS

1891	Linfield	1912	Glentoran	1938	Belfast Celtic	1967	Glentoran	1989	Linfield
1892	Linfield	1913	Glentoran	1939	Belfast Celtic	1968	Glentoran	1990	Portadown
1893	Linfield	1914	Linfield	1940	Belfast Celtic	1969	Linfield	1991	Portadown
1894	Glentoran	1915	Belfast Celtic	1948	Belfast Celtic	1970	Glentoran	1992	Glentoran
1895	Linfield	1920	Belfast Celtic	1949	Linfield	1971	Linfield	1993	Linfield
1896	Distillery	1921	Glentoran	1950	Linfield	1972	Glentoran	1994	Linfield
1897	Glentoran	1922	Linfield	1951	Glentoran	1973	Crusaders	1995	Crusaders
1898	Linfield	1923	Linfield	1952	Glenavon	1974	Coleraine	1996	Portadown
1899	Distillery	1924	Queen's Island	1953	Glentoran	1975	Linfield	1997	Crusaders
1900	Belfast Celtic	1925	Glentoran	1954	Linfield	1976	Crusaders	1998	Cliftonville
1901	Distillery	1926	Belfast Celtic	1955	Linfield	1977	Glentoran	1999	Glentoran
1902	Linfield	1927	Belfast Celtic	1956	Linfield	1978	Linfield	2000	Linfield
1903	Distillery	1928	Belfast Celtic	1957	Glentoran	1979	Linfield	2001	Linfield
1904	Linfield	1929	Belfast Celtic	1958	Ards	1980	Linfield	2002	Portadown
1905	Glentoran	1930	Linfield	1959	Linfield	1981	Glentoran	2003	Glentoran
1906	Cliftonville	1931	Glentoran	1960	Glenavon	1982	Linfield	2004	Linfield
	Distillery	1932	Linfield	1961	Linfield	1983	Linfield	2005	Glentoran
1907	Linfield	1933	Belfast Celtic	1962	Linfield	1984	Linfield	2006	Linfield
1908	Linfield	1934	Linfield	1963	Distillery	1985	Linfield	2007	Linfield
1909	Linfield	1935	Linfield	1964	Glentoran	1986	Linfield	2008	Linfield
1910	Cliftonville	1936	Belfast Celtic	1965	Derry City	1987	Linfield	2009	Glentoran
1911	Linfield	1937	Belfast Celtic	1966	Linfield	1988	Glentoran		

LADBROKES.COM CHAMPIONSHIP (Previously First Division)

1996	Coleraine	2001	Ards	2006	Crusaders
1997	Ballymena United	2002	Lisburn Distillery	2007	Institute
1998	Newry Town	2003	Dungannon Swifts	2008	Loughgall
1999	Distillery	2004	Loughgall	2009	Portadown
2000	Omagh Town	2005	Armagh City		

SETANTA SPORTS CUP

(Results continued from 2007–08 season)

GROUP 1

Cliftonville v Cork City	0-2
Drogheda United v Dungannon Swifts	3-0
Drogheda United v Cork City	1-1
Dungannon Swifts v Cliftonville	2-4
Cliftonville v Drogheda United	0-2
Cork City v Dungannon Swifts	4-1

GROUP 1 TABLE

	P	W	D	L	F	A	Pts
Drogheda United	6	4	2	0	13	3	14
Cork City	6	4	2	0	11	2	14
Cliftonville	6	1	1	4	6	11	4
Dungannon Swifts	6	0	1	5	3	17	1

GROUP 2

Derry City v Glentoran	2-0
Linfield v St Patrick's Athletic	1-1
Linfield v Glentoran	1-4
St Patrick's Athletic v Derry City	0-1
Derry City v Linfield	3-0
Glentoran v St Patrick's Athletic	1-0

GROUP 2 TABLE

	P	W	D	L	F	A	Pts
Derry City	6	4	1	1	10	4	13
Glentoran	6	2	2	2	10	10	8
Linfield	6	2	1	3	8	12	7
St Patrick's Athletic	6	1	2	3	6	8	5

SEMI-FINALS

Drogheda United 0, Glentoran 1
Derry City 0, Cork City 1

FINAL

11 November 2008

Cork City 2 *(Murray 57, Kearney 75)*

Glentoran 1 *(Neill 14)*

(at Turner's Cross, Cork).
Cork City: McNulty; Horgan, Sullivan, Murray, Danny
Murphy, O'Connor, Gamble, Darren Murphy, Kearney
(Ryan 89), Behan, Dudfield.\r\
Glentoran: Morris; Nixon, Simpson, Ward, Jon Taylor,
Scullion (Waterworth 58), Fordyce (Fitzgerald 77),
McCabe, Neill, Hamilton, Halliday (McGovern 70).
Referee: T. Stokes (Dublin).

SETANTA SPORTS CUP WINNERS

2004–05 Linfield	2006–07 Drogheda United	2007–08 Cork City
2005–06 Drogheda United		

CO-OPERATIVE INSURANCE IRISH LEAGUE CUP

QUARTER-FINALS FIRST LEG

Portadown v Linfield	2-0
Newry City v Loughgall	3-2
Glenavon v Lisburn Distillery	1-1
Glentoran v Coleraine	1-1

QUARTER-FINALS SECOND LEG

Loughgall v Newry City	5-6
Lisburn Distillery v Glenavon	1-0
Coleraine v Glentoran	0-2
Linfield v Portadown	0-1

SEMI-FINALS

Newry City v Lisburn Distillery	3-2
(at Mourneview Park).	
Glentoran v Portadown	1-2
(at Windsor Park).	

**CO-OPERATIVE INSURANCE
IRISH LEAGUE CUP FINAL 2008–09**

(at Windsor Park, 28 February 2009)

Newry City 0

Portadown 1 *(McCutcheon 30)*   4000

Newry City: Coleman; Donegan, Feeney C, Friars, Black
(King 81), Keegan, Clarke, Garrett, Ferguson, Morgan,
Feeney L (Anderson 81).

Portadown: Miskelly; O'Hara, Redman, Hunter,
Convery, Boyle, McCullough, McCluskey, Teggart A
(Mouncey 74), Braniff (Lecky 79), McCutcheon (Topley
87).

Referee: D. Malcolm (Bangor).

JJB SPORTS IRISH CUP 2008–09

FIFTH ROUND

Ballymena United v Crusaders	0-1
Cliftonville v Donegal Celtic	2-0
Glenavon v Linfield	1-3
Glentoran v Coleraine	2-1
Institute v Dungannon Swifts	1-0
Lisburn Distillery v Tobermore United	1-0
Newry City v Bangor	1-0
Portadown v Loughgall	5-0

QUARTER-FINALS

Glentoran v Cliftonville	0-1
Institute v Newry City	2-1
Linfield v Lisburn Distillery	3-0
Portadown v Crusaders	2-5

SEMI-FINALS

Cliftonville v Linfield	0-0, 3-2
Crusaders v Institute	4-1

JJB SPORTS IRISH CUP FINAL 2008–09

(at Windsor Park, 9 May 2009)

Crusaders 1 *(Dickson 48)*

Cliftonville 0 7500

Crusaders: Keenan; McKeown, McBride, Black, Smyth G, Coates, Owens (Coulter 66), Doherty, Dickson (Arthurs 71), Rainey, Donnelly (Caddell 87).

Cliftonville: Connolly; Scannell R, Johnston B, O'Hara, Holland M (Hamill 75), Scannell C, Smyth A, Donaghy, Holland B, Catney (Downey 65), O'Connor.

Referee: A. McCourt (Belfast).

IRISH CUP FINALS (from 1946–47)

1946–47	Belfast Celtic 1, Glentoran 0
1947–48	Linfield 3, Coleraine 0
1948–49	Derry City 3, Glentoran 1
1949–50	Linfield 2, Distillery 1
1950–51	Glentoran 3, Ballymena U 1
1951–52	Ards 1, Glentoran 0
1952–53	Linfield 5, Coleraine 0
1953–54	Derry City 1, Glentoran 0
1954–55	Dundela 3, Glenavon 0
1955–56	Distillery 1, Glentoran 0
1956–57	Glenavon 2, Derry City 0
1957–58	Ballymena U 2, Linfield 0
1958–59	Glenavon 2, Ballymena U 0
1959–60	Linfield 5, Ards 1
1960–61	Glenavon 5, Linfield 1
1961–62	Linfield 4, Portadown 0
1962–63	Linfield 2, Distillery 1
1963–64	Derry City 2, Glentoran 0
1964–65	Coleraine 2, Glenavon 1
1965–66	Glentoran 2, Linfield 0
1966–67	Crusaders 3, Glentoran 1
1967–68	Crusaders 2, Linfield 0
1968–69	Ards 4, Distillery 2
1969–70	Linfield 2, Ballymena U 1
1970–71	Distillery 3, Derry City
1971–72	Coleraine 2, Portadown 1
1972–73	Glentoran 3, Linfield 2
1973–74	Ards 2, Ballymena U 1
1974–75	Coleraine 1:0:1, Linfield 1:0:0
1975–76	Carrick Rangers 2, Linfield 1
1976–77	Coleraine 4, Linfield 1
1977–78	Linfield 3, Ballymena U 1
1978–79	Cliftonville 3, Portadown 2
1979–80	Linfield 2, Crusaders 0

1980–81	Ballymena U 1, Glenavon 0
1981–82	Linfield 2, Coleraine 1
1982–83	Glentoran 1:2, Linfield 1:1
1983–84	Ballymena U 4, Carrick Rangers 1
1984–85	Glentoran 1:1, Linfield 1:0
1985–86	Glentoran 2, Coleraine 1
1986–87	Glentoran 1, Larne 0
1987–88	Glentoran 1, Glenavon 0
1988–89	Ballymena U 1, Larne 0
1989–90	Glentoran 3, Portadown 0
1990–91	Portadown 2, Glenavon 1
1991–92	Glenavon 2, Linfield 1
1992–93	Bangor 1:1:1, Ards 1:1:0
1993–94	Linfield 2, Bangor 0
1994–95	Linfield 3, Carrick Rangers 1
1995–96	Glentoran 1, Glenavon 0
1996–97	Glenavon 1, Cliftonville 0
1997–98	Glentoran 1, Glenavon 0
1998–99	*Portadown awarded trophy after Cliftonville were eliminated for using an ineligible player in semi-final.*
1999–2000	Glentoran 1, Portadown 0
2000–01	Glentoran 1, Linfield 0
2001–02	Linfield 2, Portadown 1
2002–03	Coleraine 1, Glentoran 0
2003–04	Glentoran 1, Coleraine 0
2004–05	Portadown 5, Larne 1
2005–06	Linfield 2, Glentoran 1
2006–07	Linfield 2, Dungannon Swifts 2 *(aet; Linfield won 3-2 on penalties).*
2007–08	Linfield 2, Coleraine 1
2008–09	Crusaders 1, Cliftonville 0

CREST WEAR COUNTY ANTRIM SHIELD

COUNTY ANTRIM SHIELD FINAL

(at Windsor Park, 5 November 2008)

Linfield 1 *(Miskimmin 79)*

Cliftonville 2 *(Scannell C 64, Murphy 67 (pen))* 2625

Linfield: Addis; Burns, Murphy (Patterson 94), Bailie, Harkness (Miskimmin 77), Carvill, McAreavey (Mulgrew 61), Curran, O'Kane, Munster (Hagan 65), Ferguson.

Cliftonville: Connolly; Holland B, Donaghy, O'Hara, Scannell R, Holland M, McMullan (Catney 40), O'Connor, Murphy, Hamill (O'Neill 82), Scannell C.

Referee: D. Malcolm (Bangor).

ULSTER CUP WINNERS

1949 Linfield	1962 Linfield	1975 Coleraine	1988 Glentoran	2001 *No competition*
1950 Larne	1963 Crusaders	1976 Glentoran	1989 Glentoran	2002 *No competition*
1951 Glentoran	1964 Linfield	1977 Linfield	1990 Portadown	2003 Dungannon Swifts
1952 *No competition*	1965 Coleraine	1978 Linfield	1991 Bangor	*(Confined to*
1953 Glentoran	1966 Glentoran	1979 Linfield	1992 Linfield	*First Division clubs)*
1954 Crusaders	1967 Linfield	1980 Ballymena U	1993 Crusaders	2004 *No competition*
1955 Glenavon	1968 Coleraine	1981 Glentoran	1994 Bangor	2005 *No competition*
1956 Linfield	1969 Coleraine	1982 Glentoran	1995 Portadown	2006 *No competition*
1957 Linfield	1970 Linfield	1983 Glentoran	1996 Portadown	2007 *No competition*
1958 Distillery	1971 Linfield	1984 Linfield	1997 Coleraine	2008 *No competition*
1959 Glenavon	1972 Coleraine	1985 Coleraine	1998 Ballyclare Comrades	2009 *No competition*
1960 Linfield	1973 Ards	1986 Coleraine	1999 Distillery	
1961 Ballymena U	1974 Linfield	1987 Larne	2000 *No competition*	

ROLL OF HONOUR SEASON 2008–09

Competition	*Winner*	*Runner-up*
JJB Sports Premier Division	Glentoran	Linfield
Ladbrokes.Com Championship	Portadown	Donegal Celtic
JJB Sports Irish Cup	Crusaders	Cliftonville
Co-Operative Insurance Cup	Portadown	Newry City
Steel & Sons Cup	Ards	Carrick Rangers
WKD Intermediate Cup	Knockbreda	Donegal Celtic
Coca-Cola Irish Junior Cup	Immaculata	Enniskillen Town
Mid Ulster Cup	Dungannon Swifts	Loughgall
Northwest Senior Cup	Institute	Limavady
The Harry Cavan Youth Cup	Ballymena United III	Linfield Rangers
George Wilson Memorial Cup	Linfield Swifts	Cliftonville Olympic
Irish League Youth Cup	Linfield Rangers	Ballymoney U Colts
County Antrim Junior Shield	Immaculata	Ballyvea Rec
Irish League Interim Cup	H&W Welders	Dundela

AWARDS

ULSTER FOOTBALLER OF THE YEAR
(Castlereagh Glentoran Supporters Award)
Chris Scannell *(Cliftonville)*

NORTHERN IRELAND PLAYER OF THE YEAR
(Football Writers Association)
Chris Scannell *(Cliftonville)*

YOUNG PLAYER
Martin Donnelly *(Crusaders)*

MANAGER OF THE YEAR
Alan McDonald *(Glentoran)*

OUTSTANDING NON SENIOR TEAM
Knockbreda

INTERNATIONAL PERSONALITY
Jonny Evans *(Manchester United)*

SUNDAY LIFE LEADING SCORER
Premier Division
Chris Scannell *(Cliftonville)*   27

TEAM OF THE YEAR
Matthews *(Lisburn Distillery)*
McKeown *(Crusaders)*
Coates *(Crusaders)*
Magowan *(Crusaders)*
R Scannell *(Cliftonville)*
Carson *(Coleraine)*
McCabe *(Glentoran)*
Mulgrew *(Linfield)*
Donnelly *(Crusaders)*
C Scannell *(Cliftonville)*
Allen *(Lisburn Distillery)*

HARP LAGER PLAYER OF THE MONTH

Month	*Player*	*Team*
September	Mark Dickinson	Crusaders
October	Tommy McCallion	Coleraine
November	Martin Donnelly	Crusaders
December	Phillip Matthews	Lisburn Distillery
January	Mark Holland	Cliftonville
February	Stephen Carson	Coleraine
March	Chris Scannell	Cliftonville
April	Colin Nixon	Glentoran

HARP LAGER MANAGER OF THE MONTH

Month	*Player*	*Team*
September	Alan McDonald	Glentoran
October	Alan McDonald	Glentoran
November	Stephen McBride	Glenavon
December	Roy Walker	Ballymena United
January	David Jeffrey	Linfield
February	David Platt	Coleraine
March	Stephen Baxter	Crusaders
April	Alan McDonald	Glentoran

CHAMPIONS LEAGUE REVIEW 2008–09

History was not repeated for the Champions League final in Rome on 27 May, but how Chelsea and indeed Guus Hiddink must have rued using the wrong tactics in the semi-final when they had Barcelona at their mercy leading against ten men. So Manchester United was left with the task of retaining their title won a year previously in Moscow against the Blues.

One doubts whether Barcelona had a more difficult task than the one presented by Chelsea whose rearguard action in the Catalan city gave the return match at the Bridge a real edge to it.

But to the final and United opened the more confident to dominate proceedings in the opening ten minutes. The nearest to taking the lead came from Cristiano Ronaldo. It was not his best such effort, but it produced a spill from the Barcelona goalkeeper Victor Valdes. Unfortunately the follow-up was not accurate.

In their first real attempt at an attack Barcelona took the lead. Samuel Eto'o cut inside and with just a glimpse of an opening in front of goal stabbed at the ball which went in off Erwin Van der Sar's hand inside his near post. That was enough to stabilise the Catalans and they started to take control. Although it was twenty minutes from time before they added to the score, the goal exposed the Manchester United marking. Xavi Hernandez found Lionel Messi with a pin-point lofted diagonal which the diminutive forward despatched with a twisting header which caught the goalkeeper off his line.

If Manchester United were to fail at the last hurdle, Scotland's Rangers fell in the second qualifying round beaten by Kaunas. Meanwhile Barcelona had started in the third such stage beating Wisla Krakow 4-0. Liverpool managed a draw at Standard Liege and Arsenal beat Steve McClaren's Twente in Holland 2-0. Barca did lose to a goal in Poland but Arsenal scored four in the second leg. Standard pushed Liverpool to extra time.

At the group stage Chelsea finished second to Roma in Group A, Barcelona just ahead of Sporting Lisbon in Group C, Liverpool undefeated in Group D as were Manchester United in Group E though drawing four of their games in the process. Celtic had a wretched time of it, too, bottom with their sole win achieved when they were already eliminated. Panathinaikos surprisingly led Internazionale in Group B, Bayern Munich edged Lyon out of top place in Group F as did Porto ahead of Arsenal in Group G. Group H had Juventus and Real Madrid level.

Knock-out stage and a Robin Van Persie penalty gave Arsenal a 1-0 lead over Roma, while United drew away to Internazionale and Chelsea completed an Italian hat trick of ties by taking a slender lead of their own against Juventus. Liverpool pulled off an excellent win in Spain against Real Madrid and Bayern signalled their intention scoring five in Lisbon against Sporting.

The Germans did even better at home in a 7-1 win, Liverpool hit Real for four and Barcelona were 5-2 winners over Lyon. United early in each half had two goals better than Internazionale but Arsenal had to win a shoot-out against Roma. Chelsea earned a draw in Italy.

Quarter-final time and a formidable eight remaining teams, four of them English but not favoured with the draw as Chelsea were paired with Liverpool. Manchester United were held 2-2 at Old Trafford by Porto, but Arsenal managed to finish level at Villarreal. Barcelona put on their best to hit Bayern for four goals, but the shock came at Anfield where Chelsea were worth the 3-1 scoreline.

In Munich, Barcelona drew their second leg but Liverpool gave everything at Chelsea and almost pulled it off before ending a classic 4-4. The Gunners were three goals better than Villarreal at the Emirates and an early Ronaldo goal in Portugal saw Manchester United through. United proved themselves too good for Arsenal winning 1-0 at home, 3-1 in London. Sadly it was to herald their swansong.

Chelsea's Branislav Ivanovic (2) concedes a penalty by fouling Liverpool's Xabi Alonso (grounded) during the epic Champions League quarter-final second leg at Stamford Bridge. A see-saw match eventually ended 4-4 seeing Chelsea through 7-5 on aggregate. (Action Images/John Sibley)

EUROPEAN CUP FINALS

EUROPEAN CUP FINALS 1956–1992

Year	Winners	Runners-up	Venue	Attendance	Referee
1956	Real Madrid 4	Reims 3	Paris	38,000	Ellis (E)
1957	Real Madrid 2	Fiorentina 0	Madrid	124,000	Horn (Ho)
1958	Real Madrid 3	AC Milan 2 *(aet)*	Brussels	67,000	Alsteen (Bel)
1959	Real Madrid 2	Reims 0	Stuttgart	80,000	Dutsch (WG)
1960	Real Madrid 7	Eintracht Frankfurt 3	Glasgow	135,000	Mowat (S)
1961	Benfica 3	Barcelona 2	Berne	28,000	Dienst (Sw)
1962	Benfica 5	Real Madrid 3	Amsterdam	65,000	Horn (Ho)
1963	AC Milan 2	Benfica 1	Wembley	45,000	Holland (E)
1964	Internazionale 3	Real Madrid 1	Vienna	74,000	Stoll (A)
1965	Internazionale 1	Benfica 0	Milan	80,000	Dienst (Sw)
1966	Real Madrid 2	Partizan Belgrade 1	Brussels	55,000	Kreitlein (WG)
1967	Celtic 2	Internazionale 1	Lisbon	56,000	Tschenscher (WG)
1968	Manchester U 4	Benfica 1 *(aet)*	Wembley	100,000	Lo Bello (I)
1969	AC Milan 4	Ajax 1	Madrid	50,000	Ortiz (Sp)
1970	Feyenoord 2	Celtic 1 *(aet)*	Milan	50,000	Lo Bello (I)
1971	Ajax 2	Panathinaikos 0	Wembley	90,000	Taylor (E)
1972	Ajax 2	Internazionale 0	Rotterdam	67,000	Helies (F)
1973	Ajax 1	Juventus 0	Belgrade	93,500	Guglovic (Y)
1974	Bayern Munich 1	Atletico Madrid 1	Brussels	49,000	Loraux (Bel)
Replay	Bayern Munich 4	Atletico Madrid 0	Brussels	23,000	Delcourt (Bel)
1975	Bayern Munich 2	Leeds U 0	Paris	50,000	Kitabdjian (F)
1976	Bayern Munich 1	St Etienne 0	Glasgow	54,864	Palotai (H)
1977	Liverpool 3	Moenchengladbach 1	Rome	57,000	Wurtz (F)
1978	Liverpool 1	FC Brugge 0	Wembley	92,000	Corver (Ho)
1979	Nottingham F 1	Malmo 0	Munich	57,500	Linemayr (A)
1980	Nottingham F 1	Hamburg 0	Madrid	50,000	Garrido (P)
1981	Liverpool 1	Real Madrid 0	Paris	48,360	Palotai (H)
1982	Aston Villa 1	Bayern Munich 0	Rotterdam	46,000	Konrath (F)
1983	Hamburg 1	Juventus 0	Athens	80,000	Rainea (R)
1984	Liverpool 1	Roma 1	Rome	69,693	Fredriksson (Se)
	(aet; Liverpool won 4-2 on penalties)				
1985	Juventus 1	Liverpool 0	Brussels	58,000	Daina (Sw)
1986	Steaua Bucharest 0	Barcelona 0	Seville	70,000	Vautrot (F)
	(aet; Steaua won 2-0 on penalties)				
1987	Porto 2	Bayern Munich 1	Vienna	59,000	Ponnet (Bel)
1988	PSV Eindhoven 0	Benfica 0	Stuttgart	70,000	Agnolin (I)
	(aet; PSV won 6-5 on penalties)				
1989	AC Milan 4	Steaua Bucharest 0	Barcelona	97,000	Tritschler (WG)
1990	AC Milan 1	Benfica 0	Vienna	57,500	Kohl (A)
1991	Red Star Belgrade 0	Marseille 0	Bari	56,000	Lanese (I)
	(aet; Red Star won 5-3 on penalties)				
1992	Barcelona 1	Sampdoria 0 *(aet)*	Wembley	70,827	Schmidhuber (G)

UEFA CHAMPIONS LEAGUE FINALS 1993–2009

Year	Winners	Runners-up	Venue	Attendance	Referee
1993	Marseille* 1	AC Milan 0	Munich	64,400	Rothlisberger (Sw)
1994	AC Milan 4	Barcelona 0	Athens	70,000	Don (E)
1995	Ajax 1	AC Milan 0	Vienna	49,730	Craciunescu (R)
1996	Juventus 1	Ajax 1	Rome	67,000	Vega (Sp)
	(aet; Juventus won 4-2 on penalties)				
1997	Borussia Dortmund 3	Juventus 1	Munich	59,000	Puhl (H)
1998	Real Madrid 1	Juventus 0	Amsterdam	47,500	Krug (G)
1999	Manchester U 2	Bayern Munich 1	Barcelona	90,000	Collina (I)
2000	Real Madrid 3	Valencia 0	Paris	78,759	Braschi (I)
2001	Bayern Munich 1	Valencia 1	Milan	71,500	Jol (Ho)
	(aet; Bayern Munich won 5-4 on penalties)				
2002	Real Madrid 2	Leverkusen 1	Glasgow	52,000	Meier (Sw)
2003	AC Milan 0	Juventus 0	Manchester	63,215	Merk (G)
	(aet; AC Milan won 3-2 on penalties)				
2004	Porto 3	Monaco 0	Gelsenkirchen	52,000	Nielsen (D)
2005	Liverpool 3	AC Milan 3	Istanbul	65,000	González (Sp)
	(aet; Liverpool won 3-2 on penalties)				
2006	Barcelona 2	Arsenal 1	Paris	79,500	Hauge (N)
2007	AC Milan 2	Liverpool 1	Athens	74,000	Fandel (G)
2008	Manchester U 1	Chelsea 1	Moscow	69,552	Michel (Slo)
	(aet; Manchester U won 6-5 on penalties)				
2009	Barcelona 2	Manchester U 0	Rome	62,467	Busacca (Sw)

Subsequently stripped of title.

UEFA CHAMPIONS LEAGUE 2008-09

■ *Denotes player sent off.*

FIRST QUALIFYING ROUND FIRST LEG

Tuesday, 15 July 2008

Anorthosis (0) 1 *(Frousos 71 (pen))*
Pyunik (0) 0   6685
Anorthosis: Beqaj; Katsavakis, Nicolaou (Laban 80), Leiwakabessy, Ocokoljic, Constantinou, Dobrasinovic, Skopelitis, Sosin, Tsitaishvili (Tiquinho 55), Bardon (Frousos 65).
Pyunik: Meliksetian; Khachatrian, Hovespian, Yedigarian (Chilingarian 76), Dokhoyan, Andrikian, Mkrtchian, Ghazarian, Sahakian, Mikhitarian (Petrosian 80), Gharabaghtsian (Yuspashian 53).

BATE Borisov (0) 2 *(Bliznyuk 73, 78)*
Valur (0) 0   5200
BATE Borisov: Veremko; Sosnovsky, Khagush, Rzhevskiy, Yurevich, Likhtarovich, Krivets (Sivakov 85), Zhavnerchik, Stasevich (Nekhaychik 83), Bliznyuk, Rodionov (Skavysh 90).
Valur: Sturluson; Smith, Thorarinsson, Marteinsson, Eriksson, Bett, Adalsteinsson (Hafsteinsson 75), Carlsen, Benediktsson (Vilhjalmsson 79), Hansen, Sigurdsson (Ingason 88).

Dinamo Tirana (0) 0
Modrica (0) 2 *(Miljkovic 65, Stokic 79)*   2200
Dinamo Tirana: Bertoya; Sina, Palladino, Pisha, Kaushi (Ferraj 59), Gonzalez, Poci, Allmuca, Diop, Campozano (Sefa 53), Xhafaj.
Modrica: Hadzidulbic; Vasiljevic, Jolovic, Vasic, Cosic, Bogicevic, Zafirovic (Bojic 83), Stokic, Miljkovic (Joksimovic 89), Savic (Zivkovic 90), Ristanic.

F91 Dudelange (0) 0
Domzale (0) 1 *(Benko 47)*   1313
F91 Dudelange: Joubert; Mouny, Bigard (Da Mota 71), Franceschi, Guthleber, Louadj (Walter 71), Bellini (Gruszczynski 71), Remy, Hug, Ronny, Coquelet.
Domzale: Nemec; Aljancic, Hanzic, Knezovic, Elsner, Kirm, Zinko, Kavusevic (Semler 46), Brezic, Benko (Zec 90), Zatkovic (Pokorn 74).

Inter Baku (0) 0
Rabotnicki (0) 0   8000
Inter Baku: Simeonov; Abbasov, Levin, Ismailov, Gurbanov (Shishkin 67), Imamaliev (Mammadov A 73), Cervenka, Zlatinov, Mammadov E (Huseynov 90), Petrovic, Guglielmone.
Rabotnicki: Kmetovski; Lazarevski, Krstevski, Babatunde, Itoua, Osmani (Nuhiji 85), Mihajlovic, Velkovski (Ljamcevski 77), Muarem (Ristevski 50), Aksentiev, Iluoski.

Llanelli (1) 1 *(Jones S 12)*
Ventspils (0) 0   942
Llanelli: Roberts; Corbisiero, Jones S, Jones M (Holland 66), Thomas, Mumford, Jones C (Pritchard 55), Legg, Evans (Williams 71), Bowen, Griffiths.
Ventspils: Vanins; Savcenkovs, Cilinsek, Dubenskiy, Zangaryeev, Kacanovs, Menteshashvili (Butriks 65), Zizilevs (Rugins 86), Tigirlas, Rimkus, Kolesnicenko (Kosmacovs 72).

Murata (0) 0
IFK Gothenberg (3) 5 *(Soder 20, Alexandersson N 27, Wernbloom 32, Jonsson 57, Selakovic 88)*   1868
Murata: Scalabrelli; Fretta, Aldair, Valentini, Vitaioli (Bollini G 46), D'Orsi, Teodorani, Pari, Vannoni (Bollini F 60), Protti, Manuel Marani (Di Giuli 67).
IFK Gothenberg: Christensen; Bjarsmyr, Johansson, Jonsson (Eriksson 77), Sigurdsson, Hysen, Olsson, Alexandersson N (Selakovic 61), Svensson, Wernbloom, Soder (Wallerstedt 53).

Santa Coloma (0) 1 *(Alvarez 58 (pen))*
Kaunas (3) 4 *(Pilibaitis 12, 41 (pen), Gaucho 28, 79)*   444
Santa Coloma: Ricardo Fernandez; Juli Fernandez, Albanell, Alex Rodriguez (Victor Rodriguez 46), Antunes, Ayala, Maicon, Alvarez (Juli Sanchez 69), Sonejee, Urbani N, Urbani M (Jimenez 71).
Kaunas: Kello; Radzius, Mrowiec, Kancelskis, Manchkhava, Zelmikas, Baguzis, Pilibaitis (Zubavicius 73), Luksa (Valskis 67), Grigalevicius (Mamic 76), Gaucho.

Tampere United (1) 2 *(Niemi 24, James 51 (pen))*
Buducnost (0) 1 *(Beciraj 88)*   5113
Tampere United: Kaven; Lindstrom, Myntti, Jarvinen, Ojanpera, Kujala, James (Savolainen 86), Pohja, Saarinen, Rafinha (Petrescu 64), Niemi.
Buducnost: Vujadinovic; Vukcevic N, Rajovic (Vukovic I 79), Kabarkapa, Giuliano, Ajkovic, Vukcevic P, Lopez (Sekulic 52), Vukovic N, Zec (Delic 32), Beciraj.

Valletta (0) 0
Artmedia (0) 2 *(Cisovsky 73, 79)*   1080
Valletta: Hogg; Grioli, Dimech, Bezzina, Mifsud, Camilleri (Agius E 65), Pace (Mattocks 83), Falzon (Frendo 77), Giglio, Agius G, Zammit.
Artmedia: Kamenar; Dosoudil, Salata, Cisovsky, Szabo, Anderson, Fodrek (Mraz 83), Kozak, Durica (Obzera 78), Piroska (Cleber 66), Pospech.

Wednesday, 16 July 2008

Aktobe (0) 1 *(Smakov 47 (pen))*
Serif (0) 0   12,500
Aktobe: Morev; Badlo, Smakov, Kenzhisariev, Mitrofanov (Lavrik 64), Khayrullin, Golovskoy, Asanbaev (Bogomolov 77), Logvinenko, Khokhlov, Strukov.
Serif: Namasco; Testimitanu (Erokhin 54), Tarkhnishvili, Eninful, Corneencov, Balima (Gorodetchi 90), Rouamba, Arbanas, Rodriguez, Kuchuk, Alexeev (Radu 78).

Dinamo Tbilisi (3) 3 *(Kashia G 7, Gvelesiani 10, Odikadze 30 (pen))*
Runavik (0) 0   1423
Dinamo Tbilisi: Ovono Ebang; Intsckirveli, Kashia G, Nergadze, Kashia S, Khmaladze (Tomashvili 81), Merebashvili (Phirtskhalava 53), Gvelesiani, Odikadze, Digmelashvili, Akieremy (Vatsadze 53).
Runavik: Thomsen■; Hansen O, Davidsen, Hansen ET, Dalbud (Justinussen 86), Pandurevic, Pejcic (Jacobsen S 81), Stankovic, Elttor, Lokin, Potemkin (Jacobsen S 46).

Drogheda United (0) 2 *(Cahill 50, Kudozovic 68)*
Levadia (1) 1 *(Kink 23)*   2135
Drogheda United: Connor; Kendrick, Gartland, Maher, Robinson, Hughes, Baker, Byrne, Keegan (Zayed 51), Cahill, Kudozovic.
Levadia: Kaalma; Kalimullin, Sisov, Lemsalu, Nahk, Malov, Petrenka (Marmor 82), Puri (Leitan 67), Teniste, Kink, Andrejev (Zelinski 90).

Linfield (0) 0
Dinamo Zagreb (1) 2 *(Mandzukic 19, Morales 90)*   2900
Linfield: Mannus; Douglas, Murphy, Bailie, Lindsay (Burns 73), Gault, Hagan, McAreavey (Thompson 76), O'Kane, Mulgrew, Downey.
Dinamo Zagreb: Butina; Carlos, Vrdoljak, Drpic, Etto, Chago (Badelj 57), Mikic (Sammir 46), Biscan, Morales, Balaban (Tadic 78), Mandzukic.

FIRST QUALIFYING ROUND, SECOND LEG

Tuesday, 22 July 2008

Kaunas (2) 3 *(Pilibaitis 16, 90, Zelmikas 22)*
Santa Coloma (1) 1 *(Urbani N 33 (pen))*   1000
Kaunas: Kello; Radzius, Mendy (Miklinevicius 46), Kancelskis, Manchkava, Zelmikas, Fridrikas, Pilibaitis, Luksa (Mamic 46), Zubavicius, Grigalevicius (Valskis 70).
Santa Coloma: Ricardo Fernandez; Juli Fernandez, Albanell, Victor Rodriguez, Antunes (Maicon 46), Gil, Ayala, Jimenez■, Sonejee (Aguirre 71), Urbani N (Alvarez 74), Urbani M■.

Rabotnicki (0) 1 *(Velkovski 47)*
Inter Baku (0) 1 *(Cervenka 77)* 4000
Rabotnicki: Kmetovski; Lazarevski, Krstevski▪, Ljamcevski (Muarem 67), Babatunde, Itoua, Osmani, Ristevski, Velkovski, Aksentiev, Iluoski (Nuhiji 71).
Inter Baku: Simeonov; Abbasov, Levin, Ismailov, Gurbanov, Cervenka, Zlatinov (Mammadov A 77), Shishkin (Arnaut 53), Petrovic, Mammadov E (Huseynov 65), Guglielmone▪.

Runavik (1) 1 *(Elttor 16)*
Dinamo Tbilisi (0) 0 310
Runavik: Knudsen; Hansen O, Davidsen, Hansen E, Dalbud (Olsen 83), Pandurevic, Pejcic (Jacobsen S 75), Stankovic, Elttor, Lokin, Potemkin (Jacobsen F 83).
Dinamo Tbilisi: Ovono Ebang; Intskirveli, Kashia G, Nergadze, Kashia S, Khmaladze, Gvelesiani (Jishkariani 90), Phirtskhalava (Krsko 46), Odikadze, Digmelashvili, Vatsadze (Kantaria 80).

Serif (0) 4 *(Kuchuk 65, Alexeev 76, Erokhin 78, Picusceac 90)*
Aktobe (0) 0 5715
Serif: Namasco; Da Costa, Tarkhnishvili, Corneencov, Balima, Rouamba, Arbanas, Rodriguez, Fred (Erokhin 61), Kuchuk (Picusceac 82), Radu (Alexeev 46).
Aktobe: Morev; Badlo, Smakov, Kenzhisariev, Khayrullin, Golovskoy, Asanbaev (Bogomolov 71), Logvinenko, Khokhlov (Mitrofanov 80), Lavrik, Strukov.

Ventspils (2) 4 *(Kosmacovs 28, Rimkus 30, 75, Butriks 69)*
Llanelli (0) 0 2000
Ventspils: Pavlovs; Soleicuks (Bespalovs 84), Savcenkovs, Dubenskiy, Kosmacovs, Zangaryeev, Kacanovs, Menteshashvili, Tigirlas, Rimkus (Tedov 77), Butriks (Rugins 82).
Llanelli: Roberts; Corbisiero, Jones S, Jones M, Thomas, Mumford (Pritchard 62), Holloway (Williams 55), Legg, Evans, Bowen (Jones C 79), Griffiths.

Wednesday, 23 July 2008

Artmedia (1) 1 *(Farkas 33)*
Valletta (0) 0 826
Artmedia: Kamenar; Farkas, Salata, Cisovsky, Burak, Szabo, Anderson (Cleber 68), Fodrek (Urbanek 74), Kozak, Durica, Halenar (Piroska 60).
Valletta: Hogg; Grioli (Camilleri 66), Dimech, Bezzina, Scicluna, Mifsud, Agius E, Pace, Falzon (Magro 85), Giglio (Mattocks 49), Agius G.

Buducnost (0) 1 *(Beciraj 80)*
Tampere United (1) 1 *(Myntti 8)* 7278
Buducnost: Vujadinovic; Vukcevic N, Perisic, Giuliano (Rajovic 30), Ajkovic, Vukcevic P (Vukovic I 21), Vallejo (Milic 53), Lopez, Vukovic N, Sekulic, Beciraj.
Tampere United: Kaven; Lindstrom (Kuoppala 12), Myntti (Hynynen 58), Jarvinen, Ojanpera, Kujala, James, Pohja, Petrescu (Savolainen 77), Saarinen, Rafinha.

Dinamo Zagreb (1) 1 *(Mandzukic 3)*
Linfield (0) 1 *(Gault 53)* 2835
Dinamo Zagreb: Butina; Vrdoljak, Drpic, Etto, Chago (Males 59), Mikic, Badelj, Biscan, Balaban, Mandzukic (Tadic 46), Suarez (Tomic 83).
Linfield: Mannus; Douglas, Murphy, Bailie, Lindsay (Ferguson 59), Gault, Hagan, McAreavey (Kearney 82), O'Kane, Mulgrew, Downey (Miskimmin 86).

Domzale (0) 2 *(Zinko 65, 85)*
F91 Dudelange (0) 0 615
Domzale: Nemec; Aljancic, Hanzic, Knezovic, Elsner, Kirm (Pokorn 88), Juninho, Zinko, Brezic (Sviben 89), Benko, Zatkovic (Cavusevic 76).
F91 Dudelange: Joubert; Mouny, Bigard, Franceschi, Guthleber, Payal (Louadj 72), Remy (Bellini 72), Hug (Nascimento 81), Ronny, Walter, Gruszczynski.

IFK Gothenburg (1) 4 *(Johansson 15, Barkroth 52, 74, Karisik 71)*
Murata (0) 0 3746
IFK Gothenburg: Christensen; Eriksson, Bjarsmyr, Johansson (Barkroth), Jonsson, Lund, Olsson (Hysen), Karisik, Selakovic, Alexandersson D (Soder), Wallerstedt.
Murata: Scalabrelli (Donati 87); Fretta (Albani L 82), D'Orsi, Albani N, Bitaioli, Valentini, Teodorani (Casadei 65), Bollini F, Vannoni, Protti, Manuel Marani.

Levadia (0) 0
Drogheda U (0) 1 *(Gartland 47)* 1500
Levadia: Kaalma; Kalimullin, Sisov (Malov 70), Lemsalu, Leitan (Zelinski 60), Nahk, Petrenka▪, Puri (Marmor 82), Teniste, Kink, Andrejev.
Drogheda U: Ewings; Kendrick, Gartland, Maher, Hughes, Baker, Byrne, Keegan, Cahill, Kudozovic (Ristila 90), Zayed (O'Brien 88).

Modrica (0) 2 *(Zafirovic 89, Bojic 90)*
Dinamo Tirana (0) 1 *(Xhafaj 72)* 957
Modrica: Hadzidulbic; Vasiljevic, Jolovic, Vasic, Cosic, Bogicevic, Zafirovic, Stokic (Bojic 69), Miljkovic (Lukic 88), Savic (Zivkovic 85), Ristanic.
Dinamo Tirana: Kotorri; Sina, Pisha, Ferraj (Capja 84), Granic, Ahmataj, Gonzalez (Caushaj 64), Poci, Allmuca, Diop, Xhafaj.

Pyunik (0) 0
Anorthosis (1) 2 *(Tsitaishvili 29, Frousos 86)* 2500
Pyunik: Meliksetian; Khachatrian, Hovsepian, Yedigarian, Dokhoyan, Andrikian (Tadevosian 85), Mkrtchian, Ghazarian, Sahakian, Mkhitarian (Yuspashian 60), Gharabaghtsian (Petrosian 54).
Anorthosis: Beqaj; Katsavakis, Nicolaou, Leiwakabessy, Ocokoljic, Constantinou, Dobrasinovic, Skopelitis, Sosin (Frousos 72), Tsitaishvili (Laban 51), Bardon (Tiquinho 59).

Valur (0) 0
BATE Borisov (1) 1 *(Stasevich 1)* 548
Valur: Sturluson; Thorarinsson, Marteinsson, Eiriksson, Bett, Vilhjalmsson (Thorolfsson 86), Adalsteinsson, Hafsteinsson, Carlsen, Hansen, Sigurdsson (Ingason 68).
BATE Borisov: Veremko; Sosnovsky, Khagush, Rzhevskiy (Kazantsev 80), Yurevich, Likhtarovich, Krivets, Zhavnerchik, Sivakov, Stasevich (Nekhaychik 74), Rodionov (Skavysh 73).

SECOND QUALIFYING ROUND, FIRST LEG

Tuesday, 29 July 2008

Brann (0) 1 *(Demba-Nyren 87)*
Ventspils (0) 0 5972
Brann: Opdal; Dahl (Huseklepp 62), Hanstveit, Bjarnason, El-Fakiri, Solli (Einarsson 90), Moen, Bakke, Sigurdsson, Karadas, Winters (Demba-Nyren 79).
Ventspils: Vanins; Savcenkovs, Cilinsek (Mihadjuks 86), Dubenskiy, Kosmacovs, Zangaryeev, Kacanovs, Tigirlas, Lazdins (Rugins 46), Kolesnicenko (Dedov 90), Butriks.

Drogheda United (0) 1 *(Hughes 47)*
Dynamo Kiev (1) 2 *(Mikhalik 23, Aliev 86)* 4545
Drogheda United: Ewings; Kendrick, Gartland, Maher, Hughes, Baker (O'Brien 90), Byrne, Keegan (Shelley 70), Cahill, Kudozovic (Barrett 60), Zayed.
Dynamo Kiev: Shovkovsky; Betao, Diakhate, Nesmachniy, Ghioane (Shatskikh 79), Vukojevic, Aliev, Mikhalik, Ninkovic, Bangoura (Kravets 59), Milevsky (El-Kaddouri 89).

Inter Baku (0) 1 *(Zlatinov 84)*
Partizan Belgrade (1) 1 *(Bogunovic 4)* 8500
Inter Baku: Simeonov; Zagorac, Abbasov, Levin, Ismailov, Gurbanov, Belkevich, Zlatinov, Mammadov A, Petrovic, Mammadov E.
Partizan Belgrade: Bozovic D; Djordjevic, Sikimic (Miljkovic 21), Knezevic, Obradovic, Juca, Moreira, Lazic, Paunovic (Ljajic 51), Bogunovic (Cadikovski 86), Lamine.

Wednesday, 30 July 2008

Aalborg (3) 5 *(Johansson 16, Jakobsen 42, Braemer 44, Due 53, Caca 89)*

Modrica (0) 0 6043

Aalborg: Zaza; Jakobsen (Kristensen 65), Pedersen, Olfers, Bogelund (Nielsen 46), Due, Johansson, Augustinussen, Caca, Curth, Braemer.
Modrica: Hadzidulbic; Vasiljevic, Jolovic, Vasic (Zivkovic 83), Cosic, Bogicevic, Zafirovic, Stokic (Bojic 76), Miljkovic, Savic (Popovic 61), Ristanic.

Anderlecht (0) 1 *(Gillet 66)*

BATE Borisov (0) 2 *(Krivets 69 (pen), Nekhaychik 88)* 18,909

Anderlecht: Zitka; Kruiswijk, Juhasz, Wasilewski■, Polak, Chatelle (Legear 63), Goor, Losada (Suarez 82), Gillet, Kanu, Boussoufa.
BATE Borisov: Veremko; Sosnovskiy, Khagush, Rzhevskiy, Yurevich, Likhtarovich (Skavysh 80), Krivets, Zhavnerchik, Sivakov, Stasevich■ (Nekhaychik 58), Rodionov (Viskushenko 90).

Anorthosis (1) 3 *(Skopelitis 35, Sosin 47, 90)*

Rapid Vienna (0) 0 9300

Anorthosis: Beqaj; Katsavakis, Nicolaou (Tiquinho 66), Leiwakabessy, Ocokoljic, Constantinou, Dobrasinovic, Skopelitis, Sosin, Tsitaishvili (Laban 46), Bardon (Samaras 82).
Rapid Vienna: Koch; Tokic, Patocka, Katzer, Dober, Kulovits, Heikkinen, Hofmann, Kavlak, Maierhofer (Jelavic 60), Hoffer (Ketelaer 83).

Beitar Jerusalem (0) 2 *(Baruchian 60, 79)*

Wisla (1) 1 *(Pawel Brozek 29)* 17,900

Beitar Jerusalem: Kale; Alvarez, Benado, Ben Yousef, Ziv, Baruchian, Tal (Zandberg 58), Boateng, Fernandez, Tamuz (Itzhaki 46), Abreu.
Wisla: Pawelek; Baszczynski, Glowacki, Cleber, Sobolewski, Piotr Brozek, Jirsak (Lobodzinski 75), Zienczuk■, Cantoro, Boguski (Dawidowski 84), Pawel Brozek (Niedzielan 81).

Domzale (0) 0

Dinamo Zagreb (3) 3 *(Vrdoljak 11, Sammir 21 (pen), Tadic 40)* 2180

Domzale: Nemec; Aljancic, Hanzic, Knezovic, Elsner, Kirm, Zinko, Cavusevic, Brezic, Benko (Perutovic 63), Zatkovic (Juninho 56).
Dinamo Zagreb: Butina; Vrdoljak, Drpic, Hrgovic, Etto (Guela 60), Sammir (Morales 73), Mikic, Badelj (Chago 78), Biscan, Tadic, Mandzukic.

Fenerbahce (1) 2 *(Roberto Carlos 15, Selcuk 58)*

MTK (0) 0 33,591

Fenerbahce: Volkan; Lugano, Roberto Carlos, Ugur (Gurhan 66), Edu Dracena, Gokhan, Kazim-Richards (Burak 84), Alex, Selcuk, Guiza, Semih (Emre B 76).
MTK: Vegh; Balogh, Horvath, Lambulic, Pollak, Pinter, Patkai (Szabo 46), Nagy, Zsidai, Bori (Hrepka 84), Urban (Pal 56).

IFK Gothenburg (1) 1 *(Olsson 32)*

Basle (1) 1 *(Huggel 26)* 10,914

IFK Gothenburg: Christensen; Bjarsmyr, Johansson, Jonsson, Sigurdsson, Hysen (Eriksson 75), Olsson, Alexandersson N, Svensson, Wernbloom, Soder (Barkroth 83).
Basle: Costanzo; Abraham, Safari, Marque, Zanni, Gjasula, Huggel, Perovic (Stocker 58), Ergic, Carlitos, Derdiyok.

Panathinaikos (2) 3 *(Ivanschitz 17, Salpingidis 45, 74)*

Dinamo Tbilisi (0) 0 50,864

Panathinaikos: Galinovic; Sarriegi, Simao, Vintra, Spyropoulos, Mattos (Gabriel 46), Ninis, Ivanschitz, Nilsson (Christodoulopoulos 46), Salpingidis, Mantzios (Rukavina 79).
Dinamo Tbilisi: Ovono Ebang; Intsckirveli (Tomashvili 25), Kashia G, Krsko, Kashia S, Khmaladze, Gvelesiani, Phirtskhalava, Odikadze, Digmelashvili (Nergadze 66), De Juse (Spasojevic 46).

Rangers (0) 0

Kaunas (0) 0 38,283

Rangers: McGregor; Broadfoot, Papac, Dailly (Novo 46), Weir, Whittaker, Thomson, Adam, Darcheville (Boyd 66), Miller (Velicka 74), McCulloch.
Kaunas: Kello; Radzius, Mrowiec, Mendy, Kancelskis, Zelmikas, Fridrikas, Pilibaitis (Cinikas 83), Luksa, Grigalevicius (Rimkevicius 68), Gaucho (Manchkhava 62).

Serif (0) 0

Sparta Prague (0) 1 *(Kladrubsky 74)* 8300

Serif: Namasco; Da Costa, Tarkhnishvili, Eninful, Mamah, Corneencov, Balima (Radu 88), Rouamba, Arbanas, Kuchuk (Picusceac 86), Alexeev.
Sparta Prague: Kozacik; Repka, Kladrubsky, Kadlec, Kucera, Berger (Vacek 90), Kusnir (Kolar 78), Vorisek, Husek, Slepicka (Holenda 90), Matusovic.

Tampere United (1) 1 *(Niemi 18)*

Artmedia (2) 3 *(Pospech 10, Obzera 19, Piroska 86)* 9228

Tampere United: Kaven; Kuoppala, Myntti, Jarvinen, Ojanpera, Kujala, James (Savolainen 82), Pohja, Saarinen, Rafinha (Hjelm 71), Niemi.
Artmedia: Kamenar; Farkas, Salata, Cisovsky, Urbanek, Velicky, Obzera (Anderson 61), Fodrek, Kozak, Halenar (Piroska 75), Pospech (Oravec 85).

SECOND QUALIFYING ROUND, SECOND LEG

Tuesday, 5 August 2008

Kaunas (1) 2 *(Radzius 43, Pilibaitis 87)*

Rangers (1) 1 *(Thomson 33)* 5250

Kaunas: Kello; Radzius, Mrowiec, Mendy, Manchkhava, Zelmikas, Baguzis (Grigalevicius 67), Pilibaitis, Luksa (Mamic 77), Rafael (Zubavicius 89), Cinikas.
Rangers: McGregor; Broadfoot, Papac, Dailly, Weir, Thomson, Whittaker, McCulloch, Novo (Boyd 88), Miller (Lafferty 89), Adam (Velicka 66).

Ventspils (2) 2 *(Menteshashvili 6, Rimkus 44)*

Brann (0) 1 *(Bjornsson 49)* 2000

Ventspils: Vanins; Savcenkovs, Cilinsek, Dubenskiy, Kosmacovs, Zangaryeev, Kacanovs, Menteshashvili■, Tigirlas (Zizilevs 84), Rimkus, Butriks.
Brann: Opdal; Dahl (Huseklepp 79), Guntveit, Hanstveit, Bjarnason, El-Fakiri (Bjornsson 46), Moen, Bakke, Karadas, Demba-Nyren (Jaiteh 46), Winters.

Wednesday, 6 August 2008

Artmedia (3) 4 *(Kozak 9 (pen), Pospech 35, Halenar 45, Piroska 78)*

Tampere United (0) 2 *(James 72 (pen), Hjelm 79)* 1981

Artmedia: Kamenar; Farkas, Salata, Cisovsky (Obzera 46), Urbanek, Velicky (Cleber 68), Anderson, Kozak, Halenar, Piroska, Pospech (Oravec 60).
Tampere United: Kaven; Lindstrom, Kuoppala (Savolainen 46), Myntti, Aho, Jarvinen, Kujala, James, Pohja, Rafinha (Hjelm 46), Niemi.

BATE Borisov (2) 3 *(Bliznyuk 18, Rodionov 83)*

Anderlecht (1) 2 *(Biglia 22 (pen), Polak 87)* 5400

BATE Borisov: Veremko; Sosnovskiy, Khagush, Rzhevskiy, Yurevich, Likhtarovich, Krivets, Nekhaychik, Zhavnerchik (Skavysh 89), Bliznyuk (Ermakovich 38), Rodionov.
Anderlecht: Zitka; Deschacht, Juhasz, Rnic■, Biglia, Polak, Goor, Gillet, Vlcek (Chatelle 60), Kanu (Suarez 53), Boussoufa.

Basle (1) 4 *(Huggel 27, Chipperfield 71, Ergic 84, 90)*

IFK Gothenburg (1) 2 *(Wernbloom 18, Soder 52)* 18,846

Basle: Costanzo; Abraham, Safari, Marque, Zanni, Gjasula (Chipperfield 61), Huggel, Stocker (Perovic 79), Ergic, Carlitos, Derdiyok.
IFK Gothenburg: Christensen; Eriksson, Bjarsmyr, Johansson, Jonsson, Sigurdsson, Hysen (Selakovic 72), Olsson (Svensson 79), Alexandersson N, Wernbloom, Soder (Alexandersson D 74).

Dinamo Tbilisi (0) 0
Panathinaikos (0) 0   4200
Dinamo Tbilisi: Ovono Ebang; Tomashvili, Kashia G,
Krsko, Nergadze (De Juse 67), Khmaladze, Gvelesiani
(Jishkariani 77), Phirtskhalava■, Odikadze, Spasojevic
(Vatsadze 65), Akieremy.
Panathinaikos: Galinovic; Goumas, Simao, Vintra,
Spyropoulos, Mattos, Ninis (Gilberto Silva 50), Nilsson,
Salpingidis, Christodoulopoulos (Karagounis 73),
Mantzios (Rukavina 33).

Dinamo Zagreb (1) 3 *(Biscan 17, Hrgovic 50, Drpic 84)*
Domzale (1) 2 *(Brezic 30, Zec 81)*   4280
Dinamo Zagreb: Kelava; Vrdoljak, Drpic, Hrgovic, Etto,
Sammir, Mikic (Guela 65), Badelj, Biscan (Lovren 73),
Balaban (Tomic 46), Tadic.
Domzale: Nemec; Aljancic (Zec 74), Knezovic (Hanzic
79), Elsner, Kirm, Apatic, Juninho, Zinko, Cavusevic
(Semler 63), Brezic, Perutovic.

Dynamo Kiev (1) 2 *(Aliev 13, Milevski 72 (pen))*
Drogheda United (1) 2 *(Robinson 42, Gartland 88)* 11,400
Dynamo Kiev: Lutsenko; Betao, Diakhate, Ghioane,
Vukojevic, Aliev, Mikhalik, El-Kaddouri, Ninkovic
(Morozyuk 83), Bangoura (Milevski 46), Kravets
(Shatskikh 79).
Drogheda United: Ewings; Kendrick, Gartland, Shelley,
Robinson, Hughes, Baker (Kudozovic 77), Byrne,
Keegan, Cahill, Zayed (Thiam 77).

MTK (0) 0
Fenerbahce (1) 5 *(Semih 5, 61, 79, 81, Emre B 67)* 2048
MTK: Vegh; Balogh, Horvath, Lambulic, Pollak, Pinter,
Nagy, Zsidai, Bori, Pal (Kulcsar 71), Urban.
Fenerbahce: Volkan; Lugano, Roberto Carlos, Edu
Dracena, Ugur, Gokhan, Kazim-Richards (Emre B 65),
Alex (Burak 65), Selcuk, Guiza (Parlak 75), Semih.

Modrica (0) 1 *(Bojic 72)*
Aalborg (1) 2 *(Due 12, Risgard 62)*   270
Modrica: Hadzidulbic; Vasiljevic, Jolovic, Vasic, Cosic,
Bogicevic, Stokic, Miljkovic (Joksimovic 76), Savic
(Ristanic 71), Popovic (Lukic 66), Bojic.
Aalborg: Zaza; Jakobsen, Pedersen, Olfers, Bogelund
(Beauchamp 68), Due (Enevoldsen 66), Johansson
(Braemer 75), Augustinussen, Caca, Risgard, Curth.

Partizan Belgrade (0) 2 *(Juca 61, Lamine 83)*
Inter Baku (0) 0   19,221
Partizan Belgrade: Bozovic D; Stevanovic, Djordjevic,
Knezevic, Obradovic, Juca (Ljajic 86), Moreira, Lazic,
Paunovic (Petrovic 80), Bogunovic (Marinkovic 71),
Lamine.
Inter Baku: Simeonov; Rahimov, Zagorac (Abbasov 65),
Levin, Ismailov, Gurbanov, Imamaliev, Zlatinov
(Shishkin 78), Mammadov A, Petrovic, Mammadov E
(Huseynov 46).

Rapid Vienna (1) 3 *(Hoffer 22, Maierhofer 63, 67)*
Anorthosis (1) 1 *(Laban 13)*   16,720
Rapid Vienna: Koch; Tokic, Patocka, Katzer, Dober
(Thonhofer 34), Heikkinen, Hofmann, Kavlak (Jelavic
66), Boskovic (Drazan 57), Maierhofer, Hoffer.
Anorthosis: Beqaj; Katsavakis, Leiwakabessy (Nicolaou
46), Ocokoljic, Constantinou, Dellas (Tiquinho 58),
Dobrasinovic, Skopelitis, Laban, Sosin, Bardon (Samaras
46).

Sparta Prague (1) 2 *(Vorisek 45, Slepicka 49)*
Serif (0) 0   11,479
Sparta Prague: Kozacik; Repka, Kladrubsky, Kucera,
Berger (Vacek 85), Kusnir, Vorisek, Husek, Slepicka
(Holenda 80), Kadlec, Kulic (Kolar 63).
Serif: Namasco; Da Costa, Tarkhnishvili, Mamah,
Corneencov, Balima, Erokhin (Fred 71), Rouamba
(Nadson 80), Arbanas, Alexeev, Picusceac■ (Kuchuk 52).

Wisla (3) 5 *(Cantoro 9, Cleber 25 (pen), Pawel Brozek 36,*
Diaz 57, Niedzielan 87)
Beitar Jerusalem (0) 0   9500
Wisla: Pawelek; Baszczynski, Diaz, Cleber, Sobolewski,
Piotr Brozek, Jirsak (Niedzielan 67), Cantoro,
Lobodzinski (Malecki 71), Boguski (Dawidowski 78),
Pawel Brozek.
Beitar Jerusalem: Kale; Alvarez, Benado, Ben Yousef,
Ziv, Baruchian, Tal (Tamuz 60), Zandberg (Fernandez
46), Boateng, Abreu, Ohayon (Itzhaki 46).

THIRD QUALIFYING ROUND, FIRST LEG

Tuesday, 12 August 2008

Fiorentina (1) 2 *(Mutu 3, Gilardino 57)*
Slavia Prague (0) 0   32,146
Fiorentina: Frey; Kroldrup, Dainelli, Vargas (Almiron
64), Zauri, Gobbi, Kuzmanovic, Santana, Melo, Mutu
(Osvaldo 76), Gilardino (Pazzini 76).
Slavia Prague: Vaniak; Brabec, Hubacek, Suchy, Selassie
(Belaid 53), Tavares, Latka, Janda (Krajcik 73), Jarolim
(Necid 60), Svento, Senkerik.

Wednesday, 13 August 2008

Aalborg (0) 2 *(Caca 71, Curth 86)*
Kaunas (0) 0   6310
Aalborg: Zaza; Jakobsen, Pedersen, Olfers, Bogelund,
Johansson, Augustinussen, Risgard, Enevoldsen (Due
72), Saganowski (Caca 69), Curth.
Kaunas: Kello; Radzius, Mrowiec, Mendy, Manchkhava,
Baguzis, Fridrikas (Zubavicius 80), Pilibaitis, Luksa
(Rafael 46), Grigalevicius (Mamic 65), Cinikas.

Anorthosis (2) 3 *(Torosidis 5 (og), Sosin 19, Laban 87)*
Olympiakos (0) 0   9000
Anorthosis: Beqaj; Katsavakis, Nicolaou (Paulo Costa
47), Leiwakabessy (Samaras 65), Ocokoljic, Dellas,
Dobrasinovic, Skopelitis, Laban, Sosin, Bardon
(Constantinou 64).
Olympiakos: Nikopolidis (Kovac 47); Patsatzoglou,
Leonardo, Zewlakow, Torosidis, Stoltidis, Galletti, Oscar
(Mitroglou 57), Djordjevic (Leto 74), Papadopoulos,
Kovacevic.

Barcelona (2) 4 *(Eto'o 17, 83, Xavi 24, Henry 49)*
Wisla (0) 0   56,786
Barcelona: Victor Valdes; Marquez, Puyol, Dani Alves
(Pique 76), Abidal, Xavi, Iniesta, Keita, Eto'o, Henry
(Hleb 84), Pedrito (Toure Yaya 61).
Wisla: Pawelek; Baszczynski, Diaz, Cleber, Sobolewski,
Piotr Brozek, Jirsak (Kmiecik 46), Cantoro, Lobodzinski
(Rado 84), Boguski (Niedzielan 67), Pawel Brozek.

Brann (0) 0
Marseille (1) 1 *(Cheyrou 40)*   11,197
Brann: Opdal; Saevarsson (Moen 71), Dahl, Hanstveit,
Bjarnason, El-Fakiri, Huseklepp, Bakke (Jaiteh 54),
Sigurdsson, Karadas, Demba-Nyren (Winters 76).
Marseille: Mandanda; Taiwo, Hilton, Zubar, Bonnart,
Cheyrou, Cana (Kabore 47), Ben Arfa, M'Bami, Niang
(Cisse 79), Kone.

Galatasaray (1) 2 *(Nonda 18, 47)*
Steaua (2) 2 *(Moreno 4, Nicolita 12)*   19,636
Galatasaray: Aykut; Emre G (Sabri 67), Fernando Meira,
Emre A, Hakan Balta, Servet, Lincoln, Hasan Sas
(Erhan 78), Mehmet T (Baris 46), Arda, Nonda.
Steaua: Zapata; Goian, Golanski (Nesu 74), Radoi,
Marin, Petre (Neaga 61), Moreno, Toja, Nicolita, Lovin
(Tiago 81), Arthuro.

Guimaraes (0) 0
Basle (0) 0   21,452
Guimaraes: Nilson; Luciano Amaral, Arnolin,
Andrezinho, Fajardo (Jean Coral 61), Moreno,
Desmarets, Flavio Meireles, Joao Alves, Marquinho
(Carlitos 46), Douglas (Roberto 76).
Basle: Costanzo; Abraham, Safari, Marque, Zanni,
Gelabert, Huggel, Stocker (Perovic 71), Ergic, Carlitos
(Rubio 87), Derdiyok (Mustafi 80).

Juventus (3) 4 *(Camoranesi 7, Del Piero 26, Chiellini 39, Legrottaglie 90)*
Artmedia (0) 0 23,102
Juventus: Buffon; Chiellini, Grygera (Iaquinta 16), Molinaro, Legrottaglie, Salihamidzic, Camoranesi, Poulsen, Sissoko, Del Piero (Amauri 73), Trezeguet.
Artmedia: Kamenar; Salata, Cisovsky, Urbanek, Velicky, Anderson, Fodrek, Kozak, Halenar (Cleber 69), Piroska (Obzera 46), Pospech (Oravec 83).

Levski (0) 0
BATE Borisov (0) 1 *(Rzhevskiy 60)* 16,294
Levski: Petkov; Milanov, Rabeh, Vagner, Tiberkanin (Ze Soares 46), Ivanov M (Tasevski 57), Bystron, Ivanov G, Hristov, Dimitrov, Krastovchev (Jean Carlos 66).
BATE Borisov: Veremko; Khagush, Kazantsev, Rzhevskiy, Yurevich, Likhtarovich (Skavysh 89), Krivets, Sivakov, Stasevich (Zhavnerchik 59), Bliznyuk (Nekhaychik 73), Rodionov.

Partizan Belgrade (2) 2 *(Paunovic 11, Bogunovic 14)*
Fenerbahce (1) 2 *(Alex 45 (pen), Guiza 50)* 22,274
Partizan Belgrade: Bozovic D; Stevanovic, Djordjevic, Sikimic, Knezevic, Obradovic, Lazic (Cadikovski 88), Petrovic (Maletic 72), Paunovic, Bogunovic (Marinkovic 78), Lamine.
Fenerbahce: Volkan; Lugano, Roberto Carlos, Edu Dracena, Ugur (Maldonado 84), Gokhan, Kazim-Richards (Burak 55), Alex, Selcuk, Guiza, Semih (Emre B 61).

Schalke (1) 1 *(Pander 30)*
Atletico Madrid (0) 0 54,142
Schalke: Schober; Westermann, Bordon, Howedes, Pander, Ernst, Rakatic (Asamoah 79), Jones, Engelaar, Farfan (Halil Altintop 70), Kuranyi.
Atletico Madrid: Leo Franco; Antonio Lopez[■], Heitinga, Ujfalusi, Perea, Raul Garcia, Maxi Rodriguez, Paulo Assuncao, Simao (Pernia 85), Forlan, Sinama-Pongolle (Luis Garcia 67).

Shakhtar Donetsk (2) 2 *(Srna 3, Jadson 31)*
Dinamo Zagreb (0) 0 24,810
Shakhtar Donetsk: Pyatov; Hubschman, Kucher, Rat, Chigrinskiy, Fernandinho, Jadson, Willian (Duljaj 55), Srna, Gladkiy (Moreno 71), Brandao.
Dinamo Zagreb: Kelava; Vrdoljak, Drpic, Hrgovic, Etto, Sammir (Morales 69), Mikic, Badelj, Biscan (Lovren 29), Tadic, Mandzukic.

Sparta Prague (1) 1 *(Kulic 30)*
Panathinaikos (1) 2 *(Kucera 24 (og), Simao 60)* 14,478
Sparta Prague: Kozacik; Repka, Kladrubsky (Zeman 84), Kucera, Kadlec (Kolar 67), Berger, Kusnir, Vorisek, Husek, Slepicka, Kulic (Holenda 72).
Panathinaikos: Galinovic; Sarriegi, Gabriel, Simao, Vintra, Spyropoulos, Gilberto Silva, Karagounis (Ivanschitz 90), Tziolis (Ninis 57), Souza, Salpingidis (Nilsson 69).

Spartak Moscow (1) 1 *(Bazhenov 4)*
Dynamo Kiev (2) 4 *(Bangura 28, 46, Milevsky 45, 85)* 32,600
Spartak Moscow: Pletikosa; Stranzl (Filipenko 49), Fathi, Jiranek, Kovac, Shishkin, Mozart, Bystrov, Parshivlyuk (Maidana 60), Pavlyuchenko (Dzyuba 74), Bazhenov.
Dynamo Kiev: Shovkovskiy; Betao, Diakhate, Nesmachny, Vukojevic, Aliev (Ghioane 76), Mikhalik, El-Kaddouri, Ninkovic, Bangoura (Kravets 88), Milevsky (Morozyuk 90).

Standard Liege (0) 0
Liverpool (0) 0 26,000
Standard Liege: Aragon; Bonfim, Mikulic (Nicaise 90), Camozzato, Sarr, Dalmat, Defour, Fellaini, Witsel, Mbokani, De Camargo.
Liverpool: Reina; Arbeloa, Dossena, Xabi Alonso, Carragher, Agger, Kuyt (El Zhar 83), Plessis, Torres, Keane (Gerrard 67), Benayoun.

Twente (0) 0
Arsenal (0) 2 *(Gallas 63, Adebayor 82)* 26,000
Twente: Boschker; Wielaert, Braafheid, Douglas, Brama, Wilkshire, Tiote, Janssen (Heubach 90), Denneboom, Elia (Huysegems 86), Arnautovic (Gerritsen 90).
Arsenal: Almunia; Sagna, Clichy, Denilson, Djourou, Gallas, Eboue, Ramsey, Adebayor, Van Persie (Bendtner 88), Walcott (Randall 84).

THIRD QUALIFYING ROUND, SECOND LEG

Tuesday, 26 August 2008

Artmedia (1) 1 *(Fodrek 14)*
Juventus (1) 1 *(Amauri 25)* 13,451
Artmedia: Kamenar; Farkas, Salata, Cisovsky, Burak, Velicky, Obzera (Piroska 66), Anderson (Halenar 85), Fodrek, Kozak, Pospech (Cleber 80).
Juventus: Buffon; Mellberg, Grygera, Molinaro, Legrottaglie (Ariaudo 84), Nedved (Giovinco 72), Camoranesi (Sissoko 71), Poulsen, Marchisio, Amauri, Iaquinta.

Panathinaikos (0) 1 *(Souza 90)*
Sparta Prague (0) 0 59,659
Panathinaikos: Galinovic; Sarriegi, Simao, Vintra, Spyropoulos, Cleyton (Ninis 66), Gilberto Silva, Karagounis, Nilsson, Souza, Salpingidis (Gabriel 81).
Sparta Prague: Kozacik; Repka, Kladrubsky, Kucera, Kadlec, Berger, Kusnir (Zeman 61), Vorisek, Vacek (Dosek 46), Slepicka, Kulic (Holenda 77).

Wisla (0) 1 *(Cleber 52)*
Barcelona (0) 0 12,000
Wisla: Pawelek; Singlar, Baszczynski, Diaz, Cleber, Piotr Brozek, Jirsak, Zienczuk (Dawidowski 90), Lobodzinski (Malecki 82), Boguski (Niedzielan 68), Pawel Brozek.
Barcelona: Victor Valdes; Pique, Puyol, Dani Alves, Abidal, Xavi (Gudjohnsen 57), Iniesta (Hleb 66), Keita, Toure Yaya, Eto'o (Bojan 75), Henry.

Wednesday, 27 August 2008

Arsenal (1) 4 *(Nasri 27, Gallas 52, Walcott 66, Bendtner 89)*
Twente (0) 0 59,583
Arsenal: Almunia; Sagna, Clichy, Denilson, Djourou, Gallas, Nasri (Eboue 46), Fabregas (Song Billong 68), Bendtner, Van Persie (Adebayor 65), Walcott.
Twente: Michailov; Wielaert, Braafheid (Rajkovic 87), Heubach (Wellenberg 46), Douglas, Brama, Tiote, Janssen, Denneboom, Huysegems, Elia.

Atletico Madrid (1) 4 *(Aguero 18, Forlan 51, Luis Garcia 83, Maxi Rodgriguez 86 (pen))*
Schalke (0) 0 47,321
Atletico Madrid: Leo Franco; Pernia, Heitinga, Ujfalusi, Perea, Raul Garcia, Maxi Rodriguez, Maniche (Paulo Assuncao 73), Simao, Forlan (Luis Garcia 71), Aguero (Sinama Pongolle 86).
Schalke: Schober; Westermann, Bordon, Howedes, Pander[■], Kobiashvili (Rafinha 65), Ernst, Rakatic (Krstajic 90), Jones (Asamoah 78), Halil Altintop, Kuranyi.

Basle (1) 2 *(Stocker 11, Derdiyok 54)*
Guimaraes (1) 1 *(Fajardo 15 (pen))* 30,002
Basle: Costanzo; Abraham, Safari, Marque, Zanni, Gelabert (Chipperfield 64), Huggel, Stocker, Ergic (Ferati 89), Carlitos, Derdiyok.
Guimaraes: Nilson; Amaral, Arnolin, Andrezinho, Fajardo (Roberto 70), Moreno, Desmarets, Flavio Meireles, Joao Alves (Jean Coral 62), Marquinho (Luis Filipe 56), Douglas.

BATE Borisov (1) 1 *(Sosnovskiy 14)*
Levski (1) 1 *(Gadzhev 38)* 5603
BATE Borisov: Gutor; Sosnovskiy, Khagush, Rzhevskiy, Yurevich, Likhtarovich (Volodko 56), Krivets (Zhavnerchik 84), Sivakov (Nekhaychik 84), Stasevich, Bliznyuk[■], Rodionov.
Levski: Kish; Rabeh, Vagner (Minev 62), Ivanov M (Tiberkanin 67), Bystron, Gadzhev, Ivanov G (Jean Carlos 73), Hristov, Ze Soares, Dimitrov.

Dinamo Zagreb (0) 1 *(Balaban 57)*
Shakhtar Donetsk (1) 3 *(Luiz Adriano 42, Brandao 59, Willian 70)*   13,655
Dinamo Zagreb: Kelava; Vrdoljak, Drpic, Hrgovic, Sammir, Mikic (Lovren 46), Badelj (Chago 35), Biscan, Morales (Ibanez 67), Balaban, Mandzukic.
Shakhtar Donetsk: Pyatov; Hubschman (Ishchenko 71), Kucher, Shevchuk, Chigrinskiy, Duljaj, Fernandinho (Jadson 72), Willian, Srna, Luiz Adriano (Moreno 61), Brandao.

Dynamo Kiev (2) 4 *(Yussuf 4, Bangoura 24, Milevsky 49, 78)*
Spartak Moscow (0) 1 *(Dzyuba 47)*   14,000
Dynamo Kiev: Bogush; Betao, Diakhate, Vukojevic, Aliev (Moroziuk 81), Mikhalik, El-Kaddouri, Ninkovic (Ghioane 72), Yussuf, Bangoura (Kravets 78), Milevsky.
Spartak Moscow: Pletikosa; Jiranek (Dedura 61), Kovac, Shishkin, Ivanov, Filipenko, Mozart, Maidana (Saenko 46), Bystrov, Bazhenov (Pavlenko 37), Dzyuba.

Fenerbahce (1) 2 *(Semih 28, Alex 58)*
Partizan Belgrade (0) 1 *(Tosic 76)*   36,765
Fenerbahce: Volkan; Lugano, Roberto Carlos, Yasin (Baris 88), Ugur (Gurhan 61), Gokhan, Kazim-Richards, Alex, Maldonado, Guiza, Semih (Onder Turaci 71).
Partizan Belgrade: Bozovic D; Stevanovic, Djordjevic, Knezevic, Obradovic, Fejsa (Lazic 73), Juca, Moreira, Tosic, Paunovic (Bogunovic 58), Lamine.

Kaunas (0) 0
Aalborg (0) 2 *(Risgard 75, 90)*   3000
Kaunas: Dreer; Radzius, Mrowiec (Miklinevicius 80), Mendy, Manchkhava, Zelmikas, Baguzis, Pilibaitis■, Luksa (Zubavicius 65), Grigalevicius■, Rimkevicius (Valskis 65).
Aalborg: Zaza; Jakobsen, Pedersen, Olfers, Bogelund, Johansson, Augutinussen, Risgard, Enevoldsen (Due 85), Saganowski (Caca 73), Curth.

Liverpool (0) 1 *(Kuyt 118)*
Standard Liege (0) 0   43,889
Liverpool: Reina; Arbeloa, Fabio Aurelio, Xabi Alonso, Carragher, Skrtel, Kuyt, Gerrard, Torres (Plessis 120), Keane (El Zhar 83), Benayoun (Babel 61).

Standard Liege: Aragon; Bonfim, Onyewu, Camozzato, Sarr, Dalmat (Jovanovic 86), Defour (Nicaise 118), Fellaini, Witsel, Mbokani, De Camargo (Toama 101). *aet.*

Marseille (0) 2 *(Niang 65, 90)*
Brann (0) 1 *(Sigurdsson 74)*   44,641
Marseille: Mandanda; Taiwo, Hilton, Zubar, Bonnart, Ziani (Zenden 78), Cana (Cheyrou 82), Ben Arfa, M'Bami, Niang, Grandin (Kone 78).
Brann: Opdal; Dahl, Hanstveit, Bjarnason, El Fakiri, Einarsson (Jaiteh 64), Solli, Huseklepp, Sigurdsson, Karadas (Bjornsson 90), Demba-Nyren (Saevarsson 67).

Olympiakos (0) 1 *(Belluschi 54)*
Anorthosis (0) 0   27,922
Olympiakos: Nikopolidis; Leonardo, Antzas (Patsatzoglou 69), Torosidis, Stoltidis, Galletti, Cearense (Mitroglou 46), Papadopoulos, Leto (Dordevic 63), Belluschi, Kovacevic.
Anorthosis: Beqaj; Katsavakis, Leiwakabessy, Ocokoljic, Constantinou, Dellas, Dobrasinovic, Paulo Costa (Nicolaou 72), Laban, Sosin (Samaras 82), Bardon (Tiquinho 58).

Slavia Prague (0) 0
Fiorentina (0) 0   14,943
Slavia Prague: Vaniak; Brabec, Siklic, Suchy, Tavares, Janda (Svento 46), Krajcik, Belaid, Cerny (Jarolim 71), Toleski (Senkerik 46), Necid.
Fiorentina: Frey; Dainelli, Gamberini, Vargas, Zauri, Gobbi, Kuzmanovic (Donadel 63), Santana, Melo, Osvaldo (Jovetic 71), Gilardino (Pazzini 79).

Steaua (0) 1 *(Nicolita 57)*
Galatasaray (0) 0   22,850
Steaua: Zapata; Goian, Radoi, Nesu, Marin, Petre (Baciu 86), Moreno, Toja (Ghionea 65), Nicolita, Lovin, Arthuro (Stancu 77).
Galatasaray: Aykut; Fernando Meira, Hakan Balta, Servet, Linderoth (Aydin 77), Lincoln (Hasan Sas 70), Mehmet T, Ayhan (Umit K 55), Kewell, Arda, Nonda.

GROUP STAGE

GROUP A

Tuesday, 16 September 2008

Chelsea (2) 4 *(Lampard 14, Cole J 30, Malouda 82, Anelka 90)*
Bordeaux (0) 0   39,635
Chelsea: Cech; Bosingwa, Cole A, Mikel, Terry, Ricardo Carvalho, Deco (Ballack 61), Lampard, Anelka, Cole J (Belletti 74), Malouda (Kalou 84).
Bordeaux: Rame; Jurietti, Placente, Diawara, Planus, Diarra, Fernando (Ducasse 74), Gourcuff, Wendel, Gouffran (Cavenaghi 66), Chamakh (Obertan 66).

Roma (1) 1 *(Panucci 16)*
Cluj (1) 2 *(Culio 27, 49)*   25,382
Roma: Doni; Panucci (Loria 47), Cicinho, Cassetti, Aquilani, Taddei (Montella 77), De Rossi, Riise (Totti 52), Julio Baptista, Tonetto, Vucinic.
Cluj: Stancioiu; Hugo Alcantara, Muresan, Cadu, Galiassi, Trica (Peralta 67), Culio, Dani, Pereira, Dubarbier (Panin 89), Kone Y.

Wednesday, 1 October 2008

Bordeaux (1) 1 *(Gourcuff 18)*
Roma (0) 3 *(Vucinic 64, Julio Baptista 71, 83)*   26,920
Bordeaux: Valverde; Henrique■, Jurietti (Gouffran 78), Diawara, Chalme, Diarra, Fernando, Gourcuff, Jussie (Wendel 37), Obertan (Planus 40), Chamakh.
Roma: Doni; Panucci, Cicinho, Mexes, Aquilani (Chuka Okaka 63), Taddei, De Rossi, Riise, Perrotta, Vucinic (Brighi 84), Menez (Julio Baptista 51).

Cluj (0) 0
Chelsea (0) 0   20,320
Cluj: Stancioiu; Hugo Alcantara, Muresan, Cadu, Galiassi, Trica (Didi 89), Culio, Dani, Pereira, Dubarbier, Kone Y.
Chelsea: Cech; Bosingwa, Bridge, Mikel, Terry, Alex, Ballack, Lampard, Drogba (Belletti 58), Kalou (Anelka 46), Malouda (Di Santo 74).

Wednesday, 22 October 2008

Bordeaux (0) 1 *(Cadu 53 (og))*
Cluj (0) 0   26,213
Bordeaux: Rame; Jurietti, Diawara, Chalme, Planus, Diarra, Fernando, Gourcuff, Bellion (Wendel 61), Obertan (Gouffran 61), Chamakh.
Cluj: Stancioiu; Hugo Alcantara, Muresan, Cadu, Galiassi, Peralta, Trica■, Culio, Pereira, Dubarbier (Didi 75), Kone Y (Kone E 86).

Chelsea (0) 1 *(Terry 77)*
Roma (0) 0   41,002
Chelsea: Cech; Bosingwa, Bridge, Mikel, Terry, Ricardo Carvalho, Deco, Lampard, Anelka (Paulo Ferreira 90), Kalou (Di Santo 77), Malouda (Belletti 46).
Roma: Doni; Panucci, Cicinho, Mexes, Aquilani (Perrotta 61), Taddei (Menez 81), De Rossi, Riise (Tonetto 82), Brighi, Vucinic, Totti.

Tuesday, 4 November 2008

Cluj (1) 1 *(Dani 9)*
Bordeaux (2) 2 *(Gourcuff 6, Wendel 38)*   19,380
Cluj: Stancioiu; Hugo Alcantara (Panin 64), Muresan, Cadu, Galiassi (Deac 78), Peralta (Kone E 68), Culio, Dani, Pereira, Dubarbier, Kone Y.
Bordeaux: Valverde; Jurietti, Diawara, Chalme, Planus, Diarra, Fernando, Gourcuff, Wendel (Bellion 77), Gouffran (Obertan 77), Chamakh.

Roma (1) 3 *(Panucci 34, Vucinic 48, 58)*
Chelsea (0) 1 *(Terry 75)*   35,038
Roma: Doni; Panucci, Cicinho, Juan, Mexes, Pizarro, De Rossi, Perrotta (Taddei 72), Brighi, Vucinic (Riise 88), Totti (Julio Baptista 62).
Chelsea: Cech; Bosingwa (Kalou 63), Bridge, Mikel, Terry, Alex, Deco▪, Lampard, Anelka, Cole J (Drogba 46), Malouda (Belletti 46).

Wednesday, 26 November 2008

Bordeaux (0) 1 *(Diarra 82)*
Chelsea (0) 1 *(Anelka 59)*   32,486
Bordeaux: Valverde; Jurietti, Diawara, Chalme, Planus, Diarra, Fernando, Gourcuff, Wendel (Obertan 75), Gouffran (Cavenaghi 67), Chamakh.
Chelsea: Cech; Bosingwa, Cole A, Mikel, Terry, Ivanovic, Ballack, Lampard▪, Anelka (Drogba 63), Cole J (Paulo Ferreira 85), Malouda.

Cluj (1) 1 *(Kone Y 30)*
Roma (2) 3 *(Brighi 11, 64, Totti 23)*   19,292
Cluj: Stancioiu; Panin, Muresan, Cadu, Galiassi, Trica (Deac 84), Culio, Dani (Peralta 72), Pereira, Dubarbier (Kone E 70), Kone Y.
Roma: Doni; Juan, Mexes, Cassetti, Taddei, De Rossi, Julio Baptista, Perrotta (Pizarro 90), Tonetto (Riise 86), Brighi, Totti (Vucinic 81).

Tuesday, 9 December 2008

Chelsea (1) 2 *(Kalou 39, Drogba 71)*
Cluj (0) 1 *(Kone Y 54)*   41,060
Chelsea: Cech; Bosingwa, Cole A, Mikel (Bridge 76), Terry, Alex, Deco, Kalou (Drogba 64), Anelka, Cole J (Belletti 74), Ballack.
Cluj: Nuno Claro; Panin, Muresan, Hugo Alcantara, Cadu, Trica (Peralta 72), Culio, Dani, Pereira, Dubarbier (Kone E 61), Kone Y.

Roma (0) 2 *(Brighi 61, Totti 79)*
Bordeaux (0) 0   38,926
Roma: Doni; Panucci, Juan, Mexes, Riise, De Rossi, Julio Baptista, Perrotta (Pizarro 89), Brighi, Totti (Vucinic 87), Menez (Cicinho 80).
Bordeaux: Rame; Jurietti, Diawara, Chalme, Planus, Diarra, Fernando, Gourcuff, Wendel (Jussie 69), Gouffran (Cavenaghi 58), Chamakh (Bellion 69).

Group A Final Table

	P	W	D	L	F	A	Pts
Roma	6	4	0	2	12	6	12
Chelsea	6	3	2	1	9	5	11
Bordeaux	6	2	1	3	5	11	7
Cluj	6	1	1	4	5	9	4

GROUP B

Tuesday, 16 September 2008

Panathinaikos (0) 0
Internazionale (1) 2 *(Mancini 26, Adriano 85)*   58,378
Panathinaikos: Galinovic; Goumas, Simao, Vintra, Moon (Souza 82), Mattos, Cleyton, Gilberto Silva, Karagounis (Ivanschitz 36), Nilsson (Christodoulopous 72), Salpingidis.
Internazionale: Julio Cesar; Cordoba, Zanetti, Maxwell, Maicon, Materazzi, Vieira (Ali Muntari 63), Cambiasso, Mancini (Adriano 82), Quaresma (Figo 62), Ibrahimovic.

Werder Bremen (0) 0
Anorthosis (0) 0   34,690
Werder Bremen: Wiese; Boenisch, Naldo, Fritz, Mertesacker, Diego, Ozil, Jensen, Frings, Rosenberg (Sanogo 57), Pizarro (Hugo Almeida 65).
Anorthosis: Beqaj; Katsavakis, Nicolaou, Leiwakabessy, Constantinou, Dellas, Paulo Costa (Hawar 46), Savio, Laban, Sosin (Panagi 58), Bardon (Tsitaishvili 70).

Wednesday, 1 October 2008

Anorthosis (2) 3 *(Sarriegi 11 (og), Dobrasinovic 15, Hawar 78)*
Panathinaikos (1) 1 *(Salpingidis 28 (pen))*   19,259
Anorthosis: Beqaj; Katsavakis, Nicolaou, Leiwakabessy, Constantinou, Dellas, Dobrasinovic, Paulo Costa (Bardon 46), Savio (Panagi 82), Laban, Sosin (Hawar 64).
Panathinaikos: Galinovic; Sarriegi, Goumas, Vintra, Spyropoulos, Moon (Souza 67), Mattos, Cleyton, Gilberto Silva (Tziolis 87), Salpingidis, Christodoulopoulos (Ivanschitz 72).

Internazionale (1) 1 *(Maicon 13)*
Werder Bremen (0) 1 *(Pizarro 62)*   32,965
Internazionale: Julio Cesar; Cordoba, Zanetti, Maicon, Materazzi (Burdisso 19), Stankovic (Quaresma 72), Cambiasso, Ali Muntari, Ibrahimovic, Adriano (Cruz 78), Balotelli.
Werder Bremen: Wiese; Pasanen, Naldo, Baumann, Prodl (Fritz 86), Mertesacker, Diego, Ozil (Jensen 82), Frings, Rosenberg (Hunt 77), Pizarro.

Wednesday, 22 October 2008

Internazionale (1) 1 *(Adriano 43)*
Anorthosis (0) 0   27,247
Internazionale: Toldo; Cordoba, Zanetti, Maicon, Chivu, Stankovic, Cambiasso (Burdisso 83), Ali Muntari, Mancini (Quaresma 63), Ibrahimovic, Adriano (Cruz 83).
Anorthosis: Beqaj; Katsavakis, Leiwakabessy, Ocokoljic, Constantinou, Dellas, Dobrasinovic (Frousos 89), Savio, Laban, Sosin (Hawar 46), Bardon (Tsitaishvili 75).

Panathinaikos (1) 2 *(Mantzios 36, 68)*
Werder Bremen (1) 2 *(Mertesacker 20, Hugo Almeida 23)*   54,089
Panathinaikos: Tzorvas; Sarriegi, Gabriel, Simao, Vintra, Spyropoulos (Ivanschitz 46), Gilberto Silva, Karagounis (Cleyton 72), Nilsson, Salpingidis, Mantzios (Rukavina 82).
Werder Bremen: Vander; Pasanen (Boenisch 80), Naldo, Baumann, Prodl, Mertesacker, Diego, Ozil, Frings, Hugo Almeida (Sanogo 90), Pizarro (Rosenberg 26).

Tuesday, 4 November 2008

Anorthosis (2) 3 *(Bardon 30, Panagi 45, Frousos 49)*
Internazionale (2) 3 *(Balotelli 13, Materazzi 44, Cruz 80)*   17,140
Anorthosis: Beqaj; Katsavakis, Leiwakabessy, Constantinou, Georgiou, Dobrasinovic, Paul Costa (Panagi 43), Hawar, Laban, Frousos (Skopelitis 65), Bardon (Ocokoljic 78).
Internazionale: Julio Cesar; Zanetti, Maicon, Burdisso (Vieira 57), Materazzi, Stankovic (Cruz 57), Cambiasso, Mancini (Maxwell 58), Quaresma, Ibrahimovic, Balotelli.

Werder Bremen (0) 0
Panathinaikos (0) 3 *(Mantzios 58, Karagounis 70, Tziolis 83)*   35,968
Werder Bremen: Wiese; Pasanen, Naldo, Baumann, Prodl (Fritz 46) (Sanogo 68), Mertesacker, Vranjes (Hunt 64), Diego, Ozil, Rosenberg, Pizarro.
Panathinaikos: Galinovic; Sarriegi, Gabriel (Moon 75), Simao, Vintra, Spyropoulos, Gilberto Silva, Karagounis (Goumas 79), Tziolis, Nilsson, Mantzios (Salpingidis 88).

Wednesday, 26 November 2008

Anorthosis (0) 2 *(Nicolaou 62, Savio 68)*
Werder Bremen (0) 2 *(Diego 71 (pen), Hugo Almeida 88)*
                                                18,461
Anorthosis: Nagy; Katsavakis, Leiwakabessy, Ocokoljic (Frousos 56), Constantinou, Dellas, Dobrasinovic, Skopelitis (Nicolaou 46), Savio (Panagi 71), Hawar, Laban.
Werder Bremen: Vander; Naldo, Tosic, Baumann (Hunt 59), Fritz (Boenisch 76), Mertesacker, Diego, Ozil, Frings, Hugo Almeida, Pizarro (Rosenberg 79).

Internazionale (0) 0
Panathinaikos (0) 1 *(Sarriegi 68)*   34,955
Internazionale: Julio Cesar; Cordoba, Zanetti, Maxwell (Cruz 75), Maicon, Materazzi, Figo (Balotelli 73), Cambiasso, Ali Muntari (Quaresma 46), Ibrahimovic, Adriano.
Panathinaikos: Galinovic; Sarriegi, Goumas, Gabriel (Tziolis 84), Simao, Vintra, Spyropoulos, Gilberto Silva, Karagounis (Salpingidis 63), Nilsson, Mantzios (Rukavina 90).

Tuesday, 9 December 2008

Panathinaikos (0) 1 *(Karagounis 69)*
Anorthosis (0) 0   59,872
Panathinaikos: Galinovic; Sarriegi, Goumas, Simao, Vintra, Spyropoulos, Cleyton (Salpingidis 65), Gilberto Silva, Karagounis (Ivanschitz 90), Tziolis, Mantzios (Rukavina 82).
Anorthosis: Beqaj (Nagy 46); Katsavakis, Nicolaou, Leiwakabessy, Constantinou, Dellas (Frousos 46), Dobrasinovic, Skopelitis, Hawar (Paulo Costa 70), Laban, Bardon.

Werder Bremen (0) 2 *(Pizarro 63, Rosenberg 81)*
Internazionale (0) 1 *(Ibrahimovic 88)*   35,000
Werder Bremen: Wiese; Boenisch, Fritz, Prodl, Mertesacker, Vranjes (Niemeyer 89), Ozil (Jensen 90), Frings, Rosenberg, Hunt, Pizarro.
Internazionale: Julio Cesar; Cordoba, Zanetti, Maicon, Burdisso, Materazzi (Maxwell 46), Cambiasso, Ali Muntari (Balotelli 71), Mancini, Quaresma, Adriano (Ibrahimovic 46).

Group B Final Table	P	W	D	L	F	A	Pts
Panathinaikos	6	3	1	2	8	7	10
Internazionale	6	2	2	2	8	7	8
Werder Bremen	6	1	4	1	7	9	7
Anorthosis	6	1	3	2	8	8	6

GROUP C

Tuesday, 16 September 2008

Barcelona (1) 3 *(Marquez 21, Eto'o 60 (pen), Xavi 87)*
Sporting Lisbon (0) 1 *(Tonel 72)*   58,354
Barcelona: Victor Valdes; Pique, Marquez, Puyol (Sylvinho 88), Dani Alves, Xavi, Iniesta, Keita, Eto'o (Toure Yaya 66), Messi, Henry (Pedrito 75).
Sporting Lisbon: Rui Patricio; Polga, Caneira (Pereirinha 79), Tonel, Abel, Izmailov, Rochemback, Joao Moutinho, Romagnoli (Miguel Veloso 65), Derlei, Yannick Djalo (Helder Postiga 62).

Basle (0) 1 *(Abraham 90)*
Shakhtar Donetsk (2) 2 *(Fernandinho 25, Jadson 45)*
                                                34,820
Basle: Costanzo; Hodel, Abraham, Marque, Zanni, Gelabert (Rubio 62), Huggel, Chipperfield, Stocker (Eduardo 46), Carlitos, Derdiyok (Mustafi 46).
Shakhtar Donetsk: Pyatov; Hubschman, Kucher, Ilsinho (Willian 65), Shevchuk, Chigrinskiy, Fernandinho (Fedetskiy 81), Jadson, Srna, Luiz Adriano (Seleznov 73), Brandao.

Wednesday, 1 October 2008

Shakhtar Donetsk (1) 1 *(Ilsinho 45)*
Barcelona (0) 2 *(Messi 87, 90)*   25,300
Shakhtar Donetsk: Pyatov; Hubschman, Ilsinho (Willian

86), Shevchuk, Chigrinskiy, Ishchenko, Duljaj (Lewandowski 90), Fernandinho, Srna, Luiz Adriano (Seleznov 72), Brandao.
Barcelona: Victor Valdes; Pique, Marquez, Puyol, Dani Alves, Xavi, Iniesta, Keita (Gudjohnsen 81), Toure Yaya, Eto'o (Bojan 74), Henry (Messi 60).

Sporting Lisbon (0) 2 *(Zanni 55 (og), Derlei 86)*
Basle (0) 0   22,638
Sporting Lisbon: Rui Patricio; Polga, Tonel, Grimi, Abel, Miguel Veloso, Rochemback (Vukcevic 46), Joao Moutinho, Romagnoli (Pereirinha 88), Derlei, Helder Postiga (Yannick Djalo 72).
Basle: Costanzo; Abraham, Safari, Ferati, Zanni, Gelabert (Ergic 60), Gjasula, Huggel, Chipperfield (Perovic 82), Carlitos, Streller (Mustafi 79).

Wednesday, 22 October 2008

Basle (0) 0
Barcelona (3) 5 *(Messi 4, Busquets 14, Bojan 22, 46, Xavi 48)*   37,500
Basle: Costanzo; Abraham, Safari, Marque, Zanni, Huggel, Chipperfield (Gjasula 54), Ergic, Streller (Eduardo 71), Rubio (Stocker 46), Derdiyok.
Barcelona: Victor Valdes; Marquez (Martin Caceres 53), Puyol, Sylvinho, Dani Alves, Xavi (Henry 57), Busquets, Hleb, Toure Yaya (Sanchez 67), Messi, Bojan.

Shakhtar Donetsk (0) 0
Sporting Lisbon (0) 1 *(Liedson 76)*   23,120
Shakhtar Donetsk: Pyatov; Hubschman (Gay 83), Kucher, Rat, Chigrinskiy, Duljaj, Fernandinho, Jadson (Willian 72), Srna, Brandao, Moreno (Gladkiy 72).
Sporting Lisbon: Rui Patricio; Polga, Tonel, Abel, Izmailov (Grimi 74), Miguel Veloso, Rochemback, Joao Moutinho, Romagnoli (Pereirinha 68), Derlei (Helder Postiga 89), Liedson.

Tuesday, 4 November 2008

Barcelona (0) 1 *(Messi 62)*
Basle (0) 1 *(Derdiyok 82)*   49,479
Barcelona: Victor Valdes; Pique, Marquez, Puyol, Sylvinho, Iniesta (Eto'o 67), Hleb, Sanchez (Messi 60), Busquets, Bojan (Xavi 60), Henry.
Basle: Costanzo; Safari, Marque, Ferati, Zanni, Huggel, Perovic (Eduardo 59), Stocker (Gelabert 83), Ergic, Carlitos, Streller (Derdiyok 70).

Sporting Lisbon (0) 1 *(Derlei 73)*
Shakhtar Donetsk (0) 0   24,282
Sporting Lisbon: Rui Patricio; Polga, Caneira, Grimi, Abel, Izmailov (Pereirinha 90), Miguel Veloso, Rochemback, Joao Moutinho, Helder Postiga (Derlei 69), Liedson.
Shakhtar Donetsk: Pyatov; Hubschman (Lewandowski 81), Kucher, Rat, Chigrinskiy, Fernandinho, Jadson (Luiz Adriano 75), Willian, Srna, Brandao, Moreno.

Wednesday, 26 November 2008

Shakhtar Donetsk (1) 5 *(Jadson 33, 65, 73, Willian 50, Seleznov 75)*
Basle (0) 0   15,000
Shakhtar Donetsk: Pyatov; Hubschman, Kucher, Rat, Ishchenko, Fernandinho (Duljaj 73), Jadson, Gay, Willian, Srna (Yezerskiy 77), Luiz Adriano (Seleznov 46).
Basle: Costanzo; Abraham, Safari, Marque, Zanni, Huggel, Stocker, Ergic, Carlitos (Frei 69), Eduardo (Mustafi 65), Derdiyok.

Sporting Lisbon (0) 2 *(Miguel Veloso 65, Liedson 66)*
Barcelona (2) 5 *(Henry 14, Pique 17, Messi 50, Caneira 67 (og), Bojan 73 (pen))*   31,765
Sporting Lisbon: Rui Patricio*; Daniel Carrico, Polga, Caneira, Grimi, Miguel Veloso, Pereirinha, Joao Moutinho, Romagnoli (Derlei 46), Yannick Djalo (Tiago 71), Liedson (Helder Postiga 79).
Barcelona: Victor Valdes; Martin Caceres, Pique, Marquez, Dani Alves, Xavi (Keita 74), Hleb, Busquets, Gudjohnsen, Messi (Pedrito 57), Henry (Bojan 46).

Tuesday, 9 December 2008

Barcelona (0) 2 *(Sylvinho 58, Busquets 83)*

Shakhtar Donetsk (1) 3 *(Gladkiy 31, 57, Fernandinho 75)*
                                       22,763

Barcelona: Jonquera; Martin Caceres, Pique, Sylvinho, Keita, Hleb, Busquets, Sanchez, Vasquez, Bojan, Pedro (Gudjohnsen 77).
Shakhtar Donetsk: Pyatov; Hubschman, Kucher, Rat, Chigrinskiy, Fernandinho (Luiz Adriano 78), Jadson (Brandao 66), Gay, Willian, Srna, Gladkiy.

Basle (0) 0

Sporting Lisbon (1) 1 *(Yannick Djalo 19)*   30,248

Basle: Costanzo; Morganella, Safari, Marque, Ferati, Huggel, Chipperfield (Stocker 46), Frei (Perovic 78), Ergic, Carlitos, Streller (Derdiyok 66).
Sporting Lisbon: Tiago; Daniel Carrico, Polga, Caneira, Izmailov, Vukcevic (Abel 45), Pereirinha (Adrien Silva 46), Rochemback (Miguel Veloso 73), Joao Moutinho, Derlei, Yannick Djalo.

Group C Final Table	P	W	D	L	F	A	Pts
Barcelona	6	4	1	1	18	8	13
Sporting Lisbon	6	4	0	2	8	8	12
Shakhtar Donetsk	6	3	0	3	11	7	9
Basle	6	0	1	5	2	16	1

GROUP D

Tuesday, 16 September 2008

Marseille (1) 1 *(Cana 23)*

Liverpool (2) 2 *(Gerrard 26, 32 (pen))*   44,841

Marseille: Mandanda; Taiwo, Hilton, Zubar, Bonnart, Cheyrou, Cana, Ben Arfa (Ziani 57), M'Bami (Valbuena 41), Niang, Kone (Samassa 75).
Liverpool: Reina; Arbeloa, Dossena, Mascherano, Carragher, Skrtel, Lucas, Gerrard (Benayoun 69), Torres (Riera 65), Kuyt (Keane 86), Babel.

PSV Eindhoven (0) 0

Atletico Madrid (2) 3 *(Aguero 9, 36, Maniche 54)* 29,000

PSV Eindhoven: Isaksson; Salcido, Brechet (Rodriguez 74), Pieters, Marcellis, Simons, Mendez, Culina (Bakkal 46), Afellay (Lazovic 70), Koevermans, Amrabat.
Atletico Madrid: Leo Franco; Antonio Lopez, Heitinga, Ujfalusi, Perea, Luis Garcia, Paulo Assuncao, Maniche (Banega 65), Simao, Forlan (Sinama-Pongolle 31), Aguero (Raul Garcia 63).

Wednesday, 1 October 2008

Atletico Madrid (2) 2 *(Aguero 4, Raul Garcia 22)*

Marseille (1) 1 *(Niang 16)*   39,898

Atletico Madrid: Leo Franco; Pernia, Heitinga, Ujfalusi, Perea, Raul Garcia, Maxi Rodriguez (Banega 81), Paulo Assuncao, Miguel (Luis Garcia 80), Aguero, Sinama-Pongolle (Maniche 66).
Marseille: Mandanda; Taiwo, Hilton, Erbate (Zubar 46), Bonnart, Ziani, Cheyrou, Cana, Ben Arfa (Zenden 51), Valbuena (Kone 76), Niang.

Liverpool (2) 3 *(Kuyt 4, Keane 34, Gerrard 76)*

PSV Eindhoven (0) 1 *(Koevermans 78)*   41,097

Liverpool: Reina; Arbeloa, Fabio Aurelio, Xabi Alonso, Carragher, Skrtel, Kuyt, Gerrard (Babel 81), Torres, Keane (Lucas 75), Riera (Benayoun 68).
PSV Eindhoven: Isaksson; Kromkamp, Salcido, Brechet (Pieters 46), Marcellis, Simons, Mendez (Dzsudzsak 76), Culina, Bakkal, Wuytens (Koevermans 60), Amrabat.

Wednesday, 22 October 2008

Atletico Madrid (0) 1 *(Simeo 83)*

Liverpool (1) 1 *(Keane 15)*   48,769

Atletico Madrid: Leo Franco; Seitaridis, Antonio Lopez, Perea, Dominguez, Luis Garcia (Aguero 46), Maniche, Simao, Camacho (Raul Garcia 73), Forlan, Sinama Pongolle (Miguel 75).
Liverpool: Reina; Arbeloa, Dossena, Xabi Alonso (Lucas 75), Carragher, Agger, Benayoun, Gerrard (Babel 61), Keane (Kuyt 53), Mascherano, Riera.

PSV Eindhoven (0) 2 *(Koevermans 71, 85)*

Marseille (0) 0   29,000

PSV Eindhoven: Isaksson; Salcido, Rodriguez, Brechet, Marcellis, Simons, Mendez, Afellay (Addo 89), Bakkal (Culina 76), Wuytens (Dzsudzsak 78), Koevermans.
Marseille: Mandanda; Taiwo, Hilton, Zubar, Bonnart, Ziani (Kabore 62), Cheyrou (Zenden 82), Cana, Ben Arfa (Valbuena 73), Niang, Kone.

Tuesday, 4 November 2008

Liverpool (0) 1 *(Gerrard 90 (pen))*

Atletico Madrid (1) 1 *(Maxi Rodriguez 37)* 42,010

Liverpool: Reina; Arbeloa, Fabio Aurelio, Xabi Alonso, Carragher, Agger, Mascherano (Lucas 77), Gerrard, Kuyt, Keane (N'Gog 71), Riera (Babel 61).
Atletico Madrid: Leo Franco; Antonio Lopez, Pernia, Heitinga, Perea, Raul Garcia, Maxi Rodriguez, Paulo Assuncao, Maniche, Simao (Luis Garcia 89), Forlan (Aguero 70).

Marseille (1) 3 *(Kone 29, Niang 63, 71)*

PSV Eindhoven (0) 0   48,777

Marseille: Mandanda; Taiwo, Hilton, Bonnart, Ziani, Cheyrou, Cana, Ben Arfa (Kabore 74), M'Bami, Niang (Grandin 86), Kone (Valbuena 82).
PSV Eindhoven: Isaksson; Salcido, Marcellis, Simons, Mendez, Culina, Addo (Kromkamp 66), Afellay (Nijland 78), Bakkal (Dzsudzsak 61), Wuytens, Koevermans.

Wednesday, 26 November 2008

Atletico Madrid (2) 2 *(Simao 14, Maxi Rodriguez 28)*

PSV Eindhoven (0) 1 *(Koevermans 47)*

Atletico Madrid: Coupet; Seitaridis, Pernia, Heitinga (Ibanez 51), Ujfalusi, Raul Garcia (Paulo Assuncao 80), Maxi Rodriguez, Maniche, Simao, Forlan, Aguero (Sinama-Pongolle 66).
PSV Eindhoven: Isaksson; Salcido, Rodriguez, Brechet, Pieters (Culina 46), Simons, Mendez (Nijland 86), Afellay (Bakkal 28), Dzsudzsak, Lazovic, Koevermans.
Behind closed doors.

Liverpool (0) 1 *(Gerrard 22)*

Marseille (0) 0   42,010

Liverpool: Reina; Arbeloa, Fabio Aurelio (Dossena 46), Xabi Alonso, Carragher, Agger, Mascherano, Gerrard, Torres, Kuyt (Lucas 85), Riera (Benayoun 64).
Marseille: Mandanda; Taiwo, Hilton, Zubar, Bonnart (Samassa 89), Ziani, Cheyrou, Cana, Ben Arfa, Niang, Kone (Valbuena 78).

Tuesday, 9 December 2008

Marseille (0) 0

Atletico Madrid (0) 0   49,663

Marseille: Mandanda; Taiwo, Hilton, Zubar, Bonnart, Ziani (Kabore 77), Zenden, Cana, Ben Arfa, Kone (Cheyrou 80), Samassa (Valbuena 29).
Atletico Madrid: Coupet; Seitaridis, Antonio Lopez, Perea, Ibanez, Raul Garcia, Luis Garcia (Miguel 76), Maxi Rodriguez (Maniche 62), Banega, Aguero (Forlan 55), Sinama-Pongolle.

PSV Eindhoven (1) 1 *(Lazovic 35)*

Liverpool (1) 3 *(Babel 45, Riera 68, N'Gog 77)* 33,500

PSV Eindhoven: Isaksson; Salcido, Brechet, Marcellis, Simons, Mendez (Manco 80), Culina, Dzsudzsak, Bakkal (Nijland 83), Lazovic, Amrabat (Koevermans 72).
Liverpool: Cavalieri; Arbeloa (Darby 69), Dossena, Mascherano, Carragher (Kelly 82), Agger, Riera (Spearing 76), Lucas, N'Gog, Keane, Babel.

Group D Final Table	P	W	D	L	F	A	Pts
Liverpool	6	4	2	0	11	5	14
Atletico Madrid	6	3	3	0	9	4	12
Marseille	6	1	1	4	5	7	4
PSV Eindhoven	6	1	0	5	5	14	3

GROUP E

Wednesday, 17 September 2008

Celtic (0) 0
Aalborg (0) 0   58,754
Celtic: Boruc; Hinkel, Naylor, Brown S, Caldwell, McManus, Nakamura, Maloney (Vennegoor 72), McDonald (McGeady 63), Samaras, Robson.
Aalborg: Zaza; Jakobsen, Pedersen, Beauchamp■, Olfers, Johansson, Augustinussen, Risgard, Enevoldsen, Saganowski, Curth (Nielsen 86).

Manchester United (0) 0
Villarreal (0) 0   74,944
Manchester United: Van der Sar; Neville, Evra, Hargreaves (Anderson 62), Evans, Ferdinand, Park (Ronaldo 62), Fletcher, Rooney, Tevez (Giggs 81), Nani.
Villarreal: Diego Lopez; Gonzalo, Edmilson, Godin, Capdevila, Angel, Pires (Ibagaza 67), Cani (Cazorla 46), Matias Fernandez, Eguren, Guille Franco (Llorente 77).

Tuesday, 30 September 2008

Aalborg (0) 0
Manchester United (1) 3 *(Rooney 22, Berbatov 55, 79)*
                                                     10,346
Aalborg: Zaza; Pedersen, Beauchamp (Caca 38), Olfers, Bogelund, Johansson, Augustinussen, Risgard, Enevoldsen, Saganowski, Curth.
Manchester United: Van der Sar; Rafael (Brown 66), Evra, O'Shea, Ferdinand, Vidic, Ronaldo, Scholes (Giggs 16), Berbatov, Rooney (Tevez 59), Nani.

Villarreal (0) 1 *(Senna 67)*
Celtic (0) 0   21,515
Villarreal: Diego Lopez; Gonzalo, Godin, Capdevila, Angel, Pires (Bruno 83), Cazorla (Cani 90), Senna, Eguren, Llorente, Rossi (Ibagaza 77).
Celtic: Boruc; Wilson, Naylor, Hartley (Vennegoor 82), Caldwell, McManus, Nakamura (Robson 74), Brown S, Samaras, Maloney (McDonald 72), McGeady.

Tuesday, 21 October 2008

Manchester United (1) 3 *(Berbatov 30, 51, Rooney 77)*
Celtic (0) 0   74,655
Manchester United: Van der Sar; Neville (Brown 60), O'Shea, Anderson, Evans, Vidic, Ronaldo (Park 82), Fletcher, Berbatov (Tevez 60), Rooney, Nani.
Celtic: Boruc; Wilson, Naylor, Loovens, Caldwell, McManus, Nakamura (Hartley 61), Brown S, McDonald (Sheridan 77), Robson (Maloney 61), McGeady.

Villarreal (2) 6 *(Rossi 27, Capdevila 32, Llorente 66, 69, 83, Pires 78)*
Aalborg (2) 3 *(Saganowski 19, Enevoldsen 35, Johansson 77)*
                                                     15,959
Villarreal: Diego Lopez; Gonzalo, Edmilson (Bruno 65), Capdevila, Angel, Fuentes, Cazorla, Matias Fernandez (Pires 65), Senna, Guille Franco (Llorente 46), Rossi.
Aalborg: Zaza; Jakobsen, Pedersen, Olfers, Bogelund, Due, Johansson, Augustinussen, Enevoldsen, Saganowski, Curth.

Wednesday, 5 November 2008

Aalborg (0) 2 *(Curth 55, Due 81)*
Villarreal (1) 2 *(Rossi 41, Guille Franco 75)* 10,355
Aalborg: Zaza; Jakobsen, Pedersen, Olfers, Bogelund (Nielsen 75), Due, Johansson, Augustinussen, Caca (Risgard 79), Enevoldsen, Curth (Saganowski 72).
Villarreal: Diego Lopez; Gonzalo, Edmilson (Matias Fernandez 83), Godin, Capdevila, Javi Venta, Pires (Cani 62), Cazorla, Senna, Llorente, Rossi (Guille Franco 64).

Celtic (1) 1 *(McDonald 13)*
Manchester United (0) 1 *(Giggs 83)*   58,903
Celtic: Boruc; Hinkel, Wilson, Hartley, Caldwell, McManus, Robson, Brown S, McDonald (Hutchinson 81), Sheridan (Donati 64), Maloney (O'Dea 75).
Manchester United: Foster; Rafael (Evra 65), O'Shea, Carrick, Ferdinand, Vidic, Nani (Berbatov 46), Fletcher, Ronaldo, Tevez (Rooney 69), Giggs.

Tuesday, 25 November 2008

Aalborg (0) 2 *(Caca 73, Caldwell 87 (og))*
Celtic (0) 1 *(Robson 53)*   10,096
Aalborg: Zaza; Jakobsen, Pedersen (Kristensen 81), Olfers, Bogelund, Johansson, Augustinussen, Caca, Risgard, Enevoldsen (Due 70), Curth (Saganowski 70).
Celtic: Boruc; Hinkel, Wilson (Maloney 90), Loovens, Caldwell, McManus, Nakamura, Brown S, McDonald, Samaras (Sheridan 69), Robson.

Villarreal (0) 0
Manchester United (0) 0   22,529
Villarreal: Diego Lopez; Gonzalo, Capdevila■, Javi Venta, Fuentes, Eguren, Pires (Matias Fernandez 65), Cazorla, Ibagaza, Senna (Bruno 46), Rossi (Guille Franco 78).
Manchester United: Kuszczak; O'Shea, Evra, Carrick (Tevez 86), Ferdinand, Evans, Ronaldo, Anderson, Rooney, Fletcher (Gibson 80), Nani (Park 84).

Wednesday, 10 December 2008

Celtic (2) 2 *(Maloney 14, McGeady 45)*
Villarreal (0) 0   58,104
Celtic: Boruc; Hinkel, Wilson (O'Dea 81), Hartley, Caldwell, McManus, Nakamura, Brown S, Samaras (McDonald 81), Maloney, McGeady (McGowen 74).
Villarreal: Viera; Gonzalo, Edmilson, Angel, Fuentes, Cani, Ibagaza (Cazorla 60), Matias Fernandez, Senna (Nihat 46), Bruno, Guille Franco■.

Manchester United (1) 2 *(Tevez 3, Rooney 52)*
Aalborg (2) 2 *(Jakobsen 31, Curth 45)*   74,382
Manchester United: Kuszczak; Neville (Rafael 77), O'Shea, Anderson, Ferdinand, Evans, Nani, Gibson (Park 46), Rooney, Tevez, Giggs (Scholes 46).
Aalborg: Zaza; Jakobsen, Pedersen (Sorensen 76), Olfers, Bogelund, Due (Kristensen 66), Augustinussen, Risgard, Enevoldsen, Saganowski, Curth (Caca 75).

Group E Final Table	P	W	D	L	F	A	Pts
Manchester United	6	2	4	0	9	3	10
Villarreal	6	2	3	1	9	7	9
Aalborg	6	1	3	2	9	14	6
Celtic	6	1	2	3	4	7	5

GROUP F

Wednesday, 17 September 2008

Lyon (0) 2 *(Piquionne 73, Benzema 86)*
Fiorentina (2) 2 *(Gilardino 12, 42)*   37,500
Lyon: Lloris; Boumsong, Reveillere, Bodmer, Kallstrom, Juninho, Makoun (Ederson 60), Toulalan, Fred (Piquionne 65), Benzema, Govou (Mounier 89).
Fiorentina: Frey; Kroldrup, Dainelli, Vargas, Zauri (Jorgensen 76), Montolivo, Kuzmanovic (Santana 64), Almiron, Melo, Mutu, Gilardino (Pazzini 81).

Steaua (0) 0
Bayern Munich (1) 1 *(Van Buyten 15)*   13,379
Steaua: Zapata; Ogararu, Goian, Marin, Ghionea, Szekely (Kapetanos 82), Moreno, Toja (Petre 77), Lovin, Semedo, Arthuro (Stancu 71).
Bayern Munich: Rensing; Lucio, Van Buyten, Demichelis, Lahm, Lell, Ze Roberto (Ottl 75), Van Bommel, Schweinsteiger (Borowski 83), Toni, Klose (Podolski 46).

Tuesday, 30 September 2008

Bayern Munich (0) 1 *(Ze Roberto 52)*
Lyon (1) 1 *(Demichelis 25 (og))*   64,000
Bayern Munich: Rensing; Lucio, Demichelis, Lahm, Oddo, Breno, Ribery (Borowski 82), Ze Roberto, Schweinsteiger, Toni, Klose.
Lyon: Lloris; Cris, Mensah, Reveillere, Bodmer, Juninho (Boumsong 86), Makoun (Toulalan 74), Benzema, Govou (Ederson 36).

Fiorentina (0) 0
Steaua (0) 0   25,383
Fiorentina: Frey; Dainelli, Gamberini, Vargas, Montolivo (Pazzini 81), Jorgensen (Zauri 46), Santana, Almiron (Kuzmanovic 74), Melo, Mutu, Gilardino.
Steaua: Zapata; Ogararu, Goian, Radoi, Marin, Ghionea, Moreno (Tiago Gomes 86), Nicolita, Lovin, Semedo (Kapetanos 90), Stancu (Szekely 77).

Tuesday, 21 October 2008

Bayern Munich (2) 3 *(Klose 5, Schweinsteiger 25, Ze Roberto 90)*
Fiorentina (0) 0   66,000
Bayern Munich: Rensing; Lucio, Demichelis, Lahm (Lell 46), Oddo, Ribery, Ze Roberto, Van Bommel, Schweinsteiger (Borowski 65), Toni (Podolski 57), Klose.
Fiorentina: Frey; Dainelli, Gamberini, Vargas (Gobbi 74), Zauri, Montolivo, Kuzmanovic, Santana (Jovetic 64), Melo, Mutu, Gilardino.

Steaua (3) 3 *(Arthuro 8, Goian 11, Petre 45)*
Lyon (2) 5 *(Keita 23, Benzema 33, 71, Fred 69, 90)* 15,239
Steaua: Zapata; Ogararu, Goian, Radoi, Marin, Petre (Ghionea 57), Moreno, Nicolita, Lovin (Kapetanos 82), Semedo (Toja 65), Arthuro.
Lyon: Lloris; Cris, Boumsong, Grosso, Reveillere, Ederson, Juninho (Kallstrom 87), Makoun, Toulalan, Benzema (Mounier 81), Keita (Fred 67).

Wednesday, 5 November 2008

Fiorentina (1) 1 *(Mutu 10)*
Bayern Munich (0) 1 *(Borowski 78)*   37,034
Fiorentina: Frey; Dainelli, Gamberini, Zauri, Montolivo, Gobbi, Kuzmanovic (Osvaldo 79), Santana (Almiron 62), Melo, Mutu, Gilardino.
Bayern Munich: Rensing; Lucio, Demichelis, Oddo, Ribery, Ze Roberto, Van Bommel, Borowski, Schweinsteiger (Kroos 79), Podolski (Ottl 88), Klose.

Lyon (1) 2 *(Juninho 44, Reveillere 89)*
Steaua (0) 0   37,243
Lyon: Lloris; Cris, Boumsong, Grosso, Reveillere, Ederson (Kallstrom 70), Juninho, Makoun, Toulalan, Benzema (Piquionne 83), Keita (Delgado 70).
Steaua: Zapata; Ogararu, Goian, Radoi, Marin, Ghionea, Szekely (Semedo 46) (Arthuro 81), Nicolita, Tiago Gomes (Moreno 60), Kapetanos.

Tuesday, 25 November 2008

Bayern Munich (0) 3 *(Klose 57, 71, Toni 61)*
Steaua (0) 0   64,000
Bayern Munich: Rensing; Lucio (Breno 78), Van Buyten, Lahm, Oddo, Ribery, Ze Roberto, Van Bommel, Schweinsteiger, Toni (Borowski 82), Klose.
Steaua: Zapata; Goian, Golanski, Radoi, Marin, Ghionea, Szekely (Semedo 63), Petre (Lovin 66), Moreno, Nicolita, Stancu (Tiago Gomes 78).

Fiorentina (1) 1 *(Gilardino 45)*
Lyon (2) 2 *(Makoun 15, Benzema 26)*   23,736
Fiorentina: Frey; Dainelli (Kroldrup 46), Gamberini, Vargas, Zauri, Montolivo, Kuzmanovic, Santana (Jovetic 54), Melo (Osvaldo 79), Mutu, Gilardino.
Lyon: Lloris; Cris, Boumsong, Grosso, Mensah, Juninho, Makoun, Toulalan, Benzema (Piquionne 90), Govou, Keita (Ederson 80).

Wednesday, 10 December 2008

Lyon (0) 2 *(Govou 52, Benzema 68)*
Bayern Munich (3) 3 *(Klose 12, 37, Ribery 34)*   38,349
Lyon: Lloris; Boumsong, Grosso, Mensah, Gasamma (Kallstrom 64), Ederson (Delgado 77), Makoun, Toulalan, Benzema, Govou, Mounier (Fred 64).
Bayern Munich: Rensing; Van Buyten, Demichelis, Lahm, Oddo (Breno 90), Ribery, Van Bommel, Borowski, Schweinsteiger (Hamit Altintop 88), Toni, Klose (Ottl 69).

Steaua (0) 0
Fiorentina (0) 1 *(Gilardino 66)*   14,862
Steaua: Zapata; Golanski[■], Radoi, Baciu, Marin, Petre, Moreno, Toja, Nicolita, Tiago Gomes (Plesan 88), Semedo (Lovin 57).
Fiorentina: Frey; Kroldrup, Gamberini, Vargas, Zauri, Donadel, Montolivo (Masi 90), Santana (Almiron 78), Melo, Mutu, Gilardino (Osvaldo 83).

Group F Final Table	P	W	D	L	F	A	Pts
Bayern Munich	6	4	2	0	12	4	14
Lyon	6	3	2	1	14	10	11
Fiorentina	6	1	3	2	5	8	6
Steaua	6	0	1	5	3	12	1

GROUP G

Wednesday, 17 September 2008

Dynamo Kiev (0) 1 *(Bangoura 64 (pen))*
Arsenal (0) 1 *(Gallas 88)*   16,800
Dynamo Kiev: Bogush; Betao, Diakhate, Nesmachni, Vukojevic, Aliev, Eremenko, Mikhalik, Ninkovic, Ayila (Asatiani 90), Bangoura (Kravets 90).
Arsenal: Almunia; Sagna (Eboue 78), Clichy, Denilson, Toure, Gallas, Song Billong (Bendtner 70), Fabregas, Adebayor, Van Persie (Vela 84), Walcott.

Porto (2) 3 *(Lisandro 11, Gonzalez L 14, Lino 90)*
Fenerbahce (1) 1 *(Guiza 30)*   38,709
Porto: Helton; Bruno Alves, Nelson Benitez, Rolando, Sapunaru, Gonzalez L, Rodriguez (Lino 89), Gonzalez M (Hulk 61), Raul Meireles (Tomas Costa 68), Fernando, Lisandro.
Fenerbahce: Volkan; Lugano, Roberto Carlos, Yasin, Ugur (Kazim-Richards 76), Gokhan G, Emre B, Alex, Selcuk (Josico 46) (Burak 53), Maldonado, Guiza.

Tuesday, 30 September 2008

Arsenal (2) 4 *(Van Persie 31, 48, Adebayor 40, 71 (pen))*
Porto (0) 0   59,623
Arsenal: Almunia; Sagna, Clichy, Denilson, Toure, Gallas, Nasri (Eboue 65), Fabregas, Adebayor, Van Persie (Bendtner 65), Walcott (Vela 72).
Porto: Helton; Bruno Alves, Nelson Benitez, Rolando, Sapunaru, Guarin, Rodriguez (Candeias 79), Raul Meireles (Hulk 64), Tomas Costa, Fernando (Gonzalez L 46), Lisandro.

Fenerbahce (0) 0
Dynamo Kiev (0) 0   35,112
Fenerbahce: Volkan; Lugano, Roberto Carlos, Edu Dracena, Gokhan G, Emre B (Ugur 85), Kazim-Richards, Alex (Burak 77), Selcuk, Maldonado, Guiza.
Dynamo Kiev: Bogush; Betao, Diakhate, Ghioane, Vukojevic, Aliev (Asatiani 89), Eremenko, Mikhalik, El-Kaddouri (Nesmachni 62), Ninkovic, Bangoura (Shatskikh 46).

Tuesday, 21 October 2008

Fenerbahce (1) 2 *(Silvestre 19 (og), Guiza 78)*
Arsenal (3) 5 *(Adebayor 10, Walcott 11, Diaby 22, Song Billong 49, Ramsey 90)*   42,619
Fenerbahce: Volkan; Lugano, Roberto Carlos, Edu Dracena, Ugur, Gokhan G (Burak 79), Alex, Selcuk, Maldonado (Ali Bilgin 52), Guiza, Semih.
Arsenal: Almunia; Song Billong, Clichy, Denilson, Eboue, Silvestre, Diaby (Ramsey 73), Fabregas, Adebayor (Vela 86), Walcott (Djourou 86), Nasri.

Porto (0) 0
Dynamo Kiev (1) 1 *(Aliev 27)*   32,209
Porto: Nuno; Bruno Alves, Rolando, Lino, Sapunaru, Gonzalez L, Rodriguez (Sektioui 62), Gonzalez M (Tomas Costa 68), Raul Meireles, Fernando (Hulk 46), Lisandro.
Dynamo Kiev: Bogush; Betao, Diakhate, Nesmachni, Ghioane (Eremenko 60), Vukojevic, Aliev, Mikhalik, El-Kaddouri, Ninkovic (Asatiani 83), Bangoura (Milevskiy 46).

Wednesday, 5 November 2008

Arsenal (0) 0

Fenerbahce (0) 0   60,003

Arsenal: Fabianski; Toure, Clichy, Denilson, Djourou, Silvestre (Song Billong 82), Ramsey (Diaby 59), Fabregas, Bendtner (Vela 59), Van Persie, Nasri.
Fenerbahce: Volkan; Lugano, Roberto Carlos (Wederson 68), Edu Dracena, Ugur, Gokhan G, Kazim-Richards (Ali Bilgin 59), Selcuk, Maldonado (Josico 67), Guiza, Semih.

Dynamo Kiev (1) 1 *(Milevskiy 21)*

Porto (0) 2 *(Ronaldo 69, Gonzalez L 90)*   16,300

Dynamo Kiev: Bogush; Betao, Diakhate, Nesmachni, Ghioane (Bangoura 60), Vukojevic, Aliev, Eremenko, Mikhalik, El-Kaddouri, Milevskiy.
Porto: Helton; Bruno Alves, Pedro Emanuel (Lino 78), Rolando, Sapunaru (Pele 68), Gonzalez L■, Rodriguez, Raul Meireles, Sektioui (Hulk 46), Fernando, Lisandro.

Tuesday, 25 November 2008

Arsenal (0) 1 *(Bendtner 85)*

Dynamo Kiev (0) 0   59,374

Arsenal: Almunia; Gallas, Clichy, Denilson, Djourou, Silvestre, Song Billong, Fabregas, Vela (Wilshere 76), Van Persie, Ramsey (Bendtner 68).
Dynamo Kiev: Bogush; Betao, Diakhate, Ghioane, Vukojevic, Aliev■, Eremenko, El-Kaddouri, Asatiani, Bangoura, Milevskiy.

Fenerbahce (0) 1 *(Kazim-Richards 62)*

Porto (2) 2 *(Lisandro 18, 27)*   38,120

Fenerbahce: Volkan; Roberto Carlos, Edu Dracena, Ugur, Yasin, Gokhan, Emre B (Kazim-Richards 46), Alex, Josico, Guiza, Deivid (Burak 77).
Porto: Helton; Bruno Alves, Pedro Emanuel, Fucile, Rolando, Rodriguez (Gonzalez M 74), Raul Meireles, Tomas Costa (Guarin 61), Fernando, Lisandro, Hulk (Pele 79).

Wednesday, 10 December 2008

Dynamo Kiev (1) 1 *(Eremenko 20)*

Fenerbahce (0) 0   14,000

Dynamo Kiev: Bogush; Betao, Diakhate, Nesmachni, Ghioane, Vukojevic, Eremenko, Mikhalik, Cernat (Asatiani 46), Bangoura (Kravets 55), Milevskiy.
Fenerbahce: Volkan; Lugano, Roberto Carlos, Edu Dracena, Ugur (Parlak 73), Gokhan G, Alex (Ali Bilgin 64), Josico, Selcuk (Maldonado■ 59), Guiza, Deivid.

Porto (1) 2 *(Bruno Alves 38, Lisandro 53)*

Arsenal (0) 0   37,602

Porto: Helton; Bruno Alves, Pedro Emanuel, Fucile, Rolando, Gonzalez L (Gonzalez M 78), Rodriguez (Tomas Costa 78), Raul Meireles, Fernando, Lisandro, Hulk (Guarin 88).
Arsenal: Almunia; Eboue, Djourou, Denilson, Silvestre, Gallas, Song Billong (Randall 78), Ramsey (Wilshere 59), Vela, Bendtner, Diaby (Gibbs 60).

Group G Final Table	P	W	D	L	F	A	Pts
Porto	6	4	0	2	9	8	12
Arsenal	6	3	2	1	11	5	11
Dynamo Kiev	6	2	2	2	4	4	8
Fenerbahce	6	0	2	4	4	11	2

GROUP H

Wednesday, 17 September 2008

Juventus (0) 1 *(Del Piero 76)*

Zenit (0) 0   20,853

Juventus: Buffon; Chiellini, Grygera, Molinaro (De Ceglie 57), Legrottaglie, Nedved, Camoranesi (Salihamidzic 32), Poulsen, Sissoko, Del Piero, Trezeguet (Amauri 87).
Zenit: Malafeev; Krizanac, Anyukov, Puygrenier, Sirl, Zyryanov (Dominguez 80), Timoshchuk, Pogrebnyak, Arshavin, Danny, Denisov.

Real Madrid (1) 2 *(Sergio Ramos 11, Van Nistelrooy 57)*

BATE Borisov (0) 0   55,099

Real Madrid: Casillas; Sergio Ramos, Cannavaro, Marcelo, Heinze, Gago (Diarra 36), Guti (Higuain 68), Van der Vaart, Raul, Robben (Drenthe 60), Van Nistelrooy.
BATE Borisov: Veremko; Sosnovskiy, Khagush■, Rzhevskiy, Yurevich, Likhtarovich (Volodko 58), Krivets, Nekhaychik, Sivakov, Stasevich (Zhavnerchik 46), Mirchev (Baga 64).

Tuesday, 30 September 2008

BATE Borisov (2) 2 *(Krivets 17, Stasevich 23)*

Juventus (2) 2 *(Iaquinta 29, 45)*   31,400

BATE Borisov: Veremko; Sosnovskiy, Kazantsev, Rzhevskiy, Yurevich, Likhtarovich (Sivakov 70), Volodko, Krivets, Nekhaychik (Mirchev 86), Stasevich, Rodionov (Pecha 90).
Juventus: Manninger; Chiellini, Grygera, Legrottaglie (Knezevic 18), Nedved, Camoranesi (Marchisio 46), Sissoko, De Ceglie, Iaquinta (Amauri 81), Del Piero, Giovinco.

Zenit (1) 1 *(Danny 25)*

Real Madrid (2) 2 *(Hubocan 4 (og), Van Nistelrooy 31)*
                                                 21,075

Zenit: Malafeev; Hubocan (Dominguez 73), Anyukov, Puygrenier, Sirl, Zyryanov, Timoshchuk, Pogrebnyak (Fatih 73), Arshavin, Danny, Denisov.
Real Madrid: Casillas; Pepe, Sergio Ramos, Cannavaro, Heinze, Diarra, De la Red, Van der Vaart (Javi Garcia 62), Robben (Drenthe 82), Van Nistelrooy, Higuain (Saviola 88).

Tuesday, 21 October 2008

Juventus (1) 2 *(Del Piero 6, Amauri 48)*

Real Madrid (0) 1 *(Van Nistelrooy 66)*   25,813

Juventus: Manninger; Chiellini, Grygera, Molinaro, Legrottaglie (Mellberg 46), Nedved, Marchisio (Salihamidzic 37), Sissoko, Marchionni, Amauri (Iaquinta 78), Del Piero.
Real Madrid: Casillas; Pepe, Sergio Ramos, Cannavaro, Heinze, Gago, Sneijder, Van der Vaart (Drenthe 76), Raul, Van Nistelrooy, Higuain (Robben 54).

Zenit (0) 1 *(Fatih 78)*

BATE Borisov (0) 1 *(Nekhaychik 52)*   19,500

Zenit: Malafeev; Krizanac (Dominguez 69), Anyukov, Sirl, Shirokov, Zyryanov (Pogrebnyak 76), Timoshchuk, Fatih, Arshavin, Danny, Denisov.
BATE Borisov: Veremko; Sosnovskiy, Khagush, Rzhevskiy, Yurevich, Likhtarovich (Sivakov 67), Volodko, Krivets (Mirchev 85), Stasevich (Nekhaychik 46), Bliznyuk, Rodionov.

Wednesday, 5 November 2008

BATE Borisov (0) 0

Zenit (1) 2 *(Pogrebnyak 34, Danny 90)*   28,793

BATE Borisov: Veremko; Sosnovskiy, Khagush (Sivakov 79), Rzhevskiy (Kazantsev 58), Yurevich, Likhtarovich, Krivets, Nekhaychik (Mirchev 76), Stasevich, Bliznyuk, Rodionov.
Zenit: Malafeev; Krizanac, Anyukov, Puygrenier■, Sirl, Zyryanov, Timoshchuk, Pogrebnyak (Shirokov 89), Arshavin (Hubocan 78), Danny, Denisov.

Real Madrid (0) 0

Juventus (1) 2 *(Del Piero 17, 67)*   71,560

Real Madrid: Casillas; Sergio Ramos, Cannavaro, Marcelo, Drenthe, Heinze (Van der Vaart 81), Diarra, Sneijder (Higuain 65), Guti, Raul, Van Nistelrooy (Saviola 81).
Juventus: Manninger; Chiellini, Mellberg, Molinaro, Legrottaglie, Nedved, Sissoko, Tiago, Marchionni, Amauri (Iaquinta 83), Del Piero (De Ceglie 90).

Tuesday, 25 November 2008

BATE Borisov (0) 0

Real Madrid (1) 1 *(Raul 7)* 30,500

BATE Borisov: Veremko; Sosnovskiy, Khagush, Kazantsev, Yurevich, Likhtarovich (Skavysh 70), Volodko (Sivakov 65), Krivets, Stasevich (Nekhaychik 46), Bliznyuk, Rodionov.
Real Madrid: Casillas; Pepe, Sergio Ramos, Drenthe, Heinze, Gago, Sneijder, Guti (Van der Vaart 79), Torres, Raul (Javi Garcia 85), Saviola (Bueno 89).

Zenit (0) 0

Juventus (0) 0 20,155

Zenit: Malafeev; Krizanac, Lombaerts, Anyukov, Sirl, Zyryanov, Timoshchuk, Pogrebnyak, Arshavin (Fayzulin 70), Danny, Denisov.
Juventus: Manninger; Chiellini, Mellberg, Grygera, Molinaro, Nedved, Camoranesi (Marchionni 84), Marchisio, Sissoko, Iaquinta (Amauri 88), Del Piero (Giovinco 78).

Wednesday, 10 December 2008

Juventus (0) 0

BATE Borisov (0) 0 5753

Juventus: Manninger; Mellberg, Grygera, Molinaro, Legrottaglie, Zanetti, Nedved (Castiglia 90), De Ceglie, Marchionni, Amauri (Del Piero 57), Giovinco (Esposito 87).
BATE Borisov: Veremko; Sosnovskiy, Khagush, Kazantsev, Yurevich, Likhtarovich (Volodko 57), Krivets (Ermakovich 89), Sivakov, Stasevich (Nekhaychik 61), Bliznyuk, Rodionov.

Real Madrid (1) 3 *(Raul 25, 57, Robben 50)*

Zenit (0) 0 46,265

Real Madrid: Dudek; Michel Salgado, Sergio Ramos, Cannavaro, Marcelo, Gago, Guti (Javi Garcia 52), Van der Vaart (Metzelder 46), Raul (Saviola 61), Robben, Higuain.
Zenit: Malafeev; Krizanac, Lombaerts (Dominguez 76), Anyukov, Sirl, Zyryanov, Timoshchuk, Pogrebnyak (Fatih 72), Arshavin, Danny, Denisov.

Group H Final Table	P	W	D	L	F	A	Pts
Juventus	6	3	3	0	7	3	12
Real Madrid	6	4	0	2	9	5	12
Zenit	6	1	2	3	6	7	5
BATE Borisov	6	0	3	3	3	8	3

KNOCK-OUT STAGE

KNOCK-OUT ROUND, FIRST LEG

Tuesday, 24 February 2009

Arsenal (1) 1 *(Van Persie 36 (pen))*

Roma (0) 0 60,003

Arsenal: Almunia; Sagna, Clichy, Denilson, Toure, Gallas, Eboue (Ramsey 82), Diaby (Song Billong 62), Bendtner (Vela 67), Van Persie, Nasri.
Roma: Doni; Mexes, Motta, Loria (Diamoutene 70), Riise, Taddei, De Rossi, Julio Baptista (Vucinic 82), Perrotta, Brighi (Pizarro 57), Totti.

Atletico Madrid (2) 2 *(Maxi Rodriguez 3, Forlan 45)*

Porto (1) 2 *(Lisandro 22, 72)* 47,000

Atletico Madrid: Leo Franco; Seitaridis, Antonio Lopez, Ujfalusi, Ibanez, Raul Garcia (Maniche 67), Maxi Rodriguez (Miguel 80), Paulo Assuncao, Simao, Forlan, Aguero (Sinama-Pongolle 56).
Porto: Helton; Bruno Alves, Rolando, Sapunaru (Pedro Emanuel 79), Cissokho, Gonzalez L, Rodriguez, Raul Meireles (Sektioui 90), Fernando, Lisandro (Tomas Costa 90), Hulk.

Internazionale (0) 0

Manchester United (0) 0 80,018

Internazionale: Julio Cesar; Zanetti, Maicon, Rivas (Cordoba 46), Chivu, Santon, Stankovic, Cambiasso, Ali Muntari (Cruz 77), Ibrahimovic, Adriano (Balotelli 77).
Manchester United: Van der Sar; O'Shea, Evra, Carrick, Ferdinand, Evans, Ronaldo, Fletcher, Berbatov, Giggs, Park (Rooney 83).

Lyon (1) 1 *(Juninho 7)*

Barcelona (0) 1 *(Henry 67)* 39,258

Lyon: Lloris; Cris, Boumsong, Gross, Mensah, Ederson (Delgado 65), Juninho (Kallstrom 79), Makoun, Toulalan, Benzema, Keita (Pjanic 88).
Barcelona: Victor Valdes; Pique, Marquez, Puyol, Dani Alves, Xavi, Toure Yaya, Busquets (Keita 77), Eto'o, Messi, Henry.

Wednesday, 25 February 2009

Chelsea (1) 1 *(Drogba 12)*

Juventus (0) 0 38,079

Chelsea: Cech; Bosingwa, Cole A, Mikel, Terry, Alex, Ballack (Mancienne 81), Lampard, Anelka, Drogba, Kalou (Malouda 72).
Juventus: Buffon; Chiellini, Mellberg, Molinaro, Legrottaglie, Nedved, Camoranesi (Marchionni 52), Sissoko (Trezeguet 86), Tiago (Marchisio 62), Amauri, Del Piero.

Real Madrid (0) 0

Liverpool (0) 1 *(Benayoun 82)* 71,579

Real Madrid: Casillas; Pepe, Sergio Ramos, Cannavaro, Marcelo (Guti 46), Heinze, Gago, Diarra, Raul, Robben, Higuain.
Liverpool: Reina; Arbeloa, Fabio Aurelio, Xabi Alonso, Carragher, Skrtel, Benayoun, Mascherano, Torres (Babel 62), Kuyt (Lucas 90), Riera (Gerrard 88).

Sporting Lisbon (0) 0

Bayern Munich (1) 5 *(Ribery 42, 63 (pen), Klose 57, Toni 84, 90)* 35,163

Sporting Lisbon: Tiago; Polga, Caneira, Tonel, Abel (Pereirinha 61), Izmailov (Vukcevic 60), Rochemback, Joao Moutinho, Romagnoli, Derlei (Yannick Djalo 72), Liedson.
Bayern Munich: Rensing; Lucio (Van Buyten 78), Demichelis, Lahm, Oddo (Lell 66), Ribery, Ze Roberto, Van Bommel, Schweinsteiger (Hamit Altintop 71), Toni, Klose.

Villarreal (0) 1 *(Rossi 67 (pen))*

Panathinaikos (0) 1 *(Karagounis 59)* 21,810

Villarreal: Diego Lopez; Godin, Angel, Fuentes, Eguren (Pires 62), Cazorla, Ibagaza (Cani 70), Senna, Bruno, Llorente (Nihat 62), Rossi.
Panathinaikos: Galinovic; Sarriegi, Goumas (Gabriel 46), Simao, Vintra, Wawrzyniak, Spyropoulos, Gilberto Silva, Karagounis (Salpingidis 84), Nilsson, Mantzios (Rukavina 90).

KNOCK-OUT ROUND, SECOND LEG

Tuesday, 10 March 2009

Bayern Munich (4) 7 *(Podolski 7, 34,
Anderson Polga 39 (og), Schweinsteiger 43,
Van Bommel 74, Klose 82 (pen), Muller 90)*
Sporting Lisbon (1) 1 *(Joao Moutinho 42)*   65,000
Bayern Munich: Butt; Lucio (Breno 46), Van Buyten,
Lahm, Lell, Ze Roberto (Sosa 46), Ottl, Van Bommel,
Schweinsteiger (Muller 72), Podolski, Klose.
Sporting Lisbon: Rui Patricio; Polga, Pedro Silva, Tonel,
Adrien Silva (Caneira 74), Vukcevic, Miguel Veloso
(Abel 46), Pereirinha (Izmailov 46), Joao Moutinho,
Derlei, Yannick Djalo.

Juventus (1) 2 *(Iaquinta 19, Del Piero 74 (pen))*
Chelsea (1) 2 *(Essien 45, Drogba 83)*   27,319
Juventus: Buffon; Chiellini■, Mellberg, Grygera,
Molinaro, Nedved (Salihamidzic 13), Marchisio, Tiago,
Iaquinta (Giovinco 61), Del Piero, Trezeguet (Amauri
79).
Chelsea: Cech; Bosingwa, Cole A, Mikel, Terry, Alex
(Ricardo Carvalho 89), Essien (Belletti 66), Lampard,
Anelka, Drogba, Ballack.

Liverpool (2) 4 *(Torres 16, Gerrard 28 (pen), 47,
Dossena 88)*
Real Madrid (0) 0   42,550
Liverpool: Reina; Arbeloa, Fabio Aurelio, Xabi Alonso
(Lucas 61), Carragher, Skrtel, Mascherano, Gerrard
(Spearing 73), Torres (Dossena 84), Kuyt, Babel.
Real Madrid: Casillas; Pepe, Sergio Ramos, Cannavaro
(Van der Vaart 64), Heinze, Diarra, Gago (Guti 77),
Sneijder, Raul, Robben (Marcelo 46), Higuain.

Panathinaikos (0) 1 *(Mantzios 55)*
Villarreal (0) 2 *(Ibagaza 49, Llorente 70)*   60,616
Panathinaikos: Galinovic; Sarriegi, Gabriel
(Christodoulopoulos 74), Simao, Vintra, Wawrzyniak
(Rukavina 86), Gilberto Silva, Karagounis, Nilsson,
Salpingidis, Mantzios.
Villarreal: Diego Lopez; Godin, Capdevila, Angel (Javi
Venta 29), Fuentes, Eguren, Cazorla, Ibagaza (Bruno
75), Senna, Nihat (Llorente 46), Rossi.

Wednesday, 11 March 2009

Barcelona (4) 5 *(Henry 25, 27, Messi 40, Eto'o 43, Keita 90)*
Lyon (1) 2 *(Makoun 44, Juninho 48)*   86,368
Barcelona: Victor Valdes; Pique, Marguez, Sylvinho,
Dani Alves, Xavi, Iniesta (Hleb 90), Toure Yaya, Eto'o
(Bojan 87), Messi, Henry (Keita 75).
Lyon: Lloris; Clerc (Bodmer 46), Cris, Boumsong,
Grosso, Ederson (Keita 85), Juninho■, Makoun (46),
Toulalan, Benzema, Delgado (Kallstrom 61).

Manchester United (1) 2 *(Vidic 4, Ronaldo 49)*
Internazionale (0) 0   74,769
Manchester United: Van der Sar; O'Shea, Evra, Carrick,
Ferdinand, Vidic, Ronaldo, Scholes (Anderson 70),
Berbatov, Rooney (Park 84), Giggs.
Internazionale: Julio Cesar; Cordoba, Zanetti, Maicon,
Samuel, Santon, Stankovic (Adriano 58), Vieira (Ali
Muntari 46), Cambiasso, Ibrahimovic, Balotelli (Figo 70).

Porto (0) 0
Atletico Madrid (0) 0   46,509
Porto: Helton; Bruno Alves, Rolando, Sapunaru (Tomas
Costa 83), Cissokho, Gonzalez L, Rodriguez, Raul
Meireles, Fernando, Lisandro (Farias 90), Hulk
(Gonzalez M 89).
Atletico Madrid: Leo Franco; Antonio Lopez, Ujfalusi,
Perea, Ibanez, Raul Garcia (Maniche 73), Maxi
Rodriguez (Forlan 54), Paulo Assuncao, Simao, Aguero,
Sinama-Pongolle (Miguel 79).

Roma (1) 1 *(Juan 9)*
Arsenal (0) 0   62,383
Roma: Doni; Juan (Julio Baptista 28), Motta, Riise,
Diamoutene, Pizarro, Taddei (Aquilani 90), Tonetto,
Brighi (Montella 120), Vucinic, Totti.
Arsenal: Almunia; Sagna, Clichy, Denilson, Toure,
Gallas, Eboue (Walcott 74), Diaby, Bendtner (Eduardo
85), Van Persie, Nasri.
*aet; Arsenal won 7-6 on penalties: Eduardo saved; Pizarro
scored; Van Persie scored; Vucinic saved; Walcott scored;
Julio Baptista scored; Nasri scored; Montella scored;
Denilson scored; Totti scored; Toure scored; Aquilani
scored; Sagna scored; Riise scored; Diaby scored; Tonetto
missed.*

QUARTER-FINALS, FIRST LEG

Tuesday, 7 April 2009

Manchester United (1) 2 *(Rooney 15, Tevez 85)*
Porto (1) 2 *(Rodriguez 4, Gonzalez M 89)*   74,517
Manchester United: Van der Sar; O'Shea, Evra, Carrick,
Evans (Neville 72), Vidic, Ronaldo, Scholes (Tevez 72),
Rooney, Fletcher, Park (Giggs 59).
Porto: Helton; Bruno Alves, Rolando, Sapunaru,
Cissokho, Gonzalez L, Rodriguez (Gonzalez M 79), Raul
Meireles (Tomas Costa 79) (Madrid 90), Fernando,
Lisandro, Hulk.

Villarreal (1) 1 *(Senna 10)*
Arsenal (0) 1 *(Adebayor 65)*   21,577
Villarreal: Diego Lopez; Gonzalo, Godin, Capdevila,
Angel, Eguren, Cani (Matias Fernandez 46), Ibagaza
(Guille Franco 78), Senna, Llorente (Pires 70), Rossi.
Arsenal: Almunia (Fabianski 27); Sagna, Clichy,
Denilson, Toure, Gallas (Djourou 43), Song Billong,
Fabregas, Adebayor, Walcott (Eboue 78), Nasri.

Wednesday, 8 April 2009

Barcelona (4) 4 *(Messi 9, 38, Eto'o 13, Henry 43)*
Bayern Munich (0) 0   93,219
Barcelona: Victor Valdes; Pique, Marquez, Puyol, Dani
Alves, Xavi, Iniesta, Toure Yaya (Busquets 81), Eto'o
(Bojan 89), Messi, Henry (Keita 74).
Bayern Munich: Butt; Demichelis, Oddo, Lell, Breno,
Ribery, Hamit Altintop (Ottl 46), Ze Roberto (Sosa 77),
Van Bommel, Schweinsteiger, Toni.

Liverpool (1) 1 *(Torres 6)*
Chelsea (1) 3 *(Ivanovic 39, 62, Drogba 67)*   42,543
Liverpool: Reina; Arbeloa, Fabio Aurelio (Dossena 75),
Xabi Alonso, Carragher, Skrtel, Lucas (Babel 79),
Gerrard, Torres, Kuyt, Riera (Benayoun 68).
Chelsea: Cech; Ivanovic, Cole A, Essien, Terry, Alex,
Ballack, Lampard, Drogba (Anelka 80), Kalou, Malouda.

QUARTER-FINALS, SECOND LEG

Tuesday, 14 April 2009

Bayern Munich (0) 1 *(Ribery 47)*
Barcelona (0) 1 *(Keita 73)*   65,000
Bayern Munich: Butt; Lucio, Demichelis, Lahm, Lell,
Ribery, Ze Roberto (Hamit Altintop 78), Ottl, Van
Bommel, Sosa (Borowski 78), Toni.
Barcelona: Victor Valdes; Pique, Puyol, Dani Alves,
Abidal, Xavi, Iniesta (Hleb 78), Keita, Toure Yaya,
Eto'o, Messi.

Chelsea (0) 4 *(Drogba 51, Alex 57, Lampard 76, 89)*
Liverpool (2) 4 *(Fabio Aurelio 19, Xabi Alonso 28 (pen),
Lucas 81, Kuyt 83)*   38,286
Chelsea: Cech; Ivanovic, Cole A, Essien, Alex, Ricardo
Carvalho, Ballack, Lampard, Drogba (Di Santo 90),
Kalou (Anelka 36), Malouda.
Liverpool: Reina; Arbeloa (Babel 85), Fabio Aurelio,
Xabi Alonso, Carragher, Skrtel, Benayoun, Mascherano
(Riera 70), Torres (N'Gog 80), Kuyt, Lucas.

Wednesday, 15 April 2009

Arsenal (1) 3 *(Walcott 11, Adebayor 60, Van Persie 69 (pen))*

Villarreal (0) 0   58,233

Arsenal: Fabianski; Eboue, Gibbs, Nasri, Toure, Silvestre, Song Billong, Fabregas, Adebayor (Bendtner 83), Van Persie (Diaby 77), Walcott (Denilson 77).
Villarreal: Diego Lopez; Gonzalo, Godin, Capdevila, Angel, Eguren■, Pires, Cani (Pablo 70), Fernandez (Nihat 64), Bruno (Ibagaza 64), Rossi.

Porto (0) 0

Manchester United (1) 1 *(Ronaldo 6)*   50,000

Porto: Helton; Bruno Alves, Rolando, Sapunaru (Tomas Costa 80), Cissokho, Gonzalez L (Gonzalez M 32), Rodriguez (Farias 64), Raul Meireles, Fernando, Lisandro, Hulk.
Manchester United: Van der Sar; O'Shea, Evra, Carrick, Ferdinand, Vidic, Ronaldo, Anderson (Scholes 78), Berbatov (Nani 68), Rooney, Giggs.

SEMI-FINALS, FIRST LEG

Tuesday, 28 April 2009

Barcelona (0) 0

Chelsea (0) 0   95,231

Barcelona: Victor Valdes; Pique, Marquez (Puyol 52), Dani Alves, Abidal, Xavi, Iniesta, Toure Yaya, Eto'o (Bojan 82), Messi, Henry (Hleb 87).
Chelsea: Cech; Ivanovic, Bosingwa, Mikel, Terry, Alex, Essien, Lampard (Belletti 71), Drogba, Ballack (Anelka 90), Malouda.

Wednesday, 29 April 2009

Manchester United (1) 1 *(O'Shea 17)*

Arsenal (0) 0   74,517

Manchester United: Van der Sar; O'Shea, Evra, Carrick, Ferdinand (Evans 88), Vidic, Ronaldo, Anderson (Berbatov 67), Rooney, Tevez (Giggs 67), Fletcher.
Arsenal: Almunia; Sagna, Gibbs, Diaby, Toure, Silvestre, Song Billong, Fabregas, Adebayor (Eduardo 83), Walcott (Bendtner 71), Nasri.

SEMI-FINALS, SECOND LEG

Tuesday, 5 May 2009

Arsenal (0) 1 *(Van Persie 76 (pen))*

Manchester United (2) 3 *(Park 8, Ronaldo 11, 61)* 59,867

Arsenal: Almunia; Sagna, Gibbs (Eboue 46), Song Billong, Djourou, Toure, Walcott (Bendtner 63), Fabregas, Adebayor, Van Persie (Vela 80), Nasri.
Manchester United: Van der Sar; O'Shea, Evra (Rafael 65), Carrick, Ferdinand, Vidic, Ronaldo, Fletcher■, Rooney (Berbatov 66), Anderson (Giggs 63), Park.

Wednesday, 6 May 2009

Chelsea (1) 1 *(Essien 9)*

Barcelona (0) 1 *(Iniesta 90)*   37,857

Chelsea: Cech; Bosingwa, Cole A, Essien, Terry, Alex, Ballack, Lampard, Anelka, Drogba (Belletti 72), Malouda.
Barcelona: Victor Valdes; Pique, Dani Alves, Abidal■, Xavi, Iniesta (Sylvinho 90), Keita, Toure Yaya, Busquets (Bojan 85), Messi, Eto'o (Gudjohnsen 90).

UEFA CHAMPIONS LEAGUE FINAL 2009

Wednesday, 27 May 2009

Manchester U (0) 0   Barcelona (1) 2 *(Eto'o 10, Messi 70)*

(in Rome, 62,467)

Manchester U: Van der Sar; O'Shea, Evra, Carrick, Ferdinand, Vidic, Park (Berbatov 66), Anderson (Tevez 46), Ronaldo, Rooney, Giggs (Scholes 75).

Barcelona: Victor Valdes; Puyol, Sylvinho, Busquets, Pique, Toure Yaya, Eto'o, Xavi, Henry (Keita 72), Messi, Iniesta (Pedrito 90).

Referee: Busacca (Switzerland).

Diminutive Lionel Messi leaves Manchester United keeper Edwin Van der Sar open-mouthed as he leaps to head home Barcelona's second and decisive goal in the Champions League Final in Rome. (PA Photos)

EUROPEAN CUP-WINNERS' CUP
FINALS 1961–99

Year	Winners	Runners-up	Venue	Attendance	Referee
1961	Fiorentina 2	Rangers 0 *(1st Leg)*	Glasgow	80,000	Steiner (A)
	Fiorentina 2	Rangers 1 *(2nd Leg)*	Florence	50,000	Hernadi (H)
1962	Atletico Madrid 1	Fiorentina 1	Glasgow	27,389	Wharton (S)
Replay	Atletico Madrid 3	Fiorentina 0	Stuttgart	38,000	Tschenscher (WG)
1963	Tottenham Hotspur 5	Atletico Madrid 1	Rotterdam	49,000	Van Leuwen (Ho)
1964	Sporting Lisbon 3	MTK Budapest 3 *(aet)*	Brussels	3000	Van Nuffel (Bel)
Replay	Sporting Lisbon 1	MTK Budapest 0	Antwerp	19,000	Versyp (Bel)
1965	West Ham U 2	Munich 1860 0	Wembley	100,000	Szolt (H)
1966	Borussia Dortmund 2	Liverpool 1 *(aet)*	Glasgow	41,657	Schwinte (F)
1967	Bayern Munich 1	Rangers 0 *(aet)*	Nuremberg	69,480	Lo Bello (I)
1968	AC Milan 2	Hamburg 0	Rotterdam	53,000	Ortiz (Sp)
1969	Slovan Bratislava 3	Barcelona 2	Basle	19,000	Van Ravens (Ho)
1970	Manchester C 2	Gornik Zabrze 1	Vienna	8,000	Schiller (A)
1971	Chelsea 1	Real Madrid 1 *(aet)*	Athens	42,000	Scheurer (Sw)
Replay	Chelsea 2	Real Madrid 1 *(aet)*	Athens	35,000	Bucheli (Sw)
1972	Rangers 3	Moscow Dynamo 2	Barcelona	24,000	Ortiz (Sp)
1973	AC Milan 1	Leeds U 0	Salonika	45,000	Mihas (Gr)
1974	Magdeburg 2	AC Milan 0	Rotterdam	4000	Van Gemert (Ho)
1975	Dynamo Kiev 3	Ferencvaros 0	Basle	13,000	Davidson (S)
1976	Anderlecht 4	West Ham U 2	Brussels	58,000	Wurtz (F)
1977	Hamburg 2	Anderlecht 0	Amsterdam	65,000	Partridge (E)
1978	Anderlecht 4	Austria/WAC 0	Paris	48,679	Adlinger (WG)
1979	Barcelona 4	Fortuna Dusseldorf 3 *(aet)*	Basle	58,000	Palotai (H)
1980	Valencia 0	Arsenal 0	Brussels	36,000	Christov (Cz)
	(aet; Valencia won 5-4 on penalties)				
1981	Dynamo Tbilisi 2	Carl Zeiss Jena 1	Dusseldorf	9000	Lattanzi (I)
1982	Barcelona 2	Standard Liege 1	Barcelona	100,000	Eschweiler (WG)
1983	Aberdeen 2	Real Madrid 1 *(aet)*	Gothenburg	17,804	Menegali (I)
1984	Juventus 2	Porto 1	Basle	60,000	Prokop (EG)
1985	Everton 3	Rapid Vienna 1	Rotterdam	50,000	Casarin (I)
1986	Dynamo Kiev 3	Atletico Madrid 0	Lyon	39,300	Wohrer (A)
1987	Ajax 1	Lokomotiv Leipzig 0	Athens	35,000	Agnolin (I)
1988	Mechelen 1	Ajax 0	Strasbourg	39,446	Pauly (WG)
1989	Barcelona 2	Sampdoria 0	Berne	45,000	Courtney (E)
1990	Sampdoria 2	Anderlecht 0	Gothenburg	20,103	Galler (Sw)
1991	Manchester U 2	Barcelona 1	Rotterdam	42,000	Karlsson (Se)
1992	Werder Bremen 2	Monaco 0	Lisbon	16,000	D'Elia (I)
1993	Parma 3	Antwerp 1	Wembley	37,393	Assenmacher (G)
1994	Arsenal 1	Parma 0	Copenhagen	33,765	Krondl (CzR)
1995	Zaragoza 2	Arsenal 1	Paris	42,424	Ceccarini (I)
1996	Paris St Germain 1	Rapid Vienna 0	Brussels	37,500	Pairetto (I)
1997	Barcelona 1	Paris St Germain 0	Rotterdam	45,000	Merk (G)
1998	Chelsea 1	Stuttgart 0	Stockholm	30,216	Braschi (I)
1999	Lazio 2	Mallorca 1	Villa Park	33,021	Benko (A)

INTER-CITIES FAIRS CUP FINALS 1958–71

(Winners in italics)

Year	First Leg	Attendance	Second Leg	Attendance
1958	London 2 Barcelona 2	45,466	*Barcelona* 6 London 0	62,000
1960	Birmingham C 0 Barcelona 0	40,500	*Barcelona* 4 Birmingham C 1	70,000
1961	Birmingham C 2 Roma 2	21,005	*Roma* 2 Birmingham C 0	60,000
1962	Valencia 6 Barcelona 2	65,000	Barcelona 1 *Valencia* 1	60,000
1963	Dynamo Zagreb 1 Valencia 2	40,000	*Valencia* 2 Dynamo Zagreb 0	55,000
1964	*Zaragoza* 2 Valencia 1	50,000	(in Barcelona)	
1965	*Ferencvaros* 1 Juventus 0	25,000	(in Turin)	
1966	Barcelona 0 Zaragoza 1	70,000	Zaragoza 2 *Barcelona* 4	70,000
1967	Dynamo Zagreb 2 Leeds U 0	40,000	Leeds U 0 *Dynamo Zagreb* 0	35,604
1968	Leeds U 1 Ferencvaros 0	25,368	Ferencvaros 0 *Leeds U* 0	70,000
1969	Newcastle U 3 Ujpest Dozsa 0	60,000	Ujpest Dozsa 2 *Newcastle U* 3	37,000
1970	Anderlecht 3 Arsenal 1	37,000	*Arsenal* 3 Anderlecht 0	51,612
1971	Juventus 0 Leeds U 0 *(abandoned 51 minutes)*	42,000		
	Juventus 2 Leeds U 2	42,000	*Leeds U* 1* Juventus 1	42,483

UEFA CUP FINALS 1972–97

(Winners in italics)

Year	First Leg	Attendance	Second Leg	Attendance
1972	Wolverhampton W 1 Tottenham H 2	45,000	*Tottenham H* 1 Wolverhampton W 1	48,000
1973	Liverpool 0 Moenchengladbach 0 *(abandoned 27 minutes)*	44,967		
	Liverpool 3 Moenchengladbach 0	41,169	Moenchengladbach 2 *Liverpool* 0	35,000
1974	Tottenham H 2 Feyenoord 2	46,281	*Feyenoord* 2 Tottenham H 0	68,000
1975	Moenchengladbach 0 Twente 0	45,000	Twente 1 *Moenchengladbach* 5	24,500
1976	Liverpool 3 FC Brugge 2	56,000	FC Brugge 1 *Liverpool* 1	32,000
1977	Juventus 1 Athletic Bilbao 0	75,000	Athletic Bilbao 2 *Juventus* 1*	43,000
1978	Bastia 0 PSV Eindhoven 0	15,000	*PSV Eindhoven* 3 Bastia 0	27,000
1979	Red Star Belgrade 1 Moenchengladbach 1	87,500	*Moenchengladbach* 1 Red Star Belgrade 0	45,000
1980	Moenchengladbach 3 Eintracht Frankfurt 2	25,000	*Eintracht Frankfurt* 1* Moenchengladbach 0	60,000
1981	Ipswich T 3 AZ 67 Alkmaar 0	27,532	AZ 67 Alkmaar 4 *Ipswich T* 2	28,500
1982	Gothenburg 1 Hamburg 0	42,548	Hamburg 0 *Gothenburg* 3	60,000
1983	Anderlecht 1 Benfica 0	45,000	Benfica 1 *Anderlecht* 1	80,000
1984	Anderlecht 1 Tottenham H 1	40,000	*Tottenham H* 1[1] Anderlecht 1	46,258
1985	Videoton 0 Real Madrid 3	30,000	*Real Madrid* 0 Videoton 1	98,300
1986	Real Madrid 5 Cologne 1	80,000	Cologne 2 *Real Madrid* 0	15,000
1987	Gothenburg 1 Dundee U 0	50,023	Dundee U 1 *Gothenburg* 1	20,911
1988	Espanol 3 Bayer Leverkusen 0	42,000	*Bayer Leverkusen* 3[2] Espanol 0	22,000
1989	Napoli 2 Stuttgart 1	83,000	Stuttgart 3 *Napoli* 3	67,000
1990	Juventus 3 Fiorentina 1	45,000	Fiorentina 0 *Juventus* 0	32,000
1991	Internazionale 2 Roma 0	68,887	Roma 1 *Internazionale* 0	70,901
1992	Torino 2 Ajax 2	65,377	*Ajax* 0* Torino 0	40,000
1993	Borussia Dortmund 1 Juventus 3	37,000	*Juventus* 3 Borussia Dortmund 0	62,781
1994	Salzburg 0 Internazionale 1	47,500	*Internazionale* 1 Salzburg 0	80,326
1995	Parma 1 Juventus 0	23,000	Juventus 1 *Parma* 1	80,750
1996	Bayern Munich 2 Bordeaux 0	62,000	Bordeaux 1 *Bayern Munich* 3	36,000
1997	Schalke 1 Internazionale 0	56,824	Internazionale 1 *Schalke* 0[3]	81,670

*won on away goals   [1]aet; Tottenham H won 4-3 on penalties   [2]aet; Bayer Leverkusen won 3-2 on penalties
[3]aet; Schalke won 4-1 on penalties

UEFA CUP FINALS 1998–2009

Year	Winners	Runners-up	Venue	Attendance	Referee
1998	Internazionale 3	Lazio 0	Paris	42,938	Nieto (Sp)
1999	Parma 3	Marseille 0	Moscow	61,000	Dallas (S)
2000	Galatasaray 0 *(aet; Galatasaray won 4-1 on penalties)*	Arsenal 0	Copenhagen	38,919	Nieto (Sp)
2001	Liverpool 5 *(aet; Liverpool won on sudden death)*	Alaves 4	Dortmund	65,000	Veissiere (F)
2002	Feyenoord 3	Borussia Dortmund 2	Rotterdam	45,000	Pereira (P)
2003	Porto 3 *(aet)*	Celtic 2	Seville	52,972	Michel (Slo)
2004	Valencia 2	Marseille 0	Gothenburg	40,000	Collina (I)
2005	CSKA Moscow 3	Sporting Lisbon 1	Lisbon	48,000	Poll (E)
2006	Sevilla 4	Middlesbrough 0	Eindhoven	36,500	Fandel (G)
2007	Sevilla 2 *(aet; Sevilla won 3-1 on penalties)*	Espanyol 2	Glasgow	50,670	Busacca (Sw)
2008	Zenit St Petersburg 2	Rangers 0	Manchester	43,878	Fröjdfeldt (Se)
2009	Shakhtar Donetsk 2	Werder Bremen 1	Istanbul	40,000	Chantalejo (Sp)

UEFA CUP 2008–09

■ *Denotes player sent off.*

FIRST QUALIFYING ROUND, FIRST LEG
Thursday, 17 July 2008

Ararat (0) 0
Bellinzona (1) 1 *(Mangiarratti 21)* 3000
Ararat: Prazian; Emilio (Navoian 64), Minasian V,
Renato, Antonian, Mkoian, Artur H Minasian, Petrosian,
Marcos, Nranian (Artur S Minasian 66), Henrique
(Movsisian 54).
Bellinzona: Gritti; Mangiarratti, La Rocca, Raso,
Sermeter, Gashi (Wahab 75), Mehmeti, Miccolis, Garrido
(Roux 84), Neri, Lustrinelli (Conti 60).

Bangor City (1) 1 *(Davies 24)*
Midtjylland (2) 6 *(Florescu 19, Reid 40,
Christensen 53, 58, 63, Thygesen 71)* 703
Bangor City: Smith; Swanick (Hoy 68), Beattie, Johnston,
Brewerton, Sergeant, Limbert, Walsh (Fowler 68),
Davies, Stott, Noon (Edwards 62).
Midtjylland: Heinze; Afriyie, Califf, Poulsen, Reid (Ipsa
76), Borring, Florescu, Thygesen, Salami, Olsen PF
(Olsen D 60), Fagerberg (Christensen 48).

Brondby (0) 1 *(Von Schlebrugge 50)*
B36 (0) 0 7105
Brondby: Andersen; Rasmussen M (Katongo 41),
Lorentzen (Williams 72), Rasmussen T, Von Schlebrugge,
Holmen, Farnerud, Jonsson, Mikkelsen (Madsen 59),
Gislason, Wass.
B36: Joensen; Alex, Jankovic, Matras, Olsen S, Midjord,
Gunnarsson J, Faero, Thorleifsson, Olsen M, Maisom
(Ellingsgaard 90).

Chernomore (0) 4 *(Aleksandrov 84, 89, Manolov 88,
Bachev 90)*
Sant Julia (0) 0 1500
Chernomore: Ilchev; Petkov, Bachev, Manolov, Georgiev
(Stoyanov 56), Alexandrov, Pires (Andanov 56),
Yurukov, Aleksandrov, Rusev, Domakinov (Dyakov 76).
Sant Julia: Tremonti; Xinos, Romero, Veriz, Miraglia
(Nastri 68), Wagner, Peppe, Spano (Adaime 86), Fontan■,
Varela, Peralta (Diaby 74).

Cliftonville (0) 0
FC Copenhagen (1) 4 *(Norregaard 22, Junior 67, 82,
Pospech 77)* 800
Cliftonville: Connolly; Fleming, Scannell R, Holland B,
O'Hara, Smyth (Murphy 77), Donaghy, Catney,
O'Connor (Patterson 82), Holland M, Scannell C (O'Neill
82).
FC Copenhagen: Christiansen; Pospech, Laursen, Wendt
(Jensen N 61), Jorgensen, Norregaard, Kvist (Kristensen
69), Hutchinson, Sionko, Ailton (Junior 61), Nordstrand.

Cork City (0) 2 *(Mooney 64, Murray 67)*
Haka (1) 2 *(Mahlakaarto 17, Lehtinen 52)* 3791
Cork City: Devine; Horgan, Murray, Sullivan, Danny
Murphy, Gamble, Healy, Darren Murphy, Kearney,
Behan, Mooney.
Haka: Doybnya; Kangaskorpi, Okkonen, Innanen
(Minkenen 84), Kauppila, Manninen (Mattila 79),
Mahlakaarto (Viljanen 66), Fowler, Parviainen, Lehtinen,
Holopainen.

Dacia (0) 1 *(Bulat 50)*
Borac (0) 1 *(Stojanovic 84 (pen))* 4000
Dacia: Romanenco; Calin, Japalau, Korgalidze,
Orbeldaze, Dvali, Bulat, Onica, Mardari, Andronic,
Boicenco (Orbu 78).
Borac: Grahovac; Dragutinovic, Stojanovic, Kosic,
Krnjinac, Antic, Stojcev, Pejovic (Mugosa 63), Grkajac
(Djokovic 81), Ignjatovic, Lazovic (Pavlovic 75).

Djurgaarden (0) 0
Flora (0) 0 5386
Djurgaarden: Tourray; Haginge, Kuivasto, Tauer, Ekong,
Cardoso (Batan 59), Komac, Davids, Rajalakso (Quirino
72), Kusi-Asare, Oremo (Dahlberg 57).
Flora: Aksalu; Vanna, Kasimir, Vunk, Hakola, Sidorenkov,
Hurt, Kams, Reim, Anier (Post 65), Ahjupera.

EB/Streymur (0) 0
Manchester City (2) 2 *(Petrov 9, Hamann 28)* 5400
EB/Streymur: Torgard; Jacobsen (Brian Olsen 76),
Foldgast (Davidsen 85), Clementsen, Djurhuus, Bardur
Olsen, Hansen L, Bo, Hansen A, Niclasen, Samuelsen
(Eliasen 76).
Manchester City: Hart; Onuoha, Ball, Dunne, Richards,
Johnson, Ireland, Hamann (Gelson 73), Jo (Evans 73),
Vassell, Petrov.

Glentoran (1) 1 *(Halliday 29)*
Metalurgs Liepajas (1) 1 *(Surnins 15)* 300
Glentoran: Morris; Nixon, Neill (Burrows 85), Leeman,
Ward, Hill, McCabe, Fordyce (McGovern 78), Boyce
(Fitzgerald 78), Halliday, Hamilton.
Metalurgs Liepajas: Spole; Klava, Zirnis, Antonio,
Jemelins, Tamosauskas, Surnins, Solonicins, Miceika,
Beniusis (Grebis 64), Karlsons.

Gyor (0) 1 *(Boor 58)*
Zestafoni (1) 1 *(Supic 45 (og))* 4000
Gyor: Stevanovic; Kovacs, Boor, Bajzat, Jozsi, Jakl,
Nikolov, Bicak (Koltai 46), Stark, Pinter (Volgyi 67), Supic.
Zestafoni: Kvaskhvadze R; Santos, Gotsiridze,
Lobzhanidze, Dzaria (Ionanidze 82), Daushvili, Gelashvili
(Chassern 70), Vieira, Todua, Kvaskhvadze N (Boyomo
46), Oniani.

Hafnarfjordur (1) 3 *(Gudmundsson T 40 (pen), 60,
Gunlaugsson A 50)*
Grevenmacher (2) 2 *(Steimetz 19, Maric 25)* 700
Hafnarfjordur: Sigurdsson; Eriksson (Saevarsson 86),
Siim, Nielsen, Valgardsson, Asgeirsson, Vidarsson D,
Gudmundsson T, Gudnason (Gudmundsson M 84),
Gunnlaugsson A (Vilhjalmsson 84), Bjornsson.
Grevenmacher: Oberweis; Schmitt (Helbig 46), Janisch,
Maric, Makhloufi, Steimetz, Siebenaler, Stojadinovic
(Wolff 83), Hoffmann, Fleck, Bozic (Thimmesch 58).

Hajduk Split (2) 4 *(Ibricic 3, Kalinic 24, Busic 55,
Ticinovic 71)*
Birkirkara (0) 0 20,000
Hajduk Split: Subasic; Buljat J, Zivkovic (Jertec 63),
Pandza, Linic, Ibricic, Gabric (Ticinovic 58), Strinic, Rubil
(Bartolovic 75), Kalinic, Busic.
Birkirkara: Borg O; Hartvig, Lombardi, Yanchev, Fenech,
Anastasi, Bajada (Buhagiar 62), Zerafa, Mallia, Galea
(Sammut 90), Tabone (Triganza 77).

Hapoel Tel Aviv (3) 3 *(Srur 16, 32, Antebi 26)*
Juvenes (0) 0 2350
Hapoel Tel Aviv: Enyeama; Douglas (Luz 59), Badir,
Antebi, Abutbul, Kende, Topuzakov, Telkiyski, Srur
(Yeboah 67), Natcho (Lala 77), Zehavi.
Juvenes: Montanari; Renzi, Ceci, Marzocchi, Perrotta
(Santini 87), Galli, Gamberini (Fantini 46), Tasso, Selva,
Zonzini (Rossini 76), Rossi F.

Hertha Berlin (5) 8 *(Pantelic 16, 38, Raffael 22, 71,
Piszczek 33, 42, 80, Stein 68)*
Otaci (0) 1 *(Andrei Tcaciuc 78)* 12,373
Hertha Berlin: Drobny; Kaka, Von Bergen, Chahed
(Radjabali-Fardi 71), Dardai, Stein, Ebert, Kacar
(Lustenberger 67), Pantelic (Domovchiysni 46), Raffael,
Piszczek.
Otaci: Piliuga; Mekang, Oyinloye, Soltanici, Lyba
(Suruceanu 39), Malitskyy (Velesco 73), Tymchenko
(Roslach 66), Savchenko, Groshev, Andrei Tcaciuc,
Alexandr Tcaciuc.

Honka (2) 3 *(Koskela 25, Heilala 29 (pen), Otaru 55)*
IA Akranes (0) 0   2372
Honka: Maanoja; Heilala, Jalasto, Hakanpaa, Koskela, Otaru (Vasara 60), Perovuo, Turunen, Vuorinen, Haarala (Koskinen 64), Kokko (Puustinen 66).
IA Akranes: Madsen; Gudmundsson, Einarsson, Magnusson (Akason 68), Cingel, Gudjonsson A, Hauksson (Sigurdsson 68), Sveinsson (Gudjonsson T 82), Gudjonsson B, Petursson, Svadjmovic.

Ironi Kiryat (1) 1 *(Peretz 18)*
Mogren (0) 1 *(Neric 82)*   1500
Ironi Kiryat: Amos; Bakhar, Lavi■, Nussbaum■, Kojok, Tzarfati, Shabtai, Hasarma, Avidor (Swisa 70), Peretz (Biton 50), Agouda.
Mogren: Janjusevic; Pejovic, Radovic, Janicic, Bozovic, Jovanovic, Rakic, Vujovic M (Zec 46), Stojakovic (Neric 80), Vujovic N, Gluscevic (Kalezic 86).

Koper (0) 1 *(Viler 69)*
Vllaznia (2) 2 *(Sukaj 7, 45)*   800
Koper: Hasic; Handanagic (Chibuke Ibeji 46), Secic (Kreft 46), Rajcevic, Rastovac, Djukic (Ipavec 63), Cruz Vitagliano, Smon, Viler, Bozicic, Amusan.
Vllaznia: Olsi; Teli, Osja, Basic (Hoti 80), Belisha, Beqiri, Smajlaj, Kaci (Lici 90), Nalbani, Lika, Sukaj.

Legia (0) 0
Gomel (0) 0   6000
Legia: Mucha; Szala, Choto, Rzezniczak, Giza (Guerreiro 62), Iwanski (Rocki 74), Kielbowicz, Vukovic, Rybus, Radovic, Arruabarrena (Chinyama 62).
Gomel: Lohvinov; Nadievskiy, Etiege, Rybak, Misyuk, Kondrashuk, Bressan (Tigranian 76), Baranok, Dragun (Dashuk 77), Mkrtchian, Rogerio (Matveichyk 40).

Lenkoran (0) 0
Lech (0) 1 *(Lewandowski 75)*   27,000
Lenkoran: Kramarenko; Denis, Diego Souza, Todorov, Bamba, Bakhshiyev (Gurbanov 77), Ramazanov, Abdullayev (Sultanov 80), Shukurov, Amirguliyev, Veikutis.
Lech: Kotorowski; Arboleda, Henriquez, Rengifo (Cueto 90), Bosacki, Peszko, Bandrowski (Lewandowski 46), Djurdjevic, Injac, Wojtkowiak, Stilic (Wilk 89).

MTZ-Ripo (0) 2 *(Kamara 17, Nicholas 52 (pen))*
Zilina (0) 2 *(Vladavic 41, Jez 90 (pen))*   5300
MTZ-Ripo: Sulima; Zrnanovich, Valkanov, Kamara, Strakhanovich, Sashcheko (Kvaratskhelia 46), Shchegrikovich (Pehlic 75), Bordachev, Eremchuk, Kontsevoy, Nicholas (Bubnov 82).
Zilina: Pernis; Vomacka, Leitner, Pekarik, Sourek, Strba, Jez, Styvar, Vladavic, Rilke (Belak 64), Adauto (Karoglan 46) (Lietava 83).

Marsaxlokk (0) 0
Slaven (3) 4 *(Kristic 15, Poldrugac 29, Tepuric 34, Vrucina 78)*   500
Marsaxlokk: Darmanin; Julio Cesar (Brincat 89), Renato, Licari, Sammut, Mamo, Sciberras (Wellman 76), Templeman, Barbara (Pereira 46), Said, Cassar.
Slaven: Rodic; Posavec, Kristic, Kresinger (Vrucina 59), Caval, Bosnjak (Kokalovic 63), Poldrugac, Poljak (Lapic 72), Tepuric, Gregurina, Rogulj.

Olimps Riga (0) 0
St Patrick's Ath (0) 1 *(Guy 76)*   1000
Olimps Riga: Ikstens; Petrenko, Kandov, Junior, Kostjuks (Sinelnikovs 59), Zolotarjovs (Jakovlevs 66), Tarasovs, Perepechko (Mendez 78), Dubra, Shtolcers■, Fertovs.
St Patrick's Ath: Barry Ryan; Kirby (Fitzpatrick 58), Fahey, Paisley, Quigley, Guy, Dempsey, Harris, Byrne, Lynch, O'Brien (Bobby Ryan 72).

Omonia (1) 2 *(Kukaj 19 (og), Zlogar 64)*
Milano (0) 0   17,000
Omonia: Georgallides; Duro, Clayton (Pavlou 84), Charalambous, Christofi (Bangura 72), Kaseka, Wenzel, Pletsch, Maris, Zlogar, Cafu (Vasconcelos 79).
Milano: Nuredinoski; Gasi, Kukaj, Trajcev, Gligorovski (Sali 59), Lazarevski, Manevski (Cuculi 89), Isufi, Alimi (Ljimani 78), Ristov, Gancev.

Pelister (0) 0
Apoel (0) 0   4000
Pelister: Nikov; Petkovski, Stepanovski, Dimov, Todorovski, Presilski, Adriano (Momirovski 65), Ristevski, Blazevski, Glavevski (Spirovski 83), Junior (Simonovski 89).
Apoel: Chiotis; Florea, Seghiri, Nuno Morais, Charalambides, Broerse, Paulista (Papathanasiou 81), Kontis, Michael (Poursaitidis 87), Zewlakow, Mirosavljevic (Haxhi 57).

Racing (0) 0
Kalmar (1) 3 *(Dauda 32, 79, Elm R 90)*   486
Racing: Oster; Zenanne, Liotte, Willemin, Feller, Schnell, Belabed, Carvalho (Belli 64), Martine (Muhovic 90), Pupovac, Bilon (Centrone 72).
Kalmar: Wasta; Lantz (Sorin 64), Lindberg, Eklund, Larsson, Rydstrom, Ingelsten (Sobralense 60), Elm V, Elm R, Johansson, Dauda (Sacramento 81).

Salzburg (4) 7 *(Tchoyi 22, 38, N'Gwat-Mahop 28, 46,*
Zickler 34 (pen), 65, Obster 48)
Banants (0) 0   7315
Salzburg: Ochs; Gercaliu, Sekagya, Kovac, Tchoyi, Boussaidi (Bodnar 62), Aufhauser, Zickler, Nelisse, Obster (Jezek 62), N'Gwat-Mahop (Vonlanthen 62).
Banants: Matiughin; Dagbashian, Burdian, Grigorian, Khachatrian (Gyozalian 86), Krumov, Bareghamian (Kakosian 46), Karapetian, Markov, Balabekian, Zlatev (Hayrapetian 73).

Shakter Karaganda (0) 1 *(Peric 63)*
Debrecen (0) 1 *(Rudolf 61)*   6000
Shakter Karaganda: Loria; Djordjevic, Rusnac, Kislitsyn, Samchenko (Suyumagambetov 50), Kornienko, Nosadze (Glushko 69), Ashirbekov (Kenetaev 83), Lovchev, Pacanda, Peric.
Debrecen: Csernyanszki; Szucs, Takacs, Komlosi, Bernath, Leandro, Dombi (Huszak 46), Kiss, Czvitkovics, Varga (Kerekes 57), Rudolf (Demjen 83).

Siroki (0) 0
Partizani (0) 0   3000
Siroki: Vasilj; Bozic, Juric, Barisic, Silic, Carmo, Lago, Prlic, Marciano (Kozul 53), Bubalo (Raguz 76), Emerson (Zovko 64).
Partizani: Edvan Bakaj; Osmani, Beqiri, Hallaci, Pinari, Gjyla, Muzaka (Cajku 78), Karapici (Capo 58), Dhembi, Ngjela (Perlleshi 63), Elis Bakaj.

Spartak Trnava (0) 2 *(Kozuch 75, 90)*
WIT Georgia (2) 2 *(Lomaia 14, Razmadze 43 (pen))* 3200
Spartak Trnava: Rybansky; Cifersky, Dolezaj, Poncak, Carlos Perez (Hruska 46), Duris (Guldan 65), Jelenkovic, Kopunek, Hanzel, Kozuch, Filipovic (Bernath 56).
WIT Georgia: Bediashvili; Lomaia, Japaridze, Bechvaia, Kvakhadze, Razmadze, Melkadze (Kvaginadze 67), Datunaishvili G, Lipartia (Guelashvili 82), Kvaratskelia (Guchashvili 69), Klimiashvili.

Suduva (0) 1 *(Koziuberda 88)*
The New Saints (0) 0   2500
Suduva: Vitkauskas; Skinderis, Mikuckis, Slavickas V, Koziuberda, Barevicius (Slavickas G 62), Bozinovski, Luksys (Urbsys 77), Lukjanovis, Leimonas, Radavicius.
The New Saints: Harrison; Baker, Courtney, Ruscoe (Toner 68), Wood, Holmes, Beck, Leah, Wilde (Whitfield 78), Hogan (Darlington 56), Taylor.

Tobol (0) 1 *(Golban 59)*
FK Austria (0) 0 8000
Tobol: Aleksandr Petukhov; Dimitrov, Tarasenko, Irismetov, Mukanov, Nurdauletov, Zhumaskaliyev, Kharabara (Sabalakov 85), Baltiev, Aleksandr A Petukhov (Yakovlev 72), Golban (Nurgaliev 88).
FK Austria: Safar; Troyansky, Bak, Schiemer, Dragovic (Hattenberger 83), Netzer (Sun 70), Krammer, Acimovic, Standfest, Okotie, Bazina (Topic 80).

VMK (0) 0
Nordsjaelland (1) 3 *(Lundberg 28, Bernburg 49 (pen), 87)* 3000
VMK: Teles; Volodin (Jurgenson 63), Saviauk, Sarajev, Ratnikov D, Dmitrijev (Jegorov 46), Anniste (Kulatsenko 63), Borissov, Konsa, Gussev, Terehhov.
Nordsjaelland: Hansen; Cagara, Kildentoft, Lundberg, Jensen, Karlsen, Dahl (Christensen 69), Richter (Bernier 78), Bernburg, Nakajima-Farran, Pedersen N (Fetai 62).

Vaduz (1) 1 *(Fischer 32)*
Zrinjski (1) 2 *(Djuric 23, Iten 90 (og))* 720
Vaduz: Sommer; Iten, Dzombic, Ritzberger, Cerrone, Mea Vitali, Bellon, Polverino, Gaspar, Grossklaus (Willian 54), Fischer (Sutter 79).
Zrinjski: Melher; Nikolic, Zurzinov, Sunjic, Serdarusic, Ivankovic, Stojanovic (Anicic 83), Zizovic, Djuric, Matko (Susic 90), Selimovic (Zadro 70).

Vetra (0) 1 *(Ostap 14)*
Viking (0) 0 500
Vetra: Smisko; Barovskis, Kijanskas, Jankauskas, Butrimavicius, Sernas (Grigaitis 90), Lemezis, Vezevicius (Butavicius 64), Ostap, Cvetanovski, Razulis (Blazys 46).
Viking: Myhre; Bertelsen, Soma, Ross, Klingbeil, Gaarde, Stokholm, Danielsen, Fillo, Andersen (Ödegaard 70), Samuelsen (Nisja 80).

Vojvodina (0) 1 *(Duric 59)*
Olimpik Baku (0) 0 3000
Vojvodina: Brkic; Mijatovic, Popovic, Duric, Lazetic (Aleksic 46), Pavlovic, Grozdanovski (Pantelic 18), Trivunovic (Buac 80), Vukajilovic, Tadic, Stosic.
Olimpik Baku: Mehdiyev; Choruzi (Dashdemirov 73), Abuzarov (Dos Santos 87), Akhmedov, Guliyev, Nabiyev, Mogaadi (Musaev 58), Nduka, Khutsishvili, Akhalkatsi, Lascencov.

Zeta (1) 1 *(Knezevic 28)*
Interblock (0) 1 *(Jolic 90)* 4000
Zeta: Saskavcevic; Kaludjerovic M, Colakovic, Gutic, Ivanovic (Boljevic 81), Pelicic, Duric, Mendes (Culafic 75), Savio, Burzanovic, Knezevic (Djalac 70).
Interblock: Rozman; Grabus, Geric, Elsner, Zeljkovic (Rendulic 84), Matic, Salkic, Grabic, Rodic (Pregelj 65), Rakovic, Zahora (Jolic 75).

FIRST QUALIFYING ROUND, SECOND LEG

Tuesday, 29 July 2008

Nordsjaelland (2) 5 *(Bernier 5, Bernburg 53 (pen), 54, Dahl 66, Pode 89)*
VMK (0) 0 2518
Nordsjaelland: Hansen (Rasmussen T 46), Kildentoft, Lundberg, Richter, Bernier (Dahl 26), Nielsen, Christensen, Petersen, Bernburg, Thomsen, Fetai (Pode 58).
VMK: Teles; Volodin, Saviauk, Sarajev, Borissov (Jegorov 69), Ratnikov D (Kulatsenko 65), Jurgenson, Ratnikov E, Konsa (Ahven 82), Gussev, Terehhov.

Thursday, 31 July 2008

Apoel (0) 1 *(Michael 82 (pen))*
Pelister (0) 0 5000
Apoel: Chiotis; Florea (Haxhi 75), Seghiri, Nuno Morais, Charalambides, Broerse, Paulista (Poursaitidis 86), Helio Pinto (Papathanasiou 60), Kontis, Michael, Mirosavljevic.
Pelister: Nikov; Petkovski, Stepanovski, Dimov, Simonovski (Glavevski 46), Todorovski, Presilski, Adriano, Ristevski[a], Blazevski (Micevski 79), Junior (Momirovski 67).

B36 (0) 0
Brondby (0) 2 *(Wass 51, Holmen 90)* 839
B36: Joensen; Alex, Jankovic, Faero, Thorleifsson, Midjord (Hermansen 87), Gunnarsson J, Jacobsen R (Hojsted 75), Olsen M, Matras, Malson (Ellingsgaard 80).
Brondby: Andersen, Schlebrugge, Rasmussen T (Madsen 60), Jonsson, Wass, Gislason, Holmen, Kristiansen (Mikkelsen 77), Lorentzen, Rasmussen M, Williams (Katongo 60).

Banants (0) 0
Salzburg (0) 3 *(Nelisse 56, Ilic 61, Obster 68)* 800
Banants: Matiughin; Dagbashian, Burdian, Grigorian, Hayrapetian, Khachatrian (Zlatev 76), Karapetian, Kakosian, Markov, Balabekian (Bareghamian 63), Tsyhalka (Muradian 84).
Salzburg: Ochs; Gercaliu, Opdam, Sekagya, Jezek, Tchoyi (N'Gwat-Mahop 71), Pitak (Obster 46), Boussaidi, Ilic, Nelisse (Leitgeb 71), Vonlanthen.

Bellinzona (3) 3 *(Garrido 22, Sermeter 31, Roux 45)*
Ararat (0) 1 *(Mkoian 53)* 3127
Bellinzona: Bucchi; Belotti, Mangiarratti, La Rocca, Raso, Sermeter, Wahab, Garrido (Ferrazza 82), Conti, Lustrinelli (Gashi 62), Roux (Neri 72).
Ararat: Prazian; Emilio, Artur S Minasian, Renato, Antonian, Mkoian, Navoian, Artur H Minasian (Safarian 44), Petrosian (Megrabian 49), Marcos, Nranian (Henrique 46).

Birkirkara (0) 0
Hajduk Split (2) 3 *(Strinic 5, Bartolovic 45, Ibricic 90)* 2000
Birkirkara: Paris B; Hartvig, Yanchev, Paris T (Sammut 78), Fenech, Anastasi, Zerafa, Mallia, Galea (Sciberras L 84), Tabone (Triganza 60), Buhagiar.
Hajduk Split: Tomic; Zivkovic, Buljat M, Linic, Gabric, Strinic (Ibricic 46), Maloca, Ticinovic, Rubil (Pezo 75), Kalinic (Oremus 46), Bartolovic.

Borac (1) 3 *(Lazovic 17, Kosic 57, Grkajac 82)*
Dacia (1) 1 *(Korgalidze 3)* 3500
Borac: Grahovac; Dragutinovic, Ignjatovic, Dmitrovic, Antic, Stojcev (Pavlovic 65), Krnjinac, Kosic, Lazovic, Grkajac (Djokovic 87), Stojanovic (Obradovic 89).
Dacia: Romanenco (Chirilov 28); Orbeladze, Andronic, Calin, Martin, Bulat, Boicenco (Gusila 78), Onica[a], Japalau (Orbu 68), Korgalidze, Dvali.

Debrecen (1) 1 *(Rudolf 38)*
Shakter Karaganda (0) 0 8000
Debrecen: Poleksic; Bernath, Komlusi (Szucs 21), Meszaros, Takacs, Huszak (Dombi 70), Kiss, Leandro, Czvitkovics, Bogdanovic (Kerekes 46), Rudolf.
Shakter Karaganda: Loria; Djordjevic, Kornienko, Kislitsyn, Rusnak, Glushko, Lovhev, Ashirbekov (Kozhushko 72), Kenecajev (Samchenko 41), Pacanda, Peric.

FC Copenhagen (3) 7 *(Ailton 23, Junior 25, 60, Hutchinson 45, Kvist 46, Nordstrand 55 (pen), Kristensen 57)*
Cliftonville (0) 0 10,695
FC Copenhagen: Coe; Pospech (Jensen D 46), Janka, Wendt (Albrechtsen 71), Jensen N, Kristensen, Kvist, Nordstrand, Hutchinson (Norregaard 46), Ailton, Junior.
Cliftonville: Connolly; Scannell R, Holland B, O'Hara (McAlinden 69), Holland M, Hamill (Patterson 69), Scannell G, McMullan (Boyd 69), Donaghy, Catney, O'Connor.

FK Austria (1) 2 *(Acimovic 28 (pen), Krammer 52)*
Tobol (0) 0 6404
FK Austria: Safar; Majstorovic, Bak, Schiemer, Sun (Madl 69), Hattenberger, Krammer, Acimovic, Standfest, Okotie (Topic 81), Bazina.
Tobol: Aleksandr Petukhov; Dimitrov, Tarasenko, Irismetov, Mukanov, Nurdauletov[a], Nurgaliev (Yakovlev 68), Zhumaskaliyev (Skorykh 90), Kharabara (Aleksandr A Petukhov 85), Baltiev, Golban.

Flora (0) 2 *(Post 81, 83)*
Djurgaarden (1) 2 *(Cardoso 23, Ekong 54)* 2000
Flora: Aksalu; Vanna (Anier 62), Allas, Kasimir, Vunk, Hakola, Sidorenkov, Hurt (Mosnikov 75), Kams, Reim (Post 46), Ahjupera.
Djurgaarden: Tourray; Haginge (Davids 68), Kuivasto, Tauer, Johannesson, Ekong, Cardoso, Sjolund (Komac 82), Kusi-Asare, Dahlberg, Oremo (Quirino 46).

Gomel (1) 1 *(Bressan 20)*
Legia (1) 4 *(Iwanski 26 (pen), 62, Szalachowski 52, 66)*
8000
Gomel: Lohvinov; Etiege, Rybak, Kuzmianok (Prokharau 64), Misyuk, Bressan (Tigranian 62), Baranok, Matveyenko, Matveichyk, Mkrtchian, Rogerio (Barsukov 46).
Legia: Mucha; Szala, Choto, Rzezniczak, Guerreiro, Giza (Borysiuk 70), Iwanski, Kielbowicz, Rybus (Arruabarrena 79), Radovic, Rocki (Szalachowski 46).

Grevenmacher (1) 1 *(Hoffmann 30)*
Hafnarfjordur (1) 5 *(Gudnason 13, 57, Gudmundsson T 65, 74, Sverrisson B 88)* 1100
Grevenmacher: Oberweis; Janisch, Lorig, Albrecht, Makhloufi, Steimetz, Di Domenico (Thimmesch 71), Siebenaler, Stojadinovic (Munoz■ 61), Hoffmann, Bozic (Helbig 77).
Hafnarfjordur: Sigurdsson; Sverrisson B, Eriksson (Saevarsson 77), Nielsen, Valgardsson, Asgeirsson (Siim 62), Vidarsson D, Gudmundsson T, Vilhjalmsson, Gudnason (Gudmundsson M 73), Bjornsson.

Haka (2) 4 *(Mahlakaarto 10, Popovitch 15, Manninen 70, Minkenen 78)*
Cork City (0) 0 3200
Haka: Dovbnya; Kangaskorpi, Viljanen (Minkenen 61), Okkonen, Kauppila, Manninen (Nikkila 85), Mahlakaarto, Fowler, Parviainen, Lehtinen (Mattila 52), Popovitch.
Cork City: Devine; Murray, Lordan (Behan■ 46), Sullivan, Danny Murphy, Gamble, Healy, Darren Murphy, Kearney (Ryan 61), Mooney (O'Flynn 81).

IA Akranes (1) 2 *(Magnusson 16, Sigurbjornsson 49)*
Honka (0) 1 *(Vasara 72)* 650
IA Akranes: Sigurbjornsson; Gudmundsson, Magnusson, Svadjumovic (Leosson 83), Bilokapic, Thordarson, Cingel, Pjetursson AI (Pjetursson AY 71), Akason (Gudjonsson T 63), Sigurdarson, Gudjonsson B.
Honka: Maanoja, Jalasto, Turunen, Heilala, Koskinen, Weckstrom (Kukko 73), Perovuo, Koskela, Haarala, Puustinen (Vasara 64), Vuorinen (Backman 88).

Interblock (0) 1 *(Zahora 83)*
Zeta (0) 0 800
Interblock: Rozman; Geric, Pregelj (Grabus 46), Elsner, Matic, Rendulic■, Jukan, Salkic, Grabic (Zavrl 67), Rakovic, Zahora (Jolic 88).
Zeta: Saskavcevic; Kaludjerovic M, Colakovic, Gutic, Ivanovic, Djuric, Mendes, Burzanovic (Pelicic 65), Precheski (Djalac 51), Knezevic, Culafic (Djurovic 78).

Juvenes (0) 0
Hapoel Tel Aviv (2) 2 *(Antebi 5, Douglas 8)* 500
Juvenes: Montanari; Renzi, Ceci, Marzocchi, Fantini (Gamberini 46), Perrotta (Ercolani 90), Galli, Santini, Zonzini (Di Luigi 46), Selva, Casadei.
Hapoel Tel Aviv: Enyeama; Douglas, Topuzakov (Duani 73), Yeboah (Luz 62), Srur (Natcho 62), Badir, Zehavi, Abutbul, Antebi, Kende, Telkiyski.

Kalmar (3) 7 *(Elm R 7, Lindberg 9, Israelsson 41, Dauda 46, Larsson 61, Sobralense 65 (pen), 68)*
Racing (0) 1 *(Bilon 90)* 2034
Kalmar: Wasta; Sorin, Lindberg, Eklund (Lennartsson 33), Larsson, Rosengren, Rydstrom, Ingelsten (Augustsson 67), Elm R, Israelsson, Dauda (Sobralense 59).
Racing: Oster; Zenanne, Liotte, Willemin, Feller, Schnell, Belli (Camara 46), Belabed (Omerovic 69), Carvalho (Centrone 66), Pupovac, Bilon.

Lech (1) 4 *(Stilic 35, Murawski 52, Injac 64, Reiss 82)*
Lenkoran (1) 1 *(Ramazanov 45)* 17,000
Lech: Kotorowski; Arboleda, Bosacki, Wojtkowiak, Henriquez, Stilic (Lewandowski 68), Murawski, Peszko, Injac (Cueto 78), Bandrowski, Rengifo (Reiss 73).
Lenkoran: Kramarenko; Denis, Shukurov, Veikutis, Bakhshiev■, Amirguliyev, Todorov, Abdullayev (Martins 53), Diego Souza (Gurbanov 86), Ramazanov, Bamba.

Manchester City (0) 2 *(Petrov 48, Vassell 90)*
EB/Streymur (0) 0 7334
Manchester City: Hart; Corluka, Ball, Dunne, Richards, Johnson, Gelson (Hamann 62), Sturridge (Evans 70), Elano, Vassell, Petrov (Etuhu 69).
EB/Streymur: Torgard; Jacobsen (Thomassen 77), Clementsen, Bo, Djurhuus, Bardur Olsen, Foldgast (Brian Olsen 55), Anghel, Samuelsen, Hansen A (Balog 61), Niclasen.
at Barnsley.

Metalurgs Liepajas (1) 2 *(Karlsons 36, 86)*
Glentoran (0) 0 3500
Metalurgs Liepajas: Krucs■; Klava, Zirnis, Antonio, Jemelins (Spole 7), Tamosauskas, Surnins, Solonicins (Kamess 89), Miceika, Beniusis (Grebis 61), Karlsons.
Glentoran: Morris; Nixon, Neill (Carson 80), Leeman, Ward, Hill (Burrows■ 73), McCabe■, Fordyce, Boyce (Fitzgerald 61), Halliday, Hamilton.

Midtjylland (2) 4 *(Nworuh 3, 34, Sivebaek 56, Babatunde 77)*
Bangor City (0) 0 4069
Midtjylland: Raska; Kristensen J, Klimpl, Ipsa, Marcic, Olsen PF (Oliseh 46), Flinta, Akilu, Sivebaek (Gnanou 70), Babatunde, Nworuh (Thygesen 70).
Bangor City: Smith; Swanick, Beattie, Johnson, Brewerton, Seargeant, Limbert (Fowler 63), Walsh (Hoy 70), Davies, Noon, Edwards (Stott 57).

Milano (1) 1 *(Statovci 17)*
Omonia (0) 2 *(Christofi 77, Cafu 85)* 800
Milano: Nuredinoski; Lazarevski, Statovci, Kukaj (Gancev 46), Ristov, Manevski, Isufi (Gesovski 78), Trajcev, Gasi, Alimi, Gligorovski (Sali 59).
Omonia: Georgallides; Ndikumana, Wenzel, Pletsch (Alabi 78), Zlogar, Kaseka, Duro (Bangura 46), Charalambous, Aguirre (Cafu 63), Clayton, Christofi.

Mogren (0) 0
Ironi Kiryat (1) 3 *(Nussbaum 31, Peretz 53, Tzarfati 68)* 2800
Mogren: Janjulevic; Stojakovic (Kalezic 57), Jovanovic, Gluscevic, Vujovic N (Neric 73), Rakic, Bozovic, Radovic, Pejovic, Janicic, Vujovic M (Zec 46).
Ironi Kiryat: Amos; Agouda, Tzarfati (Ben Zaken 79), Kozuch (Elgarbeli 83), Nussbaum, Peretz (Shabtai 72), Suan, Avidor, Hasarma, Biton, Bakhar.

Olimpik Baku (0) 1 *(Akhalkatsi 49)*
Vojvodina (0) 1 *(Djuric 86)* 5000
Olimpik Baku: Mehdiyev; Lascencov (Nabiyev 73), Nduka, Diano, Guliyev, Akhmedov, Choruzi, Mògaadi, Akhalkatsi (Dashdemirov 70), Khutsishvili (Musaev 90), Gomesh.
Vojvodina: Babalj; Kizito, Mijatovic, Stosic, Djuric, Vukajilovic (Aleksic 58), Popovic, Tumbasevic, Grozdanovski, Pantelic (Korac 73), Buac (Pavlovic 90).

Otaci (0) 0
Hertha Berlin (0) 0 700
Otaci: Kosov; Mekang, Oyinloye, Soltanici, Suruceanu, Malitskyy (Roslach 79), Savchenko, Velesco (Carabulea 65), Groshev, Andrei Tcaciuc, Alexandr Tcaciuc.
Hertha Berlin: Drobny; Kaka, Friedrich, Radjabali-Fardi, Chahed (Stein 46), Dardai (Riedel 63), Nicu, Lustenberger, Hartmann, Pantelic (Bigalke 46), Domovchiyski.

Partizani (1) 1 *(Muzaka 40 (pen))*
Siroki (2) 3 *(Alexandre 10, 45, Silic 82)* 31,708
Partizani: Ed Bakaj; Hallaci, Pinari, Osmani, Beqiri, Gjyla, Karapici (Cajku 67), Capo, Muzaka (Tafaj 80), El Bakaj (Perlleshi 32), Ngjela.
Siroki: Vasilj; Lago, Marciano (Kozul 53), Juric, Bozic, Silic, Barisic, Bubalo (Raguz 76), Alexandre, Emerson (Zovko 64), Prlic.

Sant Julia (0) 0
Chernomore (3) 5 *(Varela 22 (og), Yurukov 39, Manolov 41, 50, Andonov 64)* 900
Sant Julia: Tremonti; Wagner, Abdian, Nastri (Diaby 53), Varela, Xinos (Goldschmidt 61), Miraglia, Peppe, Spano, Romero (Adaime 80), Peralta.
Chernomore: Ilchev; Domakinov, Bachev (Pires 46), Stoyanov (Dyakov 61), Andre, Andonov■, Alexandrov, Iliev, Petkov, Yurukov, Manolov (Atanasov 61).

Slaven (1) 4 *(Bilen 24, Caval 72, Vrucina 74, 90)*
Marsaxlokk (0) 0 2500
Slaven: Rodic; Puric, Kokalovic, Kristic, Caval, Poldrugac, Jajalo, Posavec (Vrucina 64), Bilen, Sehic (Juric 50), Kresinger (Gregurina 69).
Marsaxlokk: Darmanin; Licari, Renato (Said 46), Camenzuli, Mamo, Sammut, Sciberras (Pereira 73), Pullicino, Templeman, Wellman, Julio Cesar (Cassar 46).

St Patrick's Ath (1) 2 *(Harris 41, Quigley 71 (pen))*
Olimps Riga (0) 0 3000
St Patrick's Ath: Barry Ryan; Byrne, Lynch, Harris, Paisley, Dempsey, Fahey (O'Cearuill 90), O'Brien (Kirby 76), Quigley (Bobby Ryan 81), Fitzpatrick, Guy.
Olimps Riga: Ikstens; Junior, Petrenko, Kazura, Kandov (Sinelnikovs 64), Zolotarjovs, Fertovs, Jakovlev (Sputajs 61), Tarasovs, Perepecko (Turkovs 72), Zils.

The New Saints (0) 0
Suduva (0) 1 *(Lukjanovs 85)* 879
The New Saints: Harrison; Courtney, Baker (Carter 51), Taylor, Holmes, Ruscoe, Wilde, Beck, Wood, Toner (Darlington 65), Hogan.
Suduva: Vitkauskas; Skinderis, Mikuckis, Leimonas, Slavickas V, Bozinovski, Koziuberda, Barevicius (Jasaitis 64), Radavicius (Slavickas G 79), Luksys (Gardzijauskas 86), Lukjanovs.

Viking (2) 2 *(Stokholm 3, 33 (pen))*
Vetra (0) 0 5650
Viking: Myhre; Bertelsen, Soma (Steenslid 42), Ross (Nisja 50), Klingbeil, Gaarde, Stokholm, Danielsen, Fillo, Ijeh (Samuelsen 66), Odegaard.
Vetra: Smisko; Barovskis, Kijanskas, Jankauskas, Milosevski, Butrimavicius, Sernas, Vezevicius (Stankevicius 46), Ostap (Butavicius 46), Cvetanovski, Grigaitis (Blazys 76).

Vllaznia (0) 0
Koper (0) 0 5000
Vllaznia: Olsi; Beqiri, Belisha, Kaci (Kousal 87), Lika, Nallbani (Kapaj 75), Basic, Osja, Teli, Smajlaj (Lici 80), Sukaj.
Koper: Hasic; Amusan, Bozicic, Handanagic (Ipavec 62), Cruz Vitagliano, Nwankwo, Mertelj, Rastovac, Secic (Smon 68), Rajcevic, Viler (Pahor 90).

WIT Georgia (0) 1 *(Razmadze 90)*
Spartak Trnava (0) 0 2000
WIT Georgia: Bediashvili; Lomaia, Japaridze, Bechvaia, Kvakhadze, Razmadze, Melkadze, Datunaishvili G, Lipartia (Beriashvili 67), Kvaratskelia (Maisashvili 88), Klimiashvili (Kvaginadze 80).
Spartak Trnava: Hrdina; Dolezaj, Hanzel, Poncak, Niang, Duris (Filipovic 75), Jelenkovic, Kopunek (Prochazka 65), Hruska (Guldan 46), Kopacka, Kozuch.

Zestafoni (0) 1 *(Gotsiridze 51)*
Gyor (0) 2 *(Jakl 52, Pakolicz 66)* 4000
Zestafoni: Kvaskhvadze R; Lobzhanidze■, Todua, Boyomo, Oniani (Santos 82), Dzaria (Kvakhvadze 59), Daushvili, Vieira, Gelashvili, Gotsiridze, Chassern (Ionanidze 71).

Gyor: Stevanovic; Pinter■, Nikolov (Pakolicz 55), Supic, Bank, Jakl, Jozsi (Kovacs I 55), Bicak, Koltai, Bajzat (Kovacs II 69), Tokody.

Zilina (0) 1 *(Jez 90)*
MTZ-Ripo (0) 0 5380
Zilina: Pernis; Vomacka, Pekarik, Piacek, Sourek, Strba, Jez, Styvar, Belak (Rilke 46), Vladavic, Karoglan (Adauto 33) (Pecalka 88).
MTZ-Ripo: Sulima; Zrnanovic, Valkanov, Kamara (Nicholas 57), Strakhanovich, Sashcheko (Bubnov 81), Shchegrikovich (Pehlic 72), Bordachev, Eremchuk, Kvaratskhelia, Kontsevoy.

Zrinjski (2) 3 *(Djuric 7, Sunjic 26, Matko 77)*
Vaduz (0) 0 8000
Zrinjski: Melher; Nikolic, Zurzinov, Sunjic, Serdarusic, Ivankovic, Stojanovic, Zizovic (Anicic 80), Djuric (Susic 88), Matko (Bubalo 90), Selimovic.
Vaduz: Sommer; Reinmann, Dzombic (Bevacqua 57), Ritzberger, Cerrone, Mea Vitali (Fejzulahi 46), Bellon, Polverino, Sutter, Gaspar (Willian 46), Grossklaus.

SECOND QUALIFYING ROUND, FIRST LEG

Thursday, 14 August 2008

AEK Athens (0) 0
Omonia (1) 1 *(Cafu 40)* 35,000
AEK Athens: Saja; Edson Ramos, Majstorovic, Alexopoulus, Juanfran, Kafes, Rikka (Hetemaj 62), Zorbas (Pavlis 46), Rivaldo (Lagos 78), Blanco, Scocco.
Omonia: Georgallides; Ndikumana, Wenzel, Pletsch, Zlogar, Kaseke, Duro (Kaiafas 76), Charalambous, Clayton (Aloneftis 80), Christofi (Okkas 85), Cafu.

Apoel (1) 2 *(Broerse 34, Kosowski 47)*
Red Star Belgrade (1) 2 *(Edgar 9, Burzanovic 62)* 15,000
Apoel: Chiotis; Florea, Seghiri, Nuno Morais, Charalambides, Kosowski (Helio Pinto 69), Broerse, Paulista (Onwuachi 81), Kontis, Michael (Mirosavljevic 74), Zewlakow.
Red Star Belgrade: Radivojevic; Bronowicki (Ninkov 40), Markovic, Gueye, Jakovic, Milijas, Burzanovic, Bogdanovic, Blazic (Koroman 84), Edgar, Subasic (Trickovski 65).

Aris Salonika (0) 1 *(Koke 55)*
Slaven (0) 0 20,000
Aris Salonika: Kelemen; Lembo, Aurelio, Jahic, Vangjeli (Wlodarczyk 52), Calvo (Javito 52), Garcia, Regueiro, Battion, Thiago Gentil (Neto 65), Koke.
Slaven: Rodic; Bosnjak, Rogulj, Bilen (Gregurina 67), Lapic, Caval, Poldrugac, Jajalo, Juric (Kresinger 78), Posavec, Vrucina (Sehic 78).

Borac (0) 1 *(Pavlovic 47)*
Lokomotiv Sofia (0) 0 3500
Borac: Grahovac; Ignjatovic, Dmitrovic, Antic, Maric, Stojcev (Djokovic 69), Krnjinac, Pavlovic, Kosic (Mugosa 82), Grkajac, Stojanovic (Obradovic 90).
Lokomotiv Sofia: Bondzulic; Dzaferovic, Markov, Dobrev, Bandalovski, Ivanov, Zlatinski, Spisic (Bogdanovic 60), Dyakov (Atanasov 82), Mitev (Djilas 60), Baldovaliev.

Braga (0) 1 *(Linz 68)*
Zrinjski (0) 0 6500
Braga: Eduardo; Rodriguez, Moises, Evaldo, Frechaut, Joao Pereira, Mossoro (Matheus 46), Luis Aguiar, Meyong (Wender 80), Linz, Alan (Vandinho 83).
Zrinjski: Melher; Zurzinov, Anicic (Susic 49), Sunjic, Serdarusic, Ivankovic, Stojanovic (Kordic 81), Zizovic, Djuric, Matko, Selimovic.

Djurgaarden (1) 2 *(Oremo 37, Cardoso 90)*
Rosenborg (0) 1 *(Sapara 76)* 6947
Djurgaarden: Tourray; Quivasto, Tauer, Johannesson, Magnusson, Ekong, Sjolund (Cardoso 60), Komac (Dahlberg 79), Davids (Haginge 70), Kusi-Asare, Oremo.
Rosenborg: Jarstein; Lustig, Stadsgaard, Lago, Nordvik, Tettey, Skjelbred, Sapara, Berisha (Storflor 76), Konan, Iversen.

Dnepr (1) 3 *(Kalinichenko 10, Nazarenko 47, Kornilenko 78)*
Bellinzona (0) 2 *(Kalu 64, Sermeter 75 (pen))* 10,000
Dnepr: Kernozenko; Shershun, Eshchenko, Rusol, Lisitski (Lepa 70), Shelayev, Kalinichenko, Nazarenko, Rotan (Morais 78), Pashaev, Vorobei (Kornilenko 60).
Bellinzona: Gritti; Siqueira Barras, Mangiarretti, La Rocca, Raso, Sermeter, Gashi (Ferrazza 90), Wahab, Garrido, Kalu (De Zenzo 82), Lustrinelli (Roux 71).

Elfsborg (2) 2 *(Ishizaki 24 (pen), Karlsson 29)*
St Patrick's Ath (0) 2 *(Quigley 57 (pen), Dempsey 82)*
3918
Elfsborg: Wiland; Floren, Karlsson, Mobaeck, Lucic, Augustsson, Svensson A, Bajrami (Nordmark 79), Ishizaki, Nilsson, Berglund (Floren 71).
St Patrick's Ath: Barry Ryan; Lynch (Bobby Ryan 67), O'Cearuill, Harris, Gavin, Paisley, Fahey, Dempsey, Quigley, Murphy, Guy.

FC Copenhagen (1) 3 *(Santin 1, Junior 79, Nordstrand 85)*
Lillestrom (0) 1 *(Kippe 90)* 13,099
FC Copenhagen: Christiansen; Pospech, Larsson, Wendt, Jorgensen, Norregaard (Kvist 67), Hutchinson, Kristensen, Ailton (Junior 59), Nordstrand, Santin (Jensen N 85).
Lillestrom: Moldskred; Pedersen, Bertheussen, Stensaas, Kippe, Bjorkoy, Brenne (Sogard 81), Mouelhi, Sundgot (Feltus 81), Essediri (Myklebust 88), Occean.

Gent (0) 2 *(Thijs 62, Azofeifa 86)*
Kalmar (0) 1 *(Ingelsten 81)* 6597
Gent: Jorgacevic; Smoje, Suler, Thompson, Duarte, Thijs, Rosales, Maric (Azofeifa 80), Webnje (Olufade 54), Foley, Ruiz.
Kalmar: Wasta; Sorin, Lindberg, Eklund, Larsson (Sobralense 79), Rosengren, Rydstrom, Ingelsten, Elm V, Elm R, Elm D (Dauda 79).

Hafnarfjordur (1) 1 *(Gudmundsson M 45)*
Aston Villa (3) 4 *(Barry 4, Young A 7, Agbonlahor 38, Laursen 64)* 2200
Hafnarfjordur: Sigurdsson; Sverrisson B, Eriksson (Saevarsson 75), Siim, Nielsen, Valgardsson, Vidarsson D (Asgeirsson 63), Gudmundsson M, Gudmundsson T, Vilhjalmsson, Gudnason (Gardarsson 75).
Aston Villa: Friedel; Gardner, Shorey, Reo-Coker, Davies, Laursen, Petrov (Salifou 66), Agbonlahor (Delfouneso 76), Harewood, Barry, Young A (Routledge 71).

Haka (0) 0
Brondby (1) 4 *(Rasmussen M 30, Lorentzen 70, Williams 76, Madsen 82 (pen))* 1900
Haka: Doybnya; Kangaskorpi, Okkonen, Kauppila, Manninen (Nikkila 82), Mahlakaarto, Fowler (Minkenen 48), Parviainen, Lehtinen, Popovitch, Mattila (Gilmour 60).
Brondby: Andersen; Schlebrugge, Jonsson, Rasmussen T, Wass, Holmen, Lorentzen, Mikkelsen, Gislason (Kanstrup 77), Kristiansen (Williams 65), Rasmussen M (Madsen 69).

Honka (0) 0
Viking (0) 0 2230
Honka: Peltonen; Koskinen, Heilala, Jalasto, Hakanpaa, Weckstrom, Perovuo (Lepola 21), Turunen, Haarala, Vasara, Kokko (Puustinen 79).
Viking: Myhre; Steenslid, Pereira (Bertelsen 74), Soma, Ross, Gaarde, Stokholm, Danielsen, Fillo (Odegaard 77), Samuelsen, Ijeh (Austnes 86).

Interblock (0) 0
Hertha Berlin (1) 2 *(Pantelic 16, 81)* 2000
Interblock: Rozman; Grabus, Lazic, Ntame, Pregelj (Zeljkovic 59), Elsner, Matic, Grabic, Rodic (Jolic 46), Rakovic (Jukan 77), Zahora.
Hertha Berlin: Drobny; Kaka, Von Bergen, Cicero (Hartmann 72), Stein, Ebert, Piszczek, Lustenberger (Simunic 69), Pantelic, Raffael (Nicu 63), Chermiti.

La Coruna (0) 0
Hajduk Split (0) 0 12,000
La Coruna: Adrian (Omar Bravo 57); Aranzubia, Manuel Pablo, Luis Filipe, Lopo, Ze Castro (De Guzman 75), Sergio, Guardado, Valeron (Xisco 67), Juan Rodriguez, Riki.
Hajduk Split: Subasic; Zivkovic, Ibricic (Buljat J 89), Andric, Gabric, Oremus (Linic 61), Skoko, Maloca, Ticinovic (Strinic 70), Rubil, Kalinic.

Lech (2) 6 *(Rengifo 4, Lewandowski 14, 56, Vallori 76 (og), Injac 84, Peszko 88)*
Grasshoppers (0) 0 16,500
Lech: Kotorowski; Arboleda, Bosacki, Wojtkowiak, Henriquez, Stilic (Cueto 90), Murawski, Peszko, Bandrowski, Lewandowski (Injac 80), Rengifo (Reiss 86).
Grasshoppers: Jakupovic; Voser, Vallori, Colina, Daprela (Mikari 85), Lulic, Calla (Bobadilla 46), Cabanas, Salatic, Toure (Zuber 46), Sabanovic.

Legia (0) 1 *(Guerreiro 66)*
FC Moscow (0) 2 *(Cesnauskis 53, Samedov 63)* 4000
Legia: Mucha; Szala, Choto (Kumbev 17), Rzezniczak, Guerreiro, Iwanski, Kielbowicz, Vukovic, Rybus (Szalachowski 46), Radovic, Chinyama (Giza 66).
FC Moscow: Zhevnov; Godunok, Nababkin, Jop, Kaleshin, Bystrov, Cizek (Epureanu 85), Rebko (Samedov 59), Ivanov, Cesnauskis, Stavpets (Bracamonte 46).

Litex (0) 0
Ironi Kiryat (0) 0 2500
Litex: Golubovic; Barthe, Cambon, Venkov, Manolev, Bertin, Wellington (Eduardo 88), Sandrinho, Angelov (Bibishkov 76), Niflore (Dudu 46), Popov.
Ironi Kiryat: Amos; Bakhar, Lavi, Nussbaum, Kojok (Ruchet 85), Tzarfati, Cespedes, Hasarma, Suan, Avidor (Biton 90), Agouda (Maicon 65).

Maccabi Netanya (1) 1 *(Kioyo 27)*
Chernomore (1) 1 *(Aleksandrov 43)* 4000
Maccabi Netanya: Strauber; Saban, Bivian, Dayan, Hermon (Cohen 56), Haymovich, Gazal, Menashe (Maabi 77), Kioyo, Awudu, Yampolsky (Dego 46).
Chernomore: Ilchev; Domakinov, Bachev, Andre, Alexandrov, Petkov, Georgiev (Stoyanov 31), Yurukov (Pires 90), Fernandez, Aleksandrov (Dyakov 90), Manolov.

Manchester City (0) 0
Midtjylland (1) 1 *(Olsen D 15)* 17,200
Manchester City: Hart; Corluka, Richards, Dunne, Ben Haim, Johnson, Caicedo (Bojinov 64), Gelson, Sturridge, Elano (Etuhu 67), Petrov.
Midtjylland: Heinze; Afriyie, Califf, Poulsen, Reid, Borring, Florescu, Thygesen, Olsen D (Madsen 73), Salami (Flinta 84), Nworuh (Babatunde 55).

Metalurgs Liepajas (0) 0
Vaslui (0) 2 *(N'Doye 70, Ghenchev 73)* 3000
Metalurgs Liepajas: Steinbors; Klava, Zirnis, Antonio, Tamosauskas, Surnins, Solonicins, Dobrecovs (Kamess 68), Beniusis (Prohorenkovs 79), Grebis, Karlsons.
Vaslui: Kuciak; Buhus, Luz, Canu, Munteanu, Ghenchev, Aliuta (Gheorghiu 76), Ljubinkovic, N'Doye, Burdujan (Zmeu 65), Tamwanjera (Jovanovic N 78).

Queen of the South (1) 1 *(O'Connor 27)*
Nordsjaelland (2) 2 *(Kibebe 2, Bernier 32)* 4406
Queen of the South: Halliwell; Reid (Harris 77), McQuilken, Barr, Thomson, MacFarlane (Adams 69), Tosh, Burns, Kean, O'Connor, Arbuckle (Dobbie 46).
Nordsjaelland: Hansen; Kibebe, Kildentoft, Lundberg, Richter, Karlsen, Bernier, Christensen (Nakajima-Farran 65), Petersen (Pode 70), Bernburg (Dahl 80), Fetai.

Siroki (0) 1 *(Silic 90)*
Besiktas (1) 2 *(Delgado 19, Nobre 83)* 6500
Siroki: Vasilj; Bozic, Topic, Kozul, Juric, Barisic, Silic, Carmo (Raguz 64), Lago (Zovko 81), Marciano, Bubalo (Cruz 54).
Besiktas: Rustu; Gokhan, Cisse (Serdar K 75), Sivok, Ugur, Delgado, Tello, Aydin (Serdar O 71), Ali, Bobo (Nobre 66), Holosko.

Slovan (0) 1 *(Frejlach 85)*
Zilina (1) 2 *(Adauto 44, Jez 58)* 7750
Slovan: Zlamal; Kostal, Janu, Bilek, Holenak, Dockal, Papousek (Dittrich 58), Keric, Radzinevicius, Nezmar (Smetana 75), Dort (Frejlach 62).
Zilina: Pernis; Vomacka, Pekarik, Tesak, Pecalka, Strba, Jez, Styvar (Lietava 77), Vladavic, Rilke (Belak 75), Adauto (Durica 86).

Stabaek (1) 2 *(Kjolo 37, 71)*
Rennes (0) 1 *(Sow 77)* 2809
Stabaek: Knudsen; Kjolo, Skjonsberg, Holmvik, Annan, Keller, Farnerud, Alanzinho, Gunnarsson (Palmason 87), Nannskog, Andersson (Stenvoll 80).
Rennes: Douchez; Bocanegra, Fanni, Hansson, Dembele, Mangane, Marveaux (Leroy 68), Cheyrou, Danze, Gyan (Sow 46), Thomert (Pagis 60).

Stuttgart (2) 2 *(Tasci 13, Marica 33)*
Gyor (1) 1 *(Boor 45)* 11,000
Stuttgart: Lehmann; Osorio, Tasci, Magnin, Lanig (Hitzlsperger 81), Simak, Basturk (Pardo 81), Hilbert, Khedira, Marica (Fischer 81), Gomez.
Gyor: Stevanovic; Kovacs I, Supic, Bank, Jakl (Pakolicz 85), Jozsi, Boor, Volgyi (Nikolov 46), Koltai, Bajzat (Kovacs II 76), Tokody.

Suduva (1) 1 *(Luksys 31)*
Salzburg (1) 4 *(Sekagya 42, Janko 57 (pen), 62 (pen),*
N'Gwat-Mahop 72) 3500
Suduva: Vitkauskas; Gnedojus, Mikuckis, Skinderis, Barevicius (Slavickas G 49), Koziuberda, Radavicius, Bozinovski (Jasaitis 82), Slavickas V, Luksys (Maciulevicius 79), Lukjanovs.
Salzburg: Ochs; Bodnar, Opdam, Sekagya, Traoui (Obster 84), Jezek, Boussaidi, Ilic (Janocko 79), Aufhauser, Vonlanthen, Janko (N'Gwat-Mahop 71).

Vllaznia (0) 0
Napoli (1) 3 *(Inacio Pia 28, 47, Denis 75)* 20,000
Vllaznia: Olsi; Teli, Osja (Hoti 82), Basic, Belisha (Lici 46), Beqiri, Smajli (Boadu 65), Kaci, Nalbani, Lika, Sukaj.
Napoli: Iezzo; Cannavaro, Contini, Rinaudo, Vitale (Grava 76), Pazienza, Blasi, Maggio, Hamsik (Montervino 80), Denis, Inacio Pia (De Zerbi 69).

Vojvodina (0) 0
Hapoel Tel Aviv (0) 0 9000
Vojvodina: Brkic; Kizito, Mijatovic, Stosic, Djuric, Vukajilovic (Korac 71), Popovic, Tumbasevic (Pantelic 57), Grozdanovski, Buac, Aleksic (Sepuya 78).
Hapoel Tel Aviv: Enyeama; Douglas, Topuzakov, Antebi, Badir, Vermouth (Srur 80), Abutbul, Cohen, Telkiyski (Luz 64), Yeboah, Zahavi (Natcho 64).

WIT Georgia (0) 0
FK Austria (0) 0
Match not played; unrest in Georgia. Tie to be decided on second leg.

Young Boys (1) 4 *(Schneuwly 41, 77, Regazzoni 68, 87)*
Debrecen (1) 1 *(Rudolf 17)* 6646
Young Boys: Wolfli; Ghezal, Schneider, Portillo, Raimondi (Luscher 80), Bastians, Varela, Hochstrasser, Yapi-Yapo, Eudis (Regazzoni 66), Schneuwly (Kulaksizoglu 84).
Debrecen: Poleksic; Szucs, Takacs, Bernath, Leandro, Meszaros, Demjen, Kiss, Czvitkovics (Szakaly 79), Rudolf, Olah (Omagbemi 53).

Zurich (1) 1 *(Hassli 13)*
Sturm Graz (0) 1 *(Haas 78 (pen))* 8700
Zurich: Leoni; Lampi, Stahel, Rochat, Barmettler, Tihinen, Aegerter, Nikci (Alphonse 70), Djuric, Abdi, Hassli (Mehmedi 85).
Sturm Graz: Schicklgruber; Sonnleitner, Feldhofer, Shashiashvili (Lamotte 22), Kandelaki, Hlinka, Muratovic, Holzl, Stankovic (Jantscher 64), Haas (Sereinig 89), Kienzl.

SECOND QUALIFYING ROUND, SECOND LEG

Tuesday, 26 August 2008

Lokomotiv Sofia (1) 1 *(Atanasov 18)*
Borac (1) 1 *(Stojanovic 37 (pen))* 4000
Lokomotiv Sofia: Bondzulic; Dzaferovic, Markov, Dobrev, Bandalovski, Ivanov (Zlatinski 65), Spisic, Atanasov, Bogdanovic (Mitev 63), Antunovic (Djilas 76), Baldovaliev.
Borac: Grahovac; Dragutinovic, Ignjatovic, Dmitrovic, Antic, Maric, Stojcev (Pavlovic 78), Krnjinac, Mugosa (Djokovic 90), Grkajac (Lazovic 44), Stojanovic.

Nordsjaelland (0) 2 *(Bernburg 85, 89)*
Queen of the South (1) 1 *(Harris 2)* 3452
Nordsjaelland: Hansen; Kibebe, Kildentoft, Lundberg, Richter S, Karlsen (Dahl 46), Bernier, Christensen (Nielsen 86), Petersen (Fetai 68), Richter J, Bernburg.
Queen of the South: Bell; Reid, Barr, Thomson, Harris, MacFarlane (Robertson 79), Tosh, Burns, Adams (Dobbie 64), Kean (McQuilken 69), O'Connor.

Thursday, 28 August 2008

Aston Villa (1) 1 *(Gardner 27)*
Hafnarfjordur (1) 1 *(Bjornsson 30)* 25,000
Aston Villa: Friedel; Gardner, Salifou, Reo-Coker, Davies, Knight, Osbourne, Harewood, Agbonlahor (Delfouneso 62), Barry, Routledge.
Hafnarfjordur: Sigurdsson; Sverrisson B (Gardarsson 85), Siim, Nielsen, Valgardsson, Asgeirsson, Vidarsson D, Gudmundsson M, Gudmundsson T (Saevarsson 83), Vilhjalmsson, Bjornsson (Gudnason 58).

Bellinzona (1) 2 *(Gashi 1, La Rocca 76)*
Dnepr (1) 1 *(Samodin 9)* 4200
Bellinzona: Gritti; Bernardet, Sigueira Barras, Mangiarratti, La Rocca, Sermeter, Gashi (Conti 87), Wahab, Garrido (Roux 73), Kalu, Lustrinelli (Mehmeti 90).
Dnepr: Startsev; Shershun, Eshchenko, Rusol, Pashaev, Lisitski (Morais 79), Shelayev, Kalinichenko (Lepa 79), Nazarenko, Rotan (Vorobei 65), Samodin.

Besiktas (1) 4 *(Ugur 14, Serdar O 49, Bobo 58, Tello 85)*
Siroki (0) 0 30,000
Besiktas: Rustu; Serdar K, Zapotocny, Cisse, Sivok, Ugur, Delgado (Emre O 77), Tello, Serdar O (Ekrem 65), Bobo (Batuhan 88), Holosko.
Siroki: Vasilj; Bozic, Topic, Kozul, Juric, Barisic, Silic, Carmo (Zovko 62), Lago, Marciano (Zelenika 53), Bubalo (Cruz 63).

Brondby (2) 2 *(Madsen 30, Holmen 41)*
Haka (0) 0 5100
Brondby: Andersen; Schlebrugge, Jonsson (Berthelsen 46), Rasmussen T, Wass, Holmen, Lorentzen, Ericsson (Williams 65), Gislason, Kristiansen (Mikkelsen 46), Madsen.
Haka: Doybnya; Kangaskorpi■, Viljanen, Okkonen, Kauppila, Manninen (Gilmour 62), Mahlakaarto, Fowler, Minkenen (Mattila 62), Lehtinen, Popovitch.

Chernomore (1) 2 *(Aleksandrov 10, Andre 77)*
Maccabi Netanya (0) 0 2000
Chernomore: Ilchev (Kolev 46); Pires, Dyakov, Stoyanov, Alexandrov, Iliev, Petkov, Yurukov, Fernandez (Andre 70), Aleksandrov, Manolov (Georgiev 90).
Maccabi Netanya: Strauber; Luis Marin, Saban, Bivian, Dayan, Hermon, Haimovich (Shechter 46), Gazal, Menashe (Tazamata 79), Kioyo, Awudu (Dego 79).

Debrecen (1) 2 *(Olah 42, Omagbemi 73)*
Young Boys (1) 3 *(Schneuwly 33, Regazzoni 56,*
Yapi-Yapo 67) 6000
Debrecen: Poleksic; Takacs, Biro, Bernath, Leandro, Dombi, Meszaros, Kiss, Varga (Omagbemi 61), Kerekes (Czvitkovics 66), Olah (Eterovic 84).
Young Boys: Wolfli; Ghezal, Schneider, Portillo, Raimondi (Bastians 71), Hochstrasser (Kulaksizoglu 64), Yapi-Yapo, Doumbia, Regazzoni, Luscher, Schneuwly (Varela 64).

FC Moscow (1) 2 *(Strelkov 6, Kuzmin 50)*
Legia (0) 0 3500
FC Moscow: Zhevnov; Godunok, Cheshukov, Nababkin, Epureanu, Kuzmin, Jop, Kaleshin, Bystrov (Stavpets 76), Samedov (Ivanov 70), Strelkov (Bracamonte 58).
Legia: Mucha; Szala, Wawrzyniak, Rzezniczak, Guerreiro■, Giza, Kielbowicz, Vukovic (Borysiuk 46), Szalachowski (Edson 68), Radovic, Rocki (Chinyama 46).

FK Austria (1) 2 *(Hattenberger 26, Okotie 74)*
WIT Georgia (0) 0 6200
FK Austria: Safar; Majstorovic, Bak (Madl 87), Schiemer, Hattenberger, Sulimani, Blanchard, Krammer, Acimovic (Sun 85), Diabang (Bazina 77), Okotie.
WIT Georgia: Bediashvili; Lomaia, Japaridze, Bechvaia, Kvakhadze, Razmadze, Melkadze (Maisashvili 90), Datunaishvili G, Lipartia, Kvaratskelia (Guchashvili 67), Klimiashvili (Kvaginadze 82).
One match tie because of uncertain civil situation in Georgia.

Grasshoppers (0) 0
Lech (0) 0 2300
Grasshoppers: Jakupovic; Vallori, Colina, Smiljanic, Feltscher, Cabanas (Calla 75), Lalombongo (Berisha 46), Toko, Toure, Bobadilla, Zuber (Lulic 67).
Lech: Kotorowski; Arboleda, Bosacki, Wojtkowiak, Henriquez, Stilic (Wilk 82), Murawski, Peszko (Lewandowski 58), Injac, Bandrowski, Rengifo (Reiss 88).

Gyor (0) 1 *(Bajzat 81)*
Stuttgart (2) 4 *(Lanig 31, Hitzlsperger 41, Gomez 55, 60)*
8000
Gyor: Stevanovic; Kovacs I, Nikolov, Supic, Bank (Kovacs II 46), Jakl (Volgyi 58), Jozsi, Boor (Brnovic 73), Koltai, Bajzat, Tokody.
Stuttgart: Lehmann; Osorio, Tasci, Boka (Boulahrouz 46), Delpierre, Lanig, Basturk, Hitzlsperger, Pardo (Mandjeck 63), Marica, Gomez (Ljuboja 63).

Hajduk Split (0) 0
La Coruna (1) 2 *(Riki 42, Verdu 87 (pen))* 35,000
Hajduk Split: Subasic; Buljat J (Linic 46), Zivkovic, Buljat M, Andric■, Gabric, Skoko, Maloca, Ticinovic (Ibricic 58), Kalinic, Bartolovic (Oremus 72).
La Coruna: Aranzubia; Luis Felipe, Lopo, Laure, Adrian (Ze Castro 69), De Guzman■, Antonio Tomas, Guardado, Valeron (Verdu 59), Juan Rodriguez, Riki (Mista 81).

Hapoel Tel Aviv (1) 3 *(Yeboah 29, Zahavi 58, Abutbul 76 (pen))*
Vojvodina (0) 0 5000
Hapoel Tel Aviv: Enyeama; Douglas, Topuzakov, Antebi, Badir, Vermouth, Abutbul, Cohen, Telkiyski (Luz 77), Yeboah (Lala 82), Zahavi (Natcho 64).
Vojvodina: Brkic; Kizito, Lovric, Stosic, Djuric, Vukajilovic (Aleksic 59), Popovic, Tumbasevic (Trivunovic 40), Tadic, Buac (Pantelic 64), Lazetic.

Hertha Berlin (1) 1 *(Ebert 3)*
Interblock (0) 0 11,849
Hertha Berlin: Drobny; Friedrich, Simunic, Radjabali-Fardi, Chahed, Ebert, Nicu, Lustenberger, Kacar (Cicero 60), Pantelic (Raffael 46), Chermiti (Domovchiyski 11).
Interblock: Strajnar; Lazic, Ntame, Elsner (Pregelj 75), Zeljkovic, Rendulic, Jukan, Salkic, Grabic, Zahora (Matic 46), Jolic (Rodic 64).

Ironi Kiryat (1) 1 *(Tzarfati 8)*
Litex (1) 2 *(Popov 21, Sandrinho 53)* 500
Ironi Kiryat: Betzalel; Bakhar, Lavi, Nussbaum, Tzarfati, Cespedes, Hasarma, Suan, Avidor, Peretz (Elgarbeli 80), Agouda (Maicon 59).
Litex: Golubovic; Barthe, Cambon, Venkov, Manolev, Bertin■, Wellington, Dudu, Sandrinho, Niflore (Angelov 66) (Nikolov 89), Popov (Eduardo 77).

Kalmar (1) 4 *(Suler 4 (og), Ingelsten 54, 86, 90)*
Gent (0) 0 2600
Kalmar: Azinovic; Sorin, Lantz, Lindberg, Augustsson (Larsson 76), Nouri, Rydstrom, Ingelsten, Elm V, Elm R, Johansson.
Gent: Gorgacevic; Smoje (Duarte 46), Suler, Thompson, Grondin, Thijs, Azofeifa (Maric 64), Rosales (Olufade 57), Foley, Ruiz, Ljubijankic.

Lillestrom (1) 2 *(Occean 29, Brenne 75)*
FC Copenhagen (2) 4 *(Santin 10, Ailton 29, Hutchinson 79, Junior 86)* 2500
Lillestrom: Fredrikson; Pedersen, Bertheussen (Sogard 46), Stensaas, Kippe, Bjorkoy, Brenne, Mouelhi, Sundgot (Riseth 46), Essediri (Myklebust 68), Occean.
FC Copenhagen: Christiansen; Pospech, Laursen, Larsson (Jorgensen 19), Wendt, Norregaard, Kvist, Hutchinson, Kristensen (Sionko 46), Ailton, Santin (Junior 60).

Midtjylland (0) 0
Manchester City (0) 1 *(Califf 90 (og))* 9552
Midtjylland: Heinze; Afriyie, Calff, Poulsen, Reid, Borring, Florescu, Thygesen (Madsen 78), Olsen D (Christensen 88), Salami, Nworuh (Babatunde 66).
Manchester City: Hart; Corluka, Ball, Dunne, Ben Haim (Hamann 58), Richards, Ireland, Johnson, Jo (Evans 80), Elano (Sturridge 57), Petrov.
aet; Manchester City won 4-2 on penalties.

Napoli (1) 5 *(Rinaudo 42, 54, Inacio Pia 52, Lavezzi 80, Hamsik 87)*
Vllaznia (0) 0 30,000
Napoli: Gianello; Grava, Santacroce, Cannavaro, Rinaudo, Montervino, Pazienza, Gargano, Dalla Bona (Hamsik 60), Inacio Pia (Lavezzi 67), Zalayeta (Denis 67).
Vllaznia: Grimaj; Osja, Basic, Belisha (Hoti 85), Beqiri, Doci, Smajlaj, Lici, Nallbani, Sinani, Boadu (Kaci 84).

Omonia (1) 2 *(Duro 11, 70)*
AEK Athens (1) 2 *(Blanco 16, Pavlis 89)* 10,000
Omonia: Georgallides; Ndikumana, Wenzel, Pletsch, Zlogar, Kaseke, Duro, Charalambous, Clayton (Aloneftis 77), Christofi (Okkas 66), Cafu (Niculescu 89).
AEK Athens: Saja; Edson Ramos, Majstorovic, Juanfran■, Kyrgiakos, Kafes (Lagos 75), Basinas, Rikka (Zorbas 75), Edinho (Pavlis 79), Blanco, Scocco■.

Red Star Belgrade (0) 3 *(Subasic 76, Milijas 79, 111 (pen))*
Apoel (0) 3 *(Kosowski 53, Helio Pinto 56, Mirosavljevic 116)* 15,000
Red Star Belgrade: Radivojevic; Tomovic, Markovic, Gueye, Ninkov, Milijas, Koroman (Perovic 63), Burzanovic, Bogdanovic, Edgar, Trickovski (Subasic 73).
Apoel: Chiotis■; Christou, Florea, Seghiri, Nuno Morais, Poursaitidis, Charalambides, Kosowski, Paulista (Helio Pinto 6), Michael (Morris 101), Zewlakow (Mirosavljevic 65).
aet.

Rennes (1) 2 *(Leroy 38, 81)*
Stabaek (0) 0 12,000
Rennes: Douchez; Bocanegra, Hansson, Mangane, Leroy, Cheyrou, Lemoine, Danze, Thomert, Sow (Fanni 60), Briand (Kembo 90).
Stabaek: Knudsen; Kjolo (Sandberg 36), Skjonsberg, Holmvik, Annan, Keller, Farnerud, Alanzinho, Gunnarsson, Nannskog, Andersson (Palmason 77).

Rosenborg (1) 5 *(Iversen 43, 67 (pen), 86 (pen), Konen 65, Skjelbred 73)*
Djurgaarden (0) 0   7500
Rosenborg: Jarstein (Lund Hansen 74); Lustig, Demidov, Stadsgaard, Strand, Tettey, Skjelbred, Sapara, Berisha (Konan 46), Iversen, Storflor (Traore 57).
Djurgaarden: Tourray; Haginge, Tauer, Johannesson, Ekong, Cardoso (Ceesay 79), Sjolund, Komac (Dahlberg 58), Davids, Kusi-Asare, Oremo (Rajalakso 71).

Salzburg (0) 0
Suduva (0) 1 *(Jasaitis 78)*   5500
Salzburg: Ochs; Bodnar (Gercaliu 28), Sekagya, Jezek, Tchoyi, Boussaidi, Leitgeb, Aufhauser, Nelisse, Vonlanthen (Obster 76), N'Gwat-Mahop (Janocko 66).
Suduva: Vitkauskas; Thiago (Skinderis 65), Mikuckis, Barevicius (Luksys 71), Koziuberda, Slavickas G, Leimonas, Bozinovski, Jasaitis, Gardzijauskas (Radavicius 58), Lukjanovs.

Slaven (1) 2 *(Vrucina 14, 65)*
Aris Salonika (0) 0   3500
Slaven: Rodic; Rogulj, Lapic, Caval, Poldrugac, Puric, Jajalo, Gregurina (Nynkeu 72), Juric (Sehic 80), Posavec (Bilen 65), Vrucina.
Aris Salonika: Kelemen; Ronaldo, Aurelio, Jahic, Vangjeli (Neto 33), Calvo (Javito 65), Garcia, Regueiro, Prittas (Felipe 67), Thiago Gentil, Koke.

St Patrick's Ath (0) 2 *(Gavin 87, Fitzpatrick 90)*
Elfsborg (0) 1 *(Ishizaki 63)*   3000
St Patrick's Ath: Barry Ryan; Byrne (O'Brien 82), Lynch, Gavin, Paisley, Fahey, Bobby Ryan (Kirby 74), Dempsey, O'Neill (Fitzpatrick 69), Quigley, Guy.
Elfsborg: Wiland; Floren, Karlsson, Mobaek, Lucic, Augustsson, Svensson, Avdic (Berglund 59), Bajrami (Keene 65), Ishizaki (Kurbegovic 82), Nilsson.

Sturm Graz (1) 1 *(Holzl 12)*
Zurich (1) 1 *(Abdi 5)*   15,200
Sturm Graz: Schicklgruber; Sonnleitner, Feldhofer, Shashiashvili, Kandelaki, Hlinka, Muratovic (Beichler 98), Holzl (Lamotte 109), Stankovic (Jantscher 46), Haas, Kienzl.
Zurich: Leoni; Stahel, Stucki (Lampi 40), Barmettler, Tihinen (Koch 90), Aegerter, Okonkwo, Djuric (Nikci 62), Abdi, Alphonse, Hassli.
aet; Zurich won 4-2 on penalties.

Vaslui (3) 3 *(Burdujan 5, Canu 7, N'Doye 30)*
Metalurgs Liepajas (0) 1 *(Antonio 85)*   7000
Vaslui: Kuciak; Buhus, Luz, Canu, Munteanu, Genchev (Jovanovic N 66), Aliuta, Ljubinkovic, N'Doye (Zmeu 46), Burdujan, Tamwanjera (Buhaescu 46).
Metalurgs Liepajas: Spole; Klava, Zirnis, Antonio, Jemelins (Beniusis 31), Tamosauskas, Surnins, Solonicins, Miceika (Rafalskis 81), Dobrecovs (Zuravlovs■ 46), Karlsons.

Viking (1) 1 *(Gaarde 8)*
Honka (1) 2 *(Hakanpaa 20, Lepola 56)*   4400
Viking: Nicht; Bertelsen, Soma, Ross, Gaarde, Stokholm (Samuelsen 33), Austnes, Danielsen (Nisja 67), Fillo, Ijeh, Odegaard.
Honka: Peltonen; Koskinen, Heilala, Jalasto, Hakanpaa, Weckstrom, Perovuo (Lepola 17), Turunen, Haarala, Vasara (Aalto 85), Kokko (Puustinen 74).

Zilina (0) 2 *(Belak 81, Jez 87)*
Slovan (0) 1 *(Nezmar 90)*   7500
Zilina: Pernis; Vomacka, Pekarik, Tesak, Pecalka (Piacek 89), Strba, Jez, Vladavic, Lietava (Styvar 31), Rilke■, Adauto (Belak 65).
Slovan: Hauzr; Polak, Kostal, Vulin (Smetana 65), Bilek (Papousek 76), Holenak, Dockal, Frejlach, Keric, Radzinevicius, Blazek (Nezmar 58).

Zrinjski (0) 0
Braga (0) 2 *(Cesar Peixoto 56, Matheus 90)*   7000
Zrinjski: Melher; Nikolic, Zurzinov, Anicic, Sunjic, Serdarusic, Stojanovic (Kordic 75), Zizovic, Djuric, Matko, Selimovic (Vukovic 79).
Braga: Eduardo; Rodriguez, Moises, Evaldo, Joao Pereira, Stelvio, Cesar Peixoto (Linz 76), Luis Aguiar, Paulo Cesar, Meyong (Matheus 65), Alan (Mossoro 46).

FIRST ROUND, FIRST LEG

Tuesday, 16 September 2008

Apoel (0) 1 *(Mirosavljevic 71)*
Schalke (3) 4 *(Westermann 24, Rakitic 35, Sanchez 40, Halil Altintop 86)*   6500
Apoel: Morfis; Christou, Nuno Morais, Poursaitidis (Alexandrou 64), Charalambides, Kosowski (Onwuachi 83), Broerse, Helio Pinto, Kontis, Haxhi, Zewlakow (Mirosavljevic 64).
Schalke: Fahrmann; Westermann, Bordon, Rafinha, Krstajic (Howedes 60), Kobiashvili, Rakitic, Engelaar, Asamoah (Halil Altintop 73), Farfan, Sanchez (Lovenkrands 81).

Hertha Berlin (0) 2 *(Nicu 50, Cicero 76)*
St Patrick's Ath (0) 0   13,045
Hertha Berlin: Drobny; Kaka, Friedrich, Simunic, Cicero, Dardai (Nicu 46), Stein, Piszczek, Kacar (Lustenberger 46), Pantelic (Domovchiysti 83), Voronin.
St Patrick's Ath: Barry Ryan; Byrne, Lynch, Harris, Gavin, Kirby (Bobby Ryan 63), Fahey, Dempsey (Bialek 90), O'Neill (Fitzpatrick 83), Quigley, Guy.

Nordsjaelland (0) 0
Olympiakos (0) 2 *(Mitroglou 73, Leto 90)*   5184
Nordsjaelland: Hansen; Kibebe, Kildentoft, Lundberg, Richter S (Storm 83), Karlsen, Bernier, Dahl (Pedersen N 76), Richter J, Bernburg, Nakajima-Farran (Christensen 64).
Olympiakos: Nikopolidis; Patsatzoglou, Domi, Leonardo, Antzas, Torosidis, Stoltidis■, Galletti (Diogo 61), Papadopoulos, Belluschi (Dudu Cearense 85), Mitroglou (Leto 81).

Thursday, 18 September 2008

AC Milan (1) 3 *(Stahel 45 (og), Pato 56, Borriello 74)*
Zurich (0) 1 *(Djuric 77)*   25,000
AC Milan: Dida; Kaladze, Jankulovski, Bonera, Seedorf, Kaka, Ambrosini (Emerson 68), Antonini, Flamini, Pato (Borriello 65), Schevchenko (Ronaldinho 75).
Zurich: Leoni; Stahel, Stucki, Barmettler, Tihinen, Aegerter, Okonkwo, Djuric, Abdi (Mehmedi 88), Alphonse, Hassli (Nikci 77).

Banik Ostrava (0) 0
Spartak Moscow (0) 1 *(Fathi 56)*   4120
Banik Ostrava: Vasek; Reznik, Bolf, Marek, Tchur, Neuwirth, Otepka, Galasek, Micola (Licka 76), Strihavka, Sverkos.
Spartak Moscow: Pletikosa; Fathi, Jiranek, Rodriguez (Ryzhkov 46), Kovac, Shishkin, Filipenko, Mozart, Bystrov (Parshivlyuk 77), Prudnikov, Saenko.

Bellinzona (1) 3 *(Lustrinelli 32, Sermeter 47, La Rocca 89)*
Galatasaray (1) 4 *(Kewell 39, Baros 52, 80, Lincoln 90)*
                                                         12,300
Bellinzona: Gritti; Bernardet, Siqueira-Barras, Mangiarratti, La Rocca, Sermeter (Raso 90), Gashi■, Dauda Wahab, Garrido (Diarra 68), Kalu, Lustrinelli (Neri 74).
Galatasaray: De Sanctis; Fernando Meira, Emre A, Volkan, Servet, Lincoln, Ayhan, Kewell, Fatih (Yaser 73), Baros, Nonda (Aydin 62).

Besiktas (0) 1 *(Holosko 58)*
Metalist Kharkiv (0) 0   18,000
Besiktas: Rustu; Serdar K, Seric, Zapotocny, Cisse, Sivok, Ugur, Delgado (Ekrem 87), Tello (Serdar O 73), Marcio Nobre (Bobo 72), Holosko.
Metalist Kharkiv: Goryianov; Konyushenko (Bordian 51), Obradovic, Maidana, Gueye, Valyaev, Edmar, Slyusar (Rykun 72), Trisovic, Devic (Babich 90), Jaja.

Borac (0) 1 *(Lazovic 51)*
Ajax (2) 4 *(Sulejmani 13, Suarez 36, Huntelaar 71, 86)*
                                              5000
Borac: Grahovac; Dragutinovic, Ignjatovic, Dmitrovic, Antic, Prtenjak (Stojcev 64), Maric, Mugosa (Kocic 46), Lazovic, Stojanovic, Milovanovic (Krnjinac 73).
Ajax: Stekelenburg; Oleguer, Vermaelen, Vertonghen, Van der Wiel, Emanuelson, Sno (Lindgren 46), Sarpong (De Jong 75), Huntelaar, Sulejmani (Leonardo 79), Suarez.

Borussia Dortmund (0) 0
Udinese (2) 2 *(Flores 8, Inler 34)*   52,400
Borussia Dortmund: Weidenfeller; Lee, Subotic, Rukavina, Hummels (Felipe Santana 83), Kehl, Kringe, Blaszczykowski, Hajnal (Frei 63), Valdez, Zidan (Tinga 10).
Udinese: Handanovic; Domizzi, Coda, Lukovic, Ferronetti (Motta 83), Isla, D'Agostino, Inler, Pepe, Sanchez (Di Natale 68), Flores (Quagliarella 77).

Braga (3) 4 *(Evaldo 3, Meyong 17, 30 (pen), 76)*
Artmedia (0) 0   9227
Braga: Eduardo; Rodriguez, Moises, Evaldo, Joao Pereira, Mossoro (Luis Aguiar 59), Cesar Peixoto, Vandinho (Frechaut 79), Renteria (Linz 59), Meyong, Alan.
Artmedia: Kamenar; Farkas, Guede, Salata, Urbanek (Mraz 28), Velicky, Fodrek, Kozak, Durica (Hasek 39), Piroska, Pospech (Oravec 82).

Brann (2) 2 *(Bjarnason 25 (pen), Solli 39)*
La Coruna (0) 0   8777
Brann: Udjus; Dahl, Austin, Hanstveit, Bjarnason, Bjornsson, Einarsson (Jaiteh 74), Solli (Guntveit 88), Moen, Huseklepp (Winters 90), Sigurdsson.
La Coruna: Aranzubia; Lopo, Laure, Colotto (Filipe 60), Adrian, Sergio, Lafita (Cristian 78), Guardado, Valeron, Juan Rodriguez, Omar Bravo.

Brondby (0) 1 *(Krohn-Dehli 63)*
Rosenborg (1) 2 *(Sapara 29, Skjelbred 56)* 11,909
Brondby: Andersen; Von Schlebrugge, Jonsson, Rasmussen T, Wass, Holmen, Farnerud (Ericsson 69), Gislason, Krohn-Dehli, Kristiansen (Duncan 46), Madsen (Jallow 46).
Rosenborg: Hansen; Lustig, Dorsin (Nordvik 90), Demidov, Stadsgaard, Strand, Tettey, Skjelbred, Sapara (Lago 81), Konan (Traore 69), Iversen.

Chernomore (1) 1 *(Dyakov 42)*
Stuttgart (0) 2 *(Gomez 66, 81)*   2000
Chernomore: Hmaruc; Peris, Domakinov, Dyakov, Andre, Aleksandrov I (Manolov 72), Iliev, Petkov (Stoyanov 85), Yurukov, Fernandez (Georgiev 89), Aleksandrov II.
Stuttgart: Lehmann; Osorio (Hilbert 46), Boulahrouz, Tasci, Delpierre, Magnin, Lanig, Simak (Cacau 47), Hitzlsperger, Khedira, Gomez (Ljuboja 88).

Dinamo Zagreb (0) 0
Sparta Prague (0) 0   12,000
Dinamo Zagreb: Butina; Ibanez, Vrdoljak, Drpic, Sammir (Tadic 56), Chago (Badelj 78), Mikic, Biscan, Morales (Lovren 85), Balaban, Mandzukic.
Sparta Prague: Kozacik; Repka, Had, Kisel, Vorisek, Kudela, Vacek (Pecnik 90), Husek, Slepicka (Dosek 88), Matusovic, Kulic (Kolar 74).

Everton (2) 2 *(Yakubu 23, Castillo 38)*
Standard Liege (2) 2 *(Mbokani 8, Yobo 34 (og))* 28,312
Everton: Howard; Neville, Lescott, Yobo, Jagielka, Castillo, Osman, Anichebe (Vaughan 64), Yakubu, Cahill, Arteta.
Standard Liege: Aragon; Dante, Onyewu, Camozzato, Sarr, Dalmat, Defour, Witsel, Mbokani, De Camargo (Nicaise 86), Jovanovic.

FC Moscow (0) 1 *(Samedov 89)*
FC Copenhagen (1) 2 *(Nordstrand 45 (pen), Sionko 90)*
                                              6000
FC Moscow: Amelichenko; Godunok, Nababkin, Kuzmin, Jop, Bystrov, Ivanov, Cesnauskis E (Stavpets 62), Maxi Lopez (Bracamonte 56), Samedov, Strelkov (Baiano 69).
FC Copenhagen: Christiansen; Pospech, Laursen, Wendt, Jorgensen, Norregaard, Kvist, Hutchinson, Christensen, Nordstrand (Sionko 70), Cesar Santin (Ailton 82).

FK Austria (0) 2 *(Schiemer 64, 76)*
Lech (0) 1 *(Rengifo 65)*   7500
FK Austria: Safar; Majstorovic, Bak, Schiemer, Hattenberger, Blanchard, Krammer (Sulimani 79), Acimovic (Sun 90), Standfest, Diabang (Bazina 50), Okotie.
Lech: Kotorowski; Arboleda, Tanevski, Bosacki, Wojtkowiak, Stilic (Peszko 81), Murawski, Injac, Bandrowski, Lewandowski (Wilk 90), Rengifo.

Feyenoord (0) 0
Kalmar (0) 1 *(Elm V 71)*   22,000
Feyenoord: Timmer; Lucius, Hofland (Greene 67), Bahia, De Cler, Van Bronckhorst, Wijnaldum, Fer, De Guzman (Biseswar 61), Tomasson, Mols (Makaay 72).
Kalmar: Wasta; Sorin, Lantz, Lindberg, Augustsson (Larsson 81), Nouri, Rydstrom, Ingelsten (Dauda 90), Elm V (Elm D 90), Elm R, Johansson.

Hamburg (0) 0
Unirea (0) 0   39,010
Hamburg: Rost; Alex Silva, Reinhardt, Jansen (Atouba 86), De Jong, Jarolim, Trochowski, Demel, Thiago Neves (Pitroipa 59), Guerrero, Olic (Petric 64).
Unirea: Arlauskis; Mehmedovic, Galamaz, Nicu, Bordeanu, Balan (Todoran 81), Mara, Paduretu, Apostol, Bilasco (Danalache 89), Onofras (Burns 90).

Hapoel Tel Aviv (0) 0 *(Lala 88)*
St Etienne (0) 2 *(Payet 7, Feindouno 60)* 12,000
Hapoel Tel Aviv: Enyeama; Douglas, Topuzakov, Antebi, Natcho (Yadin 65), Vermouth, Abutbul, Cohen, Telkiyski (Srur 60), Yeboah, Zahavi (Lala 46).
St Etienne: Viviani; Tavlaridis (Varrault 46), Dabo (Sauget 65), Monsoreau, Dernis, Matuidi, Feindouno, Landrin, Perrin, Payet (Hautcoeur 78), Gomis.

Kyseri (0) 1 *(Toledo 87)*
Paris St Germain (1) 2 *(Kezman 5, Luyindula 90)* 20,000
Kyseri: Hamidou; Durmus, Ali, Toledo, Eren, Saidou, Umut (Olembe 70), Mehmet T, Abdullah (Turgay 70), Aghahowa, Mehmet B.
Paris St Germain: Landreau; Ceara, Bourillon, Traore, Armand, Clement (Makelele 61), Rothen, Sankhare, Luyindula, Pancrate, Kezman (Arnaud 78).

Litex (1) 1 *(Popov 10)*
Aston Villa (1) 3 *(Reo-Coker 45, Barry 72 (pen), Petrov 90)* 7000
Litex: Golubovic; Cambon■, Venkov■, Manolev, Nikolov, Berberovic, Wellington (Angelov 85), Dudu (Barthe 62), Sandrinho, Niflore (Acedo 74), Popov.
Aston Villa: Friedel; Young L, Shorey, Reo-Coker (Routledge 74), Laursen, Cuellar, Petrov, Gardner (Harewood 68), Agbonlahor, Barry (Salifou 78), Milner.

Maritimo (0) 0
Valencia (1) 1 *(Morientes 12)*   3000
Maritimo: Marcos; Leandro (Manu 59), Cardozo, Briguel,
Joao Guilherme, Miguelito, Fernandes, Olberdam, Joao
Luiz, Marcinho, Pedro Moutinho (Fogaca 57).
Valencia: Renan; Helguera, Alexis, Miguel, Del Horno,
Albelda, Angulo, Pablo Hernandez, Edu (Manuel
Fernandes 71), Morientes (Villa 79), Zigic (Mata 64).

NEC Nijmegen (0) 1 *(Van Beukering 57)*
Dinamo Bucharest (0) 0   11,750
NEC Nijmegen: Babos; Zomer, Wisgerhof, El-Akchaoui,
Fernandez, Davids, Schone (Worm 69), Sibum,
Radomski, Van Beukering (Tshibamba 76), Ntibazonkiza.
Dinamo Bucharest: Lobont; Pulhac, Homei, Tamas, Julio
Cesar, Bostina (Diakite 80), Adrian Cristea, Ropotan, Ze
Kalanga (Torje 46), Danciulescu, Bratu (Niculae 60).

Nancy (1) 1 *(Berenguer 42)*
Motherwell (0) 0   16,094
Nancy: Bracigliano; Helder (Dia 56), Macaluso, Chretien,
Calve, Ouaddou, Malonga (Fortune 56), Berenguer, Feret
(N'Guemo 87), Brison, Žerka.
Motherwell: Smith G; Quinn, Hammell, Reynolds,
Craigan, Malcolm (Smith D 67), Hughes, Fitzpatrick,
Sutton (Porter 67), Clarkson (Murphy 82), Lasley.

Napoli (2) 3 *(Vitale 18, Denis 20, Maggio 55)*
Benfica (1) 2 *(Suazo 16, Luisao 59)*   51,597
Napoli: Navarro; Santacroce, Cannavaro, Contini, Vitale,
Blasi (Pazienza 46), Maggio, Hamsik (Pia 75), Gargano,
Lavezzi, Denis (Zalayeta 66).
Benfica: Quim; Luisao, Leo, Sidnei, Maxi Pereira, Di
Maria (Nuno Gomes 63), Martins (Katsouranis 55),
Yebda, Suazo, Reyes, Urretaviscaya (Balboa 46).

Omonia (0) 1 *(Duro 49)*
Manchester City (0) 2 *(Jo 59, 72)*   15,907
Omonia: Georgallides; Ndikumana, Wenzel, Pletsch,
Kaseke, Duro, Charalambous, Aguirre, Okkas (Clayton
81), Aloneftis (Niculescu 74), Christofi.
Manchester City: Hart; Zabaleta, Richards, Dunne,
Garrido, Kompany (Gelson 84), Ireland, Robinho, Jo
(Sturridge 76), Elano (Hamman 85), Wright-Phillips.

Portsmouth (1) 2 *(Diarra 39, Defoe 60)*
Guimaraes (0) 0   19,612
Portsmouth: James; Johnson, Traore A (Hreidarsson 90),
Diarra, Campbell, Distin, Davis, Utaka (Diop 73), Crouch
(Kanu 90), Defoe, Belhadj.
Guimaraes: Nilson; Arnolin, Danilo, Andrezinho, Mornha
(Amaral 55), Wenio, Fajardo (Jean Coral 64), Moreno,
Desmarets, Joao Alves, Roberto.

Rennes (1) 2 *(M'Bia 36, Bocanegra 49)*
Twente (1) 1 *(Denneboom 13)*   12,893
Rennes: Douchez; Bocanegra, Fanni, Hansson, Mangane,
Leroy, M'Bia, Sorlin, Danze (Pagis 57), Wiltord (Echiejile
85), Briand (Sow 70).
Twente: Boschker; Wielaert, Braafheid, Douglas, Brama,
Stam (Wellenberg 75), Tiote, Denneboom (Huysegems
84), Perez (Hersi 75), Elia, Arnautovic.

Sampdoria (3) 5 *(Bonazzoli 14, 22, Cassano 36, 57,
Fornaroli 90)*
Kaunas (0) 0   16,870
Sampdoria: Mirante; Lucchini, Bottinelli, Stankevicius,
Gastaldello, Pieri (Ziegler 47), Palombo (Dessena 79),
Sammarco, Delvecchio, Bonazzoli, Cassano (Fornaroli
60).
Kaunas: Dreer; Radzius (Cinikas 71), Mendy, Kancelskis,
Manchkhava, Zelmikas, Baguzis (Rimkevicius 47),
Luksa■, Zubavicius, Ivaskevicius (Arouri 79), Rafael.

Santander (0) 1 *(Pereira 46)*
Honka (0) 0   18,637
Santander: Coltorti; Oriol, Garay, Cesar Navas, Sepsi
(Canales 72), Luccin, Edu Bedia, Juanjo (Tchite 82),
Serrano, Goncalves (Munitis 62), Pereira.
Honka: Peltonen; Koskinen, Heilala, Jalasto, Hakanpaa,

Weckstrom, Perovuo (Lepola 57), Turunen, Vuorinen
(Kokko 81), Haarala, Vasara.

Setubal (0) 1 *(Leandro Carrijo 67)*
Heerenveen (0) 1 *(Elyounoussi 90)*   3000
Setubal: Bruno Vale; Robson, Janicio, Auri, Aly
Cissokho, Sandro, Elias, Ricardo Chaves (Bruno Gama
65), Leandro Lima (Mateus 79), Laionel, Leandro Carrijo
(Danilo Portugal 82).
Heerenveen: Vandenbussche; Breuer, Dingsdag, Svec,
Fellinga (Paulo Henrique 74), Vayrynen, Berrens
(Elyounoussi 74), Pranjic, Jong-a-Pin, Grindheim, Sibon
(Smarason 90).

Sevilla (1) 2 *(Capel 6, Adriano 90)*
Salzburg (0) 0   40,000
Sevilla: Palop; Javi Navarro, Squillaci, Prieto, Fazio, Jesus
Navas, Maresca (Kanoute 46), Capel (Adriano 59),
Romaric, Konko, Luis Fabiano (Chevanton 68).
Salzburg: Ochs; Bodnar, Dudic, Opdam, Sekagya, Kovac,
Tchoyi (N'Gwat-Mahop 46), Leitgeb, Aufhauser
(Janocko 75), Zickler, Nelisse.

Slaven (1) 1 *(Juric 43)*
CSKA Moscow (0) 2 *(Vagner Love 81, 89 (pen))*   3000
Slaven: Rodic; Kaja, Lapic, Caval (Maras 81), Poldrugac,
Puric, Gregurina (Bilen 71), Juric (Sehic 69), Posavec,
Vrucina, Niverge.
CSKA Moscow: Akinfeev; Ignashevich, Berezutski A,
Odiah (Semberas 60), Berezutski V, Mamaev (Ryzhov
90), Krasic, Zhirkov, Aldonin (Dzagoev 46), Rahimic,
Vagner Love.

Slavia Prague (0) 0
Vaslui (0) 0   7781
Slavia Prague: Vaniak; Brabec, Hubacek, Suchy, Tavares,
Jarolim (Smicer 89), Svento, Krajcik, Belaid (Ivana 62),
Cerny, Necid (Latka 86).
Vaslui: Kuciak; Markovic, Buhus, Panait, Munteanu
(Andronic 29), Genchev, Gheorghiu (Aliuta 79),
Ljubinkovic, N'Doye, Jovanovic P (Zmeu 85),
Temwanjira.

Timisoara (1) 1 *(Bucur 25)*
Partizan Belgrade (1) 2 *(Tosic 35, Bogunovic 69)*   18,000
Timisoara: Pantilimon; Sretenovic, Luchin, Milhazes,
Alexa, Karamian (Borbely 83), Badoi (Stancu 46),
Agunbiade, Bucur, Rusic (Goga 58), Magera.
Partizan Belgrade: Bozovic; Stevanovic, Djordjevic,
Knezevic, Obradovic, Juca, Moreira, Tosic, Petrovic
(Ljajic 46), Bogunovic (Peric 90), Lamine (Cadikovski 90).

Tottenham Hotspur (1) 2 *(Bentley 33, Bent 73)*
Wisla (1) 1 *(Jirsak 34)*   35,751
Tottenham Hotspur: Gomes; Gunter (O'Hara 57), Bale,
Zokora, Woodgate, King, Bentley, Jenas, Giovani
(Assou-Ekotto 70), Bent, Lennon (Campbell 57).
Wisla: Pawelek; Singlar, Baszcznyski, Diaz, Cleber,
Sobolewski, Jirsak (Lobodzinski 61), Zienczuk, Cantoro,
Boguski (Malecki 72), Pawel Brozek (Niedzielan 79).

Wolfsburg (1) 1 *(Grafite 45 (pen))*
Rapid Bucharest (0) 0   16,245
Wolfsburg: Benaglio; Schafer, Madlung, Barzagli, Josue,
Misimovic (Dejagah 71), Hasebe, Riether, Gentner,
Dzeko (Krzynowek 90), Grafite (Saglik 71).
Rapid Bucharest: Urko; Ricardo Fernandes, Vella,
Bozovic, Constantin, Maftei, Cesinha (Julio Cesar 58),
Paulista, Herea, Juliano (Djalovic 71), Claudio Pitbull
(Grigore 82).

Young Boys (1) 2 *(Schneuwly 16, Doumbia 88)*
Club Brugge (1) 2 *(Sonck 36, Clement 72)*   10,204
Young Boys: Wolfli; Ghezal, Schneider, Portillo,
Raimondi, Bastians (Doumbia 67), Degen (Haberli 46),
Hochstrasser, Yapi-Yapo, Regazzoni, Schneuwly
(Luscher 78).
Club Brugge: Stijnen; Ciman, Evens, Klukowski, Clement,
Alcaraz, Vargas, Geraerts, Dirar, Sonck, Akpala (Chavez
70).

Zilina (0) 1 *(Vladavic 49 (pen))*
Levski (0) 1 *(Joaozinho 64)* 7581
Zilina: Pernis; Vomacka, Leitner, Pekarik, Pecalka, Strba, Jez■, Styvar (Piacek 81), Belak, Vladavic (Tesak 90), Adauto (Karoglan 71).
Levski: Petkov; Milanov, Rabeh, Vagner, Tiberkanine (Tasevski 59), Sarmov, Joaozinho, Bystron, Gadzhev (Ivanov M 60), Ivanov G, Ze Soares (Baltanov 90).

FIRST ROUND, SECOND LEG

Tuesday, 30 September 2008

CSKA Moscow (1) 1 *(Berezutski A 36)*
Slaven (0) 0 5000
CSKA Moscow: Akinfeev; Semberas, Ignashevich, Berezutski A, Berezutski V, Grigoriev, Krasic (Mamaev 46), Aldonin (Rahimic 87), Dzagoev, Erkin (Zhirkov 71), Vagner Love.
Slaven: Rodic; Kokalovic, Kaja, Maras (Puric 70), Caval, Poldrugac, Jajalo, Juric, Posavec, Vrucina (Kresinger 70), Niverge (Safaric 63).

St Patrick's Ath (0) 0
Hertha Berlin (0) 0 3021
St Patrick's Ath: Barry Ryan; Lynch■, Rogers, Harris, Gavin, Kirby (O'Brien 80), Fahey, Dempsey (O'Cearuill 90), Quigley, Fitzpatrick (Murphy 80), Guy.
Hertha Berlin: Drobny; Friedrich, Von Bergen, Simunic, Chahed, Cicero, Nicu, Piszczek (Stein 90), Lustenberger (Dardai 71), Raffael (Domovchiyski 65), Voronin.

Thursday, 2 October 2008

Ajax (0) 2 *(Sarpong 71, Suarez 90)*
Borac (0) 0 17,500
Ajax: Vermeer; Silva, Vermaelen, Vertonghen (Lindgren 54), Van der Wiel, Schilder, Enoh (Anita 60), Sno (Sarpong 46), Huntelaar, Suarez, Cvitanich.
Borac: Grahovac; Dragutinovic (Djokovic 46), Ignjatovic, Dmitrovic, Antic, Maric, Krnjinac, Mugosa, Lazovic (Grkajac 80), Stojanovic, Milovanovic (Prtenjak 90).

Artmedia (0) 0
Braga (2) 2 *(Luis Aguiar 11 (pen), 31)* 1120
Artmedia: Kamenar; Guede, Dosoudil, Salata, Velicky, Szabo, Czinege, Fodrek (Durica 66), Kozak (Anderson 71), Piroska (Kleber 54), Oravec.
Braga: Eduardo; Rodriguez, Moises, Evaldo, Joao Pereira (Frechaut 74), Luis Aguiar, Vandinho (Stelvio 67), Paulo Cesar, Jorginho, Renteria (Meyong 60), Matheus.

Aston Villa (1) 1 *(Harewood 27)*
Litex (0) 1 *(Niflore 53 (pen))* 27,230
Aston Villa: Friedel; Young L, Shorey, Cuellar, Knight, Salifou, Petrov, Young A (Osbourne 85), Harewood, Milner, Routledge.
Litex: Todorov; Barthe, Manolev, Nikolov, Zanev, Berberovic, Wellington (Angelov 78), Dudu (Tsvetanov 46), Sandrinho, Niflore, Popov (Du Bala 85).

Benfica (0) 2 *(Reyes 57, Nuno Gomes 84)*
Napoli (0) 0 56,506
Benfica: Quim; Luisao, Jorge Ribeiro, Sidnei, Katsouranis, Maxi Pereira, Amorim (Martins 72), Di Maria (Urretaviscaya 78), Yebda (Binya 77), Reyes, Nuno Gomes.
Napoli: Gianello; Cannavaro, Contini, Rinaudo, Vitale (Mannini 78), Blasi, Maggio, Hamsik (Russotto 67), Gargano, Lavezzi (Denis 72), Zalayeta.

Club Brugge (2) 2 *(Akpala 17, Sonck 29)*
Young Boys (0) 0 17,230
Club Brugge: Stijnen; Ciman, Evens, Klukowski, Alcaraz, Simaeys, Vargas (Leko 87), Geraerts, Dirar (Blondel 75), Sonck, Akpala (Chavez 90).
Young Boys: Wolfli; Ghezal, Portillo, Affolter, Kulaksizoglu, Bastians, Varela, Degen (Schwegler 45), Yapi-Yapo (Schneuwly 58), Regazzoni, Haberli (Doumbia 66).

Dinamo Bucharest (0) 0
NEC Nijmegen (0) 0 12,000
Dinamo Bucharest: Lobont; Pulhac, Blay (Torje 77), Tamas (Goian 67), Julio Cesar, Bostina, Adrian Cristea, Ropotan, Danciulescu, Bratu, Andrei Cristea (Mitea 55).
NEC Nijmegen: Babos; Zomer, Wisgerhof (Pothuizen 66), El-Akchaoui, Fernandez, Davids, Sibum, Radomski, Van Beukering (Kivuvu 68), Tshibamba (Schone 61), Ntibazonkiza.

FC Copenhagen (0) 1 *(Sheshukov 54 (og))*
FC Moscow (1) 1 *(Bracamonte 37)* 18,338
FC Copenhagen: Christiansen; Pospech, Laursen, Wendt, Jorgensen, Norregaard, Kvist, Hutchinson, Kristensen, Nordstrand (Sionko 70), Cesar Santin.
FC Moscow: Zhevnov; Godunok, Sheshukov, Nababkin, Epureanu, Kuzmin, Baiano (Cesnauskis E 65), Bystrov (Rebko 88), Ivanov, Samedov (Strelkov 65), Bracamonte.

Galatasaray (1) 2 *(Baros 24 (pen), Yaser 85)*
Bellinzona (0) 1 *(Sermeter 53 (pen))* 35,000
Galatasaray: De Sanctis; Fernando Meira, Hakan Balta, Volkan, Servet, Lincoln, Mehmet T (Yaser 73), Ayhan, Serkan (Emre A 89), Arda (Alparslan 32), Baros.
Bellinzona: Gritti; Siqueira-Barras, Mangiarratti (Mehmeti 64), La Rocca, Raso, Sermeter, Dauda Wahab (Miccolis 46), Garrido, Diarra, Conti (Roux 72), Lustrinelli.

Guimaraes (2) 2 *(Douglas 19, Joao Alves 32)*
Portsmouth (0) 2 *(Crouch 105, 111)* 12,000
Guimaraes: Nilson; Amaral (Fajardo 79), Arnolin, Danilo, Andrezinho, Wenio, Desmarets, Meireles, Joao Alves, Roberto (Carlitos 62) (Jean Coral 76), Douglas.
Portsmouth: James; Johnson, Pamarot, Diarra, Campbell, Distin, Davis (Mvuemba 73), Hughes (Belhadj 99), Crouch, Defoe (Kaboul 106), Traore A.
aet.

Heerenveen (3) 5 *(Paulo Henrique 4, Sibon 11, 24, Elyounoussi 50, 68)*
Setubal (0) 2 *(Bruno Gama 57, Ricardo Chaves 64)* 23,000
Heerenveen: Vandenbussche; Breuer, Dingsdag, Vayrynen, Berrens, Pranjic (Smarason 90), Jong-a-Pin (Fellinga 77), Grindheim, Paulo Henrique (Kopic 69), Elyounoussi, Sibon.
Setubal: Bruno Vale; Robson, Janicio, Auri, Aly Cissokho, Sandro, Elias (Bruno Gama 46), Ricardo Chaves (Carrijo 69), Mateus, Laionel (Leandro Lima 69), Bruno Moraes.

Honka (0) 0
Santander (1) 1 *(Edu Bedia 4)* 9106
Honka: Peltonen; Koskinen (Otaru 58), Heilala, Jalasto, Hakanpaa, Perovuo (Koskela 58), Turunen, Vuorinen (Weckstrom 46), Haarala, Vasara, Kokko.
Santander: Tono; Garay, Cesar Navas, Pinillos, Marcano, Luccin (Colsa 85), Lacen, Edu Bedia, Juanjo, Serrano (Valera 81), Pereira (Sepsi 46).

Kalmar (0) 1 *(Johansson 46)*
Feyenoord (1) 2 *(Wijnaldum 17, Nouri 51 (og))* 8000
Kalmar: Wasta; Lantz, Lindberg, Augustsson (Sobralense 80), Rosengren, Nouri, Rydstrom, Ingelsten (Dauda 80), Elm V, Elm R, Johansson (Elm D 80).
Feyenoord: Van Dijk; Hofland, Bahia, De Cler, Greene, Van Bronckhorst, Bruins (El Ahmadi 73), Wijnaldum, Fer, Makaay, Biseswar.

Kaunas (1) 1 *(Zelmikas 17)*
Sampdoria (0) 2 *(Fornaroli 50, Bonazzoli 58)* 2500
Kaunas: Kurskis; Radzius, Mendy, Zelmikas, Arouri, Fridrikas, Zubavicius (Valskis 46), Miklinevicius, Ivaskevicius (Manchkhava 70), Rafael, Mamic (Petkus 65).
Sampdoria: Castellazzi; Bottinelli, Stankevicius (Lucchini 69), Gastaldello, Ziegler, Padalino, Sammarco, Delvecchio (Bellucci 64), Dessena, Fornaroli, Bonazzoli.

La Coruna (1) 2 *(Colotto 18, 76)*
Brann (0) 0 7500
La Coruna: Aranzubia; Filipe, Lopo, Colotto, Adrian, Sergio, Antonio Tomas (Verdu 75), Lafita, Valeron (Guardado 62), Omar Bravo (Mista 55), Riki■.
Brann: Udjus; Dahl, Austin, Hanstveit, Bjarnason, Bjornsson (Karadas 70), Einarsson (Bakke 46), Solli, Moen, Huseklepp (Saevarsson 81), Sigurdsson.
aet; La Coruna won 3-2 on penalties.

Lech (1) 4 *(Rengifo 10, Peszko 84, Lewandowski 98, Murawski 120)*
FK Austria (0) 2 *(Acimovic 60 (pen), Hattenberger 100)* 24,000
Lech: Kotorowski; Arboleda, Tanevski (Djurdjevic 112), Wojtkowiak, Wilk, Stilic, Murawski, Peszko, Injac (Reiss 84), Lewandowski, Rengifo.
FK Austria: Safar; Majstorovic, Bak, Schiemer■, Hattenberger, Sulimani (Krammer 70), Blanchard, Acimovic, Standfest, Okotie (Diabang 102), Bazina (Madl 107).
aet.

Levski (0) 0
Zilina (0) 1 *(Adauto 60)* 12,000
Levski: Petkov; Milanov, Rabeh, Vagner, Tiberkanine (Hristov 68), Sarmov (Bemvindo 79), Joaozinho, Tasevski, Bystron, Gadzhev (Ivanov M 46), Ivanov G.
Zilina: Pernis; Vomacka, Leitner, Pekarik, Sourek, Tesak, Pecalka, Strba, Styvar (Vladavic 90), Belak (Durica 8), Adauto (Piacek 90).

Manchester City (0) 2 *(Elano 48, Wright-Phillips 55)*
Omonia (0) 1 *(Alabi 78)* 25,304
Manchester City: Hart; Zabaleta, Garrido, Kompany (Hamann 66), Richards, Ben Haim, Wright-Phillips, Robinho (Petrov 70), Jo (Evans 67), Elano, Ireland.
Omonia: Georgallides; Ndikumana, Wenzel, Pletsch, Zlogar, Kaiafas (Alabi 46), Bangura (Clayton 59), Charalambous, Okkas, Aloneftis, Christofi (Cafu 82).

Metalist Kharkiv (2) 4 *(Jaja 16, 70, Devic 25, Gancarczyk 75)*
Besiktas (0) 1 *(Marcio Nobre 90)* 20,000
Metalist Kharkiv: Goryainov; Gancarczyk, Obradovic, Maidana, Gueye, Valyaev, Edmar, Slyusar, Trisovic (Bordian 38), Devic (Fomin 87), Jaja (Babich 90).
Besiktas: Hakan; Serdar K, Gokhan, Seric, Zapotocny, Ibrahim (Emre O 47), Cisse, Delgado, Tello (Aydin 77), Bobo, Holosko (Marcio Nobre 72).

Motherwell (0) 0
Nancy (2) 2 *(Fortune 18, Gavanon 23)* 11,318
Motherwell: Smith G; Quinn, Hammell, Reynolds, Craigan (Smith D 75), Malcolm (Murphy 32), Lasley (Sutton 64), Hughes, Porter, Clarkson, McGarry.
Nancy: Bracigliano; Sami (Ouaddou 20), Andre Luiz, Macaluso, Chretien, Hadji, Brison, Gavanon (N'Guemo 66), N'Diaye, Zerka, Fortune (Berenguer 75).

Olympiakos (3) 5 *(Torosidis 11, Diogo 30, 43, Kovacevic 72, 80)*
Nordsjaelland (0) 0 27,000
Olympiakos: Nikopolidis; Domi, Zewlakow, Antzas (Djordjevic 73), Torosidis, Galitsios, Mendrinos, Papadopoulos, Leto, Belluschi (Oscar 66), Diogo (Kovacevic 79).
Nordsjaelland: Hansen; Kibebe, Kildentoft, Lundberg, Richter S, Karlsen (Christensen 67), Bernier, Storm, Dahl■, Richter J (Cagara 83), Pedersen N (Fetai 63).

Paris St Germain (0) 0
Kayseri (0) 0 20,000
Paris St Germain: Landreau; Ceara, Bourillon, Camara, Armand, Sessegnon (Sammut 73), Clement, Rothen, Mulumbu, Hoarau (Luyindula 82), Pancrate (Sankhare 90).
Kayseri: Hamidou; Durmus (Cangele 73), Ali, Toledo (Bilal 84), Eren, Saidou, Ragip, Turgay, Abdullah (Umit K 59), Aghahowa, Mehmet B.

Partizan Belgrade (0) 1 *(Stevanovic 69)*
Timisoara (0) 0 22,000
Partizan Belgrade: Bozovic; Stevanovic, Djordjevic, Knezevic, Obradovic, Juca, Moreira, Tosic, Lazic (Petrovic 60), Bogunovic (Marinkovic 78), Lamine (Cadikovski 90).
Timisoara: Pantilimon; Brezinsky, Luchin (Karamian 81), Mihazes, Stancu (Rusic 72), Alexa, Borbely, Goga, Badoi, Bucur, Magera.

Rapid Bucharest (0) 1 *(Maftei 70)*
Wolfsburg (1) 1 *(Grafite 16)* 7000
Rapid Bucharest: Elinton; Ricardo Fernandes, Barioni, Bozovic, Constantin (Grigore 46), Maftei (Julio Cesar 73), Paulista, Lazar, Juliano (Pinto 62), Boya, Claudio Pitbull.
Wolfsburg: Benaglio; Schafer, Ricardo Costa, Barzagli, Josue, Misimovic (Madlung 88), Hasebe (Zaccardo 90), Riether, Gentner (Dejagah 64), Dzeko, Grafite.

Rosenborg (1) 3 *(Konan 14, Skjelbred 73, Sapara 85 (pen))*
Brondby (2) 2 *(Duncan 22, Kristiansen 36)* 16,460
Rosenborg: Jarstein; Lustig, Dorsin, Demidov, Stadsgaard, Strand (Lago 90), Tettey, Skjelbred, Sapara, Konan, Berisha (Pelu 61).
Brondby: Andersen; Von Schlebrugge, Rasmussen T, Bischoff (Howard 75), Holmen (Mikkelsen 90), Lorentzen (Ericsson 75), Gislason, Krohn-Dehli, Kristiansen, Duncan, Jallow.

Salzburg (0) 0
Sevilla (1) 2 *(Kanoute 38, 57 (pen))* 22,500
Salzburg: Ochs; Bodnar, Gercaliu, Opdam, Sekagya, Kovac, Jezek, Tchoyi, Zickler (N'Gwat-Mahop 65), Nelisse (Janocko 73), Janko.
Sevilla: Palop; Squillaci, Escude, Fernando Navarro, Crespo, Duscher, Adriano (De Mul 79), Jesus Navas (Acosta 61), Renato, Romaric, Kanoute (Chevanton 71).

Schalke (0) 1 *(Pander 57)*
Apoel (1) 1 *(Helio Pinto 6)* 52,214
Schalke: Neuer; Bordon, Rafinha, Howedes, Pander (Kobiashvili 79), Ernst (Westermann 64), Rakitic, Engelaar, Asamoah (Kenia 64), Halil Altintop, Kuranyi.
Apoel: Chiotis; Christou (Haxhi 59), Elia, Nuno Morais, Charalambides, Kosowski, Broerse, Helio Pinto (Alexandrou 36), Kontis, Michael, Onwuachi (Zewlakow 67).

Sparta Prague (2) 3 *(Kulic 19, Kladrubsky 21, 82 (pen))*
Dinamo Zagreb (2) 3 *(Pedro Morales 17, Lovren 30, Badelj 65)* 11,934
Sparta Prague: Kozacik; Repka, Had (Dosek 67), Kladrubsky, Kucera, Kisel, Vorisek, Husek, Slepicka, Matusovic, Kulic (Pecnik 80).
Dinamo Zagreb: Butina (Kelava 12); Ibanez, Lovren, Carlos Santos, Vrdoljak, Drpic, Sammir (Badelj 58), Mikic, Biscan, Pedro Morales (Hrgovic 85), Mandzukic.

Spartak Moscow (1) 1 *(Bazhenov 3)*
Banik Ostrava (1) 1 *(Otepka 32)* 10,000
Spartak Moscow: Pletikosa; Rodriguez, Kovac, Dedura, Filipenko, Mozart, Maidana (Bystrov 65), Parshivlyuk, Prudnikov (Pavlenko 57), Saenko, Bazhenov.
Banik Ostrava: Vasek; Reznik (Lukes 82), Bolf, Marek, Tchur, Neuwirth, Otepka, Galasek, Micola (Licka 82), Strihavka (Zeher 56), Sverkos.

St Etienne (1) 2 *(Gomis 27, 76)*
Hapoel Tel Aviv (0) 0 27,347
St Etienne: Viviani; Tavlaridis, Dabo, Bilos, Dernis (Varrault 59), Matuidi, Landrin (Machado 46), Perrin, Payet (Sangat 77), Ilan, Gomis.
Hapoel Tel Aviv: Enyeama; Douglas, Topuzakov, Antebi (Shaish 77), Natcho, Badir, Abutbul, Kende (Srur 65), Telkiyski (Lala 52), Yeboah, Zahavi.

Standard Liege (1) 2 *(Nicaise 23, Jovanovic 79 (pen))*
Everton (0) 1 *(Jagielka 67)* 27,406
Standard Liege: Aragon; Dante, Onyewu, Camozzato, Sarr, Dalmat, Defour, Nicaise, Witsel, Mbokani, Jovanovic.
Everton: Howard; Hibbert (Anichebe 63), Baines, Neville (Yobo 88), Jagielka, Lescott, Osman, Saha (Pienaar 70), Yakubu, Cahill, Arteta.

Stuttgart (0) 2 *(Hitzlsperger 81, Gomez 90)*
Chernomore (0) 2 *(Yurukov 47, Iliev 80)* 10,000
Stuttgart: Lehmann; Osorio, Tasci, Boka, Lanig (Magnin 72), Hitzlsperger, Rudy (Mandjeck 86), Hilbert, Khedira, Marica (Cacau 64), Gomez.
Chernomore: Ilchev; Peris, Domakinov, Dyakov, Hristov, Stoyanov, Andre, Iliev, Petkov (Fernandez 66), Georgiev, Yurukov.

Twente (0) 1 *(Nkufo 68)*
Rennes (0) 0 20,300
Twente: Boschker; Wielaert, Braafheid, Douglas, Brama, Stam, Janssen (Tiote 8), Denneboom (Huysegems 90), Nkufo, Perez (Wellenberg 74), Elia.
Rennes: Douchez; Bocanegra (Wiltord 84), Fanni, Hansson, Mangane, Leroy (Sow 77), M'Bia, Lemoine, Danze (Pagis 70), Thomert, Briand.

Udinese (0) 0
Borussia Dortmund (1) 2 *(Hajnal 45, 90)* 13,000
Udinese: Handanovic; Domizzi, Coda, Pasquale (Lukovic 54), Ferronetti, Isla, D'Agostino, Inler, Pepe, Di Natale (Sanchez 90), Flores (Quagliarella 68).
Borussia Dortmund: Weidenfeller; Lee, Subotic, Kovac, Schmelzer, Kehl, Kringe (Sadrijaj 84), Tinga (Valdez 68), Blaszczykowski, Hajnal, Frei (Sahin 78).
aet; Udinese won 4-3 on penalties.

Unirea (0) 0
Hamburg (1) 2 *(Petric 27, 50)* 6000
Unirea: Arlauskis; Mehmedovic, Galamaz, Nicu, Brandan (Frunza 69), Bordeanu, Balan, Mara, Burns (Apostol 58), Bilasco, Onofras (Danalache 68).
Hamburg: Rost; Atouba, Reinhardt, Mathijsen, Jansen (Benjamin 85), De Jong, Jarolim, Trochowski (Torun 90), Demel, Guerrero (Olic 79), Petric.

Valencia (0) 2 *(Del Horno 78, Villa 90 (pen))*
Maritimo (1) 1 *(Marcinho 41)* 28,000
Valencia: Guaita; Albiol (Albelda 26), Marchena, Helguera (Villa 59), Del Horno, Hugo Viana, Maduro, Angulo, Vicente (Mata 69), Pablo Hernandez, Manuel Fernandes.
Maritimo: Marcos; Cardozo, Joao Guilherme, Miguelito, Paulo Jorge, Bruno, Olberdam, Djalma (Pedro Moutinho 79), Luis Olim, Marcinho (Goncalo 67), Manu (Fogaca 84).

Vaslui (1) 1 *(Burdujan 21)*
Slavia Prague (0) 1 *(Brabec 49)* 8750
Vaslui: Kuciak; Buhus, Panait, Luz (Balace 84), Genchev, Aliuta (Buhaescu 85), Ljubinkovic, N'Doye, Jovanovic P (Jovanovic N 65), Burdujan, Temwanjira.
Slavia Prague: Vaniak; Brabec, Hubacek, Suchy, Tavares, Krajcik, Belaid, Volesak (Latka 83), Cerny (Janda 73), Necid, Litteri (Ivana 10).

Wisla (0) 1 *(Pawel Brozek 83)*
Tottenham Hotspur (0) 1 *(Glowacki 58 (og))* 15,000
Wisla: Pawelek; Baszczynski, Glowacki, Diaz, Cleber, Sobolewski, Piotr Brozek, Jirsak (Lobodzinski 32), Cantoro (Zienczuk 66), Boguski (Marcelo 82), Pawel Brozek.
Tottenham Hotspur: Gomes; Gunter, Bale, Zokora, Woodgate, King, Lennon (Dawson 88), Modric (Huddlestone 77), Bent, Campbell (O'Hara 68), Jenas.

Zurich (0) 0
AC Milan (0) 1 *(Shevchenko 70)* 24,100
Zurich: Leoni; Stahel, Stucki (Lampi 79), Barmettler, Tihinen, Aegerter, Okonkwo, Djuric, Abdi, Alphonse (Tahirovic 82), Hassli.
AC Milan: Dida; Kaladze (Maldini 31), Bonera, Emerson, Seedorf (Gattuso 76), Zambrotta, Ambrosini (Kaka 61), Antonini, Ronaldinho, Flamini, Shevchenko.

GROUP STAGE

GROUP A

Thursday, 23 October 2008

Schalke (2) 3 *(Mabiala 12 (og), Kuranyi 39, Halil Altintop 69)*
Paris St Germain (0) 1 *(Chantome 90)* 48,919
Schalke: Neuer; Westermann (Krstajic 64), Bordon (Howedes 54), Rafinha, Kobiashvili, Ernst (Rakitic 72), Jones, Engelaar, Farfan, Halil Altintop, Kuranyi.
Paris St Germain: Landreau; Traore, Mabiala, Armand, Chantome, Clement, Ngoyi, Sankhare (Rothen 76), Mulumbu (Sakho 46), Kezman, Arnaud (Luyindula 76).

Twente (1) 1 *(Denneboom 7)*
Santander (0) 0 21,000
Twente: Boschker; Wielaert, Heubach, Douglas, Brama, Stam (Wellenberg 66), Tiote, Denneboom (Arnautovic 88), Nkufo, Perez (Hersi 73), Elia.
Santander: Coltorti; Cesar Navas, Sepsi, Pinillos (Valera 46), Marcano, Cosa, Luccin (Juanjo 60), Edu Bedia (Serrano 46), Tchite, Munitis, Goncalves.

Thursday, 6 November 2008

Manchester City (1) 3 *(Wright-Phillips 6, Robinho 57, Mwaruwari 62)*
Twente (1) 2 *(Elia 17, Wielaert 65)* 21,247
Manchester City: Hart; Zabaleta, Richards, Gelson, Garrido, Dunne, Wright-Phillips, Robinho, Jo (Mwaruwari 59), Vassell (Elano 66), Ireland.
Twente: Boschker; Wielaert, Braafheid, Douglas, Brama (Wellenberg 64), Stam, Hersi, Tiote (Janssen 79), Nkufo, Elia, Arnautovic (Huysegems 31).

Santander (0) 1 *(Tchite 59)*
Schalke (0) 1 *(Engelaar 63)* 15,500
Santander: Tono; Cesar Navas, Sepsi, Pinillos, Marcano, Colsa, Lacen, Tchite, Munitis, Serrano, Pereira.
Schalke: Neuer; Westermann, Bordon, Rafinha, Kobiashvili, Streit, Ernst (Jones 86), Rakitic (Halil Altintop 65), Engelaar, Farfan, Kuranyi (Asamoah 81).

Thursday, 27 November 2008

Paris St Germain (2) 2 *(Kezman 5, Luyindula 32)*
Santander (1) 2 *(Traore 40 (og), Colsa 55)* 25,000
Paris St Germain: Landreau; Ceara, Sakho, Bourillon, Traore, Armand, Rothen (Hoarau 76), Sankhare (Makelele 65), Luyindula, Pancrate (Sessegnon 71), Kezman.
Santander: Tono; Garay, Cesar Navas, Marcano, Colsa, Valera, Lacen (Goncalves 66), Tchite (Luccin 79), Munitis, Serrano, Pereira.

Schalke (0) 0
Manchester City (1) 2 *(Mwaruwari 32, Ireland 67)* 54,142
Schalke: Neuer; Westermann, Bordon (Howedes 73), Rafinha, Pander, Rakitic (Asamoah 63), Jones, Engelaar, Farfan, Halil Altintop (Sanchez 80), Kuranyi.
Manchester City: Hart; Kompany, Garrido (Ball 46), Hamann, Richards, Dunne, Wright-Phillips, Vassell, Mwaruwari (Jo 84), Sturridge, Ireland.

Wednesday, 3 December 2008
Manchester City (0) 0
Paris St Germain (0) 0 25,626
Manchester City: Hart; Zabaleta, Garrido, Kompany, Ben Haim, Dunne, Ireland, Vassell (Hamann 76), Elano (Mwaruwari 49), Jo (Evans 65), Sturridge.
Paris St Germain: Landreau; Sakho, Bourillon, Traore, Camara, Makelele (Armand 59), Clement, Rothen, Luyindula, Pancrate (Giuly 69), Kezman (Hoarau 69).

Twente (1) 2 *(Wielaert 2, Perez 55)*
Schalke (0) 1 *(Asamoah 77)* 24,000
Twente: Boschker; Wielaert, Braafheid, Douglas, Brama, Stam (Wellenberg 63), Janssen, Nkufo, Perez (Tiote 75), Elia, Arnautovic (Denneboom 90).
Schalke: Neuer; Westermann, Rafinha, Krstajic, Howedes, Ernst, Jones (Halil Altintop 69), Engelaar, Asamoah, Farfan, Kuranyi.

Thursday, 18 December 2008
Paris St Germain (2) 4 *(Luyindula 8, 86, Sessegnon 23, Kezman 84)*
Twente (0) 0 25,000
Paris St Germain: Landreau; Ceara, Sakho, Bourillon, Camara (Chantome 62), Armand, Sessegnon (Hoarau 62), Clement, Luyindula, Pancrate (Giuly 72), Kezman.
Twente: Boschker; Wielaert, Braafheid, Douglas, Brama, Stam (Wellenberg 71), Tiote, Janssen (Perez 76), Denneboom, Huysegems, Arnautovic.

Santander (2) 3 *(Pereira 20, Serrano 30, Valera 54)*
Manchester City (0) 1 *(Caicedo 90)* 18,360
Santander: Coltorti; Garay, Cesar Navas, Marcano, Colsa (Lacen 77), Luccin, Valera, Tchite, Munitis, Serrano, Pereira (Juanjo 83).
Manchester City: Schmeichel; Zabaleta, Garrido, Gelson, Richards, Ben Haim, Hamann, Vassell, Evans (Caicedo 75), Robinho (Ireland 46), Elano (Kompany 60).

Group A Final Table	P	W	D	L	F	A	Pts
Manchester City	4	2	1	1	6	5	7
Twente	4	2	0	2	5	8	6
Paris St Germain	4	1	2	1	7	5	5
Santander	4	1	2	1	6	5	5
Schalke	4	1	1	2	5	6	4

GROUP B

Thursday, 23 October 2008
Galatasaray (1) 1 *(Kewell 25)*
Olympiakos (0) 0 23,500
Galatasaray: De Sanctis; Fernando Meira, Emre A, Hakan Balta, Sabri, Servet, Lincoln, Ayhan (Volkan 71), Kewell (Mehmet G 86), Arda, Baros (Nonda 78).
Olympiakos: Nikopolidis; Patsatzoglou (Oscar 74), Domi, Zewlakow, Antzas, Torosidis, Galletti (Kovacevic 79), Papadopoulos, Belluschi, Pantos (Leto 58), Diogo.

Hertha Berlin (0) 1 *(Pantelic 74)*
Benfica (0) 1 *(Di Maria 51)* 26,144
Hertha Berlin: Drobny; Friedrich (Kaka 53), Simunic, Chahed, Cicero, Dardai (Kacar 46), Stein (Pantelic 66), Nicu, Lustenberger, Raffael, Voronin.
Benfica: Quim; Luisao, Jorge Ribeiro, Sidnei, Katsouranis (Martins 66), Maxi Pereira, Di Maria, Yebda, Reyes (Urretaviscaya 72), Cardozo (Suazo 46), Nuno Gomes.

Thursday, 6 November 2008
Benfica (0) 0
Galatasaray (0) 2 *(Emre A 51, Umit K 69)* 30,000
Benfica: Quim; Luisao, Jorge Ribeiro, Sidnei, Katsouranis, Maxi Pereira, Di Maria, Yebda (Martins 64), Reyes (Aimar 57), Nuno Gomes (Cardozo 60), Suazo.
Galatasaray: De Sanctis; Fernando Meira, Emre A, Hakan Balta, Sabri, Servet, Lincoln, Ayhan, Arda (Volkan 90), Baros (Mehmet G 81), Umit K (Yaser 84).

Metalist Kharkiv (0) 0
Hertha Berlin (0) 0 35,000
Metalist Kharkiv: Goryainov; Gancarczyk, Obradovic, Maidana, Gueye, Bordian, Valyaev, Edmar, Slyusar (Trisovic 58), Devic (Fomin 82), Jaja.
Hertha Berlin: Drobny; Kaka, Friedrich, Simunic, Chahed, Cicero, Dardai, Stein, Kacar (Lustenberger 77), Pantelic, Voronin (Raffael 82).

Thursday, 27 November 2008
Galatasaray (0) 0
Metalist Kharkiv (0) 1 *(Edmar 81)* 20,000
Galatasaray: De Sanctis; Fernando Meira, Emre A (Baris 46), Sabri, Volkan, Servet, Lincoln, Ayhan, Kewell (Aydin 78), Arda, Baros (Umit K 70).
Metalist Kharkiv: Goryainov; Gancarczyk, Obradovic, Maidana, Gueye, Bordian (Konyushenko 90), Valyaev, Edmar, Slyusar, Devic (Trisovic 63), Jaja (Fomin 80).

Olympiakos (4) 5 *(Galletti 1, Patsatzoglou 17, Diogo 24, 53, Belluschi 44)*
Benfica (1) 1 *(David Luiz 33)* 33,000
Olympiakos: Nikopolidis; Patsatzoglou, Domi, Antzas, Galletti (Leto 59), Djordjevic, Dudu Cearense, Papadopoulos, Belluschi (Oscar 76), Pantos, Diogo (Kovacevic 69).
Benfica: Quim; David Luiz, Jorge Ribeiro, Sidnei, Maxi Pereira, Amorim (Balboa 59), Binya, Yebda (Martins 76), Reyes, Nuno Gomes (Urretaviscaya 56), Suazo.

Wednesday, 3 December 2008
Hertha Berlin (0) 0
Galatasaray (0) 1 *(Baros 69 (pen))* 62,612
Hertha Berlin: Drobny; Friedrich, Simunic, Chahed (Von Bergen 46), Dardai, Stein, Ebert (Domovchiyski 71), Kacar, Pantelic (Cicero 65), Raffael, Voronin.
Galatasaray: De Sanctis; Fernando Meira, Hakan Balta, Sabri (Emre G 79), Servet, Baris, Lincoln, Mehmet T, Kewell, Arda (Volkan 90), Baros (Nonda 85).

Metalist Kharkiv (0) 1 *(Edmar 87)*
Olympiakos (0) 0 25,000
Metalist Kharkiv: Goryainov; Gancarczyk (Konyushenko 90), Obradovic, Maidana, Gueye, Bordian, Valyaev, Edmar, Slyusar, Fomin (Trisovic 82), Jaja (Babich 90).
Olympiakos: Nikopolidis; Patsatzoglou, Domi, Antzas, Torosidis (Pantos 80), Galletti (Mitroglou 72), Djordjevic, Dudu Cearense, Papadopoulos, Belluschi, Diogo.

Thursday, 18 December 2008
Benfica (0) 0
Metalist Kharkiv (0) 1 *(Rykun 84)* 10,000
Benfica: Moreira; David Luiz, Sidnei, Vitor, Bastos (Balboa 55), Maxi Pereira, Binya, Yebda, Cardozo, Urretaviscaya, Nuno Gomes (Di Maria 70).
Metalist Kharkiv: Goryainov; Gancarczyk, Obradovic, Maidana, Gueye, Bordian, Edmar, Slyusar, Trisovic (Rykun 64), Fomin (Devic 46), Jaja (Konyushenko 79).

Olympiakos (0) 4 *(Dudu Cearense 54, Galletti 67 (pen), Torosidis 87, Diogo 89)*
Hertha Berlin (0) 0 33,000
Olympiakos: Nikopolidis; Patsatzoglou, Domi, Zewlakow, Torosidis, Galletti (Pantos 74), Djordjevic (Leto 60), Dudu Cearense, Papadopoulos, Belluschi (Kovacevic 84), Diogo.
Hertha Berlin: Drobny; Kaka, Friedrich, Von Bergen (Domovchiyski 68), Cicero, Dardai, Stein, Nicu (Lucio 88), Lustenberger, Pantelic (Chermiti 74), Raffael.

Group B Final Table	P	W	D	L	F	A	Pts
Metalist Kharkiv	4	3	1	0	3	0	10
Galatasaray	4	3	0	1	4	1	9
Olympiakos	4	2	0	2	9	3	6
Hertha Berlin	4	0	2	2	1	6	2
Benfica	4	0	1	3	2	9	1

GROUP C

Thursday, 23 October 2008

Partizan Belgrade (1) 1 *(Lamine 34)*

Sampdoria (1) 2 *(Bonazzoli 20, Dessena 55)*   23,780

Partizan Belgrade: Bozovic; Stevanovic (Miljkovic 46), Jovanovic, Knezevic, Obradovic, Fejsa (Lazic 65), Juca, Moreira, Tosic, Paunovic (Bogunovic 58), Lamine.
Sampdoria: Castellazzi; Accardi, Lucchini, Bottinelli, Stankevicius, Ziegler, Franceschini, Delvecchio (Sammarco 73), Dessena, Bonazzoli (Fornaroli 87), Cassano (Bellucci 61).

Sevilla (2) 2 *(Romaric 15, Renato 16)*

Stuttgart (0) 0   35,000

Sevilla: Palop; Squillaci, Escude, Fernando Navarro, Fazio, Adriano, Jesus Navas (Fernando 75), Renato (Maresca 62), Acosta (De Mul 20), Romaric, Konko.
Stuttgart: Lehmann; Boulahrouz, Boka (Rudy 73), Delpierre, Magnin, Lanig (Elson 57), Hitzlsperger, Pardo, Hilbert, Trasch (Marica 46), Gomez.

Thursday, 6 November 2008

Standard Liege (1) 1 *(Mbokani 38)*

Sevilla (0) 0   26,500

Standard Liege: Aragon; Dante, Onyewu, Camozzato, Sarr, Dalmat (Benko 90), Defour, Witsel, Mbokani, De Camargo, Jovanovic.
Sevilla: Palop; Escude, Prieto, Fernando Navarro, Adriano (Fernando 80), Jesus Navas, Maresca, Renato, Romaric (De Mul 60), Konko (Crespo 78), Luis Fabiano.

Stuttgart (0) 2 *(Gomez 76, 80)*

Partizan Belgrade (0) 0   20,500

Stuttgart: Lehmann; Osorio, Delpierre, Magnin, Lanig, Pardo, Hilbert (Hitzlsperger 62), Elson (Boka 80), Trasch, Marica (Cacau 67), Gomez.
Partizan Belgrade: Bozovic; Stevanovic, Djordjevic, Knezevic, Obradovic, Juca (Fejsa 83), Moreira, Tosic, Petrovic, Bogunovic (Paunovic 75), Lamine.

Thursday, 27 November 2008

Partizan Belgrade (0) 0

Standard Liege (1) 1 *(De Camargo 36)*   14,210

Partizan Belgrade: Bozovic; Stevanovic, Djordjevic, Knezevic, Fejsa (Lazic 78), Juca, Moreira, Tosic, Ljajic (Jovanovic 46), Bogunovic (Paunovic 69), Lamine.
Standard Liege: Aragon; Goreux (Nicaise 67), Dante, Onyewu, Camozzato, Sarr, Defour, Witsel, Mbokani, De Camargo, Jovanovic (Mulemo 79).

Sampdoria (1) 1 *(Sammarco 39)*

Stuttgart (1) 1 *(Marica 9)*   15,500

Sampdoria: Castellazzi; Accardi, Lucchini (Campagnaro 72), Stankevicius (Ziegler 86), Gastaldello, Pieri, Franceschini, Sammarco, Delvecchio, Bonazzoli (Bellucci 68), Cassano.
Stuttgart: Lehmann; Osorio, Boulahrouz, Tasci, Magnin (Boka 12), Hitzlsperger, Pardo, Hilbert, Elson (Lanig 46) (Trasch 76), Marica, Gomez.

Wednesday, 3 December 2008

Sevilla (1) 3 *(Luis Fabiano 32 (pen), 73, Renato 46)*

Partizan Belgrade (0) 0   25,000

Sevilla: Palop; Dragutinovic, Escude, Prieto, Duscher, Jesus Navas (Fernando Navarro 80), Maresca (Romaric 78), Renato, Capel (De Mul 69), Konko, Luis Fabiano.
Partizan Belgrade: Bozovic; Stevanovic, Jovanovic, Knezevic, Obradovic, Fejsa, Moreira (Lazic 6) (Paunovic 74), Tosic, Petrovic, Ljajic, Lamine (Bogunovic 87).

Standard Liege (3) 3 *(De Camargo 23, Onyewu 34, Jovanovic 42)*

Sampdoria (0) 0   26,833

Standard Liege: Aragon (De Vriendt 83), Goreux, Dante, Onyewu, Camozzato, Sarr, Defour, Witsel, Mbokani, De Camargo (Nicaise 72), Jovanovic (Mangala 88).
Sampdoria: Castellazzi; Lucchini, Bottinelli, Campagnaro (Gastaldello 55), Stankevicius (Pieri 65), Ziegler, Franceschini. Delvecchio, Dessena, Fornaroli (Cassano 54), Bonazzoli.

Thursday, 18 December 2008

Sampdoria (0) 1 *(Bottinelli 75)*

Sevilla (0) 0   20,000

Sampdoria: Castellazzi; Lucchini (Bottinelli 62), Campagnaro, Gastaldello, Pieri (Ziegler 46), Franceschini, Padalino, Sammarco, Delvecchio, Bellucci (Stankevicius 90), Cassano.
Sevilla: Palop; Dragutinovic, Escude, Prieto, Fazio, Adriano (Capel 67), Jesus Navas, Maresca (Romaric 79), Renato, Konko (Mosquera 54), Luis Fabiano.

Stuttgart (1) 3 *(Khedira 4, Hilbert 49, Marica 72)*

Standard Liege (0) 0   28,000

Stuttgart: Lehmann; Tasci, Boka, Delpierre, Lanig, Hitzlsperger, Hilbert (Boulahrouz 70), Khedira (Pardo 77), Trasch, Marica, Gomez (Cacau 81).
Standard Liege: Aragon; Goreux, Onyewu, Mulemo, Sarr, Dalmat (Carcela-Gonzalez 65), Defour, Witsel, Mbokani (Nicaise 78), De Camargo (Mangala 74), Jovanovic.

Group C Final Table	P	W	D	L	F	A	Pts
Standard Liege	4	3	0	1	5	3	9
Stuttgart	4	2	1	1	6	3	7
Sampdoria	4	2	1	1	4	5	7
Sevilla	4	2	0	2	5	2	6
Partizan Belgrade	4	0	0	4	1	8	0

GROUP D

Thursday, 23 October 2008

Dinamo Zagreb (1) 3 *(Mandzukic 3, Balaban 81, Vrdoljak 84)*

NEC Nijmegen (1) 2 *(Carlos Santos 24 (og), Janssen 78)*   15,000

Dinamo Zagreb: Kelava; Ibanez, Lovren, Carlos Santos, Vrdoljak, Sammir (Hrgovic 66), Mikic, Badelj (Suarez 80), Biscan, Morales (Balaban 46), Mandzukic.
NEC Nijmegen: Babos; Zomer, Wisgerhof, El-Akchaoui, Fernandez, Davids, Schone (Bouaouzan 86), Sibum, Radomski (Van Beukering 86), Janssen, Ntibazonkiza.

Udinese (1) 2 *(Di Natale 24 (pen), Pepe 86)*

Tottenham Hotspur (0) 0   22,000

Udinese: Handanovic; Domizzi, Coda, Motta, Lukovic (Pasquale 89), Isla, D'Agostino, Inler, Di Natale, Sanchez (Pepe 79), Quagliarella (Flores 86).
Tottenham Hotspur: Gomes; Hutton, Assou-Ekotto (Modric 46), Zokora, Woodgate (Giovani 63), King, Lennon, Jenas, O'Hara[■], Bent, Bale.

Thursday, 6 November 2008

Spartak Moscow (1) 1 *(Rodriguez 17)*

Udinese (1) 2 *(Quagliarella 12, 60 (pen))*   25,000

Spartak Moscow: Pletikosa; Fatih, Jiranek, Rodriguez, Kovac, Shishkin, Pavlenko (Maidana 62), Bystrov, Parshivlyuk, Prudnikov (Dzyuba 76), Bazhenov.
Udinese: Handanovic; Domizzi, Coda, Motta, Pasquale[■], Obodo (D'Agostino 60), Isla, Inler, Pepe (Ferronetti 84), Sanchez (Flores 74), Quagliarella.

Tottenham Hotspur (2) 4 *(Bent 30, 33, 70, Huddlestone 59)*

Dinamo Zagreb (0) 0   16,295

Tottenham Hotspur: Gomes; Hutton, Bale, Zokora, Woodgate (Gunter 85), Dawson, Lennon, Huddlestone, Bent, Modric (Campbell 75), Bentley (Bostock 79).
Dinamo Zagreb: Kelava; Ibanez, Lovren, Vrdoljak, Drpic (Etto 46), Hrgovic, Sammir (Morales 43), Mikic, Biscan, Balaban (Badelj 60), Manduzic.

Thursday, 27 November 2008

Dinamo Zagreb (0) 0

Spartak Moscow (0) 1 *(Saenko 75)*   12,000

Dinamo Zagreb: Butina; Ibanez (Sammir 80), Lovren (Etto 69), Vrdoljak, Drpic, Hrgovic, Mikic, Badelj, Biscan, Morales (Balaban 42), Mandzukic.
Spartak Moscow: Pletikosa; Fathi, Jiranek, Rodriguez, Kovac, Pavlenko (Zotov 78), Covalciuc, Parshivlyuk, Prudnikov (Maloyan 59), Saenko, Bazhenov (Grigoriev 84).

NEC Nijmegen (0) 0
Tottenham Hotspur (1) 1 *(O'Hara 14)*   12,500

NEC Nijmegen: Babos; Zomer, Wisgerhof, El-Akchaoui, Fernandez (Tshibamba 81), El Kabir, Davids, Schone, Sibum (Bouaouzan 65), Radomski (Kivuvu 46), Van Beukering.
Tottenham Hotspur: Gomes; Gunter, Bale, Zokora, Woodgate, Dawson, Bentley (Mason 90), Huddlestone, Campbell (Obika 83), Bent (Lennon 71), O'Hara.

Wednesday, 3 December 2008

Spartak Moscow (1) 1 *(Covalciuc 2)*
NEC Nijmegen (0) 2 *(Van Beukering 84, Schone 87)*
     12,000
Spartak Moscow: Pletikosa; Fathi, Jiranek, Shishkin, Pavlenko (Maidana 73), Covalciuc, Parshivlyuk, Maloyan (Prudnikov 59), Zotov (Ivanov 46), Saenko, Bazhenov.
NEC Nijmegen: Babos; Zomer, Wisgerhof, El-Akchaoui, Fernandez, Davids, Schone, Sibum (John 64), El Kabir (Worm 74), Bouaouzan, Tshibamba (Van Beukering 46).

Udinese (1) 2 *(Quagliarella 5, Obodo 77)*
Dinamo Zagreb (0) 1 *(Biscan 90)*   18,000
Udinese: Handanovic; Domizzi, Felipe, Lukovic (D'Agostino 74), Nef (Motta 70), Sala, Obodo, Inler, Pepe (Sanchez 80), Di Natale, Quagliarella.
Dinamo Zagreb: Butina; Ibanez (Badelj 46), Vrdoljak, Drpic, Hrgovic, Etto (Sokota 63), Tomic, Sammir, Mikic, Biscan, Balaban (Tadic 56).

Thursday, 18 December 2008

NEC Nijmegen (0) 2 *(John 75, Van Beukering 78)*
Udinese (0) 0   12,500
NEC Nijmegen: Babos; Zomer, Wisgerhof, El-Akchaoui, Fernandez, Davids, Schone, Sibum, Van Beukering (Janssen 90), Bouaouzan, Ntibazonkiza (John 46).
Udinese: Belardi; Domizzi, Coda, Felipe (Inler 22), Motta (D'Agostino 69), Nef, Pasquale, Obodo, Isla (Lukovic 61), Sanchez, Flores.

Tottenham Hotspur (0) 2 *(Modric 67, Huddlestone 74)*
Spartak Moscow (2) 2 *(Dzyuba 23, 33)*   28,906
Tottenham Hotspur: Gomes; Gunter, Bale, Huddlestone, Zokora, Dawson, Bentley, O'Hara, Campbell, Modric, Gilberto (Lennon 46).
Spartak Moscow: Pletikosa; Fathi, Jiranek, Rodriguez, Shishkin (Bazhenov 85), Covalciuc, Parshivlyuk, Maloyan (Zotov 73), Ryzhkov (Grigoriev 60), Saenko, Dzyuba.

Group D Final Table	P	W	D	L	F	A	Pts
Udinese	4	3	0	1	6	4	9
Tottenham Hotspur	4	2	1	1	7	4	7
NEC Nijmegen	4	2	0	2	6	5	6
Spartak Moscow	4	1	1	2	5	6	4
Dinamo Zagreb	4	1	0	3	4	9	3

GROUP E

Thursday, 23 October 2008

Braga (1) 3 *(Luis Aguiar 8, Renteria 46, Alan 87)*
Portsmouth (0) 0   12,000
Braga: Eduardo; Rodriguez, Moises, Evaldo, Frechaut, Luis Aguiar, Vandinho (Paulo Cesar 86), Renteria (Stelvio 83), Meyong, Alan, Matheus (Cesar Peixoto 63).
Portsmouth: James; Pamarot, Hreidarsson (Belhadj 46), Davis, Campbell, Distin, Little, Diop, Crouch, Defoe, Traore A (Kanu 62).

Heerenveen (0) 1 *(Pranjic 86 (pen))*
AC Milan (2) 3 *(Jong-a-Pin 19 (og), Gattuso 23, Inzaghi 69)*   25,600
Heerenveen: Vandenbussche; Breuer, Dingsdag, Vayrynen, Beerens, Pranjic, Jong-a-Pin, Grindheim, Popov (Paulo Henrique 60), Elyounoussi (Kalou 60), Sibon.
AC Milan: Dida; Favalli, Bonera, Emerson, Gattuso, Zambrotta, Kaka (Ronaldinho 78), Antonini, Flamini, Inzaghi (Jankulovski 72), Shevchenko (Pato 72).

Thursday, 6 November 2008

AC Milan (0) 1 *(Ronaldinho 90)*
Braga (0) 0   10,608
AC Milan: Dida; Kaladze, Jankulovski, Senderos, Emerson (Seedorf 68), Gattuso, Antonini, Flamini, Pato (Ronaldinho 63), Inzaghi, Shevchenko.
Braga: Eduardo; Rodriguez, Moises, Evaldo, Frechaut, Cesar Peixoto (Matheus 74), Luis Aguiar, Vandinho, Renteria, Meyong (Paulo Cesar 46), Alan (Joao Pereira 89).

Wolfsburg (2) 5 *(Dzeko 34, 60, Grafite 39, Misimovic 53, Krzynowek 71)*
Heerenveen (1) 1 *(Vayrynen 31)*   15,615
Wolfsburg: Benaglio; Schafer, Madlung, Reither, Barzagli, Josue (Ricardo Costa 73), Misimovic (Gentner 62), Krzynowek, Dejagah, Dzeko, Grafite (Saglik 70).
Heerenveen: Steppe; Kopic (Smarason 65), Breuer, Dinsdag, Svec, Vayrynen, Pranjic, Grindheim, Popov (Jong-a-Pin 61), Paulo Henrique (Deekman 76), Sibon.

Thursday, 27 November 2008

Braga (1) 2 *(Ricardo Costa 6 (og), Meyong 49)*
Wolfsburg (1) 3 *(Dzeko 24, Misimovic 83 (pen), 90)* 7294
Braga: Eduardo; Rodriguez, Moises, Evaldo, Frechaut, Cesar Peixoto, Vandinho, Renteria (Linz 71), Meyong (Orlando Sa 90), Alan, Matheus (Luis Aguiar 64).
Wolfsburg: Benaglio; Zaccardo, Schafer, Ricardo Costa, Riether (Saglik 67), Barzagli, Josue, Misimovic, Dejagah (Krzynowek 77), Gentner, Dzeko.

Portsmouth (0) 2 *(Kaboul 62, Kanu 73)*
AC Milan (0) 2 *(Ronaldinho 84, Inzaghi 90)*   20,403
Portsmouth: James; Johnson, Belhadj, Hughes, Kaboul, Distin, Little (Mvuemba 65), Diop, Crouch, Kanu (Davis 81), Traore A.
AC Milan: Dida; Favalli, Senderos, Emerson, Gattuso (Seedorf 65), Zambrotta, Kaka (Ronaldinho 74), Antonini, Flamini, Inzaghi, Shevchenko (Pato 74).

Thursday, 4 December 2008

Heerenveen (1) 1 *(Sibon 19)*
Braga (1) 2 *(Renteria 35, Luis Aguiar 56)*   25,500
Heerenveen: Steppe; Nielsen, Breuer, Dingsdag, Svec, Vayrynen (Paulo Henrique 28), Beerens, Pranjic (Smarason 70), Grindheim, Popov, Sibon (Elyounoussi 79).
Braga: Eduardo; Moises, Evaldo, Andre Leone, Joao Pereira, Luis Aguiar, Vandinho, Renteria (Paulo Cesar 78), Meyong (Frechaut 87), Alan, Matheus (Cesar Peixoto 41).

Wolfsburg (2) 3 *(Dzeko 3, Gentner 23, Misimovic 74)*
Portsmouth (2) 2 *(Defoe 11, Mvuemba 14)*   21,015
Wolfsburg: Benaglio; Zaccardo (Hasebe 37), Schafer, Ricardo Costa, Riether (Madlung 46), Barzagli, Josue, Misimovic (Simunek 88), Gentner, Dzeko.
Portsmouth: James; Johnson, Traore A, Davis, Campbell, Distin, Hughes, Mvuemba (Crouch 67), Belhadj (Pamarot 46), Defoe, Kranjcar (Kanu 77).

Wednesday, 17 December 2008

AC Milan (1) 2 *(Ambrosini 15, Pato 56)*
Wolfsburg (0) 2 *(Zaccardo 55, Saglik 81)*   5420
AC Milan: Dida; Jankulovski, Favalli, Senderos (Kaladze 9), Seedorf, Zambrotta, Pirlo (Pato 46), Ambrosini, Antonini, Inzaghi, Shevchenko.
Wolfsburg: Benaglio; Zaccardo, Schafer, Ricardo Costa, Barzagli, Josue, Misimovic (Rodrigo Alvim 84), Hasebe (Saglik 75), Dejagah, Gentner (Krzynowek 38), Dzeko.

Portsmouth (2) 3 *(Crouch 40, 42, Hreidarsson 90)*
Heerenveen (0) 0   19,612
Portsmouth: Ashdown; Wilson, Belhadj, Mvuemba, Pamarot, Hreidarsson, Hughes, Diop (Davis 84), Crouch, Kanu, Traore A (Little 62).
Heerenveen: Vandenbussche; Nielsen, Breuer (Smarason 30), Dingsdag, Svec, Vayrynen, Beerens (Elyounoussi 46), Grindheim (Janmaat 84), Popov, Paulo Henrique, Sibon.

Group E Final Table	P	W	D	L	F	A	Pts
Wolfsburg	4	3	1	0	13	7	10
AC Milan	4	2	2	0	8	5	8
Braga	4	2	0	2	7	5	6
Portsmouth	4	1	1	2	7	8	4
Heerenveen	4	0	0	4	3	13	0

GROUP F

Thursday, 23 October 2008

Aston Villa (2) 2 *(Laursen 8, Barry 45)*

Ajax (1) 1 *(Vermaelen 22)*   36,657

Aston Villa: Friedel; Young L, Shorey, Reo-Coker (Gardner 81), Cuellar, Laursen, Petrov, Young A, Agbonlahor (Davies 90), Milner, Barry.
Ajax: Vermeer; Silva, Oleguer (Van der Wiel 78), Vermaelen, Vertonghen, Lindgren, Emanuelson, Gabri, Sarpong (Cvitanich 55), Huntelaar, Suarez (Leonardo 60).

Zilina (0) 1 *(Rilke 69)*

Hamburg (2) 2 *(Petric 15, Olic 45)*   9871

Zilina: Pernis; Vomacka, Pekarik, Piacek (Leitner 86), Sourek (Durica 54), Tesak, Strba, Styvar, Vladavic, Karoglan (Rilke 67), Adauto.
Hamburg: Rost; Atouba (Boateng 83), Reinhardt, Mathijsen, Benjamin, Jarolim, Trochowski, Demel, Guerrero (Pitroipa 75), Petric, Olic.

Thursday, 6 November 2008

Ajax (1) 1 *(Suarez 41)*

Zilina (0) 0   20,000

Ajax: Vermeer; Oleguer, Vermaelen, Vertonghen, Van der Weil, Lindgren (Schilder 72), Emanuelson, Gabri, De Jong (Kennedy 46), Huntelaar, Suarez.
Zilina: Pernis; Vomacka, Pekarik, Sourek, Tesak, Pecalka (Durica 73), Strba, Jez (Piacek 88), Vladavic, Adauto, Styvar (Rilke 73).

Slavia Prague (0) 0

Aston Villa (1) 1 *(Carew 26)*   20,322

Slavia Prague: Vaniak; Brabec, Hubacek (Senkerik 66), Suchy, Tavares, Jarolim, Smicer (Svento 41), Krajcik, Volesak (Belaid 46), Cerny, Necid.
Aston Villa: Guzan; Shorey, Cuellar, Davies, Knight, Salifou, Sidwell, Young A, Agbonlahor (Barry 89), Carew (Delfouneso 90), Gardner.

Thursday, 27 November 2008

Hamburg (0) 0

Ajax (0) 1 *(Leonardo 77)*   51,200

Hamburg: Rost; Alex Silva, Reinhardt, Mathijsen, Aogo, Jarolim, Trochowski (Pitroipa 68), Demel, Thiago Neves (Torun 84), Guerrero (Petric 74), Olic.
Ajax: Vermeer; Oleguer, Vermaelen, Vertonghen, Van der Wiel, Lindgren, Emanuelson, Enoh (Gabri 61), Kennedy (Sno 73), Sulejmani (Leonardo 61), Suarez.

Zilina (0) 0

Slavia Prague (0) 0   8789

Zilina: Pernis; Vomacka, Leitner, Pekarik, Sourek, Pecalka, Strba, Jez, Vladavic, Rilke (Styvar 84), Adauto.
Slavia Prague: Vaniak; Brabec, Hubacek, Suchy, Latka, Jarolim (Janda 71), Svento (Volesak 83), Krajcik, Belaid, Ivana (Senkerik 89), Necid.

Thursday, 4 December 2008

Aston Villa (1) 1 *(Delfouneso 28)*

Zilina (2) 2 *(Leitner 16, Styvar 19)*   28,797

Aston Villa: Guzan; Young L, Salifou (Barry 68), Reo-Coker, Knight, Cuellar, Osbourne (Milner 65), Young A, Harewood, Delfouneso (Agbonlahor 76), Gardner.
Zilina: Pernis; Vomacka, Leitner■, Pekarik, Piacek, Sourek, Pecalka, Strba, Jez (Tesak 90), Adauto (Vladavic 70), Styvar (Rilke 86).

Slavia Prague (0) 0

Hamburg (1) 2 *(Olic 30, Petric 90 (pen))*   17,368

Slavia Prague: Vaniak■; Brabec, Hubacek (Smicer 46), Suchy, Tavares, Jarolim, Svento, Krajcik, Belaid (Ivana 69), Cerny, Necid (Toleski 73).
Hamburg: Rost; Alex Silva, Reinhardt (Boateng 76), Mathijsen, Jansen, Benjamin, Aogo, Jarolim, Demel, Petric (Guerrero 90), Olic.

Wednesday, 17 December 2008

Ajax (1) 2 *(Vertonghen 4, Suarez 90 (pen))*

Slavia Prague (2) 2 *(Cerny 13, Van der Wiel 41 (og))*   30,000

Ajax: Vermeer; Oleguer, Vermaelen, Vertonghen, Van der Wiel, Anita, Emanuelson (Blind 46), De Jong, Sulejmani, Suarez, Cvitanich (Leonardo 75).
Slavia Prague: Divis; Brabec, Hubacek, Suchy, Tavares, Janda (Ivana 72), Jarolim, Krajcik, Belaid, Cerny (Cisse 89), Senkerik (Smicer 82).

Hamburg (2) 3 *(Petric 18, Olic 30, 57)*

Aston Villa (0) 1 *(Delfouneso 83)*   49,121

Hamburg: Rost; Reinhardt, Mathijsen, Jansen, Boateng, Benjamin, Aogo, Jarolim, Trochowski (Ben-Hatira 89), Petric (Thiago Neves 78), Olic (Guerrero 67).
Aston Villa: Guzan; Young L, Shorey, Salifou, Knight, Cuellar, Sidwell■, Reo-Coker, Harewood, Delfouneso, Gardner (Bannan 61).

Group F Final Table	P	W	D	L	F	A	Pts
Hamburg	4	3	0	1	7	3	9
Ajax	4	2	1	1	5	4	7
Aston Villa	4	2	0	2	5	6	6
Zilina	4	1	1	2	3	4	4
Slavia Prague	4	0	2	2	2	5	2

GROUP G

Thursday, 23 October 2008

FC Copenhagen (0) 1 *(Cesar Santin 59)*

St Etienne (2) 3 *(Gomis 2, Perrin 36, Payet 65)*   17,187

FC Copenhagen: Christiansen; Pospech, Laursen, Wendt, Jorgensen, Norregaard (Kvist 58), Hutchinson, Kristensen (Junior 74), Sionko, Nordstrand (Ailton 58), Cesar Santin.
St Etienne: Viviani; Varrault, Tavlaridis, Sauget, Monsoreau, Dernis (Benalouane 90), Matuidi, Perrin, Machado, Payet (Hautcoeur 84), Gomis (Mirallas 88).

Rosenborg (0) 0

Club Brugge (0) 0   12,166

Rosenborg: Jarstein; Lustig (Berisha 90), Dorsin, Demidov, Stadsgaard, Strand (Traore 80), Tettey, Skjelbred, Sapara, Konan (Pelu 84), Iversen.
Club Brugge: Stijnen; Ciman, Klukowski, Clement, Alcaraz, Simaeys, Vargas (Leko 60), Geraerts, Dirar, Sonck, Akpala (Blondel 90).

Thursday, 6 November 2008

St Etienne (0) 3 *(Ilan 59, Machado 63, Mirallas 76)*

Rosenborg (0) 0   24,006

St Etienne: Viviani; Varrault, Tavlaridis, Sauget, Benalouane, Dernis, Matuidi, Machado, Payet (Linganzi Koumba 82), Ilan (Hautcoeur 66), Gomis (Mirallas 74).
Rosenborg: Jarstein; Lustig (Nordvik 89), Dorsin, Demidov, Lago, Strand, Tettey, Skjelbred, Sapara (Aas 80), Konan, Iversen (Traore 65).

Valencia (0) 1 *(Morientes 61)*

FC Copenhagen (0) 1 *(Cesar Santin 85)*   20,000

Valencia: Renan; Albiol, Marchena, Miguel, Del Horno, Baraja (Manuel Fernandes 66), Vicente, Pablo Hernandez, Edu, Hugo Viana (Mata 56), Morientes (Villa 71).
FC Copenhagen: Christiansen; Pospech, Antonsson, Wendt, Jorgensen, Norregaard, Kvist, Hutchinson, Kristensen (Sionko 63), Ailton (Nordstrand 88), Cesar Santin (Wurtz 87).

Thursday, 27 November 2008

Club Brugge (0) 1 *(Vargas 50)*
St Etienne (1) 1 *(Gigliotti 44)* 21,381
Club Brugge: Stijnen; Klukowski, Clement (Geraerts 63), Alcaraz, Simaeys, Leko (Daerden 69), Vargas, De Mets, Dirar, Sonck, Akpala (Chavez 83).
St Etienne: Janot; Varrault, Benalouane, Andreu, Matuidi, Hautcoeur, Matsui (Gomis 81), Machado, Payet (Perrin 72), Gigliotti (Ilan 67), Mirallas.

Rosenborg (0) 0
Valencia (1) 4 *(Mata 21, Pablo Hernandez 76, Baraja 88, Joaquin 90)* 14,549
Rosenborg: Jarstein; Lustig (Basma 85), Dorsin, Demidov, Lago, Strand (Traore 73), Tettey, Skjelbred, Konan, Pelu (Jamtfall 64), Iversen.
Valencia: Renan; Albiol, Marchena, Miguel, Del Horno, Albelda (Maduro 78), Manuel Fernandes (Baraja 58), Pablo Hernandez, Edu, Morientes, Mata (Joaquin 46).

Thursday, 4 December 2008

FC Copenhagen (0) 1 *(Antonsson 85)*
Rosenborg (1) 1 *(Iversen 33)* 18,184
FC Copenhagen: Christiansen; Pospech, Laursen, Antonsson, Wendt, Kvist (Norregaard 71), Hutchinson (Junior 71), Kristensen, Sionko, Nordstrand, Cesar Santin.
Rosenborg: Jarstein; Lustig, Dorsin, Demidov, Lago, Nordvik, Strand (Storflor 75), Tettey, Skjelbred, Konan (Pelu 62), Iversen (Aas 84).

Valencia (0) 1 *(Zigic 60)*
Club Brugge (1) 1 *(Alcaraz 19)* 18,000
Valencia: Guaita; Curro Torres, Marchena, Helguera, Del Horno, Jaume (Vicente 55), Maduro (Albiol 64), Pablo Hernandez, Hugo Viana, Morientes (Manuel Fernandes 73), Zigic.
Club Brugge: Stijnen; Ciman, Klukowski, Clement, Alcaraz, Daerden, Simaeys, Vargas (Van Heerden 90), Geraerts, Dirar, Sonck (Akpala 82).

Wednesday, 17 December 2008

Club Brugge (0) 0
FC Copenhagen (0) 1 *(Cesar Santin 58)* 20,000
Club Brugge: Stijnen; Evens, Klukowski (Ciman 46), Clement, Alcaraz (Leko 46), Daerden, Vargas, Geraerts, De Mets, Dirar, Sonck (Akpala 61).
FC Copenhagen: Christiansen; Pospech, Laursen, Antonsson, Wendt, Norregaard (Wurtz 88), Kvist, Hutchinson, Kristensen (Jorgensen 82), Nordstrand (Sionko 66), Cesar Santin.

St Etienne (2) 2 *(Ilan 29, 44)*
Valencia (1) 2 *(Morientes 33, Zigic 71)* 28,000
St Etienne: Janot; Varrault, Bayal Sall, Benalouane, Andreu, Dernis, Matuidi, Machado, Payet (Grax 90), Ilan (Riviere 90), Mirallas (Gigliotti 83).
Valencia: Guaita; Torres (Miguel 64), Marchena, Del Horno, Maduro, Albelda, Vicente, Joaquin (Zigic 62), Manuel Fernandes, Hugo Viana, Morientes (Silva 76).

Group G Final Table

	P	W	D	L	F	A	Pts
St Etienne	4	2	2	0	9	4	8
Valencia	4	1	3	0	8	4	6
FC Copenhagen	4	1	2	1	4	5	5
Club Brugge	4	0	3	1	2	3	3
Rosenborg	4	0	2	2	1	8	2

GROUP H

Thursday, 23 October 2008

CSKA Moscow (2) 3 *(Dzagoev 9, 12, Vagner Love 61)*
La Coruna (0) 0 13,060
CSKA Moscow: Akinfeev; Semberas, Ignashevich, Berezutski A, Berezutski V, Grigoriev, Krasic, Zhirkov (Shchennikov 87), Aldonin (Rahimic 73), Dzagoev (Ramon 66), Vagner Love.

La Coruna: Aranzubia; Manuel Pablo, Filipe (Adrian 79), Lopo, Ze Castro, De Guzman (Sergio 64), Antonio Tomas, Guardado, Valeron, Omar Bravo (Mista 72), Cristian.

Nancy (0) 3 *(Zerka 48, Feret 54, Helder 84)*
Feyenoord (0) 0 11,512
Nancy: Bracigilano; Helder, Biancalani, Macaluso, Ouaddou, Malonga (Gavanon 46), Feret, N'Guemo, N'Diaye, Dia (Fortune 46), Zerka (Andre Luiz 86).
Feyenoord: Timmer; Hofland, Bahia, De Cler (Makaay 70), Greene, El Ahmadi, Van Bronckhorst, Wijnaldum, Fer, Mols (Erasmus 84), Biseswar.

Thursday, 6 November 2008

Feyenoord (1) 1 *(Van Bronckhorst 29)*
CSKA Moscow (2) 3 *(Van Bronckhorst 14 (og), Vagner Love 40, 81)* 25,000
Feyenoord: Timmer; Hofland, Bahia, De Cler, Tiendalli, El Ahmadi (Mols 79), Van Bronckhorst, Wijnaldum, Fer, Makaay, Biseswar.
CSKA Moscow: Akinfeev; Semberas, Ingashevich, Berezutski A, Berezutski V, Grigoriev, Krasic (Rahimic 85), Zhirkov, Aldonin■, Dzagoev (Mamaev 68), Vagner Love.

Lech (2) 2 *(Peszko 4, Stilic 21)*
Nancy (1) 2 *(Malonga 10, Zerka 81)* 25,000
Lech: Turina; Arboleda, Bosacki, Wojtkowiak, Djurdjevic, Wilk, Stilic, Murawski (Kucharski 90), Peszko (Lewandowski 79), Injac (Bandrowski 63), Rengifo.
Nancy: Bracigliano; Andre Luiz, Calve, Ouaddou, Malonga (Helder 86), Feret, Brison, Gavanon (Berenguer 69), N'Diaye (N'Guemo 63), Dia, Zerka.

Thursday, 27 November 2008

CSKA Moscow (2) 2 *(Dzagoev 31, Zhirkov 45)*
Lech (0) 1 *(Stilic 66)* 10,800
CSKA Moscow: Akinfeev; Semberas, Ignashevich, Berezutski A, Berezutski V, Grigoriev (Rahimic 70), Mamaev, Krasic, Zhirkov, Dzagoev (Erkin 83), Vagner Love.
Lech: Turina; Arboleda, Tanevski, Wojtkowiak, Djurdjevic, Wilk, Stilic, Peszko (Bandrowski 46), Injac, Lewandowski, Rengifo.

La Coruna (1) 3 *(Lopo 30, Hofland 50 (og), Guardado 51)*
Feyenoord (0) 0 20,000
La Coruna: Aranzubia; Manuel Pablo, Filipe, Lopo, Colotto, Sergio, Guardado (Lafita 51), Valeron, Juan Rodriguez (Antonio Tomas 60), Mista (Omar Bravo 69), Cristian.
Feyenoord: Timmer; Hofland, Bahia, De Cler, Tiendalli (Lucius 46), El Ahmadi (Leerdam 55), Van Bronckhorst, Bruins, Wijnaldum (Slory 62), Fer, Makaay.

Thursday, 4 December 2008

Lech (1) 1 *(Rengifo 41)*
La Coruna (1) 1 *(Colotto 2)* 23,000
Lech: Turina; Arboleda, Tanevski, Wojtkowiak, Djurdjevic, Wilk, Stilic, Murawski, Peszko (Lewandowski 80), Bandrowski, Rengifo.
La Coruna: Aranzubia; Filipe, Lopo, Adrian, Colotto, De Guzman, Sergio (Verdu 78), Guardado (Lafita 71), Valeron, Mista (Riki 59), Cristian.

Nancy (1) 3 *(Zerka 5, Feret 72, Camerling 79)*
CSKA Moscow (2) 4 *(Vagner Love 23, 62, 88, Ramon 33)* 14,074
Nancy: Bracigliano; Andre Luiz, Macaluso, Calve, Feret, Brison, N'Guemo, N'Diaye (Camerling 76), Dia (Berenguer 68), Zerka, Fortune (Helder 85).
CSKA Moscow: Akinfeev; Semberas, Ignashevich, Grigoriev, Krasic (Shchennikov 90), Zhirkov, Aldonin, Rahimic, Erkin (Mamaev 67), Ramon (Dzagoev 56), Vagner Love.

Wednesday, 17 December 2008

Feyenoord (0) 0
Lech (1) 1 *(Djurdjevic 27)*   23,000
Feyenoord: Timmer; Lucius, Bahia, Tiendalli, Derijck, El Ahmadi (Leerdam 56), Bruins, Wijnaldum (Erasmus 65), Fer (Janota 65), Wattamaleo, Makaay.
Lech: Turina; Arboleda, Tanevski, Wojtkowiak, Djurdjevic, Wilk, Stilic (Bandrowski 71), Murawski, Peszko, Lewandowski (Reiss 90), Rengifo (Kikut 90).

La Coruna (0) 1 *(Bodipo 73)*
Nancy (0) 0   15,000
La Coruna: Aranzubia; Manuel Pablo, Filipe, Lopo, Colotto, Sergio, Antonio Tomas (Riki 75), Lafita, Guardado (Bodipo 65), Valeron, Omar Bravo (Juan Rodriguez 79).
Nancy: Bracigliano; Andre Luiz, Biancalani (Brison 86), Macaluso, Chretien, Berenguer, Hadji, Feret, Gavanon (Fortune 76), Dia, Zerka.

Group H Final Table	P	W	D	L	F	A	Pts
CSKA Moscow	4	4	0	0	12	5	12
La Coruna	4	2	1	1	5	4	7
Lech	4	1	2	1	5	5	5
Nancy	4	1	1	2	8	7	4
Feyenoord	4	0	0	4	1	10	0

KNOCK-OUT STAGE

THIRD ROUND FIRST LEG

Wednesday, 18 February 2009

Aalborg (0) 3 *(Due 53, 71, Jakobsen 90 (pen))*
La Coruna (0) 0   7987
Aalborg: Zaza; Jakobsen, Beauchamp, Waehler, Bogelund, Due (Risgard 81), Johansson, Augustinussen, Caca (Kristensen 75), Enevoldsen, Shelton (Curth 66).
La Coruna: Aranzubia; Filipe, Lopo, Ze Castro, Adrian, Sergio, Pablo Alvarez, Antonio Tomas (Lafita 76), Valeron (Verdu 65), Juan Rodriguez, Mista (Omar Bravo 62).

Aston Villa (0) 1 *(Carew 69)*
CSKA Moscow (1) 1 *(Vagner Love 14)*   38,038
Aston Villa: Guzan; Young L, Shorey, Gardner, Davies, Knight, Petrov, Young A, Agbonlahor, Carew, Barry.
CSKA Moscow: Akinfeev; Ignashevich, Berezutski A, Berezutski V, Shchennikov, Krasic, Zhirkov (Mamaev 90), Aldonin (Erkin 90), Rahimic, Dzagoev (Daniel Carvalho 90), Vagner Love.

Bordeaux (0) 0
Galatasaray (0) 0   21,813
Bordeaux: Rame; Henrique, Jurietti, Placente (Tremoulinas 84), Diawara, Diarra, Gourcuff, Wendel (Fernando 75), Cavenaghi, Jussie, Chamakh (Gouffran 70).
Galatasaray: De Sanctis; Fernando Meira, Emre A, Servet, Baris, Lincoln (Mehmet G 86), Mehmet T, Ayhan, Kewell (Sabri 64), Arda, Baros (Nonda 46).

Braga (2) 3 *(Renteria 17, Andre Leone 27, Luis Aguiar 84)*
Standard Liege (0) 0   9406
Braga: Eduardo; Evaldo, Frechaut, Andre Leone, Joao Pereira, Cesar Peixoto (Orlando Sa 80), Luis Aguiar, Vandinho, Renteria, Meyong (Matheus 70), Alan (Stelvio 88).
Standard Liege: Aragon; Onyewu, Mikulic, Camozzato, Dalmat, Defour (Nicaise 11), Mangala (Mulemo 64), Witsel, Mbokani, De Camargo, Jovanovic (Benteke 90).

Dynamo Kiev (0) 1 *(Albiol 63 (og))*
Valencia (1) 1 *(Silva 8)*   16,800
Dynamo Kiev: Bogush; Betao, Mikhalik, Nesmachny, El-Kaddouri, Ghioane (Cernat 46), Vukojevic, Eremenko, Kravchenko (Ninkovic 66), Kravets (Correa 90), Milevskiy*.
Valencia: Cesar Sanchez; Albiol, Marchena, Del Horno, Maduro, Albelda, Manuel Fernandes (Baraja 82), Pablo Hernandez (Joaquin 70), Silva (Villa 67), Morientes, Mata.

NEC Nijmegen (0) 0
Hamburg (2) 3 *(Trochowski 41, Alex Silva 45, Olic 75)*   12,500
NEC Nijmegen: Babos; Zomer, Koenders, El-Akchaoui, Pothuizen (Kivuvu 78), Davids, Schone (El Kabir 46), Sibum, Radomski, Van Beukering (Tshibamba 70), Ntibazonkiza.
Hamburg: Rost; Alex Silva, Mathijsen, Jansen (Torun 86), Gravgaard (Benjamin 62), Aogo, Jarolim, Trochowski, Demel, Petric, Olic (Pitroipa 80).

Olympiakos (0) 1 *(Djordjevic 64 (pen))*
St Etienne (2) 3 *(Ilan 12, Dernis 43, Gomis 90)*   33,000
Olympiakos: Nikopolidis; Patsatzoglou, Domi, Antzas, Torosidis, Galletti (Derbyshire 65), Djordjevic (Oscar 77), Dudu Cearense, Papadopoulos (Zewlakow 46), Belluschi, Diogo.
St Étienne: Janot; Varrault, Tavlaridis (Benalouane 76), Dabo, Bayal Sall, Dernis (Hautcoeur 55), Matuidi, Machado, Payet, Ilan (Gomis 46), Mirallas.

Paris St Germain (0) 2 *(Hoarau 81, 85)*
Wolfsburg (0) 0   27,447
Paris St Germain: Edel; Sakho, Traore, Camara, Armand, Chantome, Makonda (Sessegnon 64), Rothen, Luyindula (Partouche 72), Hoarau, Pancrate (Mabiala 83).
Wolfsburg: Benaglio; Schafer, Simunek, Riether (Caiuby 87), Barzagli, Josue, Misimovic (Okubo 62), Hasebe (Ricardo Costa 79), Gentner, Schindzielorz, Dzeko.

Sampdoria (0) 0
Metalist Kharkiv (1) 1 *(Oleynik 45)*   14,774
Sampdoria: Castellazzi; Lucchini, Stankevicius, Raggi, Ziegler (Marilungo 74), Palombo, Franceschini (Sammarco 58), Padalino, Dessena (Pieri 58), Bellucci, Cassano.
Metalist Kharkiv: Goryainov; Obradovic, Maidana, Gueye, Bordian, Valyaev, Edmar (Gancarczyk 90), Slyusar, Oleynik, Rykun (Berezovchuk 89), Jaja (Devic 79).

Werder Bremen (0) 1 *(Diego 84)*
AC Milan (1) 1 *(Inzaghi 36)*   36,151
Werder Bremen: Wiese; Boenisch, Naldo, Baumann (Jensen 63), Fritz (Harnik 74), Mertesacker, Diego, Ozil, Tziolis, Hugo Almeida, Pizarro.
AC Milan: Dida; Favalli, Senderos, Bonera, Seedorf (Jankulovski 87), Zambrotta, Pirlo, Ambrosini, Ronaldinho (Beckham 89), Flamini, Inzaghi.

Zenit (2) 2 *(Huszti 2, Tymoshchuk 45)*
Stuttgart (1) 1 *(Gomez 15)*   17,585
Zenit: Malafeev; Krizanac, Anyukov, Sirl, Shirokov, Zyryanov (Fatih 75), Semshov, Huszti (Fayzulin 88), Tymoshchuk, Pogrebnyak, Danny.
Stuttgart: Lehmann; Osorio, Boulahrouz, Tasci, Magnin, Lanig, Hitzlsperger, Hilbert, Khedira (Boka 72), Marica (Schieber 76), Gomez.

Thursday, 19 February 2009

FC Copenhagen (0) 2 *(Ailton 56, Vingaard 90)*
Manchester C (1) 2 *(Onuoha 29, Ireland 61)*   30,159
FC Copenhagen: Christiansen; Pospech, Laursen, Antonsson, Wendt, Norregaard (Gronkjaer 70), Kvist (Vingaard 60), Hutchinson, Kristensen, Ailton, Cesar Santin (N'Doye 59).
Manchester C: Given; Richards, Bridge, Kompany, Onuoha, Dunne, Zabaleta, Robinho (Caicedo 89), Bellamy, Ireland, Wright-Phillips.

Fiorentina (0) 0
Ajax (0) 1 *(Kennedy 60)*   19,018
Fiorentina: Frey; Dainelli, Gamberini, Zauri, Pasqual, Semioli (Jovetic 57), Montolivo, Gobbi (Kuzmanovic 58), Melo, Mutu, Gilardino.
Ajax: Stekelenburg; Oleguer, Vermaelen, Van der Wiel, Anita, Schilder (Sno 77), Lindgren, Emanuelson, Kennedy, Sulejmani (Leonardo 58), Suarez.

Lech (0) 2 *(Rengifo 81, Arboleda 84)*
Udinese (0) 2 *(Quagliarella 50, Arboleda 55 (og))*   17,000
Lech: Turina; Arboleda, Bosacki, Wojtkowiak, Djurdjevic, Wilk (Bandrowski 67), Stilic, Murawski, Injac, Lewandowski, Rengifo.
Udinese: Handanovic; Zapata, Domizzi, Coda, Pasquale, Isla (Obodo 73), D'Agostino, Inler, Sanchez (Pepe 85), Asamoah, Quagliarella.

Marseille (0) 0
Twente (1) 1 *(Arnautovic 22)*   30,000
Marseille: Mandanda; Taiwo, Hilton, Mears, Zubar, Cheyrou, Kabore (Ben Arfa 31), M'Bami, Valbuena (Zenden 80), Niang (Samassa 65), Kone.
Twente: Boschker; Braafheid, Rajkovic, Douglas, Brama, Stam, Tiote, Nkufo, Perez (Heubach 90), Elia (Janssen 90), Arnautovic (Denneboom 53).

Shakhtar Donetsk (0) 2 *(Seleznov 79, Jadson 88)*
Tottenham H (0) 0   25,000
Shakhtar Donetsk: Pyatov; Ilsinho (Luiz Adriano 68), Rat, Chigrinskiy, Ishchenko, Fernandinho, Jadson, Lewandowski, Willian, Srna, Gladkiy (Seleznov 78).
Tottenham H: Gomes; Chimbonda, Gunter, Zokora, Dawson, Parrett (Bostock 89), Bentley, Jenas, Campbell, Huddlestone, Giovani (Bent 69).

THIRD ROUND, SECOND LEG

Thursday, 26 February 2009

AC Milan (2) 2 *(Pirlo 26 (pen), Pato 32)*
Werder Bremen (0) 2 *(Pizarro 68, 78)*   23,280
AC Milan: Dida; Maldini, Favalli (Jankulovski 77), Senderos, Seedorf (Flamini 54), Zambrotta, Pirlo, Ambrosini, Beckham, Pato, Inzaghi (Shevchenko 62).
Werder Bremen: Vander; Pasanen (Boenisch 67), Naldo, Fritz, Mertesacker, Diego, Ozil (Jensen 90), Tziolis, Frings, Hugo Almeida (Rosenberg 61), Pizarro.

Ajax (0) 1 *(Leonardo 88)*
Fiorentina (0) 1 *(Gilardino 61)*   42,779
Ajax: Vermeer; Oleguer, Vermaelen, Vertonghen, Van der Wiel, Lindgren (Leonardo 70), Emanueleson, Gabri (Anita 79), Enoh, Sulejmani (Alderweireld 90), Suarez.
Fiorentina: Frey; Kroldrup, Gamberini, Zauri (Jovetic 90), Pasqual, Donadel (Almiron 72), Semioli (Jorgensen 68), Montolivo, Melo, Mutu, Gilardino.

CSKA Moscow (0) 2 *(Zhirkov 61, Vagner Love 90)*
Aston Villa (0) 0   25,650
CSKA Moscow: Akinfeev; Semberas, Ignashevich, Berezutski A, Berezutski V, Shchennikov, Krasic, Zhirkov, Rahimic, Dzagoev, Vagner Love.
Aston Villa: Guzan; Young L, Shorey, Salifou (Harewood 46), Davies (Osbourne 84), Knight, Gardner, Sidwell, Delfouneso, Bannan, Albrighton.

Galatasaray (2) 4 *(Arda 43, 65, Kewell 45, Sabri 90)*
Bordeaux (1) 3 *(Bellion 1, Chamakh 74, Cavenaghi 75)*
                                                          19,000
Galatasaray: De Sanctis; Fernando Meira, Emre A, Hakan Balta (Nonda 77), Sabri, Baris (Mehmet G 82), Lincoln, Mehmet T (Kewell 19), Ayhan, Arda, Baros.
Bordeaux: Rame; Henrique, Placente, Diawara, Chalme, Diarra, Fernando, Wendel (Cavenaghi 55), Traore (Jussie 55), Bellion (Gouffran 76), Chamakh.

Hamburg (1) 1 *(Olic 9)*
NEC Nijmegen (0) 0   31,537
Hamburg: Rost; Mathijsen, Jansen (Alex Silva 46), Gravgaard, Boateng (Pitroipa 46), Benjamin, Aogo, Jarolim, Rincon, Petric, Olic (Guerrero 79).
NEC Nijmegen: Babos; Zomer, Koenders (Otten 46), Kivuvu, El-Akchaoui, Pothuizen (Fernandez 46), Davids, El Kabir, Worm (Janssen 72), Tshibamba, Ntibazonkiza.

La Coruna (1) 1 *(Sergio 38)*
Aalborg (3) 3 *(Shelton 41, Johansson 44, Enevoldsen 45)*
                                                          16,000
La Coruna: Aranzubia; Filipe (Juanan 69), Ze Castro, Piscu, Colotto, De Guzman (Pablo Alvarez 46), Sergio, Antonio Tomas, Lafita, Valeron, Bodipo (Omar Bravo 9).
Aalborg: Zaza; Jakobsen, Beauchamp, Waehler (Nielsen 53), Bogelund, Due, Johansson, Augustinussen, Caca, Enevoldsen (Risgard 77), Shelton (Curth 56).

Manchester City (0) 2 *(Bellamy 73, 80)*
FC Copenhagen (0) 1 *(Vingaard 90)*   26,018
Manchester City: Given; Richards, Bridge, Kompany, Onuoha, Dunne, Zabaleta (Elano 82), Robinho, Bellamy, Ireland, Wright-Phillips.
FC Copenhagen: Christiansen; Pospech, Antonsson, Wendt, Jorgensen, Norregaard (Vingaard 76), Kvist, Hutchinson, Kristensen (Sionko 46), Ailton, N'Doye (Gronkjaer 59).

Metalist Kharkiv (2) 2 *(Valyaev 32, Jaja 40)*
Sampdoria (0) 0   30,000
Metalist Kharkiv: Goryainov; Gancarczyk, Obradovic, Maidana, Gueye, Valyaev, Edmar, Slyusar, Oleynik (Berezovchuk 86), Rykun (Devic 57), Jaja (Bordian 78).
Sampdoria: Mirante; Campagnaro, Stankevicius (Franceschini 63), Gastaldello, Da Costa, Ziegler, Padalino (Mustacchio 82), Sammarco (Pieri 65), Dessena, Bellucci, Marilungo.

St Etienne (1) 2 *(Payet 45, Ilan 58)*
Olympiakos (0) 1 *(Oscar 75)*   30,511
St Etienne: Janot; Varrault (Sauget 81), Tavlaridis, Dabo, Bayal Sall, Dernis, Matuidi (Benalouane 72), Machado, Payet (Gigliotti 62), Ilan, Mirallas.
Olympiakos: Nikopolidis; Patsatzoglou, Zewlakow, Antzas, Torosidis (Derbyshire 46), Galitsios, Oscar, Dudu Caerense (Mendrinos 76), Leto, Pantos, Diogo (Mitroglou 65).

Standard Liege (0) 1 *(Mbokani 79)*
Braga (0) 1 *(Luis Aguiar 88)*   26,356
Standard Liege: Bolat (Aragon 46); Goreux (Carcela-Gonzalez 73), Onyewu, Mulemo, Camozzato, Sarr, Dalmat (Benteke 86), Defour, Witsel, Mbokani, De Camargo.
Braga: Eduardo; Evaldo, Andre Leone, Joao Pereira, Stelvio, Cesar Peixoto, Luis Aguiar, Vandinho, Jorginho (Alan 55), Renteria (Orlando Sa 90), Meyong (Paulo Cesar 69).

Stuttgart (0) 1 *(Gebhart 80)*
Zenit (1) 2 *(Semshov 42, Fayzulin 86)*   34,500
Stuttgart: Lehmann; Osorio, Boulahrouz, Tasci, Simak (Gebhart 60), Hitzlsperger, Hilbert (Elson 60), Khedira (Marica 76), Trasch, Cacau, Gomez.
Zenit: Malafeev; Krizanac, Kim, Anyukov, Shirokov, Zyryanov, Semshov, Huszti (Fayzulin 73), Pogrebnyak, Danny, Denisov.

Tottenham Hotspur (0) 1 *(Giovani 55)*
Shakhtar Donetsk (0) 1 *(Fernandinho 86)* 30,595
Tottenham Hotspur: Gomes; Chimbonda, Bale, Palacios, Gunter, Huddlestone, Gilberto (Bostock 77), Obika, Giovani, Campbell, O'Hara (Parrett 71).
Shakhtar Donetsk: Pyatov; Ilsinho (Gay 80), Rat, Chigrinskiy, Ishchenko, Fernandinho, Jadson, Lewandowski, Willian (Hubschman 46), Srna, Gladkiy (Moreno 61).

Twente (0) 0
Marseille (1) 1 *(Ben Arfa 24)* 24,000
Twente: Boschker; Braafheid, Rajkovic, Douglas, Brama (Janssen 79), Stam (Wellenberg 116), Tiote, Denneboom (Hersi 110), Nkufo, Perez, Arnautovic.
Marseille: Mandanda; Civelli, Taiwo, Hilton (Zubar 31), Bonnart, Ziani, Cheyrou, Cana (M'Bami 94), Ben Arfa, Niang, Samassa (Kone 97).
aet; Marseille won 7-6 on penalties.

Udinese (0) 2 *(Pepe 57, Di Natale 90)*
Lech (1) 1 *(Rengifo 13)* 11,662
Udinese: Belardi; Zapata, Domizzi, Coda, Pasquale (Lukovic 77), D'Agostino, Inler, Pepe (Isla 63), Di Natale, Asamoah, Quagliarella (Flores 46).
Lech: Turina; Arboleda, Bosacki, Wojtkowiak (Kikut 83), Djurdjevic, Stilic, Murawski, Injac (Wilk 71), Bandrowski, Lewandowski, Rengifo.

Valencia (1) 2 *(Marchena 45, Del Horno 54)*
Dynamo Kiev (1) 2 *(Kravets 34, 73)* 30,000
Valencia: Cesar Sanchez; Albiol, Marchena (Baraja 81), Alexis, Del Horno, Maduro, Manuel Fernandes, Silva, Villa, Morientes (Joaquin 59), Mata (Vicente 68).
Dynamo Kiev: Bogush; Betao, Mikhalik, Nesmachny, El-Kaddouri, Vukojevic, Correa (Ghioane 78), Aliev, Eremenko, Kravchenko (Cernat 65) (Sablic 88), Kravets.

Wolfsburg (0) 1 *(Hasebe 63)*
Paris St Germain (1) 3 *(Luyindula 38 (pen), 74, Rothen 59)* 20,205
Wolfsburg: Lenz; Zaccardo, Schafer, Simunek, Barzagli, Misimovic, Hasebe, Gentner, Schindzielorz (Dejagah 46), Dzeko, Caiuby (Okubo 46).
Paris St Germain: Landreau; Ceara (Mabiala 78), Traore, Camara, Armand, Sessegnon (Sakho 72), Chantome, Clement, Rothen (Makonda 62), Luyindula, Pancrate.

FOURTH ROUND, FIRST LEG

Thursday, 12 March 2009

CSKA Moscow (0) 1 *(Vagner Love 50 (pen))*
Shakhtar Donetsk (0) 0 19,700
CSKA Moscow: Akinfeev; Semberas, Ignashevich, Berezutski A, Berezutski V, Shchennikov, Dzagoev, Krasic (Kalouda 89), Zhirkov (Erkin 70), Rahimic (Mamaev 46), Vagner Love.
Shakhtar Donetsk: Pyatov; Hubschman, Ilsinho (Willian 67), Rat, Chigrinskiy, Ishchenko, Duljaj, Fernandinho, Jadson (Gay 85), Srna, Luiz Adriano (Moreno 72).

Dynamo Kiev (0) 1 *(Vukojevic 54)*
Metalist Kharkiv (0) 0 17,800
Dynamo Kiev: Bogush; Betao, Sablic, Mikhalik, Vukojevic, Correa, Aliev, Eremenko, Ninkovic (Ghioane 90), Kravets (Gusev 85), Milevskiy.
Metalist Kharkiv: Goryainov; Gancarczyk, Obradovic, Maidana, Gueye, Valyaev, Edmar, Slyusar, Oleynik (Devic 60), Acevedo (Berezovchuk 46), Jaja.

Hamburg (0) 1 *(Jansen 49)*
Galatasaray (1) 1 *(Ayhan 32)* 52,000
Hamburg: Rost; Alex Silva (Pitroipa 84), Mathijsen, Jansen, Boateng, Benjamin, Aogo (Olic 71), Jarolim, Trochowski, Guerrero, Petric.
Galatasaray: De Sanctis; Emre A■, Hakan Balta, Sabri, Volkan, Baris, Lincoln (Mehmet G 59), Ayhan, Kewell, Arda (Hasan Sas 83), Nonda (Umit K 74).

Manchester City (2) 2 *(Caicedo 8, Wright-Phillips 30)*
Aalborg (0) 0 24,502
Manchester City: Given; Richards, Bridge, Caicedo (Evans 63), Onuoha, Dunne, Zabaleta, Ireland, Elano, Robinho, Wright-Phillips (Etuhu 87).
Aalborg: Zaza; Jakobsen (Nielsen 86), Beauchamp, Bogelund, Due (Curth 66), Johansson, Augustinussen, Caca, Enevoldsen (Risgard 76), Shelton, Kristensen.

Marseille (2) 2 *(Cheyrou 19, Niang 33)*
Ajax (1) 1 *(Suarez 36 (pen))* 27,829
Marseille: Mandanda; Civelli, Taiwo, Hilton, Bonnart, Cheyrou, Cana (M'Bami 46), Ben Arfa (Zenden 67), Valbuena, Niang, Kone (Samassa 75).
Ajax: Vermeer; Oleguer, Vermaelen, Van der Wiel■, Alderweireld, Lindgren (Schilder 22), Emanuelson (Silva 43), Aissati, Enoh, Sulejmani, Suarez (Leonardo 83).

Paris St Germain (0) 0
Braga (0) 0 35,000
Paris St Germain: Edel; Ceara, Traore, Camara, Armand, Makelele (Giuly 58), Sessegnon, Chantome (Kezman 69), Clement, Rothen, Luyindula (Hoarau 58).
Braga: Eduardo; Rodriguez, Evaldo, Andre Leone, Joao Pereira, Cesar Peixoto (Stelvio 58), Luis Aguiar, Vandinho, Jorginho (Paulo Cesar 70), Renteria (Mossoro 84), Alan.

Udinese (0) 2 *(Quagliarella 85, Di Natale 90 (pen))*
Zenit (0) 0 20,000
Udinese: Handanovic; Zapata, Domizzi, Coda (Felipe 84), Pasquale, D'Agostino, Inler (Obodo 80), Pepe (Isla 88), Di Natale, Asamoah, Quagliarella.
Zenit: Malafeev; Anyukov, Krizanac, Sirl, Shirokov■, Zyryanov (Ionov 86), Huszti (Semshov 62), Tymoshchuk, Pogrebnyak (Fatih 63), Danny, Denisov.

Werder Bremen (1) 1 *(Naldo 20)*
St Etienne (0) 0 30,116
Werder Bremen: Wiese; Boenisch, Pasanen, Naldo, Baumann, Diego, Tziolis, Jensen (Hunt 13), Frings, Hugo Almeida (Rosenberg 59), Pizarro.
St Etienne: Janot; Varrault, Dabo (Matuidi 46), Sauget, Bayal Sall, Benalaoune, Dernis (Payet 81), Hautcoeur, Machado (Riviere 72), Mirallas, Gomis.

FOURTH ROUND, SECOND LEG

Wednesday, 18 March 2009

Ajax (1) 2 *(Enoh 33, Sulejmani 74)*
Marseille (1) 2 *(Niang 35, Mears 110)* 47,650
Ajax: Vermeer; Silva■, Oleguer, Anita, Alderweireld, Schilder, Emanuelson, Aissati (Leonardo 97), Enoh (De Jong 112), Sulejmani (Cvitanich 104), Suarez.
Marseille: Mandanda; Taiwo, Rodriguez, Hilton, Mears, Cheyrou, Kone, M'Bami, Valbuena (Ziani 52), Niang (Samassa 59), Kone (Ben Arfa 77).

St Etienne (0) 2 *(Benalouane 64, Grax 90)*
Werder Bremen (2) 2 *(Prodl 6, Pizarro 28)* 33,522
St Etienne: Janot; Varrault, Tavlaridis, Sauget, Bayal Sall, Benalouane, Dernis, Hautcoeur (Monsoreau 72), Matsui (Payet 80), Mirallas (Grax 63), Gomis.
Werder Bremen: Wiese; Boenisch, Naldo, Prodl, Mertesacker, Diego (Hunt 75), Ozil, Frings, Niemeyer (Tziolis 72), Rosenberg, Pizarro (Hugo Almeida 87).

Thursday, 19 March 2009

Aalborg (0) 2 *(Shelton 85, Jakobsen 90 (pen))*
Manchester City (0) 0 10,734
Aalborg: Zaza; Jakobsen, Beauchamp, Bogelund, Nielsen, Due (Nomvethe 46), Johansson, Augustinussen, Caca (Kristensen 106), Risgard (Tracy 77), Shelton.
Manchester City: Given; Richards, Bridge (Garrido 55), Kompany (Elano 107), Onuoha, Dunne, Zabaleta, Ireland, Evans, Robinho (97), Wright-Phillips.
aet; Manchester City won 4-3 on penalties: Jakobsen scored; Evans scored; Johansson scored; Elano scored; Augustinussen saved; Wright-Phillips scored; Nomvethe scored; Dunne saved; Shelton saved.

Braga (0) 0
Paris St Germain (0) 1 *(Hoarau 81)*   16,371
Braga: Eduardo; Rodriguez, Evaldo, Andre Leone, Joao Pereira, Cesar Peixoto (Orlando Sa 84), Luis Aguiar, Vandinho, Paulo Cesar (Jorginho 87), Renteria, Alan (Mossoro 72).
Paris St Germain: Landreau; Sakho (Ceara 46), Traore, Camara, Armand, Sessegnon, Chantome, Clement, Luyindula, Pancrate (Mabiala 87), Kezman (Hoarau 77).

Galatasaray (1) 2 *(Kewell 42 (pen), Baros 48)*
Hamburg (0) 3 *(Guerrero 57, 60, Olic 89)*   23,500
Galatasaray: De Sanctis; Hakan Balta, Sabri (Nonda 86), Volkan, Baris, Lincoln (Umit K 66), Ayhan, Kewell, Serkan (Hasan Sas 77), Arda, Baros.
Hamburg: Rost; Alex Silva, Mathijsen, Jansen, Boateng, Benjamin (Gravgaard 81), Aogo, Jarolim, Pitroipa, Guerrero, Olic (Rincon 90).

Metalist Kharkiv (1) 3 *(Slyusar 29, Jaja 56, Acevedo 70)*
Dynamo Kiev (0) 2 *(Sablic 68, Ninkovic 79)*   26,000
Metalist Kharkiv: Goryainov; Obradovic, Maidana, Gueye, Bordian (Berezovchuk 72), Valyaev (Zezeto 83), Edmar, Slyusar, Acevedo, Devic (Oleynik 58), Jaja.
Dynamo Kiev: Bogush; Betao, Sablic, Mikhalik, Nesmachny (Gusev 68), El-Kaddouri, Correa (Ninkovic 60), Aliev, Eremenko, Kravets (Ayila 85), Milevskiy.

Shakhtar Donetsk (0) 2 *(Fernandinho 54 (pen), Luiz Adriano 70)*
CSKA Moscow (0) 0   25,000
Shakhtar Donetsk: Pyatov; Kucher, Shevchuk, Ishchenko, Duljaj, Fernandinho (Willian 90), Jadson (Ilsinho 77), Lewandowski, Srna, Luiz Adriano (Seleznov 83), Gladkiy.
CSKA Moscow: Akinfeev; Semberas, Ignashevich, Berezutski A, Berezutski V, Shchennikov, Dzagoev (Aldonin 65), Mamaev (Ryzhov 76), Krasic, Erkin (Daniel Carvalho 66), Vagner Love.

Zenit (1) 1 *(Tymoshchuk 34)*
Udinese (0) 0   19,500
Zenit: Malafeev; Krizanac, Kim, Sirl (Huszti 71), Zyryanov, Fayzulin (Fatih 71), Semshov, Tymoshchuk, Pogrebnyak, Danny, Denisov.
Udinese: Handanovic; Zapata, Felipe, Lukovic (Isla 60), Pasquale, D'Agostino, Inler, Pepe, Di Natale (Obodo 90), Asamoah, Quagliarella.

QUARTER-FINALS, FIRST LEG

Thursday, 9 April 2009

Hamburg (1) 3 *(Mathijsen 9, Trochowski 63 (pen), Guerrero 79)*
Manchester City (1) 1 *(Ireland 1)*   50,500
Hamburg: Rost; Mathijsen, Jansen, Gravgaard, Benjamin, Aogo, Jarolim, Trochowski, Pitriopa, Petric, Olic (Guerrero 71).
Manchester City: Given; Richards, Bridge (Garrido 46), Ireland, Onuoha, Dunne, Zabaleta, Robinho, Bellamy, Sturridge (Mwaruwari 62), Wright-Phillips (Gelson 83).

Paris St Germain (0) 0
Dynamo Kiev (0) 0   33,140
Paris St Germain: Landreau; Ceara, Traore, Camara, Sessegnon (Pancrate 88), Chantome, Clement, Makonda, Rothen, Luyindula (Kezman 61), Hoarau (Maurice 75).
Dynamo Kiev: Bogush; Betao, Sablic, El-Kaddouri, Vukojevic, Correa (Gusev 84), Aliev (Cernat 73), Eremenko, Ninkovic, Ayila, Milevskiy.

Shakhtar Donetsk (1) 2 *(Hubschman 39, Jadson 65)*
Marseille (0) 0   24,700
Shakhtar Donetsk: Pyatov; Hubschman, Ilsinho (Willian 63), Rat, Chigrinskiy, Ishchenko, Fernandinho (Lewandowski 80), Jadson, Gay, Srna, Luiz Adriano (Gladkiy 89).
Marseille: Mandanda; Civelli, Taiwo, Hilton, Mears, Cheyrou, Zenden (Samassa 78), Cana, M'Bami (Valbuena 68), Niang, Kone.

Werder Bremen (1) 3 *(Diego 34, 67, Hugo Almeida 69)*
Udinese (0) 1 *(Quagliarella 87)*   32,548
Werder Bremen: Wiese; Boenisch (Pasanen 81), Naldo, Fritz, Mertesacker, Diego, Ozil (Niemeyer 76), Tziolis, Frings, Hugo Almeida (Hunt 71), Pizarro.
Udinese: Handanovic; Zapata, Domizzi, Felipe, Pasquale, D'Agostino, Inler (Obodo 84), Pepe (Flores 72), Sanchez, Asamoah, Quagliarella.

QUARTER-FINALS, SECOND LEG

Thursday, 16 April 2009

Dynamo Kiev (2) 3 *(Bangoura 4, Landreau 16 (og), Vukojevic 61)*
Paris St Germain (0) 0   16,873
Dynamo Kiev: Bogush; Betao, Sablic, El-Kaddouri, Vukojevic, Aliev, Eremenko, Ninkovic (Ghioane 83), Ayila (Nesmachny 82), Bangoura (Correa 69), Milevskiy.
Paris St Germain: Landreau; Ceara, Traore (Bourillon 17), Camara, Armand, Makelele, Sessegnon, Chantome, Clement (Rothen 46), Luyindula, Hoarau (Giuly 68).

Manchester City (1) 2 *(Elano 16 (pen), Caicedo 50)*
Hamburg (1) 1 *(Guerrero 12)*   47,009
Manchester City: Given; Richards, Bridge, Kompany, Onuoha, Dunne■, Zabaleta (Gelson 77), Robinho, Elano (Sturridge 85), Caicedo, Ireland.
Hamburg: Rost; Mathijsen, Jansen, Gravgaard, Boateng, Aogo, Jarolim, Trochowski (Petric 73), Pitroipa, Guerrero, Olic.

Marseille (1) 1 *(Ben Arfa 43)*
Shakhtar Donetsk (1) 2 *(Fernandinho 30, Luiz Adriano 90)*   60,000
Marseille: Mandanda; Civelli, Taiwo (Zenden 46), Hilton, Cheyrou, Kabore, Cana, Ben Arfa, Valbuena (Samassa 66), Niang, Kone.
Shakhtar Donetsk: Pyatov; Hubschman, Kucher, Ilsinho (Willian 56), Rat, Chigrinskiy, Duljaj (Gay 46), Fernandinho (Lewandowski 75), Jadson, Srna, Luiz Adriano.

Udinese (3) 3 *(Inler 15, Quagliarella 30, 38)*
Werder Bremen (1) 3 *(Diego 28, 60, Pizarro 73)*   20,000
Udinese: Handanovic; Zapata (Obodo 84), Domizzi, Felipe, Pasquale, D'Agostino (Isla 83), Inler, Sanchez (Pepe 33), Asamoah, Quagliarella, Flores.
Werder Bremen: Wiese; Pasanen (Boenisch 67), Naldo, Fritz, Mertesacker, Diego (Niemeyer 83), Ozil, Tziolis, Frings, Hugo Almeida (Rosenberg 86), Pizarro.

SEMI-FINALS, FIRST LEG

Thursday, 30 April 2009

Dynamo Kiev (1) 1 *(Chigrinskiy 22 (og))*
Shakhtar Donetsk (0) 1 *(Fernandinho 68)*   16,700
Dynamo Kiev: Bogush; Betao, Sablic, El-Kaddouri, Vukojevic, Correa (Cernat 83), Aliev, Ninkovic, Ayila, Bangoura (Ghioane 46), Milevskiy.
Shakhtar Donetsk: Pyatov; Hubschman, Kucher, Ilsinho (Willian 56), Rat, Chigrinskiy, Duljaj, Fernandinho, Jadson (Lewandowski 76), Srna, Luiz Adriano (Gladkiy 46).

Werder Bremen (0) 0
Hamburg (1) 1 *(Trochowski 28)*   37,500
Werder Bremen: Wiese; Boenisch, Naldo, Fritz (Prodl 85), Mertesacker, Diego, Ozil, Tziolis, Frings, Hugo Almeida (Rosenberg 61), Pizarro.
Hamburg: Rost; Alex Silva (Boateng 75), Mathijsen, Gravgaard, Aogo (Benjamin 79), Jarolim, Trochowski, Demel, Pitroipa, Guerrero, Olic (Torun 90).

SEMI-FINALS, SECOND LEG

Thursday, 7 May 2009

Hamburg (1) 2 *(Olic 13, 87)*

Werder Bremen (1) 3 *(Diego 29, Pizarro 66, Baumann 83)*
51,000

Hamburg: Rost; Alex Silva (Benjamin 72), Mathijsen, Jansen (Aogo 77), Gravgaard, Jarolim, Trochowski, Demel (Boateng 62), Pitroipa, Petric, Olic.
Werder Bremen: Wiese; Boenisch, Naldo, Baumann, Fritz, Mertesacker (Prodl 54), Diego, Ozil, Frings, Rosenberg (Hugo Almeida 61), Pizarro (Niemeyer 90).

Shakhtar Donetsk (1) 2 *(Jadson 17, Ilsinho 89)*
Dynamo Kiev (0) 1 *(Bangoura 47)* 24,300
Shakhtar Donetsk: Pyatov; Hubschman, Ilsinho (Lewandowski 90), Rat, Chigrinskiy, Ishchenko, Fernandinho, Jadson, Gay (Willian 70), Srna, Adriano (Gladkiy 70).
Dynamo Kiev: Bogush; Betao, Sablic, El-Kaddouri, Vukojevic, Aliev, Eremenko (Correa 76), Ninkovic, Ayila, Bangoura, Milevskiy.

UEFA CUP FINAL 2009

Wednesday, 20 May 2009

(in Istanbul, attendance 40,000)

Shakhtar Donetsk (1) 2 *(Luiz Adriano 26, Jadson 97)*   **Werder Bremen (1) 1** *(Naldo 35)*

Shakhtar Donetsk: Pyatov; Kucher, Ilsinho (Gay 100), Rat, Chigrinskiy, Fernandinho, Jadson (Duljaj 112), Lewandowski, Willian, Srna, Luiz Adriano (Gladkiy 90).

Werder Bremen: Wiese; Boenisch, Naldo, Baumann, Fritz (Pasanen 95), Prodl, Ozil, Frings, Niemeyer (Tziolis 103), Rosenberg (Hunt 78), Pizarro.

aet.

Referee: Chantalejo (Spain).

Louis Fernandinho (right) of Shakthtar Donetsk in action against Werder Bremen's Frank Baumann in the UEFA Cup Final at the Sukru Saracoglu Stadium in Istanbul. (Action Images/Keith Williams)

UEFA CHAMPIONS LEAGUE 2009–10

PARTICIPATING CLUBS

FC Barcelona (ESP)
Liverpool FC (ENG)
Chelsea FC (ENG)
Manchester United FC (ENG)
Sevilla FC (ESP)
AC Milan (ITA)
FC Bayern München (GER)
FC Internazionale Milano (ITA)
Real Madrid CF (SPA)
PFC CSKA Moskva (RUS)
FC Porto (POR)
AZ Alkmaar (NED)
Juventus (ITA)
Rangers FC (SCO)
Olympique de Marseille (FRA)
FC Dynamo Kyiv (UKR)
FC Girondins de Bordeaux (FRA)
Beşiktaş JK (TUR)
VfL Wolfsburg (GER)
R. Standard de Liège (BEL)
FC Rubin Kazan (RUS)
AFC Unirea Urziceni (ROU)
Arsenal FC (ENG)
Olympique Lyonnais (FRA)
VfB Stuttgart (GER)

ACF Fiorentina (ITA)
Club Atlético de Madrid (SPA)
FC Shakhtar Donetsk (UKR)
Sporting Clube de Portugal (POR)
Panathinaikos FC (GRE)
Celtic FC (SCO)
RSC Anderlecht (BEL)
AC Sparta Praha (CZE)
FC Dinamo 1948 Bucureşti (ROU)
FC Twente (NED)
FC Dinamo Moskva (RUS)
Sivasspor (TUR)
Olympiacos CFP (GRE)
SK Slavia Praha (CZE)
FC Zürich (SUI)
FC København (DEN)
PFC Levski Sofia (BUL)
FK Partizan (SRB)
Maccabi Haifa FC (ISR)
NK Dinamo Zagreb (CRO)
Wisla Kraków (POL)
FC BATE Borisov (BLR)
FC Salzburg (AUS)
Kalmar FF (SWE)
APOEL FC (CYP)
Stabæk IF (NOR)

ŠK Slovan Bratislava (SVK)
FK Ventspils (LVA)
NK Maribor (SVN)
FH Hafnarfjördur (ISL)
FC International Turku (FIN)
FK Ekranas (LTU)
Bohemian FC (IRL)
NK Zrinjski (BIH)
Debreceni VSC (LTU)
FC Sheriff (MDA)
FC WIT Georgia (GEO)
FK Makedonija GP Skopje (MKD)
FK Bakı (AZE)
FC Levdia Tallinn (EST)
KF Tirana (ALB)
FK Aktobe (KAZ)
FC Pyunik (ARM)
Rhyl FC (WAL)
Glentoran FC (NIR)
EB/Streymur (FRO)
F91 Dudelange (LUX)
FK Mogren (MNE)
UE Sant Julià (AND)
Hibernians FC (MLT)
SP Tre Fiori (SMR)

UEFA EUROPA LEAGUE 2009–10

PARTICIPATING CLUBS

Everton FC (ENG)
Aston Villa FC (ENG)
Villarreal CF (ESP)
Valencia CF (ESP)
S.S. Lazio (ITA) *
Genoa CFC (ITA)
EA Guingamp (FRA) *
Toulouse FC (FRA)
Werder Bremen (GER) *
Hertha BSC Berlin (GER)
FC Amkar Perm (RUS)
FC Zenit St. Petersburg (RUS)
CFR 1907 Cluj (ROU)
FC Dinamo 1948 Bucureşti (ROU)
SL Benfica (POR)
CD Nacional (POR)
SC Heerenveen (NED) *
AFC Ajax (NED)
Heart of Midlothian FC (SCO)
Trabzonspor (TUR)
FC Vorskla Poltava (UKR) *
KRC Genk (BEL) *
AEK Athens FC (GRE)
FK Teplice (CZE) *
FC Sion (SUI) *
PFC Litex Lovech (BUL) *
Fulham FC (ENG)
Athletic Club Bilbao (ESP) **
AS Roma (ITA)
LOSC Lille Métropole (FRA)
Hamburger SV (GER)
PFC Krylya Sovetov Samara (RUS)
SC Vaslui (ROU)
SC Braga (POR)
PSV Eindhoven (NED)
Aberdeen FC (SCO)
Fenerbahçe SK (TUR)
FC Metalist Kharkiv (UKR)
Club Brugge KV (BEL)
PAOK FC (GRE)
FC Slovan Liberec (CZE)
BSC Young Boys (SUI)
PFC CSKA Sofia (BUL)
Vålerenga Fotball (NOR) *
Fredrikstad FK (NOR)
Odense BK (DEN)
FK Austria Wien (AUT) *
FK Vojvodina (SRB)
Hapoel Tel-Aviv FC (ISR)
IFK Göteborg (SWE) *
MFK Košice (SVK) *
KKS Lech Poznań (POL) *
Budapest Honvéd FC (HUN) *

HNK Hajduk Split (CRO)
APOP/Kinyras Peyias FC (CYP) *
NK IB Ljubljana (SVN) *
FC Steaua Bucureşti (ROU)
FC Paços de Ferreira (POR) **
NAC Breda (NED)
Falkirk FC (SCO) **
Galatasaray AŞ (TUR)
FC Metalurh Donetsk (UKR)
KAA Gent (BEL)
Larissa FC (GRE)
SK Sigma Olomouc (CZE)
FC Basel 1893 (SUI)
PFC Cherno More Varna (BUL)
Tromsø IL (NOR)
Brøndby IF (DEN)
Aalborg BK (DEN) **
SK Rapid Wien (AUT)
SK Sturm Graz (AUT)
FK Crvena Zvezda (SRB)
FK Sevojno (SRB) **
Maccabi Netanya FC (ISR)
IF Elfsborg (SWE)
MŠK Žilina (SVK)
Legia Warszawa (POL)
Újpest FC (HUN)
HNK Rijeka (CRO)
AC Omonia (CYP)
NK Gorica (SVN)
HJK Helsinki (FIN) *
FC Honka Espoo (FIN)
SK Liepājas Metalurgs (LVA)
Skonto FC (LVA)
FK Slavija Sarajevo (BIH) *
FK Sarajevo (BIH)
FK Sūdūva (LTU) *
FBK Kaunas (LTU)
FC Dacia Chişinău (MDA)
FC Iskra-Stali (MDA)
Saint Patrick's Athletic FC (IRL)
Derry City FC (IRL)
FK Rabotnicki (MKD) *
FK Milano (MKD)
KR Reykjavík (ISL) *
FC Dinamo Tbilisi (GEO) *
FC Vaduz (LIE) *
FC Naftan Novopolotsk (BLR) *
FC Flora (EST) *
FK Qarabağ (AZE) *
KS Flamurtari (ALB) *
FC Gandzasar Kapan (ARM)
FC Tobol Kostanay (KAZ)
Crusaders FC (NIR) *
Bangor City FC (WAL) *

HB Tórshavn (FRO)
FC Differdange 03 (LUX)
Sliema Wanderers FC (MLT) *
FK Petrovac (MNE) *
FC Santa Coloma (AND) *
AC Juvenes-Dogana (SMR) *
Randers FC (DEN) ***
Rosenborg BK (NOR) ***
Motherwell FC (SCO) ***
Bnei Yehuda Tel-Aviv FC (ISR)
Helsingborgs IF (SWE)
FC Spartak Trnava (SVK)
KSP Polonia Warszawa (POL)
Haladás FC (HUN)
NK Slaven Koprivnica (CRO)
Anorthosis Famagusta FC (CYP)
NK Rudar Velenje (SVN)
FC Lahti (FIN)
FC Dinaburg (LVA)
NK Široki Brijeg (BIH)
FK Vėtra (LTU)
FC Zimbru Chişinău (MDA)
Sligo Rovers FC (IRL)
FK Renova (MKD)
Keflavík (ISL)
Fram Reykjavík (ISL)
FC Olimpi Rustavi (GEO)
FC Zestafoni (GEO)
FC Dinamo Minsk (BLR)
FC MTZ-RIPO Minsk (BLR)
JK Trans Narva (EST)
JK Nõmme Kalju (EST)
FC Inter Bakı (AZE)
Simurq PFC (AZE)
KS Vllaznia (ALB)
KS Dinamo Tirana (ALB)
FC MIKA (ARM)
FC Banants (ARM) **
FC Irtysh Pavlodar (KAZ)
FC Okzhetpes Kokshetau (KAZ)
Linfield FC (NIR)
Lisburn Distillery FC (NIR)
Llanelli AFC (WAL)
The New Saints FC (WAL)
B36 Tórshavn (FRO) **
NSÍ Runavík (FRO)
CS Grevenmacher (LUX)
UN Käerjéng 97 (LUX) **
Valletta FC (MLT)
Birkirkara FC (MLT)
FK Budućnost Podgorica (MNE)
FK Sutjeska (MNE)

cup winners **losing cup finalists* ***Fair Play winners*

SUMMARY OF APPEARANCES

EUROPEAN CUP AND CHAMPIONS LEAGUE (1955–2009)

ENGLISH CLUBS
20 Manchester U
19 Liverpool
13 Arsenal
7 Chelsea
4 Everton, Leeds U
3 Derby Co, Wolverhampton W, Aston Villa, Newcastle U, Nottingham F
1 Burnley, Tottenham H, Ipswich T, Manchester C, Blackburn R

SCOTTISH CLUBS
27 Rangers
24 Celtic
3 Aberdeen, Hearts
1 Dundee, Dundee U, Kilmarnock, Hibernian

WELSH CLUBS
6 Barry T
3 TNS
1 Cwmbran T, Rhyl, Llanelli

NORTHERN IRELAND CLUBS
24 Linfield
11 Glentoran
3 Crusaders, Portadown
1 Glenavon, Ards, Distillery, Derry C, Coleraine, Cliftonville

REPUBLIC OF IRELAND CLUBS
7 Shamrock R, Dundalk
6 Shelbourne, Waterford
4 Bohemians
3 Drumcondra, St Patrick's Ath, Derry C*
2 Sligo R, Limerick, Athlone T, Cork City
1 Cork Hibs, Cork Celtic, Drogheda U

Winners: Celtic 1966–67; Manchester U 1967–68, 1998–99; 2007–08; Liverpool 1976–77, 1977–78, 1980–81, 1983–84, 2004–05; Nottingham F 1978–79, 1979–80; Aston Villa 1981–82
Finalists: Celtic 1969–70; Leeds U 1974–75; Liverpool 1984–85, 2006–07; Arsenal 2005–06; Chelsea 2007–08; Manchester U 2008–09

EUROPEAN CUP-WINNERS' CUP (1960–99)

ENGLISH CLUBS
6 Tottenham H
5 Manchester U, Liverpool, Chelsea
4 West Ham U
3 Arsenal, Everton
2 Manchester C
1 Wolverhampton W, Leicester C, WBA, Leeds U, Sunderland, Southampton, Ipswich T, Newcastle U

SCOTTISH CLUBS
10 Rangers
8 Aberdeen, Celtic
3 Hearts
2 Dunfermline Ath, Dundee U
1 Dundee, Hibernian, St Mirren, Motherwell, Airdrieonians, Kilmarnock

WELSH CLUBS
14 Cardiff C
8 Wrexham
7 Swansea C
3 Bangor C
1 Borough U, Newport Co, Merthyr Tydfil, Barry T, Llansantffraid, Cwmbran T

NORTHERN IRELAND CLUBS
9 Glentoran
5 Glenavon
4 Ballymena U, Coleraine
3 Crusaders, Linfield
2 Ards, Bangor
1 Derry C, Distillery, Portadown, Carrick Rangers, Cliftonville

REPUBLIC OF IRELAND CLUBS
6 Shamrock R
4 Shelbourne
3 Limerick, Waterford, Dundalk, Bohemians
2 Cork Hibs, Galway U, Derry C*, Cork City
1 Cork Celtic, St Patrick's Ath, Finn Harps, Home Farm, University College Dublin, Bray W, Sligo R

Winners: Tottenham H 1962–63; West Ham U 1964–65; Manchester C 1969–70; Chelsea 1970–71, 1997–98; Rangers 1971–72; Aberdeen 1982–83; Everton 1984–85; Manchester U 1990–91; Arsenal 1993–94
Finalists: Rangers 1960–61, 1966–67; Liverpool 1965–66; Leeds U 1972–73; West Ham U 1975–76; Arsenal 1979–80, 1994–95

EUROPEAN FAIRS CUP & UEFA CUP (1955–2009)

ENGLISH CLUBS
13 Leeds U
12 Liverpool
11 Aston Villa
10 Ipswich T, Newcastle U
9 Arsenal, Everton, Tottenham H
7 Manchester U
6 Southampton, Chelsea, Blackburn R, Manchester C
5 Nottingham F
4 Birmingham C, Wolverhampton W, WBA
3 Sheffield W
2 Stoke C, Derby Co, QPR, Leicester C, Middlesbrough, West Ham U, Bolton W
1 Burnley, Coventry C, Millwall, Norwich C, London Rep XI, Watford, Fulham, Portsmouth

SCOTTISH CLUBS
19 Dundee U
16 Hibernian, Aberdeen, Rangers
15 Celtic
13 Hearts
7 Kilmarnock, Dunfermline Ath
5 Dundee
3 St Mirren, Motherwell
2 Partick T, St Johnstone
1 Morton, Raith R, Livingston, Gretna, Queen of S

WELSH CLUBS
6 TNS
5 Bangor C
3 Inter Cardiff (formerly Inter Cable-Tel), Cwmbran T, Rhyl

2 Newtown, Carmarthen T, Barry T
1 Afan Lido, Haverfordwest, Llanelli

NORTHERN IRELAND CLUBS
18 Glentoran
9 Linfield
8 Coleraine, Portadown
7 Glenavon
3 Crusaders
1 Ards, Ballymena U, Bangor, Dungannon Swifts, Cliftonville

REPUBLIC OF IRELAND CLUBS
12 Bohemians
7 Shelbourne
6 Dundalk, Cork City
5 Shamrock R, St Patrick's Ath
4 Derry C*
3 Finn Harps, Longford T, Drogheda U
2 Drumcondra
1 Cork Hibs, Athlone T, Limerick, Galway U, Bray Wanderers

Winners: Leeds U 1967–68, 1970–71; Newcastle U 1968–69; Arsenal 1969–70; Tottenham H 1971–72, 1983–84; Liverpool 1972–73, 1975–76, 2000–01; Ipswich T 1980–81
Finalists: London 1955–58, Birmingham C 1958–60, 1960–61; Leeds U 1966–67; Wolverhampton W 1971–72; Tottenham H 1973–74; Celtic 2002–03; Middlesbrough 2005–06; Rangers 2007–08

Now play in League of Ireland

INTERTOTO CUP 2008

FIRST ROUND, FIRST LEG
Mika 2, Tiraspol 2
Lisburn Distillery 2, TPS Turku 3
Etzella 0, Lokomotiv Tbilisi 0
Riga 1, Fylkir 2
Hibernians 0, Gorica 3
Neftchi 2, Nitra 0
Cracovia 1, Soligorsk 2
Rijeka 0, Renova 0
Celik 3, Grbalj 2
Bohemian 5, Rhyl 1
Besa 0, Ethnikos 0
Zhetysu 1, Honved 2
Ekranas 1, Trans 0
HB Torshavn 1, Elfsborg 4

FIRST ROUND, SECOND LEG
Elfsborg 0, HB Torshavn 0
Rhyl 2, Bohemian 4
Trans 0, Ekranas 3
Ethnikos 1, Besa 1
Renova 2, Rijeka 0
Tiraspol 0, Mika 0
Nitra 3, Neftchi 1
Lokomotiv Tbilisi 2, Etzella 2
Grbalj 2, Celik 1
Honved 4, Zhetysu 2
Gorica 0, Hibernians 0
Soligorsk 3, Cracovia 0
TPS Turku 3, Lisburn Distillery 1
Fylkir 0, Riga 2

SECOND ROUND, FIRST LEG
Saturn 7, Etzella 0
Grasshoppers 2, Besa 1
Grbalj 2, Sivasspor 0
Sturm Graz 2, Soligorsk 0
Teplice 1, Honved 3

Tiraspol 0, Tavriya 0
Chernomorets 1, Gorica 1
Beerschot 1, Neftchi 1
Hibernian 0, Elfsborg 2
Ekranas 1, Rosenborg 3
OFK Belgrade 1, Panionios 0
Riga 1, Bohemian 0
TPS Turku 1, Odense 2
Renova 1, Bnei Sachnin 2

SECOND ROUND, SECOND LEG
Elfsborg 2, Hibernian 0
Besa 0, Grasshoppers 3
Neftchi 1, Beerschot 0
Honved 0, Teplice 2
Bnei Sachnin 1, Renova 0
Gorica 0, Chernomorets 2
Bohemian 2, Riga 1
Rosenborg 4, Ekranas 0
Soligorsk 0, Sturm Graz 0
Panionios 3, OFK Belgrade 1
Etzella 1, Saturn 1
Tavriya 3, Tiraspol 1
Sivasspor 1, Grbalj 0
Odense 2, TPS Turku 0

THIRD ROUND, FIRST LEG
Bnei Sachnan 1, La Coruna 2
Panionios 0, Napoli 1
Sivasspor 0, Braga 2
Grasshoppers 3, Chernomorets 0
Saturn 1, Stuttgart 0
Neftchi 2, Vaslui 1
Rennes 1, Tavriya 0
Sturm Graz 0, Honved 0
NAC Breda 1, Rosenborg 2
Odense 2, Aston Villa 2
Elfsborg 1, Riga 0

THIRD ROUND, SECOND LEG
La Coruna 1, Bnei Sachnan 0
Napoli 1, Panionios 0
Braga 3, Sivasspor 0
Chernomorets 0, Grasshoppers 1
Stuttgart 3, Saturn 0
Vaslui 2, Neftchi 0
Tavriya 1, Rennes 0
Rennes won 10-9 on penalties.
Honved 1, Sturm Graz 2
Rosenborg 2, NAC Breda 0
Aston Villa 1, Odense 0
Riga 0, Elfsborg 0

Odense (1) 2 *(Sidwell 25 og, Christensen 90)*

Aston Villa (1) 2 *(Carew 7, Laursen 76)*   11,350

Aston Villa: Taylor; Gardner, Bouma, Reo-Coker, Knight, Laursen, Young A, Sidwell (Routledge 82), Agbonlahor, Carew, Petrov.

Aston Villa (0) 1 *(Young 51)*
Odense (0) 0   31,423

Aston Villa: Taylor; Gardner, Bouma (Barry 14), Reo-Coker, Knight, Laursen, Young A, Sidwell, Agbonlahor, Carew, Petrov.

WORLD CLUB CHAMPIONSHIP

Played annually up to 1974 and intermittently since then between the winners of the European Cup and the winners of the South American Champions Cup — known as the Copa Libertadores. In 1980 the winners were decided by one match arranged in Tokyo in February 1981 which remained the venue until 2004, when the match was superseded by the FIFA Club World Championship. AC Milan replaced Marseille who had been stripped of their European Cup title in 1993.

1960 Real Madrid beat Penarol 0-0, 5-1
1961 Penarol beat Benfica 0-1, 5-0, 2-1
1962 Santos beat Benfica 3-2, 5-2
1963 Santos beat AC Milan 2-4, 4-2, 1-0
1964 Inter-Milan beat Independiente 0-1, 2-0, 1-0
1965 Inter-Milan beat Independiente 3-0, 0-0
1966 Penarol beat Real Madrid 2-0, 2-0
1967 Racing Club beat Celtic 0-1, 2-1, 1-0
1968 Estudiantes beat Manchester United 1-0, 1-1
1969 AC Milan beat Estudiantes 3-0, 1-2
1970 Feyenoord beat Estudiantes 2-2, 1-0
1971 Nacional beat Panathinaikos* 1-1, 2-1
1972 Ajax beat Independiente 1-1, 3-0
1973 Independiente beat Juventus* 1-0
1974 Atlético Madrid* beat Independiente 0-1, 2-0
1975 Independiente and Bayern Munich could not agree dates; no matches.
1976 Bayern Munich beat Cruzeiro 2-0, 0-0
1977 Boca Juniors beat Borussia Moenchengladbach* 2-2, 3-0
1978 Not contested
1979 Olimpia beat Malmö* 1-0, 2-1
1980 Nacional beat Nottingham Forest 1-0
1981 Flamengo beat Liverpool 3-0
1982 Penarol beat Aston Villa 2-0
1983 Gremio Porto Alegre beat SV Hamburg 2-1
1984 Independiente beat Liverpool 1-0

1985 Juventus beat Argentinos Juniors 4-2 on penalties after a 2-2 draw
1986 River Plate beat Steaua Bucharest 1-0
1987 FC Porto beat Penarol 2-1 after extra time
1988 Nacional (Uru) beat PSV Eindhoven 7-6 on penalties after 1-1 draw
1989 AC Milan beat Atletico Nacional (Col) 1-0 after extra time
1990 AC Milan beat Olimpia 3-0
1991 Red Star Belgrade beat Colo Colo 3-0
1992 Sao Paulo beat Barcelona 2-1
1993 Sao Paulo beat AC Milan 3-2
1994 Velez Sarsfield beat AC Milan 2-0
1995 Ajax beat Gremio Porto Alegre 4-3 on penalties after 0-0 draw
1996 Juventus beat River Plate 1-0
1997 Borussia Dortmund beat Cruzeiro 2-0
1998 Real Madrid beat Vasco da Gama 2-1
1999 Manchester U beat Palmeiras 1-0
2000 Boca Juniors beat Real Madrid 2-1
2001 Bayern Munich beat Boca Juniors 1-0 after extra time
2002 Real Madrid beat Olimpia 2-0
2003 Boca Juniors beat AC Milan 3-1 on penalties after 1-1 draw
2004 Porto beat Once Caldas 8-7 on penalties after 0-0 draw

*European Cup runners-up; winners declined to take part.

EUROPEAN SUPER CUP 2008

Played annually between the winners of the European Champions' Cup and the European Cup-Winners' Cup (UEFA Cup from 2000). AC Milan replaced Marseille in 1993–94.

EUROPEAN SUPER CUP 2008
29 August 2008, Monaco (attendance 18,064)

Manchester U (0) 1 *(Vidic 73)* **Zenit (1) 2** *(Pogrebnyak 44, Danny 59)*

Manchester U: Van der Sar; Neville, Evra, Anderson (Park 60), Ferdinand, Vidic, Fletcher (O'Shea 60), Scholes▪, Rooney, Tevez, Nani.

Zenit: Malafeev; Krizanac (Radimov 71), Dominguez (Arshavin 46), Pogrebnyak, Sirl, Zyryanov, Danny, Anyukov, Denisov, Puygrenier (Shirokov 62), Tymoshchuk.

Referee: Bo Larsen (Denmark).

PREVIOUS MATCHES

1972	Ajax beat Rangers 3-1, 3-2	1990	AC Milan beat Sampdoria 1-1, 2-0
1973	Ajax beat AC Milan 0-1, 6-0	1991	Manchester U beat Red Star Belgrade 1-0
1974	Not contested	1992	Barcelona beat Werder Bremen 1-1, 2-1
1975	Dynamo Kiev beat Bayern Munich 1-0, 2-0	1993	Parma beat AC Milan 0-1, 2-0
1976	Anderlecht beat Bayern Munich 4-1, 1-2	1994	AC Milan beat Arsenal 0-0, 2-0
1977	Liverpool beat Hamburg 1-1, 6-0	1995	Ajax beat Zaragoza 1-1, 4-0
1978	Anderlecht beat Liverpool 3-1, 1-2	1996	Juventus beat Paris St Germain 6-1, 3-1
1979	Nottingham F beat Barcelona 1-0, 1-1	1997	Barcelona beat Borussia Dortmund 2-0, 1-1
1980	Valencia beat Nottingham F 1-0, 1-2	1998	Chelsea beat Real Madrid 1-0
1981	Not contested	1999	Lazio beat Manchester U 1-0
1982	Aston Villa beat Barcelona 0-1, 3-0	2000	Galatasaray beat Real Madrid 2-1
1983	Aberdeen beat Hamburg 0-0, 2-0	2001	Liverpool beat Bayern Munich 3-2
1984	Juventus beat Liverpool 2-0	2002	Real Madrid beat Feyenoord 3-1
1985	Juventus v Everton not contested due to UEFA ban on English clubs	2003	AC Milan beat Porto 1-0
		2004	Valencia beat Porto 2-1
1986	Steaua Bucharest beat Dynamo Kiev 1-0	2005	Liverpool beat CSKA Moscow 3-1
1987	FC Porto beat Ajax 1-0, 1-0	2006	Sevilla beat Barcelona 3-0
1988	KV Mechelen beat PSV Eindhoven 3-0, 0-1	2007	AC Milan beat Sevilla 3-1
1989	AC Milan beat Barcelona 1-1, 1-0	2008	Zenit beat Manchester U 2-1

FIFA CLUB WORLD CUP 2008

Formerly known as the FIFA Club World Championship, this tournament is played annually between the champion clubs from all 6 continental confederations, although since 2007 the champions of Oceania must play a qualifying play-off against the champion club of the permanent host country Japan.

FIFA CLUB WORLD CUP 2008
(Finals in Japan)

PLAY-OFF FOR QUARTER-FINAL
Adelaide United (1) 2 *(Mullen 39, Dodd 83)*
Waitakere United (1) 1 *(Seaman 34)*   19,777

Al Ahly (2) 2 *(Pinto 28 (og), Flavio 45)*
Pachuca (0) 4 *(Montes 47, Gimenez 73, 110, Alvarez 98)*   30,158

Adelaide United (0) 0
Gamba Osaka (1) 1 *(Endo 23)*   38,141

SEMI-FINAL
Pachuca (0) 0
Liga De Quito (2) 2 *(Bieler 4, Bolanos 26)*   33,366

Gamba Osaka (0) 3 *(Yamazaki 74, Endo 85 (pen), Hashimoto 90)*   67,618
Manchester United (2) 5 *(Vidic 28, Ronaldo 45, Rooney 75, 79, Fletcher 78)*

MATCH FOR THIRD PLACE
Pachuca (0) 0
Gamba Osaka (1) 1 *(Yamazaki 29)*   62,619

MATCH FOR FIFTH/SIXTH PLACE
Al Ahly (0) 0
Adelaide United (1) 1 *(Cristiano 7)*   35,154

FIFA CLUB WORLD CUP FINAL 2008
Sunday 21 December, Yokohama, Japan (attendance 68,682)

Liga De Quito (0) 0
Manchester United (0) 1 *(Rooney 73)*

Liga De Quito: Cevallos; Araujo N, Calle (Ambrosi 77), Bolanos (Navia 87), Urrutia, Reasco (Larrea 82), Calderon, Araujo W, Bieler, Manso, Campos.

Manchester United: Van der Sar; Rafael (Neville 85), Evra, Carrick, Ferdinand, Vidic▪, Ronaldo, Anderson (Fletcher 88), Rooney, Tevez (Evans 51), Park.

Referee: Irmatov (Uzbekistan).

PREVIOUS MATCHES

2000	Corinthians beat Vaso de Gama 4-3 on penalties after 0-0 draw	2006	Internacional beat Barcelona 1-0
2005	Sao Paulo beat Liverpool 1-0	2007	AC Milan beat Boca Juniors 4-2
		2008	Manchester U beat Liga De Quito 1-0

▪ *Denotes player sent off.*

INTERNATIONAL DIRECTORY

The latest available information has been given regarding numbers of clubs and players registered with FIFA, the world governing body. Where known, official colours are listed. With European countries, League tables show a number of signs. * indicates relegated teams, + play-offs, *+ relegated after play-offs, ++ promoted.

There are 207 member associations. The four home countries, England, Scotland, Northern Ireland and Wales, are dealt with elsewhere in the Yearbook; but basic details appear in this directory. The following countries are not members of FIFA: Gibraltar, Gozo, Kosovo, and Northern Cyprus.

EUROPE

ALBANIA

The Football Association of Albania, Rruga Labinoti, Pallati Perballe Shkolles 'Gjuhet e Huaja'.
Founded: 1930; *National Colours:* Red shirts, black shorts, red stockings.

International matches 2008
Poland (h) 0-1, Liechtenstein (h) 2-0, Sweden (h) 0-0, Malta (h) 3-0, Hungary (a) 0-2, Portugal (h) 0-0, Azerbaijan (a) 1-1.

League Championship wins (1930–37; 1945–2009)
SK Tirana 24 (including 17 Nentori 8); Dinamo Tirana 17; Partizani Tirana 15; Vllaznia 9; Elbasan 2 (including Labinoti 1); Flamurtari 1; Skenderbeu 1; Teuta 1.

Cup wins (1948–2009)
Partizani Tirana 15; Dinamo Tirana 13; SK Tirana 13 (including 17 Nentori 8); Vllaznia 6; Teuta 3; Flamurtari 3; Elbasan 2 (including Labinoti 1); Apolonia 1, Besa 1.

Final League Table 2008–09

	P	W	D	L	F	A	Pts
SK Tirana	33	19	11	3	58	27	68
Vllaznia	33	19	7	7	49	29	64
Dinamo Tirana	33	14	10	9	48	34	52
Teuta	33	12	8	13	32	34	44
Shkumbini	33	12	8	13	32	38	44
Flamurtari	33	10	12	11	33	33	42
Besa	33	10	10	13	31	41	40
Apolonia	33	11	5	17	36	43	38
Bylis+	33	9	10	14	28	38	37
Partizani+	33	9	9	15	27	36	36
Lushnja*	33	8	12	13	25	35	36
Elbasan*	33	7	14	12	28	39	35

Top scorer: Memelli (SK Tirana) 22.
Cup Final: Flamurtari 2, SK Tirana 1.

ANDORRA

Federacio Andorrana de Futbol, Avinguda Carlemany 67, 3er Pis, Apartado postal 65, Escaldes-Engordany, Principat D'Andorra.
Founded: 1994; *National Colours:* Yellow shirts, red shorts, blue stockings.

International matches 2008
Latvia (h) 0-3, Azerbaijan (h) 1-2, Kazakhstan (a) 0-3, England (h) 0-2, Belarus (h) 1-3, Croatia (a) 0-4.

League Championship wins (1996–2009)
FC Santa Coloma 4; Principat 3; Encamp 2; Ranger's 2; St Julia 2; Constelacio 1.

Cup wins (1991–2009)
FC Santa Coloma 8; Principat 6; Constelacio 1; Lusitanos 1; St Julia 1.

Qualifying League Table 2008–09

	P	W	D	L	F	A	Pts
St Julia	14	11	2	1	69	10	35
FC Santa Coloma	14	10	3	1	58	5	33
Lusitanos	14	10	0	4	36	17	30
Principat	14	8	1	5	32	31	25
UE Santa Coloma	14	6	3	5	35	28	21
Engordany	14	3	0	11	21	75	9
Inter Club	14	2	1	11	12	48	7
Ranger's	14	1	0	13	22	71	3

Championship Play-Offs	P	W	D	L	F	A	Pts
St Julia	20	16	2	2	84	15	50
FC Santa Coloma	20	15	3	2	75	12	48
Principat	20	10	1	9	38	47	31
Lusitanos	20	10	0	10	39	30	30

Relegation Play-Offs	P	W	D	L	F	A	Pts
UE Santa Coloma	20	12	3	5	65	31	39
Engordany	20	7	0	13	39	88	21

| Inter | 19 | 3 | 1 | 15 | 21 | 66 | 10 |
| Ranger's* | 19 | 1 | 0 | 18 | 24 | 96 | 3 |

Ranger's v Inter not played.
Top scorer: Urbani (Santa Coloma) 22.
Cup Final: FC Santa Coloma 6, Lusitanos 1.

ARMENIA

Football Federation of Armenia, Saryan 38, Yerevan, 375 010, Armenia.
Founded: 1992; *National Colours:* Red shirts, blue shorts, orange stockings.

International matches 2008
Malta (a) 1-0, Belarus (n) 2-1, Iceland (n) 0-2, Kazakhstan (h) 1-0, Moldova (a) 2-2, Greece (h) 0-0, Turkey (h) 0-2, Spain (a) 0-4, Belgium (a) 0-2, Bosnia (a) 1-4.

League Championship wins (1992–2008)
Pyunik 11 (including Homenetmen 3); Shirak Gyumri 4*; Ararat Yerevan 2*; Araks 2 (including Tsement); FC Yerevan 1.
*Includes one unofficial title.

Cup wins (1992–2009)
Mika 5; Ararat Yerevan 5; Pyunik (formerly Homenetmen) 4; Tsement 2; Banants 2.

Final League Table 2008

	P	W	D	L	F	A	Pts
Ararat	28	18	5	5	48	23	59
Pyunik	28	18	5	5	40	18	59
Grandzasar	28	13	8	7	39	27	47
Mika	28	13	7	8	38	28	46
Banants	28	11	8	9	34	25	41
Ulysses	28	7	8	13	19	29	29
Shirak	28	5	4	19	15	40	19
Kilikia	28	2	5	21	21	64	11

Championship Play-Off: Pyunik 2, Ararat 1.
Top scorer: Pizzelli (Ararat) 17.
Cup Final: Pyunik 1, Banants 0.

AUSTRIA

Oesterreichischer Fussball-Bund, Ernst-Happel Stadion – Sektor A/F, Postfach 340, Meierestrasse 7, Wien 1021.
Founded: 1904; *National Colours:* White shirts, black shorts, white stockings.

International matches 2008
Germany (h) 0-3, Holland (h) 3-4, Nigeria (h) 1-1, Malta (h) 5-1, Croatia (h) 0-1, Poland (h) 1-1, Germany (h) 0-1, Italy (h) 2-2, France (h) 3-1, Lithuania (a) 0-2, Faeroes (a) 1-1, Serbia (h) 1-3, Turkey (h) 2-4.

League Championship wins (1912–2009)
Rapid Vienna 32; FK Austria (formerly Amateure) 23; Tirol-Svarowski-Innsbruck 10; Admira-Energie-Wacker 8; First Vienna 6; Austria Salzburg 5; Wiener Sportklub 3; Sturm Graz 2; WAC 1; FAC 1; Hakoah 1; Linz ASK 1; WAF 1; Voest Linz 1; Graz 1; WAC 1; Wacker 1.

Cup wins (1919–2009)
FK Austria (formerly Amateure) 27; Rapid Vienna 14; TS Innsbruck (formerly Wacker Innsbruck) 7; Admira-Energie-Wacker (formerly Sportklub Admira & Admira-Energie) 5; Graz 4; First Vienna 3; WAC 3; Sturm Graz 3; Linz ASK 1; Wacker Vienna 1; WAF 1; Wiener Sportklub 1; Kremser 1; Stockerau 1; Ried 1; Karnten 1; WAC 1; Kremser 1, Horn 1.

Final League Table 2008–09

	P	W	D	L	F	A	Pts
Salzburg	36	23	5	8	86	50	74
Rapid Vienna	36	21	7	8	89	43	70
FK Austria	36	17	11	8	59	46	62
Sturm Graz	36	17	9	10	68	45	60

Ried	36	17	9	10	58	38	60
Karnten	36	11	8	17	47	57	41
Linz	36	11	4	21	35	67	37
Kapfenberger	36	10	6	20	48	81	36
Mattersburg	36	8	9	19	42	71	33
Altach*	36	8	6	22	56	90	30

Top scorer: Janko (Salzburg) 39.
Cup Final: FK Austria 3, Trenkwalder 1.

AZERBAIJAN

Association of Football Federations of Azerbaijan, 42 Gussi Gadjiev Street, Baku 370 009.
Founded: 1992; *National Colours:* White shirts, blue shorts, white stockings.

International matches 2008
Kazakhstan (h) 0-0, Lithuania (a) 0-1, Bosnia (a) 0-1, Andorra (a) 2-1, Iceland (a) 1-1, Iran (a) 0-1, Wales (a) 0-1, Liechtenstein (h) 0-0, Finland (a) 0-1, Bahrain (a) 2-1, Albania (h) 1-1.

League Championship wins (1992–2009)
Neftchi 5; Kapaz 3; Shamkir 3; Baku 2; Karabakh 1; Turan 1; Xazar 1; Inter 1.
Includes one unofficial title for Shamkir in 2002.

Cup wins (1992–2009)
Neftchi 5; Kapaz 4; Karabakh 3; Xazar 2; Inshatchi 1; Shafa 1; Baku 1.

Final League Table 2008–09
	P	W	D	L	F	A	Pts
Baku	26	20	2	4	54	13	62
Inter	26	18	7	1	54	16	61
Simurq	26	16	5	5	39	20	53
Xazar	26	15	5	6	49	21	50
Karabakh	26	14	7	5	35	22	49
Olimpik	26	12	8	6	32	18	44
Standard	26	12	3	11	30	31	39
Neftchi	26	9	9	8	30	21	36
Karvan	26	10	4	12	28	33	34
Kabala	26	9	6	11	28	21	33
Turan	26	5	5	16	19	45	20
Mugan	26	4	2	20	19	53	14
Bakili*	26	3	3	20	14	65	12
OMIK*	26	1	2	23	12	64	5

Salyan renamed Mugan.
Top scorer: Guglielmone (Inter) 17.
Cup Final: Karabakh 1, Inter 0.

BELARUS

Belarus Football Federation, Kirova Street 8/2, Minsk 220 600, Belarus.
Founded: 1992; *National Colours:* Red shirts, green shorts, red stockings.

International matches 2008
Iceland (n) 2-0, Armenia (n) 1-2, Malta (a) 1-0, Turkey (h) 2-2, Germany (a) 2-2, Finland (a) 1-1, Argentina (h) 0-0, Ukraine (a) 0-1, Andorra (a) 2-1, England (h) 1-3, Cyprus (a) 1-2.

League Championship wins (1992–2008)
Dynamo Minsk 7; BATE Borisov 5; Slavia Mozyr (formerly MPKC Mozyr) 2; Dnepr Mogilev 1; Belshina 1; Gomel 1; Shakhtyor 1.

Cup wins (1992–2009)
Belshina 3; Dynamo Minsk 3; Slavia Mozyr (formerly MPKC Mozyr) 2; MTZ-RIPA 2; Neman 1; Dynamo 93 Minsk 1; Lokomotiv 96 1; Gomel 1; Shakhtyor 1; BATE Borisov 1; Dynamo Brest 1; Naftan 1.

Final League Table 2008
	P	W	D	L	F	A	Pts
BATE Borisov	30	19	10	1	54	20	67
Dynamo Minsk	30	19	5	6	49	29	62
MTZ-Ripo	30	17	6	7	65	38	57
Shakhtyor	30	15	6	9	51	35	51
FK Viebsk	30	14	9	7	39	27	51
Dynamo Brest	30	13	8	9	40	34	47
Naftan	30	13	7	10	41	35	46
Smorgon	30	10	9	11	27	39	39
Dnepr	30	9	11	10	45	42	38
Granit	30	8	12	10	35	34	36
Neman	30	8	9	13	36	40	33
Gomel	30	9	6	15	36	40	33
Torpedo Zhodino	30	7	10	13	25	37	31
Lokomotiv Minsk	30	6	7	17	28	50	25
Savit	30	5	6	19	28	61	21
Daryda*	30	4	7	19	25	56	19

*Top scorer*s: Bliznyuk (BATE Borisov), Rodionov (BATE Borisov) 16.
Cup Final: Naftan 2, Shakhtyor 1.

BELGIUM

Union Royale Belge Des Societes De Football Association, 145 Avenue Houba de Strooper, B-1020 Bruxelles.
Founded: 1895; *National Colours:* All red.

International matches 2008
Morocco (h) 1-4, Italy (a) 1-3, Germany (a) 0-2, Estonia (h) 3-2, Turkey (a) 1-1, Armenia (h) 2-0, Spain (h) 1-2, Luxembourg (a) 1-1.

League Championship wins (1896–2009)
Anderlecht 29; Club Brugge 13; Union St Gilloise 11; Standard Liege 10; Beerschot 7; RC Brussels 6; FC Liege 5; Daring Brussels 5; Antwerp 4; Mechelen 4; Lierse SK 4; Cercle Brugge 3; Beveren 2; Genk 2; RWD Molenbeek 1.

Cup wins (1912–14; 1927; 1935; 1954–2009)
Club Brugge 10; Anderlecht 8; Standard Liege 6; Racing Genk 3; Beerschot (became Germinal) 2; Waterschei (became Racing Genk) 2; Beveren 2; Gent 2; Antwerp 2; Lierse SK 2; Union St Gilloise 2; Cercle Brugge 2; Mechelen 1; FC Liege 1; Ekeren (became Germinal) 1; Westerlo 1; La Louviere 1; Zulte-Waregem 1; Daring 1; Germinal 1; Tournai 1; Racing 1; Waregem 1.

Final League Table 2008–09
	P	W	D	L	F	A	Pts
Anderlecht	34	24	5	5	75	30	77
Standard Liege	34	24	5	5	66	26	77
Club Brugge	34	18	5	11	59	50	59
Gent	34	17	8	9	67	42	59
Waregem	34	16	7	11	55	36	55
Westerlo	34	15	7	12	42	38	52
Lokeren	34	13	12	9	40	32	51
Genk	34	15	5	14	48	51	50
CS Brugge	34	14	5	15	48	53	47
Mechelen	34	12	10	12	46	52	46
Mouscron	34	12	8	14	42	49	44
Charleroi	34	12	7	15	43	48	43
Beerschot	34	11	9	14	44	42	42
Kortrijk	34	9	11	14	37	55	38
Dender*+	34	9	8	17	44	58	35
Roeselare+	34	8	6	20	33	59	30
Tubize*	34	7	6	21	35	77	27
Mons*	34	3	10	21	31	57	19

Championship Play-Off: Anderlecht 1, 0, Standard Liege 1, 1.
Top scorer: Ruiz (Westerlo) 17.
Cup Final: Genk 2, Mechelen 0.

BOSNIA-HERZEGOVINA

Football Federation of Bosnia & Herzegovina, Ferhadija 30, Sarajevo 71000.
Founded: 1992; *National Colours:* White shirts, blue shorts, white stockings.

International matches 2008
Japan (a) 0-3, Macedonia (h) 2-2, Azerbaijan (h) 1-0, Bulgaria (h) 1-2, Spain (a) 0-1, Estonia (h) 7-0, Armenia (h) 4-1, Turkey (h) 1-2, Slovenia (a) 4-3.

League Championship wins (1998–2009)
Zeljeznicar 3; Siroki 2; Sarajevo 2; Zrinjski 2; Brotnjo 1; Leotar 1; Modrica 1.

Cup wins (1998–2009)
Sarajevo 3; Zeljeznicar 3; Modrica 1; Orasje 1; Siroki 1; Zrinjski 1; Slavija 1.

Final League Table 2008–09
	P	W	D	L	F	A	Pts
Zrinjski	30	16	3	9	50	37	57
Slavija	30	15	7	8	36	28	52
Sloboda	30	15	5	10	32	26	50
Sarajevo	30	14	7	9	43	30	49
Borac	30	15	4	11	45	26	49
Siroki	30	14	3	13	47	38	45
Svijezda	30	11	10	9	43	38	43
Laktasi	30	12	6	12	43	39	42
Zeljeznicar	30	13	3	14	30	35	42
Celik	30	12	5	13	30	32	41
Leotar	30	12	3	15	32	43	39
Velez	30	11	4	15	42	45	37
Modrica	30	10	7	13	37	41	37

Travnik	30	11	4	15	38	53	37
Orasje*	30	9	7	14	33	43	34
Posusje*	30	5	8	17	31	58	23

Top scorer: Spalevic (Slavija) 17.
Cup Final: Sloboda 2, 0, Slavija 0, 2.
Slavija won 4-3 on penalties.

BULGARIA

Bulgarian Football Union, Karnigradska Street 19, BG-1000 Sofia.
Founded: 1923; *National Colours:* White shirts, green shorts, white stockings.

International matches 2008
Northern Ireland (a) 1-0, Finland (h) 2-1, Bosnia (a) 2-1, Montenegro (a) 2-2, Italy (h) 0-0, Georgia (a) 0-0, Serbia (a) 1-6.

League Championship wins (1925–2009)
CSKA Sofia 31; Levski Sofia 26; Slavia Sofia 7; Vladislav Varna 3; Lokomotiv Sofia 3; Litex 2; Botev Plovdiv (includes Trakija) 2; AC 23 Sofia 1; SC Sofia 1; Sokol Varna 1; Spartak Plovdiv 1; Tichka Varna 1; JSZ Sofia 1; Beroe Stara Zagora 1; Etur 1; Lokomotiv Plovdiv 1.

Cup wins (1946–2009)
Levski Sofia 24; CSKA Sofia 18; Slavia Sofia 7; Lokomotiv Sofia 4; Litex 4; Botev Plovdiv (includes Trakija) 2; Spartak Plovdiv 1; Septemvri Sofia 1; Marek Dupnica 1; Spartak Varna 1; Sliven 1.

Final League Table 2008–09
	P	W	D	L	F	A	Pts
Levski Sofia	30	21	6	3	57	18	69
CSKA Sofia	30	21	5	4	54	22	68
Cherno Varna	30	18	6	6	48	19	60
Litex	30	17	7	6	53	26	58
Lokomotiv Sofia	30	16	6	8	52	29	54
Lokomotiv Plovdiv	30	12	7	11	40	43	43
Chernomorets	30	11	10	9	41	37	43
Lokomotiv Mezdra	30	10	7	13	39	41	37
Slavia Sofia	30	11	4	15	41	38	37
Pirin	30	10	5	15	35	50	35
Minjor	30	9	8	13	24	39	35
Sliven	30	8	8	14	32	40	32
Botev Plovdiv	30	8	6	16	31	50	30
Vihren*	30	8	2	20	29	50	26
Spartak Varna*	30	5	10	15	19	46	25
Belasitsa*	30	4	5	21	24	71	17

Top scorer: Kamburov (Lokomotiv Sofia) 17.
Cup Final: Litex 3, Pirin 0.

CROATIA

Croatian Football Federation, Rusanova 13, Zagreb, 10 3000, Croatia.
Founded: 1912; *National Colours:* Red & white shirts, white shorts, blue stockings.

International matches 2008
Holland (h) 0-3, Scotland (h) 1-1, Moldova (h) 1-0, Hungary (a) 1-1, Austria (a) 1-0, Germany (n) 2-1, Poland (n) 1-0, Turkey (n) 1-1, Slovenia (a) 3-2, Kazakhstan (h) 3-0, England (h) 1-4, Ukraine (a) 0-0, Andorra (h) 4-0.

League Championship wins (1941–46; 1992–2009)
Dinamo Zagreb (formerly Croatia Zagreb) 11; Hajduk Split 8; Gradjanski 1; Concordia 1; Zagreb 1.

Cup wins (1992–2009)
Dinamo Zagreb (formerly Croatia Zagreb) 10; Hajduk Split 4; Rijeka 2, Inker Zapresic 1; Osijek 1.

Final League Table 2008–09
	P	W	D	L	F	A	Pts
Dinamo Zagreb	33	23	5	5	71	26	74
Hajduk Split	33	21	5	7	59	25	68
Rijeka	33	17	5	11	50	44	56
Slaven	33	16	7	10	46	39	55
Zagreb	33	13	8	12	38	39	47
Sibenik	33	13	7	13	44	35	46
Osijek	33	10	11	12	40	41	41
Cibalia	33	10	8	15	33	53	38
Inter	33	9	9	15	41	50	36
Varteks	33	10	5	18	41	55	35
Zadar	33	7	8	18	28	49	29
Sesvete+	33	6	8	19	31	66	26

Top scorer: Mandzukic (Dinamo Zagreb) 16.
Cup Final: Dinamo Zagreb 3, 0, Hajduk Split 0, 3.
aet; Dinamo Zagreb won 4-3 on penalties.

CYPRUS

Cyprus Football Association, 1 Stasinos Str., Engomi, P.O. Box 25071, Nicosia 2404.
Founded: 1934; *National Colours:* Blue shirts, white shorts, blue stockings.

International matches 2008
Ukraine (h) 1-1, Greece (a) 0-2, Switzerland (a) 1-4, Italy (h) 1-2, Georgia (a) 1-1, Republic of Ireland (a) 0-1, Belarus (h) 2-1.

League Championship wins (1935–2009)
Apoel 20; Omonia 19; Anorthosis 13; AEL 5; EPA 3; Olympiakos 3; Apollon 3; Pezoporikos 2; Cetinkaya 1; Trast 1.

Cup wins (1935–2009)
Apoel 19; Omonia 12; Anorthosis 10; AEL 6; EPA 5; Apollon 5; Trast 3; Cetinkaya 2; Olympiakos 1; Pezoporikos 1; Salamina 1; AEK 1; Apop 1.

Final League Table 2008–09
	P	W	D	L	F	A	Pts
Apoel	26	22	3	1	53	14	69
Omonia	26	21	1	4	61	18	64
Anorthosis	26	20	2	4	49	19	62
AEL	26	13	4	9	34	30	43
Apollon	26	13	4	9	53	34	43
Apop	26	12	4	10	35	35	40
Ethnikos Achnas	26	11	7	8	34	32	40
Doxa	26	8	7	11	37	39	31
AEP	26	5	12	9	30	38	27
ENP	26	6	7	13	23	43	25
Apep	26	5	8	13	28	44	23
Alki	26	4	7	15	27	50	19
AEK*	26	3	6	17	27	45	15
Atromitos*	26	1	4	21	19	69	7

Play-Offs League Table 2008–09
Group A	P	W	D	L	F	A	Pts
Apoel	32	26	4	1	62	17	82
Omonia	32	25	1	5	70	22	76
Anorthosis	32	21	4	7	52	26	67
AEL	32	13	5	14	38	41	44

Group B	P	W	D	L	F	A	Pts
Apollon	32	17	6	9	68	42	57
Ethnikos Achnas	32	13	8	11	47	45	47
Apop	32	13	6	13	45	49	39
Doxa	32	10	8	14	46	51	38

Apop deducted six points.

Group C	P	W	D	L	F	A	Pts
AEP	32	7	15	10	39	44	36
ENP	32	8	8	16	27	51	32
Apep	32	7	10	15	33	51	31
Alki*	32	6	9	17	39	59	27

Top scorer: Serjao (Doxa) 24.
Cup Final: Apop 2, AEL 0.

CZECH REPUBLIC

Football Association of Czech Republic, Diskarska 100, Prague 6 16017 – Strahov, Czech Republic.
Founded: 1901; *National Colours:* Red shirts, white shorts, blue stockings.

International matches 2008
Poland (a) 0-2, Denmark (a) 1-1, Lithuania (h) 2-0, Scotland (h) 3-1, Switzerland (a) 1-0, Portugal (n) 1-3, Turkey (n) 2-3, England (a) 2-2, Northern Ireland (a) 0-0, Poland (a) 1-2, Slovenia (h) 1-0, San Marino (a) 3-0.

League Championship wins (1925–93)
Sparta Prague 19; Dukla Prague (prev. UDA, now Marila Pribram) 11; Slavia Prague 9; Slovan Bratislava (formerly NV Bratislava) 8; Spartak Trnava 5; Banik Ostrava 3; Inter-Bratislava 1; Spartak Hradec Kralove 1; Viktoria Zizkov 1; Zbrojovka Brno 1; Bohemians 1; Vitkovice 1.

Cup wins (1961–93)
Dukla Prague 8; Sparta Prague 8; Slovan Bratislava 5; Spartak Trnava 4; Banik Ostrava 3; Lokomotiva Kosice 2; TJ Gottwaldov 1; Dunajska Streda 1; Kosice 1.
From 1993–94, there were two separate countries; the Czech Republic and Slovakia.

League Championship wins (1994–2009)
Sparta Prague 10; Slavia Prague 3; Slovan Liberec 2; Banik Ostrava 1.

Cup wins (1994–2009)
Sparta Prague 4; Slavia Prague 4; Viktoria Zizkov 2; Teplice 2; Spartak Hradec Kralove 1; Jablonec 1; Slovan Liberec 1; Banik Ostrava 1.

Final League Table 2008-09

	P	W	D	L	F	A	Pts
Slavia Prague	30	18	8	4	57	25	62
Sparta Prague	30	16	8	6	48	25	56
Slovan Liberec	30	14	10	6	41	28	52
Sigma Olomouc	30	13	9	8	39	36	48
Jablonec	30	14	4	12	43	37	46
Mlada	30	12	10	8	39	38	46
Teplice	30	12	7	11	33	25	43
Viktoria Plzen	30	11	10	9	45	38	43
Banik Ostrava	30	11	6	13	38	36	39
Ceske	30	7	15	8	30	37	36
Brno	30	9	8	13	32	36	35
Pribram	30	9	7	14	30	40	34
Bohemians	30	10	4	16	33	46	34
Kladno	30	8	7	15	21	41	31
Zlin*	30	7	8	15	26	49	29
Viktoria Zizkov*	30	5	7	18	27	45	22

Top scorer: Keric (Slovan Liberec) 15.
Cup Final: Teplice 1, Slovacko 0.

DENMARK

Danish Football Association, Idraettens Hus, Brondby Stadion 20, DK-2605, Brondby.
Founded: 1889; *National Colours:* Red shirts, white shorts, red stockings.

International matches 2008
Slovenia (a) 2-1, Czech Republic (h) 1-1, Holland (a) 1-1, Poland (a) 1-1, Spain (h) 0-3, Hungary (a) 0-0, Portugal (a) 3-2, Malta (h) 3-0, Wales (h) 0-1.

League Championship wins (1913–2009)
KB Copenhagen 15; Brondby 10; B 93 Copenhagen 9; AB (Akademisk) 9; B 1903 Copenhagen 7; Frem 6; FC Copenhagen 7; Esbjerg BK 5; Vejle BK 5; AGF Aarhus 5; Hvidovre 3; OB Odense 3; AaB Aalborg 3; B 1909 Odense 2; Koge BK 2; Lyngby 2; Silkeborg 1; Herfolge 1.

Cup wins (1955–2009)
AGF Aarhus 9; Vejle BK 6; Brondby 6; OB Odense 5; Randers Freja 4; FC Copenhagen 4; Lyngby 3; B 1909 Odense 2; Aab Aalborg 2; Esbjerg BK 2; Frem 2; B 1903 Copenhagen 2; B 93 Copenhagen 1; KB Copenhagen 1; Vanlose 1; Hvidovre 1; B1913 Odense 1, AB (Akademisk) 1, Viborg 1; Silkeborg 1.

Final League Table 2008-09

	P	W	D	L	F	A	Pts
FC Copenhagen	33	23	5	5	67	26	74
Odense	33	21	6	6	65	31	69
Brondby	33	21	5	7	55	31	68
Midtjylland	33	16	7	10	55	46	55
Randers	33	11	13	9	52	50	46
Aarhus	33	13	6	14	39	44	45
Aalborg	33	9	12	12	40	49	39
Nordsjaelland	33	9	8	16	44	53	35
Esbjerg	33	7	11	15	32	41	32
Sonderjyske	33	5	13	15	30	56	28
Vejle*	33	4	13	16	30	50	25
Horsens*	33	5	9	19	35	58	24

Top scorers: Nordstrand (FC Copenhagen), Nygaard (Randers) 16.
Cup Final: FC Copenhagen 1, Aalborg 0.

ENGLAND

The Football Association, 25 Soho Square, London W1D 4FA.
Founded: 1863; *National Colours:* White shirts with navy blue collar, navy shorts, white stockings.

ESTONIA

Estonian Football Association, Rapia 8/10, Tallinn 11312.
Founded: 1921; *National Colours:* Blue shirts, black shorts, white stockings.

International matches 2008
Poland (a) 0-2, Canada (h) 2-0, Georgia (h) 1-1, Latvia (a) 0-1, Lithuania (h) 0-1, Faeroes (h) 4-3, Malta (h) 2-1, Belgium (a) 2-3, Bosnia (a) 0-7, Spain (h) 0-3, Turkey (h) 0-0, Latvia (h) 1-1, Moldova (h) 1-1, Lithuania (h) 1-1.

League Championship wins (1921–40; 1992–2008)
Sport 9; Flora Tallinn 7; Levadia Tallinn (includes Levadia Maardu) 7; Estonia 5; Tallinn JK 2; Norma 2; Lantana (formerly Nikol) 2; Kalev 2; Olimpia 1; VMK Tallinn 1.

Cup wins (1993–2009)
Levadia Tallinn (includes Levadia Maardu) 5; Flora Tallinn 4; Sadam 2; VMV Tallinn 2; Lantana (formerly Nikol) 1; Trans 1; Levadia Tallinn (pre-2004) 1; Norma 1.

Final League Table 2008

	P	W	D	L	F	A	Pts
Levadia Tallinn	36	29	6	1	105	22	93
Flora	36	28	7	1	113	28	91
VMK	36	20	6	10	91	47	66
Trans	36	16	8	12	62	54	56
Kalju	36	16	7	13	65	64	55
Kalev Sillamae	36	13	6	17	49	79	45
Maag	36	9	4	23	45	76	31
Tulevik	36	9	4	23	31	74	31
Kalev Tallinn	36	6	8	22	37	70	26
Vaprus*+	36	5	2	29	41	125	17

Top scorer: Teever (Kalju) 23.
Cup Final: Flora 0, Kalju 0.
aet; Flora won 4-3 on penalties.

FAEROE ISLANDS

Fotboltssamband Foroya, The Faeroes' Football Assn., Gundalur, P.O. Box 3028, FR-110, Torshavn.
Founded: 1979; *National Colours:* White shirts, blue shorts, white stockings.

International matches 2008
Iceland (a) 0-3, Estonia (a) 3-4, Portugal (a) 0-5, Serbia (a) 0-2, Romania (h) 0-1, Austria (h) 1-1, Lithuania (a) 0-1.

League Championship wins (1942–2008)
HB Torshavn 19; KI Klaksvik 17; B36 Torshavn 8; TB Tvoroyri 7; GI Gotu 6; B68 Toftir 3; SI Sorvag 1; IF Fuglafjordur 1; B71 Sandur 1; VB Vagur 1; NSI Runavik 1; EB/Streymur 1.

Cup wins (1955–2008)
HB Torshavn 26; GI Gotu 6; KI Klaksvik 5; TB Tvoroyri 5; B36 Torshavn 5; NSI Runavik 2; EB/Streymur 2; VB Vagur 1; B71 Sandur 1.

Final League Table 2008

	P	W	D	L	F	A	Pts
EB/Streymur	27	17	4	6	54	33	55
HB	27	14	7	6	57	22	49
B36	27	14	6	7	34	25	48
NSI	27	14	5	8	41	33	47
Vikingur	27	12	6	9	43	33	42
B68	27	11	3	13	24	38	36
IF	27	9	4	14	32	46	31
KI	27	7	7	13	31	39	28
B71*	27	6	5	16	26	47	23
Skala*	27	4	7	16	22	48	19

GI and LIF merged to become Vikingur.
Top scorer: Hansen (EB/Streymur) 20.
Cup Final: EB/Streymur 3, B36 2.

FINLAND

Suomen Palloliitto Finlands Bollfoerbund, Urheilukatu 5, P.O. Box 191, Helsinki 00251.
Founded: 1907; *National Colours:* White shirts, blue shorts, white stockings.

International matches 2008
Greece (a) 1-2, Bulgaria (a) 1-2, Turkey (h) 0-2, Belarus (h) 1-1, Israel (h) 2-0, Germany (h) 3-3, Azerbaijan (h) 1-0, Russia (a) 0-3, Switzerland (a) 0-1.

League Championship wins (1908–2008)
HJK Helsinki 21; Haka Valkeakoski 9; HPS Helsinki 9; TPS Turku 8; HIFK Helsinki 7; Tampere United (includes IKIssat and Ilves) 5; KuPS Kuopio 5; Kuusysi Lahti 5; KIF Helsinki 4; AIFK Turku 3; Reipas Lahti 3; VIFK Vaasa 3; Jazz Pori 3; KTP Kotka 2; OPS Oulu 2; VPS Vaasa 1; Unitas Helsinki 1; PUS Helsinki 1; Sudet Viipuri 1; HT Helsinki 1; Pyrkiva Turku 1; KPV Kokkola 1; TPV Tampere 1; MyPa Anjalankoski 1; Inter 1.

Cup wins (1955–2008)
Haka Valkeakoski 12; HJK Helsinki 10; Reipas Lahti 7; KTP Kotka 4; MyPa Anjalankoski 3; Tampere United (includes Ilves) 3; KuPS Kuopio 2; Kuusysi Lahti 2; Mikkeli 2; TPS Turku 2; PPojat 1; Drott (renamed Jaro) 1; HPS Helsinki 1; AIFK Turku 1; RoPS Rovaniemi 1; Jokerit (formerly PK-35) 1; Allianssi (formerly Atlantis) 1.

Final League Table 2008

	P	W	D	L	F	A	Pts
Inter	26	15	9	2	46	12	54
Honka	26	15	5	6	46	23	50
Lahti	26	15	3	8	44	24	48
HJK Helsinki	26	14	5	7	47	29	47
MyPa	26	11	9	6	33	21	42
TPS Turku	26	12	6	8	45	36	42
Tampere U	26	9	9	8	41	34	36
Haka	26	10	5	11	31	37	35
Jaro	26	10	5	11	36	47	35
RoPS Rovaniemi	26	8	6	12	31	37	30
VPS	26	6	11	9	18	29	29
Mariehamn	26	7	5	14	24	40	26
KuPS+	26	4	7	15	26	56	19
KooTeePee*	26	1	5	20	14	57	8

Top scorers: Kokko (Honka) 13, Myntti (Tampere U) 13.
Cup Final: HJK Helsinki 2, Honka 1.

FRANCE

Federation Francaise De Football, 60 Bis Avenue d'Iena, Paris 75116.
Founded: 1919; *National Colours:* Blue shirts, white shorts, red stockings.

International matches 2008

Spain (a) 0-1, England (h) 1-0, Ecuador (h) 2-0, Paraguay (h) 0-0, Colombia (h) 1-0, Romania (n) 0-0, Holland (n) 1-4, Italy (n) 0-2, Sweden (a) 3-2, Austria (a) 1-3, Serbia (h) 2-1, Romania (a) 2-2, Tunisia (h) 3-1, Uruguay (h) 0-0.

League Championship wins (1933–2009)

Saint Etienne 10; Olympique Marseille 8; Nantes 8; AS Monaco 7; Lyon 7; Stade de Reims 6; Girondins de Bordeaux 6; OGC Nice 4; Lille OSC (includes Olympique Lillois) 3; Paris St Germain 2; FC Sete 2; Sochaux 2; Racing Club Paris 1; Roubaix-Tourcoing 1; Strasbourg 1; Auxerre 1; Lens 1.

Cup wins (1918–2009)

Olympique Marseille 10; Paris St Germain 7; Saint Etienne 6; AS Monaco 5; Lille OSC 5; Racing Club Paris 5; Red Star 5; Auxerre 4; Lyon 4; Girondins de Bordeaux 3; OGC Nice 3; Nantes 3; Strasbourg 3; CAS Genereaux 2; Nancy 2; Sedan 2; FC Sete 2; Stade de Reims 2; SO Montpellier 2; Stade Rennes 2; Metz 2; Sochaux 2; AS Cannes 1; Club Français 1; Excelsior Roubaix 1; Le Havre 1; Olympique de Pantin 1; CA Paris 1; Toulouse 1; Bastia 1; Lorient 1; Guingamp 1.

Final League Table 2008–09

	P	W	D	L	F	A	Pts
Bordeaux	38	24	8	6	64	34	80
Marseille	38	22	11	5	67	35	77
Lyon	38	20	11	7	52	29	71
Toulouse	38	16	16	6	45	27	64
Lille	38	17	13	8	51	39	64
Paris St Germain	38	19	7	12	49	38	64
Rennes	38	15	16	7	42	34	61
Auxerre	38	16	7	15	35	35	55
Nice	38	13	11	14	40	41	50
Lorient	38	10	15	13	47	47	45
Monaco	38	11	12	15	41	45	45
Valenciennes	38	10	14	14	35	42	44
Grenoble	38	10	14	14	24	37	44
Sochaux	38	10	12	16	40	48	42
Nancy	38	10	12	16	38	47	42
Le Mans	38	10	10	18	43	54	40
St Etienne	38	11	7	20	40	56	40
Caen*	38	8	13	17	42	49	37
Nantes*	38	9	10	19	33	54	37
Le Havre*	38	7	5	26	30	67	26

Top scorer: Gignac (Toulouse) 24.
Cup Final: Guingamp 2, Rennes 1.

GEORGIA

Georgian Football Federation, 76a Tchavtchavadze Avenue, Tbilisi 380062.
Founded: 1990; *National Colours:* All white.

International matches 2008

Latvia (h) 1-3, Northern Ireland (a) 1-4, Estonia (a) 1-1, Portugal (h) 0-2, Wales (a) 2-1, Republic of Ireland (h) 1-2, Italy (a) 0-2, Cyprus (h) 1-1, Bulgaria (h) 0-0, Romania (a) 1-2.

League Championship wins (1990–2009)

Dinamo Tbilisi 13; Torpedo Kutaisi 3; WIT Georgia 2; Sioni 1; Olimpi 1.

Cup wins (1990–2009)

Dinamo Tbilisi 9; Lokomotivi 3; Torpedo Kutaisi 2; Ameri 2; Dynamo Batumi 1; Guria 1; Zestafoni 1.

Final League Table 2008–09

	P	W	D	L	F	A	Pts
WIT	30	20	9	1	57	19	69
Dinamo Tbilisi	30	19	6	5	70	21	63
Olimpi	30	16	9	5	40	20	57
Zestafoni	30	16	4	10	43	27	55
Sioni	30	11	11	8	35	29	44
Lokomotivi	30	10	8	12	35	33	38
Mglebi	30	10	6	14	36	41	36
Meskheti	30	7	8	15	23	42	29
Gagra	30	7	7	16	23	48	28
Spartaki+	30	6	7	17	28	46	25
Borjomi*	30	2	7	21	21	85	13

Ameri withdrew for financial reasons; Magharoeli replaced by Gagra.
Top scorer: Gelashvili (Zestafoni) 20.
Cup Final: Dinamo Tbilisi 1, Olimpi 1.
aet; Dinamo Tbilisi won 2-0 on penalties.

GERMANY

Deutscher Fussball-Bund, Otto-Fleck-Schneise 6, Postfach 710265, Frankfurt Am Main 60492.
Founded: 1900; *National Colours:* White shirts, black shorts, white stockings.

International matches 2008

Austria (a) 3-0, Switzerland (a) 4-0, Belarus (h) 2-2, Serbia (h) 2-1, Poland (n) 2-0, Croatia (n) 1-2, Austria (a) 1-0, Portugal (n) 3-2, Turkey (n) 3-2, Spain (n) 0-1, Belgium (h) 2-0, Liechtenstein (a) 6-0, Finland (a) 3-3, Russia (h) 2-1, Wales (h) 1-0, England (h) 1-2.

League Championship wins (1903–2009)

Bayern Munich 21; 1.FC Nuremberg 9; Schalke 04 7; Borussia Dortmund 6; SV Hamburg 6; Borussia Moenchengladbach 5; VfB Stuttgart 5; 1.FC Kaiserslautern 4; Werder Bremen 4; VfB Leipzig 3; SpVgg Furth 3; 1.FC Cologne 3; Viktoria Berlin 2; Hertha Berlin 2; Hannover 96 2; Dresden SC 2; Munich 1860 1; Union Berlin 1; FC Freiburg 1; Phoenix Karlsruhe 1; Karlsruher FV 1; Holstein Kiel 1; Fortuna Dusseldorf 1; Rapid Vienna 1; VfR Mannheim 1; Rot-Weiss Essen 1; Eintracht Frankfurt 1; Eintracht Brunswick 1; Wolfsburg 1.

Cup wins (1935–2009)

Bayern Munich 14; Werder Bremen 6; 1.FC Cologne 4; Eintracht Frankfurt 4; Schalke 04 4; 1.FC Nuremberg 4; SV Hamburg 3; Moenchengladbach 3; VfB Stuttgart 3; Dresden SC 2; Fortuna Dusseldorf 2; Karlsruhe SC 2; Munich 1860 2; Borussia Dortmund 2; 1.FC Kaiserslautern 2; First Vienna 1; VfB Leipzig 1; Kickers Offenbach 1; Rapid Vienna 1; Rot-Weiss Essen 1; SW Essen 1; Bayer Uerdingen 1; Hannover 96 1; Leverkusen 1.

Final League Table 2008–09

	P	W	D	L	F	A	Pts
Wolfsburg	34	21	6	7	80	41	69
Bayern Munich	34	20	7	7	71	42	67
Stuttgart	34	19	7	8	63	43	64
Hertha Berlin	34	19	6	9	48	41	63
Hamburg	34	19	4	11	49	47	61
Borussia Dortmund	34	15	14	5	60	37	59
Hoffenheim	34	15	10	9	63	49	55
Schalke	34	14	8	12	47	35	50
Leverkusen	34	14	7	13	59	46	49
Werder Bremen	34	12	9	13	64	50	45
Hannover	34	10	10	14	49	69	40
Cologne	34	11	6	17	35	50	39
Eintracht Frankfurt	34	8	9	17	39	60	33
Bochum	34	7	11	16	39	55	32
Moenchengladbach	34	8	7	19	39	62	31
Energie*+	34	8	6	20	30	57	30
Karlsruhe*	34	8	5	21	30	54	29
Arminia*	34	4	16	14	29	56	28

Top scorer: Grafite (Wolfsburg) 28.
Cup Final: Werder Bremen 1, Leverkusen 0.

GIBRALTAR

Gibraltar Football Association, 32a Rosia Road, Gibraltar.
Founded: 1905. *National Colours:* Red shirts, white shorts, white stockings.

International matches 2008

Jersey (a) 1-2.

League Championship wins (1896–2009)

Prince of Wales 19; Glacis United 17; Britannia 14; Gibraltar United 11; Lincoln 9; Manchester United 7; Europa 6; Newcastle (formerly Lincoln) 5; St Theresas 3; Chief Construction 2; Exiles 2; Gibraltar FC 2; Jubilee 2; South United 2; Albion 1; Athletic 1; Commander of the Yard 1; Royal Soverign 1; St Joseph's 1.

Cup wins (1896–2009)

St Joseph's 7; Lincoln 6; Europa 5; Glacis United 5; Newcastle (formerly Lincoln) 4; Britannia 3; Gibraltar United 3; Manchester United 3; AARA 1; Gibraltar FC 1; HMS Hood 1; Lincoln ABG 1; Lincoln Reliance 1; Manchester United Reserves 1; Prince of Wales 1; St Theresas 1; 2nd Battalion RGS 1; 2nd Battalion The King's Regiment 1; 4th Battalion Royal Scots 1; RAF Gibraltar 1; RAF New Camp 1.

Final League Table 2008–09

	P	W	D	L	F	A	Pts
Lincoln	12	10	1	1	41	16	31
Shamrock 101	11	6	2	3	19	17	20
Glacis U	12	6	1	5	27	22	19
St Joseph's	12	6	1	5	25	22	19
PWC Laguna	12	3	4	5	22	23	13
Gibraltar U	12	2	2	8	13	28	8
Manchester U	11	2	1	8	9	28	7

No relegation; League extended to eight clubs for 2009–10.
Cup Final: Lincoln 4, Shamrock 101 0.

GOZO

Gozo Football Association, Gozo Stadium, Mgarr Road, Xewkija, VCT 111, Gozo, Malta.
Founded: 1936.

League Championship wins (1938-2009)

Nadur Youngsters 10; Victoria Hotspurs 10; Sannat Lions 9; Ghajnsielem 6; Salesian Youths 6; Victoria Athletics 4; Xaghra United 4; Xewkija Tigers 4; Calypcians 1; Kercem Ajax 1; Victoria City 1; Victoria Stars 1; Victoria United 1; Xaghra Blue Stars 1; Xaghra Young Stars 1; Zebbug Rovers 1.

Cup wins (1972–2009)

Sannat Lions 8; Xewkija Tigers 7; Nadur Youngsters 6; Ghajnsielem 5; Xaghra United 4; S.K. Calyptians 1; Calypsians Bosco Youths 1; Victoria Hotspurs 1; Kercem Ajax 1; Quala St. Joseph 1; Victoria Wanderers 1.

Final League Table 2008-09

	P	W	D	L	F	A	Pts
Sannat Lions	18	11	3	4	32	16	36
Ghajnsielem	18	9	6	3	34	26	33
Victoria Hotspurs	18	9	2	7	34	28	29
Victoria Wanderers	18	6	6	6	21	17	24
Nadur Youngsters	18	5	6	7	20	21	21
Kercem Ajax+	18	4	7	7	29	35	19
Kala St Joseph*	18	1	6	11	14	41	9

Top scorers: Hanus (Victoria Hotspurs).
Cup Final: Victoria Wanderers 5, Victoria Hotspurs 2.

GREECE

Hellenic Football Federation, Singrou Avenue 137, Nea Smirni, 17121 Athens.
Founded: 1926; *National Colours:* Blue shirts, white shorts, blue stockings.

International matches 2008

Finland (h) 2-1, Portugal (a) 2-1, Cyprus (h) 2-0, Hungary (a) 2-3, Armenia (a) 0-0, Sweden (n) 0-2, Russia (n) 0-1, Spain (n) 1-2, Slovakia (a) 2-0, Luxembourg (a) 3-0, Latvia (a) 2-0, Moldova (h) 3-0, Switzerland (h) 1-2, Italy (h) 1-1.

League Championship wins (1928–2009)

Olympiakos 37; Panathinaikos 19; AEK Athens 11; Aris Salonika 3; PAOK Salonika 2; Larisa 1.

Cup wins (1932–2009)

Olympiakos 24; Panathinaikos 16; AEK Athens 13; PAOK Salonika 4; Panionios 2; Larisa 2; Aris Salonika 1; Ethnikos 1; Iraklis 1; Kastoria 1; OFI Crete 1.

Final League Table 2008–09

	P	W	D	L	F	A	Pts
Olympiakos	30	23	5	3	50	14	71
PAOK Salonika	30	18	9	3	39	16	63
Panathinaikos	30	17	10	3	51	18	61
AEK Athens	30	14	13	3	40	24	55
Larissa	30	12	13	5	36	26	49
Aris Salonika	30	13	8	9	30	31	47
Xanthi	30	9	11	10	25	21	38
Panionios	30	10	7	13	40	40	37
Ergotelis	30	9	9	12	31	39	36
Iraklis	30	8	9	13	22	38	33
Panthrakikos	30	9	6	15	23	37	33
Asteras	30	7	12	11	33	31	33
Levadiakos	30	9	5	16	28	36	32
OFI Crete*	30	5	9	16	30	50	24
Panserraikos*	30	5	9	16	19	45	24
Thrasyvoulos*	30	3	5	22	22	53	14

Top scorers: Blanco (AEK Athens), Galletti (Olympiakos) 14.
Cup Final: Olympiakos 4, AEK Athens 4.
aet; Olympiakos won 15-14 on penalties.

HOLLAND

Koninklijke Nederlandsche Voetbalbond, Woudenbergseweg 56–58, Postbus 515, NL-3700 AM, Zeist.
Founded: 1889; *National Colours:* Orange shirts, black shorts, orange stockings.

International matches 2008

Croatia (a) 3-0, Austria (a) 4-3, Ukraine (h) 3-0, Denmark (h) 1-1, Wales (h) 2-0, Italy (n) 3-0, France (n) 4-1, Romania (n) 2-0, Russia (n) 1-3, Russia (a) 1-1, Australia (h) 1-2, Macedonia (a) 2-1, Iceland (h) 2-0, Norway (a) 1-0, Sweden (h) 3-1.

League Championship wins (1898–2009)

Ajax Amsterdam 29; PSV Eindhoven 21; Feyenoord 14; HVV The Hague 8; Sparta Rotterdam 6; Go Ahead Deventer 4; HBS The Hague 3; Willem II Tilburg 3; RAP Amsterdam 2; RCH Heemstede 2; Heracles 2; ADO The Hague 2; AZ 67 Alkmaar 2; Quick The Hague 1; BVV Den Bosch 1; NAC Breda 1; Eindhoven 1; Enschede 1; Volewijckers Amsterdam 1; Limburgia 1; Rapid JC Den Heerlen 1; DOS Utrecht 1; DWS Amsterdam 1; Haarlem 1; SVV Schiedam 1; Be Quick Groningen 1..

Cup wins (1899–2009)

Ajax Amsterdam 17; Feyenoord 11; PSV Eindhoven 8; Quick The Hague 4; AZ 67 Alkmaar 3; Sparta Rotterdam 3; Utrecht 3; HFC Haarlem 3; DFC 2; Fortuna Geleen 2; Haarlem 2; HBS The Hague 2; RCH Haarlem 2; Roda JC 2; VOC 2; Wageningen 2; Willem II Tilburg 2; FC Den Haag (includes ADO) 2; Twente Enschede 2; Concordia Delft 1; CVV 1; Eindhoven 1; HVV The Hague 1; Longa 1; Quick Nijmegen 1; RAP Amsterdam 1; Roermond 1; Schoten 1; Velocitas Breda 1; Velocitas Groningen 1; VSV 1; VUC 1; VVV Groningen 1; ZFC Zaandam 1; NAC Breda 1; Heerenveen 1.

Final League Table 2008–09

	P	W	D	L	F	A	Pts
AZ	34	25	5	4	66	22	80
Twente	34	20	9	5	62	31	69
Ajax	34	21	5	8	74	41	68
PSV Eindhoven	34	19	8	7	71	33	65
Heerenveen	34	17	9	8	66	57	60
Groningen	34	17	5	12	53	36	56
Feyenoord	34	12	9	13	54	54	45
NAC Breda	34	13	6	15	44	54	45
Utrecht	34	11	11	12	41	44	44
Vitesse	34	11	10	13	41	48	43
NEC Nijmegen	34	9	15	10	41	40	42
Willem II	34	10	7	17	35	58	37
Sparta	34	9	8	17	46	66	35
Den Haag	34	8	8	18	41	58	32
Heracles	34	7	11	16	35	53	32
Roda JC+	34	7	9	18	38	58	30
De Graafschap*+	34	7	9	18	24	58	30
Volendam*	34	7	8	19	38	67	29

Top scorer: El Hamdaoui (AZ) 23.
Cup Final: Heerenveen 2, Twente 2.
aet; Heerenveen won 5-4 on penalties.

HUNGARY

Hungarian Football Federation, Robert Karoly krt 61-65, Robert Haz Budapest 1134.
Founded: 1901; *National Colours:* Red shirts, white shorts, green stockings.

International matches 2008

Slovakia (h) 1-1, Slovenia (h) 0-1, Greece (h) 3-2, Croatia (h) 1-1, Montenegro (h) 3-3, Denmark (h) 0-0, Sweden (a) 1-2, Albania (h) 2-0, Malta (a) 1-0, Northern Ireland (a) 2-0.

League Championship wins (1901–2009)
Ferencvaros 28; MTK-Hungaria Budapest 23; Ujpest 20; Kispest Honved 13; Vasas Budapest 6; Csepel 4; Debrecen 4; Raba Gyor 3; BTC 2; Nagyvarad 1; Vac 1; Dunaferr 1; Zalaegerszeg 1.

Cup wins (1910–2009)
Ferencvaros 20; MTK-Hungaria Budapest 12; Ujpest 8; Kispest Honved 7; Raba Gyor 4; Vasas Budapest 4; Debrecen 3; Diösgyör 2; Bocskai 1; III Ker 1; Soroksar 1; Szolnoki MAV 1; Siofok Banyasz 1; Bekescsaba 1; Pecsi 1; Matav 1; Fehervar 1.
Cup not regularly held until 1964.

Final League Table 2008–09

	P	W	D	L	F	A	Pts
Debrecen	30	21	5	4	70	29	68
Ujpest	30	17	8	5	61	38	59
Szombathelyi	30	16	5	9	44	29	53
Zalaegerszeg	30	15	7	8	52	44	52
Kecskemeti	30	14	6	10	55	44	48
Fehervar	30	14	6	10	42	34	48
MTK	30	13	6	11	43	41	45
Gyor	30	11	10	9	57	41	43
Kaposvari	30	11	7	12	51	46	40
Vasas	30	11	5	14	42	52	38
Paksi	30	9	8	13	38	51	35
Diosgyor	30	9	6	15	29	45	33
Nyiregyhaza	30	7	11	12	32	41	32
Honved	30	8	8	14	31	46	32
Siofok*	30	8	2	20	30	56	26
Rakospalotai*	30	3	6	21	33	73	15

Top scorer: Bajzat (Gyor) 20.
Cup Final: Honved 0, 1, Gyor 0, 0.

ICELAND

Knattspyrnusamband Island, Laugardal, 104 Reykjavik.
Founded: 1929; *National Colours;* All blue.

International matches
Belarus (n) 0-2, Malta (a) 0-1, Armenia (n) 2-0, Faeroes (h) 3-0, Slovakia (a) 2-1, Wales (h) 0-1, Azerbaijan (h) 1-1, Norway (a) 2-2, Scotland (h) 1-2, Holland (a) 0-2, Macedonia (h) 1-0, Malta (a) 1-0.

League Championship wins (1912–2008)
KR 24; Valur 20; Fram 18; IA Akranes 18; Vikingur 5; IBK Keflavik 4; FH Hafnarfjordur 4; IBV Vestmannaeyjar 3; KA Akureyri 1.

Cup wins (1960–2008)
KR 11; Valur 9; IA Akranes 9; Fram 7; IBV Vestmannaeyjar 4; IBK Keflavik 4; Fylkir 2; IBA Akureyri 1; Vikingur 1; FH Hafnarfjordur 1.

Final League Table 2008

	P	W	D	L	F	A	Pts
FH	22	15	2	5	50	25	47
Keflavik	22	14	4	4	54	31	46
Fram	22	13	1	8	31	21	40
KR	22	12	3	7	38	23	39
Valur	22	11	2	9	34	28	35
Fjolnir	22	10	1	11	39	33	31
Grindavik	22	9	4	9	29	36	31
Breidblik	22	8	6	8	41	36	30
Fylkir	22	6	4	12	24	40	22
Trottur	22	5	7	10	28	46	22
HK*	22	5	3	14	26	47	18
IA*	22	2	7	13	18	46	13

Top scorer: Steinarsson (Keflavik) 16.
Cup Final: KR 1, Fjolnir 0.

REPUBLIC OF IRELAND

The Football Association of Ireland (Cumann Peile Na H-Eireann), 80 Merrion Square, South Dublin 2.
Founded: 1921; *National Colours:* Green shirts, white shorts, green and white stockings.

League Championship wins (1922–2008)
Shamrock Rovers 15; Shelbourne 13; Bohemians 10; Dundalk 9; Cork Athletic (formerly Cork United) 7; St Patrick's Athletic 7; Waterford 6; Drumcondra 5; St James's Gate 2; Sligo Rovers 2; Limerick 2; Athlone Town 2; Derry City 2; Cork City 2; Dolphin 1; Cork Hibernians 1; Cork Celtic 1; Drogheda United 1.

Cup wins (1922–2008)
Shamrock Rovers 24; Dundalk 9; Bohemians 7; Shelbourne 7; Drumcondra 5; Cork Athletic (formerly Cork United) 4; Derry City 4; Cork City 2; St James's Gate 2; St Patrick's Athletic 2; Cork Hibernians 2; Limerick 2; Waterford 2; Bray Wanderers 2; Longford Town 2; Alton United 1; Athlone Town 1; Fordsons 1; Cork 1; Transport 1; Finn Harps 1; Home Farm 1; UCD 1; Galway United 1; Drogheda United 1.

Final League Table 2008

	P	W	D	L	F	A	Pts
Bohemians	33	27	4	2	55	13	85
St Patrick's Ath	33	20	6	7	48	24	66
Derry City	33	16	10	7	46	25	58
Sligo Rovers	33	12	12	9	41	28	48
Cork City	33	15	11	7	45	28	46
Bray Wanderers	33	11	6	16	28	52	39
Shamrock Rovers	33	8	13	12	33	35	37
Drogheda United	33	12	9	12	38	32	35
Galway United	33	8	8	17	34	49	32
Finn Harps*	33	9	4	20	26	53	31
Cobh Ramblers*	33	6	8	19	27	55	26
UCD*	33	4	9	20	19	46	21

Cork City and Drogheda United ten points deducted for financial reasons. Competition reduced to ten clubs for 2009.

Top scorers: Mooney (Cork City) 15, Quigley (St Patrick's Ath) 15, Farren (Derry C) 15.
Cup Final: Bohemians 2, Derry City 2.
aet; Bohemians won 4-2 on penalties.

ISRAEL

Israel Football Association, Ramat-Gan Stadium, 299 Aba Hilell Street, Ramat-Gan 52134.
Founded: 1948; *National Colours:* Blue shirts, white shorts, blue stockings.

International matches 2008
Romania (h), Chile (h) 1-0, Finland (a) 0-2, Switzerland (h) 2-2, Moldova (a) 2-1, Luxembourg (h) 3-1, Latvia (a) 1-1, Ivory Coast (h) 2-2.

League Championship wins (1932–2009)
Maccabi Tel Aviv 18; Maccabi Haifa 11; Hapoel Tel Aviv 10; Hapoel Petah Tikva 6; Beitar Jerusalem 6; Maccabi Netanya 5; Hakoah Ramat Gan 2; Hapoel Beersheba 2; Bnei Yehouda 1; British Police 1; Hapoel Kfar Saba 1; Hapoel Ramat Gan 1; Hapoel Haifa 1.

Cup wins (1928–2009)
Maccabi Tel Aviv 22; Hapoel Tel Aviv 13; Beitar Jerusalem 7; Maccabi Haifa 5; Hapoel Haifa 3; Hapoel Kfar Saba 2; Beitar Tel Aviv 2; Bnei Yehouda 2; Hakoah Ramat Gan 2; Hapoel Petah Tikva 2; Maccabi Petah Tikva 2; Maccabi Hashmonai Jerusalem 1; British Police 1; Gunners 1; Hapoel Jerusalem 1; Hapoel Yehud 1; Hapoel Lod 1; Maccabi Netanya 1; Hapoel Beersheba 1; Hapoel Ramat Gan 1; Hapoel Bnei Sakhnin 1.

Final League Table 2008–09

	P	W	D	L	F	A	Pts
Maccabi Haifa	33	19	10	4	49	25	67
Hapoel Tel Aviv	33	17	10	6	49	28	61
Beitar Jerusalem	33	16	12	5	47	28	57
Maccabi Netanya	33	14	12	7	40	32	54
Bnei Yehouda	33	14	7	12	38	31	49
Maccabi Tel Aviv	33	11	11	11	36	35	44
Maccabi Petah Tikva	33	8	15	10	26	33	39
Ashdod	33	10	8	15	41	48	38
Bnei Sakhnin	33	7	12	14	26	41	33
Hapoel Petah Tikva	33	8	7	18	30	42	31
Hakoah-Amidar*+	33	6	11	16	26	46	29
Ironi*	33	6	9	18	24	44	27

Top scorers: Yitzhaki (Beitar Jerusalem), Abuhatzira (Hapoel Petah Tikva), Elran Atar (Bnei Yehouda) 14.
Cup Final: Beitar Jerusalem 2, Maccabi Haifa 1.

ITALY

Federazione Italiana Giuoco Calcio, Via Gregorio Allegri 14, Roma 00198.
Founded: 1898; *National Colours:* Blue shirts, white shorts, blue stockings.

International matches 2008
Portugal (h) 3-1, Spain (a) 0-1, Belgium (h) 3-1, Holland (n) 0-3, Romania (n) 1-1, France (n) 2-0, Spain (n) 0-0, Austria (a) 2-2, Cyprus (a) 2-1, Georgia (h) 2-0, Bulgaria (a) 0-0, Montenegro (h) 2-1, Greece (a) 1-1.

League Championship wins (1898–2009)
Juventus 27 (excludes two titles revoked); AC Milan 17; Internazionale 17 (includes one title awarded); Genoa 9;

Torino 7 (excludes one title revoked); Pro Vercelli 7; Bologna 7; AS Roma 3; Fiorentina 2; Lazio 2; Napoli 2; Casale 1; Novese 1; Cagliari 1; Verona 1; Sampdoria 1.

Cup wins (1928–2009)
AS Roma 9; Juventus 9; Fiorentina 6; AC Milan 5; Internazionale 5; Torino 5; Lazio 5; Sampdoria 4; Napoli 3; Parma 3; Bologna 2; Atalanta 1; Genoa 1; Vado 1; Venezia 1; Vicenza 1.

Final League Table 2008–09

	P	W	D	L	F	A	Pts
Internazionale	38	25	9	4	70	32	84
Juventus	38	21	11	6	69	37	74
AC Milan	38	22	8	8	70	35	74
Fiorentina	38	21	5	12	53	38	68
Genoa	38	19	11	8	56	39	68
Roma	38	18	9	11	64	61	63
Udinese	38	16	10	12	61	50	58
Palermo	38	17	6	15	57	50	57
Cagliari	38	15	8	15	49	50	53
Lazio	38	15	5	18	46	55	50
Atalanta	38	13	8	17	45	48	47
Napoli	38	12	10	16	43	45	46
Sampdoria	38	11	13	14	49	52	46
Siena	38	12	8	18	33	44	44
Catania	38	12	7	19	41	51	43
Chievo	38	8	14	16	35	49	38
Bologna	38	9	10	19	43	62	37
Torino*	38	8	10	20	37	61	34
Reggina*	38	6	13	19	30	62	31
Lecce*	38	5	15	18	37	67	30

Top scorer: Ibrahimovic (Internazionale) 25.
Cup Final: Lazio 1, Sampdoria 1.
aet; Lazio won 6-5 on penalties.

KAZAKHSTAN

The Football Union of Kazakhstan, Satpayev Street, 29/3 Almaty 480 072, Kazakhstan.
Founded: 1914; *National Colours:* Blue shirts, blue shorts, yellow stockings.

International matches 2008
Azerbaijan (a) 0-0, Moldova (a) 0-1, Armenia (a) 0-1, Russia (a) 0-6, Montenegro (a) 0-3, Andorra (h) 3-0, Croatia (a) 0-3, Ukraine (h) 1-3, England (a) 1-5.

League Championship wins (1992–2008)
Irtysh (includes Ansat) 5; Aqtobe 4; Yelimai 3; Astana (includes Zhenis) 3; Kairat 2; Taraz 1.

Cup wins (1992–2008)
Kairat 5; Astana (includes Zhenis) 3; Dostyk 1; Vostok 1; Yelimai 1; Irtysh 1; Kaisar 1; Taraz 1; Almaty 1; Tobol 1; Aqtobe 1.

Final League Table 2008

	P	W	D	L	F	A	Pts
Aqtobe	30	20	7	3	61	18	67
Tobol	30	20	7	3	58	21	67
Yertis	30	18	8	4	58	28	54
Qaysar	30	13	10	7	29	22	49
MegaSport	30	12	6	12	33	38	42
Jetisu	30	11	8	11	28	27	41
Shakhtyor	29	11	13	5	41	26	37
Almaty	30	10	7	13	33	39	37
Oqjetpes	30	10	5	15	32	48	35
Qayrat	30	9	10	11	25	28	34
Astana	30	8	11	11	37	33	32
Odabasy	30	7	9	14	25	44	30
Yesil-Bogatyr*	30	4	12	14	21	42	24
Energetik*	30	5	8	17	21	43	19
Atyrau*	30	3	10	17	22	54	19
Vostok*	29	10	5	14	35	48	35

Yesil-Bogatyr, Atyrau and Vostok remain in the League as Almaty, MegaSport and Qayrat excluded for 2009.
Astana renamed Lokomotiv Astana.
Astana, Qayrat and Shakhtyor points deducted; Vostok thrown out of League after 25 matches, their remaining fixtures awarded as 3-0 defeats.
Energetik formerly Yekibastuzets; Qazaqmis promoted but replaced by Oqjetpes.
Top scorer: Tleshev (Yertis) 13.
Cup Final: Aqtobe 3, Almaty 1.

KOSOVO

Football Federation Kosova, Agim Ramadani 45, Prishtina, Kosovo 10000.
Founded: 1946; *National Colours:* Blue shirts, white shorts, blue stockings.

League Championship wins (1945–2009)
Prishtina 12; Vellaznimi 9; Trepca 6; Liria 5; Buduqnosti

4; Red Star 3; Rudari 3; Besa 3; Fushe-Kosova 2; Jedinstvo 2; Kosova Prishtina 2; Obiliqi 2; Slloga 2; Besiana 1; Drita 1; Dukagjini 1; KNI Ramiz Sadiku 1; KXEK Kosova 1; Proletari 1; Rudniku 1.

Cup wins (1992–2009)
Flamurtari 2; Liria 2; Prishtina 2; Besa 1; Besiana 1; Drita 1; Gjilani 1; KEK-u 1; Kosova Prishtina 1; Trepca 1; Vellaznimi 1; Hysi 1.

Final League Table

	P	W	D	L	F	A	Pts
Prishtina	30	16	9	5	46	25	57
Besa	30	14	8	8	43	31	50
Vëllaznimi	30	13	10	7	43	30	49
Trepça	30	14	7	9	46	44	49
Kosova	30	13	9	8	42	30	48
Gjilani	30	14	5	11	40	32	47
Hysi	30	13	7	10	53	35	46
Ferizaj	30	14	4	12	56	51	46
Flamurtari	30	14	4	12	45	45	46
Drenica	30	13	6	11	49	39	45
Trepça '89*	30	11	9	10	36	31	42
Ulpiana*	30	11	3	16	35	47	36
Istogu*	30	9	5	16	38	53	32
2 Korriku*	30	8	5	17	38	56	29
Besiana*	30	6	2	20	26	69	26
Drita*	30	6	5	19	34	52	23

Cup Final: Hysi 2, Prishtina 1.

LATVIA

Latvian Football Federation, Augsiela 1, LV-1009, Riga.
Founded: 1921; *National Colours:* Carmine red shirts, white shorts, carmine red stockings.

International matches 2008
Georgia (a) 3-1, Andorra (a) 3-0, Estonia (h) 1-0, Lithuania (h) 2-1, Romania (a) 0-1, Moldova (a) 2-1, Greece (h) 0-2, Switzerland (a) 1-2, Israel (h) 1-1, Estonia (a) 1-1.

League Championship wins (1922–2008)
Skonto Riga 14; ASK Riga 9; RFK Riga 8; Olympija Liepaya 7; Sarkanais Metalurgs Liepaya 7; VEF Riga 6; Energija Riga 4; Elektrons Riga 3; Torpedo Riga 3; FK Ventspils 3; Daugava Liepaya 2; ODO Riga 2; Khimikis Daugavpils 2; RAF Yelgava 2; Keisermezhs Riga 2; Dinamo Riga 1; Zhmilyeva Team 1; Darba Rezervi 1; RER Riga 1; Starts Brotseni 1; Venta Ventspils 1; Yurnieks Riga 1; Alta Riga 1; Gauja Valmiera 1; Metalurgs Liepaya 1.

Cup wins (1937–2008)
Elektrons Riga 7; Skonto Riga 7; Sarkanais Metalurgs Liepaya 5; FK Ventspils 4; ODO Riga 3; VEF Riga 3; ASK Riga 3; Tseltnieks Riga 3; RAF Yelgava 3; RFK Riga 2; Daugava Liepaya 2; Starts Brotseni 2; Selmash Liepaya 2; Yurnieks Riga 2; Khimikis Daugavpils 2; Rigas Vilki 1; Dinamo Liepaya 1; Dinamo Riga 1; RER Riga 1; Voulkan Kouldiga 1; Baltika Liepaya 1; Venta Ventspils 1; Pilots Riga 1; Lielupe Yurmala 1; Energija Riga 1; Torpedo Riga 1; Daugava SKIF Riga 1; Tseltnieks Daugavpils 1; Olympija Riga 1; FK Riga 1; Metalurgs Liepaya 1; Daugava Daugavpils 1.

First Stage Final League Table 2008

	P	W	D	L	F	A	Pts
FK Ventspils	18	12	4	2	33	6	40
Skonto Riga	18	11	3	4	28	19	36
Dinaburg	18	9	5	4	22	13	32
FK Riga	18	9	3	6	28	27	30
Metalurgs Liepaya	18	7	9	2	27	17	30
Daugava Daugavpils	18	6	6	6	27	22	24
Vindava	18	4	5	9	14	27	17
Jurmala	18	3	7	8	15	27	16
Blazna	18	2	4	12	8	26	10
Olimps Riga	18	1	6	11	12	30	9

Championship Play-Off

	P	W	D	L	F	A	Pts
FK Ventspils	28	19	6	3	53	14	63
Metalurgs Liepaya	28	14	11	3	48	25	53
Skonto Riga	28	15	7	6	43	31	52
Dinaburg	28	10	8	10	32	31	38
Daugava Daugavpils	28	10	7	11	40	35	37
FK Riga	28	10	3	15	36	55	33

Relegation Table

	P	W	D	L	F	A	Pts
Jurmala	30	10	10	10	35	34	40
Vindava	30	9	9	12	27	41	36
Blazma+	30	5	8	17	20	43	23
Olimps Riga*	30	2	11	17	22	47	17

Top scorer: Rimkus (FK Ventspils) 14.
Cup Final: Daugava Daugavpils 1, FK Ventspils 1.
aet; Daugava Daugavpils won 3-0 on penalties.

LIECHTENSTEIN

Liechtensteiner Fussball-Verband, Malbuner Huus Altenbach 11, Postfach 165, 9490 Vaduz.
Founded: 1934; *National Colours:* Blue shirts, red shorts, blue stockings.

International matches 2008

Malta (a) 1-7, Switzerland (a) 0-3, Albania (a) 0-2, Germany (h) 0-6, Azerbaijan (a) 0-0, Wales (a) 0-2, Slovakia (a) 0-4.
Liechtenstein has no national league. Teams compete in Swiss regional leagues.

Cup wins (1937–2009)

Vaduz 38; Balzers 11; Triesen 8; Eschen/Mauren 4; Schaan 3.
Cup Final: Vaduz 2, Eschen/Mauren 1.

LITHUANIA

Lithuanian Football Federation, Seimyniskiu str. 15, 2005 Vilnius.
Founded: 1922; *National Colours:* Yellow shirts, green shorts, yellow stockings.

International matches 2008

Azerbaijan (h) 1-0, Czech Republic (a) 0-2, Estonia (a) 1-0, Latvia (a) 1-2, Russia (h) 1-4, Moldova (h) 3-0, Romania (a) 3-0, Austria (h) 2-0, Serbia (a) 0-3, Faeroes (h) 1-0, Moldova (a) 1-1, Estonia (a) 1-1.

League Championship wins (1990–2008)

FBK Kaunas 8 (including Zalgiris Kaunas 1); Zalgiris Vilnius 3; Ekranas Panevezys 3; Kareda 2; Inkaras Kaunas 2; Sirijus Klaipeda 1; ROMAR Mazeikiai 1.

Cup wins (1990–2009)

Zalgiris Vilnius 5; FBK Kaunas 4; Kareda 2; Ekranas Panevezys 2; Atlantas 2; Suduva 2; Sirijus Klaipeda 1; Lietuvos Makabi Vilnius 1; Inkaras Kaunas 1.

Final League Table 2008

	P	W	D	L	F	A	Pts
Ekranas	28	20	5	3	46	12	65
FBK Kaunas	28	16	7	5	51	17	55
Suduva	28	14	6	8	35	25	48
Vetra	28	14	6	8	33	24	48
Atlantas	28	7	7	14	31	44	28
Zalgiris	28	6	10	12	27	41	28
Siauliai	28	5	9	14	24	41	24
Silute	28	3	4	21	19	62	13

Vilnius wihdrew before start of season.
Top scorer: Ledesma (FBK Kaunas) 14.
Cup Final: Suduva 1, Tauras 0.

LUXEMBOURG

Federation Luxembourgeoise De Football (F.L.F.), 68 Rue De Gasperich, Luxembourg 1617.
Founded: 1908; *National Colours:* All red.

International matches 2008

Saudi Arabia (a) 1-2, Wales (h) 0-2, Cape Verde Islands (h) 1-1, Macedonia (h) 1-4, Greece (h) 0-3, Switzerland (a) 2-1, Israel (h) 1-3, Moldova (h) 0-0, Belgium (h) 1-1.

League Championship wins (1910–2009)

Jeunesse Esch 27; Spora Luxembourg 11; Stade Dudelange 10; F91 Dudelange 8; Red Boys Differdange 6; Union Luxembourg 6; Avenir Beggen 6; US Hollerich-Bonnevoie 5; Fola Esch 5; Aris Bonnevoie 3; Progres Niedercorn 3; Sporting Club 2; Racing Club 1; National Schifflange 1; Grevenmacher 1.

Cup wins (1922–2009)

Red Boys Differdange 15; Jeunesse Esch 12; Union Luxembourg 10; Spora Luxembourg 8; Avenir Beggen 7; Stade Dudelange 4; Progres Niedercorn 4; Grevenmacher 4; F91 Dudelange 4; Fola Esch 3; Alliance Dudelange 2; US Rumelange 2; Aris Bonnevoie 1; US Dudelange 1; Jeunesse Hautcharage 1; National Schifflange 1; Racing Club 1; SC Tetange 1; Swift Hesperange 1; Etzella Ettelbruck 1; CS Petange 1.

Final League Table 2008–09

	P	W	D	L	F	A	Pts
F91 Dudelange	26	19	5	2	70	18	62
Differdange	26	15	6	5	51	37	51
Grevenmacher	26	12	10	4	55	29	46
Jeunesse Esch	26	12	10	4	45	27	46
Fola Esch	26	11	6	9	43	42	39
Hamm Benfica	26	10	7	9	38	29	37
Progres	26	9	9	8	53	44	36
Etzella	26	8	8	10	43	48	32
Kaerjeng	26	9	4	13	39	42	31
Union Luxembourg	26	8	6	12	45	48	30
Hesperange	26	8	5	13	29	41	29
Rumelange+	26	7	6	13	34	48	37
Sporting*	26	5	6	15	21	54	21
Avenir Beggen*	26	3	4	19	16	75	13

Top scorer: Piskor (Differdange) 30.
Cup Final: F91 Dudelange 5, Kaerjeng 0.

MACEDONIA

Football Association of Macedonia, VIII-ma Udarna Brigada 31-A, Skopje 1000.
Founded: 1948; *National Colours:* All red.

International matches 2008

Serbia (h) 1-1, Bosnia (a) 2-2, Poland (h) 1-1, Luxembourg (a) 4-1, Scotland (h) 1-0, Holland (h) 1-2, Iceland (a) 0-1, Montenegro (a) 1-2.

League Championship wins (1993–2009)

Vardar 5; Sileks 3; Sloga Jugomagnat 3; Rabotnicki 3; Pobeda 2; Makedonija 1.

Cup wins (1993–2009)

Vardar 5; Sloga Jugomagnat 3; Sileks 2; Rabotnicki 2; Pelister 1; Pobeda 1; Cement 1; Baskimi 1; Makedonija 1.

Final League Table 2008–09

	P	W	D	L	F	A	Pts
Makedonija	30	17	10	3	46	15	61
Milano	30	17	4	9	48	35	55
Renova	30	14	12	4	41	26	54
Rabotnicki	30	13	8	9	40	25	47
Vardar	30	11	12	7	35	23	45
Turnovo	30	9	10	11	25	39	37
Sileks	30	9	9	12	38	41	36
Pobeda	30	8	8	14	31	47	32
Metalurg	30	6	11	13	25	35	29
Pelister	30	7	7	16	25	42	28
Napredok	30	4	9	17	26	52	21

Top scorer: Gligorovski (Milano) 16.
Cup Final: Rabotnicki 1, Makedonija 1.
aet; Rabotnicki won 6-5 on penalties.

MALTA

Malta Football Association, 280 St Paul Street, Valletta VLT07.
Founded: 1900; *National Colours:* Red shirts, white shorts, red stockings.

International matches 2008

Armenia (h) 0-1, Iceland (h) 1-0, Belarus (h) 0-1, Liechtenstein (h) 7-1, Austria (a) 1-5, Estonia (a) 1-2, Portugal (h) 0-4, Albania (a) 0-3, Denmark (a) 0-3, Hungary (h) 0-1, Iceland (h) 0-1.

League Championship wins (1910–2009)

Sliema Wanderers 26; Floriana 25; Valletta 19; Hibernians 10; Hamrun Spartans 7; Rabat Ajax 2; Birkirkara 1; St George's 1; KOMR 1; Marsaxlokk 1.

Cup wins (1935–2009)

Sliema Wanderers 20; Floriana 18; Valletta 11; Hibernians 8; Hamrun Spartans 6; Birkirkara 4; Gzira United 1; Melita 1; Zurrieq 1; Rabat Ajax 1.

Qualifying League Table 2008–09

	P	W	D	L	F	A	Pts
Hibernians	18	13	2	3	49	19	41
Valletta	18	11	7	0	31	11	40
Birkirkara	18	9	5	4	31	28	32
Sliema Wanderers	18	7	5	6	24	24	26
Floriana	18	6	4	8	18	21	22
Marsaxlokk	18	6	4	8	28	33	22
Msida St Joseph	18	6	3	9	20	28	21
Hamrun Spartans	18	5	2	11	24	37	17
Qormi	18	3	6	9	16	26	15
Tarxien Rainbows	18	4	2	12	22	36	14

Final League Table 2008–09

	P	W	D	L	F	A	Pts
Hibernians	28	19	5	4	73	25	42
Valletta	28	17	9	2	50	18	40
Birkirkara	28	12	7	9	43	45	27
Marsaxlokk	28	10	6	12	46	52	25
Sliema Wanderers	28	10	8	10	33	41	25
Floriana	28	7	6	15	25	44	16

Relegation Table 2008–09

	P	W	D	L	F	A	Pts
Qormi	24	7	6	11	30	31	20
Msida St Joseph*+	24	7	5	12	25	40	16
Tarxien Rainbows+	24	6	5	13	32	44	16
Hamrun Spartans*	24	7	3	14	31	48	16

Top scorer: Scerri (Hibernians) 26.
Cup Final: Valletta 3, Sliema Wanderers 3.
aet; Sliema Wanderers won 4-3 on penalties.

MOLDOVA

Football Association of Moldova, 39 Tricolorului Str, 2012, Chisinau.
Founded: 1990; *National Colours:* Red shirts, blue shorts, red stockings.

International matches 2008
Kazakhstan (h) 1-0, Croatia (a) 0-1, Armenia (h) 2-2, Lithuania (a) 0-3, Latvia (h) 1-2, Israel (h) 1-2, Greece (a) 0-3, Luxembourg (a) 0-0, Estonia (a) 0-1, Lithuania (h) 1-1.

League Championship wins (1992–2009)
Sheriff 9; Zimbru Chisinau 8; Constructorul 1.

Cup wins (1992–2009)
Sheriff 6; Zimbru Chisinau 5; Tiligul 3; Constructorul 2; Comrat 1; Nistru Otaci 1.

Final League Table 2008–09

	P	W	D	L	F	A	Pts
Sheriff	30	25	3	2	61	15	78
Dacia	30	20	3	7	47	17	63
Iscra-Stali	30	14	10	6	28	15	52
Zimbru Chisinau	30	13	7	10	42	30	46
Dinamo	30	11	9	10	42	45	42
Olimpia	30	11	7	12	30	32	40
Tiraspol	30	9	5	16	30	36	32
Otaci	30	8	6	16	30	43	30
Rapid Ghidighici**	30	7	8	15	28	47	29
Tiligul	30	7	4	19	24	60	25
Academia	30	6	6	18	27	49	24

***Politehnica withdrew on 1st July; Steaua and Rapid merged to become Rapid Ghidighici.*
Top scorer: Andronic (Zimbru Chisinau) 16.
Cup Final: Sheriff 2, Dacia 0.

MONTENEGRO

Football Association of Montenegro, Ulica "19 decembra" bb 81000 Podgorica.
Founded: 1931; *National Colours:* All red and gold.

International matches 2008
Norway (h) 3-1, Kazakhstan (h) 3-0, Romania (a) 0-4, Hungary (a) 3-3, Bulgaria (h) 2-2, Republic of Ireland (h) 0-0, Italy (a) 1-2, Macedonia (h) 2-1.

League Championship wins (2006–09)
Buducnost 1; Zeta 1; Mogren.

Cup wins (2006–09)
Mogren 1; Rudar 1; Petrovac 1.

Final League Table 2008–09

	P	W	D	L	F	A	Pts
Mogren	33	23	5	5	62	24	74
Buducnost	33	21	7	5	72	34	70
Sutjeska	33	18	9	6	45	23	63
Grbalj	33	15	5	13	47	34	50
Rudar	33	12	5	16	40	37	41
Petrovac	33	12	5	16	42	57	41
Lovcen	33	10	10	13	23	25	40
Kom	33	10	7	16	34	44	37
Zeta	33	13	7	13	36	41	36
Jezero*+	33	9	6	18	30	62	33
Decic+	33	9	4	20	24	46	31
Jedinstvo*	33	7	8	18	28	56	29

Top scorer: Becirag (Buducnost) 18.
Cup Final: Petrovac 1, Lovcen 0.

NORTHERN CYPRUS

Turkish Republic of Northern Cyprus.
Founded: 1955; *National Colours:* All red with white trim.

League Championship wins (1956–63; 1969–74; 1976–2009)
Cetinkaya 12; Gonyeli 9; Magusa 7; Dogan 6; Yenicami 5; BAF Ulku 4; Kucuk 3; Akincilar 1; Binatli 1.

Cup wins (1956-2009)
Cetinkaya 16; Gonyeli 7; Kucuk 6; Magusa 5; Yenicami 5; Turk Ocagi 4; Binatli 1; Dogan 1; Genclik 1; Lefke 1; Yalova 1.

Final League Table 2008–09

	P	W	D	L	F	A	Pts
Gonyeli	26	18	5	3	51	13	56
Tatlisu	26	14	5	7	45	35	47
Turk Ocagi	26	13	5	8	52	40	44
Bostanci	26	12	8	6	44	35	44
Magusa	26	13	1	12	53	38	40
Turkmenkoy	26	11	7	8	39	28	40
Cetinkaya	26	12	3	11	45	43	39
Ozankoy	26	10	7	9	42	36	37
Lapta	26	11	4	11	38	38	37
Kucuk	26	9	7	10	50	38	34
Cihangir	26	8	8	10	34	30	32
Yeni*	26	10	2	14	40	59	32
Alsancak*	26	5	6	15	36	63	21
Binatli*	26	1	2	23	16	89	5

Gonyeli three points deducted.
Cup Final: Gonyeli 3, Kucuk 0.

NORTHERN IRELAND

Irish Football Association Ltd, 20 Windsor Avenue, Belfast BT9 6EE.
Founded: 1880; *National Colours:* Green shirts, white shorts, green stockings.

NORWAY

Norges Fotballforbund, Ullevaal Stadion, Sognsveien 75J, Serviceboks 1, Oslo 0855.
Founded: 1902; *National Colours:* Red shirts, white shorts, blue stockings.

International matches 2008
Wales (a) 0-3, Montenegro (a) 1-3, Uruguay (h) 2-2, Republic of Ireland (h) 1-1, Iceland (h) 2-2, Scotland (a) 0-0, Holland (h) 0-1, Ukraine (a) 0-1.

League Championship wins (1938–2008)
Rosenborg Trondheim 20; Fredrikstad 9; Viking Stavanger 8; Lillestrom 5; Valerenga 5; Larvik Turn 3; Brann Bergen 3; Lyn Oslo 2; IK Start 2; Freidig 1; Fram 1; Skeid Oslo 1; Strömsgodset Drammen 1; Moss 1; Stabaek 1.

Cup wins (1902–2008)
Odd Grenland 12; Fredrikstad 11; Rosenborg Trondheim 9; Lyn Oslo 8; Skeid Oslo 8; Rosenborg Trondheim 8; Sarpsborg 6; Brann Bergen 6; Viking Stavanger 5; Lillestrom 5; Orn Horten 4; Strömsgodset Drammen 4; Valerenga 4; Frigg 3; Mjondalen 3; Bodo/Glimt 2; Mercantile 2; Tromso 2; Molde 2; Grane Nordstrand 1; Kvik Halden 1; Sparta 1; Gjovik/Lyn 1; Moss 1; Bryne 1; Stabaek 1.
(Known as the Norwegian Championship for HM The King's Trophy).

Final League Table 2008

	P	W	D	L	F	A	Pts
Stabaek	26	16	6	4	58	24	54
Fredrikstad	26	14	6	6	38	28	48
Tromso	26	12	8	6	36	23	44
Bodo Glimt	26	12	6	8	37	38	42
Rosenborg	26	11	6	9	40	34	39
Viking	26	11	6	9	38	32	39
Lyn	26	11	5	10	38	34	38
Brann	26	8	9	9	36	36	33
Molde	26	7	10	9	39	43	31
Valerenga	26	8	6	12	31	37	30
Stromsgodset	26	8	5	13	33	44	29
Lillestrom	26	7	7	12	30	40	28
Aalesunds+	26	7	4	15	29	42	25
Hamark*	26	5	6	15	22	50	21

Top scorer: Nannskog (Stabaek) 16.
Cup Final: Valerenga 4, Stabaek 1.

POLAND

Polish Football Association, Polski Zwiazek Pilki Noznej, Miodowa 1, Warsaw 00-080.
Founded: 1919; *National Colours:* White shirts, red shorts, white stockings.

International matches 2008
Czech Republic (h) 2-0, Estonia (h) 2-0, USA (h) 0-3,

Macedonia (a) 1-1, Albania (a) 1-0, Denmark (h) 1-1, Germany (n) 0-2, Austria (a) 1-1, Croatia (n) 0-1, Ukraine (a) 0-1, Slovenia (h) 1-1, San Marino (a) 2-0, Czech Republic (h) 2-1, Slovakia (a) 1-2, Republic of Ireland (a) 3-2, Serbia (a) 1-0.

League Championship wins (1921–2009)
Gornik Zabrze 14; Ruch Chorzow 14; Wisla Krakow 13; Legia Warsaw 8; Cracovia 5; Lech Poznan 5; Pogon Lwow 4; Widzew Lodz 4; Warta Poznan 2; Polonia Bytom 2; Stal Mielec 2; LKS Lodz 2; Polonia Warsaw 2; Zaglebie Lubin 2; Garbarnia Krakow 1; Slask Wroclaw 1; Szombierki Bytom 1.

Cup wins (1951–2009)
Legia Warsaw 13; Gornik Zabrze 6; Lech Poznan 5; Zaglebie Sosnowiec 4; GKS Katowice 3; Ruch Chorzow 3; Amica Wronki 3; Wisla Krakow 3; Slask Wroclaw 2; Polonia Warsaw 2; Groclin 2; Gwardia Warsaw 1; LKS Lodz 1; Stal Rzeszow 1; Arka Gdynia 1; Lechia Gdansk 1; Widzew Lodz 1; Miedz Legnica 1; Wisla Plock 1.

Final League Table 2008–09

	P	W	D	L	F	A	Pts
Wisla	30	19	7	4	53	21	64
Legia	30	18	7	5	52	17	61
Lech	30	16	11	3	51	24	59
Polonia Warsaw	30	15	9	6	40	23	54
GKS Belchatow	30	17	3	10	40	28	54
Slask	30	11	12	7	40	34	45
Polonia Bytom	30	10	5	15	30	46	35
LKS Lodz	30	10	5	15	27	43	35
Jagiellonia	30	9	7	14	28	34	34
Ruch	30	9	7	14	22	32	34
Piast	30	9	6	15	17	26	33
Lechia	30	9	5	16	30	44	32
Odra	30	8	8	14	23	40	32
Arka	30	7	9	14	27	39	30
Cracovia+	30	7	9	14	24	40	30
Gornik Zabrze*	30	7	8	15	20	33	29

Top scorers: Pawel Brosek (Wisla), Chinyama (Legia) 19.
Cup Final: Lech 1, Ruch 0.

PORTUGAL
Federacao Portuguesa De Futebol, Praca De Alegria N.25, Apartado 21.100, P-1127, Lisboa 1250-004.
Founded: 1914; *National Colours:* Red shirts, green shorts, red stockings.

International matches 2008
Italy (a) 1-3, Greece (h) 1-2, Georgia (h) 2-0, Turkey (n) 2-0, Czech Republic (n) 3-1, Switzerland (a) 0-2, Germany (n) 2-3, Faeroes (h) 5-0, Malta (a) 4-0, Denmark (h) 2-3, Sweden (a) 0-0, Albania (h) 0-0, Brazil (a) 2-6.

League Championship wins (1935–2009)
Benfica 31; FC Porto 24; Sporting Lisbon 18; Belenenses 1; Boavista 1.

Cup wins (1939–2009)
Benfica 24; Sporting Lisbon 15; FC Porto 14; Boavista 5; Belenenses 3; Vitoria Setubal 3; Academica Coimbra 1; Leixoes 1; Sporting Braga 1; Estrela Amadora 1; Beira Mar 1.

Final League Table 2008–09

	P	W	D	L	F	A	Pts
Porto	30	21	7	2	61	18	70
Sporting Lisbon	30	20	6	4	45	20	66
Benfica	30	17	8	5	54	32	59
Nacional	30	15	7	8	47	32	52
Braga	30	13	11	6	38	21	50
Leixoes	30	12	9	9	30	31	46
Academica	30	10	9	11	28	32	39
Guimaraes	30	10	8	12	32	36	38
Maritimo	30	9	10	11	35	36	37
Ferreira	30	9	7	14	37	42	34
Amadora	30	8	10	12	26	38	34
Rio Ave	30	8	6	16	20	35	30
Naval	30	7	8	15	25	39	29
Setubal	30	7	5	18	21	46	26
Belenenses*	30	5	9	16	28	52	24
Trofense*	30	5	8	17	25	42	23

Top scorer: Nene (Nacional) 20.
Cup Final: Porto 1, Ferreira 0.

ROMANIA
Federatia Romana De Fotbal, House of Football, Str. Serg. Serbanica Vasile 12, Bucharest 73412.
Founded: 1909; *National Colours:* All yellow.

International matches 2008
Israel (a) 0-1, Russia (h) 3-0, Montenegro (h) 4-0, France (n) 0-0, Italy (n) 1-1, Holland (n) 0-2, Latvia (h) 1-0, Lithuania (h) 0-3, Faeroes (a) 1-0, France (h) 2-2, Georgia (h) 2-1.

League Championship wins (1910–2009)
Steaua Bucharest 23; Dinamo Bucharest 18; Venus Bucharest 8; Chinezul Timisoara 6; UT Arad 6; Ripensia Timisoara 4; Uni Craiova 4; Petrolul Ploiesti 3; Rapid Bucharest 3; Olimpia Satu Mare 2; Colentina Bucharest 2; Arges Pitesti 2; ICO Oradea 1; Romano-Americana Bucharest 1; Prahova Ploiesti 1; Coltea Brasov 1; Juventus Bucharest 1; Metalochimia Resita 1; United Ploiesti 1; Unirea Tricolor 1; Cluj 1; Unirea 1.

Cup wins (1934–2009)
Steaua Bucharest 21; Rapid Bucharest 13; Dinamo Bucharest 12; Uni Craiova 6; UT Arad 2; Ripensia Timisoara 2; Politehnica Timisoara 2; Petrolul Ploiesti 2; Cluj 2; Metalochimia Resita 1; Universitata Cluj (includes Stiinta) 1; CFR Turnu Severin 1; Chimia Ramnicu Vilcea 1; Jiul Petrosani 1; Progresul Bucharest 1; Progresul Oradea (formerly ICO) 1; Ariesul Turda 1; Gloria Bistrita 1.

Final League Table 2008–09

	P	W	D	L	F	A	Pts
Unirea	34	21	7	6	51	20	70
Dinamo Bucharest	34	20	5	9	56	30	65
Timisoara	34	20	7	7	58	38	61
Cluj	34	16	11	7	44	26	59
Vaslui	34	17	6	11	44	37	57
Steaua	34	14	14	6	44	27	56
Uni Craiova	34	15	11	8	44	25	56
Rapid Bucharest	34	16	7	11	44	34	55
Brasov	34	14	13	7	35	25	55
2005 Pitesti	34	12	8	14	41	47	44
Pandurii	34	11	10	13	27	36	43
Otelul	34	11	7	16	37	48	40
Gloria	34	11	5	18	32	44	38
Iasi	34	10	7	17	32	47	37
Gaz Metan*	34	10	6	18	36	51	36
Farul*	34	8	6	20	27	56	30
Otopeni*	34	5	7	22	32	54	22
Buzau*	34	4	5	25	23	62	17

Timisoara 6 points deducted by FIFA for misuse of club name.
Top scorers: Bucur (Timisoara), Costea (Uni Craiova) 17.
Cup Final: Cluj 3, Timisoara 0.

RUSSIA
Football Union of Russia; Luzhnetskaya Naberezyhnaja 8, Moscow 119 992.
Founded: 1912; *National Colours:* All white.

International matches 2008
Romania (a) 0-3, Kazakhstan (h) 6-0, Serbia (h) 2-1, Lithuania (a) 4-1, Spain (n) 1-4, Greece (n) 1-0, Sweden (n) 2-0, Holland (n) 3-1, Spain (n) 0-3, Holland (h) 1-1, Wales (h) 2-1, Germany (a) 1-2, Finland (h) 3-0.

League Championship wins (1936–2008)
Spartak Moscow 21; Dynamo Kiev 13; Dynamo Moscow 11; CSKA Moscow 10; Torpedo Moscow 3; Dinamo Tbilisi 2; Dnepr Dnepropetrovsk 2; Lokomotiv Moscow 2; Saria Voroshilovgrad 1; Ararat Erevan 1; Dynamo Minsk 1; Spartak Vladikavkaz 1; Rubin 1.

Cup wins (1936–2009)
Spartak Moscow 13; CSKA Moscow 10; Dynamo Kiev 9; Torpedo Moscow 7; Dynamo Moscow 7; Lokomotiv Moscow 7; Shakhtar Donetsk 4; Dinamo Tbilisi 2; Ararat Erevan 2; Zenit St Petersburg (formerly Zenit Leningrad) 2; Karpaty Lvov 1; SKA Rostov 1; Metalist Kharkov 1; Dnepr 1; Terek Groznyi 1.

Final League Table 2008

	P	W	D	L	F	A	Pts
Rubin	30	18	6	6	44	26	60
CSKA Moscow	30	16	8	6	53	24	56
Dynamo Moscow	30	15	9	6	41	29	54
Amkar	30	14	9	7	31	22	51
Zenit	30	12	12	6	59	37	48
Krylia Sovekov	30	12	12	6	46	28	48
Lokomotiv Moscow	30	13	8	9	37	32	47
Spartak Moscow	30	11	11	8	43	39	44
FK Moscow	30	9	11	10	34	36	38
Terek	30	9	8	13	28	42	35
Saturn	30	7	12	11	26	30	33

Spartak Nalchik	30	8	8	14	30	39	32
Tomsk	30	7	8	15	23	39	29
Khimki	30	6	9	15	34	54	27
Shinnik*	30	5	7	18	25	48	22
Luch-Energia*	30	3	12	15	24	53	21

Top scorer: Vagner Love (CSKA Moscow) 20.
Cup Final: CSKA Moscow 1, Rubin 0.

SAN MARINO
Federazione Sammarinese Giuoco Calcio, Viale Campo dei Giudei, 14; Rep. San Marino 47890.
Founded: 1931; *National Colours:* All light blue.

International matches 2008
Poland (h) 0-2, Slovakia (h) 1-3, Northern Ireland (a) 0-4, Czech Republic (h) 0-3.

League Championship wins (1986–2009)
Tre Fiori 5; Domagnono 4; Faetano 3; Folgore Falciano 3; Murata 3; La Fiorita 2; Montevito 1; Libertas 1; Cosmos 1; Pennarossa 1.

Cup wins (1937–2009)
Libertas 10; Domagnono 8; Juvenes 5; Tre Fiore 5; Tre Penne 5; Cosmos 4; Caetano 3; Murata 3; Dogana 2; Pennarossa 2; La Fiorita 1; Juvenes/Dogana 1.

Qualifying League Table 2008–09

Group A	P	W	D	L	F	A	Pts
Virtus	20	10	5	5	34	22	35
Tre Penne	20	9	8	3	25	24	35
Juvenes/Dogana	20	9	7	4	25	13	34
Pennarossa	20	10	4	6	35	24	34
La Fiorita	20	9	4	7	35	28	31
Libertas	20	8	4	8	30	31	28
Domagnono	20	5	2	13	23	38	17

Group B	P	W	D	L	F	A	Pts
Tre Penne	21	14	5	2	53	20	47
Murata	21	11	5	5	38	20	38
Faetano	21	9	7	5	39	34	34
Cosmos	21	11	1	9	44	37	34
Folgore/Falciano	21	6	6	9	28	30	24
Cailungo	21	6	5	10	23	30	23
Fiorentino	21	3	2	16	21	61	11
San Giovanni	21	0	3	18	19	70	3

Play-Offs: Tre Penne 1, Faetano 0; Murata 0, Juvenes/Dogana 1; Murata 5, Faetano 4; Juvenes/Dogana 2, Tre Penne 0; Murata 2, Tre Penne 0; Virtus 0, Tre Fiore 2; Murata 3, Virtus 2; Juvenes/Dogana 1, Tre Fiore 1 (Tre Fiore won 5-4 on penalties); Murata 1, Juvenes/Dogana 3.
Final: Tre Fiore 0, Juvenes/Dogana 0 (Tre Fiore won 3-1 on penalties).
Top scorer: Casadel (Murata) 22.
Cup Final: Juvenes/Dogana 2, Domagnono 1.

SCOTLAND
The Scottish Football Association Ltd, Hampden Park, Glasgow G42 9AY.
Founded: 1873; *National Colours:* Dark blue shirts, white shorts, dark blue stockings.

SERBIA
Football Association of Serbia, Terazije 35, P.O. Box 263, 11000 Beograd.
Founded: 1919; *National Colours:* Blue shirts, white shorts, red stockings.

International matches 2008
Macedonia (a) 1-1, Ukraine (a) 0-2, Republic of Ireland (a) 1-1, Russia (a) 1-2, Germany (a) 1-2, Faeroes (h) 2-0, France (a) 1-2, Lithuania (h) 3-0, Austria (a) 3-1, Bulgaria (h) 6-1, Poland (h) 0-1.

League Championship wins (1923–2009)
Red Star Belgrade 25; Partizan Belgrade 21; Hajduk Split 9; Gradjanski Zagreb 5; BSK Belgrade 5; Dinamo Zagreb 4; Jugoslavija Belgrade 2; Concordia Zagreb 2; FC Sarajevo 2; Vojvodina Novi Sad 2; HASK Zagreb 1; Zeljeznicar 1; Obilic 1.

Cup wins (1947–2009)
Red Star Belgrade 22; Partizan Belgrade 11; Hajduk Split 9; Dinamo Zagreb 8; BSK Belgrade (includes OFK) 2; Rijeka 2; Velez Mostar 2; Vardar Skopje 1; Borac Banjaluka 1; Sartid 1; Zeleznik 1.

Final League Table 2008–09

	P	W	D	L	F	A	Pts
Partizan Belgrade	33	25	5	3	63	15	80
Vojvodina	33	18	7	8	46	25	61
Red Star Belgrade	33	17	8	8	59	32	59
Habitpharm	33	13	14	6	39	27	53
Borac	33	9	13	11	28	35	40
Napredak	33	10	8	15	28	37	38
Hajduk Kula	33	9	11	13	23	34	38
Rad	33	7	15	11	27	35	36
Cukaricki	33	9	8	16	30	39	35
Jagodina	33	10	4	19	28	47	34
OFK Belgrade	33	8	9	16	28	54	33
Banat*	33	7	10	16	21	40	31

Mladost withdrew for financial reasons; Banat restored.
Top scorer: Diarra (Partizan Belgrade) 19.
Cup Final: Partizan Belgrade 3, Ševojno 0.

SLOVAKIA
Slovak Football Association, Junacka 6, 83280 Bratislava, Slovakia.
Founded: 1993; *National Colours:* All blue and white.

International matches 2008
Hungary (a) 1-1, Turkey (a) 0-1, Switzerland (a) 0-2, Iceland (h) 1-2, Greece (h) 0-2, Northern Ireland (h) 2-1, Slovenia (a) 1-2, San Marino (a) 3-1, Poland (a) 2-1, Liechtenstein (h) 4-0.

League Championship wins (1939–44; 1994–2009)
Slovan Bratislava 9; Zilina 4; Kosice 2; Inter Bratislava 2; Artmedia Petrzalka 2; Bystrica 1; OAP Bratislava 1; Ruzomberok 1.

Cup wins (1994–2009)
Inter Bratislava 3; Slovan Bratislava 3; Artmedia Petrzalka 2; Spartak Trnava 1; Koba Senec 1; Matador Puchov 1; Bystrica 1; Ruzomberok 1; ViOn Zlate 1; Kosice 1.

Final League Table 2008–09

	P	W	D	L	F	A	Pts
Slovan Bratislava	33	21	7	5	69	25	70
Zilina	33	18	8	7	56	26	62
Spartak Trnava	33	15	10	8	45	38	55
Kosice	33	14	10	9	48	42	52
Ruzomberok	33	12	11	10	48	34	47
Artmedia	33	12	11	10	50	38	47
Tatran	33	10	11	12	40	50	41
Dubnica	33	10	7	16	43	49	37
Dunajska	33	9	9	15	32	59	36
Bystrica	33	9	8	16	30	39	35
Nitra	33	9	8	16	34	53	35
Moravce*	33	5	8	20	21	63	23

Senec merged with Dunajska.
Top scorer: Masaryk (Slovan Bratislava) 15.
Cup Final: Kosice 1, Artmedia 1.

SLOVENIA
Football Association of Slovenia, Nogometna zveza Slovenije, Cerinova 4, P.P. 3986, 1001 Ljubljana, Slovenia.
Founded: 1920; *National Colours:* White shirts with green sleeves, white shorts, white stockings.

International matches 2008
Denmark (h) 1-2, Hungary (a) 1-0, Sweden (a) 0-1, Croatia (h) 2-3, Poland (a) 1-1, Slovakia (h) 2-0, Czech Republic (a) 0-1, Bosnia (h) 3-4.

League Championship wins (1992–2009)
Maribor 8; SCT Olimpija 4; Gorica 4; Domzale 2.

Cup wins (1992–2009)
Maribor 5; SCT Olimpija 4; Gorica 2; Koper 2; Interblock 2; Mura 1; Rudar 1; Publikum 1.

Final League Table 2008–09

	P	W	D	L	F	A	Pts
Maribor	36	17	12	7	62	44	63
Gorica	36	17	5	14	60	55	56
Rudar	36	16	7	13	44	39	55
Celje	36	15	8	13	48	39	53
Domzale	36	12	14	10	44	40	50
Interblock	36	13	8	15	52	51	47
Nafta	36	11	10	15	36	52	43
Koper	36	10	12	14	39	47	42
Drava+	36	12	6	18	47	53	42
Primorje*	36	9	14	13	36	48	41

Top scorer: Velikonja (Gorica) 17.
Cup Final: Interblock 2, Koper 1.

SPAIN
Real Federacion Espanola De Futbol, Ramon y Cajal, s/n, Apartado Postale 385, Madrid 28230.
Founded: 1913; *National Colours:* Red shirts, blue shorts, blue stockings with red, blue and yellow border.

International matches 2008
France (h) 1-0, Italy (h) 1-0, Peru (h) 2-1, USA (h) 1-0, Russia (n) 4-1, Sweden (n) 2-1, Greece (n) 2-1, Italy (n) 0-0, Russia (n) 3-0, Germany (n) 1-0, Denmark (a) 3-0, Bosnia (h) 1-0, Armenia (h) 4-0, Estonia (a) 3-0, Belgium (a) 2-1, Chile (h) 3-0.

League Championship wins (1929–36; 1940–2009)
Real Madrid 31; Barcelona 19; Atletico Madrid 9; Athletic Bilbao 8; Valencia 6; Real Sociedad 2; Real Betis 1; Sevilla 1; La Coruna 1.

Cup wins (1994–2009)
Barcelona 25; Athletic Bilbao 23; Real Madrid 17; Atletico Madrid 9; Valencia 7; Real Zaragoza 6; Espanyol 4; Sevilla 4; Real Union de Irun 3; La Coruna 2; Real Sociadad (includes Ciclista) 2; Real Betis 2; Arenas 1; Racing de Irun 1; Vizcaya Bilbao 1; Real Sociedad 1; Mallorca 1.

Final League Table 2008–09

	P	W	D	L	F	A	Pts
Barcelona	38	27	6	5	105	35	87
Real Madrid	38	25	3	10	83	52	78
Sevilla	38	21	7	10	54	39	70
Atletico Madrid	38	20	7	11	80	57	67
Villarreal	38	18	11	9	61	54	65
Valencia	38	18	8	12	68	54	62
La Coruna	38	16	10	12	48	47	58
Malaga	38	15	10	13	55	59	55
Mallorca	38	14	9	15	53	60	51
Espanyol	38	12	11	15	46	49	47
Santander	38	12	10	16	49	48	46
Almeria	38	13	7	18	45	61	46
Athletic Bilbao	38	12	8	18	47	62	44
Osasuna	38	10	13	15	41	47	43
Valladolid	38	12	7	19	46	58	43
Gijon	38	14	1	23	47	79	43
Getafe	38	10	12	16	50	56	42
Betis*	38	10	12	16	51	58	42
Numancia*	38	10	5	23	38	69	35
Recreativo*	38	8	9	21	34	57	33

Top scorer: Forlan (Atletico Madrid) 32.
Cup Final: Barcelona 4, Athletic Bilbao 1.

SWEDEN

Svenska Fotbollfoerbundet, Box 1216, S-17123 Solna.
Founded: 1904; *National Colours:* Yellow shirts, blue shorts, yellow stockings.

International matches 2008
Costa Rica (a) 1-0, USA (a) 0-2, Turkey (a) 0-0, Brazil (h) 0-1, Slovenia (h) 1-0, Ukraine (h) 0-1, Greece (n) 2-0, Spain (n) 1-2, Russia (n) 0-2, France (h) 2-3, Albania (a) 0-0, Hungary (h) 2-1, Portugal (h) 0-0, Holland (a) 1-3.

League Championship wins (1896–2008)
IFK Gothenburg 19; Malmo FF 15; Orgryte 14; IFK Norrköping 12; Djurgaarden 11; AIK Stockholm 10; GAIS Gothenburg 6; IF Helsingborg 6; IF Elfsborg 5; Oster Vaxjo 4; Halmstad 4; Atvidaberg 2; IFK Eskilstuna 1; IF Gavic Brynas 1; IF Gothenburg 1; Fassbergs 1; IK Sleipner 1; Hammarby 1; Kalmar 1.

Cup wins (1941–2008)
Malmo FF 14; AIK Stockholm 7; IFK Norrköping 6; IFK Gothenburg 5; Djurgaarden 4; Helsingborg 3; Kalmar 3; Atvidaberg 2; IF Elfsborg 2; GAIS Gothenburg 1; IF Raa 1; Landskrona 1; Oster Vaxjo 1; Degerfors 1; Halmstad 1; Orgryte 1.

Final League Table 2008

	P	W	D	L	F	A	Pts
Kalmar	30	20	4	6	70	32	64
Elfsborg	30	19	6	5	49	18	63
IFK Gothenburg	30	15	9	6	50	26	54
Helsingborg	30	16	6	8	54	41	54
AIK	30	12	9	9	36	32	45
Malmo	30	12	8	10	51	46	44
Orebro	30	11	9	10	36	39	42
Halmstad	30	11	8	11	41	38	41
Hammarby	30	11	8	11	44	51	41
Trelleborg	30	9	13	8	33	31	40
GAIS Gothenburg	30	9	11	10	30	36	38
Djurgaarden	30	9	9	12	30	41	36
Gefle	30	7	7	16	33	42	28
Ljungskile*+	30	6	6	18	23	52	24
Sundsvall*	30	5	7	18	26	54	22

Norrkoping* | | 30 | 4 | 8 | 18 | 31 | 58 | 20
Top scorer: Ingelsten (Kalmar) 19.
Cup Final: IFK Gothenburg 0, Kalmar 0.
aet; IFK Gothenburg won 5-4 on penalties.

SWITZERLAND

Schweizerisher Fussballverband, Postfach 3000, Berne 15.
Founded: 1895; *National Colours:* Red shirts, white shorts, red stockings.

International matches 2008
England (a) 1-2, Germany (h) 0-4, Slovakia (h) 2-0, Liechtenstein (h) 3-0, Czech Republic (h) 0-1, Turkey (h) 1-2, Portugal (h) 2-0, Cyprus (h) 4-1, Israel (a) 2-2, Luxembourg (h) 1-2, Latvia (h) 2-1, Greece (a) 2-1, Finland (h) 1-0.

League Championship wins (1898–2009)
Grasshoppers 26; Servette 17; FC Basle 12; FC Zurich 12; Young Boys Berne 11; Lausanne 7; La Chaux-de-Fonds 3; FC Lugano 3; Winterthur 3; FC Aarau 3; Neuchatel Xamax 2; Sion 2; St Gallen 2; FC Anglo-American Club 1; FC Brühl 1; Cantonal-Neuchatel 1; Biel-Bienne 1; Bellinzona 1; FC Etoile La Chaux-de-Fonds 1; Lucerne 1.

Cup wins (1926–2009)
Grasshoppers 18; FC Sion 11; Lausanne 9; FC Basle 9; Servette 7; FC Zurich 7; La Chaux-de-Fonds 6; Young Boys Berne 6; FC Lugano 3; Lucerne 2; FC Grenchen 1; St Gallen 1; Urania Geneva 1; Young Fellows Zurich 1; FC Aarau 1; Wil 1.

Final League Table 2008–09

	P	W	D	L	F	A	Pts
Zurich	36	24	7	5	80	36	79
Young Boys	36	22	7	7	85	46	73
Basle	36	22	6	8	72	44	72
Grasshoppers	36	12	14	10	57	48	50
Aarau	36	11	11	14	35	51	44
Bellinzona	36	11	10	15	44	51	43
Neuchatel Xamax	36	10	10	16	50	57	40
Sion	36	9	10	17	44	60	37
Lucerne+	36	9	8	19	45	62	35
Vaduz*	36	5	7	24	28	85	22

Top scorer: Doumia (Young Boys) 20.
Cup Final: Sion 3, Young Boys 2.

TURKEY

Turkiye Futbol Federasyonu, Konaklar Mah. Ihlamurlu Sok. 9, 4 Levent, Istanbul 80620.
Founded: 1923; *National Colours:* All white.

International matches 2008
Sweden (h) 0-0, Belarus (a) 2-2, Slovakia (h) 1-0, Uruguay (h) 2-3, Finland (a) 2-0, Portugal (n) 0-2, Switzerland (n) 2-1, Czech Republic (n) 3-2, Croatia (n) 1-1, Germany (n) 2-3, Chile (h) 1-0, Armenia (a) 2-0, Belgium (h) 1-1, Bosnia (h) 2-1, Estonia (a) 0-0, Austria (a) 4-2.

League Championship wins (1959–2009)
Fenerbahce 17; Galatasaray 17; Besiktas 11; Trabzonspor 6.

Cup wins (1963–2009)
Galatasaray 14; Besiktas 8; Trabzonspor 7; Fenerbahce 4; Goztepe Izmir 2; Altay Izmir 2; Ankaragucu 2; Genclerbirligi 2; Kocaelispor 2; Eskisehirspor 1; Bursaspor 1; Sakaryaspor 1; Kayseri 1.

Final League Table 2008–09

	P	W	D	L	F	A	Pts
Besiktas	34	21	8	5	60	30	71
Sivas	34	19	9	6	54	28	66
Trabzonspor	34	19	8	7	54	34	65
Fenerbahce	34	18	7	9	60	36	61
Galatasaray	34	18	7	9	57	39	61
Bursa	34	16	10	8	47	37	58
Kayseri	34	13	11	10	38	26	50
Gaziantep	34	12	11	11	46	48	47
Istanbul	34	12	6	16	37	46	42
Ankara	34	11	8	15	36	42	41
Eskisehir	34	10	10	14	45	49	40
Antalya	34	10	10	14	34	42	40
Ankaragucu	34	11	6	17	36	47	39
Genclerbirligi	34	10	8	16	38	50	38
Denizli	34	11	5	18	39	52	38
Konya*	34	10	8	16	35	46	38

Kocaeli*	34	8	5	21	47	73	29
Hacettepe*	34	5	7	22	24	63	22

Top scorer: Baros (Galatasaray 20).
Cup Final: Besiktas 4, Fenerbahce 2.

UKRAINE

Football Federation of Ukraine, Laboratorna Str. 1, P.O. Box 293, Kiev 03150.
Founded: 1991; *National Colours:* All yellow and blue.

International matches 2008
Cyprus (a) 1-1, Serbia (h) 2-0, Holland (a) 0-3, Sweden (a) 1-0, Poland (h) 1-0, Belarus (h) 1-0, Kazakhstan (a) 3-1, Croatia (h) 0-0, Norway (h) 1-0.

League Championship wins (1992–2009)
Dynamo Kiev 13; Shakhtar Donetsk 4; Tavriya Simferopol 1.

Cup wins (1992–2009)
Dynamo Kiev 9; Shakhtar Donetsk 6; Chernomorets Odessa 2; Vorskla 1.

Final League Table 2008–09

	P	W	D	L	F	A	Pts
Dynamo Kiev	30	26	1	3	71	19	79
Shakhtar Donetsk	30	19	7	4	47	16	64
Metalist	30	17	8	5	44	25	59
Metalurg Donetsk	30	14	7	9	36	27	49
Vorskla	30	14	7	9	32	26	49
Dnepr	30	13	9	8	34	25	48
Metalurg Zapor	30	12	9	9	29	30	45
Tavriya	30	10	7	13	41	45	37
Karpaty	30	8	10	12	33	39	34
Chernomorets	30	12	2	16	34	42	32
Arsenal Kiev	30	8	8	14	26	33	32
Krivbas	30	8	8	14	21	36	32
Zorya	30	8	7	15	29	45	31
Illichivets	30	7	5	18	31	54	26
Lvov*	30	6	8	16	24	39	26
Kharkiv*	30	2	9	19	19	59	50

Chernomorets deducted six points.
Top scorer: Kovpak (Tavriya) 17.
Cup Final: Vorskla 1, Shakhtar Donetsk 0.

WALES

The Football Association of Wales Limited, Plymouth Chambers, 3 Westgate Street, Cardiff, CF10 1DP.
Founded: 1876; *National Colours:* All red.

SOUTH AMERICA

ARGENTINA

Asociacion Del Futbol Argentina, Viamonte 1366/76, 1053 Buenos Aires.
Founded: 1893; *National Colours:* Light blue and white vertical striped shirts, dark blue shorts, white stockings.
International matches 2008
Egypt (a) 2-0, Mexico (a) 4-1, USA (a) 0-0, Ecuador (h) 1-1, Brazil (a) 0-0, Belarus (a) 0-0, Paraguay (h) 1-1, Peru (a) 1-1, Uruguay (h) 2-1, Chile (a) 0-1, Scotland (a) 1-0.

BOLIVIA

Federacion Boliviana De Futbol, Av. Libertador Bolivar No. 1168, Casilla de Correo 484, Cochabamba, Bolivia.
Founded: 1925; *National Colours:* Green shirts, white shorts, green stockings.
International matches 2008
Peru (h) 2-1, Venezuela (a) 1-0, Chile (h) 0-2, Paraguay (h) 4-2, Guatemala (a) 0-3, Panama (h) 1-0, Ecuador (a) 1-3, Brazil (a) 0-0, Peru (h) 3-0, Uruguay (h) 2-2, El Salvador (h) 0-2.

BRAZIL

Confederacao Brasileira De Futebol, Rua Victor Civita 66, Bloco 1-Edificio 5-5 Andar, Barra da Tijuca, Rio De Janeiro 22775-040.
Founded: 1914; *National Colours:* Yellow shirts with green collar and cuffs, blue shorts, white stockings with green and yellow border.
International matches 2008
Republic of Ireland (a) 1-0, Sweden (a) 1-0, Canada (h) 3-2, Venezuela (h) 0-2, Paraguay (a) 0-2, Argentina (h) 0-0, Chile (a) 3-0, Bolivia (h) 0-0, Venezuela (a) 4-0, Colombia (h) 0-0, Portugal (h) 6-2.

CHILE

Federacion De Futbol De Chile, Avda. Quillin No. 5635, Casilla postal 3733, Correo Central, Santiago de Chile.
Founded: 1895; *National Colours:* Red shirts with blue collar and cuffs, blue shorts, white stockings.
International matches 2008
Japan (a) 0-0, South Korea (a) 1-0, Israel (a) 0-1, Guatemala (h) 2-0, Panama (h) 0-0, Bolivia (a) 2-0, Venezuela (a) 3-2, Turkey (a) 0-1, Brazil (h) 0-3, Colombia (h) 4-0, Mexico (a) 1-0, Spain (a) 0-3, Ecuador (a) 0-1, Argentina (h) 1-0.

COLOMBIA

Federacion Colombiana De Futbol, Avenida 32, No. 16–22 piso 4o. Apartado Aereo 17602, Santafe de Bogota.
Founded: 1924; *National Colours:* Yellow shirts, blue shorts, red stockings.
International matches 2008
Uruguay (a) 2-2, Honduras (h) 1-2, Venezuela (h) 5-2, Republic of Ireland (a) 0-1, France (a) 0-1, Peru (a) 1-1, Ecuador (a) 0-0, Ecuador (h) 0-1, Uruguay (h) 0-1, Chile (a) 0-4, Paraguay (h) 0-1, Brazil (a) 0-0, Nigeria (h) 1-0.

ECUADOR

Federacion Ecuatoriana del Futbol, km 4 1/2 via a la Costa (Avda. del Bombero), PO Box 09-01-7447 Guayaquil.
Founded: 1925; *National Colours:* Yellow shirts, blue shorts, red stockings.
International matches 2008
Haiti (h) 3-1, France (a) 0-2, Argentina (a) 1-1, Colombia (h) 0-0, Colombia (a) 1-0, Bolivia (h) 3-1, Uruguay (a) 0-0, Chile (h) 1-0, Venezuela (a) 1-3, Mexico (h) 1-2, Iran (a) 1-0.

PARAGUAY

Asociacion Paraguaya de Futbol, Estadio De Los Defensores del Chaco, Calles Mayor Martinez 1393, Asuncion.
Founded: 1906; *National Colours:* Red and white shirts, blue shorts, blue stockings.
International matches 2008
Honduras (h) 0-2, South Africa (a) 0-3, Ivory Coast (a) 1-1, Japan (a) 0-0, France (a) 0-0, Brazil (h) 2-0, Bolivia (a) 2-4, Saudi Arabia (a) 1-1, Venezuela (h) 2-0, Colombia (a) 1-0, Peru (h) 1-0, Oman (a) 1-0.

PERU

Federacion Peruana De Futbol, Av. Aviacion 2085, San Luis, Lima 30.
Founded: 1922; *National Colours:* White shirts with red stripe, white shorts with red lines, white stockings with red line.
International matches 2008
Bolivia (a) 1-2, Costa Rica (h) 3-1, Spain (a) 1-3, Mexico (a) 0-4, Colombia (h) 1-1, Uruguay (a) 0-6, Venezuela (h) 1-0, Argentina (h) 1-1, Bolivia (a) 0-3, Paraguay (a) 0-1.

URUGUAY

Asociacion Uruguaya De Futbol, Guayabo 1531, 11200 Montevideo.
Founded: 1900; *National Colours:* Sky blue shirts with white collar/cuffs, black shorts and stockings with sky blue borders.
International matches 2008
Colombia (h) 2-2, Turkey (a) 3-2, Norway (a) 2-2, Venezuela (h) 1-1, Peru (h) 6-0, Japan (a) 3-1, Colombia (a) 1-0, Ecuador (h) 0-0, France (a) 0-0, Argentina (a) 1-2, Bolivia (a) 2-2.

VENEZUELA

Federacion Venezolana De Futbol, Avda. Santos Erminy Ira, Calle las Delicias Torre Mega II, P.H. Sabana Grande, Caracas 1050.
Founded: 1926; *National Colours:* Burgundy shirts, white shorts and stockings.
International matches 2008
Haiti (h) 1-0, Haiti (h) 1-1, El Salvador (h) 1-0, Bolivia (h) 0-1, Colombia (a) 2-5, Brazil (a) 2-0, Netherlands Antilles (a) 1-0, Uruguay (a) 1-1, Chile (h) 2-3, Syria (h) 4-1, Peru (a) 0-1, Paraguay (a) 0-2, Brazil (h) 0-4, Ecuador (h) 3-1, Angola (h) 0-0.

ASIA

AFGHANISTAN

Afghanistan Football Federation, PO Box 5099, Kabul.
Founded: 1933; *National Colours:* All white with red lines.
International matches 2008
Bangladesh (a) 0-0, Kyrgyzstan (a) 1-0, Sri Lanka (a) 2-2, Bangladesh (a) 2-2, Bhutan (h) 1-3, India (a) 0-1, Turkmenistan (h) 0-5, Tajikistan (h) 0-4, Nepal (a) 2-2, Malaysia (a) 0-6.

AUSTRALIA

Soccer Australia Ltd, Level 3, East Stand, Stadium Australia, Edwin Flack Avenue, Homebush, NSW 2127.
Founded: 1961; *National Colours:* All green with gold trim.
International matches 2008
Qatar (h) 3-0, Singapore (a) 0-0, China (a) 0-0, Ghana (h) 1-0, Iraq (h) 1-0, Iraq (a) 0-1, Qatar (a) 3-1, China (h) 0-1, South Africa (h) 2-2, Holland (a) 2-1, Uzbekistan (a) 1-0, Qatar (h) 4-0, Bahrain (a) 1-0.

BAHRAIN

Bahrain Football Association, P.O. Box 5464, Manama.
Founded: 1957; *National Colours:* All red.
International matches 2008
Kuwait (h) 1-0, Syria (h) 1-2, Yemen (h) 2-1, Oman (a) 1-0, Qatar (a) 2-1, Iran (h) 1-0, Japan (h) 1-0, Singapore (a) 1-0, Thailand (a) 3-2, Thailand (h) 1-1, Oman (h) 1-1, Japan (a) 0-1, Burkina Faso (h) 3-1, UAE (a) 3-2, Japan (h) 2-3, Qatar (a) 1-1, Azerbaijan (h) 1-2, Saudi Arabia (a) 0-4, Australia (h) 0-1, Saudi Arabia (h) 1-0.

BANGLADESH

Bangladesh Football Federation, Bangabandhu National Stadium-1, Dhaka 1000.
Founded: 1972; *National Colours:* Orange shirts, white shorts, green stockings.
International matches 2008
Afghanistan (h) 0-0, Kyrgyzstan (a) 1-2, Bhutan (h) 1-1, Afghanistan (h) 2-2, Sri Lanka (a) 0-1, Burma (a) 0-1, Vietnam (h) 2-2, Burma (a) 0-0, Indonesia (h) 0-2.

BHUTAN

Bhutan Football Federation, P.O. Box 365, Thimphu.
Founded: 1983; *National Colours:* All yellow and red.
International matches 2008
Tajikistan (h) 1-3, Brunei (h) 1-1, Philippines (a) 0-3, Bangladesh (a) 1-1, Sri Lanka (a) 0-2, Afghanistan (a) 3-1, India (a) 1-2.

BRUNEI DARUSSALAM

The Football Association of Brunei Darussalam, P.O. Box 2010, 1920 Bandar Seri Begawan BS 8674.
Telephone: 00673-2/382 761; *Fax:* 00673-2/382 760.
Founded: 1959; *Number of Clubs:* 22; *Number of Players:* 830; *National Colours:* Yellow shirts, black shorts, black and white stockings.
International matches 2008
Philippines (a) 0-1, Bhutan (a) 1-1, Tajikistan (h) 0-4, Philippines (h) 1-1, Timor-Leste (a) 4-1, Laos (a) 2-3, Cambodia (a) 1-2.

BURMA

Myanmar Football Federation, Youth Training Centre, Thingankyun Township, Yangon.
Founded: 1947; *National Colours:* Red shirts, white shorts, red stockings.
International matches 2008
Nepal (h) 3-0, Sri Lanka (a) 3-1, North Korea (a) 0-1, India (a) 0-1, North Korea (h) 0-4, Cambodia (a) 7-1, Indonesia (a) 0-4, Vietnam (a) 3-2, Turkmenistan (h) 1-2, Bangladesh (h) 1-0, Malaysia (a) 0-4, Bangladesh (h) 1-0, Indonesia (h) 2-1, Malaysia (h) 4-1, Indonesia (h) 1-0, Indonesia (a) 0-3, Singapore (a) 1-3, Cambodia (h) 3-2.

CAMBODIA

Cambodian Football Federation, Chaeng Maeng Village, Rd. Kab Srov, Sangkat Samrong Krom, Khan Dangkor, Phnom-Penh .
Founded: 1933; *National Colours:* All blue.
International matches 2008
Nepal (h) 0-1, Macao (h) 3-1, Indonesia (a) 0-7, Burma (h) 1-7, Laos (h) 3-2, Timor-Leste (h) 2-2, Philippines (h) 2-3, Brunei (h) 2-1, Singapore (a) 0-5, Indonesia (a) 0-4, Burma (a) 2-3.

CHINA PR

Football Association of The People's Republic of China, 9 Tiyuguan Road, Beijing 100763.
Founded: 1924; *National Colours:* All white.
International matches 2008
UAE (a) 0-0, Lebanon (h) 0-0, Syria (h) 2-1, Iraq (a) 1-1, South Korea (h) 2-3, Japan (h) 0-1, North Korea (h) 3-1, Thailand (h) 3-3, Australia (h) 0-0, Mexico (a) 0-1, El Salvador (a) 2-2, Jordan (h) 2-0, Qatar (a) 0-0, Qatar (h) 0-1, Iraq (h) 1-2, Australia (a) 1-0, Oman (a) 1-3, Iran (h) 0-2, Jordan (a) 1-0.

CHINESE TAIPEI

Chinese Taipei Football Association, 2F No. Yu Men St., Taipei, Taiwan 104.
Founded: 1936; *National Colours:* Blue shirts and shorts, white stockings.
International matches 2008
Pakistan (h) 1-2, Guam (h) 4-1, Sri Lanka (h) 2-2, India (a) 0-3, India (a) 2-2.

GUAM

Guam Football Association, P.O.Box 5093, Agana, Guam 96932.
Founded: 1975; *National Colours:* Blue shirts, white shorts, blue stockings.
International matches 2008
Sri Lanka (h) 1-5, Chinese Taipei (a) 1-4, Pakistan (a) 2-8.

HONG KONG

The Hong Kong Football Association Ltd, 55 Fat Kwong Street, Homantin, Kowloon, Hong Kong.
Founded: 1914; *National Colours:* All red.
International matches 2008
Macao (a) 9-1.

INDIA

All India Football Federation, Nehru Stadium (West Stand), Fatorda Margao-Goa 403 602.
Founded: 1937; *National Colours:* Sky blue shirts, navy blue shorts, sky and navy blue stockings.
International matches 2008
Chinese Taipei (h) 3-0, Chinese Taipei (h) 2-2, Nepal (h) 4-0, Pakistan (h) 2-1, Maldives (a) 1-0, Bhutan (h) 2-1, Maldives (h) 0-1, Malaysia (h) 1-1, Afghanistan (h) 1-0, Tajikistan (h) 1-1, Turkmenistan (h) 2-1, Burma (h) 1-0, Tajikistan (h) 4-1.

INDONESIA

Football Association of Indonesia, Gelora Bung Karno, Pintu X-XI, Jakarta 10270.
Founded: 1930; *National Colours:* Red shirts, white shorts, red stockings.
International matches 2008
Yemen (h) 1-0, Malaysia (h) 1-1, Vietnam (h) 1-0, Cambodia (h) 7-0, Burma (h) 4-0, Bangladesh (a) 2-0, Burma (a) 1-2, Burma (a) 1-2, Burma (h) 3-0, Cambodia (h) 4-0, Singapore (h) 0-2, Thailand (h) 0-1, Thailand (a) 1-2.

IRAN

IR Iran Football Federation, No. 16-4th deadend, Pakistan Street, PO Box 15316-6967 Shahid Beheshti Avenue, Tehran 15316.
Founded: 1920; *National Colours:* All white.
International matches 2008
Qatar (a) 0-0, Costa Rica (h) 0-0, Syria (h) 0-0, Bahrain (a) 0-1, Kuwait (a) 2-2, Zambia (h) 3-2, UAE (h) 0-0, UAE (a) 1-0, Syria (a) 2-0, Kuwait (h) 2-0, Palestine (h) 3-0, Qatar (h) 6-1, Syria (h) 2-0, Jordan (h) 2-1, Azerbaijan (h) 1-0, Saudi Arabia (a) 1-1, North Korea (h) 2-1, Qatar (a) 1-0, UAE (a) 1-1, Ecuador (a) 0-1, China (a) 2-0.

IRAQ

Iraqi Football Association, Olympic Committee Building, Palestine Street, PO Box 484, Baghdad.
Founded: 1948; *National Colours:* All black.
International matches 2008
Jordan (a) 1-1, UAE (a) 1-0, China (h) 1-1, Kuwait (a) 0-0, Qatar (a) 0-2, Syria (a) 1-2, Thailand (a) 1-2, Australia (a) 0-1, Australia (h) 1-0, China (a) 2-1, Qatar (h) 0-1, UAE (a) 2-2.

JAPAN

Japan Football Association, JFA House, 3-10-15, Hongo, Bunkyo-ku, Tokyo 113-0033.
Founded: 1921; *National Colours:* Blue shirts, white shorts, blue stockings.
International matches 2008
Chile (h) 0-0, Bosnia (h) 3-0, Thailand (h) 4-1, North Korea (h) 1-1, China (a) 1-0, South Korea (h) 1-1, Bahrain (a) 0-1, Ivory Coast (h) 1-0, Paraguay (h) 0-0, Oman (h) 3-0, Oman (a) 1-1, Thailand (a) 3-0, Bahrain (h) 1-0, Uruguay (h) 1-3, Bahrain (a) 3-2, UAE (h) 1-1, Uzbekistan (h) 1-1, Qatar (a) 3-0, Syria (h) 3-1.

JORDAN

Jordan Football Association, P.O. Box 962024 Al Hussein Sports City, 11196 Amman.
Founded: 1949; *National Colours:* All white and red.
International matches 2008
Iraq (h) 1-1, Singapore (h) 2-1, Lebanon (h) 4-1, North Korea (h) 0-1, Qatar (a) 1-2, Uzbekistan (a) 1-4, Turkmenistan (a) 2-0, China (a) 0-2, South Korea (a) 2-2, South Korea (h) 0-1, North Korea (a) 0-2, Turkmenistan (h) 2-0, Syria (h) 0-0, Oman (h) 3-1, Qatar (h) 3-0, Iran (a) 1-2, South Korea (a) 0-1, Palestine (a) 1-1, Oman (a) 0-2, China (h) 0-1.

KOREA, NORTH

Football Association of The Democratic People's Rep. of Korea, Kumsong-dong, Kwangbok Street, Mangyongdae Distr, PO Box 56, Pyongyang FNJ-PRK.
Founded: 1945; *National Colours:* All white.
International matches 2008
Jordan (a) 1-0, Japan (a) 1-1, South Korea (h) 1-1, China (a) 1-3, South Korea (h) 0-0, Turkmenistan (a) 0-0, Turkmenistan (h) 1-0, Jordan (h) 2-0, South Korea (a) 0-0, Sri Lanka (h) 3-0, Nepal (a) 1-0, Burma (h) 1-0, Tajikistan (h) 0-1, Burma (a) 4-0, Qatar (a) 1-2, Uzbekistan (a) 0-0, UAE (a) 2-1, South Korea (h) 1-1, Iran (a) 1-2, Thailand (a) 0-1, Vietnam (a) 0-0.

KOREA, SOUTH

Korea Football Association, 1-131 Sinmunno, 2-ga, Jongno-Gu, Seoul 110-062.
Founded: 1928; *National Colours:* Red shirts, blue shorts, red stockings.
International matches 2008
Chile (h) 0-1, Turkmenistan (h) 4-0, China (a) 3-2, North Korea (a) 1-1, Japan (a) 1-1, North Korea (a) 0-0, Jordan (h) 2-2, Jordan (a) 1-0, Turkmenistan (a) 3-1, North Korea (h) 0-0, Jordan (h) 1-0, North Korea (a) 1-1, Uzbekistan (h) 3-0, UAE (h) 4-1, Qatar (a) 1-1, Saudi Arabia (a) 2-0.

KUWAIT

Kuwait Football Association, P.O. Box 2029, Udiliya, Block 4 Al-Ittihad Street, Safat 13021.
Founded: 1952; *National Colours:* All blue.
International matches 2008
Lebanon (h) 3-2, Ivory Coast (h) 0-2, Bahrain (a) 0-1, Singapore (h) 0-2, Oman (a) 1-1, UAE (a) 0-2, Iran (h) 2-2, Iraq (h) 0-0, Qatar (a) 1-1, Saudi Arabia (a) 1-2, Syria (a) 0-1, Syria (h) 4-2, UAE (h) 2-3, Iran (a) 0-2.

KYRGYZSTAN

Football Federation of Kyrgyz Republic, PO Box 1484, Kurenkeeva Street 195, Bishkek 720040, Kyrgyzstan.
Founded: 1992; *National Colours:* Red shirts, white shorts, red stockings.
International matches 2008
Oman (a) 0-2, Afghanistan (h) 0-1, Bangladesh (h) 2-1.

LAOS

Federation Lao de Football, National Stadium, Kounboulo Street, PO Box 3777, Vientiane 856-21, Laos.
Founded: 1951; *National Colours:* All red.
International matches 2008
Cambodia (a) 2-3, Philippines (a) 2-1, Brunei (h) 3-2, Timor-Leste (h) 2-1, Malaysia (a) 0-3, Thailand (a) 0-6, Vietnam (a) 0-4.

LEBANON

Federation Libanaise De Football-Association, P.O. Box 4732, Verdun Street, Bristol, Radwan Centre Building, Beirut.
Founded: 1933; *National Colours:* Red shirts, white shorts, red stockings.

International matches 2008
Kuwait (a) 2-3, China (a) 0-0, Jordan (a) 1-4, Uzbekistan (h) 0-1, Singapore (a) 0-2, Maldives (h) 4-0, Maldives (a) 2-1, Qatar (a) 1-2, Saudi Arabia (a) 1-4, Saudi Arabia (h) 1-2, Uzbekistan (a) 0-3, Singapore (h) 1-2.

MACAO

Associacao De Futebol De Macau (AFM), Ave. da Amizade 405, Seng Vo Kok, 13 Andar "A", Macau.
Founded: 1939; *National Colours:* All green.
International matches 2008
Nepal (a) 2-3, Cambodia (a) 1-3, Hong Kong (h) 1-0.

MALAYSIA

Football Association of Malaysia, 3rd Floor, Wisma Fam, Jalan, SSA/9, Kelana Jaya Selangor Darul Ehsan 47301.
Founded: 1933; *National Colours:* All yellow and black.
International matches 2008
Pakistan (h) 4-1, Nepal (h) 4-0, Afghanistan (h) 6-0, Burma (h) 4-0, Burma (a) 1-4, Singapore (h) 2-2, Laos (h) 3-0, Vietnam (h) 2-3, Thailand (a) 0-3.

MALDIVES REPUBLIC

Football Association of Maldives, National Stadium G. Banafsaa Magu 20-04, Male.
Founded: 1982; *National Colours:* Red shirts, Green shorts, white stockings.
International matches 2008
Lebanon (a) 0-4, Lebanon (h) 1-2, Pakistan (h) 3-0, Nepal (h) 4-1, India (h) 0-1, Sri Lanka (a) 1-0, India (a) 1-0.

MONGOLIA

Mongolia Football Federation, PO Box 259 Ulaan-Baatar 210646.
National Colours: White shirts, red shorts, white stockings.

NEPAL

All-Nepal Football Association, AMFA House, Ward No. 4, Bishalnagar, PO Box 12582, Kathmandu.
Founded: 1951; *National Colours:* All red.
International matches 2008
Pakistan (h) 2-1, Pakistan (h) 0-2, Thailand (a) 0-7, Macao (h) 3-2, Cambodia (a) 1-0, India (a) 0-4, Maldives (a) 1-4, Pakistan (a) 4-1, Burma (a) 0-3, North Korea (h) 0-1, Sri Lanka (h) 3-0, Nepal (h) 4-0, Afghanistan (h) 2-2.

OMAN

Oman Football Association, P.O. Box 3462, Ruwi Postal Code 112.
Founded: 1978; *National Colours:* All white.
International matches 2008
Singapore (h) 2-0, Kuwait (h) 1-1, Bahrain (h) 0-1, UAE (h) 1-1, Thailand (a) 1-0, Liberia (h) 1-0, Kyrgyzstan (h) 2-0, Yemen (h) 0-0, Syria (a) 1-2, Turkmenistan (h) 2-1, Japan (a) 0-3, Japan (h) 1-1, Bahrain (a) 1-1, Thailand (h) 2-1, Syria (a) 1-2, Jordan (a) 1-3, Uzbekistan (h) 2-0, Morocco (h) 0-0, Zimbabwe (h) 3-2, Jordan (h) 2-0, Paraguay (h) 0-1, China (h) 3-1, Ecuador (h) 2-0.

PAKISTAN

Pakistan Football Federation, 6 National Hockey Stadium, Feroze Pure Road, Lahore, Pakistan.
Founded: 1948; *National Colours:* All green and white.
International matches 2008
Nepal (a) 1-2, Nepal (a) 2-0, Chinese Taipei (a) 2-1, Sri Lanka (h) 1-7, Guam (h) 9-2, Maldives (a) 0-3, India (a) 1-2, Nepal (h) 1-4, Malaysia (a) 1-4.

PALESTINE

Palestinian Football Federation, Al-Yarmouk, Gaza.
Founded: 1928; *National Colours:* White shirts, black shorts, white stockings.
International matches 2008
Iran (a) 0-3, Qatar (h) 0-1, Jordan (h) 1-1.

PHILIPPINES

Philippine Football Federation, Room 405, Building V, Philsports Complex, Meralco Avenue, Pasig City, Metro Manila.
Founded: 1907; *National Colours:* All blue.
International matches 2008
Brunei (h) 1-0, Tajikistan (h) 0-0, Bhutan (h) 3-0, Timor-Leste (h) 1-0, Brunei (a) 1-1, Laos (h) 1-2, Cambodia (a) 3-2.

QATAR

Qatar Football Association, 7th Floor, QNOC Building, Cornich, P.O. Box 5333, Doha.
Founded: 1960; *National Colours:* All white.
International matches 2008
Iran (h) 0-0, Syria (a) 0-0, Australia (a) 0-3, Iraq (h) 2-0, Bahrain (h) 1-2, Jordan (h) 2-1, Kuwait (h) 1-1, Lebanon (h) 2-1, China (h) 0-0, China (a) 1-0, Australia (h) 1-3, Iraq (a) 1-0, Palestine (a) 1-0, Iran (a) 1-6, Jordan (a) 0-3, Tajikistan (h) 5-0, North Korea (h) 2-1, Saudi Arabia (a) 1-2, Uzbekistan (h) 3-0, Bahrain (h) 1-1, Australia (a) 0-4, Iran (h) 0-1, South Korea (h) 1-1, Japan (h) 0-3.

SAUDI ARABIA

Saudi Arabian Football Federation, Al Mather Quarter (Olympic Complex), Prince Faisal Bin Fahad Street, P.O. Box 5844, Riyadh 11432.
Founded: 1959; *National Colours:* White shirts, green shorts, white stockings.
International matches 2008
Luxembourg (h) 2-1, Singapore (h) 2-0, Uzbekistan (a) 0-3, Syria (h) 1-0, Kuwait (h) 2-1, Lebanon (h) 4-1, Lebanon (a) 2-1, Singapore (a) 3-0, Uzbekistan (h) 4-0, Paraguay (h) 1-1, Qatar (h) 2-1, Iran (h) 1-1, UAE (a) 2-1, Thailand (h) 1-0, Bahrain (h) 4-0, South Korea (h) 0-2, Bahrain (a) 0-1, Syria (h) 1-1.

SINGAPORE

Football Association of Singapore, Jalan Besar Stadium, 100 Tyrwhitt Road, Singapore 207542.
Founded: 1892; *National Colours:* All red.
International matches 2008
Kuwait (a) 2-0, Oman (a) 0-2, Jordan (a) 1-2, Saudi Arabia (a) 0-2, Australia (h) 0-0, Lebanon (h) 2-0, Bahrain (h) 0-1, Uzbekistan (h) 3-7, Uzbekistan (a) 0-3, Saudi Arabia (h) 0-3, Lebanon (a) 2-1, Vietnam (a) 0-0, Malaysia (a) 2-2, Cambodia (h) 5-0, Burma (h) 3-1, Indonesia (a) 2-0, Vietnam (a) 0-0, Vietnam (h) 0-1.

SRI LANKA

Football Federation of Sri Lanka, 100/9, Independence Avenue, Colombo 07.
Founded: 1939; *National Colours:* All white.
International matches 2008
Guam (a) 5-1, Pakistan (a) 7-1, Chinese Taipei (a) 2-2, Afghanistan (h) 2-2, Bhutan (h) 2-0, Bangladesh (h) 1-0, Maldives (h) 0-1, North Korea (h) 0-3, Burma (h) 1-3, Nepal (a) 0-3.

SYRIA

Syrian Football Federation, PO Box 421, Maysaloon Street, Damascus.
Founded: 1936; *National Colours:* All red.
International matches 2008
Qatar (h) 0-0, Bahrain (h) 2-1, China (a) 1-2, Iran (a) 0-0, UAE (h) 1-1, Oman (h) 2-1, Iraq (h) 2-1, Saudi Arabia (a) 0-1, Kuwait (h) 1-0, Kuwait (a) 2-4, Iran (h) 0-2, UAE (a) 3-1, Jordan (a) 0-0, Oman (h) 2-1, Iran (a) 0-2, Venezuela (a) 1-4, Japan (a) 1-3, Saudi Arabia (a) 1-1.

TAJIKISTAN

Tajikistan Football Federation, 22 Shotemur Ave., Dushanbe 734 025.
Founded: 1991; *National Colours:* All white.
International matches 2008
Bhutan (a) 3-1, Philippines (a) 0-0, Brunei (a) 4-0, Turkmenistan (a) 0-0, India (a) 1-1, Afghanistan (h) 4-0, North Korea (a) 1-0, India (a) 1-4, Qatar (a) 0-5.

THAILAND

The Football Association of Thailand, Gate 3, Rama I Road, Patumwan, Bangkok 10330.
Founded: 1916; *National Colours:* All red.
International matches 2008
Japan (a) 1-4, China (a) 3-3, Oman (h) 0-1, Nepal (h) 7-0, Iraq (h) 2-1, Bahrain (h) 2-3, Bahrain (a) 1-1, Japan (h) 0-3, Oman (a) 1-2, North Korea (h) 1-0, Saudi Arabia (a) 0-1, Vietnam (a) 2-2, Vietnam (h) 2-0, Laos (h) 6-0, Malaysia (h) 3-0, Indonesia (a) 1-0, Indonesia (h) 2-1, Vietnam (h) 1-2, Vietnam (h) 1-1 .

TIMOR-LESTE

Federacao Futebol Timor-Leste, Rua 12 de Novembro Str., Cruz, Dili.
Founded: 2002; *National Colours:* Red shirts, black shorts, red stockings.

International matches 2008
Philippines (a) 0-1, Cambodia (a) 2-2, Brunei (h) 1-4, Laos (a) 1-2.

TURKMENISTAN

Football Association of Turkmenistan, 32 Belinskiy Street, Stadium Kopetdag, Ashgabat 744 001.
Founded: 1992; *National Colours:* Green shirts, white shorts, green stockings.
International matches 2008
South Korea (a) 0-4, Jordan (h) 0-2, Oman (a) 1-2, North Korea (h) 0-0, North Korea (a) 0-1, South Korea (h) 1-3, Jordan (a) 0-2, Tajikistan (h) 0-0, Afghanistan (a) 5-0, India (a) 1-2, Burma (a) 2-1, Vietnam (a) 3-2.

UNITED ARAB EMIRATES

United Arab Emirates Football Association, P.O. Box 916, Abu Dhabi.
Founded: 1971; *National Colours:* All white.
International matches 2008
China (h) 0-0, Iraq (h) 0-1, Kuwait (h) 2-0, Oman (a) 1-1, Syria (a) 1-1, Iran (a) 0-0, Iran (h) 0-1, Kuwait (a) 3-2, Syria (h) 1-3, Algeria (a) 0-1, Bahrain (h) 2-3, North Korea (h) 1-2, Saudi Arabia (h) 1-2, Japan (a) 1-1, South Korea (a) 1-4, Iran (h) 1-1, Iraq (h) 2-2.

UZBEKISTAN

Uzbekistan Football Federation, Massiv Almazar Furkat Street 15/1, 700003 Tashkent, Uzbekistan.
Founded: 1946; *National Colours:* All white.
International matches 2008
Lebanon (a) 1-0, Jordan (h) 4-1, Saudi Arabia (h) 3-0, Singapore (a) 7-3, Singapore (h) 3-0, Lebanon (h) 3-0, Saudi Arabia (a) 0-4, Oman (a) 0-2, North Korea (h) 0-0, Qatar (a) 0-3, Australia (h) 0-1, South Korea (a) 0-3, Japan (a) 1-1.

VIETNAM

Vietnam Football Federation, 18 Ly van Phuc, Dong Da District, Hanoi 844.
Founded: 1962; *National Colours:* All red.
International matches 2008
Indonesia (a) 0-1, Burma (h) 2-3, Turkmenistan (h) 2-3, Singapore (h) 0-0, North Korea (h) 0-0, Thailand (h) 2-2, Thailand (a) 0-2, Malaysia (a) 3-2, Laos (h) 4-0, Singapore (h) 0-0, Singapore (a) 1-0, Thailand (a) 2-1, Thailand (h) 1-1.

YEMEN

Yemen Football Association, Quarter of Sport – Al Jeraf, Behind the Stadium of Ali Mushsen, Al Moreissy in the Sport, Al-Thawra City.
Founded: 1962; *National Colours:* All green.
International matches 2008
Bahrain (a) 1-2, Tanzania (h) 2-1, Indonesia (a) 0-1, Oman (a) 0-0, Sudan (h) 1-1.

CONCACAF

ANGUILLA

Anguilla Football Association, P.O. Box 1318, The Valley, Anguilla, BWI.
Founded: 1990; *National Colours:* Turquoise, white, orange and blue shirts and shorts, turquoise and orange stockings.
International matches 2008
El Salvador (a) 0-12, El Salvador (h) 0-4, St Vincent (h) 1-3, Martinique (a) 1-3.

ANTIGUA & BARBUDA

The Antigua/Barbuda Football Association, Newgate Street, P.O. Box 773, St John's.
Founded: 1928; *National Colours:* Red, black, yellow and blue shirts, black shorts and stockings.
International matches 2008
Barbados (a) 2-3, Aruba (a) 3-0, Aruba (h) 1-0, St Lucia (h) 6-1, St Kitts (h) 2-0, Cuba (h) 3-4, Cuba (a) 0-4, Bermuda (h) 4-0, Cayman Islands (a) 1-1, St Martin (h) 3-2, Guyana (h) 3-0, Trinidad & Tobago (a) 2-3, Guyana (h) 2-1, St Kitts (h) 4-3, Haiti (h) 1-1, Cuba (h) 0-3, Guadeloupe (h) 2-2.

ARUBA

Arubaanse Voetbal Bond, Ferguson Street, Z/N P.O. Box 376, Oranjestad, Aruba.
Founded: 1932; *National Colours:* Yellow shirts, blue shorts, yellow and blue stockings.

International matches 2008
Antigua (h) 0-3, Antigua (a) 0-1, Netherlands Antilles (a) 0-0, Grenada (h) 1-3.

BAHAMAS

Bahamas Football Association, Plaza on the Way, West Bay Street, P.O. Box N 8434, Nassau, NP.
Founded: 1967; *National Colours:* Yellow shirts, black shorts, yellow stockings.
International matches 2008
British Virgin Islands (h) 1-1, British Virgin Islands (a) 2-2, Jamaica (a) 0-7, Jamaica (h) 0-6.

BARBADOS

Barbados Football Association, Hildor No. 4, 10th Avenue, P.O. Box 1362, Belleville-St. Michael, Barbados.
Founded: 1910; *National Colours:* Royal blue and gold shirts, gold shorts, white, gold and blue stockings.
International matches 2008
Antigua (h) 3-2, Dominica (a) 1-1, St Vincent (a) 2-0, Grenada (a) 1-1, Dominica (h) 1-0, Trinidad & Tobago (a) 0-3, Bermuda (a) 1-2, Bermuda (a) 0-3, USA (a) 0-8, USA (h) 0-1, British Virgin Islands (h) 2-1, St Kitts (a) 3-1, Surinam (h) 3-2, Cuba (a) 1-1, Netherlands Antilles (h) 2-1, Jamaica (a) 2-1, Trinidad & Tobago (h) 1-2, Grenada (h) 2-4.

BELIZE

Belize National Football Association, 26 Hummingbird Highway, Belmopan, P.O. Box 1742, Belize City.
Founded: 1980; *National Colours:* Red, white and black shirts, black shorts, red and black stockings.
International matches 2008
El Salvador (h) 0-1, St Kitts (h) 3-1, St Kitts (a) 1-1, Honduras (a) 0-2, Mexico (h) 0-2, Mexico (a) 0-7.

BERMUDA

The Bermuda Football Association, 48 Cedar Avenue, Hamilton HM12.
Founded: 1928; *National Colours:* All blue.
International matches 2008
Puerto Rico (h) 0-1, Cayman Islands (h) 1-1, Cayman Islands (a) 3-1, Barbados (h) 2-1, Barbados (h) 3-0, Trinidad & Tobago (a) 2-1, Trinidad & Tobago (h) 0-2, Antigua (h) 0-4, St Martin (h) 7-0, Cayman Islands (a) 0-0.

BRITISH VIRGIN ISLANDS

British Virgin Islands Football Association, P.O. Box 29, Road Town, Tortola, BVI.
National Colours: Gold and green shirts, green shorts, green stockings.
International matches 2008
US Virgin Islands (h) 0-0, US Virgin Islands (h) 1-1, Bahamas (a) 1-1, Bahamas (h) 2-2, St Kitts (a) 0-4, Barbados (h) 1-2.

US VIRGIN ISLANDS

USVI Soccer Federation Inc., 54, Castle Coakley, PO Box 2346, Kingshill, St Croix 00851.
National Colours: Royal blue and gold shirts, royal blue shorts and stockings.
International matches 2008
British Virgin Islands (a) 0-0, British Virgin Islands (a) 1-1, Grenada (a) 0-10.

CANADA

The Canadian Soccer Association, Place Soccer Canada, 237 Metcalfe Street, Ottawa, ONT K2P 1R2.
Founded: 1912; *National Colours:* All red.
International matches 2008
Estonia (a) 0-2, Brazil (h) 2-3, Panama (h) 2-2, St Vincent (a) 3-0, St Vincent (h) 4-1, Jamaica (h) 1-1, Honduras (h) 1-2, Mexico (a) 1-2, Honduras (a) 1-3, Mexico (h) 2-2, Jamaica (a) 0-3.

CAYMAN ISLANDS

Cayman Islands Football Association, PO Box 178 GT, Truman Bodden Sports Complex, Olympic Way Off Walkers Rd, George Town, Grand Cayman, Cayman Islands WI.
Founded: 1966; *National Colours:* Red and white shirts, blue and white shorts, white and red stockings.
International matches 2008
Bermuda (a) 1-1, Bermuda (h) 1-3, St Martin (h) 3-0, Antigua (h) 1-1, Bermuda (h) 0-0, Guadeloupe (a) 1-7, Martinique (h) 0-1, Grenada (h) 2-4, Jamaica (h) 0-2.

COSTA RICA

Federacion Costarricense De Futbol, Costado Norte Estatua Leon Cortes, San Jose 670-1000.
Founded: 1921; *National Colours:* Red shirts, blue shorts, white stockings.
International matches 2008
Sweden (h) 0-1, Iran (a) 0-0, Jamaica (a) 1-1, Peru (a) 1-3, Grenada (a) 2-2, Grenada (h) 3-0, El Salvador (h) 1-0, Surinam (h) 7-0, Haiti (a) 3-1, Surinam (a) 4-1, Haiti (h) 2-0, El Salvador (a) 3-1.

CUBA

Asociacion de Futbol de Cuba, Calle 13 No. 661, Esq. C. Vedado, ZP 4, La Habana.
Founded: 1924; *National Colours:* All red, white and blue.
International matches 2008
Guyana (a) 1-2, Guyana (h) 0-0, Antigua (a) 4-3, Antigua (h) 4-0, St Vincent (h) 1-0, Trinidad & Tobago (h) 1-3, USA (h) 0-1, Guatemala (a) 1-4, USA (a) 1-6, Guatemala (h) 2-1, Netherlands Antilles (h) 7-1, Barbados (h) 1-1, Surinam (h) 6-0, Trinidad & Tobago (a) 0-3, Guadeloupe (h) 2-1, Antigua (h) 3-0, Haiti (h) 0-1, Grenada (h) 2-2, Guadeloupe (h) 0-0.

DOMINICA

Dominica Football Association, 33 Great Marlborough Street, Roseau.
Founded: 1970; *National Colours:* Emerald green shirts, black shorts, green stockings.
International matches 2008
Guadeloupe (h) 0-3, Barbados (h) 1-1, Barbados (a) 0-1, Guyana (a) 0-3, Surinam (h) 1-3.

DOMINICAN REPUBLIC

Federacion Dominicana De Futbol, Centro Olimpico Juan Pablo Duarte, Ensanche Miraflores, Apartado De Correos No. 1953, Santo Domingo.
Founded: 1953; *National Colours:* Navy blue shirts, white shorts, red stockings.
International matches 2008
Haiti (h) 1-2, Haiti (h) 0-2, Puerto Rico (a) 0-1, Trinidad & Tobago (a) 0-9.

EL SALVADOR

Federacion Salvadorena De Futbol, Primera Calle Poniente No. 2025, San Salvador CA1029.
Founded: 1935; *National Colours:* All blue.
International matches 2008
Belize (a) 1-0, Haiti (a) 0-0, Haiti (a) 0-0, Anguilla (h) 12-0, Trinidad & Tobago (a) 0-1, Venezuela (a) 0-1, Anguilla (a) 4-0, China (h) 2-2, Guatemala (h) 0-0, Panama (a) 0-1, Panama (h) 3-1, Guatemala (h) 0-0, Jamaica (h) 0-0, Trinidad & Tobago (h) 1-3, Costa Rica (a) 0-1, Haiti (h) 5-0, Surinam (a) 2-0, Haiti (a) 0-0, Surinam (h) 3-0, Bolivia (h) 2-0, Costa Rica (h) 1-3.

GRENADA

Grenada Football Association, P.O. Box 326, National Stadium, Queens Park, St George's, Grenada, W.I.
Founded: 1924; *National Colours:* Green and yellow striped shirts, red shorts, yellow stockings.
International matches 2008
Guyana (a) 2-1, St Vincent (a) 2-1, Barbados (h) 1-1, US Virgin Islands (h) 10-0, Trinidad & Tobago (a) 0-2, Jamaica (h) 2-1, Costa Rica (h) 2-2, Costa Rica (a) 0-3, Aruba (h) 3-1, Netherlands Antilles (a) 0-2, Martinique (h) 2-2, Guadeloupe (a) 1-2, Cayman Islands (h) 4-2, Trinidad & Tobago (h) 2-1, Jamaica (a) 4-0, Barbados (h) 4-2, Cuba (h) 2-2, Jamaica (a) 0-2.

GUADELOUPE

Ligue Guadeloupeenne de Football, Rue de la Ville D'Orly, Bergevin, 97110, Pointe-a-Pitre.
Not affiliated to FIFA.
International matches 2008
Dominica (a) 3-0, Trinidad & Tobago (a) 0-0, St Vincent (h) 1-2, Martinique (h) 1-1, New Caledonia (h) 4-0, Tahiti (h) 1-0, Guyana (h) 4-0, Cayman Islands (h) 7-1, Grenada (h) 2-1, Martinique (h) 3-1, Cuba (h) 1-2, Haiti (h) 3-2, Antigua (h) 2-2, Jamaica (a) 0-2, Cuba (h) 0-0.

GUATEMALA

Federacion Nacional de Futbol de Guatemala, 2a Calle 15-57, Zona 15, Boulevard Vista Hermosa, Guatemala City 01009.

Founded: 1946; *National Colours:* Blue shirts, white shorts, blue stockings.
International matches 2008
Haiti (h) 1-0, El Salvador (a) 0-0, Panama (h) 0-1, Chile (a) 0-2, St Lucia (h) 6-0, St Lucia (a) 3-1, El Salvador (a) 0-0, Bolivia (h) 3-0, USA (h) 1-0, Trinidad & Tobago (a) 1-1, Cuba (h) 4-1, Trinidad & Tobago (h) 0-0, Cuba (a) 1-2, USA (a) 0-2.

GUYANA

Guyana Football Federation, 159 Rupununi Street, Bel Air Park, P.O. Box 10727, Georgetown.
Founded: 1902; *National Colours:* Green shirts and shorts, yellow stockings.
International matches 2008
St Vincent (h) 1-0, Grenada (h) 1-2, St Vincent (a) 2-2, Cuba (h) 2-1, Cuba (h) 0-0, Surinam (a) 0-1, Surinam (h) 1-2, Trinidad & Tobago (a) 0-2, Dominica (h) 3-0, Surinam (h) 1-1, Trinidad & Tobago (a) 0-3, Antigua (a) 0-3, St Kitts (h) 1-1, Antigua (h) 1-2, Trinidad & Tobago (a) 1-1.

HAITI

Federation Haitienne De Football, 128 Avenue Christiophe, P.O. Box 2258, Port-Au-Prince.
Founded: 1904; *National Colours:* Blue shirts, red shorts, blue stockings.
International matches 2008
El Salvador (h) 0-0, El Salvador (h) 0-0, Venezuela (a) 0-1, Venezuela (a) 1-1, Dominican Republic (a) 2-1, Dominican Republic (a) 2-0, Ecuador (a) 1-3, Guatemala (a) 0-1, Honduras (a) 1-3, Netherlands Antilles (h) 0-0, Netherlands Antilles (a) 1-0, Trinidad & Tobago (a) 0-2, Trinidad & Tobago (h) 1-0, Surinam (h) 2-2, El Salvador (a) 0-5, Costa Rica (h) 1-3, El Salvador (h) 0-0, Costa Rica (a) 0-2, Surinam (a) 1-1, Antigua (h) 1-1, Guadeloupe (h) 2-3, Cuba (h) 1-0.

HONDURAS

Federacion Nacional Autonoma De Futbol De Honduras, Colonia Florencia Norte, Ave Roble, Edificio Plaza America, Ave. Roble 1 y 2 Nivel, Tegucigalpa, D.C.
Founded: 1951; *National Colours:* All white.
International matches 2008
Paraguay (h) 2-0, Colombia (h) 2-1, Belize (h) 2-0, Venezuela (h) 1-1, Haiti (h) 3-1, Puerto Rico (h) 4-0, Puerto Rico (a) 2-2, Mexico (a) 1-2, Canada (a) 2-1, Jamaica (h) 2-0, Canada (h) 3-1, Jamaica (a) 0-1, Mexico (h) 1-0.

JAMAICA

Jamaica Football Federation Ltd, 20 St Lucia Crescent, Kingston 5.
Founded: 1910; *National Colours:* Gold shirts, black shorts, gold stockings.
International matches 2008
Costa Rica (h) 1-1, Trinidad & Tobago (h) 2-2, St Vincent (h) 5-1, Trinidad & Tobago (a) 2-1, Grenada (a) 1-2, Bahamas (h) 7-0, Bahamas (a) 6-0, El Salvador (a) 0-0, Canada (a) 1-1, Mexico (a) 0-3, Honduras (a) 0-2, Mexico (h) 1-0, Honduras (h) 1-0, Cayman Islands (a) 2-0, Canada (h) 3-0, Barbados (h) 2-1, Grenada (h) 4-0, Trinidad & Tobago (h) 1-1, Guadeloupe (h) 2-0, Grenada (h) 2-0.

MARTINIQUE

2, Rue Saint John Perse, Nome Tartenson, BP 307, 97203 Fort de France.
Not affiliated to FIFA.
International matches 2008
St Vincent (h) 3-0, Anguilla (h) 3-1, Guadeloupe (h) 1-1, Tahiti (h) 1-0, New Caledonia (h) 1-1, Reunion (h) 0-1, Grenada (h) 2-2, Cayman Islands (h) 1-0, Guadeloupe (a) 1-3.

MEXICO

Federacion Mexicana De Futbol Asociacion, A.C., Colima No. 373, Colonia Roma Mexico DF 06700.
Founded: 1927; *National Colours:* Green shirts with white collar, white shorts, red stockings.
International matches 2008
USA (a) 2-2, Ghana (h) 2-1, China (h) 1-0, Argentina (h) 1-4, Peru (h) 4-0, Belize (h) 2-0, Belize (h) 7-0, Honduras (h) 2-1, Jamaica (h) 3-0, Canada (h) 2-1, Chile (h) 0-1, Jamaica (a) 0-1, Canada (a) 2-2, Ecuador (h) 2-1, Honduras (a) 0-1.

MONSERRAT

Monserrat Football Association Inc., P.O. Box 505, Woodlands, Monserrat.
Founded: 1994; *National Colours:* Green shirts with black and white stripes, green shorts with white stripes, green stockings with black and white stripes.
International matches 2008
Surinam (a) 1-7.

NETHERLANDS ANTILLES

Nederlands Antiliaanse Voetbal Unie, Bonamweg 49, Curacao, NA.
Founded: 1921; *National Colours:* White shirts with red and blue stripes, red shorts with blue and white stripes, white stockings with red stripes.
International matches 2008
Nicaragua (a) 1-0, Nicaragua (h) 2-0, Surinam (h) 2-1, Venezuela (h) 0-1, Haiti (a) 0-0, Haiti (h) 0-1, Trinidad & Tobago (a) 0-2, Aruba (h) 0-0, Grenada (h) 2-0, Cuba (a) 1-7, Surinam (h) 1-2, Barbados (h) 1-2.

NICARAGUA

Federacion Nicaraguense De Futbol, Hospital Pautista 1, Cuadra avajo, 1 cuada al Sur y 1/2, Cuadra Abajo, Managua 976.
Founded: 1931; *National Colours:* Blue shirts, white shorts, blue stockings.
International matches 2008
Netherlands Antilles (h) 0-1, Netherlands Antilles (a) 0-2.

PANAMA

Federacion Panamena De Futbol, Estadio Rommel Fernandez, Puerta 24, Ave. Jose Aeustin Araneo, Apartado Postal 8-391, Zona 8, Panama.
Founded: 1937; *National Colours:* All red.
International matches 2008
Guatemala (h) 1-0, Canada (h) 2-2, Chile (a) 0-0, El Salvador (h) 1-0, El Salvador (a) 1-3, Bolivia (a) 0-1.

PUERTO RICO

Federacion Puertorriquena De Futbol, P.O. Box 193590 San Juan 00919.
Founded: 1940; *National Colours:* Red, blue and white shirts and shorts, red and blue stockings.
International matches 2008
Bermuda (a) 1-0, Trinidad & Tobago (h) 2-2, Dominican Republic (h) 1-0, Honduras (a) 0-4, Honduras (h) 2-2.

ST KITTS & NEVIS

St Kitts & Nevis Football Association, P.O. Box 465, Warner Park, Basseterre, St Kitts, W.I.
Founded: 1932; *National Colours:* Green and yellow shirts, red shorts, yellow stockings.
International matches 2008
Belize (a) 1-3, Belize (h) 1-1, Antigua (a) 0-2, British Virgin Islands (h) 4-0, Barbados (h) 1-3, Guyana (h) 1-1, Trinidad & Tobago (a) 1-3, Antigua (h) 3-4.

ST LUCIA

St Lucia National Football Association, PO Box 255, Sans Souci, Castries, St Lucia.
Founded: 1979; *National Colours:* White shirts and shorts with yellow, blue and black stripes, white, blue and yellow stockings.
International matches 2008
Turks & Caicos (a) 1-2, Turks & Caicos (h) 2-0, Antigua (a) 1-6, Guatemala (a) 0-6, Guatemala (h) 1-3.

ST MARTIN

Comite de Football des Iles du Nord, PO Box 811, S-M 97059.
Not affiliated to FIFA.
International matches 2008
Cayman Islands (h) 0-3, Bermuda (a) 0-7, Antigua (a) 2-3.

ST VINCENT & THE GRENADINES

St Vincent & The Grenadines Football Federation, Sharpe Street, PO Box 1278, Saint George.
Founded: 1979; *National Colours:* Green shirts with yellow border, blue shorts, yellow stockings.
International matches 2008
Guyana (a) 0-1, Guyana (h) 2-2, Grenada (h) 1-2, Guadeloupe (a) 2-1, Barbados (h) 0-2, Jamaica (a) 1-5,

Cuba (a) 0-1, Canada (h) 0-3, Canada (a) 1-4, Martinique (a) 0-3, Anguilla (h) 3-1.

SURINAM

Surinaamse Voetbal Bond, Letitia Vriesde Laan 7, P.O. Box 1223, Paramaribo.
Founded: 1920; *National Colours:* White, green and red shirts, green and white shirts and stockings.
International matches 2008
Monserrat (h) 7-1, Netherlands Antilles.(a) 1-2, Guyana (h) 1-0, Guyana (a) 2-1, Dominica (h) 3-1, Guyana (a) 1-1, Haiti (a) 2-2, Costa Rica (a) 0-7, El Salvador (h) 0-2, Costa Rica (h) 1-4, El Salvador (a) 0-3, Barbados (h) 2-3, Netherlands Antilles (h) 2-1, Cuba (a) 0-6, Haiti (h) 1-1.

TRINIDAD & TOBAGO

Trinidad & Tobago Football Federation, 24–26 Dundonald Street, PO Box 400, Port of Spain.
Founded: 1908; *National Colours:* Red shirts, black shorts, white stockings.
International matches 2008
Puerto Rico (a) 2-2, Guadeloupe (h) 0-0, El Salvador (h) 1-0, Jamaica (a) 2-2, Grenada (h) 2-0, Barbados (h) 3-0, England (h) 0-3, Jamaica (h) 1-2, Bermuda (h) 1-2, Bermuda (a) 2-0, Guyana (h) 2-0, Netherlands Antilles (h) 2-0, Haiti (h) 2-0, Haiti (a) 0-1, El Salvador (a) 3-1, Cuba (a) 3-1, Guyana (h) 3-0, Guatemala (h) 1-1, USA (a) 0-3, Dominican Republic (h) 9-0, Guatemala (a) 0-0, USA (h) 2-1, Antigua (h) 3-2, St Kitts (h) 3-1, Guyana (h) 1-1, Cuba (h) 3-0, Grenada (h) 1-2, Barbados (h) 2-1, Jamaica (a) 1-1.

TURKS & CAICOS

Turks & Caicos Islands Football Association, P.O. Box 626, Tropicana Plaza, Leeward Highway, Providenciales.
Founded: 1996; *National Colours:* All white.
International matches 2008
St Lucia (h) 2-1, St Lucia (a) 0-2.

USA

US Soccer Federation, US Soccer House, 1801–1811 S. Prairie Avenue, Chicago, Illinois 60616.
Founded: 1913; *National Colours:* White shirts, blue shorts, white stockings.
International matches 2008
Sweden (h) 2-0, Mexico (h) 2-2, Poland (a) 3-0, England (a) 0-2, Spain (a) 0-2, Argentina (a) 0-0, Barbados (h) 8-0, Barbados (a) 1-0, Guatemala (h) 1-1, Cuba (a) 1-0, Trinidad & Tobago (h) 3-0, Cuba (h) 6-1, Trinidad & Tobago (a) 1-2, Guatemala (h) 2-0.

OCEANIA

AMERICAN SAMOA

American Samoa Football Association, P.O. Box 282, Pago Pago AS 96799.
Founded: 1984; *National Colours:* Navy blue shirts, white shorts, red stockings.

COOK ISLANDS

Cook Islands Football Association, Victoria Road, Tupapa, P.O. Box 29, Avarua, Rarotonga, Cook Islands.
Founded: 1971; *National Colours:* Green shirts with white sleeves, green shorts, white stockings.

FIJI

Fiji Football Association, PO Box 2514, Government Buildings, Suva.
Founded: 1938; *National Colours:* White shirts, blue shorts and stockings.
International matches 2008
Vanuatu (h) 2-0, Vanuatu (a) 1-2, New Zealand (a) 2-0.

NEW CALEDONIA

Federation Caledonienne de Football, 7 bis, Rue Suffren Quartien latin, BP 560, 99845 Noumea, New Caledonia.
Founded: 1928; *National Colours:* Grey shirts, red shorts, grey stockings.
International matches 2008
Vanuatu (a) 1-1, Vanuatu (h) 3-0, New Zealand (h) 1-3, New Zealand (a) 0-3, Tahiti (h) 1-0.

NEW ZEALAND

New Zealand Soccer Inc., PO Box 301 043, Albany, Auckland, New Zealand.
Founded: 1891; *National Colours:* All white.

International matches 2008
New Caledonia (a) 3-1, New Caledonia (h) 3-0, Fiji (h) 0-2.

PAPUA NEW GUINEA

Papua New Guinea Football Association, PO Box 957, Room II Level I, Haus Tisa, Lae.
Founded: 1962; *National Colours:* Red and yellow shirts, black shorts, yellow stockings.

SAMOA

The Samoa Football Soccer Federation, P.O. Box 960, Apia.
Founded: 1968; *National Colours:* Blue, white and red shirts, blue and white shorts, red and blue stockings.

SOLOMON ISLANDS

Solomon Islands Football Federation, PO Box 854, Honiara, Solomon Islands.
Founded: 1978; *National Colours:* Gold and blue shirts, blue and white shorts, white and blue stockings.

TAHITI

Federation Tahitienne de Football, Rue Coppenrath Stade de Fautana, PO Box 50858 Pirae 98716.
Founded: 1989; *National Colours:* Red shirts, white shorts, red stockings.
International matches 2008
New Caledonia (a) 0-1.

TONGA

Tonga Football Association, Tungi Arcade, Taufa'Ahau Road, P.O. Box 852, Nuku'Alofa, Tonga.
Founded: 1965; *National Colours:* Red shirts, white shorts, red stockings.

TUVALU

Not affiliated to FIFA.

VANUATU

Vanuatu Football Federation, P.O. Box 266, Port Vila, Vanuatu.
Founded: 1934; *National Colours:* Gold and black shirts, black shorts, gold and black stockings.
International matches 2008
New Caledonia (h) 1-1, New Caledonia (a) 0-3, Fiji (a) 0-2, Fiji (h) 2-1.

AFRICA

ALGERIA

Federation Algerienne De Foot-ball, Chemin Ahmed Ouaked, Boite Postale No. 39, Dely-Ibrahim-Alger.
Founded: 1962; *National Colours:* Green shirts, white shorts, green stockings.
International matches 2008
DR Congo (h) 1-1, Senegal (a) 0-1, Liberia (h) 3-0, Gambia (a) 0-1, Gambia (h) 1-0, UAE (h) 1-0, Senegal (h) 3-2, Liberia (a) 0-0, Mali (h) 1-1.

ANGOLA

Federation Angolaise De Football, Compl. da Cidadela Desportiva, B.P. 3449, Luanda.
Founded: 1979; *National Colours:* Red shirts, black shorts, red stockings.
International matches 2008
Egypt (h) 3-3, Morocco (a) 1-2, South Africa (a) 1-1, Senegal (a) 3-1, Tunisia (a) 0-0, Egypt (a) 1-2, Benin (h) 3-0, Niger (a) 1-1, Uganda (a) 1-3, Uganda (h) 0-0, Tunisia (a) 1-1, Benin (a) 2-3, Niger (h) 3-1, Venezuela (a) 0-0.

BENIN

Federation Beninoise De Football, Stade Rene Pleven d'Akpakpa, B.P. 965, Cotonou 01.
Founded: 1962; *National Colours:* Green shirts, Yellow shorts, red stockings.
International matches 2008
Senegal (h) 1-2, Angola (a) 0-3, Uganda (h) 4-1, Niger (a) 2-0, Niger (h) 2-0, Morocco (a) 1-3, Angola (h) 3-2, Uganda (a) 1-2, Egypt (a) 1-5.

BOTSWANA

Botswana Football Association, P.O. Box 1396, Gabarone.
Founded: 1970; *National Colours:* Blue, white and black striped shirts, blue, white and black shorts and stockings.

International matches 2008
South Africa (a) 1-2, Swaziland (a) 4-1, Zimbabwe (h) 0-1, Madagascar (h) 0-0, Mozambique (a) 2-1, Ivory Coast (h) 1-1, Ivory Coast (a) 0-4, Mozambique (h) 0-2, Zimbabwe (a) 0-1, Lesotho (h) 1-0, Madagascar (a) 0-1, Madagascar (h) 0-1.

BURKINA FASO
Federation Burkinabe De Foot-Ball, 01 B.P. 57, Ouagadougou 01.
Founded: 1960; *National Colours:* All green, red and white.
International matches 2008
Cape Verde Islands (h) 0-1, Tunisia (a) 2-1, Burundi (h) 2-0, Seychelles (a) 3-2, Seychelles (h) 4-1, Bahrain (a) 1-3, Tunisia (h) 0-0, Burundi (a) 3-1.

BURUNDI
Federation De Football Du Burundi, Bulding Nyogozi, Boulevard de l'Uprona, B.P. 3426, Bujumbura.
Founded: 1948; *National Colours:* Red and white shirts, white and red shorts, green stockings.
International matches 2008
Rwanda (h) 0-0, Seychelles (h) 1-0, Burkina Faso (a) 0-2, Tunisia (h) 0-1, Tunisia (a) 1-2, Seychelles (a) 2-1, Burkina Faso (h) 1-3.

CAMEROON
Federation Camerounaise De Football, B.P. 1116, Yaounde.
Founded: 1959; *National Colours:* Green shirts, red shorts, yellow stockings.
International matches 2008
Egypt (a) 2-4, Zambia (h) 5-1, Sudan (h) 3-0, Tunisia (h) 3-2, Ghana (a) 1-0, Egypt (a) 0-1, Cape Verde Islands (h) 2-0, Mauritius (a) 3-0, Tanzania (a) 0-0, Tanzania (h) 2-1, Cape Verde Islands (a) 2-1, Mauritius (h) 5-0, South Africa (a) 2-3.

CAPE VERDE ISLANDS
Federacao Cabo-Verdiana De Futebol, Praia Cabo Verde, FCF CX, P.O. Box 234, Praia.
Founded: 1982; *National Colours:* Blue and white shirts and shorts, blue and red stockings.
International matches 2008
Burkina Faso (a) 1-0, Luxembourg (a) 1-1, Cameroon (h) 0-2, Tanzania (h) 1-0, Mauritius (a) 1-0, Mauritius (h) 3-1, Cameroon (h) 1-2, Tanzania (a) 1-3.

CENTRAL AFRICAN REPUBLIC
Federation Centrafricaine De Football, Immeuble Soca Constructa, B.P. 344, Bangui.
Founded: 1937; *National Colours:* Blue and white shirts, white shorts, blue stockings.

CHAD
Federation Tchadienne de Football, B.P. 886, N'Djamena.
Founded: 1962; *National Colours:* Blue shirts, yellow shorts, red stockings.
International matches 2008
Mali (h) 1-2, Congo (h) 2-1, Congo (a) 0-2, Libya (a) 0-3, Sudan (a) 2-1, Sudan (h) 1-3, Mali (a) 1-2.

COMOROS
Federation Comorienne de Football, BP 798, Moroni.
Founded: 1979; *National Colours:* All green.
International matches 2008
Namibia (h) 0-3, Malawi (h) 0-1, Lesotho (h) 0-1.

CONGO
Federation Congolaise De Football, 80 Rue Eugene-Etienne, Centre Ville, PO Box 11, Brazzaville.
Founded: 1962; *National Colours:* Green shirts, yellow shorts, red stockings.
International matches 2008
Mali (a) 2-4, Sudan (h) 1-0, Chad (a) 1-2, Chad (h) 2-0, Mali (h) 1-0, Sudan (a) 0-2.

CONGO DR
Federation Congolaise De Football-Association, Av. de l'Enseignemt 210, C/Kasa-Vubu, Kinshasa 1.
Founded: 1919; *National Colours:* Blue and yellow shirts, yellow and blue shorts, white and blue stockings.
International matches 2008
Gabon (a) 0-0, Algeria (a) 1-1, Egypt (a) 1-2, Malawi (h) 1-0, Djibouti (a) 6-0, Djibouti (h) 5-1, Togo (h) 2-1, Egypt (h) 0-1, Malawi (a) 1-2.

DJIBOUTI
Federation Djiboutienne de Football, Stade el Haoj Hassan Gouled, B.P. 2694, Djibouti.
Founded: 1977; *National Colours:* Green shirts, white shorts, blue stockings.
International matches 2008
Malawi (a) 1-8, Malawi (h) 0-4, Congo DR (h) 0-6, Congo DR (a) 1-5, Malawi (h) 0-3, Egypt (a) 0-4.

EGYPT
Egyptian Football Association, 5 Gabalaya Street, Guezira, El Borg Post Office, Cairo.
Founded: 1921; *National Colours:* Red shirts, white shorts, black stockings.
International matches 2008
Namibia (h) 3-0, Mali (h) 1-0, Angola (a) 3-3, Cameroon (h) 4-2, Sudan (h) 3-0, Zambia (h) 1-1, Angola (h) 2-1, Ivory Coast (a) 4-1, Cameroon (h) 1-0, Argentina (h) 0-2, Congo DR (h) 2-1, Djibouti (a) 4-0, Malawi (a) 0-1, Malawi (h) 2-0, Sudan (a) 0-4, DR Congo (a) 1-0, Djibouti (h) 4-0, Benin (h) 5-1.

ERITREA
The Eritrean National Football Federation, Sematat Avenue 29–31, P.O. Box 3665, Asmara.
Founded: 1996; *National Colours:* Blue shirts, red shorts, green stockings.

ETHIOPIA
Ethiopia Football Federation, Addis Ababa Stadium, P.O. Box 1080, Addis Ababa.
Founded: 1943; *National Colours:* Green shirts, yellow shorts, red stockings.
International matches 2008
Morocco (a) 0-3, Rwanda (h) 1-2, Mauritania (a) 1-0, Mauritania (h) 6-1.

GABON
Federation Gabonaise De Football, B.P. 181, Libreville.
Founded: 1962; *National Colours:* Green, yellow and blue shirts, blue and yellow shorts, white stockings with tri-colour trims.
International matches 2008
Congo DR (h) 0-0, Libya (a) 0-1, Ghana (h) 2-0, Ghana (a) 0-2, Lesotho (h) 2-0, Mali (h) 1-0, Lesotho (a) 3-0, Libya (h) 1-0, Guinea (h) 3-3.

GAMBIA
Gambia Football Association, Independence Stadium, Bakau, P.O. Box 523, Banjul.
Founded: 1952; *National Colours:* All red, blue and white.
International matches 2008
Liberia (a) 1-1, Senegal (h) 0-0, Algeria (h) 1-0, Algeria (a) 0-1, Liberia (h) 3-0, Senegal (a) 1-1.

GHANA
Ghana Football Association, National Sports Council, P.O. Box 1272, Accra.
Founded: 1957; *National Colours:* All yellow.
International matches 2008
Guinea (h) 2-1, Namibia (h) 1-0, Morocco (h) 2-0, Nigeria (h) 2-1, Cameroon (h) 0-1, Ivory Coast (h) 4-2, Mexico (h) 1-2, Australia (a) 0-1, Libya (h) 3-0, Lesotho (a) 3-2, Gabon (a) 0-2, Gabon (h) 2-0, Tanzania (a) 1-1, Libya (a) 0-1, Lesotho (h) 3-0, South Africa (a) 1-2, Tunisia (h) 0-0.

GUINEA
Federation Guineenne De Football, P.O. Box 3645, Conakry.
Founded: 1959; *National Colours:* Red shirts, yellow shorts, green stockings.
International matches 2008
Sudan (h) 6-0, Ghana (a) 1-2, Morocco (h) 3-2, Namibia (h) 1-1, Ivory Coast (a) 0-5, Zimbabwe (h) 0-0, Kenya (a) 0-2, Namibia (a) 2-1, Namibia (h) 4-0, Ivory Coast (h) 1-2, Zimbabwe (a) 0-0, South Africa (a) 1-0, Kenya (h) 3-2, Gabon (h) 3-3.

GUINEA-BISSAU
Federacao De Football Da Guinea-Bissau, Alto Bandim (Nova Sede), PO Box 375 Bissau 1035.
Founded: 1974; *National Colours:* Red, green and yellow shirts, green and yellow shorts, red, green and yellow stockings.

GUINEA, EQUATORIAL

Federacion Ecuatoguineana De Futbol, c/P Patricio Lumumba (Estadio La Paz), Malabo 1071.
Founded: 1986; *National Colours:* All red.
International matches 2008
Sierra Leone (h) 2-0, South Africa (a) 1-4, Nigeria (h) 0-1, Nigeria (a) 0-2, Sierra Leone (a) 1-2, South Africa (h) 0-1.

IVORY COAST

Federation Ivoirienne De Football, 01 PO Box 1202, Abidjan 01.
Founded: 1960; *National Colours:* Orange shirts, black shorts, green stockings.
International matches 2008
Kuwait (a) 2-0, Nigeria (a) 1-0, Benin (h) 4-1, Mali (h) 3-0, Guinea (h) 5-0, Egypt (h) 1-4, Ghana (a) 2-4, Tunisia (a) 0-2, Paraguay (n) 1-1, Japan (n) 0-1, Mozambique (h) 1-0, Madagascar (a) 0-0, Botswana (a) 1-1, Botswana (h) 4-0, Guinea (a) 2-1, Mozambique (a) 1-1, Madagascar (h) 3-0, Israel (a) 2-2.

KENYA

Kenya Football Federation, Nyayo National Stadium, P.O. Box 40234, Nairobi.
Founded: 1960; *National Colours:* All red.
International matches 2008
Namibia (a) 1-2, Guinea (h) 2-0, Zimbabwe (h) 2-0, Zimbabwe (a) 0-0, Malawi (a) 0-0, Namibia (h) 1-0, Guinea (a) 2-3.

LESOTHO

Lesotho Football Association, P.O. Box 1879, Maseru-100, Lesotho.
Founded: 1932; *National Colours:* Blue shirts, green shorts, white stockings.
International matches 2008
Swaziland (a) 2-2, Mozambique (a) 3-2, Swaziland (h) 1-1, Ghana (h) 2-3, Libya (h) 0-1, Libya (a) 0-4, Gabon (a) 0-2, Malawi (h) 0-1, Namibia (h) 1-1, Comoros (a) 1-0, Botswana (a) 1-0, Gabon (h) 0-3, Ghana (a) 0-3.

LIBERIA

Liberia Football Association, Broad and Center Streets, PO Box 10-1066, Monrovia 1000.
Founded: 1936; *National Colours:* Blue shirts, white shorts, red stockings.
International matches 2008
Sudan (h) 2-0, Oman (a) 0-1, Sierra Leone (h) 3-1, Libya (a) 2-4, Gambia (h) 1-1, Algeria (h) 0-3, Senegal (h) 2-2, Senegal (a) 1-3, Gambia (a) 0-3, Algeria (h) 0-0.

LIBYA

Libyan Football Federation, Asayadi Street, Near Janat Al-Areet, P.O. Box 5137, Tripoli.
Founded: 1963; *National Colours:* Green and black shirts, black shorts and stockings.
International matches 2008
Uganda (a) 1-1, Zambia (h) 2-2, Liberia (h) 4-2, Ghana (a) 0-3, Gabon (h) 1-0, Lesotho (a) 1-1, Lesotho (h) 4-0, Senegal (h) 0-0, Chad (h) 3-0, Niger (h) 6-2, Ghana (h) 1-0, Gabon (a) 0-1.

MADAGASCAR

Federation Malagasy de Football, Immeuble Preservatrice Vie-Lot IBF-9B, Rue Rabearivelo-Antsahavola, PO Box 4409, Antananarivo 101.
Founded: 1961; *National Colours:* Red and green shirts, white and green shorts, green and white stockings.
International matches 2008
Mauritius (a) 2-1, Botswana (a) 0-0, Ivory Coast (h) 0-0, Mozambique (h) 1-1, Mozambique (a) 0-3, Swaziland (h) 1-1, Seychelles (h) 1-1, Mauritius (h) 2-1, Mozambique (h) 1-2, Zambia (h) 0-2, Botswana (h) 1-0, Ivory Coast (a) 0-3.

MALAWI

Football Association of Malawi, Mpira House, Old Chileka Road, P.O. Box 865, Blantyre.
Founded: 1966; *National Colours:* Red shirts, white shorts, red and black stockings.
International matches 2008
Namibia (a) 3-1, Tanzania (a) 1-1, Djibouti (h) 8-1, Congo DR (a) 0-1, Egypt (h) 1-0, Egypt (a) 0-2, Kenya (h) 0-0, Lesotho (a) 1-0, Comoros (a) 1-0, Namibia (h) 0-1, Djibouti (a) 3-0, South Africa (a) 0-3, Congo DR (h) 2-1.

MALI

Federation Malienne De Football, Avenue du Mali, Hamdallaye ACI 2000, PO Box 1020, Bamako 12582.
Founded: 1960; *National Colours:* Green shirts, yellow shorts, red stockings.
International matches 2008
Egypt (a) 0-1, Benin (h) 1-0, Nigeria (a) 0-0, Ivory Coast (a) 0-3, Congo (h) 4-2, Chad (a) 2-1, Sudan (a) 2-3, Sudan (h) 3-0, Gabon (h) 0-1, Congo (a) 1-2, Chad (h) 2-1, Algeria (a) 1-1.

MAURITANIA

Federation De Foot-Ball De La Rep. Islamique. De Mauritanie, B.P. 566, Nouakchott.
Founded: 1961; *National Colours:* Green and yellow shirts, yellow shorts, green stockings.
International matches 2008
Rwanda (a) 0-3, Morocco (h) 1-4, Ethiopia (h) 0-1, Ethiopia (a) 1-6, Rwanda (h) 0-1, Morocco (a) 1-4.

MAURITIUS

Mauritius Football Association, Chancery House, 2nd Floor Nos. 303–305, 14 Lislet Geoffroy Street, Port Louis.
Founded: 1952; *National Colours:* All red.
International matches 2008
Tanzania (a) 1-1, Cameroon (h) 0-3, Cape Verde Islands (h) 0-1, Cape Verde Islands (a) 1-3, Seychelles (h) 0-7, Swaziland (h) 1-1, Madagascar (a) 1-2, Tanzania (h) 1-4, Cameroon (a) 0-5.

MOROCCO

Federation Royale Marocaine De Football, 51 Bis Av. Ibn Sina, PO Box 51, Agdal, Rabat 10 000.
Founded: 1955; *National Colours:* All green, white and red.
International matches 2008
Zambia (h) 2-0, Angola (h) 2-1, Namibia (a) 5-1, Guinea (a) 2-3, Ghana (a) 0-2, Belgium (a) 4-1, Ethiopia (h) 3-0, Mauritania (a) 4-1, Rwanda (a) 1-3, Rwanda (h) 2-0, Benin (h) 3-1, Oman (a) 0-0, Mauritania (h) 4-1, Zambia (h) 3-0.

MOZAMBIQUE

Federacao Mocambicana De Futebol, Av. Samora Machel 11-2, Caixa Postal 1467, Maputo.
Founded: 1978; *National Colours:* Red shirts, black shorts, red and black stockings.
International matches 2008
South Africa (a) 0-2, Lesotho (h) 2-3, Ivory Coast (a) 0-1, Botswana (h) 1-2, Madagascar (a) 1-1, Madagascar (h) 3-0, Botswana (a) 2-0, Madagascar (a) 2-1, Swaziland (h) 3-0, Ivory Coast (h) 1-1, Botswana (a) 1-0, Tanzania (a) 0-1.

NAMIBIA

Namibia Football Association, Abraham Mashego Street 8521, Katurua Council of Churches in Namibia, P.O. Box 1345, Windhoek 9000, Namibia.
Founded: 1990; *National Colours:* All red.
International matches 2008
Egypt (a) 0-3, Senegal (a) 1-3, Morocco (h) 1-5, Ghana (a) 0-1, Guinea (h) 1-1, Kenya (h) 2-1, Zimbabwe (a) 0-2, Guinea (h) 1-2, Guinea (a) 0-4, Comoros (a) 3-0, Lesotho (a) 1-1, Malawi (a) 1-0, Kenya (a) 0-1, Zimbabwe (h) 4-2.

NIGER

Federation Nigerienne De Football, Rue de la Tapoa, PO Box 10299, Niamey.
Founded: 1967; *National Colours:* Orange shirts, white shorts, green stockings.
International matches 2008
Uganda (a) 0-1, Angola (h) 1-2, Benin (h) 0-2, Benin (h) 0-2, Libya (a) 2-6, Uganda (h) 3-1, Angola (a) 1-3.

NIGERIA

Nigeria Football Association, Plot 2033, Olusegun, Obasanjo Way, Zone 7, Wuse Abuja, PO Box 5101 Garki, Abuja, Nigeria.
Founded: 1945; *National Colours:* All green and white.
International matches 2008
Sudan (h) 2-0, Ivory Coast (h) 0-1, Mali (h) 0-0, Benin (h) 2-0, Ghana (a) 1-2, Austria (a) 1-1, South Africa (h) 2-0, Sierra Leone (a) 1-0, Guinea Equatorial (a) 1-0, Guinea Equatorial (h) 2-0, South Africa (a) 1-0, Sierra Leone (h) 4-1, Colombia (a) 0-1.

RWANDA

Federation Rwandaise De Football Amateur, B.P. 2000, Kigali.
Founded: 1972; *National Colours:* Red, green and yellow shirts, green shorts, red stockings.
International matches 2008
Burundi (a) 0-0, Mauritania (h) 3-0, Ethiopia (a) 2-1, Ethiopia (h) 3-1, Morocco (a) 0-2, Mauritania (a) 1-0, Togo (a) 0-1.

SENEGAL

Federation Senegalaise De Football, Stade Leopold Sedar Senghor, Route De L'Aeroport De Yoff, B.P. 130 21, Dakar.
Founded: 1960; *National Colours:* All white and green.
International matches 2008
Namibia (h) 3-1, Benin (a) 2-1, Tunisia (a) 2-2, Angola (h) 1-3, South Africa (h) 1-1, Algeria (h) 1-0, Gambia (a) 0-0, Liberia (a) 2-2, Liberia (h) 3-1, Libya (a) 0-0, Algeria (a) 2-3, Gambia (h) 1-1.

SEYCHELLES

Seychelles Football Federation, P.O. Box 843, People's Stadium, Victoria-Mahe, Seychelles.
Founded: 1979; *National Colours:* Red and green shirts and shorts, red stockings.
International matches 2008
Burundi (a) 0-1, Tunisia (h) 0-2, Burkina Faso (h) 2-3, Burkina Faso (a) 1-4, Mauritius (a) 7-0, Madagascar (a) 1-1, Swaziland (h) 0-1, Burundi (h) 1-2, Tunisia (a) 0-5.

ST THOMAS AND PRINCIPE

Federation Santomense De Futebol, Rua Ex-Joao de Deus No. QXXIII-426/26, PO Box 440, Sao Tome.
Founded: 1975; *National Colours:* Green and red shirts, yellow shorts, green stockings.

SIERRA LEONE

Sierra Leone Football Association, 21 Battery Street, Kingtorn, P.O. Box 672, National Stadium, Brookfields, Freetown.
Founded: 1967; *National Colours:* Green and blue shirts, green, blue and white shorts and stockings.
International matches 2008
Liberia (a) 1-3, Equatorial Guinea (a) 0-2, Nigeria (h) 0-1, South Africa (h) 1-0, South Africa (a) 0-0, Equatorial Guinea (h) 2-1, Nigeria (a) 1-4.

SOMALIA

Somali Football Federation, PO Box 222, Mogadishu BN 03040.
Founded: 1951; *National Colours:* Sky blue and white shirts and shorts, white and sky blue stockings.

SOUTH AFRICA

South African Football Association, First National Bank Stadium, PO Box 910, Johannesburg 2000, South Africa.
Founded: 1991; *National Colours:* White shirts with yellow striped sleeves, white shorts with yellow stripes, white stockings.
International matches 2008
Mozambique (h) 2-0, Botswana (h) 2-1, Angola (h) 1-1, Tunisia (a) 1-3, Senegal (h) 1-1, Zimbabwe (h) 2-1, Paraguay (h) 3-0, Nigeria (a) 0-2, Equatorial Guinea (h) 4-1, Sierra Leone (a) 0-1, Sierra Leone (h) 0-0, Australia (a) 2-2, Nigeria (h) 0-1, Guinea (h) 0-1, Malawi (h) 3-0, Equatorial Guinea (a) 1-0, Ghana (h) 2-1, Cameroon (h) 3-2.

SUDAN

Sudan Football Association, Bladia Street, Khartoum.
Founded: 1936; *National Colours:* Red shirts, white shorts, black stockings.
International matches 2008
Nigeria (a) 0-2, Guinea (a) 0-6, Zambia (h) 0-3, Egypt (a) 0-3, Cameroon (a) 0-3, Yemen (a) 1-1, Congo (a) 0-1, Mali (h) 3-2, Mali (a) 0-3, Egypt (h) 4-0, Chad (h) 1-2, Chad (a) 3-1, Congo (h) 2-0, Kenya (a) 0-0.

SWAZILAND

National Football Association of Swaziland, Sigwaca House, Plot 582, Sheffield Road, PO Box 641, Mbabane H100.
Founded: 1968; *National Colours:* Blue shirts, gold shorts, red stockings.
International matches 2008
Botswana (h) 1-4, Lesotho (h) 2-2, Lesotho (h) 1-1, Togo (h) 2-1, Zambia (h) 0-0, Zambia (a) 0-1, Madagascar (a) 1-1, Mauritius (a) 1-1, Seychelles (a) 1-0, Togo (a) 0-6.

TANZANIA

Football Association of Tanzania, Uhuru/Shaurimoyo Road, Karume Memorial Stadium, P.O. Box 1574, Ilala/Dar Es Salaam.
Founded: 1930; *National Colours:* Green, yellow and blue shirts, black shorts, green stockings with horizontal stripe.
International matches 2008
Yemen (a) 1-2, Malawi (h) 1-1, Mauritius (h) 1-1, Cape Verde Islands (a) 0-1, Cameroon (h) 0-0, Cameroon (a) 1-2, Ghana (h) 1-1, Mauritius (a) 4-1, Cape Verde Islands (h) 3-1, Mozambique (h) 1-0.

TOGO

Federation Togolaise De Football, C.P. 5, Lome.
Founded: 1960; *National Colours:* White shirts, green shorts, red stockings with yellow and green stripes.
International matches 2008
Guinea (h) 0-2, Zambia (h) 1-0, Swaziland (a) 1-2, Congo DR (a) 1-2, Zambia (a) 0-1, Swaziland (h) 6-0, Rwanda (h) 1-0.

TUNISIA

Federation Tunisienne De Football, Maison des Federations Sportives, Cite Olympique, Tunis 1003.
Founded: 1956; *National Colours:* Red shirts, white shorts, red stockings.
International matches 2008
Zambia (h) 1-2, Zambia (h) 1-0, Senegal (h) 2-2, South Africa (h) 3-1, Angola (h) 0-0, Cameroon (h) 2-3, Ivory Coast (h) 2-0, Burkina Faso (h) 1-2, Seychelles (a) 2-0, Burundi (a) 1-0, Burundi (h) 2-1, Angola (h) 1-1, Burkina Faso (a) 0-0, Seychelles (h) 5-0, France (a) 1-3, Ghana (a) 0-0.

UGANDA

Federation of Uganda Football Associations, Plot No. 879, Kyadondo Block 8, Mengo Wakaliga Road, P.O. Box 22518, Kampala.
Founded: 1924; *National Colours:* All yellow, red and white.
International matches 2008
Libya (h) 1-1, Niger (h) 1-0, Benin (a) 1-4, Angola (h) 3-1, Angola (a) 0-0, Niger (a) 1-3, Benin (h) 2-1.

ZAMBIA

Football Association of Zambia, Football House, Alick Nkhata Road, P.O. Box 34751, Lusaka.
Founded: 1929; *National Colours:* White and green shirts, green and white shorts, white and green stockings.
International matches 2008
Tunisia (a) 2-1, Tunisia (a) 0-1, Morocco (a) 0-2, Sudan (a) 3-0, Cameroon (a) 1-5, Egypt (a) 1-1, Libya (a) 2-2, Iran (a) 2-3, Togo (a) 0-1, Swaziland (a) 0-0, Swaziland (h) 1-0, Zimbabwe (h) 0-0, Madagascar (a) 2-0, Togo (h) 1-0, Morocco (a) 0-3.

ZIMBABWE

Zimbabwe Football Association, P.O. Box CY 114, Causeway, Harare.
Founded: 1965; *National Colours:* All green and gold.
International matches 2008
South Africa (a) 1-2, Botswana (a) 1-0, Guinea (a) 0-0, Namibia (h) 2-0, Kenya (a) 0-2, Kenya (h) 0-0, Zambia (a) 0-0, Botswana (h) 1-0, Guinea (h) 0-0, Oman (a) 2-3, Namibia (a) 2-4.

WORLD CUP 2010 QUALIFYING COMPETITION

EUROPE

■ *Denotes player sent off.*

GROUP 1

Tirana, 6 September 2008, 13,522
Albania (0) 0
Sweden (0) 0
Albania: Beqaj; Vangeli, Dallku, Curri, Beqiri, Skela (Teli 82), Lala, Hyka, Duro, Cana, Salihi (Berisha 75).
Sweden: Isaksson; Wendt (Stoor 78), Mellberg, Majstorovic, Hansson, Nilsson, Linderoth (Larsson S 6), Kallstrom (Holmen 84), Andersson D, Larsson H, Ibrahimovic.
Referee: Mallenco (Spain).

Budapest, 6 September 2008, 18,984
Hungary (0) 0
Denmark (0) 0
Hungary: Babos; Vanczak, Szelesi, Juhasz, Bodnar, Vadocz, Huszti (Rudolf 90), Hajnal, Dzsudzsak (Torghelle 46), Dardai, Gera.
Denmark: Andersen; Christopher Poulsen, Laursen, Jacobsen L, Agger, Christian Poulsen, Jensen D, Vingaard (Borring 61), Tomasson (Retov 68), Rommedahl, Bendtner (Nygaard 87).
Referee: Hamer (Luxembourg).

Ta'Qali, 6 September 2008, 11,000
Malta (0) 0
Portugal (1) 4 *(Said 25 (og), Hugo Almeida 61, Simao 71, Nani 78)*
Malta: Haber; Said, Dimech, Pace, Briffa, Bajada, Woods (Mallia 59), Scerri (Barbara 70), Sammut, Mifsud, Agius G (Fenech 80).
Portugal: Quim; Ricardo Carvalho, Pepe, Bosingwa, Antunes, Raul Meireles, Nani, Deco, Carlos Martins (Maniche 63), Simao (Joao Moutinho 75), Hugo Almeida (Nuno Gomes 67).
Referee: Blom (Holland).

Tirana, 10 September 2008, 7400
Albania (1) 3 *(Dallku 45, 90, Duro 84)*
Malta (0) 0
Albania: Beqaj; Curri, Dallku, Duro (Berisha 86), Hyka, Lala, Skela, Agolli, Cana, Bulku (Beqiri 54), Bogdani (Salihi 73).
Malta: Haber; Dimech, Xuereb, Bajada, Barbara (Frendo 46), Briffa, Pace, Agius G (Scerri 85), Mifsud, Sammut, Schembri.
Referee: Schorgenhofer (Austria).

Lisbon, 10 September 2008, 33,000
Portugal (1) 2 *(Nani 42, Deco 86 (pen))*
Denmark (0) 3 *(Bendtner 63, Christian Poulsen 88, Jensen D 90)*
Portugal: Quim; Bosingwa, Pepe, Ricardo Carvalho, Paulo Ferreira, Raul Meireles, Nani (Joao Moutinho 81), Maniche, Hugo Almeida (Danny 72), Deco, Simao (Nuno Gomes 72).
Denmark: Andersen; Christian Poulsen, Laursen, Agger, Andreasen (Bernburg 87), Jacobsen L (Silberbauer 46), Jensen D, Lovenkrands (Borring 72), Tomasson, Rommedahl, Bendtner.
Referee: Webb (England).

Stockholm, 10 September 2008, 28,177
Sweden (0) 2 *(Kallstrom 55, Holmen 64)*
Hungary (0) 1 *(Rudolf 90)*
Sweden: Isaksson; Hansson, Mellberg, Majstorovic, Holmen, Andersson D, Nilsson, Larsson S, Kallstrom, Ibrahimovic (Rosenberg 81), Larsson H.
Hungary: Babos; Vanczak, Szelesi, Juhasz, Hajnal, Dardai (Rudolf 70), Bodor (Dzsudzsak 80), Vadocz, Huszti, Gera, Torghelle.
Referee: Meyer (Germany).

Copenhagen, 11 October 2008, 33,124
Denmark (2) 3 *(Larsen 9, 47, Agger 29 (pen))*
Malta (0) 0
Denmark: Sorensen; Bogelund, Laursen, Agger, Kahlenberg (Krohn-Dehli 60), Christian Poulsen, Jensen D (Kristensen 82), Rasmussen T, Rommedahl, Nordstrand, Larsen (Rasmussen M 76).
Malta: Haber; Dimech, Caruana, Azzopardi, Xuereb, Pace, Briffa, Schembri (Barbara 60), Mifsud (Scerri 87), Agius G (Nwoko 80), Woods.
Referee: Paniashvili (Georgia).

Budapest, 11 October 2008, 18,000
Hungary (0) 2 *(Torghelle 49, Juhasz 81)*
Albania (0) 0
Hungary: Fulop; Vanczak, Szelesi, Juhasz, Bodnar, Huszti (Vadocz 86), Halmosi, Hajnal (Buzsaky 61), Dzsudzsak, Dardai, Torghelle (Rudolf 90).
Albania: Beqaj; Vangeli (Hyka 54) (Bulku 83), Dallku, Curri, Beqiri (Kapllani 74), Skela, Lala, Duro, Cana, Agolli, Bogdani.
Referee: Circhetta (Switzerland).

Stockholm, 11 October 2008, 33,241
Sweden (0) 0
Portugal (0) 0
Sweden: Isaksson; Majstorovic, Hansson, Safari, Nilsson, Larsson S, Kallstrom, Holmen, Andersson D, Elmander, Ibrahimovic.
Portugal: Quim; Fernando Meira, Pepe, Paulo Ferreira, Bruno Alves, Bosingwa, Raul Meireles, Nani (Danny 86), Joao Moutinho, Ronaldo, Hugo Almeida (Quaresma 65).
Referee: Rosetti (Italy).

Ta'Qali, 15 October 2008, 4797
Malta (0) 0
Hungary (1) 1 *(Torghelle 23)*
Malta: Haber; Xuereb, Dimech, Caruana (Briffa 36), Pace, Barbara (Nwoko 77), Bajada, Woods, Schembri, Scerri (Agius G 63), Mifsud.
Hungary: Fulop; Bodnar, Vanczak, Juhasz, Halmosi, Dzsudzsak (Buzsaky 70), Dardai (Toth 86), Bodor, Huszti, Gera, Torghelle.
Referee: Valgeirsson (Iceland).

Braga, 15 October 2008, 29,500
Portugal (0) 0
Albania (0) 0
Portugal: Quim; Miguel (Maniche 75), Pepe, Paulo Ferreira, Bruno Alves, Manuel Fernandes, Raul Meireles, Joao Moutinho (Quaresma 55), Hugo Almeida, Danny (Nani 55), Ronaldo.
Albania: Beqaj; Vangeli, Curri, Beqiri (Teli■ 24), Skela, Lala, Duro (Berisha 77), Bulku, Agolli, Cana, Bogdani (Vrapi 46).
Referee: Kircher (Germany).

Ta'Qali, 11 February 2009, 2041
Malta (0) 0
Albania (0) 0
Malta: Haber; Dimech, Muscat A (Failla 81), Bajada, Agius A, Agius G (Fenech 69), Schembri, Scerri (Briffa 69), Sammut, Mifsud, Cohen.
Albania: Hidi; Beqiri, Vrapi, Dallku, Curri, Agolli (Vangeli 46) (Lila 80), Skela, Duro, Bulku, Lika, Bogdani (Berisha 79).
Referee: Deaconu (Romania).

Tirana, 28 March 2009, 12,000
Albania (0) 0
Hungary (1) 1 *(Torghelle 38)*
Albania: Hidi; Dallku, Vangeli, Curri, Skela, Lala, Duro, Cana, Lika (Bakaj 70), Salihi, Berisha.
Hungary: Babos; Vasko, Bodor, Vanczak, Szelesi, Dardai, Huszti, Halmosi (Gera 90), Hajnal (Vadocz 80), Torghelle (Priskin 86), Rudolf.
Referee: Kuipers (Holland).

Ta'Qali, 28 March 2009, 6235

Malta (0) 0

Denmark (2) 3 *(Larsen 12, 23, Nordstrand 89)*

Malta: Haber; Dimech, Caruana (Muscat A 69), Pace, Briffa (Barbara 84), Bajada, Bogdanovic, Schembri (Agius G 72), Mifsud, Agius A, Cohen.
Denmark: Sorensen; Jakobsen, Kroldrup, Jacobsen, Agger, Jorgensen, Christian Poulsen, Jensen D (Andreasen 63), Rommedahl, Larsen (Nordstrand 82), Bendtner (Borring 30).
Referee: Mikulski (Poland).

Porto, 28 March 2009, 40,200

Portugal (0) 0

Sweden (0) 0

Portugal: Eduardo; Ricardo Carvalho, Pepe, Bruno Alves, Bosingwa (Rolando 46), Tiago (Deco 62), Duda, Raul Meireles, Simao, Danny (Hugo Almeida 66), Ronaldo.
Sweden: Isaksson; Johansson, Mellberg, Majstorovic, Elm R, Anders Svensson (Larsson S 81), Kallstrom, Holmen (Wilhelmsson 58), Nilsson, Larsson H, Elmander (Berg 86).
Referee: De Bleeckere (Belgium).

Copenhagen, 1 April 2009, 24,320

Denmark (2) 3 *(Andreasen 31, Larsen 38, Poulsen C 80)*

Albania (0) 0

Denmark: Sorensen; Jakobsen, Jacobsen, Andreasen, Agger, Christian Poulsen, Kahlenberg, Jorgensen (Poulsen J 46), Jensen D (Bendtner 34), Rommedahl (Borring 71), Larsen.
Albania: Hidi; Vangeli, Dallku, Curri, Skela, Bylykbashi, Duro, Bulku (Salihi 46), Agolli, Lika, Berisha (Memelli 85).
Referee: Skomina (Slovenia).

Budapest, 1 April 2009, 35,800

Hungary (1) 3 *(Hajnal 6, Gera 80, Juhasz 90)*

Malta (0) 0

Hungary: Fulop; Bodnar, Vanczak, Szelesi, Juhasz, Huszti, Halmosi (Toth 90), Hajnal (Gera 46), Dzsudzsak (Vadocz 79), Bodor, Torghelle.
Malta: Haber; Caruana, Muscat A, Briffa (Fenech 85), Bajada, Agius A, Bogdanovic (Barbara 89), Agius G, Schembri (Scerri 46), Mifsud, Cohen.
Referee: Sukhina (Russia).

Tirana, 6 June 2009, 13,320

Albania (1) 1 *(Bogdani 28)*

Portugal (1) 2 *(Hugo Almeida 27, Bruno Alves 90)*

Albania: Hidi; Vrapi, Vangeli, Curri, Beqiri, Skela (Bylykbashi 90), Duro (Berisha 87), Cana, Bulku, Agolli, Bogdani (Salihi 65).
Portugal: Eduardo; Pepe, Ricardo Carvalho (Nani 76), Bosingwa, Bruno Alves, Raul Meireles, Duda, Deco, Boa Morte (Simao 46), Ronaldo, Hugo Almeida (Edinho 69).
Referee: F. Meyer (Germany).

Stockholm, 6 June 2009, 33,619

Sweden (0) 0

Denmark (1) 1 *(Kahlenberg 22)*

Sweden: Isaksson; Johansson, Mellberg, Majstorovic, Elm R, Andersson D (Elm V 68), Wilhelmsson (Elmander 58), Nilsson (Larsson S 80), Kallstrom, Ibrahimovic, Larsson H.
Denmark: Sorensen; Jacobsen, Agger, Kjaer, Christian Poulsen (Augustinussen 72), Jorgensen (Gronkjaer 56), Kvist, Kahlenberg, Poulsen J, Bendtner (Bernburg 84), Rommedahl.
Referee: Riley (England).

Gothenburg, 10 June 2009, 25,271

Sweden (1) 4 *(Kallstrom 21, Majstorovic 52, Ibrahimovic 56, Berg 58)*

Malta (0) 0

Sweden: Isaksson; Johansson, Mellberg, Majstorovic, Kallstrom, Elm V (Holmen 80), Elm R (Larsson S 78), Anders Svensson, Safari, Ibrahimovic, Berg (Hysen 78).
Malta: Hogg; Dimech, Caruana, Muscat A (Sammut 89), Briffa, Bajada, Pace, Hutchinson, Agius A (Muscat M 85), Bogdanovic, Schembri (Fenech 78).
Referee: Murray (Scotland).

Group 1 Table	P	W	D	L	F	A	Pts
Denmark	6	5	1	0	13	2	16
Hungary	6	4	1	1	8	2	13
Portugal	6	2	3	1	8	4	9
Sweden	6	2	3	1	6	2	9
Albania	8	1	3	4	4	8	6
Malta	8	0	1	7	0	21	1

GROUP 2

Tel Aviv, 6 September 2008, 29,600

Israel (0) 2 *(Benayoun 73, Sahar 90)*

Switzerland (1) 2 *(Yakin 45, Nkufo 56)*

Israel: Awat; Kozokin, Ben Haim, Ziv, Strool, Kayal (Ohayon 62), Cohen, Benayoun, Toema, Golan (Barda 60), Colautti (Sahar 46).
Switzerland: Benaglio; Lichtsteiner, Grichting, Djourou, Magnin, Inler, Huggel, Behrami (Spycher 87), Barnetta (Vonlanthen 71), Yakin (Abdi 75), Nkufo.
Referee: Hansson (Sweden).

Luxembourg, 6 September 2008, 4596

Luxembourg (0) 0

Greece (2) 3 *(Torosidis 36, Gekas 45, Charisteas 75 (pen))*

Luxembourg: Joubert; Hoffmann, Kintziger, Strasser, Peters, Mutsch, Lombardelli (Lang 68), Leweck F (Da Mota 58), Bettmer, Payal, Kitenge (Joachim 81).
Greece: Chalkias; Torosidis, Seitaridis, Kyrgiakos, Dellas, Katsouranis, Karagounis, Basinas (Salpingidis 46), Lyberopoulos (Patsatzoglou 66), Gekas, Charisteas.
Referee: Hermansen (Denmark).

Tiraspol, 6 September 2008, 4300

Moldova (0) 1 *(Alexeev 76)*

Latvia (2) 2 *(Karlsons 8, Astafjevs 22)*

Moldova: Calancea; Rebeja, Lascencov, Golovatenco, Epureanu, Bordian, Corneencov, Andronic (Alexeev 61), Suvorov (Tigirlas 67), Picusciac, Frunza.
Latvia: Vanins; Stepanovs, Klava, Gorkss, Solonicins, Pereplotkins (Kolesnicenko 83), Laizans, Kacanovs (Zirnis 90), Astafjevs, Verpakovskis (Rubins 75), Karlsons.
Referee: Courtney (Northern Ireland).

Riga, 10 September 2008, 8600

Latvia (0) 0

Greece (1) 2 *(Gekas 10, 49)*

Latvia: Vanins; Stepanovs, Gorkss, Klava, Astafjevs, Kacanovs, Laizans, Pereplotkins (Visnakovs 79), Solonicins (Rubins 65), Verkpakovskis, Karlsons (Grebis 60).
Greece: Chalkias; Seitaridis, Torosidis, Dellas, Kyrgiakos, Papadopoulos, Katsouranis, Karagounis (Basinas 61), Samaras (Lyberopoulos 88), Charisteas, Gekas (Salpingidis 76).
Referee: Chapron (France).

Chisinau, 10 September 2008, 10,500

Moldova (1) 1 *(Picusciac 1)*

Israel (2) 2 *(Golan 39, Saban 45)*

Moldova: Namasco; Lascencov, Rebeja, Bordian, Golovatenco, Epureanu, Corneencov (Savinov 27), Comlionoc (Andronic 76), Frunza (Alexeev 69), Suvorov, Picusciac.
Israel: Awat; Kozokin (Saban 38), Ziv, Ben Haim, Keinan, Cohen (Kayal 68), Ohayon, Toema, Benayoun, Golan, Sahar (Buzaglo 4).
Referee: Fernandez (Spain).

Zurich, 10 September 2008, 20,500

Switzerland (1) 1 *(Nkufo 43)*

Luxembourg (1) 2 *(Strasser 27, Leweck F 87)*

Switzerland: Benaglio; Nef (Vonlanthen 73), Djourou, Grichting, Magnin, Inler, Yakin (Abdi 65), Barnetta, Inler, Nkufo, Frei (Lustrinelli 65).
Luxembourg: Joubert; Hoffmann, Kintziger, Lang (Leweck F 44), Lombardelli (Gerson 76), Mutsch, Payal, Peters, Strasser, Bettmer, Kitenge (Joachim 66).
Referee: Filipovic (Serbia).

Piraeus, 11 October 2008, 13,684

Greece (2) 3 *(Charisteas 31, 51, Katsouranis 40)*

Moldova (0) 0

Greece: Chalkias; Torosidis, Seitaridis, Kyrgiakos, Dellas, Papadopoulos, Katsouranis (Patsatzoglou 72), Basinas, Samaras (Amanatidis 70), Gekas (Salpingidis 46), Charisteas.
Moldova: Calancea; Epureanu, Rebeja, Bordian, Armas, Tigirlas, Savinov, Corneencov (Andronic 79), Cebotaru, Bugaiov (Suvorov 68), Alexeev (Picusciac 46).
Referee: Berntsen (Norway).

Luxembourg, 11 October 2008, 3562

Luxembourg (1) 1 *(Peters 14)*

Israel (1) 3 *(Benayoun 2 (pen), Golan 54, Toema 81)*

Luxembourg: Joubert; Wagner, Reiter, Kintziger, Peters, Payal, Mutsch, Leweck F, Bettmer, Bensi (Da Mota 67), Bossi (Joachim 67).
Israel: Awat; Ben Dayan, Saban, Keinan, Ben Haim, Toema (Sahar 81), Kayal, Benayoun (Buzaglo 87), Alberman (Ohayon 90), Golan, Barda.
Referee: Egorov (Russia).

St Gallen, 11 October 2008, 18,026

Switzerland (0) 2 *(Frei 63, Nkufo 73)*

Latvia (0) 1 *(Ivanovs 71)*

Switzerland: Benaglio; Spycher, Lichtsteiner, Grichting, Djourou (Eggimann 46), Inler, Huggel, Behrami, Barnetta (Gelson 84), Nkufo, Frei (Yakin 78).
Latvia: Vanins; Ivanovs, Savcenkovs, Gorkss, Cauna (Rubins 59), Solonicins (Visnakovs 81), Pereplotkins (Kolesnicenko 69), Laizans■, Kacanovs, Astafjevs, Karlsons.
Referee: Baptista (Portugal).

Piraeus, 15 October 2008, 28,810

Greece (0) 1 *(Charisteas 68)*

Switzerland (1) 2 *(Frei 41 (pen), Nkufo 77)*

Greece: Chalkias; Torosidis, Seitaridis, Kyrgiakos (Patsatzoglou 30), Dellas, Papadopoulos, Katsouranis, Basinas, Samaras (Karagounis 62), Gekas (Lyberopoulos 46), Charisteas.
Switzerland: Benaglio; Spycher, Lichtsteiner, Grichting, Eggimann, Inler, Huggel, Behrami, Barnetta (Gelson 33), Nkufo (Derdiyok 86), Frei (Yakin 75).
Referee: Cantalejo (Spain).

Riga, 15 October 2008, 7100

Latvia (0) 1 *(Kolesnicenko 89)*

Israel (0) 1 *(Benayoun 50)*

Latvia: Vanins; Astafjevs, Klava, Ivanovs, Kacanovs, Kolesnicenko, Rubins, Karlsons (Cauna 61), Gorkss, Pereplotkins (Grebis 61), Solonicins (Visnakovs 75).
Israel: Awat; Saban, Ben Haim, Alberman, Toema, Kayal (Ohayon 67), Ben Dayan, Barda (Buzaglo 90), Golan (Sahar 83), Keinan, Benayoun.
Referee: Hrinak (Slovakia).

Luxembourg, 15 October 2008, 2157

Luxembourg (0) 0

Moldova (0) 0

Luxembourg: Joubert; Kintziger, Hoffmann, Strasser, Peters, Payal (Lombardelli 46), Mutsch, Leweck F (Joachim 69), Bettmer, Kitenge, Bossi (Gerson 46).
Moldova: Calancea; Rebeja, Lascencov, Epureanu, Bordian, Armas, Corneencov (Cebotaru 72), Suvorov, Picusciac (Tigirlas 65), Frunza, Bugaiov (Bulat 53).
Referee: Borski (Poland).

Tel Aviv, 28 March 2009, 38,000

Israel (0) 1 *(Golan 55)*

Greece (1) 1 *(Gekas 42)*

Israel: Awat; Saban, Keinan, Ben Haim, Ben Dayan, Cohen (Vermouth 85), Benayoun (Kayal 77), Alberman, Barda (Itzhaki 61), Sahar, Golan.
Greece: Chalkias; Torosidis, Seitaridis, Kyrgiakos, Dellas, Tziolis (Patsatzoglou 88), Papadopoulos, Karagounis, Basinas (Samaras 62), Gekas, Charisteas.
Referee: Rosetti (Italy).

Luxembourg, 28 March 2009, 2516

Luxembourg (0) 0

Latvia (1) 4 *(Karlsons 25, Cauna 48, Visnakovs 71, Pereplotkins 86)*

Luxembourg: Joubert; Janisch, Hoffmann, Plein, Strasser, Peters, Payal (Gerson 46), Mutsch, Leweck F (Lombardelli 66), Bettmer, Bensi (Kitenge 70).
Latvia: Vanins; Klava, Ivanovs, Gorkss, Cauna (Rubins 77), Kolesnicenko, Kacanovs, Astafjevs, Zigajevs (Visnakovs 66), Verpakovskis (Pereplotkins 72), Karlsons.
Referee: Whitby (Wales).

Chisinau, 28 March 2009, 10,500

Moldova (0) 0

Switzerland (1) 2 *(Frei 32, Gelson 90)*

Moldova: Namasco; Armas (Manaliu 87), Golovatenco, Epureanu, Lascencov, Ionita (Cebotaru 56), Gatcan, Savinov, Calincov, Bugaev, Alexeev.
Switzerland: Benaglio; Senderos, Magnin, Lichtsteiner, Grichting, Padalino (Gelson 79), Inler, Huggel, Barnetta (Djourou 90), Nkufo (Derdiyok 79), Frei.
Referee: McDonald (Scotland).

Iraklion, 1 April 2009, 22,794

Greece (1) 2 *(Salpingidis 32, Samaras 67 (pen))*

Israel (0) 1 *(Golan 59)*

Greece: Chalkias; Torosidis, Seitaridis, Moras, Kyrgiakos, Katsouranis, Karagounis (Patsatzoglou 70), Papadopoulos, Gekas (Samaras 64), Charisteas (Basinas 84), Salpingidis.
Israel: Awat; Ziv (Barda 40), Saban, Keinan, Ben Haim, Ben Dayan, Kayal, Alberman, Shechter (Itzhaki 74), Sahar (Benayoun 46), Golan.
Referee: Benquerenca (Portugal).

Riga, 1 April 2009, 6700

Latvia (1) 2 *(Zigajevs 44, Verpakovskis 76)*

Luxembourg (0) 0

Latvia: Vanins; Klava, Ivanovs, Gorkss, Kolesnicenko, Kacanovs, Cauna, Astafjeves, Zigajevs (Solonicins 87), Verpakovskis, Karlsons (Pereplotkins 20) (Rubins 69).
Luxembourg: Joubert; Kintziger, Janisch, Hoffmann (Bensi 80), Strasser, Peters, Payal (Ferreira 83), Mutsch, Lombardelli (Leweck F 60), Bettmer, Kitenge.
Referee: Firat (Turkey).

Geneva, 1 April 2009, 20,100

Switzerland (1) 2 *(Nkufo 21, Frei 52)*

Moldova (0) 0

Switzerland: Benaglio; Senderos, Magnin, Lichtsteiner, Grichting, Padalino (Abdi 87), Inler, Huggel (Dzemaili 71), Barnetta, Nkufo (Derdiyok 84), Frei.
Moldova: Namasco; Lascencov, Golovatenco, Gatcan (Alexeev 57), Onica, Cebotaru, Bulat, Savinov, Calincov (Andronic 78), Manaliu (Tigirlas 79), Bugaev.
Referee: Rocchi (Italy).

Group 2 Table	P	W	D	L	F	A	Pts
Greece	6	4	1	1	12	4	13
Switzerland	6	4	1	1	11	6	13
Latvia	6	3	1	2	10	6	10
Israel	6	2	3	1	10	8	9
Luxembourg	6	1	1	4	3	13	4
Moldova	6	0	1	5	2	11	1

GROUP 3

Wroclaw, 6 September 2008, 8400

Poland (1) 1 *(Zewlakow 17 (pen))*

Slovenia (1) 1 *(Dedic 35)*

Poland: Fabianski; Zewlakow, Wasilewski, Kowalczyk, Bosacki (Jop 50), Roger (Saganowski 71), Piszczek, Murawski (Bandrowski 46), Lewandowski M, Krzynowek, Blaszczykowski.
Slovenia: Handanovic; Suler, Kirm (Birsa 70), Ilic, Cesar, Brecko, Koren, Komac (Zlogar 84), Sisic, Novakovic, Dedic (Matic 90).
Referee: Jakobsson (Iceland).

Bratislava, 6 September 2008, 5445

Slovakia (0) 2 *(Skrtel 46, Hamsik 70)*

Northern Ireland (0) 1 *(Durica 81 (og))*

Slovakia: Senecky; Skrtel, Petras, Pekarik, Durica, Sapara, Kozak, Karhan (Zabavnik 75), Hamsik, Vittek (Mintal 84), Jakubko (Svento 59).
Northern Ireland: Taylor; Baird (Shiels 78), McCartney, Evans, Hughes, Craigan, Davis, Clingan, Gillespie (Feeney 53), Healy, Paterson (Brunt 66).
Referee: Ivanov (Russia).

Belfast, 10 September 2008, 12,882

Northern Ireland (0) 0

Czech Republic (0) 0

Northern Ireland: Taylor; Evans, Hughes, McCartney, Baird, Craigan, Brunt, Clingan (O'Connor 46), Feeney (Paterson 72), Gillespie (Shiels 83), Healy.
Czech Republic: Cech; Jankulovski, Kovac R, Rozehnal, Ujfalusi, Grygera, Plasil, Polak, Sionko (Pospech 67), Sirl, Baros (Slepicka 77).
Referee: Bebek (Croatia).

Serravalle, 10 September 2008, 2374

San Marino (0) 0

Poland (1) 2 *(Smolarek 36, Lewandowski R 68)*

San Marino: Simoncini A (Valentini F 73); Vitaioli F, Albani N, Berretti (Mauro Marani 80), Simoncini D, Valentini C, Bollini (Vannucci 46), Bugli, Michele Marani, Manuel Marani, Selva A.
Poland: Fabianski; Jop, Kowalczyk (Krzynowek 28), Zewlakow, Wojtkowiak, Blaszczykowski, Lewandowski M, Piszczek (Murawski 88), Roger, Saganowski (Lewandowski R 58), Smolarek.
Referee: Zografos (Greece).

Maribor, 10 September 2008, 11,000

Slovenia (1) 2 *(Novakovic 22, 81)*

Slovakia (0) 1 *(Jakubko 83)*

Slovenia: Handanovic; Brecko, Komac, Suler, Cesar, Sisic (Zlogar 85), Koren, Novakovic, Dedic (Ljubijankic 76), Kirm (Matic 90), Ilic.
Slovakia: Senecky; Petras, Skrtel, Pekarik, Karhan (Jakubko 58), Sapara, Vittek, Holosko (Svento 46), Strba, Durica (Kozak 78), Hamsik.
Referee: Moen (Norway).

Chorzow, 11 October 2008, 38,293

Poland (1) 2 *(Pawel Brozek 26, Blaszczykowski 52)*

Czech Republic (0) 1 *(Fenin 87)*

Poland: Boruc; Wawrzyniak (Krzynowek 43), Zewlakow, Wasilewski, Dudka, Roger, Murawski (Jodlowiec 90), Lewandowski M, Blaszczykowski, Smolarek, Pawel Brozek (Lewandowski R 69).
Czech Republic: Cech; Ujfalusi, Rozehnal, Pospech, Kovac R, Jankulovski, Grygera (Sionko 58), Sirl, Plasil, Slepicka (Sverkos 58), Baros (Fenin 81).
Referee: Stark (Germany).

Serravalle, 11 October 2008, 1037

San Marino (1) 1 *(Selva A 45)*

Slovakia (2) 3 *(Sestak 32, Kozak 39, Karhan 50)*

San Marino: Simoncini A; Della Valle, Vannucci, Valentini C, Simoncini D (Vitaioli M 84), Berretti (Bonini 72), Bacciocchi (Albani N 46), Michele Marani, Mauro Marani, Selva A, Manuel Marani.
Slovakia: Kamenar; Jendrisek, Cech, Petras, Kratochvil*, Krajcik, Borbely (Karhan 46), Mintal (Jakubko 62), Kozak, Vittek, Sestak (Petras 85).
Referee: Kever (Switzerland).

Maribor, 11 October 2008, 12,385

Slovenia (0) 2 *(Novakovic 84, Ljubijankic 85)*

Northern Ireland (0) 0

Slovenia: Handanovic; Suler, Kirm (Matic 90), Ilic, Cesar, Brecko, Koren, Komac, Novakovic, Sisic (Birsa 81), Dedic (Ljubijankic 69).
Northern Ireland: Taylor; Baird, McCartney, McAuley, Hughes, Evans, Gillespie, McCann (McGivern 73), Lafferty, Healy, Davis.
Referee: Gonzalez (Spain).

Teplice, 15 October 2008, 15,220

Czech Republic (0) 1 *(Sionko 62)*

Slovenia (0) 0

Czech Republic: Zitka; Ujfalusi, Rozehnal, Rajnoch, Pospech, Jankulovski, Sionko, Plasil, Jarolim (Sirl 66), Fenin (Sverkos 81), Baros (Kladrubsky 90).
Slovenia: Handanovic; Moerec, Suler, Kirm, Ilic, Brecko (Mejak 87), Koren, Sisic (Birsa 65), Novakovic, Dedic (Jokic 79).
Referee: Atkinson (England).

Belfast, 15 October 2008, 12,957

Northern Ireland (2) 4 *(Healy 31, McCann 43, Lafferty 56, Davis 75)*

San Marino (0) 0

Northern Ireland: Taylor; Baird, McCartney, McCann (Paterson 73), McAuley (McGivern 61), Hughes, Gillspie, O'Connor, Lafferty (Feeney 82), Healy, Davis.
San Marino: Valentini F; Della Valle, Vannucci, Valentini C, Bacciocchi, Albani N, Michele Marani, Mauro Marani*, Bonini (Vitaioli F 77), Selva A (Vitaioli M 46), Manuel Marani (Cibelli 86).
Referee: Kari (Finland).

Bratislava, 15 October 2008, 17,650

Slovakia (0) 2 *(Sestak 85, 86)*

Poland (0) 1 *(Smolarek 70)*

Slovakia: Senecky; Jendrisek (Obzera 80), Petras, Pekarik, Durica, Cech, Zabavnik (Kozak 83), Sapara (Jakubko 73), Hamsik, Vittek, Sestak.
Poland: Boruc; Zewlakow, Wasilewski, Wojtkowiak, Roger (Lewandowski R 89), Murawski (Gargula 65), Lewandowski M, Dudka, Blaszczykowski, Smolarek, Pawel Brozek (Krzynowek 84).
Referee: Layec (France).

Serravalle, 19 November 2008, 1318

San Marino (0) 0

Czech Republic (0) 3 *(Kovac R 48, Pospech 53, Necid 83)*

San Marino: Simoncini A; Della Valle, Vannucci, Simoncini D, Berretti, Bacciocchi, Muccioli (Andreini 70), Michele Marani (Cibelli 81), Bonini, Vitaioli M (Rinaldi 87), Manuel Marani.
Czech Republic: Zitka; Ujfalusi, Rozehnal, Pospech, Kovac R, Jankulovski, Sirl, Sionko, Polak (Jarolim 70), Fenin (Necid 66), Baros (Bednar 81).

Serravalle, 11 February 2009, 1942

San Marino (0) 0

Northern Ireland (2) 3 *(McAuley 7, McCann 33, Brunt 63)*

San Marino: Valentini F; Della Valle, Berretti, Bacciocchi (Vitaioli F 73), Vannucci, Valentini C, Simoncini D, Muccioli (Bugli 66), Michele Marani, Vitaioli M (Casadei 87), Manuel Marani*.
Northern Ireland: Taylor; Hughes (McCourt 80), McCartney, McCann, McAuley, Craigan, Johnson, Davis, Lafferty (Brunt 55), Healy, Paterson (Feeney 77).
Referee: Stankovic (Serbia).

Belfast, 28 March 2009, 13,357

Northern Ireland (1) 3 *(Feeney 10, Evans 47, Michal Zewlakow 61 (og))*

Poland (1) 2 *(Jelen 27, Saganowski 90)*

Northern Ireland: Taylor; McAuley, Evans, Craigan, Hughes, Clingan, Johnson, McCann, Feeney (Baird 84), Healy (Little 90), Brunt.
Poland: Boruc; Wasilewski, Michal Zewlakow (Bosacki 65), Wawrzyniak, Roger, Bandrowski (Blaszczykowski 60), Lewandowski M, Krzynowek, Dudka, Jelen (Saganowski 71), Lewandowski R.
Referee: Hansson (Sweden).

Maribor, 28 March 2009, 12,500

Slovenia (0) 0

Czech Republic (0) 0

Slovenia: Handanovic; Mavric, Kirm, Cesar, Filekovic, Koren, Jokic, Komac (Mejak 85), Dedic (Ljubijankic 67), Sisic (Zlogar 83), Novakovic.
Czech Republic: Cech; Ujfalusi, Rozehnal, Jankulovski, Grygera, Sirl (Kadlec 76), Sionko, Polak, Plasil, Sverkos (Necid 79), Baros (Fenin 90).
Referee: Proenca (Portugal).

Prague, 1 April 2009, 20,000
Czech Republic (1) 1 *(Jankulovski 30)*
Slovakia (1) 2 *(Sestak 22, Jendrisek 83)*

Czech Republic: Cech; Rozehnal, Kovac R (Pospech 72), Jankulovski, Grygera, Sionko (Lafata 84), Polak, Plasil, Jarolim, Necid (Fenin 79), Baros.
Slovakia: Mucha; Skrtel, Pekarik, Durica, Strba, Hamsik (Sapara 88), Zabavnik, Karhan, Sestak (Stoch 74), Jendrisek (Vittek 90), Holosko.
Referee: Mallenco (Spain).

Belfast, 1 April 2009, 15,000
Northern Ireland (0) 1 *(Feeney 73)*
Slovenia (0) 0

Northern Ireland: Taylor; Hughes, McCartney (McGivern 44), McCann, McAuley (Baird 16), Evans, Davis, Clingan, Feeney, Healy, Johnson.
Slovenia: Handanovic; Mavric, Kirm (Pecnik 77), Cesar, Brecko (Mejac 85), Koren, Komac, Jokic, Filekovic, Novakovic, Dedic (Ljubijankic 64).
Referee: Yefet (Israel).

Kielce, 1 April 2009, 15,200
Poland (4) 10 *(Boguski 1, 28, Smolarek 18, 59, 72, 81, Lewandowski R 43, Jelen 51, Lewandowski M 62, Saganowski 88)*

San Marino (0) 0

Poland: Fabianski; Wasilewski, Bosacki, Roger, Boguski (Saganowski 80), Lewandowski M, Krzynowek, Dudka, Jelen (Blaszczykowski 71), Smolarek, Lewandowski R (Sosin 66).
San Marino: Valentini F; Della Valle, Vitaioli F (Berretti 64), Simoncini D, Bacciocchi, Andreini (Vannucci 82), Albani N, Rinaldi, Michele Marani, Bugli, Bonini (Selva A 53).
Referee: Kulbakou (Belarus).

Bratislava, 6 June 2009, 6652
Slovakia (5) 7 *(Cech 3, 32, Pekarik 12, Stoch 35, Kozak 42, Jakubko 63, Hanzel 69)*

San Marino (0) 0

Slovakia: Mucha; Pekarik, Durica (Salata 46), Cech, Kozak, Hanzel, Hamsik (Novak 46), Karhan, Vittek, Stoch (Borbely 63), Jakubko.
San Marino: Simoncini A; Vitaioli, Vannucci, Simoncini D, Berretti (Andreini 79), Bacciocchi, Rinaldi (Ciacci 65), Michele Marani (Bonini 86), Mauro Marani, Bugli, Selva A.
Referee: Nzolo (Belgium).

Group 3 Table	P	W	D	L	F	A	Pts
Slovakia	6	5	0	1	17	6	15
Northern Ireland	7	4	1	2	12	6	13
Poland	6	3	1	2	18	7	10
Czech Republic	6	2	2	2	6	4	8
Slovenia	6	2	2	2	5	4	8
San Marino	7	0	0	7	1	32	0

GROUP 4

Vaduz, 6 September 2008, 7842
Liechtenstein (0) 0
Germany (1) 6 *(Podolski 21, 48, Rolfes 65, Schweinsteiger 66, Hitzlsperger 76, Westermann 86)*

Liechtenstein: Jehle; Martin Stocklasa, Ritzberger, D'Elia, Polverino (Rohrer 64), Gerster, Burgmeier, Buchel M, Frick M, Fischer (Buchel R 87), Christen (Beck R 74).
Germany: Enke; Westermann, Tasci, Lahm, Fritz, Trochowski, Schweinsteiger, Rolfes (Marin 69), Hitzlsperger, Podolski (Kuranyi 76), Klose (Gomez 64).
Referee: Gomes (Portugal).

Cardiff, 6 September 2008, 17,106
Wales (0) 1 *(Vokes 83)*
Azerbaijan (0) 0

Wales: Hennessey; Morgan, Gunter, Williams A, Bale, Edwards D (Vokes 72), Ledley, Fletcher, Earnshaw (Evans C 62), Davies S, Koumas (Robinson 89).
Azerbaijan: Agayev; Yunisoglu, Malikov, Mammadov N (Nduka 78), Abbasov, Rashad Sadikhov, Mammadov E, Fabio*, Bakhshiyev, Subasic, Huseynov (Nabiyev 46).
Referee: Stavrev (Macedonia).

Baku, 10 September 2008, 25,000
Azerbaijan (0) 0
Liechtenstein (0) 0

Azerbaijan: Agayev; Malikov, Yunisoglu, Bakhshiyev, Gurbanov (Zeynalov 71), Chertoganov, Abbasov, Subasic, Javadov (Huseynov 46), Rashad Sadikhov, Mammadov E (Gomesh 65).
Liechtenstein: Jehle; Ritzberger (Oehri 20), D'Elia, Gerster, Martin Stocklasa, Fischer, Frick M, Burgmeier, Buchel M, Christen (Beck T 68), Polverino (Rohrer 46).
Referee: Georgiev (Bulgaria).

Helsinki, 10 September 2008, 37,150
Finland (2) 3 *(Johansson 33, Vayrynen 43, Sjolund 53)*
Germany (2) 3 *(Klose 38, 45, 82)*

Finland: Jaaskelainen; Lampi, Kallio, Hyypia, Pasanen, Kolkka, Heikkinen, Eremenko R, Vayrynen (Kuqi N 75), Johansson, Forssell (Sjolund 41).
Germany: Enke; Tasci, Lahm, Westermann, Fritz (Hinkel 82), Schweinsteiger, Rolfes (Helmes 82), Hitzlsperger (Gomez 68), Trochowski, Podolski, Klose.
Referee: Kassai (Hungary).

Moscow, 10 September 2008, 28,000
Russia (1) 2 *(Pavlyuchenko 22 (pen), Pogrebnyak 81)*
Wales (0) 1 *(Ledley 67)*

Russia: Akinfeev; Anyukov, Ignashevich (Bystrov 90), Kolodin, Semak (Pogrebnyak 74), Semshov, Torbinskiy (Saenko 61), Zhirkov, Zyryanov, Arshavin, Pavlyuchenko.
Wales: Hennessey; Morgan, Gunter, Bale, Robinson (Ricketts 46), Edwards D (Evans S 76), Fletcher, Ledley, Williams A, Davies S, Vokes (Evans C 62).
Referee: Skomina (Slovenia).

Helsinki, 11 October 2008, 22,124
Finland (0) 1 *(Forssell 61 (pen))*
Azerbaijan (0) 0

Finland: Jaaskelainen; Tihinen, Pasanen, Kallio, Hyypia, Vayrynen, Tainio (Litmanen 79), Sjolund, Eremenko R (Heikkinen 90), Roiha (Pohja 62), Forssell.
Azerbaijan: Agayev; Shukurov, Yunisoglu, Malikov, Abbasov, Zeynalov, Rashad Sadikhov, Mammadov E (Huseynov 59), Chertoganov (Abdullayev 79), Subasic (Ponomarev 73), Gomesh.
Referee: Collum (Scotland).

Dortmund, 11 October 2008, 65,607
Germany (2) 2 *(Podolski 9, Ballack 28)*
Russia (0) 1 *(Arshavin 51)*

Germany: Adler; Westermann, Mertesacker, Lahm, Friedrich A, Trochowski (Frings 83), Schweinsteiger, Hitzlsperger (Rolfes 90), Ballack, Podolski, Klose (Gomez 71).
Russia: Akinfeev; Berezutski V, Ignashevich, Anyukov, Zhirkov, Yanbaev (Dzagoev 46), Semak (Sychev 84), Zyryanov, Denisov, Pogrebnyak, Arshavin.
Referee: Frojdfeldt (Sweden).

Cardiff, 11 October 2008, 13,356
Wales (1) 2 *(Edwards D 42, Frick M 80 (og))*
Liechtenstein (0) 0

Wales: Hennessey; Morgan, Gunter, Bale, Williams A, Koumas, Fletcher (Robinson 56), Edwards D, Davies S, Bellamy (Collins J 80), Vokes (Evans C 51).
Liechtenstein: Jehle; Martin Stocklasa, Ritzberger (Christen 67), D'Elia, Polverino (Buchel R 80), Gerster, Burgmeier, Buchel M, Frick M, Fischer, Beck T.
Referee: Vejlgaard (Denmark).

Moenchengladbach, 15 October 2008, 45,000
Germany (0) 1 *(Trochowski 72)*
Wales (0) 0

Germany: Adler; Westermann, Mertesacker, Lahm, Friedrich A (Fritz 65), Trochowski, Schweinsteiger, Hitzlsperger, Ballack, Podolski (Gomez 82), Klose (Helmes 46).
Wales: Hennessey; Gunter (Ricketts 86), Bale, Fletcher (Robinson 77), Morgan, Williams A, Davies S, Collins J, Bellamy, Koumas, Edwards D (Evans C 77).
Referee: Duhamel (France).

Moscow, 15 October 2008, 28,000
Russia (1) 3 *(Pasanen 23 (og), Lampi 65 (og), Arshavin 88)*
Finland (0) 0

Russia: Akinfeev; Ignashevich, Berezutski V, Anyukov, Zyryanov, Zhirkov, Semshov, Semak, Pogrebnyak (Saenko 60), Denisov, Arshavin (Dzagoev 90).
Finland: Jaaskelainen; Tihinen, Pasanen, Lampi, Hyypia, Vayrynen (Pohja 69), Sjolund (Litmanen 85), Kolkka, Heikkinen, Eremenko R (Tainio 66), Forssell.
Referee: Vassaras (Greece).

Leipzig, 28 March 2009, 43,368
Germany (2) 4 *(Ballack 4, Jansen 9, Schweinsteiger 48, Podolski 50)*
Liechtenstein (0) 0

Germany: Enke; Tasci, Mertesacker, Lahm, Jansen (Helmes 46), Beck, Schweinsteiger (Rolfes 88), Hitzlsperger (Marin 78), Ballack, Podolski, Gomez.
Liechtenstein: Jehle; Michael Stocklasa, Vogt, Martin Stocklasa, Ritzberger, Oehri, Rohrer, Gerster, Frick M, Buchel R, Beck T (Beck R 74).
Referee: Ishchenko (Ukraine).

Moscow, 28 March 2009, 62,000
Russia (1) 2 *(Pavlyuchenko 32, Zyryanov 71)*
Azerbaijan (0) 0

Russia: Akinfeev; Ignashevich, Berezutski V, Anyukov, Zyryanov, Zhirkov, Semshov, Semak (Dzagoev 56), Pavlyuchenko (Pogrebnyak 72), Denisov, Arshavin.
Azerbaijan: Veliyev; Shukurov, Melikov, Abbasov, Yunisoglu, Rashad Sadikhov, Fabio (Gomesh 61), Bakhshiyev, Maharramov, Subasic (Javadov 46), Nadyrov.
Referee: Gumienny (Belgium).

Cardiff, 28 March 2009, 22,604
Wales (0) 0

Finland (1) 2 *(Johansson 42, Kuqi S 90)*
Wales: Hennessey; Gunter, Bale, Edwards D (Ramsey 56), Nyatanga, Collins J, Koumas, Fletcher (Robinson 65), Bellamy, Davies S, Ledley (Earnshaw 71).
Finland: Jaaskelainen; Tihinen, Pasanen, Kallio, Hyypia, Eremenko R, Heikkinen, Eremenko A (Sjolund 78), Litmanen (Porokara 90), Johansson, Forssell (Kuqi S 89).
Referee: Gonzalez (Spain).

Vaduz, 1 April 2009, 5679
Liechtenstein (0) 0

Russia (1) 1 *(Zyryanov 38)*
Liechtenstein: Jehle; Vogt (D'Elia 60), Michael Stocklasa, Martin Stocklasa, Ritzberger, Oehri (Rohrer 46), Polverino, Gerster, Burgmeier, Buchel M (Beck T 75), Frick M.
Russia: Akinfeev; Ignashevich, Berezutski V, Anyukov, Zyryanov, Zhirkov, Torbinskiy (Semak 66), Semchov, Pavlyuchenko (Pogrebnyak 84), Denisov, Arshavin.
Referee: McKeon (Republic of Ireland).

Cardiff, 1 April 2009, 26,064
Wales (0) 0

Germany (1) 2 *(Ballack 11, Williams A 48 (og))*
Wales: Hennessey; Ricketts (Gunter 54), Bale, Williams A, Nyatanga (Cotterill 75), Collins J, Davies S, Ramsey, Vokes (Evans C 62), Earnshaw, Ledley.
Germany: Enke; Tasci, Mertesacker, Lahm, Beck, Schweinsteiger (Helmes 86), Rolfes (Westermann 79), Hitzlsperger, Ballack, Podolski (Trochowski 72), Gomez.
Referee: Hauge (Norway).

Baku, 6 June 2009, 25,000
Azerbaijan (0) 0

Wales (1) 1 *(Edwards D 41)*
Azerbaijan: Veliyev; Shukurov, Melikov, Levin, Nabiyev (Huseynov 50), Rashad Sadikhov, Fabio (Subasic 46), Zeynalov, Bakhshiyev, Javadov, Akhtyamov (Nadyrov 60).
Wales: Hennessey; Gunter, Eardley, Nyatanga, Morgan, Williams A, Ramsey, Edwards D, Ledley, Earnshaw (Vokes 70), Church (Tudur-Jones 83).
Referee: Strombergsson (Sweden).

Helsinki, 6 June 2009, 20,319
Finland (1) 2 *(Forssell 33, Johansson 71)*
Liechtenstein (1) 1 *(Frick M 14)*

Finland: Jaaskelainen; Tihinen, Pasanen (Lampi 46), Kallio, Hyypia, Tainio (Heikkenen 67), Eremenko R, Eremenko A, Litmanen (Kuqi S 72), Johansson, Forssell.
Liechtenstein: Jehle; Vogt (Rohrer 66), Michael Stocklasa, Martin Stocklasa, Ritzberger, Polverino, Buchel M (Christen 58), Burgmeier, Frick M, Fischer, Buchel R (Buchel S 76).
Referee: Kovarik (Czech Republic).

Helsinki, 10 June 2009, 37,028
Finland (0) 0

Russia (1) 3 *(Kerzhakov 26, 53, Zyryanov 71)*
Finland: Jaaskelainen; Tihinen, Pasanen, Kallio (Moisander 54), Hyypia, Heikkinen, Eremenko R, Eremenko A (Kolkka 61), Litmanen (Tainio 69), Johansson, Forssell.
Russia: Akinfeev; Kolodin, Ignashevich, Berezutski V, Zyryanov, Zhirkov, Semshov, Bystrov (Semak 77), Kerzhakov (Pavlyuchenko 67), Denisov, Arshavin.
Referee: Plautz (Austria).

Group 4 Table	P	W	D	L	F	A	Pts
Germany	6	5	1	0	18	4	16
Russia	6	5	0	1	12	3	15
Finland	6	3	1	2	8	10	10
Wales	7	3	0	4	5	7	9
Azerbaijan	5	0	1	4	0	5	1
Liechtenstein	6	0	1	5	1	15	1

GROUP 5

Erevan, 6 September 2008, 30,000
Armenia (0) 0

Turkey (0) 2 *(Tuncay 60, Semih 78)*
Armenia: Berezovskiy; Tadevosian, Hovsepian, Arzumanian (Khachatrian 35), Arakelian, Voskanian, Pachajian, Mkrtchian, Mikhitarian (Zebelian 65), Manucharian (Arm Karamian 76), Art Karamian.
Turkey: Volkan; Gokhan Z, Gokhan G, Servet, Hakan Balta, Arda, Mehmet Aurelio, Emre B, Semih (Gokhan U 82), Tuncay (Ayhan 66), Mevlut (Kazim-Richards 55).
Referee: Ovrebo (Norway).

Liege, 6 September 2008, 17,992
Belgium (1) 3 *(Sonck 40, 80, Defour 75)*
Estonia (0) 2 *(Zenjov 57, Oper 90)*

Belgium: Stijnen; Vermaelen (Van Damme 70), Van Buyten, Kompany, Witsel, Vertonghen, Simons, Fellaini, Defour, Sonck (Huysegems 90), Mirallas (De Sutter 76).
Estonia: Londak; Piiroja (Stepanov 43), Kruglov, Klavan, Jaager, Barengrub, Lindpere, Dmitrijev, Zenjov (Vunk 60), Oper, Kink (Puri 78).
Referee: Dean (England).

Murcia, 6 September 2008, 29,152
Spain (0) 1 *(Villa 57)*
Bosnia (0) 0

Spain: Casillas; Sergio Ramos, Albiol, Puyol, Capdevila, Xavi, Senna, Iniesta, Fabregas (Xabi Alonso 64), Capel (Cazorla 72), Villa (Guiza 84).
Bosnia: Hasagic; Radeljic, Nadarevic, Berberovic (Ibisevic 65), Salihovic, Rahimic, Muratovic, Misimovic, Damjanovic (Ibricic 80), Vladavic, Dzeko (Pjanic 84).
Referee: Thomson (Scotland).

Zenica, 10 September 2008, 15,000

Bosnia (2) 7 *(Misimovic 24, 30 (pen), 56, Muslimovic 59, Dzeko 60, 72, Ibricic 88)*

Estonia (0) 0

Bosnia: Hasagic; Berberovic, Spahic, Muratovic (Ibricic 73), Rahimic, Damjanovic, Muslimovic (Ibisevic 71), Misimovic (Pjanic 66), Dzeko, Nadarevic, Salihovic.
Estonia: Londak (Aksalu 71); Rahn, Barengrub, Dmitrijev (Saag 65), Purje, Oper, Lindpere (Kruglov 65), Vunk, Vassiljev, Klavan, Jaager.
Referee: Balaj (Romania).

Albacete, 10 September 2008, 16,996

Spain (2) 4 *(Capdevila 7, Villa 16, 79, Senna 83)*

Armenia (0) 0

Spain: Casillas; Capdevila, Sergio Ramos, Albiol, Puyol, Xavi (Fabregas 74), Senna, Iniesta, Cazorla (Krkic 65), Guiza (Xabi Alonso 56), Villa.
Armenia: Berezovskiy; Tadevosian, Hovsepian, Arzumanian, Arakelian, Aleksanian (Khachatrian 79), Voskanian, Pachajyan, Mkrtchian, Art Karamian (Arm Karamian 52), Melkonian (Manucharian 46).
Referee: Asumaa (Finland).

Istanbul, 10 September 2008, 25,000

Turkey (0) 1 *(Emre B 74 (pen))*

Belgium (1) 1 *(Sonck 32)*

Turkey: Volkan; Servet, Caglar, Gokhan Z, Emre B, Gokhan G, Arda, Mehmet Topal (Merlut 69), Semih, Tuncay (Halil Altintop 14), Kazim-Richards (Mehmet Topuz 46).
Belgium: Stijnen; Simons, Kompany, Defour (Mudingayi 46), Witsel (Daems 76), Sonck (De Sutter 85), Vermaelen, Vertonghen, Swertz, Fellaini, Dembele.
Referee: Lannoy (France).

Brussels, 11 October 2008, 20,949

Belgium (2) 2 *(Sonck 21, Fellaini 37)*

Armenia (0) 0

Belgium: Stijnen; Van Damme, Kompany, Gillet, Witsel, Vertonghen, Simons, Fellaini, Defour (Huysegems 72), Sonck (De Sutter 87), Dembele.
Armenia: Berezovskiy; Tadevosian, Hovsepian, Arzumanian, Arakelian, Aleksanian (Ara Hakobian 64), Voskanian, Pachajian, Mkrtchian, Art Karamian (Mikhitarian 85), Zebelian (Melkonian 80).
Referee: Rasmussen (Denmark).

Tallinn, 11 October 2008, 9200

Estonia (0) 0

Spain (2) 3 *(Juanito 34, Villa 38, Puyol 69)*

Estonia: Londak; Piiroja, Kruglov, Jaager, Barengrub, Vunk, Vassiljev, Lindpere (Klavan 75), Dmitrijev, Voskobionikov (Saag 73), Kink (Puri 59).
Spain: Casillas; Sergio Ramos (Iraola 54), Puyol, Juanito, Capdevila, Xavi, Xabi Alonso, Iniesta (Riera 79), Cazorla, Torres, Villa (Fabregas 70).
Referee: Eriksson (Sweden).

Istanbul, 11 October 2008, 23,628

Turkey (0) 2 *(Arda 51, Mevlut 66)*

Bosnia (1) 1 *(Dzeko 26)*

Turkey: Volkan; Sabri, Ibrahim K, Servet, Hakan Balta, Ayhan (Halil Altintop 63), Arda, Mehmet Aurelio, Kazim-Richards, Mevlut (Yusuf 79), Batuhan (Nuri 38).
Bosnia: Hasagic (Brasnic 74); Berberovic, Spahic, Radeljic (Ibisevic 63), Salihovic, Rahimic, Muratovic (Pjanic 80), Misimovic, Ibricic, Damjanovic, Dzeko.
Referee: Baskakov (Russia).

Brussels, 15 October 2008, 45,888

Belgium (1) 1 *(Sonck 7)*

Spain (1) 2 *(Iniesta 36, Villa 88)*

Belgium: Stijnen; Simons, Kompany, Van Buyten (Daems 46), Defour (Van Damme 73), Witsel, Sonck, Vermaelen, Vertonghen, Vanden Borre (Gillet 87), Fellaini.
Spain: Casillas; Juanito, Puyol, Iniesta (Guiza 84), Villa, Xavi, Torres (Fabregas 16), Capdevila, Sergio Ramos, Senna, Cazorla (Xabi Alonso 64).
Referee: Michel (Slovakia).

Zenica, 15 October 2008, 13,000

Bosnia (2) 4 *(Spahic 31, Dzeko 39, Muslimovic 56, 89)*

Armenia (0) 1 *(Minasian 85)*

Bosnia: Brasnic; Berberovic (Vladavic 61), Spahic (Vasilic 68), Muratovic, Rahimic, Damjanovic, Misimovic, Dzeko, Mravac, Ibisevic (Muslimovic 46), Salihovic.
Armenia: Berezovskiy; Yedigarian (Minasian 59), Hovsepian, Arzumanian, Voskanian, Zebelian (Ara Hakobian 73), Arm Karamian, Melkonian (Arakelian 41), Pachajian, Mkrtchian, Tadevosian.
Referee: Kenan (Israel).

Tallinn, 15 October 2008, 6500

Estonia (0) 0

Turkey (0) 0

Estonia: Londak; Shishov, Piiroja, Kruglov, Klavan, Barengrub, Vunk (Puri 77), Vassiljev, Dmitrijev, Voskoboinikov (Zenjov 63), Oper.
Turkey: Volkan; Sabri, Ibrahim K, Servet, Hakan Balta, Arda, Nuri (Mevlut 35), Mehmet Aurelio, Kazim-Richards (Ugur 72), Ayhan (Yusuf 60), Halil Altintop.
Referee: Malek (Poland).

Erevan, 28 March 2009, 3000

Armenia (1) 2 *(Mkhitarian 32, Yedigarian 88)*

Estonia (1) 2 *(Vassiljev 36, Zenjov 67)*

Armenia: Berezovskiy; Minasian, Hovsepian, Arzumanian, Arakelian, Voskanian (Ghazarian 46), Pachajian (Yedigarian 83), Mkrtchian, Mkhitarian, Art Karamian, Arm Karamian (Manucharian 52).
Estonia: Pareiko; Rahn, Piiroja, Klavan, Jaager, Vunk, Vassiljev (Saag 75), Lindpere (Puri 74), Dmitrijev, Voskoboinikov (Zenjov 63), Kink.
Referee: Wilmes (Luxembourg).

Genk, 28 March 2009, 20,041

Belgium (0) 2 *(Dembele 67, Sonck 89 (pen))*

Bosnia (1) 4 *(Dzeko 11, Jahic 74, Bajramovic 81, Misimovic 86)*

Belgium: Stijnen; Daems (De Sutter 80), Vermaelen, Swerts, Mudingayi, Fellaini, Defour (Pocognoli 60), Simons, Dembele, De Camargo (Hazard 46), Sonck.
Bosnia: Supic; Pandza, Jahic, Spahic (Mravac 60), Nadarevic, Berberovic, Muratovic, Misimovic, Ibricic, Muslimovic (Bajramovic 70), Dzeko (Pjanic 89).
Referee: Ivanov (Russia).

Madrid, 28 March 2009, 73,820

Spain (0) 1 *(Pique 60)*

Turkey (0) 0

Spain: Casillas; Capdevila, Pique, Sergio Ramos, Albiol, Cazorla (Silva 78), Xavi, Xabi Alonso, Senna, Torres (Llorente 88), Villa (Mata 63).
Turkey: Volkan; Ibrahim U, Emre A, Gokhan G, Hakan Balta, Arda (Gokhan U 77), Emre B (Sabri 84), Mehmet Aurelio, Tuncay, Nihat, Semih (Ayhan 57).
Referee: Busacca (Switzerland).

Zenica, 1 April 2009, 13,800

Bosnia (2) 2 *(Dzeko 12, 20)*

Belgium (0) 1 *(Swerts 88)*

Bosnia: Supic; Spahic, Pandza, Nadarevic, Jahic, Berberovic, Rahimic, Muratovic (Bajramovic 87), Misimovic, Ibricic (Pjanic 77), Dzeko (Topic 90).
Belgium: Stijnen; Vermaelen, Kompany, Swerts, Witsel■, Simons, Mudingayi (De Sutter 55), Fellaini, Sonck (Gillet 90), Mirallas (Hazard 73), Dembele.
Referee: Hrinak (Slovakia).

Tallinn, 1 April 2009, 5200

Estonia (0) 0 1 *(Puri 83)*

Armenia (0) 0

Estonia: Pareiko; Rahn, Piiroja, Klavan, Jaager, Puri, Vassiljev, Dmitrijev, Viikmae (Zenjov 62), Voskoboinikov (Vunk 87), Kink (Lindpere 69).
Armenia: Kasparov; Yedigarian (Arm Karamian 84), Minasian, Hovsepian, Arzumanian, Arakelian, Manucharian, Pachajian, Mkrtchian, Mkhitarian, Art Karamian (Ghazarian 89).
Referee: Zimmermann (Switzerland).

Istanbul, 1 April 2009, 19,617
Turkey (1) 1 *(Semih 26)*
Spain (0) 2 *(Xabi Alonso 62 (pen), Riera 90)*

Turkey: Volkan; Ibrahim U, Gokhan G, Hakan Balta, Emre A, Arda (Nuri 88), Mehmet Aurelio, Emre B, Semih (Sabri 81), Tuncay, Nihat (Batuhan 77).
Spain: Casillas; Sergio Ramos, Marchena, Capdevila, Pique, Xavi, Xabi Alonso, Riera, Senna (Cazorla 67), Torres (Guiza 85), Villa (Busquets 74).
Referee: Riley (England).

Group 5 Table	P	W	D	L	F	A	Pts
Spain	6	6	0	0	13	2	18
Bosnia	6	4	0	2	18	7	12
Turkey	6	2	2	2	6	5	8
Belgium	6	2	1	3	10	11	7
Estonia	6	1	2	3	5	15	5
Armenia	6	0	1	5	3	15	1

GROUP 6

Almaty, 20 August 2008, 7700
Kazakhstan (3) 3 *(Ostapenko 14, 30, Uzdenov 45)*
Andorra (0) 0

Kazakhstan: Loriya; Kuchma, Irismetov, Asanbayev (Baizhanov 78), Baltiyev, Zhumaskaliev, Smakov, Nurdauletov, Skorykh (Karpovich 68), Uzdenov (Byakov 63), Ostapenko.
Andorra: Gomes; Lima T, Lima I, Pujol (Somoza 82), Bernaus, Ayala (Escura 15), Xavi, Vieira, Toscano (Txema 72), Vales, Fernando Silva.
Referee: Banari (Moldova).

Barcelona, 6 September 2008, 10,300
Andorra (0) 0
England (0) 2 *(Cole J 48, 55)*

Andorra: Koldo; Lima T (Juli Fernandez 90), Lima I, Txema, Xavi, Vieira, Pujol (Vales 90), Ayala, Jimenez, Sonejee, Fernando Silva (Toscano 65).
England: James; Johnson G, Cole A, Barry, Terry, Lescott, Walcott, Lampard (Beckham 80), Rooney, Defoe (Heskey 46), Downing (Cole J 46).
Referee: Cuneyt (Turkey).

Zagreb, 6 September 2008, 17,424
Croatia (2) 3 *(Kovac N 13, Modric 36, Petric 81)*
Kazakhstan (0) 0

Croatia: Pletikosa; Kovac R, Corluka, Simunic, Modric (Pokrivac 85), Kovac N, Srna, Rakitic, Pranjic, Olic (Leko 88), Klasnic (Petric 64).
Kazakhstan: Loriya; Kuchma, Irismetov, Zhalmagambetov, Smakov, Byakov, Baizhanov (Chichulin 57), Baltiyev, Zhumaskaliev, Skorykh (Karpovich 81), Ostapenko (Uzdenov 84).
Referee: Johannesson (Sweden).

Lvov, 6 September 2008, 24,000
Ukraine (0) 1 *(Shevchenko 90 (pen))*
Belarus (0) 0

Ukraine: Pyatov; Shevchuk, Rusol, Yarmash, Tymoshchuk, Nazarenko, Mikhalik, Kravchenko, Kalinichenko (Aliev 46), Voronin (Seleznov 58), Milevsky (Shevchenko 74).
Belarus: Zhevnov; Verkhovtsov, Omelyanchuk, Filipenko, Strakanovich, Putsilo (Pavlov 80), Kulchiy, Korytko (Chukhley 67), Hleb A, Kutuzov, Bulyga (Hleb V 72).
Referee: Rizzoli (Italy).

La Vella, 10 September 2008, 200
Andorra (0) 1 *(Pujol 67 (pen))*
Belarus (1) 3 *(Verkhovtsov 37, Rodionov 79, Hleb V 90)*

Andorra: Koldo; Ayala, Escura, Sonejee, Lima T, Lima I, Pujol (Toscano 82), Vieira (Vales 62), Fernando Silva (Moreno 86), Jimenez, Xavi.
Belarus: Veremko; Kulchi, Filipenko, Omelyanchuk, Pavlov (Rodionov 57), Korytko, Bulyga (Hleb V 63), Strakanovich (Sitko 87), Hleb A, Kutuzov, Verkhovtsov.
Referee: Evans (Wales).

Zagreb, 10 September 2008, 35,218
Croatia (0) 1 *(Mandzukic 78)*
England (1) 4 *(Walcott 26, 59, 82, Rooney 63)*

Croatia: Pletikosa; Corluka, Simunic, Kovac R■, Srna, Rakitic, Pranjic, Modric, Kovac N (Pokrivac 62), Petric (Knezevic 56), Olic (Mandzukic 73).
England: James; Terry (Upson 89), Ferdinand, Cole A, Brown, Lampard, Cole J (Jenas 56), Barry, Walcott (Beckham 85), Rooney, Heskey.
Referee: Michel (Slovakia).

Almaty, 10 September 2008, 17,000
Kazakhstan (0) 1 *(Ostapenko 68)*
Ukraine (1) 3 *(Nazarenko 45, 80, Shevchenko 54)*

Kazakhstan: Loriya; Irismetov, Kuchma, Azovskiy, Karpovich, Smakov, Zhumaskaliyev, Asanbayev (Baizhanov 73), Baltiyev (Uzdenov 88), Skorykh, Ostapenko.
Ukraine: Pyatov; Shevchuk, Yarmash, Kucher, Aliev, Tymoshchuk, Levchenko, Mikhalik, Nazarenko (Kravchenko 81), Seleznov (Homenyuk 87), Shevchenko (Voronin 88).
Referee: Brych (Germany).

Wembley, 11 October 2008, 89,107
England (0) 5 *(Ferdinand 52, Rooney 76, 86, Defoe 90, Kuchma 64 (og))*
Kazakhstan (0) 1 *(Kukeyev 68)*

England: James; Brown, Cole A, Gerrard, Ferdinand, Upson, Walcott (Beckham 79), Lampard, Heskey, Rooney (Defoe 86), Barry (Wright-Phillips 46).
Kazakhstan: Mokin; Kuchma, Kislitsyn, Kirov (Sabalakov 85), Kukeyev, Baltiyev, Logvinenko, Ibrayev, Skorykh, Ostapenko (Maltsev 76), Nusserbayev.
Referee: Allaerts (Belgium).

Kharkiv, 11 October 2008, 38,500
Ukraine (0) 0
Croatia (0) 0

Ukraine: Pyatov; Chigrinskiy, Yarmash, Shevchuk, Aliev, Golaydo, Tymoshchuk, Nazarenko, Mikhalik, Levchenko (Kravchenko 84), Shevchenko.
Croatia: Pletikosa; Krizanac, Corluka, Simunic, Vukojevic, Srna, Rakitic (Mandzukic 84), Pranjic, Modric, Kovac N, Olic.
Referee: Braamhaar (Holland).

Minsk, 15 October 2008, 32,000
Belarus (1) 1 *(Sitko 28)*
England (1) 3 *(Gerrard 11, Rooney 50, 74)*

Belarus: Zhevnov; Verkhovtsov, Filipenko, Omelyanchuk, Molosh, Kulchi, Sitko, Putsilo (Rodionov 67), Stasevich (Hleb V 90), Kutuzov (Strakanovich 77), Bulyga.
England: James; Brown, Bridge, Gerrard, Ferdinand, Upson, Walcott (Wright-Phillips 68), Lampard, Heskey (Crouch 70), Rooney (Beckham 87), Barry.
Referee: Hauge (Norway).

Zagreb, 15 October 2008, 14,441
Croatia (2) 4 *(Rakitic 16, 86 (pen), Olic 32, Modric 75)*
Andorra (0) 0

Croatia: Pletikosa; Krizanac (Knezevic 78), Simunic, Corluka, Vukojevic (Leko 61), Rakitic, Pranjic, Modric, Petric, Olic (Mandzukic 68), Klasnic.
Andorra: Koldo; Rodriguez, Lima I, Escura (Txema 81), Vieira, Pujol, Ayala, Xavi, Vales, Jimenez (Somoza 87), Fernando Silva (Toscano 90).
Referee: Vad (Hungary).

La Vella, 1 April 2009, 1000
Andorra (0) 0
Croatia (2) 2 *(Klasnic 15, Eduardo 35)*

Andorra: Koldo; Lima T, Escura (Rodriguez 90), Vieira, Pujol, Bernaus, Andorra, Vales, Sonejee, Jimenez (Moreno 81), Fernando Silva (Moreira 78).
Croatia: Pletikosa; Vejic, Krizanac, Cale (Vukojevic 69), Corluka, Kranjcar, Juric (Pokrivac 64), Srna, Rakitic, Eduardo, Klasnic (Kalinic 77).
Referee: Trattou (Cyprus).

Wembley, 1 April 2009, 87,548

England (1) 2 *(Crouch 29, Terry 85)*

Ukraine (0) 1 *(Shevchenko 74)*

England: James; Johnson G, Cole A, Barry, Terry, Ferdinand (Jagielka 88), Lennon (Beckham 58), Lampard, Crouch (Wright-Phillips 79), Rooney, Gerrard.
Ukraine: Pyatov; Chigrinskiy, Shevchuk, Yarmash, Mikhalik, Valyaev (Nazarenko 61), Slyusar (Kalinichenko 89), Aliev, Tymoshchuk, Voronin (Shevchenko 55), Milevskiy.
Referee: Bo Larsen (Denmark).

Almaty, 1 April 2009, 19,000

Kazakhstan (1) 1 *(Abdulin 10)*

Belarus (0) 5 *(Hleb A 48, Kalachev 53, 63, Stasevich 57, Kovel 88)*

Kazakhstan: Loriya; Irismetov, Abdulin, Kislitsyn, Smakov, Logvinenko, Kukeev, Karpovich (Ibraev 63), Baltiev (Nurgaliev 81), Ostapenko, Nuserbaev.
Belarus: Zhevnov; Sosnovskiy, Yurevich, Shitov, Stasevich (Kovel 80), Kulchiy (Kashevski 75), Kalachev, Bordachev, Hleb A, Rodionov, Kutuzov (Bliznyuk 86).
Referee: Jech (Czech Republic).

Grodno, 6 June 2009, 8500

Belarus (2) 5 *(Bliznyuk 3, 75, Kalachev 44, Kornilenko 50, 65)*

Andorra (0) 1 *(Lima T 90 (pen))*

Belarus: Zhevnov; Yurevich, Sosnovskiy, Shitov (Rudik 66), Verkhovtsov, Stasevich, Kalachev, Hleb A, Kashevski (Kovel 66), Bliznyuk, Kornilenko (Rodionov 80).
Andorra: Koldo; Lima T (Juli Fernandez 90), Lima I, Escura, Ayala, Andorra (Rodriguez 82), Vales, Sonejee, Fernando Silva, Moreno, Moreira (Jimenez 76).
Referee: Krajnc (Slovenia).

Zagreb, 6 June 2009, 32,073

Croatia (1) 2 *(Petric 2, Modric 68)*

Ukraine (1) 2 *(Shevchenko 13, Gay 54)*

Croatia: Runje; Simunic, Kovac R, Corluka, Juric (Vukojevic 46), Rakitic (Leko 46), Pranjic, Modric, Srna, Petric, Olic (Mandzukic 60).
Ukraine: Pyatov; Chigrinskiy, Mandzyuk, Kucher, Shevchuk, Rotan, Gay, Nazarenko (Kalinichenko 75), Tymoshchuk (Rusol 88), Shevchenko (Seleznov 23), Milevskiy.
Referee: Hauge (Norway).

Almaty, 6 June 2009, 24,000

Kazakhstan (0) 0

England (2) 4 *(Barry 39, Heskey 45, Rooney 72, Lampard 78 (pen))*

Kazakhstan: Mokin; Abdulin, Kirov, Kislitsyn, Karpovich, Logvinenko, Kukeev, Skorykh, Averchenko (Erbes 74), Ostapenko (Ibraev 27), Nuserbaev.
England: Green; Johnson G (Beckham 76), Cole A, Barry, Terry, Upson, Gerrard, Lampard, Heskey (Defoe 81), Rooney, Walcott (Wright-Phillips 46).
Referee: Jakobsson (Iceland).

Wembley, 10 June 2009, 57,897

England (3) 6 *(Rooney 4, 38, Lampard 29, Defoe 73, 75, Crouch 80)*

Andorra (0) 0

England: Green; Johnson G, Cole A (Bridge 63), Beckham, Terry, Lescott, Gerrard (Young A 46), Lampard, Crouch, Rooney (Defoe 46), Walcott.
Andorra: Koldo (Gomes 89); Lima T (Vales 47), Txema, Ayala, Lima I, Andorra, Vieira, Jimenez, Sonejee, Moreno, Fernando Silva (Juli Fernandez 79).
Referee: Nijhuis (Holland).

Kiev, 10 June 2009, 11,500

Ukraine (1) 2 *(Nazarenko 33, 47)*

Kazakhstan (1) 1 *(Nuserbaev 18)*

Ukraine: Bogush; Chigrinskiy, Mandzyuk, Shevchuk, Rusol, Gay, Rotan (Kalinichenko 81), Tymoshchuk, Nazarenko, Milevskiy, Voronin (Seleznov 68).
Kazakhstan: Mokin; Abudlin, Kirov (Irismetov 70), Kislitsyn, Erbes (Averchenko 74), Karpovich, Skorykh, Logvinenko, Kukeev, Khizhinchenko, Nuserbaev (Travin 63).
Referee: Paixao (Portugal).

Group 6 Table	P	W	D	L	F	A	Pts
England	7	7	0	0	26	4	21
Croatia	6	3	2	1	12	6	11
Ukraine	6	3	2	1	9	6	11
Belarus	5	3	0	2	14	7	9
Kazakhstan	7	1	0	6	7	22	3
Andorra	7	0	0	7	2	25	0

GROUP 7

Vienna, 6 September 2008, 48,000

Austria (2) 3 *(Janko 8, Aufhauser 41, Ivanschitz 72 (pen))*

France (0) 1 *(Govou 61)*

Austria: Manninger; Scharner, Prodl, Pogatetz, Garics, Stranzl, Ivanschitz (Leitgeb 81), Fuchs, Aufhauser, Janko (Maierhofer 88), Harnik (Standfest 90).
France: Mandanda; Sagna (Gourcuff 71), Mexes, Gallas, Evra, Toulalan, Nasri (Anelka 79), Diarra L, Henry, Govou, Benzema.
Referee: Bo Larsen (Denmark).

Cluj, 6 September 2008, 14,000

Romania (0) 0

Lithuania (1) 3 *(Stankevicius 31, Mikoliunas 69, Kalonas 86)*

Romania: Lobont; Sapunaru, Radu (Niculae M 46), Radoi (Lazar 72), Goian, Contra, Tamas, Dica, Cocis, Niculae D, Marica (Bratu 53).
Lithuania: Karcemarskas; Stankevicius, Semberas, Klimavicius, Dedura, Zelmikas, Pilibaitis (Savenas 74), Mikoliunas, Ksanavicius (Kalonas 62), Cesnauskis D, Danilevicius (Cesnauskis E 80).
Referee: Kelly (Republic of Ireland).

Belgrade, 6 September 2008, 9615

Serbia (1) 2 *(Jacobsen J 30 (og), Zigic 88)*

Faeroes (0) 0

Serbia: Disljenkovic; Obradovic, Vidic, Rukavina, Dragutinovic, Tosic (Jankovic 75), Stankovic, Milijas (Ilic 61), Krasic, Pantelic (Lazovic 56), Zigic.
Faeroes: Mikkelsen; Naes■, Jacobsen J, Davidsen, Danielsen, Bo, Thomassen, Samuelsen (Lokin 69), Jacobsen C, Flotum, Borg.
Referee: Nikolaev (Russia).

Torshavn, 10 September 2008, 805

Faeroes (0) 0

Romania (0) 1 *(Cocis 59)*

Faeroes: Mikkelsen; Bo, Danielsen, Davidsen, Jacobsen J, Jacobsen P (Lokin 80), Samuelsen, Thomassen, Borg (Eliasen 90), Flotum (Olsen A 76), Jacobsen C.
Romania: Lobont; Radoi (Ghionea■ 18), Goian, Contra, Nesu, Aliuta (Moti 68), Cocis, Codrea, Lazar, Costea, Niculae M (Bratu 70).
Referee: Strahonja (Croatia).

Paris, 10 September 2008, 53,027

France (0) 2 *(Henry 53, Anelka 63)*

Serbia (0) 1 *(Ivanovic 75)*

France: Mandanda; Abidal, Gallas, Sagna, Clichy, Toulalan, Diarra A, Benzema (Anelka 46), Gourcuff (Flamini 90), Govou (Diarra L 82), Henry.
Serbia: Stojkovic; Krstajic, Vidic, Ivanovic, Stankovic (Kacar 4), Tosic, Ergic (Zigic 56), Jankovic, Kuzmanovic, Sulejmani (Krasic 68), Pantelic.
Referee: Benquerenca (Portugal).

Marijampole, 10 September 2008, 4500

Lithuania (0) 2 *(Danilevicius 52, 58)*

Austria (0) 0

Lithuania: Karcemarskas; Semberas, Klimavicius, Dedura, Zelmikas, Stankevicius, Pilibaitis (Cesnauskis E 72), Mikolunas, Ksanavicius (Zaliukas 75), Cesnauskis D (Kalonas 66), Danilevicius.
Austria: Manninger; Prodl, Pogatetz, Garics, Stranzl, Scharner (Hoffer 66), Ivanschitz, Fuchs, Aufhauser (Saumel 55), Maierhofer, Harnik.
Referee: Tagliavento (Italy).

Torshavn, 11 October 2008, 1890
Faeroes (0) 1 *(Lokin 47)*
Austria (0) 1 *(Stranzl 49)*

Faeroes: Mikkelsen; Naes, Jacobsen J, Davidsen, Danielsen, Bo, Thomassen (Benjaminsen 37), Hansen A, Holst, Jacobsen C, Borg (Lokin 32) (Flotum 74).
Austria: Manninger; Stranzl, Scharner, Prodl, Pogatetz, Garics (Kienast 67), Ivanschitz, Fuchs, Janko (Arnautovic 80), Hoffer, Harnik (Holzl 25).
Referee: Ceferin (Slovenia).

Constanta, 11 October 2008, 12,800
Romania (2) 2 *(Petre 5, Goian 16)*
France (1) 2 *(Ribery 36, Gourcuff 68)*

Romania: Lobont; Rat, Ogararu, Chivu, Tamas, Goian, Muresan, Cocis, Petre (Costea 75), Mutu (Bucur 75), Marica.
France: Mandanda; Abidal, Boumsong, Sagna, Evra, Malouda (Benzema 37), Toulalan, Ribery (Briand 90), Gourcuff, Diarra A, Henry.
Referee: De Bleeckere (Belgium).

Belgrade, 11 October 2008, 22,000
Serbia (2) 3 *(Ivanovic 6, Krasic 34, Zigic 82)*
Lithuania (0) 0

Serbia: Stojkovic; Obradovic, Dragutinovic (Krstajic 24), Vidic, Ivanovic (Kuzmanovic 57), Stankovic, Milijas, Krasic (Jankovic 72), Jovanovic, Zigic, Pantelic.
Lithuania: Karcemarskas; Zelmikas, Stankevicius, Semberas, Klimavicius■, Dedura, Pilibaitis (Skerla 79), Papeckys (Kalonas 46), Mikoliunas (Jankauskas 46), Ksanavicius, Danilevicius.
Referee: Gonzalez (Spain).

Vienna, 15 October 2008, 48,000
Austria (0) 1 *(Janko 80)*
Serbia (3) 3 *(Krasic 14, Jovanovic 18, Obradovic 24)*

Austria: Manninger; Stranzl (Gercaliu 18), Scharner, Prodl, Pogatetz, Garics, Ivanschitz, Fuchs, Aufhauser (Saumel 60), Janko, Hoffer (Arnautovic 46).
Serbia: Stojkovic; Lukovic, Obradovic, Vidic, Ivanovic, Stankovic (Jankovic 76), Milijas (Kuzmanovic 53), Krasic, Jovanovic, Zigic, Pantelic (Tosic 64).
Referee: Riley (England).

Kaunas, 15 October 2008, 5000
Lithuania (1) 1 *(Danilevicius 20)*
Faeroes (0) 0

Lithuania: Karcemarskas; Alunderis, Stankevicius, Skerla, Semberas, Dedura, Pilibaitis (Zaliukas 90), Mikoliunas, Ksanavicius (Kalonas A 58), Velicka (Poskus 69), Danilevicius.
Faeroes: Mikkelsen; Naes, Jacobsen J, Davidsen, Danielsen, Bo, Benjaminsen (Jacobsen R 87), Samuelsen (Hojsted 81), Lokin (Hansen 85), Jacobsen C, Holst.
Referee: Kapitanis (Cyprus).

Kaunas, 28 March 2009, 8700
Lithuania (0) 0
France (0) 1 *(Ribery 67)*

Lithuania: Karcemarskas; Dedura, Skerla, Semberas, Klimavicius, Cesnauskis E (Mikoliunas 85), Cesnauskis D, Sernas, Panka (Poskus 81), Savenas (Ivaskevicius 65), Danilevicius.
France: Mandanda; Squillaci, Sagna, Gallas, Evra, Toulalan, Ribery, Gourcuff (Nasri 78), Diarra L, Luyindula (Benzema 64), Henry.
Referee: Braamhaar (Holland).

Constanta, 28 March 2009, 12,000
Romania (0) 2 *(Marica 50, Stoica 74)*
Serbia (2) 3 *(Jovanovic 18, Stoica 44 (og), Ivanovic 59)*

Romania: Lobont; Stoica, Tamas, Rat, Radoi, Contra, Cocis (Niculae M 76), Codrea (Tanase 46), Mutu, Marica, Costea (Bucur 63).
Serbia: Stojkovic; Obradovic, Vidic, Ivanovic, Dragutinovic, Stankovic, Milijas, Krasic, Jovanovic (Jankovic 62), Zigic, Pantelic (Subotic 66).
Referee: Trefoloni (Italy).

Klagenfurt, 1 April 2009, 23,000
Austria (2) 2 *(Hoffer 25, 44)*
Romania (1) 1 *(Tanase 24)*

Austria: Gspurning; Schiemer, Prodl, Pogatetz, Ortlechner, Beichler (Holzl 78), Pehlivan, Scharner, Maierhofer, Hoffer (Okotie 54), Arnautovic (Korkmaz 70).
Romania: Lobont; Tamas, Rat, Radoi (Stoica 46), Goian, Contra, Tanase, Nicolita (Nicu 84), Cocis, Marica, Bucur (Niculae M 68).
Referee: Thomson (Scotland).

Paris, 1 April 2009, 79,543
France (0) 1 *(Ribery 75)*
Lithuania (0) 0

France: Mandanda; Squillaci, Sagna, Gallas, Evra, Ribery, Gourcuff (Benzema 57), Diarra L, Diarra A, Luyindula (Gignac 68), Henry.
Lithuania: Karcemarskas; Skerla, Semberas, Klimavicius, Alunderis, Zaliukas, Sernas, Pilibaitis (Velicka 82), Mikoliunas (Cesnauskis E 65), Kalonas (Savenas 59), Danilevicius.
Referee: Webb (England).

Marijampole, 6 June 2009, 5850
Lithuania (0) 0
Romania (1) 1 *(Marica 38)*

Lithuania: Karcemarskas; Skerla, Klimavicius (Luksys 84), Stankevicius, Semberas, Cesnauskis E, Kalonas (Mikolunas 64), Zaliukas, Sernas, Pilibaitis (Dedura 81), Danilevicius.
Romania: Coman; Shivu, Apostol, Sapunaru, Rat, Radoi, Tanase, Ghioane (Lazar 90), Marica (Niculae M 85), Mara (Roman 72), Danciulescu.
Referee: Eriksson (Sweden).

Belgrade, 6 June 2009, 50,000
Serbia (1) 1 *(Milijas 7 (pen))*
Austria (0) 0

Serbia: Stojkovic; Subotic, Ivanovic, Dragutinovic, Vidic (Rukavina 46), Milijas, Krasic (Kacar 82), Stankovic, Jovanovic, Lazovic (Jankovic 56), Pantelic.
Austria: Gspurning; Ortlechner, Stranzl, Schiemer, Dragovic, Pehlivan, Scharner, Jantscher, Holzl (Lexa 66), Maierhofer (Janko 56), Hoffer (Okotie 56).
Referee: Vink (Holland).

Torshavn, 10 June 2009, 2896
Faeroes (0) 0
Serbia (1) 2 *(Jovanovic 44, Subotic 62)*

Faeroes: Mikkelsen; Gregersen, Naes, Davidsen, Danielsen, Bo, Olsen S (Petersen 78), Benjaminsen, Samuelsen (Jacobsen C 68), Lokin, Holst (Flotum 87).
Serbia: Stojkovic; Kolarov, Subotic, Lukovic, Ivanovic, Krasic (Kacar 83), Milijas, Kuzmanovic, Jovanovic (Sulejmani 77), Zigic, Pantelic (Lazovic 65).
Referee: Levi (Israel).

Group 7 Table	P	W	D	L	F	A	Pts
Serbia	7	6	0	1	15	5	18
France	5	3	1	1	7	6	10
Lithuania	7	3	0	4	6	6	9
Austria	6	2	3	1	9	7	7
Romania	6	2	1	3	7	10	7
Faeroes	5	0	1	4	1	7	1

GROUP 8

Larnaca, 6 September 2008, 6000
Cyprus (1) 1 *(Aloneftis 29)*
Italy (1) 2 *(Di Natale 8, 90)*

Cyprus: Georgallides; Christou, Charalambous, Charalambides, Nicolaou, Michael (Yiasoumi 72), Makrides, Garpozis, Aloneftis, Okkas (Pavlou 74), Konstantinou (Christofi 63).
Italy: Buffon; Cannavaro, Grosso (Cassetti 18), Gamberini (Barzagli 4), De Rossi, Camoranesi, Zambrotta, Pirlo, Di Natale, Toni (Gattuso 46), Gilardino.
Referee: Vink (Holland).

Mainz, 6 September 2008, 4500
Georgia (0) 1 *(Kenia 90)*
Republic of Ireland (1) 2 *(Doyle K 13, Whelan 70)*
Georgia: Loria; Shashiashvili, Lobjanidze, Khizanishvili (Asatiani 83), Kaladze, Odikadze, Menteshashvili, Kobiashvili, Kenia, Aleksidze (Siradze 61), Iashvili (Mchedlidze 77).
Republic of Ireland: Given; Finnan (McShane 80), O'Shea, Dunne, Rowlands, Whelan, Kilbane, Hunt, Keane, Doyle K (Miller 77), McGeady (Keogh A 87).
Referee: Szabo (Hungary).

Podgorica, 6 September 2008, 9000
Montenegro (0) 2 *(Vucinic 61, Jovetic 82 (pen))*
Bulgaria (1) 2 *(Petrov S 11, Georgiev 90)*
Montenegro: Poleksic; Pavicevic, Batak, Tanasijevic, Drincic, Bozovic, Boskovic (Burzanovic 83), Pekovic, Jovetic, Bogavac (Vukcevic 53), Vucinic (Djalovic 86).
Bulgaria: Ivankov; Milanov (Tomasic 48), Iliev, Angelov S■, Tunchev, Genchev (Georgiev 66), Petrov S, Lazarov, Dimitrov, Berbatov, Popov (Yankov 40).
Referee: Oriekhov (Ukraine).

Udine, 10 September 2008, 27,164
Italy (1) 2 *(De Rossi 17, 89)*
Georgia (0) 0
Italy: Buffon; Dossena, Cannavaro, Legrottaglie, Zambrotta, Aquilani, Camoranesi, De Rossi, Pirlo (Palombo 46), Di Natale (Del Piero 56), Toni (Iaquinta 70).
Georgia: Loria; Salukvadze, Kaladze, Lobjanidze, Eliava (Kvirkvelia 46), Khmaladze, Menteshashvili (Odikadze 68), Kobiashvili, Kenia, Iashvili, Mchedlidze (Siradze 55).
Referee: Einwaller (Austria).

Podgorica, 10 September 2008, 12,000
Montenegro (0) 0
Republic of Ireland (0) 0
Montenegro: Poleksic; Batak, Jovanovic, Pavicevic, Tanasijevic, Zverotic, Bozovic (Vukcevic 54), Drincic, Pekovic, Jovetic, Vucinic.
Republic of Ireland: Given; Finnan, Hunt, Dunne, O'Shea, Whelan, Reid A, Doyle K, Keane, Kilbane, McGeady.
Referee: Kaldma (Estonia).

Sofia, 11 October 2008, 35,000
Bulgaria (0) 0
Italy (0) 0
Bulgaria: Ivankov; Wagner (Ivanov I 37), Tunchev, Milanov, Iliev, Petrov M (Popov 90), Yankov, Petrov S, Georgiev, Berbatov, Dimitrov.
Italy: Amelia; Cannavaro, Chiellini, Dossena, Montolivo (Perrotta 68), Zambrotta, Gattuso, De Rossi, Pepe, Gilardino (Toni 73), Di Natale (Rossi 68).
Referee: Lannoy (France).

Tbilisi, 11 October 2008, 40,000
Georgia (0) 1 *(Kobiashvili 73)*
Cyprus (0) 1 *(Konstantinou 67)*
Georgia: Lomaia; Shashiashvili, Salukvadze, Lobjanidze, Khizanishvili, Menteshashvili, Kobiashvili, Kenia (Gotsiridze 65), Razmadze, Iashvili, Mchedlidze (Aleksidze 76).
Cyprus: Georgallides; Elia (Lambrou 83), Constantinou, Charalambides, Michael (Nicolaou 37), Makrides, Charalambous, Aloneftis (Panagi 90), Konstantinou, Garpozis, Okkas.
Referee: Matejek (Czech Republic).

Tbilisi, 15 October 2008, 35,250
Georgia (0) 0
Bulgaria (0) 0
Georgia: Lomaia; Kvakhadze, Shashiashvili, Salukvadze, Lobjanidze, Menteshashvili, Kobiashvili, Razmadze, Mchedlidze (Siradze 32), Iashvili (Merebashvili 71), Gotsiridze (Odikadze 84).
Bulgaria: Petkov; Ivanov I, Tunchev, Milanov, Iliev, Yankov (Angelov S 56), Petrov S, Petrov M (Popov 29), Georgiev, Dimitrov (Rangelov 73), Berbatov.
Referee: Kuipers (Holland).

Lecce, 15 October 2008, 20,162
Italy (2) 2 *(Aquilani 8, 29)*
Montenegro (1) 1 *(Vucinic 19)*
Italy: Amelia; Cannavaro, Zambrotta, Chiellini, Dossena (Bonera 59), Gattuso, De Rossi, Aquilani (Perrotta 65), Di Natale (Quagliarella 76), Gilardino, Pepe.
Montenegro: Poleksic, Jovanovic, Pavicevic, Batak, Zverotic (Novakovic 89), Boskovic (Bozovic 81), Vukcevic, Drincic, Jovetic, Tanasijevic, Vucinic (Damjanovic 90).
Referee: Proenca (Portugal).

Dublin, 15 October 2008, 55,833
Republic of Ireland (1) 1 *(Keane 5)*
Cyprus (0) 0
Republic of Ireland: Given; McShane, Kilbane, Dunne, O'Shea, Whelan, Gibson, Doyle K (Folan 90), Keane, Duff, McGeady.
Cyprus: Georgallides; Elia, Constantinou, Marangos (Panagi 52), Charalambous, Lambrou (Papathanasiou 46), Makrides, Konstantinou (Yiasoumi 79), Garpozis, Christofi, Okkas.
Referee: Tudor (Romania).

Dublin, 11 February 2009, 45,000
Republic of Ireland (0) 2 *(Keane 73 (pen), 78)*
Georgia (1) 1 *(Iashvili 1)*
Republic of Ireland: Given; Kelly, O'Shea, Whelan, Dunne, Andrews, Duff (Hunt S 80), Doyle K, Keane, Kilbane, McGeady.
Georgia: Lomaia; Lobjanidze, Kvirkvelia, Khizanishvili, Kaladze, Siradze (Aleksidze 77), Menteshashvili (Khmaladze 70), Kobiashvili, Razmadze, Iashvili, Gotsiridze (Merebashvili 68).
Referee: Hyytia (Finland).

Larnaca, 28 March 2009, 1500
Cyprus (1) 2 *(Konstantinou 33, Christofi 56)*
Georgia (0) 1 *(Kobiashvili 71 (pen))*
Cyprus: Georgallides; Elia, Christou, Satsias (Avraam 82), Michael, Charalambous (Yiasoumi 90), Garpozis, Alexandrou, Konstantinou, Christofi, Aloneftis (Panagi 69).
Georgia: Lomaia; Shashiashvili, Lobjanidze, Kvakhadze, Khizanishvili, Odikadze, Kobiashvili, Razmadze, Mchedlidze (Siradze 28), Iashvili, Gotsiridze.
Referee: Fautrel (France).

Podgorica, 28 March 2009, 10,500
Montenegro (0) 0
Italy (1) 2 *(Pirlo 11 (pen), Pazzini 73)*
Montenegro: Poleksic; Pavicevic, Batak, Basa, Drincic, Bozovic, Boskovic, Vukcevic (Zverotic 89), Pekovic (Vujovic 79), Jovetic, Djalovic (Beciraj 71).
Italy: Buffon; Chiellini, Cannavaro, Grosso, De Rossi, Pirlo (Brighi 81), Zambrotta, Palombo, Quagliarella, Iaquinta (Pazzini 59), Di Natale (Pepe 9).
Referee: Atkinson (England).

Dublin, 28 March 2009, 60,002
Republic of Ireland (1) 1 *(Dunne 1)*
Bulgaria (0) 1 *(Kilbane 74 (og))*
Republic of Ireland: Given; McShane, O'Shea, Whelan, Dunne, Andrews, Kilbane, Hunt S, Keane, Doyle K, McGeady (Keogh A 90).
Bulgaria: Ivankov; Manolev, Angelov S, Stoianov, Milanov (Kishishev 24), Tomasic, Petrov S, Georgiev (Makriev 66), Telkiyski, Popov I (Dimitrov 46), Rangelov.
Referee: Bebek (Croatia).

Sofia, 1 April 2009, 16,916
Bulgaria (1) 2 *(Popov I 80, Makriev 90)*
Cyprus (0) 0
Bulgaria: Ivankov; Manolev, Kishishev, Angelov S, Tomasic, Stoianov, Georgiev, Telkiyski (Dimitrov 62), Petrov S, Popov I (Todorov 74), Rangelov (Makriev 90).
Cyprus: Georgallides; Elia, Christou, Satsias, Michael (Marangos 76), Charalambous, Garpozis, Konstantinou, Christofi (Yiasoumi 59), Aloneftis, Alexandrou (Avraam 65).
Referee: Ingvarsson (Sweden).

Tbilisi, 1 April 2009, 16,000

Georgia (0) 0

Montenegro (0) 0

Georgia: Lomaia; Kvirkvelia, Kvakhadze, Kashia, Salukvadze, Kobiashvili, Khmaladze, Odikadze (Klimiashvili 66), Merebashvili, Gotsiridze (Siradze 78), Iashvili.
Montenegro: Poleksic; Batak, Basa, Zverotic (Vujovic 87), Tanasijevic, Pejovic, Drincic, Boskovic, Pekovic, Djalovic (Beciraj 68), Jovetic.
Referee: Malcolm (Northern Ireland).

Bari, 1 April 2009, 41,000

Italy (1) 1 *(Iaquinta 9)*

Republic of Ireland (0) 1 *(Keane 89)*

Italy: Buffon; Grosso, Chiellini, Cannavaro, Zambrotta, Pirlo (Palombo 44), De Rossi, Brighi, Pepe (Dossena 55), Pazzini[a], Iaquinta (Quagliarella 90).
Republic of Ireland: Given; McShane, O'Shea, Whelan, Dunne, Andrews (Gibson 54), Kilbane, Hunt S, Keane, Doyle K (Hunt N 63), McGeady.
Referee: Stark (Germany).

Sofia, 6 June 2009, 38,000

Bulgaria (1) 1 *(Telkiyski 29)*

Republic of Ireland (1) 1 *(Dunne 24)*

Bulgaria: Ivankov; Kishishev, Angelov S, Tomasic, Stoianov, Milanov, Telkiyski (Dimitrov 81), Petrov S, Petrov M (Georgiev 61), Bojinov (Makriev 59), Berbatov.
Republic of Ireland: Given; O'Shea (Kelly 82), Kilbane, Dunne, St Ledger-Hall, Whelan, Hunt S (McGeady 71), Andrews, Folan, Keane (Best 74), Duff.
Referee: Bo Larsen (Denmark).

Larnaca, 6 June 2009, 3000

Cyprus (2) 2 *(Konstantinou 13, Michael 45 (pen))*

Montenegro (0) 2 *(Damjanovic 65, 78)*

Cyprus: Georgallides (Morfis 34); Elia, Christou, Michael, Makrides, Charalambous, Nicolaou (Charalambides 78), Garpozis (Satsias 68), Konstantinou, Aloneftis, Okkas.
Montenegro: Poleksic; Tanasijevic, Pejovic (Fatic 86), Pavicevic, Djudovic, Batak, Novakovic (Zverotic 19), Kascelan, Drincic (Damjanovic 46), Vujovic, Vucinic.
Referee: Carballo (Spain).

Group 8 Table

	P	W	D	L	F	A	Pts
Italy	6	4	2	0	9	3	14
Republic of Ireland	7	3	4	0	8	5	13
Bulgaria	6	1	5	0	6	4	8
Cyprus	6	1	2	3	6	9	5
Montenegro	6	0	4	2	5	8	4
Georgia	7	0	3	4	4	9	3

GROUP 9

Skopje, 6 September 2008, 9000

Macedonia (1) 1 *(Naumoski 5)*

Scotland (0) 0

Macedonia: Milosevski; Sedloski, Petrov (Grncarov 79), Noveski, Mitreski, Lazarevski, Sumulikoski, Grozdanovski, Pandev (Tasevski 83), Naumoski (Trajanov 69), Maznov.
Scotland: Gordon; Alexander G, Naysmith, Hartley (Commons 66), Caldwell G, McManus, Fletcher D, Brown S, McFadden, Miller (Boyd 81), Robson (Maloney 76).
Referee: Kralovec (Czech Republic).

Oslo, 6 September 2008, 17,254

Norway (1) 2 *(Iversen 36 (pen), 50)*

Iceland (1) 2 *(Helguson 39, Gudjohnsen 69)*

Norway: Jarstein; Riise JA, Reginiussen, Hogli, Hangeland, Winsnes, Skjelbred (Grindheim 70), Andresen, Iversen, Helstad, Carew (Pedersen 65).
Iceland: Sturluson; Steinsson, Saevarsson, Hreidarsson, Eiriksson, Sigurdsson K, Hallfredsson (Steinarsson 74), Gunnarsson A (Palmason 68), Gislason, Helguson (Gunnarsson V 85), Gudjohnsen E.
Referee: Yefet (Israel).

Reykjavik, 10 September 2008, 9767

Iceland (0) 1 *(Gudjohnsen 77)*

Scotland (1) 2 *(Broadfoot 18, Robson 59)*

Iceland: Sturulson; Eiriksson (Sigurdsson I 46), Hreidarsson, Saevarsson (Gunnarsson V 78), Steinsson, Gislason, Gunnarsson A (Palmason 64), Sigurdsson K, Hallfredsson, Gudjohnsen E, Helguson.
Scotland: Gordon; Broadfoot, Naysmith, Brown S, Caldwell G, McManus[a], Fletcher D, Maloney (Alexander G 79), McFadden (Hartley 79), Robson, Commons (Miller 63).
Referee: Gumienny (Belgium).

Skopje, 10 September 2008, 11,000

Macedonia (0) 1 *(Pandev 77)*

Holland (0) 2 *(Heitinga 46, Van der Vaart 60)*

Macedonia: Milosevski; Sedloski, Noveski, Mitreski, Lazarevski (Petrov 58), Trajanov (Ristic 83), Sumulikoski, Grozdanovski, Pandev, Naumoski, Maznov (Tasevski 62).
Holland: Stekelenburg; Ooijer (Boulahrouz 28), Mathijsen, Heitinga, Van der Vaart, Van Bommel, De Jong, Van Persie (Kuyt 70), Robben (Afellay 82), Huntelaar.
Referee: Gilewski (Poland).

Rotterdam, 11 October 2008, 37,500

Holland (1) 2 *(Mathijsen 15, Huntelaar 64)*

Iceland (0) 0

Holland: Van der Sar; Ooijer, Mathijsen, Marcellis, Van der Vaart (Sneijder 81), Van Bronckhorst, Van Bommel, De Jong (De Zeeuw 14), Kuyt, Huntelaar, Babel (Afellay 68).
Iceland: Gunnleifsson; Sigurdsson R (Bjarnason 73), Sigurdsson I, Saevarsson, Hreidarsson, Gunnarsson B (Gunnarsson A 73), Sigurdsson K, Hallfredsson (Smarason 87), Gislason, Gunnarsson V, Gudjohnsen E.
Referee: Trefoloni (Italy).

Glasgow, 11 October 2008, 50,205

Scotland (0) 0

Norway (0) 0

Scotland: Gordon; Broadfoot, Naysmith, Morrison (Fletcher S 56), Caldwell G, Weir, Robson, Brown, Fletcher D, McFadden (Iwelumo 56), Maloney.
Norway: Knudsen; Hoiland, Waehler, Hangeland, Riise JA, Grindheim, Stromstad (Pedersen 76), Riise BH (Braaten 56), Winsnes, Carew, Iversen.
Referee: Busacca (Switzerland).

Reykjavik, 15 October 2008, 5527

Iceland (1) 1 *(Gunnarsson V 15)*

Macedonia (0) 0

Iceland: Gunnleifsson; Steinsson, Sigurdsson I, Saevarsson, Hreidarsson, Gunnarsson B (Gunnarsson A 26), Sigurdsson K, Hallfredsson, Gislason, Gunnarsson V (Palmason 65), Gudjohnsen E (Bjarnason 80).
Macedonia: Milosevski; Sedloski, Petrov (Trajanov 52), Noveski, Mitreski, Lazarevski, Tasevski (Ristic 78), Sumulikoski, Grozdanovski, Pandev, Maznov (Stojkov 60).
Referee: Selcuk (Turkey).

Oslo, 15 October 2008, 23,840

Norway (0) 0

Holland (0) 1 *(Van Bommel 62)*

Norway: Knudsen; Riise JA, Hangeland, Hoiland, Winsnes, Waehler, Grindheim, Hauger (Helstad 84), Iversen, Carew, Pedersen (Elyounoussi 77).
Holland: Van der Sar; Ooijer, Mathijsen, Marcellis, Van Bronckhorst, Van Bommel, De Zeeuw, Van der Vaart (Sneijder 75), Babel (Afellay 25), Kuyt, Huntelaar (Van Persie 56).
Referee: Plautz (Austria).

Amsterdam, 28 March 2009, 49,552

Holland (2) 3 *(Huntelaar 30, Van Persie 45, Kuyt 76 (pen))*

Scotland (0) 0

Holland: Stekelenburg; Ooijer, Mathijsen, Van der Wiel, De Jong (Afellay 79), Van Bronckhorst, Van Bommel, Kuyt, Huntelaar (Schaars 79), Van Persie (Sneijder 64), Robben.

Scotland: McGregor; Alexander G (Hutton 73), Naysmith, Berra, Caldwell G, Ferguson, Teale (Morrison 84), Fletcher D, McCormack, Miller (Fletcher S 70), Brown S.
Referee: Duhamel (France).

Amsterdam, 1 April 2009, 47,750

Holland (3) 4 *(Kuyt 15, 40, Huntelaar 24, Van der Vaart 87)*
Macedonia (0) 0

Holland: Stekelenburg; Van der Wiel, Ooijer, Mathijsen, Van Bronckhorst, Van Bommel, Sneijder (Van der Vaart 76), De Jong, Robben (Babel 46), Kuyt (Afellay 80), Huntelaar.
Macedonia: Pachovski; Sedloski, Noveski, Mitreski, Popov, Grozdanovski (Lazarevski 57), Trajanov (Polozani 63), Tasevski (Maznov 89), Sumulikoski, Naumoski, Pandev.
Referee: Rasmussen (Denmark).

Glasgow, 1 April 2009, 42,259

Scotland (1) 2 *(McCormack 39, Fletcher S 65)*
Iceland (0) 1 *(Sigurdsson I 54)*

Scotland: Gordon; Hutton, Naysmith, Morrison (Rae 90), Caldwell G, McManus, Fletcher D, Brown S, Fletcher S (Teale 78), Miller, McCormack.
Iceland: Gunnleifsson; Eiriksson, Steinsson, Sigurdsson I (Bjarnason 81), Gunnarsson A (Jonsson E 70), Danielsson, Sigurdsson K, Palmason, Helguson, Gudjohnsen E, Smarason.
Referee: Einwaller (Austria).

Reykjavik, 6 June 2009, 9635

Iceland (0) 1 *(Sigurdsson K 88)*
Holland (2) 2 *(De Jong 8, Von Bommel 16)*

Iceland: Gunnleifsson; Saevarsson, Steinsson, Sigurdsson I, Hreidarsson, Eiriksson (Smarason 76), Danielsson (Gunnarsson B 46), Sigurdsson K, Palmason, Gislason (Gunnarsson A 67), Gudjohnsen E.
Holland: Stekelenburg; Ooijer, Mathijsen, Heitinga, Van der Vaart (Babel 75), Van Bommel, De Jong (Mendes 80), Van Bronckhorst, Van Persie, Robben, Kuyt (Huntelaar 67).
Referee: Dean (England).

Skopje, 6 June 2009, 7000

Macedonia (0) 0
Norway (0) 0

Macedonia: Nikolovski; Grncarov, Sedloski, Mitreski, Georgievski, Popov, Despotovski, Sumulikoski (Maznov 63), Naumoski (Ristic 75), Stojkov (Grozdanovski 81), Pandev.
Norway: Knudsen; Waehler, Riise JA, Hoiland, Hangeland, Winsnes, Skjelbred (Riise BH 46), Grindheim (Hauger 73), Pedersen, Carew, Braaten (Huseklepp 57).
Referee: Tagliavento (Italy).

Rotterdam, 10 June 2009, 45,600

Holland (1) 2 *(Ooijer 32, Robben 51)*
Norway (0) 0

Holland: Stekelenburg; Ooijer, Mathijsen, Heitinga, Van der Vaart, Van Bommel, Van Bronckhorst (Braafheid 46), Schaars, Robben (Babel 78), Kuyt, Van Persie (Huntelaar 83).
Norway: Knudsen; Hoiland, Waehler, Riise JA, Hauger, Grindheim (Skjelbred 67), Fevang, Pedersen, Winsnes (Tettey 79), Riise BH (Braaten 42), Carew.
Referee: Baskakov (Russia).

Skopje, 10 June 2009, 7000

Macedonia (1) 2 *(Stojkov 9, Ivanovski 86)*
Iceland (0) 0

Macedonia: Nikolovski (Pachovski 74); Sedloski, Mitreski, Lazarevski, Popov, Georgievski, Despotovski, Sumulikoski (Grozdanovski 80), Naumoski, Stojkov (Ivanovski 66), Pandev.
Iceland: Gunnleifsson; Ottesen, Steinsson, Gunnarsson B, Eiriksson, Sigurdsson K, Palmason (Gudmundsson J 74), Jonsson E (Saevarsson 60), Hallfredsson, Gislason, Smarason.
Referee: Ennjimi (France).

Group 9 Table	P	W	D	L	F	A	Pts
Holland	7	7	0	0	16	2	21
Scotland	5	2	1	2	4	6	7
Macedonia	6	2	1	3	4	7	7
Iceland	7	1	1	5	6	12	4
Norway	5	0	3	2	2	5	3

England's Theo Walcott rounds off a fine individual performance by striking his hat-trick and his country's fourth goal in the 4-1 victory over Croatia in Zagreb. (PA Photos)

SOUTH AMERICA

Buenos Aires, 13 October 2007, 55,000

Argentina (2) 2 *(Riquelme 27, 45)*

Chile (0) 0

Argentina: Abbondanzieri; Zanetti, Milito, Demichelis, Heinze, Riquelme, Cambiasso, Mascherano, Maxi Rodriguez (Gago 68), Tevez (Aguero 74), Messi (Saviola 84).
Chile: Bravo; Alvarez■, Riffo, Vidal, Ponce, Fernandez, Iturra (Maldonado 63), Gonzalez, Fierro (Droguett 37), Suazo, Rubio (Salas 46).
Referee: Vazquez (Uruguay).

Montevideo, 13 October 2007, 25,200

Uruguay (2) 5 *(Suarez 5, Forlan 38, Abreu 48, Sanchez 68, Bueno 83)*

Bolivia (0) 0

Uruguay: Carini; Fucile, Godin, Garcia, Perez, Scotti, Pereira M, Rodriguez, Abreu (Bueno 73), Suarez (Regueiro 66), Forlan (Sanchez 66).
Bolivia: Galarza; Raldes, Amador, Soliz (Cabrera 46), Hoyos (Suarez N 75), Alvarez, Lima, Vaca, Garcia R■, Martins, Moreno J (Cardozo 59).
Referee: Selman (Chile).

Bogota, 14 October 2007, 41,000

Colombia (0) 0

Brazil (0) 0

Colombia: Agustin; Zuniga, Velez, Mosquera, Moreno W, Amaya, Ferreira (Ramirez 55), Sanchez, Castrillon (Grisales 55), Garcia (Perea 81), Renteria.
Brazil: Julio Cesar; Maicon, Juan, Lucio, Ronaldinho, Kaka (Afonso 84), Gilberto Silva, Gilberto, Mineiro, Vagner Love (Josue 70), Robinho (Julio Baptista 62).
Referee: Amarilla (Paraguay).

Quito, 14 October 2007, 29,644

Ecuador (0) 0

Venezuela (0) 1 *(Rey 68)*

Ecuador: Viteri; Hurtado I, Espinoza, Bagui (Quiroz 76), Mendez, Castillo, Lara (Ayovi 46), Valencia (Borja 71), De La Cruz, Tenorio C, Benitez.
Venezuela: Vega; Rouga, Rojas, Rey, Cichero, Vallenilla, Arango (Guerra 65), Vera, Paez (Gonzalez H 77), Mea Vitali (Vielma 80), Maldonado.
Referee: Ortube (Bolivia).

Lima, 14 October 2007, 50,000

Peru (0) 0

Paraguay (0) 0

Peru: Butron; Acasiete, Vargas (Chiroque 83), Galliquio (Maestri 73), Rodriguez, Vilchez, Solano, De La Haza, Quinteros (Jayo 88), Farfan, Pizarro.
Paraguay: Villar; Morel, Caceres J, Da Silva, Caniza, Vera, Barreto (Britez 87), Riveros, Caceres V, Cabanas (Achucarro 76), Valdez (Cardozo 69).
Referee: Simon (Brazil).

La Paz, 17 October 2007, 19,469

Bolivia (0) 0

Colombia (0) 0

Bolivia: Galarza; Amador, Ribeiro, Raldes, Verduguez, Reyes L■, Mojica, Campos (Cabrera 55), Arce (Gutierrez R 72), Andaveris (Vaca 46), Limberg Gutierrez.
Colombia: Agustin; Arizala, Mosquera, Vallejo, Moreno W, Amaya, Sanchez, Ferreira (Ramirez 55), Anchico (Banguero 85), Valencia (Castrillon 63), Renteria.
Referee: Reinoso (Ecuador).

Maracaibo, 17 October 2007, 10,600

Venezuela (0) 0

Argentina (2) 2 *(Milito 16, Messi 43)*

Venezuela: Vega; Rojas, Vallenilla (Rosales 46), Rey, Cichero, Rouga, Arango, Seijas (Guerra 53), Paez, Mea Vitali, Maldonado (Arismendi 66).
Argentina: Abbondanzieri; Ibarra (Gago 63), Milito, Demichelis, Zanetti, Burdisso (Diaz 73), Riquelme, Cambiasso, Mascherano, Messi, Tevez (Denis 80).
Referee: Simon (Brazil).

Rio de Janeiro, 18 October 2007, 87,000

Brazil (1) 5 *(Vagner Love 19, Ronaldinho 62, Kaka 77, 85, Elano 83)*

Ecuador (0) 0

Brazil: Julio Cesar; Juan, Maicon, Lucio, Mineiro, Gilberto Silva, Gilberto, Ronaldinho, Kaka (Diego 89), Vagner Love (Elano 76), Robinho.
Ecuador: Viteri; Hurtado I, Bagui, Espinoza, Ayovi (Guerron 77), Mendez, De La Cruz, Castillo, Urrutia, Quiroz (Tenorio C 46), Benitez (Lara 82).
Referee: Larrionda (Uruguay).

Santiago, 18 October 2007, 58,000

Chile (1) 2 *(Suazo 11, Fernandez 52)*

Peru (0) 0

Chile: Bravo; Droguett, Riffo, Vidal, Ponce, Fernandez, Iturra, Gonzalez, Fierro (Fuentes 89), Suazo (Rubio 83), Salas (Jimenez 87).
Peru: Butron; Vilchez (Bazalar 73), Vargas, Galliquio, Acasiete, Rodriguez, De La Haza (Quinteros 46), Jayo, Solano, Pizarro, Farfan.
Referee: Ruiz (Colombia).

Asuncion, 18 October 2007, 23,200

Paraguay (1) 1 *(Valdez 15)*

Uruguay (0) 0

Paraguay: Villar; Morel, Caceres J, Da Silva, Caniza, Riveros, Caceres V, Vera, Barreto (Santana 86), Cabanas (Achucarro 79), Valdez (Cardozo 66).
Uruguay: Carini; Godin, Fucile, Lugano, Rodriguez (Bueno 79), Perez (Gonzalez A 68), Garcia, Pereira M, Scotti, Forlan, Suarez (Sanchez 62).
Referee: Baldassi (Argentina).

Buenos Aires, 17 November 2007, 43,308

Argentina (1) 3 *(Aguero 41, Riquelme 57, 74)*

Bolivia (0) 0

Argentina: Abbondanzieri; Milito, Zanetti, Demichelis, Ibarra, Mascherano, Cambiasso (Gago 69), Riquelme, Messi, Tevez (Denis 82), Aguero (Maxi Rodriguez 75).
Bolivia: Arias; Luis Gutierrez, Hoyos, Raldes, Garcia R, Vaca, Mendez, Suarez, Moreno J (Gutierrez R 61), Limberg Gutierrez (Arce 61), Cabrera (Martins 80).
Referee: Rivera (Peru).

Bogota, 17 November 2007, 28,273

Colombia (0) 1 *(Bustos 82)*

Venezuela (0) 0

Colombia: Agustin; Mosquera, Bustos, Velez, Moreno W, Ramirez (Torres 46), Castrillon, Amaya, Sanchez (Grisales 71), Renteria, Garcia (Moreno M 50).
Venezuela: Morales; Rojas, Vielma, Rey, Vallenilla, Rouga, Arango, Paez (Gonzalez C 67), Mea Vitali, Maldonado (Guerra 56), Fedor (Cichero 79).
Referee: Selman (Chile).

Asuncion, 18 November 2007, 30,000

Paraguay (2) 5 *(Valdez 10, Riveros 28, 88, Santa Cruz 51, Ayala 83)*

Ecuador (0) 1 *(Kaviedes 80)*

Paraguay: Villar; Da Silva, Caceres J, Morel (Veron 77), Barreto, Vera, Caceres V, Riveros, Santa Cruz (Ayala 74), Valdez (Bonet 60), Cabanas.
Ecuador: Elizaga; Montano, Guagua, Bagui, Espinoza, Ayovi, Urrutia (Campos 46), Castillo, Mendez, Ordonez (Kaviedes 63), Benitez (Caicedo 74).
Referee: Lopes (Brazil).

Lima, 18 November 2007, 45,847

Peru (0) 1 *(Vargas 72)*

Brazil (1) 1 *(Kaka 40)*

Peru: Penny; Acasiete, Salas, Rodriguez, Vargas, Lobaton (De La Haza 66), Jayo (Mendoza 63), Solano, Pizarro, Guerrero (Palacios 46), Farfan.
Brazil: Julio Cesar; Maicon, Juan, Lucio, Mineiro, Gilberto, Gilberto Silva, Ronaldinho, Kaka, Robinho (Elano 74), Vagner Love (Luis Fabiano 69).
Referee: Torres (Paraguay).

Montevideo, 18 November 2007, 45,000

Uruguay (1) 2 *(Suarez 42, Abreu 81)*

Chile (0) 2 *(Salas 59, 69 (pen))*

Uruguay: Carini; Godin, Fucile, Lugano, Rodriguez, Gargano, Perez (Arevalo 46), Scotti (Pereira M 61), Abreu, Sanchez (Gonzalez I 65), Suarez.
Chile: Bravo; Alvarez (Fuentes 60), Jara, Droguett, Riffo, Vidal, Ponce, Fernandez, Suazo (Moya 72), Salas, Rubio (Villanueva 46).
Referee: Pezzotta (Argentina).

San Cristobal, 20 November 2007, 24,000

Venezuela (2) 5 *(Arismendi 20, 40, Guerra 81, Maldonado 89, 90)*

Bolivia (2) 3 *(Arce 27, Martins 19, 77)*

Venezuela: Morales; Rey, Cichero, Rojas, Arango, Vera (Mea Vitali 59), Seijas (Perez 64), Paez (Guerra 74), Rosales, Maldonado, Arismendi.
Bolivia: Arias; Raldes, Luis Gutierrez, Ribeiro, Vaca (Lima 46), Mendez, Garcia R, Gomez, Mojica (Limberg Gutierrez 70), Arce, Martins (Moreno J 79).
Referee: Fagundes (Brazil).

Bogota, 21 November 2007, 45,000

Colombia (0) 2 *(Bustos 62, Moreno D 82)*

Argentina (1) 1 *(Messi 36)*

Colombia: Agustin; Velez, Moreno W, Bustos, Mosquera, Ferreira (Torres 46), Castrillon (Grisales 46), Sanchez, Amaya, Renteria, Moreno M (Moreno D 72).
Argentina: Abbondanzieri; Milito, Demichelis, Zanetti, Ibarra, Gago, Cambiasso (Maxi Rodriguez 74), Mascherano, Riquelme, Messi, Tevez[*].
Referee: Larrionda (Uruguay).

Quito, 21 November 2007, 28,557

Ecuador (3) 5 *(Ayovi 10, 48, Kaviedes 24, Mendez 44, 62)*

Peru (0) 1 *(Mendoza 86)*

Ecuador: Elizaga (Villafuerte 66); Espinoza, De Jesus, Ambrosi, Hurtado I, Quiroz, Mendez, Castillo, Ayovi, Kaviedes (Urrutia 68), Benitez (Montero 84).
Peru: Penny; Salas, Vilchez (Solis 9), Acasiete, Gomez, Palacios, Bazalar (Mendoza 58), Lobaton, Garcia, Mostto, Pizarro (Farfan 58).
Referee: Chandia (Chile).

Sao Paulo, 22 November 2007, 70,000

Brazil (1) 2 *(Luis Fabiano 44, 64)*

Uruguay (0) 1 *(Abreu 8)*

Brazil: Julio Cesar; Maicon (Daniel Alves 86), Juan, Alex, Ronaldinho (Josue 60), Mineiro, Kaka, Gilberto Silva, Gilberto, Robinho (Vagner Love 73), Luis Fabiano.
Uruguay: Carini; Lugano, Godin, Fucile, Rodriguez, Pereira M, Gonzalez I (Bueno 82), Gonzalez A, Gargano, Suarez (Sanchez 71), Abreu.
Referee: Baldassi (Argentina).

Santiago, 22 November 2007, 52,320

Chile (0) 0

Paraguay (2) 3 *(Cabanas 24, Da Silva 45, 57)*

Chile: Bravo; Riffo, Ponce, Droguett, Alvarez, Maldonado, Iturra (Jimenez 46), Fernandez, Suazo, Salas, Rubio (Villanueva 46).
Paraguay: Villa; Morel, Da Silva, Caceres J, Vera, Santana, Riveros (Barreto 80), Caceres V, Bonet, Valdez (Achucarro 67), Cabanas (Santa Cruz 57).
Referee: Ruiz (Colombia).

Montevideo, 14 June 2008, 25,000

Uruguay (1) 1 *(Lugano 12)*

Venezuela (0) 1 *(Vargas 56)*

Uruguay: Carini; Caceres, Lugano, Godin, Gargano, Perez, Pereira M (Silva 76), Gonzalez I, Forlan (Sanchez 65), Abreu, Suarez (Bueno 65).
Venezuela: Vega; Hernandez, Rey, Vielma, Rojas (Seijas 79), Mea Vitali, Chacon, Vargas (Rondon 74), Rincon, Arango, Maldonado (Boada 87).
Referee: Intriago (Ecuador).

Buenos Aires, 15 June 2008, 41,167

Argentina (0) 1 *(Palacio 89)*

Ecuador (0) 1 *(Urrutia 69)*

Argentina: Abbondanzieri; Demichelis, Burdisso, Zanetti, Heinze, Veron (Palacio 85), Maxi Rodriguez (Gago 46), Riquelme, Mascherano (Cruz 63), Aguero, Messi.
Ecuador: Cevallos; De Jesus, Mina, Hurtado I, Espinoza, Castillo, Ayovi (Bolanos 85), Valencia, Urrutia, Tenorio C (De La Cruz 88), Guerron (Benitez 88).
Referee: Artube (Bolivia).

La Paz, 15 June 2008, 27,722

Bolivia (0) 0

Chile (1) 2 *(Medel 28, 76)*

Bolivia: Galarza; Alvarez (Ribeiro 46), Raldes, Hoyos (Saucedo 78), Luis Gutierrez, Reyes A, Reyes L, Campos (Botero 65), Martins, Limberg Gutierrez, Arce.
Chile: Bravo; Cereceda, Medel, Jara, Fuentes, Morales (Villanueva 55), Fuenzalida (Estrada 46), Carmona, Beausejour (Gonzalez 58), Sanchez, Suazo.
Referee: Rivera (Peru).

Asuncion, 15 June 2008, 38,000

Paraguay (1) 2 *(Santa Cruz 26, Cabanas 49)*

Brazil (0) 0

Paraguay: Villar; Caniza, Caceres J, Veron[*], Da Silva, Barreto, Vera, Santana, Cabanas (Torres 74), Valdez (Caceres V 52), Santa Cruz (Cardozo 81).
Brazil: Julio Cesar; Juan, Maicon, Lucio, Josue (Anderson 46), Gilberto Silva, Gilberto, Diego (Julio Baptista 69), Mineiro (Adriano 60), Robinho, Luis Fabiano.
Referee: Larrionda (Uruguay).

Lima, 15 June 2008, 25,000

Peru (1) 1 *(Marino 40)*

Colombia (1) 1 *(Rodallega 8)*

Peru: Butron; Neira (Rengifo 76), Vilchez, Vargas, Rodriguez, Prado, Hidalgo (Cominges 59), Torres R, Marino, Solano, Guerrero.
Colombia: Agustin; Bustos, Zapata, Velez (Zuniga 72), Moreno W, Vargas (Grisales 60), Guarin, Torres (Portocarrero 86), Sanchez, Rodallega, Perea.
Referee: Torres (Paraguay).

La Paz, 18 June 2008, 8561

Bolivia (2) 4 *(Botero 23, 70, Garcia R 25, Martins 76)*

Paraguay (0) 2 *(Santa Cruz 66, Valdez 82)*

Bolivia: Arias; Ribeiro, Raldes, Luis Gutierrez, Torrico, Garcia R (Gutierrez R 46), Vaca, Reyes A (Rivero 67), Reyes L, Martins, Botero (Saucedo 73).
Paraguay: Bobadilla; Morel, Da Silva, Caceres J, Vera (Zeballos 46), Riveros, Caceres V, Bonet, Barreto, Cardozo (Valdez 62), Cabanas (Santa Cruz 62).
Referee: Gaciba (Brazil).

Quito, 18 June 2008, 25,000

Ecuador (0) 0

Colombia (0) 0

Ecuador: Cevallos; Hurtado I, Ambrosi, Urrutia (Guerron 46), Tenorio C (Caicedo 81), Benitez, De Jesus, Castillo, Ayovi (Bolanos 72), Valencia, Espinoza.
Colombia: Agustin; Moreno W, Mosquera, Gonzalez, Escobar (Moreno D 54), Guarin, Rodallega, Amaya, Torres (Hernandez 63), Soto (Sanchez 80), Zuniga.
Referee: Baldassi (Argentina).

Montevideo, 18 June 2008, 20,016

Uruguay (2) 6 *(Forlan 8, 37 (pen), 56, Bueno 61, 69, Abreu 90)*

Peru (0) 0

Uruguay: Castillo; Silva, Lugano, Godin, Caceres, Rodriguez, Perez (Eguren 69), Gonzalez I (Suarez 72), Gargano, Forlan, Bueno (Abreu 79).
Peru: Butron; Villalta, Vargas (Rengifo 46), Rodriguez, Prado, Hidalgo (Salas 67), Cevasco, Torres R, Solano, Marino (Cruzado 71), Guerrero[*].
Referee: Pozo (Chile).

Belo Horizonte, 19 June 2008, 65,000

Brazil (0) 0

Argentina (0) 0

Brazil: Julio Cesar; Maicon, Lucio, Juan, Mineiro, Julio Baptista, Gilberto Silva, Gilberto, Anderson (Diego 34) (Daniel Alves 79), Adriano (Luis Fabiano 70), Robinho.
Argentina: Abbondanzieri; Zanetti, Heinze, Coloccini, Burdisso, Riquelme (Battaglia 83), Mascherano, Gutierrez, Gago, Messi (Palacio 90), Cruz (Aguero 67).
Referee: Ruiz (Colombia).

Puerto La Cruz, 20 June 2008, 38,000

Venezuela (0) 2 *(Maldonado 59, Arango 80)*

Chile (0) 3 *(Suazo 54 (pen), 90, Jara 73)*

Venezuela: Vega; Vielma, Rojas, Rey, Hernandez, Arango, Vargas (Rincon 59), Mea Vitali (Seijas 80), Chacon, Rondon (Arismendi 55), Maldonado.
Chile: Bravo; Medel, Jara, Fuentes, Cereceda (Ponce 76), Beausejor (Gonzalez 59), Morales (Gazale 60), Estrada, Carmona, Suazo, Sanchez.
Referee: Silvera (Uruguay).

Buenos Aires, 6 September 2008, 46,250

Argentina (0) 1 *(Aguero 60)*

Paraguay (1) 1 *(Heinze 13 (og))*

Argentina: Abbondanzieri (Carrizo 14); Zanetti, Heinze (Diaz 46), Demichelis, Coloccini, Di Maria (Aguero 46), Riquelme, Mascherano, Cambiasso, Tevez■, Messi.
Paraguay: Villar; Veron, Morel (Torres 46), Da Silva, Caceres J, Vera, Santana, Riveros, Barreto, Valdez, Cardozo (Lopez 71).
Referee: Simon (Brazil).

Quito, 6 September 2008, 35,000

Ecuador (1) 3 *(Caicedo 21, Mendez 51 (pen), Benitez 72)*

Bolivia (1) 1 *(Botero 40)*

Ecuador: Cevallos; Reasco (De Jesus 28), Hurtado I, Espinoza, Mendez, Castillo, Ayovi, Guerron, Caicedo (Palacios 76), Bolanos (Urrutia 75), Benitez.
Bolivia: Arias; Garcia I, Rivero, Raldes, Hoyos, Vaca (Saucedo 88), Gomez■, Garcia R, Robles, Escobar (Pena 67), Botero (Martins 64).
Referee: Pozo (Chile).

Bogota, 7 September 2008, 35,024

Colombia (0) 0

Uruguay (1) 1 *(Eguren 15)*

Colombia: Agustin; Perea, Zuniga, Velez, Mosquera, Vargas (Torres 46), Sanchez, Hernandez (Moreno M 63), Guarin, Rodallega, Garcia (Moreno D 60).
Uruguay: Castillo; Silva (Gonzalez A 80), Lugano, Godin, Fucile, Rodriguez, Pereira M, Gargano, Eguren (Scotti 90), Suarez (Sanchez 68), Forlan.
Referee: Gaciba (Brazil).

Lima, 7 September 2008, 25,000

Peru (1) 1 *(Alva Niezen 39)*

Venezuela (0) 0

Peru: Butron; Zambrano, Vargas, Rodriguez, Prado, Torres R, Solano (Quinteros 62), De La Haza, Fano (Rengifo 80), Chavez (La Rosa 90), Alva Niezen.
Venezuela: Vega; Rojas (Moreno 55), Rey, Hernandez, Boada, Vargas (Guerra 66), Rincon, Mea Vitali (Vielma 71), Chacon, Arango, Maldonado.
Referee: Maldonado (Bolivia).

Santiago, 8 September 2008, 60,239

Chile (0) 0

Brazil (2) 3 *(Luis Fabiano 21, 83, Robinho 44)*

Chile: Bravo; Vidal (Cereceda 46), Medel, Jara, Droguett (Beausejour 46), Gonzalez (Valdivia■ 46), Fernandez, Estrada, Carmona, Suazo, Sanchez.
Brazil: Julio Cesar; Maicon, Lucio, Kleber■, Ronaldinho (Juan Jr 54), Josue, Gilberto Silva, Diego (Elano 78), Robinho, Luis Fabiano (Jo 86).
Referee: Torres (Paraguay).

Asuncion, 10 September 2008, 31,867

Paraguay (2) 2 *(Riveros 28, Valdez 45)*

Venezuela (0) 0

Paraguay: Villar; Morel, Manzur, Da Silva, Riveros, Caceres V, Bonet, Barreto (Torres 79), Santana (Caniza 73), Valdez (Lopez 63), Santa Cruz.
Venezuela: Vega; Rey, Hernandez (Fuenmayor 55), Boada, Mea Vitali, Guerra, Chacon (Lucena 35), Arango, Rincon, Moreno, Maldonado (Torrealba 71).
Referee: Baldassi (Argentina).

Montevideo, 10 September 2008, 45,000

Uruguay (0) 0

Ecuador (0) 0

Uruguay: Castillo; Silva, Lugano, Godin, Caceres, Rodriguez, Gonzalez I (Suarez 60), Gargano (Pereira M 46), Eguren, Forlan, Bueno (Abreu 70).
Ecuador: Cevallos; Mina, Hurtado I, Espinoza, De Jesus, Valencia, Mendez, Castillo, Ayovi, Guerron (Cortez 82), Caicedo (Borja 79).
Referee: Ruiz (Colombia).

Rio de Janeiro, 11 September 2008, 31,422

Brazil (0) 0

Bolivia (0) 0

Brazil: Julio Cesar; Maicon, Lucio, Juan Jr, Luisao, Lucas (Julio Baptista 60), Josue, Diego (Elano 76), Ronaldinho (Nilmar 76), Robinho, Luis Fabiano.
Bolivia: Arias; Raldes, Rivero, Hoyos, Garcia I■, Garcia R, Flores, Vaca (Cabrera 89), Robles, Moreno J (Luis Gutierrez 56), Martins (Escobar 78).
Referee: Intriago (Ecuador).

Santiago, 11 September 2008, 47,459

Chile (2) 4 *(Jara 26, Suazo 38, Fuentes 48, Fernandez 71)*

Colombia (0) 0

Chile: Bravo; Vidal, Medel, Jara, Fuentes, Cereceda (Contreras 78), Gonzalez, Fernandez, Estrada, Suazo (Morales 85), Sanchez (Fierro 81).
Colombia: Agustin; Perea, Portocarrero, Mosquera, Sanchez, Hernandez (Moreno D 46), Armero, Anchico (Zuniga 54), Amaya, Rodallega (Rodriguez 75), Moreno M.
Referee: Larrionda (Uruguay).

Lima, 11 September 2008, 40,000

Peru (0) 1 *(Fano 90)*

Argentina (0) 1 *(Cambiasso 82)*

Peru: Butron; Zambrano, Vilchez, Vargas, Prado, Torres R, Solano, De La Haza, Fano, Chavez (Rengifo 75), Alva Niezen (Salas 66).
Argentina: Carrizo; Zanetti, Diaz, Demichelis, Coloccini, Riquelme, Guttierez (Battaglia 16), Gago, Cambiasso (Zabaleta 87), Messi, Aguero (Denis 63).
Referee: Amarilla (Paraguay).

Buenos Aires, 11 October 2008, 42,421

Argentina (2) 2 *(Messi 5, Aguero 12)*

Uruguay (1) 1 *(Lugano 39)*

Argentina: Carrizo; Heinze, Demichelis, Burdisso, Zanetti, Mascherano, Cambiasso, Riquelme (Ledesma 72), Messi (Diaz 88), Aguero (Milito 71), Tevez.
Uruguay: Castillo; Lugano, Godin, Fucile (Cavani 23), Caceres, Pereira M, Eguren, Rodriguez (Bueno 74), Perez, Abreu (Chevanton 73), Suarez.
Referee: Torres (Paraguay).

La Paz, 11 October 2008, 23,147

Bolivia (2) 3 *(Botero 3, 16, Garcia R 81)*

Peru (0) 0

Bolivia: Arias; Raldes (Luis Gutierrez 83), Vargas, Rivero, Reyes L, Garcia R, Flores, Vaca (Torrico 81), Martins (Escobar 64), Botero, Robles.
Peru: Butron; Prado, Zambrano, Vilchez, Vargas, Torres R, Marino, De La Haza, Fano (Rengifo 85), Chavez (Guizasola 46), Alva Niezen (Aguirre 62).
Referee: Buitrago (Colombia).

Bogota, 12 October 2008, 26,000

Colombia (0) 0

Paraguay (1) 1 *(Cabanas 9)*

Colombia: Agustin; Yepes, Bedoya, Zuniga, Perea, Vargas, Hernandez (Ferreira 55), Guarin (Ramos 73), Armero, Montero (Quintero 55), Renteria.
Paraguay: Villar; Veron, Da Silva, Caceres J, Vera, Torres, Riveros, Caceres V, Barreto (Bonet 82), Valdez (Bogado 76), Cabanas (Cardozo 86).
Referee: Lunati (Argentina).

Quito, 12 October 2008, 33,079

Ecuador (0) 1 *(Benitez 70)*

Chile (0) 0

Ecuador: Elizaga; Espinoza, De Jesus, Ambrosi (Bolanos 46), Hurtado I, Castillo (Urrutia 43), Ayovi, Valencia▪, Caicedo (Hidalgo 85), Benitez, Guerron.
Chile: Bravo; Jara▪, Fuentes▪, Cereceda (Estrada 53), Vidal, Medel, Gonzalez, Fernandez (Contreras 23), Carmona, Suazo (Morales 58), Sanchez.
Referee: Vazquez (Uruguay).

San Cristobal, 12 October 2008, 38,000

Venezuela (0) 0

Brazil (3) 4 *(Kaka 6, Robinho 9, 66, Adriano 19)*

Venezuela: Vega; Rey, Boada, Vielma, Rojas, Mea Vitali (Lucena 70), Guerra (Moreno 61), Chacon, Arango, Vargas (Seijas 55), Maldonado.
Brazil: Julio Cesar; Kleber, Juan (Thiago Silva 46), Maicon, Lucio, Kaka (Alex 71), Josue (Mancini 78), Gilberto Silva, Elano, Adriano, Robinho.
Referee: Rivera (Peru).

La Paz, 14 October 2008, 21,075

Bolivia (2) 2 *(Martins 15, 41)*

Uruguay (0) 2 *(Bueno 64, Abreu 88)*

Bolivia: Arias; Raldes, Vargas, Rivero, Garcia I, Vaca (Torrico 64), Reyes A, Flores, Robles, Martins (Parada 88), Botero (Escobar 71).
Uruguay: Castillo; Silva, Lugano, Caceres, Arismendi, Scotti, Rodriguez (Abreu 70), Gonzalez A (Pereira M 55), Gargano, Sanchez, Bueno.
Referee: Baldassi (Argentina).

Asuncion, 15 October 2008, 31,545

Paraguay (0) 1 *(Cardozo 81)*

Peru (0) 0

Paraguay: Villar; Morel, Da Silva, Caceres J, Santana (Benitez 67), Riveros, Caceres V, Bonet, Barreto (Martinez 46), Valdez (Cardozo 67), Cabanas.
Peru: Butron; Contreras, Vilchez, Vargas, Prado, Torres R, Solano, Marino (Alva Niezen 70), De La Haza (Quinteros 84), Rengifo, Fano (Chavez 82).
Referee: Fagundes (Brazil).

Rio de Janeiro, 16 October 2008, 54,910

Brazil (0) 0

Colombia (0) 0

Brazil: Julio Cesar; Maicon, Lucio, Kleber, Juan (Thiago Silva 46), Kaka, Josue, Gilberto Silva, Elano (Mancini 57), Robinho (Alexandre Pato 63), Jo.
Colombia: Agustin; Zuniga, Perea, Bedoya (Aguilar 66), Yepes, Toja, Guarin, Vargas, Armero, Renteria (Ramos 75), Quintero (Moreno D 70).
Referee: Selman (Chile).

Santiago, 16 October 2008, 65,000

Chile (1) 1 *(Orellana 35)*

Argentina (0) 0

Chile: Bravo; Medel, Contreras, Ponce (Vidal 87), Gonzalez (Droguett 20), Fernandez, Estrada, Carmona, Beausejour, Orellana (Martinez 87), Suazo.
Argentina: Carrizo; Heinze, Demichelis, Burdisso (Diaz 20), Zanetti, Mascherano, Ledesma, Cambiasso (Sand 85), Aguero, Milito (Bergessio 46), Messi.
Referee: Ruiz (Colombia).

Puerto La Cruz, 16 October 2008, 10,581

Venezuela (0) 3 *(Maldonado 48, Moreno 56, Arango 67)*

Ecuador (1) 1 *(Mina 12)*

Venezuela: Vega; Cichero, Rey, Fuenmayor, Rosales, Rincon, Gonzalez C (Rojas 70), Arango, Lucena, Moreno (Boada 79), Maldonado (Arismendi 74).
Ecuador: Cevallos; Mina, Hurtado I (Castro 36), Espinoza, De Jesus, Cortez, Urrutia, Mendez, Ayovi (Bolanos 60), Guerron (Borja 65), Caicedo.
Referee: Osses (Chile).

Buenos Aires, 28 March 2009, 46,085

Argentina (1) 4 *(Messi 26, Tevez 47, Rodriguez 51, Aguero 73)*

Venezuela (0) 0

Argentina: Carrizo; Angeleri, Zanetti, Heinze, Maxi Rodriguez (Di Maria 75), Mascherano, Gutierrez, Gago, Tevez (Veron 71), Messi, Aguero (Milito 78).
Venezuela: Vega; Rojas (Acosta 84), Fuenmayor, Cichero, Velasquez, Rosales (Moreno 50), Rincon, Gonzalez C, Chacon, Arango, Maldonado (Flores 78).
Referee: Rivera (Peru).

Montevideo, 28 March 2009, 45,000

Uruguay (1) 2 *(Forlan 28, Lugano 57)*

Paraguay (0) 0

Uruguay: Viera; Lugano, Godin (Silva 82), Caceres, Pereira M, Eguren, Pereira A, Rodriguez (Martinez 72), Perez, Forlan (Abreu 78), Suarez.
Paraguay: Villar; Da Silva, Caceres J, Veron, Barreto, Estigarribia (Aquino 46), Vera (Cardozo 69), Torres (Samudio 58), Riveros, Cabanas, Valdez.
Referee: Simon (Brazil).

Bogota, 29 March 2009, 22,044

Colombia (1) 2 *(Torres 26, Renteria 88)*

Bolivia (0) 0

Colombia: Ospina; Marin, Zuniga, Zapata, Yepes, Vargas, Torres (Motta 70), Armero, Aguilar, Quintero (Rodallega 79), Garcia (Renteria 70).
Bolivia: Arias; Rivero, Pena, Hoyos, Luis Gutierrez, Vaca (Hurtado 77), Garcia R, Flores, Robles (Torrico 46), Escobar, Cabrera (Castillo▪ 67).
Referee: Intriago (Ecuador).

Quito, 29 March 2009, 40,000

Ecuador (0) 1 *(Noboa 89)*

Brazil (0) 1 *(Julio Baptista 72)*

Ecuador: Cevallos; Reasco, Hurtado I, Espinoza, Valencia, Mendez, Castillo, Ayovi, Guerron (Noboa 75), Caicedo (Palacios 90), Benitez.
Brazil: Julio Cesar; Lucio, Marcelo, Maicon (Daniel Alves 24), Lucas, Gilberto Silva, Elano (Josue 61), Felipe Melo, Ronaldinho (Julio Baptista 71), Robinho, Luis Fabiano.
Referee: Chandia (Chile).

Lima, 30 March 2009, 48,700

Peru (1) 1 *(Fano 34)*

Chile (2) 3 *(Sanchez 2, Suazo 32 (pen), Fernandez 70)*

Peru: Butron; Zambrano, Vargas▪, Rodriguez, Prado, Torres M (De La Haza 46), Ramirez, Torres R, Solano (Sanchez 79), Fano, Chavez (Alva 60).
Chile: Bravo; Ponce, Jara, Cereceda, Isla (Contreras 63), Gonzalez, Fernandez (Tello 72), Carmona (Estrada 76), Beausejour, Suazo, Sanchez.
Referee: Amarilla (Paraguay).

La Paz, 1 April 2009, 30,487

Bolivia (3) 6 *(Martins 11, Botero 34 (pen), 53, 66, Da Rosa 45, Torrico 87)*

Argentina (1) 1 *(Gonzalez L 25)*

Bolivia: Arias; Rivero, Ribeiro, Pena, Da Rosa (Saucedo 69), Torrico, Reyes L, Reyes A (Garcia I 53), Martins, Botero, Garcia R (Flores 79).
Argentina: Carrizo; Zanetti, Heinze, Demichelis, Papa▪, Gonzalez L (Angeleri 69), Maxi Rodriguez (Di Maria▪ 57), Mascherano, Gago, Tevez (Montenegro 76), Messi.
Referee: Vazquez (Uruguay).

Quito, 1 April 2009, 36,853
Ecuador (0) 1 _(Noboa 64)_
Paraguay (0) 1 _(Benitez 90)_
Ecuador: Cevallos; Ambrosi, Reasco, Hurtado I, Espinoza, Castillo, Valencia (Urrutia 86), Mendez, Caicedo (Calderon 46), Benitez, Guerron (Noboa 62).
Paraguay: Villar; Veron, Manzur, Da Silva■, Caniza, Vera (Bonet 80), Riveros, Caceres V, Aquino (Martinez 75), Valdez (Benitez 70), Cabanas.
Referee: Roldan (Colombia).

Puerto Ordaz, 1 April 2009, 35,000
Venezuela (0) 2 _(Fedor 78, Arango 82)_
Colombia (0) 0
Venezuela: Vega; Fuenmayor, Lucena, Gonzalez C (Pena 65), Arango (Acosta 85), Velasquez, Salazar, Rosales, Rincon, Moreno, Maldonado (Fedor 74).
Colombia: Ospina; Marin, Bedoya, Nunez (Mosquera 46), Zuniga, Zapata, Yepes, Aguilar■, Torres (Rodallega 74), Garcia, Quintero (Marrugo 57).
Referee: Pozo (Chile).

Porto Alegre, 2 April 2009, 55,000
Brazil (2) 3 _(Luis Fabiano 18 (pen), 27, Felipe Melo 63)_
Peru (0) 0
Brazil: Julio Cesar; Luisao (Miranda 12), Lucio, Kleber, Daniel Alves, Kaka, Gilberto Silva, Felipe Melo, Elano (Ronaldinho 76), Robinho (Alexandre Pato 70), Luis Fabiano.
Peru: Butron; Zambrano, Vilchez, Rodriguez, Prado, Torres R, Solano (Fernandez 69), Ramirez (Alva 79), La Rosa, Garcia (Sanchez 62), Fano.
Referee: Pezzotta (Argentina).

Santiago, 2 April 2009, 55,000
Chile (0) 0
Uruguay (0) 0
Chile: Bravo; Ponce, Jara, Contreras, Isla■, Gonzalez, Fernandez (Orellana 60), Carmona, Beausejour (Iturra 39) (Cereceda 46), Suazo, Sanchez.
Uruguay: Viera; Lugano, Godin, Caceres, Rodriguez (Cavani 85), Perez (Fernandez 41), Pereira M, Pereira A (Abreu 72), Eguren, Suarez, Forlan.
Referee: Baldassi (Argentina).

Buenos Aires, 6 June 2009, 55,000
Argentina (0) 1 _(Diaz 55)_
Colombia (0) 0
Argentina: Andujar; Diaz, Demichelis, Heinze, Gago (Zanetti 46), Veron, Mascherano, Gutierrez, Aguero (Milito 41), Tevez (Burdisso 84), Messi.
Colombia: Ospina; Marin (Ramos 66), Zuniga, Zapata, Yepes, Perea, Guarin, Armero (Quintero 82), Vargas, Garcia (Rodallega 73), Renteria.
Referee: Ortube (Bolivia).

La Paz, 6 June 2009, 23,427
Bolivia (0) 0
Venezuela (1) 1 _(Rivero 32 (og))_
Bolivia: Arias; Rivero, Raldes, Hoyos, Da Rosa, Vaca (Escobar 63), Reyes L■, Reyes A, Garcia R (Alvarez 77), Cabrera (Yecerotte 46), Martins■.
Venezuela: Romo; Perozo, Flores, Boada, Yeguez (Salazar 65), Di Giorgi, Velasquez, Seijas, Pena (Fernandez 56), Maldonado, Garcia (Rondon 70).
Referee: Vera (Ecuador).

Montevideo, 6 June 2009, 52,000
Uruguay (0) 0
Brazil (2) 4 _(Daniel Alves 12, Juan 35, Luis Fabiano 51, Kaka 74 (pen))_
Uruguay: Viera; Caceres, Valdez, Godin, Perez (Abreu 46), Pereira M■, Pereira A (Fernandez 66), Martinez, Eguren, Suarez (Cavani 75), Forlan.
Brazil: Julio Cesar; Daniel Alves, Lucio, Kleber, Juan, Felipe Melo, Elano (Ramires 66), Kaka (Julio Baptista 85), Gilberto Silva, Robinho (Josue 85), Luis Fabiano■.
Referee: Laverni (Argentina).

Asuncion, 7 June 2009, 34,000
Paraguay (0) 0
Chile (1) 2 _(Fernandez 13, Suazo 51)_
Paraguay: Villar; Caceres M, Manzur, Caniza, Caceres J, Vera (Ledesma 58), Riveros, Caceres V, Barreto (Martinez 48), Valdez, Cardozo (Benitez 60).

Chile: Bravo; Ponce, Medel, Jara, Gonzalez (Millar 46), Fernandez, Estrada, Carmona, Beausejour, Suazo (Mancilla 72), Sanchez (Orellana 88).
Referee: Pezzotta (Argentina).

Lima, 7 June 2009, 17,050
Peru (0) 1 _(Vargas 51)_
Ecuador (1) 2 _(Montero 37, Tenorio C 58)_
Peru: Fernandez; Zambrano, Vilchez, Vargas, Rodriguez, Prado (Sanchez 72), De La Haza, Torres R (Ballon 80), Ramirez (Merino 46), Guerrero, Fano.
Ecuador: Elizaga; Fleitas, Reasco, Guagua, Castillo, Ayovi, Noboa, Mendez, Montero (Mina 83), Tenorio C (Hidalgo 88), Palacios (Guerron 51).
Referee: Torres (Paraguay).

Quito, 10 June 2009, 36,359
Ecuador (0) 2 _(Ayovi 72, Palacios 83)_
Argentina (0) 0
Ecuador: Elizaga; Reasco, Hurtado I, Espinoza, Valencia, Noboa (Palacios 46), Mendez, Castillo, Ayovi, Tenorio C (Montero 13), Caicedo (Guerron 79).
Argentina: Andujar; Otamendi, Zanetti, Heinze (Milito 82), Demichelis, Rodriguez, Gutierrez, Gago (Veron 75), Battaglia, Tevez (Bergessio 67), Messi.
Referee: Chandia (Chile).

Recife, 11 June 2009, 56,682
Brazil (1) 2 _(Robinho 41, Nilmar 50)_
Paraguay (1) 1 _(Cabanas 25)_
Brazil: Julio Cesar; Kleber, Lucio, Juan, Daniel Alves, Elano (Ramires 60), Felipe Melo, Kaka, Gilberto Silva, Robinho (Kleberson 85), Nilmar (Alexandre Pato 74).
Paraguay: Villar; Caceres J, Veron, Da Silva, Caniza, Martinez (Lopez 77), Ledesma (Aquino 61), Caceres V, Bonet (Benitez 70), Riveros, Cabanas.
Referee: Ruiz (Colombia).

Santiago, 11 June 2009, 60,214
Chile (1) 4 _(Beausejour 44, Estrada 74, Sanchez 78, 89)_
Bolivia (0) 0
Chile: Bravo; Ponce, Medel, Jara, Millar (Isla 83), Gonzalez, Fernandez (Valdivia 68), Estrada, Beausejour, Suazo (Mancilla 83), Sanchez.
Bolivia: Arias; Rivero, Raldes, Pena, Garcia I■, Torrico (Reyes A 57), Garcia R, Da Rosa (Yecerotte 46), Robles (Vaca 83), Escobar.
Referee: Silvera (Uruguay).

Medellin, 11 June 2009, 32,300
Colombia (1) 1 _(Garcia 26)_
Peru (0) 0
Colombia: Ospina; Zapata, Marin, Zuniga, Yepes, Perea, Guarin, Vargas (Aguilar 54), Torres (Pino 67), Garcia, Renteria (Rodallega 46).
Peru: Butron; Zambrano, Vilchez, Vargas (Trujillo 21), Rodriguez, De La Haza, Ballon (Sanchez 81), Ramirez, La Rosa, Guerrero (Rengifo 87), Fano.
Referee: Simon (Brazil).

Puerto Ordaz, 11 June 2009, 37,000
Venezuela (1) 2 _(Maldonado 9, Rey 74)_
Uruguay (0) 2 _(Suarez 60, Forlan 72)_
Venezuela: Vega; Fuenmayor, Rey, Gonzalez C (Pena 68), Chacon (Velasquez 61), Arango, Salazar, Rincon, Lucena, Moreno, Maldonado (Fedor 84).
Uruguay: Castillo; Caceres (Cavani 80), Lugano, Godin, Fucile, Fernandez (Rodriguez 46), Amado, Perez, Pereira A, Suarez (Abreu 65), Forlan.
Referee: Fagundes (Brazil).

SOUTH AMERICA TABLE	P	W	D	L	F	A	Pts
Brazil	14	7	6	1	25	6	27
Chile	14	8	2	4	23	14	26
Paraguay	14	7	3	4	20	13	24
Argentina	14	6	4	4	19	15	22
Ecuador	14	5	5	4	18	20	20
Uruguay	14	4	6	4	23	16	18
Colombia	14	4	5	5	7	11	17
Venezuela	14	5	2	7	17	24	17
Bolivia	14	3	3	8	19	30	12
Peru	14	1	4	9	7	29	7

OCEANIA

GROUP A

Tahiti 0, New Caledonia 1; Fiji 16, Tuvalu 0; New Caledonia 1, Tuvalu 0; Fiji 4, Cook Islands 0; Tahiti 1, Tuvalu 1; New Caledonia 3, Cook Islands 0; Cook Islands 4, Tuvalu 1; Fiji 4, Tahiti 0; Fiji 1, New Caledonia 1; Tahiti 1, Cook Islands 0.
Fiji and New Caledonia qualify for semi-finals.

GROUP B

Solomon Islands 12, American Samoa 1; Samoa 0, Vanuatu 4; Solomon Islands 4, Tonga 0; Samoa 7, American Samoa 0; Vanuatu 15, American Samoa 0; Samoa 2, Tonga 1; Tonga 4, American Samoa 0; Solomon Islands 2, Vanuatu 0; Samoa 0, Solomon Islands 3; Vanuatu 4, Tonga 1.
Solomon Islands and Vanuatu qualify for semi-finals.

SEMI-FINALS

Solomon Islands 2, New Caledonia 3; Fiji 3, Vanuatu 0.

THIRD PLACE

Vanuatu 2, Solomon Islands 0.

FINAL

Fiji 0, New Caledonia 1.

FINAL ROUND

Fiji 0, New Zealand 2; Vanuatu 1, New Zealand 2; Fiji 3, New Caledonia 3; New Zealand 4, Vanuatu 1; New Caledonia 4, Fiji 0; Vanuatu 1, New Caledonia 1; New Zealand 0, Fiji 2; New Caledonia 3, Vanuatu 0; Fiji 2, Vanuatu 0; New Caledonia 1, New Zealand 3; Vanuatu 2, Fiji 1; New Zealand 3, New Caledonia 0; New Zealand 0, Fiji 2.

ASIA

FIRST ROUND

Bangalesh 1, Tajikistan 1; Tajikistan 5, Bangalesh 0; Thailand 6, Macao 1; Macao 1, Thailand 7; Vietnam 0, UAE 1; UAE 5, Vietnam 0; Oman 2, Nepal 0; Nepal 0, Oman 2; Syria 3, Afganistan 0; Afganistan 1, Syria 2; Palestine 0, Singapore 4; Singapore v Palestine awarded 3-0; Lebanon 4, India 1; India 2, Lebanon 2; Yemen 3, Maldives 0; Maldives 0, Yemen 0; Cambodia 0, Turkmenistan 1; Turkmenistan 4, Cambodia 1; Uzbekistan 9, Taiwan 0; Taiwan 0, Uzbekistan 2; Kyrgyzstan 2, Jordan 0; Jordan 2, Kyrgyzstan 0 - Jordan won 6-5 on penalties; Mongolia 1, North Korea 4; North Korea 5, Mongolia 1; Timor-Leste 2, Hong Kong 3; Hong Kong 8, Timor-Leste 1; Sri Lanka 0, Qatar 1; Qatar 5, Sri Lanka 0; China 7, Myanmar 0; Myanmar 0, China 4; Bahrain 4, Malaysia 1; Malaysia 0, Bahrain 0; Pakistan 0, Iraq 7; Iraq 0, Pakistan 0.

SECOND ROUND

Singapore 2, Tajikistan 0; Tajikistan 1, Singapore 1; Indonesia 1, Syria 4; Syria 7, Indonesia 0; Yemen 1, Thailand 1; Thailand 1, Yemen 0; Hong Kong 0, Turkmenistan 0; Turkmenistan 3, Hong Kong 0.

GROUP 1

Australia 3, Qatar 0; Iraq 1, China 1; China 0, Australia 0; Qatar 2, Iraq 0; Australia 1, Iraq 0; Qatar 0, China 0; China 0, Qatar 1; Iraq 1, Australia 0; China 1, Iraq 2; Qatar1, Australia 3; Australia 0, China 1; Iraq 0, Qatar 1.

GROUP 2

Japan 4, Thailand 1; Oman 0, Bahrain 1; Thailand 0, Oman 1; Bahrain 1, Japan 0; Japan 3, Oman 0; Thailand 2, Bahrain 3; Oman 1, Japan 1; Bahrain 1, Thailand 1; Thailand 0, Japan 3; Bahrain 1, Oman 1; Japan 1, Bahrain 0; Oman 2, Thailand 1.

GROUP 3

South Korea 4, Turkmenistan 0; Jordan 0, North Korea 1; North Korea 0, South Korea 0; Turkmenistan 0, Jordan 2;

South Korea 2, Jordan 2; Turkmenistan 0, North Korea 0; North Korea 1, Turkmenistan 0; Jordan 0, South Korea 1; North Korea 2, Jordan 0; South Korea 1, North Korea 0; South Korea 0, North Korea 0; Jordan 2, Turkmenistan 0.

GROUP 4

Lebanon 0, Uzbekistan 1; Saudi Arabia 2, Singapore 0; Uzbekistan 3, Saudi Arabia 0; Singapore 2, Lebanon 0; Singapore 3, Uzbekistan 7; Saudi Arabia 4, Lebanon 1; Uzbekistan 1, Singapore 0; Lebanon 1, Saudi Arabia 2; Singapore 0, Saudi Arabia 2; Uzbekistan 3, Lebanon 0; Lebanon 1, Singapore 2; Saudi Arabia 4, Uzbekistan 0.

GROUP 5

Iran 0, Syria 0; UAE 2, Kuwait 0; Syria 1, UAE 1; Kuwait 2, Iran 2; Iran 0, UAE 0; Syria 1, Kuwait 0; UAE 0, Iran 1; Kuwait 4, Syria 2; Kuwait 2, UAE 3; Syria 0, Iran 2; Iran 2, Kuwait 0; UAE 1, Syria 3.

GROUP A

Bahrain 2, Japan 3; Qatar 3, Uzbekistan 0; Uzbekistan 0, Australia 1; Qatar 1, Bahrain 1; Australia 4, Qatar 0; Japan 1, Uzbekistan 1; Bahrain 0, Australia 1; Qatar 0, Japan 3; Japan 0, Australia 0; Uzbekistan 0, Bahrain 1; Japan 1, Bahrain 0; Uzbekistan 4, Qatar 0; Australia 2, Uzbekistan 0; Bahrain 1, Japan 1; Uzbekistan 0, Japan 1; Qatar 0, Australia 0; Japan 1, Qatar 1; Australia 2, Bahrain 0; Bahrain 1, Uzbekistan 0; Australia 2, Japan 1.

GROUP B

UAE 1, North Korea 2; Saudi Arabia 1, Iran 1; North Korea 1, South Korea 1; UAE 1, Saudi Arabia 2; South Korea 4, UAE 1; Iran 2, North Korea 1; UAE 1, Iran 1; Saudi Arabia 0, South Korea 2; North Korea 1, Saudi Arabia 0; Iran 1, South Korea 1; North Korea 2, UAE 0; Iran 1, Saudi Arabia 2; South Korea 1, North Korea 0; Saudi Arabia 3, UAE 2; UAE 0, South Korea 2; North Korea 0, Iran 0; South Korea 0, Saudi Arabia 0; Iran 1, UAE 0; South Korea 1, Iran 1; Saudi Arabia 0, North Korea 0.

CONCACAF

FIRST ROUND

Dominican Republic v Puerto Rico not played; Puerto Rico 1, Dominican Republic 0; US Virgin Islands v Grenada not played; Grenada 10, US Virgin Islands 0; Surinam v Monserrat not played; Monserrat 1, Surinam 7; Bermuda 1, Cayman Islands 1; Cayman Islands 1, Bermuda 3; Belize 3, St Kitts & Nevis 1; St Kitts & Nevis 1, Belize 1; Nicaragua 0, Netherlands Antilles 1; Netherlands Antilles 2, Nicaragua 0; Dominica 1, Barbados 1; Barbados 1, Dominica 0; Aruba 0, Antigua & Barbuda 3; Antigua & Barbuda 1, Aruba 0; Turks & Caicos 2, St Lucia 1; St Lucia 2, Turks & Caicos 0; El Salvador 12, Anguilla 0; Anguilla 0, El Salvador 4; Bahamas 1, British Virgin Islands 1; British Virgin Islands 2, Bahamas 2.

SECOND ROUND

Honduras 4, Puerto Rico 0; Puerto Rico 2, Honduras 0; Belize 0, Mexico 2; Mexico 7, Belize 0; Surinam 1, Guyana 0; Guyana 1, Surinam 2; Grenada 2, Costa Rica 2; Costa Rica 3, Grenada 0; Guatemala 6, St Lucia 0; St Lucia 1, Guatemala 3; St Vincent & the Grenadines 0,

Canada 3; Canada 4, St Vincent & the Grenadines 1; Trinidad & Tobago 1, Bermuda 2; Bermuda 0, Trinidad & Tobago 2; Haiti 0, Netherlands Antilles 0; Netherlands Antilles 0, Haiti 1; USA 8, Barbados 0; Barbados 0, USA 1; Panama 1, El Salvador 0; El Salvador 3, Panama 1; Antigua & Barbuda 3, Cuba 4; Cuba 4, Antigua & Barbuda 0; Jamaica 7, Bahamas 0; Bahamas 0, Jamaica 6.

SEMI-FINAL

GROUP A

Cuba 1, Trinidad & Tobago 3; Guatemala 0, USA 1; Trinidad & Tobago 1, Guatemala 1; Cuba 0, USA 1; USA 3, Trinidad & Tobago 0; Guatemala 4, Cuba 1; USA 6, Cuba 1; Guatemala 0, Trinidad & Tobago 0; Cuba 2, Guatemala 1; Trinidad & Tobago 2, USA 1; USA 2, Guatemala 0; Trinidad & Tobago 3, Cuba 0.

GROUP B

Canada 1, Jamaica 1; Mexico 2, Honduras 1; Mexico 3, Jamaica 0; Canada 1, Honduras 2; Mexico 2, Canada 1; Honduras 2, Jamaica 0; Jamaica 1, Mexico 0; Honduras 3,

Canada 1; Jamaica 1, Honduras 0; Canada 2, Mexico 2; Jamaica 3, Canada 0; Honduras 1, Mexico 0.

GROUP C
Haiti 2, Surinam 2; Costa Rica 1, El Salvador 0; Costa Rica 7, Surinam 0; El Salvador 5, Haiti 0; Surinam 0, El Salvador 2; Haiti 1, Costa Rica 3; Surinam 1, Costa Rica 4; Haiti 0, El Salvador 0; Costa Rica 2, Haiti 0; El Salvador 3, Surinam 0; .El Salvador 1, Costa Rica 3; Surinam 1, Haiti 1.

FINAL ROUND
USA 2, Mexico 0; El Salvador 2, Trinidad & Tobago 2; Costa Rica 2, Honduras 0; Trinidad & Tobago 1,

Honduras 1; Mexico 2, Costa Rica 0; El Salvador 2, USA 2; USA 3, Trinidad & Tobago 0; Honduras 3, Mexico 1; Costa Rica 1, El Salvador 0; Costa Rica 3, USA 1; Trinidad & Tobago 2, Costa Rica 3; El Salvador2, Mexico 1; USA 2, Honduras 1; Mexico 2, Trinidad & Tobago 1; Honduras 1, El Salvador 0. *Remaining Fixtures:* Honduras v Costa Rica; Trinidad & Tobago v El Salvador; Mexico v USA; Honduras v Trinidad & Tobago; USA v El Salvador; Costa Rica v Mexico; El Salvador v Costa Rica; Mexico v Honduras; Trinidad & Tobago v USA; Costa Rica v Trinidad & Tobago; Mexico v El Salvador; Honduras v USA; USA v Costa Rica; Trinidad & Tobago v Mexico; El Salvador v Honduras.

AFRICA

FIRST ROUND
Madagascar 6, Comoros 2; Comoros 0, Madagascar 4; Sierra Leone 1, Guinea-Bissau 0; Guinea-Bissau 0, Sierra Leone 0; Djibouti 1, Somalia 0; Somalia v Djibouti not played.

GROUP 1
Tanzania 1, Mauritius 1; Cameroon 2, Cape Verde Islands 0; Cape Verde Islands 1, Tanzania 0; Mauritius 0, Cameroon 3; Tanzania 0, Cameroon 0; Mauritius 0, Cape Verde Islands 1; Cameroon 2, Tanzania 1; Cape Verde Islands 3, Mauritius 1; Mauritius 1, Tanzania 4; Cape Verde Islands 1, Cameroon 2; Tanzania 3, Cape Verde Islands 1; Cameroon 5, Mauritius 0.

GROUP 2
Namibia 2, Kenya 1; Guinea 0, Zimbabwe 0; Kenya 2, Guinea 0; Zimbabwe 2, Namibia 0; Kenya 2, Zimbabwe 0; Namibia 1, Guinea 2; Guinea 4, Namibia 0; Zimbabwe 0, Kenya 0; Kenya 1, Namibia 0; Zimbabwe 0, Guinea 0; Namibia 4, Zimbabwe 2; Guinea 3, Kenya 2.

GROUP 3
Uganda 1, Niger 0; Angola 3, Benin 0; Niger 1, Angola 2; Benin 4, Uganda 1; Uganda 3, Angola 1; Niger 0, Benin 2; Angola 0, Uganda 0; Benin 2, Niger 0; Benin 3, Angola 2; Niger 3, Uganda 1; Uganda 2, Benin 1; Angola 3, Niger 1.

GROUP 4
Equatorial Guinea 2, Sierra Leone 0; Nigeria 2, South Africa 0; South Africa 4, Equatorial Guinea 1; Sierra Leone 0, Nigeria 1; Sierra Leone 1, South Africa 0; Equatorial Guinea 0, Nigeria 1; Nigeria 2, Equatorial Guinea 0; South Africa 0, Sierra Leone 0; South Africa 0, Nigeria 1; Sierra Leone 2, Equatorial Guinea 1; Equatorial Guinea 0, South Africa 1; Nigeria 4, Sierra Leone 1.

GROUP 5
Gabon v Lesotho not played; Ghana 3, Libya 0; Libya 1, Gabon 0; Lesotho 2, Ghana 3; Gabon 2, Ghana 0; Lesotho 0, Libya 1; Ghana 2, Gabon 0; Libya 4, Lesotho 0; Gabon 2, Lesotho 0; Libya 1, Ghana 0; Lesotho 0, Gabon 3; Gabon 1, Libya 0; Ghana 3, Lesotho 0.

GROUP 6
Senegal 1, Algeria 0; Liberia 1, Gambia 1; Algeria 3, Liberia 0; Gambia 0, Senegal 0; Gambia 1, Algeria 0; Liberia 2, Senegal 2; Algeria 1, Gambia 0; Senegal 3, Liberia 1; Algeria 3, Senegal 2; Gambia 3, Liberia 0; Liberia 0, Algeria 0; Senegal 1, Gambia 1.

GROUP 7
Botswana 0, Madagascar 0; Ivory Coast 1, Mozambique 0; Madagascar 0, Ivory Coast 0; Mozambique 1, Botswana 2; Botswana 1, Ivory Coast 1; Madagascar 1, Mozambique 1; Ivory Coast 4, Botswana 0; Mozambique 3, Madagascar 0; Madagascar 1, Botswana 1; Mozambique 1, Ivory Coast 1; Botswana 0, Mozambique 1; Ivory Coast 3, Madagascar 0.

GROUP 8
Rwanda 3, Mauritania 0; Morocco 3, Ethiopia 0; Mauritania 1, Morocco 4; Ethiopia 1, Rwanda 2; Mauritania 0, Ethiopia 1; Rwanda 3, Morocco 1; Ethiopia 6, Mauritania 1; Morocco 2, Rwanda 0; Mauritania 0, Rwanda 1; Morocco 4, Mauritania 1.

GROUP 9
Burundi 1, Seychelles 0; Tunisia 1, Burkina Faso 2; Seychelles 0, Tunisia 2; Burkina Faso 2, Burundi 0; Seychelles 2, Burkina Faso 3; Burundi 0, Tunisia 1; Burkina Faso 4, Seychelles 1; Tunisia 2, Burundi 1; Seychelles 1, Burundi 2; Burkina Faso 0, Tunisia 0; Tunisia 5, Seychelles 0; Burundi 1, Burkina Faso 3.

GROUP 10
Sudan v Chad not played; Mali 4, Congo 2; Chad 1, Mali 2; Congo 1, Sudan 0; Chad 2, Congo 1; Sudan 3, Mali 2; Congo 2, Chad 0; Mali 3, Sudan 0; Sudan 1, Chad 2; Congo 1, Mali 0; Chad 1, Sudan 3; Sudan 2, Congo 0; Mali 2, Chad 1.

GROUP 11
Togo 1, Zambia 0; Swaziland 2, Togo 1; Swaziland 0, Zambia 0; Zambia 1, Swaziland 0; Zambia 1, Togo 0; Togo 6, Swaziland 0.

GROUP 12
Malawi 8, Djibouti 1; Egypt 2, Congo DR 1; Djibouti 0, Egypt 4; Congo DR 1, Malawi 0; Djibouti 0, Congo DR 6; Malawi 1, Egypt 0; Egypt 2, Malawi 0; Congo DR 5, Djibouti 1; Djibouti 0, Malawi 3; Congo DR 0, Egypt 1; Malawi 2, DR Congo 1; Egypt 4, Djibouti 0.

GROUP A
Togo 1, Cameroon 0; Morocco 1, Gabon 2; Cameroon 0, Morocco 0; Gabon 3, Togo 0; Morocco 0, Togo 0. *Remaining Fixtures:* Gabon v Cameroon; Cameroon v Gabon; Togo v Morocco; Cameroon v Togo; Gabon v Morocco; Morocco v Cameroon; Togo v Gabon.

GROUP B
Kenya 1, Tunisia 2; Mozambique 0, Nigeria 0; Tunisia 2, Mozambique 0; Nigeria 3, Kenya 0; Tunisia 0, Nigeria 0; Kenya 2, Mozambique 1. *Remaining Fixtures:* Mozambique v Kenya; Nigeria v Tunisia; Tunisia v Kenya; Nigeria v Mozambique; Kenya v Nigeria; Mozambique v Tunisia.

GROUP C
Rwanda 0, Algeria 0; Egypt 1, Zambia 1; Zambia 1, Rwanda 0; Algeria 3, Egypt 1; Zambia 0, Algeria 2. *Remaining Fixtures:* Egypt v Rwanda, Algeria v Zambia; Rwanda v Egypt; Zambia v Egypt; Algeria v Rwanda; Egypt v Algeria; Rwanda v Zambia.

GROUP D
Sudan 1, Mali 1; Ghana 1, Benin 0; Benin 1, Sudan 0; Mali 0, Ghana 2; Mali 3, Benin 1; Sudan 0, Ghana 2. *Remaining Fixtures:* Benin v Mali; Ghana v Sudan; Benin v Ghana; Mali v Sudan; Sudan v Benin; Ghana v Mali.

GROUP E
Burkina Faso 4, Guinea 2; Ivory Coast 5, Malawi 0; Malawi 0, Burkina Faso 1; Guinea1, Ivory Coast 2; Burkina Faso 2, Ivory Coast 3; Guinea 2, Malawi 1. *Remaining Fixtures:* Ivory Coast v Burkina Faso; Malawi v Guinea; Guinea v Burkina Faso; Malawi v Ivory Coast; Burkina Faso v Malawi; Ivory Coast v Guinea.

WORLD CUP 2010 – OTHER QUALIFIERS

AUSTRALIAN GAMES

Denotes player sent off.

Melbourne, 6 February 2008, 50,969
Australia (3) 3 *(Kennedy 10, Cahill 18, Bresciano 33)*
Qatar (0) 0
Australia: Schwarzer; Neill, Moore (Holman 77), Cahill (Valeri 67), Culina, Emerton, Wilkshire, Kennedy (Aloisi 70), McDonald, Carney, Bresciano.

Kunming, 26 March 2008, 32,000
China (0) 0   Australia (0) 0
Australia: Schwarzer; Neill, North, Culina, Beauchamp, Valeri, Wilkshire, Thompson (Holman 10), Carney, Grella, Bresciano.

Brisbane, 1 June 2008, 48,678
Australia (0) 1 *(Kewell 47)*   **Iraq (0) 0**
Australia: Schwarzer; Beauchamp, North, Culina, Emerton, Wilkshire, McDonald (Holman 65), Kewell (Djite 77), Carney, Grella, Bresciano (Valeri 62).

Dubai, 7 June 2008, 8000
Iraq (0) 1 *(Mohammed 27)*   **Australia (0) 0**
Australia: Schwarzer; Coyne (Kennedy 64), Beauchamp, North, Culina, Valeri, Emerton, Wilkshire, Kewell (McDonald), Carney, Grella (Holman 46).

Doha, 14 June 2008, 12,000
Qatar (0) 1 *(Al Khalfan 90)*   **Australia (1) 3** *(Emerton 17, 56, Kewell 75)*
Australia: Schwarzer; Beauchamp, North, Culina, Valeri, Emerton, Wilkshire, Kewell (Djite 85), Carney, Holman, Bresciano.

Sydney, 22 June 2008, 70,054
Australia (0) 0   China (1) 1 *(Sun 11)*
Australia: Petkovic; Topor-Stanley, Spiranovic, North, Zadkovich, Valeri, Jedinak (Kilkenny 79), Holland (Williams), Djite, Kewell, Troisi (Sarkies 83).

Tashkent, 10 September 2008, 34,000
Uzbekistan (0) 0   Australia (1) 1 *(Chipperfield 26)*
Australia: Schwarzer; Neill, Chipperfield, Burns, Emerton, Wilkshire, Kewell (Djite 90), Coyne, Valeri, Holman (Sterjovski 77), Bresciano (Carney 73).

Brisbane, 15 October 2008, 34,320
Australia (2) 4 *(Cahill 8, Emerton 17 (pen), 58, Kennedy 76)*
Qatar (0) 0
Australia: Schwarzer; Neill, Moore, Cahill, Culina, Emerton (Burns 86), Wilkshire, Kennedy, Carney, Chipperfield (Sterjovski 46), McDonald (Holman 68).

Manama, 19 November 2008, 10,000
Bahrain (0) 0   Australia (0) 1 *(Bresciano 90)*
Australia: Schwarzer; Neill, Cahill (Sterjovski 86), Culina, Wilkshire, Kennedy, Kewell (Holman 71), Carney, Coyne (North 69), Valeri, Bresciano.

Yokohama, 11 February 2009, 66,000
Japan (0) 0   Australia (0) 0
Japan: Tsuzuki; Nakazawa, Tanaka MT, Uchida, Endo, Matsui (Okubo 57), Tanaka T (Okazaki 83), Nakamura S, Tamada, Nagatomo, Hasebe.
Australia: Schwarzer; Neill, Moore, Cahill (Kennedy 85), Culina, Wilkshire, Chipperfield, Grella, Holman (Garcia 64), Valeri, Bresciano (Carney 90).

Sydney, 1 April 2009, 57,292
Australia (0) 2 *(Kennedy 66, Kewell 73 (pen))*
Uzbekistan (0) 0
Australia: Schwarzer; Neill, Culina, Beauchamp, Wilkshire, Kewell (Holman 75), Chipperfield, Garcia, Valeri (Jedinak 82), McDonald (Kennedy 61), Bresciano.

Doha, 6 June 2009, 7000
Qatar (0) 0   Australia (0) 0
Australia: Schwarzer; Neill, Cahill (Garcia 90), Culina, Coyne, Kennedy, Kewell, Chipperfield, Grella (North 73), Valeri, Bresciano (Holman 77).

Sydney, 10 June 2009, 39,540
Australia (0) 2 *(Sterjovski 55, Carney 88)*   **Bahrain (0) 0**
Australia: Schwarzer; Milligan, Carney, Culina, Coyne (North 73), Jedinak (Grella 63), Wilkshire, Kewell, Holman (Carle 84), Sterjovski, McDonald.

Melbourne, 17 June 2009, 69,238
Australia (0) 2 *(Cahill 59, 77)*
Japan (1) 1 *(Tanaka MT 39)*
Australia: Schwarzer; Neill, Stefanutto, Cahill (Vidosic 84), Culina, Kennedy, Carle (Burns 77), Grella, Williams (McDonald 77), Sterjovski, North.
Japan: Narazaki; Abe, Tanaka MT, Uchida, Hashimoto (Kohrogi 84), Konno, Okazaki, Matsui (Yano 67), Tamada, Nakamura K, Nagatomo.

JAPANESE GAMES

Saitama, 6 February 2008, 35,130
Japan (1) 4 *(Endo 21, Okubo 54, Nakazawa 66, Maki 90)*
Thailand (1) 1 *(Winothai 22)*
Japan: Kawaguchi; Nakazawa, Komano, Abe, Endo, Uchida, Yamase (Maki 68), Suzuki, Nakamura K, Okubo (Hanyu 87), Takahara (Bando 77).

Manama, 26 March 2008, 26,000
Bahrain (0) 1 *(Hubail 78)*   **Japan (0) 0**
Japan: Kawaguchi; Nakazawa, Komano, Yasuda (Yamagishi 71), Abe (Tamada 81), Maki, Suzuki, Nakamura K, Konno, Okubo.

Yokohama, 2 June 2008, 46,764
Japan (2) 3 *(Nakazawa 10, Okubo 22, Nakamura 49)*
Oman (0) 0
Japan: Narazaki; Nakazawa, Komano, Tanaka MT, Nagatomo (Konno 83), Endo, Matsui, Nakamura S, Tamada (Maki 79), Okubo (Kagawa 72), Hasebe.

Muscat, 7 June 2008, 6500
Oman (1) 1 *(Mubarak 12)*   **Japan (0) 1** *(Endo 53 (pen))*
Japan: Narazaki; Nakazawa, Komano, Tanaka MT, Uchida (Konno 90), Endo, Matsui (Yamase 78), Nakamura S, Tamada (Yano 90), Okubo*, Hasebe.

Bangkok, 14 June 2008, 25,000
Thailand (0) 0   Japan (2) 3 *(Tanaka MT 23, Nakazawa 38, Nakamura K 88)*
Japan: Narazaki; Nakazawa, Komano, Tanaka MT, Uchida, Endo, Nagatomo (Konno 82), Matsui (Nakamura K 70), Nakamura S (Yano 70), Tamada, Hasebe.

Saitama, 22 June 2008, 51,180
Japan (0) 1 *(Uchida 90)*   **Bahrain (0) 0**
Japan: Narazaki; Nakazawa, Tanaka MT, Uchida, Endo, Sato (Yamase 64), Nakamura S, Tamada, Nakamura K, Yasuda (Konno 73), Honda (Maki 80).

Manama, 6 September 2008, 20,000
Bahrain (0) 2 *(Isa 87, Tanaka MT 89 (og))*   **Japan (2) 3**
(Nakamura S 18, Endo 44 (pen), Nakamura K 85)
Japan: Narazaki; Nakazawa, Uchida, Tanaka MT, Abe,
Endo, Matsui (Nakamura K 70), Nakamura S, Tamada,
Tanaka T, Hasebe (Konno 84).

Saitama, 15 October 2008, 55,142
Japan (1) 1 *(Tamada 40)*   **Uzbekistan (1) 1** *(Shatskikh 27)*
Japan: Narazaki; Nakazawa, Tanaka MT, Abe, Endo,
Nakamura S, Tamada (Kohrogi 81), Kagawa (Inamoto
76), Uchida, Okubo (Okazaki 62), Hasebe.

Doha, 19 November 2008, 13,000
Qatar (0) 0   Japan (1) 3 *(Tanaka T 19, Tamada 47,*
Tanaka MT 68)
Japan: Kawaguchi; Terada, Uchida, Tanaka MT, Endo,
Tanaka T (Matsui 71), Nakamura S, Tamada (Sato 90),
Nagatomo, Okubo (Okazaki 86), Hasebe.

Saitama, 28 March 2009, 57,276
Japan (0) 1 *(Nakamura S 47)*   **Bahrain (0) 0**
Japan: Narazaki; Nakazawa, Tanaka MT, Uchida, Endo,
Tanaka T (Okazaki 86), Nakamura S, Tamada (Matsui
79), Nagatomo, Okubo, Hasebe (Hashimoto 76).

Tashkent, 6 June 2009, 34,000
Uzbekistan (0) 0   Japan (1) 1 *(Okazaki 9)*
Japan: Narazaki; Nakazawa, Komano, Tanaka MT,
Endo, Okazaki, Nakamura S (Abe 90), Nakamura K
(Honda 66), Nagatomo, Okubo (Yano 69), Hasebe■.

Yokohama, 10 June 2009, 60,256
Japan (1) 1 *(Albinali 3 (og))*   **Qatar (0) 1** *(Yahya 53 (pen))*
Japan: Narazaki; Nakazawa, Tanaka MT, Abe (Matsui
58), Uchida, Hashimoto, Okazaki, Nakamura S (Honda
81), Tamada (Kohrogi 67), Nakamura K, Konno.

SOUTH KOREAN GAMES

Seoul, 6 February 2008, 25,738
South Korea (1) 4 *(Kwak TH 43, Seol 57, 85, Park JS 70)*
Turkmenistan (0) 0
South Korea: Jung; Oh BS, Cho YH (Park WJ 85), Kim
N (Lee KW 77), Park JS, Park CY, Seol, Lee YP, Kang,
Kwak TH, Yeom (Kim DH 31).

Shanghai, 26 March 2008, 20,000
North Korea (0) 0   South Korea (0) 0
North Korea: Ri MG; Ri J, Ri KH. An YH, Hong, Mun,
Jong TS (Pak NC 90), Pak SC, Han (Cha 27), Kim YJ,
Nam.
South Korea: Jung; Oh BS, Cho WH, Kim N (Kim DH
27), Park JS, Cho JJ (Yeom 46), Park CY, Seol (Han 81),
Lee YP, Kang, Lee JS.

Seoul, 31 May 2008, 50,000
South Korea (1) 2 *(Park JS 39, Park CY 48)*
Jordan (0) 2 *(Mahmoud 73, 81)*
South Korea: Kim YD; Oh BS, Cho WH, Kim N (Cho
YH 76), Kwak HJ, Park JS, Park CY, Lee YP, Lee CY
(Kim DH 55), Lee JS, Ahn (Ko 86).

Amman, 7 June 2008, 8000
Jordan (0) 0   South Korea (1) 1 *(Park CY 24 (pen))*
South Korea: Jung; Oh BS, Cho WH, Kim N, Kwak HJ,
Park JS, Park CY, Seol (Cho YH 46), Lee YP (Lee JS
68), Lee KH (Ahn 80), Kang.

Ashgabat, 14 June 2008, 11,000
Turkmenistan (0) 1 *(Ovekov 77 (pen))*   **South Korea (1)**
3 *(Kim BH 14, 81, 90 (pen))*
South Korea: Jung; Oh BS (Lee JS 29), Cho WH (Choi
HJ 46), Cho YH, Kim N, Lee KH (Lee CY 80), Kim DH,
Park CY, Seol, Kim CW, Kang.

Seoul, 22 June 2008, 48,519
South Korea (0) 0   North Korea (0) 0
South Korea: Jung; Kim CW, Oh JE (Lee KH 78), Kim
DH, Ahn (Park CY 60), Ko, Choi HJ, Kang, Lee JS, Kim
JW (Kim N 71), Lee CY.
North Korea: Ri MG; Cha, Ri J, Ri KC, An YH, Hong
(Choe 10), Mun, Jong TS, Pak CJ, Kim YJ (Pak NC 63),
Nam.

Shanghai, 10 September 2008, 3000
North Korea (0) 1 *(Hong 64 (pen))*
South Korea (0) 1 *(Ki 69)*
North Korea: Ri MG; Cha, Ri J, Ri KC, An YH, Hong,
Mun, Jong TS, Park CJ, Kim YJ (Choe 71) (Kim K 89),
Nam.
South Korea: Jung; Oh BS (Choi HJ 79), Kim DJ, Kim N,
Kim JK, Choi SK (Lee CS 60), Kim DH, Cho JJ (Seol
60), Kim CW, Kang, Ki.

Seoul, 15 October 2008, 30,000
South Korea (2) 4 *(Lee KH 20, 80, Park JS 26,*
Kwak TH 89)   **UAE (0) 1** *(Al Hammadi 72)*
South Korea: Jung; Cho YH, Kim DJ, Ki (Cho WH 80),
Park JS, Lee CY (Kim HB 55), Lee KH (Shin 88), Lee
YP, Kim JW, Jeong, Kwak TH.

Riyadh, 19 November 2008, 60,000
Saudi Arabia (0) 0   South Korea (0) 2 *(Lee KH 76,*
Park CY 90)
South Korea: Lee WJ; Oh BS, Cho YH, Ki, Park JS, Kim
JW, Jeong (Park CY 74), Lee KH (Yeom 89), Lee YP,
Kang, Lee CY (Cho WH 90).

Tehran, 11 February 2009, 75,000
Iran (0) 1 *(Nekounam 58)*
South Korea (0) 1 *(Park JS 81)*
South Korea: Lee WJ; Oh BS, Kang, Cho YH, Park JS
(Park CY 84), Kim JW, Jeong (Yeom 41), Lee KH, Lee
YP (Kim DJ 70), Ki, Lee CY.

Seoul, 1 April 2009, 48,000
South Korea (0) 1 *(Kim CW 86)*   **North Korea (0) 0**
South Korea: Lee WJ; Oh BS, Kang, Cho WH, Hwang
(Lee JS 53), Park JS, Park CY, Lee KH (Kim CW 77),
Lee YP (Kim DJ 59), Ki, Lee CY.
North Korea: Ri MK; Cha, Ri J, Pak NC, Ri KC, Ji (Nam
SC 80), Hong, Mun, Jong TS, Pak CJ, Kim YJ (Choe 83).

Dubai, 6 June 2009, 4000
UAE (0) 0   South Korea (2) 2 *(Park CY 9, Ki 37)*
South Korea: Lee WJ; Oh BS, Cho YH, Park JS, Kim
JW■, Park CY (Bae 82), Lee KH (Cho WH 51), Lee YP
(Kim DJ 59), Lee JS, Ki, Lee CY.

Seoul, 10 June 2009, 32,510
South Korea (0) 0   Saudi Arabia (0) 0
South Korea: Lee WJ; Cho WH, Cho YH, Kim DJ, Park
JS, Park CY (Yang 73), Lee KH (Choi TU 84), Lee JS,
Kim H, Ki, Lee CY.

Seoul, 17 June 2009, 40,000
South Korea (0) 1 *(Park JS 82)*   **Iran (0) 1** *(Shojaei 52)*
South Korea: Lee WJ; Oh BS, Cho YH, Kim DJ (Lee YP
70), Park JS, Kim JW, Park CY, Lee KH, Lee JS, Ki
(Yang 75), Lee CY (Cho WH 46).

NORTH KOREAN GAMES

Ulaan-Baatar, 21 October 2007, 4870
Mongolia (0) 1 *(Selenge 90)*
North Korea (3) 4 *(Pak CM 14, Jong CM, 24, 32, 78)*
North Korea: Ri MG (Ju 46); Ri J, Pak NC, Pak CM, Pak SC, Jon, Ri CM (Jong SH 76), Jong CM, Kim KJ, Kim K (So 30), Yun.

Pyongyang, 28 October 2007, 5000
North Korea (3) 5 *(Park CM 3, 74, Kim KJ 10, Jong CM 36, Jon 90)*
Mongolia (1) 1 *(Donorov 41)*
North Korea: Ju; Cha, Ri J (Ri KH 65), Pak NC, Pak CM, Pak SC, Jon, Ri CM■, Jong CM (So 79), Kim KJ (Ri HR 46), Yun.

Amman, 6 February 2008,16,000
Jordan (0) 0
North Korea (1) 1 *(Hong 44)*
North Korea: Ri MG; Ri J, Ri KC, An YH, Hong, Mun, Jong TS, Pak CJ (Cha 60), Han, Kim YJ (Ryang 40) (Pak NC 90), Nam SC.

Ashgabat, 2 June 2008, 20,000
Turkmenistan (0) 0
North Korea (0) 0
North Korea: Ri MG; Cha (Han 57), Ri J, Ri KC, An YH, Hong, Mun, Jong TS, Pak CJ, Kim YJ (Pak NC 64), Nam SC.

Pyongyang, 7 June 2008, 25,000
North Korea (0) 1 *(Choe 72)*
Turkmenistan (0) 0
North Korea: Ri MG; Cha, Ri J, Pak NC, Ri KC, An YH (Kim YJ 60), Hong (Kim MW 87), Mun, Pak CJ (Han 28), Nam SC, Choe.

Pyongyang, 14 June 2008, 28,000
North Korea (1) 2 *(Hong 44, 72)*
Jordan (0) 0
North Korea: Ri MG; Cha, Ri J, Pak NC (Choe 88), Ri KC, An YH, Hong, Mun, Jong TS, Han, Nam SC.

Abu Dhabi, 6 September 2008, 10,000
UAE (0) 1 *(Basheer Saeed 85)*
North Korea (0) 2 *(Choe 72, An 80)*
North Korea: Ri MG; Cha, Ri J, Ri KC, An YH, Hong (Kim K 71), Mun, Pak CJ, Kim YJ (An CH 29), Nam SC, Choe (Kim MW 86).

Tehran, 15 October 2008, 60,000
Iran (1) 2 *(Mahdavikia 9, Nekounam 63)*
North Korea (0) 1 *(Jong TS 72)*
North Korea: Ri MG; Cha, Ri J, Ri KC, An YH, Hong, Mun (Pak NC 90), Jong TS, Pak CJ, Kim YJ (Choe 46), Nam SC.

Pyongyang, 11 February 2009, 48,000
North Korea (1) 1 *(Mun 29)*
Saudi Arabia (0) 0
North Korea: Ri MG; Cha, Ri J, Pak NC, Ri KC, Ji, An YH (An CH 67) (Kim MW 85), Hong, Mun, Jong TS, Pak CJ.

Pyongyang, 28 March 2009, 50,000
North Korea (0) 2 *(Pak NC 51, Mun 90)*
UAE (0) 0
North Korea: Ri MG; Cha, Ri J, Pak NC, Ri KC, Ji, An YH, Hong (Choe 88), Mun, Jong TS, Pak CJ.

Pyongyang, 6 June 2009, 30,000
North Korea (0) 0
Iran (0) 0
North Korea: Ri MG; Cha, Ri J, Pak NC, Ri KC, Ji, An YH, Hong, Mun (Kim YJ 88), Jong TS, Pak CJ.

Riyadh, 7 June 2009, 65,000
Saudi Arabia (0) 0
North Korea (0) 0
North Korea: Ri MG; Cha, Ri J, Pak NC, Ri KC, Ji, An YH, Hong (An CH 60), Mun (Kim K 74), Jong TS (Kim YJ■ 89), Pak CJ.

OLYMPIC FOOTBALL TOURNAMENT 2008

(Finals in China)

GROUP A
Australia 1, Serbia 1
Ivory Coast 1, Argentina 2
Argentina 1, Australia 0
Serbia 2, Ivory Coast 4
Ivory Coast 1, Australia 0
Argentina 2, Serbia 0
Australia 0, Ivory Coast 1
Serbia 0, Argentina 2

GROUP B
Japan 0, USA 1
Holland 0, Nigeria 0
Nigeria 2, Japan 1
USA 2, Holland 2
Holland 1, Japan 0
Nigeria 2, USA 1
Holland 1, Japan 0
Nigeria 2, USA 1

GROUP C
Brazil 1, Belgium 0
China 1, New Zealand 1
New Zealand 0, Brazil 5
Belgium 2, China 0
China 0, Brazil 3
New Zealand 0, Belgium 1
Brazil 3, China 0
Belgium 1, New Zealand 0

GROUP D
Honduras 0, Italy 3
South Korea 1, Cameroon 1

Cameroon 1, Honduras 0
Italy 3, South Korea 0
South Korea 1, Honduras 0
Cameroon 0, Italy 0

QUARTER-FINALS
Nigeria 2, Ivory Coast 0
Italy 2, Belgium 3
Argentina 2, Holland 1
Brazil 2, Cameroon 0

SEMI-FINALS
Nigeria 4, Belgium 1
Argentina 3, Brazil 0

MATCH FOR THIRD PLACE
Belgium 0, Brazil 3

FINAL IN BEIJING

Nigeria (0) 0
Argentina (0) 1 *(Di Maria 58)*   89,102
Nigeria: Vanzekin; Okonkwo, Apdam, Adeleye, James, Obinna, Isaac (Ekpo 70), Okoronkwo (Anichebe 64), Ajilore, Adefemi, Odemwingie.
Argentina: Romero; Garay, Monzon, Zabaleta, Gago, Riquelme, Di Maria (Banega 88), Pareja, Mascherano, Messi, Aguero (Sosa 79).
Referee: Kassai (Hungary).

WORLD CUP 2010 QUALIFYING COMPETITION
(Remaining fixtures)

EUROPE

GROUP 1
05.09.09 Denmark v Portugal; Hungary v Sweden.
09.09.09 Albania v Denmark; Malta v Sweden;
Hungary v Portugal.
10.10.09 Denmark v Sweden; Portugal v Hungary.
14.10.09 Sweden v Albania; Denmark v Hungary;
Portugal v Malta.

GROUP 2
05.09.09 Switzerland v Greece; Israel v Latvia;
Moldova v Luxembourg.
09.09.09 Moldova v Greece; Israel v Luxembourg;
Latvia v Switzerland.
10.10.09 Greece v Latvia; Israel v Moldova;
Luxembourg v Switzerland.
14.10.09 Greece v Luxembourg; Switzerland v Israel;
Latvia v Moldova.

GROUP 3
19.08.09 Slovenia v San Marino.
05.09.09 Poland v Northern Ireland;
Slovakia v Czech Republic.
09.09.09 Northern Ireland v Slovakia; Slovenia v Poland;
Czech Republic v San Marino.
10.10.09 Czech Republic v Poland; Slovakia v Slovenia.
14.10.09 San Marino v Slovenia;
Czech Republic v Northern Ireland;
Poland v Slovakia.

GROUP 4
19.08.09 Azerbaijan v Germany.
05.09.09 Azerbaijan v Finland; Russia v Liechtenstein.
09.09.09 Wales v Russia; Germany v Azerbaijan;
Liechtenstein v Finland.
10.10.09 Liechtenstein v Azerbaijan; Finland v Wales;
Russia v Germany.
14.10.09 Azerbaijan v Russia; Germany v Finland;
Liechtenstein v Wales.

GROUP 5
05.09.09 Armenia v Bosnia; Spain v Belgium;
Turkey v Estonia.
09.09.09 Armenia v Belgium; Bosnia v Turkey;
Spain v Estonia.
10.10.09 Armenia v Spain; Belgium v Turkey;
Estonia v Bosnia.
14.10.09 Turkey v Armenia; Estonia v Belgium;
Bosnia v Spain.

GROUP 6
19.08.09 Belarus v Croatia.
05.09.09 Ukraine v Andorra; Croatia v Belarus.
09.09.09 Andorra v Kazakhstan; Belarus v Ukraine;
England v Croatia.
10.09.09 Ukraine v Kazakhstan.
10.10.09 Belarus v Kazakhstan; Ukraine v England.
14.10.09 Andorra v Ukraine; England v Belarus;
Kazakhstan v Croatia.

GROUP 7
19.08.09 Faeroes v France.
05.09.09 Austria v Faeroes; France v Romania.
09.09.09 Faeroes v Lithuania; Serbia v France;
Romania v Austria.
10.10.09 France v Faeroes; Austria v Lithuania;
Serbia v Romania.
14.10.09 Romania v Faeroes; France v Austria;
Lithuania v Serbia.

GROUP 8
05.09.09 Bulgaria v Montenegro; Georgia v Italy;
Cyprus v Eire.
09.09.09 Italy v Bulgaria; Montenegro v Cyprus.
10.10.09 Montenegro v Georgia; Cyprus v Bulgaria;
Eire v Italy.
14.10.09 Bulgaria v Georgia; Eire v Montenegro;
Italy v Cyprus.

GROUP 9
19.08.09 Norway v Scotland.
05.09.09 Iceland v Norway; Scotland v Macedonia.
09.09.09 Norway v Macedonia; Scotland v Holland.

SOUTH AMERICA

05.09.09 Paraguay v Bolivia; Argentina v Brazil;
Colombia v Ecuador; Peru v Uruguay;
Chile v Venezuela.
09.09.09 Paraguay v Argentina; Brazil v Chile;
Uruguay v Colombia; Bolivia v Ecuador;
Venezuela v Peru.

10.10.09 Bolivia v Brazil; Colombia v Chile;
Venezuela v Paraguay; Argentina v Peru;
Ecuador v Uruguay.
14.10.09 Uruguay v Argentina; Peru v Bolivia;
Paraguay v Colombia; Chile v Ecuador;
Brazil v Venezuela.

THE WORLD CUP 1930–2006

Year	Winners		Runners-up		Venue	Attendance	Referee
1930	Uruguay	4	Argentina	2	Montevideo	90,000	Langenus (B)
1934	Italy*	2	Czechoslovakia	1	Rome	50,000	Eklind (Se)
1938	Italy	4	Hungary	2	Paris	45,000	Capdeville (F)
1950	Uruguay	2	Brazil	1	Rio de Janeiro	199,854	Reader (E)
1954	West Germany	3	Hungary	2	Berne	60,000	Ling (E)
1958	Brazi	5	Sweden	2	Stockholm	49,737	Guigue (F)
1962	Brazil	3	Czechoslovakia	1	Santiago	68,679	Latychev (USSR)
1966	England*	4	West Germany	2	Wembley	93,802	Dienst (Sw)
1970	Brazil	4	Italy	1	Mexico City	107,412	Glockner (EG)
1974	West Germany	2	Holland	1	Munich	77,833	Taylor (E)
1978	Argentina*	3	Holland	1	Buenos Aires	77,000	Gonella (I)
1982	Italy	3	West Germany	1	Madrid	90,080	Coelho (Br)
1986	Argentina	3	West Germany	2	Mexico City	114,580	Filho (Br)
1990	West Germany	1	Argentina	0	Rome	73,603	Mendez (Mex)
1994	Brazil*	0	Italy	0	Los Angeles	94,194	Puhl (H)
	(Brazil won 3-2 on penalties)						
1998	France	3	Brazil	0	St-Denis	75,000	Belqola (Mor)
2002	Brazil	2	Germany	0	Yokohama	69,029	Collina (I)
2006	Italy*	1	France	1	Berlin	69,000	Elizondo (Arg)
	(Italy won 5-3 on penalties)						
(*After extra time)							

GOALSCORING AND ATTENDANCES IN WORLD CUP FINAL ROUNDS

Venue	Matches	Goals (av)	Attendance (av)
1930 Uruguay	18	70 (3.9)	434,500 (24,138)
1934 Italy	17	70 (4.1)	395,000 (23,235)
1938 France	18	84 (4.6)	483,000 (26,833)
1950 Brazil	22	88 (4.0)	1,337,000 (60,772)
1954 Switzerland	26	140 (5.4)	943,000 (36,270)
1958 Sweden	35	126 (3.6)	868,000 (24,800)
1962 Chile	32	89 (2.8)	776,000 (24,250)
1966 England	32	89 (2.8)	1,614,677 (50,458)
1970 Mexico	32	95 (2.9)	1,673,975 (52,311)
1974 West Germany	38	97 (2.5)	1,774,022 (46,684)
1978 Argentina	38	102 (2.7)	1,610,215 (42,374)
1982 Spain	52	146 (2.8)	2,064,364 (38,816)
1986 Mexico	52	132 (2.5)	2,441,731 (46,956)
1990 Italy	52	115 (2.2)	2,515,168 (48,368)
1994 USA	52	141 (2.7)	3,567,415 (68,604)
1998 France	64	171 (2.6)	2,775,400 (43,366)
2002 Japan/S. Korea	64	161 (2.5)	2,705,566 (42,274)
2006 Germany	64	147 (2.3)	3,354,646 (52,416)

LEADING GOALSCORERS

Year	Player	Goals
1930	Guillermo Stabile (Argentina)	8
1934	Angelo Schiavio (Italy), Oldrich Nejedly (Czechoslovakia), Edmund Conen (Germany)	4
1938	Leonidas da Silva (Brazil)	8
1950	Ademir (Brazil)	9
1954	Sandor Kocsis (Hungary)	11
1958	Just Fontaine (France)	13
1962	Valentin Ivanov (USSR), Leonel Sanchez (Chile), Garrincha, Vava (both Brazil), Florian Albert (Hungary), Drazen Jerkovic (Yugoslavia)	4
1966	Eusebio (Portugal)	9
1970	Gerd Muller (West Germany)	10
1974	Grzegorz Lato (Poland)	7
1978	Mario Kempes (Argentina)	6
1982	Paolo Rossi (Italy)	6
1986	Gary Lineker (England)	6
1990	Salvatore Schillaci (Italy)	6
1994	Oleg Salenko (Russia), Hristo Stoichkov (Bulgaria)	6
1998	Davor Suker (Croatia)	6
2002	Ronaldo (Brazil)	8
2006	Miroslav Klose (Germany)	5

EUROPEAN FOOTBALL CHAMPIONSHIP

(formerly EUROPEAN NATIONS' CUP)

Year	Winners		Runners-up		Venue	Attendance
1960	USSR	2	Yugoslavia	1	Paris	17,966
1964	Spain	2	USSR	1	Madrid	120,000
1968	Italy	2	Yugoslavia	0	Rome	60,000
	After 1-1 draw					75,000
1972	West Germany	3	USSR	0	Brussels	43,437
1976	Czechoslovakia	2	West Germany	2	Belgrade	45,000
	(Czechoslovakia won on penalties)					
1980	West Germany	2	Belgium	1	Rome	47,864
1984	France	2	Spain	0	Paris	48,000
1988	Holland	2	USSR	0	Munich	72,308
1992	Denmark	2	Germany	0	Gothenburg	37,800
1996	Germany	2	Czech Republic	1	Wembley	73,611
	(Germany won on sudden death)					
2000	France	2	Italy	1	Rotterdam	50,000
	(France won on sudden death)					
2004	Greece	1	Portugal	0	Lisbon	62,865
2008	Spain	1	Germany	0	Vienna	51,428

CONFEDERATIONS CUP 2009

(In South Africa)

GROUP A

Johannesburg, 14 June 2009, 48,837
South Africa (0) 0
Iraq (0) 0
South Africa: Khune; Gaxa, Masilela, Mokoena, Mhlongo, Sibaya, Modise, Dikgacoi, Booth, Parker (Pienaar 85), Fanteni (Mashego 78).
Iraq: Mohammed Kassid; Mohammed Ali Kareem, Basem Abbas, Fareed Majeed, Nashat Akram, Emad Mohammed (Alaa Abdul Zahra 76), Younis Mahmoud, Karrar Jasim (Hawar Mulla Mohammed 74), Salam Shaker, Ali Hussein Rehema, Mahdi Kareem (Salih Sadir 88).

Rustenburg, 14 June 2009, 21,649
New Zealand (0) 0
Spain (4) 5 *(Torres 6, 14, 17, Fabregas 24, Villa 48)*
New Zealand: Moss; Lochhead, Vicelich, Elliott, Brown, Smeltz (James 76), Killen (Wright 85), Bertos, Brockie (Christie 27), Mulligan, Boyens.
Spain: Casillas; Sergio Ramos (Arbeloa 54), Albiol, Xabi Alonso, Puyol, Capdevila, Xavi (Cazorla 54), Fabregas, Torres (David Silva 70), Villa, Riera.

Mangaung/Bloemfontein, 17 June 2009, 30,512
Spain (0) 1 *(Villa 55)*
Iraq (0) 0
Spain: Casillas; Sergio Ramos, Pique, Xabi Alonso, Marchena, Capdevila, Xavi (Busquets 82), Mata, Torres, Villa (Guiza 74), Cazorla (David Silva 67).
Iraq: Mohammed Kassid; Mohammed Ali Kareem, Basem Abbas, Fareed Majeed, Nashat Akram, Hawar Mulla Mohammed (Karrar Jasim 69), Salam Shaker, Ali Hussein Rehema, Alaa Abdul Zahra (Younis Mahmoud 80), Samer Saeed (Mahdi Kareem 60).

Rustenburg, 17 June 2009, 36,598
South Africa (1) 2 *(Parker 21, 52)*
New Zealand (0) 0
South Africa: Khune; Gaxa, Masilela, Mokoena, Sibaya, Pienaar, Modise, Dikgacoi, Booth, Parker (Tshabalala 81), Fanteni (Mashego 62).
New Zealand: Moss; Lochhead, Vicelich, Elliott, Brown (Oughton 55), Smeltz, Killen (Wood 75), Bertos (James 66), Christie, Mulligan, Boyens.

Johannesburg, 20 June 2009, 23,295
Iraq (0) 0
New Zealand (0) 0
Iraq: Mohammed Kassid; Mohammed Ali Kareem, Basem Abbas, Nashat Akram, Emad Mohammed (Alaa Abdul Zahra 56), Younis Mahmoud, Hawar Mulla Mohammed (Fareed Majeed 46), Karrar Jasim, Salam Shaker, Ali Hussein Rehema, Mahdi Kareem (Salih Sadir 67).
New Zealand: Moss; Scott (Mulligan 85), Lochhead, Sigmund (Boyens 71), Vicelich, Elliott, Brown, Smeltz, Killen, Bertos, Brockie (Christie 68).

Mangaung/Bloemfontein, 20 June 2009, 38,212
Spain (0) 2 *(Villa 52, Llorente 72)*
South Africa (0) 0
Spain: Reina; Arbeloa, Pique, Albiol, Puyol, Busquets, Xavi, Fabregas, Torres (Llorente 60), Villa (Pablo Hernandez 60), Riera (Cazorla 81).
South Africa: Khune; Gaxa, Masilela, Mokoena, Mhlongo, Sibaya (Mashego 83), Pienaar, Modise, Dikgacoi, Booth, Parker (Tshabalala 90).

GROUP B

Mangaung/Bloemfontein, 15 June 2009, 27,851
Brazil (3) 4 *(Kaka 5, 90 (pen), Luis Fabiano 12, Juan 37)*
Egypt (1) 3 *(Zidan 9, 55, Shawky 54)*
Brazil: Julio Cesar; Lucio, Daniel Alves, Juan, Kleber (Andre Santos 83), Gilberto Silva, Kaka, Robinho (Ramires 62), Elano (Alexandre Pato 62), Luis Fabiano.
Egypt: El Hadary; Ahmed Said, Hani Said, Ahmed Fathi, Abd Rabbou (Al Muhamadi 75), Zidan, Shawky, Moawad, Ahmed Hassan (Ahmed Eid 51), Gomaa Aboutrika.

Tshwane/Pretoria, 15 June 2009, 34,341
USA (1) 1 *(Donovan 41 (pen))*
Italy (0) 3 *(Rossi 58, 90, De Rossi 72)*
USA: Howard; Bornstein (Kljestan 86), Onyewu, Dempsey, Donovan, Bradley, Clark[■], DeMerit, Altidore (Davies 66), Spector, Feilhaber (Beasley 72).
Italy: Buffon; Grosso, Chiellini, De Rossi, Legrottaglie, Zambrotta, Pirlo, Camoranesi (Rossi 57), Gattuso (Montolivo 57), Iaquinta, Gilardino (Toni 69).

Tshwane/Pretoria, 18 June 2009, 39,617
USA (0) 0
Brazil (2) 3 *(Felipe Melo 7, Robinho 20, Maicon 62)*
USA: Howard; Bornstein, Onyewu, Beasley (Casey 46), Dempsey, Donovan, Bradley, DeMerit, Kljestan[■], Altidore (Feilhaber 60), Spector.
Brazil: Julio Cesar; Maicon, Lucio (Luisao 70), Felipe Melo, Miranda, Andre Santos, Gilberto Silva, Kaka (Julio Baptista 69), Robinho, Ramires, Luis Fabiano (Nilmar 69).

Johannesburg, 18 June 2009, 52,150
Egypt (1) 1 *(Homos 40)*
Italy (0) 0
Egypt: El Hadary; Ahmed Said, Hani Said, Ahmed Fathi (Ahmed Hassan 80), Abd Rabbou, Zidan (Ahmed Eid 57), Shawky, Homos, Moawad (Farag 69), Gomaa, Aboutrika.
Italy: Buffon; Zambrotta, Grosso, Chiellini, Cannavaro, De Rossi, Rossi (Montolivo 58), Pirlo, Gattuso (Toni 58), Quagliarella (Pepe 64), Iaquinta.

Tshwane/Pretoria, 21 June 2009, 41,195
Italy (0) 0
Brazil (3) 3 *(Luis Fabiano 37, 43, Dossena 45 (og))*
Italy: Buffon; Zambrotta, Dossena, Chiellini, Cannavaro, De Rossi, Camoranesi, Pirlo, Toni (Gilardino 57), Iaquinta (Rossi 38), Montolivo (Pepe 46).
Brazil: Julio Cesar; Maicon, Lucio, Juan (Luisao 24), Felipe Melo, Andre Santos, Gilberto Silva (Kleberson 84), Kaka, Robinho, Luis Fabiano, Ramires (Josue 86).

Rustenburg, 21 June 2009, 23,140
Egypt (0) 0
USA (1) 3 *(Davies 21, Bradley 63, Dempsey 71)*
Egypt: El Hadary; Al Muhamadi, Hani Said, Ahmed Fathi (Ahmed Said 56), Abd Rabbou, Ahmed Eid (Ahmed Hassan 50), Shawky, Farag, Abdelghani (Abougrisha 62), Gomaa, Aboutrika.
USA: Guzan; Bornstein, Onyewu, Dempsey, Davies (Casey 82), Donovan, Bradley, Clark, DeMerit, Altidore (Feilhaber 69), Spector.

SEMI-FINALS

Mangaung/Bloemfontein, 24 June 2009, 35,369

Spain (0) 0

USA (1) 2 *(Altidore 27, Dempsey 74)*

Spain: Casillas; Sergio Ramos, Pique, Capdevila, Xavi, Puyol, Xabi Alonso, Fabregas (Cazorla 68), Torres, Villa, Riera (Mata 78).
USA: Howard; Bocanegra, Onyewu, Dempsey (Bornstein 88), Davies (Feilhaber 69), Donovan, Bradley■, Clark, DeMerit, Altidore (Casey 83), Spector.

Johannesburg, 25 June 2009, 48,049

Brazil (0) 1 *(Daniel Alves 88)*

South Africa (0) 0

Brazil: Julio Cesar; Maicon, Lucio, Felipe Melo, Luisao, Gilberto Silva, Andre Santos (Daniel Alves 82), Ramires, Kaka, Robinho, Luis Fabiano (Kleberson 90).
South Africa: Khune; Gaxa, Masilela, Mokoena, Mhlongo, Tshabalala (Mashego 90), Pienaar (Van Heerden 90), Modise (Mphela 90), Dikgacoi, Booth, Parker.

MATCH FOR THIRD PLACE

Rustenburg, 28 June 2009, 31,788

Spain (0) 3 *(Guiza 68, 89, Xabi Alonso 107)*

South Africa (0) 2 *(Mphela 73, 90)*

Spain: Casillas; Albiol, Pique, Xabi Alonso, Arbeloa, Capdevila, Busquets (Llorente 81), Cazorla, Villa (Guiza 57), Torres (David Silva 57), Riera.
South Africa: Khune; Gaxa, Masilela, Mokoena, Sibaya, Tshabalala (Mhlongo 84), Pienaar (Mphela 64), Modise (Van Heerden 69), Dikgacoi, Booth, Parker.
aet.

CONFEDERATION CUP FINAL 2009

Johannesburg, 28 June 2009, 52,291

USA (2) 2 *(Dempsey 10, Donovan 27)*   **Brazil (0) 3** *(Luis Fabiano 46, 74, Lucio 84)*

USA: Howard; Bocanegra, Onyewu, Dempsey, Davies, Donovan, Clark (Casey 88), DeMerit, Altidore (Bornstein 75), Spector, Feilhaber (Kljestan 75).

Brazil: Julio Cesar; Maicon, Lucio, Felipe Melo, Gilberto Silva, Luisao, Andre Santos (Daniel Alves 66), Kaka, Robinho, Ramires (Elano 67), Luis Fabiano.

Referee: M. Hansson (Sweden).

GOLDEN BALL WINNER
Kaka

GOLDEN SHOE WINNER
Luis Fabiano

GOLDEN GLOVE WINNER
Tim Howard

FIFA FAIR PLAY AWARD
Brazil

PREVIOUS TOURNAMENTS

Year	Winners		Runners-up		Venue
1992	Argentina	3	Saudi Arabia	1	Saudi Arabia
1995	Denmark	2	Argentina	0	Saudi Arabia
1997	Brazil	6	Australia	0	Saudi Arabia
1999	Mexico	4	Brazil	3	Mexico
2001	France	1	Japan	0	Korea/Japan
2003	France	1	Cameroon	0	France
2005	Brazil	4	Argentina	1	Germany
2009	Brazil	3	USA	2	South Africa

BRITISH AND IRISH INTERNATIONAL RESULTS 1872–2009

Note: In the results that follow, wc=World Cup, ec=European Championship, ui=Umbro International Trophy. tf = Tournoi de France. For Ireland, read Northern Ireland from 1921. *After extra time.

ENGLAND v SCOTLAND

Played: 110; England won 45, Scotland won 41, Drawn 24. Goals: England 192, Scotland 169.

Year	Date	Venue	E	S	Year	Date	Venue	E	S
1872	30 Nov	Glasgow	0	0	1932	9 Apr	Wembley	3	0
1873	8 Mar	Kennington Oval	4	2	1933	1 Apr	Glasgow	1	2
1874	7 Mar	Glasgow	1	2	1934	14 Apr	Wembley	3	0
1875	6 Mar	Kennington Oval	2	2	1935	6 Apr	Glasgow	0	2
1876	4 Mar	Glasgow	0	3	1936	4 Apr	Wembley	1	1
1877	3 Mar	Kennington Oval	1	3	1937	17 Apr	Glasgow	1	3
1878	2 Mar	Glasgow	2	7	1938	9 Apr	Wembley	0	1
1879	5 Apr	Kennington Oval	5	4	1939	15 Apr	Glasgow	2	1
1880	13 Mar	Glasgow	4	5	1947	12 Apr	Wembley	1	1
1881	12 Mar	Kennington Oval	1	6	1948	10 Apr	Glasgow	2	0
1882	11 Mar	Glasgow	1	5	1949	9 Apr	Wembley	1	3
1883	10 Mar	Sheffield	2	3	wc1950	15 Apr	Glasgow	1	0
1884	15 Mar	Glasgow	0	1	1951	14 Apr	Wembley	2	3
1885	21 Mar	Kennington Oval	1	1	1952	5 Apr	Glasgow	2	1
1886	31 Mar	Glasgow	1	1	1953	18 Apr	Wembley	2	2
1887	19 Mar	Blackburn	2	3	wc1954	3 Apr	Glasgow	4	2
1888	17 Mar	Glasgow	5	0	1955	2 Apr	Wembley	7	2
1889	13 Apr	Kennington Oval	2	3	1956	14 Apr	Glasgow	1	1
1890	5 Apr	Glasgow	1	1	1957	6 Apr	Wembley	2	1
1891	6 Apr	Blackburn	2	1	1958	19 Apr	Glasgow	4	0
1892	2 Apr	Glasgow	4	1	1959	11 Apr	Wembley	1	0
1893	1 Apr	Richmond	5	2	1960	9 Apr	Glasgow	1	1
1894	7 Apr	Glasgow	2	2	1961	15 Apr	Wembley	9	3
1895	6 Apr	Everton	3	0	1962	14 Apr	Glasgow	0	2
1896	4 Apr	Glasgow	1	2	1963	6 Apr	Wembley	1	2
1897	3 Apr	Crystal Palace	1	2	1964	11 Apr	Glasgow	0	1
1898	2 Apr	Glasgow	3	1	1965	10 Apr	Wembley	2	2
1899	8 Apr	Birmingham	2	1	1966	2 Apr	Glasgow	4	3
1900	7 Apr	Glasgow	1	4	ec1967	15 Apr	Wembley	2	3
1901	30 Mar	Crystal Palace	2	2	ec1968	24 Jan	Glasgow	1	1
1902	3 Mar	Birmingham	2	2	1969	10 May	Wembley	4	1
1903	4 Mar	Sheffield	1	2	1970	25 Apr	Glasgow	0	0
1904	9 Apr	Glasgow	1	0	1971	22 May	Wembley	3	1
1905	1 Apr	Crystal Palace	1	0	1972	27 May	Glasgow	1	0
1906	7 Apr	Glasgow	1	2	1973	14 Feb	Glasgow	5	0
1907	6 Apr	Newcastle	1	1	1973	19 May	Wembley	1	0
1908	4 Apr	Glasgow	1	1	1974	18 May	Glasgow	0	2
1909	3 Apr	Crystal Palace	2	0	1975	24 May	Wembley	5	1
1910	2 Apr	Glasgow	0	2	1976	15 May	Glasgow	1	2
1911	1 Apr	Everton	1	1	1977	4 June	Wembley	1	2
1912	23 Mar	Glasgow	1	1	1978	20 May	Glasgow	1	0
1913	5 Apr	Chelsea	1	0	1979	26 May	Wembley	3	1
1914	14 Apr	Glasgow	1	3	1980	24 May	Glasgow	2	0
1920	10 Apr	Sheffield	5	4	1981	23 May	Wembley	0	1
1921	9 Apr	Glasgow	0	3	1982	29 May	Glasgow	1	0
1922	8 Apr	Aston Villa	0	1	1983	1 June	Wembley	2	0
1923	14 Apr	Glasgow	2	2	1984	26 May	Glasgow	1	1
1924	12 Apr	Wembley	1	1	1985	25 May	Glasgow	0	1
1925	4 Apr	Glasgow	0	2	1986	23 Apr	Wembley	2	1
1926	17 Apr	Manchester	0	1	1987	23 May	Glasgow	0	0
1927	2 Apr	Glasgow	2	1	1988	21 May	Wembley	1	0
1928	31 Mar	Wembley	1	5	1989	27 May	Glasgow	2	0
1929	13 Apr	Glasgow	0	1	ec1996	15 June	Wembley	2	0
1930	5 Apr	Wembley	5	2	ec1999	13 Nov	Glasgow	2	0
1931	28 Mar	Glasgow	0	2	ec1999	17 Nov	Wembley	0	1

ENGLAND v WALES

Played: 99; England won 64, Wales won 14, Drawn 21. Goals: England 242, Wales 90.

Year	Date	Venue	E	W	Year	Date	Venue	E	W
1879	18 Jan	Kennington Oval	2	1	1882	13 Mar	Wrexham	3	5
1880	15 Mar	Wrexham	3	2	1883	3 Feb	Kennington Oval	5	0
1881	26 Feb	Blackburn	0	1	1884	17 Mar	Wrexham	4	0

			E	W
1885	14 Mar	Blackburn	1	1
1886	29 Mar	Wrexham	3	1
1887	26 Feb	Kennington Oval	4	0
1888	4 Feb	Crewe	5	1
1889	23 Feb	Stoke	4	1
1890	15 Mar	Wrexham	3	1
1891	7 May	Sunderland	4	1
1892	5 Mar	Wrexham	2	0
1893	13 Mar	Stoke	6	0
1894	12 Mar	Wrexham	5	1
1895	18 Mar	Queen's Club, Kensington	1	1
1896	16 Mar	Cardiff	9	1
1897	29 Mar	Sheffield	4	0
1898	28 Mar	Wrexham	3	0
1899	20 Mar	Bristol	4	0
1900	26 Mar	Cardiff	1	1
1901	18 Mar	Newcastle	6	0
1902	3 Mar	Wrexham	0	0
1903	2 Mar	Portsmouth	2	1
1904	29 Feb	Wrexham	2	2
1905	27 Mar	Liverpool	3	1
1906	19 Mar	Cardiff	1	0
1907	18 Mar	Fulham	1	1
1908	16 Mar	Wrexham	7	1
1909	15 Mar	Nottingham	2	0
1910	14 Mar	Cardiff	1	0
1911	13 Mar	Millwall	3	0
1912	11 Mar	Wrexham	2	0
1913	17 Mar	Bristol	4	3
1914	16 Mar	Cardiff	2	0
1920	15 Mar	Highbury	1	2
1921	14 Mar	Cardiff	0	0
1922	13 Mar	Liverpool	1	0
1923	5 Mar	Cardiff	2	2
1924	3 Mar	Blackburn	1	2
1925	28 Feb	Swansea	2	1
1926	1 Mar	Crystal Palace	1	3
1927	12 Feb	Wrexham	3	3
1927	28 Nov	Burnley	1	2
1928	17 Nov	Swansea	3	2
1929	20 Nov	Chelsea	6	0
1930	22 Nov	Wrexham	4	0
1931	18 Nov	Liverpool	3	1
1932	16 Nov	Wrexham	0	0
1933	15 Nov	Newcastle	1	2

			E	W
1934	29 Sept	Cardiff	4	0
1936	5 Feb	Wolverhampton	1	2
1936	17 Oct	Cardiff	1	2
1937	17 Nov	Middlesbrough	2	1
1938	22 Oct	Cardiff	2	4
1946	13 Nov	Manchester	3	0
1947	18 Oct	Cardiff	3	0
1948	10 Nov	Aston Villa	1	0
wc1949	15 Oct	Cardiff	4	1
1950	15 Nov	Sunderland	4	2
1951	20 Oct	Cardiff	1	1
1952	12 Nov	Wembley	5	2
wc1953	10 Oct	Cardiff	4	1
1954	10 Nov	Wembley	3	2
1955	27 Oct	Cardiff	1	2
1956	14 Nov	Wembley	3	1
1957	19 Oct	Cardiff	4	0
1958	26 Nov	Aston Villa	2	2
1959	17 Oct	Cardiff	1	1
1960	23 Nov	Wembley	5	1
1961	14 Oct	Cardiff	1	1
1962	21 Oct	Wembley	4	0
1963	12 Oct	Cardiff	4	0
1964	18 Nov	Wembley	2	1
1965	2 Oct	Cardiff	0	0
EC1966	16 Nov	Wembley	5	1
EC1967	21 Oct	Cardiff	3	0
1969	7 May	Wembley	2	1
1970	18 Apr	Cardiff	1	1
1971	19 May	Wembley	0	0
1972	20 May	Cardiff	3	0
wc1972	15 Nov	Cardiff	1	0
wc1973	24 Jan	Wembley	1	1
1973	15 May	Wembley	3	0
1974	11 May	Cardiff	2	0
1975	21 May	Wembley	2	2
1976	24 Mar	Wrexham	2	1
1976	8 May	Cardiff	1	0
1977	31 May	Wembley	0	1
1978	3 May	Cardiff	3	1
1979	23 May	Wembley	0	0
1980	17 May	Wrexham	1	4
1981	20 May	Wembley	0	0
1982	27 Apr	Cardiff	1	0
1983	23 Feb	Wembley	2	1
1984	2 May	Wrexham	0	1
wc2004	9 Oct	Old Trafford	2	0
wc2005	3 Sept	Cardiff	1	0

ENGLAND v IRELAND

Played: 98; England won 75, Ireland won 7, Drawn 16. Goals: England 323, Ireland 81.

			E	I
1882	18 Feb	Belfast	13	0
1883	24 Feb	Liverpool	7	0
1884	23 Feb	Belfast	8	1
1885	28 Feb	Manchester	4	0
1886	13 Mar	Belfast	6	1
1887	5 Feb	Sheffield	7	0
1888	31 Mar	Belfast	5	1
1889	2 Mar	Everton	6	1
1890	15 Mar	Belfast	9	1
1891	7 Mar	Wolverhampton	6	1
1892	5 Mar	Belfast	2	0
1893	25 Feb	Birmingham	6	1
1894	3 Mar	Belfast	2	2
1895	9 Mar	Derby	9	0
1896	7 Mar	Belfast	2	0
1897	20 Feb	Nottingham	6	0
1898	5 Mar	Belfast	3	2
1899	18 Feb	Sunderland	13	2
1900	17 Mar	Dublin	2	0
1901	9 Mar	Southampton	3	0
1902	22 Mar	Belfast	1	0

			E	I
1903	14 Feb	Wolverhampton	4	0
1904	12 Mar	Belfast	3	1
1905	25 Feb	Middlesbrough	1	1
1906	17 Feb	Belfast	5	0
1907	16 Feb	Everton	1	0
1908	15 Feb	Belfast	3	1
1909	13 Feb	Bradford	4	0
1910	12 Feb	Belfast	1	1
1911	11 Feb	Derby	2	1
1912	10 Feb	Dublin	6	1
1913	15 Feb	Belfast	1	2
1914	14 Feb	Middlesbrough	0	3
1919	25 Oct	Belfast	1	1
1920	23 Oct	Sunderland	2	0
1921	22 Oct	Belfast	1	1
1922	21 Oct	West Bromwich	2	0
1923	20 Oct	Belfast	1	2
1924	22 Oct	Everton	3	1
1925	24 Oct	Belfast	0	0
1926	20 Oct	Liverpool	3	3
1927	22 Oct	Belfast	0	2

			E	I
1928	22 Oct	Everton	2	1
1929	19 Oct	Belfast	3	0
1930	20 Oct	Sheffield	5	1
1931	17 Oct	Belfast	6	2
1932	17 Oct	Blackpool	1	0
1933	14 Oct	Belfast	3	0
1935	6 Feb	Everton	2	1
1935	19 Oct	Belfast	3	1
1936	18 Nov	Stoke	3	1
1937	23 Oct	Belfast	5	1
1938	16 Nov	Manchester	7	0
1946	28 Sept	Belfast	7	2
1947	5 Nov	Everton	2	2
1948	9 Oct	Belfast	6	2
wc1949	16 Nov	Manchester	9	2
1950	7 Oct	Belfast	4	1
1951	14 Nov	Aston Villa	2	0
1952	4 Oct	Belfast	2	2
wc1953	11 Nov	Everton	3	1
1954	2 Oct	Belfast	2	0
1955	2 Nov	Wembley	3	0
1956	10 Oct	Belfast	1	1
1957	6 Nov	Wembley	2	3
1958	4 Oct	Belfast	3	3
1959	18 Nov	Wembley	2	1
1960	8 Oct	Belfast	5	2
1961	22 Nov	Wembley	1	1
1962	20 Oct	Belfast	3	1
1963	20 Nov	Wembley	8	3
1964	3 Oct	Belfast	4	3
1965	10 Nov	Wembley	2	1
EC1966	20 Oct	Belfast	2	0
EC1967	22 Nov	Wembley	2	0
1969	3 May	Belfast	3	1
1970	21 Apr	Wembley	3	1
1971	15 May	Belfast	1	0
1972	23 May	Wembley	0	1
1973	12 May	Everton	2	1
1974	15 May	Wembley	1	0
1975	17 May	Belfast	0	0
1976	11 May	Wembley	4	0
1977	28 May	Belfast	2	1
1978	16 May	Wembley	1	0
EC1979	7 Feb	Wembley	4	0
1979	19 May	Belfast	2	0
EC1979	17 Oct	Belfast	5	1
1980	20 May	Wembley	1	1
1982	23 Feb	Wembley	4	0
1983	28 May	Belfast	0	0
1984	24 Apr	Wembley	1	0
wc1985	27 Feb	Belfast	1	0
wc1985	13 Nov	Wembley	0	0
EC1986	15 Oct	Wembley	3	0
EC1987	1 Apr	Belfast	2	0
wc2005	26 Mar	Old Trafford	4	0
wc2005	7 Sept	Belfast	0	1

SCOTLAND v WALES

Played: 103; Scotland won 60, Wales won 20, Drawn 23. Goals: Scotland 238, Wales 116.

			S	W
1876	25 Mar	Glasgow	4	0
1877	5 Mar	Wrexham	2	0
1878	23 Mar	Glasgow	9	0
1879	7 Apr	Wrexham	3	0
1880	3 Apr	Glasgow	5	1
1881	14 Mar	Wrexham	5	1
1882	25 Mar	Glasgow	5	0
1883	12 Mar	Wrexham	3	0
1884	29 Mar	Glasgow	4	1
1885	23 Mar	Wrexham	8	1
1886	10 Apr	Glasgow	4	1
1887	21 Mar	Wrexham	2	0
1888	10 Mar	Edinburgh	5	1
1889	15 Apr	Wrexham	0	0
1890	22 Mar	Paisley	5	0
1891	21 Mar	Wrexham	4	3
1892	26 Mar	Edinburgh	6	1
1893	18 Mar	Wrexham	8	0
1894	24 Mar	Kilmarnock	5	2
1895	23 Mar	Wrexham	2	2
1896	21 Mar	Dundee	4	0
1897	20 Mar	Wrexham	2	2
1898	19 Mar	Motherwell	5	2
1899	18 Mar	Wrexham	6	0
1900	3 Feb	Aberdeen	5	2
1901	2 Mar	Wrexham	1	1
1902	15 Mar	Greenock	5	1
1903	9 Mar	Cardiff	1	0
1904	12 Mar	Dundee	1	1
1905	6 Mar	Wrexham	1	3
1906	3 Mar	Edinburgh	0	2
1907	4 Mar	Wrexham	0	1
1908	7 Mar	Dundee	2	1
1909	1 Mar	Wrexham	2	3
1910	5 Mar	Kilmarnock	1	0
1911	6 Mar	Cardiff	2	2
1912	2 Mar	Tynecastle	1	0
1913	3 Mar	Wrexham	0	0
1914	28 Feb	Glasgow	0	0
1920	26 Feb	Cardiff	1	1
1921	12 Feb	Aberdeen	2	1
1922	4 Feb	Wrexham	1	2
1923	17 Mar	Paisley	2	0
1924	16 Feb	Cardiff	0	2
1925	14 Feb	Tynecastle	3	1
1925	31 Oct	Cardiff	3	0
1926	30 Oct	Glasgow	3	0
1927	29 Oct	Wrexham	2	2
1928	27 Oct	Glasgow	4	2
1929	26 Oct	Cardiff	4	2
1930	25 Oct	Glasgow	1	1
1931	31 Oct	Wrexham	3	2
1932	26 Oct	Edinburgh	2	5
1933	4 Oct	Cardiff	2	3
1934	21 Nov	Aberdeen	3	2
1935	5 Oct	Cardiff	1	1
1936	2 Dec	Dundee	1	2
1937	30 Oct	Cardiff	1	2
1938	9 Nov	Edinburgh	3	2
1946	19 Oct	Wrexham	1	3
1947	12 Nov	Glasgow	1	2
wc1948	23 Oct	Cardiff	3	1
1949	9 Nov	Glasgow	2	0
1950	21 Oct	Cardiff	3	1
1951	14 Nov	Glasgow	0	1
wc1952	18 Oct	Cardiff	2	1
1953	4 Nov	Glasgow	3	3
1954	16 Oct	Cardiff	1	0
1955	9 Nov	Glasgow	2	0
1956	20 Oct	Cardiff	2	2
1957	13 Nov	Glasgow	1	1
1958	18 Oct	Cardiff	3	0
1959	4 Nov	Glasgow	1	1
1960	20 Oct	Cardiff	0	2
1961	8 Nov	Glasgow	2	0
1962	20 Oct	Cardiff	3	2
1963	20 Nov	Glasgow	2	1
1964	3 Oct	Cardiff	2	3
EC1965	24 Nov	Glasgow	4	1
EC1966	22 Oct	Cardiff	1	1

			S	W
1967	22 Nov	Glasgow	3	2
1969	3 May	Wrexham	5	3
1970	22 Apr	Glasgow	0	0
1971	15 May	Cardiff	0	0
1972	24 May	Glasgow	1	0
1973	12 May	Wrexham	2	0
1974	14 May	Glasgow	2	0
1975	17 May	Cardiff	2	2
1976	6 May	Glasgow	3	1
wc1976	17 Nov	Glasgow	1	0
1977	28 May	Wrexham	0	0

			S	W
wc1977	12 Oct	Liverpool	2	0
1978	17 May	Glasgow	1	1
1979	19 May	Cardiff	0	3
1980	21 May	Glasgow	1	0
1981	16 May	Swansea	0	2
1982	24 May	Glasgow	1	0
1983	28 May	Cardiff	2	0
1984	28 Feb	Glasgow	2	1
wc1985	27 Mar	Glasgow	0	1
wc1985	10 Sept	Cardiff	1	1
1997	27 May	Kilmarnock	0	1
2004	18 Feb	Cardiff	0	4

SCOTLAND v IRELAND

Played: 94; Scotland won 62, Ireland won 15, Drawn 17. Goals: Scotland 257, Ireland 81.

			S	I
1884	26 Jan	Belfast	5	0
1885	14 Mar	Glasgow	8	2
1886	20 Mar	Belfast	7	2
1887	19 Feb	Glasgow	4	1
1888	24 Mar	Belfast	10	2
1889	9 Mar	Glasgow	7	0
1890	29 Mar	Belfast	4	1
1891	28 Mar	Glasgow	2	1
1892	19 Mar	Belfast	3	2
1893	25 Mar	Glasgow	6	1
1894	31 Mar	Belfast	2	1
1895	30 Mar	Glasgow	3	1
1896	28 Mar	Belfast	3	3
1897	27 Mar	Glasgow	5	1
1898	26 Mar	Belfast	3	0
1899	25 Mar	Glasgow	9	1
1900	3 Mar	Belfast	3	0
1901	23 Feb	Glasgow	11	0
1902	1 Mar	Belfast	5	1
1902	9 Aug	Belfast	3	0
1903	21 Mar	Glasgow	0	2
1904	26 Mar	Dublin	1	1
1905	18 Mar	Glasgow	4	0
1906	17 Mar	Dublin	1	0
1907	16 Mar	Glasgow	3	0
1908	14 Mar	Dublin	5	0
1909	15 Mar	Glasgow	5	0
1910	19 Mar	Belfast	0	1
1911	18 Mar	Glasgow	2	0
1912	16 Mar	Belfast	4	1
1913	15 Mar	Dublin	2	1
1914	14 Mar	Belfast	1	1
1920	13 Mar	Glasgow	3	0
1921	26 Feb	Belfast	2	0
1922	4 Mar	Glasgow	2	1
1923	3 Mar	Belfast	1	0
1924	1 Mar	Glasgow	2	0
1925	28 Feb	Belfast	3	0
1926	27 Feb	Glasgow	4	0
1927	26 Feb	Belfast	2	0
1928	25 Feb	Glasgow	0	1
1929	23 Feb	Belfast	7	3
1930	22 Feb	Glasgow	3	1
1931	21 Feb	Belfast	0	0
1931	19 Sept	Glasgow	3	1
1932	12 Sept	Belfast	4	0
1933	16 Sept	Glasgow	1	2

			S	I
1934	20 Oct	Belfast	1	2
1935	13 Nov	Edinburgh	2	1
1936	31 Oct	Belfast	3	1
1937	10 Nov	Aberdeen	1	1
1938	8 Oct	Belfast	2	0
1946	27 Nov	Glasgow	0	0
1947	4 Oct	Belfast	0	2
1948	17 Nov	Glasgow	3	2
1949	1 Oct	Belfast	8	2
1950	1 Nov	Glasgow	6	1
1951	6 Oct	Belfast	3	0
1952	5 Nov	Glasgow	1	1
1953	3 Oct	Belfast	3	1
1954	3 Nov	Glasgow	2	2
1955	8 Oct	Belfast	1	2
1956	7 Nov	Glasgow	1	0
1957	5 Oct	Belfast	1	1
1958	5 Nov	Glasgow	2	2
1959	3 Oct	Belfast	4	0
1960	9 Nov	Glasgow	5	2
1961	7 Oct	Belfast	6	1
1962	7 Nov	Glasgow	5	1
1963	12 Oct	Belfast	1	2
1964	25 Nov	Glasgow	3	2
1965	2 Oct	Belfast	2	3
1966	16 Nov	Glasgow	2	1
1967	21 Oct	Belfast	0	1
1969	6 May	Glasgow	1	1
1970	18 Apr	Belfast	1	0
1971	18 May	Glasgow	0	1
1972	20 May	Glasgow	2	0
1973	16 May	Glasgow	1	2
1974	11 May	Glasgow	0	1
1975	20 May	Glasgow	3	0
1976	8 May	Glasgow	3	0
1977	1 June	Glasgow	3	0
1978	13 May	Glasgow	1	1
1979	22 May	Glasgow	1	0
1980	17 May	Belfast	0	1
wc1981	25 Mar	Glasgow	1	1
1981	19 May	Glasgow	2	0
wc1981	14 Oct	Belfast	0	0
1982	28 Apr	Belfast	1	1
1983	24 May	Glasgow	0	0
1983	13 Dec	Belfast	0	2
1992	19 Feb	Glasgow	1	0
2008	20 Aug	Glasgow	0	0

WALES v IRELAND

Played: 93; Wales won 43, Ireland won 27, Drawn 23. Goals: Wales 187, Ireland 131.

			W	I
1882	25 Feb	Wrexham	7	1
1883	17 Mar	Belfast	1	1
1884	9 Feb	Wrexham	6	0
1885	11 Apr	Belfast	8	2

			W	I
1886	27 Feb	Wrexham	5	0
1887	12 Mar	Belfast	1	4
1888	3 Mar	Wrexham	11	0
1889	27 Apr	Belfast	3	1

			W	I					W	I
1890	8 Feb	Shrewsbury	5	2		1938	16 Mar	Belfast	0	1
1891	7 Feb	Belfast	2	7		1939	15 Mar	Wrexham	3	1
1892	27 Feb	Bangor	1	1		1947	16 Apr	Belfast	1	2
1893	8 Apr	Belfast	3	4		1948	10 Mar	Wrexham	2	0
1894	24 Feb	Swansea	4	1		1949	9 Mar	Belfast	2	0
1895	16 Mar	Belfast	2	2		wc1950	8 Mar	Wrexham	0	0
1896	29 Feb	Wrexham	6	1		1951	7 Mar	Belfast	2	1
1897	6 Mar	Belfast	3	4		1952	19 Mar	Swansea	3	0
1898	19 Feb	Llandudno	0	1		1953	15 Apr	Belfast	3	2
1899	4 Mar	Belfast	0	1		wc1954	31 Mar	Wrexham	1	2
1900	24 Feb	Llandudno	2	0		1955	20 Apr	Belfast	3	2
1901	23 Mar	Belfast	1	0		1956	11 Apr	Cardiff	1	1
1902	22 Mar	Cardiff	0	3		1957	10 Apr	Belfast	0	0
1903	28 Mar	Belfast	0	2		1958	16 Apr	Cardiff	1	1
1904	21 Mar	Bangor	0	1		1959	22 Apr	Belfast	1	4
1905	18 Apr	Belfast	2	2		1960	6 Apr	Wrexham	3	2
1906	2 Apr	Wrexham	4	4		1961	12 Apr	Belfast	5	1
1907	23 Feb	Belfast	3	2		1962	11 Apr	Cardiff	4	0
1908	11 Apr	Aberdare	0	1		1963	3 Apr	Belfast	4	1
1909	20 Mar	Belfast	3	2		1964	15 Apr	Swansea	2	3
1910	11 Apr	Wrexham	4	1		1965	31 Mar	Belfast	5	0
1911	28 Jan	Belfast	2	1		1966	30 Mar	Cardiff	1	4
1912	13 Apr	Cardiff	2	3		EC1967	12 Apr	Belfast	0	0
1913	18 Jan	Belfast	1	0		EC1968	28 Feb	Wrexham	2	0
1914	19 Jan	Wrexham	1	2		1969	10 May	Belfast	0	0
1920	14 Feb	Belfast	2	2		1970	25 Apr	Swansea	1	0
1921	9 Apr	Swansea	2	1		1971	22 May	Belfast	0	1
1922	4 Apr	Belfast	1	1		1972	27 May	Wrexham	0	0
1923	14 Apr	Wrexham	0	3		1973	19 May	Everton	0	1
1924	15 Mar	Belfast	1	0		1974	18 May	Wrexham	1	0
1925	18 Apr	Wrexham	0	0		1975	23 May	Belfast	0	1
1926	13 Feb	Belfast	0	3.		1976	14 May	Swansea	1	0
1927	9 Apr	Cardiff	2	2		1977	3 June	Belfast	1	1
1928	4 Feb	Belfast	2	1		1978	19 May	Wrexham	1	0
1929	2 Feb	Wrexham	2	2		1979	25 May	Belfast	1	1
1930	1 Feb	Belfast	0	7		1980	23 May	Cardiff	0	1
1931	22 Apr	Wrexham	3	2		1982	27 May	Wrexham	3	0
1931	5 Dec	Belfast	0	4		1983	31 May	Belfast	1	0
1932	7 Dec	Wrexham	4	1		1984	22 May	Swansea	1	1
1933	4 Nov	Belfast	1	1		wc2004	8 Sept	Cardiff	2	2
1935	27 Mar	Wrexham	3	1		wc2005	8 Oct	Belfast	3	2
1936	11 Mar	Belfast	2	3		2007	6 Feb	Belfast	0	0
1937	17 Mar	Wrexham	4	1						

OTHER BRITISH INTERNATIONAL RESULTS 1908–2008

ENGLAND

		v ALBANIA	E	A					E	A
wc1989	8 Mar	Tirana	2	0		1983	15 June	Brisbane	1	0
wc1989	26 Apr	Wembley	5	0		1983	18 June	Melbourne	1	1
wc2001	28 Mar	Tirana	3	1		1991	1 June	Sydney	1	0
wc2001	5 Sept	Newcastle	2	0		2003	12 Feb	West Ham	1	3
		v ANDORRA	E	A				**v AUSTRIA**	E	A
EC2006	2 Sept	Old Trafford	5	0		1908	6 June	Vienna	6	1
EC2007	28 Mar	Barcelona	3	0		1908	8 June	Vienna	11	1
wc2008	6 Sept	Barcelona	2	0		1909	1 June	Vienna	8	1
wc2009	10 June	Wembley	6	0		1930	14 May	Vienna	0	0
						1932	7 Dec	Chelsea	4	3
		v ARGENTINA	E	A		1936	6 May	Vienna	1	2
1951	9 May	Wembley	2	1		1951	28 Nov	Wembley	2	2
1953	17 May	Buenos Aires	0	0		1952	25 May	Vienna	3	2
(abandoned after 21 mins)						wc1958	15 June	Boras	2	2
wc1962	2 June	Rancagua	3	1		1961	27 May	Vienna	1	3
1964	6 June	Rio de Janeiro	0	1		1962	4 Apr	Wembley	3	1
wc1966	23 July	Wembley	1	0		1965	20 Oct	Wembley	2	3
1974	22 May	Wembley	2	2		1967	27 May	Vienna	1	0
1977	12 June	Buenos Aires	1	1		1973	26 Sept	Wembley	7	0
1980	13 May	Wembley	3	1		1979	13 June	Vienna	3	4
wc1986	22 June	Mexico City	1	2		wc2004	4 Sept	Vienna	2	2
1991	25 May	Wembley	2	2		wc2005	8 Oct	Old Trafford	1	0
wc1998	30 June	St Etienne	2	2		2007	16 Nov	Vienna	1	0
2000	23 Feb	Wembley	0	0						
wc2002	7 June	Sapporo	1	0				**v AZERBAIJAN**	E	A
2005	12 Nov	Geneva	3	2		wc2004	13 Oct	Baku	1	0
						wc2005	30 Mar	Newcastle	2	0
		v AUSTRALIA	E	A				**v BELARUS**	E	B
1980	31 May	Sydney	2	1		wc2008	15 Oct	Minsk	3	1
1983	11 June	Sydney	0	0						

		v BELGIUM	E	B
1921	21 May	Brussels	2	0
1923	19 Mar	Highbury	6	1
1923	1 Nov	Antwerp	2	2
1924	8 Dec	West Bromwich	4	0
1926	24 May	Antwerp	5	3
1927	11 May	Brussels	9	1
1928	19 May	Antwerp	3	1
1929	11 May	Brussels	5	1
1931	16 May	Brussels	4	1
1936	9 May	Brussels	2	3
1947	21 Sept	Brussels	5	2
1950	18 May	Brussels	4	1
1952	26 Nov	Wembley	5	0
wc1954	17 June	Basle	4	4*
1964	21 Oct	Wembley	2	2
1970	25 Feb	Brussels	3	1
EC1980	12 June	Turin	1	1
wc1990	27 June	Bologna	1	0*
1998	29 May	Casablanca	0	0
1999	10 Oct	Sunderland	2	1

		v BOHEMIA	E	B
1908	13 June	Prague	4	0

		v BRAZIL	E	B
1956	9 May	Wembley	4	2
wc1958	11 June	Gothenburg	0	0
1959	13 May	Rio de Janeiro	0	2
wc1962	10 June	Vina del Mar	1	3
1963	8 May	Wembley	1	1
1964	30 May	Rio de Janeiro	1	5
1969	12 June	Rio de Janeiro	1	2
wc1970	7 June	Guadalajara	0	1
1976	23 May	Los Angeles	0	1
1977	8 June	Rio de Janeiro	0	0
1978	19 Apr	Wembley	1	1
1981	12 May	Wembley	0	1
1984	10 June	Rio de Janeiro	2	0
1987	19 May	Wembley	1	1
1990	28 Mar	Wembley	1	0
1992	17 May	Wembley	1	1
1993	13 June	Washington	1	1
UI1995	11 June	Wembley	1	3
TF1997	10 June	Paris	0	1
2000	27 May	Wembley	1	1
wc2002	21 June	Shizuoka	1	2
2007	1 June	Wembley	1	1

		v BULGARIA	E	B
wc1962	7 June	Rancagua	0	0
1968	11 Dec	Wembley	1	1
1974	1 June	Sofia	1	0
EC1979	6 June	Sofia	3	0
EC1979	22 Nov	Wembley	2	0
1996	27 Mar	Wembley	1	0
EC1998	10 Oct	Wembley	0	0
EC1999	9 June	Sofia	1	1

		v CAMEROON	E	C
wc1990	1 July	Naples	3	2*
1991	6 Feb	Wembley	2	0
1997	15 Nov	Wembley	2	0
2002	26 May	Kobe	2	2

		v CANADA	E	C
1986	24 May	Burnaby	1	0

		v CHILE	E	C
wc1950	25 June	Rio de Janeiro	2	0
1953	24 May	Santiago	2	1
1984	17 June	Santiago	0	0
1989	23 May	Wembley	0	0
1998	11 Feb	Wembley	0	2

		v CHINA	E	C
1996	23 May	Beijing	3	0

		v CIS	E	C
1992	29 Apr	Moscow	2	2

		v COLOMBIA	E	C
1970	20 May	Bogota	4	0
1988	24 May	Wembley	1	1
1995	6 Sept	Wembley	0	0
wc1998	26 June	Lens	2	0
2005	31 May	New Jersey	3	2

		v CROATIA	E	C
1996	24 Apr	Wembley	0	0
2003	20 Aug	Ipswich	3	1
EC2004	21 June	Lisbon	4	2
EC2006	11 Oct	Zagreb	0	2
EC2007	21 Nov	Wembley	2	3
wc2008	10 Sept	Zagreb	4	1

		v CYPRUS	E	C
EC1975	16 Apr	Wembley	5	0
EC1975	11 May	Limassol	1	0

		v CZECHOSLOVAKIA	E	C
1934	16 May	Prague	1	2
1937	1 Dec	Tottenham	5	4
1963	29 May	Bratislava	4	2
1966	2 Nov	Wembley	0	0
wc1970	11 June	Guadalajara	1	0
1973	27 May	Prague	1	1
EC1974	30 Oct	Wembley	3	0
EC1975	30 Oct	Bratislava	1	2
1978	29 Nov	Wembley	1	0
wc1982	20 June	Bilbao	2	0
1990	25 Apr	Wembley	4	2
1992	25 Mar	Prague	2	2

		v CZECH REPUBLIC	E	C
1998	18 Nov	Wembley	2	0
2008	20 Aug	Wembley	2	2

		v DENMARK	E	D
1948	26 Sept	Copenhagen	0	0
1955	2 Oct	Copenhagen	5	1
wc1956	5 Dec	Wolverhampton	5	2
wc1957	15 May	Copenhagen	4	1
1966	3 July	Copenhagen	2	0
EC1978	20 Sept	Copenhagen	4	3
EC1979	12 Sept	Wembley	1	0
EC1982	22 Sept	Copenhagen	2	2
EC1983	21 Sept	Wembley	0	1
1988	14 Sept	Wembley	1	0
1989	7 June	Copenhagen	1	1
1990	15 May	Wembley	1	0
EC1992	11 June	Malmo	0	0
1994	9 Mar	Wembley	1	0
wc2002	15 June	Niigata	3	0
2003	16 Nov	Old Trafford	2	3
2005	17 Aug	Copenhagen	1	4

		v ECUADOR	E	Ec
1970	24 May	Quito	2	0
wc2006	25 June	Stuttgart	1	0

		v EGYPT	E	Eg
1986	29 Jan	Cairo	4	0
wc1990	21 June	Cagliari	1	0

		v ESTONIA	E	Es
EC2007	6 June	Tallinn	3	0
EC2007	13 Oct	Wembley	3	0

		v FIFA	E	FIFA
1938	26 Oct	Highbury	3	0
1953	21 Oct	Wembley	4	4
1963	23 Oct	Wembley	2	1

		v FINLAND	E	F
1937	20 May	Helsinki	8	0
1956	20 May	Helsinki	5	1
1966	26 June	Helsinki	3	0
wc1976	13 June	Helsinki	4	1
wc1976	13 Oct	Wembley	2	1
1982	3 June	Helsinki	4	1
wc1984	17 Oct	Wembley	5	0
wc1985	22 May	Helsinki	1	1
1992	3 June	Helsinki	2	1

			E	F
wc2000	11 Oct	Helsinki	0	0
wc2001	24 Mar	Liverpool	2	1

v FRANCE			E	F
1923	10 May	Paris	4	1
1924	17 May	Paris	3	1
1925	21 May	Paris	3	2
1927	26 May	Paris	6	0
1928	17 May	Paris	5	1
1929	9 May	Paris	4	1
1931	14 May	Paris	2	5
1933	6 Dec	Tottenham	4	1
1938	26 May	Paris	4	2
1947	3 May	Highbury	3	0
1949	22 May	Paris	3	1
1951	3 Oct	Highbury	2	2
1955	15 May	Paris	0	1
1957	27 Nov	Wembley	4	0
EC1962	3 Oct	Sheffield	1	1
EC1963	27 Feb	Paris	2	5
wc1966	20 July	Wembley	2	0
1969	12 Mar	Wembley	5	0
wc1982	16 June	Bilbao	3	1
1984	29 Feb	Paris	0	2
1992	19 Feb	Wembley	2	0
EC1992	14 June	Malmo	0	0
TF1997	7 June	Montpellier	1	0
1999	10 Feb	Wembley	0	2
2000	2 Sept	Paris	1	1
EC2004	13 June	Lisbon	1	2
2008	26 Mar	Paris	0	1

v GEORGIA			E	G
wc1996	9 Nov	Tbilisi	2	0
wc1997	30 Apr	Wembley	2	0

v GERMANY			E	G
1930	10 May	Berlin	3	3
1935	4 Dec	Tottenham	3	0
1938	14 May	Berlin	6	3
1991	11 Sept	Wembley	0	1
1993	19 June	Detroit	1	2
EC1996	26 June	Wembley	1	1*
EC2000	17 June	Charleroi	1	0
wc2000	7 Oct	Wembley	0	1
wc2001	1 Sept	Munich	5	1
2007	22 Aug	Wembley	1	2
2008	19 Nov	Berlin	2	1

v EAST GERMANY			E	EG
1963	2 June	Leipzig	2	1
1970	25 Nov	Wembley	3	1
1974	29 May	Leipzig	1	1
1984	12 Sept	Wembley	1	0

v WEST GERMANY			E	WG
1954	1 Dec	Wembley	3	1
1956	26 May	Berlin	3	1
1965	12 May	Nuremberg	1	0
1966	23 Feb	Wembley	1	0
wc1966	30 July	Wembley	4	2*
1968	1 June	Hanover	0	1
wc1970	14 June	Leon	2	3*
EC1972	29 Apr	Wembley	1	3
EC1972	13 May	Berlin	0	0
1975	12 Mar	Wembley	2	0
1978	22 Feb	Munich	1	2
wc1982	29 June	Madrid	0	0
1982	13 Oct	Wembley	1	2
1985	12 June	Mexico City	3	0
1987	9 Sept	Dusseldorf	1	3
wc1990	4 July	Turin	1	1*

v GREECE			E	G
EC1971	21 Apr	Wembley	3	0
EC1971	1 Dec	Piraeus	2	0
EC1982	17 Nov	Salonika	3	0
EC1983	30 Mar	Wembley	0	0
1989	8 Feb	Athens	2	1
1994	17 May	Wembley	5	0
wc2001	6 June	Athens	2	0

			E	G
wc2001	6 Oct	Old Trafford	2	2
2006	16 Aug	Old Trafford	4	0

v HOLLAND			E	H
1935	18 May	Amsterdam	1	0
1946	27 Nov	Huddersfield	8	2
1964	9 Dec	Amsterdam	1	1
1969	5 Nov	Amsterdam	1	0
1970	14 Jun	Wembley	0	0
1977	9 Feb	Wembley	0	2
1982	25 May	Wembley	2	0
1988	23 Mar	Wembley	2	2
EC1988	15 June	Dusseldorf	1	3
wc1990	16 June	Cagliari	0	0
2005	9 Feb	Villa Park	0	0
wc1993	28 Apr	Wembley	2	2
wc1993	13 Oct	Rotterdam	0	2
EC1996	18 June	Wembley	4	1
2001	15 Aug	Tottenham	0	2
2002	13 Feb	Amsterdam	1	1
2006	15 Nov	Amsterdam	1	1

v HUNGARY			E	H
1908	10 June	Budapest	7	0
1909	29 May	Budapest	4	2
1909	31 May	Budapest	8	2
1934	10 May	Budapest	1	2
1936	2 Dec	Highbury	6	2
1953	25 Nov	Wembley	3	6
1954	23 May	Budapest	1	7
1960	22 May	Budapest	0	2
wc1962	31 May	Rancagua	1	2
1965	5 May	Wembley	1	0
1978	24 May	Wembley	4	1
wc1981	6 June	Budapest	3	1
wc1982	18 Nov	Wembley	1	0
EC1983	27 Apr	Wembley	2	0
EC1983	12 Oct	Budapest	3	0
1988	27 Apr	Budapest	0	0
1990	12 Sept	Wembley	1	0
1992	12 May	Budapest	1	0
1996	18 May	Wembley	3	0
1999	28 Apr	Budapest	1	1
2006	30 May	Old Trafford	3	1

v ICELAND			E	I
1982	2 June	Reykjavik	1	1
2004	5 June	City of Manchester	6	1
EC2007	24 Mar	Tel Aviv	0	0

v REPUBLIC OF IRELAND			E	RI
1946	30 Sept	Dublin	1	0
1949	21 Sept	Everton	0	2
wc1957	8 May	Wembley	5	1
wc1957	19 May	Dublin	1	1
1964	24 May	Dublin	3	1
1976	8 Sept	Wembley	1	1
EC1978	25 Oct	Dublin	1	1
EC1980	6 Feb	Wembley	2	0
1985	26 Mar	Wembley	2	1
EC1988	12 June	Stuttgart	0	1
wc1990	11 June	Cagliari	1	1
EC1990	14 Nov	Dublin	1	1
EC1991	27 Mar	Wembley	1	1
1995	15 Feb	Dublin	0	1
(abandoned after 27 mins)				

v ISRAEL			E	I
1986	26 Feb	Ramat Gan	2	1
1988	17 Feb	Tel Aviv	0	0
EC2007	24 Mar	Tel Aviv	0	0
EC2007	8 Sept	Wembley	3	0

v ITALY			E	I
1933	13 May	Rome	1	1
1934	14 Nov	Highbury	3	2
1939	13 May	Milan	2	2
1948	16 May	Turin	4	0
1949	30 Nov	Tottenham	2	0
1952	18 May	Florence	1	1
1959	6 May	Wembley	2	2
1961	24 May	Rome	3	2

			E	I
1973	14 June	Turin	0	2
1973	14 Nov	Wembley	0	1
1976	28 May	New York	3	2
wc1976	17 Nov	Rome	0	2
wc1977	16 Nov	Wembley	2	0
EC1980	15 June	Turin	0	1
1985	6 June	Mexico City	1	2
1989	15 Nov	Wembley	0	0
wc1990	7 July	Bari	1	2
wc1997	12 Feb	Wembley	0	1
TF1997	4 June	Nantes	2	0
wc1997	11 Oct	Rome	0	0
2000	15 Nov	Turin	0	1
2002	27 Mar	Leeds	1	2

v JAMAICA			E	J
2006	3 June	Old Trafford	6	0

v JAPAN			E	J
UI1995	3 June	Wembley	2	1
2004	1 June	City of Manchester	1	1

v KAZAKHSTAN			E	K
wc2008	11 Oct	Wembley	5	1
wc2009	6 June	Almaty	4	0

v KUWAIT			E	K
wc1982	25 June	Bilbao	1	0

v LIECHTENSTEIN			E	L
EC2003	29 Mar	Vaduz	2	0
EC2003	10 Sept	Old Trafford	2	0

v LUXEMBOURG			E	L
1927	21 May	Esch-sur-Alzette	5	2
wc1960	19 Oct	Luxembourg	9	0
wc1961	28 Sept	Highbury	4	1
wc1977	30 Mar	Wembley	5	0
wc1977	12 Oct	Luxembourg	2	0
EC1982	15 Dec	Wembley	9	0
EC1983	16 Nov	Luxembourg	4	0
EC1998	14 Oct	Luxembourg	3	0
EC1999	4 Sept	Wembley	6	0

v MACEDONIA			E	M
EC2002	16 Oct	Southampton	2	2
EC2003	6 Sept	Skopje	2	1
EC2006	6 Sept	Skopje	1	0
EC2006	7 Oct	Old Trafford	0	0

v MALAYSIA			E	M
1991	12 June	Kuala Lumpur	4	2

v MALTA			E	M
EC1971	3 Feb	Valletta	1	0
EC1971	12 May	Wembley	5	0
2000	3 June	Valletta	2	1

v MEXICO			E	M
1959	24 May	Mexico City	1	2
1961	10 May	Wembley	8	0
wc1966	16 July	Wembley	2	0
1969	1 June	Mexico City	0	0
1985	9 June	Mexico City	0	1
1986	17 May	Los Angeles	3	0
1997	29 Mar	Wembley	2	0
2001	25 May	Derby	4	0

v MOLDOVA			E	M
wc1996	1 Sept	Chisinau	3	0
wc1997	10 Sept	Wembley	4	0

v MOROCCO			E	M
wc1986	6 June	Monterrey	0	0
1998	27 May	Casablanca	1	0

v NEW ZEALAND			E	NZ
1991	3 June	Auckland	1	0
1991	8 June	Wellington	2	0

v NIGERIA			E	N
1994	16 Nov	Wembley	1	0
wc2002	12 June	Osaka	0	0

v NORWAY			E	N
1937	14 May	Oslo	6	0
1938	9 Nov	Newcastle	4	0
1949	18 May	Oslo	4	1
1966	29 June	Oslo	6	1

			E	N
wc1980	10 Sept	Wembley	4	0
wc1981	9 Sept	Oslo	1	2
wc1992	14 Oct	Wembley	1	1
wc1993	2 June	Oslo	0	2
1994	22 May	Wembley	0	0
1995	11 Oct	Oslo	0	0

v PARAGUAY			E	P
wc1986	18 June	Mexico City	3	0
2002	17 Apr	Liverpool	4	0
wc2006	10 June	Frankfurt	1	0

v PERU			E	P
1959	17 May	Lima	1	4
1962	20 May	Lima	4	0

v POLAND			E	P
1966	5 Jan	Everton	1	1
1966	5 July	Chorzow	1	0
wc1973	6 June	Chorzow	0	2
wc1973	17 Oct	Wembley	1	1
wc1986	11 June	Monterrey	3	0
wc1989	3 June	Wembley	3	0
wc1989	11 Oct	Katowice	0	0
EC1990	17 Oct	Wembley	2	0
EC1991	13 Nov	Poznan	1	1
wc1993	29 May	Katowice	1	1
wc1993	8 Sept	Wembley	3	0
wc1996	9 Oct	Wembley	2	1
wc1997	31 May	Katowice	2	0
EC1999	27 Mar	Wembley	3	1
EC1999	8 Sept	Warsaw	0	0
wc2004	8 Sept	Katowice	2	1
wc2005	12 Oct	Old Trafford	2	1

v PORTUGAL			E	P
1947	25 May	Lisbon	10	0
1950	14 May	Lisbon	5	3
1951	19 May	Everton	5	2
1955	22 May	Oporto	1	3
1958	7 May	Wembley	2	1
wc1961	21 May	Lisbon	1	1
wc1961	25 Oct	Wembley	2	0
1964	17 May	Lisbon	4	3
1964	4 June	São Paulo	1	1
wc1966	26 July	Wembley	2	1
1969	10 Dec	Wembley	1	0
1974	3 Apr	Lisbon	0	0
EC1974	20 Nov	Wembley	0	0
EC1975	19 Nov	Lisbon	1	1
wc1986	3 June	Monterrey	0	1
1995	12 Dec	Wembley	1	1
1998	22 Apr	Wembley	3	0
EC2000	12 June	Eindhoven	2	3
2002	7 Sept	Villa Park	1	1
2004	18 Feb	Faro	1	1
EC2004	24 June	Lisbon	2	2*
wc2006	1 July	Gelsenkirchen	0	0

v ROMANIA			E	R
1939	24 May	Bucharest	2	0
1968	6 Nov	Bucharest	0	0
1969	15 Jan	Wembley	1	1
wc1970	2 June	Guadalajara	1	0
wc1980	15 Oct	Bucharest	1	2
wc1981	29 April	Wembley	0	0
wc1985	1 May	Bucharest	0	0
wc1985	11 Sept	Wembley	1	1
1994	12 Oct	Wembley	1	1
wc1998	22 June	Toulouse	1	2
EC2000	20 June	Charleroi	2	3

v RUSSIA			E	R
EC2007	12 Sept	Wembley	3	0
EC2007	17 Oct	Moscow	1	2

v SAN MARINO			E	SM
wc1992	17 Feb	Wembley	6	0
wc1993	17 Nov	Bologna	7	1

v SAUDI ARABIA			E	SA
1988	16 Nov	Riyadh	1	1
1998	23 May	Wembley	0	0

v SERBIA-MONTENEGRO			E	S-M
2003	3 June	Leicester	2	1

		v SLOVAKIA	E	S
EC2002	12 Oct	Bratislava	2	1
EC2003	11 June	Middlesbrough	2	1
2009	28 Mar	Wembley	4	0
		v SOUTH AFRICA	E	SA
1997	24 May	Old Trafford	2	1
2003	22 May	Durban	2	1
		v SOUTH KOREA	E	SK
2002	21 May	Seoguipo	1	1
		v SPAIN	E	S
1929	15 May	Madrid	3	4
1931	9 Dec	Highbury	7	1
wc1950	2 July	Rio de Janeiro	0	1
1955	18 May	Madrid	1	1
1955	30 Nov	Wembley	4	1
1960	15 May	Madrid	0	3
1960	26 Oct	Wembley	4	2
1965	8 Dec	Madrid	2	0
1967	24 May	Wembley	2	0
EC1968	3 Apr	Wembley	1	0
EC1968	8 May	Madrid	2	1
1980	26 Mar	Barcelona	2	0
EC1980	18 June	Naples	2	1
1981	25 Mar	Wembley	1	2
wc1982	5 July	Madrid	0	0
1987	18 Feb	Madrid	4	2
1992	9 Sept	Santander	0	1
EC 1996	22 June	Wembley	0	0
2001	28 Feb	Villa Park	3	0
2004	17 Nov	Madrid	0	1
2007	7 Feb	Old Trafford	0	1
2009	11 Feb	Seville	0	2
		v SWEDEN	E	S
1923	21 May	Stockholm	4	2
1923	24 May	Stockholm	3	1
1937	17 May	Stockholm	4	0
1947	19 Nov	Highbury	4	2
1949	13 May	Stockholm	1	3
1956	16 May	Stockholm	0	0
1959	28 Oct	Wembley	2	3
1965	16 May	Gothenburg	2	1
1968	22 May	Wembley	3	1
1979	10 June	Stockholm	0	0
1986	10 Sept	Stockholm	0	1
wc1988	19 Oct	Wembley	0	0
wc1989	6 Sept	Stockholm	0	0
EC1992	17 June	Stockholm	1	2
uI1995	8 June	Leeds	3	3
EC1998	5 Sept	Stockholm	1	2
EC1999	5 June	Wembley	0	0
2001	10 Nov	Old Trafford	1	1
wc2002	2 June	Saitama	1	1
2004	31 Mar	Gothenburg	0	1
wc2006	20 June	Cologne	2	2
		v SWITZERLAND	E	S
1933	20 May	Berne	4	0
1938	21 May	Zurich	1	2
1947	18 May	Zurich	0	1
1948	2 Dec.	Highbury	6	0
1952	28 May	Zurich	3	0
wc1954	20 June	Berne	2	0
1962	9 May	Wembley	3	1
1963	5 June	Basle	8	1
EC1971	13 Oct	Basle	3	2
EC1971	10 Nov	Wembley	1	1
1975	3 Sept	Basle	2	1
1977	7 Sept	Wembley	0	0
wc1980	19 Nov	Wembley	2	1
wc1981	30 May	Basle	1	2
1988	28 May	Lausanne	1	0
1995	15 Nov	Wembley	3	1
EC1996	8 June	Wembley	1	1
1998	25 Mar	Berne	1	1

			E	S
EC2004	17 June	Coimbra	3	0
2008	6 Feb	Wembley	2	1
		v TRINIDAD & TOBAGO	E	Tr
wc2006	15 June	Nuremberg	2	0
2008	2 June	Port of Spain	3	0
		v TUNISIA	E	T
1990	2 June	Tunis	1	1
wc1998	15 June	Marseilles	2	0
		v TURKEY	E	T
wc1984	14 Nov	Istanbul	8	0
			E	T
wc1985	16 Oct	Wembley	5	0
EC1987	29 Apr	Izmir	0	0
EC1987	14 Oct	Wembley	8	0
EC1991	1 May	Izmir	1	0
EC1991	16 Oct	Wembley	1	0
wc1992	18 Nov	Wembley	4	0
wc1993	31 Mar	Izmir	2	0
EC2003	2 Apr	Sunderland	2	0
EC2003	11 Oct	Istanbul	0	0
		v UKRAINE	E	U
2000	31 May	Wembley	2	0
2004	18 Aug	Newcastle	3	0
wc2009	1 Apr	Wembley	2	1
		v URUGUAY	E	U
1953	31 May	Montevideo	1	2
wc1954	26 June	Basle	2	4
1964	6 May	Wembley	2	1
wc1966	11 July	Wembley	0	0
1969	8 June	Montevideo	2	1
1977	15 June	Montevideo	0	0
1984	13 June	Montevideo	0	2
1990	22 May	Wembley	1	2
1995	29 Mar	Wembley	0	0
2006	1 Mar	Liverpool	2	1
		v USA	E	USA
wc1950	29 June	Belo Horizonte	0	1
1953	8 June	New York	6	3
1959	28 May	Los Angeles	8	1
1964	27 May	New York	10	0
1985	16 June	Los Angeles	5	0
1993	9 June	Foxboro	0	2
1994	7 Sept	Wembley	2	0
2005	28 May	Chicago	2	1
2008	28 May	Wembley	2	0
		v USSR	E	USSR
1958	18 May	Moscow	1	1
wc1958	8 June	Gothenburg	2	2
wc1958	17 June	Gothenburg	0	1
1958	22 Oct	Wembley	5	0
1967	6 Dec	Wembley	2	2
EC1968	8 June	Rome	2	0
1973	10 June	Moscow	2	1
1984	2 June	Wembley	0	2
1986	26 Mar	Tbilisi	1	0
EC1988	18 June	Frankfurt	1	3
1991	21 May	Wembley	3	1
		v YUGOSLAVIA	E	Y
1939	18 May	Belgrade	1	2
1950	22 Nov	Highbury	2	2
1954	16 May	Belgrade	0	1
1956	28 Nov	Wembley	3	0
1958	11 May	Belgrade	0	5
1960	11 May	Wembley	3	3
1965	9 May	Belgrade	1	1
1966	4 May	Wembley	2	0
EC1968	5 June	Florence	0	1
1972	11 Oct	Wembley	1	1
1974	5 June	Belgrade	2	2
EC1986	12 Nov	Wembley	2	0
EC1987	11 Nov	Belgrade	4	1
1989	13 Dec	Wembley	2	1

SCOTLAND

v ARGENTINA			S	A
1977	18 June	Buenos Aires	1	1
1979	2 June	Glasgow	1	3
1990	28 Mar	Glasgow	1	0
2008	19 Nov	Glasgow	0	1

v AUSTRALIA			S	A
wc1985	20 Nov	Glasgow	2	0
wc1985	4 Dec	Melbourne	0	0
1996	27 Mar	Glasgow	1	0
2000	15 Nov	Glasgow	0	2

v AUSTRIA			S	A
1931	16 May	Vienna	0	5
1933	29 Nov	Glasgow	2	2
1937	9 May	Vienna	1	1
1950	13 Dec	Glasgow	0	1
1951	27 May	Vienna	0	4
wc1954	16 June	Zurich	0	1
1955	19 May	Vienna	4	1
1956	2 May	Glasgow	1	1
1960	29 May	Vienna	1	4
1963	8 May	Glasgow	4	1
(*abandoned after 79 mins*)				
wc1968	6 Nov	Glasgow	2	1
wc1969	5 Nov	Vienna	0	2
EC1978	20 Sept	Vienna	2	3
EC1979	17 Oct	Glasgow	1	1
1994	20 Apr	Vienna	2	1
wc1996	31 Aug	Vienna	0	0
wc1997	2 Apr	Celtic Park	2	0
2003	30 Apr	Glasgow	0	2
2005	17 Aug	Graz	2	2
2007	30 May	Vienna	1	0

v BELARUS			S	B
wc1997	8 June	Minsk	1	0
wc1997	7 Sept	Aberdeen	4	1
wc2005	8 June	Minsk	0	0
wc2005	8 Oct	Glasgow	0	1

v BELGIUM			S	B
1947	18 May	Brussels	1	2
1948	28 Apr	Glasgow	2	0
1951	20 May	Brussels	5	0
EC1971	3 Feb	Liège	0	3
EC1971	10 Nov	Aberdeen	1	0
1974	2 June	Brussels	1	2
EC1979	21 Nov	Brussels	0	2
EC1979	19 Dec	Glasgow	1	3
EC1982	15 Dec	Brussels	2	3
EC1983	12 Oct	Glasgow	1	1
EC1987	1 Apr	Brussels	1	4
EC1987	14 Oct	Glasgow	2	0
wc2001	24 Mar	Glasgow	2	2
wc2001	5 Sept	Brussels	0	2

v BOSNIA			S	B
EC1999	4 Sept	Sarajevo	2	1
EC1999	5 Oct	Glasgow	1	0

v BRAZIL			S	B
1966	25 June	Glasgow	1	1
1972	5 July	Rio de Janeiro	0	1
1973	30 June	Glasgow	0	1
wc1974	18 June	Frankfurt	0	0
1977	23 June	Rio de Janeiro	0	2
wc1982	18 June	Seville	1	4
1987	26 May	Glasgow	0	2
wc1990	20 June	Turin	0	1
wc1998	10 June	Saint-Denis	1	2

v BULGARIA			S	B
1978	22 Feb	Glasgow	2	1
EC1986	10 Sept	Glasgow	0	0
EC1987	11 Nov	Sofia	1	0
EC1990	14 Nov	Sofia	1	1
EC1991	27 Mar	Glasgow	1	1
2006	11 May	Kobe	5	1

v CANADA			S	C
1983	12 June	Vancouver	2	0
1983	16 June	Edmonton	3	0
1983	20 June	Toronto	2	0
1992	21 May	Toronto	3	1
2002	15 Oct	Easter Road	3	1

v CHILE			S	C
1977	15 June	Santiago	4	2
1989	30 May	Glasgow	2	0

v CIS			S	C
EC1992	18 June	Norrkoping	3	0

v COLOMBIA			S	C
1988	17 May	Glasgow	0	0
1996	30 May	Miami	0	1
1998	23 May	New York	2	2

v COSTA RICA			S	CR
wc1990	11 June	Genoa	0	1

v CROATIA			S	C
wc2000	11 Oct	Zagreb	1	1
wc2001	1 Sept	Glasgow	0	0
2008	26 Mar	Glasgow	1	1

v CYPRUS			S	C
wc1968	17 Dec	Nicosia	5	0
wc1969	11 May	Glasgow	8	0
wc1989	8 Feb	Limassol	3	2
wc1989	26 Apr	Glasgow	2	1

v CZECHOSLOVAKIA			S	C
1937	22 May	Prague	3	1
1937	8 Dec	Glasgow	5	0
wc1961	14 May	Bratislava	0	4
wc1961	26 Sept	Glasgow	3	2
wc1961	29 Nov	Brussels	2	4*
1972	2 July	Porto Alegre	0	0
wc1973	26 Sept	Glasgow	2	1
wc1973	17 Oct	Prague	0	1
wc1976	13 Oct	Prague	0	2
wc1977	21 Sept	Glasgow	3	1

v CZECH REPUBLIC			S	C
EC1999	31 Mar	Glasgow	1	2
EC1999	9 June	Prague	2	3
2008	30 May	Prague	1	3

v DENMARK			S	D
1951	12 May	Glasgow	3	1
1952	25 May	Copenhagen	2	1
1968	16 Oct	Copenhagen	1	0
EC1970	11 Nov	Glasgow	1	0
EC1971	9 June	Copenhagen	0	1
wc1972	18 Oct	Copenhagen	4	1
wc1972	15 Nov	Glasgow	2	0
EC1975	3 Sept	Copenhagen	1	0
EC1975	29 Oct	Glasgow	3	1
wc1986	4 June	Nezahualcayotl	0	1
1996	24 Apr	Copenhagen	0	2
1998	25 Mar	Glasgow	0	1
2002	21 Aug	Glasgow	0	1
2004	28 Apr	Copenhagen	0	1

v ECUADOR			S	E
1995	24 May	Toyama	2	1

v EGYPT			S	E
1990	16 May	Aberdeen	1	3

v ESTONIA			S	E
wc1993	19 May	Tallinn	3	0
wc1993	2 June	Aberdeen	3	1
wc1997	11 Feb	Monaco	0	0
wc1997	29 Mar	Kilmarnock	2	0
EC1998	10 Oct	Edinburgh	3	2
EC1999	8 Sept	Tallinn	0	0
2004	27 May	Tallinn	1	0

v FAEROES

			S	F
EC1994	12 Oct	Glasgow	5	1
EC1995	7 June	Toftir	2	0
EC1998	14 Oct	Aberdeen	2	1
EC1999	5 June	Toftir	1	1
EC2002	7 Sept	Toftir	2	2
EC2003	6 Sept	Glasgow	3	1
EC2006	2 Sept	Celtic Park	6	0
EC2007	6 June	Toftir	2	0

v FINLAND

			S	F
1954	25 May	Helsinki	2	1
wc1964	21 Oct	Glasgow	3	1
wc1965	27 May	Helsinki	2	1
1976	8 Sept	Glasgow	6	0
1992	25 Mar	Glasgow	1	1
EC1994	7 Sept	Helsinki	2	0
EC1995	6 Sept	Glasgow	1	0
1998	22 Apr	Edinburgh	1	1

v FRANCE

			S	F
1930	18 May	Paris	2	0
1932	8 May	Paris	3	1
1948	23 May	Paris	0	3
1949	27 Apr	Glasgow	2	0
1950	27 May	Paris	1	0
1951	16 May	Glasgow	1	0
wc1958	15 June	Orebro	1	2
1984	1 June	Marseilles	0	2
wc1989	8 Mar	Glasgow	2	0
wc1989	11 Oct	Paris	0	3
1997	12 Nov	St Etienne	1	2
2000	29 Mar	Glasgow	0	2
2002	27 Mar	Paris	0	5
EC2006	7 Oct	Glasgow	1	0
EC2007	12 Sept	Paris	1	0

v GEORGIA

			S	G
EC2007	24 Mar	Glasgow	2	1
EC2007	17 Oct	Tblisi	0	2

v GERMANY

			S	G
1929	1 June	Berlin	1	1
1936	14 Oct	Glasgow	2	0
EC1992	15 June	Norrkoping	0	2
1993	24 Mar	Glasgow	0	1
1998	28 Apr	Bremen	1	0
EC2003	7 June	Glasgow	1	1
EC2003	10 Sept	Dortmund	1	2

v EAST GERMANY

			S	EG
1974	30 Oct	Glasgow	3	0
1977	7 Sept	East Berlin	0	1
EC1982	13 Oct	Glasgow	2	0
EC1983	16 Nov	Halle	1	2
1985	16 Oct	Glasgow	0	0
1990	25 Apr	Glasgow	0	1

v WEST GERMANY

			S	WG
1957	22 May	Stuttgart	3	1
1959	6 May	Glasgow	3	2
1964	12 May	Hanover	2	2
wc1969	16 Apr	Glasgow	1	1
wc1969	22 Oct	Hamburg	2	3
1973	14 Nov	Glasgow	1	1
1974	27 Mar	Frankfurt	1	2
wc1986	8 June	Queretaro	1	2

v GREECE

			S	G
EC1994	18 Dec	Athens	0	1
EC1995	16 Aug	Glasgow	1	0

v HOLLAND

			S	H
1929	4 June	Amsterdam	2	0
1938	21 May	Amsterdam	3	1
1959	27 May	Amsterdam	2	1
1966	11 May	Glasgow	0	3
1968	30 May	Amsterdam	0	0
1971	1 Dec	Rotterdam	1	2
wc1978	11 June	Mendoza	3	2
1982	23 Mar	Glasgow	2	1
1986	29 Apr	Eindhoven	0	0
EC1992	12 June	Gothenburg	0	1
1994	23 Mar	Glasgow	0	1
1994	27 May	Utrecht	1	3
EC1996	10 June	Birmingham	0	0
2000	26 Apr	Arnhem	0	0
EC2003	15 Nov	Glasgow	1	0
EC2003	19 Nov	Amsterdam	0	6
wc2009	28 Mar	Amsterdam	0	3

v HONG KONG XI

			S	HK
†2002	23 May	Hong Kong	4	0

†match not recognised by FIFA

v HUNGARY

			S	H
1938	7 Dec	Glasgow	3	1
1954	8 Dec	Glasgow	2	4
1955	29 May	Budapest	1	3
1958	7 May	Glasgow	1	1
1960	5 June	Budapest	3	3
1980	31 May	Budapest	1	3
1987	9 Sept	Glasgow	2	0
2004	18 Aug	Glasgow	0	3

v ICELAND

			S	I
wc1984	17 Oct	Glasgow	3	0
wc1985	28 May	Reykjavik	1	0
EC2002	12 Oct	Reykjavik	2	0
EC2003	29 Mar	Glasgow	2	1
wc2008	10 Sept	Reykjavik	2	1
wc2009	1 Apr	Glasgow	2	1

v IRAN

			S	I
wc1978	7 June	Cordoba	1	1

v REPUBLIC OF IRELAND

			S	RI
wc1961	3 May	Glasgow	4	1
wc1961	7 May	Dublin	3	0
1963	9 June	Dublin	0	1
1969	21 Sept	Dublin	1	1
EC1986	15 Oct	Dublin	0	0
EC1987	18 Feb	Glasgow	0	1
2000	30 May	Dublin	2	1
2003	12 Feb	Glasgow	0	2

v ISRAEL

			S	I
wc1981	25 Feb	Tel Aviv	1	0
wc1981	28 Apr	Glasgow	3	1
1986	28 Jan	Tel Aviv	1	0

v ITALY

			S	I
1931	20 May	Rome	0	3
wc1965	9 Nov	Glasgow	1	0
wc1965	7 Dec	Naples	0	3
1988	22 Dec	Perugia	0	2
wc1992	18 Nov	Glasgow	0	0
wc1993	13 Oct	Rome	1	3
wc2005	26 Mar	Milan	0	2
wc2005	3 Sept	Glasgow	1	1
EC2007	28 Mar	Bari	0	2
EC2007	17 Nov	Glasgow	3	1

v JAPAN

			S	J
1995	21 May	Hiroshima	0	0
2006	13 May	Saitama	0	0

v LATVIA

			S	L
wc1996	5 Oct	Riga	2	0
wc1997	11 Oct	Glasgow	2	0
wc2000	2 Sept	Riga	1	0
wc2001	6 Oct	Glasgow	2	1

v LITHUANIA

			S	L
EC1998	5 Sept	Vilnius	0	0
EC1999	9 Oct	Glasgow	3	0
EC2003	2 Apr	Kaunas	0	1
EC2003	11 Oct	Glasgow	1	0
EC2006	6 Sept	Kaunas	2	1
EC2007	8 Sept	Glasgow	3	1

v LUXEMBOURG

			S	L
1947	24 May	Luxembourg	6	0
EC1986	12 Nov	Glasgow	3	0
EC1987	2 Dec	Esch	0	0

v MACEDONIA		S	M
wc2008	6 Sept Skopje	0	1

v MALTA		S	M
1988	22 Mar Valletta	1	1
1990	28 May Valletta	2	1
wc1993	17 Feb Glasgow	3	0
wc1993	17 Nov Valletta	2	0
1997	1 June Valletta	3	2

v MOLDOVA		S	M
EC2004	13 Oct Chisinau	1	1
EC2005	4 June Glasgow	2	0

v MOROCCO		S	M
wc1998	23 June St Etienne	0	3

v NEW ZEALAND		S	NZ
wc1982	15 June Malaga	5	2
2003	27 May Tynecastle	1	1

v NIGERIA		S	N
2002	17 Apr Aberdeen	1	2

v NORWAY		S	N
1929	28 May Oslo	7	3
1954	5 May Glasgow	1	0
1954	19 May Oslo	1	1
1963	4 June Bergen	3	4
1963	7 Nov Glasgow	6	1
1974	6 June Oslo	2	1
EC1978	25 Oct Glasgow	3	2
EC1979	7 June Oslo	4	0
wc1988	14 Sept Oslo	2	1
wc1989	15 Nov Glasgow	1	1
1992	3 June Oslo	0	0
wc1998	16 June Bordeaux	1	1
2003	20 Aug Oslo	0	0
wc2004	9 Oct Glasgow	0	1
wc2005	7 Sept Oslo	2	1
wc2008	11 Oct Glasgow	0	0

v PARAGUAY		S	P
wc1958	11 June Norrkoping	2	3

v PERU		S	P
1972	26 Apr Glasgow	2	0
wc1978	3 June Cordoba	1	3
1979	12 Sept Glasgow	1	1

v POLAND		S	P
1958	1 June Warsaw	2	1
1960	4 June Glasgow	2	3
wc1965	23 May Chorzow	1	1
wc1965	13 Oct Glasgow	1	2
1980	28 May Poznan	0	1
1990	19 May Glasgow	1	1
2001	25 Apr Bydgoszcz	1	1

v PORTUGAL		S	P
1950	21 May Lisbon	2	2
1955	4 May Glasgow	3	0
1959	3 June Lisbon	0	1
1966	18 June Glasgow	0	1
EC1971	21 Apr Lisbon	0	2
EC1971	13 Oct Glasgow	2	1
1975	13 May Glasgow	1	0
EC1978	29 Nov Lisbon	0	1
EC1980	26 Mar Glasgow	4	1
wc1980	15 Oct Glasgow	0	0
wc1981	18 Nov Lisbon	1	2
wc1992	14 Oct Glasgow	0	0
wc1993	28 Apr Lisbon	0	5
2002	20 Nov Braga	0	2

v ROMANIA		S	R
EC1975	1 June Bucharest	1	1
EC1975	17 Dec Glasgow	1	1
1986	26 Mar Glasgow	3	0
EC1990	12 Sept Glasgow	2	1
EC1991	16 Oct Bucharest	0	1
2004	31 Mar Glasgow	1	2

v RUSSIA		S	R
EC1994	16 Nov Glasgow	1	1
EC1995	29 Mar Moscow	0	0

v SAN MARINO		S	SM
EC1991	1 May Serravalle	2	0
EC1991	13 Nov Glasgow	4	0
EC1995	26 Apr Serravalle	2	0
EC1995	15 Nov Glasgow	5	0
wc2000	7 Oct Serravalle	2	0
wc2001	28 Mar Glasgow	4	0

v SAUDI ARABIA		S	SA
1988	17 Feb Riyadh	2	2

v SLOVENIA		S	Sl
wc2004	8 Sept Glasgow	0	0
wc2005	12 Oct Celje	3	0

v SOUTH AFRICA		S	SA
2002	20 May Hong Kong	0	2
2007	22 Aug Aberdeen	1	0

v SOUTH KOREA		S	SK
2002	16 May Busan	1	4

v SPAIN		S	Sp
wc1957	8 May Glasgow	4	2
wc1957	26 May Madrid	1	4
1963	13 June Madrid	6	2
1965	8 May Glasgow	0	0
EC1974	20 Nov Glasgow	1	2
EC1975	5 Feb Valencia	1	1
1982	24 Feb Valencia	0	3
wc1984	14 Nov Glasgow	3	1
wc1985	27 Feb Seville	0	1
1988	27 Apr Madrid	0	0
2004	3 Sept Valencia	1	1

Match abandoned afer 60 minutes; floodlight failure.

v SWEDEN		S	Sw
1952	30 May Stockholm	1	3
1953	6 May Glasgow	1	2
1975	16 Apr Gothenburg	1	1

		S	Sw
1977	27 Apr Glasgow	3	1
wc1980	10 Sept Stockholm	1	0
wc1981	9 Sept Glasgow	2	0
wc1990	16 June Genoa	2	1
1995	11 Oct Stockholm	0	2
wc1996	10 Nov Glasgow	1	0
wc1997	30 Apr Gothenburg	1	2
2004	17 Nov Edinburgh	1	4

v SWITZERLAND		S	Sw
1931	24 May Geneva	3	2
1948	17 May Berne	1	2
1950	26 Apr Glasgow	3	1
wc1957	19 May Basle	2	1
wc1957	6 Nov Glasgow	3	2
1973	22 June Berne	0	1
1976	7 Apr Glasgow	1	0
EC1982	17 Nov Berne	0	2
EC1983	30 May Glasgow	2	2
EC1990	17 Oct Glasgow	2	1
EC1991	11 Sept Berne	2	2
wc1992	9 Sept Berne	1	3
wc1993	8 Sept Aberdeen	1	1
wc1996	18 June Birmingham	1	0
2006	1 Mar Glasgow	1	3

v TRINIDAD & TOBAGO		S	TT
2004	30 May Edinburgh	4	1

v TURKEY		S	T
1960	8 June Ankara	2	4

v UKRAINE		S	U
EC2006	11 Oct Kiev	0	2
EC2007	13 Oct Glasgow	3	1

v URUGUAY			S	U
wc1954	19 June	Basle	0	7
1962	2 May	Glasgow	2	3
1983	21 Sept	Glasgow	2	0
wc1986	13 June	Nezahualcoyotl	0	0

v USA			S	USA
1952	30 Apr	Glasgow	6	0
1992	17 May	Denver	1	0
1996	26 May	New Britain	1	2
1998	30 May	Washington	0	0
2005	11 Nov	Glasgow	1	1

v USSR			S	USSR
1967	10 May	Glasgow	0	2
1971	14 June	Moscow	0	1

			S	USSR
wc1982	22 June	Malaga	2	2
1991	6 Feb	Glasgow	0	1

v YUGOSLAVIA			S	Y
1955	15 May	Belgrade	2	2
1956	21 Nov	Glasgow	2	0
wc1958	8 June	Vasteras	1	1
1972	29 June	Belo Horizonte	2	2
wc1974	22 June	Frankfurt	1	1
1984	12 Sept	Glasgow	6	1
wc1988	19 Oct	Glasgow	1	1
wc1989	6 Sept	Zagreb	1	3

v ZAIRE			S	Z
wc1974	14 June	Dortmund	2	0

WALES

v ALBANIA			W	A
EC1994	7 Sept	Cardiff	2	0
EC1995	15 Nov	Tirana	1	1

v ARGENTINA			W	A
1992	3 June	Tokyo	0	1
2002	13 Feb	Cardiff	1	1

v ARMENIA			W	A
wc2001	24 Mar	Erevan	2	2
wc2001	1 Sept	Cardiff	0	0

v AUSTRIA			W	A
1954	9 May	Vienna	0	2

			W	A
EC1955	23 Nov	Wrexham	1	2
EC1974	4 Sept	Vienna	1	2
1975	19 Nov	Wrexham	1	0
1992	29 Apr	Vienna	1	1
EC2005	26 Mar	Cardiff	0	2
EC2005	30 Mar	Vienna	0	1

v AZERBAIJAN			W	A
EC2002	20 Nov	Baku	2	0
EC2003	29 Mar	Cardiff	4	0
wc2004	4 Sept	Baku	1	1
wc2005	12 Oct	Cardiff	2	0
wc2008	6 Sept	Cardiff	1	0
wc2009	6 June	Baku	1	0

v BELARUS			W	B
EC1998	14 Oct	Cardiff	3	2
EC1999	4 Sept	Minsk	2	1
wc2000	2 Sept	Minsk	1	2
wc2001	6 Oct	Cardiff	1	0

v BELGIUM			W	B
1949	22 May	Liège	1	3
1949	23 Nov	Cardiff	5	1
EC1990	17 Oct	Cardiff	3	1
EC1991	27 Mar	Brussels	1	1
wc1992	18 Nov	Brussels	0	2
wc1993	31 Mar	Cardiff	2	0
wc1997	29 Mar	Cardiff	1	2
wc1997	11 Oct	Brussels	2	3

v BOSNIA			W	B
2003	12 Feb	Cardiff	2	2

v BRAZIL			W	B
wc1958	19 June	Gothenburg	0	1
1962	12 May	Rio de Janeiro	1	3
1962	16 May	São Paulo	1	3
1966	14 May	Rio de Janeiro	1	3
1966	18 May	Belo Horizonte	0	1
1983	12 June	Cardiff	1	1
1991	11 Sept	Cardiff	1	0
1997	12 Nov	Brasilia	0	3
2000	23 May	Cardiff	0	3
2006	5 Sept	Cardiff	0	2

v BULGARIA			W	B
EC1983	27 Apr	Wrexham	1	0
EC1983	16 Nov	Sofia	0	1
EC1994	14 Dec	Cardiff	0	3
EC1995	29 Mar	Sofia	1	3
2006	15 Aug	Swansea	0	0
2007	22 Aug	Burgas	1	0

v CANADA			W	C
1986	10 May	Toronto	0	2
1986	20 May	Vancouver	3	0
2004	30 May	Wrexham	1	0

v CHILE			W	C
1966	22 May	Santiago	0	2

v COSTA RICA			W	CR
1990	20 May	Cardiff	1	0

v CROATIA			W	C
2002	21 Aug	Varazdin	1	1

v CYPRUS			W	C
wc1992	14 Oct	Limassol	1	0
wc1993	13 Oct	Cardiff	2	0
2005	16 Nov	Limassol	0	1
EC2006	11 Oct	Cardiff	3	1
EC2007	13 Oct	Nicosia	1	3

v CZECHOSLOVAKIA			W	C
wc1957	1 May	Cardiff	1	0
wc1957	26 May	Prague	0	2
EC1971	21 Apr	Swansea	1	3
EC1971	27 Oct	Prague	0	1
wc1977	30 Mar	Wrexham	3	0
wc1977	16 Nov	Prague	0	1
wc1980	19 Nov	Cardiff	1	0
wc1981	9 Sept	Prague	0	2
EC1987	29 Apr	Wrexham	1	1
EC1987	11 Nov	Prague	0	2
wc1993	28 Apr	Ostrava†	1	1
wc1993	8 Sept	Cardiff†	2	2

†Czechoslovakia played as RCS (Republic of Czechs and Slovaks).

v CZECH REPUBLIC			W	CR
2002	27 Mar	Cardiff	0	0
EC2006	2 Sept	Teplice	1	2
EC2007	2 June	Cardiff	0	0

v DENMARK			W	D
wc1964	21 Oct	Copenhagen	0	1
wc1965	1 Dec	Wrexham	4	2
EC1987	9 Sept	Cardiff	1	0
EC1987	14 Oct	Copenhagen	0	1
1990	11 Sept	Copenhagen	0	1
EC1998	10 Oct	Copenhagen	2	1
EC1999	9 June	Liverpool	0	2
2008	19 Nov	Brondby	1	0

		v ESTONIA	W	E
1994	23 May	Tallinn	2	1
2009	29 May	Llanelli	1	0

		v FINLAND	W	F
EC1971	26 May	Helsinki	1	0
EC1971	13 Oct	Swansea	3	0
EC1987	10 Sept	Helsinki	1	1
EC1987	1 Apr	Wrexham	4	0
wc1988	19 Oct	Swansea	2	2
wc1989	6 Sept	Helsinki	0	1
2000	29 Mar	Cardiff	1	2
EC2002	7 Sept	Helsinki	2	0
EC2003	10 Sept	Cardiff	1	1
wc2009	28 Mar	Cardiff	0	2

		v FAEROES	W	F
wc1992	9 Sept	Cardiff	6	0
wc1993	6 June	Toftir	3	0

		v FRANCE	W	F
1933	25 May	Paris	1	1
1939	20 May	Paris	1	2
1953	14 May	Paris	1	6
1982	2 June	Toulouse	1	0

		v GEORGIA	W	G
EC1994	16 Nov	Tbilisi	0	5
EC1995	7 June	Cardiff	0	1
2008	20 Aug	Swansea	1	2

		v GERMANY	W	G
EC1995	26 Apr	Dusseldorf	1	1
EC1995	11 Oct	Cardiff	1	2
2002	14 May	Cardiff	1	0
EC2007	8 Sept	Cardiff	0	2
EC2007	21 Nov	Frankfurt	0	0
wc2008	15 Oct	Moenchengladbach	0	1
wc2009	1 Apr	Cardiff	0	2

		v EAST GERMANY	W	EG
wc1957	19 May	Leipzig	1	2
wc1957	25 Sept	Cardiff	4	1
wc1969	16 Apr	Dresden	1	2
wc1969	22 Oct	Cardiff	1	3

		v WEST GERMANY	W	WG
1968	8 May	Cardiff	1	1
1969	26 Mar	Frankfurt	1	1
1976	6 Oct	Cardiff	0	2
1977	14 Dec	Dortmund	1	1
EC1979	2 May	Wrexham	0	2
EC1979	17 Oct	Cologne	1	5
wc1989	31 May	Cardiff	0	0
wc1989	15 Nov	Cologne	1	2
EC1991	5 June	Cardiff	1	0
EC1991	16 Oct	Nuremberg	1	4

		v GREECE	W	G
wc1964	9 Dec	Athens	0	2
wc1965	17 Mar	Cardiff	4	1

		v HOLLAND	W	H
wc1988	14 Sept	Amsterdam	0	1
wc1989	11 Oct	Wrexham	1	2
1992	30 May	Utrecht	0	4
wc1996	5 Oct	Cardiff	1	3
wc1996	9 Nov	Eindhoven	1	7
2008	1 June	Rotterdam	0	2

		v HUNGARY	W	H
wc1958	8 June	Sanviken	1	1
wc1958	17 June	Stockholm	2	1
1961	28 May	Budapest	2	3
EC1962	7 Nov	Budapest	1	3
EC1963	20 Mar	Cardiff	1	1
EC1974	30 Oct	Cardiff	2	0
EC1975	16 Apr	Budapest	2	1
1985	16 Oct	Cardiff	0	3
2004	31 Mar	Budapest	2	1
2005	9 Feb	Cardiff	2	0

		v ICELAND	W	I
wc1980	2 June	Reykjavik	4	0
wc1981	14 Oct	Swansea	2	2
wc1984	12 Sept	Reykjavik	0	1
wc1984	14 Nov	Cardiff	2	1
1991	1 May	Cardiff	1	0
2008	28 May	Reykjavik	1	0

		v IRAN	W	I
1978	18 Apr	Teheran	1	0

		v REPUBLIC OF IRELAND	W	RI
1960	28 Sept	Dublin	3	2
1979	11 Sept	Swansea	2	1
1981	24 Feb	Dublin	3	1
1986	26 Mar	Dublin	1	0
1990	28 Mar	Dublin	0	1
1991	6 Feb	Wrexham	0	3
1992	19 Feb	Dublin	1	0
1993	17 Feb	Dublin	1	2
1997	11 Feb	Cardiff	0	0
EC2007	24 Mar	Dublin	0	1
EC2007	17 Nov	Cardiff	2	2

		v ISRAEL	W	I
wc1958	15 Jan	Tel Aviv	2	0
wc1958	5 Feb	Cardiff	2	0
1984	10 June	Tel Aviv	0	0
1989	8 Feb	Tel Aviv	3	3

		v ITALY	W	I
1965	1 May	Florence	1	4
wc1968	23 Oct	Cardiff	0	1
wc1969	4 Nov	Rome	1	4
1988	4 June	Brescia	1	0
1996	24 Jan	Terni	0	3
EC1998	5 Sept	Liverpool	0	2
EC1999	5 June	Bologna	0	4
EC2002	16 Oct	Cardiff	2	1
EC2003	6 Sept	Milan	0	4

		v JAMAICA	W	J
1998	25 Mar	Cardiff	0	0

		v JAPAN	W	J
1992	7 June	Matsuyama	1	0

		v LATVIA	W	L
2004	18 Aug	Riga	2	0

		v LIECHTENSTEIN	W	L
2006	14 Nov	Swansea	4	0
wc2008	11 Oct	Cardiff	2	0

		v KUWAIT	W	K
1977	6 Sept	Wrexham	0	0
1977	20 Sept	Kuwait	0	0

		v LUXEMBOURG	W	L
EC1974	20 Nov	Swansea	5	0
EC1975	1 May	Luxembourg	3	1
EC1990	14 Nov	Luxembourg	1	0
EC1991	13 Nov	Cardiff	1	0
2008	26 Mar	Luxembourg	2	0

		v MALTA	W	M
EC1978	25 Oct	Wrexham	7	0
EC1979	2 June	Valletta	2	0
1988	1 June	Valletta	3	2
1998	3 June	Valletta	3	0

		v MEXICO	W	M
wc1958	11 June	Stockholm	1	1
1962	22 May	Mexico City	1	2

		v MOLDOVA	W	M
EC1994	12 Oct	Kishinev	2	3
EC1995	6 Sept	Cardiff	1	0

		v NEW ZEALAND	W	NZ
2007	26 May	Wrexham	2	2

v NORWAY			W	N
EC1982	22 Sept	Swansea	1	0
EC1983	21 Sept	Oslo	0	0
1984	6 June	Trondheim	0	1
1985	26 Feb	Wrexham	1	1
1985	5 June	Bergen	2	4
1994	9 Mar	Cardiff	1	3
wc2000	7 Oct	Cardiff	1	1
wc2001	5 Sept	Oslo	2	3
2004	27 May	Oslo	0	0
2008	6 Feb	Wrexham	3	0

v PARAGUAY			W	P
2006	1 Mar	Cardiff	0	0

v POLAND			W	P
wc1973	28 Mar	Cardiff	2	0
wc1973	26 Sept	Katowice	0	3
1991	29 May	Radom	0	0
wc2000	11 Oct	Warsaw	0	0
wc2001	2 June	Cardiff	1	2
wc2004	13 Oct	Cardiff	2	3
wc2005	7 Sept	Warsaw	0	1
2009	11 Feb	Vila Real	0	1

v PORTUGAL			W	P
1949	15 May	Lisbon	2	3
1951	12 May	Cardiff	2	1
2000	2 June	Chaves	0	3

v QATAR			W	Q
2000	23 Feb	Doha	1	0

v ROMANIA			W	R
EC1970	11 Nov	Cardiff	0	0
EC1971	24 Nov	Bucharest	0	2
1983	12 Oct	Wrexham	5	0
wc1992	20 May	Bucharest	1	5
wc1993	17 Nov	Cardiff	1	2

v RUSSIA			W	R
EC2003	15 Nov	Moscow	0	0
EC2003	19 Nov	Cardiff	0	1
wc2008	10 Sept	Moscow	1	2

v SAN MARINO			W	SM
wc1996	2 June	Serravalle	5	0
wc1996	31 Aug	Cardiff	6	0
EC2007	28 Mar	Cardiff	3	0
EC2007	17 Oct	Serravalle	2	1

v SAUDI ARABIA			W	SA
1986	25 Feb	Dahran	2	1

v SERBIA-MONTENEGRO			W	SM
EC2003	20 Aug	Belgrade	0	1
EC2003	11 Oct	Cardiff	2	3

v SLOVAKIA			W	S
EC2006	7 Oct	Cardiff	1	5
EC2007	12 Sept	Trnava	5	2

v SLOVENIA			W	Sl
2005	17 Aug	Swansea	0	0

v SPAIN			W	S
wc1961	19 Apr	Cardiff	1	2

			W	S
wc1961	18 May	Madrid	1	1
1982	24 Mar	Valencia	1	1
wc1984	17 Oct	Seville	0	3
wc1985	30 Apr	Wrexham	3	0

v SWEDEN			W	S
wc1958	15 June	Stockholm	0	0
1988	27 Apr	Stockholm	1	4
1989	26 Apr	Wrexham	0	2
1990	25 Apr	Stockholm	2	4
1994	20 Apr	Wrexham	0	2

v SWITZERLAND			W	S
1949	26 May	Berne	0	4
1951	16 May	Wrexham	3	2
1996	24 Apr	Lugano	0	2
EC1999	31 Mar	Zurich	0	2
EC1999	9 Oct	Wrexham	0	2

v TRINIDAD & TOBAGO			W	TT
2006	27 May	Graz	2	1

v TUNISIA			W	T
1998	6 June	Tunis	0	4

v TURKEY			W	T
EC1978	29 Nov	Wrexham	1	0
EC1979	21 Nov	Izmir	0	1
wc1980	15 Oct	Cardiff	4	0
wc1981	25 Mar	Ankara	1	0
wc1996	14 Dec	Cardiff	0	0
wc1997	20 Aug	Istanbul	4	6

v REST OF UNITED KINGDOM			W	UK
1951	5 Dec	Cardiff	3	2
1969	28 July	Cardiff	0	1

v UKRAINE			W	U
wc2001	28 Mar	Cardiff	1	1
wc2001	6 June	Kiev	1	1

v USA			W	USA
2003	27 May	San Jose	0	2

v URUGUAY			W	U
1986	21 Apr	Wrexham	0	0

v USSR			W	USSR
wc1965	30 May	Moscow	1	2
wc1965	27 Oct	Cardiff	2	1
wc1981	30 May	Wrexham	0	0
wc1981	18 Nov	Tbilisi	0	3
1987	18 Feb	Swansea	0	0

v YUGOSLAVIA			W	Y
1953	21 May	Belgrade	2	5
1954	22 Nov	Cardiff	1	3

			W	Y
EC1976	24 Apr	Zagreb	0	2
EC1976	22 May	Cardiff	1	1
EC1982	15 Dec	Titograd	4	4
EC1983	14 Dec	Cardiff	1	1
1988	23 Mar	Swansea	1	2

NORTHERN IRELAND

v ALBANIA			NI	A
wc1965	7 May	Belfast	4	1
wc1965	24 Nov	Tirana	1	1
EC1982	15 Dec	Tirana	0	0
EC1983	27 Apr	Belfast	1	0
wc1992	9 Sept	Belfast	3	0
wc1993	17 Feb	Tirana	2	1
wc1996	14 Dec	Belfast	2	0
wc1997	10 Sept	Zurich	0	1

v ALGERIA			NI	A
wc1986	3 June	Guadalajara	1	1

v ARGENTINA			NI	A
wc1958	11 June	Halmstad	1	3

v ARMENIA			NI	A
wc1996	5 Oct	Belfast	1	1
wc1997	30 Apr	Erevan	0	0
EC2003	29 Mar	Erevan	0	1
EC2003	10 Sept	Belfast	0	1

v AUSTRALIA			NI	A
1980	11 June	Sydney	2	1
1980	15 June	Melbourne	1	1
1980	18 June	Adelaide	2	1

v AUSTRIA			NI	A
wc1982	1 July	Madrid	2	2
EC1982	13 Oct	Vienna	0	2
EC1983	21 Sept	Belfast	3	1
EC1990	14 Nov	Vienna	0	0

			NI	A
EC1991	16 Oct	Belfast	2	1
EC1994	12 Oct	Vienna	2	1
EC1995	15 Nov	Belfast	5	3
wc2004	13 Oct	Belfast	3	3
wc2005	12 Oct	Vienna	0	2

		v AZERBAIJAN	NI	A
wc2004	9 Oct	Baku	0	0
wc2005	3 Sept	Belfast	2	0

		v BARBADOS	NI	B
2004	30 May	Waterford	1	1

		v BELGIUM	NI	B
wc1976	10 Nov	Liège	0	2
wc1977	16 Nov	Belfast	3	0
1997	11 Feb	Belfast	3	0

		v BRAZIL	NI	B
wc1986	12 June	Guadalajara	0	3

		v BULGARIA	NI	B
wc1972	18 Oct	Sofia	0	3
wc1973	26 Sept	Sheffield	0	0
EC1978	29 Nov	Sofia	2	0
EC1979	2 May	Belfast	2	0
wc2001	28 Mar	Sofia	3	4
wc2001	2 June	Belfast	0	1
2008	6 Feb	Belfast	0	1

		v CANADA	NI	C
1995	22 May	Edmonton	0	2
1999	27 Apr	Belfast	1	1
2005	9 Feb	Belfast	0	1

		v CHILE	NI	C
1989	26 May	Belfast	0	1
1995	25 May	Edmonton	1	2

		v COLOMBIA	NI	C
1994	4 June	Boston	0	2

		v CYPRUS	NI	C
EC1971	3 Feb	Nicosia	3	0
EC1971	21 Apr	Belfast	5	0
wc1973	14 Feb	Nicosia	0	1
wc1973	8 May	London	3	0
2002	21 Aug	Belfast	0	0

		v CZECHOSLOVAKIA	NI	C
wc1958	8 June	Halmstad	1	0
wc1958	17 June	Malmo	2	1*

*After extra time

		v CZECH REPUBLIC	NI	C
wc2001	24 Mar	Belfast	0	1
wc2001	6 June	Teplice	1	3
wc2008	10 Sept	Belfast	0	0

		v DENMARK	NI	D
EC1978	25 Oct	Belfast	2	1
EC1979	6 June	Copenhagen	0	4
1986	26 Mar	Belfast	1	1
EC1990	17 Oct	Belfast	1	1
EC1991	13 Nov	Odense	1	2
wc1992	18 Nov	Belfast	0	1
wc1993	13 Oct	Copenhagen	0	1
wc2000	7 Oct	Belfast	1	1
wc2001	1 Sept	Copenhagen	1	1
EC2006	7 Oct	Copenhagen	0	0
EC2007	17 Nov	Belfast	2	1

		v ESTONIA	NI	E
2004	31 Mar	Tallinn	1	0
2006	1 Mar	Belfast	1	0

		v FAEROES	NI	F
EC1991	1 May	Belfast	1	1
EC1991	11 Sept	Landskrona	5	0

		v FINLAND	NI	F
wc1984	27 May	Pori	0	1
wc1984	14 Nov	Belfast	2	1
EC1998	10 Oct	Belfast	1	0
EC1998	9 Oct	Helsinki	1	4

			NI	F
2003	12 Feb	Belfast	0	1
2006	16 Aug	Helsinki	2	1

		v FRANCE	NI	F
1928	21 Feb	Paris	0	4
1951	12 May	Belfast	2	2
1952	11 Nov	Paris	1	3
wc1958	19 June	Norrkoping	0	4
1982	24 Mar	Paris	0	4
wc1982	4 July	Madrid	1	4
1986	26 Feb	Paris	0	0
1988	27 Apr	Belfast	0	0
1999	18 Aug	Belfast	0	1

		v GEORGIA	NI	G
2008	26 Mar	Belfast	4	1

		v GERMANY	NI	G
1992	2 June	Bremen	1	1
1996	29 May	Belfast	1	1
wc1996	9 Nov	Nuremberg	1	1
wc1997	20 Aug	Belfast	1	3
EC1999	27 Mar	Belfast	0	3
EC1999	8 Sept	Dortmund	0	4
2005	4 June	Belfast	1	4

		v WEST GERMANY	NI	WG
wc1958	15 June	Malmo	2	2
wc1960	26 Oct	Belfast	3	4
wc1961	10 May	Hamburg	1	2
1966	7 May	Belfast	0	2
1977	27 Apr	Cologne	0	5
EC1982	17 Nov	Belfast	1	0
EC1983	16 Nov	Hamburg	1	0

		v GREECE	NI	G
wc1961	3 May	Athens	1	2
wc1961	17 Oct	Belfast	2	0
1988	17 Feb	Athens	2	3
EC2003	2 Apr	Belfast	0	2
EC2003	11 Oct	Athens	0	1

		v HOLLAND	NI	H
1962	9 May	Rotterdam	0	4
wc1965	17 Mar	Belfast	2	1
wc1965	7 Apr	Rotterdam	0	0
wc1976	13 Oct	Rotterdam	2	2
wc1977	12 Oct	Belfast	0	1

		v HONDURAS	NI	H
wc1982	21 June	Zaragoza	1	1

		v HUNGARY	NI	H
wc1988	19 Oct	Budapest	0	1
wc1989	6 Sept	Belfast	1	2
2000	26 Apr	Belfast	0	1
2008	19 Nov	Belfast	0	2

		v ICELAND	NI	I
wc1977	11 June	Reykjavik	0	1
wc1977	21 Sept	Belfast	2	0
wc2000	11 Oct	Reykjavik	0	1
wc2001	5 Sept	Belfast	3	0
EC2006	2 Sept	Belfast	0	3
EC2007	12 Sept	Reykjavik	1	2

		v REPUBLIC OF IRELAND	NI	RI
EC1978	20 Sept	Dublin	0	0
EC1979	21 Nov	Belfast	1	0
wc1988	14 Sept	Belfast	0	0
wc1989	11 Oct	Dublin	0	3
wc1993	31 Mar	Dublin	0	3
wc1993	17 Nov	Belfast	1	1
EC1994	16 Nov	Belfast	0	4
EC1995	29 Mar	Dublin	1	1
1999	29 May	Dublin	1	0

		v ISRAEL	NI	I
1968	10 Sept	Jaffa	3	2
1976	3 Mar	Tel Aviv	1	1
wc1980	26 Mar	Tel Aviv	0	0
wc1981	18 Nov	Belfast	1	0
1984	16 Oct	Belfast	3	0
1987	18 Feb	Tel Aviv	1	1

v ITALY			NI	I
wc1957	25 Apr	Rome	0	1
1957	4 Dec	Belfast	2	2
wc1958	15 Jan	Belfast	2	1
1961	25 Apr	Bologna	2	3
1997	22 Jan	Palermo	0	2
2003	3 June	Campobasso	0	2
2009	6 June	Pisa	0	3

v LATVIA			NI	L
wc1993	2 June	Riga	2	1
wc1993	8 Sept	Belfast	2	0
EC1995	26 Apr	Riga	1	0
EC1995	7 June	Belfast	1	2
EC2006	11 Oct	Belfast	1	0
EC2007	8 Sept	Riga	0	1

v LIECHTENSTEIN			NI	L
EC1994	20 Apr	Belfast	4	1
EC1995	11 Oct	Eschen	4	0
2002	27 Mar	Vaduz	0	0
EC2007	24 Mar	Vaduz	4	1
EC2007	22 Aug	Belfast	3	1

v LITHUANIA			NI	L
wc1992	28 Apr	Belfast	2	2
wc1993	25 May	Vilnius	1	0

v LUXEMBOURG			NI	L
2000	23 Feb	Luxembourg	3	1

v MALTA			NI	M
wc1988	21 May	Belfast	3	0
wc1989	26 Apr	Valletta	2	0
2000	28 Mar	Valletta	3	0
wc2000	2 Sept	Belfast	1	0
wc2001	6 Oct	Valletta	1	0
2005	17 Aug	Ta'Qali	1	1

v MEXICO			NI	M
1966	22 June	Belfast	4	1
1994	11 June	Miami	0	3

v MOLDOVA			NI	M
EC1998	18 Nov	Belfast	2	2
EC1999	31 Mar	Chisinau	0	0

v MOROCCO			NI	M
1986	23 Apr	Belfast	2	1

v NORWAY			NI	N
1922	25 May	Bergen	1	2
EC1974	4 Sept	Oslo	1	2
EC1975	29 Oct	Belfast	3	0
1990	27 Mar	Belfast	2	3
1996	27 Mar	Belfast	0	2
2001	28 Feb	Belfast	0	4
2004	18 Feb	Belfast	1	4

v POLAND			NI	P
EC1962	10 Oct	Katowice	2	0
EC1962	28 Nov	Belfast	2	0
1988	23 Mar	Belfast	1	1
1991	5 Feb	Belfast	3	1
2002	13 Feb	Limassol	1	4
EC2004	4 Sept	Belfast	0	3
EC2005	30 Mar	Warsaw	0	1
wc2009	28 Mar	Belfast	3	2

v PORTUGAL			NI	P
wc1957	16 Jan	Lisbon	1	1
wc1957	1 May	Belfast	3	0
wc1973	28 Mar	Coventry	1	1
wc1973	14 Nov	Lisbon	1	1
wc1980	19 Nov	Lisbon	0	1
wc1981	29 Apr	Belfast	1	0
EC1994	7 Sept	Belfast	1	2
EC1995	3 Sept	Lisbon	1	1
wc1997	29 Mar	Belfast	0	0
wc1997	11 Oct	Lisbon	0	1
2005	15 Nov	Belfast	1	1

v ROMANIA			NI	R
wc1984	12 Sept	Belfast	3	2
wc1985	16 Oct	Bucharest	1	0

			NI	R
1994	23 Mar	Belfast	2	0
2006	27 May	Chicago	0	2

v SAN MARINO			NI	SM
wc2008	15 Oct	Belfast	4	0
wc2009	11 Feb	Serravalle	3	0

v ST KITTS & NEVIS			NI	SK
2004	2 June	Basseterre	2	0

v SERBIA-MONTENEGRO			NI	SM
2004	28 Apr	Belfast	1	1

v SLOVAKIA			NI	S
1998	25 Mar	Belfast	1	0
wc2008	6 Sept	Bratislava	1	2

v SLOVENIA			NI	S
wc2008	11 Oct	Maribor	0	2
wc2009	1 Apr	Belfast	1	0

v SOUTH AFRICA			NI	SA
1924	24 Sept	Belfast	1	2

v SPAIN			NI	S
1958	15 Oct	Madrid	2	6
1963	30 May	Bilbao	1	1
1963	30 Oct	Belfast	0	1
EC1970	11 Nov	Seville	0	3
EC1972	16 Feb	Hull	1	1
wc1982	25 June	Valencia	1	0
1985	27 Mar	Palma	0	0
wc1986	7 June	Guadalajara	1	2
wc1988	21 Dec	Seville	0	4
wc1989	8 Feb	Belfast	0	2
wc1992	14 Oct	Belfast	0	0
wc1993	28 Apr	Seville	1	3
1998	2 June	Santander	1	4
2002	17 Apr	Belfast	0	5
EC2002	12 Oct	Albacete	0	3
EC2003	11 June	Belfast	0	0
EC2006	6 Sept	Belfast	3	2
EC2007	21 Nov	Las Palmas	0	1

v SWEDEN			NI	S
EC1974	30 Oct	Solna	2	0
EC1975	3 Sept	Belfast	1	2
wc1980	15 Oct	Belfast	3	0
wc1981	3 June	Solna	0	1
1996	24 Apr	Belfast	1	2
EC2007	28 Mar	Belfast	2	1
EC2007	17 Oct	Stockholm	1	1

v SWITZERLAND			NI	S
wc1964	14 Oct	Belfast	1	0
wc1964	14 Nov	Lausanne	1	2
1998	22 Apr	Belfast	1	0
2004	18 Aug	Zurich	0	0

v THAILAND			NI	T
1997	21 May	Bangkok	0	0

v TRINIDAD & TOBAGO			NI	TT
2004	6 June	Bacolet	3	0

v TURKEY			NI	T
wc1968	23 Oct	Belfast	4	1
wc1968	11 Dec	Istanbul	3	0
EC1983	30 Mar	Belfast	2	1
EC1983	12 Oct	Ankara	0	1
wc1985	1 May	Belfast	2	0
wc1985	11 Sept	Izmir	0	0
EC1986	12 Nov	Izmir	0	0
EC1987	11 Nov	Belfast	1	0
EC1998	5 Sept	Istanbul	0	3
EC1999	4 Sept	Belfast	0	3

v UKRAINE			NI	U
wc1996	31 Aug	Belfast	0	1
wc1997	2 Apr	Kiev	1	2
EC2002	16 Oct	Belfast	0	0
EC2003	6 Sept	Donetsk	0	0

v URUGUAY			NI	U
1964	29 Apr	Belfast	3	0
1990	18 May	Belfast	1	0
2006	21 May	New Jersey	0	1

v USSR			NI	USSR
wc1969	19 Sept	Belfast	0	0
wc1969	22 Oct	Moscow	0	2
EC1971	22 Sept	Moscow	0	1
EC1971	13 Oct	Belfast	1	1

v YUGOSLAVIA			NI	Y
EC1975	16 Mar	Belfast	1	0
EC1975	19 Nov	Belgrade	0	1
wc1982	17 June	Zaragoza	0	0
EC1987	29 Apr	Belfast	1	2
EC1987	14 Oct	Sarajevo	0	3
EC1990	12 Sept	Belfast	0	2
EC1991	27 Mar	Belgrade	1	4
2000	16 Aug	Belfast	1	2

REPUBLIC OF IRELAND

v ALBANIA			RI	A
wc1992	26 May	Dublin	2	0
wc1993	26 May	Tirana	2	1
EC2003	2 Apr	Tirana	0	0
EC2003	7 June	Dublin	2	1

v ALGERIA			RI	A
1982	28 Apr	Algiers	0	2

v ANDORRA			RI	A
wc2001	28 Mar	Barcelona	3	0
wc2001	25 Apr	Dublin	3	1

v ARGENTINA			RI	A
1951	13 May	Dublin	0	1
†1979	29 May	Dublin	0	0
1980	16 May	Dublin	0	1
1998	22 Apr	Dublin	0	2

†*Not considered a full international.*

v AUSTRALIA			RI	A
2003	19 Aug	Dublin	2	1

v AUSTRIA			RI	A
1952	7 May	Vienna	0	6
1953	25 Mar	Dublin	4	0
1958	14 Mar	Vienna	1	3
1962	8 Apr	Dublin	2	3
EC1963	25 Sept	Vienna	0	0
EC1963	13 Oct	Dublin	3	2
1966	22 May	Vienna	0	1
1968	10 Nov	Dublin	2	2
EC1971	30 May	Dublin	1	4
EC1971	10 Oct	Linz	0	6
EC1995	11 June	Dublin	1	3
EC1995	6 Sept	Vienna	1	3

v BELGIUM			RI	B
1928	12 Feb	Liège	4	2
1929	30 Apr	Dublin	4	0
1930	11 May	Brussels	3	1
wc1934	25 Feb	Dublin	4	4
1949	24 Apr	Dublin	0	2
1950	10 May	Brussels	1	5
1965	24 Mar	Dublin	0	2
1966	25 May	Liège	3	2
wc1980	15 Oct	Dublin	1	1
wc1981	25 Mar	Brussels	0	1
EC1986	10 Sept	Brussels	2	2
EC1987	29 Apr	Dublin	0	0
wc1997	29 Oct	Dublin	1	1
wc1997	16 Nov	Brussels	1	2

v BOLIVIA			RI	B
1994	24 May	Dublin	1	0
1996	15 June	New Jersey	3	0
2007	26 May	Boston	1	1

v BRAZIL			RI	B
1974	5 May	Rio de Janeiro	1	2
1982	27 May	Uberlandia	0	7
1987	23 May	Dublin	1	0
2004	18 Feb	Dublin	0	0
2008	6 Feb	Dublin	0	1

v BULGARIA			RI	B
wc1977	1 June	Sofia	1	2
wc1977	12 Oct	Dublin	0	0
EC1979	19 May	Sofia	0	1
EC1979	17 Oct	Dublin	3	0

			RI	B
wc1987	1 Apr	Sofia	1	2
wc1987	14 Oct	Dublin	2	0
2004	18 Aug	Dublin	1	1
wc2009	28 Mar	Dublin	1	1
wc2009	6 June	Sofia	1	1

v CAMEROON			RI	C
wc2002	1 June	Niigata	1	1

v CANADA			RI	C
2003	18 Nov	Dublin	3	0

v CHILE			RI	C
1960	30 Mar	Dublin	2	0
1972	21 June	Recife	1	2
1974	12 May	Santiago	2	1
1982	22 May	Santiago	0	1
1991	22 May	Dublin	1	1
2006	24 May	Dublin	0	1

v CHINA			RI	C
1984	3 June	Sapporo	1	0
2005	29 Mar	Dublin	1	0

v COLOMBIA			RI	C
2008	29 May	Fulham	1	0

v CROATIA			RI	C
1996	2 June	Dublin	2	2
EC1998	5 Sept	Dublin	2	0
EC1999	4 Sept	Zagreb	0	1
2001	15 Aug	Dublin	2	2
2004	16 Nov	Dublin	1	0

v CYPRUS			RI	C
wc1980	26 Mar	Nicosia	3	2
wc1980	19 Nov	Dublin	6	0
wc2001	24 Mar	Nicosia	4	0
wc2001	6 Oct	Dublin	4	0
wc2004	4 Sept	Dublin	3	0
wc2005	8 Oct	Nicosia	1	0
EC2006	7 Oct	Nicosia	2	5
EC2007	17 Oct	Dublin	1	1
2008	15 Oct	Dublin	1	0

v CZECHOSLOVAKIA			RI	C
1938	18 May	Prague	2	2
EC1959	5 Apr	Dublin	2	0
EC1959	10 May	Bratislava	0	4
wc1961	8 Oct	Dublin	1	3
wc1961	29 Oct	Prague	1	7
EC1967	21 May	Dublin	0	2
EC1967	22 Nov	Prague	2	1
wc1969	4 May	Dublin	1	2
wc1969	7 Oct	Prague	0	3
1979	26 Sept	Prague	1	4
1981	29 Apr	Dublin	3	1
1986	27 May	Reykjavik	1	0

v CZECH REPUBLIC			RI	C
1994	5 June	Dublin	1	3
1996	24 Apr	Prague	0	2
1998	25 Mar	Olomouc	1	2
2000	23 Feb	Dublin	3	2
2004	31 Mar	Dublin	2	1
EC2006	11 Oct	Dublin	1	1
EC2007	12 Sept	Prague	0	1

v DENMARK			RI	D
wc1956	3 Oct	Dublin	2	1
wc1957	2 Oct	Copenhagen	2	0
wc1968	4 Dec	Dublin	1	1
(abandoned after 51 mins)				

			RI	D
wc1969	27 May	Copenhagen	0	2
wc1969	15 Oct	Dublin	1	1
EC1978	24 May	Copenhagen	3	3
EC1979	2 May	Dublin	2	0
wc1984	14 Nov	Copenhagen	0	3
wc1985	13 Nov	Dublin	1	4
wc1992	14 Oct	Copenhagen	0	0
wc1993	28 Apr	Dublin	1	1
2002	27 Mar	Dublin	3	0
2007	22 Aug	Copenhagen	4	0

v ECUADOR

			RI	E
1972	19 June	Natal	3	2
2007	23 May	New Jersey	1	1

v EGYPT

			RI	E
wc1990	17 June	Palermo	0	0

v ENGLAND

			RI	E
1946	30 Sept	Dublin	0	1
1949	21 Sept	Everton	2	0
wc1957	8 May	Wembley	1	5
wc1957	19 May	Dublin	1	1
1964	24 May	Dublin	1	3
1976	8 Sept	Wembley	1	1
EC1978	25 Oct	Dublin	1	1
EC1980	6 Feb	Wembley	0	2
1985	26 Mar	Wembley	1	2
EC1988	12 June	Stuttgart	1	0
wc1990	11 June	Cagliari	1	1
EC1990	14 Nov	Dublin	1	1
EC1991	27 Mar	Wembley	1	1
1995	15 Feb	Dublin	1	0

(abandoned after 27 mins)

v ESTONIA

			RI	E
wc2000	11 Oct	Dublin	2	0
wc2001	6 June	Tallinn	2	0

v FAEROES

			RI	F
EC2004	13 Oct	Dublin	2	0
EC2005	8 June	Toftir	2	0

v FINLAND

			RI	F
wc1949	8 Sept	Dublin	3	0
wc1949	9 Oct	Helsinki	1	1
1990	16 May	Dublin	1	1
2000	15 Nov	Dublin	3	0
2002	21 Aug	Helsinki	3	0

v FRANCE

			RI	F
1937	23 May	Paris	2	0
1952	16 Nov	Dublin	1	1
wc1953	4 Oct	Dublin	3	5
wc1953	25 Nov	Paris	0	1
wc1972	15 Nov	Dublin	2	1
wc1973	19 May	Paris	1	1
wc1976	17 Nov	Paris	0	2
wc1977	30 Mar	Dublin	1	0
wc1980	28 Oct	Paris	0	2
wc1981	14 Oct	Dublin	3	2
1989	7 Feb	Dublin	0	0
wc2004	9 Oct	Paris	0	0
wc2005	7 Sept	Dublin	0	1

v GEORGIA

			RI	G
EC2003	29 Mar	Tbilisi	2	1
EC2003	11 June	Dublin	2	0
wc2008	6 Sept	Mainz	2	1
wc2009	11 Feb	Dublin	2	1

v GERMANY

			RI	G
1935	8 May	Dortmund	1	3
1936	17 Oct	Dublin	5	2
1939	23 May	Bremen	1	1
1994	29 May	Hanover	2	0
wc2002	5 June	Ibaraki	1	1
EC2006	2 Sept	Stuttgart	0	1
EC2007	13 Oct	Dublin	0	0

v WEST GERMANY

			RI	WG
1951	17 Oct	Dublin	3	2
1952	4 May	Cologne	0	3
1955	28 May	Hamburg	1	2
1956	25 Nov	Dublin	3	0
1960	11 May	Dusseldorf	1	0
1966	4 May	Dublin	0	4
1970	9 May	Berlin	1	2
1975	1 Mar	Dublin	1	0†
1979	22 May	Dublin	1	3

			RI	WG
1981	21 May	Bremen	0	3†
1989	6 Sept	Dublin	1	1

†v West Germany 'B'

v GREECE

			RI	G
2000	26 Apr	Dublin	0	1
2002	20 Nov	Athens	0	0

v HOLLAND

			RI	N
1932	8 May	Amsterdam	2	0
1934	8 Apr	Amsterdam	2	5
1935	8 Dec	Dublin	3	5
1955	1 May	Dublin	1	0
1956	10 May	Rotterdam	4	1
wc1980	10 Sept	Dublin	2	1
wc1981	9 Sept	Rotterdam	2	2
EC1982	22 Sept	Rotterdam	1	2
EC1983	12 Oct	Dublin	2	3
EC1988	18 June	Gelsenkirchen	0	1
wc1990	21 June	Palermo	1	1
1994	20 Apr	Tilburg	1	0
wc1994	4 July	Orlando	0	2
EC1995	13 Dec	Liverpool	0	2
1996	4 June	Rotterdam	1	3
wc2000	2 Sept	Amsterdam	2	2
wc2001	1 Sept	Dublin	1	0
2004	5 June	Amsterdam	1	0
2006	16 Aug	Dublin	0	4

v HUNGARY

			RI	H
1934	15 Dec	Dublin	2	4
1936	3 May	Budapest	3	3
1936	6 Dec	Dublin	2	3
1939	19 Mar	Cork	2	2
1939	18 May	Budapest	2	2
wc1969	8 June	Dublin	1	2
wc1969	5 Nov	Budapest	0	4
wc1989	8 Mar	Budapest	0	0
wc1989	4 June	Dublin	2	0
1991	11 Sept	Gyor	2	1

v ICELAND

			RI	I
EC1962	12 Aug	Dublin	4	2
EC1962	2 Sept	Reykjavik	1	1
EC1982	13 Oct	Dublin	2	0
EC1983	21 Sept	Reykjavik	3	0
1986	25 May	Reykjavik	2	1
wc1996	10 Nov	Dublin	0	0
wc1997	6 Sept	Reykjavik	4	2

v IRAN

			RI	I
1972	18 June	Recife	2	1
wc2001	10 Nov	Dublin	2	0
wc2001	15 Nov	Tehran	0	1

v N. IRELAND

			RI	NI
EC1978	20 Sept	Dublin	0	0
EC1979	21 Nov	Belfast	0	1
wc1988	14 Sept	Belfast	0	0
wc1989	11 Oct	Dublin	3	0
wc1993	31 Mar	Dublin	3	0
wc1993	17 Nov	Belfast	1	1
EC1994	16 Nov	Belfast	4	0
EC1995	29 Mar	Dublin	1	1
1999	29 May	Dublin	0	1

v ISRAEL

			RI	I
1984	4 Apr	Tel Aviv	0	3
1985	27 May	Tel Aviv	0	0
1987	10 Nov	Dublin	5	0
EC2005	26 Mar	Tel Aviv	1	1
EC2005	4 June	Dublin	2	2

v ITALY

			RI	I
1926	21 Mar	Turin	0	3
1927	23 Apr	Dublin	1	2
EC1970	8 Dec	Rome	0	3
EC1971	10 May	Dublin	1	2
1985	5 Feb	Dublin	1	2
wc1990	30 June	Rome	0	1
1992	4 June	Foxboro	0	2
wc1994	18 June	New York	1	0
2005	17 Aug	Dublin	1	2
wc2009	1 Apr	Bari	1	1

v JAMAICA

			RI	J
2004	2 June	Charlton	1	0

v LATVIA

			RI	L
wc1992	9 Sept	Dublin	4	0
wc1993	2 June	Riga	2	1
EC1994	7 Sept	Riga	3	0
EC1995	11 Oct	Dublin	2	1

v LIECHTENSTEIN

			RI	L
EC1994	12 Oct	Dublin	4	0
EC1995	3 June	Eschen	0	0
wc1996	31 Aug	Eschen	5	0
wc1997	21 May	Dublin	5	0

v LITHUANIA

			RI	L
wc1993	16 June	Vilnius	1	0
wc1993	8 Sept	Dublin	2	0
wc1997	20 Aug	Dublin	0	0
wc1997	10 Sept	Vilnius	2	1

v LUXEMBOURG

			RI	L
1936	9 May	Luxembourg	5	1
wc1953	28 Oct	Dublin	4	0
wc1954	7 Mar	Luxembourg	1	0
EC1987	28 May	Luxembourg	2	0
EC1987	9 Sept	Dublin	2	1

v MACEDONIA

			RI	M
wc1996	9 Oct	Dublin	3	0
wc1997	2 Apr	Skopje	2	3
EC1999	9 June	Dublin	1	0
EC1999	9 Oct	Skopje	1	1

v MALTA

			RI	M
EC1983	30 Mar	Valletta	1	0
EC1983	16 Nov	Dublin	8	0
wc1989	28 May	Dublin	2	0
wc1989	15 Nov	Valletta	2	0
1990	2 June	Valletta	3	0
EC1998	14 Oct	Dublin	5	0
EC1999	8 Sept	Valletta	3	2

v MEXICO

			RI	M
1984	8 Aug	Dublin	0	0
wc1994	24 June	Orlando	1	2
1996	13 June	New Jersey	2	2
1998	23 May	Dublin	0	0
2000	4 June	Chicago	2	2

v MONTENEGRO

			RI	M
wc2008	10 Sept	Podgorica	0	0

v MOROCCO

			RI	M
1990	12 Sept	Dublin	1	0

v NIGERIA

			RI	N
2002	16 May	Dublin	1	2
2004	29 May	Charlton	0	3
2009	29 May	Fulham	1	1

v NORWAY

			RI	N
wc1937	10 Oct	Oslo	2	3
wc1937	7 Nov	Dublin	3	3
1950	26 Nov	Dublin	2	2
1951	30 May	Oslo	3	2
1954	8 Nov	Dublin	2	1
1955	25 May	Oslo	3	1
1960	6 Nov	Dublin	3	1
1964	13 May	Oslo	4	1
1973	6 June	Oslo	1	1
1976	24 Mar	Oslo	3	0
1978	21 May	Oslo	0	0
wc1984	17 Oct	Oslo	0	1
wc1985	1 May	Dublin	0	0
1988	1 June	Oslo	0	0
wc1994	28 June	New York	0	0
2003	30 Apr	Dublin	1	0
2008	20 Aug	Oslo	1	1

v PARAGUAY

			RI	P
1999	10 Feb	Dublin	2	0

v POLAND

			RI	P
1938	22 May	Warsaw	0	6
1938	13 Nov	Dublin	3	2
1958	11 May	Katowice	2	2
1958	5 Oct	Dublin	2	2
1964	10 May	Kracow	1	3
1964	25 Oct	Dublin	3	2
1968	15 May	Dublin	2	2
1968	30 Oct	Katowice	0	1
1970	6 May	Dublin	1	2
1970	23 Sept	Dublin	0	2
1973	16 May	Wroclaw	0	2
1973	21 Oct	Dublin	1	0
1976	26 May	Poznan	2	0
1977	24 Apr	Dublin	0	0
1978	12 Apr	Lodz	0	3
1981	23 May	Bydgoszcz	0	3
1984	23 May	Dublin	0	0
1986	12 Nov	Warsaw	0	1
1988	22 May	Dublin	3	1
EC1991	1 May	Dublin	0	0
EC1991	16 Oct	Poznan	3	3
2004	28 Apr	Bydgoszcz	0	0
2008	19 Nov	Dublin	2	3

v PORTUGAL

			RI	P
1946	16 June	Lisbon	1	3
1947	4 May	Dublin	0	2
1948	23 May	Lisbon	0	2
1949	22 May	Dublin	1	0
1972	25 June	Recife	1	2
1992	7 June	Boston	2	0
EC1995	26 Apr	Dublin	1	0
EC1995	15 Nov	Lisbon	0	3
1996	29 May	Dublin	0	1
wc2000	7 Oct	Lisbon	1	1
wc2001	2 June	Dublin	1	1
2005	9 Feb	Dublin	1	0

v ROMANIA

			RI	R
1988	23 Mar	Dublin	2	0
wc1990	25 June	Genoa	0	0*
wc1997	30 Apr	Bucharest	0	1
wc1997	11 Oct	Dublin	1	1
2004	27 May	Dublin	1	0

v RUSSIA

			RI	R
1994	23 Mar	Dublin	0	0
1996	27 Mar	Dublin	0	2
2002	13 Feb	Dublin	2	0
EC2002	7 Sept	Moscow	2	4
EC2003	6 Sept	Dublin	1	1

v SAN MARINO

			RI	SM
EC2006	15 Nov	Dublin	5	0
EC2007	7 Feb	Serravalle	2	1

v SAUDI ARABIA

			RI	SA
wc2002	11 June	Yokohama	3	0

v SERBIA

			RI	S
2008	24 May	Dublin	1	1

v SCOTLAND

			RI	S
wc1961	3 May	Glasgow	1	4
wc1961	7 May	Dublin	0	3
1963	9 June	Dublin	1	0
1969	21 Sept	Dublin	1	1
EC1986	15 Oct	Dublin	0	0
EC1987	18 Feb	Glasgow	1	0
2000	30 May	Dublin	1	2
2003	12 Feb	Glasgow	2	0

v SLOVAKIA

			RI	S
EC2007	28 Mar	Dublin	1	0
EC2007	8 Sept	Bratislava	2	2

v SOUTH AFRICA

			RI	SA
2000	11 June	New Jersey	2	1

v SPAIN

			RI	S
1931	26 Apr	Barcelona	1	1
1931	13 Dec	Dublin	0	5
1946	23 June	Madrid	1	0
1947	2 Mar	Dublin	3	2
1948	30 May	Barcelona	1	2
1949	12 June	Dublin	1	4
1952	1 June	Madrid	0	6
1955	27 Nov	Dublin	2	2
EC1964	11 Mar	Seville	1	5
EC1964	8 Apr	Dublin	0	2
wc1965	5 May	Dublin	1	0
wc1965	27 Oct	Seville	1	4
wc1965	10 Nov	Paris	0	1
EC1966	23 Oct	Dublin	0	0

			RI	S
EC1966	7 Dec	Valencia	0	2
1977	9 Feb	Dublin	0	1
EC1982	17 Nov	Dublin	3	3
EC1983	27 Apr	Zaragoza	0	2
1985	26 May	Cork	0	0
wc1988	16 Nov	Seville	0	2
wc1989	26 Apr	Dublin	1	0
wc1992	18 Nov	Seville	0	0
wc1993	13 Oct	Dublin	1	3
wc2002	16 June	Suwon	1	1

v SWEDEN			RI	S
wc1949	2 June	Stockholm	1	3
wc1949	13 Nov	Dublin	1	3
1959	1 Nov	Dublin	3	2
1960	18 May	Malmo	1	4
EC1970	14 Oct	Dublin	1	1
EC1970	28 Oct	Malmo	0	1
1999	28 Apr	Dublin	2	0
2006	1 Mar	Dublin	3	0

v SWITZERLAND			RI	S
1935	5 May	Basle	0	1
1936	17 Mar	Dublin	1	0
1937	17 May	Berne	1	0
1938	18 Sept	Dublin	4	0
1948	5 Dec	Dublin	0	1
EC1975	11 May	Dublin	2	1
EC1975	21 May	Berne	0	1

			RI	S
1980	30 Apr	Dublin	2	0
wc1985	2 June	Dublin	3	0
wc1985	11 Sept	Berne	0	0
1992	25 Mar	Dublin	2	1
EC2002	16 Oct	Dublin	1	2
EC2003	11 Oct	Basle	0	2
wc2004	8 Sept	Basle	1	1
wc2005	12 Oct	Dublin	0	0

v TRINIDAD & TOBAGO			RI	TT
1982	30 May	Port of Spain	1	2

v TUNISIA			RI	T
1988	19 Oct	Dublin	4	0

v TURKEY			RI	T
EC1966	16 Nov	Dublin	2	1
EC1967	22 Feb	Ankara	1	2
EC1974	20 Nov	Izmir	1	1
EC1975	29 Oct	Dublin	4	0

			RI	T
1976	13 Oct	Ankara	3	3
1978	5 Apr	Dublin	4	2
1990	26 May	Izmir	0	0
EC1990	17 Oct	Dublin	5	0
EC1991	13 Nov	Istanbul	3	1
EC2000	13 Nov	Dublin	1	1
EC2000	17 Nov	Bursa	0	0
2003	9 Sept	Dublin	2	2

v URUGUAY			RI	U
1974	8 May	Montevideo	0	2
1986	23 Apr	Dublin	1	1

v USA			RI	USA
1979	29 Oct	Dublin	3	2
1991	1 June	Boston	1	1
1992	29 Apr	Dublin	4	1
1992	30 May	Washington	1	3
1996	9 June	Boston	1	2
2000	6 June	Boston	1	1
2002	17 Apr	Dublin	2	1

v USSR			RI	USSR
wc1972	18 Oct	Dublin	1	2
wc1973	13 May	Moscow	0	1
EC1974	30 Oct	Dublin	3	0
EC1975	18 May	Kiev	1	2
wc1984	12 Sept	Dublin	1	0
wc1985	16 Oct	Moscow	0	2
EC1988	15 June	Hanover	1	1
1990	25 Apr	Dublin	1	0

v WALES			RI	W
1960	28 Sept	Dublin	2	3
1979	11 Sept	Swansea	1	2
1981	24 Feb	Dublin	1	3
1986	26 Mar	Dublin	0	1
1990	28 Mar	Dublin	1	0
1991	6 Feb	Wrexham	3	0
1992	19 Feb	Dublin	0	1
1993	17 Feb	Dublin	2	1
1997	11 Feb	Cardiff	0	0
EC2007	24 Mar	Dublin	1	0
EC2007	17 Nov	Cardiff	2	2

v YUGOSLAVIA			RI	Y
1955	19 Sept	Dublin	1	4
1988	27 Apr	Dublin	2	0
EC1998	18 Nov	Belgrade	0	1
EC1999	1 Sept	Dublin	2	1

The England team line up before the World Cup qualifying match against Croatia in Zagreb. A fine individual performance from Theo Walcott netted him a hat-trick with England going on to win 4-1. (PA Photos)

OTHER BRITISH AND IRISH INTERNATIONAL MATCHES 2008–09

FRIENDLIES

Wembley, 20 August 2008, 69,738

England (1) 2 *(Brown 45, Cole J 90)*

Czech Republic (1) 2 *(Baros 22, Jankulovski 48)*

England: James; Brown, Cole A, Barry, Ferdinand (Woodgate 58), Terry, Beckham (Jenas 79), Lampard (Bentley 79), Defoe (Heskey 46), Rooney (Downing 68), Gerrard (Cole J 58).
Czech Republic: Cech; Grygera (Pospech 46), Ujfalusi, Rozehnal, Jankulovski, Vlcek (Jarolim 46), Kovac R (Rajnoch 76), Polak, Plasil (Papadopoulos 90), Sirl (Kadlac 76), Baros (Sverkos 46).
Referee: T. Hauge (Norway).

Berlin, 19 November 2008, 74,244

Germany (0) 1 *(Helmes 63)*

England (1) 2 *(Upson 23, Terry 84)*

Germany: Adler (Wiese 46); Friedrich (Tasci 68), Rolfes, Mertesacker, Westermann, Compper (Schafer 77), Schweinsteiger, Trochowski, Jones (Helmes 46), Klose (Marin 46), Gomez (Podolski 57).
England: James (Carson 46); Johnson, Bridge, Barry, Upson, Terry, Wright-Phillips (Crouch 90), Carrick, Defoe (Bent D 46), Agbonlahor (Young A 77), Downing.
Referee: Busacca (Switzerland).

Seville, 11 February 2009

Spain (1) 2 *(Villa 36, Llorente 82)*

England (0) 0

Spain: Casillas (Reina 46); Sergio Ramos, Albiol (Marchena 75), Pique, Xabi Alonso, Iniesta, Villa (Silva 56), Xavi (Guiza 85), Torres (Llorente 64), Capdevila (Arbeloa 46), Senna.
England: James (Green 46); Johnson G, Cole A, Carrick, Jagielka (Upson 46), Terry, Wright-Phillips, Barry (Lampard 46), Agbonlahor (Cole C 75), Heskey (Crouch 46), Downing (Beckham 46).
Referee: S. Lannoy (France).

Wembley, 28 March 2009, 85,512

England (1) 4 *(Heskey 7, Rooney 70, 90, Lampard 82)*

Slovakia (0) 0

England: James (Foster 46); Johnson G, Cole A, Barry, Upson, Terry, Lennon (Beckham 46), Lampard, Heskey (Cole C 15), Crouch (Carrick 74), Rooney, Gerrard (Downing 46).
Slovakia: Senecky; Pekarik, Valachovic, Skrtel, Cech (Jendrisik 46), Karhan (Strba 83), Zabanik, Sestak (Jakubko 72), Kozak (Sapara 62), Hamsik (Mintal 79), Vittek (Holosko 46).
Referee: A. Hamer.

Hampden Park, 20 August 2008, 28,072

Scotland (0) 0

Northern Ireland (0) 0

Scotland: Gordon (McGregor 46); Alexander G, McManus (Barr 46), Weir (Berra 72), Naysmith, Brown S, Thomson (Robson 46), Fletcher D (Stewart 69), Morrison (Commons 62), Miller K, McFadden.
Northern Ireland: Taylor; McAuley (Duff 76), Evans J, Craigan, McGivern, Baird, Clingan (O'Connor 58), Davis, Brunt (Feeney 55), Healy, Paterson (Shiels 46).
Referee: N. Vollquartz (Denmark).

Hampden Park, 19 November 2008, 32,492

Scotland (0) 0

Argentina (0) 1 *(Rodriguez 8)*

Scotland: McGregor; Hutton, Broadfoot, Hartley (Maloney 59), Caldwell G, McManus (Berra 75), Brown S (Alexander G 83), Ferguson (Robertson 59), Iwelumo (Miller L 46), McFadden (Clarkson 67), Commons.
Argentina: Carrizo; Zanetti, Demichelis, Heinze, Papa (Cata Diaz 86), Rodriguez (Sosa 90), Mascherano, Gago, Gutierrez (Gonzalez 71), Lavezzi (Denis 75), Tevez.
Referee: F. Brych (Germany).

Liberty Stadium, Swansea, 20 August 2008, 6435

Wales (1) 1 *(Koumas 16)*

Georgia (0) 2 *(Kenia 66, Gotsiridze 90)*

Wales: Myhill; Erdley, Ricketts, Williams A, Morgan, Robinson, Davies S, Fletcher, Eastwood (Earnshaw 80), Koumas, Parry (Vaughan 70).
Georgia: Loria; Lobjanidze, Iashvili (Gotsiradze 79), Khizanishvili, Asatiani, Menteshashvili, Mujiri (Khmaladze 46), Kvakhadze, Odikadze (Devdariani 85), Kenia (Klimiashvili 77), Mchedlidze.
Referee: M. Jug (Slovenia).

Brondby, 19 November 2008, 10,271

Denmark (0) 0

Wales (0) 1 *(Bellamy 77)*

Denmark: Sorensen; Bogelund (Larsen 46), Kroldrup (Jorgensen 60), Agger, Rasmussen T (Andreasen 46), Norregaard, Kristensen (Retov 71), Nordstrand (Mtiliga 46), Bendtner, Romedahl, Krohn-Dehli (Vingaard 60).
Wales: Myhill; Gunter, Bale (Eardley 87), Williams A, Collins J, Nyatanga, Edwards D (Ricketts 46), Bellamy, Evans C (Vokes 60), Ramsey (Tudur-Jones 88), Collison.
Referee: M. Weiner (Germany).

Vila Real, 11 February 2009

Poland (0) 1 *(Guerreiro 79)*

Wales (0) 0

Poland: Fabianski (Boruc 46); Wawrzyniak, Lewandowski R (Pawel Brozek 62), Dudka, Krzynowek (Smolarek 46), Boguski (Lobodzinski 46), Murawski (Tralka 75), Wasilewski, Zewlakow, Gargula (Guerreiro 46), Lewandowski M.
Wales: Hennessey (Myhill 46); Gunter, Bale, Ricketts, Williams A, Nyatanga, Collison (Fletcher 46), Bellamy (Cotterill 46), Edwards D, Evans C (Vokes 46), Ledley (Ramsey 46).
Referee: B. Paixao (Portugal).

Llanelli, 29 May 2009, 4071

Wales (1) 1 *(Earnshaw 26 (pen))*

Estonia (0) 0

Wales: Myhill (Hennessey 46); Gunter, Bale, Williams A, Morgan, Nyatanga, Ledley, Ramsey (Edwards D 67), Vokes (Church 59), Earnshaw (Evans C 59) (King A 88), Collison (Allen 80).
Estonia: Kotenko; Sisov, Morozov, Barengrub, Kruglov (Puri E 78), Teniste, Puri S (Kams 65), Dupikov (Marmor 72), Gussev (Konsa 65), Vunk, Vassiljev.
Referee: M. Thorisson (Iceland).

Matthew Upson scores for England in the international friendly against Germany at the Olympic Stadium in Berlin.
(Action Images/Carl Recine)

Oslo, 20 August 2008, 16,037

Norway (0) 1 *(Reginiussen 61)*

Republic of Ireland (1) 1 *(Keane 44)*

Norway: Jarstein; Reginiussen, Hangeland, Winsnes, Riise JA, Stromstad (Haestad 44), Andresen, Hogli, Abdellaoui (Grindheim 80), Helstad (Nevland 57), Holm F (Pedersen 46).
Republic of Ireland: Given (Kiely 46); Finnan (Kelly 69), O'Shea, Dunne, Kilbane, Whelan, McGeady (Hunt N 69), Reid S, Duff, Doyle K (Murphy 64), Keane.
Referee: M. Whitery.

Dublin, 15 October 2008, 55,833

Republic of Ireland (1) 1 *(Keane 5)*

Cyprus (0) 0

Republic of Ireland: Given; McShane, O'Shea, Dunne, Kilbane, McGeady, Gibson, Whelan, Duff, Keane, Doyle K (Folan 90).
Cyprus: Georgallides; Elia, Constantinou A, Lambrou (Papathanasiou 46), Charalambous, Christofi, Maragkos (Panagi 52), Makridis, Garpozis, Okkas, Contantinou M (Yiasoumi 79).
Referee: A. Tudor (Romania).

Croke Park, 19 November 2008, 60,000

Republic of Ireland (0) 2 *(Hunt S 88 (pen), Andrews 90)*

Poland (2) 3 *(Lewandowski M 3, Lewandowski R 89, Guerreiro 47)*

Republic of Ireland: Given; McShane (Bruce 61), Kilbane, Whelan, O'Shea, Dunne, Keogh (Hunt S 61), Gibson (Andrews 73), Folan, Doyle K (Hunt N 60), Duff (Long 66).
Poland: Fabianski; Wasilewski, Dudka, Bosacki, Wawrzyniak, Blaszcyzkowski (Lewandowski R 46), Gargula, Lewandowski M, Krzynowek (Jodlowiec 81), Boguski (Peszko 70), Pawel Brozek (Guerreiro 46).
Referee: K. Jakobsson (Iceland).

Fulham, 29 May 2009

Nigeria (1) 1 *(Eneramo 30)*

Republic of Ireland (1) 1 *(Keane 38)*

Nigeria: Ejide; Adefemi, Sodje, Mohammed, Olofinjana, Aluko (Obinna 61), Uche, Adeleye, Utaka, Akpala (Odemwingie 61), Eneramo.
Republic of Ireland: Given (Westwood 46); Foley (McShane 71), Dunne, St Ledger-Hall, Nolan, Lawrence (Hunt S 81), Miller, Andrews (Whelan 59), Duff (McGeady 46), Keane (Long 46), Best.
Referee: W. Collum.

Windsor Park, 19 November 2008, 6251

Northern Ireland (0) 0

Hungary (0) 2 *(Torghelle 57, Gera 71)*

Northern Ireland: Taylor (Tuffey 46); Duff (McGinn 54), McGivern, Baird, Evans J, Clingan, Gillespie, O'Connor (Feeney 82), Healy (Thompson 88), Lafferty (Shiels 46), Brunt (Paterson 70).
Hungary: Babos; Bodnar, Vanczak, Guhasz, Rudolf, Toth, Halmosi, Vadocz (Dardai 88), Torghelle (Feczesin 81), Gera, Huszti (Dzsudzsak 84).
Referee: R. Schoergenhofer (Austria).

Pisa, 6 June 2009

Italy (1) 3 *(Rossi 20, Foggia 52, Pellissier 72)*

Northern Ireland (0) 0

Italy: Marchetti; Santon, Gamberini, Legrottaglie, Grosso (Dossena 46), D'Agostino (Galloppa 75), Gattuso (Palombo 46), Montolivo (Brighi 46), Mascara (Foggia 46), Pazzini (Pellissier 62), Rossi.
Northern Ireland: Tuffey (Mannus 62); Johnson, Casement, Coates, McGivern, Little (Donnelly 82), O'Connor (Garrett 62), McCann, Evans C (Ferguson 78), Carson (Lawrie 70), Healy (McGinn 46).
Referee: K. Blom (Holland).

B INTERNATIONALS 2009

Cumbernauld, 6 May 2009, 2110
Scotland (1) 3 *(Webster 47, Boyd 75, Griffiths L 84)*
Northern Ireland (0) 0
Scotland: Marshall (Turner 78); Cuthbert (Ross 46), Hammell (Easton 46), Arfield (Black 46), Webster, Reynolds, Burke (Bannan 68), Hughes, Clarkson (Griffiths L 74), Naismith, Boyd.
Northern Ireland: Tuffey (Carson 53); Weir (Gibb 46), Casement, McGivern, Lafferty (Duffy 53), McGinn (Norwood 70), Evans C, O'Connor (Garrett 70), McCourt (Ferguson 70), McQuoid (Lawrie 35), Little.

BRITISH & IRISH INTERNATIONAL MANAGERS

England
Walter Winterbottom 1946–1962 (after period as coach); Alf Ramsey 1963–1974; Joe Mercer (caretaker) 1974; Don Revie 1974–1977; Ron Greenwood 1977–1982; Bobby Robson 1982–1990; Graham Taylor 1990–1993; Terry Venables (coach) 1994–1996; Glenn Hoddle 1996–1999; Kevin Keegan 1999–2000; Sven-Goran Eriksson 2001–2006; Steve McClaren 2006–07; Fabio Capello from January 2008.

Northern Ireland
Peter Doherty 1951–1952; Bertie Peacock 1962–1967; Billy Bingham 1967–1971; Terry Neill 1971–1975; Dave Clements (player-manager) 1975–1976; Danny Blanchflower 1976–1979; Billy Bingham 1980–1994; Bryan Hamilton 1994–1998; Lawrie McMenemy 1998–1999; Sammy McIlroy 2000–2003; Lawrie Sanchez 2004–2007; Nigel Worthington from June 2007.

Scotland (since 1967)
Bobby Brown 1967–1971; Tommy Docherty 1971–1972; Willie Ormond 1973–1977; Ally MacLeod 1977–1978; Jock Stein 1978–1985; Alex Ferguson (caretaker) 1985–1986 Andy Roxburgh (coach) 1986–1993; Craig Brown 1993–2001; Berti Vogts 2002–2004; Walter Smith 2004–2007; Alex McLeish 2007; George Burley from January 2008.

Wales (since 1974)
Mike Smith 1974–1979; Mike England 1980–1988; David Williams (caretaker) 1988; Terry Yorath 1988–1993; John Toshack 1994 for one match; Mike Smith 1994–1995; Bobby Gould 1995–1999; Mark Hughes 1999–2004; John Toshack from November 2004.

Republic of Ireland
Liam Tuohy 1971–1972; Johnny Giles 1973–1980 (after period as player-manager); Eoin Hand 1980–1985; Jack Charlton 1986–1996; Mick McCarthy 1996–2002; Brian Kerr 2003–2006; Steve Staunton 2006–07; Giovanni Trapattoni from February 2008.

England manager Fabio Capello applauds his team after the 2-1 win over Germany in a friendly international in Berlin.
(PA Photos)

INTERNATIONAL APPEARANCES 1872–2009

This is a list of full international appearances by Englishmen, Irishmen, Scotsmen and Welshmen in matches against the Home Countries and against foreign nations. It does not include unofficial matches against Commonwealth and Empire countries. The year indicated refers to the player's international debut season; i.e. 2005 is the 2004–05 season.

As at July 2009.

ENGLAND

Abbott, W. 1902 (Everton)	1
A'Court, A. 1958 (Liverpool)	5
Adams, T. A. 1987 (Arsenal)	66
Adcock, H. 1929 (Leicester C)	5
Agbonlahor, G. 2009 (Aston Villa)	2
Alcock, C. W. 1875 (Wanderers)	1
Alderson, J. T. 1923 (C Palace)	1
Aldridge, A. 1888 (WBA, Walsall Town Swifts)	2
Allen, A. 1888 (Aston Villa)	1
Allen, A. 1960 (Stoke C)	3
Allen, C. 1984 (QPR, Tottenham H)	5
Allen, H. 1888 (Wolverhampton W)	5
Allen, J. P. 1934 (Portsmouth)	2
Allen, R. 1952 (WBA)	5
Alsford, W. J. 1935 (Tottenham H)	1
Amos, A. 1885 (Old Carthusians)	2
Anderson, R. D. 1879 (Old Etonians)	1
Anderson, S. 1962 (Sunderland)	2
Anderson, V. A. 1979 (Nottingham F, Arsenal, Manchester U)	30
Anderton, D. R. 1994 (Tottenham H)	30
Angus, J. 1961 (Burnley)	1
Armfield, J. C. 1959 (Blackpool)	43
Armitage, G. H. 1926 (Charlton Ath)	1
Armstrong, D. 1980 (Middlesbrough, Southampton)	3
Armstrong, K. 1955 (Chelsea)	1
Arnold, J. 1933 (Fulham)	1
Arthur, J. W. H. 1885 (Blackburn R)	7
Ashcroft, J. 1906 (Woolwich Arsenal)	3
Ashmore, G. S. 1926 (WBA)	1
Ashton, C. T. 1926 (Corinthians)	1
Ashton, D. 2008 (West Ham U)	1
Ashurst, W. 1923 (Notts Co)	5
Astall, G. 1956 (Birmingham C)	2
Astle, J. 1969 (WBA)	5
Aston, J. E. 1949 (Manchester U)	17
Athersmith, W. C. 1892 (Aston Villa)	12
Atyeo, P. J. W. 1956 (Bristol C)	6
Austin, S. W. 1926 (Manchester C)	1
Bach, P. 1899 (Sunderland)	1
Bache, J. W. 1903 (Aston Villa)	7
Baddeley, T. 1903 (Wolverhampton W)	5
Bagshaw, J. J. 1920 (Derby Co)	1
Bailey, G. R. 1985 (Manchester U)	2
Bailey, H. P. 1908 (Leicester Fosse)	5
Bailey, M. A. 1964 (Charlton Ath)	2
Bailey, N. C. 1878 (Clapham Rovers)	19
Baily, E. F. 1950 (Tottenham H)	9
Bain, J. 1877 (Oxford University)	1
Baker, A. 1928 (Arsenal)	1
Baker, B. H. 1921 (Everton, Chelsea)	2
Baker, J. H. 1960 (Hibernian, Arsenal)	8
Ball, A. J. 1965 (Blackpool, Everton, Arsenal)	72
Ball, J. 1928 (Bury)	1
Ball, M. J. 2001 (Everton)	1
Balmer, W. 1905 (Everton)	1
Bamber, J. 1921 (Liverpool)	1
Bambridge, A. L. 1881 (Swifts)	3
Bambridge, E. C. 1879 (Swifts)	18
Bambridge, E. H. 1876 (Swifts)	1
Banks, G. 1963 (Leicester C, Stoke C)	73
Banks, H. E. 1901 (Millwall)	1
Banks, T. 1958 (Bolton W)	6
Bannister, W. 1901 (Burnley, Bolton W)	2
Barclay, R. 1932 (Sheffield U)	3

Bardsley, D. J. 1993 (QPR)	2
Barham, M. 1983 (Norwich C)	2
Barkas, S. 1936 (Manchester C)	5
Barker, J. 1935 (Derby Co)	11
Barker, R. 1872 (Herts Rangers)	1
Barker, R. R. 1895 (Casuals)	1
Barlow, R. J. 1955 (WBA)	1
Barmby, N. J. 1995 (Tottenham H, Middlesbrough, Everton, Liverpool)	23
Barnes, J. 1983 (Watford, Liverpool)	79
Barnes, P. S. 1978 (Manchester C, WBA, Leeds U)	22
Barnet, H. H. 1882 (Royal Engineers)	1
Barrass, M. W. 1952 (Bolton W)	3
Barrett, A. F. 1930 (Fulham)	1
Barrett, E. D. 1991 (Oldham Ath, Aston Villa)	3
Barrett, J. W. 1929 (West Ham U)	1
Barry, G. 2000 (Aston Villa)	30
Barry, L. 1928 (Leicester C)	5
Barson, F. 1920 (Aston Villa)	1
Barton, J. 1890 (Blackburn R)	1
Barton, J. 2007 (Manchester C)	1
Barton, P. H. 1921 (Birmingham)	7
Barton, W. D. 1995 (Wimbledon, Newcastle U)	3
Bassett, W. I. 1888 (WBA)	16
Bastard, S. R. 1880 (Upton Park)	1
Bastin, C. S. 1932 (Arsenal)	21
Batty, D. 1991 (Leeds U, Blackburn R, Newcastle U, Leeds U)	42
Baugh, R. 1886 (Stafford Road, Wolverhampton W)	2
Bayliss, A. E. J. M. 1891 (WBA)	1
Baynham, R. L. 1956 (Luton T)	3
Beardsley, P. A. 1986 (Newcastle U, Liverpool, Newcastle U)	59
Beasant, D. J. 1990 (Chelsea)	2
Beasley, A. 1939 (Huddersfield T)	1
Beats, W. E. 1901 (Wolverhampton W)	2
Beattie, J. S. 2003 (Southampton)	5
Beattie, T. K. 1975 (Ipswich T)	9
Beckham, D. R. J. 1997 (Manchester U, Real Madrid, LA Galaxy)	112
Becton, F. 1895 (Preston NE, Liverpool)	2
Bedford, H. 1923 (Blackpool)	2
Bell, C. 1968 (Manchester C)	48
Bennett, W. 1901 (Sheffield U)	2
Benson, R. W. 1913 (Sheffield U)	1
Bent, D. A. 2006 (Charlton Ath, Tottenham H)	4
Bentley, D. M. 2008 (Blackburn R, Tottenham H)	7
Bentley, R. T. F. 1949 (Chelsea)	12
Beresford, J. 1934 (Aston Villa)	1
Berry, A. 1909 (Oxford University)	1
Berry, J. J. 1953 (Manchester U)	4
Bestall, J. G. 1935 (Grimsby T)	1
Betmead, H. A. 1937 (Grimsby T)	1
Betts, M. P. 1877 (Old Harrovians)	1
Betts, W. 1889 (Sheffield W)	1
Beverley, J. 1884 (Blackburn R)	3
Birkett, R. H. 1879 (Clapham Rovers)	1
Birkett, R. J. E. 1936 (Middlesbrough)	1
Birley, F. H. 1874 (Oxford University, Wanderers)	2
Birtles, G. 1980 (Nottingham F)	3
Bishop, S. M. 1927 (Leicester C)	4
Blackburn, F. 1901 (Blackburn R)	3
Blackburn, G. F. 1924 (Aston Villa)	1
Blenkinsop, E. 1928 (Sheffield W)	26
Bliss, H. 1921 (Tottenham H)	1
Blissett, L. L. 1983 (Watford, AC Milan)	14

Blockley, J. P. 1973 (Arsenal)	1
Bloomer, S. 1895 (Derby Co, Middlesbrough)	23
Blunstone, F. 1955 (Chelsea)	5
Bond, R. 1905 (Preston NE, Bradford C)	8
Bonetti, P. P. 1966 (Chelsea)	7
Bonsor, A. G. 1873 (Wanderers)	2
Booth, F. 1905 (Manchester C)	1
Booth, T. 1898 (Blackburn R, Everton)	2
Bould, S. A. 1994 (Arsenal)	2
Bowden, E. R. 1935 (Arsenal)	6
Bower, A. G. 1924 (Corinthians)	5
Bowers, J. W. 1934 (Derby Co)	3
Bowles, S. 1974 (QPR)	5
Bowser, S. 1920 (WBA)	1
Bowyer, L. D. 2003 (Leeds U)	1
Boyer, P. J. 1976 (Norwich C)	1
Boyes, W. 1935 (WBA, Everton)	3
Boyle, T. W. 1913 (Burnley)	1
Brabrook, P. 1958 (Chelsea)	3
Bracewell, P. W. 1985 (Everton)	3
Bradford, G. R. W. 1956 (Bristol R)	1
Bradford, J. 1924 (Birmingham)	12
Bradley, W. 1959 (Manchester U)	3
Bradshaw, F. 1908 (Sheffield W)	1
Bradshaw, T. H. 1897 (Liverpool)	1
Bradshaw, W. 1910 (Blackburn R)	4
Brann, G. 1886 (Swifts)	3
Brawn, W. F. 1904 (Aston Villa)	2
Bray, J. 1935 (Manchester C)	6
Brayshaw, E. 1887 (Sheffield W)	1
Bridge W. M. 2002 (Southampton, Chelsea, Manchester C)	33
Bridges, B. J. 1965 (Chelsea)	4
Bridgett, A. 1905 (Sunderland)	11
Brindle, T. 1880 (Darwen)	2
Brittleton, J. T. 1912 (Sheffield W)	5
Britton, C. S. 1935 (Everton)	9
Broadbent, P. F. 1958 (Wolverhampton W)	7
Broadis, I. A. 1952 (Manchester C, Newcastle U)	14
Brockbank, J. 1872 (Cambridge University)	1
Brodie, J. B. 1889 (Wolverhampton W)	3
Bromilow, T. G. 1921 (Liverpool)	5
Bromley-Davenport, W. E. 1884 (Oxford University)	2
Brook, E. F. 1930 (Manchester C)	18
Brooking, T. D. 1974 (West Ham U)	47
Brooks, J. 1957 (Tottenham H)	3
Broome, F. H. 1938 (Aston Villa)	7
Brown, A. 1882 (Aston Villa)	3
Brown, A. 1971 (WBA)	1
Brown, A. S. 1904 (Sheffield U)	2
Brown, G. 1927 (Huddersfield T, Aston Villa)	9
Brown, J. 1881 (Blackburn R)	5
Brown, J. H. 1927 (Sheffield W)	6
Brown, K. 1960 (West Ham U)	1
Brown, W. 1924 (West Ham U)	1
Brown, W. M. 1999 (Manchester U)	21
Bruton, J. 1928 (Burnley)	3
Bryant, W. I. 1925 (Clapton)	1
Buchan, C. M. 1913 (Sunderland)	6
Buchanan, W. S. 1876 (Clapham R)	1
Buckley, F. C. 1914 (Derby Co)	1
Bull, S. G. 1989 (Wolverhampton W)	13
Bullock, F. E. 1921 (Huddersfield T)	1
Bullock, N. 1923 (Bury)	3
Burgess, H. 1904 (Manchester C)	4
Burgess, H. 1931 (Sheffield W)	4
Burnup, C. J. 1896 (Cambridge University)	1
Burrows, H. 1934 (Sheffield W)	3
Burton, F. E. 1889 (Nottingham F)	1
Bury, L. 1877 (Cambridge University, Old Etonians)	2
Butcher, T. 1980 (Ipswich T, Rangers)	77
Butler, J. D. 1925 (Arsenal)	1
Butler, W. 1924 (Bolton W)	1
Butt, N. 1997 (Manchester U, Newcastle U)	39
Byrne, G. 1963 (Liverpool)	2

Byrne, J. J. 1962 (C Palace, West Ham U)	11
Byrne, R. W. 1954 (Manchester U)	33
Callaghan, I. R. 1966 (Liverpool)	4
Calvey, J. 1902 (Nottingham F)	1
Campbell, A. F. 1929 (Blackburn R, Huddersfield T)	8
Campbell, S. 1996 (Tottenham H, Arsenal, Portsmouth)	73
Camsell, G. H. 1929 (Middlesbrough)	9
Capes, A. J. 1903 (Stoke)	1
Carr, J. 1905 (Newcastle U)	2
Carr, J. 1920 (Middlesbrough)	2
Carr, W. H. 1875 (Owlerton, Sheffield)	1
Carragher, J. L. 1999 (Liverpool)	34
Carrick, M. 2001 (West Ham U, Tottenham H, Manchester U)	17
Carson, S. P. 2008 (Liverpool, WBA)	3
Carter, H. S. 1934 (Sunderland, Derby Co)	13
Carter, J. H. 1926 (WBA)	3
Catlin, A. E. 1937 (Sheffield W)	5
Chadwick, A. 1900 (Southampton)	2
Chadwick, E. 1891 (Everton)	7
Chamberlain, M. 1983 (Stoke C)	8
Chambers, H. 1921 (Liverpool)	8
Channon, M. R. 1973 (Southampton, Manchester C)	46
Charles, G. A. 1991 (Nottingham F)	2
Charlton, J. 1965 (Leeds U)	35
Charlton, R. 1958 (Manchester U)	106
Charnley, R. O. 1963 (Blackpool)	1
Charsley, C. C. 1893 (Small Heath)	1
Chedgzoy, S. 1920 (Everton)	8
Chenery, C. J. 1872 (C Palace)	3
Cherry, T. J. 1976 (Leeds U)	27
Chilton, A. 1951 (Manchester U)	2
Chippendale, H. 1894 (Blackburn R)	1
Chivers, M. 1971 (Tottenham H)	24
Christian, E. 1879 (Old Etonians)	1
Clamp, E. 1958 (Wolverhampton W)	4
Clapton, D. R. 1959 (Arsenal)	1
Clare, T. 1889 (Stoke)	4
Clarke, A. J. 1970 (Leeds U)	19
Clarke, H. A. 1954 (Tottenham H)	1
Clay, T. 1920 (Tottenham H)	4
Clayton, R. 1956 (Blackburn R)	35
Clegg, J. C. 1872 (Sheffield W)	1
Clegg, W. E. 1873 (Sheffield W, Sheffield Albion)	2
Clemence, R. N. 1973 (Liverpool, Tottenham H)	61
Clement, D. T. 1976 (QPR)	5
Clough, B. H. 1960 (Middlesbrough)	2
Clough, N. H. 1989 (Nottingham F)	14
Coates, R. 1970 (Burnley, Tottenham H)	4
Cobbold, W. N. 1883 (Cambridge University, Old Carthusians)	9
Cock, J. G. 1920 (Huddersfield T, Chelsea)	2
Cockburn, H. 1947 (Manchester U)	13
Cohen, G. R. 1964 (Fulham)	37
Cole, A. 2001 (Arsenal, Chelsea)	73
Cole, A. A. 1995 (Manchester U)	15
Cole, C. 2009 (West Ham U)	2
Cole, J. J. 2001 (West Ham U, Chelsea)	53
Colclough, H. 1914 (C Palace)	1
Coleman, E. H. 1921 (Dulwich Hamlet)	1
Coleman, J. 1907 (Woolwich Arsenal)	1
Collymore, S. V. 1995 (Nottingham F, Aston Villa)	3
Common, A. 1904 (Sheffield U, Middlesbrough)	3
Compton, L. H. 1951 (Arsenal)	2
Conlin, J. 1906 (Bradford C)	1
Connelly, J. M. 1960 (Burnley, Manchester U)	20
Cook, T. E. R. 1925 (Brighton)	1
Cooper, C. T. 1995 (Nottingham F)	2
Cooper, N. C. 1893 (Cambridge University)	1
Cooper, T. 1928 (Derby Co)	15
Cooper, T. 1969 (Leeds U)	20
Coppell, S. J. 1978 (Manchester U)	42
Copping, W. 1933 (Leeds U, Arsenal, Leeds U)	20

Corbett, B. O. 1901 (Corinthians)	1
Corbett, R. 1903 (Old Malvernians)	1
Corbett, W. S. 1908 (Birmingham)	3
Corrigan, J. T. 1976 (Manchester C)	9
Cottee, A. R. 1987 (West Ham U, Everton)	7
Cotterill, G. H. 1891 (Cambridge University, Old Brightonians)	4
Cottle, J. R. 1909 (Bristol C)	1
Cowan, S. 1926 (Manchester C)	3
Cowans, G. S. 1983 (Aston Villa, Bari, Aston Villa)	10
Cowell, A. 1910 (Blackburn R)	1
Cox, J. 1901 (Liverpool)	3
Cox, J. D. 1892 (Derby Co)	1
Crabtree, J. W. 1894 (Burnley, Aston Villa)	14
Crawford, J. F. 1931 (Chelsea)	1
Crawford, R. 1962 (Ipswich T)	2
Crawshaw, T. H. 1895 (Sheffield W)	10
Crayston, W. J. 1936 (Arsenal)	8
Creek, F. N. S. 1923 (Corinthians)	1
Cresswell, W. 1921 (South Shields, Sunderland, Everton)	7
Crompton, R. 1902 (Blackburn R)	41
Crooks, S. D. 1930 (Derby Co)	26
Crouch, P. J. 2005 (Southampton, Liverpool, Portsmouth)	34
Crowe, C. 1963 (Wolverhampton W)	1
Cuggy, F. 1913 (Sunderland)	2
Cullis, S. 1938 (Wolverhampton W)	12
Cunliffe, A. 1933 (Blackburn R)	2
Cunliffe, D. 1900 (Portsmouth)	1
Cunliffe, J. N. 1936 (Everton)	1
Cunningham, L. 1979 (WBA, Real Madrid)	6
Curle, K. 1992 (Manchester C)	3
Currey, E. S. 1890 (Oxford University)	2
Currie, A. W. 1972 (Sheffield U, Leeds U)	17
Cursham, A. W. 1876 (Notts Co)	6
Cursham, H. A. 1880 (Notts Co)	8
Daft, H. B. 1889 (Notts Co)	5
Daley, A. M. 1992 (Aston Villa)	7
Danks, T. 1885 (Nottingham F)	1
Davenport, P. 1985 (Nottingham F)	1
Davenport, J. K. 1885 (Bolton W)	2
Davis, G. 1904 (Derby Co)	2
Davis, H. 1903 (Sheffield W)	3
Davison, J. E. 1922 (Sheffield W)	1
Dawson, J. 1922 (Burnley)	2
Day, S. H. 1906 (Old Malvernians)	3
Dean, W. R. 1927 (Everton)	16
Deane, B. C. 1991 (Sheffield U)	3
Deeley, N. V. 1959 (Wolverhampton W)	2
Defoe, J. C. 2004 (Tottenham H, Portsmouth, Tottenham H)	34
Devey, J. H. G. 1892 (Aston Villa)	2
Devonshire, A. 1980 (West Ham U)	8
Dewhurst, F. 1886 (Preston NE)	9
Dewhurst, G. P. 1895 (Liverpool Ramblers)	1
Dickinson, J. W. 1949 (Portsmouth)	48
Dimmock, J. H. 1921 (Tottenham H)	3
Ditchburn, E. G. 1949 (Tottenham H)	6
Dix, R. W. 1939 (Derby Co)	1
Dixon, J. A. 1885 (Notts Co)	1
Dixon, K. M. 1985 (Chelsea)	8
Dixon, L. M. 1990 (Arsenal)	22
Dobson, A. T. C. 1882 (Notts Co)	4
Dobson, C. F. 1886 (Notts Co)	1
Dobson, J. M. 1974 (Burnley, Everton)	5
Doggart, A. G. 1924 (Corinthians)	1
Dorigo, A. R. 1990 (Chelsea, Leeds U)	15
Dorrell, A. R. 1925 (Aston Villa)	4
Douglas, B. 1958 (Blackburn R)	36
Downing, S. 2005 (Middlesbrough)	23
Downs, R. W. 1921 (Everton)	1
Doyle, M. 1976 (Manchester C)	5
Drake, E. J. 1935 (Arsenal)	5

Dublin, D. 1998 (Coventry C, Aston Villa)	4
Ducat, A. 1910 (Woolwich Arsenal, Aston Villa)	6
Dunn, A. T. B. 1883 (Cambridge University, Old Etonians)	4
Dunn, D. J. I. 2003 (Blackburn R)	1
Duxbury, M. 1984 (Manchester U)	10
Dyer, K. C. 2000 (Newcastle U, West Ham U)	33
Earle, S. G. J. 1924 (Clapton, West Ham U)	2
Eastham, G. 1963 (Arsenal)	19
Eastham, G. R. 1935 (Bolton W)	1
Eckersley, W. 1950 (Blackburn R)	17
Edwards, D. 1955 (Manchester U)	18
Edwards, J. H. 1874 (Shropshire Wanderers)	1
Edwards, W. 1926 (Leeds U)	16
Ehiogu, U. 1996 (Aston Villa, Middlesbrough)	4
Ellerington, W. 1949 (Southampton)	2
Elliott, G. W. 1913 (Middlesbrough)	3
Elliott, W. H. 1952 (Burnley)	5
Evans, R. E. 1911 (Sheffield U)	4
Ewer, F. H. 1924 (Casuals)	2
Fairclough, P. 1878 (Old Foresters)	1
Fairhurst, D. 1934 (Newcastle U)	1
Fantham, J. 1962 (Sheffield W)	1
Fashanu, J. 1989 (Wimbledon)	2
Felton, W. 1925 (Sheffield W)	1
Fenton, M. 1938 (Middlesbrough)	1
Fenwick, T. W. 1984 (QPR, Tottenham H)	20
Ferdinand, L. 1993 (QPR, Newcastle U, Tottenham H)	17
Ferdinand, R. G. 1998 (West Ham U, Leeds U, Manchester U)	73
Field, E. 1876 (Clapham Rovers)	2
Finney, T. 1947 (Preston NE)	76
Fleming, H. J. 1909 (Swindon T)	11
Fletcher, A. 1889 (Wolverhampton W)	2
Flowers, R. 1955 (Wolverhampton W)	49
Flowers, T. D. 1993 (Southampton, Blackburn R)	11
Forman, Frank 1898 (Nottingham F)	9
Forman, F. R. 1899 (Nottingham F)	3
Forrest, J. H. 1884 (Blackburn R)	11
Fort, J. 1921 (Millwall)	1
Foster, B. 2007 (Manchester U)	2
Foster, R. E. 1900 (Oxford University, Corinthians)	5
Foster, S. 1982 (Brighton & HA)	3
Foulke, W. J. 1897 (Sheffield U)	1
Foulkes, W. A. 1955 (Manchester U)	1
Fowler, R. B. 1996 (Liverpool, Leeds U)	26
Fox, F. S. 1925 (Millwall)	1
Francis, G. C. J. 1975 (QPR)	12
Francis, T. 1977 (Birmingham C, Nottingham F, Manchester C, Sampdoria)	52
Franklin, C. F. 1947 (Stoke C)	27
Freeman, B. C. 1909 (Everton, Burnley)	5
Froggatt, J. 1950 (Portsmouth)	13
Froggatt, R. 1953 (Sheffield W)	4
Fry, C. B. 1901 (Corinthians)	1
Furness, W. I. 1933 (Leeds U)	1
Galley, T. 1937 (Wolverhampton W)	2
Gardner, A. 2004 (Tottenham H)	1
Gardner, T. 1934 (Aston Villa)	2
Garfield, B. 1898 (WBA)	1
Garraty, W. 1903 (Aston Villa)	1
Garrett, T. 1952 (Blackpool)	3
Gascoigne, P. J. 1989 (Tottenham H, Lazio, Rangers, Middlesbrough)	57
Gates, E. 1981 (Ipswich T)	2
Gay, L. H. 1893 (Cambridge University, Old Brightonians)	3
Geary, F. 1890 (Everton)	2
Geaves, R. L. 1875 (Clapham Rovers)	1
Gee, C. W. 1932 (Everton)	3
Geldard, A. 1933 (Everton)	4

George, C. 1977 (Derby Co)	1	Hall, J. 1956 (Birmingham C)	17
George, W. 1902 (Aston Villa)	3	Halse, H. J. 1909 (Manchester U)	1
Gerrard, S. G. 2000 (Liverpool)	74	Hammond, H. E. D. 1889 (Oxford University)	1
Gibbins, W. V. T. 1924 (Clapton)	2	Hampson, J. 1931 (Blackpool)	3
Gidman, J. 1977 (Aston Villa)	1	Hampton, H. 1913 (Aston Villa)	4
Gillard, I. T. 1975 (QPR)	3	Hancocks, J. 1949 (Wolverhampton W)	3
Gilliat, W. E. 1893 (Old Carthusians)	1	Hapgood, E. 1933 (Arsenal)	30
Goddard, P. 1982 (West Ham U)	1	Hardinge, H. T. W. 1910 (Sheffield U)	1
Goodall, F. R. 1926 (Huddersfield T)	25	Hardman, H. P. 1905 (Everton)	4
Goodall, J. 1888 (Preston NE, Derby Co)	14	Hardwick, G. F. M. 1947 (Middlesbrough)	13
Goodhart, H. C. 1883 (Old Etonians)	3	Hardy, H. 1925 (Stockport Co)	1
Goodwyn, A. G. 1873 (Royal Engineers)	1	Hardy, S. 1907 (Liverpool, Aston Villa)	21
Goodyer, A. C. 1879 (Nottingham F)	1	Harford, M. G. 1988 (Luton T)	2
Gosling, R. C. 1892 (Old Etonians)	5	Hargreaves, F. W. 1880 (Blackburn R)	3
Gosnell, A. A. 1906 (Newcastle U)	1	Hargreaves, J. 1881 (Blackburn R)	2
Gough, H. C. 1921 (Sheffield U)	1	Hargreaves, O. 2002 (Bayern Munich, Manchester U)	42
Goulden, L. A. 1937 (West Ham U)	14	Harper, E. C. 1926 (Blackburn R)	1
Graham, L. 1925 (Millwall)	2	Harris, G. 1966 (Burnley)	1
Graham, T. 1931 (Nottingham F)	2	Harris, P. P. 1950 (Portsmouth)	2
Grainger, C. 1956 (Sheffield U, Sunderland)	7	Harris, S. S. 1904 (Cambridge University,	
Gray, A. A. 1992 (C Palace)	1	Old Westminsters)	6
Gray, M. 1999 (Sunderland)	3	Harrison, A. H. 1893 (Old Westminsters)	2
Greaves, J. 1959 (Chelsea, Tottenham H)	57	Harrison, G. 1921 (Everton)	2
Green, F. T. 1876 (Wanderers)	1	Harrow, J. H. 1923 (Chelsea)	2
Green, G. H. 1925 (Sheffield U)	8	Hart, C. 2008 (Manchester C)	1
Green, R. P. 2005 (Norwich C, West Ham U)	4	Hart, E. 1929 (Leeds U)	8
Greenhalgh, E. H. 1872 (Notts Co)	2	Hartley, F. 1923 (Oxford C)	1
Greenhoff, B. 1976 (Manchester U, Leeds U)	18	Harvey, A. 1881 (Wednesbury Strollers)	1
Greenwood, D. H. 1882 (Blackburn R)	2	Harvey, J. C. 1971 (Everton)	1
Gregory, J. 1983 (QPR)	6	Hassall, H. W. 1951 (Huddersfield T, Bolton W)	5
Grimsdell, A. 1920 (Tottenham H)	6	Hateley, M. 1984 (Portsmouth, AC Milan, Monaco,	
Grosvenor, A. T. 1934 (Birmingham)	3	Rangers)	32
Gunn, W. 1884 (Notts Co)	2	Hawkes, R. M. 1907 (Luton T)	5
Guppy, S. 2000 (Leicester C)	1	Haworth, G. 1887 (Accrington)	5
Gurney, R. 1935 (Sunderland)	1	Hawtrey, J. P. 1881 (Old Etonians)	2
		Haygarth, E. B. 1875 (Swifts)	1
Hacking, J. 1929 (Oldham Ath)	3	Haynes, J. N. 1955 (Fulham)	56
Hadley, H. 1903 (WBA)	1	Healless, H. 1925 (Blackburn R)	2
Hagan, J. 1949 (Sheffield U)	1	Hector, K. J. 1974 (Derby Co)	2
Haines, J. T. W. 1949 (WBA)	1	Hedley, G. A. 1901 (Sheffield U)	1
Hall, A. E. 1910 (Aston Villa)	1	Hegan, K. E. 1923 (Corinthians)	4
Hall, G. W. 1934 (Tottenham H)	10	Hellawell, M. S. 1963 (Birmingham C)	2

England and Liverpool star Steven Gerrard receives the Football Writers' Association player of the season award for 2008–09. (Action Images/Matthew Childs)

Hendrie, L. A. 1999 (Aston Villa) 1
Henfrey, A. G. 1891 (Cambridge University,
  Corinthians) 5
Henry, R. P. 1963 (Tottenham H) 1
Heron, F. 1876 (Wanderers) 1
Heron, G. H. H. 1873 (Uxbridge, Wanderers) 5
Heskey, E. W. I. 1999 (Leicester C, Liverpool,
  Birmingham C, Wigan Ath, Aston Villa) 53
Hibbert, W. 1910 (Bury) 1
Hibbs, H. E. 1930 (Birmingham) 25
Hill, F. 1963 (Bolton W) 2
Hill, G. A. 1976 (Manchester U) 6
Hill, J. H. 1925 (Burnley, Newcastle U) 11
Hill, R. 1983 (Luton T) 3
Hill, R. H. 1926 (Millwall) 1
Hillman, J. 1899 (Burnley) 1
Hills, A. F. 1879 (Old Harrovians) 1
Hilsdon, G. R. 1907 (Chelsea) 8
Hinchcliffe, A. G. 1997 (Everton, Sheffield W) 7
Hine, E. W. 1929 (Leicester C) 6
Hinton, A. T. 1963 (Wolverhampton W, Nottingham F)
  3
Hirst, D. E. 1991 (Sheffield W) 3
Hitchens, G. A. 1961 (Aston Villa, Internazionale) 7
Hobbis, H. H. F. 1936 (Charlton Ath) 2
Hoddle, G. 1980 (Tottenham H, Monaco) 53
Hodge, S. B. 1986 (Aston Villa, Tottenham H,
  Nottingham F) 24
Hodgetts, D. 1888 (Aston Villa) 6
Hodgkinson, A. 1957 (Sheffield U) 5
Hodgson, G. 1931 (Liverpool) 3
Hodkinson, J. 1913 (Blackburn R) 3
Hogg, W. 1902 (Sunderland) 3
Holdcroft, G. H. 1937 (Preston NE) 2
Holden, A. D. 1959 (Bolton W) 5
Holden, G. H. 1881 (Wednesbury OA) 4
Holden-White, C. 1888 (Corinthians) 2
Holford, T. 1903 (Stoke) 1
Holley, G. H. 1909 (Sunderland) 10
Holliday, E. 1960 (Middlesbrough) 3
Hollins, J. W. 1967 (Chelsea) 1
Holmes, R. 1888 (Preston NE) 7
Holt, J. 1890 (Everton, Reading) 10
Hopkinson, E. 1958 (Bolton W) 14
Hossack, A. H. 1892 (Corinthians) 2
Houghton, W. E. 1931 (Aston Villa) 7
Houlker, A. E. 1902 (Blackburn R, Portsmouth,
  Southampton) 5
Howarth, R. H. 1887 (Preston NE, Everton) 5
Howe, D. 1958 (WBA) 23
Howe, J. R. 1948 (Derby Co) 3
Howell, L. S. 1873 (Wanderers) 1
Howell, R. 1895 (Sheffield U, Liverpool) 2
Howey, S. N. 1995 (Newcastle U) 4
Hudson, A. A. 1975 (Stoke C) 2
Hudson, J. 1883 (Sheffield) 1
Hudspeth, F. C. 1926 (Newcastle U) 1
Hufton, A. E. 1924 (West Ham U) 6
Hughes, E. W. 1970 (Liverpool, Wolverhampton W) 62
Hughes, L. 1950 (Liverpool) 3
Hulme, J. H. A. 1927 (Arsenal) 9
Humphreys, P. 1903 (Notts Co) 1
Hunt, G. S. 1933 (Tottenham H) 3
Hunt, Rev. K. R. G. 1911 (Leyton) 2
Hunt, R. 1962 (Liverpool) 34
Hunt, S. 1984 (WBA) 2
Hunter, J. 1878 (Sheffield Heeley) 7
Hunter, N. 1966 (Leeds U) 28
Hurst, G. C. 1966 (West Ham U) 49

Ince, P. E. C. 1993 (Manchester U, Internazionale,
  Liverpool, Middlesbrough) 53
Iremonger, J. 1901 (Nottingham F) 2

Jack, D. N. B. 1924 (Bolton W, Arsenal) 9

Jackson, E. 1891 (Oxford University) 1
Jagielka, P. N. 2008 (Everton) 3
James, D. B. 1997 (Liverpool, Aston Villa, West Ham U,
  Manchester C, Portsmouth) 48
Jarrett, B. G. 1876 (Cambridge University) 3
Jefferis, F. 1912 (Everton) 2
Jeffers, F. 2003 (Arsenal) 1
Jenas, J. A. 2003 (Newcastle U, Tottenham H) 20
Jezzard, B. A. G. 1954 (Fulham) 2
Johnson, A. 2005 (C Palace, Everton) 8
Johnson, D. E. 1975 (Ipswich T, Liverpool) 8
Johnson, E. 1880 (Saltley College, Stoke) 2
Johnson, G. M. C. 2004 (Chelsea, Portsmouth) 15
Johnson, J. A. 1937 (Stoke C) 5
Johnson, S. A. M. 2001 (Derby Co) 1
Johnson, T. C. F. 1926 (Manchester C, Everton) 5
Johnson, W. H. 1900 (Sheffield U) 6
Johnston, H. 1947 (Blackpool) 10
Jones, A. 1882 (Walsall Swifts, Great Lever) 3
Jones, H. 1923 (Nottingham F) 1
Jones, H. 1927 (Blackburn R) 6
Jones, M. D. 1965 (Sheffield U, Leeds U) 3
Jones, R. 1992 (Liverpool) 8
Jones, W. 1901 (Bristol C) 1
Jones, W. H. 1950 (Liverpool) 2
Joy, B. 1936 (Casuals) 1

Kail, E. I. L. 1929 (Dulwich Hamlet) 3
Kay, A. H. 1963 (Everton) 1
Kean, F. W. 1923 (Sheffield W, Bolton W) 9
Keegan, J. K. 1973 (Liverpool, SV Hamburg,
  Southampton) 63
Keen, E. R. L. 1933 (Derby Co) 4
Kelly, R. 1920 (Burnley, Sunderland, Huddersfield T) 14
Kennedy, A. 1984 (Liverpool) 2
Kennedy, R. 1976 (Liverpool) 17
Kenyon-Slaney, W. S. 1873 (Wanderers) 1
Keown, M. R. 1992 (Everton, Arsenal) 43
Kevan, D. T. 1957 (WBA) 14
Kidd, B. 1970 (Manchester U) 2
King, L. B. 2002 (Tottenham H) 19
King, R. S. 1882 (Oxford University) 1
Kingsford, R. K. 1874 (Wanderers) 1
Kingsley, M. 1901 (Newcastle U) 1
Kinsey, G. 1892 (Wolverhampton W, Derby Co) 4
Kirchen, A. J. 1937 (Arsenal) 3
Kirkland, C. E. 2007 (Liverpool) 1
Kirton, W. J. 1922 (Aston Villa) 1
Knight, A. E. 1920 (Portsmouth) 1
Knight, Z. 2005 (Fulham) 2
Knowles, C. 1968 (Tottenham H) 4
Konchesky, P. M. 2003 (Charlton Ath, West Ham U) 2

Labone, B. L. 1963 (Everton) 26
Lampard, F. J. 2000 (West Ham U, Chelsea) 71
Lampard, F. R. G. 1973 (West Ham U) 2
Langley, E. J. 1958 (Fulham) 3
Langton, R. 1947 (Blackburn R, Preston NE, Bolton W)
  11
Latchford, R. D. 1978 (Everton) 12
Latheron, E. G. 1913 (Blackburn R) 2
Lawler, C. 1971 (Liverpool) 4
Lawton, T. 1939 (Everton, Chelsea, Notts Co) 23
Leach, T. 1931 (Sheffield W) 2
Leake, A. 1904 (Aston Villa) 5
Lee, E. A. 1904 (Southampton) 1
Lee, F. H. 1969 (Manchester C) 27
Lee, J. 1951 (Derby Co) 1
Lee, R. M. 1995 (Newcastle U) 21
Lee, S. 1983 (Liverpool) 14
Leighton, J. E. 1886 (Nottingham F) 1
Lennon, A. J. 2006 (Tottenham H) 11
Lescott, J. P. 2008 (Everton) 7
Le Saux, G. P. 1994 (Blackburn R, Chelsea) 36
Le Tissier, M. P. 1994 (Southampton) 8

Lilley, H. E. 1892 (Sheffield U)	1	Middleditch, B. 1897 (Corinthians)	1
Linacre, H. J. 1905 (Nottingham F)	2	Milburn, J. E. T. 1949 (Newcastle U)	13
Lindley, T. 1886 (Cambridge University, Nottingham F)		Miller, B. G. 1961 (Burnley)	1
	13	Miller, H. S. 1923 (Charlton Ath)	1
Lindsay, A. 1974 (Liverpool)	4	Mills, D. J. 2001 (Leeds U)	19
Lindsay, W. 1877 (Wanderers)	1	Mills, G. R. 1938 (Chelsea)	3
Lineker, G. 1984 (Leicester C, Everton, Barcelona,		Mills, M. D. 1973 (Ipswich T)	42
Tottenham H)	80	Milne, G. 1963 (Liverpool)	14
Lintott, E. H. 1908 (QPR, Bradford C)	7	Milton, C. A. 1952 (Arsenal)	1
Lipsham, H. B. 1902 (Sheffield U)	1	Milward, A. 1891 (Everton)	4
Little, B. 1975 (Aston Villa)	1	Mitchell, C. 1880 (Upton Park)	5
Lloyd, L. V. 1971 (Liverpool, Nottingham F)	4	Mitchell, J. F. 1925 (Manchester C)	1
Lockett, A. 1903 (Stoke)	1	Moffat, H. 1913 (Oldham Ath)	1
Lodge, L. V. 1894 (Cambridge University, Corinthians)		Molyneux, G. 1902 (Southampton)	4
	5	Moon, W. R. 1888 (Old Westminsters)	7
Lofthouse, J. M. 1885 (Blackburn R, Accrington,		Moore, H. T. 1883 (Notts Co)	2
Blackburn R)	7	Moore, J. 1923 (Derby Co)	1
Lofthouse, N. 1951 (Bolton W)	33	Moore, R. F. 1962 (West Ham U)	108
Longworth, E. 1920 (Liverpool)	5	Moore, W. G. B. 1923 (West Ham U)	1
Lowder, A. 1889 (Wolverhampton W)	1	Mordue, J. 1912 (Sunderland)	2
Lowe, E. 1947 (Aston Villa)	3	Morice, C. J. 1872 (Barnes)	1
Lucas, T. 1922 (Liverpool)	3	Morley, A. 1982 (Aston Villa)	6
Luntley, E. 1880 (Nottingham F)	2	Morley, H. 1910 (Notts Co)	1
Lyttelton, Hon. A. 1877 (Cambridge University)	1	Morren, T. 1898 (Sheffield U)	1
Lyttelton, Hon. E. 1878 (Cambridge University)	1	Morris, F. 1920 (WBA)	2
		Morris, J. 1949 (Derby Co)	3
Mabbutt, G. 1983 (Tottenham H)	16	Morris, W. W. 1939 (Wolverhampton W)	3
Macaulay, R. H. 1881 (Cambridge University)	1	Morse, H. 1879 (Notts Co)	1
McCall, J. 1913 (Preston NE)	5	Mort, T. 1924 (Aston Villa)	3
McCann, G. P. 2001 (Sunderland)	1	Morten, A. 1873 (C Palace)	1
McDermott, T. 1978 (Liverpool)	25	Mortensen, S. H. 1947 (Blackpool)	25
McDonald, C. A. 1958 (Burnley)	8	Morton, J. R. 1938 (West Ham U)	1
Macdonald, M. 1972 (Newcastle U)	14	Mosforth, W. 1877 (Sheffield W, Sheffield Albion,	
McFarland, R. L. 1971 (Derby Co)	28	Sheffield W)	9
McGarry, W. H. 1954 (Huddersfield T)	4	Moss, F. 1922 (Aston Villa)	5
McGuinness, W. 1959 (Manchester U)	2	Moss, F. 1934 (Arsenal)	4
McInroy, A. 1927 (Sunderland)	1	Mosscrop, E. 1914 (Burnley)	2
McMahon, S. 1988 (Liverpool)	17	Mozley, D. 1950 (Derby Co)	3
McManaman, S. 1995 (Liverpool, Real Madrid)	37	Mullen, J. 1947 (Wolverhampton W)	12
McNab, R. 1969 (Arsenal)	4	Mullery, A. P. 1965 (Tottenham H)	35
McNeal, R. 1914 (WBA)	2	Murphy, D. B. 2002 (Liverpool)	9
McNeil, M. 1961 (Middlesbrough)	9		
Macrae, S. 1883 (Notts Co)	5	Neal, P. G. 1976 (Liverpool)	50
Maddison, F. B. 1872 (Oxford University)	1	Needham, E. 1894 (Sheffield U)	16
Madeley, P. E. 1971 (Leeds U)	24	Neville, G. A. 1995 (Manchester U)	85
Magee, T. P. 1923 (WBA)	5	Neville, P. J. 1996 (Manchester U, Everton)	59
Makepeace, H. 1906 (Everton)	4	Newton, K. R. 1966 (Blackburn R, Everton)	27
Male, C. G. 1935 (Arsenal)	19	Nicholls, J. 1954 (WBA)	2
Mannion, W. J. 1947 (Middlesbrough)	26	Nicholson, W. E. 1951 (Tottenham H)	1
Mariner, P. 1977 (Ipswich T, Arsenal)	35	Nish, D. J. 1973 (Derby Co)	5
Marsden, J. T. 1891 (Darwen)	1	Norman, M. 1962 (Tottenham H)	23
Marsden, W. 1930 (Sheffield W)	3	Nugent, D. J. 2007 (Preston NE)	1
Marsh, R. W. 1972 (QPR, Manchester C)	9	Nuttall, H. 1928 (Bolton W)	3
Marshall, T. 1880 (Darwen)	2		
Martin, A. 1981 (West Ham U)	17	Oakley, W. J. 1895 (Oxford University, Corinthians)	16
Martin, H. 1914 (Sunderland)	1	O'Dowd, J. P. 1932 (Chelsea)	3
Martyn, A. N. 1992 (C Palace, Leeds U)	23	O'Grady, M. 1963 (Huddersfield T, Leeds U)	2
Marwood, B. 1989 (Arsenal)	1	Ogilvie, R. A. M. M. 1874 (Clapham R)	1
Maskrey, H. M. 1908 (Derby Co)	1	Oliver, L. F. 1929 (Fulham)	1
Mason, C. 1887 (Wolverhampton W)	3	Olney, B. A. 1928 (Aston Villa)	2
Matthews, R. D. 1956 (Coventry C)	5	Osborne, F. R. 1923 (Fulham, Tottenham H)	4
Matthews, S. 1935 (Stoke C, Blackpool)	54	Osborne, R. 1928 (Leicester C)	1
Matthews, V. 1928 (Sheffield U)	2	Osgood, P. L. 1970 (Chelsea)	4
Maynard, W. J. 1872 (1st Surrey Rifles)	2	Osman, R. 1980 (Ipswich T)	11
Meadows, J. 1955 (Manchester C)	1	Ottaway, C. J. 1872 (Oxford University)	2
Medley, L. D. 1951 (Tottenham H)	6	Owen, J. R. B. 1874 (Sheffield)	1
Meehan, T. 1924 (Chelsea)	1	Owen, M. J. 1998 (Liverpool, Real Madrid, Newcastle U)	
Melia, J. 1963 (Liverpool)	2		89
Mercer, D. W. 1923 (Sheffield U)	2	Owen, S. W. 1954 (Luton T)	3
Mercer, J. 1939 (Everton)	5		
Merrick, G. H. 1952 (Birmingham C)	23	Page, L. A. 1927 (Burnley)	7
Merson, P. C. 1992 (Arsenal, Middlesbrough,		Paine, T. L. 1963 (Southampton)	19
Aston Villa)	21	Pallister, G. A. 1988 (Middlesbrough, Manchester U)	22
Metcalfe, V. 1951 (Huddersfield T)	2	Palmer, C. L. 1992 (Sheffield W)	18
Mew, J. W. 1921 (Manchester U)	1	Pantling, H. H. 1924 (Sheffield U)	1

Paravicini, P. J. de 1883 (Cambridge University)	3
Parker, P. A. 1989 (QPR, Manchester U)	19
Parker, S. M. 2004 (Charlton Ath, Chelsea, Newcastle U)	3
Parker, T. R. 1925 (Southampton)	1
Parkes, P. B. 1974 (QPR)	1
Parkinson, J. 1910 (Liverpool)	2
Parlour, R. 1999 (Arsenal)	10
Parr, P. C. 1882 (Oxford University)	1
Parry, E. H. 1879 (Old Carthusians)	3
Parry, R. A. 1960 (Bolton W)	2
Patchitt, B. C. A. 1923 (Corinthians)	2
Pawson, F. W. 1883 (Cambridge University, Swifts)	2
Payne, J. 1937 (Luton T)	1
Peacock, A. 1962 (Middlesbrough, Leeds U)	6
Peacock, J. 1929 (Middlesbrough)	3
Pearce, S. 1987 (Nottingham F, West Ham U)	78
Pearson, H. F. 1932 (WBA)	1
Pearson, J. H. 1892 (Crewe Alex)	1
Pearson, J. S. 1976 (Manchester U)	15
Pearson, S. C. 1948 (Manchester U)	8
Pease, W. H. 1927 (Middlesbrough)	1
Pegg, D. 1957 (Manchester U)	1
Pejic, M. 1974 (Stoke C)	4
Pelly, F. R. 1893 (Old Foresters)	3
Pennington, J. 1907 (WBA)	25
Pentland, F. B. 1909 (Middlesbrough)	5
Perry, C. 1890 (WBA)	3
Perry, T. 1898 (WBA)	1
Perry, W. 1956 (Blackpool)	3
Perryman, S. 1982 (Tottenham H)	1
Peters, M. 1966 (West Ham U, Tottenham H)	67
Phelan, M. C. 1990 (Manchester U)	1
Phillips, K. 1999 (Sunderland)	8
Phillips, L. H. 1952 (Portsmouth)	3
Pickering, F. 1964 (Everton)	3
Pickering, J. 1933 (Sheffield U)	1
Pickering, N. 1983 (Sunderland)	1
Pike, T. M. 1886 (Cambridge University)	1
Pilkington, B. 1955 (Burnley)	1
Plant, J. 1900 (Bury)	1
Platt, D. 1990 (Aston Villa, Bari, Juventus, Sampdoria, Arsenal)	62
Plum, S. L. 1923 (Charlton Ath)	1
Pointer, R. 1962 (Burnley)	3
Porteous, T. S. 1891 (Sunderland)	1
Powell, C. G. 2001 (Charlton Ath)	5
Priest, A. E. 1900 (Sheffield U)	1
Prinsep, J. F. M. 1879 (Clapham Rovers)	1
Puddefoot, S. C. 1926 (Blackburn R)	2
Pye, J. 1950 (Wolverhampton W)	1
Pym, R. H. 1925 (Bolton W)	3
Quantrill, A. 1920 (Derby Co)	4
Quixall, A. 1954 (Sheffield W)	5
Radford, J. 1969 (Arsenal)	2
Raikes, G. B. 1895 (Oxford University)	4
Ramsey, A. E. 1949 (Southampton, Tottenham H)	32
Rawlings, A. 1921 (Preston NE)	1
Rawlings, W. E. 1922 (Southampton)	2
Rawlinson, J. F. P. 1882 (Cambridge University)	1
Rawson, H. E. 1875 (Royal Engineers)	1
Rawson, W. S. 1875 (Oxford University)	2
Read, A. 1921 (Tufnell Park)	1
Reader, J. 1894 (WBA)	1
Reaney, P. 1969 (Leeds U)	3
Redknapp, J. F. 1996 (Liverpool)	17
Reeves, K. P. 1980 (Norwich C, Manchester C)	2
Regis, C. 1982 (WBA, Coventry C)	5
Reid, P. 1985 (Everton)	13
Revie, D. G. 1955 (Manchester C)	6
Reynolds, J. 1892 (WBA, Aston Villa)	8
Richards, C. H. 1898 (Nottingham F)	1
Richards, G. H. 1909 (Derby Co)	1

Richards, J. P. 1973 (Wolverhampton W)	1
Richards, M. 2007 (Manchester C)	11
Richardson, J. R. 1933 (Newcastle U)	2
Richardson, K. 1994 (Aston Villa)	1
Richardson, K. E. 2005 (Manchester U)	8
Richardson, W. G. 1935 (WBA)	1
Rickaby, S. 1954 (WBA)	1
Ricketts, M. B. 2002 (Bolton W)	1
Rigby, A. 1927 (Blackburn R)	5
Rimmer, E. J. 1930 (Sheffield W)	4
Rimmer, J. J. 1976 (Arsenal)	1
Ripley, S. E. 1994 (Blackburn R)	2
Rix, G. 1981 (Arsenal)	17
Robb, G. 1954 (Tottenham H)	1
Roberts, C. 1905 (Manchester U)	3
Roberts, F. 1925 (Manchester C)	4
Roberts, G. 1983 (Tottenham H)	6
Roberts, H. 1931 (Arsenal)	1
Roberts, H. 1931 (Millwall)	1
Roberts, R. 1887 (WBA)	3
Roberts, W. T. 1924 (Preston NE)	2
Robinson, J. 1937 (Sheffield W)	4
Robinson, J. W. 1897 (Derby Co, New Brighton Tower, Southampton)	11
Robinson, P. W. 2003 (Leeds U, Tottenham H, Blackburn R)	41
Robson, B. 1980 (WBA, Manchester U)	90
Robson, R. 1958 (WBA)	20
Rocastle, D. 1989 (Arsenal)	14
Rooney, W. 2003 (Everton, Manchester U)	52
Rose, W. C. 1884 (Swifts, Preston NE, Wolverhampton W)	5
Rostron, T. 1881 (Darwen)	2
Rowe, A. 1934 (Tottenham H)	1
Rowley, J. F. 1949 (Manchester U)	6
Rowley, W. 1889 (Stoke)	2
Royle, J. 1971 (Everton, Manchester C)	6
Ruddlesdin, H. 1904 (Sheffield W)	3
Ruddock, N. 1995 (Liverpool)	1
Ruffell, J. W. 1926 (West Ham U)	6
Russell, B. B. 1883 (Royal Engineers)	1
Rutherford, J. 1904 (Newcastle U)	11
Sadler, D. 1968 (Manchester U)	4
Sagar, C. 1900 (Bury)	2
Sagar, E. 1936 (Everton)	4
Salako, J. A. 1991 (C Palace)	5
Sandford, E. A. 1933 (WBA)	1
Sandilands, R. R. 1892 (Old Westminsters)	5
Sands, J. 1880 (Nottingham F)	1
Sansom, K. G. 1979 (C Palace, Arsenal)	86
Saunders, F. E. 1888 (Swifts)	1
Savage, A. H. 1876 (C Palace)	1
Sayer, J. 1887 (Stoke)	1
Scales, J. R. 1995 (Liverpool)	3
Scattergood, E. 1913 (Derby Co)	1
Schofield, J. 1892 (Stoke)	3
Scholes, P. 1997 (Manchester U)	66
Scott, L. 1947 (Arsenal)	17
Scott, W. R. 1937 (Brentford)	1
Seaman, D. A. 1989 (QPR, Arsenal)	75
Seddon, J. 1923 (Bolton W)	6
Seed, J. M. 1921 (Tottenham H)	5
Settle, J. 1899 (Bury, Everton)	6
Sewell, J. 1952 (Sheffield W)	6
Sewell, W. R. 1924 (Blackburn R)	1
Shackleton, L. F. 1949 (Sunderland)	5
Sharp, J. 1903 (Everton)	2
Sharpe, L. S. 1991 (Manchester U)	8
Shaw, G. E. 1932 (WBA)	1
Shaw, G. L. 1959 (Sheffield U)	5
Shea, D. 1914 (Blackburn R)	2
Shearer, A. 1992 (Southampton, Blackburn R, Newcastle U)	63
Shellito, K. J. 1963 (Chelsea)	1

Shelton A. 1889 (Notts Co) — 6
Shelton, C. 1888 (Notts Rangers) — 1
Shepherd, A. 1906 (Bolton W, Newcastle U) — 2
Sheringham, E. P. 1993 (Tottenham H, Manchester U, Tottenham H) — 51
Sherwood, T. A. 1999 (Tottenham H) — 3
Shilton, P. L. 1971 (Leicester C, Stoke C, Nottingham F, Southampton, Derby Co) — 125
Shimwell, E. 1949 (Blackpool) — 1
Shorey, N. 2007 (Reading) — 2
Shutt, G. 1886 (Stoke) — 1
Silcock, J. 1921 (Manchester U) — 3
Sillett, R. P. 1955 (Chelsea) — 3
Simms, E. 1922 (Luton T) — 1
Simpson, J. 1911 (Blackburn R) — 8
Sinclair, T. 2002 (West Ham U, Manchester C) — 12
Sinton, A. 1992 (QPR, Sheffield W) — 12
Slater, W. J. 1955 (Wolverhampton W) — 12
Smalley, T. 1937 (Wolverhampton W) — 1
Smart, T. 1921 (Aston Villa) — 5
Smith, A. 1891 (Nottingham F) — 3
Smith, A. 2001 (Leeds U, Manchester U, Newcastle U) — 19
Smith, A. K. 1872 (Oxford University) — 1
Smith, A. M. 1989 (Arsenal) — 13
Smith, B. 1921 (Tottenham H) — 2
Smith, C. E. 1876 (C Palace) — 1
Smith, G. O. 1893 (Oxford University, Old Carthusians, Corinthians) — 20
Smith, H. 1905 (Reading) — 4
Smith, J. 1920 (WBA) — 2
Smith, Joe 1913 (Bolton W) — 5
Smith, J. C. R. 1939 (Millwall) — 2
Smith, J. W. 1932 (Portsmouth) — 3
Smith, Leslie 1939 (Brentford) — 1
Smith, Lionel 1951 (Arsenal) — 6
Smith, R. A. 1961 (Tottenham H) — 15
Smith, S. 1895 (Aston Villa) — 1
Smith, S. C. 1936 (Leicester C) — 1
Smith, T. 1960 (Birmingham C) — 2
Smith, T. 1971 (Liverpool) — 1
Smith, W. H. 1922 (Huddersfield T) — 3
Sorby, T. H. 1879 (Thursday Wanderers, Sheffield) — 1
Southgate, G. 1996 (Aston Villa, Middlesbrough) — 57
Southworth, J. 1889 (Blackburn R) — 3
Sparks, F. J. 1879 (Herts Rangers, Clapham Rovers) — 3
Spence, J. W. 1926 (Manchester U) — 2
Spence, R. 1936 (Chelsea) — 2
Spencer, C. W. 1924 (Newcastle U) — 2
Spencer, H. 1897 (Aston Villa) — 6
Spiksley, F. 1893 (Sheffield W) — 7
Spilsbury, B. W. 1885 (Cambridge University) — 3
Spink, N. 1983 (Aston Villa) — 1
Spouncer, W. A. 1900 (Nottingham F) — 1
Springett, R. D. G. 1960 (Sheffield W) — 33
Sproston, B. 1937 (Leeds U, Tottenham H, Manchester C) — 11
Squire, R. T. 1886 (Cambridge University) — 3
Stanbrough, M. H. 1895 (Old Carthusians) — 1
Staniforth, R. 1954 (Huddersfield T) — 8
Starling, R. W. 1933 (Sheffield W, Aston Villa) — 2
Statham, D. J. 1983 (WBA) — 3
Steele, F. C. 1937 (Stoke C) — 6
Stein, B. 1984 (Luton T) — 1
Stephenson, C. 1924 (Huddersfield T) — 1
Stephenson, G. T. 1928 (Derby Co, Sheffield W) — 3
Stephenson, J. E. 1938 (Leeds U) — 2
Stepney, A. C. 1968 (Manchester U) — 1
Sterland, M. 1989 (Sheffield W) — 1
Steven, T. M. 1985 (Everton, Rangers, Marseille) — 36
Stevens, G. A. 1985 (Tottenham H) — 7
Stevens, M. G. 1985 (Everton, Rangers) — 46
Stewart, J. 1907 (Sheffield W, Newcastle U) — 3
Stewart, P. A. 1992 (Tottenham H) — 3
Stiles, N. P. 1965 (Manchester U) — 28

Stoker, J. 1933 (Birmingham) — 3
Stone, S. B. 1996 (Nottingham F) — 9
Storer, H. 1924 (Derby Co) — 2
Storey, P. E. 1971 (Arsenal) — 19
Storey-Moore, I. 1970 (Nottingham F) — 1
Strange, A. H. 1930 (Sheffield W) — 20
Stratford, A. H. 1874 (Wanderers) — 1
Streten, B. 1950 (Luton T) — 1
Sturgess, A. 1911 (Sheffield U) — 2
Summerbee, M. G. 1968 (Manchester C) — 8
Sunderland, A. 1980 (Arsenal) — 1
Sutcliffe, J. W. 1893 (Bolton W, Millwall) — 5
Sutton, C. R. 1998 (Blackburn R) — 1
Swan, P. 1960 (Sheffield W) — 19
Swepstone, H. A. 1880 (Pilgrims) — 6
Swift, F. V. 1947 (Manchester C) — 19

Tait, G. 1881 (Birmingham Excelsior) — 1
Talbot, B. 1977 (Ipswich T, Arsenal) — 6
Tambling, R. V. 1963 (Chelsea) — 3
Tate, J. T. 1931 (Aston Villa) — 3
Taylor, E. 1954 (Blackpool) — 1
Taylor, E. H. 1923 (Huddersfield T) — 8
Taylor, J. G. 1951 (Fulham) — 2
Taylor, P. H. 1948 (Liverpool) — 3
Taylor, P. J. 1976 (C Palace) — 4
Taylor, T. 1953 (Manchester U) — 19
Temple, D. W. 1965 (Everton) — 1
Terry, J. G. 2003 (Chelsea) — 53
Thickett, H. 1899 (Sheffield U) — 2
Thomas, D. 1975 (QPR) — 8
Thomas, D. 1983 (Coventry C) — 2
Thomas, G. R. 1991 (C Palace) — 9
Thomas, M. L. 1989 (Arsenal) — 2
Thompson, A. 2004 (Celtic) — 1
Thompson, P. 1964 (Liverpool) — 16
Thompson, P. B. 1976 (Liverpool) — 42
Thompson T. 1952 (Aston Villa, Preston NE) — 2
Thomson, R. A. 1964 (Wolverhampton W) — 8
Thornewell, G. 1923 (Derby Co) — 4
Thornley, I. 1907 (Manchester C) — 1
Tilson, S. F. 1934 (Manchester C) — 4
Titmuss, F. 1922 (Southampton) — 2
Todd, C. 1972 (Derby Co) — 27
Toone, G. 1892 (Notts Co) — 2
Topham, A. G. 1894 (Casuals) — 1
Topham, R. 1893 (Wolverhampton W, Casuals) — 2
Towers, M. A. 1976 (Sunderland) — 3
Townley, W. J. 1889 (Blackburn R) — 2
Townrow, J. E. 1925 (Clapton Orient) — 2
Tremelling, D. R. 1928 (Birmingham) — 1
Tresadern, J. 1923 (West Ham U) — 2
Tueart, D. 1975 (Manchester C) — 6
Tunstall, F. E. 1923 (Sheffield U) — 7
Turnbull, R. J. 1920 (Bradford) — 1
Turner, A. 1900 (Southampton) — 2
Turner, H. 1931 (Huddersfield T) — 2
Turner, J. A. 1893 (Bolton W, Stoke, Derby Co) — 3
Tweedy, G. J. 1937 (Grimsby T) — 1

Ufton, D. G. 1954 (Charlton Ath) — 1
Underwood, A. 1891 (Stoke C) — 2
Unsworth, D. G. 1995 (Everton) — 1
Upson, M. J. 2003 (Birmingham C, West Ham U) — 15
Urwin, T. 1923 (Middlesbrough, Newcastle U) — 4
Utley, G. 1913 (Barnsley) — 1

Vassell, D. 2002 (Aston Villa) — 22
Vaughton, O. H. 1882 (Aston Villa) — 5
Veitch, C. C. M. 1906 (Newcastle U) — 6
Veitch, J. G. 1894 (Old Westminsters) — 1
Venables, T. F. 1965 (Chelsea) — 2
Venison, B. 1995 (Newcastle U) — 2
Vidal, R. W. S. 1873 (Oxford University) — 1
Viljoen, C. 1975 (Ipswich T) — 2

Viollet, D. S. 1960 (Manchester U) 2
Von Donop 1873 (Royal Engineers) 2

Wace, H. 1878 (Wanderers) 3
Waddle, C. R. 1985 (Newcastle U, Tottenham H, Marseille) 62
Wadsworth, S. J. 1922 (Huddersfield T) 9
Wainscoat, W. R. 1929 (Leeds U) 1
Waiters, A. K. 1964 (Blackpool) 5
Walcott, T. J. 2006 (Arsenal) 8
Walden, F. I. 1914 (Tottenham H) 2
Walker, D. S. 1989 (Nottingham F, Sampdoria, Sheffield W) 59
Walker, I. M. 1996 (Tottenham H, Leicester C) 4
Walker, W. H. 1921 (Aston Villa) 18
Wall, G. 1907 (Manchester U) 7
Wallace, C. W. 1913 (Aston Villa) 3
Wallace, D. L. 1986 (Southampton) 1
Walsh, P. A. 1983 (Luton T) 5
Walters, A. M. 1885 (Cambridge University, Old Carthusians) 9
Walters, K. M. 1991 (Rangers) 1
Walters, P. M. 1885 (Oxford University, Old Carthusians) 13
Walton, N. 1890 (Blackburn R) 1
Ward, J. T. 1885 (Blackburn Olympic) 1
Ward, P. 1980 (Brighton & HA) 1
Ward, T. V. 1948 (Derby Co) 2
Waring, T. 1931 (Aston Villa) 5
Warner, C. 1878 (Upton Park) 1
Warnock, S. 2008 (Blackburn R) 1
Warren, B. 1906 (Derby Co, Chelsea) 22
Waterfield, G. S. 1927 (Burnley) 1
Watson, D. 1984 (Norwich C, Everton) 12
Watson, D. V. 1974 (Sunderland, Manchester C, Werder Bremen, Southampton, Stoke C) 65
Watson, V. M. 1923 (West Ham U) 5
Watson, W. 1913 (Burnley) 3
Watson, W. 1950 (Sunderland) 4
Weaver, S. 1932 (Newcastle U) 3
Webb, G. W. 1911 (West Ham U) 2
Webb, N. J. 1988 (Nottingham F, Manchester U) 26
Webster, M. 1930 (Middlesbrough) 3
Wedlock, W. J. 1907 (Bristol C) 26
Weir, D. 1889 (Bolton W) 2
Welch, R. de C. 1872 (Wanderers, Harrow Chequers) 2
Weller, K. 1974 (Leicester C) 4
Welsh, D. 1938 (Charlton Ath) 3
West, G. 1969 (Everton) 3
Westwood, R. W. 1935 (Bolton W) 6
Whateley, O. 1883 (Aston Villa) 2
Wheeler, J. E. 1955 (Bolton W) 1
Wheldon, G. F. 1897 (Aston Villa) 4
White, D. 1993 (Manchester C) 1
White, T. A. 1933 (Everton) 1
Whitehead, J. 1893 (Accrington, Blackburn R) 2
Whitfeld, H. 1879 (Old Etonians) 1
Whitham, M. 1892 (Sheffield U) 1
Whitworth, S. 1975 (Leicester C) 7
Whymark, T. J. 1978 (Ipswich T) 1
Widdowson, S. W. 1880 (Nottingham F) 1
Wignall, F. 1965 (Nottingham F) 2
Wilcox, J. M. 1996 (Blackburn R, Leeds U) 3

Wilkes, A. 1901 (Aston Villa) 5
Wilkins, R. C. 1976 (Chelsea, Manchester U, AC Milan) 84
Wilkinson, B. 1904 (Sheffield U) 1
Wilkinson, L. R. 1891 (Oxford University) 1
Williams, B. F. 1949 (Wolverhampton W) 24
Williams, O. 1923 (Clapton Orient) 2
Williams, S. 1983 (Southampton) 6
Williams, W. 1897 (WBA) 6
Williamson, E. C. 1923 (Arsenal) 2
Williamson, R. G. 1905 (Middlesbrough) 7
Willingham, C. K. 1937 (Huddersfield T) 12
Willis, A. 1952 (Tottenham H) 1
Wilshaw, D. J. 1954 (Wolverhampton W) 12
Wilson, C. P. 1884 (Hendon) 2
Wilson, C. W. 1879 (Oxford University) 2
Wilson, G. 1921 (Sheffield W) 12
Wilson, G. P. 1900 (Corinthians) 2
Wilson, R. 1960 (Huddersfield T, Everton) 63
Wilson, T. 1928 (Huddersfield T) 1
Winckworth, W. N. 1892 (Old Westminsters) 2
Windridge, J. E. 1908 (Chelsea) 8
Wingfield-Stratford, C. V. 1877 (Royal Engineers) 1
Winterburn, N. 1990 (Arsenal) 2
Wise, D. F. 1991 (Chelsea) 21
Withe, P. 1981 (Aston Villa) 11
Wollaston, C. H. R. 1874 (Wanderers) 4
Wolstenholme, S. 1904 (Everton, Blackburn R) 3
Wood, H. 1890 (Wolverhampton W) 3
Wood, R. E. 1955 (Manchester U) 3
Woodcock, A. S. 1978 (Nottingham F, Cologne, Arsenal) 42
Woodgate, J. S. 1999 (Leeds U, Newcastle U, Real Madrid, Tottenham H) 8
Woodger, G. 1911 (Oldham Ath) 1
Woodhall, G. 1888 (WBA) 2
Woodley, V. R. 1937 (Chelsea) 19
Woods, C. C. E. 1985 (Norwich C, Rangers, Sheffield W) 43
Woodward, V. J. 1903 (Tottenham H, Chelsea) 23
Woosnam, M. 1922 (Manchester C) 1
Worrall, F. 1935 (Portsmouth) 2
Worthington, F. S. 1974 (Leicester C) 8
Wreford-Brown, C. 1889 (Oxford University, Old Carthusians) 4
Wright, E. G. D. 1906 (Cambridge University) 1
Wright, I. E. 1991 (C Palace, Arsenal, West Ham U) 33
Wright, J. D. 1939 (Newcastle U) 1
Wright, M. 1984 (Southampton, Derby Co, Liverpool) 45
Wright, R. I. 2000 (Ipswich T, Arsenal) 2
Wright, T. J. 1968 (Everton) 11
Wright, W. A. 1947 (Wolverhampton W) 105
Wright-Phillips, S. C. 2005 (Manchester C, Chelsea, Manchester C) 25
Wylie, J. G. 1878 (Wanderers) 1

Yates, J. 1889 (Burnley) 1
York, R. E. 1922 (Aston Villa) 2
Young, A. 1933 (Huddersfield T) 9
Young, A. S. 2008 (Aston Villa) 5
Young, G. M. 1965 (Sheffield W) 1
Young, L. P. 2005 (Charlton Ath) 7

NORTHERN IRELAND

Addis, D. J. 1922 (Cliftonville) 1
Aherne, T. 1947 (Belfast C, Luton T) 4
Alexander, T. E. 1895 (Cliftonville) 1
Allan, C. 1936 (Cliftonville) 1
Allen, J. 1887 (Limavady) 1
Anderson, J. 1925 (Distillery) 1
Anderson, T. 1973 (Manchester U, Swindon T, Peterborough U) 22
Anderson, W. 1898 (Linfield, Cliftonville) 4

Andrews, W. 1908 (Glentoran, Grimsby T) 3
Armstrong, G. J. 1977 (Tottenham H, Watford, Real Mallorca, WBA, Chesterfield) 63
Baird, C. P. 2003 (Southampton, Fulham) 40
Baird, G. 1896 (Distillery) 3
Baird, H. C. 1939 (Huddersfield T) 1
Balfe, J. 1909 (Shelbourne) 2
Bambrick, J. 1929 (Linfield, Chelsea) 11

Banks, S. J. 1937 (Cliftonville) 1
Barr, H. H. 1962 (Linfield, Coventry C) 3
Barron, J. H. 1894 (Cliftonville) 7
Barry, J. 1888 (Cliftonville) 3
Barry, J. 1900 (Bohemians) 1
Baxter, R. A. 1887 (Distillery) 1
Baxter, S. N. 1887 (Cliftonville) 1
Bennett, L. V. 1889 (Dublin University) 1
Best, G. 1964 (Manchester U, Fulham) 37
Bingham, W. L. 1951 (Sunderland, Luton T, Everton,
   Port Vale) 56
Black, K. T. 1988 (Luton T, Nottingham F) 30
Black, T. 1901 (Glentoran) 1
Blair, H. 1928 (Portadown, Swansea T) 4
Blair, J. 1907 (Cliftonville) 5
Blair, R. V. 1975 (Oldham Ath) 5
Blanchflower, J. 1954 (Manchester U) 12
Blanchflower, R. D. 1950 (Barnsley, Aston Villa,
   Tottenham H) 56
Blayney, A. 2006 (Doncaster R) 1
Bookman, L. J. O. 1914 (Bradford C, Luton T) 4
Bothwell, A. W. 1926 (Ards) 5
Bowler, G. C. 1950 (Hull C) 3
Boyle, P. 1901 (Sheffield U) 5
Braithwaite, R. M. 1962 (Linfield, Middlesbrough) 10
Breen, T. 1935 (Belfast C, Manchester U) 9
Brennan, B. 1912 (Bohemians) 1
Brennan, R. A. 1949 (Luton T, Birmingham C, Fulham)
    5
Briggs, W. R. 1962 (Manchester U, Swansea T) 2
Brisby, D. 1891 (Distillery) 1
Brolly, T. H. 1937 (Millwall) 4
Brookes, E. A. 1920 (Shelbourne) 1
Brotherston, N. 1980 (Blackburn R) 27
Brown, J. 1921 (Glenavon, Tranmere R) 3
Brown, J. 1935 (Wolverhampton W, Coventry C,
   Birmingham C) 10
Brown, N. M. 1887 (Limavady) 1
Brown, W. G. 1926 (Glenavon) 1
Browne, F. 1887 (Cliftonville) 5
Browne, R. J. 1936 (Leeds U) 6
Bruce, A. 1925 (Belfast C) 1
Bruce, W. 1961 (Glentoran) 2
Brunt, C. 2005 (Sheffield W, WBA) 23
Buckle, H. R. 1903 (Cliftonville, Sunderland, Bristol R)
    3
Buckle, J. 1882 (Cliftonville) 1
Burnett, J. 1894 (Distillery, Glentoran) 5
Burnison, J. 1901 (Distillery) 2
Burnison, S. 1908 (Distillery, Bradford, Distillery) 8
Burns, J. 1923 (Glenavon) 1
Burns, W. 1925 (Glentoran) 1
Butler, M. P. 1939 (Blackpool) 1

Campbell, A. C. 1963 (Crusaders) 2
Campbell, D. A. 1986 (Nottingham F, Charlton Ath) 10
Campbell, James 1897 (Cliftonville) 14
Campbell, John 1896 (Cliftonville) 1
Campbell, J. P. 1951 (Fulham) 2
Campbell, R. M. 1982 (Bradford C) 2
Campbell, W. G. 1968 (Dundee) 6
Capaldi, A. C. 2004 (Plymouth Arg, Cardiff C) 22
Carey, J. J. 1947 (Manchester U) 7
Carroll, E. 1925 (Glenavon) 1
Carroll, R. E. 1997 (Wigan Ath, Manchester U,
   West Ham U) 19
Carson, S. 2009 (Coleraine) 1
Casement, C. 2009 (Ipswich T) 1
Casey, T. 1955 (Newcastle U, Portsmouth) 12
Caskey, W. 1979 (Derby Co, Tulsa R) 8
Cassidy, T. 1971 (Newcastle U, Burnley) 24
Caughey, M. 1986 (Linfield) 2
Chambers, R. J. 1921 (Distillery, Bury, Nottingham F)
    12
Chatton, H. A. 1925 (Partick Th) 3

Christian, J. 1889 (Linfield) 1
Clarke, C. J. 1986 (Bournemouth, Southampton, QPR,
   Portsmouth) 38
Clarke, R. 1901 (Belfast C) 2
Cleary, J. 1982 (Glentoran) 5
Clements, D. 1965 (Coventry C, Sheffield W, Everton,
   New York Cosmos) 48
Clingan, S. G. 2006 (Nottingham F, Norwich C) 21
Clugston, J. 1888 (Cliftonville) 14
Clyde, M. G. 2005 (Wolverhampton W) 3
Coates, C. 2009 (Crusaders) 1
Cochrane, D. 1939 (Leeds U) 12
Cochrane, G. 1903 (Cliftonville) 1
Cochrane, G. T. 1976 (Coleraine, Burnley,
   Middlesbrough, Gillingham) 26
Cochrane, M. 1898 (Distillery, Leicester Fosse) 8
Collins, F. 1922 (Celtic) 1
Collins, R. 1922 (Cliftonville) 1
Condy, J. 1882 (Distillery) 3
Connell, T. E. 1978 (Coleraine) 1
Connor, J. 1901 (Glentoran, Belfast C) 13
Connor, M. J. 1903 (Brentford, Fulham) 3
Cook, W. 1933 (Celtic, Everton) 15
Cooke, S. 1889 (Belfast YMCA, Cliftonville) 3
Coote, A. 1999 (Norwich C) 6
Coulter, J. 1934 (Belfast C, Everton, Grimsby T,
   Chelmsford C) 11
Cowan, J. 1970 (Newcastle U) 1
Cowan, T. S. 1925 (Queen's Island) 1
Coyle, F. 1956 (Coleraine, Nottingham F) 4
Coyle, L. 1989 (Derry C) 1
Coyle, R. I. 1973 (Sheffield W) 5
Craig, A. B. 1908 (Rangers, Morton) 9
Craig, D. J. 1967 (Newcastle U) 25
Craigan, S. J. 2003 (Partick Th, Motherwell) 40
Crawford, A. 1889 (Distillery, Cliftonville) 7
Croft, T. 1922 (Queen's Island) 3
Crone, R. 1889 (Distillery) 4
Crone, W. 1882 (Distillery) 12
Crooks, W. J. 1922 (Manchester U) 1
Crossan, E. 1950 (Blackburn R) 3
Crossan, J. A. 1960 (Sparta-Rotterdam, Sunderland,
   Manchester C, Middlesbrough) 24
Crothers, C. 1907 (Distillery) 1
Cumming, L. 1929 (Huddersfield T, Oldham Ath) 3
Cunningham, W. 1892 (Ulster) 4
Cunningham, W. E. 1951 (St Mirren, Leicester C,
   Dunfermline Ath) 30
Curran, S. 1926 (Belfast C) 4
Curran, J. J. 1922 (Glenavon, Pontypridd, Glenavon) 5
Cush, W. W. 1951 (Glenavon, Leeds U, Portadown) 26

Dalrymple, J. 1922 (Distillery) 1
Dalton, W. 1888 (YMCA, Linfield) 11
D'Arcy, S. D. 1952 (Chelsea, Brentford) 5
Darling, J. 1897 (Linfield) 22
Davey, H. H. 1926 (Reading, Portsmouth) 5
Davis, S. 2005 (Aston Villa, Fulham, Rangers) 34
Davis, T. L. 1937 (Oldham Ath) 1
Davison, A. J. 1996 (Bolton W, Bradford C, Grimsby T)
    3
Davison, J. R. 1882 (Cliftonville) 8
Dennison, R. 1988 (Wolverhampton W) 18
Devine, A. O. 1886 (Limavady) 1
Devine, J. 1990 (Glentoran) 1
Dickson, D. 1970 (Coleraine) 4
Dickson, T. A. 1957 (Linfield) 1
Dickson, W. 1951 (Chelsea, Arsenal) 12
Diffin, W. J. 1931 (Belfast C) 1
Dill, A. H. 1882 (Knock, Down Ath, Cliftonville) 9
Doherty, I. 1901 (Belfast C) 1
Doherty, J. 1928 (Portadown) 1
Doherty, J. 1933 (Cliftonville) 2
Doherty, L. 1985 (Linfield) 2
Doherty, M. 1938 (Derry C) 1

Doherty, P. D. 1935 (Blackpool, Manchester C,
  Derby Co, Huddersfield T, Doncaster R)   16
Doherty, T. E. 2003 (Bristol C)   9
Donaghey, B. 1903 (Belfast C)   1
Donaghy, M. M. 1980 (Luton T, Manchester U, Chelsea)   91
Donnelly, L. 1913 (Distillery)   1
Donnelly, M. 2009 (Crusaders)   1
Doran, J. F. 1921 (Brighton)   3
Dougan, A. D. 1958 (Portsmouth, Blackburn R,
  Aston Villa, Leicester C, Wolverhampton W)   43
Douglas, J. P. 1947 (Belfast C)   1
Dowd, H. O. 1974 (Glenavon, Sheffield W)   3
Dowie, I. 1990 (Luton T, West Ham U, Southampton,
  C Palace, West Ham U, QPR)   59
Duff, M. J. 2002 (Cheltenham T, Burnley)   22
Duggan, H. A. 1930 (Leeds U)   8
Dunlop, G. 1985 (Linfield)   4
Dunne, J. 1928 (Sheffield U)   7

Eames, W. L. E. 1885 (Dublin U)   3
Eglington, T. J. 1947 (Everton)   6
Elder, A. R. 1960 (Burnley, Stoke C)   40
Elleman, A. R. 1889 (Cliftonville)   2
Elliott, S. 2001 (Motherwell, Hull C)   39
Elwood, J. H. 1929 (Bradford)   2
Emerson, W. 1920 (Glentoran, Burnley)   11
English, S. 1933 (Rangers)   2
Enright, J. 1912 (Leeds C)   1
Evans, C. J. 2009 (Manchester U)   1
Evans, J. G. 2007 (Manchester U)   17

Falloon, E. 1931 (Aberdeen)   2
Farquharson, T. G. 1923 (Cardiff C)   7
Farrell, P. 1901 (Distillery)   2
Farrell, P. 1938 (Hibernian)   1
Farrell, P. D. 1947 (Everton)   7
Feeney, J. M. 1947 (Linfield, Swansea T)   2
Feeney, W. 1976 (Glentoran)   1
Feeney, W. J. 2002 (Bournemouth, Luton T, Cardiff C)   32
Ferguson, G. 1999 (Linfield)   5
Ferguson, S. 2009 (Newcastle U)   1
Ferguson, W. 1966 (Linfield)   2
Ferris, J. 1920 (Belfast C, Chelsea, Belfast C)   6
Ferris, R. O. 1950 (Birmingham C)   3
Fettis, A. W. 1992 (Hull C, Nottingham F, Blackburn R)   25
Finney, T. 1975 (Sunderland, Cambridge U)   14
Fitzpatrick, J. C. 1896 (Bohemians)   2
Flack, H. 1929 (Burnley)   1
Fleming, J. G. 1987 (Nottingham F, Manchester C,
  Barnsley)   31
Forbes, G. 1888 (Limavady, Distillery)   3
Forde, J. T. 1959 (Ards)   4
Foreman, T. A. 1899 (Cliftonville)   1
Forsythe, J. 1888 (YMCA)   2
Fox, W. T. 1887 (Ulster)   2
Frame, T. 1925 (Linfield)   1
Fulton, R. P. 1928 (Larne, Belfast C)   21

Gaffikin, G. 1890 (Linfield Ath)   15
Galbraith, W. 1890 (Distillery)   1
Gallagher, P. 1920 (Celtic, Falkirk)   11
Gallogly, C. 1951 (Huddersfield T)   2
Gara, A. 1902 (Preston NE)   3
Gardiner, A. 1930 (Cliftonville)   5
Garrett, J. 1925 (Distillery)   1
Garrett, R. 2009 (Linfield)   1
Gaston, R. 1969 (Oxford U)   1
Gaukrodger, G. 1895 (Linfield)   1
Gault, M. 2008 (Linfield)   1
Gaussen, A. D. 1884 (Moyola Park, Magherafelt)   6
Geary, J. 1931 (Glentoran)   2
Gibb, J. T. 1884 (Wellington Park, Cliftonville)   10

Gibb, T. J. 1936 (Cliftonville)   1
Gibson W. K. 1894 (Cliftonville)   14
Gillespie, K. R. 1995 (Manchester U, Newcastle U,
  Blackburn R, Leicester C, Sheffield U)   86
Gillespie, S. 1886 (Hertford)   6
Gillespie, W. 1889 (West Down)   1
Gillespie, W. 1913 (Sheffield U)   25
Goodall, A. L. 1899 (Derby Co, Glossop)   10
Goodbody, M. F. 1889 (Dublin University)   2
Gordon, H. 1895 (Linfield)   3
Gordon R. W. 1891 (Linfield)   7
Gordon, T. 1894 (Linfield)   2
Gorman, W. C. 1947 (Brentford)   4
Gough, J. 1925 (Queen's Island)   1
Gowdy, J. 1920 (Glentoran, Queen's Island, Falkirk)   6
Gowdy, W. A. 1932 (Hull C, Sheffield W, Linfield,
  Hibernian)   6
Graham, W. G. L. 1951 (Doncaster R)   14
Gray, P. 1993 (Luton T, Sunderland, Nancy, Luton T,
  Burnley, Oxford U)   26
Greer, W. 1909 (QPR)   3
Gregg, H. 1954 (Doncaster R, Manchester U)   25
Griffin, D. J. 1996 (St Johnstone, Dundee U,
  Stockport Co)   29

Hall, G. 1897 (Distillery)   1
Halligan, W. 1911 (Derby Co, Wolverhampton W)   2
Hamill, M. 1912 (Manchester U, Belfast C,
  Manchester C)   7
Hamill, R. 1999 (Glentoran)   1
Hamilton, B. 1969 (Linfield, Ipswich T, Everton,
  Millwall, Swindon T)   50
Hamilton, G. 2003 (Portadown)   5
Hamilton, J. 1882 (Knock)   2
Hamilton, R. 1928 (Rangers)   5
Hamilton, W. D. 1885 (Dublin Association)   1
Hamilton, W. J. 1885 (Dublin Association)   1
Hamilton, W. J. 1908 (Distillery)   1
Hamilton, W. R. 1978 (QPR, Burnley, Oxford U)   41
Hampton, H. 1911 (Bradford C)   9
Hanna, J. 1912 (Nottingham F)   2
Hanna, J. D. 1899 (Royal Artillery, Portsmouth)   1
Hannon, D. J. 1908 (Bohemians)   6
Harkin, J. T. 1968 (Southport, Shrewsbury T)   5
Harland, A. I. 1922 (Linfield)   2
Harris, J. 1921 (Cliftonville, Glenavon)   2
Harris, V. 1906 (Shelbourne, Everton)   20
Harvey, M. 1961 (Sunderland)   34
Hastings, J. 1882 (Knock, Ulster)   7
Hatton, S. 1963 (Linfield)   2
Hayes, W. E. 1938 (Huddersfield T)   4
Healy, D. J. 2000 (Manchester U, Preston NE, Leeds U,
  Fulham, Sunderland)   74
Healy, P. J. 1982 (Coleraine, Glentoran)   4
Hegan, D. 1970 (WBA, Wolverhampton W)   7
Henderson, J. 1885 (Ulster)   3
Hewison, G. 1885 (Moyola Park)   2
Hill, C. F. 1990 (Sheffield U, Leicester C, Trelleborg,
  Northampton T)   27
Hill, M. J. 1959 (Norwich C, Everton)   7
Hinton, E. 1947 (Fulham, Millwall)   7
Holmes, S. P. 2002 (Wrexham)   1
Hopkins, J. 1926 (Brighton)   1
Horlock, K. 1995 (Swindon T, Manchester C)   32
Houston, J. 1912 (Linfield, Everton)   6
Houston, W. 1933 (Linfield)   1
Houston, W. J. 1885 (Moyola Park)   2
Hughes, A. W. 1998 (Newcastle U, Aston Villa, Fulham)   66
Hughes, J. 2006 (Lincoln C)   2
Hughes, M.A. 2006 (Oldham Ath)   2
Hughes, M. E. 1992 (Manchester C, Strasbourg,
  West Ham U, Wimbledon, C Palace)   71
Hughes, P. A. 1987 (Bury)   3

Hughes, W. 1951 (Bolton W) — 1
Humphries, W. M. 1962 (Ards, Coventry C, Swansea T) — 14

Hunter, A. 1905 (Distillery, Belfast C) — 8
Hunter, A. 1970 (Blackburn R, Ipswich T) — 53
Hunter, B. V. 1995 (Wrexham, Reading) — 15
Hunter, R. J. 1884 (Cliftonville) — 3
Hunter, V. 1962 (Coleraine) — 2

Ingham, M. G. 2005 (Sunderland, Wrexham) — 3
Irvine, R. J. 1962 (Linfield, Stoke C) — 8
Irvine, R. W. 1922 (Everton, Portsmouth, Connah's Quay, Derry C) — 15
Irvine, W. J. 1963 (Burnley, Preston NE, Brighton & HA) — 23
Irving, S. J. 1923 (Dundee, Cardiff C, Chelsea) — 18

Jackson, T. A. 1969 (Everton, Nottingham F, Manchester U) — 35
Jamison, J. 1976 (Glentoran) — 1
Jenkins, I. 1997 (Chester C, Dundee U) — 6
Jennings, P. A. 1964 (Watford, Tottenham H, Arsenal, Tottenham H) — 119
Johnson, D. M. 1999 (Blackburn R, Birmingham C) — 52
Johnston, H. 1927 (Portadown) — 1
Johnston, R. S. 1882 (Distillery) — 5
Johnston, R. S. 1905 (Distillery) — 1
Johnston, S. 1890 (Linfield) — 4
Johnston, W. 1885 (Oldpark) — 2
Johnston, W. C. 1962 (Glenavon, Oldham Ath) — 2
Jones, J. 1930 (Linfield, Hibernian, Glenavon) — 23
Jones, J. 1956 (Glenavon) — 3
Jones, S. 1934 (Distillery, Blackpool) — 2
Jones, S. G. 2003 (Crewe Alex, Burnley) — 29
Jordan, T. 1895 (Linfield) — 2

Kavanagh, P. J. 1930 (Celtic) — 1
Keane, T. R. 1949 (Swansea T) — 1
Kearns, A. 1900 (Distillery) — 6
Kee, P. V. 1990 (Oxford U, Ards) — 9
Keith, R. M. 1958 (Newcastle U) — 23
Kelly, H. R. 1950 (Fulham, Southampton) — 4
Kelly, J. 1896 (Glentoran) — 1
Kelly, J. 1932 (Derry C) — 11
Kelly, P. J. 1921 (Manchester C) — 1
Kelly, P. M. 1950 (Barnsley) — 1
Kennedy, A. L. 1923 (Arsenal) — 2
Kennedy, P. H. 1999 (Watford, Wigan Ath) — 20
Kernaghan, N. 1936 (Belfast C) — 3
Kirk, A. R. 2000 (Hearts, Boston U, Northampton T) — 8
Kirkwood, H. 1904 (Cliftonville) — 1
Kirwan, J. 1900 (Tottenham H, Chelsea, Clyde) — 17

Lacey, W. 1909 (Everton, Liverpool, New Brighton) — 23
Lafferty, K. 2006 (Burnley, Rangers) — 20
Lawrie, J. 2009 (Port Vale) — 1
Lawther, I. 1888 (Glentoran) — 2
Lawther, W. I. 1960 (Sunderland, Blackburn R) — 4
Leatham, J. 1939 (Belfast C) — 1
Ledwidge, J. J. 1906 (Shelbourne) — 2
Lemon, J. 1886 (Glentoran, Belfast YMCA) — 3
Lennon, N. F. 1994 (Crewe Alex, Leicester C, Celtic) — 40
Leslie, W. 1887 (YMCA) — 1
Lewis, J. 1899 (Glentoran, Distillery) — 4
Little, A. 2009 (Rangers) — 2
Lockhart, H. 1884 (Rossall School) — 1
Lockhart, N. H. 1947 (Linfield, Coventry C, Aston Villa) — 8
Lomas, S. M. 1994 (Manchester C, West Ham U) — 45
Loyal, J. 1891 (Clarence) — 1
Lutton, R. J. 1970 (Wolverhampton W, West Ham U) — 6
Lynas, R. 1925 (Cliftonville) — 1
Lyner, D. R. 1920 (Glentoran, Manchester U, Kilmarnock) — 6
Lytle, J. 1898 (Glentoran) — 1

McAdams, W. J. 1954 (Manchester C, Bolton W, Leeds U) — 15
McAlery, J. M. 1882 (Cliftonville) — 2
McAlinden, J. 1938 (Belfast C, Portsmouth, Southend U) — 4
McAllen, J. 1898 (Linfield) — 9
McAlpine, S. 1901 (Cliftonville) — 1
McArthur, A. 1886 (Distillery) — 1
McAuley, G. 2005 (Lincoln C, Leicester C) — 16
McAuley, J. L. 1911 (Huddersfield T) — 6
McAuley, P. 1900 (Belfast C) — 1
McBride, S. D. 1991 (Glenavon) — 4
McCabe, J. J. 1949 (Leeds U) — 6
McCabe, W. 1891 (Ulster) — 1
McCambridge, J. 1930 (Ballymena, Cardiff C) — 4
McCandless, J. 1912 (Bradford) — 5
McCandless, W. 1920 (Linfield, Rangers) — 9
McCann, G. S. 2002 (West Ham U, Cheltenham T, Barnsley, Scunthorpe U) — 22
McCann, P. 1910 (Belfast C, Glentoran) — 7
McCarthy, J. D. 1996 (Port Vale, Birmingham C) — 18
McCartney, A. 1903 (Ulster, Linfield, Everton, Belfast C, Glentoran) — 15
McCartney, G. 2002 (Sunderland, West Ham U, Sunderland) — 31
McCashin, J. W. 1896 (Cliftonville) — 5
McCavana, W. T. 1955 (Coleraine) — 3
McCaw, J. H. 1927 (Linfield) — 6
McClatchey, J. 1886 (Distillery) — 3
McClatchey, T. 1895 (Distillery) — 1
McCleary, J. W. 1955 (Cliftonville) — 1
McCleery, W. 1922 (Cliftonville, Linfield) — 10
McClelland, J. 1980 (Mansfield T, Rangers, Watford, Leeds U) — 53
McClelland, J. T. 1961 (Arsenal, Fulham) — 6
McCluggage, A. 1922 (Cliftonville, Bradford, Burnley) — 13
McClure, G. 1907 (Cliftonville, Distillery) — 4
McConnell, E. 1904 (Cliftonville, Glentoran, Sunderland, Sheffield W) — 12
McConnell, P. 1928 (Doncaster R, Southport) — 2
McConnell, W. G. 1912 (Bohemians) — 6
McConnell, W. H. 1925 (Reading) — 8
McCourt, F. J. 1952 (Manchester C) — 6
McCourt, P. J. 2002 (Rochdale, Celtic) — 2
McCoy, R. K. 1987 (Coleraine) — 1
McCoy, S. 1896 (Distillery) — 1
McCracken, E. 1928 (Barking) — 1
McCracken, R. 1921 (C Palace) — 4
McCracken, R. 1922 (Linfield) — 1
McCracken, W. R. 1902 (Distillery, Newcastle U, Hull C) — 16
McCreery, D. 1976 (Manchester U, QPR, Tulsa R, Newcastle U, Hearts) — 67
McCrory, S. 1958 (Southend U) — 1
McCullough, K. 1935 (Belfast C, Manchester C) — 5
McCullough, W. J. 1961 (Arsenal, Millwall) — 10
McCurdy, C. 1980 (Linfield) — 1
McDonald, A. 1986 (QPR) — 52
McDonald, R. 1930 (Rangers) — 2
McDonnell, J. 1911 (Bohemians) — 4
McElhinney, G. M. A. 1984 (Bolton W) — 6
McEvilly, L. R. 2002 (Rochdale) — 1
McFaul, W. S. 1967 (Linfield, Newcastle U) — 6
McGarry, J. K. 1951 (Cliftonville) — 3
McGaughey, M. 1985 (Linfield) — 1
McGibbon, P. C. G. 1995 (Manchester U, Wigan Ath) — 7
McGinn, N. 2009 (Celtic) — 2
McGivern, R. 2009 (Manchester C) — 6
McGrath, R. C. 1974 (Tottenham H, Manchester U) — 21
McGregor, S. 1921 (Glentoran) — 1
McGrillen, J. 1924 (Clyde, Belfast C) — 2
McGuire, E. 1907 (Distillery) — 1
McGuire, J. 1928 (Linfield) — 1
McIlroy, H. 1906 (Cliftonville) — 1

Priestley, T. J. M. 1933 (Coleraine, Chelsea)   2
Pyper, Jas. 1897 (Cliftonville)   7
Pyper, John 1897 (Cliftonville)   9
Pyper, M. 1932 (Linfield)   1

Quinn, J. M. 1985 (Blackburn R, Swindon T, Leicester C, Bradford C, West Ham U, Bournemouth, Reading)   46
Quinn, S. J. 1996 (Blackpool, WBA, Willem II, Sheffield W, Peterborough U, Northampton T)   50

Rafferty, P. 1980 (Linfield)   1
Ramsey, P. C. 1984 (Leicester C)   14
Rankine, J. 1883 (Alexander)   2
Rattray, D. 1882 (Avoniel)   3
Rea, R. 1901 (Glentoran)   1
Redmond, R. 1884 (Cliftonville)   1
Reid, G. H. 1923 (Cardiff C)   1
Reid, J. 1883 (Ulster)   6
Reid, S. E. 1934 (Derby Co)   3
Reid, W. 1931 (Hearts)   1
Reilly, M. M. 1900 (Portsmouth)   2
Renneville, W. T. J. 1910 (Leyton, Aston Villa)   4
Reynolds, J. 1890 (Distillery, Ulster)   5
Reynolds, R. 1905 (Bohemians)   1
Rice, P. J. 1969 (Arsenal)   49
Roberts, F. C. 1931 (Glentoran)   1
Robinson, P. 1920 (Distillery, Blackburn R)   2
Robinson, S. 1997 (Bournemouth, Luton T)   7
Rogan, A. 1988 (Celtic, Sunderland, Millwall)   18
Rollo, D. 1912 (Linfield, Blackburn R)   16
Roper, E. O. 1886 (Dublin University)   1
Rosbotham, A. 1887 (Cliftonville)   7
Ross, W. E. 1969 (Newcastle U)   1
Rowland, K. 1994 (West Ham U, QPR)   19
Rowley, R. W. M. 1929 (Southampton, Tottenham H)   6
Rushe, F. 1925 (Distillery)   1
Russell, A. 1947 (Linfield)   1
Russell, S. R. 1930 (Bradford C, Derry C)   3
Ryan, R. A. 1950 (WBA)   1

Sanchez, L. P. 1987 (Wimbledon)   3
Scott, E. 1920 (Liverpool, Belfast C)   31
Scott, J. 1958 (Grimsby)   2
Scott, J. E. 1901 (Cliftonville)   1
Scott, L. J. 1895 (Dublin University)   2
Scott, P. W. 1975 (Everton, York C, Aldershot)   10
Scott, T. 1894 (Cliftonville)   13
Scott, W. 1903 (Linfield, Everton, Leeds City)   25
Scraggs, M. J. 1921 (Glentoran)   2
Seymour, H. C. 1914 (Bohemians)   1
Seymour, J. 1907 (Cliftonville)   2
Shanks, T. 1903 (Woolwich Arsenal, Brentford)   3
Sharkey, P. G. 1976 (Ipswich T)   1
Sheehan, Dr G. 1899 (Bohemians)   3
Sheridan, J. 1903 (Everton, Stoke C)   6
Sherrard, J. 1885 (Limavady)   3
Sherrard, W. C. 1895 (Cliftonville)   3
Sherry, J. J. 1906 (Bohemians)   2
Shields, R. J. 1957 (Southampton)   1
Shiels, D. 2006 (Hibernian)   8
Silo, M. 1888 (Belfast YMCA)   1
Simpson, W. J. 1951 (Rangers)   12
Sinclair, J. 1882 (Knock)   2
Slemin, J. C. 1909 (Bohemians)   1
Sloan, A. S. 1925 (London Caledonians)   1
Sloan, D. 1969 (Oxford U)   2
Sloan, H. A. de B. 1903 (Bohemians)   8
Sloan, J. W. 1947 (Arsenal)   1
Sloan, T. 1926 (Cardiff C, Linfield)   11
Sloan, T. 1979 (Manchester U)   3
Small, J. M. 1887 (Clarence, Cliftonville)   4
Smith, A. W. 2003 (Glentoran, Preston NE)   18
Smith, E. E. 1921 (Cardiff C)   1
Smith, J. E. 1901 (Distillery)   2

Smyth, R. H. 1886 (Dublin University)   1
Smyth, S. 1948 (Wolverhampton W, Stoke C)   9
Smyth, W. 1949 (Distillery)   4
Snape, A. 1920 (Airdrieonians)   1
Sonner, D. J. 1998 (Ipswich T, Sheffield W, Birmingham C, Nottingham F, Peterborough U)   13
Spence, D. W. 1975 (Bury, Blackpool, Southend U)   29
Spencer, S. 1890 (Distillery)   6
Spiller, E. A. 1883 (Cliftonville)   5
Sproule, I. 2006 (Hibernian, Bristol C)   11
Stanfield, O. M. 1887 (Distillery)   30
Steele, A. 1926 (Charlton Ath, Fulham)   4
Stevenson, A. E. 1934 (Rangers, Everton)   17
Stewart, A. 1967 (Glentoran, Derby Co)   7
Stewart, D. C. 1978 (Hull C)   1
Stewart, I. 1982 (QPR, Newcastle U)   31
Stewart, R. K. 1890 (St Columb's Court, Cliftonville)   11
Stewart, T. C. 1961 (Linfield)   1
Swan, S. 1899 (Linfield)   1

Taggart, G. P. 1990 (Barnsley, Bolton W, Leicester C)   51
Taggart, J. 1899 (Walsall)   1
Taylor, M. S. 1999 (Fulham, Birmingham C)   77
Thompson, F. W. 1910 (Cliftonville, Linfield, Bradford C, Clyde)   12
Thompson, J. 1897 (Distillery)   1
Thompson, P. 2006 (Linfield, Stockport Co)   8
Thompson, R. 1928 (Queen's Island)   1
Thompson, W. 1889 (Belfast Ath)   1
Thunder, P. J. 1911 (Bohemians)   1
Todd, S. J. 1966 (Burnley, Sheffield W)   11
Toner, C. 2003 (Leyton Orient)   2
Toner, J. 1922 (Arsenal, St Johnstone)   8
Torrans, R. 1893 (Linfield)   1
Torrans, S. 1889 (Linfield)   26
Trainor, D. 1967 (Crusaders)   1
Tuffey, J. 2009 (Partick T)   2
Tully, C. P. 1949 (Celtic)   10
Turner, A. 1896 (Cliftonville)   1
Turner, E. 1896 (Cliftonville)   1
Turner, W. 1886 (Cliftonville)   3
Twomey, J. F. 1938 (Leeds U)   2

Uprichard, W. N. M. C. 1952 (Swindon T, Portsmouth)   18

Vernon, J. 1947 (Belfast C, WBA)   17

Waddell, T. M. R. 1906 (Cliftonville)   1
Walker, J. 1955 (Doncaster R)   1
Walker, T. 1911 (Bury)   1
Walsh, D. J. 1947 (WBA)   9
Walsh, W. 1948 (Manchester C)   5
Waring, J. 1899 (Cliftonville)   1
Warren, P. 1913 (Shelbourne)   2
Watson, J. 1883 (Ulster)   9
Watson, P. 1971 (Distillery)   1
Watson, T. 1926 (Cardiff C)   1
Wattie, J. 1899 (Distillery)   1
Webb, C. G. 1909 (Brighton & HA)   3
Webb, S. M. 2006 (Ross Co)   4
Weir, E. 1939 (Clyde)   1
Welsh, E. 1966 (Carlisle U)   4
Whiteside, N. 1982 (Manchester U, Everton)   38
Whiteside, T. 1891 (Distillery)   1
Whitfield, E. R. 1886 (Dublin University)   1
Whitley, Jeff 1997 (Manchester C, Sunderland, Cardiff C)   20
Whitley, Jim 1998 (Manchester C)   3
Williams, J. R. 1886 (Ulster)   2
Williams, M. S. 1999 (Chesterfield, Watford, Wimbledon, Stoke C, Wimbledon, Milton Keynes D)   36
Williams, P. A. 1991 (WBA)   1
Williamson, J. 1890 (Cliftonville)   3

Willighan, T. 1933 (Burnley) 2
Willis, G. 1906 (Linfield) 4
Wilson, D. J. 1987 (Brighton & HA, Luton T, Sheffield W) 24
Wilson, H. 1925 (Linfield) 2
Wilson, K. J. 1987 (Ipswich T, Chelsea, Notts Co, Walsall) 42
Wilson, M. 1884 (Distillery) 3
Wilson, R. 1888 (Cliftonville) 1
Wilson, S. J. 1962 (Glenavon, Falkirk, Dundee) 12

Wilton, J. M. 1888 (St Columb's Court, Cliftonville, St Columb's Court) 7
Wood, T. J. 1996 (Walsall) 1
Worthington, N. 1984 (Sheffield W, Leeds U, Stoke C) 66
Wright, J. 1906 (Cliftonville) 6
Wright, T. J. 1989 (Newcastle U, Nottingham F, Manchester C) 31

Young, S. 1907 (Linfield, Airdrieonians, Linfield) 9

SCOTLAND

Adam, C. G. 2007 (Rangers) 2
Adams, J. 1889 (Hearts) 3
Agnew, W. B. 1907 (Kilmarnock) 3
Aird, J. 1954 (Burnley) 4
Aitken, A. 1901 (Newcastle U, Middlesbrough, Leicester Fosse) 14
Aitken, G. G. 1949 (East Fife, Sunderland) 8
Aitken, R. 1886 (Dumbarton) 2
Aitken, R. 1980 (Celtic, Newcastle U, St Mirren) 57
Aitkenhead, W. A. C. 1912 (Blackburn R) 1
Albiston, A. 1982 (Manchester U) 14
Alexander, D. 1894 (East Stirlingshire) 2
Alexander, G. 2002 (Preston NE, Burnley) 38
Alexander, N. 2006 (Cardiff C) 3
Allan, D. S. 1885 (Queen's Park) 3
Allan, G. 1897 (Liverpool) 1
Allan, H. 1902 (Hearts) 1
Allan, J. 1887 (Queen's Park) 2
Allan, T. 1974 (Dundee) 2
Ancell, R. F. D. 1937 (Newcastle U) 2
Anderson, A. 1933 (Hearts) 23
Anderson, F. 1874 (Clydesdale) 1
Anderson, G. 1901 (Kilmarnock) 1
Anderson, H. A. 1914 (Raith R) 1
Anderson, J. 1954 (Leicester C) 1
Anderson, K. 1896 (Queen's Park) 3
Anderson, R. 2003 (Aberdeen, Sunderland) 11
Anderson, W. 1882 (Queen's Park) 6
Andrews, P. 1875 (Eastern) 1
Archibald, A. 1921 (Rangers) 8
Archibald, S. 1980 (Aberdeen, Tottenham H, Barcelona) 27
Armstrong, M. W. 1936 (Aberdeen) 3
Arnott, W. 1883 (Queen's Park) 14
Auld, J. R. 1887 (Third Lanark) 3
Auld, R. 1959 (Celtic) 3

Baird, A. 1892 (Queen's Park) 2
Baird, D. 1890 (Hearts) 3
Baird, H. 1956 (Airdrieonians) 1
Baird, J. C. 1876 (Vale of Leven) 3
Baird, S. 1957 (Rangers) 7
Baird, W. U. 1897 (St Bernard) 1
Bannon, E. J. 1980 (Dundee U) 11
Barbour, A. 1885 (Renton) 1
Barker, J. B. 1893 (Rangers) 2
Barr, D. 1887 (Falkirk) 1
Barrett, F. 1894 (Dundee) 2
Battles, B. 1901 (Celtic) 3
Battles, B. jun. 1931 (Hearts) 1
Bauld, W. 1950 (Hearts) 3
Baxter, J. C. 1961 (Rangers, Sunderland) 34
Baxter, R. D. 1939 (Middlesbrough) 3
Beattie, A. 1937 (Preston NE) 7
Beattie, C. 2006 (Celtic, WBA) 7
Beattie, R. 1939 (Preston NE) 1
Begbie, I. 1890 (Hearts) 4
Bell, A. 1912 (Manchester U) 1
Bell, J. 1890 (Dumbarton, Everton, Celtic) 10
Bell, M. 1901 (Hearts) 1
Bell, W. J. 1966 (Leeds U) 2
Bennett, A. 1904 (Celtic, Rangers) 11
Bennie, R. 1925 (Airdrieonians) 3

Bernard, P. R. J. 1995 (Oldham Ath) 2
Berra, C. 2008 (Hearts, Wolverhampton W) 4
Berry, D. 1894 (Queen's Park) 3
Berry, W. H. 1888 (Queen's Park) 4
Bett, J. 1982 (Rangers, Lokeren, Aberdeen) 25
Beveridge, W. W. 1879 (Glasgow University) 3
Black, A. 1938 (Hearts) 3
Black, D. 1889 (Hurlford) 1
Black, E. 1988 (Metz) 2
Black, I. H. 1948 (Southampton) 1
Blackburn, J. E. 1873 (Royal Engineers) 1
Blacklaw, A. S. 1963 (Burnley) 3
Blackley, J. 1974 (Hibernian) 7
Blair, D. 1929 (Clyde, Aston Villa) 8
Blair, J. 1920 (Sheffield W, Cardiff C) 8
Blair, J. 1934 (Motherwell) 1
Blair, J. A. 1947 (Blackpool) 1
Blair, W. 1896 (Third Lanark) 1
Blessington, J. 1894 (Celtic) 4
Blyth, J. A. 1978 (Coventry C) 2
Bone, J. 1972 (Norwich C) 2
Booth, S. 1993 (Aberdeen, Borussia Dortmund, Twente) 21
Bowie, J. 1920 (Rangers) 2
Bowie, W. 1891 (Linthouse) 1
Bowman, D. 1992 (Dundee U) 6
Bowman, G. A. 1892 (Montrose) 1
Boyd, J. M. 1934 (Newcastle U) 1
Boyd, K. 2006 (Rangers) 15
Boyd, R. 1889 (Mossend Swifts) 2
Boyd, T. 1991 (Motherwell, Chelsea, Celtic) 72
Boyd, W. G. 1931 (Clyde) 2
Bradshaw, T. 1928 (Bury) 1
Brand, R. 1961 (Rangers) 8
Brandon, T. 1896 (Blackburn R) 1
Brazil, A. 1980 (Ipswich T, Tottenham H) 13
Breckenridge, T. 1888 (Hearts) 1
Bremner, D. 1976 (Hibernian) 1
Bremner, W. J. 1965 (Leeds U) 54
Brennan, F. 1947 (Newcastle U) 7
Breslin, B. 1897 (Hibernian) 1
Brewster, G. 1921 (Everton) 1
Broadfoot, K. 2009 (Rangers) 3
Brogan, J. 1971 (Celtic) 4
Brown, A. 1890 (St Mirren) 2
Brown, A. 1904 (Middlesbrough) 1
Brown, A. D. 1950 (East Fife, Blackpool) 14
Brown, G. C. P. 1931 (Rangers) 19
Brown, H. 1947 (Partick Th) 3
Brown, J. B. 1939 (Clyde) 1
Brown, J. G. 1975 (Sheffield U) 1
Brown, R. 1884 (Dumbarton) 2
Brown, R. 1890 (Cambuslang) 1
Brown, R. 1947 (Rangers) 3
Brown, R. jun. 1885 (Dumbarton) 1
Brown, S. 2006 (Hibernian, Celtic) 16
Brown, W. D. F. 1958 (Dundee, Tottenham H) 28
Browning, J. 1914 (Celtic) 1
Brownlie, J. 1909 (Third Lanark) 16
Brownlie, J. 1971 (Hibernian) 7
Bruce, D. 1890 (Vale of Leven) 1
Bruce, R. F. 1934 (Middlesbrough) 1
Buchan, M. M. 1972 (Aberdeen, Manchester U) 34

Buchanan, J. 1889 (Cambuslang)	1
Buchanan, J. 1929 (Rangers)	2
Buchanan, P. S. 1938 (Chelsea)	1
Buchanan, R. 1891 (Abercorn)	1
Buckley, P. 1954 (Aberdeen)	3
Buick, A. 1902 (Hearts)	2
Burchill, M. J. 2000 (Celtic)	6
Burke, C. 2006 (Rangers)	2
Burley, C. W. 1995 (Chelsea, Celtic, Derby Co)	46
Burley, G. E. 1979 (Ipswich T)	11
Burns, F. 1970 (Manchester U)	1
Burns, K. 1974 (Birmingham C, Nottingham F)	20
Burns, T. 1981 (Celtic)	8
Busby, M. W. 1934 (Manchester C)	1
Cairns, T. 1920 (Rangers)	8
Calderhead, D. 1889 (Q of S Wanderers)	1
Calderwood, C. 1995 (Tottenham H)	36
Calderwood, R. 1885 (Cartvale)	3
Caldow, E. 1957 (Rangers)	40
Caldwell, G. 2002 (Newcastle U, Hibernian, Celtic)	33
Caldwell, S. 2001 (Newcastle U, Sunderland)	9
Callaghan, P. 1900 (Hibernian)	1
Callaghan, W. 1970 (Dunfermline Ath)	2
Cameron, C. 1999 (Hearts, Wolverhampton W)	28
Cameron, J. 1886 (Rangers)	1
Cameron, J. 1896 (Queen's Park)	1
Cameron, J. 1904 (St Mirren, Chelsea)	2
Campbell, C. 1874 (Queen's Park)	13
Campbell, H. 1889 (Renton)	1
Campbell, Jas 1913 (Sheffield W)	1
Campbell, J. 1880 (South Western)	1
Campbell, J. 1891 (Kilmarnock)	2
Campbell, John 1893 (Celtic)	12
Campbell, John 1899 (Rangers)	4
Campbell, K. 1920 (Liverpool, Partick Th)	8
Campbell, P. 1878 (Rangers)	2
Campbell, P. 1898 (Morton)	1
Campbell, R. 1947 (Falkirk, Chelsea)	5
Campbell, W. 1947 (Morton)	5
Canero, P. 2004 (Leicester C)	1
Carabine, J. 1938 (Third Lanark)	3
Carr, W. M. 1970 (Coventry C)	6
Cassidy, J. 1921 (Celtic)	4
Chalmers, S. 1965 (Celtic)	5
Chalmers, W. 1885 (Rangers)	1
Chalmers, W. S. 1929 (Queen's Park)	1
Chambers, T. 1894 (Hearts)	1
Chaplin, G. D. 1908 (Dundee)	1
Cheyne, A. G. 1929 (Aberdeen)	5
Christie, A. J. 1898 (Queen's Park)	3
Christie, R. M. 1884 (Queen's Park)	1
Clark, J. 1966 (Celtic)	4
Clark, R. B. 1968 (Aberdeen)	17
Clarke, S. 1988 (Chelsea)	6
Clarkson, D. 2008 (Motherwell)	2
Cleland, J. 1891 (Royal Albert)	1
Clements, R. 1891 (Leith Ath)	1
Clunas, W. L. 1924 (Sunderland)	2
Collier, W. 1922 (Raith R)	1
Collins, J. 1988 (Hibernian, Celtic, Monaco, Everton)	58
Collins, R. Y. 1951 (Celtic, Everton, Leeds U)	31
Collins, T. 1909 (Hearts)	1
Colman, D. 1911 (Aberdeen)	4
Colquhoun, E. P. 1972 (Sheffield U)	9
Colquhoun, J. 1988 (Hearts)	2
Combe, J. R. 1948 (Hibernian)	3
Commons, K. 2009 (Derby Co)	4
Conn, A. 1956 (Hearts)	1
Conn, A. 1975 (Tottenham H)	2
Connachan, E. D. 1962 (Dunfermline Ath)	2
Connelly, G. 1974 (Celtic)	2
Connolly, J. 1973 (Everton)	1
Connor, J. 1886 (Airdrieonians)	1
Connor, J. 1930 (Sunderland)	4
Connor, R. 1986 (Dundee, Aberdeen)	4
Cook, W. L. 1934 (Bolton W)	3
Cooke, C. 1966 (Dundee, Chelsea)	16
Cooper, D. 1980 (Rangers, Motherwell)	22
Cormack, P. B. 1966 (Hibernian, Nottingham F)	9
Cowan, J. 1896 (Aston Villa)	3
Cowan, J. 1948 (Morton)	25
Cowan, W. D. 1924 (Newcastle U)	1
Cowie, D. 1953 (Dundee)	20
Cox, C. J. 1948 (Hearts)	1
Cox, S. 1949 (Rangers)	24
Craig, A. 1929 (Motherwell)	3
Craig, J. 1977 (Celtic)	1
Craig, J. P. 1968 (Celtic)	1
Craig, T. 1927 (Rangers)	8
Craig, T. B. 1976 (Newcastle U)	1
Crainey, S. D. 2002 (Celtic, Southampton)	6
Crapnell, J. 1929 (Airdrieonians)	9
Crawford, D. 1894 (St Mirren, Rangers)	3
Crawford, J. 1932 (Queen's Park)	5
Crawford, S. 1995 (Raith R, Dunfermline Ath,	
Plymouth Arg)	25
Crerand, P. T. 1961 (Celtic, Manchester U)	16
Cringan, W. 1920 (Celtic)	5
Crosbie, J. A. 1920 (Ayr U, Birmingham)	2
Croal, J. A. 1913 (Falkirk)	3
Cropley, A. J. 1972 (Hibernian)	2
Cross, J. H. 1903 (Third Lanark)	1
Cruickshank, J. 1964 (Hearts)	6
Crum, J. 1936 (Celtic)	2
Cullen, M. J. 1956 (Luton T)	1
Cumming, D. S. 1938 (Middlesbrough)	1
Cumming, J. 1955 (Hearts)	9
Cummings, G. 1935 (Partick Th, Aston Villa)	9
Cummings, W. 2002 (Chelsea)	1
Cunningham, A. N. 1920 (Rangers)	12
Cunningham, W. C. 1954 (Preston NE)	8
Curran, H. P. 1970 (Wolverhampton W)	5
Dailly, C. 1997 (Derby Co, Blackburn R, West Ham U,	
Rangers)	67
Dalglish, K. 1972 (Celtic, Liverpool)	102
Davidson, C. I. 1999 (Blackburn R, Leicester C)	17
Davidson, D. 1878 (Queen's Park)	5
Davidson, J. A. 1954 (Partick Th)	8
Davidson, S. 1921 (Middlesbrough)	1
Dawson, A. 1980 (Rangers)	5
Dawson, J. 1935 (Rangers)	14
Deans, J. 1975 (Celtic)	2
Delaney, J. 1936 (Celtic, Manchester U)	13
Devine, A. 1910 (Falkirk)	1
Devlin, P. J. 2003 (Birmingham C)	10
Dewar, G. 1888 (Dumbarton)	2
Dewar, N. 1932 (Third Lanark)	3
Dick, J. 1959 (West Ham U)	1
Dickie, M. 1897 (Rangers)	3
Dickov, P. 2001 (Manchester C, Leicester C,	
Blackburn R)	10
Dickson, W. 1888 (Dundee Strathmore)	1
Dickson, W. 1970 (Kilmarnock)	5
Divers, J. 1895 (Celtic)	1
Divers, J. 1939 (Celtic)	1
Dobie, R. S. 2002 (WBA)	6
Docherty, T. H. 1952 (Preston NE, Arsenal)	25
Dodds, D. 1984 (Dundee U)	2
Dodds, J. 1914 (Celtic)	3
Dodds, W. 1997 (Aberdeen, Dundee U, Rangers)	26
Doig, J. E. 1887 (Arbroath, Sunderland)	5
Donachie, W. 1972 (Manchester C)	35
Donaldson, A. 1914 (Bolton W)	6
Donnachie, J. 1913 (Oldham Ath)	3
Donnelly, S. 1997 (Celtic)	10
Dougal, J. 1939 (Preston NE)	1
Dougall, C. 1947 (Birmingham C)	1
Dougan, R. 1950 (Hearts)	1

Douglas, A. 1911 (Chelsea)	1
Douglas, J. 1880 (Renfrew)	1
Douglas, R. 2002 (Celtic, Leicester C)	19
Dowds, P. 1892 (Celtic)	1
Downie, R. 1892 (Third Lanark)	1
Doyle, D. 1892 (Celtic)	8
Doyle, J. 1976 (Ayr U)	1
Drummond, J. 1892 (Falkirk, Rangers)	14
Dunbar, M. 1886 (Cartvale)	1
Duncan, A. 1975 (Hibernian)	6
Duncan, D. 1933 (Derby Co)	14
Duncan, D. M. 1948 (East Fife)	3
Duncan, J. 1878 (Alexandra Ath)	2
Duncan, J. 1926 (Leicester C)	1
Duncanson, J. 1947 (Rangers)	1
Dunlop, J. 1890 (St Mirren)	1
Dunlop, W. 1906 (Liverpool)	1
Dunn, J. 1925 (Hibernian, Everton)	6
Durie, G. S. 1988 (Chelsea, Tottenham H, Rangers)	43
Durrant, I. 1988 (Rangers, Kilmarnock)	20
Dykes, J. 1938 (Hearts)	2
Easson, J. F. 1931 (Portsmouth)	3
Elliott, M. S. 1998 (Leicester C)	18
Ellis, J. 1892 (Mossend Swifts)	1
Evans, A. 1982 (Aston Villa)	4
Evans, R. 1949 (Celtic, Chelsea)	48
Ewart, J. 1921 (Bradford C)	1
Ewing, T. 1958 (Partick Th)	2
Farm, G. N. 1953 (Blackpool)	10
Ferguson, B. 1999 (Rangers, Blackburn R, Rangers)	45
Ferguson, D. 1988 (Rangers)	2
Ferguson, D. 1992 (Dundee U, Everton)	7
Ferguson, I. 1989 (Rangers)	9
Ferguson, J. 1874 (Vale of Leven)	6
Ferguson, R. 1966 (Kilmarnock)	7
Fernie, W. 1954 (Celtic)	12
Findlay, R. 1898 (Kilmarnock)	1
Fitchie, T. T. 1905 (Woolwich Arsenal, Queen's Park)	4
Flavell, R. 1947 (Airdrieonians)	2
Fleck, R. 1990 (Norwich C)	4
Fleming, C. 1954 (East Fife)	1
Fleming, J. W. 1929 (Rangers)	3
Fleming, R. 1886 (Morton)	1
Fletcher, D. B. 2004 (Manchester U)	42
Fletcher, S. 2008 (Hibernian)	4
Forbes, A. R. 1947 (Sheffield U, Arsenal)	14
Forbes, J. 1884 (Vale of Leven)	5
Ford, D. 1974 (Hearts)	3
Forrest, J. 1966 (Rangers, Aberdeen)	5
Forrest, J. 1958 (Motherwell)	1
Forsyth, A. 1972 (Partick Th, Manchester U)	10
Forsyth, C. 1964 (Kilmarnock)	4
Forsyth, T. 1971 (Motherwell, Rangers)	22
Foyers, R. 1893 (St Bernards)	2
Fraser, D. M. 1968 (WBA)	2
Fraser, J. 1891 (Moffat)	1
Fraser, M. J. E. 1880 (Queen's Park)	5
Fraser, J. 1907 (Dundee)	1
Fraser, W. 1955 (Sunderland)	2
Freedman, D. A. 2002 (C Palace)	2
Fulton, W. 1884 (Abercorn)	1
Fyfe, J. H. 1895 (Third Lanark)	1
Gabriel, J. 1961 (Everton)	2
Gallacher, H. K. 1924 (Airdrieonians, Newcastle U, Chelsea, Derby Co)	20
Gallacher, K. W. 1988 (Dundee U, Coventry C, Blackburn R, Newcastle U)	53
Gallacher, P. 1935 (Sunderland)	1
Gallacher, P. 2002 (Dundee U)	8
Gallagher, P. 2004 (Blackburn R)	1
Galloway, M. 1992 (Celtic)	1
Galt, J. H. 1908 (Rangers)	2

Gardiner, I. 1958 (Motherwell)	1
Gardner, D. R. 1897 (Third Lanark)	1
Gardner, R. 1872 (Queen's Park, Clydesdale)	5
Gemmell, T. 1955 (St Mirren)	2
Gemmell, T. 1966 (Celtic)	18
Gemmill, A. 1971 (Derby Co, Nottingham F, Birmingham C)	43
Gemmill, S. 1995 (Nottingham F, Everton)	26
Gibb, W. 1873 (Clydesdale)	1
Gibson, D. W. 1963 (Leicester C)	7
Gibson, J. D. 1926 (Partick Th, Aston Villa)	8
Gibson, N. 1895 (Rangers, Partick Th)	14
Gilchrist, J. E. 1922 (Celtic)	1
Gilhooley, M. 1922 (Hull C)	1
Gillespie, G. 1880 (Rangers, Queen's Park)	7
Gillespie, G. T. 1988 (Liverpool)	13
Gillespie, Jas 1898 (Third Lanark)	1
Gillespie, John 1896 (Queen's Park)	1
Gillespie, R. 1927 (Queen's Park)	4
Gillick, T. 1937 (Everton)	5
Gilmour, J. 1931 (Dundee)	1
Gilzean, A. J. 1964 (Dundee, Tottenham H)	22
Glass, S. 1999 (Newcastle U)	1
Glavin, R. 1977 (Celtic)	1
Glen, A. 1956 (Aberdeen)	2
Glen, R. 1895 (Renton, Hibernian)	3
Goram, A. L. 1986 (Oldham Ath, Hibernian, Rangers)	43
Gordon, C. S. 2004 (Hearts, Sunderland)	36
Gordon, J. E. 1912 (Rangers)	10
Gossland, J. 1884 (Rangers)	1
Goudie, J. 1884 (Abercorn)	1
Gough, C. R. 1983 (Dundee U, Tottenham H, Rangers)	61
Gould, J. 2000 (Celtic)	2
Gourlay, J. 1886 (Cambuslang)	2
Govan, J. 1948 (Hibernian)	6
Gow, D. R. 1888 (Rangers)	1
Gow, J. J. 1885 (Queen's Park)	1
Gow, J. R. 1888 (Rangers)	1
Graham, A. 1978 (Leeds U)	11
Graham, G. 1972 (Arsenal, Manchester U)	12
Graham, J. 1884 (Annbank)	1
Graham, J. A. 1921 (Arsenal)	1
Grant, J. 1959 (Hibernian)	2
Grant, P. 1989 (Celtic)	2
Gray, A. 1903 (Hibernian)	1
Gray, A. D. 2003 (Bradford C)	2
Gray, A. M. 1976 (Aston Villa, Wolverhampton W, Everton)	20
Gray, D. 1929 (Rangers)	10
Gray, E. 1969 (Leeds U)	12
Gray, F. T. 1976 (Leeds U, Nottingham F, Leeds U)	32
Gray, W. 1886 (Pollokshields Ath)	1
Green, A. 1971 (Blackpool, Newcastle U)	6
Greig, J. 1964 (Rangers)	44
Groves, W. 1888 (Hibernian, Celtic)	3
Gulliland, W. 1891 (Queen's Park)	4
Gunn, B. 1990 (Norwich C)	6
Haddock, H. 1955 (Clyde)	6
Haddow, D. 1894 (Rangers)	1
Haffey, F. 1960 (Celtic)	2
Hamilton, A. 1885 (Queen's Park)	4
Hamilton, A. W. 1962 (Dundee)	24
Hamilton, G. 1906 (Port Glasgow Ath)	1
Hamilton, G. 1947 (Aberdeen)	5
Hamilton, J. 1892 (Queen's Park)	3
Hamilton, J. 1924 (St Mirren)	1
Hamilton, R. C. 1899 (Rangers, Dundee)	11
Hamilton, T. 1891 (Hurlford)	1
Hamilton, T. 1932 (Rangers)	1
Hamilton, W. M. 1965 (Hibernian)	1
Hammell, S. 2005 (Motherwell)	1
Hannah, A. B. 1888 (Renton)	1

Lawrence, T. 1963 (Liverpool) 3
Lawson, D. 1923 (St Mirren) 1
Leckie, R. 1872 (Queen's Park) 1
Leggat, G. 1956 (Aberdeen, Fulham) 18
Leighton, J. 1983 (Aberdeen, Manchester U, Hibernian, Aberdeen) 91
Lennie, W. 1908 (Aberdeen) 2
Lennox, R. 1967 (Celtic) 10
Leslie, L. G. 1961 (Airdrieonians) 5
Levein, C. 1990 (Hearts) 16
Liddell, W. 1947 (Liverpool) 28
Liddle, D. 1931 (East Fife) 3
Lindsay, D. 1903 (St Mirren) 1
Lindsay, J. 1880 (Dumbarton) 8
Lindsay, J. 1888 (Renton) 3
Linwood, A. B. 1950 (Clyde) 1
Little, R. J. 1953 (Rangers) 1
Livingstone, G. T. 1906 (Manchester C, Rangers) 2
Lochhead, A. 1889 (Third Lanark) 1
Logan, J. 1891 (Ayr) 1
Logan, T. 1913 (Falkirk) 1
Logie, J. T. 1953 (Arsenal) 1
Loney, W. 1910 (Celtic) 2
Long, H. 1947 (Clyde) 1
Longair, W. 1894 (Dundee) 1
Lorimer, P. 1970 (Leeds U) 21
Love, A. 1931 (Aberdeen) 3
Low, A. 1934 (Falkirk) 1
Low, J. 1891 (Cambuslang) 1
Low, T. P. 1897 (Rangers) 1
Low, W. L. 1911 (Newcastle U) 5
Lowe, J. 1887 (St Bernards) 1
Lundie, J. 1886 (Hibernian) 1
Lyall, J. 1905 (Sheffield W) 1

McAdam, J. 1880 (Third Lanark) 1
McAllister, B. 1997 (Wimbledon) 3
McAllister, G. 1990 (Leicester C, Leeds U, Coventry C) 57
McAllister, J. R. 2004 (Livingston) 1
Macari, L. 1972 (Celtic, Manchester U) 24
McArthur, D. 1895 (Celtic) 3
McAtee, A. 1913 (Celtic) 1
McAulay, J. 1884 (Arthurlie) 1
McAulay, J. D. 1882 (Dumbarton) 9
McAulay, R. 1932 (Rangers) 2
Macauley, A. R. 1947 (Brentford, Arsenal) 7
McAvennie, F. 1986 (West Ham U, Celtic) 5
McBain, E. 1894 (St Mirren) 1
McBain, N. 1922 (Manchester U, Everton) 3
McBride, J. 1967 (Celtic) 2
McBride, P. 1904 (Preston NE) 6
McCall, A. 1888 (Renton) 1
McCall, A. S. M. 1990 (Everton, Rangers) 40
McCall, J. 1886 (Renton) 5
McCalliog, J. 1967 (Sheffield W, Wolverhampton W) 5
McCallum, N. 1888 (Renton) 1
McCann, N. 1999 (Hearts, Rangers, Southampton) 26
McCann, R. J. 1959 (Motherwell) 5
McCartney, W. 1902 (Hibernian) 1
McClair, B. 1987 (Celtic, Manchester U) 30
McClory, A. 1927 (Motherwell) 3
McCloy, P. 1924 (Ayr U) 2
McCloy, P. 1973 (Rangers) 4
McCoist, A. 1986 (Rangers, Kilmarnock) 61
McColl, I. M. 1950 (Rangers) 14
McColl, R. S. 1896 (Queen's Park, Newcastle U, Queen's Park) 13
McColl, W. 1895 (Renton) 1
McCombie, A. 1903 (Sunderland, Newcastle U) 4
McCorkindale, J. 1891 (Partick Th) 1
McCormack, R. 2008 (Motherwell, Cardiff C) 3
McCormick, R. 1886 (Abercorn) 1
McCrae, D. 1929 (St Mirren) 2
McCreadie, A. 1893 (Rangers) 2

McCreadie, E. G. 1965 (Chelsea) 23
McCulloch, D. 1935 (Hearts, Brentford, Derby Co) 7
McCulloch, L. 2005 (Wigan Ath, Rangers) 15
MacDonald, A. 1976 (Rangers) 1
McDonald, J. 1886 (Edinburgh University) 1
McDonald, J. 1956 (Sunderland) 2
MacDougall, E. J. 1975 (Norwich C) 7
McDougall, J. 1877 (Vale of Leven) 5
McDougall, J. 1926 (Airdrieonians) 1
McDougall, J. 1931 (Liverpool) 2
McEveley, J. 2008 (Derby Co) 3
McFadden, J. 2002 (Motherwell, Everton, Birmingham C) 42
McFadyen, W. 1934 (Motherwell) 2
Macfarlane, A. 1904 (Dundee) 5
Macfarlane, W. 1947 (Hearts) 1
McFarlane, R. 1896 (Greenock Morton) 1
McGarr, E. 1970 (Aberdeen) 2
McGarvey, F. P. 1979 (Liverpool, Celtic) 7
McGeoch, A. 1876 (Dumbreck) 4
McGhee, J. 1886 (Hibernian) 1
McGhee, M. 1983 (Aberdeen) 4
McGinlay, J. 1994 (Bolton W) 13
McGonagle, W. 1933 (Celtic) 6
McGrain, D. 1973 (Celtic) 62
McGregor, A. 2007 (Rangers) 4
McGregor, J. C. 1877 (Vale of Leven) 4
McGrory, J. 1928 (Celtic) 7
McGrory, J. E. 1965 (Kilmarnock) 3
McGuire, W. 1881 (Beith) 2
McGurk, F. 1934 (Birmingham) 1
McHardy, H. 1885 (Rangers) 1
McInally, A. 1989 (Aston Villa, Bayern Munich) 8
McInally, J. 1987 (Dundee U) 10
McInally, T. B. 1926 (Celtic) 2
McInnes, D. 2003 (WBA) 2
McInnes, T. 1889 (Cowlairs) 1
McIntosh, W. 1905 (Third Lanark) 1
McIntyre, A. 1878 (Vale of Leven) 2
McIntyre, H. 1880 (Rangers) 1
McIntyre, J. 1884 (Rangers) 1
MacKay, D. 1959 (Celtic) 14
Mackay, D. C. 1957 (Hearts, Tottenham H) 22
Mackay, G. 1988 (Hearts) 4
Mackay, M. 2004 (Norwich C) 5
McKay, J. 1924 (Blackburn R) 1
McKay, R. 1928 (Newcastle U) 1
McKean, R. 1976 (Rangers) 1
McKenzie, D. 1938 (Brentford) 1
Mackenzie, J. A. 1954 (Partick Th) 9
McKeown, M. 1889 (Celtic) 2
McKie, J. 1898 (East Stirling) 1
McKillop, T. R. 1938 (Rangers) 1
McKimmie, S. 1989 (Aberdeen) 40
McKinlay, D. 1922 (Liverpool) 2
McKinlay, T. 1996 (Celtic) 22
McKinlay, W. 1994 (Dundee U, Blackburn R) 29
McKinnon, A. 1874 (Queen's Park) 1
McKinnon, R. 1966 (Rangers) 28
McKinnon, R. 1994 (Motherwell) 3
McKinnon, W. 1883 (Dumbarton) 4
MacKinnon, W. W. 1872 (Queen's Park) 9
McLaren, A. 1929 (St Johnstone) 5
McLaren, A. 1947 (Preston NE) 4
McLaren, A. 1992 (Hearts, Rangers) 24
McLaren, A. 2001 (Kilmarnock) 1
McLaren, J. 1888 (Hibernian, Celtic) 3
McLean, A. 1926 (Celtic) 4
McLean, D. 1896 (St Bernards) 2
McLean, D. 1912 (Sheffield W) 1
McLean, G. 1968 (Dundee) 1
McLean, T. 1969 (Kilmarnock) 6
McLeish, A. 1980 (Aberdeen) 77
McLeod, D. 1905 (Celtic) 4
McLeod, J. 1888 (Dumbarton) 5

MacLeod, J. M. 1961 (Hibernian)	4
MacLeod, M. 1985 (Celtic, Borussia Dortmund, Hibernian)	20
McLeod, W. 1886 (Cowlairs)	1
McLintock, A. 1875 (Vale of Leven)	3
McLintock, F. 1963 (Leicester C, Arsenal)	9
McLuckie, J. S. 1934 (Manchester C)	1
McMahon, A. 1892 (Celtic)	6
McManus, S. 2007 (Celtic)	18
McMenemy, J. 1905 (Celtic)	12
McMenemy, J. 1934 (Motherwell)	1
McMillan, I. L. 1952 (Airdrieonians, Rangers)	6
McMillan, J. 1897 (St Bernards)	1
McMillan, T. 1887 (Dumbarton)	1
McMullan, J. 1920 (Partick Th, Manchester C)	16
McNab, A. 1921 (Morton)	2
McNab, A. 1937 (Sunderland, WBA)	2
McNab, C. D. 1931 (Dundee)	6
McNab, J. S. 1923 (Liverpool)	1
McNair, A. 1906 (Celtic)	15
McNamara, J. 1997 (Celtic, Wolverhampton W)	33
McNamee, D. 2004 (Livingston)	4
McNaught, W. 1951 (Raith R)	5
McNaughton, K. 2002 (Aberdeen, Cardiff C)	4
McNeill, W. 1961 (Celtic)	29
McNiel, H. 1874 (Queen's Park)	10
McNiel, M. 1876 (Rangers)	2
McPhail, J. 1950 (Celtic)	5
McPhail, R. 1927 (Airdrieonians, Rangers)	17
McPherson, D. 1892 (Kilmarnock)	1
McPherson, D. 1989 (Hearts, Rangers)	27
McPherson, J. 1875 (Clydesdale)	1
McPherson, J. 1879 (Vale of Leven)	8
McPherson, J. 1888 (Kilmarnock, Cowlairs, Rangers)	9
McPherson, J. 1891 (Hearts)	1
McPherson, R. 1882 (Arthurlie)	1
McQueen, G. 1974 (Leeds U, Manchester U)	30
McQueen, M. 1890 (Leith Ath)	2
McRorie, D. M. 1931 (Morton)	1
McSpadyen, A. 1939 (Partick Th)	2
McStay, P. 1984 (Celtic)	76
McStay, W. 1921 (Celtic)	13
McSwegan, G. 2000 (Hearts)	2
McTavish, J. 1910 (Falkirk)	1
McWattie, G. C. 1901 (Queen's Park)	2
McWilliam, P. 1905 (Newcastle U)	8
Madden, J. 1893 (Celtic)	2
Main, F. R. 1938 (Rangers)	1
Main, J. 1909 (Hibernian)	1
Maley, W. 1893 (Celtic)	2
Maloney, S. R. 2006 (Celtic, Aston Villa, Celtic)	15
Malpas, M. 1984 (Dundee U)	55
Marshall, D. J. 2005 (Celtic)	2
Marshall, G. 1992 (Celtic)	1
Marshall, H. 1899 (Celtic)	2
Marshall, J. 1885 (Third Lanark)	4
Marshall, J. 1921 (Middlesbrough, Llanelly)	7
Marshall, J. 1932 (Rangers)	3
Marshall, R. W. 1892 (Rangers)	2
Martin, B. 1995 (Motherwell)	2
Martin, F. 1954 (Aberdeen)	6
Martin, N. 1965 (Hibernian, Sunderland)	3
Martis, J. 1961 (Motherwell)	1
Mason, J. 1949 (Third Lanark)	7
Massie, A. 1932 (Hearts, Aston Villa)	18
Masson, D. S. 1976 (QPR, Derby Co)	17
Mathers, D. 1954 (Partick Th)	1
Matteo, D. 2001 (Leeds U)	6
Maxwell, W. S. 1898 (Stoke C)	1
May, J. 1906 (Rangers)	5
Meechan, P. 1896 (Celtic)	1
Meiklejohn, D. D. 1922 (Rangers)	15
Menzies, A. 1906 (Hearts)	1
Mercer, R. 1912 (Hearts)	2
Middleton, R. 1930 (Cowdenbeath)	1

Millar, J. 1897 (Rangers)	3
Millar, J. 1963 (Rangers)	2
Miller, A. 1939 (Hearts)	1
Miller, C. 2001 (Dundee U)	1
Miller, J. 1931 (St Mirren)	5
Miller, K. 2001 (Rangers, Wolverhampton W, Celtic, Derby Co, Rangers)	42
Miller, L. 2006 (Dundee U, Aberdeen)	2
Miller, P. 1882 (Dumbarton)	3
Miller, T. 1920 (Liverpool, Manchester U)	3
Miller, W. 1876 (Third Lanark)	1
Miller, W. 1947 (Celtic)	6
Miller, W. 1975 (Aberdeen)	65
Mills, W. 1936 (Aberdeen)	3
Milne, J. V. 1938 (Middlesbrough)	2
Mitchell, D. 1890 (Rangers)	5
Mitchell, J. 1908 (Kilmarnock)	3
Mitchell, R. C. 1951 (Newcastle U)	2
Mochan, N. 1954 (Celtic)	3
Moir, W. 1950 (Bolton W)	1
Moncur, R. 1968 (Newcastle U)	16
Morgan, H. 1898 (St Mirren, Liverpool)	2
Morgan, W. 1968 (Burnley, Manchester U)	21
Morris, D. 1923 (Raith R)	6
Morris, H. 1950 (East Fife)	1
Morrison, J. C. 2008 (WBA)	5
Morrison, T. 1927 (St Mirren)	1
Morton, A. L. 1920 (Queen's Park, Rangers)	31
Morton, H. A. 1929 (Kilmarnock)	2
Mudie, J. K. 1957 (Blackpool)	17
Muir, W. 1907 (Dundee)	1
Muirhead, T. A. 1922 (Rangers)	8
Mulhall, G. 1960 (Aberdeen, Sunderland)	3
Munro, A. D. 1937 (Hearts, Blackpool)	3
Munro, F. M. 1971 (Wolverhampton W)	9
Munro, I. 1979 (St Mirren)	7
Munro, N. 1888 (Abercorn)	2
Murdoch, J. 1931 (Motherwell)	1
Murdoch, R. 1966 (Celtic)	12
Murphy, F. 1938 (Celtic)	1
Murray, I. 2003 (Hibernian, Rangers)	6
Murray, J. 1895 (Renton)	1
Murray, J. 1958 (Hearts)	5
Murray, J. W. 1890 (Vale of Leven)	1
Murray, P. 1896 (Hibernian)	2
Murray, S. 1972 (Aberdeen)	1
Murty, G. S. 2004 (Reading)	4
Mutch, G. 1938 (Preston NE)	1
Naismith, S. J. 2007 (Kilmarnock, Rangers)	2
Napier, C. E. 1932 (Celtic, Derby Co)	5
Narey, D. 1977 (Dundee U)	35
Naysmith, G. A. 2000 (Hearts, Everton, Sheffield U)	46
Neil, R. G. 1896 (Hibernian, Rangers)	2
Neill, R. W. 1876 (Queen's Park)	5
Neilson, R. 2007 (Hearts)	1
Nellies, P. 1913 (Hearts)	2
Nelson, J. 1925 (Cardiff C)	4
Nevin, P. K. F. 1986 (Chelsea, Everton, Tranmere R)	28
Niblo, T. D. 1904 (Aston Villa)	1
Nibloe, J. 1929 (Kilmarnock)	11
Nicholas, C. 1983 (Celtic, Arsenal, Aberdeen)	20
Nicholson, B. 2001 (Dunfermline Ath)	3
Nicol, S. 1985 (Liverpool)	27
Nisbet, J. 1929 (Ayr U)	3
Niven, J. B. 1885 (Moffat)	1
O'Connor, G. 2002 (Hibernian, Lokomotiv Moscow, Birmingham C)	15
O'Donnell, F. 1937 (Preston NE, Blackpool)	6
O'Donnell, P. 1994 (Motherwell)	1
Ogilvie, D. H. 1934 (Motherwell)	1
O'Hare, J. 1970 (Derby Co)	13
O'Neil, B. 1996 (Celtic, Wolfsburg, Derby Co, Preston NE)	7

O'Neil, J. 2001 (Hibernian)   1
Ormond, W. E. 1954 (Hibernian)   6
O'Rourke, F. 1907 (Airdrieonians)   1
Orr, J. 1892 (Kilmarnock)   1
Orr, R. 1902 (Newcastle U)   2
Orr, T. 1952 (Morton)   2
Orr, W. 1900 (Celtic)   3
Orrock, R. 1913 (Falkirk)   1
Oswald, J. 1889 (Third Lanark, St Bernards, Rangers)   3

Parker, A. H. 1955 (Falkirk, Everton)   15
Parlane, D. 1973 (Rangers)   12
Parlane, R. 1878 (Vale of Leven)   3
Paterson, G. D. 1939 (Celtic)   1
Paterson, J. 1920 (Leicester C)   1
Paterson, J. 1931 (Cowdenbeath)   3
Paton, A. 1952 (Motherwell)   2
Paton, D. 1896 (St Bernards)   1
Paton, M. 1883 (Dumbarton)   5
Paton, R. 1879 (Vale of Leven)   2
Patrick, J. 1897 (St Mirren)   2
Paul, H. McD. 1909 (Queen's Park)   3
Paul, W. 1888 (Partick Th)   3
Paul, W. 1891 (Dykebar)   1
Pearson, S. P. 2004 (Motherwell, Celtic, Derby Co)   10
Pearson, T. 1947 (Newcastle U)   2
Penman, A. 1966 (Dundee)   1
Pettigrew, W. 1976 (Motherwell)   5
Phillips, J. 1877 (Queen's Park)   3
Plenderleith, J. B. 1961 (Manchester C)   1
Porteous, W. 1903 (Hearts)   1
Pressley, S. J. 2000 (Hearts)   32
Pringle, C. 1921 (St Mirren)   1
Provan, D. 1964 (Rangers)   5
Provan, D. 1980 (Celtic)   10
Pursell, P. 1914 (Queen's Park)   1

Quashie, N. F. 2004 (Portsmouth, Southampton, WBA)   14
Quinn, J. 1905 (Celtic)   11
Quinn, P. 1961 (Motherwell)   4

Rae, G. 2001 (Dundee, Rangers, Cardiff C)   14
Rae, J. 1889 (Third Lanark)   2
Raeside, J. S. 1906 (Third Lanark)   1
Raisbeck, A. G. 1900 (Liverpool)   8
Rankin, G. 1890 (Vale of Leven)   2
Rankin, R. 1929 (St Mirren)   3
Redpath, W. 1949 (Motherwell)   9
Reid, J. G. 1914 (Airdrieonians)   3
Reid, R. 1938 (Brentford)   2
Reid, W. 1911 (Rangers)   9
Reilly, L. 1949 (Hibernian)   38
Rennie, H. G. 1900 (Hearts, Hibernian)   13
Renny-Tailyour, H. W. 1873 (Royal Engineers)   1
Rhind, A. 1872 (Queen's Park)   1
Richmond, A. 1906 (Queen's Park)   1
Richmond, J. T. 1877 (Clydesdale, Queen's Park)   3
Ring, T. 1953 (Clyde)   12
Rioch, B. D. 1975 (Derby Co, Everton, Derby Co)   24
Riordan, D. G. 2006 (Hibernian)   1
Ritchie, A. 1891 (East Stirlingshire)   1
Ritchie, H. 1923 (Hibernian)   2
Ritchie, J. 1897 (Queen's Park)   1
Ritchie, P. S. 1999 (Hearts, Bolton W, Walsall)   7
Ritchie, W. 1962 (Rangers)   1
Robb, D. T. 1971 (Aberdeen)   5
Robb, W. 1926 (Rangers, Hibernian)   2
Robertson, A. 1955 (Clyde)   5
Robertson, D. 1992 (Rangers)   3
Robertson, G. 1910 (Motherwell, Sheffield W)   4
Robertson, G. 1938 (Kilmarnock)   1
Robertson, H. 1962 (Dundee)   1
Robertson, J. 1931 (Dundee)   1
Robertson, J. 1991 (Hearts)   16

Robertson, J. N. 1978 (Nottingham F, Derby Co)   28
Robertson, J. G. 1965 (Tottenham H)   1
Robertson, J. T. 1898 (Everton, Southampton, Rangers)   16
Robertson, P. 1903 (Dundee)   1
Robertson, S. 2009 (Dundee U)   1
Robertson, T. 1889 (Queen's Park)   4
Robertson, T. 1898 (Hearts)   1
Robertson, W. 1887 (Dumbarton)   2
Robinson, R. 1974 (Dundee)   4
Robson, B. 2008 (Dundee U, Celtic)   6
Ross, M. 2002 (Rangers)   13
Rough, A. 1976 (Partick Th, Hibernian)   53
Rougvie, D. 1984 (Aberdeen)   1
Rowan, A. 1880 (Caledonian, Queen's Park)   2
Russell, D. 1895 (Hearts, Celtic)   6
Russell, J. 1890 (Cambuslang)   1
Russell, W. F. 1924 (Airdrieonians)   2
Rutherford, E. 1948 (Rangers)   1

St John, I. 1959 (Motherwell, Liverpool)   21
Sawers, W. 1895 (Dundee)   1
Scarff, P. 1931 (Celtic)   1
Schaedler, E. 1974 (Hibernian)   1
Scott, A. S. 1957 (Rangers, Everton)   16
Scott, J. 1966 (Hibernian)   1
Scott, J. 1971 (Dundee)   2
Scott, M. 1898 (Airdrieonians)   1
Scott, R. 1894 (Airdrieonians)   1
Scoular, J. 1951 (Portsmouth)   9
Sellar, W. 1885 (Battlefield, Queen's Park)   9
Semple, W. 1886 (Cambuslang)   1
Severin, S. D. 2002 (Hearts, Aberdeen)   15
Shankly, W. 1938 (Preston NE)   5
Sharp, G. M. 1985 (Everton)   12
Sharp, J. 1904 (Dundee, Woolwich Arsenal, Fulham)   5
Shaw, D. 1947 (Hibernian)   8
Shaw, F. W. 1884 (Pollokshields Ath)   2
Shaw, J. 1947 (Rangers)   4
Shearer, D. 1994 (Aberdeen)   7
Shearer, R. 1961 (Rangers)   4
Sillars, D. C. 1891 (Queen's Park)   5
Simpson, J. 1895 (Third Lanark)   3
Simpson, J. 1935 (Rangers)   14
Simpson, N. 1983 (Aberdeen)   5
Simpson, R. C. 1967 (Celtic)   5
Sinclair, G. L. 1910 (Hearts)   3
Sinclair, J. W. E. 1966 (Leicester C)   1
Skene, L. H. 1904 (Queen's Park)   1
Sloan, T. 1904 (Third Lanark)   1
Smellie, R. 1887 (Queen's Park)   6
Smith, A. 1898 (Rangers)   20
Smith, D. 1966 (Aberdeen, Rangers)   2
Smith, G. 1947 (Hibernian)   18
Smith, H. G. 1988 (Hearts)   3
Smith, J. 1924 (Ayr U)   1
Smith, J. 1935 (Rangers)   2
Smith, J. 1968 (Aberdeen, Newcastle U)   4
Smith, J. 2003 (Celtic)   2
Smith, J. E. 1959 (Celtic)   2
Smith, Jas 1872 (Queen's Park)   1
Smith, John 1877 (Mauchline, Edinburgh University, Queen's Park)   10
Smith, N. 1897 (Rangers)   12
Smith, R. 1872 (Queen's Park)   2
Smith, T. M. 1934 (Kilmarnock, Preston NE)   2
Somers, J. 1905 (Celtic)   4
Somers, W. S. 1879 (Third Lanark, Queen's Park)   3
Somerville, G. 1886 (Queen's Park)   1
Souness, G. J. 1975 (Middlesbrough, Liverpool, Sampdoria)   54
Speedie, D. R. 1985 (Chelsea, Coventry C)   10
Speedie, F. 1903 (Rangers)   3
Speirs, J. H. 1908 (Rangers)   1
Spencer, J. 1995 (Chelsea, QPR)   14

Stanton, P. 1966 (Hibernian)	16
Stark, J. 1909 (Rangers)	2
Steel, W. 1947 (Morton, Derby Co, Dundee)	30
Steele, D. M. 1923 (Huddersfield)	3
Stein, C. 1969 (Rangers, Coventry C)	21
Stephen, J. F. 1947 (Bradford)	2
Stevenson, G. 1928 (Motherwell)	12
Stewart, A. 1888 (Queen's Park)	2
Stewart, A. 1894 (Third Lanark)	1
Stewart, D. 1888 (Dumbarton)	1
Stewart, D. 1893 (Queen's Park)	3
Stewart, D. S. 1978 (Leeds U)	1
Stewart, G. 1906 (Hibernian, Manchester C)	4
Stewart, J. 1977 (Kilmarnock, Middlesbrough)	2
Stewart, M. J. 2002 (Manchester U, Hearts)	4
Stewart, R. 1981 (West Ham U)	10
Stewart, W. G. 1898 (Queen's Park)	2
Stockdale, R. K. 2002 (Middlesbrough)	5
Storrier, D. 1899 (Celtic)	3
Strachan, G. D. 1980 (Aberdeen, Manchester U, Leeds U)	50
Sturrock, P. 1981 (Dundee U)	20
Sullivan, N. 1997 (Wimbledon, Tottenham H)	28
Summers, W. 1926 (St Mirren)	1
Symon, J. S. 1939 (Rangers)	1
Tait, T. S. 1911 (Sunderland)	1
Taylor, J. 1872 (Queen's Park)	6
Taylor, J. D. 1892 (Dumbarton, St Mirren)	4
Taylor, W. 1892 (Hearts)	1
Teale, G. 2006 (Wigan Ath, Derby Co)	13
Telfer, P. N. 2000 (Coventry C)	1
Telfer, W. 1933 (Motherwell)	2
Telfer, W. D. 1954 (St Mirren)	1
Templeton, R. 1902 (Aston Villa, Newcastle U, Woolwich Arsenal, Kilmarnock)	11
Thompson, S. 2002 (Dundee U, Rangers)	16
Thomson, A. 1886 (Arthurlie)	1
Thomson, A. 1889 (Third Lanark)	1
Thomson, A. 1909 (Airdrieonians)	1
Thomson, A. 1926 (Celtic)	3
Thomson, C. 1904 (Hearts, Sunderland)	21
Thomson, C. 1937 (Sunderland)	1
Thomson, D. 1920 (Dundee)	1
Thomson, J. 1930 (Celtic)	4
Thomson, J. J. 1872 (Queen's Park)	3
Thomson, J. R. 1933 (Everton)	1
Thomson, K. 2009 (Rangers)	1
Thomson, R. 1932 (Celtic)	1
Thomson, R. W. 1927 (Falkirk)	1
Thomson, S. 1884 (Rangers)	2
Thomson, W. 1892 (Dumbarton)	4
Thomson, W. 1896 (Dundee)	1
Thomson, W. 1980 (St Mirren)	7
Thornton, W. 1947 (Rangers)	7
Toner, W. 1959 (Kilmarnock)	2
Townsley, T. 1926 (Falkirk)	1
Troup, A. 1920 (Dundee, Everton)	5
Turnbull, E. 1948 (Hibernian)	8
Turner, T. 1884 (Arthurlie)	1
Turner, W. 1885 (Pollokshields Ath)	2
Ure, J. F. 1962 (Dundee, Arsenal)	11
Urquhart, D. 1934 (Hibernian)	1
Vallance, T. 1877 (Rangers)	7
Venters, A. 1934 (Cowdenbeath, Rangers)	3
Waddell, T. S. 1891 (Queen's Park)	6
Waddell, W. 1947 (Rangers)	17

Wales, H. M. 1933 (Motherwell)	1
Walker, A. 1988 (Celtic)	3
Walker, F. 1922 (Third Lanark)	1
Walker, G. 1930 (St Mirren)	4
Walker, J. 1895 (Hearts, Rangers)	5
Walker, J. 1911 (Swindon T)	9
Walker, J. N. 1993 (Hearts, Partick Th)	2
Walker, R. 1900 (Hearts)	29
Walker, T. 1935 (Hearts)	20
Walker, W. 1909 (Clyde)	2
Wallace, I. A. 1978 (Coventry C)	3
Wallace, W. S. B. 1965 (Hearts, Celtic)	7
Wardhaugh, J. 1955 (Hearts)	2
Wark, J. 1979 (Ipswich T, Liverpool)	29
Watson, J. 1903 (Sunderland, Middlesbrough)	6
Watson, J. 1948 (Motherwell, Huddersfield T)	2
Watson, J. A. K. 1878 (Rangers)	1
Watson, P. R. 1934 (Blackpool)	1
Watson, R. 1971 (Motherwell)	1
Watson, W. 1898 (Falkirk)	1
Watt, F. 1889 (Kilbirnie)	4
Watt, W. W. 1887 (Queen's Park)	1
Waugh, W. 1938 (Hearts)	1
Webster, A. 2003 (Hearts)	22
Weir, A. 1959 (Motherwell)	6
Weir, D. G. 1997 (Hearts, Everton, Rangers)	63
Weir, J. 1887 (Third Lanark)	1
Weir, J. B. 1872 (Queen's Park)	4
Weir, P. 1980 (St Mirren, Aberdeen)	6
White, John 1922 (Albion R, Hearts)	2
White, J. A. 1959 (Falkirk, Tottenham H)	22
White, W. 1907 (Bolton W)	2
Whitelaw, A. 1887 (Vale of Leven)	2
Whyte, D. 1988 (Celtic, Middlesbrough, Aberdeen)	12
Wilkie, L. 2002 (Dundee)	11
Williams, G. 2002 (Nottingham F)	5
Wilson, A. 1907 (Sheffield W)	6
Wilson, A. 1954 (Portsmouth)	1
Wilson, A. N. 1920 (Dunfermline, Middlesbrough)	12
Wilson, D. 1900 (Queen's Park)	1
Wilson, D. 1913 (Oldham Ath)	1
Wilson, D. 1961 (Rangers)	22
Wilson, G. W. 1904 (Hearts, Everton, Newcastle U)	6
Wilson, Hugh 1890 (Newmilns, Sunderland, Third Lanark)	4
Wilson, I. A. 1987 (Leicester C, Everton)	5
Wilson, J. 1888 (Vale of Leven)	4
Wilson, P. 1926 (Celtic)	4
Wilson, P. 1975 (Celtic)	1
Wilson, R. P. 1972 (Arsenal)	2
Winters, R. 1999 (Aberdeen)	1
Wiseman, W. 1927 (Queen's Park)	2
Wood, G. 1979 (Everton, Arsenal)	4
Woodburn, W. A. 1947 (Rangers)	24
Wotherspoon, D. N. 1872 (Queen's Park)	2
Wright, K. 1992 (Hibernian)	1
Wright, S. 1993 (Aberdeen)	2
Wright, T. 1953 (Sunderland)	3
Wylie, T. G. 1890 (Rangers)	1
Yeats, R. 1965 (Liverpool)	2
Yorston, B. C. 1931 (Aberdeen)	1
Yorston, H. 1955 (Aberdeen)	1
Young, A. 1905 (Everton)	2
Young, A. 1960 (Hearts, Everton)	8
Young, G. L. 1947 (Rangers)	53
Young, J. 1906 (Celtic)	1
Younger, T. 1955 (Hibernian, Liverpool)	24

WALES

Adams, H. 1882 (Berwyn R, Druids) 4
Aizlewood, M. 1986 (Charlton Ath, Leeds U, Bradford
  C, Bristol C, Cardiff C) 39
Allchurch, I. J. 1951 (Swansea T, Newcastle U, Cardiff C,
  Swansea T) 68
Allchurch, L. 1955 (Swansea T, Sheffield U) 11
Allen, B. W. 1951 (Coventry C) 2
Allen, J. M. 2009 (Swansea C) 1
Allen, M. 1986 (Watford, Norwich C, Millwall,
  Newcastle U) 14
Arridge, S. 1892 (Bootle, Everton, New Brighton Tower)
  8
Astley, D. J. 1931 (Charlton Ath, Aston Villa, Derby Co,
  Blackpool) 13
Atherton, R. W. 1899 (Hibernian, Middlesbrough) 9

Bailiff, W. E. 1913 (Llanelly) 4
Baker, C. W. 1958 (Cardiff C) 7
Baker, W. G. 1948 (Cardiff C) 1
Bale, G. 2006 (Southampton, Tottenham H) 20
Bamford, T. 1931 (Wrexham) 5
Barnard, D. S. 1998 (Barnsley, Grimsby T) 22
Barnes, W. 1948 (Arsenal) 22
Bartley, T. 1898 (Glossop NE) 1
Bastock, A. M. 1892 (Shrewsbury T) 1
Beadles, G. H. 1925 (Cardiff C) 2
Bell, W. S. 1881 (Shrewsbury Engineers, Crewe Alex) 5
Bellamy, C. D. 1998 (Norwich C, Coventry C,
  Newcastle U, Blackburn R, Liverpool, West Ham U,
  Manchester C) 56
Bennion, S. R. 1926 (Manchester U) 10
Berry, G. F. 1979 (Wolverhampton W, Stoke C) 5
Blackmore, C. G. 1985 (Manchester U, Middlesbrough)
  39
Blake, N. A. 1994 (Sheffield U, Bolton W, Blackburn R,
  Wolverhampton W) 29
Blew, H. 1899 (Wrexham) 22
Boden, T. 1880 (Wrexham) 1
Bodin, P. J. 1990 (Swindon T, C Palace, Swindon T) 23
Boulter, L. M. 1939 (Brentford) 1
Bowdler, H. E. 1893 (Shrewsbury T) 1
Bowdler, J. C. H. 1890 (Shrewsbury T,
  Wolverhampton W, Shrewsbury T) 4
Bowen, D. L. 1955 (Arsenal) 19
Bowen, E. 1880 (Druids) 2
Bowen, J. P. 1994 (Swansea C, Birmingham C) 2
Bowen, M. R. 1986 (Tottenham H, Norwich C,
  West Ham U) 41
Bowsher, S. J. 1929 (Burnley) 1
Boyle, T. 1981 (C Palace) 2
Britten, T. J. 1878 (Parkgrove, Presteigne) 2
Brookes, S. J. 1900 (Llandudno) 2
Brown, A. I. 1926 (Aberdare Ath) 1
Brown, J. R. 2006 (Gillingham, Blackburn R) 3
Browning, M. T. 1996 (Bristol R, Huddersfield T) 5
Bryan, T. 1886 (Oswestry) 2
Buckland, T. 1899 (Bangor) 1
Burgess, W. A. R. 1947 (Tottenham H) 32
Burke, T. 1883 (Wrexham, Newton Heath) 8
Burnett, T. B. 1877 (Ruabon) 1
Burton, A. D. 1963 (Norwich C, Newcastle U) 9
Butler, J. 1893 (Chirk) 3
Butler, W. T. 1900 (Druids) 2

Cartwright, L. 1974 (Coventry C, Wrexham) 7
Carty, T. See McCarthy (Wrexham).
Challen, J. B. 1887 (Corinthians, Wellingborough GS) 4
Chapman, T. 1894 (Newtown, Manchester C, Grimsby T)
  7
Charles, J. M. 1981 (Swansea C, QPR, Oxford U) 19
Charles, M. 1955 (Swansea T, Arsenal, Cardiff C) 31
Charles, W. J. 1950 (Leeds U, Juventus, Leeds U,
  Cardiff C) 38

Church, S. R. 2009 (Reading) 2
Clarke, R. J. 1949 (Manchester C) 22
Coleman, C. 1992 (C Palace, Blackburn R, Fulham) 32
Collier, D. J. 1921 (Grimsby T) 1
Collins, D. L. 2005 (Sunderland) 7
Collins, J. M. 2004 (Cardiff C, West Ham U) 29
Collins, W. S. 1931 (Llanelly) 1
Collison, J. D. 2008 (West Ham U) 5
Conde, C. 1884 (Chirk) 3
Cook, F. C. 1925 (Newport Co, Portsmouth) 8
Cornforth, J. M. 1995 (Swansea C) 2
Cotterill, D. R. G. B. 2006 (Bristol C, Wigan Ath,
  Sheffield U) 13
Coyne, D. 1996 (Tranmere R, Grimsby T, Leicester C,
  Burnley, Tranmere R) 16
Crofts, A. L. 2006 (Gillingham) 12
Crompton, W. 1931 (Wrexham) 3
Cross, E. A. 1876 (Wrexham) .2
Crosse, K. 1879 (Druids) 3
Crossley, M. G. 1997 (Nottingham F, Middlesbrough,
  Fulham) 8
Crowe, V. H. 1959 (Aston Villa) 16
Cumner, R. H. 1939 (Arsenal) 3
Curtis, A. T. 1976 (Swansea C, Leeds U, Swansea C,
  Southampton, Cardiff C) 35
Curtis, E. R. 1928 (Cardiff C, Birmingham) 3

Daniel, R. W. 1951 (Arsenal, Sunderland) 21
Darvell, S. 1897 (Oxford University) 2
Davies, A. 1876 (Wrexham) 2
Davies, A. 1904 (Druids, Middlesbrough) 2
Davies, A. 1983 (Manchester U, Newcastle U,
  Swansea C, Bradford C) 13
Davies, A. O. 1885 (Barmouth, Swifts, Wrexham,
  Crewe Alex) 9
Davies, A. R. 2006 (Yeovil T) 1
Davies, A. T. 1891 (Shrewsbury T) 1
Davies, C. 1972 (Charlton Ath) 1
Davies, C. M. 2006 (Oxford U, Verona, Oldham Ath) 5
Davies, D. 1904 (Bolton W) 3
Davies, D. C. 1899 (Brecon, Hereford) 2
Davies, D. W. 1912 (Treharris, Oldham Ath) 2
Davies, E. Lloyd 1904 (Stoke, Northampton T) 16
Davies, E. R. 1953 (Newcastle U) 6
Davies, G. 1980 (Fulham, Manchester C) 16
Davies, Rev. H. 1928 (Wrexham) 1
Davies, Idwal 1923 (Liverpool Marine) 1
Davies, J. E. 1885 (Oswestry) 1
Davies, Jas 1878 (Wrexham) 1
Davies, John 1879 (Wrexham) 1
Davies, Jos 1888 (Newton Heath, Wolverhampton W) 7
Davies, Jos 1889 (Everton, Chirk, Ardwick, Sheffield U,
  Manchester C, Millwall, Reading) 11
Davies, J. P. 1883 (Druids) 2
Davies, Ll. 1907 (Wrexham, Everton, Wrexham) 13
Davies, L. S. 1922 (Cardiff C) 23
Davies, O. 1890 (Wrexham) 1
Davies, R. 1883 (Wrexham) 3
Davies, R. 1885 (Druids) 1
Davies, R. O. 1892 (Wrexham) 2
Davies, R. T. 1964 (Norwich C, Southampton,
  Portsmouth) 29
Davies, R. W. 1964 (Bolton W, Newcastle U,
  Manchester C, Manchester U, Blackpool) 34
Davies, S. 2001 (Tottenham H, Everton, Fulham) 57
Davies, S. I. 1996 (Manchester U) 1
Davies, Stanley 1920 (Preston NE, Everton, WBA,
  Rotherham U) 18
Davies, T. 1886 (Oswestry) 1
Davies, T. 1903 (Druids) 4
Davies, W. 1884 (Wrexham) 1
Davies, W. 1924 (Swansea T, Cardiff C, Notts Co) 17
Davies, William 1903 (Wrexham, Blackburn R) 11

Davies, W. C. 1908 (C Palace, WBA, C Palace) 4
Davies, W. D. 1975 (Everton, Wrexham, Swansea C) 52
Davies, W. H. 1876 (Oswestry) 4
Davis, G. 1978 (Wrexham) 3
Davis, W. O. 1913 (Millwall Ath) 5
Day, A. 1934 (Tottenham H) 1
Deacy, N. 1977 (PSV Eindhoven, Beringen) 12
Dearson, D. J. 1939 (Birmingham) 3
Delaney, M. A. 2000 (Aston Villa) 36
Derrett, S. C. 1969 (Cardiff C) 4
Dewey, F. T. 1931 (Cardiff Corinthians) 2
Dibble, A. 1986 (Luton T, Manchester C) 3
Doughty, J. 1886 (Druids, Newton Heath) 8
Doughty, R. 1888 (Newton Heath) 2
Duffy, R. M. 2006 (Portsmouth) 13
Durban, A. 1966 (Derby Co) 27
Dwyer, P. J. 1978 (Cardiff C) 10

Eardley, N, 2008 (Oldham Ath) 10
Earnshaw, R. 2002 (Cardiff C, WBA, Norwich C,
  Derby Co, Nottingham F) 45
Easter, J. M. 2007 (Wycombe W, Plymouth Arg) 7
Eastwood, F. 2008 (Wolverhampton W) 10
Edwards, C. 1878 (Wrexham) 1
Edwards, C. N. H. 1996 (Swansea C) 1
Edwards, D. 2008 (Wolverhampton W) 14
Edwards, G. 1947 (Birmingham C, Cardiff C) 12
Edwards, H. 1878 (Wrexham Civil Service, Wrexham) 8
Edwards, J. H. 1876 (Wanderers) 1
Edwards, J. H. 1895 (Oswestry) 3
Edwards, J. H. 1898 (Aberystwyth) 1
Edwards, L. T. 1957 (Charlton Ath) 2
Edwards, R. I. 1978 (Chester, Wrexham) 4
Edwards, R. O. 2003 (Aston Villa, Wolverhampton W) 15
Edwards, R. W. 1998 (Bristol C) 4
Edwards, T. 1932 (Linfield) 1
Egan, W. 1892 (Chirk) 1
Ellis, B. 1932 (Motherwell) 6
Ellis, E. 1931 (Nunhead, Oswestry) 3
Emanuel, W. J. 1973 (Bristol C) 2
England, H. M. 1962 (Blackburn R, Tottenham H) 44
Evans, B. C. 1972 (Swansea C, Hereford U) 7
Evans, C. M. 2008 (Manchester C) 10
Evans, D. G. 1926 (Reading, Huddersfield T) 4
Evans, H. P. 1922 (Cardiff C) 6
Evans, I. 1976 (C Palace) 13
Evans, J. 1893 (Oswestry) 3
Evans, J. 1912 (Cardiff C) 8
Evans, J. H. 1922 (Southend U) 4
Evans, Len 1927 (Aberdare Ath, Cardiff C, Birmingham) 4
Evans, M. 1884 (Oswestry) 1
Evans, P. S. 2002 (Brentford, Bradford C) 2
Evans, R. 1902 (Clapton) 1
Evans, R. E. 1906 (Wrexham, Aston Villa, Sheffield U) 10
Evans, R. O. 1902 (Wrexham, Blackburn R, Coventry C) 10
Evans, R. S. 1964 (Swansea T) 1
Evans, S. J. 2007 (Wrexham) 7
Evans, T. J. 1927 (Clapton Orient, Newcastle U) 4
Evans, W. 1933 (Tottenham H) 6
Evans, W. A. W. 1876 (Oxford University) 2
Evans, W. G. 1890 (Bootle, Aston Villa) 3
Evelyn, E. C. 1887 (Crusaders) 1
Eyton-Jones, J. A. 1883 (Wrexham) 4

Farmer, G. 1885 (Oswestry) 2
Felgate, D. 1984 (Lincoln C) 1
Finnigan, R. J. 1930 (Wrexham) 1
Fletcher, C. N. 2004 (Bournemouth, West Ham U,
  Crystal Palace) 36
Flynn, B. 1975 (Burnley, Leeds U, Burnley) 66
Ford, T. 1947 (Swansea T, Aston Villa, Sunderland,
  Cardiff C) 38

Foulkes, H. E. 1932 (WBA) 1
Foulkes, W. I. 1952 (Newcastle U) 11
Foulkes, W. T. 1884 (Oswestry) 2
Fowler, J. 1925 (Swansea T) 6
Freestone, R. 2000 (Swansea C) 1

Gabbidon, D. L. 2002 (Cardiff C, West Ham U) 40
Garner, G. 2006 (Leyton Orient) 1
Garner, J. 1896 (Aberystwyth) 1
Giggs, R. J. 1992 (Manchester U) 64
Giles, D. C. 1980 (Swansea C, C Palace) 12
Gillam, S. G. 1889 (Wrexham, Shrewsbury, Clapton) 5
Glascodine, G. 1879 (Wrexham) 1
Glover, E. M. 1932 (Grimsby T) 7
Godding, G. 1923 (Wrexham) 2
Godfrey, B. C. 1964 (Preston NE) 3
Goodwin, U. 1881 (Ruthin) 1
Goss, J. 1991 (Norwich C) 9
Gough, R. T. 1883 (Oswestry White Star) 1
Gray, A. 1924 (Oldham Ath, Manchester C,
  Manchester Central, Tranmere R, Chester) 24
Green, A. W. 1901 (Aston Villa, Notts Co,
  Nottingham F) 8
Green, C. R. 1965 (Birmingham C) 15
Green, G. H. 1938 (Charlton Ath) 4
Green, R. M. 1998 (Wolverhampton W) 2
Grey, Dr W. 1876 (Druids) 2
Griffiths, A. T. 1971 (Wrexham) 17
Griffiths, F. J. 1900 (Blackpool) 2
Griffiths, G. 1887 (Chirk) 1
Griffiths, J. H. 1953 (Swansea T) 1
Griffiths, L. 1902 (Wrexham) 1
Griffiths, M. W. 1947 (Leicester C) 11
Griffiths, P. 1884 (Chirk) 6
Griffiths, P. H. 1932 (Everton) 1
Griffiths, T. P. 1927 (Everton, Bolton W, Middlesbrough,
  Aston Villa) 21
Gunter, C. 2007 (Cardiff C, Tottenham H) 16

Hall, G. D. 1988 (Chelsea) 9
Hallam, J. 1889 (Oswestry) 1
Hanford, H. 1934 (Swansea T, Sheffield W) 7
Harrington, A. C. 1956 (Cardiff C) 11
Harris, C. S. 1976 (Leeds U) 24
Harris, W. C. 1954 (Middlesbrough) 6
Harrison, W. C. 1899 (Wrexham) 5
Hartson, J. 1995 (Arsenal, West Ham U, Wimbledon,
  Coventry, Celtic) 51
Haworth, S. O. 1997 (Cardiff C, Coventry C) 5
Hayes, A. 1890 (Wrexham) 2
Hennessey, W. R. 2007 (Wolverhampton W) 19
Hennessey, W. T. 1962 (Birmingham C, Nottingham F,
  Derby Co) 39
Hersee, A. M. 1886 (Bangor) 2
Hersee, R. 1886 (Llandudno) 1
Hewitt, R. 1958 (Cardiff C) 5
Hewitt, T. J. 1911 (Wrexham, Chelsea, South Liverpool) 8
Heywood, D. 1879 (Druids) 1
Hibbott, H. 1880 (Newtown Excelsior, Newtown) 3
Higham, G. G. 1878 (Oswestry) 2
Hill, M. R. 1972 (Ipswich T) 2
Hockey, T. 1972 (Sheffield U, Norwich C, Aston Villa) 9
Hoddinott, T. F. 1921 (Watford) 2
Hodges, G. 1984 (Wimbledon, Newcastle U, Watford,
  Sheffield U) 18
Hodgkinson, A. V. 1908 (Southampton) 1
Holden, A. 1984 (Chester C) 1
Hole, B. G. 1963 (Cardiff C, Blackburn R, Aston Villa,
  Swansea C) 30
Hole, W. J. 1921 (Swansea T) 9
Hollins, D. M. 1962 (Newcastle U) 11
Hopkins, I. J. 1935 (Brentford) 12
Hopkins, J. 1983 (Fulham, C Palace) 16

Hopkins, M. 1956 (Tottenham H)   34
Horne, B. 1988 (Portsmouth, Southampton, Everton,
    Birmingham C)   59
Howell, E. G. 1888 (Builth)   3
Howells, R. G. 1954 (Cardiff C)   2
Hugh, A. R. 1930 (Newport Co)   1
Hughes, A. 1894 (Rhos)   2
Hughes, A. 1907 (Chirk)   1
Hughes, C. M. 1992 (Luton T, Wimbledon)   8
Hughes, E. 1899 (Everton, Tottenham H)   14
Hughes, E. 1906 (Wrexham, Nottingham F, Wrexham,
    Manchester C)   16
Hughes, F. W. 1882 (Northwich Victoria)   6
Hughes, I. 1951 (Luton T)   4
Hughes, J. 1877 (Cambridge University, Aberystwyth)   2
Hughes, J. 1905 (Liverpool)   3
Hughes, J. I. 1935 (Blackburn R)   1
Hughes, L. M. 1984 (Manchester U, Barcelona,
    Manchester U, Chelsea, Southampton)   72
Hughes, P. W. 1887 (Bangor)   3
Hughes, W. 1891 (Bootle)   3
Hughes, W. A. 1949 (Blackburn R)   5
Hughes, W. M. 1938 (Birmingham)   10
Humphreys, J. V. 1947 (Everton)   1
Humphreys, R. 1888 (Druids)   1
Hunter, A. H. 1887 (FA of Wales Secretary)   1

Jackett, K. 1983 (Watford)   31
Jackson, W. 1899 (St Helens Rec)   1
James, E. 1893 (Chirk)   8
James, E. G. 1966 (Blackpool)   9
James, L. 1972 (Burnley, Derby Co, QPR, Burnley,
    Swansea C, Sunderland)   54
James, R. M. 1979 (Swansea C, Stoke C, QPR,
    Leicester C, Swansea C)   47
James, W. 1931 (West Ham U)   2
Jarrett, R. H. 1889 (Ruthin)   2
Jarvis, A. L. 1967 (Hull C)   3
Jenkins, E. 1925 (Lovell's Ath)   1
Jenkins, J. 1924 (Brighton &_HA)   8
Jenkins, R. W. 1902 (Rhyl)   1
Jenkins, S. R. 1996 (Swansea C, Huddersfield T)   16
Jenkyns, C. A. L. 1892 (Small Heath, Woolwich Arsenal,
    Newton Heath, Walsall)   8
Jennings, W. 1914 (Bolton W)   11
John, R. F. 1923 (Arsenal)   15
John, W. R. 1931 (Walsall, Stoke C, Preston NE,
    Sheffield U, Swansea T)   14
Johnson, A. J. 1999 (Nottingham F, WBA)   15
Johnson, M. G. 1964 (Swansea T)   1
Jones, A. 1987 (Port Vale, Charlton Ath)   6
Jones, A. F. 1877 (Oxford University)   1
Jones, A. T. 1905 (Nottingham F, Notts Co)   2
Jones, Bryn 1935 (Wolverhampton W, Arsenal)   17
Jones, B. S. 1963 (Swansea T, Plymouth Arg, Cardiff C)
    15
Jones, Charlie 1926 (Nottingham F, Arsenal)   8
Jones, Cliff 1954 (Swansea T, Tottenham H, Fulham)   59
Jones, C. W. 1935 (Birmingham)   2
Jones, D. 1888 (Chirk, Bolton W, Manchester C)   14
Jones, D. E. 1976 (Norwich C)   8
Jones, D. O. 1934 (Leicester C)   7
Jones, Evan 1910 (Chelsea, Oldham Ath, Bolton W)   7
Jones, F. R. 1885 (Bangor)   3
Jones, F. W. 1893 (Small Heath)   1
Jones, G. P. 1907 (Wrexham)   2
Jones, H. 1902 (Aberaman)   1
Jones, Humphrey 1885 (Bangor, Queen's Park,
    East Stirlingshire, Queen's Park)   14
Jones, Ivor 1920 (Swansea T, WBA)   10
Jones, Jeffrey 1908 (Llandrindod Wells)   3
Jones, J. 1876 (Druids)   1
Jones, J. 1883 (Berwyn Rangers)   3
Jones, J. 1925 (Wrexham)   1
Jones, J. L. 1895 (Sheffield U, Tottenham H)   21

Jones, J. Love 1906 (Stoke, Middlesbrough)   2
Jones, J. O. 1901 (Bangor)   2
Jones, J. P. 1976 (Liverpool, Wrexham, Chelsea,
    Huddersfield T)   72
Jones, J. T. 1912 (Stoke, C Palace)   15
Jones, K. 1950 (Aston Villa)   1
Jones, Leslie J. 1933 (Cardiff C, Coventry C, Arsenal   11
Jones, M. A. 2007 (Wrexham)   2
Jones, M. G. 2000 (Leeds U, Leicester C)   13
Jones, P. L. 1997 (Liverpool, Tranmere R)   2
Jones, P. S. 1997 (Stockport Co, Southampton,
    Wolverhampton W, QPR)   50
Jones, P. W. 1971 (Bristol R)   1
Jones, R. 1887 (Bangor, Crewe Alex)   3
Jones, R. 1898 (Leicester Fosse)   1
Jones, R. 1899 (Druids)   1
Jones, R. 1900 (Bangor)   2
Jones, R. 1906 (Millwall)   2
Jones, R. A. 1884 (Druids)   4
Jones, R. A. 1994 (Sheffield W)   1
Jones, R. S. 1894 (Everton)   1
Jones, S. 1887 (Wrexham, Chester)   2
Jones, S. 1893 (Wrexham, Burton Swifts, Druids)   6
Jones, T. 1926 (Manchester U)   4
Jones, T. D. 1908 (Aberdare)   1
Jones, T. G. 1938 (Everton)   17
Jones, T. J. 1932 (Sheffield W)   2
Jones, V. P. 1995 (Wimbledon)   9
Jones, W. E. A. 1947 (Swansea T, Tottenham H)   4
Jones, W. J. 1901 (Aberdare, West Ham U)   4
Jones, W. Lot 1905 (Manchester C, Southend U)   20
Jones, W. P. 1889 (Druids, Wynnstay)   4
Jones, W. R. 1897 (Aberystwyth)   1

Keenor, F. C. 1920 (Cardiff C, Crewe Alex)   32
Kelly, F. C. 1899 (Wrexham, Druids)   3
Kelsey, A. J. 1954 (Arsenal)   41
Kenrick, S. L. 1876 (Druids, Oswestry, Shropshire
    Wanderers)   5
Ketley, C. F. 1882 (Druids)   1
King, A. (Leicester C)   (1)
King, J. 1955 (Swansea T)   1
Kinsey, N. 1951 (Norwich C, Birmingham C)   7
Knill, A. R. 1989 (Swansea C)   1
Koumas, J. 2001 (Tranmere R, WBA, Wigan Ath)   34
Krzywicki, R. L. 1970 (WBA, Huddersfield T)   8

Lambert, R. 1947 (Liverpool)   5
Latham, G. 1905 (Liverpool, Southport Central,
    Cardiff C)   10
Law, B. J. 1990 (QPR)   1
Lawrence, E. 1930 (Clapton Orient, Notts Co)   2
Lawrence, S. 1932 (Swansea T)   8
Lea, A. 1889 (Wrexham)   4
Lea, C. 1965 (Ipswich T)   2
Leary, P. 1889 (Bangor)   1
Ledley, J. C. 2006 (Cardiff C)   29
Leek, K. 1961 (Leicester C, Newcastle U, Birmingham C,
    Northampton T)   13
Legg, A. 1996 (Birmingham C, Cardiff C)   6
Lever, A. R. 1953 (Leicester C)   1
Lewis, B. 1891 (Chester, Wrexham, Middlesbrough,
    Wrexham)   10
Lewis, D. 1927 (Arsenal)   3
Lewis, D. 1983 (Swansea C)   1
Lewis, D. J. 1933 (Swansea C)   2
Lewis, D. M. 1890 (Bangor)   2
Lewis, J. 1906 (Bristol R)   1
Lewis, J. 1926 (Cardiff C)   1
Lewis, T. 1881 (Wrexham)   2
Lewis, W. 1885 (Bangor, Crewe Alex, Chester,
    Manchester C, Chester)   27
Lewis, W. L. 1927 (Swansea T, Huddersfield T)   6
Llewellyn, C. M. 1998 (Norwich C, Wrexham)   6
Lloyd, B. W. 1976 (Wrexham)   3

Lloyd, J. W. 1879 (Wrexham, Newtown) 2
Lloyd, R. A. 1891 (Ruthin) 2
Lockley, A. 1898 (Chirk) 1
Lovell, S. 1982 (C Palace, Millwall) 6
Lowndes, S. R. 1983 (Newport Co, Millwall, Barnsley) 10
Lowrie, G. 1948 (Coventry C, Newcastle U) 4
Lucas, P. M. 1962 (Leyton Orient) 4
Lucas, W. H. 1949 (Swansea T) 7
Lumberg, A. 1929 (Wrexham, Wolverhampton W) 4

McCarthy, T. P. 1889 (Wrexham) 1
McMillan, R. 1881 (Shrewsbury Engineers) 2
Maguire, G. T. 1990 (Portsmouth) 7
Mahoney, J. F. 1968 (Stoke C, Middlesbrough, Swansea C) 51
Mardon, P. J. 1996 (WBA) 1
Margetson, M. W. 2004 (Cardiff C) 1
Marriott, A. 1996 (Wrexham) 5
Martin, T. J. 1930 (Newport Co) 1
Marustik, C. 1982 (Swansea C) 6
Mates, J. 1891 (Chirk) 3
Matthews, R. W. 1921 (Liverpool, Bristol C, Bradford) 3
Matthews, W. 1905 (Chester) 2
Matthias, J. S. 1896 (Brymbo, Shrewsbury T, Wolverhampton W) 5
Matthias, T. J. 1914 (Wrexham) 12
Mays, A. W. 1929 (Wrexham) 1
Medwin, T. C. 1953 (Swansea T, Tottenham H) 30
Melville, A. K. 1990 (Swansea C, Oxford U, Sunderland, Fulham, West Ham U) 65
Meredith, S. 1900 (Chirk, Stoke, Leyton) 8
Meredith, W. H. 1895 (Manchester C, Manchester U) 48
Mielczarek, R. 1971 (Rotherham U) 1
Millership, H. 1920 (Rotherham Co) 6
Millington, A. H. 1963 (WBA, C Palace, Peterborough U, Swansea C) 21
Mills, T. J. 1934 (Clapton Orient, Leicester C) 4
Mills-Roberts, R. H. 1885 (St Thomas' Hospital, Preston NE, Llanberis) 8
Moore, G. 1960 (Cardiff C, Chelsea, Manchester U, Northampton T, Charlton Ath) 21
Morgan, C. 2007 (Milton Keynes D, Peterborough U) 15
Morgan, J. R. 1877 (Cambridge University, Derby School Staff) 10
Morgan, J. T. 1905 (Wrexham) 1
Morgan-Owen, H. 1902 (Oxford University, Corinthians) 4
Morgan-Owen, M. M. 1897 (Oxford University, Corinthians) 13
Morley, E. J. 1925 (Swansea T, Clapton Orient) 4
Morris, A. G. 1896 (Aberystwyth, Swindon T, Nottingham F) 21
Morris, C. 1900 (Chirk, Derby Co, Huddersfield T) 27
Morris, E. 1893 (Chirk) 3
Morris, H. 1894 (Sheffield U, Manchester C, Grimsby T) 3
Morris, J. 1887 (Oswestry) 1
Morris, J. 1898 (Chirk) 1
Morris, R. 1900 (Chirk, Shrewsbury T) 6
Morris, R. 1902 (Newtown, Druids, Liverpool, Leeds C, Grimsby T, Plymouth Arg) 11
Morris, S. 1937 (Birmingham) 5
Morris, W. 1947 (Burnley) 5
Moulsdale, J. R. B. 1925 (Corinthians) 1
Murphy, J. P. 1933 (WBA) 15
Myhill, G. O. 2008 (Hull C) 5

Nardiello, D. 1978 (Coventry C) 2
Nardiello, D. A. 2007 (Barnsley, QPR) 3
Neal, J. E. 1931 (Colwyn Bay) 2
Neilson, A. B. 1992 (Newcastle U, Southampton) 5
Newnes, J. 1926 (Nelson) 1
Newton, L. F. 1912 (Cardiff Corinthians) 1
Nicholas, D. S. 1923 (Stoke, Swansea T) 3

Nicholas, P. 1979 (C Palace, Arsenal, C Palace, Luton T, Aberdeen, Chelsea, Watford) 73
Nicholls, J. 1924 (Newport Co, Cardiff C) 4
Niedzwiecki, E. A. 1985 (Chelsea) 2
Nock, W. 1897 (Newtown) 1
Nogan, L. M. 1992 (Watford, Reading) 2
Norman, A. J. 1986 (Hull C) 5
Nurse, M. T. G. 1960 (Swansea T, Middlesbrough) 12
Nyatanga, L. J. 2006 (Derby Co) 27

O'Callaghan, E. 1929 (Tottenham H) 11
Oliver, A. 1905 (Bangor, Blackburn R) 2
Oster, J. M. 1998 (Everton, Sunderland) 13
O'Sullivan, P. A. 1973 (Brighton & HA) 3
Owen, D. 1879 (Oswestry) 1
Owen, E. 1884 (Ruthin Grammar School) 3
Owen, G. 1888 (Chirk, Newton Heath, Chirk) 4
Owen, J. 1892 (Newton Heath) 1
Owen, T. 1879 (Oswestry) 1
Owen, Trevor 1899 (Crewe Alex) 2
Owen, W. 1884 (Chirk) 16
Owen, W. P. 1880 (Ruthin) 12
Owens, J. 1902 (Wrexham) 1

Page, M. E. 1971 (Birmingham C) 28
Page, R. J. 1997 (Watford, Sheffield U, Cardiff C, Coventry C) 41
Palmer, D. 1957 (Swansea T) 3
Parris, J. E. 1932 (Bradford) 1
Parry, B. J. 1951 (Swansea T) 1
Parry, C. 1891 (Everton, Newtown) 13
Parry, E. 1922 (Liverpool) 5
Parry, M. 1901 (Liverpool) 16
Parry, P. I. 2004 (Cardiff C) 12
Parry, T. D. 1900 (Oswestry) 7
Parry, W. 1895 (Newtown) 1
Partridge, D. W. 2005 (Motherwell, Bristol C) 7
Pascoe, C. 1984 (Swansea C, Sunderland) 10
Paul, R. 1949 (Swansea T, Manchester C) 33
Peake, E. 1908 (Aberystwyth, Liverpool) 11
Peers, E. J. 1914 (Wolverhampton W, Port Vale) 12
Pembridge, M. A. 1992 (Luton T, Derby Co, Sheffield W, Benfica, Everton, Fulham) 54
Perry, E. 1938 (Doncaster R) 3
Perry, J. 1994 (Cardiff C) 1
Phennah, E. 1878 (Civil Service) 1
Phillips, C. 1931 (Wolverhampton W, Aston Villa) 13
Phillips, D. 1984 (Plymouth Arg, Manchester C, Coventry C, Norwich C, Nottingham F) 62
Phillips, L. 1971 (Cardiff C, Aston Villa, Swansea C, Charlton Ath) 58
Phillips, T. J. S. 1973 (Chelsea) 4
Phoenix, H. 1882 (Wrexham) 1
Pipe, D. R. 2003 (Coventry C) 1
Poland, G. 1939 (Wrexham) 2
Pontin, K. 1980 (Cardiff C) 2
Powell, A. 1947 (Leeds U, Everton, Birmingham C) 8
Powell, D. 1968 (Wrexham, Sheffield U) 11
Powell, I. V. 1947 (QPR, Aston Villa) 8
Powell, J. 1878 (Druids, Bolton W, Newton Heath) 15
Powell, Seth 1885 (Oswestry, WBA) 1
Price, H. 1907 (Aston Villa, Burton U, Wrexham) 5
Price, J. 1877 (Wrexham) 12
Price, L. P. 2006 (Ipswich T, Derby Co) 6
Price, P. 1980 (Luton T, Tottenham H) 25
Pring, K. D. 1966 (Rotherham U) 3
Pritchard, H. K. 1985 (Bristol C) 1
Pryce-Jones, A. W. 1895 (Newtown) 1
Pryce-Jones, W. E. 1887 (Cambridge University) 5
Pugh, A. 1889 (Rhostyllen) 1
Pugh, D. H. 1896 (Wrexham, Lincoln C) 7
Pugsley, J. 1930 (Charlton Ath) 1
Pullen, W. J. 1926 (Plymouth Arg) 1

Ramsey, A. 2009 (Arsenal) 6

Rankmore, F. E. J. 1966 (Peterborough U) 1
Ratcliffe, K. 1981 (Everton, Cardiff C) 59
Rea, J. C. 1894 (Aberystwyth) 9
Ready, K. 1997 (QPR) 5
Reece, G. I. 1966 (Sheffield U, Cardiff C) 29
Reed, W. G. 1955 (Ipswich T) 2
Rees, A. 1984 (Birmingham C) 1
Rees, J. M. 1992 (Luton T) 1
Rees, R. R. 1965 (Coventry C, WBA, Nottingham F) 39
Rees, W. 1949 (Cardiff C, Tottenham H) 4
Richards, A. 1932 (Barnsley) 1
Richards, D. 1931 (Wolverhampton W, Brentford, Birmingham) 21
Richards, G. 1899 (Druids, Oswestry, Shrewsbury T) 6
Richards, R. W. 1920 (Wolverhampton W, West Ham U, Mold) 9
Richards, S. V. 1947 (Cardiff C) 1
Richards, W. E. 1933 (Fulham) 1
Ricketts, S. 2005 (Swansea C, Hull C) 34
Roach, J. 1885 (Oswestry) 1
Robbins, W. W. 1931 (Cardiff C, WBA) 11
Roberts, A. M. 1993 (QPR) 2
Roberts, D. F. 1973 (Oxford U, Hull C) 17
Roberts, G. W. 2000 (Tranmere R) 9
Roberts, I. W. 1990 (Watford, Huddersfield T, Leicester C, Norwich C) 15
Roberts, Jas 1913 (Wrexham) 2
Roberts, J. 1879 (Corwen, Berwyn R) 7
Roberts, J. 1881 (Ruthin) 2
Roberts, J. 1906 (Bradford C) 2
Roberts, J. G. 1971 (Arsenal, Birmingham C) 22
Roberts, J. H. 1949 (Bolton W) 1
Roberts, N. W. 2000 (Wrexham, Wigan Ath) 4
Roberts, P. S. 1974 (Portsmouth) 4
Roberts, R. 1884 (Druids, Bolton W, Preston NE) 9
Roberts, R. 1886 (Wrexham) 3
Roberts, R. 1891 (Rhos, Crewe Alex) 2
Roberts, R. L. 1890 (Chester) 1
Roberts, S. W. 2005 (Wrexham) 1
Roberts, W. 1879 (Llangollen, Berwyn R) 6
Roberts, W. 1883 (Rhyl) 1
Roberts, W. 1886 (Wrexham) 4
Roberts, W. H. 1882 (Ruthin, Rhyl) 6
Robinson, C. P. 2000 (Wolverhampton W, Portsmouth, Sunderland, Norwich C, Toronto Lynx) 52
Robinson, J. R. C. 1996 (Charlton Ath) 30
Rodrigues, P. J. 1965 (Cardiff C, Leicester C, Sheffield W) 40
Rogers, J. P. 1896 (Wrexham) 3
Rogers, W. 1931 (Wrexham) 2
Roose, L. R. 1900 (Aberystwyth, London Welsh, Stoke, Everton, Stoke, Sunderland) 24
Rouse, R. V. 1959 (C Palace) 1
Rowlands, A. C. 1914 (Tranmere R) 1
Rowley, T. 1959 (Tranmere R) 1
Rush, I. 1980 (Liverpool, Juventus, Liverpool) 73
Russell, M. R. 1912 (Merthyr T, Plymouth Arg) 23

Sabine, H. W. 1887 (Oswestry) 1
Saunders, D. 1986 (Brighton & HA, Oxford U, Derby Co, Liverpool, Aston Villa, Galatasaray, Nottingham F, Sheffield U, Benfica, Bradford C) 75
Savage, R. W. 1996 (Crewe Alex, Leicester C, Birmingham C) 39
Savin, G. 1878 (Oswestry) 1
Sayer, P. A. 1977 (Cardiff C) 7
Scrine, F. H. 1950 (Swansea T) 2
Sear, C. R. 1963 (Manchester C) 1
Shaw, E. G. 1882 (Oswestry) 3
Sherwood, A. T. 1947 (Cardiff C, Newport Co) 41
Shone, W. W. 1879 (Oswestry) 1
Shortt, W. W. 1947 (Plymouth Arg) 12
Showers, D. 1975 (Cardiff C) 2
Sidlow, C. 1947 (Liverpool) 7
Sisson, H. 1885 (Wrexham Olympic) 3

Slatter, N. 1983 (Bristol R, Oxford U) 22
Smallman, D. P. 1974 (Wrexham, Everton) 7
Southall, N. 1982 (Everton) 92
Speed, G. A. 1990 (Leeds U, Everton, Newcastle U, Bolton W) 85
Sprake, G. 1964 (Leeds U, Birmingham C) 37
Stansfield, F. 1949 (Cardiff C) 1
Stevenson, B. 1978 (Leeds U, Birmingham C) 15
Stevenson, N. 1982 (Swansea C) 4
Stitfall, R. F. 1953 (Cardiff C) 2
Sullivan, D. 1953 (Cardiff C) 17
Symons, C. J. 1992 (Portsmouth, Manchester C, Fulham, C Palace) 37

Tapscott, D. R. 1954 (Arsenal, Cardiff C) 14
Taylor, G. K. 1996 (C Palace, Sheffield U, Burnley, Nottingham F) 15
Taylor, J. 1898 (Wrexham) 1
Taylor, O. D. S. 1893 (Newtown) 4
Thatcher, B. D. 2004 (Leicester C, Manchester C) 7
Thomas, C. 1899 (Druids) 2
Thomas, D. A. 1957 (Swansea T) 2
Thomas, D. S. 1948 (Fulham) 4
Thomas, E. 1925 (Cardiff Corinthians) 1
Thomas, G. 1885 (Wrexham) 2
Thomas, H. 1927 (Manchester U) 1
Thomas, Martin R. 1987 (Newcastle U) 1
Thomas, Mickey 1977 (Wrexham, Manchester U, Everton, Brighton & HA, Stoke C, Chelsea, WBA) 51
Thomas, R. J. 1967 (Swindon T, Derby Co, Cardiff C) 50
Thomas, T. 1898 (Bangor) 2
Thomas, W. R. 1931 (Newport Co) 2
Thomson, D. 1876 (Druids) 1
Thomson, G. F. 1876 (Druids) 2
Toshack, J. B. 1969 (Cardiff C, Liverpool, Swansea C) 40
Townsend, W. 1887 (Newtown) 2
Trainer, H. 1895 (Wrexham) 3
Trainer, J. 1887 (Bolton W, Preston NE) 20
Trollope, P. J. 1997 (Derby Co, Fulham, Coventry C, Northampton T) 9
Tudur-Jones, O. 2008 (Swansea C) 4
Turner, H. G. 1937 (Charlton Ath) 8
Turner, J. 1892 (Wrexham) 1
Turner, R. E. 1891 (Wrexham) 2
Turner, W. H. 1887 (Wrexham) 5

Van Den Hauwe, P. W. R. 1985 (Everton) 13
Vaughan, D. O. 2003 (Crewe Alex, Real Sociedad, Blackpool) 14
Vaughan, Jas 1893 (Druids) 4
Vaughan, John 1879 (Oswestry, Druids, Bolton W) 11
Vaughan, J. O. 1885 (Rhyl) 4
Vaughan, N. 1983 (Newport Co, Cardiff C) 10
Vaughan, T. 1885 (Rhyl) 1
Vearncombe, G. 1958 (Cardiff C) 2
Vernon, T. R. 1957 (Blackburn R, Everton, Stoke C) 32
Villars, A. K. 1974 (Cardiff C) 3
Vizard, E. T. 1911 (Bolton W) 22
Vokes, S. M. 2008 (Bournemouth, Wolverhampton W) 10

Walley, J. T. 1971 (Watford) 1
Walsh, I. P. 1980 (C Palace, Swansea C) 18
Ward, D. 1959 (Bristol R, Cardiff C) 2
Ward, D. 2000 (Notts Co, Nottingham F) 5
Warner, J. 1937 (Swansea T, Manchester U) 2
Warren, F. W. 1929 (Cardiff C, Middlesbrough, Hearts) 6
Watkins, A. E. 1898 (Leicester Fosse, Aston Villa, Millwall) 5
Watkins, W. M. 1902 (Stoke, Aston Villa, Sunderland, Stoke) 10
Webster, C. 1957 (Manchester U) 4
Weston, R. D. 2000 (Arsenal, Cardiff C) 7

Whatley, W. J. 1939 (Tottenham H)	2
White, P. F. 1896 (London Welsh)	1
Wilcock, A. R. 1890 (Oswestry)	1
Wilding, J. 1885 (Wrexham Olympians, Bootle, Wrexham)	9
Williams, A. 1994 (Reading, Wolverhampton W, Reading)	13
Williams, A. E. 2008 (Stockport Co, Swansea C)	13
Williams, A. L. 1931 (Wrexham)	1
Williams, A. P. 1998 (Southampton)	2
Williams, B. 1930 (Bristol C)	1
Williams, B. D. 1928 (Swansea T, Everton)	10
Williams, D. G. 1988 (Derby Co, Ipswich T)	13
Williams, D. M. 1986 (Norwich C)	5
Williams, D. R. 1921 (Merthyr T, Sheffield W, Manchester U)	8
Williams, E. 1893 (Crewe Alex)	2
Williams, E. 1901 (Druids)	5
Williams, G. 1893 (Chirk)	6
Williams, G. E. 1960 (WBA)	26
Williams, G. G. 1961 (Swansea T)	5
Williams, G. J. 2006 (West Ham U, Ipswich T)	2
Williams, G. J. J. 1951 (Cardiff C)	1
Williams, G. O. 1907 (Wrexham)	1

Williams, H. J. 1965 (Swansea T)	3
Williams, H. T. 1949 (Newport Co, Leeds U)	4
Williams, J. H. 1884 (Oswestry)	1
Williams, J. J. 1939 (Wrexham)	1
Williams, J. T. 1925 (Middlesbrough)	1
Williams, J. W. 1912 (C Palace)	2
Williams, R. 1935 (Newcastle U)	2
Williams, R. P. 1886 (Caernarvon)	1
Williams, S. G. 1954 (WBA, Southampton)	43
Williams, W. 1876 (Druids, Oswestry, Druids)	11
Williams, W. 1925 (Northampton T)	1
Witcomb, D. F. 1947 (WBA, Sheffield W)	3
Woosnam, A. P. 1959 (Leyton Orient, West Ham U, Aston Villa)	17
Woosnam, G. 1879 (Newtown Excelsior)	1
Worthington, T. 1894 (Newtown)	1
Wynn, G. A. 1909 (Wrexham, Manchester C)	11
Wynn, W. 1903 (Chirk)	1

Yorath, T. C. 1970 (Leeds U, Coventry C, Tottenham H, Vancouver W)	59
Young, E. 1990 (Wimbledon, C Palace, Wolverhampton W)	21

REPUBLIC OF IRELAND

Aherne, T. 1946 (Belfast C, Luton T)	16
Aldridge, J. W. 1986 (Oxford U, Liverpool, Real Sociedad, Tranmere R)	69
Ambrose, P. 1955 (Shamrock R)	5
Anderson, J. 1980 (Preston NE, Newcastle U)	16
Andrews, K. J. 2009 (Blackburn R)	6
Andrews, P. 1936 (Bohemians)	1
Arrigan, T. 1938 (Waterford)	1

Babb, P. A. 1994 (Coventry C, Liverpool, Sunderland)	35
Bailham, E. 1964 (Shamrock R)	1
Barber, E. 1966 (Shelbourne, Birmingham C)	2
Barrett, G. 2003 (Arsenal, Coventry C)	6
Barry, P. 1928 (Fordsons)	2
Beglin, J. 1984 (Liverpool)	15
Bennett, A. J. 2007 (Reading)	2
Bermingham, J. 1929 (Bohemians)	1
Bermingham, P. 1935 (St James' Gate)	1
Best, L. J. B. 2009 (Coventry C)	2
Bonner, P. 1981 (Celtic)	80
Braddish, S. 1978 (Dundalk)	2
Bradshaw, P. 1939 (St James' Gate)	5
Brady, F. 1926 (Fordsons)	2
Brady, T. R. 1964 (QPR)	6
Brady, W. L. 1975 (Arsenal, Juventus, Sampdoria, Internazionale, Ascoli, West Ham U)	72
Branagan, K. G. 1997 (Bolton W)	1
Breen, G. 1996 (Birmingham C, Coventry C, West Ham U, Sunderland)	63
Breen, T. 1937 (Manchester U, Shamrock R)	5
Brennan, F. 1965 (Drumcondra)	1
Brennan, S. A. 1965 (Manchester U, Waterford)	19
Brown, J. 1937 (Coventry C)	2
Browne, W. 1964 (Bohemians)	3
Bruce, A. S. 2007 (Ipswich T)	2
Buckley, L. 1984 (Shamrock R, Waregem)	2
Burke, F. 1952 (Cork Ath)	1
Burke, J. 1929 (Shamrock R)	1
Burke, J. 1934 (Cork)	1
Butler, P. J. 2000 (Sunderland)	1
Butler, T. 2003 (Sunderland)	2
Byrne, A. B. 1970 (Southampton)	14
Byrne, D. 1929 (Shelbourne, Shamrock R, Coleraine)	3
Byrne, J. 1928 (Bray Unknowns)	1
Byrne, J. 1985 (QPR, Le Havre, Brighton & HA, Sunderland, Millwall)	23
Byrne, J. 2004 (Shelbourne)	2

Byrne, P. 1931 (Dolphin, Shelbourne, Drumcondra)	3
Byrne, P. 1984 (Shamrock R)	8
Byrne, S. 1931 (Bohemians)	1

Campbell, A. 1985 (Santander)	3
Campbell, N. 1971 (St Patrick's Ath, Fortuna Cologne)	11
Cannon, H. 1926 (Bohemians)	2
Cantwell, N. 1954 (West Ham U, Manchester U)	36
Carey, B. P. 1992 (Manchester U, Leicester C)	3
Carey, J. J. 1938 (Manchester U)	29
Carolan, J. 1960 (Manchester U)	2
Carr, S. 1999 (Tottenham H, Newcastle U)	44
Carroll, B. 1949 (Shelbourne)	2
Carroll, T. R. 1968 (Ipswich T, Birmingham C)	17
Carsley, L. K. 1998 (Derby Co, Blackburn R, Coventry C, Everton)	39
Cascarino, A. G. 1986 (Gillingham, Millwall, Aston Villa, Celtic, Chelsea, Marseille, Nancy)	88
Chandler, J. 1980 (Leeds U)	2
Chatton, H. A. 1931 (Shelbourne, Dumbarton, Cork)	3
Clarke, C. R. 2004 (Stoke C)	2
Clarke, J. 1978 (Drogheda U)	1
Clarke, K. 1948 (Drumcondra)	2
Clarke, M. 1950 (Shamrock R)	1
Clinton, T. J. 1951 (Everton)	3
Coad, P. 1947 (Shamrock R)	11
Coffey, T. 1950 (Drumcondra)	1
Colfer, M. D. 1950 (Shelbourne)	2
Colgan, N. 2002 (Hibernian, Barnsley)	9
Collins, F. 1927 (Jacobs)	1
Conmy, O. M. 1965 (Peterborough U)	5
Connolly, D. J. 1996 (Watford, Feyenoord, Wolverhampton W, Excelsior, Feyenoord, Wimbledon, West Ham U, Wigan Ath)	41
Connolly, H. 1937 (Cork)	1
Connolly, J. 1926 (Fordsons)	1
Conroy, G. A. 1970 (Stoke C)	27
Conway, J. P. 1967 (Fulham, Manchester C)	20
Corr, P. J. 1949 (Everton)	4
Courtney, E. 1946 (Cork U)	1
Coyle, O. C. 1994 (Bolton W)	1
Coyne, T. 1992 (Celtic, Tranmere R, Motherwell)	22
Crowe, G. 2003 (Bohemians)	2
Cummins, G. P. 1954 (Luton T)	19
Cuneen, T. 1951 (Limerick)	1
Cunningham, K. 1996 (Wimbledon, Birmingham C)	72

Curtis, D. P. 1957 (Shelbourne, Bristol C, Ipswich T, Exeter C) 17
Cusack, S. 1953 (Limerick) 1

Daish, L. S. 1992 (Cambridge U, Coventry C) 5
Daly, G. A. 1973 (Manchester U, Derby Co, Coventry C, Birmingham C, Shrewsbury T) 48
Daly, J. 1932 (Shamrock R) 2
Daly, M. 1978 (Wolverhampton W) 2
Daly, P. 1950 (Shamrock R) 1
Davis, T. L. 1937 (Oldham Ath, Tranmere R) 4
Deacy, E. 1982 (Aston Villa) 4
Delaney, D. F. 2008 (QPR) 2
Delap, R. J. 1998 (Derby Co, Southampton) 11
De Mange, K. J. P. P. 1987 (Liverpool, Hull C) 2
Dempsey, J. T. 1967 (Fulham, Chelsea) 19
Dennehy, J. 1972 (Cork Hibernians, Nottingham F, Walsall) 11
Desmond, P. 1950 (Middlesbrough) 4
Devine, J. 1980 (Arsenal, Norwich C) 13
Doherty, G. M. T. 2000 (Luton T, Tottenham H, Norwich C) 34
Donnelly, J. 1935 (Dundalk) 10
Donnelly, T. 1938 (Drumcondra, Shamrock R) 2
Donovan, D. C. 1955 (Everton) 5
Donovan, T. 1980 (Aston Villa) 2
Douglas, J. 2004 (Blackburn R, Leeds U) 8
Dowdall, C. 1928 (Fordsons, Barnsley, Cork) 3
Doyle, C. 1959 (Shelbourne) 1
Doyle, Colin 2007 (Birmingham C) 1
Doyle, D. 1926 (Shamrock R) 1
Doyle, K. E. 2006 (Reading) 26
Doyle, L. 1932 (Dolphin) 1
Doyle, M. P. 2004 (Coventry C) 1
Duff, D. A. 1998 (Blackburn R, Chelsea, Newcastle U) 74
Duffy, B. 1950 (Shamrock R) 1
Duggan, H. A. 1927 (Leeds U, Newport Co) 5
Dunne, A. P. 1962 (Manchester U, Bolton W) 33
Dunne, J. 1930 (Sheffield U, Arsenal, Southampton, Shamrock R) 15
Dunne, J. C. 1971 (Fulham) 1
Dunne, L. 1935 (Manchester C) 2
Dunne, P. A. J. 1965 (Manchester U) 5
Dunne, R. P. 2000 (Everton, Manchester C) 52
Dunne, S. 1953 (Luton T) 15
Dunne, T. 1956 (St Patrick's Ath) 3
Dunning, P. 1971 (Shelbourne) 2
Dunphy, E. M. 1966 (York C, Millwall) 23
Dwyer, N. M. 1960 (West Ham U, Swansea T) 14

Eccles, P. 1986 (Shamrock R) 1
Egan, R. 1929 (Dundalk) 1
Eglington, T. J. 1946 (Shamrock R, Everton) 24
Elliott, S. W. 2005 (Sunderland) 9
Ellis, P. 1935 (Bohemians) 7
Evans, M. J. 1998 (Southampton) 1

Fagan, E. 1973 (Shamrock R) 1
Fagan, F. 1955 (Manchester C, Derby Co) 8
Fagan, J. 1926 (Shamrock R) 1
Fairclough, M. 1982 (Dundalk) 2
Fallon, S. 1951 (Celtic) 8
Fallon, W. J. 1935 (Notts Co, Sheffield W) 9
Farquharson, T. G. 1929 (Cardiff C) 4
Farrell, P. 1937 (Hibernian) 2
Farrell, P. D. 1946 (Shamrock R, Everton) 28
Farrelly, G. 1996 (Aston Villa, Everton, Bolton W) 6
Feenan, J. J. 1937 (Sunderland) 2
Finnan, S. 2000 (Fulham, Liverpool, Espanyol) 53
Finucane, A. 1967 (Limerick) 11
Fitzgerald, F. J. 1955 (Waterford) 2
Fitzgerald, P. J. 1961 (Leeds U, Chester) 5
Fitzpatrick, K. 1970 (Limerick) 1
Fitzsimons, A. G. 1950 (Middlesbrough, Lincoln C) 26

Fleming, C. 1996 (Middlesbrough) 10
Flood, J. J. 1926 (Shamrock R) 5
Fogarty, A. 1960 (Sunderland, Hartlepools U) 11
Folan, C. C. 2009 (Hull C) 4
Foley, D. J. 2000 (Watford) 6
Foley, J. 1934 (Cork, Celtic) 7
Foley, K. P. 2009 (Wolverhampton W) 1
Foley, M. 1926 (Shelbourne) 1
Foley, T. C. 1964 (Northampton T) 9
Foy, T. 1938 (Shamrock R) 2
Fullam, J. 1961 (Preston NE, Shamrock R) 11
Fullam, R. 1926 (Shamrock R) 2

Gallagher, C. 1967 (Celtic) 2
Gallagher, M. 1954 (Hibernian) 1
Gallagher, P. 1932 (Falkirk) 1
Galvin, A. 1983 (Tottenham H, Sheffield W, Swindon T) 29
Gamble, J. 2007 (Cork C) 2
Gannon, E. 1949 (Notts Co, Sheffield W, Shelbourne) 14
Gannon, M. 1972 (Shelbourne) 1
Gaskins, P. 1934 (Shamrock R, St James' Gate) 7
Gavin, J. T. 1950 (Norwich C, Tottenham H, Norwich C) 7
Geoghegan, M. 1937 (St James' Gate) 2
Gibbons, A. 1952 (St Patrick's Ath) 4
Gibson, D. T. D. 2008 (Manchester U) 5
Gilbert, R. 1966 (Shamrock R) 1
Giles, C. 1951 (Doncaster R) 1
Giles, M. J. 1960 (Manchester U, Leeds U, WBA, Shamrock R) 59
Given, S. J. J. 1996 (Blackburn R, Newcastle U, Manchester C) 96
Givens, D. J. 1969 (Manchester U, Luton T, QPR, Birmingham C, Neuchatel X) 56
Gleeson, S. M. 2007 (Wolverhampton W) 2
Glen, W. 1927 (Shamrock R) 8
Glynn, D. 1952 (Drumcondra) 2
Godwin, T. F. 1949 (Shamrock R, Leicester C, Bournemouth) 13
Golding, J. 1928 (Shamrock R) 2
Goodman, J. 1997 (Wimbledon) 4
Goodwin, J. 2003 (Stockport Co) 1
Gorman, W. C. 1936 (Bury, Brentford) 13
Grace, J. 1926 (Drumcondra) 1
Grealish, A. 1976 (Orient, Luton T, Brighton & HA, WBA) 45
Gregg, E. 1978 (Bohemians) 8
Griffith, R. 1935 (Walsall) 1
Grimes, A. A. 1978 (Manchester U, Coventry C, Luton T) 18

Hale, A. 1962 (Aston Villa, Doncaster R, Waterford) 14
Hamilton, T. 1959 (Shamrock R) 2
Hand, E. K. 1969 (Portsmouth) 20
Harrington, W. 1936 (Cork) 5
Harte, I. P. 1996 (Leeds U, Levante) 64
Hartnett, J. B. 1949 (Middlesbrough) 2
Haverty, J. 1956 (Arsenal, Blackburn R, Millwall, Celtic, Bristol R, Shelbourne) 32
Hayes, A. W. P. 1979 (Southampton) 1
Hayes, W. E. 1947 (Huddersfield T) 2
Hayes, W. J. 1949 (Limerick) 1
Healey, R. 1977 (Cardiff C) 2
Healy, C. 2002 (Celtic, Sunderland) 13
Heighway, S. D. 1971 (Liverpool, Minnesota K) 34
Henderson, B. 1948 (Drumcondra) 2
Henderson, W. C. P. 2006 (Brighton & HA, Preston NE) 6
Hennessy, J. 1965 (Shelbourne, St Patrick's Ath) 5
Herrick, J. 1972 (Cork Hibernians, Shamrock R) 3
Higgins, J. 1951 (Birmingham C) 1
Holland, M. R. 2000 (Ipswich T, Charlton Ath) 49
Holmes, J. 1971 (Coventry C, Tottenham H, Vancouver W) 30

Hoolahan, W. 2008 (Blackpool) 1
Horlacher, A. F. 1930 (Bohemians) 7
Houghton, R. J. 1986 (Oxford U, Liverpool, Aston Villa,
  C Palace, Reading) 73
Howlett, G. 1984 (Brighton & HA) 1
Hoy, M. 1938 (Dundalk) 6
Hughton, C. 1980 (Tottenham H, West Ham U) 53
Hunt, N. 2009 (Reading) 2
Hunt, S. P. 2007 (Reading) 20
Hurley, C. J. 1957 (Millwall, Sunderland, Bolton W) 40
Hutchinson, F. 1935 (Drumcondra) 2

Ireland S J. 2006 (Manchester C) 6
Irwin, D. J. 1991 (Manchester U) 56

Jordan, D. 1937 (Wolverhampton W) 2
Jordan, W. 1934 (Bohemians) 2

Kavanagh, G. A. 1998 (Stoke C, Cardiff C, Wigan Ath)
   16
Kavanagh, P. J. 1931 (Celtic) 2
Keane, R. D. 1998 (Wolverhampton W, Coventry C,
  Internazionale, Leeds U, Tottenham H, Liverpool,
  Tottenham H) 90
Keane, R. M. 1991 (Nottingham F, Manchester U) 67
Keane, T. R. 1949 (Swansea T) 4
Kearin, M. 1972 (Shamrock R) 1
Kearns, F. T. 1954 (West Ham U) 1
Kearns, M. 1971 (Oxford U, Walsall, Wolverhampton W)
   18
Kelly, A. T. 1993 (Sheffield U, Blackburn R) 34
Kelly, D. T. 1988 (Walsall, West Ham U, Leicester C,
  Newcastle U, Wolverhampton W, Sunderland,
  Tranmere R) 26
Kelly, G. 1994 (Leeds U) 52
Kelly, J. 1932 (Derry C) 4
Kelly, J. A. 1957 (Drumcondra, Preston NE) 47
Kelly, J. P. V. 1961 (Wolverhampton W) 5
Kelly, M. J. 1988 (Portsmouth) 4
Kelly, N. 1954 (Nottingham F) 1
Kelly, S. M. 2006 (Tottenham H, Birmingham C) 14
Kendrick, J. 1927 (Everton, Dolphin) 4
Kenna, J. J. 1995 (Blackburn R) 27
Kennedy, M. F. 1986 (Portsmouth) 2
Kennedy, M. J. 1996 (Liverpool, Wimbledon,
  Manchester C, Wolverhampton W) 34
Kennedy, W. 1932 (St James' Gate) 3
Kenny, P. 2004 (Sheffield U) 7
Keogh, A. D. 2007 (Wolverhampton W) 11
Keogh, J. 1966 (Shamrock R) 1
Keogh, S. 1959 (Shamrock R) 1
Kernaghan, A. N. 1993 (Middlesbrough, Manchester C)
   22
Kiely, D. L. 2000 (Charlton Ath, WBA) 11
Kiernan, F. W. 1951 (Shamrock R, Southampton) 5
Kilbane, K. D. 1998 (WBA, Sunderland, Everton,
  Wigan Ath, Hull C) 96
Kinnear, J. P. 1967 (Tottenham H, Brighton & HA) 26
Kinsella, J. 1928 (Shelbourne) 1
Kinsella, M. A. 1998 (Charlton Ath, Aston Villa, WBA)
   48
Kinsella, O. 1932 (Shamrock R) 2
Kirkland, A. 1927 (Shamrock R) 1

Lacey, W. 1927 (Shelbourne) 3
Langan, D. 1978 (Derby Co, Birmingham C, Oxford U)
   26
Lapira, J. 2007 (Notre Dame) 1
Lawler, J. F. 1953 (Fulham) 8
Lawlor, J. C. 1949 (Drumcondra, Doncaster R) 3
Lawlor, M. 1971 (Shamrock R) 5
Lawrence, L. 2009 (Stoke C) 1
Lawrenson, M. 1977 (Preston NE, Brighton & HA,
  Liverpool) 39
Lee, A. D. 2003 (Rotherham U, Cardiff C, Ipswich T) 10

Leech, M. 1969 (Shamrock R) 8
Lennon, C. 1935 (St James' Gate) 3
Lennox, G. 1931 (Dolphin) 2
Long, S. P. 2007 (Reading) 10
Lowry, D. 1962 (St Patrick's Ath) 1
Lunn, R. 1939 (Dundalk) 2
Lynch, J. 1934 (Cork Bohemians) 1

McAlinden, J. 1946 (Portsmouth) 2
McAteer, J. W. 1994 (Bolton W, Liverpool, Blackburn R,
  Sunderland) 52
McCann, J. 1957 (Shamrock R) 1
McCarthy, J. 1926 (Bohemians) 3
McCarthy, M. 1932 (Shamrock R) 1
McCarthy, M. 1984 (Manchester C, Celtic, Lyon,
  Millwall) 57
McConville, T. 1972 (Dundalk, Waterford) 6
McDonagh, Jacko 1984 (Shamrock R) 3
McDonagh, J. 1981 (Everton, Bolton W, Notts Co,
  Wichita Wings) 25
McEvoy, M. A. 1961 (Blackburn R) 17
McGeady, A. 2004 (Celtic) 26
McGee, P. 1978 (QPR, Preston NE) 15
McGoldrick, E. J. 1992 (C Palace, Arsenal) 15
McGowan, D. 1949 (West Ham U) 3
McGowan, J. 1947 (Cork U) 1
McGrath, M. 1958 (Blackburn R, Bradford) 22
McGrath, P. 1985 (Manchester U, Aston Villa,
  Derby Co) 83
McGuire, W. 1936 (Bohemians) 1
Macken, A. 1977 (Derby Co) 1
Macken J. P. 2005 (Manchester C) 1
McKenzie, G. 1938 (Southend U) 9
Mackey, G. 1957 (Shamrock R) 3
McLoughlin, A. F. 1990 (Swindon T, Southampton,
  Portsmouth) 42
McLoughlin, F. 1930 (Fordsons, Cork) 2
McMillan, W. 1946 (Belfast C) 2
McNally, J. B. 1959 (Luton T) 3
McPhail, S. 2000 (Leeds U) 10
McShane, P. D. 2007 (WBA, Sunderland) 17
Madden, O. 1936 (Cork) 1
Maguire, J. 1929 (Shamrock R) 1
Mahon, A. J. 2000 (Tranmere R) 2
Malone, G. 1949 (Shelbourne) 1
Mancini, T. J. 1974 (QPR, Arsenal) 5
Martin, C. 1927 (Bo'ness) 1
Martin, C. J. 1946 (Glentoran, Leeds U, Aston Villa) 30
Martin, M. P. 1972 (Bohemians, Manchester U, WBA,
  Newcastle U) 52
Maybury, A. 1998 (Leeds U, Hearts, Leicester C) 10
Meagan, M. K. 1961 (Everton, Huddersfield T,
  Drogheda) 17
Meehan, P. 1934 (Drumcondra) 1
Miller, L. W. P. 2004 (Celtic, Manchester U, Sunderland)
   20
Milligan, M. J. 1992 (Oldham Ath) 1
Monahan, P. 1935 (Sligo R) 2
Mooney, J. 1965 (Shamrock R) 2
Moore, A. 1996 (Middlesbrough) 8
Moore, P. 1931 (Shamrock R, Aberdeen, Shamrock R) 9
Moran, K. 1980 (Manchester U, Sporting Gijon,
  Blackburn R) 71
Moroney, T. 1948 (West Ham U, Evergreen U) 12
Morris, C. B. 1988 (Celtic, Middlesbrough) 35
Morrison, C. H. 2002 (C Palace, Birmingham C,
  C Palace) 36
Moulson, C. 1936 (Lincoln C, Notts Co) 5
Moulson, G. B. 1948 (Lincoln C) 3
Muckian, C. 1978 (Drogheda U) 1
Muldoon, T. 1927 (Aston Villa) 1
Mulligan, P. M. 1969 (Shamrock R, Chelsea, C Palace,
  WBA, Shamrock R) 50
Munroe, L. 1954 (Shamrock R) 1
Murphy, A. 1956 (Clyde) 1

Murphy, B. 1986 (Bohemians)	1
Murphy, D. 2007 (Sunderland)	9
Murphy, J. 1980 (C Palace)	3
Murphy, J. 2004 (WBA)	1
Murphy, P. M. 2007 (Carlisle U)	1
Murray, T. 1950 (Dundalk)	1
Newman, W. 1969 (Shelbourne)	1
Nolan. E. W. 2009 (Preston NE)	1
Nolan, R. 1957 (Shamrock R)	10
O'Brien, A. 2007 (Newcastle U)	5
O'Brien, A. J. 2001 (Newcastle U, Portsmouth)	26
O'Brien, F. 1980 (Philadelphia F)	3
O'Brien J. M. 2006 (Bolton W)	3
O'Brien, L. 1986 (Shamrock R, Manchester U, Newcastle U, Tranmere R)	16
O'Brien, M. T. 1927 (Derby Co, Walsall, Norwich C, Watford)	4
O'Brien, R. 1976 (Notts Co)	5
O'Byrne, L. B. 1949 (Shamrock R)	1
O'Callaghan, B. R. 1979 (Stoke C)	6
O'Callaghan, K. 1981 (Ipswich T, Portsmouth)	21
O'Cearuill, J. 2007 (Arsenal)	2
O'Connell, A. 1967 (Dundalk, Bohemians)	2
O'Connor, T. 1950 (Shamrock R)	4
O'Connor, T. 1968 (Fulham, Dundalk, Bohemians)	7
O'Driscoll, J. F. 1949 (Swansea T)	3
O'Driscoll, S. 1982 (Fulham)	3
O'Farrell, F. 1952 (West Ham U, Preston NE)	9
O'Flanagan, K. P. 1938 (Bohemians, Arsenal)	10
O'Flanagan, M. 1947 (Bohemians)	1
O'Halloran, S. E. 2007 (Aston Villa)	2
O'Hanlon, K. G. 1988 (Rotherham U)	1
O'Kane, P. 1935 (Bohemians)	3
O'Keefe, E. 1981 (Everton, Port Vale)	5
O'Keefe, T. 1934 (Cork, Waterford)	3
O'Leary, D. 1977 (Arsenal)	68
O'Leary, P. 1980 (Shamrock R)	7
O'Mahoney, M. T. 1938 (Bristol R)	6
O'Neill, F. S. 1962 (Shamrock R)	20
O'Neill, J. 1952 (Everton)	17
O'Neill, J. 1961 (Preston NE)	1
O'Neill, K. P. 1996 (Norwich C, Middlesbrough)	13
O'Neill, W. 1936 (Dundalk)	11
O'Regan, K. 1984 (Brighton & HA)	4
O'Reilly, J. 1932 (Brideville, Aberdeen, Brideville, St James' Gate)	20
O'Reilly, J. 1946 (Cork U)	2
O'Shea, J. F. 2002 (Manchester U)	54
Peyton, G. 1977 (Fulham, Bournemouth, Everton)	33
Peyton, N. 1957 (Shamrock R, Leeds U)	6
Phelan, T. 1992 (Wimbledon, Manchester C, Chelsea, Everton, Fulham)	42
Potter, D. M. 2007 (Wolverhampton W)	5
Quinn, A. 2003 (Sheffield W, Sheffield U)	8
Quinn, B. S. 2000 (Coventry C)	4
Quinn, N. J. 1986 (Arsenal, Manchester C, Sunderland)	91
Reid, A. M. 2004 (Nottingham F, Tottenham H, Charlton Ath, Sunderland)	27
Reid, C. 1931 (Brideville)	1
Reid, S. J. 2002 (Millwall, Blackburn R)	23
Richardson, D. J. 1972 (Shamrock R, Gillingham)	3

Rigby, A. 1935 (St James' Gate)	3
Ringstead, A. 1951 (Sheffield U)	20
Robinson, J. 1928 (Bohemians, Dolphin)	2
Robinson, M. 1981 (Brighton & HA, Liverpool, QPR)	24
Roche, P. J. 1972 (Shelbourne, Manchester U)	8
Rogers, E. 1968 (Blackburn R, Charlton Ath)	19
Rowlands, M. C. 2004 (QPR)	3
Ryan, G. 1978 (Derby Co, Brighton & HA)	18
Ryan, R. A. 1950 (WBA, Derby Co)	16
Sadlier, R. T. 2002 (Millwall)	1
Savage, D. P. T. 1996 (Millwall)	5
Saward, P. 1954 (Millwall, Aston Villa, Huddersfield T)	18
Scannell, T. 1954 (Southend U)	1
Scully, P. J. 1989 (Arsenal)	1
Sheedy, K. 1984 (Everton, Newcastle U)	46
Sheridan, J. J. 1988 (Leeds U, Sheffield W)	34
Slaven, B. 1990 (Middlesbrough)	7
Sloan, J. W. 1946 (Arsenal)	2
Smyth, M. 1969 (Shamrock R)	1
Squires, J. 1934 (Shelbourne)	1
Stapleton, F. 1977 (Arsenal, Manchester U, Ajax, Le Havre, Blackburn R)	71
Staunton, S. 1989 (Liverpool, Aston Villa, Liverpool, Aston Villa)	102
St Ledger-Hall, S. P. 2009 (Preston NE)	2
Stevenson, A. E. 1932 (Dolphin, Everton)	7
Stokes, A. 2007 (Sunderland)	3
Strahan, F. 1964 (Shelbourne)	5
Sullivan, J. 1928 (Fordsons)	1
Swan, M. M. G. 1960 (Drumcondra)	1
Synnott, N. 1978 (Shamrock R)	3
Taylor, T. 1959 (Waterford)	1
Thomas, P. 1974 (Waterford)	2
Thompson, J. 2004 (Nottingham F)	1
Townsend, A. D. 1989 (Norwich C, Chelsea, Aston Villa, Middlesbrough)	70
Traynor, T. J. 1954 (Southampton)	8
Treacy, R. C. P. 1966 (WBA, Charlton Ath, Swindon T, Preston NE, WBA, Shamrock R)	42
Tuohy, L. 1956 (Shamrock R, Newcastle U, Shamrock R)	8
Turner, C. J. 1936 (Southend U, West Ham U)	10
Turner, P. 1963 (Celtic)	2
Vernon, J. 1946 (Belfast C)	2
Waddock, G. 1980 (QPR, Millwall)	21
Walsh, D. J. 1946 (Linfield, WBA, Aston Villa)	20
Walsh, J. 1982 (Limerick)	1
Walsh, M. 1976 (Blackpool, Everton, QPR, Porto)	21
Walsh, M. 1982 (Everton)	4
Walsh, W. 1947 (Manchester C)	9
Waters, J. 1977 (Grimsby T)	2
Watters, F. 1926 (Shelbourne)	1
Weir, E. 1939 (Clyde)	3
Westwood, K. 2009 (Coventry C)	1
Whelan, G. D. 2008 (Stoke C)	12
Whelan, R. 1964 (St Patrick's Ath)	2
Whelan, R. 1981 (Liverpool, Southend U)	53
Whelan, W. 1956 (Manchester U)	4
White, J. J. 1928 (Bohemians)	1
Whittaker, R. 1959 (Chelsea)	1
Williams, J. 1938 (Shamrock R)	1

BRITISH AND IRISH INTERNATIONAL GOALSCORERS SINCE 1872

Where two players with the same surname and initials have appeared for the same country, and one or both have scored, they have been distinguished by reference to the club which appears *first* against their name in the international appearances section.

ENGLAND

Name		Name		Name		Name	
A'Court, A.	1	Bull, S. G.	4	Fowler, R. B.	7	Kennedy, R.	3
Adams, T. A.	5	Bullock, N.	2	Francis, G. C. J.	3	Kenyon-Slaney, W. S.	2
Adcock, H.	1	Burgess, H.	4	Francis, T.	12	Keown, M. R.	2
Alcock, C. W.	1	Butcher, T.	3	Freeman, B. C.	3	Kevan, D. T.	8
Allen, A.	3	Byrne, J. J.	8	Froggatt, J.	2	Kidd, B.	1
Allen, R.	2			Froggatt, R.	2	King, L. B.	1
Amos, A.	1	Campbell, S. J.	1			Kingsford, R. K.	1
Anderson, V.	2	Camsell, G. H.	18	Galley, T.	1	Kirchen, A. J.	2
Anderton, D. R.	7	Carter, H. S.	7	Gascoigne, P. J.	10	Kirton, W. J.	1
Astall, G.	1	Carter, J. H.	4	Geary, F.	3		
Athersmith, W. C.	3	Chadwick, E.	3	Gerrard, S. G.	14	Lampard, F. J.	17
Atyeo, P. J. W.	5	Chamberlain, M.	1	Gibbins, W. V. T.	3	Langton, R.	1
		Chambers, H.	5	Gilliatt, W. E.	3	Latchford, R. D.	5
Bache, J. W.	4	Channon, M. R.	21	Goddard, P.	1	Latheron, E. G.	1
Bailey, N. C.	2	Charlton, J.	6	Goodall, J.	12	Lawler, C.	1
Baily, E. F.	5	Charlton, R.	49	Goodyer, A. C.	1	Lawton, T.	22
Baker, J. H.	3	Chenery, C. J.	1	Gosling, R. C.	2	Lee, F.	10
Ball, A. J.	8	Chivers, M.	13	Goulden, L. A.	4	Lee, J.	1
Bambridge, A. L.	1	Clarke, A. J.	10	Grainger, C.	3	Lee, R. M.	2
Bambridge, E. C.	11	Cobbold, W. N.	6	Greaves, J.	44	Lee, S.	2
Barclay, R.	2	Cock, J. G.	2	Grovesnor, A. T.	2	Le Saux, G. P.	1
Barmby, N. J.	4	Cole, A.	1	Gunn, W.	1	Lindley, T.	14
Barnes, J.	11	Cole, J. J.	10			Lineker, G.	48
Barnes, P. S.	4	Common, A.	2	Haines, J. T. W.	2	Lofthouse, J. M.	3
Barry, G.	2	Connelly, J. M.	7	Hall, G. W.	9	Lofthouse, N.	30
Barton, J.	1	Coppell, S. J.	7	Halse, H. J.	2	Hon. A. Lyttelton	1
Bassett, W. I.	8	Cotterill, G. H.	2	Hampson, J.	5		
Bastin, C. S.	12	Cowans, G.	2	Hampton, H.	2	Mabbutt, G.	1
Beardsley, P. A.	9	Crawford, R.	1	Hancocks, J.	2	Macdonald, M.	6
Beasley, A.	1	Crawshaw, T. H.	1	Hardman, H. P.	1	Mannion, W. J.	11
Beattie, T. K.	1	Crayston, W. J.	1	Harris, S. S.	2	Mariner, P.	13
Beckham, D. R. J.	17	Creek, F. N. S.	1	Hassall, H. W.	4	Marsh, R. W.	1
Becton, F.	2	Crooks, S. D.	7	Hateley, M.	9	Matthews, S.	11
Bedford, H.	1	Crouch, P. J.	16	Haynes, J. N.	18	Matthews, V.	1
Bell, C.	9	Currey, E. S.	2	Hegan, K. E.	4	McCall, J.	1
Bentley, R. T. F.	9	Currie, A. W.	3	Henfrey, A. G.	2	McDermott, T.	3
Bishop, S. M.	1	Cursham, A. W.	2	Heskey, E. W.	7	McManaman, S.	3
Blackburn, F.	1	Cursham, H. A.	5	Hilsdon, G. R.	14	Medley, L. D.	1
Blissett, L.	3			Hine, E. W.	4	Melia, J.	1
Bloomer, S.	28	Daft, H. B.	3	Hinton, A. T.	1	Mercer, D. W.	1
Bond, R.	2	Davenport, J. K.	2	Hirst, D. E.	1	Merson, P. C.	3
Bonsor, A. G.	1	Davis, G.	1	Hitchens, G. A.	5	Milburn, J. E. T.	10
Bowden, E. R.	1	Davis, H.	1	Hobbis, H. H. F.	1	Miller, H. S.	1
Bowers, J. W.	2	Day, S. H.	2	Hoddle, G.	8	Mills, G. R.	3
Bowles, S.	1	Dean, W. R.	18	Hodgetts, D.	1	Milward, A.	3
Bradford, G. R. W.	1	Defoe, J. C.	8	Hodgson, G.	1	Mitchell, C.	5
Bradford, J.	7	Devey, J. H. G.	1	Holley, G. H.	8	Moore, J.	1
Bradley, W.	2	Dewhurst, F.	11	Houghton, W. E.	5	Moore, R. F.	2
Bradshaw, F.	3	Dix, W. R.	1	Howell, R.	1	Moore, W. G. B.	2
Brann, G.	1	Dixon, K. M.	4	Hughes, E. W.	1	Morren, T.	1
Bridge, W. M.	1	Dixon, L. M.	1	Hulme, J. H. A.	4	Morris, F.	1
Bridges, B. J.	1	Dorrell, A. R.	1	Hunt, G. S.	1	Morris, J.	3
Bridgett, A.	3	Douglas, B.	11	Hunt, R.	18	Mortensen, S. H.	23
Brindle, T.	1	Drake, E. J.	6	Hunter, N.	2	Morton, J. R.	1
Britton, C. S.	1	Ducat, A.	1	Hurst, G. C.	24	Mosforth, W.	3
Broadbent, P. F.	2	Dunn, A. T. B.	2			Mullen, J.	6
Broadis, I. A.	8			Ince, P. E. C.	2	Mullery, A. P.	1
Brodie, J. B.	1	Eastham, G.	2			Murphy, D. B	1
Bromley-Davenport, W.	2	Edwards, D.	5	Jack, D. N. B.	3		
Brook, E. F.	10	Ehiogu, U.	1	Jeffers, F.	1	Neal, P. G.	5
Brooking, T. D.	5	Elliott, W. H.	3	Jenas, J. A.	1	Needham, E.	3
Brooks, J.	2	Evans, R. E.	1	Johnson, D. E.	6	Nicholls, J.	1
Broome, F. H.	3			Johnson, E.	2	Nicholson, W. E.	1
Brown, A.	4	Ferdinand, L.	5	Johnson, J. A.	2	Nugent, D. J.	1
Brown, A. S.	1	Ferdinand, R. G.	3	Johnson, T. C. F.	5		
Brown, G.	5	Finney, T.	30	Johnson, W. H.	1	O'Grady, M.	3
Brown, J.	3	Fleming, H. J.	9			Osborne, F. R.	3
Brown, W.	1	Flowers, R.	10	Kail, E. I. L.	2	Owen, M. J.	40
Brown, W. M.	1	Forman, Frank	1	Kay, A. H.	1	Own goals	29
Buchan, C. M.	4	Forman, Fred	3	Keegan, J. K.	21		
		Foster, R. E.	3	Kelly, R.	8	Page, L. A.	1

Name	
Taggart, G. P.	7
Thompson, F. W.	2
Torrans, S.	1
Tully, C. P.	3
Turner, A.	1
Walker, J.	1
Walsh, D. J.	5
Welsh, E.	1
Whiteside, N.	9
Whiteside, T.	1
Whitley, Jeff	2
Williams, J. R.	1
Williams, M. S.	1
Williamson, J.	1
Wilson, D. J.	1
Wilson, K. J.	6
Wilson, S. J.	7
Wilton, J. M.	2
Young, S.	1

N.B. In 1914 Young goal should be credited to Gillespie W v Wales

SCOTLAND

Name	
Aitken, R. (*Celtic*)	1
Aitken, R. (*Dumbarton*)	1
Aitkenhead, W. A. C.	2
Alexander, D.	1
Allan, D. S.	4
Allan, J.	2
Anderson, F.	1
Anderson, W.	4
Andrews, P.	1
Archibald, A.	1
Archibald, S.	4
Baird, D.	2
Baird, J. C.	2
Baird, S.	2
Bannon, E.	1
Barbour, A.	1
Barker, J. B.	4
Battles, B. Jr	1
Bauld, W.	2
Baxter, J. C.	3
Beattie, C.	1
Bell, J.	5
Bennett, A.	2
Berry, D.	1
Bett, J.	1
Beveridge, W. W.	1
Black, A.	3
Black, D.	1
Bone, J.	1
Booth, S.	6
Boyd, K	7
Boyd, R.	2
Boyd, T.	1
Boyd, W. G.	1
Brackenridge, T.	1
Brand, R.	8
Brazil, A.	1
Bremner, W. J.	3
Broadfoot, K.	1
Brown, A. D.	6
Buchanan, P. S.	1
Buchanan, R.	1
Buckley, P.	1
Buick, A.	2
Burke, C.	2
Burley, C. W.	3
Burns, K.	1
Cairns, T.	1
Caldwell, G.	2
Calderwood, C.	1
Calderwood, R.	2
Caldow, E.	4
Cameron, C.	2
Campbell, C.	1
Campbell, John (*Celtic*)	5
Campbell, John (*Rangers*)	4
Campbell, J. (*South Western*)	1
Campbell, P.	2
Campbell, R.	1
Cassidy, J.	1
Chalmers, S.	3
Chambers, T.	1
Cheyne, A. G.	4
Christie, A. J.	1
Clarkson, D.	1
Clunas, W. L.	1
Collins, J.	12
Collins, R. Y.	10
Combe, J. R.	1
Conn, A.	1
Cooper, D.	6
Craig, J.	1
Craig, T.	1
Crawford, S.	4
Cunningham, A. N.	5
Curran, H. P.	1
Daily, C.	6
Dalglish, K.	30
Davidson, D.	1
Davidson, J. A.	1
Delaney, J.	3
Devine, A.	1
Dewar, G.	1
Dewar, N.	4
Dickov, P.	1
Dickson, W.	4
Divers, J.	1
Dobie, R. S.	1
Docherty, T. H.	1
Dodds, D.	1
Dodds, W.	7
Donaldson, A.	1
Donnachie, J.	1
Dougall, J.	1
Drummond, J.	2
Dunbar, M.	1
Duncan, D.	7
Duncan, D. M.	1
Duncan, J.	1
Dunn, J.	2
Durie, G. S.	7
Easson, J. F.	1
Elliott, M. S.	1
Ellis, J.	1
Ferguson, B.	3
Ferguson, J.	6
Fernie, W.	1
Fitchie, T. T.	1
Flavell, R.	2
Fleming, C.	2
Fleming, J. W.	3
Fletcher, D.	4
Fletcher, S.	1
Fraser, M. J. E.	1
Freedman, D. A.	1
Gallacher, H. K.	23
Gallacher, K. W.	9
Gallacher, P.	1
Galt, J. H.	1
Gemmell, T. (*St Mirren*)	1
Gemmell, T. (*Celtic*)	1
Gemmill, A.	8
Gemmill, S.	1
Gibb, W.	1
Gibson, D. W.	1
Gibson, J. D.	1
Gibson, N.	1
Gillespie, Jas.	3
Gillick, T.	3
Gilzean, A. J.	12
Gossland, J.	2
Goudie, J.	1
Gough, C. R.	6
Gourlay, J.	1
Graham, A.	2
Graham, G.	3
Gray, A.	7
Gray, E.	3
Gray, F.	1
Greig, J.	3
Groves, W.	4
Hamilton, G.	4
Hamilton, J. (*Queen's Park*)	3
Hamilton, R. C.	15
Harper, J. M.	2
Hartley, P. J.	1
Harrower, W.	5
Hartford, R. A.	4
Heggie, C. W	4
Henderson, J. G.	1
Henderson, W.	5
Hendry, E. C. J.	3
Herd, D. G.	3
Herd, G.	1
Hewie, J. D.	2
Higgins, A. (*Newcastle U*)	1
Higgins, A. (*Kilmarnock*)	4
Highet, T. C.	1
Holt, G.J.	1
Holton, J. A.	2
Hopkin, D.	2
Houliston, W.	2
Howie, H.	1
Howie, J.	2
Hughes, J.	1
Hunter, W.	1
Hutchison, D.	6
Hutchison, T.	1
Hutton, J.	1
Hyslop, T.	1
Imrie, W. N.	1
Jackson, A.	8
Jackson, C.	1
Jackson, D.	4
James, A. W.	4
Jardine, A.	1
Jenkinson, T.	1
Jess, E.	2
Johnston, A.	2
Johnston, L. H.	1
Johnston, M.	14
Johnstone, D.	2
Johnstone, J.	4
Johnstone, Jas.	1
Johnstone, R.	10
Johnstone, W.	1
Jordan, J.	11
Kay, J. L.	5
Keillor, A.	3
Kelly, J.	1
Kelso, R.	1
Ker, G.	10
King, A.	1
King, J.	1
Kinnear, D.	1
Kyle, K.	1
Lambert, P.	1
Lambie, J.	1
Lambie, W. A.	5
Lang, J. J.	2
Latta, A.	2
Law, D.	30
Leggat, G.	8
Lennie, W.	1
Lennox, R.	3
Liddell, W.	6
Lindsay, J.	6
Linwood, A. B.	1
Logan, J.	1
Lorimer, P.	4
Love, A.	1
Low, J. (*Cambuslang*)	1
Lowe, J. (*St Bernards*)	1
Macari, L.	5
MacDougall, E. J.	3
MacFarlane, A.	1
MacLeod, M.	1
Mackay, D. C.	4
Mackay, G.	1
MacKenzie, A.	1
MacKinnon, W. W.	5
Madden, J.	5
Maloney, S.	1
Marshall, H.	1
Marshall, J.	1
Mason, J.	4
Massie, A.	1
Masson, D. S.	5
McAdam, J.	1
McAllister, G.	5
McAulay, J. D.	1
McAvennie, F.	1
McCall, J.	1
McCall, S. M.	1
McCalliog, J.	1
McCallum, N.	1
McCann, N.	3
McClair, B. J.	2
McCoist, A.	19
McColl, R. S.	13
McCormack, R.	1
McCulloch, D.	3
McCulloch, L.	1
McDougall, J.	4
McFadden, J.	13
McFadyen, W.	2
McGhee, M.	2
McGinlay, J.	4
McGregor, J.	1
McGrory, J.	6
McGuire, W.	1
McInally, A.	3
McInnes, T.	2
McKie, J.	2
McKimmie, S.	1
McKinlay, W.	4
McKinnon, A.	1
McKinnon, R.	1
McLaren, A.	4
McLaren, J.	1
McLean, A.	1
McLean, T.	1
McLintock, F.	1
McMahon, A.	6
McManus, S.	1
McMenemy, J.	5
McMillan, I. L.	2
McNeill, W.	3
McNiel, H.	5
McPhail, J.	3
McPhail, R.	7
McPherson, J.	5
McPherson, J. (*Vale of Leven*)	1
McPherson, R.	1
McQueen, G.	5
McStay, P.	9
McSwegan, G.	1
Meiklejohn, D. D.	3
Millar, J.	2
Miller, K.	11
Miller, T.	2
Miller, W.	1
Mitchell, R. C.	1
Morgan, W.	1
Morris, D.	1
Morris, H.	3
Morton, A. L.	5
Mudie, J. K.	9
Mulhall, G.	1

Name	
Munro, A. D.	1
Munro, N.	2
Murdoch, R.	5
Murphy, F.	1
Murray, J.	1
Napier, C. E.	3
Narey, D.	1
Naysmith, G. A.	1
Neil, R. G.	2
Nevin, P. K. F.	5
Nicholas, C.	5
Nisbet, J.	2
O'Connor, G.	4
O'Donnell, F.	2
O'Hare, J.	5
Ormond, W. E.	2
O'Rourke, F.	1
Orr, R.	1
Orr, T.	1
Oswald, J.	1
Own goals	16
Parlane, D.	1
Paul, H. McD.	2
Paul, W.	5
Pettigrew, W.	2
Provan, D.	1
Quashie, N. F.	1
Quinn, J.	7
Quinn, P.	1
Rankin, G.	2
Rankin, R.	2
Reid, W.	4
Reilly, L.	22
Renny-Tailyour, H. W.	1
Richmond, J. T.	1
Ring, T.	2
Rioch, B. D.	6
Ritchie, J.	1
Ritchie, P. S.	1
Robertson, A.	2
Robertson, J.	3
Robertson, J. N.	8
Robertson, J. T.	2
Robertson, T.	1
Robertson, W.	1
Robson, B.	1
Russell, D.	1
Scott, A. S.	5
Sellar, W.	4
Sharp, G.	1
Shaw, F. W.	1
Shearer, D.	2
Simpson, J.	1
Smith, A.	5
Smith, G.	4
Smith, J.	1
Smith, John	13
Somerville, G.	1
Souness, G. J.	4
Speedie, F.	2
St John, I.	9
Steel, W.	12
Stein, C.	10
Stevenson, G.	4
Stewart, A.	1
Stewart, R.	1
Stewart, W. E.	1
Strachan, G.	5
Sturrock, P.	3
Taylor, J. D.	1
Templeton, R.	1
Thompson, S.	3
Thomson, A.	1
Thomson, C.	4
Thomson, R.	1
Thomson, W.	1

Name	
Thornton, W.	1
Waddell, T. S.	1
Waddell, W.	6
Walker, J.	2
Walker, R.	7
Walker, T.	9
Wallace, I. A.	1
Wark, J.	7
Watson, J. A. K.	1
Watt, F.	2
Watt, W. W.	1
Webster, A.	1
Weir, A.	1
Weir, D.	1
Weir, J. B.	2
White, J. A.	3
Wilkie, L.	1
Wilson, A.	2
Wilson, A. N.	13
Wilson, D. (*Queen's Park*)	2
Wilson, D. (*Rangers*)	9
Wilson, H.	1
Wylie, T. G.	1
Young, A.	5

WALES

Name	
Allchurch, I. J.	23
Allen, M.	3
Astley, D. J.	12
Atherton, R. W.	2
Bale, G.	2
Bamford, T.	1
Barnes, W.	1
Bellamy, C. D.	16
Blackmore, C. G.	1
Blake, N. A.	4
Bodin, P. J.	3
Boulter, L. M.	1
Bowdler, J. C. H.	3
Bowen, D. L.	1
Bowen, M.	3
Boyle, T.	1
Bryan, T.	1
Burgess, W. A. R.	1
Burke, T.	1
Butler, W. T.	1
Chapman, T.	2
Charles, J.	1
Charles, M.	6
Charles, W. J.	15
Clarke, R. J.	5
Coleman, C.	4
Collier, D. J.	1
Collins, J.	1
Crosse, K.	1
Cumner, R. H.	1
Curtis, A.	6
Curtis, E. R.	3
Davies, D. W.	1
Davies, E. Lloyd	1
Davies, G.	2
Davies, L. S.	6
Davies, R. T.	9
Davies, R. W.	6
Davies, Simon	6
Davies, Stanley	5
Davies, W.	6
Davies, W. H.	1
Davies, William	5
Davis, W. O.	1
Deacy, N.	4
Doughty, J.	6
Doughty, R.	2
Durban, A.	2
Dwyer, P.	2

Name	
Earnshaw, R.	14
Eastwood, F.	4
Edwards, D.	2
Edwards, G.	2
Edwards, R. I.	4
England, H. M.	4
Evans, C.	2
Evans, I.	1
Evans, J.	1
Evans, R. E.	2
Evans, W.	1
Eyton-Jones, J. A.	1
Fletcher, C.	1
Flynn, B.	7
Ford, T.	23
Foulkes, W. I.	1
Fowler, J.	3
Giles, D.	2
Giggs, R. J.	12
Glover, E. M.	7
Godfrey, B. C.	2
Green, A. W.	3
Griffiths, A. T.	6
Griffiths, M. W.	2
Griffiths, T. P.	3
Harris, C. S.	1
Hartson, J.	14
Hersee, R.	1
Hewitt, R.	1
Hockey, T.	1
Hodges, G.	2
Hole, W. J.	1
Hopkins, I. J.	2
Horne, B.	2
Howell, E. G.	3
Hughes, L. M.	16
James, E.	2
James, L.	10
James, R.	7
Jarrett, R. H.	3
Jenkyns, C. A.	1
Jones, A.	1
Jones, Bryn	6
Jones, B. S.	2
Jones, Cliff	16
Jones, C. W.	1
Jones, D. E.	1
Jones, Evan	1
Jones, H.	1
Jones, I.	1
Jones, J. L.	1
Jones, J. O.	1
Jones, J. P.	1
Jones, Leslie J.	1
Jones, R. A.	2
Jones, W. L.	6
Keenor, F. C.	2
Koumas, J.	10
Krzywicki, R. L.	1
Ledley, J.	2
Leek, K.	5
Lewis, B.	4
Lewis, D. M.	2
Lewis, W.	8
Lewis, W. L.	1
Llewelyn, C. M	1
Lovell, S.	1
Lowrie, G.	2
Mahoney, J. F.	1
Mays, A. W.	1
Medwin, T. C.	6
Melville, A. K	3
Meredith, W. H.	11
Mills, T. J.	1
Moore, G.	1

Name	
Morgan, J. R.	2
Morgan-Owen, H.	1
Morgan-Owen, M. M.	2
Morris, A. G.	9
Morris, H.	2
Morris, R.	1
Morris, S.	2
Nicholas, P.	2
O'Callaghan, E.	3
O'Sullivan, P. A.	1
Owen, G.	2
Owen, W.	4
Owen, W. P.	6
Own goals	14
Palmer, D.	3
Parry, P. I.	1
Parry, T. D.	3
Paul, R.	1
Peake, E.	1
Pembridge, M.	6
Perry, E.	1
Phillips, C.	5
Phillips, D.	2
Powell, A.	1
Powell, D.	1
Price, J.	4
Price, P.	1
Pryce-Jones, W. E.	3
Pugh, D. H.	2
Reece, G. I.	2
Rees, R. R.	3
Richards, R. W.	1
Roach, J.	2
Robbins, W. W.	4
Roberts, J. (*Corwen*)	1
Roberts, Jas.	1
Roberts, P. S.	1
Roberts, R. (*Druids*)	1
Roberts, W. (*Llangollen*)	2
Roberts, W. (*Wrexham*)	1
Roberts, W. H.	1
Robinson, C. P.	1
Robinson, J. R. C.	3
Rush, I.	28
Russell, M. R.	1
Sabine, H. W.	1
Saunders, D.	22
Savage, R. W.	2
Shaw, E. G.	2
Sisson, H.	4
Slatter, N.	2
Smallman, D. P.	1
Speed, G. A.	7
Symons, C. J.	2
Tapscott, D. R.	4
Taylor, G. K.	1
Thomas, M.	4
Thomas, T.	1
Toshack, J. B.	12
Trainer, H.	2
Vaughan, John	2
Vernon, T. R.	8
Vizard, E. T.	1
Vokes, S. M.	1
Walsh, I.	7
Warren, F. W.	3
Watkins, W. M.	4
Wilding, J.	4
Williams, A.	1
Williams, D. R.	2
Williams, G. E.	1
Williams, G. G.	1
Williams, W.	1
Woosnam, A. P.	3

Wales and Manchester United's Ryan Giggs with the PFA Players Player of the Year award for 2009.
(PA Photos)

SOUTH AMERICA

COPA SUDAMERICANA 2008

PRELIMINARY ROUND FIRST LEG
River Plate (Uru) 2, Univ Catolica 0
Universitario 0, Dep Quito 0
UA Maracaibo 0, America (Col) 0
Olimpia 4, Blooming 2

PRELIMINARY ROUND SECOND LEG
Univ Catolica 4, River Plate (Uru) 0
Dep Quito 2, Universitario 1
America (Col) 4, UA Maracaibo 2
Blooming 1, Olimpia 0

FIRST ROUND FIRST LEG
Independiente 2, Estudiantes 1
Argentinos Juniors 0, San Lorenzo 0
At Paranaense 0, Sao Paulo 0
Internacional 1, Gremio 1
Vasco da Gama 3, Palmeiras 1
Botafogo 3, At Mineiro 1
America (Col) 2, Dep Cali (Col) 0
LDU Quito 4, Bolivar 2
Defensor 2, Libertad 1
Arsenal 4, Motagua 0
San Luis 3, Dep Quito 1
Aragua 1, Guadalajara 2
Univ Catolica 4, Olimpia 0
Nublense 1, Sport Ancash 0

FIRST ROUND SECOND LEG
Estudiantes 2, Independiente 1
Estudiantes won 5-3 on penalties.
San Lorenzo 0, Argentinos Juniors 2
Sao Paulo 0, At Paranaense 0
At Paranaense won 4-3 on penalties.
Gremio 2, Internacional 2
Palmeiras 3, Vasco da Gama 0
At Mineiro 2, Botafogo 5
Dep Cali (Col) 1, America (Col) 0
Bolivar 2, LDU Quito 1
Libertad 3, Defensor 3
Motagua 1, Arsenal 2
Dep Quito 3, San Luis 2
Guadalajara 1, Aragua 1
Olimpia 2, Univ Catolica 2
Sport Ancash 4, Nublense 0
Byes: River Plate (Arg), Boca Juniors.

SECOND ROUND FIRST LEG
Boca Juniors 4, LDU Quito 0

Estudiantes 2, Arsenal 1
Guadalajara 2, At Paranaense 2
Sport Ancash 0, Palmeiras 0
San Luis 2, Argentinos Juniors 1
America (Col) 1, Botafogo 0
Univ Catolica 1, Internacional 2
Defensor 1, River Plate (Arg) 2

SECOND ROUND SECOND LEG
LDU Quito 1, Boca Juniors 1
Arsenal 0, Estudiantes 0
At Paranaense 3, Guadalajara 4
Palmeiras 1, Sport Ancash 0
Argentinos Juniors 2, San Luis 0
Botafogo 3, America (Col) 1
Internacional 0, Univ Catolica 0
River Plate (Arg) 2, Defensor 1

QUARTER-FINALS FIRST LEG
Estudiantes 2, Botafogo 0
Palmeiras 0, Argentinos Juniors 1
River Plate (Arg) 1, Guadalajara 2
Internacional 2, Boca Juniors 0

QUARTER-FINALS SECOND LEG
Botafogo 2, Estudiantes 2
Argentinos Juniors 2, Palmeiras 0
Guadalajara 2, River Plate (Arg) 2
Boca Juniors 1, Internacional 2

SEMI-FINALS FIRST LEG
Guadalajara 0, Internacional 2
Argentinos Juniors 1, Estudiantes 1

SEMI-FINALS SECOND LEG
Internacional 4, Guadalajara 0
Estudiantes 1, Argentinos Juniors 0

FINAL FIRST LEG
Estudiantes 0, Internacional 1

FINAL SECOND LEG
Internacional 1, Estudiantes 1

LEADING GOALSCORERS
Alex (Internacional)   5
Nilmar (Internacional)   5

COPA LIBERTADORES 2009

PRELIMINARY ROUND FIRST LEG
El Nacional 0, Nacional 5
Independiente 4, Penarol 0
Univ de Chile 1, Pachuca 0
Dep Anzoategui 2, Dep Cuenca 0
Sporting Cristal 2, Estudiantes 1
Palmeiras 5, Real Potosi 1

PRELIMINARY ROUND SECOND LEG
Nacional 3, El Nacional 3
Penarol 0, Independiente 0
Pachuca 2, Univ de Chile 1
Dep Cuenca 3, Dep Anzoategui 0
Estudiantes 1, Sporting Cristal 0
Real Potosi 0, Palmeiras 2

Group 1	P	W	D	L	F	A	Pts
Sport	6	4	1	1	10	7	13
Palmeiras	6	3	1	2	9	7	10
Colo Colo	6	2	1	3	9	7	7
LDU Quito	6	1	1	4	6	13	4

Group 2	P	W	D	L	F	A	Pts
Boca Juniors	6	5	0	1	11	3	15
Dep Cuenca	6	3	1	2	9	4	10
Dep Tachira	6	3	0	3	6	9	9
Guarani	6	0	1	5	5	15	1

Group 3	P	W	D	L	F	A	Pts
Nacional (Uru)	6	4	2	0	12	3	14
Univ San Martin	6	2	2	2	7	9	8
River Plate	6	2	1	3	7	9	7
Nacional (Par)	6	1	1	4	7	12	4

Group 4	P	W	D	L	F	A	Pts
Sao Paulo	6	4	1	1	10	6	13
Defensor	6	2	2	2	6	6	8
Independiente Medellin	6	1	4	1	7	7	7
America (Col)	6	0	3	3	3	7	3

Group 5	P	W	D	L	F	A	Pts
Cruzeiro	6	4	1	1	9	5	13
Estudiantes	6	3	1	2	9	4	10
Dep Quito	6	2	2	2	6	9	8
Universitario (Bol)	6	0	2	4	2	8	2

Group 6	P	W	D	L	F	A	Pts
Caracas	6	3	1	2	7	4	10
Guadalajara	6	2	3	1	9	6	9
Everton	6	2	2	2	7	10	8
Lanus	6	0	4	2	5	8	4

Group 7	P	W	D	L	F	A	Pts
Gremio	6	5	1	0	11	1	16
Univ de Chile	6	3	1	2	8	6	10
Boyaca	6	3	0	3	8	8	9
Aurora	6	0	0	6	3	15	0

Group 8	P	W	D	L	F	A	Pts
Libertad	6	4	0	2	7	5	12
San Luis	6	2	2	2	7	7	8
Universitario (Peru)	6	2	2	2	6	7	8
San Lorenzo	6	2	0	4	6	7	6

SECOND ROUND FIRST LEG
Palmeiras 1, Sport 0
Univ San Martin 1, Gremio 3
Dep Cuenca 2, Caracas 1
Univ de Chile 1, Cruzeiro 2
Estudiantes 3, Libertad 0
Defensor 2, Boca Juniors 2
San Luis v Nacional, Guadalajara v
Sao Paulo; both Mexican clubs with-
drew due to outbreak of swine flu.

SECOND ROUND SECOND LEG
Sport 1, Palmeiras 0
Palmeiras won 3-1 on penalties.
Gremio 2, Univ San Martin 0
Caracas 4, Dep Cuenca 0
Cruzeiro 1, Univ de Chile 0
Libertad 0, Estudiantes 0
Boca Juniors 0, Defensor 1

QUARTER-FINALS FIRST LEG
Caracas 1, Gremio 1
Cruzeiro 2, Sao Paulo 1
Palmeiras 1, Nacional 1
Defensor 0, Estudiantes 1

QUARTER-FINALS SECOND LEG
Gremio 0, Caracas 0
Sao Paulo 0, Cruzeiro 2
Nacional 0, Palmeiras 0
Estudiantes 1, Defensor 0

SEMI-FINALS FIRST LEG
Cruzeiro 3, Gremio 1
Estudiantes 1, Nacional 0

SEMI-FINALS SECOND LEG
Gremio 2, Cruzeiro 2
Nacional 1, Estudiantes 2

FINAL FIRST LEG
Estudiantes 0, Cruzeiro 0

FINAL SECOND LEG
Cruzeiro v Estudiantes
See Stop Press

LEADING GOALSCORERS
Jorge Nunez (Nacional (Par))   7
Rodrigo Teixeira (Dep Cuenca)   7
Keirrison (Palmeiras)   6

NORTH AMERICA

MAJOR LEAGUE SOCCER 2008

EASTERN CONFERENCE

	P	W	D	L	F	A	Pts
Columbus Crew	30	17	6	7	50	36	57
Chicago Fire	30	13	7	10	44	33	46
New England Rev	30	12	7	11	40	43	43
Kansas City Wizards	30	11	9	10	37	39	42
New York Red Bulls	30	10	9	11	42	48	39
DC United	30	11	4	15	43	51	37
Toronto	30	9	8	13	34	43	35

WESTERN CONFERENCE

	P	W	D	L	F	A	Pts
Houston Dynamo	30	13	12	5	45	32	51
Chivas USA	30	12	7	11	40	41	43
Real Salt Lake	30	10	10	10	40	39	40
Colorado Rapids	30	11	5	14	44	45	38
FC Dallas	30	8	12	10	45	41	36
Los Angeles Galaxy	30	8	9	13	55	62	33
San Jose Earthquakes	30	8	9	13	32	38	33

QUARTER-FINALS FIRST LEG

New England Rev v Chicago Fire   0-0
Kansas City Wizards v Columbus Crew   1-1
Real Salt Lake v Chivas USA   1-0
New York Red Bulls v Houston Dynamo   1-1

QUARTER-FINALS SECOND LEG

Chicago Fire v New England Rev   3-0
Houston Dynamo v New York Red Bulls   0-3
Chivas USA v Real Salt Lake   2-2
Columbus Crew v Kansas City Wizards   2-0

SEMI-FINALS

Columbus Crew v Chicago Fire   2-1
Real Salt Lake v New York Red Bulls   0-1

MLS CUP 2008

Columbus Crew v New York Red Bulls   3-1

AFRICAN NATIONS CHAMPIONSHIP 2009

FINALS HELD IN IVORY COAST (Restricted to players active in Africa)

PRELIMINARY ROUND FIRST LEG
Libya 1, Tunisia 1
Gambia 1, Mauritania 1
Ghana 2, Niger 0
Central African Republic 0, Gabon 2
Rwanda 1, Burundi 0
Kenya 1, Tanzania 0
Eritrea 2, Uganda 2
Malawi 2, Mozambique 1
Swaziland 1, Zambia 1

PRELIMINARY ROUND SECOND LEG
Tunisia 1, Libya 1
Libya won 6-5 on penalties.
Mauritania 0, Gambia 0
Niger 1, Ghana 2
Gabon w.o. v Central African Republic withdrew
Burundi 0, Rwanda 0
Tanzania 2, Kenya 0
Uganda 3, Eritrea 0
Mozambique 1, Malawi 0
Zambia 3, Swaziland 1
Togo w.o. v Benin withdrew
Congo w.o. v Chad disqualified

FIRST ROUND FIRST LEG
Algeria 1, Morocco 1
Senegal 0, Mali 0
Mauritania 2, Guinea 2
Nigeria 2, Burkina Faso 0
Ghana 2, Togo 0
Cameroon 1, Gabon 2
DR Congo 3, Congo 0
Sudan 4, Rwanda 0
Tanzania 2, Uganda 0
Mozambique 1, Angola 1
Botswana 1, Zambia 0
Zimbabwe 0, Namibia 0

FIRST ROUND SECOND LEG
Morocco 1, Algeria 1
Morocco won 3-1 on penalties.
Mali 0, Senegal 0
Senegal won 5-4 on penalties.
Guinea 1, Mauritania 1
Burkina Faso 1, Nigeria 2
Togo 2, Ghana 2
Gabon 0, Cameroon 2
Congo 2, DR Congo 1
Rwanda 1, Sudan 1
Uganda 1, Tanzania 1

Angola 1, Mozambique 0
Zambia 3, Botswana 0
Namibia 0, Zimbabwe 1
Libya w.o. v Egypt withdrew
South Africa w.o. v Mauritius with-
drew

SECOND ROUND FIRST LEG
Libya 3, Morocco 0
Guinea 1, Senegal 0
Ghana 3, Nigeria 2
Cameroon 0, DR Congo 2
Sudan 1, Tanzania 2
Angola 0, Zambia 1
South Africa 0, Zimbabwe 1

SECOND ROUND SECOND LEG
Morocco 3, Libya 1
Senegal 1, Guinea 0
Senegal won 3-1 on penalties.
Nigeria 0, Ghana 0
DR Congo 1, Cameroon 0
Tanzania 3, Sudan 1
Zambia 2, Angola 1
Zimbabwe 2, South Africa 0

FINAL TOURNAMENT IN IVORY COAST

Group A	P	W	D	L	F	A	Pts
Zambia	3	1	2	0	4	1	5
Senegal	3	1	2	0	1	0	5
Tanzania	3	1	1	1	2	2	4
Ivory Coast	3	0	1	2	0	4	1

Group B	P	W	D	L	F	A	Pts
Ghana	3	1	2	0	6	3	5
DR Congo	3	1	1	1	3	4	4
Zimbabwe	3	0	3	0	3	3	3
Libya	3	0	2	1	1	3	2

SEMI-FINALS
Ghana 1, Senegal 1
aet; Ghana won 7-6 on penalties.
Zambia 1, DR Congo 2

THIRD PLACE MATCH
Zambia 2, Senegal 1

FINAL
Ghana 0, DR Congo 2

ASIAN CHAMPIONS LEAGUE 2008

Group A	P	W	D	L	F	A	Pts
Quruvchi	6	4	1	1	8	2	13
Al-Ittihad (Jeddah)	6	3	0	3	6	5	9
Sepahan	6	2	1	3	5	8	7
Al-Ittihad (Aleppo)	6	2	0	4	4	8	6

Group B	P	W	D	L	F	A	Pts
Saipa	6	3	3	0	7	3	12
Quwa Al-Jawiya	6	2	2	2	5	5	8
Al-Wasl	6	2	1	3	5	7	7
Al-Kuwait	6	1	2	3	4	6	5

Group C	P	W	D	L	F	A	Pts
Al-Karama	6	3	2	1	8	3	11
Al-Wahda	6	2	3	1	6	7	9
Al-Sadd	6	1	3	2	6	8	6
Al-Ahly	6	0	4	2	5	7	4

Group D	P	W	D	L	F	A	Pts
Al-Qadissiyah	6	3	2	1	8	7	11
Pakhtakor	6	3	2	1	13	6	11
Arbil	6	2	2	2	8	11	8
Al-Gharrafa	6	0	2	4	3	8	2

*Al-Qadissiyah topped group because of results
against Pakhtakor.*

Group E	P	W	D	L	F	A	Pts
Adelaide United	6	4	2	0	9	2	14
Changchun	6	3	3	0	10	3	12
Pohang	6	1	2	3	6	7	5
B. Binh	6	0	1	5	4	17	1

Group F	P	W	D	L	F	A	Pts
Kashima	6	5	0	1	28	3	15
Beijing	6	4	0	2	14	9	12
Krung	6	2	1	3	20	27	7
DPM	6	0	1	5	4	27	1

Group G	P	W	D	L	F	A	Pts
Gamba	6	4	2	0	14	8	14
Melbourne Victory	6	2	1	3	10	11	7
Chunnam	6	1	3	2	8	10	6
Chonburi	6	1	2	3	7	10	5

*Urawa (the holders) bye to Quarter-Finals; Quruvchi
changed name to Bunyodkor.*

QUARTER-FINALS FIRST LEG	
Saipa v Bunyodkor	2-2
Kashima v Adelaide United	1-1
Al-Qadissiyah v Urawa	3-2
Al-Karama v Gamba	1-2

QUARTER-FINALS SECOND LEG	
Bunyodkor v Saipa	5-1
Adelaide United v Kashima	1-0
Urawa v Al-Qadissiyah	2-0
Gamba v Al-Karama	2-0

SEMI-FINALS FIRST LEG	
Adelaide United v Bunyodkor	3-0
Gamba v Urawa	1-1

SEMI-FINALS SECOND LEG	
Bunyodkor v Adelaide United	1-0
Urawa v Gamba	1-3

FINAL FIRST LEG	
Gamba v Adelaide United	3-0

FINAL SECOND LEG	
Adelaide United v Gamba	0-2

GULF CUP 2009

IN OMAN

Group A	P	W	D	L	F	A	Pts
Oman	3	2	1	0	6	0	7
Kuwait	3	1	2	0	2	1	5
Bahrain	3	1	0	2	3	4	3
Iraq	3	0	1	2	2	8	1

Group B	P	W	D	L	F	A	Pts
Saudi Arabia	3	2	1	0	9	0	7
Qatar	3	1	2	0	2	1	5
UAE	3	1	1	1	3	4	4
Yemen	3	0	0	3	2	11	0

SEMI-FINALS
Oman 1, Qatar 0
Saudi Arabia 1, Kuwait 0

FINAL
Oman 0, Saudi Arabia 0
aet; Oman won 6-5 on penalties.

UEFA UNDER-21 CHAMPIONSHIP 2007–09

Qualifying Competition

GROUP 1
Italy 4, Albania 0
Greece 4, Azerbaijan 1
Croatia 2, Faeroes 0
Croatia 3, Greece 2
Albania 1, Faeroes 0
Azerbaijan 0, Greece 2
Italy 2, Faeroes 1
Albania 1, Croatia 0
Albania 0, Italy 1
Croatia 3, Azerbaijan 2
Faeroes 0, Greece 2
Italy 2, Croatia 0
Faeroes 1, Azerbaijan 0
Greece 2, Italy 2
Azerbaijan 1, Albania 1
Faeroes 1, Croatia 2
Italy 5, Azerbaijan 0
Faeroes 0, Albania 5
Greece 3, Croatia 4
Azerbaijan 0, Croatia 1
Faeroes 0, Italy 1
Greece 2, Albania 1
Azerbaijan 0, Italy 2
Albania 1, Greece 1
Croatia 4, Albania 0
Italy 1, Greece 1
Azerbaijan 2, Faeroes 2
Croatia 1, Italy 1
Greece 1, Faeroes 0
Albania 0, Azerbaijan 0

GROUP 2
Armenia 1, Liechtenstein 0
Ukraine 1, Turkey 2
Ukraine 4, Armenia 0
Armenia 1, Czech Republic 1
Liechtenstein 2, Turkey 3
Czech Republic 8, Liechtenstein 0
Armenia 0, Ukraine 2
Liechtenstein 0, Czech Republic 4
Turkey 2, Ukraine 0
Liechtenstein 1, Ukraine 3
Czech Republic 3, Armenia 0
Czech Republic 1, Turkey 1
Ukraine 5, Liechtenstein 0
Liechtenstein 1, Armenia 4
Ukraine 0, Czech Republic 2
Turkey 3, Liechtenstein 0
Armenia 2, Turkey 1
Turkey 2, Czech Republic 0
Czech Republic 0, Ukraine 1
Turkey 4, Armenia 0

GROUP 3
Bulgaria 1, Montenegro 2
Republic of Ireland 0, Portugal 2
Montenegro 0, England 3
Bulgaria 0, England 2
Portugal 4, Montenegro 0
Bulgaria 1, Portugal 0
England 1, Montenegro 0
Montenegro 1, Portugal 2
Republic of Ireland 0, England 3
Montenegro 1, Republic of Ireland 0
England 2, Bulgaria 0
Republic of Ireland 1, Bulgaria 0
Portugal 1, England 1
England 3, Republic of Ireland 0
Republic of Ireland 1, Montenegro 1
Portugal 2, Bulgaria 0
Bulgaria 2, Republic of Ireland 0
England 2, Portugal 0
Montenegro 0, Bulgaria 0
Portugal 2, Republic of Ireland 2

GROUP 4
Georgia 0, Spain 1
Kazakhstan 0, Russia 3
Poland 3, Georgia 1

Georgia 2, Kazakhstan 1
Russia 1, Poland 0
Poland 1, Kazakhstan 0
Spain 4, Georgia 0
Russia 4, Kazakhstan 0
Poland 0, Spain 2
Kazakhstan 4, Georgia 1
Poland 0, Russia 1
Spain 3, Poland 0
Georgia 2, Russia 0
Spain 5, Kazakhstan 0
Kazakhstan 3, Poland 0
Russia 1, Spain 2
Russia 4, Georgia 0
Kazakhstan 1, Spain 2
Georgia 0, Poland 5
Spain 2, Russia 0

GROUP 5
Estonia 0, Norway 1
Macedonia 0, Holland 1
Norway 0, Holland 1
Switzerland 1, Macedonia 1
Macedonia 1, Estonia 0
Norway 2, Switzerland 1
Estonia 0, Holland 3
Macedonia 1, Norway 1
Estonia 0, Switzerland 4
Holland 1, Macedonia 0
Switzerland 5, Estonia 0
Norway 2, Estonia 0
Macedonia 2, Switzerland 1
Holland 3, Estonia 0
Holland 0, Switzerland 1
Estonia 1, Macedonia 0
Switzerland 2, Norway 0
Holland 1, Norway 1
Switzerland 1, Holland 0
Norway 0, Macedonia 0

GROUP 6
Slovenia 2, Lithuania 1
Denmark 0, Finland 1
Denmark 4, Lithuania 0
Finland 3, Scotland 2
Lithuania 0, Slovenia 0
Scotland 0, Denmark 0
Scotland 3, Lithuania 0
Finland 1, Slovenia 0
Slovenia 1, Denmark 3
Lithuania 0, Finland 1
Lithuania 0, Denmark 3
Slovenia 0, Scotland 4
Denmark 1, Slovenia 0
Finland 2, Lithuania 1
Scotland 2, Finland 1
Lithuania 0, Scotland 3
Scotland 3, Slovenia 1
Finland 2, Denmark 1
Slovenia 0, Finland 0
Denmark 1, Scotland 0

GROUP 7
Iceland 0, Cyprus 1
Slovakia 2, Iceland 2
Belgium 0, Austria 1
Slovakia 1, Austria 1
Iceland 0, Belgium 0
Austria 2, Cyprus 1
Belgium 4, Slovakia 2
Iceland 1, Austria 1
Slovakia 4, Cyprus 1
Cyprus 1, Slovakia 2
Austria 3, Belgium 2
Cyprus 1, Austria 2
Belgium 1, Iceland 2
Cyprus 2, Iceland 0
Cyprus 0, Belgium 2
Austria 1, Slovakia 0
Slovakia 1, Belgium 1

Austria 1, Iceland 0
Iceland 1, Slovakia 1
Belgium 3, Cyprus 2

GROUP 8
Serbia 1, Latvia 1
Belarus 1, Hungary 0
Hungary 1, Latvia 0
San Marino 0, Belarus 3
Belarus 2, Latvia 1
San Marino 1, Hungary 6
Serbia 3, Belarus 1
Latvia 2, San Marino 0
Hungary 2, Serbia 1
Serbia 3, San Marino 0
Hungary 0, Belarus 1
Latvia 0, Serbia 2
Belarus 6, San Marino 0
Latvia 1, Hungary 0
Belarus 1, Serbia 1
San Marino 0, Serbia 5
Hungary 5, San Marino 0
San Marino 0, Latvia 1
Serbia 8, Hungary 0
Latvia 0, Belarus 0

GROUP 9
Moldova 0, Northern Ireland 1
Israel 3, Luxembourg 0
Northern Ireland 0, Germany 3
Moldova 1, Israel 0
Luxembourg 1, Northern Ireland 2
Israel 2, Germany 2
Luxembourg 0, Moldova 2
Germany 3, Moldova 0
Northern Ireland 1, Israel 3
Northern Ireland 5, Luxembourg 0
Luxembourg 0, Germany 7
Northern Ireland 3, Moldova 0
Israel 2, Northern Ireland 1
Germany 6, Luxembourg 0
Israel 1, Moldova 0
Moldova 1, Germany 0
Luxembourg 0, Israel 5

Germany 3, Northern Ireland 0
Moldova 2, Luxembourg 0
Germany 0, Israel 0

GROUP 10
France 1, Romania 1
Malta 0, Romania 1
France 1, Wales 0
Bosnia 4, Malta 0
Romania 3, Bosnia 0
Malta 0, France 2
France 4, Bosnia 0
Romania 0, France 0
Wales 3, Malta 1
Romania 4, Malta 0
Wales 4, Bosnia 0
Malta 2, Bosnia 1
Wales 4, France 2
Malta 0, Wales 4
Bosnia 1, Wales 2
Wales 0, Romania 1
France 5, Malta 0
Bosnia 1, Romania 1
Romania 0, Wales 3
Bosnia 0, France 1

PLAY-OFFS FIRST LEG
Wales 2, England 3
Germany 1, France 1
Turkey 1, Belarus 0
Austria 2, Finland 1
Switzerland 2, Spain 1
Denmark 0, Serbia 1
Italy 0, Israel 0

PLAY-OFFS SECOND LEG
Spain 3, Switzerland 1 *(aet.)*
England 2, Wales 2
Belarus 2, Turkey 0
Finland 2, Austria 1 *(aet; Finland won 4-2 on penalties)*
Israel 1, Italy 3
France 0, Germany 1
Serbia 1, Denmark 0

Final Tournament in Sweden

GROUP A GROUP A
Sweden 5, Belarus 1
Italy 0, Serbia 0
Sweden 1, Italy 2
Belarus 0, Serbia 0
Serbia 1, Sweden 3
Belarus 1, Italy 2

GROUP B
England 2, Finland 1
Spain 0, Germany 0
Germany 2, Finland 0
Spain 0, England 2
Finland 0, Spain 2
Germany 1, England 1

SEMI-FINALS
England 3, Sweden 3
England won 5-4 on penalties: Milner missed; Berg saved; Hart scored; Elm scored; Cattermole scored; Bjarsmyr scored; Johnson scored; Lustig scored; Walcott scored; Bengtsson R scored; Gibbs scored; Molins hit post.
Italy 0, Germany 1

FINAL

Malmo, 29 June 2009, 18,769

Germany (1) 4 *(Castro 23, Ozil 48, Wagner 79, 84)*

England (0) 0

Germany: Neuer; Beck, Boenisch, Howedes, Boateng, Khedira, Ozil (Schmelzer 89), Wagner, Johnson (Schwaab 69), Hummels (Aogo 83), Castro.
England: Loach; Cranie (Gardner 79), Gibbs, Cattermole, Richards, Onuoha (Mancienne 46), Milner, Noble, Walcott, Johnson A, Muamba (Rodwell 78).
Referee: B. Kuipers (Holland).

UEFA UNDER-17 CHAMPIONSHIP 2008–09

(Finals in Germany)

GROUP A
Spain 0, Italy 0
France 1, Switzerland 1
Spain 0, France 0
Italy 1, Switzerland 3
Switzerland 0, Spain 0
Italy 2, France 1

GROUP B
England 1, Holland 1
Germany 3, Turkey 1

Germany 4, England 0
Turkey 1, Holland 2
Holland 0, Germany 2
Turkey 1, England 0
Semi-Finals
Switzerland 1, Holland 2
Germany 2, Italy 0

FINAL
Holland 1, Germany 2 *(aet.)*

UEFA UNDER-19 CHAMPIONSHIP 2008-09

Qualifying Competition

GROUP 1

Scotland v Azerbaijan	1-1
Hungary v San Marino	6-0
Scotland v San Marino	8-0
Azerbaijan v Hungary	0-1
Hungary v Scotland	0-1
San Marino v Azerbaijan	0-5

GROUP 2

Belgium v Kazakhstan	2-1
Croatia v Estonia	1-4
Croatia v Kazakhstan	4-0
Estonia v Belgium	0-5
Belgium v Croatia	2-2
Kazakhstan v Estonia	1-2

GROUP 3

Italy v Latvia	2-2
Russia v Moldova	2-0
Italy v Moldova	2-2
Latvia v Russia	0-3
Russia v Italy	1-0
Moldova v Latvia	0-1

GROUP 4

Republic of Ireland v Malta	2-0
France v Liechtenstein	4-0
Republic of Ireland v Liechtenstein	1-0
Malta v France	0-3
France v Republic of Ireland	2-0
Liechtenstein v Malta	1-1

GROUP 5

Norway v Slovenia	4-2
Slovakia v Armenia	3-1
Slovakia v Slovenia	0-2
Armenia v Norway	0-1
Norway v Slovakia	0-1
Slovenia v Armenia	3-2

GROUP 6

Holland v Lithuania	4-1
Germany v Luxembourg	3-0
Germany v Lithuania	5-0
Luxembourg v Holland	2-3
Holland v Germany	1-2
Lithuania v Luxembourg	3-0

GROUP 7

Czech Republic v Cyprus	1-1
Georgia v Denmark	2-2
Czech Republic v Denmark	0-0

Cyprus v Georgia	0-0
Georgia v Czech Republic	0-1
Denmark v Cyprus	2-1

GROUP 8

Sweden v Iceland	3-3
Austria v Macedonia	2-2
Sweden v Macedonia	4-0
Iceland v Austria	0-3
Austria v Sweden	1-1
Macedonia v Iceland	1-0

GROUP 9

Serbia v Northern Ireland	3-1
England v Albania	3-0
Serbia v Albania	5-0
Northern Ireland v England	1-3
England v Serbia	1-4
Albania v Northern Ireland	1-2

GROUP 10

Greece v Bosnia	1-2
Poland v Montenegro	2-1
Greece v Montenegro	1-0
Bosnia v Poland	2-2
Poland v Greece	0-2
Montenegro v Bosnia	0-0

GROUP 11

Romania v Wales	3-2
Turkey v Andorra	4-0
Andorra v Romania	0-2
Turkey v Wales	3-0
Romania v Turkey	1-2
Wales v Andorra	6-0

GROUP 12

Israel v Finland	1-2
Portugal v Bulgaria	1-1
Israel v Bulgaria	3-1
Finland v Portugal	0-2
Portugal v Israel	3-0
Bulgaria v Finland	1-3

GROUP 13

Spain v Faeroes	5-0
Switzerland v Belarus	1-2
Switzerland v Faeroes	3-1
Belarus v Spain	0-4
Spain v Switzerland	0-2
Faeroes v Belarus	0-1

Elite Round

GROUP 1

Hungary v Austria	2-3
Serbia v Finland	1-1
Finland v Hungary	1-2
Serbia v Austria	3-0
Hungary v Serbia	0-1
Austria v Finland	0-2

GROUP 2

Russia v Slovenia	3-3
Holland v Belarus	0-0
Russia v Belarus	2-2
Slovenia v Holland	1-1
Holland v Russia	2-1
Belarus v Slovenia	0-2

GROUP 3

Turkey v Greece	1-0
Portugal v Denmark	3-0
Turkey v Denmark	1-0
Greece v Portugal	0-1
Portugal v Turkey	0-4
Denmark v Greece	1-0

GROUP 4

Belgium v Republic of Ireland	1-0
Switzerland v Sweden	3-1
Belgium v Sweden	5-0

Republic of Ireland v Switzerland	1-6
Switzerland v Belgium	1-1
Sweden v Republic of Ireland	1-2

GROUP 5

Romania v Lativa	2-0
France v Norway	1-2
France v Latvia	4-1
Norway v Romania	1-1
Romania v France	0-3
Latvia v Norway	0-0

GROUP 6

Scotland v Slovakia	2-1
England v Bosnia	2-0
Scotland v Bosnia	3-0
Slovakia v England	1-4
England v Scotland	2-1
Bosnia v Slovakia	0-1

GROUP 7

Spain v Czech Republic	5-1
Germany v Estonia	5-0
Germany v Czech Republic	1-0
Estonia v Spain	0-3
Spain v Germany	1-0
Czech Republic v Estonia	5-1

Competition still being played.

ENGLAND UNDER-21 RESULTS 1976–2009
EC UEFA Competition for Under-21 Teams

v ALBANIA

Year	Date		Venue	Eng	Alb
EC1989	Mar	7	Shkroda	2	1
EC1989	April	25	Ipswich	2	0
EC2001	Mar	27	Tirana	1	0
EC2001	Sept	4	Middlesbrough	5	0

v ANGOLA

Year	Date		Venue	Eng	Ang
1995	June	10	Toulon	1	0
1996	May	28	Toulon	0	2

v ARGENTINA

Year	Date		Venue	Eng	Arg
1998	May	18	Toulon	0	2
2000	Feb	22	Fulham	1	0

v AUSTRIA

Year	Date		Venue	Eng	Aus
1994	Oct	11	Kapfenberg	3	1
1995	Nov	14	Middlesbrough	2	1
EC2004	Sept	3	Krems	2	0
EC2005	Oct	7	Leeds	1	2

v AZERBAIJAN

Year	Date		Venue	Eng	Az
EC2004	Oct	12	Baku	0	0
EC2005	Mar	29	Middlesbrough	2	0
2009	June	8	Milton Keynes	7	0

v BELGIUM

Year	Date		Venue	Eng	Bel
1994	June	5	Marseille	2	1
1996	May	24	Toulon	1	0

v BRAZIL

Year	Date		Venue	Eng	B
1993	June	11	Toulon	0	0
1995	June	6	Toulon	0	2
1996	June	1	Toulon	1	2

v BULGARIA

Year	Date		Venue	Eng	Bul
EC1979	June	5	Pernik	3	1
EC1979	Nov	20	Leicester	5	0
1989	June	5	Toulon	2	3
EC1998	Oct	9	West Ham	1	0
EC1999	June	8	Vratsa	1	0
EC2007	Sept	11	Sofia	2	0
EC2007	Nov	16	Milton Keynes	2	0

v CROATIA

Year	Date		Venue	Eng	Cro
1996	Apr	23	Sunderland	0	1
2003	Aug	19	West Ham	0	3

v CZECHOSLOVAKIA

Year	Date		Venue	Eng	Cz
1990	May	28	Toulon	2	1
1992	May	26	Toulon	1	2
1993	June	9	Toulon	1	1

v CZECH REPUBLIC

Year	Date		Venue	Eng	CzR
1998	Nov	17	Ipswich	0	1
EC2007	June	11	Arnhem	0	0
2008	Nov	18	Bramall Lane	2	0

v DENMARK

Year	Date		Venue	Eng	Den
EC1978	Sept	19	Hvidovre	2	1
EC1979	Sept	11	Watford	1	0
EC1982	Sept	21	Hvidovre	4	1
EC1983	Sept	20	Norwich	4	1
EC1986	Mar	12	Copenhagen	1	0
EC1986	Mar	26	Manchester	1	1
1988	Sept	13	Watford	0	0
1994	Mar	8	Brentford	1	0
1999	Oct	8	Bradford	4	1
2005	Aug	16	Herning	1	0

v EAST GERMANY

Year	Date		Venue	Eng	EG
EC1980	April	16	Sheffield	1	2
EC1980	April	23	Jena	0	1

v EQUADOR

Year	Date		Venue	Eng	E
2009	Feb	10	Malaga	2	3

v FINLAND

Year	Date		Venue	Eng	Fin
EC1977	May	26	Helsinki	1	0
EC1977	Oct	12	Hull	8	1
EC1984	Oct	16	Southampton	2	0
EC1985	May	21	Mikkeli	1	3
EC2000	Oct	10	Valkeakoski	2	2
EC2001	Mar	23	Barnsley	4	0
EC2009	June	15	Halmstad	2	1

v FRANCE

Year	Date		Venue	Eng	Fra
EC1984	Feb	28	Sheffield	6	1
EC1984	Mar	28	Rouen	1	0
1987	June	11	Toulon	0	2
EC1988	April	13	Besancon	2	4
EC1988	April	27	Highbury	2	2
1988	June	12	Toulon	2	4
1990	May	23	Toulon	7	3
1991	June	3	Toulon	1	0
1992	May	28	Toulon	0	0
1993	June	15	Toulon	1	0
1994	May	31	Aubagne	0	3
1995	June	10	Toulon	0	2
1998	May	14	Toulon	1	1
1999	Feb	9	Derby	2	1
EC2005	Nov	11	Tottenham	1	1
EC2005	Nov	15	Nancy	1	2
2009	Mar	31	Nottingham	0	2

v GEORGIA

Year	Date		Venue	Eng	Geo
EC1996	Nov	8	Batumi	1	0
EC1997	April	29	Charlton	0	0
2000	Aug	31	Middlesbrough	6	1

v GERMANY

Year	Date		Venue	Eng	Ger
1991	Sept	10	Scunthorpe	2	1
EC2000	Oct	6	Derby	1	1
EC2001	Aug	31	Frieburg	2	1
2005	Mar	25	Hull	2	2
2005	Sept	6	Mainz	1	1
EC2006	Oct	6	Coventry	1	0
EC2006	Oct	10	Leverkusen	2	0
EC2009	June	22	Halmstad	1	1
EC2009	June	29	Malmo	0	4

v GREECE

Year	Date		Venue	Eng	Gre
EC1982	Nov	16	Piraeus	0	1
EC1983	Mar	29	Portsmouth	2	1
1989	Feb	7	Patras	0	1
EC1997	Nov	13	Heraklion	0	2
EC1997	Dec	17	Norwich	4	2
EC2001	June	5	Athens	1	3
EC2001	Oct	5	Ewood Park	2	1

v HOLLAND

Year	Date		Venue	Eng	H
EC1993	April	27	Portsmouth	3	0
EC1993	Oct	12	Utrecht	1	1
2001	Aug	14	Reading	4	0
EC2001	Nov	9	Utrecht	2	2
EC2001	Nov	13	Derby	1	0
2004	Feb	17	Hull	3	2
2005	Feb	8	Derby	1	2
2006	Nov	14	Alkmaar	1	0
EC2007	June	20	Heerenveen	1	1

v HUNGARY

Year	Date		Venue	Eng	Hun
EC1981	June	5	Keszthely	2	1
EC1981	Nov	17	Nottingham	2	0
EC1983	April	26	Newcastle	1	0
EC1983	Oct	11	Nyiregyhaza	2	0
1990	Sept	11	Southampton	3	1
1992	May	12	Budapest	2	2
1999	April	27	Budapest	2	2

			v REPUBLIC OF IRELAND	Eng	RoI
1981	Feb	25	Liverpool	1	0
1985	Mar	25	Portsmouth	3	2
1989	June	9	Toulon	0	0
EC1990	Nov	13	Cork	3	0
EC1991	Mar	26	Brentford	3	0
1994	Nov	15	Newcastle	1	0
1995	Mar	27	Dublin	2	0
EC2007	Oct	16	Cork	3	0
EC2008	Feb	5	Southampton	3	0

			v ITALY	Eng	Italy
EC1978	Mar	8	Manchester	2	1
EC1978	April	5	Rome	0	0
EC1984	April	18	Manchester	3	1
EC1984	May	2	Florence	0	1
EC1986	April	9	Pisa	0	2
EC1986	April	23	Swindon	1	1
EC1997	Feb	12	Bristol	1	0
EC1997	Oct	10	Rieti	1	0
EC2000	May	27	Bratislava	0	2
2000	Nov	14	Monza*	0	0
2002	Mar	26	Valley Parade	1	1
EC2002	May	20	Basle	1	2
2003	Feb	11	Pisa	0	1
2007	Mar	24	Wembley	3	3
EC2007	June	14	Arnhem	2	2

*Abandoned 11 mins; fog.

			v ISRAEL	Eng	Isr
1985	Feb	27	Tel Aviv	2	1

			v LATVIA	Eng	Lat
1995	April	25	Riga	1	0
1995	June	7	Burnley	4	0

			v LUXEMBOURG	Eng	Lux
EC1998	Oct	13	Greven Macher	5	0
EC1999	Sept	3	Reading	5	0

			v MACEDONIA	Eng	M
EC2002	Oct	15	Reading	3	1
EC2003	Sept	5	Skopje	1	1

			v MALAYSIA	Eng	Mal
1995	June	8	Toulon	2	0

			v MEXICO	Eng	Mex
1988	June	5	Toulon	2	1
1991	May	29	Toulon	6	0
1992	May	25	Toulon	1	1
2001	May	24	Leicester	3	0

			v MOLDOVA	Eng	Mol
EC1996	Aug	31	Chisinau	2	0
EC1997	Sept	9	Wycombe	1	0
EC2006	Aug	15	Ipswich	2	2

			v MONTENEGRO	Eng	M
EC2007	Sept	7	Podgorica	3	0
EC2007	Oct	12	Leicester	1	0

			v MOROCCO	Eng	Mor
1987	June	7	Toulon	2	0
1988	June	9	Toulon	1	0

			v NORWAY	Eng	Nor
EC1977	June	1	Bergen	2	1
EC1977	Sept	6	Brighton	6	0
1980	Sept	9	Southampton	3	0
1981	Sept	8	Drammen	0	0
EC1992	Oct	13	Peterborough	0	2
EC1993	June	1	Stavanger	1	1
1995	Oct	10	Stavanger	2	2
2006	Feb	28	Reading	3	1
2009	Mar	27	Sandefjord	5	0

			v POLAND	Eng	Pol
EC1982	Mar	17	Warsaw	2	1
EC1982	April	7	West Ham	2	2
EC1989	June	2	Plymouth	2	1
EC1989	Oct	10	Jastrzebie	3	1
EC1990	Oct	16	Tottenham	0	1
EC1991	Nov	12	Pila	1	2
EC1993	May	28	Zdroj	4	1
EC1993	Sept	7	Millwall	1	2
EC1996	Oct	8	Wolverhampton	0	0
EC1997	May	30	Katowice	1	1
EC1999	Mar	26	Southampton	5	0
EC1999	Sept	7	Plock	1	3
EC2004	Sept	7	Rybnik	3	1
EC2005	Oct	11	Hillsborough	4	1
2008	Mar	25	Wolverhampton	0	0

			v PORTUGAL	Eng	Por
1987	June	13	Toulon	0	0
1990	May	21	Toulon	0	1
1993	June	7	Toulon	2	0
1994	June	7	Toulon	2	0
EC1994	Sept	6	Leicester	0	0
1995	Sept	2	Lisbon	0	2
1996	May	30	Toulon	1	3
2000	Apr	16	Stoke	0	1
EC2002	May	22	Zurich	1	3
EC2003	Mar	28	Rio Major	2	4
EC2003	Sept	9	Everton	1	2
EC2008	Nov	20	Agueda	1	1
2008	Sept	5	Wembley	2	0

			v ROMANIA	Eng	Rom
EC1980	Oct	14	Ploesti	0	4
EC1981	April	28	Swindon	3	0
EC1985	April	30	Brasov	0	0
EC1985	Sept	10	Ipswich	3	0
2007	Aug	21	Bristol	1	1

			v RUSSIA	Eng	Rus
1994	May	30	Bandol	2	0

			v SAN MARINO	Eng	SM
EC1993	Feb	16	Luton	6	0
EC1993	Nov	17	San Marino	4	0

			v SENEGAL	Eng	Sen
1989	June	7	Toulon	6	1
1991	May	27	Toulon	2	1

			v SERBIA	Eng	Ser
EC2007	June	17	Nijmegen	2	0

			v SERBIA-MONTENEGRO	Eng	S-M
2003	June	2	Hull	3	2

			v SCOTLAND	Eng	Sco
1977	April	27	Sheffield	1	0
EC1980	Feb	12	Coventry	2	1
EC1980	Mar	4	Aberdeen	0	0
EC1982	April	19	Glasgow	1	0
EC1982	April	28	Manchester	1	1
EC1988	Feb	16	Aberdeen	1	0
EC1988	Mar	22	Nottingham	1	0
1993	June	13	Toulon	1	0

			v SLOVAKIA	Eng	Slo
EC2002	June	1	Bratislava	0	2
EC2002	Oct	11	Trnava	4	0
EC2003	June	10	Sunderland	2	0
2007	June	5	Norwich	5	0

			v SLOVENIA	Eng	Slo
2000	Feb	12	Nova Gorica	1	0
2008	Aug	19	Hull	2	1

			v SOUTH AFRICA	Eng	SA
1998	May	16	Toulon	3	1

			v SPAIN	Eng	Spa
EC1984	May	17	Seville	1	0
EC1984	May	24	Sheffield	2	0
1987	Feb	18	Burgos	2	1
1992	Sept	8	Burgos	1	0
2001	Feb	27	Birmingham	0	4
2004	Nov	16	Alcala	0	1
2007	Feb	6	Derby	2	2
EC2009	June	18	Gothenburg	2	0

			v SWEDEN	Eng	Swe
1979	June	9	Vasteras	2	1
1986	Sept	9	Ostersund	1	1
EC1988	Oct	18	Coventry	1	1
EC1989	Sept	5	Uppsala	0	1
EC1998	Sept	4	Sundvall	2	0
EC1999	June	4	Huddersfield	3	0
2004	Mar	30	Kristiansund	2	2
EC2009	June	26	Gothenburg	3	3

			v SWITZERLAND	Eng	Swit
EC1980	Nov	18	Ipswich	5	0
EC1981	May	31	Neuenburg	0	0
1988	May	28	Lausanne	1	1
1996	April	1	Swindon	0	0
1998	Mar	24	Brugglifeld	0	2
EC2002	May	17	Zurich	2	1
EC2006	Sept	6	Lucerne	3	2

			v TURKEY	Eng	Tur
EC1984	Nov	13	Bursa	0	0
EC1985	Oct	15	Bristol	3	0
EC1987	April	28	Izmir	0	0
EC1987	Oct	13	Sheffield	1	1
EC1991	April	30	Izmir	2	2
1991	Oct	15	Reading	2	0
EC1992	Nov	17	Orient	0	1
EC1993	Mar	30	Izmir	0	0
EC2000	May	29	Bratislava	6	0
EC2003	April	1	Newcastle	1	1
EC2003	Oct	10	Istanbul	0	1

			v UKRAINE	Eng	Uk
2004	Aug	17	Middlesbrough	3	1

			v USA	Eng	USA
1989	June	11	Toulon	0	2
1994	June	2	Toulon	3	0

			v USSR	Eng	USSR
1987	June	9	Toulon	0	0
1988	June	7	Toulon	1	0
1990	May	25	Toulon	2	1
1991	May	31	Toulon	2	1

			v WALES	Eng	Wales
1976	Dec	15	Wolverhampton	0	0
1979	Feb	6	Swansea	1	0
1990	Dec	5	Tranmere	0	0
EC2004	Oct	8	Blackburn	2	0
EC2005	Sept	2	Wrexham	4	0
2008	May	5	Wrexham	2	0
EC2008	Oct	10	Cardiff	3	2
EC2008	Oct	14	Villa Park	2	2

			v WEST GERMANY	Eng	WG
EC1982	Sept	21	Sheffield	3	1
EC1982	Oct	12	Bremen	2	3
1987	Sept	8	Ludenscheid	0	2

			v YUGOSLAVIA	Eng	Yugo
EC1978	April	19	Novi Sad	1	2
EC1978	May	2	Manchester	1	1
EC1986	Nov	11	Peterborough	1	1
EC1987	Nov	10	Zemun	5	1
EC2000	Mar	29	Barcelona	3	0
2002	Sept	6	Bolton	1	1

ENGLAND C 2008–09

16 Sept

Bosnia A2 6 *(Mikelini 6, Zizovic 25, 89, Savic 30, 33, Bekric 75)*

England 2 *(Moore 57, Day 62)*

(in Sarajevo).
England: Cronin; Day, Wright (Stevens 55), Foster, Robinson, Smith, Arnold, D'Laryea (Bailey 59), Brodie (Harrad 55), Moore, Cole.

12 Nov

Italy 2 *(Dionisi 36, Statella 71)*

England 2 *(Simpson 58, Constable 82)*

(in Benevento).
England: Bartlett; Gleeson, Tremarco (Wright 73), Smith, Simpson, Geohaghan, Penn (Robinson 73), D'Laryea (Bostwick 56), Constable, Cole, Pitman (Harrad 56).

17 Feb

Malta U21 0

England 4 *(Brown 6, Borg 52 (og), Densmore 56, Newton 89)*

(in Paola).
England: Roberts (Arnold 46); Densmore, Newton, Byrom, Wroe, Riley (Doe 46), Tomlin, McMahon (Shaw T 46), Clayton, Walker (Boyes 46), Brown P (Welsh 46).

19 May

England 0

Belgium U21 1 *(Capon 64)*   2842

(at Oxford).
England: Bartlett; Densmore, Geohaghan, Charles, Laird (Newton 76), Penn (Welsh 77), Wroe, Byrom (Fleming 56), Tomlin, Constable, Clayton (Hearn 69).

BRITISH AND IRISH UNDER-21 TEAMS 2008-09

■ *Denotes player sent off.*

ENGLAND

Hull, 19 August 2008, 9733
England (2) 2 *(Richards 25, Milner 38)*
Slovenia (1) 1 *(Velikonja 12)*
England: Lewis (Heaton 46); Richards (Cranie 73), Taylor A, Huddlestone (Muamba 61), Mancienne, Onuoha (Wheater 84), Lennon (Johnson A 73), Noble, Derbyshire, Johnson M (Campbell 61), Milner (Kightly 46).

Wembley, 5 September 2008, 27,732
England (1) 2 *(Milner 44 (pen), Agbonlahor 63)*
Portugal (0) 0
England: Hart; Cranie, Taylor A, Muamba (Cattermole 56), Taylor S, Mancienne, Milner, Huddlestone, Agbonlahor (Campbell 76), Noble, Johnson A (Kightly 86).

Sheffield, 18 November 2008, 18,735
England (1) 2 *(Campbell 10, Gardner 55)*
Czech Republic (0) 0
England: Lewis (Fielding 31); Cranie (Norton 60), O'Hara (Bertrand 80), Muamba (Cork 60), Stearman, Onuoha, Lennon, Gardner (Delph 86), Campbell (Ebanks-Blake 69), Vaughan (Lallana 86), Kightly.

Malaga, 10 February 2009
Ecuador (0) 3 *(Guerron 53, Palacios 54, Caicedo 82)*
England (2) 2 *(Johnson A 14, Campbell 41)*
England: Heaton (Loach 88); Taylor S, Mattock (Gibbs 61), Mancienne, Richards (Cork 46), Stearman, Kightly (Gardner 61), Huddlestone, Campbell, Cattermole (Naughton 76), Johnson A (Welbeck).

Sandefjord, 27 March 2009, 2014
Norway (0) 0
England (2) 5 *(Campbell 17, Johnson 29, Huddlestone 73, Derbyshire 78, 80)*
England: Hart (Loach 78); Gardiner, Taylor A (Gibbs 46), Muamba (Mancienne 46), Wheater, Onuoha (Derbyshire 46), Cattermole (Milner 67), Huddlestone, Campbell, O'Hara (Cranie 78), Johnson A.

Nottingham Forest, 31 March 2009, 23,632
England (0) 0
France (2) 2 *(Obertan 26, Sissoko 35)*
England: Hart; Cranie (Rodwell 85), Taylor A (O'Hara 85), Mancienne, Wheater (Muamba 46), Onuoha, Milner (Welbeck 71), Huddlestone, Derbyshire (Campbell 60), Noble (Gardner 71), Johnson A.

Milton Keynes, 8 June 2009, 12,020
England (3) 7 *(Mancienne 1, Sadigov 26 (og), Gardner 31, Cattermole 55, Gibbs 64, 70, Rodwell 90)*
Azerbaijan (0) 0
England: Hart (Loach 82); Cranie, Gibbs, Muamba (Rodwell 46), Tomkins, Mancienne, Gardner (Taylor A 46), Cattermole (Lewis 76), Campbell (Stearman 62), Noble (Rose 55), Johnson A.

Halmstad, 15 June 2009
England (1) 2 *(Cattermole 15, Richards 53)*
Finland (1) 1 *(Sparv 33 (pen))*
England: Hart; Cranie, Cattermole, Milner, Agbonlahor (Rodwell 86), Noble, Muamba, Walcott (Campbell 46), Richards (Tomkins 89), Mancienne, Gibbs.

Gothenburg, 18 June 2009
Spain (0) 0
England (0) 2 *(Campbell 67, Milner 73)*
England: Hart; Cranie, Gibbs, Noble, Richards, Onuoha, Milner (Gardner 84), Muamba, Agbonlahor (Campbell 39), Cattermole, Johnson A (Walcott 62).

Halmstad, 22 June 2009
Germany (1) 1 *(Castro 5)*
England (1) 1 *(Rodwell 30)*
England: Loach (Lewis 46); Stearman, Taylor A, Tomkins, Mancienne, Gardner, Johnson A, Rodwell, Campbell (Walcott 58), Rose, Driver (Gibbs 71).

Gothenburg, 26 June 2009
England (3) 3 *(Cranie 1, Onuoha 27, Bjarsmyr 38 (og))*
Sweden (0) 3 *(Berg 68, 81, Toivonen 75)*
aet; England won 5-4 on penalties.
England: Hart; Cranie, Gibbs, Noble (Rodwell 70), Richards, Onuoha, Milner, Muamba (Johnson A 116), Walcott, Agbonlahor (Campbell 60), Cattermole.

Malmo, 29 June 2009
Germany (1) 4 *(Castro 23, Ozil 48, Wagner 79, 84)*
England (0) 0
England: Loach; Cranie (Gardner 79), Gibbs, Noble, Richards, Onuoha (Mancienne 46), Milner, Cattermole, Walcott, Muamba (Rodwell 78), Johnson A.

UEFA UNDER-21 PLAY-OFF

FIRST LEG

Ninian Park, 10 October 2008, 10,500
Wales (2) 2 *(Church 13, 45)*
England (2) 3 *(Wheater 19, Johnson A 35, Agbonlahor 62)*
Wales: fon Williams; Eardley, Wiggins, Collison, Blake, Adams (Allen 59), King, Church, Ramsey, MacDonald (Brown 76), Nyatanga.
England: Hart; Wheater, O'Hara, Cattermole, Taylor S, Mancienne, Milner, Huddlestone, Agbonlahor (Campbell 76), Noble, Johnson A.

SECOND LEG

Villa Park, 14 October 2008, 23,812
England (2) 2 *(Huddlestone 14, Vokes 35 (og))*
Wales (2) 2 *(Ramsey 24, Church 29)*
England: Hart; Wheater, O'Hara, Cattermole (Muamba 31), Taylor S, Mancienne, Milner, Huddlestone■, Agbonlahor (Campbell 46), Noble, Johnson A.
Wales: fon Williams; Eardley, Wiggins, Collison, Blake, Jacobson, King (Bradley 60), Church, Ramsey, MacDonald (Adams 83), Vokes.

SCOTLAND

Marijampole, 20 August 2008, 1000
Lithuania (0) 0
Scotland (2) 3 *(Arfield 5, McCormack 40, McDonald 60)*
Scotland: MacDonald; Caddis, Wallace, McArthur, Cuthbert, Considine, Lennon, Arfield (Robertson 65), McCormack, McDonald (Dorrans 83), Mulgrew (Elliot 29).

Falkirk, 4 September 2008
Scotland (2) 3 *(Fletcher 1, 63, Kenneth 42)*
Slovenia (0) 1 *(Matavz 54)*
Scotland: MacDonald; Cuthbert, Kenneth, Considine, Wallace, Lennon   (Hamill 77), Arfield, McDonald (Robertson 87), Mulgrew McCormack, Fletcher (Elliot 87).

Aalborg, 9 September 2008, 3659
Denmark (1) 1 *(Pedersen 27)*
Scotland (0) 0
Scotland: MacDonald; Cuthbert (Hamill 72), Wallace, Arfield, Kenneth, Reynolds, Lennon, McDonald (Murphy 84), Elliot (Dorrans 62), Mulgrew, McCormack.

Hamilton, 18 November 2008
Scotland (1) 1 *(Murphy 3)*
Northern Ireland (2) 3 *(McQuoid 9, 26, Little 49)*
Scotland: Martin (Gallacher 12); Gray (Mitchell 80), Easton, Duff (Goodwillie 46), Pearce, Arfield (Millar 75),

Caddis, Maguire (Loy 70), Murphy, McDonald (Coutts 46), Stevenson (Lennon 75).
Northern Ireland: Carson; Chapman (McMenamin 46), Lafferty (Flynn 46), Casement, Cathcart, Evans C (Magee 86), Shroot (Lawrie 46), Weir, Little, McQuoid (McQuilken 67), Ferguson (Colligan 80).

Elbasani, 28 March 2009, 1600
Albania (0) 0
Scotland (0) 1 *(Maguire 85 (pen))*
Scotland: Martin; Hanlon, Caddis, Scobbie, Mitchell, Arfield, Shinnie, McDonald, Murphy (Maguire 67), Goodwillie, Bannan (Loy 89).

Falkirk,1 April 2009, 3000
Scotland (1) 5 *(Goodwillie 36, Maguire 50, Shinnie 53, Murphy 74, McGinn 90)*
Albania (0) 2 *(Hyka 72, Vila 87)*
Scotland: Martin; Caddis, Scobbie, Mitchell, Hanlon, Arfield, Shinnie, McDonald (McGinn 65), Maguire, Goodwillie (Murphy 71), Bannan (Fleck 63).

WALES

Wrexham, 20 August 2008, 3118
Wales (0) 0

Romania (0) 1 *(Ropotan 65)*
Wales: Hennessey; Blake, Bale, Edwards D, Gunter, Williams R, MacDonald (Brown J 85), Ramsey (Bradley 65), Vokes, Evans C, Wiggins (Church 74).

Iasi, 9 September 2008
Romania (0) 0
Wales (1) 3 *(Williams R 9, Church 55, Wiggins 64)*
Wales: fon Williams; Blake (Mike Williams 19), Wiggins, Ramsey, Eardley, Williams R, King, Bradley, Church, MacDonald, Adams.

Ettelbruck, 27 March 2009, 520
Luxembourg (0) 0
Wales (0) 0
Wales: Maxwell; James (Brown J 62), Basey (Taylor 69), Eardley, Wilson, Williams R, King, Bradley, Church, MacDonald, Allen.

Llanelli, 31 March 2009, 2924
Wales (4) 5 *(Eardley 10 (pen), Brown 11, King 23, Church 41, Wilson 79)*
Luxembourg (0) 1 *(Polldori 57)*
Wales: Taylor R; Eardley, Taylor N, Bradley, Morris, Williams R (Wilson 55), Allen (Craig 61), King (Partington 46), Church, Brown J, MacDonald.

NORTHERN IRELAND

Kiev, 19 August 2008
Poland (0) 1 *(Wilczek 53)*
Northern Ireland (0) 0
Northern Ireland: Carson; Casement, Flynn, Cathcart (McMenamin 46), Lafferty, Evans C (O'Kane 72), Chapman, Lowry, Lawrie (McQuoid 46), Little, McLean (McKay 89).

Kiev, 20 August 2008
Ukraine (0) 4
Northern Ireland (1) 1 *(Casement 27)*
Northern Ireland: Carson; Casement, Flynn, Cathcart, Lafferty (McQuoid), McLean (McMenamin), Lowrie (Evans C), O'Kane, Stewart (Chapman), Little (Lawrie), McKay.

Wuppertal, 5 September 2008, 5550
Germany (2) 3 *(Kroos 11, Halfar 38, Aogo 61)*
Northern Ireland (0) 0
Northern Ireland: Carson; Casement, Lafferty (O'Kane 77), Chapman, O'Flynn, Cathcart, Little, Evans C, McAllister (McMenamin 46), Lowry, McLean (McKay 64).

Portadown, 31 March 2009
Northern Ireland (0) 1 *(Casement 72)*
Ukraine (1) 1 *(Konopilenka 36 (pen))*
Northern Ireland: Carson; Casement, Cathcart, Gibb, Lafferty, Evans C, Garrett, Chapman, McQuoid, Shroot, Allen.

REPUBLIC OF IRELAND

Vienna, 19 August 2008
Austria (0) 1 *(Stanislaw 90)*
Republic of Ireland (1) 1 *(Treacy 14)*
Republic of Ireland: Redmond (Henderson 46); Coleman, Liddle (Madden 73), Spillane, Dennehy (Breen 46), Ryan, Judge, Gleeson (O'Keefe 46), Jackson (Amond 63), Berrett, Treacy (Moore 51).

Sofia, 5 September 2008
Bulgaria (1) 2 *(Kyrdov 44, Tseytanov 77)*
Republic of Ireland (0) 0
Republic of Ireland: Redmond; Coleman, Liddle, Nolan, Dennehy, Ryan, Judge, Berrett (Amond 70), Scannell, Garvan, Treacy.

Madeira, 9 September 2008
Portugal (2) 2 *(Vaz Te, Fernandes 45)*
Republic of Ireland (0) 2 *(Garvan 49, 65)*
Republic of Ireland: Redmond; Coleman, Liddle, Spillane, Nolan, Ryan (Gleeson 46), Judge (Madden 79), McCarthy, Garvan, Amond (Moore 46), Scannell.

Teisiai, 14 October, 2008
Lithuania (0) 0
Republic of Ireland (0) 3 *(Ryan 74, Gordej 83 (og), Garvan 88)*
Republic of Ireland: Redmond (Henderson 46); Coleman, Bermingham, Spillane (Dennehy 89), Nolan, Scannell (Amond 67), Garvan, Gleeson, Ryan (Berrett 75), Jay O'Shea, Pilkington (Liddle 83).

Cork, 10 February 2009
Republic of Ireland (1) 1 *(Spillane 26)*
Germany (1) 1 *(Wagner)*
Republic of Ireland: Redmond (Henderson 46); Moloney, Spillane, Lowry, Liddle, Gleeson, Meyler, Garvan, Judge, Sheridan, Scannell (Carey 86).

Waterford, 27 March 2009, 1760
Republic of Ireland (1) 2 *(O'Shea J 37, Judge 58)*
Spain (0) 1 *(Bolado 63)*
Republic of Ireland: Redmond (Henderson 46); Coleman (Carey 55), Nolan, Dennehy, Moloney, Gleeson (O'Toole 75), Meyler, Garvan, Judge (Fagan 76), Sheridan, Jay O'Shea.

Cork, 31 March 2009
Republic of Ireland (0) 0
Turkey (2) 3 *(Yilmaz 15, Ozcan 40, Sismanoglu 90)*
Republic of Ireland: Redmond; Moloney, Nolan, Dennehy, Bermingham, Gleeson, Meyler (McCarthy 46), Garvan, Judge (Fagan 81), Sheridan, Jay O'Shea (Carey 73).

Rio Ferdinand a graduate of the England under-21 set up, here seen in Premiership action for Manchester United. Ferdinand, now a fixture in Fabio Capello's senior side, made his under-21 debut in 1997 going on to make five appearances. (PA Photos)

BRITISH UNDER-21 APPEARANCES 1976–2009

ENGLAND

Ablett, G. 1988 (Liverpool)	1	Bywater, S. 2001 (West Ham U)	6
Adams, N. 1987 (Everton)	1		
Adams, T. A. 1985 (Arsenal)	5	Cadamarteri, D. L. 1999 (Everton)	3
Agbonlahor, G. 2007 (Aston Villa)	16	Caesar, G. 1987 (Arsenal)	3
Allen, B. 1992 (QPR)	8	Cahill, G. J. 2007 (Aston Villa)	3
Allen, C. 1980 (QPR, C Palace)	3	Callaghan, N. 1983 (Watford)	9
Allen, C. A. 1995 (Oxford U)	2	Camp, L. M. J. 2005 (Derby Co)	5
Allen, M. 1987 (QPR)	2	Campbell, A. P. 2000 (Middlesbrough)	4
Allen, P. 1985 (West Ham U, Tottenham H)	3	Campbell, F. L. 2008 (Manchester U)	14
Allen, R. W. 1998 (Tottenham H)	3	Campbell, K. J. 1991 (Arsenal)	4
Alnwick, B. R. 2008 (Tottenham H)	1	Campbell, S. 1994 (Tottenham H)	11
Ambrose, D. P. F. 2003 (Ipswich T, Newcastle U,		Carbon, M. P. 1996 (Derby Co)	4
Charlton Ath)	10	Carr, C. 1985 (Fulham)	1
Ameobi, F. 2001 (Newcastle U)	19	Carr, F. 1987 (Nottingham F)	9
Anderson, V. A. 1978 (Nottingham F)	1	Carragher, J. L. 1997 (Liverpool)	27
Anderton, D. R. 1993 (Tottenham H)	12	Carlisle, C. J. 2001 (QPR)	3
Andrews, I. 1987 (Leicester C)	1	Carrick, M. 2001 (West Ham U)	14
Ardley, N. C. 1993 (Wimbledon)	10	Carson, S. P. 2004 (Leeds U, Liverpool)	29
Ashcroft, L. 1992 (Preston NE)	1	Casper, C. M. 1995 (Manchester U)	1
Ashton, D. 2004 (Crewe Alex, Norwich C)	9	Caton, T. 1982 (Manchester C)	14
Atherton, P. 1992 (Coventry C)	1	Cattermole, L. B. 2008 (Middlesbrough, Wigan Ath)	13
Atkinson, B. 1991 (Sunderland)	6	Chadwick, L. H. 2000 (Manchester U)	13
Awford, A. T. 1993 (Portsmouth)	9	Challis, T. M. 1996 (QPR)	2
		Chamberlain, M. 1983 (Stoke C)	4
Bailey, G. R. 1979 (Manchester U)	14	Chaplow, R. D. 2004 (Burnley)	1
Baines, L. J. 2005 (Wigan Ath)	16	Chapman, L. 1981 (Stoke C)	1
Baker, G. E. 1981 (Southampton)	2	Charles, G. A. 1991 (Nottingham F)	7
Ball, M. J. 1999 (Everton)	8	Chettle, S. 1988 (Nottingham F)	12
Barker, S. 1985 (Blackburn R)	4	Chopra, R. M. 2004 (Newcastle U)	1
Barmby, N. J. 1994 (Tottenham H, Everton)	4	Clark, L. R. 1992 (Newcastle U)	11
Bannister, G. 1982 (Sheffield W)	1	Clarke, P. M. 2003 (Everton)	8
Barnes, J. 1983 (Watford)	2	Christie, M. N. 2001 (Derby Co)	11
Barnes, P. S. 1977 (Manchester C)	9	Clegg, M. J. 1998 (Manchester U)	2
Barrett, E. D. 1990 (Oldham Ath)	4	Clemence, S. N. 1999 (Tottenham H)	1
Barry, G. 1999 (Aston Villa)	27	Clough, N. H. 1986 (Nottingham F)	15
Barton, J. 2004 (Manchester C)	2	Cole, A. 2001 (Arsenal)	4
Bart-Williams, C. G. 1993 (Sheffield W)	16	Cole, A. A. 1992 (Arsenal, Bristol C, Newcastle U)	8
Batty, D. 1988 (Leeds U)	7	Cole, C. 2003 (Chelsea)	19
Bazeley, D. S. 1992 (Watford)	1	Cole, J. J. 2000 (West Ham U)	8
Beagrie, P. 1988 (Sheffield U)	2	Coney, D. 1985 (Fulham)	4
Beardsmore, R. 1989 (Manchester U)	5	Connor, T. 1987 (Brighton & HA)	1
Beattie, J. S. 1999 (Southampton)	5	Cooke, R. 1986 (Tottenham H)	1
Beckham, D. R. J. 1995 (Manchester U)	9	Cooke, T. J. 1996 (Manchester U)	4
Bent, D. A. 2003 (Ipswich T, Charlton Ath)	14	Cooper, C. T. 1988 (Middlesbrough)	8
Bent, M. N. 1998 (C Palace)	2	Cork, J. F. P. 2009 (Chelsea)	2
Bentley, D. M. 2004 (Arsenal, Blackburn R)	8	Corrigan, J. T. 1978 (Manchester C)	8
Beeston, C 1988 (Stoke C)	1	Cort, C. E. R. 1999 (Wimbledon)	12
Benjamin, T. J. 2001 (Leicester C)	1	Cottee, A. R. 1985 (West Ham U)	8
Bertrand, R. 2009 (Chelsea)	1	Couzens, A. J. 1995 (Leeds U)	4
Bertschin, K. E. 1977 (Birmingham C)	3	Cowans, G. S. 1979 (Aston Villa)	5
Birtles, G. 1980 (Nottingham F)	2	Cox, N. J. 1993 (Aston Villa)	6
Blackstock, D. A. 2008 (QPR)	2	Cranie, M. J. 2008 (Portsmouth)	16
Blackwell, D. R. 1991 (Wimbledon)	6	Cranson, I. 1985 (Ipswich T)	5
Blake, M. A. 1990 (Aston Villa)	9	Cresswell, R. P. W. 1999 (York C, Sheffield W)	4
Blissett, L. L. 1979 (Watford)	4	Croft, G. 1995 (Grimsby T)	4
Booth, A. D. 1995 (Huddersfield T)	3	Crooks, G. 1980 (Stoke C)	4
Bothroyd, J. 2001 (Coventry C)	1	Crossley, M. G. 1990 (Nottingham F)	3
Bowyer, L. D. 1996 (Charlton Ath, Leeds U)	13	Crouch, P. J. 2002 (Portsmouth, Aston Villa)	5
Bracewell, P. 1983 (Stoke C)	13	Cundy, J. V. 1991 (Chelsea)	3
Bradbury, L. M. 1997 (Portsmouth, Manchester C)	3	Cunningham, L. 1977 (WBA)	6
Bramble, T. M. 2001 (Ipswich T, Newcastle U)	10	Curbishley, L. C. 1981 (Birmingham C)	1
Branch, P. M. 1997 (Everton)	1	Curtis, J. C. K. 1998 (Manchester U)	16
Bradshaw, P. W. 1977 (Wolverhampton W)	4		
Breacker, T. 1986 (Luton T)	2	Daniel, P. W. 1977 (Hull C)	7
Brennan, M. 1987 (Ipswich T)	5	Dann, S. 2008 (Coventry C)	2
Bridge, W. M. 1999 (Southampton)	8	Davenport, C. R. P. 2005 (Tottenham H)	8
Bridges, M. 1997 (Sunderland, Leeds U)	3	Davies, A. J. 2004 (Middlesbrough)	1
Brightwell, I. 1989 (Manchester C)	4	Davies, C. E. 2006 (WBA)	3
Briscoe, L. S. 1996 (Sheffield W)	5	Davies, K. C. 1998 (Southampton, Blackburn R,	
Brock, K. 1984 (Oxford U)	4	Southampton)	3
Broomes, M. C. 1997 (Blackburn R)	2	Davis, K. G. 1995 (Luton T)	3
Brown, M. R. 1996 (Manchester C)	4	Davis, P. 1982 (Arsenal)	11
Brown, W. M. 1999 (Manchester U)	4	Davis, S. 2001 (Fulham)	11
Bull, S. G. 1989 (Wolverhampton W)	5	Dawson, M. R. 2003 (Nottingham F, Tottenham H)	13
Bullock, M. J. 1998 (Barnsley)	1	Day, C. N. 1996 (Tottenham H, C Palace)	6
Burrows, D. 1989 (WBA, Liverpool)	7	D'Avray, M. 1984 (Ipswich T)	2
Butcher, T. I. 1979 (Ipswich T)	7	Deehan, J. M. 1977 (Aston Villa)	7
Butt, N. 1995 (Manchester U)	7	Defoe, J. C. 2001 (West Ham U)	23
Butters, G. 1989 (Tottenham H)	3	Delph, F. 2009 (Leeds U)	1
Butterworth, I. 1985 (Coventry C, Nottingham F)	8	Dennis, M. E. 1980 (Birmingham C)	3

Derbyshire, M. A. 2007 (Blackburn R)	14
Dichio, D. S. E. 1996 (QPR)	1
Dickens, A. 1985 (West Ham U)	1
Dicks, J. 1988 (West Ham U)	4
Digby, F. 1987 (Swindon T)	5
Dillon, K. P. 1981 (Birmingham C)	1
Dixon, K. M. 1985 (Chelsea)	1
Dobson, A. 1989 (Coventry C)	4
Dodd, J. R. 1991 (Southampton)	8
Donowa, L. 1985 (Norwich C)	3
Dorigo, A. R. 1987 (Aston Villa)	11
Downing, S. 2004 (Middlesbrough)	8
Dozzell, J. 1987 (Ipswich T)	9
Draper, M. A. 1991 (Notts Co)	3
Driver, A. 2009 (Hearts)	1
Duberry, M. W. 1997 (Chelsea)	5
Dunn, D. J. I. 1999 (Blackburn R)	20
Duxbury, M. 1981 (Manchester U)	7
Dyer, B. A. 1994 (C Palace)	10
Dyer, K. C. 1998 (Ipswich T, Newcastle U)	11
Dyson, P. I. 1981 (Coventry C)	4
Eadie, D. M. 1994 (Norwich C)	7
Ebanks-Blake, S. 2009 (Wolverhampton W)	1
Ebbrell, J. 1989 (Everton)	14
Edghill, R. A. 1994 (Manchester C)	3
Ehiogu, U. 1992 (Aston Villa)	15
Elliott, P. 1985 (Luton T)	3
Elliott, R. J. 1996 (Newcastle U)	2
Elliott, S. W. 1998 (Derby Co)	3
Etherington, N. 2002 (Tottenham H)	4
Euell, J. J. 1998 (Wimbledon)	6
Evans, R. 2003 (Chelsea)	2
Fairclough, C. 1985 (Nottingham F, Tottenham H)	7
Fairclough, D. 1977 (Liverpool)	1
Fashanu, J. 1980 (Norwich C, Nottingham F)	11
Fear, P. 1994 (Wimbledon)	3
Fenton, G. A. 1995 (Aston Villa)	1
Fenwick, T. W. 1981 (C Palace, QPR)	11
Ferdinand, A. J. 2005 (West Ham U)	17
Ferdinand, R. G. 1997 (West Ham U)	5
Fereday, W. 1985 (QPR)	5
Fielding, F. D. 2009 (Blackburn R)	1
Flitcroft, G. W. 1993 (Manchester C)	10
Flowers, T. D. 1987 (Southampton)	3
Ford, M. 1996 (Leeds U)	1
Forster, N. M. 1995 (Brentford)	4
Forsyth, M. 1988 (Derby Co)	1
Foster, S. 1980 (Brighton & HA)	1
Fowler, R. B. 1994 (Liverpool)	8
Fox, D. J. 2008 (Coventry C)	1
Froggatt, S. J. 1993 (Aston Villa)	2
Futcher, P. 1977 (Luton T, Manchester C)	11
Gabbiadini, M. 1989 (Sunderland)	2
Gale, A. 1982 (Fulham)	1
Gallen, K. A. 1995 (QPR)	4
Gardner, A. 2002 (Tottenham H)	1
Gardner, C. 2008 (Aston Villa)	14
Gascoigne, P. J. 1987 (Newcastle U)	13
Gayle, H. 1984 (Birmingham C)	3
Gernon, T. 1983 (Ipswich T)	1
Gerrard, P. W. 1993 (Oldham Ath)	18
Gerrard, S. G. 2000 (Liverpool)	4
Gibbs, K. J. R. 2009 (Arsenal)	9
Gibbs, N. 1987 (Watford)	5
Gibson, C. 1982 (Aston Villa)	1
Gilbert, W. A. 1979 (C Palace)	11
Goddard, P. 1981 (West Ham U)	8
Gordon, D. 1987 (Norwich C)	4
Gordon, D. D. 1994 (C Palace)	13
Grant, A. J. 1996 (Everton)	1
Grant, L. A. 2003 (Derby Co)	4
Granville, D. P. 1997 (Chelsea)	3
Gray, A. 1988 (Aston Villa)	2
Greening, J. 1999 (Manchester U, Middlesbrough)	18
Griffin, A. 1999 (Newcastle U)	3
Guppy, S. A. 1998 (Leicester C)	1
Haigh, P. 1977 (Hull C)	1
Hall, M. T. J. 1997 (Coventry C)	8
Hall, R. A. 1992 (Southampton)	11
Hamilton, D. V. 1997 (Newcastle U)	1
Harding, D. A. 2005 (Brighton & HA)	4
Hardyman, P. 1985 (Portsmouth)	2

Hargreaves, O. 2001 (Bayern Munich)	3
Harley, J. 2000 (Chelsea)	3
Hart, C. 2007 (Manchester C)	21
Hateley, M. 1982 (Coventry C, Portsmouth)	10
Hayes, M. 1987 (Arsenal)	3
Hazell, R. J. 1979 (Wolverhampton W)	1
Heaney, N. A. 1992 (Arsenal)	6
Heath, A. 1981 (Stoke C, Everton)	8
Heaton, T. D. 2008 (Manchester U)	3
Hendon, I. M. 1992 (Tottenham H)	7
Hendrie, L. A. 1996 (Aston Villa)	13
Hesford, I. 1981 (Blackpool)	7
Heskey, E. W. I. 1997 (Leicester C, Liverpool)	16
Hilaire, V. 1980 (C Palace)	9
Hill, D. R. L. 1995 (Tottenham H)	4
Hillier, D. 1991 (Arsenal)	1
Hinchcliffe, A. 1989 (Manchester C)	1
Hinshelwood, P. A. 1978 (C Palace)	2
Hirst, D. E. 1988 (Sheffield W)	7
Hislop, N. S. 1998 (Newcastle U)	1
Hoddle, G. 1977 (Tottenham H)	12
Hodge, S. B. 1983 (Nottingham F, Aston Villa)	8
Hodgson, D. J. 1981 (Middlesbrough)	6
Holdsworth, D. 1989 (Watford)	1
Holland, C. J. 1995 (Newcastle U)	10
Holland, P. 1995 (Mansfield T)	4
Holloway, D. 1998 (Sunderland)	1
Horne, B. 1989 (Millwall)	5
Howe, E. J. F. 1998 (Bournemouth)	2
Hoyte, J. R. 2004 (Arsenal)	18
Hucker, P. 1984 (QPR)	2
Huckerby, D. 1997 (Coventry C)	4
Huddlestone, T. A. 2005 (Derby Co, Tottenham H)	33
Hughes, S. J. 1997 (Arsenal)	8
Humphreys, R. J. 1997 (Sheffield W)	3
Hunt, N. B. 2004 (Bolton W)	10
Impey, A. R. 1993 (QPR)	1
Ince, P. E. C. 1989 (West Ham U)	2
Jackson, M. A. 1992 (Everton)	10
Jagielka, P. N. 2003 (Sheffield U)	6
James, D. B. 1991 (Watford)	10
James, J. C. 1990 (Luton T)	2
Jansen, M. B. 1999 (C Palace, Blackburn R)	6
Jeffers, F. 2000 (Everton, Arsenal)	16
Jemson, N. B. 1991 (Nottingham F)	1
Jenas, J. A. 2002 (Newcastle U)	9
Jerome, C. 2006 (Cardiff C, Birmingham C)	10
Joachim, J. K. 1994 (Leicester C)	9
Johnson, A. 2008 (Middlesbrough)	19
Johnson, G. M. C. 2003 (West Ham U, Chelsea)	14
Johnson, M. 2008 (Manchester C)	2
Johnson, S. A. M. 1999 (Crewe Alex, Derby Co, Leeds U)	
	15
Johnson, T. 1991 (Notts Co, Derby Co)	7
Johnston, C. P. 1981 (Middlesbrough)	2
Jones, D. R. 1977 (Everton)	1
Jones, C. H. 1978 (Tottenham H)	1
Jones, D. F. L. 2004 (Manchester U)	1
Jones, R. 1993 (Liverpool)	2
Keegan, G. A. 1977 (Manchester C)	1
Kenny, W. 1993 (Everton)	1
Keown, M. R. 1987 (Aston Villa)	8
Kerslake, D. 1986 (QPR)	1
Kightly, M. J. 2008 (Wolverhampton W)	7
Kilcline, B. 1983 (Notts C)	2
Kilgallon, M. 2004 (Leeds U)	5
King, A. E. 1977 (Everton)	2
King, L. B. 2000 (Tottenham H)	12
Kirkland, C. E. 2001 (Coventry C, Liverpool)	8
Kitson, P. 1991 (Leicester C, Derby Co)	7
Knight, A. 1983 (Portsmouth)	2
Knight, I. 1987 (Sheffield W)	2
Knight, Z. 2002 (Fulham)	4
Konchesky, P. M. 2002 (Charlton Ath)	15
Kozluk, R. 1998 (Derby Co)	2
Lake, P. 1989 (Manchester C)	5
Lallana, A. D. 2009 (Southampton)	1
Lampard, F. J. 1998 (West Ham U)	19
Langley, T. W. 1978 (Chelsea)	1
Leadbitter, G. 2008 (Sunderland)	3
Lee, D. J. 1990 (Chelsea)	10
Lee, R. M. 1986 (Charlton Ath)	2

Shearer, A. 1991 (Southampton)	11
Shelton, G. 1985 (Sheffield W)	1
Sheringham, E. P. 1988 (Millwall)	1
Sheron, M. N. 1992 (Manchester C)	16
Sherwood, T. A. 1990 (Norwich C)	4
Shipperley, N. J. 1994 (Chelsea, Southampton)	7
Sidwell, S. J. 2003 (Reading)	5
Simonsen, S. P. A. 1998 (Tranmere R, Everton)	4
Simpson, P. 1986 (Manchester C)	5
Sims, S. 1977 (Leicester C)	10
Sinclair, T. 1994 (QPR, West Ham U)	5
Sinnott, L. 1985 (Watford)	1
Slade, S. A. 1996 (Tottenham H)	4
Slater, S. I. 1990 (West Ham U)	3
Small, B. 1993 (Aston Villa)	12
Smith, A. 2000 (Leeds U)	10
Smith, D. 1988 (Coventry C)	10
Smith, M. 1981 (Sheffield W)	5
Smith, M. 1995 (Sunderland)	1
Smith, T. W. 2001 (Watford)	1
Snodin, I. 1985 (Doncaster R)	4
Soares, T. J. 2006 (C Palace)	4
Statham, B. 1988 (Tottenham H)	3
Statham, D. J. 1978 (WBA)	6
Stead, J. G. 2004 (Blackburn R, Sunderland)	11
Stearman, R. J. 2009 (Wolverhampton W)	4
Stein, B. 1984 (Luton T)	3
Sterland, M. 1984 (Sheffield W)	7
Steven, T. M. 1985 (Everton)	2
Stevens, G. A. 1983 (Brighton & HA, Tottenham H)	8
Stewart, J. 2003 (Leicester C)	1
Stewart, P. 1988 (Manchester C)	1
Stockdale, R. K. 2001 (Middlesbrough)	1
Stuart, G. C. 1990 (Chelsea)	5
Stuart, J. C. 1996 (Charlton Ath)	4
Suckling, P. 1986 (Coventry C, Manchester C, C Palace)	10
Summerbee, N. J. 1993 (Swindon T)	3
Sunderland, A. 1977 (Wolverhampton W)	1
Surman, A. R. E. 2008 (Southampton)	4
Sutch, D. 1992 (Norwich C)	4
Sutton, C. R. 1993 (Norwich C)	13
Swindlehurst, D. 1977 (C Palace)	1
Talbot, B. 1977 (Ipswich T)	1
Taylor, A. D. 2007 (Middlesbrough)	13
Taylor, M. 2001 (Blackburn R)	1
Taylor, M. S. 2003 (Portsmouth)	3
Taylor, R. A. 2006 (Wigan Ath)	4
Taylor, S. J. 2002 (Arsenal)	3
Taylor, S. V. 2004 (Newcastle U)	29
Terry, J. G. 2001 (Chelsea)	9
Thatcher, B. D. 1996 (Millwall, Wimbledon)	4
Thelwell, A. A. 2001 (Tottenham H)	1
Thirlwell, P. 2001 (Sunderland)	1
Thomas, D. 1981 (Coventry C, Tottenham H)	7
Thomas, J. W. 2006 (Charlton Ath)	2
Thomas, M. 1986 (Luton T)	3
Thomas, M. L. 1988 (Arsenal)	12
Thomas, R. E. 1990 (Watford)	1
Thompson, A. 1995 (Bolton W)	2
Thompson, D. A. 1997 (Liverpool)	7
Thompson, G. L. 1981 (Coventry C)	6
Thorn, A. 1988 (Wimbledon)	5
Thornley, B. L. 1996 (Manchester U)	3
Tiler, C. 1990 (Barnsley, Nottingham F)	13

Tomkins, J. O. C. 2009 (West Ham U)	3
Tonge, M. W. E. 2004 (Sheffield U)	2
Unsworth, D. G. 1995 (Everton)	6
Upson, M. J. 1999 (Arsenal)	11
Vassell, D. 1999 (Aston Villa)	11
Vaughan, J. O. 2007 (Everton)	2
Venison, B. 1983 (Sunderland)	10
Vernazza, P. A. P. 2001 (Arsenal, Watford)	2
Vinnicombe, C. 1991 (Rangers)	12
Waddle, C. R. 1985 (Newcastle U)	1
Walcott, T. J. 2007 (Arsenal)	20
Wallace, D. L. 1983 (Southampton)	14
Wallace, Ray 1989 (Southampton)	4
Wallace, Rod 1989 (Southampton)	11
Walker, D. 1985 (Nottingham F)	7
Walker, I. M. 1991 (Tottenham H)	9
Walsh, G. 1988 (Manchester U)	2
Walsh, P. A. 1983 (Luton T)	4
Walters, K. 1984 (Aston Villa)	9
Ward, P. 1978 (Brighton & HA)	2
Warhurst, P. 1991 (Oldham Ath, Sheffield W)	8
Watson, B. 2007 (C Palace)	1
Watson, D. 1984 (Norwich C)	7
Watson, D. N. 1994 (Barnsley)	5
Watson, G. 1991 (Sheffield W)	2
Watson, S. C. 1993 (Newcastle U)	12
Weaver, N. J. 2000 (Manchester C)	10
Webb, N. J. 1985 (Portsmouth, Nottingham F)	3
Welbeck, D. 2009 (Manchester U)	2
Welsh, J. J. 2004 (Liverpool, Hull C)	8
Wheater, D. J. 2008 (Middlesbrough)	11
Whelan, P. J. 1993 (Ipswich T)	3
Whelan, N. 1995 (Leeds U)	2
Whittingham, P. 2004 (Aston Villa, Cardiff C)	17
White, D. 1988 (Manchester C)	6
Whyte, C. 1982 (Arsenal)	4
Wicks, S. 1982 (QPR)	1
Wilkins, R. C. 1977 (Chelsea)	1
Wilkinson, P. 1985 (Grimsby T, Everton)	4
Williams, D. 1998 (Sunderland)	2
Williams, P. 1989 (Charlton Ath)	4
Williams, P. D. 1991 (Derby Co)	6
Williams, S. C. 1977 (Southampton)	14
Wilson, M. A. 2001 (Manchester U, Middlesbrough)	6
Winterburn, N. 1986 (Wimbledon)	1
Wise, D. F. 1988 (Wimbledon)	1
Woodcock, A. S. 1978 (Nottingham F)	2
Woodgate, J. S. 2000 (Leeds U)	1
Woodhouse, C. 1999 (Sheffield U)	4
Woods, C. C. E. 1979 (Nottingham F, QPR, Norwich C)	6
Wright, A. G. 1993 (Blackburn R)	2
Wright, M. 1983 (Southampton)	4
Wright, R. I. 1997 (Ipswich T)	15
Wright, S. J. 2001 (Liverpool)	10
Wright, W. 1979 (Everton)	6
Wright-Phillips, S. C. 2002 (Manchester C)	6
Yates, D. 1989 (Notts Co)	5
Young, A. S. 2007 (Watford, Aston Villa)	10
Young, L. P. 1999 (Tottenham H, Charlton Ath)	12
Zamora, R. L. 2002 (Brighton & HA)	6

NORTHERN IRELAND

Allen, C. 2009 (Lisburn Distillery)	1
Armstrong, D. T. 2007 (Hearts)	1
Bailie, N. 1990 (Linfield)	2
Baird, C. P. 2002 (Southampton)	6
Beatty, S. 1990 (Chelsea, Linfield)	2
Black, J. 2003 (Tottenham H)	1
Black, K. T. 1990 (Luton T)	1
Black, R. Z. 2002 (Morecambe)	1
Blackledge, G. 1978 (Portadown)	1
Blayney, A. 2003 (Southampton)	4
Boyle, W. S. 1998 (Leeds U)	7
Braniff, K. R. 2002 (Millwall)	11
Brotherston, N. 1978 (Blackburn R)	1
Browne, G. 2003 (Manchester C)	5
Brunt, C. 2005 (Sheffield W)	2
Buchanan, D. T. H. 2006 (Bury)	15

Buchanan, W. B. 2002 (Bolton W, Lisburn Distillery)	5
Burns, L. 1998 (Port Vale)	13
Callaghan, A. 2006 (Limavady U, Ballymena U, Derry C)	15
Campbell, S. 2003 (Ballymena U)	1
Capaldi, A. C. 2002 (Birmingham C, Plymouth Arg)	14
Carlisle, W. T. 2000 (C Palace)	9
Carroll, R. E. 1998 (Wigan Ath)	11
Carson, S. 2000 (Rangers, Dundee U)	2
Carson, T. 2007 (Sunderland)	11
Carvill, M. D. 2008 (Wrexham)	7
Casement, C. 2007 (Ipswich T)	14
Cathcart, C. 2007 (Manchester U)	11
Catney, R. 2007 (Lisburn Distillery)	1
Chapman, A. 2008 (Sheffield U)	6
Clarke, L. 2003 (Peterborough U)	4
Clarke, R. 2006 (Newry C)	7

Clarke, R. D. J. 1999 (Portadown)	5
Clingan, S. G. 2003 (Wolverhampton W, Nottingham F)	11
Close, B. 2002 (Middlesbrough)	10
Clyde, M. G. 2002 (Wolverhampton W)	5
Colligan, L. 2009 (Ballymena U)	1
Connell, T. E. 1978 (Coleraine)	1
Coote, A. 1998 (Norwich C)	12
Convery, J. 2000 (Celtic)	4
Davey, H. 2004 (UCD)	3
Davis, S. 2004 (Aston Villa)	3
Devine, D. 1994 (Omagh T)	1
Devine, J. 1990 (Glentoran)	1
Dickson, H. 2002 (Wigan Ath)	4
Doherty, M. 2007 (Hearts)	2
Dolan, J. 2000 (Millwall)	6
Donaghy, M. M. 1978 (Larne)	1
Donnelly, M. 2007 (Sheffield U, Crusaders)	2
Dowie, I. 1990 (Luton T)	1
Duff, S. 2003 (Cheltenham T)	1
Elliott, S. 1999 (Glentoran)	3
Ervin, J. 2005 (Linfield)	2
Evans, C. J. 2009 (Manchester U)	5
Evans, J. 2006 (Manchester U)	3
Feeney, L. 1998 (Linfield, Rangers)	8
Feeney, W. 2002 (Bournemouth)	8
Ferguson, M. 2000 (Glentoran)	2
Ferguson, S. 2009 (Newcastle U)	1
Fitzgerald, D. 1998 (Rangers)	4
Flynn, J. J. 2009 (Blackburn R)	5
Fordyce, D. T. 2007 (Portsmouth, Glentoran)	12
Friars, E. C. 2005 (Notts Co)	7
Friars, S. M. 1998 (Liverpool, Ipswich T)	21
Garrett, R. 2007 (Stoke C, Linfield)	11
Gault, S. 2005 (Linfield)	2
Gibb, S. 2009 (Falkirk)	1
Gilfillan, B. J. 2005 (Gretna, Peterhead)	9
Gillespie, K. R. 1994 (Manchester U)	1
Glendinning, M. 1994 (Bangor)	1
Graham, G. L. 1999 (C Palace)	5
Graham, R. S. 1999 (QPR)	15
Gray, P. 1990 (Luton T)	1
Griffin, D. J. 1998 (St Johnstone)	10
Hamilton, G. 2000 (Blackburn R, Portadown)	12
Hamilton, W. R. 1978 (Linfield)	1
Harkin, M. P. 2000 (Wycombe W)	9
Harvey, J. 1978 (Arsenal)	1
Hawe, S. 2001 (Blackburn R)	2
Hayes, T. 1978 (Luton T)	1
Hazley, M. 2007 (Stoke C)	3
Healy, D. J. 1999 (Manchester U)	8
Herron, C. J. 2003 (QPR)	2
Higgins, R. 2006 (Derry C)	1
Holmes, S. 2000 (Manchester C, Wrexham)	13
Howland, D. 2007 (Birmingham C)	4
Hughes, J. 2006 (Lincoln C)	7
Hughes, M. A. 2003 (Tottenham H, Oldham Ath)	12
Hughes, M. E. 1990 (Manchester C)	1
Hunter, M. 2002 (Glentoran)	1
Ingham, M. G. 2001 (Sunderland)	4
Johnson, D. M. 1998 (Blackburn R)	11
Johnston, B. 1978 (Cliftonville)	1
Julian, A. A. 2005 (Brentford)	1
Kane, A. M. 2008 (Blackburn R)	5
Kee, P. V. 1990 (Oxford U)	1
Kelly, D. 2000 (Derry C)	11
Kelly, N. 1990 (Oldham Ath)	1
Kirk, A. R. 1999 (Hearts)	9
Lafferty, D. 2009 (Celtic)	5
Lafferty, K. 2006 (Burnley)	2
Lawrie, J. 2009 (Port Vale)	3
Lennon, N. F. 1990 (Manchester C, Crewe Alex)	2
Lindsay, K. 2006 (Larne)	1
Little, A. 2009 (Rangers)	4
Lowry, P. 2009 (Institute)	4
Lyttle, G. 1998 (Celtic, Peterborough U)	8
Magee, J. 1994 (Bangor)	1

Magee, J. 2009 (Lisburn Distillery)	1
Magilton, J. 1990 (Liverpool)	1
Matthews, N. P. 1990 (Blackpool)	1
McAllister, M. 2007 (Dungannon Swifts)	.4
McArdle, R. A. 2006 (Sheffield W, Rochdale)	19
McAreavey, P. 2000 (Swindon T)	7
McBride, J. 1994 (Glentoran)	1
McCaffrey, D. 2006 (Hibernian)	8
McCallion, E. 1998 (Coleraine)	1
McCann, G. S. 2000 (West Ham U)	11
McCann, P. 2003 (Portadown)	1
McCann, R. 2002 (Rangers, Linfield)	2
McCartney, G. 2001 (Sunderland)	5
McChrystal, M. 2005 (Derry C)	9
McCourt, P. J. 2002 (Rochdale, Derry C)	8
McCoy, R. K. 1990 (Coleraine)	1
McCreery, D. 1978 (Manchester U)	1
McEvilly, L. R. 2003 (Rochdale)	9
McFlynn, T. M. 2000 (QPR, Woking, Margate)	19
McGibbon, P. C. G. 1994 (Manchester U)	1
McGlinchey, B. 1998 (Manchester C, Port Vale, Gillingham)	14
McGovern, M. 2005 (Celtic)	10
McGowan, M. V. 2006 (Clyde)	2
McIlroy, T. 1994 (Linfield)	1
McKay, W. 2009 (Leicester C)	3
McKenna, K. 2007 (Tottenham H)	6
McKnight, P. 1998 (Rangers)	3
McLean, B. S. 2006 (Rangers)	1
McLean, J. 2009 (Derry C)	4
McMahon, G. J. 2002 (Tottenham H)	1
McMenamin, L. A. 2009 (Sheffield W)	4
McQuilken, J. 2009 (Tescoma Zlin)	1
McQuoid, J. J. B. 2009 (Bournemouth)	4
McVeigh, A. 2002 (Ayr U)	1
McVeigh, P. M. 1998 (Tottenham H)	11
McVey, K. 2006 (Coleraine)	8
Meenan, D. 2007 (Finn Harps, Monaghan U)	3
Melaugh, G. M. 2002 (Aston Villa, Glentoran)	11
Millar, W. P. 1990 (Port Vale)	1
Miskelly, D. T. 2000 (Oldham Ath)	10
Moreland, V. 1978 (Glentoran)	1
Morgan, M. P. T. 1999 (Preston NE)	1
Morris, E. J. 2002 (WBA, Glentoran)	8
Morrison, O. 2001 (Sheffield W, Sheffield U)	7
Morrow, A. 2001 (Northampton T)	1
Morrow, S. 2005 (Hibernian)	4
Mulgrew, J. 2007 (Linfield)	10
Mulryne, P. P. 1999 (Manchester U, Norwich C)	5
Murray, W. 1978 (Linfield)	1
Murtagh, C. 2005 (Hearts)	1
Nicholl, J. M. 1978 (Manchester U)	1
Nixon, C. 2000 (Glentoran)	1
O'Connor, M. J. 2008 (Crewe Alex)	3
O'Hara, G. 1994 (Leeds U)	1
O'Kane, E. 2009 (Everton)	3
O'Neill, J. P. 1978 (Leicester C)	1
O'Neill, M. A. M. 1994 (Hibernian)	1
O'Neill, S. 2009 (Ballymena U)	1
Paterson, M. A. 2007 (Stoke C)	2
Paterson, D. J. 1994 (C Palace)	1
Quinn, S. J. 1994 (Blackpool)	1
Ramsey, K. 2006 (Institute)	1
Robinson, S. 1994 (Tottenham H)	1
Scullion, D. 2006 (Dungannon Swifts)	8
Shiels, D. 2005 (Hibernian)	6
Shroot, R. 2009 (Harrow B, Birmingham C)	2
Simms, G. 2001 (Hartlepool U)	14
Skates, G. 2000 (Blackburn R)	4
Sloan, T. 1978 (Ballymena U)	1
Smylie, D. 2006 (Newcastle U, Livingston)	6
Stewart, S. 2009 (Aberdeen)	1
Stewart, T. 2006 (Wolverhampton W, Linfield)	19
Taylor, J. 2007 (Hearts, Glentoran)	9
Taylor, M. S. 1998 (Fulham)	1
Teggart, N. 2005 (Sunderland)	2
Thompson, P. 2006 (Linfield)	4
Toner, C. 2000 (Tottenham H, Leyton Orient)	17
Tuffey, J. 2007 (Partick T)	13

Turner, C. 2007 (Sligo R, Bohemians)   12

Ward, J. J. 2006 (Aston Villa, Chesterfield)   7
Ward, M. 2006 (Dungannon Swifts)   1
Ward, S. 2005 (Glentoran)   10
Waterman, D. G. 1998 (Portsmouth)   14

Waterworth, A. 2008 (Lisburn Distillery, Hamilton A)   7
Webb, S. M. 2004 (Ross Co, St Johnstone, Ross Co)   6
Weir, R. J. 2009 (Sunderland)   1
Wells, D. P. 1999 (Barry T)   1
Whitley, J. 1998 (Manchester C)   17
Willis, P. 2006 (Liverpool)   1

SCOTLAND

Adam, C. G. 2006 (Rangers)   5
Adams, J. 2007 (Kilmarnock)   1
Aitken, R. 1977 (Celtic)   16
Albiston, A. 1977 (Manchester U)   5
Alexander, N. 1997 (Stenhousemuir, Livingston)   10
Anderson, I. 1997 (Dundee, Toulouse)   15
Anderson, R. 1997 (Aberdeen)   15
Anthony, M. 1997 (Celtic)   3
Archdeacon, O. 1987 (Celtic)   1
Archibald, A. 1998 (Partick Th)   5
Archibald, S. 1980 (Aberdeen, Tottenham H)   5
Arfield, S. 2008 (Falkirk)   11

Bagen, D. 1997 (Kilmarnock)   4
Bain, K. 1993 (Dundee)   4
Baker, M. 1993 (St Mirren)   10
Baltacha, S. S. 2000 (St Mirren)   3
Bannan, B. 2009 (Aston Villa)   2
Bannon, E. J. 1979 (Hearts, Chelsea, Dundee U)   7
Beattie, C. 2004 (Celtic)   7
Beattie, J. 1992 (St Mirren)   4
Beaumont, D. 1985 (Dundee U)   1
Bell, D. 1981 (Aberdeen)   2
Bernard, P. R. J. 1992 (Oldham Ath)   15
Berra, C. 2005 (Hearts)   6
Bett, J. 1981 (Rangers)   7
Black, E. 1983 (Aberdeen)   8
Blair, A. 1980 (Coventry C, Aston Villa)   5
Bollan, G. 1992 (Dundee U, Rangers)   17
Bonar, P. 1997 (Raith R)   4
Booth, S. 1991 (Aberdeen)   14
Bowes, M. J. 1992 (Dunfermline Ath)   1
Bowman, D. 1985 (Hearts)   1
Boyack, S. 1997 (Rangers)   1
Boyd, K. 2003 (Kilmarnock)   1
Boyd, T. 1987 (Motherwell)   5
Brazil, A. 1978 (Hibernian)   1
Brazil, A. 1979 (Ipswich T)   8
Brebner, G. I. 1997 (Manchester U, Reading, Hibernian)   18
Brighton, T. 2005 (Rangers, Clyde)   7
Broadfoot, K. 2005 (St Mirren)   5
Brough, J. 1981 (Hearts)   1
Brown, A. H. 2004 (Hibernian)   1
Brown, S. 2005 (Hibernian)   10
Browne, P. 1997 (Raith R)   1
Bryson, C. 2006 (Clyde)   1
Buchan, J. 1997 (Aberdeen)   13
Burchill, M. J. 1998 (Celtic)   15
Burke, A. 1997 (Kilmarnock)   4
Burke, C. 2004 (Rangers)   3
Burley, C. W. 1992 (Chelsea)   7
Burley, G. E. 1977 (Ipswich T)   5
Burns, H. 1985 (Rangers)   2
Burns, T. 1977 (Celtic)   5

Caddis, P. 2008 (Celtic, Dundee U)   5
Caldwell, G. 2000 (Newcastle U)   19
Caldwell, S. 2001 (Newcastle U)   4
Cameron, G. 2008 (Dundee U)   3
Campbell, R. 2008 (Hibernian)   6
Campbell, S. 1989 (Dundee)   3
Campbell, S. P. 1998 (Leicester C)   15
Canero, P. 2000 (Kilmarnock)   17
Carey, L. A. 1998 (Bristol C)   1
Casey, J. 1978 (Celtic)   1
Christie, M. 1992 (Dundee)   3
Clark, R. B. 1977 (Aberdeen)   3
Clarke, S. 1984 (St Mirren)   8
Clarkson, D. 2004 (Motherwell)   13
Cleland, A. 1990 (Dundee U)   11
Collins, J. 1988 (Hibernian)   8
Collins, N. 2005 (Sunderland)   7
Connolly, P. 1991 (Dundee U)   3
Connor, R. 1981 (Ayr U)   2
Conroy, R. 2007 (Celtic)   4
Considine, A. 2007 (Aberdeen)   5

Cooper, D. 1977 (Clydebank, Rangers)   6
Cooper, N. 1982 (Aberdeen)   13
Coutts, P. A. 2009 (Peterborough U)   1
Crabbe, S. 1990 (Hearts)   2
Craig, M. 1998 (Aberdeen)   2
Craig, T. 1977 (Newcastle U)   1
Crainey, S. D. 2000 (Celtic)   7
Crainie, D. 1983 (Celtic)   1
Crawford, S. 1994 (Raith R)   19
Creaney, G. 1991 (Celtic)   11
Cummings, W. 2000 (Chelsea)   8
Cuthbert, S. 2007 (Celtic, St Mirren)   13

Dailly, C. 1991 (Dundee U)   34
Dalglish, P. 1999 (Newcastle U, Norwich C)   6
Dargo, C. 1998 (Raith R)   10
Davidson, C. I. 1997 (St Johnstone)   2
Davidson, H. N. 2000 (Dundee U)   3
Dawson, A. 1979 (Rangers)   8
Deas, P. A. 1992 (St Johnstone)   2
Dempster, J. 2004 (Rushden & D)   1
Dennis, S. 1992 (Raith R)   1
Diamond, A. 2004 (Aberdeen)   12
Dickov, P. 1992 (Arsenal)   4
Dixon, P. 2008 (Dundee)   2
Dodds, D. 1978 (Dundee U)   1
Dods, D. 1997 (Hibernian)   5
Doig, C. R. 2000 (Nottingham F)   13
Donald, G. S. 1992 (Hibernian)   3
Donnelly, S. 1994 (Celtic)   11
Dorrans, G. 2007 (Livingston)   6
Dow, A. 1993 (Dundee, Chelsea)   3
Dowie, A. J. 2003 (Rangers, Partick Th)   14
Duff, J. 2009 (Inverness CT)   1
Duff, S. 2003 (Dundee U)   9
Duffy, D. A. 2005 (Falkirk, Hull C)   8
Duffy, J. 1987 (Dundee)   3
Durie, G. S. 1987 (Chelsea)   4
Durrant, I. 1987 (Rangers)   4
Doyle, J. 1981 (Partick Th)   2

Easton, B. 2009 (Hamilton A)   1
Easton, C. 1997 (Dundee U)   21
Elliot, B. 1998 (Celtic)   2
Elliot, C. 2006 (Hearts)   9
Esson, R. 2000 (Aberdeen)   7

Fagan, S. M. 2005 (Motherwell)   1
Ferguson, B. 1997 (Rangers)   12
Ferguson, D. 1987 (Rangers)   5
Ferguson, D. 1992 (Dundee U)   7
Ferguson, D. 1992 (Manchester U)   5
Ferguson, I. 1983 (Dundee)   4
Ferguson, I. 1987 (Clyde, St Mirren, Rangers)   6
Ferguson, R. 1977 (Hamilton A)   1
Findlay, W. 1991 (Hibernian)   5
Fitzpatrick, A. 1977 (St Mirren)   5
Fitzpatrick, M. 2007 (Motherwell)   4
Flannigan, C. 1993 (Clydebank)   1
Fleck, J. 2009 (Rangers)   2
Fleck, R. 1987 (Rangers, Norwich C)   6
Fleming, G. 2008 (Gretna)   1
Fletcher, D. B. 2003 (Manchester U)   2
Fletcher, S. 2007 (Hibernian)   7
Foster, R. M. 2005 (Aberdeen)   5
Fotheringham, M. M. 2004 (Dundee)   3
Fowler, J. 2002 (Kilmarnock)   3
Foy, R. A. 2004 (Liverpool)   5
Fraser, S. T. 2000 (Luton T)   4
Freedman, D. A. 1995 (Barnet, C Palace)   8
Fridge, L. 1989 (St Mirren)   2
Fullarton, J. 1993 (St Mirren)   17
Fulton, M. 1980 (St Mirren)   5
Fulton, S. 1991 (Celtic)   5

Gallacher, K. W. 1987 (Dundee U)   7

Meldrum, C. 1996 (Kilmarnock) 6
Melrose, J. 1977 (Partick Th) 8
Millar, M, 2009 (Celtic) 1
Miller, C. 1995 (Rangers) 8
Miller, J. 1987 (Aberdeen, Celtic) 7
Miller, K. 2000 (Hibernian, Rangers) 7
Miller, W. 1978 (Aberdeen) 2
Miller, W. 1991 (Hibernian) 7
Milne, K. 2000 (Hearts) 1
Milne, R. 1982 (Dundee U) 3
Mitchell, C. 2008 (Falkirk) 4
Money, I. C. 1987 (St Mirren) 3
Montgomery, N. A. 2003 (Sheffield U) 2
Morrison, S. A. 2004 (Aberdeen, Dunfermline Ath) 12
Muir, L. 1977 (Hibernian) 1
Mulgrew, C. P. 2006 (Celtic, Wolverhampton W, Aberdeen) 14

Murphy J. 2009 (Motherwell) 4
Murray, H. 2000 (St Mirren) 3
Murray, I. 2001 (Hibernian) 15
Murray, N. 1993 (Rangers) 16
Murray, R. 1993 (Bournemouth) 1
Murray, S. 2004 (Kilmarnock) 2

Narey, D. 1977 (Dundee U) 4
Naismith, S. J. 2006 (Kilmarnock, Rangers) 15
Naysmith, G. A. 1997 (Hearts) 22
Neilson, R. 2000 (Hearts) 1
Nevin, P. 1985 (Chelsea) 5
Nicholas, C. 1981 (Celtic, Arsenal) 6
Nicholson, B. 1999 (Rangers) 7
Nicol, S. 1981 (Ayr U, Liverpool) 14
Nisbet, J. 1989 (Rangers) 5
Noble, D. J. 2003 (West Ham U) 2
Notman, A. M. 1999 (Manchester U) 10

O'Brien, B. 1999 (Blackburn R, Livingston) 6
O'Connor, G. 2003 (Hibernian) 8
O'Donnell, P. 1992 (Motherwell) 8
O'Leary, R. 2008 (Kilmarnock) 2
O'Neil, B. 1992 (Celtic) 7
O'Neil, J. 1991 (Dundee U) 1
O'Neill, M. 1995 (Clyde) 6
Orr, N. 1978 (Morton) 7

Parker, K. 2001 (St Johnstone) 1
Parlane, D. 1977 (Rangers) 2
Paterson, C. 1981 (Hibernian) 2
Paterson, J. 1997 (Dundee U) 9
Payne, G. 1978 (Dundee U) 3
Peacock, L. A. 1997 (Carlisle U) 1
Pearce, A. J. 2008 (Reading) 2
Pearson, S. P. 2003 (Motherwell) 8
Pressley, S. J. 1993 (Rangers, Coventry C, Dundee U) 26
Provan, D. 1977 (Kilmarnock) 1
Prunty, B. 2004 (Aberdeen) 6

Quinn, P. C. 2004 (Motherwell) 3
Quinn, R. 2006 (Celtic) 9

Rae, A. 1991 (Millwall) 8
Rae, G. 1999 (Dundee) 6
Redford, I. 1981 (Rangers) 2
Reid, B. 1991 (Rangers) 4
Reid, C. 1993 (Hibernian) 3
Reid, M. 1982 (Celtic) 2
Reid, R. 1977 (St Mirren) 3
Reilly, A. 2004 (Wycombe W) 1
Renicks, S. 1997 (Hamilton A) 1
Reynolds, M. 2007 (Motherwell) 9
Rice, B. 1985 (Hibernian) 1
Richardson, L. 1980 (St Mirren) 2
Riordan, D. G. 2004 (Hibernian) 5
Ritchie, A. 1980 (Morton) 1
Ritchie, P. S. 1996 (Hearts) 7
Robertson, A. 1991 (Rangers) 1
Robertson, C. 1977 (Rangers) 1
Robertson, D. 1987 (Aberdeen) 7
Robertson, D. 2007 (Dundee U) 4
Robertson, G. A. 2004 (Nottingham F, Rotherham U) 15
Robertson, H. 1994 (Aberdeen) 2
Robertson, J. 1985 (Hearts) 2
Robertson, L. 1993 (Rangers) 3
Robertson, S. 1998 (St Johnstone) 2
Roddie, A. 1992 (Aberdeen) 5
Ross, G. 2007 (Dunfermline Ath) 1

Ross, T. W. 1977 (Arsenal) 1
Rowson, D. 1997 (Aberdeen) 5
Russell, R. 1978 (Rangers) 3

Salton, D. B. 1992 (Luton T) 6
Samson, C. I. 2004 (Kilmarnock) 6
Scobbie, T. 2008 (Falkirk) 5
Scott, M. 2006 (Livingston) 1
Scott, P. 1994 (St Johnstone) 4
Scrimgour, D. 1997 (St Mirren) 3
Seaton, A. 1998 (Falkirk) 1
Severin, S. D. 2000 (Hearts) 10
Shannon, R. 1987 (Dundee) 7
Sharp, G. M. 1982 (Everton) 1
Sharp, R. 1990 (Dunfermline Ath) 4
Sheerin, P. 1996 (Southampton) 1
Shields, G. 1997 (Rangers) 2
Shinnie, A. 2009 (Dundee) 2
Simmons, S. 2003 (Hearts) 1
Simpson, N. 1982 (Aberdeen) 11
Sinclair, G. 1977 (Dumbarton) 1
Skilling, M. 1993 (Kilmarnock) 2
Smith, B. M. 1992 (Celtic) 5
Smith, C. 2008 (St Mirren) 2
Smith, D. L. 2006 (Motherwell) 2
Smith, G. 1978 (Rangers) 1
Smith, G. 2004 (Rangers) 8
Smith, H. G. 1987 (Hearts) 2
Smith, S. 2007 (Rangers) 1
Sneddon, A. 1979 (Celtic) 1
Snodgrass, R. 2008 (Livingston) 2
Soutar, D. 2003 (Dundee) 11
Speedie, D. R. 1985 (Chelsea) 1
Spencer, J. 1991 (Rangers) 3
Stanton, P. 1977 (Hibernian) 1
Stark, W. 1985 (Aberdeen) 1
Stephen, R. 1983 (Dundee) 1
Stevens, G. 1977 (Motherwell) 1
Stevenson, L. 2008 (Hibernian) 8
Stewart, C. 2002 (Kilmarnock) 1
Stewart, J. 1978 (Kilmarnock, Middlesbrough) 3
Stewart, M. J. 2000 (Manchester U) 17
Stewart, M. 1979 (Dundee U, West Ham U) 12
Stillie, D. 1995 (Aberdeen) 14
Strachan, G. D. 1980 (Aberdeen) 1
Strachan, G. D. 1998 (Coventry C) 7
Sturrock, P. 1977 (Dundee U) 9
Sweeney, P. H. 2004 (Millwall) 8
Sweeney, S. 1991 (Clydebank) 7

Tarrant, N. K. 1999 (Aston Villa) 5
Teale, G. 1997 (Clydebank, Ayr U) 6
Telfer, P. N. 1993 (Luton T) 3
Thomas, K. 1993 (Hearts) 8
Thompson, S. 1997 (Dundee U) 12
Thomson, K. 2005 (Hibernian) 6
Thomson, W. 1977 (Partick Th, St Mirren) 10
Tolmie, J. 1980 (Morton) 1
Tortolano, J. 1987 (Hibernian) 2
Turner, I. 2005 (Everton) 6
Tweed, S. 1993 (Hibernian) 3

Wales, G. 2000 (Hearts) 1
Walker, A. 1988 (Celtic) 1
Wallace, I. A. 1978 (Coventry C) 1
Wallace, L. 2007 (Hearts) 10
Wallace, R. 2004 (Celtic, Sunderland) 4
Walsh, C. 1984 (Nottingham F) 5
Wark, J. 1977 (Ipswich T) 8
Watson, A. 1981 (Aberdeen) 4
Watson, K. 1977 (Rangers) 1
Watt, M. 1991 (Aberdeen) 12
Watt. S. M. 2005 (Chelsea) 5
Webster, A. 2003 (Hearts) 2
Whiteford, A. 1997 (St Johnstone) 1
Whittaker, S. G. 2005 (Hibernian) 18
Whyte, D. 1987 (Celtic) 9
Wilkie, L. 2000 (Dundee) 6
Will, J. A. 1992 (Arsenal) 3
Williams, G. 2002 (Nottingham F) 9
Wilson, M. 2004 (Dundee U, Celtic) 19
Wilson, S. 1999 (Rangers) 7
Wilson, T. 1983 (St Mirren) 1
Wilson, T. 1988 (Nottingham F) 4
Winnie, D. 1988 (St Mirren) 1
Woods, M. 2006 (Sunderland) 2

Wright, P. 1989 (Aberdeen, QPR)	3
Wright, S. 1991 (Aberdeen)	14
Wright, T. 1987 (Oldham Ath)	1

Young, Darren 1997 (Aberdeen)	8
Young, Derek 2000 (Aberdeen)	5

WALES

Adams, N. W. 2008 (Bury, Leicester C)	5
Aizlewood, M. 1979 (Luton T)	2
Allen, J. M. 2008 (Swansea C)	10
Anthony, B. 2005 (Cardiff C)	8
Baddeley, L. M. 1996 (Cardiff C)	2
Balcombe, S. 1982 (Leeds U)	1
Bale, G. 2006 (Southampton, Tottenham H)	4
Barnhouse, D. J. 1995 (Swansea C)	3
Basey, G. W. 2009 (Charlton Ath)	1
Bater, P. T. 1977 (Bristol R)	2
Beevers, L. J. 2005 (Boston U, Lincoln C)	7
Bellamy, C. D. 1996 (Norwich C)	8
Birchall, A. S. 2003 (Arsenal, Mansfield T)	12
Bird, A. 1993 (Cardiff C)	6
Blackmore, C. 1984 (Manchester U)	3
Blake, D. J. 2007 (Cardiff C)	10
Blake, N. A. 1991 (Cardiff C)	5
Blaney, S. D. 1997 (West Ham U)	3
Bodin, P. J. 1983 (Cardiff C)	1
Bowen, J. P. 1993 (Swansea C)	5
Bowen, M. R. 1983 (Tottenham H)	3
Boyle, T. 1982 (C Palace)	1
Brace, D. P. 1995 (Wrexham)	6
Bradley, M. S. 2007 (Walsall)	10
Brough, M. 2003 (Notts Co)	3
Brown, J. D. 2008 (Cardiff C)	6
Brown, J. R. 2003 (Gillingham)	7
Byrne, M. T. 2003 (Bolton W)	1
Calliste, R. T. 2005 (Manchester U, Liverpool)	15
Carpenter, R. E. 2005 (Burnley)	1
Cegielski, K. 1977 (Wrexham)	2
Chapple, S. R. 1992 (Swansea C)	8
Charles, J. M. 1979 (Swansea C)	3
Church, S. R. 2008 (Reading)	12
Clark, J. 1978 (Manchester U, Derby Co)	7
Coates, J. S. 1996 (Swansea C)	5
Coleman, C. 1990 (Swansea C)	3
Collins, J. M. 2003 (Cardiff C)	7
Collins, M. J. 2007 (Fulham, Swansea C)	2
Collison, J. D. 2008 (West Ham U)	7
Cotterill, D. R. G. B. 2005 (Bristol C, Wigan Ath)	11
Coyne, D. 1992 (Tranmere R)	2
Craig, N. L. 2009 (Everton)	1
Critchell, K. A. R. 2005 (Southampton)	3
Crofts, A. L. 2005 (Gillingham)	10
Crowell, M. T. 2004 (Wrexham)	7
Curtis, A. T. 1977 (Swansea C)	1
Davies, A. 1982 (Manchester U)	6
Davies, A. G. 2006 (Cambridge U)	6
Davies, A. R. 2005 (Southampton, Yeovil T)	14
Davies, C. M. 2005 (Oxford U, Verona, Oldham Ath)	9
Davies, D. 1999 (Barry T)	1
Davies, G. M. 1993 (Hereford U, C Palace)	1
Davies, I. C. 1978 (Norwich C)	1
Davies, L. 2005 (Bangor C)	1
Davies, R. J. 2006 (WBA)	4
Davies, S. 1999 (Peterborough U, Tottenham H)	10
Day, R. 2000 (Manchester C, Mansfield T)	11
Deacy, N. 1977 (PSV Eindhoven)	1
De-Vulgt, L. S. 2002 (Swansea C)	2
Dibble, A. 1983 (Cardiff C)	3
Doyle, S. C. 1979 (Preston NE, Huddersfield T)	2
Duffy, R. M. 2005 (Portsmouth)	7
Dwyer, P. J. 1979 (Cardiff C)	1
Eardley, N. 2007 (Oldham Ath)	9
Earnshaw, R. 1999 (Cardiff C)	10
Easter, D. J. 2006 (Cardiff C)	1
Ebdon, M. 1990 (Everton)	1
Edwards, C. N. H. 1996 (Swansea C)	7
Edwards, D. A. 2006 (Shrewsbury T, Luton T, Wolverhampton W)	9
Edwards, R. I. 1977 (Chester)	2
Edwards, R. W. 1991 (Bristol C)	13
Evans, A. 1977 (Bristol R)	1

Evans, C. 2007 (Manchester C)	9
Evans, K. 1999 (Leeds U, Cardiff C)	4
Evans, P. S. 1996 (Shrewsbury T)	1
Evans, S. J. 2001 (C Palace)	2
Evans, T. 1995 (Cardiff C)	3
Fish, N. 2005 (Cardiff C)	2
Fleetwood, S. 2005 (Cardiff C)	5
Flynn, C. P. 2007 (Crewe Alex)	1
Folland, R. W. 2000 (Oxford U)	1
Foster, M. G. 1993 (Tranmere R)	1
Fowler, L. A. 2003 (Coventry C, Huddersfield T)	9
Freestone, R. 1990 (Chelsea)	1
Gabbidon, D. L. 1999 (WBA, Cardiff C)	17
Gale, D. 1983 (Swansea C)	2
Gall, K. A. 2002 (Bristol R, Yeovil T)	8
Gibson, N. D. 1999 (Tranmere R, Sheffield W)	11
Giggs, R. J. 1991 (Manchester U)	1
Gilbert, P. 2005 (Plymouth Arg)	12
Giles, D. C. 1977 (Cardiff C, Swansea C, C Palace)	4
Giles, P. 1982 (Cardiff C)	3
Graham, D. 1991 (Manchester U)	1
Green, R. M. 1998 (Wolverhampton W)	16
Griffith, C. 1990 (Cardiff C)	1
Griffiths, C. 1991 (Shrewsbury T)	1
Grubb, D. 2007 (Bristol C)	1
Gunter, C. 2006 (Cardiff C, Tottenham H)	8
Haldane, L. O. 2007 (Bristol R)	1
Hall, G. D. 1990 (Chelsea)	1
Hartson, J. 1994 (Luton T, Arsenal)	9
Haworth, S. O. 1997 (Cardiff C, Coventry C, Wigan Ath)	12
Hennessey, W. R. 2006 (Wolverhampton W)	6
Hillier, I. M. 2001 (Tottenham H, Luton T)	5
Hodges, G. 1983 (Wimbledon)	5
Holden, A. 1984 (Chester C)	1
Holloway, C. D. 1999 (Exeter C)	2
Hopkins, J. 1982 (Fulham)	5
Hopkins, S. A. 1999 (Wrexham)	1
Huggins, D. S. 1996 (Bristol C)	1
Hughes, D. 2005 (Kaiserslautern, Regensburg)	2
Hughes, D. R. 1994 (Southampton)	1
Hughes, I. 1992 (Bury)	11
Hughes, L. M. 1983 (Manchester U)	5
Hughes, R. D. 1996 (Aston Villa, Shrewsbury T)	13
Hughes, W. 1977 (WBA)	3
Jackett, K. 1981 (Watford)	2
Jacobson, J. M. 2006 (Cardiff C, Bristol R)	15
James, L. R. S. 2006 (Southampton)	10
James, R. M. 1977 (Swansea C)	3
Jarman, L. 1996 (Cardiff C)	10
Jeanne, L. C. 1999 (QPR)	8
Jelleyman, G. A. 1999 (Peterborough U)	1
Jenkins, L. D. 1998 (Swansea C)	9
Jenkins, S. R. 1993 (Swansea C)	2
Jones, C. T. 2007 (Swansea C)	1
Jones, E. P. 2000 (Blackpool)	1
Jones, F. 1981 (Wrexham)	1
Jones, J. A. 2001 (Swansea C)	3
Jones, L. 1982 (Cardiff C)	3
Jones, M. A. 2004 (Wrexham)	4
Jones, M. G. 1998 (Leeds U)	7
Jones, P. L. 1992 (Liverpool)	12
Jones, R. A. 1994 (Sheffield W)	3
Jones, S. J. 2005 (Swansea C)	2
Jones, V. 1979 (Bristol R)	2
Kendall, L. M. 2001 (C Palace)	2
Kendall, M. 1978 (Tottenham H)	1
Kenworthy, J. R. 1994 (Tranmere R)	3
King, A. 2008 (Leicester C)	6
Knott, G. R. 1996 (Tottenham H)	1
Law, B. J. 1990 (QPR)	2
Lawless, A. 2006 (Torquay U)	1
Ledley, J. C. 2005 (Cardiff C)	5

Letheran, G. 1977 (Leeds U)	2
Letheran, K. C. 2006 (Swansea C)	1
Lewis, D. 1982 (Swansea C)	9
Lewis, J. 1983 (Cardiff C)	1
Llewellyn, C. M. 1998 (Norwich C)	14
Loveridge, J. 1982 (Swansea C)	3
Low, J. D. 1999 (Bristol R, Cardiff C)	1
Lowndes, S. R. 1979 (Newport Co, Millwall)	4
MacDonald, S. B. 2006 (Swansea C)	18
McCarthy, A. J. 1994 (QPR)	3
McDonald, C. 2006 (Cardiff C)	3
Mackin, L. 2006 (Wrexham)	1
Maddy, P. 1982 (Cardiff C)	2
Margetson, M. W. 1992 (Manchester C)	7
Martin, A. P. 1999 (C Palace)	1
Martin, D. A. 2006 (Notts Co)	1
Marustik, C. 1982 (Swansea C)	7
Maxwell, C. 2009 (Wrexham)	2
Maxwell, L. J. 1999 (Liverpool, Cardiff C)	14
Meaker, M. J. 1994 (QPR)	2
Melville, A. K. 1990 (Swansea C, Oxford U)	2
Micallef, C. 1982 (Cardiff C)	3
Morgan, A. M. 1995 (Tranmere R)	4
Morgan, C. 2004 (Wrexham, Milton Keynes D)	12
Morris, A. J. 2009 (Cardiff C)	1
Moss, D. M. 2003 (Shrewsbury T)	6
Mountain, P. D. 1997 (Cardiff C)	2
Mumford, A. O. 2003 (Swansea C)	4
Nardiello, D. 1978 (Coventry C)	1
Neilson, A. B. 1993 (Newcastle U)	7
Nicholas, P. 1978 (C Palace, Arsenal)	3
Nogan, K. 1990 (Luton T)	2
Nogan, L. M. 1991 (Oxford U)	1
Nyatanga, L. J. 2005 (Derby Co)	10
Oster, J. M. 1997 (Grimsby T, Everton)	9
Owen, G. 1991 (Wrexham)	8
Page, R. J. 1995 (Watford)	4
Parslow, D. 2005 (Cardiff C)	4
Partington, J. M. 2009 (Bournemouth)	1
Partridge, D. W. 1997 (West Ham U)	1
Pascoe, C. 1983 (Swansea C)	4
Pearce, S. 2006 (Bristol C)	3
Pejic, S. M. 2003 (Wrexham)	6
Pembridge, M. A. 1991 (Luton T)	1
Perry, J. 1990 (Cardiff C)	3
Peters, M. 1992 (Manchester C, Norwich C)	3
Phillips, D. 1984 (Plymouth Arg)	3
Phillips, G. R. 2001 (Swansea C)	3
Phillips, L. 1979 (Swansea C, Charlton Ath)	2
Pipe, D. R. 2003 (Coventry C, Notts Co)	12
Pontin, K. 1978 (Cardiff C)	1
Powell, I. 1991 (Southampton)	4
Powell, L. 2004 (Leicester C)	3
Powell, R. 2006 (Bolton W)	2
Price, J. J. 1998 (Swansea C)	7
Price, L. P. 2005 (Ipswich T)	10
Price, M. D. 2001 (Everton, Hull C, Scarborough)	13
Price, P. 1981 (Luton T)	1
Pritchard, M. O. 2006 (Swansea C)	2
Pugh, D. 1982 (Doncaster R)	2
Pugh, S. 1993 (Wrexham)	2
Pulis, A. J. 2006 (Stoke C)	5
Ramasut, M. W. T. 1997 (Bristol R)	4
Ramsey, A. J. 2008, (Cardiff C, Arsenal)	11
Ratcliffe, K. 1981 (Everton)	2
Ready, K. 1992 (QPR)	5
Rees, A. 1984 (Birmingham C)	1
Rees, J. M. 1990 (Luton T)	3
Rees, M. R. 2003 (Millwall)	4
Ribeiro, C. M. 2008 (Bristol C)	3

Roberts, A. M. 1991 (QPR)	2
Roberts, C. J. 1999 (Cardiff C)	1
Roberts, G. 1983 (Hull C)	1
Roberts, G. W. 1997 (Liverpool, Panionios, Tranmere R)	11
Roberts, J. G. 1977 (Wrexham)	1
Roberts, N. W. 1999 (Wrexham)	3
Roberts, P. 1997 (Porthmadog)	1
Roberts, S. I. 1999 (Swansea C)	13
Roberts, S. W. 2000 (Wrexham)	3
Robinson, C. P. 1996 (Wolverhampton W)	6
Robinson, J. R. C. 1992 (Brighton & HA, Charlton Ath)	5
Rowlands, A. J. R. 1996 (Manchester C)	5
Rush, I. 1981 (Liverpool)	2
Savage, R. W. 1995 (Crewe Alex)	3
Sayer, P. A. 1977 (Cardiff C)	2
Searle, D. 1991 (Cardiff C)	6
Slatter, D. 2000 (Chelsea)	6
Slatter, N. 1983 (Bristol R)	6
Somner, M. J. 2004 (Brentford)	2
Speed, G. A. 1990 (Leeds U)	3
Spender, S. 2005 (Wrexham)	6
Stevenson, N. 1982 (Swansea C)	2
Stevenson, W. B. 1977 (Leeds U)	3
Stock, B. B. 2003 (Bournemouth)	4
Symons, C. J. 1991 (Portsmouth)	2
Taylor, G. K. 1995 (Bristol R)	4
Taylor, N. J. 2008 (Wrexham)	5
Taylor, R. F. 2008 (Chelsea)	1
Thomas, D. G. 1977 (Leeds U)	3
Thomas, D. J. 1998 (Watford)	2
Thomas, J. A. 1996 (Blackburn R)	21
Thomas, Martin R. 1979 (Bristol R)	2
Thomas, Mickey R. 1977 (Wrexham)	2
Thomas, S. 2001 (Wrexham)	5
Tibbott, L. 1977 (Ipswich T)	2
Tipton, M. J. 1998 (Oldham Ath)	6
Tolley, J. C. 2001 (Shrewsbury T)	12
Tudur-Jones, O. 2006 (Swansea C)	3
Twiddy, C. 1995 (Plymouth Arg)	3
Valentine, R. D. 2001 (Everton, Darlington)	8
Vaughan, D. O. 2003 (Crewe Alex)	8
Vaughan, N. 1982 (Newport Co)	2
Vokes, S. M. 2007 (Bournemouth, Wolverhampton W)	11
Walsh, D. 2000 (Wrexham)	8
Walsh, I. P. 1979 (C Palace, Swansea C)	2
Walton, M. 1991 (Norwich C.)	1
Ward, D. 1996 (Notts Co)	2
Warlow, O. J. 2007 (Lincoln C)	2
Weston, R. D. 2001 (Arsenal, Cardiff C)	4
Whitfield, P. M. 2003 (Wrexham)	1
Wiggins, R. 2006 (C Palace)	9
Williams, A. P. 1998 (Southampton)	9
Williams, A. S. 1996 (Blackburn R)	16
Williams, D. 1983 (Bristol R)	1
Williams, D. I. L. 1998 (Liverpool, Wrexham)	9
Williams, D. T. 2006 (Yeovil T)	1
Williams, E. 1997 (Caernarfon T)	2
Williams, G. 1983 (Bristol R)	2
Williams, G. A. 2003 (C Palace)	5
Williams, M. 2001 (Manchester U)	10
Williams, M. P. 2006 (Wrexham)	14
Williams, M. R. 2006 (Wrexham)	2
Williams, O. fon 2007 (Crewe Alex, Stockport Co)	11
Williams, R. 2007 (Middlesbrough)	10
Williams, S. J. 1995 (Wrexham)	4
Wilmot, R. 1982 (Arsenal)	6
Wilson, J. S. 2009 (Bristol C)	2
Worgan, L. J. 2005 (Milton Keynes D, Rushden & D)	5
Wright, A. A. 1998 (Oxford U)	3
Young, S. 1996 (Cardiff C)	5

FA SCHOOLS & YOUTH GAMES 2008–09

ENGLAND UNDER-16

Afobe, Aneke, Rees (Arsenal); Butland (Birmingham C); Billington (Blackburn R); Cousins, Morris (Charlton Ath); Blackman, Chalobah, Deen-Conteh, McEachran (Chelsea); Barkley, Bidwell (Everton); Wickham (Ipswich T); Garbutt (Leeds U); Coady, Robinson, Wisdom (Liverpool); Johnstone, Keane, Morrison, Thorpe (Manchester U); Atkinson, Fowler, Pilatos (Middlesbrough); Laing (Sunderland); Berahino, Thorne (West Bromwich Albion); Fanimo, Hall (West Ham U); Ismail (Wolverhampton W).

SKY SPORTS VICTORY SHIELD

3 Oct *(in Ballymena).*

Northern Ireland 0   England 6 *(Afobe 7, 57, Oliver 42 (og), Barkley 53, Fowler 74, Morrison 80)*

England: Butland; Pilatos (Morris 51), Garbutt, McEachran, Lang, Thorpe (Chalobah 51), Ismail (Hall 41), Barkley, Afobe (Fowler 64), Aneke (Rees 41), Morrison.

31 Oct *(in Llanelli).*

Wales 0   England 1 *(Afobe 75)*

England: Blackman; Morris (Pilatos 41), Robinson, Rees (Chalobah 74), Laing, Wisdom, Fowler (Ismail 41), Barkley, Afobe, Hall (Wickham 64), Deen-Conteh (Thorne 58).

28 Nov *(in Lincoln).*

England 2 *(Afobe 11, Wickham 43)*   **Scotland 0**   5119

England: Johnstone; Atkinson (Wisdom 41), Garbutt, Thorne (Fanimo 76), Laing, Thorpe, Pilatos, Barkley (Cousins 71), Afobe, Wickham (Berahino 64), Deen-Conteh (Ismail 41).

Scotland 2, Wales 1
Scotland 2, Northern Ireland 2
Northern Ireland 0, Wales 1

	P	W	D	L	F	A	GD	Pts
England	3	3	0	0	9	0	9	9
Scotland	3	1	1	1	4	5	–1	4
Wales	3	1	0	2	2	3	–1	3
Northern Ireland	3	0	1	2	2	9	–7	1

MONTAIGU TOURNAMENT

8 Apr

England 3 *(Berahino 3, 56, Bidwell 33)*   **Russia 1**

England: Butland; Pilatos, Bidwell, Barkley, Thorpe, Chalobah, Thorne, Aneke (Cousins), Berahino (Keane), McEachran (Fowler), Hall (Coady).

10 Apr

England 3 *(Keane 45, Barkley 64, Berahino 66)*   **UAE 0**

England: Butland; Pilatos, Atkinson (Thorpe), Barkley, Billington, Chalobah, Keane (Bidwell), Cousins, Berahino (Aneke), Fowler (Hall), Coady.

11 Apr

England 3 *(Hall 21, Cousins 44, Bidwell 67 (pen))*
Ivory Coast 0

England: Blackman; Atkinson, Bidwell, Thorpe, Billington, Coady, Thorne, Cousins (Chalobah), Aneke (Pilatos), Fowler (Berahino), Hall.

13 Apr

England 0   Germany 0

(England won 2-1 on penalties).
England: Butland; Pilatos, Bidwell, Barkley, Thorpe, Chalobah, Aneke (Hall 70), Berahino, Keane, Atkinson, Coady.

ENGLAND UNDER-17

Afobe, Aneke, Banton, Freeman, Frimpong, Nicholas, Wilshere (Arsenal); Gardner (Aston Villa); Hitchcock (Blackburn R); Jenkinson, Shelvey (Charlton Ath); Knott, McEachran (Chelsea); Baxter (Everton); Marsh-Brown (Fulham); Wickham (Ipswich T); Garbutt, McCann (Leeds U); Parkes (Leicester C); Chamberlain, Ince (Liverpool); Benali (Manchester C); Fryers, Johnstone, Lingard, Tunnicliffe (Manchester U); Edwards, Park (Middlesbrough); Habergham, Steer (Norwich C); Head (Plymouth Arg); Hurst (Portsmouth); Baggie, Walcott (Reading); Alnwick, Laing (Sunderland); Bostock (Tottenham H); Oshodi (Watford); Allsopp, Mantom, Elford-Alliyu (West Bromwich Albion); Mendez-Laing, Reckord (Wolverhampton W).

NORDIC TOURNAMENT (in Sweden)

28 July *(in Stenungsund).*

England 1 *(Knott 5)*   **Finland 0**

England: Allsop; Reckord (Garbutt 52), Hurst, Nicholas, Parkes, Mendez-Laing (Wickham 57), Aneke (McCann 40), Walcott (Lingard 82), Freeman (Marsh-Brown 71), Edwards, Knott (Banton 71).

29 July *(in Kungshamn).*

England 1 *(Wickham 61)*   **Iceland 0**

England: Alnwick; Marsh-Brown, Nicholas, Parkes, Garbutt, McCann (Edwards 40), Mendez-Laing (Freeman 51), Lingard (Knott 51), Aneke (Reckord 74), Wickham (Hurst 67), Banton (Walcott 51).

31 July *(in Stromstad).*

England 0   Norway 0   551

England: Allsop; Reckord (Garbutt 72), Hurst, Nicholas, Parkes, Aneke, Walcott (Banton 75), Freeman (Mendez-Laing 68), Wickham, Edwards (Marsh-Brown 79), Knott.

2 Aug *(in Kungshamn).*

England 1 *(Walcott 19)*   **Denmark 6** *(Dumec 8, Hvilsom 46, Eriksen 53, Boilsen 67 (pen), Green 79, Larsen 81)*

England: Alnwick; Marsh-Brown, Reckord, Hurst, Nicholas, Walcott, Banton (Wickham 65), Garbutt (Parkes 53), Lingard (Aneke 53), McCann (Freeman 53), Edwards (Mendez-Laing 63).

27 Aug *(at Rushden).*

England 1 *(Tunnicliffe 13)*   **Portugal 2** *(Barros 40, 44)*
1039

England: Allsop; Marsh-Brown, Tunnicliffe, Oshodi, Mendez-Laing, Bostock, Walcott (Hitchcock 74), Fryers, Edwards (Benali 56), Parkes, Park (Baggie 65).

29 Aug *(at Peterborough).*

England 1 *(Walcott 77)*   **Israel 0**   2002

England: Chamberlain; Reckord, Oshodi, Mantom, Mendez-Laing (Park 57), Benali, Hitchcock (Walcott 72), Bostock, Baggie (Tunnicliffe 60), Jenkinson, Parkes.

31 Aug *(at Northampton).*

England 2 *(Tunnicliffe 27, 80)*   **Italy 0**   1378

England: Allsop; Marsh-Brown, Oshodi (Mantom 70), Parkes, Fryers, Walcott, Tunnicliffe, Bostock, Edwards, Park (Mendez-Laing 78), Hitchcock (Benali 74).

22 Oct *(in Tenerife).*

Armenia 0   England 0

England: Steer; Marsh-Brown, Fryers, Frimpong, Tunnicliffe, Wilshere, Baxter, Bostock (Walcott 68), Freeman (Knott 54), Shelvey, Parkes.

24 Oct *(in Tenerife).*

Estonia 0   England 7 *(Parkes 19, Baxter 36, Shelvey 49, Freeman 51, Tamm 62 (og), Head 63, Tunnicliffe 80)*

England: Allsop; Hurst, Oshodi, Parkes, Reckord, Frimpong (Shelvey 41), Tunnicliffe, Wilshere (Walcott 55), Baxter, Knott, Freeman (Head 51).

27 Oct *(in Tenerife).*
Spain 1 *(Fryers 80 (og))* **England 1** *(Walcott 10)*
England: Steer; Hurst (Marsh-Brown 82), Ashodi, Parkes, Reckord, Frimpong, Wilshere, Baxter, Shelvey, Knott (Fryers 63), Walcott (Bostock 76).

UEFA UNDER-17 CHAMPIONSHIP

21 Feb *(in Albufeira).*
Portugal 2 *(Barros 2)* **England 0**
England: Johnstone; Marsh-Brown, Parkes (Oshodi 70), Baxter, Tunnicliffe (Frimpong 60), Afobe (Elford-Alliyu 46), Walcott (McCann 56), Ince, Freeman (Benali 46), Laing, Fryers (Reckord 56).

22 Feb *(in Lagos).*
France 2 *(Gadi 2, Situ 17)* **England 0**
England: Steer; Reckord (Fryers 71), Oshodi, Parkes (Marsh-Brown 65), Tunnicliffe, Walcott (Ince 41), Freeman (Afobe 41), Frimpong, Laing, Benali, Elford-Alliyu (McCann 58).

24 Feb *(in Ferreiras).*
Israel 0   England 4 *(Elford-Alliyu 13, Baxter 35, Afobe 61, Freeman 67)*
England: Johnstone; Marsh-Brown, McCann, Oshodi, Parkes (Laing 73), Baxter, Afobe (Walcott 64), Freeman, Frimpong (Tunnicliffe 53), Fryers, Elford-Alliyu (Ince 73).

25 Mar *(in Szombathely).*
Portugal 0   England 1 *(Freeman 58)*
England: Steer; Hurst, Garbutt (Habergham), Gardner, Laing, Parkes, Shelvey, Baxter, Freeman (Afobe), Bostock, Elford-Alliyu.

27 Mar *(in Szombathely).*
England 2 *(Freeman 40, Afobe 77)* **Serbia 1**
England: Steer; Hurst, Garbutt, Gardner, Laing, Parkes, Shelvey, Baxter, Freeman, Bostock, Elford-Alliyu (Afobe).

30 Mar *(in Szombathely).*
Hungary 0   England 2 *(Walcott 57, Afobe 60)*
England: Johnstone; Hurst (Freeman 67), Gardner (Elford-Alliyu 41), Parkes, Afobe, Ince, McEachran, Bostock, Oshodi, Walcott, Habergham.

6 May *(in Gera).*
England 1 *(Garbutt 70)*
Holland 1 *(Ozyakup 3)*
England: Steer; Hurst, Garbutt, Gardner, Parkes, Bostock (Tunnicliffe 68), Baxter, Wilshere, Freeman (Afobe 76), Oshodi, Elford-Alliyu (Shelvey 58).

ENGLAND UNDER-19

Gibbs, Hoyte G, Lansbury, Murphy, Thomas, Wilshere (Arsenal); Baker, Delfouneso (Aston Villa); Pearce (Birmingham C); Obadeyi (Bolton W); Bertrand, Cork, Mellis, Sinclair, Woods (Chelsea); Elito (Colchester U); Hills, Moses (Crystal Palace); Gosling, Rodwell (Everton); Briggs, (Fulham); Smithies (Huddersfield T); Delph, White (Leeds U); Chambers, Mattock (Leicester C); Kelly (Liverpool); Mee, Sturridge, Trippier, Tutte (Manchester U); Amos, Drinkwater, James, Rose, Welbeck (Manchester U); Franks, Steele (Middlesbrough); Ranger (Newcastle U); Reid (Nottingham F); Walker (Sheffield U); Chandler, Henderson, Waghorn (Sunderland); Button, Obika, Parrett (Tottenham H); Sears, Spence, Tomkins (West Ham U).

UEFA CHAMPIONSHIP 2008

14 July *(in Jablonec).*
Czech Republic 2 *(Necid 55, 58)* **England 0** 6153
England: Button; Cork, Gosling (Chandler 78), Tomkins, Pearce, Sinclair (Obadeyi 64), Gibbs, Sturridge, Sears, Rose, Bertrand.

17 July *(in Jablonec).*
England 0   Italy 0
England: Button; Cork, Tomkins, Pearce, Gibbs, Sturridge, Sears (Sinclair 88), Rose (Delph 78), Bertrand, Moses, Mee.

20 July *(in Liberec).*
England 3 *(Mee 48, Sears 68 (pen), Sturridge 85)*
Greece 0 1047
England: Button; Cork, Mattock, Pearce, Gibbs, Sturridge, Sears (Sinclair 83), Rose, Bertrand (Gosling 87), Moses (Delph 73), Mee.

9 Sept *(at Shrewsbury).*
England 2 *(Murphy 68, 70)* **Holland 1** *(Wijnaldum 41)* 4260
England Steele; Trippier, Hills (Briggs 78), Rodwell (Woods 46), Pearce, Hoyte, Franks (Thomas 60), Lansbury, Welbeck, Murphy, Moses (Elito 73).

8 Oct *(in Coleraine).*
England 3 *(Drinkwater 6, Delfouneso 39, Lansbury 78)*
Albania 0
England: Steele; Trippier, Hoyte, Spence, Hills, Woods, Drinkwater, Moses, Murphy (Elito 67), Lansbury, Welbeck (Delfouneso 20).

10 Oct *(in Belfast).*
Northern Ireland 1 *(Lawrie 2)* **England 3** *(Lansbury 25, 39 (pen), Murphy 84)*
England: Steele; Trippier (Pearce 46), Hoyte, Spence, Hills, Woods, Drinkwater (Rodwell 85), Moses, Murphy, Lansbury, Delfouneso.

13 Oct *(in Newry).*
England 1 *(Moses 28)* **Serbia 4** *(Krsticic 8, Ljajic 19, Aleksic 38, Ignjovski 63)*
England: Amos; Briggs (Hoyte 77), Spence, Rodwell, Pearce, Emmanuel-Thomas (Drinkwater 46), Woods, Lansbury, Moses, Delfouneso, Elito (Hills 46).

18 Nov *(at Colchester).*
England 1 *(Lansbury 29)* **Germany 0** 9692
England: Amos; Trippier (Spence 87), Hills, Rodwell, Hoyte, Baker, Lansbury (Woods 76), Drinkwater, Welbeck (Delfouneso 46), Mellis (Murphy), Moses (Franks 68).

FRIENDLY

10 Feb *(at Bournemouth).*
England 0   Spain 3 *(Falque 5, Jordi 30, Ruiz 61)* 8202
England: Smithies; Trippier (Walker 70), Hills (Reid 70), Rodwell, Spence, Hoyte (Kelly 46), Drinkwater, Gosling (Tutte▪ 61), Delfouneso, (Waghorn 60), Lansbury (Chambers 78), Wilshere.

25 Mar *(at Walsall).*
England 0   Czech Republic 0
England: Steele; Walker, Mattock (White 73), Rodwell, Hoyte, Kelly, Henderson (Tutte 80), Drinkwater, Delfouneso, Obika (Sears 46), Gosling.

UEFA CHAMPIONSHIP 2009

27 May *(at Doncaster).*
England 2 *(Rose 40, Ranger 75)* **Bosnia 0** 1071
England: Steele; Trippier, Mattock, James, Spence, Kelly, Tutte (Moses 59), Drinkwater, Delfouneso (Waghorn 89), Ranger, Rose (Parrett 82).

29 May *(at Bradford).*
England 4 *(Ranger 29, 52, Delfouneso 88, 90)*
Slovakia 1 *(Gal-Andrezy 58)* 3833
England: Steele; Trippier, Mattock, James, Kelly, Hoyte, Moses, Drinkwater (Parrett 88), Delfouneso, Ranger, Rose.

1 June *(at Bramall Lane).*
England 2 *(Ranger 66, Moses 73)*
Scotland 1 *(McDonald 82 (pen))* 2817
England: Steele; Trippier (Spence 76), Mattock (Briggs 80), James, Kelly, Drinkwater (Parrett 46), Delfouneso, Ranger, Rose, Moses, Hoyte.

▪ *Denotes player sent off.*

ENGLAND UNDER-20

Gibbs (Arsenal); Clarke, Albrighton (Aston Villa); Obadeyi (Bolton W); Bertrand, Sinclair (Chelsea); Smalling (Fulham); Clayton, Mee, Sturridge, Vidal (Manchester C); Amos (Manchester U); Walker (Middlesbrough); Colback (Sunderland); Button (Tottenham H); Sears, Stanislaus, Tomkins (West Ham U).

31 Mar *(at QPR)*.
England 2 *(Clarke 20, Sturridge 30)* **Italy 0**   6297
England: Button (Amos 46); Vidal, Bertrand (Mee 76), Walker (Clayton 67), Tomkins (Smalling 46), Clarke, Albrighton (Colback 79), Gibbs, Sturridge (Obadeyi 82), Sears, Sinclair (Stanislaus 65).

SCHOOLS FOOTBALL 2008–09

BOODLES INDEPENDENT SCHOOLS FA CUP 2008-09

FIRST ROUND
Aldenham 0, RGS Newcastle 1
Ardingly 1, Latymer Upper 2
Bolton 2, Grange 2
Bolton won 4-2 on penalties.
Bradfield 2, Brentwood 0
Bristol GS 1, Winchester 4
Charterhouse 2, Bedford Modern 1
Cheadle Hume 1, John Lyon 0
Dulwich College 4, Chigwell 2
Grammar School at Leeds 0, King's School, Chester 2
Haileybury 1, Shrewsbury 6
Highgate 2, City of London 1
Kimbolton 0, Bury GS 1
KES Whitley 3, KCS Wimbledon 2
Manchester GS 6, Westminster 1
QEGS Blackburn 5, Colfe's 0
QEH Bristol 0, St Mary's College, Crosby 5
St Edmund's, Canterbury 0, Hampton 5
St Columba's College 1, Oldham Hume GS 0
Wolverhampton GS 2, Alleyn's 1

SECOND ROUND
Bury GS 7, Dover College 0
Dulwich College 2, Birkdale 6
Frensham Heights 2, Winchester 6
Hampton 5, Highgate 0
KES Whitley 4, Ibstock Place 2
Lancing 3, Charterhouse 0
Malvern 3, Cheadle Hume 2
Manchester GS 3, St Bede's College, Manchester 2
Millfield 4, King's School, Chester 1
QEGS Blackburn 2, Eton 1
Repton 1, RGS Newcastle 1
RGS Newcastle won 9-8 on penalties.
Shrewsbury 3, Forest 4
St Columba's College 4, Bradfield 2
St Mary's College, Crosby 0, Bolton 1
St Bede's School (Hailsham) 10, Norwich 0
Wolverhampton GS 1, Latymer Upper 0

THIRD ROUND
Birkdale 0, Hampton 3
KES Whitley 0, Winchester 1

Lancing 2, Millfield 5
Manchester GS 3, St Bede's School (Hailsham) 2
QEGS Blackburn 2, Forest 0
RGS Newcastle 2, Bury GS 1
St Columba's College 1, Bolton 2
Wolverhampton GS 2, Malvern 1

FOURTH ROUND
Hampton 1, Bolton 1
Hampton won 4-3 on penalties.
QEGS Blackburn 1, Manchester GS 3
RGS Newcastle 0, Millfield 2
Winchester 1, Wolverhampton GS 1
Winchester won 7-6 on penalties.

SEMI-FINALS
Winchester 0, Millfield 7
Hampton 1, Manchester GS 0

FINAL (at Cheltenham Town FC)
Millfield 2 *(Beacher, Dunk (pen))*
Hampton 0
Millfield: A. Norman; L Ellis, D. O'Hare, P. Hartnup, H. Dunk, J. Metters, S. Boulter (A. Amato), C. Laird (J. Gritt), J. Beacher, J. Moss (H. Clarke), E. Thomas.
Hampton: B. Frank; T. Callaghan, T. Page, J. Meldram, D. Mitchell, I. Prowse, S. Highton (T. Michel), J. Parker, M. Richmond (J. Barwick), L. Wells, T. Loffler (J. Halket).
Referee: H. Webb (Yorkshire).

RENSBURG SHEPPARDS ISFA UNDER-16 CUP FINAL

Manchester GS 3, Eton 0
(at Burton Albion).

RENSBURG SHEPPARDS ISFA UNDER-13 CUP FINAL

Grange School 2, Alleyn's School 1
(at Burton Albion).

UNIVERSITY FOOTBALL 2008–09

125th UNIVERSITY MATCH

(at Craven Cottage, 29 March 2009)

Oxford 1   Cambridge 0

Oxford: D. Whylly; T Wherry*, T Squires* (M Flood 90), T Hodgson*, L Farr*, L Weston, C Knight*, J Kelly, R McCrickerd, S Hall (K Desai 90), A Toogood*.
Scorer: S. Hall 10.

Cambridge (squad): S Ferguson, C Maynard, M Little, Ali Hakimi*, J Brown, E Burrows, M Baxter*, M Stark, M Amos*, M Johnson* J Rutt(c)*, M Leung, C Ellis, J Day, P Hartley, S Harrison.

*denotes Old Blue
Oxford have won 49 games, Cambridge 48 and 28 drawn.
Both teams have now scored exactly 197 goals.

WOMEN'S FOOTBALL 2008–09

On the domestic front Vic Akers, arguably the mightiest ever giant of women's football has stepped down after twenty years as manager of Arsenal Ladies. His final season was rewarded with yet another triumphant triple success as his Gunners swept to the Women's Premier League Championship, the Women's Premier league Cup and the Women's FA Cup. In all Akers masterminded 31 domestic and one European Trophy during his stewardship taking Arsenal's success to a level that will be almost impossible to match. He is succeeded at the helm by Tony Gervaise.

Arsenal's league triumph was the closest yet seen in the National Division with the Gunners going into the last game knowing that if their opponents Everton were to beat them, they would lose their crown. In the end Arsenal triumphed by 1-0 and annexed the title on goal difference, the margin being by 17 goals. In all other respects the two teams' statistics were identical which established how far Everton Ladies have progressed. Indeed during the season they became the first team to beat the Gunners in a league match since 16 October 2003. In the Premier League Liverpool who finished 11th and WFC Fulham a place below them were relegated.

In the Northern Division Sunderland were top by a point from Ooh Lincoln and the Wearsiders were thus promoted whilst the bottom two Rotherham United and Tranmere Rovers were relegated.

The Southern Division saw promoted Millwall Lionesses have a renaissance beating second placed Barnet by all of fourteen points. The relegated sides were Ipswich Town and Truro City. The Women's Premier Reserve Division One title was taken by Chelsea with Arsenal second. The Division Two Champions were West Ham with Reading as runners-up. The Mids/North Division One Champions were Leeds with the runners-up being Everton; whilst the Mids/North Division Two honours went to Sunderland with Nottingham Forest coming second.

The FA Women's Cup final sponsored by E.ON played on Monday 4 May 2009 saw Arsenal record their tenth success in ten appearances. The match at Derby's Pride Park saw the Gunners beat Sunderland 2-1 with goals from Katie Chapman after 32 minutes and Karen Little in second half stoppage time during which Sunderland's Kelly McDougall scored an even later consolation effort.

Earlier in the season (26 February 2009) the Tesco Women's Premier League Cup was also annexed by Arsenal. The game played at Gosford Park, Scunthorpe United's ground, ended with a 5-0 victory for the Gunners, over probably their oldest rivals, Doncaster Rovers Belles. The goal-scorers were Kelly Smith who opened the scoring on 5 minutes then added a second on 32 minutes, completing her hat-trick in the 58th minute. The wrap-up came when Alex Scott netted on 67 minutes, with substitute Suzanne Grant claiming the fifth in the 89th minute.

England Ladies continued to progress well on the international scene with Senior Team under Coach Hope Powell having an unbeaten run. They had excellent victories over the Czech Republic, Finland, South Africa, Scotland, Canada and particularly Norway whilst securing creditable draws with France, Spain and Finland. The Under 23s with Coach Brent Hills only played two games beating Norway and losing to the powerful USA. The Under 19s coached by Everton's Mo Marley had an excellent campaign winning 8 matches drawing 3 and losing to two of the top sides namely Germany and the USA. The Under 17s played as many as 12 games and recorded 4 wins with 2 draws and 6 defeats.

The popularity of Women's football still continues to grow and the FA report that it remains the biggest female team sport in the country with over 1.35 million women and girls playing recreational football of which more than 150,000 are playing in affiliated school or club teams. Other happenings of significance included:

- The four County FAs from Yorkshire running in April and May 2009 a wide range of events to promote the development of coaches and support staff for the future demands of the game.
- Sir Trevor Brooking attending to present prizes to Derbyshire's best young female footballers in their Weekend Football Festival.
- The FA and Tesco hosted a Girl's Football Week from 22–28 June inclusive in nine regional events to promote the "next generation of players".
- The Football Association's National Game Strategy was published during the 2008–09 season and its "Women and Girls Strategy" sets out its vision for female football in England over the next four years.
- The intended English Summer Soccer League has been postponed for a further year and will go ahead in 2011.
- There has also been an extension in the experiment involving "mixed football" whereby girls can play with and against boys in the age groups of Under 12, 13 and 14. This experiment will continue until the end of season 2009–10 after which it will receive a full evaluation.
- The Football Association is holding workshops to increase the involvement of female officials, because of the 24,000 registered referees only 1,066 are female. This created the impetus for the innovation of these workshops.
- The Isle of Man Cup Final was this season refereed by all female officials.

There was little doubting that the main recipient at the end of season's FA Women's Football Awards Ceremony would be Vic Ackers. He received the "FA Special Achievement Award" whilst Arsenal took the title of Tesco "Club of the Year" trophy. Other notable achievements recorded were "Player of the Year" Fara Williams (Everton); "Young Player of the Year" Toni Duggan (Everton); and "Manager of the Year" Mick Mulhern (Sunderland). The full list of the recipients was as follows:

Umbro Top Goal Scorer (National Division)	Kelly Smith (Arsenal)
Umbro Top Goal Scorer (Southern Division)	Sam Pittuck (West Ham)
Umbro Top Goal Scorer (Northern Division)	Jodie Michalska (Lincoln)
The FA Young Player of the Year	Toni Duggan (Everton)
The FA Club Media Award	Leeds Carnegie LFC
The FA Club Marketing Award	Nottingham Forest LFC
Tesco Manager of the Year	Mick Mulhern (Sunderland)
Tesco Club of the Year	Arsenal LFC
The FA Best Programme Award	Keynsham Town LFC
The FA Fair Play Award	Rotherham LFC
The FA National Media Award	The Guardian
The FA Regional Media Award	BBC Radio Leeds
Nationwide International Player of the Year	Fara Williams (Everton)
Tesco Players' Player of the Year	Fara Williams (Everton)
The FA Special Achievement Award	Vic Akers (Arsenal)
The FA Tesco Community Award	Sport England National Sports Foundation

KEN GOLDMAN

FA WOMEN'S PREMIER LEAGUE 2008–09

NATIONAL DIVISION

	P	W	D	L	F	A	GD	Pts
Arsenal	22	20	1	1	89	14	75	61
Everton	22	20	1	1	68	10	58	61
Chelsea	22	16	2	4	55	23	32	50
Doncaster R Belles	22	9	6	7	43	36	7	33
Birmingham C	22	10	3	9	39	43	–4	33
Leeds Carnegie	22	8	4	10	32	40	–8	28
Watford	22	7	4	11	31	40	–9	25
Bristol Academy	22	5	8	9	39	49	–10	23
Blackburn R	22	5	3	14	27	52	–25	18
Nottingham F	22	5	2	15	25	59	–34	17
Liverpool	22	4	4	14	28	63	–35	16
WFC Fulham	22	1	6	15	17	64	–47	9

SOUTHERN DIVISION

	P	W	D	L	F	A	GD	Pts
Millwall Lionesses	22	17	3	2	61	14	47	54
Barnet	22	11	7	4	58	33	25	40
West Ham U	22	10	9	3	41	20	21	39
Charlton Ath	22	10	6	6	37	28	9	36
Portsmouth	22	9	6	7	50	36	14	33
Colchester U	22	8	6	8	37	41	–4	30
Cardiff C	22	8	5	9	40	38	2	29
Keynsham T	22	8	3	11	34	49	–15	27
Crystal Palace	22	5	8	9	31	43	–12	23
Brighton & HA	22	5	5	12	28	44	–16	20
Ipswich T	22	5	3	14	19	64	–45	18
Truro C	22	3	5	14	32	58	–26	14

NORTHERN DIVISION

	P	W	D	L	F	A	GD	Pts
Sunderland	22	17	2	3	95	16	79	53
Ooh Lincoln	22	16	4	2	79	15	64	52
Manchester C	22	13	4	5	42	22	20	43
Newcastle U	22	12	5	5	58	28	30	41
Leicester C	22	12	4	6	54	33	21	40
Reading	22	9	6	7	43	31	12	33
Aston Villa	22	10	2	10	49	50	–1	32
Preston NE	22	7	3	12	37	51	–14	24
Sheffield W	22	6	0	16	37	72	–35	18
Curzon Ashton	22	4	4	14	35	70	–35	16
Tranmere R	22	4	2	16	28	76	–48	14
Rotherham U	22	3	2	17	17	110	–93	11

NATIONAL DIVISION RESULTS 2008–09

	Arsenal	Birmingham C	Blackburn R	Bristol Academy	Chelsea	Doncaster R Belles	Everton	Leeds Carnegie	Liverpool	Nottingham F	Watford	WFC Fulham
Arsenal	—	6-2	4-0	3-0	4-1	6-1	0-3	4-0	2-0	5-0	6-1	7-0
Birmingham C	1-3	—	1-1	2-1	0-1	2-2	0-1	3-2	0-1	4-0	3-2	3-1
Blackburn R	0-4	4-1	—	2-2	1-2	1-2	1-3	2-2	0-1	0-3	1-4	1-2
Bristol Academy	1-4	4-2	3-1	—	1-2	1-1	1-3	1-2	6-0	4-2	2-2	1-1
Chelsea	0-2	3-3	4-0	3-0	—	4-1	0-4	3-1	5-0	3-1	1-0	4-1
Doncaster R Belles	0-0	3-1	2-0	4-0	0-1	—	0-3	0-3	2-3	2-1	2-1	7-0
Everton	0-1	4-2	4-2	5-0	1-0	1-0	—	5-0	5-0	7-0	3-1	6-0
Leeds Carnegie	1-6	1-2	0-2	1-1	0-2	3-3	0-0	—	4-1	4-1	1-0	2-1
Liverpool	2-11	2-3	1-2	2-3	1-1	2-5	1-2	1-3	—	1-2	0-1	2-2
Nottingham F	1-5	0-1	0-1	2-2	1-5	1-4	0-3	1-0	2-2	—	1-2	1-0
Watford	0-1	1-2	4-1	3-3	1-5	2-2	0-1	1-0	0-3	3-2	—	2-0
WFC Fulham	0-5	0-1	3-4	2-2	0-5	0-0	1-4	0-2	2-2	1-3	0-0	—

NATIONAL DIVISION LEAGUE – PREVIOUS WINNERS

1992–93	Arsenal	1998–99	Croydon	2004–05	Arsenal
1993–94	Doncaster Belles	1999–00	Croydon	2005–06	Arsenal
1994–95	Arsenal	2000–01	Arsenal	2006–07	Arsenal
1995–96	Croydon	2001–02	Arsenal	2007–08	Arsenal
1996–97	Arsenal	2002–03	Fulham	2008–09	Arsenal
1997–98	Everton	2003–04	Arsenal		

FA TESCO WOMEN'S COMMUNITY SHIELD 2008

Arsenal 1 *(Smith 72)*
Everton 0   1494

(at Macclesfield).
Arsenal: Byrne; Scott, Tracey, Ludlow, Flaherty, Grant C, Smith (Little 75), Yankey, Davison, Carney, Bassett.
Everton: Brown; Easton, Unitt, Williams, Westwood (Hinnigan 81), Johnson, Duggan (Christiansen 90), Scott, Dowie, Potter (Boyle 64), Evans.
Referee: S. Ihringova.

THE FA TESCO WOMEN'S PREMIER LEAGUE CUP 2008–09

FIRST ROUND

Colchester United v Portsmouth Ladies	5-6
Newcastle United v Preston North End	1-2
Reading Women v Barnet Ladies	0-2
Sunderland v Sheffield Wednesday	4-1

SECOND ROUND

Arsenal v Charlton Athletic	6-2
Brighton & Hove Albion v Truro City	3-2
Bristol Academy v Keynsham Town	3-0
Cardiff City v Fulham	1-2
Chelsea v Barnet Ladies	4-0
Millwall Lionesses v Ipswich Town	7-1
Watford v Crystal Palace	3-0
West Ham United v Portsmouth Ladies	1-2
Blackburn Rovers v Rotherham United	7-2
Everton v Birmingham City	2-1
Leeds Carnegie v Manchester City	1-0
Leicester City v Aston Villa	6-2
Preston North End v Curzon Ashton	5-3
Nottingham Forest v Liverpool	4-2
Ooh Lincoln v Sunderland	3-1
Tranmere Rovers v Doncaster Rovers Belles	1-6

THIRD ROUND

Ooh Lincoln v Watford	2-3
Blackburn Rovers v Portsmouth	4-4
Portsmouth won 4-3 on penalties.	
Arsenal v Everton	3-1

Preston North End v Brighton & Hove Albion	1-0
Chelsea v Leeds Carnegie	3-2
Millwall Lionesses v Leicester City	1-3
Fulham v Bristol Academy	4-2
Nottingham Forest v Doncaster Rovers Belles	0-4

QUARTER-FINALS

Leicester City v Arsenal	0-7
Doncaster Rovers Belles v Watford	3-0
Portsmouth v Preston North End	0-1
Chelsea v Fulham	3-0

SEMI-FINALS

Doncaster Rovers Belles v Preston North End	3-1
Chelsea v Arsenal	0-4

FINAL (at Scunthorpe)

Arsenal (2) 5 *(Smith 5, 32, 58, Scott 67, Grant S 89)*	
Doncaster Rovers Belles (0) 0	2753

Arsenal: Byrne; Scott, Ludlow, Grant C, Smith (Bruton 88), Yankey, Davison (Grant S 77), Bassett (Flaherty 81), Little, Chapman, Fahey.
Doncaster Rovers Belles: Hobbs; Weston, Leat, Williams, Utley, Turner, Heckler, Exley, Stevens (Shaw 77), Hughes, Johnson (Chadwick 88).
Referee: S. Rowntree.

THE FA WOMEN'S CUP 2008–09
SPONSORED BY E.ON

PRELIMINARY ROUND

Newcastle Medics v Prudhoe Youth Club	1-4
Teesside Athletic v East Durham United	2-4
Tynedale v St Francis 2000	0-9
Wigan v Morecambe Ladies	4-1
Lancaster City v Wigan Athletic Ladies	0-9
Guiseley Ladies v Sheffield United Community	3-2
Keighley Ladies v Kirklees	4-1
Sheffield Ladies v Barnsley	1-3
Heather St Johns v Oadby & Wigston Girls & Ladies	1-0
Friar Lane & Epworth v Huncote Sports & Social	9-0
Welbeck Welfare Ladies v Marlborough Rovers	14-1
Long Eaton United v Loughborough Foxes	0-4
Oadby Town Women v Clifton Ladies	1-6
West Bridgford v West Bridgford Colts	2-4
Worcester City v Pegasus Ladies	2-3
Hereford Phoenix Ladies v Tipton Town Ladies	14-0
Fairfield Villa v Stoke City	0-3
Ferndale Ladies v Leamington Lions	2-5
Cambridge University v Histon Hornets	1-0
Swanton United Ladies v Hethersett Athletic	0-5
Peterborough v Peterborough Azure	2-2
Peterborough won 5-2 on penalties.	
Woodbridge Town v Thorpe United	7-0
Haverhill Rovers v West Lynn	0-5
Leighton Linslade Ladies v Bedford Ladies	0-6
Arlesey Town Ladies v Daventry Town	8-2
Leighton United v Kingsthorpe Ladies & Girls	6-2
Kettering Town v Woodford United	11-0
St Martins v AFC Kempston Rovers	4-3
Sandy Ladies v Brackley Sports	5-0
Raunds Town v Flitwick Eagles Ladies	3-1
Hitchin Hearts v Runwell Hospital	6-0
Hemel Hempstead Town v Billericay	5-2
Harlow Athletic withdrew v Sawbridgeworth Town w.o.	
Tempest v Runwell & Rayleigh Raiders	2-2
Rayleigh Raiders won 6-5 on penalties.	
Braintree Town v Tring Athletic	2-0
Great Berry Ladies v Royston Town	5-7
Saffron Walden Town w.o. v Stevenage Borough Vixens withdrew.	
Hutton Ladies v Hawkwell Athletic Ladies	1-2
Hoddesdon Owls v Dagenham & Redbridge	0-2
West Bergholt v Barking	1-2
Old Actonians v The Comets	7-0
Panthers v Denham United	5-3
London Corinthians v Aylesford	4-0
Crawley Wasps v Crowborough Athletic	1-3

Ramsgate v Deal Town Ladies	0-4
Seahaven Harriers Ladies & Girls v Haywards Heath Town	0-2
Rottingdean Village v Eastbourne Town	0-1
Eastleigh Ladies v Aldershot Town	0-5
Horley Town v Bisley Ladies	3-2
Abbey Rangers v Shanklin	0-18
Chichester City United v Merstham Ladies	4-2
Littlehampton Town Devils & Ladies v Wandgas	1-3
MK Wanderers v Salisbury City	3-1
Cheltenham Town Ladies v Newbury Ladies & Girls	5-0
Stoke Lane Athletic v Swindon Supermarine Ladies	4-3
Maidenhead United Ladies v Chalfont St Peter	5-1
Reading Girls v Brize Norton	4-0
Alphington v Frome Town	1-7
Poole Town v Weymouth Ladies	0-5

FIRST QUALIFYING ROUND

Lumley Ladies v East Durham United	2-2
Lumley Ladies won 3-2 on penalties.	
Norton & Stockton Ancients w.o. v Stokesley Ladies withdrew.	
Whitley Bay Women v Boldon Ladies	12-0
St Francis 2000 Ladies v York City	1-3
Forest Hall Women's YPC v Gateshead Cleveland Hall	2-1
Prudhoe Youth Club v Blyth Spartans	0-5
Spennymoor Town v North Shields Ladies	4-1
Darlington RA v Birtley Town Ladies	5-3
Windscale v Wigan Athletic Ladies	1-6
Winsford Ladies v Preston Rangers	3-4
Bury Girls & Ladies v Whitehaven Ladies	4-1
Warrington Town v Sefton Peronni	3-3
Sefton Peronni won 4-3 on penalties.	
Liverpool Feds v Chester City	2-1
Wigan v Bolton Wanderers	6-1
Accrington Stanley Ladies v Middleton Colts	1-5
Penrith AFC v Wirral	3-1
Winterton Rangers v Guiseley Ladies	2-12
Barnsley v Keighley Ladies	5-0
Sheffield United Ladies v Huddersfield Town	0-1
Ossett Albion v Dearne & District Ladies	4-1
Hinckley United Ladies v Friar Lane & Epworth	2-7
Clifton Ladies v Harborough Town Ladies 2007	5-0
Lynby v Sandiacre Town	0-10
Welbeck Welfare Ladies w.o. v St Patricks Ladies withdrew.	
Mansfield Town v Loughborough Foxes	4-2

Heather St Johns v Gedling Town Ladies	2-4
Loughborough Dynamo v Rolls Royce Leisure	1-2
Buxton v West Bridgford Colts	4-0
Studley v Hereford Phoenix Ladies	2-1
Birmingham Athletic v Wednesfield	9-0
Stafford Town Ladies v Redditch United Women s	6-2
Stoke City v Bourne United	4-0
Walsall v Leamington Lions	0-4
Pegasus Ladies v Lichfield Diamonds	0-3
Tamworth Lionesses v Stourport Swifts	5-3
Stratford Town v Dudley United	0-3
Woodbridge Town v Cambridge University	9-0
Peterborough v Hethersett Athletic	1-0
Cambridge United v West Lynn	1-2
Huntingdon Town Ladies v March Town United	5-0
Kettering Town v Bedford Ladies	0-1
Leighton United v Arlesey Town Ladies	1-5
Sandy Ladies v St Martins	1-2
Corby S&L v Raunds Town	4-2
Dagenham & Redbridge v Hemel Hempstead Town	3-3
Dagenham & Redbridge won 4-3 on penalties.	
Braintree Town v Brentwood Town	2-5
Sherrardswood Ladies v Saffron Walden Town	1-7
Sawbridgeworth Town v C&K Basildon	2-4
Garston v Runwell & Rayleigh Raiders	12-0
Hitchin Hearts v Hannakins Ladies	2-4
Barking v London Colney	2-1
Hawkwell Athletic Ladies v Royston Town	2-6
Battersea v Panthers	0-2
Hampstead v Tower Hamlets	3-4
Brentford v One Wish Ladies	21-0
Regents Park Rangers v Wingate & Finchley	2-1
Uxbridge United Ladies v Haringey Borough	0-15
Old Actonians v Hampton	6-0
Manford Way Ladies w.o. v London United Ladies	
withdrew.	
AFC Wimbledon Ladies v Joybabe	5-0
Haywards Heath Town v London Corinthians	1-2
Deal Town Ladies v Crowborough Athletic	4-3
Ebbsfleet United v Eastbourne Town	3-2
Maidstone Town v Canterbury City	2-1
Chichester City United v Aldershot Town	1-5
Shanklin v Horley Town	1-1
Horley Town won 3-2 on penalties.	
Andover New Street v Wandgas	3-1
Southampton Saints v Havant & Waterlooville	0-2
Oxford United v Swindon Spitfires	0-1
Aylesbury United v Maidenhead United Ladies	0-11
Chinnor Ladies w.o. v Carterton withdrew.	
Tetbury Town v Bitton Ladies	3-2
Oldland Abbotonians v Wycombe Wanderers	0-1
Reading Girls v MK Wanderers	2-6
Woodley Saints v Slough	3-2
Stoney Stratford Town v Launton	0-4
Marlow Ladies v Bracknell Town	1-7
Banbury United v Newent Town Ladies	4-0
Chippenham Town Ladies v Henley Town	1-0
Stoke Lane Athletic v Cheltenham Town Ladies	3-6
Cullompton Rangers v Frome Town	1-2
Launceston v Weymouth Ladies	2-2
Launceston won 3-1 on penalties.	
Illminster Town v Purbeck Ladies	5-2
Larkhall Athletic v Keynsham Town Development	4-0

SECOND QUALIFYING ROUND

York City v Lumley Ladies	4-0
Whitley Bay Women v Norton & Stockton Ancients	3-0
Blyth Spartans v Forest Hall Women's FC	11-0
Darlington RA v Spennymoor Town	8-1
Sefton Peronni v Wigan Athletic Ladies	0-1
Bury Girls & Ladies v Preston Rangers	9-2
Wigan v Liverpool Feds	1-7
Penrith AFC Ladies v Middleton Colts	2-1
Huddersfield Town v Ossett Albion	2-4
Barnsley v Guiseley Ladies	2-3
Welbeck Welfare Ladies v Friar Lane & Epworth	3-5
Sandiacre Town v Clifton Ladies	3-2
Gedling Town Ladies v Mansfield Town	2-5
Buxton v Rolls Royce Leisure	1-4
Stoke City v Studley	3-0
Stafford Town Ladies v Birmingham Athletic	5-2
Lichfield Diamonds v Leamington Lions	1-0
Dudley United v Tamworth Lionesses	3-1
West Lynn v Huntingdon Town Ladies	7-0
Peterborough v Woodbridge Town	2-2
Peterborough won 5-4 on penalties.	

St Martins v Corby S&L	1-2
Arlesey Town Ladies v Bedford Ladies	1-4
C&K Basildon v Dagenham & Redbridge	2-5
Saffron Walden Town v Brentwood Town	1-4
Hannakins Ladies v Garston	0-3
Royston Town v Barking	1-2
Regents Park Rangers v Panthers	0-3
Brentford v Tower Hamlets	0-5
Old Actonians v Haringey Borough	1-4
AFC Wimbledon Ladies v Manford Way Ladies	7-0
Ebbsfleet United v Maidstone Town	1-0
Deal Town Ladies v London Corinthians	2-4
Andover New Street v Havant & Waterlooville	1-6
Horley Town v Aldershot Town	5-1
Maidenhead United Ladies v Tetbury Town	6-0
Cheltenham Town Ladies v Launton	3-1
Bracknell Town v Chippenham Town Ladies	4-0
Chinnor Ladies v Banbury United	3-1
Swindon Spitfires v MK Wanderers	3-2
Woodley Saints v Wycombe Wanderers	0-4
Illminster Town v Larkhall Athletic	3-6
Launceston v Frome Town	1-4

THIRD QUALIFYING ROUND

Blyth Spartans v Darlington RA	6-10
Whitley Bay Women v York City	0-2
Liverpool Feds v Penrith AFC Ladies	4-0
Bury Girls & Ladies v Wigan Athletic Ladies	3-1
Guiseley Ladies v Ossett Albion	4-2
Mansfield Town v Rolls Royce Leisure	2-1
Sandiacre Town v Friar Lane & Epworth	7-0
Lichfield Diamonds v Dudley United	1-1
Lichfield Diamonds won 4-3 on penalties.	
Stafford Town Ladies v Stoke City	1-3
Peterborough v West Lynn	4-1
Bedford Ladies v Corby S&L	4-0
Garston v Barking	0-2
Brentwood Town v Dagenham & Redbridge	0-1
Haringey Borough v AFC Wimbledon Ladies	2-3
Tower Hamlets v Panthers	2-1
London Corinthians v Ebbsfleet United	1-5
Horley Town v Havant & Waterloovillle	0-5
Swindon Spitfires v Bracknell Town	0-8
Maidenhead United Ladies v Chinnor Ladies	7-3
Wycombe Wanderers v Cheltenham Town Ladies	3-3
Cheltenham Town Ladies won 4-3 on penalties.	
Frome Town v Larkhall Athletic	1-0

FIRST ROUND

Leeds City Vixens v Crewe Alexandra	4-0
West Auckland Town v Middlesbrough	0-2
Liverpool Feds v Salford SV Ladies	4-2
Guiseley Ladies v Peterlee Town	4-1
Bury Girls & Ladies v Rochdale AFC Ladies	3-5
Stockport County v Bradford City	0-1
Morley Spurs v Blackpool Wren Rovers	2-4
Scunthorpe United v Darlington RA	1-2
Derby County v Mansfield Town	4-0
Leafield Athletic v West Bromwich Albion	3-3
Leafield Athletic won 5-3 on penalties.	
Stoke City v Peterborough	6-2
Coventry City v Copsewood (Coventry)	3-2
Lichfield Diamonds v Leicester City Ladies	3-4
Loughborough Students v Sandiacre Town	3-2
Cambridge City v Wolverhampton Wanderers	0-4
Lewes v Tower Hamlets	9-0
Ebbsfleet United v Wellingborough Diamonds	1-3
Enfield Town v Queens Park Rangers	3-0
Dagenham & Redbridge v Luton Town Ladies	2-3
Tottenham Hotspur v Oxford City	3-1
Welwyn Garden City v Chesham United	0-2
Bedford Town Belles v Reading Royals	2-0
Havant & Waterlooville v Barking	2-0
Norwich City Ladies v AFC Wimbledon Ladies	1-0
Northampton Town v Bedford Ladies	4-1
Maidenhead United Ladies v Swindon Town	0-1
Frome Town v Forest Green Rovers	2-4
TNS & Shrewsbury Town v Bracknell Town	5-0
Yeovil Town v Plymouth Argyle	2-8
AFC Team Bath Ladies v Weston St Johns	2-0
Byes: Cheltenham Town Ladies, York City	

SECOND ROUND

Guiseley Ladies v Derby County	0-2
York City v Liverpool Feds	2-1
Leeds City Vixens v Bradford City	6-4

Middlesbrough v Darlington RA	3-2
Blackpool Wren Rovers v Rochdale AFC Ladies	3-1
Wellingborough Diamonds v Leicester City Ladies	6-1
TNS & Shrewsbury Town v Coventry City	2-2

Coventry City won 4-1 on penalties.

Leafield Athletic v Wolverhampton Wanderers	0-3
Stoke City v Loughborough Students	1-2
Tottenham Hotspur v Northampton Town	1-4
Swindon Town v Luton Town Ladies	2-6
Lewes v Bedford Town Belles	6-0
Enfield Town v Norwich City Ladies	1-0
Havant & Waterlooville v Chesham United	1-2
Forest Green Rovers v Cheltenham Town Ladies	2-0
AFC Team Bath Ladies v Plymouth Argyle	0-6

THIRD ROUND

Leeds City Vixens v Sunderland	1-6
Sheffield Wednesday v Preston North End	4-5
Curzon Ashton v Blackpool Wren Rovers	5-0
Rotherham United v York City	2-1
Manchester City v Newcastle United	3-3

Manchester City won 7-6 on penalties.

Tranmere Rovers v Middlesbrough	1-3
Aston Villa v Wolverhampton Wanderers	4-1
Loughborough Students v Ooh Lincoln Ladies	0-2
Wellingborough Diamonds v Derby County	1-5
Leicester City v Coventry City	3-1
Enfield Town v Colchester United	0-1
Brighton & Hove Albion v Luton Town Ladies	0-1
Millwall Lionesses v West Ham United	2-0
Northampton Town v Barnet Ladies	0-5
Charlton Athletic v Ipswich Town	2-1
Lewes v Chesham United	3-3

Lewes won 3-2 on penalties.

Crystal Palace v Reading Women	4-3
Cardiff City v Keynsham Town	1-1

Cardiff City won 4-3 on penalties.

Plymouth Argyle v Forest Green Rovers	0-2
Truro City Ladies v Portsmouth	0-4

FOURTH ROUND

Derby County v Lewes	3-3

Derby County won 4-3 on penalties.

Leeds Carnegie Ladies v Forest Green Rovers	7-0
Arsenal v Colchester United	7-0
Watford v Bristol Academy	1-3
Crystal Palace v Aston Villa	1-2
Manchester City v Preston North End	4-3

Blackburn Rovers v Luton Town Ladies	3-0
Everton v Fulham	4-0
Doncaster Rovers Belles v Millwall Lionesses	0-1
Ooh Lincoln Ladies v Curzon Ashton	0-1

Tie awarded to Ooh Lincoln Ladies – Curzon Ashton removed.

Nottingham Forest v Liverpool	0-1

Tie awarded to Nottingham Forest – Liverpool removed.

Charlton Athletic v Birmingham City	0-6
Barnet Ladies v Portsmouth	2-1
Sunderland v Cardiff City	4-1
Leicester City v Middlesbrough	2-4
Chelsea v Rotherham United	9-1

FIFTH ROUND

Sunderland v Barnet Ladies	5-0
Middlesbrough v Arsenal	0-4
Millwall Lionesses v Blackburn Rovers	0-1
Manchester City v Everton	0-4
Ooh Lincoln Ladies v Nottingham Forest	3-1
Derby County v Chelsea	0-2
Aston Villa v Leeds Carnegie Ladies	0-3
Bristol Academy v Birmingham City	2-2

Bristol Academy won 4-3 on penalties.

SIXTH ROUND

Chelsea v Ooh Lincoln Ladies	3-1
Arsenal v Leeds Carnegie Ladies	3-1
Blackburn Rovers v Everton	0-2
Sunderland v Bristol Academy	4-2

SEMI-FINALS

Arsenal v Everton	3-1
Sunderland v Chelsea	3-0

FINAL (at DERBY)

Monday, 4 May 2009

Arsenal 2 *(Chapman 32, Little 89)*

Sunderland 1 *(McDougall 90)*   23,291

Arsenal: Byrne; Bassett (White 90), Grant C, Flaherty, Fahey, Davison (Ross 82), Ludlow, Chapman, Yankey, Little, Grant S (Lander 62).
Sunderland: Alderson; Bronze, Greenwell, Bannon, Halliday, Staniforth, McDougall, Nobbs, Williams (Devine 62), Gutteridge (Danby 83), Stokes.
Referee: A. Ihringova.

UEFA WOMEN'S CUP 2008–09

FIRST QUALIFYING ROUND

GROUP 1

Femina 3, KI 1	
Zvezda 8, Gintra 0	
Zvezda 8, KI 0	
Gintra 2, Femina 0	
Femina 0, Zvezda 1	
KI 2, Gintra 2	

GROUP 2

AZ 1, Glasgow 1
Masinac 15, Narta 1
Masinac 0, Glasgow 4
Narta 0, AZ 7
AZ 4, Masinac 1
Glasgow 11, Narta 0

GROUP 3

Sparta 3, Tienen 0
Levante 9, Shkiponjat 0
Sparta 9, Shkiponjat 0
Tienen 2, Levante 9
Levante 0, Sparta 0
Shkiponjat 2, Tienen 8

GROUP 4

Sofia v Iveria
cancelled.
Roa 2, Honka 0
Roa v Iveria
cancelled.
Honka 6, Sofia 0

Sofia 0, Roa 7
Iveria v Honka
cancelled.

GROUP 5

Valur 8, Cardiff 1
Holon 1, Sala 1
Valur 6, Sala 2
Cardiff 1, Holon 2
Holon 0, Valur 9
Sala 0, Cardiff 0

GROUP 6

Alma 3, Osijek 1
Clujana 6, Glentoran 0
Alma 8, Glentoran 0
Osijek 1, Clujana 3
Clujana 1, Alma 3
Glentoran 1, Osijek 1

GROUP 7

1st Dezembro 7, Vamos 1
Neulengbach 6, ZNK KRKA 0
ZNK KRKA 1, 1st Dezembro 1
Neulengbach 8, Vamos 0
Vamos 0, ZNK KRKA 9
1st Dezembro 0, Neulengbach 4

GROUP 8

PAOK 3, Levadia 0
Wroclaw 0, Naftokhimik 1
Wroclaw 4, Levadia 0
Naftokhimik 1, PAOK 0

PAOK 0, Wroclaw 4
Levadia 1, Naftokhimik 2

GROUP 9

Vitebsk 1, Zurich 1
Sarajevo 0, Gallway 0
Vitebsk 0, Gallway 2
Zurich 3, Sarajevo 2
Sarajevo 1, Vitebsk 2
Gallway 0, Zurich 2

SECOND QUALIFYING ROUND

GROUP 1

Frankfurt 0, Zvezda 1
Glasgow 1, Roa 6
Frankfurt 3, Roa 1
Zvezda 1, Glasgow 0
Glasgow 1, Frankfurt 3
Roa 1, Zvezda 3

GROUP 2

Bardolino 2, Alma 1
Umea 5, Valur 1
Valur 2, Bardolino 3
Umea 6, Alma 0
Alma 0, Valur 8
Bardolino 0, Umea 4

GROUP 3

Arsenal 7, Zurich 2
Lyon 8, Neulengbach 2

Arsenal 6, Neulengbach 0
Zurich 1, Lyon 7
Lyon 3, Arsenal 0
Neulengbach 5, Zurich 3

GROUP 4
Brondby 1, Levante 0
Duisburg 5, Naftokhimik 1
Brondby 5, Naftokhimik 1
Levante 0, Duisburg 5
Duisburg 4, Brondby 1
Naftokhimik 1, Levante 4

QUARTER-FINALS FIRST LEG
Brondby 2, Zvezda 4
Frankfurt 1, Duisburg 3
Arsenal 3, Umea 2
Bardolino 0, Lyon 5

QUARTER-FINALS SECOND LEG
Umea 6, Arsenal 0
Zvezda 3, Brondby 1
Duisburg 2, Frankfurt 0
Lyon 4, Bardolino 1

SEMI-FINALS FIRST LEG
Lyon 1, Duisburg 1
Zvezda 2, Umea 0

SEMI-FINALS SECOND LEG
Duisburg 3, Lyon 1
Umea 2, Zvezda 2

FINAL FIRST LEG
Zvezda 0, Duisburg 6

FINAL SECOND LEG
Duisburg 1, Zvezda 1

UEFA WOMEN'S CHAMPIONSHIP 2006–09

PRELIMINARY ROUND

GROUP A1
Northern Ireland 5, Croatia 1
Turkey 9, Georgia 0
Croatia 2, Turkey 1
Georgia 0, Northern Ireland 4
Croatia 6, Georgia 0
Northern Ireland 0, Turkey 1

GROUP A2
Bosnia 2, Israel 5
Armenia 1, Latvia 0
Israel 1, Armenia 0
Latvia 1, Bosnia 4
Israel 3, Latvia 0
Bosnia 1, Armenia 1

GROUP A3
Malta 0, Slovakia 8
Lithuania 1, Luxembourg 1
Slovakia 3, Lithuania 0
Luxembourg 4, Malta 2
Slovakia 4, Luxembourg 0
Malta 0, Lithuania 0

GROUP A4
Estonia 0, Romania 5
Bulgaria 1, Azerbaijan 0
Azerbaijan 3, Estonia 2
Romania 2, Bulgaria 0
Romania 4, Azerbaijan 1
Estonia 0, Bulgaria 5

GROUP A5
Kazakhstan 1, Wales 2
Macedonia 0, Faeroes 7
Wales 6, Macedonia 0
Faeroes 0, Kazakhstan 1
Wales 2, Faeroes 1
Kazakhstan 1, Macedonia 0

QUALIFYING ROUND

GROUP 1
England 4, Northern Ireland 0
Northern Ireland 1, Czech Republic 3
Belarus 0, Spain 3
Belarus 5, Northern Ireland 0
Belarus 1, Czech Republic 4
Czech Republic 2, Spain 2
England 4, Belarus 0
England 1, Spain 0
Spain 4, Northern Ireland 0
Northern Ireland 0, England 2
England 0, Czech Republic 0
Czech Republic 4, Northern Ireland 0
Spain 6, Belarus 1
Spain 4, Czech Republic 1
Belarus 1, England 6
Northern Ireland 0, Spain 3
Northern Ireland 1, Belarus 1
Czech Republic 3, Belarus 1
Spain 2, England 2
Czech Republic 1, England 5

GROUP 2
Republic of Ireland 2, Hungary 1
Hungary 3, Romania 3
Italy 0, Sweden 2
Republic of Ireland 1, Italy 2
Romania 0, Sweden 7
Sweden 7, Hungary 0
Romania 0, Republic of Ireland 2
Hungary 1, Italy 3
Italy 5, Romania 0
Republic of Ireland 2, Romania 1
Italy 4, Republic of Ireland 1
Hungary 0, Republic of Ireland 2
Hungary 0, Sweden 6
Sweden 1, Italy 0
Romania 1, Italy 6
Romania 3, Hungary 1
Republic of Ireland 0, Sweden 5
Italy 3, Hungary 0
Sweden 1, Republic of Ireland 0
Sweden 2, Romania 0

GROUP 3
France 6, Greece 0
Slovenia 0, Serbia 5
France 6, Slovenia 0
Greece 0, Iceland 3
Iceland 1, France 0
Iceland 5, Serbia 0
Slovenia 2, Iceland 1
Serbia 0, France 8
Slovenia 0, France 2
Serbia 1, Greece 2
Greece 0, France 5
Serbia 0, Slovenia 3
France 2, Serbia 0
Slovenia 3, Greece 1
Serbia 0, Iceland 4
Iceland 7, Greece 0
Iceland 5, Slovenia 0
Greece 4, Slovenia 6
France 2, Iceland 1
Greece 0, Serbia 5

GROUP 4
Germany 5, Holland 1
Switzerland 1, Belgium 0
Switzerland 2, Holland 2
Wales 0, Germany 6
Germany 7, Switzerland 0
Holland 2, Wales 1
Wales 0, Switzerland 2
Germany 3, Belgium 0
Belgium 1, Wales 0
Holland 0, Germany 1
Wales 0, Belgium 1
Wales 0, Holland 1
Belgium 2, Holland 2
Belgium 3, Switzerland 1
Belgium 0, Germany 5
Switzerland 2, Wales 0
Germany 4, Wales 0
Switzerland 0, Germany 3
Holland 3, Belgium 0
Holland 1, Switzerland 1

GROUP 5
Slovakia 2, Portugal 1
Scotland 0, Portugal 0
Slovakia 0, Ukraine 4
Ukraine 2, Scotland 1
Ukraine 5, Slovakia 0
Denmark 5, Portugal 1
Slovakia 0, Scotland 3
Portugal 0, Slovakia 1
Portugal 0, Ukraine 1
Scotland 0, Denmark 1
Slovakia 1, Denmark 4
Denmark 2, Scotland 1
Portugal 1, Scotland 4
Portugal 0, Denmark 4
Scotland 0, Ukraine 1
Denmark 6, Slovakia 1
Ukraine 1, Denmark 0
Denmark 1, Ukraine 0
Scotland 6, Slovakia 0
Ukraine 1, Portugal 1

GROUP 6
Austria 0, Poland 1
Israel 2, Poland 2
Israel 0, Russia 6
Israel 0, Norway 3
Poland 4, Israel 1
Austria 1, Russia 5
Austria 5, Israel 0
Norway 3, Russia 0
Russia 3, Poland 1
Norway 3, Austria 0
Norway 7, Israel 0
Norway 3, Poland 0
Poland 2, Austria 4
Israel 0, Austria 2
Poland 0, Norway 3
Austria 0, Norway 4
Russia 4, Israel 0
Russia 0, Norway 0
Poland 1, Russia 4
Russia 3, Austria 1

**PLAY-OFF FOR FINAL
TOURNAMENT**

FIRST LEG
Spain 0, Holland 2
Czech Republic 0, Italy 1
Republic of Ireland 1, Iceland 1
Scotland 2, Russia 3
Slovenia 0, Ukraine 3

SECOND LEG
Holland 2, Spain 0
Italy 2, Czech Republic 1
Iceland 3, Republic of Ireland 0
Russia 1, Scotland 2
Ukraine 2, Slovenia 0
Finals in Finland August 2009.

ENGLAND WOMEN'S INTERNATIONAL MATCHES 2008–09

EUROPEAN CHAMPIONSHIP QUALIFIERS

28 Sept (in Prague)
Czech Republic 1 *(Doskova 28)* 1054
England 5 *(Westwood 61, Smith K 79, 86, Carney 81, Scott J 83)*

England: Brown; Scott A, Stoney (Unitt 84), Scott J, Johnson, Asante, Carney, Williams, Sanderson (Westwood 46), Smith K, Yankey (Smith S 64).

2 Oct (in Zamora)
Spain 2 *(Boquette 9, Bermudez 42)*
England 2 *(Carney 55, Smith K 77)*

England: Brown; Scott A, Stoney, Scott J, Johnson, Asante, Carney, Williams, Aluko (Westwood 46), Smith K, Yankey (Smith S 82).

6 Apr
Spain 2 *(Lambarri 58, Gonzalez 63)*
England 0

7 Apr
England 0
Czech Republic 1 *(Vonkova 18)*

CYPRUS CUP
(in Larnaca)

6 Mar
England 6 *(Williams 18, Sanderson 19, Smith K 42, Houghton 87, Chapman 90)*
South Africa 0

England: Chamberlain; Scott A, Stoney, Williams, Asante, Houghton, Carney (Clarke 62), Scott J (Chapman 46), Sanderson (Aluko 74), Smith K (Westwood 46) (Buet 72), Smith S (Yankey 46).

7 Mar
England 2 *(Carney 28, Stoney 75)*
France 2 *(Franco 15, Thomis 72)*

England: Brown; Johnson (Scott A 46), Stoney, Asante, Houghton, Scott J, Williams, Carney, Westwood (Chapman 68), Smith S, Smith K (Aluko 56).

11 Mar
England 3 *(Aluko 40, Westwood 66, Clarke 83)*
Scotland 0

England: Chamberlain; Scott A, Johnson, Yorston, Unitt, Chapman, Buet, Clarke, Westwood, Yankey, Aluko (Sanderson 82).

12 Mar
England 3 *(Sanderson 32, Smith K 40, Williams 45)*
Canada 1 *(Sinclair 14)*

England: Brown; Scott A, Stoney, Williams, Asante, Houghton, Carney, Scott J, Sanderson (Aluko 71), Smith K, Smith S.

WOMEN'S UNDER-23 CHAMPIONSHIP

2 Feb
England 2 *(Clarke 2)* **Norway 0**

6 Feb
England 0 **USA 3**

FIFA UNDER-20 WOMEN'S WORLD CUP
(played in Chile)

Chile 0 **England 2** *(Chaplen 54, Duggan 80)*

Nigeria 1 *(Orji 71)* **England 1** *(Dowie 45)*

New Zealand 1 *(McLaughlin 27)* **England 1** *(Duggan 90)*

USA 3 *(Winters 53, Leroux 81, 90)* **England 0**
England fielded Under-19 team.

FIFA UNDER-17 WOMEN'S WORLD CUP
(played in New Zealand)

Brazil 0 **England 3** *(Carter 71, 89, Bruton 75)*

Nigeria 0 **England 1** *(Holbrook 79)*

South Korea 3 *(So Yun 8, Kyung Yeon 16, Ari 71)*
England 0

Japan 2 *(Kira 8, Iwabuchi 82)*
England 2 *(Staniforth 45, Christiansen 90)*
England won 5-4 on penalties.

North Korea 2 *(Ho Un Byol 19, Jon Myong Hwa 44)*
England 1 *(Jane 75)*

Germany 3 *(Wesely 11, Knaak 74, Mester 88)*
England 0

UEFA UNDER-17 WOMEN'S CHAMPIONSHIP

Greece 0 **England 4** *(Cole 7, Bruton 28, Carter 47, Eli 69)*

Estonia 0 **England 3** *(Bruton 16, Gardener 70, Carter 80)*

Norway 2 *(Haavi 42, Vassbo 47)* **England 1** *(Eli 85)*

FRIENDLIES

17 July (in Unterhaching)

Germany 3 *(Smisek 15, Prinz 55, Behringer 70 (pen))*

England 0   *9185*

England: Brown; Scott A (Johnson 60), Stoney, Williams, White, Asante, Carney (Smith S 77), Scott J, Sanderson (Westwood 61), Smith K, Yankey.

9 Feb (in Larnaca)

England 2 *(Smith K 2 (pen), Sanderson 3)*

Finland 2 *(Puranen, Makinen)*

England: Telford; Stoney (Houghton), Unitt, Asante, Johnson, Bassett, Carney, Williams, Sanderson (Handley), Smith K (Scott A), Smith S.

13 Feb (in Larnaca)

England 4 *(White 40, Westwood 42, Smith K 44 (pen), Yankey 55)*

Finland 1

England: Brown; Scott A, Yorston (Hickmott), Williams, White (Asante), Houghton, Carney, Westwood (Johnson), Sanderson, Smith K (Smith S), Yankey.

23 Apr (at Shrewsbury)

England 3 *(Williams 18, 81, Johnson 39)*

Norway 0   *4468*

England: Brown; Scott A, Stoney, Williams, Johnson, Asante, Carney, Scott J, Aluko (Chapman 66), Smith K, Smith S (Clarke 79).

WOMEN'S OLYMPIC FOOTBALL TOURNAMENT 2008

(Finals in China)

GROUP E
Argentina 1, Canada 2
China 2, Sweden 1
Sweden 1, Argentina 0
Canada 1, China 1
China 2, Argentina 0
Sweden 2, Canada 1

GROUP F
Germany 0, Brazil 0
North Korea 1, Nigeria 0
Nigeria 0, Germany 1
Brazil 2, North Korea 1
North Korea 0, Germany 1
Nigeria 1, Brazil 3

GROUP G
Japan 2, New Zealand 2

Norway 2, USA 0
USA 1, Japan 0
New Zealand 0, Norway 1
Norway 1, Japan 5
USA 4, New Zealand 0

QUARTER-FINALS
Brazil 2, Norway 1
Sweden 0, Germany 2
China 0, Japan 2
USA 2, Canada 1

SEMI-FINALS
Brazil 4, Germany 1
Japan 2, USA 4

MATCH FOR THIRD PLACE
Germany 2, Japan 0

FINAL IN BEIJING

Brazil (0) 0

USA (0) 1 *(Lloyd 96)*   51,612

Brazil: Barbara; Simone (Rosana 104), Tania, Renata Costa, Maycon, Daniela (Fabiana 77), Formiga (Francielle 106), Ester, Marta, Cristiane, Erika.

USA: Solo; Mitts, Rampone, Tarpley (Cheney 71), Boxx, Rodriguez (Cox 120), O'Reilly (Kai 101), Lloyd, Markgraf, Hucles, Chalupny.

aet.

Referee: Damkova (Czech Republic).

Arsenal's Kim Little (centre) battles with Stephanie Bannon (left) and Lucy Bronze (right) of Sunderland during the FA Women's Cup Final at Pride Park. Arsenal defeated a brave Sunderland 2-1. (The FA/Action Images/Paul Harding)

NATIONAL LEAGUE SYSTEMS CUP 2009–10

PRELIMINARY ROUND

Nottinghamshire Senior League v Teesside Football League	0-1
Cumberland County League v Yorkshire Old Boys League	4-5
Midland Football Combination (Div 1) v West Yorkshire Football League	1-0
Isle of Man League v Manchester Football League	1-0
Wearside League v Cambridgeshire County League	1-2
Northamptonshire Combination v Peterborough & District League	2-1
Brighton & Hove District League v Dorset Premier League	0-3
Guernsey Senior County League v Kent County League	6-0
Mid Sussex League v Bedfordshire Football League	0-4
Jersey Football Combination v Spartan South Midlands League (Div 2)	2-0
Reading Football League v Middlesex County League	4-1
Northampton Town League v Hampshire Premier League	2-1

Competition still being played.

UEFA REGIONS' CUP

PRELIMINARY ROUND

GROUP 1

South-Eastern v San Marino	1-1
Liechtenstein v Drava *match cancelled.*	
San Marino v Drava	1-0
Liechtenstein v South-Eastern *match cancelled.*	
San Marino v Liechtenstein *match cancelled.*	
Drava v South-Eastern	2-0

GROUP 2

Gwent County v Zur Salom	1-4
Bohemia v Malta	0-3
Zur Salom v Malta	0-1
Bohemia v Gwent County	4-3
Zur Salom v Bohemia	2-0
Malta v Gwent County	2-0

GROUP 3

Marmara Region v Alytis	1-1
Vaxjo BK Smaland v Tbilisi	0-1
Alytis v Tbilisi	3-3
Vaxjo BK Smaland v Marmara Region	0-2
Alytis v Vaxjo BK Smaland	2-0
Tbilisi v Marmara Region	0-1

INTERMEDIARY ROUND

GROUP 1

FV Niederhein v Kempen	0-2
Eastern Region v Malta	2-1
FV Niederhein v Malta	5-2
Kempen v Eastern Region	2-1
Malta v Kempen	1-0
FV Niederhein v Eastern Region	0-0

GROUP 2

Southern v Region I	0-0
Piemonte v East of Scotland	3-1
Region I v Piemonte	2-2
East of Scotland v Southern	0-3
East of Scotland v Region I	1-5
Piemonte v Southern	0-0

GROUP 3

Zagreb v MNZ Lendava	2-0
District West v Ticino	0-0
Zagreb v District West	2-1
MNZ Lendava v Ticino	0-1
Ticino v Zagreb	1-2
MNZ Lendava v District West	1-3

GROUP 4

Atlantique v San Marino	1-1
Castilla y Leon v Braga	1-0
Atlantique v Castilla y Leon	0-3
San Marino v Braga	1-5
Braga v Atlantique	2-2
San Marino v Castilla y Leon	0-4

GROUP 5

Marmara Region v Larisas	1-1
Privolzhie v Brest Region	6-1
Brest Region v Larisas	2-0
Privolzhie v Marmara Region	5-2
Larisas v Privolzhie	0-2
Brest Region v Marmara Region	0-2

GROUP 6

Oltenia v South-East Region	0-0
AT Ialoveni v Odessa	1-5
Oltenia v AT Ialoveni	4-0
South-East Region v Odessa	1-1
Odessa v Oltenia	1-2
South-East Region v AT Ialoveni	1-2

GROUP 7

Eastern Serbia v Savez Gradiska	0-0
Wielkopolski v Uusimaa	3-0
Eastern Serbia v Wielkopolski	0-0
Savez Gradiska v Uusimaa	2-0
Uusimaa v Eastern Serbia	1-4
Savez Gradiska v Wielkopolski	1-0

GROUP 8

Bratislava v Avey	4-2
Ararat v Kurzemes	0-1
Bratislava v Ararat	2-0
Avey v Kurzemes	1-1
Kurzemes v Bratislava	0-4
Avey v Ararat	2-0

FINAL TOURNAMENT

GROUP A

Oltenia v Zagreb	1-1
Bratislava v Privolzhie	0-5
Zagreb v Privolzhie	0-2
Bratislava v Oltenia	0-2
Zagreb v Bratislava	2-0
Privolzhie v Oltenia	0-2

GROUP B

Castilla y Leon v Savez Gradiska	1-0
Kempen v Region 1	2-1
Savez Gradiska v Region 1	0-3
Kempen v Castilla y Leon	1-4
Savez Gradiska v Kempen	0-1
Region 1 v Casillla y Leon	0-2

FINAL

Oltenia v Castillas y Leon	1-2

UNIBOND LEAGUE 2008–09

UNIBOND PREMIER DIVISION 2008–09

			Home				Away					Total					
	P	W	D	L	F	A	W	D	L	F	A	W	D	L	F	A	GD	Pts
1 Eastwood Town	42	15	5	1	49	19	10	7	4	33	18	25	12	5	82	37	45	87
2 Ilkeston Town	42	13	5	3	35	17	10	8	3	24	17	23	13	6	59	34	25	82
3 Nantwich Town	42	12	4	5	43	23	10	6	5	40	18	22	10	10	83	41	42	76
4 Guiseley	42	11	4	6	46	27	11	6	4	52	33	22	10	10	98	60	38	76
5 Kendal Town	42	11	5	5	50	30	10	6	5	35	33	21	11	10	85	63	22	74
6 FC United of Manchester	42	11	6	4	47	29	10	3	8	35	29	21	9	12	82	58	24	72
7 Bradford Park Avenue	42	12	5	4	39	23	8	7	6	35	29	20	12	10	74	52	22	72
8 Hednesford Town	42	10	3	8	39	27	11	3	7	39	25	21	6	15	78	52	26	69
9 Ashton United	42	11	7	3	45	26	5	3	13	26	49	16	10	16	71	75	–4	58
10 North Ferriby United	42	9	4	8	44	29	7	2	12	23	36	16	6	20	67	65	2	54
11 Frickley Athletic	42	7	10	4	25	23	6	5	10	25	35	13	15	14	50	58	–8	54
12 Ossett Town	42	8	5	8	38	38	7	3	11	33	36	15	8	19	71	74	–3	53
13 Marine	42	7	4	10	28	34	8	2	11	26	41	15	6	21	54	75	–21	51
14 Buxton	42	7	7	7	25	23	6	3	12	31	35	13	10	19	56	58	–2	49
15 Matlock Town	42	9	6	6	35	28	3	7	11	30	46	12	13	17	65	74	–9	49
16 Boston United	42	6	5	10	22	27	6	8	7	16	25	12	13	17	38	52	–14	49
17 Worksop Town	42	6	7	8	24	38	6	5	10	24	49	12	12	18	48	87	–39	48
18 Cammell Laird	42	7	5	9	29	30	5	6	10	29	40	12	11	19	58	70	–12	47
19 Whitby Town	42	8	4	9	27	28	4	6	11	31	43	12	10	20	58	71	–13	46
20 Witton Albion	42	6	4	11	29	36	6	2	13	24	37	12	6	24	53	73	–20	42
21 Leigh Genesis	42	5	2	14	19	54	6	5	10	23	34	11	7	24	42	88	–46	40
22 Prescot Cables	42	4	4	13	28	49	1	8	12	24	58	5	12	25	52	107	–55	27

UNIBOND FIRST DIVISION NORTH 2008–09

	P	W	D	L	F	A	GD	Pts
Durham City	40	25	12	3	98	41	57	87
Skelmersdale United	40	26	8	6	96	51	45	86
Newcastle Blue Star	40	21	10	9	93	54	39	73
Colwyn Bay	40	23	7	10	72	49	23	73
Curzon Ashton	40	20	8	12	66	44	22	68
Ossett Albion	40	19	9	12	76	61	15	66
Lancaster City	40	19	8	13	69	64	5	65
FC Halifax Town	40	17	12	11	71	52	19	63
Wakefield FC	40	16	8	16	65	62	3	56
Mossley	40	16	7	17	64	76	–12	55
Bamber Bridge	40	16	5	19	69	78	–9	53
Clitheroe	40	15	7	18	64	76	–12	52
Woodley Sports	40	16	3	21	57	74	–17	51
Chorley	40	13	8	19	56	66	–10	47
Trafford	40	13	7	20	72	83	–11	46
Garforth Town	40	13	5	22	77	99	–22	44
Radcliffe Borough	40	12	6	22	51	66	–15	42
Harrogate Railway Athletic	40	13	3	24	58	82	–24	42
Warrington Town	40	11	8	21	50	73	–23	41
Salford City	40	10	6	24	59	107	–48	36
Rossendale United	40	8	10	22	53	83	–30	34

UNIBOND FIRST DIVISION SOUTH 2008–09

	P	W	D	L	F	A	GD	Pts
Retford United	38	24	9	5	88	34	54	81
Belper Town	38	24	9	5	79	41	38	81
Stocksbridge Park Steels	38	23	6	9	92	44	48	75
Carlton Town	38	20	10	8	83	50	33	70
Rushall Olympic	38	20	8	10	63	42	21	68
Glapwell	38	21	5	12	78	58	20	68
Stamford	38	15	16	7	65	51	14	61
Shepshed Dynamo	38	16	8	14	61	61	0	56
Leek Town	38	14	12	12	63	60	3	54
Lincoln United	38	14	9	15	58	65	–7	51
Sheffield	38	14	8	16	67	69	–2	50
Quorn	38	13	9	16	54	63	–9	48
Grantham Town	38	12	11	15	49	65	–16	47
Loughborough Dynamo	38	11	13	14	45	58	–13	46
Kidsgrove Athletic	38	12	5	21	49	62	–13	41
Willenhall Town	38	10	8	20	55	74	–19	38
Spalding United	38	10	7	21	41	82	–41	37
Goole AFC	38	13	5	20	62	85	–23	33
Gresley Rovers	38	6	7	25	41	78	–37	25
Brigg Town	38	3	5	30	41	92	–51	14

LEADING GOALSCORERS

Premier Division	Lge	Cup	Total
Michael Lennon (Nantwich Town)	27	7	34
Ross Dyer (Hednesford Town)	21	8	29
Dave Walker (Nantwich Town)	19	10	29
Tyrone Barnett (Hednesford Town)	20	6	26
Aidan Savory (Ossett Town)	23	2	25
Mark Reed (Buxton)	20	5	25
Craig Hobson (Kendal Town)	18	7	25
Kyle Wilson (FC United of Mcr)	21	3	24
Mark Bett (Bradford PA)	20	4	24
Elliott Durrell (Hednesford Town)	17	7	24
Ian Holmes (Eastwood Town)	20	3	23
Gavin Knight (Buxton)	16	7	23
Tom Cahill (Ilkeston Town)	12	11	23

First Division North	Lge	Cup	Total
Paul Brayson (Newcastle BS)	33	14	47
Scott Barlow (Trafford)	28	12	40
Michael Norton (Curzon Ashton)	28	10	38
Steven Richardson (Durham City)	21	9	30
George Donnelly (Skelmersdale Utd)	19	11	30
Mark Horton (Skelmersdale Utd))	19	7	26
Adam Johnston (Durham City)	12	12	24
Rob Hopley (Colwyn Bay))	19	4	23
Gavin Salmon (Woodley Sports)	17	6	23
Gavin Cogden (Durham City)	15	8	23
Andy Hayward (Garforth Town)	11	12	23

First Division South	Lge	Cup	Total
Mick Godber (Retford United)	29	11	40
Lee Stevenson (Belper Town)	22	7	29
Ian Brown (Glapwell)	26	2	28
Mark Ward (Stocksbridge PS)	19	7	26
Jamie Clarke (Stamford)	15	10	25
Daryl Thomas (Carlton Town)	23	1	24
Ben Walker (Belper Town)	15	9	24
Sean Cann (Lincoln Utd)	20	2	22
Jamie Vardy (Stocksbridge PS)	16	6	22

UNIBOND LEAGUE ATTENDANCES 2008–09

PREMIER	Highest Average	2152	FC United of Manchester
	Division Highest	3719	FC United of Manchester v Bradford PA (25 April 2009)
DIVISION ONE NORTH	Highest Average	1165	Halifax Town
	Division Highest	1675	Halifax Town v Ossett Albion (26 December 2008)
DIVISION ONE SOUTH	Highest Average	349	Sheffield FC
	Division Highest	760	Sheffield FC v Retford United (1 January 2009)

UNIBOND LEAGUE CHALLENGE CUP 2008–09

PRELIMINARY ROUND

FC Halifax Town v Wakefield	2-1

FIRST ROUND

Salford City v Mossley	2-0
Harrogate Railway Athletic v Durham City	0-2
Newcastle Blue Star v Ossett Albion	2-1
Bamber Bridge v Chorley	2-1
Belper Town v Gresley Rovers	4-2
Brigg Town v Sheffield	0-5
Clitheroe v Garforth Town	2-4
Goole v Stocksbridge Park Steels	2-3
Leek Town v Rushall Olympic	0-1
Loughborough Dynamo v Carlton Town	4-1
Radcliffe Borough v Lancaster City	2-0
Retford United v Glapwell	2-1
Rossendale United v Woodley Sports	0-2
Shepshed Dynamo v Quorn	4-0
Spalding United v Grantham Town	3-0
Trafford v Skelmersdale United	1-3
Warrington Town v Colwyn Bay	0-2
Kidsgrove Athletic v Willenhall Town	3-3
Kidsgrove Athletic won 4-3 on penalties.	
Stamford v Lincoln United	6-4
FC Halifax Town v Curzon Ashton	1-2

SECOND ROUND

Loughborough Dynamo v Stamford	3-1
Spalding United v Shepshed Dynamo	1-0
Woodley Sports v Radcliffe Borough	2-1
Colwyn Bay v Skelmersdale United	2-6
Curzon Ashton v Garforth Town	0-1
Belper Town v Stocksbridge Park Steels	1-3
Retford United v Newcastle Blue Star	2-3
Sheffield v Durham City	3-2
Bamber Bridge v Salford City	2-1
Kidsgrove Athletic v Rushall Olympic	3-0

THIRD ROUND

Spalding United v Boston United	1-6

Witton Albion v Cammell Laird	2-1
Newcastle Blue Star v Whitby Town	2-7
Ashton United v Leigh Genesis	3-1
Buxton v Matlock Town	2-3
Skelmersdale United v Bamber Bridge	10-0
Woodley Sports v FC United of Manchester	3-0
Kidsgrove Athletic v Hednesford Town	1-3
Frickley Athletic v Garforth Town	0-1
Guiseley v Bradford Park Avenue	2-0
Kendal Town v Nantwich Town	4-1
Loughborough Town v Ilkeston Town	1-2
Ossett Town v Worksop Town	0-3
Prescot Cables v Marine	2-2
Marine won 4-1 on penalties.	
Sheffield v North Ferriby United	5-2
Stocksbridge Park Steels v Eastwood Town	0-1

FOURTH ROUND

Garforth Town v Whitby Town	1-3
Ilkeston Town v Sheffield	3-0
Kendal Town v Woodley Sports	3-2
Eastwood Town v Boston United	0-4
Guiseley v Ashton United	3-0
Hednesford Town v Skelmersdale United	2-3
Witton Albion v Marine	2-1
Worksop Town v Matlock Town	1-3

QUARTER-FINALS

Witton Albion v Guiseley	2-3
Kendal Town v Skelmersdale United	1-5
Boston United v Ilkeston Town	3-4
Whitby Town v Matlock Town	3-3
Whitby Town won 4-2 on penalties.	

SEMI-FINALS

Guiseley v Skelmersdale United	5-0
Whitby Town v Ilkeston Town	3-5

FINAL

Guiseley v Ilkeston Town	3-2

PRESIDENT'S CUP 2008–09

FIRST ROUND

Brigg Town v Spalding United	3-2
Chorley v Clitheroe	1-1
Chorley won 3-2 on penalties.	
Glapwell v Shepshed Dynamo	0-4
Gresley Rovers v Leek Town	4-0
Ossett Albion v FC Halifax Town	3-4
Sheffield v Goole	2-1
Skelmersdale United v Kidsgrove Athletic	4-3
Durham City v Garforth Town	2-1
Woodley Sports v Salford City	3-3
Woodley Sports won 4-1 on penalties.	
Woodley Sports dismissed for fielding an ineligible player.	

SECOND ROUND

Rushall Olympic v Belper Town	1-2
Chorley v Lancaster City	2-0
Grantham v Stamford	1-4
Gresley Rovers v Willenhall Town	1-3
Lincoln United v Brigg Town	6-2
Mossley v Radcliffe Borough	2-1
Quorn v Loughborough Dynamo	3-1
Retford United v Stocksbridge Park Steels	4-3
Shepshed Dynamo v Carlton Town	4-2
Wakefield v Harrogate Railway Athletic	5-1
Colwyn Bay v Trafford	0-3
Skelmersdale United v Warrington Town	1-0
Rossendale United v Bamber Bridge	3-4
FC Halifax Town v Sheffield	3-1

Durham City v Newcastle Blue Star	2-4
Curzon Ashton v Salford City	2-3

THIRD ROUND

Chorley v Mossley	1-2
FC Halifax Town v Retford United	0-2
Lincoln United v Stamford	2-2
Lincoln United won 6-5 on penalties.	
Lincoln United dismissed for fielding an ineligible player.	
Salford City v Skelmersdale United	2-4
Bamber Bridge v Trafford	1-4
Belper Town v Willenhall Town	2-2
Willenhall Town won 3-2 on penalties.	
Shepshed Dynamo v Quorn	2-3
Newcastle Blue Star v Wakefield	4-3

QUARTER-FINALS

Mossley v Retford United	2-1
Quorn v Stamford	1-1
Quorn won 4-3 on penalties.	
Willenhall Town v Trafford	1-3
Skelmersdale United v Newcastle Blue Star	3-0

SEMI-FINALS

Skelmersdale United v Quorn	0-2
Trafford v Mossley	2-1

FINAL

Quorn v Trafford	0-2

CHAIRMAN'S CUP 2008–09

FINAL

Durham City v Retford United	2-1

PETER SWALES MEMORIAL SHELD 2008–09

Eastwood Town v Durham City	2-1

UNIBOND LEAGUE PROMOTION PLAY-OFFS 2008–09

PREMIER DIVISION

SEMI-FINALS

Ilkeston Town 4, Kendal Town 3 (*aet.*)
Nantwich Town 2, Guiseley 1 (*aet.*)

FINAL

Ilkeston 2, Nantwich Town 1 (*aet.*)

FIRST DIVISION SOUTH

SEMI-FINALS

Stocksbridge Park Steels 5, Carlton Town 2
Belper Town 1, Rushall Olympic 0

FINAL

Belper Town 0, Stocksbridge Park Steels 1

FIRST DIVISION NORTH

SEMI-FINALS

Skelmersdale United 0, Curzon Ashton 1
Newcastle Blue Star 2, Colwyn Bay 2 (*aet.*)
Newcastle Blue Star won 4-2 on penalties.

FINAL

Newcastle Blue Star 4 Curzon Ashton 1

SOUTHERN LEAGUE 2008–09

BRITISH GAS BUSINESS LEAGUE PREMIER DIVISION 2008–09

			Home			Away			Total						
		P	W	D	L	W	D	L	W	D	L	F	A	GD	Pts
1	Corby Town	42	10	6	5	15	3	3	25	9	8	85	38	47	84
2	Farnborough	42	14	5	2	9	9	3	23	14	5	67	36	31	83
3	Gloucester City	42	12	4	5	9	8	4	21	12	9	80	45	35	75
4	Cambridge City	42	14	1	6	7	9	5	21	10	11	62	40	22	73
5	Hemel Hempstead Town	42	12	5	4	9	2	10	21	7	14	71	48	23	70
6	Oxford City	42	11	4	6	8	6	7	19	10	13	76	55	21	67
7	Merthyr Tydfil	42	11	5	5	8	5	8	19	10	13	66	55	11	67
8	Chippenham Town (–3)*	42	12	5	4	8	3	10	20	8	14	64	51	13	65
9	Evesham United	42	8	8	5	8	5	8	16	13	13	48	39	9	61
10	Halesowen Town (–3)*	42	11	2	8	8	4	9	19	6	17	65	73	–8	60
11	Brackley Town	42	10	4	7	5	8	8	15	12	15	69	62	7	57
12	Tiverton Town	42	7	6	8	9	3	9	16	9	17	51	50	1	57
13	Swindon Supermarine	42	7	7	7	8	5	8	15	12	15	59	61	–2	57
14	Bashley	42	10	6	5	5	6	10	15	12	15	52	58	–6	57
15	Bedford Town	42	10	7	4	4	1	16	14	8	20	44	55	–11	50
16	Stourbridge	42	8	6	7	5	5	11	13	11	18	62	78	–16	50
17	Rugby Town	42	7	5	9	4	5	12	11	10	21	63	71	–8	43
18	Clevedon Town	42	7	4	10	4	6	11	11	10	21	51	80	–29	43
19	Banbury United	42	10	3	8	1	5	15	11	8	23	43	83	–40	41
20	Hitchin Town	42	5	9	7	5	1	15	10	10	22	57	79	–22	40
21	Yate Town	42	7	4	10	2	5	14	9	9	24	54	91	–37	36
22	Mangotsfield United	42	7	2	12	3	4	14	10	6	26	39	80	–41	36

* points deducted for breach of rules.

BRITISH GAS BUSINESS LEAGUE ONE MIDLANDS DIVISION 2008–09

			Home			Away			Total						
		P	W	D	L	W	D	L	W	D	L	F	A	GD	Pts
1	Leamington	42	16	1	4	16	4	1	32	5	5	114	44	70	101
2	Nuneaton Town	42	14	3	4	14	5	2	28	8	6	85	31	54	92
3	Atherstone Town	42	11	8	2	13	5	3	24	13	5	82	45	37	85
4	Chasetown	42	13	5	3	12	4	5	25	9	8	67	31	36	84
5	Chesham United	42	9	6	6	13	4	4	22	10	10	70	38	32	76
6	Sutton Coldfield Town	42	12	2	7	12	2	7	24	4	14	79	62	17	76
7	Bury Town	42	12	4	5	10	5	6	22	9	11	88	41	47	75
8	Leighton Town	42	10	6	5	8	7	6	18	13	11	57	46	11	67
9	Marlow	42	12	4	5	7	5	9	19	9	14	65	53	12	66
10	Aylesbury United	42	11	2	8	8	5	8	19	7	16	65	58	7	64
11	Romulus	42	10	4	7	7	6	8	17	10	15	60	42	18	61
12	AFC Sudbury	42	8	8	5	9	2	10	17	10	15	66	65	1	61
13	Bromsgrove Rovers	42	10	1	10	5	7	9	15	8	19	58	53	5	53
14	Bedworth United	42	6	4	11	8	3	10	14	7	21	50	66	–16	49
15	Soham Town Rangers	42	6	4	11	7	3	11	13	7	22	48	79	–31	46
16	Stourport Swifts	42	4	4	13	6	6	9	10	10	22	46	74	–28	40
17	Barton Rovers	42	5	3	13	7	1	13	12	4	26	50	79	–29	40
18	Arlesey Town	42	6	1	14	5	4	12	11	5	26	40	70	–30	38
19	Rothwell Town	42	5	8	8	3	4	14	8	12	22	35	79	–44	36
20	Woodford United	42	2	3	16	7	4	10	9	7	26	38	80	–42	34
21	Dunstable Town (–13)*	42	9	2	10	2	1	18	11	3	28	54	89	–35	23
22	Malvern Town	42	1	7	13	1	3	17	2	10	30	27	119	–92	16

* points deducted for breach of rules.

BRITISH GAS BUSINESS LEAGUE ONE SOUTH & WEST DIVISION 2008–09

			Home			Away			Total						
		P	W	D	L	W	D	L	W	D	L	F	A	GD	Pts
1	Truro City	42	12	6	3	17	2	2	29	8	5	120	49	71	95
2	Windsor & Eton	42	12	5	4	14	2	5	26	7	9	77	44	33	85
3	AFC Totton	42	14	5	2	9	8	4	23	13	6	89	39	50	82
4	Beaconsfield SYCOB	42	15	4	2	9	5	7	24	9	9	77	44	33	81
5	Didcot Town	42	11	5	5	10	5	6	21	10	11	91	52	39	73
6	Thatcham Town	42	12	3	6	8	5	8	20	8	14	74	58	16	68
7	Bridgwater Town	42	11	6	4	8	2	11	19	8	15	69	56	13	65
8	North Leigh	42	11	3	7	6	7	8	17	10	15	68	64	4	61
9	AFC Hayes	42	10	4	7	8	3	10	18	7	17	80	92	–12	61
10	Paulton Rovers	42	10	2	9	6	8	7	16	10	16	65	62	3	58
11	Cinderford Town	42	6	5	10	9	6	6	15	11	16	71	75	–4	56
12	Gosport Borough	42	9	2	10	6	8	7	15	10	17	64	67	–3	55
13	Uxbridge	42	8	7	6	7	2	12	15	9	18	76	72	4	54
14	Cirencester Town	42	9	5	7	5	5	11	14	10	18	78	79	–1	52
15	Abingdon United	42	10	3	8	5	4	12	15	7	20	63	77	–14	52
16	Slough Town	42	7	9	5	4	3	14	11	12	19	62	91	–29	45
17	Burnham	42	7	6	8	5	3	13	12	9	21	52	83	–31	45
18	Bishops Cleeve	42	8	4	9	2	9	10	10	13	19	51	71	–20	43
19	Andover	42	5	5	11	5	7	9	10	12	20	58	102	–44	42
20	Taunton Town	42	6	6	10	3	4	14	9	9	24	50	85	–35	36
21	Bracknell Town	42	6	4	11	3	4	14	9	8	25	39	75	–36	35
22	Winchester City (–3)*	42	6	6	9	4	2	15	10	8	24	47	84	–37	35

* points deducted for breach of rules.

SOUTHERN LEAGUE PLAY-OFFS 2008–09

PREMIER DIVISION PLAY-OFF FINAL
Saturday 2 May 2009
Farnborough 0
Gloucester City 1 *(Rose 25)*   1715

DIVISION ONE MIDLANDS PLAY–OFF FINAL
Saturday 2 May 2009
Nuneaton Town 1 *(Mackey 17)*
Chasetown 0   3111

DIVISION ONE SOUTH & WEST PLAY-OFF FINAL
Saturday 2 May 2009
AFC Totton 1 *(Bennett 67)*
Didcot Town 2 *(Williams 40, John 96)*   646
aet.

SOUTHERN LEAGUE LEADING GOALSCORERS 2008–09

(Includes League and League Cup goals only)

PREMIER DIVISION

David Kolodynski (Rugby Town)	26
Ben Mackey (Brackley Town)	21
Alexander Sykes (Gloucester City)	21
Leon Broadhurst (Stourbridge)	19
Michael Charles (Farnborough)	19
Stephen Diggin (Corby Town)	19
David Pratt (Chippenham Town)	17

DIVISION ONE MIDLANDS

Mark Bellingham (Leamington)	39
Daniel Burnell (Chesham United)	30

Tyrone Fagan (Romulus)	21
Dean Perrow (Chasetown)	21
Luke Corbett (Leamington)	20
Lee Reed (Bury Town)	20

DIVISION ONE SOUTH & WEST

Bradley Bubb (Beaconsfield SYCOB)	32
Stewart Yetton (Truro City)	32
Liam Hope (North Leigh)	26
James Taylor (AFC Totton)	26
Dean Papali (AFC Hayes)	25
Jody Bevan (Cinderford Town)	23
Jemel Johnson (Thatcham Town)	23

SOUTHERN LEAGUE ATTENDANCES 2008–09

PREMIER	**Highest Average**	799	Farnborough
	Division Highest	2230	Farnborough 3 Corby Town 3 (21 March 2009)
DIVISION ONE MIDLANDS	**Highest Average**	798	Nuneaton Town
	Division Highest	2302	Bedworth United 1 Nuneaton Town 2 (27 December 2008)
DIVISION ONE SOUTH & WEST	**Highest Average**	493	Truro City
	Division Highest	1119	Truro City 4 Windsor & Eton 2 (24 March 2009)

ERREA SOUTHERN LEAGUE CUP 2008–09

PRELIMINARY ROUND

Chippenham Town v Oxford City	2-2
Chippenham Town won 5-4 on penalties.	
Sutton Coldfield Town v Halesowen Town	1-1
Halesowen Town won 6-5 on penalties.	

FIRST ROUND

Corby Town v Rothwell Town	0-1
Malvern Town v Cirencester Town	1-2
Aylesbury United v Burnham	3-0
Beaconsfield SYCOB v Marlow	4-1
Abingdon United v Banbury United	1-1
Abingdon United won 5-3 on penalties.	
Andover v Farnborough	2-2
Andover won 3-0 on penalties.	
Atherstone Town v Nuneaton Town	2-2
Atherstone Town won 4-3 on penalties.	
Barton Rovers v Dunstable Town	0-3
Bracknell Town v Windsor & Eton	0-0, 0-1
Abandoned 64 minutes:	
Bridgwater Town v Taunton Town	4-3
Bromsgrove Rovers v Romulus	0-1
Bury Town v AFC Sudbury	2-0
Chasetown v Leamington	1-3
Chippenham Town v Brackley Town	1-3
Didcot Town v Swindon Supermarine	1-2
Evesham United v Gloucester City	0-3
Gosport Borough v AFC Totton	1-0
Halesowen Town v Stourbridge	1-0
Hemel Hempstead Town v Bedford Town	3-0
Hitchin Town v Arlesey Town	4-0
Leighton Town v Slough Town	3-0
Mangotsfield United v Clevedon Town	3-1
Merthyr Tydfil v Bishop's Cleeve	4-2
Rugby Town v Bedworth United	1-2
Soham Town Rangers v Cambridge City	3-4
Stourport Swifts v Cinderford Town	3-4
Thatcham Town v Chesham United	2-4
Tiverton Town v Truro City	3-4
Uxbridge v AFC Hayes	3-4
Winchester City v Bashley	3-4
Woodford United v North Leigh	0-1

SECOND ROUND

Andover v Bashley	2-1
Atherstone Town v Leamington	2-1

Aylesbury United v Windsor & Eton	1-2
Bedworth United v Halesowen Town	0-2
Brackley Town v Romulus	3-2
Cinderford Town v Merthyr Tydfil	4-3
Gloucester City v Abingdon United	3-0
Gosport Borough v Beaconsfield SYCOB	1-2
AFC Hayes v Chesham United	2-4
Hemel Hempstead Town v Dunstable Town	4-4
Dunstable Town won 5-4 on penalties.	
Hitchin Town v Cambridge City	1-0
Leighton Town v Bury Town	1-3
Mangotsfield United v Yate Town	1-2
North Leigh v Rothwell Town	4-0
Swindon Supermarine v Cirencester Town	1-0
Truro City v Bridgwater Town	0-3

THIRD ROUND

Brackley Town v North Leigh	3-0
Bury Town v Hitchin Town	2-0
Chesham United v Beaconsfield SYCOB	4-1
Cinderford Town v Bridgwater Town	2-2
Bridgwater Town won 5-3 on penalties.	
Dunstable Town v Windsor & Eton	1-2
Gloucester City v Yate Town	3-0
Halesowen Town v Atherstone Town	0-2
Andover v Swindon Supermarine	2-6

FOURTH ROUND

Bridgwater Town v Gloucester City	2-1
Bury Town v Chesham United	3-1
Atherstone Town v Brackley Town	2-0
Swindon Supermarine v Windsor & Eton	3-0

SEMI-FINALS

Atherstone Town v Bury Town	2-2
Atherstone Town won 3-1 on penalties.	
Bridgwater Town v Swindon Supermarine	3-0

FINAL FIRST LEG

Atherstone Town v Bridgwater Town	2-1

FINAL SECOND LEG

Bridgwater Town v Atherstone Town (att. 533)	1-3

RYMAN LEAGUE 2008–09

RYMAN LEAGUE PREMIER DIVISION 2008–09

		P	Home W	D	L	F	A	Away W	D	L	F	A	Total W	D	L	F	A	GD	Pts
1	Dover Athletic	42	18	2	1	55	17	15	3	3	36	17	33	5	4	91	34	57	104
2	Staines Town	42	15	5	1	45	18	8	8	5	30	23	23	13	6	75	41	34	82
3	Tonbridge Angels	42	10	5	6	40	28	10	8	3	42	26	20	13	9	82	54	28	73
4	Carshalton Athletic	42	6	5	10	26	39	13	6	2	38	24	19	11	12	64	63	1	68
5	Sutton United	42	11	9	1	33	19	7	4	10	24	34	18	13	11	57	53	4	67
6	AFC Hornchurch	42	12	2	7	32	21	7	6	8	28	30	19	8	15	60	51	9	65
7	Wealdstone	42	11	4	6	37	22	7	4	10	33	34	18	8	16	70	56	14	62
8	Dartford	42	9	6	6	39	24	8	5	8	23	25	17	11	14	62	49	13	62
9	Tooting & Mitcham United	42	10	4	7	36	28	6	6	9	21	29	16	10	16	57	57	0	58
10	Ashford Town (Middx)	42	11	2	8	34	27	7	0	14	30	39	18	2	22	64	66	-2	56
11	Billericay Town	42	9	8	4	34	27	6	3	12	20	39	15	11	16	54	66	-12	56
12	Canvey Island	42	10	4	7	39	31	6	3	12	26	39	16	7	19	65	70	-5	55
13	Horsham	42	8	4	9	24	25	8	3	10	25	35	16	7	19	49	60	-11	55
14	Harrow Borough	42	7	6	8	33	34	7	6	8	23	39	14	12	16	56	73	-17	54
15	Maidstone United	42	6	6	9	18	24	8	5	8	28	27	14	11	17	46	51	-5	53
16	Hendon	42	8	4	9	38	27	7	2	12	31	38	15	6	21	69	65	4	51
17	Hastings United	42	6	4	11	23	33	8	3	10	29	35	14	7	21	52	68	-16	49
18	Boreham Wood	42	6	2	13	20	28	6	10	5	28	33	12	12	18	48	61	-13	48
19	Margate	42	8	4	9	29	29	5	3	13	22	35	13	7	22	51	64	-13	46
20	Harlow Town (-3)*	42	5	4	12	31	37	8	2	11	30	40	13	6	23	61	77	-16	42
21	Heybridge Swifts	42	4	6	11	20	34	6	5	10	21	29	10	11	21	41	63	-22	41
22	Ramsgate (-4)*	42	5	5	11	26	37	3	6	12	21	42	8	11	23	47	79	-32	31

* points deducted for breach of rules.

RYMAN LEAGUE DIVISION ONE NORTH 2008–09

		P	Home W	D	L	F	A	Away W	D	L	F	A	Total W	D	L	F	A	GD	Pts
1	Aveley	42	13	5	3	43	24	16	4	1	38	16	29	9	4	81	40	41	96
2	East Thurrock United	42	12	2	4	58	21	15	3	3	54	29	30	5	7	112	50	62	95
3	Brentwood Town	42	13	4	4	40	15	13	6	2	37	17	26	10	6	77	32	45	88
4	Waltham Abbey	42	15	1	5	52	16	10	6	5	33	29	25	7	10	85	45	40	82
5	Concord Rangers	42	10	6	5	38	19	13	4	4	45	15	23	10	9	83	34	49	79
6	Northwood	42	14	4	3	39	15	8	8	5	26	24	22	12	8	65	39	26	78
7	Wingate & Finchley	42	12	4	5	36	22	7	6	8	31	29	19	10	13	67	51	16	67
8	Redbridge	42	9	6	6	32	29	9	4	8	29	21	18	10	14	61	50	11	64
9	Ware	42	10	1	10	35	36	9	3	9	34	39	19	4	19	69	75	-6	61
10	Chatham Town	42	9	3	9	28	20	9	3	9	30	32	18	6	18	58	60	-2	60
11	Tilbury	42	9	7	5	29	20	7	3	11	33	33	16	10	16	62	53	9	58
12	Enfield Town	42	9	5	7	35	33	8	2	11	36	35	17	7	18	71	68	3	58
13	Great Wakering Rovers	42	10	5	6	35	28	6	5	10	21	34	16	10	16	56	62	-6	58
14	Cheshunt	42	8	3	10	30	30	9	2	10	30	41	17	5	20	60	71	-11	56
15	Leyton	42	7	9	5	35	22	5	6	10	28	34	12	15	15	63	56	7	51
16	Maldon Town (-3)*	42	7	2	12	22	28	6	7	8	26	35	13	9	20	48	63	-15	45
17	Ilford	42	8	2	11	14	20	4	3	14	13	48	12	5	25	27	68	-41	41
18	Thamesmead Town	42	8	6	8	31	36	5	2	14	15	37	10	10	22	46	73	-27	40
19	Potters Bar Town (-1)*	42	4	6	11	24	37	5	4	12	28	36	9	10	23	52	73	-21	36
20	Waltham Forest	42	5	4	12	23	41	4	3	14	16	40	9	7	26	39	81	-42	34
21	Witham Town	42	3	5	13	21	57	3	4	14	16	46	6	9	27	37	103	-66	27
22	Hillingdon Borough	42	3	0	18	20	57	1	4	16	15	50	4	4	34	35	107	-72	16

* points deducted for breach of rules.

RYMAN LEAGUE DIVISION ONE SOUTH 2008–09

		P	Home W	D	L	F	A	Away W	D	L	F	A	Total W	D	L	F	A	GD	Pts
1	Kingstonian	42	12	4	5	43	21	14	4	3	48	27	26	8	8	91	48	43	86
2	Cray Wanderers	42	15	2	4	47	25	9	5	7	40	29	24	7	11	87	54	33	79
3	Fleet Town	42	9	9	3	41	21	12	6	3	41	22	21	15	6	82	43	39	78
4	Metropolitan Police	42	9	10	2	37	21	12	4	5	35	24	21	14	7	72	45	27	77
5	Worthing	42	9	7	5	41	26	12	6	3	36	22	21	13	8	77	48	29	76
6	Sittingbourne	42	7	6	8	29	31	12	7	2	34	23	19	13	10	63	54	9	70
7	Ashford Town	42	10	6	5	37	23	6	9	6	31	31	16	15	11	68	54	14	63
8	Merstham (-1)*	42	9	7	5	30	22	9	3	9	27	32	18	10	14	57	54	3	63
9	Godalming Town	42	10	4	7	37	22	7	7	7	34	28	17	11	14	71	50	21	62
10	Croydon Athletic	42	7	7	7	27	23	9	7	5	40	31	16	14	12	67	54	13	62
11	Folkestone Invicta	42	10	3	8	25	21	6	8	7	29	25	16	11	15	54	46	8	59
12	Dulwich Hamlet (-3)*	42	9	7	5	37	30	6	8	7	27	20	15	15	12	64	50	14	57
13	Eastbourne Town	42	9	2	10	34	38	8	4	9	32	34	17	6	19	66	72	-6	57
14	Walton & Hersham	42	6	6	9	18	22	7	5	9	28	33	13	11	18	46	55	-9	50
15	Leatherhead	42	8	4	9	31	32	6	4	11	26	42	14	8	20	57	74	-17	50
16	Whitstable Town	42	8	4	9	34	37	6	4	11	24	40	14	8	20	58	77	-19	50
17	Walton Casuals	42	7	4	10	19	28	5	4	12	24	32	12	8	22	43	60	-17	44
18	Whyteleafe	42	7	3	11	23	30	4	7	10	25	34	11	10	21	48	64	-16	43
19	Burgess Hill Town	42	6	8	7	24	28	4	5	12	25	38	10	13	19	49	66	-17	43
20	Corinthian Casuals	42	6	6	9	33	56	5	4	12	28	35	11	10	21	61	91	-30	43
21	Chipstead	42	4	7	10	30	51	4	5	12	27	45	8	12	22	57	96	-39	36
22	Crowborough Athletic (-3)*	42	3	2	16	28	67	1	2	18	14	58	4	4	34	42	125	-83	13

* points deducted for breach of rules.

RYMAN LEAGUE PLAY-OFFS 2008–09

PREMIER DIVISION PLAY-OFF FINAL
Saturday 2 May 2009
Staines Town 1 *(S. Taylor)*
Carshalton Athletic 0   1198
aet.

DIVISION ONE SOUTH PLAY-OFF FINAL
Saturday 2 May 2009
Cray Wanderers 1 *(S. Osborn)*
Metropolitan Police 0   659

DIVISION ONE NORTH FINAL
Saturday 2 May 2009
Waltham Abbey 1 *(H. Elmes)*
Concord Rangers 1 *(F. Batchelor)*   459
aet; Waltham Abbey won 5-4 on penalties.

RYMAN LEAGUE ATTENDANCES 2008–09

PREMIER	**Highest Average**	1289	Dover Athletic
	Division Highest	2760	Dover Athletic v Tooting and Mitcham United (16 December 2008)
DIVISION ONE NORTH	**Highest Average**	216	Enfield Town
	Division Highest	534	Aveley v Ilford (11 October 2008)
DIVISION ONE SOUTH	**Highest Average**	338	Kingstonian
	Division Highest	746	Kingstonian v Cray Wanderers (13 April 2009)

RYMAN LEAGUE LEADING GOALSCORERS 2008–09

PREMIER LEAGUE		Games played	Goals scored
Jolly R	Carshalton Athletic	42	30
Rook C	Tonbridge Angels	36	25
Collin F	Dover Athletic	35	21
Harrison B	Ashford Town (Middx)	41	20
Butler R	Staines Town	38	19
Ashe R	Wealdstone	40	16
Vines P	Tooting & Mitcham U	37	16
Welford S	Dover Athletic	40	16
Bricknell B	Billericay Town	32	15
Sawyer F	Hastings United	36	15
Araba H	Redbridge	23	17
Richmond N	Aveley	39	17
Barnett L	Chatham Town	20	16
Elbi P	Aveley	34	16
Cable R	Thamesmead Town	37	15
Elmes H	Waltham Abbey	28	15

DIVISION ONE NORTH			
Tuohy M	East Thurrock United	40	39
Holland B	Waltham Abbey	39	20
Stanley S	Brentwood Town	33	20
Stowe C	Tilbury	31	19
Heale D	Concord Rangers	41	18
Newby K	East Thurrock United	39	18

DIVISION ONE SOUTH			
Traynor S	Kingstonian	41	32
Dryden J	Folkestone Invicta	42	21
Stanley G	Godalming Town	36	21
Brady R	Sittingbourne	29	18
Harper S	Burgess Hill Town	39	17
Hamici L	Sutton United	27	16
Hutchings T	Leatherhead	39	16
Wilson-Denis C	Kingstonian	39	16
Cory D	Whitstable Town	33	15
Gordon G	Merstham	33	15

ISTHMIAN LEAGUE CUP 2008–09

FIRST ROUND
Brentwood Town v Potters Bar Town	0-1
Great Wakering Rovers v East Thurrock United	0-1

SECOND ROUND
Croydon Athletic v Sutton United	0-2
Crowborough Athletic v Eastbourne Town	0-4
Dulwich Hamlet v Cray Wanderers	3-2
Worthing v Horsham	1-2
Whyteleafe v Chipstead	0-3
Burgess Hill Town v Hastings United	3-2
Merstham v Tonbridge Angels	2-5
Tooting & Mitcham United v Carshalton Athletic	2-5
Godalming Town v Walton & Hersham	1-0
Walton Casuals v Fleet Town	1-6
Hendon v Harrow Borough	0-2
Leatherhead v Ashford Town (Middlesex)	0-2
Hillingdon Borough v Kingstonian	0-3
Wealdstone v Metropolitan Police	5-2
Northwood v Corinthian Casuals	4-1
Wingate & Finchley v Staines Town	0-3
Ashford Town v Thamesmead Town	1-2
Ramsgate v Chatham Town	4-0
Sittingbourne v Whitstable Town	0-1
Folkestone Invicta v Tilbury	1-2
Aveley v Maidstone United	3-1
Dover Athletic v Canvey Island	4-1
Concord Rangers v East Thurrock United	5-3
Dartford v Margate	3-2
Heybridge Swifts v Maldon Town	2-1
Harlow Town v Cheshunt	4-2
Witham Town v Waltham Forest	0-5
AFC Hornchurch v Potters Bar Town	4-0
Ilford v Redbridge	0-1
Billericay Town v Enfield Town	4-1
Leyton v Ware	0-2
Boreham Wood v Waltham Abbey	2-3

THIRD ROUND
Ashford Town (Middlesex) v Kingstonian	2-1
Godalming Town v Harrow Borough	1-2
Harlow Town v Heybridge Swifts	3-2
Northwood v Fleet Town	2-0
Staines Town v Wealdstone	2-1
Sutton United v Horsham	2-3
Waltham Abbey v Billericay Town	2-3
Whitstable Town v Tilbury	1-2
Eastbourne Town v Chipstead	4-0
Thamesmead Town v Ramsgate	0-4
AFC Hornchurch v Waltham Forest	2-0
Aveley v Dover Athletic	1-4
Carshalton Athletic v Tonbridge Angels	3-0
Burgess Hill Town v Dulwich Hamlet	1-3
Concord Rangers v Dartford	1-3
Ware v Redbridge	2-5

FOURTH ROUND
Carshalton Athletic v Eastbourne Town	5-1
Harlow Town v Harrow Borough	1-2
Staines Town v Northwood	5-2
Billericay Town v AFC Hornchurch	1-0
Dulwich Hamlet v Dover Athletic	0-2
Redbridge v Ashford Town (Middlesex)	1-2
Tilbury v Ramsgate	3-0
Horsham v Dartford	3-2

QUARTER-FINALS
Billericay Town v Dover Athletic	3-2
Harrow Borough v Horsham	4-1
Carshalton Athletic v Ashford Town (Middlesex)	2-3
Tilbury v Staines Town	1-1
Tilbury won 4-2 on penalties.	

SEMI-FINALS
Harrow Borough v Ashford Town (Middlesex)	3-1
Tilbury v Billericay Town	2-0

FINAL
Harrow Borough v Tilbury (att. 284)	0-2

THE FA TROPHY 2008–09
IN PARTNERSHIP WITH CARLSBERG

PRELIMINARY ROUND

Trafford v Rossendale United	8-1
Retford United v Kidsgrove Athletic	1-2
Clitheroe v Grantham Town	4-1
Brigg Town v Willenhall Town	4-0
Durham City v Curzon Ashton	1-1, 2-1
Romulus v Loughborough Dynamo	3-2
Goole v Nuneaton Town	1-1, 1-0
Spalding United v Wakefield	2-1
Lancaster City v Leek Town	1-0
Rushall Olympic v Ossett Albion	2-1
Garforth Town v Belper Town	2-0
Skelmersdale United v Shepshed Dynamo	2-1
Chorley v Warrington Town	0-0, 0-3
Woodley Sports v Quorn	0-1
Harrogate Railway v FC Halifax Town	2-1
Carlton Town v Atherstone Town	2-1
Sheffield v Bamber Bridge	5-3
Mossley v Stocksbridge Park Steels	1-5
Salford City v Gresley Rovers	2-0
Aveley v Ilford	2-0
Waltham Forest v AFC Sudbury	1-4
Wingate & Finchley v Ware	2-1
Great Wakering Rovers v Ashford Town	5-3
Northwood v Whyteleafe	2-0
Merstham v Arlesey Town	4-1
Metropolitan Police v Waltham Abbey	0-0, 2-1
Kingstonian v Whitstable Town	2-3
Rothwell Town v Tilbury	2-2, 0-2
Leatherhead v Sittingbourne	1-2
Leighton Town v Chipstead	7-1
Bury Town v Barton Rovers	2-1
Maldon Town v Cheshunt	0-1
Crowborough Athletic v Eastbourne Town	3-0
Folkestone Invicta v Chatham Town	1-1, 0-2
Leyton v Dulwich Hamlet	1-4
Potters Bar Town v Brentwood Town	0-2
East Thurrock United v Thamesmead Town	2-1
Concord Rangers v Woodford United	4-1
Walton Casuals v Hillingdon Borough	4-3
Godalming Town v Enfield Town	1-5
Corinthian Casuals v Worthing	1-3
Soham Town Rangers v Redbridge	1-0
Burgess Hill Town v Dunstable Town	3-1
Bracknell Town v Malvern Town	2-0
Aylesbury United v Bridgwater Town	2-0
Didcot Town v Andover	1-2
Winchester City v Taunton Town	3-0
Fleet Town v Beaconsfield SYCOB	3-1
Cinderford Town v Truro City	2-4
Paulton Rovers v Thatcham Town	1-1, 0-2
Marlow v Cirencester Town	2-0

FIRST QUALIFYING ROUND

Romulus v Garforth Town	1-1, 4-3
Harrogate Railway v Leigh Genesis	0-1
Stourbridge v Salford City	6-0
Rushall Olympic v Bedworth United	0-0, 1-4
Witton Albion v Worksop Town	0-1
Whitby Town v Trafford	3-2
Hednesford Town v Quorn	3-1
Ashton United v Lincoln United	2-1
Matlock Town v Warrington Town	0-1
FC United of Manchester v Radcliffe Borough	1-0
Brigg Town v Marine	1-5
Boston United v Kidsgrove Athletic	6-0
Skelmersdale United v Sheffield	1-0
Guiseley v Ossett Town	0-1
Glapwell v Leamington	3-2
Colwyn Bay v Chasetown	2-2, 1-2
Stocksbridge Park Steels v Goole	3-1
Lancaster City v Rugby Town	3-3, 0-2
Spalding United v North Ferriby United	0-0, 0-2
Frickley Athletic v Nantwich Town	0-2
Prescot Cables v Cammell Laird	0-3
Stamford v Kendal Town	3-0
Durham City v Halesowen Town	4-4, 1-0
Bradford Park Avenue v Clitheroe	1-2

Eastwood Town v Ilkeston Town	0-2
Newcastle Blue Star v Sutton Coldfield Town	2-2, 1-4
Buxton v Carlton Town	5-3
Concord Rangers v Billericay Town	3-1
Uxbridge v Walton & Hersham	2-1
Walton Casuals v Heybridge Swifts	0-0, 2-3
Whitstable Town v Brackley Town	3-4
Worthing v Merstham	2-0
Maidstone United v AFC Hornchurch	1-1, 2-1
Crowborough Athletic v Northwood	0-2
Wingate & Finchley v Ashford Town (Middlesex)	1-1, 4-2
Brentwood Town v AFC Sudbury	2-3
Wealdstone v Croydon Athletic	1-0
Bedford Town v Corby Town	1-2
Hemel Hempstead Town v AFC Hayes	6-0
Metropolitan Police v Dulwich Hamlet	0-2
Soham Town Rangers v Witham Town	6-0
Aveley v Hitchin Town	1-2
Tilbury v Cray Wanderers	1-1, 0-1
Harrow Borough v Chatham Town	2-1
Staines Town v Dover Athletic	0-2
Boreham Wood v Burgess Hill Town	2-0
Tonbridge Angels v Ramsgate	2-3
Dartford v Harlow Town	2-1
Bury Town v Leighton Town	1-0
Enfield Town v Great Wakering Rovers	0-2
Cambridge City v Canvey Island	1-1, 0-0
Cambridge City won 4-2 on penalties.	
Cheshunt v East Thurrock United	1-2
Horsham v Sittingbourne	4-2
Margate v Hendon	0-1
Hastings United v Carshalton Athletic	3-1
Sutton United v Tooting & Mitcham United	2-0
Tiverton Town v North Leigh	5-2
Mangotsfield United v Bashley	0-2
Yate Town v Stourport Swifts	1-1, 3-1
Andover v Gosport Borough	3-2
Banbury United v Burnham	0-1
Merthyr Tydfil v Bishop's Cleeve	4-1
Bromsgrove Rovers v Gloucester City	1-4
Evesham United v Clevedon Town	4-0
Winchester City v Windsor & Eton	0-5
Bracknell Town v Swindon Supermarine	2-4
Farnborough v Marlow	4-0
Thatcham Town v Slough Town	5-4
Truro City v Chesham United	3-3, 1-2
Oxford City v Aylesbury United	3-1
AFC Totton v Abingdon United	3-2
Chippenham Town v Fleet Town	2-1

SECOND QUALIFYING ROUND

Worksop Town v FC United of Manchester	0-3
Chasetown v North Ferriby United	1-1, 4-1
Buxton v Skelmersdale United	0-1
Ossett Town v Bedworth United	1-0
Ashton United v Ilkeston Town	0-2
Clitheroe v Boston United	2-4
Marine v Durham City	1-2
Romulus v Warrington Town	2-2, 1-3
Stourbridge v Evesham United	2-1
Leigh Genesis v Cammell Laird	1-5
Sutton Coldfield Town v Glapwell	2-3
Rugby Town v Nantwich Town	1-3
Stamford v Hednesford Town	3-4
Stocksbridge Park Steels v Whitby Town	0-2
Swindon Supermarine v Maidstone United	2-0
Great Wakering Rovers v AFC Sudbury	1-1, 3-4
Soham Town Rangers v Farnborough	0-5
East Thurrock United v Gloucester City	4-2
Boreham Wood v Uxbridge	1-2
Northwood v Brackley Town	1-4
Hendon v Sutton United	1-2
Harrow Borough v Hastings United	2-3
Dover Athletic v Cambridge City	2-3
abandoned 58 minutes; waterlogged pitch.	
Heybridge Swifts v Chippenham Town	0-0, 1-2
Andover v Merthyr Tydfil	3-2
Burnham v Windsor & Eton	0-5

Dulwich Hamlet v Bury Town	0-3
Dartford v Oxford City	3-3, 4-2
Horsham v Cray Wanderers	1-2
Hitchin Town v Ramsgate	3-6
Corby Town v Chesham United	2-3
Yate Town v Bashley	1-3
Thatcham Town v AFC Totton	0-4
Concord Rangers v Hemel Hempstead Town	1-3
Wealdstone v Tiverton Town	1-2
Wingate & Finchley v Worthing	1-0

THIRD QUALIFYING ROUND

Hinckley United v Burscough	1-2
King's Lynn v Stafford Rangers	3-2
Solihull Moors v Durham City	1-2
Ossett Town v Fleetwood Town	3-1
Whitby Town v Stalybridge Celtic	0-3
Redditch United v Cammell Laird	1-1, 2-0
Tamworth v Workington	0-1
Warrington Town v Nantwich Town	0-1
FC United of Manchester v Boston United	1-3
Vauxhall Motors v Southport	0-0, 1-2
Chasetown v Ilkeston Town	1-2
Farsley Celtic v Droylsden	2-0
Gainsborough Trinity v AFC Telford United	0-2
Hyde United v Hednesford Town	1-1, 0-5
Blyth Spartans v Alfreton Town	3-4
Stourbridge v Hucknall Town	3-2
Gateshead v Harrogate Town	0-2
Glapwell v Skelmersdale United	0-1
Uxbridge v Dorchester Town	2-1
Fisher Athletic v Havant & Waterlooville	0-2
Weston-Super-Mare v AFC Sudbury	1-2
Team Bath v Windsor & Eton	2-1
Swindon Supermarine v Bromley	1-0
Braintree Town v Farnborough	1-1, 2-6
Basingstoke Town v East Thurrock United	1-0
Cambridge City v Hastings United	1-0
Bath City v East Thurrock United	5-1
Wingate & Finchley v Sutton United	1-1, 2-2
Wingate & Finchley won 4-3 on penalties.	
Maidenhead United v Chesham United	2-4
St Albans City v Dartford	0-0, 1-1
St Albans City won 4-2 on penalties.	
Hampton & Richmond Borough v Bury Town	1-2
Cray Wanderers v Brackley Town	0-4
Eastleigh v Bashley	0-2
Andover v Newport County	0-3
Worcester City v AFC Wimbledon	1-3
Ramsgate v Bognor Regis Town	0-2
Hayes & Yeading United v Chelmsford City	4-1
Welling United v AFC Totton	1-1, 2-1
Hemel Hempstead Town v Heybridge Swifts	5-1
Bishop's Stortford v Tiverton Town	0-0, 0-1

FIRST ROUND

Altrincham v Southport	1-4
Durham City v Harrogate Town	2-0
Northwich Victoria v York City	0-2
Wrexham v Mansfield Town	2-1
Hednesford Town v Nantwich Town	3-2
Burton Albion v Farsley Celtic	1-1, 2-2
Burton Albion won 3-2 on penalties.	
Ilkeston Town v Ossett Town	3-2
Barrow v Skelmersdale United	2-1
Alfreton Town v Redditch United	0-1
Kidderminster Harriers v Burscough	3-2
Workington v King's Lynn	4-3
Stourbridge v Stalybridge Celtic	1-6
Boston United v AFC Telford United	1-2
Swindon Supermarine v Eastbourne Borough	1-0
Stevenage Borough v St Albans City	4-1
Cambridge City v Kettering Town	1-4
AFC Sudbury v Oxford United	0-2

Bashley v Tiverton Town	2-2, 1-2
Welling United v Weymouth	2-0
Histon v Cambridge United	2-3
Forest Green Rovers v Hemel Hempstead Town	5-1
Bognor Regis Town v Ebbsfleet United	0-2
Farnborough v Wingate & Finchley	3-1
Uxbridge v AFC Wimbledon	2-1
Hayes & Yeading United v Grays Athletic	2-0
Havant & Waterlooville v Bury Town	3-1
Torquay United v Bath City	2-0
Woking v Salisbury City	1-2
Basingstoke Town v Brackley Town	3-1
Newport County v Rushden & Diamonds	1-1, 1-1
Rushden & Diamonds won 5-3 on penalties.	
Chesham United v Crawley Town	2-4
Team Bath v Lewes	1-2

SECOND ROUND

Lewes v Havant & Waterlooville	3-3, 3-4
Ilkeston Town v Kidderminster Harriers	3-5
Burton Albion v Salisbury City	3-0
Basingstoke Town v Wrexham	1-2
Hednesford Town v Welling United	4-3
Forest Green Rovers v Redditch United	5-0
Tiverton Town v Kettering Town	1-1, 1-1
Kettering Town won 4-1 on penalties.	
Durham City v Southport	1-1, 1-3
AFC Telford United v Hayes & Yeading United	4-0
Farnborough v Stevenage Borough	0-2
Torquay United v Rushden & Diamonds	1-0
Ebbsfleet United v Stalybridge Celtic	2-1
Barrow v Workington	0-3
Uxbridge v Swindon Supermarine	1-6
Oxford United v York City	1-2
Cambridge United v Crawley Town	0-5

THIRD ROUND

Kettering Town v AFC Telford United	0-1
Kidderminster Harriers v York City	1-1, 1-1
York City won 13-12 on penalties.	
Workington v Wrexham	1-3
Forest Green Rovers v Hednesford Town	1-0
Ebbsfleet United v Swindon Supermarine	2-0
Havant & Waterlooville v Crawley Town	2-0
Southport v Torquay United	3-0
Stevenage Borough v Burton Albion	4-0

FOURTH ROUND

Wrexham v Ebbsfleet United	0-0, 1-3
Stevenage Borough v Forest Green Rovers	4-0
AFC Telford United v Southport	2-2, 1-0
York City v Havant & Waterlooville	2-0

SEMI-FINALS (two legs)

Stevenage Borough v Ebbsfleet United	3-2, 1-0
AFC Telford United v York City	0-2, 1-2

FINAL (at Wembley)

Saturday 9 May 2009

Stevenage Borough (0) 2 *(Morison 69, Boylan 90)*

York City (0) 0   27,198

Stevenage Borough: Day; Wilson, Roberts, Bostwick, Henry, Murphy, Drury, Mills, Morison, Boylan, Vincenti (Anaclet 86).

York City: Ingham; Purkiss, Pejic, Mackin, McGurk, Parslow, Rusk (Russell 77), Greaves (McWilliams 72), McBreen (Sodje 60), Brodie, Boyes.

Referee: M. Jones (Cheshire).

THE FA VASE 2008-09

IN PARTNERSHIP WITH CARLSBERG

FIRST QUALIFYING ROUND

Guisborough Town v Pontefract Collieries	5-0
Northallerton Town v Marske United	0-1
Spennymoor Town v Norton & Stockton Ancients	3-2
Whickham v Stokesley SC	0-0, 1-4
Brandon United v Bottesford Town	2-0
Chester-Le-Street Town v South Shields	3-1
Seaham Red Star v Glasshoughton Welfare	4-1
Easington Colliery v Silsden	1-3
Crook Town v Billingham Synthonia	3-2
Washington v Sunderland Nissan	1-2
Willington v Thackley	1-6
Jarrow Roofing BCA v Bishop Auckland	0-3
Penrith v Atherton LR	2-1
Worsborough Bridge Athletic v Cheadle Town	5-2
Flixton v Congleton Town	0-2
Atherton Collieries v Chadderton	3-2
Colne v Darwen	3-2
Goodrich v Pelsall Villa	1-7
Bridgnorth Town v Stratford Town	1-4
Oadby Town v Staveley MW	3-0
Clipstone Welfare v Highgate United	1-3
Cadbury Athletic v Heather St Johns	4-2
Pershore Town v Graham St Prims	2-1
Ellistown w.o. v Stapenhill withdrew.	
Gedling MW v Norton United	1-2
Hinckley Downes v Gedling Town	0-1
Heanor Town v Rolls Royce Leisure	5-4
Pegasus Juniors v Barwell	0-5
Wednesfield v Coventry Copsewood	2-0
Bardon Hill Sports v Holwell Sports	2-1
Bromyard Town v Blackwell MW	2-3
Brockton v Calverton MW	2-2, 1-4
Coleshill Town v Bolehall Swifts	3-2
Glossop North End v Sporting Khalsa	5-0
Causeway United v Ollerton Town	0-0, 2-1
Dudley Sports v Rainworth MW	0-1
Sutton Town v Rocester	1-4
New Mills v Wolverhampton Casuals	6-0
Shirebrook Town v Castle Vale	2-3
Teversal v Nuneaton Griff	3-0
Newark Town v Meir KA	3-1
Birstall United v Long Eaton United	2-4
GSA Sports v Mickleover Sports	2-4
Barrow Town v Wellington	3-0
Bartley Green v Saffron Dynamo	3-1
Kimberley Town v Gornal Athletic	0-2
Haverhill Rovers v Ely City	1-0
Leiston v Bourne Town	4-0
Lincoln Moorlands Railway v Sleaford Town	1-0
Debenham LC v Fakenham Town	4-0
Mildenhall Town v Godmanchester Rovers	3-0
Gorleston v Deeping Rangers	2-0
Wisbech Town v Swaffham Town	5-0
Clapton v Thrapston Town	2-3
Welwyn Garden City v Daventry Town	1-6
London Colney v Hatfield Town	5-2
Cranfield United v Haringey Borough	3-1
Bedfont v Ampthill Town	2-1
Burnham Ramblers v Harwich & Parkeston	3-1
Rushden & Higham United v Feltham	4-0
Basildon United v Wootton Blue Cross	2-1
Hoddesdon Town v Colney Heath	0-1
Bedford v Hullbridge Sports	1-2
Southend Manor v Harpenden Town	3-1
Broxbourne Borough V&E w.o. v Beaumont Athletic removed.	
Hanwell Town v Barking	1-1, 6-0
Stansted v Brimsdown Rovers	2-1
London APSA v Oxhey Jets	1-3
Saffron Walden Town v Sporting Bengal United	4-2
Langford v Cockfosters	5-1
Tring Athletic v Leverstock Green	0-2
Dorking v Sidley United	3-1
Oakwood v Chertsey Town	3-3, 2-3
Hassocks v Three Bridges	4-3
Southwick v Mile Oak	2-2, 0-1
Bookham v Hailsham Town	5-0
Selsey v Holmesdale	1-1, 3-2
Wick v Erith Town	2-3

Eastbourne United v Banstead Athletic	1-5
Chessington & Hook United v Steyning Town	4-3
Epsom & Ewell v Colliers Wood United	4-2
Herne Bay v Lingfield	1-2
Peacehaven & Telscombe v Littlehampton Town	4-1
Worthing United v Crawley Down	0-2
Malmesbury Victoria v Cheltenham Saracens	2-1
Hamble ASSC v Harrow Hill	1-4
Petersfield Town w.o. v Tadley Calleva withdrew.	
Downton v Westbury United	1-4
Newport Pagnell Town v Totton & Eling	1-1, 1-2
Amesbury Town v Marlow United	6-3
Bournemouth v Calne Town	2-3
Christchurch v Hartley Wintney	3-1
Highworth Town v Thame United	3-0
Longwell Green Sports v Shrewton United	3-2
Moneyfields v Shortwood United	0-1
Alresford Town v Romsey Town	3-2
Ringwood Town v Cowes Sports	0-4
Bicester Town v Wantage Town	1-5
Lydney Town v Fairford Town	1-5
Buckingham Athletic v Wootton Bassett Town	3-5
Reading Town v Pewsey Vale	4-1
Blackfield & Langley v Corsham Town	2-1
Milton United v Brockenhurst	2-1
Fareham Town v Bristol Manor Farm	0-3
Bristol Manor Farm expelled for fielding ineligible player.	
Minehead v Launceston	1-2
Newquay v Wadebridge Town	2-3
Porthleven v St Blazey	3-1
Saltash United v Liskeard Athletic	3-1
Gillingham Town v Larkhall Athletic	0-2
Newton Abbot v Budley Salterton	2-0
Penryn Athletic v Hamworthy United	0-2
Bridport v Brislington	0-4
Ilfracombe Town v Wellington Town	3-7
Bishop Sutton v Bodmin Town	1-3
Penzance v Welton Rovers	0-1
Runcorn Linnets v Padiham	4-3

SECOND QUALIFYING ROUND

Horden CW v Sunderland Nissan	1-2
Peterlee Town v Billingham Town	2-0
Leeds Carnegie v Brandon United	3-0
Darlington Railway Athletic v Morpeth Town	0-3
Selby Town v Seaham Red Star	5-1
Thornaby v Thackley	4-5
Barton Town Old Boys v Crook Town	1-2
Ashington v North Shields	2-0
Birtley Town v Scarborough Athletic	2-3
West Auckland Town v Sunderland RCA	2-4
Tow Law Town v Spennymoor Town	2-4
Esh Winning v Team Northumbria	2-1
Hall Road Rangers v Ryton	1-4
Armthorpe Welfare v Guisborough Town	3-6
Yorkshire Amateur v Shildon	0-7
West Allotment Celtic v Silsden	2-1
Eccleshill United v Bedlington Terriers	0-1
Marske United v Bishop Auckland	4-1
Stokesley SC v Chester-Le-Street Town	3-2
Hebburn Town v Tadcaster Albion	1-2
Abbey Hey v Parkgate	2-1
St Helens Town v Ashton Athletic	1-2
Nostell MW v Poulton Victoria	2-1
AFC Blackpool v Squires Gate	1-2
Rossington Main v Daisy Hill	2-0
Holker Old Boys v Colne	2-2, 0-5
Worsborough Bridge Athletic v Ramsbottom United	1-3
Penrith v Dinnington Town	2-0
Hallam v Winsford United	3-2
Congleton Town v Maltby Main	3-0
Brodsworth MW v Ashton Town	3-0
AFC Emley v Oldham Town	2-6
Atherton Collieries v Bootle	0-3
Cradley Town v Warstones Wanderers	1-1
Warstones Wanderers won 2-1 on penalties.	
Pilkington XXX v Cadbury Athletic	2-1
Pelsall Villa v Castle Vale	0-2

Anstey Nomads v Shifnal Town	0-1
Greenwood Meadows v Dosthill Colts	0-3
Stone Dominoes v Tividale	4-1
New Mills v Ellistown	3-2
Dunkirk v Heath Hayes	4-0
Kirby Muxloe v Wednesfield	1-0
Bewdley Town v Long Eaton United	1-3
Barwell v AFC Wulfrunians	2-0
Radford v Leek CSOB	0-2
Bartley Green v St Andrews	1-1, 3-2
Calverton MW v Glossop North End	1-4
Coleshill Town v Ibstock United	4-3
Darlaston Town v Oadby Town	3-0
Mickleover Sports v Biddulph Victoria	1-2
Blaby & Whetstone Athletic v Arnold Town	2-6
Friar Lane & Epworth v Coalville Town	0-2
Stratford Town v Gedling Town	3-1
Norton United v Heanor Town	2-3
Dudley Town v Southam United	2-0
Ellesmere Rangers v Borrowash Victoria	1-3
Westfields v Blackwell MW	4-0
Bardon Hill Sports v Teversal	1-3
Pershore Town v Rothley Imperial	2-3
Loughborough University v Ledbury Town	2-0
Barrow Town v Lye Town	1-2
Holbrook Miners Welfare v Eccleshall	1-1, 0-1
Racing Club Warwick v Rocester	3-1
Oldbury United v Highgate United	1-2
Radcliffe Olympic v Alvechurch	3-4
Causeway United w.o. v Brierley Hill & Withymoor withdrew.	
Leiston v Huntingdon Town	5-1
Felixstowe & Walton United v Whitton United	4-3
Cornard United v Eynesbury Rovers	3-1
Walsham Le Willows v Wisbech Town	2-4
St Neots Town v Great Yarmouth Town	1-0
Woodbridge Town v Yaxley	0-1
Holbeach United v Gorleston	2-1
Lincoln Moorlands Railway v Diss Town	1-5
Haverhill Rovers v Long Melford	0-1
Newmarket Town v March Town United	3-0
Debenham LC v Stowmarket Town	1-0
Kirklee & Pakefield v Norwich United	1-0
Ipswich Wanderers v Hadleigh United	0-6
Mildenhall Town v Thetford Town	2-0
Thrapston Town v Burnham Ramblers	2-1
North Greenford United v Sport London E Benfica	0-3
Saffron Walden Town v Biggleswade United	0-1
Potton United v Bugbrooke St Michaels	5-0
Halstead Town v Hanwell Town	4-1
Southend Manor v Royston Town	2-3
London Colney v Daventry Town	0-4
AFC Kempston Rovers v Kentish Town	1-3
Langford v Cogenhoe United	1-2
Wellingborough Town v Cranfield United	6-0
Rushden & Higham United v Daventry United	0-1
Oxhey Jets v Sileby Rangers	3-1
Bedfont v Codicote	2-3
Crawley Green v Leverstock Green	2-3
FC Clacton v Tokyngton Manor	6-2
Bedfont Green v Rothwell Corinthians	6-1
St Margaretsbury v Colney Heath	5-1
Stewarts & Lloyds v Enfield 1893	1-0
Tiptree United v Broxbourne Borough V&E	3-1
Wembley v Basildon United	0-4
Kingsbury London Tigers v Raunds Town	1-2
Northampton Spencer v Hullbridge Sports	2-0
Dorking v Selsey	3-5
East Grinstead Town v Lancing	2-1
Faversham Town v Tunbridge Wells	0-1
Bagshot Lea v Pagham	4-3
Egham Town v Crawley Down	4-2
Lingfield v Horley Town	1-2
Hassocks v Chertsey Town	2-3
Slade Green v Redhill	1-3
Lordswood v Ringmer	4-0
Wealden v Mile Oak	0-5
Erith Town v Rye United	3-4
Ash United v Sevenoaks Town	1-0
Croydon v Haywards Heath Town	4-0
South Park v Shoreham	1-2
Raynes Park Vale v Chessington & Hook United	1-2
St Francis Rangers v Westfield	4-3
Farnham Town v Peacehaven & Telscombe	1-3
Newhaven v Banstead Athletic	1-3
Chichester City United v Sleaford Town	4-0

Saltdean United v Epsom & Ewell	0-1
Deal Town v Cobham	0-3
Andover New Street v Totton & Eling	0-1
Farnborough North End v Bemerton Heath Harlequins	0-2
Abingdon Town v Flackwell Heath	1-2
Hallen v Reading Town	1-3
Wantage Town v Binfield	1-2
Holyport v Sandhurst Town	0-2
Christchurch v Petersfield Town	2-0
Ardley United v Harrow Hill	2-3
Henley Town v Wootton Bassett Town	0-6
Hayling United v Carterton	1-0
Shortwood United v Devizes Town	4-0
Milton United v Clanfield 85	2-2, 1-1
Clanfield 85 won 4-2 on penalties.	
Aylesbury Vale v Alton Town	3-1
Fairford Town v Hook Norton	1-1, 1-3
Warminster Town v Lavestock & Ford	2-1
Highworth Town v New Milton Town	1-2
Amesbury Town v Melksham Town	0-2
Kidlington v Chalfont Wasps	2-1
Cowes Sports v Calne Town	1-3
Blackfield & Langley v Longwell Green Sports	0-1
Buckingham Town v AFC Wallingford	4-0
Westbury United v Malmsbury Victoria	2-2, 1-3
Fareham Town v Alresford Town	2-1
Wadebridge Town v Bodmin Town	0-4
Shaftesbury v Shepton Mallet	3-1
Tavistock v Wellington Town	2-0
Radstock Town v Hamworthy United	1-4
Welton Rovers v Cullompton Rangers	0-2
Street v Falmouth Town	6-2
Barnstaple Town v Newton Abbot	3-1
Porthleven v Buckland Athletic	4-3
Launceston v Keynsham Town	3-1
Odd Down v Brislington	0-2
Saltash United v Portishead	6-1
Clevedon United v Elmore	1-0
Chard Town v Sherborne Town	1-2
Larkhall Athletic v Plymouth Parkway	2-1
Runcorn Linnets v Bacup Borough	4-0
Erith & Belvedere v Sidlesham	7-0
Bookham v Frimley Green	2-2, 1-4
Newark Town v Gornal Athletic	3-3, 1-0
Rainworth MW v Walsall Wood	2-0
Brimsdown Rovers v Eton Manor	0-1

FIRST ROUND

Esh Winning v Scarborough Athletic	1-2
Guisborough Town v Ryton	1-1, 1-10
Crook Town v Shildon	2-4
Bedlington Terriers v Stokesley SC	1-1, 1-3
Winterton Rangers v Selby Town	2-1
Sunderland Nissan v Morpeth Town	0-0, 4-3
Thackley v Liversedge	3-0
Ashington v Leeds Carnegie	3-1
Sunderland RCA v Marske United	1-2
Tadcaster Albion v Spennymoor Town	1-5
Bridlington Town v West Allotment Celtic	6-1
Newcastle Benfield v Peterlee Town	4-1
Ashton Athletic v Nostell MW	2-2, 1-3
Oldham Town v Congleton Town	1-0
Alsager Town v Hallam	2-2, 3-1
Colne v Abbey Hey	2-3
Maine Road v Runcorn Linnets	3-3, 1-2
Bootle v Ramsbottom United	2-1
Rossington Main v Brodsworth MW	1-4
Penrith v Squires Gate	2-1
Borrowash Victoria v Arnold Town	1-3
Kirby Muxloe v Pilkington XXX	1-3
Dosthill Colts v Loughborough University	2-1
Castle Vale v Stone Dominoes	1-2
Coalville Town v Newark Town	4-0
Market Drayton Town v Teversal	3-0
Darlaston Town v Eccleshall	3-1
Warstones Wanderers v Long Eaton United	0-4
Alvechurch v Causeway United	1-3
Bartley Green v Barwell	1-2
Dudley Town v Rothley Imperial	2-0
Racing Club Warwick v Heanor Town	1-2
Newcastle Town v Highgate United	5-0
Westfields v Lye Town	2-1
Leek CSOB v Boldmere St Michaels	1-2

New Mills v Glossop North End	1-4
Shifnal Town v Biddulph Victoria	0-1
Rainworth MW v Dunkirk	1-3
Stratford Town v Coleshill Town	6-0
Cornard United v Wisbech Town	2-0
Hadleigh United v Debenham LC	0-1
Dereham Town v Newmarket Town	4-2
Holbeach United v Felixstowe & Walton United	1-1, 1-0
Wroxham v Leiston	0-2
Mildenhall Town v Diss Town	4-2
Yaxley v Kirklee & Pakefield	3-3, 1-5
Long Melford v St Neots Town	0-2
Kentish Town v Thrapston Town	5-2
Cogenhoe United v Codicote	6-0
Eton Manor v Sport London E Benfica	1-2
Halstead Town v Raunds Town	2-4
Leverstock Green v Northampton Spencer	2-3
Biggleswade United v Desborough Town	3-0
Biggleswade Town v Berkhamsted Town	2-0
Potton United v Wivenhoe Town	1-3
Daventry Town v Daventry United	2-0
Stewarts & Lloyds v Oxhey Jets	3-0
FC Clacton v Bedfont Green	4-1
Basildon United v Stotfold	4-4, 4-1
Barkingside v Bowers & Pitsea	2-2, 2-0
Royston Town v Wellingborough Town	1-3
Tiptree United v Hertford Town	8-0
St Margaretsbury v Romford	1-2
Chessington & Hook United v Shoreham	0-3
Banstead Athletic v Erith & Belvedere	2-1
East Preston v Whitehawk	0-2
Molesey v Bagshot Lea	2-1
Hythe Town v Egham Town	0-3
Frimley Green v Redhill	2-1
East Grinstead Town v Rye United	4-2
Guildford City v Selsey	1-3
Chichester City United v Epsom & Ewell	2-0
Horsham YMCA v Peacehaven & Telscombe	1-4
Horley Town v Croydon	2-4
Arundel v Chertsey Town	1-0
Mile Oak v Cobham	1-0
Lordswood v St Francis Rangers	1-5
Tunbridge Wells v Ash United	4-1
Melksham Town v New Milton Town	0-1
Longwell Green Sports v Clanfield 85	0-1
Newport (IW) v Witney United	0-1
Almondsbury Town v Reading Town	1-0
Fareham Town v Binfield	0-0, 2-3
Aylesbury Vale v Harrow Hill	5-0
Bemerton Heath Harlequins v Shortwood United	3-0
Chalfont St Peter v Totton & Eling	5-2
Buckingham Town v Malmsbury Victoria	2-0
VT v Calne Town	6-1
Sandhurst Town v Warminster Town	2-1
Cove v Christchurch	1-2
Hayling Town v Brading Town	3-0
Wootton Bassett Town v Kidlington	3-2
Flackwell Heath v Hook Norton	1-6
Porthleven v Larkhall Athletic	1-2
Frome Town v Tavistock	2-1
Street v Clevedon United	1-1, 4-2
Sherborne Town v Saltash United	2-4
Barnstaple Town v Hamworthy United	1-2
Shaftesbury v Wimborne Town	0-3
Cullompton Rangers v Willand Rovers	0-0, 0-1
Brislington v Bodmin Town	3-2
Dawlish Town v Launceston	5-1

SECOND ROUND

Spennymoor Town v Stokesley SC	2-1
Alsager Town v Runcorn Linnets	1-1, 2-2
Runcorn Linnets won 5-4 on penalties.	
Bootle v Oldham Town	5-3
Winterton Rangers v Ashington	3-1
Consett v Marske United	0-1
Ryton v Nostell MW	2-2, 1-4
Bridlington Town v Penrith	0-2
AFC Fylde v Newcastle Benfield	1-0
Scarborough Athletic v Sunderland Nissan	3-2
Whitley Bay v Abbey Hey	5-2
Brodsworth Miners Welfare v Pickering Town	0-2
Formby v Dunston Federation	0-4
Thackley v Shildon	0-1
Dosthill Colts v Coalville Town	2-5
Arnold Town v Pilkington XXX	4-0

Stone Dominoes v Coventry Sphinx	1-0
Glossop North End v Biddulph Victoria	4-0
Blackstones v Dunkirk	2-0
Shawbury United v Westfields	2-2, 2-2
Westfields won 5-4 on penalties.	
Market Drayton Town v Newcastle Town	2-1
Daventry Town v Dudley Town	3-1
Stratford Town v Causeway United	4-2
Tipton Town v Boldmere St Michaels	1-0
Stewarts & Lloyds v Heanor Town	5-1
Darlaston Town v Long Eaton United	0-3
Boston Town v Cogenhoe United	1-2
Barwell v Studley	3-3, 2-2
Barwell won 4-3 on penalties.	
Sport London E Benfica v St Neots Town	0-5
Wellingborough Town v Long Buckby	0-3
FC Clacton v Basildon United	4-0
St Ives Town v Romford	2-1
Lowestoft Town v Tiptree United	2-0
Kirklee & Pakefield v Dereham Town	0-1
Raunds Town v Holbeach United	1-2
Leiston v Debenham LC	1-0
VCD Athletic v Mildenhall Town	2-1
Harefield United v Barkingside	2-1
Needham Market v Northampton Spencer	1-0
Wivenhoe Town v Cornard United	3-0
Kentish Town v Biggleswade Town	2-6
Biggleswade United v Stanway Rovers	0-3
Chalfont St Peter v Clanfield 85	2-0
Molesey v St Francis Rangers	3-0
Frimley Green v Binfield	1-0
Banstead Athletic v Arundel	1-2
Aylesbury Vale v East Grinstead Town	4-0
Sandhurst Town v Witney United	1-2
Christchurch v Tunbridge Wells	1-0
Chichester City United v Shoreham	0-4
Croydon v Mile Oak	3-0
Selsey v Whitehawk	2-0
Hook Norton v VT	1-1, 0-4
Egham Town v Buckingham Town	0-1
Hayling United v New Milton Town	2-4
Camberley Town v Peacehaven & Telscombe	4-3
Larkhall Athletic v Lymington Town	4-1
Bitton v Poole Town	4-2
Wimborne Town v Wootton Bassett Town	3-4
Dawlish Town v Street	3-4
Shrivenham v Hamworthy United	2-2, 1-4
Willand Rovers v Bemerton Heath Harlequins	2-1
Almondsbury Town v Hungerford Town	0-2
Brislington v Bideford	2-4
Frome Town v Saltash United	4-1

THIRD ROUND

Glossop North End v Winterton Rangers	2-1
Barwell v Coalville Town	0-1
Market Drayton Town v Arnold Town	1-1, 2-0
Spennymoor Town v Shildon	3-2
Marske United v Pickering Town	7-0
Penrith v Whitley Bay	0-1
Long Eaton United v Bootle	0-1
Scarborough Athletic v Blackstones	6-1
AFC Fylde v Runcorn Linnets	4-1
Stratford Town v Westfields	1-1, 1-0
Tipton Town v Dunston Federation	0-3
Stone Dominoes v Nostell MW	1-0
Long Buckby v St Ives Town	1-2
Needham Market v St Neots Town	4-3
Stanway Rovers v Shoreham	1-0
Leiston v Aylesbury Vale	4-1
Lowestoft Town v Harefield United	2-1
Croydon v Camberley Town	3-1
Stewarts & Lloyds v Daventry Town	2-1
FC Clacton v Holbeach United	4-3
Arundel v Cogenhoe United	1-4
Biggleswade Town v Wivenhoe Town	6-0
Dereham Town v Molesey	3-1
Selsey v Chalfont St Peter	0-2
Frimley Green v VCD Athletic	0-0, 0-4
Larkhall Athletic v Wimborne Town	3-1
VT v Willand Rovers	1-0
Witney United v Buckingham Town	2-1
Hamworthy United v Hungerford Town	1-3
Christchurch v New Milton Town	3-0
Street v Bitton	0-0, 1-2
Bideford v Frome Town	2-1

FOURTH ROUND

Bitton v Cogenhoe United	2-1
VCD Athletic v Marske United	2-3
Biggleswade Town v Croydon	2-1
St Ives Town v Stanway Rovers	0-0, 2-0
Market Drayton Town v VT	2-1
Coalville Town v Spennymoor Town	1-1, 1-1
Spennymoor Town won 5-4 on penalties.	
Needham Market v AFC Fylde	0-0, 2-1
Christchurch v FC Clacton	4-0
Stratford Town v Stone Dominoes	3-2
Bideford v Scarborough Athletic	1-0
Larkhall Athletic v Dereham Town	2-4
Hungerford Town v Leiston	3-2
Bootle v Whitley Bay	1-3
Dunston Federation v Chalfont St Peter	5-6
Glossop North End v Stewarts & Lloyds	2-1
Lowestoft Town v Witney United	1-0

FIFTH ROUND

St Ives Town v Marske United	0-3
Lowestoft Town v Hungerford Town	4-3
Chalfont St Peter v Christchurch	4-0
Biggleswade Town v Market Drayton Town	4-2
Bitton v Glossop North End	0-2
Bideford v Spennymoor Town	2-0
Whitley Bay v Stratford Town	2-0
Needham Market v Dereham Town	2-1

SIXTH ROUND

Whitley Bay v Biggleswade Town	5-2
Lowestoft Town v Bideford	4-0
Needham Market v Chalfont St Peter	0-0, 0-0
Chalfont St Peter won 6-5 on penalties.	
Glossop North End v Marske United	5-2

SEMI-FINAL (two legs)

Chalfont St Peter v Glossop North End	3-3, 2-2
Glossop North End won 6-5 on penalties.	
Whitley Bay v Lowestoft Town	2-1, 1-1

FINAL (at Wembley)

Sunday 10 May 2009

Whitley Bay (2) 2 *(Kerr 36, Chow 45)* 12,212

Glossop North End (0) 0

Glossop North End: Cooper; Young, Kay, Lugsden, Yates, Gorton, Bailey R (Hind 56), Morris, Allen (Balfe 65), Hamilton (Bailey T 72), Hodges.
Whitley Bay: Burke; Taylor, Picton, McFarlane (Fawcett 59), Coulson, Ryan, Moore, Robson, Kerr, Chow (Robinson 73), Johnstone (Bell 59).
Referee: K. Friend (Leicestershire).

THE FA COUNTY YOUTH CUP 2008–09

FIRST QUALIFYING ROUND

Liverpool v Manchester	2-1
Hertfordshire v Worcestershire	2-3
North Riding v Lincolnshire	1-5
Nottinghamshire v Staffordshire	3-0
Somerset v Amateur Football Alliance	3-4
London v Herefordshire	4-1
Surrey v Oxfordshire	2-2
Oxfordshire won 5-4 on penalties.	
Jersey v Kent	0-2
Sheffield & Hallamshire v Cheshire	0-2
Westmoreland v Cumberland	3-1
Durham v Derbyshire	6-0
Berks & Bucks v Cornwall	4-5
Northamptonshire v Huntingdonshire	1-2
Essex v Devon	2-1
Dorset v Guernsey	2-1

SECOND ROUND

East Riding v Liverpool	1-2
Lincolnshire v Leicestershire & Rutland	0-2
Westmoreland v Lancashire	1-2
West Riding v Northumberland	5-0
Shropshire v Birmingham	1-5
Durham v Cheshire	5-4
Nottinghamshire v Isle of Man	0-3
Cornwall v Worcestershire	4-5
Wiltshire v Amateur Football Alliance	2-1
Essex v Middlesex	0-3
Dorset v Kent	0-4
Sussex v Oxfordshire	1-4
Huntingdonshire v Suffolk	0-6
Norfolk v Hampshire	1-2

Cambridgeshire v Gloucestershire	5-1
London v Bedfordshire	3-0

THIRD ROUND

Oxfordshire v Kent	0-5
Worcestershire v Suffolk	0-1
Birmingham v Middlesex	3-2
Durham v Liverpool	
abandoned 87 minutes at 2-3; injured player.	
Tie awarded to Durham, Liverpool removed.	
Isle of Man v London	2-1
Lancashire v Cambridgeshire	1-7
Leicestershire & Rutland v West Riding	2-1
Hampshire v Wiltshire	3-5

FOURTH ROUND

Cambridgeshire v Wiltshire	1-4
Suffolk v Isle of Man	1-2
Kent v Durham	2-1
Birmingham v Leicestershire & Rutland	1-0

SEMI-FINALS

Birmingham v Wiltshire	2-1
Isle of Man v Kent	2-2
Kent won on penalties.	

FINAL (at Gillingham FC)

Kent (1) 1 *(Cliff 40)*

Birmingham (1) 2 *(Johnson 4, Doyle 82)*

THE FA YOUTH CUP 2008–09

SPONSORED BY E.ON

PRELIMINARY ROUND

Seaham Red Star v Walker Central	1-2
Leigh Genesis v Nantwich Town	0-2
Colne v AFC Blackpool	4-0
Stalybridge Celtic v Wrexham	2-3
Liversedge v Stocksbridge Park Steels	2-1
Sheffield v Bradford Park Avenue	6-1
Stapenhill withdrew v Retford United w.o.	
Lincoln United v Holwell Sports	2-0
Mansfield Town v Bourne Town	13-0
Teversall v Mickleover Sports	2-5
Walsall Wood v Coventry Sphinx	2-5
Coventry Copsewood withdrew v Boldmere St Michaels w.o.	
Rocester v Sutton Coldfield Town	1-2
Bromsgrove Rovers v Tipton Town	3-1
Redditch United v Pelsall Villa	2-1
Southam United withdrew v Nuneaton Town w.o.	
Norton United v Stone Dominoes	5-0
Chasetown w.o. v Wolverhampton Casuals withdrew.	
Long Melford v Debenham LC	1-3
Wroxham v Great Yarmouth Town	0-2
Yaxley v AFC Kempston Rovers	1-3
Kettering Town v Rothwell Corinthians	1-2
Cheshunt v Boreham Wood	0-6
Bishop's Stortford v Tiptree United	3-1
St Margaretsbury v Hullbridge Sports	4-1
Waltham Abbey v Tring Athletic	2-1
Welwyn Garden City v Billericay Town	1-3
Halstead Town v Southend Manor	0-4
Ilford v Ware	1-4
Kingsbury London Tigers withdrew v Leyton w.o.	
Hampton & Richmond Borough v Dulwich Hamlet	5-0
Northwood v Redbridge	2-4
Hanwell Town v AFC Wimbledon	2-4
Mile Oak v Tonbridge Angels	1-5
Chipstead v Haywards Heath Town	4-1
Lordswood w.o. v Erith & Belvedere withdrew.	
Deal Town v Lewes	0-5
Whyteleafe w.o. v Warlingham withdrew.	
Hassocks v Walton & Hersham	3-0
Arundel withdrew v Cobham w.o.	
Carshalton Athletic v Oakwood	4-5
Aylesbury Vale w.o. v North Leigh withdrew.	
Wokingham Town & Emmbrook v AFC Wallingford	3-0
Chalfont St Peter v Burnham	3-1
Binfield v Beaconsfield SYCOB	2-5
Cove v Fleet Town	1-3
Farnborough v Maidenhead United	2-4
Portishead v Bath City	2-3
Forest Green Rovers v Mangotsfield United	3-2
Radstock Town v Team Bath	1-2
Stourport Swifts v Willenhall Town	3-1
Bromyard Town v Rugby Town	4-3
Stourbridge v Racing Club Warwick	4-0
Burgess Hill Town v Bisley	6-1
Weston-Super-Mare v Cheltenham Saracens	2-3
Worcester City w.o v Eccleshall withdrew.	
March Town United v Witton United	0-4
Waltham Forest withdrew v Witham Town w.o.	
Kentish Town v Uxbridge	2-1
Chesham United v Thatcham Town	2-1
Newport County v Brislington	10-0
Bitton v Torquay United	1-1
Torquay United won 5-4 on penalties.	
Hebburn Town v Dunston Federation	2-5
York City v Sunderand RCA	5-0
Eastbourne Borough v Folkestone Invicta	3-2

Bury Town v Kirklee & Pakefield	5-0
Corinthian Casuals v North Greenford United	0-2
Reading Town v Kidlington	1-3
Rushden & Diamonds v Raunds Town	5-0
Brackley Town v Bugbrooke St Michaels	4-3
Grays Athletic v Colney Heath	2-4
Ebbsfleet United v Redhill	14-0
Westfield v Epsom & Ewell	0-3
Cammell Laird v Altrincham	5-1
Silsden v FC Halifax Town	4-3
Blaby & Whetstone Athletic v New Mills	2-0
Oadby Town v Alfreton Town	2-1
Rainworth MW v Long Eaton United	0-2
Stafford Rangers v Newcastle Town	4-0
Dosthill Colts v Lye Town	4-2
Malvern Town v Burton Albion	3-1
Highgate United v Nuneaton Griff	4-2
Hednesford Town v Bedworth United	3-2
Wednesfield v Ellesmere Rangers	2-6
AFC Telford United v Bewdley Town	3-1
Mildenhall Town v Cornard United	1-4
Arlesey Town v Sileby Rangers	0-8
Canvey Island v AFC Hornchurch	2-1
Hoddesdon Town v FC Clacton	4-0
Royston Town v Thurrock	0-4
Harefield United v Wingate & Finchley	4-1
Welling United v Wealdstone	1-4
Ashford Town (Middlesex) v Haringey Borough	2-1
Faversham Town v VCD Athletic	4-4
Faversham Town won 3-2 on penalties.	
Tooting & Mitcham United v Worthing	1-1
Worthing won 3-2 on penalties.	
Sandhurst Town v Carterton	0-1
Henley Town v Aylesbury United	5-1
King's Lynn v Woodbridge Town	1-4
Wallsend BC v Ryton	13-0
Horsham YMCA v Kingstonian	1-9
Prudhoe Town v Whitley Bay	1-6
Merthyr Tydfil v Chard Town	1-0
Loughborough Dynamo v Grantham Town	10-0
Gornal Athletic v Pershore Town	3-0
Newmarket Town v Histon	0-5
Soham Town Rangers v Leiston	1-0
Walsham Le Willows v Ipswich Wanderers	3-0
Diss Town v Stowmarket Town	1-3
Dunstable Town v Daventry Town	5-1
St Albans City v Romford	8-1
Chatham Town v Horley Town	1-0
Godalming Town v Three Bridges	2-2
Three Bridges won 4-2 on penalties.	
Pagham v Molesey	2-0
Alton Town v Marlow	1-3
Sherborne Town v Havant & Waterlooville	1-5
Gateshead v West Allotment Celtic	3-2
Vauxhall Motors v Woodley Sports	3-2
Ringmer v Margate	3-5
Farsley Celtic v Hall Road Rangers	0-1

FIRST QUALIFYING ROUND

Warrington Town v Prescot Cables	2-1
Wallsend BC v Dunston Federation	2-1
Formby v Vauxhall Motors	5-0
Loughborough Dynamo v Mansfield Town	0-9
Barrow Town withdrew v Shirebrook Town w.o.	
Rolls Royce Leisure v Retford United	0-2
Bromyard Town v Stratford Town	3-5
Hednesford Town v Redditch United	2-0
Coventry Sphinx v Norton United	5-2

Wellington v Gornal Athletic	2-1
Sutton Coldfield Town v Chasetown	2-1
Wroxham v Histon	1-7
Hoddesdon Town v Hitchin Town	3-1
Colney Heath v Chelmsford City	3-1
Hampton & Richmond Borough v AFC Wimbledon	3-2
Leyton v Fisher Athletic	0-3
North Greenford United v Hayes & Yeading United	1-6
Rye United v Tonbridge Angels	0-6
Whyteleafe w.o. v Tunbridge Wells withdrew.	
Milton United withdrew v Buckingham Town w.o.	
Fleet Town v Oxford United	0-8
Thame United v Wokingham Town & Emmbrook	4-0
Tadley Calleva withdrew v Beaconsfield SYCOB w.o.	
Marlow v Basingstoke Town	1-3
Stourbridge v Nuneaton Town	3-1
Boldmere St Michaels v Dosthill Colts	2-0
Rothwell Corinthians v Northampton Spencer	3-4
Stevenage Borough v Bishop's Stortford	7-2
Chalfont St Peter v Andover	3-0
Bishop's Cleeve v Team Bath	1-3
Selby Town v Eccleshill United	1-4
Glasshoughton Welfare v Liversedge	1-2
Ossett Albion v Thackley	1-4
Bromsgrove Rovers v Alvechurch	3-1
AFC Telford United v Stourport Swifts	5-2
Thurrock v Burnham Ramblers	4-0
Kentish Town v Staines Town	1-2
Camberley Town v Worthing	1-5
Aylesbury Vale v Newport Pagnell Town	1-2
Workington v Ashton Town	1-2
Chester-Le-Street Town v Walker Central	4-5
Eastbourne Borough v Lingfield	7-0
Salford City v Nantwich Town	4-5
Hall Road Rangers v Ossett Town	4-0
Rothwell Town v Cranfield United	1-3
Rushden & Diamonds v Leighton Town	9-2
Bromley v South Park	6-1
Winchester City v Eastleigh	0-2
Bridgwater Town v Torquay United	0-2
Bath City v Wootton Bassett Town	5-1
Northwich Victoria v Wrexham	0-7
Lancaster City v Daisy Hill	1-3
Barwell v Staveley MW	2-4
Oadby Town v Rothley Imperial	4-1
Matlock Town v Stamford	1-2
Blaby & Whetstone Athletic v Birstall United	7-3
Sileby Rangers v Thrapston Town	12-0
Merstham v Lordswood	1-3
Epsom & Ewell v Hassocks	5-0
Chertsey Town v Woking	0-3
Christchurch v Weymouth	0-1
Cheltenham Saracens v Westbury United	5-0
Cirencester Town v Paulton Rovers	7-0
Padiham v Fleetwood Town	0-1
Congleton Town v Curzon Ashton	0-0
Curzon Ashton won 5-4 on penalties.	
Chorley v Marine	0-2
Sheffield v Garforth Town	0-1
Silsden AFC v Yorkshire Amateur	1-4
North Ferriby United v Wakefield	2-3
Deeping Rangers v Lincoln United	0-2
Gresley Rovers v Boston United	1-3
Malvern Town v Solihull Moors	1-6
Highgate United v Worcester City	2-5
Witton United v Walsham Le Willows	1-3
Debenham LC v Needham Market	2-0
Stowmarket Town v Woodbridge Town	0-5
Cambridge United v Felixstowe & Walton United	8-2
Stotfold v Brackley Town	5-0
Cogenhoe United v Dunstable Town	4-3
Braintree Town v St Albans City	0-6
Canvey Island v Leverstock Green	1-3

Billericay Town v Waltham Abbey	0-1
Ware v Hemel Hempstead Town	2-4
Wivenhoe Town v St Margaretsbury	1-4
Southend Manor v Maldon Town	2-3
Ashford Town (Middlesex) v Harefield United	6-2
Croydon Athletic v Enfield Town	2-2
Croydon Athletic won 4-2 on penalties.	
Faversham Town v Lewes	2-4
Sutton United v Pagham	5-0
Three Bridges v Shoreham	2-0
Kingstonian v Colliers Wood United	5-4
Maidenhead United v Oxford City	6-0
Henley Town v Banbury United	3-3
Banbury United won 9-8 on penalties.	
Poole Town v Gosport Borough	2-3
Bournemouth v Moneyfields	1-2
Dorchester Town v Shaftesbury	3-1
Gateshead v Guisborough Town	5-0
York City v Whitley Bay	5-0
Ashton Athletic v Burscough	1-3
FCV Reds v Stewarts & Lloyds	2-1
Boreham Wood v Brentwood Town	3-2
Ebbsfleet United v East Grinstead Town	3-1
Chipstead v Croydon	2-1
Cobham v Burgess Hill Town	0-8
Colne v Bootle	2-1
Long Eaton United v Carlton Town	1-5
Mickleover Sports v Arnold Town	4-0
Glossop North End v Hinckley United	2-4
Stafford Rangers v Ellesmere Rangers	1-2
Fakenham Town v Bury Town	0-5
Soham Town Rangers v Dereham Town	2-1
Cornard United v Lowestoft Town	1-4
AFC Kempston Rovers v Wellingborough Town	2-3
Bowers & Pitsea v Witham Town	2-3
Thamesmead Town v Redbridge	2-1
Cockfosters v Wealdstone	2-1
Ramsgate v Dover Athletic	2-3
Maidstone United v Dartford	1-0
Chatham Town v Sittingbourne	12-2
Oakwood v Horsham	4-3
Kidlington v Chesham United	3-2
Didcot Town v Bracknell Town	2-1
Carterton v Windsor & Eton	0-1
VT v Havant & Waterlooville	1-2
Forest Green Rovers v Elmore	4-0
Tiverton Town v Newport County	2-3
Merthyr Tydfil v Yate Town	3-4
Margate v Hastings United	2-3
Cammell Laird v Southport	2-2
Cammell Laird won 4-2 on penalties.	
AFC Totton v Salisbury City	2-3
Bashley v Hamworthy United	2-3
Guiseley v Worksop Town	1-2

SECOND QUALIFYING ROUND

Gateshead v York City	0-1
Walker Central v Wallesend BC	3-2
Warrington Town v Nantwich Town	0-3
Daisy Hill v Formby	0-5
Ashton Town v Fleetwood Town	1-4
Marine v Wrexham	2-4
Colne v Cammell Laird	2-3
Curzon Ashton v Burscough	2-1
Wakefield v Garforth Town	4-3
Yorkshire Amateur v Thackley	4-2
Liversedge v Hall Road Rangers	3-0
Worksop Town v Eccleshill United	3-0
Mickleover Sports v Retford United	2-0
Shirebrook Town v Lincoln United	4-3
Hinckley United v Staveley MW	3-1
Stamford v Mansfield Town	2-6

Oadby Town v Blaby & Whetstone Athletic	3-3
Oadby Town won 5-4 on penalties.	
Carlton Town v Boston United	0-5
Solihull Moors v Wellington	18-0
Hednesford Town v AFC Telford United	3-3
Hednesford Town won 4-3 on penalties.	
Worcester City v Stourbridge	3-4
Bromsgrove Rovers v Boldmere St Michaels	2-3
Coventry Sphinx v Ellesmere Rangers	3-2
Stratford Town v Sutton Coldfield Town	1-3
Lowestoft Town v Walsham Le Willows	1-4
Debenham LC v Cambridge United	0-4
Histon v Soham Town Rangers	2-1
Woodbridge Town v Bury Town	3-5
Sileby Rangers v Rushden & Diamonds	2-3
Wellingborough Town v FCV Reds	0-2
Stotfold v Northampton Spencer	1-3
Cogenhoe United v Cranfield United	3-0
Hoddesdon Town v Stevenage Borough	3-5
Witham Town v St Margaretsbury	3-2
Thurrock v St Albans City	3-2
Hemel Hempstead Town v Waltham Abbey	2-1
Colney Heath v Boreham Wood	0-2
Leverstock Green v Maldon Town	1-2
Hayes & Yeading United v Hampton & Richmond Borough	2-0
Staines Town v Croydon Athletic	1-1
Croydon Athletic won 4-3 on penalties.	
Ashford Town (Middlesex) v Fisher Athletic	3-1
Cockfosters v Thamesmead Town	3-5
Ebbsfleet United v Tonbridge Angels	2-1
Maidstone United v Lordswood	1-0
Whyteleafe v Dover Athletic	2-5
Bromley v Lewes	2-3
Chipstead v Chatham Town	0-1
Hastings United v Eastbourne Borough	1-6
Oakwood v Burgess Hill Town	0-3
Three Bridges v Woking	1-2
Epsom & Ewell v Kingstonian	1-1
Kingstonian won 4-2 on penalties.	
Worthing v Sutton United	0-4
Maidenhead United v Thame United	1-4
Didcot Town v Beaconsfield SYCOB	3-3
Didcot Town won 8-7 on penalties.	
Windsor & Eton v Buckingham Town	0-6
Banbury United v Kidlington	4-2
Chalfont St Peter v Newport Pagnell Town	0-3
Oxford United v Basingstoke Town	2-3
Weymouth v Moneyfields	4-1
Salisbury City v Dorchester Town	9-1
Havant & Waterlooville v Hamworthy United	3-1
Eastleigh v Gosport Borough	5-4
Cheltenham Saracens v Forest Green Rovers	1-3
Bath City v Cirencester Town	0-2
Newport County v Yate Town	4-0
Team Bath v Torquay United	3-4

THIRD QUALIFYING ROUND

York City v Walker Central	8-0
Cammell Laird v Curzon Ashton	0-4
Formby v Fleetwood Town	2-3
Nantwich Town v Wrexham	1-0
Yorkshire Amateur v Worksop Town	0-1
Wakefield v Liversedge	2-1
Oadby Town v Boston United	2-2
Oadby Town won 5-3 on penalties.	
Shirebrook Town v Hinckley United	0-2
Mickleover Sports v Mansfield Town	0-7
Coventry Sphinx v Sutton Coldfield Town	3-2
Hednesford Town v Stourbridge	4-0
Solihull Moors v Boldmere St Michaels	3-0
Cambridge United v Bury Town	3-0
Walsham Le Willows v Histon	1-5

FCV Reds v Cogenhoe United	2-1
Rushden & Diamonds v Northampton Spencer	7-0
Boreham Wood v Maldon Town	4-2
Witham Town v Thurrock	1-5
Stevenage Borough v Hemel Hempstead Town	2-1
Croydon Athletic v Thamesmead Town	6-2
Hayes & Yeading United v Ashford Town (Middlesex)	2-1
Chatham Town v Eastbourne Borough	0-2
Maidstone United v Dover Athletic	0-6
Ebbsfleet United v Lewes	2-4
Woking v Sutton United	3-1
Burgess Hill Town v Kingstonian	4-3
Newport Pagnell Town v Basingstoke Town	1-4
Didcot Town v Buckingham Town	3-1
Thame United v Banbury United	1-2
Salisbury City v Eastleigh	1-5
Weymouth v Havant & Waterlooville	1-2
Cirencester Town v Torquay United	5-2
Forest Green Rovers v Newport County	3-4

FIRST ROUND

Grimsby Town v Lincoln City	0-1
Bradford City v Scunthorpe United	1-0
Rochdale v Huddersfield Town	1-0
Hartlepool United v Carlisle United	1-4
Bury v Crewe Alexandra	0-2
Worksop Town v Rotherham United	0-3
Darlington v Tranmere Rovers	2-3
Nantwich Town v Curzon Ashton	5-0
York City v Stockport County	2-3
Chester City v Leeds United	0-2
Macclesfield Town v Morecambe	4-1
Accrington Stanley v Wakefield	3-1
Fleetwood Town v Oldham Athletic	0-3
Shrewsbury Town v Chesterfield	2-0
Leicester City v Port Vale	2-1
Coventry Sphinx v Milton Keynes Dons	2-3
Solihull Moors v FCV Reds	2-0
Oadby Town v Hinckley United	2-1
Mansfield Town v Peterborough United	3-2
Rushden & Diamonds v Northampton Town	1-2
Walsall v Hednesford Town	5-3
Millwall v Luton Town	2-0
Gillingham v Eastbourne Borough	3-0
Brighton & Hove Albion v Dover Athletic	5-1
Southend United v Brentford	3-3
Brentford won 9-8 on penalties.	
Stevenage Borough v Thurrock	2-3
Banbury United v Dagenham & Redbridge	1-2
Cambridge United v Colchester United	4-1
Lewes v Histon	2-0
Boreham Wood v Leyton Orient	0-5
Hayes & Yeading United v Croydon Athletic	1-2
Burgess Hill Town v Wycombe Wanderers	0-2
Basingstoke Town v Barnet	0-2
Aldershot Town v Havant & Waterlooville	1-4
Didcot Town v Cirencester Town	2-2
Cirencester Town won 4-1 on penalties.	
Cheltenham Town v Newport County	5-1
AFC Bournemouth v Bristol Rovers	0-1
Swindon Town v Eastleigh	4-1
Yeovil Town v Hereford United	4-1
Woking v Exeter City	1-2

SECOND ROUND

Accrington Stanley v Carlisle United	0-3
Oldham Athletic v Rotherham United	2-0
Walsall v Rochdale	4-3
Solihull Moors v Tranmere Rovers	0-2
Nantwich Town v Macclesfield Town	2-1

Stockport County v Crewe Alexandra	3-3
Crewe Alexandra won 4-2 on penalties.	
Lincoln City v Mansfield Town	3-1
Shrewsbury Town v Bradford City	2-0
Oadby Town v Leeds United	0-3
Leicester City v Milton Keynes Dons	3-1
Swindon Town v Exeter City	3-0
Yeovil Town v Cirencester Town	1-2
Cambridge United v Northampton Town	0-2
Lewes v Croydon Athletic	3-0
Barnet v Havant & Waterlooville	3-1
Brentford v Thurrock	6-2
Bristol Rovers v Brighton & Hove Albion	3-1
Millwall v Dagenham & Redbridge	5-1
Cheltenham Town v Gillingham	0-1
Wycombe Wanderers v Leyton Orient	1-2

THIRD ROUND

Swansea City v Manchester City	0-3
Brentford v Middlesbrough	1-2
Manchester United v Chelsea	2-3
Cardiff City v Blackpool	3-0
Swindon Town v Crystal Palace	1-5
Reading v Preston North End	0-1
Tottenham Hotspur v Sheffield United	3-0
Portsmouth v Gillingham	2-1
Leyton Orient v Watford	0-4
Barnsley v Walsall	2-3
Norwich City v Wigan Athletic	1-0
Sunderland v Cirencester Town	2-1
Leeds United v Liverpool	1-2
Carlisle United v Crewe Alexandra	1-3
Sheffield Wednesday v Millwall	1-3
Coventry City v Stoke City	2-3
Ipswich Town v Shrewsbury Town	1-0
Bolton Wanderers v Doncaster Rovers	2-0
Burnley v West Bromwich Albion	3-1
Northampton Town v Tranmere Rovers	0-3
Aston Villa v Arsenal	2-3
Southampton v Derby County	3-1
Barnet v Bristol Rovers	1-2
Plymouth Argyle v Fulham	2-1
Newcastle United v Oldham Athletic	2-1
Lewes v Hull City	1-2
Queens Park Rangers v Bristol City	5-3
Everton v Nantwich Town	2-0
Birmingham City v Lincoln City	2-1
Leicester City v Wolverhampton Wanderers	2-3
Charlton Athletic v Blackburn Rovers	2-1
Nottingham Forest v West Ham United	3-1

FOURTH ROUND

Ipswich Town v Crystal Palace	4-2
Arsenal v Wolverhampton Wanderers	3-1
Preston North End v Sunderland	0-1
Chelsea v Walsall	5-1
Queens Park Rangers v Newcastle United	1-3
Norwich City v Stoke City	1-1
Norwich City won 4-2 on penalties.	
Southampton v Watford	0-1
Plymouth Argyle v Millwall	3-2
Bristol Rovers v Liverpool	2-2
Liverpool won 4-2 on penalties.	

Bolton Wanderers v Hull City	4-0
Burnley v Everton	1-3
Middlesbrough v Nottingham Forest	1-2
Charlton Athletic v Tottenham Hotspur	0-3
Birmingham City v Crewe Alexandra	3-2
Portsmouth v Manchester City	0-1
Cardiff City v Tranmere Rovers	0-0
Cardiff City won 5-4 on penalties.	

FIFTH ROUND

Ipswich Town v Watford	2-3
Liverpool v Chelsea	1-0
Sunderland v Arsenal	0-4
Plymouth Argyle v Tottenham Hotspur	0-3
Everton v Norwich City	1-1
Norwich City won 3-1 on penalties.	
Manchester City v Newcastle United	4-2
Nottingham Forest v Bolton Wanderers	0-1
Cardiff City v Birmingham City	0-2

SIXTH ROUND

Manchester City v Norwich City	1-0
Tottenham Hotspur v Arsenal	1-3
Liverpool v Bolton Wanderers	4-2
Birmingham City v Watford	1-0

SEMI-FINALS (TWO LEGS)

Manchester City v Arsenal	1-2, 1-4
Birmingham City v Liverpool	0-3, 1-3

FINAL FIRST LEG

22 MAY

Arsenal (2) 4 *(Sunu 21, Wilshere 35 (pen), Watt 57, Emmanuel-Thomas 66)*

Liverpool (1) 1 *(Kacaniklic 37)*   33,662

Arsenal: Shea; Eastmond, Cruise, Frimpong (Watt 17), Bartley, Ayling, Lansbury, Coquelin, Sunu (Murphy 75), Wilshere (Henderson 90), Emmanuel-Thomas.
Liverpool: Bouzanis; Clair, Buchtmann, Ayala, Kennedy, Wisdom, Amoo, Irwin, Dalla Valle (Robinson 80), Ince, Kacaniklic (Eccleston 64).
Referee: L. Mason (Lancashire).

FINAL SECOND LEG

26 MAY

Liverpool (0) 1 *(Dalla Valle 52)*

Arsenal (1) 2 *(Watt 25, Ayala 70 (og))*   7792

Liverpool: Bouzanis; Irwin, Robinson (Clair 83), Ayala, Kennedy, Wisdom, Amoo, Buchtmann, Della Valle, Ince, Kacaniklic (Eccleston 46).
Arsenal: Shea; Eastmond, Cruise, Wilshere, Bartley, Ayling (Cooper 83), Lansbury, Coquelin (Ozyakup 83), Sunu (Murphy 68), Watt, Emannuel-Thomas (Henderson 83).
Referee: L. Mason (Lancashire).

THE FA SUNDAY CUP 2008–09

IN PARTNERSHIP WITH CARLSBERG

PRELIMINARY ROUND

Sporting Dynamo v Scots Grey	0-13
Sandy (Sunday) v Gossoms End	3-0
Cube v Shelford Falcons	3-4
Bedfont Sunday v Battersby Ironsides	3-0

FIRST ROUND

Brow v Swanfield	2-3
Bolton Woods v Allerton	3-3
Bolton Woods won 6-5 on penalties.	
Dock v Crossflatts	2-0
Barry's v Hartlepool Lion Hillcarter	3-5
BRNESC v Rawdon	3-3
BRNESC won 3-1 on penalties.	
Britannia v Poulton Royal	2-0
Queens Park v Pocklington Town	4-0
Canada v Hartlepool Athletic Rugby	2-0
Hessle Rangers v Western Approaches	0-2
Dawdon Colliery Welfare v Dengo United	4-0
Heywood Irish Centre v Home & Bargain	2-2
Heywood Irish Centre won 4-2 on penalties.	
Hartlepool Rovers Quoit v Ford Motors	0-2
Murton Victoria v Sandon Dock	3-2
Halton Moore v Paddock	0-2
Beverley United v Lobster	2-3
Sunderland RCA Barnes v Lee Jones	4-0
Nicosia v Oyster Martyrs	4-7
Shankhouse United v Thornhill Lees	2-3
Queensbury v Witton Park Rose & Crown	0-5
West Lee v Obiter Fabs 4	2-3
Elland AFC v Seaburn	1-0
Tower v Royal Standard	2-0
JOB v The View	2-4
Silsden (Sunday) v Jolly Miller	2-0
Fforde Green Brazil v Seymour KFCA	2-1
Grey Horse (Failsworth) v Sandstone	2-3
Warstones Wanderers (Sunday) v Leicester Polska	5-1
Belt Road v Bartley Green Sunday	2-2
Bartley Green Sunday won 4-3 on penalties.	
Harp 2003 v Keresley RFC	6-1
Bulls Head (Dawley Bank) v Grosvenor Park	4-1
Victoria v Travellers	1-2
Kingshurst Sporting Club v Scots Grey	1-2
Magnet Tavern v Grafham	8-0
Springfield Lions v Wisbech St Mary	1-2
Hawkins Sports v Birstall Stamford	3-6
Duke of Rutland v Plough Barfly's	2-0
St Margarets v Crawley Green (Sunday)	3-0
61 (Sunday) v Sandy (Sunday)	3-3
61 (Sunday) won 4-3 on penalties.	
Hammer v Celtic SC (Luton)	1-4
AC Sportsmen & Ravensborough v Shelford Falcons	0-1
Heyford United w.o. v Brache Green Man withdrew.	
Risden Wood v AFC Black Swan OB	3-0
London Maccabi Lions v Bury Park Saracens	3-1
Belstone v Luton Old Boys (Sunday)	3-0
St Joseph's South Oxhey v Moat	1-2
Partizan v Club Lewsey	0-6
Enfield Rangers v Greengate	3-1
Brantham Athletic (Sunday) v FC Houghton Centre	9-2
Nirankari Sports Sabha withdrew v Stanbridge & Tilsworth w.o.	
Loughton Nu Bar v St Joseph's (Luton)	3-4
CB Hounslow United (Sunday) v Brixton United	1-3
Wycombe Town v Bedfont Sunday	3-1
Broadfields United v Sutton Athletic	3-2
Sunbury Athletic v Kerria Sports	2-3
Hanham Sunday v Bucks SU	3-1
Ashton v Richfield Rovers	2-1
Seven Allstars v Lebeq Tavern Courage	1-2
Rapid Moorfields v Bristol Athletic	1-0
Ajax LA v Brook	1-0
Whitenap v Bournemouth Electric	0-1
Lakeside Athletic v Poole Borough	5-1
Totton Town v Knighton Arms	2-4

SECOND ROUND

Swanfield v BRNESC	3-3
BRNESC won 4-3 on penalties.	
Bolton Woods v Britannia	2-1
Paddock v Queens Park	2-2
Queens Park won 2-0 on penalties.	

Hartlepool Lion Hillcarter v Canada	1-2
Western Approaches v Heywood Irish Centre	2-3
Dawdon Colliery Welfare v Sunderland RCA Barnes	1-2
Hetton Lyons Cricket Club v Lobster	3-2
Dock v Thornhill Lees	1-2
Elland AFC v Sandstone	1-3
Tower v Fforde Green Brazil	3-6
Coundon Conservative v Murton Victoria	2-0
Ford Motors v Oyster Martyrs	1-3
Witton Park Rose & Crown v The View	1-0
Obiter Fabs 4 v Silsden (Sunday)	1-2
Warstones Wanderers (Sunday) v Harp 2003	2-1
Bartley Green Sunday v Bulls Head (Dawley Bank)	1-2
Wisbech St Mary v St Margarets	2-6
Birstall Stamford v Scots Grey	4-4
Scots Grey won 4-3 on penalties.	
Magnet Tavern v Travellers	4-0
Duke of Rutland v London Maccabi Lions	0-2
Heyford United v Club Lewsey	0-4
61 (Sunday) v Belstone	0-0
Belstone won 4-3 on penalties.	
Enfield Rangers v Celtic SC (Luton)	3-1
Shelford Falcons v Moat	4-1
Risden Wood v Stanbridge & Tilsworth	2-4
Brantham Athletic (Sunday) v St Joseph's (Luton)	2-1
Kerria Sports v Wycombe Town	3-5
Lebeq Tavern Courage v Rapid Moorfields	6-1
Brixton United v Broadfields United	1-3
Hanham Sunday v Ashton	3-2
Bournemouth Electric v Ajax LA	5-1
Knighton Arms v Lakeside Athletic	2-3

THIRD ROUND

Canada v BRNESC	7-0
Bolton Woods v Queens Park	0-5
Thornhill Lees v Hetton Lyons Cricket Club	1-8
Sunderland RCA Barnes v Heywood Irish Centre	0-4
Fforde Green Brazil v Sandstone	3-1
Witton Park Rose & Crown v Silsden (Sunday)	4-2
Oyster Martyrs v Coundon Conservative	3-1
Bulls Head (Dawley Bank) v Shelford Falcons	5-2
Magnet Tavern v Warstones Wanderers (Sunday)	6-1
Scots Grey v St Margarets	6-2
Club Lewsey v Brantham Athletic (Sunday)	3-3
Club Lewsey won 7-6 on penalties.	
Stanbridge & Tilsworth v London Maccabi Lions	3-1
Enfield Rangers v Belstone	2-2
Enfield Rangers won 7-6 on penalties.	
Hanham Sunday v Wycombe Town	1-2
Lebeq Tavern Courage v Broadfields United	7-2
Lakeside Athletic v Bournemouth Electric	5-1

FOURTH ROUND

Bulls Head (Dawley Bank) v Heywood Irish Centre	0-4
Queens Park v Fforde Green Brazil	2-5
Magnet Tavern v Oyster Martyrs	1-2
Scots Grey v Hetton Lyons Cricket Club	1-0
Canada v Witton Park Rose & Crown	2-5
Wycombe Town v Club Lewsey	4-1
Stanbridge & Tillsworth v Enfield Rangers	5-0
Lakeside Athletic v Lebeq Tavern Courage	1-0

FIFTH ROUND

Fforde Green Brazil v Stanbridge & Tillsworth	2-1
Scots Grey v Heywood Irish Centre	3-1
Oyster Martyrs v Witton Park Rose & Crown	1-0
Wycombe Town v Lakeside Athletic	1-1
Lakeside Athletic won 5-4 on penalties.	

SEMI-FINALS

Scots Grey v Lakeside Athletic	1-0
Fforde Green Brazil v Oyster Martyrs	2-3

FINAL (at Liverpool FC)

Scots Grey 4 *(Bignall 16, Staples 90, Jeffries 98, 118)*
Oyster Martyrs 3 *(Latham 35, Rooney 57, Lipson 120)*
(aet.)   2559

FA PREMIER RESERVE LEAGUES 2008–09

FA PREMIER RESERVE LEAGUE – NORTH SECTION

	P	W	D	L	GD	Pts	Leading Goalscorers	(excludes Play-off)	
Sunderland	20	13	4	3	18	43	Federico Macheda	Manchester U	9
Manchester U	20	10	6	4	16	36	Thomas Craddock	Middlesbrough	7
Blackburn R	20	9	6	5	11	33	Nile Ranger	Newcastle U	7
Newcastle U	20	9	5	6	4	32	David Ball	Manchester C	6
Manchester C	20	10	0	10	3	30	Mark Doninger	Newcastle U	6
Wigan Ath	20	7	3	10	–11	24	David Dowson	Sunderland	6
Liverpool	20	5	7	8	0	22	Tomasz Cywka	Wigan Ath	6
Everton	20	5	7	8	–6	22	Alan Judge	Blackburn R	5
Hull C	20	6	4	10	–16	22	Carlos Villanueva		
Middlesbrough	20	6	3	11	–7	21	Rolland	Blackburn R	5
Bolton W	20	6	3	11	–16	21	James Vaughan	Everton	5
							Andrew Carroll	Newcastle U	5

RESULTS 2008–09

	BR	BW	E	HC	L	MC	MU	M	NU	S	WA
Blackburn R	—	5–1	2–1	2–0	1–1	0–1	2–1	3–0	0–1	0–0	1–1
Bolton W	1–1	—	1–1	2–1	2–1	1–5	0–3	1–1	3–0	0–1	0–2
Everton	1–1	0–3	—	0–1	1–1	1–0	1–1	2–2	1–0	0–0	2–0
Hull C	1–5	2–0	1–2	—	1–2	1–4	2–1	3–2	1–1	0–3	1–0
Liverpool	0–1	3–4	2–3	0–0	—	1–2	2–2	2–0	5–1	0–2	1–0
Manchester C	1–2	2–1	3–1	1–2	1–0	—	0–3	3–1	3–0	0–3	3–2
Manchester U	0–0	2–0	2–0	4–0	0–0	2–1	—	1–0	1–1	2–0	1–2
Middlesbrough	1–0	3–0	1–0	2–2	0–1	2–0	0–1	—	1–4	4–2	2–0
Newcastle U	2–1	3–0	2–1	1–1	1–1	2–1	3–3	3–2	—	1–2	5–0
Sunderland	4–0	2–0	0–0	2–1	2–1	2–0	1–0	3–1	1–2	—	2–0
Wigan Ath	1–3	0–2	2–1	2–1	2–2	2–1	4–5	2–1	2–1	1–1	—

FA PREMIER RESERVE LEAGUE – SOUTH SECTION

	P	W	D	L	GD	Pts	Leading Goalscorers	(excludes Play-off)	
Aston Villa	16	11	3	2	16	36	Thomas Kilbey	Portsmouth	5
Tottenham H	16	10	1	5	7	31	Fred Sears	West Ham U	5
Fulham	16	7	5	4	8	26	Mark Randall	Arsenal	4
Portsmouth	16	8	1	7	–7	25	Jonathan Hogg	Aston Villa	4
West Ham U	16	7	1	8	–7	22	Fabio Borini	Chelsea	4
Arsenal	16	5	4	7	–5	19	Michael Uwezu	Fulham	4
Chelsea	16	5	3	8	2	18	Giles Barnes	Fulham	4
Stoke C	16	4	2	10	–5	14	Adel Taarabt	Tottenham H	4
WBA	16	4	2	10	–9	14	Lateef Elford-Alliyu	WBA	4

RESULTS 2008–09

	A	AV	C	F	P	SC	TH	WBA	WH
Arsenal	—	1–4	2–3	2–0	2–0	3–2	0–3	2–0	0–1
Aston V	0–0	—	4–3	2–1	6–1	1–0	1–0	2–0	0–0
Chelsea	0–0	0–1	—	1–1	6–0	0–2	3–0	2–2	2–0
Fulham	3–0	1–1	2–1	—	1–3	3–1	1–1	2–0	4–1
Portsmouth	0–1	2–0	0–2	2–2	—	1–0	0–1	1–0	1–0
Stoke C	2–2	1–2	3–2	2–2	0–1	—	0–1	2–0	0–2
Tottenham H	2–1	2–1	4–0	0–3	2–3	0–2	—	3–2	2–0
WBA	1–1	1–2	1–0	3–0	0–3	2–1	1–2	—	4–2
West Ham U	1–0	0–2	4–3	0–2	2–0	1–0	1–3	4–3	—

PREMIER RESERVE LEAGUE PLAY-OFF

Aston Villa (1) 3 *(Delfouneso 25, Collins 57, Lowry 86)*
Sunderland (1) 1 *(Waghorn 28)*
at Villa Park. 5337

Aston Villa: Parish; Lichaj, Lowry, Hogg, Clark, Roome, Albrighton, Bannan (Gardner 86), Weimann (Collins 52), Delfouneso, Hofbauer (Herd 85).

Sunderland: Colgan; Kay, Adams, Meyler, M'voto, Hartley, Weir (Noble 74), Cook (Chandler 84), Dowson, Colback, Waghorn.

TOTESPORT.COM RESERVE LEAGUES 2008–09

TOTESPORT.COM LEAGUE

CENTRAL DIVISION

	P	W	D	L	F	A	GD	Pts
Shrewsbury T	16	12	3	1	49	13	26	39
Nottingham F	16	10	4	2	37	12	25	34
Sheffield U	16	6	3	7	27	25	2	21
Sheffield W	16	6	3	7	24	27	–3	21
Walsall	16	6	3	7	23	31	–8	21
Port Vale	16	6	2	8	24	26	–2	20
Lincoln C	16	5	4	7	28	35	–7	19
Macclesfield T	16	3	5	8	21	47	–26	14
Mansfield T	16	4	1	11	15	32	–17	13

WEST DIVISION

	P	W	D	L	F	A	GD	Pts
Burnley	18	11	4	3	42	18	24	37
Manchester C	18	10	1	7	39	27	12	31
Morecambe	18	9	3	6	31	29	2	30
Carlisle U	18	8	5	5	38	27	11	29
Preston NE	18	8	3	7	28	19	9	27
Blackpool	18	6	4	8	33	43	–10	22
Rochdale	18	6	4	8	28	44	–16	22
Tranmere R	18	4	7	7	25	30	–5	19
Bury	18	4	5	9	19	32	–13	17
Accrington S	18	4	4	10	21	35	–14	16

EAST DIVISION

	P	W	D	L	F	A	GD	Pts
Leeds U	16	13	0	3	27	8	19	39
Huddersfield T	16	11	4	1	46	22	24	37
Hartlepool U	16	10	2	4	40	30	10	32
Scunthorpe U	16	5	5	6	29	24	5	20
Bradford C	16	5	1	10	27	26	1	16
Rotherham U	16	4	4	8	27	37	–10	16
Barnsley	16	4	4	8	33	45	–12	16
Grimsby T	16	4	3	9	27	39	–12	15
York C	16	3	3	10	21	46	–25	12

SEMI–FINALS
Accrington S 0, Sunderland 2
Derby Co 3, Grimsby T 1

FINAL
Derby Co 1, Sunderland 3

TOTESPORT.COM COMBINATION

CENTRAL DIVISION

	P	W	D	L	GD	Pts
Reading	18	13	3	2	52	42
Millwall	18	11	1	6	23	34
Crystal Palace	18	10	2	6	4	32
Southampton	18	9	3	6	–2	30
Brighton & HA	18	9	2	7	2	29
QPR	18	8	4	6	1	28
Charlton Ath	18	7	2	9	0	23
Aldershot T	18	4	5	9	–2	17
Gillingham	18	3	6	9	–15	15
Lewes	18	1	2	15	–63	5

EAST DIVISION

	P	W	D	L	GD	Pts
Luton T	18	8	7	3	10	31
Watford	18	9	3	6	4	30
Wycombe W	18	7	7	4	2	28
Ipswich T	18	7	5	6	22	26

	P	W	D	L	F	A	GD	Pts
Peterborough U	18	6	6	6	7			24
Colchester U	18	7	2	9	2			23
Southend U	18	7	2	9	–11			23
Leyton Orient	18	6	4	8	–14			22
Northampton T	18	6	3	9	–6			21
Stevenage B	18	6	3	9	–16			21

WALES & WEST DIVISION

	P	W	D	L	GD	Pts
Plymouth Arg	18	11	5	2	19	38
Swindon T	18	9	6	3	13	33
Bristol C	18	9	4	5	18	31
Exeter C	18	10	0	8	10	30
Bournemouth	18	7	4	7	–7	25
Swansea C	18	6	5	7	–5	23
Salisbury C	18	6	3	9	–16	21
Forest Green R	18	6	2	10	–21	20
Yeovil T	18	6	1	11	–1	19
Cheltenham T	18	4	2	12	–10	14

CUP COMPETITION

GROUP A

	P	W	D	L	GD	Pts
Reading	4	3	1	0	10	10
Bristol C	4	2	1	1	4	7
Southampton	4	2	0	2	–2	6
Plymouth Arg	4	1	1	2	–4	4
Swansea C	4	0	1	3	–8	1

GROUP B

	P	W	D	L	GD	Pts
Crystal Palace	3	3	0	0	6	9
Charlton Ath	4	1	2	1	2	5
Ipswich T	3	1	1	1	0	4
Watford	3	1	0	2	–5	3
QPR	3	0	1	2	–3	1

Unplayed matches cancelled.

TOTESPORT.COM LEAGUE CUP

GROUP ONE

	P	W	D	L	F	A	GD	Pts
Sunderland	3	3	0	0	15	0	15	9
Newcastle U	3	2	0	1	8	5	3	6
Carlisle U	4	2	0	2	8	15	–7	6
Sheffield U	4	1	1	2	5	8	–3	4
Hartlepool U	4	0	1	3	4	12	–8	1

GROUP TWO

	P	W	D	L	F	A	GD	Pts
Grimsby T	3	2	1	0	5	3	2	7
Middlesbrough	3	1	2	0	7	2	5	5
Sheffield W	3	1	0	2	5	7	–2	3
Bradford C	3	0	1	2	2	7	–5	1

GROUP THREE

	P	W	D	L	F	A	GD	Pts
Derby Co	3	2	1	0	10	6	4	7
Oldham Ath	3	2	0	1	5	5	0	6
Walsall	3	1	1	1	6	6	0	4
Mansfield T	3	0	0	3	6	10	–4	0

GROUP FOUR

	P	W	D	L	F	A	GD	Pts
Accrington S	3	3	0	0	8	4	4	9
Rochdale	4	1	2	1	6	6	0	5
Morecambe	4	1	1	2	10	11	–1	4
Tranmere R	3	1	1	1	6	7	–1	4
Macclesfield T	4	1	0	3	6	8	–2	3

Unplayed matches declared void.

FA ACADEMY UNDER 18 LEAGUE 2008–09

GROUP A

	P	W	D	L	GD	Pts
Arsenal	28	22	4	2	40	70
Norwich C	28	13	6	9	4	45
Ipswich T	28	14	2	12	2	44
Crystal Palace	28	12	4	12	4	40
West Ham U	28	10	8	10	13	38
Southampton	28	12	2	14	–7	38
Portsmouth	28	10	5	13	–4	35
Chelsea	28	10	4	14	–8	34
Fulham	28	8	9	11	–1	33
Charlton Ath	28	6	4	18	–33	22

GROUP B

	P	W	D	L	GD	Pts
Tottenham H	28	19	7	2	49	64
Leicester C	28	19	3	6	42	60
Aston Villa	28	16	6	6	24	54
Coventry C	28	15	8	5	16	53
Reading	28	10	5	13	–8	35
Bristol C	28	9	6	13	–4	33
Cardiff C	28	7	7	14	–15	28
Watford	28	7	4	17	–15	25
Birmingham C	28	7	4	17	–34	25
Milton Keynes D	28	3	4	21	–55	13

GROUP C

	P	W	D	L	GD	Pts
Manchester C	28	22	6	0	55	72
Manchester U	28	15	8	5	31	53
WBA	28	13	5	10	18	44
Liverpool	28	13	5	10	7	44
Everton	28	11	8	9	10	41
Stoke C	28	11	7	10	–11	40
Wolverhampton W	28	10	9	9	–3	39
Crewe Alex	28	11	5	12	1	38
Blackburn R	28	8	6	14	–14	30
Bolton W	28	7	2	19	–29	23

GROUP D

	P	W	D	L	GD	Pts
Sunderland	28	22	2	4	32	68
Newcastle U	28	13	7	8	9	46
Derby Co	28	11	7	10	4	40
Sheffield U	28	8	11	9	–9	35
Nottingham F	28	10	3	15	–10	33
Leeds U	28	9	5	14	–2	32
Barnsley	28	7	7	14	–30	28
Sheffield W	28	6	6	16	–20	24
Huddersfield T	28	5	9	14	–32	24
Middlesbrough	28	5	8	15	–17	23

SEMI–FINALS
Sunderland 1, Tottenham H 2
Manchester C 1, Arsenal 2

FINAL
Tottenham H 0, Arsenal 1

PUMA YOUTH ALLIANCE 2008–09

NORTH WEST CONFERENCE

	P	W	D	L	F	A	GD	Pts
Wrexham	27	19	7	1	55	26	29	64
Burnley	27	19	3	5	73	37	36	60
Carlisle U	27	18	3	6	63	29	34	57
Preston NE	27	17	2	8	75	43	32	53
Macclesfield T	27	12	7	8	43	36	7	43
Walsall	27	13	4	10	59	54	5	43
Wigan Ath	27	12	6	9	43	37	6	42
Oldham Ath	27	11	6	10	51	39	12	39
Port Vale	27	12	1	14	60	55	5	37
Rochdale	27	11	4	12	47	58	–11	37
Shrewsbury T	27	11	3	13	36	45	–9	36
Tranmere R	27	9	8	10	46	38	8	35
Stockport Co	27	10	5	12	43	47	–4	35
Bury	27	7	5	15	43	52	–9	26
Morecambe	27	6	7	14	41	69	–28	25
Chester C	27	7	3	17	36	53	–17	24
Blackpool	27	6	4	17	29	75	–46	22
Accrington S	27	3	2	22	19	69	–50	11

NORTH EAST CONFERENCE

	P	W	D	L	F	A	GD	Pts
Chesterfield	24	16	3	5	40	29	11	51
Hull C	24	15	3	6	49	26	23	48
Grimsby T	24	13	5	6	48	27	21	44
Scunthorpe U	24	13	4	7	44	23	21	43
Darlington	24	12	5	7	51	35	16	41
York C	24	11	7	6	35	21	14	40
Lincoln C	24	9	8	7	39	32	7	35
Mansfield T	24	11	2	11	40	36	4	35
Bradford C	24	9	2	13	32	44	–12	29
Doncaster R	24	6	4	14	30	48	–18	22
Hartlepool U	24	6	3	15	28	41	–13	21
Rotherham U	24	4	6	14	33	65	–32	18
Boston U	24	3	4	17	26	68	–42	13

SOUTH WEST CONFERENCE

	P	W	D	L	F	A	GD	Pts
Swindon T	20	15	2	3	57	21	36	47
Plymouth Arg	20	13	6	1	45	22	23	45
Swansea C	20	11	4	5	38	22	16	37
Exeter C	20	11	3	6	40	21	19	36
Bournemouth	20	9	4	7	35	31	4	31
Yeovil T	20	7	7	6	28	30	–2	28
Bristol R	20	5	8	7	41	33	8	23
Torquay U	20	5	3	12	31	46	–15	18
Cheltenham T	20	5	3	12	21	43	–22	18
Oxford U	20	5	2	13	20	44	–24	17
Hereford U	20	2	2	16	19	62	–43	8

SOUTH EAST CONFERENCE

	P	W	D	L	F	A	GD	Pts
Southend U	22	15	5	2	40	21	19	50
QPR	22	14	4	4	38	30	8	46
Millwall	22	13	4	5	49	28	21	43
Wycombe W	22	12	4	6	49	33	16	40
Brighton & HA	22	12	4	6	38	23	15	40
Colchester U	22	12	4	6	37	31	6	40
Peterborough U	22	11	2	9	37	29	8	35
Rushden & D	22	10	2	10	37	27	10	32
Brentford	22	9	5	8	32	23	9	32
Leyton Orient	22	8	5	9	35	37	–2	29
Gillingham	22	7	5	10	27	32	–5	26
Luton T	22	7	3	12	36	55	–19	24
Northampton T	22	6	4	12	27	33	–6	22
Dagenham & R	22	2	7	13	20	40	–20	13
Aldershot T	22	4	1	17	30	54	–24	13
Barnet	22	3	3	16	17	53	–36	12

THE PUMA YOUTH ALLIANCE CUP 2008–09

SOUTHERN SECTION

GROUP 1

	P	W	D	L	Pts
Swindon T	5	5	0	0	15
Bournemouth	5	3	0	2	9
Cheltenham T	5	2	1	2	7
Oxford U	5	2	1	2	7
Hereford U	5	1	0	4	6
Aldershot T	5	1	0	4	3

GROUP 2

	P	W	D	L	Pts
Swansea C	5	4	0	1	12
Exeter C	5	3	0	2	9
Bristol R	5	2	2	1	8
Plymouth Arg	5	2	1	2	7
Torquay U	5	1	1	3	4
Yeovil T	5	1	0	4	3

GROUP 3

	P	W	D	L	Pts
Colchester U	4	3	1	0	10
Brentford	4	2	2	0	8
Brighton & HA	4	1	1	2	4
Dagenham & R	4	1	1	2	4
Barnet	4	0	1	3	1

GROUP 4

	P	W	D	L	Pts
Gillingham	4	3	0	1	9
Peterborough U	4	2	1	1	7
Leyton Orient	4	1	1	2	4
Northampton T	4	1	1	2	4
Luton T	4	0	3	1	3

GROUP 5

	P	W	D	L	Pts
Southend U	4	2	1	1	7
Wycombe W	4	2	1	1	7
QPR	4	2	0	2	6
Millwall	4	1	1	2	4
Rushden & D	4	1	1	2	4

ROUND TWO

Bristol R 1, Bournemouth 1
Bristol R won 4-2 on penalties.
Cheltenham T 1, QPR 2
Exeter C 2, Swansea C 5
Oxford U 1, Leyton O 1
Leyton O won 6-5 on penalties.
Peterborough U 2, Brentford 3
Southend 2, Gillingham 3
Swindon T 2, Colchester U 1
Wycombe W 0, Brighton & HA 1

NORTHERN SECTION

ROUND ONE

Boston U, Scunthorpe U 1
Burnley 4, Rotherham U 0
Bury 1, Rochdale 2
Carlisle U 2, Wrexham 1
Chester C 0, Hartlepool U 1
Chesterfield 3, Accrington S 0
Doncaster R 1, Mansfield T 4
Grimsby T 1, Hull C 1
Grimsby T won on penalties.
Lincoln C 1, Macclesfield T 2
Morecambe 3, Bradford C 2
Oldham Ath 3, Walsall 2
Shrewsbury T 2, Port Vale 0
Stockport Co 0, Tranmere R 1
Wigan Ath 0, Darlington 3

ROUND TWO

Carlisle U 2, Mansfield T 1
Chesterfield 1 York C 0
Darlington 2 Macclesfield T 0
Oldham Ath 3, Morecambe 3
Morcambe won 4-3 on penalties.
Rochdale 2, Hartlepool 4
Scarborough 2, Grimsby T 3
Shrewsbury T 2, Burnley 2
Shrewsbury T won 9-8 on penalties.
Tranmere R 3, Blackpool 0

QUARTER–FINALS

Shrewsbury T 1, Morecambe 1
Morecambe won 4-3 on penalties.
Swansea C 0, Swindon T 5
Tranmere R 1, Carlisle U 0
Brighton & HA 0, QPR 1
Gillingham 3, Brentford 5
Chesterfield 1, Darlington 2
Hartlepool U 0, Grimsby T 0
Grimsby T won 5–4 on penalties.
Leyton Orient 2, Bristol R 2
Leyton Orient won 4–2 on penalties.

AREA SEMI–FINALS

Gillingham 3, Swindon T 0
Morecambe 0, Grimsby T 2
QPR 2, Leyton Orient 1
Tranmere R 2, Darlington 0

AREA FINALS

QPR 3, Gillingham 0
Grimsby T 1, Tranmere R 1
Grimsby T won 4-3 on penalties.

FINAL

QPR 1, Grimsby T 2

NON-LEAGUE TABLES 2008–09

NATIONAL LEAGUE SYSTEM – STEP 5

SKILLTRAININGLTD NORTHERN LEAGUE
DIVISION ONE

	P	W	D	L	F	A	GD	Pts
Newcastle Benfield	42	25	9	8	78	42	36	84
Consett	42	25	8	9	91	51	40	83
Whitley Bay	42	25	7	10	108	58	50	82
Spennymoor Town	42	24	10	8	78	49	29	82
Sunderland Nissan	42	23	9	10	93	56	37	78
Dunston Federation	42	20	13	9	77	48	29	73
Penrith	42	21	8	13	90	62	28	71
Shildon	42	18	15	9	84	58	26	69
West Allotment Celtic	42	19	11	12	66	60	6	68
Ryton	42	18	8	16	81	77	4	62
Tow Law Town	42	17	11	14	73	69	4	62
Morpeth Town	42	19	4	19	64	68	–4	61
Chester Le Street Town	42	17	7	18	74	72	2	58
Bedlington Terriers	42	15	9	18	66	76	–10	54
Billingham Synthonia	42	12	11	19	68	75	–7	47
Ashington	42	13	8	21	63	83	–20	47
Billingham Town	42	11	8	23	63	96	–33	41
Bishop Auckland	42	9	11	22	56	85	–29	38
South Shields	42	9	10	23	52	79	–27	37
West Auckland Town	42	8	7	27	50	99	–49	31
Seaham Red Star	42	8	7	27	42	94	–52	31
Northallerton Town	42	8	5	29	50	110	–60	29

SUSSEX COUNTY LEAGUE DIVISION ONE

	P	W	D	L	F	A	GD	Pts
Eastbourne United Assoc	38	23	6	9	79	37	42	75
Arundel	38	21	10	7	96	53	43	73
Horsham YMCA	38	23	4	11	72	53	19	73
Wick	38	21	8	9	77	60	17	71
Three Bridges	38	20	7	11	75	51	24	67
Shoreham	38	18	11	9	63	45	18	65
Chichester City United	38	19	5	14	74	70	4	62
Redhill	38	16	13	9	70	43	27	61
Lingfield	38	14	15	9	62	51	11	57
Ringmer (–10)	38	19	5	14	86	60	26	52
Selsey	38	14	9	15	59	48	11	51
Pagham	38	13	9	16	51	59	–8	48
St Francis Rangers	38	13	8	17	64	65	–1	47
Whitehawk	38	13	8	17	62	64	–2	47
Hailsham Town	38	12	7	19	54	92	–38	43
Hassocks	38	10	10	18	49	61	–12	40
East Grinstead Town	38	8	9	21	54	84	–30	33
East Preston	38	9	5	24	53	85	–32	32
Oakwood	38	8	5	25	43	97	–54	29
Worthing United	38	4	10	24	42	107	–65	22

CHERRY RED COMBINED COUNTIES
PREMIER DIVISION

	P	W	D	L	F	A	GD	Pts
Bedfont Green	42	29	9	4	116	55	61	96
North Greenford United	42	22	13	7	99	66	33	79
Chertsey Town	42	23	8	11	96	58	38	77
Epsom & Ewell	42	22	11	9	85	55	30	77
Camberley Town	42	21	12	9	99	56	43	75
Cove (–1)	42	19	14	9	81	56	25	70
Badshot Lea	42	21	6	15	87	91	–4	69
Raynes Park Vale	42	20	4	18	80	80	0	64
Ash United	42	17	11	14	78	70	8	62
Banstead Athletic	42	18	7	17	78	80	–2	61
Molesey	42	16	10	16	77	62	15	58
Horley Town	42	15	13	14	56	53	3	58
Egham Town	42	16	8	18	62	66	–4	56
Colliers Wood United	42	15	8	19	81	73	8	53
Bookham	42	14	10	18	75	85	–10	52
Sandhurst Town	42	14	9	19	63	81	–18	51
Wembley	42	12	10	20	61	81	–20	46
Bedfont	42	12	9	21	58	85	–27	45
Chessington & Hook United	42	10	14	18	61	78	–17	44
Guildford City	42	11	11	20	55	95	–40	44
Hartley Wintney	42	4	10	28	50	112	–62	22
Cobham	42	4	7	31	48	108	–60	19

EAGLE BITTER UNITED COUNTIES LEAGUE
PREMIER DIVISION

	P	W	D	L	F	A	GD	Pts
Stewarts & Lloyds Corby	40	27	7	6	95	40	55	88
Stotfold	40	27	3	10	106	63	43	84
Newport Pagnell Town	40	24	10	6	84	40	44	82
Deeping Rangers	40	24	8	8	96	50	46	80
Boston Town	40	23	11	6	79	51	28	80
St Ives Town (–3)	40	24	7	9	76	44	32	76
Daventry Town (–3)	40	22	7	11	83	51	32	70
Long Buckby	40	20	7	13	78	52	26	67
Cogenhoe United	40	15	13	12	58	55	3	58

Raunds Town	40	16	8	16	60	68	–8	56
Desborough Town	40	15	6	19	62	68	–6	51
Northampton Spencer	40	14	9	17	64	71	–7	51
Blackstones	40	13	11	16	60	63	–3	50
Yaxley	40	14	7	19	47	55	–8	49
Sleaford Town	40	13	9	18	57	74	–17	48
Holbeach United	40	12	11	17	56	60	–4	47
St Neots Town	40	12	7	21	66	75	–9	43
Wellingborough Town	40	7	8	25	30	66	–36	29
Bourne Town	40	6	9	25	47	99	–52	27
Potton United	40	4	7	29	38	116	–78	19
Rothwell Corinthians	40	3	5	32	36	117	–81	14

FTL FUTBOL HELLENIC LEAGUE PREMIER DIVISION

	P	W	D	L	F	A	GD	Pts
Hungerford Town	42	29	9	4	103	38	65	96
Shortwood United	42	29	9	4	99	45	54	96
Witney United	42	28	7	7	105	55	50	91
Almondsbury Town (–1)	42	28	7	7	106	41	65	90
Ardley United	42	23	11	8	85	58	27	80
Highworth Town	42	24	5	13	88	60	28	77
Chalfont Wasps	42	22	4	16	77	70	7	70
Reading Town	42	19	10	13	88	49	39	67
Kidlington	42	17	9	16	70	65	5	60
Pegasus Juniors	42	17	4	21	73	82	–9	55
Wantage Town	42	17	3	22	71	69	2	54
Carterton	42	15	8	19	70	79	–9	53
Hook Norton	42	14	10	18	69	81	–12	52
Fairford Town	42	13	12	17	62	67	–5	51
Marlow United	42	16	3	23	69	98	–29	51
Flackwell Heath (–3)	42	16	5	21	80	86	–6	50
Old Woodstock Town	42	13	10	19	59	70	–11	49
Shrivenham	42	12	4	26	49	87	–38	40
Abingdon Town	42	11	5	26	43	86	–43	38
Bicester Town	42	10	6	26	48	114	–66	36
Milton United	42	8	6	28	52	105	–53	30
Harrow Hill	42	4	7	31	46	107	–61	19

ASPIRE MIDLAND FOOTBALL ALLIANCE

	P	W	D	L	F	A	GD	Pts
Market Drayton Town	42	31	6	5	111	31	80	99
Barwell	42	27	10	5	91	36	55	91
Coalville Town	42	25	7	10	88	51	37	82
Boldmere St Michaels	42	25	6	11	98	54	44	81
Tipton Town	42	23	9	10	82	44	38	78
Stratford Town	42	21	11	10	92	65	27	74
Coventry Sphinx	42	23	5	14	96	78	18	74
Shifnal Town (–3)	42	20	10	12	73	56	17	67
Causeway United	42	19	7	16	62	47	15	64
Alvechurch	42	16	15	11	73	55	18	63
Coleshill Town	42	18	9	15	70	59	11	63
Bridgnorth Town	42	17	8	17	76	85	–9	59
Highgate United	42	15	9	18	67	75	–8	54
Studley	42	15	6	21	55	77	–22	51
Friar Lane & Epworth	42	14	9	19	70	96	–26	51
Cradley Town	42	14	8	20	69	81	–12	50
Westfields	42	13	10	19	75	79	–4	49
Biddulph Victoria	42	12	8	22	57	102	–45	44
Oadby Town	42	9	10	23	43	73	–30	37
Rocester	42	8	9	25	49	88	–39	33
Racing Club Warwick	42	4	6	32	31	131	–100	18
Oldbury United (–1)	42	1	6	35	33	98	–65	8

VODKAT NORTH WEST COUNTIES LEAGUE
PREMIER DIVISION

	P	W	D	L	F	A	GD	Pts
AFC Fylde	42	33	5	4	122	35	87	104
New Mills	42	34	2	6	92	33	59	104
Newcastle Town	42	26	9	7	91	33	58	87
Congleton Town	42	26	8	8	85	44	41	86
Glossop North End	42	25	7	10	83	49	34	82
Ashton Athletic	42	18	7	17	67	68	–1	61
Alsager Town	42	18	5	19	66	72	–6	59
Bacup Borough	42	16	10	16	71	71	0	58
Silsden	42	16	10	16	62	67	–5	58
Squires Gate	42	14	15	13	56	56	0	57
Runcorn Linnets	42	16	7	19	64	84	–20	55
Atherton LR	42	12	15	15	70	77	–7	51
Maine Road	42	14	9	19	60	74	–14	51
Formby	42	15	3	24	57	67	–10	48
Ramsbottom United (–4)	42	13	12	17	56	72	–16	47
St Helens Town	42	14	4	24	64	97	–33	46
Nelson	42	11	12	19	68	86	–18	45
Colne	42	11	10	21	64	75	–11	43
Flixton	42	9	14	19	58	86	–28	41
Winsford United	42	9	13	20	52	82	–30	39
Abbey Hey	42	11	5	26	60	89	–29	38
Atherton Collieries	42	7	8	27	42	93	–51	29

KOOLSPORT NORTHERN COUNTIES EAST LEAGUE
PREMIER DIVISION

	P	W	D	L	F	A	GD	Pts
Mickleover Sports	38	28	4	6	108	47	61	88
Long Eaton United	38	25	6	7	76	40	36	81
Selby Town	38	25	5	8	89	40	49	80
Bridlington Town	38	23	7	8	105	51	54	76
Winterton Rangers	38	19	7	12	74	49	25	64
Arnold Town	38	17	13	8	58	46	12	64
Thackley	38	20	2	16	87	62	25	62
Dinnington Town	38	19	5	14	73	60	13	62
Pickering Town	38	17	7	14	81	64	17	58
Hallam	38	17	5	16	78	69	9	56
Parkgate	38	15	6	17	67	79	−12	51
Maltby Main (−3)	38	15	7	16	63	67	−4	49
Nostell Miners Welfare	38	12	13	13	45	51	−6	49
Liversedge (−3)	38	14	7	17	60	64	−4	46
Armthorpe Welfare	38	14	3	21	61	58	3	45
Hall Road Rangers	38	11	6	21	53	94	−41	39
Shirebrook Town	38	9	4	25	47	85	−38	31
Lincoln Moorlands Railway	38	9	3	26	45	93	−48	30
Brodsworth Welfare	38	5	8	25	46	92	−46	23
Eccleshill United	38	6	2	30	48	153	−105	20

RIDGEONS EASTERN COUNTIES LEAGUE
PREMIER DIVISION

	P	W	D	L	F	A	GD	Pts
Lowestoft Town	40	32	4	4	114	46	68	100
CRC	40	26	5	9	86	54	32	83
Needham Market	40	26	3	11	94	64	30	81
Dereham Town	40	25	4	11	108	67	41	79
Wroxham	40	24	6	10	86	52	34	78
Kirkley & Pakefield	40	23	7	10	78	44	34	76
Leiston	40	22	9	9	90	41	49	75
Tiptree United	40	20	5	15	90	72	18	65
Stanway Rovers	40	19	7	14	81	65	16	64
Walsham Le Willows	40	15	9	16	60	62	−2	54
Mildenhall Town	40	16	5	19	75	81	−6	53
Felixstowe & Walton United	40	16	1	23	75	110	−35	49
Histon Reserves	40	14	6	20	77	88	−11	48
Ely City	40	12	6	22	59	82	−23	42
King's Lynn Reserves	40	11	8	21	57	81	−24	41
Wisbech Town	40	11	6	23	59	82	−23	39
Wivenhoe Town	40	12	2	26	65	105	−40	38
Woodbridge Town	40	9	10	21	52	77	−25	37
Norwich United	40	8	10	22	46	74	−28	34
Harwich & Parkeston	40	9	6	25	47	98	−51	33
Haverhill Rovers	40	7	7	26	42	96	−54	28

MOLTEN SPARTAN SOUTH MIDLANDS
PREMIER DIVISION

	P	W	D	L	F	A	GD	Pts
Biggleswade Town	40	27	4	9	100	41	59	85
Harefield United	40	26	7	7	103	45	58	85
Chalfont St Peter	40	23	9	8	99	56	43	78
Broxbourne Borough V&E	40	20	8	12	76	63	13	68
Kingsbury London Tigers	40	18	12	10	68	52	16	66
Leverstock Green	40	18	10	12	90	60	30	64
Hanwell Town	40	17	11	12	81	53	28	62
Tring Athletic	40	18	8	14	81	67	14	62
Welwyn Garden City	40	18	7	15	69	75	−6	61
Hertford Town	40	15	13	12	61	46	15	58
Langford	40	16	9	15	81	82	−1	57
Colney Heath	40	16	8	16	67	71	−4	56
Oxhey Jets	40	15	10	15	77	82	−5	55
St Margaretsbury	40	15	8	17	54	62	−8	53
Aylesbury Vale	40	14	7	19	56	74	−18	49
Biggleswade United	40	13	6	21	52	82	−30	45
Brimsdown Rovers	40	10	11	19	59	77	−18	41
Haringey Borough	40	10	7	23	50	83	−33	37
Cockfosters	40	9	6	25	62	101	−39	33
Holmer Green	40	6	10	24	36	80	−44	28
Kentish Town	40	7	7	26	58	128	−70	28

SYDENHAMS WESSEX LEAGUE PREMIER DIVISION

	P	W	D	L	F	A	GD	Pts
Poole Town	42	38	2	2	144	34	110	116
VT	42	31	8	3	141	35	106	101
Moneyfields	42	29	4	9	99	44	55	91
Wimborne Town	42	26	9	7	115	41	74	87
Brockenhurst	42	24	10	8	71	41	30	82
Newport (IW)	42	24	5	13	87	64	23	77
Christchurch	42	22	8	12	77	48	29	74
Hamworthy United	42	21	5	16	77	73	4	68
New Milton Town	42	18	10	14	72	55	17	64
Fareham Town	42	16	13	13	64	53	11	61
Romsey Town	42	16	12	14	65	75	−10	60
Bemerton Heath Harlequins	42	16	5	21	56	67	−11	53
Cowes Sports	42	13	11	18	65	78	−13	50
Brading Town	42	13	8	21	62	70	−8	47
Bournemouth	42	12	8	22	60	89	−29	44
Hayling United	42	11	8	23	66	96	−30	41
Alresford Town	42	11	7	24	53	88	−35	40
Lymington Town	42	10	8	24	58	104	−46	38
Alton Town	42	9	9	24	56	105	−49	36
Laverstock & Ford	42	8	7	27	49	106	−57	31
Hamble ASSC	42	5	6	31	30	121	−91	21
Horndean	42	5	5	32	45	125	−80	20

TOOLSTATION WESTERN LEAGUE PREMIER

	P	W	D	L	F	A	GD	Pts
Bitton	40	26	6	8	85	32	53	84
Frome Town	40	23	7	10	74	44	30	76
Willand Rovers	40	20	13	7	72	49	23	73
Dawlish Town	40	23	3	14	93	52	41	72
Bristol Manor Farm	40	22	6	12	75	53	22	72
Bideford	40	20	9	11	68	43	25	69
Wellington	40	20	7	13	87	53	34	67
Welton Rovers	40	19	9	12	64	52	12	66
Hallen	40	19	8	13	57	40	17	65
Brislington	40	18	6	16	62	54	8	60
Melksham Town	40	15	14	11	59	53	6	59
Sherborne Town	40	17	8	15	55	59	−4	59
Street	40	13	7	20	55	65	−10	46
Ilfracombe Town	40	11	11	18	48	70	−22	44
Bishop Sutton	40	9	16	15	48	48	0	43
Calne Town	40	11	10	19	70	78	−8	43
Radstock Town	40	12	6	22	56	95	−39	42
Barnstaple Town	40	10	9	21	49	82	−33	39
Corsham Town	40	10	8	22	37	80	−43	38
Chard Town	40	9	5	26	30	77	−47	32
Devizes Town	40	5	8	27	41	106	−65	23

ESSEX SENIOR LEAGUE

	P	W	D	L	F	A	GD	Pts
Romford	30	21	8	1	79	25	54	71
Enfield	30	21	1	8	62	29	33	64
Takeley	30	19	4	7	59	37	22	61
Southend Manor	30	16	7	7	65	41	24	55
Barkingside	30	13	7	10	48	51	−3	46
Eton Manor	30	12	8	10	52	40	12	44
Burnham Ramblers	30	12	7	11	62	50	12	43
Basildon United (−3)	30	14	3	13	53	50	3	42
Hullbridge Sports	30	11	8	11	44	46	−2	41
Stansted	30	12	4	14	57	50	7	40
Bowers & Pitsea (−3)	30	11	7	12	35	35	0	37
Barking	30	8	7	15	45	62	−17	31
Sawbridgeworth Town	30	8	5	17	43	70	−27	29
London APSA (−1)	30	7	5	18	34	67	−33	25
Mauritius Sports	30	4	8	18	42	76	−34	20
Clapton	30	5	3	22	40	91	−51	18

BULMERS CIDER KENT LEAGUE PREMIER DIVISION

	P	W	D	L	F	A	GD	Pts
VCD Athletic	32	22	4	6	68	24	44	70
Hythe Town	32	21	4	7	71	39	32	67
Greenwich Borough (−1)	32	20	4	8	60	45	15	63
Faversham Town	32	20	2	10	83	40	43	62
Holmesdale	32	18	7	7	57	30	27	61
Herne Bay	32	19	3	10	68	50	18	60
Erith Town (+2)	32	14	10	8	59	39	20	54
Erith & Belvedere	32	16	5	11	67	50	17	53
Croydon	32	15	4	13	58	40	18	49
Tunbridge Wells	32	13	6	13	53	50	3	45
Norton Sports	32	12	4	16	44	57	−13	40
Deal Town	32	10	8	14	57	53	4	38
Slade Green	32	11	4	17	53	66	−13	37
Sevenoaks Town	32	9	4	19	44	67	−23	31
Beckenham Town	32	8	4	20	54	76	−22	28
Lordswood	32	6	3	23	43	79	−36	21
Sporting Bengal United	32	0	0	32	26	160	−134	0

NATIONAL LEAGUE SYSTEM – STEP 6
SKILLTRAININGLTD NORTHERN
DIVISION TWO

	P	W	D	L	F	A	GD	Pts
Horden Colliery Welfare	38	24	8	6	92	44	48	80
Norton & Stockton Ancients	38	24	8	6	79	36	43	80
Esh Winning	38	23	8	7	89	59	30	77
Sunderland Ryhope CA	38	21	8	9	88	46	42	71
Marske United	38	18	8	12	63	59	4	62
Brandon United	38	18	7	13	85	67	18	61
Guisborough Town	38	18	7	13	71	53	18	61
Birtley Town	38	18	7	13	73	62	11	61
Crook Town	38	17	7	14	68	71	−3	58
Hebburn Town	38	15	10	13	71	83	−12	55
Whitehaven	38	15	8	15	57	52	5	53
Team Northumbria	38	13	12	13	75	66	9	51
Stokesley SC	38	14	7	17	63	67	−4	49
Whickham	38	14	7	17	55	73	−18	49
North Shields	38	13	6	19	53	76	−23	45
Jarrow Roofing Boldon CA	38	11	4	23	50	78	−28	37
Washington (−3)	38	10	4	24	61	78	−17	33
Darlington Railway Athletic	38	10	2	26	45	80	−35	32
Prudhoe Town	38	5	11	22	47	88	−41	26
Thornaby	38	5	7	26	50	97	−47	22

SUSSEX COUNTY LEAGUE DIVISION TWO

	P	W	D	L	F	A	GD	Pts
Peacehaven & Telscombe	34	25	5	4	104	31	73	80
Mile Oak	34	24	3	7	92	35	57	75
Crawley Down	34	19	10	5	77	33	44	67
Rustington	34	20	4	10	66	39	27	64
Westfield	34	17	8	9	57	46	11	59
Rye United	34	16	8	10	66	45	21	56
Seaford Town	34	17	5	12	61	56	5	56
Sidley United	34	12	9	13	49	57	–8	45
Lancing	34	12	6	16	55	65	–10	42
Loxwood	34	11	8	15	44	49	–5	41
Southwick	34	12	5	17	58	71	–13	41
Storrington	34	12	5	17	43	58	–15	41
Steyning Town	34	11	6	17	42	67	–25	39
Littlehampton Town	34	9	10	15	65	82	–17	37
Wealden	34	10	6	18	57	69	–12	36
Midhurst & Easebourne	34	9	6	19	46	74	–28	33
Bexhill United	34	8	6	20	45	67	–22	30
Sidlesham	34	3	8	23	27	110	–83	17

CHERRY RED COMBINED COUNTIES LEAGUE DIVISION ONE

	P	W	D	L	F	A	GD	Pts
Staines Lammas	34	22	5	7	78	39	39	71
Hanworth Villa	34	21	7	6	79	44	35	70
Dorking	34	22	4	8	78	45	33	70
Mole Valley SCR	34	22	4	8	87	55	32	70
Knaphill	34	22	3	9	86	55	31	69
Worcester Park	34	20	7	7	72	38	34	67
Feltham	34	15	7	12	62	53	9	52
Farnham Town	34	16	3	15	85	74	11	51
Sheerwater	34	15	3	16	64	71	–7	48
CB Hounslow United	34	13	6	15	48	52	–4	45
Warlingham	34	12	8	14	62	70	–8	44
Farleigh Rovers	34	11	8	15	49	61	–12	41
Westfield	34	11	5	18	50	67	–17	38
South Park	34	11	4	19	59	68	–9	37
Crescent Rovers	34	8	9	17	48	70	–22	33
Frimley Green	34	10	3	21	40	74	–34	33
Coulsdon United	34	4	8	22	56	95	–39	20
Chobham	34	2	4	28	43	115	–72	10

EAGLE BITTER UNITED COUNTIES LEAGUE DIVISION ONE

	P	W	D	L	F	A	GD	Pts
Peterborough Northern Star	30	24	2	4	94	24	70	74
Daventry United	30	19	5	6	81	40	41	62
Northampton Sileby Rangers	30	16	4	10	67	47	20	52
Northampton ON Cheneks	30	16	3	11	63	52	11	51
AFC Kempston Rovers	30	13	8	9	66	64	2	47
Rushden & Higham United	30	11	13	6	50	37	13	46
Whitworths	30	12	9	9	56	47	9	45
Buckingham Town	30	14	3	13	56	60	–4	45
Eynesbury Rovers (–6)	30	13	10	7	59	48	11	43
Bugbrooke St Michaels	30	10	9	11	61	53	8	39
Thrapston Town (–3)	30	12	5	13	54	58	–4	38
Wootton Blue Cross	30	8	5	17	49	71	–22	29
Burton Park Wanderers	30	7	6	17	41	71	–30	27
Huntingdon Town	30	6	8	16	37	62	–25	26
Olney Town	30	8	1	21	41	69	–28	25
Irchester United	30	3	5	22	33	105	–72	14

FTL FUTBOL HELLENIC LEAGUE DIVISION ONE EAST

	P	W	D	L	F	A	GD	Pts
Binfield	34	29	3	2	89	18	71	90
Ascot United	34	25	4	5	91	35	56	79
Newbury	34	20	11	3	100	41	59	71
Wokingham & Emmbrook	34	20	6	8	86	44	42	66
Holyport	34	16	9	9	76	60	16	57
South Kilburn	34	15	8	11	68	62	6	53
Henley Town	34	13	13	8	65	43	22	52
Chinnor	34	14	9	11	51	48	3	51
Thame United	34	13	10	11	64	45	19	49
Kintbury Rangers	34	15	4	15	69	58	11	49
Finchampstead	34	12	12	10	64	43	21	48
Penn & Tylers Green	34	10	9	15	46	59	–13	39
Englefield Green Rovers	34	9	9	16	52	73	–21	36
Rayners Lane	34	8	7	19	45	63	–18	31
Launton Sports	34	7	5	22	45	91	–46	26
Bisley	34	5	10	19	42	74	–32	25
Prestwood	34	5	4	25	29	130	–101	19
Eton Wick	34	1	5	28	25	120	–95	8

FTL FUTBOL HELLENIC LEAGUE DIVISION ONE WEST

	P	W	D	L	F	A	GD	Pts
Hardwicke	32	27	3	2	93	18	75	84
Malmesbury Victoria	32	21	6	5	91	45	46	69
Oxford City Nomads	32	20	4	8	80	51	29	64
Wootton Bassett Town	32	17	9	6	61	30	31	60
Letcombe	32	17	6	9	88	52	36	57
Purton	32	17	6	9	85	59	26	57
Winterbourne United	32	15	5	12	77	54	23	50

LYDNEY TOWN / TYTHERINGTON ROCKS (continued)

	P	W	D	L	F	A	GD	Pts
Lydney Town	32	14	7	11	45	45	0	49
Tytherington Rocks (–1)	32	13	8	11	48	40	8	46
Headington Amateurs	32	11	8	13	72	64	8	41
Clanfield	32	11	6	15	51	63	–12	39
Cheltenham Saracens	32	10	7	15	52	63	–11	37
Easington Sports	32	9	6	17	45	69	–24	33
Trowbridge Town	32	10	2	20	40	67	–27	32
Cricklade Town	32	7	3	22	50	97	–47	24
Cirencester United	32	4	3	25	34	130	–96	15
Pewsey Vale	32	3	3	26	31	96	–65	12

MIDLAND COMBINATION LEAGUE PREMIER DIVISION

	P	W	D	L	F	A	GD	Pts
Loughborough University	40	31	3	6	96	34	62	96
Castle Vale	40	27	8	5	84	42	42	89
Southam United	40	24	10	6	83	36	47	82
Oldbury Athletic	40	26	4	10	101	55	46	82
Heather St John	40	18	12	10	68	45	23	66
Nuneaton Griff	40	18	10	12	64	51	13	64
Walsall Wood	40	18	9	13	59	50	9	63
Pilkington XXX	40	17	6	17	79	83	–4	57
Coventry Copsewood	40	16	8	16	75	66	9	56
Heath Hayes	40	17	5	18	56	79	–23	56
Cadbury Athletic	40	16	7	17	62	57	5	55
Knowle	40	13	11	16	50	64	–14	50
Pershore Town	40	13	10	17	59	81	–22	49
GSA Sports	40	13	6	21	64	84	–20	45
Massey Ferguson	40	11	11	18	61	72	–11	44
Brocton	40	11	8	21	60	71	–11	41
Continental Star	40	11	7	22	70	84	–14	40
Bartley Green (–3)	40	11	8	21	58	81	–23	38
Bolehall Swifts	40	10	7	23	43	71	–28	37
Meir KA	40	9	8	23	52	87	–35	35
Coton Green	40	5	12	23	59	110	–51	27

VODKAT NORTH WEST COUNTIES LEAGUE DIVISION ONE

	P	W	D	L	F	A	GD	Pts
Bootle	34	25	5	4	78	27	51	80
Padiham	34	22	7	5	93	41	52	73
Stone Dominoes	34	23	2	9	85	51	34	71
AFC Liverpool	34	22	3	9	82	39	43	69
Wigan Robin Park (–3)	34	18	5	11	61	49	12	56
Oldham Town	34	16	5	13	60	54	6	53
Cheadle Town	34	16	4	14	54	44	10	52
Irlam	34	13	13	8	51	43	8	52
Holker Old Boys	34	14	8	12	59	61	–2	50
Chadderton	34	14	6	14	60	54	6	48
Eccleshall	34	14	5	15	44	44	0	47
Norton United	34	12	6	16	63	60	3	42
Darwen	34	11	7	16	51	74	–23	40
Leek CSOB	34	7	10	17	51	72	–21	31
AFC Blackpool	34	7	8	19	34	59	–25	29
Rochdale Town	34	6	6	22	55	91	–36	24
Daisy Hill	34	6	4	24	39	101	–62	22
Ashton Town	34	4	8	22	35	91	–56	20

KOOLSPORT NORTHERN COUNTIES EAST LEAGUE DIVISION ONE

	P	W	D	L	F	A	GD	Pts
Scarborough Athletic	36	29	5	2	121	24	97	92
Rainworth Miners Welfare	36	23	9	4	90	42	48	78
Askern Villa	36	21	9	6	65	34	31	72
Staveley Miners Welfare	36	20	8	8	77	43	34	68
Barton Town Old Boys	36	20	7	9	76	53	23	67
Bottesford Town	36	20	2	14	77	62	15	62
Leeds Carnegie	36	17	10	9	79	41	38	61
AFC Emley	36	17	9	10	59	48	11	60
Pontefract Collieries	36	16	5	15	62	56	6	53
Hemsworth Miners Welfare	36	13	11	12	57	52	5	50
Rossington Main	36	12	7	17	53	67	–14	43
Appleby Frodingham	36	11	9	16	58	79	–21	42
Grimsby Borough	36	11	7	18	52	68	–16	40
Teversal	36	12	3	21	59	86	–27	39
Brighouse Town	36	9	8	19	55	73	–18	35
Worsborough Bridge Athletic	36	9	5	22	45	86	–41	32
Tadcaster Albion	36	9	4	23	47	94	–47	31
Yorkshire Amateur	36	7	4	25	52	83	–31	25
Glasshoughton Welfare	36	0	6	30	29	118	–89	6

RIDGEONS EASTERN COUNTIES LEAGUE DIVISION ONE

	P	W	D	L	F	A	GD	Pts
Newmarket Town	38	29	4	5	85	29	56	91
Hadleigh United	38	26	4	8	79	40	39	82
Debenham LC	38	25	3	10	91	36	55	78
Halstead Town	38	23	9	6	97	47	50	78
Great Yarmouth Town	38	22	7	9	79	46	33	73
Gorleston	38	21	8	9	87	59	28	71
FC Clacton	38	22	4	12	97	58	39	70
Brantham Athletic	38	20	6	12	81	57	24	66
Diss Town	38	17	8	13	78	63	15	59

	P	W	D	L	F	A	GD	Pts
Godmanchester Rovers	38	15	7	16	58	57	1	52
Cornard United	38	14	8	16	62	63	-1	50
Stowmarket Town	38	13	11	14	52	67	-15	50
March Town United	38	13	6	19	62	74	-12	45
Saffron Walden Town	38	10	14	14	48	51	-3	44
Downham Town	38	9	7	22	48	95	-47	34
Thetford Town	38	9	6	23	55	84	-29	33
Ipswich Wanderers	38	7	8	23	57	84	-27	29
Swaffham Town	38	7	6	25	38	102	-64	27
Long Melford	38	6	5	27	33	104	-71	23
Fakenham Town	38	4	5	29	39	110	-71	17

MOLTEN SPARTAN SOUTH MIDLANDS LEAGUE DIVISION ONE

	P	W	D	L	F	A	GD	Pts
Royston Town	40	33	4	3	138	30	108	103
Kings Langley	40	26	9	5	93	34	59	87
Hatfield Town	40	26	4	10	97	55	42	82
Bedford Town Reserves	40	20	12	8	68	39	29	72
Hoddesdon Town	40	21	8	11	73	41	32	71
New Bradwell St Peter	40	20	10	10	80	56	24	70
Amersham Town	40	20	10	10	88	66	22	70
Harpenden Town	40	20	7	13	95	60	35	67
London Colney	40	19	8	13	94	57	37	65
Cranfield United	40	20	4	16	84	65	19	64
Tokyngton Manor	40	17	7	16	71	84	-13	58
Winslow United	40	16	8	16	71	88	-17	56
Stony Stratford Town	40	15	6	19	83	91	-8	51
Bedford	40	12	8	20	61	95	-34	44
Ampthill Town	40	12	6	22	63	74	-11	42
Crawley Green	40	10	9	21	60	70	-10	39
Arlesey Athletic	40	10	6	24	57	114	-57	36
Sport London E Benfica	40	9	8	23	64	99	-35	35
Buckingham Athletic	40	7	6	27	45	78	-33	27
Sun Postal Sports (-3)	40	7	7	26	51	106	-55	25
Brache Sparta	40	5	3	32	48	182	-134	18

SYDENHAMS WESSEX LEAGUE DIVISION ONE

	P	W	D	L	F	A	GD	Pts
Totton & Eling	40	31	8	1	124	34	90	101
Blackfield & Langley	40	28	7	5	102	35	67	91
United Services Portsmouth	40	23	8	9	119	66	53	77
Petersfield Town	40	22	10	8	86	56	30	76
Warminster Town	40	22	8	10	98	47	51	74
Whitchurch United	40	21	10	9	102	62	40	73
Hythe & Dibden	40	19	10	11	101	78	23	67
Farnborough North End	40	18	12	10	66	49	17	66
Fawley	40	18	8	14	84	59	25	62
Stockbridge	40	16	12	12	68	66	2	60
Ringwood Town	40	17	6	17	86	80	6	57
Amesbury Town	40	15	8	17	83	90	-7	53
Verwood Town	40	14	9	17	65	75	-10	51
AFC Aldermaston	40	12	6	22	64	91	-27	42
Shaftesbury	40	11	9	20	61	92	-31	42
Tadley Calleva	40	11	6	23	66	102	-36	39
Downton	40	9	10	21	56	91	-35	37
East Cowes Victoria Athletic	40	8	8	24	48	109	-61	32
AFC Portchester	40	6	11	23	49	106	-57	29
Andover New Street	40	7	6	27	58	111	-53	27
Fleet Spurs	40	3	6	31	36	123	-87	15

TOOLSTATION WESTERN LEAGUE DIVISION ONE

	P	W	D	L	F	A	GD	Pts
Larkhall Athletic	38	30	5	3	127	27	100	95
Longwell Green Sports	38	27	4	7	78	40	38	85
Bradford Town	38	22	6	10	106	55	51	72
Cadbury Heath (-3)	38	21	8	9	84	54	30	68
Keynsham Town	38	19	9	10	62	46	16	66
Hengrove Athletic	38	19	4	15	57	52	5	61
Oldland Abbotonians	38	17	8	13	65	60	5	59
Shrewton United (-1)	38	18	4	16	73	66	7	57
Westbury United (-1)	38	16	8	14	71	50	21	55
Wells City	38	14	10	14	54	70	-16	52
Portishead Town	38	14	9	15	56	59	-3	51
Gillingham Town	38	14	8	16	71	72	-1	50
Bridport	38	14	7	17	51	65	-14	49
Elmore	38	12	7	19	72	104	-32	43
Clevedon United	38	11	7	20	60	78	-18	40
Roman Glass St George	38	8	15	15	58	77	-19	39
Shepton Mallet	38	10	6	22	51	88	-37	36
Almondsbury	38	8	11	19	70	91	-21	35
Odd Down	38	7	9	22	51	80	-29	30
Minehead	38	5	3	30	33	116	-83	18

WEST MIDLANDS (REGIONAL) LEAGUE PREMIER DIVISION

	P	W	D	L	F	A	GD	Pts
AFC Wulfrunians	40	28	3	9	89	47	42	87
Bloxwich United	40	27	4	9	123	50	73	85
Bewdley Town	40	26	7	7	107	52	55	85
Ellesmere Rangers	40	25	7	8	105	45	60	82
Dudley Town	40	24	7	9	91	55	36	79
Wellington	40	21	6	13	76	62	14	69
Darlaston Town	40	20	6	14	67	58	9	66

	P	W	D	L	F	A	GD	Pts
Heath Town Rangers	40	19	4	17	68	68	0	61
Wednesfield	40	16	11	13	68	59	9	59
Shawbury United	40	16	9	15	59	66	-7	57
Lye Town	40	16	7	17	69	62	7	55
Dudley Sports	40	15	10	15	53	55	-2	55
Tividale	40	15	8	17	63	64	-1	53
Bromyard Town	40	14	8	18	61	67	-6	50
Gornal Athletic	40	13	10	17	56	60	-4	49
Goodrich	40	10	11	19	58	88	-30	41
Ludlow Town	40	12	5	23	66	99	-33	41
Pelsall Villa	40	7	13	20	53	72	-19	34
Wolverhampton Casuals	40	10	2	28	60	113	-53	32
Ledbury Town	40	8	7	25	68	128	-60	31
Bustleholme	40	4	3	33	39	129	-90	15

CARLSBERG SOUTH WEST PENINSULA LEAGUE PREMIER DIVISION

	P	W	D	L	F	A	GD	Pts
Bodmin Town	36	27	5	4	88	25	63	86
Plymouth Parkway	36	22	7	7	99	46	53	73
Buckland Athletic	36	21	9	6	79	39	40	72
Ivybridge Town	36	21	8	7	88	61	27	71
Saltash United	36	20	8	8	98	53	45	68
Tavistock (-2)	36	20	5	11	70	58	12	63
Dartmouth	36	18	5	13	72	70	2	59
Cullompton Rangers	36	18	2	16	80	70	10	56
Torpoint Athletic	36	16	5	15	75	79	-4	53
Launceston	36	14	6	16	72	70	2	48
Witheridge	36	13	8	15	64	54	10	47
St Blazey	36	11	10	15	64	74	-10	43
Wadebridge Town	36	11	8	17	54	71	-17	41
Falmouth Town	36	10	6	20	48	73	-25	36
Holsworthy	36	9	6	21	48	103	-55	33
Liskeard Athletic	36	9	5	22	69	99	-30	32
Clyst Rovers	36	9	4	23	58	104	-46	31
Elburton Villa	36	7	6	23	55	88	-33	27
Newton Abbot Spurs	36	7	5	24	36	80	-44	26

Newton Abbot Spurs – record expunged.

EAST MIDLANDS COUNTIES LEAGUE

	P	W	D	L	F	A	GD	Pts
Kirby Muxloe SC	34	23	6	5	83	38	45	75
Borrowash Victoria	34	21	9	4	80	37	43	72
Holbrook Miners Welfare	34	20	9	5	68	29	39	69
Gedling Town	34	20	7	7	84	49	35	67
Dunkirk	34	18	7	9	59	38	21	61
Barrow Town	34	18	4	12	67	58	9	58
Holwell Sports	34	17	6	11	68	42	26	57
Gedling Miners Welfare	34	15	4	15	55	60	-5	49
St Andrews	34	13	6	15	64	64	0	45
Hinckley Downes	34	14	2	18	54	57	-3	44
Greenwood Meadows	34	11	9	14	47	61	-14	42
Heanor Town	34	12	4	18	53	63	-10	40
Graham Street Prims	34	11	6	17	58	72	-14	39
Radford	34	9	7	18	47	79	-32	34
Ibstock United	34	8	9	17	34	61	-27	33
Ellistown	34	8	8	18	57	72	-15	32
Bardon Hill Sports	34	9	5	20	48	76	-28	32
Blackwell Miners Welfare	34	3	4	27	20	90	-70	13

SCOTTISH

SCOT-ADS HIGHLAND FOOTBALL LEAGUE

	P	W	D	L	F	A	GD	Pts
Cove Rangers	28	22	4	2	96	26	70	70
Deveronvale	28	18	7	3	78	31	47	61
Inverurie Loco Works	28	18	3	7	75	33	42	57
Keith	28	18	2	8	62	35	27	56
Wick Academy	28	16	3	9	54	46	8	51
Buckie Thistle	28	15	4	9	61	38	23	49
Fraserburgh	28	13	8	7	62	47	15	47
Huntly	28	14	4	10	50	43	7	46
Forres Mechanics	28	12	7	9	64	42	22	43
Nairn County	28	12	5	11	44	45	-1	41
Clachnacuddin	28	8	7	13	53	58	-5	31
Lossiemouth	28	7	4	17	31	55	-24	25
Rothes	28	2	4	22	24	80	-56	10
Brora Rangers	28	2	3	23	21	91	-70	9
Fort William	28	0	1	27	16	121	-105	1

IMAGE PRINTERS EAST OF SCOTLAND LEAGUE PREMIER DIVISION

	P	W	D	L	F	A	GD	Pts
Spartans	22	16	4	2	73	26	47	52
Dalbeattie Star	22	14	4	4	61	26	35	46
Lothian Thistle	22	11	3	8	66	26	20	36
Edinburgh University	22	9	7	6	37	18	19	34
Whitehill Welfare	22	8	6	8	38	28	10	32
Preston Athletic	22	9	5	8	36	31	5	32
Heriot-Watt University	22	9	3	10	33	31	2	30
Edinburgh City	22	8	5	9	45	34	11	29
Coldstream	22	8	4	10	29	30	-1	28
Selkirk	22	8	3	11	19	55	-36	27
Easthouses Lily MW	22	7	2	13	40	40	0	23
Peebles	22	1	0	21	12	124	-112	3

AMATEUR FOOTBALL ALLIANCE 2008–09

AFA SENIOR CUP

aet; †won after extra time and penalties

ROUND 1
Albanian 2, Old Actonians Association* 4
HSBC w/o, Bethwin SE w/d
St Albans Rangers 2, Ibis 6
Old Buckwellians 0, Weirside Rangers 8
Old Foresters 2, Old Malvernians 1
Old Brentwoods 1, Economicals 2
Egbertians 1, Kew Association 5
Kings Old Boys 0, Honourable Artillery Company 2
Old Westminster Citizens 2, Old Parmiterians 5
BB Eagles 3, Southgate Olympic 0
Wood Green Old Boys 2, Old Finchleians 1
Old Dorkinians 2, Old Kolsassians 5
East Barnet Old Grammarians 3, Old Uffingtonians 4
Old Manorians 2, Brent 3
Merton 2, Carshalton 0
Bank of England 3, William Fitt 2
Fulham Compton Old Boys 2, Old Chigwellians 0
Mill Hill Village 2, Latymer Old Boys 4
Old Tiffinians 5, Old Latymerians 1
Old Lyonians 2, Old Elizabethans 4
Norsemen 3, Old Pauline 2
Parkfield 0, Civil Service 2
Sinjuns Grammarians 1, Southgate County 2
Polytechnic 8, Hale End Athletic 0
Lloyds TSB Bank 5, Old Bromleians† 5
Glyn Old Boys 2, Enfield Old Grammarians 4

ROUND 2
Old Edmontonians 1, Alexandra Park 3
Latymer Old Boys 0, Old Suttonians 2
Old Carthusians 1, Old Parmiterians 5
Old Actonians Association* 5, Old Esthameians 2
West Wickham w/o, Hampstead Heathens w/d
Old Salesians 6, South Bank Cuaco 2
Weirside Rangers 2, Leyton County Old Boys† 2
Mill Hill County Old Boys 3, Old Guildfordians 2
Old Hamptonians 0, Old Ignatians 2
Old Salvatorians 1, Old Minchendenians 3
Broomfield 3, Old Thorntonians 1
Old Challoners 1, Centymca 0
Polytechnic 4, Alleyn Old Boys 1
Old Parkonians 0, Crouch End Vampires 2
Old Bromleians 0, Nottsborough 8
Old Owens 3, Old Aloysians 4
Bealonians 4, Old Salopians 0
Old Cholmeleians 2, Brent 1
Kew Association 1, Old Meadonians 2
Old Stationers 0, Fulham Compton Old Boys 3
Old Wilsonians 4, HSBC 1
Wake Green Amateur 3, Ibis 1
Wandsworth Borough 1, Old Elizabethans 3
Winchmore Hill 6, Enfield Old Grammarians 1
BB Eagles 1, Old Belgravians 4
Honourable Artillery Company 0, UCL Academicals 1
Old Isleworthians 4, Old Foresters 3
Southgate County 1, Norsemen 4
Bank of England 1, Wood Green Old Boys 2
Old Kolsassians 1, Civil Service 3
Old Tiffinians 2, Merton 6
Old Uffingtonians 4, Economicals 3

ROUND 3
Old Suttonians 1, Merton* 3
Old Parmiterians w/o, Old Elizabethans w/d
Broomfield 3, West Wickham 2
Wake Green Amateur w/o, Old Isleworthians w/d
Bealonians 1, Old Aloysians 0
Leyton County Old Boys 3, Old Challoners 2
Winchmore Hill 10, Old Ignatians 0
Norsemen 4, Old Uffingtonians 3
Civil Service† 1, Old Cholmeleians 1
Polytechnic 5, Wood Green Old Boys 0
Old Salesians 2, UCL Academicals 3
Old Belgravians 0, Old Meadonians 3
Fulham Compton Old Boys 0, Crouch End Vampires 2
Old Actonians Association 4, Alexandra Park 2
Old Minchendenians 6, Mill Hill County Old Boys 3
Old Wilsonians 0, Nottsborough 2

ROUND 4
Old Parmiterians 6, Leyton County Old Boys 0
Merton 1, Crouch End Vampires† 1

Civil Service* 3, Wake Green Amateur 1
Broomfield 1, Nottsborough 2
Old Minchendenians 1, Norsemen* 3
Old Actonians Association 0, UCL Academicals 1
Old Meadonians 1, Winchmore Hill 5
Polytechnic† 1, Bealonians 1

QUARTER-FINALS
Norsemen 1, Old Parmiterians 2
Polytechnic 2, Crouch End Vampires 1
Winchmore Hill 3, UCL Academicals 0
Civil Service 0, Nottsborough 2

SEMI-FINALS
Winchmore Hill 0, Polytechnic† 0
Nottsborough 3, Old Parmiterians 1

FINAL
Polytechnic 0, Nottsborough 1

SOUTHERN AMATEUR LEAGUE

SENIOR SECTION

DIVISION ONE	P	W	D	L	F	A	Pts
Nottsborough	20	13	5	2	49	15	44
Winchmore Hill	20	11	4	5	33	17	37
Old Salesians	20	9	6	5	35	24	33
Old Owens	20	9	5	6	34	26	32
West Wickham	20	9	4	7	27	24	31
Polytechnic	20	8	6	6	34	35	30
Old Wilsonians	20	8	5	7	32	29	29
Weirside Rangers	20	5	7	8	29	31	22
Old Actonians Association	20	5	6	9	32	41	21
Old Esthameians	20	4	2	14	25	55	14
Alleyn Old Boys	20	2	4	14	21	54	10

AMATEUR FOOTBALL COMBINATION

PREMIER DIVISION	P	W	D	L	F	A	Pts
Bealonians	18	13	1	4	45	19	40
Old Aloysians	18	10	3	5	35	25	33
Honorable Artillery Co.	18	9	3	6	35	35	30
Old Hamptonians	18	7	5	6	33	25	26
Albanian	18	7	5	6	32	32	26
Old Meadonians	18	7	3	8	38	33	24
Parkfield	18	7	3	8	32	42	24
Old Salvatorians	18	6	4	8	31	37	22
Old Parmitarians	18	5	4	9	34	39	19
UCL Academicals	18	3	1	14	24	50	10

ARTHURIAN LEAGUE

PREMIER DIVISION	P	W	D	L	F	A	Pts
Old Carthusians	18	13	3	2	51	20	42
Old Harrovians	18	12	1	5	51	42	37
Old Brentwoods	18	9	1	8	32	30	28
Old Cholmeleians	18	8	3	7	33	34	27
King's Wimbledon Old Boys	18	7	4	7	32	34	25
Old Westminsters	18	6	6	6	33	30	24
Lancing Old Boys	18	5	4	9	31	37	19
Old Foresters*	18	6	2	10	34	35	17
Old Etonians	18	4	4	10	31	41	16
Old Malvernians	18	3	6	9	23	48	15
*Points deducted.							

INTERMEDIATE SECTION
Div 1 – 11 teams – Won by Nottsborough Res
Div 2 – 11 teams – Won by Old Actonians Association Res
Div 3 – 11 teams – Won by Old Westminster Citizens Res

JUNIOR SECTION
Div 1 – 11 teams – Won by Winchmore Hill 3rd
Div 2 – 11 teams – Won by Old Westminster Citizens 3rd
Div 3 – 11 teams – Won by Old Parkonians 3rd

MINOR SECTION
Div 1 – 11 teams – Won by Civil Service 5th
Div 2 North – 11 teams – Won by Old Parkonians 4th
Div 2 South – 10 teams – Won by Polytechnic 5th
Div 3 North – 11 teams – Won by Alexandra Park 5th
Div 3 South – 10 teams – Old Actonians Association 6th
Div 4 North – 11 teams – Won by Broomfield 5th
Div 4 South – 9 teams – Won by BB Eagles 5th
Div 5 North – 11 teams – Won by Norsemen 9th
Div 5 South – 10 teams – Won by Old Westminster Citizens
  5th

IMPORTANT ADDRESSES

The Football Association: The Secretary, 25 Soho Square, London W1D 4FA. *020 7745 4545*

Scotland: David Taylor, Hampden Park, Glasgow G42 9AY. *0141 616 6000*
Northern Ireland (Irish FA): Chief Executive, 20 Windsor Avenue, Belfast BT9 6EG. *028 9066 9458*
Wales: 11/12 Neptune Court, Vanguard Way, Cardiff CF24 5PJ. *029 2043 5830*
Republic of Ireland National Sports Campus, Abbotstown, Dublin 15. *00 353 1 8999 500*

International Federation (FIFA): P. O. Box 85 8030 Zurich, Switzerland. *00 41 43 222 7777. Fax: 00 411 384 9696*
Union of European Football Associations: Secretary, Route de Geneve 46, Case Postale CH-1260 Nyon, Switzerland. *00 41 848 00 2727. Fax: 0041 22 994 44 88*

THE LEAGUES

The Premier League: M. Foster, 30 Gloucester Place, London W1A 8PL. *0207 864 9000*
The Football League: Secretary, The Football League, Unit 5, Edward VII Quay, Navigation Way, Preston, Lancashire PR2 2YF. *0870 442 0 1888. Fax 0870 442 0 1188*
Scottish Premier League: R. Mitchell, Hampden Park, Somerville Drive, Glasgow G42 9BA. *0141 646 6962*
The Scottish League: P. Donald, Hampden Park, Glasgow G42 9EB. *0141 620 4160*
The Irish League: Secretary, 96 University Street, Belfast BT7 1HE. *028 9024 2888*
Football League of Ireland: D. Crowther, 80 Merrion Square, Dublin 2. *00353 16765120*
Football Conference: 3rd Floor, Wellington House, 31–34 Waterloo Street, Birmingham B2 5TJ. *0121 214 1950*
Southern League: J. Mills, 8 College Yard, Worcester WR1 2LA. *01905 330 444*
Northern Premier League: R.D. Bayley, 22 Woburn Drive, Hale, Altrincham, Cheshire WA15 8LZ. *0161 980 7007*
Isthmian League: B. Badcock, 18 Calford Drive, Hanchett Village, Haverhill, Suffolk CB9 7WQ. *01440 708 064*
Eastern Counties League: N. Spurling, 16 Thanet Road, Ipswich, Suffolk IP4 5LB. *01473 720 893*
Essex Senior League: D. Walls, 2 Hillsfield Cottage, Layer, Breton, Essex CO2 0PS. *01206 330 146*
Hellenic League: B. King, 83 Queens Road, Carterton, Oxon OX18 3YF. *01993 212 738.*

Kent League: R. Vinter, Bakery House, The Street, Chilham, Canterbury, Kent CT4 8BX. *01227 730 457*
Midland Alliance: J. Shaw, 176 Springthorpe Road, Erdington, Birmingham B24 0SN. *0121 350 5869*
North West Counties League: J. Deal, 24 The Pastures, Crossens, Southport PR9 8RH. *01704 211 955*
Northern Counties East: B. Gould, 42 Thirlmere Drive, Dronfield, Derbyshire S18 2HW. *01246 415 928*
Northern League: T. Golightly, 85 Park Road North, Chester-le-Street, Co. Durham DH3 3SA. *0191 388 2056*
Spartan South Midlands League: M. Mitchell, 26 Leighton Court, Dunstable, Beds LU6 1EW. *01582 667 291*
Sussex County League: P. Beard, 2 Van Gogh Place, Bersted, Bognor Regis, West Sussex PO22 9BG. *01243 822 063*
United Counties League: A. Crick, Daisy Cottage, Shore Road, Freiston, Boston PE22 0LN. *01205 760 162*
Wessex League: I. Craig, 7 Old River, Denmead, Hampshire PO7 6UX. *02392 230 973*
Western League: K.A. Clarke, 32 Westmead Lane, Chippenham, Wilts SN15 3HZ. *01249 464 467*
Suburban League (Formerly Combined Counties): M.J. Bidmead, 55 Grange Road, Chessington, Surrey KT9 1EZ
Midland Combination: N. Wood, 30 Glalsdale Lane, Hall Green, Birmingham B28 8PX. *0121 244 6412*
West Midlands League: N.R. Juggins, 14 Badger Way, Blackwell, Bromsgrove, Worcs B60 1EX. *0121 445 2953*

OTHER USEFUL ADDRESSES

Amateur Football Alliance: M. L. Brown, 55 Islington Park Street, London N1 1QB. *020 7359 3493*
English Schools FA: J. Read, 4 Parker Court, Staffordshire Technology Park, Stafford ST18 0WP. *01785 785 970*
British Universities Sports Association: G. Gregory-Jones, Chief Executive: BUSA, 20–24 King's Bench Street, London SE1 0QX. *0207 633 5050*
The Football Supporters Federation: The Fans Stadium, Kingsmeadow, Jack Goodchild Way, 422a Kingston Road, Kingston-upon-Thames KT1 3PB. *0208 547 3577*
National Playing Fields Association: 57b, 25 Ovington Square, London SW3 1LQ. *0207 584 6445*
Professional Footballers' Association: G. Taylor, 2 Oxford Court, Bishopsgate, Off Lower Mosley Street, Manchester M2 3WQ. *0161 236 0575*
Referees' Association: A. Smith, 1 Westhill Road, Coundon, Coventry CV6 2AD. *024 7660 1701*
Women's Football Alliance: Miss K. Doyle, The Football Association, 25 Soho Square, London W1D 4FA. *020 7745 4545*
Women's Football Conference: M. Appleby, 25 Soho Square, London W1D 4FA. *0207 745 4589*
League Managers Association: The Camkin Suite, 1 Pegasus House, Pegasus Court, Tachbrook Park, Warwick CV34 6LW. *01926 831 556. Fax: 01926 429 781*
Institute of Football Management and Administration: K. Verity, Camkin House, 8 Charles Court, Budbrooke Road, Warwick CV34 5LZ. *01926 411 884.*
World Cup (1966) Association: Hon. Secretary, David Duncan, 96 Glenlea Road, Eltham, London SE9 1DZ
The Ninety-Two Club: 104 Gilda Crescent, Whitchurch, Bristol BS14 9LD
The Football Trust: Second Floor, Walkden House, 10 Melton Street, London NW1 2EJ. *020 7388 4504*

Association of Provincial Football Supporters Clubs in London: Stephen Moon, 32 Westminster Gardens, Barking, Essex IG11 0BJ. *020 8594 2367*
World Association of Friends of English Football: Carlisle Hill, Gluck, Habichthof 2, D24939 Flensburg, Germany. *0049 461 4700222*
Football Postcard Collectors Club: PRO: Bryan Horsnell, 275 Overdown Road, Tilehurst, Reading RG31 6NX. *0118 942 4448 (and fax)*
UK Programme Collectors Club: Secretary, John Litster, 46 Milton Road, Kirkcaldy, Fife KY1 1TL. *01592 268718. Fax: 01592 595069*
Programme Monthly & Football Collectable Magazine: P.O. Box 3236 Norwich NR7 7BE
Scottish Football Historians Association: 43 Lady Nairn Avenue, Kirkcaldy KY1 2AW
Phil Gould (Licensed Football Agent), c/o Whoppit Management Ltd, P. O. Box 27204, London N11 2WS. *07071 732 468. Fax: 07070 732 469*
The Scandinavian Union of Supporters of British Football: Postboks, 15 Stovner, N-0913 Oslo, Norway
Football Writers' Association: Executive Secretary, Ken Montgomery, 6 Chase Lane, Barkingside, Essex IG6 1BH. *0208 554 2455 (and fax)*
Programme Promotions: 47 The Beeches, Lampton Road, Hounslow, Middlesex TW3 4DF.
Web: www.footballprogrammes.com
Football Safety Officers Association: C/O J. Sidney, Nottingham Forest F.C., City Ground, Pavilion Road, Nottingham NG2 5FG. *0115 952 6000*
Football Foundation: 30 Gloucester Place, London W1U 8FF. *0845 345 4555*
Football Licensing Authority: 27 Harcourt House, 19 Cavendish Square, London W1G 0PL. *0207 491 7191*
Sport England: 16 Upper Woburn Place, London WC1H 0QP. *0207 388 1277.*

FOOTBALL CLUB CHAPLAINCY

With chaplaincy now firmly established among Premier and Football League clubs, the question that is sometimes posed enquires whether the same is true further down the footballing pyramid.

Perhaps surprisingly, the answer to the question is that it is not! The involvement of a chaplain appears to be something of a rarity beyond the two major leagues in our country.

Of course, there is the occasional "seepage", when a club with a chaplain is relegated from League Two into the Conference and the respected and perhaps long-serving chaplain naturally continues to serve his club at the lower level. But it has more often been the case that a former chaplain from a Premier or Football League club, who has moved to a new responsibility in a different area and suggested to the local non-league club the possibility of him working there, has had his offer rejected or ignored.

However, the discerning Northern League appointed the Rev Leo Osborn as chaplain to *all* its clubs some years ago.... But some vision and sensitivity is, so far at least, unique in the game.

Nevertheless, it remains the hope and prayer of everyone concerned with and for football chaplaincy, that the concept *will* increasingly be welcomed and accepted by non-league clubs just as it has been in the Premier and Football Leagues.

THE REV

OFFICIAL CHAPLAINS TO FA PREMIERSHIP AND FOOTBALL LEAGUE CLUBS

Rev Ken Baker – Aston Villa; Rev Ken Howles – Blackburn R; Rev Philip Mason – Bolton W; Rev Matt Baker – Charlton Ath; Rev Henry Corbett and Rev Harry Ross (Co-Chaplains) – Everton; Rev Gary Piper – Fulham; Rev Bill Bygroves – Liverpool; Rev Chris Howitz – Manchester C; Rev John Boyers – Manchester U; Rev David Tully – Newcastle U; Rev Jonathan Jeffrey and Mr Mick Mellows (Co-Chaplains) – Portsmouth; The Ven Elwin Cockett and Rev Alan Bolding (Co-Chaplains) – West Ham U; Rev Peter Amos – Barnsley; Rev Michael Ward – Blackpool; Rev John Moore – Boston U; Rev Andy Rimmer – Bournemouth; Rev Andy Bowerman – Bradford C; Rev Lewis Allen – Brentford; Rev Derek Cleave – Bristol C; Rev Dave Jeal – Bristol R; Rev Mark Hirst – Burnley; Rev John O'Dwyer – Bury; Rev Alun Jones – Carlisle U; Mr Paul Bennett and Rev John O'Dwyer (Co-Chaplains) – Cheltenham T; Rev Jim McGlade – Chesterfield; Rev Steve Clapham – Crewe Alex; Rev Chris Roe – Crystal Palace; Pastor Jon Burns – Darlington; Rev Tony Luke – Derby Co; Rev Richard Hayton – Gillingham; Rev Allen Bagshawe – Hull C; Rev Kevan McCormack – Ipswich T; Rev Paul C. Welch and Fr Steven Billington (Co-Chaplains) – Leeds U; Rev Richard Gamble – Leicester C; Rev Alan Comfort – Leyton Orient; Rev Andrew Vaughan – Lincoln C; Rev Alan West – Luton T; Rev Jeremy Tear – Macclesfield T; Rev Timothy Mitchell – Mansfield T; Fr Owen Beament – Millwall; Rev Ron Smith – Milton Keynes D; Rev Ken Baker – Northampton T; Revs Bert Cadmore and Arthur W. Bowles (Co-Chaplains) – Norwich C; Rev Steve Sylvester – Nottingham F; Rev Mark Tanner – Notts Co; Rev Richard Longfoot – Peterborough U; Rev Jeff Howden – Plymouth Arg; Rev John M Hibberts – Port Vale; Rev Chris Nelson – Preston NE; Rev Bob Mayo and Rev Cameron Collington (Co-Chaplains) – Queens Park Rangers; Steve Prince – Reading; Rev Alan Wright – Scunthorpe U; Rev Peter Allen – Sheffield W; Rev Ian Johnson – Southampton; Rev Billy Montgomery – Stockport Co; Rev Kevin Johns – Swansea C; Rev Simon Stevenette – Swindon T; Fr Gerald Courell – Tranmere R; Rev Martin Butt – Walsall; Rev Clive Ross – Watford; Rev John Hall-Matthews and Rev Steve Davies (Co-Chaplains) – Wolverhampton W; Rev Jim Pearce – Yeovil T; Rev Peter Wyatt – Dagenham & Redbridge; Rev Stephen Clark – Doncaster Rovers; Rev Chris Sims – Shrewsbury Town; Rev Stephen Taylor – Sunderland; Rev Ken Hipkiss – West Bromwich Albion; Rev John Roberts and Rev Tim O'Brien (Co-Chaplains) – Wycombe Wanderers; Rev Mike Pusey – Aldershot Town.

NON-LEAGUE CLUBS

Mr John Maxwell – Abingdon T; Rev Andrew Barclay-Watt – Altrincham; Rev David Hughes – Barnstaple T; Deacon Tom Luke – Barrow; Rev Stuart Wood – Cambridge U; Mr John Maxwell – Cirencester T; The Ven Paul Taylor – Dorchester T; Rev Kevin Johns – Garden Village; Rev Ken Hipkiss – Halesowen T; Paul Barker – Hampton & Richmond B; Capt Howard Evans – Hinckley U; Rev Ron Day – Histon; Philip Hearn – Kidderminster H; Rev Keith Beardmore – Newport Co; Rev Clive Jones – Nuneaton B; Canon Roger Knight – Rushden & D; Fr Ronald Crane – Solihull Moors; Rev Martin Abrams –Southport; Rev Ken Hawkings – Sutton T; Rev David Wright – Telford U; Rev Lee Gilbert – Warrington T; Rev Chris Cullwick – York C; Rev Leo Osborn – Chaplain to the Northern League.

The chaplains hope that those who read this page will see the value and benefit of chaplaincy work in football and will take appropriate steps to spread the word where this is possible. They would also like to thank the editors of the Football Yearbook *for their continued support for this specialist and growing area of work.*

For further information, please contact: SCORE (Sports Chaplaincy Offering Resources and Encouragement), PO Box 123, Sale, Cheshire M33 4ZA). Telephone 0161 969 1762 or email JKBSCOREUK@aol.com

Obituary

The Rev Canon John Hester, chaplain at Brighton & Hove Albion FC 1975–97, died 10 February 2008 aged 80.

OBITUARIES

Peter Aldis (Born King's Norton, Birmingham, 11 April 1927. Died 13 November 2008.) Peter Aldis signed professional forms for Aston Villa in May 1949, but it was not until the 1953–54 campaign that he established himself in the line-up. He formed a solid defensive partnership with Stan Lynn and was a member of the team that defeated Manchester United at Wembley to lift the FA Cup in 1957. On leaving Villa Park he played for Hinckley Athletic and then spent several seasons in Australia, before eventually returning to live in the Midlands.

Alex Alston (Born Preston, 26 February 1937. Died Blackpool, 20 February 2009.) Centre forward Alex Alston joined Preston North End in the summer of 1955, making his first-team debut against Sunderland during the 1957–58 campaign. He made over 100 appearances during his stay at Deepdale and later turned out for Bury, Barrow and Fleetwood.

David Anderson (Born January 1948. Died March 2009.) Goalkeeper David Anderson was capped by Scotland at Schoolboy and Junior levels, making his senior debut for Hearts in a Summer Cup tie against local rivals Hibs towards the end of the 1963–64 campaign when just 16 years of age. However, he made only two more first-team appearances during his stay at Tynecastle, later turning out for a string of clubs including Dunfermline, Dumbarton, Berwick Rangers and Hamilton.

Ian Anderson (Born 11 September 1954. Died Edinburgh, 5 November 2008.) Ian Anderson was a hard-tackling midfield player who spent four years on the books of Dundee before moving on to St Johnstone, for whom he was leading scorer in 1976–77. He subsequently enjoyed a successful career in the NASL firstly with Houston Hurricane and then Tampa Bay Rowdies.

Ted Ballard (Born Brentford, Middlesex, 16 June 1920. Died Hastings, 10 June 2008.) Wing half Ted Ballard joined Leyton Orient towards the end of the 1945–46 campaign, having previously made a handful of wartime appearances for Brentford. He stayed just a season at Brisbane Road, before moving on to Southampton where he spent five years, principally as an understudy to the likes of Joe Mallett and Alf Ramsey. His best spell for the Saints was at the start of the 1950–51 campaign, when he was a regular in the left-back slot.

Bill Baxter (Born Edinburgh, 23 April 1939. Died Dunfermline, 25 May 2009.) Bill Baxter was a tough defender who broke into the Ipswich Town first team during the 1960–61 season, helping the club win the Second Division title and then the Football League championship 12 months later. Initially a wing half, he was transformed into an effective central defender, making over 450 senior appearances during his stay at Portman Road. In March 1971 Bill moved on to Hull and then spent the 1972–73 season as player-manager of Northampton Town.

Jock Bayne (Born Glasgow, 1917. Died Boston, 16 March 2009.) Goalkeeper Jock Bayne was on Brentford's books in the 1938–39 campaign without breaking into the first team. He subsequently joined St Mirren, featuring in just one senior game, the final match before war broke out in September 1939. Jock was later on the books of Third Lanark before signing for non-League Boston United in 1946 and serving as the Midland League club's regular 'keeper for the early post-war period.

Keith Bentley (Born Hull, 27 July 1936. Died Hessle, East Yorkshire, 15 September 2008.) Keith Bentley was an inside forward who enjoyed a single season as a professional with Hull City, playing in a run of six successive games in December 1957. He later had spells in non-League football with Scarborough, Goole Town and Bridlington Town.

Ray Bilcliff (Born Barlow, Blaydon-on-Tyne, 24 May 1931. Died Blidworth, Notts., March 2009.) Full back Ray Bilcliff was a regular in the Middlesbrough line-up in the second half of the 1950s. Solid and consistent, he eventually moved on to Hartlepools in January 1961 where he spent a further three seasons. Ray made a total of 299 Football League appearances without scoring a single goal.

Paul Birch (Born West Bromwich, 20 November 1962. Died Sutton Coldfield, 2 February 2009.) Paul Birch was an honest, hard-working and committed midfield player who began his career with Aston Villa. After making his first-team debut in January 1983 he went on to establish himself in the line-up, becoming a great favourite of the club's fans for his wholehearted performances in the centre of the park. He was a near ever-present during the 1987–88 campaign, when Villa won promotion from the old Second Division, but in February 1991 he signed for Wolves. After five years at Molineux he moved on and subsequently played for Doncaster Rovers, Exeter City and Halesowen Town before leaving football for a while, although he later became involved in coaching and had a spell working on the staff at Birmingham City.

Paddy Bonham (Died Australia, December 2008.) Full back Paddy Bonham was an important figure for the successful Shelbourne team of the early 1960s. He gained a number of domestic honours and was also capped for the League of Ireland.

Paul Borland (Born Rutherglen, Lanarkshire, 28 June 1979. Died Castlemilk, Glasgow, 28 July 2008.) Defender Paul Borland was capped by Scotland at U18 level and spent four seasons on the books of Celtic without making

Bill Baxter

the first team. At Queen's Park he was a member of the team that won the Third Division title in 1999–2000, but he subsequently left the game when just 22 years of age.

Andy Bowman (Born Pittenweem, Fife, 7 March 1934. Died Dundee, 2 March 2009.) Andy Bowman was a tough-tackling defensive half back who began his career with Chelsea, but after making just one appearance in four seasons at Stamford Bridge, he returned to Scotland, signing for Hearts. After Dave McKay had been sold to Spurs, Andy took over his place in the line-up and he was a key figure in the side that won the Scottish League title and the League Cup in 1959–60. Andy later played for Newport County, Tonbridge and Hamilton Academical before leaving the senior game.

Jimmy (Jake) Bradley (Born Greenock, 21 March 1927. Died United States, 26 November 2008.) Jimmy Bradley made his senior debut at outside left for Hibs in the Scottish League Cup final of 1950–51, covering for injuries, but despite a useful individual performance his team lost out to Motherwell. He subsequently featured for Third Lanark and Shrewsbury without making a significant impact and later emigrated to the United States where he played for a number of clubs before turning to coaching.

Ken Branagan (Born Salford, Lancs., 27 July 1930. Died 9 August 2008.) Ken Branagan joined Manchester City as a teenager and went on to enjoy a lengthy spell as City's regular right back in the early 1950s, although he missed out on a place in the line-up for both the 1955 and 1956 FA Cup finals. A speedy and reliable full back, he remained on the books at Maine Road until October 1960, making more than 200 first-team appearances before joining Oldham Athletic. Ken assisted the Latics to gain promotion from the Fourth Division in 1962–63.

Ronnie Briggs (Born Belfast, 29 March 1943. Died Bristol, 28 August 2008.) Ronnie Briggs was capped at Schoolboy level by Northern Ireland and subsequently joined the groundstaff at Manchester United, switching to professional status on reaching his 17th birthday. Although only on the fringes of first-team action at Old Trafford, he fared better during spells with Swansea and Bristol Rovers. Ronnie gained two full caps for his country and another two at U23 level.

Bert 'Sailor' Brown (Born Great Yarmouth, 7 November 1915. Died Forres, Morayshire, 27 December 2008.) Sailor Brown joined Charlton Athletic in the summer of 1934, and after making his debut he became a regular in the line-up. He served in the RAF during the war, although despite this it was a fruitful period for him, as he featured in three Wembley finals and also appeared in six unofficial internationals for England, scoring four goals. When peacetime football resumed, he gained an FA Cup runners-up medal with Charlton, who lost out to Derby in the 1946 final, then enjoyed spells with Nottingham Forest and Villa before injury terminated his senior career.

Jimmy Brown (Born Buckhaven, Fife, 19 July 1925. Died Cellardyke, Fife, 7 November 2008.) Jimmy Brown signed for Hearts during the war and went on to become the club's regular 'keeper, making over 200 appearances and retaining his place until 1952, when he was sidelined by an injury. He later enjoyed considerable success with Kilmarnock, for whom he featured in two Scottish Cup finals (1957 and 1960) and one League Cup final (1960–61) although finishing on the losing side on each occasion. He subsequently had brief spells with a number of clubs including St Mirren and East Fife, and also spent time in Canada, before retiring from the game.

Len Browning (Born Doncaster, 30 March 1928. Died 27 September 2008.) Forward Len Browning won a regular place in the forward line for Leeds United during the 1948–49 season but after just over 100 games for the Elland Road club he was sold to Sheffield United in November 1951. Len was a member of the Blades' team that won the Second Division title in 1952–53, but was forced to retire soon afterwards after contracting tuberculosis.

Cameron Buchanan (Born Chapelhall, Airdrie, Lanarkshire, 31 July 1928. Died 10 September 2008.) Cameron Buchanan won fame as the youngest-ever player to appear in senior football in England when he lined up for Wolves against West Bromwich Albion at Molineux in September 1942 when just 14 years and 57 days old. He played a total of 18 wartime games for Wolves and later spent five years on the books at Dean Court where he added a further 88 appearances. Cameron subsequently spent time in Canada, before returning home for a brief spell with Norwich.

Paddy Buckley (Born Leith, 31 January 1925. Died Tranent, East Lothian, 4 November 2008.) Paddy Buckley became a prolific goalscorer with St Johnstone, leading the charts in the four seasons he played for the Muirton Park club. Transferred to Aberdeen in April 1952 he continued to find the net regularly and was leading scorer with 17 goals in 1954–55 when the Dons won the Scottish League title for the first time in their history. He went on to assist the club to victory in the Scottish League Cup in October 1955 before a knee injury led to his retirement.

David Burns (Born 19 July 1956. Died 2 January 2009.) David Burns trained as a solicitor and later became company secretary of Airtours. Between 2000 and August 2002 he served as chief executive of the Football League, before returning to work in the leisure industry. In recent years he had also been a director of Altrincham FC.

Bryan Bush (Born Bristol, 25 April 1925. Died Bristol, 25 August 2008.) Bryan Bush was a speedy winger who signed for Bristol Rovers in October 1947. He went on to make 122 senior appearances for the club and was a regular in the side that won the Division Three South championship in 1952–53, in which he scored 12 goals including two in the 5–3 win at Walsall. A leg injury eventually curtailed his career, although he went on to help Trowbridge Town win the 1955–56 Western League championship.

Bobby Campbell (Born Glasgow, 28 June 1922. Died Bristol, 3 May 2009.) A wartime player with Falkirk and Queens Park Rangers, winger Bobby Campbell signed for Chelsea in May 1947. He spent the next seven seasons at Stamford Bridge, accumulating more than 200 first-team appearances and gaining a total of five caps for Scotland. Bobby subsequently spent a further four seasons on the books of Reading and served Dumbarton as manager in 1961–62 before beginning an 18-year association with Bristol Rovers both as coach and manager.

Jack Capper (Born Wrexham, 23 July 1931. Died Wrexham, 10 March 2009.) Centre half Jack Capper made almost 50 Football League appearances for Wrexham then played in the Southern League for Headington (now Oxford) United. In January 1956 he signed for Lincoln City, for whom he was principally an understudy for Tony Emery, before concluding his senior career at Chester.

Tommy Casey (Born Comber, Co Down, 11 March 1930. Died Nailsea, Somerset, 11 January 2009.) Tommy Casey signed for Leeds United in the summer of 1949. However, he was given few chances at Elland Road, and it was only when he dropped down a division to play for Bournemouth that he began to show his full potential. Two successful seasons on the South Coast earned him a transfer to Newcastle, where he gained a reputation as a dynamic midfield player and he

earned an FA Cup winners' medal when he appeared for United in their success over Manchester City in the 1955 final. Tommy won 12 caps for Northern Ireland, featuring in the team that reached the quarter-finals of the World Cup in 1958. He later played for Portsmouth, Bristol City and Gloucester City (where he was player-manager) and also had spells as manager of Distillery and Grimsby Town.

Stan Challis (Born Lympstone, Devon, 22 April 1918. Died Exeter, 16 October 2008.) Stan Challis was a winger who made four wartime appearances for Crystal Palace while serving in the Royal Marines. He went on to spend two seasons on the books of Exeter City, scoring 11 goals from 18 games during the 1945–46 campaign and also featuring in a handful of games the following season.

Willie Clark (Born 27 September 1918. Died 28 December 2008.) Willie Clark signed for Hibs shortly before the outbreak of war and went on to spend over a decade on the books at Easter Road, principally as a reserve right back, although he enjoyed a more extended involvement in the 1952–53 season. He later spent two seasons with St Johnstone before retiring from football.

Cec Coldwell (Born Dungworth, Sheffield, 12 January 1929. Died Poynton, Cheshire, 9 November 2008.) Cec Coldwell joined Sheffield United in September 1951 and went on to spend the next 16 years as a player at Bramall Lane. He established himself in the line-up in 1955 and was appointed captain in 1957, leading the team to promotion from the Second Division in 1960–61. A dedicated, reliable defender he made over 450 appearances for the Blades, and after retiring as a player he remained at the club in a coaching capacity until 1983, twice serving briefly as caretaker-manager.

Cec Coldwell

Alfie Conn (Born Prestonpans, East Lothian, 2 October 1926. Died Dunfermline, 7 January 2009.) Alfie Conn joined Hearts as a 17-year-old and went on to become one of the key figures in the club's successful team of the 1950s, forming a famous forward line with Willie Bauld and Jimmy Wardhaugh known as 'The Terrible Trio'. Alfie scored one of the goals that enabled Hearts to defeat Celtic in the Scottish Cup final of 1956 and remains the fourth-highest goalscorer for Hearts in the post-war period. He wound down his career with a spell at Raith and also played in South Africa before leaving the game.

Ernie Cooksey (Born Bishop's Stortford, 11 June 1980. Died 3 July 2008.) Ernie Cooksey was a tenacious midfield player full of grit and determination with an infectious enthusiasm for the game. A former trainee with Colchester United, he developed in non-League football before stepping up to the Football League in the summer of 2003 when he signed for Oldham Athletic. He later played for Rochdale and Boston United, taking his tally of senior appearances to more than 150. In the summer of 2007 Ernie signed for Grays Athletic of the Blue Square Premier League, but sadly he made his final appearance as a professional against Exeter City in February of 2008. His untimely death was a result of skin cancer.

Willie Cotter (Born circa 1922. Died Cork, Republic of Ireland, 15 November 2008.) Willie Cotter was a prominent League of Ireland player in the 1940s and 1950s, featuring in four different championship sides with Cork United (1942–43, 1943–44) and Cork Athletic (1949–50 and 1950–51). In addition he gained FAI Cup winners' medals in 1951 and 1953. Willie also won five caps for the League of Ireland representative side.

Charlie Cox (Born Glasgow, 19 February 1926. Died Glasgow, 15 December 2008.) Charlie Cox was a skilful right half who made over 150 appearances for Hearts in the immediate post-war period before moving on to Motherwell at the end of 1951. He was a member of the team that defeated Dundee 4–0 to win the Scottish Cup final in 1951, and later was a near ever-present in the team that won the Division B title in 1953–54.

Bob Crampsey (Born Glasgow, 8 July 1930. Died Glasgow, 27 July 2008.) A schoolteacher by profession, Bob Crampsey won the BBC's Brain of Britain title in 1965. He was also a highly respected journalist who covered the game for radio, television and newspapers in Scotland for some 40 years. In addition, Bob was well known for his football writing, which included a biography of Jock Stein and a history of the Scottish League.

Vic Crowe (Born Abercynon, 31 January 1932. Died Sutton Coldfield, 21 January 2009.) Vic Crowe spent a decade as a first-team member at Aston Villa, featuring in the side that won the Division Two title in 1959–60 and in both legs of the inaugural Football League Cup final of 1960–61. A combative midfield player, full of grit and determination, he won 16 caps for Wales. Vic made over 350 senior appearances during his stay at Villa Park, then moved on to Peterborough, helping Posh reach the semi-finals of the Football League Cup in 1965–66. He subsequently had a spell in the USA with Atlanta Chiefs then returned to England and joined the backroom staff at Villa Park, serving as manager for the period January 1970 to May 1974, and leading Villa to the Third Division championship in 1971–72.

John Cumming (Born Carluke, Lanarkshire, 17 March 1930. Died Carluke, Lanarkshire, 6 December 2008.) John Cumming was one of the great figures in the post-war history of Hearts and, along with Dave Mackay, a driving force in the club's successes of the late 1950s and early '60s. After winning a regular place in the side in the 1953–54 campaign, he established himself as a powerful and effective wing half who possessed tremendous spirit and stamina. Known as the 'Iron Man', John led Hearts to Scottish League titles in 1957–58 and 1959–60, also winning the Scottish Cup once, in 1956, and the League Cup on four occasions.

Bobby Cummings (Born Ashington, 17 November 1935. Died 26 August 2008.) Centre forward Bobby Cummings had a spell on Newcastle's books as a youngster but failed to make the grade and after dropping down to play for Ashington he returned to senior football with Aberdeen in February 1960. He proved a regular scorer for the Dons, netting 49 goals from 86 appearances. Bobby returned to Newcastle in October 1963 and went on to lead the team to promotion from the old Second Division in 1964–65. He subsequently played for Darlington and Hartlepools, helping both clubs win promotion from the Fourth Division, then had a spell in South Africa with Port Elizabeth City.

Dermot Curtis (Born Dublin, 26 August 1932. Died Exeter, 1 November 2008.) Dermot Curtis was a legendary figure in the modern history of Exeter City, helping the club to win their first-ever promotion in the 1963–64 campaign and he was also the first player on the club's books to be capped at full international level. A robust centre forward who was an excellent header of the ball, he had played for Shelbourne, Bristol City and Ipswich Town before arriving at St James Park. Dermot won a total of 17 caps for the Republic of Ireland, scoring eight goals.

Alan Daley (Born Mansfield, 11 October 1927. Died Bedford, 24 June 2008.) Alan Daley was a fast and direct winger who enjoyed a very varied career regularly changing clubs, often alternating between League and non-League clubs. He enjoyed lengthy spells with Mansfield, Stockport and Coventry City in the 1950s, the highlight of his career coming when he assisted Coventry to promotion from the Fourth Division in 1958–59.

Vic Crowe

Kenny Davies (Born Doncaster, 20 September 1923. Died Exeter, 14 November 2008.) Kenny Davies was a left winger who made 40 wartime appearances for Wolves before moving on to Walsall. Although he was a regular at Fellows Park in the opening half of the 1946–47 campaign he only stayed a season before moving on to Brighton.

Reg Davies (Born Cymmer, nr. Port Talbot, Glamorgan, 27 May 1929. Died Perth, Australia, 9 February 2009.) Reg Davies was a slight but talented inside forward who rejected the option of a career in singing for life as a footballer. He went on to make over 400 Football League appearances in a journey that encompassed spells with Southend, Newcastle, Swansea and Carlisle United. Reg was capped six times by Wales in the 1950s.

Alex Devanney (Born 25 July 1930. Died Alloa, May 2009.) Goalkeeper Alex Devanney made his bow in senior football with Celtic at the start of the 1951–52 campaign. He later served Berwick Rangers, Northampton (where he was a reserve) and Alloa Athletic before leaving senior football at the end of the 1960–61 campaign.

Ray Deakin (Born Liverpool, 19 June 1959. Died 24 December 2008.) Ray Deakin was a left-sided defender who was an apprentice with Everton then spent a season at Port Vale, before moving on to Bolton where he switched from left back to a more central role in the defence. The best years of his career were spent at Burnley. He led the team to safety from relegation at the end of the 1986–87 season and went on to captain the side that lost to Wolves at Wembley in the final of the Associate Members Cup 12 months later.

Johnny Dixon (Born Hebburn, Co Durham, 10 December 1923. Died Sutton Coldfield, 20 January 2009.) Johnny Dixon made almost 40 appearances for Newcastle United in the wartime emergency competitions before signing professional terms for Aston Villa in January 1946. He was a regular in the first-team line-up for the best part of a decade, amassing some 430 appearances and scoring 144 goals. A creative, inspirational inside forward, the great highlight of his career came when he captained Villa to a 2–1 victory over favourites Manchester United in the 1957 FA Cup final.

George Dobbie (Born Edinburgh, 1932. Died Livingston, 19 January 2009.) Centre forward George Dobbie spent six seasons on the books of Third Lanark in the early 1950s, one of the highlights of his spell coming when he scored four times in a 10–0 victory away to Alloa in a Scottish League Cup tie in August 1953. George subsequently played for Hearts and Raith before injury ended his career.

Jamie Dolan (Born Salsburgh, Lanarkshire, 22 February 1969. Died Bathgate, West Lothian, 31 August 2008.) Jamie Dolan was a hard-tackling midfield dynamo who was a mainstay of the successful Motherwell team of the mid-1990s. A regular in the side from the 1991–92 campaign, he made over 200 senior appearances for the club. Later in his career he enjoyed the distinction of winning promotion to the SPL in three consecutive seasons with different clubs: Dunfermline (1999–2000), Livingston (2000–01) and Partick (2001–02). His premature death came after he suffered a heart attack when out jogging.

Bill Ealing (Born Tamworth, Staffs., 12 March 1930. Died Sutton Coldfield, West Midlands, 21 October 2008.) Centre forward Bill Ealing had a spell on the books of Blackburn, although he failed to break into the first team at Ewood Park. After signing for Walsall he was included in the line-up for the opening game of the 1952–53 season but had the misfortune to suffer an injury that effectively ended his career.

George Edwards (Born Treherbert, Glamorgan, 2 December 1920. Died Cardiff, 22 October 2008.) George Edwards was capped for Wales Amateurs against England as a teenager and also featured for Swansea as an amateur before the war. He subsequently played three times for Wales in unofficial internationals during the hostilities and won 12 full caps for his country. George went on to assist Birmingham City to the Football League South title in 1945–46 and the Division

Two championship in 1947–48. He later helped Cardiff win promotion to the First Division in 1951–52. George served as a director at Ninian Park from 1957 to 1976 and again from 1981 to 1986, and was also a member of the Sports Council of Wales.

John Elsworthy (Born Nantyderry, Monmouthshire, 26 July 1931. Died 3 May 2009.) John Elsworthy was a big powerful half back who had the distinction of assisting Ipswich Town to four separate Football League titles: Division Three South in 1953–54 and 1956–57, Division Two in 1960–61 and Division One in 1961–62. In total he spent 15 years on the club's books, making 435 appearances and scoring 53 goals.

David Evans (Born Edmonton, Middlesex, 23 April 1935. Died Harpenden, 22 October 2008.) David Evans was a self-made millionaire who was MP for Welwyn & Hatfield and also chairman of Luton Town from 1984 to 1989. During this time at Kenilworth Road he was instrumental in bringing in a controversial membership scheme that effectively barred away fans from entry and also replaced the playing surface with an artificial pitch. The Hatters also won their only major honour to date during this time when they won the Football League Cup in 1988.

Dudley Forbes (Born Johannesburg, South Africa, 19 April 1926. Died Johannesburg, South Africa, 15 May 2009.) Dudley Forbes toured Australia and New Zealand in 1947 with South Africa, and at the end of the year he signed for Charlton Athletic, becoming, with Sid O'Linn, the first of a number of South African players to join the club in the 1940s and '50s. A wing half, he made 57 Football League appearances for the Addicks before returning home in 1953 when he rejoined his former club Marist OB.

Tommy Fowler (Born Prescot, Lancs., 16 December 1924. Died 4 May 2009.) Winger Tommy Fowler played a few wartime games for Everton, but after being wounded in action he signed for Northampton Town. He stayed with the Cobblers for the next 16 years, establishing a new club record of 552 League and Cup appearances, including a remarkable run of 237 consecutive first-team appearances between April 1952 and March 1957. Tommy eventually left the County Ground in December 1961 and concluded his career with a couple of seasons at Aldershot.

Friaça (Born Porciúncula, Rio de Janeiro, Brazil, 20 October 1924. Died Itaperuna, Rio de Janeiro, Brazil, 12 January 2009.) Friaça was a forward who featured for Brazil in the 1950 World Cup tournament, scoring in the 2–1 defeat by Uruguay in the group match that decided the destination of the trophy (the tournament that year was concluded with a final group of four rather than knock-out stages leading to a final).

Colin Gale (Born Pontypridd, 31 August 1932. Died Rhydyfelin, nr. Pontypridd, 27 October 2008.) Colin Gale was principally a reserve defender in a six-year spell at Cardiff. However, when he dropped down the divisions to sign for Northampton Town he went straight in the line-up at centre half and retained his place in the side for the next five seasons. Colin was a member of the team that defeated Arsenal in an FA Cup third-round tie in 1957–58 and in 1960–61 he assisted the Cobblers to promotion from the Fourth Division.

Ted Gaskell (Born Bredbury, Cheshire, 19 December 1916. Died 10 February 2009.) Goalkeeper Ted Gaskell spent almost 15 years on the books of Brentford, but due to the war he had to wait some ten years before making his senior debut and in total made just 34 Football League appearances.

Régis Genaux (Born Charleroi, Belgium, 31 August 1973. Died Chaudfontaine, Belgium, 8 November 2008.) Régis Genaux developed in Belgium with the Standard Liège club, for whom he made over 150 appearances and was a member of the team that won the domestic cup in 1993. In a brief spell with Coventry in 1996–97 he never really settled and he was soon on his way to Udinese. Regis recovered his form in Serie A before his career was cut short by injury. He subsequently returned to Belgium where he became involved in coaching.

Michael Gliksten (Born circa 1938. Died Cambridge, 5 February 2009.) Michael Gliksten joined the board of directors at Charlton in 1957, succeeding his father as club chairman five years later. He stayed in post for some 20 years and his departure in 1982 marked the end of a 50-year old family dynasty at the club.

Ralph Graham (Born Durham, 29 December 1929. Died Vancouver, Canada, 20 March 2009.) Outside left Ralph Graham signed for Doncaster Rovers in the close season of 1947, but was mostly used as a back-up player and in 1950 he moved on to Southport. In two seasons at Haig Avenue he made 29 Football League appearances before drifting into the non-League game. He later emigrated to Canada where he played for a number of clubs and was also involved in coaching.

Alick Grant (Born Peasedown, Somerset, 11 August 1916. Died September 2008.) Goalkeeper Alick Grant had been on the books of both Sheffield United and Bury before he made his bow in senior football for Aldershot shortly before the outbreak of war. He went on to make almost 100 wartime appearances for Leicester and subsequently played for Derby, Newport, Leeds and York before leaving the game.

Edward Grayson (Born 1 March 1925. Died 23 September 2008.) Edward Grayson was a barrister called to the Bar in 1948 with a strong interest in sport who went on to contribute to the development of a legal framework for sport in modern society. In 1973 he became the founder president fro the British Society for Sport and the Law and he also wrote extensively on the subject, including for this publication. In court he extended the boundaries of the law in a number of areas, notably in two football-related cases, O'Neill v Fashanu and Wimbledon FC and Elliott v Saunders and Liverpool FC.

Ian Greaves (Born Crompton, Lancs., 26 May 1932. Died Ainsworth, Lancs., 2 January 2009.) Ian Greaves was a full back who was one of the young Busby Babes at Old Trafford before the Munich tragedy pushed him into the limelight and a place in the first team. He won an FA Cup runners-up medal in 1958, appearing in the defeat by Bolton at Wembley that year, and later had spells with Lincoln, Oldham and Altrincham before turning to coaching. Ian went on to become a successful manager, winning the Second Division title with Huddersfield (1969–70) and Bolton (1977–78), and also taking Mansfield to promotion from the Fourth Division (1985–86) and success in the Associate Members Cup (1987). An astute and inspirational manager, he also had spells in charge of Oxford and Wolves.

Mick Green (Born Southend, 20 November 1957. Died February 2009.) Mick Green was a midfield player for Exeter City, who made a single first-team appearance as a substitute in the 1976–77 season. He later became an academic at Loughborough University, gaining a PhD and working as a lecturer.

Ken Griffiths (Born Stoke-on-Trent, 2 April 1930. Died Stoke-on-Trent, 10 August 2008.) Ken Griffiths was associated with Port Vale from 1945, although it was five years before he turned professional. An inside left, he was a member of the side that won the Division Three North title and reached the FA Cup semi-final in 1953–54. He went on to have a brief spell with Mansfield in the second half of the 1958–59 campaign before switching to the non-League game.

Neville Hamilton (Born Leicester, 19 April 1960. Died Leicester, 9 February 2009.) Neville Hamilton was an enthusiastic midfielder who began his career with Leicester City. He later spent some two-and-a-half seasons as a regular in the Mansfield Town midfield, making 79 Football League appearances, and then enjoyed a further three seasons with Rochdale as a regular in the line-up. Neville signed for Second Division Wolves in the summer of 1984, but he had the misfortune to suffer a heart attack in pre-season training and retired from playing on medical advice. He subsequently gained FA coaching qualifications and after a spell as Community Development Officer at Filbert Street he coached at a number of clubs in the Midlands.

Joe Haverty (Born Dublin, 17 February 1936. Died London, 7 February 2009.) A diminutive but skilful winger who joined Arsenal from St Patrick's Athletic in the summer of 1954, Joe Haverty made over 100 senior appearances for the Gunners and also won 32 caps for the Republic of Ireland. His career also included spells with Blackburn, Millwall and Bristol Rovers, while in recent years he had served Arsenal as a scout.

Ken Hawden (Born Huddersfield, 16 September 1931. Died Derby, 13 June 2008.) Ken Hawden was a centre forward who played twice for Derby County in the 1953–54 season and later turned out for Matlock and Belper Town.

Jimmy Hernon (Born Cleland, Lanarkshire, 6 December 1924. Died Hastings, 7 March 2009.) Jimmy Hernon was a skilful inside forward who joined Leicester City during wartime and went on to make a total of 31 Football League appearances for the club. He later spent three seasons at Bolton before moving on to Grimsby Town and then Watford, where his career was ended by a knee injury.

Gilbert Heron (Born Kingston, Jamaica, 9 April 1922. Died Detroit, USA, 27 November 2008.) Gilbert Heron was one of the pioneer black players in senior British football in the 1950s. Spotted by Celtic during their 1951 tour of North America, when he was playing for Detroit Corinthians, he made five appearances for the Parkhead club and a further seven for Third Lanark in 1952–53. A forward with tremendous pace, he also had a spell with Kidderminster Harriers before returning to the USA to play in Detroit.

Billy Hewison (Born Burnopfield, Co Durham, 31 December 1919. Died 9 November 2008.) Billy Hewison was a centre half who made 35 wartime appearances for Sunderland during the war and featured in both legs of the League War Cup final against Wolves in May 1942.

Bill Hiftle (Born Byker-on-Tyne, 16 January 1917. Died Newcastle upon Tyne, 30 October 2008.) Bill Hiftle was an outside left who had been on Charlton Athletic's books as a youngster without breaking into the first team. He spent the final two pre-war seasons on the books of Doncaster Rovers, making a total of ten Division Three North appearances.

Mick Hill (Born Hereford, 3 December 1947. Died Hereford, 22 June 2008.) Mick Hill signed for Sheffield United shortly before his 18th birthday, spent four years at Bramall Lane before Bobby Robson brought him to Ipswich in October 1969. Mick enjoyed a useful spell at Portman Road, earning two caps for Wales and then concluded his senior career at Crystal Palace. A versatile forward, he later played in South Africa for Cape Town City.

Joseph Hodgetts (Born Forest Town, Mansfield, circa 1916. Died Sutton-in-Ashfield, Notts., August 2008.) Joseph Hodgetts was an outside left who spent the second half of the 1937–38 campaign with Brighton. Although he failed to make the first team at the Goldstone Ground he managed a single senior appearance for Mansfield Town the following season and also played three times during the emergency competitions in World War Two.

Ken Hollyman (Born Cardiff, 18 November 1922. Died Cardiff, 14 May 2009.) A dependable right half, Ken Hollyman joined Cardiff City during the war and went on to feature in the side that won the Division Three South title in 1946–47. He made over 200 appearances during his stay at Ninian Park before joining Newport County in November 1953 where he spent six seasons as a first-team regular. Ken was also an international baseball player for Wales.

Peter Horridge (Born Manchester, 31 May 1934. Died Newton Heath, Manchester, 26 November 2008.) Peter Horridge was a product of local football who spent almost seven years on the books of Manchester City, for whom he was principally a reserve. A left back, his three first-team appearances came during the 1958–59 season when he deputised occasionally for Cliff Sear.

Keith Houliston (Born 15 July 1949. Died 10 October 2008.) Forward Keith Houliston featured regularly for Queen of the South during the 1970–71 season, when he also won three caps for Scotland's Amateurs. A successful local businessman, he was later a director of the club from April 1994 until his death.

Fred Jenkins (Born Stockton, 5 December 1925. Died Castletown, Sunderland, 7 May 2009.) Fred Jenkins was a speedy winger who featured for Sunderland during the war and later signed for Queen of the South. He spent two seasons with the Doonhamers before being sold to Chelsea for a club record fee of £10,000. However, he was principally a reserve at Stamford Bridge and eventually returned to Queen of the South after spells with a number of clubs including Barry Town, Kettering and Leicester.

Tommy Johnston (Born Loanhead, Midlothian, 18 August 1927. Died Shoalhaven, New South Wales, Australia, 4 September 2008.) Tommy Johnston was a forward who became a cult figure at Leyton Orient during two spells at the club (1956–58 and 1959–61). During this time he won a Third Division championship medal in 1956–57 and established club records for most goals in a season (35 in 1957–58) and the highest career total (121). Earlier in his career he had played for Kilmarnock, Darlington, Oldham, Norwich and Newport County, while he also had spells at Blackburn and Gillingham. In total he made some 429 Football and Scottish League appearances, scoring 255 goals.

David Jones (Born Onllwyn, nr. Neath, Glamorgan, 18 January 1946. Died 15 October 2008.) Goalkeeper David Jones was on Derby County's books as a youngster, but failed to break into the first team. He later moved on to Burton Albion before enjoying a brief spell with Newport County, during which he made three first-team appearances.

Tommy Jover (Born 27 July 1917. Died 25 August 2008.) Tommy Jover was a flying winger who made a single wartime appearance for Luton Town against Leicester City in October 1941. A legendary figure in the history of Dulwich Hamlet,

for whom he played for 20 years, Tommy was also a top class sprinter, representing Great Britain in the sprint relay at the 1948 European Championships in Oslo.

Mike Keen (Born High Wycombe, 19 March 1940. Died 11 April 2009.) Mike Keen made his senior debut for Queens Park Rangers in September 1959 and by the end of the season he had firmly established himself at right half in the line-up. He did not miss a first-team game between March 1962 and September 1968, a remarkable run of 286 competitive matches and after being appointed club captain he led the club to the Third Division title and the Football League Cup in 1966–67. The following season he took Rangers into the First Division for the first time in their history, before moving on to play for Luton and then Watford. Mike later served both Watford and Northampton Town as manager.

Alan Kelly (Born Dublin, 5 July 1936. Died Maryland, United States, 20 May 2009.) Goalkeeper Alan Kelly made his name with Drumcondra, where he gained FAI and League of Ireland winners' medals before signing for Preston North End in April 1958. He stayed at Deepdale for 14 years, making a total of 447 Football League appearances and featuring in the side that lost out to West Ham in the 1964 FA Cup final. Alan won 47 caps for the Republic of Ireland, for whom he was the regular 'keeper for most of the 1960s. On retiring as a player he turned to coaching and was assistant to Johnny Giles as manager of the national team before eventually moving to coach in the USA.

Tommy Johnston

Hugh Kelly (Born Valleyfield, Fife, 23 July 1923. Died St Anne's, Lancs., 28 March 2009.) Hugh Kelly signed for Blackpool during the war, but it was not until the 1947–48 campaign that he won a regular place in the line-up at left half. He was on the losing side in both the 1948 and 1951 FA Cup finals, but missed out in 1953 through injury. He became captain of the side leading the Seasiders to a best ever position of runners-up in the Football League in 1955–56 and made over 400 Football League appearances before leaving the club in 1961. Hugh won a single cap for Scotland against the USA in 1952.

Jim Kerr (Born circa 1942. Died Sanquhar, 8 November 2008.) Jim Kerr was a tough, no-nonsense defender who joined Queen of the South shortly after the start of the 1959–60 season. He went on to become a regular for the Dumfries club throughout the 1960s, making some 400 first-team appearances.

Willie Kilmarnock (Born Irvine, Ayrshire, 16 January 1922. Died Irvine, Ayrshire, 7 June 2009.) Willie Kilmarnock was tremendous servant for Motherwell, joining the club shortly before the outbreak of war and remaining until November 1956. He made 418 peacetime appearances for 'Well, assisting the club to victory in the Scottish League Cup in 1950–51, the Scottish Cup the following season and the Second Division title in 1953–54. Willie also appeared for Scotland in a wartime international and was capped for the Scottish League. He concluded his career with a spell at Airdrieonians before leaving the senior game.

Tommy Kinsella (Born Dublin, 1941. Died Dublin, 6 February 2009.) Tommy Kinsella was on Arsenal's books as a youngster without breaking into the first team, and subsequently played for a number of clubs including Distillery, Coleraine and Shamrock Rovers. A winger he was a member of the Coleraine team that won the Irish Cup in 1965 and also won representative honours for the Irish League.

Frank Kirkup (Born Spennymoor, 12 January 1939. Died Spennymoor, 2009.) Outside left Frank Kirkup had a spell on the books of Blackburn without making the first team, but went on to make over 250 appearances for Workington, Carlisle and Notts County before retiring from the senior game in 1967.

Bill Lawton (Born Ashton-under-Lyne, Lancashire, 4 June 1920. Died Brighton, 14 August 2008.) Bill Lawton spent four years on the books of Oldham Athletic, for whom he was a regular in 1945–46, the final season of wartime football. He spent the summer months playing as a cricket professional in the northern leagues, making two first class appearances for Lancashire. Bill later retired to run a hotel in Brighton with his wife, the well-known actress Dora Bryan.

Don Leeson (Born Askern, Yorkshire, 25 August 1935. Died Grimsby, 15 February 2009.) Don Leeson succeeded Harry Hough as first-choice 'keeper for Barnsley in the second half of the 1958–59 campaign, retaining the jersey for the next two seasons and making over 100 first-team appearances.

Gordon Lennon (Born Larne, Co. Antrim, 15 February 1983. Died Dingwall, 7 June 2009.) Gordon Lennon was an effective defender who began his carer with Albion Rovers in the 2005–06 campaign. He later had spells with Partick Thistle and Stenhousemuir before signing for Dumbarton at the beginning of 2008. Gordon captained Dumbarton to the Scottish League Third Division title in 2008–09, but was tragically killed in a car crash shortly afterwards.

Gerry Lightowler (Born Bradford, 5 September 1940. Died 26 July 2008.) Gerry Lightowler was a full back who made over 200 appearances for Bradford Park Avenue between 1959 and 1968. After a spell in the USA with Los Angeles Wolves, he returned home for a final season with Bradford City.

George Lindsay (Born circa 1943. Died Wishaw, Lanarkshire, 27 March 2009.) George Lindsay was a speedy winger who spent eight seasons on the books of Motherwell, making over 150 first-team appearances. He moved on to Queen of the South in the summer of 1968 and later also had a brief spell with East Stirlingshire before leaving senior football.

Adam Little (Born Blantyre, Lanarkshire, 1 September 1919. Died 12 June 2008.) Capped by Scotland at Schoolboy international level, Adam Little went on to study medicine at Glasgow University, whilst also turning out for Rangers for whom he played a handful of first-team games in the pre-war period. He featured regularly as a wing half for the Ibrox club during the hostilities, adding a further 150 appearances, and also guested for Arsenal and Airdrieonians. He later joined Morton, featuring regularly in their line-up in the early 1950s. Adam made one appearance for Scotland in the unofficial international against England in October 1943.

Eddie Lowe (Born Halesowen, 11 July 1925. Died Nottingham, 10 March 2009.) Eddie Lowe was a regular for Aston Villa in the early post-war seasons, when he also won three England caps. However, in the summer of 1950 he moved south to join Fulham along with his brother Reg and he was to remain at Craven Cottage until the start of the 1963–64 season. A talented, creative left half, Eddie went on to make over 500 appearances during his stay, featuring in the side that won promotion to the old First Division in 1958–59. He later had two seasons as player-manager of Notts County before leaving the game.

Bert Loxley (Born Bonsall, nr. Matlock, Derbyshire, 3 February 1934. Died 9 October 2008.) Bert Loxley made his debut for Notts County in the final game of the 1954–55 season and eventually established himself in the line-up at wing half, switching to centre half early in 1959. Bert went on to make over 250 appearances during his stay at Meadow Lane, assisting the Magpies to promotion from the Fourth Division in 1959–60. After a spell out of the League he joined Lincoln City in 1966, remaining at Sincil Bank until 1987 and serving the Imps as trainer, manager and physio.

Brian Lucas (Born Farnborough, 31 January 1961. Died 23 March 2009.) Brian Lucas was a skilful midfield player who made over 100 Football League appearances for Aldershot between 1980 and 1984 before dropping into non-League football. After spells with a number of clubs he joined the newly formed Aldershot Town and featured in their first-ever competitive game against Clapton in August 1992.

Stewart McCallum (Born Bearsden, Glasgow, 9 May 1927. Died Bodelwyddan, Rhyl, Denbighshire, 2008.) Stewart McCallum was one of a small group of Scots who turned out for Newells Old Boys in Argentina in 1948. He returned to Britain and spent almost a decade as a professional with Wrexham, Workington, Coventry City, Hartlepools and Southport, accumulating almost 100 senior appearances.

Ian McColl (Born Alexandria, Dunbartonshire, 7 June 1927. Died 25 October 2008.) Ian McColl signed for Queen's Park during the war, making some 57 appearances in the emergency competitions before joining Rangers. He quickly established himself in the side at Ibrox, playing at right half in the famous 'Iron Curtain' defence of the early post-war years. Ian was an intelligent player with plenty of skill, and he went on to win six League titles with Rangers and five Scottish Cup victories, captaining the side from 1957. In November 1960 he was appointed as Scotland manager, retaining the post with some success until resigning in May 1965. He was then manager of Sunderland until February 1968, where his signings included the iconic midfielder Jim Baxter. He won 14 caps for Scotland during his playing career.

Andy McCreesh (Born Billingham, 8 September 1962. Died 5 February 2009.) Andy McCreesh was a defender who made two first-team appearances for Middlesbrough at the start of the 1981–82 but was released shortly before the end of that campaign. He later played in South Africa and Australia before returning to the Teesside where he turned out for a number of clubs in the Northern League.

Jock Macdonald, OBE (Born Inverness, 2 November 1930. Died Inverness, 17 December 2008.) A whisky executive by profession, Jock Macdonald was a motivating figure in the formation of Inverness Caledonian Thistle and the club's first chairman. A former player and director for Inverness Thistle, his enthusiasm also contributed to the club's election to the Scottish League. Jock represented the North of Scotland on the SFA for many years and also served on the International Committee.

Charlie McFadyen (Born circa 1934. Died Glasgow, October 2008.) Charlie McFadyen joined St Johnstone in the summer of 1955 and went on to make over 300 appearances, spending more than a decade at Muirton Park. A solid, dependable right back, he was a member of two Second Division title-winning sides (1959–60 and 1962–63) and also appeared in two Scottish Cup semi-finals.

Desmond McLean (Born Glasgow, 20 May 1931. Died 29 December 2008.) Goalkeeper Desmond McLean served Celtic and Queen's Park as an amateur before joining the professional ranks at Arsenal. However, it was only when he returned to Scotland to play for Airdrieonians at the start of 1952–53 that he made the breakthrough to first-team football. He later had spells with Dundee United and Dumbarton, although he remained principally a reserve at all his clubs.

Ron Mann (Born Nottingham, 8 October 1932. Died Nottingham, 30 November 2008.) Ron Mann was capped by England Boys' Clubs and went on to have a six-year spell on the books of Notts County, although he made just one first-team appearance for the Magpies. He enjoyed better fortunes during his stay at Aldershot where he had a lengthy run in the side at left back in the first half of the 1956–57 campaign.

Gordon Marsland (Born Blackpool, 20 March 1945. Died Blackpool, 4 January 2009.) Gordon Marsland never made the first team for Blackpool, but after moving on to Carlisle in the summer of 1965 he became a regular at left half. After recovering from a broken leg, which kept him out of action for a year, he resumed his place in the side making 71 senior appearances before moving on to Bristol Rovers.

Eric Massey (Born Derby, 11 September 1923. Died 3 May 2009.) Eric Massey joined Bury immediately after the war and made over 200 first-team appearances during the next decade. A forward in his early days with the club, he later reverted to playing at full back, before moving on to join Macclesfield Town in 1957.

Les Melville (Born Ormskirk, Cheshire, 29 November 1930. Died Stockport, 1 February 2009.) Wing half Les Melville was on Everton's books as a youngster, but never made the first team at Goodison Park. He later featured at first-team level for Bournemouth and Oldham Athletic. However, perhaps his greatest achievement in football came when he joined Worcester City in the 1958 close season. Here he was converted into a solid, unspectacular centre half and was an important member of the team that enjoyed a glorious run in the FA Cup, famously defeating Liverpool 2–1 in a third round tie, a feat which remains one of the greatest Cup upsets of all time.

George Miller (Born Larkhall, Lanarkshire, 20 May 1939. Died Wishaw, North Lanarkshire, 26 December 2008.) George Miller was a member of the Dunfermline team that defeated Celtic to win the Scottish Cup in 1961 and went on to bring

European football to East End Park. A big money transfer to Wolves followed, but he never really settled in the Midlands and was soon back north of the Border, playing for Hearts. He appeared for the Tynecastle club in the 1968 Scottish Cup final, when they lost out to Dunfermline, and concluded his playing career at Falkirk. George later had spells as manager of both Dunfermline and Falkirk.

Brookes Mileson (Born Sunderland, 13 November 1947. Died Carlisle, 3 November 2008.) Brookes Mileson was a wealthy businessman who sponsored the Northern League and after failing in a bid to take over Carlisle United he transformed Gretna following a takeover in 2003. Three promotions took the club to the SPL and a place in the Scottish Cup final for 2006, when they lost to Hearts. However, Mileson then fell ill, withdrew his financial support and the club went out of business in the summer of 2008.

Bryce Morrison (Born circa 1952. Died 21 March 2009.) Bryce Morrison had been employed by Liverpool FC since 1992 and was club secretary at the time of his sudden and unexpected death.

George Morton (Born Liverpool, 30 September 1943. Died Liverpool, 15 January 2009.) George Morton began his career on the groundstaff at Everton, graduating to the professional ranks on reaching the age of 17. However, he never made it beyond the reserve team at Goodison before moving on to Rochdale in the summer of 1962. A prolific inside right he scored 55 goals in 161 first team appearances during his stay at Spotland before switching to non-League football with New Brighton and then Bangor City.

Bob Mountford (Born Stoke-on-Trent, 23 February 1952. Died Merewether, Newcastle, New South Wales, Australia, 25 August 2008.) Centre forward Bob Mountford began his career with Port Vale, making his senior debut whilst still an apprentice with the club. However, in October 1974 he was sold to Rochdale, where he led the club's scoring charts in three consecutive seasons. After a brief spell at Huddersfield he joined Halifax, where he was member of the team that knocked Manchester City out of the FA Cup in January 1980. Bob later turned out for Crewe and Stockport before emigrating to Australia.

George Muir (Born 1937. Died Taunton, 21 December 2008.) George Muir spent a decade on the books of Hibs as a full back during the 1950s, making 60 first-team appearances. He later moved south to play for Yeovil Town where he was a member of the team that won the Southern League championship and reached the FA Cup third round in 1963–64.

Ian Muir (Born Motherwell, 16 June 1929. Died Bristol, 22 February 2009.) A tall defender, Ian Muir was restricted to a handful of appearances at Motherwell, before joining Bristol Rovers in the 1953 close season. He made 26 appearances in four seasons for the Pirates and was then a regular for Oldham during the 1957–58 campaign before leaving senior football.

Eddie Mulvey (Born Dublin, 29 December 1934. Died Glasnevin, Dublin, 11 February 2009.) Inside forward Eddie Mulvey joined Stockport from Glentoran in November 1957 and in just under two seasons at Edgeley Park he made 26 Football League appearances. He was released by County in the summer of 1960 and returned to Ireland, spending six seasons on the books of Limerick.

Alex Munro (Born Glasgow, 3 October 1944. Died St Austell, Cornwall, 24 May 2009.) Alex Munro was a powerful, aggressive defender who spent almost a decade on the books of Bristol Rovers after signing from Drumchapel Boys' Club at the start of the 1962–63 season. He settled into the side at left back, making 169 appearances for the Pirates before moving to South Africa where he played for a number of clubs including Durban City, East London United and Hellenic.

Eddie Murphy (Born Hamilton, 13 May 1924. Died 28 January 2009.) Eddie Murphy began his senior career on the books of Hibs without making the first team. He later signed for Morton where he impressed with some cool skills and clever play up front, hitting a last-minute winner against Celtic in the Scottish Cup semi-final of 1948, before going on to win a runners-up medal as the team went down to Rangers in the replayed final. Eddie subsequently moved south, making almost 200 first-team appearances for Northampton, Barnsley and Exeter.

Jimmy Murray (Born Elvington, Kent, 11 October 1935. Died Lichfield, Staffs., 27 September 2008.) Jimmy Murray was prolific centre forward who was a key member of the successful Wolves side of the late 1950s, helping the club win back-to-back Football League titles in 1957–58 and 1958–59 and the FA Cup in 1960. He later played for Manchester City, where he contributed to the 1965–66 Division Two championship side, and Walsall. Jimmy won a single cap for the Football League representative side and appeared twice for England U23s.

Les Mynard (Born Bewdley, Worcs., 19 December 1925. Died 25 July 2008.) Winger Les Mynard made a handful of appearances for Wolves in the early post-war years. A pacy winger who could play on either flank, he fared better in spells at Derby and Scunthorpe before leaving the senior game at the end of the 1952–53 season.

Jimmy Neighbour (Born Chingford, Essex, 15 November 1950. Died Buckhurst Hill, Essex, 11 April 2009.) Jimmy Neighbour was an old-fashioned style wing man who made his first-team debut for Tottenham in October 1970. Later that season he featured at outside left when Spurs overcame Aston Villa to win the Football League Cup. He subsequently had spells with Norwich City and Seattle Sounders before returning home to finish his senior career at West Ham, where he gained a League Cup runners-up medal in 1981.

George Niven (Born Blairhall, Fife, 11 June 1929. Died Kingussie, Highland, 17 July 2008.) Goalkeeper George Niven joined Rangers as an 18-year-old and went on to win five Scottish League titles, two Scottish Cups and one League Cup during his stay at Ibrox. Later he enjoyed several seasons as Partick Thistle's regular custodian before leaving the professional game, although he was still turning out in local football when in his 50s. George was capped seven times by the Scottish League representative side.

Tommy Northcott (Born Torquay, 5 December 1931. Died 26 September 2008.) Tommy Northcott won Youth international honours for England, and after developing his career at Torquay he joined First Division Cardiff City. After a short but successful spell with Lincoln City, he returned to Torquay in November 1957 where he led the club's scoring charts for four consecutive seasons and helped the team win promotion from the Fourth Division in 1959–60. In total he made over 400 Football League appearances for the Gulls, scoring 136 goals.

Christy O'Callaghan (Died Dublin, 18 January 2009.) Goalkeeper Christy O'Callaghan was a member of the successful Shamrock Rovers team of the 1950s, winning both domestic league and cup honours with the club. Christy was also capped by the League of Ireland. His twin brother Danny, also a League international, pre-deceased him.

Elkanah Onyeali (Born Imo State, Nigeria, 7 June 1939. Died Mbieri, Imo State, Nigeria, 10 August 2008.) Elkanah Onyeali came to England to study and linked up with Tranmere Rovers with some success, scoring nine goals from 16 outings. A pacy, powerful forward, he was capped on a number of occasions by Nigeria, featuring in the qualifying rounds for the 1960 Olympic Games.

Noel O'Reilly (Born circa 1948. Died Dublin, 26 September 2008.) Noel O'Reilly was one of the most influential figures in the game in Ireland. A coach with Shamrock Rovers and St Patrick's Athletic, where he worked with Brian Kerr, Noel joined the FAI set up in 1999. When Kerr was appointed as head of the senior team in 2003, Noel became his deputy and even after Kerr had departed he retained a strong influence, holding the post of FAI Senior Coach Educator at the time of his death.

Harry Oscroft (Born Mansfield, 10 March 1926. Died Suffolk, 31 December 2008.) Outside left Harry Oscroft signed for Mansfield soon after the war and quickly became a popular figure at Field Mill before being sold to Stoke. He went on to score over a century of goals during his stay at the Victoria Ground, finishing as the Potters leading scorer in 1952–53 and 1954–55, before concluding his career with a couple of seasons at local rivals Port Vale.

Harry Parkes (Born Erdington, Birmingham, 4 January 1920. Died Solihull, 4 March 2009.) Harry Parkes was one of the most popular figures in the post-war history of Aston Villa. A versatile player and one-club man, he made over 400 first-team appearances in a 16-year spell at Villa Park after originally signing during the war. A half back or defender, he was a member of the team that won the Football League War Cup North in 1943–44. Harry remained well known in local sporting circles running a busy sports-outfitters store in Birmingham city centre for over 30 years before eventually retiring.

Bill Pearson (Born Clonmel, Irish Free State, 23 October 1921. Died 2009.) Although born in Ireland, Bill Pearson was brought up in York and signed for Grimsby Town in 1943 when serving as a PT Instructor. He guested for Aberdeen, Manchester City and York during the hostilities and went on to make 35 Football League appearances for the Mariners before concluding his career with a season at Chester.

Alan Philpott (Born Stoke-on-Trent, 8 November 1942. Died Fenton, Stoke-on-Trent, 26 May 2009.) Alan Philpott was a versatile player who developed through the youth system at Stoke, making over 50 appearances during the 1960s. Later he spent two seasons at Oldham before joining non-League Stafford Rangers. Alan died after suffering a heart attack while umpiring a local cricket match.

Albert Pounder (Born Charlton, 27 July 1931. Died 11 December 2008.) Albert Pounder was a winger who made just a single appearance for Charlton before moving on to Queens Park Rangers. He enjoyed several useful spells on the right flank for Rangers, making a total of 55 senior appearances, before departing for Sittingbourne.

Aubrey Powell (Born Swansea, 19 April 1918. Died Methley, West Yorkshire, 27 January 2009.) Aubrey Powell was a neat inside forward who recovered well after suffering a broken leg early on in his professional career with Leeds. A PT instructor during the war years, he found time to make over 100 appearances for United in the emergency competitions and also played four times for Wales in unofficial internationals during the hostilities. He was a regular in the Leeds side in the first two war years, later moving on to Everton for a substantial fee before winding down his career with a spell at Birmingham. Aubrey also won a total of eight caps for Wales in peacetime.

Harold Prince (Born Stoke-on-Trent, 4 December 1921. Died Bucknall, Stoke-on-Trent, 17 February 2009.) Goalkeeper Harold Prince spent the war years on the books of Port Vale and Wolves, making a total of 55 appearances in the emergency competitions. When peacetime football resumed he was on the books of Vale once more, but although he spent the next three seasons at Vale Park he was principally a reserve only occasionally deputising in the first team.

Albert Quinn (Born Lanchester, Co Durham, 18 April 1920. Died 26 June 2008.) Inside forward Albert Quinn played a handful of first-team games for Sunderland during the 1947–48 season, scoring twice in a 5–1 victory over Liverpool. He later signed for Darlington where he led the scoring charts in both 1948–49 and 1949–50, netting 44 goals in 91 appearances during a three-year stay at Feethams.

Colin Rawson (Born Langwith, Derbys., 12 November 1926. Died Sutton-in-Ashfield, Notts., April 2009.) Colin Rawson began his career at Nottingham Forest, where he made just one appearance before moving on to Peterborough United, then members of the Midland League. He returned to senior football with Rotherham, where he was an ever-present at left half in the team that won the Division Three North title in 1950–51. Colin subsequently played for Sheffield United, Millwall (where he was club captain) and Torquay United before retiring from the game in 1962.

Jimmy Rayner (Born Cornsay, Durham, 31 March 1935. Died Durham, 5 January 2009.) Jimmy Rayner enjoyed a varied career, interspersing spells in senior football with long periods in the semi-professional game. At senior level he turned out for Grimsby, Barrow, Peterborough and Notts County, making over a century of appearances as a wing half for Posh. In non-League football he proved to be a prolific centre forward, notably with Grantham and Boston United. He eventually returned to live in the North East where he played for Durham City and Gateshead, and was later Chairman of Durham City.

John Ryan (Born Alloa, 16 October 1930. Died Swindon, 12 August 2008.) John Ryan was a forward who began his career with Charlton Athletic in 1954. A regular goalscorer, the highlight of his career at The Valley came when he scored the last-minute winner in an amazing 7–6 win over Huddersfield Town in December 1957. He subsequently moved to Newcastle, but never made the first team at St James' Park, and later concluded his career with a season at Bristol City.

Dicky Robinson (Born South Shields, 19 January 1927. Died Barrow, 19 April 2009.) Dicky Robinson was a versatile full back who made almost 400 Football league appearances for Middlesbrough between 1946 and 1959. He later made a century of appearances for Barrow and also won representative honours for the Football League.

Pete Sampson (Born Pitsea, Essex, 9 July 1927. Died Congresbury, Bristol, 16 May 2009.) Peter Sampson was a wing half who spent 12 seasons with Bristol Rovers, making 339 Football League appearances. A loyal and consistent performer, he was an ever-present for three consecutive seasons including 1952–53 when Rovers won the Division Three South title.

Roy Saunders (Born Salford, 4 September 1930. Died 29 January 2009.) Wing half Roy Saunders won England Youth honours and went on to make some 144 first-team appearances for Liverpool between 1953 and 1959. Later he enjoyed a further four years with Swansea, where he was a member of the team that won the Welsh Cup in 1961.

Jack Scott (Born Larkhall, Lanarkshire, 17 February 1923. Died Larkhall, Lanarkshire, 29 December 2008.) Jack Scott signed for Hamilton in September 1943 and went on to make 11 wartime appearances for the Accies and a further three as a guest for East Fife. He also had a very brief spell on the books of Tranmere Rovers from March 1947 without breaking into the first team.

Alan Shackleton (Born Padiham, Lancs., 3 February 1934. Died Bromley, Kent, 25 April 2009.) Centre forward Alan Shackleton made his debut for Burnley in 1957, but although he had a good scoring record at Turf Moor he was unable to dislodge Ray Pointer from the side and he moved on to Leeds. He later had spells with Everton and Oldham Athletic, finishing with highly respectable career figures of 97 Football League appearances and 51 goals.

Bill Shorthouse (Born Bilston, Staffs., 27 May 1922. Died Wolverhampton, 6 September 2008.) Bill Shorthouse joined Wolves in 1941, graduating to the professional ranks some five years later. A tough tackling centre half, he was one of the cornerstones of the club's successful team of the early 1950s, gaining an FA Cup winners' medal in 1949 and contributing to the Football League championship campaign in 1953–54. Solid and dependable, he was rarely absent from the line-up until retiring at the end of the 1956–57 season. He subsequently joined the backroom staff at Molineux and later also coached the youth teams of Birmingham City and Aston Villa.

Bill Shorthouse

Joe Sibley (Born Southend, 6 October 1919. Died: Southend, 20 February 2008.) Inside forward Joe Sibley joined Southend United in May 1938 but it was not until after the war had ended that he made his senior debut. He moved to Newcastle United in February 1947 and although highly regarded, injury blighted his three seasons at St James' Park. He returned to Southend in the summer of 1950, adding a further 200-plus appearances and playing a significant role in the club's fortunes in the period to 1956.

Geoff Sidebottom (Born Mapplewell, nr. Barnsley, 29 December 1936. Died Scunthorpe, 3 November 2008.) A product of the Wolves' nursery club, Wath Wanderers, goalkeeper Geoff Sidebottom went on to sign professional terms shortly before his 18th birthday. He subsequently enjoyed a lengthy career in the game making over 200 senior appearances for Wolves, Aston Villa, Scunthorpe and Brighton. Geoff was a member of the Villa team that won the inaugural Football League Cup competition of 1960–61, featuring in the decisive second leg of the final against Rotherham.

Alex Simpson (Born Glasgow, 24 November 1924. Died Wombourne, Staffs., 16 June 2008.) Wing half Alex Simpson never got much of a look in during a two-year spell at Wolves, but thereafter experienced regular first-team football at Notts County, Southampton and Shrewsbury during the 1950s. At Meadow Lane he helped County win the Division Three South title in 1949–50.

Jimmy Sirrel (Born Glasgow, 2 February 1922. Died Nottingham, 25 September 2008.) Jimmy Sirrel was one of the legendary figures in the history of Notts County, serving the club as manager on three separate occasions and gaining three promotions: as Division Four champions in 1970–71, then up to the Second Division in 1972–73 and finally to the old First Division in 1980–81. As a player he was a skilful inside forward, beginning his senior career with Celtic towards the end of 1945. Jimmy then played for Bradford Park Avenue, Brighton and Aldershot before obtaining his coaching qualifications. His first managerial job came when he took over at Brentford. In addition to his time at Meadow Lane he also served Sheffield United as manager.

John Sjoberg (Born Aberdeen, 12 June 1941. Died 2 October 2008.) John Sjoberg signed for Leicester City in the summer of 1958, although it was not until midway through the 1962–63 campaign that he took over from Len Chalmers at right back for City, retaining his place for the FA Cup final defeat by Manchester United that season. He went on to make over 400 first-team appearances for City. John was a member of the team that defeated Stoke to win the Football League Cup in 1962–63 and also appeared in the following season's final when they lost out to Chelsea over two legs. After switching to centre half he was a key member of the Foxes' defence as they won the Second Division title in 1970–71. John wound down his career with a brief spell at Rotherham before leaving the game to focus on his printing business.

Geoff Slack (Born Morecambe, 13 July 1934. Died Carnforth, Lancs., 8 January 2009.) Winger Geoff Slack joined Stockport County from Morecambe soon after the start of the 1958–59 campaign, but never managed to establish himself in the County line-up and after making eight first-team appearances he returned to non-League football, later turning out for Lancaster City and Netherfield.

Billy Smith (Born circa 1930. Died Johannesburg, South Africa, 24 April 2009.) Billy Smith was a tenacious full back who made his debut for Aberdeen in January 1952. A member of the Dons' team that won the Scottish League title in 1954–55, he later played for Third Lanark before joining Highland League club Deveronvale as player coach.

Dean Smith (Born Leicester, 28 November 1958. Died April 2009.) Dean Smith was a powerful striker who served an apprenticeship with Leicester City before signing professional forms. He made ten Football League appearances for the Foxes and later enjoyed a successful spell with Brentford, netting 16 goals from 54 appearances before dropping into non-League football.

Cec Smyth (Born Belfast, 4 May 1941. Died 7 November 2008.) Full back Cec Smyth began his career with Distillery before joining Exeter in August 1962. He went on to enjoy seven years of regular first-team football with the Grecians, making exactly 300 senior appearances and helping the team secure promotion from the Fourth Division in 1963–64. Cec later spent a season with Torquay and also played for Barnstaple Town.

David Stacey (Born 1929. Died 3 April 2009.) David Stacey was one of the key individuals in the world of football programme collecting, producing the Football Programme Directory and organising the annual International Programme Fair in London. He also served Arsenal as a cheerleader in the 1950s and early '60s.

Len Staples (Born Leicester, 23 January 1926. Died Cumbria, 2 September 2008.) Len Staples played a handful of wartime games for Leicester City, but when peacetime football returned he was unable to win a place in the first team at Filbert Street. An inside forward or wing half, he enjoyed regular first-team with Newport County after signing in August 1949, making 176 first-team appearances during his stay at Somerton Park.

Jim Stevenson (Born circa 1935. Died Mitcheldean, nr. Cheltenham, 2 March 2009.) Jim Stevenson was a talented half back for Dundee and Dunfermline Athletic in the 1950s. He missed out on a place in the Pars' Scottish Cup winning team of 1961 due to a broken leg, but remained at East End Park until 1963, when he moved south to sign for Cheltenham Town.

Alan Suddick

Tom Stimpson (Born Stanton Hill, Notts., 9 April 1907. Died Sutton-in-Ashfield, Notts., 8 February 2009.) Although he never played in the Football League, Tom Stimpson featured in the Midland League for Mansfield Town in the 1929–30 season and later played for Scunthorpe United in the same competition. At the age of 101, he was the oldest surviving player for both clubs at the time of his death.

Ron Stitfall (Born Cardiff, 14 December 1925. Died Cardiff, 22 June 2008.) Ron Stitfall made his debut for Cardiff City during the wartime emergency fixtures, eventually signing professional forms in 1947. He went on to become a key figure in the side at full back, amassing over 400 senior appearances and helping the club win promotion to the First Division in 1951–52 and 1959–60. Ron won two caps for Wales during his career.

Alan Suddick (Born Chester-le-Street, Co Durham, 2 May 1944. Died Manchester, 16 March 2009.) Alan Suddick was a forward with tremendous skills on the ball who began his professional career with Newcastle United, featuring in the team that won the Second Division title in 1964–65. He was sold to Blackpool in December 1966 and went on to achieve legendary status amongst the Seasiders' fans, who christened him 'The King of Bloomfield Road'. In a decade at Bloomfield Road he scored 64 goals in 310 appearances, helping the club win promotion to the First Division in 1969–70 and the Anglo Italian Cup in 1971. Alan also had brief spells with Stoke and Bury before leaving full-time football.

Jack Swindells (Born Manchester, 12 April 1937. Died Cornwall, 23 June 2009.) Jack Swindells enjoyed a lengthy career as something of a journeyman centre forward scoring 63 Football League goals from a total of 190 appearances for Blackburn, Accrington Stanley, Barnsley, Workington, Torquay and Newport. He later spent several seasons in non-League football with Altrincham, netting 82 goals from 63 games in the 1965–66 campaign.

Des Tennant (Born Aberdare, Glamorgan, 17 October 1925. Died 12 January 2009.) Des Tennant was a versatile defender, although essentially a right back, who made over 400 appearances for Brighton between 1948 and 1959. He was a key member of the Seagulls' side that won the Division Three South title in 1957–58, thus gaining promotion to the old Second Division for the first time in the club's history.

Eddie Thompson, OBE (Born Glasgow, 16 July 1940. Died Dundee, 15 October 2008.) Eddie Thompson was a businessman who made his money building up and then selling on a chain of convenience stores. He was a popular chairman of Dundee United after taking over the club in 2002 and he remained at the helm until his death. During this time he restored the club to financial health, whilst ensuring that the fans, through the club's supporters' trust, were the second largest shareholding group. He also served on the SPL Board.

Jim Thompson (Born circa 1933. Died Aylesford, Kent, 16 January 2009.) Jim Thompson was chairman of Maidstone when the club won promotion to the Football League in 1989. Prior to this he had been an active figure in building the non-League pyramid and had served as chairman of the Football Conference, having been a leading light in its formation.

Chic Thomson (Born Perth, 2 March 1930. Died Nottingham, 6 January 2009.) Chic Thomson began his career with Clyde but found his time at Shawfield interrupted by National Service. After being demobilised he signed for Chelsea, where he went on to win a Football League championship medal as the club clinched the title for the first time in their history in the 1954–55 season. Later he spent four seasons at Nottingham Forest, for whom he produced a solid display in the 1959 FA Cup final as they held on to beat Luton and lift the trophy.

Peter Tilley (Born Lurgan, Co Armagh, 13 January 1930. Died 11 August 2008.) Peter Tilley signed for Arsenal in the summer of 1952, but he was mostly a reserve during his stay at Highbury, making just a single first-team appearance. He subsequently returned north, enjoying several regular seasons of regular first-team football with Bury and Halifax, making close to 300 appearances before leaving senior football in the summer of 1963.

Ray Tumbridge (Born Hampstead, London, 6 March 1955. Died 4 June 2009.) Left back Ray Tumbridge made 48 senior appearances for Charlton in the early 1970s before leaving The Valley in the summer of 1975. He moved on to Weymouth and then played for a string of non-League clubs including Dartford, Gravesend & Northfleet and Tonbridge, eventually retiring as a player in 1991.

Johnny Urquhart (Born Kirkcaldy, Fife, 3 February 1925. Died Kirkcaldy, Fife, 12 December 2008.) Johnny Urquhart joined Hearts during the war and went on to become a first-team regular at outside left in the early 1950s. A member of the team that won the Scottish League Cup in 1954–55, he was also capped for the Scottish League against the Irish League during the same season. After leaving Tynecastle he added a further 200 appearances for Raith, and continued to serve the Kirkcaldy club after his playing career was over as a director, club chairman and, from 1994, president.

Jim Vigden (Born circa 1927. Died Brixham, Devon, 22 March 2009.) Jim Vigden was a goalkeeper on the books of Torquay United in 1945–46, the final wartime season, when he made five appearances. He later enjoyed a lengthy career in local non-League football.

Billy Waugh (Born Edinburgh, 27 November 1921. Died Felixstowe, 26 March 2009.) A versatile winger, Billy Waugh signed for Luton in 1944 and was a near ever-present during the first three post-war seasons. He later had spells with Queens Park Rangers and Bournemouth, finishing with a career tally of 230 Football League appearances.

Jack Wheeler

Harry Webster (Born Sheffield, 22 August 1930. Died 2 April 2008.) Harry Webster joined Bolton as a teenager and won a regular place in the line-up during the 1950–51 campaign. Injury kept him out of the 1953 FA Cup final, but he went on to make over 100 first-team appearances for the Trotters as a versatile forward. He subsequently spent two seasons with Chester before winding down his career with Chorley. Harry was a member of the FA squad that toured Australia in 1951, playing in one of the five test matches.

Selwyn Whalley (Born Stoke-on-Trent, 24 February 1934. Died Stoke-on-Trent, 8 August 2008.) Selwyn Whalley was a right half or right back who spent 13 years on the books of Port Vale, throughout his career combining football with a job as a PE teacher in local secondary schools. He made a total of 194 appearances for Vale, scoring eight goals.

Jack Wheeler (Born Evesham, Worcs., 13 July 1919. Died Nottingham, 10 January 2009.) Goalkeeper Jack Wheeler joined Birmingham towards the end of the 1937–38 campaign, but after making a handful of appearances his career was interrupted by the war. After demobilisation he was unable to dislodge Gil Merrick as the club's first-choice 'keeper and moved on to Huddersfield, where he was an ever-present in the team that won promotion to the top flight in 1952–53. Jack left for Kettering Town in the summer of 1956 and then took up a post as trainer of Notts County in 1957. He remained there until 1983, also serving as caretaker-manager for the period September 1968 to November 1969.

Billy Whiteside (Born Glasgow, 27 June 1948. Died Australia, 2008.) Goalkeeper Bill Whiteside was first-choice 'keeper for Stranraer for three seasons in the early 1970s, making over 100 senior appearances. He also had spells with Raith Rovers and Hamilton before emigrating to Australia.

George Wiseman (Born East Dereham, Norfolk, 23 May 1921. Died Exeter, 5 October 2008.) George Wiseman was spotted whilst serving in the RAF and made 20 appearances for Notts County in the wartime emergency competitions. He spent the 1946–47 season with Norwich where he was one of five 'keepers used during the campaign and was restricted to just eight Football League outings.

Jim Wooldridge (Born Rossington, Yorkshire, 28 September 1918. Died 10 November 2008.) Jim Wooldridge was a full back who made over 100 wartime appearances for Doncaster, also guesting for Mansfield Town during the hostilities. Rovers romped away with the Division Three North title in 1946–47, but Jim missed most of the second half of the campaign through injury. On leaving Belle Vue he went on to play for Frickley Colliery and Brodsworth Colliery.

Andy Young (Born Oakley, Fife, 21 June 1925. Died Dunfermline, 17 October 2008.) Andy Young was one of the all-time greats for Raith Rovers, forming a memorable half-back line alongside Willie McNaught and Andy Leigh in the 1950s. He played briefly for Celtic during the war before signing for Raith early in 1945, making over 500 appearances for the club in a career that lasted until 1961. Andy was a member of the Rovers team that reached the Scottish League Cup final and also won the Second Division title in 1948–49.

Ian Nannestad
www.soccer-history.co.uk

THE FOOTBALL RECORDS

BRITISH FOOTBALL RECORDS

ALL-TIME PREMIER LEAGUE CHAMPIONSHIP SEASONS ON POINTS AVERAGE

	Team	Season	P	W	D	L	F	A	Pts	Pts Av
1	Chelsea	2004–05	38	29	8	1	72	15	95	2.50
2	Manchester U	1999–2000	38	28	7	3	97	45	91	2.39
3	Chelsea	2005–06	38	29	4	5	72	22	91	2.39
4	Arsenal	2003–04	38	26	12	0	73	26	90	2.36
	Manchester U	2008–09	38	28	6	4	68	24	90	2.36
6	Manchester U	2006–07	38	28	5	5	83	27	89	2.34
7	Arsenal	2001–02	38	26	9	3	79	36	87	2.28
	Manchester U	2007–08	38	27	6	5	80	22	87	2.28
9	Manchester U	1993–94	42	27	11	4	80	38	92	2.19
10	Manchester U	2002–03	38	25	8	5	74	34	83	2.18
11	Manchester U	1995–96	38	25	7	6	73	35	82	2.15
12	Blackburn R	1994–95	42	27	8	7	80	39	89	2.11
13	Manchester U	2000–01	38	24	8	6	79	31	80	2.10
14	Manchester U	1998–99	38	22	13	3	80	37	79	2.07
15	Arsenal	1997–98	38	23	9	6	68	33	78	2.05
16	Manchester U	1992–93	42	24	12	6	67	31	84	2.00
17	Manchester U	1996–97	38	21	12	5	76	44	75	1.97

PREMIER LEAGUE EVER-PRESENT CLUBS

	P	W	D	L	F	A	Pts
Manchester U	658	422	143	93	1288	563	1409
Arsenal	658	352	180	126	1116	585	1236
Chelsea	658	335	176	147	1045	630	1181
Liverpool	658	331	168	159	1069	634	1161
Aston Villa	658	247	198	213	836	772	939
Tottenham H	658	237	174	247	884	892	885
Everton	658	228	179	251	813	845	863

TOP TEN PREMIERSHIP APPEARANCES

1	David James	547	6	Emile Heskey	438
2	Gary Speed	535	7	Frank Lampard	432
3	Ryan Giggs	523	8	Gareth Southgate	426
4	Sol Campbell	485	9	Teddy Sheringham	418
5	Alan Shearer	441	10	Paul Scholes	416

TOP TEN PREMIERSHIP GOALSCORERS

1	Alan Shearer	260	6	Teddy Sheringham	146
2	Andy Cole	187	7	Michael Owen	144
3	Thierry Henry	174	8	Jimmy Floyd Hasselbaink	127
4	Robbie Fowler	163	9	Dwight Yorke	123
5	Les Ferdinand	149	10	Robbie Keane	115

PREMIERSHIP GOAL MILESTONES

Goal	Date	Scorer	Match
1	15.8.92	Brian Deane	Sheffield U v Manchester U
100	25.8.92	Mark Walters	Liverpool v Ipswich T
1000	7.4.93	Mike Newell	Blackburn R v Nottingham F
5000	7.12.96	Andy Townsend	Aston Villa v Southampton
10,000	15.12.01	Les Ferdinand	Tottenham H v Fulham
11,000	7.12.02	Jay-Jay Okocha	Bolton W v Blackburn R
12,000	13.12.03	Alan Shearer	Newcastle U v Tottenham H
13,000	28.11.04	Frederic Kanoute	Tottenham H v Middlesbrough
14,000	26.12.05	Jermain Defoe	Tottenham H v Birmingham C
15,000	30.12.06	Moritz Volz	Fulham v Chelsea

EUROPEAN CUP AND CHAMPIONS LEAGUE RECORDS

CHAMPIONS LEAGUE ATTENDANCES AND GOALS FROM GROUP STAGES ONWARDS

Season	Attendances	Average	Goals	Games
1992–93	873,251	34,930	56	25
1993–94	1,202,289	44,529	71	27
1994–95	2,328,515	38,172	140	61
1995–96	1,874,316	30,726	159	61
1996–97	2,093,228	34,315	161	61
1997–98	2,868,271	33,744	239	85
1998–99	3,608,331	42,451	238	85
1999–2000	5,490,709	34,973	442	157
2000–01	5,773,486	36,774	449	157
2001–02	5,417,716	34,508	393	157
2002–03	6,461,112	41,154	431	157
2003–04	4,611,214	36,890	309	125
2004–05	4,946,820	39,575	331	125
2005–06	5,291,187	42,330	285	125
2006–07	5,591,463	44,732	309	125
2007–08	5,454,718	43,638	330	125
2008–09	5,003,754	40,030	322	125

HIGHEST AVERAGE ATTENDANCE IN ONE EUROPEAN CUP SEASON
1959–60 50,545 from a total attendance of 2,780,000.

HIGHEST SCORE IN A EUROPEAN CUP MATCH
Feyenoord (Holland)12, KR Reykjavik (Iceland) 0
(First Round First Leg 1969–70)

HIGHEST AGGREGATE
Benfica (Portugal) 18, Dudelange (Luxembourg) 0
(Preliminary Round 1965–66)

MOST GOALS OVERALL
64 Raul (Real Madrid) 1995–2009.
60 Ruud Van Nistelrooy (PSV Eindhoven, Manchester United and Real Madrid) 1998–2009.
58 Filippo Inzaghi (Juventus, AC Milan) 1995–2009.
56 Andriy Shevchenko (Dynamo Kiev, AC Milan and Chelsea) 1994–2009.

CHAMPIONS LEAGUE BIGGEST WINS
Liverpool 8 Besiktas 0 6.11.2007
Juventus 7, Olympiakos 0 10.12.2003
Marseille 6, CKSA Moscow 0 17.3.93

FIRST TEAM TO SCORE SEVEN GOALS
Paris St Germain 7, Rosenborg 2 24.10.2000

HIGHEST AGGREGATE OF GOALS
Monaco 8, La Coruna 3 05.11.2003

HIGHEST SCORING DRAW
Hamburg 4, Juventus 4 13.9.2000

GREATEST COMEBACKS
Werder Bremen beat Anderlecht 5-3 after being three goals down in 33 minutes on 8.12.1993. They scored five goals in 23 second-half minutes.
La Coruna beat Paris St Germain 4-3 after being three goals down in 55 minutes on 7.3.2001. They scored four goals in 27 second-half minutes.
Liverpool after being three goals down in the first half on 25.5.2005 in the Champions League Final. They scored three goals in five second-half minutes and won the penalty shoot-out after extra time 3-2.
Liverpool 3 goals down to Basle in 29 minutes on 12.11.2002. They scored three second half goals in 24 minutes to draw 3-3.

MOST GOALS IN CHAMPIONS LEAGUE MATCH
4, Marco Van Basten, AC Milan v IFK Gothenburg (33, 53 (pen), 61, 62 mins) 4-0 25.11.1992.
4, Simone Inzaghi, Lazio v Marseille (17, 37, 38, 71 mins) 5-1 14.3.2000.
4, Ruud Van Nistelrooy, Manchester U v Sparta Prague (14, 25 (pen), 60, 90 mins) 4-1 3.11.2004.
4, Dado Prso, Monaco v La Coruna (26, 30, 45, 49, 23 mins) 8-3 5.11.2003.
4, Andriy Shevchenko, AC Milan at Fenerbahce (16, 52, 70, 76,60 mins) 4-0 23.11.2005.

MOST WINS WITH DIFFERENT CLUBS
Clarence Seedorf (Ajax) 1995; (Real Madrid) 1998; (AC Milan) 2003, 2007.

MOST WINNERS MEDALS
6 Francisco Gento (Real Madrid) 1956, 1957, 1958, 1959, 1960, 1966.
5 Alfredo Di Stefano (Real Madrid) 1956, 1957, 1958, 1959, 1960.
5 Jose Maria Zarraga (Real Madrid) 1956, 1957, 1958, 1959, 1960.

4 Jose-Hector Rial (Real Madrid) 1956, 1957, 1958, 1959.
4 Marquitos (Real Madrid) 1956, 1957, 1959, 1960.
4 Phil Neal (Liverpool) 1977, 1978, 1981, 1984.

MOST GOALS SCORED IN FINALS
7 Alfredo Di Stefano (Real Madrid), 1956 (1), 1957 (1 pen), 1958 (1), 1959 (1), 1960 (3).
7 Ferenc Puskas (Real Madrid), 1960 (4), 1962 (3).

MOST FINAL APPEARANCES PER COUNTRY
Italy 25 (11 wins, 14 defeats).
Spain 21 (12 wins, 9 defeats)
England 17 (11 wins, 6 defeats)
Germany 13 (6 wins, 7 defeats)

MOST CLUB FINAL WINNERS
Real Madrid (Spain)   9   1956, 1957, 1958, 1959, 1960, 1966, 1998, 2000, 2002.
AC Milan (Italy)   7   1963, 1969, 1989, 1990, 1994, 2003, 2007.

MOST APPEARANCES IN FINAL
Real Madrid 12; AC Milan 11.

MOST EUROPEAN CUP APPEARANCES
Paolo Maldini (AC Milan)

Season	European Cup	UEFA Cup	Super Cup	WCC
1985–86	0	6	0	0
1987–88	0	2	0	0
1988–89	7	0	0	0
1989–90	8	0	2	1
1990–91	4	0	1	1
1992–93	10	0	0	0
1993–94	10	0	2	1
1994–95	11	0	1	1
1995–96	0	8	0	0
1996–97	6	0	0	0
1999–2000	6	0	0	0
2000–01	14	0	0	0
2001–02	0	4	0	0
2002–03	19	0	0	0
2003–04	9	0	1	1
2004–05	13	0	0	0
2005–06	9	0	0	0
2006–07	9	0	0	0
2007–08	4	0	0	0
2008–09	2	0	0	0
Total	141	20	7	5

MOST SUCCESSFUL MANAGER
Bob Paisley (Liverpool) 1977, 1978, 1981.

FASTEST GOALS SCORED IN CHAMPIONS LEAGUE
10.2 sec   Roy Makaay for Bayern Munich v Real Madrid 7 March 2007.
20.07 sec   Gilberto Silva for Arsenal at PSV Eindhoven 25 September 2002.
20.12 sec   Alessandro Del Piero for Juventus at Manchester United 1 October 1997.

YOUNGEST CHAMPIONS LEAGUE GOALSCORER
Peter Ofori-Quaye for Olympiakos v Rosenborg at 17 years 195 days in 1997–98.

FASTEST HAT-TRICK SCORED IN CHAMPIONS LEAGUE
Mike Newell, 9 mins for Blackburn R v Rosenborg (4-1) 6.12.95.

MOST SUCCESSIVE CHAMPIONS LEAGUE APPEARANCES
Manchester U (England) 13 1996–97 – 2008–09.

MOST SUCCESSIVE EUROPEAN CUP APPEARANCES
Real Madrid (Spain) 15 1955–56 – 1969–70.

MOST SUCCESSIVE WINS IN THE CHAMPIONS LEAGUE
Barcelona (Spain) 11 2002–03.

LONGEST UNBEATEN RUN IN THE CHAMPIONS LEAGUE
Manchester U (England) 25 2007–08 – 2009 (Final).

REINSTATED WINNERS EXCLUDED FROM NEXT COMPETITION
1993 Marseille originally stripped of title. This was rescinded but they were not allowed to compete the following season.

TOP TEN PREMIER LEAGUE AVERAGE ATTENDANCES 2008–09

1	Manchester U	75,304
2	Arsenal	60,040
3	Newcastle U	48,750
4	Liverpool	43,611
5	Manchester C	42,899
6	Chelsea	41,589
7	Sunderland	40,168
8	Aston Villa	39,812
9	Tottenham H	35,929
10	Everton	35,667

TOP TEN FOOTBALL LEAGUE AVERAGE ATTENDANCES 2008–09

1	Derby Co	29,440
2	Sheffield U	26,023
3	Norwich C	24,543
4	Wolverhampton W	24,153
5	Nottingham F	22,299
6	Sheffield W	21,542
7	Ipswich T	20,961
8	Charlton Ath	20,894
9	Reading	19,942
10	Birmingham C	19,090

TOP TEN AVERAGE ATTENDANCES

1	Manchester United	2006–07	75,826
2	Manchester United	2007–08	75,691
3	Manchester United	2008–09	75,308
4	Manchester United	2005–06	68,765
5	Manchester United	2004–05	67,871
6	Manchester United	2003–04	67,641
7	Manchester United	2002–03	67,630
8	Manchester United	2001–02	67,586
9	Manchester United	2000–01	67,544
10	Arsenal	2008–09	60,070

TOP TEN AVERAGE WORLD CUP FINAL CROWDS

1	In USA	1994	68,604
2	In Brazil	1950	60,772
3	In Germany	2006	52,416
4	In Mexico	1970	52,311
5	In England	1966	50,458
6	In Italy	1990	48,368
7	In Mexico	1986	46,956
8	In West Germany	1974	46,684
9	In France	1998	43,366
10	In Argentina	1978	42,374

TOP TEN ALL-TIME ENGLAND CAPS

1	Peter Shilton	125
2	David Beckham	112
3	Bobby Moore	108
4	Bobby Charlton	106
5	Billy Wright	105
6	Bryan Robson	90
7	Michael Owen	89
8	Kenny Sansom	86
9	Gary Neville	85
10	Ray Wilkins	84

TOP TEN ALL-TIME ENGLAND GOALSCORERS

1	Bobby Charlton	49
2	Gary Lineker	48
3	Jimmy Greaves	44
4	Michael Owen	40
5	Tom Finney	30
6	Nat Lofthouse	30
7	Alan Shearer	30
8	Vivian Woodward	29
9	Steve Bloomer	28
10	David Platt	27

GOALKEEPING RECORDS
(without conceding a goal)

BRITISH RECORD (all competitive games)
Chris Woods, Rangers, in 1196 minutes from 26 November 1986 to 31 January 1987.

FA PREMIER LEAGUE
Edwin Van der Sar (Manchester U) in 1311 minutes during the 2008–09 season.

FOOTBALL LEAGUE
Steve Death, Reading, 1103 minutes from 24 March to 18 August 1979.

MOST CLEAN SHEETS IN A SEASON
Peter Cech (Chelsea) 24 2004–05

MOST CLEAN SHEETS OVERALL IN PREMIER LEAGUE
David James (Liverpool, Aston Villa, West Ham U, Manchester C and Portsmouth) 168 games.

MOST GOALS FOR IN A SEASON

FA PREMIER LEAGUE		Goals	Games
1999–2000	Manchester U	97	38

FOOTBALL LEAGUE Division 4			
1960–61	Peterborough U	134	46

SCOTTISH PREMIER LEAGUE			
2003–04	Celtic	105	38

SCOTTISH LEAGUE Division 2			
1937–38	Raith R	142	34

MOST GOALS AGAINST IN A SEASON

FA PREMIER LEAGUE		Goals	Games
1993–94	Swindon T	100	42

FOOTBALL LEAGUE Division 2			
1898–99	Darwen	141	34

SCOTTISH PREMIER LEAGUE			
1999–2000	Aberdeen	83	36

SCOTTISH LEAGUE Division 2			
1931–32	Edinburgh C	146	38

MOST LEAGUE GOALS IN A SEASON

FA PREMIER LEAGUE		Goals	Games
1993–94	Andy Cole (Newcastle U)	34	40
1994–95	Alan Shearer (Blackburn R)	34	42

FOOTBALL LEAGUE Division 1			
1927–28	Dixie Dean (Everton)	60	39

Division 2			
1926–27	George Camsell (Middlesbrough)	59	37

Division 3(S)			
1936–37	Joe Payne (Luton T)	55	39

Division 3(N)			
1936–37	Ted Harston (Mansfield T)	55	41

Division 3			
1959–60	Derek Reeves (Southampton)	39	46

Division 4			
1960–61	Terry Bly (Peterborough U)	52	46

FA CUP			
1887–88	Jimmy Ross (Preston NE)	20	8

LEAGUE CUP			
1986–87	Clive Allen (Tottenham H)	12	9

SCOTTISH PREMIER LEAGUE			
2000–01	Henrik Larsson (Celtic)	35	37

SCOTTISH LEAGUE Division 1			
1931–32	William McFadyen (Motherwell)	52	34

Division 2			
1927–28	Jim Smith (Ayr U)	66	38

MOST FA CUP FINAL GOALS

Ian Rush (Liverpool) 5: 1986(2), 1989(2), 1992(1)

SCORED IN EVERY PREMIERSHIP GAME

Arsenal 2001–02 38 matches

FEWEST GOALS FOR IN A SEASON

FA PREMIER LEAGUE		Goals	Games
2007–08	Derby Co	20	38

FOOTBALL LEAGUE Division 2			
1899–1900	Loughborough T	18	34

SCOTTISH PREMIER LEAGUE			
2001–02	St Johnstone	24	38

SCOTTISH LEAGUE New Division 1			
1980–81	Stirling Alb	18	39

FEWEST GOALS AGAINST IN A SEASON

FA PREMIER LEAGUE		Goals	Games
2004–05	Chelsea	15	38

FOOTBALL LEAGUE Division 1			
1978–79	Liverpool	16	42

SCOTTISH PREMIER LEAGUE			
2001–02	Celtic	18	38

SCOTTISH LEAGUE Division 1			
1913–14	Celtic	14	38

MOST LEAGUE GOALS IN A CAREER

FOOTBALL LEAGUE Arthur Rowley	Goals	Games	Season
WBA	4	24	1946–48
Fulham	27	56	1948–50
Leicester C	251	303	1950–58
Shrewsbury T	152	236	1958–65
	434	619	

SCOTTISH LEAGUE Jimmy McGrory			
Celtic	1	3	1922–23
Clydebank	13	30	1923–24
Celtic	396	375	1924–25
	410	408	

MOST HAT-TRICKS

Career
34 Dixie Dean (Tranmere R, Everton, Notts Co, England)

Division 1 (one season post-war)
6 Jimmy Greaves (Chelsea), 1960–61

Three for one team one match
West, Spouncer, Hooper, Nottingham F v Leicester Fosse, Division 1, 21 April 1909
Barnes, Ambler, Davies, Wrexham v Hartlepools U, Division 4, 3 March 1962
Adcock, Stewart, White, Manchester C v Huddersfield T, Division 2, 7 Nov 1987
Loasby, Smith, Wells, Northampton T v Walsall, Division 3S, 5 Nov 1927
Bowater, Hoyland, Readman, Mansfield T v Rotherham U, Division 3N, 27 Dec 1932

MOST CUP GOALS IN A CAREER

FA CUP (Pre-Second World war)
Henry Cursham 48 (Notts Co)

FA CUP (post-war)
Ian Rush 43 (Chester, Liverpool)

LEAGUE CUP
Geoff Hurst 49 (West Ham U, Stoke C)
Ian Rush 49 (Chester, Liverpool, Newcastle U)

GOALS PER GAME (Football League to 1991–92)

Goals per game	Division 1		Division 2		Division 3		Division 4		Division 3(S)		Division 3(N)	
	Games	Goals	Games	Goals	Games	Goals	Games	Goals	Games	Goals	Games	Goals
0	2465	0	2665	0	1446	0	1438	0	997	0	803	0
1	5606	5606	5836	5836	3225	3225	3106	3106	2073	2073	1914	1914
2	8275	16550	8609	17218	4569	9138	4441	8882	3314	6628	2939	5878
3	7731	23193	7842	23526	3784	11352	4041	12123	2996	8988	2922	8766
4	6229	24920	5897	23588	2837	11348	2784	11136	2445	9780	2410	9640
5	3752	18755	3634	18170	1566	7830	1506	7530	1554	7770	1599	7995
6	2137	12822	2007	12042	769	4614	786	4716	870	5220	930	5580
7	1092	7644	1001	7007	357	2499	336	2352	451	3157	461	3227
8	542	4336	376	3008	135	1080	143	1144	209	1672	221	1768
9	197	1773	164	1476	64	576	35	315	76	684	102	918
10	83	830	68	680	13	130	8	80	33	330	45	450
11	37	407	19	209	2	22	7	77	15	165	15	165
12	12	144	17	204	1	12	0	0	7	84	8	96
13	4	52	4	52	0	0	0	0	2	26	4	52
14	2	28	1	14	0	0	0	0	0	0	0	0
17	0	0	0	0	0	0	0	0	0	0	1	17
	38164	117061	38140	113030	18768	51826	18631	51461	15042	46577	14374	46466

New Overall Totals (since 1992)		Totals (up to 1991–92)		Complete Overall Totals (since 1888–89)	
Games	34588	Games	143119	Games	177707
Goals	88902	Goals	426421	Goals	515323

Extensive research by statisticians has unearthed seven results from early years of the Football League which differ from the original scores. These are 26 January 1889 Wolverhampton W 5 Everton 0 (not 4-0), 16 March 1889 Notts Co 3 Derby Co 5 (not 2-5), 4 January 1896 Arsenal 5 Loughborough 0 (not 6-0), 28 November 1896 Leicester Fosse 4 Walsall 2 (not 4-1), 21 April 1900 Burslem Port Vale v Lincoln City 2-1 (not 2-0), 25 December 1902 Glossop NE 3 Stockport Co 0 (not 3-1), 26 April 1913 Hull C 2 Leicester C 0 (not 2-1).

GOALS PER GAME (from 1992–93)

Goals per game	Premier		Championship/Div 1		League One/Div 2		League Two/Div 3	
	Games	Goals	Games	Goals	Games	Goals	Games	Goals
0	592	0	796	0	746	0	746	0
1	1274	1274	1762	1762	1763	1763	1786	1786
2	1664	3328	2385	4770	2405	4810	2335	4670
3	1368	4104	1995	5985	2053	6159	1987	5961
4	949	3796	1286	5144	1299	5196	1205	4820
5	472	2360	708	3540	677	3385	609	3045
6	234	1404	314	1884	270	1620	288	1728
7	97	679	98	686	121	847	107	749
8	45	360	30	240	32	256	37	296
9	9	81	5	45	15	135	10	90
10	1	10	3	30	3	30	3	30
11	1	11	2	22	0	0	1	11
	6706	17407	9384	24108	9384	24201	9114	23186

A CENTURY OF LEAGUE AND CUP GOALS IN CONSECUTIVE SEASONS

George Camsell   *League*   *Cup*   *Season*
Middlesbrough   59   5   1926–27
(101 goals)   33   4   1927–28
(*Camsell's cup goals were all scored in the FA Cup.*)

Steve Bull
Wolverhampton W   34   18   1987–88
(102 goals)   37   13   1988–89
(*Bull had 12 in the Sherpa Van Trophy, 3 Littlewoods Cup, 3 FA Cup in 1987–88; 11 Sherpa Van Trophy, 2 Littlewoods Cup in 1988–89.*)

PENALTIES

Most in a Season (individual)
Division 1   *Goals*   *Season*
Francis Lee (Manchester C)   13   1971–72

Most awarded in one game
Five   Crystal Palace (4 – 1 scored, 3 missed)
       v Brighton & HA (1 scored), Div 2   1988–89

Most saved in a Season
Division 1
Paul Cooper (Ipswich T)   8 (of 10)   1979–80

MOST GOALS IN A GAME

FA PREMIER LEAGUE
19 Sept 1999 Alan Shearer (Newcastle U)
              5 goals v Sheffield W
4 Mar 1995   Andy Cole (Manchester U)
              5 goals v Ipswich T

FOOTBALL LEAGUE
Division 1
14 Dec 1935 Ted Drake (Arsenal) 7 goals v Aston V
Division 2
5 Feb 1955   Tommy Briggs (Blackburn R)
              7 goals v Bristol R
23 Feb 1957   Neville Coleman (Stoke C) 7 goals v
              Lincoln C
Division 3(S)
13 April 1936 Joe Payne (Luton T) 10 goals v Bristol R
Division 3(N)
26 Dec 1935   Bunny Bell (Tranmere R)
              9 goals v Oldham Ath
Division 3
16 Sept 1969 Steve Earle (Fulham) 5 goals v Halifax T
24 April 1965 Barrie Thomas (Scunthorpe U)
              5 goals v Luton T
20 Nov 1965   Keith East (Swindon T)
              5 goals v Mansfield T
2 Oct 1971   Alf Wood (Shrewsbury T)
              5 goals v Blackburn R
10 Sept 1983 Tony Caldwell (Bolton W)
              5 goals v Walsall
4 May 1987   Andy Jones (Port Vale)
              5 goals v Newport Co
3 April 1990 Steve Wilkinson (Mansfield T)
              5 goals v Birmingham C
5 Sept 1998   Giuliano Grazioli (Peterborough U)
              5 goals v Barnet
6 April 2002 Lee Jones (Wrexham)
              5 goals v Cambridge U
Division 4
26 Dec 1962   Bert Lister (Oldham Ath)
              6 goals v Southport

FA CUP
20 Nov 1971   Ted MacDougall (Bournemouth)
              9 goals v Margate (*1st Round*)
LEAGUE CUP
25 Oct 1989   Frankie Bunn (Oldham Ath)
              6 goals v Scarborough

SCOTTISH LEAGUE
Premier Division
17 Nov 1984   Paul Sturrock (Dundee U)
              5 goals v Morton
Premier League
23 Aug 1996   Marco Negri (Rangers) 5 goals v
              Dundee U
Division 1
14 Sept 1928 Jimmy McGrory (Celtic)
              8 goals v Dunfermline Ath
Division 2
1 Oct 1927   Owen McNally (Arthurlie)
              8 goals v Armadale
2 Jan 1930   Jim Dyet (King's Park)
              8 goals v Forfar Ath
18 April 1936 John Calder (Morton)
              8 goals v Raith R
20 Aug 1937   Norman Hayward (Raith R)
              8 goals v Brechin C

SCOTTISH CUP
12 Sept 1885 John Petrie (Arbroath)
              13 goals v Bon Accord (*1st Round*)

LONGEST SEQUENCE OF CONSECUTIVE SCORING (Individual)

FA PREMIER LEAGUE
Ruud Van Nistelrooy
(Manchester U)   15 in 10 games   2003–04
FOOTBALL LEAGUE RECORD
Tom Phillipson
(Wolverhampton W)   23 in 13 games   1926–27

LONGEST UNBEATEN SEQUENCE

FA PREMIER LEAGUE	*Team*	*Games*
May 2003–October 2004	Arsenal	49
FOOTBALL LEAGUE		
Division 1		
Nov 1977–Dec 1978	Nottingham F	42

LONGEST UNBEATEN CUP SEQUENCE

Liverpool 25 rounds League/Milk Cup 1980–84

LONGEST UNBEATEN SEQUENCE IN A SEASON

FA PREMIER LEAGUE	*Team*	*Games*
2003–04	Arsenal	38
FOOTBALL LEAGUE		
Division 1		
1920–21	Burnley	30

LONGEST UNBEATEN START TO A SEASON

FA PREMIER LEAGUE	*Team*	*Games*
2003–04	Arsenal	38
FOOTBALL LEAGUE		
Division 1		
1973–74	Leeds U	29
1987–88	Liverpool	29

LONGEST SEQUENCE WITHOUT A WIN IN A SEASON

FA PREMIER LEAGUE	*Team*	*Games*
2007–08	Derby Co	32
FOOTBALL LEAGUE	*Team*	*Games*
Division 2		
1983–84	Cambridge U	31

LONGEST SEQUENCE WITHOUT A WIN FROM SEASON'S START

FOOTBALL LEAGUE	*Team*	*Games*
Division 4		
1970–71	Newport Co	25

LONGEST SEQUENCE OF CONSECUTIVE DEFEATS

FOOTBALL LEAGUE	*Team*	*Games*
Division 2		
1898–99	Darwen	18

East Stirling 24 in 2003–04.

LONGEST WINNING SEQUENCE

FA PREMIER LEAGUE	*Team*	*Games*
2001–02 and 2002–03	Arsenal	14
FOOTBALL LEAGUE		
Division 2		
1904–05	Manchester U	14
1905–06	Bristol C	14
1950–51	Preston NE	14
FROM SEASON'S START		
Division 3		
1985–86	Reading	13
SCOTTISH PREMIER LEAGUE		
2003–04	Celtic	25

HIGHEST WINS

Highest win in a First-Class Match
(*Scottish Cup 1st Round*)
Arbroath 36 Bon Accord 0 12 Sept 1885

Highest win in an International Match
England 13 Ireland 0 18 Feb 1882

Highest win in a FA Cup Match
Preston NE 26 Hyde U 0 15 Oct 1887
(*1st Round*)

Highest win in a League Cup Match
West Ham U 10 Bury 0 25 Oct 1983
(*2nd Round, 2nd Leg*)
Liverpool 10 Fulham 0 23 Sept 1986
(*2nd Round, 1st Leg*)

Highest win in an FA Premier League Match
Manchester U 9 Ipswich T 0 4 Mar 1995
Nottingham F 1 Manchester U 8 6 Feb 1999

Highest win in a Football League Match
Division 2 – highest home win
Newcastle U 13 Newport Co 0 5 Oct 1946
Division 3(N) – highest home win
Stockport Co 13 Halifax T 0 6 Jan 1934
Division 2 – highest away win
Burslem Port Vale 0 Sheffield U 10 10 Dec 1892

Highest wins in a Scottish League Match
Scottish Premier League – highest home win
Rangers 7 St Johnstone 0 8 Nov 1998
Celtic 7 Aberdeen 0 16 Oct 1999
Celtic 7 Aberdeen 0 2 Nov 2002
Hibernian 7 Livingston 0 8 Feb 2006
Scottish Division 2 – highest home win
Airdrieonians 15 Dundee Wanderers 1 Dec 1894
Scottish Premier League – away win
Hamilton A 0 Celtic 8 5 Nov 1988

MOST HOME WINS IN A SEASON

Brentford won all 21 games in Division 3(S), 1929–30

RECORD AWAY WINS IN A SEASON

Doncaster R won 18 of 21 games in Division 3(N), 1946–47

CONSECUTIVE AWAY WINS

FA PREMIER LEAGUE
Chelsea 9 games 2004–05

FOOTBALL LEAGUE
Division 1
Tottenham H 10 games (1959–60 (2), 1960–61 (8))

MOST WINS IN A SEASON

	Wins	Games
FA PREMIER LEAGUE		
2004–05　Chelsea	29	38
2005–06　Chelsea	29	38
FOOTBALL LEAGUE		
Division 3(N)		
1946–47　Doncaster R	33	42
SCOTTISH PREMIER LEAGUE		
2001–02　Celtic	33	38
SCOTTISH LEAGUE		
Division 1		
1920–21　Rangers	35	42

MOST POINTS IN A SEASON
(under old system of two points for a win)

	Points	Games
FOOTBALL LEAGUE		
Division 4		
1975–76　Lincoln C	74	46
SCOTTISH LEAGUE		
Division 1		
1920–21　Rangers	76	42

FEWEST WINS IN A SEASON

	Wins	Games
FA PREMIER LEAGUE		
2007–08　Derby Co	1	38
FOOTBALL LEAGUE		
Division 2		
1899–1900　Loughborough T	1	34
SCOTTISH PREMIER LEAGUE		
1998–99　Dunfermline Ath	4	36
SCOTTISH LEAGUE		
Division 1		
1891–92　Vale of Leven	0	22

UNDEFEATED AT HOME OVERALL

Liverpool 85 games (63 League, 9 League Cup, 7 European, 6 FA Cup), Jan 1978–Jan 1981

UNDEFEATED AT HOME LEAGUE

Chelsea 86 games, March 2004–October 2008

UNDEFEATED IN A SEASON

FA PREMIER LEAGUE
2003–04 Arsenal 38 games

FOOTBALL LEAGUE
1889–90 Preston NE 22 games
Division 2
1893–94 Liverpool 22 games

UNDEFEATED AWAY

Arsenal 19 games FA Premier League 2001–02 and 2003–04 (only Preston NE with 11 in 1888–89 had previously remained unbeaten away) in the top flight

HIGHEST AGGREGATE SCORES

FA PREMIER LEAGUE
Portsmouth 7 Reading 4 29 Sept 2007

Highest Aggregate Score England
Division 3(N)
Tranmere R 13 Oldham Ath 4 26 Dec 1935

Highest Aggregate Score Scotland
Division 2
Airdrieonians 15 Dundee Wanderers 1 1 Dec 1894

MOST POINTS IN A SEASON
(three points for a win)

	Points	Games
FA PREMIER LEAGUE		
2004–05　Chelsea	95	38
FOOTBALL LEAGUE		
Championship		
2005–06　Reading	106	46
SCOTTISH PREMIER LEAGUE		
2001–02　Celtic	103	38
SCOTTISH LEAGUE		
New Division 3		
2004–05　Gretna	98	36

FEWEST POINTS IN A SEASON

	Points	Games
FA PREMIER LEAGUE		
2007–08　Derby Co	11	38
FOOTBALL LEAGUE		
Division 2		
1904–05　Doncaster R	8	34
1899–1900　Loughborough T	8	34
SCOTTISH PREMIER LEAGUE		
2005–06　Livingston	18	38
SCOTTISH LEAGUE		
Division 1		
1954–55　Stirling Alb	6	30

ONE DEFEAT IN A SEASON

FA PREMIER LEAGUE		*Defeats*	*Games*
2004–05	Chelsea	1	38

FOOTBALL LEAGUE
Division 1

1990–91	Arsenal	1	38

SCOTTISH PREMIER LEAGUE

2001–02	Celtic	1	38

SCOTTISH LEAGUE
Premier Division
Division 1

1920–21	Rangers	1	42

Division 2

1956–57	Clyde	1	36
1962–63	Morton	1	36
1967–68	St Mirren	1	36

New Division 2

1975–76	Raith R	1	26

MOST DEFEATS IN A SEASON

FA PREMIER LEAGUE		*Defeats*	*Games*
1994–95	Ipswich T	29	42
2005–06	Sunderland	29	38
2007–08	Derby Co	29	38

FOOTBALL LEAGUE
Division 3

1997–98	Doncaster R	34	46

SCOTTISH PREMIER LEAGUE

2005–06	Livingston	28	38

SCOTTISH LEAGUE
New Division 1

1992–93	Cowdenbeath	34	44

NO DEFEATS IN A SEASON

FA PREMIER LEAGUE

2003–04	Arsenal	won 26, drew 12

FOOTBALL LEAGUE
Division 1

1888–89	Preston NE	won 18, drew 4

Division 2

1893–94	Liverpool	won 22, drew 6

SCOTTISH LEAGUE DIVISION 1

1898–99	Rangers	won 18

SENDINGS-OFF

SEASON
451 (League alone)   2003–04
(Before rescinded cards taken into account)

DAY
19 (League)   13 Dec 2003

FA CUP FINAL
Kevin Moran, Manchester U v Everton   1985
Jose Antonio Reyes, Arsenal v Manchester U   2005

QUICKEST
FA Premier League
Andreas Johansson Wigan Ath v Arsenal 7 May 2006
and Keith Gillespie Sheffield U v Reading 20 January
2007 both in 10 seconds
Football League
Walter Boyd, Swansea C v Darlington Div 3 as
substitute in zero seconds   23 Nov 1999

MOST IN ONE GAME
Five: Chesterfield (2) v Plymouth Arg (3) 22 Feb 1997
Five: Wigan Ath (1) v Bristol R (4)   2 Dec 1997
Five: Exeter C (3) v Cambridge U (2)   23 Nov 2002

MOST IN ONE TEAM
Wigan Ath (1) v Bristol R (4)   2 Dec 1997
Hereford U (4) v Northampton T (0)   6 Sept 1992

MOST DRAWN GAMES IN A SEASON

FA PREMIER LEAGUE		*Draws*	*Games*
1993–94	Manchester C	18	42
1993–94	Sheffield U	18	42
1994–95	Southampton	18	42

FOOTBALL LEAGUE
Division 1

1978–79	Norwich C	23	42

Division 3

1997–98	Cardiff C	23	46
1997–98	Hartlepool U	23	46

Division 4

1986–87	Exeter C	23	46

SCOTTISH PREMIER LEAGUE

1998–99	Dunfermline Ath	16	38

SCOTTISH LEAGUE
Premier Division

1993–94	Aberdeen	21	44

New Division 1

1986–87	East Fife	21	44

NEW WEMBLEY RECORDS

ENGLAND UNDER-21 INTERNATIONALS
24.3.07 England Under-21 v Italy Under-21 55,700

TROPHY FINAL
12.5.07 Stevenage B v Kidderminster H   53,262

VASE FINAL
13.5.07 Truro C v AFC Totton   27,754

FA CUP FINAL
19.5.07 Chelsea v Manchester U   89,826

CONFERENCE PLAY-OFF
20.5.07 Morecambe v Exeter C   40,043

LEAGUE 2 PLAY-OFF
26.5.07 Bristol R v Shrewsbury T   61,589

LEAGUE 1 PLAY-OFF
27.5.07 Blackpool v Yeovil T   59,313

CHAMPIONSHIP PLAY-OFF
28.5.07 Derby Co v WBA 74,993

ENGLAND INTERNATIONALS
1.6.07 England v Brazil 88,745

MOST SUCCESSFUL MANAGERS

Sir Alex Ferguson CBE
Manchester U
22 major trophies in 18 seasons:
11 Premier League, 5 FA Cup, 3 League Cup,
2 European Cup, 1 Cup-Winners' Cup.

Aberdeen
1976–86 – 9 trophies:
3 League, 4 Scottish Cup, 1 League Cup, 1 Cup-
Winners' Cup.

Bob Paisley – Liverpool
1974–83 – 13 trophies:
6 League, 3 European Cup, 3 League Cup, 1 UEFA
Cup.

Bill Struth – Rangers
1920–54 – 30 trophies:
18 League, 10 Scottish Cup, 2 League Cup

LEAGUE CHAMPIONSHIP HAT-TRICKS

Huddersfield T	1923–24 to 1925–26
Arsenal	1932–33 to 1934–35
Liverpool	1981–82 to 1983–84
Manchester U	1998–99 to 2000–01
Manchester U	2006–07 to 2008–09

MOST LEAGUE MEDALS

Ryan Giggs (Manchester U) 11: 1993, 1994, 1996, 1997,
1999, 2000, 2001, 2003, 2007, 2008 and 2009

MOST LEAGUE APPEARANCES
(750+ matches)

1005 Peter Shilton (286 Leicester City, 110 Stoke City, 202 Nottingham Forest, 188 Southampton, 175 Derby County, 34 Plymouth Argyle, 1 Bolton Wanderers, 9 Leyton Orient) 1966–97

931 Tony Ford (355 Grimsby T, 9 Sunderland (loan), 112 Stoke C, 114 WBA, 68 Grimsby T, 5 Bradford C (loan), 76 Scunthorpe U, 103 Mansfield T, 89 Rochdale) 1975–2002

909 Graeme Armstrong (204 Stirling A, 83 Berwick R, 353 Meadowbank T, 268 Stenhousemuir, 1 Alloa) 1975–2001

863 Tommy Hutchison (165 Blackpool, 314 Coventry City, 46 Manchester City, 92 Burnley, 178 Swansea City, 68 Alloa) 1965–91

824 Terry Paine (713 Southampton, 111 Hereford United) 1957–77

790 Neil Redfearn (35 Bolton W, 10 Lincoln C (loan), 90 Lincoln C, 46 Doncaster R, 57 Crystal Palace, 24 Watford, 62 Oldham Ath, 292 Barnsley, 30 Charlton Ath, 17 Bradford C, 22 Wigan Ath, 42 Halifax T, 54 Boston U, 9 Rochdale) 1982–2004

782 Robbie James (484 Swansea C, 48 Stoke C, 87 QPR, 23 Leicester C, 89 Bradford C, 51 Cardiff C) 1973–94

777 Alan Oakes (565 Manchester C, 211 Chester C, 1 Port Vale) 1959–84

774 Dave Beasant (340 Wimbledon, 20 Newcastle U, 133 Chelsea, 6 Grimsby T (loan), 4 Wolverhampton W (loan), 88 Southampton, 139 Nottingham F, 27 Portsmouth, 1 Tottenham H (loan), 16 Brighton & HA) 1979–2003

771 John Burridge (27 Workington, 134 Blackpool, 65 Aston Villa, 6 Southend U (loan), 88 Crystal Palace, 39 QPR, 74 Wolverhampton W, 6 Derby Co (loan), 109 Sheffield U, 62 Southampton, 67 Newcastle U, 65 Hibernian, 3 Scarborough, 4 Lincoln C, 3 Aberdeen, 3 Dumbarton, 3 Falkirk, 4 Manchester C, 3 Darlington, 6 Queen of the South) 1968–96

770 John Trollope (all for Swindon Town) 1960–80†

764 Jimmy Dickinson (all for Portsmouth) 1946–65

763 Stuart McCall (395 Bradford C, 103 Everton, 194 Rangers, 71 Sheffield U) 1982–2004

761 Roy Sproson (all for Port Vale) 1950–72

760 Mick Tait (64 Oxford U, 106 Carlisle U, 33 Hull C, 240 Portsmouth, 99 Reading, 79 Darlington, 139 Hartlepool U) 1975–97

758 Ray Clemence (48 Scunthorpe United, 470 Liverpool, 240 Tottenham Hotspur) 1966–87

758 Billy Bonds (95 Charlton Ath, 663 West Ham U) 1964–88

757 Pat Jennings (48 Watford, 472 Tottenham Hotspur, 237 Arsenal) 1963–86

757 Frank Worthington (171 Huddersfield T, 210 Leicester C, 84 Bolton W, 75 Birmingham C, 32 Leeds U, 19 Sunderland, 34 Southampton, 31 Brighton & HA, 59 Tranmere R, 23 Preston NE, 19 Stockport Co) 1966–88

752 Wayne Allison (84 Halifax T, 7 Watford, 195 Bristol C, 101 Swindon T, 74 Huddersfield T, 103 Tranmere R, 73 Sheffield U, 115 Chesterfield)

† record for one club

CONSECUTIVE
401 Harold Bell (401 Tranmere R; 459 in all games) 1946–55

MOST SENIOR MATCHES
1390 Peter Shilton (1005 League, 86 FA Cup, 102 League Cup, 125 Internationals, 13 Under-23, 4 Football League XI, 20 European Cup, 7 Texaco Cup, 5 Simod Cup, 4 European Super Cup, 4 UEFA Cup, 3 Screen Sport Super Cup, 3 Zenith Data Systems Cup, 2 Autoglass Trophy, 2 Charity Shield, 2 Full Members Cup, 1 Anglo-Italian Cup, 1 Football League play-offs, 1 World Club Championship)

MOST FA CUP APPEARANCES
88 Ian Callaghan (79 Liverpool, 7 Swansea C, 2 Crewe Alex)

YOUNGEST PLAYERS

FA Premier League appearance
Matthew Briggs, 16 years 65 days, Fulham v Middlesbrough, 13.5.2007.

FA Premier League scorer
James Vaughan, 16 years 271 days, Everton v Crystal Palace 10.4.2005

Football League appearance
Reuben Noble-Lazarus 15 years 45 days, Barnsley v Ipswich T, FL Championship 30.9.2008

Football League scorer
Ronnie Dix, 15 years 180 days, Bristol Rovers v Norwich City, Division 3S, 3.3.28.

Division 1 appearance
Derek Forster, 15 years 185 days, Sunderland v Leicester City, 22.8.64.

Division 1 scorer
Jason Dozzell, 16 years 57 days as substitute Ipswich Town v Coventry City, 4.2.84

Division 1 hat-tricks
Alan Shearer, 17 years 240 days, Southampton v Arsenal, 9.4.88
Jimmy Greaves, 17 years 10 months, Chelsea v Portsmouth, 25.12.57

FA Cup appearance (any round)
Andy Awford, 15 years 88 days as substitute Worcester City v Boreham Wood, 3rd Qual. rd, 10.10.87

FA Cup proper appearance
Luke Freeman, 15 years 273 days, Gillingham v Barnet 10.11.2007

FA Cup Final appearance
Curtis Weston, 17 years 119 days, Millwall v Manchester U, 2004

FA Cup Final scorer
Norman Whiteside, 18 years 18 days, Manchester United v Brighton & Hove Albion, 1983

FA Cup Final captain
David Nish, 21 years 212 days, Leicester City v Manchester City, 1969

League Cup appearance
Chris Coward, 16 years 30 days, Stockport Co v Sheffield W, 2005

League Cup Final scorer
Norman Whiteside, 17 years 324 days, Manchester United v Liverpool, 1983

League Cup Final captain
Barry Venison, 20 years 7 months 8 days, Sunderland v Norwich City, 1985

OLDEST PLAYERS

FA Premier League appearance
John Burridge 43 years 5 months, Manchester C v QPR 14.5.1995

Football League appearance
Neil McBain, 52 years 4 months, New Brighton v Hartlepools United, Div 3N, 15.3.47 (McBain was New Brighton's manager and had to play in an emergency)

Division 1 appearance
Stanley Matthews, 50 years 5 days, Stoke City v Fulham, 6.2.65

INTERNATIONAL RECORDS

MOST GOALS IN AN INTERNATIONAL

Record/World Cup	Archie Thompson (Australia) 13 goals v American Samoa	11.4.2001
England	Malcolm Macdonald (Newcastle U) 5 goals v Cyprus, at Wembley	16.4.1975
	Willie Hall (Tottenham H) 5 goals v Ireland, at Old Trafford	16.11.1938
	Steve Bloomer (Derby Co) 5 goals v Wales, at Cardiff	16.3.1896
	Howard Vaughton (Aston Villa) 5 goals v Ireland, at Belfast	18.2.1882
Northern Ireland	Joe Bambrick (Linfield) 6 goals v Wales, at Belfast	1.2.1930
Wales	John Price (Wrexham) 4 goals v Ireland, at Wrexham	25.2.1882
	Mel Charles (Cardiff C) 4 goals v Ireland, at Cardiff	11.4.1962
	Ian Edwards (Chester) 4 goals v Malta, at Wrexham	25.10.1978

MOST GOALS IN AN INTERNATIONAL CAREER

		Goals	Games
England	Bobby Charlton (Manchester U)	49	106
Scotland	Denis Law (Huddersfield T, Manchester C, Torino, Manchester U)	30	55
	Kenny Dalglish (Celtic, Liverpool)	30	102
Northern Ireland	David Healy (Manchester U, Preston NE, Leeds U, Fulham, Sunderland)	35	74
Wales	Ian Rush (Liverpool, Juventus)	28	73
Republic of Ireland	Robbie Keane (Wolverhampton W, Coventry C, Internazionale, Leeds U, Tottenham H, Liverpool, Tottenham H)	39	90

HIGHEST SCORES

Record/World Cup Match	Australia	31	American Samoa	0	2001
European Championship	San Marino	0	Germany	13	2006
Olympic Games	Denmark	17	France	1	1908
	Germany	16	USSR	0	1912
Other International Match	Libya	21	Oman	0	1966
European Cup	Feyenoord	12	K R Reykjavik	2	1969
European Cup-Winners' Cup	Sporting Lisbon	16	Apoel Nicosia	1	1963
Fairs & UEFA Cups	Ajax	14	Red Boys	0	1984

GOALSCORING RECORDS

World Cup Final	Geoff Hurst (England) 3 goals v West Germany	1966
World Cup Final tournament	Just Fontaine (France) 13 goals	1958
Career	Artur Friedenreich (Brazil) 1329 goals	1910–30
	Pele (Brazil) 1281 goals	*1956–78
	Franz 'Bimbo' Binder (Austria, Germany) 1006 goals	1930–50
World Cup Finals fastest	Hakan Sukur (Turkey) 10.8 secs v South Korea	2002

Pele subsequently scored two goals in Testimonial matches making his total 1283.

MOST CAPPED INTERNATIONALS IN THE BRITISH ISLES

England	Peter Shilton	125 appearances	1970–90
Northern Ireland	Pat Jennings	119 appearances	1964–86
Scotland	Kenny Dalglish	102 appearances	1971–86
Wales	Neville Southall	92 appearances	1982–97
Republic of Ireland	Steve Staunton	102 appearances	1988–2002

LONDON INTERNATIONAL VENUES

Eleven different venues in the London area have staged full England international games: Kennington Oval, Richmond Athletic Ground, Queen's Club, Crystal Palace, Craven Cottage, The Den, Stamford Bridge, Highbury, Wembley, Selhurst Park, White Hart Lane and Upton Park.

FOOTBALL TITLES FOR YOUR REFERENCE LIBRARY

THE MEN WHO NEVER WERE by Jack Rollin & Tony Brown
The expunged Football League season of 1939–40
ISBN 978-1-905891-11-5.   £12

THE FORGOTTEN CUP by Jack Rollin & Tony Brown
The FA Cup competition of 1945–46
ISBN 978-1-899468-86-7.   £10

CHAMPIONS ALL! by Tony Brown
Results, players, line-ups and review of the Football League and
Premiership champions 1889–2007
ISBN 978-1-905891-02-3.   £32 (signed limited edition)

FOOTBALL LEAGUE PLAYERS' RECORDS 1888–1939
by Michael Joyce
Career details of all Football League players in this period.
ISBN 978-1-899468-67-6.   £25
Three volumes of Scottish players' records are also available.

THE DEFINITIVE NEWTON HEATH by Alan Shury and
Brian Landamore
The story of the club that became Manchester United in 1902,
with contemporary press reports, results, line-ups and player
details
ISBN 978-1-899468-16-4.   £8.99

THE FA CUP COMPLETE RESULTS by Tony Brown
Every result to 2006, including the qualifying rounds.
ISBN 978-1-899468-71-3.   £24
Other "complete results" titles include the FA Amateur Cup,
FA Vase, FA Trophy, Football League Cup and Lancashire Cup.

FOOTBALL LEAGUE & PREMIERSHIP RESULTS AND
DATES
Every result and final table from 1888 to 2006.
ISBN 978-1-899468-00-3.   £16

THE EARLY FA CUP FINALS & THE SOUTHERN
AMATEURS by Keith Warsop
A definitive account of the finals from 1872 to 1883, and the men
who played in them.
ISBN 978-1-899468-78-2.   £15

THE FOOTBALL LEAGUE MATCH BY MATCH 1888–1970
A set of 55 volumes giving detailed results, scorers and line-up
grids for all Football League seasons prior to the first Rothmans
Yearbook of 1970.   £12 per volume.

SoccerData publications are available from Tony Brown, 4 Adrian Close, Beeston,
Nottingham NG9 6FL. Please visit the web site at www.soccerdata.com. 10% of the value
of your order will be a welcome contribution to postage costs. Cheques should be
payable to Tony Brown please.

THE FA BARCLAYS PREMIERSHIP AND COCA-COLA FOOTBALL LEAGUE FIXTURES 2009–10

Reproduced under licence from Football DataCo Limited. All rights reserved. Licence number PRINT/SKYSPOAN/17004a Copyright © and Database Right 2009[/10] The Football Association Premier League Ltd / The Football League Ltd. All rights reserved. No part of this publication may be reproduced, stored in a retrieval system or transmitted in any way or by any means (including photocopying, recording or storing it in any medium by electronic means), without the written permission of the copyright/database right owner. Applications for written permission should be addressed c/o Football DataCo Ltd, 30 Gloucester Place, London W1U 8PL.

*Sky Sports   All fixtures subject to change.

Friday, 7 August 2009
Coca-Cola Football League Championship
Middlesbrough v Sheffield U* (8.00)

Saturday, 8 August 2009
Coca-Cola Football League Championship
Cardiff C v Scunthorpe U
Crystal Palace v Plymouth Arg
Derby Co v Peterborough U
Leicester C v Swansea C
Preston NE v Bristol C
QPR v Blackpool
Reading v Nottingham F
Sheffield W v Barnsley
Watford v Doncaster R
WBA v Newcastle U

Coca-Cola Football League One
Brighton & HA v Walsall
Bristol R v Leyton Orient
Carlisle U v Brentford
Charlton Ath v Wycombe W
Gillingham v Swindon T
Leeds U v Exeter C
Milton Keynes D v Hartlepool U
Norwich C v Colchester U
Oldham Ath v Stockport Co
Southampton v Millwall* (12.45)
Southend v Huddersfield T
Yeovil T v Tranmere R

Coca-Cola Football League Two
Aldershot T v Darlington
Bury v Bournemouth
Cheltenham T v Grimsby T
Crewe Alex v Dagenham & R
Lincoln C v Barnet
Morecambe v Hereford U
Northampton T v Macclesfield T
Notts Co v Bradford C
Port Vale v Rochdale
Rotherham U v Accrington S
Shrewsbury T v Burton Albion
Torquay U v Chesterfield

Sunday, 9 August 2009
Coca-Cola Football League Championship
Coventry C v Ipswich T* (12.45)

Saturday, 15 August 2009
Barclays Premier League
Aston Villa v Wigan Ath
Blackburn R v Manchester C
Bolton W v Sunderland
Chelsea v Hull C* (12.45)
Everton v Arsenal
Portsmouth v Fulham
Stoke C v Burnley
Wolverhampton W v West Ham U

Coca-Cola Football League Championship
Barnsley v Coventry C
Blackpool v Cardiff C
Bristol C v Crystal Palace
Doncaster R v Preston NE
Ipswich T v Leicester C
Newcastle U v Reading* (5.20)
Nottingham F v WBA
Peterborough U v Sheffield W
Plymouth Arg v QPR
Scunthorpe U v Derby Co
Sheffield U v Watford
Swansea C v Middlesbrough

Coca-Cola Football League One
Brentford v Brighton & HA
Colchester U v Yeovil T
Exeter C v Norwich C
Hartlepool U v Charlton Ath
Huddersfield T v Southampton
Leyton Orient v Oldham Ath
Millwall v Carlisle U
Stockport Co v Bristol R
Swindon T v Milton Keynes D
Tranmere R v Gillingham
Walsall v Southend
Wycombe W v Leeds U

Coca-Cola Football League Two
Accrington S v Lincoln C
Barnet v Shrewsbury T
Bournemouth v Rotherham U
Bradford C v Port Vale
Burton Albion v Morecambe
Chesterfield v Northampton T
Dagenham & R v Torquay U
Darlington v Bury
Grimsby T v Crewe Alex
Hereford U v Cheltenham T
Macclesfield T v Notts Co
Rochdale v Aldershot T

Sunday, 16 August 2009
Barclays Premier League
Manchester U v Birmingham C* (1.30)
Tottenham H v Liverpool* (4.00)

Tuesday, 18 August 2009
Barclays Premier League
Arsenal v Bolton W
Birmingham C v Portsmouth
Burnley v Manchester U
Fulham v Blackburn R
Hull C v Tottenham H
Sunderland v Chelsea
West Ham U v Aston Villa
Wigan Ath v Wolverhampton W

Coca-Cola Football League Championship
Barnsley v Preston NE
Blackpool v Derby Co
Bristol C v QPR

Doncaster R v Coventry C
Ipswich T v Crystal Palace
Nottingham F v Watford
Peterborough U v WBA
Plymouth Arg v Cardiff C
Scunthorpe U v Middlesbrough
Sheffield U v Leicester C
Swansea C v Reading

Coca-Cola Football League One
Brentford v Norwich C
Colchester U v Gillingham
Exeter C v Yeovil T
Hartlepool U v Bristol R
Huddersfield T v Brighton & HA
Leyton Orient v Charlton Ath
Millwall v Oldham Ath
Stockport Co v Carlisle U
Swindon T v Southampton
Tranmere R v Milton Keynes D
Walsall v Leeds U
Wycombe W v Southend

Coca-Cola Football League Two
Accrington S v Northampton T
Barnet v Morecambe
Bournemouth v Aldershot T
Bradford C v Lincoln C
Burton Albion v Torquay U
Dagenham & R v Shrewsbury T
Darlington v Crewe Alex
Grimsby T v Rotherham U
Hereford U v Bury
Macclesfield T v Port Vale
Rochdale v Cheltenham T

Wednesday, 19 August 2009
Barclays Premier League
Liverpool v Stoke C
Manchester C v Everton

Coca-Cola Football League Championship
Newcastle U v Sheffield W

Coca-Cola Football League Two
Chesterfield v Notts Co

Saturday, 22 August 2009
Barclays Premier League
Arsenal v Portsmouth
Birmingham C v Stoke C
Burnley v Everton
Hull C v Bolton W
Liverpool v Aston Villa
Manchester C v Wolverhampton W
Sunderland v Blackburn R
West Ham U v Tottenham H
Wigan Ath v Manchester U

Coca-Cola Football League Championship
Cardiff C v Bristol C
Coventry C v Swansea C

Crystal Palace v Newcastle U
Derby Co v Plymouth Arg
Leicester C v Barnsley
Middlesbrough v Doncaster R
Preston NE v Peterborough U
QPR v Nottingham F
Reading v Sheffield U
Sheffield W v Scunthorpe U
Watford v Blackpool
WBA v Ipswich T* (5.20)

Coca-Cola Football League One
Brighton & HA v Stockport Co
Bristol R v Huddersfield T
Carlisle U v Exeter C
Charlton Ath v Walsall
Gillingham v Hartlepool U
Leeds U v Tranmere R
Milton Keynes D v Colchester U
Norwich C v Wycombe W
Oldham Ath v Swindon T
Southampton v Brentford
Southend v Millwall
Yeovil T v Leyton Orient

Coca-Cola Football League Two
Aldershot T v Accrington S
Bury v Grimsby T
Cheltenham T v Bradford C
Crewe Alex v Hereford U
Lincoln C v Burton Albion
Morecambe v Macclesfield T
Northampton T v Bournemouth
Notts Co v Dagenham & R
Port Vale v Darlington
Rotherham U v Rochdale
Shrewsbury T v Chesterfield
Torquay U v Barnet

Sunday, 16 August 2009
Barclays Premier League
Fulham v Chelsea* (4.00)

Saturday, 29 August 2009
Barclays Premier League
Blackburn R v West Ham U
Bolton W v Liverpool
Chelsea v Burnley
Everton v Wigan Ath
Manchester U v Arsenal* (5.15)
Stoke C v Sunderland
Tottenham H v Birmingham C
Wolverhampton W v Hull C

**Coca-Cola Football League
Championship**
Barnsley v Reading
Blackpool v Coventry C
Bristol C v Middlesbrough
Doncaster R v Cardiff C
Ipswich T v Preston NE
Nottingham F v Derby Co
Plymouth Arg v Sheffield W
Scunthorpe U v QPR
Sheffield U v WBA
Swansea C v Watford

Coca-Cola Football League One
Brentford v Oldham Ath
Colchester U v Leeds U
Exeter C v Milton Keynes D
Hartlepool U v Yeovil T
Huddersfield T v Norwich C
Leyton Orient v Carlisle U
Millwall v Brighton & HA
Stockport Co v Southampton
Swindon T v Southend
Tranmere R v Charlton Ath
Walsall v Gillingham
Wycombe W v Bristol R

Coca-Cola Football League Two
Accrington S v Shrewsbury T
Barnet v Notts Co
Bournemouth v Crewe Alex
Bradford C v Torquay U
Burton Albion v Northampton T
Chesterfield v Morecambe
Dagenham & R v Lincoln C
Darlington v Cheltenham T
Grimsby T v Aldershot T
Hereford U v Port Vale
Macclesfield T v Rotherham U
Rochdale v Bury

Sunday, 30 August 2009
Barclays Premier League
Portsmouth v Manchester C* (1.30)
Aston Villa v Fulham* (4.00)

Monday, 31 August 2009
**Coca-Cola Football League
Championship**
Peterborough U v Crystal Palace*
(5.15)
Newcastle U v Leicester C* (7.45)

Saturday, 5 September 2009
Coca-Cola Football League One
Brighton & HA v Wycombe W
Bristol R v Millwall
Carlisle U v Tranmere R
Charlton Ath v Brentford* (12.15)
Gillingham v Exeter C
Leeds U v Stockport Co
Milton Keynes D v Huddersfield T
Norwich C v Walsall
Oldham Ath v Hartlepool U
Southampton v Colchester U
Southend v Leyton Orient
Yeovil T v Swindon T

Coca-Cola Football League Two
Aldershot T v Hereford U
Bury v Accrington S
Cheltenham T v Dagenham & R
Crewe Alex v Macclesfield T
Lincoln C v Darlington
Morecambe v Rochdale
Northampton T v Barnet
Notts Co v Burton Albion
Port Vale v Grimsby T
Rotherham U v Chesterfield
Shrewsbury T v Bradford C
Torquay U v Bournemouth

Saturday, 12 September 2009
Barclays Premier League
Blackburn R v Wolverhampton W
Liverpool v Burnley
Manchester C v Arsenal
Portsmouth v Bolton W
Stoke C v Chelsea
Sunderland v Hull C
Tottenham H v Manchester U
Wigan Ath v West Ham U

**Coca-Cola Football League
Championship**
Coventry C v Bristol C
Crystal Palace v Scunthorpe U
Derby Co v Sheffield U
Leicester C v Blackpool
Middlesbrough v Ipswich T
Preston NE v Swansea C
QPR v Peterborough U
Reading v Doncaster R
Sheffield W v Nottingham F
Watford v Barnsley
WBA v Plymouth Arg

Coca-Cola Football League One
Bristol R v Oldham Ath
Carlisle U v Brighton & HA
Charlton Ath v Southampton
Gillingham v Millwall
Hartlepool U v Wycombe W
Huddersfield T v Brentford
Leyton Orient v Exeter C
Southend v Leeds U
Swindon T v Colchester U
Tranmere R v Walsall
Yeovil T v Stockport Co

Coca-Cola Football League Two
Accrington S v Darlington
Aldershot T v Port Vale
Bournemouth v Lincoln C
Bradford C v Burton Albion
Bury v Cheltenham T
Dagenham & R v Chesterfield
Grimsby T v Hereford U
Macclesfield T v Barnet
Notts Co v Northampton T
Rochdale v Torquay U
Rotherham U v Morecambe
Shrewsbury T v Crewe Alex

Sunday, 13 September 2009
Barclays Premier League
Birmingham C v Aston Villa* (12.00)
Fulham v Everton* (4.15)

**Coca-Cola Football League
Championship**
Cardiff C v Newcastle U* (2.05)

Monday, 14 September 2009
Coca-Cola Football League One
Milton Keynes D v Norwich C* (7.45)

Tuesday, 15 September 2009
**Coca-Cola Football League
Championship**
Coventry C v Sheffield U
Derby Co v Barnsley
Ipswich T v Nottingham F
Leicester C v Peterborough U
Plymouth Arg v Watford
QPR v Crystal Palace
Reading v Cardiff C
Scunthorpe U v Preston NE
Sheffield W v Middlesbrough
Swansea C v Bristol C
WBA v Doncaster R

Wednesday, 16 September 2009
**Coca-Cola Football League
Championship**
Blackpool v Newcastle U

Friday, 18 September 2009
**Coca-Cola Football League
Championship**
Sheffield U v Sheffield W* (7.45)

Saturday, 19 September 2009
Barclays Premier League
Arsenal v Wigan Ath
Aston Villa v Portsmouth
Bolton W v Stoke C
Burnley v Sunderland* (12.45)
Everton v Blackburn R
Hull C v Birmingham C
West Ham U v Liverpool
Wolverhampton W v Fulham

**Coca-Cola Football League
Championship**
Barnsley v Swansea C
Bristol C v Scunthorpe U
Cardiff C v QPR

Crystal Palace v Derby Co
Doncaster R v Ipswich T
Middlesbrough v WBA
Newcastle U v Plymouth Arg
Nottingham F v Blackpool
Peterborough U v Reading
Preston NE v Coventry C
Watford v Leicester C

Coca-Cola Football League One
Brentford v Bristol R
Brighton & HA v Southend
Colchester U v Hartlepool U
Exeter C v Tranmere R
Leeds U v Gillingham
Millwall v Huddersfield T
Norwich C v Charlton Ath
Oldham Ath v Carlisle U
Southampton v Yeovil T
Stockport Co v Leyton Orient
Walsall v Swindon T
Wycombe W v Milton Keynes D

Coca-Cola Football League Two
Barnet v Bradford C
Burton Albion v Dagenham & R
Cheltenham T v Rotherham U
Chesterfield v Macclesfield T
Crewe Alex v Aldershot T
Darlington v Bournemouth
Hereford U v Accrington S
Lincoln C v Shrewsbury T
Morecambe v Notts Co
Northampton T v Rochdale
Port Vale v Bury
Torquay U v Grimsby T

Sunday, 20 September 2009
Barclays Premier League
Manchester U v Manchester C* (1.30)
Chelsea v Tottenham H* (4.00)

Saturday, 26 September 2009
Barclays Premier League
Birmingham C v Bolton W
Blackburn R v Aston Villa
Fulham v Arsenal
Liverpool v Hull C
Manchester C v West Ham U
Portsmouth v Everton* (12.45)
Stoke C v Manchester U
Tottenham H v Burnley
Wigan Ath v Chelsea

Coca-Cola Football League Championship
Blackpool v Peterborough U
Coventry C v Middlesbrough
Derby Co v Bristol C
Ipswich T v Newcastle U
Leicester C v Preston NE
QPR v Barnsley
Reading v Watford
Scunthorpe U v Doncaster R
Sheffield W v Cardiff C
Swansea C v Sheffield U
WBA v Crystal Palace

Coca-Cola Football League One
Bristol R v Brighton & HA
Carlisle U v Southampton
Charlton Ath v Exeter C
Gillingham v Norwich C
Hartlepool U v Walsall
Huddersfield T v Stockport Co
Leyton Orient v Millwall
Milton Keynes D v Leeds U
Southend v Oldham Ath
Swindon T v Wycombe W
Tranmere R v Colchester U
Yeovil T v Brentford

Coca-Cola Football League Two
Accrington S v Crewe Alex
Aldershot T v Cheltenham T
Bournemouth v Burton Albion
Bradford C v Chesterfield
Bury v Lincoln C
Dagenham & R v Morecambe
Grimsby T v Darlington
Macclesfield T v Torquay U
Notts Co v Port Vale
Rochdale v Hereford U
Rotherham U v Barnet
Shrewsbury T v Northampton T

Sunday, 27 September 2009
Barclays Premier League
Sunderland v Wolverhampton W*
  (4.00)

Coca-Cola Football League Championship
Plymouth Arg v Nottingham F* (1.15)

Tuesday, 29 September 2009
Coca-Cola Football League Championship
Barnsley v WBA
Bristol C v Blackpool
Cardiff C v Derby Co
Crystal Palace v Sheffield W
Doncaster R v Swansea C
Middlesbrough v Leicester C
Nottingham F v Scunthorpe U
Peterborough U v Plymouth Arg
Preston NE v Reading
Sheffield U v Ipswich T
Watford v Coventry C

Coca-Cola Football League One
Brentford v Southend
Brighton & HA v Gillingham
Colchester U v Charlton Ath
Exeter C v Swindon T
Leeds U v Carlisle U
Millwall v Yeovil T
Norwich C v Leyton Orient
Oldham Ath v Milton Keynes D
Southampton v Bristol R
Stockport Co v Hartlepool U
Walsall v Huddersfield T
Wycombe W v Tranmere R

Coca-Cola Football League Two
Barnet v Dagenham & R
Burton Albion v Macclesfield T
Cheltenham T v Shrewsbury T
Crewe Alex v Bury
Darlington v Rochdale
Hereford U v Bournemouth
Lincoln C v Notts Co
Morecambe v Bradford C
Northampton T v Rotherham U
Port Vale v Accrington S
Torquay U v Aldershot T

Wednesday, 30 September 2009
Coca-Cola Football League Championship
Newcastle U v QPR

Coca-Cola Football League Two
Chesterfield v Grimsby T

Saturday, 3 October 2009
Barclays Premier League
Aston Villa v Manchester C
Bolton W v Tottenham H
Burnley v Birmingham C
Everton v Stoke C
Hull C v Wigan Ath
Manchester U v Sunderland

West Ham U v Fulham
Wolverhampton W v Portsmouth

Coca-Cola Football League Championship
Barnsley v Ipswich T
Coventry C v Leicester C
Crystal Palace v Blackpool
Derby Co v Sheffield W
Newcastle U v Bristol C
Peterborough U v Nottingham F
Plymouth Arg v Scunthorpe U
Preston NE v WBA* (12.45)
Reading v Middlesbrough
Sheffield U v Doncaster R
Swansea C v QPR
Watford v Cardiff C

Coca-Cola Football League One
Brentford v Swindon T
Brighton & HA v Milton Keynes D
Colchester U v Huddersfield T
Exeter C v Hartlepool U
Leeds U v Charlton Ath
Millwall v Tranmere R
Norwich C v Bristol R
Oldham Ath v Yeovil T
Southampton v Gillingham
Stockport Co v Southend
Walsall v Carlisle U
Wycombe W v Leyton Orient

Coca-Cola Football League Two
Barnet v Grimsby T
Burton Albion v Rochdale
Cheltenham T v Notts Co
Chesterfield v Accrington S
Crewe Alex v Rotherham U
Darlington v Macclesfield T
Hereford U v Dagenham & R
Lincoln C v Aldershot T
Morecambe v Shrewsbury T
Northampton T v Bradford C
Port Vale v Bournemouth
Torquay U v Bury

Sunday, 4 October 2009
Barclays Premier League
Arsenal v Blackburn R* (1.30)
Chelsea v Liverpool* (4.00)

Saturday, 10 October 2009
Coca-Cola Football League One
Bristol R v Leeds U
Carlisle U v Norwich C
Charlton Ath v Oldham Ath
Gillingham v Wycombe W
Hartlepool U v Brentford
Huddersfield T v Exeter C
Leyton Orient v Colchester U
Milton Keynes D v Walsall
Southend v Southampton
Swindon T v Millwall
Yeovil T v Brighton & HA

Coca-Cola Football League Two
Accrington S v Cheltenham T
Aldershot T v Morecambe
Bournemouth v Chesterfield
Bradford C v Crewe Alex
Bury v Northampton T
Dagenham & R v Darlington
Grimsby T v Burton Albion
Macclesfield T v Lincoln C
Notts Co v Torquay U
Rochdale v Barnet
Rotherham U v Hereford U
Shrewsbury T v Port Vale

Monday, 12 October 2009
Coca-Cola Football League One
Tranmere R v Stockport Co* (7.45)

Saturday, 17 October 2009
Barclays Premier League
Arsenal v Birmingham C
Aston Villa v Chelsea* (12.45)
Everton v Wolverhampton W
Fulham v Hull C
Manchester U v Bolton W
Portsmouth v Tottenham H
Stoke C v West Ham U
Sunderland v Liverpool

Coca-Cola Football League
Championship
Blackpool v Plymouth Arg
Bristol C v Peterborough U
Cardiff C v Crystal Palace
Doncaster R v Barnsley
Ipswich T v Swansea C
Leicester C v Derby Co
Middlesbrough v Watford
Nottingham F v Newcastle U* (5.20)
QPR v Preston NE
Scunthorpe U v Sheffield U
Sheffield W v Coventry C
WBA v Reading

Coca-Cola Football League One
Charlton Ath v Huddersfield T
Leyton Orient v Brentford
Milton Keynes D v Gillingham
Oldham Ath v Southampton
Southend v Bristol R
Stockport Co v Millwall
Swindon T v Hartlepool U
Tranmere R v Brighton & HA
Walsall v Exeter C
Wycombe W v Colchester U
Yeovil T v Carlisle U

Coca-Cola Football League Two
Accrington S v Bournemouth
Aldershot T v Bury
Burton Albion v Barnet
Cheltenham T v Macclesfield T
Crewe Alex v Port Vale
Dagenham & R v Bradford C
Darlington v Shrewsbury T
Grimsby T v Rochdale
Hereford U v Chesterfield
Northampton T v Lincoln C
Rotherham U v Notts Co
Torquay U v Morecambe

Sunday, 18 October 2009
Barclays Premier League
Blackburn R v Burnley* (1.00)
Wigan Ath v Manchester C* (4.00)

Monday, 19 October 2009
Coca-Cola Football League One
Leeds U v Norwich C* (7.45)

Tuesday, 20 October 2009
Coca-Cola Football League
Championship
Blackpool v Sheffield U
Bristol C v Plymouth Arg
Cardiff C v Coventry C
Doncaster R v Peterborough U
Ipswich T v Watford
Leicester C v Crystal Palace
Middlesbrough v Derby Co
Nottingham F v Barnsley
QPR v Reading
Scunthorpe U v Newcastle U
Sheffield W v Preston NE
WBA v Swansea C

Saturday, 24 October 2009
Barclays Premier League
Birmingham C v Sunderland
Bolton W v Everton
Burnley v Wigan Ath
Chelsea v Blackburn R
Hull C v Portsmouth
Manchester C v Fulham
Tottenham H v Stoke C
Wolverhampton W v Aston Villa*
(12.45)

Coca-Cola Football League
Championship
Barnsley v Bristol C
Coventry C v WBA
Crystal Palace v Nottingham F
Derby Co v QPR
Newcastle U v Doncaster R
Peterborough U v Scunthorpe U
Plymouth Arg v Ipswich T
Preston NE v Middlesbrough
Reading v Leicester C
Sheffield U v Cardiff C
Swansea C v Blackpool
Watford v Sheffield W

Coca-Cola Football League One
Brentford v Stockport Co
Brighton & HA v Oldham Ath
Bristol R v Yeovil T
Carlisle U v Southend
Colchester U v Walsall
Exeter C v Wycombe W
Gillingham v Charlton Ath
Hartlepool U v Tranmere R
Huddersfield T v Leyton Orient
Millwall v Leeds U
Norwich C v Swindon T
Southampton v Milton Keynes D

Coca-Cola Football League Two
Barnet v Darlington
Bournemouth v Grimsby T
Bradford C v Hereford U
Bury v Rotherham U
Chesterfield v Burton Albion
Lincoln C v Torquay U
Macclesfield T v Dagenham & R
Morecambe v Northampton T
Notts Co v Crewe Alex
Port Vale v Cheltenham T
Rochdale v Accrington S
Shrewsbury T v Aldershot T

Sunday, 25 October 2009
Barclays Premier League
Liverpool v Manchester U* (2.00)
West Ham U v Arsenal* (4.15)

Friday, 30 October 2009
QPR v Leicester C* (7.45)

Saturday, 31 October 2009
Barclays Premier League
Arsenal v Tottenham H* (12.45)
Bolton W v Chelsea
Burnley v Hull C
Everton v Aston Villa
Fulham v Liverpool
Manchester U v Blackburn R
Portsmouth v Wigan Ath
Stoke C v Wolverhampton W
Sunderland v West Ham U

Coca-Cola Football League
Championship
Bristol C v Sheffield W
Cardiff C v Nottingham F
Coventry C v Reading
Doncaster R v Blackpool

Ipswich T v Derby Co
Middlesbrough v Plymouth Arg
Peterborough U v Barnsley
Preston NE v Crystal Palace
Scunthorpe U v Swansea C
WBA v Watford

Coca-Cola Football League One
Brighton & HA v Hartlepool U
Carlisle U v Charlton Ath
Exeter C v Brentford
Leeds U v Yeovil T
Leyton Orient v Southampton
Millwall v Colchester U
Milton Keynes D v Bristol R
Oldham Ath v Huddersfield T
Southend v Gillingham
Stockport Co v Norwich C
Tranmere R v Swindon T
Wycombe W v Walsall

Coca-Cola Football League Two
Bournemouth v Rochdale
Burton Albion v Bury
Cheltenham T v Crewe Alex
Chesterfield v Barnet
Dagenham & R v Port Vale
Grimsby T v Accrington S
Hereford U v Darlington
Macclesfield T v Bradford C
Morecambe v Lincoln C
Notts Co v Shrewsbury T
Rotherham U v Aldershot T
Torquay U v Northampton T

Sunday, 1 November 2009
Barclays Premier League
Birmingham C v Manchester C* (4.00)

Monday, 2 November 2009
Coca-Cola Football League
Championship
Sheffield U v Newcastle U* (7.45)

Friday, 6 November 2009
Coca-Cola Football League
Championship
Derby Co v Coventry C* (7.45)

Saturday, 7 November 2009
Barclays Premier League
Aston Villa v Bolton W
Blackburn R v Portsmouth
Liverpool v Birmingham C
Manchester C v Burnley
Tottenham H v Sunderland
West Ham U v Everton
Wigan Ath v Fulham
Wolverhampton W v Arsenal

Coca-Cola Football League
Championship
Barnsley v Sheffield U
Blackpool v Scunthorpe U
Crystal Palace v Middlesbrough
Leicester C v WBA
Newcastle U v Peterborough U
Nottingham F v Bristol C
Plymouth Arg v Doncaster R
Reading v Ipswich T
Sheffield W v QPR
Swansea C v Cardiff C* (12.45)
Watford v Preston NE

Sunday, 8 November 2009
Barclays Premier League
Hull C v Stoke C* (1.30)
Chelsea v Manchester U* (4.00)

Saturday, 14 November 2009
Coca-Cola Football League One
Brentford v Millwall
Bristol R v Carlisle U
Charlton Ath v Milton Keynes D
Colchester U v Exeter C
Gillingham v Oldham Ath
Hartlepool U v Leyton Orient
Huddersfield T v Wycombe W
Norwich C v Tranmere R
Southampton v Brighton & HA
Swindon T v Leeds U
Walsall v Stockport Co
Yeovil T v Southend

Coca-Cola Football League Two
Accrington S v Dagenham & R
Aldershot T v Macclesfield T
Barnet v Hereford U
Bradford C v Bournemouth
Bury v Notts Co
Crewe Alex v Morecambe
Darlington v Burton Albion
Lincoln C v Cheltenham T
Northampton T v Grimsby T
Port Vale v Rotherham U
Rochdale v Chesterfield
Shrewsbury T v Torquay U

Saturday, 21 November 2009
Barclays Premier League
Birmingham C v Fulham
Burnley v Aston Villa
Chelsea v Wolverhampton W
Hull C v West Ham U
Liverpool v Manchester C* (12.45)
Manchester U v Everton
Sunderland v Arsenal
Tottenham H v Wigan Ath

Coca-Cola Football League Championship
Barnsley v Cardiff C
Coventry C v Crystal Palace
Doncaster R v QPR
Ipswich T v Sheffield W
Leicester C v Plymouth Arg
Middlesbrough v Nottingham F
Preston NE v Newcastle U
Reading v Blackpool
Sheffield U v Peterborough U
Swansea C v Derby Co
Watford v Scunthorpe U
WBA v Bristol C

Coca-Cola Football League One
Brentford v Walsall
Brighton & HA v Leeds U
Bristol R v Gillingham
Carlisle U v Swindon T
Huddersfield T v Hartlepool U
Leyton Orient v Tranmere R
Millwall v Wycombe W
Oldham Ath v Colchester U
Southampton v Norwich C
Southend v Milton Keynes D
Stockport Co v Exeter C
Yeovil T v Charlton Ath

Coca-Cola Football League Two
Barnet v Port Vale
Bradford C v Accrington S
Burton Albion v Hereford U
Chesterfield v Darlington
Dagenham & R v Rochdale
Lincoln C v Grimsby T
Macclesfield T v Bournemouth
Morecambe v Cheltenham T
Northampton T v Crewe Alex
Notts Co v Aldershot T
Shrewsbury T v Bury
Torquay U v Rotherham U

Sunday, 22 November 2009
Barclays Premier League
Bolton W v Blackburn R* (1.30)
Stoke C v Portsmouth* (4.00)

Tuesday, 24 November 2009
Coca-Cola Football League One
Charlton Ath v Bristol R
Colchester U v Stockport Co
Exeter C v Millwall
Gillingham v Yeovil T
Hartlepool U v Southampton
Leeds U v Leyton Orient
Milton Keynes D v Carlisle U
Norwich C v Brighton & HA
Swindon T v Huddersfield T
Tranmere R v Southend
Walsall v Oldham Ath
Wycombe W v Brentford

Coca-Cola Football League Two
Accrington S v Macclesfield T
Aldershot T v Northampton T
Bournemouth v Dagenham & R
Bury v Chesterfield
Cheltenham T v Barnet
Crewe Alex v Burton Albion
Darlington v Morecambe
Grimsby T v Bradford C
Hereford U v Shrewsbury T
Port Vale v Torquay U
Rochdale v Notts Co
Rotherham U v Lincoln C

Saturday, 28 November 2009
Barclays Premier League
Aston Villa v Tottenham H
Blackburn R v Stoke C
Fulham v Bolton W
Manchester C v Hull C
Portsmouth v Manchester U
West Ham U v Burnley
Wigan Ath v Sunderland
Wolverhampton W v Birmingham C

Coca-Cola Football League Championship
Blackpool v Preston NE
Bristol C v Sheffield U
Cardiff C v Ipswich T
Crystal Palace v Watford
Derby Co v Reading
Newcastle U v Swansea C
Nottingham F v Doncaster R
Peterborough U v Middlesbrough
Plymouth Arg v Barnsley
QPR v Coventry C
Scunthorpe U v Leicester C
Sheffield W v WBA

Sunday, 29 November 2009
Barclays Premier League
Everton v Liverpool* (1.30)
Arsenal v Chelsea* (4.00)

Tuesday, 1 December 2009
Coca-Cola Football League One
Brentford v Colchester U
Brighton & HA v Charlton Ath
Bristol R v Exeter C
Carlisle U v Hartlepool U
Huddersfield T v Tranmere R
Leyton Orient v Gillingham
Millwall v Milton Keynes D
Oldham Ath v Leeds U
Southampton v Wycombe W
Southend v Norwich C
Stockport Co v Swindon T
Yeovil T v Walsall

Coca-Cola Football League Two
Barnet v Bournemouth
Bradford C v Rochdale
Burton Albion v Accrington S
Dagenham & R v Aldershot T
Lincoln C v Port Vale
Macclesfield T v Grimsby T
Morecambe v Bury
Northampton T v Hereford U
Notts Co v Darlington
Shrewsbury T v Rotherham U
Torquay U v Cheltenham T

Wednesday, 2 December 2009
Coca-Cola Football League Two
Chesterfield v Crewe Alex

Saturday, 5 December 2009
Barclays Premier League
Arsenal v Stoke C
Aston Villa v Hull C
Blackburn R v Liverpool
Everton v Tottenham H
Fulham v Sunderland
Manchester C v Chelsea
Portsmouth v Burnley
West Ham U v Manchester U
Wigan Ath v Birmingham C
Wolverhampton W v Bolton W

Coca-Cola Football League Championship
Blackpool v Barnsley
Bristol C v Ipswich T
Cardiff C v Preston NE
Crystal Palace v Doncaster R
Derby Co v WBA
Newcastle U v Watford
Nottingham F v Leicester C
Peterborough U v Swansea C
Plymouth Arg v Sheffield U
QPR v Middlesbrough
Scunthorpe U v Coventry C
Sheffield W v Reading

Coca-Cola Football League One
Charlton Ath v Southend
Colchester U v Bristol R
Exeter C v Brighton & HA
Gillingham v Carlisle U
Hartlepool U v Millwall
Leeds U v Huddersfield T
Milton Keynes D v Yeovil T
Norwich C v Oldham Ath
Swindon T v Leyton Orient
Tranmere R v Brentford
Walsall v Southampton
Wycombe W v Stockport Co

Coca-Cola Football League Two
Accrington S v Torquay U
Aldershot T v Chesterfield
Bournemouth v Shrewsbury T
Bury v Barnet
Cheltenham T v Northampton T
Crewe Alex v Lincoln C
Darlington v Bradford C
Grimsby T v Dagenham & R
Hereford U v Notts Co
Port Vale v Morecambe
Rochdale v Macclesfield T
Rotherham U v Burton Albion

Tuesday, 8 December 2009
Coca-Cola Football League Championship
Barnsley v Scunthorpe U
Coventry C v Newcastle U
Doncaster R v Sheffield W
Ipswich T v Peterborough U
Leicester C v Bristol C

Middlesbrough v Blackpool
Preston NE v Derby Co
Reading v Crystal Palace
Sheffield U v Nottingham F
Swansea C v Plymouth Arg
Watford v QPR
WBA v Cardiff C

Saturday, 12 December 2009
Barclays Premier League
Birmingham C v West Ham U
Bolton W v Manchester C
Burnley v Fulham
Chelsea v Everton
Hull C v Blackburn R
Liverpool v Arsenal
Manchester U v Aston Villa
Stoke C v Wigan Ath
Sunderland v Portsmouth
Tottenham H v Wolverhampton W

Coca-Cola Football League Championship
Barnsley v Newcastle U
Coventry C v Peterborough U
Doncaster R v Bristol C
Ipswich T v Blackpool
Leicester C v Sheffield W
Middlesbrough v Cardiff C
Preston NE v Plymouth Arg
Reading v Scunthorpe U
Sheffield U v Crystal Palace
Swansea C v Nottingham F
Watford v Derby Co
WBA v QPR

Coca-Cola Football League One
Brentford v Leeds U
Brighton & HA v Colchester U
Bristol R v Swindon T
Carlisle U v Wycombe W
Huddersfield T v Gillingham
Leyton Orient v Milton Keynes D
Millwall v Walsall
Oldham Ath v Exeter C
Southampton v Tranmere R
Southend v Hartlepool U
Stockport Co v Charlton Ath
Yeovil T v Norwich C

Coca-Cola Football League Two
Barnet v Crewe Alex
Bradford C v Rotherham U
Burton Albion v Aldershot T
Chesterfield v Cheltenham T
Dagenham & R v Bury
Lincoln C v Rochdale
Macclesfield T v Hereford U
Morecambe v Bournemouth
Northampton T v Port Vale
Notts Co v Accrington S
Shrewsbury T v Grimsby T
Torquay U v Darlington

Tuesday, 15 December 2009
Barclays Premier League
Birmingham C v Blackburn R
Bolton W v West Ham U
Burnley v Arsenal
Hull C v Everton
Manchester U v Wolverhampton W
Stoke C v Fulham
Sunderland v Aston Villa
Tottenham H v Manchester C

Wednesday, 16 December 2009
Barclays Premier League
Chelsea v Portsmouth
Liverpool v Wigan Ath

Saturday, 19 December 2009
Barclays Premier League
Arsenal v Hull C
Aston Villa v Stoke C
Blackburn R v Tottenham H
Everton v Birmingham C
Fulham v Manchester U
Manchester C v Sunderland
Portsmouth v Liverpool
West Ham U v Chelsea
Wigan Ath v Bolton W
Wolverhampton W v Burnley

Coca-Cola Football League Championship
Blackpool v WBA
Bristol C v Reading
Cardiff C v Leicester C
Crystal Palace v Barnsley
Derby Co v Doncaster R
Newcastle U v Middlesbrough
Nottingham F v Preston NE
Peterborough U v Watford
Plymouth Arg v Coventry C
QPR v Sheffield U
Scunthorpe U v Ipswich T
Sheffield W v Swansea C

Coca-Cola Football League One
Charlton Ath v Millwall
Colchester U v Carlisle U
Exeter C v Southend
Gillingham v Stockport Co
Hartlepool U v Yeovil T
Leeds U v Southampton
Milton Keynes D v Brentford
Norwich C v Huddersfield T
Swindon T v Brighton & HA
Tranmere R v Bristol R
Walsall v Leyton Orient
Wycombe W v Oldham Ath

Coca-Cola Football League Two
Accrington S v Barnet
Aldershot T v Bradford C
Bournemouth v Notts Co
Bury v Macclesfield T
Cheltenham T v Burton Albion
Crewe Alex v Torquay U
Darlington v Northampton T
Grimsby T v Morecambe
Hereford U v Lincoln C
Port Vale v Chesterfield
Rochdale v Shrewsbury T
Rotherham U v Dagenham & R

Saturday, 26 December 2009
Barclays Premier League
Arsenal v Aston Villa
Birmingham C v Chelsea
Burnley v Bolton W
Fulham v Tottenham H
Hull C v Manchester U
Liverpool v Wolverhampton W
Manchester C v Stoke C
Sunderland v Everton
West Ham U v Portsmouth
Wigan Ath v Blackburn R

Coca-Cola Football League Championship
Cardiff C v Plymouth Arg
Coventry C v Doncaster R
Crystal Palace v Ipswich T
Derby Co v Blackpool
Leicester C v Sheffield U
Middlesbrough v Scunthorpe U
Preston NE v Barnsley
QPR v Bristol C
Reading v Swansea C
Sheffield W v Newcastle U

Watford v Nottingham F
WBA v Peterborough U

Coca-Cola Football League One
Brighton & HA v Leyton Orient
Bristol R v Walsall
Carlisle U v Huddersfield T
Charlton Ath v Swindon T
Gillingham v Brentford
Leeds U v Hartlepool U
Milton Keynes D v Stockport Co
Norwich C v Millwall
Oldham Ath v Tranmere R
Southampton v Exeter C
Southend v Colchester U
Yeovil T v Wycombe W

Coca-Cola Football League Two
Aldershot T v Barnet
Bury v Bradford C
Cheltenham T v Bournemouth
Crewe Alex v Rochdale
Lincoln C v Chesterfield
Morecambe v Accrington S
Northampton T v Dagenham & R
Notts Co v Grimsby T
Port Vale v Burton Albion
Rotherham U v Darlington
Shrewsbury T v Macclesfield T
Torquay U v Hereford U

Monday, 28 December 2009
Barclays Premier League
Aston Villa v Liverpool
Blackburn R v Sunderland
Bolton W v Hull C
Chelsea v Fulham
Everton v Burnley
Manchester U v Wigan Ath
Portsmouth v Arsenal
Stoke C v Birmingham C
Tottenham H v West Ham U
Wolverhampton W v Manchester C

Coca-Cola Football League Championship
Barnsley v Middlesbrough
Blackpool v Sheffield W
Bristol C v Watford
Doncaster R v Leicester C
Ipswich T v QPR
Newcastle U v Derby Co
Nottingham F v Coventry C
Peterborough U v Cardiff C
Plymouth Arg v Reading
Scunthorpe U v WBA
Sheffield U v Preston NE
Swansea C v Crystal Palace

Coca-Cola Football League One
Brentford v Charlton Ath
Colchester U v Southampton
Exeter C v Gillingham
Hartlepool U v Oldham Ath
Huddersfield T v Milton Keynes D
Leyton Orient v Southend
Millwall v Bristol R
Stockport Co v Leeds U
Swindon T v Yeovil T
Tranmere R v Carlisle U
Walsall v Norwich C
Wycombe W v Brighton & HA

Coca-Cola Football League Two
Accrington S v Bury
Barnet v Northampton T
Bournemouth v Torquay U
Bradford C v Shrewsbury T
Burton Albion v Notts Co
Chesterfield v Rotherham U
Dagenham & R v Cheltenham T
Darlington v Lincoln C

Grimsby T v Port Vale
Hereford U v Aldershot T
Macclesfield T v Crewe Alex
Rochdale v Morecambe

Saturday, 2 January 2010
Coca-Cola Football League One
Brentford v Southampton
Colchester U v Milton Keynes D
Exeter C v Carlisle U
Hartlepool U v Gillingham
Huddersfield T v Bristol R
Leyton Orient v Yeovil T
Millwall v Southend
Stockport Co v Brighton & HA
Swindon T v Oldham Ath
Tranmere R v Leeds U
Walsall v Charlton Ath
Wycombe W v Norwich C

Coca-Cola Football League Two
Accrington S v Aldershot T
Barnet v Torquay U
Bournemouth v Northampton T
Bradford C v Cheltenham T
Burton Albion v Lincoln C
Chesterfield v Shrewsbury T
Dagenham & R v Notts Co
Darlington v Port Vale
Grimsby T v Bury
Hereford U v Crewe Alex
Macclesfield T v Morecambe
Rochdale v Rotherham U

Saturday, 9 January 2010
Barclays Premier League
Arsenal v Everton
Birmingham C v Manchester U
Burnley v Stoke C
Fulham v Portsmouth
Hull C v Chelsea
Liverpool v Tottenham H
Manchester C v Blackburn R
Sunderland v Bolton W
West Ham U v Wolverhampton W
Wigan Ath v Aston Villa

Coca-Cola Football League
Championship
Cardiff C v Blackpool
Coventry C v Barnsley
Crystal Palace v Bristol C
Derby Co v Scunthorpe U
Leicester C v Ipswich T
Middlesbrough v Swansea C
Preston NE v Doncaster R
QPR v Plymouth Arg
Reading v Newcastle U
Sheffield W v Peterborough U
Watford v Sheffield U
WBA v Nottingham F

Coca-Cola Football League One
Brighton & HA v Brentford
Bristol R v Stockport Co
Carlisle U v Millwall
Charlton Ath v Hartlepool U
Gillingham v Tranmere R
Leeds U v Wycombe W
Milton Keynes D v Swindon T
Norwich C v Exeter C
Oldham Ath v Leyton Orient
Southampton v Huddersfield T
Southend v Walsall
Yeovil T v Colchester U

Coca-Cola Football League Two
Aldershot T v Rochdale
Bury v Darlington
Cheltenham T v Hereford U
Crewe Alex v Grimsby T

Lincoln C v Accrington S
Morecambe v Burton Albion
Northampton T v Chesterfield
Notts Co v Macclesfield T
Port Vale v Bradford C
Rotherham U v Bournemouth
Shrewsbury T v Barnet
Torquay U v Dagenham & R

Saturday, 16 January 2010
Barclays Premier League
Aston Villa v West Ham U
Blackburn R v Fulham
Bolton W v Arsenal
Chelsea v Sunderland
Everton v Manchester C
Manchester U v Burnley
Portsmouth v Birmingham C
Stoke C v Liverpool
Tottenham H v Hull C
Wolverhampton W v Wigan Ath

Coca-Cola Football League
Championship
Barnsley v Sheffield W
Blackpool v QPR
Bristol C v Preston NE
Doncaster R v Watford
Ipswich T v Coventry C
Newcastle U v WBA
Nottingham F v Reading
Peterborough U v Derby Co
Plymouth Arg v Crystal Palace
Scunthorpe U v Cardiff C
Sheffield U v Middlesbrough
Swansea C v Leicester C

Coca-Cola Football League One
Brentford v Carlisle U
Colchester U v Norwich C
Exeter C v Leeds U
Hartlepool U v Milton Keynes D
Huddersfield T v Southend
Leyton Orient v Bristol R
Millwall v Southampton
Stockport Co v Oldham Ath
Swindon T v Gillingham
Tranmere R v Yeovil T
Walsall v Brighton & HA
Wycombe W v Charlton Ath

Coca-Cola Football League Two
Accrington S v Rotherham U
Barnet v Lincoln C
Bournemouth v Bury
Bradford C v Notts Co
Burton Albion v Shrewsbury T
Chesterfield v Torquay U
Dagenham & R v Crewe Alex
Darlington v Aldershot T
Grimsby T v Cheltenham T
Hereford U v Morecambe
Macclesfield T v Northampton T
Rochdale v Port Vale

Saturday, 23 January 2010
Coca-Cola Football League One
Brighton & HA v Huddersfield T
Bristol R v Hartlepool U
Carlisle U v Stockport Co
Charlton Ath v Leyton Orient
Gillingham v Colchester U
Leeds U v Walsall
Milton Keynes D v Tranmere R
Norwich C v Brentford
Oldham Ath v Millwall
Southampton v Swindon T
Southend v Wycombe W
Yeovil T v Exeter C

Coca-Cola Football League Two
Aldershot T v Bournemouth
Bury v Hereford U
Cheltenham T v Rochdale
Crewe Alex v Darlington
Lincoln C v Bradford C
Morecambe v Barnet
Northampton T v Accrington S
Notts Co v Chesterfield
Port Vale v Macclesfield T
Rotherham U v Grimsby T
Shrewsbury T v Dagenham & R
Torquay U v Burton Albion

Tuesday, 26 January 2010
Barclays Premier League
Bolton W v Burnley
Manchester U v Hull C
Portsmouth v West Ham U
Stoke C v Manchester C
Tottenham H v Fulham
Wolverhampton W v Liverpool

Coca-Cola Football League
Championship
Barnsley v Leicester C
Blackpool v Watford
Bristol C v Cardiff C
Doncaster R v Middlesbrough
Ipswich T v WBA
Nottingham F v QPR
Peterborough U v Preston NE
Plymouth Arg v Derby Co
Scunthorpe U v Sheffield W
Sheffield U v Reading
Swansea C v Coventry C

Wednesday, 27 January 2010
Barclays Premier League
Aston Villa v Arsenal
Blackburn R v Wigan Ath
Chelsea v Birmingham C
Everton v Sunderland

Coca-Cola Football League
Championship
Newcastle U v Crystal Palace

Saturday, 30 January 2010
Barclays Premier League
Arsenal v Manchester U
Birmingham C v Tottenham H
Burnley v Chelsea
Fulham v Aston Villa
Hull C v Wolverhampton W
Liverpool v Bolton W
Manchester C v Portsmouth
Sunderland v Stoke C
West Ham U v Blackburn R
Wigan Ath v Everton

Coca-Cola Football League
Championship
Cardiff C v Doncaster R
Coventry C v Blackpool
Crystal Palace v Peterborough U
Derby Co v Nottingham F
Leicester C v Newcastle U
Middlesbrough v Bristol C
Preston NE v Ipswich T
QPR v Scunthorpe U
Reading v Barnsley
Sheffield W v Plymouth Arg
Watford v Swansea C
WBA v Sheffield U

Coca-Cola Football League One
Brighton & HA v Millwall
Bristol R v Wycombe W
Carlisle U v Leyton Orient
Charlton Ath v Tranmere R

Gillingham v Walsall
Leeds U v Colchester U
Milton Keynes D v Exeter C
Norwich C v Hartlepool U
Oldham Ath v Brentford
Southampton v Stockport Co
Southend v Swindon T
Yeovil T v Huddersfield T

Coca-Cola Football League Two
Aldershot T v Grimsby T
Bury v Rochdale
Cheltenham T v Darlington
Crewe Alex v Bournemouth
Lincoln C v Dagenham & R
Morecambe v Chesterfield
Northampton T v Burton Albion
Notts Co v Barnet
Port Vale v Hereford U
Rotherham U v Macclesfield T
Shrewsbury T v Accrington S
Torquay U v Bradford C

Saturday, 6 February 2010
Barclays Premier League
Birmingham C v Wolverhampton W
Bolton W v Fulham
Burnley v West Ham U
Chelsea v Arsenal
Hull C v Manchester C
Liverpool v Everton
Manchester U v Portsmouth
Stoke C v Blackburn R
Sunderland v Wigan Ath
Tottenham H v Aston Villa

Coca-Cola Football League Championship
Barnsley v Watford
Blackpool v Leicester C
Bristol C v Coventry C
Doncaster R v Reading
Ipswich T v Middlesbrough
Newcastle U v Cardiff C
Nottingham F v Sheffield W
Peterborough U v QPR
Plymouth Arg v WBA
Scunthorpe U v Crystal Palace
Sheffield U v Derby Co
Swansea C v Preston NE

Coca-Cola Football League One
Brentford v Gillingham
Colchester U v Southend
Exeter C v Southampton
Hartlepool U v Leeds U
Huddersfield T v Carlisle U
Leyton Orient v Brighton & HA
Millwall v Norwich C
Stockport Co v Milton Keynes D
Swindon T v Charlton Ath
Tranmere R v Oldham Ath
Walsall v Bristol R
Wycombe W v Yeovil T

Coca-Cola Football League Two
Accrington S v Morecambe
Barnet v Aldershot T
Bournemouth v Cheltenham T
Bradford C v Bury
Burton Albion v Port Vale
Chesterfield v Lincoln C
Dagenham & R v Northampton T
Darlington v Rotherham U
Grimsby T v Notts Co
Hereford U v Torquay U
Macclesfield T v Shrewsbury T
Rochdale v Crewe Alex

Tuesday, 9 February 2010
Barclays Premier League
Arsenal v Liverpool
Fulham v Burnley
Portsmouth v Sunderland
West Ham U v Birmingham C
Wigan Ath v Stoke C
Wolverhampton W v Tottenham H

Coca-Cola Football League Championship
Cardiff C v Peterborough U
Coventry C v Nottingham F
Crystal Palace v Swansea C
Derby Co v Newcastle U
Leicester C v Doncaster R
Middlesbrough v Barnsley
Preston NE v Sheffield U
QPR v Ipswich T
Reading v Plymouth Arg
Sheffield W v Blackpool
Watford v Bristol C
WBA v Scunthorpe U

Wednesday, 10 February 2010
Barclays Premier League
Aston Villa v Manchester U
Blackburn R v Hull C
Everton v Chelsea
Manchester C v Bolton W

Saturday, 13 February 2010
Coca-Cola Football League Championship
Barnsley v Plymouth Arg
Coventry C v QPR
Doncaster R v Nottingham F
Ipswich T v Cardiff C
Leicester C v Scunthorpe U
Middlesbrough v Peterborough U
Preston NE v Blackpool
Reading v Derby Co
Sheffield U v Bristol C
Swansea C v Newcastle U
Watford v Crystal Palace
WBA v Sheffield W

Coca-Cola Football League One
Brentford v Wycombe W
Brighton & HA v Norwich C
Bristol R v Charlton Ath
Carlisle U v Milton Keynes D
Huddersfield T v Swindon T
Leyton Orient v Leeds U
Millwall v Exeter C
Oldham Ath v Walsall
Southampton v Hartlepool U
Southend v Tranmere R
Stockport Co v Colchester U
Yeovil T v Gillingham

Coca-Cola Football League Two
Barnet v Cheltenham T
Bradford C v Grimsby T
Burton Albion v Crewe Alex
Chesterfield v Bury
Dagenham & R v Bournemouth
Lincoln C v Rotherham U
Macclesfield T v Accrington S
Morecambe v Darlington
Northampton T v Aldershot T
Notts Co v Rochdale
Shrewsbury T v Hereford U
Torquay U v Port Vale

Tuesday, 16 February 2010
Coca-Cola Football League Championship
Blackpool v Middlesbrough
Bristol C v Leicester C
Cardiff C v WBA

Crystal Palace v Reading
Derby Co v Preston NE
Nottingham F v Sheffield U
Peterborough U v Ipswich T
Plymouth Arg v Swansea C
QPR v Watford
Scunthorpe U v Barnsley
Sheffield W v Doncaster R

Wednesday, 17 February 2010
Coca-Cola Football League Championship
Newcastle U v Coventry C

Saturday, 20 February 2010
Barclays Premier League
Arsenal v Sunderland
Aston Villa v Burnley
Blackburn R v Bolton W
Everton v Manchester U
Fulham v Birmingham C
Manchester C v Liverpool
Portsmouth v Stoke C
West Ham U v Hull C
Wigan Ath v Tottenham H
Wolverhampton W v Chelsea

Coca-Cola Football League Championship
Blackpool v Reading
Bristol C v WBA
Cardiff C v Barnsley
Crystal Palace v Coventry C
Derby Co v Swansea C
Newcastle U v Preston NE
Nottingham F v Middlesbrough
Peterborough U v Sheffield U
Plymouth Arg v Leicester C
QPR v Doncaster R
Scunthorpe U v Watford
Sheffield W v Ipswich T

Coca-Cola Football League One
Charlton Ath v Yeovil T
Colchester U v Oldham Ath
Exeter C v Stockport Co
Gillingham v Bristol R
Hartlepool U v Huddersfield T
Leeds U v Brighton & HA
Milton Keynes D v Southend
Norwich C v Southampton
Swindon T v Carlisle U
Tranmere R v Leyton Orient
Walsall v Brentford
Wycombe W v Millwall

Coca-Cola Football League Two
Accrington S v Bradford C
Aldershot T v Notts Co
Bournemouth v Macclesfield T
Bury v Shrewsbury T
Cheltenham T v Morecambe
Crewe Alex v Northampton T
Darlington v Chesterfield
Grimsby T v Lincoln C
Hereford U v Burton Albion
Port Vale v Barnet
Rochdale v Dagenham & R
Rotherham U v Torquay U

Tuesday, 23 February 2010
Coca-Cola Football League One
Charlton Ath v Brighton & HA
Colchester U v Brentford
Exeter C v Bristol R
Gillingham v Leyton Orient
Hartlepool U v Carlisle U
Leeds U v Oldham Ath
Milton Keynes D v Millwall
Norwich C v Southend
Swindon T v Stockport Co

Tranmere R v Huddersfield T
Walsall v Yeovil T
Wycombe W v Southampton

Coca-Cola Football League Two
Accrington S v Burton Albion
Aldershot T v Dagenham & R
Bournemouth v Barnet
Bury v Morecambe
Cheltenham T v Torquay U
Crewe Alex v Chesterfield
Darlington v Notts Co
Grimsby T v Macclesfield T
Hereford U v Northampton T
Port Vale v Lincoln C
Rochdale v Bradford C
Rotherham U v Shrewsbury T

Saturday, 27 February 2010
Barclays Premier League
Birmingham C v Wigan Ath
Bolton W v Wolverhampton W
Burnley v Portsmouth
Chelsea v Manchester C
Hull C v Aston Villa
Liverpool v Blackburn R
Manchester U v West Ham U
Stoke C v Arsenal
Sunderland v Fulham
Tottenham H v Everton

Coca-Cola Football League
Championship
Barnsley v Blackpool
Coventry C v Scunthorpe U
Doncaster R v Crystal Palace
Ipswich T v Bristol C
Leicester C v Nottingham F
Middlesbrough v QPR
Preston NE v Cardiff C
Reading v Sheffield W
Sheffield U v Plymouth Arg
Swansea C v Peterborough U
Watford v Newcastle U
WBA v Derby Co

Coca-Cola Football League One
Brentford v Tranmere R
Brighton & HA v Exeter C
Bristol R v Colchester U
Carlisle U v Gillingham
Huddersfield T v Leeds U
Leyton Orient v Swindon T
Millwall v Hartlepool U
Oldham Ath v Norwich C
Southampton v Walsall
Southend v Charlton Ath
Stockport Co v Wycombe W
Yeovil T v Milton Keynes D

Coca-Cola Football League Two
Barnet v Bury
Bradford C v Darlington
Burton Albion v Rotherham U
Chesterfield v Aldershot T
Dagenham & R v Grimsby T
Lincoln C v Crewe Alex
Macclesfield T v Rochdale
Morecambe v Port Vale
Northampton T v Cheltenham T
Notts Co v Hereford U
Shrewsbury T v Bournemouth
Torquay U v Accrington S

Saturday, 6 March 2010
Barclays Premier League
Arsenal v Burnley
Aston Villa v Sunderland
Blackburn R v Birmingham C
Everton v Hull C
Fulham v Stoke C

Manchester C v Tottenham H
Portsmouth v Chelsea
West Ham U v Bolton W
Wigan Ath v Liverpool
Wolverhampton W v Manchester U

Coca-Cola Football League
Championship
Blackpool v Ipswich T
Bristol C v Doncaster R
Cardiff C v Middlesbrough
Crystal Palace v Sheffield U
Derby Co v Watford
Newcastle U v Barnsley
Nottingham F v Swansea C
Peterborough U v Coventry C
Plymouth Arg v Preston NE
QPR v WBA
Scunthorpe U v Reading
Sheffield W v Leicester C

Coca-Cola Football League One
Charlton Ath v Stockport Co
Colchester U v Brighton & HA
Exeter C v Oldham Ath
Gillingham v Huddersfield T
Hartlepool U v Southend
Leeds U v Brentford
Milton Keynes D v Leyton Orient
Norwich C v Yeovil T
Swindon T v Bristol R
Tranmere R v Southampton
Walsall v Millwall
Wycombe W v Carlisle U

Coca-Cola Football League Two
Accrington S v Notts Co
Aldershot T v Burton Albion
Bournemouth v Morecambe
Bury v Dagenham & R
Cheltenham T v Chesterfield
Crewe Alex v Barnet
Darlington v Torquay U
Grimsby T v Shrewsbury T
Hereford U v Macclesfield T
Port Vale v Northampton T
Rochdale v Lincoln C
Rotherham U v Bradford C

Saturday, 13 March 2010
Barclays Premier League
Birmingham C v Everton
Bolton W v Wigan Ath
Burnley v Wolverhampton W
Chelsea v West Ham U
Hull C v Arsenal
Liverpool v Portsmouth
Manchester U v Fulham
Stoke C v Aston Villa
Sunderland v Manchester C
Tottenham H v Blackburn R

Coca-Cola Football League
Championship
Barnsley v Crystal Palace
Coventry C v Plymouth Arg
Doncaster R v Derby Co
Ipswich T v Scunthorpe U
Leicester C v Cardiff C
Middlesbrough v Newcastle U
Preston NE v Nottingham F
Reading v Bristol C
Sheffield U v QPR
Swansea C v Sheffield W
Watford v Peterborough U
WBA v Blackpool

Coca-Cola Football League One
Brentford v Milton Keynes D
Brighton & HA v Swindon T
Bristol R v Tranmere R
Carlisle U v Colchester U

Huddersfield T v Norwich C
Leyton Orient v Walsall
Millwall v Charlton Ath
Oldham Ath v Wycombe W
Southampton v Leeds U
Southend v Exeter C
Stockport Co v Gillingham
Yeovil T v Hartlepool U

Coca-Cola Football League Two
Barnet v Accrington S
Bradford C v Aldershot T
Burton Albion v Cheltenham T
Chesterfield v Port Vale
Dagenham & R v Rotherham U
Lincoln C v Hereford U
Macclesfield T v Bury
Morecambe v Grimsby T
Northampton T v Darlington
Notts Co v Bournemouth
Shrewsbury T v Rochdale
Torquay U v Crewe Alex

Tuesday, 16 March 2010
Coca-Cola Football League
Championship
Barnsley v Nottingham F
Coventry C v Cardiff C
Crystal Palace v Leicester C
Derby Co v Middlesbrough
Peterborough U v Doncaster R
Plymouth Arg v Bristol C
Preston NE v Sheffield W
Reading v QPR
Sheffield U v Blackpool
Swansea C v WBA
Watford v Ipswich T

Wednesday, 17 March 2010
Coca-Cola Football League
Championship
Newcastle U v Scunthorpe U

Saturday, 20 March 2010
Barclays Premier League
Arsenal v West Ham U
Aston Villa v Wolverhampton W
Blackburn R v Chelsea
Everton v Bolton W
Fulham v Manchester C
Manchester U v Liverpool
Portsmouth v Hull C
Stoke C v Tottenham H
Sunderland v Birmingham C
Wigan Ath v Burnley

Coca-Cola Football League
Championship
Blackpool v Crystal Palace
Bristol C v Newcastle U
Cardiff C v Watford
Doncaster R v Sheffield U
Ipswich T v Barnsley
Leicester C v Coventry C
Middlesbrough v Reading
Nottingham F v Peterborough U
QPR v Swansea C
Scunthorpe U v Plymouth Arg
Sheffield W v Derby Co
WBA v Preston NE

Coca-Cola Football League One
Charlton Ath v Gillingham
Leeds U v Millwall
Leyton Orient v Huddersfield T
Milton Keynes D v Southampton
Oldham Ath v Brighton & HA
Southend v Carlisle U
Stockport Co v Brentford
Swindon T v Norwich C
Tranmere R v Hartlepool U

Walsall v Colchester U
Wycombe W v Exeter C
Yeovil T v Bristol R

Coca-Cola Football League Two
Accrington S v Rochdale
Aldershot T v Shrewsbury T
Burton Albion v Chesterfield
Cheltenham T v Port Vale
Crewe Alex v Notts Co
Dagenham & R v Macclesfield T
Darlington v Barnet
Grimsby T v Bournemouth
Hereford U v Bradford C
Northampton T v Morecambe
Rotherham U v Bury
Torquay U v Lincoln C

Tuesday, 23 March 2010
Coca-Cola Football League Championship
Blackpool v Swansea C
Bristol C v Barnsley
Cardiff C v Sheffield U
Doncaster R v Newcastle U
Ipswich T v Plymouth Arg
Leicester C v Reading
Middlesbrough v Preston NE
Nottingham F v Crystal Palace
QPR v Derby Co
Scunthorpe U v Peterborough U
Sheffield W v Watford
WBA v Coventry C

Saturday, 27 March 2010
Barclays Premier League
Birmingham C v Arsenal
Bolton W v Manchester U
Burnley v Blackburn R
Chelsea v Aston Villa
Hull C v Fulham
Liverpool v Sunderland
Manchester C v Wigan Ath
Tottenham H v Portsmouth
West Ham U v Stoke C
Wolverhampton W v Everton

Coca-Cola Football League Championship
Barnsley v Doncaster R
Coventry C v Sheffield W
Crystal Palace v Cardiff C
Derby Co v Leicester C
Newcastle U v Nottingham F
Peterborough U v Bristol C
Plymouth Arg v Blackpool
Preston NE v QPR
Reading v WBA
Sheffield U v Scunthorpe U
Swansea C v Ipswich T
Watford v Middlesbrough

Coca-Cola Football League One
Brentford v Leyton Orient
Brighton & HA v Tranmere R
Bristol R v Southend
Carlisle U v Yeovil T
Colchester U v Wycombe W
Exeter C v Walsall
Gillingham v Milton Keynes D
Hartlepool U v Swindon T
Huddersfield T v Charlton Ath
Millwall v Stockport Co
Norwich C v Leeds U
Southampton v Oldham Ath

Coca-Cola Football League Two
Barnet v Burton Albion
Bournemouth v Accrington S
Bradford C v Dagenham & R
Bury v Aldershot T

Chesterfield v Hereford U
Lincoln C v Northampton T
Macclesfield T v Cheltenham T
Morecambe v Torquay U
Notts Co v Rotherham U
Port Vale v Crewe Alex
Rochdale v Grimsby T
Shrewsbury T v Darlington

Saturday, 3 April 2010
Barclays Premier League
Arsenal v Wolverhampton W
Birmingham C v Liverpool
Bolton W v Aston Villa
Burnley v Manchester C
Everton v West Ham U
Fulham v Wigan Ath
Manchester U v Chelsea
Portsmouth v Blackburn R
Stoke C v Hull C
Sunderland v Tottenham H

Coca-Cola Football League Championship
Bristol C v Nottingham F
Cardiff C v Swansea C
Coventry C v Derby Co
Doncaster R v Plymouth Arg
Ipswich T v Reading
Middlesbrough v Crystal Palace
Peterborough U v Newcastle U
Preston NE v Watford
QPR v Sheffield W
Scunthorpe U v Blackpool
Sheffield U v Barnsley
WBA v Leicester C

Coca-Cola Football League One
Brighton & HA v Southampton
Carlisle U v Bristol R
Exeter C v Colchester U
Leeds U v Swindon T
Leyton Orient v Hartlepool U
Millwall v Brentford
Milton Keynes D v Charlton Ath
Oldham Ath v Gillingham
Southend v Yeovil T
Stockport Co v Walsall
Tranmere R v Norwich C
Wycombe W v Huddersfield T

Coca-Cola Football League Two
Bournemouth v Bradford C
Burton Albion v Rotherham U
Cheltenham T v Lincoln C
Chesterfield v Rochdale
Dagenham & R v Accrington S
Grimsby T v Northampton T
Hereford U v Barnet
Macclesfield T v Aldershot T
Morecambe v Crewe Alex
Notts Co v Bury
Rotherham U v Port Vale
Torquay U v Shrewsbury T

Monday, 5 April 2010
Coca-Cola Football League Championship
Barnsley v Peterborough U
Blackpool v Doncaster R
Crystal Palace v Preston NE
Derby Co v Ipswich T
Leicester C v QPR
Newcastle U v Sheffield U
Nottingham F v Cardiff C
Plymouth Arg v Middlesbrough
Reading v Coventry C
Sheffield W v Bristol C
Swansea C v Scunthorpe U
Watford v WBA

Coca-Cola Football League One
Brentford v Exeter C
Bristol R v Milton Keynes D
Charlton Ath v Carlisle U
Colchester U v Millwall
Gillingham v Southend
Hartlepool U v Brighton & HA
Huddersfield T v Oldham Ath
Norwich C v Stockport Co
Southampton v Leyton Orient
Swindon T v Tranmere R
Walsall v Wycombe W
Yeovil T v Leeds U

Coca-Cola Football League Two
Accrington S v Grimsby T
Aldershot T v Rotherham U
Barnet v Chesterfield
Bradford C v Macclesfield T
Bury v Burton Albion
Crewe Alex v Cheltenham T
Darlington v Hereford U
Lincoln C v Morecambe
Northampton T v Torquay U
Port Vale v Dagenham & R
Rochdale v Bournemouth
Shrewsbury T v Notts Co

Saturday, 10 April 2010
Barclays Premier League
Aston Villa v Everton
Blackburn R v Manchester U
Chelsea v Bolton W
Hull C v Burnley
Liverpool v Fulham
Manchester C v Birmingham C
Tottenham H v Arsenal
West Ham U v Sunderland
Wigan Ath v Portsmouth
Wolverhampton W v Stoke C

Coca-Cola Football League Championship
Barnsley v Derby Co
Bristol C v Swansea C
Cardiff C v Reading
Crystal Palace v QPR
Doncaster R v WBA
Middlesbrough v Sheffield W
Newcastle U v Blackpool
Nottingham F v Ipswich T
Peterborough U v Leicester C
Preston NE v Scunthorpe U
Sheffield U v Coventry C
Watford v Plymouth Arg

Coca-Cola Football League One
Brentford v Huddersfield T
Brighton & HA v Carlisle U
Colchester U v Swindon T
Exeter C v Leyton Orient
Leeds U v Southend
Millwall v Gillingham
Norwich C v Milton Keynes D
Oldham Ath v Bristol R
Southampton v Charlton Ath
Stockport Co v Yeovil T
Walsall v Tranmere R
Wycombe W v Hartlepool U

Coca-Cola Football League Two
Barnet v Macclesfield T
Burton Albion v Bradford C
Cheltenham T v Bury
Chesterfield v Dagenham & R
Crewe Alex v Shrewsbury T
Darlington v Accrington S
Hereford U v Grimsby T
Lincoln C v Bournemouth
Morecambe v Rotherham U
Northampton T v Notts Co

Port Vale v Aldershot T
Torquay U v Rochdale

Tuesday, 13 April 2010
Coca-Cola Football League One
Bristol R v Southampton
Carlisle U v Leeds U
Charlton Ath v Colchester U
Gillingham v Brighton & HA
Hartlepool U v Stockport Co
Huddersfield T v Walsall
Leyton Orient v Norwich C
Milton Keynes D v Oldham Ath
Southend v Brentford
Swindon T v Exeter C
Tranmere R v Wycombe W
Yeovil T v Millwall

Coca-Cola Football League Two
Accrington S v Port Vale
Aldershot T v Torquay U
Bournemouth v Hereford U
Bradford C v Morecambe
Bury v Crewe Alex
Dagenham & R v Barnet
Grimsby T v Chesterfield
Macclesfield T v Burton Albion
Notts Co v Lincoln C
Rochdale v Darlington
Rotherham U v Northampton T
Shrewsbury T v Cheltenham T

Saturday, 17 April 2010
Barclays Premier League
Birmingham C v Hull C
Blackburn R v Everton
Fulham v Wolverhampton W
Liverpool v West Ham U
Manchester C v Manchester U
Portsmouth v Aston Villa
Stoke C v Bolton W
Sunderland v Burnley
Tottenham H v Chelsea
Wigan Ath v Arsenal

Coca-Cola Football League
Championship
Blackpool v Nottingham F
Coventry C v Preston NE
Derby Co v Crystal Palace
Ipswich T v Doncaster R
Leicester C v Watford
Plymouth Arg v Newcastle U
QPR v Cardiff C
Reading v Peterborough U
Scunthorpe U v Bristol C
Sheffield W v Sheffield U
Swansea C v Barnsley
WBA v Middlesbrough

Coca-Cola Football League One
Bristol R v Brentford
Carlisle U v Oldham Ath
Charlton Ath v Norwich C
Gillingham v Leeds U
Hartlepool U v Colchester U
Huddersfield T v Millwall
Leyton Orient v Stockport Co
Milton Keynes D v Wycombe W
Southend v Brighton & HA
Swindon T v Walsall
Tranmere R v Exeter C
Yeovil T v Southampton

Coca-Cola Football League Two
Accrington S v Hereford U
Aldershot T v Crewe Alex
Bournemouth v Darlington
Bradford C v Barnet
Bury v Port Vale
Dagenham & R v Burton Albion

Grimsby T v Torquay U
Macclesfield T v Chesterfield
Notts Co v Morecambe
Rochdale v Northampton T
Rotherham U v Cheltenham T
Shrewsbury T v Lincoln C

Saturday, 24 April 2010
Barclays Premier League
Arsenal v Manchester C
Aston Villa v Birmingham C
Bolton W v Portsmouth
Burnley v Liverpool
Chelsea v Stoke C
Everton v Fulham
Hull C v Sunderland
Manchester U v Tottenham H
West Ham U v Wigan Ath
Wolverhampton W v Blackburn R

Coca-Cola Football League
Championship
Barnsley v QPR
Bristol C v Derby Co
Cardiff C v Sheffield W
Crystal Palace v WBA
Doncaster R v Scunthorpe U
Middlesbrough v Coventry C
Newcastle U v Ipswich T
Nottingham F v Plymouth Arg
Peterborough U v Blackpool
Preston NE v Leicester C
Sheffield U v Swansea C
Watford v Reading

Coca-Cola Football League One
Brentford v Yeovil T
Brighton & HA v Bristol R
Colchester U v Tranmere R
Exeter C v Charlton Ath
Leeds U v Milton Keynes D
Millwall v Leyton Orient
Norwich C v Gillingham
Oldham Ath v Southend
Southampton v Carlisle U
Stockport Co v Huddersfield T
Walsall v Hartlepool U
Wycombe W v Swindon T

Coca-Cola Football League Two
Barnet v Rotherham U
Burton Albion v Bournemouth
Cheltenham T v Aldershot T
Chesterfield v Bradford C
Crewe Alex v Accrington S
Darlington v Grimsby T
Hereford U v Rochdale
Lincoln C v Bury
Morecambe v Dagenham & R
Northampton T v Shrewsbury T
Port Vale v Notts Co
Torquay U v Macclesfield T

Saturday, 1 May 2010
Barclays Premier League
Birmingham C v Burnley
Blackburn R v Arsenal
Fulham v West Ham U
Liverpool v Chelsea
Manchester C v Aston Villa
Portsmouth v Wolverhampton W
Stoke C v Everton
Sunderland v Manchester U
Tottenham H v Bolton W
Wigan Ath v Hull C

Coca-Cola Football League One
Bristol R v Norwich C
Carlisle U v Walsall
Charlton Ath v Leeds U
Gillingham v Southampton

Hartlepool U v Exeter C
Huddersfield T v Colchester U
Leyton Orient v Wycombe W
Milton Keynes D v Brighton & HA
Southend v Stockport Co
Swindon T v Brentford
Tranmere R v Millwall
Yeovil T v Oldham Ath

Coca-Cola Football League Two
Accrington S v Chesterfield
Aldershot T v Lincoln C
Bournemouth v Port Vale
Bradford C v Northampton T
Bury v Torquay U
Dagenham & R v Hereford U
Grimsby T v Barnet
Macclesfield T v Darlington
Notts Co v Cheltenham T
Rochdale v Burton Albion
Rotherham U v Crewe Alex
Shrewsbury T v Morecambe

Sunday, 2 May 2010
Coca-Cola Football League
Championship
Blackpool v Bristol C
Coventry C v Watford
Derby Co v Cardiff C
Ipswich T v Sheffield U
Leicester C v Middlesbrough
Plymouth Arg v Peterborough U
QPR v Newcastle U
Reading v Preston NE
Scunthorpe U v Nottingham F
Sheffield W v Crystal Palace
Swansea C v Doncaster R
WBA v Barnsley

Saturday, 8 May 2010
Coca-Cola Football League One
Brentford v Hartlepool U
Brighton & HA v Yeovil T
Colchester U v Leyton Orient
Exeter C v Huddersfield T
Leeds U v Bristol R
Millwall v Swindon T
Norwich C v Carlisle U
Oldham Ath v Charlton Ath
Southampton v Southend
Stockport Co v Tranmere R
Walsall v Milton Keynes D
Wycombe W v Gillingham

Coca-Cola Football League Two
Barnet v Rochdale
Burton Albion v Grimsby T
Cheltenham T v Accrington S
Chesterfield v Bournemouth
Crewe Alex v Bradford C
Darlington v Dagenham & R
Hereford U v Rotherham U
Lincoln C v Macclesfield T
Morecambe v Aldershot T
Northampton T v Bury
Port Vale v Shrewsbury T
Torquay U v Notts Co

Sunday, 9 May 2010
Barclays Premier League
Arsenal v Fulham
Aston Villa v Blackburn R
Bolton W v Birmingham C
Burnley v Tottenham H
Chelsea v Wigan Ath
Everton v Portsmouth
Hull C v Liverpool
Manchester U v Stoke C
West Ham U v Manchester C
Wolverhampton W v Sunderland

BLUE SQUARE PREMIER FIXTURES 2009–10

Saturday, 8 August 2009
AFC Wimbledon v Luton T
Altrincham T v Ebbsfleet U
Cambridge U v Barrow
Forest Green R v Kettering T
Gateshead v Histon
Grays Ath v Chester C
Kidderminster H v Hayes &
Yeading U
Mansfield T v Crawley T
Oxford U v York C
Rushden & D'monds v Salisbury C
Stevenage B v Tamworth
Wrexham v Eastbourne B

Tuesday, 11 August 2009
Barrow v Altrincham T
Chester C v Gateshead
Crawley T v Forest Green R
Eastbourne B v AFC Wimbledon
Ebbsfleet U v Cambridge U
Hayes & Yeading U v Stevenage B
Histon v Grays Ath
Kettering T v Oxford U
Luton T v Mansfield T
Salisbury C v Kidderminster H
Tamworth v Wrexham
York C v Rushden & D'monds

Saturday, 15 August 2009
Barrow v Stevenage B
Chester C v Cambridge U
Crawley T v Wrexham
Eastbourne B v Rushden & D'monds
Ebbsfleet U v Kidderminster H
Hayes & Yeading U v Altrincham T
Histon v Oxford U
Kettering T v AFC Wimbledon
Luton T v Gateshead
Salisbury C v Mansfield T
Tamworth v Grays Ath
York C v Forest Green R

Tuesday, 18 August 2009
AFC Wimbledon v Salisbury C
Altrincham T v Histon
Cambridge U v Crawley T
Forest Green R v Luton T
Gateshead v Tamworth
Grays Ath v Eastbourne B
Kidderminster H v Kettering T
Mansfield T v Barrow
Oxford U v Chester C
Rushden & D'monds v Hayes &
Yeading U
Stevenage B v Ebbsfleet U
Wrexham v York C

Saturday, 22 August 2009
Altrincham T v AFC Wimbledon
Crawley T v Gateshead
Eastbourne B v Barrow
Grays Ath v Kidderminster H
Hayes & Yeading U v York C
Histon v Salisbury C
Luton T v Chester C
Mansfield T v Ebbsfleet U
Oxford U v Stevenage B
Rushden & D'monds v
Forest Green R
Tamworth v Cambridge U
Wrexham v Kettering T

Saturday, 29 August 2009
AFC Wimbledon v Oxford U
Barrow v Tamworth
Cambridge U v Gateshead
Chester C v Mansfield T
Crawley T v Grays Ath
Ebbsfleet U v Hayes & Yeading U
Forest Green R v Wrexham
Kettering T v Luton T
Kidderminster H v Altrincham T
Salisbury C v Eastbourne B
Stevenage B v Rushden & D'monds
York C v Histon

Monday, 31 August 2009
Altrincham T v Chester C
Eastbourne B v Ebbsfleet U
Gateshead v York C
Grays Ath v AFC Wimbledon
Hayes & Yeading U v Salisbury C
Histon v Stevenage B
Mansfield T v Kettering T
Oxford U v Forest Green R
Rushden & D'monds v Cambridge U
Tamworth v Kidderminster H
Wrexham v Barrow

Tuesday, 1 September 2009
Luton T v Crawley T

Saturday, 5 September 2009
Barrow v Rushden & D'monds
Cambridge U v Forest Green R
Chester C v Histon
Ebbsfleet U v Oxford U
Gateshead v Hayes & Yeading U
Grays Ath v Mansfield T
Kettering T v Altrincham T
Kidderminster H v Eastbourne B
Salisbury C v Luton T
Stevenage B v Wrexham
Tamworth v AFC Wimbledon
York C v Crawley T

Tuesday, 8 September 2009
AFC Wimbledon v Wrexham
Barrow v York C
Cambridge U v Altrincham T
Chester C v Tamworth
Crawley T v Histon
Ebbsfleet U v Rushden & D'monds
Forest Green R v Hayes & Yeading U
Kettering T v Gateshead
Kidderminster H v Mansfield T
Oxford U v Luton T
Salisbury C v Grays Ath
Stevenage B v Eastbourne B

Saturday, 12 September 2009
AFC Wimbledon v Cambridge U
Altrincham T v Crawley T
Eastbourne B v Chester C
Forest Green R v Ebbsfleet U
Gateshead v Salisbury C
Hayes & Yeading U v Tamworth
Histon v Kidderminster H
Luton T v Barrow
Mansfield T v Stevenage B
Rushden & D'monds v Grays Ath
Wrexham v Oxford U
York C v Kettering T

Saturday, 19 September 2009
Barrow v Forest Green R

Cambridge U v Wrexham
Chester C v Stevenage B
Crawley T v Kettering T
Ebbsfleet U v AFC Wimbledon
Grays Ath v Altrincham T
Hayes & Yeading U v Histon
Kidderminster H v Gateshead
Luton T v York C
Oxford U v Eastbourne B
Rushden & D'monds v Mansfield T
Tamworth v Salisbury C

Tuesday, 22 September 2009
AFC Wimbledon v Crawley T
Altrincham T v Tamworth
Eastbourne B v Hayes & Yeading U
Forest Green R v Kidderminster H
Gateshead v Rushden & D'monds
Histon v Ebbsfleet U
Kettering T v Barrow
Mansfield T v Oxford U
Salisbury C v Chester C
Stevenage B v Grays Ath
Wrexham v Luton T
York C v Cambridge U

Saturday, 26 September 2009
AFC Wimbledon v Histon
Cambridge U v Luton T
Crawley T v Rushden & D'monds
Eastbourne B v Tamworth
Forest Green R v Grays Ath
Gateshead v Oxford U
Kettering T v Ebbsfleet U
Mansfield T v Hayes & Yeading U
Salisbury C v Barrow
Stevenage B v Altrincham T
Wrexham v Chester C
York C v Kidderminster H

Tuesday, 29 September 2009
Altrincham T v Gateshead
Barrow v Mansfield T
Chester C v Forest Green R
Ebbsfleet U v Salisbury C
Grays Ath v Cambridge U
Hayes & Yeading U v Kettering T
Histon v Eastbourne B
Kidderminster H v Wrexham
Luton T v Stevenage B
Oxford U v Crawley T
Rushden & D'monds v
AFC Wimbledon
Tamworth v York C

Saturday, 3 October 2009
AFC Wimbledon v Kidderminster H
Barrow v Oxford U
Eastbourne B v Kettering T
Ebbsfleet U v Crawley T
Grays Ath v Gateshead
Hayes & Yeading U v Chester C
Histon v Cambridge U
Luton T v Tamworth
Mansfield T v Forest Green R
Rushden & D'monds v Altrincham T
Wrexham v Salisbury C
York C v Stevenage B

Saturday, 10 October 2009
Altrincham T v Mansfield T
Cambridge U v Ebbsfleet U
Chester C v Rushden & D'monds

Crawley T v Barrow
Forest Green R v AFC Wimbledon
Gateshead v Eastbourne B
Kettering T v Wrexham
Kidderminster H v Luton T
Oxford U v Grays Ath
Salisbury C v York C
Stevenage B v Hayes & Yeading U
Tamworth v Histon

Saturday, 17 October 2009
AFC Wimbledon v Kettering T
Altrincham T v Luton T
Barrow v Ebbsfleet U
Eastbourne B v Mansfield T
Gateshead v Chester C
Hayes & Yeading U v Cambridge U
Histon v Forest Green R
Kidderminster H v Crawley T
Rushden & D'monds v Tamworth
Stevenage B v Salisbury C
Wrexham v Grays Ath
York C v Oxford U

Saturday, 31 October 2009
Cambridge U v Kidderminster H
Chester C v AFC Wimbledon
Crawley T v York C
Ebbsfleet U v Wrexham
Forest Green R v Eastbourne B
Grays Ath v Barrow
Kettering T v Stevenage B
Luton T v Rushden & D'monds
Mansfield T v Histon
Oxford U v Altrincham T
Salisbury C v Gateshead
Tamworth v Hayes & Yeading U

Saturday, 14 November 2009
Altrincham T v Forest Green R
Barrow v AFC Wimbledon
Cambridge U v Kettering T
Crawley T v Mansfield T
Eastbourne B v Salisbury C
Grays Ath v Luton T
Kidderminster H v Oxford U
Rushden & D'monds v Histon
Stevenage B v Gateshead
Tamworth v Chester C
Wrexham v Hayes & Yeading U
York C v Ebbsfleet U

Saturday, 21 November 2009
AFC Wimbledon v York C
Chester C v Altrincham T
Ebbsfleet U v Tamworth
Forest Green R v Stevenage B
Gateshead v Grays Ath
Hayes & Yeading U v Crawley T
Histon v Wrexham
Kettering T v Kidderminster H
Luton T v Cambridge U
Mansfield T v Eastbourne B
Oxford U v Barrow
Salisbury C v Rushden & D'monds

Tuesday, 24 November 2009
AFC Wimbledon v Ebbsfleet U
Barrow v Grays Ath
Cambridge U v Rushden & D'monds
Crawley T v Salisbury C
Eastbourne B v Histon
Forest Green R v Oxford U
Kettering T v Hayes & Yeading U
Mansfield T v Luton T
Stevenage B v Chester C
Tamworth v Altrincham T

Wrexham v Kidderminster H
York C v Gateshead

Saturday, 28 November 2009
Altrincham T v Kettering T
Chester C v Eastbourne B
Ebbsfleet U v Mansfield T
Gateshead v Crawley T
Grays Ath v Tamworth
Hayes & Yeading U v Forest Green R
Histon v York C
Kidderminster H v Barrow
Luton T v AFC Wimbledon
Oxford U v Cambridge U
Rushden & D'monds v Wrexham
Salisbury C v Stevenage B

Tuesday, 1 December 2009
Altrincham T v Barrow
Cambridge U v Chester C
Crawley T v Oxford U
Ebbsfleet U v Stevenage B
Gateshead v Mansfield T
Grays Ath v Histon
Hayes & Yeading U v Eastbourne B
Kidderminster H v Tamworth
Luton T v Kettering T
Rushden & D'monds v York C
Salisbury C v AFC Wimbledon
Wrexham v Forest Green R

Saturday, 5 December 2009
AFC Wimbledon v Gateshead
Barrow v Hayes & Yeading U
Chester C v Luton T
Eastbourne B v Cambridge U
Forest Green R v
    Rushden & D'monds
Histon v Altrincham T
Kettering T v Salisbury C
Mansfield T v Grays Ath
Oxford U v Ebbsfleet U
Stevenage B v Kidderminster H
Tamworth v Crawley T
York C v Wrexham

Tuesday, 8 December 2009
Oxford U v Hayes & Yeading U

Saturday, 19 December 2009
Altrincham T v Eastbourne B
Cambridge U v Oxford U
Crawley T v AFC Wimbledon
Ebbsfleet U v Histon
Gateshead v Kettering T
Grays Ath v York C
Hayes & Yeading U v
    Kidderminster H
Luton T v Forest Green R
Rushden & D'monds v Chester C
Salisbury C v Tamworth
Stevenage B v Barrow
Wrexham v Mansfield T

Saturday, 26 December 2009
AFC Wimbledon v Hayes &
    Yeading U
Barrow v Gateshead
Cambridge U v Stevenage B
Crawley T v Eastbourne B
Ebbsfleet U v Grays Ath
Forest Green R v Salisbury C
Kettering T v Tamworth
Kidderminster H v Chester C
Luton T v Histon
Oxford U v Rushden & D'monds

Wrexham v Altrincham T
York C v Mansfield T

Monday, 28 December 2009
Altrincham T v York C
Chester C v Barrow
Eastbourne B v Luton T
Gateshead v Wrexham
Grays Ath v Crawley T
Hayes & Yeading U v Ebbsfleet U
Histon v Kettering T
Mansfield T v Cambridge U
Rushden & D'monds v
    Kidderminster H
Salisbury C v Oxford U
Stevenage B v AFC Wimbledon
Tamworth v Forest Green R

Friday, 1 January 2010
Altrincham T v Wrexham
Chester C v Kidderminster H
Eastbourne B v Crawley T
Gateshead v Barrow
Grays Ath v Ebbsfleet U
Hayes & Yeading U v
    AFC Wimbledon
Histon v Luton T
Mansfield T v York C
Rushden & D'monds v Oxford U
Salisbury C v Forest Green R
Stevenage B v Cambridge U
Tamworth v Kettering T

Saturday, 16 January 2010
AFC Wimbledon v Mansfield T
Barrow v Histon
Cambridge U v Eastbourne B
Crawley T v Chester C
Ebbsfleet U v Altrincham T
Forest Green R v Gateshead
Kettering T v Rushden & D'monds
Kidderminster H v Grays Ath
Luton T v Salisbury C
Oxford U v Tamworth
Wrexham v Stevenage B
York C v Hayes & Yeading U

Tuesday, 19 January 2010
AFC Wimbledon v Grays Ath
Barrow v Wrexham
Chester C v Salisbury C
Eastbourne B v Stevenage B
Forest Green R v Crawley T
Histon v Rushden & D'monds
Kettering T v Cambridge U
Kidderminster H v Ebbsfleet U
Mansfield T v Altrincham T
Tamworth v Gateshead
York C v Luton T

Saturday, 23 January 2010
Altrincham T v Hayes & Yeading U
Cambridge U v York C
Crawley T v Kidderminster H
Ebbsfleet U v Forest Green R
Gateshead v Luton T
Grays Ath v Oxford U
Mansfield T v Chester C
Rushden & D'monds v Barrow
Salisbury C v Histon
Stevenage B v Kettering T
Tamworth v Eastbourne B
Wrexham v AFC Wimbledon

Saturday, 30 January 2010
AFC Wimbledon v Barrow
Altrincham T v Stevenage B

Chester C v Grays Ath
Eastbourne B v Gateshead
Forest Green R v Mansfield T
Hayes & Yeading U v Rushden &
  D'monds
Histon v Tamworth
Kettering T v Crawley T
Kidderminster H v Cambridge U
Luton T v Ebbsfleet U
Oxford U v Wrexham
York C v Salisbury C

Tuesday, 2 February 2010
Gateshead v Altrincham T

Saturday, 6 February 2010
AFC Wimbledon v Forest Green R
Altrincham T v Salisbury C
Barrow v Luton T
Chester C v Ebbsfleet U
Crawley T v Cambridge U
Eastbourne B v Wrexham
Grays Ath v Rushden & D'monds
Histon v Hayes & Yeading U
Kettering T v York C
Mansfield T v Gateshead
Oxford U v Kidderminster H
Tamworth v Stevenage B

Tuesday, 9 February 2010
Ebbsfleet U v Kettering T
Forest Green R v Chester C
Hayes & Yeading U v Grays Ath
Kidderminster H v AFC Wimbledon
Luton T v Oxford U
Rushden & D'monds v Eastbourne B
Salisbury C v Crawley T
Stevenage B v Mansfield T
Wrexham v Tamworth
York C v Barrow

Saturday, 13 February 2010
Barrow v Kettering T
Cambridge U v AFC Wimbledon
Chester C v Wrexham
Crawley T v Altrincham T
Ebbsfleet U v York C
Grays Ath v Salisbury C
Hayes & Yeading U v Gateshead
Kidderminster H v Forest Green R
Luton T v Eastbourne B
Oxford U v Histon
Rushden & D'monds v Stevenage B
Tamworth v Mansfield T

Saturday, 20 February 2010
AFC Wimbledon v Tamworth
Barrow v Kidderminster H
Eastbourne B v Altrincham T
Forest Green R v Cambridge U
Gateshead v Ebbsfleet U
Histon v Chester C
Kettering T v Grays Ath
Mansfield T v Rushden & D'monds
Salisbury C v Hayes & Yeading U
Stevenage B v Oxford U
Wrexham v Crawley T

Tuesday, 23 February 2010
Grays Ath v Hayes & Yeading U
Oxford U v AFC Wimbledon
York C v Chester C

Saturday, 27 February 2010
Altrincham T v Grays Ath
Cambridge U v Tamworth
Chester C v Oxford U
Crawley T v Luton T
Ebbsfleet U v Barrow
Gateshead v Forest Green R
Hayes & Yeading U v Mansfield T
Kidderminster H v Histon
Rushden & D'monds v Kettering T
Salisbury C v Wrexham
York C v Eastbourne B

Saturday, 6 March 2010
AFC Wimbledon v Altrincham T
Barrow v Cambridge U
Eastbourne B v Kidderminster H
Forest Green R v York C
Hayes & Yeading U v Luton T
Histon v Gateshead
Kettering T v Chester C
Mansfield T v Salisbury C
Stevenage B v Crawley T
Tamworth v Rushden & D'monds
Wrexham v Ebbsfleet U

Saturday, 13 March 2010
AFC Wimbledon v Eastbourne B
Cambridge U v Histon
Chester C v Hayes & Yeading U
Crawley T v Ebbsfleet U
Forest Green R v Barrow
Grays Ath v Stevenage B
Kidderminster H v York C
Luton T v Wrexham
Mansfield T v Tamworth
Oxford U v Kettering T
Rushden & D'monds v Gateshead
Salisbury C v Altrincham T

Tuesday, 16 March 2010
Cambridge U v Salisbury C
Luton T v Kidderminster H
Stevenage B v Histon

Saturday, 20 March 2010
Altrincham T v Rushden & D'monds
Barrow v Crawley T
Eastbourne B v Grays Ath
Ebbsfleet U v Luton T
Gateshead v Stevenage B
Histon v Mansfield T
Kettering T v Forest Green R
Tamworth v Oxford U
Wrexham v Cambridge U
York C v AFC Wimbledon

Saturday, 27 March 2010
AFC Wimbledon v Rushden &
  D'monds
Barrow v Eastbourne B
Cambridge U v Grays Ath
Crawley T v Stevenage B
Ebbsfleet U v Chester C
Forest Green R v Altrincham T
Kettering T v Mansfield T
Kidderminster H v Salisbury C
Luton T v Hayes & Yeading U
Oxford U v Gateshead
Wrexham v Histon
York C v Tamworth

Saturday, 3 April 2010
Altrincham T v Kidderminster H
Chester C v York C
Eastbourne B v Forest Green R
Gateshead v Cambridge U
Grays Ath v Kettering T
Hayes & Yeading U v Oxford U
Histon v AFC Wimbledon
Mansfield T v Wrexham
Rushden & D'monds v Crawley T
Salisbury C v Ebbsfleet U
Stevenage B v Luton T
Tamworth v Barrow

Monday, 5 April 2010
AFC Wimbledon v Stevenage B
Barrow v Chester C
Cambridge U v Mansfield T
Crawley T v Hayes & Yeading U
Ebbsfleet U v Eastbourne B
Forest Green R v Tamworth
Kettering T v Histon
Kidderminster H v Rushden &
  D'monds
Luton T v Grays Ath
Oxford U v Salisbury C
Wrexham v Gateshead
York C v Altrincham T

Saturday, 10 April 2010
Altrincham T v Oxford U
Chester C v Kettering T
Eastbourne B v York C
Gateshead v Kidderminster H
Grays Ath v Wrexham
Hayes & Yeading U v Barrow
Histon v Crawley T
Mansfield T v AFC Wimbledon
Rushden & D'monds v Ebbsfleet U
Salisbury C v Cambridge U
Stevenage B v Forest Green R
Tamworth v Luton T

Saturday, 17 April 2010
AFC Wimbledon v Chester C
Barrow v Salisbury C
Cambridge U v Hayes & Yeading U
Crawley T v Tamworth
Ebbsfleet U v Gateshead
Forest Green R v Histon
Kettering T v Eastbourne B
Kidderminster H v Stevenage B
Luton T v Altrincham T
Oxford U v Mansfield T
Wrexham v Rushden & D'monds
York C v Grays Ath

Saturday, 24 April 2010
Altrincham T v Cambridge U
Chester C v Crawley T
Eastbourne B v Oxford U
Gateshead v AFC Wimbledon
Grays Ath v Forest Green R
Hayes & Yeading U v Wrexham
Histon v Barrow
Mansfield T v Kidderminster H
Rushden & D'monds v Luton T
Salisbury C v Kettering T
Stevenage B v York C
Tamworth v Ebbsfleet U

THE SCOTTISH PREMIER LEAGUE AND FOOTBALL LEAGUE FIXTURES 2009–10

Reproduced under licence from Football DataCo Limited. All rights reserved. Licence number PRINT/SKYSPOAN/17004a Copyright © and Database Right 2009[/10] The Scottish Premier League / The Scottish Football League Limited 2008. All rights reserved. No part of this publication may be reproduced, stored in a retrieval system or transmitted in any way or by any means (including photocopying, recording or storing it in any medium by electronic means), without the written permission of the copyright/database right owner. Applications for written permission should be addressed c/o Football DataCo Ltd, 30 Gloucester Place, London W1U 8PL.

Saturday, 8 August 2009
Irn-Bru First Division
Ayr U v Partick Th
Dundee v Morton
Dunfermline Ath v Inverness CT
Queen of the S v Raith R
Ross Co v Livingston

Irn-Bru Second Division
Airdrie Utd v Arbroath
Dumbarton v Alloa Ath
East Fife v Brechin C
Peterhead v Clyde
Stirling Alb v Stenhousemuir

Irn-Bru Third Division
Berwick R v Annan Ath
East Stirlingshire v Cowdenbeath
Montrose v Elgin C
Queen's Park v Forfar Ath
Stranraer v Albion

Saturday, 15 August 2009
Clydesdale Bank Premier League
Aberdeen v Celtic
Dundee U v Hearts
Hibernian v St Mirren
Kilmarnock v Hamilton A
Rangers v Falkirk
St Johnstone v Motherwell

Irn-Bru First Division
Inverness CT v Ayr U
Livingston v Queen of the S
Morton v Dunfermline Ath
Partick Th v Ross Co
Raith R v Dundee

Irn-Bru Second Division
Alloa Ath v Peterhead
Arbroath v Dumbarton
Brechin C v Airdrie Utd
Clyde v Stirling Alb
Stenhousemuir v East Fife

Irn-Bru Third Division
Albion v Berwick R
Annan Ath v East Stirlingshire
Cowdenbeath v Montrose
Elgin C v Queen's Park
Forfar Ath v Stranraer

Saturday, 22 August 2009
Clydesdale Bank Premier League
Celtic v St Johnstone
Falkirk v Hibernian
Hamilton A v Aberdeen
Motherwell v Kilmarnock
St Mirren v Dundee U

Irn-Bru First Division
Ayr U v Morton
Dundee v Inverness CT
Dunfermline Ath v Livingston

Queen of the S v Partick Th
Ross Co v Raith R

Irn-Bru Second Division
Airdrie Utd v Alloa Ath
Dumbarton v Clyde
East Fife v Arbroath
Peterhead v Stenhousemuir
Stirling Alb v Brechin C

Irn-Bru Third Division
Berwick R v Cowdenbeath
East Stirlingshire v Elgin C
Montrose v Forfar Ath
Stranraer v Annan Ath

Sunday, 23 August 2009
Clydesdale Bank Premier League
Hearts v Rangers

Irn-Bru Third Division
Queen's Park v Albion

Saturday, 29 August 2009
Clydesdale Bank Premier League
Aberdeen v Motherwell
Dundee U v Falkirk
Hibernian v Celtic
Kilmarnock v St Mirren
Rangers v Hamilton A

Irn-Bru First Division
Dunfermline Ath v Raith R
Inverness CT v Ross Co
Livingston v Dundee
Partick Th v Morton
Queen of the S v Ayr U

Irn-Bru Second Division
Brechin C v Dumbarton
Clyde v Alloa Ath
East Fife v Airdrie Utd
Stenhousemuir v Arbroath
Stirling Alb v Peterhead

Irn-Bru Third Division
Albion v Cowdenbeath
Berwick R v Queen's Park
Elgin C v Annan Ath
Forfar Ath v East Stirlingshire
Stranraer v Montrose

Sunday, 30 August 2009
Clydesdale Bank Premier League
St Johnstone v Hearts

Saturday, 12 September 2009
Clydesdale Bank Premier League
Celtic v Dundee U
Falkirk v Aberdeen
Hearts v Kilmarnock
Motherwell v Rangers
St Mirren v St Johnstone

Irn-Bru First Division
Ayr U v Livingston
Dundee v Dunfermline Ath
Morton v Inverness CT
Raith R v Partick Th
Ross Co v Queen of the S

Irn-Bru Second Division
Airdrie Utd v Clyde
Alloa Ath v Stirling Alb
Arbroath v Brechin C
Dumbarton v Stenhousemuir
Peterhead v East Fife

Irn-Bru Third Division
Annan Ath v Forfar Ath
Berwick R v Stranraer
Cowdenbeath v Elgin C
East Stirlingshire v Queen's Park
Montrose v Albion

Sunday, 13 September 2009
Clydesdale Bank Premier League
Hamilton A v Hibernian

Saturday, 19 September 2009
Clydesdale Bank Premier League
Aberdeen v St Mirren
Celtic v Hearts
Dundee U v Motherwell
Hamilton A v Falkirk
Hibernian v St Johnstone
Kilmarnock v Rangers

Irn-Bru First Division
Livingston v Inverness CT
Partick Th v Dunfermline Ath
Queen of the S v Dundee
Raith R v Morton
Ross Co v Ayr U

Irn-Bru Second Division
Arbroath v Peterhead
Clyde v Brechin C
Dumbarton v Airdrie Utd
Stenhousemuir v Alloa Ath
Stirling Alb v East Fife

Irn-Bru Third Division
Albion v Forfar Ath
Elgin C v Berwick R
Montrose v East Stirlingshire
Queen's Park v Annan Ath
Stranraer v Cowdenbeath

Saturday, 26 September 2009
Clydesdale Bank Premier League
Falkirk v Kilmarnock
Hearts v Hamilton A
Motherwell v Hibernian
Rangers v Aberdeen
St Johnstone v Dundee U
St Mirren v Celtic

Irn-Bru First Division
Ayr U v Raith R
Dundee v Ross Co
Dunfermline Ath v Queen of the S
Inverness CT v Partick Th
Morton v Livingston

Irn-Bru Second Division
Airdrie Utd v Stirling Alb
Alloa Ath v Arbroath
Brechin C v Stenhousemuir
East Fife v Clyde
Peterhead v Dumbarton

Irn-Bru Third Division
Annan Ath v Albion
Berwick R v Montrose
Cowdenbeath v Queen's Park
East Stirlingshire v Stranraer
Forfar Ath v Elgin C

Saturday, 3 October 2009
Clydesdale Bank Premier League
Hamilton A v St Johnstone
Hibernian v Dundee U
Kilmarnock v Aberdeen
Motherwell v Falkirk
Rangers v Celtic
St Mirren v Hearts

Irn-Bru First Division
Ayr U v Dundee
Partick Th v Livingston
Queen of the S v Morton
Raith R v Inverness CT
Ross Co v Dunfermline Ath

Irn-Bru Second Division
Alloa Ath v East Fife
Arbroath v Clyde
Dumbarton v Stirling Alb
Peterhead v Brechin C
Stenhousemuir v Airdrie Utd

Irn-Bru Third Division
Albion v East Stirlingshire
Berwick R v Forfar Ath
Cowdenbeath v Annan Ath
Montrose v Queen's Park
Stranraer v Elgin C

Saturday, 10 October 2009
Irn-Bru First Division
Dundee v Partick Th
Dunfermline Ath v Ayr U
Inverness CT v Queen of the S
Livingston v Raith R
Morton v Ross Co

Irn-Bru Second Division
Airdrie Utd v Peterhead
Brechin C v Alloa Ath
Clyde v Stenhousemuir
East Fife v Dumbarton
Stirling Alb v Arbroath

Irn-Bru Third Division
Annan Ath v Montrose
East Stirlingshire v Berwick R
Elgin C v Albion
Forfar Ath v Cowdenbeath
Queen's Park v Stranraer

Saturday, 17 October 2009
Clydesdale Bank Premier League
Aberdeen v Hearts
Celtic v Motherwell

Dundee U v Hamilton A
Falkirk v St Mirren
Hibernian v Kilmarnock
St Johnstone v Rangers

Irn-Bru First Division
Inverness CT v Dunfermline Ath
Livingston v Ross Co
Morton v Dundee
Partick Th v Ayr U
Raith R v Queen of the S

Irn-Bru Second Division
Alloa Ath v Dumbarton
Arbroath v Airdrie Utd
Brechin C v East Fife
Clyde v Peterhead
Stenhousemuir v Stirling Alb

Irn-Bru Third Division
Albion v Queen's Park
Annan Ath v Stranraer
Cowdenbeath v Berwick R
Elgin C v East Stirlingshire
Forfar Ath v Montrose

Saturday, 24 October 2009
Clydesdale Bank Premier League
Aberdeen v Dundee U
Hamilton A v Celtic
Hearts v Falkirk
Kilmarnock v St Johnstone
Rangers v Hibernian
St Mirren v Motherwell

Irn-Bru First Division
Ayr U v Inverness CT
Dundee v Raith R
Dunfermline Ath v Morton
Queen of the S v Livingston
Ross Co v Partick Th

Irn-Bru Second Division
Airdrie Utd v Brechin C
Dumbarton v Arbroath
East Fife v Stenhousemuir
Peterhead v Alloa Ath
Stirling Alb v Clyde

Saturday, 31 October 2009
Clydesdale Bank Premier League
Celtic v Kilmarnock
Dundee U v Rangers
Hibernian v Aberdeen
Motherwell v Hearts
St Johnstone v Falkirk
St Mirren v Hamilton A

Irn-Bru First Division
Dunfermline Ath v Dundee
Inverness CT v Morton
Livingston v Ayr U
Partick Th v Raith R
Queen of the S v Ross Co

Irn-Bru Second Division
Airdrie Utd v East Fife
Alloa Ath v Clyde
Arbroath v Stenhousemuir
Dumbarton v Brechin C
Peterhead v Stirling Alb

Irn-Bru Third Division
Berwick R v Albion
East Stirlingshire v Annan Ath
Montrose v Cowdenbeath

Queen's Park v Elgin C
Stranraer v Forfar Ath

Saturday, 7 November 2009
Clydesdale Bank Premier League
Aberdeen v St Johnstone
Falkirk v Celtic
Hamilton A v Motherwell
Hearts v Hibernian
Kilmarnock v Dundee U
Rangers v St Mirren

Irn-Bru First Division
Ayr U v Queen of the S
Dundee v Livingston
Morton v Partick Th
Raith R v Dunfermline Ath
Ross Co v Inverness CT

Irn-Bru Second Division
Brechin C v Arbroath
Clyde v Airdrie Utd
East Fife v Peterhead
Stenhousemuir v Dumbarton
Stirling Alb v Alloa Ath

Irn-Bru Third Division
Albion v Montrose
Elgin C v Cowdenbeath
Forfar Ath v Annan Ath
Queen's Park v East Stirlingshire
Stranraer v Berwick R

Saturday, 14 November 2009
Irn-Bru First Division
Ayr U v Ross Co
Dundee v Queen of the S
Dunfermline Ath v Partick Th
Inverness CT v Livingston
Morton v Raith R

Irn-Bru Second Division
Airdrie Utd v Dumbarton
Alloa Ath v Stenhousemuir
Brechin C v Clyde
East Fife v Stirling Alb
Peterhead v Arbroath

Irn-Bru Third Division
Annan Ath v Elgin C
Berwick R v Queen's Park
Cowdenbeath v Albion
East Stirlingshire v Forfar Ath
Montrose v Stranraer

Saturday, 21 November 2009
Clydesdale Bank Premier League
Dundee U v Celtic
Falkirk v Hamilton A
Hearts v St Johnstone
Motherwell v Aberdeen
Rangers v Kilmarnock
St Mirren v Hibernian

Irn-Bru First Division
Livingston v Morton
Partick Th v Inverness CT
Queen of the S v Dunfermline Ath
Raith R v Ayr U
Ross Co v Dundee

Irn-Bru Second Division
Arbroath v Alloa Ath
Clyde v East Fife
Dumbarton v Peterhead
Stenhousemuir v Brechin C
Stirling Alb v Airdrie Utd

Irn-Bru Third Division
Albion v Annan Ath
Elgin C v Forfar Ath
Montrose v Berwick R
Queen's Park v Cowdenbeath
Stranraer v East Stirlingshire

Saturday, 28 November 2009
Clydesdale Bank Premier League
Aberdeen v Rangers
Celtic v St Mirren
Hibernian v Falkirk
Kilmarnock v Hearts
Motherwell v Dundee U
St Johnstone v Hamilton A

Saturday, 5 December 2009
Clydesdale Bank Premier League
Celtic v Aberdeen
Dundee U v St Mirren
Falkirk v Rangers
Hamilton A v Hearts
Hibernian v Motherwell
St Johnstone v Kilmarnock

Irn-Bru First Division
Ayr U v Dunfermline Ath
Partick Th v Dundee
Queen of the S v Inverness CT
Raith R v Livingston
Ross Co v Morton

Irn-Bru Second Division
Airdrie Utd v Stenhousemuir
Brechin C v Peterhead
Clyde v Arbroath
East Fife v Alloa Ath
Stirling Alb v Dumbarton

Irn-Bru Third Division
Annan Ath v Queen's Park
Berwick R v Elgin C
Cowdenbeath v Stranraer
East Stirlingshire v Montrose
Forfar Ath v Albion

Saturday, 12 December 2009
Clydesdale Bank Premier League
Aberdeen v Hamilton A
Hearts v Dundee U
Kilmarnock v Hibernian
Motherwell v Celtic
Rangers v St Johnstone
St Mirren v Falkirk

Irn-Bru First Division
Dundee v Ayr U
Dunfermline Ath v Ross Co
Inverness CT v Raith R
Livingston v Partick Th
Morton v Queen of the S

Irn-Bru Second Division
Alloa Ath v Brechin C
Arbroath v Stirling Alb
Dumbarton v East Fife
Peterhead v Airdrie Utd
Stenhousemuir v Clyde

Irn-Bru Third Division
Albion v Elgin C
Berwick R v East Stirlingshire
Cowdenbeath v Forfar Ath
Montrose v Annan Ath
Stranraer v Queen's Park

Saturday, 19 December 2009
Clydesdale Bank Premier League
Aberdeen v Hibernian
Hamilton A v Dundee U
Hearts v Celtic
Kilmarnock v Falkirk
Rangers v Motherwell
St Johnstone v St Mirren

Irn-Bru First Division
Ayr U v Partick Th
Dundee v Morton
Dunfermline Ath v Inverness CT
Queen of the S v Raith R
Ross Co v Livingston

Irn-Bru Second Division
Airdrie Utd v Arbroath
Dumbarton v Alloa Ath
East Fife v Brechin C
Peterhead v Clyde
Stirling Alb v Stenhousemuir

Irn-Bru Third Division
Annan Ath v Cowdenbeath
East Stirlingshire v Albion
Elgin C v Stranraer
Forfar Ath v Berwick R
Queen's Park v Montrose

Saturday, 26 December 2009
Clydesdale Bank Premier League
Celtic v Hamilton A
Dundee U v Kilmarnock
Falkirk v Hearts
Hibernian v Rangers
Motherwell v St Johnstone
St Mirren v Aberdeen

Irn-Bru First Division
Inverness CT v Dundee
Livingston v Dunfermline Ath
Morton v Ayr U
Partick Th v Queen of the S
Raith R v Ross Co

Irn-Bru Second Division
Alloa Ath v Airdrie Utd
Arbroath v East Fife
Brechin C v Stirling Alb
Clyde v Dumbarton
Stenhousemuir v Peterhead

Irn-Bru Third Division
Albion v Stranraer
Annan Ath v Berwick R
Cowdenbeath v East Stirlingshire
Elgin C v Montrose
Forfar Ath v Queen's Park

Wednesday, 30 December 2009
Clydesdale Bank Premier League
Aberdeen v Falkirk
Hamilton A v St Mirren
Hearts v Motherwell
Kilmarnock v Celtic
Rangers v Dundee U
St Johnstone v Hibernian

Saturday, 2 January 2010
Clydesdale Bank Premier League
Celtic v Rangers
Dundee U v Aberdeen
Falkirk v St Johnstone
Hibernian v Hearts
Motherwell v Hamilton A
St Mirren v Kilmarnock

Irn-Bru First Division
Dunfermline Ath v Raith R
Inverness CT v Ross Co
Livingston v Dundee
Partick Th v Morton
Queen of the S v Ayr U

Irn-Bru Second Division
Airdrie Utd v Clyde
Alloa Ath v Stirling Alb
Arbroath v Brechin C
Dumbarton v Stenhousemuir
Peterhead v East Fife

Irn-Bru Third Division
Berwick R v Cowdenbeath
East Stirlingshire v Elgin C
Montrose v Forfar Ath
Queen's Park v Albion
Stranraer v Annan Ath

Saturday, 9 January 2010
Irn-Bru Third Division
Annan Ath v Forfar Ath
Berwick R v Stranraer
Cowdenbeath v Elgin C
East Stirlingshire v Queen's Park
Montrose v Albion

Saturday, 16 January 2010
Clydesdale Bank Premier League
Celtic v Falkirk
Dundee U v Hibernian
Hamilton A v Rangers
Hearts v St Mirren
Kilmarnock v Motherwell
St Johnstone v Aberdeen

Irn-Bru First Division
Ayr U v Livingston
Morton v Inverness CT
Raith R v Partick Th
Ross Co v Queen of the S

Irn-Bru Second Division
Brechin C v Dumbarton
Clyde v Alloa Ath
East Fife v Airdrie Utd
Stenhousemuir v Arbroath
Stirling Alb v Peterhead

Irn-Bru Third Division
Albion v Cowdenbeath
Elgin C v Annan Ath
Forfar Ath v East Stirlingshire
Queen's Park v Berwick R
Stranraer v Montrose

Sunday, 17 January 2010
Irn-Bru First Division
Dundee v Dunfermline Ath

Saturday, 23 January 2010
Clydesdale Bank Premier League
Aberdeen v Kilmarnock
Falkirk v Dundee U
Hibernian v Hamilton A
Motherwell v St Mirren
Rangers v Hearts
St Johnstone v Celtic

Irn-Bru First Division
Livingston v Inverness CT
Partick Th v Dunfermline Ath
Queen of the S v Dundee
Raith R v Morton
Ross Co v Ayr U

Irn-Bru Second Division
Arbroath v Peterhead
Clyde v Brechin C
Dumbarton v Airdrie Utd
Stenhousemuir v Alloa Ath
Stirling Alb v East Fife

Irn-Bru Third Division
Albion v Forfar Ath
Elgin C v Berwick R
Montrose v East Stirlingshire
Queen's Park v Annan Ath
Stranraer v Cowdenbeath

Wednesday, 27 January 2010
Clydesdale Bank Premier League
Celtic v Hibernian
Dundee U v St Johnstone
Falkirk v Motherwell
Hamilton A v Kilmarnock
Hearts v Aberdeen
St Mirren v Rangers

Saturday, 30 January 2010
Clydesdale Bank Premier League
Aberdeen v Motherwell
Hamilton A v Celtic
Hibernian v St Mirren
Kilmarnock v Dundee U
Rangers v Falkirk
St Johnstone v Hearts

Irn-Bru First Division
Ayr U v Raith R
Dundee v Ross Co
Dunfermline Ath v Queen of the S
Inverness CT v Partick Th
Morton v Livingston

Irn-Bru Second Division
Airdrie Utd v Stirling Alb
Alloa Ath v Arbroath
Brechin C v Stenhousemuir
East Fife v Clyde
Peterhead v Dumbarton

Irn-Bru Third Division
Annan Ath v Albion
Berwick R v Montrose
Cowdenbeath v Queen's Park
East Stirlingshire v Stranraer
Forfar Ath v Elgin C

Saturday, 6 February 2010
Irn-Bru Second Division
Airdrie Utd v Peterhead
Brechin C v Alloa Ath
Clyde v Stenhousemuir
East Fife v Dumbarton
Stirling Alb v Arbroath

Irn-Bru Third Division
Annan Ath v Montrose
East Stirlingshire v Berwick R
Elgin C v Albion
Forfar Ath v Cowdenbeath
Queen's Park v Stranraer

Wednesday, 10 February 2010
Clydesdale Bank Premier League
Celtic v Hearts
Dundee U v Hamilton A
Falkirk v Kilmarnock
Hibernian v Aberdeen
Motherwell v Rangers
St Mirren v St Johnstone

Saturday, 13 February 2010
Clydesdale Bank Premier League
Aberdeen v Celtic
Hamilton A v Motherwell
Hearts v Falkirk
Kilmarnock v St Johnstone
Rangers v Hibernian
St Mirren v Dundee U

Irn-Bru First Division
Ayr U v Dundee
Partick Th v Livingston
Queen of the S v Morton
Raith R v Inverness CT
Ross Co v Dunfermline Ath

Irn-Bru Second Division
Alloa Ath v East Fife
Arbroath v Clyde
Dumbarton v Stirling Alb
Peterhead v Brechin C
Stenhousemuir v Airdrie Utd

Irn-Bru Third Division
Albion v East Stirlingshire
Berwick R v Forfar Ath
Cowdenbeath v Annan Ath
Montrose v Queen's Park
Stranraer v Elgin C

Saturday, 20 February 2010
Clydesdale Bank Premier League
Celtic v Dundee U
Falkirk v Aberdeen
Hearts v Hamilton A
Kilmarnock v St Mirren
Motherwell v Hibernian
St Johnstone v Rangers

Irn-Bru First Division
Dundee v Partick Th
Dunfermline Ath v Ayr U
Inverness CT v Queen of the S
Livingston v Raith R
Morton v Ross Co

Irn-Bru Second Division
Airdrie Utd v Alloa Ath
Dumbarton v Clyde
East Fife v Arbroath
Peterhead v Stenhousemuir
Stirling Alb v Brechin C

Irn-Bru Third Division
Berwick R v Annan Ath
East Stirlingshire v Cowdenbeath
Montrose v Elgin C
Queen's Park v Forfar Ath
Stranraer v Albion

Saturday, 27 February 2010
Clydesdale Bank Premier League
Aberdeen v Hearts
Dundee U v Falkirk
Hibernian v St Johnstone
Motherwell v Kilmarnock
Rangers v Celtic
St Mirren v Hamilton A

Irn-Bru First Division
Inverness CT v Ayr U
Livingston v Queen of the S
Morton v Dunfermline Ath
Partick Th v Ross Co
Raith R v Dundee

Irn-Bru Second Division
Alloa Ath v Peterhead
Arbroath v Dumbarton
Brechin C v Airdrie Utd
Clyde v Stirling Alb
Stenhousemuir v East Fife

Irn-Bru Third Division
Albion v Berwick R
Annan Ath v East Stirlingshire
Cowdenbeath v Montrose
Elgin C v Queen's Park
Forfar Ath v Stranraer

Saturday, 6 March 2010
Clydesdale Bank Premier League
Falkirk v Celtic
Hamilton A v Aberdeen
Hibernian v Kilmarnock
Rangers v St Mirren
St Johnstone v Motherwell

Irn-Bru First Division
Ayr U v Morton
Dundee v Inverness CT
Dunfermline Ath v Livingston
Queen of the S v Partick Th
Ross Co v Raith R

Irn-Bru Second Division
Airdrie Utd v East Fife
Alloa Ath v Clyde
Arbroath v Stenhousemuir
Dumbarton v Brechin C
Peterhead v Stirling Alb

Irn-Bru Third Division
Annan Ath v Elgin C
Cowdenbeath v Albion
East Stirlingshire v Forfar Ath
Montrose v Stranraer
Queen's Park v Berwick R

Sunday, 7 March 2010
Clydesdale Bank Premier League
Dundee U v Hearts

Saturday, 13 March 2010
Irn-Bru First Division
Dunfermline Ath v Dundee
Inverness CT v Morton
Livingston v Ayr U
Partick Th v Raith R
Queen of the S v Ross Co

Irn-Bru Second Division
Brechin C v Arbroath
Clyde v Airdrie Utd
East Fife v Peterhead
Stenhousemuir v Dumbarton
Stirling Alb v Alloa Ath

Irn-Bru Third Division
Albion v Montrose
Elgin C v Cowdenbeath
Forfar Ath v Annan Ath
Queen's Park v East Stirlingshire
Stranraer v Berwick R

Saturday, 20 March 2010
Clydesdale Bank Premier League
Aberdeen v Dundee U
Celtic v St Johnstone
Hamilton A v Falkirk
Hearts v Hibernian
Kilmarnock v Rangers
St Mirren v Motherwell

Irn-Bru First Division
Ayr U v Queen of the S
Dundee v Livingston
Morton v Partick Th
Raith R v Dunfermline Ath
Ross Co v Inverness CT

Irn-Bru Second Division
Airdrie Utd v Dumbarton
Alloa Ath v Stenhousemuir
Brechin C v Clyde
East Fife v Stirling Alb
Peterhead v Arbroath

Irn-Bru Third Division
Annan Ath v Queen's Park
Berwick R v Elgin C
Cowdenbeath v Stranraer
East Stirlingshire v Montrose
Forfar Ath v Albion

Tuesday, 23 March 2010
Irn-Bru First Division
Dundee v Queen of the S
Dunfermline Ath v Partick Th
Inverness CT v Livingston
Morton v Raith R

Wednesday, 24 March 2010
Clydesdale Bank Premier League
Hibernian v Dundee U
Kilmarnock v Hamilton A
Motherwell v Hearts
Rangers v Aberdeen
St Johnstone v Falkirk
St Mirren v Celtic

Irn-Bru First Division
Ayr U v Ross Co

Saturday, 27 March 2010
Clydesdale Bank Premier League
Aberdeen v St Mirren
Celtic v Kilmarnock
Dundee U v Motherwell
Falkirk v Hibernian
Hamilton A v St Johnstone
Hearts v Rangers

Irn-Bru First Division
Livingston v Morton
Partick Th v Inverness CT
Queen of the S v Dunfermline Ath
Raith R v Ayr U
Ross Co v Dundee

Irn-Bru Second Division
Arbroath v Alloa Ath
Clyde v East Fife
Dumbarton v Peterhead
Stenhousemuir v Brechin C
Stirling Alb v Airdrie Utd

Irn-Bru Third Division
Albion v Annan Ath

Elgin C v Forfar Ath
Montrose v Berwick R
Queen's Park v Cowdenbeath
Stranraer v East Stirlingshire

Saturday, 3 April 2010
Clydesdale Bank Premier League
Hibernian v Celtic
Kilmarnock v Aberdeen
Motherwell v Falkirk
Rangers v Hamilton A
St Johnstone v Dundee U
St Mirren v Hearts

Irn-Bru First Division
Dundee v Ayr U
Dunfermline Ath v Ross Co
Inverness CT v Raith R
Livingston v Partick Th
Morton v Queen of the S

Irn-Bru Second Division
Airdrie Utd v Stenhousemuir
Brechin C v Peterhead
Clyde v Arbroath
East Fife v Alloa Ath
Stirling Alb v Dumbarton

Irn-Bru Third Division
Annan Ath v Cowdenbeath
East Stirlingshire v Albion
Elgin C v Stranraer
Forfar Ath v Berwick R
Queen's Park v Montrose

Saturday, 10 April 2010
Clydesdale Bank Premier League
Aberdeen v St Johnstone
Celtic v Motherwell
Dundee U v Rangers
Falkirk v St Mirren
Hamilton A v Hibernian
Hearts v Kilmarnock

Irn-Bru First Division
Ayr U v Dunfermline Ath
Partick Th v Dundee
Queen of the S v Inverness CT
Raith R v Livingston
Ross Co v Morton

Irn-Bru Second Division
Alloa Ath v Brechin C
Arbroath v Stirling Alb
Dumbarton v East Fife
Peterhead v Airdrie Utd
Stenhousemuir v Clyde

Irn-Bru Third Division
Albion v Elgin C
Berwick R v East Stirlingshire
Cowdenbeath v Forfar Ath
Montrose v Annan Ath
Stranraer v Queen's Park

Saturday, 17 April 2010
Irn-Bru First Division
Inverness CT v Dunfermline Ath
Livingston v Ross Co
Morton v Dundee
Partick Th v Ayr U
Raith R v Queen of the S

Irn-Bru Second Division
Alloa Ath v Dumbarton
Arbroath v Airdrie Utd
Brechin C v East Fife
Clyde v Peterhead
Stenhousemuir v Stirling Alb

Irn-Bru Third Division
Albion v Queen's Park
Annan Ath v Stranraer
Cowdenbeath v Berwick R
Elgin C v East Stirlingshire
Forfar Ath v Montrose

Saturday, 24 April 2010
Irn-Bru First Division
Ayr U v Inverness CT
Dundee v Raith R
Dunfermline Ath v Morton
Queen of the S v Livingston
Ross Co v Partick Th

Irn-Bru Second Division
Airdrie Utd v Brechin C
Dumbarton v Arbroath
East Fife v Stenhousemuir
Peterhead v Alloa Ath
Stirling Alb v Clyde

Irn-Bru Third Division
Berwick R v Albion
East Stirlingshire v Annan Ath
Montrose v Cowdenbeath
Queen's Park v Elgin C
Stranraer v Forfar Ath

Saturday, 1 May 2010
Irn-Bru First Division
Inverness CT v Dundee
Livingston v Dunfermline Ath
Morton v Ayr U
Partick Th v Queen of the S
Raith R v Ross Co

Irn-Bru Second Division
Alloa Ath v Airdrie Utd
Arbroath v East Fife
Brechin C v Stirling Alb
Clyde v Dumbarton
Stenhousemuir v Peterhead

Irn-Bru Third Division
Albion v Stranraer
Annan Ath v Berwick R
Cowdenbeath v East Stirlingshire
Elgin C v Montrose
Forfar Ath v Queen's Park

OTHER FIXTURES 2009–10

JULY 2009

15 Wed	UEFA Champions League 2Q (1)
	UEFA Europa League 2Q (1)
22 Wed	UEFA Champions League 2Q (2)
	UEFA Europa League 2Q (2)
25 Sat	
29 Wed	UEFA Champions League 3Q (1)
	UEFA Europa League 3Q (1)

AUGUST 2009

05 Wed	UEFA Champions League 3Q (2)
	UEFA Europa League 3Q (2)
08 Sat	Football League commences
09 Sun	FA Community Shield
12 Wed	Holland v England – International Friendly
	Football League Cup 1
15 Sat	The FA Cup Sponsored by E.On EP
	Premier League commences
19 Wed	UEFA Champions League Play-Off (1)
	UEFA Europa League Play-Off (1)
26 Wed	UEFA Champions League Play-Off (2)
	UEFA Europa League Play-Off (2)
	Football League Cup 2
28 Fri	UEFA Super Cup
29 Sat	The FA Cup Sponsored by E.On P

SEPTEMBER 2009

02 Wed	Football League Trophy 1
05 Sat	England v Slovenia – International Qualifier
	The FA Carlsberg Vase 1Q
07 Mon	The FA Youth Cup Sponsored by E.On P†
09 Wed	England v Croatia – World Cup Qualifier
12 Sat	The FA Cup Sponsored by E.On 1Q
13 Sun	The FA Women's Cup Sponsored by E.On P
16 Wed	UEFA Champions League MD1
	UEFA Europa League MD1
19 Sat	The FA Carlsberg Vase 2Q
20 Sun	The FA Carlsberg Sunday Cup P
21 Mon	The FA Youth Cup Sponsored by E.On 1Q†
23 Wed	Football League Cup 3
26 Sat	The FA Cup Sponsored by E.On 2Q
	The FA Carlsberg National League System Cup 1*
27 Sun	The FA Women's Cup Sponsored by E.On 1Q
30 Wed	UEFA Champions League MD2
	UEFA Europa League MD2

OCTOBER 2009

03 Sat	The FA Carlsberg Trophy P
	The FA Carlsberg Vase 1p
05 Mon	The FA Youth Cup Sponsored by E.On 2Q†
07 Wed	Football League Trophy 2
10 Sat	Ukraine v England – World Cup Qualifier
	The FA Cup Sponsored by E.On 3Q
11 Sun	The FA Women's Cup Sponsored by E.On 2Q
14 Wed	England v Belarus – World Cup Qualifier
17 Sat	The FA Carlsberg Trophy 1Q
18 Sun	The FA Carlsberg Sunday Cup 1
	The FA County Youth Cup 1*
19 Mon	The FA Youth Cup Sponsored by E.On 3Q†
21 Wed	UEFA Champions League MD3
	UEFA Europa League MD3
24 Sat	The FA Cup Sponsored by E.On 4Q
25 Sun	The FA Women's Cup Sponsored by E.On 3Q
28 Wed	Football League Cup 4
31 Sat	The FA Carlsberg Trophy 2Q

NOVEMBER 2009

04 Wed	UEFA Champions League MD4
	UEFA Europa League MD4
07 Sat	The FA Cup Sponsored by E.On 1p
	The FA Youth Cup Sponsored by E.On 1p*
08 Sun	The FA Women's Cup Sponsored by E.On 1p
11 Wed	Football League Trophy AQF
14 Sat	International Play-Off Matches
	The FA Carlsberg Vase 2p
15 Sun	The FA Carlsberg Sunday Cup 2
	The FA County Youth Cup 2*
18 Wed	International Play-Off Matches
	The FA Cup Sponsored by E.On 1p Replay
21 Sat	The FA Carlsberg Trophy 3Q
	The FA Youth Cup Sponsored by E.On 2p*
25 Wed	UEFA Champions League MD5
28 Sat	The FA Cup Sponsored by E.On 2p
29 Sun	The FA Women's Cup Sponsored by E.On 2p

DECEMBER 2009

02 Wed	UEFA Europa League MD5
	Football League Cup 5
05 Sat	The FA Carlsberg Vase 3p
06 Sun	The FA Carlsberg Sunday Cup 3
09 Wed	UEFA Champions League MD6
	The FA Cup Sponsored by E.On 2p Replay
12 Sat	The FA Carlsberg Trophy 1p
	The FA Youth Cup Sponsored by E.On 3p*
	The FA Carlsberg National League System Cup 2*
13 Sun	The FA Women's Cup Sponsored by E.On 3p
16 Wed	UEFA Europa League MD6
	Football League Trophy Asf
20 Sun	The FA County Youth Cup 3*

JANUARY 2010

02 Sat	The FA Cup Sponsored by E.On 3p
06 Wed	Football League Cup SF1
09 Sat	The FA Carlsberg Trophy 2p

10 Sun	The FA Women's Cup Sponsored by E.On 4p
13 Wed	The FA Cup Sponsored by E.On 3p Replay
16 Sat	The FA Carlsberg Vase 4p
	The FA Youth Cup Sponsored by E.On 4p*
17 Sun	The FA Carlsberg Sunday Cup 4
20 Wed	Football League Cup SF2
	Football League Trophy Af1
23 Sat	The FA Cup Sponsored by E.On 4p
24 Sun	The FA County Youth Cup 4*
	The FA Women's Cup Sponsored by E.On 5p
30 Sat	The FA Carlsberg Trophy 3p
	The FA Youth Cup Sponsored by E.On 5p*

FEBRUARY 2010

03 Wed	The FA Cup Sponsored by E.On 4p Replay
06 Sat	The FA Carlsberg Vase 5p
13 Sat	The FA Cup Sponsored by E.On 5p
	The FA Youth Cup Sponsored by E.On 6p*
14 Sun	The FA Women's Cup Sponsored by E.On 6p
17 Wed	UEFA Champions League 16
	UEFA Europa League 32 (1)
	Football League Trophy Af2
20 Sat	The FA Carlsberg Trophy 4p
	The FA Carlsberg National League System Cup 3*
21 Sun	The FA Carlsberg Sunday Cup 5
24 Wed	UEFA Champions League 16
	UEFA Europa League 32 (2)
	The FA Cup Sponsored by E.On 5p Replay
27 Sat	The FA Carlsberg Vase 6p
28 Sun	Football League Cup Final
	The FA County Youth Cup SF*

MARCH 2010

03 Wed	International Friendly
06 Sat	The FA Cup Sponsored by E.On 6p
	The FA Youth Cup Sponsored by E.On SF1*
10 Wed	UEFA Champions League 16
	UEFA Europa League 16 (1)
13 Sat	The FA Carlsberg Trophy SF1
14 Sun	The FA Women's Cup Sponsored by E.On SF
17 Wed	UEFA Champions League 16
	UEFA Europa League 16 (2)
	The FA Cup Sponsored by E.On 6p Replay

20 Sat	The FA Carlsberg Trophy SF2
	The FA Youth Cup Sponsored by E.On SF2*
21 Sun	The FA Carlsberg Sunday Cup SF
27 Sat	The FA Carlsberg Vase SF1
28 Sun	Football League Trophy Final
31 Wed	UEFA Champions League Qf (1)
	UEFA Europa League Qf (1)

APRIL 2010

03 Sat	The FA Carlsberg Vase SF2
07 Wed	UEFA Champions League Qf (2)
	UEFA Europa League Qf (2)
10 Sat	The FA Cup Sponsored by E.On SF
11 Sun	The FA Cup Sponsored by E.On SF
21 Wed	UEFA Champions League SF (1)
	UEFA Europa League SF (1)
24 Sat	The FA County Youth Cup Final (Prov)
25 Sun	The FA Carlsberg Sunday Cup Final (Prov)
28 Wed	UEFA Champions League SF (2)
	UEFA Europa League SF (2)

MAY 2010

01 Sat	The FA County Youth Cup Final (Prov)
02 Sun	Championship Season Finish
	The FA Carlsberg Sunday Cup Final (Prov)
	The FA Women's Cup Sponsored by E.On Final
08 Sat	The FA Carlsberg Trophy Final (Prov)
	Championship Play-Off SF1
	League 1 & League 2 Finishes
09 Sun	Premier League Season Finish
	The FA Carlsberg Vase Final (Prov)
10 Mon	The FA Carlsberg National League System Cup SF*
12 Wed	UEFA Europa League Final
	Championship Play-Off SF2
15 Sat	The FA Cup Sponsored by E.On Final
	League1 & League 2 Play-Off SF1
19 Wed	League 1 & League 2 Play-Off SF2
22 Sat	UEFA Champions League Final
	Championship Play-Off Final (Prov)
	FA Youth Cup Final 1st leg
23 Sun	Championship Play-Off Final (Prov)
26 Wed	FA Youth Cup Final 2nd leg
29 Sat	League 1 Play-Off Final
30 Sun	League 2 Play-Off Final

JUNE 2010

| 11 Fri | World Cup Commences |

† Ties to be played in week commencing
* Closing date of round

STOP PRESS

Tevez moves next door ... Adebayor joins him ... Man City take overall spending to £200m ... Man Utd get Owen for nothing ... Estudiantes beat Cruzeiro 2-1 in Copa Libertadores final ... Europa League starts ... 80,000 at Ronaldo unveiling ... Saints appoint Pardew ... Appointment: Irish FA Chief Executive Patrick Nelson ...

Summer transfers completed and pending:
Premier League: Arsenal: Thomas Vermaelen (Ajax) undisclosed. **Aston Villa:** Stewart Downing (Middlesbrough) undisclosed. **Birmingham C:** Cristian Benitez (Santos Laguna) undisclosed; Giovanni Espinoza (Barcelona SC) undisclosed; Roger Johnson (Cardiff C) £5m; Scott Dann (Coventry C) undisclosed; Joe Hart (Manchester C) Loan; Lee Bowyer (West Ham U) Free; Barry Ferguson (Rangers) undisclosed. **Blackburn R:** Gael Givet (Marseille) undisclosed; Steven N'Zonzi (Amiens) undisclosed; Elrio Van Heerden (Club Brugge) Free; Lars Jacobsen (Everton) Free. **Bolton W:** Sean Davis (Portsmouth) Free; Paul Robinson (WBA) Loan. **Burnley:** Tyrone Mears (Derby Co) undisclosed; Steven Fletcher (Hibernian) £3m; David Edgar (Newcastle U) Free; Richard Eckersley (Manchester U) undisclosed; Brian Easton (Hamilton A) £350,000. **Chelsea:** Daniel Sturridge (Manchester C) undisclosed; Ross Turnbull (Middlesbrough) Free; Yuri Zhirkov (CSKA Moscow) undisclosed. **Everton:** Anton Peterlin (Ventura County Fusion) Free; Jo (Manchester C) Loan. **Fulham:** Stephen Kelly (Birmingham C) undisclosed. **Hull C:** Steven Mouvokolo (Bologne) undisclosed. **Liverpool:** Glen Johnson (Portsmouth) undisclosed. **Manchester C:** Gareth Barry (Aston Villa) £12m; Roque Santa Cruz (Blackburn R) £17m; Stuart Taylor (Aston Villa) undisclosed; Carlos Tevez (Corinthians) £25m; Emmanuel Adebayor (Arsenal) £25m. **Manchester U:** Michael Owen (Newcastle U) Free; Antonio Valencia (Wigan Ath) undisclosed; Gabriel Obertan (Bordeaux) undisclosed. **Portsmouth:** Aaron Mokoena (Blackburn R) Free. **Sunderland:** Fraizer Campbell (Manchester U) £3,500,000; Paulo Da Silva (Toluca) Free. **West Ham U:** Luis Jimenez (Internazionale) Loan; Herita Ilunga (Toulouse) undisclosed; Peter Kurucz (Ujpest) undisclosed. **Wigan Ath:** Hendry Thomas (Olimpia) undisclosed; Jordi Gomez (Espanyol) undisclosed; Jason Scotland (Swansea C) £2,000,000. **Wolverhampton W:** Ronald Zubar (Marseille) undisclosed; Greg Halford (Sunderland) undisclosed; Nenad Milijas (Red Star Belgrade) undisclosed; Marcus Hahnemann (Reading) Free; Andrew Surman (Southampton) undisclosed; Kevin Doyle (Reading) undisclosed.

Football League Championship: Barnsley: Onome Sodje (York C) Free. **Bristol C:** Dean Gerken (Colchester U) undisclosed; Andre Blackman (Portsmouth) Free; Paul Hartley (Celtic) Free; David Clarkson (Motherwell) Free; Lewin Nyatanga (Derby Co) undisclosed; Danny Haynes (Ipswich T) undisclosed. **Cardiff C:** Paul Quinn (Motherwell) undisclosed; Anthony Gerrard (Walsall) undisclosed; Mark Hudson (Charlton Ath) undisclosed; David Marshall (Norwich C) undisclosed; Michael Chopra (Sunderland) £4m. **Crystal Palace:** Freddie Sears (West Ham U) Loan; Darren Ambrose (Charlton Ath) Free. **Derby Co:** Lee Croft (Norwich C) Free; Dean Moxey (Exeter C) undisclosed; Jake Buxton (Burton Alb) undisclosed. **Ipswich T:** Damien Delaney (QPR) undisclosed; Lee Martin (Manchester U) undisclosed. **Leicester C:** Chris Weale (Bristol C) Free; Dany N'Guessan (Lincoln C) undisclosed; Richard Wellens (Doncaster R) £1,200,000; Wayne Brown (Hull C) Free; Robbie Neilson (Hearts) Free; Jack Hobbs (Liverpool) undisclosed. **Middlesbrough:** Mark Yeates (Colchester U) undisclosed; Danny Coyne (Tranmere R) Free. **Nottingham F:** Lee Camp (QPR) undisclosed; David McGoldrick (Southampton) undisclosed; Paul Anderson (Liverpool) £250,000; Dele Adebola (Bristol C) Free; Chris Gunter (Tottenham H) £1,750,000; Paul McKenna (Preston NE) £750,000. **Peterborough U:** Tommy Rowe (Stockport Co) undisclosed; Lee Frecklington (Lincoln C) undisclosed; Toumani Diagouraga (Hereford U) undisclosed; Krystian Pearce (Birmingham C) Loan. **Plymouth Arg:** Carl Fletcher (Crystal Palace) Free; Bradley Wright-Phillips (Southampton) Free. **Scunthorpe U:** Rob Jones (Hibernian) undisclosed; Josh Wright (Charlton Ath) Free; Michael O'Connor (Crewe Alex) undisclosed. **Sheffield U:** Kyel Reid (West Ham U) Free; Lee Williamson (Watford) undisclosed; Andy Taylor (Tranmere R) undisclosed. **Sheffield W:** Tommy Miller (Ipswich T) Free; Darren Purse (Cardiff C) Free; Darren Potter (Wolverhampton W) undisclosed. **Swansea C:** Steven Dobbie (Queen of the South) Free; Jordi Lopez (Mallorca) undisclosed. **Watford:** Danny Graham (Carlisle U) Free; Scott Severin (Aberdeen) Free; Jure Travner (Publikum) undisclosed. **WBA:** Simon Cox (Swindon T) £1,500,000.

Football League 1: Brentford: Myles Weston (Notts Co) undisclosed; Sam Saunders, Danny Foster and Ben Strevens (all Dagenham & R) Free. **Brighton & HA:** Mark Wright (Milton Keynes D) Free; Gary Dicker (Stockport Co) Free; Graeme Smith (Motherwell) Free; James Tunnicliffe (Stockport Co) undisclosed; Liam Dickinson (Derby Co) undisclosed. **Bristol R:** Dominic Blizzard (Stockport Co) Free. **Carlisle U:** Adam Collin (Workington) Free; Matty Robson (Hartlepool U) Free; Tom Taiwo (Chelsea) Loan; Tony Kane (Blackburn R) Free. **Charlton Ath:** Miguel Angel Llera (Milton Keynes D) Free; Frazer Richardson (Leeds U) Free; Bakary Soro (Lorient) undisclosed. **Colchester U:** Lee Beevers (Lincoln C) Free. **Exeter C:** Scott Golbourne (Reading) Free; Barry Corr (Swindon T) Free; Joe Burnell (Oxford U) Free. **Gillingham:** Kevin Maher (Oldham Ath) Free; Chris Palmer (Walsall) Free. **Hartlepool U:** Peter Hartley (Sunderland) Free; Scott Flinders (Crystal Palace) Free; Neil Austin (Darlington) Free; Jon-Andre Fredriksen (Sarpsborg) Free. **Huddersfield T:** Theo Robinson (Watford) undisclosed; Antony Kay (Tranmere R) Free; Peter Clarke (Southend U) Free; Lee Peltier

(Yeovil T) undisclosed; Robbie Simpson (Coventry C) undisclosed. **Leeds U:** Shan. (Cheltenham T) Free; Jason Crowe (Northampton T) Free. **Leyton Orient:** Scott McGleish (Wycom. W) Free; Jimmy Smith (Chelsea) Free. **Millwall:** John Sullivan (Brighton & HA) undisclosed; Jason Price (Doncaster R) Free. **Milton Keynes D:** Dan Woodards (Crewe Alex) Free; David McCracken (Wycombe W) Free; Jermaine Easter (Plymouth Arg) undisclosed; Stuart Searle (Watford) Free; Lewis Gobern (Wolverhampton W) Free. **Norwich C:** Owain Tudur-Jones (Swansea C) undisclosed; Michael Nelson (Hartlepool U) Free; Matthew Gill (Exeter C) Free; Michael Theoklitos (Melbourne Victory) Free. **Oldham Ath:** Jon Worthington (Huddersfield T) Free; Joe Jacobson (Bristol R) Free; Pawel Abbott (Darlington) Free; Robert Purdie (Darlington) Free. **Southend U:** Lee Sawyer (Chelsea) Loan. **Swindon T:** Gordon Greer (Doncaster R) Free; David Lucas (Leeds U) Free; Jonathan Douglas (Leeds U) Free; Alan O'Brien (Hibernian) Free; Scott Cuthbert (Celtic) undisclosed. **Tranmere R:** Alan Mahon (Burnley) Free; Ryan France (Hull C) Free; John Welsh (Hull C) Free. **Walsall:** Steve Jones (Burnley) Free; Mark Hughes (Northampton T) Free; Josh O'Keefe (Blackburn R) Free. **Wycombe W:** Michael Duberry (Reading) Free; Chris Westwood (Peterborough U) Free; Ian Westlake (Cheltenham T) Free; Stuart Green (Blackpool) Free. **Yeovil T:** Stefan Stam (Oldham Ath) Free; Scott Murray (Bristol C) Free.

Football League 2: Accrington S: Michael Symes (Shrewsbury T) Free; Luke Joyce (Carlisle U) Free. **Barnet:** Micah Hyde (Woking) Free; Jake Cole (QPR) Free. **Bradford C:** Gareth Evans (Macclesfield T) undisclosed; Zesh Rehman (QPR) Free; Simon Ramsden (Rochdale) Free. **Burton Albion:** Paul Boertien (Walsall) Free; Richard Walker (Bristol R) Free; Robin Shroot (Birmingham C) Loan; Martin Butler (Grimsby T) undisclosed; Guy Branston (Kettering T) undisclosed; Shane Redmond (Nottingham F) Loan. **Bury:** Danny Carlton (Carlisle U) Free. **Cheltenham T:** Justin Richards (Kidderminster H) Free; Barry Hayles (Leicester C) Free; Julian Alsop (Bishops Cleeve) Free. **Chesterfield:** Ian Breckin (Nottingham F) Free. **Crewe Alexandra:** Patrick Ada (Histon) undisclosed. **Dagenham & R:** Danny Green (Bishop's Stortford) undisclosed; Joshua Scott (Hayes & Yeading) Free; Stuart Thurgood (Grays Ath) Free; Will Antwi (Wycombe W) Free. **Darlington:** Dean Windass (Hull C) Free. **Grimsby T:** Peter Sweeney (Leeds U) Free; Joe Widdowson (West Ham U) Free; Michael Leary (Barnet) Free; Nick Colgan (Sunderland) Free. **Hereford U:** Glen Southam (Dagenham & R) Free; Adam Bartlett (Kidderminster H) Free; Marc Pugh (Shrewsbury T) Free; Kenny Lunt (Sheffield W) Free; Jamie Tolley (Macclesfield T) Free; Darren Jones (Forest Green R) undisclosed. **Lincoln C:** Joe Heath (Nottingham F) Loan. **Macclesfield T:** Paul Morgan (Bury) Free; Ben Wright (Lincoln C) Free; Steve Reed (Weymouth) undisclosed; Nat Brown (Wrexham) Free; Hamza Bencherif (Nottingham F) Free; Ross Draper (Hednesford T) undisclosed; Colin Daniel (Crewe Alex) Free. **Northampton T:** Dean Beckwith (Hereford U) Free; Steve Guinan (Hereford U) Free. **Notts Co:** Ben Davies (Shrewsbury T) Free; Graeme Lee (Bradford C) undisclosed; Brendan Moloney (Nottingham F) Loan. **Port Vale:** Doug Loft (Brighton & HA) Free; Adam Yates (Morecambe) Free; Tommy Fraser (Brighton & HA) undisclosed. **Rochdale:** Kenny Arthur (Accrington S) Free; Matthew Edwards (Leeds U) Free. **Rotherham U:** Jamie Annerson (Sheffield U) Free; Nicky Law (Sheffield U) Free; Paul Warne (Yeovil T) Free. **Shrewsbury T:** Lewis Neal (Carlisle U) Free; Chris Neal (Preston NE) nominal; Dean Holden (Falkirk) Free. **Torquay U:** Ben Joyce (Swindon T) Free.

Scottish Premier League: Celtic: Marc-Antoine Fortune (Nancy) undisclosed; Lukasz Zaluska (Dundee U) Free; Landry N'Guemo (Nancy) Loan. **Dundee U:** Danny Cadamarteri (Huddersfield T) Free; Jennison Myrie-Williams (Bristol C) Free; Steve Banks (Hearts) Free; Andy Webster (Rangers) Loan. **Falkirk:** Brian McLean (Motherwell) Free; Sean Fraser (Coventry C) Free; Alex MacDonald (Burnley) Loan; Mark Twaddle (Partick T) undisclosed; Ryan Flynn (Liverpool) Loan. **Hibernian:** Kevin McBride (Falkirk) Free. **Kilmarnock:** Graeme Owens (Middlesbrough) Free. **Motherwell:** Chris Humphrey (Shrewsbury T) Free; Steven Jennings (Tranmere R) Free. **St Johnstone:** Collin Samuel (Toronto) undisclosed; Euan McLean (Dundee U) undisclosed; Gavin Swankie (Dundee) undisclosed; Graham Gartland (Drogheda U) undisclosed; Graeme Smith (Rangers) Free; Danny Grainger (Dundee U) undisclosed. **St Mirren:** Lee Mair (Aberdeen) undisclosed; Michael Higdon (Falkirk) Free.

Leaving the country: **Arsenal:** Havard Nordtveit (Lillestrom) Loan. **Birmingham C:** Mehdi Nafti (Aris Salonika) Free. **Blackburn R:** Matt Derbyshire (Olympiakos) undisclosed; Andre Ooijer (PSV Eindhoven) Free. **Chelsea:** Ben Sahar (Espanyol) undisclosed; Slobodan Rajkovic (Twente) Loan. **Fulham:** Collins John (Roeselare) Free. **Liverpool:** Jermaine Pennant (Real Zaragoza) Free; Sebastian Leto (Panathinaikos) £1,300,000; Sami Hyypia (Leverkusen) Free. **Manchester C:** Gelson (St Etienne) undisclosed; Darius Vassell (Ankaragucu) Free. **Manchester U:** Cristiano Ronaldo (Real Madrid) £80,000,000; Rodrigo Possebon (Braga) Loan. **Portsmouth:** Andrea Mbuyi-Mutombo (Standard Liege) Free; Arnold Mvuemba (Lorient) Loan. **Tottenham H:** Didier Zokora (Sevilla) undisclosed. **Barnsley:** Dennis Souza (Katar) Free. **Bristol C:** Peter Styvar (Xanthi) Loan. **Derby Co:** Emanuel Villa (Cruz Azul) undisclosed. **Plymouth Arg:** Emile Mpenza (Sion) Free. **Colchester U:** Chris Coyne (Perth Glory) Free. **Crewe Alex:** Julien Baudet (Colorado Rapids) Free. **Celtic:** Shunsuke Nakamura (Espanyol) Free.

Now you can buy any of these other bestselling sports titles from your bookshop or *direct from the publisher.*

FREE P&P AND UK DELIVERY
(Overseas and Ireland £3.50 per book)

Playfair Football Annual 2009–2010	Glenda Rollin and Jack Rollin	£6.99
1966 and All That	Geoff Hurst	£7.99
Psycho	Stuart Pearce	£7.99
Gazza: My Story	Paul Gascoigne	£7.99
Vinnie	Vinnie Jones	£7.99
The Doc	Tommy Docherty	£8.99
Black and Blue	Paul Canoville	£7.99
Left Foot Forward	Garry Nelson	£6.99
My Defence	Ashley Cole	£7.99
The Autobiography	Niall Quinn	£7.99
Determined	Norman Whiteside	£7.99
Cloughie	Brian Clough	£7.99
My Manchester United Years	Bobby Charlton	£8.99
My England Years	Bobby Charlton	£7.99
Fallen Idle	Peter Marinello	£6.99
Being Gazza	Paul Gascoigne	£6.99
The Autobiography	Alan Mullery	£7.99

TO ORDER SIMPLY CALL THIS NUMBER

01235 400 414

or visit our website:
www.headline.co.uk

Prices and availability subject to change without notice.